LEXI-COMP'S

Drug Information Handbook

P•O•C•K•E•T

2004-2005

LEXI-COMP

APhA

Drug Information Handbook

P·O·C·K·E·T

2004-2005

Charles F. Lacy, PharmD, FCSHP
Vice President, Information Technologies
Director, Drug Information Services
Professor, Pharmacy Practice
Nevada College of Pharmacy
Las Vegas, Nevada

Lora L. Armstrong, PharmD, BCPS
Director, Pharmacy & Therapeutics Formulary Process
Caremark, Inc.
Northbrook, Illinois

Morton P. Goldman, PharmD, BCPS
Assistant Director, Pharmacotherapy Services
Department of Pharmacy
Cleveland Clinic Foundation
Cleveland, Ohio

Leonard L. Lance, RPh, BSPharm
Pharmacist
Lexi-Comp, Inc.
Hudson, Ohio

NOTICE

This handbook is intended to serve the user as a handy quick reference and not as a complete drug information resource. It does not include information on every therapeutic agent available. The publication covers commonly used drugs and is specifically designed to present certain important aspects of drug data in a more concise format than is generally found in medical literature or product material supplied by manufacturers.

The nature of drug information is that it is constantly evolving because of ongoing research and clinical experience and is often subject to interpretation. While great care has been taken to ensure the accuracy of the information presented, the reader is advised that the authors, editors, reviewers, contributors, and publishers cannot be responsible for the continued currency of the information or for any errors, omissions, or the application of this information, or for any consequences arising therefrom. Therefore, the author(s) and/or the publisher shall have no liability to any person or entity with regard to claims, loss, or damage caused, or alleged to be caused, directly or indirectly, by the use of information contained herein. Because of the dynamic nature of drug information, readers are advised that decisions regarding drug therapy must be based on the independent judgment of the clinician, changing information about a drug (eg, as reflected in the literature and manufacturer's most current product information), and changing medical practices. The editors are not responsible for any inaccuracy of quotation or for any false or misleading implication that may arise due to the text or formulas as used or due to the quotation of revisions no longer official. Further, the reader/user, herewith, is advised that information shown under the heading **Dosage** is provided only as an indication of the amount of the drug typically given or taken during therapy. Actual dosing amount for any specific drug should be based on an in-depth evaluation of the individual patient's therapy requirement and strong consideration given to such issues as contraindications, warnings, precautions, adverse reactions, along with the interaction of other drugs. The manufacturers most current product information or other standard recognized references should always be consulted for such detailed information prior to drug use.

The editors, authors, and contributors have written this book in their private capacities. No official support or endorsement by any federal agency or pharmaceutical company is intended or inferred.

The publishers have made every effort to trace the copyright holders for borrowed material. If they have inadvertently overlooked any, they will be pleased to make the necessary arrangements at the first opportunity.

If you have any suggestions or questions regarding any information presented in this handbook, please contact our drug information pharmacist at

1-877-837-LEXI (5394)

This manual was produced using the FormuLex™ Program — a complete publishing service of Lexi-Comp Inc.

1100 Terex Road
Hudson, Ohio 44236
(330) 650-6506

ISBN 1-59195-085-6

TABLE OF CONTENTS

ABOUT THE AUTHORS

Charles F. Lacy, PharmD, FCSHP

Dr Lacy is the Vice President for Information Technologies and Professor of Pharmacy Practice at the Nevada College of Pharmacy. In his capacity at the college, Dr. Lacy oversees the Library and Learning Resources Center, the Computer Information Systems, and the Drug Information Service. This college-based service provides drug use policy services in addition to traditional drug information resources to the college's affiliated institutions. Prior to his promotion, Dr. Lacy was the Facilitative Officer for Clinical Programs where he managed the clinical curriculum, clinical faculty activities, student experiential programs, pharmacy residency programs, and the college's continuing education programs. Currently, Dr. Lacy is also the Chairman of the Eureka Development Foundation, a philanthropic group supporting the students at the college and plans and develops new programs for the college.

Prior to coming to the Nevada College of Pharmacy, Dr Lacy was the Clinical Coordinator for the Department of Pharmacy at Cedars-Sinai Medical Center. With over 19 years of clinical experience at one of the nation's largest teaching hospitals, he has developed a reputation as an acknowledged expert in drug information and critical care drug therapy.

Dr Lacy received his doctorate from the University of Southern California School of Pharmacy. Presently, Dr Lacy holds teaching affiliations with the Nevada College of Pharmacy, the University of Southern California School of Pharmacy, the University of California at San Francisco School of Pharmacy, the University of the Pacific School of Pharmacy, Western University of Health Sciences School of Pharmacy, and the University of Alberta at Edmonton, School of Pharmacy and Health Sciences.

Dr Lacy is an active member of numerous professional associations including the American Society of Health-System Pharmacists (ASHP), the American College of Clinical Pharmacy (ACCP), the American Society of Consultant Pharmacists (ASCP), the American Association of Colleges of Pharmacy (AACP), American Pharmacists Association (APhA), the Nevada Pharmacy Alliance (NPA), and the California Society of Hospital Pharmacists (CSHP), through which he has chaired many committees and subcommittees.

Lora L. Armstrong, PharmD, BCPS

Dr Armstrong received her bachelor's degree in pharmacy from Ferris State University and her Doctor of Pharmacy degree from Midwestern University. Dr Armstrong is a Board-Certified Pharmacotherapy Specialist (BCPS).

In her current position, Dr Armstrong serves as the Director of the Pharmacy & Therapeutics Committee process at Caremark, Inc, Prescription Services Division. Caremark is a prescription benefit management company (PBM). Dr Armstrong is responsible for coordination of the Caremark National Pharmacy & Therapeutics Committee and the Caremark Pharmacy & Therapeutics Subcommittee. Dr Armstrong is also responsible for monitoring the pharmaceutical product pipeline, monitoring drug surveillance, and communicating Pharmacy & Therapeutics Committee Formulary information to Caremark's internal and external customers.

Prior to joining Caremark, Inc, Dr Armstrong served as the Director of Drug Information Services at the University of Chicago Hospitals. She obtained 17 years of experience in a variety of clinical settings including critical care, hematology, oncology, infectious diseases, and clinical pharmacokinetics. Dr Armstrong played an active role in the education and training of medical, pharmacy, and nursing staff. She coordinated the Drug Information Center, the medical center's Adverse Drug Reaction Monitoring Program, and the continuing Education Program for pharmacists. She also maintained the hospital's strict formulary program and was the editor of the University of Chicago Hospitals' *Formulary of Accepted Drugs* and the drug information center's monthly newsletter *Topics in Drug Therapy.*

Dr Armstrong is an active member of the Academy of Managed Care Pharmacy (AMCP), the American Society of Health-Systems Pharmacists (ASHP), the American Pharmaceutical Association (APhA), the American College of Clinical Pharmacy (ACCP), and the Pharmacy & Therapeutics Society (P & T Society). Dr Armstrong wrote the chapter entitled "Drugs and Hormones Used in Endocrinology" in the 4th edition of the textbook *Endocrinology.* She is an Adjunct Clinical Instructor of Pharmacy Practice at Midwestern University. Dr Armstrong currently serves on the Drug Information Advisory Board for pharmacist.com and on the American Pharmaceutical Association Scientific Review Panel for Evaluations of Drug Interactions (EDI).

Morton P. Goldman, PharmD, BCPS

Dr Goldman received his bachelor's degree in pharmacy from the University of Pittsburgh, College of Pharmacy and his Doctor of Pharmacy degree from the University of Cincinnati, Division of Graduate Studies and Research. He completed his concurrent 2-year hospital pharmacy residency at the VA Medical Center in Cincinnati. Dr Goldman is presently the Assistant Director of Pharmacotherapy Services for the Department of Pharmacy at the Cleveland Clinic Foundation (CCF) after having spent over 4 years at CCF as an Infectious Disease pharmacist and 4 years as Clinical Manager. He holds faculty appointments from The University of Toledo, College of Pharmacy and Case Western Reserve University, College of Medicine and is the Pharmacology Curriculum Coordinator for the new Cleveland Clinic Lerner College of Medicine. Dr Goldman is a Board-Certified Pharmacotherapy Specialist (BCPS) with added qualifications in infectious diseases.

In his capacity as Assistant Director of Pharmacotherapy Services at CCF, Dr Goldman remains actively involved in patient care and clinical research with the Department of Infectious Disease, as well as the continuing education of the medical and pharmacy staff. He is an editor of CCF's *Guidelines for Antibiotic Use* and participates in their annual Antimicrobial Review retreat. He is a member of the Pharmacy and Therapeutics Committee and many of its subcommittees. Dr Goldman has authored numerous journal articles and lectures locally and nationally on infectious diseases topics and current drug therapies. He is currently a reviewer for the *Annals of Pharmacotherapy* and the *Journal of the American Medical Association*, an editorial board member of the *Journal of Infectious Disease Pharmacotherapy*, and coauthor of the *Infectious Diseases Handbook* and the *Drug Information Handbook for the Allied Health Professional* produced by Lexi-Comp, Inc. He also provides technical support to Lexi-Comp's Clinical Reference Library™ publications.

Dr Goldman is an active member of the Ohio College of Clinical Pharmacy, the Society of Infectious Disease Pharmacists, the American College of Clinical Pharmacy (and is a Fellow of the College), and the American Society of Health-Systems Pharmacists.

Leonard L. Lance, RPh, BSPharm

Leonard L. (Bud) Lance has been directly involved in the pharmaceutical industry since receiving his bachelor's degree in pharmacy from Ohio Northern University in 1970. Upon graduation from ONU, Mr Lance spent four years as a navy pharmacist in various military assignments and was instrumental in the development and operation of the first whole hospital I.V. admixture program in a military (Portsmouth Naval Hospital) facility.

After completing his military service, he entered the retail pharmacy field and has managed both an independent and a home I.V. franchise pharmacy operation. Since the late 1970s, Mr Lance has focused much of his interest on using computers to improve pharmacy service. The independent pharmacy he worked for was one of the first retail pharmacies in the State of Ohio to computerize (1977).

His love for computers and pharmacy lead him to Lexi-Comp, Inc. in 1988. He developed Lexi-Comp's first drug database in 1989 and was involved in the editing and publishing of Lexi-Comp's first *Drug Information Handbook* in 1990.

As a result of his strong publishing interest, he presently serves in the capacity of pharmacy editor and technical advisor as well as pharmacy (information) database coordinator for Lexi-Comp. Along with authoring the *Drug Information Handbook for the Allied Health Professional* and *Lippincott Williams & Wilkins Quick Look Drug Book*, he provides technical support to Lexi-Comp's reference publications. Mr Lance also assists approximately 200 major hospitals in producing their own formulary (pharmacy) publications through Lexi-Comp's custom publishing service.

Mr Lance is a member and past president (1984) of the Summit Pharmaceutical Association (SPA). He is also a member of the Ohio Pharmacists Association (OPA), the American Pharmaceutical Association (APhA), and the American Society of Health-System Pharmacists (ASHP).

EDITORIAL ADVISORY PANEL

EDITORIAL ADVISORY PANEL *(Continued)*

David S. Jacobs, MD
President, Pathologists Chartered
Consultant in Pathology and Laboratory Medicine
Overland Park, Kansas

Bernard L. Kasten, Jr, MD, FCAP
Vice-President/Chief Medical Officer
Quest Diagnostics Inc
Teteroboro, New Jersey

Polly E. Kintzel, PharmD, BCPS, BCOP
Clinical Specialist for Stem Cell Transplantation
Detroit Medical Center
Harper Hospital
Detroit, Michigan

Jill Kolesar, PharmD, FCCP, BCPS
Associate Professor of Pharmacy
University of Wisconsin
Madison, Wisconsin

Donna M. Kraus, PharmD, FAPhA
Associate Professor of Pharmacy Practice
Departments of Pharmacy Practice and Pediatrics
Pediatric Clinical Pharmacist
University of Illinois
Chicago, Illinois

Daniel L. Krinsky, RPh, MS
Director, Pharmacotherapy Sales and Marketing
Lexi-Comp, Inc
Hudson, Ohio

Kay Kyllonen, PharmD
Clinical Specialist
The Cleveland Clinic Children's Hospital
Cleveland, Ohio

Charles Lacy, RPh, PharmD, FCSHP
Facilitative Officer, Clinical Programs
Nevada College of Pharmacy
Las Vegas, Nevada

Brenda R. Lance, RN, MSN
Manager of Service Integration
Ritzman Infusion Services
Akron, Ohio

Leonard L. Lance, RPh, BSPharm
Clinical Pharmacist
Lexi-Comp Inc
Hudson, Ohio

Jerrold B. Leikin, MD, FACP, FACEP, FACMT, FAACT
Director, Medical Toxicology
Evanston Northwestern Healthcare-OMEGA
Glenbrook Hospital
Glenview, Illinois
Associate Director
Toxikon Consortium at Cook County Hospital
Chicago, Illinois
Professor of Medicine
Pharmacology and Health Systems Management
Rush Medical College
Chicago, Ilinois
Professor of Medicine
Feinberg School of Medicine
Northwestern University
Chicago, Ilinois

7

EDITORIAL ADVISORY PANEL *(Continued)*

A.J. (Fred) Remillard, PharmD
Assistant Dean, Research and Graduate Affairs
College of Pharmacy and Nutrition
University of Saskatchewan
Saskatoon, Saskatchewan

Martha Sajatovic, MD
Associate Professor of Psychiatry
Case Western Reserve University
Cleveland, Ohio

Todd P. Semla, PharmD
Associate Professor of Clinical Psychiatry
Feinberg School of Medicine
Northwestern University
Evanston, Illinois

Francis G. Serio, DMD, MS
Professor & Chairman
Department of Periodontics
University of Mississippi
Jackson, Mississippi

Stephen Shalansky, PharmD, FCSHP
Research Coordinator, Pharmacy Department
St Paul's Hospital
Vancouver, British Columbia

Dominic A. Solimando, Jr, MA
Oncology Pharmacist
President, Oncology Pharmacy Services, Inc
Arlington, VA

Joni Lombardi Stahura, BS, PharmD, RPh
Pharmacotherapy Specialist
Lexi-Comp, Inc
Hudson, Ohio

Carol K. Taketomo, PharmD
Pharmacy Manager
Children's Hospital of Los Angeles
Los Angeles, California

Mary Temple, PharmD
Pediatric Clinical Research Specialist
Hillcrest Hospital
Mayfield Heights, Ohio

Liz Tomsik, PharmD, BCPS
Pharmacotherapy Specialist
Lexi-Comp, Inc
Hudson, Ohio

Beatrice B. Turkoski, RN, PhD
Associate Professor, Graduate Faculty,
Advanced Pharmacology
College of Nursing
Kent State University
Kent, Ohio

Anne Marie Whelan, PharmD
College of Pharmacy
Dalhousie University
Halifax, Nova Scotia

Richard L. Wynn, PhD
Professor of Pharmacology
Baltimore College of Dental Surgery
Dental School
University of Maryland Baltimore
Baltimore, Maryland

PREFACE

Over the past decade, the Food and Drug Administration approved more than 300 new drugs and vaccines that prevent and treat over 150 conditions. Pharmaceutical companies have been working to dramatically advance the treatment of disease. At the end of 2002, 28% more medicines were being investigated by pharmaceutical companies for approval than was true the decade before. As we are all aware, innovative medicines save lives, relieve symptoms, and cure and prevent diseases. These drugs can also improve the quality of life by reducing the need for surgery and hospitalization, allowing people to stay with their families and in their communities for longer periods. They can also help people avoid disability and nursing home care, thus maintaining the individual's independence and autonomy. We are fortunate to live in an era where medications are readily available to prevent, treat, and cure a wide variety of conditions. With the great potential for continued pharmaceutical breakthroughs, new medications will continue to play an important role in improving the health of people the world over. Even as overall healthcare expenditures increase, drug therapies continue to represent a sensible option for the treatment of disease.

Along with new discoveries in drug treatments comes the need for each of us to be ever vigilant to stay abreast of these changes in the pharmaceutical armamentarium. As the world of pharmaceutical products expands, so does the increased potential for drug-related problems such as drug interactions, reactions, and mishaps. As such, it is our duty to analyze the potential risks along with the potential benefits these medications may produce. The enormous volume of available literature on pharmacotherapeutics continues to explode, which poses a significant challenge for all practitioners in healthcare.

It remains the goal of the authors of the *Drug Information Handbook, Pocket Edition* to provide you, the user, with the critical information currently available regarding these agents in a comprehensive, yet concise compendium, that is easy-to-use and practical to carry. With this explosion of information, it becomes even more important for a handbook to provide the depth desired and yet be able to stay within the required size constraints of portability. It is our goal to provide you with the most comprehensive collection of drug information that we can offer, with the hope that you can use it in your therapeutic decision-making.

— Charles F. Lacy, PharmD, FCSHP

ACKNOWLEDGMENTS

The *Drug Information Handbook, Pocket Edition* exists in its present form as the result of the concerted efforts of the following individuals: Robert D. Kerscher, publisher and president of Lexi-Comp, Inc; Mark Bonfiglio, PharmD, director of pharmacotherapy resources; Stacy S. Robinson, editorial manager; Barbara F. Kerscher, production manager; David C. Marcus, director of information systems; Kristin M. Thompson, product manager; Alexandra Hart, composition specialist; Tracey J. Henterly, graphic designer; and Julian I. Graubart, American Pharmaceutical Association (APhA), Director of Books and Electronic Products.

Special acknowledgment goes to all Lexi-Comp staff for their contributions to this handbook.

Much of the material contained in this book was a result of pharmacy contributors throughout the United States and Canada. Lexi-Comp has assisted many medical institutions to develop hospital-specific formulary manuals that contain clinical drug information as well as dosing. Working with these clinical pharmacists, hospital pharmacy and therapeutics committees, and hospital drug information centers, Lexi-Comp has developed an evolutionary drug database that reflects the practice of pharmacy in these major institutions.

In addition, the authors wish to thank their families, friends, and colleagues who supported them in their efforts to complete this handbook.

In particular, Dr Lacy would like to thank Kevin Landa for his assistance in composition evaluation and Edna M. Chan, RPh, PharmD, a clinical pharmacist at Children's Hospital of Los Angeles for her contribution as an editorial advisor.

DESCRIPTION OF SECTIONS AND FIELDS USED IN THIS HANDBOOK

The *Drug Information Handbook, Pocket Edition* is divided into four sections.

The first section is a compilation of introductory text pertinent to the use of this book.

The drug information section of the handbook, in which all drugs are listed alphabetically, details information pertinent to each drug. Extensive cross-referencing is provided by U.S. brand names and synonyms. Many combination monographs have been added to this edition; however, they have been condensed with only brand names and forms available. For more information on these products, see the individual components.

The third section is an extracted version of the *Drug Information Handbook, 12th Edition* appendix which offering a compilation of tables, guidelines, nomograms, algorithms, and conversion information which can be helpful when considering patient care.

The last section of this handbook contains a Therapeutic Category & Key Word Index which lists all drugs in this handbook in their unique therapeutic class; also listed are controlled substances by their restriction class.

The **Alphabetical Listing of Drugs** is presented in a consistent format and provides the following fields of information:

Generic Name	U.S. adopted name
Pronunciation	Phonetic pronunciation guide
Related Information	Cross-reference to other pertinent drug information found elsewhere in this handbook
U.S. Brand Names	Trade names (manufacturer-specific) found in the United States. The symbol [DSC] appears after trade names that have been recently discontinued.
Synonyms	Other names or accepted abbreviations of the generic drug
Therapeutic Category	Unique systematic classification of medications
Use	Information pertaining to appropriate FDA-approved indications of the drug.
Unlabeled/ Investigational Use	Information pertaining to non-FDA approved and investigational indications of the drug.
Restrictions	The controlled substance classification from the Drug Enforcement Agency (DEA). U.S. Schedules are I-V. Schedules vary by country and sometimes state (ie, Massachusetts uses I-VI)
Pregnancy Risk Factor	Five categories established by the FDA to indicate the potential of a systemically absorbed drug for causing birth defects.
Contraindications	Information pertaining to inappropriate use of the drug
Warnings/Precautions	Precautionary considerations, hazardous conditions related to use of the drug, and disease states or patient populations in which the drug should be cautiously used
Common Adverse Reactions	Only side effects >1% are included and are grouped by percentage of incidence (if known) and/or body system
Drug Interactions	
Cytochrome P450 Effect	Describes which cytochrome P450 enzymes are responsible for metabolizing the drug and/or which enzymes might be induced or inhibited by the drug.
Increased Effect/ Toxicity	Drug combinations that result in an increased or toxic therapeutic effect between the drug listed in the monograph and other drugs or drug classes.
Decreased Effect	Drug combinations that result in a decreased therapeutic effect between the drug listed in the monograph and other drugs or drug classes.
Mechanism of Action	How the drug works in the body to elicit a response

Pharmacodynamics/ Kinetics	The magnitude of a drug's effect depends on the drug concentration at the site of action. The pharmacodynamics are expressed in terms of onset of action and duration of action. Pharmacokinetics are expressed in terms of absorption, distribution (including appearance in breast milk and crossing of the placenta), protein binding, metabolism, bioavailability, half-life, time to peak serum concentration, and elimination.
Dosage	The amount of the drug to be typically given or taken during therapy for children and adults; also includes any dosing adjustment/comments for renal impairment or hepatic impairment and other suggested dosing adjustments (eg, hematological toxicity)
Administration	Information regarding the recommended final concentrations, rates of administration for parenteral drugs, or other guidelines when giving the medication
Monitoring Parameters	Laboratory tests and patient physical parameters that should be monitored for safety and efficacy of drug therapy
Reference Range	Therapeutic and toxic serum concentrations listed including peak and trough levels
Patient Information	Specific information pertinent for the patient
Dosage Forms	Information with regard to form and strength of the drug. Information is strung with the forms in all caps and bolded and uses the following abbreviations: AERO = aerosol; CAP = capsule; CONC = concentrate; CRM = cream; CRYST = crystals; ELIX = elixir; GRAN = granules; INF = infusion; INJ = injection; LIQ = liquid; LOZ = lozenge; OINT = ointment; SHAMP = shampoo; SOLN = solution; SUPP = suppository; SUSP = suspension; SYR = syrup; TAB = tablet.

FDA PREGNANCY CATEGORIES

Throughout this book there is a field labeled Pregnancy Risk Factor (PRF) and the letter A, B, C, D or X immediately following which signifies a category. The FDA has established these five categories to indicate the potential of a systemically absorbed drug for causing birth defects. The key differentiation among the categories rests upon the reliability of documentation and the risk:benefit ratio. Pregnancy Category X is particularly notable in that if any data exists that may implicate a drug as a teratogen and the risk:benefit ratio is clearly negative, the drug is contraindicated during pregnancy.

These categories are summarized as follows:

A   Controlled studies in pregnant women fail to demonstrate a risk to the fetus in the first trimester with no evidence of risk in later trimesters. The possibility of fetal harm appears remote.

B   Either animal-reproduction studies have not demonstrated a fetal risk but there are no controlled studies in pregnant women, or animal-reproduction studies have shown an adverse effect (other than a decrease in fertility) that was not confirmed in controlled studies in women in the first trimester and there is no evidence of a risk in later trimesters.

C   Either studies in animals have revealed adverse effects on the fetus (teratogenic or embryocidal effects or other) and there are no controlled studies in women, or studies in women and animals are not available. Drugs should be given only if the potential benefits justify the potential risk to the fetus.

D   There is positive evidence of human fetal risk, but the benefits from use in pregnant women may be acceptable despite the risk (eg, if the drug is needed in a life-threatening situation or for a serious disease for which safer drugs cannot be used or are ineffective).

X   Studies in animals or human beings have demonstrated fetal abnormalities or there is evidence of fetal risk based on human experience, or both, and the risk of the use of the drug in pregnant women clearly outweighs any possible benefit. The drug is contraindicated in women who are or may become pregnant.

SAFE WRITING

Health professionals and their support personnel frequently produce handwritten copies of information they see in print; therefore, such information is subjected to even greater possibilities for error or m sinterpretation on the part of others. Thus, particular care must be given to how drug names and strengths are expressed when creating written healthcare documents.

The following are a few examples of safe writing rules suggested by the Institute for Safe Medication Practices, Inc.*

1. There should be a space between a number and its units as it is easier to read. There should be no periods after the abbreviations mg or mL.

Correct	Incorrect
10 mg	10mg
100 mg	100mg

2. Never place a decimal and a zero after a whole number (2 mg is correct and 2.0 mg is **incorrect**). If the decimal point is not seen because it falls on a line or because individuals are working from copies where the decimal point is not seen, this causes a tenfold overdose.

3. Just the opposite is true for numbers less than one. Always place a zero before a naked decimal (0.5 mL is correct, .5 mL is **incorrect**).

4. Never abbreviate the word unit. The handwritten U or u, looks like a 0 (zero), and may cause a tenfold overdose error to be made.

5. IU is not a safe abbreviation for international units. The handwritten IU looks like IV. Write out international units or use int. units.

6. Q.D. is not a safe abbreviation for once daily, as when the Q is followed by a sloppy dot, it looks like QID which means four times daily.

7. O.D. is not a safe abbreviation for once daily, as it is properly interpreted as meaning "right eye" and has caused liquid medications such as saturated solution of potassium iodide and Lugol's solution to be administered incorrectly. There is no safe abbreviation for once daily. It must be written out in full.

8. Do not use chemical names such as 6-mercaptopurine or 6-thioguanine, as sixfold overdoses have been given when these were not recognized as chemical names. The proper names of these drugs are mercaptopurine or thioguanine.

9. Do not abbreviate drug names (5FC, 6MP, 5-ASA, MTX, HCTZ, CPZ, PBZ, etc) as they are misinterpreted and cause error.

10. Do not use the apothecary system or symbols.

11. Do not abbreviate microgram as μg; instead use mcg as there is less likelihood of misinterpretation.

12. When writing an outpatient prescription, write a complete prescription. A complete prescription can prevent the prescriber, the pharmacist, and/or the patient from making a mistake and can eliminate the need for further clarification. The legible prescriptions should contain:

    a. patient's full name

    b. for pediatric or geriatric patients: their age (or weight where applicable)

    c. drug name, dosage form and strength; if a drug is new or rarely prescribed, print this information

    d. number or amount to be dispensed

    e. complete instructions for the patient, including the purpose of the medication

    f. when there are recognized contraindications for a prescribed drug, indicate to the pharmacist that you are aware of this fact (ie, when prescribing a potassium salt for a patient receiving an ACE inhibitor, write "K serum level being monitored")

*From "Safe Writing" by Davis NM, PharmD and Cohen MR, MS, Lecturers and Consultants for Safe Medication Practices, 1143 Wright Drive, Huntington Valley, PA 19006. Phone: (215) 947-7566.

FDA NAME DIFFERENTIATION PROJECT
THE USE OF TALL-MAN LETTERS

Confusion between similar drug names is an important cause of medication errors. For years, The Institute For Safe Medication Practices (ISMP), has urged generic manufacturers to use a combination of large and small letters as well as bolding (ie, chlorpro**MAZINE** and chlorpro**PAMIDE**) to help distinguish drugs with look-alike names, especially when they share similar strengths. Recently the FDA's Division of Generic Drugs began to issue recommendation letters to manufacturers suggesting this novel way to label their products to help reduce this drug name confusion. Although this project has had marginal success, the method has successfully eliminated problems with products such as diphenhydr**AMINE** and dimenhy**DRINATE**. Hospitals should also follow suit by making similar changes in their own labels, preprinted order forms, computer screens and printouts, and drug storage location labels.

Lexi-Comp Medical Publishing will use "Tall-Man" letters for the drugs suggested by the FDA.

The following is a list of product names and recommended FDA revisions.

Drug Product	Recommended Revision
acetazolamide	aceta**ZOLAMIDE**
acetohexamide	aceto**HEXAMIDE**
bupropion	bu**PROP**ion
buspirone	bus**PIR**one
chlorpromazine	chlorpro**MAZINE**
chlorpropamide	chlorpro**PAMIDE**
clomiphene	clomi**PHENE**
clomipramine	clomi**PRAMINE**
cycloserine	cyclo**SERINE**
cyclosporine	cyclo**SPORINE**
daunorubicin	**DAUNO**rubicin
dimenhydrinate	dimenhy**DRINATE**
diphenhydramine	diphenhydr**AMINE**
dobutamine	**DOBUT**amine
dopamine	**DOP**amine
doxorubicin	**DOXO**rubicin
glipizide	glipi**ZIDE**
glyburide	gly**BURIDE**
hydralazine	hydr**ALAZINE**
hydroxyzine	hydr**OXY**zine
medroxyprogesterone	medroxy**PROGESTER**one
methylprednisolone	methyl**PREDNIS**olone
methyltestosterone	methyl**TESTOSTER**one
nicardipine	ni**CAR**dipine
nifedipine	**NIFE**dipine
prednisolone	predniso**LONE**
prednisone	predni**SONE**
sulfadiazine	sulfa**DIAZINE**
sulfisoxazole	sulfi**SOXAZOLE**
tolazamide	**TOLAZ**amide
tolbutamide	**TOLBUT**amide
vinblastine	vin**BLAS**tine
vincristine	vin**CRIS**tine

Institute for Safe Medication Practices. "New Tall-Man Lettering Will Reduce Mix-Ups Due to Generic Drug Name Confusion," *ISMP Medication Safety Alert*, September 19, 2001. Available at: http://www.ismp.org.

Institute for Safe Medication Practices. "Prescription Mapping, Can Improve Efficiency While Minimizing Errors With Look-Alike Products," *ISMP Medication Safety Alert*, October 6, 1999. Available at: http://www.ismp.org.

U.S. Pharmacopeia, "USP Quality Review: Use Caution-Avoid Confusion," March 2001, No. 76. Available at: http://www.usp.org.

ALPHABETICAL LISTING OF DRUGS

+ **1370-999-397** *see* Anagrelide *on page 99*
+ **A200® Lice [OTC]** *see* Permethrin *on page 984*
+ **A-200® Maximum Strength [OTC]** *see* Pyrethrins and Piperonyl Butoxide *on page 1065*
+ **A and D® Ointment [OTC]** *see* Vitamin A and Vitamin D *on page 1311*

Abacavir (a BAK a veer)
Related Information
Antiretroviral Therapy for HIV Infection *on page 1448*
Management of Healthcare Worker Exposures to HBV, HCV, and HIV *on page 1421*
U.S. Brand Names Ziagen®
Therapeutic Category Antiretroviral Agent, Nucleoside Reverse Transcriptase Inhibitor (NRTI) [Guanosine Analog]
Use Treatment of HIV infections in combination with other antiretroviral agents
Pregnancy Risk Factor C
Contraindications Hypersensitivity to abacavir (or carbovir) or any component of the formulation (do not rechallenge patients who have experienced hypersensitivity to abacavir); moderate-to-severe hepatic impairment
Warnings/Precautions Should always be used as a component of a multidrug regimen. Fatal hypersensitivity reactions have occurred. **Patients exhibiting symptoms of fever, skin rash, fatigue, respiratory symptoms (eg, pharyngitis, dyspnea, cough) and GI symptoms (eg, abdominal pain, nausea, vomiting) should discontinue therapy immediately and call for medical attention. Abacavir should be permanently discontinued if hypersensitivity cannot be ruled out, even when other diagnoses are possible. Abacavir SHOULD NOT be restarted because more severe symptoms may occur within hours, including LIFE-THREATENING HYPOTENSION AND DEATH. Fatal hypersensitivity reactions have occurred following the reintroduction of abacavir in patients whose therapy was interrupted (interruption in drug supply, temporary discontinuation while treating other conditions). Reactions occurred within hours. In some cases, signs of hypersensitivity may have been previously present, but attributed to other medical conditions (acute onset respiratory diseases, gastroenteritis, reactions to other medications). If abacavir is restarted following an interruption in therapy, evaluate the patient for previously unsuspected symptoms of hypersensitivity. Do not restart if hypersensitivity is suspected or if hypersensitivity cannot be ruled out. To report these events on abacavir hypersensitivity, a registry has been established (1-800-270-0425).** Use with caution in patients with mild hepatic dysfunction (contraindicated in moderate-to-severe dysfunction); prior liver disease, prolonged use, and obesity may be risk factors for development of lactic acidosis and severe hepatomegaly with steatosis.
Common Adverse Reactions Note: Hypersensitivity reactions, which may be fatal, occur in ~5% of patients (see Warnings/Precautions). Symptoms may include anaphylaxis, fever, rash (including erythema multiforme), fatigue, diarrhea, abdominal pain, respiratory symptoms (eg, pharyngitis, dyspnea, cough, adult respiratory distress syndrome, or respiratory failure), headache, malaise, lethargy, myalgia, myolysis, arthralgia, edema, paresthesia, nausea and vomiting, mouth ulcerations, conjunctivitis, lymphadenopathy, hepatic failure, and renal failure.

Rates of adverse reactions were defined during combination therapy with lamivudine. Adverse reaction rates attributable to abacavir alone are not available.

Adults:
  Central nervous system: Insomnia (7%)
  Endocrine & metabolic: Hyperglycemia, hypertriglyceridemia (25%)
  Gastrointestinal: Nausea (47%), vomiting (16%), diarrhea (12%), anorexia (11%), pancreatitis
  Neuromuscular & skeletal: Weakness
  Miscellaneous: Transaminases increased, hypersensitivity reaction (5%)
Children:
  Central nervous system: Fever (19%), headache (16%)
  Dermatologic: Rash (11%)
  Gastrointestinal: Nausea (38%), vomiting (38%), diarrhea (16%), anorexia (9%)
  Miscellaneous: Hypersensitivity reaction (5%)
Drug Interactions
Increased Effect/Toxicity: Ethanol may increase the risk of toxicity. Abacavir increases the blood levels of amprenavir. Abacavir may decrease the serum concentration of methadone in some patients. Concomitant use of ribavirin and nucleoside analogues may increase the risk of developing lactic acidosis (includes adefovir, didanosine, lamivudine, stavudine, zalcitabine, zidovudine).
Mechanism of Action Nucleoside reverse transcriptase inhibitor. Abacavir is a guanosine analogue which is phosphorylated to carbovir triphosphate which interferes with HIV viral RNA dependent DNA polymerase resulting in inhibition of viral replication.
Pharmacodynamics/Kinetics
Absorption: Rapid and extensive absorption
Distribution: V_d: 0.86 L/kg
Protein binding: 27% to 33%
Metabolism: Hepatic via alcohol dehydrogenase and glucuronyl transferase to inactive carboxylate and glucuronide metabolites
Bioavailability: 83%
Half-life elimination: 1.5 hours
Time to peak: 0.7-1.7 hours
Excretion: Primarily urine (as metabolites, 1.2% as unchanged drug); feces (16% total dose)

Dosage Oral:
> Children: 3 months to 16 years: 8 mg/kg body weight twice daily (maximum 300 mg twice daily) in combination with other antiretroviral agents
> Adults: 300 mg twice daily in combination with other antiretroviral agents
> **Dosage adjustment in hepatic impairment:**
>> Mild dysfunction (Child-Pugh score 5-6): 200 mg twice daily
>> Moderate-to-severe dysfunction: Safety and efficacy not established; use is contraindicated by the manufacturer

Administration May be administered with or without food.

Patient Information This is not a cure for HIV infection, nor will it reduce the risk of transmission to others. Long-term effects are not known. You will need frequent blood tests to adjust dosage for maximum therapeutic effect. Take as directed, for full course of therapy; do not discontinue (even if feeling better). You may experience headache or muscle pain or weakness. If you experience any of the following: Fever, skin rash, fatigue, nausea, vomiting, diarrhea, abdominal pain, contact your prescriber **immediately**. If you are instructed to stop the medication, **do not take this medication in the future.** Do not restart without specific instructions by your prescriber.

Dosage Forms SOLN, oral: 20 mg/mL (240 mL). **TAB:** 300 mg

Abacavir, Lamivudine, and Zidovudine
(a BAK a veer, la MI vyoo deen, & zye DOE vyoo deen)

U.S. Brand Names Trizivir®

Synonyms Azidothymidine, Abacavir, and Lamivudine; AZT, Abacavir, and Lamivudine; Compound S, Abacavir, and Lamivudine; Lamivudine, Abacavir, and Zidovudine; 3TC, Abacavir, and Zidovudine; ZDV, Abacavir, and Lamivudine; Zidovudine, Abacavir, and Lamivudine

Therapeutic Category Antiretroviral Agent, Reverse Transcriptase Inhibitor (Combination)

Use Treatment of HIV infection (either alone or in combination with other antiretroviral agents) in patients whose regimen would otherwise contain the components of Trizivir®

Pregnancy Risk Factor C

Dosage Oral: Adolescents and Adults: 1 tablet twice daily; **Note:** Not recommended for patients <40 kg
> **Dosage adjustment in renal impairment:** Because lamivudine and zidovudine require dosage adjustment in renal impairment, Trizivir® should not be used in patients with Cl_{cr} ≤50 mL/minute
> Elderly: Use with caution

Dosage Forms TAB, film coated: Abacavir 300 mg, lamivudine 150 mg, and zidovudine 300 mg

Abarelix (a ba REL iks)

U.S. Brand Names Plenaxis™

Therapeutic Category Gonadotropin Releasing Hormone Antagonist

Use Palliative treatment of advanced symptomatic prostate cancer; treatment is limited to men who are not candidates for LHRH therapy, refuse surgical castration, and have one or more of the following complications due to metastases or local encroachment: 1) risk of neurological compromise, 2) ureteral or bladder outlet obstruction, or 3) severe bone pain (persisting despite narcotic analgesia)

Restrictions Abarelix is not distributed through retail pharmacies. Prescribing and distribution of abarelix is limited to physicians and hospital pharmacies participating in the Plenaxis™ PLUS program. See Additional Information, or contact Praecis Pharmaceuticals at www.plenaxisplus.com or by calling 1-877-772-3247.

Pregnancy Risk Factor X

Contraindications Hypersensitivity to abarelix or any component of the formulation

Warnings/Precautions Has been associated with immediate-onset allergic reactions; may occur with initial dose and risk increases with duration of treatment. Observe for signs/symptoms of allergic reactions (which may include hypotension and/or syncope) for at least 30 minutes following each injection. Abarelix may cause prolongation of the QT interval; consider risk:benefit in patients with baseline QT_c values >450 msec or patients receiving concurrent medications which prolong the QT_c interval (class Ia and class III antiarrhythmics). Efficacy may diminish during prolonged treatment, particularly in patients weighing >225 pounds; monitor serum testosterone levels to identify treatment failures. Monitor transaminase levels and hepatic function during therapy. Extended treatment may result in a decrease in bone mineral density. Not indicated for use in women or children.

Common Adverse Reactions
> >10%:
>> Cardiovascular: Hot flushes (79%), peripheral edema (15%)
>> Central nervous system: Sleep disturbance (44%), pain (31%), dizziness (12%), headache (12%)
>> Endocrine & metabolic: Breast enlargement (30%), nipple discharge/tenderness (20%)
>> Gastrointestinal: Constipation (15%), diarrhea (11%)
>> Neuromuscular & skeletal: Back pain (17%)
>> Respiratory: Upper respiratory infection (12%)
> 1% to 10%:
>> Central nervous system: Fatigue (10%)
>> Endocrine & metabolic: Serum triglycerides increased (10%)
>> Gastrointestinal: Nausea (10%)

(Continued)

Abarelix *(Continued)*

Genitourinary: Dysuria (10%), micturition frequency (10%), urinary retention (10%), urinary tract infection (10%)

Hepatic: Transaminase levels increased (2% to 8%)

Miscellaneous: Allergic reactions (urticaria, pruritus, syncope, hypotension): risk increases with prolonged treatment (in clinical trials, cumulative risk increased from 0.5% at 56 days to 2.9% at 676 days of therapy)

Drug Interactions

Increased Effect/Toxicity: When used with other QT_c-prolonging agents, additive effects QT_c prolongation may occur with concurrent therapy. Life-threatening ventricular arrhythmias may result; example drugs include class Ia and class III antiarrhythmics, cisapride, selected quinolones, erythromycin, pimozide, mesoridazine, and thioridazine. Consider risk:benefit when deciding to initiate therapy in patients receiving these drugs.

Mechanism of Action Competes with naturally occurring GnRH for binding on receptors of the pituitary. Suppresses LH and FSH, resulting in decreased testosterone. Unlike LHRH agonists, does not induce an initial rise in serum testosterone.

Pharmacodynamics/Kinetics

Distribution: V_d: 4040 liters (± 1607)

Metabolism: Hepatic, via peptide hydrolysis

Half-life elimination: 13 days

Time to peak, serum: 3 days (following I.M. administration)

Excretion: Urine (13% unchanged drug)

Dosage I.M.: Male prostate cancer: 100 mg administered on days 1, 15, 29 (week 4), and every 4 weeks thereafter.

Monitor serum testosterone (to identify treatment failure) just prior to abarelix administration, beginning on day 29 and every 8 weeks thereafter.

Administration Administer intramuscularly (to the buttock); monitor for signs/symptoms of allergic reaction for at least 30 minutes after each injection

Monitoring Parameters Signs/symptoms of allergic reaction (for at least 30 minutes after each injection). Obtain transaminase levels at baseline and periodically during treatment. Serum testosterone (to identify treatment failure) just prior to abarelix administration, beginning on day 29 and every 8 weeks thereafter. PSA and bone mineral density may be monitored as needed.

Reference Range Efficacy is monitored by suppression of serum testosterone <50 ng/dL

Dosage Forms INJ, powder for reconstitution [preservative free]: 113 mg

♦ **Abbokinase®** *see Urokinase on page 1283*

♦ **Abbott-43818** *see Leuprolide on page 724*

♦ **Abbreviations and Measurements** *see page 1339*

♦ **ABCD** *see Amphotericin B Cholesteryl Sulfate Complex on page 90*

Abciximab *(ab SIK si mab)*

Related Information

Glycoprotein Antagonists *on page 1376*

U.S. Brand Names ReoPro®

Synonyms C7E3; 7E3

Therapeutic Category Antiplatelet Agent, Glycoprotein IIb/IIIa Inhibitor; Glycoprotein IIb/IIIa Inhibitor; Platelet Aggregation Inhibitor

Use Prevention of acute cardiac ischemic complications in patients at high risk for abrupt closure of the treated coronary vessel and patients at risk of restenosis; an adjunct with heparin to prevent cardiac ischemic complications in patients with unstable angina not responding to conventional therapy when a percutaneous coronary intervention is scheduled within 24 hours

Pregnancy Risk Factor C

Contraindications Hypersensitivity to abciximab, to murine proteins, or any component of the formulation; active internal hemorrhage or recent (within 6 weeks) clinically significant GI or GU bleeding; history of cerebrovascular accident within 2 years or cerebrovascular accident with significant neurological deficit; clotting abnormalities or administration of oral anticoagulants within 7 days unless prothrombin time (PT) is ≤1.2 times control PT value; thrombocytopenia (<100,000 cells/µL); recent (within 6 weeks) major surgery or trauma; intracranial tumor, arteriovenous malformation, or aneurysm; severe uncontrolled hypertension; history of vasculitis; use of dextran before PTCA or intent to use dextran during PTCA; concomitant use of another parenteral GP IIb/IIIa inhibitor

Warnings/Precautions Administration of abciximab is associated with a significantly increased frequency of major bleeding complications including retroperitoneal bleeding, spontaneous GI or GU bleeding and bleeding at the arterial access site

Clinical data indicate that the risk of major bleeding due to abciximab therapy may be elevated in the following settings:

Patients weighing <75 kilograms

Elderly patients (>65 years of age)

History of previous gastrointestinal disease

Recent thrombolytic therapy

Increased risk of hemorrhage during or following angioplasty is associated with the following factors; these risks may be additive to that associated with abciximab therapy:

Unsuccessful PTCA

PTCA procedure >70 minutes duration

PTCA performed within 12 hours of symptom onset for acute myocardial infarction

The safety and efficacy of readministering abciximab has not yet been established; administration of abciximab may result in human antichimeric antibody formation that can cause hypersensitivity reactions (including anaphylaxis), thrombocytopenia, or diminished efficacy. Anticoagulation, such as with heparin, may contribute to the risk of bleeding.

Common Adverse Reactions As with all drugs which may affect hemostasis, bleeding is associated with abciximab. Hemorrhage may occur at virtually any site. Risk is dependent on multiple variables, including the concurrent use of multiple agents which alter hemostasis and patient susceptibility.

>10%:
Cardiovascular: Hypotension (14%), chest pain (11%)
Gastrointestinal: Nausea (14%)
Hematologic: Minor bleeding (4% to 17%)
Neuromuscular & skeletal: Back pain (18%)
1% to 10%:
Cardiovascular: Bradycardia (5%), peripheral edema (2%)
Central nervous system: Headache (7%)
Gastrointestinal: Vomiting (7%), abdominal pain (3%)
Hematologic: Major bleeding (1% to 14%), thrombocytopenia: <100,000 cells/mm^3 (3% to 6%); <50,000 cells/mm^3 (0.4% to 2%)
Local: Injection site pain (4%)

Drug Interactions
Increased Effect/Toxicity: The risk of bleeding is increased when abciximab is given with heparin, other anticoagulants, thrombolytics, or antiplatelet drugs. However, aspirin and heparin were used concurrently in the majority of patients in the major clinical studies of abciximab. Allergic reactions may be increased in patients who have received diagnostic or therapeutic monoclonal antibodies due to the presence of HACA antibodies. Concomitant use of other glycoprotein IIb/IIIa antagonists is contraindicated.

Mechanism of Action Fab antibody fragment of the chimeric human-murine monoclonal antibody 7E3; this agent binds to platelet IIb/IIIa receptors, resulting in steric hindrance, thus inhibiting platelet aggregation

Pharmacodynamics/Kinetics Half-life elimination: ~30 minutes

Dosage I.V.: 0.25 mg/kg bolus administered 10-60 minutes before the start of intervention followed by an infusion of 0.125 mcg/kg/minute (to a maximum of 10 mcg/minute) for 12 hours
Patients with unstable angina not responding to conventional medical therapy and who are planning to undergo percutaneous coronary intervention within 24 hours may be treated with abciximab 0.25 mg/kg intravenous bolus followed by an 18- to 24-hour intravenous infusion of 10 mcg/minute, concluding 1 hour after the percutaneous coronary intervention.

Administration Abciximab is intended for coadministration with aspirin postangioplasty and heparin infused and weight adjusted to maintain a therapeutic bleeding time (eg, ACT 300-500 seconds)

Bolus dose: Aseptically withdraw the necessary amount of abciximab (2 mg/mL) for the bolus dose through a 0.22-micron filter into a syringe; the bolus should be administered 10-60 minutes before the procedure

Continuous infusion: Aseptically withdraw 4.5 mL (9 mg) of abciximab for the infusion through a 0.22 micron filter into a syringe; inject this into 250 mL of NS or D$_5$W to make a solution with a final concentration of 35 mcg/mL. Infuse at a rate of 17 mL/hour (10 mcg/minute) for 12 hours via pump; **filter all infusions**.

Monitoring Parameters Prothrombin time, activated partial thromboplastin time, hemoglobin, hematocrit, platelet count, fibrinogen, fibrin split products, transfusion requirements, signs of hypersensitivity reactions, guaiac stools, and Hematix® urine

Dosage Forms INJ, solution: 2 mg/mL (5 mL)

♦ **Abelcet**® see Amphotericin B (Lipid Complex) on page 92
♦ **Abilify**™ see Aripiprazole on page 114
♦ **ABLC** see Amphotericin B (Lipid Complex) on page 92
♦ **A/B Otic** see Antipyrine and Benzocaine on page 107
♦ **Abreva**® [OTC] see Docosanol on page 397
♦ **Absorbine Jr.**® **Antifungal [OTC]** see Tolnaftate on page 1241

Acarbose (AY car bose)
Related Information
Hypoglycemic Drugs & Thiazolidinedione Information on page 1378
U.S. Brand Names Precose®
Therapeutic Category Alpha-Glucosidase Inhibitor; Antidiabetic Agent, Alpha-glucosidase Inhibitor; Hypoglycemic Agent, Oral
Use
Monotherapy, as indicated as an adjunct to diet to lower blood glucose in patients with type 2 diabetes mellitus (noninsulin dependent, NIDDM) whose hyperglycemia cannot be managed on diet alone
Combination with a sulfonylurea, metformin, or insulin in patients with type 2 diabetes mellitus (noninsulin dependent, NIDDM) when diet plus acarbose do not result in adequate glycemic control. The effect of acarbose to enhance glycemic control is additive to that of other hypoglycemic agents when used in combination.
Pregnancy Risk Factor B
(Continued)

Acarbose *(Continued)*

Contraindications Hypersensitivity to acarbose or any component of the formulation; patients with diabetic ketoacidosis or cirrhosis; patients with inflammatory bowel disease, colonic ulceration, partial intestinal obstruction, or in patients predisposed to intestinal obstruction; patients who have chronic intestinal diseases associated with marked disorders of digestion or absorption, and in patients who have conditions that may deteriorate as a result of increased gas formation in the intestine

Warnings/Precautions Acarbose may increase the hypoglycemic potential of sulfonylureas. Oral glucose (dextrose) should be used in the treatment of mild to moderate hypoglycemia. Severe hypoglycemia may require the use of either intravenous glucose infusion or glucagon injection.

Treatment-emergent elevations of serum transaminases (AST and/or ALT) occurred in 15% of acarbose-treated patients in long-term studies. These serum transaminase elevations appear to be dose related. At doses >100 mg 3 times/day, the incidence of serum transaminase elevations greater than 3 times the upper limit of normal was 2-3 times higher in the acarbose group than in the placebo group. These elevations were asymptomatic, reversible, more common in females, and, in general, were not associated with other evidence of liver dysfunction.

When diabetic patients are exposed to stress such as fever, trauma, infection, or surgery, a temporary loss of control of blood glucose may occur. At such times, temporary insulin therapy may be necessary.

Common Adverse Reactions >10%:

Gastrointestinal: Abdominal pain (21%) and diarrhea (33%) tend to return to pretreatment levels over time, and the frequency and intensity of flatulence (77%) tend to abate with time

Hepatic: Elevated liver transaminases

Drug Interactions

Increased Effect/Toxicity: Acarbose may increase the risk of hypoglycemia when used with oral hypoglycemics. See Warnings/Precautions.

Decreased Effect: The effect of acarbose is antagonized/decreased by thiazide and related diuretics, corticosteroids, phenothiazines, thyroid products, estrogens, oral contraceptives, phenytoin, nicotinic acid, sympathomimetics, calcium channel-blocking drugs, isoniazid, intestinal adsorbents (eg, charcoal), and digestive enzyme preparations (eg, amylase, pancreatin). Acarbose decreases the absorption/serum concentration of digoxin.

Mechanism of Action Competitive inhibitor of pancreatic α-amylase and intestinal brush border α-glucosidases, resulting in delayed hydrolysis of ingested complex carbohydrates and disaccharides and absorption of glucose; dose-dependent reduction in postprandial serum insulin and glucose peaks; inhibits the metabolism of sucrose to glucose and fructose

Pharmacodynamics/Kinetics

Absorption: <2% as active drug

Metabolism: Exclusively via GI tract, principally by intestinal bacteria and digestive enzymes; 13 metabolites identified

Bioavailability: Low systemic bioavailability of parent compound; acts locally in GI tract

Excretion: Urine (~34%)

Dosage Oral:

Adults: Dosage must be individualized on the basis of effectiveness and tolerance while not exceeding the maximum recommended dose

Initial dose: 25 mg 3 times/day with the first bite of each main meal

Maintenance dose: Should be adjusted at 4- to 8-week intervals based on 1-hour postprandial glucose levels and tolerance. Dosage may be increased from 25 mg 3 times/day to 50 mg 3 times/day. Some patients may benefit from increasing the dose to 100 mg 3 times/day.

Maintenance dose ranges: 50-100 mg 3 times/day.

Maximum dose:

≤60 kg: 50 mg 3 times/day

>60 kg: 100 mg 3 times/day

Patients receiving sulfonylureas: Acarbose given in combination with a sulfonylurea will cause a further lowering of blood glucose and may increase the hypoglycemic potential of the sulfonylurea. If hypoglycemia occurs, appropriate adjustments in the dosage of these agents should be made.

Dosing adjustment in renal impairment: Cl_{cr} <25 mL/minute: Peak plasma concentrations were 5 times higher and AUCs were 6 times larger than in volunteers with normal renal function; however, long-term clinical trials in diabetic patients with significant renal dysfunction have not been conducted and treatment of these patients with acarbose is not recommended.

Administration Should be administered with the first bite of each main meal.

Monitoring Parameters Postprandial glucose, glycosylated hemoglobin levels, serum transaminase levels should be checked every 3 months during the first year of treatment and periodically thereafter

Patient Information Take this medication exactly as directed, with the first bite of each main meal. It is important to continue to adhere to dietary instructions, a regular exercise program, and regular testing of urine and/or blood glucose. The risk of hypoglycemia, its symptoms and treatment, and conditions that predispose to its development should be well understood by patients and responsible family members. A source of glucose (dextrose) should be readily available to treat symptoms of low blood glucose when taking acarbose in combination with a sulfonylurea or insulin. If side effects occur, they usually develop during the first few weeks of therapy and are most often mild to moderate gastrointestinal effects, such as flatulence, diarrhea, or abdominal discomfort and generally diminish in frequency and intensity with time.

Dosage Forms TAB: 25 mg, 50 mg, 100 mg

Acebutolol (a se BYOO toe lole)

Related Information
Beta-Blockers Comparison *on page 1368*

U.S. Brand Names Sectral®

Synonyms Acebutolol Hydrochloride

Therapeutic Category Antiarrhythmic Agent, Class II; Antihypertensive Agent; Beta Blocker, Intrinsic Sympathomimetic Activity (ISA)

Use Treatment of hypertension, ventricular arrhythmias, angina

Pregnancy Risk Factor B (manufacturer); D (2nd and 3rd trimesters - expert analysis)

Contraindications Hypersensitivity to beta-blocking agents; uncompensated congestive heart failure; cardiogenic shock; bradycardia or second- and third-degree heart block (except in patients with a functioning artificial pacemaker); sinus node dysfunction; pregnancy (2nd and 3rd trimesters)

Warnings/Precautions Abrupt withdrawal of drug **should be avoided.** May result in an exaggerated cardiac responsiveness such as tachycardia, hypertension, ischemia, angina, myocardial infarction, and sudden death. It is recommended that patients be gradually tapered off beta-blockers (over a 2-week period) rather than via abrupt discontinuation. Although acebutolol primarily blocks beta$_1$-receptors, high doses can result in beta$_2$-receptor blockage. Use with caution in diabetic patients. Beta-blockers may impair glucose tolerance, potentiate hypoglycemia, and/or mask symptoms of hypoglycemia in a diabetic patient. Use with caution in bronchospastic lung disease and renal dysfunction (especially the elderly). Beta-blockers with intrinsic sympathomimetic activity do not appear to be of benefit in CHF and should be avoided. See Dosage - Renal/Hepatic Impairment.

Common Adverse Reactions
>10%: Central nervous system: Fatigue (11%)
1% to 10%:
   Cardiovascular: Chest pain (2%), edema (2%), bradycardia, hypotension, CHF
   Central nervous system: Headache (6%), dizziness (6%), insomnia (3%), depression (2%), abnormal dreams (2%), anxiety, hyperesthesia, hypoesthesia, impotence
   Dermatologic: Rash (2%), pruritus
   Gastrointestinal: Constipation (4%), diarrhea (4%), dyspepsia (4%), nausea (4%), flatulence (3%), vomiting, abdominal pain
   Genitourinary: Micturition frequency (3%), dysuria, nocturia, impotence (2%)
   Neuromuscular & skeletal: Arthralgia (2%), myalgia (2%), back pain, joint pain
   Ocular: Abnormal vision (2%), conjunctivitis, dry eyes, eye pain
   Respiratory: Dyspnea (4%), rhinitis (2%), cough (1%), pharyngitis, wheezing

Potential adverse effects (based on experience with other beta-blocking agents) include reversible mental depression, disorientation, catatonia, short-term memory loss, emotional lability, slightly clouded sensorium, laryngospasm, respiratory distress, allergic reactions, erythematous rash, agranulocytosis, purpura, thrombocytopenia, mesenteric artery thrombosis, ischemic colitis, alopecia, Peyronie's disease, claudication

Drug Interactions
Cytochrome P450 Effect: Inhibits CYP2D6 (weak)

Increased Effect/Toxicity: Acebutolol may increase the effects of other drugs which slow AV conduction (digoxin, verapamil, diltiazem), alpha-blockers (prazosin, terazosin), and alpha-adrenergic stimulants (epinephrine, phenylephrine). Acebutolol may mask the tachycardia from hypoglycemia caused by insulin and oral hypoglycemics. In patients receiving concurrent therapy, the risk of hypertensive crisis is increased when either clonidine or the beta-blocker is withdrawn. Reserpine has been shown to enhance the effect of acebutolol. Beta-blockers may increase the action or levels of ethanol, disopyramide, nondepolarizing muscle relaxants, and theophylline although the effects are difficult to predict.

Decreased Effect: Decreased effect of acebutolol with aluminum salts, barbiturates, calcium salts, cholestyramine, colestipol, NSAIDs, penicillins (ampicillin), rifampin, and salicylates due to decreased bioavailability and plasma levels. The effect of sulfonylureas may be decreased by beta-blockers; however, the decreased effect has not been shown with tolbutamide.

Mechanism of Action Competitively blocks beta$_1$-adrenergic receptors with little or no effect on beta$_2$-receptors except at high doses; exhibits membrane stabilizing and intrinsic sympathomimetic activity

Pharmacodynamics/Kinetics
Onset of action: 1-2 hours
Duration: 12-24 hours
Absorption: Oral: 40%
(Continued)

Acebutolol (Continued)

Protein binding: 5% to 15%
Metabolism: Extensive first-pass effect
Half-life elimination: 6-7 hours
Time to peak: 2-4 hours
Excretion: Feces (~55%); urine (35%)

Dosage Oral:

Adults:

Hypertension: 400-800 mg/day (larger doses may be divided); maximum: 1200 mg/day
Ventricular arrhythmias: Initial: 400 mg/day; maintenance: 600-1200 mg/day in divided doses

Elderly: Initial: 200-400 mg/day; dose reduction due to age related decrease in Cl_{cr} will be necessary; do not exceed 800 mg/day

Dosing adjustment in renal impairment:

Cl_{cr} 25-49 mL/minute/1.73 m^2: Reduce dose by 50%.
Cl_{cr} <25 mL/minute/1.73 m^2: Reduce dose by 75%.

Dosing adjustment in hepatic impairment: Use with caution.

Administration To discontinue therapy, taper dose gradually. May be administered without regard to meals.

Monitoring Parameters Blood pressure, orthostatic hypotension, heart rate, CNS effects, ECG

Patient Information Do not discontinue abruptly; consult pharmacist or prescriber before taking with other adrenergic drugs (eg, cold medications); notify prescriber if CHF symptoms become worse or if other side effects occur; take at the same time each day; use with caution while driving or performing tasks requiring alertness; may mask signs of hypoglycemia in diabetics; may be taken without regard to meals

Dosage Forms CAP: 200 mg, 400 mg

♦ **Acebutolol Hydrochloride** see Acebutolol on page 23

♦ **Aceon®** see Perindopril Erbumine on page 983

♦ **Acephen® [OTC]** see Acetaminophen on page 24

Acetaminophen (a seet a MIN oh fen)

Related Information

Acetaminophen Toxicity Nomogram on page 1499

U.S. Brand Names Acephen® [OTC]; Aspirin Free Anacin® Maximum Strength [OTC]; Cetafen® [OTC]; Cetafen Extra® [OTC]; Comtrex® Sore Throat Maximum Strength [OTC]; ElixSure™ Fever/Pain [OTC]; Feverall® [OTC]; Genapap® [OTC]; Genapap® Children [OTC]; Genapap® Extra Strength [OTC]; Genapap® Infant [OTC]; Genebs® [OTC]; Genebs® Extra Strength [OTC]; Mapap® [OTC]; Mapap® Arthritis [OTC]; Mapap® Children's [OTC]; Mapap® Extra Strength [OTC]; Mapap® Infants [OTC]; Redutemp® [OTC]; Silapap® Children's [OTC]; Silapap® Infants [OTC]; Tylenol® [OTC]; Tylenol® 8 Hour [OTC]; Tylenol® Arthritis Pain [OTC]; Tylenol® Children's [OTC]; Tylenol® Extra Strength [OTC]; Tylenol® Infants [OTC]; Tylenol® Junior Strength [OTC]; Tylenol® Sore Throat [OTC]; Valorin [OTC]; Valorin Extra [OTC]

Synonyms APAP; N-Acetyl-P-Aminophenol; Paracetamol

Therapeutic Category Analgesic, Non-narcotic; Antimigraine Agent, Prophylaxis; Antipyretic

Use Treatment of mild to moderate pain and fever (antipyretic/analgesic); does not have anti-rheumatic or anti-inflammatory effects

Pregnancy Risk Factor B

Contraindications Hypersensitivity to acetaminophen or any component of the formulation

Warnings/Precautions May cause severe hepatic toxicity on acute overdose; in addition, chronic daily dosing in adults of 5-8 g of acetaminophen over several weeks or 3-4 g/day of acetaminophen for one year have resulted in liver damage. Use with caution in patients with alcoholic liver disease; consuming ≥3 alcoholic drinks/day may increase the risk of liver damage. Use caution in patients with known G6PD deficiency.

OTC labeling: When used for self-medication, patients should be instructed to contact healthcare provider if used for fever lasting >3 days or for pain lasting >10 days in adults or >5 days in children.

Common Adverse Reactions Frequency not defined.

Dermatologic: Rash
Endocrine & metabolic: May increase chloride, uric acid, glucose; may decrease sodium, bicarbonate, calcium
Hematologic: Anemia; blood dyscrasias (neutropenia, pancytopenia, leukopenia)
Hepatic: May increase bilirubin, alkaline phosphatase
Renal: May increase ammonia, nephrotoxicity with chronic overdose, analgesic nephropathy
Miscellaneous: Hypersensitivity reactions (rare)

Drug Interactions

Cytochrome P450 Effect: Substrate (minor) of CYP1A2, 2A6, 2C8/9, 2D6, 2E1, 3A4; **Inhibits** CYP3A4 (weak)

Increased Effect/Toxicity: Barbiturates, carbamazepine, hydantoins, isoniazid, rifampin, sulfinpyrazone may increase the hepatotoxic potential of acetaminophen; chronic ethanol abuse increases risk for acetaminophen toxicity; effect of warfarin may be enhanced

Decreased Effect: Barbiturates, carbamazepine, hydantoins, rifampin, sulfinpyrazone may decrease the analgesic effect of acetaminophen; cholestyramine may decrease acetaminophen absorption (separate dosing by at least 1 hour)

Mechanism of Action Inhibits the synthesis of prostaglandins in the central nervous system and peripherally blocks pain impulse generation; produces antipyresis from inhibition of hypothalamic heat-regulating center

Pharmacodynamics/Kinetics

Onset of action: <1 hour

Duration: 4-6 hours

Absorption: Incomplete; varies by dosage form

Protein binding: 8% to 43% at toxic doses

Metabolism: At normal therapeutic dosages, hepatic to sulfate and glucuronide metabolites, while a small amount is metabolized by CYP to a highly reactive intermediate (acetylimidoquinone) which is conjugated with glutathione and inactivated; at toxic doses (as little as 4 g daily) glutathione conjugation becomes insufficient to meet the metabolic demand causing an increase in acetylimidoquinone concentration, which may cause hepatic cell necrosis

Half-life elimination: Prolonged following toxic doses

Neonates: 2-5 hours

Adults: 1-3 hours

Time to peak, serum: Oral: 10-60 minutes; may be delayed in acute overdoses

Excretion: Urine (2% to 5% unchanged); 55% as glucuronide metabolites; 30% as sulphate metabolites)

Dosage Oral, rectal:

Children <12 years: 10-15 mg/kg/dose every 4-6 hours as needed; do **not** exceed 5 doses (2.6 g) in 24 hours; alternatively, the following age-based doses may be used; see table.

Acetaminophen Dosing

Age	Dosage (mg)	Age	Dosage (mg)
0-3 mo	40	4-5 y	240
4-11 mo	80	6-8 y	320
1-2 y	120	9-10 y	400
2-3 y	160	11 y	480

Note: Higher rectal doses have been studied for use in preoperative pain control in children. However, specific guidelines are not available and dosing may be product dependent. The safety and efficacy of alternating acetaminophen and ibuprofen dosing has not been established.

Adults: 325-650 mg every 4-6 hours or 1000 mg 3-4 times/day; do **not** exceed 4 g/day

Dosing interval in renal impairment:

Cl$_{cr}$ 10-50 mL/minute: Administer every 6 hours

Cl$_{cr}$ <10 mL/minute: Administer every 8 hours (metabolites accumulate)

Hemodialysis: Moderately dialyzable (20% to 50%)

Dosing adjustment/comments in hepatic impairment: Use with caution. Limited, low-dose therapy usually well tolerated in hepatic disease/cirrhosis. However, cases of hepatotoxicity at daily acetaminophen dosages <4 g/day have been reported. Avoid chronic use in hepatic impairment.

Administration

Suppositories: Do not freeze

Suspension, oral: Shake well before pouring a dose

Monitoring Parameters Relief of pain or fever

Reference Range

Therapeutic concentration (analgesic/antipyretic): 10-30 µg/mL

Toxic concentration (acute ingestion) with probable hepatotoxicity: >200 µg/mL at 4 hours or 50 µg/mL at 12 hours after ingestion

Dosage Forms CAP: 500 mg. **CAPLET:** 500 mg. **CAPLET, extended release:** 650 mg. **ELIX:** 160 mg/5 mL (120 mL, 480 mL, 3780 mL). **GELCAP:** 500 mg. **GELTAB:** 500 mg. **GELTAB, extended release:** 650 mg. **LIQ, oral:** 160 mg/5 mL (120 mL, 240 mL, 480 mL); 500 mg/15 mL (120 mL, 240 mL). **SOLN, oral drops:** 80 mg/0.8 mL (15 mL, 30 mL). **SOLN, oral:** 160 mg/5 mL (120 mL, 480 mL). **SUPP, rectal:** 120 mg, 325 mg, 650 mg. **SUSP, oral:** 160 mg/5 mL (120 mL, 240 mL). **SUSP, oral drops:** 80 mg/0.8 mL (15 mL, 30 mL). **SYR, oral:** 160 mg/5 mL (120 mL). **TAB:** 325 mg, 500 mg. **TAB, chewable:** 80 mg, 160 mg

♦ **Acetaminophen and Chlorpheniramine** *see* Chlorpheniramine and Acetaminophen *on page 262*

Acetaminophen and Codeine (a seet a MIN oh fen & KOE deen)

U.S. Brand Names Capital® and Codeine; Tylenol® With Codeine

Synonyms Codeine and Acetaminophen

Therapeutic Category Analgesic Combination, Narcotic

Use Relief of mild to moderate pain

Restrictions C-III; C-V

Pregnancy Risk Factor C

Dosage Doses should be adjusted according to severity of pain and response of the patient. Adult doses ≥60 mg codeine fail to give commensurate relief of pain but merely prolong analgesia and are associated with an appreciably increased incidence of side effects. Oral:

Children: Analgesic:

Codeine: 0.5-1 mg codeine/kg/dose every 4-6 hours

(Continued)

Acetaminophen and Codeine *(Continued)*

Acetaminophen: 10-15 mg/kg/dose every 4 hours up to a maximum of 2.6 g/24 hours for children <12 years; **alternatively, the following can be used:**

3-6 years: 5 mL 3-4 times/day as needed of elixir

7-12 years: 10 mL 3-4 times/day as needed of elixir

>12 years: 15 mL every 4 hours as needed of elixir

Adults:

Antitussive: Based on codeine (15-30 mg/dose) every 4-6 hours (maximum: 360 mg/24 hours based on codeine component)

Analgesic: Based on codeine (30-60 mg/dose) every 4-6 hours (maximum: 4000 mg/24 hours based on acetaminophen component)

Dosing adjustment in renal impairment: See individual monographs for Acetaminophen and Codeine

Dosage Forms ELIX, oral [C-V]: Acetaminophen 120 mg and codeine phosphate 12 mg per 5 mL (5 mL, 10 mL, 12.5 mL, 15 mL, 120 mL, 480 mL); (Tylenol® with Codeine) [DSC]: Acetaminophen 120 mg and codeine phosphate 12 mg per 5 mL (480 mL). **SUSP, oral** [C-V] (Capital® and Codeine): Acetaminophen 120 mg and codeine phosphate 12 mg per 5 mL (480 mL). **TAB** [C-III]: #2: Acetaminophen 300 mg and codeine phosphate 15 mg; #3 (Tylenol® with Codeine): Acetaminophen 300 mg and codeine phosphate 30 mg; #4 (Tylenol® with Codeine): Acetaminophen 300 mg and codeine phosphate 60 mg

Acetaminophen and Diphenhydramine

(a seet a MIN oh fen & dye fen HYE dra meen)

U.S. Brand Names Anacin PM Aspirin Free [OTC] [DSC]; Excedrin® P.M. [OTC]; Goody's PM® Powder; Legatrin PM® [OTC]; Percogesic® Extra Strength [OTC]; Tylenol® PM Extra Strength [OTC]; Tylenol® Severe Allergy [OTC]

Synonyms Diphenhydramine and Acetaminophen

Therapeutic Category Analgesic, Non-narcotic and Antihistamine

Use Aid in the relief of insomnia accompanied by minor pain

Dosage Oral: Adults: 50 mg of diphenhydramine HCl (76 mg diphenhydramine citrate) at bedtime or as directed by physician; do not exceed recommended dosage; not for use in children <12 years of age

Dosage Forms CAPLET: Acetaminophen 500 mg and diphenhydramine 12.5 mg; acetaminophen 500 mg and diphenhydramine 25 mg; acetaminophen 500 mg and diphenhydramine citrate 38 mg; acetaminophen 500 mg and diphenhydramine 50 mg. **GELCAP:** Acetaminophen 500 mg and diphenhydramine 25 mg. **GELTAB:** Acetaminophen 500 mg and diphenhydramine hydrochloride 25 mg; acetaminophen 500 mg and diphenhydramine citrate 38 mg. **POWDER, oral solution:** Acetaminophen 500 mg and diphenhydramine citrate 38 mg. **TAB:** Acetaminophen 500 mg and diphenhydramine hydrochloride 25 mg; acetaminophen 500 mg and diphenhydramine citrate 38 mg

♦ **Acetaminophen and Hydrocodone** *see* Hydrocodone and Acetaminophen *on page 627* *on page 627*

♦ **Acetaminophen and Oxycodone** *see* Oxycodone and Acetaminophen *on page 945* *on page 945*

Acetaminophen and Phenyltoloxamine

(a seet a MIN oh fen & fen il to LOKS a meen)

U.S. Brand Names Genesec® [OTC]; Percogesic® [OTC]; Phenylgesic® [OTC]

Synonyms Phenyltoloxamine and Acetaminophen

Therapeutic Category Analgesic, Non-narcotic

Use Relief of mild to moderate pain

Pregnancy Risk Factor B

Dosage Oral:

Analgesic: Based on acetaminophen component:

Children: 10-15 mg/kg/dose every 4-6 hours as needed; do **not** exceed 5 doses/24 hours

Adults: 325-650 every 4-6 hours as needed; do **not** exceed 4 g/day

Product labeling:

Percogesic®:

Children 6-12 years: 1 tablet every 4 hours; do **not** exceed 4 tablets/24 hours

Adults: 1-2 tablets every 4 hours; do **not** exceed 8 tablets/24 hours

Dosage Forms TAB: Acetaminophen 325 mg and phenyltoloxamine citrate 30 mg

Acetaminophen and Pseudoephedrine

(a seet a MIN oh fen & soo doe e FED rin)

U.S. Brand Names Alka-Seltzer Plus® Cold and Sinus Liquigels [OTC]; Cetafen Cold® [OTC]; Genapap™ Sinus Maximum Strength [OTC]; Mapap Sinus Maximum Strength [OTC]; Medi-Synal [OTC]; Ornex® [OTC]; Ornex® Maximum Strength [OTC]; Sinus-Relief® [OTC]; Sinutab® Sinus [OTC]; Sudafed® Sinus and Cold [OTC]; Sudafed® Sinus Headache [OTC]; SudoGest Sinus [OTC]; Tylenol® Cold, Infants [OTC]; Tylenol® Sinus, Children's [OTC]; Tylenol® Sinus Day Non-Drowsy [OTC]

Synonyms Pseudoephedrine and Acetaminophen

Therapeutic Category Alpha/Beta Agonist

Use Relief of mild to moderate pain; relief of congestion

Dosage Oral:

Analgesic: Based on acetaminophen component:

Children: 10-15 mg/kg/dose every 4-6 hours as needed; do **not** exceed 5 doses in 24 hours

Adults: 325-650 mg every 4-6 hours as needed; do **not** exceed 4 g/day

Decongestant: Based on pseudoephedrine component:
Children:
2-6 years: 15 mg every 4 hours; do **not** exceed 90 mg/day
6-12 years: 30 mg every 4 hours; do **not** exceed 180 mg/day
Children >12 years and Adults: 60 mg every 4 hours; do **not** exceed 360 mg/day
Product labeling:
Alka-Seltzer Plus® Cold and Sinus:
Children 6-12 years: 1 dose with water every 4 hours (maximum: 4 doses/24 hours)
Adults: 2 doses with water every 4 hours (maximum: 4 doses/24 hours)
Children's Tylenol® Sinus: Children:
Liquid:
2-5 years (24-47 lb): 1 teaspoonful every 4-6 hours (maximum: 4 doses/24 hours)
6-11 years (48-95 lb): 2 teaspoonfuls every 4-6 hours (maximum: 4 doses/24 hours)
Tablet, chewable:
2-5 years (24-47 lb): 2 tablets every 4-6 hours (maximum: 4 doses/24 hours)
6-11 years (48-95 lb): 4 tablets every 4-6 hours (maximum: 4 doses/24 hours)
Sinutab® Sinus: Children >12 years and Adults: 2 doses every 6 hours (maximum: 8 doses/24 hours)
Dosage Forms CAP, liquid: Acetaminophen 325 mg and pseudoephedrine 30 mg. **CAPLET:** Acetaminophen 325 mg and pseudoephedrine 30 mg; acetaminophen 500 mg and pseudoephedrine 30 mg. **GELCAP:** Acetaminophen 500 mg and pseudoephedrine 30 mg. **GELTAB:** Acetaminophen 500 mg and pseudoephedrine 30 mg. **SUSP:** Acetaminophen 160 mg and pseudoephedrine 15 mg/5 mL. **LIQ, oral drops:** Acetaminophen 80 mg/0.8 mL and pseudoephedrine 7.5 mg/0.8 mL. **TAB:** Acetaminophen 325 mg and pseudoephedrine 30 mg; acetaminophen 500 mg and pseudoephedrine 30 mg

Acetaminophen and Tramadol (a seet a MIN oh fen & TRA ma dole)

U.S. Brand Names Ultracet™
Synonyms APAP and Tramadol; Tramadol Hydrochloride and Acetaminophen
Therapeutic Category Analgesic, Non-narcotic
Use Short-term (≤5 days) management of acute pain
Pregnancy Risk Factor C
Dosage Oral: Adults: Acute pain: Two tablets every 4-6 hours as needed for pain relief (maximum: 8 tablets/day); treatment should not exceed 5 days
Dosage adjustment in renal impairment: Cl_{cr} <30 mL/minute: Maximum of 2 tablets every 12 hours; treatment should not exceed 5 days
Dosage adjustment in hepatic impairment: Not recommended.
Dosage Forms TAB: Acetaminophen 325 mg and tramadol 37.5 mg

Acetaminophen, Aspirin, and Caffeine

(a seet a MIN oh fen, AS pir in, & KAF een)
U.S. Brand Names Excedrin® Extra Strength [OTC]; Excedrin® Migraine [OTC]; Fem-Prin® [OTC]; Genaced™ [OTC]; Goody's® Extra Strength Headache Powder [OTC]; Goody's® Extra Strength Pain Relief [OTC]; Pain-Off [OTC]; Vanquish® Extra Strength Pain Reliever [OTC]
Synonyms Aspirin, Acetaminophen, and Caffeine; Caffeine and Acetaminophen; Caffeine, Acetaminophen, and Aspirin; Caffeine, Aspirin, and Acetaminophen
Therapeutic Category Analgesic, Non-narcotic
Use Relief of mild to moderate pain; mild to moderate pain associated with migraine headache
Pregnancy Risk Factor D
Dosage Oral: Adults:
Analgesic:
Based on **acetaminophen** component:
Mild to moderate pain: 325-650 mg every 4-6 hours as needed; do **not** exceed 4 g/day
Mild to moderate pain associated with migraine headache: 500 mg/dose (in combination with 500 mg aspirin and 130 mg caffeine) every 6 hours while symptoms persist; do not use for longer than 48 hours
Based on **aspirin** component:
Mild to moderate pain: 325-650 mg every 4-6 hours as needed; do **not** exceed 4 g/day
Mild to moderate pain associated with migraine headache: 500 mg/dose (in combination with 500 mg acetaminophen and 130 mg caffeine) every 6 hours; do not use for longer than 48 hours

Product labeling:
Excedrin® Extra Strength, Excedrin® Migraine: Children >12 years and Adults: 2 doses every 6 hours (maximum: 8 doses/24 hours)
Note: When used for migraine, do not use for longer than 48 hours
Goody's® Extra Strength Headache Powder: Children >12 years and Adults: 1 powder, placed on tongue or dissolved in water, every 4-6 hours (maximum: 4 powders/24 hours)
Goody's® Extra Strength Pain Relief Tablets: Children >12 years and Adults: 2 tablets every 4-6 hours (maximum: 8 tablets/24 hours)
Vanquish® Extra Strength Pain Reliever: Children >12 years and Adults: 2 tablets every 4 hours (maximum: 12 tablets/24 hours)
Dosage Forms CAPLET: Acetaminophen 194 mg, aspirin 227 mg, and caffeine 33 mg; acetaminophen 250 mg, aspirin 250 mg, and caffeine 65 mg. **GELTAB:** Acetaminophen 250 mg, aspirin 250 mg, and caffeine 65 mg. **POWDER:** Acetaminophen 260 mg, aspirin 520 mg, and caffeine 32.5 mg. **TAB:** Acetaminophen 250 mg, aspirin 250 mg, and caffeine 65 mg

♦ **Acetaminophen, Butalbital, and Caffeine** *see Butalbital, Acetaminophen, and Caffeine on page 194*

♦ **Acetaminophen, Caffeine, Hydrocodone, Chlorpheniramine, and Phenylephrine** *see Hydrocodone, Chlorpheniramine, Phenylephrine, Acetaminophen, and Caffeine on page 632*

Acetaminophen, Chlorpheniramine, and Pseudoephedrine
(a seet a MIN oh fen, klor fen IR a meen, & soo doe e FED rin)

U.S. Brand Names Actifed® Cold and Sinus [OTC]; Alka-Seltzer® Plus Cold Liqui-Gels® [OTC]; Children's Tylenol® Plus Cold [OTC]; Comtrex® Maximum Strength Sinus and Nasal Decongestant [OTC]; Sinutab® Sinus Allergy Maximum Strength [OTC]; Thera-Flu® Cold and Sore Throat Night Time [OTC]; Tylenol® Allergy Sinus [OTC]

Synonyms Acetaminophen, Pseudoephedrine, and Chlorpheniramine; Chlorpheniramine, Acetaminophen, and Pseudoephedrine; Chlorpheniramine, Pseudoephedrine, and Acetaminophen; Pseudoephedrine, Acetaminophen, and Chlorpheniramine; Pseudoephedrine, Chlorpheniramine, and Acetaminophen

Therapeutic Category Antihistamine; Antihistamine/Decongestant/Analgesic

Use Temporary relief of sinus symptoms

Pregnancy Risk Factor B

Dosage Oral:
Analgesic: Based on **acetaminophen** component:
Children: 10-15 mg/kg/dose every 4-6 hours as needed; do **not** exceed 5 doses in 24 hours
Adults: 325-650 mg every 4-6 hours as needed; do **not** exceed 4 g/day
Antihistamine: Based on **chlorpheniramine maleate** component:
Children:
2-6 years: 1 mg every 4-6 hours (maximum: 6 mg/24 hours)
6-12 years: 2 mg every 4-6 hours (maximum: 12 mg/24 hours)
Children >12 years and Adults: 4 mg every 4-6 hours (maximum: 24 mg/24 hours)
Decongestant: Based on **pseudoephedrine** component:
Children:
2-6 years: 15 mg every 4 hours (maximum: 90 mg/24 hours)
6-12 years: 30 mg every 4 hours (maximum: 180 mg/24 hours)
Children >12 years and Adults: 60 mg every 4 hours (maximum: 360 mg/24 hours)

Product labeling:
Alka-Seltzer® Plus Cold Medicine Liqui-Gels®:
Children 6-12 years: 1 softgel every 4 hours with water (maximum: 4 doses/24 hours)
Children >12 years and Adults: 2 softgels every 4 hours with water (maximum: 4 doses/24 hours)
Sinutab® Sinus Allergy Maximum Strength: Children >12 years and Adults: 2 tablets/caplets every 6 hours (maximum: 8 doses/24 hours)
Thera-Flu® Cold and Sore Throat Night Time: Children >12 years and Adults: 1 packet dissolved in hot water every 6 hours (maximum: 4 packets/24 hours)

Dosage Forms CAP, liquid: Acetaminophen 325 mg, chlorpheniramine 2 mg, and pseudoephedrine 30 mg. **CAPLET:** Acetaminophen 500 mg, chlorpheniramine 2 mg, and pseudoephedrine 30 mg. **GELCAP:** Acetaminophen 500 mg, chlorpheniramine 2 mg, and pseudoephedrine 30 mg. **GELTAB:** Acetaminophen 500 mg, chlorpheniramine 2 mg, and pseudoephedrine 30 mg. **LIQ:** Acetaminophen 160 mg, chlorpheniramine 1 mg, and pseudoephedrine 15 mg per 5 mL (120 mL). **POWDER, oral solution** [packet]: Acetaminophen 650 mg, chlorpheniramine 4 mg, and pseudoephedrine 60 mg. **TAB:** Acetaminophen 500 mg, chlorpheniramine 2 mg, and pseudoephedrine 30 mg. **TAB, chewable:** Acetaminophen 80 mg, chlorpheniramine 0.5 mg, and pseudoephedrine 7.5 mg

Acetaminophen, Dextromethorphan, and Pseudoephedrine
(a seet a MIN oh fen, deks troe meth OR fan, & soo doe e FED rin)

U.S. Brand Names Alka-Seltzer® Plus Flu Liqui-Gels® [OTC]; Comtrex® Non-Drowsy Cold and Cough Relief [OTC]; Contac® Severe Cold and Flu/Non-Drowsy [OTC]; Infants' Tylenol® Cold Plus Cough Concentrated Drops [OTC]; Sudafed® Severe Cold [OTC]; Thera-Flu® Severe Cold Non-Drowsy [OTC] [DSC]; Triaminic® Cough and Sore Throat Formula [OTC]; Tylenol® Cold Day Non-Drowsy [OTC]; Tylenol® Flu Non-Drowsy Maximum Strength [OTC]; Vicks® DayQuil® Multi-Symptom Cold and Flu [OTC]

Synonyms Dextromethorphan, Acetaminophen, and Pseudoephedrine; Pseudoephedrine, Acetaminophen, and Dextromethorphan; Pseudoephedrine, Dextromethorphan, and Acetaminophen

Therapeutic Category Antihistamine

Use Treatment of mild to moderate pain and fever; symptomatic relief of cough and congestion

Dosage Oral:
Analgesic: Based on acetaminophen component:
Children: 10-15 mg/kg/dose every 4-6 hours as needed; do **not** exceed 5 doses/24 hours
Adults: 325-650 mg every 4-7 hours as needed; do **not** exceed 4 g/day
Cough suppressant: Based on dextromethorphan component:
Children 6-12 years: 15 mg every 6-8 hours; do **not** exceed 60 mg/24 hours
Children >12 years and Adults: 10-20 mg every 4-8 hours **or** 30 mg every 8 hours; do **not** exceed 120 mg/24 hours
Decongestant: Based on pseudoephedrine component:
Children:
2-6 years: 15 mg every 4 hours (maximum: 90 mg/24 hours)
6-12 years: 30 mg every 4 hours (maximum: 180 mg/24 hours)
Children >12 years and Adults: 60 mg every 4 hours (maximum: 360 mg/24 hours)

Product labeling:
Alka-Seltzer Plus® Cold and Flu Liqui-Gels®:
  Children 6-12 years: 1 dose every 4 hours (maximum: 4 doses/24 hours)
  Children >12 years and Adults: 2 dose every 4 hours (maximum: 4 doses/24 hours)
Infants' Tylenol® Cold Plus Cough Concentrated Drops: Children 2-3 years (24-55 lb): 2 dropperfuls every 4-6 hours (maximum: 4 doses/24 hours)
Sudafed® Severe Cold, Thera-Flu® Non-Drowsy Maximum Strength (gelcap), Tylenol® Flu Non-Drowsy Maximum Strength: Children >12 years and Adults: 2 every 6 hours (maximum: 8 doses/24 hours)
Tylenol® Cold Non-Drowsy:
  Children 6-11 years: 1 dose every 6 hours (maximum: 4 doses/24 hours)
  Children ≥12 years and Adults: 2 doses every 6 hours (maximum: 8 doses/24 hours)
Thera-Flu® Non-Drowsy Maximum Strength: Children >12 years and Adults: 1 packet dissolved in hot water every 6 hours (maximum: 4 packets/24 hours)

Dosage Forms CAP, liquid: Acetaminophen 250 mg, dextromethorphan 10 mg, and pseudoephedrine 30 mg; acetaminophen 325 mg, dextromethorphan 10 mg, and pseudoephedrine 30 mg. **CAPLET:** Acetaminophen 325 mg, dextromethorphan 15 mg, and pseudoephedrine 30 mg; acetaminophen 500 mg, dextromethorphan 15 mg, and pseudoephedrine 30 mg. **DROPS, oral concentrate:** Acetaminophen 160 mg, dextromethorphan 5 mg, and pseudoephedrine 15 mg per 1.6 mL (15 mL). **GELCAP:** Acetaminophen 325 mg, dextromethorphan 15 mg, and pseudoephedrine 30 mg; acetaminophen 500 mg, dextromethorphan 15 mg, and pseudoephedrine 30 mg. **LIQ:** Acetaminophen 160 mg, dextromethorphan 7.5 mg, and pseudoephedrine 15 mg per 5 mL (120 mL, 240 mL); acetaminophen 325 mg, dextromethorphan 10 mg, and pseudoephedrine 30 mg per 15 mL (175 mL). **POWDER, oral solution** [packet]: Acetaminophen 1000 mg, dextromethorphan 30 mg, and pseudoephedrine 60 mg. **TAB:** Acetaminophen 325 mg, dextromethorphan 15 mg, and pseudoephedrine 30 mg

♦ **Acetaminophen, Dichloralphenazone, and Isometheptene** see Acetaminophen, Isometheptene, and Dichloralphenazone on page 29

Acetaminophen, Isometheptene, and Dichloralphenazone
(a seet a MIN oh fen, eye soe me THEP teen, & dye KLOR al FEN a zone)
U.S. Brand Names I.D.A.; Midrin®; Migrin-A
Synonyms Acetaminophen, Dichloralphenazone, and Isometheptene; Dichloralphenazone, Acetaminophen, and Isometheptene; Dichloralphenazone, Isometheptene, and Acetaminophen; Isometheptene, Acetaminophen, and Dichloralphenazone; Isometheptene, Dichloralphenazone, and Acetaminophen
Therapeutic Category Analgesic, Non-narcotic; Antimigraine Agent, Prophylaxis
Use Relief of migraine and tension headache
Restrictions C-IV
Pregnancy Risk Factor B
Dosage Oral: Adults:
  Migraine headache: 2 capsules to start, followed by 1 capsule every hour until relief is obtained (maximum: 5 capsules/12 hours)
  Tension headache: 1-2 capsules every 4 hours (maximum: 8 capsules/24 hours)
Dosage Forms CAP: Acetaminophen 325 mg, isometheptene mucate 65 mg, dichloralphenazone 100 mg

♦ **Acetaminophen, Pseudoephedrine, and Chlorpheniramine** see Acetaminophen, Chlorpheniramine, and Pseudoephedrine on page 28
♦ **Acetaminophen Toxicity Nomogram** see page 1499
♦ **Acetasol® HC** see Acetic Acid, Propylene Glycol Diacetate, and Hydrocortisone on page 31

AcetaZOLAMIDE (a set a ZOLE a mide)
Related Information
  Anticonvulsants by Seizure Type on page 1358
  Epilepsy on page 1477
  Glaucoma Drug Therapy Comparison on page 1481
  Sulfonamide Derivatives on page 1404
U.S. Brand Names Diamox® Sequels®
Therapeutic Category Anticonvulsant, Miscellaneous; Carbonic Anhydrase Inhibitor; Diuretic, Carbonic Anhydrase Inhibitor
Use Treatment of glaucoma (chronic simple open-angle, secondary glaucoma, preoperatively in acute angle-closure); drug-induced edema or edema due to congestive heart failure (adjunctive therapy); centrencephalic epilepsies (immediate release dosage form); prevention or amelioration of symptoms associated with acute mountain sickness
Unlabeled/Investigational Use Urine alkalinization; respiratory stimulant in COPD
Pregnancy Risk Factor C
Contraindications Hypersensitivity to acetazolamide, sulfonamides, or any component of the formulation; hepatic disease or insufficiency; decreased sodium and/or potassium levels; adrenocortical insufficiency, cirrhosis; hyperchloremic acidosis, severe renal disease or dysfunction; severe pulmonary obstruction; long-term use in noncongestive angle-closure glaucoma
Warnings/Precautions Use in impaired hepatic function may result in coma. Use with caution in patients with respiratory acidosis and diabetes mellitus. Impairment of mental alertness and/or physical coordination may occur. Chemical similarities are present among sulfonamides, sulfonylureas, carbonic anhydrase inhibitors, thiazides, and loop diuretics (except ethacrynic acid). Use in patients with sulfonamide allergy is specifically contraindicated in product
(Continued)

AcetaZOLAMIDE *(Continued)*

labeling, however, a risk of cross-reaction exists in patients with allergy to any of these compounds; avoid use when previous reaction has been severe.

I.M. administration is painful because of the alkaline pH of the drug; use by this route is not recommended

Drug may cause substantial increase in blood glucose in some diabetic patients; malaise and complaints of tiredness and myalgia are signs of excessive dosing and acidosis in the elderly

Common Adverse Reactions Frequency not defined.

Cardiovascular: Flushing

Central nervous system: Ataxia, confusion, convulsions, depression, dizziness, drowsiness, excitement, fatigue, headache, malaise

Dermatologic: Allergic skin reactions, photosensitivity, Stevens-Johnson syndrome, toxic epidermal necrolysis, urticaria

Endocrine & metabolic: Electrolyte imbalance, growth retardation (children), hyperglycemia, hypoglycemia, hypokalemia, hyponatremia, metabolic acidosis

Gastrointestinal: Appetite decreased, diarrhea, melena, nausea, taste alternation, vomiting

Genitourinary: Crystalluria, glycosuria, hematuria, polyuria, renal failure

Hematologic: Agranulocytosis, aplastic anemia, leukopenia, thrombocytopenia, thrombocytopenic purpura

Hepatic: Cholestatic jaundice, fulminant hepatic necrosis, hepatic insufficiency, liver function tests abnormal

Neuromuscular & skeletal: Flaccid paralysis, paresthesia

Ocular: Myopia

Otic: Hearing disturbance, tinnitus

Miscellaneous: Anaphylaxis

Drug Interactions

Cytochrome P450 Effect: Inhibits CYP3A4 (weak)

Increased Effect/Toxicity: Concurrent use with diflunisal may increase the effect of acetazolamide causing a significant decrease in intraocular pressure. Cyclosporine concentrations may be increased by acetazolamide. Salicylate use may result in carbonic anhydrase inhibitor accumulation and toxicity. Acetazolamide-induced hypokalemia may increase the risk of toxicity with digoxin.

Decreased Effect: Use of acetazolamide may increase lithium excretion and alter excretion of other drugs by alkalinization of urine (eg, amphetamines, quinidine, methenamine, salicylates). Primidone serum concentrations may be decreased.

Mechanism of Action Reversible inhibition of the enzyme carbonic anhydrase resulting in reduction of hydrogen ion secretion at renal tubule and an increased renal excretion of sodium, potassium, bicarbonate, and water to decrease production of aqueous humor; also inhibits carbonic anhydrase in central nervous system to retard abnormal and excessive discharge from CNS neurons

Pharmacodynamics/Kinetics

Onset of action: Capsule, extended release: 2 hours; I.V.: 2 minutes

Peak effect: Capsule, extended release: 8-12 hours; I.V.: 15 minutes; Tablet: 2-4 hours

Duration: Inhibition of aqueous humor secretion: Capsule, extended release: 18-24 hours; I.V.: 4-5 hours; Tablet: 8-12 hours

Distribution: Erythrocytes, kidneys; blood-brain barrier and placenta; distributes into milk (~30% of plasma concentrations)

Excretion: Urine (70% to 100% as unchanged drug)

Dosage Note: I.M. administration is not recommended because of pain secondary to the alkaline pH

Children:

Glaucoma:

Oral: 8-30 mg/kg/day or 300-900 mg/m^2/day divided every 8 hours

I.V.: 20-40 mg/kg/24 hours divided every 6 hours, not to exceed 1 g/day

Edema: Oral, I.V.: 5 mg/kg or 150 mg/m^2 once every day

Epilepsy: Oral: 8-30 mg/kg/day in 1-4 divided doses, not to exceed 1 g/day; sustained release capsule is not recommended for treatment of epilepsy

Adults:

Glaucoma:

Chronic simple (open-angle): Oral: 250 mg 1-4 times/day or 500 mg sustained release capsule twice daily

Secondary, acute (closed-angle): I.V.: 250-500 mg, may repeat in 2-4 hours to a maximum of 1 g/day

Edema: Oral, I.V.: 250-375 mg once daily

Epilepsy: Oral: 8-30 mg/kg/day in 1-4 divided doses; **sustained release capsule is not recommended for treatment of epilepsy**

Mountain sickness: Oral: 250 mg every 8-12 hours (or 500 mg extended release capsules every 12-24 hours)

Therapy should begin 24-48 hours before and continue during ascent and for at least 48 hours after arrival at the high altitude

Urine alkalinization (unlabeled use): Oral: 5 mg/kg/dose repeated 2-3 times over 24 hours

Respiratory stimulant in COPD (unlabeled use): Oral, I.V.: 250 mg twice daily

Elderly: Oral: Initial: 250 mg twice daily; use lowest effective dose

Dosing adjustment in renal impairment:

Cl_{cr} 10-50 mL/minute: Administer every 12 hours

Cl_{cr} <10 mL/minute: Avoid use (ineffective)

Hemodialysis: Moderately dialyzable (20% to 50%)

Peritoneal dialysis: Supplemental dose is not necessary

Administration Oral: May cause an alteration in taste, especially carbonated beverages; short-acting tablets may be crushed and suspended in cherry or chocolate syrup to disguise the bitter taste of the drug, do not use fruit juices, alternatively submerge tablet in 10 mL of hot water and add 10 mL honey or syrup

Monitoring Parameters Intraocular pressure, potassium, serum bicarbonate; serum electrolytes, periodic CBC with differential

Patient Information Report numbness or tingling of extremities; do not crush, chew, or swallow contents of long-acting capsule, but may be opened and sprinkled on soft food; ability to perform tasks requiring mental alertness and/or physical coordination may be impaired; take with food; drug may cause substantial increase in blood glucose in some diabetic patients

Dosage Forms CAP, sustained release (Diamox® Sequels®): 500 mg. **INJ, powder for reconstitution:** 500 mg. **TAB:** 125 mg, 250 mg

Acetic Acid (a SEE tik AS id)

U.S. Brand Names VoSol®

Synonyms Ethanoic Acid

Therapeutic Category Antibacterial, Otic; Antibacterial, Topical; Topical Skin Product

Use Irrigation of the bladder; treatment of superficial bacterial infections of the external auditory canal

Pregnancy Risk Factor C

Dosage

Irrigation (note dosage of an irrigating solution depends on the capacity or surface area of the structure being irrigated):

For continuous irrigation of the urinary bladder with 0.25% acetic acid irrigation, the rate of administration will approximate the rate of urine flow; usually 500-1500 mL/24 hours

For periodic irrigation of an indwelling urinary catheter to maintain patency, about 50 mL of 0.25% acetic acid irrigation is required

Otic: Insert saturated wick; keep moist 24 hours; remove wick and instill 5 drops 3-4 times/day

Dosage Forms SOLN, irrigation: 0.25% (250 mL, 500 mL, 1000 mL). **SOLN, otic** (VōSol®): 2% (15 mL)

♦ **Acetic Acid and Aluminum Acetate Otic** *see* Aluminum Acetate and Acetic Acid *on page 66*

♦ **Acetic Acid, Hydrocortisone, and Propylene Glycol Diacetate** *see* Acetic Acid, Propylene Glycol Diacetate, and Hydrocortisone *on page 31*

Acetic Acid, Propylene Glycol Diacetate, and Hydrocortisone

(a SEE tik AS id, PRO pa leen GLY kole dye AS e tate, & hye droe KOR ti sone)

U.S. Brand Names Acetasol® HC; VōSoL® HC

Synonyms Acetic Acid, Hydrocortisone, and Propylene Glycol Diacetate; Hydrocortisone, Acetic Acid, and Propylene Glycol Diacetate; Hydrocortisone, Propylene Glycol Diacetate, and Acetic Acid; Propylene Glycol Diacetate, Acetic Acid, and Hydrocortisone; Propylene Glycol Diacetate, Hydrocortisone, and Acetic Acid

Therapeutic Category Antibiotic/Corticosteroid, Otic

Use Treatment of superficial infections of the external auditory canal caused by organisms susceptible to the action of the antimicrobial, complicated by swelling

Dosage Adults: Otic: Instill 4 drops in ear(s) 3-4 times/day

Dosage Forms SOLN, otic drops: Acetic acid 2%, propylene glycol 3%, and hydrocortisone 1% (10 mL)

AcetoHEXAMIDE (a set oh HEKS a mide)

Related Information

Hypoglycemic Drugs & Thiazolidinedione Information *on page 1378*

Sulfonamide Derivatives *on page 1404*

Synonyms Dymelor [DSC]

Therapeutic Category Antidiabetic Agent, Sulfonylurea; Hypoglycemic Agent, Oral; Sulfonylurea Agent

Use Adjunct to diet for the management of mild to moderately severe, stable, type 2 diabetes mellitus (noninsulin dependent, NIDDM)

Pregnancy Risk Factor D

Dosage Oral: Adults (elderly patients may be more sensitive and should be started at a lower dosage initially):

Initial: 250 mg/day; increase in increments of 250-500 mg daily at intervals of 5-7 days up to 1.5 g/day. Patients on ≤1 g/day can be controlled with once daily administration. Patients receiving 1.5 g/day usually benefit from twice daily administration before the morning and evening meals. Doses >1.5 g daily are not recommended.

Dosing adjustment in renal impairment: Cl_{cr} <50 mL/minute: Not recommended due to increased potential for developing hypoglycemia

Dosing adjustment in hepatic impairment: Initiate therapy at lower than recommended doses; further dosage adjustment may be necessary because acetohexamide is extensively metabolized but no specific guidelines are available

Dosage Forms TAB: 250 mg, 500 mg

♦ **Acetoxymethylprogesterone** *see* MedroxyPROGESTERone *on page 781*

Acetylcholine (a se teel KOE leen)

U.S. Brand Names Miochol-E®

Synonyms Acetylcholine Chloride

Therapeutic Category Cholinergic Agent; Cholinergic Agent, Ophthalmic; Ophthalmic Agent, Miotic

Use Produces complete miosis in cataract surgery, keratoplasty, iridectomy and other anterior segment surgery where rapid miosis is required

Pregnancy Risk Factor C

Contraindications Hypersensitivity to acetylcholine chloride or any component of the formulation; acute iritis and acute inflammatory disease of the anterior chamber

Warnings/Precautions Systemic effects rarely occur but can cause problems for patients with acute cardiac failure, bronchial asthma, peptic ulcer, hyperthyroidism, GI spasm, urinary tract obstruction, and Parkinson's disease; open under aseptic conditions only

Common Adverse Reactions Frequency not defined.

Cardiovascular: Bradycardia, hypotension, flushing

Central nervous system: Headache

Ocular: Altered distance vision, decreased night vision, transient lenticular opacities

Respiratory: Dyspnea

Miscellaneous: Diaphoresis

Drug Interactions

Increased Effect/Toxicity: Effect may be prolonged or enhanced in patients receiving tacrine.

Decreased Effect: May be decreased with flurbiprofen and suprofen, ophthalmic.

Mechanism of Action Causes contraction of the sphincter muscles of the iris, resulting in miosis and contraction of the ciliary muscle, leading to accommodation spasm

Pharmacodynamics/Kinetics

Onset of action: Rapid

Duration: ~10 minutes

Dosage Adults: Intraocular: 0.5-2 mL of 1% injection (5-20 mg) instilled into anterior chamber before or after securing one or more sutures

Administration Open under aseptic conditions only.

Patient Information May sting on instillation; use caution while driving at night or performing hazardous tasks; do not touch dropper to eye

Dosage Forms POWDER, intraocular solution: 1:100 [10 mg/mL] (2 mL)

♦ **Acetylcholine Chloride** see Acetylcholine on page 32

Acetylcysteine (a se teel SIS teen)

U.S. Brand Names Mucomyst®; Mucosil™ [DSC]

Synonyms Acetylcysteine Sodium; Mercapturic Acid; NAC; N-Acetylcysteine; N-Acetyl-L-cysteine

Therapeutic Category Antidote, Acetaminophen; Mucolytic Agent

Use Adjunctive mucolytic therapy in patients with abnormal or viscid mucous secretions in acute and chronic bronchopulmonary diseases; pulmonary complications of surgery and cystic fibrosis; diagnostic bronchial studies; antidote for acute acetaminophen toxicity (oral)

Unlabeled/Investigational Use Prevention of radiocontrast-induced renal dysfunction (oral); antidote for acute acetaminophen toxicity (I.V.)

Pregnancy Risk Factor B

Contraindications Hypersensitivity to acetylcysteine or any component of the formulation

Warnings/Precautions Since increased bronchial secretions may develop after inhalation, percussion, postural drainage and suctioning should follow; if bronchospasm occurs, administer a bronchodilator; discontinue acetylcysteine if bronchospasm progresses

Common Adverse Reactions

Inhalation:

>10%:

Stickiness on face after nebulization

Miscellaneous: Unpleasant odor during administration

1% to 10%:

Central nervous system: Drowsiness, chills, fever

Gastrointestinal: Vomiting, nausea, stomatitis

Local: Irritation

Respiratory: Bronchospasm, rhinorrhea, hemoptysis

Miscellaneous: Clamminess

Systemic:

1% to 10%:

Central nervous system: Fever, drowsiness

Gastrointestinal: Nausea, vomiting

Drug Interactions

Decreased Effect: Adsorbed by activated charcoal; clinical significance is minimal, though, once a pure acetaminophen ingestion requiring N-acetylcysteine is established; further charcoal dosing is unnecessary once the appropriate initial charcoal dose is achieved (5-10 g:g acetaminophen)

Mechanism of Action Exerts mucolytic action through its free sulfhydryl group which opens up the disulfide bonds in the mucoproteins thus lowering mucous viscosity. The exact mechanism of action in acetaminophen toxicity is unknown; thought to act by providing substrate for conjugation with the toxic metabolite.

Pharmacodynamics/Kinetics

Onset of action: Inhalation: 5-10 minutes
Duration: Inhalation: >1 hour
Distribution: Oral: 0.33-0.47 L/kg
Protein binding, plasma: Oral: 50%
Half-life elimination: Reduced acetylcysteine: 2 hours; Total acetylcysteine: 5.5 hours
Time to peak, plasma: Oral: 1-2 hours
Excretion: Urine

Dosage

Acetaminophen poisoning: Children and Adults:
Oral: 140 mg/kg; followed by 17 doses of 70 mg/kg every 4 hours; repeat dose if emesis occurs within 1 hour of administration; therapy should continue until all doses are administered even though the acetaminophen plasma level has dropped below the toxic range
I.V. (unlabeled): Loading dose: 140 mg/kg, followed by 70 mg/kg every 4 hours, for a total of 13 doses (loading dose and 48 hours of treatment); infuse each dose over 1 hour
Inhalation: Acetylcysteine 10% and 20% solution (Mucomyst®) (dilute 20% solution with sodium chloride or sterile water for inhalation); 10% solution may be used undiluted
Infants: 1-2 mL of 20% solution or 2-4 mL 10% solution until nebulized given 3-4 times/day
Children: 3-5 mL of 20% solution or 6-10 mL of 10% solution until nebulized given 3-4 times/day
Adolescents: 5-10 mL of 10% to 20% solution until nebulized given 3-4 times/day
Note: Patients should receive an aerosolized bronchodilator 10-15 minutes prior to acetylcysteine
Meconium ileus equivalent: Children and Adults: 100-300 mL of 4% to 10% solution by irrigation or orally
Prevention of radiocontrast-induced renal dysfunction (unlabeled use): Adults: Oral: 600 mg twice daily for 2 days (beginning the day before the procedure); may be given as powder in capsules, some centers use solution (diluted in cola beverage or juice). Hydrate patient with saline concurrently.

Administration Recommended procedure for I.V. administration of oral N-acetylcysteine:
Obtain informed consent.
Using D$_5$W, dilute acetylcysteine 20% oral solution to a 3% solution.
Administer loading dose of NAC: 140 mg/kg infused through a peripheral intravenous catheter over 1 hour using an in-line 0.2-µ millipore filter
Administer maintenance doses of NAC (first maintenance dose 4 hours after initiating the loading dose): 70 mg/kg/dose: Doses administered every 4 hours, each infused over 1 hour through an in-line 0.2-µ millipore filter for a total of 13 doses (loading dose and 48 hours of treatment)

Reference Range Determine acetaminophen level as soon as possible, but no sooner than 4 hours after ingestion (to ensure peak levels have been obtained); administer for acetaminophen level >150 µg/mL at 4 hours following ingestion; toxic concentration with probable hepatotoxicity: >200 µg/mL at 4 hours or 50 µg at 12 hours

Patient Information Clear airway by coughing deeply before using aerosol.

Dosage Forms SOLN: 10% [100 mg/mL] (4 mL, 10 mL, 30 mL); 20% [200 mg/mL] (4 mL, 10 mL, 30 mL)

♦ **Acetylcysteine Sodium** *see* Acetylcysteine *on page 32*
♦ **Acetylsalicylic Acid** *see* Aspirin *on page 120*
♦ **Achromycin** *see* Tetracycline *on page 1206*
♦ **Aciclovir** *see* Acyclovir *on page 35*
♦ **Acidulated Phosphate Fluoride** *see* Fluoride *on page 535*
♦ **Aciphex®** *see* Rabeprazole *on page 1077*

Acitretin (a si TRE tin)

U.S. Brand Names Soriatane®
Therapeutic Category Retinoid-Like Compund
Use Treatment of severe psoriasis
Pregnancy Risk Factor X
Contraindications Hypersensitivity to acitretin, other retinoids, or any component of the formulation; patients who are pregnant or intend on becoming pregnant; ethanol ingestion; severe hepatic or renal dysfunction; chronically elevated blood lipid levels; concomitant use with methotrexate or tetracycline

Acitretin is contraindicated in females of childbearing potential unless all of the following conditions apply:
1) Patient has severe psoriasis unresponsive to other therapy or if clinical condition contraindicates other treatments.
2) Patient must have two negative urine or serum pregnancy tests prior to therapy.
3) Patient must commit to using two effective forms of birth control starting one month prior to acitretin treatment and for 3 years after discontinuation.
4) Patient is reliable in understanding and carrying out instructions.
5) Patient has received, and acknowledged understanding of a careful oral and printed explanation of the hazards of fetal exposure to acitretin and the risk of possible contraception failure; this explanation may include showing a line drawing to the patient of an infant with the characteristic external deformities resulting from retinoid exposure during pregnancy. Patient must sign an agreement/informed consent document stating that she
(Continued)

Acitretin *(Continued)*

understands these risks and that she should not consume ethanol during therapy or for 2 months after discontinuation.

6) All patients (male and female) should not donate blood during and for 3 years following treatment with acitretin.

Warnings/Precautions Not for use by women who want to become pregnant; patient should not get pregnant for at least 3 years after discontinuation. All patients (male and female) should abstain from ethanol or ethanol-containing products during therapy and for 2 months after discontinuation. All patients should be advised not to donate blood during therapy or for 3 years following completion of therapy. Monitor for hepatotoxicity; discontinue if elevations of liver enzymes occur. Use with caution in patients at risk of hypertriglyceridemias. Rarely associated with pseudotumor cerebri. Discontinue if visual changes occur. May cause a decrease in night vision or decreased tolerance to contact lenses. All patients must be provided with a medication guide each time acitretin is dispensed. Female patients must also sign an informed consent prior to therapy. Safety and efficacy for pediatric patients have not been established; growth potential may be affected.

Common Adverse Reactions

>10%:

Central nervous system: Hyperesthesia (10% to 25%)

Dermatologic: Cheilitis (>75%), alopecia (50% to 75%), skin peeling (50% to 75%), dry skin (25% to 50%), nail disorder (25% to 50%), pruritus (25% to 50%), erythematous rash (10% to 25%), skin atrophy (10% to 25%), sticky skin (10% to 25%), paronychia (10% to 25%)

Endocrine & metabolic: Hypercholesterolemia (25% to 50%), hypertriglyceridemia (50% to 75%), HDL decreased (25% to 50%), phosphorus increased (10% to 25%), potassium increased (10% to 25%), sodium increased (10% to 25%), magnesium increased/decreased (10% to 25%), fasting blood sugar increased (25% to 50%), fasting blood sugar decreased (10% to 25%)

Gastrointestinal: Xerostomia (10% to 25%)

Hematologic: Reticulocytes increased (25% to 50%), hematocrit decreased (10% to 25%), hemoglobin decreased (10% to 25%), WBC increased/decreased (10% to 25%), haptoglobin increased (10% to 25%), neutrophils increased (10% to 25%)

Hepatic: Liver function tests increased (25% to 50%), alkaline phosphatase increased (10% to 25%), direct bilirubin increased (10% to 25%), GGTP increased (10% to 25%)

Neuromuscular & skeletal: Paresthesia (10% to 25%), arthralgia (10% to 25%), rigors (10% to 25%), CPK increased (25% to 50%), spinal hyperostosis progression (10% to 25%)

Ocular: Xerophthalmia (10% to 25%),

Renal: Uric acid increased (10% to 25%), acetonuria (10% to 25%), hematuria (10% to 25%), RBC in urine (10% to 25%)

Respiratory: Rhinitis (25% to 50%), epistaxis (10% to 25%)

1% to 10%:

Cardiovascular: Flushing, edema

Central nervous system: Headache, pain, depression, insomnia, somnolence, fatigue

Dermatologic: Skin odor, change in hair texture, bullous eruption, dermatitis, increased diaphoresis, psoriasiform rash, purpura, pyogenic granuloma, rash, seborrhea, ulcers, fissures, sunburn

Endocrine & metabolic: Hot flashes, potassium decreased, phosphorus decreased, sodium decreased, calcium increased or decreased, chloride increased or decreased

Gastrointestinal: Gingival bleeding, gingivitis, increased saliva, stomatitis, thirst, ulcerative stomatitis, abdominal pain, diarrhea, nausea, taste disturbance, anorexia, increased appetite, tongue disorder

Hepatic: Total bilirubin increased

Neuromuscular & skeletal: Arthritis, back pain, hypertonia, myalgia, osteodynia, peripheral joint hyperostosis, Bell's palsy

Ocular: Blurred vision, blepharitis, conjunctivitis, night blindness, photophobia, corneal epithelial abnormality, eye pain, eyebrow or eyelash loss, diplopia, cataract

Otic: Earache, tinnitus

Renal: BUN increased, creatinine increased, glycosuria, proteinuria

Respiratory: Sinusitis

Drug Interactions

Increased Effect/Toxicity: Additive toxic effects with vitamin A or other systemic retinoids, methotrexate, or tetracycline. Ethanol may lead to formation of teratogenic metabolite. Glucose-lowering effect of sulfonylureas may be potentiated.

Decreased Effect: Acitretin causes decreased efficacy of progestin "mini-pill" preparations.

Pharmacodynamics/Kinetics Etretinate has been detected in serum for up to 3 years following therapy, possibly due to storage in adipose tissue.

Onset: May take 2-3 months for full effect; improvement may be seen within 8 weeks.

Absorption: Oral: ~72% absorbed when given with food

Protein binding: >99% bound, primarily to albumin

Metabolism: Metabolized to *cis*-acitretin; both compounds are further metabolized. Concomitant ethanol use leads to the formation of etretinate (active).

Half-life elimination: Acitretin: 49 hours (range: 33-96); *cis*-acitretin: 63 hours (range: 28-157); etretinate: 120 days (range: 84-168 days)

Excretion: Feces (34% to 54%); urine (16% to 53%)

Dosage Oral: Adults: Individualization of dosage is required to achieve maximum therapeutic response while minimizing side effects

Initial therapy: Therapy should be initiated at 25-50 mg/day, given as a single dose with the main meal

Maintenance doses of 25-50 mg/day may be given after initial response to treatment; the maintenance dose should be based on clinical efficacy and tolerability

Monitoring Parameters Lipid profile (baseline and at 1- to 2-week intervals for 4-8 weeks); liver function tests (baseline, and at 1- to 2-week intervals until stable, then as clinically indicated); blood glucose in patients with diabetes; bone abnormalities (with long-term use)

Patient Information Take with food. Do not drink alcohol during therapy and for 2 months after discontinuation. Use contraception for 1 month before, during, and for 3 years after discontinuation. You may not be able to tolerate contact lenses during treatment. Do not donate blood during treatment and for 3 years after discontinuation (male and female patients). Avoid exposure to sunlight. Wear protective clothing and sunscreens. Avoid use of other vitamin A products. Females: Use two effective forms of birth control. If you have had your tubes tied, then use an additional form of birth control. If you become pregnant, contact your prescriber immediately.

Dosage Forms CAP: 10 mg, 25 mg

♦ **Aclovate**® *see Alclometasone on page 47*

Acrivastine and Pseudoephedrine (AK ri vas teen & soo doe e FED rin)

U.S. Brand Names Semprex®-D
Synonyms Pseudoephedrine and Acrivastine
Therapeutic Category Antihistamine/Decongestant
Use Temporary relief of nasal congestion, decongest sinus openings, running nose, itching of nose or throat, and itchy, watery eyes due to hay fever or other upper respiratory allergies
Pregnancy Risk Factor B
Dosage Oral: Adults: 1 capsule 3-4 times/day
   Dosing comments in renal impairment: Do not use
Dosage Forms CAP: Acrivastine 8 mg and pseudoephedrine 60 mg

♦ **ACT** *see Dactinomycin on page 334*
♦ **ACT**® **[OTC]** *see Fluoride on page 535*
♦ **Act-D** *see Dactinomycin on page 334*
♦ **ActHIB**® *see Haemophilus b Conjugate Vaccine on page 607*
♦ **Acticin**® *see Permethrin on page 984*
♦ **Actidose-Aqua**® **[OTC]** *see Charcoal on page 253*
♦ **Actidose**® **with Sorbitol [OTC]** *see Charcoal on page 253*
♦ **Actifed**® **Cold and Allergy [OTC]** *see Triprolidine and Pseudoephedrine on page 1273*
♦ **Actifed**® **Cold and Sinus [OTC]** *see Acetaminophen, Chlorpheniramine, and Pseudoephedrine on page 28*
♦ **Actigall**® *see Ursodiol on page 1284*
♦ **Actimmune**® *see Interferon Gamma-1b on page 682*
♦ **Actinomycin** *see Dactinomycin on page 334*
♦ **Actinomycin Cl** *see Dactinomycin on page 334*
♦ **Actinomycin D** *see Dactinomycin on page 334*
♦ **Actiq**® *see Fentanyl on page 514*
♦ **Activase**® *see Alteplase on page 63*
♦ **Activated Carbon** *see Charcoal on page 253*
♦ **Activated Charcoal** *see Charcoal on page 253*
♦ **Activated Ergosterol** *see Ergocalciferol on page 449*
♦ **Activated Protein C, Human, Recombinant** *see Drotrecogin Alfa on page 418*
♦ **Activella**™ *see Estradiol and Norethindrone on page 463*
♦ **Actonel**® *see Risedronate on page 1100*
♦ **Actos**® *see Pioglitazone on page 1004*
♦ **ACU-dyne**® **[OTC]** *see Povidone-Iodine on page 1025*
♦ **Acular**® *see Ketorolac on page 706*
♦ **Acular LS**™ *see Ketorolac on page 706*
♦ **Acular**® **PF** *see Ketorolac on page 706*
♦ **ACV** *see Acyclovir on page 35*
♦ **Acycloguanosine** *see Acyclovir on page 35*

Acyclovir (ay SYE kloe veer)

U.S. Brand Names Zovirax®
Synonyms Aciclovir; ACV; Acycloguanosine
Therapeutic Category Antiviral Agent; Antiviral Agent, Parenteral; Antiviral Agent, Topical
Use Treatment of genital herpes simplex virus (HSV), herpes labialis (cold sores), herpes zoster (shingles), HSV encephalitis, neonatal HSV, mucocutaneous HSV, varicella-zoster (chickenpox)
Unlabeled/Investigational Use Prevention of HSV reactivation in HIV positive patients; prevention of HSV reactivation in hematopoietic stem cell transplant (HSCT); prevention of CMV infection after bone marrow transplants in HSV and CMV seropositive individuals
Pregnancy Risk Factor B
(Continued)

Acyclovir *(Continued)*

Contraindications Hypersensitivity to acyclovir, valacyclovir, or any component of the formulation

Warnings/Precautions Use with caution in immunocompromised patients; thrombocytopenic purpura/hemolytic uremic syndrome (TTP/HUS) has been reported. Use caution in the elderly, pre-existing renal disease or in those receiving other nephrotoxic drugs. Maintain adequate hydration during I.V. therapy. Use I.V. preparation with caution in patients with underlying neurologic abnormalities, serious hepatic or electrolyte abnormalities, or substantial hypoxia.

Chickenpox: Treatment should begin within 24 hours of appearance of rash; oral route not recommended for routine use in otherwise healthy children with varicella, but may be effective in patients at increased risk of moderate to severe infection (>12 years of age, chronic cutaneous or pulmonary disorders, long-term salicylate therapy, corticosteroid therapy).

Genital herpes: Physical contact should be avoided when lesions are present; transmission may also occur in the absence of symptoms. Treatment should begin with the first signs or symptoms.

Herpes labialis: For external use only to the lips and face; do not apply to eye or inside the mouth or nose. Treatment should begin with the first signs or symptoms.

Herpes zoster: Acyclovir should be started within 72 hours of appearance of rash to be effective.

Common Adverse Reactions
Systemic: Oral:
1% to 10%:
Central nervous system: Lightheadedness, headache
Gastrointestinal: Diarrhea, nausea, vomiting, abdominal pain
Systemic: Parenteral:
>10%:
Central nervous system: Lightheadedness
Gastrointestinal: Anorexia
1% to 10%:
Dermatologic: Hives, itching, rash
Gastrointestinal: Nausea, vomiting
Hepatic: Liver function tests increased
Local: Inflammation at injection site or phlebitis
Renal: Acute renal failure, BUN increased, creatinine increased
Topical:
>10%: Mild pain, burning, or stinging
1% to 10%: Itching

Drug Interactions
Increased Effect/Toxicity: Increased CNS side effects when taken with zidovudine or probenecid.

Mechanism of Action Acyclovir is converted to acyclovir monophosphate by virus-specific thymidine kinase then further converted to acyclovir triphosphate by other cellular enzymes. Acyclovir triphosphate inhibits DNA synthesis and viral replication by competing with deoxyguanosine triphosphate for viral DNA polymerase and being incorporated into viral DNA.

Pharmacodynamics/Kinetics
Absorption: Oral: 15% to 30%
Distribution: Widely (ie, brain, kidney, lungs, liver, spleen, muscle, uterus, vagina, CSF)
Protein binding: 9% to 33%
Metabolism: Converted by viral enzymes to acyclovir monophosphate, and further converted to diphosphate then triphosphate (active form) by cellular enzymes
Bioavailability: Oral: 10% to 20% with normal renal function (bioavailability decreases with increased dose)
Half-life elimination: Terminal: Neonates: 4 hours; Children 1-12 years: 2-3 hours; Adults: 3 hours
Time to peak, serum: Oral: Within 1.5-2 hours
Excretion: Urine (62% to 90% as unchanged drug and metabolite)

Dosage Note: Obese patients should be dosed using ideal body weight

Genital HSV:
I.V.: Children ≥12 years and Adults (immunocompetent): Initial episode, severe: 5 mg/kg every 8 hours for 5-7 days
Oral:
Children:
Initial episode (unlabeled use): 40-80 mg/kg/day divided into 3-4 doses for 5-10 days (maximum: 1 g/day)
Chronic suppression (unlabeled use; limited data): 80 mg/kg/day in 3 divided doses (maximum: 1 g/day), re-evaluate after 12 months of treatment
Adults:
Initial episode: 200 mg every 4 hours while awake (5 times/day) for 10 days (per manufacturer's labeling); 400 mg 3 times/day for 5-10 days has also been reported
Recurrence: 200 mg every 4 hours while awake (5 times/day) for 5 days (per manufacturer's labeling; begin at earliest signs of disease); 400 mg 3 times/day for 5 days has also been reported

Chronic suppression: 400 mg twice daily or 200 mg 3-5 times/day, for up to 12 months followed by re-evaluation (per manufacturer's labeling); 400-1200 mg/day in 2-3 divided doses has also been reported

Topical: Adults (immunocompromised): Ointment: Initial episode: ½" ribbon of ointment for a 4" square surface area every 3 hours (6 times/day) for 7 days

Herpes labialis (cold sores): Topical: Children ≥12 years and Adults: Cream: Apply 5 times/day for 4 days

Herpes zoster (shingles):
Oral: Adults (immunocompetent): 800 mg every 4 hours (5 times/day) for 7-10 days
I.V.:
Children <12 years (immunocompromised): 20 mg/kg/dose every 8 hours for 7 days
Children ≥12 years and Adults (immunocompromised): 10 mg/kg/dose or 500 mg/m²/dose every 8 hours for 7 days

HSV encephalitis: I.V.:
Children 3 months to 12 years: 20 mg/kg/dose every 8 hours for 10 days (per manufacturer's labeling); dosing for 14-21 days also reported
Children ≥12 years and Adults: 10 mg/kg/dose every 8 hours for 10 days (per manufacturer's labeling); 10-15 mg/kg every 8 hours for 14-21 days also reported

Mucocutaneous HSV:
I.V.:
Children <12 years (immunocompromised): 10 mg/kg/dose every 8 hours for 7 days
Children ≥12 years and Adults (immunocompromised): 5 mg/kg/dose every 8 hours for 7 days (per manufacturer's labeling); dosing for up to 14 days also reported
Oral: Adults (immunocompromised, unlabeled use): 400 mg 5 times a day for 7-14 days
Topical: Ointment: Adults (nonlife-threatening, immunocompromised): ½" ribbon of ointment for a 4" square surface area every 3 hours (6 times/day) for 7 days

Neonatal HSV: I.V.: Neonate: Birth to 3 months: 10 mg/kg/dose every 8 hours for 10 days (manufacturer's labeling); 15 mg/kg/dose or 20 mg/kg/dose every 8 hours for 14-21 days has also been reported

Varicella-zoster (chickenpox): Begin treatment within the first 24 hours of rash onset:
Oral:
Children ≥2 years and ≤40 kg (immunocompetent): 20 mg/kg/dose (up to 800 mg/dose) 4 times/day for 5 days
Children >40 kg and Adults (immunocompetent): 800 mg/dose 4 times a day for 5 days
I.V.:
Children <1 year (immunocompromised, unlabeled use): 10 mg/kg/dose every 8 hours for 7-10 days
Children ≥1 year and Adults (immunocompromised, unlabeled use): 1500 mg/m²/day divided every 8 hours or 10 mg/kg/dose every 8 hours for 7-10 days

Prevention of HSV reactivation in HIV-positive patients, for use only when recurrences are frequent or severe (unlabeled use): Oral:
Children: 80 mg/kg/day in 3-4 divided doses
Adults: 200 mg 3 times/day or 400 mg 2 times/day

Prevention of HSV reactivation in HSCT (unlabeled use): Note: Start at the beginning of conditioning therapy and continue until engraftment or until mucositis resolves (~30 days)
Oral: Adults: 200 mg 3 times/day
I.V.:
Children: 250 mg/m²/dose every 8 hours or 125 mg/m²/dose every 6 hours
Adults: 250 mg/m²/dose every 12 hours

Bone marrow transplant recipients (unlabeled use): I.V.: Children and Adults: Allogeneic patients who are HSV and CMV seropositive: 500 mg/m²/dose (10 mg/kg) every 8 hours; for clinically-symptomatic CMV infection, consider replacing acyclovir with ganciclovir

Dosing adjustment in renal impairment:
Oral:
Cl_cr 10-25 mL/minute: Normal dosing regimen 800 mg every 4 hours: Administer 800 mg every 8 hours
Cl_cr <10 mL/minute:
Normal dosing regimen 200 mg every 4 hours, 200 mg every 8 hours, or 400 mg every 12 hours: Administer 200 mg every 12 hours
Normal dosing regimen 800 mg every 4 hours: Administer 800 mg every 12 hours
I.V.:
Cl_cr 25-50 mL/minute: Administer recommended dose every 12 hours
Cl_cr 10-25 mL/minute: Administer recommended dose every 24 hours
Cl_cr <10 mL/minute: Administer 50% of recommended dose every 24 hours
Hemodialysis: Administer dose after dialysis
Peritoneal dialysis: No supplemental dose needed
CAVH: 3.5 mg/kg/day
CVVHD/CVVH: Adjust dose based upon Cl_cr 30 mL/minute
Administration
Oral: May be administered with or without food.
I.V.: Avoid rapid infusion; infuse over 1 hour to prevent renal damage; maintain adequate hydration of patient; check for phlebitis and rotate infusion sites
(Continued)

Acyclovir *(Continued)*

Topical: Not for use in the eye. Apply using a finger cot or rubber glove to avoid transmission to other parts of the body or to other persons.

Monitoring Parameters Urinalysis, BUN, serum creatinine, liver enzymes, CBC

Patient Information This is not a cure for herpes (recurrences tend to continually reappear every 3-6 months after original infection), nor will this medication reduce the risk of transmission to others when lesions are present; avoid sexual intercourse when visible lesions are present. Take as directed for full course of therapy; do not discontinue even if feeling better. Oral doses may be taken with food.

Dosage Forms CAP: 200 mg. **CRM, topical:** 5% (2 g). **INJ, powder for reconstitution:** 500 mg, 1000 mg. **INJ, solution** [preservative free]: 25 mg/mL (20 mL, 40 mL); 50 mg/mL (10 mL, 20 mL). **OINT, topical:** 5% (3 g, 15 g). **SUSP, oral:** 200 mg/5 mL (480 mL). **TAB:** 400 mg, 800 mg

♦ **AD3L** *see* Valrubicin *on page 1291*

♦ **Adagen®** *see* Pegademase Bovine *on page 962*

♦ **Adalat® CC** *see* NIFEdipine *on page 903*

Adalimumab *(a da LIM yoo mab)*

U.S. Brand Names Humira™

Synonyms Antitumor Necrosis Factor Apha (Human); D2E7; Human Antitumor Necrosis Factor-alpha

Therapeutic Category Antirheumatic, Disease Modifying; Monoclonal Antibody

Use Treatment of active rheumatoid arthritis (moderate to severe) in patients with inadequate response to one or more disease-modifying antirheumatic drugs (DMARDs)

Pregnancy Risk Factor B

Contraindications Hypersensitivity to adalimumab or any component of the formulation

Warnings/Precautions Use caution with chronic infection, history of recurrent infection, or predisposition to infection; do not give with a clinically-important, active infection. May affect defenses against infections and malignancies; serious infections (including sepsis and fatal infections) have been reported. Many of the serious infections have occurred in patients on concomitant immunosuppressive therapy. Patients should be evaluated for latent tuberculosis infection with a tuberculin skin test prior to therapy. Treatment of latent tuberculosis should be initiated before adalimumab is used. Reactivation of tuberculosis and opportunistic infection may occur during treatment. Use caution in patients residing in regions where histoplasmosis is endemic. Discontinue if serious infection or sepsis develops during treatment. Impact on the development and course of malignancies is not fully defined.

May exacerbate pre-existing or recent-onset demyelinating CNS disorders. Patients should be brought up to date with all immunizations before initiating therapy. Live vaccines should not be given concurrently. Safety and efficacy have not been established in pediatric patients.

Common Adverse Reactions
>10%:
Central nervous system: Headache (12%)
Dermatologic: Rash (12%)
Respiratory: Upper respiratory tract infection (17%), sinusitis (11%)
5% to 10%:
Cardiovascular: Hypertension (5%)
Endocrine & metabolic: Hyperlipidemia (7%), hypercholesterolemia (6%)
Gastrointestinal: Nausea (9%), abdominal pain (7%)
Genitourinary: Urinary tract infection (8%)
Local: Injection site reaction (8%)
Neuromuscular & skeletal: Back pain (6%)
Renal: Hematuria (5%)
Miscellaneous: Accidental injury (10%), flu-like syndrome (7%)

Mechanism of Action Adalimumab is a recombinant monoclonal antibody that binds to human tumor necrosis factor alpha (TNF-alpha) receptor sites, thereby interfering with endogenous TNF-alpha activity. Elevated TNF levels in the synovial fluid are involved in the pathologic pain and joint destruction in rheumatoid arthritis. Adalimumab decreases signs and symptoms of rheumatoid arthritis and inhibits progression of structural damage.

Pharmacodynamics/Kinetics
Distribution: V_d: 4.7-6 L; Synovial fluid concentrations: 31% to 95% of serum
Bioavailability: Absolute: 64%
Half-life elimination: Terminal: ~2 weeks (range 10-20 days)
Time to peak, serum: S.C.: 131 ± 56 hours
Excretion: Clearance increased in the presence of anti-adalimumab antibodies; decreased in patients 40 to >75 years

Dosage S.C.: Adults: Rheumatoid arthritis: 40 mg every other week; may be administered with other DMARDs; patients not taking methotrexate may increase dose to 40 mg/weekly

Administration For S.C. injection; rotate injection sites. Do not use if solution is discolored. Do not administer to skin which is red, tender, bruised, or hard.

Monitoring Parameters Improvement of symptoms; signs of infection; place and read PPD before initiation

Patient Information This medication may be administered by S.C. injection only. May cause headache, nausea, or stomach pain. Notify prescriber of any signs of infection.

Dosage Forms INJ, solution [preservative free]: 40 mg/0.8 mL (1 mL)

♦ **Adamantanamine Hydrochloride** *see Amantadine on page 68*

Adapalene (a DAP a leen)
U.S. Brand Names Differin®
Therapeutic Category Acne Product
Use Treatment of acne vulgaris
Pregnancy Risk Factor C
Contraindications Hypersensitivity to adapalene or any component in the vehicle gel
Warnings/Precautions Use with caution in patients with eczema; avoid excessive exposure to sunlight and sunlamps; avoid contact with abraded skin, mucous membranes, eyes, mouth, angles of the nose

Certain cutaneous signs and symptoms such as erythema, dryness, scaling, burning or pruritus may occur during treatment; these are most likely to occur during the first 2-4 weeks and will usually lessen with continued use

Common Adverse Reactions >10%: Dermatologic: Erythema, scaling, dryness, pruritus, burning, pruritus or burning immediately after application
Mechanism of Action Retinoid-like compound which is a modulator of cellular differentiation, keratinization and inflammatory processes, all of which represent important features in the pathology of acne vulgaris
Pharmacodynamics/Kinetics
    Absorption: Topical: Minimal
    Excretion: Bile
Dosage Topical: Children >12 years and Adults: Apply once daily at bedtime; therapeutic results should be noticed after 8-12 weeks of treatment
Patient Information Thoroughly wash hands after applying; avoid hydration of skin immediately before application; minimize exposure to sunlight; avoid washing face more frequently than 2-3 times/day; if severe irritation occurs, discontinue medication temporarily and adjust dose when irritation subsides; avoid using topical preparations with high alcoholic content during treatment period; do not exceed prescribed dose
Dosage Forms CRM, topical: 0.1% (15 g, 45 g). **GEL, topical:** 0.1% (15 g, 45 g). **PLEDGET, topical:** 0.1% (60s). **SOLN, topical:** 0.1% (30 mL)

♦ **Adderall®** *see Dextroamphetamine and Amphetamine on page 363*
♦ **Adderall XR™** *see Dextroamphetamine and Amphetamine on page 363*

Adefovir (a DEF o veer)
U.S. Brand Names Hepsera™
Synonyms Adefovir Dipivoxil
Therapeutic Category Antiretroviral Agent, Reverse Transcriptase Inhibitor (Nucleoside); Antiviral Agent, Hepatitis
Use Treatment of chronic hepatitis B with evidence of active viral replication (based on persistent elevation of ALT/AST or histologic evidence), including patients with lamivudine-resistant hepatitis B
Pregnancy Risk Factor C
Contraindications Hypersensitivity to adefovir or any component of the formulation
Warnings/Precautions Use with caution in patients with renal dysfunction or in patients at risk of renal toxicity (including concurrent nephrotoxic agents or NSAIDs). Chronic administration may result in nephrotoxicity. Dosage adjustment is required in patients with renal dysfunction or in patients who develop renal dysfunction during therapy. May cause the development of resistance in patients with unrecognized or untreated HIV infection. Lactic acidosis and severe hepatomegaly with steatosis (sometimes fatal) have occurred with antiretroviral nucleoside analogues; female gender, obesity, and prolonged treatment may increase the risk of hepatotoxicity. Treatment should be discontinued in patients with lactic acidosis or signs/symptoms of hepatotoxicity (which may occur without marked transaminase elevations). Acute exacerbations of hepatitis may occur (in up to 25% of patients) when antihepatitis therapy is discontinued. Exacerbations typically occur within 12 weeks; monitor patients following discontinuation of therapy. Safety and efficacy in pediatric patients have not been established.
Common Adverse Reactions
    >10%: Renal: Hematuria (11% vs. 10% in placebo-treated)
    1% to 10%:
        Central nervous system: Fever, headache,
        Dermatologic: Rash, pruritus
        Gastrointestinal: Dyspepsia (3%), nausea, vomiting, flatulence, diarrhea, abdominal pain
        Hepatic: AST/ALT increased, abnormal liver function, hepatic failure
        Neuromuscular & skeletal: Weakness
        Renal: Serum creatinine increased (4%), renal failure, renal insufficiency
            Note: In patients with baseline renal dysfunction, frequency of increased serum creatinine has been observed to be as high as 26% to 37%; the role of adefovir in these changes could not be established.
        Respiratory: Cough increased, sinusitis, pharyngitis
Drug Interactions
    Increased Effect/Toxicity: Ibuprofen increases the bioavailability of adefovir. Concurrent use of nephrotoxic agents (including aminoglycosides, cyclosporine, NSAIDs, tacrolimus, vancomycin) may increase the risk of nephrotoxicity.
    (Continued)

Adefovir *(Continued)*

Mechanism of Action Acyclic nucleotide reverse transcriptase inhibitor (adenosine analog) which interferes with HBV viral RNA dependent DNA polymerase resulting in inhibition of viral replication.

Pharmacodynamics/Kinetics
Distribution: 0.35-0.39 L/kg
Protein binding: ≤4%
Metabolism: Prodrug; rapidly converted to adefovir (active metabolite) in intestine
Bioavailability: 59%
Half-life elimination: 7.5 hours; prolonged in renal impairment
Time to peak: 1.75 hours
Excretion: Urine (45% as active metabolite within 24 hours)

Dosage Oral: Adults: 10 mg once daily
Dosage adjustment in renal impairment:
Cl_{cr} 20-49 mL/minute: 10 mg every 48 hours
Cl_{cr} 10-19 mL/minute: 10 mg every 72 hours
Hemodialysis: 10 mg every 7 days (following dialysis)

Administration May be administered without regard to food.

Monitoring Parameters HIV status (prior to initiation of therapy); serum creatinine (prior to initiation and during therapy)

Patient Information Not a cure for hepatitis B, nor will it reduce the risk of transmission. Report persistent lethargy, acute headache, severe nausea or vomiting, difficulty breathing, loss of sensation, or rash. Do not discontinue unless instructed by prescriber; additional monitoring is required after discontinuation to ensure the disease does not recur.

Dosage Forms TAB: 10 mg

♦ **Adefovir Dipivoxil** *see Adefovir on page 39*
♦ **Adenine Arabinoside** *see Vidarabine on page 1304*
♦ **Adenocard®** *see Adenosine on page 40*
♦ **Adenoscan®** *see Adenosine on page 40*

Adenosine *(a DEN oh seen)*

U.S. Brand Names Adenocard®; Adenoscan®

Synonyms 9-Beta-D-ribofuranosyladenine

Therapeutic Category Antiarrhythmic Agent, Class IV; Diagnostic Agent

Use
Adenocard®: Treatment of paroxysmal supraventricular tachycardia (PSVT) including that associated with accessory bypass tracts (Wolff-Parkinson-White syndrome); when clinically advisable, appropriate vagal maneuvers should be attempted prior to adenosine administration; **not effective in atrial flutter, atrial fibrillation, or ventricular tachycardia**
Adenoscan®: Pharmacologic stress agent used in myocardial perfusion thallium-201 scintigraphy

Pregnancy Risk Factor C

Contraindications Hypersensitivity to adenosine or any component of the formulation; second- or third-degree AV block or sick sinus syndrome (except in patients with a functioning artificial pacemaker), atrial flutter, atrial fibrillation, and ventricular tachycardia (this drug is not effective in converting these arrhythmias to sinus rhythm). The manufacturer states that Adenoscan® should be avoided in patients with known or suspected bronchoconstrictive or bronchospastic lung disease.

Warnings/Precautions Patients with pre-existing S-A nodal dysfunction may experience prolonged sinus pauses after adenosine. There have been reports of atrial fibrillation/flutter in patients with PSVT associated with accessory conduction pathways after adenosine. Adenosine decreases conduction through the AV node and may produce a short-lasting first-, second-, or third-degree heart block. Because of the very short half-life, the effects are generally self-limiting. Rare, prolonged episodes of asystole have been reported, with fatal outcomes in some cases. At the time of conversion to normal sinus rhythm, a variety of new rhythms may appear on the ECG. A limited number of patients with asthma have received adenosine and have not experienced exacerbation of their asthma. Adenosine may cause bronchoconstriction in patients with asthma, and should be used cautiously in patients with obstructive lung disease not associated with bronchoconstriction (eg, emphysema, bronchitis).

Common Adverse Reactions
>10%:
Cardiovascular: Facial flushing (18%), palpitations, chest pain, hypotension
Central nervous system: Headache
Respiratory: Dyspnea (12%)
Miscellaneous: Diaphoresis
1% to 10%:
Central nervous system: Dizziness
Gastrointestinal: Nausea (3%)
Neuromuscular & skeletal: Paresthesia, numbness
Respiratory: Chest pressure (7%)

Drug Interactions
Increased Effect/Toxicity: Dipyridamole potentiates effects of adenosine. Use with carbamazepine may increase heart block.
Decreased Effect: Methylxanthines (eg, caffeine, theophylline) antagonize the effect of adenosine.

Mechanism of Action Slows conduction time through the AV node, interrupting the re-entry pathways through the AV node, restoring normal sinus rhythm

Pharmacodynamics/Kinetics
Onset of action: Rapid
Duration: Very brief
Metabolism: Blood and tissue to inosine then to adenosine monophosphate (AMP) and hypoxanthine
Half-life elimination: <10 seconds

Dosage
Adenocard®: **Rapid I.V. push (over 1-2 seconds) via peripheral line:**
Infants and Children:
Manufacturer's recommendation:
<50 kg: 0.05 to 0.1 mg/kg. If conversion of PSVT does not occur within 1-2 minutes, may increase dose by 0.05 to 0.1 mg/kg. May repeat until sinus rhythm is established or to a maximum single dose of 0.3 mg/kg or 12 mg. Follow each dose with normal saline flush.
≥50 kg: Refer to Adults dosing
Pediatric advanced life support (PALS): Treatment of SVT: I.V., I.O.: 0.1 mg/kg; if not effective, administer 0.2 mg/kg of PSVT; medium dose required: 0.15 mg/kg; maximum single dose: 12 mg. Follow each dose with normal saline flush.
Adults: 6 mg; if not effective within 1-2 minutes, 12 mg may be given; may repeat 12 mg bolus if needed
Maximum single dose: 12 mg
Follow each I.V. bolus of adenosine with normal saline flush
Note: Preliminary results in adults suggest adenosine may be administered via a central line at lower doses (ie, initial adult dose: 3 mg).

Adenoscan®: Continuous I.V. infusion via peripheral line: 140 mcg/kg/minute for 6 minutes using syringe or columetric infusion pump; total dose: 0.84 mg/kg. Thallium-201 is injected at midpoint (3 minutes) of infusion.

Hemodialysis: Significant drug removal is unlikely based on physiochemical characteristics.
Peritoneal dialysis: Significant drug removal is unlikely based on physiochemical characteristics.
Note: Higher doses may be needed for administration via peripheral versus central vein.

Administration For rapid bolus I.V. use only; administer I.V. push over 1-2 seconds at a peripheral I.V. site as proximal as possible to trunk (not in lower arm, hand, lower leg, or foot); follow each bolus with normal saline flush. **Note:** Preliminary results in adults suggest adenosine may be administered via central line at lower doses (eg, adults initial dose: 3 mg)

Monitoring Parameters ECG monitoring, heart rate, blood pressure

Dosage Forms INJ, solution [preservative free]: (Adenocard®): 3 mg/mL (2 mL, 4 mL); (Adenoscan®): 3 mg/mL (20 mL, 30 mL)

Agalsidase Beta (aye GAL si days BAY ta)
U.S. Brand Names Fabrazyme®
Synonyms Alpha-Galactosidase-A (Human, Recombinant); r-h α-GAL
Therapeutic Category Enzyme
Use Replacement therapy for Fabry disease
Pregnancy Risk Factor B
(Continued)

Agalsidase Beta *(Continued)*

Contraindications No known contraindications

Warnings/Precautions Infusion reactions are common, and may be severe; pretreatment with antipyretics is advised. Use caution in cardiovascular disease (risk related to infusion reactions may be increased). A registry has been created to monitor therapeutic responses and adverse effects during long-term treatment; patients should be encouraged to register (www.fabryregistry.com or 1-800-745-4447). Safety and efficacy in pediatric patients have not been established (studies limited to patients ≤16 years of age).

Common Adverse Reactions Note: The most common and serious adverse reactions are infusion reactions (symptoms may include fever, tachycardia, hypertension, throat tightness, dyspnea, chills, abdominal pain, pruritus, urticaria, vomiting).

>10%:
   Cardiovascular: Edema (21%), chest pain (17%), hypotension (14%)
   Central nervous system: Fever (48%), headache (45%), anxiety (28%), pain (21%), dizziness (14%), paresthesia (14%)
   Dermatologic: Pallor (14%)
   Gastrointestinal: Nausea (28%)
   Miscellaneous: Infusion reactions (alteration of temperature sensation 17%)
   Neuromuscular & skeletal: Rigors (52%), skeletal pain (21%)
   Respiratory: Rhinitis (38%), pharyngitis (28%)

1% to 10%:
   Cardiovascular: Cardiomegaly (10%), hypertension (10%)
   Central nervous system: Depression (10%)
   Gastrointestinal: Dyspepsia (10%)
   Genitourinary: Testicular pain (7%)
   Neuromuscular & skeletal: Arthrosis (10%)
   Respiratory: Bronchitis (10%), bronchospasm (7%), laryngitis (7%), sinusitis (7%)

Other reported severe reactions (frequency not established): Arrhythmia, ataxia, bradycardia, cardiac arrest, cardiac output decreased, nephritic syndrome, stroke, vertigo

Mechanism of Action Agalsidase beta is a recombinant form of the enzyme alpha-galactosidase-A, which is required for the hydrolysis of GL-3 and other glycosphingolipids. The compounds may accumulate (over many years) within the tissues of patients with Fabry disease, leading to renal and cardiovascular complications. In clinical trials of limited duration, agalsidase been noted to reduce tissue inclusions of a key sphingolipid (GL-3). It is believed that long-term enzyme replacement may reduce clinical manifestations of renal failure, cardiomyopathy, and stroke. However, the relationship to a reduction in clinical manifestations has not been established.

Pharmacodynamics/Kinetics Half-life elimination: 42-102 minutes (nonlinear)

Dosage I.V.: Adults: 1 mg/kg every 2 weeks

Dosage adjustment in renal impairment: No dosage adjustment required

Administration Antipyretics should be administered prior to infusion. Initial infusion rate should not exceed 0.25 mg/minute (15 mg/hour). Decrease rate in the event of an infusion reaction. After patient tolerance to the infusion is established, rate may be increased in increments of 0.05-0.08 mg/minute (3-5 mg/hour) with each subsequent infusion. A 0.2 micron low protein-binding filter may be used.

Monitoring Parameters Development of IgG or IgE antibodies in patients with suspected allergic reactions (test available from manufacturer).

Dosage Forms INJ, powder for reconstitution: 35 mg

- ◆ **AK-Trol**® *see Neomycin, Polymyxin B, and Dexamethasone on page 892*
- ◆ **Alamag [OTC]** *see Aluminum Hydroxide and Magnesium Hydroxide on page 67*
- ◆ **Alamag Plus [OTC]** *see Aluminum Hydroxide, Magnesium Hydroxide, and Simethicone on page 68*
- ◆ **Alamast**™ *see Pemirolast on page 969*
- ◆ **Alatrofloxacin Mesylate** *see Trovafloxacin on page 1277*
- ◆ **Alavert**™ **[OTC]** *see Loratadine on page 759*
- ◆ **Albalon**® *see Naphazoline on page 881*

Albendazole (al BEN da zole)

U.S. Brand Names Albenza®

Therapeutic Category Anthelmintic

Use Treatment of parenchymal neurocysticercosis caused by *Taenia solium* and cystic hydatid disease of the liver, lung, and peritoneum caused by *Echinococcus granulosus*

Unlabeled/Investigational Use Albendazole has activity against *Ascaris lumbricoides* (roundworm); *Ancylostoma caninum*; *Ancylostoma duodenale* and *Necator americanus* (hookworms); cutaneous larva migrans; *Enterobius vermicularis* (pinworm); *Gnathostoma spinigerum*; *Gongylonema* sp; *Hymenolepis nana* sp (tapeworms); *Mansonella perstans* (filariasis); *Opisthorchis sinensis* and *Opisthorchis viverrini* (liver flukes); *Strongyloides stercoralis* and *Trichuris trichiura* (whipworm); visceral larva migrans (toxocariasis); activity has also been shown against the liver fluke *Clonorchis sinensis*, *Giardia lamblia*, *Cysticercus cellulosae*, and *Echinococcus multilocularis*. Albendazole has also been used for the treatment of intestinal microsporidiosis (*Encephalitozoon intestinalis*), disseminated microsporidiosis (*E. hellem, E. cuniculi, E. intestinalis, Pleistophora* sp, *Trachipleistophora* sp, *Brachiola vesicularum*), and ocular microsporidiosis (*E. hellem, E. cuniculi, Vittaforma corneae*).

Pregnancy Risk Factor C

Contraindications Hypersensitivity to albendazole or any component of the formulation

Warnings/Precautions Discontinue therapy if LFT elevations are significant; may restart treatment when decreased to pretreatment values. Becoming pregnant within 1 month following therapy is not advised.

Neurocysticercosis: Corticosteroids should be administered 1-2 days before albendazole therapy to minimize inflammatory reactions. Steroid and anticonvulsant therapy should be used concurrently during the first week of therapy to prevent cerebral hypertension. If retinal lesions exist, weigh risk of further retinal damage due to albendazole-induced changes to the retinal lesion vs benefit of disease treatment.

Common Adverse Reactions

N = Neurocysticercosis; H = Hydatid disease

>10%:
    Central nervous system: Headache (11% - N; 1% - H)
    Hepatic: LFTs Increased (~15% - H; <1% - N)
1% to 10%:
    Central nervous system: Dizziness, vertigo, fever (≤1%); intracranial pressure increased (1% - N), meningeal signs (1% - N)
    Dermatologic: Alopecia (2% - H; <1% - N)
    Gastrointestinal: Abdominal pain (6% - H; 0% - N); nausea/vomiting (3% to 6%)
    Hematologic: Leukopenia (reversible) (<1%)
    Miscellaneous: Allergic reactions (<1%)

Drug Interactions

Cytochrome P450 Effect: Substrate (minor) of CYP1A2, 3A4; **Inhibits** CYP1A2 (weak)

Increased Effect/Toxicity: Albendazole serum levels are increased when taken with dexamethasone, praziquantel.

Decreased Effect: Cimetidine may increase albendazole metabolism.

Mechanism of Action Active metabolite, albendazole, causes selective degeneration of cytoplasmic microtubules in intestinal and tegmental cells of intestinal helminths and larvae; glycogen is depleted, glucose uptake and cholinesterase secretion are impaired, and desecratory substances accumulate intracellulary. ATP production decreases causing energy depletion, immobilization, and worm death.

Pharmacodynamics/Kinetics

Absorption: <5%; may increase up to 4-5 times when administered with a fatty meal
Distribution: Well inside hydatid cysts and CSF
Protein binding: 70%
Metabolism: Hepatic; extensive first-pass effect; pathways include rapid sulfoxidation (major), hydrolysis, and oxidation
Half-life elimination: 8-12 hours
Time to peak, serum: 2-2.4 hours
Excretion: Urine (<1% as active metabolite); feces

Dosage Oral:
Children:
    Cysticercus cellulosae (unlabeled use): 15 mg/kg/day (maximum: 800 mg/day) in 2 divided doses for 8-30 days; may be repeated as necessary
    Echinococcus granulosus (tapeworm) (unlabeled use): 15 mg/kg/day (maximum: 800 mg) divided twice daily for 1-6 months
Children and Adults:
    Neurocysticercosis:
        <60 kg: 15 mg/kg/day in 2 divided doses (maximum: 800 mg/day) for 8-30 days
(Continued)

Albendazole *(Continued)*

>=60 kg: 400 mg twice daily for 8-30 days

Note: Give concurrent anticonvulsant and steroid therapy during first week.

Hydatid:

<60 kg: 15 mg/kg/day in 2 divided doses (maximum: 800 mg/day)

>=60 kg: 400 mg twice daily

Note: Administer dose for three 28-day cycles with a 14-day drug-free interval in between.

Ancylostoma caninum, Ascaris lumbricoides (roundworm), *Ancylostoma duodenale,* and *Necator americanus* (hookworms) (unlabeled use): 400 mg as a single dose

Clonorchis sinensis (Chinese liver fluke) (unlabeled use): 10 mg/kg for 7 days

Cutaneous larva migrans (unlabeled use): 400 mg once daily for 3 days

Enterobius vermicularis (pinworm) (unlabeled use): 400 mg as a single dose; may repeat in 2 weeks

Gnathostoma spinigerum (unlabeled use): 400 mg twice daily for 21 days

Gongylonemiasis (unlabeled use): 10 mg/kg/day for 3 days

Mansonella perstans (unlabeled use): 400 mg twice daily for 10 days

Visceral larva migrans (toxocariasis) (unlabeled use): 400 mg twice daily for 5 days

Adults:

Cysticercus cellulosae (unlabeled use): 400 mg twice daily for 8-30 days; may be repeated as necessary

Disseminated microsporidiosis (unlabeled use): 400 mg twice daily

Echinococcus granulosus (tapeworm) (unlabeled use): 400 mg twice daily for 1-6 months

Intestinal microsporidiosis (unlabeled use): 400 mg twice daily for 21 days

Ocular microsporidiosis (unlabeled use): 400 mg twice daily, in combination with fumagillin

Administration Administer with meals; administer anticonvulsant and steroid therapy during first week of neurocysticercosis therapy

Monitoring Parameters Monitor fecal specimens for ova and parasites for 3 weeks after treatment; if positive, retreat; monitor LFTs, and clinical signs of hepatotoxicity; CBC at start of each 28-day cycle and every 2 weeks during therapy

Dosage Forms TAB: 200 mg

♦ **Albenza**® *see* Albendazole *on page 43*

♦ **Albumarc**® *see* Albumin *on page 44*

Albumin *(al BYOO min)*

U.S. Brand Names Albumarc®; Albuminar®; Albutein®; Buminate®; Plasbumin®

Synonyms Albumin (Human); Normal Human Serum Albumin; Normal Serum Albumin (Human); Salt Poor Albumin; SPA

Therapeutic Category Blood Product Derivative; Plasma Volume Expander, Colloid

Use Plasma volume expansion and maintenance of cardiac output in the treatment of certain types of shock or impending shock; may be useful for burn patients, ARDS, and cardiopulmonary bypass; other uses considered by some investigators (but not proven) are retroperitoneal surgery, peritonitis, and ascites; unless the condition responsible for hypoproteinemia can be corrected, albumin can provide only symptomatic relief or supportive treatment

Unlabeled/Investigational Use In cirrhotics, administered with diuretics to help facilitate diuresis; large volume paracentesis; volume expansion in dehydrated, mildly-hypotensive cirrhotics

Pregnancy Risk Factor C

Contraindications Hypersensitivity to albumin or any component of the formulation; patients with severe anemia or cardiac failure

Warnings/Precautions Use with caution in patients with hepatic or renal failure because of added protein load; rapid infusion of albumin solutions may cause vascular overload. All patients should be observed for signs of hypervolemia such as pulmonary edema. Use with caution in those patients for whom sodium restriction is necessary. Avoid 25% concentration in preterm infants due to risk of intraventricular hemorrhage. Nutritional supplementation is not an appropriate indication for albumin.

Common Adverse Reactions Frequency not defined.

Cardiovascular: CHF precipitation, edema, hypertension, hypervolemia, hypotension, tachycardia

Central nervous system: Chills, fever, headache

Dermatologic: Pruritus, rash, urticaria

Gastrointestinal: Nausea, vomiting

Respiratory: Bronchospasm, pulmonary edema

Miscellaneous: Anaphylaxis

Drug Interactions

Increased Effect/Toxicity: ACE inhibitors: May have increased risk of atypical reactions; withhold ACEIs for at least 24 hours prior to plasma exchanges using large volumes of albumin

Mechanism of Action Provides increase in intravascular oncotic pressure and causes mobilization of fluids from interstitial into intravascular space

Dosage I.V.:

5% should be used in hypovolemic patients or intravascularly-depleted patients

25% should be used in patients in whom fluid and sodium intake must be minimized

Dose depends on condition of patient:
 Children: Hypovolemia: 0.5-1 g/kg/dose (10-20 mL/kg/dose of albumin 5%); maximum dose: 6 g/kg/day
 Adults: Usual dose: 25 g; initial dose may be repeated in 15-30 minutes if response is inadequate; no more than 250 g should be administered within 48 hours
  Hypoproteinemia: 0.5-1 g/kg/dose; repeat every 1-2 days as calculated to replace ongoing losses
  Hypovolemia: 0.5-1 g/kg/dose; repeat as needed; maximum dose: 6 g/kg/day

Administration For I.V. administration only. Use within 4 hours after opening vial; discard unused portion. In emergencies, may administer as rapidly as necessary to improve clinical condition. After initial volume replacement:
 5%: Do not exceed 2-4 mL/minute in patients with normal plasma volume; 5-10 mL/minute in patients with hypoproteinemia
 25%: Do not exceed 1 mL/minute in patients with normal plasma volume; 2-3 mL/minute in patients with hypoproteinemia

Monitoring Parameters Blood pressure, pulmonary edema, hematocrit

Dosage Forms INJ, human: 5% [50 mg/mL] (50 mL, 250 mL); 25% [250 mg/mL] (50 mL, 100 mL). (Albumarc®): 5% [50 mg/mL] (250 mL, 500 mL); 25% [250 mg/mL] (50 mL, 100 mL). (Albuminar®): 5% [50 mg/mL] (50 mL, 250 mL, 500 mL, 1000 mL); 25% [250 mg/mL] (20 mL, 50 mL, 100 mL). (Albutein®, Buminate®): 5% [50 mg/mL]: (250 mL, 500 mL); 25% [250 mg/mL] (20 mL, 50 mL, 100 mL). (Plasbumin®): 5% [50 mg/mL] (50 mL, 250 mL, 500 mL); 25% [250 mg/mL] (20 mL, 50 mL, 100 mL)

♦ **Albuminar®** *see* Albumin *on page 44*
♦ **Albumin (Human)** *see* Albumin *on page 44*
♦ **Albutein®** *see* Albumin *on page 44*

Albuterol (al BYOO ter ole)

Related Information
 Bronchodilators, Comparison of Inhaled Sympathomimetics *on page 1370*

U.S. Brand Names AccuNeb™; Proventil®; Proventil® HFA; Proventil® Repetabs®; Ventolin® [DSC]; Ventolin® HFA; Volmax®; VoSpire ER™

Synonyms Albuterol Sulfate; Salbutamol

Therapeutic Category Beta₂-Adrenergic Agonist; Bronchodilator; Sympathomimetic Agent

Use Bronchodilator in reversible airway obstruction due to asthma or COPD; prevention of exercise-induced bronchospasm

Pregnancy Risk Factor C

Contraindications Hypersensitivity to albuterol, adrenergic amines, or any component of the formulation

Warnings/Precautions Optimize anti-inflammatory treatment before initiating maintenance treatment with albuterol. Do not use as a component of chronic therapy without an anti-inflammatory agent. Only the mildest forms of asthma (Step 1 and/or exercise-induced) would not require concurrent use based upon asthma guidelines. Patient must be instructed to seek medical attention in cases where acute symptoms are not relieved or a previous level of response is diminished. The need to increase frequency of use may indicate deterioration of asthma, and treatment must not be delayed.

Use caution in patients with cardiovascular disease (arrhythmia or hypertension or CHF), convulsive disorders, diabetes, glaucoma, hyperthyroidism, or hypokalemia. Beta agonists may cause elevation in blood pressure, heart rate, and result in CNS stimulation/excitation. Beta₂ agonists may increase risk of arrhythmia, increase serum glucose, or decrease serum potassium.

Do not exceed recommended dose; serious adverse events including fatalities, have been associated with excessive use of inhaled sympathomimetics. Rarely, paradoxical broncho-spasm may occur with use of inhaled bronchodilating agents; this should be distinguished from inadequate response. All patients should utilize a spacer device when using a metered-dose inhaler; in addition, face masks should be used in children <4 years of age.

Because of its minimal effect on beta₁-receptors and its relatively long duration of action, albuterol is a rational choice in the elderly when an inhaled beta agonist is indicated. Oral use should be avoided in the elderly due to adverse effects. Patient response may vary between inhalers that contain chlorofluorocarbons and those which are chlorofluorocarbon-free.

Common Adverse Reactions Incidence of adverse effects is dependent upon age of patient, dose, and route of administration.
 Cardiovascular: Angina, atrial fibrillation, chest discomfort, extrasystoles, flushing, hypertension, palpitations, tachycardia
 Central nervous system: CNS stimulation, dizziness, drowsiness, headache, insomnia, irritability, lightheadedness, migraine, nervousness, nightmares, restlessness, sleeplessness, tremor
 Dermatologic: Angioedema, erythema multiforme, rash, Stevens-Johnson syndrome, urticaria
 Endocrine & metabolic: Hypokalemia, serum glucose increased, serum potassium decreased
 Gastrointestinal: Diarrhea, dry mouth, gastroenteritis, nausea, unusual taste, vomiting, tooth discoloration
 Genitourinary: Micturition difficulty
 Neuromuscular & skeletal: Muscle cramps, weakness
 Otic: Otitis media, vertigo
 Respiratory: Asthma exacerbation, bronchospasm, cough, epistaxis, laryngitis, oropharyngeal drying/irritation, oropharyngeal edema
(Continued)

Albuterol *(Continued)*

Miscellaneous: Allergic reaction, lymphadenopathy

Drug Interactions

Cytochrome P450 Effect: Substrate of CYP3A4 (major)

Increased Effect/Toxicity: When used with inhaled ipratropium, an increased duration of bronchodilation may occur. Cardiovascular effects are potentiated in patients also receiving MAO inhibitors, tricyclic antidepressants, and sympathomimetic agents (eg, amphetamine, dopamine, dobutamine). Albuterol may increase the risk of malignant arrhythmias with inhaled anesthetics (eg, enflurane, halothane).

Decreased Effect: When used with nonselective beta-adrenergic blockers (eg, propranolol) the effect of albuterol is decreased. CYP3A4 inducers may decrease the levels/effects of albuterol; example inducers include aminoglutethimide, carbamazepine, nafcillin, nevirapine, phenobarbital, phenytoin, and rifamycins.

Mechanism of Action Relaxes bronchial smooth muscle by action on beta$_2$-receptors with little effect on heart rate

Pharmacodynamics/Kinetics

Onset of action: Peak effect: Nebulization/oral inhalation: 0.5-2 hours; Oral: 2-3 hours

Duration: Nebulization/oral inhalation: 3-4 hours; Oral: 4-6 hours

Metabolism: Hepatic to an inactive sulfate

Half-life elimination: Inhalation: 3.8 hours; Oral: 3.7-5 hours

Excretion: Urine (30% as unchanged drug)

Dosage

Oral:

Children: Bronchospasm (treatment):

2-6 years: 0.1-0.2 mg/kg/dose 3 times/day; maximum dose not to exceed 12 mg/day (divided doses)

6-12 years: 2 mg/dose 3-4 times/day; maximum dose not to exceed 24 mg/day (divided doses)

Extended release: 4 mg every 12 hours; maximum dose not to exceed 24 mg/day (divided doses)

Children >12 years and Adults: Bronchospasm (treatment): 2-4 mg/dose 3-4 times/day; maximum dose not to exceed 32 mg/day (divided doses)

Extended release: 8 mg every 12 hours; maximum dose not to exceed 32 mg/day (divided doses). A 4 mg dose every 12 hours may be sufficient in some patients, such as adults of low body weight.

Elderly: Bronchospasm (treatment): 2 mg 3-4 times/day; maximum: 8 mg 4 times/day

Inhalation: MDI 90 mcg/puff:

Children ≤12 years:

Bronchospasm (acute): 4-8 puffs every 20 minutes for 3 doses, then every 1-4 hours; spacer/holding-chamber device should be used

Exercise-induced bronchospasm (prophylaxis): 1-2 puffs 5 minutes prior to exercise

Children >12 years and Adults:

Bronchospasm (acute): 4-8 puffs every 20 minutes for up to 4 hours, then every 1-4 hours as needed

Exercise-induced bronchospasm (prophylaxis): 2 puffs 5-30 minutes prior to exercise

Children ≥4 years and Adults: Bronchospasm (chronic treatment): 1-2 inhalations every 4-6 hours; maximum: 12 inhalations/day

NIH guidelines: 2 puffs 3-4 times a day as needed; may double dose for mild exacerbations

Nebulization:

Children ≤12 years:

Bronchospasm (treatment): 0.05 mg/kg every 4-6 hours; minimum dose: 1.25 mg, maximum dose: 2.5 mg

2-12 years: AccuNeb™: 0.63 mg or 1.25 mg 3-4 times/day, as needed, delivered over 5-15 minutes

Children >40 kg, patients with more severe asthma, or children 11-12 years: May respond better with a 1.25 mg dose

Bronchospasm (acute): Solution 0.5%: 0.15 mg/kg (minimum dose: 2.5 mg) every 20 minutes for 3 doses, then 0.15-0.3 mg/kg (up to 10 mg) every 1-4 hours as needed; may also use 0.5 mg/kg/hour by continuous infusion. Continuous nebulized albuterol at 0.3 mg/kg/hour has been used safely in the treatment of severe status asthmaticus in children; continuous nebulized doses of 3 mg/kg/hour ± 2.2 mg/kg/hour in children whose mean age was 20.7 months resulted in no cardiac toxicity; the optimal dosage for continuous nebulization remains to be determined.

Note: Use of the 0.5% solution should be used for bronchospasm (acute or treatment) in children <15 kg. AccuNeb™ has not been studied for the treatment of acute bronchospasm; use of the 0.5% concentrated solution may be more appropriate.

Children >12 years and Adults:

Bronchospasm (treatment): 2.5 mg, diluted to a total of 3 mL, 3-4 times/day over 5-15 minutes

NIH guidelines: 1.25-5 mg every 4-8 hours

Bronchospasm (acute) in intensive care patients: 2.5-5 mg every 20 minutes for 3 doses, then 2.5-10 mg every 1-4 hours as needed, **or** 10-15 mg/hour continuously

Hemodialysis: Not removed

Peritoneal dialysis: Significant drug removal is unlikely based on physiochemical characteristics

Administration
Inhalation: MDI: Shake well before use; prime prior to first use, and whenever inhaler has not been used for >2 weeks, by releasing 4 test sprays into the air (away from face)
Oral: Do not crush or chew extended release tablets.

Monitoring Parameters FEV$_1$, peak flow, and/or other pulmonary function tests; blood pressure, heart rate; CNS stimulation; serum glucose, serum potassium; asthma symptoms; arterial or capillary blood gases (if patients condition warrants)

Patient Information Do not exceed recommended dosage; rinse mouth with water following each inhalation to help with dry throat and mouth; follow specific instructions accompanying inhaler; if more than one inhalation is necessary, wait at least 1 full minute between inhalations. May cause nervousness, restlessness, insomnia; if these effects continue after dosage reduction, notify prescriber; also report palpitations, tachycardia, chest pain, muscle tremors, dizziness, headache, flushing or if breathing difficulty persists.

Dosage Forms AERO, oral: 90 mcg/dose (17 g); (Proventil®): 90 mcg/dose (17 g); (Ventolin® [DSC]): 90 mcg/dose (6.8 g, 17 g). **AERO, oral** [chlorofluorocarbon free]: (Proventil® HFA): 90 mcg/dose (6.7 g); (Ventolin® HFA): 90 mcg/dose (18 g). **SOLN, oral inhalation:** 0.083% (3 mL); 0.5% (20 mL); (AccuNeb™): 0.63 mg/3 mL (3 mL), 1.25 mg/3 mL (3 mL); (Proventil®): 0.083% (3 mL), 0.5% (20 mL). **SYR:** 2 mg/5 mL (480 mL). **TAB:** 2 mg, 4 mg. **TAB, extended release:** (Proventil® Repetabs®): 4 mg; (Volmax®, VoSpire™): 4 mg, 8 mg

♦ **Albuterol and Ipratropium** see Ipratropium and Albuterol *on page 686*
♦ **Albuterol Sulfate** see Albuterol *on page 45*
♦ **Alcaine®** see Proparacaine *on page 1050*
♦ **Alcalak [OTC]** see Calcium Carbonate *on page 203*

Alclometasone (al kloe MET a sone)

Related Information
Corticosteroids Comparison *on page 1372*

U.S. Brand Names Aclovate®

Synonyms Alclometasone Dipropionate

Therapeutic Category Anti-inflammatory Agent; Corticosteroid, Topical (Low Potency)

Use Treatment of inflammation of corticosteroid-responsive dermatosis (low potency topical corticosteroid)

Pregnancy Risk Factor C

Contraindications Hypersensitivity to alclometasone or any component of the formulation; viral, fungal, or tubercular skin lesions

Warnings/Precautions Adverse systemic effects may occur when used on large areas of the body, denuded areas, for prolonged periods of time, with an occlusive dressing, and/or in infants or small children (not for use in children <1 year of age)

Common Adverse Reactions 1% to 10%:
Dermatologic: Itching, erythema, dryness papular rashes
Local: Burning, irritation

Mechanism of Action Stimulates the synthesis of enzymes needed to decrease inflammation, suppress mitotic activity, and cause vasoconstriction

Dosage Topical: Apply a thin film to the affected area 2-3 times/day. Therapy should be discontinued when control is achieved; if no improvement is seen, reassessment of diagnosis may be necessary.

Administration For external use only; do not use on open wounds; apply sparingly to occlusive dressings; should not be used in the presence of open or weeping lesions

Patient Information Before applying, gently wash area to reduce risk of infection; apply a thin film to cleansed area and rub in gently and thoroughly until medication vanishes; avoid exposure to sunlight, severe sunburn may occur

Dosage Forms CRM: 0.05% (15 g, 45 g, 60 g). **OINT:** 0.05% (15 g, 45 g, 60 g)

♦ **Alclometasone Dipropionate** see Alclometasone *on page 47*
♦ **Aldactazide®** see Hydrochlorothiazide and Spironolactone *on page 627*
♦ **Aldactone®** see Spironolactone *on page 1158*
♦ **Aldara™** see Imiquimod *on page 657*

Aldesleukin (al des LOO kin)

U.S. Brand Names Proleukin®

Synonyms Epidermal Thymocyte Activating Factor; ETAF; IL-2; Interleukin-2; Lymphocyte Mitogenic Factor; NSC-373364; T-Cell Growth Factor; TCGF; Thymocyte Stimulating Factor

Therapeutic Category Biological Response Modulator; Interleukin

Use Treatment of metastatic renal cell cancer, melanoma

Unlabeled/Investigational Use Investigational: Multiple myeloma, HIV infection, and AIDS; may be used in conjunction with lymphokine-activated killer (LAK) cells, tumor-infiltrating lymphocyte (TIL) cells, interleukin-1, and interferons; colorectal cancer; non-Hodgkin's lymphoma

Pregnancy Risk Factor C

Contraindications Hypersensitivity to aldesleukin or any component of the formulation; patients with abnormal thallium stress or pulmonary function tests; patients who have had an organ allograft; retreatment in patients who have experienced sustained ventricular tachycardia (≥5 beats); refractory cardiac rhythm disturbances, recurrent chest pain with ECG changes consistent with angina or myocardial infarction, intubation ≥72 hours, pericardial
(Continued)

Aldesleukin *(Continued)*

tamponade, renal dialysis for ≥72 hours, coma or toxic psychosis lasting ≥48 hours, repetitive or refractory seizures, bowel ischemia/perforation, GI bleeding requiring surgery

Warnings/Precautions High-dose aldesleukin therapy has been associated with capillary leak syndrome (CLS); CLS results in hypotension and reduced organ perfusion which may be severe and can result in death; therapy should be restricted to patients with normal cardiac and pulmonary functions as defined by thallium stress and formal pulmonary function testing; extreme caution should be used in patients with normal thallium stress tests and pulmonary functions tests who have a history of prior cardiac or pulmonary disease. Patients must have a serum creatinine of ≤1.5 mg/dL prior to treatment.

Adverse effects are frequent and sometimes fatal. May exacerbate pre-existing or initial presentation of autoimmune diseases and inflammatory disorders. Patients should be evaluated and treated for CNS metastases and have a negative scan prior to treatment. Mental status changes (irritability, confusion, depression) can occur and may indicate bacteremia, hypoperfusion, CNS malignancy, or CNS toxicity.

Intensive aldesleukin treatment is associated with impaired neutrophil function (reduced chemotaxis) and with an increased risk of disseminated infection, including sepsis and bacterial endocarditis, in treated patients. Consequently, pre-existing bacterial infections should be adequately treated prior to initiation of therapy. Additionally, all patients with indwelling central lines should receive antibiotic prophylaxis effective against *S. aureus*. Antibiotic prophylaxis which has been associated with a reduced incidence of staphylococcal infections in aldesleukin studies includes the use of oxacillin, nafcillin, ciprofloxacin, or vancomycin.

Standard prophylactic supportive care during high-dose aldesleukin treatment includes acetaminophen to relieve constitutional symptoms and an H_2 antagonist to reduce the risk of GI ulceration and/or bleeding.

Common Adverse Reactions

>10%:
  Cardiovascular: Hypotension (85%), dose-limiting, possibly fatal; sinus tachycardia (70%); arrhythmias (22%); edema (47%); angina
  Central nervous system: Mental status changes (transient memory loss, confusion, drowsiness) (73%); dizziness (17%); cognitive changes, fatigue, malaise, somnolence and disorientation (25%); headaches, insomnia, paranoid delusion
  Dermatologic: Macular erythematous rash (100% of patients on high-dose therapy); pruritus (48%); erythema (41%); rash (26%); exfoliative dermatitis (14%); dry skin (15%)
  Endocrine & metabolic: Fever and chills (89%); low electrolyte levels (magnesium, calcium, phosphate, potassium, sodium) (1% to 15%)
  Gastrointestinal: Nausea and vomiting (87%); diarrhea (76%); stomatitis (32%); GI bleeding (13%); weight gain (23%), anorexia (27%)
  Hematologic: Anemia (77%); thrombocytopenia (64%); leukopenia (34%) - may be dose-limiting; coagulation disorders (10%)
  Hepatic: Transient elevations of bilirubin (64%) and enzymes (56%); jaundice (11%)
  Neuromuscular & skeletal: Weakness; rigors - respond to acetaminophen, diphenhydramine, an NSAID, or meperidine
  Renal: Oliguria/anuria (63%, severe in 5% to 6%), proteinuria (12%); renal failure (dose-limiting toxicity) manifested as oliguria noted within 24-48 hours of initiation of therapy; marked fluid retention, azotemia, and increased serum creatinine seen, which may return to baseline within 7 days of discontinuation of therapy; hypophosphatemia
  Respiratory: Congestion (54%); dyspnea (27% to 52%)
  Miscellaneous: Pain (54%), infection (including sepsis and endocarditis) due to neutrophil impairment (23%)

1% to 10%:
  Cardiovascular: Capillary leak syndrome, including peripheral edema, ascites, pulmonary infiltration, and pleural effusion (2% to 4%), may be dose-limiting and potentially fatal; myocardial infarction (2%)
  Central nervous system: Seizures (1%)
  Endocrine & metabolic: Hypo- and hyperglycemia (2%); increased electrolyte levels (magnesium, calcium, phosphate, potassium, sodium) (1%), hypothyroidism
  Hepatic: Ascites (4%)
  Neuromuscular & skeletal: Arthralgia (6%), myalgia (6%)
  Renal: Hematuria (9%), increased creatinine (5%)
  Respiratory: Pleural effusions, edema (10%)

Drug Interactions

Increased Effect/Toxicity: Aldesleukin may affect central nervous function; therefore, interactions could occur following concomitant administration of psychotropic drugs (eg, narcotics, analgesics, antiemetics, sedatives, tranquilizers).

Concomitant administration of drugs possessing nephrotoxic (eg, aminoglycosides, indomethacin), myelotoxic (eg, cytotoxic chemotherapy), cardiotoxic (eg, doxorubicin), or hepatotoxic (eg, methotrexate, asparaginase) effects with aldesleukin may increase toxicity in these organ systems. The safety and efficacy of aldesleukin in combination with chemotherapies has not been established.

Beta-blockers and other antihypertensives may potentiate the hypotension seen with aldesleukin.

Decreased Effect: Corticosteroids have been shown to decrease toxicity of aldesleukin, but have not been used since there is concern that they may reduce the efficacy of the lymphokine.

Mechanism of Action Aldesleukin promotes proliferation, differentiation, and recruitment of T and B cells, natural killer (NK) cells, and thymocytes; aldesleukin also causes cytolytic activity in a subset of lymphocytes and subsequent interactions between the immune system and malignant cells; aldesleukin can stimulate lymphokine-activated killer (LAK) cells and tumor-infiltrating lymphocytes (TIL) cells. LAK cells (which are derived from lymphocytes from a patient and incubated in aldesleukin) have the ability to lyse cells which are resistant to NK cells; TIL cells (which are derived from cancerous tissue from a patient and incubated in aldesleukin) have been shown to be 50% more effective than LAK cells in experimental studies.

Pharmacodynamics/Kinetics
Distribution: V_d: 4-7 L; primarily in plasma and then in the lymphocytes
Bioavailability: I.M.: 37%
Half-life elimination: Initial: 6-13 minutes; Terminal: 80-120 minutes

Dosage Refer to individual protocols.
I.V.:
Renal cell carcinoma: 600,000 int. units/kg every 8 hours for a maximum of 14 doses; repeat after 9 days of rest for a total of 28 doses per course. Re-evaluate at 4 weeks. Retreat if needed 7 weeks after hospital discharge from previous course.
Melanoma:
Single-agent use: 600,000 int. units/kg every 8 hours for a maximum of 14 doses; repeat after 9 days of rest for a total of 28 doses per course. Re-evaluate at 4 weeks. Retreat if needed 7 weeks after hospital discharge from previous course.
In combination with cytotoxic agents: 24 million int. units/m^2 days 12-16 and 19-23
S.C.:
Single-agent doses: 3-18 million int. units/day for 5 days weekly and repeated weekly up to 6 weeks
In combination with interferon:
5 million int. units/m^2 3 times/week
1.8 million int. units/m^2 twice daily 5 days/week for 6 weeks
Investigational regimen: S.C.: 11 million int. units (flat dose) daily x 4 days per week for 4 consecutive weeks; repeat every 6 weeks

Administration Administer as I.V. infusion over 15 minutes; may be administered by S.C. injection
Management of symptoms related to vascular leak syndrome:
If actual body weight increases >10% above baseline, or rales or rhonchi are audible:
Administer furosemide at dosage determined by patient response
Administer dopamine hydrochloride 2-4 mcg/kg/minute to maintain renal blood flow and urine output
If patient has dyspnea at rest: Administer supplemental oxygen by face mask
If patient has severe respiratory distress: Intubate patient and provide mechanical ventilation; administer ranitidine (as the hydrochloride salt), 50 mg I.V. every 8-12 hours as prophylaxis against stress ulcers

Monitoring Parameters
The following clinical evaluations are recommended for all patients prior to beginning treatment and then frequently during drug administration:
Standard hematologic tests including CBC, differential, and platelet counts; blood chemistries including electrolytes, renal and hepatic function tests
Chest x-rays
Monitoring during therapy should include vital signs (temperature, pulse, blood pressure, and respiration rate) and weight; in a patient with a decreased blood pressure, especially <90 mm Hg, cardiac monitoring for rhythm should be conducted. If an abnormal complex or rhythm is seen, an ECG should be performed; vital signs in these hypotension patients should be taken hourly and central venous pressure (CVP) checked.
During treatment, pulmonary function should be monitored on a regular basis.

Dosage Forms INJ, powder for reconstitution: 22 x 10^6 int. units

- **Aldomet** *see* Methyldopa *on page 820*
- **Aldoril®** *see* Methyldopa and Hydrochlorothiazide *on page 821*
- **Aldoril® D** *see* Methyldopa and Hydrochlorothiazide *on page 821*
- **Aldroxicon I [OTC]** *see* Aluminum Hydroxide, Magnesium Hydroxide, and Simethicone *on page 68*
- **Aldroxicon II [OTC]** *see* Aluminum Hydroxide, Magnesium Hydroxide, and Simethicone *on page 68*
- **Aldurazyme®** *see* Laronidase *on page 718*

Alefacept (a LE fa sept)
U.S. Brand Names Amevive®
Synonyms B 9273; BG 9273; Human LFA-3/IgG(1) Fusion Protein; LFA-3/IgG(1) Fusion Protein, Human
Therapeutic Category Monoclonal Antibody
Use Treatment of moderate to severe plaque psoriasis in adults who are candidates for systemic therapy or phototherapy
Restrictions Alefacept will be distributed directly to physician offices or to a specialty pharmacy; injections are intended to be administered in the physician's office
Pregnancy Risk Factor B
(Continued)

Alefacept *(Continued)*

Contraindications Hypersensitivity to alefacept or any component of the formulation; patients with a pretreatment depression in CD4 T-lymphocytes; history of severe malignancy; clinically-important infection

Warnings/Precautions Alefacept induces a decline in circulating T-lymphocytes (CD4+ and CD8+); CD4+ lymphocyte counts should be monitored weekly throughout therapy. Do not initiate in pre-existing depression of CD4+ lymphocytes and withhold treatment in any patient who develops a depressed CD4+ lymphocyte count (<250 cells/μL) during treatment; permanently discontinue if CD4+ lymphocyte counts remain <250 cells/μL for 1 month.

Alefacept may increase the risk of malignancies; use caution in patients at high risk for malignancy. Discontinue if malignancy develops during therapy. Alefacept may increase the risk of infection and may reactivate latent infection; monitor for new infections. Avoid use in patients receiving other immunosuppressant drugs or phototherapy. Safety and efficacy of live or attenuated vaccines have not been evaluated. Not indicated for use in pediatric patients.

Common Adverse Reactions

≥10%:

Hematologic: Lymphopenia (up to 10% of patients required temporary discontinuation, up to 17% during a second course of therapy)

Local: Injection site reactions (up to 16% of patients; includes pain, inflammation, bleeding, edema, or other reaction)

1% to 10%:

Central nervous system: Chills (6%; primarily during intravenous administration), dizziness

Dermatologic: Pruritus

Gastrointestinal: Nausea

Neuromuscular & skeletal: Myalgia

Respiratory: Pharyngitis, cough increased

Miscellaneous: Malignancies (1% vs 0.2% in placebo), antibodies to alefacept (3%; significance unknown), infections (1% to 2% requiring hospitalization)

Drug Interactions

Increased Effect/Toxicity: No formal drug interaction studies have been completed.

Decreased Effect: No formal drug interaction studies have been completed.

Mechanism of Action Binds to CD2, a receptor on the surface of lymphocytes, inhibiting their interaction with leukocyte functional antigen 3 (LFA-3). Interaction between CD2 and LFA-3 is important for the activation of T-lymphocytes in psoriasis. Activated T-lymphocytes secrete a number of inflammatory mediators, including interferon gamma, which are involved in psoriasis. Since CD2 is primarily expressed on T-lymphocytes, treatment results in a reduction in CD4+ and CD8+ T-lymphocytes, with lesser effects on other cell populations (NK- and B-lymphocytes).

Pharmacodynamics/Kinetics

Distribution: V_d: 0.094 L/kg

Bioavailability: 63% (following I.M. administration)

Half-life: 270 hours (following I.V. administration)

Excretion: Clearance: 0.25 mL/hour/kg

Dosage Adults:

I.M.: 15 mg once weekly; usual duration of treatment: 12 weeks

I.V.: 7.5 mg once weekly; usual duration of treatment: 12 weeks

A second course of treatment may be initiated at least 12 weeks after completion of the initial course of treatment, provided CD4+ T-lymphocyte counts are within the normal range.

Note: CD4+ T-lymphocyte counts should be monitored before initiation of treatment and weekly during therapy. Dosing should be withheld if CD4+ counts are <250 cells/μL, and dosing should be permanently discontinued if CD4+ lymphocyte counts remain at <250 cell/μL for longer than 1 month.

Elderly: Refer to Adults dosing

Dosage adjustment in renal impairment: No dosage adjustment required

Administration Do not filter alefacept solutions.

I.M. injections should be administered at least 1 inch from previous administration sites.

I.V. administration set should be primed with 3 mL NS and the line should be flushed with 3 mL NS following the dose. Administer over ≤5 seconds.

Monitoring Parameters Baseline lymphocyte counts prior to initiation and weekly during treatment course; severity of psoriatic lesions; signs and symptoms of infection

Patient Information This drug can only be administered by injection or infusion. Report headache or unusual fatigue; increased nausea or abdominal pain; cough, runny nose, difficulty breathing; chest pain or persistent dizziness; fatigue, muscle pain or weakness, back pain; fever or chills; mouth sores; vaginal itching or discharge; sore throat; unhealed sores; or frequent infections. It is important to keep appointments for blood cell monitoring. Notify prescriber if pregnancy occurs during therapy or within 8 weeks of treatment.

Dosage Forms INJ, powder for reconstitution: [I.V. administration]: 7.5 mg [DSC]. **INJ, powder for reconstitution:** [I.M. administration]: 15 mg

Alemtuzumab *(ay lem TU zoo mab)*

U.S. Brand Names Campath®

Synonyms Campath-1H; DNA-derived Humanized Monoclonal Antibody; Humanized IgG1 Anti-CD52 Monoclonal Antibody

Therapeutic Category Antineoplastic Agent, Monoclonal Antibody

Use Treatment of B-cell chronic lymphocytic leukemia (B-CLL)

Unlabeled/Investigational Use Treatment of refractory T-cell prolymphocytic leukemia (T-PLL); rheumatoid arthritis; graft versus host disease; multiple myeloma

Pregnancy Risk Factor C

Contraindications Known type 1 hypersensitivity or anaphylactic reaction to alemtuzumab or any component of the formulation; hypersensitivity to another monoclonal antibody; active systemic infections; underlying immunodeficiency (eg, seropositive for HIV); single doses >30 mg or cumulative doses >90 mg/week; administration by I.V. push or bolus

Warnings/Precautions Serious infections may occur. Prophylactic therapy against PCP pneumonia and herpes viral infections is recommended. Premedicate with an antihistamine and acetaminophen prior to dosing. Gradual escalation to the recommended maintenance dose is required at initiation and if therapy is interrupted for ≥7 days. Irradiation of any blood products administered during lymphopenia is recommended. Discontinue therapy during serious infection, serious hematologic or other serious toxicity until the event resolves. Permanently discontinue if autoimmune anemia or autoimmune thrombocytopenia occurs. Patients should not be immunized with live, viral vaccines during or recently after treatment. Women of childbearing potential and men of reproductive potential should use effective contraceptive methods during treatment and for a minimum of 6 months following therapy. Safety and efficacy have not been established in pediatric patients.

Common Adverse Reactions

>10%:

Cardiovascular: Hypotension (15% to 32%, infusion-related), peripheral edema (13%), hypertension (11%), tachycardia/SVT (11%)

Central nervous system: Drug-related fever (83%, infusion-related), fatigue (22% to 34%, infusion-related), headache (13% to 24%), dysthesias (15%), dizziness (12%), neutropenic fever (10%)

Dermatologic: Rash (30% to 40%, infusion-related), urticaria (22% to 30%, infusion-related), pruritus (14% to 24%, infusion-related)

Gastrointestinal: Nausea (47% to 54%), vomiting (33% to 41%), anorexia (20%), diarrhea (13% to 22%), stomatitis/mucositis (14%), abdominal pain (11%)

Hematologic: Lymphopenia, severe neutropenia (64% to 70%); severe anemia (38% to 47%) and severe thrombocytopenia (50% to 52%) may be prolonged and dose-limiting

Neuromuscular & skeletal: Rigors (89%, infusion-related), skeletal muscle pain (24%), weakness (13%), myalgia (11%)

Respiratory: Dyspnea (17% to 26%, infusion-related), cough (25%), bronchitis/pneumonitis (21%), pharyngitis (12%)

Miscellaneous: Infection (43% including sepsis, pneumonia, opportunistic infections; received PCP pneumonia and herpes prophylaxis); diaphoresis (19%)

1% to 10%:

Cardiovascular: Chest pain (10%)

Central nervous system: Insomnia (10%), malaise (9%), depression (7%), temperature change sensation (5%), somnolence (5%)

Dermatologic: Purpura (8%)

Gastrointestinal: Dyspepsia (10%), constipation (9%)

Hematologic: Pancytopenia /marrow hypoplasia (6%), positive Coombs' test without hemolysis (2%), autoimmune thrombocytopenia (2%), antibodies to alemtuzumab (2%), autoimmune hemolytic anemia (1%)

Neuromuscular & skeletal: Back pain (10%), tremor (7%)

Respiratory: Bronchospasm (9%), epistaxis (7%), rhinitis (7%)

Mechanism of Action Recombinant monoclonal antibody binds to CD52, a nonmodulating antigen present on the surface of B and T lymphocytes, a majority of monocytes, macrophages, NK cells and a subpopulation of granulocytes. After binding to CD52+ cells, an antibody-dependent lysis occurs.

Pharmacodynamics/Kinetics Half-life elimination: 12 days

Dosage Note: **Dose escalation is required**; usually accomplished in 3-7 days. Do not exceed single doses >30 mg or cumulative doses >90 mg/week. Premedicate with diphenhydramine and acetaminophen 30 minutes before initiation of infusion. Start anti-infective prophylaxis. Discontinue therapy during serious infection, serious hematologic or other serious toxicity until the event resolves. Permanently discontinue if evidence of autoimmune anemia or autoimmune thrombocytopenia occurs.

I.V. infusion: Adults: B-CLL:

Initial: 3 mg/day as a 2-hour infusion; increase to 10 mg/day, then to 30 mg/day as tolerated

Maintenance: 30 mg/day 3 times/week on alternate days for up to 12 weeks

Dosage adjustment for hematologic toxicity (severe neutropenia or thrombocytopenia, not autoimmune):

First occurrence: ANC <250/μL and/or platelet count ≤25,000/μL: Hold therapy; resume at same dose when ANC ≥500/μL and platelet count ≥50,000/μL. If delay between dosing is ≥7 days, restart at 3 mg/day and escalate as tolerated.

Second occurrence: ANC <250/μL and/or platelet count ≤25,000/μL: Hold therapy; resume at 10 mg/day when ANC ≥500/μL and platelet count ≥50,000/μL. If delay between dosing is ≥7 days, restart at 3 mg/day and escalate as tolerated.

Third occurrence: ANC <250/μL and/or platelet count ≤25,000/μL: Permanently discontinue therapy

Patients with a baseline ANC ≤500/μL and/or a baseline platelet count ≤25,000/μL at initiation of therapy: If ANC and/or platelet counts decreased to ≤50% of the baseline value, hold therapy. When ANC and/or platelet count return to baseline, resume therapy. If delay between dosing is ≥7 days, restart at 3 mg/day and escalate as tolerated.

(Continued)

Alemtuzumab *(Continued)*

Administration Administer by I.V. infusion only over 2 hours. Premedicate with diphenhydramine and acetaminophen 30 minutes before initiation of infusion. Start anti-infective prophylaxis. Other drugs should not be added to or simultaneously infused through the same I.V. line. Do not give I.V. bolus or push.

Monitoring Parameters Vital signs; carefully monitor BP especially in patient with ischemic heart disease or on antihypertensive medications; CBC and platelets weekly (more frequent monitoring needed if any hematologic abnormality occurs); signs and symptoms of infection; CD4+ lymphocyte counts

Patient Information This medication can only be administered I.V. During infusion, you will be closely monitored. You will need frequent laboratory tests during course of therapy. Do not use any prescription or OTC medications unless approved by your prescriber. Maintain adequate hydration (2-3 L/day unless otherwise instructed) and nutrition (frequent small meals will help). You may experience abdominal pain, mouth sores, nausea, or vomiting (small frequent meals, good mouth care with soft toothbrush or swabs, sucking lozenges or chewing gum, and avoidance of spicy or salty foods may help). Report unresolved gastrointestinal problems, persistent fever, chills, muscle pain, skin rash, unusual bleeding or bruising, signs of infection (mouth sores, sore throat, white plaques in mouth or perianal area, burning on urination); swelling of extremities; difficulty breathing; chest pain or palpitations; or other persistent adverse reactions.

Dosage Forms INJ, solution: 10 mg/mL (3 mL)

Alendronate *(a LEN droe nate)*

U.S. Brand Names Fosamax®
Synonyms Alendronate Sodium
Therapeutic Category Bisphosphonate Derivative
Use Treatment and prevention of osteoporosis in postmenopausal females; treatment of osteoporosis in males; Paget's disease of the bone in patients who are symptomatic, at risk for future complications, or with alkaline phosphatase ≥2 times the upper limit of normal; treatment of glucocorticoid-induced osteoporosis in males and females with low bone mineral density who are receiving a daily dosage ≥7.5 mg of prednisone (or equivalent)
Pregnancy Risk Factor C
Contraindications Hypersensitivity to alendronate, other bisphosphonates, or any component of the formulation; hypocalcemia; abnormalities of the esophagus which delay esophageal emptying such as stricture or achalasia; inability to stand or sit upright for at least 30 minutes
Warnings/Precautions Use caution in patients with renal impairment; hypocalcemia must be corrected before therapy initiation; ensure adequate calcium and vitamin D intake. May cause irritation to upper gastrointestinal mucosa. Esophagitis, esophageal ulcers, esophageal erosions, and esophageal stricture (rare) have been reported; risk increases in patients unable to comply with dosing instructions. Use with caution in patients with dysphagia, esophageal disease, gastritis, duodenitis, or ulcers (may worsen underlying condition).
Common Adverse Reactions Note: Incidence of adverse effects increases significantly in patients treated for Paget's disease at 40 mg/day, mostly GI adverse effects.

>10%: Endocrine & metabolic: Hypocalcemia (transient, mild, 18%); hypophosphatemia (transient, mild, 10%)

1% to 10%:
Central nervous system: Headache (0.2% to 3%)
Gastrointestinal: Abdominal pain (1% to 7%), acid reflux (1% to 5%), dyspepsia (1% to 4%), nausea (1% to 4%), flatulence (0.2% to 4%), diarrhea (0.6% to 3%), constipation (0.3% to 3%), esophageal ulcer (0.1% to 2%), abdominal distension (0.2% to 1%), gastritis (0.2% to 1%), vomiting (0.2% to 1%), dysphagia (0.1% to 1%), gastric ulcer (1%), melena (1%)
Neuromuscular & skeletal: Musculoskeletal pain (0.4% to 4%), muscle cramps (0.2% to 1%)

Drug Interactions
Increased Effect/Toxicity: I.V. ranitidine has been shown to double the bioavailability of alendronate. Estrogen replacement therapy, in combination with alendronate, may enhance the therapeutic effects of both agents on the maintenance of bone mineralization. An increased incidence of adverse GI effects has been noted when >10 mg alendronate is used in patients taking aspirin-containing products.
Decreased Effect: Oral medications (especially those containing multivalent cations, including calcium and antacids): May interfere with alendronate absorption; wait at least 30 minutes after taking alendronate before taking any oral medications
Mechanism of Action A bisphosphonate which inhibits bone resorption via actions on osteoclasts or on osteoclast precursors; decreases the rate of bone resorption direction, leading to an indirect decrease in bone formation
Pharmacodynamics/Kinetics
Distribution: 28 L (exclusive of bone)
Protein binding: ~78%
Metabolism: None
Bioavailability: Fasting: Female: 0.7%; Male: 0.6%; reduced 60% with food or drink
Half-life elimination: Exceeds 10 years
Excretion: Urine; feces (as unabsorbed drug)
Dosage Oral: Adults:
Osteoporosis in postmenopausal females:
Prophylaxis: 5 mg once daily or 35 mg once weekly
Treatment: 10 mg once daily or 70 mg once weekly

Osteoporosis in males: 10 mg once daily **or** 70 mg once weekly
Paget's disease of bone: 40 mg once daily for 6 months
  Retreatment: Relapses during the 12 months following therapy occurred in 9% of patients who responded to treatment. Specific retreatment data are not available. Retreatment with alendronate may be considered, following a 6-month post-treatment evaluation period, in patients who have relapsed based on increases in serum alkaline phosphatase, which should be measured periodically. Retreatment may also be considered in those who failed to normalize their serum alkaline phosphatase.
Glucocorticoid-induced osteoporosis: Treatment: 5 mg once daily; a dose of 10 mg once daily should be used in postmenopausal females who are not receiving estrogen. Patients treated with glucocorticoids should receive adequate amounts of calcium and vitamin D.
Elderly: No dosage adjustment is necessary
Dosage adjustment in renal impairment:
  Cl$_{cr}$ 35-60 mL/minute: None necessary
  Cl$_{cr}$ <35 mL/minute: Alendronate is not recommended due to lack of experience
Dosage adjustment in hepatic impairment: None necessary
Administration Alendronate must be taken with plain water (tablets 6-8 oz; oral solution 2 oz) first thing in the morning and ≥30 minutes before the first food, beverage, or other medication of the day. Patients should be instructed to stay upright (not to lie down) for at least 30 minutes **and** until after first food of the day (to reduce esophageal irritation). Patients should receive supplemental calcium and vitamin D if dietary intake is inadequate.
Monitoring Parameters Alkaline phosphatase should be periodically measured; serum calcium and phosphorus; monitor pain and fracture rate; hormonal status (male and female) prior to therapy; bone mineral density (should be done prior to initiation of therapy and after 6-12 months of combined glucocorticoid and alendronate treatment)
Reference Range Calcium (total): Adults: 9.0-11.0 mg/dL (2.05-2.54 mmol/L), may slightly decrease with aging; phosphorus: 2.5-4.5 mg/dL (0.81-1.45 mmol/L)
Patient Information Take as directed, with a full glass of water first thing in the morning and at least 30 minutes before the first food or beverage of the day. Wait at least 30 minutes after taking alendronate before taking anything else. Stay in sitting or standing position for 30 minutes following administration and until after the first food of the day to reduce potential for esophageal irritation. Consult prescriber to determine necessity of lifestyle changes (eg, decreased smoking, decreased alcohol intake, dietary supplements of calcium, or increased dietary vitamin D).
Dosage Forms SOLN, oral, as monosodium trihydrate: 70 mg/75 mL. **TAB:** 5 mg, 10 mg, 35 mg, 40 mg, 70 mg

◆ **Alendronate Sodium** see Alendronate on page 52
◆ **Alenic Alka Tablet [OTC]** see Aluminum Hydroxide and Magnesium Trisilicate on page 67
◆ **Aler-Dryl [OTC]** see DiphenhydrAMINE on page 383
◆ **Alesse®** see Ethinyl Estradiol and Levonorgestrel on page 484
◆ **Aleve® [OTC]** see Naproxen on page 882
◆ **Alfenta®** see Alfentanil on page 53

Alfentanil (al FEN ta nil)

Related Information
  Narcotic Agonists Comparison on page 1395
U.S. Brand Names Alfenta®
Synonyms Alfentanil Hydrochloride
Therapeutic Category Analgesic, Narcotic
Use Analgesic adjunct given by continuous infusion or in incremental doses in maintenance of anesthesia with barbiturate or N$_2$O or a primary anesthetic agent for the induction of anesthesia in patients undergoing general surgery in which endotracheal intubation and mechanical ventilation are required
Restrictions C-II
Pregnancy Risk Factor C
Contraindications Hypersensitivity to alfentanil hydrochloride, to narcotics, or any component of the formulation; increased intracranial pressure, severe respiratory depression
Warnings/Precautions Use with caution in patients with drug dependence, head injury, acute asthma and respiratory conditions; hypotension has occurred in neonates with respiratory distress syndrome; use caution when administering to patients with bradyarrhythmias; rapid I.V. infusion may result in skeletal muscle and chest wall rigidity, impaired ventilation, or respiratory distress/arrest; inject slowly over 3-5 minutes. Alfentanil may produce more hypotension compared to fentanyl, therefore, be sure to administer slowly and ensure patient has adequate hydration.
Common Adverse Reactions
  >10%:
    Cardiovascular: Bradycardia, peripheral vasodilation
    Central nervous system: Drowsiness, sedation, increased intracranial pressure
    Gastrointestinal: Nausea, vomiting, constipation
    Endocrine & metabolic: Antidiuretic hormone release
    Ocular: Miosis
  1% to 10%:
    Cardiovascular: Cardiac arrhythmias, orthostatic hypotension
    Central nervous system: Confusion, CNS depression
    Ocular: Blurred vision
(Continued)

Alfentanil *(Continued)*

Drug Interactions
Cytochrome P450 Effect: Substrate of CYP3A4 (major)

Increased Effect/Toxicity: Dextroamphetamine may enhance the analgesic effect of morphine and other opiate agonists. CNS depressants (eg, benzodiazepines, barbiturates, tricyclic antidepressants), erythromycin, reserpine, beta-blockers may increase the toxic effects of alfentanil. CYP3A4 inhibitors may increase the levels/effects of alfentanil; example inhibitors include azole antifungals, ciprofloxacin, clarithromycin, diclofenac, doxycycline, erythromycin, imatinib, isoniazid, nefazodone, nicardipine, propofol, protease inhibitors, quinidine, and verapamil.

Mechanism of Action Binds with stereospecific receptors at many sites within the CNS, increases pain threshold, alters pain perception, inhibits ascending pain pathways; is an ultra short-acting narcotic

Pharmacodynamics/Kinetics
Onset of action: Rapid

Duration (dose dependent): 30-60 minutes

Distribution: V_d: Newborns, premature: 1 L/kg; Children: 0.163-0.48 L/kg; Adults: 0.46 L/kg

Half-life elimination: Newborns, premature: 5.33-8.75 hours; Children: 40-60 minutes; Adults: 83-97 minutes

Dosage Doses should be titrated to appropriate effects; wide range of doses is dependent upon desired degree of analgesia/anesthesia

Children <12 years: Dose not established

Adults: Dose should be based on ideal body weight as follows (see table):

Alfentanil

Indication	Approx Duration of Anesthesia (min)	Induction Period (Initial Dose) (mcg/kg)	Maintenance Period (Increments/ Infusion)	Total Dose (mcg/kg)	Effects
Incremental injection	≤30	8-20	3-5 mcg/kg or 0.5-1 mcg/kg/min	8-40	Spontaneously breathing or assisted ventilation when required.
	30-60	20-50	5-15 mcg/kg	Up to 75	Assisted or controlled ventilation required. Attenuation of response to laryngoscopy and intubation.
Continuous infusion	>45	50-75	0.5-3 mcg/kg/min average infusion rate 1-1.5 mcg/ kg/min	Dependent on duration of procedure	Assisted or controlled ventilation required. Some attenuation of response to intubation and incision, with intraoperative stability.
Anesthetic induction	>45	130-245	0.5-1.5 mcg/kg/ min or general anesthetic	Dependent on duration of procedure	Assisted or controlled ventilation required. Administer slowly (over 3 minutes). Concentration of inhalation agents reduced by 30% to 50% for initial hour.

Administration Administer I.V. slowly over 3-5 minutes or by I.V. continuous infusion.

Monitoring Parameters Respiratory rate, blood pressure, heart rate

Reference Range 100-340 ng/mL (depending upon procedure)

Dosage Forms INJ, solution [preservative free]: 500 mcg/mL (2 mL, 5 mL, 10 mL, 20 mL)

♦ **Alfentanil Hydrochloride** *see Alfentanil on page 53*

♦ **Alferon® N** *see Interferon Alfa-n3 on page 679*

Alfuzosin (al FYOO zoe sin)

U.S. Brand Names Uroxatral™

Synonyms Alfuzosin Hydrochloride

Therapeutic Category Alpha-Adrenergic Blocking Agent, Oral

Use Treatment of the functional symptoms of benign prostatic hyperplasia (BPH)

Pregnancy Risk Factor B

Contraindications Hypersensitivity to alfuzosin or any component of the formulation; moderate or severe hepatic insufficiency (Child-Pugh class B and C); potent CYP3A4 inhibitors (eg, itraconazole, ketoconazole, ritonavir)

Warnings/Precautions Not intended for use as an antihypertensive drug. May cause orthostasis, syncope, or dizziness. Patients should avoid situations where injury may occur as a result of syncope. Discontinue if symptoms of angina occur or worsen. Use caution with history of QT prolongation or use with medications which may prolong the QT interval. Rule out prostatic carcinoma before beginning therapy. Use caution with renal or mild hepatic impairment.

Drug Interactions
Cytochrome P450 Effect: Substrate of CYP3A4 (major)

Increased Effect/Toxicity: CYP3A4 inhibitors may increase serum level and/or toxicity of alfuzosin. Potent inhibitors (itraconazole, ketoconazole, ritonavir) lead to threefold increase in concentrations; concurrent use is contraindicated. Administration with diltiazem, a less potent inhibitor, leads to an approximate 1.5-fold increase in concentrations of both agents.

Decreased Effect: CYP3A4 inducers may decrease the levels/effects of alfuzosin; example inducers include aminoglutethimide, carbamazepine, nafcillin, nevirapine, phenobarbital, phenytoin, and rifamycins.

Mechanism of Action An antagonist of alpha₁ adrenoreceptors in the lower urinary tract. Smooth muscle tone is mediated by the sympathetic nervous stimulation of alpha₁ adrenoreceptors, which are abundant in the prostate, prostatic capsule, prostatic urethra, and bladder neck. Blockade of these adrenoreceptors can cause smooth muscles in the bladder neck and prostate to relax, resulting in an improvement in urine flow rate and a reduction in symptoms of BPH.

Pharmacodynamics/Kinetics
Absorption: Decreased 50% under fasting conditions
Distribution: V_d: 3.2 L/kg
Protein binding: 82% to 90%
Metabolism: Hepatic, primarily via CYP3A4; metabolism includes oxidation, O-demethylation and N-dealkylation; forms metabolites (inactive)
Bioavailability: 49% following a meal
Half-life elimination: 10 hours
Time to peak, plasma: 8 hours following a meal
Excretion: Feces (69%); urine (24%)

Dosage Oral: Adults: 10 mg once daily
Dosage adjustment in renal impairment: Bioavailability and maximum serum concentrations are increased by ~50% with mild, moderate, or severe renal impairment
Note: Safety has not been evaluated in patients with creatinine clearances <30 mL/minute.
Dosage adjustment in hepatic impairment:
Mild hepatic impairment: Use has not been studied
Moderate or severe hepatic impairment (Child-Pugh class B and C): Clearance is decreased $\frac{1}{3}$ to $\frac{1}{4}$ and serum concentration is increased three- to fourfold; use is contraindicated

Administration Tablet should be swallowed whole; do not crush or chew. Administer once daily (with a meal); should be taken at the same time each day.

Monitoring Parameters Urine flow; blood pressure

Patient Information Take following a meal at the same time each day. Swallow whole, do not crush or chew. May cause drowsiness, dizziness, or impaired judgment (use caution when driving or engaging in tasks that require alertness until response to drug is known); postural hypotension (use caution when rising from sitting or lying position or when climbing stairs).

Dosage Forms TAB, extended release: 10 mg

♦ **Alfuzosin Hydrochloride** *see Alfuzosin on page 54*

Alglucerase (al GLOO ser ase)

U.S. Brand Names Ceredase®
Synonyms Glucocerebrosidase
Therapeutic Category Enzyme, Glucocerebrosidase
Use Replacement therapy for Gaucher's disease (type 1)
Pregnancy Risk Factor C
Contraindications Hypersensitivity to any component of the formulation
Warnings/Precautions Prepared from pooled human placental tissue that may contain the causative agents of some viral diseases. Patients who develop IgG antibodies are at a higher risk for developing hypersensitivity. Use caution with androgen sensitive malignancies or prior allergies to hCG. May cause early virilization in males <10 years of age.
Common Adverse Reactions Frequency not defined.
Cardiovascular: Peripheral edema
Central nervous system: Chills, fatigue, fever, headache, lightheadedness
Endocrine & metabolic: Hot flashes, menstrual abnormalities
Gastrointestinal: Abdominal discomfort, diarrhea, nausea, oral ulcerations, vomiting
Local: Injection site: Abscess, burning, discomfort, pruritus, swelling
Neuromuscular & skeletal: Backache, weakness
Miscellaneous: Dysosmia; hypersensitivity reactions (abdominal cramping, angioedema, chest discomfort, flushing, hypotension, nausea, pruritus, respiratory symptoms, urticaria); IgG antibody formation (~13%)
Mechanism of Action Glucocerebrosidase is an enzyme prepared from human placental tissue. Gaucher's disease is an inherited metabolic disorder caused by the defective activity of beta-glucosidase and the resultant accumulation of glucosyl ceramide laden macrophages in the liver, bone, and spleen; acts by replacing the missing enzyme associated with Gaucher's disease.
Pharmacodynamics/Kinetics Half-life elimination: ~3-11 minutes
Dosage I.V.: Children and Adults: Dosing is individualized based on disease severity; average dose: 60 units/kg every 2 weeks. Range: 2.5 units/kg 3 times/week to 60 units/kg 1-4 times/week. Once patient response is well established, dose may be reduced every 3-6 months to determine maintenance therapy.
Administration I.V.: Infuse I.V. over 1-2 hours; use of an in-line filter is recommended; do not shake solution as it denatures the enzyme
Monitoring Parameters CBC, platelets, liver function tests, IgG antibody formation, acid phosphatase (AP)
Dosage Forms INJ, solution, [preservative free]: 10 units/mL (5 mL); 80 units/mL (5 mL)

♦ **Alinia**™ *see Nitazoxanide on page 907*

Alitretinoin (a li TRET i noyn)
U.S. Brand Names Panretin®
Therapeutic Category Antineoplastic Agent, Miscellaneous; Retinoic Acid Derivative
Use Orphan drug: Topical treatment of cutaneous lesions in AIDS-related Kaposi's sarcoma
Unlabeled/Investigational Use Cutaneous T-cell lymphomas
Pregnancy Risk Factor D
Contraindications Hypersensitivity to alitretinoin, other retinoids, or any component of the formulation; pregnancy
Warnings/Precautions May cause fetal harm if absorbed by a woman who is pregnant. May be photosensitizing (based on experience with other retinoids); minimize sun or other UV exposure of treated areas. Do not use concurrently with topical products containing DEET (increased toxicity may result). Safety in pediatric patients or geriatric patients has not been established.
Common Adverse Reactions
> 10%:
    Central nervous system: Pain (0% to 34%)
    Dermatologic: Rash (25% to 77%), pruritus (8% to 11%)
    Neuromuscular & skeletal: Paresthesia (3% to 22%)
5% to 10%:
    Cardiovascular: Edema (3% to 8%)
    Dermatologic: Exfoliative dermatitis (3% to 9%), skin disorder (0% to 8%)
Drug Interactions
Increased Effect/Toxicity: Increased toxicity of DEET may occur if products containing this compound are used concurrently with alitretinoin. Due to limited absorption after topical application, interaction with systemic medications is unlikely.
Mechanism of Action Binds to retinoid receptors to inhibit growth of Kaposi's sarcoma
Pharmacodynamics/Kinetics Absorption: Not extensive
Dosage Topical: Apply gel twice daily to cutaneous Kaposi's sarcoma or T-cell lymphoma (unlabeled use) lesions
Administration Do not use occlusive dressings.
Patient Information For external use only; avoid UV light exposure (sun or sunlamps) of treated areas; avoid DEET-containing products
Dosage Forms GEL: 0.1% (60 g tube)

♦ **Alka-Mints**® [OTC] *see Calcium Carbonate on page 203*

♦ **Alka-Seltzer Plus**® **Cold and Cough [OTC]** *see Chlorpheniramine, Phenylephrine, and Dextromethorphan on page 264*

♦ **Alka-Seltzer Plus**® **Cold and Sinus Liquigels [OTC]** *see Acetaminophen and Pseudoephedrine on page 26*

♦ **Alka-Seltzer**® **Plus Cold Liqui-Gels**® **[OTC]** *see Acetaminophen, Chlorpheniramine, and Pseudoephedrine on page 28*

♦ **Alka-Seltzer**® **Plus Flu Liqui-Gels**® **[OTC]** *see Acetaminophen, Dextromethorphan, and Pseudoephedrine on page 28*

♦ **Alkeran**® *see Melphalan on page 786*

♦ **Allbee**® **C-800 [OTC]** *see Vitamin B Complex Combinations on page 1311*

♦ **Allbee**® **C-800 + Iron [OTC]** *see Vitamin B Complex Combinations on page 1311*

♦ **Allbee**® **with C [OTC]** *see Vitamin B Complex Combinations on page 1311*

♦ **Allegra**® *see Fexofenadine on page 521*

♦ **Allegra-D**® *see Fexofenadine and Pseudoephedrine on page 522*

♦ **Allerest**® **Maximum Strength Allergy and Hay Fever [OTC]** *see Chlorpheniramine and Pseudoephedrine on page 263*

♦ **Allerfrim**® **[OTC]** *see Triprolidine and Pseudoephedrine on page 1273*

♦ **Allergen**® *see Antipyrine and Benzocaine on page 107*

♦ **AllerMax**® **[OTC]** *see DiphenhydrAMINE on page 383*

♦ **Allerphed**® **[OTC]** *see Triprolidine and Pseudoephedrine on page 1273*

♦ **Allersol**® *see Naphazoline on page 881*

Allopurinol (al oh PURE i nole)
U.S. Brand Names Aloprim™; Zyloprim®
Synonyms Allopurinol Sodium
Therapeutic Category Antigout Agent; Xanthine Oxidase Inhibitor
Use
    Oral: Prevention of attack of gouty arthritis and nephropathy; treatment of secondary hyperuricemia which may occur during treatment of tumors or leukemia; prevention of recurrent calcium oxalate calculi
    I.V.: Treatment of elevated serum and urinary uric acid levels when oral therapy is not tolerated in patients with leukemia, lymphoma, and solid tumor malignancies who are receiving cancer chemotherapy
Pregnancy Risk Factor C

Contraindications Hypersensitivity to allopurinol or any component of the formulation

Warnings/Precautions Do not use to treat asymptomatic hyperuricemia. Discontinue at first signs of rash; reduce dosage in renal insufficiency, reinstate with caution in patients who have had a previous mild allergic reaction, use with caution in children; monitor liver function and complete blood counts before initiating therapy and periodically during therapy, use with caution in patients taking diuretics concurrently. Risk of skin rash may be increased in patients receiving amoxicillin or ampicillin. The risk of hypersensitivity may be increased in patients receiving thiazides, and possibly ACE inhibitors. Use caution with mercaptopurine or azathioprine; dosage adjustment required.

Common Adverse Reactions The most common adverse reaction to allopurinol is a skin rash (usually maculopapular; however, more severe reactions, including Stevens-Johnson syndrome, have also been reported). While some studies cite an incidence of these reactions as high as >10% of cases (often in association with ampicillin or amoxicillin), the product labeling cites a much lower incidence, reflected below. Allopurinol should be discontinued at the first appearance of a rash or other sign of hypersensitivity.

>1%:

Dermatologic: Rash (1.5%)

Gastrointestinal: Nausea (1.3%), vomiting (1.2%)

Renal: Renal failure/impairment (1.2%)

Drug Interactions

Increased Effect/Toxicity: Allopurinol may increase the effects of azathioprine, chlorpropamide, mercaptopurine, theophylline, and oral anticoagulants. An increased risk of bone marrow suppression may occur when given with myelosuppressive agents (cyclophosphamide, possibly other alkylating agents). Amoxicillin/ampicillin, ACE inhibitors, and thiazide diuretics have been associated with hypersensitivity reactions when combined with allopurinol (rare), and the incidence of rash may be increased with penicillins (ampicillin, amoxicillin). Urinary acidification with large amounts of vitamin C may increase kidney stone formation.

Decreased Effect: Ethanol decreases effectiveness.

Mechanism of Action Allopurinol inhibits xanthine oxidase, the enzyme responsible for the conversion of hypoxanthine to xanthine to uric acid. Allopurinol is metabolized to oxypurinol which is also an inhibitor of xanthine oxidase; allopurinol acts on purine catabolism, reducing the production of uric acid without disrupting the biosynthesis of vital purines.

Pharmacodynamics/Kinetics

Onset of action: Peak effect: 1-2 weeks

Absorption: Oral: ~80%; Rectal: Poor and erratic

Distribution: V_d: ~1.6 L/kg; V_{ss}: 0.84-0.87 L/kg; enters breast milk

Protein binding: <1%

Metabolism: ~75% to active metabolites, chiefly oxypurinol

Bioavailability: 49% to 53%

Half-life elimination:

Normal renal function: Parent drug: 1-3 hours; Oxypurinol: 18-30 hours

End-stage renal disease: Prolonged

Time to peak, plasma: Oral: 30-120 minutes

Excretion: Urine (76% as oxypurinol, 12% as unchanged drug)

Allopurinol and oxypurinol are dialyzable

Dosage

Oral: Doses >300 mg should be given in divided doses.

Children ≤10 years: Secondary hyperuricemia associated with chemotherapy: 10 mg/kg/day in 2-3 divided doses **or** 200-300 mg/m²/day in 2-4 divided doses, maximum: 800 mg/24 hours

Alternative (manufacturer labeling): <6 years: 150 mg/day in 3 divided doses; 6-10 years: 300 mg/day in 2-3 divided doses

Children >10 years and Adults:

Secondary hyperuricemia associated with chemotherapy: 600-800 mg/day in 2-3 divided doses for prevention of acute uric acid nephropathy for 2-3 days starting 1-2 days before chemotherapy

Gout: Mild: 200-300 mg/day; Severe: 400-600 mg/day; to reduce the possibility of acute gouty attacks, initiate dose at 100 mg/day and increase weekly to recommended dosage.

Recurrent calcium oxalate stones: 200-300 mg/day in single or divided doses

Elderly: Initial: 100 mg/day, increase until desired uric acid level is obtained

I.V.: Hyperuricemia secondary to chemotherapy: Intravenous daily dose can be given as a single infusion or in equally divided doses at 6-, 8-, or 12-hour intervals. A fluid intake sufficient to yield a daily urinary output of at least 2 L in adults and the maintenance of a neutral or, preferably, slightly alkaline urine are desirable.

Children ≤10 years: Starting dose: 200 mg/m²/day

Children >10 years and Adults: 200-400 mg/m²/day (max: 600 mg/day)

Dosing adjustment in renal impairment: Must be adjusted due to accumulation of allopurinol and metabolites:

Oral: Removed by hemodialysis; adult maintenance doses of allopurinol (mg) based on creatinine clearance (mL/minute): See table on next page.

Hemodialysis: Administer dose posthemodialysis or administer 50% supplemental dose

I.V.:

Cl_{cr} 10-20 mL/minute: 200 mg/day

Cl_{cr} 3-10 mL/minute: 100 mg/day

Cl_{cr} <3 mL/minute: 100 mg/day at extended intervals

(Continued)

Allopurinol *(Continued)*

Adult Maintenance Doses of Allopurinol[1]

Creatinine Clearance (mL/min)	Maintenance Dose of Allopurinol (mg)
140	400 qd
120	350 qd
100	300 qd
80	250 qd
60	200 qd
40	150 qd
20	100 qd
10	100 q2d
0	100 q3d

[1]This table is based on a standard maintenance dose of 300 mg of allopurinol per day for a patient with a creatinine clearance of 100 mL/min.

Administration
Oral: Should administer oral forms after meals with plenty of fluid.

I.V.: The rate of infusion depends on the volume of the infusion. Whenever possible, therapy should be initiated at 24-48 hours before the start of chemotherapy known to cause tumor lysis (including adrenocorticosteroids). I.V. daily dose can be administered as a single infusion or in equally divided doses at 6-, 8-, or 12-hour interval.

Monitoring Parameters CBC, serum uric acid levels, I & O, hepatic and renal function, especially at start of therapy

Reference Range Uric acid, serum: An increase occurs during childhood
Adults:
Male: 3.4-7 mg/dL or slightly more
Female: 2.4-6 mg/dL or slightly more

Values >7 mg/dL are sometimes arbitrarily regarded as hyperuricemia, but there is no sharp line between normals on the one hand, and the serum uric acid of those with clinical gout. Normal ranges cannot be adjusted for purine ingestion, but high purine diet increases uric acid. Uric acid may be increased with body size, exercise, and stress.

Patient Information Take after meals with plenty of fluid (at least 10-12 glasses of fluids per day); discontinue the drug and contact prescriber at first sign of rash, painful urination, blood in urine, irritation of the eyes, or swelling of the lips or mouth; may cause drowsiness; alcohol decreases effectiveness

Dosage Forms INJ, powder for reconstitution (Aloprim™): 500 mg. **TAB** (Zyloprim®): 100 mg, 300 mg

♦ **Allopurinol Sodium** *see* Allopurinol *on page 56*

♦ **All-*trans*-Retinoic Acid** *see* Tretinoin (Oral) *on page 1258*

♦ **Almacone® [OTC]** *see* Aluminum Hydroxide, Magnesium Hydroxide, and Simethicone *on page 68*

♦ **Almacone Double Strength® [OTC]** *see* Aluminum Hydroxide, Magnesium Hydroxide, and Simethicone *on page 68*

♦ **Almora® [OTC]** *see* Magnesium Gluconate *on page 769*

Almotriptan *(al moh TRIP tan)*

Related Information
Antimigraine Drugs Comparison *on page 1363*

U.S. Brand Names Axert™

Synonyms Almotriptan Malate

Therapeutic Category Antimigraine Agent, Prophylaxis; Serotonin 5-HT$_{1D}$ Receptor Agonist

Use Acute treatment of migraine with or without aura

Pregnancy Risk Factor C

Contraindications Hypersensitivity to almotriptan or any component of the formulation; use as prophylactic therapy for migraine; hemiplegic or basilar migraine; cluster headache; known or suspected ischemic heart disease (angina pectoris, MI, documented silent ischemia, coronary artery vasospasm, Prinzmetal's variant angina); peripheral vascular syndromes (including ischemic bowel disease); uncontrolled hypertension; use within 24 hours of another 5-HT$_1$ agonist; use within 24 hours of ergotamine derivative; concurrent administration or within 2 weeks of discontinuing an MAO inhibitor (specifically MAO type A inhibitors)

Warnings/Precautions Almotriptan is indicated only in patients ≥18 years of age with a clear diagnosis of migraine headache. If a patient does not respond to the first dose, the diagnosis of migraine should be reconsidered. Do not give to patients with risk factors for CAD until a cardiovascular evaluation has been performed; if evaluation is satisfactory, the healthcare provider should administer the first dose and cardiovascular status should be periodically re-evaluated. Cardiac events (coronary artery vasospasm, transient ischemia, myocardial infarction, ventricular tachycardia/fibrillation, cardiac arrest, and death), cerebral/subarachnoid hemorrhage, stroke, peripheral vascular ischemia and colonic ischemia have been reported with 5-HT$_1$ agonist administration. Significant elevation in blood pressure, including hypertensive crisis, has also been reported on rare occasions in patients with and without a history of hypertension. Use with caution in liver or renal dysfunction. Safety and efficacy in pediatric patients have not been established.

Common Adverse Reactions 1% to 10%:
Central nervous system: Headache (>1%), dizziness (>1%), somnolence (>1%)
Gastrointestinal: Nausea (1% to 2%), xerostomia (1%)
Neuromuscular & skeletal: Paresthesia (1%)

Drug Interactions
Cytochrome P450 Effect: Substrate (minor) of CYP2D6, 3A4
Increased Effect/Toxicity: Ergot-containing drugs prolong vasospastic reactions; ketoconazole and CYP3A4 inhibitors increase almotriptan serum concentration; select serotonin reuptake inhibitors may increase symptoms of hyper-reflexia, weakness, and incoordination; MAO inhibitors may increase toxicity

Mechanism of Action Selective agonist for serotonin (5-HT$_{1B}$, 5-HT$_{1D}$, 5-HT$_{1F}$ receptors) in cranial arteries; causes vasoconstriction and reduce sterile inflammation associated with antidromic neuronal transmission correlating with relief of migraine

Pharmacodynamics/Kinetics
Absorption: Well absorbed
Distribution: V$_d$: 180-200 L
Protein binding: ~35%
Metabolism: MAO type A oxidative deamination (~27% of dose); via CYP3A4 and 2D6 (~12% of dose) to inactive metabolites
Bioavailability: 70%
Half-life elimination: 3-4 hours
Time to peak: 1-3 hours
Excretion: Urine (40% as unchanged drug); feces (13% unchanged and metabolized)

Dosage Oral: Adults: Migraine: Initial: 6.25-12.5 mg in a single dose; if the headache returns, repeat the dose after 2 hours; no more than 2 doses in 24-hour period
Note: If the first dose is ineffective, diagnosis needs to be re-evaluated. Safety of treating more than 4 migraines/month has not been established.
Dosage adjustment in renal impairment: Initial: 6.25 mg in a single dose; maximum daily dose: ≤12.5 mg
Dosage adjustment in hepatic impairment: Initial: 6.25 mg in a single dose; maximum daily dose: ≤12.5 mg

Patient Information This drug is to be used to reduce your migraine not to prevent or reduce the number of attacks. Take exactly as directed. If headache returns or is not fully resolved, the dose may be repeated after 2 hours. Do not use more than two doses in 24 hours. Do not take within 24 hours of other migraine medication without consulting prescriber. You may experience dizziness, fatigue, or drowsiness (use caution when driving or engaging in tasks that require alertness until response to drug is known). Report immediately chest pain, palpitations, feeling of tightness or pressure in chest, jaw, or throat; acute headache or dizziness; muscle cramping, pain, or tremors; skin rash; hallucinations, anxiety, panic; or other adverse reactions.

Dosage Forms TAB: 6.25 mg, 12.5 mg

Alprazolam (al PRAY zoe lam)

Related Information
Benzodiazepines Comparison on page 1366
U.S. Brand Names Alprazolam Intensol®; Xanax®; Xanax XR®
Therapeutic Category Antianxiety Agent; Benzodiazepine
Use Treatment of anxiety disorder (GAD); panic disorder, with or without agoraphobia; anxiety associated with depression
Unlabeled/Investigational Use Anxiety in children
Restrictions C-IV
Pregnancy Risk Factor D
Contraindications Hypersensitivity to alprazolam or any component of the formulation (cross-sensitivity with other benzodiazepines may exist); narrow-angle glaucoma; concurrent use with ketoconazole or itraconazole; pregnancy
Warnings/Precautions Rebound or withdrawal symptoms, including seizures may occur 18 hours to 3 days following abrupt discontinuation or large decreases in dose (more common in patients receiving >4 mg/day or prolonged treatment). Dose reductions or tapering must be approached with extreme caution. Breakthrough anxiety may occur at the end of dosing
(Continued)

Alprazolam *(Continued)*

interval. Use with caution in patients receiving concurrent CYP3A4 inhibitors, particularly when these agents are added to therapy. Has weak uricosuric properties, use with caution in renal impairment or predisposition to urate nephropathy. Use with caution in elderly or debilitated patients, patients with hepatic disease (including alcoholics), renal impairment, or obese patients.

Causes CNS depression (dose-related) resulting in sedation, dizziness, confusion, or ataxia, which may impair physical and mental capabilities. Patients must be cautioned about performing tasks that require mental alertness (eg, operating machinery or driving). Use with caution in patients receiving other CNS depressants or psychoactive agents. Effects with other sedative drugs or ethanol may be potentiated. Benzodiazepines have been associated with falls and traumatic injury and should be used with extreme caution in patients who are at risk of these events (especially the elderly). Use with caution in patients with respiratory disease or impaired gag reflex.

Use caution in patients with depression, particularly if suicidal risk may be present. Episodes of mania or hypomania have occurred in depressed patients treated with alprazolam. May cause physical or psychological dependence - use with caution in patients with a history of drug dependence. Acute withdrawal, including seizures, may be precipitated in patients after administration of flumazenil to patients receiving long-term benzodiazepine therapy.

Benzodiazepines have been associated with anterograde amnesia. Paradoxical reactions, including hyperactive or aggressive behavior, have been reported with benzodiazepines, particularly in adolescent/pediatric or psychiatric patients. Does not have analgesic, antidepressant, or antipsychotic properties.

Common Adverse Reactions
>10%:
  Central nervous system: Drowsiness, fatigue, ataxia, lightheadedness, memory impairment, dysarthria, irritability, sedation, depression
  Endocrine & metabolic: Libido decreased, menstrual disorders
  Gastrointestinal: Xerostomia, salivation decreased, appetite increased/decreased, weight gain/loss
  Genitourinary: Micturition difficulties
1% to 10%:
  Cardiovascular: Hypotension
  Central nervous system: Confusion, derealization, dizziness, disinhibition, akathisia, nightmares
  Dermatologic: Dermatitis, rash
  Endocrine & metabolic: Libido increased
  Gastrointestinal: Salivation increased, dyspepsia
  Genitourinary: Sexual dysfunction, incontinence
  Neuromuscular & skeletal: Rigidity, tremor, muscle cramps, ataxia, arthralgia
  Otic: Tinnitus
  Respiratory: Nasal congestion, dyspnea
  Miscellaneous: Diaphoresis

Drug Interactions
Cytochrome P450 Effect: Substrate of CYP3A4 (major)

Increased Effect/Toxicity: Alprazolam potentiates the CNS depressant effects of narcotic analgesics, barbiturates, phenothiazines, ethanol, antihistamines, MAO inhibitors, sedative-hypnotics, and cyclic antidepressants. Alprazolam increases plasma concentrations of imipramine and desipramine; monitor. CYP3A4 inhibitors may increase the levels/effects of alprazolam. Example inhibitors include azole antifungals, ciprofloxacin, clarithromycin, diclofenac, doxycycline, erythromycin, imatinib, isoniazid, nefazodone, nicardipine, propofol, protease inhibitors, quinidine, and verapamil.

Decreased Effect: Carbamazepine, rifampin, rifabutin, cigarette smoking, and phenobarbital may enhance the metabolism of alprazolam and decrease its therapeutic effect. CYP3A4 inducers may decrease the levels/effects of alprazolam; example inducers include aminoglutethimide, carbamazepine, nafcillin, nevirapine, phenobarbital, phenytoin, and rifamycins.

Mechanism of Action Binds to stereospecific benzodiazepine receptors on the postsynaptic GABA neuron at several sites within the central nervous system, including the limbic system, reticular formation. Enhancement of the inhibitory effect of GABA on neuronal excitability results by increased neuronal membrane permeability to chloride ions. This shift in chloride ions results in hyperpolarization (a less excitable state) and stabilization.

Pharmacodynamics/Kinetics
Distribution: V_d: 0.9-1.2 L/kg; enters breast milk
Protein binding: 80%
Metabolism: Hepatic via CYP3A4; forms 2 active metabolites (4-hydroxyalprazolam and α-hydroxyalprazolam)
Bioavailability: 90%
Half-life elimination:
  Adults: 11.2 hours (range: 6.3-26.9)
  Elderly: 16.3 hours (range: 9-26.9 hours)
  Alcoholic liver disease: 19.7 hours (range: 5.8-65.3 hours)
  Obesity: 21.8 hours (range: 9.9-40.4 hours)
Time to peak, serum: 1-2 hours
Excretion: Urine (as unchanged drug and metabolites)

Dosage Oral: **Note:** Treatment >4 months should be re-evaluated to determine the patient's continued need for the drug

Children: Anxiety (unlabeled use): Immediate release: Initial: 0.005 mg/kg/dose or 0.125 mg/dose 3 times/day; increase in increments of 0.125-0.25 mg, up to a maximum of 0.02 mg/kg/dose or 0.06 mg/kg/day (0.375-3 mg/day)

Adults:

Anxiety: Immediate release: Effective doses are 0.5-4 mg/day in divided doses; the manufacturer recommends starting at 0.25-0.5 mg 3 times/day; titrate dose upward; maximum: 4 mg/day

Anxiety associated with depression: Immediate release: Average dose required: 2.5-3 mg/day in divided doses

Ethanol withdrawal (unlabeled use): Immediate release: Usual dose: 2-2.5 mg/day in divided doses

Panic disorder:

Immediate release: Initial: 0.5 mg 3 times/day; dose may be increased every 3-4 days in increments ≤1 mg/day; many patients obtain relief at 2 mg/day, as much as 10 mg/day may be required

Extended release: 0.5-1 mg once daily; may increase dose every 3-4 days in increments ≤1 mg/day (range: 3-6 mg/day)

Switching from immediate release to extended release: Patients may be switched to extended release tablets by taking the total daily dose of the immediate release tablets and giving it once daily using the extended release preparation.

Dose reduction: Abrupt discontinuation should be avoided. Daily dose may be decreased by 0.5 mg every 3 days, however, some patients may require a slower reduction. If withdrawal symptoms occur, resume previous dose and discontinue on a less rapid schedule.

Elderly: Elderly patients may be more sensitive to the effects of alprazolam including ataxia and oversedation. The elderly may also have impaired renal function leading to decreased clearance. The smallest effective dose should be used. Titrate gradually, if needed.

Immediate release: Initial 0.25 mg 2-3 times/day

Extended release: Initial: 0.5 mg once daily

Dosing adjustment in hepatic impairment: Reduce dose by 50% to 60% or avoid in cirrhosis

Administration

Immediate release preparations: Can be administered sublingually with comparable onset and completeness of absorption.

Extended release tablet: Should be taken once daily in the morning; do not crush, break or chew.

Monitoring Parameters Respiratory and cardiovascular status

Patient Information Avoid alcohol and other CNS depressants; avoid activities needing good psychomotor coordination until CNS effects are known; drug may cause physical or psychological dependence; avoid abrupt discontinuation after prolonged use; do not crush, break, or chew extended release tablets

Dosage Forms SOLN, oral (Alprazolam Intensol®): 1 mg/mL (30 mL). **TAB** (Xanax®): 0.25 mg, 0.5 mg, 1 mg, 2 mg. **TAB, extended release** (Xanax XR®): 0.5 mg, 1 mg, 2 mg, 3 mg

♦ **Alprazolam Intensol®** *see* Alprazolam *on page 59*

Alprostadil (al PROS ta dill)

U.S. Brand Names Caverject®; Caverject® Impulse™; Edex®; Muse®; Prostin VR Pediatric®

Synonyms PGE$_1$; Prostaglandin E$_1$

Therapeutic Category Prostaglandin

Use

Prostin VR Pediatric®: Temporary maintenance of patency of ductus arteriosus in neonates with ductal-dependent congenital heart disease until surgery can be performed. These defects include cyanotic (eg, pulmonary atresia, pulmonary stenosis, tricuspid atresia, Fallot's tetralogy, transposition of the great vessels) and acyanotic (eg, interruption of aortic arch, coarctation of aorta, hypoplastic left ventricle) heart disease

Caverject®: Treatment of erectile dysfunction of vasculogenic, psychogenic, or neurogenic etiology; adjunct in the diagnosis of erectile dysfunction

Edex®, Muse®: Treatment of erectile dysfunction of vasculogenic, psychogenic, or neurogenic etiology

Unlabeled/Investigational Use Investigational: Treatment of pulmonary hypertension in infants and children with congenital heart defects with left-to-right shunts

Pregnancy Risk Factor X/C (Muse®)

Contraindications Hypersensitivity to alprostadil or any component of the formulation; hyaline membrane disease or persistent fetal circulation and when a dominant left-to-right shunt is present; respiratory distress syndrome; conditions predisposing patients to priapism (sickle cell anemia, multiple myeloma, leukemia); patients with anatomical deformation of the penis, penile implants; use in men for whom sexual activity is inadvisable or contraindicated; pregnancy

Warnings/Precautions Use cautiously in neonates with bleeding tendencies; apnea may occur in 10% to 12% of neonates with congenital heart defects, especially in those weighing <2 kg at birth; apnea usually appears during the first hour of drug infusion.

When used in erectile dysfunction: priapism may occur; treat immediately to avoid penile tissue damage and permanent loss of potency; discontinue therapy if signs of penile fibrosis develop (penile angulation, cavernosal fibrosis, or Peyronie's disease). When used in erectile dysfunction (Muse®), syncope occurring within 1 hour of administration, has been reported; the
(Continued)

Alprostadil *(Continued)*

potential for drug-drug interactions may occur when Muse® is prescribed concomitantly with antihypertensives.

Common Adverse Reactions

Intraurethral:

>10%: Genitourinary: Penile pain, urethral burning

2% to 10%:

Central nervous system: Headache, dizziness, pain

Genitourinary: Vaginal itching (female partner), testicular pain, urethral bleeding (minor)

Intracavernosal injection:

>10%: Genitourinary: Penile pain

1% to 10%:

Cardiovascular: Hypertension

Central nervous system: Headache, dizziness

Genitourinary: Prolonged erection (>4 hours, 4%), penile fibrosis, penis disorder, penile rash, penile edema

Local: Injection site hematoma and/or bruising

Intravenous:

>10%:

Cardiovascular: Flushing

Central nervous system: Fever

Respiratory: Apnea

1% to 10%:

Cardiovascular: Bradycardia, hypotension, hypertension, tachycardia, cardiac arrest, edema

Central nervous system: Seizures, headache, dizziness

Endocrine & metabolic: Hypokalemia

Gastrointestinal: Diarrhea

Hematologic: Disseminated intravascular coagulation

Neuromuscular & skeletal: Back pain

Respiratory: Upper respiratory infection, flu syndrome, sinusitis, nasal congestion, cough

Miscellaneous: Sepsis, localized pain in structures other than the injection site

Drug Interactions

Increased Effect/Toxicity: Risk of hypotension and syncope may be increased with antihypertensives.

Mechanism of Action
Causes vasodilation by means of direct effect on vascular and ductus arteriosus smooth muscle; relaxes trabecular smooth muscle by dilation of cavernosal arteries when injected along the penile shaft, allowing blood flow to and entrapment in the lacunar spaces of the penis (ie, corporeal veno-occlusive mechanism)

Pharmacodynamics/Kinetics

Onset of action: Rapid

Duration: <1 hour

Distribution: Insignificant following penile injection

Protein binding, plasma: 81% to albumin

Metabolism: ~75% by oxidation in one pass via lungs

Half-life elimination: 5-10 minutes

Excretion: Urine (90% as metabolites) within 24 hours

Dosage

Patent ductus arteriosus (Prostin VR Pediatric®):

I.V. continuous infusion into a large vein, or alternatively through an umbilical artery catheter placed at the ductal opening: 0.05-0.1 mcg/kg/minute with therapeutic response, rate is reduced to lowest effective dosage; with unsatisfactory response, rate is increased gradually; maintenance: 0.01-0.4 mcg/kg/minute

PGE_1 is usually given at an infusion rate of 0.1 mcg/kg/minute, but it is often possible to reduce the dosage to $1/2$ or even $1/10$ without losing the therapeutic effect. The mixing schedule is as follows. Infusion rates deliver 0.1 mcg/kg/minute: See table.

Alprostadil

Add 1 Ampul (500 mcg) to:	Concentration (mcg/mL)	Infusion Rate	
		mL/min/kg Needed to Infuse 0.1 mcg/kg/min	mL/kg/24 h
250 mL	2	0.05	72
100 mL	5	0.02	28.8
50 mL	10	0.01	14.4
25 mL	20	0.005	7.2

Therapeutic response is indicated by increased pH in those with acidosis or by an increase in oxygenation (PO_2) usually evident within 30 minutes

Erectile dysfunction:

Caverject®, Edex®: Intracavernous: Individualize dose by careful titration; doses >40 mcg (Edex®) or >60 mcg (Caverject®) are not recommended: Initial dose must be titrated in physicians office. Patient must stay in the physician's office until complete detumescence occurs; if there is no response, then the next higher dose may be given within 1 hour; if there is still no response, a 1-day interval before giving the next dose is recommended;

increasing the dose or concentration in the treatment of impotence results in increasing pain and discomfort

Vasculogenic, psychogenic, or mixed etiology: Initiate dosage titration at 2.5 mcg, increasing by 2.5 mcg to a dose of 5 mcg and then in increments of 5-10 mcg depending on the erectile response until the dose produces an erection suitable for intercourse, not lasting >1 hour; if there is absolutely no response to initial 2.5 mcg dose, the second dose may be increased to 7.5 mcg, followed by increments of 5-10 mcg

Neurogenic etiology (eg, spinal cord injury): Initiate dosage titration at 1.25 mcg, increasing to a dose of 2.5 mcg and then 5 mcg; increase further in increments 5 mcg until the dose is reached that produces an erection suitable for intercourse, not lasting >1 hour

Maintenance: Once appropriate dose has been determined, patient may self-administer injections at a frequency of no more than 3 times/week with at least 24 hours between doses

Muse® Pellet: Intraurethral:

Initial: 125-250 mcg

Maintenance: Administer as needed to achieve an erection; duration of action is about 30-60 minutes; use only two systems per 24-hour period

Elderly: Elderly patients may have a greater frequency of renal dysfunction; lowest effective dose should be used. In clinical studies with Edex®, higher minimally effective doses and a higher rate of lack of effect were noted.

Administration Erectile dysfunction: Use a ½ inch, 27- to 30-gauge needle. Inject into the dorsolateral aspect of the proximal third of the penis, avoiding visible veins; alternate side of the penis for injections.

Monitoring Parameters Arterial pressure, respiratory rate, heart rate, temperature, degree of penile pain, length of erection, signs of infection

Patient Information Store in refrigerator; if self-injecting for the treatment of impotence, dilute with the supplied diluent and use immediately after diluting; see prescriber at least every 3 months to ensure proper technique and for dosage adjustment. Alternate sides of the penis with each injection; do not inject more than 3 times/week, allowing at least 24 hours between each dose; dispose of the syringe, needle, and vial properly; discard single-use vials after each use; report moderate to severe penile pain or erections lasting >4 hours to a prescriber immediately; inform a prescriber as soon as possible if any new penile pain, nodules, hard tissue or signs of infection develop; the risk of transmission of blood-borne diseases is increased with use of alprostadil injections since a small amount of bleeding at the injection site is possible. Do not share this medication or needles/syringes; do not drive or operate heavy machinery within 1 hour of administration.

Dosage Forms INJ, powder for reconstitution: (Caverject®): 10 mcg, 20 mcg, 40 mcg; (Caverject® Impulse™): 10 mcg, 20 mcg; (Edex®): 10 mcg, 20 mcg, 40 mcg. **INJ, solution:** (Caverject® [DSC]): 20 mcg/mL (2 mL); (Prostin VR Pediatric®): 500 mcg/mL (1 mL). **PELLET, urethral** (Muse®): 125 mcg, 250 mcg, 500 mcg, 1000 mcg

♦ **Alrex®** see Loteprednol on page 764

♦ **Altace®** see Ramipril on page 1079

♦ **Altamist [OTC]** see Sodium Chloride on page 1146

Alteplase (AL te plase)

U.S. Brand Names Activase®; Cathflo™ Activase®

Synonyms Alteplase, Recombinant; Alteplase, Tissue Plasminogen Activator, Recombinant; tPA

Therapeutic Category Fibrinolytic Agent

Use Management of acute myocardial infarction for the lysis of thrombi in coronary arteries; management of acute massive pulmonary embolism (PE) in adults

Acute myocardial infarction (AMI): Chest pain ≥20 minutes, ≤12-24 hours; S-T elevation ≥0.1 mV in at least two ECG leads

Acute pulmonary embolism (APE): Age ≤75 years: As soon as possible within 5 days of thrombotic event. Documented massive pulmonary embolism by pulmonary angiography or echocardiography or high probability lung scan with clinical shock.

Cathflo™ Activase®: Restoration of central venous catheter function

Unlabeled/Investigational Use Acute peripheral arterial occlusive disease

Pregnancy Risk Factor C

Contraindications Hypersensitivity to alteplase or any component of the formulation

Treatment of acute MI or PE: Active internal bleeding; history of CVA; recent intracranial or intraspinal surgery or trauma; intracranial neoplasm; arteriovenous malformation or aneurysm; known bleeding diathesis; severe uncontrolled hypertension

Treatment of acute ischemic stroke: Evidence of intracranial hemorrhage or suspicion of subarachnoid hemorrhage on pretreatment evaluation; recent (within 3 months) intracranial or intraspinal surgery; prolonged external cardiac massage; suspected aortic dissection; serious head trauma or previous stroke; history of intracranial hemorrhage; uncontrolled hypertension at time of treatment (eg, >185 mm Hg systolic or >110 mm Hg diastolic); seizure at the onset of stroke; active internal bleeding; intracranial neoplasm; arteriovenous malformation or aneurysm; known bleeding diathesis including but not limited to: current use of anticoagulants or an INR >1.7, administration of heparin within 48 hours preceding the onset of stroke and an elevated aPTT at presentation, platelet count <100,000/mm³.

(Continued)

Alteplase *(Continued)*

Other exclusion criteria (NINDS recombinant tPA study): Stroke or serious head injury within 3 months, major surgery or serious trauma within 2 weeks, GI or urinary tract hemorrhage within 3 weeks, aggressive treatment required to lower blood pressure, glucose level <50 mg/dL or >400 mg/dL, arterial puncture at a noncompressible site or lumbar puncture within 1 week, clinical presentation suggesting post-MI pericarditis, pregnancy; breast-feeding.

Warnings/Precautions Concurrent heparin anticoagulation may contribute to bleeding. Monitor all potential bleeding sites. Doses >150 mg are associated with increased risk of intracranial hemorrhage. Intramuscular injections and nonessential handling of the patient should be avoided. Venipunctures should be performed carefully and only when necessary. If arterial puncture is necessary, use an upper extremity vessel that can be manually compressed. If serious bleeding occurs then the infusion of alteplase and heparin should be stopped.

For the following conditions the risk of bleeding is higher with use of thrombolytics and should be weighed against the benefits of therapy: recent major surgery (eg, CABG, obstetrical delivery, organ biopsy, previous puncture of noncompressible vessels), cerebrovascular disease, recent gastrointestinal or genitourinary bleeding, recent trauma, hypertension (systolic BP >175 mm Hg and/or diastolic BP >110 mm Hg), high likelihood of left heart thrombus (eg, mitral stenosis with atrial fibrillation), acute pericarditis, subacute bacterial endocarditis, hemostatic defects including ones caused by severe renal or hepatic dysfunction, significant hepatic dysfunction, pregnancy, diabetic hemorrhagic retinopathy or other hemorrhagic ophthalmic conditions, septic thrombophlebitis or occluded AV cannula at seriously infected site, advanced age (eg, >75 years), patients receiving oral anticoagulants, any other condition in which bleeding constitutes a significant hazard or would be particularly difficult to manage because of location.

Coronary thrombolysis may result in reperfusion arrhythmias. In treatment of patients with acute ischemic stroke more than 3 hours after symptom onset is not recommended; treatment of patients with minor neurological deficit or with rapidly improving symptoms is not recommended.

Cathflo™ Activase®: When used to restore catheter function, use Cathflo™ cautiously in those patients with known or suspected catheter infections. Evaluate catheter for other causes of dysfunction before use. Avoid excessive pressure when instilling into catheter. Use of Cathflo™ in children <2 years of age (or weighing <10 kg) has not been adequately evaluated.

Common Adverse Reactions As with all drugs which may affect hemostasis, bleeding is the major adverse effect associated with alteplase. Hemorrhage may occur at virtually any site. Risk is dependent on multiple variables, including the dosage administered, concurrent use of multiple agents which alter hemostasis, and patient predisposition. Rapid lysis of coronary artery thrombi by thrombolytic agents may be associated with reperfusion-related atrial and/or ventricular arrhythmias. **Note:** Lowest rate of bleeding complications expected with dose used to restore catheter function.

1% to 10%:
Cardiovascular: Hypotension
Central nervous system: Fever
Dermatologic: Bruising (1%)
Gastrointestinal: GI hemorrhage (5%), nausea, vomiting
Genitourinary: GU hemorrhage (4%)
Local: Bleeding at catheter puncture site (15.3%, accelerated administration)
Hematologic: Bleeding (0.5% major, 7% minor: GUSTO trial)

Additional cardiovascular events associated **with use in myocardial infarction:** AV block, cardiogenic shock, heart failure, cardiac arrest, recurrent ischemia/infarction, myocardial rupture, electromechanical dissociation, pericardial effusion, pericarditis, mitral regurgitation, cardiac tamponade, thromboembolism, pulmonary edema, asystole, ventricular tachycardia, bradycardia, ruptured intracranial AV malformation, seizure, hemorrhagic bursitis, cholesterol crystal embolization

Additional events associated **with use in pulmonary embolism:** Pulmonary re-embolization, pulmonary edema, pleural effusion, thromboembolism

Additional events associated **with use in stroke:** Cerebral edema, cerebral herniation, seizure, new ischemic stroke

Drug Interactions

Increased Effect/Toxicity: The potential for hemorrhage with alteplase is increased by oral anticoagulants (warfarin), heparin, low molecular weight heparins, and drugs which affect platelet function (eg, NSAIDs, dipyridamole, ticlopidine, clopidogrel, IIb/IIIa antagonists). Concurrent use with aspirin and heparin may increase the risk of bleeding. However, aspirin and heparin were used concomitantly with alteplase in the majority of patients in clinical studies.

Decreased Effect: Aminocaproic acid (an antifibrinolytic agent) may decrease the effectiveness of thrombolytic therapy. Nitroglycerin may increase the hepatic clearance of alteplase, potentially reducing lytic activity (limited clinical information).

Mechanism of Action Initiates local fibrinolysis by binding to fibrin in a thrombus (clot) and converts entrapped plasminogen to plasmin

Pharmacodynamics/Kinetics

Duration: >50% present in plasma cleared ~5 minutes after infusion terminated, ~80% cleared within 10 minutes

Excretion: Clearance: Rapidly from circulating plasma (550-650 mL/minute), primarily hepatic; >50% present in plasma is cleared within 5 minutes after the infusion is terminated, ~80% cleared within 10 minutes

Dosage

I.V.:

Coronary artery thrombi: Front loading dose (weight-based):

Patients >67 kg: Total dose: 100 mg over 1.5 hours; infuse 15 mg (30 mL) over 1-2 minutes. Infuse 50 mg (100 mL) over 30 minutes. See "Note."

Patients ≤67 kg: Total dose: 1.25 mg/kg; infuse 15 mg I.V. bolus over 1-2 minutes, then infuse 0.75 mg/kg (not to exceed 50 mg) over next 30 minutes, followed by 0.5 mg/kg over next 60 minutes (not to exceed 35 mg). See "Note."

Note: Concurrently, begin heparin 60 units/kg bolus (maximum: 4000 units) followed by continuous infusion of 12 units/kg/hour (maximum: 1000 units/hour) and adjust to aPTT target of 1.5-2 times the upper limit of control. Infuse remaining 35 mg (70 mL) of alteplase over the next hour.

Acute pulmonary embolism: 100 mg over 2 hours.

Acute ischemic stroke: Doses should be given within the first 3 hours of the onset of symptoms; recommended total dose: 0.9 mg/kg (maximum dose should not exceed 90 mg) infused over 60 minutes.

Load with 0.09 mg/kg (10% of the 0.9 mg/kg dose) as an I.V. bolus over 1 minute, followed by 0.81 mg/kg (90% of the 0.9 mg/kg dose) as a continuous infusion over 60 minutes. Heparin should not be started for 24 hours or more after starting alteplase for stroke.

Intracatheter: Central venous catheter clearance: Cathflo™ Activase®:

Patients ≥10 to <30 kg: 110% of the internal lumen volume of the catheter (≤2 mg [1 mg/mL]); retain in catheter for ≤2 hours; may instill a second dose if catheter remains occluded

Patients ≥30 kg: 2 mg (1 mg/mL); retain in catheter for ≤2 hours; may instill a second dose if catheter remains occluded

Intra-arterial: Acute peripheral arterial occlusive disease (unlabeled use): 0.02-0.1 mg/kg/hour for up to 36 hours

Advisory Panel to the Society for Cardiovascular and Interventional Radiology on Thrombolytic Therapy recommendation: ≤2 mg/hour and subtherapeutic heparin (aPTT <1.5 times baseline)

Administration

Activase®: Acute MI: Accelerated infusion:

Bolus dose may be prepared by one of three methods:

1) removal of 15 mL reconstituted (1 mg/mL) solution from vial

2) removal of 15 mL from a port on the infusion line after priming

3) programming an infusion pump to deliver a 15 mL bolus at the initiation of infusion

Remaining dose may be administered as follows:

50 mg vial: Either PVC bag or glass vial and infusion set

100 mg vial: Insert spike end of the infusion set through the same puncture site created by transfer device and infuse from vial

If further dilution is desired, may be diluted in equal volume of 0.9% sodium chloride or D₅W to yield a final concentration of 0.5 mg/mL AD

Cathflo™ Activase®: Intracatheter: Instill dose into occluded catheter. Do not force solution into catheter. After a 30-minute dwell time, assess catheter function by attempting to aspirate blood. If catheter is functional, aspirate 4-5 mL of blood to remove Cathflo™ Activase® and residual clots. Gently irrigate the catheter with NS. If catheter remains nonfunctional, let Cathflo™ Activase® dwell for another 90 minutes (total dwell time: 120 minutes) and reassess function. If catheter function is not restored, a second dose may be instilled.

Monitoring Parameters

When using for central venous catheter clearance: Assess catheter function by attempting to aspirate blood.

When using for management of acute myocardial infarction: Assess for evidence of cardiac reperfusion through resolution of chest pain, resolution of baseline ECG changes, preserved left ventricular function, cardiac enzyme washout phenomenon, and/or the appearance of reperfusion arrhythmias; assess for bleeding potential through clinical evidence of GI bleeding, hematuria, gingival bleeding, fibrinogen levels, fibrinogen degradation products, prothrombin times, and partial thromboplastin times.

Reference Range

Not routinely measured; literature supports therapeutic levels of 0.52-1.8 µg/mL

Fibrinogen: 200-400 mg/dL

Activated partial thromboplastin time (aPTT): 22.5-38.7 seconds

Prothrombin time (PT): 10.9-12.2 seconds

Dosage Forms INJ, powder for reconstitution, recombinant: (Activase®): 50 mg, 100 mg; (Cathflo™ Activase®): 2 mg

♦ **Alteplase, Recombinant** see Alteplase on page 63

♦ **Alteplase, Tissue Plasminogen Activator, Recombinant** see Alteplase on page 63

♦ **ALternaGel® [OTC]** see Aluminum Hydroxide on page 66

♦ **Altinac™** see Tretinoin (Topical) on page 1260

♦ **Altocor™** see Lovastatin on page 764

Altretamine (al TRET a meen)

U.S. Brand Names Hexalen®
Synonyms Hexamethylmelamine; HEXM; HMM; HXM; NSC-13875
Therapeutic Category Antineoplastic Agent, Miscellaneous
Use Palliative treatment of persistent or recurrent ovarian cancer
Pregnancy Risk Factor D
Contraindications Hypersensitivity to altretamine or any component of the formulation; pre-existing severe bone marrow suppression or severe neurologic toxicity; pregnancy
Warnings/Precautions The U.S. Food and Drug Administration (FDA) currently recommends that procedures for proper handling and disposal of antineoplastic agents be considered. Peripheral blood counts and neurologic examinations should be done routinely before and after drug therapy. Use with caution in patients previously treated with other myelosuppressive drugs or with pre-existing neurotoxicity; use with caution in patients with renal or hepatic dysfunction; altretamine may be slightly mutagenic.

Common Adverse Reactions
>10%:
    Central nervous system: Peripheral sensory neuropathy, neurotoxicity (21%; may be progressive and dose-limiting)
    Gastrointestinal: Nausea/vomiting (50% to 70%), anorexia (48%), diarrhea (48%)
    Hematologic: Anemia, thrombocytopenia (31%), leukopenia (62%), neutropenia
1% to 10%:
    Central nervous system: Seizures
    Gastrointestinal: Stomach cramps
    Hepatic: Alkaline phosphatase increased

Drug Interactions
Increased Effect/Toxicity: Altretamine may cause severe orthostatic hypotension when administered with MAO inhibitors. Cimetidine may decrease metabolism of altretamine.
Decreased Effect: Phenobarbital may increase metabolism of altretamine which may decrease the effect.
Mechanism of Action Although altretamine clinical antitumor spectrum resembles that of alkylating agents, the drug has demonstrated activity in alkylator-resistant patients. The drug selectively inhibits the incorporation of radioactive thymidine and uridine into DNA and RNA, inhibiting DNA and RNA synthesis; reactive intermediates covalently bind to microsomal proteins and DNA; can spontaneously degrade to demethylated melamines and formaldehyde which are also cytotoxic.

Pharmacodynamics/Kinetics
Absorption: Well absorbed (75% to 89%)
Distribution: Highly concentrated hepatically and renally; low in other organs
Metabolism: Hepatic; rapid and extensive demethylation; active metabolites
Half-life elimination: 13 hours
Time to peak, plasma: 0.5-3 hours
Excretion: Urine (<1% as unchanged drug)

Dosage Refer to individual protocols. Oral:
Adults: 4-12 mg/kg/day in 3-4 divided doses for 21-90 days
    Alternatively: 240-320 mg/m^2/day in 3-4 divided doses for 21 days, repeated every 6 weeks
    Alternatively: 260 mg/m^2/day for 14-21 days of a 28-day cycle in 4 divided doses
    Alternatively: 150 mg/m^2/day in 3-4 divided doses for 14 days of a 28-day cycle

Administration Administer total daily dose as 3-4 divided doses after meals and at bedtime.
Patient Information Report any numbness or tingling in extremities; nausea and vomiting may occur
Dosage Forms GELCAP: 50 mg

♦ Alu-Cap® [OTC] *see* Aluminum Hydroxide *on page 66*

Aluminum Acetate and Acetic Acid
(a LOO mi num AS e tate & a SEE tik AS id)

U.S. Brand Names Otic Domeboro®
Synonyms Acetic Acid and Aluminum Acetate Otic; Burow's Otic
Therapeutic Category Antibiotic, Otic; Otic Agent, Anti-infective
Use Treatment of superficial infections of the external auditory canal
Dosage Instill 4-6 drops in ear(s) every 2-3 hours; insert saturated wick, keep moist for 24 hours

Aluminum Hydroxide (a LOO mi num hye DROKS ide)

U.S. Brand Names ALternaGel® [OTC]; Alu-Cap® [OTC]
Therapeutic Category Antacid; Antidote, Hyperphosphatemia
Use Treatment of hyperacidity; hyperphosphatemia
Pregnancy Risk Factor C
Contraindications Hypersensitivity to aluminum salts or any component of the formulation
Warnings/Precautions Hypophosphatemia may occur with prolonged administration or large doses; aluminum intoxication and osteomalacia may occur in patients with uremia. Use with caution in patients with CHF, renal failure, edema, cirrhosis, and low sodium diets, and patients who have recently suffered gastrointestinal hemorrhage; uremic patients not receiving dialysis may develop osteomalacia and osteoporosis due to phosphate depletion.

Elderly may be predisposed to constipation and fecal impaction. Careful evaluation of possible drug interactions must be done. When used as an antacid in ulcer treatment, consider buffer capacity (mEq/mL) to calculate dose.

Common Adverse Reactions Frequency not defined.

Gastrointestinal: Constipation, stomach cramps, fecal impaction, nausea, vomiting, discoloration of feces (white speckles)

Endocrine & metabolic: Hypophosphatemia, hypomagnesemia

Drug Interactions

Decreased Effect: Aluminum hydroxide may decrease the absorption of allopurinol, antibiotics (tetracyclines, quinolones, some cephalosporins), bisphosphonate derivatives, corticosteroids, cyclosporine, delavirdine, iron salts, imidazole antifungals, isoniazid, mycophenolate, penicillamine, phosphate supplements, phenytoin, phenothiazines, trientine. Absorption of aluminum hydroxide may be decreased by citric acid derivatives.

Mechanism of Action Neutralizes hydrochloride in stomach to form Al $(Cl)_3$ salt $+ H_2O$

Dosage Oral:

Hyperphosphatemia:

Children: 50-150 mg/kg/24 hours in divided doses every 4-6 hours, titrate dosage to maintain serum phosphorus within normal range

Adults: Initial: 300-600 mg 3 times/day with meals

Antacid: Adults: 600-1200 mg between meals and at bedtime

Administration Oral: Dose should be followed with water.

Monitoring Parameters Monitor phosphorous levels periodically when patient is on chronic therapy

Patient Information Do not take oral drugs within 1-2 hours of administration; notify prescriber if relief is not obtained or if there are any signs to suggest bleeding from the GI tract

Dosage Forms CAP (Alu-Cap®): 400 mg. **SUSP, oral:** 320 mg/5 mL (473 mL); (ALternaGel®): 600 mg/5 mL (360 mL)

Aluminum Hydroxide and Magnesium Carbonate
(a LOO mi num hye DROKS ide & mag NEE zhum KAR bun nate)

U.S. Brand Names Gaviscon® Extra Strength [OTC]; Gaviscon® Liquid [OTC]

Synonyms Magnesium Carbonate and Aluminum Hydroxide

Therapeutic Category Antacid

Use Temporary relief of symptoms associated with gastric acidity

Dosage Oral: Adults:

Liquid:

Gaviscon® Regular Strength: 15-30 mL 4 times/day after meals and at bedtime

Gaviscon® Extra Strength Relief: 15-30 mL 4 times/day after meals

Tablet (Gaviscon® Extra Strength Relief): Chew 2-4 tablets 4 times/day

Dosage Forms LIQ: Aluminum 31.7 mg and magnesium 119.3 mg per 5 mL (355 mL); aluminum 84.6 mg and magnesium 79.1 mg per 5 mL (355 mL). **TAB, chewable:** Aluminum 160 mg and magnesium 105 mg

Aluminum Hydroxide and Magnesium Hydroxide
(a LOO mi num hye DROKS ide & mag NEE zhum hye DROK side)

U.S. Brand Names Alamag [OTC]; Maalox® [OTC] [DSC]; Maalox® TC (Therapeutic Concentrate) [OTC] [DSC]; Rulox; Rulox No. 1

Synonyms Magnesium Hydroxide and Aluminum Hydroxide

Therapeutic Category Antacid

Use Antacid, hyperphosphatemia in renal failure

Pregnancy Risk Factor C

Dosage Oral: 5-10 mL 4-6 times/day, between meals and at bedtime; may be used every hour for severe symptoms

Maalox®: 10-20 mL 4 times/day

Dosage Forms SUSP: Aluminum 225 mg and magnesium 200 mg per 5 mL (150 mL, 360 mL, 780 mL); (Alamag, Rulox): Aluminum hydroxide 225 mg and magnesium hydroxide 200 mg per 5 mL (360 mL); (Maalox® [DSC]): Aluminum hydroxide 225 mg and magnesium hydroxide 200 mg per 5 mL (150 mL, 360 mL, 780 mL). **SUSP, high potency** (Maalox® TC) [DSC]: Aluminum 600 mg and magnesium 300 mg per 5 mL (360 mL). **TAB, chewable:** (Alamag): Aluminum hydroxide 300 mg and magnesium hydroxide 150 mg; (Rulox No. 1): Aluminum hydroxide 200 mg and magnesium hydroxide 200 mg

Aluminum Hydroxide and Magnesium Trisilicate
(a LOO mi num hye DROKS ide & mag NEE zhum trye SIL i kate)

U.S. Brand Names Alenic Alka Tablet [OTC]; Gaviscon® Tablet [OTC]; Genaton Tablet [OTC]

Synonyms Magnesium Trisilicate and Aluminum Hydroxide

Therapeutic Category Antacid

Use Temporary relief of hyperacidity

Pregnancy Risk Factor C

Dosage Oral: Adults: Chew 2-4 tablets 4 times/day or as directed by healthcare provider

Dosage Forms TAB, chewable: Aluminum 80 mg and magnesium 20 mg

Aluminum Hydroxide, Magnesium Hydroxide, and Simethicone

(a LOO mi num hye DROKS ide, mag NEE zhum hye DROKS ide, & sye METH i kone)

U.S. Brand Names Alamag Plus [OTC]; Aldroxicon I [OTC]; Aldroxicon II [OTC]; Almacone® [OTC]; Almacone Double Strength® [OTC]; Maalox® [OTC]; Maalox® Max [OTC]; Mylanta® Liquid [OTC]; Mylanta® Maximum Strength Liquid [OTC]

Synonyms Magnesium Hydroxide, Aluminum Hydroxide, and Simethicone; Simethicone, Aluminum Hydroxide, and Magnesium Hydroxide

Therapeutic Category Antacid; Antiflatulent

Use Temporary relief of hyperacidity associated with gas; may also be used for indications associated with other antacids

Pregnancy Risk Factor C

Dosage Oral: Adults: 10-20 mL or 2-4 tablets 4-6 times/day between meals and at bedtime; may be used every hour for severe symptoms

Dosage Forms LIQ: Aluminum hydroxide 200 mg, magnesium hydroxide 200 mg, and simethicone 20 mg per 5 mL (360 mL); aluminum hydroxide 400 mg, magnesium hydroxide 400 mg, and simethicone 40 mg per 5 mL (360 mL); (Aldroxicon I): Aluminum hydroxide 200 mg, magnesium hydroxide 200 mg, and simethicone 20 mg per 5 mL (30 mL); (Aldroxicon II): Aluminum hydroxide 400 mg, magnesium hydroxide 400 mg, and simethicone 40 mg per 5 mL (30 mL); (Almacone®): Aluminum hydroxide 200 mg, magnesium hydroxide 200 mg, and simethicone 20 mg per 5 mL (360 mL); (Almacone Double Strength): Aluminum hydroxide 400 mg, magnesium hydroxide 400 mg, and simethicone 40 mg per 5 mL (360 mL); (Maalox®): Aluminum hydroxide 200 mg, magnesium hydroxide 200 mg, and simethicone 20 mg per 5 mL (360 mL, 770 mL); (Maalox® Max): Aluminum hydroxide 400 mg, magnesium hydroxide 400 mg, and simethicone 40 mg per 5 mL (360 mL, 770 mL); (Mylanta®): Aluminum hydroxide 200 mg, magnesium hydroxide 200 mg, and simethicone 20 mg per 5 mL (180 mL, 360 mL, 720 mL); (Mylanta® Maximum Strength): Aluminum hydroxide 400 mg, magnesium hydroxide 400 mg, and simethicone 40 mg per 5 mL (180 mL, 360 mL, 720 mL). **SUSP:** (Alamag Plus): Aluminum hydroxide 225 mg, magnesium hydroxide 200 mg, and simethicone 25 mg per 5 mL (360 mL)' **TAB, chewable:** Aluminum hydroxide 200 mg, magnesium hydroxide 200 mg, and simethicone 25 mg; (Alamag Plus): Aluminum hydroxide 200 mg, magnesium hydroxide 200 mg, and simethicone 25 mg; (Almacone®): Aluminum hydroxide 200 mg, magnesium hydroxide 200 mg, and simethicone 20 mg

♦ **Aluminum Sucrose Sulfate, Basic** see Sucralfate on page 1167

Aluminum Sulfate and Calcium Acetate

(a LOO mi num SUL fate & KAL see um AS e tate)

U.S. Brand Names Domeboro® [OTC]; Pedi-Boro® [OTC]

Synonyms Calcium Acetate and Aluminum Sulfate

Therapeutic Category Topical Skin Product

Use Astringent wet dressing for relief of inflammatory conditions of the skin and to reduce weeping that may occur in dermatitis

Dosage Topical: Soak affected area in the solution for 15-30 minutes or apply wet dressing soaked in the solution for more extended periods; rewet dressing with solution every 15-30 minutes

Dosage Forms POWDER, for topical solution: (Domeboro®): Aluminum sulfate 1191 mg and calcium acetate 938 mg per packet (12s, 100s); (Pedi-Boro®): Aluminum sulfate 49% and calcium acetate 51% per packet (12s, 100s). **TAB, effervescent, for topical solution** (Domeboro®): Aluminum sulfate 878 mg and calcium acetate 604 mg

♦ **Alupent®** see Metaproterenol on page 803

♦ **Alustra™** see Hydroquinone on page 636

Amantadine (a MAN ta deen)

Related Information

Community-Acquired Pneumonia in Adults on page 1457

Parkinson's Agents Comparison on page 1402

U.S. Brand Names Symmetrel®

Synonyms Adamantanamine Hydrochloride; Amantadine Hydrochloride

Therapeutic Category Anti-Parkinson's Agent, Dopamine Agonist; Antiviral Agent; Antiviral Agent, Influenza; Dopaminergic Agent, Antiparkinson's

Use Prophylaxis and treatment of influenza A viral infection; treatment of parkinsonism; treatment of drug-induced extrapyramidal symptoms

Unlabeled/Investigational Use Creutzfeldt-Jakob disease

Pregnancy Risk Factor C

Contraindications Hypersensitivity to amantadine or any component of the formulation

Warnings/Precautions Use with caution in patients with liver disease, a history of recurrent and eczematoid dermatitis, uncontrolled psychosis or severe psychoneurosis, seizures and in those receiving CNS stimulant drugs; reduce dose in renal disease; when treating Parkinson's disease, do not discontinue abruptly. In many patients, the therapeutic benefits of amantadine are limited to a few months. Elderly patients may be more susceptible to the CNS effects (using 2 divided daily doses may minimize this effect). Use with caution in patients with CHF, peripheral edema, or orthostatic hypotension. Avoid in angle closure glaucoma.

Common Adverse Reactions 1% to 10%:
Cardiovascular: Orthostatic hypotension, peripheral edema
Central nervous system: Insomnia, depression, anxiety, irritability, dizziness, hallucinations, ataxia, headache, somnolence, nervousness, dream abnormality, agitation, fatigue, confusion
Dermatologic: Livedo reticularis
Gastrointestinal: Nausea, anorexia, constipation, diarrhea, xerostomia
Respiratory: Dry nose

Drug Interactions
Increased Effect/Toxicity: Anticholinergics (benztropine and trihexyphenidyl) may potentiate CNS side effects of amantadine. Hydrochlorothiazide, triamterene, and/or trimethoprim may increase toxicity of amantadine; monitor for altered response.

Mechanism of Action As an antiviral, blocks the uncoating of influenza A virus preventing penetration of virus into host; antiparkinsonian activity may be due to its blocking the reuptake of dopamine into presynaptic neurons or by increasing dopamine release from presynaptic fibers

Pharmacodynamics/Kinetics
Onset of action: Antidyskinetic: Within 48 hours
Absorption: Well absorbed
Distribution: V_d: Normal: 1.5-6.1 L/kg; Renal failure: 5.1 ± 0.2 L/kg; in saliva, tear film, and nasal secretions; in animals, tissue (especially lung) concentrations higher than serum concentrations; crosses blood-brain barrier
Protein binding: Normal renal function: ~67%; Hemodialysis: ~59%
Metabolism: Not appreciable; small amounts of an acetyl metabolite identified
Bioavailability: 86% to 90%
Half-life elimination: Normal renal function: 16 ± 6 hours (9-31 hours); End-stage renal disease: 7-10 days
Excretion: Urine (80% to 90% unchanged) by glomerular filtration and tubular secretion
Total clearance: 2.5-10.5 L/hour

Dosage Oral:
Children:
Influenza A treatment:
1-9 years: 5 mg/kg/day in 2 divided doses (manufacturers range: 4.4-8.8 mg/kg/day); maximum dose: 150 mg/day
≥10 years and <40 kg: 5 mg/kg/day; maximum dose: 150 mg/day
10-12 years and ≥40 kg: 100 mg twice daily.
≥13 years: Refer to Adults dosing
Note: Initiate within 24-48 hours after onset of symptoms; discontinue as soon as possible based on clinical response (generally within 3-5 days or within 24-48 hours after symptoms disappear)
Influenza A prophylaxis: Refer to "Influenza A treatment" dosing
Note: Continue treatment throughout the peak influenza activity in the community or throughout the entire influenza season in patients who cannot be vaccinated. Development of immunity following vaccination takes ~2 weeks; amantadine therapy should be considered for high-risk patients from the time of vaccination until immunity has developed. For children <9 years receiving influenza vaccine for the first time, amantadine prophylaxis should continue for 6 weeks (4 weeks after the first dose and 2 weeks after the second dose)
Adults:
Drug-induced extrapyramidal symptoms: 100 mg twice daily; may increase to 300-400 mg/day, if needed
Parkinson's disease or Creutzfeldt-Jakob disease (unlabeled use): 100 mg twice daily as sole therapy; may increase to 400 mg/day if needed with close monitoring; initial dose: 100 mg/day if with other serious illness or with high doses of other anti-Parkinson drugs
Influenza A viral infection: 100 mg twice daily; initiate within 24-48 hours after onset of symptoms; discontinue as soon as possible based on clinical response (generally within 3-5 days or within 24-48 hours after symptoms disappear)
Influenza A prophylaxis: 100 mg twice daily
Note: Continue treatment throughout the peak influenza activity in the community or throughout the entire influenza season in patients who cannot be vaccinated. Development of immunity following vaccination takes ~2 weeks; amantadine therapy should be considered for high-risk patients from the time of vaccination until immunity has developed
Elderly:
Influenza A treatment: ≤100 mg/day; initiate within 24-48 hours after onset of symptoms; discontinue as soon as possible based on clinical response (generally within 3-5 days or within 24-48 hours after symptoms disappear)
Influenza A prophylaxis: ≤100 mg/day
Note: Continue treatment throughout the peak influenza activity in the community or throughout the entire influenza season in patients who cannot be vaccinated. Development of immunity following vaccination takes ~2 weeks; amantadine therapy should be considered for high-risk patients from the time of vaccination until immunity has developed.

Dosing interval in renal impairment:
Cl_{cr} 30-50 mL/minute: Administer 200 mg on day 1, then 100 mg/day
Cl_{cr} 15-29 mL/minute: Administer 200 mg on day 1, then 100 mg on alternate days
Cl_{cr} <15 mL/minute: Administer 200 mg every 7 days
(Continued)

Amantadine *(Continued)*

Hemodialysis: Administer 200 mg every 7 days
Peritoneal dialysis: No supplemental dose is needed
Continuous arterio-venous or venous-venous hemofiltration: No supplemental dose is needed

Monitoring Parameters Renal function, Parkinson's symptoms, mental status, influenza symptoms, blood pressure

Patient Information Do not abruptly discontinue therapy, it may precipitate a parkinsonian crisis; may impair ability to perform activities requiring mental alertness or coordination; must take throughout flu season or for at least 10 days following vaccination for effective prophylaxis; take second dose of the day in early afternoon to decrease incidence of insomnia

Dosage Forms CAP: 100 mg. **SYR** (Symmetrel®): 50 mg/5 mL (480 mL). **TAB** (Symmetrel®): 100 mg

♦ **Amantadine Hydrochloride** *see Amantadine on page 68*

♦ **Amaryl**® *see Glimepiride on page 590*

♦ **Ambien**® *see Zolpidem on page 1333*

♦ **AmBisome**® *see Amphotericin B (Liposomal) on page 93*

Amcinonide *(am SIN oh nide)*

Related Information
Corticosteroids Comparison *on page 1372*

U.S. Brand Names Cyclocort®

Therapeutic Category Anti-inflammatory Agent; Corticosteroid, Topical (High Potency)

Use Relief of the inflammatory and pruritic manifestations of corticosteroid-responsive dermatoses (high potency corticosteroid)

Pregnancy Risk Factor C

Contraindications Hypersensitivity to amcinonide or any component of the formulation; use on the face, groin, or axilla

Warnings/Precautions Adverse systemic effects may occur when used on large areas of the body, denuded areas, for prolonged periods of time, with an occlusive dressing, and/or in infants or small children; occlusive dressings should not be used in presence of infection or weeping lesions

Common Adverse Reactions Frequency not defined.
Dermatologic: Acne, hypopigmentation, allergic dermatitis, maceration of the skin, skin atrophy, striae, miliaria, telangiectasia
Endocrine & metabolic: HPA suppression, Cushing's syndrome, growth retardation
Local: Burning, itching, irritation, dryness, folliculitis, hypertrichosis
Systemic: Suppression of HPA axis, Cushing's syndrome, hyperglycemia; these reactions occur more frequently with occlusive dressings
Miscellaneous: Secondary infection

Mechanism of Action Stimulates the synthesis of enzymes needed to decrease inflammation, suppress mitotic activity, and cause vasoconstriction

Pharmacodynamics/Kinetics
Absorption: Adequate through intact skin; increases with skin inflammation or occlusion
Metabolism: Hepatic
Excretion: Urine and feces

Dosage Topical: Adults: Apply in a thin film 2-3 times/day. Therapy should be discontinued when control is achieved; if no improvement is seen, reassessment of diagnosis may be necessary.

Patient Information Before applying, gently wash area to reduce risk of infection; apply a thin film to cleansed area and rub in gently and thoroughly until medication vanishes; avoid exposure to sunlight, severe sunburn may occur

Dosage Forms CRM: 0.1% (15 g, 30 g, 60 g). **LOTION:** 0.1% (60 mL); (Cyclocort®): 0.1% (20 mL, 60 mL). **OINT:** 0.1% (30 g, 60 g); (Cyclocort®): 0.1% (15 g, 30 g, 60 g)

♦ **Amerge**® *see Naratriptan on page 884*

♦ **Americaine**® **[OTC]** *see Benzocaine on page 154*

♦ **Americaine**® **Anesthetic Lubricant** *see Benzocaine on page 154*

♦ **A-Methapred**® *see MethylPREDNISolone on page 824*

♦ **Amethocaine Hydrochloride** *see Tetracaine on page 1206*

♦ **Amethopterin** *see Methotrexate on page 815*

♦ **Amevive**® *see Alefacept on page 49*

♦ **Amfepramone** *see Diethylpropion on page 372*

♦ **Amibid LA** *see Guaifenesin on page 603*

♦ **Amicar**® *see Aminocaproic Acid on page 74*

♦ **Amidate**® *see Etomidate on page 497*

Amifostine *(am i FOS teen)*

U.S. Brand Names Ethyol®

Synonyms Ethiofos; Gammaphos; WR2721; YM-08310

Therapeutic Category Antidote, Cisplatin

Use Reduce the incidence of moderate to severe xerostomia in patients undergoing postoperative radiation treatment for head and neck cancer, where the radiation port includes a substantial portion of the parotid glands. Reduce the cumulative renal toxicity associated with repeated administration of cisplatin in patients with advanced ovarian cancer or nonsmall cell lung cancer.

Pregnancy Risk Factor C

Contraindications Hypersensitivity to aminothiol compounds, mannitol, or any component of the formulation

Warnings/Precautions Patients who are hypotensive or in a state of dehydration should not receive amifostine. Interrupt antihypertensive therapy for 24 hours before amifostine. Patients receiving antihypertensive therapy that cannot be stopped for 24 hours preceding amifostine treatment also should not receive amifostine. Patients should be adequately hydrated prior to amifostine infusion and kept in a supine position during the infusion. Blood pressure should be monitored every 5 minutes during the infusion. If hypotension requiring interruption of therapy occurs, patients should be placed in the Trendelenburg position and given an infusion of normal saline using a separate I.V. line.

It is recommended that antiemetic medication, including dexamethasone 20 mg I.V. and a serotonin 5-HT$_3$ receptor antagonist be administered prior to and in conjunction with amifostine. Rare hypersensitivity reactions, including anaphylaxis and severe cutaneous reaction, have been reported with a higher frequency in patients receiving amifostine as a radioprotectant. Discontinue if allergic reaction occurs; do not rechallenge.

Reports of clinically relevant hypocalcemia are rare, but serum calcium levels should be monitored in patients at risk of hypocalcemia, such as those with nephrotic syndrome.

Common Adverse Reactions >10%:
Cardiovascular: Flushing; hypotension (62%)
Central nervous system: Chills, dizziness, somnolence
Gastrointestinal: Nausea/vomiting (may be severe)
Respiratory: Sneezing
Miscellaneous: Feeling of warmth/coldness, hiccups

Drug Interactions
Increased Effect/Toxicity: Special consideration should be given to patients receiving antihypertensive medications or other drugs that could potentiate hypotension.

Mechanism of Action Prodrug that is dephosphorylated by alkaline phosphatase in tissues to a pharmacologically active free thiol metabolite. The free thiol is available to bind to, and detoxify, reactive metabolites of cisplatin; and can also act as a scavenger of free radicals that may be generated in tissues.

Pharmacodynamics/Kinetics
Distribution: V$_d$: 3.5 L
Metabolism: Hepatic dephosphorylation to two metabolites (active-free thiol and disulfide)
Half-life elimination: 9 minutes
Excretion: Urine
Clearance, plasma: 2.17 L/minute

Dosage Adults:
Cisplatin-induced renal toxicity, reduction: I.V.: 740-910 mg/m^2 once daily 30 minutes prior to cytotoxic therapy
Note: Doses >740 mg/m^2 are associated with a higher incidence of hypotension and may require interruption of therapy or dose modification for subsequent cycles. For 910 mg/m^2 doses, the manufacturer suggests the following blood pressure-based adjustment schedule:
The infusion of amifostine should be interrupted if the systolic blood pressure decreases significantly from baseline, as defined below:
Decrease of 20 mm Hg if baseline systolic blood pressure <100
Decrease of 25 mm Hg if baseline systolic blood pressure 100-119
Decrease of 30 mm Hg if baseline systolic blood pressure 120-139
Decrease of 40 mm Hg if baseline systolic blood pressure 140-179
Decrease of 50 mm Hg if baseline systolic blood pressure ≥180
If the blood pressure returns to normal within 5 minutes (assisted by fluid administration and postural management) and the patient is asymptomatic, the infusion may be restarted so that the full dose of amifostine may be administered. If the full dose of amifostine cannot be administered, the dose of amifostine for subsequent cycles should be 740 mg/m^2.
Xerostomia from head and neck cancer, reduction:
I.V.: 200mg/m^2/day during radiation therapy **or**
S.C.: 500 mg/day during radiation therapy

Administration I.V.: Administer over 3-15 minutes; administration as a longer infusion is associated with a higher incidence of side effects

Monitoring Parameters Blood pressure should be monitored every 5 minutes during the infusion

Patient Information This I.V. medication is given to help reduce side effects of your chemotherapy. Report immediately lightheadedness, dizziness, fainting, or any nausea; you will be given medication. Report chills, severe dizziness, tremors or shaking, or sudden onset of hiccups.

Dosage Forms INJ, powder for reconstitution: 500 mg

♦ **Amigesic**® *see* Salsalate *on page 1122*

Amikacin (am i KAY sin)
Related Information
Aminoglycoside Dosing and Monitoring *on page 1350*
Antimicrobial Drugs of Choice *on page 1440*
(Continued)

Amikacin *(Continued)*

Tuberculosis Treatment Guidelines *on page 1466*

U.S. Brand Names Amikin®

Synonyms Amikacin Sulfate

Therapeutic Category Antibiotic, Aminoglycoside

Use Treatment of serious infections due to organisms resistant to gentamicin and tobramycin including *Pseudomonas*, *Proteus*, *Serratia*, and other gram-positive bacilli (bone infections, respiratory tract infections, endocarditis, and septicemia); documented infection of mycobacterial organisms susceptible to amikacin

Pregnancy Risk Factor C

Contraindications Hypersensitivity to amikacin sulfate or any component of the formulation; cross-sensitivity may exist with other aminoglycosides

Warnings/Precautions Dose and/or frequency of administration must be monitored and modified in patients with renal impairment; drug should be discontinued if signs of ototoxicity, nephrotoxicity, or hypersensitivity occur; ototoxicity is proportional to the amount of drug given and the duration of treatment; tinnitus or vertigo may be indications of vestibular injury and impending bilateral irreversible damage; renal damage is usually reversible

Common Adverse Reactions 1% to 10%:

Central nervous system: Neurotoxicity

Otic: Ototoxicity (auditory), ototoxicity (vestibular)

Renal: Nephrotoxicity

Drug Interactions

Increased Effect/Toxicity: Amikacin may increase or prolong the effect of neuromuscular blocking agents. Concurrent use of amphotericin (or other nephrotoxic drugs) may increase the risk of amikacin-induced nephrotoxicity. The risk of ototoxicity from amikacin may be increased with other ototoxic drugs.

Mechanism of Action Inhibits protein synthesis in susceptible bacteria by binding to 30S ribosomal subunits

Pharmacodynamics/Kinetics

Absorption: I.M.: May be delayed in the bedridden patient

Distribution: Primarily into extracellular fluid (highly hydrophilic); penetrates blood-brain barrier when meninges inflamed; crosses placenta

Relative diffusion of antimicrobial agents from blood into CSF: Good only with inflammation (exceeds usual MICs)

CSF:blood level ratio: Normal meninges: 10% to 20%; Inflamed meninges: 15% to 24%

Half-life elimination (renal function and age dependent):

Infants: Low birth weight (1-3 days): 7-9 hours; Full-term >7 days: 4-5 hours

Children: 1.6-2.5 hours

Adults: Normal renal function: 1.4-2.3 hours; Anuria/end-stage renal disease: 28-86 hours

Time to peak, serum: I.M.: 45-120 minutes

Excretion: Urine (94% to 98%)

Dosage Individualization is critical because of the low therapeutic index

Use of ideal body weight (IBW) for determining the mg/kg/dose appears to be more accurate than dosing on the basis of total body weight (TBW)

In morbid obesity, dosage requirement may best be estimated using a dosing weight of IBW + 0.4 (TBW - IBW)

Initial and periodic peak and trough plasma drug levels should be determined, particularly in critically-ill patients with serious infections or in disease states known to significantly alter aminoglycoside pharmacokinetics (eg, cystic fibrosis, burns, or major surgery)

Infants, Children, and Adults: I.M., I.V.: 5-7.5 mg/kg/dose every 8 hours

Some clinicians suggest a daily dose of 15-20 mg/kg for all patients with normal renal function. This dose is at least as efficacious with similar, if not less, toxicity than conventional dosing.

Dosing interval in renal impairment: Some patients may require larger or more frequent doses if serum levels document the need (ie, cystic fibrosis or febrile granulocytopenic patients)

Cl_{cr} ≥60 mL/minute: Administer every 8 hours

Cl_{cr} 40-60 mL/minute: Administer every 12 hours

Cl_{cr} 20-40 mL/minute: Administer every 24 hours

Cl_{cr} <20 mL/minute: Loading dose, then monitor levels

Hemodialysis: Dialyzable (50% to 100%); administer dose postdialysis or administer ⅔ normal dose as a supplemental dose postdialysis and follow levels

Peritoneal dialysis: Dose as Cl_{cr} <20 mL/minute: Follow levels

Continuous arteriovenous or venovenous hemodiafiltration effects: Dose as for Cl_{cr} 10-40 mL/minute and follow levels

Administration Administer I.M. injection in large muscle mass

Monitoring Parameters Urinalysis, BUN, serum creatinine, appropriately timed peak and trough concentrations, vital signs, temperature, weight, I & O, hearing parameters

Reference Range

Sample size: 0.5-2 mL blood (red top tube) or 0.1-1 mL serum (separated)

Therapeutic levels:

Peak:

Life-threatening infections: 25-30 µg/mL

Serious infections: 20-25 µg/mL

Urinary tract infections: 15-20 µg/mL

Trough:

Serious infections: 1-4 µg/mL

Life-threatening infections: 4-8 µg/mL
Toxic concentration: Peak: >35 µg/mL; Trough: >10 µg/mL
Timing of serum samples: Draw peak 30 minutes after completion of 30-minute infusion or at 1 hour following initiation of infusion or I.M. injection; draw trough within 30 minutes prior to next dose

Patient Information Report loss of hearing, ringing or roaring in the ears, or feeling of fullness in head

Dosage Forms INJ, solution: 50 mg/mL (2 mL, 4 mL); 62.5 mg/mL (8 mL); 250 mg/mL (2 mL, 4 mL)

♦ **Amikacin Sulfate**   *see Amikacin on page 71*

♦ **Amikin®**   *see Amikacin on page 71*

Amiloride (a MIL oh ride)

U.S. Brand Names Midamor® [DSC]
Synonyms Amiloride Hydrochloride
Therapeutic Category Diuretic, Potassium-Sparing
Use Counteracts potassium loss induced by other diuretics in the treatment of hypertension or edematous conditions including CHF, hepatic cirrhosis, and hypoaldosteronism; usually used in conjunction with more potent diuretics such as thiazides or loop diuretics
Unlabeled/Investigational Use Investigational: Cystic fibrosis; reduction of lithium-induced polyuria
Pregnancy Risk Factor B
Contraindications Hypersensitivity to amiloride or any component of the formulation; presence of elevated serum potassium levels (>5.5 mEq/L); if patient is receiving other potassium-conserving agents (eg, spironolactone, triamterene) or potassium supplementation (medicine, potassium-containing salt substitutes, potassium-rich diet); anuria; acute or chronic renal insufficiency; evidence of diabetic nephropathy. Patients with evidence of renal impairment or diabetes mellitus should not receive this medicine without close, frequent monitoring of serum electrolytes and renal function.
Warnings/Precautions Use cautiously in patients with severe hepatic insufficiency; may cause hyperkalemia (serum levels >5.5 mEq/L) which, if uncorrected, is potentially fatal; medication should be discontinued if potassium level are >6.5 mEq/L
Common Adverse Reactions 1% to 10%:
Central nervous system: Headache, fatigue, dizziness
Endocrine & metabolic: Hyperkalemia (up to 10%; risk reduced in patients receiving kaliuretic diuretics), hyperchloremic metabolic acidosis, dehydration, hyponatremia, gynecomastia
Gastrointestinal: Nausea, diarrhea, vomiting, abdominal pain, gas pain, appetite changes, constipation
Genitourinary: Impotence
Neuromuscular & skeletal: Muscle cramps, weakness
Respiratory: Cough, dyspnea
Drug Interactions
Increased Effect/Toxicity: Increased risk of amiloride-associated hyperkalemia with triamterene, spironolactone, ACE inhibitors or angiotensin receptor antagonists, potassium preparations, cyclosporine, tacrolimus, and indomethacin. Amiloride may increase the toxicity of amantadine and lithium by reduction of renal excretion. Quinidine and amiloride together may increase risk of malignant arrhythmias.
Decreased Effect: Decreased effect of amiloride with use of NSAIDs. Amoxicillin's absorption may be reduced with concurrent use.
Mechanism of Action Interferes with potassium/sodium exchange (active transport) in the distal tubule, cortical collecting tubule and collecting duct by inhibiting sodium, potassium-ATPase; decreases calcium excretion; increases magnesium loss
Pharmacodynamics/Kinetics
Onset of action: 2 hours
Duration: 24 hours
Absorption: ~15% to 25%
Distribution: V_d: 350-380 L
Protein binding: 23%
Metabolism: No active metabolites
Half-life elimination: Normal renal function: 6-9 hours; End-stage renal disease: 8-144 hours
Time to peak, serum: 6-10 hours
Excretion: Urine and feces (equal amounts as unchanged drug)
Dosage Oral:
Children: Although safety and efficacy in children have not been established by the FDA, a dosage of 0.625 mg/kg/day has been used in children weighing 6-20 kg.
Adults: 5-10 mg/day (up to 20 mg)
Elderly: Initial: 5 mg once daily or every other day
Dosing adjustment in renal impairment:
Cl_{cr} 10-50 mL/minute: Administer at 50% of normal dose.
Cl_{cr} <10 mL/minute: Avoid use.
Administration Administer with food or meals to avoid GI upset.
Monitoring Parameters I & O, daily weights, blood pressure, serum electrolytes, renal function
Patient Information Report any muscle cramps, weakness, nausea, or dizziness; use caution operating machinery or performing other tasks requiring alertness
Dosage Forms TAB: 5 mg

Amiloride and Hydrochlorothiazide
(a MIL oh ride & hye droe klor oh THYE a zide)
U.S. Brand Names Moduretic® [DSC]
Synonyms Hydrochlorothiazide and Amiloride
Therapeutic Category Antihypertensive Agent, Combination
Use Potassium-sparing diuretic; antihypertensive
Pregnancy Risk Factor B
Dosage Adults: Oral: Start with 1 tablet/day, then may be increased to 2 tablets/day if needed; usually given in a single dose
Dosage Forms TAB: Amiloride 5 mg and hydrochlorothiazide 50 mg

♦ **Amiloride Hydrochloride** *see Amiloride on page 73*

♦ **2-Amino-6-Mercaptopurine** *see Thioguanine on page 1215*

♦ **2-Amino-6-Trifluoromethoxy-benzothiazole** *see Riluzole on page 1098*

♦ **Aminobenzylpenicillin** *see Ampicillin on page 95*

Aminocaproic Acid (a mee noe ka PROE ik AS id)
U.S. Brand Names Amicar®
Therapeutic Category Hemostatic Agent
Use Treatment of excessive bleeding from fibrinolysis
Pregnancy Risk Factor C
Contraindications Disseminated intravascular coagulation; evidence of an intravascular clotting process
Warnings/Precautions Rapid I.V. administration of the undiluted drug is not recommended. Aminocaproic acid may accumulate in patients with decreased renal function. Intrarenal obstruction may occur secondary to glomerular capillary thrombosis or clots in the renal pelvis and ureters. Do not use in hematuria of upper urinary tract origin unless possible benefits outweigh risks. Use with caution in patients with cardiac, renal, or hepatic disease. Do not administer without a definite diagnosis of laboratory findings indicative of hyperfibrinolysis. Inhibition of fibrinolysis may promote clotting or thrombosis. Subsequently, use with great caution in patients with or at risk for veno-occlusive disease of the liver. Benzyl alcohol is used as a preservative, therefore, these products should not be used in the neonate. Do not administer with factor IX complex concentrates or anti-inhibitor coagulant complexes.
Common Adverse Reactions 1% to 10%:
Cardiovascular: Hypotension, bradycardia, arrhythmia
Central nervous system: Dizziness, headache, malaise, fatigue
Dermatologic: Rash
Gastrointestinal: GI irritation, nausea, cramps, diarrhea
Hematologic: Decreased platelet function, elevated serum enzymes
Neuromuscular & skeletal: Myopathy, weakness
Otic: Tinnitus
Respiratory: Nasal congestion
Drug Interactions
  Increased Effect/Toxicity: Increased risk of hypercoagulability with oral contraceptives, estrogens. Should not be administered with factor IX complex concentrated or anti-inhibitor complex concentrates due to an increased risk of thrombosis.
Mechanism of Action Competitively inhibits activation of plasminogen to plasmin, also, a lesser antiplasmin effect
Pharmacodynamics/Kinetics
Onset of action: ~1-72 hours
Distribution: Widely through intravascular and extravascular compartments
Metabolism: Minimally hepatic
Half-life elimination: 1-2 hours
Time to peak: Oral: Within 2 hours
Excretion: Urine (68% to 86% as unchanged drug)
Dosage In the management of acute bleeding syndromes, oral dosage regimens are the same as the I.V. dosage regimens in adults and children
Chronic bleeding: Oral, I.V.: 5-30 g/day in divided doses at 3- to 6-hour intervals
Acute bleeding syndrome:
  Children: Oral, I.V.: 100 mg/kg or 3 g/m^2 during the first hour, followed by continuous infusion at the rate of 33.3 mg/hour or 1 g/m^2/hour; total dosage should not exceed 18 g/m^2/24 hours
  Traumatic hyphema: Oral: 100 mg/kg/dose every 6-8 hours
  Adults:
    Oral: For elevated fibrinolytic activity, administer 5 g during first hour, followed by 1-1.25 g/hour for approximately 8 hours or until bleeding stops
    I.V.: 4-5 g in 250 mL of diluent during first hour followed by continuous infusion at the rate of 1-1.25 g/hour in 50 mL of diluent, continue for 8 hours or until bleeding stops
    Maximum daily dose: Oral, I.V.: 30 g
Dosing adjustment in renal impairment: Oliguria or ESRD: Reduce to 15% to 25% of usual dose
Administration Administration by infusion using appropriate I.V. solution (dextrose 5% or 0.9% sodium chloride); rapid I.V. injection (IVP) should be avoided since hypotension, bradycardia,

and arrhythmia may result. Aminocaproic acid may accumulate in patients with decreased renal function.

Monitoring Parameters Fibrinogen, fibrin split products, creatine phosphokinase (with long-term therapy)

Reference Range Therapeutic concentration: >130 µg/mL (concentration necessary for inhibition of fibrinolysis)

Patient Information Report any signs of bleeding; change positions slowly to minimize dizziness

Dosage Forms INJ, solution: 250 mg/mL (20 mL). **SYR:** 1.25 g/5 mL (240 mL, 480 mL). (Amicar®): 1.25 g/5 mL (480 mL); **TAB [scored]:** 500 mg

♦ **Amino-Cerv**™ *see Urea on page 1282*

Aminoglutethimide (a mee noe gloo TETH i mide)
U.S. Brand Names Cytadren®
Synonyms AG; AGT; BA-16038; Elipten
Therapeutic Category Adrenal Steroid Inhibitor; Antiadrenal Agent; Antineoplastic Agent, Miscellaneous
Use Suppression of adrenal function in selected patients with Cushing's syndrome
Pregnancy Risk Factor D
Dosage Adults: Oral: 250 mg every 6 hours may be increased at 1- to 2-week intervals to a total of 2 g/day
  Dosing adjustment in renal impairment: Dose reduction may be necessary
Dosage Forms TAB: [scored] 250 mg

♦ **Aminoglycoside Dosing and Monitoring** *see page 1350*

Aminolevulinic Acid (a MEE noh lev yoo lin ik AS id)
U.S. Brand Names Levulan® Kerastick®
Synonyms Aminolevulinic Acid Hydrochloride
Therapeutic Category Photosensitizing Agent, Topical; Porphyrin Agent, Topical; Topical Skin Product
Use Treatment of minimally to moderately thick actinic keratoses (grade 1 or 2) of the face or scalp; to be used in conjunction with blue light illumination
Pregnancy Risk Factor C
Contraindications Hypersensitivity to aminolevulinic acid or any component of the formulation; individuals with cutaneous photosensitivity at wavelengths of 400-450 nm; porphyria; allergy to porphyrins
Warnings/Precautions For external use only. Do not apply to eyes or mucous membranes. Treatment site will become photosensitive following application. Patients should be instructed to avoid exposure to sunlight, bright indoor lights, or tanning beds during the period prior to blue light treatment. Should be applied by a qualified health professional to avoid application to perilesional skin. Has not been tested in individuals with coagulation defects (acquired or inherited).

Common Adverse Reactions
Transient stinging, burning, itching, erythema, and edema result from the photosensitizing properties of this agent. Symptoms subside between 1 minute and 24 hours after turning off the blue light illuminator. Severe stinging or burning was reported in at least 50% of patients from at least 1 lesional site treatment.
>10%: Dermatologic: Severe stinging or burning (50%), scaling of the skin/crusted skin (64% to 71%), hyperpigmentation/hypopigmentation (22% to 36%), itching (14% to 25%), erosion (2% to 14%)
1% to 10%:
  Central nervous system: Dysesthesia (up to 2%)
  Dermatologic: Skin ulceration (2% to 4%), vesiculation (4% to 5%), pustular drug eruption (up to 4%), skin disorder (5% to 12%)
  Hematologic: Bleeding/hemorrhage (2% to 4%)
  Local: Wheal/flare (2% to 7%), local pain (1%), tenderness (1% to 2%), edema (1%), scabbing (up to 2%), ulceration (2% to 4%), excoriation (1%)

Drug Interactions
Increased Effect/Toxicity: Photosensitizing agents such as griseofulvin, thiazide diuretics, sulfonamides, sulfonylureas, phenothiazines, and tetracyclines theoretically may increase the photosensitizing potential of aminolevulinic acid.
Mechanism of Action Aminolevulinic acid is a metabolic precursor of protoporphyrin IX (PpIX), which is a photosensitizer. Photosensitization following application of aminolevulinic acid topical solution occurs through the metabolic conversion to PpIX. When exposed to light of appropriate wavelength and energy, accumulated PpIX produces a photodynamic reaction.
Pharmacodynamics/Kinetics
PpIX:
  Peak fluorescence intensity: 11 hours ± 1 hour
  Half-life, mean clearance for lesions: 30 ± 10 hours
Dosage Adults: Topical: Apply to actinic keratoses (**not** perilesional skin) followed 14-18 hours later by blue light illumination. Application/treatment may be repeated at a treatment site after 8 weeks.
Administration Dab lesion gently with wet applicator tip. Do not apply to periorbital area, ocular tissue, or mucosal surfaces. Allow to dry then reapply to same lesion. Apply to either scalp or (Continued)

Aminolevulinic Acid *(Continued)*

facial lesions, but not to both simultaneously. Follow application with blue light exposure in 14-18 hours.

Patient Information Solution will be applied by prescriber. Once solution is applied, affected skin will be sensitive to light. Wear protective clothing when exposed to light and avoid bright lights (including tanning beds) and sunlight. Sunscreens will not prevent phototoxic reactions. Solution will be applied directly to lesions; blue light exposure should follow 14-18 hours later. Do not wash solution off skin during this time. If you are not able to return for blue light therapy, avoid sunlight and other bright light for at least 40 hours following application of solution.

Dosage Forms POWDER for topical solution: 20% (1s, 6s) [2-component system containing aminolevulinic acid hydrochloride 354 mg (powder) and diluent containing ethanol 48% (1.5 mL) packaged together in an applicator tube]

♦ **Aminolevulinic Acid Hydrochloride** *see Aminolevulinic Acid on page 75*

♦ **Aminophylline** *see Theophylline Salts on page 1210*

♦ **Aminosalicylate Sodium** *see Aminosalicylic Acid on page 76*

Aminosalicylic Acid *(a mee noe sal i SIL ik AS id)*

U.S. Brand Names Paser®

Synonyms Aminosalicylate Sodium; 4-Aminosalicylic Acid; Para-Aminosalicylate Sodium; PAS; Sodium PAS

Therapeutic Category Salicylate

Use Adjunctive treatment of tuberculosis used in combination with other antitubercular agents

Unlabeled/Investigational Use Crohn's disease

Pregnancy Risk Factor C

Contraindications Hypersensitivity to aminosalicylic acid or any component of the formulation

Warnings/Precautions Use with caution in patients with hepatic or renal dysfunction and patients with gastric ulcer.

Common Adverse Reactions Frequency not defined.

Cardiovascular: Pericarditis, vasculitis

Central nervous system: Encephalopathy, fever

Dermatologic: Skin eruptions

Endocrine & metabolic: Goiter (with or without myxedema), hypoglycemia

Gastrointestinal: Abdominal pain, diarrhea, nausea, vomiting

Hematologic: Agranulocytosis, anemia (hemolytic), leukopenia, thrombocytopenia

Hepatic: Hepatitis, jaundice

Ocular: Optic neuritis

Respiratory: Eosinophilic pneumonia

Drug Interactions

Decreased Effect: Aminosalicylic acid may decrease serum levels of digoxin and vitamin B_{12}.

Mechanism of Action Aminosalicylic acid (PAS) is a highly specific bacteriostatic agent active against *M. tuberculosis*. Structurally related to para-aminobenzoic acid (PABA) and its mechanism of action is thought to be similar to the sulfonamides, a competitive antagonism with PABA; disrupts plate biosynthesis in sensitive organisms.

Pharmacodynamics/Kinetics

Absorption: Readily, >90%

Protein binding: 50% to 60%

Metabolism: Hepatic (>50%) via acetylation

Half-life elimination: Reduced with renal impairment

Time to peak, serum: 6 hours

Excretion: Urine (>80% as unchanged drug and metabolites)

Dosage Oral:

Children: Tuberculosis: 200-300 mg/kg/day in 3-4 equally divided doses

Adults:

Tuberculosis: 150 mg/kg/day in 2-3 equally divided doses

Crohn's disease (unlabeled use): 1.5 g/day

Dosing adjustment in renal impairment:

Cl_{cr} 10-50 mL/minute: Administer 50% to 75% of dose

Cl_{cr} <10 mL/minute: Administer 50% of dose

Administer after hemodialysis: Administer 50% of dose

Continuous arteriovenous hemofiltration: Dose for Cl_{cr} <10 mL/minute

Administration Do not use granules if packet is swollen or if granules are discolored (ie, brown or purple). Granules may be sprinkled on applesauce or yogurt (do not chew) or suspended in tomato or orange juice.

Patient Information Notify prescriber if persistent sore throat, fever, unusual bleeding or bruising, persistent nausea, vomiting, or abdominal pain occurs; do not stop taking before consulting your prescriber; take with food or meals; do not use products that are brown or purple; store in a cool, dry place away from sunlight

Dosage Forms GRAN: 4 g/packet (30s)

♦ **4-Aminosalicylic Acid** *see Aminosalicylic Acid on page 76*

♦ **5-Aminosalicylic Acid** *see Mesalamine on page 798*

♦ **Aminoxin® [OTC]** *see Pyridoxine on page 1067*

Amiodarone (a MEE oh da rone)

U.S. Brand Names Cordarone®; Pacerone®

Synonyms Amiodarone Hydrochloride

Therapeutic Category Antiarrhythmic Agent, Class III

Use

Oral: Management of life-threatening recurrent ventricular fibrillation (VF) or hemodynamically unstable ventricular tachycardia (VT)

I.V.: Initiation of treatment and prophylaxis of frequency recurring VF and unstable VT in patients refractory to other therapy. Also, used for patients when oral amiodarone is indicated, but who are unable to take oral medication.

Unlabeled/Investigational Use

Conversion of atrial fibrillation to normal sinus rhythm; maintenance of normal sinus rhythm

Prevention of postoperative atrial fibrillation during cardiothoracic surgery

Paroxysmal supraventricular tachycardia (SVT)

Control of rapid ventricular rate due to accessory pathway conduction in pre-excited atrial arrhythmias [ACLS guidelines]

After defibrillation and epinephrine in cardiac arrest with persistent ventricular tachycardia (VT) or ventricular fibrillation (VF) [ACLS guidelines]

Control of hemodynamically stable VT, polymorphic VT or wide-complex tachycardia of uncertain origin [ACLS guidelines]

Pregnancy Risk Factor D

Contraindications Hypersensitivity to amiodarone or any component of the formulation; severe sinus-node dysfunction; second- and third-degree heart block (except in patients with a functioning artificial pacemaker); bradycardia causing syncope (except in patients with a functioning artificial pacemaker); pregnancy

Warnings/Precautions Monitor for pulmonary toxicity, liver toxicity, or exacerbation of the arrhythmia. Use very cautiously and with close monitoring in patients with thyroid or liver disease. Significant heart block or sinus bradycardia can occur. Patients should be hospitalized when amiodarone is initiated. Amiodarone is a potent inhibitor of CYP enzymes, and may lead to increased serum concentrations/toxicity of a number of medications. Particular caution must be used when a drug with QT_c-prolonging potential relies on metabolism via these enzymes, since the effect of elevated concentrations may be additive with the effect of amiodarone.

Pre-existing pulmonary disease does not increase risk of developing pulmonary toxicity, but if pulmonary toxicity develops then the prognosis is worse. Due to complex pharmacokinetics, it is difficult to predict when an arrhythmia or interaction with a subsequent treatment will occur following discontinuation of amiodarone. May cause optic neuropathy and/or optic neuritis, usually resulting in visual impairment. Corneal microdeposits occur in a majority of patients, and may cause visual disturbances in some patients (blurred vision, halos); these are not generally considered a reason to discontinue treatment.

Caution in surgical patients; may enhance hemodynamic effect of anesthetics; associated with increased risk of adult respiratory distress syndrome (ARDS) postoperatively. Injection contains benzyl alcohol, which has been associated with "gasping syndrome" in neonates.

Common Adverse Reactions In a recent meta-analysis, patients taking lower doses of amiodarone (152-330 mg daily for at least 12 months) were more likely to develop thyroid, neurologic, skin, ocular, and bradycardic abnormalities than those taking placebo (Vorperian, 1997). Pulmonary toxicity was similar in both the low dose amiodarone group and in the placebo group but there was a trend towards increased toxicity in the amiodarone group. Gastrointestinal and hepatic events were seen to a similar extent in both the low dose amiodarone group and placebo group.

>10%:

Cardiovascular: Hypotension (I.V. 16%, refractory in rare cases)

Central nervous system (3% to 40%): Abnormal gait/ataxia, dizziness, fatigue, headache, malaise, impaired memory, involuntary movement, insomnia, poor coordination, peripheral neuropathy, sleep disturbances, tremor

Dermatologic: Photosensitivity (10% to 75%)

Endocrine & Metabolic: Hypothyroidism (1% to 22%)

Gastrointestinal: Nausea, vomiting, anorexia and constipation (10% to 33%), AST or ALT level >2X normal (15% to 50%)

1% to 10%:

Cardiovascular: Congestive heart failure (3%), bradycardia (3% to 5%), AV block (5%), conduction abnormalities, SA node dysfunction (1% to 3%), cardiac arrhythmias, flushing, edema. Additional effects associated with I.V. administration include asystole, cardiac arrest, electromechanical dissociation, ventricular tachycardia, and cardiogenic shock.

Dermatologic: Slate blue skin discoloration (<10%)

Endocrine & metabolic: Hyperthyroidism (<3%), libido decreased

Gastrointestinal: Abdominal pain, abnormal salivation, abnormal taste (oral)

Hematologic: Coagulation abnormalities

Hepatic: Hepatitis and cirrhosis (<3%)

Local: Phlebitis (I.V., with concentrations >3 mg/mL)

Ocular: Visual disturbances (2% to 9%), corneal microdeposits (occur in a majority of patients and lead to visual disturbance in ~10%), halo vision (<5% occurring especially at night), optic neuritis (1%)

Respiratory: Pulmonary toxicity has been estimated to occur at a frequency between 2% and 7% of patients (some reports indicate a frequency as high as 17%). Toxicity may present as hypersensitivity pneumonitis; pulmonary fibrosis (cough, fever, malaise);

(Continued)

Amiodarone *(Continued)*

pulmonary inflammation; interstitial pneumonitis; or alveolar pneumonitis. ARDS has been reported in up to 2% of patients receiving I. V. amiodarone, and postoperatively in patients receiving oral amiodarone.

Miscellaneous: Abnormal smell (oral)

Drug Interactions

Cytochrome P450 Effect: Substrate of CYP1A2 (minor), 2C8/9 (major), 2C19 (minor), 2D6 (minor), 3A4 (minor); **Inhibits** CYP1A2 (strong), 2A6 (moderate), 2B6 (weak), 2C8/9 (moderate), 2C19 (weak), 2D6 (moderate), 3A4 (moderate)

Increased Effect/Toxicity: The effect of drugs which prolong the QT interval, including amitriptyline, astemizole, bepridil, cisapride, disopyramide, erythromycin, gatifloxacin, halo-peridol, imipramine, moxifloxacin, quinidine, pimozide, procainamide, sotalol, sparfloxacin, theophylline, and thioridazine may be increased. Cisapride, gatifloxacin, moxifloxacin, and sparfloxacin are contraindicated.

Note: Due to the long half-life of amiodarone, drug interactions may take 1 or more weeks to develop. Use of amiodarone with diltiazem, verapamil, digoxin, beta-blockers, and other drugs which delay AV conduction may cause excessive AV block (amiodarone may also decrease the metabolism of some of these agents - see below). CYP2C8/9 inhibitors may increase the levels/effects of amiodarone; example inhibitors include delavirdine, fluconazole, gemfibrozil, ketoconazole, nicardipine, NSAIDs, pioglitazone, and sulfonamides Amprenavir, cimetidine, nelfinavir, and ritonavir increase amiodarone levels. Amiodarone may increase the levels of digoxin (reduce dose by 50% on initiation), clonazepam, cyclosporine, flecainide (decrease dose up to 33%), metoprolol, phenothiazines, phenytoin, procainamide (reduce dose), propranolol, quinidine, tricyclic antidepressants, and warfarin. Concurrent use of fentanyl may lead to bradycardia, sinus arrest, and hypotension. Amiodarone may increase lovastatin- or simvastatin-induced myopathy; concurrent use not recommended. Amiodarone may alter thyroid function and response to thyroid supplements. Amiodarone enhances the myocardial depressant and conduction defects of inhalation anesthetics (monitor).

Decreased Effect: CYP2C8/9 inducers may decrease the levels/effects of amiodarone; example inducers include carbamazepine, phenobarbital, phenytoin, rifampin, rifapentine, and secobarbital. Amiodarone may alter thyroid function and response to thyroid supplements; monitor closely.

Mechanism of Action Class III antiarrhythmic agent which inhibits adrenergic stimulation, prolongs the action potential and refractory period in myocardial tissue; decreases AV conduction and sinus node function

Pharmacodynamics/Kinetics

Onset of action: Oral: 3 days to 3 weeks; I.V.: May be more rapid

Peak effect: 1 week to 5 months

Duration after discontinuing therapy: 7-50 days

Note: Mean onset of effect and duration after discontinuation may be shorter in children than adults

Distribution: V_d: 66 L/kg (range: 18-148 L/kg); crosses placenta; enters breast milk in concentrations higher than maternal plasma concentrations

Protein binding: 96%

Metabolism: Hepatic, major metabolite active; possible enterohepatic recirculation

Bioavailability: ~50%

Half-life elimination: 40-55 days (range: 26-107 days); shorter in children than adults

Excretion: Feces; urine (<1% as unchanged drug)

Dosage Note: Lower loading and maintenance doses are preferable in women and all patients with low body weight.

Oral:

Children (calculate doses for children <1 year on body surface area): Loading dose: 10-15 mg/kg/day or 600-800 mg/1.73 m²/day for 4-14 days or until adequate control of arrhythmia or prominent adverse effects occur (this loading dose may be given in 1-2 divided doses/day). Dosage should then be reduced to 5 mg/kg/day or 200-400 mg/1.73 m²/day given once daily for several weeks. If arrhythmia does not recur, reduce to lowest effective dosage possible. Usual daily minimal dose: 2.5 mg/kg/day; maintenance doses may be given for 5 of 7 days/week.

Adults: Ventricular arrhythmias: 800-1600 mg/day in 1-2 doses for 1-3 weeks, then when adequate arrhythmia control is achieved, decrease to 600-800 mg/day in 1-2 doses for 1 month; maintenance: 400 mg/day. Lower doses are recommended for supraventricular arrhythmias.

I.V.:

Children (safety and efficacy of amiodarone use in children has not been fully established): Ventricular arrhythmias: A multicenter study (Perry, 1996; n=40; mean age 5.4 years with 24 of 40 children <2 years of age) used an I.V. loading dose of 5 mg/kg that was divided into five 1 mg/kg aliquots, with each aliquot given over 5-10 minutes. Additional 1-5 mg/kg doses could be administered 30 minutes later in a similar fashion if needed. The mean loading dose was 6.3 mg/kg. A maintenance dose (continuous infusion of 10-15 mg/kg/day) was administered to 21 of the 40 patients. Further studies are needed.

Note: I.V. administration at low flow rates (potentially associated with use in pediatrics) may result in leaching of plasticizers (DEHP) from intravenous tubing. DEHP may adversely affect male reproductive tract development. Alternative means of dosing and administration (1 mg/kg aliquots) may need to be considered.

Adults:
Breakthrough VF or VT: 150 mg supplemental doses in 100 mL D_5W over 10 minutes

Pulseless VF or VT: I.V. push: Initial: 300 mg in 20-30 mL NS or D_5W; if VF or VT recurs, supplemental dose of 150 mg followed by infusion of 1 mg/minute for 6 hours, then 0.5 mg/minute (maximum daily dose: 2.2 g)

Note: When switching from I.V. to oral therapy, use the following as a guide:
<1-week I.V. infusion: 800-1600 mg/day
1- to 3-week I.V. infusion: 600-800 mg/day
>3-week I.V. infusion: 400 mg/day

Recommendations for conversion to intravenous amiodarone after oral administration: During long-term amiodarone therapy (ie, ≥4 months), the mean plasma-elimination half-life of the active metabolite of amiodarone is 61 days. Replacement therapy may not be necessary in such patients if oral therapy is discontinued for a period <2 weeks, since any changes in serum amiodarone concentrations during this period may **not** be clinically significant.

Unlabeled uses:
Prophylaxis of atrial fibrillation following open heart surgery (unlabeled use): **Note:** A variety of regimens have been used in clinical trials, including oral and intravenous regimens:
Oral: 400 mg twice daily (starting in postop recovery) for up to 7 days. An alternative regimen of amiodarone 600 mg/day for 7 days prior to surgery, followed by 200 mg/day until hospital discharge, has also been shown to decrease the risk of postoperative atrial fibrillation.

I.V.: 1000 mg infused over 24 hours (starting at postop recovery) for 2 days has been shown to reduce the risk of postoperative atrial fibrillation

Recurrent atrial fibrillation (unlabeled use): No standard regimen defined; examples of regimens include: Oral: Initial: 10 mg/kg/day for 14 days; followed by 300 mg/day for 4 weeks, followed by maintenance dosage of 100-200 mg/day (see Roy D, 2000). Other regimens have been described and are used clinically (ie, 400 mg 3 times/day for 5-7 days, then 400 mg/day for 1 month, then 200 mg/day).

Stable VT or SVT (unlabeled use): First 24 hours: 1000 mg according to following regimen
Step 1: 150 mg (100 mL) over first 10 minutes (mix 3 mL in 100 mL D_5W)
Step 2: 360 mg (200 mL) over next 6 hours (mix 18 mL in 500 mL D_5W): 1 mg/minute
Step 3: 540 mg (300 mL) over next 18 hours: 0.5 mg/minute
Note: After the first 24 hours: 0.5 mg/minute utilizing concentration of 1-6 mg/mL

Dosing in elderly patients: No specific guidelines available. Dose selection should be cautious, at low end of dosage range, and titration should be slower to evaluate response.

Dosing adjustment in hepatic impairment: Probably necessary in substantial hepatic impairment. No specific guidelines available.

Hemodialysis: Not dialyzable (0% to 5%); supplemental dose is not necessary.

Peritoneal dialysis effects: Not dialyzable (0% to 5%); supplemental dose is not necessary.

Administration
Oral: Administer consistently with regard to meals. Take in divided doses with meals if high daily dose or if GI upset occurs. If GI intolerance occurs with single-dose therapy, use twice daily dosing.

I.V.: Give I.V. therapy using an infusion pump through a central line or a peripheral line at a concentration of <2 mg/mL. Slow the infusion rate if hypotension develops. **Note:** I.V. administration at low flow rates (potentially associated with use in pediatrics) may result in leaching of plasticizers (DEHP) from intravenous tubing. DEHP may adversely affect male reproductive tract development. Alternative means of dosing and administration (1 mg/kg aliquots) may need to be considered.

Monitoring Parameters Monitor heart rate (ECG) and rhythm throughout therapy; assess patient for signs of thyroid dysfunction (thyroid function tests and liver enzymes), lethargy, edema of the hands, feet, weight loss, and pulmonary toxicity (baseline pulmonary function tests)

Reference Range Therapeutic: 0.5-2.5 mg/L (SI: 1-4 µmol/L) (parent); desethyl metabolite is active and is present in equal concentration to parent drug

Patient Information Take with food; use sunscreen or stay out of sun to prevent burns; skin discoloration is reversible; photophobia may make sunglasses necessary; do not discontinue abruptly; regular blood work for thyroid functions tests and ophthalmologic exams are necessary; notify prescriber if persistent dry cough or shortness of breath occurs

Dosage Forms INJ, solution: 50 mg/mL (3 mL, 18 mL); (Cordarone®): 50 mg/mL (30 mL).
TAB [scored]: 200 mg; (Cordarone®): 200 mg; (Pacerone®): 200 mg, 400 mg

♦ **Amiodarone Hydrochloride** *see* Amiodarone *on page 77*

♦ **Ami-Tex PSE** *see* Guaifenesin and Pseudoephedrine *on page 605*

♦ **Amitone® [OTC]** *see* Calcium Carbonate *on page 203*

Amitriptyline (a mee TRIP ti leen)
Related Information
Antidepressant Agents Comparison *on page 1359*
U.S. Brand Names Elavil® [DSC]
Synonyms Amitriptyline Hydrochloride
Therapeutic Category Antidepressant, Tricyclic (Tertiary Amine); Antimigraine Agent, Prophylaxis
Use Relief of symptoms of depression
(Continued)

Amitriptyline *(Continued)*

Unlabeled/Investigational Use Analgesic for certain chronic and neuropathic pain; prophylaxis against migraine headaches; treatment of depressive disorders in children

Pregnancy Risk Factor C

Contraindications Hypersensitivity to amitriptyline or any component of the formulation (cross-sensitivity with other tricyclics may occur); use of MAO inhibitors within past 14 days; acute recovery phase following myocardial infarction; concurrent use of cisapride

Warnings/Precautions Often causes drowsiness/sedation, resulting in impaired performance of tasks requiring alertness (eg, operating machinery or driving). Sedative effects may be additive with other CNS depressants and/or ethanol. The degree of sedation is very high relative to other antidepressants. May worsen psychosis in some patients or precipitate a shift to mania or hypomania in patients with bipolar disease. May cause hyponatremia/SIADH. May increase the risks associated with electroconvulsive therapy. This agent should be discontinued, when possible, prior to elective surgery. Therapy should not be abruptly discontinued in patients receiving high doses for prolonged periods.

May cause orthostatic hypotension; the risk of this problem is very high relative to other antidepressants. Use with caution in patients at risk of hypotension or in patients where transient hypotensive episodes would be poorly tolerated (cardiovascular disease or cerebrovascular disease). The degree of anticholinergic blockade produced by this agent is very high relative to other cyclic antidepressants; use with caution in patients with urinary retention, benign prostatic hyperplasia, narrow-angle glaucoma, xerostomia, visual problems, constipation, or a history of bowel obstruction. May alter glucose control - use with caution in patients with diabetes.

The possibility of a suicide attempt is inherent in major depression and may persist until remission occurs. Use caution in high-risk patients during initiation of therapy. Prescriptions should be written for the smallest quantity consistent with good patient care. Use with caution in patients with a history of cardiovascular disease (including previous MI, stroke, tachycardia, or conduction abnormalities). The risk of conduction abnormalities with this agent is high relative to other antidepressants. May lower seizure threshold - use caution in patients with a previous seizure disorder or condition predisposing to seizures such as brain damage, alcoholism, or concurrent therapy with other drugs which lower the seizure threshold. Use with caution in hyperthyroid patients or those receiving thyroid supplementation. Use with caution in patients with hepatic or renal dysfunction and in elderly patients. Not recommended for use in patients <12 years of age.

Common Adverse Reactions Anticholinergic effects may be pronounced; moderate to marked sedation can occur (tolerance to these effects usually occurs).

Frequency not defined.

Cardiovascular: Orthostatic hypotension, tachycardia, nonspecific ECG changes, changes in AV conduction, cardiomyopathy (rare), MI, stroke, heart block, arrhythmias, syncope, hypertension, palpitation

Central nervous system: Restlessness, dizziness, insomnia, sedation, fatigue, anxiety, impaired cognitive function, seizures, extrapyramidal symptoms, coma, hallucinations, confusion, disorientation, impaired coordination, ataxia, headache, nightmares, hyperpyrexia

Dermatologic: Allergic rash, urticaria, photosensitivity, alopecia

Endocrine & metabolic: Syndrome of inappropriate ADH secretion

Gastrointestinal: Weight gain, xerostomia, constipation, paralytic ileus, nausea, vomiting, anorexia, stomatitis, peculiar taste, diarrhea, black tongue

Genitourinary: Urinary retention

Hematologic: Bone marrow depression, purpura, eosinophilia

Ocular: Blurred vision, mydriasis, ocular pressure increased

Otic: Tinnitus

Neuromuscular & skeletal: Numbness, paresthesia, peripheral neuropathy, tremor, weakness

Miscellaneous: Diaphoresis; withdrawal reactions (nausea, headache, malaise)

Drug Interactions

Cytochrome P450 Effect: Substrate of CYP1A2 (minor), 2B6 (minor), 2C8/9 (minor), 2C19 (minor), 2D6 (major), 3A4 (minor); **Inhibits** CYP1A2 (weak), 2C8/9 (weak), 2C19 (weak), 2D6 (weak), 2E1 (weak)

Increased Effect/Toxicity: Amitriptyline increases the effects of amphetamines, anticholinergics, other CNS depressants (sedatives, hypnotics, or ethanol), carbamazepine, tolazamide, chlorpropamide, and warfarin. When used with MAO inhibitors, hyperpyrexia, hypertension, tachycardia, confusion, seizures, and **deaths have been reported** (serotonin syndrome). Serotonin syndrome has also been reported with ritonavir (rare). CYP2D6 inhibitors may increase the levels/effects of amitriptyline; example inhibitors include chlorpromazine, delavirdine, fluoxetine, miconazole, paroxetine, pergolide, quinidine, quinine, ritonavir, and ropinirole. Cimetidine, fenfluramine, grapefruit juice, indinavir, methylphenidate, diltiazem, valproate, and verapamil may increase the serum concentrations of TCAs. Use of lithium with a TCA may increase the risk for neurotoxicity. Phenothiazines may increase concentration of some TCAs and TCAs may increase the concentration of phenothiazines. Pressor response to I.V. epinephrine, norepinephrine, and phenylephrine may be enhanced in patients receiving TCAs (**Note:** Effect is unlikely with epinephrine or levonordefrin dosages typically administered as infiltration in combination with local anesthetics). Combined use of beta-agonists or drugs which prolong QT_c (including quinidine, procainamide, disopyramide, cisapride, sparfloxacin, gatifloxacin, moxifloxacin) with TCAs may predispose patients to cardiac arrhythmias.

Decreased Effect: Carbamazepine, phenobarbital, and rifampin may increase the metabolism of amitriptyline resulting in a decreased effect of amitriptyline. Amitriptyline inhibits the antihypertensive response to bethanidine, clonidine, debrisoquin, guanadrel, guanethidine, guanabenz, or guanfacine. Cholestyramine and colestipol may bind TCAs and reduce their absorption.

Mechanism of Action Increases the synaptic concentration of serotonin and/or norepinephrine in the central nervous system by inhibition of their reuptake by the presynaptic neuronal membrane

Pharmacodynamics/Kinetics

Onset of action: Migraine prophylaxis: 6 weeks, higher dosage may be required in heavy smokers because of increased metabolism; Depression: 4-6 weeks, reduce dosage to lowest effective level

Distribution: Crosses placenta; enters breast milk

Metabolism: Hepatic to nortriptyline (active), hydroxy and conjugated derivatives; may be impaired in the elderly

Half-life elimination: Adults: 9-27 hours (average: 15 hours)

Time to peak, serum: ~4 hours

Excretion: Urine (18% as unchanged drug); feces (small amounts)

Dosage

Children:

Chronic pain management (unlabeled use): Oral: Initial: 0.1 mg/kg at bedtime, may advance as tolerated over 2-3 weeks to 0.5-2 mg/kg at bedtime

Depressive disorders (unlabeled use): Oral: Initial doses of 1 mg/kg/day given in 3 divided doses with increases to 1.5 mg/kg/day have been reported in a small number of children (n=9) 9-12 years of age; clinically, doses up to 3 mg/kg/day (5 mg/kg/day if monitored closely) have been proposed

Migraine prophylaxis (unlabeled use): Oral: Initial: 0.25 mg/kg/day, given at bedtime; increase dose by 0.25 mg/kg/day to maximum 1 mg/kg/day. Reported dosing ranges: 0.1-2 mg/kg/day; maximum suggested dose: 10 mg

Adolescents: Depressive disorders: Oral: Initial: 25-50 mg/day; may administer in divided doses; increase gradually to 100 mg/day in divided doses

Adults:

Depression:

Oral: 50-150 mg/day single dose at bedtime or in divided doses; dose may be gradually increased up to 300 mg/day

I.M.: 20-30 mg 4 times/day

Migraine prophylaxis (unlabeled use): Oral: Initial: 10-25 mg at bedtime; usual dose: 150 mg; reported dosing ranges: 10-400 mg/day

Pain management (unlabeled use): Oral: Initial: 25 mg at bedtime; may increase as tolerated to 100 mg/day

Elderly: Depression: Oral: Initial: 10-25 mg at bedtime; dose should be increased in 10-25 mg increments every week if tolerated; dose range: 25-150 mg/day

Dosing interval in hepatic impairment: Use with caution and monitor plasma levels and patient response

Hemodialysis: Nondialyzable

Administration Not recommended for I.V.

Monitoring Parameters Monitor blood pressure and pulse rate prior to and during initial therapy; evaluate mental status; monitor weight; ECG in older adults and patients with cardiac disease

Reference Range Therapeutic: Amitriptyline and nortriptyline 100-250 ng/mL (SI: 360-900 nmol/L); nortriptyline 50-150 ng/mL (SI: 190-570 nmol/L); Toxic: >0.5 µg/mL; plasma levels do not always correlate with clinical effectiveness

Patient Information Avoid alcohol; do not discontinue medication abruptly; may cause urine to turn blue-green; may cause drowsiness; full effect may not occur for 3-6 weeks; dry mouth may be helped by sips of water, sugarless gum, or hard candy

Dosage Forms INJ: 10 mg/mL (10 mL) [DSC]. **TAB:** 10 mg, 25 mg, 50 mg, 75 mg, 100 mg, 150 mg

Amitriptyline and Chlordiazepoxide
(a mee TRIP ti leen & klor dye az e POKS ide)

U.S. Brand Names Limbitrol®; Limbitrol® DS

Synonyms Chlordiazepoxide and Amitriptyline

Therapeutic Category Antidepressant, Tricyclic Combination

Use Treatment of moderate to severe anxiety and/or agitation and depression

Restrictions C-IV

Pregnancy Risk Factor D

Dosage Initial: 3-4 tablets in divided doses; this may be increased to 6 tablets/day as required; some patients respond to smaller doses and can be maintained on 2 tablets

Dosage Forms TAB: 5-12.5 (Limbitrol®): Amitriptyline 12.5 mg and chlordiazepoxide 5 mg; 10-25 (Limbitrol® DS): Amitriptyline 25 mg and chlordiazepoxide 10 mg

Amitriptyline and Perphenazine (a mee TRIP ti leen & per FEN a zeen)

U.S. Brand Names Triavil®

Synonyms Perphenazine and Amitriptyline

Therapeutic Category Antidepressant, Tricyclic Combination

Use Treatment of patients with moderate to severe anxiety and depression

(Continued)

Amitriptyline and Perphenazine *(Continued)*

Unlabeled/Investigational Use Depression with psychotic features

Pregnancy Risk Factor D

Dosage Oral: 1 tablet 2-4 times/day

Dosage Forms TAB: 2-10 (Triavil®): Amitriptyline 10 mg and perphenazine 2 mg; 2-25 (Triavil®): Amitriptyline 25 mg and perphenazine 2 mg; 4-10 Amitriptyline 10 mg and perphenazine 4 mg; 4-25 (Triavil®): Amitriptyline 25 mg and perphenazine 4 mg; 4-50: Amitriptyline 50 mg and perphenazine 4 mg

♦ **Amitriptyline Hydrochloride** *see* Amitriptyline *on page 79*

Amlexanox *(am LEKS an oks)*

U.S. Brand Names Aphthasol®

Therapeutic Category Anti-inflammatory Agent

Use Treatment of aphthous ulcers (ie, canker sores)

Unlabeled/Investigational Use Allergic disorders

Pregnancy Risk Factor B

Dosage Administer (0.5 cm - $^1/_4$") directly on ulcers 4 times/day following oral hygiene, after meals, and at bedtime

Dosage Forms PASTE: 5% (5 g)

Amlodipine *(am LOE di peen)*

Related Information

Calcium Channel Blockers Comparison *on page 1371*

U.S. Brand Names Norvasc®

Synonyms Amlodipine Besylate

Therapeutic Category Antihypertensive Agent; Calcium Channel Blocker

Use Treatment of hypertension and angina

Pregnancy Risk Factor C

Contraindications Hypersensitivity to amlodipine or any component of the formulation

Warnings/Precautions Use with caution and titrate dosages for patients with impaired renal or hepatic function; use caution when treating patients with CHF, sick-sinus syndrome, severe left ventricular dysfunction, hypertrophic cardiomyopathy (especially obstructive), concomitant therapy with beta-blockers or digoxin, edema, or increased intracranial pressure with cranial tumors; do not abruptly withdraw (may cause chest pain); elderly may experience hypotension and constipation more readily.

Common Adverse Reactions

>10%: Cardiovascular: Peripheral edema (2% to 15% dose-related)

1% to 10%:

Cardiovascular: Flushing (1% to 3%), palpitations (1% to 4%)

Central nervous system: Headache (7%; similar to placebo 8%), dizziness (1% to 3%), fatigue (4%), somnolence (1% to 2%)

Dermatologic: Rash (1% to 2%), pruritus (1% to 2%)

Endocrine & metabolic: Male sexual dysfunction (1% to 2%)

Gastrointestinal: Nausea (3%), abdominal pain (1% to 2%), dyspepsia (1% to 2%), gingival hyperplasia

Neuromuscular & skeletal: Muscle cramps (1% to 2%), weakness (1% to 2%)

Respiratory: Dyspnea (1% to 2%), pulmonary edema (15% from PRAISE trial, CHF population)

Drug Interactions

Cytochrome P450 Effect: Substrate of CYP3A4 (major); **Inhibits** CYP1A2 (moderate), 2A6 (weak), 2B6 (weak), 2C8/9 (weak), 2D6 (weak), 3A4 (weak)

Increased Effect/Toxicity: CYP3A4 inhibitors may increase the levels/effects of amlodipine; example inhibitors include azole antifungals, ciprofloxacin, clarithromycin, diclofenac, doxycycline, erythromycin, imatinib, isoniazid, nefazodone, nicardipine, propofol, protease inhibitors, quinidine, and verapamil. Cyclosporine levels may be increased by amlodipine. Blood pressure-lowering effects of sildenafil, tadalafil, and vardenafil are additive with amlodipine (use caution).

Decreased Effect: Rifampin (and potentially other enzyme inducers) increase the metabolism of amlodipine. Calcium may reduce the calcium channel blocker's hypotensive effects. CYP3A4 inducers may decrease the levels/effects of amlodipine; example inducers include aminoglutethimide, carbamazepine, nafcillin, nevirapine, phenobarbital, phenytoin, and rifamycins.

Mechanism of Action Inhibits calcium ion from entering the "slow channels" or select voltage-sensitive areas of vascular smooth muscle and myocardium during depolarization, producing a relaxation of coronary vascular smooth muscle and coronary vasodilation; increases myocardial oxygen delivery in patients with vasospastic angina

Pharmacodynamics/Kinetics

Onset of action: 30-50 minutes

Peak effect: 6-12 hours

Duration: 24 hours

Absorption: Oral: Well absorbed

Protein binding: 93%

Metabolism: Hepatic (>90%) to inactive metabolite

Bioavailability: 64% to 90%

Half-life elimination: 30-50 hours

Excretion: Urine
Dosage Oral:
Children 6-17 years: Hypertension: 2.5-5 mg once daily
Adults:
Hypertension: Initial dose: 5 mg once daily; maximum dose: 10 mg once daily. In general, titrate in 2.5 mg increments over 7-14 days. Usual dosage range (JNC-7): 2.5-10 mg once daily.
Angina: Usual dose: 5-10 mg
Elderly: Dosing should start at the lower end of dosing range due to possible increased incidence of hepatic, renal, or cardiac impairment. Elderly patients also show decreased clearance of amlodipine.
Hypertension: 2.5 mg once daily
Angina: 5 mg once daily
Dialysis: Hemodialysis and peritoneal dialysis does not enhance elimination. Supplemental dose is not necessary.
Dosage adjustment in hepatic impairment:
Angina: Administer 5 mg once daily.
Hypertension: Administer 2.5 mg once daily.
Administration May be administered without regard to meals.
Patient Information Take as prescribed; do not stop abruptly without consulting prescriber. You may experience headache (if unrelieved, consult prescriber), nausea or vomiting (frequent small meals may help), or constipation (increased dietary bulk and fluids may help). May cause drowsiness; use caution when driving or engaging in tasks that require alertness until response to drug is known. Report unrelieved headache, vomiting, constipation, palpitations, peripheral or facial swelling, weight gain >5 lb/week, or respiratory changes.
Dosage Forms TAB [equivalent to amlodipine base] 2.5 mg, 5 mg, 10 mg

Amlodipine and Benazepril (am LOE di peen & ben AY ze pril)
U.S. Brand Names Lotrel®
Synonyms Benazepril and Amlodipine
Therapeutic Category Angiotensin-Converting Enzyme (ACE) Inhibitor/Calcium Channel Blocker Combination; Antihypertensive Agent, Combination
Use Treatment of hypertension
Pregnancy Risk Factor C/D (2nd and 3rd trimesters)
Dosage Oral:
Adults: Dose is individualized, given once daily
Elderly: Initial dose: 2.5 mg based on amlodipine component
Dosage adjustment in renal impairment: Cl_{cr} ≤30 mL/minute: Use of combination product is not recommended.
Dosage adjustment in hepatic impairment: Initial dose: 2.5 mg based on amlodipine component
Dosage Forms CAP: Amlodipine 2.5 mg and benazepril 10 mg; amlodipine 5 mg and benazepril 10 mg; amlodipine 5 mg and benazepril 20 mg; amlodipine 10 mg and benazepril 20 mg

♦ **Amlodipine Besylate** see Amlodipine on page 82
♦ **Ammonapse** see Sodium Phenylbutyrate on page 1151

Ammonium Chloride (a MOE nee um KLOR ide)
Therapeutic Category Electrolyte Supplement, Parenteral; Metabolic Alkalosis Agent; Urinary Acidifying Agent
Use Diuretic or systemic and urinary acidifying agent; treatment of hypochloremic states
Pregnancy Risk Factor C
Contraindications Severe hepatic and renal dysfunction; patients with primary respiratory acidosis
Warnings/Precautions Safety and efficacy not established in children, use with caution in infants
Common Adverse Reactions Frequency not defined.
Central nervous system: Headache (with large doses), coma, mental confusion
Dermatologic: Rash
Endocrine & metabolic: Hypokalemia (with large doses), metabolic acidosis, potassium and sodium may be decreased, hyperchloremia
Gastrointestinal: Vomiting, gastric irritation, nausea
Hepatic: Ammonia may be increased
Local: Pain at site of injection
Respiratory: Hyperventilation (with large doses)
Mechanism of Action Increases acidity by increasing free hydrogen ion concentration
Pharmacodynamics/Kinetics
Absorption: Well absorbed; complete within 3-6 hours
Metabolism: Hepatic
Excretion: Urine
Dosage Metabolic alkalosis: The following equations represent different methods of correction utilizing either the serum HCO_3^-, the serum chloride, or the base excess
Dosing of mEq NH_4Cl via the chloride-deficit method (hypochloremia):
Dose of mEq NH_4Cl = [0.2 L/kg x body weight (kg)] x [103 - observed serum chloride]; administer 100% of dose over 12 hours, then re-evaluate
(Continued)

Ammonium Chloride *(Continued)*

Note: 0.2 L/kg is the estimated chloride space and 103 is the average normal serum chloride concentration

Dosing of mEq NH$_4$Cl via the bicarbonate-excess method (refractory hypochloremic metabolic alkalosis):

Dose of NH$_4$Cl = [0.5 L/kg x body weight (kg)] x (observed serum HCO$_3^-$ - 24); administer 50% of dose over 12 hours, then re-evaluate

Note: 0.5 L/kg is the estimated bicarbonate space and 24 is the average normal serum bicarbonate concentration

Dosing of mEq NH$_4$Cl via the base-excess method:

Dose of NH$_4$Cl = [0.3 L/kg x body weight (kg)] x measured base excess (mEq/L); administer 50% of dose over 12 hours, then re-evaluate

Note: 0.3 L/kg is the estimated extracellular bicarbonate and base excess is measured by the chemistry lab and reported with arterial blood gases

These equations will yield different requirements of ammonium chloride

Equation #1 is inappropriate to use if the patient has severe metabolic alkalosis without hypochloremia or if the patient has uremia

Equation #3 is the most useful for the first estimation of ammonium chloride dosage

Children: Urinary acidifying agents: Oral, I.V.: 75 mg/kg/day in 4 divided doses; maximum daily dose: 6 g

Adults: Urinary acidifying agent/diuretic:

Oral: 1-2 g every 4-6 hours

I.V.: 1.5 g/dose every 6 hours

Administration Dilute to 0.2 mEq/mL and infuse I.V. over 3 hours; maximum concentration: 0.4 mEq/mL; maximum rate of infusion: 1 mEq/kg/hour; rapid I.V. injection may increase the likelihood of ammonia toxicity

Patient Information Take oral dose after meals

Dosage Forms INJ: 26.75% [5 mEq/mL] (20 mL). **TAB:** 500 mg. **TAB, enteric coated:** 486 mg

♦ **Amnesteem**™ *see Isotretinoin on page 696*

Amobarbital *(am oh BAR bi tal)*

U.S. Brand Names Amytal®

Synonyms Amylobarbitone

Therapeutic Category Anticonvulsant, Barbiturate; Barbiturate; Hypnotic; Sedative

Use Hypnotic in short-term treatment of insomnia; reduce anxiety and provide sedation preoperatively

Unlabeled/Investigational Use Therapeutic or diagnostic "Amytal® Interviewing"; Wada test

Restrictions C-II

Pregnancy Risk Factor D

Dosage

Children:

Sedative: I.M., I.V. : 6-12 years: Manufacturer's dosing range: 65- 500 mg

Hypnotic: I.M.: 2-3 mg/kg (maximum: 500 mg)

Adults:

Hypnotic: I.M., I.V.: 65-200 mg at bedtime (maximum I.M. dose: 500 mg)

Sedative: I.M., I.V.: 30-50 mg 2-3 times/day

"Amytal® interview" (unlabeled use): I.V.: 50-100 mg/minute for total dose of 200-1000 mg or until patient experiences drowsiness, impaired attention, slurred speech, or nystagmus

Wada test (unlabeled use): Intra-arterial: 100 mg over 4-5 seconds via percutaneous transfemoral catheter

Dosing adjustment in renal/hepatic impairment: Dosing should be reduced; specific recommendations not available.

Dosage Forms INJ, powder for reconstitution: 500 mg

Amobarbital and Secobarbital *(am oh BAR bi tal & see koe BAR bi tal)*

U.S. Brand Names Tuinal® [DSC]

Synonyms Secobarbital and Amobarbital

Therapeutic Category Barbiturate

Use Short-term treatment of insomnia

Restrictions C-II

Pregnancy Risk Factor D

Dosage Adults: Oral: 1-2 capsules at bedtime

Dosage Forms CAP: Amobarbital 50 mg and secobarbital 50 mg

Amoxapine *(a MOKS a peen)*

Related Information

Antidepressant Agents Comparison *on page 1359*

Synonyms Asendin [DSC]

Therapeutic Category Antidepressant, Tricyclic (Secondary Amine)

Use Treatment of depression, psychotic depression, depression accompanied by anxiety or agitation

Pregnancy Risk Factor C

Contraindications Hypersensitivity to amoxapine or any component of the formulation; use of MAO inhibitors within past 14 days; acute recovery phase following myocardial infarction

Warnings/Precautions May cause sedation, resulting in impaired performance of tasks requiring alertness (eg, operating machinery or driving). Sedative effects may be additive with other CNS depressants and/or ethanol. The degree of sedation is moderate relative to other antidepressants. May worsen psychosis in some patients or precipitate a shift to mania or hypomania in patients with bipolar disease. May increase the risks associated with electroconvulsive therapy. This agent should be discontinued, when possible, prior to elective surgery. Therapy should not be abruptly discontinued in patients receiving high doses for prolonged periods.

May cause extrapyramidal symptoms, including pseudoparkinsonism, acute dystonic reactions, akathisia, and tardive dyskinesia (risk of these reactions is low). May be associated with neuroleptic malignant syndrome.

May cause orthostatic hypotension (risk is moderate relative to other antidepressants) - use with caution in patients at risk of hypotension or in patients where transient hypotensive episodes would be poorly tolerated (cardiovascular disease or cerebrovascular disease). The degree of anticholinergic blockade produced by this agent is moderate relative to other cyclic antidepressants - use caution in patients with urinary retention, benign prostatic hyperplasia, narrow-angle glaucoma, xerostomia, visual problems, constipation, or history of bowel obstruction.

The possibility of a suicide attempt is inherent in major depression and may persist until remission occurs. Use caution in high-risk patients during initiation of therapy. Prescriptions should be written for the smallest quantity consistent with good patient care. Use with caution in patients with a history of cardiovascular disease (including previous MI, stroke, tachycardia, or conduction abnormalities). The risk of conduction abnormalities with this agent is moderate relative to other antidepressants. May lower seizure threshold - use caution in patients with a previous seizure disorder or condition predisposing to seizures such as brain damage, alcoholism, or concurrent therapy with other drugs which lower the seizure threshold. Use with caution in hyperthyroid patients or those receiving thyroid supplementation. Use with caution in patients with hepatic or renal dysfunction and in elderly patients. Tolerance develops in 1-3 months in some patients; close medical follow-up is essential.

Common Adverse Reactions
>10%:
  Central nervous system: Drowsiness
  Gastrointestinal: Xerostomia, constipation
1% to 10%:
  Central nervous system: Dizziness, headache, confusion, nervousness, restlessness, insomnia, ataxia, excitement, anxiety
  Dermatologic: Edema, skin rash
  Endocrine: Elevated prolactin levels
  Gastrointestinal: Nausea
  Neuromuscular & skeletal: Tremor, weakness
  Ocular: Blurred vision
  Miscellaneous: Diaphoresis

Drug Interactions
Cytochrome P450 Effect: Substrate of CYP2D6 (major)
  Increased Effect/Toxicity: Amoxapine increases the effects of amphetamines, anticholinergics, other CNS depressants (sedatives, hypnotics, or ethanol), chlorpropamide, tolazamide, and warfarin. When used with MAO inhibitors, hyperpyrexia, hypertension, tachycardia, confusion, seizures, and **deaths have been reported** (serotonin syndrome). Serotonin syndrome has also been reported with ritonavir (rare). CYP2D6 inhibitors may increase the levels/effects of amoxapine; example inhibitors include chlorpromazine, delavirdine, fluoxetine, miconazole, paroxetine, pergolide, quinidine, quinine, ritonavir, and ropinirole. Use of lithium with a TCA may increase the risk for neurotoxicity. Phenothiazines may increase concentration of some TCAs and TCAs may increase the concentration of phenothiazines. Pressor response to I.V. epinephrine, norepinephrine, and phenylephrine may be enhanced in patients receiving TCAs (**Note:** Effect is unlikely with epinephrine or levonordefrin dosages typically administered as infiltration in combination with local anesthetics). Combined use of beta-agonists or drugs which prolong QT$_c$ (including quinidine, procainamide, disopyramide, cisapride, sparfloxacin, gatifloxacin, moxifloxacin) with TCAs may predispose patients to cardiac arrhythmias.
  Decreased Effect: Amoxapine inhibits the antihypertensive effects of bethanidine, clonidine, debrisoquin, guanadrel, guanethidine, guanabenz, or guanfacine. Cholestyramine and colestipol may bind TCAs and reduce their absorption.

Mechanism of Action Reduces the reuptake of serotonin and norepinephrine. The metabolite, 7-OH-amoxapine has significant dopamine receptor blocking activity similar to haloperidol.

Pharmacodynamics/Kinetics
Onset of antidepressant effect: Usually occurs after 1-2 weeks, but may require 4-6 weeks
Absorption: Rapid and well absorbed
Distribution: V$_d$: 0.9-1.2 L/kg; enters breast milk
Protein binding: 80%
Metabolism: Primarily hepatic
Half-life elimination: Parent drug: 11-16 hours; Active metabolite (8-hydroxy): Adults: 30 hours
Time to peak, serum: 1-2 hours
Excretion: Urine (as unchanged drug and metabolites)

Dosage Oral:
Children: Not established in children <16 years of age.
(Continued)

Amoxapine *(Continued)*

Adolescents: Initial: 25-50 mg/day; increase gradually to 100 mg/day; may administer as divided doses or as a single dose at bedtime

Adults: Initial: 25 mg 2-3 times/day, if tolerated, dosage may be increased to 100 mg 2-3 times/day; may be given in a single bedtime dose when dosage <300 mg/day

Elderly: Initial: 25 mg at bedtime increased by 25 mg weekly for outpatients and every 3 days for inpatients if tolerated; usual dose: 50-150 mg/day, but doses up to 300 mg may be necessary

Maximum daily dose:

Inpatient: 600 mg

Outpatient: 400 mg

Administration May be administered with food to decrease GI distress.

Monitoring Parameters Monitor blood pressure and pulse rate prior to and during initial therapy evaluate mental status; monitor weight; ECG in older adults

Reference Range Therapeutic: Amoxapine: 20-100 ng/mL (SI: 64-319 nmol/L); 8-OH amoxapine: 150-400 ng/mL (SI: 478-1275 nmol/L); both: 200-500 ng/mL (SI: 637-1594 nmol/L)

Patient Information Dry mouth may be helped by sips of water, sugarless gum, or hard candy; avoid alcohol; very important to maintain established dosage regimen; photosensitivity to sunlight can occur, do not discontinue abruptly; full effect may not occur for 3-4 weeks; full dosage may be taken at bedtime to avoid daytime sedation

Dosage Forms TAB: 25 mg, 50 mg, 100 mg, 150 mg

Amoxicillin (a moks i SIL in)

Related Information

Antimicrobial Drugs of Choice *on page 1440*

Community-Acquired Pneumonia in Adults *on page 1457*

Prevention of Bacterial Endocarditis *on page 1429*

U.S. Brand Names Amoxil®; DisperMox™; Moxilin®; Trimox®

Synonyms Amoxicillin Trihydrate; Amoxycillin; *p*-Hydroxyampicillin

Therapeutic Category Antibiotic, Penicillin

Use Treatment of otitis media, sinusitis, and infections caused by susceptible organisms involving the respiratory tract, skin, and urinary tract; prophylaxis of bacterial endocarditis in patients undergoing surgical or dental procedures; as part of a multidrug regimen for *H. pylori* eradication

Unlabeled/Investigational Use Postexposure prophylaxis for anthrax exposure with documented susceptible organisms

Pregnancy Risk Factor B

Contraindications Hypersensitivity to amoxicillin, penicillin, or any component of the formulation

Warnings/Precautions In patients with renal impairment, doses and/or frequency of administration should be modified in response to the degree of renal impairment; a high percentage of patients with infectious mononucleosis have developed rash during therapy with amoxicillin; a low incidence of cross-allergy with other beta-lactams and cephalosporins exists

Common Adverse Reactions Frequency not defined.

Central nervous system: Hyperactivity, agitation, anxiety, insomnia, confusion, convulsions, behavioral changes, dizziness

Dermatologic: Acute exanthematous pustulosis, erythematous maculopapular rashes, erythema multiforme, Stevens-Johnson syndrome, exfoliative dermatitis, toxic epidermal necrolysis, hypersensitivity vasculitis, urticaria

Gastrointestinal: Nausea, vomiting, diarrhea, hemorrhagic colitis, pseudomembranous colitis, tooth discoloration (brown, yellow, or gray; rare)

Hematologic: Anemia, hemolytic anemia, thrombocytopenia, thrombocytopenia purpura, eosinophilia, leukopenia, agranulocytosis

Hepatic: Elevated AST (SGOT) and ALT (SGPT), cholestatic jaundice, hepatic cholestasis, acute cytolytic hepatitis

Drug Interactions

Increased Effect/Toxicity: Disulfiram and probenecid may increase amoxicillin levels. Amoxicillin may increase the effects of oral anticoagulants (warfarin). Theoretically, allopurinol taken with amoxicillin has an additive potential for amoxicillin rash. Penicillins may increase the exposure to methotrexate during concurrent therapy; monitor.

Decreased Effect: Decreased effectiveness with tetracyclines and chloramphenicol. Although anecdotal reports suggest oral contraceptive efficacy could be reduced by penicillins, this has been refuted by more rigorous scientific and clinical data.

Mechanism of Action Inhibits bacterial cell wall synthesis by binding to one or more of the penicillin binding proteins (PBPs); which in turn inhibits the final transpeptidation step of peptidoglycan synthesis in bacterial cell walls, thus inhibiting cell wall biosynthesis. Bacteria eventually lyse due to ongoing activity of cell wall autolytic enzymes (autolysins and murein hydrolases) while cell wall assembly is arrested.

Pharmacodynamics/Kinetics

Absorption: Oral: Rapid and nearly complete; food does not interfere

Distribution: Widely to most body fluids and bone; poor penetration into cells, eyes, and across normal meninges

Pleural fluids, lungs, and peritoneal fluid; high urine concentrations are attained; also into synovial fluid, liver, prostate, muscle, and gallbladder; penetrates into middle ear effusions, maxillary sinus secretions, tonsils, sputum, and bronchial secretions; crosses placenta; low concentrations enter breast milk

CSF:blood level ratio: Normal meninges: <1%; Inflamed meninges: 8% to 90%
Protein binding: 17% to 20%
Metabolism: Partially hepatic
Half-life elimination:
 Neonates, full-term: 3.7 hours
 Infants and Children: 1-2 hours
 Adults: Normal renal function: 0.7-1.4 hours
 Cl_{cr} <10 mL/minute: 7-21 hours
Time to peak: Capsule: 2 hours; Suspension: 1 hour
Excretion: Urine (80% as unchanged drug); lower in neonates

Dosage Oral:
 Children ≤3 months: 20-30 mg/kg/day divided every 12 hours
 Children: >3 months and <40 kg: Dosing range: 20-50 mg/kg/day in divided doses every 8-12 hours
  Ear, nose, throat, genitourinary tract, or skin/skin structure infections:
   Mild to moderate: 25 mg/kg/day in divided doses every 12 hours **or** 20 mg/kg/day in divided doses every 8 hours
   Severe: 45 mg/kg/day in divided doses every 12 hours **or** 40 mg/kg/day in divided doses every 8 hours
  Acute otitis media due to highly-resistant strains of *S. pneumoniae:* Doses as high as 80-90 mg/kg/day divided every 12 hours have been used
  Lower respiratory tract infections: 45 mg/kg/day in divided doses every 12 hours **or** 40 mg/kg/day in divided doses every 8 hours
  Subacute bacterial endocarditis prophylaxis: 50 mg/kg 1 hour before procedure
  Anthrax exposure (unlabeled use): **Note:** Postexposure prophylaxis only with documented susceptible organisms:
   <40 kg: 15 mg/kg every 8 hours
   ≥40 kg: 500 mg every 8 hours

 Adults: Dosing range: 250-500 mg every 8 hours or 500-875 mg twice daily; maximum dose: 2-3 g/day
  Ear, nose, throat, genitourinary tract or skin/skin structure infections:
   Mild to moderate: 500 mg every 12 hours **or** 250 mg every 8 hours
   Severe: 875 mg every 12 hours **or** 500 mg every 8 hours
  Lower respiratory tract infections: 875 mg every 12 hours **or** 500 mg every 8 hours
  Endocarditis prophylaxis: 2 g 1 hour before procedure
  Helicobacter pylori eradication: 1000 mg twice daily; requires combination therapy with at least one other antibiotic and an acid-suppressing agent (proton pump inhibitor or H_2 blocker)
  Anthrax exposure (unlabeled use): **Note:** Postexposure prophylaxis only with documented susceptible organisms: 500 mg every 8 hours

 Dosing interval in renal impairment: The 875 mg tablet should not be used in patients with Cl_{cr} <30 mL/minute.
  Cl_{cr} 10-30 mL/minute: 250-500 mg every 12 hours
  Cl_{cr} <10 mL/minute: 250-500 mg every 24 hours
  Dialysis: Moderately dialyzable (20% to 50%) by hemo- or peritoneal dialysis; approximately 50 mg of amoxicillin per liter of filtrate is removed by continuous arteriovenous or venovenous hemofiltration; dose as per Cl_{cr} <10 mL/minute guidelines

Administration Administer around-the-clock to promote less variation in peak and trough serum levels. The appropriate amount of suspension may be mixed with formula, milk, fruit juice, water, ginger ale or cold drinks; administer dose immediately after mixing.
 DisperMox™: Dissolve 1 tablet in ~10 mL of water immediately before administration. Rinse container with additional water and drink entire contents to ensure that complete dose is taken. Do not chew or swallow tablet whole.

Monitoring Parameters With prolonged therapy, monitor renal, hepatic, and hematologic function periodically; assess patient at beginning and throughout therapy for infection; monitor for signs of anaphylaxis during first dose

Patient Information Report diarrhea promptly; entire course of medication (10-14 days) should be taken to ensure eradication of organism; females should report symptoms of vaginitis; pediatric drops may be placed on child's tongue or added to formula, milk, etc

Dosage Forms CAP: 250 mg, 500 mg; (Amoxil®, Moxilin®, Trimox®): 250 mg, 500 mg.
 POWDER, oral suspension: 125 mg/5 mL (80 mL, 100 mL, 150 mL); 200 mg/5 mL (50 mL, 75 mL, 100 mL); 250 mg/5 mL (80 mL, 100 mL, 150 mL); 400 mg/5 mL (50 mL, 75 mL, 100 mL); (Amoxil®): 125 mg/5 mL (150 mL); 200 mg/5 mL (5 mL, 50 mL, 75 mL, 100 mL); 250 mg/5 mL (100 mL, 150 mL); 400 mg/5 mL (5 mL, 50 mL, 75 mL, 100 mL); (Moxilin®): 250 mg/5 mL (100 mL, 150 mL); (Trimox®): 125 mg/5 mL (80 mL, 100 mL, 150 mL); 250 mg/5 mL (80 mL, 100 mL, 150 mL). **POWDER, oral suspension [drops]** (Amoxil®): 50 mg/mL (15 mL, 30 mL).
 TAB, chewable: 125 mg, 200 mg, 250 mg, 400 mg; (Amoxil®): 200 mg, 400 mg. **TAB, film coated** (Amoxil®): 500 mg, 875 mg. **TAB, for oral suspension** (DisperMox™): 200 mg, 400 mg

Amoxicillin and Clavulanate Potassium

 (a moks i SIL in & klav yoo LAN ate poe TASS ee um)

Related Information
 Antimicrobial Drugs of Choice *on page 1440*
U.S. Brand Names Augmentin®; Augmentin ES-600®; Augmentin XR™
Synonyms Amoxicillin and Clavulanic Acid
 (Continued)

Amoxicillin and Clavulanate Potassium *(Continued)*

Therapeutic Category Antibiotic, Anaerobic; Antibiotic, Penicillin & Beta-lactamase Inhibitor

Use Treatment of otitis media, sinusitis, and infections caused by susceptible organisms involving the lower respiratory tract, skin and skin structure, and urinary tract; spectrum same as amoxicillin with additional coverage of beta-lactamase producing *B. catarrhalis*, *H. influenzae*, *N. gonorrhoeae*, and *S. aureus* (not MRSA). The expanded coverage of this combination makes it a useful alternative when amoxicillin resistance is present and patients cannot tolerate alternative treatments.

Pregnancy Risk Factor B

Contraindications Hypersensitivity to amoxicillin, clavulanic acid, penicillin, or any component of the formulation; history of cholestatic jaundice or hepatic dysfunction with amoxicillin/clavulanate potassium therapy

Warnings/Precautions Prolonged use may result in superinfection. In patients with renal impairment, doses and/or frequency of administration should be modified in response to the degree of renal impairment; high percentage of patients with infectious mononucleosis have developed rash during therapy; a low incidence of cross-allergy with other beta-lactams and cephalosporins exists; incidence of diarrhea is higher than with amoxicillin alone. Due to differing content of clavulanic acid, not all formulations are interchangeable. Some products contain phenylalanine.

Common Adverse Reactions
>10%: Gastrointestinal: Diarrhea (3% to 34%; incidence varies upon dose and regimen used)
1% to 10%:
Dermatologic: Diaper rash, skin rash, urticaria
Gastrointestinal: Abdominal discomfort, loose stools, nausea, vomiting
Genitourinary: Vaginitis
Miscellaneous: Moniliasis

Additional adverse reactions seen with **ampicillin-class antibiotics:** Agitation, agranulocytosis, ALT elevated, anaphylaxis, anemia, angioedema, anxiety, AST elevated, behavioral changes, black "hairy" tongue, confusion, convulsions, dizziness, enterocolitis, eosinophilia, erythema multiforme, exanthematous pustulosis, exfoliative dermatitis, gastritis, glossitis, hematuria, hemolytic anemia, hemorrhagic colitis, indigestion, insomnia, hyperactivity, interstitial nephritis, leukopenia, mucocutaneous candidiasis, pruritus, pseudomembranous colitis, serum sickness-like reaction, Stevens-Johnson syndrome, stomatitis, thrombocytopenia, thrombocytopenic purpura, tooth discoloration, toxic epidermal necrolysis

Drug Interactions
Increased Effect/Toxicity: Probenecid may increase amoxicillin levels. Increased effect of anticoagulants with amoxicillin. Allopurinol taken with Augmentin® has an additive potential for rash. Penicillins may increase the exposure to methotrexate during concurrent therapy; monitor.

Decreased Effect: Although anecdotal reports suggest oral contraceptive efficacy could be reduced by penicillins, this has been refuted by more rigorous scientific and clinical data.

Mechanism of Action Clavulanic acid binds and inhibits beta-lactamases that inactivate amoxicillin resulting in amoxicillin having an expanded spectrum of activity. Amoxicillin inhibits bacterial cell wall synthesis by binding to one or more of the penicillin binding proteins (PBPs); which in turn inhibits the final transpeptidation step of peptidoglycan synthesis in bacterial cell walls, thus inhibiting cell wall biosynthesis. Bacteria eventually lyse due to ongoing activity of cell wall autolytic enzymes (autolysins and murein hydrolases) while cell wall assembly is arrested.

Pharmacodynamics/Kinetics Amoxicillin pharmacokinetics are not affected by clavulanic acid.
Amoxicillin: See Amoxicillin monograph.
Clavulanic acid:
Metabolism: Hepatic
Excretion: Urine (30% to 40% as unchanged drug)

Dosage Note: Dose is based on the amoxicillin component; see "Augmentin® Product-Specific Considerations" table on next page.
Infants <3 months: 30 mg/kg/day divided every 12 hours using the 125 mg/5 mL suspension
Children ≥3 months and <40 kg:
Otitis media: 90 mg/kg/day divided every 12 hours for 10 days
Lower respiratory tract infections, severe infections, sinusitis: 45 mg/kg/day divided every 12 hours **or** 40 mg/kg/day divided every 8 hours
Less severe infections: 25 mg/kg/day divided every 12 hours or 20 mg/kg/day divided every 8 hours
Children >40 kg and Adults: 250-500 mg every 8 hours or 875 mg every 12 hours
Children ≥16 years and Adults:
Acute bacterial sinusitis: Extended release tablet: Two 1000 mg tablets every 12 hours for 10 days
Community-acquired pneumonia: Extended release tablet: Two 1000 mg tablets every 12 hours for 7-10 days
Dosing interval in renal impairment:
Cl_{cr} <30 mL/minute: Do not use 875 mg tablet or extended release tablets
Cl_{cr} 10-30 mL/minute: 250-500 mg every 12 hours
Cl_{cr} <10 mL/minute: 250-500 every 24 hours
Hemodialysis: Moderately dialyzable (20% to 50%)
250-500 mg every 24 hours; administer dose during and after dialysis. Do not use extended release tablets.

Peritoneal dialysis: Moderately dialyzable (20% to 50%)
   Amoxicillin: Administer 250 mg every 12 hours
   Clavulanic acid: Dose for Cl_{cr} <10 mL/minute
Continuous arteriovenous or venovenous hemofiltration effects:
   Amoxicillin: ~50 mg of amoxicillin/L of filtrate is removed
   Clavulanic acid: Dose for Cl_{cr} <10 mL/minute

Augmentin® Product-Specific Considerations

Strength	Form	Consideration
125 mg	CT, S	q8h dosing
	S	For adults having difficulty swallowing tablets, 125 mg/5 mL suspension may be substituted for 500 mg tablet.
200 mg	CT, S	q12h dosing
	CT	Contains phenylalanine
	S	For adults having difficulty swallowing tablets, 200 mg/5 mL suspension may be substituted for 875 mg tablet.
250 mg	CT, S, T	q8h dosing
	CT	Contains phenylalanine
	T	Not for use in patients <40 kg
	CT, T	Tablet and chewable tablet are not interchangeable due to differences in clavulanic acid.
	S	For adults having difficulty swallowing tablets, 250 mg/5 mL suspension may be substituted for 500 mg tablet.
400 mg	CT, S	q12h dosing
	CT	Contains phenylalanine
	S	For adults having difficulty swallowing tablets, 400 mg/5 mL suspension may be substituted for 875 mg tablet.
500 mg	T	q8h or q12h dosing
600 mg	S	q12 h dosing
		Contains phenylalanine
		Not for use in adults or children ≥40 kg
		600 mg/5 mL suspension is not equivalent to or interchangeable with 200 mg/5 mL or 400 mg/5 mL due to differences in clavulanic acid.
875 mg	T	q12 h dosing; not for use in Cl_{cr} <30 mL/minute
1000 mg	XR	q12h dosing
		Not for use in children <16 years of age
		Not interchangeable with two 500 mg tablets
		Not for use in Cl_{cr} <30 mL/minute or hemodialysis

Legend: CT = chewable tablet, S = suspension, T = tablet, XR = extended release.

Administration Administer around-the-clock to promote less variation in peak and trough serum levels. Administer with food to decrease stomach upset; shake suspension well before use. Extended release tablets should be administered with food.

Monitoring Parameters Assess patient at beginning and throughout therapy for infection; with prolonged therapy, monitor renal, hepatic, and hematologic function periodically; monitor for signs of anaphylaxis during first dose

Patient Information Take extended release tablets with food. Report diarrhea promptly; entire course of medication (10-14 days) should be taken to ensure eradication of organism; females should report onset of symptoms of candidal vaginitis

Dosage Forms POWDER, oral suspension: 200: Amoxicillin 200 mg and clavulanate potassium 28.5 mg per 5 mL (100 mL); 400: Amoxicillin 400 mg and clavulanate potassium 57 mg per 5 mL (100 mL); (Augmentin®): 125: Amoxicillin trihydrate 125 mg and clavulanate potassium 31.25 mg per 5 mL (75 mL, 100 mL, 150 mL); 200: Amoxicillin 200 mg and clavulanate potassium 28.5 mg per 5 mL (50 mL, 75 mL, 100 mL); 250: Amoxicillin trihydrate 250 mg and clavulanate potassium 62.5 mg per 5 mL (75 mL, 100 mL, 150 mL); 400: Amoxicillin 400 mg and clavulanate potassium 57 mg per 5 mL (50 mL, 75 mL, 100 mL); (Augmentin ES-600®): Amoxicillin 600 mg and clavulanic potassium 42.9 mg per 5 mL (75 mL, 125 mL, 200 mL). **TAB:** 500: Amoxicillin trihydrate 500 mg and clavulanate potassium 125 mg; 875: Amoxicillin trihydrate 875 mg and clavulanate potassium 125 mg; (Augmentin®): 250: Amoxicillin trihydrate 250 mg and clavulanate potassium 125 mg; 500: Amoxicillin trihydrate 500 mg and clavulanate potassium 125 mg; 875: Amoxicillin trihydrate 875 mg and clavulanate potassium 125 mg. **TAB, chewable:** 200: Amoxicillin trihydrate 200 mg and clavulanate potassium 28.5 mg; 400: Amoxicillin trihydrate 400 mg and clavulanate potassium 57 mg; (Augmentin®): 125: Amoxicillin trihydrate 125 mg and clavulanate potassium 31.25 mg; 200: Amoxicillin trihydrate 200 mg and clavulanate potassium 28.5 mg; 250: Amoxicillin trihydrate 250 mg and clavulanate potassium 62.5 mg; 400: Amoxicillin trihydrate 400 mg and clavulanate potassium 57 mg. **TAB, extended release** (Augmentin XR™): Amoxicillin 1000 mg and clavulanic acid 62.5 mg

♦ **Amoxicillin and Clavulanic Acid** *see* Amoxicillin and Clavulanate Potassium *on page 87*
♦ **Amoxicillin, Lansoprazole, and Clarithromycin** *see* Lansoprazole, Amoxicillin, and Clarithromycin *on page 717*
♦ **Amoxicillin Trihydrate** *see* Amoxicillin *on page 86*
♦ **Amoxil®** *see* Amoxicillin *on page 86*
♦ **Amoxycillin** *see* Amoxicillin *on page 86*

- **Amphetamine and Dextroamphetamine** *see* Dextroamphetamine and Amphetamine *on page 363*
- **Amphocin®** *see* Amphotericin B (Conventional) *on page 90*
- **Amphotec®** *see* Amphotericin B Cholesteryl Sulfate Complex *on page 90*

Amphotericin B Cholesteryl Sulfate Complex
(am foe TER i sin bee kole LES te ril SUL fate KOM plecks)

U.S. Brand Names Amphotec®

Synonyms ABCD; Amphotericin B Colloidal Dispersion

Therapeutic Category Antifungal Agent, Parental; Antifungal Agent, Systemic

Use Treatment of invasive aspergillosis in patients who have failed amphotericin B deoxycholate treatment, or who have renal impairment or experience unacceptable toxicity which precludes treatment with amphotericin B deoxycholate in effective doses.

Unlabeled/Investigational Use Effective in patients with serious *Candida* species infections

Pregnancy Risk Factor B

Contraindications Hypersensitivity to amphotericin B or any component of the formulation

Warnings/Precautions Anaphylaxis has been reported with amphotericin B-containing drugs. If severe respiratory distress occurs, the infusion should be immediately discontinued. During the initial dosing, the drug should be administered under close clinical observation. Infusion reactions, sometimes, severe, usually subside with continued therapy - manage with decreased rate of infusion and pretreatment with antihistamines/corticosteroids.

Common Adverse Reactions
>10%: Central nervous system: Chills, fever
1% to 10%:
Cardiovascular: Hypotension, tachycardia
Central nervous system: Headache
Dermatologic: Rash
Endocrine & metabolic: Hypokalemia, hypomagnesemia
Gastrointestinal: Nausea, diarrhea, abdominal pain
Hematologic: Thrombocytopenia
Hepatic: LFT change
Neuromuscular & skeletal: Rigors
Renal: Elevated creatinine
Respiratory: Dyspnea

Note: Amphotericin B colloidal dispersion has an improved therapeutic index compared to conventional amphotericin B, and has been used safely in patients with amphotericin B-related nephrotoxicity; however, continued decline of renal function has occurred in some patients.

Drug Interactions
Increased Effect/Toxicity: Toxic effect with other nephrotoxic drugs (eg, cyclosporine and aminoglycosides) may be additive. Corticosteroids may increase potassium depletion caused by amphotericin. Amphotericin B may predispose patients receiving digitalis glycosides or neuromuscular blocking agents to toxicity secondary to hypokalemia.
Decreased Effect: Pharmacologic antagonism may occur with azole antifungals (ketoconazole, miconazole, etc).

Mechanism of Action Binds to ergosterol altering cell membrane permeability in susceptible fungi and causing leakage of cell components with subsequent cell death. Proposed mechanism suggests that amphotericin causes an oxidation-dependent stimulation of macrophages (Lyman, 1992).

Pharmacodynamics/Kinetics
Distribution: V_d: Total volume increases with higher doses, reflects increasing uptake by tissues (with 4 mg/kg/day = 4 L/kg); predominantly distributed in the liver; concentrations in kidneys and other tissues are lower than observed with conventional amphotericin B
Half-life elimination: 28-29 hours; prolonged with higher doses

Dosage Children and Adults: I.V.:
Premedication: For patients who experience chills, fever, hypotension, nausea, or other nonanaphylactic infusion-related immediate reactions, premedicate with the following drugs, 30-60 minutes prior to drug administration: a nonsteroidal (eg, ibuprofen, choline magnesium trisalicylate, etc) with or without diphenhydramine; or acetaminophen with diphenhydramine; or hydrocortisone 50-100 mg. If the patient experiences rigors during the infusion, meperidine may be administered.
Range: 3-4 mg/kg/day (infusion of 1 mg/kg/hour); maximum: 7.5 mg/kg/day

Monitoring Parameters Liver function tests, electrolytes, BUN, Cr, temperature, CBC, I/O, signs of hypokalemia (muscle weakness, cramping, drowsiness, ECG changes)

Dosage Forms INJ, powder for reconstitution: 50 mg, 100 mg

- **Amphotericin B Colloidal Dispersion** *see* Amphotericin B Cholesteryl Sulfate Complex *on page 90*

Amphotericin B (Conventional) (am foe TER i sin bee con VEN sha nal)
Related Information
Antifungal Agents Comparison *on page 1362*
U.S. Brand Names Amphocin®; Fungizone®
Synonyms Amphotericin B Desoxycholate
Therapeutic Category Antifungal Agent, Parental; Antifungal Agent, Systemic; Antifungal Agent, Topical

Use Treatment of severe systemic and central nervous system infections caused by susceptible fungi such as *Candida* species, *Histoplasma capsulatum*, *Cryptococcus neoformans*, *Aspergillus* species, *Blastomyces dermatitidis*, *Torulopsis glabrata*, and *Coccidioides immitis*; fungal peritonitis; irrigant for bladder fungal infections; and topically for cutaneous and mucocutaneous candidal infections; used in fungal infection in patients with bone marrow transplantation, amebic meningoencephalitis, ocular aspergillosis (intraocular injection), candidal cystitis (bladder irrigation), chemoprophylaxis (low-dose I.V.), immunocompromised patients at risk of aspergillosis (intranasal/nebulized), refractory meningitis (intrathecal), coccidioidal arthritis (intra-articular/I.M.).

Low-dose amphotericin B 0.1-0.25 mg/kg/day has been administered after bone marrow transplantation to reduce the risk of invasive fungal disease. Alternative routes of administration and extemporaneous preparations have been used when standard antifungal therapy is not available (eg, inhalation, intraocular injection, subconjunctival application, intracavitary administration into various joints and the pleural space).

Pregnancy Risk Factor B

Contraindications Hypersensitivity to amphotericin or any component of the formulation

Warnings/Precautions Anaphylaxis has been reported with amphotericin B-containing drugs. During the initial dosing, the drug should be administered under close clinical observation. Avoid additive toxicity with other nephrotoxic drugs; drug-induced renal toxicity usually improves with interrupting therapy, decreasing dosage, or increasing dosing interval. I.V. amphotericin is used primarily for the treatment of patients with progressive and potentially fatal fungal infections; topical preparations may stain clothing. Infusion reactions are most common 1-3 hours after starting the infusion and diminish with continued therapy. Use amphotericin B with caution in patients with decreased renal function.

Common Adverse Reactions
>10%:
  Central nervous system: Fever, chills, headache, malaise, general pain
  Endocrine & metabolic: Hypokalemia, hypomagnesemia
  Gastrointestinal: Anorexia
  Hematologic: Anemia
  Renal: Nephrotoxicity
1% to 10%:
  Cardiovascular: Hypotension, hypertension, flushing
  Central nervous system: Delirium, arachnoiditis, pain along lumbar nerves
  Gastrointestinal: Nausea, vomiting
  Genitourinary: Urinary retention
  Hematologic: Leukocytosis
  Local: Thrombophlebitis
  Neuromuscular & skeletal: Paresthesia (especially with I.T. therapy)
  Renal: Renal tubular acidosis, renal failure

Drug Interactions
  Increased Effect/Toxicity: Use of amphotericin with other nephrotoxic drugs (eg, cyclosporine and aminoglycosides) may result in additive toxicity. Amphotericin may increase the toxicity of flucytosine. Antineoplastic agents may increase the risk of amphotericin-induced nephrotoxicity, bronchospasms, and hypotension. Corticosteroids may increase potassium depletion caused by amphotericin. Amphotericin B may predispose patients receiving digitalis glycosides or neuromuscular-blocking agents to toxicity secondary to hypokalemia.
  Decreased Effect: Pharmacologic antagonism may occur with azole antifungal agents (ketoconazole, miconazole).

Mechanism of Action Binds to ergosterol altering cell membrane permeability in susceptible fungi and causing leakage of cell components with subsequent cell death. Proposed mechanism suggests that amphotericin causes an oxidation-dependent stimulation of macrophages (Lyman, 1992).

Pharmacodynamics/Kinetics
  Distribution: Minimal amounts enter the aqueous humor, bile, CSF (inflamed or noninflamed meninges), amniotic fluid, pericardial fluid, pleural fluid, and synovial fluid
  Protein binding, plasma: 90%
  Half-life elimination: Biphasic: Initial: 15-48 hours; Terminal: 15 days
  Time to peak: Within 1 hour following a 4- to 6-hour dose
  Excretion: Urine (2% to 5% as biologically active form); ~40% eliminated over a 7-day period and may be detected in urine for at least 7 weeks after discontinued use

Dosage
  I.V.: Premedication: For patients who experience chills, fever, hypotension, nausea, or other nonanaphylactic infusion-related immediate reactions, premedicate with the following drugs, 30-60 minutes prior to drug administration: a nonsteroidal (eg, ibuprofen, choline magnesium trisalicylate, etc) with or without diphenhydramine; or acetaminophen with diphenhydramine; or hydrocortisone 50-100 mg. If the patient experiences rigors during the infusion, meperidine may be administered.
  Infants and Children:
    Test dose: I.V.: 0.1 mg/kg/dose to a maximum of 1 mg; infuse over 30-60 minutes. Many clinicians believe a test dose is unnecessary.
    Maintenance dose: 0.25-1 mg/kg/day given once daily; infuse over 2-6 hours. Once therapy has been established, amphotericin B can be administered on an every-other-day basis at 1-1.5 mg/kg/dose; cumulative dose: 1.5-2 g over 6-10 week.
  Adults:
    Test dose: 1 mg infused over 20-30 minutes. Many clinicians believe a test dose is unnecessary.
(Continued)

Amphotericin B (Conventional) *(Continued)*

Maintenance dose: Usual: 0.25-1.5 mg/kg/day; 1-1.5 mg/kg over 4-6 hours every other day may be given once therapy is established; aspergillosis, mucormycosis, rhinocerebral phycomycosis often require 1-1.5 mg/kg/day; do not exceed 1.5 mg/kg/day

Duration of therapy varies with nature of infection: Usual duration is 4-12 weeks or cumulative dose of 1-4 g

I.T.: Meningitis, coccidioidal or cryptococcal:

Children.: 25-100 mcg every 48-72 hours; increase to 500 mcg as tolerated

Adults: Initial: 25-300 mcg every 48-72 hours; increase to 500 mcg to 1 mg as tolerated; maximum total dose: 15 mg has been suggested

Oral: 1 mL (100 mg) 4 times/day

Topical: Apply to affected areas 2-4 times/day for 1-4 weeks of therapy depending on nature and severity of infection

Bladder irrigation: Candidal cystitis: Irrigate with 50 mcg/mL solution instilled periodically or continuously for 5-10 days or until cultures are clear

Dosing adjustment in renal impairment: If renal dysfunction is due to the drug, the daily total can be decreased by 50% or the dose can be given every other day; I.V. therapy may take several months

Dialysis: Poorly dialyzed; no supplemental dosage necessary when using hemo- or peritoneal dialysis or continuous arteriovenous or venovenous hemodiafiltration effects

Administration in dialysate: Children and Adults: 1-2 mg/L of peritoneal dialysis fluid either with or without low-dose I.V. amphotericin B (a total dose of 2-10 mg/kg given over 7-14 days). Precipitate may form in ionic dialysate solutions.

Monitoring Parameters Renal function (monitor frequently during therapy), electrolytes (especially potassium and magnesium), liver function tests, temperature, PT/PTT, CBC; monitor input and output; monitor for signs of hypokalemia (muscle weakness, cramping, drowsiness, ECG changes, etc)

Reference Range Therapeutic: 1-2 µg/mL (SI: 1-2.2 µmol/L)

Patient Information Amphotericin cream may slightly discolor skin and stain clothing; good personal hygiene may reduce the spread and recurrence of lesions; avoid covering topical applications with occlusive bandages; most skin lesions require 1-3 weeks of therapy; report any cramping, muscle weakness, or pain at or near injection site

Dosage Forms CRM: 3% (20 g). **INJ, powder for reconstitution:** 50 mg. **LOTION:** 3% (30 mL)

◆ **Amphotericin B Desoxycholate** *see* Amphotericin B (Conventional) *on page 90*

Amphotericin B (Lipid Complex) (am foe TER i sin bee LIP id KOM pleks)

U.S. Brand Names Abelcet®

Synonyms ABLC

Therapeutic Category Antifungal Agent, Parental; Antifungal Agent, Systemic

Use Treatment of aspergillosis or any type of progressive fungal infection in patients who are refractory to or intolerant of conventional amphotericin B therapy

Unlabeled/Investigational Use Effective in patients with serious *Candida* species infections

Pregnancy Risk Factor B

Contraindications Hypersensitivity to amphotericin or any component of the formulation

Warnings/Precautions Anaphylaxis has been reported with amphotericin B-containing drugs. If severe respiratory distress occurs, the infusion should be immediately discontinued. During the initial dosing, the drug should be administered under close clinical observation. Acute reactions (including fever and chills) may occur 1-2 hours after starting an intravenous infusion. These reactions are usually more common with the first few doses and generally diminish with subsequent doses.

Common Adverse Reactions Nephrotoxicity and infusion-related hyperpyrexia, rigor, and chilling are reduced relative to amphotericin deoxycholate.

>10%:

Central nervous system: Chills, fever

Renal: Increased serum creatinine

1% to 10%:

Cardiovascular: Hypotension, cardiac arrest

Central nervous system: Headache, pain

Dermatologic: Rash

Endocrine & metabolic: Bilirubinemia, hypokalemia, acidosis

Gastrointestinal: Nausea, vomiting, diarrhea, gastrointestinal hemorrhage, abdominal pain

Renal: Renal failure

Respiratory: Respiratory failure, dyspnea, pneumonia

Drug Interactions

Increased Effect/Toxicity: See Drug Interactions - Increased Effect/Toxicity in Amphotericin B (Conventional) *on page 90.*

Decreased Effect: See Drug Interactions - Decreased Effect in Amphotericin B (Conventional) *on page 90.*

Mechanism of Action Binds to ergosterol altering cell membrane permeability in susceptible fungi and causing leakage of cell components with subsequent cell death. Proposed mechanism suggests that amphotericin causes an oxidation-dependent stimulation of macrophages (Lyman, 1992).

Pharmacodynamics/Kinetics
Distribution: V_d: Increases with higher doses; reflects increased uptake by tissues (131 L/kg with 5 mg/kg/day)
Half-life elimination: ~24 hours
Excretion: Clearance: Increases with higher doses (5 mg/kg/day): 400 mL/hour/kg

Dosage Children and Adults: I.V.:
Premedication: For patients who experience chills, fever, hypotension, nausea, or other nonanaphylactic infusion-related immediate reactions, premedicate with the following drugs, 30-60 minutes prior to drug administration: a nonsteroidal (eg, ibuprofen, choline magnesium trisalicylate, etc) with or without diphenhydramine; or acetaminophen with diphenhydramine; or hydrocortisone 50-100 mg. If the patient experiences rigors during the infusion, meperidine may be administered.
Range: 2.5-5 mg/kg/day as a single infusion
Dosing adjustment in renal impairment: None necessary; effects of renal impairment are not currently known
Hemodialysis: No supplemental dosage necessary
Peritoneal dialysis: No supplemental dosage necessary
Continuous arteriovenous or venovenous hemofiltration: No supplemental dosage necessary

Administration For a patient who experiences chills, fever, hypotension, nausea, or other nonanaphylactic infusion-related reactions, premedication with the following drugs, 30-60 minutes prior to drug administration: A nonsteroidal (ibuprofen, choline magnesium trisalicylate, etc) with or without diphenhydramine; or acetaminophen with diphenhydramine, or hydrocortisone 50-100 mg. If the patient experiences rigors during the infusion, meperidine may be administered. If infusion time exceeds 2 hours, mix contents by shaking infusion bag every 2 hours.

Monitoring Parameters Renal function (monitor frequently during therapy), electrolytes (especially potassium and magnesium), liver function tests, temperature, PT/PTT, CBC; monitor input and output; monitor for signs of hypokalemia (muscle weakness, cramping, drowsiness, ECG changes, etc)

Dosage Forms INJ, suspension: 5 mg/mL (20 mL)

Amphotericin B (Liposomal) (am foe TER i sin bee lye po SO mal)

U.S. Brand Names AmBisome®
Synonyms L-AmB
Therapeutic Category Antifungal Agent, Parental; Antifungal Agent, Systemic
Use Empirical therapy for presumed fungal infection in febrile, neutropenic patients. Treatment of patients with *Aspergillus* species, *Candida* species and/or *Cryptococcus* species infections refractory to amphotericin B desoxycholate, or in patients where renal impairment or unacceptable toxicity precludes the use of amphotericin B desoxycholate. Treatment of cryptococcal meningitis in HIV-infected patients. Treatment of visceral leishmaniasis.
Unlabeled/Investigational Use Effective in patients with serious *Candida* species infections
Pregnancy Risk Factor B
Contraindications Hypersensitivity to amphotericin B or any component of the formulation unless, in the opinion of the treating physician, the benefit of therapy outweighs the risk
Warnings/Precautions Although amphotericin B (liposomal) has been shown to be significantly less toxic than amphotericin B desoxycholate, adverse events may still occur. Patients should be under close clinical observation during initial dosing. As with other amphotericin B-containing products, anaphylaxis has been reported. Facilities for cardiopulmonary resuscitation should be available during administration, and the drug should be administered by medically-trained personnel. Acute reactions (including fever and chills) may occur 1-2 hours after starting infusions; reactions are more common with the first few doses and generally diminish with subsequent doses. Immediately discontinue infusion if severe respiratory distress occurs; the patient should not receive further infusions. Safety and efficacy have not been established in patients <1 year of age.
Common Adverse Reactions Percentage of adverse reactions is dependent upon population studied and may vary with respect to premedications and underlying illness. Incidence of decreased renal function and infusion-related events are lower than rates observed with amphotericin B deoxycholate.
>10%:
Cardiovascular: Peripheral edema (15%), edema (12% to 14%), tachycardia (9% to 18%), hypotension (7% to 14%), hypertension (8% to 20%), chest pain (8% to 12%), hypervolemia (8% to 12%)
Central nervous system: Chills (29% to 48%), insomnia (17% to 22%), headache (9% to 20%), anxiety (7% to 14%), pain (14%), confusion (9% to 13%)
Dermatologic: Rash (5% to 25%), pruritus (11%)
Endocrine & metabolic: Hypokalemia (31% to 51%), hypomagnesemia (15% to 50%), hyperglycemia (8% to 23%), hypocalcemia (5% to 18%), hyponatremia (8% to 12%)
Gastrointestinal: Nausea (16% to 40%), vomiting (10% to 32%), diarrhea (11% to 30%), abdominal pain (7% to 20%), constipation (15%), anorexia (10% to 14%)
Hematologic: Anemia (27% to 48%), blood transfusion reaction (9% to 18%), leukopenia (15% to 17%), thrombocytopenia (6% to 13%)
Hepatic: Increased alkaline phosphatase (7% to 22%), increased BUN (7% to 21%), bilirubinemia (9% to 18%), increased ALT (15%), increased AST (13%), abnormal liver function tests (not specified) (4% to 13%)
Local: Phlebitis (9% to 11%)
Neuromuscular & skeletal: Weakness (6% to 13%), back pain (12%)
Renal: Increased creatinine (18% to 40%), hematuria (14%)
(Continued)

Amphotericin B (Liposomal) *(Continued)*

Respiratory: Dyspnea (18% to 23%), lung disorder (14% to 18%), increased cough (2% to 18%), epistaxis (8% to 15%), pleural effusion (12%), rhinitis (11%)

Miscellaneous: Sepsis (7% to 14%), infection (11% to 12%)

2% to 10%:

Cardiovascular: Arrhythmia, atrial fibrillation, bradycardia, cardiac arrest, cardiomegaly, facial swelling, flushing, postural hypotension, valvular heart disease, vascular disorder

Central nervous system: Agitation, abnormal thinking, coma, convulsion, depression, dysesthesia, dizziness (7% to 8%), hallucinations, malaise, nervousness, somnolence

Dermatologic: Alopecia, bruising, cellulitis, dry skin, maculopapular rash, petechia, purpura, skin discoloration, skin disorder, skin ulcer, urticaria, vesiculobullous rash

Endocrine & metabolic: Acidosis, increased amylase, fluid overload, hypernatremia (4%), hyperchloremia, hyperkalemia, hypermagnesemia, hyperphosphatemia, hypophosphatemia, hypoproteinemia, increased lactate dehydrogenase, increased nonprotein nitrogen

Gastrointestinal: Constipation, dry mouth, dyspepsia, enlarged abdomen, eructation, fecal incontinence, flatulence, gastrointestinal hemorrhage (10%), hematemesis, hemorrhoids, gum/oral hemorrhage, ileus, mucositis, rectal disorder, stomatitis, ulcerative stomatitis

Genitourinary: Vaginal hemorrhage

Hematologic: Coagulation disorder, hemorrhage, decreased prothrombin, thrombocytopenia

Hepatic: Hepatocellular damage, hepatomegaly, veno-occlusive liver disease

Local: Injection site inflammation

Neuromuscular & skeletal: Arthralgia, bone pain, dystonia, myalgia, neck pain, paresthesia, rigors, tremor

Ocular: Conjunctivitis, dry eyes, eye hemorrhage

Renal: Abnormal renal function, acute kidney failure, dysuria, kidney failure, toxic nephropathy, urinary incontinence

Respiratory: Asthma, atelectasis, cough, dry nose, hemoptysis, hyperventilation, lung edema, pharyngitis, pneumonia, respiratory alkalosis, respiratory insufficiency, respiratory failure, sinusitis, hypoxia (6% to 8%)

Miscellaneous: Allergic reaction, cell-mediated immunological reaction, flu-like syndrome, graft versus host disease, herpes simplex, hiccup, procedural complication (8% to 10%), diaphoresis (7%)

Drug Interactions

Increased Effect/Toxicity: Drug interactions have not been studied in a controlled manner; however, drugs that interact with conventional amphotericin B may also interact with amphotericin B liposome for injection. See Drug Interactions - Increased Effect/Toxicity in Amphotericin B (Conventional) monograph.

Mechanism of Action Binds to ergosterol altering cell membrane permeability in susceptible fungi and causing leakage of cell components with subsequent cell death. Proposed mechanism suggests that amphotericin causes an oxidation-dependent stimulation of macrophages (Lyman, 1992).

Pharmacodynamics/Kinetics

Distribution: V_d: 131 L/kg

Half-life elimination: Terminal: 174 hours

Dosage Children and Adults: I.V.:

Note: Premedication: For patients who experience chills, fever, hypotension, nausea, or other nonanaphylactic infusion-related immediate reactions, premedicate with the following drugs, 30-60 minutes prior to drug administration: a nonsteroidal (eg, ibuprofen, choline magnesium trisalicylate, etc) with or without diphenhydramine; or acetaminophen with diphenhydramine; or hydrocortisone 50-100 mg. If the patient experiences rigors during the infusion, meperidine may be administered.

Empiric therapy: Recommended initial dose: 3 mg/kg/day

Systemic fungal infections (*Aspergillus, Candida, Cryptococcus*): Recommended initial dose of 3-5 mg/kg/day

Cryptococcal meningitis in HIV-infected patients: 6 mg/kg/day

Treatment of visceral leishmaniasis:

Immunocompetent patients: 3 mg/kg/day on days 1-5, and 3 mg/kg/day on days 14 and 21; a repeat course may be given in patients who do not achieve parasitic clearance

Immunocompromised patients: 4 mg/kg/day on days 1-5, and 4 mg/kg/day on days 10, 17, 24, 31, and 38

Dosing adjustment in renal impairment: None necessary; effects of renal impairment are not currently known

Hemodialysis: No supplemental dosage necessary

Peritoneal dialysis effects: No supplemental dosage necessary

Continuous arteriovenous or venovenous hemofiltration: No supplemental dosage necessary

Administration Should be administered by intravenous infusion, using a controlled infusion device, over a period of approximately 2 hours. Infusion time may be reduced to approximately 1 hour in patients in whom the treatment is well-tolerated. If the patient experiences discomfort during infusion, the duration of infusion may be increased. Administer at a rate of 2.5 mg/kg/hour. Existing intravenous line should be flushed with D_5W prior to infusion (if not feasible, administer through a separate line). An in-line membrane filter (not less than 1 micron) may be used.

Monitoring Parameters Renal function (monitor frequently during therapy), electrolytes (especially potassium and magnesium), liver function tests, temperature, PT/PTT, CBC; monitor input and output; monitor for signs of hypokalemia (muscle weakness, cramping, drowsiness, ECG changes, etc)

Dosage Forms INJ, powder for reconstitution: 50 mg

Ampicillin (am pi SIL in)
Related Information
Antimicrobial Drugs of Choice *on page 1440*
Community-Acquired Pneumonia in Adults *on page 1457*
Prevention of Bacterial Endocarditis *on page 1429*

U.S. Brand Names Principen®

Synonyms Aminobenzylpenicillin; Ampicillin Sodium; Ampicillin Trihydrate

Therapeutic Category Antibiotic, Penicillin

Use Treatment of susceptible bacterial infections (nonbeta-lactamase-producing organisms); susceptible bacterial infections caused by streptococci, pneumococci, nonpenicillinase-producing staphylococci, *Listeria*, meningococci; some strains of *H. influenzae*, *Salmonella*, *Shigella*, *E. coli*, *Enterobacter*, and *Klebsiella*

Pregnancy Risk Factor B

Contraindications Hypersensitivity to ampicillin, any component of the formulation, or other penicillins

Warnings/Precautions Dosage adjustment may be necessary in patients with renal impairment; a low incidence of cross-allergy with other beta-lactams exists; high percentage of patients with infectious mononucleosis have developed rash during therapy with ampicillin. Appearance of a rash should be carefully evaluated to differentiate a nonallergic ampicillin rash from a hypersensitivity reaction. Ampicillin rash occurs in 5% to 10% of children receiving ampicillin and is a generalized dull red, maculopapular rash, generally appearing 3-14 days after the start of therapy. It normally begins on the trunk and spreads over most of the body. It may be most intense at pressure areas, elbows, and knees.

Common Adverse Reactions Frequency not defined.
Central nervous system: Fever, penicillin encephalopathy, seizures
Dermatologic: Erythema multiforme, exfoliative dermatitis, rash, urticaria
> Note: Appearance of a rash should be carefully evaluated to differentiate (if possible) nonallergic ampicillin rash from hypersensitivity reaction. Incidence is higher in patients with viral infections, *Salmonella* infections, lymphocytic leukemia, or patients that have hyperuricemia.

Gastrointestinal: black hairy tongue, diarrhea, enterocolitis, glossitis, nausea, pseudomembranous colitis, sore mouth or tongue, stomatitis, vomiting
Hematologic: Agranulocytosis, anemia, hemolytic anemia, eosinophilia, leukopenia, thrombocytopenia purpura
Hepatic: AST increased
Renal: Interstitial nephritis (rare)
Respiratory: Laryngeal stridor
Miscellaneous: Anaphylaxis, serum sickness-like reaction

Drug Interactions
Increased Effect/Toxicity: Ampicillin increases the effect of disulfiram and anticoagulants. Probenecid may increase penicillin levels. Theoretically, allopurinol taken with ampicillin has an additive potential for rash. Penicillins may increase the exposure to methotrexate during concurrent therapy; monitor.

Decreased Effect: Although anecdotal reports suggest oral contraceptive efficacy could be reduced by penicillins, this has been refuted by more rigorous scientific and clinical data.

Mechanism of Action Inhibits bacterial cell wall synthesis by binding to one or more of the penicillin binding proteins (PBPs); which in turn inhibits the final transpeptidation step of peptidoglycan synthesis in bacterial cell walls, thus inhibiting cell wall biosynthesis. Bacteria eventually lyse due to ongoing activity of cell wall autolytic enzymes (autolysins and murein hydrolases) while cell wall assembly is arrested.

Pharmacodynamics/Kinetics
Absorption: Oral: 50%
Distribution: Bile, blister, and tissue fluids; penetration into CSF occurs with inflamed meninges only, good only with inflammation (exceeds usual MICs)
Normal meninges: Nil; Inflamed meninges: 5% to 10%
Protein binding: 15% to 25%
Half-life elimination:
Children and Adults: 1-1.8 hours
Anuria/end-stage renal disease: 7-20 hours
Time to peak: Oral: Within 1-2 hours
Excretion: Urine (~90% as unchanged drug) within 24 hours

Dosage
Infants and Children:
Mild-to-moderate infections:
I.M., I.V.: 100-150 mg/kg/day in divided doses every 6 hours (maximum: 2-4 g/day)
Oral: 50-100 mg/kg/day in doses divided every 6 hours (maximum: 2-4 g/day)
Severe infections/meningitis: I.M., I.V.: 200-400 mg/kg/day in divided doses every 6 hours (maximum: 6-12 g/day)
Endocarditis prophylaxis: I.M., I.V.:
Dental, oral, respiratory tract, or esophageal procedures: 50 mg/kg within 30 minutes prior to procedure in patients unable to take oral amoxicillin
Genitourinary and gastrointestinal tract (except esophageal) procedures:
High-risk patients: 50 mg/kg (maximum: 2 g) within 30 minutes prior to procedure, followed by ampicillin 25 mg/kg (or amoxicillin 25 mg/kg orally) 6 hours later; must be used in combination with gentamicin.

(Continued)

Ampicillin *(Continued)*

Moderate-risk patients: 50 mg/kg within 30 minutes prior to procedure

Adults:
Susceptible infections:
Oral: 250-500 mg every 6 hours
I.M., I.V.: 250-500 mg every 6 hours
Sepsis/meningitis: I.M., I.V.: 150-250 mg/kg/24 hours divided every 3-4 hours (range: 6-12 g/day)
Endocarditis prophylaxis: I.M., I.V.:
Dental, oral, respiratory tract, or esophageal procedures: 2 g within 30 minutes prior to procedure in patients unable to take oral amoxicillin
Genitourinary and gastrointestinal tract (except esophageal) procedures:
High-risk patients: 2 g within 30 minutes prior to procedure, followed by ampicillin 1 g (or amoxicillin 1 g orally) 6 hours later; must be used in combination with gentamicin
Moderate-risk patients: 2 g within 30 minutes prior to procedure

Dosing interval in renal impairment:
Cl_{cr} >50 mL/minute: Administer every 6 hours
Cl_{cr} 10-50 mL/minute: Administer every 6-12 hours
Cl_{cr} <10 mL/minute: Administer every 12-24 hours
Hemodialysis: Moderately dialyzable (20% to 50%); administer dose after dialysis
Peritoneal dialysis: Moderately dialyzable (20% to 50%)
Administer 250 mg every 12 hours
Continuous arteriovenous or venovenous hemofiltration effects: Dose as for Cl_{cr} 10-50 mL/minute; ~50 mg of ampicillin per liter of filtrate is removed

Administration Administer around-the-clock to promote less variation in peak and trough serum levels.
Oral: Administer on an empty stomach (ie, 1 hour prior to, or 2 hours after meals) to increase total absorption.
I.V.: Administer over 3-5 minutes (125-500 mg) or over 10-15 minutes (1-2 g). More rapid infusion may cause seizures.

Monitoring Parameters With prolonged therapy monitor renal, hepatic, and hematologic function periodically; observe signs and symptoms of anaphylaxis during first dose

Patient Information Report diarrhea promptly; entire course of medication should be taken to ensure eradication of organism; females should report onset of symptoms of candidal vaginitis

Dosage Forms CAP (Principen®) 250 mg, 500 mg. **INJ, powder for reconstitution:** 125 mg, 250 mg, 500 mg, 1 g, 2 g, 10 g. **POWDER, oral suspension** (Principen®): 125 mg/5 mL (100 mL, 200 mL); 250 mg/5 mL (100 mL, 200 mL)

Ampicillin and Sulbactam (am pi SIL in & SUL bak tam)

Related Information
Antimicrobial Drugs of Choice *on page 1440*
Community-Acquired Pneumonia in Adults *on page 1457*
U.S. Brand Names Unasyn®
Synonyms Sulbactam and Ampicillin
Therapeutic Category Antibiotic, Anaerobic; Antibiotic, Penicillin & Beta-lactamase Inhibitor
Use Treatment of susceptible bacterial infections involved with skin and skin structure, intra-abdominal infections, gynecological infections; spectrum is that of ampicillin plus organisms producing beta-lactamases such as *S. aureus*, *H. influenzae*, *E. coli*, *Klebsiella*, *Acinetobacter*, *Enterobacter*, and anaerobes
Pregnancy Risk Factor B
Contraindications Hypersensitivity to ampicillin, sulbactam, penicillins, or any component of the formulations
Warnings/Precautions Dosage adjustment may be necessary in patients with renal impairment; a low incidence of cross-allergy with other beta-lactams exists; high percentage of patients with infectious mononucleosis have developed rash during therapy with ampicillin. Appearance of a rash should be carefully evaluated to differentiate a nonallergic ampicillin rash from a hypersensitivity reaction.
Common Adverse Reactions Also see Ampicillin monograph
>10%: Local: Pain at injection site (I.M.)
1% to 10%:
Dermatologic: Rash
Gastrointestinal: Diarrhea
Local: Pain at injection site (I.V.), thrombophlebitis
Miscellaneous: Allergic reaction (may include serum sickness, urticaria, bronchospasm, hypotension, etc)
Drug Interactions
Increased Effect/Toxicity: Disulfiram or probenecid can increase ampicillin levels. Theoretically, allopurinol taken with ampicillin has an additive potential for rash. Penicillins may increase the exposure to methotrexate during concurrent therapy; monitor.
Decreased Effect: Although anecdotal reports suggest oral contraceptive efficacy could be reduced by penicillins, this has been refuted by more rigorous scientific and clinical data.
Mechanism of Action Sulbactam has very little antibacterial activity by itself. The addition of sulbactam, a beta-lactamase inhibitor, to ampicillin extends the spectrum of ampicillin to include some beta-lactamase producing organisms; inhibits bacterial cell wall synthesis by binding to one or more of the penicillin binding proteins (PBPs); which in turn inhibits the final transpeptidation step of peptidoglycan synthesis in bacterial cell walls, thus inhibiting cell wall

biosynthesis. Bacteria eventually lyse due to ongoing activity of cell wall autolytic enzymes (autolysins and murein hydrolases) while cell wall assembly is arrested.

Pharmacodynamics/Kinetics

Ampicillin: See Ampicillin monograph.

Sulbactam:

Distribution: Bile, blister, and tissue fluids

Protein binding: 38%

Half-life elimination: Normal renal function: 1-1.3 hours

Excretion: Urine (~75% to 85% as unchanged drug) within 8 hours

Dosage Unasyn® (ampicillin/sulbactam) is a combination product. Dosage recommendations for Unasyn® are based on the ampicillin component.

Children ≥1 year: I.V.:

Mild-to-moderate infections: 100-150 mg ampicillin/kg/day (150-300 mg Unasyn®) divided every 6 hours; maximum: 8 g ampicillin/day (12 g Unasyn®)

Severe infections: 200-400 mg ampicillin/kg/day divided every 6 hours; maximum: 8 g ampicillin/day (12 g Unasyn®)

Adults: I.M., I.V.: 1-2 g ampicillin (1.5-3 g Unasyn®) every 6 hours; maximum: 8 g ampicillin/day (12 g Unasyn®)

Dosing interval in renal impairment:

Cl_{cr} 15-29 mL/minute: Administer every 12 hours

Cl_{cr} 5-14 mL/minute: Administer every 24 hours

Administration Administer around-the-clock to promote less variation in peak and trough serum levels. Administer by slow injection over 10-15 minutes or I.V. over 15-30 minutes.

Monitoring Parameters With prolonged therapy, monitor hematologic, renal, and hepatic function; monitor for signs of anaphylaxis during first dose

Dosage Forms INJ, powder for reconstitution: 3 g [ampicillin sodium 2 g and sulbactam sodium 1 g]; 15 g [ampicillin sodium 10 g and sulbactam sodium 5 g]; (Unasyn®): 1.5 g [ampicillin sodium 1 g and sulbactam sodium 0.5 g]; 3 g [ampicillin sodium 2 g and sulbactam sodium 1 g]; 15 g [ampicillin sodium 10 g and sulbactam sodium 5 g]

♦ **Ampicillin Sodium** *see* Ampicillin *on page 95*

♦ **Ampicillin Trihydrate** *see* Ampicillin *on page 95*

Amprenavir (am PREN a veer)

Related Information

Antiretroviral Therapy for HIV Infection *on page 1448*

Management of Healthcare Worker Exposures to HBV, HCV, and HIV *on page 1421*

U.S. Brand Names Agenerase®

Therapeutic Category Antiretroviral Agent, Protease Inhibitor; Protease Inhibitor

Use Treatment of HIV infections in combination with at least two other antiretroviral agents; oral solution should only be used when capsules or other protease inhibitors are not therapeutic options

Pregnancy Risk Factor C

Contraindications Hypersensitivity to amprenavir or any component of the formulation; concurrent therapy with cisapride, ergot derivatives, midazolam, pimozide, and triazolam; severe previous allergic reaction to sulfonamides; oral solution is contraindicated in infants or children <4 years of age, pregnant women, patients with renal or hepatic failure, and patients receiving concurrent metronidazole or disulfiram

Warnings/Precautions Because of hepatic metabolism and effect on cytochrome P450 enzymes, amprenavir should be used with caution in combination with other agents metabolized by this system (see Contraindications and Drug Interactions). Avoid use of lovastatin or simvastatin (risk of rhabdomyolysis increases). Avoid concurrent use of hormonal contraceptives, rifampin, and/or St John's wort (may lead to loss of virologic response and/or resistance). Use with caution in patients with diabetes mellitus, sulfonamide allergy, hepatic impairment, or hemophilia. Additional vitamin E supplements should be avoided. Certain ethnic populations (Asians, Eskimos, Native Americans) may be at increased risk of propylene glycol-associated adverse effects; therefore, use of the oral solution of amprenavir should be avoided. Use oral solution only when capsules or other protease inhibitors are not options.

Common Adverse Reactions Protease inhibitors cause dyslipidemia which includes elevated cholesterol and triglycerides and a redistribution of body fat centrally to cause increased abdominal girth, buffalo hump, facial atrophy, and breast enlargement. These agents also cause hyperglycemia.

>10%:

Dermatologic: Rash (28%)

Endocrine & metabolic: Hyperglycemia (37% to 41%), hypertriglyceridemia (36% to 47%)

Gastrointestinal: Nausea (38% to 73%), vomiting (20% to 29%), diarrhea (33% to 56%)

Miscellaneous: Perioral tingling/numbness

1% to 10%:

Central nervous system: Depression (4% to 15%), headache, paresthesia, fatigue

Dermatologic: Stevens-Johnson syndrome (1% of total, 4% of patients who develop a rash)

Endocrine & metabolic: Hypercholesterolemia (4% to 9%)

Gastrointestinal: Taste disorders (1% to 10%)

Drug Interactions

Cytochrome P450 Effect: Substrate of CYP2C8/9 (minor), 3A4 (major); **Inhibits** CYP2C19 (weak), 3A4 (strong)

(Continued)

Amprenavir *(Continued)*

Increased Effect/Toxicity: Concurrent use of cisapride, pimozide, and quinidine is contra-indicated. Serum concentrations/effect of many benzodiazepines may be increased; concurrent use of midazolam or triazolam is contraindicated. Concurrent use of ergot alkaloids (dihydroergotamine, ergotamine, ergonovine, methylergonovine) with amprenavir is also contraindicated (may cause vasospasm and peripheral ischemia).

Concurrent use of oral solution with disulfiram or metronidazole is contraindicated (risk of propylene glycol toxicity). Serum concentrations of amiodarone, bepridil, lidocaine, quinidine and other antiarrhythmics may be increased, potentially leading to toxicity; when amprenavir is coadministered with ritonavir, flecainide and propafenone are contraindicated. HMG-CoA reductase inhibitors serum concentrations may be increased by amprenavir, increasing the risk of myopathy/rhabdomyolysis; lovastatin and simvastatin are not recommended; fluvastatin and pravastatin may be safer alternatives. Serum concentrations/effect of benzodiazepines, calcium channel blockers, cyclosporine, itraconazole, ketoconazole, rifabutin, tacrolimus, tricyclic antidepressants may be increased. May increase warfarin's effects, monitor INR.

Sildenafil, tadalafil, and/or vardenafil serum concentrations may be increased by amprenavir. When used concurrently with sildenafil, do not exceed a maximum sildenafil dose of 25 mg in a 48-hour period. When used concurrently with tadalafil, do not exceed a maximum tadalafil dose of 10 mg in a 72-hour period. When used concurrently with vardenafil, do not exceed vardenafil dose of 2.5 mg in a 24-hour period (2.5 mg in a 72-hour period if used with ritonavir). Concurrent therapy with ritonavir may result in increased serum concentrations: dosage adjustment is recommended. Clarithromycin, indinavir, nelfinavir may increase serum concentrations of amprenavir.

Decreased Effect: CYP3A4 inducers may decrease the levels/effects of amprenavir; example inducers include aminoglutethimide, carbamazepine, nafcillin, nevirapine, phenobarbital, phenytoin, and rifamycins. The administration of didanosine (buffered formulation) should be separated from amprenavir by 1 hour to limit interaction between formulations. Serum concentrations of estrogen (oral contraceptives) may be decreased, use alternative (nonhormonal) forms of contraception. Dexamethasone may decrease the therapeutic effect of amprenavir. Serum concentrations of delavirdine may be decreased; may lead to loss of virologic response and possible resistance to delavirdine; concomitant use is not recommended. Efavirenz and nevirapine may decrease serum concentrations of amprenavir (dosing for combinations not established). Avoid St John's wort (may lead to subtherapeutic concentrations of amprenavir). Effect of amprenavir may be diminished when administered with methadone (consider alternative antiretroviral); in addition, effect of methadone may be reduced (dosage increase may be required).

Mechanism of Action Binds to the protease activity site and inhibits the activity of the enzyme. HIV protease is required for the cleavage of viral polyprotein precursors into individual functional proteins found in infectious HIV. Inhibition prevents cleavage of these polyproteins, resulting in the formation of immature, noninfectious viral particles.

Pharmacodynamics/Kinetics

Absorption: 63%

Distribution: 430 L

Protein binding: 90%

Metabolism: Hepatic via CYP (primarily CYP3A4)

Bioavailability: Not established; increased sixfold with high-fat meal

Half-life elimination: 7.1-10.6 hours

Time to peak: 1-2 hours

Excretion: Feces (75%); urine (14% as metabolites)

Dosage Oral: **Note:** Capsule and oral solution are **not** interchangeable on a mg-per-mg basis.

Capsule:

Children 4-12 years and older (<50 kg): 20 mg/kg twice daily or 15 mg/kg 3 times daily; maximum: 2400 mg/day

Children >13 years (>50 kg) and Adults: 1200 mg twice daily

Note: Dosage adjustments for amprenavir when administered in combination therapy:

Efavirenz: Adjustments necessary for both agents:

Amprenavir 1200 mg 3 times/day (single protease inhibitor) **or**

Amprenavir 1200 mg twice daily plus ritonavir 200 mg twice daily

Ritonavir: Adjustments necessary for both agents:

Amprenavir 1200 mg plus ritonavir 200 mg once daily **or**

Amprenavir 600 mg plus ritonavir 100 mg twice daily

Solution:

Children 4-12 years or older (up to 16 years weighing <50 kg): 22.5 mg/kg twice daily or 17 mg/kg 3 times daily; maximum: 2800 mg/day

Children 13-16 years (weighing at least 50 kg) or >16 years and Adults: 1400 mg twice daily

Dosage adjustment in renal impairment: Oral solution is contraindicated in renal failure.

Dosage adjustment in hepatic impairment:

Child-Pugh score between 5-8:

Capsule: 450 mg twice daily

Solution: 513 mg twice daily; contraindicated in hepatic failure

Child-Pugh score between 9-12:

Capsule: 300 mg twice daily

Solution: 342 mg twice daily; contraindicated in hepatic failure

Patient Information Advise prescriber of any previous reactions to sulfonamides. Do not take this medication with antacids or high-fat meals. Do not take additional vitamin E supplements.

Do not take any prescription medications, over-the-counter products or herbal products, especially St John's wort, without consulting prescriber. For women using oral contraceptives, an alternative method of contraception should be used.

Dosage Forms CAP: 50 mg, 150 mg. **SOLN, oral** [use only when there are no other options]: 15 mg/mL (240 mL)

♦ **AMPT**   see Metyrosine on page 833

♦ **Amrinone Lactate**   see Inamrinone on page 661

Amyl Nitrite   (AM il NYE trite)

Synonyms Isoamyl Nitrite

Therapeutic Category Antidote, Cyanide; Vasodilator, Coronary

Use Coronary vasodilator in angina pectoris; adjunct in treatment of cyanide poisoning; produce changes in the intensity of heart murmurs

Pregnancy Risk Factor X

Dosage Nasal inhalation:

Cyanide poisoning: Children and Adults: Inhale the vapor from a 0.3 mL crushed ampul every minute for 15-30 seconds until I.V. sodium nitrite infusion is available

Angina: Adults: 1-6 inhalations from 1 crushed ampul; may repeat in 3-5 minutes

Dosage Forms INH, vapor [crushable glass perles]: 0.3 mL

♦ **Amylobarbitone**   see Amobarbital on page 84

♦ **Amytal®**   see Amobarbital on page 84

♦ **Anacin PM Aspirin Free [OTC] [DSC]**   see Acetaminophen and Diphenhydramine on page 26

♦ **Anadrol®**   see Oxymetholone on page 946

♦ **Anafranil®**   see ClomiPRAMINE on page 297

Anagrelide   (an AG gre lide)

U.S. Brand Names Agrylin®

Synonyms   1370-999-397;   Anagrelide   Hydrochloride;   BL4162A; 6,7-Dichloro-1,5-Dihydroimidazo [2,1b] quinazolin-2(3H)-one Monohydrochloride

Therapeutic Category Platelet Reducing Agent

Use Treatment of essential thrombocythemia (ET) and thrombocythemia associated with chronic myelogenous leukemia (CML), polycythemia vera, and other myeloproliferative disorders

Pregnancy Risk Factor C

Dosage Adults: Oral: 0.5 mg 4 times/day or 1 mg twice daily

Maintain for ≥1 week, then adjust to the lowest effective dose to reduce and maintain platelet count <600,000/μL ideally to the normal range; the dose must not be increased by >0.5 mg/day in any 1 week; maximum dose: 10 mg/day or 2.5 mg/dose

Elderly: There are no special requirements for dosing in the elderly

Dosage Forms CAP: 0.5 mg, 1 mg

♦ **Anagrelide Hydrochloride**   see Anagrelide on page 99

Anakinra   (an a KIN ra)

U.S. Brand Names Kineret®

Synonyms IL-1Ra; Interleukin-1 Receptor antagonist

Therapeutic Category Antirheumatic, Disease Modifying; Interleukin-1 Receptor Antagonist

Use Reduction of signs and symptoms of moderately- to severely-active rheumatoid arthritis in adult patients who have failed one or more disease-modifying antirheumatic drugs (DMARDs); may be used alone or in combination with DMARDs (other than tumor necrosis factor-blocking agents)

Pregnancy Risk Factor B

Contraindications Hypersensitivity to E. coli-derived proteins, anakinra, or any component of the formulation; patients with active infections (including chronic or local infection)

Warnings/Precautions Anakinra may affect defenses against infections and malignancies. Safety and efficacy in patients with immunosuppression or chronic infections have not been evaluated. Discontinue administration if patient develops a serious infection. Do not start drug administration in patients with an active infection. Patients with asthma may be at an increased risk of serious infections. Should not be used in combination with tumor necrosis factor antagonists, unless no satisfactory alternatives exist, and then only with extreme caution. Impact on the development and course of malignancies is not fully defined.

Use caution in patients with a history of significant hematologic abnormalities; has been associated with uncommon, but significant decreases in hematologic parameters (particularly neutrophil counts). Patients must be advised to seek medical attention if they develop signs and symptoms suggestive of blood dyscrasias. Discontinue if significant hematologic abnormalities are confirmed.

Patients should be brought up to date with all immunizations before initiating therapy. Live vaccines should not be given concurrently. Patients with a significant exposure to varicella virus should temporarily discontinue anakinra. Hypersensitivity reactions may occur. Impact on the development and course of malignancies is not fully defined. The safety of anakinra has not been studied in children <18 years of age.

Common Adverse Reactions

>10%:

Central nervous system: Headache (12%)

(Continued)

Anakinra *(Continued)*

Local: Injection site reaction (majority mild, typically lasting 14-28 days, characterized by erythema, ecchymosis, inflammation and pain; up to 71%)

Miscellaneous: Infection (40% versus 35% in placebo; serious infections in 2% to 7%)

1% to 10%:

Gastrointestinal: Nausea (8%), diarrhea (7%), abdominal pain (5%)

Hematologic: Decreased WBCs (8%)

Respiratory: Sinusitis (7%)

Miscellaneous: Flu-like symptoms (6%)

Drug Interactions

Increased Effect/Toxicity: Concurrent use of anakinra and etanercept has been associated with an increased risk of serious infection while American College of Rheumatology (ACR) response rates were not improved, as compared to etanercept alone. Use caution with other drugs known to block or decrease the activity of tumor necrosis factor (TNF); includes infliximab and thalidomide.

Mechanism of Action Binds to the interleukin-1 (IL-1) receptor. IL-1 is induced by inflammatory stimuli and mediates a variety of immunological responses, including degradation of cartilage (loss of proteoglycans) and stimulation of bone resorption.

Pharmacodynamics/Kinetics

Bioavailability: S.C.: 95%

Half-life elimination: Terminal: 4-6 hours

Time to peak: S.C.: 3-7 hours

Dosage Adults: S.C.: Rheumatoid arthritis: 100 mg once daily (administer at approximately the same time each day)

Dosage adjustment in renal impairment: No specific guidelines for adjustment (clearance decreased by 70% to 75% in patients with Cl_{cr} <30 mL/minute)

Administration Rotate injection sites (thigh, abdomen, upper arm); injection should be given at least 1 inch away from previous injection site. Do not shake. Provided in single-use, preservative free syringes with 27 gauge needles; discard any unused portion.

Monitoring Parameters Neutrophil counts should be assessed prior to initiation of treatment, and repeated every month for the first 3 months of treatment, then quarterly up to 1 year.

Patient Information If self-injecting, follow instructions for injection and disposal of needles exactly. If redness, swelling, or irritation appears at the injection site, contact prescriber. Do not have any vaccinations while using this medication without consulting prescriber first. Immediately report skin rash, unusual muscle or bone weakness, or signs of respiratory flu or other infection (eg, chills, fever, sore throat, easy bruising or bleeding, mouth sores, unhealed sores).

Dosage Forms INJ [preservative free]: 100 mg/0.67mL (1 mL)

♦ **Analpram-HC®** *see* Pramoxine and Hydrocortisone *on page 1028*

♦ **Anaprox®** *see* Naproxen *on page 882*

♦ **Anaprox® DS** *see* Naproxen *on page 882*

♦ **Anaspaz®** *see* Hyoscyamine *on page 641*

Anastrozole *(an AS troe zole)*

U.S. Brand Names Arimidex®

Synonyms ICI-D1033; ZD1033

Therapeutic Category Antineoplastic Agent, Aromatase Inactivator; Aromatase Inhibitor

Use Treatment of locally-advanced or metastatic breast cancer (ER-positive or hormone receptor unknown) in postmenopausal women; treatment of advanced breast cancer in postmenopausal women with disease progression following tamoxifen therapy; adjuvant treatment of early ER-positive breast cancer in postmenopausal women

Pregnancy Risk Factor D

Contraindications Hypersensitivity to anastrozole or any component of the formulation; pregnancy

Warnings/Precautions Use with caution in patients with hyperlipidemias; total cholesterol and LDL-cholesterol increase in patients receiving anastrozole; exclude pregnancy before initiating therapy. Tamoxifen should not be used concurrently. Safety and efficacy in pediatric patients have not been established.

Common Adverse Reactions

>10%:

Cardiovascular: Vasodilatation (25% to 35%)

Central nervous system: Pain (11% to 15%), headache (9% to 13%), depression (5% to 11%)

Endocrine & metabolic: Hot flashes (12% to 35%)

Neuromuscular & skeletal: Weakness (16% to 17%), arthritis (14%), arthralgia (13%), back pain (8% to 12%), bone pain (5% to 11%)

Respiratory: Cough increased (7% to 11%), pharyngitis (6% to 12%)

1% to 10%:

Cardiovascular: Peripheral edema (5% to 10%), hypertension (5% to 9%), chest pain (5% to 7%)

Central nervous system: Insomnia (6% to 9%), dizziness (6%), anxiety (5%), lethargy (1%), fever, malaise, confusion, nervousness, somnolence

Dermatologic: Rash (6% to 10%), alopecia, pruritus

Endocrine & metabolic: Hypercholesteremia (7%)

Gastrointestinal: Vomiting (8% to 9%), constipation (7% to 9%), abdominal pain (7% to 8%), diarrhea (7% to 8%), anorexia (5% to 7%), xerostomia (6%), dyspepsia (5%), weight gain (2% to 8%), weight loss

Genitourinary: Urinary tract infection (6%), vulvovaginitis (6%), vaginal bleeding (5%) leukorrhea (2%), vaginal hemorrhage (2%), vaginal dryness (2%)

Hematologic: Anemia, leukopenia

Hepatic: Liver function tests increased, alkaline phosphatase increased

Local: Deep vein thrombosis, thrombophlebitis

Neuromuscular & skeletal: Osteoporosis (7%), fracture (7%), arthrosis (6%), paresthesia (5% to 6%), hypertonia (3%), myalgia, arthralgia

Ocular: Cataracts (4%)

Respiratory: Dyspnea (6% to 10%), sinusitis, bronchitis, rhinitis

Miscellaneous: Lymph edema (9%), infection (7%), flu-syndrome (5% to 7%), diaphoresis (2% to 4%)

Drug Interactions

Cytochrome P450 Effect: Inhibits CYP1A2 (weak), 2C8/9 (weak), 3A4 (weak)

Decreased Effect:

Estrogens: Concurrent use may decrease efficacy of anastrozole.

Tamoxifen: Decreased plasma concentration of anastrozole; avoid concurrent use.

Mechanism of Action Potent and selective nonsteroidal aromatase inhibitor. By inhibiting aromatase, the conversion of androstenedione to estrone, and testosterone to estradiol, is prevented. Anastrozole causes an 85% decrease in estrone sulfate levels.

Pharmacodynamics/Kinetics

Onset of estradiol reduction: 24 hours

Duration of estradiol reduction: 6 days

Absorption: Well absorbed (80%); not affected by food

Protein binding, plasma: 40%

Metabolism: Extensively hepatic (85%) via N-dealkylation, hydroxylation, and glucuronidation; primary metabolite inactive

Half-life elimination: 50 hours

Excretion: Urine (10% as unchanged drug; 60% as metabolites)

Dosage Breast cancer: Adults: Oral (refer to individual protocols): 1 mg once daily

Dosage adjustment in renal impairment: Dosage adjustment not necessary

Dosage adjustment in hepatic impairment: Plasma concentrations in subjects with stable hepatic cirrhosis were within the range concentrations in normal subjects across all clinical trials; therefore, no dosage adjustment is needed

Dosage Forms TAB: 1 mg

Anthralin (AN thra lin)

U.S. Brand Names Drithocreme®; Dritho-Scalp®; Psoriatec™

Synonyms Dithranol

Therapeutic Category Antipsoriatic Agent, Topical; Keratolytic Agent

Use Treatment of psoriasis (quiescent or chronic psoriasis)

Pregnancy Risk Factor C

Dosage Children (unlabeled) and Adults: Topical: Generally, apply once a day or as directed. The irritant potential of anthralin is directly related to the strength being used and each (Continued)

Anthralin *(Continued)*

patient's individual tolerance. Always commence treatment using a short, daily contact time (5-10 minutes) for at least 1 week using the lowest strength possible. Contact time may be gradually increased (to 20-30 minutes) as tolerated.

Skin application: Apply sparingly only to psoriatic lesions and rub gently and carefully into the skin until absorbed. Avoid applying an excessive quantity which may cause unnecessary soiling and staining of the clothing or bed linen.

Scalp application: Comb hair to remove scalar debris, wet hair and, after suitably parting, rub cream well into the lesions, taking care to prevent the cream from spreading onto the forehead,

Remove by washing or showering; optimal period of contact will vary according to the strength used and the patient's response to treatment. Continue treatment until the skin is entirely clear (ie, when there is nothing to feel with the fingers and the texture is normal).

Dosage Forms CRM: (Dritho-Cream®, Psoriatec™): 1% (50 g); (Dritho-Scalp®): 0.5% (50 g)

Anthrax Vaccine Adsorbed *(AN thraks vak SEEN ad SORBED)*

U.S. Brand Names BioThrax™

Synonyms AVA

Therapeutic Category Vaccine

Use Immunization against *Bacillus anthracis*. Recommended for individuals who may come in contact with animal products which come from anthrax endemic areas and may be contaminated with *Bacillus anthracis* spores; recommended for high-risk persons such as veterinarians and other handling potentially infected animals. Routine immunization for the general population is not recommended.

The Department of Defense is implementing an anthrax vaccination program against the biological warfare agent anthrax, which will be administered to all active duty and reserve personnel.

Unlabeled/Investigational Use Postexposure prophylaxis in combination with antibiotics

Restrictions Not commercially available in the U.S.; presently, all anthrax vaccine lots are owned by the U.S. Department of Defense. The Centers for Disease Control (CDC) does not currently recommend routine vaccination of the general public.

Pregnancy Risk Factor D

Contraindications Hypersensitivity to anthrax vaccine or any component of the formulation; severe anaphylactic reaction to a previous dose of anthrax vaccine; history of anthrax; history of Guillain-Barré syndrome; pregnancy

Warnings/Precautions Immediate treatment for anaphylactic/anaphylactoid reaction should be available during vaccine use. Patients with a history of Guillain-Barré syndrome should not be given the vaccine unless there is a clear benefit that outweighs the potential risk of recurrence. Defer dosing during acute respiratory disease or other active infection; defer dosing during short-term corticosteroid therapy, chemotherapy or radiation; additional dose required in patients on long-term corticosteroid therapy; discontinue immunization in patients with chills or fever associated with administration; use caution with latex allergy; immune response may be decreased with immunodeficiency; safety and efficacy in children <18 years of age or adults >65 years of age have not been established

Common Adverse Reactions (Includes pre- and post-licensure data; systemic reactions reported more often in women than in men)

>10%:

Central nervous system: Malaise (4% to 11%)

Local: Tenderness (58% to 71%), erythema (12% to 43%), subcutaneous nodule (4% to 39%), induration (8% to 21%), warmth (11% to 19%), local pruritus (7% to 19%)

Neuromuscular & skeletal: Arm motion limitation (7% to 12%)

1% to 10%:

Central nervous system: Headache (4% to 7%), fever (<1% to 7%)

Gastrointestinal: Anorexia (4%), vomiting (4%), nausea (<1% to 4%)

Local: Mild local reactions (edema/induration <30mm) (9%), edema (8%)

Neuromuscular & skeletal: Myalgia (4% to 7%)

Respiratory: Respiratory difficulty (4%)

Drug Interactions

Decreased Effect: Effect of vaccine may be decreased with chemotherapy, corticosteroids (high doses, ≥14 days), immunosuppressant agents and radiation therapy; consider waiting at least 3 months between discontinuing therapy and administering vaccine.

Mechanism of Action Active immunization against *Bacillus anthracis*. The vaccine is prepared from a cell-free filtrate of *B. anthracis*, but no dead or live bacteria.

Pharmacodynamics/Kinetics Duration: Unknown; may be 1-2 years following two inoculations based on animal data

Dosage S.C.:

Children <18 years: Safety and efficacy have not been established

Children ≥18 years and Adults:

Primary immunization: Three injections of 0.5 mL each given 2 weeks apart, followed by three additional injections given at 6-, 12-, and 18 months; it is not necessary to restart the series if a dose is not given on time; resume as soon as practical

Subsequent booster injections: 0.5 mL at 1-year intervals are recommended for immunity to be maintained

Elderly: Safety and efficacy have not been established for patients >65 years of age

Administration Administer S.C.; shake well before use. Do not use if discolored or contains particulate matter. Do not use the same site for more than one injection. Do not mix with other injections. After administration, massage injection site to disperse the vaccine. Federal law requires that the date of administration, the vaccine manufacturer, lot number of vaccine, and the administering person's name, title and address be entered into the patient's permanent medical record.

Monitoring Parameters Monitor for local reactions, chills, fever, anaphylaxis

Patient Information The anthrax vaccine is used to protect against anthrax disease. Anthrax disease can be a skin disease, caused by contact with infected animals or animal products. It can also be caused by inhalation of anthrax spores. Immunization using the vaccine consists of a series of 6 injections. The vaccine should be used by people who may be exposed to the anthrax bacteria, such as laboratory workers, veterinarians, and military personnel. You should not use the vaccine if you have already had anthrax disease. Most people receiving the vaccine will experience soreness, redness, or itching at the injection site, which should clear up within 48 hours. Contact your prescriber immediately if you experience a fever, difficulty breathing, hoarseness, wheezing, fast heart beat, hives, dizziness, paleness, or swelling of the throat.

Dosage Forms INJ, suspension: 5 mL

- **AntibiOtic® Ear** see Neomycin, Polymyxin B, and Hydrocortisone on page 892
- **Anti-CD11a** see Efalizumab on page 424
- **Anti-CD20 Monoclonal Antibody** see Rituximab on page 1106
- **Anti-CD20-Murine Monoclonal Antibody I-131** see Tositumomab and Iodine I 131 Tositumomab on page 1248
- **Anticoagulants, Injectable** see page 1357
- **Anticonvulsants by Seizure Type** see page 1358
- **Antidepressant Agents Comparison** see page 1359
- **Antidigoxin Fab Fragments, Ovine** see Digoxin Immune Fab on page 376
- **Antidiuretic Hormone** see Vasopressin on page 1298
- **Antifungal Agents Comparison** see page 1362

Antihemophilic Factor (Human) (an tee hee moe FIL ik FAK tor HYU man)

U.S. Brand Names Alphanate®; Hemofil® M; Humate-P®; Koāte®-DVI; Monarc® M; Monoclate-P®

Synonyms AHF (Human); Factor VIII (Human)

Therapeutic Category Antihemophilic Agent; Blood Product Derivative

Use Management of hemophilia A for patients in whom a deficiency in factor VIII has been demonstrated; can be of significant therapeutic value in patients with acquired factor VIII inhibitors not exceeding 10 Bethesda units/mL

Humate-P®: In addition, indicated as treatment of spontaneous bleeding in patients with severe von Willebrand disease and in mild and moderate von Willebrand disease where desmopressin is known or suspected to be inadequate

Orphan status: Alphanate®: Management of von Willebrand disease

Pregnancy Risk Factor C

Contraindications Hypersensitivity to any component of the formulation or to mouse protein (Monoclate-P® M, Hemofil® M)

Warnings/Precautions Risk of viral transmission is not totally eradicated. Because antihemophilic factor is prepared from pooled plasma, it may contain the causative agent of viral hepatitis and other viral diseases. Hepatitis B vaccination is recommended for all patients. Hepatitis A vaccination is also recommended for seronegative patients. Antihemophilic factor contains trace amounts of blood groups A and B isohemagglutinins and when large or frequently repeated doses are given to individuals with blood groups A, B, and AB, the patient should be monitored for signs of progressive anemia and the possibility of intravascular hemolysis should be considered. Natural rubber latex is a component of Hemofil® M packaging. Products vary by preparation method; final formulations contain human albumin.

Mechanism of Action Protein (factor VIII) in normal plasma which is necessary for clot formation and maintenance of hemostasis; activates factor X in conjunction with activated factor IX; activated factor X converts prothrombin to thrombin, which converts fibrinogen to fibrin, and with factor XIII forms a stable clot

Pharmacodynamics/Kinetics Half-life elimination: Mean: 12-17 hours with hemophilia A; consult specific product labeling

Dosage Children and Adults: I.V.: Individualize dosage based on coagulation studies performed prior to treatment and at regular intervals during treatment; 1 AHF unit is the activity present in 1 mL of normal pooled human plasma; dosage should be adjusted to actual vial size currently stocked in the pharmacy. (General guidelines presented; consult individual product labeling for specific dosing recommendations.)

Dosage based on desired factor VIII increase (%):

To calculate dosage needed based on desired factor VIII increase (%):

Body weight (kg) x 0.5 int. units/kg x desired factor VIII increase (%) = int. units factor VIII required

For example:

50 kg x 0.5 int. units/kg x 30 (% increase) = 750 int. units factor VIII

Dosage based on expected factor VIII increase (%):

It is also possible to calculate the **expected** % factor VIII increase:

(# int. units administered x 2%/int. units/kg) divided by body weight (kg) = expected % factor VIII increase

(Continued)

Antihemophilic Factor (Human) *(Continued)*

For example:

(1400 int. units x 2%/int. units/kg) divided by 70 kg = 40%

General guidelines:

Minor Hemorrhage: Required peak postinfusion AHF level: 20% to 40% (10-20 int. units/kg), repeat dose every 12-24 hours for 1-3 days until bleeding is resolved or healing achieved; mild superficial or early hemorrhages may respond to a single dose

Moderate hemorrhage: Required peak postinfusion AHF level: 30% to 60% (15-30 int. units/kg): Infuse every 12-24 hours for ≥3 days until pain and disability are resolved

Alternatively, a loading dose to achieve 50% (25 int. units/kg) may be given, followed by 10-15 int. units/kg dose given every 8-12 hours; may be needed for >7 days

Severe/life-threatening hemorrhage: Required peak postinfusion AHF level: 60% to 100% (30-50 int. units/kg): Infuse every 8-24 hours until threat is resolved

Alternatively, a loading dose to achieve 80% to 100% (40-50 int. units/kg) may be given, followed by 20-25 int. units/kg dose given every 8-12 hours for ≥14 days

Minor surgery: Required peak postinfusion AHF level: 30% to 80% (15-40 int. units/kg): Highly dependent upon procedure and specific product recommendations; for some procedures, may be administered as a single infusion plus oral antifibrinolytic therapy within 1 hour; in other procedures, may repeat dose every 12-24 hours as needed

Major surgery: Required peak pre- and postsurgery AHF level: 80% to 100% (40-50 int. units/kg): Administer every 6-24 hours until healing is complete (10-14 days)

Prophylaxis: May also be given on a regular schedule to prevent bleeding

If bleeding is not controlled with adequate dose, test for presence of inhibitor. It may not be possible or practical to control bleeding if inhibitor titers >10 Bethesda units/mL; antihemophilic factor (porcine) may be considered as an alternative

von Willebrand disease:

Treatment of hemorrhage in von Willebrand disease (Humate-P®): 1 int. units of factor VIII per kg of body weight would be expected to raise circulating vWF:RC of approximately 3.5-4 int. units/dL

Type 1, mild (if desmopressin is not appropriate): Major hemorrhage:

Loading dose: 40-60 int. units/kg

Maintenance dose: 40-50 int. units/kg every 8-12 hours for 3 days, keeping vWF:RC of nadir >50%; follow with 40-50 int. units/kg daily for up to 7 days

Type 1, moderate or severe:

Minor hemorrhage: 40-50 int. units/kg for 1-2 doses

Major hemorrhage:

Loading dose: 50-75 int. units/kg

Maintenance dose: 40-60 int. units/kg daily for up to 7 days

Types 2 and 3:

Minor hemorrhage: 40-50 int. units/kg for 1-2 doses

Major hemorrhage:

Loading dose: 60-80 int. units/kg

Maintenance dose: 40-60 int. units/kg every 8-12 hours for 3 days, keeping vWF:RC of nadir >50%; follow with 40-60 int. units/kg daily for up to 7 days

Elderly: Response in the elderly is not expected to differ from that of younger patients; dosage should be individualized

Administration Total dose may be administered over 5-10 minutes (maximum: 10 mL/minute); infuse Monoclate-P® at 2 mL/minute; adapt based on patient response

Monitoring Parameters Heart rate and blood pressure (before and during I.V. administration); AHF levels prior to and during treatment; in patients with circulating inhibitors, the inhibitor level should be monitored; hematocrit; monitor for signs and symptoms of intravascular hemolysis; bleeding

Reference Range Average normal antihemophilic factor plasma activity ranges: 50% to 150%

Level to prevent spontaneous hemorrhage: 5%

Required peak postinfusion AHF activity in blood (as % of normal or units/dL plasma):

Early hemarthrosis, muscle bleed, or oral bleed: 20% to 40%

More extensive hemarthrosis, muscle bleed, or hematoma: 30% to 60%

Life-threatening bleeds (such as head injury, throat bleed, severe abdominal pain): 80% to 100%

Minor surgery, including tooth extraction: 60% to 80%

Major surgery: 80% to 100% (pre- and postoperative)

Patient Information This medication can only be given intravenously. Report sudden-onset headache, rash, chest or back pain, wheezing, or respiratory difficulties, hives, itching, low grade fever, nausea, vomiting, tiredness, decreased appetite to prescriber. Wear identification indicating that you have a hemophilic condition.

Dosage Forms INJ, human: Labeling on cartons and vials indicates number of int. units

Antihemophilic Factor (Porcine) *(an tee hee moe FIL ik FAK ter POR seen)*

U.S. Brand Names Hyate:C®

Synonyms AHF (Porcine); Factor VIII (Porcine)

Therapeutic Category Antihemophilic Agent; Blood Product Derivative

Use Management of hemophilia A in patients with antibodies to human factor VIII (consider use of human factor VIII in patients with antibody titer of <5 Bethesda units/mL); management of previously nonhemophilic patients with spontaneously-acquired inhibitors to human factor VIII, regardless of initial antihuman inhibitor titer

Pregnancy Risk Factor C

Contraindications Hypersensitivity to porcine or any component of the formulation

Warnings/Precautions Rarely administration has been associated with anaphylaxis; epineph-rine, hydrocortisone, and facilities for cardiopulmonary resuscitation should be available in case such a reaction occurs; infusion may be followed by a rise in plasma levels of antibody to both human and porcine factor VIII; inhibitor levels should be monitored both pre- and post-treatment

Common Adverse Reactions Reactions tend to lessen in frequency and severity as further infusions are given; hydrocortisone and/or antihistamines may help to prevent or alleviate side effects and may be prescribed as precautionary measures.

1% to 10%:
    Central nervous system: Fever, headache, chills
    Dermatologic: Rashes
    Gastrointestinal: Nausea, vomiting

Mechanism of Action Factor VIII is the coagulation portion of the factor VIII complex in plasma. Factor VIII acts as a cofactor for factor IX to activate factor X in the intrinsic pathway of blood coagulation.

Pharmacodynamics/Kinetics Half-life elimination: 10-11 hours (patients without detectable inhibitors)

Dosage Clinical response should be used to assess efficacy

Initial dose:
    Antibody level to human factor VIII <50 Bethesda units/mL: 100-150 porcine units/kg (body weight) is recommended
    Antibody level to human factor VIII >50 Bethesda units/mL: Activity of the antibody to antihemophilic (porcine) should be determined; **an antiporcine antibody level** >20 Bethesda units/mL indicates that the patient is unlikely to benefit from treatment; for lower titers, a dose of 100-150 porcine units/kg is recommended
    The initial dose may also be calculated using the following method:
    1. Determine patient's antibody titer against porcine factor VIII
    2. Calculate average plasma volume:
        (body weight kg) (average blood volume) (1 - hematocrit) = plasma volume
        (body weight kg) (80 mL/kg) (1 - hematocrit) = plasma volume
        Note: A hematocrit of 50% = 0.5 for the equation
    3. Neutralizing dose:
        (plasma volume mL) (antibody titer Bethesda units/mL) = neutralizing dose units
        This is the predicted dose required to neutralize the circulating antibodies. An incre-mental dose must be added to the neutralizing dose in order to increase the plasma factor VIII to the desired level.
    4. Incremental dose:
        (desired plasma factor VIII level) (body weight) divided by 1.5 = incremental dose units
    5. Total dose = neutralizing dose + incremental dose = total dose units
    If a patient has previously been treated with Hyate:C®, this may provide a guide to his likely response and, therefore, assist in estimation of the preliminary dose

Subsequent doses: Following administration of the initial dose, if the recovery of factor VIII in the patient's plasma is not sufficient, another larger dose should be administered; if recovery after the second dose is still insufficient, a third and larger dose may prove effective. Once appropriate factor VIII levels are achieved, dosing can be repeated every 6-8 hours.

Administration Administer by I.V. route only; infuse slowly, 2-5 mL/minute

Monitoring Parameters Factor VIII levels pre- and postinfusion; inhibitor levels to human and/or porcine factor VIII pre- and postinfusion; heart rate and blood pressure (before and during I.V. administration); bleeding
    Antibody levels to human factor VIII >50 Bethesda units/mL: Activity of the antibody to antihe-mophilic (porcine) should be determined
    Antiporcine antibody level >20 Bethesda units/mL: Patient may not benefit from treatment

Reference Range
    Average normal antihemophilic factor plasma activity range: 50% to 150%
    Level to prevent spontaneous hemorrhage: 5%

Patient Information This medication can only be given intravenously. Report sudden-onset headache, rash, chest or back pain, or respiratory difficulties to prescriber. Wear identification indicating that you have a hemophilic condition.

Dosage Forms INJ, powder for reconstitution: 400-700 porcine units

Antihemophilic Factor (Recombinant)
(an tee hee moe FIL ik FAK tor ree KOM be nant)

U.S. Brand Names Advate; Helixate® FS; Kogenate® FS; Recombinate™; ReFacto®

Synonyms AHF (Recombinant); Factor VIII (Recombinant); rAHF

Therapeutic Category Antihemophilic Agent

Use Management of hemophilia A (classic hemophilia) for patients in whom a deficiency in factor VIII has been demonstrated; prevention and control of bleeding episodes; perioperative management of hemophilia A; can be of significant therapeutic value in patients with acquired factor VIII inhibitors not exceeding 10 Bethesda units/mL

Pregnancy Risk Factor C
(Continued)

Antihemophilic Factor (Recombinant) *(Continued)*

Contraindications Hypersensitivity to mouse or hamster protein (Advate, Helixate® FS, Kogenate® FS); hypersensitivity to mouse, hamster, or bovine protein (Recombinate™, ReFacto®); hypersensitivity to any component of the formulation

Warnings/Precautions Monitor for signs of formation of antibodies to factor VIII; may occur at anytime but more common in young children with severe hemophilia. Monitor for allergic hypersensitivity reactions. Products vary by preparation method. Recombinate™ is stabilized using human albumin. Helixate® FS and Kogenate® FS are stabilized with sucrose.

Mechanism of Action Protein (factor VIII) in normal plasma which is necessary for clot formation and maintenance of hemostasis; activates factor X in conjunction with activated factor IX; activated factor X converts prothrombin to thrombin, which converts fibrinogen to fibrin, and with factor XIII forms a stable clot

Pharmacodynamics/Kinetics Half-life elimination: Mean: 14-16 hours

Dosage Children and Adults: I.V.: Individualize dosage based on coagulation studies performed prior to treatment and at regular intervals during treatment; 1 AHF unit is the activity present in 1 mL of normal pooled human plasma; dosage should be adjusted to actual vial size currently stocked in the pharmacy. (General guidelines presented; consult individual product labeling for specific dosing recommendations.)

Dosage based on desired factor VIII increase (%):
To calculate dosage needed based on desired factor VIII increase (%):
Body weight (kg) x 0.5 int. units/kg x desired factor VIII increase (%) = int. units factor VIII required
For example:
50 kg x 0.5 int. units/kg x 30 (% increase) = 750 int. units factor VIII

Dosage based on expected factor VIII increase (%):
It is also possible to calculate the **expected** % factor VIII increase:
(# int. units administered x 2%/int. units/kg) divided by body weight (kg) = expected % factor VIII increase
For example:
(1400 int. units x 2%/int. units/kg) divided by 70 kg = 40%

General guidelines:
Minor hemorrhage: Required peak postinfusion AHF level: 20% to 40% (10-20 int. units/kg); mild superficial or early hemorrhages may respond to a single dose; may repeat dose every 12-24 hours for 1-3 days until bleeding is resolved or healing achieved

Moderate hemorrhage/minor surgery: Required peak postinfusion AHF level: 30% to 60% (15-30 int. units/kg); repeat dose at 12-24 hours if needed; some products suggest continuing for ≥3 days until pain and disability are resolved

Severe/life-threatening hemorrhage: Required peak postinfusion AHF level: Initial dose: 80% to 100% (40-50 int. units/kg); maintenance dose: 40% to 50% (20-25 int. units/kg) every 8-12 hours until threat is resolved

Major surgery: Required peak pre- and postsurgery AHF level: ~100% (50 int. units/kg) give first dose prior to surgery and repeat every 6-12 hours until healing complete (10-14 days)

Prophylaxis: May also be given on a regular schedule to prevent bleeding

If bleeding is not controlled with adequate dose, test for presence of inhibitor. It may not be possible or practical to control bleeding if inhibitor titers >10 Bethesda units/mL; antihemophilic factor (porcine) may be considered as an alternative

Elderly: Response in the elderly is not expected to differ from that of younger patients; dosage should be individualized

Administration Total dose may be administered over 5-10 minutes (maximum: 10 mL/minute); adapt based on patient response
Advate: Infuse over ≤5 minutes (maximum: 10 mL/minute)

Monitoring Parameters Heart rate and blood pressure (before and during I.V. administration); AHF levels prior to and during treatment; development of factor VIII inhibitors; bleeding

Reference Range Average normal antihemophilic factor plasma activity ranges: 50% to 150%
Level to prevent spontaneous hemorrhage: 5%
Required peak postinfusion AHF activity in blood (as % of normal or units/dL plasma):
Early hemarthrosis, muscle bleed, or oral bleed: 20% to 40%
More extensive hemarthrosis, muscle bleed, or hematoma: 30% to 60%
Life-threatening bleeds (such as head injury, throat bleed, severe abdominal pain): 80% to 100%
Minor surgery, including tooth extraction: 60% to 80%
Major surgery: 80% to 100% (pre- and postoperative)

Patient Information This medication can only be given intravenously. Report hives, itching, wheezing, sudden-onset headache, rash, chest or back pain, or other respiratory difficulties to prescriber. Wear identification indicating that you have a hemophilic condition.

Dosage Forms INJ, powder for reconstitution, recombinant [preservative free]: (Advate): 250 int. units, 500 int. units, 1000 int. units, 1500 int. units [plasma/albumin free]. (Helixate® FS, Kogenate® FS): 250 int. units, 500 int. units, 1000 int. units; (Recombinate™): 250 int. units, 500 units, 1000 int. units; (ReFacto®): 250 int. units, 500 units, 1000 int. units, 2000 int. units

Anti-inhibitor Coagulant Complex

(an tee-in HI bi tor coe AG yoo lant KOM pleks)
U.S. Brand Names Autoplex® T; Feiba VH®
Synonyms Coagulant Complex Inhibitor

Therapeutic Category Antihemophilic Agent; Blood Product Derivative

Use Patients with factor VIII inhibitors who are to undergo surgery or those who are bleeding

Pregnancy Risk Factor C

Contraindications Disseminated intravascular coagulation; patients with normal coagulation mechanism

Warnings/Precautions Products are prepared from pooled human plasma; such plasma may contain the causative agents of viral diseases. Tests used to control efficacy such as APTT, WBCT, and TEG do not correlate with clinical efficacy. Dosing to normalize these values may result in DIC. Identification of the clotting deficiency as caused by factor VIII inhibitors is essential prior to starting therapy. Use with extreme caution in patients with impaired hepatic function.

Dosage Dosage range: 25-100 factor VIII correctional units per kg depending on the severity of hemorrhage

Dosage Forms INJ: (Autoplex® T): Each bottle is labeled with correctional units of factor VIII [with heparin 2 units/mL]; (Feiba VH®): Each bottle is labeled with correctional units of factor VIII [heparin free]

♦ **Antimicrobial Drugs of Choice** *see page 1440*
♦ **Antimigraine Drugs Comparison** *see page 1363*
♦ **Antipsychotic Agents Comparison** *see page 1364*

Antipyrine and Benzocaine (an tee PYE reen & BEN zoe kane)

U.S. Brand Names A/B Otic; Allergen®; Aurodex; Auroto

Synonyms Benzocaine and Antipyrine

Therapeutic Category Otic Agent, Analgesic; Otic Agent, Cerumenolytic

Use Temporary relief of pain and reduction of swelling associated with acute congestive and serous otitis media, swimmer's ear, otitis externa; facilitates ear wax removal

Pregnancy Risk Factor C

Dosage Otic: Fill ear canal; moisten cotton pledget, place in external ear, repeat every 1-2 hours until pain and congestion are relieved; for ear wax removal instill drops 3-4 times/day for 2-3 days

Dosage Forms SOLN, otic: Antipyrine 5.4% and benzocaine 1.4% (15 mL); (A/B Otic, Allergen®, Aurodex, Auroto): Antipyrine 5.4% and benzocaine 1.4% (15 mL)

♦ **Antiretroviral Therapy for HIV Infection** *see page 1448*

Antithrombin III (an tee THROM bin three)

U.S. Brand Names Thrombate III®

Synonyms AT III; Heparin Cofactor I

Therapeutic Category Anticoagulant; Blood Product Derivative

Use Treatment of hereditary antithrombin III deficiency in connection with surgical or obstetrical procedures; thromboembolism

Unlabeled/Investigational Use Acquired antithrombin III deficiencies related to disseminated intravascular coagulation (DIC)

Pregnancy Risk Factor B

Contraindications Hypersensitivity to any component of the formulation

Warnings/Precautions Product is prepared from pooled human plasma; may contain the causative agents of viral diseases.

Common Adverse Reactions 1% to 10%: Central nervous system: Dizziness (2%)

Drug Interactions

Increased Effect/Toxicity: Heparin's anticoagulant effects are potentiated by antithrombin III (half-life of antithrombin III is decreased by heparin). Risk of hemorrhage with antithrombin III may be increased by drotrecogin, thrombolytic agents, oral anticoagulants (warfarin), and drugs which affect platelet function (eg, aspirin, NSAIDs, dipyridamole, ticlopidine, clopidogrel, and IIb/IIIa antagonists).

Mechanism of Action Antithrombin III is the primary physiologic inhibitor of *in vivo* coagulation. It is an $alpha_2$-globulin. Its principal actions are the inactivation of thrombin, plasmin, and other active serine proteases of coagulation, including factors IXa, Xa, XIa, XIIa, and VIIa. The inactivation of proteases is a major step in the normal clotting process. The strong activation of clotting enzymes at the site of every bleeding injury facilitates fibrin formation and maintains normal hemostasis. Thrombosis in the circulation would be caused by active serine proteases if they were not inhibited by antithrombin III after the localized clotting process. Patients with congenital deficiency are in a prethrombotic state, even if asymptomatic, as evidenced by elevated plasma levels of prothrombin activation fragment, which are normalized following infusions of antithrombin III concentrate.

Pharmacodynamics/Kinetics Half-life elimination: Biologic: 2.5 days (immunologic assay); 3.8 days (functional AT-III assay)

Dosage Adults:

Initial dose: Dosing is individualized based on pretherapy AT-III levels. The initial dose should raise antithrombin III levels (AT-III) to 120% and may be calculated based on the following formula:

Initial dosage (int. units) = [desired AT-III level % - baseline AT-III level %] x body weight (kg) divided by 1.4%/int. units/kg (eg, if a 70 kg adult patient had a baseline AT-III level of 57%, the initial dose would be (120% - 57%) x 70/1.4%/int. units/kg = 3150 int. units).

Maintenance dose: Subsequent dosing should be targeted to keep levels between 80% to 120% which may be achieved by administering 60% of the initial dose every 24 hours. (Continued)

Antithrombin III *(Continued)*

Adjustments may be made by adjusting dose or interval. Maintain level within normal range for 2-8 days depending on type of surgery or procedure.

Administration Infuse over 10-20 minutes

Monitoring Parameters Monitor antithrombin III levels (pre-infusion and 20 minutes post-infusion for each dose); liver function tests

Reference Range Maintain antithrombin III level in plasma >80%

Dosage Forms INJ, powder for reconstitution [preservative free]: 500 int. units, 1000 int. units

Antithymocyte Globulin (Equine) (an te THY moe site GLOB yu lin, E kwine)

U.S. Brand Names Atgam®

Synonyms Antithymocyte Immunoglobulin; ATG; Horse Antihuman Thymocyte Gamma Globulin; Lymphocyte Immune Globulin

Therapeutic Category Immunosuppressant Agent

Use Prevention and treatment of acute renal allograft rejection; treatment of moderate to severe aplastic anemia in patients not considered suitable candidates for bone marrow transplantation

Unlabeled/Investigational Use Prevention and treatment of other solid organ allograft rejection; prevention of graft-versus-host disease following bone marrow transplantation

Pregnancy Risk Factor C

Contraindications Hypersensitivity to lymphocytic immune globulin, any component of the formulation, or other equine gamma globulins

Warnings/Precautions Must be administered via central line due to chemical phlebitis; should only be used by physicians experienced in immunosuppressive therapy or management of solid organ or bone marrow transplant patients; adequate laboratory and supportive medical resources must be readily available in the facility for patient management; rash, dyspnea, hypotension, or anaphylaxis precludes further administration of the drug. Discontinue if severe and unremitting thrombocytopenia and/or leukopenia occur. Dose must be administered over at least 4 hours; patient may need to be pretreated with an antipyretic, antihistamine, and/or corticosteroid. Intradermal skin testing is recommended prior to first-dose administration.

Common Adverse Reactions

>10%:
  Central nervous system: Fever, chills
  Dermatologic: Pruritus, rash, urticaria
  Hematologic: Leukopenia, thrombocytopenia

1% to 10%:
  Cardiovascular: Bradycardia, chest pain, CHF, edema, encephalitis, hypotension, hypertension, myocarditis, tachycardia
  Central nervous system: Agitation, headache, lethargy, lightheadedness, listlessness, seizures
  Gastrointestinal: Diarrhea, nausea, stomatitis, vomiting
  Hepatic: Hepatosplenomegaly, liver function tests abnormal
  Local: Pain at injection site, phlebitis, thrombophlebitis, burning soles/palms
  Neuromuscular & skeletal: Myalgia, back pain, arthralgia
  Ocular: Periorbital edema
  Renal: Abnormal renal function tests
  Respiratory: Dyspnea, respiratory distress
  Miscellaneous: Anaphylaxis, serum sickness, viral infection, night sweats, diaphoresis, lymphadenopathy

Mechanism of Action May involve elimination of antigen-reactive T-lymphocytes (killer cells) in peripheral blood or alteration of T-cell function

Pharmacodynamics/Kinetics

Distribution: Poorly into lymphoid tissues; binds to circulating lymphocytes, granulocytes, platelets, bone marrow cells
Half-life elimination, plasma: 1.5-12 days
Excretion: Urine (~1%)

Dosage An intradermal skin test is recommended prior to administration of the initial dose of ATG; use 0.1 mL of a 1:1000 dilution of ATG in normal saline. A positive skin reaction consists of a wheal ≥10 mm in diameter. If a positive skin test occurs, the first infusion should be administered in a controlled environment with intensive life support immediately available. A systemic reaction precludes further administration of the drug. The absence of a reaction does **not** preclude the possibility of an immediate sensitivity reaction.

Premedication with diphenhydramine, hydrocortisone, and acetaminophen is recommended prior to first dose.

Children: I.V.:
  Aplastic anemia protocol: 10-20 mg/kg/day for 8-14 days; then administer every other day for 7 more doses; addition doses may be given every other day for 21 total doses in 28 days
  Renal allograft: 5-25 mg/kg/day
Adults: I.V.:
  Aplastic anemia protocol: 10-20 mg/kg/day for 8-14 days, then administer every other day for 7 more doses, for a total of 21 doses in 28 days
  Renal allograft:
    Rejection prophylaxis: 15 mg/kg/day for 14 days followed by 14 days of alternative day therapy at the same dose; the first dose should be administered within 24 hours before or after transplantation

Rejection treatment: 10-15 mg/kg/day for 14 days, then administer every other day for 10-14 days up to 21 doses in 28 days

Administration Infuse dose over at least 4 hours. Any severe systemic reaction to the skin test such as generalized rash, tachycardia, dyspnea, hypotension, or anaphylaxis should preclude further therapy. Epinephrine and resuscitative equipment should be nearby. Patient may need to be pretreated with an antipyretic, antihistamine, and corticosteroid. Mild itching and erythema can be treated with antihistamines. Infuse into a vascular shunt, arterial venous fistula or high-flow central vein through a 0.2-1 micron in-line filter

First dose: Premedicate with diphenhydramine orally 30 minutes prior to and hydrocortisone I.V. 15 minutes prior to infusion and acetaminophen 2 hours after start of infusion.

Monitoring Parameters Lymphocyte profile, CBC with differential and platelet count, vital signs during administration

Dosage Forms INJ, solution: 50 mg (5 mL)

Antithymocyte Globulin (Rabbit) (an te THY moe site GLOB yu lin (RAB bit)
U.S. Brand Names Thymoglobulin®
Synonyms Antithymocyte Immunoglobulin; ATG
Therapeutic Category Immunosuppressant Agent
Use Treatment of renal transplant acute rejection in conjunction with concomitant immunosuppression

Contraindications Patients with history of allergy or anaphylaxis to rabbit proteins, or who have an acute viral illness

Warnings/Precautions Infusion may produce fever and chills. To minimize, the first dose should be infused over a minimum of 6 hours into a high-flow vein. Also, premedication with corticosteroids, acetaminophen, and/or an antihistamine and/or slowing the infusion rate may reduce reaction incidence and intensity.

Prolonged use or overdosage of Thymoglobulin® in association with other immunosuppressive agents may cause over-immunosuppression resulting in severe infections and may increase the incidence of lymphoma or post-transplant lymphoproliferative disease (PTLD) or other malignancies. Appropriate antiviral, antibacterial, antiprotozoal, and/or antifungal prophylaxis is recommended.

Thymoglobulin® should only be used by physicians experienced in immunosuppressive therapy for the treatment of renal transplant patients. Medical surveillance is required during the infusion. In rare circumstances, anaphylaxis has been reported with use. In such cases, the infusion should be terminated immediately. Medical personnel should be available to treat patients who experience anaphylaxis. Emergency treatment such as 0.3-0.5 mL aqueous epinephrine (1:1000 dilution) subcutaneously and other resuscitative measures including oxygen, intravenous fluids, antihistamines, corticosteroids, pressor amines, and airway management, as clinically indicated, should be provided. Thymoglobulin® or other rabbit immunoglobulins should not be administered again for such patients. Thrombocytopenia or neutropenia may result from cross-reactive antibodies and is reversible following dose adjustments.

Common Adverse Reactions
>10%:
Central nervous system: Fever, chills, headache
Dermatologic: Rash
Endocrine & metabolic: Hyperkalemia
Gastrointestinal: Abdominal pain, diarrhea
Hematologic: Leukopenia, thrombocytopenia
Neuromuscular & skeletal: Weakness
Respiratory: Dyspnea
Miscellaneous: Systemic infection, pain
1% to 10%:
Gastrointestinal: Gastritis
Respiratory: Pneumonia
Miscellaneous: Sensitivity reactions: Anaphylaxis may be indicated by hypotension, respiratory distress, serum sickness, viral infection

Mechanism of Action May involve elimination of antigen-reactive T-lymphocytes (killer cells) in peripheral blood or alteration of T-cell function

Pharmacodynamics/Kinetics Half-life elimination, plasma: 2-3 days

Dosage I.V.: 1.5 mg/kg/day for 7-14 days

Administration For I.V. use only; administer via central line; use of high flow veins will minimize the occurrence of phlebitis and thrombosis; administer by slow I.V. infusion through an in-line filter with pore size of 0.2 micrometer over a minimum of 6 hours for the first infusion and over at least 4 hours on subsequent days of therapy.

Monitoring Parameters Lymphocyte profile, CBC with differential and platelet count, vital signs during administration

Dosage Forms INJ, powder for reconstitution: 25 mg vial

- **Anusol-HC®** *see* Hydrocortisone *on page 632*
- **Anusol® HC-1 [OTC]** *see* Hydrocortisone *on page 632*
- **Anzemet®** *see* Dolasetron *on page 400*
- **APAP** *see* Acetaminophen *on page 24*
- **APAP and Tramadol** *see* Acetaminophen and Tramadol *on page 27*
- **Apatate® [OTC]** *see* Vitamin B Complex Combinations *on page 1311*
- **Aphedrid™ [OTC]** *see* Triprolidine and Pseudoephedrine *on page 1273*
- **Aphthasol®** *see* Amlexanox *on page 82*
- **Aplisol®** *see* Tuberculin Tests *on page 1279*
- **Aplonidine** *see* Apraclonidine *on page 110*
- **APPG** *see* Penicillin G Procaine *on page 974*

Apraclonidine (a pra KLOE ni deen)
Related Information
Glaucoma Drug Therapy Comparison *on page 1481*
U.S. Brand Names Iopidine®
Synonyms Aplonidine; Apraclonidine Hydrochloride; p-Aminoclonidine
Therapeutic Category Alpha$_2$-Adrenergic Agonist, Ophthalmic; Sympathomimetic Agent, Ophthalmic
Use Prevention and treatment of postsurgical intraocular pressure (IOP) elevation; short-term, adjunctive therapy in patients who require additional reduction of IOP
Pregnancy Risk Factor C
Dosage Adults: Ophthalmic:
0.5%: Instill 1-2 drops in the affected eye(s) 3 times/day
1%: Instill 1 drop in operative eye 1 hour prior to anterior segment laser surgery, second drop in eye immediately upon completion of procedure
Dosing adjustment in renal impairment: Although the topical use of apraclonidine has not been studied in renal failure patients, structurally related clonidine undergoes a significant increase in half-life in patients with severe renal impairment; close monitoring of cardiovascular parameters in patients with impaired renal function is advised.
Dosing adjustment in hepatic impairment: Close monitoring of cardiovascular parameters in patients with impaired liver function is advised because the systemic dosage form of clonidine is partially metabolized in the liver
Dosage Forms SOLN, ophthalmic: 0.5% (5 mL, 10 mL); 1% (0.1 mL)

- **Apraclonidine Hydrochloride** *see* Apraclonidine *on page 110*

Aprepitant (ap RE pi tant)
U.S. Brand Names Emend®
Synonyms L 754030; MK 869
Therapeutic Category Antiemetic; Substance P/Neurokinin 1 Receptor Antagonist
Use Prevention of acute and delayed nausea and vomiting associated with highly-emetogenic chemotherapy in combination with a corticosteroid and 5-HT$_3$ receptor antagonist
Pregnancy Risk Factor B
Contraindications Hypersensitivity to aprepitant or any component of the formulation; use with astemizole, cisapride, pimozide, or terfenadine
Warnings/Precautions Aprepitant is a substrate, inhibitor, and inducer of CYP3A4 and an inducer of CYP2C9. Use caution with agents primarily metabolized via CYP3A4. Use caution with hepatic impairment. Not intended for treatment of nausea and vomiting or for chronic continuous therapy. Safety and efficacy in pediatric patients have not been established.
Common Adverse Reactions Percentages reported as part of combination therapy.
>10%:
Central nervous system: Fatigue (18%)
Gastrointestinal: Nausea (13%)
Neuromuscular & skeletal: Weakness (18%)
Miscellaneous: Hiccups (11%)
1% to 10%:
Central nervous system: Dizziness (7%)
Endocrine & metabolic: Dehydration (6%)
Gastrointestinal: Diarrhea (10%), abdominal pain (5%), epigastric discomfort (4%), gastritis (4%)
Hepatic: ALT increased (6%), AST increased (3%)
Renal: BUN increased (5%), proteinuria (7%)
Drug Interactions
Cytochrome P450 Effect: Substrate of CYP1A2 (minor), 2C19 (minor), 3A4 (major); **Inhibits** CYP2C8/9 (weak), 3A4 (weak); **Induces** CYP2C9 (weak), 3A4 (weak)
Increased Effect/Toxicity: Aprepitant may inhibit the metabolism and increase plasma levels of agents metabolized via CYP3A4. Use with astemizole, cisapride, pimozide, or terfenadine is contraindicated. CYP3A4 inhibitors may increase the levels/effects of aprepitant; example inhibitors include azole antifungals, ciprofloxacin, clarithromycin, diclofenac, doxycycline, erythromycin, imatinib, isoniazid, nefazodone, nicardipine, propofol, protease inhibitors, quinidine, and verapamil. Aprepitant may increase the bioavailability of corticosteroids; dose adjustment of dexamethasone and methylprednisolone is needed.
Decreased Effect: CYP3A4 inducers may decrease the levels/effects of aprepitant; example inducers include aminoglutethimide, carbamazepine, nafcillin, nevirapine, phenobarbital,

phenytoin, and rifamycins. Metabolism of warfarin may be induced; monitor INR following the start of each cycle. Efficacy of oral contraceptives may be decreased (plasma levels of ethinyl estradiol and norethindrone decreased with concomitant use). Plasma levels of both paroxetine and aprepitant are decreased with concomitant use.

Mechanism of Action Prevents acute and delayed vomiting by selectively inhibiting the substance P/neurokinin 1 (NK_1) receptor.

Pharmacodynamics/Kinetics

Distribution: V_d: 70 L; crosses the blood brain barrier

Protein binding: >95%

Metabolism: Extensively hepatic via CYP3A4 (major); CYP1A2 and CYP2C19 (minor); forms seven metabolites (weakly active)

Bioavailability: 60% to 65%

Half-life elimination: Terminal: 9-13 hours

Time to peak, plasma: 4 hours

Dosage Oral: Adults: 125 mg on day 1, followed by 80 mg on days 2 and 3; should be used in combination with a corticosteroid and 5-HT$_3$ receptor antagonist

In clinical trials, the following regimen was used:

Aprepitant: Oral: 125 mg day 1, followed by 80 mg on days 2 and 3

Dexamethasone: Oral: 12 mg on day 1, followed 8 mg on days 2, 3, and 4

Ondansetron: I.V.: 32 mg on day 1

Dosage adjustment in renal impairment: No dose adjustment necessary in patients with renal disease or end-stage renal disease maintained on hemodialysis.

Dosage adjustment in hepatic impairment:

Mild to moderate impairment (Child-Pugh score 5-9): No adjustment necessary

Severe impairment (Child-Pugh score >9): No data available

Administration May be administered with or without food. First dose should be given 1 hour prior to chemotherapy; subsequent doses should be given in the morning.

Patient Information May be taken with or without food. Common side effects include diarrhea, hiccups, loss of appetite, tiredness or weakness. This medicine may not mix well with other medicines; check medicines with prescriber.

Dosage Forms CAP: 80 mg, 125 mg; (combination package): 80 mg (2 capsules) and 125 mg (1 capsule)

◆ **Apresazide [DSC]** *see* Hydralazine and Hydrochlorothiazide *on page 625*

◆ **Apresoline [DSC]** *see* HydrALAZINE *on page 624*

◆ **Apri**® *see* Ethinyl Estradiol and Desogestrel *on page 477*

◆ **Aprodine**® **[OTC]** *see* Triprolidine and Pseudoephedrine *on page 1273*

Aprotinin (a proe TYE nin)

U.S. Brand Names Trasylol®

Therapeutic Category Blood Product Derivative; Hemostatic Agent

Use Reduction or prevention of blood loss in patients undergoing coronary artery bypass surgery when a high risk of excessive bleeding exists, including open heart reoperation, pre-existing coagulopathies, operations on the great vessels, and when a patient's beliefs prohibit blood transfusions

Pregnancy Risk Factor B

Contraindications Hypersensitivity to aprotinin or any component of the formulation

Warnings/Precautions Anaphylactic reactions are possible. Hypersensitivity reactions are more common with repeated use especially when re-exposure is within 6 months. All patients should receive a test dose at least 10 minutes before loading dose. Patients with a history of allergic reactions to drugs or other agents may be more likely to develop a reaction.

Common Adverse Reactions 1% to 10%: Atrial fibrillation, atrial flutter, bronchoconstriction, dyspnea, fever, heart failure, hypotension, increased potential for postoperative renal dysfunction, mental confusion, myocardial infarction, phlebitis, supraventricular tachycardia, ventricular tachycardia

Drug Interactions

Increased Effect/Toxicity: Heparin and aprotinin prolong ACT; the ACT becomes a poor measure of adequate anticoagulation with the concurrent use of these drugs. Use with succinylcholine or tubocurarine may produce prolonged or recurring apnea.

Decreased Effect: Aprotinin blocks the fibrinolytic activity of thrombolytic agents (alteplase, streptokinase). The antihypertensive effects of captopril (and other ACE inhibitors) may be blocked; avoid concurrent use.

Mechanism of Action Serine protease inhibitor; inhibits plasmin, kallikrein, and platelet activation producing antifibrinolytic effects; a weak inhibitor of plasma pseudocholinesterase. It also inhibits the contact phase activation of coagulation and preserves adhesive platelet glycoproteins making them resistant to damage from increased circulating plasmin or mechanical injury occurring during bypass

Pharmacodynamics/Kinetics

Half-life elimination: 2.5 hours

Excretion: Urine

Dosage

Test dose: **All** patients should receive a 1 mL I.V. test dose at least 10 minutes prior to the loading dose to assess the potential for allergic reactions. **Note:** To avoid physical incompatibility with heparin when adding to pump-prime solution, each agent should be added during recirculation to assure adequate dilution.

(Continued)

Aprotinin *(Continued)*

Regimen A (standard dose):
2 million units (280 mg) loading dose I.V. over 20-30 minutes
2 million units (280 mg) into pump prime volume
500,000 units/hour (70 mg/hour) I.V. during operation
Regimen B (low dose):
1 million units (140 mg) loading dose I.V. over 20-30 minutes
1 million units (140 mg) into pump prime volume
250,000 units/hour (35 mg/hour) I.V. during operation

Administration All intravenous doses should be administered through a central line

Monitoring Parameters Bleeding times, prothrombin time, activated clotting time, platelet count, red blood cell counts, hematocrit, hemoglobin and fibrinogen degradation products; for toxicity also include renal function tests and blood pressure

Reference Range Antiplasmin effects occur when plasma aprotinin concentrations are 125 KIU/mL and antikallikrein effects occur when plasma levels are 250-500 KIU/mL; it remains unknown if these plasma concentrations are required for clinical benefits to occur during cardiopulmonary bypass; **Note:** KIU = Kallikrein inhibitor unit

Dosage Forms INJ, solution: 1.4 mg/mL [10,000 KIU/mL] (100 mL, 200 mL)

◆ **Aquacare®** [OTC] *see* Urea *on page 1282*
◆ **Aquachloral® Supprettes®** *see* Chloral Hydrate *on page 254*
◆ **Aqua Gem E®** [OTC] *see* Vitamin E *on page 1311*
◆ **AquaMEPHYTON®** [DSC] *see* Phytonadione *on page 1000*
◆ **Aquanil™ HC** [OTC] *see* Hydrocortisone *on page 632*
◆ **Aquaphilic® With Carbamide** [OTC] *see* Urea *on page 1282*
◆ **Aquasol A®** *see* Vitamin A *on page 1309*
◆ **Aquasol E®** [OTC] *see* Vitamin E *on page 1311*
◆ **Aquatab®** *see* Guaifenesin and Pseudoephedrine *on page 605*
◆ **Aquatab® C** *see* Guaifenesin, Pseudoephedrine, and Dextromethorphan *on page 606*
◆ **Aquatab® D Dose Pack** *see* Guaifenesin and Pseudoephedrine *on page 605*
◆ **Aquatab® DM** *see* Guaifenesin and Dextromethorphan *on page 604*
◆ **Aquatensen®** *see* Methyclothiazide *on page 820*
◆ **Aquazide® H** *see* Hydrochlorothiazide *on page 625*
◆ **Aqueous Procaine Penicillin G** *see* Penicillin G Procaine *on page 974*
◆ **Ara-A** *see* Vidarabine *on page 1304*
◆ **Arabinofuranosyladenine** *see* Vidarabine *on page 1304*
◆ **Arabinosylcytosine** *see* Cytarabine *on page 329*
◆ **Ara-C** *see* Cytarabine *on page 329*
◆ **Aralen®** *see* Chloroquine *on page 260*
◆ **Aramine®** [DSC] *see* Metaraminol *on page 805*
◆ **Aranesp™** *see* Darbepoetin Alfa *on page 343*
◆ **Arava®** *see* Leflunomide *on page 719*
◆ **Aredia®** *see* Pamidronate *on page 952*

Argatroban *(ar GA troh ban)*

Therapeutic Category Anticoagulant, Thrombin Inhibitor

Use Prophylaxis or treatment of thrombosis in adults with heparin-induced thrombocytopenia; adjunct to percutaneous coronary intervention (PCI) in patients who have or are at risk of thrombosis associated with heparin-induced thrombocytopenia

Pregnancy Risk Factor B

Contraindications Hypersensitivity to argatroban or any component of the formulation; overt major bleeding

Warnings/Precautions Hemorrhage can occur at any site in the body. Extreme caution should be used when there is an increased danger of hemorrhage, such as severe hypertension, immediately following lumbar puncture, spinal anesthesia, major surgery (including brain, spinal cord, or eye surgery), congenital or acquired bleeding disorders, and gastrointestinal ulcers. Use caution with hepatic dysfunction. Concomitant use with warfarin will cause increased prolongation of the PT and INR greater than that of warfarin alone; alternative guidelines for monitoring therapy should be followed. Safety and efficacy for use with other thrombolytic agents has not been established. Discontinue all parenteral anticoagulants prior to starting therapy. Allow reversal of heparin's effects before initiation. Patients with hepatic dysfunction may require >4 hours to achieve full reversal of argatroban's anticoagulant effect following treatment. Avoid use during PCI in patients with elevations of ALT/AST (>3 times ULN); the use of argatroban in these patients has not been evaluated. For adult use; safety and efficacy in children <18 years of age have not been established.

Common Adverse Reactions As with all anticoagulants, bleeding is the major adverse effect of argatroban. Hemorrhage may occur at virtually any site. Risk is dependent on multiple variables, including the intensity of anticoagulation and patient susceptibility.

>10%:
Gastrointestinal: Gastrointestinal bleed (minor, 14%; <1% in PCI)
Genitourinary: Genitourinary bleed and hematuria (minor, 12%)

1% to 10%:
    Cardiovascular: Hypotension (7%), cardiac arrest (6%), ventricular tachycardia (5%), atrial fibrillation (3%), cerebrovascular disorder (2%)
    Central nervous system: Fever (7%), pain (5%), intracranial bleeding (1%, only observed in patients also receiving streptokinase or tissue plasminogen activator)
    Gastrointestinal: Diarrhea (6%), nausea (5%), vomiting (4%), abdominal pain (3%), bleeding (major, 2%)
    Genitourinary: Urinary tract infection (5%)
    Hematologic: Decreased hemoglobin <2 g/dL and hematocrit (minor, 10%)
    Local: Bleeding at the injection site (minor, 2% to 5%)
    Renal: Abnormal renal function (3%)
    Respiratory: Dyspnea (8% to 10%), coughing (3% to 10%), hemoptysis (minor, 3%), pneumonia (3%)
    Miscellaneous: Sepsis (6%), infection (4%)

Drug Interactions

Cytochrome P450 Effect: Substrate of CYP3A4 (minor)

Increased Effect/Toxicity: Drugs which affect platelet function (eg, aspirin, NSAIDs, dipyridamole, ticlopidine, clopidogrel), anticoagulants, or thrombolytics may potentiate the risk of hemorrhage. Sufficient time must pass after heparin therapy is discontinued; allow heparin's effect on the aPTT to decrease

Concomitant use of argatroban with warfarin increases PT and INR greater than that of warfarin alone. Argatroban is commonly continued during the initiation of warfarin therapy to assure anticoagulation and to protect against possible transient hypercoagulability.

Mechanism of Action A direct, highly selective thrombin inhibitor. Reversibly binds to the active thrombin site of free and clot-associated thrombin. Inhibits fibrin formation; activation of coagulation factors V, VIII, and XIII; protein C; and platelet aggregation.

Pharmacodynamics/Kinetics

Onset of action: Immediate
Distribution: 174 mL/kg
Protein binding: Albumin: 20%; α_1-acid glycoprotein: 35%
Metabolism: Hepatic via hydroxylation and aromatization. Metabolism via CYP3A4/5 to four known metabolites plays a minor role. Unchanged argatroban is the major plasma component. Plasma concentration of metabolite M1 is 0% to 20% of the parent drug and is three-to fivefold weaker.
Half-life elimination: 39-51 minutes; Hepatic impairment: ≤181 minutes
Time to peak: Steady-state: 1-3 hours
Excretion: Feces (65%); urine (22%); low quantities of metabolites M2-4 in urine

Dosage I.V.: Adults:

Heparin-induced thrombocytopenia:

Initial dose: 2 mcg/kg/minute
Maintenance dose: Measure aPTT after 2 hours, adjust dose until the steady-state aPTT is 1.5-3.0 times the initial baseline value, not exceeding 100 seconds; dosage should not exceed 10 mcg/kg/minute
Conversion to oral anticoagulant: Because there may be a combined effect on the INR when argatroban is combined with warfarin, loading doses of warfarin should not be used. Warfarin therapy should be started at the expected daily dose.
Patients receiving ≤2 mcg/kg/minute of argatroban: Argatroban therapy can be stopped when the combined INR on warfarin and argatroban is >4; repeat INR measurement in 4-6 hours; if INR is below therapeutic level, argatroban therapy may be restarted. Repeat procedure daily until desired INR on warfarin alone is obtained.
Patients receiving >2 mcg/kg/minute of argatroban: Reduce dose of argatroban to 2 mcg/kg/minute; measure INR for argatroban and warfarin 4-6 hours after dose reduction; argatroban therapy can be stopped when the combined INR on warfarin and argatroban is >4. Repeat INR measurement in 4-6 hours; if INR is below therapeutic level, argatroban therapy may be restarted. Repeat procedure daily until desired INR on warfarin alone is obtained.

Percutaneous coronary intervention (PCI):

Initial: Begin infusion of 25 mcg/kg/minute and administer bolus dose of 350 mcg/kg (over 3-5 minutes). ACT should be checked 5-10 minutes after bolus infusion; proceed with procedure if ACT >300 seconds. Following initial bolus:
    ACT <300 seconds: Give an additional 150 mcg/kg bolus, and increase infusion rate to 30 mcg/kg/minute (recheck ACT in 5-10 minutes)
    ACT >450 seconds: Decrease infusion rate to 15 mcg/kg/minute (recheck ACT in 5-10 minutes)
    Once a therapeutic ACT (300-450 seconds) is achieved, infusion should be continued at this dose for the duration of the procedure.
Impending abrupt closure, thrombus formation during PCI, or inability to achieve ACT >300 sec: An additional bolus of 150 mcg/kg, followed by an increase in infusion rate to 40 mcg/kg/minute may be administered.

Dosage adjustment in renal impairment: No adjustment is necessary
Dosage adjustment in hepatic impairment: Decreased clearance and increased elimination half-life are seen with hepatic impairment; dose should be reduced. Initial dose for moderate hepatic impairment is 0.5 mcg/kg/minute. **Note:** During PCI, avoid use in patients with elevations of ALT/AST (>3 times ULN); the use of argatroban in these patients has not been evaluated.

Elderly: No adjustment is necessary for patients with normal liver function

Administration Solution **must be diluted to 1 mg/mL** prior to administration.
(Continued)

Argatroban *(Continued)*

Monitoring Parameters Obtain baseline aPTT prior to start of therapy. Check aPTT 2 hours after start of therapy to adjust dose, keeping the steady-state aPTT 1.5-3 times the initial baseline value (not exceeding 100 seconds). Monitor hemoglobin, hematocrit, signs and symptoms of bleeding.

Patient Information This drug can only be administered by injection. You may have a tendency to bleed easily while taking this drug; brush teeth with soft brush, floss with waxed floss, use electric razor, avoid scissors or sharp knives, and potentially harmful activities. Report fever, confusion, persistent nausea or GI upset, unusual bleeding (including bleeding gums, nosebleed, blood in urine, dark stool), bruising, pain in joints or back, swelling or pain at injection site.

Dosage Forms INJ, solution: 100 mg/mL (2.5 mL)

Arginine *(AR ji neen)*

U.S. Brand Names R-Gene®

Synonyms Arginine Hydrochloride

Therapeutic Category Diagnostic Agent, Pituitary Function; Metabolic Alkalosis Agent

Use Pituitary function test (growth hormone)

Unlabeled/Investigational Use Management of severe, uncompensated, metabolic alkalosis (pH ≥7.55) **after** optimizing therapy with sodium and potassium supplements

Pregnancy Risk Factor B

Dosage I.V.: Pituitary function test:
Children: 500 mg kg/dose administered over 30 minutes
Adults: 30 g (300 mL) administered over 30 minutes

Dosage Forms INJ, solution: 10% [100 mg/mL = 950 mOsm/L] (300 mL)

♦ **Arginine Hydrochloride** *see Arginine on page 114*

♦ **8-Arginine Vasopressin** *see Vasopressin on page 1298*

♦ **Aricept®** *see Donepezil on page 401*

♦ **Arimidex®** *see Anastrozole on page 100*

Aripiprazole *(ay ri PIP ray zole)*

Related Information
Antipsychotic Agents Comparison *on page 1364*

U.S. Brand Names Abilify™

Synonyms BMS 337039; OPC-14597

Therapeutic Category Antipsychotic Agent, Dopamine Stabilizer; Antipsychotic Agent, Quinolinone; Antipsychotic Agent, Atypical

Use Treatment of schizophrenia

Unlabeled/Investigational Use Psychosis, bipolar disorder

Pregnancy Risk Factor C

Contraindications Hypersensitivity to aripiprazole or any component of the formulation

Warnings/Precautions May be sedating, use with caution in disorders where CNS depression is a feature. May cause orthostatic hypotension (although reported rates are similar to placebo); use caution in patients at risk of this effect or those who would not tolerate transient hypotensive episodes (cerebrovascular disease, cardiovascular disease, or other medications which may predispose).

Use caution in patients with Parkinson's disease; hemodynamic instability; bone marrow suppression; predisposition to seizures; subcortical brain damage; severe cardiac, hepatic, renal, or respiratory disease. Esophageal dysmotility and aspiration have been associated with antipsychotic use; use caution in patients at risk of pneumonia (ie, Alzheimer's disease). May alter temperature regulation or mask toxicity of other drugs due to antiemetic effects. Use caution in patients with a history of drug abuse.

Other atypical antipsychotics have been associated with development of hyperglycemia (not documented with aripiprazole); use caution in patients with diabetes or other disorders of glucose regulation.

May cause extrapyramidal symptoms, including pseudoparkinsonism, acute dystonic reactions, akathisia, and tardive dyskinesia (risk of these reactions is very low relative to typical/conventional antipsychotics, frequencies reported are similar to placebo). May be associated with neuroleptic malignant syndrome (NMS).

Common Adverse Reactions
>10%:
Central nervous system: Headache (32%), anxiety (25%), insomnia (24%), lightheadedness (11%), somnolence (11%)
Endocrine & metabolic: Weight gain (8% to 30%; highest frequency in patients with BMI <23)
Gastrointestinal: Nausea (14%), vomiting (12%)
1% to 10%:
Cardiovascular: Edema (peripheral, 1%), chest pain (1%), hypertension (1%), tachycardia (1%), hypotension (1%), bradycardia (1%)
Central nervous system: Akathisia (10%), extrapyramidal symptoms (6%; similar to placebo), fever (2%), depression (1%), nervousness (1%), mania (1%), confusion (1%)
Dermatologic: Rash (6%), ecchymosis (1%), pruritus (1%)
Endocrine & metabolic: Hypothyroidism (1%), weight loss (1%)

Gastrointestinal: Constipation (10%), anorexia (1%)

Genitourinary: Urinary incontinence (1%)

Hematologic: Anemia (1%)

Neuromuscular & skeletal: Weakness (7%), tremor (3%), neck pain (1%), neck rigidity (1%), muscle cramp (1%), cogwheel rigidity (1%), CPK increased (1%)

Ocular: Blurred vision (3%), conjunctivitis (1%)

Respiratory: Rhinitis (4%), cough (3%), dyspnea (1%), pneumonia (1%)

Miscellaneous: Flu-like syndrome (1%)

Drug Interactions

Cytochrome P450 Effect: Substrate (major) of CYP2D6, 3A4

Increased Effect/Toxicity:

CYP2D6 inhibitors may increase the levels/effects of aripiprazole; example inhibitors include chlorpromazine, delavirdine, fluoxetine, miconazole, paroxetine, pergolide, quinidine, quinine, ritonavir, and ropinirole.

Inhibitors of CYP3A4 may increase serum concentrations of aripiprazole (metabolite concentrations are decreased). Manufacturer recommends a 50% reduction in dose during concurrent ketoconazole therapy. Similar reductions in dose may be required with other potent inhibitors. Inhibitors include amiodarone, cimetidine, clarithromycin, erythromycin, delavirdine, diltiazem, dirithromycin, disulfiram, fluoxetine, fluvoxamine, grapefruit juice, indinavir, itraconazole, ketoconazole, nefazodone, nevirapine, propoxyphene, quinupristin-dalfopristin, ritonavir, saquinavir, verapamil, zafirlukast, zileuton.

Decreased Effect: CYP3A4 inducers may decrease serum concentrations of aripiprazole (and metabolite). Manufacturer recommends a doubling of the aripiprazole dose when carbamazepine is added. Similar increases may be required with other inducers. Inducers include phenobarbital, phenytoin, rifampin and rifabutin. Withdrawal of an inducing agent may require a decrease in aripiprazole dose.

Mechanism of Action Aripiprazole exhibits high affinity for D_2, D_3, $5-HT_{1A}$, and $5-HT_{2A}$ receptors; moderate affinity for D_4, $5-HT_{2C}$, $5-HT_7$, alpha, and H_1 receptors. It also possesses moderate affinity for the serotonin reuptake transporter; has no affinity for muscarinic receptors. Aripiprazole functions as a partial agonist at the D_2 and $5-HT_{1A}$ receptors, and as an antagonist at the $5-HT_{2A}$ receptor.

Pharmacodynamics/Kinetics

Onset: Initial: 1-3 weeks

Absorption: Well absorbed

Distribution: V_d: 4.9 L/kg

Protein binding: 99%, primarily to albumin

Metabolism: Hepatic, via CYP2D6, CYP3A4 (dehydro-aripiprazole metabolite has affinity for D2 receptors similar to the parent drug and represents 40% of the parent drug exposure in plasma)

Bioavailability: 87%

Half-life: Aripiprazole: 75 hours; dehydro-aripiprazole: 94 hours

Time to peak, plasma: 3-5 hours

Excretion: Feces (55%), urine (25%); primarily as metabolites

Dosage Oral:

Adults: 10-15 mg once daily; may be increased to a maximum of 30 mg once daily (efficacy at dosages above 10-15 mg has not been shown to be increased). Dosage titration should not be more frequent than every 2 weeks.

Elderly: Refer to Adults dosing

Dosage adjustment in renal/hepatic impairment: No dosage adjustment required

Administration May be administered with or without food.

Monitoring Parameters Vital signs, lipid profile, fasting blood glucose/Hgb A_{1c}; BMI; mental status, abnormal involuntary movement scale (AIMS), extrapyramidal symptoms (EPS)

Dosage Forms TAB: 5 mg, 10 mg, 15 mg, 20 mg, 30 mg

♦ **Aristocort®** *see* Triamcinolone *on page 1261*

♦ **Aristocort® A** *see* Triamcinolone *on page 1261*

♦ **Aristocort® Forte** *see* Triamcinolone *on page 1261*

♦ **Aristospan®** *see* Triamcinolone *on page 1261*

♦ **Arixtra®** *see* Fondaparinux *on page 560*

♦ **A.R.M® [OTC]** *see* Chlorpheniramine and Pseudoephedrine *on page 263*

♦ **Armour® Thyroid** *see* Thyroid *on page 1222*

♦ **Aromasin®** *see* Exemestane *on page 500*

Arsenic Trioxide (AR se nik tri OKS id)

U.S. Brand Names Trisenox™

Synonyms NSC-706363

Therapeutic Category Antineoplastic Agent, Miscellaneous

Use Induction of remission and consolidation in patients with acute promyelocytic leukemia (APL) which is specifically characterized by t(15;17) translocation or PML/RAR-alpha gene expression. Should be used only in those patients who have relapsed or are refractory to retinoid and anthracycline chemotherapy.

Orphan drug: Treatment of myelodysplastic syndrome; multiple myeloma; chronic myeloid leukemia (CML); acute myelocytic leukemia (AML)

Pregnancy Risk Factor D

Contraindications Hypersensitivity to arsenic or any component of the formulation; pregnancy

(Continued)

Arsenic Trioxide *(Continued)*

Warnings/Precautions The U.S. Food and Drug Administration (FDA) currently recommends that procedures for proper handling and disposal of antineoplastic agents be considered. For use only by physicians experienced with the treatment of acute leukemia. A baseline 12-lead ECG, serum electrolytes (potassium, calcium, magnesium), and creatinine should be obtained. Correct electrolyte abnormalities prior to treatment and monitor potassium and magnesium levels during therapy (potassium should stay >4 mEq/dL and magnesium >1.8 mg/dL). Correct QT_c >500 msec prior to treatment. Discontinue therapy and hospitalize patient if QT_c >500 msec, syncope or irregular heartbeats develop during therapy. May prolong the QT interval. May lead to torsade de pointes or complete AV block. Risk factors for torsade de pointes include CHF, a history of torsade de pointes, pre-existing QT interval prolongation, patients taking potassium-wasting diuretics, and conditions which cause hypokalemia or hypomagnesemia. If possible, discontinue all medications known to prolong the QT interval. May cause retinoic-acid-acute promyelocytic leukemia (RA-APL) syndrome or APL differentiation syndrome. High-dose steroids have been used for treatment. May lead to the development of hyperleukocytosis. Use with caution in renal impairment. Safety and efficacy in children <5 years of age have not been established (limited experience with children 5-16 years of age).

Common Adverse Reactions

>10%:

Cardiovascular: Tachycardia (55%), edema (40%), QT interval >500 msec (38%), chest pain (25%), hypotension (25%)

Central nervous system: Fatigue (63%), fever (63%), headache (60%), insomnia (43%), anxiety (30%), dizziness (23%), depression (20%), pain (15%)

Dermatologic: Dermatitis (43%), pruritus (33%), bruising (20%), dry skin (13%)

Endocrine & metabolic: Hypokalemia (50%), hyperglycemia (45%), hypomagnesemia (45%), hyperkalemia (18%)

Gastrointestinal: Nausea (75%), abdominal pain (58%), vomiting (58%), diarrhea (53%), sore throat (40%), constipation (28%), anorexia (23%), decreased appetite (15%), weight gain (13%)

Genitourinary: Vaginal hemorrhage (13%)

Hematologic: Leukocytosis (50%), APL differentiation syndrome (23%), thrombocytopenia (19%), anemia (14%), febrile neutropenia (13%)

Hepatic: Elevated ALT (20%), elevated AST (13%)

Local: Injection site: Pain (20%), erythema (13%)

Neuromuscular & skeletal: Rigors (38%), arthralgia (33%), paresthesia (33%), myalgia (25%), bone pain (23%), back pain (18%), limb pain (13%), neck pain (13%), tremor (13%)

Respiratory: Cough (65%), dyspnea (53%), epistaxis (25%), hypoxia (23%), pleural effusion (20%), sinusitis (20%), postnasal drip (13%), upper respiratory tract infection (13%), wheezing (13%)

Miscellaneous: Herpes simplex (13%)

1% to 10%:

Cardiovascular: Hypotension (10%), flushing (10%), pallor (10%), palpitations (10%), facial edema (8%), abnormal ECG (not QT prolongation) (7%)

Central nervous system: Convulsion (8%), somnolence (8%), agitation (5%), coma (5%), confusion (5%)

Dermatologic: Erythema (10%), hyperpigmentation (8%), petechia (8%), skin lesions (8%), urticaria (8%), local exfoliation (5%)

Endocrine & metabolic: Hypocalcemia (10%), hypoglycemia (8%), acidosis (5%)

Gastrointestinal: Dyspepsia (10%), loose stools (10%), abdominal distension (8%), abdominal tenderness (8%), dry mouth (8%), fecal incontinence (8%), gastrointestinal hemorrhage (8%), hemorrhagic diarrhea (8%), oral blistering (8%), weight loss (8%), oral candidiasis (5%)

Genitourinary: Intermenstrual bleeding (8%), incontinence (5%)

Hematologic: Neutropenia (10%), DIC (8%), hemorrhage (8%), lymphadenopathy (8%)

Neuromuscular & skeletal: Weakness (5%)

Ocular: Blurred vision (10%), eye irritation (10%), dry eye (8%), eyelid edema (5%), painful eye (5%)

Otic: Earache (8%), tinnitus (5%)

Renal: Renal failure (8%), renal impairment (8%), oliguria (5%)

Respiratory: Crepitations (10%), decreased breath sounds (10%), rales (10%), hemoptysis (8%), rhonchi (8%), tachypnea (8%), nasopharyngitis (5%)

Miscellaneous: Increased diaphoresis (10%), injection site edema (10%), bacterial infection (8%), herpes zoster (8%), night sweats (8%), hypersensitivity (5%), sepsis (5%)

Drug Interactions

Increased Effect/Toxicity: Use caution with medications causing hypokalemia or hypomagnesemia (ampho B, aminoglycosides, diuretics, cyclosporin). Use caution with medications that prolong the QT interval, avoid concurrent use if possible: includes type Ia and type III antiarrhythmic agents, selected quinolones (sparfloxacin, gatifloxacin, moxifloxacin, grepafloxacin), cisapride, thioridazine, and other agents.

Mechanism of Action Not fully understood; causes *in vitro* morphological changes and DNA fragmentation to NB4 human promyelocytic leukemia cells; also damages or degrades the fusion protein PML-RAR alpha

Pharmacodynamics/Kinetics

Metabolism: Hepatic; pentavalent arsenic is reduced to trivalent arsenic (active) by arsenate reductase; trivalent arsenic is methylated to monomethylarsinic acid, which is then converted to dimethylarsinic acid via methyltransferases

Excretion: Urine (as methylated metabolite); disposition not yet studied

Dosage I.V.: Children >5 years and Adults:

Induction: 0.15 mg/kg/day; administer daily until bone marrow remission; maximum induction: 60 doses

Consolidation: 0.15 mg/kg/day starting 3-6 weeks after completion of induction therapy; maximum consolidation: 25 doses over 5 weeks

Dosage adjustment in renal impairment: Safety and efficacy have not been established; use with caution due to renal elimination

Dosage adjustment in hepatic impairment: Safety and efficacy have not been established

Elderly: Safety and efficacy have not been established; clinical trials included patients ≤72 years of age; use with caution due to the increased risk of renal impairment in the elderly

Administration Dilute in 100-250 mL D_5W or 0.9% sodium chloride. Does not contain a preservative; properly discard unused portion. Do not mix with other medications. Infuse over 1-2 hours. If acute vasomotor reactions occur, may infuse over a maximum of 4 hours. Does not require administration via a central venous catheter.

Monitoring Parameters Baseline then weekly 12-lead ECG, baseline then twice weekly serum electrolytes, hematologic and coagulation profiles at least twice weekly; more frequent monitoring may be necessary in unstable patients

Patient Information Check other medications with prescriber. Some medications may not mix well. Avoid homeopathic, herbal, or over-the-counter medications during treatment without approval of prescriber. You may not be alert. Avoid driving, doing other tasks or hobbies until until response to drug is known. May cause fatigue, fever, nausea, vomiting, diarrhea, cough, or headache. Contact prescriber immediately for unexplained fever, shortness of breath, lightheadedness, passing out, rapid heartbeats, or weight gain. ECG and blood tests will be performed regularly during treatment.

Dosage Forms INJ, solution: [preservative free] 1 mg/mL (10 mL)

♦ **Artane** *see* Trihexyphenidyl *on page 1268*
♦ **Arthropan® [OTC] [DSC]** *see* Choline Salicylate *on page 271*
♦ **Arthrotec®** *see* Diclofenac and Misoprostol *on page 368*
♦ **ASA** *see* Aspirin *on page 120*
♦ **5-ASA** *see* Mesalamine *on page 798*
♦ **Asacol®** *see* Mesalamine *on page 798*

Ascorbic Acid (a SKOR bik AS id)

U.S. Brand Names C-500-GR™ [OTC]; Cecon® [OTC]; Cevi-Bid® [OTC]; C-Gram [OTC]; Dull-C® [OTC]; Vita-C® [OTC]

Synonyms Vitamin C

Therapeutic Category Urinary Acidifying Agent; Vitamin, Water Soluble

Use Prevention and treatment of scurvy and to acidify the urine

Unlabeled/Investigational Use Investigational: In large doses to decrease the severity of "colds"; dietary supplementation; a 20-year study was recently completed involving 730 individuals which indicates a possible decreased risk of death by stroke when ascorbic acid at doses ≥45 mg/day was administered

Pregnancy Risk Factor A/C (dose exceeding RDA recommendation)

Warnings/Precautions Diabetics and patients prone to recurrent renal calculi (eg, dialysis patients) should not take excessive doses for extended periods of time (some studies point to as little as 100 mg/day)

Common Adverse Reactions

1% to 10%: Renal: Hyperoxaluria with large doses

Drug Interactions

Increased Effect/Toxicity: Ascorbic acid enhances iron absorption from the GI tract. Concomitant ascorbic acid taken with oral contraceptives may increase contraceptive effect.

Decreased Effect: Ascorbic acid and fluphenazine may decrease fluphenazine levels. Ascorbic acid and warfarin may decrease anticoagulant effect. Changes in dose of ascorbic acid when taken with oral contraceptives may reduce the contraceptive effect.

Mechanism of Action Not fully understood; necessary for collagen formation and tissue repair; involved in some oxidation-reduction reactions as well as other metabolic pathways, such as synthesis of carnitine, steroids, and catecholamines and conversion of folic acid to folinic acid

Pharmacodynamics/Kinetics

Absorption: Oral: Readily absorbed; an active process thought to be dose dependent

Distribution: Large

Metabolism: Hepatic via oxidation and sulfation

Excretion: Urine (with high blood levels)

Dosage Oral, I.M., I.V., S.C.:

Recommended daily allowance (RDA):

<6 months: 30 mg

6 months to 1 year: 35 mg

1-3 years: 15 mg; upper limit of intake should not exceed 400 mg/day

4-8 years: 25 mg; upper limit of intake should not exceed 650 mg/day

9-13 years: 45 mg; upper limit of intake should not exceed 1200 mg/day

14-18 years: Upper limit of intake should not exceed 1800 mg/day

Male: 75 mg

Female: 65 mg

Adults: Upper limit of intake should not exceed 2000 mg/day

(Continued)

Ascorbic Acid *(Continued)*

Male: 90 mg
Female: 75 mg;
Pregnant female:
≤18 years: 80 mg; upper limit of intake should not exceed 1800 mg/day
19-50 years: 85 mg; upper limit of intake should not exceed 2000 mg/day
Lactating female:
≤18 years: 15 mg; upper limit of intake should not exceed 1800 mg/day
19-50 years: 20 mg; upper limit of intake should not exceed 2000 mg/day
Adult smoker: Add an additional 35 mg/day
Children:
Scurvy: 100-300 mg/day in divided doses for at least 2 weeks
Urinary acidification: 500 mg every 6-8 hours
Dietary supplement: 35-100 mg/day
Adults:
Scurvy: 100-250 mg 1-2 times/day for at least 2 weeks
Urinary acidification: 4-12 g/day in 3-4 divided doses
Prevention and treatment of colds: 1-3 g/day
Dietary supplement: 50-200 mg/day
Administration Avoid rapid I.V. injection
Monitoring Parameters Monitor pH of urine when using as an acidifying agent
Dosage Forms CAP: 500 mg, 1000 mg. **CAP, timed release:** 500 mg. **CRYST:** 4 g/teaspoonful (100 g). **INJ, solution:** 250 mg/mL (2 mL, 30 mL); 500 mg/mL (50 mL); (Cenolate®): 500 mg/mL (1 mL, 2 mL). **POWDER, solution:** 4 g/teaspoonful (100 g, 500 g). **SOLN, oral:** 90 mg/mL (50 mL). **TAB:** 100 mg, 250 mg, 500 mg, 1000 mg. **TAB, chewable:** 100 mg, 250 mg, 500 mg. **TAB, timed release:** 500 mg, 1000 mg, 1500 mg

- ◆ **Ascorbic Acid and Ferrous Sulfate** *see Ferrous Sulfate and Ascorbic Acid on page 521*
- ◆ **Ascriptin® [OTC]** *see Aspirin on page 120*
- ◆ **Ascriptin® Arthritis Pain [OTC]** *see Aspirin on page 120*
- ◆ **Ascriptin® Enteric [OTC]** *see Aspirin on page 120*
- ◆ **Ascriptin® Extra Strength [OTC]** *see Aspirin on page 120*
- ◆ **Asendin [DSC]** *see Amoxapine on page 84*

Asparaginase *(a SPEAR a ji nase)*

U.S. Brand Names Elspar®
Synonyms *E. coli* Asparaginase; *Erwinia* Asparaginase; L-asparaginase; NSC-106977 (*Erwinia*); NSC-109229 (*E. coli*)
Therapeutic Category Antineoplastic Agent, Protein Synthesis Inhibitor
Use Treatment of acute lymphocytic leukemia, lymphoma
Pregnancy Risk Factor C
Contraindications Hypersensitivity to asparaginase or any component of the formulation; history of anaphylaxis to asparaginase; if a reaction occurs to Elspar®, obtain **Erwinia L-asparaginase** and use with caution; pancreatitis (active or any history of)
Warnings/Precautions The U.S. Food and Drug Administration (FDA) currently recommends that procedures for proper handling and disposal of antineoplastic agents be considered. Monitor for severe allergic reactions. May alter hepatic function. Use cautiously in patients with an underlying coagulopathy.

Risk factors for allergic reactions:
Route of administration: I.V. administration is more likely to cause a reaction than I.M. or S.C.
Prolonged therapy dose: Doses >6000-12,000 units/m^2 increase the risk of a reaction.
Previous therapy: Patients who have received previous cycles of asparaginase have an increased risk.
Intermittent therapy: Intervals of even a few days between doses increase the risk.

Up to 33% of patients who have an allergic reaction to *E. coli* asparaginase will also react to the *Erwinia* form or pegaspargase.

A test dose is often recommended prior to the first dose of asparaginase, or prior to restarting therapy after a hiatus of several days. Most commonly, 0.1-0.2 mL of a 20-250 units/mL (2-50 units) is injected intradermally, and the patient observed for 15-30 minutes. **False-negative rates of up to 80% to test doses of 2-50 units are reported.** Desensitization may be performed in patients found to be hypersensitive by the intradermal test dose or who have received previous courses of therapy with the drug.
Common Adverse Reactions Note: Immediate effects: Fever, chills, nausea, and vomiting occur in 50% to 60% of patients.

>10%:
Central nervous system: Fatigue, somnolence, depression, hallucinations, agitation, disorientation or convulsions (10% to 60%), stupor, confusion, coma (25%)
Endocrine & metabolic: Fever, chills (50% to 60%), hyperglycemia (10%)
Gastrointestinal: Nausea, vomiting (50% to 60%), anorexia, abdominal cramps (70%), acute pancreatitis (15%, may be severe in some patients)
Hematologic: Hypofibrinogenemia and depression of clotting factors V and VIII, variable decreased in factors VII and IX, severe protein C deficiency and decrease in antithrombin III (may be dose-limiting or fatal)
Hepatic: Transient elevations of transaminases, bilirubin, and alkaline phosphatase

Hypersensitivity: Acute allergic reactions (fever, rash, urticaria, arthralgia, hypotension, angioedema, bronchospasm, anaphylaxis (15% to 35%); may be dose-limiting in some patients, may be fatal)
Renal: Azotemia (66%)
1% to 10%:
Endocrine & metabolic: Hyperuricemia
Gastrointestinal: Stomatitis

Drug Interactions
Increased Effect/Toxicity: Increased toxicity has been noticed when asparaginase is administered with vincristine (neuropathy) and prednisone (hyperglycemia). Decreased metabolism when used with cyclophosphamide. Increased hepatotoxicity when used with mercaptopurine.
Decreased Effect: Asparaginase terminates methotrexate action.

Mechanism of Action Asparaginase inhibits protein synthesis by hydrolyzing asparagine to aspartic acid and ammonia. Leukemia cells, specially lymphoblasts, require exogenous asparagine; normal cells can synthesize asparagine. Asparaginase is cycle-specific for the G_1 phase.

Pharmacodynamics/Kinetics
Absorption: I.M.: Produces peak blood levels 50% lower than those from I.V. administration
Distribution: V_d: 4-5 L/kg; 70% to 80% of plasma volume; does not penetrate CSF
Metabolism: Systemically degraded
Half-life elimination: 8-30 hours
Excretion: Urine (trace amounts)
Clearance: Unaffected by age, renal or hepatic function

Dosage Refer to individual protocols.
Children:
I.V.:
Infusion for induction: 1000 units/kg/day for 10 days
Consolidation: 6000-10,000 units/m²/day for 14 days
I.M.: 6000 units/m² on days 4, 7, 10, 13, 16, 19, 22, 25, 28
Adults:
I.V. infusion single agent for induction:
200 units/kg/day for 28 days **or**
5000-10,000 units/m²/day for 7 days every 3 weeks **or**
10,000-40,000 units every 2-3 weeks
I.M. as single agent: 6000-12,000 units/m²; reconstitution to 10,000 units/mL may be necessary

Some institutions recommended the following precautions for asparaginase administration: Have parenteral epinephrine, diphenhydramine, and hydrocortisone available at the bedside. Have a freely running I.V. in place. Have a physician readily accessible. Monitor the patient closely for 30-60 minutes. Avoid administering the drug at night.

Some practitioners recommend a desensitization regimen for patients who react to a test dose, or are being retreated following a break in therapy. Doses are doubled and given every 10 minutes until the total daily dose for that day has been administered. See table.

Asparaginase Desensitization

Injection No.	Elspar Dose (IU)	Accumulated Total Dose
1	1	1
2	2	3
3	4	7
4	8	15
5	16	31
6	32	63
7	64	127
8	128	255
9	256	511
10	512	1023
11	1024	2047
12	2048	4095
13	4096	8191
14	8192	16,383
15	16,384	32,767
16	32,768	65,535
17	65,536	131,071
18	131,072	262,143

For example, if a patient was to receive a total dose of 4000 units, he/she would receive injections 1 through 12 during the desensitization
Administration May be administered I.M., I.V., or S.C.
I.M.: Doses should be given as a deep intramuscular injection into a large muscle
(Continued)

Asparaginase *(Continued)*

I.V.: I.V. infusion in 50-250 mL of D$_5$W or NS over at least 60 minutes; a small test dose (0.1 mL of a dilute 20 unit/mL solution) should be given first

Occasionally, gelatinous fiber-like particles may develop on standing; filtration through a 5-micron filter during administration will remove the particles with no loss of potency; some loss of potency has been observed with the use of a 0.2 micron filter

Monitoring Parameters Vital signs during administration, CBC, urinalysis, amylase, liver enzymes, prothrombin time, renal function tests, urine dipstick for glucose, blood glucose, uric acid

Patient Information This medication can be given I.M., I.V., or subcutaneously. It is vital to maintain good hydration (2-3 L/day of fluids unless instructed to restrict fluid intake) and good nutritional status (small frequent meals may help). You may experience acute gastric disturbances (eg, nausea or vomiting); frequent mouth care or lozenges may help or antiemetic may be prescribed. Report any respiratory difficulty, skin rash, or acute anxiety immediately. Report unusual fever or chills, confusion, agitation, depression, yellowing of skin or eyes, unusual bleeding or bruising, unhealed sores, or vaginal discharge. Contraceptive measures are recommended during therapy.

Dosage Forms INJ, powder for reconstitution: 10,000 units

- ◆ **Aspercin [OTC]** *see Aspirin on page 120*
- ◆ **Aspercin Extra [OTC]** *see Aspirin on page 120*
- ◆ **Aspergum® [OTC]** *see Aspirin on page 120*

Aspirin *(AS pir in)*

Related Information

Salicylates *on page 1500*

U.S. Brand Names Ascriptin® [OTC]; Ascriptin® Arthritis Pain [OTC]; Ascriptin® Enteric [OTC]; Ascriptin® Extra Strength [OTC]; Aspercin [OTC]; Aspercin Extra [OTC]; Aspergum® [OTC]; Bayer® Aspirin [OTC]; Bayer® Aspirin Extra Strength [OTC]; Bayer® Aspirin Regimen Adult Low Strength [OTC]; Bayer® Aspirin Regimen Adult Low Strength with Calcium [OTC]; Bayer® Aspirin Regimen Children's [OTC]; Bayer® Aspirin Regimen Regular Strength [OTC]; Bayer® Plus Extra Strength [OTC]; Bufferin® [OTC]; Bufferin® Arthritis Strength [OTC]; Bufferin® Extra Strength [OTC]; Easprin®; Ecotrin® [OTC]; Ecotrin® Low Adult Strength [OTC]; Ecotrin® Maximum Strength [OTC]; Halfprin® [OTC]; St. Joseph® Pain Reliever [OTC]; Sureprin 81™ [OTC]; ZORprin®

Synonyms Acetylsalicylic Acid; ASA

Therapeutic Category Analgesic, Salicylate; Anti-inflammatory Agent; Antiplatelet Agent; Antipyretic; Nonsteroidal Anti-inflammatory Drug (NSAID), Oral; Platelet Aggregation Inhibitor; Salicylate

Use Treatment of mild to moderate pain, inflammation, and fever; may be used as prophylaxis of myocardial infarction; prophylaxis of stroke and/or transient ischemic episodes; management of rheumatoid arthritis, rheumatic fever, osteoarthritis, and gout (high dose); adjunctive therapy in revascularization procedures (coronary artery bypass graft [CABG], percutaneous transluminal coronary angioplasty [PTCA], carotid endarterectomy)

Unlabeled/Investigational Use Low doses have been used in the prevention of pre-eclampsia, recurrent spontaneous abortions, prematurity, fetal growth retardation (including complications associated with autoimmune disorders such as lupus or antiphospholipid syndrome)

Pregnancy Risk Factor C/D (full-dose aspirin in 3rd trimester - expert analysis)

Contraindications Hypersensitivity to salicylates, other NSAIDs, or any component of the formulation; asthma; rhinitis; nasal polyps; inherited or acquired bleeding disorders (including factor VIII and factor IX deficiency); do not use in children (<16 years of age) for viral infections (chickenpox or flu symptoms), with or without fever, due to a potential association with Reye's syndrome; pregnancy (3rd trimester especially)

Warnings/Precautions Use with caution in patients with platelet and bleeding disorders, renal dysfunction, dehydration, erosive gastritis, or peptic ulcer disease. Heavy ethanol use (>3 drinks/day) can increase bleeding risks. Avoid use in severe renal failure or in severe hepatic failure. Discontinue use if tinnitus or impaired hearing occurs. Caution in mild-moderate renal failure (only at high dosages). Patients with sensitivity to tartrazine dyes, nasal polyps and asthma may have an increased risk of salicylate sensitivity. Surgical patients should avoid ASA if possible, for 1-2 weeks prior to surgery, to reduce the risk of excessive bleeding.

When used for self-medication (OTC labeling): Children and teenagers who have or are recovering from chickenpox or flu-like symptoms should not use this product. Changes in behavior (along with nausea and vomiting) may be an early sign of Reye's syndrome; patients should be instructed to contact their healthcare provider if these occur.

Common Adverse Reactions As with all drugs which may affect hemostasis, bleeding is associated with aspirin. Hemorrhage may occur at virtually any site. Risk is dependent on multiple variables including dosage, concurrent use of multiple agents which alter hemostasis, and patient susceptibility. Many adverse effects of aspirin are dose-related, and are rare at low dosages. Other serious reactions are idiosyncratic, related to allergy or individual sensitivity. Accurate estimation of frequencies is not possible. The reactions listed below have been reported for aspirin (frequency not defined).

Cardiovascular: Hypotension, tachycardia, dysrhythmias, edema
Central nervous system: Fatigue, insomnia, nervousness, agitation, confusion, dizziness, headache, lethargy, cerebral edema, hyperthermia, coma

Dermatologic: Rash, angioedema, urticaria

Endocrine & metabolic: Acidosis, hyperkalemia, dehydration, hypoglycemia (children), hyperglycemia, hypernatremia (buffered forms)

Gastrointestinal: Nausea, vomiting, dyspepsia, epigastric discomfort, heartburn, stomach pains, gastrointestinal ulceration (6% to 31%), gastric erosions, gastric erythema, duodenal ulcers

Hematologic: Anemia, disseminated intravascular coagulation, prolongation of prothrombin times, coagulopathy, thrombocytopenia, hemolytic anemia, bleeding, iron deficiency anemia

Hepatic: Hepatotoxicity, increased transaminases, hepatitis (reversible)

Neuromuscular & skeletal: Rhabdomyolysis, weakness, acetabular bone destruction (OA)

Otic: Hearing loss, tinnitus

Renal: Interstitial nephritis, papillary necrosis, proteinuria, renal impairment, renal failure (including cases caused by rhabdomyolysis), increased BUN, increased serum creatinine

Respiratory: Asthma, bronchospasm, dyspnea, laryngeal edema, hyperpnea, tachypnea, respiratory alkalosis, noncardiogenic pulmonary edema

Miscellaneous: Anaphylaxis, prolonged pregnancy and labor, stillbirths, low birth weight, peripartum bleeding, Reye's syndrome

Drug Interactions

Cytochrome P450 Effect: Substrate of CYP2C8/9 (minor)

Increased Effect/Toxicity: Aspirin may increase methotrexate serum levels/toxicity and may displace valproic acid from binding sites which can result in toxicity. NSAIDs and aspirin increase GI adverse effects (ulceration). Aspirin with oral anticoagulants (warfarin), thrombolytic agents, heparin, low molecular weight heparins, and antiplatelet agents (ticlopidine, clopidogrel, dipyridamole, NSAIDs, and IIb/IIIa antagonists) may increase risk of bleeding. Bleeding times may be additionally prolonged with verapamil. The effects of older sulfonylurea agents (tolazamide, tolbutamide) may be potentiated due to displacement from plasma proteins. This effect does not appear to be clinically significant for newer sulfonylurea agents (glyburide, glipizide, glimepiride).

Decreased Effect: The effects of ACE inhibitors may be blunted by aspirin administration (may be significant only at higher aspirin dosages). Aspirin may decrease the effects of beta-blockers, loop diuretics (furosemide), thiazide diuretics, and probenecid. Aspirin may cause a decrease in NSAIDs serum concentration and decrease the effects of probenecid. Increased serum salicylate levels when taken with with urine acidifiers (ammonium chloride, methionine).

Mechanism of Action Inhibits prostaglandin synthesis, acts on the hypothalamus heat-regulating center to reduce fever, blocks prostaglandin synthetase action which prevents formation of the platelet-aggregating substance thromboxane A_2

Pharmacodynamics/Kinetics

Duration: 4-6 hours

Absorption: Rapid

Distribution: V_d: 10 L; readily into most body fluids and tissues

Metabolism: Hydrolyzed to salicylate (active) by esterases in GI mucosa, red blood cells, synovial fluid, and blood; metabolism of salicylate occurs primarily by hepatic conjugation; metabolic pathways are saturable

Bioavailability: 50% to 75% reaches systemic circulation

Half-life elimination: Parent drug: 15-20 minutes; Salicylates (dose dependent): 3 hours at lower doses (300-600 mg), 5-6 hours (after 1 g), 10 hours with higher doses

Time to peak, serum: ~1-2 hours

Excretion: Urine (75% as salicyluric acid, 10% as salicylic acid)

Dosage

Children:

Analgesic and antipyretic: Oral, rectal: 10-15 mg/kg/dose every 4-6 hours, up to a total of 4 g/day

Anti-inflammatory: Oral: Initial: 60-90 mg/kg/day in divided doses; usual maintenance: 80-100 mg/kg/day divided every 6-8 hours; monitor serum concentrations

Antiplatelet effects: Adequate pediatric studies have not been performed; pediatric dosage is derived from adult studies and clinical experience and is not well established; suggested doses have ranged from 3-5 mg/kg/day to 5-10 mg/kg/day given as a single daily dose. Doses are rounded to a convenient amount (eg, $\frac{1}{2}$ of 80 mg tablet).

Mechanical prosthetic heart valves: 6-20 mg/kg/day given as a single daily dose (used in combination with an oral anticoagulant in children who have systemic embolism despite adequate oral anticoagulation therapy (INR 2.5-3.5) and used in combination with low-dose anticoagulation (INR 2-3) and dipyridamole when full-dose oral anticoagulation is contraindicated)

Blalock-Taussig shunts: 3-5 mg/kg/day given as a single daily dose

Kawasaki disease: Oral: 80-100 mg/kg/day divided every 6 hours; monitor serum concentrations; after fever resolves: 3-5 mg/kg/day once daily; in patients without coronary artery abnormalities, give lower dose for at least 6-8 weeks or until ESR and platelet count are normal; in patients with coronary artery abnormalities, low-dose aspirin should be continued indefinitely

Antirheumatic: Oral: 60-100 mg/kg/day in divided doses every 4 hours

Adults:

Analgesic and antipyretic: Oral, rectal: 325-650 mg every 4-6 hours up to 4 g/day

Anti-inflammatory: Oral: Initial: 2.4-3.6 g/day in divided doses; usual maintenance: 3.6-5.4 g/day; monitor serum concentrations

Myocardial infarction prophylaxis: 75-325 mg/day; use of a lower aspirin dosage has been recommended in patients receiving ACE inhibitors

(Continued)

Aspirin *(Continued)*

Acute myocardial infarction: 160-325 mg/day

CABG: 325 mg/day starting 6 hours following procedure

PTCA: Initial: 80-325 mg/day starting 2 hours before procedure; longer pretreatment durations (up to 24 hours) should be considered if lower dosages (80-100 mg) are used

Carotid endarterectomy: 81-325 mg/day preoperatively and daily thereafter

Acute stroke : 160-325 mg/day, initiated within 48 hours (in patients who are not candidates for thrombolytics and are not receiving systemic anticoagulation)

Stroke prevention/TIA: 30-325 mg/day (dosages up to 1300 mg/day in 2-4 divided doses have been used in clinical trials)

Pre-eclampsia prevention (unlabeled use): 60-80 mg/day during gestational weeks 13-26 (patient selection criteria not established)

Dosing adjustment in renal impairment: Cl_{cr} <10 mL/minute: Avoid use.

Hemodialysis: Dialyzable (50% to 100%)

Dosing adjustment in hepatic disease: Avoid use in severe liver disease.

Administration Do not crush sustained release or enteric coated tablet. Administer with food or a full glass of water to minimize GI distress

Reference Range Timing of serum samples: Peak levels usually occur 2 hours after ingestion. Salicylate serum concentrations correlate with the pharmacological actions and adverse effects observed. The serum salicylate concentration (mcg/mL) and the corresponding clinical correlations are as follows: See table.

Serum Salicylate: Clinical Correlations

Serum Salicylate Concentration (mcg/mL)	Desired Effects	Adverse Effects/Intoxication
~100	Antiplatelet Antipyresis Analgesia	GI intolerance and bleeding, hypersensitivity, hemostatic defects
150-300	Anti-inflammatory	Mild salicylism
250-400	Treatment of rheumatic fever	Nausea/vomiting, hyperventilation, salicylism, flushing, sweating, thirst, headache, diarrhea, and tachycardia
>400-500		Respiratory alkalosis, hemorrhage, excitement, confusion, asterixis, pulmonary edema, convulsions, tetany, metabolic acidosis, fever, coma, cardiovascular collapse, renal and respiratory failure

Patient Information Watch for bleeding gums or any signs of GI bleeding; take with food or milk to minimize GI distress, notify prescriber if ringing in ears or persistent GI pain occurs; avoid other concurrent aspirin or salicylate-containing products

Dosage Forms CAPLET, buffered: 325 mg, 500 mg. **GELCAP:** 325 mg, 500 mg. **GUM:** 227 mg. **SUPP, rectal:** 60 mg, 120 mg, 125 mg, 200 mg, 300 mg, 325 mg, 600 mg, 650 mg. **TAB:** 325 mg, 500 mg. **TAB, film coated:** 325 mg. **TAB, buffered:** 325 mg, 500 mg. **TAB, chewable:** 81 mg. **TAB, controlled release** (ZORprin®): 800 mg. **TAB, enteric coated:** 81 mg, 162 mg, 325 mg, 500 mg, 650 mg, 975 mg; (Easprin®): 975 mg

♦ **Aspirin, Acetaminophen, and Caffeine** *see* Acetaminophen, Aspirin, and Caffeine *on page 27*

♦ **Aspirin and Carisoprodol** *see* Carisoprodol and Aspirin *on page 222*

Aspirin and Codeine *(AS pir in & KOE deen)*

Synonyms Codeine and Aspirin

Therapeutic Category Analgesic Combination, Narcotic

Use Relief of mild to moderate pain

Restrictions C-III

Pregnancy Risk Factor D

Dosage Oral:

Children:

Aspirin: 10 mg/kg/dose every 4 hours

Codeine: 0.5-1 mg/kg/dose every 4 hours

Adults: 1-2 tablets every 4-6 hours as needed for pain

Dosing adjustment in renal impairment:

Cl_{cr} 10-50 mL/minute: Administer 75% of dose

Cl_{cr} <10 mL/minute: Avoid use

Dosing interval in hepatic disease: Avoid use in severe liver disease

Dosage Forms TAB: #3: Aspirin 325 mg and codeine 30 mg; #4: Aspirin 325 mg and codeine 60 mg

Aspirin and Dipyridamole *(AS pir in & dye peer ID a mole)*

U.S. Brand Names Aggrenox®

Synonyms Aspirin and Extended-Release Dipyridamole; Dipyridamole and Aspirin

Therapeutic Category Antiplatelet Agent

Use Reduction in the risk of stroke in patients who have had transient ischemia of the brain or completed ischemic stroke due to thrombosis

Pregnancy Risk Factor B (dipyridamole); D (aspirin)

Contraindications Hypersensitivity to dipyridamole, aspirin, or any component of the formulation; allergy to NSAIDs; patients with asthma, rhinitis, and nasal polyps; bleeding disorders (factor VII or IX deficiencies); children <16 years of age with viral infections; pregnancy (aspirin)

Warnings/Precautions Patients who consume ≥3 alcoholic drinks per day are at risk of bleeding. Cautious use in patients with inherited or acquired bleeding disorders including those of liver disease or vitamin K deficiency. Watch for signs and symptoms of GI ulcers and bleeding. Avoid use in patients with active peptic ulcer disease. Discontinue use if dizziness, tinnitus, or impaired hearing occurs. Stop 1-2 weeks before elective surgical procedures to avoid bleeding. Use caution in the elderly who are at high risk for adverse events. Cautious use in patients with hypotension, patients with unstable angina, recent MI, and hepatic dysfunction. Avoid in patients with severe renal failure. Safety and efficacy in children have not been established.

Common Adverse Reactions
>10%:
  Central nervous system: Headache (38%)
  Gastrointestinal: Dyspepsia, abdominal pain (18%), nausea (16%), diarrhea (13%)
1% to 10%:
  Cardiovascular: Cardiac failure (2%)
  Central nervous system: Pain (6%), seizures (2%), fatigue (6%), malaise (2%), syncope (1%), amnesia (2%), confusion (1%), somnolence (1%)
  Dermatologic: Purpura (1%)
  Gastrointestinal: Vomiting (8%), bleeding (4%), rectal bleeding (2%), hemorrhoids (1%), hemorrhage (1%), anorexia (1%)
  Hematologic: Anemia (2%)
  Neuromuscular & skeletal: Back pain (5%), weakness (2%), arthralgia (6%), arthritis (2%), arthrosis (1%), myalgia (1%)
  Respiratory: Cough (2%), upper respiratory tract infections (1%), epistaxis (2%)

Drug Interactions
  Cytochrome P450 Effect: Aspirin: **Substrate** of CYP2C8/9 (minor)
  Increased Effect/Toxicity: See individual agents.
  Decreased Effect: See individual agents.

Mechanism of Action The antithrombotic action results from additive antiplatelet effects. Dipyridamole inhibits the uptake of adenosine into platelets, endothelial cells, and erythrocytes. Aspirin inhibits platelet aggregation by irreversible inhibition of platelet cyclooxygenase and thus inhibits the generation of thromboxane A2.

Pharmacodynamics/Kinetics
  Aggrenox®:
    Half-life elimination: Salicylic acid: 1.71 hours
    Time to peak: 0.63 hours
  Aspirin: See Aspirin monograph.
  Dipyridamole:
    Distribution: V_d: 92 L
    Protein binding: 99%
    Metabolism: Hepatic via conjugation with glucuronic acid
    Half-life elimination: 13.6 hours
    Time to peak: 2 hours
    Excretion: Feces (95% as glucuronide metabolite); urine (5%)

Dosage Adults: Oral: 1 capsule (dipyridamole 200 mg, aspirin 25 mg) twice daily.
  Dosage adjustment in renal impairment: Avoid use in patients with severe renal dysfunction (Cl_{cr} <10 mL/minute). Studies have not been done in patients with renal impairment.
  Dosage adjustment in hepatic impairment: Avoid use in patients with severe hepatic impairment; studies have not been done in patients with varying degrees of hepatic impairment
  Elderly: Plasma concentrations were 40% higher, but specific dosage adjustments have not been recommended

Administration Capsule should be swallowed whole; do not crush or chew. May be given with or without food.

Monitoring Parameters Hemoglobin, hematocrit, signs or symptoms of bleeding, signs or symptoms of stroke or transient ischemic attack

Patient Information Swallow capsule whole without chewing or crushing; monitor for signs and symptoms of bleeding or another stroke or transient ischemic attack

Dosage Forms CAP: Dipyridamole (extended release) 200 mg and aspirin 25 mg

◆ **Aspirin and Extended-Release Dipyridamole** *see* Aspirin and Dipyridamole *on page 122*
◆ **Aspirin and Hydrocodone** *see* Hydrocodone and Aspirin *on page 628*

Aspirin and Meprobamate (AS pir in & me proe BA mate)

U.S. Brand Names Equagesic®

Synonyms Meprobamate and Aspirin

Therapeutic Category Analgesic/Skeletal Muscle Relaxant; Antianxiety Agent

Use Adjunct to treatment of skeletal muscular disease in patients exhibiting tension and/or anxiety

Restrictions C-IV

Pregnancy Risk Factor D

(Continued)

Aspirin and Meprobamate *(Continued)*

Dosage Oral: 1 tablet 3-4 times/day

Dosage Forms TAB: Aspirin 325 mg and meprobamate 200 mg

♦ **Aspirin and Oxycodone** *see* Oxycodone and Aspirin *on page 945*

Aspirin and Pravastatin *(AS pir in & PRA va stat in)*

U.S. Brand Names Pravigard™ PAC

Synonyms Buffered Aspirin and Pravastatin Sodium; Pravastatin and Aspirin

Therapeutic Category Antilipemic Agent, HMG-CoA Reductase Inhibitor; Salicylate

Use Combination therapy in patients who need treatment with aspirin and pravastatin to reduce the incidence of cardiovascular events, including myocardial infarction, stroke, and death.

Pregnancy Risk Factor X

Dosage Oral: Adults:

Initial: Pravastatin 40 mg with aspirin (either 81 mg or 325 mg); both medications taken once daily. If pravastatin 40 mg does not achieve the desired cholesterol result, dosage may be increased to 80 mg once daily with aspirin (either 81 mg or 325 mg) once daily. Some patients may achieve/maintain goal cholesterol levels at a pravastatin dosage of 20 mg.

See Pravastatin *on page 1028* for dosing in renal or hepatic impairment, as well as, dosing with concurrent immunosuppressant therapy.

Dosage Forms TAB, combination package (Pravigard™ PAC) [each administration card contains]: (81/20): Aspirin, buffered 81 mg (5/card) and Pravachol® (pravastatin) 20 mg (5/card); (81/40): Aspirin, buffered 81 mg (5/card) and Pravachol® (pravastatin) 40 mg (5/card); (81/80): Aspirin, buffered 81 mg (5/card) and Pravachol® (pravastatin) 80 mg (5/card); (325/20): Aspirin, buffered 325 mg (5/card) and Pravachol® (pravastatin) 20 mg (5/card); (325/40): Aspirin, buffered 325 mg (5/card) and Pravachol® (pravastatin) 40 mg (5/card); (325/80): Aspirin, buffered 325 mg (5/card) and Pravachol® (pravastatin) 80 mg (5/card)

♦ **Aspirin, Caffeine and Acetaminophen** *see* Acetaminophen, Aspirin, and Caffeine *on page 27*

♦ **Aspirin, Caffeine, and Butalbital** *see* Butalbital, Aspirin, and Caffeine *on page 195*

♦ **Aspirin, Caffeine, and Propoxyphene** *see* Propoxyphene, Aspirin, and Caffeine *on page 1054*

♦ **Aspirin, Carisoprodol, and Codeine** *see* Carisoprodol, Aspirin, and Codeine *on page 222*

♦ **Aspirin Free Anacin® Maximum Strength [OTC]** *see* Acetaminophen *on page 24*

♦ **Aspirin, Orphenadrine, and Caffeine** *see* Orphenadrine, Aspirin, and Caffeine *on page 933*

♦ **Assessment of Renal Function** *see page 1348*

♦ **Astelin®** *see* Azelastine *on page 138*

♦ **Astramorph/PF™** *see* Morphine Sulfate *on page 861*

♦ **Atacand®** *see* Candesartan *on page 208*

♦ **Atacand HCT™** *see* Candesartan and Hydrochlorothiazide *on page 209*

♦ **Atarax®** *see* HydrOXYzine *on page 640*

Atazanavir *(at a za NA veer)*

Related Information

Antiretroviral Therapy for HIV Infection *on page 1448*

U.S. Brand Names Reyataz™

Synonyms Atazanavir Sulfate; BMS-232632

Therapeutic Category Antiretroviral Agent, Protease Inhibitor

Use Treatment of HIV-1 infections in combination with at least two other antiretroviral agents

Pregnancy Risk Factor B

Contraindications Hypersensitivity to atazanavir or any component of the formulation. Concurrent therapy with: Bepridil; cisapride; ergot derivatives (dihydroergotamine, ergonovine, ergotamine, methylergonovine); indinavir; irinotecan; lovastatin; midazolam; pimozide; proton pump inhibitors (esomeprazole, lansoprazole, omeprazole); rifampin; simvastatin; St John's wort; or triazolam.

Warnings/Precautions Atazanavir is hepatically metabolized and has multiple drug interactions. Use caution with medications metabolized by CYP3A4 and/or UGT1A1 (many are contraindicated). Additional CYP3A4 substrates include calcium channel blockers, immunosuppressants, and sildenafil.

Atazanavir may prolong P-R interval, use with caution in patients with pre-existing conduction abnormalities or with medications which prolong A-V conduction (dosage adjustment required with some agents). May exacerbate pre-existing hepatic dysfunction; use caution in patients with hepatitis B or C or in patients with cirrhosis. Asymptomatic elevations in bilirubin (unconjugated) occur commonly during therapy with atazanavir; consider alternative therapy if bilirubin is >5 times ULN. Evaluate alternative etiologies if transaminase elevations also occur.

Use with caution in patients with hemophilia A or B; increased bleeding during protease inhibitor therapy has been reported. Changes in glucose tolerance, hyperglycemia, exacerbation of diabetes, DKA, and new-onset diabetes mellitus have been reported in patients receiving protease inhibitors. May be associated with fat redistribution (buffalo hump, increased abdominal girth, breast enlargement, facial atrophy). Optimal dosing in pediatric patients has not been established; do not use in children <3 months of age due to potential for kernicterus.

Common Adverse Reactions Protease inhibitors cause dyslipidemia which includes elevated cholesterol and triglycerides and a redistribution of body fat centrally to cause increased abdominal girth, buffalo hump, facial atrophy, and breast enlargement. These agents also cause hyperglycemia.

>10%:
  Central nervous system: Headache (10% to 14%)
  Gastrointestinal: Nausea (10% to 16%)
  Hepatic: Bilirubin increased (>2.6 times ULN): 35% to 47%), amylase increased (14%)
3% to 10%:
  Central nervous system: Fever (4% to 5%), depression (4% to 8%), insomnia (1% to 3%), dizziness (1% to 3%), peripheral neuropathy (1% to 8%), fatigue (2% to 5%), pain (1% to 3%)
  Dermatologic: Rash (9% to 10%)
  Endocrine & metabolic: Lipodystrophy (1% to 8%)
  Gastrointestinal: Abdominal pain (6% to 8%), vomiting (6% to 8%), diarrhea (6% to 8%)
  Hepatic: Jaundice (7% to 8%), transaminases increased (2% to 9%)
  Neuromuscular & skeletal: Back pain (2% to 6%), arthralgia (4%)
  Respiratory: Cough increased (3% to 5%)

Drug Interactions

Cytochrome P450 Effect: Substrate of CYP3A4 (major); **Inhibits** CYP1A2 (weak), 2C9 (weak), 3A4 (strong)

Increased Effect/Toxicity: CYP3A4 inhibitors may increase the levels/effects of atazanavir; example inhibitors include azole antifungals, ciprofloxacin, clarithromycin, diclofenac, doxycycline, erythromycin, imatinib, isoniazid, nefazodone, nicardipine, propofol, protease inhibitors, quinidine, and verapamil. Serum concentrations of medications significantly metabolized by CYP3A4 or UGT1A1 may be elevated by atazanavir. Concurrent therapy with bepridil, cisapride, ergot derivatives (dihydroergotamine, ergonovine, ergotamine, methylergonovine), indinavir, irinotecan, lovastatin, midazolam, pimozide, simvastatin or triazolam is contraindicated (or not recommended, per manufacturer). Serum concentrations of antiarrhythmics (amiodarone, lidocaine, and quinidine) may be increased; monitor serum concentrations of these agents. Serum concentrations of calcium channel blockers, immunosuppressants (cyclosporine, sirolimus, tacrolimus), tricyclic antidepressants may be increased.

Serum concentrations of atazanavir are increased by ritonavir. Specific dosing adjustment of atazanavir in combination with ritonavir and efavirenz has been established. Serum concentrations of saquinavir may be increased by atazanavir. Dosing recommendations for the combination have not been established. Sildenafil serum concentration may be substantially increased (do not exceed single sildenafil doses of 25 mg in 48 hours). When used concurrently with tadalafil, do not exceed a maximum tadalafil dose of 10 mg in a 72-hour period. Specific guidelines for vardenafil are not established; recommendations for other strong CYP3A4 inhibitors include vardenafil dose not to exceed 2.5 mg in 24 hours. Concurrent use of indinavir may increase the risk of hyperbilirubinemia. Concurrent administration is not recommended.

Atazanavir may increase warfarin's hypoprothrombinemic effect; monitor INR closely. Serum levels of the hormones in oral contraceptives may increase significantly with administration of atazanavir; use with caution at lowest effective dose. Atazanavir may increase serum concentrations of clarithromycin, potentially increasing the risk of QT_c prolongation. A 50% reduction in clarithromycin dose or an alternative agent (except in *M. avium* complex infections) should be considered. An increase in rifabutin plasma AUC (>200%) has been observed when coadministered with atazanavir (decrease rifabutin's dose by up to 75%).

Decreased Effect: Concurrent use of proton pump inhibitors may reduce atazanavir absorption; avoid concurrent use. Antacids and buffered formulations (ie, didanosine buffered tablets) may reduce the serum concentrations of atazanavir. Administer atazanavir 2 hours before or 1 hour after these medications. H_2 antagonists may reduce the absorption of atazanavir; avoid concurrent use or administer at least 12 hours apart.

CYP3A4 inducers may decrease the levels/effects of atazanavir; example inducers include aminoglutethimide, carbamazepine, nafcillin, nevirapine, phenobarbital, phenytoin, and rifamycins.

Anticonvulsants (phenobarbital and carbamazepine) may decrease serum levels and consequently effectiveness of atazanavir. Rifampin decreases bioavailability of protease inhibitors by ~90%; loss of virologic response and resistance may occur; the two drugs should not be administered together. St John's wort (*Hypericum perforatum*) decreases serum concentrations of protease inhibitors and may lead to treatment failures; concurrent use is contraindicated. Tenofovir may decrease serum concentrations of atazanavir, resulting in a loss of virologic response (specific atazanavir dosing recommendations provided by manufacturer).

Mechanism of Action Inhibits the HIV-1 protease; inhibition of the viral protease prevents cleavage of the gag-pol polyprotein resulting in the production of immature, noninfectious virus

Pharmacodynamics/Kinetics
  Protein binding: 86%
  Metabolism: Hepatic, via multiple pathways including CYP3A4
  Half-life elimination: 6.5 hours
  Time to peak, plasma: 2.5 hours
  Excretion: Feces (79% as metabolites, 20% as unchanged drug); urine (13% as metabolites, 7% as unchanged drug)

Dosage Oral: Adults: 400 mg once daily; administer with food

Coadministration with efavirenz: It is recommended that atazanavir 300 mg plus ritonavir 100 mg be given with efavirenz 600 mg (all as a single daily dose); administer with food (Continued)

Atazanavir *(Continued)*

Coadministration with didanosine buffered formulations: Administer atazanavir 2 hours before or 1 hour after didanosine buffered formulations

Coadministration with tenofovir: The manufacturer recommends that atazanavir 300 mg plus ritonavir 100 mg be given with tenofovir 300 mg (all as a single daily dose); administer with food

Dosage adjustment in renal impairment: No recommendation

Dosage adjustment in hepatic impairment:
Moderate hepatic insufficiency (Child-Pugh Class B): Reduce dose to 300 mg once daily
Severe hepatic insufficiency (Child-Pugh Class C): Avoid use

Administration Administer with food.

Monitoring Parameters Viral load, CD4, serum glucose; liver function tests, bilirubin

Patient Information This drug may interact with many medications. Check with prescriber before taking any medication, including OTC and herbal medicines. This drug is not a cure for HIV and has not been shown to reduce the risk of transmitting HIV to others. Do not miss doses. If you miss a dose, take as soon as possible and return to your regular schedule (never take a double dose). Frequent blood tests may be required with prolonged therapy. May cause nausea or vomiting (small, frequent meals, frequent mouth care, chewing gum, or sucking lozenges may help). Report rash; difficulty breathing; CNS changes (migraine, confusion, suicidal ideation); muscular or skeletal pain, weakness, or tremors; or other adverse reactions.

Dosage Forms CAP, as sulfate: 100 mg, 150 mg, 200 mg

♦ **Atazanavir Sulfate** *see Atazanavir on page 124*

Atenolol *(a TEN oh lole)*

Related Information
Beta-Blockers Comparison *on page 1368*

U.S. Brand Names Tenormin®

Therapeutic Category Antianginal Agent; Antihypertensive Agent; Antimigraine Agent; Prophylaxis; Beta Blocker, Beta₁ Selective

Use Treatment of hypertension, alone or in combination with other agents; management of angina pectoris, postmyocardial infarction patients

Unlabeled/Investigational Use Acute ethanol withdrawal, supraventricular and ventricular arrhythmias, and migraine headache prophylaxis

Pregnancy Risk Factor D

Contraindications Hypersensitivity to atenolol or any component of the formulation; sinus bradycardia; sinus node dysfunction; heart block greater than first-degree (except in patients with a functioning artificial pacemaker); cardiogenic shock; uncompensated cardiac failure; pulmonary edema; pregnancy

Warnings/Precautions Safety and efficacy in children have not been established. Administer cautiously in compensated heart failure and monitor for a worsening of the condition (efficacy of atenolol in heart failure has not been established). Beta-blocker therapy should not be withdrawn abruptly (particularly in patients with CAD), but gradually tapered to avoid acute tachycardia, hypertension, and/or ischemia. Use caution with concurrent use of beta-blockers and either verapamil or diltiazem; bradycardia or heart block can occur. Avoid concurrent I.V. use of both agents. Beta-blockers should be avoided in patients with bronchospastic disease (asthma) and peripheral vascular disease (may aggravate arterial insufficiency). Atenolol, with B1 selectivity, has been used cautiously in bronchospastic disease with close monitoring. Use cautiously in diabetics - may mask hypoglycemic symptoms. May mask signs of thyrotoxicosis. May cause fetal harm when administered in pregnancy. Use cautiously in the renally impaired (dosage adjustment required). Use care with anesthetic agents which decrease myocardial function. Caution in myasthenia gravis.

Common Adverse Reactions 1% to 10%:
Cardiovascular: Persistent bradycardia, hypotension, chest pain, edema, heart failure, second- or third-degree AV block, Raynaud's phenomenon
Central nervous system: Dizziness, fatigue, insomnia, lethargy, confusion, mental impairment, depression, headache, nightmares
Gastrointestinal: Constipation, diarrhea, nausea
Genitourinary: Impotence
Miscellaneous: Cold extremities

Drug Interactions

Increased Effect/Toxicity: Atenolol may increase the effects of other drugs which slow AV conduction (digoxin, verapamil, diltiazem), alpha-blockers (prazosin, terazosin), and alpha-adrenergic stimulants (epinephrine, phenylephrine). Atenolol may mask the tachycardia from hypoglycemia caused by insulin and oral hypoglycemics. In patients receiving concurrent therapy, the risk of hypertensive crisis is increased when either clonidine or the beta-blocker is withdrawn. Reserpine has been shown to enhance the effect of atenolol. Beta-blockers may increase the action or levels of ethanol, disopyramide, nondepolarizing muscle relaxants, and theophylline although the effects are difficult to predict.

Decreased Effect: Decreased effect of atenolol with aluminum salts, barbiturates, calcium salts, cholestyramine, colestipol, NSAIDs, penicillins (ampicillin), rifampin, salicylates, and sulfinpyrazone due to decreased bioavailability and plasma levels. Beta-blockers may decrease the effect of sulfonylureas.

Mechanism of Action Competitively blocks response to beta-adrenergic stimulation, selectively blocks beta₁-receptors with little or no effect on beta₂-receptors except at high doses

Pharmacodynamics/Kinetics
Onset of action: Peak effect: Oral: 2-4 hours
Duration: Normal renal function: 12-24 hours
Absorption: Incomplete
Distribution: Low lipophilicity; does not cross blood-brain barrier
Protein binding: 3% to 15%
Metabolism: Limited hepatic
Half-life elimination: Beta:
Neonates: ≤35 hours; Mean: 16 hours
Children: 4.6 hours; children >10 years may have longer half-life (>5 hours) compared to children 5-10 years (<5 hours)
Adults: Normal renal function: 6-9 hours, prolonged with renal impairment; End-stage renal disease: 15-35 hours
Excretion: Feces (50%); urine (40% as unchanged drug)

Dosage
Oral:
Children: 0.8-1 mg/kg/dose given daily; range of 0.8-1.5 mg/kg/day; maximum dose: 2 mg/kg/day
Adults:
Hypertension: 25-50 mg once daily, may increase to 100 mg/day. Doses >100 mg are unlikely to produce any further benefit.
Angina pectoris: 50 mg once daily, may increase to 100 mg/day. Some patients may require 200 mg/day.
Postmyocardial infarction: Follow I.V. dose with 100 mg/day or 50 mg twice daily for 6-9 days postmyocardial infarction.
I.V.:
Hypertension: Dosages of 1.25-5 mg every 6-12 hours have been used in short-term management of patients unable to take oral enteral beta-blockers
Postmyocardial infarction: Early treatment: 5 mg slow I.V. over 5 minutes; may repeat in 10 minutes. If both doses are tolerated, may start oral atenolol 50 mg every 12 hours or 100 mg/day for 6-9 days postmyocardial infarction.
Dosing interval for oral atenolol in renal impairment:
Cl_{cr} 15-35 mL/minute: Administer 50 mg/day maximum.
Cl_{cr} <15 mL/minute: Administer 50 mg every other day maximum.
Hemodialysis: Moderately dialyzable (20% to 50%) via hemodialysis; administer dose postdialysis or administer 25-50 mg supplemental dose.
Peritoneal dialysis: Elimination is not enhanced; supplemental dose is not necessary.

Administration When administered acutely for cardiac treatment, monitor ECG and blood pressure. May administer by rapid infusion (I.V. push) at a rate of 1 mg/minute or by slow infusion over ~30 minutes. Necessary monitoring for surgical patients who are unable to take oral beta-blockers (prolonged ileus) has not been defined. Some institutions require monitoring of baseline and postinfusion heart rate and blood pressure when a patient's response to beta-blockade has not been characterized (ie, the patient's initial dose or following a change in dose). Consult individual institutional policies and procedures.

Monitoring Parameters Acute cardiac treatment: Monitor ECG and blood pressure with I.V. administration; heart rate and blood pressure with oral administration

Patient Information Adhere to dosage regimen; watch for postural hypotension; **abrupt withdrawal of the drug should be avoided;** take at the same time each day; may mask diabetes symptoms; notify prescriber if any adverse effects occur; use with caution while driving or performing tasks requiring alertness; may be taken without regard to meals

Dosage Forms INJ, solution: 0.5 mg/mL (10 mL). **TAB:** 25 mg, 50 mg, 100 mg

Atenolol and Chlorthalidone (a TEN oh lole & klor THAL i done)

U.S. Brand Names Tenoretic®
Synonyms Chlorthalidone and Atenolol
Therapeutic Category Antihypertensive Agent, Combination
Use Treatment of hypertension with a cardioselective beta-blocker and a diuretic
Pregnancy Risk Factor D
Dosage Adults: Oral: Initial (based on atenolol component): 50 mg once daily, then individualize dose until optimal dose is achieved
Dosage Forms TAB: 50: Atenolol 50 mg and chlorthalidone 25 mg; 100: Atenolol 100 mg and chlorthalidone 25 mg

♦ **ATG** see Antithymocyte Globulin (Equine) on page 108
♦ **ATG** see Antithymocyte Globulin (Rabbit) on page 109
♦ **Atgam®** see Antithymocyte Globulin (Equine) on page 108
♦ **AT III** see Antithrombin III on page 107
♦ **Ativan®** see Lorazepam on page 760

Atomoxetine (AT oh mox e teen)

U.S. Brand Names Strattera™
Synonyms Atomoxetine Hydrochloride; LY139603; Methylphenoxy-Benzene Propanamine; Tomoxetine
Therapeutic Category Norepinephrine Reuptake Inhibitor, Selective
Use Treatment of attention deficit/hyperactivity disorder (ADHD)
Unlabeled/Investigational Use Treatment of depression
(Continued)

Atomoxetine *(Continued)*

Pregnancy Risk Factor C

Contraindications Hypersensitivity to atomoxetine or any component of the formulation; use of MAO inhibitors within 14 days; narrow-angle glaucoma

Warnings/Precautions Use caution with hepatic and renal impairment (dosage adjustments necessary in hepatic impairment). May cause increased heart rate or blood pressure, use caution with hypertension or other cardiovascular disease. Use caution in patients who are "poor metabolizers" (CYP2D6), bioavailability increases. May cause urinary retention/hesitancy, use caution in patients with history of urinary retention or bladder outlet obstruction. Allergic reactions (including angioneurotic edema, urticaria, and rash) may occur. Growth should be monitored during treatment. Safety and efficacy have not been evaluated in pediatric patients <6 years of age; safety and efficacy of long-term use have not been established.

Common Adverse Reactions Percentages as reported in children and adults; some adverse reactions may be increased in "poor metabolizers" (CYP2D6).

>10%:

    Central nervous system: Headache (17% to 27%), insomnia (16%)

    Gastrointestinal: Xerostomia (4% to 21%), abdominal pain (20%), vomiting (15%), appetite decreased (10% to 14%), nausea (12%)

    Respiratory: Cough (11%)

1% to 10%:

    Cardiovascular: Palpitations (4%), systolic blood pressure increased (2% to 9%), orthostatic hypotension (2%), tachycardia (2%)

    Central nervous system: Fatigue/lethargy (7% to 9%), irritability (8%), somnolence (7%), dizziness (6%), mood swings (5%), abnormal dreams (4%), sleep disturbance (4%), pyrexia (3%), rigors (3%), crying (2%)

    Dermatologic: Dermatitis (2% to 4%)

    Endocrine & metabolic: Dysmenorrhea (7%), libido decreased (6%), menstruation disturbance (3%), orgasm abnormal (2%), weight loss (2%)

    Gastrointestinal: Dyspepsia (6% to 8%), diarrhea (4%), flatulence (2%), constipation (3% to 10%)

    Genitourinary: Erectile disturbance (7%), ejaculatory disturbance (5%), prostatitis (3%), impotence (3%)

    Neuromuscular & skeletal: Paresthesia (4%), myalgia (3%)

    Otic: Ear infection (3%)

    Renal: Urinary retention/hesitation (8%)

    Respiratory: Rhinorrhea (4%), sinus headache (3%), sinusitis (6%)

    Miscellaneous: Diaphoresis increased (4%), influenza (3%)

Drug Interactions

    Cytochrome P450 Effect: Substrate of CYP2C19 (minor), 2D6 (major)

Increased Effect/Toxicity: MAO inhibitors may increase risk of CNS toxicity (combined use is contraindicated). CYP2D6 inhibitors may increase the levels/effects of atomoxetine; example inhibitors include chlorpromazine, delavirdine, fluoxetine, miconazole, paroxetine, pergolide, quinidine, quinine, ritonavir, and ropinirole. Albuterol may increase risk of cardiovascular toxicity.

Mechanism of Action Selectively inhibits the reuptake of norepinephrine (Ki 4.5nM) with little to no activity at the other neuronal reuptake pumps or receptor sites.

Pharmacodynamics/Kinetics

    Absorption: Rapid

    Distribution: V_d: I.V.: 0.85 L/kg

    Protein binding: 98%, primarily albumin

    Metabolism: Hepatic, via CYP2D6 and CYP2C19; forms metabolites (4-hydroxyatomoxetine, active, equipotent to atomoxetine; N-desmethylatomoxetine in poor metabolizers, limited activity)

    Bioavailability: 63% in extensive metabolizers; 94% in poor metabolizers

    Half-life elimination: Atomoxetine: 5 hours (up to 24 hours in poor metabolizers); Active metabolites: 4-hydroxyatomoxetine: 6-8 hours; N-desmethylatomoxetine: 6-8 hours (34-40 hours in poor metabolizers)

    Time to peak, plasma: 1-2 hours

    Excretion: Urine (80%, as conjugated 4-hydroxy metabolite); feces (17%)

Dosage Oral:

    Children and Adolescents ≤70 kg: ADHD: Initial: 0.5 mg/kg/day, increase after minimum of 3 days to ~1.2 mg/kg/day; may administer as either a single daily dose or two evenly divided doses in morning and late afternoon/early evening. Maximum daily dose: 1.4 mg/kg or 100 mg, whichever is less. In patients receiving effective CYP2D6 inhibitors (eg, paroxetine, fluoxetine, quinidine), do not exceed 1.2 mg/kg.

    Children and Adolescents >70 kg: Refer to Adults dosing

    Adults:

        ADHD: Initial: 40 mg/day, increased after minimum of 3 days to ~80 mg/day; may administer as either a single daily dose or two evenly divided doses in morning and late afternoon/early evening. May increase to 100 mg in 2-4 additional weeks to achieve optimal response. In patients receiving effective CYP2D6 inhibitors (eg, paroxetine, fluoxetine, quinidine), do not exceed 80 mg/day.

        Depression (unlabeled use): 40-65 mg/day

    Elderly: Use has not been evaluated in the elderly

    Dosage adjustment in renal impairment: No adjustment needed

Dosage adjustment in hepatic impairment:
   Moderate hepatic insufficiency (Child-Pugh class B): All doses should be reduced to 50% of normal
   Severe hepatic insufficiency (Child-Pugh class C): All doses should be reduced to 25% of normal

Administration May be administered with or without food.

Monitoring Parameters Patient growth (ensuring normal weight/height gain); attention, hyperactivity, anxiety; blood pressure, pulse

Patient Information May take with or without food; use caution when driving or operating hazardous machinery until effects of the drug are known.

Dosage Forms CAP: 10 mg, 18 mg, 25 mg, 40 mg, 60 mg

♦ **Atomoxetine Hydrochloride** *see Atomoxetine on page 127*

Atorvastatin (a TORE va sta tin)

Related Information
   Lipid-Lowering Agents *on page 1381*

U.S. Brand Names Lipitor®

Therapeutic Category Antilipemic Agent, HMG-CoA Reductase Inhibitor; HMG-CoA Reductase Inhibitor

Use Used with dietary therapy for the following:
   Hyperlipidemias: To reduce elevations in total cholesterol, LDL-C, apolipoprotein B, and triglycerides in patients with primary hypercholesterolemia (elevations of 1 or more components are present in Fredrickson type IIa, IIb, III, and IV hyperlipidemias); treatment of homozygous familial hypercholesterolemia
   Heterozygous familial hypercholesterolemia (HeFH): In adolescent patients (10-17 years of age, females >1 year postmenarche) with HeFH having LDL-C ≥190 mg/dL **or** LDL ≥160 mg/dL with positive family history of premature cardiovascular disease (CVD) or with 2 or more CVD risk factors in the adolescent patient

Pregnancy Risk Factor X

Contraindications Hypersensitivity to atorvastatin or any component of the formulation; active liver disease; unexplained persistent elevations of serum transaminases; pregnancy; breast-feeding

Warnings/Precautions Secondary causes of hyperlipidemia should be ruled out prior to therapy. Liver function must be monitored by periodic laboratory assessment. Rhabdomyolysis with acute renal failure has occurred. Risk is increased with concurrent use of clarithromycin, danazol, diltiazem, fluvoxamine, indinavir, nefazodone, nelfinavir, ritonavir, verapamil, troleandomycin, cyclosporine, fibric acid derivatives, erythromycin, niacin, or azole antifungals. Weigh the risk versus benefit when combining any of these drugs with atorvastatin. Discontinue in any patient experiencing an acute or serious condition predisposing to renal failure secondary to rhabdomyolysis. Use with caution in patients who consume large amounts of ethanol or have a history of liver disease. Safety and efficacy have not been established in patients <10 years or in premenarcheal girls.

Common Adverse Reactions
   >10%: Central nervous system: Headache (3% to 17%)
   2% to 10%:
      Cardiovascular: Chest pain, peripheral edema
      Central nervous system: Weakness (0% to 4%), insomnia, dizziness
      Dermatologic: Rash (1% to 4%)
      Gastrointestinal: Abdominal pain (0% to 4%), constipation (0% to 3%), diarrhea (0% to 4%), dyspepsia (1% to 3%), flatulence (1% to 3%), nausea
      Genitourinary: Urinary tract infection
      Neuromuscular & skeletal: Arthralgia (0% to 5%), myalgia (0% to 6%), back pain (0% to 4%), arthritis
      Respiratory: Sinusitis (0% to 6%), pharyngitis (0% to 3%), bronchitis, rhinitis
      Miscellaneous: Infection (2% to 10%), flu-like syndrome (0% to 3%), allergic reaction (0% to 3%)
   <2% (Limited to important or life-threatening symptoms): Pneumonia, dyspnea, epistaxis, face edema, fever, photosensitivity, malaise, edema, gastroenteritis, elevated transaminases, colitis, vomiting, gastritis, xerostomia, rectal hemorrhage, esophagitis, eructation, glossitis, stomatitis, anorexia, increased appetite, biliary pain, cheilitis, duodenal ulcer, dysphagia, enteritis, melena, gingival hemorrhage, tenesmus, hepatitis, pancreatitis, cholestatic jaundice, paresthesia, somnolence, abnormal dreams, decreased libido, emotional lability, incoordination, peripheral neuropathy, torticollis, facial paralysis, hyperkinesia, depression, hypesthesia, hypertonia, leg cramps, bursitis, myasthenia, myositis, tendinous contracture, pruritus, alopecia, dry skin, urticaria, acne, eczema, seborrhea, skin ulcer, cystitis, hematuria, impotence, dysuria, nocturia, epididymitis, fibrocystic breast disease, vaginal hemorrhage, nephritis, abnormal urination, amblyopia, tinnitus, deafness, glaucoma, taste loss, taste perversion, palpitation, vasodilation, syncope, migraine, postural hypotension, phlebitis, arrhythmia, angina, hypertension, hyperglycemia, gout, weight gain, hypoglycemia, ecchymosis, anemia, lymphadenopathy, thrombocytopenia, petechiae, pharyngitis, rhinitis, myopathy

Drug Interactions
   Cytochrome P450 Effect: Substrate of CYP3A4 (major); **Inhibits** CYP3A4 (weak)
   Increased Effect/Toxicity: Inhibitors of CYP3A4 (amiodarone, amprenavir, clarithromycin, cyclosporine, diltiazem, fluvoxamine, erythromycin, fluconazole, indinavir, itraconazole, ketoconazole, miconazole, nefazodone, nelfinavir, ritonavir, troleandomycin, and verapamil)
   (Continued)

Atorvastatin *(Continued)*

may increase atorvastatin blood levels and may increase the risk of atorvastatin-induced myopathy and rhabdomyolysis. The risk of myopathy and rhabdomyolysis due to concurrent use of a CYP3A4 inhibitor with atorvastatin is probably less than lovastatin or simvastatin. Cyclosporine, clofibrate, fenofibrate, gemfibrozil, and niacin also may increase the risk of myopathy and rhabdomyolysis. The effect/toxicity of levothyroxine may be increased by atorvastatin. Levels of digoxin and ethinyl estradiol may be increased by atorvastatin.

Decreased Effect: Colestipol, antacids decreased plasma concentrations but effect on LDL-cholesterol was not altered. Cholestyramine may decrease absorption of atorvastatin when administered concurrently.

Mechanism of Action Inhibitor of 3-hydroxy-3-methylglutaryl coenzyme A (HMG-CoA) reductase, the rate limiting enzyme in cholesterol synthesis (reduces the production of mevalonic acid from HMG-CoA); this then results in a compensatory increase in the expression of LDL receptors on hepatocyte membranes and a stimulation of LDL catabolism

Pharmacodynamics/Kinetics

Onset of action: Initial changes: 3-5 days; Maximal reduction in plasma cholesterol and triglycerides: 2 weeks

Absorption: Rapid

Protein binding: 98%

Metabolism: Hepatic; forms active ortho- and parahydroxylated derivates and an inactive beta-oxidation product

Half-life elimination: Parent drug: 14 hours

Time to peak, serum: 1-2 hours

Excretion: Bile; urine (2% as unchanged drug)

Dosage Oral: **Note:** Doses should be individualized according to the baseline LDL-cholesterol levels, the recommended goal of therapy, and patient response; adjustments should be made at intervals of 2-4 weeks

Children 10-17 years (females >1 year postmenarche): HeFH: 10 mg once daily (maximum: 20 mg/day)

Adults: Hyperlipidemias: Initial: 10-20 mg once daily; patients requiring >45% reduction in LDL-C may be started at 40 mg once daily; range: 10-80 mg once daily

Dosing adjustment in renal impairment: No dosage adjustment is necessary.

Dosing adjustment in hepatic impairment: Do not use in active liver disease.

Administration May be administered with food if desired; may take without regard to time of day

Monitoring Parameters Lipid levels after 2-4 weeks; LFTs, CPK

It is recommended that liver function tests (LFTs) be performed prior to and at 12 weeks following both the initiation of therapy and any elevation in dose, and periodically (eg, semiannually) thereafter

Patient Information May take with food if desired; may take without regard to time of day

Dosage Forms TAB: 10 mg, 20 mg, 40 mg, 80 mg

Atovaquone *(a TOE va kwone)*

Related Information

Malaria Treatment *on page 1464*

U.S. Brand Names Mepron®

Therapeutic Category Antiprotozoal

Use Acute oral treatment of mild to moderate *Pneumocystis carinii* pneumonia (PCP) in patients who are intolerant to co-trimoxazole; prophylaxis of PCP in patients intolerant to co-trimoxazole; treatment/suppression of *Toxoplasma gondii* encephalitis, primary prophylaxis of HIV-infected persons at high risk for developing *Toxoplasma gondii* encephalitis

Pregnancy Risk Factor C

Contraindications Life-threatening allergic reaction to the drug or formulation

Warnings/Precautions Has only been indicated in mild to moderate PCP; use with caution in elderly patients due to potentially impaired renal, hepatic, and cardiac function

Common Adverse Reactions Note: Adverse reaction statistics have been compiled from studies including patients with advanced HIV disease; consequently, it is difficult to distinguish reactions attributed to atovaquone from those caused by the underlying disease or a combination, thereof.

>10%:
   Central nervous system: Headache, fever, insomnia, anxiety
   Dermatologic: Rash
   Gastrointestinal: Nausea, diarrhea, vomiting
   Respiratory: Cough
1% to 10%:
   Central nervous system: Dizziness
   Dermatologic: Pruritus
   Endocrine & metabolic: Hypoglycemia, hyponatremia
   Gastrointestinal: Abdominal pain, constipation, anorexia, dyspepsia, increased amylase
   Hematologic: Anemia, neutropenia, leukopenia
   Hepatic: Elevated liver enzymes
   Neuromuscular & skeletal: Weakness
   Renal: Elevated BUN/creatinine
   Miscellaneous: Oral moniliasis

Drug Interactions
  Increased Effect/Toxicity: Possible increased toxicity with other highly protein-bound drugs.
  Decreased Effect: Rifamycins (rifampin) used concurrently decrease the steady-state plasma concentrations of atovaquone.
Mechanism of Action Has not been fully elucidated; may inhibit electron transport in mitochondria inhibiting metabolic enzymes
Pharmacodynamics/Kinetics
  Absorption: Significantly increased with a high-fat meal
  Distribution: 3.5 L/kg
  Protein binding: >99%
  Metabolism: Undergoes enterohepatic recirculation
  Bioavailability: Tablet: 23%; Suspension: 47%
  Half-life elimination: 2-3 days
  Excretion: Feces (94% as unchanged drug)
Dosage Oral: Adolescents 13-16 years and Adults:
  Prevention of PCP: 1500 mg once daily with food
  Treatment of mild to moderate PCP: 750 mg twice daily with food for 21 days
Patient Information Take as directed. Take with high-fat meals.
Dosage Forms SUSP, oral: 750 mg/5 mL (5 mL, 210 mL)

Atovaquone and Proguanil (a TOE va kwone & pro GWA nil)
Related Information
  Malaria Treatment *on page 1464*
U.S. Brand Names Malarone™
Synonyms Proguanil and Atovaquone
Therapeutic Category Antimalarial Agent
Use Prevention or treatment of acute, uncomplicated *P. falciparum* malaria
Pregnancy Risk Factor C
Contraindications Hypersensitivity to atovaquone, proguanil, or any component of the formulation; prophylactic use in severe renal impairment
Warnings/Precautions Not indicated for severe or complicated malaria. Absorption of atovaquone may be decreased in patients who have diarrhea or vomiting; monitor closely and consider use of an antiemetic. If severe, consider use of an alternative antimalarial. Administer with caution to patients with pre-existing renal disease. Not for use in patients <11 kg. Delayed cases of *P. falciparum* malaria may occur after stopping prophylaxis. Recrudescent infections or infections following prophylaxis with this agent should be treated with an alternative agent(s).
Common Adverse Reactions The following adverse reactions were reported in ≥5% of adults taking atovaquone/proguanil in treatment doses.

  >10%: Gastrointestinal: Abdominal pain (17%), nausea (12%), vomiting (12% adults, 10% to 13% children)
  1% to 10%:
    Central nervous system: Headache (10%), dizziness (5%)
    Dermatologic: Pruritus (6% children)
    Gastrointestinal: Diarrhea (8%), anorexia (5%)
    Neuromuscular & skeletal: Weakness (8%)

  Adverse reactions reported in placebo-controlled clinical trials when used for prophylaxis. In general, reactions were similar to (or lower than) those seen with placebo:
  >10%:
    Central nervous system: Headache (22% adults, 19% children)
    Gastrointestinal: Abdominal pain (33% children)
    Neuromuscular & skeletal: Myalgia (12% adults)
  1% to 10%:
    Central nervous system: Fever (5% adults, 6% children)
    Gastrointestinal: Abdominal pain (9% adults), diarrhea (6% adults, 2% children), dyspepsia (3% adults), gastritis (3% adults), vomiting (1% adults, 7% children)
    Neuromuscular & skeletal: Back pain (8% adults)
    Respiratory: Upper respiratory tract infection (8% adults), cough (6% adults, 9% children)
    Miscellaneous: Flu-like syndrome (2% adults, 9% children)
  In addition, 54% of adults in the placebo-controlled trials reported any adverse event (65% for placebo) and 60% of children reported adverse events (62% for placebo).
Drug Interactions
  Cytochrome P450 Effect: Proguanil: **Substrate** (minor) of 1A2, 2C19, 3A4.
  Decreased Effect: Metoclopramide decreases bioavailability of atovaquone. Rifabutin decreases atovaquone levels by 34%. Rifampin decreases atovaquone levels by 50%. Tetracycline decreases plasma concentrations of atovaquone by 40%.
Mechanism of Action
  Atovaquone: Selectively inhibits parasite mitochondrial electron transport.
  Proguanil: The metabolite cycloguanil inhibits dihydrofolate reductase, disrupting deoxythymidylate synthesis. Together, atovaquone/cycloguanil affect the erythrocytic and exoerythrocytic stages of development.
Pharmacodynamics/Kinetics
  Atovaquone: See Atovaquone monograph.
  (Continued)

Atovaquone and Proguanil *(Continued)*

Proguanil:
Absorption: Extensive
Distribution: 42 L/kg
Protein binding: 75%
Metabolism: Hepatic to active metabolites, cycloguanil (via CYP2C19) and 4-chlorophenylbiguanide
Half-life elimination: 12-21 hours
Excretion: Urine (40% to 60%)

Dosage Oral:
Children (dosage based on body weight):
Prevention of malaria: Start 1-2 days prior to entering a malaria-endemic area, continue throughout the stay and for 7 days after returning. Take as a single dose, once daily.
11-20 kg: Atovaquone/proguanil 62.5 mg/25 mg
21-30 kg: Atovaquone/proguanil 125 mg/50 mg
31-40 kg: Atovaquone/proguanil 187.5 mg/75 mg
>40 kg: Atovaquone/proguanil 250 mg/100 mg
Treatment of acute malaria: Take as a single dose, once daily for 3 consecutive days.
11-20 kg: Atovaquone/proguanil 250 mg/100 mg
21-30 kg: Atovaquone/proguanil 500 mg/200 mg
31-40 kg: Atovaquone/proguanil 750 mg/300 mg
>40 kg: Atovaquone/proguanil 1 g/400 mg

Adults:
Prevention of malaria: Atovaquone/proguanil 250 mg/100 mg once daily; start 1-2 days prior to entering a malaria-endemic area, continue throughout the stay and for 7 days after returning
Treatment of acute malaria: Atovaquone/proguanil 1 g/400 mg as a single dose, once daily for 3 consecutive days
Elderly: Use with caution due to possible decrease in renal and hepatic function, as well as possible decreases in cardiac function, concomitant diseases, or other drug therapy.

Dosage adjustment in renal impairment: Should not be used as prophylaxis in severe renal impairment (Cl_{cr} <30 mL/minute). Alternative treatment regimens should be used in patients with Cl_{cr} <30 mL/minute. No dosage adjustment required in mild to moderate renal impairment.

Dosage adjustment in hepatic impairment: No dosage adjustment required in mild to moderate hepatic impairment. No data available for use in severe hepatic impairment.

Administration Dose should be given at the same time each day with food or a milky drink. If vomiting occurs within 1 hour of administration, repeat the dose.

Patient Information Take at the same time each day with food or a milky drink. If vomiting occurs within 1 hour of taking your dose, you may repeat the dose. Wear protective clothing and use insect repellents and bednets to help prevent malaria exposure. Notify your prescriber if you develop a fever after returning from or while visiting a malaria-endemic area.

Dosage Forms TAB: Atovaquone 250 mg and proguanil 100 mg. **TAB, pediatric:** Atovaquone 62.5 mg and proguanil 25 mg

♦ **ATRA** *see* Tretinoin (Oral) *on page 1258*

Atracurium *(a tra KYOO ree um)*

Related Information
Neuromuscular Blocking Agents Comparison *on page 1397*

U.S. Brand Names Tracrium®

Synonyms Atracurium Besylate

Therapeutic Category Neuromuscular Blocker Agent, Nondepolarizing

Use Adjunct to general anesthesia to facilitate endotracheal intubation and to relax skeletal muscles during surgery; to facilitate mechanical ventilation in ICU patients; does not relieve pain or produce sedation

Pregnancy Risk Factor C

Contraindications Hypersensitivity to atracurium besylate or any component of the formulation

Warnings/Precautions Reduce initial dosage and inject slowly (over 1-2 minutes) in patients in whom substantial histamine release would be potentially hazardous (eg, patients with clinically important cardiovascular disease); maintenance of an adequate airway and respiratory support is critical; certain clinical conditions may result in potentiation or antagonism of neuromuscular blockade:
Potentiation: Electrolyte abnormalities, severe hyponatremia, severe hypocalcemia, severe hypokalemia, hypermagnesemia, neuromuscular diseases, acidosis, acute intermittent porphyria, renal failure, hepatic failure
Antagonism: Alkalosis, hypercalcemia, demyelinating lesions, peripheral neuropathies, diabetes mellitus

Increased sensitivity in patients with myasthenia gravis, Eaton-Lambert syndrome; resistance in burn patients (>30% of body) for period of 5-70 days postinjury; resistance in patients with muscle trauma, denervation, immobilization, infection, chronic treatment with atracurium. Cross-sensitivity with other neuromuscular-blocking agents may occur; use extreme caution in patients with previous anaphylactic reactions. Bradycardia may be more common with atracurium than with other neuromuscular-blocking agents since it has no clinically significant effects on heart rate to counteract the bradycardia produced by anesthetics.

Common Adverse Reactions Mild, rare, and generally suggestive of histamine release
1% to 10%: Cardiovascular: Flushing

Causes of prolonged neuromuscular blockade: Excessive drug administration; cumulative drug effect, decreased metabolism/excretion (hepatic and/or renal impairment); accumulation of active metabolites; electrolyte imbalance (hypokalemia, hypocalcemia, hypermagnesemia, hypernatremia); hypothermia

Drug Interactions

Increased Effect/Toxicity: Increased effects are possible with aminoglycosides, beta-blockers, clindamycin, calcium channel blockers, halogenated anesthetics, imipenem, ketamine, lidocaine, loop diuretics (furosemide), macrolides (case reports), magnesium sulfate, procainamide, quinidine, quinolones, tetracyclines, and vancomycin. May increase risk of myopathy when used with high- dose corticosteroids for extended periods.

Decreased Effect: Effect of nondepolarizing neuromuscular blockers may be reduced by carbamazepine (chronic use), corticosteroids (also associated with myopathy - see increased effect), phenytoin (chronic use), sympathomimetics, and theophylline.

Mechanism of Action Blocks neural transmission at the myoneural junction by binding with cholinergic receptor sites

Pharmacodynamics/Kinetics

Onset of action (dose dependent): 2-3 minutes

Duration: Recovery begins in 20-35 minutes following initial dose of 0.4-0.5 mg/kg under balanced anesthesia; recovery to 95% of control takes 60-70 minutes

Metabolism: Undergoes ester hydrolysis and Hofmann elimination (nonbiologic process independent of renal, hepatic, or enzymatic function); metabolites have no neuromuscular blocking properties; laudanosine, a product of Hofmann elimination, is a CNS stimulant and can accumulate with prolonged use. Laudanosine is hepatically metabolized.

Half-life elimination: Biphasic: Adults: Initial (distribution): 2 minutes; Terminal: 20 minutes

Excretion: Urine (<5%)

Dosage I.V. (not to be used I.M.): Dose to effect; doses must be individualized due to interpatient variability; use ideal body weight for obese patients

Children 1 month to 2 years: Initial: 0.3-0.4 mg/kg followed by maintenance doses as needed to maintain neuromuscular blockade

Children >2 years to Adults: 0.4-0.5 mg/kg, then 0.08-0.1 mg/kg 20-45 minutes after initial dose to maintain neuromuscular block, followed by repeat doses of 0.08-0.1 mg/kg at 15- to 25-minute intervals

Initial dose after succinylcholine for intubation (balanced anesthesia): Adults: 0.2-0.4 mg/kg

Pretreatment/priming: 10% of intubating dose given 3-5 minutes before initial dose

Continuous infusion:

Surgery: Initial: 9-10 mcg/kg/minute at initial signs of recovery from bolus dose; block usually maintained by a rate of 5-9 mcg/kg/minute under balanced anesthesia

ICU: Block usually maintained by rate of 11-13 mcg/kg/minute (rates for pediatric patients may be higher)

See table.

Atracurium Besylate Infusion Chart

Drug Delivery Rate (mcg/kg/min)	Infusion Rate (mL/kg/min) 0.2 mg/mL (20 mg/100 mL)	Infusion Rate (mL/kg/min) 0.5 mg/mL (50 mg/100 mL)
5	0.025	0.01
6	0.03	0.012
7	0.035	0.014
8	0.04	0.016
9	0.045	0.018
10	0.05	0.02

Dosage adjustment for hepatic or renal impairment is not necessary

Administration May be given undiluted as a bolus injection; not for I.M. injection due to tissue irritation; administration via infusion requires the use of an infusion pump; use infusion solutions within 24 hours of preparation

Monitoring Parameters Vital signs (heart rate, blood pressure, respiratory rate); degree of muscle relaxation (via peripheral nerve stimulator and presence of spontaneous movement); renal function (serum creatinine, BUN) and liver function when in ICU

In the ICU setting, prolonged paralysis and generalized myopathy, following discontinuation of agent, may be minimized by appropriately monitoring degree of blockade.

Patient Information May be difficult to talk because of head and neck muscle blockade

Dosage Forms INJ: 10 mg/mL (10 mL). **INJ** [preservative free]: 10 mg/mL (5 mL)

♦ **Atracurium Besylate** see Atracurium on page 132
♦ **AtroPen®** see Atropine on page 133

Atropine (A troe peen)

Related Information

Cycloplegic Mydriatics Comparison on page 1375

U.S. Brand Names AtroPen®; Atropine-Care®; Isopto® Atropine; Sal-Tropine™

(Continued)

Atropine *(Continued)*

Synonyms Atropine Sulfate

Therapeutic Category Anticholinergic Agent; Anticholinergic Agent, Ophthalmic; Antidote, Organophosphate Poisoning; Antispasmodic Agent, Gastrointestinal; Bronchodilator; Ophthalmic Agent, Mydriatic

Use

Injection: Preoperative medication to inhibit salivation and secretions; treatment of symptomatic sinus bradycardia; AV block (nodal level); ventricular asystole; antidote for organophosphate pesticide poisoning

Ophthalmic: Produce mydriasis and cycloplegia for examination of the retina and optic disc and accurate measurement of refractive errors; uveitis

Oral: Inhibit salivation and secretions

Unlabeled/Investigational Use Pulseless electric activity, asystole, neuromuscular blockade reversal; treatment of nerve agent toxicity (chemical warfare) in combination with pralidoxime

Restrictions The AtroPen® formulation is available for use primarily by the Department of Defense.

Pregnancy Risk Factor C

Contraindications Hypersensitivity to atropine or any component of the formulation; narrow-angle glaucoma; adhesions between the iris and lens; tachycardia; obstructive GI disease; paralytic ileus; intestinal atony of the elderly or debilitated patient; severe ulcerative colitis; toxic megacolon complicating ulcerative colitis; hepatic disease; obstructive uropathy; renal disease; myasthenia gravis (unless used to treat side effects of acetylcholinesterase inhibitor); asthma; thyrotoxicosis; Mobitz type II block

Warnings/Precautions Use with caution in children with spastic paralysis; use with caution in elderly patients. Low doses cause a paradoxical decrease in heart rates. Some commercial products contain sodium metabisulfite, which can cause allergic-type reactions. May accumulate with multiple inhalational administration, particularly in the elderly. Heat prostration may occur in hot weather. Use with caution in patients with autonomic neuropathy, prostatic hyperplasia, hyperthyroidism, CHF, cardiac arrhythmias, chronic lung disease, biliary tract disease; anticholinergic agents are generally not well tolerated in the elderly and their use should be avoided when possible; atropine is rarely used except as a preoperative agent or in the acute treatment of bradyarrhythmias.

AtroPen®: There are no absolute contraindications for the use of atropine in organophosphate poisonings, however, use caution in those patients where the use of atropine would be otherwise contraindicated. Formulation for use by trained personnel only.

Common Adverse Reactions Severity and frequency of adverse reactions are dose related and vary greatly; listed reactions are limited to significant and/or life-threatening.

Cardiovascular: Arrhythmia, flushing, hypotension, palpitation, tachycardia

Central nervous system: Ataxia, coma, delirium, disorientation, dizziness, drowsiness, excitement, fever, hallucinations, headache, insomnia, nervousness, weakness

Dermatologic: Anhidrosis, urticaria, rash, scarlatiniform rash

Gastrointestinal: Bloating, constipation, delayed gastric emptying, loss of taste, nausea, paralytic ileus, vomiting, xerostomia

Genitourinary: Urinary hesitancy, urinary retention

Ocular: Angle-closure glaucoma, blurred vision, cycloplegia, dry eyes, mydriasis, ocular tension increased

Respiratory: Dyspnea, laryngospasm, pulmonary edema

Miscellaneous: Anaphylaxis

Drug Interactions

Increased Effect/Toxicity: Antihistamines, phenothiazines, TCAs, and other drugs with anticholinergic activity may increase anticholinergic effects of atropine when used concurrently. Sympathomimetic amines may cause tachyarrhythmias; avoid concurrent use.

Decreased Effect: Effect of some phenothiazines may be antagonized. Levodopa effects may be decreased (limited clinical validation). Drugs with cholinergic mechanisms (metoclopramide, cisapride, bethanechol) decrease anticholinergic effects of atropine.

Mechanism of Action Blocks the action of acetylcholine at parasympathetic sites in smooth muscle, secretory glands and the CNS; increases cardiac output, dries secretions, antagonizes histamine and serotonin

Pharmacodynamics/Kinetics

Onset of action: I.V.: Rapid

Absorption: Complete

Distribution: Widely throughout the body; crosses placenta; trace amounts enter breast milk; crosses blood-brain barrier

Metabolism: Hepatic

Half-life elimination: 2-3 hours

Excretion: Urine (30% to 50% as unchanged drug and metabolites)

Dosage

Neonates, Infants, and Children: Doses <0.1 mg have been associated with paradoxical bradycardia.

Inhibit salivation and secretions (preanesthesia): Oral, I.M., I.V., S.C.:

<5 kg: 0.02 mg/kg/dose 30-60 minutes preop then every 4-6 hours as needed. Use of a minimum dosage of 0.1 mg in neonates <5 kg will result in dosages >0.02 mg/kg. There is no documented minimum dosage in this age group.

>5 kg: 0.01-0.02 mg/kg/dose to a maximum 0.4 mg/dose 30-60 minutes preop; minimum dose: 0.1 mg

Alternate dosing:
3-7 kg (7-16 lb): 0.1 mg
8-11 kg (17-24 lb): 0.15 mg
11-18 kg (24-40 lb): 0.2 mg
18-29 kg (40-65 lb): 0.3 mg
>30 kg (>65 lb): 0.4 mg

Bradycardia: I.V., intratracheal: 0.02 mg/kg, minimum dose 0.1 mg, maximum single dose: 0.5 mg in children and 1 mg in adolescents; may repeat in 5-minute intervals to a maximum total dose of 1 mg in children or 2 mg in adolescents. (**Note:** For intratracheal administration, the dosage must be diluted with normal saline to a total volume of 1-5 mL). When treating bradycardia in neonates, reserve use for those patients unresponsive to improved oxygenation and epinephrine.

Infants and Children: Nerve agent toxicity management (unlabeled use): See **"Note"** in Adults dosing.

Prehospital ("in the field"): I.M.:
Birth to <2 years: Mild-to-moderate symptoms: 0.05 mg/kg; severe symptoms: 0.1 mg/kg
2-10 years: Mild-to-moderate symptoms: 1 mg; severe symptoms: 2 mg
>10 years: Mild-to-moderate symptoms: 2 mg; severe symptoms: 4 mg

Hospital/emergency department: I.M.:
Birth to <2 years: Mild-to-moderate symptoms: 0.05 mg/kg I.M. **or** 0.02 mg/kg I.V.; severe symptoms: 0.1 mg/kg I.M. **or** 0.02 mg/kg I.V.
2-10 years: Mild-to-moderate symptoms: 1 mg; severe symptoms: 2 mg
>10 years: Mild-to-moderate symptoms: 2 mg; severe symptoms: 4 mg

Children: Organophosphate or carbamate poisoning:
I.V.: 0.03-0.05 mg/kg every 10-20 minutes until atropine effect, then every 1-4 hours for at least 24 hours
I.M. (AtroPen®): Mild symptoms: Administer dose listed below as soon as exposure is known or suspected. If severe symptoms develop after first dose, 2 additional doses should be repeated in 10 minutes; do not administer more than 3 doses. Severe symptoms: Immediately administer 3 doses as follows:
<6.8 kg (15 lbs): Use of **AtroPen® formulation not recommended;** administer atropine 0.05 mg/kg
6.8-18 kg (15-40 lbs): 0.5 mg/dose
18-41 kg (40-90 lbs): 1 mg/dose
>41 kg (>90 lbs): 2 mg/dose

Adults (doses <0.5 mg have been associated with paradoxical bradycardia):
Asystole or pulseless electrical activity: I.V.: 1 mg; repeat in 3-5 minutes if asystole persists; total dose of 0.04 mg/kg; may give intratracheally in 10 mL NS (intratracheal dose should be 2-2.5 times the I.V. dose)
Inhibit salivation and secretions (preanesthesia):
I.M., I.V., S.C.: 0.4-0.6 mg 30-60 minutes preop and repeat every 4-6 hours as needed
Bradycardia: I.V.: 0.5-1 mg every 5 minutes, not to exceed a total of 3 mg or 0.04 mg/kg; may give intratracheally in 10 mL NS (intratracheal dose should be 2-2.5 times the I.V. dose)
Neuromuscular blockade reversal: I.V.: 25-30 mcg/kg 60 seconds before neostigmine or 7-10 mcg/kg in combination with edrophonium
Organophosphate or carbamate poisoning:
I.V.: 2 mg, followed by 2 mg every 5-60 minutes until adequate atropinization has occurred; initial doses of up to 6 mg may be used in life-threatening cases
I.M. (AtroPen®): Mild symptoms: Administer 2 mg as soon as exposure is known or suspected. If severe symptoms develop after first dose, 2 additional doses should be repeated in 10 minutes; do not administer more than 3 doses. Severe symptoms: Immediately administer three 2 mg doses.
Nerve agent toxicity management (unlabeled use): I.M.: See **Note**. Prehospital ("in the field") or hospital/emergency department: Mild-to-moderate symptoms: 2-4 mg; severe symptoms: 6 mg
Note: Pralidoxime is a component of the management of nerve agent toxicity; consult pralidoxime monograph for specific route and dose. For prehospital ("in the field") management, repeat atropine I.M. (children: 0.05-0.1 mg/kg; adults: 2 mg) at 5-10 minute intervals until secretions have diminished and breathing is comfortable or airway resistance has returned to near normal. For hospital management, repeat atropine I.M. (infants 1 mg; all others: 2 mg) at 5-10 minute intervals until secretions have diminished and breathing is comfortable or airway resistance has returned to near normal.
Mydriasis, cycloplegia (preprocedure): Ophthalmic (1% solution): Instill 1-2 drops 1 hour before procedure.
Uveitis: Ophthalmic:
1% solution: Instill 1-2 drops 4 times/day
Ointment: Apply a small amount in the conjunctival sac up to 3 times/day; compress the lacrimal sac by digital pressure for 1-3 minutes after instillation
Elderly, frail patients: Nerve agent toxicity management (unlabeled use): I.M.: See **"Note"** in Adults dosing.
Prehospital ("in the field"): Mild-to-moderate symptoms: 1 mg; severe symptoms: 2-4 mg
Hospital/emergency department: Mild-to-moderate symptoms: 1 mg; severe symptoms: 2 mg

Administration
I.M.: AtroPen®: Administer to outer thigh. May be given through clothing as long as pockets at the injection site are empty. Hold auto-injector in place for 10 seconds following injection; massage the injection site.
(Continued)

Atropine *(Continued)*

I.V.: Administer undiluted by rapid I.V. injection; slow injection may result in paradoxical bradycardia.

Monitoring Parameters Heart rate, blood pressure, pulse, mental status; intravenous administration requires a cardiac monitor

Patient Information Maintain good oral hygiene habits because lack of saliva may increase chance of cavities. Observe caution while driving or performing other tasks requiring alertness, as drug may cause drowsiness, dizziness, or blurred vision. Notify prescriber if rash, flushing, or eye pain occurs, or if difficulty in urinating, constipation, or sensitivity to light becomes severe or persists. Do not allow dropper bottle or tube to touch eye during administration.

Dosage Forms INJ, solution, as sulfate: 0.05 mg/mL (5 mL); 0.1 mg/mL (5 mL, 10 mL); 0.4 mg/mL (0.5 mL, 1 mL, 20 mL); 0.5 mg/mL (1 mL); 1 mg/mL (1 mL); (AtroPen®) [prefilled auto-injector]: 0.5 mg/0.7 mL (0.7 mL); 1 mg/0.7 mL (0.7 mL); 2 mg/0.7 mL (0.7 mL). **OINT, ophthalmic:** 1% (3.5 g). **SOLN, ophthalmic:** 1% (5 mL, 15 mL); (Atropine-Care®): 1% (2 mL); (Isopto® Atropine): 1% (5 mL, 15 mL). **TAB** (Sal-Tropine™): 0.4 mg

♦ **Atropine and Difenoxin** *see Difenoxin and Atropine on page 372*

♦ **Atropine and Diphenoxylate** *see Diphenoxylate and Atropine on page 385*

♦ **Atropine-Care®** *see Atropine on page 133*

♦ **Atropine, Hyoscyamine, Scopolamine, and Phenobarbital** *see Hyoscyamine, Atropine, Scopolamine, and Phenobarbital on page 643*

♦ **Atropine Sulfate** *see Atropine on page 133*

♦ **Atrovent®** *see Ipratropium on page 685*

♦ **A/T/S®** *see Erythromycin on page 453*

♦ **Attenuvax®** *see Measles Virus Vaccine (Live) on page 776*

♦ **Augmentin®** *see Amoxicillin and Clavulanate Potassium on page 87*

♦ **Augmentin ES-600®** *see Amoxicillin and Clavulanate Potassium on page 87*

♦ **Augmentin XR™** *see Amoxicillin and Clavulanate Potassium on page 87*

Auranofin *(au RANE oh fin)*

U.S. Brand Names Ridaura®

Therapeutic Category Antirheumatic, Disease Modifying; Gold Compound

Use Management of active stage of classic or definite rheumatoid arthritis in patients that do not respond to or tolerate other agents; psoriatic arthritis; adjunctive or alternative therapy for pemphigus

Pregnancy Risk Factor C

Contraindications Renal disease, history of blood dyscrasias, congestive heart failure, exfoliative dermatitis, necrotizing enterocolitis, history of anaphylactic reactions

Warnings/Precautions NSAIDs and corticosteroids may be discontinued after starting gold therapy; therapy should be discontinued if platelet count falls to <100,000/mm³; WBC <4000, granulocytes <1500/mm³, explain possibility of adverse effects and their manifestations; use with caution in patients with renal or hepatic impairment

Common Adverse Reactions

>10%:
  Dermatologic: Itching, rash
  Gastrointestinal: Stomatitis
  Ocular: Conjunctivitis
  Renal: Proteinuria

1% to 10%:
  Dermatologic: Urticaria, alopecia
  Gastrointestinal: Glossitis
  Hematologic: Eosinophilia, leukopenia, thrombocytopenia
  Renal: Hematuria

Drug Interactions

Increased Effect/Toxicity: Toxicity of penicillamine, antimalarials, hydroxychloroquine, cytotoxic agents, and immunosuppressants may be increased.

Mechanism of Action The exact mechanism of action of gold is unknown; gold is taken up by macrophages which results in inhibition of phagocytosis and lysosomal membrane stabilization; other actions observed are decreased serum rheumatoid factor and alterations in immunoglobulins. Additionally, complement activation is decreased, prostaglandin synthesis is inhibited, and lysosomal enzyme activity is decreased.

Pharmacodynamics/Kinetics

Onset of action: Delayed; therapeutic response may require as long as 3-4 months
Duration: Prolonged
Absorption: Oral: ~20% gold in dose is absorbed
Protein binding: 60%
Half-life elimination (single or multiple dose dependent): 21-31 days
Time to peak, serum: ~2 hours
Excretion: Urine (60% of absorbed gold); remainder in feces

Dosage Oral:

Children: Initial: 0.1 mg/kg/day divided daily; usual maintenance: 0.15 mg/kg/day in 1-2 divided doses; maximum: 0.2 mg/kg/day in 1-2 divided doses

Adults: 6 mg/day in 1-2 divided doses; after 3 months may be increased to 9 mg/day in 3 divided doses; if still no response after 3 months at 9 mg/day, discontinue drug

Dosing adjustment in renal impairment:
Cl$_{cr}$ 50-80 mL/minute: Reduce dose to 50%
Cl$_{cr}$ <50 mL/minute: Avoid use

Monitoring Parameters Monitor urine for protein; CBC and platelets; monitor for mouth ulcers and skin reactions; may monitor auranofin serum levels

Reference Range Gold: Normal: 0-0.1 µg/mL (SI: 0-0.0064 µmol/L); Therapeutic: 1-3 µg/mL (SI: 0.06-0.18 µmol/L); Urine: <0.1 µg/24 hours

Patient Information Minimize exposure to sunlight; benefits from drug therapy may take as long as 3 months to appear; report pruritus, rash, sore mouth; metallic taste may occur; take shortly after a meal or light snack, can be given as bedtime dose if drowsiness occurs; optimum effect may take 2-4 weeks to be achieved; avoid alcohol; be aware of possible photosensitivity reaction; may cause painful erections; avoid sudden changes in position

Dosage Forms CAP: 3 mg [29% gold]

Azathioprine (ay za THYE oh preen)

U.S. Brand Names Azasan®; Imuran®

Synonyms Azathioprine Sodium

Therapeutic Category Antineoplastic Agent, Miscellaneous; Immunosuppressant Agent

Use Adjunct with other agents in prevention of rejection of kidney transplants; also used in severe active rheumatoid arthritis unresponsive to other agents; other autoimmune diseases (ITP, SLE, MS, Crohn's disease)

Unlabeled/Investigational Use Adjunct in prevention of rejection of solid organ (nonrenal) transplants

Pregnancy Risk Factor D

Contraindications Hypersensitivity to azathioprine or any component of the formulation; pregnancy

Warnings/Precautions Chronic immunosuppression increases the risk of neoplasia; has mutagenic potential to both men and women and with possible hematologic toxicities; use with caution in patients with liver disease, renal impairment; monitor hematologic function closely

Common Adverse Reactions Frequency not defined.
Central nervous system: Fever, chills
Dermatologic: Alopecia, erythematous or maculopapular rash
Gastrointestinal: Nausea, vomiting, anorexia, diarrhea, aphthous stomatitis, pancreatitis
Hematologic: Leukopenia, thrombocytopenia, anemia, pancytopenia (bone marrow suppression may be determined, in part, by genetic factors, ie, patients with TPMT deficiency are at higher risk)
Hepatic: Hepatotoxicity, jaundice, hepatic veno-occlusive disease
Neuromuscular & skeletal: Arthralgias
Ocular: Retinopathy
(Continued)

Azathioprine *(Continued)*

Miscellaneous: Rare hypersensitivity reactions which include myalgias, rigors, dyspnea, hypotension, serum sickness, rash; secondary infections may occur secondary to immunosuppression

Drug Interactions

Increased Effect/Toxicity: Allopurinol may increase serum levels of azathioprine's active metabolite (mercaptopurine). Decrease azathioprine dose to $1/3$ to $1/4$ of normal dose. Azathioprine and ACE inhibitors may induce severe leukopenia. Aminosalicylates (olsalazine, mesalamine, sulfasalazine) may inhibit TPMT, increasing toxicity/myelosuppression of azathioprine.

Decreased Effect: Azathioprine may result in decreased action of warfarin.

Mechanism of Action Azathioprine is an imidazolyl derivative of mercaptopurine; antagonizes purine metabolism and may inhibit synthesis of DNA, RNA, and proteins; may also interfere with cellular metabolism and inhibit mitosis

Pharmacodynamics/Kinetics

Distribution: Crosses placenta

Protein binding: ~30%

Metabolism: Extensively hepatic via xanthine oxidase to mercaptopurine (active); mercaptopurine requires detoxification by thiopurine methyltransferase (TPMT)

Half-life elimination: Parent drug: 12 minutes; mercaptopurine: 0.7-3 hours; End-stage renal disease: Slightly prolonged

Excretion: Urine (primarily as metabolites)

Dosage I.V. dose is equivalent to oral dose (dosing should be based on ideal body weight):

Children and Adults: Renal transplantation: Oral, I.V.: 2-5 mg/kg/day to start, then 1-3 mg/kg/day maintenance

Adults: Rheumatoid arthritis: Oral: 1 mg/kg/day for 6-8 weeks; increase by 0.5 mg/kg every 4 weeks until response or up to 2.5 mg/kg/day

Dosing adjustment in renal impairment:

Cl_{cr} 10-50 mL/minute: Administer 75% of normal dose daily

Cl_{cr} <10 mL/minute: Administer 50% of normal dose daily

Hemodialysis: Slightly dialyzable (5% to 20%)

Administer dose posthemodialysis: CAPD effects: Unknown; CAVH effects: Unknown

Administration Azathioprine can be administered IVP over 5 minutes at a concentration not to exceed 10 mg/mL **or** azathioprine can be further diluted with normal saline or D_5W and administered by intermittent infusion over 15-60 minutes

Monitoring Parameters CBC, platelet counts, total bilirubin, alkaline phosphatase

Patient Information Response in rheumatoid arthritis may not occur for up to 3 months; do not stop taking without the prescriber's approval; do not have any vaccinations before checking with your prescriber; check with your prescriber if you have a persistent sore throat, unusual bleeding or bruising, or fatigue. Contraceptive measures are recommended during therapy.

Dosage Forms INJ, powder for reconstitution: 100 mg. **TAB** [scored] 50 mg; (Azasan®): 25 mg, 50 mg, 75 mg, 100 mg; (Imuran®): 50 mg

♦ **Azathioprine Sodium** *see Azathioprine on page 137*

Azelaic Acid *(a zeh LAY ik AS id)*

U.S. Brand Names Azelex®; Finacea™; Finevin®

Therapeutic Category Acne Product; Topical Skin Product, Acne

Use Topical treatment of mild to moderate inflammatory acne vulgaris; treatment of mild to moderate rosacea

Finacea™: Not FDA-approved for the treatment of acne

Pregnancy Risk Factor B

Dosage Topical:

Adolescents >12 years and Adults: Acne vulgaris: After skin is thoroughly washed and patted dry, gently but thoroughly massage a thin film of azelaic acid cream into the affected areas twice daily, in the morning and evening. The duration of use can vary and depends on the severity of the acne. In the majority of patients with inflammatory lesions, improvement of the condition occurs within 4 weeks.

Adults: Rosacea: Massage gently into affected areas of the face twice daily

Dosage Forms CRM (Azelex®, Finevin®): 20% (30 g, 50 g). **GEL** (Finacea™): 15% (30 g)

Azelastine *(a ZEL as teen)*

U.S. Brand Names Astelin®; Optivar®

Synonyms Azelastine Hydrochloride

Therapeutic Category Antihistamine; Antihistamine, Nasal; Antihistamine, Ophthalmic

Use

Nasal spray: Treatment of the symptoms of seasonal allergic rhinitis such as rhinorrhea, sneezing, and nasal pruritus in children ≥5 years of age and adults; treatment of the symptoms of vasomotor rhinitis in children ≥12 years of age and adults

Ophthalmic: Treatment of itching of the eye associated with seasonal allergic conjunctivitis in children ≥3 years of age and adults

Pregnancy Risk Factor C

Contraindications Hypersensitivity to azelastine or any component of the formulation

Warnings/Precautions

Nasal spray: May cause drowsiness in some patients; instruct patient to use caution when driving or operating machinery. Effects may be additive with CNS depressants and/or ethanol.

Ophthalmic: Solution contains benzalkonium chloride; wait at least 10 minutes after instilling solution before inserting soft contact lenses. Do not use contact lenses if eyes are red.

Common Adverse Reactions

Nasal spray:

>10%:

Central nervous system: Headache (15%), somnolence (12%)

Gastrointestinal: Bitter taste (20%)

2% to 10%:

Central nervous system: Dizziness (2%), fatigue (2%)

Gastrointestinal: Nausea (3%), weight gain (2%), dry mouth (3%)

Respiratory: Nasal burning (4%), pharyngitis (4%), paroxysmal sneezing (3%), rhinitis (2%), epistaxis (2%)

<2%:

Cardiovascular: Flushing, hypertension, tachycardia

Central nervous system: Drowsiness, fatigue, vertigo, depression, nervousness, hypoesthesia, anxiety, depersonalization, sleep disorder, abnormal thinking, malaise

Dermatologic: Contact dermatitis, eczema, hair and follicle infection, furunculosis

Gastrointestinal: Constipation, gastroenteritis, glossitis, increased appetite, ulcerative stomatitis, vomiting, increased ALT, aphthous stomatitis, abdominal pain

Genitourinary: Urinary frequency, hematuria, albuminuria, amenorrhea

Neuromuscular & skeletal: Myalgia, vertigo, temporomandibular dislocation, hypoesthesia, hyperkinesia, back pain, extremity pain

Ocular: Conjunctivitis, watery eyes, eye pain

Respiratory: Bronchospasm, coughing, throat burning, laryngitis

Miscellaneous: Allergic reactions, viral infections

Ophthalmic:

>10%:

Central nervous system: Headache (15%)

Ocular: Transient burning/stinging (30%)

1% to 10%:

Central nervous system: Fatigue

Genitourinary: Bitter taste (10%)

Ocular: Conjunctivitis, eye pain, blurred vision (temporary)

Respiratory: Asthma, dyspnea, pharyngitis

Miscellaneous: Flu-like syndrome

Drug Interactions

Cytochrome P450 Effect: Substrate (minor) of CYP1A2, 2C19, 2D6, 3A4; **Inhibits** CYP2B6 (weak), 2C8/9 (weak), 2C19 (weak), 2D6 (weak), 3A4 (weak)

Increased Effect/Toxicity: May cause additive sedation when concomitantly administered with other CNS depressant medications. Cimetidine can increase the AUC and C_{max} of azelastine by as much as 65%.

Mechanism of Action Competes with histamine for H_1-receptor sites on effector cells and inhibits the release of histamine and other mediators involved in the allergic response. When used intranasally, reduces hyper-reactivity of the airways; increases the motility of bronchial epithelial cilia, improving mucociliary transport

Pharmacodynamics/Kinetics

Onset of action: Peak effect: Nasal spray: 3 hours; Ophthalmic solution: 3 minutes

Duration: Nasal spray: 12 hours; Ophthalmic solution: 8 hours

Protein binding: 88%

Metabolism: Hepatic via CYP; active metabolite, desmethylazelastine

Bioavailability: Intranasal: 40%

Half-life elimination: 22 hours

Time to peak, serum: 2-3 hours

Dosage

Children 5-11 years: Seasonal allergic rhinitis: Intranasal: 1 spray each nostril twice daily

Children ≥12 years and Adults: Seasonal allergic rhinitis or vasomotor rhinitis: Intranasal: 2 sprays (137 mcg/spray) each nostril twice daily

Children ≥3 years and Adults: Itching eyes due to seasonal allergic conjunctivitis: Ophthalmic: Instill 1 drop into affected eye(s) twice daily

Administration Intranasal: Before initial use of the nasal spray, the delivery system should be primed with 4 sprays or until a fine mist appears. If 3 or more days have elapsed since last use, the delivery system should be reprimed.

Patient Information Causes drowsiness and may impair ability to perform hazardous activities requiring mental alertness or physical coordination; avoid spraying in eyes

Dosage Forms SOLN, intranasal spray (Astelin®): 1 mg/mL [137 mcg/spray] (17 mL). **SOLN, ophthalmic** (Optivar®): 0.05% (6 mL)

Azithromycin (az ith roe MYE sin)

Related Information

Antimicrobial Drugs of Choice *on page 1440*
Community-Acquired Pneumonia in Adults *on page 1457*
Prevention of Bacterial Endocarditis *on page 1429*

U.S. Brand Names Zithromax®

Synonyms Azithromycin Dihydrate; Zithromax® TRI-PAK™; Zithromax® Z-PAK®

Therapeutic Category Antibiotic, Macrolide

Use Treatment of acute otitis media due to *H. influenzae*, *M. catarrhalis*, or *S. pneumoniae*; pharyngitis/tonsillitis due to *S. pyogenes*; treatment of mild to moderate upper and lower respiratory tract infections, infections of the skin and skin structure, community-acquired pneumonia, pelvic inflammatory disease (PID), sexually-transmitted diseases (urethritis/cervicitis), pharyngitis/tonsillitis (alternative to first-line therapy), and genital ulcer disease (chancroid) due to susceptible strains of *C. trachomatis*, *M. catarrhalis*, *H. influenzae*, *S. aureus*, *S. pneumoniae*, *Mycoplasma pneumoniae*, and *C. psittaci*; acute bacterial exacerbations of chronic obstructive pulmonary disease (COPD) due to *H. influenzae*, *M. catarrhalis*, or *S. pneumoniae*

Unlabeled/Investigational Use Prevention of (or to delay onset of) or treatment of MAC in patients with advanced HIV infection; prophylaxis of bacterial endocarditis in patients who are allergic to penicillin and undergoing surgical or dental procedures

Pregnancy Risk Factor B

Contraindications Hypersensitivity to azithromycin, other macrolide antibiotics, or any component of the formulation

Warnings/Precautions Use with caution in patients with hepatic dysfunction; hepatic impairment with or without jaundice has occurred chiefly in older children and adults; it may be accompanied by malaise, nausea, vomiting, abdominal colic, and fever; discontinue use if these occur; may mask or delay symptoms of incubating gonorrhea or syphilis, so appropriate culture and susceptibility tests should be performed prior to initiating azithromycin; pseudomembranous colitis has been reported with use of macrolide antibiotics; use caution with renal dysfunction; safety and efficacy have not been established in children <6 months of age with acute otitis media or community-acquired pneumonia, or in children <2 years of age with pharyngitis/tonsillitis.

Common Adverse Reactions 1% to 10%: Gastrointestinal: Diarrhea, nausea, abdominal pain, cramping, vomiting (especially with high single-dose regimens)

Drug Interactions

Cytochrome P450 Effect: Substrate of CYP3A4 (minor); **Inhibits** CYP3A4 (weak)

Increased Effect/Toxicity: Concurrent use of pimozide is contraindicated due to potential cardiotoxicity. The manufacturer warns that azithromycin potentially may increase levels of tacrolimus, phenytoin, ergot alkaloids, alfentanil, astemizole, bromocriptine, carbamazepine, cyclosporine, digoxin, disopyramide, and triazolam. However, azithromycin did not affect the response/levels of carbamazepine, terfenadine, theophylline, or warfarin in specific interaction studies; caution is advised when administered together. Nelfinavir may increase azithromycin serum levels (monitor for adverse effects).

Decreased Effect: Decreased azithromycin peak serum concentrations with aluminum- and magnesium-containing antacids (by 24%), however, total absorption is unaffected.

Mechanism of Action Inhibits RNA-dependent protein synthesis at the chain elongation step; binds to the 50S ribosomal subunit resulting in blockage of transpeptidation

Pharmacodynamics/Kinetics

Absorption: Rapid

Distribution: Extensive tissue; distributes well into skin, lungs, sputum, tonsils, and cervix; penetration into CSF is poor

Protein binding (concentration dependent): 7% to 50%

Metabolism: Hepatic

Bioavailability: 37%; variable effect with food (increased with oral suspension, unchanged with tablet)

Half-life elimination: Terminal: 68 hours

Time to peak, serum: 2.3-4 hours

Excretion: Feces (50% as unchanged drug); urine (~5% to 12%)

Dosage

Oral:

Children ≥6 months:

Community-acquired pneumonia: 10 mg/kg on day 1 (maximum: 500 mg/day) followed by 5 mg/kg/day once daily on days 2-5 (maximum: 250 mg/day)

Otitis media:

1-day regimen: 30 mg/kg as a single dose (maximum dose: 1500 mg)

3-day regimen: 10 mg/kg once daily for 3 days (maximum: 500 mg/day)

5-day regimen: 10 mg/kg on day 1 (maximum: 500 mg/day) followed by 5 mg/kg/day once daily on days 2-5 (maximum: 250 mg/day)

Children ≥2 years: Pharyngitis, tonsillitis: 12 mg/kg/day once daily for 5 days (maximum: 500 mg/day)

Children:

M. avium-infected patients with acquired immunodeficiency syndrome (unlabeled use): 5 mg/kg/day once daily (maximum dose: 250 mg/day) or 20 mg/kg (maximum dose: 1200 mg) once weekly given alone or in combination with rifabutin

Treatment and secondary prevention of disseminated MAC (unlabeled use): 5 mg/kg/day once daily (maximum dose: 250 mg/day) in combination with ethambutol, with or without rifabutin

Prophylaxis for bacterial endocarditis (unlabeled use): 15 mg/kg 1 hour before procedure

Uncomplicated chlamydial urethritis or cervicitis (unlabeled use): Children ≥45 kg: 1 g as a single dose

Adolescents ≥16 years and Adults:

Respiratory tract, skin and soft tissue infections: 500 mg on day 1 followed by 250 mg/day on days 2-5 (maximum: 500 mg/day)

Alternative regimen for bacterial exacerbation of COPD: 500 mg/day for a total of 3 days

Urethritis/cervicitis:

Due to *C. trachomatis*: 1 g as a single dose

Due to *N. gonorrhoeae*: 2 g as a single dose

Chancroid due to *H. ducreyi*: 1 g as a single dose

Prophylaxis of disseminated *M. avium* complex disease in patient with advanced HIV infection (unlabeled use): 1200 mg once weekly (may be combined with rifabutin)

Treatment of disseminated *M. avium* complex disease in patient with advanced HIV infection (unlabeled use): 600 mg daily (in combination with ethambutol 15 mg/kg)

Prophylaxis for bacterial endocarditis (unlabeled use): 500 mg 1 hour prior to the procedure

I.V.: Adults:

Community-acquired pneumonia: 500 mg as a single dose for at least 2 days, follow I.V. therapy by the oral route with a single daily dose of 500 mg to complete a 7-10 day course of therapy

Pelvic inflammatory disease (PID): 500 mg as a single dose for 1-2 days, follow I.V. therapy by the oral route with a single daily dose of 250 mg to complete a 7-day course of therapy

Dosage adjustment in renal impairment: Use caution in patients with Cl_{cr} <10 mL/minute

Administration

I.V.: Other medications should not be infused simultaneously through the same I.V. line.

Oral: Suspension and tablet may be taken without regard to food.

Monitoring Parameters Liver function tests, CBC with differential

Patient Information Take as directed. Take all of prescribed medication. Do not discontinue until prescription is completed. Suspension may be taken with or without food; tablet form may be taken with meals to decrease GI effects. Do not take with aluminum- or magnesium-containing antacids.

Dosage Forms INJ, powder for reconstitution: 500 mg. **POWDER, oral suspension:** 100 mg/5 mL (15 mL); 200 mg/5 mL (15 mL, 22.5 mL, 30 mL); 1 g. **TAB:** 250 mg, 500 mg, 600 mg; (Zithromax® TRI-PAK™): 500 mg (3s), (Zithromax® Z-PAK®): 250 mg (6s)

♦ **Azithromycin Dihydrate** *see* Azithromycin *on page 140*

♦ **Azmacort®** *see* Triamcinolone *on page 1261*

♦ **Azo-Gesic® [OTC]** *see* Phenazopyridine *on page 987*

♦ **Azopt®** *see* Brinzolamide *on page 180*

♦ **Azo-Standard® [OTC]** *see* Phenazopyridine *on page 987*

♦ **AZT** *see* Zidovudine *on page 1324*

♦ **AZT + 3TC** *see* Zidovudine and Lamivudine *on page 1326*

♦ **AZT, Abacavir, and Lamivudine** *see* Abacavir, Lamivudine, and Zidovudine *on page 19*

♦ **Azthreonam** *see* Aztreonam *on page 141*

Aztreonam (AZ tree oh nam)

Related Information

Antimicrobial Drugs of Choice *on page 1440*

Community-Acquired Pneumonia in Adults *on page 1457*

U.S. Brand Names Azactam®

Synonyms Azthreonam

Therapeutic Category Antibiotic, Miscellaneous

Use Treatment of patients with urinary tract infections, lower respiratory tract infections, septicemia, skin/skin structure infections, intra-abdominal infections, and gynecological infections caused by susceptible gram-negative bacilli

Pregnancy Risk Factor B

Contraindications Hypersensitivity to aztreonam or any component of the formulation

Warnings/Precautions Rare cross-allergenicity to penicillins and cephalosporins. Use caution in renal impairment; dosing adjustment required.

Common Adverse Reactions As reported in adults:

1% to 10%:

Dermatologic: Rash

Gastrointestinal: Diarrhea, nausea, vomiting

Local: Thrombophlebitis, pain at injection site

Drug Interactions

Decreased Effect: Avoid antibiotics that induce beta-lactamase production (cefoxitin, imipenem).

Mechanism of Action Inhibits bacterial cell wall synthesis by binding to one or more of the penicillin binding proteins (PBPs); which in turn inhibits the final transpeptidation step of peptidoglycan synthesis in bacterial cell walls, thus inhibiting cell wall biosynthesis. Bacteria eventually lyse due to ongoing activity of cell wall autolytic enzymes (autolysins and murein hydrolases) while cell wall assembly is arrested. Monobactam structure makes cross-allergenicity with beta-lactams unlikely.

(Continued)

141

Aztreonam *(Continued)*

Pharmacodynamics/Kinetics

Absorption: I.M.: Well absorbed; I.M. and I.V. doses produce comparable serum concentrations

Distribution: Widely to most body fluids and tissues; crosses placenta; enters breast milk

V_d: Children: 0.2-0.29 L/kg; Adults: 0.2 L/kg

Relative diffusion of antimicrobial agents from blood into CSF: Good only with inflammation (exceeds usual MICs)

CSF:blood level ratio: Meninges: Inflamed: 8% to 40%; Normal: ~1%

Protein binding: 56%

Metabolism: Hepatic (minor %)

Half-life elimination:

Children 2 months to 12 years: 1.7 hours

Adults: Normal renal function: 1.7-2.9 hours

End-stage renal disease: 6-8 hours

Time to peak: I.M., I.V. push: Within 60 minutes; I.V. infusion: 1.5 hours

Excretion: Urine (60% to 70% as unchanged drug); feces (~13% to 15%)

Dosage

Children >1 month: I.M., I.V.:

Mild-to-moderate infections: 30 mg/kg every 8 hours

Moderate-to-severe infections: 30 mg/kg every 6-8 hours; maximum: 120 mg/kg/day (8 g/day)

Cystic fibrosis: 50 mg/kg/dose every 6-8 hours (ie, up to 200 mg/kg/day); maximum: 8 g/day

Adults:

Urinary tract infection: I.M., I.V.: 500 mg to 1 g every 8-12 hours

Moderately-severe systemic infections: 1 g I.V. or I.M. or 2 g I.V. every 8-12 hours

Severe systemic or life-threatening infections (especially caused by *Pseudomonas aeruginosa*): I.V.: 2 g every 6-8 hours; maximum: 8 g/day

Dosing adjustment in renal impairment: Adults: Following initial dose, maintenance doses should be given as follows:

Cl_{cr} 10-30 mL/minute: 50% of usual dose at the usual interval

Cl_{cr} <10 mL/minute: 25% of usual dosage at the usual interval

Hemodialysis: Moderately dialyzable (20% to 50%); $1/_8$ of initial dose after each hemodialysis session (given in addition to the maintenance doses)

Peritoneal dialysis: Administer as for Cl_{cr} <10 mL/minute

Continuous arteriovenous or venovenous hemofiltration: Dose as for Cl_{cr} 10-30 mL/minute

Administration Doses >1 g should be administered I.V.

I.M.: Administer by deep injection into large muscle mass, such as upper outer quadrant of gluteus maximus or the lateral part of the thigh

I.V.: Administer by IVP over 3-5 minutes or by intermittent infusion over 20-60 minutes at a final concentration not to exceed 20 mg/mL

Monitoring Parameters Periodic liver function test; monitor for signs of anaphylaxis during first dose

Dosage Forms INF [premixed]: 1 g (50 mL); 2 g (50 mL). **INJ, powder for reconstitution:** 500 mg, 1 g, 2 g

- ◆ **Azulfidine**® *see* Sulfasalazine *on page 1174*
- ◆ **Azulfidine**® **EN-tabs**® *see* Sulfasalazine *on page 1174*
- ◆ **B1** *see* Tositumomab and Iodine I 131 Tositumomab *on page 1248*
- ◆ **B1 Antibody** *see* Tositumomab and Iodine I 131 Tositumomab *on page 1248*
- ◆ **B2036-PEG** *see* Pegvisomant *on page 968*
- ◆ **B 9273** *see* Alefacept *on page 49*
- ◆ **BA-16038** *see* Aminoglutethimide *on page 75*
- ◆ **Babee**® **Teething**® **[OTC]** *see* Benzocaine *on page 154*
- ◆ **Bacid**® **[OTC]** *see* Lactobacillus *on page 711*
- ◆ **Baciguent**® **[OTC]** *see* Bacitracin *on page 142*
- ◆ **BaciIM**® *see* Bacitracin *on page 142*
- ◆ **Bacillus Calmette-Guérin (BCG) Live** *see* BCG Vaccine *on page 148*

Bacitracin *(bas i TRAY sin)*

U.S. Brand Names AK-Tracin® [DSC]; Baciguent® [OTC]; BaciIM®

Therapeutic Category Antibiotic, Ophthalmic; Antibiotic, Topical; Antibiotic, Miscellaneous

Use Treatment of susceptible bacterial infections mainly; has activity against gram-positive bacilli; due to toxicity risks, systemic and irrigant uses of bacitracin should be limited to situations where less toxic alternatives would not be effective

Unlabeled/Investigational Use Oral administration: Successful in antibiotic-associated colitis; has been used for enteric eradication of vancomycin-resistant enterococci (VRE)

Pregnancy Risk Factor C

Contraindications Hypersensitivity to bacitracin or any component of the formulation; I.M. use is contraindicated in patients with renal impairment

Warnings/Precautions Prolonged use may result in overgrowth of nonsusceptible organisms; I.M. use may cause renal failure due to tubular and glomerular necrosis; **do not administer intravenously** because severe thrombophlebitis occurs

Common Adverse Reactions 1% to 10%:

Cardiovascular: Hypotension, edema of the face/lips, tightness of chest

Central nervous system: Pain
Dermatologic: Rash, itching
Gastrointestinal: Anorexia, nausea, vomiting, diarrhea, rectal itching
Hematologic: Blood dyscrasias
Miscellaneous: Diaphoresis

Drug Interactions

Increased Effect/Toxicity: Nephrotoxic drugs, neuromuscular blocking agents, and anesthetics (increased neuromuscular blockade).

Mechanism of Action Inhibits bacterial cell wall synthesis by preventing transfer of mucopeptides into the growing cell wall

Pharmacodynamics/Kinetics

Duration: 6-8 hours

Absorption: Poor from mucous membranes and intact or denuded skin; rapidly following I.M. administration; not absorbed by bladder irrigation, but absorption can occur from peritoneal or mediastinal lavage

Distribution: CSF: Nil even with inflammation

Protein binding, plasma: Minimal

Time to peak, serum: I.M.: 1-2 hours

Excretion: Urine (10% to 40%) within 24 hours

Dosage Do not administer I.V.:

Infants: I.M.:

≤2.5 kg: 900 units/kg/day in 2-3 divided doses

>2.5 kg: 1000 units/kg/day in 2-3 divided doses

Children: I.M.: 800-1200 units/kg/day divided every 8 hours

Adults: Oral:

Antibiotic-associated colitis: 25,000 units 4 times/day for 7-10 days

VRE eradication (unlabeled use): 25,000 units 4 times/day for 7-10 days

Children and Adults:

Topical: Apply 1-5 times/day

Ophthalmic, ointment: Instill ¼" to ½" ribbon every 3-4 hours into conjunctival sac for acute infections, or 2-3 times/day for mild to moderate infections for 7-10 days

Irrigation, solution: 50-100 units/mL in normal saline, lactated Ringer's, or sterile water for irrigation; soak sponges in solution for topical compresses 1-5 times/day or as needed during surgical procedures

Administration For I.M. administration only, **do not administer I.V.**; confirm any orders for parenteral use; pH of urine should be kept >6 by using sodium bicarbonate; bacitracin sterile powder should be dissolved in 0.9% sodium chloride injection containing 2% procaine hydrochloride; do not use diluents containing parabens

Monitoring Parameters I.M.: Urinalysis, renal function tests

Patient Information

Ophthalmic: Tilt head back, place medication in conjunctival sac and close eyes; apply light finger pressure on lacrimal sac for 1 minute following instillation. Ophthalmic ointment may cause blurred vision; do not share eye medications with others.

Topical: Do not be use for longer than 1 week unless directed by prescriber.

Dosage Forms INJ, powder for reconstitution (BaciIM®): 50,000 units. **OINT, ophthalmic** (AK-Tracin® [DSC]): 500 units/g (3.5 g). **OINT, topical:** 500 units/g (0.9 g, 15 g, 30 g, 120 g, 454 g)

Bacitracin and Polymyxin B (bas i TRAY sin & pol i MIKS in bee)

U.S. Brand Names AK-Poly-Bac®; Betadine® First Aid Antibiotics + Moisturizer [OTC]; Polysporin® Ophthalmic; Polysporin® Topical [OTC]

Synonyms Polymyxin B and Bacitracin

Therapeutic Category Antibiotic, Ophthalmic; Antibiotic, Topical

Use Treatment of superficial infections caused by susceptible organisms

Pregnancy Risk Factor C

Dosage Children and Adults:

Ophthalmic ointment: Instill ½" ribbon in the affected eye(s) every 3-4 hours for acute infections or 2-3 times/day for mild to moderate infections for 7-10 days

Topical ointment/powder: Apply to affected area 1-4 times/day; may cover with sterile bandage if needed

Dosage Forms OINT, ophthalmic: (AK-Poly-Bac®, Polysporin®): Bacitracin 500 units and polymyxin B 10,000 units per g (3.5 g). **OINT, topical:** Bacitracin 500 units and polymyxin B 10,000 units per g in white petrolatum (14 g, 15 g, 30 g). **POWDER, topical:** Bacitracin 500 units and polymyxin B 10,000 units per g (10 g)

Bacitracin, Neomycin, and Polymyxin B

(bas i TRAY sin, nee oh MYE sin, & pol i MIKS in bee)

U.S. Brand Names Mycitracin® [OTC]; Neosporin® Ophthalmic Ointment; Neosporin® Topical [OTC]; Triple Antibiotic®

Synonyms Neomycin, Bacitracin, and Polymyxin B; Polymyxin B, Bacitracin, and Neomycin

Therapeutic Category Antibiotic, Ophthalmic; Antibiotic, Topical

Use Helps prevent infection in minor cuts, scrapes and burns; short-term treatment of superficial external ocular infections caused by susceptible organisms

Pregnancy Risk Factor C

(Continued)

Bacitracin, Neomycin, and Polymyxin B *(Continued)*

Dosage Children and Adults:

Ophthalmic: Ointment: Instill ½" into the conjunctival sac every 3-4 hours for 7-10 days for acute infections; apply ½" 2-3 times/day for mild to moderate infections for 7-10 days

Topical: Apply 1-4 times/day to infected area and cover with sterile bandage as needed

Dosage Forms OINT, ophthalmic (Neosporin®): Bacitracin 400 units, neomycin 3.5 mg, and polymyxin B 10,000 units per g (3.5 g). **OINT, topical:** Bacitracin 400 units, neomycin 3.5 mg, and polymyxin B 5000 units per g (0.9 g, 14 g, 15 g, 30 g, 454 g)

Bacitracin, Neomycin, Polymyxin B, and Hydrocortisone

(bas i TRAY sin, nee oh MYE sin, pol i MIKS in bee, & hye droe KOR ti sone)

U.S. Brand Names AK-Spore® H.C. [DSC]; Cortisporin® Ointment

Synonyms Hydrocortisone, Bacitracin, Neomycin, and Polymyxin B; Neomycin, Bacitracin, Polymyxin B, and Hydrocortisone; Polymyxin B, Bacitracin, Neomycin, and Hydrocortisone

Therapeutic Category Antibiotic/Corticosteroid, Ophthalmic; Antibiotic, Otic; Antibiotic, Topical

Use Prevention and treatment of susceptible superficial topical infections

Pregnancy Risk Factor C

Dosage Children and Adults:

Ophthalmic: Ointment: Instill ½" ribbon to inside of lower lid every 3-4 hours until improvement occurs

Topical: Apply sparingly 2-4 times/day. Therapy should be discontinued when control is achieved; if no improvement is seen, reassessment of diagnosis may be necessary.

Dosage Forms OINT, ophthalmic (AK-Spore® H.C. [DSC], Cortisporin®): Bacitracin 400 units, neomycin 3.5 mg, polymyxin B 10,000 units, and hydrocortisone 10 mg per g (3.5 g). **OINT, topical** (Cortisporin®): Bacitracin 400 units, neomycin 3.5 mg, polymyxin B 5000 units, and hydrocortisone 10 mg per g (15 g)

Bacitracin, Neomycin, Polymyxin B, and Lidocaine

(bas i TRAY sin, nee oh MYE sin, pol i MIKS in bee, & LYE doe kane)

U.S. Brand Names Spectrocin Plus® [OTC]

Synonyms Lidocaine, Neomycin, Bacitracin, and Polymyxin B; Neomycin, Bacitracin, Polymyxin B, and Lidocaine; Polymyxin B, Neomycin, Bacitracin, and Lidocaine

Therapeutic Category Antibiotic, Topical

Use Prevention and treatment of susceptible superficial topical infections

Dosage Topical: Adults: Apply 1-4 times/day to infected areas; cover with sterile bandage if needed

Dosage Forms OINT, topical: Bacitracin 500 units, neomycin base 3.5 g, polymyxin B 5000 units, and lidocaine 40 mg per g (15 g, 30 g)

Baclofen (BAK loe fen)

U.S. Brand Names Lioresal®

Therapeutic Category Skeletal Muscle Relaxant

Use Treatment of reversible spasticity associated with multiple sclerosis or spinal cord lesions

Orphan drug: Intrathecal: Treatment of intractable spasticity caused by spinal cord injury, multiple sclerosis, and other spinal disease (spinal ischemia or tumor, transverse myelitis, cervical spondylosis, degenerative myelopathy)

Unlabeled/Investigational Use Intractable hiccups, intractable pain relief, bladder spasticity, trigeminal neuralgia, cerebral palsy, Huntington's chorea

Pregnancy Risk Factor C

Contraindications Hypersensitivity to baclofen or any component of the formulation

Warnings/Precautions Use with caution in patients with seizure disorder or impaired renal function. Avoid abrupt withdrawal of the drug; abrupt withdrawal of intrathecal baclofen has resulted in severe sequelae (hyperpyrexia, obtundation, rebound/exaggerated spasticity, muscle rigidity, and rhabdomyolysis), leading to organ failure and some fatalities. Risk may be higher in patients with injuries at T-6 or above, history of baclofen withdrawal, or limited ability to communicate. Elderly are more sensitive to the effects of baclofen and are more likely to experience adverse CNS effects at higher doses.

Common Adverse Reactions

>10%:

Central nervous system: Drowsiness, vertigo, psychiatric disturbances, insomnia, slurred speech, ataxia, hypotonia

Neuromuscular & skeletal: Weakness

1% to 10%:

Cardiovascular: Hypotension

Central nervous system: Fatigue, confusion, headache

Dermatologic: Rash

Gastrointestinal: Nausea, constipation

Genitourinary: Polyuria

Drug Interactions

Increased Effect/Toxicity: Baclofen may decrease the clearance of ibuprofen or other NSAIDs and increase the potential for renal toxicity. Effects may be additive with CNS depressants.

Mechanism of Action Inhibits the transmission of both monosynaptic and polysynaptic reflexes at the spinal cord level, possibly by hyperpolarization of primary afferent fiber terminals, with resultant relief of muscle spasticity

Pharmacodynamics/Kinetics
Onset of action: 3-4 days
   Peak effect: 5-10 days
Absorption (dose dependent): Oral: Rapid
Protein binding: 30%
Metabolism: Hepatic (15% of dose)
Half-life elimination: 3.5 hours
Time to peak, serum: Oral: Within 2-3 hours
Excretion: Urine and feces (85% as unchanged drug)

Dosage
Oral (avoid abrupt withdrawal of drug):
   Children:
      2-7 years: Initial: 10-15 mg/24 hours divided every 8 hours; titrate dose every 3 days in increments of 5-15 mg/day to a maximum of 40 mg/day
      ≥8 years: Maximum: 60 mg/day in 3 divided doses
   Adults: 5 mg 3 times/day, may increase 5 mg/dose every 3 days to a maximum of 80 mg/day
   Hiccups: Adults: Usual effective dose: 10-20 mg 2-3 times/day
Intrathecal:
   Test dose: 50-100 mcg, doses >50 mcg should be given in 25 mcg increments, separated by 24 hours. A screening dose of 25 mcg may be considered in very small patients. Patients not responding to screening dose of 100 mcg should not be considered for chronic infusion/implanted pump.
   Maintenance: After positive response to test dose, a maintenance intrathecal infusion can be administered via an implanted intrathecal pump. Initial dose via pump: Infusion at a 24-hour rate dosed at twice the test dose. Avoid abrupt discontinuation.
Elderly: Oral (the lowest effective dose is recommended): Initial: 5 mg 2-3 times/day, increasing gradually as needed; if benefits are not seen withdraw the drug slowly.
Dosing adjustment in renal impairment: It is necessary to reduce dosage in renal impairment but there are no specific guidelines available
Hemodialysis: Poor water solubility allows for accumulation during chronic hemodialysis. Low-dose therapy is recommended. There have been several case reports of accumulation of baclofen resulting in toxicity symptoms (organic brain syndrome, myoclonia, deceleration and steep potentials in EEG) in patients with renal failure who have received normal doses of baclofen.

Administration Intrathecal: For screening dosages, dilute with preservative-free sodium chloride to a final concentration of 50 mcg/mL for bolus injection into the subarachnoid space; for maintenance infusions, concentrations of 500-2000 mcg/mL may be used

Patient Information

Intrathecal: It is important not to miss scheduled appointments for refills. Contact prescriber immediately if symptoms of withdrawal occur (high fever, confusion, increased spasticity, or muscle rigidity).

Oral: Take with food or milk; abrupt withdrawal after prolonged use may cause anxiety, hallucinations, tachycardia or spasticity; may cause drowsiness and impair coordination and judgment.

Dosage Forms INJ, solution, intrathecal [preservative free] (Lioresal®): 50 mcg/mL (1 mL); 500 mcg/mL (20 mL); 2000 mcg/mL (5 mL). **TAB:** 10 mg, 20 mg

♦ **BactoShield® CHG [OTC]** see Chlorhexidine Gluconate on page 259
♦ **Bactrim™** see Sulfamethoxazole and Trimethoprim on page 1173
♦ **Bactrim™ DS** see Sulfamethoxazole and Trimethoprim on page 1173
♦ **Bactroban®** see Mupirocin on page 866
♦ **Bactroban® Nasal** see Mupirocin on page 866
♦ **Baking Soda** see Sodium Bicarbonate on page 1144
♦ **BAL** see Dimercaprol on page 382
♦ **BAL in Oil®** see Dimercaprol on page 382

Balsalazide (bal SAL a zide)

U.S. Brand Names Colazal®
Synonyms Balsalazide Disodium
Therapeutic Category 5-Aminosalicylic Acid Derivative; Anti-inflammatory Agent
Use Treatment of mild to moderate active ulcerative colitis
Pregnancy Risk Factor B
Contraindications Hypersensitivity to salicylates, components of the formulation, or metabolites of balsalazide
Warnings/Precautions Pyloric stenosis may prolong gastric retention of balsalazide capsules. Renal toxicity has been observed with other mesalamine (5-aminosalicylic acid) products, use with caution in patients with known renal disease. May exacerbate symptoms of colitis. Safety and efficacy of use beyond 12 weeks has not been established. For adult use; safety and efficacy in children has not been established.
Common Adverse Reactions 1% to 10%:
Central nervous system: Headache (8%), insomnia (2%), fatigue (2%), fever (2%), pain (2%), dizziness (1%)
(Continued)

Balsalazide *(Continued)*

Gastrointestinal: Abdominal pain (6%), diarrhea (5%), nausea (5%), vomiting (4%), anorexia (2%), dyspepsia (2%), flatulence (2%), rectal bleeding (2%), cramps (1%), constipation (1%), dry mouth (1%), frequent stools (1%)

Genitourinary: Urinary tract infection (1%)

Neuromuscular & skeletal: Arthralgia (4%), back pain (2%), myalgia (1%)

Respiratory: Respiratory infection (4%), cough (2%), pharyngitis (2%), rhinitis (2%), sinusitis (1%)

Miscellaneous: Flu-like syndrome (1%)

Additional adverse reactions reported with mesalamine products (limited to important or life-threatening symptoms): Acute intolerance syndrome (cramping, abdominal pain, bloody diarrhea, fever, headache, pruritus, rash), alopecia, cholestatic jaundice, cirrhosis, elevated liver function tests, eosinophilic pneumonitis, hepatocellular damage, hepatotoxicity, jaundice, Kawasaki-like syndrome, liver failure, liver necrosis, nephrotic syndrome, pancreatitis, pericarditis, and renal dysfunction

Drug Interactions

Decreased Effect: No studies have been conducted. Oral antibiotics may potentially interfere with 5-aminosalicylic acid release in the colon.

Mechanism of Action Balsalazide is a prodrug, converted by bacterial azoreduction to 5-aminosalicylic acid (active), 4-aminobenzoyl-β-alanine (inert), and their metabolites. 5-aminosalicylic acid may decrease inflammation by blocking the production of arachidonic acid metabolites topically in the colon mucosa.

Pharmacodynamics/Kinetics

Onset of action: Delayed; may require several days to weeks

Absorption: Very low and variable

Protein binding: ≥99%

Metabolism: Azoreduced in the colon to 5-aminosalicylic acid (active), 4-aminobenzoyl-β-alanine (inert), and N-acetylated metabolites

Half-life elimination: Primary effect is topical (colonic mucosa); systemic half-life not determined

Time to peak: 1-2 hours

Excretion: Feces (65% as 5-aminosalicylic acid, 4-aminobenzoyl-β-alanine, and N-acetylated metabolites); urine (25% as N-acetylated metabolites); Parent drug: Urine or feces (<1%)

Dosage Oral:

Adults: 2.25 g (three 750 mg capsules) 3 times/day for 8-12 weeks

Elderly: No specific dosage adjustment available

Dosage adjustment in renal impairment: No information available with balsalazide; renal toxicity has been observed with other 5-aminosalicylic acid products, use with caution

Dosage adjustment in hepatic impairment: No specific dosage adjustment available

Patient Information Take as directed; do not chew or open capsules. Report abdominal pain, unresolved diarrhea, severe headache, or chest pain to prescriber.

Dosage Forms CAP: 750 mg

♦ **Balsalazide Disodium** *see* Balsalazide *on page 145*

♦ **Balsam Peru, Trypsin, and Castor Oil** *see* Trypsin, Balsam Peru, and Castor Oil *on page 1278*

♦ **Bancap HC®** *see* Hydrocodone and Acetaminophen *on page 627*

♦ **Band-Aid® Hurt-Free™ Antiseptic Wash [OTC]** *see* Lidocaine *on page 742*

♦ **Banophen® [OTC]** *see* DiphenhydrAMINE *on page 383*

Basiliximab *(ba si LIK si mab)*

U.S. Brand Names Simulect®

Therapeutic Category Immunosuppressant Agent; Monoclonal Antibody

Use Prophylaxis of acute organ rejection in renal transplantation

Pregnancy Risk Factor B (manufacturer)

Contraindications Hypersensitivity basiliximab, murine proteins, or any component of the formulation

Warnings/Precautions To be used as a component of immunosuppressive regimen which includes cyclosporine and corticosteroids. Only physicians experienced in transplantation and immunosuppression should prescribe, and patients should receive the drug in a facility with adequate equipment and staff capable of providing the laboratory and medical support required for transplantation.

The incidence of lymphoproliferative disorders and/or opportunistic infections may be increased by immunosuppressive therapy. Severe hypersensitivity reactions, occurring within 24 hours, have been reported. Reactions, including anaphylaxis, have occurred both with the initial exposure and/or following re-exposure after several months. Use caution during re-exposure to a subsequent course of therapy in a patient who has previously received basiliximab. Discontinue the drug permanently if a reaction occurs. Medications for the treatment of hypersensitivity reactions should be available for immediate use. Treatment may result in the development of human antimurine antibodies (HAMA); however, limited evidence suggesting the use of muromonab-CD3 or other murine products is not precluded.

Common Adverse Reactions Administration of basiliximab did not appear to increase the incidence or severity of adverse effects in clinical trials. Adverse events were reported in 96% of both the placebo and basiliximab groups.

>10%:
  Cardiovascular: Peripheral edema, hypertension, atrial fibrillation
  Central nervous system: Fever, headache, insomnia, pain
  Dermatologic: Wound complications, acne
  Endocrine & metabolic: Hypokalemia, hyperkalemia, hyperglycemia, hyperuricemia, hypo-
    phosphatemia, hypercholesterolemia
  Gastrointestinal: Constipation, nausea, diarrhea, abdominal pain, vomiting, dyspepsia
  Genitourinary: Urinary tract infection
  Hematologic: Anemia
  Neuromuscular & skeletal: Tremor
  Respiratory: Dyspnea, infection (upper respiratory)
  Miscellaneous: Viral infection
3% to 10%:
  Cardiovascular: Chest pain, cardiac failure, hypotension, arrhythmia, tachycardia, general-
    ized edema, abnormal heart sounds, angina pectoris
  Central nervous system: Hypoesthesia, neuropathy, agitation, anxiety, depression, malaise,
    fatigue, rigors, dizziness
  Dermatologic: Cyst, hypertrichosis, pruritus, rash, skin disorder, skin ulceration
  Endocrine & metabolic: Dehydration, diabetes mellitus, fluid overload, hypercalcemia,
    hyperlipidemia, hypoglycemia, hypomagnesemia, acidosis, hypertriglyceridemia, hypocal-
    cemia, hyponatremia
  Gastrointestinal: Flatulence, gastroenteritis, GI hemorrhage, gingival hyperplasia, melena,
    esophagitis, stomatitis, enlarged abdomen, moniliasis, ulcerative stomatitis, weight gain
  Genitourinary: Impotence, genital edema, albuminuria, bladder disorder, hematuria, urinary
    frequency, oliguria, abnormal renal function, renal tubular necrosis, ureteral disorder,
    urinary retention, dysuria
  Hematologic: Hematoma, hemorrhage, purpura, thrombocytopenia, thrombosis, polycy-
    themia, leukopenia
  Neuromuscular & skeletal: Arthralgia, arthropathy, cramps, fracture, hernia, myalgia, pares-
    thesia, weakness, back pain, leg pain
  Ocular: Cataract, conjunctivitis, abnormal vision
  Respiratory: Bronchitis, bronchospasm, pneumonia, pulmonary edema, sinusitis, rhinitis,
    coughing, pharyngitis
  Miscellaneous: Accidental trauma, facial edema, sepsis, infection, increased glucocorti-
    coids, herpes infection
Drug Interactions
  Increased Effect/Toxicity: Basiliximab is an immunoglobulin; specific drug interactions
    have not been evaluated, but are not anticipated.
  Decreased Effect: Basiliximab is an immunoglobulin; specific drug interactions have not
    been evaluated, but are not anticipated. It is not known if the immune response to vaccines
    will be impaired during or following basiliximab therapy.
Mechanism of Action Chimeric (murine/human) monoclonal antibody which blocks the
  alpha-chain of the interleukin-2 (IL-2) receptor complex; this receptor is expressed on activated
  T lymphocytes and is a critical pathway for activating cell-mediated allograft rejection
Pharmacodynamics/Kinetics
  Duration: Mean: 36 days (determined by IL-2R alpha saturation)
  Distribution: Mean: V_d: Children: 5.2 ± 2.8 L; Adults: 8.6 ± 4.1 L
  Half-life elimination: Children: 9.4 days; Adults: Mean: 7.2 days
  Excretion: Clearance: Children: 20 mL/hour; Adults: Mean: 41 mL/hour
Dosage Note: Patients previously administered basiliximab should only be re-exposed to a
  subsequent course of therapy with extreme caution.
  I.V.:
    Children <35 kg: Renal transplantation: 10 mg within 2 hours prior to transplant surgery,
      followed by a second 10 mg dose 4 days after transplantation; the second dose should be
      withheld if complications occur (including severe hypersensitivity reactions or graft loss)
    Children ≥35 kg and Adults: Renal transplantation: 20 mg within 2 hours prior to transplant
      surgery, followed by a second 20 mg dose 4 days after transplantation; the second dose
      should be withheld if complications occur (including severe hypersensitivity reactions or
      graft loss)
  Dosing adjustment/comments in renal or hepatic impairment: No specific dosing adjust-
    ment recommended
Administration Intravenous infusion over 20-30 minutes via intravenous line
Monitoring Parameters Signs and symptoms of acute rejection
Dosage Forms INJ, powder for reconstitution: 10 mg, 20 mg

♦ **BayRab®**   *see* Rabies Immune Globulin (Human) *on page 1077*
♦ **BayRho-D® Full-Dose**   *see* Rh₀(D) Immune Globulin *on page 1089*
♦ **BayRho-D® Mini-Dose**   *see* Rh₀(D) Immune Globulin *on page 1089*
♦ **BayTet™**   *see* Tetanus Immune Globulin (Human) *on page 1204*
♦ **Baza® Antifungal [OTC]**   *see* Miconazole *on page 834*
♦ **Baza® Clear [OTC]**   *see* Vitamin A and Vitamin D *on page 1311*
♦ **B-Caro-T™**   *see* Beta-Carotene *on page 159*
♦ **BCG, Live**   *see* BCG Vaccine *on page 148*

BCG Vaccine (bee see jee vak SEEN)

U.S. Brand Names TheraCys®; TICE® BCG
Synonyms Bacillus Calmette-Guérin (BCG) Live; BCG, Live
Therapeutic Category Biological Response Modulator; Vaccine, Live Bacteria
Use Immunization against tuberculosis and immunotherapy for cancer; treatment of bladder cancer

BCG vaccine is not routinely recommended for use in the U.S. for prevention of tuberculosis
BCG vaccine is strongly recommended for infants and children with negative tuberculin skin tests who:

> are at high risk of intimate and prolonged exposure to persistently untreated or ineffectively treated patients with infectious pulmonary tuberculosis, and
> cannot be removed from the source of exposure, and
> cannot be placed on long-term preventive therapy
> are continuously exposed with tuberculosis who have bacilli resistant to isoniazid and rifampin

> BCG is also recommended for tuberculin-negative infants and children in groups in which the rate of new infections exceeds 1% per year and for whom the usual surveillance and treatment programs have been attempted but are not operationally feasible

Pregnancy Risk Factor C
Dosage Children >1 month and Adults:

> Immunization against tuberculosis (TICE® BCG): 0.2-0.3 mL percutaneous; initial lesion usually appears after 10-14 days consisting of small red papule at injection site and reaches maximum diameter of 3 mm in 4-6 weeks; conduct postvaccinal tuberculin test (ie, 5 TU of PPD) in 2-3 months; if test is negative, repeat vaccination

> Immunotherapy for bladder cancer:
>> Intravesical treatment: Instill into bladder for 2 hours
>> TheraCys®: One dose instilled into bladder once weekly for 6 weeks followed by one treatment at 3, 6, 12, 18, and 24 months after initial treatment
>> TICE® BCG: One dose instilled into the bladder once weekly for 6 weeks followed by once monthly for 6-12 months

Dosage Forms INJ, powder for reconstitution, intravesical: (TheraCys®): 81 mg; (TICE® BCG): 50 mg

♦ **BCNU**   *see* Carmustine *on page 222*
♦ **B Complex Combinations**   *see* Vitamin B Complex Combinations *on page 1311*
♦ **Bebulin® VH**   *see* Factor IX Complex (Human) *on page 504*

Becaplermin (be KAP ler min)

U.S. Brand Names Regranex®
Synonyms Recombinant Human Platelet-Derived Growth Factor B; rPDGF-BB
Therapeutic Category Growth Factor, Platelet-Derived; Topical Skin Product
Use Debridement adjunct for the treatment of diabetic ulcers that occur on the lower limbs and feet
Pregnancy Risk Factor C
Contraindications Hypersensitivity to becaplermin or any component of the formulation; known neoplasm(s) at the site(s) of application; active infection at ulcer site
Warnings/Precautions Concurrent use of corticosteroids, cancer chemotherapy, or other immunosuppressive agents; ulcer wounds related to arterial or venous insufficiency. Thermal, electrical, or radiation burns at wound site. Malignancy (potential for tumor proliferation, although unproven; topical absorption is minimal). Should not be used in wounds that close by primary intention. For external use only.
Mechanism of Action Recombinant B-isoform homodimer of human platelet-derived growth factor (rPDGF-BB) which enhances formation of new granulation tissue, induces fibroblast proliferation, and differentiation to promote wound healing
Pharmacodynamics/Kinetics

> Onset of action: Complete healing: 15% of patients within 8 weeks, 25% at 10 weeks
> Absorption: Minimal
> Distribution: Binds to PDGF-beta receptors in normal skin and granulation tissue

Dosage Topical: Adults:

> Diabetic ulcers: Apply appropriate amount of gel once daily with a cotton swab or similar tool, as a coating over the ulcer

> The amount of becaplermin to be applied will vary depending on the size of the ulcer area. To calculate the length of gel applied to the ulcer, measure the greatest length of the ulcer by the greatest width of the ulcer in inches. Tube size will determine the formula used in the calculation. For a 15 or 7.5 g tube, multiply length x width x 0.6. For a 2 g tube, multiply length x width x 1.3.

Note: If the ulcer does not decrease in size by ~30% after 10 weeks of treatment or complete healing has not occurred in 20 weeks, continued treatment with becaplermin gel should be reassessed.

Monitoring Parameters Ulcer volume (pressure ulcers); wound area; evidence of closure; drainage (diabetic ulcers); signs/symptoms of toxicity (erythema, local infections)

Patient Information

Hands should be washed thoroughly before applying. The tip of the tube should not come into contact with the ulcer or any other surface; the tube should be recapped tightly after each use. A cotton swab, tongue depressor, or other application aid should be used to apply gel.

Step-by-step instructions for application:

Squeeze the calculated length of gel on to a clean, firm, nonabsorbable surface (wax paper)

With a clean cotton swab, tongue depressor, or similar application aid, spread the measured gel over the ulcer area to obtain an even layer

Cover with a saline-moistened gauze dressing. After ~12 hours, the ulcer should be gently rinsed with saline or water to remove residual gel and covered with a saline-moistened gauze dressing (**without** gel).

Dosage Forms GEL, topical: 0.01% (15 g)

Beclomethasone (be kloe METH a sone)

U.S. Brand Names Beconase® [DSC]; Beconase® AQ; QVAR™; Vancenase® AQ 84 mcg [DSC]; Vancenase® Pockethaler® [DSC]; Vanceril® [DSC]

Synonyms Beclomethasone Dipropionate; Beclovent [DSC]

Therapeutic Category Anti-inflammatory Agent, Inhalant; Corticosteroid, Inhalant; Corticosteroid, Intranasal

Use

Oral inhalation: Maintenance and prophylactic treatment of asthma; includes those who require corticosteroids and those who may benefit from a dose reduction/elimination of systemically administered corticosteroids. Not for relief of acute bronchospasm

Nasal aerosol: Symptomatic treatment of seasonal or perennial rhinitis and to prevent recurrence of nasal polyps following surgery

Pregnancy Risk Factor C

Contraindications Hypersensitivity to beclomethasone or any component of the formulation; status asthmaticus

Warnings/Precautions Not to be used in status asthmaticus or for the relief of acute bronchospasm; safety and efficacy in children <6 years of age have not been established. May cause suppression of hypothalamic-pituitary-adrenal (HPA) axis, particularly in younger children or in patients receiving high doses for prolonged periods. Particular care is required when patients are transferred from systemic corticosteroids to inhaled products due to possible adrenal insufficiency or withdrawal from steroids, including an increase in allergic symptoms. Patients receiving 20 mg per day of prednisone (or equivalent) may be most susceptible. Fatalities have occurred due to adrenal insufficiency in asthmatic patients during and after transfer from systemic corticosteroids to aerosol steroids; aerosol steroids do **not** provide the systemic steroid needed to treat patients having trauma, surgery, or infections. Withdrawal and discontinuation of the corticosteroid should be done slowly and carefully.

Controlled clinical studies have shown that orally-inhaled and intranasal corticosteroids may cause a reduction in growth velocity in pediatric patients. (In studies of orally-inhaled corticosteroids, the mean reduction in growth velocity was approximately 1 centimeter per year [range 0.3-1.8 cm per year] and appears to be related to dose and duration of exposure.) The growth of pediatric patients receiving inhaled corticosteroids, should be monitored routinely (eg, via stadiometry). To minimize the systemic effects of orally-inhaled and intranasal corticosteroids, each patient should be titrated to the lowest effective dose.

May suppress the immune system, patients may be more susceptible to infection. Use with caution in patients with systemic infections or ocular herpes simplex. Avoid exposure to chickenpox and measles. Corticosteroids should be used with caution in patients with diabetes, hypertension, osteoporosis, peptic ulcer, glaucoma, cataracts, or tuberculosis. Use caution in hepatic impairment.

Common Adverse Reactions Frequency not defined.

Central nervous system: Agitation, depression, dizziness, dysphoria, headache, lightheadedness, mental disturbances

Dermatologic: Acneiform lesions, angioedema, atrophy, bruising, pruritus, purpura, striae, rash, urticaria

Endocrine & metabolic: Cushingoid features, growth velocity reduction in children and adolescents, HPA function suppression, weight gain

Gastrointestinal: Dry/irritated nose, throat and mouth, hoarseness, localized *Candida* or *Aspergillus* infections, loss of smell, loss of taste, nausea, unpleasant smell, unpleasant taste, vomiting

Local: Nasal spray: Burning, epistaxis, localized *Candida* infections, nasal septum perforation (rare), nasal stuffiness, nosebleeds, rhinorrhea, sneezing, transient irritation, ulceration of nasal mucosa (rare)

Ocular: Cataracts, glaucoma, increased intraocular pressure

Respiratory: Cough, paradoxical bronchospasm, pharyngitis, sinusitis, wheezing

Miscellaneous: Anaphylactic/anaphylactoid reactions, death (due to adrenal insufficiency, reported during and after transfer from systemic corticosteroids to aerosol in asthmatic patients), immediate and delayed hypersensitivity reactions

(Continued)

Beclomethasone *(Continued)*

Drug Interactions

Increased Effect/Toxicity: The addition of salmeterol has been demonstrated to improve response to inhaled corticosteroids (as compared to increasing steroid dosage).

Mechanism of Action Controls the rate of protein synthesis, depresses the migration of polymorphonuclear leukocytes, fibroblasts, reverses capillary permeability, and lysosomal stabilization at the cellular level to prevent or control inflammation

Pharmacodynamics/Kinetics

Onset of action: Therapeutic effect: 1-4 weeks

Absorption: Readily; quickly hydrolyzed by pulmonary esterases prior to absorption

Distribution: Beclomethasone: 20 L; active metabolite: 424 L

Protein binding: 87%

Metabolism: Hepatic via CYP3A4 to active metabolites

Bioavailability: Of active metabolite, 44% following nasal inhalation (43% from swallowed portion)

Half-life elimination: Initial: 3 hours

Excretion: Feces (60%); urine (12%)

Dosage Nasal inhalation and oral inhalation dosage forms are not to be used interchangeably

Aqueous inhalation, nasal:

Vancenase® AQ, Beconase® AQ: Children ≥6 years and Adults: 1-2 inhalations each nostril twice daily; total dose 168-336 mcg/day

Vancenase® AQ 84 mcg: Children ≥6 years and Adults: 1-2 inhalations in each nostril once daily; total dose 168-336 mcg/day

Intranasal (Vancenase®, Beconase®):

Children 6-12 years: 1 inhalation in each nostril 3 times/day; total dose 252 mcg/day

Children ≥12 years and Adults: 1 inhalation in each nostril 2-4 times/day or 2 inhalations each nostril twice daily (total dose 168-336 mcg/day); usual maximum maintenance: 1 inhalation in each nostril 3 times/day (252 mcg/day)

Oral inhalation (doses should be titrated to the lowest effective dose once asthma is controlled):

Vanceril®:

Children 6-12 years: 1-2 inhalations 3-4 times/day (alternatively: 2-4 inhalations twice daily); maximum dose: 10 inhalations/day (420 mcg)

Children ≥12 years and Adults: 2 inhalations 3-4 times/day (alternatively: 4 inhalations twice daily); maximum dose: 20 inhalations/day (840 mcg/day); patients with severe asthma: Initial: 12-16 inhalations/day (divided 3-4 times/day); dose should be adjusted downward according to patient's response

QVAR™:

Children 5-11 years: Initial: 40 mcg twice daily; maximum dose: 80 mcg twice daily

Children ≥12 years and Adults:

Patients previously on bronchodilators only: Initial dose 40-80 mcg twice daily; maximum dose: 320 mcg twice day

Patients previously on inhaled corticosteroids: Initial dose 40-160 mcg twice daily; maximum dose: 320 mcg twice daily

NIH Guidelines (NIH, 1997) (give in divided doses):

Children:

"Low" dose: 84-336 mcg/day (42 mcg/puff: 2-8 puffs/day or 84 mcg/puff: 1-4 puffs/day)

"Medium" dose: 336-672 mcg/day (42 mcg/puff: 8-16 puffs/day or 84 mcg/puff: 4-8 puffs/day)

"High" dose: >672 mcg/day (42 mcg/puff: >16 puffs/day or 84 mcg/puff >8 puffs/day)

Adults:

"Low" dose: 168-504 mcg/day (42 mcg/puff: 4-12 puffs/day or 84 mcg/puff: 2-6 puffs/day)

"Medium" dose: 504-840 mcg/day (42 mcg/puff: 12-20 puffs/day or 84 mcg/puff: 6-10 puffs/day)

"High" dose: >840 mcg/day (42 mcg/puff: >20 puffs/day or 84 mcg/puff: >10 puffs/day)

Administration

Aerosol inhalation: Shake container thoroughly before using

Aerosol inhalation, oral: Consider use of a spacer device for children <8 years of age requiring a metered dose inhaler (MDI)

Patient Information Rinse mouth and throat after use to prevent *Candida* infection; report sore throat or mouth lesions. Inhaled beclomethasone makes many asthmatics cough, to reduce chance, inhale drug slowly or use prescribed inhaled bronchodilator 5 minutes before beclomethasone is used; keep inhaler clean and unobstructed, wash in warm water and dry thoroughly; shake thoroughly before using.

Dosage Forms AERO, oral inhalation (QVAR™): 40 mcg/inhalation [100 metered doses] (7.3 g); 80 mcg/inhalation [100 metered doses] (7.3 g); (Vanceril® [DSC]): 42 mcg/inhalation [200 metered doses] (16.8 g). **AERO, intranasal** (Beconase® [DSC], Vancenase® [DSC]): 42 mcg/inhalation [80 metered doses] (6.7 g); [200 metered doses] (16.8 g). **SUSP, intranasal, aqueous** [spray] (Beconase® AQ): 42 mcg/inhalation [≥200 metered doses] (25 g); (Vancenase® AQ Double Strength [DSC]): 84 mcg per inhalation [120 actuations] (19 g)

♦ **Beclomethasone Dipropionate** *see* Beclomethasone *on page 149*

♦ **Beclovent [DSC]** *see* Beclomethasone *on page 149*

♦ **Beconase® [DSC]** *see* Beclomethasone *on page 149*

♦ **Beconase® AQ** *see* Beclomethasone *on page 149*

♦ **Behenyl Alcohol** *see* Docosanol *on page 397*

Belladonna and Opium (bel a DON a & OH pee um)

U.S. Brand Names B&O Supprettes®

Synonyms Opium and Belladonna

Therapeutic Category Analgesic Combination, Narcotic; Antispasmodic Agent, Gastrointestinal

Use Relief of moderate to severe pain associated with rectal or bladder tenesmus that may occur in postoperative states and neoplastic situations; pain associated with ureteral spasms not responsive to non-narcotic analgesics and to space intervals between injections of opiates

Restrictions C-II

Pregnancy Risk Factor C

Contraindications Glaucoma; severe renal or hepatic disease; bronchial asthma; respiratory depression; convulsive disorders; acute alcoholism; premature labor

Warnings/Precautions Usual precautions of opiate agonist therapy should be observed; infants <3 months of age are more susceptible to respiratory depression, use with caution and generally in reduced doses in this age group

Common Adverse Reactions

>10%:
Dermatologic: Dry skin
Gastrointestinal: Constipation, dry throat, xerostomia
Respiratory: Dry nose
Miscellaneous: Diaphoresis (decreased)

1% to 10%:
Dermatologic: Increased sensitivity to light
Endocrine & metabolic: Decreased flow of breast milk
Gastrointestinal: Dysphagia

Drug Interactions

Increased Effect/Toxicity: Additive effects with CNS depressants. May increase effects of digoxin and atenolol. Coadministration with other anticholinergic agents (phenothiazines, tricyclic antidepressants, amantadine, and antihistamines) may increase effects such as dry mouth, constipation, and urinary retention.

Decreased Effect: May decrease effects of drugs with cholinergic mechanisms. Antipsychotic efficacy of phenothiazines may be decreased.

Mechanism of Action Anticholinergic alkaloids act primarily by competitive inhibition of the muscarinic actions of acetylcholine on structures innervated by postganglionic cholinergic neurons and on smooth muscle; resulting effects include antisecretory activity on exocrine glands and intestinal mucosa and smooth muscle relaxation. Contains many narcotic alkaloids including morphine; its mechanism for gastric motility inhibition is primarily due to this morphine content; it results in a decrease in digestive secretions, an increase in GI muscle tone, and therefore a reduction in GI propulsion.

Pharmacodynamics/Kinetics

Opium:
Onset of action: Within 30 minutes
Metabolism: Hepatic, with formation of glucuronide metabolites

Dosage Rectal: Adults: 1 suppository 1-2 times/day, up to 4 doses/day

Patient Information May cause drowsiness and blurred vision

Dosage Forms SUPP: #15 A: Belladonna extract 16.2 mg and opium 30 mg; #16 A: Belladonna extract 16.2 mg and opium 60 mg

Belladonna, Phenobarbital, and Ergotamine

(bel a DON a, fee noe BAR bi tal, & er GOT a meen)

U.S. Brand Names Bellamine S; Bel-Phen-Ergot S®; Bel-Tabs

Synonyms Belladonna, Phenobarbital, and Ergotamine Tartrate; Ergotamine Tartrate, Belladonna, and Phenobarbital; Phenobarbital, Belladonna, and Ergotamine Tartrate

Therapeutic Category Ergot Alkaloid and Derivative

Use Management and treatment of menopausal disorders, GI disorders, and recurrent throbbing headache

Pregnancy Risk Factor X

Dosage Oral: 1 tablet each morning and evening

Dosage Forms TAB: Belladonna alkaloids 0.2 mg, phenobarbital 40 mg, and ergotamine 0.6 mg

- ♦ **Benadryl® Dye-Free Allergy [OTC]** *see* DiphenhydrAMINE *on page 383*
- ♦ **Benadryl® Gel [OTC]** *see* DiphenhydrAMINE *on page 383*
- ♦ **Benadryl® Gel Extra Strength [OTC]** *see* DiphenhydrAMINE *on page 383*
- ♦ **Benadryl® Injection** *see* DiphenhydrAMINE *on page 383*

Benazepril (ben AY ze pril)

Related Information
Angiotensin Agents Comparison *on page 1353*

U.S. Brand Names Lotensin®

Synonyms Benazepril Hydrochloride

Therapeutic Category Angiotensin-Converting Enzyme (ACE) Inhibitor; Antihypertensive Agent

Use Treatment of hypertension, either alone or in combination with other antihypertensive agents; treatment of left ventricular dysfunction after myocardial infarction

Pregnancy Risk Factor C/D (2nd and 3rd trimesters)

Contraindications Hypersensitivity to benazepril or any component of the formulation; angioedema or serious hypersensitivity related to previous treatment with an ACE inhibitor; bilateral renal artery stenosis; patients with idiopathic or hereditary angioedema; pregnancy (2nd and 3rd trimesters)

Warnings/Precautions Anaphylactic reactions can occur. Angioedema can occur at any time during treatment (especially following first dose). Angioedema may involve head and neck (potentially affecting the airway) or the intestine (presenting with abdominal pain). Careful blood pressure monitoring with first dose (hypotension can occur especially in volume depleted patients). Dosage adjustment needed in renal impairment. Use with caution in hypovolemia; collagen vascular diseases; valvular stenosis (particularly aortic stenosis); hyperkalemia; or before, during, or immediately after anesthesia. Avoid rapid dosage escalation which may lead to renal insufficiency. Hypersensitivity reactions may be seen during hemodialysis with high-flux dialysis membranes (eg, AN69). Deterioration in renal function can occur with initiation. Use with caution in unilateral renal artery stenosis and pre-existing renal insufficiency.

Common Adverse Reactions 1% to 10%:
Cardiovascular: Postural dizziness (2%)
Central nervous system: Headache (6%), dizziness (4%), fatigue (3%), somnolence (2%)
Endocrine & metabolic: Hyperkalemia (1%), increased uric acid
Gastrointestinal: Nausea (2%)
Renal: Increased serum creatinine (2%), worsening of renal function may occur in patients with bilateral renal artery stenosis or hypovolemia
Respiratory: Cough (1% to 10%)

Drug Interactions
  Increased Effect/Toxicity: Potassium supplements, co-trimoxazole (high dose), angiotensin II receptor antagonists (candesartan, losartan, irbesartan, etc), or potassium-sparing diuretics (amiloride, spironolactone, triamterene) may result in elevated serum potassium levels when combined with benazepril. ACE inhibitor effects may be increased by phenothiazines or probenecid (increases levels of captopril). ACE inhibitors may increase serum concentrations/effects of digoxin, lithium, and sulfonlyureas. Diuretics have additive hypotensive effects with ACE inhibitors, and hypovolemia increases the potential for adverse renal effects of ACE inhibitors. In patients with compromised renal function, coadministration with NSAIDs may result in further deterioration of renal function. Allopurinol and ACE inhibitors may cause a higher risk of hypersensitivity reaction when taken concurrently.

  Decreased Effect: Aspirin (high dose) may reduce the therapeutic effects of ACE inhibitors; at low dosages this does not appear to be significant. Rifampin may decrease the effect of ACE inhibitors. Antacids may decrease the bioavailability of ACE inhibitors (may be more likely to occur with captopril); separate administration times by 1-2 hours. NSAIDs, specifically indomethacin, may reduce the hypotensive effects of ACE inhibitors.

Mechanism of Action Competitive inhibition of angiotensin I being converted to angiotensin II, a potent vasoconstrictor, through the angiotensin I-converting enzyme (ACE) activity, with resultant lower levels of angiotensin II which causes an increase in plasma renin activity and a reduction in aldosterone secretion

Pharmacodynamics/Kinetics
Reduction in plasma angiotensin-converting enzyme (ACE) activity:
  Onset of action: Peak effect: 1-2 hours after 2-20 mg dose
  Duration: >90% inhibition for 24 hours after 5-20 mg dose
Reduction in blood pressure:
  Peak effect: Single dose: 2-4 hours; Continuous therapy: 2 weeks
Absorption: Rapid (37%); food does not alter significantly; metabolite (benazeprilat) itself unsuitable for oral administration due to poor absorption
Distribution: V_d: ~8.7 L
Metabolism: Rapidly and extensively hepatic to its active metabolite, benazeprilat, via enzymatic hydrolysis; extensive first-pass effect
Half-life elimination: Effective: 10-11 hours; Benazeprilat: Terminal: 22 hours
Time to peak: Parent drug: 1-1.5 hours
Excretion: Clearance: Nonrenal clearance (ie, biliary, metabolic) appears to contribute to the elimination of benazeprilat (11% to 12%), particularly patients with severe renal impairment; hepatic clearance is the main elimination route of unchanged benazepril
Dialysis: ~6% of metabolite removed in 4 hours of dialysis following 10 mg of benazepril administered 2 hours prior to procedure; parent compound not found in dialysate

Dosage Oral: Adults: Initial: 10 mg/day in patients not receiving a diuretic; 20-40 mg/day as a single dose or 2 divided doses; base dosage adjustments on peak (2-6 hours after dosing) and trough responses.

Dosing interval in renal impairment: Cl_{cr} <30 mL/minute: Administer 5 mg/day initially; maximum daily dose: 40 mg.

Hemodialysis: Moderately dialyzable (20% to 50%); administer dose postdialysis or administer 25% to 35% supplemental dose.

Peritoneal dialysis: Supplemental dose is not necessary.

Administration Discontinue diuretics 2-3 days prior to benazepril initiation; if the diuretics cannot be discontinued, begin benazepril at 5 mg

Patient Information May be taken without regard to meals. Report persistent cough or other side effects. Do not stop therapy except under prescriber advice. May cause dizziness, fainting, and lightheadedness, especially in first week of therapy. Sit and stand up slowly. May cause changes in taste or rash. Do not add a salt substitute (potassium) without advice of prescriber.

Dosage Forms TAB: 5 mg, 10 mg, 20 mg, 40 mg

♦ **Benazepril and Amlodipine** *see* Amlodipine and Benazepril *on page 83*

Benazepril and Hydrochlorothiazide
(ben AY ze pril & hye droe klor oh THYE a zide)
U.S. Brand Names Lotensin® HCT
Synonyms Hydrochlorothiazide and Benazepril
Therapeutic Category Angiotensin-Converting Enzyme (ACE) Inhibitor/Thiazide Diuretic; Antihypertensive Agent, Combination
Use Treatment of hypertension
Pregnancy Risk Factor C/D (2nd and 3rd trimesters)
Dosage Dose is individualized
Dosage Forms TAB: Benazepril 5 mg and hydrochlorothiazide 6.25 mg; benazepril 10 mg and hydrochlorothiazide 12.5 mg; benazepril 20 mg and hydrochlorothiazide 12.5 mg; benazepril 20 mg and hydrochlorothiazide 25 mg

♦ **Benazepril Hydrochloride** *see* Benazepril *on page 152*
♦ **BeneFix®** *see* Factor IX *on page 503*
♦ **Benemid [DSC]** *see* Probenecid *on page 1037*
♦ **Benicar™** *see* Olmesartan *on page 925*
♦ **Benicar HCT™** *see* Olmesartan and Hydrochlorothiazide *on page 925*

Bentoquatam (BEN toe kwa tam)
U.S. Brand Names IvyBlock® [OTC]
Synonyms Quaternium-18 Bentonite
Therapeutic Category Topical Skin Product
Use Skin protectant for the prevention of allergic contact dermatitis to poison oak, ivy, and sumac
Contraindications Hypersensitivity to bentoquatam or any component of the formulation
Warnings/Precautions Use with caution in patients with history of allergic-type responses to medications (especially topical formulations); open wounds, psoriatic lesions, or other cutaneous conditions. Use with caution in patients who are postexposure to poison oak, ivy, or sumac (lack of efficacy).
Mechanism of Action An organoclay substance which is capable of absorbing or binding to urushiol, the active principle in poison oak, ivy, and sumac. Bentoquatam serves as a barrier, blocking urushiol skin contact/absorption.
Pharmacodynamics/Kinetics Absorption: Has not been studied
Dosage Children >6 years and Adults: Topical: Apply to skin 15 minutes prior to potential exposure to poison ivy, poison oak, or poison sumac, and reapply every 4 hours
Monitoring Parameters Signs and symptoms of exposure to poison oak, ivy, or sumac (rash, swelling, blisters)
Patient Information Do not use this medication if you have had an allergic reaction to bentoquatam. Do not use this medication on children <6 years of age, unless ordered by your child's prescriber. Do not use this medication to treat a rash caused by poison ivy, oak, or sumac. Use this medication on your skin only. Read and follow the instructions on the medicine label. The medication must be used at least 15 minutes **before** you are exposed to poison ivy, poison oak, or poison sumac. Shake the bottle well before each use. Rub a thin layer of the lotion on your skin to form a smooth wet layer. When the lotion dries, you will see a clay-like coating on the protected parts of your skin. You will need to apply more lotion on your skin at least every 4 hours or sooner if the medication rubs off. Do not use the medication in or near your eyes. If you do get the medication in your eyes, rinse them well with cool water for at least 20 minutes. Tell your prescriber if you have eye redness or eye pain that does not go away.
Dosage Forms LOT: 5% (120 mL)

♦ **Bentyl®** *see* Dicyclomine *on page 369*
♦ **Benylin® Expectorant [OTC]** *see* Guaifenesin and Dextromethorphan *on page 604*
♦ **Benzamycin®** *see* Erythromycin and Benzoyl Peroxide *on page 454*
♦ **Benzamycin® Pak** *see* Erythromycin and Benzoyl Peroxide *on page 454*
♦ **Benzathine Benzylpenicillin** *see* Penicillin G Benzathine *on page 972*

♦ **Benzathine Penicillin G** *see* Penicillin G Benzathine *on page 972*

♦ **Benzazoline Hydrochloride** *see* Tolazoline *on page 1238*

♦ **Benzene Hexachloride** *see* Lindane *on page 746*

♦ **Benzhexol Hydrochloride** *see* Trihexyphenidyl *on page 1268*

♦ **Benzmethyzin** *see* Procarbazine *on page 1040*

Benzocaine (BEN zoe kane)

U.S. Brand Names Americaine® [OTC]; Americaine® Anesthetic Lubricant; Anbesol® [OTC]; Anbesol® Baby [OTC]; Anbesol® Maximum Strength [OTC]; Babee® Teething® [OTC]; Benzodent® [OTC]; Chiggerex® [OTC]; Chiggertox® [OTC]; Cylex® [OTC]; Detane® [OTC]; Foille® [OTC]; Foille® Medicated First Aid [OTC]; Foille® Plus [OTC]; HDA® Toothache [OTC]; Hurricaine®; Lanacane® [OTC]; Mycinettes® [OTC]; Orabase®-B [OTC]; Orajel® [OTC]; Orajel® Baby [OTC]; Orajel® Baby Nighttime [OTC]; Orajel® Maximum Strength [OTC]; Orasol® [OTC]; Solarcaine® [OTC]; Trocaine® [OTC]; Zilactin®-B [OTC]; Zilactin® Baby [OTC]

Synonyms Ethyl Aminobenzoate

Therapeutic Category Local Anesthetic, Ester Derivative; Local Anesthetic, Oral; Local Anesthetic, Otic; Local Anesthetic, Topical

Use Temporary relief of pain associated with local anesthetic for pruritic dermatosis, pruritus, minor burns, acute congestive and serous otitis media, swimmer's ear, otitis externa, toothache, minor sore throat pain, canker sores, hemorrhoids, rectal fissures, anesthetic lubricant for passage of catheters and endoscopic tubes; nonprescription diet aid

Pregnancy Risk Factor C

Contraindications Hypersensitivity to benzocaine, other ester-type local anesthetics, or any component of the formulation; secondary bacterial infection of area; ophthalmic use; see package labeling for specific contraindications

Warnings/Precautions Not intended for use when infections are present

Common Adverse Reactions Dose-related and may result in high plasma levels
1% to 10%:
Dermatologic: Angioedema, contact dermatitis
Local: Burning, stinging

Drug Interactions
Decreased Effect: May antagonize actions of sulfonamides.

Mechanism of Action Ester local anesthetic blocks both the initiation and conduction of nerve impulses by decreasing the neuronal membrane's permeability to sodium ions, which results in inhibition of depolarization with resultant blockade of conduction

Pharmacodynamics/Kinetics
Absorption: Topical: Poor to intact skin; well absorbed from mucous membranes and traumatized skin
Metabolism: Hepatic (to a lesser extent) and plasma via hydrolysis by cholinesterase
Excretion: Urine (as metabolites)

Dosage Children and Adults:
Mucous membranes: Dosage varies depending on area to be anesthetized and vascularity of tissues
Oral mouth/throat preparations: Refer to specific package labeling or as directed by physician
Topical: Apply to affected area as needed

Patient Information Do not eat for 1 hour after application to oral mucosa; chemical burns should be neutralized before application of benzocaine; avoid application to large areas of broken skin, especially in children

Dosage Forms AERO, oral spray: 20% (60 mL). **AERO, topical spray:** 5% (97.5 mL, 105 mL); 20% (20 mL, 90 mL, 120 mL, 135 mL). **CRM, topical:** 5% (30 g, 454 g); 20% (30 g). **GEL, oral:** 6.3% (7.5 g); 6.5% (15 mL); 7.5% (7.5 g, 10 g, 15 g); 10% (6 g, 7.5 g, 10 g); 20% (6 g, 7 g, 7.5 g, 10 g); (Hurricaine®): 20% (5 g, 30 g). **GEL, topical:** 20% (2.5 g, 28 g). **LIQ, oral:** 6.3% (9 mL, 15 mL, 30 mL); 7.5% (13 mL); 10% (13 mL); 20% (9 mL, 14 mL, 30 mL). **LIQ, topical:** 2% (30 mL). **LOT, oral:** 2.5% (15 mL). **LOZ:** 10 mg, 15 mg. **OINT, oral:** 20% (30 g). **OINT, topical:** 2% (52 g); 5% (3.5 g, 28 g). **PASTE, oral:** 20% (7 g)

♦ **Benzocaine and Antipyrine** *see* Antipyrine and Benzocaine *on page 107*

♦ **Benzocaine and Cetylpyridinium Chloride** *see* Cetylpyridinium and Benzocaine *on page 252*

Benzocaine, Butyl Aminobenzoate, Tetracaine, and Benzalkonium Chloride
(BEN zoe kane, BYOO til a meen oh BENZ oh ate, TET ra kane, & benz al KOE nee um KLOR ide)

U.S. Brand Names Cetacaine®

Synonyms Tetracaine Hydrochloride, Benzocaine Butyl Aminobenzoate, and Benzalkonium Chloride

Therapeutic Category Local Anesthetic

Use Topical anesthetic to control pain or gagging

Pregnancy Risk Factor C

Dosage Apply to affected area for approximately 1 second or less

Dosage Forms AERO, topical: Benzocaine 14%, butyl aminobenzoate 2%, tetracaine 2%, and benzalkonium 0.5% (56 g). **GEL, topical:** Benzocaine 14%, butyl aminobenzoate 2%, tetracaine 2%, and benzalkonium 0.5% (29 g). **LIQ, topical:** Benzocaine 14%, butyl aminobenzoate 2%, tetracaine 2%, and benzalkonium 0.5% (56 mL)

Benzocaine, Gelatin, Pectin, and Sodium Carboxymethylcellulose

(BEN zoe kane, JEL a tin, PEK tin, & SOW dee um kar box ee meth il SEL yoo lose)
U.S. Brand Names Orabase® With Benzocaine [OTC]
Synonyms Gelatin, Benzocaine, Pectin, and Sodium Carboxymethylcellulose; Pectin, Benzocaine, Gelatin, and Sodium Carboxymethylcellulose; Sodium Carboxymethylcellulose, Benzocaine, Gelatin, and Pectin
Therapeutic Category Local Anesthetic
Use Topical anesthetic and emollient for oral lesions
Pregnancy Risk Factor C
Dosage Apply 2-4 times/day
Dosage Forms PASTE: Benzocaine 20%, gelatin, pectin, and sodium carboxymethylcellulose (5 g, 15 g)

♦ **Benzodent® [OTC]** see Benzocaine on page 154
♦ **Benzodiazepines Comparison** see page 1366

Benzonatate (ben ZOE na tate)
U.S. Brand Names Tessalon®
Therapeutic Category Antitussive; Local Anesthetic, Oral
Use Symptomatic relief of nonproductive cough
Pregnancy Risk Factor C
Contraindications Hypersensitivity to benzonatate, related compounds (such as tetracaine), or any component of the formulation
Common Adverse Reactions 1% to 10%:
  Central nervous system: Sedation, headache, dizziness
  Dermatologic: Rash
  Gastrointestinal: GI upset
  Neuromuscular & skeletal: Numbness in chest
  Ocular: Burning sensation in eyes
  Respiratory: Nasal congestion
Mechanism of Action Tetracaine congener with antitussive properties; suppresses cough by topical anesthetic action on the respiratory stretch receptors
Pharmacodynamics/Kinetics
  Onset of action: Therapeutic: 15-20 minutes
  Duration: 3-8 hours
Dosage Children >10 years and Adults: Oral: 100 mg 3 times/day or every 4 hours up to 600 mg/day
Monitoring Parameters Monitor patient's chest sounds and respiratory pattern
Patient Information Swallow capsule whole (do not break or chew capsule); use of hard candy may increase saliva flow to aid in protecting pharyngeal mucosa
Dosage Forms CAP: 100 mg, 200 mg

♦ **Benzoyl Peroxide and Erythromycin** see Erythromycin and Benzoyl Peroxide on page 454

Benzoyl Peroxide and Hydrocortisone
(BEN zoe il peer OKS ide & hye droe KOR ti sone)
U.S. Brand Names Vanoxide-HC®
Synonyms Hydrocortisone and Benzoyl Peroxide
Therapeutic Category Acne Product
Use Treatment of acne vulgaris and oily skin
Pregnancy Risk Factor C
Dosage Topical: Shake well; apply thin film 1-3 times/day, gently massage into skin
Dosage Forms LOT: Benzoyl peroxide 5% and hydrocortisone acetate 0.5% (25 mL)

Benztropine (BENZ troe peen)
Related Information
  Parkinson's Agents Comparison on page 1402
U.S. Brand Names Cogentin®
Synonyms Benztropine Mesylate
Therapeutic Category Anticholinergic Agent; Anti-Parkinson's Agent, Anticholinergic
Use Adjunctive treatment of Parkinson's disease; treatment of drug-induced extrapyramidal symptoms (except tardive dyskinesia)
Pregnancy Risk Factor C
Contraindications Hypersensitivity to benztropine or any component of the formulation; pyloric or duodenal obstruction, stenosing peptic ulcers; bladder neck obstructions; achalasia; myasthenia gravis; children <3 years of age
Warnings/Precautions Use with caution in older children (dose has not been established). Use with caution in hot weather or during exercise. May cause anhidrosis and hyperthermia, which may be severe. The risk is increased in hot environments, particularly in the elderly, alcoholics, patients with CNS disease, and those with prolonged outdoor exposure.

Elderly patients frequently develop increased sensitivity and require strict dosage regulation - side effects may be more severe in elderly patients with atherosclerotic changes. Use with caution in patients with tachycardia, cardiac arrhythmias, hypertension, hypotension, prostatic hyperplasia (especially in the elderly), any tendency toward urinary retention, liver or kidney (Continued)

Benztropine *(Continued)*

disorders, and obstructive disease of the GI or GU tract. When given in large doses or to susceptible patients, may cause weakness and inability to move particular muscle groups.

May be associated with confusion or hallucinations (generally at higher dosages). Intensification of symptoms or toxic psychosis may occur in patients with mental disorders.

Common Adverse Reactions Frequency not defined.
Cardiovascular: Tachycardia
Central nervous system: Confusion, disorientation, memory impairment, toxic psychosis, visual hallucinations
Dermatologic: Rash
Endocrine & metabolic: Heat stroke, hyperthermia
Gastrointestinal: Xerostomia, nausea, vomiting, constipation, ileus
Genitourinary: Urinary retention, dysuria
Ocular: Blurred vision, mydriasis
Miscellaneous: Fever

Drug Interactions
Cytochrome P450 Effect: Substrate of CYP2D6 (minor)
Increased Effect/Toxicity: Central and/or peripheral anticholinergic syndrome can occur when benztropine is administered with amantadine, rimantadine, narcotic analgesics, phenothiazines and other antipsychotics (especially with high anticholinergic activity), tricyclic antidepressants, quinidine and some other antiarrhythmics, and antihistamines. Benztropine may increase the absorption of digoxin.
Decreased Effect: May increase gastric degradation of levodopa and decrease the amount of levodopa absorbed by delaying gastric emptying. Therapeutic effects of cholinergic agents (tacrine, donepezil) and neuroleptics may be antagonized.

Mechanism of Action Possesses both anticholinergic and antihistaminic effects. *In vitro* anticholinergic activity approximates that of atropine; *in vivo* it is only about half as active as atropine. Animal data suggest its antihistaminic activity and duration of action approach that of pyrilamine maleate. May also inhibit the reuptake and storage of dopamine and thereby, prolong the action of dopamine.

Pharmacodynamics/Kinetics
Onset of action: Oral: Within 1 hour; Parenteral: Within 15 minutes
Duration: 6-48 hours
Metabolism: Hepatic (N-oxidation, N-dealkylation, and ring hydroxylation)
Bioavailability: 29%

Dosage Use in children ≤3 years of age should be reserved for life-threatening emergencies
Drug-induced extrapyramidal symptom: Oral, I.M., I.V.:
Children >3 years: 0.02-0.05 mg/kg/dose 1-2 times/day
Adults: 1-4 mg/dose 1-2 times/day
Acute dystonia: Adults: I.M., I.V.: 1-2 mg
Parkinsonism: Oral:
Adults: 0.5-6 mg/day in 1-2 divided doses; if one dose is greater, administer at bedtime; titrate dose in 0.5 mg increments at 5- to 6-day intervals
Elderly: Initial: 0.5 mg once or twice daily; increase by 0.5 mg as needed at 5-6 days; maximum: 4 mg/day

Monitoring Parameters Symptoms of EPS or Parkinson's, pulse, anticholinergic effects

Patient Information Take after meals or with food if GI upset occurs. Do not discontinue drug abruptly. Report adverse GI effects, rapid or pounding heartbeat, confusion, eye pain, rash, fever, or heat intolerance. Observe caution when performing hazardous tasks or those that require alertness such as driving, as may cause drowsiness. Avoid alcohol and other CNS depressants. May cause dry mouth; adequate fluid intake or hard sugar-free candy may relieve. Difficult urination or constipation may occur; notify prescriber if effects persist; may increase susceptibility to heat stroke.

Dosage Forms INJ, solution (Cogentin®): 1 mg/mL (2 mL). **TAB:** 0.5 mg, 1 mg, 2 mg

♦ **Benztropine Mesylate** *see* Benztropine *on page 155*
♦ **Benzylpenicillin Benzathine** *see* Penicillin G Benzathine *on page 972*
♦ **Benzylpenicillin Potassium** *see* Penicillin G (Parenteral/Aqueous) *on page 973*
♦ **Benzylpenicillin Sodium** *see* Penicillin G (Parenteral/Aqueous) *on page 973*

Benzylpenicilloyl-polylysine *(BEN zil pen i SIL oyl pol i LIE seen)*

U.S. Brand Names Pre-Pen®
Synonyms Penicilloyl-polylysine; PPL
Therapeutic Category Diagnostic Agent, Penicillin Allergy Skin Test
Use Adjunct in assessing the risk of administering penicillin (penicillin or benzylpenicillin) in adults with a history of clinical penicillin hypersensitivity
Pregnancy Risk Factor C
Contraindications Known hypersensitivity to penicillin or any component of the formulation
Common Adverse Reactions Frequency not defined.
Cardiovascular: Hypotension
Dermatologic: Angioneurotic edema, pruritus, erythema, urticaria
Local: Intense local inflammatory response at skin test site, wheal (locally)
Respiratory: Dyspnea
Miscellaneous: Systemic allergic reactions occur rarely

Drug Interactions

Decreased Effect: Corticosteroids and other immunosuppressive agents may inhibit the immune response to the skin test.

Mechanism of Action Elicits IgE antibodies which produce type I accelerate urticarial reactions to penicillins

Dosage PPL is administered by a scratch technique or by intradermal injection. For initial testing, PPL should always be applied via the scratch technique. **Do not administer intradermally to patients who have positive reactions to a scratch test.** PPL test alone does not identify those patients who react to a minor antigenic determinant and does not appear to predict reliably the occurrence of late reactions.

Scratch test: Use scratch technique with a 20-gauge needle to make 3-5 mm nonbleeding scratch on epidermis, apply a small drop of solution to scratch, rub in gently with applicator or toothpick. A positive reaction consists of a pale wheal surrounding the scratch site which develops within 10 minutes and ranges from 5-15 mm or more in diameter.

Intradermal test: Use intradermal test with a tuberculin syringe with a 26- or 30-gauge short bevel needle; a dose of 0.01-0.02 mL is injected intradermally. A control of 0.9% sodium chloride should be injected at least 1.5" from the PPL test site. Most skin responses to the intradermal test will develop within 5-15 minutes.

Interpretation:

(-) Negative: No reaction

(±) Ambiguous: Wheal only slightly larger than original bleb with or without erythematous flare and larger than control site

(+) Positive: Itching and marked increase in size of original bleb

Control site should be reactionless

Administration PPL is administered by a scratch technique or by intradermal injection. For initial testing, PPL should always be applied via the scratch technique. Do not give intradermally to patients who have positive reactions to a scratch test. Have epinephrine 1:1000 immediately available.

Dosage Forms INJ, solution: 0.25 mL

Bepridil (BE pri dil)

Related Information

Calcium Channel Blockers Comparison *on page 1371*

U.S. Brand Names Vascor® [DSC]

Synonyms Bepridil Hydrochloride

Therapeutic Category Antianginal Agent; Calcium Channel Blocker

Use Treatment of chronic stable angina; due to side effect profile, reserve for patients who have been intolerant of other antianginal therapy; bepridil may be used alone or in combination with nitrates or beta-blockers

Pregnancy Risk Factor C

Contraindications Hypersensitivity to bepridil or any component of the formulation, calcium channel blockers, or adenosine; history of serious ventricular or atrial arrhythmias (especially tachycardia or those associated with accessory conduction pathways), uncompensated cardiac insufficiency, congenital QT interval prolongation, patients taking other drugs that prolong the QT interval; concurrent administration with ritonavir, amprenavir, atazanavir, or sparfloxacin

Warnings/Precautions Use with great caution in patients with history of IHSS, second or third degree AV block, cardiogenic shock; reserve for patients in whom other antianginals have failed. Carefully titrate dosages for patients with impaired renal or hepatic function; use caution when treating patients with CHF, significant hypotension, severe left ventricular dysfunction, hypertrophic cardiomyopathy (especially obstructive), concomitant therapy with beta-blockers or digoxin, edema, or increased intracranial pressure with cranial tumors; do not abruptly withdraw (may cause chest pain); elderly may experience hypotension and constipation more readily.

If dosage reduction does not maintain the QT within a safe range (not to exceed 0.52 seconds during therapy), discontinue the medication; has class I antiarrhythmic properties and can induce new arrhythmias, including VT/VF; it can also cause torsade de pointes type ventricular tachycardia due to its ability to prolong the QT interval; avoid use in patients in the immediate period postinfarction.

Common Adverse Reactions

>10%:

Central nervous system: Dizziness

Gastrointestinal: Nausea, dyspepsia

1% to 10%:

Cardiovascular: Bradycardia, edema, palpitations, QT prolongation (dose-related; up to 5% with prolongation of ≥25%), CHF (1%)

Central nervous system: Nervousness, headache (7% to 13%), drowsiness, psychiatric disturbances (<2%), insomnia (2% to 3%)

Dermatologic: Rash (≤2%)

Endocrine & metabolic: Sexual dysfunction

Gastrointestinal: Diarrhea, anorexia, xerostomia, constipation, abdominal pain, dyspepsia, flatulence

Neuromuscular & skeletal: Weakness (7% to 14%), tremor (<9%), paresthesia (3%)

Ocular: Blurred vision

Otic: Tinnitus

Respiratory: Rhinitis, dyspnea (≤9%), cough (≤2%)

(Continued)

Bepridil *(Continued)*

Miscellaneous (≤2%): Flu syndrome, diaphoresis

Drug Interactions

Cytochrome P450 Effect: Inhibits CYP2D6 (weak)

Increased Effect/Toxicity: Use with H_2 blockers may increase bioavailability of bepridil. Use of bepridil with beta-blockers may increase cardiac depressant effects on AV conduction. Bepridil may increase serum levels/effects of carbamazepine, cyclosporine, digitalis, quinidine, and theophylline. Concurrent use of fentanyl with bepridil may increase hypotension. Use with amprenavir, atazanavir, ritonavir, sparfloxacin (possibly also gatifloxacin and moxifloxacin) may increase risk of bepridil toxicity, especially its cardiotoxicity. Use with cisapride may increase the risk of malignant arrhythmias, concurrent use is contraindicated. Blood pressure-lowering effects may be additive with sildenafil, tadalafil, and vardenafil (use caution).

Mechanism of Action Bepridil, a type 4 calcium antagonist, possesses characteristics of the traditional calcium antagonists, inhibiting calcium ion from entering the "slow channels" or select voltage-sensitive areas of vascular smooth muscle and myocardium during depolarization and producing a relaxation of coronary vascular smooth muscle and coronary vasodilation. However, bepridil may also inhibit fast sodium channels (inward), which may account for some of its side effects (eg, arrhythmias); a direct bradycardia effect of bepridil has been postulated via direct action on the S-A node.

Pharmacodynamics/Kinetics

Onset of action: 1 hour

Absorption: 100%

Protein binding: >99%

Metabolism: Hepatic

Bioavailability: 60%

Half-life elimination: 24 hours

Time to peak: 2-3 hours

Excretion: Urine (as metabolites)

Dosage Adults: Oral: Initial: 200 mg/day, then adjust dose at 10-day intervals until optimal response is achieved; usual dose: 300 mg/day; maximum daily dose: 400 mg

Dosage adjustment in renal impairment: Risk of toxic reactions is greater in patients with renal impairment; dose selection should be cautious, usually starting at the low end of the dosage range

Elderly: Peak concentrations and half-life are markedly increased in the elderly (>74 years); dose selection should be cautious, usually starting at the low end of the dosage range

Monitoring Parameters ECG and serum electrolytes, blood pressure, signs and symptoms of congestive heart failure; elderly may need very close monitoring due to underlying cardiac and organ system defects

Reference Range 1-2 ng/mL

Patient Information May cause cardiac arrhythmias if potassium is low; can be taken with food or meals; maintain potassium supplementation as directed; routine ECGs will be necessary during start of therapy or dosage changes; notify prescriber if the following occur: Irregular heartbeat, shortness of breath, pronounced dizziness, constipation, or hypotension

Dosage Forms TAB: 200 mg, 300 mg

♦ **Bepridil Hydrochloride** *see Bepridil on page 157*

Beractant *(ber AKT ant)*

U.S. Brand Names Survanta®

Synonyms Bovine Lung Surfactant; Natural Lung Surfactant

Therapeutic Category Lung Surfactant

Use Prevention and treatment of respiratory distress syndrome (RDS) in premature infants

Prophylactic therapy: Body weight <1250 g in infants at risk for developing or with evidence of surfactant deficiency (administer within 15 minutes of birth)

Rescue therapy: Treatment of infants with RDS confirmed by x-ray and requiring mechanical ventilation (administer as soon as possible - within 8 hours of age)

Warnings/Precautions Rapidly affects oxygenation and lung compliance and should be restricted to a highly supervised use in a clinical setting with immediate availability of clinicians experienced with intubation and ventilatory management of premature infants. If transient episodes of bradycardia and decreased oxygen saturation occur, discontinue the dosing procedure and initiate measures to alleviate the condition; produces rapid improvements in lung oxygenation and compliance that may require immediate reductions in ventilator settings and FiO_2.

Common Adverse Reactions During the dosing procedure:

>10%: Cardiovascular: Transient bradycardia

1% to 10%: Respiratory: Oxygen desaturation

Mechanism of Action Replaces deficient or ineffective endogenous lung surfactant in neonates with respiratory distress syndrome (RDS) or in neonates at risk of developing RDS. Surfactant prevents the alveoli from collapsing during expiration by lowering surface tension between air and alveolar surfaces.

Pharmacodynamics/Kinetics Excretion: Clearance: Alveolar clearance is rapid

Dosage

Prophylactic treatment: Administer 100 mg phospholipids (4 mL/kg) intratracheal as soon as possible; as many as 4 doses may be administered during the first 48 hours of life, no more frequently than 6 hours apart. The need for additional doses is determined by evidence of continuing respiratory distress; if the infant is still intubated and requiring at least 30% inspired oxygen to maintain a PaO_2 $\leq$80 torr.

Rescue treatment: Administer 100 mg phospholipids (4 mL/kg) as soon as the diagnosis of RDS is made; may repeat if needed, no more frequently than every 6 hours to a maximum of 4 doses

Administration

For intratracheal administration only

Suction infant prior to administration; inspect solution to verify complete mixing of the suspension

Administer intratracheally by instillation through a 5-French end-hole catheter inserted into the infant's endotracheal tube

Administer the dose in four 1 mL/kg aliquots. Each quarter-dose is instilled over 2-3 seconds; each quarter-dose is administered with the infant in a different position; slightly downward inclination with head turned to the right, then repeat with head turned to the left; then slightly upward inclination with head turned to the right, then repeat with head turned to the left.

Monitoring Parameters Continuous ECG and transcutaneous O_2 saturation should be monitored during administration; frequent arterial blood gases are necessary to prevent postdosing hyperoxia and hypocarbia

Dosage Forms SUSP, inhalation: 25 mg/mL (4 mL, 8 mL)

♦ **Beta-Blockers Comparison** *see page 1368*

Beta-Carotene (BAY ta KARE oh teen)
U.S. Brand Names A-Caro-25®; B-Caro-T™; Lumitene™
Therapeutic Category Vitamin, Fat Soluble
Unlabeled/Investigational Use Prophylaxis and treatment of polymorphous light eruption; prophylaxis against photosensitivity reactions in erythropoietic protoporphyria
Pregnancy Risk Factor C
Dosage Oral:
Children <14 years: 30-150 mg/day
Adults: 30-300 mg/day
Dosage Forms CAP: 10,000 int. units (6 mg); 25,000 int. units (15 mg); (A-Caro-25®, B-Caro-T™): 25,000 int. units (15 mg); (Lumitene™): 50,000 int. units (30 mg). **TAB:** 10,000 int. units

♦ **Betadine® [OTC]** *see Povidone-Iodine on page 1025*
♦ **Betadine® First Aid Antibiotics + Moisturizer [OTC]** *see Bacitracin and Polymyxin B on page 143*
♦ **Betadine® Ophthalmic** *see Povidone-Iodine on page 1025*
♦ **9-Beta-D-ribofuranosyladenine** *see Adenosine on page 40*
♦ **Betagan®** *see Levobunolol on page 729*

Betaine Anhydrous (BAY ta een an HY drus)
U.S. Brand Names Cystadane®
Therapeutic Category Homocystinuria Agent
Use Orphan drug: Treatment of homocystinuria to decrease elevated homocysteine blood levels; included within the category of homocystinuria are deficiencies or defects in cystathionine beta-synthase (CBS), 5,10-methylenetetrahydrofolate reductase (MTHFR), and cobalamin cofactor metabolism (CBL).
Pregnancy Risk Factor C
Dosage
Children <3 years: Dosage may be started at 100 mg/kg/day and then increased weekly by 100 mg/kg increments
Children ≥3 years and Adults: Oral: 6 g/day administered in divided doses of 3 g twice daily. Dosages of up to 20 g/day have been necessary to control homocysteine levels in some patients.
Dosage in all patients can be gradually increased until plasma homocysteine is undetectable or present only in small amounts
Dosage Forms POWDER, oral solution: 1 g/scoop (180 g)

Betamethasone (bay ta METH a sone)
Related Information
Corticosteroids Comparison *on page 1372*
U.S. Brand Names Alphatrex®; Betatrex®; Beta-Val®; Celestone®; Celestone® Phosphate; Celestone® Soluspan®; Diprolene®; Diprolene® AF; Luxiq™; Maxivate®
Synonyms Betamethasone Dipropionate; Betamethasone Dipropionate, Augmented; Betamethasone Sodium Phosphate; Betamethasone Valerate; Flubenisolone
Therapeutic Category Anti-inflammatory Agent; Corticosteroid, Systemic; Corticosteroid, Topical (Low Potency); Corticosteroid, Topical (Medium Potency); Corticosteroid, Topical (High Potency); Glucocorticoid
Use Inflammatory dermatoses such as seborrheic or atopic dermatitis, neurodermatitis, anogenital pruritus, psoriasis, inflammatory phase of xerosis
Pregnancy Risk Factor C
Contraindications Hypersensitivity to betamethasone or any component of the formulation; systemic fungal infections
Warnings/Precautions Not to be used in status asthmaticus or for the relief of acute bronchospasm; topical use in patients ≤12 years of age is not recommended. May cause suppression
(Continued)

Betamethasone *(Continued)*

of hypothalamic-pituitary-adrenal (HPA) axis, particularly in younger children or in patients receiving high doses for prolonged periods. Particular care is required when patients are transferred from systemic corticosteroids to inhaled products due to possible adrenal insufficiency or withdrawal from steroids, including an increase in allergic symptoms. Patients receiving 20 mg per day of prednisone (or equivalent) may be most susceptible. Fatalities have occurred due to adrenal insufficiency in asthmatic patients during and after transfer from systemic corticosteroids to aerosol steroids; aerosol steroids do **not** provide the systemic steroid needed to treat patients having trauma, surgery, or infections. Withdrawal and discontinuation of the corticosteroid should be done slowly and carefully

Controlled clinical studies have shown that orally-inhaled and intranasal corticosteroids may cause a reduction in growth velocity in pediatric patients. (In studies of orally-inhaled corticosteroids, the mean reduction in growth velocity was approximately 1 centimeter per year [range 0.3-1.8 cm per year] and appears to be related to dose and duration of exposure.) The growth of pediatric patients receiving inhaled corticosteroids, should be monitored routinely (eg, via stadiometry). To minimize the systemic effects of orally-inhaled and intranasal corticosteroids, each patient should be titrated to the lowest effective dose.

May suppress the immune system, patients may be more susceptible to infection. Use with caution in patients with systemic infections or ocular herpes simplex. Avoid exposure to chickenpox and measles.

Use with caution in patients with hypothyroidism, cirrhosis, ulcerative colitis; do not use occlusive dressings on weeping or exudative lesions and general caution with occlusive dressings should be observed; discontinue if skin irritation or contact dermatitis should occur; do not use in patients with decreased skin circulation

Common Adverse Reactions

Systemic:

>10%:

    Central nervous system: Insomnia, nervousness

    Gastrointestinal: Increased appetite, indigestion

1% to 10%:

    Central nervous system: Dizziness or lightheadedness, headache

    Dermatologic: Hirsutism, hypopigmentation

    Endocrine & metabolic: Diabetes mellitus

    Neuromuscular & skeletal: Arthralgia

    Ocular: Cataracts, glaucoma

    Respiratory: Epistaxis

    Miscellaneous: Diaphoresis

Topical:

1% to 10%:

    Dermatologic: Itching, allergic contact dermatitis, erythema, dryness papular rashes, folliculitis, furunculosis, pustules, pyoderma, vesiculation, hyperesthesia, skin infection (secondary)

    Local: Burning, irritation

Drug Interactions

Cytochrome P450 Effect: Inhibits CYP3A4 (weak)

Increased Effect/Toxicity: Inhibitors of CYP3A4 (including erythromycin, diltiazem, itraconazole, ketoconazole, quinidine, and verapamil) may decrease metabolism of betamethasone.

Decreased Effect: May induce cytochrome P450 enzymes, which may lead to decreased effect of any drug metabolized by P450 (ie, barbiturates, phenytoin, rifampin). Decreased effectiveness of salicylates when taken with betamethasone.

Mechanism of Action Controls the rate of protein synthesis, depresses the migration of polymorphonuclear leukocytes, fibroblasts, reverses capillary permeability, and lysosomal stabilization at the cellular level to prevent or control inflammation

Pharmacodynamics/Kinetics

Protein binding: 64%

Metabolism: Hepatic

Half-life elimination: 6.5 hours

Time to peak, serum: I.V.: 10-36 minutes

Excretion: Urine (<5% as unchanged drug)

Dosage Base dosage on severity of disease and patient response

Children: Use lowest dose listed as initial dose for adrenocortical insufficiency (physiologic replacement)

    I.M.: 0.0175-0.125 mg base/kg/day divided every 6-12 hours **or** 0.5-7.5 mg base/m^2/day divided every 6-12 hours

    Oral: 0.0175-0.25 mg/kg/day divided every 6-8 hours **or** 0.5-7.5 mg/m^2/day divided every 6-8 hours

    Topical:

        ≤12 years: Use is not recommended.

        >12 years: Apply a thin film twice daily; use minimal amount for shortest period of time to avoid HPA axis suppression

Adolescents and Adults:

    Oral: 2.4-4.8 mg/day in 2-4 doses; range: 0.6-7.2 mg/day

    I.M.: Betamethasone sodium phosphate and betamethasone acetate: 0.6-9 mg/day (generally, $^1/_3$ to $^1/_2$ of oral dose) divided every 12-24 hours

Foam: Apply twice daily, once in the morning and once at night to scalp

Dosing adjustment in hepatic impairment: Adjustments may be necessary in patients with liver failure because betamethasone is extensively metabolized in the liver

Adults:

Intrabursal, intra-articular, intradermal: 0.25-2 mL

Intralesional: Rheumatoid arthritis/osteoarthritis:

Very large joints: 1-2 mL

Large joints: 1 mL

Medium joints: 0.5-1 mL

Small joints: 0.25-0.5 mL

Topical: Apply thin film 2-4 times/day. Therapy should be discontinued when control is achieved; if no improvement is seen, reassessment of diagnosis may be necessary.

Administration

Oral: Not for alternate day therapy; once daily doses should be given in the morning.

I.M.: Do **not** give injectable sodium phosphate/acetate suspension I.V.

Topical: Apply topical sparingly to areas. Not for use on broken skin or in areas of infection. Do not apply to wet skin unless directed. Do not apply to face or inguinal area. Do not cover with occlusive dressing.

Patient Information Take oral with food or milk; apply topical sparingly to areas and gently rub in until it disappears, not for use on broken skin or in areas of infection; do not apply to face or inguinal areas

Dosage Forms CRM, topical, as dipropionate: 0.05% (15 g, 45 g, 60 g); (Alphatrex®): 0.05% (15 g, 45 g); (Maxivate®): 0.05% (45 g). **CRM, topical, as dipropionate augmented** (Diprolene® AF): 0.05% (15 g, 50 g). **CRM, topical, as valerate:** 0.1% (15 g, 45 g); (Betatrex®, Beta-Val®): 0.1% (15 g, 45 g). **FOAM, topical, as valerate** (Luxiq™): 0.12% (50 g, 100 g). **GEL, topical, as dipropionate augmented** (Diprolene®): 0.05% (15 g, 50 g). **INJ, solution, as sodium phosphate** (Celestone® Phosphate): 4 mg/mL (5 mL). **INJ, suspension** (Celestone® Soluspan®): Betamethasone sodium phosphate 3 mg/mL and betamethasone acetate 3 mg/mL [6 mg/mL] (5 mL) **LOT, topical, as dipropionate:** 0.05% (20 mL, 60 mL); (Alphatrex®, Maxivate®): 0.05% (60 mL). **LOT, topical, as dipropionate augmented** (Diprolene®): 0.05% (30 mL, 60 mL). **LOT, topical, as valerate** (Beta-Val®, Betatrex®): 0.1% (60 mL). **OINT, topical, as dipropionate:** 0.05% (15 g, 45 g); (Alphatrex®, Maxivate®): 0.05% (45 g). **OINT, topical, as dipropionate augmented:** 0.05% (15 g, 45 g, 50 g); (Diprolene®): 0.05% (15 g, 50 g). **OINT, topical, as valerate** (Betatrex®): 0.1% (15 g, 45 g). **SYR, as base** (Celestone®): 0.6 mg/5 mL (118 mL). **TAB, as base** (Celestone®): 0.6 mg

Betamethasone and Clotrimazole (bay ta METH a sone & kloe TRIM a zole)

U.S. Brand Names Lotrisone®

Synonyms Clotrimazole and Betamethasone

Therapeutic Category Antifungal/Corticosteroid, Topical

Use Topical treatment of various dermal fungal infections (including tinea pedis, cruris, and corpora in patients ≥17 years of age)

Pregnancy Risk Factor C

Dosage

Children <17 years: Do not use

Children ≥17 years and Adults:

Tinea corporis, tinea cruris: Topical: Massage into affected area twice daily, morning and evening; do not use for longer than 2 weeks; re-evaluate after 1 week if no clinical improvement; do not exceed 45 g cream/week or 45 mL lotion/week

Tinea pedis: Topical: Massage into affected area twice daily, morning and evening; do not use for longer than 4 weeks; re-evaluate after 2 weeks if no clinical improvement; do not exceed 45 g cream/week or 45 mL lotion/week

Elderly: Use with caution; skin atrophy and skin ulceration (rare) have been reported in patients with thinning skin; do not use for diaper dermatitis or under occlusive dressings

Dosage Forms CRM: Betamethasone 0.05% and clotrimazole 1% (15 g, 45 g). **LOT:** Betamethasone 0.05% and clotrimazole 1% (30 mL)

♦ **Betamethasone Dipropionate** see Betamethasone on page 159

♦ **Betamethasone Dipropionate, Augmented** see Betamethasone on page 159

♦ **Betamethasone Sodium Phosphate** see Betamethasone on page 159

♦ **Betamethasone Valerate** see Betamethasone on page 159

♦ **Betapace®** see Sotalol on page 1154

♦ **Betapace AF®** see Sotalol on page 1154

♦ **Betasept® [OTC]** see Chlorhexidine Gluconate on page 259

♦ **Betaseron®** see Interferon Beta-1b on page 681

♦ **Betatrex®** see Betamethasone on page 159

♦ **Beta-Val®** see Betamethasone on page 159

Betaxolol (be TAKS oh lol)

Related Information

Beta-Blockers Comparison on page 1368

Glaucoma Drug Therapy Comparison on page 1481

U.S. Brand Names Betoptic® S; Kerlone®

Synonyms Betaxolol Hydrochloride

Therapeutic Category Antihypertensive Agent; Beta Blocker, Beta₁ Selective; Beta-Adrenergic Blocker, Ophthalmic

(Continued)

Betaxolol *(Continued)*

Use Treatment of chronic open-angle glaucoma and ocular hypertension; management of hypertension

Pregnancy Risk Factor C (manufacturer); D (2nd and 3rd trimesters - expert analysis)

Contraindications Hypersensitivity to betaxolol or any component of the formulation; sinus bradycardia; heart block greater than first-degree (except in patients with a functioning artificial pacemaker); cardiogenic shock; uncompensated cardiac failure; pulmonary edema; pregnancy (2nd and 3rd trimester)

Warnings/Precautions Administer cautiously in compensated heart failure and monitor for a worsening of the condition. Beta-blocker therapy should not be withdrawn abruptly (particularly in patients with CAD), but gradually tapered to avoid acute tachycardia, hypertension, and/or ischemia. Use caution with concurrent use of beta-blockers and either verapamil or diltiazem; bradycardia or heart block can occur. Use caution in patients with PVD (can aggravate arterial insufficiency). In general, beta-blockers should be avoided in patients with bronchospastic disease. Betaxolol, with B1 selectivity, should be used cautiously in bronchospastic disease with close monitoring. Use cautiously in diabetics because it can mask prominent hypoglycemic symptoms. Can mask signs of thyrotoxicosis. Can cause fetal harm when administered in pregnancy. Dosage adjustment required in severe renal impairment and those on dialysis. Use care with anesthetic agents which decrease myocardial function.

Common Adverse Reactions

Ophthalmic:

>10%: Ocular: Conjunctival hyperemia

1% to 10%:

Ocular: Anisocoria, corneal punctate keratitis, keratitis, corneal staining, decreased corneal sensitivity, eye pain, vision disturbances

Systemic:

>10%:

Central nervous system: Drowsiness, insomnia

Endocrine & metabolic: Decreased sexual ability

1% to 10%:

Cardiovascular: Bradycardia, palpitations, edema, CHF, reduced peripheral circulation

Central nervous system: Mental depression

Gastrointestinal: Diarrhea or constipation, nausea, vomiting, stomach discomfort

Respiratory: Bronchospasm

Miscellaneous: Cold extremities

Drug Interactions

Cytochrome P450 Effect: Substrate (major) of CYP1A2, 2D6; **Inhibits** CYP2D6 (weak)

Increased Effect/Toxicity: CYP1A2 inhibitors may increase the levels/effects of betaxolol; example inhibitors include amiodarone, ciprofloxacin, fluvoxamine, ketoconazole, lomefloxacin, ofloxacin, and rofecoxib. CYP2D6 inhibitors may increase the levels/effects of betaxolol; example inhibitors include chlorpromazine, delavirdine, fluoxetine, miconazole, paroxetine, pergolide, quinidine, quinine, ritonavir, and ropinirole. The heart rate-lowering effects of betaxolol are additive with other drugs which slow AV conduction (digoxin, verapamil, diltiazem). Reserpine increases the effects of betaxolol. Concurrent use of betaxolol may increase the effects of alpha-blockers (prazosin, terazosin), alpha-adrenergic stimulants (epinephrine, phenylephrine), and the vasoconstrictive effects of ergot alkaloids. Betaxolol may mask the tachycardia from hypoglycemia caused by insulin and oral hypoglycemics. In patients receiving concurrent therapy, the risk of hypertensive crisis is increased when either clonidine or the beta-blocker is withdrawn. Beta-blockers may increase the action or levels of ethanol, disopyramide, nondepolarizing muscle relaxants, and theophylline although the effects are difficult to predict.

Decreased Effect: CYP1A2 inducers may decrease the levels/effects of betaxolol; example inducers include aminoglutethimide, carbamazepine, phenobarbital, and rifampin. Decreased effect of betaxolol with aluminum salts, barbiturates, calcium salts, cholestyramine, colestipol, NSAIDs, penicillins (ampicillin), rifampin, salicylates, and sulfinpyrazone due to decreased bioavailability and plasma levels. Beta-blockers may decrease the effect of sulfonylureas.

Mechanism of Action Competitively blocks beta$_1$-receptors, with little or no effect on beta$_2$-receptors; ophthalmic reduces intraocular pressure by reducing the production of aqueous humor

Pharmacodynamics/Kinetics

Onset of action: Ophthalmic: 30 minutes; Oral: 1-1.5 hours

Duration: Ophthalmic: ≥12 hours

Absorption: Ophthalmic: Some systemic; Oral: ~100%

Metabolism: Hepatic to multiple metabolites

Protein binding: Oral: 50%

Bioavailability: Oral: 89%

Half-life elimination: Oral: 12-22 hours

Time to peak: Ophthalmic: ~2 hours; Oral: 1.5-6 hours

Excretion: Urine

Dosage Adults:

Ophthalmic: Instill 1 drop twice daily.

Oral: 5-10 mg/day; may increase dose to 20 mg/day after 7-14 days if desired response is not achieved. Initial dose in elderly: 5 mg/day.

Dosage adjustment in renal impairment: Administer 5 mg/day. Can increase every 2 weeks up to a maximum of 20 mg/day.

Cl_{cr} <10 mL/minute: Administer 50% of usual dose.

Administration Ophthalmic: Shake well before using. Tilt head back and instill in eye. Keep eye open and do not blink for 30 seconds. Apply gentle pressure to lacrimal sac for 1 minute. Wipe away excess from skin. Do not touch applicator to eye and do not contaminate tip of applicator.

Monitoring Parameters Ophthalmic: Intraocular pressure. Systemic: Blood pressure, pulse

Patient Information

Oral: Take exactly as prescribed and do not discontinue without consulting prescriber. May cause dizziness or blurred vision (use caution when driving engaging in tasks requiring alertness until response to drug is known); or nausea or vomiting (small, frequent meals, frequent mouth care, sucking lozenges, or chewing gum may help). Report chest pain, palpitations or irregular heartbeat; persistent GI upset (eg, nausea, vomiting, diarrhea, or constipation); unusual cough; difficulty breathing; swelling or coolness of extremities; or unusual mental depression.

Ophthalmic: Keep eye open and do not blink for 30 seconds after instillation; wear sunglasses to avoid photophobic discomfort; apply gentle pressure to lacrimal sac during and immediately following instillation (1 minute)

Dosage Forms SOLN, ophthalmic: 0.5% (5 mL, 10 mL, 15 mL). **SUSP, ophthalmic** (Betoptic® S): 0.25% (2.5 mL, 10 mL, 15 mL). **TAB** (Kerlone®): 10 mg, 20 mg

♦ **Betaxolol Hydrochloride** *see* Betaxolol *on page 161*

♦ **Betaxon®** *see* Levobetaxolol *on page 729*

Bethanechol (be THAN e kole)

U.S. Brand Names Urecholine®

Synonyms Bethanechol Chloride

Therapeutic Category Cholinergic Agent

Use Nonobstructive urinary retention and retention due to neurogenic bladder

Unlabeled/Investigational Use Treatment and prevention of bladder dysfunction caused by phenothiazines; diagnosis of flaccid or atonic neurogenic bladder; gastroesophageal reflux

Pregnancy Risk Factor C

Contraindications Hypersensitivity to bethanechol or any component of the formulation; mechanical obstruction of the GI or GU tract or when the strength or integrity of the GI or bladder wall is in question; hyperthyroidism, peptic ulcer disease, epilepsy, obstructive pulmonary disease, bradycardia, vasomotor instability, atrioventricular conduction defects, hypotension, or parkinsonism

Warnings/Precautions Potential for reflux infection if the sphincter fails to relax as bethanechol contracts the bladder; safety and efficacy in children have not been established

Common Adverse Reactions Frequency not defined.

Cardiovascular: Hypotension, tachycardia, flushed skin

Central nervous system: Headache, malaise

Gastrointestinal: Abdominal cramps, diarrhea, nausea, vomiting, salivation, eructation

Genitourinary: Urinary urgency

Ocular: Lacrimation, miosis

Respiratory: Asthmatic attacks, bronchial constriction

Miscellaneous: Diaphoresis

Drug Interactions

Increased Effect/Toxicity: Bethanechol and ganglionic blockers may cause a critical fall in blood pressure. Cholinergic drugs or anticholinesterase agents may have additive effects with bethanechol.

Decreased Effect: Procainamide, quinidine may decrease the effects of bethanechol. Anticholinergic agents (atropine, antihistamines, TCAs, phenothiazines) may decrease effects.

Mechanism of Action Stimulates cholinergic receptors in the smooth muscle of the urinary bladder and gastrointestinal tract resulting in increased peristalsis, increased GI and pancreatic secretions, bladder muscle contraction, and increased ureteral peristaltic waves

Pharmacodynamics/Kinetics

Onset of action: 30-90 minutes

Duration: Up to 6 hours

Absorption: Variable

Dosage Oral:

Children:

Urinary retention (unlabeled use): 0.6 mg/kg/day divided 3-4 times/day

Gastroesophageal reflux (unlabeled use): 0.1-0.2 mg/kg/dose given 30 minutes to 1 hour before each meal to a maximum of 4 times/day

Adults:

Urinary retention, neurogenic bladder, and/or bladder atony:

Oral: Initial: 10-50 mg 2-4 times/day (some patients may require dosages of 50-100 mg 4 times/day). To determine effective dose, may initiate at a dose of 5-10 mg, with additional doses of 5-10 mg hourly until an effective cumulative dose is reached. Cholinergic effects at higher oral dosages may be cumulative.

S.C.: Initial: 2.575 mg, may repeat in 15-30 minutes (maximum cumulative initial dose: 10.3 mg); subsequent doses may be given 3-4 times daily as needed (some patients may require more frequent dosing at 2.5- to 3-hour intervals). Chronic neurogenic atony may require doses of 7.5-10 every 4 hours.

Gastroesophageal reflux (unlabeled): Oral: 25 mg 4 times/day

Elderly: Use the lowest effective dose

(Continued)

Bethanechol *(Continued)*

Monitoring Parameters Observe closely for side effects

Patient Information Should be taken 1 hour before meals or 2 hours after meals to avoid nausea or vomiting; may cause abdominal discomfort, salivation, diaphoresis, or flushing; notify prescriber if these symptoms become pronounced; rise slowly from sitting/lying down

Dosage Forms TAB: 5 mg, 10 mg, 25 mg, 50 mg

- ◆ **Bethanechol Chloride** *see Bethanechol on page 163*
- ◆ **Betimol®** *see Timolol on page 1229*
- ◆ **Betoptic® S** *see Betaxolol on page 161*

Bexarotene *(beks AIR oh teen)*

U.S. Brand Names Targretin®

Therapeutic Category Antineoplastic Agent, Miscellaneous; Retinoic Acid Derivative; Vitamin A Derivative

Use

Oral: Treatment of cutaneous manifestations of cutaneous T-cell lymphoma in patients who are refractory to at least one prior systemic therapy

Topical: Treatment of cutaneous lesions in patients with refractory cutaneous T-cell lymphoma (stage 1A and 1B) or who have not tolerated other therapies

Pregnancy Risk Factor X

Contraindications Hypersensitivity to bexarotene or any component of the formulation; pregnancy

Warnings/Precautions Pregnancy test needed 1 week before initiation and every month thereafter. Effective contraception must be in place one month before initiation, during therapy, and for at least 1 month after discontinuation. Male patients with sexual partners who are pregnant, possibly pregnant, or who could become pregnant, must use condoms during sexual intercourse during treatment and for 1 month after last dose. Induces significant lipid abnormalities in a majority of patients (triglyceride, total cholesterol, and HDL); reversible on discontinuation. Use extreme caution in patients with underlying hypertriglyceridemia. Pancreatitis secondary to hypertriglyceridemia has been reported. Monitor for liver function test abnormalities and discontinue drug if tests are three times the upper limit of normal values for AST (SGOT), ALT (SGPT) or bilirubin. Hypothyroidism occurs in about a third of patients. Monitor for signs and symptoms of infection about 4-8 weeks after initiation (leukopenia may occur). Any new visual abnormalities experienced by the patient should be evaluated by an ophthalmologist (cataracts can form, or worsen, especially in the geriatric population). May cause photosensitization. Safety and efficacy are not established in the pediatric population. Avoid use in hepatically impaired patients. Limit additional vitamin A intake to <15,000 int. units/day. Use caution with diabetic patients; monitor for hypoglycemia.

Common Adverse Reactions First percentage is at a dose of 300 mg/m²/day; the second percentage is at a dose >300 mg/m²/day.

>10%:

Cardiovascular: Peripheral edema (13% to 11%)

Central nervous system: Headache (30% to 42%), chills (10% to 13%)

Dermatologic: Rash (17% to 23%), exfoliative dermatitis (10% to 28%)

Endocrine & metabolic: Hyperlipidemia (about 79% in both dosing ranges), hypercholesteremia (32% to 62%), hypothyroidism (29% to 53%)

Hematologic: Leukopenia (17% to 47%)

Neuromuscular & skeletal: Weakness (20% to 45%)

Miscellaneous: Infection (13% to 23%)

<10%:

Cardiovascular: Hemorrhage, hypertension, angina pectoris, right heart failure, tachycardia, cerebrovascular accident

Central nervous system: Fever (5% to 17%), insomnia (5% to 11%), subdural hematoma, syncope, depression, agitation, ataxia, confusion, dizziness, hyperesthesia

Dermatologic: Dry skin (about 10% for both dosing ranges), alopecia (4% to 11%), skin ulceration, acne, skin nodule, maculopapular rash, serous drainage, vesicular bullous rash, cheilitis

Endocrine & metabolic: Hypoproteinemia, hyperglycemia, weight loss/gain, serum amylase (elevated), breast pain

Gastrointestinal: Abdominal pain (11% to 4%), nausea (16% to 8%), diarrhea (7% to 42%), vomiting (4% to 13%), anorexia (2% to 23%), constipation, xerostomia, flatulence, colitis, dyspepsia, gastroenteritis, gingivitis, melena, pancreatitis

Genitourinary: Albuminuria, hematuria, urinary incontinence, urinary tract infection, urinary urgency, dysuria, kidney function abnormality

Hematologic: Hypochromic anemia (4% to 13%), anemia (6% to 25%), eosinophilia, thrombocythemia, coagulation time increased, lymphocytosis, thrombocytopenia

Hepatic: LDH increase (7% to 13%), hepatic failure

Neuromuscular & skeletal: Back pain (2% to 11%), arthralgia, myalgia, bone pain, myasthenia, arthrosis, neuropathy

Ocular: Dry eyes, conjunctivitis, blepharitis, corneal lesion, visual field defects, keratitis

Otic: Ear pain, otitis externa

Renal: Creatinine (elevated)

Respiratory: Pharyngitis, rhinitis, dyspnea, pleural effusion, bronchitis, increased cough, lung edema, hemoptysis, hypoxia

Miscellaneous: Flu-like syndrome (4% to 13%), bacterial infection (1% to 13%)

Topical:
Cardiovascular: Edema (10%)
Central nervous system: Headache (14%), weakness (6%), pain (30%)
Dermatologic: Rash (14% to 72%), pruritus (6% to 40%), contact dermatitis (14%), exfoliative dermatitis (6%)
Hematologic: Leukopenia (6%), lymphadenopathy (6%)
Neuromuscular & skeletal: Paresthesia (6%)
Respiratory: Cough (6%), pharyngitis (6%)
Miscellaneous: Diaphoresis (6%), infection (18%)

Drug Interactions
Cytochrome P450 Effect: Substrate of CYP3A4 (minor); **Induces** CYP3A4 (weak)
Increased Effect/Toxicity: Bexarotene plasma concentrations may be increased by azole antifungals, clarithromycin, erythromycin, fluvoxamine, nefazodone, quinine, ritonavir, gemfibrozil, or grapefruit juice. Bexarotene may increase the toxicity of DEET.
Decreased Effect: Bexarotene plasma levels may be decreased by rifampin, phenytoin, phenobarbital, or nafcillin. Bexarotene may decrease the plasma levels of hormonal contraceptives and tamoxifen.

Mechanism of Action The exact mechanism is unknown. Binds and activates retinoid X receptor subtypes. Once activated, these receptors function as transcription factors that regulate the expression of genes which control cellular differentiation and proliferation. Bexarotene inhibits the growth *in vitro* of some tumor cell lines of hematopoietic and squamous cell origin.

Pharmacodynamics/Kinetics
Absorption: Significantly improved by a fat-containing meal
Protein binding: >99%
Metabolism: Hepatic via CYP3A4 isoenzyme; four metabolites identified; further metabolized by glucuronidation
Half-life elimination: 7 hours
Time to peak: 2 hours
Excretion: Primarily feces; urine (<1% as unchanged drug and metabolites)

Dosage
Oral: 300 mg/m^2/day taken as a single daily dose. If there is no tumor response after 8 weeks and the initial dose was well tolerated, then an increase to 400 mg/m^2/day can be made with careful monitoring. Maintain as long as the patient is deriving benefit.
If the initial dose is not tolerated, then it may be adjusted to 200 mg/m^2/day, then to 100 mg/m^2/day or temporarily suspended if necessary to manage toxicity
Topical: Apply once every other day for first week, then increase on a weekly basis to once daily, 2 times/day, 3 times/day, and finally 4 times/day, according to tolerance
Dosing adjustment in renal impairment: No studies have been conducted; however, renal insufficiency may result in significant protein binding changes and alter pharmacokinetics of bexarotene
Dosing adjustment in hepatic impairment: No studies have been conducted; however, hepatic impairment would be expected to result in decreased clearance of bexarotene due to the extensive hepatic contribution to elimination

Administration
Oral: Administer capsule following a fat-containing meal.
Topical: Allow gel to dry before covering with clothing. Avoid application to normal skin. Use of occlusive dressings is not recommended.

Monitoring Parameters If female, pregnancy test 1 week before initiation then monthly while on bexarotene; lipid panel before initiation, then weekly until lipid response established and then at 8-week intervals thereafter; baseline LFTs, repeat at 1, 2, and 4 weeks after initiation then at 8-week intervals thereafter if stable; baseline and periodic thyroid function tests; baseline CBC with periodic monitoring

Patient Information

Oral: Take with a fat-containing meal. Get pregnancy test before starting therapy and then every month thereafter while on the medicine. Do not get pregnant while taking this medicine. Use 2 forms of birth control 1 month before, during, and for at least a month after completion of therapy. For male patients, protect your partner against pregnancy by wearing a condom. Continue using protection for 1 month after last dose. Take at a similar time daily. Call your prescriber if you have a fever, chills, or any signs of infection. You are at risk of infections: stay away from crowds and people with viruses. Wash your hands frequently. Check vitamin A intake with your prescriber. You should avoid large amounts of vitamin A.

Topical gel: Allow gel to dry before covering. Avoid applying to normal skin or mucous membranes. Do not use occlusive dressings.
Dosage Forms CAP: 75 mg. **GEL:** 1% (60 g)

♦ **Bextra**® *see* Valdecoxib *on page 1285*
♦ **Bexxar**® *see* Tositumomab and Iodine I 131 Tositumomab *on page 1248*
♦ **BG 9273** *see* Alefacept *on page 49*
♦ **Biaxin**® *see* Clarithromycin *on page 288*
♦ **Biaxin**® **XL** *see* Clarithromycin *on page 288*

Bicalutamide (bye ka LOO ta mide)

U.S. Brand Names Casodex®
Synonyms CDX; ICI-176334
Therapeutic Category Antiandrogen; Antineoplastic Agent, Antiandrogen
(Continued)

Bicalutamide *(Continued)*

Use In combination therapy with LHRH agonist analogues in treatment of advanced prostatic carcinoma

Pregnancy Risk Factor X

Contraindications Hypersensitivity to bicalutamide or any component of the formulation; pregnancy

Warnings/Precautions Rare cases of death or hospitalization due to hepatitis have been reported postmarketing. Use with caution in moderate to severe hepatic dysfunction. Hepatotoxicity generally occurs within the first 3-4 months of use. Baseline liver function tests should be obtained and repeated regularly during the first 4 months of treatment, and periodically thereafter. Additionally, patients should be monitored for signs and symptoms of liver dysfunction. Bicalutamide should be discontinued if patients have jaundice or ALT is two times the upper limit of normal. May cause gynecomastia in a high percentage of patients.

Common Adverse Reactions Endocrine & metabolic: Hot flashes (8% to 24% in combination with LHRH agonists), gynecomastia (23% to 62%), breast tenderness (25% to 60%)

≥2% to <5%:

Cardiovascular: Angina pectoris, CHF, edema

Central nervous system: Anxiety, depression, confusion, somnolence, nervousness, fever, chills

Dermatologic: Dry skin, pruritus, alopecia

Endocrine & metabolic: Breast pain, diabetes mellitus, decreased libido, dehydration, gout

Gastrointestinal: Anorexia, dyspepsia, rectal hemorrhage, xerostomia, melena, weight gain

Genitourinary: Polyuria, urinary impairment, dysuria, urinary retention, urinary urgency

Hepatic: Alkaline phosphatase increased

Neuromuscular & skeletal: Myasthenia, arthritis, myalgia, leg cramps, pathological fracture, neck pain, hypertonia, neuropathy

Renal: Creatinine increased

Respiratory: Cough increased, pharyngitis, bronchitis, pneumonia, rhinitis, lung disorder

Miscellaneous: Sepsis, neoplasma

Drug Interactions

Increased Effect/Toxicity: Bicalutamide may displace warfarin from protein binding sites which may result in an increased anticoagulant effect, especially when bicalutamide therapy is started after the patient is already on warfarin.

Mechanism of Action Pure nonsteroidal antiandrogen that binds to androgen receptors; specifically a competitive inhibitor for the binding of dihydrotestosterone and testosterone; prevents testosterone stimulation of cell growth in prostate cancer

Pharmacodynamics/Kinetics

Absorption: Rapid and complete

Protein binding: 96%

Metabolism: Extensively hepatic; stereospecific metabolism

Half-life elimination: Up to 10 days; active enantiomer 5.8 days

Excretion: Urine and feces (as unchanged drug and metabolites)

Dosage Adults: Oral: 50-150 mg/day

Dosage adjustment in renal impairment: None necessary as renal impairment has no significant effect on elimination

Dosage adjustment in liver impairment: Limited data in subjects with severe hepatic impairment suggest that excretion of bicalutamide may be delayed and could lead to further accumulation. Use with caution in patients with moderate to severe hepatic impairment.

Administration Dose should be taken at the same time each day with or without food; start treatment at the same time as treatment with an LHRH analog

Monitoring Parameters CBC, ECG, echocardiograms, and serum testosterone and luteinizing hormone (periodically). Liver function tests should be obtained at baseline and repeated regularly during the first 4 months of treatment, and periodically thereafter; monitor for signs and symptoms of liver dysfunction. (discontinue if jaundice is noted or ALT is two or more times the upper limit of normal).

Patient Information Take as directed and do not alter dose or discontinue without consulting prescriber. Take at the same time each day with or without food; void before taking medication. Diabetics should monitor serum glucose closely and notify prescriber of changes; this medication can alter hypoglycemic requirements. You may lose your hair and experience impotency. May cause dizziness, confusion, or drowsiness (use caution when driving or engaging in tasks that require alertness until response to drug is known); nausea or vomiting (small frequent meals, frequent mouth care, sucking lozenges, or chewing gum may help); or constipation (increased dietary fiber, fruit, or fluid and increased exercise may help). Report easy bruising or bleeding; yellowing of skin or eyes; change in color of urine or stool; unresolved CNS changes (nervousness, chills, insomnia, somnolence); skin rash, redness, or irritation; chest pain or palpitations; difficulty breathing; urinary retention or inability to void; muscle weakness, tremors, or pain; persistent nausea, vomiting, diarrhea, or constipation; or other unusual signs or adverse reactions.

Dosage Forms TAB: 50 mg

♦ **Bicillin®** C-R *see* Penicillin G Benzathine and Penicillin G Procaine *on page 972*

♦ **Bicillin®** C-R 900/300 *see* Penicillin G Benzathine and Penicillin G Procaine *on page 972*

♦ **Bicillin®** L-A *see* Penicillin G Benzathine *on page 972*

♦ **Bicitra®** *see* Sodium Citrate and Citric Acid *on page 1147*

♦ **BiCNu®** *see* Carmustine *on page 222*

♦ **Biltricide®** *see* Praziquantel *on page 1029*

Bimatoprost (bi MAT oh prost)

Related Information
Glaucoma Drug Therapy Comparison *on page 1481*

U.S. Brand Names Lumigan®

Therapeutic Category Ophthalmic Agent, Prostaglandin Derivative; Prostaglandin, Ophthalmic

Use Reduction of intraocular pressure (IOP) in patients with open-angle glaucoma or ocular hypertension; should be used in patients who are intolerant of other IOP-lowering medications or failed treatment with another IOP-lowering medication

Pregnancy Risk Factor C

Contraindications Hypersensitivity to bimatoprost or any component of the formulation

Warnings/Precautions May cause permanent changes in eye color (increases the amount of brown pigment in the iris), the eyelid skin, and eyelashes. In addition, may increase the length and/or number of eyelashes (may vary between eyes). Use caution in patients with intraocular inflammation, aphakic patients, pseudophakic patients with a torn posterior lens capsule, or patients with risk factors for macular edema. Contains benzalkonium chloride (may be adsorbed by contact lenses) Safety and efficacy have not been determined for use in patients with renal impairment, angle closure, inflammatory or neovascular glaucoma. Safety and efficacy in pediatric patients not established.

Common Adverse Reactions
>10%: Ocular (15% to 45%): Conjunctival hyperemia, growth of eyelashes, ocular pruritus
1% to 10%:
    Central nervous system: Headache (1% to 5%)
    Dermatologic: Hirsutism (1% to 5%)
    Hepatic: Abnormal liver function tests (1% to 5%)
    Neuromuscular & skeletal: Weakness (1% to 5%)
    Ocular:
        3% to 10%: Blepharitis, burning, cataract, dryness, eyelid redness, eyelash darkening, foreign body sensation, irritation, pain, pigmentation of periocular skin, superficial punctate keratitis, visual disturbance
        1% to 3%: Allergic conjunctivitis, asthenopia, conjunctival edema, discharge, increased iris pigmentation, photophobia, tearing
    Respiratory: Upper respiratory tract infection (10%)

Mechanism of Action As a synthetic analog of prostaglandin with ocular hypotensive activity, bimatoprost decreases intraocular pressure by increasing the outflow of aqueous humor.

Pharmacodynamics/Kinetics
Onset of action: Reduction of IOP: ~4 hours
    Peak effect: Maximum reduction of IOP: ~8-12 hours
Distribution: 0.67 L/kg
Protein binding: ~88%
Metabolism: Undergoes oxidation, N-demethylation, and glucuronidation after reaching systemic circulation; forms metabolites
Half-life elimination: I.V.: 45 minutes
Time to peak: 10 minutes
Excretion: Urine (67%); feces (25%)

Dosage Ophthalmic: Adult: Open-angle glaucoma or ocular hypertension: Instill 1 drop into affected eye(s) once daily in the evening; do not exceed once-daily dosing (may decrease IOP-lowering effect). If used with other topical ophthalmic agents, separate administration by at least 5 minutes.

Administration May be used with other eye drops to lower intraocular pressure. If using more than one ophthalmic product, wait at least 5 minutes in between application of each medication. Remove contact lenses prior to administration and wait 15 minutes before reinserting.

Patient Information Wash hands before instilling. Sit or lie down to instill. Open eye, look at ceiling, and instill prescribed amount of solution. Apply gentle pressure to inner corner of eye. Do not let tip of applicator touch eye; do not contaminate tip of applicator (contamination may cause eye infection leading to possible eye damage or vision loss). Contact prescriber concerning continued use of drops if eye infection develops, trauma occurs to the eye, and prior to eye surgery. This product contains benzalkonium chloride which may be adsorbed by contact lenses; remove contacts prior to administration and wait 15 minutes before reinserting. May cause permanent changes in eye color (increases the amount of brown pigment in the iris), eyelid, and eyelashes. May also increase the length and/or number of eyelashes. Changes may occur slowly (months to years). May be used with other eye drops to lower intraocular pressure. If using more than one eye drop medicine, wait at least 5 minutes in between application of each medication. Notify prescriber if conjunctivitis or eyelid reactions occur with use of this product.

Dosage Forms SOLN, ophthalmic: 0.03% (2.5 mL, 5 mL, 7.5 mL)

♦ **Biocef** *see* Cephalexin *on page 248*
♦ **Biofed [OTC]** *see* Pseudoephedrine *on page 1061*
♦ **Biolon**™ *see* Sodium Hyaluronate *on page 1148*
♦ **Bio-Statin**® *see* Nystatin *on page 919*
♦ **BioThrax**™ *see* Anthrax Vaccine Adsorbed *on page 102*
♦ **bis-chloronitrosourea** *see* Carmustine *on page 222*
♦ **Bismatrol** *see* Bismuth *on page 168*

Bismuth (BIZ muth)

Related Information
Antimicrobial Drugs of Choice *on page 1440*

U.S. Brand Names Children's Kaopectate® (reformulation) [OTC]; Colo-Fresh™ [OTC]; Devrom®; Diotame® [OTC]; Kaopectate® [OTC]; Kaopectate® Extra Strength [OTC]; Pepto-Bismol® [OTC]; Pepto-Bismol® Maximum Strength [OTC]

Synonyms Bismatrol; Bismuth Subgallate; Bismuth Subsalicylate; Pink Bismuth

Therapeutic Category Antidiarrheal

Use Symptomatic treatment of mild, nonspecific diarrhea; indigestion, nausea, control of traveler's diarrhea (enterotoxigenic *Escherichia coli*); as part of a multidrug regimen for *H. pylori* eradication to reduce the risk of duodenal ulcer recurrence; subgallate formulation to control fecal odors in colostomy, ileostomy, or fecal incontinence

Pregnancy Risk Factor C/D (3rd trimester)

Contraindications Do not use subsalicylate in patients with influenza or chickenpox because of risk of Reye's syndrome; hypersensitivity to salicylates or any component of the formulation; history of severe GI bleeding; history of coagulopathy; pregnancy (3rd trimester)

Warnings/Precautions Subsalicylate should be used with caution if patient is taking aspirin; use with caution in children, especially those <3 years of age and those with viral illness; may be neurotoxic with very large doses.

When used for self-medication (OTC labeling): Children and teenagers who have or are recovering from chickenpox or flu-like symptoms should not use subsalicylate. Changes in behavior (along with nausea and vomiting) may be an early sign of Reye's syndrome; patients should be instructed to contact their healthcare provider if these occur.

Common Adverse Reactions >10%: Gastrointestinal: Discoloration of the tongue (darkening), grayish black stools

Drug Interactions
Increased Effect/Toxicity: Toxicity of aspirin, warfarin, and/or hypoglycemics may be increased.

Decreased Effect: The effects of tetracyclines and uricosurics may be decreased.

Mechanism of Action Bismuth subsalicylate exhibits both antisecretory and antimicrobial action. This agent may provide some anti-inflammatory action as well. The salicylate moiety provides antisecretory effect and the bismuth exhibits antimicrobial directly against bacterial and viral gastrointestinal pathogens. Bismuth has some antacid properties.

Pharmacodynamics/Kinetics
Absorption: Minimal (<1%) across GI tract, salt (eg, salicylate) may be readily absorbed (80%); bismuth subsalicylate is rapidly cleaved to bismuth and salicylic acid in the stomach

Distribution: Salicylate: V_d: 170 mL/kg

Protein binding, plasma: Bismuth and salicylate: >90%

Metabolism: Bismuth: Oral: Salts undergo chemical dissociation; Salicylate: Extensively hepatic

Half-life elimination: Terminal: Bismuth: 21-72 days; Salicylate: 2-5 hours

Excretion: Bismuth: Urine and feces; Salicylate: 10% (as unchanged drug)

Clearance: Bismuth: 50 mL/minute

Dosage
Oral:
Nonspecific diarrhea: Subsalicylate (doses based on 262 mg/5 mL liquid or 262 mg tablets):
Children: Up to 8 doses/24 hours:
3-6 years: $^1/_3$ tablet or 5 mL every 30 minutes to 1 hour as needed
6-9 years: $^2/_3$ tablet or 10 mL every 30 minutes to 1 hour as needed
9-12 years: 1 tablet or 15 mL every 30 minutes to 1 hour as needed
Adults: 2 tablets or 30 mL every 30 minutes to 1 hour as needed up to 8 doses/24 hours
Prevention of traveler's diarrhea: 2.1 g/day or 2 tablets 4 times/day before meals and at bedtime
Helicobacter pylori eradication: 524 mg 4 times/day with meals and at bedtime; requires combination therapy
Control of fecal odor in ileostomy or colostomy: Subgallate: 1-2 tablets 3 times/day with meals (maximum: 5 tablets/day)
Dosing adjustment in renal impairment: Should probably be avoided in patients with renal failure

Patient Information Chew tablet well or shake suspension well before using; may darken stools; if diarrhea persists for more than 2 days, consult prescriber; can turn tongue black; tinnitus may indicate toxicity and use should be discontinued

Dosage Forms CAPLET, as subgallate (Devrom®): 200 mg. **LIQ, as subsalicylate**: 262 mg/15 mL (240 mL, 360 mL, 480 mL); 525 mg/15 mL (240 mL, 360 mL); (Children's Kaopectate®): 87 mg/5 mL (180 mL); (Diotame®): 262 mg/15 mL (30 mL); (Kaopectate®): 262 mg/15 mL (240 mL); (Kaopectate® Extra Strength): 525 mg/15 mL (240 mL); (Pepto-Bismol®): 262 mg/15 mL (120 mL, 240 mL, 360 mL, 480 mL); (Pepto-Bismol® Maximum Strength): 525 mg/15 mL (120 mL, 240 mL, 360 mL). **TAB, as subgallate** (Colo-Fresh™): 324 mg. **TAB, chewable, as subgallate** (Devrom®): 200 mg. **TAB, chewable, as subsalicylate** (Diotame®, Pepto-Bismol®): 262 mg

♦ **Bismuth Subgallate** *see Bismuth on page 168*

♦ **Bismuth Subsalicylate** *see Bismuth on page 168*

Bismuth Subsalicylate, Metronidazole, and Tetracycline
(BIZ muth sub sa LIS i late, me troe NI da zole, & tet ra SYE kleen)

U.S. Brand Names Helidac®

Synonyms Bismuth Subsalicylate, Tetracycline, and Metronidazole; Metronidazole, Bismuth Subsalicylate, and Tetracycline; Metronidazole, Tetracycline, and Bismuth Subsalicylate; Tetracycline, Bismuth Subsalicylate, and Metronidazole; Tetracycline, Metronidazole, and Bismuth Subsalicylate

Therapeutic Category Antidiarrheal

Use In combination with an H_2 antagonist, as part of a multidrug regimen for *H. pylori* eradication to reduce the risk of duodenal ulcer recurrence

Pregnancy Risk Factor D (tetracycline); B (metronidazole)

Dosage Adults: Chew 2 bismuth subsalicylate 262.4 mg tablets, swallow 1 metronidazole 250 mg tablet, and swallow 1 tetracycline 500 mg capsule 4 times/day at meals and bedtime, plus an H_2 antagonist (at the appropriate dose) for 14 days; follow with 8 oz of water; the H_2 antagonist should be continued for a total of 28 days

Dosage Forms Each package contains 14 blister cards (2-week supply); each card contains the following: **CAP:** Tetracycline: 500 mg (4). **TAB:** Bismuth subsalicylate, chewable: 262.4 mg (8); metronidazole: 250 mg (4)

♦ **Bismuth Subsalicylate, Tetracycline, and Metronidazole** *see* Bismuth Subsalicylate, Metronidazole, and Tetracycline *on page 169*

Bisoprolol (bis OH proe lol)
Related Information
Beta-Blockers Comparison *on page 1368*

U.S. Brand Names Zebeta®

Synonyms Bisoprolol Fumarate

Therapeutic Category Antihypertensive Agent; Beta Blocker, Beta$_1$ Selective

Use Treatment of hypertension, alone or in combination with other agents

Unlabeled/Investigational Use Angina pectoris, supraventricular arrhythmias, PVCs

Pregnancy Risk Factor C (manufacturer); D (2nd and 3rd trimesters - expert analysis)

Contraindications Hypersensitivity to bisoprolol or any component of the formulation; sinus bradycardia; heart block greater than first-degree (except in patients with a functioning artificial pacemaker); cardiogenic shock; uncompensated cardiac failure; pulmonary edema; pregnancy (2nd and 3rd trimesters)

Warnings/Precautions Use with caution in patients with inadequate myocardial function, bronchospastic disease, hyperthyroidism, undergoing anesthesia; and in those with impaired hepatic function. Beta-blocker therapy should not be withdrawn abruptly (particularly in patients with CAD), but gradually tapered to avoid acute tachycardia, hypertension, and/or ischemia. Use caution in patients with PVD (can aggravate arterial insufficiency). Use caution with concurrent use with verapamil or diltiazem; bradycardia or heart block can occur. Bisoprolol should be used cautiously in bronchospastic disease with close monitoring. Use cautiously in diabetics because it can mask prominent hypoglycemic symptoms. Can mask signs of thyrotoxicosis. Can cause fetal harm when administered in pregnancy. Use care with anesthetic agents which decrease myocardial function.

Common Adverse Reactions
>10%:
   Central nervous system: Drowsiness, insomnia
   Endocrine & metabolic: Decreased sexual ability
1% to 10%:
   Cardiovascular: Bradycardia, palpitations, edema, CHF, reduced peripheral circulation
   Central nervous system: Mental depression
   Gastrointestinal: Diarrhea or constipation, nausea, vomiting, stomach discomfort
   Ocular: Mild ocular stinging and discomfort, tearing, photophobia, decreased corneal sensitivity, keratitis
   Respiratory: Bronchospasm
   Miscellaneous: Cold extremities

Drug Interactions
Cytochrome P450 Effect: Substrate of CYP2D6 (minor), 3A4 (major)

Increased Effect/Toxicity: Bisoprolol may increase the effects of other drugs which slow AV conduction (digoxin, verapamil, diltiazem), alpha-blockers (prazosin, terazosin), and alpha-adrenergic stimulants (epinephrine, phenylephrine). Bisoprolol may mask the tachycardia from hypoglycemia caused by insulin and oral hypoglycemics. In patients receiving concurrent therapy, the risk of hypertensive crisis is increased when either clonidine or the beta-blocker is withdrawn. Reserpine has been shown to enhance the effect of beta-blockers. Beta-blockers may increase the action or levels of ethanol, disopyramide, nondepolarizing muscle relaxants, and theophylline although the effects are difficult to predict. CYP3A4 inhibitors may increase the levels/effects of bisoprolol; example inhibitors include azole antifungals, ciprofloxacin, clarithromycin, diclofenac, doxycycline, erythromycin, imatinib, isoniazid, nefazodone, nicardipine, propofol, protease inhibitors, quinidine, and verapamil.

Decreased Effect: Decreased effect of bisoprolol with aluminum salts, barbiturates, calcium salts, cholestyramine, colestipol, NSAIDs, penicillins (ampicillin), rifampin, and salicylates due to decreased bioavailability and plasma levels. The effect of sulfonylureas may be decreased by beta-blockers. CYP3A4 inducers may decrease the levels/effects of bisoprolol; example inducers include aminoglutethimide, carbamazepine, nafcillin, nevirapine, phenobarbital, phenytoin, and rifamycins.

(Continued)

Bisoprolol *(Continued)*

Mechanism of Action Selective inhibitor of beta$_1$-adrenergic receptors; competitively blocks beta$_1$-receptors, with little or no effect on beta$_2$-receptors at doses <10 mg

Pharmacodynamics/Kinetics

Onset of action: 1-2 hours

Absorption: Rapid and almost complete

Distribution: Widely; highest concentrations in heart, liver, lungs, and saliva; crosses blood-brain barrier; enters breast milk

Protein binding: 26% to 33%

Metabolism: Extensively hepatic; significant first-pass effect

Half-life elimination: 9-12 hours

Time to peak: 1.7-3 hours

Excretion: Urine (3% to 10% as unchanged drug); feces (<2%)

Dosage Oral:

Adults: 2.5-5 mg once daily, may be increased to 10 mg, and then up to 20 mg once daily, if necessary

Elderly: Initial dose: 2.5 mg/day; may be increased by 2.5-5 mg/day; maximum recommended dose: 20 mg/day

Dosing adjustment in renal/hepatic impairment: Cl$_{cr}$ <40 mL/minute: Initial: 2.5 mg/day; increase cautiously.

Hemodialysis: Not dialyzable

Monitoring Parameters Blood pressure, EKG, neurologic status

Patient Information Do not discontinue abruptly (angina may be precipitated); notify prescriber if CHF symptoms become worse or side effects occur; take at the same time each day; may mask diabetes symptoms; consult pharmacist or prescriber before taking with other adrenergic drugs (eg, cold medications); use with caution while driving or performing tasks requiring alertness; may be taken without regard to meals

Dosage Forms TAB: 5 mg, 10 mg

Bisoprolol and Hydrochlorothiazide

(bis OH proe lol & hye droe klor oh THYE a zide)

U.S. Brand Names Ziac®

Synonyms Hydrochlorothiazide and Bisoprolol

Therapeutic Category Antihypertensive Agent, Combination

Use Treatment of hypertension

Pregnancy Risk Factor C/D (2nd and 3rd trimesters)

Dosage Oral: Adults: Dose is individualized, given once daily

Dosage Forms TAB: Bisoprolol 2.5 mg and hydrochlorothiazide 6.25 mg; bisoprolol 5 mg and hydrochlorothiazide 6.25 mg; bisoprolol 10 mg and hydrochlorothiazide 6.25 mg

◆ **Bisoprolol Fumarate** *see* Bisoprolol *on page 169*

◆ **Bistropamide** *see* Tropicamide *on page 1277*

Bivalirudin *(bye VAL i roo din)*

U.S. Brand Names Angiomax®

Synonyms Hirulog

Therapeutic Category Anticoagulant, Thrombin Inhibitor

Use Anticoagulant used in conjunction with aspirin for patients with unstable angina undergoing percutaneous transluminal coronary angioplasty (PTCA)

Pregnancy Risk Factor B

Contraindications Hypersensitivity to bivalirudin or any component of the formulation; active major bleeding

Warnings/Precautions Safety and efficacy have not been established when used with platelet inhibitors other than aspirin, in patients with unstable angina not undergoing PTCA, in patients with other coronary syndromes, or in pediatric patients. As with all anticoagulants, bleeding may occur at any site and should be considered following an unexplained fall in blood pressure or hematocrit, or any unexplained symptom. Use with caution in patients with disease states associated with increased risk of bleeding.

Common Adverse Reactions As with all anticoagulants, bleeding is the major adverse effect of bivalirudin. Hemorrhage may occur at virtually any site. Risk is dependent on multiple variables, including the intensity of anticoagulation and patient susceptibility. Additional adverse effects are often related to idiosyncratic reactions, and the frequency is difficult to estimate.

Adverse reactions reported were generally less than those seen with heparin.

>10%:

Cardiovascular: Hypotension (12% bivalirudin vs 17% heparin)

Central nervous system: Pain (15%), headache (12%)

Gastrointestinal: Nausea (15%)

Neuromuscular & skeletal: Back pain (42% vs 44% heparin)

1% to 10%:

Cardiovascular: Hypertension (6%), bradycardia (5%)

Central nervous system: Insomnia (7%), anxiety (6%), fever (5%), nervousness (5%)

Gastrointestinal: Vomiting (6%), dyspepsia (5%), abdominal pain (5%)

Genitourinary: Urinary retention (4%)

Hematologic: Major hemorrhage (4% bivalirudin vs 9% heparin), transfusion required (2% bivalirudin vs 6% heparin)

Local: Injection site pain (8%)
Neuromuscular & skeletal: Pelvic pain (6%)

Drug Interactions
    Increased Effect/Toxicity: Aspirin may increase anticoagulant effect of bivalirudin (Note: All clinical trials included coadministration of aspirin). Limited drug interaction studies have not yet shown pharmacodynamic interactions between bivalirudin and ticlopidine, abciximab, or low molecular weight heparin (low molecular weight heparin was discontinued at least 8 hours prior to bivalirudin administration).

Mechanism of Action Bivalirudin acts as a specific and reversible direct thrombin inhibitor, binding to circulating and clot-bound thrombin. Shows linear dose- and concentration-dependent prolongation of ACT, aPTT, PT and TT.

Pharmacodynamics/Kinetics
    Onset of action: Immediate
    Duration: Coagulation times return to baseline ~1 hour following discontinuation of infusion
    Distribution: 0.2 L/kg
    Protein binding, plasma: Does not bind other than thrombin
    Half-life elimination: Normal renal function: 25 minutes; Cl_{cr} 10-29 mL/minute: 57 minutes
    Excretion: Urine, proteolytic cleavage

Dosage Adults: Anticoagulant in patients with unstable angina undergoing PTCA (treatment should be started just prior to PTCA): I.V.: Initial: Bolus: 1 mg/kg, followed by continuous infusion: 2.5 mg/kg/hour over 4 hours; if needed, infusion may be continued at 0.2 mg/kg/hour for up to 20 hours; patients should also receive aspirin 300-325 mg/day
    Dosage adjustment in renal impairment: Infusion dose should be reduced based on degree of renal impairment; initial bolus dose remains unchanged; monitor activated coagulation time (ACT)
        Cl_{cr} ≥60 mL/minute: No adjustment required
        Cl_{cr} 30-59 mL/minute: Decrease infusion dose by 20%
        Cl_{cr} 10-29 mL/minute: Decrease infusion dose by 60%
        Dialysis-dependent patients (off dialysis): Decrease infusion dose by 90%
        Clearance of bivalirudin remains 1.8-fold greater than the glomerular filtration rate, regardless of the degree in renal impairment.
    Dosage adjustment in hepatic impairment: No dosage adjustment is needed
    Elderly: No dosage adjustment is needed in elderly patients with normal renal function. Puncture site hemorrhage and catheterization site hemorrhage were seen in more patients ≥65 years of age than in patients <65 years of age

Administration For I.V. administration only. To prepare infusion, reconstitute each 250 mg vial with 5 mL sterile water for injection; further dilute with 5% dextrose in water or 0.9% sodium chloride for injection; final concentration should be 5 mg/mL for the initial continuous infusion (50 mL/250 mg vial). If needed, a lower concentration bag should be prepared for the low rate infusion; final concentration should be 0.5 mg/mL. Do not mix with other medications.

Monitoring Parameters Manufacturer recommends monitoring of ACT in patients with renal impairment. Although the ACT was checked after 5 minutes and 45 minutes in clinical trials, the bivalirudin dose was not titrated to the ACT.

Patient Information This drug can only be administered by injection. You may have a tendency to bleed easily while taking this drug; brush teeth with soft brush, floss with waxed floss, use electric razor, avoid scissors or sharp knives, and potentially harmful activities. Report chest pain; unusual bleeding or bruising (bleeding gums, nosebleed, blood in urine, dark stool); pain in joints or back; or numbness, tingling, swelling, or pain at injection site.

Dosage Forms INJ, powder for reconstitution: 250 mg

♦ **BL4162A** *see* Anagrelide *on page 99*
♦ **Blenoxane®** *see* Bleomycin *on page 171*
♦ **Bleo** *see* Bleomycin *on page 171*

Bleomycin (blee oh MYE sin)

U.S. Brand Names Blenoxane®
Synonyms Bleo; Bleomycin Sulfate; BLM; NSC-125066
Therapeutic Category Antineoplastic Agent, Antibiotic
Use Treatment of squamous cell carcinomas, melanomas, sarcomas, testicular carcinoma, Hodgkin's lymphoma, and non-Hodgkin's lymphoma
    Orphan drug: Sclerosing agent for malignant pleural effusion
Pregnancy Risk Factor D
Contraindications Hypersensitivity to bleomycin sulfate or any component of the formulation; severe pulmonary disease; pregnancy
Warnings/Precautions The U.S. Food and Drug Administration (FDA) currently recommends that procedures for proper handling and disposal of antineoplastic agents be considered. Occurrence of pulmonary fibrosis is higher in elderly patients and in those receiving >400 units total and in smokers and patients with prior radiation therapy. A severe idiosyncratic reaction consisting of hypotension, mental confusion, fever, chills and wheezing (similar to anaphylaxis) has been reported in 1% of lymphoma patients treated with bleomycin. Since these reactions usually occur after the first or second dose, careful monitoring is essential after these doses. Check lungs prior to each treatment for fine rales (1st sign). Follow manufacturer recommendations for administering O_2 during surgery to patients who have received bleomycin.
Common Adverse Reactions
    >10%:
        Cardiovascular: Raynaud's phenomenon
(Continued)

Bleomycin *(Continued)*

Dermatologic: Pain at the tumor site, phlebitis. About 50% of patients develop erythema, induration, hyperkeratosis, and peeling of the skin, particularly on the palmar and plantar surfaces of the hands and feet. Hyperpigmentation (50%), alopecia, nailbed changes may also occur. These effects appear dose-related and reversible with discontinuation of the drug.

Gastrointestinal: Stomatitis and mucositis (30%), anorexia, weight loss

Respiratory: Tachypnea, rales, acute or chronic interstitial pneumonitis and pulmonary fibrosis (5% to 10%), hypoxia and death (1%). Symptoms include cough, dyspnea, and bilateral pulmonary infiltrates. The pathogenesis is not certain, but may be due to damage of pulmonary, vascular, or connective tissue. Response to steroid therapy is variable and somewhat controversial.

Miscellaneous: Acute febrile reactions (25% to 50%); anaphylactoid reactions characterized by hypotension, confusion, fever, chills, and wheezing. Onset may be immediate or delayed for several hours.

1% to 10%:

Dermatologic: Rash (8%), skin thickening, diffuse scleroderma, onycholysis

Miscellaneous: Acute anaphylactoid reactions

Drug Interactions

Increased Effect/Toxicity: Lomustine increases severity of leukopenia. Cisplatin may decrease bleomycin elimination.

Decreased Effect: Bleomycin may decrease plasma levels of digoxin. Concomitant therapy with phenytoin results in decreased phenytoin levels.

Mechanism of Action Inhibits synthesis of DNA; binds to DNA leading to single- and double-strand breaks

Pharmacodynamics/Kinetics

Absorption: I.M. and intrapleural administration: 30% to 50% of I.V. serum concentrations; intraperitoneal and S.C. routes produce serum concentrations equal to those of I.V.

Distribution: V_d: 22 L/m^2; highest concentrations in skin, kidney, lung, heart tissues; lowest in testes and GI tract; does not cross blood-brain barrier

Protein binding: 1%

Metabolism: Via several tissues including hepatic, GI tract, skin, pulmonary, renal, and serum

Half-life elimination: Biphasic (renal function dependent):

Normal renal function: Initial: 1.3 hours; Terminal: 9 hours

End-stage renal disease: Initial: 2 hours; Terminal: 30 hours

Time to peak, serum: I.M.: Within 30 minutes

Excretion: Urine (50% to 70% as active drug)

Dosage Refer to individual protocols; 1 unit = 1 mg

May be administered I.M., I.V., S.C., or intracavitary

Children and Adults:

Test dose for lymphoma patients: I.M., I.V., S.C.: Because of the possibility of an anaphylactoid reaction, ≤2 units of bleomycin for the first 2 doses; monitor vital signs every 15 minutes; wait a minimum of 1 hour before administering remainder of dose; if no acute reaction occurs, then the regular dosage schedule may be followed

Single-agent therapy:

I.M./I.V./S.C.: Squamous cell carcinoma, lymphoma, testicular carcinoma: 0.25-0.5 units/ kg (10-20 units/m^2) 1-2 times/week

CIV: 15 units/m^2 over 24 hours daily for 4 days

Combination-agent therapy:

I.M./I.V.: 3-4 units/m^2

I.V.: ABVD: 10 units/m^2 on days 1 and 15

Maximum cumulative lifetime dose: 400 units

Pleural sclerosing: 60-240 units as a single infusion. Dose may be repeated at intervals of several days if fluid continues to accumulate (mix in 50-100 mL of D$_5$W, NS, or SWFI); may add lidocaine 100-200 mg to reduce local discomfort.

Dosing adjustment in renal impairment:

Cl$_{cr}$ 10-50 mL/minute: Administer 75% of normal dose

Cl$_{cr}$ <10 mL/minute: Administer 50% of normal dose

Administration I.V. doses should be administered slowly (manufacturer recommends giving over a period of 10 minutes); I.M. or S.C. may cause pain at injection site

Monitoring Parameters Pulmonary function tests (total lung volume, forced vital capacity, carbon monoxide diffusion), renal function, chest x-ray, temperature initially

Patient Information You may experience loss of appetite, nausea, vomiting, mouth sores; small frequent meals, frequent mouth care with soft swab, frequent mouth rinses, sucking lozenges, or chewing gum may help; if unresolved, notify prescriber. You may experience fever or chills (will usually resolve); redness, peeling, or increased color of skin, or loss of hair (reversible after cessation of therapy). Report any change in respiratory status; difficulty breathing; wheezing; air hunger; increased secretions; difficulty expectorating secretions; confusion; unresolved fever or chills; sores in mouth; vaginal itching, burning, or discharge; sudden onset of dizziness; or acute headache. Contraceptive measures are recommended during therapy.

Dosage Forms INJ, powder for reconstitution: 15 units, 30 units

♦ **BLM** *see* Bleomycin *on page 171*

♦ **Blocadren**® *see* Timolol *on page 1229*

♦ **BMS-232632** *see* Atazanavir *on page 124*

♦ **BMS 337039** *see* Aripiprazole *on page 114*

♦ **Bonine**® **[OTC]** *see* Meclizine *on page 779*

Bortezomib (bore TEZ oh mib)

U.S. Brand Names Velcade™

Synonyms LDP-341; MLN341; PS-341

Therapeutic Category Proteasome Inhibitor

Use Treatment of multiple myeloma in patients who have had two prior therapies and had disease progression during the previous therapy

Pregnancy Risk Factor D

Contraindications Hypersensitivity to bortezomib, boron, mannitol, or any component of the formulation; pregnancy

Warnings/Precautions The U.S. Food and Drug Administration (FDA) currently recommends that procedures for proper handling and disposal of antineoplastic agents be considered. May cause peripheral neuropathy, risk may be increased with previous use of neurotoxic agents or pre-existing peripheral neuropathy; adjustment of dose and schedule may be required. May cause orthostatic/postural hypotension; use caution with dehydration, history of syncope or medications associated with hypotension. Use caution with hepatic or renal impairment. Safety and efficacy have not been established in pediatric patients.

Common Adverse Reactions

>10%:

Cardiovascular: Edema (25%), hypotension (12%)

Central nervous system: Pyrexia (36%), headache (28%), insomnia (27%), dizziness (21%, excludes vertigo), anxiety (14%)

Dermatologic: Rash (21%), pruritus (11%)

Endocrine & metabolic: Dehydration (18%)

Gastrointestinal: Nausea (64%), diarrhea (51%), appetite decreased (43%), constipation (43%), vomiting (36%), abdominal pain (13%), abnormal taste (13%), dyspepsia (13%)

Hematologic: Thrombocytopenia (43%, Grade 3: 27%, Grade 4: 3%); anemia (32%, Grade 3: 9%); neutropenia (24%, Grade 3: 13%, Grade 4: 3%)

Neuromuscular & skeletal: Asthenic conditions (65%, Grade 3: 18% - includes fatigue, malaise, weakness); peripheral neuropathy (37%, Grade 3: 14%); arthralgia (26%); limb pain (26%); paresthesia and dysesthesia (23%), back pain (14%); bone pain (14%); muscle cramps (14%); myalgia (14%); rigors (12%)

Ocular: Blurred vision (11%)

Respiratory: Dyspnea (22%), upper respiratory tract infection (18%), cough (17%)

Miscellaneous: Herpes zoster (11%)

1% to 10%: Respiratory: Pneumonia (10%)

Drug Interactions

Cytochrome P450 Effect: Substrate of CYP1A2 (minor), 2C8/9 (minor), 2C19 (minor), 2D6 (minor), 3A4 (major); **Inhibits** CYP1A2 (weak), 2C8/9 (weak), 2C19 (moderate), 2D6 (weak), 3A4 (weak)

Increased Effect/Toxicity: CYP3A4 inhibitors may increase the levels/effects of bortezomib; example inhibitors include azole antifungals, ciprofloxacin, clarithromycin, diclofenac, doxycycline, erythromycin, imatinib, isoniazid, nefazodone, nicardipine, propofol, protease inhibitors, quinidine, and verapamil.

Decreased Effect: CYP3A4 inducers may decrease the levels/effects of bortezomib; example inducers include aminoglutethimide, carbamazepine, nafcillin, nevirapine, phenobarbital, phenytoin, and rifamycins.

Mechanism of Action Bortezomib inhibits proteasomes, enzyme complexes which regulate protein homeostasis within the cell. Specifically, it reversibly inhibits chymotrypsin-like activity at the 26S proteasome, leading to activation of signaling cascades, cell-cycle arrest and apoptosis.

Pharmacodynamics/Kinetics

Protein binding: ~83%

Metabolism: Hepatic via CYP 1A2, 2C9, 2C19, 2D6, 3A4; forms metabolites (inactive)

Half-life elimination: 9-15 hours

Dosage I.V.: Adults: Multiple myeloma: 1.3 mg/m^2 twice weekly for 2 weeks on days 1, 4, 8, 11, followed by a 10-day rest period on days 12-21. Consecutive doses should be separated by at least 72 hours. One treatment cycle is equal to 21 days.

Dosage adjustment in renal impairment: Specific guidelines are not available; studies did not include patients with Cl$_{cr}$ <13 mL/minute and patients on hemodialysis. Monitor closely for toxicity.

Dosage adjustment in hepatic impairment: Specific guidelines are not available; clearance may be decreased; monitor closely for toxicity

Dosage adjustment for toxicity:

Grade 3 nonhematological (excluding neuropathy) or Grade 4 hematological toxicity: Withhold until toxicity resolved; may reinitiate at a 25% reduced dose

Neuropathic pain and/or peripheral sensory neuropathy:

Grade 1 without pain or loss of function: No action needed

Grade 1 with pain or Grade 2 interfering with function but not activities of daily living: Reduce dose to 1 mg/m^2

(Continued)

Bortezomib *(Continued)*

> Grade 2 with pain or Grade 3 interfering with activities of daily living: Withhold until toxicity resolved, may reinitiate at 0.7 mg/m² once weekly
> Grade 4: Discontinue therapy

Administration Administer via rapid I.V. push

Monitoring Parameters Peripheral neuropathy, hypotension, CBC

Dosage Forms INJ, powder for reconstitution [preservative free]: 3.5 mg

Bosentan (boe SEN tan)

U.S. Brand Names Tracleer®

Therapeutic Category Endothelin Antagonist

Use Treatment of pulmonary artery hypertension (PAH) in patients with World Health Organization (WHO) Class III or IV symptoms to improve exercise capacity and decrease the rate of clinical deterioration

Unlabeled/Investigational Use Investigational: Congestive heart failure

Restrictions Bosentan (Tracleer®) is available only through a limited distribution program directly from the manufacturer (Actelion Pharmaceuticals 1-866-228-3546). It will not be available through wholesalers or individual pharmacies.

Pregnancy Risk Factor X

Contraindications Hypersensitivity to bosentan or any component of the formulation; concurrent use of cyclosporine or glyburide; pregnancy

Warnings/Precautions Avoid use in moderate to severe hepatic impairment. Avoid use in patients with elevated serum transaminases (>3 times upper limit of normal) at baseline; dosage adjustment recommended if elevations occur during therapy. Monitor hepatic function closely (at least monthly). Treatment should be stopped in patients who develop elevated transaminases (ALT or AST) in combination with symptoms of hepatic injury (unusual fatigue, jaundice, nausea, vomiting, abdominal pain, and/or fever) or elevated serum bilirubin ≥2 times upper limit of normal.

Use in pregnancy is contraindicated; exclude pregnancy prior to initiation of therapy; patients must be instructed to use effective, nonhormonal contraception throughout treatment. May cause dose-related decreases in hemoglobin and hematocrit (monitoring of hemoglobin is recommended). May cause fluid retention evidenced by signs and symptoms of CHF, weight gain, and leg edema. Safety and efficacy in pediatric patients have not been established.

Common Adverse Reactions
>10% :
  Central nervous system: Headache (16% to 22%)
  Hematologic: Hemoglobin decreased (≥1 g/dL in up to 57%; typically in first 6 weeks of therapy)
  Hepatic: Serum transaminases increased (>3 times upper limit of normal; up to 11%)
  Respiratory: Nasopharyngitis (11%)
1% to 10%:
  Cardiovascular: Flushing (7% to 9%), edema (lower limb, 8%; generalized 4%), hypotension (7%), palpitations (5%)
  Central nervous system: Fatigue (4%)
  Dermatologic: Pruritus (4%)
  Gastrointestinal: Dyspepsia (4%)
  Hematologic: Anemia (3%)
  Hepatic: Abnormal hepatic function (6% to 8%)

Drug Interactions
Cytochrome P450 Effect: Substrate (major) of CYP2C8/9, 3A4; **Induces** CYP2C8/9 (weak), 3A4 (weak)
Increased Effect/Toxicity: An increased risk of serum transaminase elevations was observed during concurrent therapy with glyburide; concurrent use is contraindicated. Cyclosporine increases serum concentrations of bosentan (approximately 3-4 times baseline). Concurrent use of cyclosporine is contraindicated. Ketoconazole may increase the serum concentrations of bosentan; concentrations are increased approximately twofold; monitor for increased effects.

CYP2C8/9 inhibitors may increase the levels/effects of bosentan; example inhibitors include delavirdine, fluconazole, gemfibrozil, ketoconazole, nicardipine, NSAIDs, pioglitazone, and sulfonamides. CYP3A4 inhibitors may increase the levels/effects of bosentan; example inhibitors include azole antifungals, ciprofloxacin, clarithromycin, diclofenac, doxycycline, erythromycin, imatinib, isoniazid, nefazodone, nicardipine, propofol, protease inhibitors, quinidine, and verapamil.

Decreased Effect: CYP2C8/9 inducers may decrease the levels/effects of bosentan; example inducers include carbamazepine, phenobarbital, phenytoin, rifampin, rifapentine, and secobarbital. Bosentan may enhance the metabolism of cyclosporine, decreasing its serum concentrations by ~50%; effect on sirolimus and/or tacrolimus has not been specifically evaluated, but may be similar. Concurrent use of cyclosporine is contraindicated. Bosentan is a weak inducer, but may increase the metabolism of drugs metabolized by CYP2C8/9. CYP3A4 inducers may decrease the levels/effects of bosentan; example inducers include aminoglutethimide, carbamazepine, nafcillin, nevirapine, phenobarbital, phenytoin, and rifamycins.Bosentan may enhance the metabolism of methadone resulting in methadone withdrawal.

Mechanism of Action Blocks endothelin receptors on vascular endothelium and smooth muscle. Stimulation of these receptors is associated with vasoconstriction. Although bosentan blocks both ET_A and ET_B receptors, the affinity is higher for the A subtype. Improvement in symptoms of pulmonary artery hypertension and a decrease in the rate of clinical deterioration have been demonstrated in clinical trials.

Pharmacodynamics/Kinetics

Distribution: V_d: 18 L

Protein binding, plasma: >98% to albumin

Metabolism: Hepatic via CYP2C9 and 3A4 to three primary metabolites (one having pharmacologic activity)

Bioavailability: 50%

Half-life elimination: 5 hours; prolonged with heart failure, possibly in PAH

Excretion: Feces (as metabolites); urine (<3% as unchanged drug)

Dosage Oral: Adults: Initial: 62.5 mg twice daily for 4 weeks; increase to maintenance dose of 125 mg twice daily; adults <40 kg should be maintained at 62.5 mg twice daily

Note: When discontinuing treatment, consider a reduction in dosage to 62.5 mg twice daily for 3-7 days (to avoid clinical deterioration).

Dosage adjustment in renal impairment: No dosage adjustment required.

Dosage adjustment in hepatic impairment: Avoid use in patients with **pretreatment** moderate to severe hepatic insufficiency.

Modification based on transaminase elevation:

If any elevation, regardless of degree, is accompanied by clinical symptoms of hepatic injury (unusual fatigue, nausea, vomiting, abdominal pain, fever, or jaundice) or a serum bilirubin ≥2 times the upper limit of normal, treatment should be stopped.

AST/ALT >3 times but ≤5 times upper limit of normal: Confirm with additional test; if confirmed, reduce dose or interrupt treatment. Monitor transaminase levels at least every 2 weeks. May continue or reintroduce treatment, as appropriate, following return to pretreatment values. Begin with initial dose (above) and recheck transaminases within 3 days

AST/ALT >5 times but ≤8 times upper limit of normal: Confirm with additional test; if confirmed, stop treatment. Monitor transaminase levels at least every 2 weeks. May reintroduce treatment, as appropriate, following return to pretreatment values.

AST/ALT >8 times upper limit of normal: Stop treatment.

Administration May be administered with or without food, once in the morning and once in the evening.

Monitoring Parameters Serum transaminase (AST and ALT) should be determined prior to the initiation of therapy and at monthly intervals thereafter. A woman of childbearing potential must have a negative pregnancy test prior to the initiation of therapy and monthly thereafter. Hemoglobin and hematocrit should be measured at baseline, at 1 month and 3 months of treatment, and every 3 months thereafter. Monitor for clinical signs and symptoms of liver injury.

Patient Information May be taken with or without food. Report unusual fatigue, nausea, vomiting, abdominal pain, and/or yellowing of the skin/eyes to prescriber immediately. Do not get pregnant while taking this medication. A woman of childbearing potential must use an effective nonhormonal method of contraception during treatment with this medication.

Dosage Forms TAB: 62.5 mg, 125 mg

♦ **B&O Supprettes**® *see Belladonna and Opium on page 151*

♦ **Botox**® *see Botulinum Toxin Type A on page 175*

♦ **Botox**® **Cosmetic** *see Botulinum Toxin Type A on page 175*

Botulinum Pentavalent (ABCDE) Toxoid

(BOT yoo lin num pen ta VAY lent [aye, bee, cee, dee, ee] TOKS oyd)

Synonyms Botulinum Toxoid, Pentavalent Vaccine (Against Types A / B / C / D / E Strains of *C. botulinum*)

Therapeutic Category Toxoid and Vaccine

Unlabeled/Investigational Use Investigational: Prophylaxis of botulism in personnel working with *C. botulinum* cultures

Botulinum Toxin Type A (BOT yoo lin num TOKS in type aye)

U.S. Brand Names Botox®; Botox® Cosmetic

Therapeutic Category Neuromuscular Blocker Agent, Toxin; Ophthalmic Agent, Toxin

Use Treatment of strabismus and blepharospasm associated with dystonia (including benign essential blepharospasm or VII nerve disorders in patients ≥12 years of age); cervical dystonia (spasmodic torticollis) in patients ≥16 years of age; temporary improvement in the appearance of lines/wrinkles of the face (moderate to severe glabellar lines associated with corrugator and/or procerus muscle activity) in adult patients ≤65 years of age

Orphan drug: Treatment of dynamic muscle contracture in pediatric cerebral palsy patients

Unlabeled/Investigational Use Treatment of oromandibular dystonia, spasmodic dysphonia (laryngeal dystonia) and other dystonias (ie, writer's cramp, focal task-specific dystonias); migraine treatment and prophylaxis

Pregnancy Risk Factor C (manufacturer)

Contraindications Hypersensitivity to albumin, botulinum toxin, or any component of the formulation; infection at the proposed injection site(s); pregnancy. Relative contraindications include diseases of neuromuscular transmission; coagulopathy including therapeutic anticoagulation; uncooperative patient

Warnings/Precautions Higher doses or more frequent administration may result in neutralizing antibody formation and loss of efficacy. Product contains albumin and may carry a remote risk of virus transmission. Use caution if there is inflammation, excessive weakness, or (Continued)

Botulinum Toxin Type A *(Continued)*

atrophy at the proposed injection site(s). Have appropriate support in case of anaphylactic reaction. Use with caution in patients with neuromuscular diseases (such as myasthenia gravis), neuropathic disorders (such as amyotrophic lateral sclerosis), or patients taking aminoglycosides or other drugs that interfere with neuromuscular transmission. Ensure adequate contraception in women of childbearing years. Long-term effects of chronic therapy unknown.

Cervical dystonia: Dysphagia is common. It may be severe requiring alternative feeding methods. Risk factors include smaller neck muscle mass, bilateral injections into the sterno-cleidomastoid muscle or injections into the levator scapulae. Dysphasia may be associated with increased risk of upper respiratory infection.

Blepharospasm: Reduced blinking from injection of the orbicularis muscle can lead to corneal exposure and ulceration.

Strabismus: Retrobulbar hemorrhages may occur from needle penetration into orbit. Spatial disorientation, double vision, or past pointing may occur if one or more extraocular muscles are paralyzed. Covering the affected eye may help. Careful testing of corneal sensation, avoidance of lower lid injections, and treatment of epithelial defects necessary.

Temporary reduction in glabellar lines: Do not use more frequently than every 3 months. Patients with marked facial asymmetry, ptosis, excessive dermatochalasis, deep dermal scarring, thick sebaceous skin, or the inability to substantially lessen glabellar lines by physically spreading them apart were excluded from clinical trials. Reduced blinking from injection of the orbicularis muscle can lead to corneal exposure and ulceration. Spatial disorientation, double vision, or past pointing may occur if one or more extraocular muscles are paralyzed.

Common Adverse Reactions Adverse effects usually occur in 1 week and may last up to several months

>10% :

Central nervous system: Headache (cervical dystonia up to 11%, reduction of glabellar lines up to 13%; can occur with other uses)

Gastrointestinal: Dysphagia (cervical dystonia 19%)

Neuromuscular & skeletal: Neck pain (cervical dystonia 11%)

Ocular: Ptosis (blepharospasm 10% to 40%, strabismus 1% to 38%, reduction of glabellar lines 1% to 5%); vertical deviation (strabismus 17%)

Respiratory: Upper respiratory infection (cervical dystonia 12%),

2% to 10%:

Central nervous system: Dizziness (cervical dystonia, reduction of glabellar lines); speech disorder (cervical dystonia), fever (cervical dystonia), drowsiness (cervical dystonia)

Gastrointestinal: Xerostomia (cervical dystonia), nausea (cervical dystonia, reduction of glabellar lines)

Local: Injection site reaction

Neuromuscular & skeletal: Back pain (cervical dystonia); hypertonia (cervical dystonia); weakness (cervical dystonia, reduction of glabellar lines); facial pain (reduction of glabellar lines)

Ocular: Dry eyes (blepharospasm 6%), superficial punctate keratitis (blepharospasm 6%)

Respiratory: Cough (cervical dystonia), rhinitis (cervical dystonia), infection (reduction of glabellar lines)

Miscellaneous: Flu syndrome (cervical dystonia, reduction of glabellar lines)

Drug Interactions

Increased Effect/Toxicity: Aminoglycosides, neuromuscular-blocking agents

Mechanism of Action Botulinum A toxin is a neurotoxin produced by *Clostridium botulinum*, spore-forming anaerobic bacillus, which appears to affect only the presynaptic membrane of the neuromuscular junction in humans, where it prevents calcium-dependent release of acetylcholine and produces a state of denervation. Muscle inactivation persists until new fibrils grow from the nerve and form junction plates on new areas of the muscle-cell walls.

Pharmacodynamics/Kinetics

Onset of action (improvement):

Blepharospasm: ~3 days

Cervical dystonia: ~2 weeks

Strabismus: ~1-2 days

Reduction of glabellar lines (Botox® Cosmetic): 1-2 days, increasing in intensity during first week

Duration:

Blepharospasm: ~3 months

Cervical dystonia: <3 months

Strabismus: ~2-6 weeks

Reduction of glabellar lines (Botox® Cosmetic): Up to 3 months

Absorption: Not expected to be present in peripheral blood at recommended doses

Time to peak:

Blepharospasm: 1-2 weeks

Cervical dystonia: ~6 weeks

Strabismus: Within first week

Dosage I.M.:

Children ≥16 years and Adults: Cervical dystonia: For dosing guidance, the mean dose is 236 units (25th to 75th percentile range 198-300 units) divided among the affected muscles in patients previously treated with botulinum toxin. Initial dose in previously untreated patients should be lower. Sequential dosing should be based on the patient's head and neck position, localization of pain, muscle hypertrophy, patient response, and previous adverse reactions. The total dose injected into the sternocleidomastoid muscles should be ≤100 units to decrease the occurrence of dysphagia.

Children ≥12 years and Adults:

Blepharospasm: Initial dose: 1.25-2.5 units injected into the medial and lateral pretarsal orbicularis oculi of the upper and lower lid; dose may be increased up to twice the previous dose if the response from the initial dose lasted ≤2 months; maximum dose per site: 5 units; cumulative dose in a 30-day period: ≤200 units. Tolerance may occur if treatments are given more often than every 3 months, but the effect is not usually permanent.

Strabismus:

Initial dose:

Vertical muscles and for horizontal strabismus <20 prism diopters: 1.25-2.5 units in any one muscle

Horizontal strabismus of 20-50 prism diopters: 2.5-5 units in any one muscle

Persistent VI nerve palsy >1 month: 1.5-2.5 units in the medial rectus muscle

Re-examine patients 7-14 days after each injection to assess the effect of that dose. Subsequent doses for patients experiencing incomplete paralysis of the target may be increased up to twice the previous administered dose. The maximum recommended dose as a single injection for any one muscle is 25 units. Do not administer subsequent injections until the effects of the previous dose are gone.

Adults ≤65 years: Reduction of glabellar lines: An effective dose is determined by gross observation of the patient's ability to activate the superficial muscles injected. The location, size and use of muscles may vary markedly among individuals. Inject 0.1 mL dose into each of five sites, two in each corrugator muscle and one in the procerus muscle (total dose 0.5 mL).

Elderly: No specific adjustment recommended

Dosage adjustment in renal impairment: No specific adjustment recommended

Dosage adjustment in hepatic impairment: No specific adjustment recommended

Administration

Cervical dystonia: Use 25-, 27-, or 30-gauge needle for superficial muscles and a longer 22-gauge needle for deeper musculature; electromyography may help localize the involved muscles

Blepharospasm: Use a 27- or 30-gauge needle without electromyography guidance. Avoid injecting near the levator palpebrae superioris (may decrease ptosis); avoid medial lower lid injections (may decrease diplopia). Apply pressure at the injection site to prevent ecchymosis in the soft eyelid tissues.

Strabismus injections: Must use surgical exposure or electromyographic guidance; use the electrical activity recorded from the tip of the injections needle as a guide to placement within the target muscle. Local anesthetic and ocular decongestant should be given before injection. The volume of injection should be 0.05-0.15 mL per muscle. Many patients will require additional doses because of inadequate response to initial dose.

Reduction of glabellar lines (Botox® Cosmetic): Use a 30-gauge needle. Ensure injected volume/dose is accurate and where feasible keep to a minimum. Avoid injection near the levator palpebrae superioris. Medial corrugator injections should be at least 1 cm above the bony supraorbital ridge. Do not inject toxin closer than 1 cm above the central eyebrow.

Patient Information This medicine is given in a clinic or hospital setting by a prescriber. It is given as an injection. It is not a cure, but may be given on a periodic basis to help with spasms. Tell your prescriber if you have any nerve diseases or any infections where the shot might be given. Patients with blepharospasm may not have been very active. Start activity slowly and increase as you see how you feel. Call prescriber as soon as possible if you have trouble swallowing, speaking, or breathing. May have double vision or other problems where covering the eye with a patch may help.

Dosage Forms INJ, powder for reconstitution: (Botox®, Botox® Cosmetic): 100 units *Clostridium botulinum* toxin type A

Botulinum Toxin Type B (BOT yoo lin num TOKS in type bee)

U.S. Brand Names Myobloc®

Therapeutic Category Neuromuscular Blocker Agent, Toxin

Use Treatment of cervical dystonia (spasmodic torticollis)

Unlabeled/Investigational Use Treatment of cervical dystonia in patients who have developed resistance to botulinum toxin type A

Pregnancy Risk Factor C (manufacturer)

Contraindications Hypersensitivity to albumin, botulinum toxin, or any component of the formulation; infection at the injection site(s); pregnancy; coadministration of agents known to potentiate neuromuscular blockade. Relative contraindications include diseases of neuromuscular transmission; coagulopathy, including therapeutic anticoagulation; inability of patient to cooperate.

Warnings/Precautions Higher doses or more frequent administration may result in neutralizing antibody formation and loss of efficacy. Product contains albumin and may carry a remote risk of virus transmission. Use caution if there is inflammation, excessive weakness, or atrophy at the proposed injection site(s). Concurrent use of botulinum toxin type A or within <4 months of type B is not recommended. Have appropriate support in case of anaphylactic reaction. Use with caution in patients taking aminoglycosides or other drugs that interfere with neuromuscular transmission. Ensure adequate contraception in women of childbearing years. Long-term effects of chronic therapy unknown. Increased risk of dysphagia and respiratory complications. Safety and efficacy in children have not been established.

(Continued)

Botulinum Toxin Type B *(Continued)*

Common Adverse Reactions

>10%:

  Central nervous system: Headache (10% to 16%), pain (6% to 13%; placebo 10%)

  Gastrointestinal: Dysphagia (10% to 25%), xerostomia (3% to 34%)

  Local: Injection site pain (12% to 16%)

  Neuromuscular & skeletal: Neck pain (up to 17%; placebo: 16%)

  Miscellaneous: Infection (13% to 19%; placebo: 15%)

1% to 10%:

  Cardiovascular: Chest pain, vasodilation, peripheral edema

  Central nervous system: Dizziness (3% to 6%), fever, malaise, migraine, anxiety, tremor, hyperesthesia, somnolence, confusion, vertigo

  Dermatologic: Pruritus, bruising

  Gastrointestinal: Nausea (3% to 10%; placebo: 5%), dyspepsia (up to 10%; placebo: 5%), vomiting, stomatitis, taste perversion

  Genitourinary: Urinary tract infection, cystitis, vaginal moniliasis

  Hematologic: Serum neutralizing activity

  Neuromuscular & skeletal: Torticollis (up to 8%; placebo: 7%), arthralgia (up to 7%; placebo: 5%), back pain (3% to 7%; placebo: 3%), myasthenia (3% to 6%; placebo: 3%), weakness (up to 6%; placebo: 4%), arthritis

  Ocular: Amblyopia, abnormal vision

  Otic: Otitis media, tinnitus

  Respiratory: Cough (3% to 7%; placebo: 3%), rhinitis (1% to 5%; placebo: 6%), dyspnea, pneumonia

  Miscellaneous: Flu-syndrome (6% to 9%), allergic reaction, viral infection, abscess, cyst

Drug Interactions

Increased Effect/Toxicity: Aminoglycosides, neuromuscular-blocking agents, botulinum toxin type A, other agents which may block neuromuscular transmission

Mechanism of Action Botulinum B toxin is a neurotoxin produced by *Clostridium botulinum*, spore-forming anaerobic bacillus. It cleaves synaptic Vesicle Association Membrane Protein (VAMP; synaptobrevin) which is a component of the protein complex responsible for docking and fusion of the synaptic vesicle to the presynaptic membrane. By blocking neurotransmitter release, botulinum B toxin paralyzes the muscle.

Pharmacodynamics/Kinetics

Duration: 12-16 weeks

Absorption: Not expected to be present in peripheral blood at recommended doses

Dosage

Children: Not established in pediatric patients

Adults: Cervical dystonia: I.M.: Initial: 2500-5000 units divided among the affected muscles in patients **previously treated** with botulinum toxin; initial dose in **previously untreated** patients should be lower. Subsequent dosing should be optimized according to patient's response.

Elderly: No dosage adjustments required, but limited experience in patients ≥75 years old

Dosage adjustment in renal impairment: No specific adjustment recommended

Dosage adjustment in hepatic impairment: No specific adjustment recommended

Patient Information This medicine is given in a clinic or hospital setting by a prescriber. It is given as an injection. It is not a cure, but may be given on a periodic basis to help with spasms. Tell your prescriber if you have any nerve diseases or any infections where the injection might be given. Call your prescriber as soon as possible if you have trouble swallowing, speaking, breathing, or any muscle weakness.

Dosage Forms INJ, solution: 5000 units/mL (0.5 mL, 1 mL, 2 mL)

♦ **Botulinum Toxoid, Pentavalent Vaccine (Against Types A / B / C / D / E Strains of *C. botulinum*)** *see* Botulinum Pentavalent (ABCDE) Toxoid *on page 175*

♦ **Bovine Lung Surfactant** *see* Beractant *on page 158*

♦ **Bravelle**™ *see* Follitropins *on page 555*

♦ **Breathe Right® Saline [OTC]** *see* Sodium Chloride *on page 1146*

♦ **Breonesin® [OTC] [DSC]** *see* Guaifenesin *on page 603*

♦ **Brethaire [DSC]** *see* Terbutaline *on page 1199*

♦ **Brethine®** *see* Terbutaline *on page 1199*

Bretylium *(bre TIL ee um)*

Synonyms Bretylium Tosylate

Therapeutic Category Antiarrhythmic Agent, Class III

Use Treatment of ventricular tachycardia and fibrillation; treatment of other serious ventricular arrhythmias resistant to lidocaine

Pregnancy Risk Factor C

Contraindications Hypersensitivity to bretylium or any component of the formulation; severe aortic stenosis; severe pulmonary hypertension

Warnings/Precautions Hypotension occurs frequently. Keep patients supine until tolerance develops. Patients with fixed cardiac output (severe pulmonary hypertension or aortic stenosis) may experience severe hypotension due to decrease in peripheral resistance without ability to increase cardiac output. Reduce dose in renal failure patients. May have prolonged half-life in the elderly. Transient hypertension and increased frequency of arrhythmias may occur initially. Rapid I.V. injection may result in transient blood pressure changes, nausea, and vomiting. Use only in areas where there is equipment and staff familiar with management of life-threatening arrhythmias. Use continuous cardiac and blood pressure monitoring. Keep patients supine (postural hypotension common). Adjust dose in patients with impaired renal function. Give to a pregnant woman only if clearly needed.

Common Adverse Reactions
>10%: Cardiovascular: Hypotension (both postural and supine)
1% to 10%: Gastrointestinal: Nausea, vomiting

Drug Interactions
Increased Effect/Toxicity: Other antiarrhythmic agents may potentiate or antagonize cardiac effects of bretylium. Toxic effects may be additive. The vasopressor effects of catecholamines may be enhanced by bretylium. Toxicity of agents which may prolong QT interval (including cisapride, tricyclic antidepressants, antipsychotics, erythromycin, Class Ia and Class III antiarrhythmics) and specific quinolones (sparfloxacin, gatifloxacin, moxifloxacin) may be increased. Digoxin toxicity may be aggravated by bretylium.

Mechanism of Action Class III antiarrhythmic; after an initial release of norepinephrine at the peripheral adrenergic nerve terminals, inhibits further release by postganglionic nerve endings in response to sympathetic nerve stimulation

Pharmacodynamics/Kinetics
Onset of action: I.M.: May require 2 hours; I.V.: 6-20 minutes
Peak effect: 6-9 hours
Duration: 6-24 hours
Protein binding: 1% to 6%
Metabolism: None
Half-life elimination: 7-11 hours; Mean: 4-17 hours; End-stage renal disease: 16-32 hours
Excretion: Urine (70% to 80% as unchanged drug) within 24 hours

Dosage Note: Patients should undergo defibrillation/cardioversion before and after bretylium doses as necessary.
Children (**Note:** Not well established, although the following dosing has been suggested):
I.M.: 2-5 mg/kg as a single dose
I.V.: Acute ventricular fibrillation: Initial: 5 mg/kg, then attempt electrical defibrillation; repeat with 10 mg/kg if ventricular fibrillation persists at 15- to 30-minute intervals to maximum total of 30 mg/kg.
Maintenance dose: I.M., I.V.: 5 mg/kg every 6 hours
Adults:
Immediate life-threatening ventricular arrhythmias (ventricular fibrillation, unstable ventricular tachycardia): Initial dose: I.V.: 5 mg/kg (undiluted) over 1 minute; if arrhythmia persists, administer 10 mg/kg (undiluted) over 1 minute and repeat as necessary (usually at 15- to 30-minute intervals) up to a total dose of 30-35 mg/kg.
Other life-threatening ventricular arrhythmias:
Initial dose: I.M., I.V.: 5-10 mg/kg, may repeat every 1-2 hours if arrhythmia persists; administer I.V. dose (diluted) over 8-10 minutes.
Maintenance dose: I.M.: 5-10 mg/kg every 6-8 hours; I.V. (diluted): 5-10 mg/kg every 6 hours; I.V. infusion (diluted): 1-2 mg/minute (little experience with doses >40 mg/kg/day)
Example dilution: 2 g/250 mL D₅W (infusion pump should be used for I.V. infusion administration)
Rate of I.V. infusion: 1-4 mg/minute
1 mg/minute = 7 mL/hour
2 mg/minute = 15 mL/hour
3 mg/minute = 22 mL/hour
4 mg/minute = 30 mL/hour

Dosing adjustment in renal impairment:
Cl_{cr} 10-50 mL/minute: Administer 25% to 50% of dose.
Cl_{cr} <10 mL/minute: Administer 25% of dose.
Dialysis: Not dialyzable (0% to 5%) via hemo- or peritoneal dialysis; supplemental doses are not needed.

Administration I.M. injection in adults should not exceed 5 mL volume in any one site

Monitoring Parameters ECG, heart rate, blood pressure; requires a cardiac monitor

Patient Information You may experience nausea or vomiting (call for assistance if this occurs, do not try to get out of bed or change position on your own).

Dosage Forms INJ, solution: 50 mg/mL (10 mL). **INJ, solution** [premixed in D₅W]: 2 mg/mL (250 mL); 4 mg/mL (250 mL)

- ♦ **Bretylium Tosylate** see Bretylium on page 178
- ♦ **Brevibloc®** see Esmolol on page 457
- ♦ **Brevicon®** see Ethinyl Estradiol and Norethindrone on page 487
- ♦ **Brevital® Sodium** see Methohexital on page 814
- ♦ **Bricanyl [DSC]** see Terbutaline on page 1199

Brimonidine (bri MOE ni deen)

Related Information
Glaucoma Drug Therapy Comparison on page 1481
U.S. Brand Names Alphagan® P
Synonyms Brimonidine Tartrate
Therapeutic Category Alpha₂-Adrenergic Agonist, Ophthalmic; Sympathomimetic Agent
Use Lowering of intraocular pressure (IOP) in patients with open-angle glaucoma or ocular hypertension
Pregnancy Risk Factor B
(Continued)

Brimonidine *(Continued)*

Dosage Ophthalmic: Children ≥2 years of age and Adults: Glaucoma (Alphagan®, Alphagan® P): Instill 1 drop in affected eye(s) 3 times/day (approximately every 8 hours)
Dosage Forms SOLN, ophthalmic (Alphagan® P): 0.15% (5 mL, 10 mL, 15 mL)

♦ **Brimonidine Tartrate** *see* Brimonidine *on page 179*

Brinzolamide *(brin ZOH la mide)*
Related Information
  Glaucoma Drug Therapy Comparison *on page 1481*
U.S. Brand Names Azopt®
Therapeutic Category Carbonic Anhydrase Inhibitor
Use Lowers intraocular pressure in patients with ocular hypertension or open-angle glaucoma
Pregnancy Risk Factor C
Dosage Ophthalmic: Adults: Instill 1 drop in affected eye(s) 3 times/day
Dosage Forms SUSP, ophthalmic: 1% (5 mL, 10 mL, 15 mL)

♦ **Brioschi® [OTC]** *see* Sodium Bicarbonate *on page 1144*
♦ **British Anti-Lewisite** *see* Dimercaprol *on page 382*
♦ **BRL 43694** *see* Granisetron *on page 601*
♦ **Brofed®** *see* Brompheniramine and Pseudoephedrine *on page 181*
♦ **Bromaline® [OTC]** *see* Brompheniramine and Pseudoephedrine *on page 181*
♦ **Bromaxefed RF** *see* Brompheniramine and Pseudoephedrine *on page 181*
♦ **Bromfed® [OTC]** *see* Brompheniramine and Pseudoephedrine *on page 181*
♦ **Bromfed-PD® [OTC]** *see* Brompheniramine and Pseudoephedrine *on page 181*
♦ **Bromfenex®** *see* Brompheniramine and Pseudoephedrine *on page 181*
♦ **Bromfenex® PD** *see* Brompheniramine and Pseudoephedrine *on page 181*

Bromocriptine *(broe moe KRIP teen)*
Related Information
  Parkinson's Agents Comparison *on page 1402*
U.S. Brand Names Parlodel®
Synonyms Bromocriptine Mesylate
Therapeutic Category Anti-Parkinson's Agent, Dopamine Agonist; Dopaminergic Agent, Antiparkinson's; Ergot Alkaloid and Derivative
Use
  Amenorrhea with or without galactorrhea; infertility or hypogonadism; prolactin-secreting adenomas; acromegaly; Parkinson's disease
  A previous indication for prevention of postpartum lactation was withdrawn voluntarily by Sandoz Pharmaceuticals Corporation.
Unlabeled/Investigational Use Neuroleptic malignant syndrome
Pregnancy Risk Factor B
Contraindications Hypersensitivity to bromocriptine, ergot alkaloids, or any component of the formulation; ergot alkaloids are contraindicated with potent inhibitors of CYP3A4 (includes protease inhibitors, azole antifungals, and some macrolide antibiotics); uncontrolled hypertension; severe ischemic heart disease or peripheral vascular disorders; pregnancy (risk to benefit evaluation must be performed in women who become pregnant during treatment for acromegaly, prolactinoma, or Parkinson's disease - hypertension during treatment should generally result in efforts to withdraw)
Warnings/Precautions Use with caution in patients with impaired renal or hepatic function, a history of psychosis, or cardiovascular disease (myocardial infarction, arrhythmia). Patients who receive bromocriptine during and immediately following pregnancy as a continuation of previous therapy (ie, acromegaly) should be closely monitored for cardiovascular effects. Discontinuation of bromocriptine in patients with macroadenomas has been associated with rapid regrowth of tumor and increased prolactin serum levels. Use with caution in patients with a history of peptic ulcer disease, dementia, or concurrent antihypertensive therapy. Pleural and peritoneal fibrosis have been reported with prolonged daily use. Cardiac valvular fibrosis has also been associated with ergot alkaloids. Safety and effectiveness in patients <15 years of age have not been established.
Common Adverse Reactions
  >10%:
    Central nervous system: Headache, dizziness
    Gastrointestinal: Nausea
  1% to 10%:
    Cardiovascular: Orthostatic hypotension
    Central nervous system: Fatigue, lightheadedness, drowsiness
    Gastrointestinal: Anorexia, vomiting, abdominal cramps, constipation
    Respiratory: Nasal congestion
Drug Interactions
  Cytochrome P450 Effect: Substrate of CYP3A4 (major); **Inhibits** CYP1A2 (weak), 3A4 (weak)
  Increased Effect/Toxicity: Effects of bromocriptine may be increased by antifungals (azole derivatives); macrolide antibiotics; protease inhibitors; MAO inhibitors. Bromocriptine may increase the effects of CYP3A4 substrates (eg, benzodiazepines, buspirone, calcium channel blockers); sibutramine; and other serotonin agonists (serotonin syndrome).

CYP3A4 inhibitors may increase the levels/effects of bromocriptine; example inhibitors include azole antifungals, ciprofloxacin, clarithromycin, diclofenac, doxycycline, erythromycin, imatinib, isoniazid, nefazodone, nicardipine, propofol, protease inhibitors, quinidine, and verapamil.

Decreased Effect: Effects of bromocriptine may be diminished by antipsychotics, metoclopramide.

Mechanism of Action Semisynthetic ergot alkaloid derivative and a dopamine receptor agonist which activates postsynaptic dopamine receptors in the tuberoinfundibular and nigrostriatal pathways

Pharmacodynamics/Kinetics
Protein binding: 90% to 96%
Metabolism: Primarily hepatic
Half-life elimination: Biphasic: Initial: 6-8 hours; Terminal: 50 hours
Time to peak, serum: 1-2 hours
Excretion: Feces; urine (2% to 6% as unchanged drug)

Dosage Oral: Adults:
Parkinsonism: 1.25 mg 2 times/day, increased by 2.5 mg/day in 2- to 4-week intervals (usual dose range is 30-90 mg/day in 3 divided doses), though elderly patients can usually be managed on lower doses
Neuroleptic malignant syndrome: 2.5-5 mg 3 times/day
Hyperprolactinemia: 2.5 mg 2-3 times/day
Acromegaly: Initial: 1.25-2.5 mg increasing as necessary every 3-7 days; usual dose: 20-30 mg/day
Prolactin-secreting adenomas: Initial: 1.25-2.5 mg/day; daily range 2.5-10 mg.
Dosing adjustment in hepatic impairment: No guidelines are available, however, may be necessary

Monitoring Parameters Monitor blood pressure closely as well as hepatic, hematopoietic, and cardiovascular function

Patient Information Take with food or milk; drowsiness commonly occurs upon initiation of therapy; limit use of alcohol; avoid exposure to cold; incidence of side effects is high (68%) with nausea the most common; hypotension occurs commonly with initiation of therapy, usually upon rising after prolonged sitting or lying

Discontinue immediately if pregnant; may restore fertility; women desiring not to become pregnant should use barrier contraceptive means

Dosage Forms CAP: 5 mg. **TAB:** 2.5 mg

♦ **Bromocriptine Mesylate** *see Bromocriptine on page 180*

Brompheniramine and Pseudoephedrine
(brome fen IR a meen & soo doe e FED rin)

U.S. Brand Names AccuHist®; Andehist NR Syrup; Brofed®; Bromaline® [OTC]; Bromaxefed RF; Bromfed® [OTC]; Bromfed-PD® [OTC]; Bromfenex®; Bromfenex® PD; Children's Dimetapp® Elixir Cold & Allergy [OTC]; Histex™ SR; Lodrane®; Lodrane® LD; Rondec® Syrup; Touro™ Allergy

Synonyms Brompheniramine Maleate and Pseudoephedrine Hydrochloride; Brompheniramine Maleate and Pseudoephedrine Sulfate; Pseudoephedrine and Brompheniramine

Therapeutic Category Antihistamine/Decongestant

Use Temporary relief of symptoms of seasonal and perennial allergic rhinitis, and vasomotor rhinitis, including nasal obstruction

Pregnancy Risk Factor C

Dosage Oral:
Capsule, sustained release:
Based on 60 mg pseudoephedrine:
Children 6-12 years: 1 capsule every 12 hours
Children ≥12 years and Adults: 1-2 capsules every 12 hours
Based on 120 mg pseudoephedrine: Children ≥12 years and Adults: 1 capsule every 12 hours
Liquid:
Based on brompheniramine 1 mg/pseudoephedrine 15 mg per 1 mL: Children:
1-3 months: 0.25 mL 4 times/day
3-6 months: 0.5 mL 4 times/day
6-12 months: 0.75 mL 4 times/day
12-24 months: 1 mL 4 times/day
Based on brompheniramine 1 mg/pseudoephedrine 15 mg per 5 mL: Children:
6-11 months (6-8 kg): 2.5 mL every 6-8 hours (maximum: 4 doses/24 hours)
12-23 months (8-10 kg): 3.75 mL every 6-8 hours (maximum: 4 doses/24 hours)
2-6 years: 5 mL every 6-8 hours (maximum: 4 doses/24 hours)
6-12 years: 10 mL every 6-8 hours (maximum: 4 doses/24 hours)
>12 years and Adults: 20 mg every 4 hours (maximum: 4 doses/24 hours)
Based on brompheniramine 4 mg/pseudoephedrine 30 mg:
Children 2-6 years: 2.5 mL 3 times/day
Children >6 years and Adults: 5 mL 3 times/day
Brompheniramine 4 mg/pseudoephedrine 45 mg per 5 mL:
Children 2-6 years: 2.5 mL 4 times/day
Children >6 years and Adults: 5 mL 4 times/day

Dosage Forms CAP, extended release: (Bromfed®, Bromfenex®): Brompheniramine maleate 12 mg and pseudoephedrine hydrochloride 120 mg; (Bromfed-PD®, Bromfenex® PD, Lodrane®
(Continued)

Brompheniramine and Pseudoephedrine *(Continued)*

LD): Brompheniramine maleate 6 mg and pseudoephedrine hydrochloride 60 mg; (Histex™): Brompheniramine maleate 10 mg anbd pseudoephedrine hydrochloride 120 mg. **CAP, sustained release** (Touro™ Allergy): Brompheniramine maleate 5.75 mg and pseudoephedrine hydrochloride 60 mg. **ELIX:** Brompheniramine maleate 1 mg and pseudoephedrine hydrochloride 15 mg per 5 mL (120 mL, 480 mL); (Children's Dimetapp® Elixir Cold & Allergy): Brompheniramine maleate 1 mg and pseudoephedrine hydrochloride 15 mg per 5 mL (240 mL). **LIQ** (Lodrane®): Brompheniramine maleate 4 mg and pseudoephedrine hydrochloride 60 mg per 5 mL (480 mL); **LIQ, oral drops** (AccuHist®): Brompheniramine maleate 1 mg and pseudoephedrine hydrochloride 15 mg per 1 mL (30 mL); **SOLN** (Bromaline®): Brompheniramine maleate 1 mg and pseudoephedrine hydrochloride 15 mg per 5 mL (120 mL, 480 mL) **SYR:** (Andehist NR): Brompheniramine maleate 4 mg and pseudoephedrine sulfate 45 mg per 5 mL (473 mL); (Brofed®): Brompheniramine maleate 4 mg and pseudoephedrine hydrochloride 30 mg per 5 mL(480 mL); (Bromaxefed RF, Rondec®): Brompheniramine maleate 4 mg and pseudoephedrine hydrochloride 45 mg per 5 mL (120 mL, 480 mL)

- **Brompheniramine Maleate and Pseudoephedrine Hydrochloride** *see* Brompheniramine and Pseudoephedrine *on page 181*
- **Brompheniramine Maleate and Pseudoephedrine Sulfate** *see* Brompheniramine and Pseudoephedrine *on page 181*
- **Bronchodilators, Comparison of Inhaled Sympathomimetics** *see page 1370*
- **Broncho Saline® [OTC]** *see* Sodium Chloride *on page 1146*
- **Brontex®** *see* Guaifenesin and Codeine *on page 604*
- **B-type Natriuretic Peptide (Human)** *see* Nesiritide *on page 894*

Budesonide *(byoo DES oh nide)*

U.S. Brand Names Entocort™ EC; Pulmicort Respules®; Pulmicort Turbuhaler®; Rhinocort® Aqua®

Therapeutic Category Corticosteroid, Inhalant; Corticosteroid, Intranasal; Corticosteroid, Topical (Medium Potency)

Use

Intranasal: Children ≥6 years of age and Adults: Management of symptoms of seasonal or perennial rhinitis

Nebulization: Children 12 months to 8 years: Maintenance and prophylactic treatment of asthma

Oral capsule: Treatment of active Crohn's disease (mild to moderate) involving the ileum and/ or ascending colon

Oral inhalation: Maintenance and prophylactic treatment of asthma; includes patients who require corticosteroids and those who may benefit from systemic dose reduction/elimination

Pregnancy Risk Factor C/B (Pulmicort Respules® and Turbuhaler®)

Contraindications Hypersensitivity to budesonide or any component of the formulation

Inhalation: Contraindicated in primary treatment of status asthmaticus, acute episodes of asthma; not for relief of acute bronchospasm

Warnings/Precautions May cause hypercorticism and/or suppression of hypothalamic-pituitary-adrenal (HPA) axis, particularly in younger children or in patients receiving high doses for prolonged periods. Particular care is required when patients are transferred from systemic corticosteroids to products with lower systemic bioavailability (ie, inhalation). May lead to possible adrenal insufficiency or withdrawal from steroids, including an increase in allergic symptoms. Patients receiving prolonged therapy of ≥20 mg per day of prednisone (or equivalent) may be most susceptible. Aerosol steroids do **not** provide the systemic steroid needed to treat patients having trauma, surgery, or infections.

Controlled clinical studies have shown that orally-inhaled and intranasal corticosteroids may cause a reduction in growth velocity in pediatric patients. (In studies of orally-inhaled corticosteroids, the mean reduction in growth velocity was approximately 1 centimeter per year [range 0.3-1.8 cm per year] and appears to be related to dose and duration of exposure.) To minimize the systemic effects of orally-inhaled and intranasal corticosteroids, each patient should be titrated to the lowest effective dose. Growth should be routinely monitored in pediatric patients.

May suppress the immune system, patients may be more susceptible to infection. Use with caution in patients with systemic infections or ocular herpes simplex. Avoid exposure to chickenpox and measles. Corticosteroids should be used with caution in patients with diabetes, hypertension, osteoporosis, peptic ulcer, glaucoma, cataracts, or tuberculosis. Use caution in hepatic impairment. Enteric-coated capsules should not be crushed or chewed.

Common Adverse Reactions Reaction severity varies by dose and duration; not all adverse reactions have been reported with each dosage form.

>10%:

Central nervous system: Oral capsule: Headache (up to 21%)

Gastrointestinal: Oral capsule: Nausea (up to 11%)

Respiratory: Respiratory infection, rhinitis

Miscellaneous: Symptoms of HPA axis suppression and/or hypercorticism (acne, easy bruising, fat redistribution, striae, edema) may occur in >10% of patients following administration of dosage forms which result in higher systemic exposure (ie, oral capsule), but may be less frequent than rates observed with comparator drugs (prednisolone). These symptoms may be rare (<1%) following administration via methods which result in lower exposures (topical).

1% to 10%:
Cardiovascular: Syncope, edema, hypertension
Central nervous system: Chest pain, dysphonia, emotional lability, fatigue, fever, insomnia, migraine, nervousness, pain, dizziness, vertigo
Dermatologic: Bruising, contact dermatitis, eczema, pruritus, pustular rash, rash
Endocrine & metabolic: Hypokalemia, adrenal insufficiency
Gastrointestinal: Abdominal pain, anorexia, diarrhea, dry mouth, dyspepsia, gastroenteritis, oral candidiasis, taste perversion, vomiting, weight gain, flatulence
Hematologic: Cervical lymphadenopathy, purpura, leukocytosis
Neuromuscular & skeletal: Arthralgia, fracture, hyperkinesis, hypertonia, myalgia, neck pain, weakness, paresthesia, back pain
Ocular: Conjunctivitis, eye infection
Otic: Earache, ear infection, external ear infection
Respiratory: Bronchitis, bronchospasm, cough, epistaxis, nasal irritation, pharyngitis, sinusitis, stridor
Miscellaneous: Allergic reaction, flu-like syndrome, herpes simplex, infection, moniliasis, viral infection, voice alteration

Drug Interactions
Cytochrome P450 Effect: Substrate of CYP3A4 (minor)

Increased Effect/Toxicity: Cimetidine may decrease the clearance and increase the bioavailability of budesonide, increasing its serum concentrations. In addition, CYP3A4 inhibitors may increase the serum level and/or toxicity of budesonide this effect was shown with ketoconazole, but not erythromycin. Other potential inhibitors include amiodarone, cimetidine, clarithromycin, delavirdine, diltiazem, dirithromycin, disulfiram, fluoxetine, fluvoxamine, grapefruit juice, indinavir, itraconazole, ketoconazole, nefazodone, nevirapine, propoxyphene, quinupristin-dalfopristin, ritonavir, saquinavir, verapamil, zafirlukast, zileuton. The addition of salmeterol has been demonstrated to improve response to inhaled corticosteroids (as compared to increasing steroid dosage).

Decreased Effect: CYP3A4 inducers (including carbamazepine, phenytoin, phenobarbital, rifampin) may decrease budesonide levels and/or effects. Theoretically, proton pump inhibitors (omeprazole, pantoprazole) alter gastric pH may affect the rate of dissolution of enteric-coated capsules. Administration with omeprazole did not alter kinetics of budesonide capsules.

Mechanism of Action Controls the rate of protein synthesis, depresses the migration of polymorphonuclear leukocytes, fibroblasts, reverses capillary permeability, and lysosomal stabilization at the cellular level to prevent or control inflammation

Pharmacodynamics/Kinetics
Onset of action: Respules®: 2-8 days; Rhinocort® Aqua®: ~10 hours; Turbuhaler®: 24 hours
Peak effect: Respules®: 4-6 weeks; Rhinocort® Aqua®: ~2 weeks; Turbuhaler®: 1-2 weeks
Absorption: Capsule: Rapid and complete
Distribution: 2.2-3.9 L/kg
Protein binding: 85% to 90%
Metabolism: Hepatic via CYP3A4 to two metabolites: 16 alpha-hydroxyprednisolone and 6 beta-hydroxybudesonide; minor activity
Bioavailability: Limited by high first-pass effect; Capsule: 9% to 21%; Respules®: 6%; Turbuhaler®: 6% to 13%; Nasal: 34%
Half-life elimination: 2-3.6 hours
Time to peak: Capsule: 30-600 minutes (variable in Crohn's disease); Respules®: 10-30 minutes; Turbuhaler®: 1-2 hours; Nasal: 1 hour
Excretion: Urine (60%) and feces as metabolites

Dosage
Nasal inhalation: (Rhinocort® Aqua®): Children ≥6 years and Adults: 64 mcg/day as a single 32 mcg spray in each nostril. Some patients who do not achieve adequate control may benefit from increased dosage. A reduced dosage may be effective after initial control is achieved. Maximum dose: Children <12 years: 128 mcg/day; Adults: 256 mcg/day

Nebulization: Children 12 months to 8 years: Pulmicort Respules®: Titrate to lowest effective dose once patient is stable; start at 0.25 mg/day or use as follows:
Previous therapy of bronchodilators alone: 0.5 mg/day administered as a single dose or divided twice daily (maximum daily dose: 0.5 mg)
Previous therapy of inhaled corticosteroids: 0.5 mg/day administered as a single dose or divided twice daily (maximum daily dose: 1 mg)
Previous therapy of oral corticosteroids: 1 mg/day administered as a single dose or divided twice daily (maximum daily dose: 1 mg)

Oral inhalation:
Children ≥6 years:
Previous therapy of bronchodilators alone: 200 mcg twice initially which may be increased up to 400 mcg twice daily
Previous therapy of inhaled corticosteroids: 200 mcg twice initially which may be increased up to 400 mcg twice daily
Previous therapy of oral corticosteroids: The highest recommended dose in children is 400 mcg twice daily
Adults:
Previous therapy of bronchodilators alone: 200-400 mcg twice initially which may be increased up to 400 mcg twice daily
Previous therapy of inhaled corticosteroids: 200-400 mcg twice initially which may be increased up to 800 mcg twice daily
(Continued)

Budesonide *(Continued)*

Previous therapy of oral corticosteroids: 400-800 mcg twice daily which may be increased up to 800 mcg twice daily

NIH Guidelines (NIH, 1997) (give in divided doses twice daily):

Children:

"Low" dose: 100-200 mcg/day

"Medium" dose: 200-400 mcg/day (1-2 inhalations/day)

"High" dose: >400 mcg/day (>2 inhalation/day)

Adults:

"Low" dose: 200-400 mcg/day (1-2 inhalations/day)

"Medium" dose: 400-600 mcg/day (2-3 inhalations/day)

"High" dose: >600 mcg/day (>3 inhalation/day)

Oral: Adults: Crohn's disease: 9 mg once daily in the morning; safety and efficacy have not been established for therapy duration >8 weeks; recurring episodes may be treated with a repeat 8-week course of treatment

Note: Treatment may be tapered to 6 mg once daily for 2 weeks prior to complete cessation. Patients receiving CYP3A4 inhibitors should be monitored closely for signs and symptoms of hypercorticism; dosage reduction may be required.

Dosage adjustment in hepatic impairment: Monitor closely for signs and symptoms of hypercorticism; dosage reduction may be required.

Administration

Inhalation: Inhaler should be shaken well immediately prior to use; while activating inhaler, deep breathe for 3-5 seconds, hold breath for ~10 seconds and allow ≥1 minute between inhalations. Rinse mouth with water after use to reduce aftertaste and incidence of candidiasis.

Nebulization: Shake well before using. Use Pulmicort Respules® with jet nebulizer connected to an air compressor; administer with mouthpiece or facemask. Do not use ultrasonic nebulizer. Do not mix with other medications in nebulizer. Rinse mouth following treatments to decrease risk of oral candidiasis (wash face if using face mask).

Oral capsule: Capsule should be swallowed whole; do not crush or chew.

Monitoring Parameters Monitor growth in pediatric patients.

Patient Information Use as directed; do not increase dosage or discontinue abruptly without consulting prescriber. Report acute nervousness or inability to sleep; severe sneezing or nosebleed; difficulty breathing, sore throat, hoarseness, or bronchitis; respiratory difficulty or bronchospasms; disturbed menstrual pattern; vision changes; loss of taste or smell perception; or worsening of condition or lack of improvement. May be more susceptible to infection; avoid exposure to chickenpox and measles unless immunity has been established

Inhalation/nebulization: This is not a bronchodilator and will not relieve acute asthma attacks. It may take several days for you to realize full effects of treatment. If you are also using an inhaled bronchodilator, wait 10 minutes before using this steroid aerosol. You may experience dizziness, anxiety, or blurred vision (rise slowly from sitting or lying position and use caution when driving or engaging in tasks requiring alertness until response to drug is known); or taste disturbance or aftertaste (frequent mouth care and mouth rinses may help). Rinse mouth with water following oral treatments to decrease risk of oral candidiasis (wash face if using face mask).

Oral capsule: Swallow whole; do not crush or chew capsule.

Dosage Forms CAP, enteric coated (Entocort™ EC): 3 mg. **POWDER, oral inhalation** (Pulmicort Turbuhaler®): 200 mcg/inhalation (104 g); (additional dosage strengths available in Canada: 100 mcg/inhalation, 400 mcg/inhalation). **SPRAY, nasal** (Rhinocort® Aqua®): 32 mcg/inhalation (8.6 g). **SUSP, oral inhalation** (Pulmicort Respules®): 0.25 mg/2 mL (30s), 0.5 mg/2 mL (30s)

♦ **Buffered Aspirin and Pravastatin Sodium** *see Aspirin and Pravastatin on page 124*

♦ **Bufferin® [OTC]** *see Aspirin on page 120*

♦ **Bufferin® Arthritis Strength [OTC]** *see Aspirin on page 120*

♦ **Bufferin® Extra Strength [OTC]** *see Aspirin on page 120*

Bumetanide *(byoo MET a nide)*

Related Information

Sulfonamide Derivatives *on page 1404*

U.S. Brand Names Bumex®

Therapeutic Category Antihypertensive Agent; Diuretic, Loop

Use Management of edema secondary to congestive heart failure or hepatic or renal disease including nephrotic syndrome; may be used alone or in combination with antihypertensives in the treatment of hypertension; can be used in furosemide-allergic patients

Pregnancy Risk Factor C (manufacturer); D (expert analysis)

Contraindications Hypersensitivity to bumetanide, any component of the formulation, or sulfonylureas; anuria; patients with hepatic coma or in states of severe electrolyte depletion until the condition improves or is corrected; pregnancy (based on expert analysis)

Warnings/Precautions Profound diuresis with fluid and electrolyte loss is possible; close medical supervision and dose evaluation is required; use caution when dosing in patients with hepatic failure; use caution in patients with known hypersensitivity to sulfonamides or thiazides (due to possible cross-sensitivity; avoid in history of severe reactions)

Chemical similarities are present among sulfonamides, sulfonylureas, carbonic anhydrase inhibitors, thiazides, and loop diuretics (except ethacrynic acid). Use in patients with sulfonylurea allergy is specifically contraindicated in product labeling, however, a risk of cross-reaction exists in patients with allergy to any of these compounds; avoid use when previous reaction has been severe.

Excessive amounts can lead to profound diuresis with fluid and electrolyte loss; close medical supervision and dose evaluation is required; *in vitro* studies using pooled sera from critically-ill neonates have shown bumetanide to be a potent displacer of bilirubin; avoid use in neonates at risk for kernicterus.

Common Adverse Reactions

>10%:

Endocrine & metabolic: Hyperuricemia (18%), hypochloremia (15%), hypokalemia (15%)

Renal: Azotemia (11%)

1% to 10%:

Central nervous system: Dizziness (1%)

Endocrine & metabolic: Hyponatremia (9%), hyperglycemia (7%), variations in phosphorus (5%), CO_2 content (4%), bicarbonate (3%), and calcium (2%)

Neuromuscular & skeletal: Muscle cramps (1%)

Otic: Ototoxicity (1%)

Renal: Increased serum creatinine (7%)

Drug Interactions

Increased Effect/Toxicity: Bumetanide-induced hypokalemia may predispose to digoxin toxicity and may increase the risk of arrhythmia with drugs which may prolong QT interval, including type Ia and type III antiarrhythmic agents, cisapride, and some quinolones (sparfloxacin, gatifloxacin, and moxifloxacin). The risk of toxicity from lithium and salicylates (high dose) may be increased by loop diuretics. Hypotensive effects and/or adverse renal effects of ACE inhibitors and NSAIDs are potentiated by bumetanide-induced hypovolemia. The effects of peripheral adrenergic-blocking drugs or ganglionic blockers may be increased by bumetanide.

Bumetanide may increase the risk of ototoxicity with other ototoxic agents (aminoglycosides, cis-platinum), especially in patients with renal dysfunction. Synergistic diuretic effects occur with thiazide-type diuretics. Diuretics tend to be synergistic with other antihypertensive agents, and hypotension may occur.

Decreased Effect: Glucose tolerance may be decreased by loop diuretics, requiring adjustment of hypoglycemic agents. Cholestyramine or colestipol may reduce bioavailability of bumetanide. Indomethacin (and other NSAIDs) may reduce natriuretic and hypotensive effects of diuretics. Hypokalemia may reduce the efficacy of some antiarrhythmics.

Mechanism of Action Inhibits reabsorption of sodium and chloride in the ascending loop of Henle and proximal renal tubule, interfering with the chloride-binding cotransport system, thus causing increased excretion of water, sodium, chloride, magnesium, phosphate and calcium; it does not appear to act on the distal tubule

Pharmacodynamics/Kinetics

Onset of action: Oral, I.M.: 0.5-1 hour; I.V.: 2-3 minutes

Duration: 6 hours

Distribution: V_d: 13-25 L/kg

Protein binding: 95%

Metabolism: Partially hepatic

Half-life elimination: Neonates: ~6 hours; Infants (1 month): ~2.4 hours; Adults: 1-1.5 hours

Excretion: Primarily urine (as unchanged drug and metabolites)

Dosage

Oral, I.M., I.V.:

Neonates (see Warnings/Precautions): 0.01-0.05 mg/kg/dose every 24-48 hours

Infants and Children: 0.015-0.1 mg/kg/dose every 6-24 hours (maximum dose: 10 mg/day)

Adults:

Edema:

Oral: 0.5-2 mg/dose (maximum dose: 10 mg/day) 1-2 times/day

I.M., I.V.: 0.5-1 mg/dose; may repeat in 2-3 hours for up to 2 doses if needed (maximum dose: 10 mg/day)

Continuous I.V. infusion: 0.9-1 mg/hour

Hypertension: Oral: 0.5 mg daily (range: 1-4 mg/day, maximum dose: 5 mg/day); for larger doses, divide into 2-3 doses daily

Administration Administer I.V. slowly, over 1-2 minutes; an alternate-day schedule or a 3-4 daily dosing regimen with rest periods of 1-2 days in between may be the most tolerable and effective regimen for the continued control of edema; reserve I.V. administration for those unable to take oral medications

Monitoring Parameters Blood pressure, serum electrolytes, renal function

Patient Information May be taken with food to reduce GI effects; rise slowly from a lying or sitting position to minimize dizziness, lightheadedness or fainting; also use extra care when exercising, standing for long periods of time, and during hot weather; take last dose of day early in the evening to prevent nocturia

Dosage Forms INJ, solution: 0.25 mg/mL (2 mL, 4 mL, 10 mL). **TAB:** 0.5 mg, 1 mg, 2 mg

♦ **Bumex**® *see* Bumetanide *on page 184*

♦ **Buminate**® *see* Albumin *on page 44*

♦ **Buphenyl**® *see* Sodium Phenylbutyrate *on page 1151*

Bupivacaine (byoo PIV a kane)

U.S. Brand Names Marcaine®; Marcaine® Spinal; Sensorcaine®; Sensorcaine®-MPF

Synonyms Bupivacaine Hydrochloride

Therapeutic Category Local Anesthetic, Injectable

Use Local anesthetic (injectable) for peripheral nerve block, infiltration, sympathetic block, caudal or epidural block, retrobulbar block

Pregnancy Risk Factor C

Contraindications Hypersensitivity to bupivacaine hydrochloride, amide-type local anesthetics (etidocaine, lidocaine, mepivacaine, prilocaine, ropivacaine) or any component of the formulation (para-aminobenzoic acid or parabens in specific formulations); not to be used for obstetrical paracervical block anesthesia

Warnings/Precautions Use with caution in patients with hepatic impairment. Some commercially available formulations contain sodium metabisulfite, which may cause allergic-type reactions; not recommended for use in children <12 years of age. The solution for spinal anesthesia should not be used in children <18 years of age. **Do not use solutions containing preservatives for caudal or epidural block.** Local anesthetics have been associated with rare occurrences of sudden respiratory arrest; convulsions due to systemic toxicity leading to cardiac arrest have also been reported, presumably following unintentional intravascular injection. The 0.75% is **not** recommended for obstetrical anesthesia. A test dose is recommended prior to epidural administration (prior to initial dose) and all reinforcing doses with continuous catheter technique.

Common Adverse Reactions Note: Incidence of adverse reactions is difficult to define. Most effects are dose-related, and are often due to accelerated absorption from the injection site, unintentional intravascular injection, or slow metabolic degradation. The development of any central nervous system symptoms may be an early indication of more significant toxicity (seizures).

Cardiovascular: Hypotension, bradycardia, palpitations, heart block, ventricular arrhythmias, cardiac arrest

Central nervous system: Restlessness, anxiety, dizziness, seizures (0.1%); rare symptoms (usually associated with unintentional subarachnoid injection during high spinal anesthesia) include persistent anesthesia, paresthesia, paralysis, headache, septic meningitis, and cranial nerve palsies

Gastrointestinal: Nausea, vomiting; rare symptoms (usually associated with unintentional subarachnoid injection during high spinal anesthesia) include fecal incontinence and loss of sphincter control

Genitourinary: Rare symptoms (usually associated with unintentional subarachnoid injection during high spinal anesthesia) include urinary incontinence, loss of perineal sensation, and loss of sexual function

Neuromuscular & skeletal: Weakness

Ocular: Blurred vision, pupillary constriction

Otic: Tinnitus

Respiratory: Apnea, hypoventilation (usually associated with unintentional subarachnoid injection during high spinal anesthesia)

Miscellaneous; Allergic reactions (urticaria, pruritus, angioedema), anaphylactoid reactions

Drug Interactions

Cytochrome P450 Effect: Substrate (minor) of CYP1A2, 2C19, 2D6, 3A4

Increased Effect/Toxicity: Increased effect if used with hyaluronidase. Bupivacaine used in conjunction with epinephrine in patients on beta-blockers, ergot-type oxytocics, MAO inhibitors, tricyclic antidepressants, phenothiazines, vasopressors, or isoproterenol may result in prolonged hypotension or hypertension.

Mechanism of Action Blocks both the initiation and conduction of nerve impulses by decreasing the neuronal membrane's permeability to sodium ions, which results in inhibition of depolarization with resultant blockade of conduction

Pharmacodynamics/Kinetics

Onset of action: Anesthesia (route dependent): 4-10 minutes

Duration: 1.5-8.5 hours

Metabolism: Hepatic

Half-life elimination (age dependent): Neonates: 8.1 hours; Adults: 1.5-5.5 hours

Excretion: Urine (~6%)

Dosage Dose varies with procedure, depth of anesthesia, vascularity of tissues, duration of anesthesia and condition of patient. Some formulations contain metabisulfites (in epinephrine-containing injection); do not use solutions containing preservatives for caudal or epidural block.

Local anesthesia: Infiltration: 0.25% infiltrated locally; maximum: 175 mg

Caudal block (with or without epinephrine, preservative free):

Children: 1-3.7 mg/kg

Adults: 15-30 mL of 0.25% or 0.5%

Epidural block (other than caudal block - with or without epinephrine, preservative free):

Administer in 3-5 mL increments, allowing sufficient time to detect toxic manifestations of inadvertent I.V. or I.T. administration:

Children: 1.25 mg/kg/dose

Adults: 10-20 mL of 0.25% or 0.5%

Surgical procedures requiring a high degree of muscle relaxation and prolonged effects only: 10-20 mL of 0.75% (**Note:** Not to be used in obstetrical cases)

Maxillary and mandibular infiltration and nerve block: 9 mg (1.8 mL) of 0.5% (with epinephrine) per injection site; a second dose may be administered if necessary to produce adequate anesthesia after allowing up to 10 minutes for onset, up to a maximum of 90 mg per dental appointment

Obstetrical anesthesia: Incremental dose: 3-5 mL of 0.5% (not exceeding 50-100 mg in any dosing interval); allow sufficient time to detect toxic manifestations or inadvertent I.V. or I.T. injection

Peripheral nerve block: 5 mL of 0.25 or 0.5%; maximum: 400 mg/day

Sympathetic nerve block: 20-50 mL of 0.25%

Retrobulbar anesthesia: 2-4 mL of 0.75%

Spinal anesthesia: Solution of 0.75% bupivacaine in 8.25% dextrose is used:

Lower extremity and perineal procedures: 1 mL

Lower abdominal procedures: 1.6 mL

Obstetrical:

Normal vaginal delivery: 0.8 mL (higher doses may be required in some patients)

Cesarean section: 1-1.4 mL

Administration Solutions containing preservatives should not be used for epidural or caudal blocks

Monitoring Parameters Monitor fetal heart rate during paracervical anesthesia

Patient Information This medication is given to reduce sensation in the injected area. You will experience decreased sensation to pain, heat, or cold in the area and/or decreased muscle strength (depending on area of application) until the effects wear off; use necessary caution to reduce incidence of possible injury until full sensation returns. If used in mouth, do not eat or drink until full sensation returns.

Dosage Forms INJ, solution [preservative free]: 0.25% [2.5 mg/mL] (20 mL, 30 mL, 50 mL), 0.5% [5 mg/mL] (20 mL, 30 mL), 0.75% [7.5 mg/mL] (20 mL, 30 mL); (Marcaine®): 0.25% [2.5 mg/mL] (10 mL, 30 mL, 50 mL), 0.5% [5 mg/mL] (10 mL, 30 mL), 0.75% [7.5 mg/mL] (10 mL, 30 mL); (Marcaine® Spinal): 0.75% [7.5 mg/mL] (2 mL); (Sensorcaine®-MPF): 0.25% [2.5 mg/mL] (10 mL, 30 mL), 0.5% [5 mg/mL] (10 mL, 30 mL), 0.75% [7.5 mg/mL] (10 mL, 30 mL). **INJ, solution:** 0.25% [2.5 mg/mL] (10 mL, 30 mL, 50 mL), 0.5% [5 mg/mL] (10 mL, 30 mL, 50 mL), 0.75% [7.5 mg/mL] (10 mL, 30 mL); (Marcaine®, Sensorcaine®): 0.25% [2.5 mg/mL] (50 mL), 0.5% [5 mg/mL] (50 mL). **INJ, solution, with epinephrine 1:200,000** [preservative free]: (Marcaine®): 0.25% [2.5 mg/mL] (10 mL, 30 mL, 50 mL), 0.5% [5 mg/mL] (3 mL, 10 mL, 30 mL), 0.75% [7.5 mg/mL] (30 mL); (Sensorcaine®-MPF): 0.25% [2.5 mg/mL] (10 mL, 30 mL), 0.5% [5 mg/mL] (5 mL, 10 mL, 30 mL). **INJ, solution, with epinephrine 1:200,000** (Marcaine®, Sensorcaine®): 0.25% [2.5 mg/mL] (50 mL); 0.5% [5 mg/mL] (50 mL)

♦ **Bupivacaine and Lidocaine** *see* Lidocaine and Bupivacaine *on page 744*

♦ **Bupivacaine Hydrochloride** *see* Bupivacaine *on page 186*

♦ **Buprenex®** *see* Buprenorphine *on page 187*

Buprenorphine (byoo pre NOR feen)

Related Information

Narcotic Agonists Comparison *on page 1395*

U.S. Brand Names Buprenex®; Subutex®

Synonyms Buprenorphine Hydrochloride

Therapeutic Category Analgesic, Narcotic; Narcotic Antagonist

Use

Injection: Management of moderate to severe pain

Tablet: Treatment of opioid dependence

Unlabeled/Investigational Use Heroin and opioid withdrawal

Restrictions Injection: C-V; Tablet: C-III

Prescribing of tablets for opioid dependence is limited to physicians who have met the qualification criteria and have received a DEA number specific to prescribing this product. Tablets will be available through pharmacies and wholesalers which normally provide controlled substances.

Pregnancy Risk Factor C

Contraindications Hypersensitivity to buprenorphine or any component of the formulation

Warnings/Precautions An opioid-containing analgesic regimen should be tailored to each patient's needs and based upon the type of pain being treated (acute versus chronic), the route of administration, degree of tolerance for opioids (naive versus chronic user), age, weight, and medical condition. The optimal analgesic dose varies widely among patients. Doses should be titrated to pain relief/prevention. Use with caution in patients with hepatic dysfunction or possible neurologic injury; may precipitate abstinence syndrome in narcotic-dependent patients; tolerance or drug dependence may result from extended use. Tablets, which are used for induction treatment of opioid dependence, should not be started until effects of withdrawal are evident.

Common Adverse Reactions

Injection:

>10%: Central nervous system: Sedation

1% to 10%:

Cardiovascular: Hypotension

Central nervous system: Respiratory depression, dizziness, headache

Gastrointestinal: Vomiting, nausea

Ocular: Miosis

Otic: Vertigo

Miscellaneous: Diaphoresis

(Continued)

Buprenorphine *(Continued)*

Tablet:
>10:
    Central nervous system: Headache (30%), pain (24%), insomnia (21% to 25%), Oralety (12%), depression (11%)
    Gastrointestinal: Nausea (10% to 14%), abdominal pain (12%), constipation (8% to 11%)
    Neuromuscular & skeletal: Back pain (14%), weakness (14%)
    Respiratory: Rhinitis (11%)
    Miscellaneous: Withdrawal syndrome (19%; placebo 37%), infection (12% to 20%), diaphoresis (12% to 13%)

1% to 10%:
    Central nervous system: Chills (6%), nervousness (6%), somnolence (5%), dizziness (4%), fever (3%)
    Gastrointestinal: Vomiting (5% to 8%), diarrhea (5%), dyspepsia (3%)
    Ocular: Lacrimation (5%)
    Respiratory: Cough (4%), pharyngitis (4%)
    Miscellaneous: Flu-like syndrome (6%)

Drug Interactions
  Cytochrome P450 Effect: Substrate of CYP3A4 (major); **Inhibits** CYP1A2 (weak), 2A6 (weak), 2C19 (weak), 2D6 (weak)
  Increased Effect/Toxicity: Barbiturate anesthetics and other CNS depressants may produce additive respiratory and CNS depression. Respiratory and CV collapse was reported in a patient who received diazepam and buprenorphine. Effects may be additive with other CNS depressants. CYP3A4 inhibitors may increase the levels/effects of buprenorphine; example inhibitors include azole antifungals, ciprofloxacin, clarithromycin, diclofenac, doxycycline, erythromycin, imatinib, isoniazid, nefazodone, nicardipine, propofol, protease inhibitors, quinidine, and verapamil.
  Decreased Effect: CYP3A4 inducers may decrease the levels/effects of buprenorphine; example inducers include aminoglutethimide, carbamazepine, nafcillin, nevirapine, phenobarbital, phenytoin, and rifamycins. Naltrexone may antagonize the effect of narcotic analgesics; concurrent use or use within 7-10 days of injection for pain relief is contraindicated.

Mechanism of Action Buprenorphine exerts its analgesic effect via high affinity binding to μ opiate receptors in the CNS; displays both agonist and antagonist activity

Pharmacodynamics/Kinetics
  Onset of action: Analgesic: 10-30 minutes
  Duration: 6-8 hours
  Absorption: I.M., S.C.: 30% to 40%
  Distribution: V_d: 97-187 L/kg
  Protein binding: High
  Metabolism: Primarily hepatic; extensive first-pass effect
  Half-life elimination: 2.2-3 hours
  Excretion: Feces (70%); urine (20% as unchanged drug)

Dosage Long-term use is not recommended
  Note: These are guidelines and do not represent the maximum doses that may be required in all patients. Doses should be titrated to pain relief/prevention. In high-risk patients (eg, elderly, debilitated, presence of respiratory disease) and/or concurrent CNS depressant use, reduce dose by one-half. Buprenorphine has an analgesic ceiling.
  Acute pain (moderate to severe):
    Children 2-12 years: I.M., slow I.V.: 2-6 mcg/kg every 4-6 hours
    Children ≥13 years and Adults:
      I.M.: Initial: Opiate-naive: 0.3 mg every 6-8 hours as needed; initial dose (up to 0.3 mg) may be repeated once in 30-60 minutes after the initial dose if needed; usual dosage range: 0.15-0.6 mg every 4-8 hours as needed
      Slow I.V.: Initial: Opiate-naive: 0.3 mg every 6-8 hours as needed; initial dose (up to 0.3 mg) may be repeated once in 30-60 minutes after the initial dose if needed
    Elderly: 0.15 mg every 6 hours; elderly patients are more likely to suffer from confusion and drowsiness compared to younger patients
  Heroin or opiate withdrawal (unlabeled use): Children ≥13 years and Adults: I.M., slow I.V.: Variable; 0.1-0.4 mg every 6 hours
  Sublingual: Children ≥16 years and Adults: Opioid dependence:
    Induction: Range: 12-16 mg/day (doses during an induction study used 8 mg on day 1, followed by 16 mg on day 2; induction continued over 3-4 days). Treatment should begin at least 4 hours after last use of heroin or short-acting opioid, preferably when first signs of withdrawal appear. Titrating dose to clinical effectiveness should be done as rapidly as possible to prevent undue withdrawal symptoms and patient drop-out during the induction period.
    Maintenance: Target dose: 16 mg/day; range: 4-24 mg/day; patients should be switched to the buprenorphine/naloxone combination product for maintenance and unsupervised therapy

Administration
  I.V.: Administer slowly, over at least 2 minutes.
  Sublingual: Tablet should be placed under the tongue until dissolved; should not be swallowed. If 2 or more tablets are needed per dose, all may be placed under the tongue at once, or 2 at a time; to ensure consistent bioavailability, subsequent doses should always be taken the same way.

Monitoring Parameters Pain relief, respiratory and mental status, CNS depression, blood pressure

Patient Information May cause drowsiness.
Dosage Forms INJ, solution (Buprenex®): 0.3 mg/mL (1 mL). **TAB, sublingual** (Subutex®): 2 mg, 8 mg

Buprenorphine and Naloxone (byoo pre NOR feen & nal OKS one)

U.S. Brand Names Suboxone®

Synonyms Buprenorphine Hydrochloride and Naloxone Hydrochloride Dihydrate; Naloxone and Buprenorphine; Naloxone Hydrochloride Dihydrate and Buprenorphine Hydrochloride

Therapeutic Category Analgesic, Narcotic

Use Treatment of opioid dependence

Restrictions C-III; Prescribing of tablets for opioid dependence is limited to physicians who have met the qualification criteria and have received a DEA number specific to prescribing this product. Tablets will be available through pharmacies and wholesalers which normally provide controlled substances.

Pregnancy Risk Factor C

Dosage Sublingual: Children ≥16 years and Adults: Opioid dependence: **Note:** This combination product is not recommended for use during the induction period; initial treatment should begin using buprenorphine oral tablets. Patients should be switched to the combination product for maintenance and unsupervised therapy.

Maintenance: Target dose (based on buprenorphine content): 16 mg/day; range: 4-24 mg/day

Dosage Forms TAB, sublingual: Buprenorphine 2 mg and naloxone 0.5 mg; buprenorphine 8 mg and naloxone 2 mg

♦ **Buprenorphine Hydrochloride** *see* Buprenorphine *on page 187*
♦ **Buprenorphine Hydrochloride and Naloxone Hydrochloride Dihydrate** *see* Buprenorphine and Naloxone *on page 189*

BuPROPion (byoo PROE pee on)

Related Information

Antidepressant Agents Comparison *on page 1359*

U.S. Brand Names Wellbutrin®; Wellbutrin SR®; Wellbutrin XL™; Zyban®

Therapeutic Category Antidepressant, Dopamine-Reuptake Inhibitor; Smoking Deterrent

Use Treatment of depression; adjunct in smoking cessation

Unlabeled/Investigational Use Attention-deficit/hyperactivity disorder (ADHD)

Pregnancy Risk Factor B

Contraindications Hypersensitivity to bupropion or any component of the formulation; seizure disorder; anorexia/bulimia; use of MAO inhibitors within 14 days; patients undergoing abrupt discontinuation of ethanol or sedatives (including benzodiazepines); patients receiving other dosage forms of bupropion

Warnings/Precautions Seizure risk is increased at total daily dosage >450 mg, individual dosages >150 mg, or by sudden, large increments in dose. The risk of seizures is increased in patients with a history of seizures, anorexia/bulimia, head trauma, CNS tumor, severe hepatic cirrhosis, abrupt discontinuation of sedative-hypnotics or ethanol, medications which lower seizure threshold (antipsychotics, antidepressants, theophyllines, systemic steroids), stimulants, or hypoglycemic agents. Discontinue and do not restart in patients experiencing a seizure. May cause CNS stimulation (restlessness, anxiety, insomnia) or anorexia. Use with caution in patients where weight loss is not desirable. The incidence of sexual dysfunction with bupropion is generally lower than with SSRIs.

Use caution in patients with cardiovascular disease, history of hypertension, or coronary artery disease; treatment-emergent hypertension (including some severe cases) has been reported, both with bupropion alone and in combination with nicotine transdermal systems.

Use with caution in patients with hepatic or renal dysfunction and in elderly patients. Elderly patients may be at greater risk of accumulation during chronic dosing. May cause motor or cognitive impairment in some patients, use with caution if tasks requiring alertness such as operating machinery or driving are undertaken. May worsen psychosis in some patients or precipitate a shift to mania or hypomania in patients with bipolar disease. The possibility of a suicide attempt is inherent in major depression and may persist until remission occurs. Use caution in high-risk patients during initiation of therapy. Prescriptions should be written for the smallest quantity consistent with good patient care.

Arthralgia, myalgia, and fever with rash and other symptoms suggestive of delayed hypersensitivity resembling serum sickness reported.

Common Adverse Reactions Frequencies, when reported, reflect highest incidence reported with sustained release product.

>10%:
   Central nervous system: Dizziness (11%), headache (25%), insomnia (16%)
   Gastrointestinal: Nausea (18%), xerostomia (24%)
   Respiratory: Pharyngitis (11%)
1% to 10%:
   Cardiovascular: Arrhythmias, chest pain (4%), flushing, hypertension (may be severe), hypotension, palpitation (5%), syncope, tachycardia
   Central nervous system: Agitation (9%), anxiety (6%), confusion, depression, euphoria, hostility, irritability (2%), memory decreased (3%), migraine, nervousness (3%), sleep disturbance, somnolence (3%)
   Dermatologic: Pruritus (4%), rash (4%), sweating increased (5%), urticaria (1%)
   Endocrine & metabolic: Hot flashes, libido decreased, menstrual complaints
(Continued)

BuPROPion *(Continued)*

Gastrointestinal: Abdominal pain, anorexia (3%), appetite increased, constipation (5%), diarrhea (7%), dyspepsia, dysphagia (2%), taste perversion (4%), vomiting (2%)

Genitourinary: Urinary frequency (5%)

Neuromuscular & skeletal: Arthralgia (4%), arthritis (2%), myalgia (6%), neck pain, paresthesia (2%), tremor (3%), twitching (2%)

Ocular: Amblyopia (2%), blurred vision

Otic: Auditory disturbance, tinnitus (6%)

Respiratory: Cough increased (2%), sinusitis (1%)

Miscellaneous: Allergic reaction (including anaphylaxis, pruritus, urticaria), infection

Note: Data for the immediate-release formulation of bupropion revealed a seizure incidence of 0.4% in patients treated at doses in the 300-450 mg/day range. The estimated seizure incidence increases almost 10-fold between 450 mg and 600 mg per day. Data for the sustained release dosage form revealed a seizure incidence of 0.1% in patients treated at a dosage range of 100-300 mg/day, and increases to ~0.4% at the maximum recommended dose of 400 mg/day.

Drug Interactions

Cytochrome P450 Effect: Substrate of CYP1A2 (minor), 2A6 (minor), 2B6 (major), 2C8/9 (minor), 2D6 (minor), 2E1 (minor), 3A4 (minor); **Inhibits** CYP2D6 (weak)

Increased Effect/Toxicity: Treatment-emergent hypertension may occur in patients treated with bupropion and nicotine patch. Cimetidine may inhibit the metabolism (increase clinical/adverse effects) of bupropion. Toxicity of bupropion is enhanced by levodopa and phenelzine (MAO inhibitors). Risk of seizures may be increased with agents that may lower seizure threshold (antipsychotics, antidepressants, theophylline, abrupt discontinuation of benzodiazepines, systemic steroids). Effect of warfarin may be altered by bupropion. Concurrent use with amantadine appears to result in a higher incidence of adverse effects; use caution. CYP2B6 inhibitors may increase the levels/effects of bupropion; example inhibitors include desipramine, paroxetine, and sertraline. Combined use of CYP2B6 inhibitors (orphenadrine, thiotepa, cyclophosphamide) with bupropion may increase serum concentrations and may result in seizures.

Decreased Effect: CYP2B6 inducers may decrease the levels/effects of bupropion; example inducers include carbamazepine, nevirapine, phenobarbital, phenytoin, and rifampin. Effect of warfarin may be altered by bupropion.

Mechanism of Action Aminoketone antidepressant structurally different from all other marketed antidepressants; like other antidepressants the mechanism of bupropion's activity is not fully understood. Bupropion is a relatively weak inhibitor of the neuronal uptake of serotonin, norepinephrine, and dopamine, and does not inhibit monoamine oxidase. Metabolite inhibits the reuptake of norepinephrine. The primary mechanism of action is thought to be dopaminergic and/or noradrenergic.

Pharmacodynamics/Kinetics

Absorption: Rapid

Distribution: V_d: 19-21 L/kg

Protein binding: 82% to 88%

Metabolism: Extensively hepatic to 3 active metabolites: Hydroxybupropion, erythrohydrobupropion, threohydrobupropion (metabolite activity ranges from $1/5$ to $1/2$ potency of bupropion)

Bioavailability: 5% to 20% in animals

Half-life:

Distribution: 3-4 hours

Elimination: 21 ± 9 hours; Metabolites: Hydroxybupropion: 20 ± 5 hours; Erythrohydrobupropion: 33 ± 13 hours

Time to peak, serum: Bupropion: ~3 hours; bupropion extended release: ~5 hours

Metabolites: Hydroxybupropion, erythrohydrobupropion, threohydrobupropion: 6 hours

Excretion: Urine (87%); feces (10%)

Dosage Oral:

Children and Adolescents: ADHD (unlabeled use): 1.4-6 mg/kg/day

Adults:

Depression:

Immediate release: 100 mg 3 times/day; begin at 100 mg twice daily; may increase to a maximum dose of 450 mg/day

Sustained release: Initial: 150 mg/day in the morning; may increase to 150 mg twice daily by day 4 if tolerated; target dose: 300 mg/day given as 150 mg twice daily; maximum dose: 400 mg/day given as 200 mg twice daily

Extended release: Initial: 150 mg/day in the morning; may increase as early as day 4 of dosing to 300 mg/day; maximum dose: 450 mg/day

Smoking cessation (Zyban®): Initiate with 150 mg once daily for 3 days; increase to 150 mg twice daily; treatment should continue for 7-12 weeks

Elderly: Depression: 50-100 mg/day, increase by 50-100 mg every 3-4 days as tolerated; there is evidence that the elderly respond at 150 mg/day in divided doses, but some may require a higher dose

Dosing adjustment/comments in renal impairment: Effect of renal disease on bupropion's pharmacokinetics has not been studied; elimination of the major metabolites of bupropion may be affected by reduced renal function. Patients with renal failure should receive a reduced dosage initially and be closely monitored.

Dosing adjustment in hepatic impairment:
Note: The mean AUC increased by ~1.5-fold for hydroxybupropion and ~2.5-fold for erythro/threohydrobupropion; median T_{max} was observed 19 hours later for hydroxybupropion, 31 hours later for erythro/threohydrobupropion; mean half-life for hydroxybupropion increased fivefold, and increased twofold for erythro/threohydrobupropion in patients with severe hepatic cirrhosis compared to healthy volunteers.

Mild to moderate hepatic impairment: Use with caution and/or reduced dose/frequency
Severe hepatic cirrhosis: Use with extreme caution; maximum dose:
Wellbutrin®: 75 mg/day
Wellbutrin SR®: 100 mg/day or 150 mg every other day
Wellbutrin XL™: 150 mg every other day
Zyban®: 150 mg every other day

Administration May be taken without regard to meals. Sustained and extended release tablets should be swallowed whole; do not crush, chew, or divide. The insoluble shell of the extended-release tablet may remain intact during GI transit and is eliminated in the feces.

Monitoring Parameters Body weight

Reference Range Therapeutic levels (trough, 12 hours after last dose): 50-100 ng/mL

Patient Information Take in equally divided doses 3-4 times/day to minimize the risk of seizures; avoid alcohol; do not take more than recommended dose or more than 150 mg in a single dose; do not discontinue without consulting prescriber; it may take 3-4 weeks for full effect; may impair driving or other motor or cognitive skills and judgment. Excessive use or abrupt discontinuation of alcohol or sedatives may alter seizure threshold.

Smoking cessation: Bupropion can provide beneficial effects, but must be taken on a regular basis. Bupropion is only part of the total remedy for smoking cessation and must be combined with behavior and lifestyle modifications.

Dosage Forms TAB (Wellbutrin®): 75 mg, 100 mg. **TAB, extended release** (Wellbutrin XL™): 150 mg, 300 mg. **TAB, sustained release:** (Wellbutrin® SR): 100 mg, 150 mg, 200 mg; (Zyban®): 150 mg

♦ **Burnamycin [OTC]** see Lidocaine on page 742
♦ **Burn Jel [OTC]** see Lidocaine on page 742
♦ **Burn-O-Jel [OTC]** see Lidocaine on page 742
♦ **Burow's Otic** see Aluminum Acetate and Acetic Acid on page 66
♦ **BuSpar®** see BusPIRone on page 191

BusPIRone (byoo SPYE rone)

U.S. Brand Names BuSpar®

Synonyms Buspirone Hydrochloride

Therapeutic Category Antianxiety Agent

Use Management of generalized anxiety disorder (GAD)

Unlabeled/Investigational Use Management of aggression in mental retardation and secondary mental disorders; major depression; potential augmenting agent for antidepressants; premenstrual syndrome

Pregnancy Risk Factor B

Contraindications Hypersensitivity to buspirone or any component of the formulation

Warnings/Precautions Safety and efficacy not established in children <18 years of age; use in hepatic or renal impairment is not recommended; does not prevent or treat withdrawal from benzodiazepines. Low potential for cognitive or motor impairment. Use with MAO inhibitors may result in hypertensive reactions.

Common Adverse Reactions
>10%: Central nervous system: Dizziness
1% to 10%:
Central nervous system: Drowsiness, EPS, serotonin syndrome, confusion, nervousness, lightheadedness, excitement, anger, hostility, headache
Dermatologic: Rash
Gastrointestinal: Diarrhea, nausea
Neuromuscular & skeletal: Muscle weakness, numbness, paresthesia, incoordination, tremor
Ocular: Blurred vision, tunnel vision
Miscellaneous: Diaphoresis, allergic reactions

Drug Interactions
Cytochrome P450 Effect: Substrate of CYP2D6 (minor), 3A4 (major)
Increased Effect/Toxicity: Concurrent use of buspirone with SSRIs or trazodone may cause serotonin syndrome. Erythromycin, clarithromycin, diltiazem, itraconazole, ketoconazole, verapamil, and grapefruit juice may result in increases in buspirone concentrations. Buspirone should not be used concurrently with an MAO inhibitor due to reports of increased blood pressure; theoretically, a selective MAO type B inhibitors (selegiline) has a lower risk of this reaction. Concurrent use of buspirone with nefazodone may increase risk of CNS adverse events; limit buspirone initial dose (eg, 2.5 mg/day). CYP3A4 inhibitors may increase the levels/effects of buspirone; example inhibitors include azole antifungals, ciprofloxacin, clarithromycin, diclofenac, doxycycline, erythromycin, imatinib, isoniazid, nefazodone, nicardipine, propofol, protease inhibitors, quinidine, and verapamil.
Decreased Effect: CYP3A4 inducers may decrease the levels/effects of buspirone; example inducers include aminoglutethimide, carbamazepine, nafcillin, nevirapine, phenobarbital, phenytoin, and rifamycins.
(Continued)

BusPIRone *(Continued)*

Mechanism of Action The mechanism of action of buspirone is unknown. Buspirone has a high affinity for serotonin 5-HT$_{1A}$ and 5-HT$_2$ receptors, without affecting benzodiazepine-GABA receptors; buspirone has moderate affinity for dopamine D$_2$ receptors

Pharmacodynamics/Kinetics
Absorption: Oral: ~100%
Distribution: V$_d$: 5.3 L/kg
Protein binding: 95%
Metabolism: Hepatic via oxidation; extensive first-pass effect
Bioavailability: ~4%
Half-life elimination: Mean: 2.4 hours (range: 2-11 hours)
Time to peak, serum: Within 0.7-1.5 hours
Excretion: Urine: 65%; feces: 35%; ~1% dose excreted unchanged

Dosage Oral:
Generalized anxiety disorder:
Children and Adolescents: Initial: 5 mg daily; increase in increments of 5 mg/day at weekly intervals as needed, to a maximum dose of 60 mg/day divided into 2-3 doses
Adults: 15 mg/day (7.5 mg twice daily); may increase in increments of 5 mg/day every 2-4 days to a maximum of 60 mg/day; target dose for most people is 30 mg/day (15 mg twice daily)
Dosing adjustment in renal or hepatic impairment: Buspirone is metabolized by the liver and excreted by the kidneys. Patients with impaired hepatic or renal function demonstrated increased plasma levels and a prolonged half-life of buspirone. Therefore, use in patients with severe hepatic or renal impairment cannot be recommended.

Monitoring Parameters Mental status, symptoms of anxiety

Patient Information Report any change in senses (ie, smelling, hearing, vision); cautious use with alcohol is recommended; cannot be substituted for benzodiazepines unless directed by prescriber; takes 2-3 weeks to see the full effect of this medication; if you miss a dose, do **not** double your next dose

Dosage Forms TAB: 5 mg, 7.5 mg, 10 mg, 15 mg, 30 mg; (BuSpar®): 5 mg, 10 mg, 15 mg, 30 mg

♦ **Buspirone Hydrochloride** *see BusPIRone on page 191*

Busulfan *(byoo SUL fan)*

U.S. Brand Names Busulfex®; Myleran®

Therapeutic Category Antineoplastic Agent, Alkylating Agent

Use
Oral: Chronic myelogenous leukemia and bone marrow disorders, such as polycythemia vera and myeloid metaplasia, conditioning regimens for bone marrow transplantation
I.V.: Combination therapy with cyclophosphamide as a conditioning regimen prior to allogeneic hematopoietic progenitor cell transplantation for chronic myelogenous leukemia

Pregnancy Risk Factor D

Contraindications Hypersensitivity to busulfan or any component of the formulation; failure to respond to previous courses; pregnancy

Warnings/Precautions The U.S. Food and Drug Administration (FDA) currently recommends that procedures for proper handling and disposal of antineoplastic agents be considered. May induce severe bone marrow hypoplasia; reduce or discontinue dosage at first sign, as reflected by an abnormal decrease in any of the formed elements of the blood; use with caution in patients recently given other myelosuppressive drugs or radiation treatment. If white blood count is high, hydration and allopurinol should be employed to prevent hyperuricemia. Use caution in patients predisposed to seizures. Discontinue if lung toxicity develops. Busulfan has been causally related to the development of secondary malignancies (tumors and acute leukemias). Busulfan has been associated with ovarian failure (including failure to achieve puberty) in females. High busulfan area under the concentration versus time curve (AUC) values (>1500 μM/minute) are associated with increased risk of hepatic veno-occlusive disease during conditioning for allogenic BMT.

Common Adverse Reactions
Fertility/carcinogenesis: Sterility, ovarian suppression, amenorrhea, azoospermia, and testicular atrophy; malignant tumors have been reported in patients on busulfan therapy.

>10%: Hematologic: Severe pancytopenia, leukopenia, thrombocytopenia, anemia, and bone marrow suppression are common and patients should be monitored closely while on therapy. Since this is a delayed effect (busulfan affects the stem cells), the drug should be discontinued temporarily at the first sign of a large or rapid fall in any blood element. Some patients may develop bone marrow fibrosis or chronic aplasia which is probably due to the busulfan toxicity. In large doses, busulfan is myeloablative and is used for this reason in BMT. Myelosuppressive:
WBC: Moderate
Platelets: Moderate
Onset: 7-10 days
Nadir: 14-21 days
Recovery: 28 days
1% to 10%:
Dermatologic: Hyperpigmentation skin (busulfan tan), urticaria, erythema, alopecia
Endocrine & metabolic: Amenorrhea
Gastrointestinal: Nausea, vomiting, diarrhea; drug has little effect on the GI mucosal lining

Neuromuscular & skeletal: Weakness

Drug Interactions

Cytochrome P450 Effect: Substrate of CYP3A4 (major)

Increased Effect/Toxicity: CYP3A4 inhibitors may increase the levels/effects of busulfan; example inhibitors include azole antifungals, ciprofloxacin, clarithromycin, diclofenac, doxycycline, erythromycin, imatinib, isoniazid, nefazodone, nicardipine, propofol, protease inhibitors, quinidine, and verapamil. Metronidazole may increase busulfan plasma levels.

Decreased Effect: CYP3A4 inducers may decrease the levels/effects of busulfan; example inducers include aminoglutethimide, carbamazepine, nafcillin, nevirapine, phenobarbital, phenytoin, and rifamycins.

Mechanism of Action Reacts with N-7 position of guanosine and interferes with DNA replication and transcription of RNA. Busulfan has a more marked effect on myeloid cells (and is, therefore, useful in the treatment of CML) than on lymphoid cells. The drug is also very toxic to hematopoietic stem cells (thus its usefulness in high doses in BMT preparative regimens). Busulfan exhibits weak immunosuppressive activity. Interferes with the normal function of DNA by alkylation and cross-linking the strands of DNA.

Pharmacodynamics/Kinetics

Duration: 28 days

Absorption: Rapid and complete

Distribution: V_d: ~1 L/kg; into CSF and saliva with levels similar to plasma

Protein binding: ~14%

Metabolism: Extensively hepatic

Half-life elimination: After first dose: 3.4 hours; After last dose: 2.3 hours

Time to peak, serum: Oral: Within 4 hours; I.V.: Within 5 minutes

Excretion: Urine (10% to 50% as metabolites) within 24 hours (<2% as unchanged drug)

Dosage Busulfan should be based on adjusted ideal body weight because actual body weight, ideal body weight, or other factors can produce significant differences in busulfan clearance among lean, normal, and obese patients; refer to individual protocols

Children:

For remission induction of CML: Oral: 0.06-0.12 mg/kg/day **OR** 1.8-4.6 mg/m²/day; titrate dosage to maintain leukocyte count above 40,000/mm³; reduce dosage by 50% if the leukocyte count reaches 30,000-40,000/mm³; discontinue drug if counts fall to ≤20,000/mm³

BMT marrow-ablative conditioning regimen:

Oral: 1 mg/kg/dose (ideal body weight) every 6 hours for 16 doses

I.V.:

≤12 kg: 1.1 mg/kg/dose (ideal body weight) every 6 hours for 16 doses

>12 kg: 0.8 mg/kg/dose (ideal body weight) every 6 hours for 16 doses

Adjust dose to desired AUC [1125 µmol(min)] using the following formula:

Adjusted dose (mg) = Actual dose (mg) x [target AUC µmol(min) / actual AUC µmol(min)]

Adults:

For remission induction of CML: Oral: 4-8 mg/day (may be as high as 12 mg/day); Maintenance doses: Controversial, range from 1-4 mg/day to 2 mg/week; treatment is continued until WBC reaches 10,000-20,000 cells/mm³ at which time drug is discontinued; when WBC reaches 50,000/mm³, maintenance dose is resumed

BMT marrow-ablative conditioning regimen:

Oral: 1 mg/kg/dose (ideal body weight) every 6 hours for 16 doses

I.V.: 0.8 mg/kg (ideal body weight or actual body weight, whichever is lower) every 6 hours for 4 days (a total of 16 doses)

I.V. dosing in morbidly obese patients: Dosing should be based on adjusted ideal body weight (AIBW) which should be calculated as ideal body weight (IBW) + 0.25 times (actual weight minus ideal body weight)

AIBW = IBW + 0.25 x (AW - IBW)

Unapproved use:

Polycythemia vera: 2-6 mg/day

Thrombocytosis: 4-6 mg/day

Administration Intravenous busulfan should be administered via a **central** venous catheter as a 2-hour infusion, every 6 hours for 4 consecutive days for a total of 16 doses; do not use polycarbonate syringes.

BMT only: Phenytoin or clonazepam should be administered prophylactically during and for at least 48 hours following completion of busulfan. Risk of seizures is increased in patients with sickle cell disease. Increased risk of VOD when busulfan AUC >3000 µmol(min)/L (mean AUC, 2012 µmol(min)/L). To facilitate ingestion of high doses, insert multiple tablets into clear gel capsules.

Monitoring Parameters CBC with differential and platelet count, hemoglobin, liver function tests

Patient Information Take oral medication as directed with chilled liquids. Maintain adequate hydration (2-3 L/day of fluids unless instructed to restrict fluid intake) to help prevent kidney complications. Avoid alcohol, acidic or spicy foods, aspirin, or OTC medications unless approved by prescriber. Brush teeth with soft toothbrush or cotton swab. You may lose head hair or experience darkening of skin color (reversible when medication is discontinued), amenorrhea, sterility, or skin rash. You may experience nausea, vomiting, anorexia, or constipation (small frequent meals, increased exercise, and increased dietary fruit or fiber may help). You will be more susceptible to infection (avoid crowds or contagious persons, and do not receive any vaccinations unless approved by prescriber). Report palpitations or chest pain, excessive

(Continued)

193

Busulfan *(Continued)*

dizziness, confusion, respiratory difficulty, numbness or tingling of extremities, unusual bruising or bleeding, pain or changes in urination, or other adverse effects. Contraceptive measures are recommended during therapy.

Dosage Forms INJ, solution (Busulfex®): 6 mg/mL (10 mL). **TAB** (Myleran®): 2 mg

♦ **Busulfex®** *see Busulfan on page 192*

Butabarbital *(byoo ta BAR bi tal)*

U.S. Brand Names Butisol Sodium®

Therapeutic Category Barbiturate; Hypnotic; Sedative

Use Sedative; hypnotic

Restrictions C-III

Pregnancy Risk Factor D

Contraindications Hypersensitivity to barbiturates or any component of the formulation; porphyria; pregnancy

Warnings/Precautions May cause CNS depression, which may impair physical or mental abilities. Patients must be cautioned about performing tasks which require mental alertness (eg, operating machinery or driving). Effects with other sedative drugs or ethanol may be potentiated. May cause respiratory depression or hypotension. Use with caution in hemodynamically unstable patients or patients with respiratory disease. Potential for drug dependency exists; abrupt cessation may precipitate withdrawal, including status epilepticus in epileptic patients. Use caution in elderly, debilitated, renally impaired, hepatic impairment, or pediatric patients. May cause paradoxical responses, including agitation and hyperactivity, particularly in acute pain and pediatric patients. Use with caution in patients with depression or suicidal tendencies, or in patients with a history of drug abuse. Tolerance, psychological and physical dependence may occur with prolonged use.

Common Adverse Reactions

>10%: Central nervous system: Dizziness, lightheadedness, drowsiness, "hangover" effect

1% to 10%:

Central nervous system: Confusion, mental depression, unusual excitement, nervousness, faint feeling, headache, insomnia, nightmares

Gastrointestinal: Constipation, nausea, vomiting

Drug Interactions

Increased Effect/Toxicity: When butabarbital is combined with other CNS depressants, ethanol, narcotic analgesics, antidepressants, or benzodiazepines, additive respiratory and CNS depression may occur. Barbiturates may enhance the hepatotoxic potential of acetaminophen overdoses. Chloramphenicol, MAO inhibitors, valproic acid, and felbamate may inhibit barbiturate metabolism. Barbiturates may impair the absorption of griseofulvin, and may enhance the nephrotoxic effects of methoxyflurane.

Decreased Effect: Barbiturates such as butabarbital are hepatic enzyme inducers, and may increase the metabolism of antipsychotics, some beta-blockers (unlikely with atenolol and nadolol), calcium channel blockers, chloramphenicol, cimetidine, corticosteroids, cyclosporine, disopyramide, doxycycline, ethosuximide, felbamate, furosemide, griseofulvin, lamotrigine, phenytoin, propafenone, quinidine, tacrolimus, TCAs, and theophylline. Barbiturates may increase the metabolism of estrogens and reduce the efficacy of oral contraceptives; an alternative method of contraception should be considered. Barbiturates inhibit the hypoprothrombinemic effects of oral anticoagulants via increased metabolism. Barbiturates may enhance the metabolism of methadone resulting in methadone withdrawal.

Mechanism of Action Interferes with transmission of impulses from the thalamus to the cortex of the brain resulting in an imbalance in central inhibitory and facilitatory mechanisms

Pharmacodynamics/Kinetics

Distribution: V_d: 0.8 L/kg

Protein binding: 26%

Metabolism: Hepatic

Half-life elimination: 1.6 days to 5.8 days

Time to peak, serum: 40-60 minutes

Excretion: Urine (as metabolites)

Dosage Oral:

Children: Preoperative sedation: 2-6 mg/kg/dose (maximum: 100 mg)

Adults:

Sedative: 15-30 mg 3-4 times/day

Hypnotic: 50-100 mg

Preop: 50-100 mg 1-1^1/$_2$ hours before surgery

Reference Range Therapeutic: Not established; Toxic: 28-73 µg/mL

Patient Information May cause drowsiness, avoid alcohol or other CNS depressants, may impair judgment and coordination; may cause physical and psychological dependence with prolonged use; do not exceed recommended dose

Dosage Forms ELIX: 30 mg/5 mL (480 mL). **TAB:** 30 mg, 50 mg

Butalbital, Acetaminophen, and Caffeine

(byoo TAL bi tal, a seet a MIN oh fen, & KAF een)

U.S. Brand Names Anolor 300; Esgic®; Esgic-Plus™; Fioricet®; Repan®; Zebutal™

Synonyms Acetaminophen, Butalbital, and Caffeine

Therapeutic Category Barbiturate

Use Relief of the symptomatic complex of tension or muscle contraction headache

Pregnancy Risk Factor D

Dosage Adults: Oral: 1-2 tablets or capsules every 4 hours; not to exceed 6/day
  Dosing interval in renal or hepatic impairment: Should be reduced

Dosage Forms CAP (Esgic®): Butalbital 50 mg, caffeine 40 mg, and acetaminophen 325 mg; (Esgic-Plus™): Butalbital 50 mg, caffeine 40 mg, and acetaminophen 500 mg. **TAB** (Fioricet®, Repan®): Butalbital 50 mg, caffeine 40 mg, and acetaminophen 325 mg

Butalbital, Aspirin, and Caffeine (byoo TAL bi tal, AS pir in, & KAF een)

U.S. Brand Names Fiorinal®

Synonyms Aspirin, Caffeine, and Butalbital; Butalbital Compound

Therapeutic Category Barbiturate

Use Relief of the symptomatic complex of tension or muscle contraction headache

Restrictions C-III

Pregnancy Risk Factor C/D (prolonged use or high doses at term)

Dosage Oral: Adults: 1-2 tablets or capsules every 4 hours; not to exceed 6/day
  Dosing interval in renal or hepatic impairment: Should be reduced

Dosage Forms CAP (Fiorinal®): Butalbital 50 mg, caffeine 40 mg, and aspirin 325 mg

♦ **Butalbital Compound** *see* Butalbital, Aspirin, and Caffeine *on page 195*

Butenafine (byoo TEN a feen)

U.S. Brand Names Lotrimin® Ultra™ [OTC]; Mentax®

Synonyms Butenafine Hydrochloride

Therapeutic Category Antifungal Agent, Topical

Use Topical treatment of tinea pedis (athlete's foot), tinea cruris (jock itch), tinea corporis (ringworm), and tinea versicolor

Pregnancy Risk Factor B

Contraindications Hypersensitivity to butenafine or any component of the formulation

Warnings/Precautions Only for topical use (not ophthalmic, vaginal, or internal routes); patients sensitive to other allylamine antifungals may cross-react with butenafine; has not been studied in immunocompromised patients

Common Adverse Reactions >1%: Dermatologic: Burning, stinging, irritation, erythema, pruritus (2%)

Mechanism of Action Butenafine exerts antifungal activity by blocking squalene epoxidation, resulting in inhibition of ergosterol synthesis (antidermatophyte and *Sporothrix schenckii* activity). In higher concentrations, the drug disrupts fungal cell membranes (anticandidal activity).

Pharmacodynamics/Kinetics
  Absorption: Minimal systemic
  Metabolism: Hepatic via hydroxylation
  Half-life elimination: 35 hours
  Time to peak, serum: 6 hours

Dosage Children >12 years and Adults: Topical:
  Tinea corporis, tinea cruris, or tinea versicolor: Apply once daily for 2 weeks to affected area and surrounding skin
  Tinea pedis: Apply once daily for 4 weeks or twice daily for 7 days to affected area and surrounding skin (7-day regimen may have lower efficacy)

Monitoring Parameters Culture and KOH exam, clinical signs of tinea pedis

Patient Information Report any signs of rash or allergy to your prescriber immediately; do not apply other topical medications on the same area as butenafine unless directed by your prescriber

Dosage Forms CRM: (Lotrimin® Ultra™ [OTC]): 1% (12 g, 24 g); (Mentax®): 1% (15 g, 30 g)

♦ **Butenafine Hydrochloride** *see* Butenafine *on page 195*

♦ **Butisol Sodium®** *see* Butabarbital *on page 194*

Butoconazole (byoo toe KOE na zole)

U.S. Brand Names Gynazole-1™; Mycelex®-3 [OTC]

Synonyms Butoconazole Nitrate

Therapeutic Category Antifungal Agent, Imidazole Derivative; Antifungal Agent, Vaginal

Use Local treatment of vulvovaginal candidiasis

Pregnancy Risk Factor C (use only in 2nd or 3rd trimester)

Contraindications Hypersensitivity to butoconazole or any component of the formulation

Warnings/Precautions If irritation or sensitization occurs, discontinue use. Contains mineral oil which may weaken latex or rubber products (condoms, vaginal contraceptive diaphragms); do not use these products within 72 hours of treatment. HIV infection should be considered in sexually-active women with difficult to eradicate recurrent vaginal yeast infections. OTC product is not for use in women with a first-time vaginal yeast infection. Safety and efficacy in females <12 years have not been established.

Common Adverse Reactions Frequency not defined.
  Gastrointestinal: Abdominal pain or cramping
  Genitourinary: Pelvic pain; vulvar/vaginal burning, itching, soreness, and swelling

Mechanism of Action Increases cell membrane permeability in susceptible fungi (*Candida*)

Pharmacodynamics/Kinetics
  Absorption: 2%
  Metabolism: Not reported
  (Continued)

Butoconazole (Continued)

Time to peak: 12-24 hours

Dosage Adults: Female:

Femstat®-3 [OTC]: Insert 1 applicatorful (~5 g) intravaginally at bedtime for 3 consecutive days

Gynazole-1™: Insert 1 applicatorful (~5 g) intravaginally as a single dose; treatment may need to be extended for up to 6 days in pregnant women (use in pregnancy during 2nd or 3rd trimester only)

Patient Information May cause burning or stinging on application; dispose of applicator after use. If symptoms of vaginitis persist, contact prescriber. Do not use OTC product if you have abdominal pain, fever, or foul-smelling discharge. Contact prescriber if infection does not clear within 3 days. Do not use tampons while using this medication. This medication contains mineral oil, which may cause damage to condoms or diaphragms; use another method of birth control during treatment.

Dosage Forms CRM, vaginal: (Mycelex®-3): 2% (20 g); (Gynazole-1™) [prefilled applicator]: 2% (5 g)

♦ **Butoconazole Nitrate** *see* Butoconazole *on page 195*

Butorphanol (byoo TOR fa nole)

Related Information

Narcotic Agonists Comparison *on page 1395*

U.S. Brand Names Stadol®; Stadol® NS

Synonyms Butorphanol Tartrate

Therapeutic Category Analgesic, Narcotic; Narcotic Antagonist

Use

Parenteral: Management of moderate to severe pain; preoperative medication; supplement to balanced anesthesia; management of pain during labor

Nasal spray: Management of moderate to severe pain, including migraine headache pain

Restrictions C-IV

Pregnancy Risk Factor C/D (prolonged use or high doses at term)

Contraindications Hypersensitivity to butorphanol or any component of the formulation; avoid use in opiate-dependent patients who have not been detoxified, may precipitate opiate withdrawal; pregnancy (prolonged use or high doses at term)

Warnings/Precautions An opioid-containing analgesic regimen should be tailored to each patient's needs and based upon the type of pain being treated (acute versus chronic), the route of administration, degree of tolerance for opioids (naive versus chronic user), age, weight, and medical condition. The optimal analgesic dose varies widely among patients. Doses should be titrated to pain relief/prevention. May cause CNS depression; use with caution in patients with hepatic/renal dysfunction, may elevate CSF pressure, may increase cardiac workload; tolerance of drug dependence may result from extended use. Concurrent use of sumatriptan nasal spray and butorphanol nasal spray may increase risk of transient high blood pressure.

Common Adverse Reactions

>10%:

Central nervous system: Drowsiness (43%), dizziness (19%), insomnia (Stadol® NS)

Gastrointestinal: Nausea/vomiting (13%)

Respiratory: Nasal congestion (Stadol® NS)

1% to 10%:

Cardiovascular: Vasodilation, palpitations

Central nervous system: Lightheadedness, headache, lethargy, anxiety, confusion, euphoria, somnolence

Dermatologic: Pruritus

Gastrointestinal: Anorexia, constipation, xerostomia, stomach pain, unpleasant aftertaste

Neuromuscular & skeletal: Tremor, paresthesia, weakness

Ocular: Blurred vision

Otic: Ear pain, tinnitus

Respiratory: Bronchitis, cough, dyspnea, epistaxis, nasal irritation, pharyngitis, rhinitis, sinus congestion, sinusitis, upper respiratory infection

Miscellaneous: Diaphoresis (increased)

Drug Interactions

Increased Effect/Toxicity: Increased toxicity with CNS depressants, phenothiazines, barbiturates, skeletal muscle relaxants, alfentanil, guanabenz, and MAO inhibitors.

Mechanism of Action Mixed narcotic agonist-antagonist with central analgesic actions; binds to opiate receptors in the CNS, causing inhibition of ascending pain pathways, altering the perception of and response to pain; produces generalized CNS depression

Pharmacodynamics/Kinetics

Onset of action: I.M.: 5-10 minutes; I.V.: <10 minutes; Nasal: Within 15 minutes

Peak effect: I.M.: 0.5-1 hour; I.V.: 4-5 minutes

Duration: I.M., I.V.: 3-4 hours; Nasal: 4-5 hours

Absorption: Rapid and well absorbed

Protein binding: 80%

Metabolism: Hepatic

Bioavailability: Nasal: 60% to 70%

Half-life elimination: 2.5-4 hours

Excretion: Primarily urine

Dosage Note: These are guidelines and do not represent the maximum doses that may be required in all patients. Doses should be titrated to pain relief/prevention. Butorphanol has an analgesic ceiling.

Adults:

Parenteral:

Acute pain (moderate to severe):

I.M.: Initial: 2 mg, may repeat every 3-4 hours as needed; usual range: 1-4 mg every 3-4 hours as needed

I.V.: Initial: 1 mg, may repeat every 3-4 hours as needed; usual range: 0.5-2 mg every 3-4 hours as needed

Preoperative medication: I.M.: 2 mg 60-90 minutes before surgery

Supplement to balanced anesthesia: I.V.: 2 mg shortly before induction and/or an incremental dose of 0.5-1 mg (up to 0.06 mg/kg), depending on previously administered sedative, analgesic, and hypnotic medications

Pain during labor (fetus >37 weeks gestation and no signs of fetal distress):

I.M., I.V.: 1-2 mg; may repeat in 4 hours

Note: Alternative analgesia should be used for pain associated with delivery or if delivery is anticipated within 4 hours

Nasal spray:

Moderate to severe pain (including migraine headache pain): Initial: 1 spray (~1 mg per spray) in 1 nostril; if adequate pain relief is not achieved within 60-90 minutes, an additional 1 spray in 1 nostril may be given; may repeat initial dose sequence in 3-4 hours after the last dose as needed

Alternatively, an initial dose of 2 mg (1 spray in each nostril) may be used in patients who will be able to remain recumbent (in the event drowsiness or dizziness occurs); additional 2 mg doses should not be given for 3-4 hours

Note: In some clinical trials, an initial dose of 2 mg (as 2 doses 1 hour apart or 2 mg initially - 1 spray in each nostril) has been used, followed by 1 mg in 1 hour; side effects were greater at these dosages

Dosage adjustment in renal impairment:

I.M., I.V.: Initial dosage should generally be $^1/_2$ of the recommended dose; repeated dosing must be based on initial response rather than fixed intervals, but generally should be at least 6 hours apart

Nasal spray: Initial dose should not exceed 1 mg; a second dose may be given after 90-120 minutes

Dosage adjustment in hepatic impairment:

I.M., I.V.: Initial dosage should generally be $^1/_2$ of the recommended dose; repeated dosing must be based on initial response rather than fixed intervals, but generally should be at least 6 hours apart

Nasal spray: Initial dose should not exceed 1 mg; a second dose may be given after 90-120 minutes

Elderly:

I.M., I.V.: Initial dosage should generally be $^1/_2$ of the recommended dose; repeated dosing must be based on initial response rather than fixed intervals, but generally should be at least 6 hours apart

Nasal Spray: Initial dose should not exceed 1 mg; a second dose may be given after 90-120 minutes

Administration Intranasal: Consider avoiding simultaneous intranasal migraine sprays; may want to separate by at least 30 minutes

Monitoring Parameters Pain relief, respiratory and mental status, blood pressure

Reference Range 0.7-1.5 ng/mL

Patient Information May cause drowsiness; avoid alcohol

Dosage Forms INJ, solution [preservative free] (Stadol®): 1 mg/mL (1 mL); 2 mg/mL (1 mL, 2 mL). **INJ, solution** [with preservative] (Stadol®): 2 mg/mL (10 mL). **SPRAY, intranasal** (Stadol® NS): 10 mg/mL (2.5 mL)

♦ **Butorphanol Tartrate** *see Butorphanol on page 196*

♦ **B Vitamin Combinations** *see Vitamin B Complex Combinations on page 1311*

♦ **BW-430C** *see Lamotrigine on page 714*

♦ **BW524W91** *see Emtricitabine on page 428*

♦ **C2B8** *see Rituximab on page 1106*

♦ **C2B8 Monoclonal Antibody** *see Rituximab on page 1106*

♦ **C7E3** *see Abciximab on page 20*

♦ **311C90** *see Zolmitriptan on page 1332*

♦ **C-500-GR™ [OTC]** *see Ascorbic Acid on page 117*

Cabergoline (ca BER goe leen)

Related Information

Parkinson's Agents Comparison *on page 1402*

U.S. Brand Names Dostinex®

Therapeutic Category Ergot Alkaloid and Derivative

Use Treatment of hyperprolactinemic disorders, either idiopathic or due to pituitary adenomas

Unlabeled/Investigational Use Adjunct for the treatment of Parkinson's disease

Pregnancy Risk Factor B

(Continued)

Cabergoline *(Continued)*

Contraindications Hypersensitivity to cabergoline, any component of the formulation, or ergot derivatives; ergot alkaloids are contraindicated with potent inhibitors of CYP3A4 (includes protease inhibitors, azole antifungals, and some macrolide antibiotics); uncontrolled hypertension

Warnings/Precautions Initial doses >1 mg may cause orthostatic hypotension. Use caution when patients are receiving other medications which may reduce blood pressure. Not indicated for the inhibition or suppression of physiologic lactation since it has been associated with cases of hypertension, stroke, and seizures. Because cabergoline is extensively metabolized by the liver, careful monitoring in patients with hepatic impairment is warranted. Female patients should instruct the physician if they are pregnant, become pregnant, or intend to become pregnant. Should not be used in patients with pregnancy-induced hypertension unless benefit outweighs potential risk. Do not give to postpartum women who are breast-feeding or planning to breast-feed. In all patients, prolactin concentrations should be monitored monthly until normalized. Pleural and peritoneal fibrosis have been reported with prolonged daily use. Cardiac valvular fibrosis has also been associated with ergot alkaloids.

Common Adverse Reactions

>10%:
   Central nervous system: Headache (26%), dizziness (17%)
   Gastrointestinal: Nausea (29%)

1% to 10%:
   Body as whole: Asthenia (6%), fatigue (5%), syncope (1%), influenza-like symptoms (1%), malaise (1%), periorbital edema (1%), peripheral edema (1%)
   Cardiovascular: Hot flashes (3%), hypotension (1%), dependent edema (1%), palpitations (1%)
   Central nervous system: Vertigo (4%), depression (3%), somnolence (2%), anxiety (1%), insomnia (1%), impaired concentration (1%), nervousness (1%)
   Dermatologic: Acne (1%), pruritus (1%)
   Endocrine: Breast pain (2%), dysmenorrhea (1%)
   Gastrointestinal: Constipation (7%), abdominal pain (5%), dyspepsia (5%), vomiting (4%), xerostomia (2%), diarrhea (2%), flatulence (2%), throat irritation (1%), toothache (1%), anorexia (1%)
   Neuromuscular & skeletal: Pain (2%), arthralgia (1%), paresthesias (2%)
   Ocular: Abnormal vision (1%)
   Respiratory: Rhinitis (1%)

Drug Interactions

Increased Effect/Toxicity: Effects of cabergoline may be increased by antifungals (azole derivatives); CYP3A4 inhibitors (eg, amiodarone, cimetidine, erythromycin, ritonavir); macrolide antibiotics; protease inhibitors; MAO inhibitors. Cabergoline may increase the effects of sibutramine and other serotonin agonists (serotonin syndrome).

Decreased Effect: Effects of cabergoline may be diminished by antipsychotics, metoclopramide.

Mechanism of Action Cabergoline is a long-acting dopamine receptor agonist with a high affinity for D_2 receptors; prolactin secretion by the anterior pituitary is predominantly under hypothalamic inhibitory control exerted through the release of dopamine

Pharmacodynamics/Kinetics

Distribution: Extensive, particularly to the pituitary
Protein binding: 40% to 42%
Metabolism: Extensively hepatic; minimal CYP
Half-life elimination: 63-69 hours
Time to peak: 2-3 hours

Dosage Initial dose: Oral: 0.25 mg twice weekly; the dose may be increased by 0.25 mg twice weekly up to a maximum of 1 mg twice weekly according to the patient's serum prolactin level. Dosage increases should not occur more rapidly than every 4 weeks. Once a normal serum prolactin level is maintained for 6 months, the dose may be discontinued and prolactin levels monitored to determine if cabergoline is still required. The durability of efficacy beyond 24 months of therapy has not been established.

Elderly: No dosage recommendations suggested, but start at the low end of the dosage range

Patient Information Patient should be instructed to notify physician if she suspects she is pregnant, becomes pregnant, or intends to become pregnant during therapy with cabergoline. A pregnancy test should be done if there is any suspicion of pregnancy and continuation of treatment should be discussed with physician.

Dosage Forms TAB: 0.5 mg

♦ **Cafergot®** *see Ergotamine on page 450*

♦ **Caffeine, Acetaminophen, and Aspirin** *see Acetaminophen, Aspirin, and Caffeine on page 27*

Caffeine and Sodium Benzoate *(KAF een & SOW dee um BEN zoe ate)*

Synonyms Sodium Benzoate and Caffeine
Therapeutic Category Diuretic, Miscellaneous
Use Emergency stimulant in acute circulatory failure, diuretic
Unlabeled/Investigational Use Relief of spinal puncture headache
Pregnancy Risk Factor C
Dosage
   Children: Stimulant: I.M., I.V., S.C.: 8 mg/kg every 4 hours as needed

Adults:
Stimulant/diuretic: I.M., I.V.: 500 mg, maximum single dose: 1 g
Spinal puncture headache (unlabeled use):
I.V.: 500 mg in 1000 mL NS infused over 1 hour, followed by 1000 mL NS infused over 1 hour; a second course of caffeine can be given for unrelieved headache pain in 4 hours.
Oral: 300 mg
Dosage Forms INJ, solution: Caffeine 121 mg and sodium benzoate 129 mg per mL (2 mL); caffeine 125 mg and sodium benzoate 125 mg per mL (2 mL)

♦ **Caffeine, Aspirin, and Acetaminophen** see Acetaminophen, Aspirin, and Caffeine on page 27
♦ **Caffeine, Hydrocodone, Chlorpheniramine, Phenylephrine, and Acetaminophen** see Hydrocodone, Chlorpheniramine, Phenylephrine, Acetaminophen, and Caffeine on page 632
♦ **Caffeine, Orphenadrine, and Aspirin** see Orphenadrine, Aspirin, and Caffeine on page 933
♦ **Caffeine, Propoxyphene, and Aspirin** see Propoxyphene, Aspirin, and Caffeine on page 1054
♦ **Calan®** see Verapamil on page 1302
♦ **Calan® SR** see Verapamil on page 1302
♦ **Calcarb 600 [OTC]** see Calcium Carbonate on page 203
♦ **Calci-Chew® [OTC]** see Calcium Carbonate on page 203

Calcifediol (kal si fe DYE ole)
U.S. Brand Names Calderol® [DSC]
Synonyms 25-HCC; 25-Hydroxycholecalciferol; 25-Hydroxyvitamin D_3
Therapeutic Category Vitamin, Fat Soluble
Use Treatment and management of metabolic bone disease associated with chronic renal failure or hypocalcemia in patients on chronic renal dialysis
Pregnancy Risk Factor C (manufacturer); A/D (dose exceeding RDA recommendation) (expert analysis)
Contraindications Hypersensitivity to calcifediol or any component of the formulation; malabsorption syndrome; hypervitaminosis D; significantly decreased renal function; hypercalcemia; pregnancy (dose exceeding RDA)
Warnings/Precautions Adequate (supplemental) dietary calcium is necessary for clinical response to vitamin D; calcium-phosphate product (serum calcium times phosphorus) must not exceed 70; avoid hypercalcemia
Common Adverse Reactions Frequency not defined.
Cardiovascular: Hypotension, cardiac arrhythmias, hypertension
Central nervous system: Irritability, headache, somnolence, seizures (rare)
Dermatologic: Pruritus
Endocrine & metabolic: Hypercalcemia, polydipsia, hypermagnesemia
Gastrointestinal: Nausea, vomiting, constipation, anorexia, pancreatitis, metallic taste, xerostomia
Hepatic: Elevated LFTs
Neuromuscular & skeletal: Myalgia, bone pain
Ocular: Conjunctivitis, photophobia
Renal: Polyuria
Drug Interactions
Increased Effect/Toxicity: The effect of calcifediol is increased with thiazide diuretics. Additive effect with antacids (magnesium).
Decreased Effect: The effect of calcifediol is decreased when taken with cholestyramine or colestipol.
Mechanism of Action Vitamin D analog that (along with calcitonin and parathyroid hormone) regulates serum calcium homeostasis by promoting absorption of calcium and phosphorus in the small intestine; promotes renal tubule resorption of phosphate; increases rate of accretion and resorption in bone minerals
Pharmacodynamics/Kinetics
Absorption: Rapid from small intestines
Distribution: Activated in kidneys; stored in liver and fat depots
Half-life elimination: 12-22 days
Time to peak: Within 4 hours
Excretion: Feces
Dosage Oral: Hepatic osteodystrophy:
Infants: 5-7 mcg/kg/day
Children and Adults: Usual dose: 20-100 mcg/day or 20-200 mcg every other day; titrate to obtain normal serum calcium/phosphate levels; increase dose at 4-week intervals; initial dose: 300-350 mcg/week, administered daily or on alternate days
Patient Information Compliance with dose, diet, and calcium supplementation is essential; avoid taking magnesium supplements or magnesium-containing antacids; report weakness, lethargy, headache, and decreased appetite
Dosage Forms CAP: 20 mcg

♦ **Calciferol™** see Ergocalciferol on page 449
♦ **Calcijex®** see Calcitriol on page 200
♦ **Calci-Mix®[OTC]** see Calcium Carbonate on page 203

Calcipotriene (kal si POE try een)
U.S. Brand Names Dovonex®
Therapeutic Category Topical Skin Product; Vitamin, Fat Soluble
Use Treatment of moderate plaque psoriasis
Pregnancy Risk Factor C
Dosage Topical: Adults: Apply in a thin film to the affected skin twice daily and rub in gently and completely
Dosage Forms CRM: 0.005% (60 g, 100 g, 120 g). **OINT:** 0.005% (60 g, 100 g, 120 g). **SOLN, topical:** 0.005% (60 mL)

Calcitonin (kal si TOE nin)
U.S. Brand Names Miacalcin®
Synonyms Calcitonin (Salmon)
Therapeutic Category Antidote, Hypercalcemia
Use Calcitonin (salmon): Treatment of Paget's disease of bone (osteitis deformans); adjunctive therapy for hypercalcemia; used in postmenopausal osteoporosis and osteogenesis imperfecta
Pregnancy Risk Factor C
Contraindications Hypersensitivity to salmon protein or gelatin diluent
Warnings/Precautions A skin test should be performed prior to initiating therapy of calcitonin salmon; have epinephrine immediately available for a possible hypersensitivity reaction
Common Adverse Reactions
>10%:
    Cardiovascular: Facial flushing
    Gastrointestinal: Nausea, diarrhea, anorexia
    Local: Edema at injection site
1% to 10%:
    Genitourinary: Polyuria
    Neuromuscular & skeletal: Back/joint pain
    Respiratory: Nasal bleeding/crusting (following intranasal administration)
Drug Interactions
Decreased Effect: Calcitonin may be antagonized by calcium and vitamin D in treating hypercalcemia.
Mechanism of Action Structurally similar to human calcitonin; it directly inhibits osteoclastic bone resorption; promotes the renal excretion of calcium, phosphate, sodium, magnesium and potassium by decreasing tubular reabsorption; increases the jejunal secretion of water, sodium, potassium, and chloride
Pharmacodynamics/Kinetics
Hypercalcemia:
    Onset of action: ~2 hours
    Duration: 6-8 hours
Distribution: Does not cross placenta
Half-life elimination: S.C.: 1.2 hours
Excretion: Urine (as inactive metabolites)
Dosage Salmon calcitonin:
Children: Dosage not established
Adults:
    Paget's disease: I.M., S.C.: Initial: 100 units/day; maintenance: 50 units/day or 50-100 units every 1-3 days
    Hypercalcemia: Initial: I.M., S.C.: 4 units/kg every 12 hours; may increase up to 8 units/kg every 12 hours to a maximum of every 6 hours
    Osteogenesis imperfecta: I.M., S.C.: 2 units/kg 3 times/week
    Postmenopausal osteoporosis:
        I.M., S.C.: 100 units/day
        Intranasal: 200 units (1 spray)/day
Monitoring Parameters Serum electrolytes and calcium; alkaline phosphatase and 24-hour urine collection for hydroxyproline excretion (Paget's disease); serum calcium
Reference Range Therapeutic: <19 pg/mL (SI: 19 ng/L) basal, depending on the assay
Patient Information Nasal spray: Notify prescriber if you develop significant nasal irritation. To activate the pump, hold the bottle upright and depress the two white side arms toward the bottle six times until a faint spray is emitted. The pump is activated once this first faint spray has been emitted; at this point, firmly place the nozzle into the bottle. It is not necessary to reactivate the pump before each daily use. Alternate nostrils with the spray formulation.
Dosage Forms INJ, solution, calcitonin-salmon: 200 int. units/mL (2 mL). **SPRAY, nasal spray, calcitonin-salmon:** 200 int. units/0.09 mL (3.7 mL)

♦ **Calcitonin (Salmon)** see Calcitonin on page 200
♦ **Cal-Citrate® 250 [OTC]** see Calcium Citrate on page 205

Calcitriol (kal si TRYE ole)
U.S. Brand Names Calcijex®; Rocaltrol®
Synonyms 1,25 Dihydroxycholecalciferol
Therapeutic Category Vitamin, Fat Soluble
Use Management of hypocalcemia in patients on chronic renal dialysis; management of secondary hyperparathyroidism in moderate to severe chronic renal failure; management of hypocalcemia in hypoparathyroidism and pseudohypoparathyroidism

Unlabeled/Investigational Use Decrease severity of psoriatic lesions in psoriatic vulgaris; vitamin D resistant rickets

Pregnancy Risk Factor C (manufacturer); A/D (dose exceeding RDA recommendation) (expert analysis)

Contraindications Hypercalcemia; vitamin D toxicity; abnormal sensitivity to the effects of vitamin D; pregnancy (dose exceeding RDA)

Warnings/Precautions Adequate dietary (supplemental) calcium is necessary for clinical response to vitamin D. Monitor serum calcium and phosphate concentrations; avoid hypercalcemia; calcium-phosphate product (serum calcium times phosphorus) must not exceed 70. Immobilization or excessive dosage may increase risk of hypercalcemia and/or hypercalciuria. Maintain adequate hydration. Use caution in patients with malabsorption syndromes (efficacy may be limited and/or response may be unpredictable).

Common Adverse Reactions

>10%: Endocrine & metabolic: Hypercalcemia (33%)

Frequency not defined:

Cardiovascular: Cardiac arrhythmias, hypertension, hypotension

Central nervous system: Headache, irritability, seizures (rare), somnolence, psychosis

Dermatologic: Pruritus, erythema multiforme

Endocrine & metabolic: Hypermagnesemia, polydipsia

Gastrointestinal: Anorexia, constipation, metallic taste, nausea, pancreatitis, vomiting, xerostomia

Hepatic: Elevated LFTs

Neuromuscular & skeletal: Bone pain, myalgia, dystrophy, soft tissue calcification

Ocular: Conjunctivitis, photophobia

Renal: Polyuria

Drug Interactions

Cytochrome P450 Effect: Induces CYP3A4 (weak)

Increased Effect/Toxicity: Risk of hypercalcemia with thiazide diuretics. Risk of hypermagnesemia with magnesium-containing antacids. Risk of digoxin toxicity may be increased (if hypercalcemia occurs).

Decreased Effect: Cholestyramine and colestipol decrease absorption/effect of calcitriol. Thiazide diuretics, enzyme inducers (phenytoin, phenobarbital), and corticosteroids may reduce the effect of calcitriol.

Mechanism of Action Promotes absorption of calcium in the intestines and retention at the kidneys thereby increasing calcium levels in the serum; decreases excessive serum phosphatase levels, parathyroid hormone levels, and decreases bone resorption; increases renal tubule phosphate resorption

Pharmacodynamics/Kinetics

Onset of action: ~2-6 hours

Duration: 3-5 days

Absorption: Oral: Rapid

Protein binding: 99.9%

Metabolism: Primarily to 1,24,25-trihydroxycholecalciferol and 1,24,25-trihydroxy ergocalciferol

Half-life elimination: 3-8 hours

Excretion: Primarily feces; urine (4% to 6%)

Dosage Individualize dosage to maintain calcium levels of 9-10 mg/dL

Renal failure:

Children:

Oral: 0.25-2 mcg/day have been used (with hemodialysis); 0.014-0.041 mcg/kg/day (not receiving hemodialysis); increases should be made at 4- to 8-week intervals

I.V.: 0.01-0.05 mcg/kg 3 times/week if undergoing hemodialysis

Adults:

Oral: 0.25 mcg/day or every other day (may require 0.5-1 mcg/day); increases should be made at 4- to 8-week intervals

I.V.: 0.5 mcg/day 3 times/week (may require from 0.5-3 mcg/day given 3 times/week) if undergoing hemodialysis

Hypoparathyroidism/pseudohypoparathyroidism: Oral (evaluate dosage at 2- to 4-week intervals):

Children:

<1 year: 0.04-0.08 mcg/kg once daily

1-5 years: 0.25-0.75 mcg once daily

Children >6 years and Adults: 0.5-2 mcg once daily

Vitamin D-dependent rickets: Children and Adults: Oral: 1 mcg once daily

Vitamin D-resistant rickets (familial hypophosphatemia): Children and Adults: Oral: Initial: 0.015-0.02 mcg/kg once daily; maintenance: 0.03-0.06 mcg/kg once daily; maximum dose: 2 mcg once daily

Hypocalcemia in premature infants: Oral: 1 mcg once daily for 5 days

Hypocalcemic tetany in premature infants: I.V.: 0.05 mcg/kg once daily for 5-12 days

Elderly: No dosage recommendations, but start at the lower end of the dosage range

Administration May be administered without regard to food. Give with meals to reduce GI problems.

Monitoring Parameters Monitor symptoms of hypercalcemia (weakness, fatigue, somnolence, headache, anorexia, dry mouth, metallic taste, nausea, vomiting, cramps, diarrhea, muscle pain, bone pain and irritability)

Reference Range Calcium (serum) 9-10 mg/dL (4.5-5 mEq/L) but do not include the I.V. dosages; phosphate: 2.5-5 mg/dL

(Continued)

Calcitriol *(Continued)*

Patient Information Compliance with dose, diet, and calcium supplementation is essential; report weakness, lethargy, headache, and decreased appetite; avoid taking magnesium supplements or magnesium-containing antacids

Dosage Forms CAP (Rocaltrol®): 0.25 mcg, 0.5 mcg. **INJ, solution:** 1 mcg/mL (1 mL), 2 mcg/mL (2 mL); (Calicjex®): 1 mcg/mL (1 mL). **SOLN, oral** (Rocaltrol®): 1 mcg/mL (15 mL)

Calcium Acetate (KAL see um AS e tate)

U.S. Brand Names PhosLo®

Therapeutic Category Antidote, Hyperphosphatemia; Calcium Salt; Electrolyte Supplement, Oral; Electrolyte Supplement, Parenteral

Use

Oral: Control of hyperphosphatemia in end-stage renal failure; does not promote aluminum absorption

I.V.: Calcium supplementation in parenteral nutrition therapy

Pregnancy Risk Factor C

Contraindications Hypersensitivity to any component of the formulation; hypercalcemia, renal calculi

Warnings/Precautions Calcium absorption is impaired in achlorhydria (common in elderly - try alternate salt, administer with food); administration is followed by increased gastric acid secretion within 2 hours of administration; while hypercalcemia and hypercalciuria may result when therapeutic replacement amounts are given for prolonged periods, they are most likely to occur in hypoparathyroid patients receiving high doses of vitamin D

Common Adverse Reactions

Mild hypercalcemia (calcium: >10.5 mg/dL to ≤12 mg/dL) may be asymptomatic or manifest itself as constipation, anorexia, nausea, and vomiting

More severe hypercalcemia (calcium: >12 mg/dL) is associated with confusion, delirium, stupor, and coma

Drug Interactions

Increased Effect/Toxicity: High doses of calcium with thiazide diuretics may result in milk-alkali syndrome and hypercalcemia; monitor response. Calcium salts may decrease T_4 absorption; separate dose from levothyroxine by at least 4 hours. Calcium acetate may potentiate digoxin toxicity.

Decreased Effect: Absorption of tetracycline, atenolol (and potentially other beta-blockers), iron, quinolone antibiotics, alendronate, sodium fluoride, and zinc absorption may be significantly decreased; space administration times. Effects of calcium channel blockers (eg, verapamil) effects may be diminished. Polystyrene sulfonate's potassium-binding ability may be reduced; avoid concurrent administration.

Mechanism of Action Combines with dietary phosphate to form insoluble calcium phosphate which is excreted in feces

Pharmacodynamics/Kinetics

Absorption: Requires vitamin D; minimal unless chronic, high doses are given; calcium is absorbed in soluble, ionized form; solubility of calcium is increased in an acid environment

Distribution: Crosses placenta; enters breast milk

Excretion: Primarily feces (as unabsorbed calcium); urine (20%)

Dosage

Dietary Reference Intake:

0-6 months: 210 mg/day

7-12 months: 270 mg/day

1-3 years: 500 mg/day

4-8 years: 800 mg/day

Adults, Male/Female:

9-18 years: 1300 mg/day

19-50 years: 1000 mg/day

≥51 years: 1200 mg/day

Female: Pregnancy: Same as for Adults, Male/Female

Female: Lactating: Same as for Adults, Male/Female

Oral: Adults, on dialysis: Initial: 1334 mg with each meal, can be increased gradually to bring the serum phosphate value <6 mg/dL as long as hypercalcemia does not develop (usual dose: 2001-2868 mg calcium acetate with each meal); do not give additional calcium supplements

I.V.: Dose is dependent on the requirements of the individual patient; in central venous total parental nutrition (TPN), calcium is administered at a concentration of 5 mEq (10 mL)/L of TPN solution; the additive maintenance dose in neonatal TPN is 0.5 mEq calcium/kg/day (1.0 mL/kg/day)

Neonates: 70-200 mg/kg/day

Infants and Children: 70-150 mg/kg/day

Adolescents: 18-35 mg/kg/day

Administration Administer with meals.

Monitoring Parameters Serum calcium, serum phosphate; for control of hypophosphatemia, serum calcium times phosphate should not exceed 66

Reference Range

Serum calcium: 8.4-10.2 mg/dL

Due to a poor correlation between the serum ionized calcium (free) and total serum calcium, particularly in states of low albumin or acid/base imbalances, direct measurement of ionized calcium is recommended

In low albumin states, the corrected **total** serum calcium may be estimated by this equation (assuming a normal albumin of 4 g/dL)

Corrected total calcium = total serum calcium + 0.8 (4.0 - measured serum albumin)
or
Corrected calcium = measured calcium - measured albumin + 4.0

Patient Information Take with meals; do not take calcium supplements within 1-2 hours of taking other medicine by mouth or eating large amounts of fiber-rich foods; do not use nonprescription antacids or drink large amounts of alcohol, caffeine-containing beverages, or use tobacco

Dosage Forms Elemental calcium listed in brackets: **GELCAP** (PhosLo®): 667 mg [169 mg].
INJ, solution: 0.5 mEq/mL (10 mL, 50 mL, 100 mL). **TAB** (PhosLo®): 667 mg [169 mg]

♦ **Calcium Acetate and Aluminum Sulfate** *see* Aluminum Sulfate and Calcium Acetate *on page 68*

Calcium Carbonate (KAL see um KAR bun ate)

U.S. Brand Names Alcalak [OTC]; Alka-Mints® [OTC]; Amitone® [OTC]; Calcarb 600 [OTC]; Calci-Chew® [OTC]; Calci-Mix®[OTC]; Cal-Gest [OTC]; Cal-Mint [OTC]; Caltrate® 600 [OTC]; Chooz® [OTC]; Florical® [OTC]; Mylanta® Children's [OTC]; Nephro-Calci® [OTC]; Os-Cal® 500 [OTC]; Oysco 500 [OTC]; Oyst-Cal 500 [OTC]; Rolaids® Extra Strength [OTC]; Titralac ™ [OTC]; Titralac™ Extra Strength [OTC]; Tums® [OTC]; Tums® 500 [OTC]; Tums® E-X [OTC]; Tums® Extra Strength Sugar Free [OTC]; Tums® Smooth Dissolve [OTC]; Tums® Ultra [OTC]

Therapeutic Category Antacid; Antidote, Hyperphosphatemia; Calcium Salt; Electrolyte Supplement, Oral

Use As an antacid, and treatment and prevention of calcium deficiency or hyperphosphatemia (eg, osteoporosis, osteomalacia, mild/moderate renal insufficiency, hypoparathyroidism, postmenopausal osteoporosis, rickets); has been used to bind phosphate

Contraindications Hypercalcemia, renal calculi, hypophosphatemia

Warnings/Precautions Calcium carbonate absorption is impaired in achlorhydria (common in elderly - use alternate salt, administer with food); administration is followed by increased gastric acid secretion within 2 hours of administration; while hypercalcemia and hypercalciuria may result when therapeutic replacement amounts are given for prolonged periods, they are most likely to occur in hypoparathyroid patients receiving high doses of vitamin D

Common Adverse Reactions Well tolerated

1% to 10%:
Central nervous system: Headache
Endocrine & metabolic: Hypophosphatemia, hypercalcemia
Gastrointestinal: Constipation, laxative effect, acid rebound, nausea, vomiting, anorexia, abdominal pain, xerostomia, flatulence
Miscellaneous: Milk-alkali syndrome with very high, chronic dosing and/or renal failure (headache, nausea, irritability, and weakness or alkalosis, hypercalcemia, renal impairment)

Drug Interactions

Increased Effect/Toxicity: High doses of calcium with thiazide diuretics may result in milk-alkali syndrome and hypercalcemia; monitor response. Calcium salts may decrease T_4 absorption; separate dose from levothyroxine by at least 4 hours. Calcium acetate may potentiate digoxin toxicity.

Decreased Effect: Absorption of tetracycline, atenolol (and potentially other beta-blockers), iron, quinolone antibiotics, alendronate, sodium fluoride, and zinc absorption may be significantly decreased; space administration times. Effects of calcium channel blockers (eg, verapamil) effects may be diminished. Polystyrene sulfonate's potassium-binding ability may be reduced; avoid concurrent administration.

Mechanism of Action As dietary supplement, used to prevent or treat negative calcium balance; in osteoporosis, it helps to prevent or decrease the rate of bone loss. The calcium in calcium salts moderates nerve and muscle performance and allows normal cardiac function. Also used to treat hyperphosphatemia in patients with advanced renal insufficiency by combining with dietary phosphate to form insoluble calcium phosphate, which is excreted in feces. Calcium salts as antacids neutralize gastric acidity resulting in increased gastric an duodenal bulb pH; they additionally inhibit proteolytic activity of peptic if the pH is increased >4 and increase lower esophageal sphincter tone.

Pharmacodynamics/Kinetics

Absorption: Requires vitamin D; minimal unless chronic, high doses are given; calcium is absorbed in soluble, ionized form; solubility of calcium is increased in an acid environment
Distribution: Crosses placenta; enters breast milk
Excretion: Primarily feces (as unabsorbed calcium); urine (20%)

Dosage Oral (dosage is in terms of elemental calcium):

Dietary Reference Intake:
0-6 months: 210 mg/day
7-12 months: 270 mg/day
1-3 years: 500 mg/day
4-8 years: 800 mg/day
Adults, Male/Female:
9-18 years: 1300 mg/day
19-50 years: 1000 mg/day
≥51 years: 1200 mg/day

(Continued)

Calcium Carbonate *(Continued)*

Female: Pregnancy: Same as for Adults, Male/Female

Female: Lactating: Same as for Adults, Male/Female

Hypocalcemia (dose depends on clinical condition and serum calcium level): Dose expressed in mg of **elemental calcium**

Neonates: 50-150 mg/kg/day in 4-6 divided doses; not to exceed 1 g/day

Children: 45-65 mg/kg/day in 4 divided doses

Adults: 1-2 g or more/day in 3-4 divided doses

Adults:

Dietary supplementation: 500 mg to 2 g divided 2-4 times/day

Antacid: Dosage based on acid-neutralizing capacity of specific product; generally, 1-2 tablets or 5-10 mL every 2 hours; maximum: 7000 mg calcium carbonate per 24 hours; specific product labeling should be consulted

Adults >51 years: Osteoporosis: 1200 mg/day

Dosing adjustment in renal impairment: Cl_{cr} <25 mL/minute: Dosage adjustments may be necessary depending on the serum calcium levels

Reference Range

Serum calcium: 8.4-10.2 mg/dL: Monitor plasma calcium levels if using calcium salts as electrolyte supplements for deficiency

Due to a poor correlation between the serum ionized calcium (free) and total serum calcium, particularly in states of low albumin or acid/base imbalances, direct measurement of ionized calcium is recommended

In low albumin states, the corrected **total** serum calcium may be estimated by: Corrected total calcium = total serum calcium + 0.8 (4.0 - measured serum albumin)

Patient Information Shake suspension well; chew tablets thoroughly; take with large quantities of water or juice; do not take calcium supplements within 1-2 hours of taking other medicine by mouth or eating large amounts of fiber-rich foods; do not take other antacids or calcium supplements or drink large amounts of alcohol or caffeine-containing beverages; if the maximum dosage of antacids is required for >2 weeks, consult your prescriber

Dosage Forms CAP: 364 mg; 1250 mg. **POWDER:** 1600 mg/teaspoonful. **SUSP, oral:** 1250 mg/5 mL. **TAB:** 364 mg; 1250 mg; 1500 mg. **TAB, chewable:** 400 mg; 420 mg; 500 mg; 650 mg; 750 mg; 850 mg; 1000 mg; 1250 mg

Calcium Carbonate and Magnesium Hydroxide

(KAL see um KAR bun ate & mag NEE zhum hye DROKS ide)

U.S. Brand Names Mylanta® Gelcaps® [OTC]; Mylanta® Supreme [OTC]; Mylanta® Ultra [OTC]; Rolaids® [OTC]; Rolaids®, Extra Strength [OTC]

Synonyms Magnesium Hydroxide and Calcium Carbonate

Therapeutic Category Antacid

Use Hyperacidity

Dosage Adults: Oral: 2-4 tablets between meals, at bedtime, or as directed by healthcare provider

Dosage Forms GELCAP: Calcium 550 mg and magnesium 125 mg. **SUSP, oral:** Calcium 400 mg and magnesium 135 mg per 5 mL (30 mL, 360 mL, 720 mL). **TAB, chewable:** Calcium 550 mg and magnesium 110 mg; calcium 675 mg and magnesium 135 mg; calcium 700 mg and magnesium 300 mg

♦ **Calcium Carbonate, Magnesium Hydroxide, and Famotidine** *see* Famotidine, Calcium Carbonate, and Magnesium Hydroxide *on page 507*

♦ **Calcium Channel Blockers Comparison** *see page 1371*

Calcium Chloride (KAL see um KLOR ide)

Therapeutic Category Calcium Salt; Electrolyte Supplement, Parenteral

Use Cardiac resuscitation when epinephrine fails to improve myocardial contractions, cardiac disturbances of hyperkalemia, hypocalcemia, or calcium channel blocking agent toxicity; emergent treatment of hypocalcemic tetany, treatment of hypermagnesemia

Pregnancy Risk Factor C

Contraindications In ventricular fibrillation during cardiac resuscitation, hypercalcemia, and in patients with risk of digitalis toxicity, renal or cardiac disease; not recommended in treatment of asystole and electromechanical dissociation

Warnings/Precautions Avoid too rapid I.V. administration (<1 mL/minute) and extravasation; use with caution in digitalized patients, respiratory failure, or acidosis; hypercalcemia may occur in patients with renal failure, and frequent determination of serum calcium is necessary; avoid metabolic acidosis (ie, administer only 2-3 days then change to another calcium salt)

Drug Interactions

Increased Effect/Toxicity: High doses of calcium with thiazide diuretics may result in milk-alkali syndrome and hypercalcemia; monitor response. Calcium may potentiate digoxin toxicity.

Decreased Effect: Effects of calcium channel blockers (eg, verapamil) effects may be diminished.

Mechanism of Action Moderates nerve and muscle performance via action potential excitation threshold regulation

Pharmacodynamics/Kinetics

Distribution: Crosses placenta; enters breast milk

Excretion: Primarily feces (as unabsorbed calcium); urine (20%)

Dosage Note: Calcium chloride is 3 times as potent as calcium gluconate

Cardiac arrest in the presence of hyperkalemia or hypocalcemia, magnesium toxicity, or calcium antagonist toxicity: I.V.:

Infants and Children: 20 mg/kg; may repeat in 10 minutes if necessary

Adults: 2-4 mg/kg (10% solution), repeated every 10 minutes if necessary

Hypocalcemia: I.V.:

Children (manufacturer's recommendation): 2.7-5 mg/kg/dose every 4-6 hours

Alternative pediatric dosing: Infants and Children: 10-20 mg/kg/dose (infants <1 mEq; children 1-7 mEq), repeat every 4-6 hours if needed

Adults: 500 mg to 1 g (7-14 mEq)/dose repeated every 4-6 hours if needed

Hypocalcemic tetany: I.V.:

Infants and Children: 10 mg/kg (0.5-0.7 mEq/kg) over 5-10 minutes; may repeat after 6-8 hours or follow with an infusion with a maximum dose of 200 mg/kg/day

Adults: 1 g over 10-30 minutes; may repeat after 6 hours

Hypocalcemia secondary to citrated blood transfusion: I.V.:

Neonates, Infants, and Children: Give 0.45 mEq **elemental** calcium for each 100 mL citrated blood infused

Adults: 1.35 mEq calcium with each 100 mL of citrated blood infused

Dosing adjustment in renal impairment: Cl_{cr} <25 mL/minute: Dosage adjustments may be necessary depending on the serum calcium levels

Administration Rapid I.V. injection at a maximum rate of 50 mg/minute; for I.V. infusion, dilute to a maximum concentration of 20 mg/mL and infuse over 1 hour or no greater than 45-90 mg/kg/hour (0.6-1.2 mEq/kg/hour); administration via a central or deep vein is preferred

Reference Range

Serum calcium: 8.4-10.2 mg/dL

Due to a poor correlation between the serum ionized calcium (free) and total serum calcium, particularly in states of low albumin or acid/base imbalances, direct measurement of ionized calcium is recommended

In low albumin states, the corrected **total** serum calcium may be estimated by this equation (assuming a normal albumin of 4 g/dL)

Corrected total calcium = total serum calcium + 0.8 (4.0 - measured serum albumin)

or

Corrected calcium = measured calcium - measured albumin + 4.0

Serum/plasma chloride: 95-108 mEq/L

Dosage Forms INJ [preservative free]: 10% [100 mg/mL] (10 mL)

Calcium Citrate (KAL see um SIT rate)

U.S. Brand Names Cal-Citrate® 250 [OTC]; Citracal® [OTC]; Citracal® Liquitab [OTC]

Therapeutic Category Calcium Salt

Use Antacid; treatment and prevention of calcium deficiency or hyperphosphatemia (eg, osteoporosis, osteomalacia, mild/moderate renal insufficiency, hypoparathyroidism, postmenopausal osteoporosis, rickets)

Pregnancy Risk Factor C

Dosage Oral: Dosage is in terms of elemental calcium

Dietary Reference Intake:

0-6 months: 210 mg/day

7-12 months: 270 mg/day

1-3 years: 500 mg/day

4-8 years: 800 mg/day

Adults, Male/Female:

9-18 years: 1300 mg/day

19-50 years: 1000 mg/day

≥51 years: 1200 mg/day

Female: Pregnancy: Same as for Adults, Male/Female

Female: Lactating: Same as for Adults, Male/Female

Dietary supplement: Usual dose: 500 mg to 2 g 2-4 times/day

Dosage Forms GRAN: 760 mg/teaspoonful (480 g). **TAB:** Elemental calcium 250 mg; (Cal-Citrate®): Elemental calcium 250 mg; (Citracal®): 950 mg. **TAB, effervescent** (Citracal® Liquitab): 2376 mg

♦ **Calcium Disodium Edetate** see Edetate Calcium Disodium on page 421

♦ **Calcium Disodium Versenate®** see Edetate Calcium Disodium on page 421

♦ **Calcium EDTA** see Edetate Calcium Disodium on page 421

Calcium Glubionate (KAL see um gloo BYE oh nate)

Therapeutic Category Calcium Salt

Use Adjunct in treatment and prevention of postmenopausal osteoporosis; treatment and prevention of calcium depletion or hyperphosphatemia (eg, osteoporosis, osteomalacia, mild/moderate renal insufficiency, hypoparathyroidism, rickets)

Pregnancy Risk Factor C

Dosage Dosage is in terms of **elemental** calcium

Dietary Reference Intake:

0-6 months: 210 mg/day

7-12 months: 270 mg/day

1-3 years: 500 mg/day

4-8 years: 800 mg/day

(Continued)

Calcium Glubionate *(Continued)*

Adults, Male/Female:
9-18 years: 1300 mg/day
19-50 years: 1000 mg/day
≥51 years: 1200 mg/day
Female: Pregnancy: Same as for Adults, Male/Female
Female: Lactating: Same as for Adults, Male/Female

Syrup is a hyperosmolar solution; dosage is in terms of calcium glubionate, elemental calcium is in parentheses
Neonatal hypocalcemia: 1200 mg (77 mg Ca^{++})/kg/day in 4-6 divided doses
Maintenance: Infants and Children: 600-2000 mg (38-128 mg Ca^{++})/kg/day in 4 divided doses up to a maximum of 9 g (575 mg Ca^{++})/day
Adults: 6-18 g (~0.5-1 g Ca^{++})/day in divided doses
Dosing adjustment in renal impairment: Cl_{cr} <25 mL/minute: Dosage adjustments may be necessary depending on the serum calcium levels
Dosage Forms SYR: 1.8 g/5 mL (480 mL)

Calcium Gluceptate *(KAL see um gloo SEP tate)*

Therapeutic Category Calcium Salt; Electrolyte Supplement, Parenteral

Use Treatment of cardiac disturbances of hyperkalemia, hypocalcemia, or calcium channel blocker toxicity; cardiac resuscitation when epinephrine fails to improve myocardial contractions; treatment of hypermagnesemia and hypocalcemia

Pregnancy Risk Factor C

Dosage Dose expressed in mg of calcium gluceptate (elemental calcium is in parentheses)
Cardiac resuscitation in the presence of hypocalcemia, hyperkalemia, magnesium toxicity, or calcium channel blocker toxicity: I.V.:
Children: 110 mg (9 mg Ca^{++})/kg/dose
Adults: 1.1-1.5 g (90-123 mg Ca^{++})
Hypocalcemia:
I.M.:
Children: 200-500 mg (16.4-41 mg Ca^{++})/kg/day divided every 6 hours
Adults: 500 mg to 1.1 g/dose as needed
I.V.: Adults: 1.1-4.4 g (90-360 mg Ca^{++}) administered slowly as needed (≤2 mL/minute)
After citrated blood administration: Children and Adults: I.V.: 0.45 mEq Ca^{++}/100 mL blood infused
Dosing adjustment in renal impairment: Cl_{cr} <25 mL/minute: Dosage adjustments may be necessary depending on the serum calcium levels

Calcium Gluconate *(KAL see um GLOO koe nate)*

Therapeutic Category Calcium Salt; Electrolyte Supplement, Oral; Electrolyte Supplement, Parenteral

Use Treatment and prevention of hypocalcemia; treatment of tetany, cardiac disturbances of hyperkalemia, cardiac resuscitation when epinephrine fails to improve myocardial contractions, hypocalcemia, or calcium channel blocker toxicity; calcium supplementation

Pregnancy Risk Factor C

Contraindications In ventricular fibrillation during cardiac resuscitation; patients with risk of digitalis toxicity, renal or cardiac disease, hypercalcemia, renal calculi, hypophosphatemia

Warnings/Precautions Avoid too rapid I.V. administration and avoid extravasation. Use with caution in digitalized patients, severe hyperphosphatemia, respiratory failure or acidosis. May produce cardiac arrest. Hypercalcemia may occur in patients with renal failure, frequent determination of serum calcium is necessary.

Drug Interactions

Increased Effect/Toxicity: High doses of calcium with thiazide diuretics may result in milk-alkali syndrome and hypercalcemia; monitor response. Oral administration of calcium salts may decrease T_4 absorption; separate dose from levothyroxine by at least 4 hours. Calcium acetate may potentiate digoxin toxicity.

Decreased Effect: Absorption of tetracycline, atenolol (and potentially other beta-blockers), iron, quinolone antibiotics, alendronate, sodium fluoride, and zinc absorption may be significantly decreased by oral calcium administration; space administration times. Effects of calcium channel blockers (eg, verapamil) effects may be diminished. Polystyrene sulfonate's potassium-binding ability may be reduced; avoid concurrent oral administration.

Mechanism of Action As dietary supplement, used to prevent or treat negative calcium balance; in osteoporosis, it helps to prevent or decrease the rate of bone loss. The calcium in calcium salts moderates nerve and muscle performance and allows normal cardiac function.

Pharmacodynamics/Kinetics
Absorption: Requires vitamin D; minimal unless chronic, high doses are given; calcium is absorbed in soluble, ionized form; solubility of calcium is increased in an acid environment
Distribution: Crosses placenta; enters breast milk
Excretion: Primarily feces (as unabsorbed calcium); urine (20%)

Dosage Dosage is in terms of **elemental** calcium
Dietary Reference Intake:
0-6 months: 210 mg/day
7-12 months: 270 mg/day
1-3 years: 500 mg/day
4-8 years: 800 mg/day

Adults, Male/Female:
   9-18 years: 1300 mg/day
   19-50 years: 1000 mg/day
   ≥51 years: 1200 mg/day
Female: Pregnancy: Same as for Adults, Male/Female
Female: Lactating: Same as for Adults, Male/Female
Dosage expressed in terms of **calcium gluconate**
Hypocalcemia: I.V.:
   Neonates: 200-800 mg/kg/day as a continuous infusion or in 4 divided doses
   Infants and Children: 200-500 mg/kg/day as a continuous infusion or in 4 divided doses
   Adults: 2-15 g/24 hours as a continuous infusion or in divided doses
Hypocalcemia: Oral:
   Children: 200-500 mg/kg/day divided every 6 hours
   Adults: 500 mg to 2 g 2-4 times/day
   Osteoporosis/bone loss: Oral: 1000-1500 mg in divided doses/day
Hypocalcemia secondary to citrated blood infusion: I.V.: Give 0.45 mEq **elemental** calcium for each 100 mL citrated blood infused
Hypocalcemic tetany: I.V.:
   Neonates: 100-200 mg/kg/dose, may follow with 500 mg/kg/day in 3-4 divided doses or as an infusion
   Infants and Children: 100-200 mg/kg/dose (0.5-0.7 mEq/kg/dose) over 5-10 minutes; may repeat every 6-8 hours **or** follow with an infusion of 500 mg/kg/day
   Adults: 1-3 g (4.5-16 mEq) may be administered until therapeutic response occurs
Calcium antagonist toxicity, magnesium intoxication, or cardiac arrest in the presence of hyperkalemia or hypocalcemia: Calcium chloride is recommended calcium salt: I.V.:
   Infants and Children: 60-100 mg/kg/dose (maximum: 3 g/dose)
   Adults: 500-800 mg; maximum: 3 g/dose
Maintenance electrolyte requirements for total parenteral nutrition: I.V.: Daily requirements:
   Adults: 8-16 mEq/1000 kcal/24 hours
Dosing adjustment in renal impairment: Cl_{cr} <25 mL/minute: Dosage adjustments may be necessary depending on the serum calcium levels
Administration Rapid I.V. injection at a maximum rate of 50 mg/minute; for I.V. infusion, dilute to a maximum concentration of 50 mg/mL and infuse over 1 hour or no greater than 120-240 mg/kg/hour (0.6-1.2 mEq calcium/kg/hour)

   Extravasation treatment example: Hyaluronidase: Add 1 mL NS to 150 unit vial to make 150 units/mL of concentration; mix 0.1 mL of above with 0.9 mL NS in 1 mL syringe to make final concentration = 15 units/mL
Reference Range
   Serum calcium: 8.4-10.2 mg/dL: Monitor plasma calcium levels if using calcium salts as electrolyte supplements for deficiency
   Due to a poor correlation between the serum ionized calcium (free) and total serum calcium, particularly in states of low albumin or acid/base imbalances, direct measurement of ionized calcium is recommended
   In low albumin states, the corrected **total** serum calcium may be estimated by: Corrected total calcium = total serum calcium + 0.8 (4.0 - measured serum albumin)
Patient Information Do not take calcium supplements within 1-2 hours of taking other medicine by mouth or eating large amounts of fiber-rich foods; do not drink large amounts of alcohol or caffeine-containing beverages; take with food
Dosage Forms INJ, solution [preservative free]: 10% [100 mg/mL] (10 mL, 50 mL, 100 mL, 200 mL). **POWDER:** 347 mg/tablespoonful (480 g). **TAB:** 500 mg, 650 mg, 975 mg

- ◆ **Calcium Leucovorin** see Leucovorin on page 723
- ◆ **CaldeCORT® [OTC]** see Hydrocortisone on page 632
- ◆ **Calderol® [DSC]** see Calcifediol on page 199

Calfactant (kaf AKT ant)
U.S. Brand Names Infasurf®
Therapeutic Category Lung Surfactant
Use Prevention of respiratory distress syndrome (RDS) in premature infants at high risk for RDS and for the treatment ("rescue") of premature infants who develop RDS

   Prophylaxis: Therapy at birth with calfactant is indicated for premature infants <29 weeks of gestational age at significant risk for RDS. Should be administered as soon as possible, preferably within 30 minutes after birth.
   Treatment: For infants ≤72 hours of age with RDS (confirmed by clinical and radiologic findings) and requiring endotracheal intubation.
Warnings/Precautions Rapidly affects oxygenation and lung compliance and should be restricted to highly supervised use in a clinical setting with immediate availability of clinicians experienced with intubation and ventilatory management of premature infants; if transient episodes of bradycardia and decreased oxygen saturation occur, discontinue the dosing procedure and initiate measures to alleviate the condition; produces rapid improvement in lung oxygenation and compliance that may require immediate reductions in ventilator settings and FiO_2; for intratracheal administration only
Common Adverse Reactions
   Cardiovascular: Bradycardia (34%), cyanosis (65%)
   Respiratory: Airway obstruction (39%), reflux (21%), requirement for manual ventilation (16%), reintubation (1% to 10%)
   (Continued)

Calfactant *(Continued)*

Mechanism of Action Endogenous lung surfactant is essential for effective ventilation because it modifies alveolar surface tension, thereby stabilizing the alveoli. Lung surfactant deficiency is the cause of respiratory distress syndrome (RDS) in premature infants and lung surfactant restores surface activity to the lungs of these infants.

Pharmacodynamics/Kinetics No human studies of absorption, biotransformation, or excretion have been performed

Dosage Intratracheal administration **only**: Each dose is 3 mL/kg body weight at birth; should be administered every 12 hours for a total of up to 3 doses

Administration Gentle swirling or agitation of the vial is often necessary for redispersion as injection suspension settles during storage; do **not** shake; visible flecks in the suspension and foaming at the surface are normal; does not require reconstitution; do not dilute or sonicate

Should be administered intratracheally through an endotracheal tube. Dose is drawn into a syringe from the single-use vial using a 20-gauge or larger needle with care taken to avoid excessive foaming. Should be administered in 2 aliquots of 1.5 mL/kg each. After each aliquot is instilled, the infant should be positioned with either the right or the left side dependent. Administration is made while ventilation is continued over 20-30 breaths for each aliquot, with small bursts timed only during the inspiratory cycles. A pause followed by evaluation of the respiratory status and repositioning should separate the two aliquots.

Monitoring Parameters Following administration, patients should be carefully monitored so that oxygen therapy and ventilatory support can be modified in response to changes in respiratory status

Dosage Forms SUSP, intratracheal: [preservative free] 35 mg/mL (6 mL)

- ♦ **Cal-Gest [OTC]** *see* Calcium Carbonate *on page 203*
- ♦ **Cal-Mint [OTC]** *see* Calcium Carbonate *on page 203*
- ♦ **Caltrate® 600 [OTC]** *see* Calcium Carbonate *on page 203*
- ♦ **Campath®** *see* Alemtuzumab *on page 50*
- ♦ **Campath-1H** *see* Alemtuzumab *on page 50*
- ♦ **Camphorated Tincture of Opium** *see* Paregoric *on page 957*
- ♦ **Camptosar®** *see* Irinotecan *on page 687*
- ♦ **Camptothecin-11** *see* Irinotecan *on page 687*
- ♦ **Canasa™** *see* Mesalamine *on page 798*
- ♦ **Cancidas®** *see* Caspofungin *on page 227*

Candesartan *(kan de SAR tan)*

Related Information
Angiotensin Agents Comparison *on page 1353*

U.S. Brand Names Atacand®

Synonyms Candesartan Cilexetil

Therapeutic Category Angiotensin II Receptor Antagonist (ARB); Antihypertensive Agent

Use Alone or in combination with other antihypertensive agents in treating essential hypertension

Unlabeled/Investigational Use Congestive heart failure

Pregnancy Risk Factor C/D (2nd and 3rd trimesters)

Contraindications Hypersensitivity to candesartan or any component of the formulation; hypersensitivity to other A-II receptor antagonists; bilateral renal artery stenosis; pregnancy (2nd and 3rd trimesters)

Warnings/Precautions Avoid use or use smaller dose in volume-depleted patients. Drugs which alter renin-angiotensin system have been associated with deterioration in renal function, including oliguria, acute renal failure and progressive azotemia. Use with caution in patients with renal artery stenosis (unilateral or bilateral) to avoid decrease in renal function; use caution in patients with pre-existing renal insufficiency (may decrease renal perfusion).

Common Adverse Reactions May be associated with worsening of renal function in patients dependent on renin-angiotensin-aldosterone system.

Cardiovascular: Flushing, tachycardia, palpitations, angina, MI
Central nervous system: Dizziness, lightheadedness, drowsiness, headache, vertigo, anxiety, depression, somnolence, fever
Dermatologic: Angioedema, rash
Endocrine & metabolic: Hyperglycemia, hypertriglyceridemia, hyperuricemia
Genitourinary: Hematuria
Neuromuscular & skeletal: Back pain, increased CPK, weakness
Respiratory: Upper respiratory tract infection, bronchitis, epistaxis
Miscellaneous: Diaphoresis (increased)

Drug Interactions

Cytochrome P450 Effect: Substrate of CYP2C8/9 (minor); **Inhibits** CYP2C8/9 (weak)

Increased Effect/Toxicity: The risk of lithium toxicity may be increased by candesartan; monitor lithium levels. Concurrent use with potassium-sparing diuretics (amiloride, spironolactone, triamterene), potassium supplements, or trimethoprim (high-dose) may increase the risk of hyperkalemia.

Mechanism of Action Candesartan is an angiotensin receptor antagonist. Angiotensin II acts as a vasoconstrictor. In addition to causing direct vasoconstriction, angiotensin II also stimulates the release of aldosterone. Once aldosterone is released, sodium as well as water are reabsorbed. The end result is an elevation in blood pressure. Candesartan binds to the AT1 angiotensin II receptor. This binding prevents angiotensin II from binding to the receptor thereby blocking the vasoconstriction and the aldosterone secreting effects of angiotensin II.

Pharmacodynamics/Kinetics
Onset of action: 2-3 hours
Peak effect: 6-8 hours
Duration: >24 hours
Distribution: V_d: 0.13 L/kg
Protein binding: 99%
Metabolism: To candesartan by the intestinal wall cells
Bioavailability: 15%
Half-life elimination (dose dependent): 5-9 hours
Time to peak: 3-4 hours
Excretion: Urine (26%)
Clearance: Total body: 0.37 mL/kg/minute; Renal: 0.19 mL/kg/minute

Dosage Adults: Oral:
Hypertension: Usual dose is 4-32 mg once daily; dosage must be individualized. Blood pressure response is dose-related over the range of 2-32 mg. The usual recommended starting dose of 16 mg once daily when it is used as monotherapy in patients who are not volume depleted. It can be administered once or twice daily with total daily doses ranging from 8-32 mg. Larger doses do not appear to have a greater effect and there is relatively little experience with such doses.
Congestive heat failure (unlabeled use): Target dose: 32 mg
Elderly: No initial dosage adjustment is necessary for elderly patients (although higher concentrations (C_{max}) and AUC were observed in these populations), for patients with mildly impaired renal function, or for patients with mildly impaired hepatic function.
Dosage adjustment in hepatic impairment: No initial dosage adjustment required in mild hepatic impairment. Consider initiation at lower dosages in moderate hepatic impairment (AUC increased by 145%). No data available concerning dosing in severe hepatic impairment.

Monitoring Parameters Supine blood pressure, electrolytes, serum creatinine, BUN, urinalysis, symptomatic hypotension, and tachycardia
Dosage Forms TAB: 4 mg, 8 mg, 16 mg, 32 mg

Candesartan and Hydrochlorothiazide
(kan de SAR tan & hye droe klor oh THYE a zide)
U.S. Brand Names Atacand HCT™
Synonyms Candesartan Cilexetil and Hydrochlorothiazide
Therapeutic Category Angiotensin II Antagonist/Thiazide Diuretic Combination
Use Treatment of hypertension; combination product should not be used for initial therapy
Pregnancy Risk Factor C/D (2nd and 3rd trimesters)
Dosage Oral: Adults: Replacement therapy: Combination product can be substituted for individual agents; maximum therapeutic effect would be expected within 4 weeks
Usual dosage range:
Candesartan: 8-32 mg/day, given once daily or twice daily in divided doses
Hydrochlorothiazide: 12.5-50 mg once daily
Dosage adjustment in renal impairment: Serum levels of candesartan are increased and the half-life of hydrochlorothiazide is prolonged in patients with renal impairment. Do not use if Cl_{cr} <30 mL/minute
Dosage adjustment in hepatic impairment: Use with caution
Elderly: No initial dosage adjustment is recommended in patients with normal renal and hepatic function; some patients may have increased sensitivity
Dosage Forms TAB: (16-12.5): Candesartan 16 mg and hydrochlorothiazide 12.5 mg; (32-12.5): Candesartan 32 mg and hydrochlorothiazide 12.5 mg

♦ **Candesartan Cilexetil** *see* Candesartan *on page 208*
♦ **Candesartan Cilexetil and Hydrochlorothiazide** *see* Candesartan and Hydrochlorothiazide *on page 209*
♦ **Cankaid® [OTC]** *see* Carbamide Peroxide *on page 216*
♦ **Capastat® Sulfate** *see* Capreomycin *on page 211*

Capecitabine (ka pe SITE a been)
U.S. Brand Names Xeloda®
Therapeutic Category Antineoplastic Agent, Antimetabolite (Pyrimidine)
Use Treatment of metastatic colorectal cancer, metastatic breast cancer
Pregnancy Risk Factor D
Contraindications Hypersensitivity to capecitabine, fluorouracil, or any component of the formulation; known deficiency of dihydropyrimidine dehydrogenase (DPD); severe renal impairment (Cl_{cr} <30 mL/minute); pregnancy
Warnings/Precautions The U.S. Food and Drug Administration (FDA) currently recommends that procedures for proper handling and disposal of antineoplastic agents be considered. Use with caution in patients with bone marrow suppression, poor nutritional status, on warfarin therapy, ≥80 years of age, or renal or hepatic dysfunction. Use with caution in patients who have received extensive pelvic radiation or alkylating therapy. Use cautiously with warfarin; altered coagulation parameters and bleeding have been reported.

Capecitabine can cause severe diarrhea; median time to first occurrence is 31 days; subsequent doses should be reduced after grade 3 or 4 diarrhea
(Continued)

Capecitabine *(Continued)*

Hand-and-foot syndrome (palmar-plantar erythrodysesthesia or chemotherapy-induced acral erythema) is characterized by numbness, dysesthesia/paresthesia, tingling, painless or painful swelling, erythema, desquamation, blistering, and severe pain. If grade 2 or 3 hand-and-foot syndrome occurs, interrupt administration of capecitabine until the event resolves or decreases in intensity to grade 1. Following grade 3 hand-and-foot syndrome, decrease subsequent doses of capecitabine.

There has been cardiotoxicity associated with fluorinated pyrimidine therapy, including myocardial infarction, angina, dysrhythmias, cardiogenic shock, sudden death, and ECG changes. These adverse events may be more common in patients with a history of coronary artery disease.

Common Adverse Reactions Frequency listed derived from monotherapy trials.
>10%:
  Cardiovascular: Edema (9% to 15%)
  Central nervous system: Fatigue (~40%), fever (12% to 18%), pain (colorectal cancer: 12%)
  Dermatologic: Palmar-plantar erythrodysesthesia (hand-and-foot syndrome) (~55%, may be dose limiting), dermatitis (27% to 37%)
  Gastrointestinal: Diarrhea (~55%, may be dose limiting), mild to moderate nausea (43% to 53%), vomiting (27% to 37%), stomatitis (~25%), decreased appetite (colorectal cancer: 26%), anorexia (23%), abdominal pain (20% to 35%), constipation (~15%)
  Hematologic: Lymphopenia (94%), anemia (72% to 80%; Grade 3/4: <1% to 3%), neutropenia (13% to 26%; Grade 3/4: 1% to 2%), thrombocytopenia (24%; Grade 3/4: 1% to 3%)
  Hepatic: Increased bilirubin (22% to 48%)
  Neuromuscular & skeletal: Paresthesia (21%)
  Ocular: Eye irritation (~15%)
  Respiratory: Dyspnea (colorectal cancer: 14%)
5% to 10%:
  Cardiovascular: Venous thrombosis (colorectal cancer: 8%), chest pain (colorectal cancer: 6%)
  Central nervous system: Headache (~10%), dizziness (~8%), insomnia (8%), mood alteration (colorectal cancer: 5%), depression (colorectal cancer: 5%)
  Dermatologic: Nail disorders (7%), skin discoloration (colorectal cancer: 7%), alopecia (colorectal cancer: 6%)
  Endocrine & metabolic: Dehydration (7%)
  Gastrointestinal: Motility disorder (colorectal cancer: 10%), oral discomfort (colorectal cancer: 10%), dyspepsia (8%), upper GI inflammatory disorders (colorectal cancer: 8%), hemorrhage (colorectal cancer: 6%), ileus (colorectal cancer: 6%), taste disturbance (colorectal cancer: 6%)
  Neuromuscular & skeletal: Back pain (colorectal cancer: 10%), myalgia (9%), neuropathy (colorectal cancer: 10%), arthralgia (colorectal cancer: 8%), limb pain (colorectal cancer: 6%)
  Respiratory: Cough (7%), sore throat (2%), epistaxis (3%)
  Ocular: Abnormal vision (colorectal cancer: 5%)
  Miscellaneous: Viral infection (colorectal cancer: 5%)

Drug Interactions
  Increased Effect/Toxicity: Response to warfarin may be increased by capecitabine.

Mechanism of Action Capecitabine is a prodrug of fluorouracil. It undergoes hydrolysis in the liver and tissues to form fluorouracil which is the active moiety. Fluorouracil is a fluorinated pyrimidine antimetabolite that inhibits thymidylate synthetase, blocking the methylation of deoxyuridylic acid to thymidylic acid, interfering with DNA, and to a lesser degree, RNA synthesis. Fluorouracil appears to be phase specific for the G_1 and S phases of the cell cycle.

Pharmacodynamics/Kinetics
  Absorption: Rapid and extensive
  Protein binding: <60%; 35% to albumin
  Metabolism: Hepatic: Inactive metabolites: 5'-deoxy-5-fluorocytidine, 5'-deoxy-5-fluorouridine; Tissue: Active metabolite: Fluorouracil
  Half-life elimination: 0.5-1 hour
  Time to peak: 1.5 hours; Fluorouracil: 2 hours
  Excretion: Urine (96%, 50% as α-fluoro-β-alanine)

Dosage Oral:
  Adults: 2500 mg/m^2/day in 2 divided doses (~12 hours apart) at the end of a meal for 2 weeks followed by a 1- or 2-week rest period
  Elderly: The elderly may be pharmacodynamically more sensitive to the toxic effects of fluorouracil. Insufficient data are available to provide dosage modifications.

  Dosing adjustment in renal impairment:
    Cl_{cr} 50-80 mL/minute: No adjustment of initial dose
    Cl_{cr} 30-50 mL/minute: Reduce dose by 25%
    Cl_{cr} <30 mL/minute: Do not use
  Dosing adjustment in hepatic impairment:
    Mild to moderate impairment: No starting dose adjustment is necessary; however, carefully monitor patients
    Severe hepatic impairment: Patients have not been studied
  Dosage modification guidelines: See table on next page.

Administration Capecitabine is administered orally, usually in two divided doses taken 12 hours apart. Doses should be taken after meals with water.

Recommended Dose Modifications

Toxicity NCI Grades	During a Course of Therapy	Dose Adjustment for Next Cycle (% of starting dose)
Grade 1	Maintain dose level	Maintain dose level
Grade 2		
1st appearance	Interrupt until resolved to grade 0-1	100%
2nd appearance	Interrupt until resolved to grade 0-1	75%
3rd appearance	Interrupt until resolved to grade 0-1	50%
4th appearance	Discontinue treatment permanently	
Grade 3		
1st appearance	Interrupt until resolved to grade 0-1	75%
2nd appearance	Interrupt until resolved to grade 0-1	50%
3rd appearance	Discontinue treatment permanently	
Grade 4		
1st appearance	Discontinue permanently or If physician deems it to be in the patient's best interest to continue, interrupt until resolved to grade 0-1	50%

Monitoring Parameters Renal function should be estimated at baseline to determine initial dose; during therapy, CBC with differential, hepatic function, and renal function should be monitored

Patient Information Take with food or within 30 minutes after meal. Avoid use of antacids within 2 hours of taking capecitabine. Do not crush, chew, or dissolve tablets. You will need frequent blood tests while taking this medication. Maintain adequate hydration (2-3 L/day of fluids unless instructed to restrict fluid intake). You may experience lethargy, dizziness, visual changes, confusion, anxiety (avoid driving or engaging in tasks requiring alertness until response to drug is known). For nausea, vomiting, loss of appetite, or dry mouth, small, frequent meals, chewing gum, or sucking lozenges may help. You may experience loss of hair (will grow back when treatment is discontinued). You may experience photosensitivity (use sunscreen, wear protective clothing and eyewear, and avoid direct sunlight). You may experience dry, itchy, skin, and dry or irritated eyes (avoid contact lenses). You will be more susceptible to infection; avoid crowds or infected persons. Report chills or fever, confusion, persistent or violent vomiting or stomach pain, persistent diarrhea, respiratory difficulty, chest pain or palpitations, unusual bleeding or bruising, bone pain, muscle spasms/tremors, or vision changes immediately.

Dosage Forms TAB: 150 mg, 500 mg

♦ **Capex™** see Fluocinolone on page 533

♦ **Capital® and Codeine** see Acetaminophen and Codeine on page 25

♦ **Capoten®** see Captopril on page 212

♦ **Capozide®** see Captopril and Hydrochlorothiazide on page 214

Capreomycin (kap ree oh MYE sin)

Related Information
Antimicrobial Drugs of Choice on page 1440
Tuberculosis Treatment Guidelines on page 1466

U.S. Brand Names Capastat® Sulfate

Synonyms Capreomycin Sulfate

Therapeutic Category Antibiotic, Miscellaneous; Antitubercular Agent

Use Treatment of tuberculosis in conjunction with at least one other antituberculosis agent

Pregnancy Risk Factor C

Contraindications Hypersensitivity to capreomycin sulfate or any component of the formulation

Warnings/Precautions Use in patients with renal insufficiency or pre-existing auditory impairment must be undertaken with great caution, and the risk of additional eighth nerve impairment or renal injury should be weighed against the benefits to be derived from therapy. Since other parenteral antituberculous agents (eg, streptomycin) also have similar and sometimes irreversible toxic effects, particularly on eighth cranial nerve and renal function, simultaneous administration of these agents with capreomycin is not recommended. Use with nonantituberculous drugs (ie, aminoglycoside antibiotics) having ototoxic or nephrotoxic potential should be undertaken only with great caution. Use caution with renal dysfunction and in the elderly.

Common Adverse Reactions
>10%:
Otic: Ototoxicity [subclinical hearing loss (11%), clinical loss (3%)], tinnitus
Renal: Nephrotoxicity (36%, increased BUN)
1% to 10%: Hematologic: Eosinophilia (dose-related, mild)
(Continued)

Capreomycin *(Continued)*

Drug Interactions
Increased Effect/Toxicity: May increase effect/duration of nondepolarizing neuromuscular blocking agents. Additive toxicity (nephrotoxicity and ototoxicity), respiratory paralysis may occur with aminoglycosides (eg, streptomycin).

Mechanism of Action Capreomycin is a cyclic polypeptide antimicrobial. It is administered as a mixture of capreomycin IA and capreomycin IB. The mechanism of action of capreomycin is not well understood. Mycobacterial species that have become resistant to other agents are usually still sensitive to the action of capreomycin. However, significant cross-resistance with viomycin, kanamycin, and neomycin occurs.

Pharmacodynamics/Kinetics
Half-life elimination: Normal renal function: 4-6 hours
Time to peak, serum: I.M.: ~1 hour
Excretion: Urine (as unchanged drug)

Dosage I.M., I.V.:
Infants and Children: 15-30 mg/kg/day, up to 1 g/day maximum
Adults: 1 g/day (not to exceed 20 mg/kg/day) for 60-120 days, followed by 1 g 2-3 times/week
Elderly: Refer to Adults dosing; use with caution due to the increased potential for pre-existing renal dysfunction or impaired hearing

Dosing interval in renal impairment: Adults:
Cl_{cr} >100 mL/minute: Administer 13-15 mg/kg every 24 hours
Cl_{cr} 80-100 mL/minute: Administer 10-13 mg/kg every 24 hours
Cl_{cr} 60-80 mL/minute: Administer 7-10 mg/kg every 24 hours
Cl_{cr} 40-60 mL/minute: Administer 11-14 mg/kg every 48 hours
Cl_{cr} 20-40 mL/minute: Administer 10-14 mg/kg every 72 hours
Cl_{cr} <20 mL/minute: Administer 4-7 mg/kg every 72 hours

Administration
I.M.: Administer by deep I.M. injection into a large muscle mass.
I.V.: Administer over 60 minutes.

Monitoring Parameters Audiometric measurements and vestibular function at baseline and during therapy; renal function at baseline and weekly during therapy; serum potassium; liver function tests

Reference Range 10 µg/mL

Patient Information Report any hearing loss immediately. Do not discontinue without notifying prescriber.

Dosage Forms INJ, powder for reconstitution: 1 g

♦ **Capreomycin Sulfate** *see* Capreomycin *on page 211*

Captopril *(KAP toe pril)*

Related Information
Angiotensin Agents Comparison *on page 1353*

U.S. Brand Names Capoten®

Synonyms ACE

Therapeutic Category Angiotensin-Converting Enzyme (ACE) Inhibitor; Antihypertensive Agent

Use Management of hypertension; treatment of congestive heart failure, left ventricular dysfunction after myocardial infarction, diabetic nephropathy

Unlabeled/Investigational Use Treatment of hypertensive crisis, rheumatoid arthritis; diagnosis of anatomic renal artery stenosis, hypertension secondary to scleroderma renal crisis; diagnosis of aldosteronism, idiopathic edema, Bartter's syndrome, postmyocardial infarction for prevention of ventricular failure; increase circulation in Raynaud's phenomenon, hypertension secondary to Takayasu's disease

Pregnancy Risk Factor C/D (2nd and 3rd trimesters)

Contraindications Hypersensitivity to captopril or any component of the formulation; angioedema related to previous treatment with an ACE inhibitor; idiopathic or hereditary angioedema; bilateral renal artery stenosis; pregnancy (2nd or 3rd trimester)

Warnings/Precautions Anaphylactic reactions can occur. Angioedema can occur at any time during treatment (especially following first dose). Angioedema may involve head and neck (potentially affecting the airway) or the intestine (presenting with abdominal pain). Careful blood pressure monitoring with first dose (hypotension can occur especially in volume depleted patients). Use with caution in collagen vascular diseases; valvular stenosis (particularly aortic stenosis); hyperkalemia; or before, during, or immediately after anesthesia. Avoid rapid dosage escalation which may lead to renal insufficiency. Neutropenia/agranulocytosis with myeloid hyperplasia can rarely occur. If patient has renal impairment then a baseline WBC with differential and serum creatinine should be evaluated and monitored closely during the first 3 months of therapy. Hypersensitivity reactions may be seen during hemodialysis with high-flux dialysis membranes (eg, AN69). Deterioration in renal function can occur with initiation.

Use with caution and decrease dosage in patients with renal impairment (especially renal artery stenosis), severe CHF, or with coadministered diuretic therapy; experience in children is limited. Severe hypotension may occur in patients who are sodium and/or volume depleted, initiate lower doses and monitor closely when starting therapy in these patients; ACE inhibitors may be preferred agents in elderly patients with CHF and diabetes mellitus (diabetic proteinuria is reduced, minimal CNS effects, and enhanced insulin sensitivity); however, due to decreased renal function, tolerance must be carefully monitored.

Common Adverse Reactions

1% to 10%:

Cardiovascular: Hypotension (1% to 3%), tachycardia (1%), chest pain (1%), palpitation (1%)

Dermatologic: Rash (maculopapular or urticarial) (4% to 7%), pruritus (2%); in patients with rash, a positive ANA and/or eosinophilia has been noted in 7% to 10%.

Endocrine & metabolic: Hyperkalemia (1% to 11%)

Hematologic: Neutropenia may occur in up to 4% of patients with renal insufficiency or or collagen-vascular disease.

Renal: Proteinuria (1%), increased serum creatinine, worsening of renal function (may occur in patients with bilateral renal artery stenosis or hypovolemia)

Respiratory: Cough (<1% to 2%)

Miscellaneous: Hypersensitivity reactions (rash, pruritus, fever, arthralgia, and eosinophilia) have occurred in 4% to 7% of patients (depending on dose and renal function); dysgeusia - loss of taste or diminished perception (2% to 4%)

Frequency not defined:

Cardiovascular: Angioedema, cardiac arrest, cerebrovascular insufficiency, rhythm disturbances, orthostatic hypotension, syncope, flushing, pallor, angina, myocardial infarction, Raynaud's syndrome, CHF

Central nervous system: Ataxia, confusion, depression, nervousness, somnolence

Dermatologic: Bullous pemphigus, erythema multiforme, Stevens-Johnson syndrome, exfoliative dermatitis

Endocrine & metabolic: Increased serum transaminases, increased serum bilirubin, increased alkaline phosphatase, gynecomastia

Gastrointestinal: Pancreatitis, glossitis, dyspepsia

Genitourinary: Urinary frequency, impotence

Hematologic: Anemia, thrombocytopenia, pancytopenia, agranulocytosis, anemia

Hepatic: Jaundice, hepatitis, hepatic necrosis (rare), cholestasis, hyponatremia (symptomatic)

Neuromuscular & skeletal: Asthenia, myalgia, myasthenia

Ocular: Blurred vision

Renal: Renal insufficiency, renal failure, nephrotic syndrome, polyuria, oliguria

Respiratory: Bronchospasm, eosinophilic pneumonitis, rhinitis

Miscellaneous: Anaphylactoid reactions

Drug Interactions

Cytochrome P450 Effect: Substrate of CYP2D6 (major)

Increased Effect/Toxicity: Potassium supplements, co-trimoxazole (high dose), angiotensin II receptor antagonists (candesartan, losartan, irbesartan, etc) or potassium-sparing diuretics (amiloride, spironolactone, triamterene) may result in elevated serum potassium levels when combined with captopril. CYP2D6 inhibitors may increase the levels/effects of captopril; example inhibitors include chlorpromazine, delavirdine, fluoxetine, miconazole, paroxetine, pergolide, quinidine, quinine, ritonavir, and ropinirole. ACE inhibitor effects may be increased by phenothiazines or probenecid (increases levels of captopril). ACE inhibitors may increase serum concentrations/effects of digoxin, lithium, and sulfonlyureas.

Diuretics have additive hypotensive effects with ACE inhibitors, and hypovolemia increases the potential for adverse renal effects of ACE inhibitors. In patients with compromised renal function, coadministration with NSAIDs may result in further deterioration of renal function. Allopurinol and ACE inhibitors may cause a higher risk of hypersensitivity reaction when taken concurrently.

Decreased Effect: Aspirin (high dose) may reduce the therapeutic effects of ACE inhibitors; at low dosages this does not appear to be significant. Rifampin may decrease the effect of ACE inhibitors. Antacids may decrease the bioavailability of ACE inhibitors (may be more likely to occur with captopril); separate administration times by 1-2 hours. NSAIDs, specifically indomethacin, may reduce the hypotensive effects of ACE inhibitors. More likely to occur in low renin or volume dependent hypertensive patients.

Mechanism of Action Competitive inhibitor of angiotensin-converting enzyme (ACE); prevents conversion of angiotensin I to angiotensin II, a potent vasoconstrictor; results in lower levels of angiotensin II which causes an increase in plasma renin activity and a reduction in aldosterone secretion

Pharmacodynamics/Kinetics

Onset of action: Peak effect: Blood pressure reduction: 1-1.5 hours after dose

Duration: Dose related, may require several weeks of therapy before full hypotensive effect

Absorption: 60% to 75%; reduced 30% to 40% by food

Protein binding: 25% to 30%

Metabolism: 50%

Half-life elimination (renal and cardiac function dependent):

Adults, healthy volunteers: 1.9 hours; Congestive heart failure: 2.06 hours; Anuria: 20-40 hours

Excretion: Urine (95%) within 24 hours

Dosage Note: Dosage must be titrated according to patient's response; use lowest effective dose. Oral:

Infants: Initial: 0.15-0.3 mg/kg/dose; titrate dose upward to maximum of 6 mg/kg/day in 1-4 divided doses; usual required dose: 2.5-6 mg/kg/day

Children: Initial: 0.5 mg/kg/dose; titrate upward to maximum of 6 mg/kg/day in 2-4 divided doses

Older Children: Initial: 6.25-12.5 mg/dose every 12-24 hours; titrate upward to maximum of 6 mg/kg/day

(Continued)

Captopril *(Continued)*

Adolescents: Initial: 12.5-25 mg/dose given every 8-12 hours; increase by 25 mg/dose to maximum of 450 mg/day

Adults:

Acute hypertension (urgency/emergency): 12.5-25 mg, may repeat as needed (may be given sublingually, but no therapeutic advantage demonstrated)

Hypertension:

Initial dose: 12.5-25 mg 2-3 times/day; may increase by 12.5-25 mg/dose at 1- to 2-week intervals up to 50 mg 3 times/day; add diuretic before further dosage increases

Maximum dose: 150 mg 3 times/day

Congestive heart failure:

Initial dose: 6.25-12.5 mg 3 times/day in conjunction with cardiac glycoside and diuretic therapy; initial dose depends upon patient's fluid/electrolyte status

Target dose: 50 mg 3 times/day

Maximum dose: 150 mg 3 times/day

LVD after MI: Initial dose: 6.25 mg followed by 12.5 mg 3 times/day; then increase to 25 mg 3 times/day during next several days and then over next several weeks to target dose of 50 mg 3 times/day

Diabetic nephropathy: 25 mg 3 times/day; other antihypertensives often given concurrently

Dosing adjustment in renal impairment:

Cl_{cr} 10-50 mL/minute: Administer at 75% of normal dose.

Cl_{cr} <10 mL/minute: Administer at 50% of normal dose.

Note: Smaller dosages given every 8-12 hours are indicated in patients with renal dysfunction; renal function and leukocyte count should be carefully monitored during therapy.

Hemodialysis: Moderately dialyzable (20% to 50%); administer dose postdialysis or administer 25% to 35% supplemental dose.

Peritoneal dialysis: Supplemental dose is not necessary.

Monitoring Parameters BUN, serum creatinine, urine dipstick for protein, complete leukocyte count, and blood pressure

Patient Information Take 1 hour before meals. Do not stop therapy except under prescriber advice. Report if you develop sore throat, fever, swelling, rash, difficult breathing, irregular heartbeats, chest pains, or cough. May cause dizziness, fainting, and lightheadedness, especially in first week of therapy; sit and stand up slowly; do not add a salt substitute (potassium) without advice of prescriber.

Dosage Forms TAB: 12.5 mg, 25 mg, 50 mg, 100 mg

Captopril and Hydrochlorothiazide

(KAP toe pril & hye droe klor oh THYE a zide)

U.S. Brand Names Capozide®

Synonyms Hydrochlorothiazide and Captopril

Therapeutic Category Angiotensin-Converting Enzyme (ACE) Inhibitor/Thiazide Diuretic; Antihypertensive Agent, Combination

Use Management of hypertension and treatment of congestive heart failure

Pregnancy Risk Factor C/D (2nd and 3rd trimesters)

Dosage Oral: Adults: Hypertension, CHF: May be substituted for previously titrated dosages of the individual components; alternatively, may initiate as follows:

Initial: Single tablet (captopril 25 mg/hydrochlorothiazide 15 mg) taken once daily; daily dose of captopril should not exceed 150 mg; daily dose of hydrochlorothiazide should not exceed 50 mg

Dosage Forms TAB: 25/15: Captopril 25 mg and hydrochlorothiazide 15 mg; 25/25: Captopril 25 mg and hydrochlorothiazide 25 mg; 50/15: Captopril 50 mg and hydrochlorothiazide 15 mg; 50/25: Captopril 50 mg and hydrochlorothiazide 25 mg

♦ **Carac**™ *see Fluorouracil on page 536*

♦ **Carafate**® *see Sucralfate on page 1167*

Carbachol (KAR ba kole)

Related Information

Glaucoma Drug Therapy Comparison *on page 1481*

U.S. Brand Names Carbastat®; Carboptic®; Isopto® Carbachol; Miostat®

Synonyms Carbacholine; Carbamylcholine Chloride

Therapeutic Category Cholinergic Agent, Ophthalmic; Ophthalmic Agent, Miotic

Use Lowers intraocular pressure in the treatment of glaucoma; cause miosis during surgery

Pregnancy Risk Factor C

Dosage Adults:

Ophthalmic: Instill 1-2 drops up to 3 times/day

Intraocular: 0.5 mL instilled into anterior chamber before or after securing sutures

Dosage Forms SOLN, intraocular (Carbastat®, Miostat®): 0.01% (1.5 mL). **SOLN, ophthalmic:** (Carboptic®): 3% (15 mL); (Isopto® Carbachol): 0.75% (15 mL); 1.5% (15 mL, 30 mL); 3% (15 mL, 30 mL)

♦ **Carbacholine** *see Carbachol on page 214*

Carbamazepine (kar ba MAZ e peen)

Related Information

Anticonvulsants by Seizure Type *on page 1358*

Epilepsy *on page 1477*

U.S. Brand Names Carbatrol®; Epitol®; Tegretol®; Tegretol®-XR

Synonyms CBZ

Therapeutic Category Anticonvulsant, Miscellaneous

Use Partial seizures with complex symptomatology (psychomotor, temporal lobe), generalized tonic-clonic seizures (grand mal), mixed seizure patterns; pain relief of trigeminal or glossopharyngeal neuralgia

Unlabeled/Investigational Use Treatment of bipolar disorders and other affective disorders, resistant schizophrenia, ethanol withdrawal, restless leg syndrome, psychotic behavior associated with dementia, post-traumatic stress disorders

Pregnancy Risk Factor D

Contraindications Hypersensitivity to carbamazepine or any component of the formulation; may have cross-sensitivity with tricyclic antidepressants; marrow depression; MAO inhibitor use; pregnancy (may harm fetus)

Warnings/Precautions MAO inhibitors should be discontinued for a minimum of 14 days before carbamazepine is begun; administer with caution to patients with history of cardiac damage or hepatic disease; potentially fatal blood cell abnormalities have been reported following treatment; early detection of hematologic change is important; advise patients of early signs and symptoms including fever, sore throat, mouth ulcers, infections, easy bruising, petechial or purpuric hemorrhage; carbamazepine is not effective in absence, myoclonic or akinetic seizures; exacerbation of certain seizure types have been seen after initiation of carbamazepine therapy in children with mixed seizure disorders. Elderly may have increased risk of SIADH-like syndrome.

Common Adverse Reactions Frequency not defined.

Cardiovascular: Edema, CHF, syncope, bradycardia, hypertension or hypotension, AV block, arrhythmias, thrombophlebitis, thromboembolism, lymphadenopathy

Central nervous system: Sedation, dizziness, fatigue, ataxia, confusion, headache, slurred speech, aseptic meningitis (case report)

Dermatologic: Rash, urticaria, toxic epidermal necrolysis, Stevens-Johnson syndrome, photosensitivity reaction, alterations in skin pigmentation, exfoliative dermatitis, erythema multiforme, purpura, alopecia

Endocrine & metabolic: Hyponatremia, SIADH, fever, chills

Gastrointestinal: Nausea, vomiting, gastric distress, abdominal pain, diarrhea, constipation, anorexia, pancreatitis

Genitourinary: Urinary retention, urinary frequency, azotemia, renal failure, impotence

Hematologic: Aplastic anemia, agranulocytosis, eosinophilia, leukopenia, pancytopenia, thrombocytopenia, bone marrow suppression, acute intermittent porphyria, leukocytosis

Hepatic: Hepatitis, abnormal liver function tests, jaundice, hepatic failure

Neuromuscular & skeletal: Peripheral neuritis

Ocular: Blurred vision, nystagmus, lens opacities, conjunctivitis

Otic: Tinnitus, hyperacusis

Miscellaneous: Hypersensitivity (including multiorgan reactions, may include vasculitis, disorders mimicking lymphoma, eosinophilia, hepatosplenomegaly), diaphoresis

Drug Interactions

Cytochrome P450 Effect: **Substrate** of CYP2C8/9 (minor), 3A4 (major); **Induces** CYP1A2 (strong), 2B6 (strong), 2C8/9 (strong), 2C19 (strong), 3A4 (strong)

Increased Effect/Toxicity: Carbamazepine levels/toxicity may be increased by amprenavir (and possibly other protease inhibitors), cimetidine, clarithromycin, danazol, diltiazem, erythromycin, felbamate, fluoxetine, fluvoxamine, isoniazid, lamotrigine, metronidazole, propoxyphene, verapamil, fluconazole, itraconazole, and ketoconazole. Carbamazepine may enhance the hepatotoxic potential of acetaminophen. Neurotoxicity may result in patients receiving lithium and carbamazepine concurrently. CYP3A4 inhibitors may increase the levels/effects of carbamazepine; example inhibitors include azole antifungals, ciprofloxacin, clarithromycin, diclofenac, doxycycline, erythromycin, imatinib, isoniazid, nefazodone, nicardipine, propofol, protease inhibitors, quinidine, and verapamil.

Decreased Effect: Carbamazepine may decrease the effect of benzodiazepines, citalopram, clozapine, corticosteroids, cyclosporine, doxycycline, ethosuximide, felbamate, felodipine, haloperidol, mebendazole, methadone, oral contraceptives, phenytoin, tacrolimus, theophylline, thyroid hormones, tricyclic antidepressants, valproic acid, and warfarin. Carbamazepine suspension is incompatible with chlorpromazine solution and thioridazine liquid. Schedule carbamazepine suspension at least 1-2 hours apart from other liquid medicinals. Mefloquine may decrease serum concentration of carbamazepine. CYP3A4 inducers may decrease the levels/effects of carbamazepine; example inducers include aminoglutethimide, nafcillin, nevirapine, phenobarbital, phenytoin, and rifamycins.

Mechanism of Action In addition to anticonvulsant effects, carbamazepine has anticholinergic, antineuralgic, antidiuretic, muscle relaxant and antiarrhythmic properties; may depress activity in the nucleus ventralis of the thalamus or decrease synaptic transmission or decrease summation of temporal stimulation leading to neural discharge by limiting influx of sodium ions across cell membrane or other unknown mechanisms; stimulates the release of ADH and potentiates its action in promoting reabsorption of water; chemically related to tricyclic antidepressants

Pharmacodynamics/Kinetics

Absorption: Slow

Distribution: V_d: Neonates: 1.5 L/kg; Children: 1.9 L/kg; Adults: 0.59-2 L/kg

Protein binding: 75% to 90%; may be decreased in newborns

Metabolism: Hepatic to active epoxide metabolite; induces hepatic enzymes to increase metabolism

Bioavailability: 85%

(Continued)

Carbamazepine (Continued)

Half-life elimination: Initial: 18-55 hours; Multiple doses: Children: 8-14 hours; Adults: 12-17 hours

Time to peak, serum: Unpredictable, 4-8 hours

Excretion: Urine (1% to 3% as unchanged drug)

Dosage Oral (dosage must be adjusted according to patient's response and serum concentrations):

Children:

<6 years: Initial: 5 mg/kg/day; dosage may be increased every 5-7 days to 10 mg/kg/day; then up to 20 mg/kg/day if necessary; administer in 2-4 divided doses

6-12 years: Initial: 100 mg twice daily or 10 mg/kg/day in 2 divided doses; increase by 100 mg/day at weekly intervals depending upon response; usual maintenance: 20-30 mg/kg/day in 2-4 divided doses (maximum dose: 1000 mg/day)

Children >12 years and Adults: 200 mg twice daily to start, increase by 200 mg/day at weekly intervals until therapeutic levels achieved; usual dose: 400-1200 mg/day in 2-4 divided doses; maximum dose: 12-15 years: 1000 mg/day, >15 years: 1200 mg/day; some patients have required up to 1.6-2.4 g/day

Trigeminal or glossopharyngeal neuralgia: Initial: 100 mg twice daily with food, gradually increasing in increments of 100 mg twice daily as needed; usual maintenance: 400-800 mg daily in 2 divided doses; maximum dose: 1200 mg/day

Elderly: 100 mg 1-2 times daily, increase in increments of 100 mg/day at weekly intervals until therapeutic level is achieved; usual dose: 400-1000 mg/day

Dosing adjustment in renal impairment: Cl_{cr} <10 mL/minute: Administer 75% of dose

Administration

Suspension dosage form must be given on a 3-4 times/day schedule versus tablets which can be given 2-4 times/day. When carbamazepine suspension has been combined with chlorpromazine or thioridazine solutions a precipitate forms which may result in loss of effect. Therefore, it is recommended that the carbamazepine suspension dosage form not be administered at the same time with other liquid medicinal agents or diluents. Since a given dose of suspension will produce higher peak levels than the same dose given as the tablet form, patients given the suspension should be started on lower doses and increased slowly to avoid unwanted side effects.

Extended release tablets should be inspected for damage. Damaged extended release tablets (without release portal) should not be administered.

Monitoring Parameters CBC with platelet count, reticulocytes, serum iron, liver function tests, urinalysis, BUN, serum carbamazepine levels, thyroid function tests, serum sodium; observe patient for excessive sedation, especially when instituting or increasing therapy

Reference Range

Timing of serum samples: Absorption is slow, peak levels occur 6-8 hours after ingestion of the first dose; the half-life ranges from 8-60 hours, therefore, steady-state is achieved in 2-5 days

Therapeutic levels: 4-12 μg/mL (SI: 25-51 μmol/L)

Toxic concentration: >15 μg/mL; patients who require higher levels of 8-12 μg/mL (SI: 34-51 μmol/L) should be watched closely. Side effects including CNS effects occur commonly at higher dosage levels. If other anticonvulsants are given therapeutic range is 4-8 μg/mL.

Patient Information Take with food; may cause drowsiness; periodic blood test monitoring required; report observe bleeding, bruising, jaundice, abdominal pain, pale stools, mental disturbances, fever, chills, sore throat, or mouth ulcers

Dosage Forms CAP, extended release (Carbatrol®): 200 mg, 300 mg. **SUSP, oral:** 100 mg/5 mL (10 mL, 450 mL); (Tegretol®): 100 mg/5 mL (450 mL). **TAB** (Epitol®, Tegretol®): 200 mg. **TAB, chewable** (Tegretol®): 100 mg. **TAB, extended release** (Tegretol®-XR): 100 mg, 200 mg, 400 mg

♦ **Carbamide** see Urea on page 1282

Carbamide Peroxide (KAR ba mide per OKS ide)

U.S. Brand Names Bausch & Lomb Earwax Removal [OTC]; Cankaid® [OTC]; Debrox® [OTC]; Dent's Ear Wax [OTC]; E•R•O [OTC]; Gly-Oxide® [OTC]; Murine® Ear [OTC]; Orajel® Perioseptic® Spot Treatment [OTC]

Synonyms Urea Peroxide

Therapeutic Category Otic Agent, Cerumenolytic

Use Relief of minor inflammation of gums, oral mucosal surfaces and lips including canker sores and dental irritation; emulsify and disperse ear wax

Pregnancy Risk Factor C

Dosage Children and Adults:

Oral solution (should not be used for >7 days): Oral preparation should not be used in children <2 years of age; apply several drops undiluted on affected area 4 times/day after meals and at bedtime; expectorate after 2-3 minutes **or** place 10 drops onto tongue, mix with saliva, swish for several minutes, expectorate

Otic:

Children <12 years: Tilt head sideways and individualize the dose according to patient size; 3 drops (range: 1-5 drops) twice daily for up to 4 days, tip of applicator should not enter ear canal; keep drops in ear for several minutes by keeping head tilted and placing cotton in ear

Children ≥12 years and Adults: Tilt head sideways and instill 5-10 drops twice daily up to 4 days, tip of applicator should not enter ear canal; keep drops in ear for several minutes by keeping head tilted and placing cotton in ear

Dosage Forms SOLN, oral: 10% (60 mL); (Cankaid®): 10% (22 mL); (Gly-Oxide®): 10% (15 mL, 60 mL); (Orajel® Perioseptic® Spot Treatment): 15% (13.3 mL). SOLN, otic: 6.5% (15 mL); (Bausch & Lomb Earwax Removal, Dent's Ear Wax, E•R•O, Murine® Ear:) 6.5% (15 mL); (Debrox®): 6.5% (15 mL, 30 mL)

♦ Carbamylcholine Chloride *see* Carbachol *on page 214*

♦ Carbastat® *see* Carbachol *on page 214*

♦ Carbatrol® *see* Carbamazepine *on page 214*

♦ Carbaxefed DM RF *see* Carbinoxamine, Pseudoephedrine, and Dextromethorphan *on page 219*

♦ Carbaxefed RF *see* Carbinoxamine and Pseudoephedrine *on page 218*

Carbenicillin (kar ben i SIL in)
U.S. Brand Names Geocillin®
Synonyms Carbenicillin Indanyl Sodium; Carindacillin
Therapeutic Category Antibiotic, Penicillin
Use Treatment of serious urinary tract infections and prostatitis caused by susceptible gram-negative aerobic bacilli
Pregnancy Risk Factor B
Contraindications Hypersensitivity to carbenicillin, penicillins, or any component of the formulation
Warnings/Precautions Do not use in patients with severe renal impairment (Cl_{cr} <10 mL/minute); dosage modification required in patients with impaired renal and/or hepatic function. Use with caution in patients with history of hypersensitivity to cephalosporins.
Common Adverse Reactions
>10%: Gastrointestinal: Diarrhea
1% to 10%: Gastrointestinal: Nausea, bad taste, vomiting, flatulence, glossitis
Drug Interactions
Increased Effect/Toxicity: Increased bleeding effects if taken with high doses of heparin or oral anticoagulants. Aminoglycosides may be synergistic against selected organisms. Penicillins may increase the exposure to methotrexate during concurrent therapy; monitor. Probenecid and disulfiram may increase levels of penicillins (carbenicillin).
Decreased Effect: Decreased effectiveness with tetracyclines. Although anecdotal reports suggest oral contraceptive efficacy could be reduced by penicillins, this has been refuted by more rigorous scientific and clinical data.
Mechanism of Action Inhibits bacterial cell wall synthesis by binding to one or more of the penicillin binding proteins (PBPs); which in turn inhibits the final transpeptidation step of peptidoglycan synthesis in bacterial cell walls, thus inhibiting cell wall biosynthesis. Bacteria eventually lyse due to ongoing activity of cell wall autolytic enzymes (autolysins and murein hydrolases) while cell wall assembly is arrested.
Pharmacodynamics/Kinetics
Absorption: 30% to 40%
Distribution: Crosses placenta; small amounts enter breast milk; distributes into bile; low concentrations attained in CSF
Protein binding: ~50%
Half-life elimination: Children: 0.8-1.8 hours; Adults: 1-1.5 hours, prolonged to 10-20 hours with renal insufficiency
Time to peak, serum: Normal renal function: 0.5-2 hours; concentrations are inadequate for treatment of systemic infections
Excretion: Urine (~80% to 99% as unchanged drug)
Dosage Oral:
Children: 30-50 mg/kg/day divided every 6 hours; maximum dose: 2-3 g/day
Adults: 1-2 tablets every 6 hours for urinary tract infections or 2 tablets every 6 hours for prostatitis
Dosing interval in renal impairment: Adults:
Cl_{cr} 10-50 mL/minute: Administer 382-764 mg every 12-24 hours
Cl_{cr} <10 mL/minute: Administer 382-764 mg every 24-48 hours
Moderately dialyzable (20% to 50%)
Monitoring Parameters Renal, hepatic, and hematologic function tests
Reference Range Therapeutic: Not established; Toxic: >250 µg/mL (SI: >660 µmol/L)
Patient Information Tablets have a bitter taste; take with a full glass of water, preferably on an empty stomach; take all medication for 7-14 days, do not skip doses
Dosage Forms TAB, film coated: 382 mg

♦ Carbenicillin Indanyl Sodium *see* Carbenicillin *on page 217*

Carbetapentane and Pseudoephedrine
(kar bay ta PEN tane & soo doe e FED rin)
U.S. Brand Names Respi-Tann™
Synonyms Carbetapentane Tannate and Pseudoephedrine Tannate; Pseudoephedrine and Carbetapentane
Therapeutic Category Antitussive/Decongestant
Use Relief of cough and congestion due to the common cold, influenza, sinusitis, or bronchitis
Pregnancy Risk Factor C
Dosage Relief of cough and congestion: Oral:
Children:
2-6 years: $1/2$ tablet or 2.5 mL suspension every 12 hours (maximum 4 doses/24 hours)
(Continued)

Carbetapentane and Pseudoephedrine *(Continued)*

6-12 years: 1 tablet or 5 mL suspension every 12 hours (maximum: 4 doses/24 hours)
>12 years: Refer to Adults dosing
Adults: 2 tablets or 10 mL suspension every 12 hours (maximum: 4 doses/24 hours)
Dosage Forms SUSP: Carbetapentane 25 mg and pseudoephedrine 75 mg per 5 mL (480 mL). **TAB, chewable:** Carbetapentane 25 mg and pseudoephedrine 75 mg

♦ **Carbetapentane, Ephedrine, Phenylephrine, and Chlorpheniramine** *see* Chlorpheniramine, Ephedrine, Phenylephrine, and Carbetapentane *on page 263*

♦ **Carbetapentane Tannate and Pseudoephedrine Tannate** *see* Carbetapentane and Pseudoephedrine *on page 217*

Carbidopa (kar bi DOE pa)

U.S. Brand Names Lodosyn®
Therapeutic Category Anti-Parkinson's Agent, Dopamine Agonist; Dopaminergic Agent, Antiparkinson's
Use Given with levodopa in the treatment of parkinsonism to enable a lower dosage of levodopa to be used and a more rapid response to be obtained and to decrease side-effects; for details of administration and dosage, see Levodopa; has no effect without levodopa
Pregnancy Risk Factor C
Dosage Oral: Adults: 70-100 mg/day; maximum daily dose: 200 mg
Dosage Forms TAB: 25 mg

♦ **Carbidopa and Levodopa** *see* Levodopa and Carbidopa *on page 732*

♦ **Carbidopa, Levodopa, and Entacapone** *see* Levodopa, Carbidopa, and Entacapone *on page 733*

Carbinoxamine (kar bi NOKS a meen)

U.S. Brand Names Histex™ CT; Histex™ I/E; Histex™ PD
Synonyms Carbinoxamine Maleate
Therapeutic Category Antihistamine
Use Seasonal and perennial allergic rhinitis; urticaria
Pregnancy Risk Factor C
Dosage Oral: Allergic rhinitis/urticaria:
Children:
3-9 months: Histex™ PD: 1 mg (1.25 mL) 4 times/day
9-18 months: Histex™ PD: 1-2 mg (1.25-2.5 mL) 4 times/day
18 months to 2 years: Histex™ PD: 2 mg (2.5 mL) 4 times/day
6-12 years:
Histex™ CT: One-half tablet every 12 hours
Histex™ PD: Refer to Adults dosing
≥12 years: Refer to Adults dosing
Adults:
Histex™ CT, Histex™ I/E: One capsule or tablet every 12 hours; maximum: 2 doses/24 hours
Histex™ PD: 4 mg (5 mL) 4 times/day
Dosage Forms CAP, variable release (Histex™ I/E): Carbinoxamine 2 mg [immediate release] and carbinoxamine 8 mg [extended release]. **LIQ:** Carbinoxamine 4 mg/5 mL (480 mL); (Histex™ PD): Carbinoxamine 4 mg/5 mL (480 mL). **TAB, timed release** (Histex™ CT): Carbinoxamine 8 mg

Carbinoxamine and Pseudoephedrine

(kar bi NOKS a meen & soo doe e FED rin)
U.S. Brand Names Andehist NR Drops; Carbaxefed RF; Hydro-Tussin™-CBX; Palgic®-D; Palgic®-DS; Rondec® Drops; Rondec® Tablets; Rondec-TR®; Sildec
Synonyms Pseudoephedrine and Carbinoxamine
Therapeutic Category Adrenergic Agonist Agent; Antihistamine; Antihistamine/Decongestant
Use Seasonal and perennial allergic rhinitis; vasomotor rhinitis
Pregnancy Risk Factor C
Dosage Oral:
Children:
Drops (Andehist NR, Carbaxefed RF, Rondec®, Sildec):
1-3 months: 0.25 mL 4 times/day
3-6 months: 0.5 mL 4 times/day
6-12 months: 0.75 mL 4 times/day
12-24 months: 1 mL 4 times/day
Syrup (Hydro-Tussin™-CBX, Palgic®-DS):
1-3 months: 1.25 mL up to 4 times/day
3-6 months: 2.5 mL up to 4 times/day
6-9 months: 3.75 mL up to 4 times/day
9-18 months: 3.75-5 mL up to 4 times/day
18 months to 6 years: 5 mL 3-4 times/day
>6 years: Refer to adult dosing.
Tablet (Rondec®): ≥6 years: Refer to adult dosing.
Tablet, sustained release:
6-12 years (Palgic®-D): One-half tablet every 12 hours
≥12 years (Palgic®-D, Rondec-TR®): Refer to adult dosing.

Adults:
Syrup (Hydro-Tussin™-CBX, Palgic®-DS): 10 mL 4 times/day
Tablet (Rondec®): 1 tablet 4 times a day
Tablets, sustained release (Palgic-TR®): 1 tablet every 12 hours

Dosage Forms SOLN, oral drops: (Andehist NR, Carbaxefed RF, Rondec®, Sildec): Carbinoxamine 1 mg and pseudoephedrine 15 mg per mL (30 mL). **SYR** (Hydro-Tussin™-CBX, Palgic®DS): Carbinoxamine 2 mg and pseudoephedrine 25 mg per 5 mL (480 mL). **TAB** (Rondec®): Carbinoxamine 4 mg and pseudoephedrine 60 mg. **TAB, sustained release:** (Palgic®-D): Carbinoxamine 8 mg and pseudoephedrine 80 mg; (Rondec-TR®): Carbinoxamine 8 mg and pseudoephedrine 120 mg

♦ **Carbinoxamine, Dextromethorphan, and Pseudoephedrine** *see* Carbinoxamine, Pseudoephedrine, and Dextromethorphan *on page 219*

♦ **Carbinoxamine Maleate** *see* Carbinoxamine *on page 218*

Carbinoxamine, Pseudoephedrine, and Dextromethorphan
(kar bi NOKS a meen, soo doe e FED rin, & deks troe meth OR fan)

U.S. Brand Names Andehist DM NR Drops; Carbaxefed DM RF; Rondec®-DM Drops; Tussafed®

Synonyms Carbinoxamine, Dextromethorphan, and Pseudoephedrine; Dextromethorphan, Carbinoxamine, and Pseudoephedrine; Dextromethorphan, Pseudoephedrine, and Carbinoxamine; Pseudoephedrine, Carbinoxamine, and Dextromethorphan; Pseudoephedrine, Dextromethorphan, and Carbinoxamine

Therapeutic Category Antihistamine/Decongestant/Antitussive

Use Relief of coughs and upper respiratory symptoms, including nasal congestion, associated with allergy or the common cold

Pregnancy Risk Factor C

Dosage Oral:
Drops: Infants and Children:
1-3 months: 1/4 mL 4 times/day
3-6 months: 1/2 mL 4 times/day
6-12 months: 3/4 mL 4 times/day
12-24 months: 1 mL 4 times/day
Syrup:
Children 18 months to 6 years: 2.5 mL 4 times/day
Children >6 years and Adults: 5 mL 4 times/day

Dosage Forms SOLN, oral (Tussafed®): Carbinoxamine 4 mg, pseudoephedrine 60 mg and dextromethorphan 15 mg per 5 mL (480 mL). **SOLN, oral drops:** (Andehist DM NR, Carbaxefed DM RF, Rondec® DM): Carbinoxamine 1 mg, pseudoephedrine 15 mg and dextromethorphan 4 mg per mL (30 mL).

♦ **Carbinoxamine, Pseudoephedrine, and Hydrocodone** *see* Hydrocodone, Carbinoxamine, and Pseudoephedrine *on page 632*

♦ **Carbocaine® [DSC]** *see* Mepivacaine *on page 793*

Carboplatin (KAR boe pla tin)
U.S. Brand Names Paraplatin®

Synonyms CBDCA

Therapeutic Category Antineoplastic Agent, Alkylating Agent; Antineoplastic Agent, Irritant

Use Treatment of ovarian cancer

Unlabeled/Investigational Use Lung cancer, head and neck cancer, endometrial cancer, esophageal cancer, bladder cancer, breast cancer, cervical cancer, CNS tumors, germ cell tumors, osteogenic sarcoma, and high-dose therapy with stem cell/bone marrow support

Pregnancy Risk Factor D

Contraindications History of severe allergic reaction to cisplatin, carboplatin, other platinum-containing formulations, mannitol, or any component of the formulation; pregnancy

Warnings/Precautions The U.S. Food and Drug Administration (FDA) currently recommends that procedures for proper handling and disposal of antineoplastic agents be considered. High doses have resulted in severe abnormalities of liver function tests. Bone marrow suppression, which may be severe, and vomiting are dose related; reduce dosage in patients with bone marrow suppression and impaired renal function. Clinically significant hearing loss has been reported to occur in pediatric patients when carboplatin was administered at higher than recommended doses in combination with other ototoxic agents. Increased risk of allergic reactions in patients previously exposed to platinum therapy. When administered as sequential infusions, taxane derivatives (docetaxel, paclitaxel) should be administered before platinum derivatives (carboplatin, cisplatin) to limit myelosuppression and to enhance efficacy.

Common Adverse Reactions
>10%:
Dermatologic: Alopecia (includes other agents in combination with carboplatin)
Endocrine & metabolic: Hypomagnesemia, hypokalemia, hyponatremia, hypocalcemia; less severe than those seen after cisplatin (usually asymptomatic)
Gastrointestinal: Nausea, vomiting, stomatitis
Hematologic: Myelosuppression is dose-related and is the dose-limiting toxicity; thrombocytopenia is the predominant manifestation, with a reported incidence of 37% in patients receiving 400 mg/m^2 as a single agent and 80% in patients receiving 520 mg/m^2; leukopenia has been reported in 27% to 38% of patients receiving carboplatin as a single agent
Nadir: ~21 days following a single dose
(Continued)

Carboplatin *(Continued)*

Hepatic: Alkaline phosphatase increased, AST increased (usually mild and reversible)

Otic: Hearing loss at high tones (above speech ranges, up to 19%); clinically-important ototoxicity is not usually seen

Renal: Increases in creatinine and BUN have been reported; most of them are mild and they are commonly reversible; considerably less nephrotoxic than cisplatin

1% to 10%:

Gastrointestinal: Diarrhea, anorexia

Hematologic: Hemorrhagic complications

Local: Pain at injection site

Neuromuscular & skeletal: Peripheral neuropathy (4% to 6%; up to 10% in older and/or previously-treated patients)

Otic: Ototoxicity

Drug Interactions

Increased Effect/Toxicity: Nephrotoxic drugs; aminoglycosides increase risk of ototoxicity. When administered as sequential infusions, observational studies indicate a potential for increased toxicity when platinum derivatives (carboplatin, cisplatin) are administered before taxane derivatives (docetaxel, paclitaxel).

Mechanism of Action Carboplatin is an alkylating agent which covalently binds to DNA; possible cross-linking and interference with the function of DNA

Pharmacodynamics/Kinetics

Distribution: V_d: 16 L/kg; Into liver, kidney, skin, and tumor tissue

Protein binding: 0%; platinum is 30% irreversibly bound

Metabolism: Minimally hepatic to aquated and hydroxylated compounds

Half-life elimination: Terminal: 22-40 hours; Cl_{cr} >60 mL/minute: 2.5-5.9 hours

Excretion: Urine (~60% to 90%) within 24 hours

Dosage IVPB, I.V. infusion, intraperitoneal (refer to individual protocols):

Children:

Solid tumor: 300-600 mg/m^2 once every 4 weeks

Brain tumor: 175 mg/m^2 weekly for 4 weeks every 6 weeks, with a 2-week recovery period between courses

Adults:

Ovarian cancer: 300-360 mg/m^2 I.V. every 3-4 weeks

Autologous BMT: I.V.: 1600 mg/m^2 (total dose) divided over 4 days **requires BMT (ie, FATAL without BMT)**

Dosing adjustment in renal impairment:

Cl_{cr} 41-59 mL/minute: Recommended dose on day 1 is 250 mg/m^2

Cl_{cr} 16-40 mL/minute: Recommended dose on day 1 is 200 mg/m^2

Cl_{cr} <15 mL/minute: The data available for patients with severely impaired kidney function are too limited to permit a recommendation for treatment

Dosing adjustment in hepatic impairment: There are no published studies available on the dosing of carboplatin in patients with impaired liver function.

Intraperitoneal: 200-650 mg/m^2 in 2 L of dialysis fluid have been administered into the peritoneum of ovarian cancer patients

Administration Administer as IVPB over 15 minutes up to a continuous intravenous infusion over 24 hours; may also be administered intraperitoneally Do not use needles or I.V. administration sets containing aluminum parts that may come in contact with carboplatin (aluminum can react causing precipitate formation and loss of potency).

Monitoring Parameters CBC (with differential and platelet count), serum electrolytes, creatinine clearance, liver function tests

Patient Information Maintain adequate nutrition (frequent small meals may help) and adequate hydration (2-3 L/day of fluids unless instructed to restrict fluid intake). Nausea and vomiting may be severe; request antiemetic. You will be susceptible to infection; avoid crowds or exposure to infection. Report sore throat, fever, chills, unusual fatigue or unusual bruising/bleeding, difficulty breathing, muscle cramps or twitching, or change in hearing acuity. Contraceptive measures are recommended during therapy.

Dosage Forms INJ, powder for reconstitution: 50 mg, 150 mg, 450 mg

♦ **Carboprost** *see* Carboprost Tromethamine *on page 220*

Carboprost Tromethamine (KAR boe prost tro METH a meen)

U.S. Brand Names Hemabate®

Synonyms Carboprost

Therapeutic Category Abortifacient; Prostaglandin

Use Termination of pregnancy and refractory postpartum uterine bleeding

Unlabeled/Investigational Use Investigational: Hemorrhagic cystitis

Pregnancy Risk Factor X

Contraindications Hypersensitivity to carboprost tromethamine or any component of the formulation; acute pelvic inflammatory disease; pregnancy

Warnings/Precautions Use with caution in patients with history of asthma, hypotension or hypertension, cardiovascular, adrenal, renal or hepatic disease, anemia, jaundice, diabetes, epilepsy or compromised uteri

Common Adverse Reactions

>10%: Gastrointestinal: Nausea (33%)

1% to 10%: Cardiovascular: Flushing (7%)

Drug Interactions
 Increased Effect/Toxicity: Toxicity may be increased by oxytocic agents.
Mechanism of Action Carboprost tromethamine is a prostaglandin similar to prostaglandin F_2 alpha (dinoprost) except for the addition of a methyl group at the C-15 position. This substitution produces longer duration of activity than dinoprost; carboprost stimulates uterine contractility which usually results in expulsion of the products of conception and is used to induce abortion between 13-20 weeks of pregnancy. Hemostasis at the placentation site is achieved through the myometrial contractions produced by carboprost.
Dosage I.M.: Adults:
 Abortion: Initial: 250 mcg, then 250 mcg at $1^{1}/_{2}$-hour to $3^{1}/_{2}$-hour intervals depending on uterine response; a 500 mcg dose may be given if uterine response is not adequate after several 250 mcg doses; do not exceed 12 mg total dose or continuous administration for >2 days
 Refractory postpartum uterine bleeding: Initial: 250 mcg; may repeat at 15- to 90-minute intervals to a total dose of 2 mg
 Bladder irrigation for hemorrhagic cystitis (refer to individual protocols): [0.4-1.0 mg/dL as solution] 50 mL instilled into bladder 4 times/day for 1 hour
Administration Do not inject I.V.; may result in bronchospasm, hypertension, vomiting, and anaphylaxis. Administer deep I.M.; rotate site if repeat injections are required.
Dosage Forms INJ, solution: Carboprost 250 mcg and tromethamine 83 mcg per mL (1 mL)

♦ **Carboptic®** see Carbachol on page 214
♦ **Cardene®** see NiCARdipine on page 900
♦ **Cardene® I.V.** see NiCARdipine on page 900
♦ **Cardene® SR** see NiCARdipine on page 900
♦ **Cardizem®** see Diltiazem on page 380
♦ **Cardizem® CD** see Diltiazem on page 380
♦ **Cardizem® LA** see Diltiazem on page 380
♦ **Cardizem® SR** see Diltiazem on page 380
♦ **Cardura®** see Doxazosin on page 406
♦ **Carimune™** see Immune Globulin (Intravenous) on page 659
♦ **Carindacillin** see Carbenicillin on page 217
♦ **Carisoprodate** see Carisoprodol on page 221

Carisoprodol (kar eye soe PROE dole)

U.S. Brand Names Soma®
Synonyms Carisoprodate; Isobamate
Therapeutic Category Skeletal Muscle Relaxant
Use Skeletal muscle relaxant
Pregnancy Risk Factor C
Contraindications Hypersensitivity to carisoprodol, meprobamate or any component of the formulation; acute intermittent porphyria
Warnings/Precautions May cause CNS depression, which may impair physical or mental abilities. Effects with other sedative drugs or ethanol may be potentiated. Use with caution in patients with hepatic/renal dysfunction. Tolerance or drug dependence may result from extended use.
Common Adverse Reactions
 >10%: Central nervous system: Drowsiness
 1% to 10%:
  Cardiovascular: Tachycardia, tightness in chest, flushing of face, syncope
  Central nervous system: Mental depression, allergic fever, dizziness, lightheadedness, headache, paradoxical CNS stimulation
  Dermatologic: Angioedema
  Gastrointestinal: Nausea, vomiting, stomach cramps
  Neuromuscular & skeletal: Trembling
  Ocular: Burning eyes
  Respiratory: Dyspnea
  Miscellaneous: Hiccups
Drug Interactions
 Cytochrome P450 Effect: Substrate of CYP2C19 (major)
 Increased Effect/Toxicity: CYP2C19 inhibitors may increase the levels/effects of carisoprodol; example inhibitors include delavirdine, fluconazole, fluvoxamine, gemfibrozil, isoniazid, omeprazole, and ticlopidine. Ethanol, CNS depressants, psychotropic drugs, and phenothiazines may increase toxicity.
Mechanism of Action Precise mechanism is not yet clear, but many effects have been ascribed to its central depressant actions
Pharmacodynamics/Kinetics
 Onset of action: ~30 minutes
 Duration: 4-6 hours
 Distribution: Crosses placenta; high concentrations enter breast milk
 Metabolism: Hepatic
 Half-life elimination: 8 hours
 Excretion: Urine
Dosage Oral: Adults: 350 mg 3-4 times/day; take last dose at bedtime; compound: 1-2 tablets 4 times/day
 (Continued)

Carisoprodol *(Continued)*

Monitoring Parameters Look for relief of pain and/or muscle spasm and avoid excessive drowsiness

Patient Information May cause drowsiness or dizziness; avoid alcohol and other CNS depressants

Dosage Forms TAB: 350 mg

Carisoprodol and Aspirin (kar eye soe PROE dole & AS pir in)

U.S. Brand Names Soma® Compound

Synonyms Aspirin and Carisoprodol

Therapeutic Category Analgesic/Skeletal Muscle Relaxant

Use Skeletal muscle relaxant

Pregnancy Risk Factor C/D (full-dose aspirin in 3rd trimester)

Dosage Oral: Adults: 1-2 tablets 4 times/day

Dosage Forms TAB: Carisoprodol 200 mg and aspirin 325 mg

Carisoprodol, Aspirin, and Codeine

(kar eye soe PROE dole, AS pir in, and KOE deen)

U.S. Brand Names Soma® Compound w/Codeine

Synonyms Aspirin, Carisoprodol, and Codeine; Codeine, Aspirin, and Carisoprodol

Therapeutic Category Analgesic/Skeletal Muscle Relaxant

Use Skeletal muscle relaxant

Restrictions C-III

Pregnancy Risk Factor C/D (full-dose aspirin in 3rd trimester)

Dosage Oral: Adults: 1 or 2 tablets 4 times/day

Dosage Forms TAB: Carisoprodol 200 mg, aspirin 325 mg, and codeine 16 mg

- ◆ **Carmol® 10 [OTC]** *see* Urea *on page 1282*
- ◆ **Carmol® 20 [OTC]** *see* Urea *on page 1282*
- ◆ **Carmol® 40** *see* Urea *on page 1282*
- ◆ **Carmol® Deep Cleaning** *see* Urea *on page 1282*
- ◆ **Carmol-HC®** *see* Urea and Hydrocortisone *on page 1282*
- ◆ **Carmol® Scalp** *see* Sulfacetamide *on page 1169*

Carmustine (kar MUS teen)

U.S. Brand Names BiCNu®; Gliadel®

Synonyms BCNU; bis-chloronitrosourea; Carmustinum; NSC-409962; WR-139021

Therapeutic Category Antineoplastic Agent, Alkylating Agent (Nitrosourea); Antineoplastic Agent, Vesicant; Vesicant

Use
Injection: Treatment of brain tumors (glioblastoma, brainstem glioma, medulloblastoma, astrocytoma, ependymoma, and metastatic brain tumors), multiple myeloma, Hodgkin's disease, non-Hodgkin's lymphomas, melanoma, lung cancer, colon cancer
Wafer (implant): Adjunct to surgery in patients with recurrent glioblastoma multiforme; adjunct to surgery and radiation in patients with high-grade malignant glioma

Pregnancy Risk Factor D

Contraindications Hypersensitivity to carmustine or any component of the formulation; myelosuppression; pregnancy

Warnings/Precautions The U.S. Food and Drug Administration (FDA) currently recommends that procedures for proper handling and disposal of antineoplastic agents be considered. Administer with caution to patients with depressed platelet, leukocyte or erythrocyte counts, renal or hepatic impairment. Diluent contains significant amounts of ethanol; use caution with aldehyde dehydrogenase-2 deficiency or history of "alcohol flushing syndrome." Do not give courses more frequently than every 6 week.

Baseline pulmonary function tests are recommended. Delayed onset pulmonary fibrosis occurring up to 17 years after treatment has been reported in children (1-16 years) who received carmustine in cumulative doses ranging from 770-1800 mg/m^2 combined with cranial radiotherapy for intracranial tumors.

Common Adverse Reactions
>10%:
Cardiovascular: Hypotension with high dose therapy, due to the alcohol content of the diluent
Central nervous system: Dizziness, ataxia; Wafers: Seizures (54%) postoperatively
Dermatologic: Pain and burning at the injection site (may be relieved by diluting the drug and infusing it through a fast-running dextrose or saline infusion); phlebitis
Gastrointestinal: Severe nausea and vomiting, usually begins within 2-4 hours of drug administration and lasts for 4-6 hours. Patients should receive a prophylactic antiemetic regimen including a serotonin (5-HT$_3$) antagonist and dexamethasone
Hematologic: Myelosuppression - cumulative, dose-related, delayed, thrombocytopenia is usually more common and more severe than leukopenia
Onset: 7-14 days
Nadir: 21-35 days
Recovery: 42-56 days
Hepatic: Reversible increases in bilirubin, alkaline phosphatase, and SGOT occur in 20% to 25% of patients

Ocular: Ocular toxicities (transient conjunctival flushing and blurred vision), retinal hemorrhages

Respiratory: Interstitial fibrosis occurs in up to 50% of patients receiving a cumulative dose >1400 mg/m², or bone marrow transplantation doses; may be delayed up to 3 years; rare in patients receiving lower doses. A history of lung disease or concomitant bleomycin therapy may increase the risk of this reaction. Patients should have baseline and periodic pulmonary function tests, patients with forced vital capacity (FVC) or carbon monoxide diffusing capacity of the lungs (DLCO) <70% of predicted are at higher risk.

1% to 10%:

Central nervous system: Wafers: Amnesia, aphasia, ataxia, cerebral edema, confusion, convulsion, depression, diplopia, dizziness, headache, hemiplegia, hydrocephalus, insomnia, meningitis, somnolence, stupor

Dermatologic: Facial flushing, probably due to the alcohol diluent; alopecia

Gastrointestinal: Anorexia, constipation, diarrhea, stomatitis

Hematologic: Anemia

Drug Interactions

Increased Effect/Toxicity: Carmustine given in combination with cimetidine is reported to cause bone marrow depression. Carmustine given in combination with etoposide is reported to cause severe hepatic dysfunction with hyperbilirubinemia, ascites, and thrombocytopenia. Diluent for infusion contains alcohol; avoid concurrent use of medications that inhibit aldehyde dehydrogenase-2 or cause disulfiram-like reactions.

Mechanism of Action Interferes with the normal function of DNA by alkylation and cross-linking the strands of DNA, and by possible protein modification

Pharmacodynamics/Kinetics

Distribution: Readily crosses blood-brain barrier producing CSF levels equal to 15% to 70% of blood plasma levels; enters breast milk; highly lipid soluble

Metabolism: Rapidly hepatic

Half-life elimination: Biphasic: Initial: 1.4 minutes; Secondary: 20 minutes (active metabolites: plasma half-life of 67 hours)

Excretion: Urine (~60% to 70%) within 96 hours; lungs (6% to 10% as CO_2)

Dosage

I.V. (refer to individual protocols):

Children: 200-250 mg/m² every 4-6 weeks as a single dose

Adults: Usual dosage (per manufacturer labeling): 150-200 mg/m² every 6 weeks as a single dose or divided into daily injections on 2 successive days

Alternative regimens:

75-120 mg/m² days 1 and 2 every 6-8 weeks **or**

50-80 mg/m² days 1,2,3 every 6-8 weeks

Primary brain cancer:

150-200 mg/m² every 6-8 weeks as a single dose **or**

75-120 mg/m² days 1 and 2 every 6-8 weeks **or**

20-65 mg/m² every 4-6 weeks **or**

0.5-1 mg/kg every 4-6 weeks **or**

40-80 mg/m²/day for 3 days every 6-8 weeks

Autologous BMT: ALL OF THE FOLLOWING DOSES ARE FATAL WITHOUT BMT

Combination therapy: Up to 300-900 mg/m²

Single-agent therapy: Up to 1200 mg/m² (fatal necrosis is associated with doses >2 g/m²)

Implantation (wafer): Adults: Recurrent glioblastoma multiforme, malignant glioma: Up to 8 wafers may be placed in the resection cavity (total dose 62.6 mg); should the size and shape not accommodate 8 wafers, the maximum number of wafers allowed should be placed

Hemodialysis: Supplemental dosing is not required

Dosing adjustment in hepatic impairment: Dosage adjustment may be necessary; however, no specific guidelines are available

Administration Injection: Significant absorption to PVC containers - should be administered in either glass or Excel® container. I.V. infusion over 1-2 hours is recommended; infusion through a free-flowing saline or dextrose infusion, or administration through a central catheter can alleviate venous pain/irritation

High-dose carmustine: Maximum rate of infusion of ≤3 mg/m²/minute to avoid excessive flushing, agitation, and hypotension; infusions should run over at least 2 hours; some investigational protocols dictate shorter infusions.

Extravasation management: Elevate extremity. Inject long-acting dexamethasone (Decadron® LA) or by hyaluronidase (Wydase®) throughout tissue with a 25- to 37-gauge needle. Apply warm, moist compresses.

Monitoring Parameters CBC with differential and platelet count, pulmonary function, liver function, and renal function tests; monitor blood pressure during administration

Wafer: Complications of craniotomy (seizures, intracranial infection, brain edema)

Patient Information Limit oral intake for 4-6 hours before therapy. Do not use alcohol, aspirin-containing products, and OTC medications without consulting prescriber. You may experience nausea or vomiting (frequent small meals, frequent mouth care, sucking lozenges, or chewing gum may help). If this is ineffective, consult prescriber for antiemetic medication. You may experience loss of hair (reversible). You will be more susceptible to infection (avoid crowds and exposure to infection as much as possible). You will be more sensitive to sunlight; use sunblock, wear protective clothing and dark glasses, or avoid direct exposure to sunlight. Frequent mouth care with soft toothbrush or cotton swabs and frequent mouth rinses may help relieve mouth sores. Report fever, chills, unusual bruising or bleeding, signs of infection, (Continued)

Carmustine (Continued)

excessive fatigue, yellowing of eyes or skin, or change in color of urine or stool. Contraceptive measures are recommended during therapy.

Dosage Forms INJ, powder for reconstitution (BiCNu®): 100 mg. **WAFER** (Gliadel®): 7.7 mg (8s)

◆ **Carmustinum** *see Carmustine on page 222*

◆ **Carnitor**® *see Levocarnitine on page 730*

◆ **Carrington Antifungal [OTC]** *see Miconazole on page 834*

Carteolol (KAR tee oh lole)

Related Information
Beta-Blockers Comparison *on page 1368*
Glaucoma Drug Therapy Comparison *on page 1481*

U.S. Brand Names Cartrol®; Ocupress®

Synonyms Carteolol Hydrochloride

Therapeutic Category Antihypertensive Agent; Beta Blocker, Intrinsic Sympathomimetic Activity (ISA); Beta-Adrenergic Blocker, Ophthalmic

Use Management of hypertension; treatment of chronic open-angle glaucoma and intraocular hypertension

Pregnancy Risk Factor C (manufacturer); D (2nd and 3rd trimesters - expert analysis)

Contraindications Hypersensitivity to carteolol or any component of the formulation; sinus bradycardia; heart block greater than first-degree (except in patients with a functioning artificial pacemaker); cardiogenic shock; bronchial asthma, bronchospasm, or COPD; uncompensated cardiac failure; pulmonary edema; pregnancy (2nd and 3rd trimesters)

Warnings/Precautions Avoid abrupt discontinuation in patients with a history of CAD; slowly wean while monitoring for signs and symptoms of ischemia. Use caution in patients with PVD (can aggravate arterial insufficiency). Use caution with concurrent use of beta-blockers and either verapamil or diltiazem; bradycardia or heart block can occur. Patients with bronchospastic disease should not receive beta-blockers. Use cautiously in diabetics because it can mask prominent hypoglycemic symptoms. Can mask signs of thyrotoxicosis. Can cause fetal harm when administered in pregnancy. Dosage adjustment is required in patients with renal dysfunction. Use care with anesthetic agents that decrease myocardial function. Beta-blockers with intrinsic sympathomimetic activity have not been demonstrated to be of value in CHF. Some products contain sulfites which can cause allergic reactions. Response diminished over time.

Common Adverse Reactions

Ophthalmic:
>10%: Ocular: Conjunctival hyperemia
1% to 10%: Ocular: Anisocoria, corneal punctate keratitis, corneal staining, decreased corneal sensitivity, eye pain, vision disturbances

Systemic:
>10%:
Central nervous system: Drowsiness, insomnia
Endocrine & metabolic: Decreased sexual ability
1% to 10%:
Cardiovascular: Bradycardia, palpitations, edema, CHF, reduced peripheral circulation
Central nervous system: Mental depression
Gastrointestinal: Diarrhea or constipation, nausea, vomiting, stomach discomfort
Respiratory: Bronchospasm
Miscellaneous: Cold extremities

Drug Interactions

Cytochrome P450 Effect: Substrate of CYP2D6 (minor)

Increased Effect/Toxicity: Carteolol may increase the effects of other drugs which slow AV conduction (digoxin, verapamil, diltiazem), alpha-blockers (prazosin, terazosin), and alpha-adrenergic stimulants (epinephrine, phenylephrine). Carteolol may mask the tachycardia from hypoglycemia caused by insulin and oral hypoglycemics. In patients receiving concurrent therapy, the risk of hypertensive crisis is increased when either clonidine or the beta-blocker is withdrawn. Reserpine has been shown to enhance the effect of beta-blockers. Beta-blockers may increase the action or levels of ethanol, disopyramide, nondepolarizing muscle relaxants, and theophylline although the effects are difficult to predict.

Decreased Effect: Decreased effect of beta-blockers with aluminum salts, barbiturates, calcium salts, cholestyramine, colestipol, NSAIDs, penicillins (ampicillin), rifampin, salicylates, and sulfinpyrazone due to decreased bioavailability and plasma levels. Beta-blockers may decrease the effect of sulfonylureas (possibly hyperglycemia). Nonselective beta-blockers blunt the effect of beta-2 adrenergic agonists (albuterol).

Mechanism of Action Blocks both beta$_1$- and beta$_2$-receptors and has mild intrinsic sympathomimetic activity; has negative inotropic and chronotropic effects and can significantly slow AV nodal conduction

Pharmacodynamics/Kinetics
Onset of action: Oral: 1-1.5 hours
Peak effect: 2 hours
Duration: 12 hours
Absorption: Oral: 80%
Protein binding: 23% to 30%

Metabolism: 30% to 50%
Half-life elimination: 6 hours
Excretion: Urine (as metabolites)

Dosage Adults:
Oral: 2.5 mg as a single daily dose, with a maintenance dose normally 2.5-5 mg once daily; doses >10 mg do not increase response and may in fact decrease effect.
Ophthalmic: Instill 1 drop in affected eye(s) twice daily.

Dosing interval in renal impairment: Oral:
Cl_{cr} >60 mL/minute/1.73 m^2: Administer every 24 hours.
Cl_{cr} 20-60 mL/minute/1.73 m^2: Administer every 48 hours.
Cl_{cr} <20 mL/minute/1.73 m^2: Administer every 72 hours.

Administration
Oral: Administer with meals.
Ophthalmic: Intended for twice daily dosing. Keep eye open and do not blink for 30 seconds after instillation. Wear sunglasses to avoid photophobic discomfort. Apply gentle pressure to lacrimal sac during and immediately following instillation (1 minute).

Monitoring Parameters Ophthalmic: Intraocular pressure; Systemic: Blood pressure, pulse, CNS status

Patient Information Oral: Take exactly as directed. Do not increase, decrease, or adjust dosage without consulting prescriber. Take pulse daily, prior to medication; follow prescriber's instruction about holding medication. Do not take with antacids and avoid taking OTC medications (eg, cold remedies) without consulting prescriber. If diabetic, monitor serum blood glucose closely (drug may alter glucose tolerance or mask signs of hypoglycemia). May cause fatigue, dizziness, or postural hypotension; use caution when changing position from lying or sitting to standing, when driving, or climbing stairs until response to medication is known. May cause alteration in sexual performance (reversible). Report unresolved swelling of extremities, difficulty breathing or new cough, unresolved fatigue, unusual weight gain, unresolved constipation, or unusual muscle weakness.

Ophthalmic: Wash hands before instilling. Sit or lie down to instill. Open eye, look at ceiling, and instill prescribed amount of medication. Close eye and apply gentle pressure to inner corner of eye. Do not let tip of applicator Temporary stinging or burning may occur. Report persistent pain, burning, vision changes, swelling, itching, or worsening of condition.

Dosage Forms SOLN, ophthalmic (Ocupress®): 1% (5 mL, 10 mL, 15 mL). **TAB** (Cartrol®): 2.5 mg, 5 mg

♦ **Carteolol Hydrochloride** see Carteolol on page 224
♦ **Cartia XT**™ see Diltiazem on page 380
♦ **Cartrol®** see Carteolol on page 224

Carvedilol (KAR ve dil ole)

Related Information
Beta-Blockers Comparison on page 1368

U.S. Brand Names Coreg®

Therapeutic Category Alpha-/Beta-Adrenergic Blocker; Antihypertensive Agent; Beta Blocker, Alpha-Blocker

Use Mild to severe heart failure of ischemic or cardiomyopathic origin (usually in addition to standardized therapy); left ventricular dysfunction following myocardial infarction (MI); management of hypertension

Unlabeled/Investigational Use Angina pectoris

Pregnancy Risk Factor C (manufacturer); D (2nd and 3rd trimesters - expert analysis)

Contraindications Hypersensitivity to carvedilol or any component of the formulation; patients with decompensated cardiac failure requiring intravenous inotropic therapy; bronchial asthma or related bronchospastic conditions; second- or third-degree AV block, sick sinus syndrome, and severe bradycardia (except in patients with a functioning artificial pacemaker); cardiogenic shock; severe hepatic impairment; pregnancy (2nd and 3rd trimesters)

Warnings/Precautions Initiate cautiously and monitor for possible deterioration in patient status (including symptoms of CHF). Adjustment of other medications (ACE inhibitors and/or diuretics) may be required. In severe chronic heart failure, trial patients were excluded if they had cardiac-related rales, ascites, or a serum creatinine >2.8 mg/dL. Patients should be advised to avoid driving or other hazardous tasks during initiation of therapy due to the risk of syncope. Avoid abrupt discontinuation (may be associated with angina, arrhythmia, or myocardial infarction). Manufacturer recommends discontinuation of therapy if liver injury occurs (confirmed by laboratory testing). Use caution in patients with PVD (can aggravate arterial insufficiency). Use caution with concurrent use of verapamil or diltiazem; bradycardia or heart block can occur. Patients with bronchospastic disease should not receive beta-blockers. Use cautiously in diabetics because it can mask prominent hypoglycemic symptoms. May mask signs of thyrotoxicosis. Use care with anesthetic agents that decrease myocardial function. Avoid abrupt discontinuation particularly in patients with coronary artery disease (taper dose over 1-2 weeks with close monitoring). Safety and efficacy in children <18 years of age have not been established.

Common Adverse Reactions Note: Frequency ranges include data from hypertension and heart failure trials. Higher rates of adverse reactions have generally been noted in patients with CHF. However, the frequency of adverse effects associated with placebo is also increased in this population. Events occurring at a frequency > placebo in clinical trials.

>10%:
Cardiovascular: Hypotension (9% to 14%)
(Continued)

Carvedilol *(Continued)*

Central nervous system: Dizziness (6% to 32%), fatigue (4% to 24%)
Endocrine & metabolic: Hyperglycemia (5% to 12%), weight gain (10% to 12%)
Gastrointestinal: Diarrhea (2% to 12%)
Neuromuscular & skeletal: Weakness (11%)

1% to 10%:
Cardiovascular: Bradycardia (2% to 10%), hypertension (3%), AV block (3%), angina (2% to 6%), postural hypotension (2%), syncope (3% to 8%), dependent edema (4%), palpitations, peripheral edema (1% to 7%), generalized edema (5% to 6%)
Central nervous system: Headache (5% to 8%), fever (3%), paresthesia (2%), somnolence (2%), insomnia (2%), malaise, hypesthesia, vertigo
Endocrine & metabolic: Gout (6%), hypercholesterolemia (4%), dehydration (2%), hyperkalemia (3%), hypervolemia (2%), hypertriglyceridemia (1%), hyperuricemia, hypoglycemia, hyponatremia
Gastrointestinal: Nausea (4% to 9%), vomiting (6%), melena, periodontitis
Genitourinary: Hematuria (3%), impotence
Hematologic: Thrombocytopenia (1% to 2%), decreased prothrombin, purpura
Hepatic: Increased transaminases, increased alkaline phosphatase
Neuromuscular & skeletal: Back pain (2% to 7%), arthralgia (6%), myalgia (3%), muscle cramps
Ocular: Blurred vision (3% to 5%)
Renal: Increased BUN (6%), abnormal renal function, albuminuria, glycosuria, increased creatinine (3%), kidney failure
Respiratory: Rhinitis (2%), increased cough (5%)
Miscellaneous: Injury (3% to 6%), increased diaphoresis (3%), allergy, sudden death

Drug Interactions
Cytochrome P450 Effect: Substrate of CYP1A2 (minor), 2C8/9 (major), 2D6 (major), 2E1 (minor), 3A4 (minor)
Increased Effect/Toxicity: CYP2C8/9 inhibitors may increase the levels/effects of carvedilol; example inhibitors include delavirdine, fluconazole, gemfibrozil, ketoconazole, nicardipine, NSAIDs, pioglitazone, and sulfonamides. CYP2D6 inhibitors may increase the levels/effects of carvedilol; example inhibitors include chlorpromazine, delavirdine, fluoxetine, miconazole, paroxetine, pergolide, quinidine, quinine, ritonavir, and ropinirole. Clonidine and cimetidine increase the serum levels and effects of carvedilol. Carvedilol may increase the levels of cyclosporine. Carvedilol may increase the effects of other drugs which slow AV conduction (digoxin, verapamil, diltiazem), alpha-blockers (prazosin, terazosin), and alpha-adrenergic stimulants (epinephrine, phenylephrine). Carvedilol may mask the tachycardia from hypoglycemia caused by insulin and oral hypoglycemics. In patients receiving concurrent therapy, the risk of hypertensive crisis is increased when either clonidine or the beta-blocker is withdrawn. Reserpine has been shown to enhance the effect of beta-blockers. Beta-blockers may increase the action or levels of disopyramide, and theophylline although the effects are difficult to predict.
Decreased Effect: CYP2C8/9 inducers may decrease the levels/effects of carvedilol; example inducers include carbamazepine, phenobarbital, phenytoin, rifampin, rifapentine, and secobarbital. Decreased effect of beta-blockers has also occurred with antacids, barbiturates, calcium channel blockers, cholestyramine, colestipol, NSAIDs, penicillins (ampicillin), and salicylates due to decreased bioavailability and plasma levels. Beta-blockers may decrease the effect of sulfonylureas. Nonselective beta-blockers blunt the effect of beta-2 adrenergic agonists (albuterol).

Mechanism of Action As a racemic mixture, carvedilol has nonselective beta-adrenoreceptor and alpha-adrenergic blocking activity. No intrinsic sympathomimetic activity has been documented. Associated effects in hypertensive patients include reduction of cardiac output, exercise- or beta agonist-induced tachycardia, reduction of reflex orthostatic tachycardia, vasodilation, decreased peripheral vascular resistance (especially in standing position), decreased renal vascular resistance, reduced plasma renin activity, and increased levels of atrial natriuretic peptide. In CHF, associated effects include decreased pulmonary capillary wedge pressure, decreased pulmonary artery pressure, decreased heart rate, decreased systemic vascular resistance, increased stroke volume index, and decreased right arterial pressure (RAP).

Pharmacodynamics/Kinetics
Onset of action: 1-2 hours
Peak antihypertensive effect: ~1-2 hours
Absorption: Rapid; food decreases rate but not extent of absorption; administration with food minimizes risks of orthostatic hypotension
Distribution: V_d: 115 L
Protein binding: >98%, primarily to albumin
Metabolism: Extensively hepatic, via **CYP2C9, 2D6**, 3A4, and 2C19 (2% excreted unchanged); three active metabolites (4-hydroxyphenyl metabolite is 13 times more potent than parent drug for beta-blockade); first-pass effect; plasma concentrations in the elderly and those with cirrhotic liver disease are 50% and 4-7 times higher, respectively
Bioavailability: 25% to 35%
Half-life elimination: 7-10 hours
Excretion: Primarily feces

Dosage Oral: Adults: Reduce dosage if heart rate drops to <55 beats/minute.
Hypertension: 6.25 mg twice daily; if tolerated, dose should be maintained for 1-2 weeks, then increased to 12.5 mg twice daily. Dosage may be increased to a maximum of 25 mg twice daily after 1-2 weeks. Maximum dose: 50 mg/day

Congestive heart failure: 3.125 mg twice daily for 2 weeks; if this dose is tolerated, may increase to 6.25 mg twice daily. Double the dose every 2 weeks to the highest dose tolerated by patient. (Prior to initiating therapy, other heart failure medications should be stabilized and fluid retention minimized.)

Maximum recommended dose:

Mild to moderate heart failure:

<85 kg: 25 mg twice daily

>85 kg: 50 mg twice daily

Severe heart failure: 25 mg twice daily

Left ventricular dysfunction following MI: Initial 3.125-6.25 mg twice daily; increase dosage incrementally (ie, from 6.25 to 12.5 mg twice daily) at intervals of 3-10 days, based on tolerance, to a target dose of 25 mg twice daily. **Note**: Should be initiated only after patient is hemodynamically stable and fluid retention has been minimized.

Angina pectoris (unlabeled use): 25-50 mg twice daily

Dosing adjustment in renal impairment: None necessary

Dosing adjustment in hepatic impairment: Use is contraindicated in severe liver dysfunction.

Administration Administer with food.

Monitoring Parameters Heart rate, blood pressure (base need for dosage increase on trough blood pressure measurements and for tolerance on standing systolic pressure 1 hour after dosing); renal studies, BUN, liver function

Patient Information Take with food to minimize the risk of hypotension; do not interrupt or discontinue using carvedilol without prescriber's advice; use care to avoid standing abruptly or standing still for long periods; lie down if dizziness or faintness occurs and consult prescriber for a reduced dosage; contact lens wearers may experience dry eyes

Dosage Forms TAB: 3.125 mg, 6.25 mg, 12.5 mg, 25 mg

♦ **Casodex®** see Bicalutamide on page 165

Caspofungin (kas poe FUN jin)

Related Information

Antifungal Agents Comparison on page 1362

U.S. Brand Names Cancidas®

Synonyms Caspofungin Acetate

Therapeutic Category Antifungal Agent, Parental; Antifungal Agent, Systemic

Use Treatment of invasive Aspergillus infections; treatment of candidemia and other Candida infections (abscesses, esophageal, intra-abdominal, peritonitis, pleural space)

Pregnancy Risk Factor C

Contraindications Hypersensitivity to caspofungin or any component of the formulation

Warnings/Precautions Has not been studied as initial therapy for fungal infection. Avoid concurrent use of cyclosporine. Limited data are available concerning treatment durations longer than 2 weeks.

Common Adverse Reactions

>10%:

Central nervous system: Headache (up to 11%), fever (3% to 26%)

Hematologic: Hemoglobin decreased (3% to 12%)

Hepatic: Serum alkaline phosphatase (3% to 11%) increased, transaminases increased (up to 13%)

Local: Infusion site reactions (2% to 12%), phlebitis (up to 16%)

1% to 10%:

Cardiovascular: Flushing (3%), facial edema (up to 3%), hypertension (2%), tachycardia (1% to 2%), hypotension (1%)

Central nervous system: Dizziness (2%), chills (up to 5%), pain (1% to 5%), insomnia (1%)

Dermatologic: Rash (<1% to 5%), pruritus (1% to 3%), erythema (1% to 2%)

Endocrine & metabolic: Hypokalemia (10%)

Gastrointestinal: Nausea (2% to 6%), vomiting (1% to 4%), abdominal pain (2% to 4%), diarrhea (1% to 4%), anorexia (1%)

Hematologic: Eosinophils increased (3%), neutrophils decreased (2% to 3%), WBC decreased (5% to 6%), anemia (up to 4%), platelet count decreased (2% to 3%)

Hepatic: Bilirubin increased (3%)

Local: Phlebitis/thrombophlebitis (4% to 6%), induration (up to 3%)

Neuromuscular & skeletal: Myalgia (up to 3%), paresthesia (1% to 3%), tremor (2%)

Renal: Nephrotoxicity (8%)*, proteinuria (5%), hematuria (2%), serum creatinine increased (<1% to 4%), urinary WBCs increased (up to 8%), urinary RBCs increased (1% to 4%), blood urea nitrogen increased (1%)

*Nephrotoxicity defined as serum creatinine ≥2X baseline value or ≥1 mg/dL in patients with serum creatinine above ULN range (patients with Cl_{cr} <30 mL/minute were excluded)

Miscellaneous: Flu-like syndrome (3%), diaphoresis (up to 1%)

(Continued)

Caspofungin *(Continued)*

Drug Interactions

Increased Effect/Toxicity: Concurrent administration of cyclosporine may increase caspofungin concentrations. In limited experience, a high frequency of elevated hepatic serum transaminases was observed.

Decreased Effect: Caspofungin may decrease blood concentrations of tacrolimus. In limited experience, some enzyme inducers decreased the serum concentrations of caspofungin. Dosage adjustment of caspofungin to 70 mg is required for patients on rifampin and should be considered when used with other inducers; includes carbamazepine, dexamethasone, efavirenz, nevirapine, and phenytoin.

Mechanism of Action Inhibits synthesis of β(1,3)-D-glucan, an essential component of the cell wall of susceptible fungi. Highest activity in regions of active cell growth. Mammalian cells do not require β(1,3)-D-glucan, limiting potential toxicity.

Pharmacodynamics/Kinetics

Protein binding: 97% to albumin

Metabolism: Slowly, via hydrolysis and *N*-acetylation as well as by spontaneous degradation, with subsequent metabolism to component amino acids. Overall metabolism is extensive.

Half-life elimination: Beta (distribution): 9-11 hours; Terminal: 40-50 hours

Excretion: Urine (41% as metabolites, 1% to 9% unchanged) and feces (35% as metabolites)

Dosage I.V.:

Children: Safety and efficacy in pediatric patients have not been established

Adults: **Note:** Duration of caspofungin treatment should be determined by patient status and clinical response.

Invasive *Aspergillus*: Initial dose: 70 mg infused over 1 hour; subsequent dosing: 50 mg/day

Invasive candidiasis: Initial dose: 70 mg infused over 1 hour; subsequent dosing: 50 mg/day

Esophageal candidiasis: 50 mg/day; **Note:** The majority of patients studied for this indication also had oropharyngeal involvement.

Concomitant use of an enzyme inducer:

Patients receiving rifampin: 70 mg caspofungin daily

Patients receiving carbamazepine, dexamethasone, efavirenz, nevirapine, **or** phenytoin (and possibly other enzyme inducers) may require an increased daily dose of caspofungin (70 mg/day).

Elderly: The number of patients >65 years of age in clinical studies was not sufficient to establish whether a difference in response may be anticipated.

Dosage adjustment in renal impairment: No specific dosage adjustment is required; supplemental dose is not required following dialysis

Dosage adjustment in hepatic impairment:

Mild hepatic insufficiency (Child-Pugh score 5-6): No adjustment necessary

Moderate hepatic insufficiency (Child-Pugh score 7-9): 35 mg/day; initial 70 mg loading dose should still be administered in treatment of invasive infections

Severe hepatic insufficiency (Child-Pugh score >9): No clinical experience

Administration Infuse slowly, over 1 hour; monitor during infusion; isolated cases of possible histamine-related reactions have occurred during clinical trials (rash, flushing, pruritus, facial edema); do not coadminister with other medications

Patient Information This medication can only be administered by infusion. Report immediately any pain, burning, or swelling at infusion site, or any signs of allergic reaction (eg, difficulty breathing or swallowing, back pain, chest tightness, rash, hives, or swelling of lips or mouth). Report nausea, vomiting, abdominal pain, or diarrhea.

Dosage Forms INJ, powder for reconstitution: 50 mg, 70 mg

Cefaclor (SEF a klor)
Related Information
Antimicrobial Drugs of Choice *on page 1440*
U.S. Brand Names Ceclor®; Ceclor® CD
Therapeutic Category Antibiotic, Cephalosporin (Second Generation)
Use Infections caused by susceptible organisms including *Staphylococcus aureus* and *H. influenzae*; treatment of otitis media, sinusitis, and infections involving the respiratory tract, skin and skin structure, bone and joint, and urinary tract
Pregnancy Risk Factor B
Contraindications Hypersensitivity to cefaclor, any component of the formulation, or other cephalosporins
Warnings/Precautions Modify dosage in patients with severe renal impairment; prolonged use may result in superinfection; use with caution in patients with a history of penicillin allergy especially IgE-mediated reactions (eg, anaphylaxis, urticaria)
Common Adverse Reactions
1% to 10%:
  Dermatologic: Rash (maculopapular, erythematous, or morbilliform) (1% to 2%)
  Gastrointestinal: Diarrhea (2%)
  Hematologic: Eosinophilia (2%)
  Hepatic: Elevated transaminases (3%)
Reactions reported with other cephalosporins include fever, abdominal pain, superinfection, renal dysfunction, toxic nephropathy, hemorrhage, cholestasis
Drug Interactions
Increased Effect/Toxicity: Probenecid may decrease cephalosporin elimination. Furosemide, aminoglycosides when taken with cefaclor may result in additive nephrotoxicity. Bleeding may occur when administered with anticoagulants.
Mechanism of Action Inhibits bacterial cell wall synthesis by binding to one or more of the penicillin-binding proteins (PBPs) which in turn inhibits the final transpeptidation step of peptidoglycan synthesis in bacterial cell walls, thus inhibiting cell wall biosynthesis. Bacteria eventually lyse due to ongoing activity of cell wall autolytic enzymes (autolysins and murein hydrolases) while cell wall assembly is arrested.
Pharmacodynamics/Kinetics
Absorption: Well absorbed, acid stable
Distribution: Widely throughout the body and reaches therapeutic concentration in most tissues and body fluids, including synovial, pericardial, pleural, peritoneal fluids; bile, sputum, and urine; bone, myocardium, gallbladder, skin and soft tissue; crosses placenta; enters breast milk
Protein binding: 25%
Metabolism: Partially hepatic
Half-life elimination: 0.5-1 hour; prolonged with renal impairment
Time to peak: Capsule: 60 minutes; Suspension: 45 minutes
Excretion: Urine (80% as unchanged drug)
Dosage Oral:
Children >1 month: 20-40 mg/kg/day divided every 8-12 hours; maximum dose: 2 g/day (total daily dose may be divided into two doses for treatment of otitis media or pharyngitis)
Adults: 250-500 mg every 8 hours
  Extended release tablets:
    500 mg every 12 hours for 7 days for acute bacterial exacerbations of or secondary infections with chronic bronchitis
    375 mg every 12 hours for 10 days for pharyngitis or tonsillitis, or for uncomplicated skin and skin structure infections
Dosing adjustment in renal impairment: Cl_{cr} <50 mL/minute: Administer 50% of dose
Hemodialysis: Moderately dialyzable (20% to 50%)
Monitoring Parameters Assess patient at beginning and throughout therapy for infection; monitor for signs of anaphylaxis during first dose
Patient Information Chilling of the oral suspension improves flavor (do not freeze); report persistent diarrhea; entire course of medication (10-14 days) should be taken to ensure eradication of organism; may interfere with oral contraceptives; females should report symptoms of vaginitis
Dosage Forms CAP: 250 mg, 500 mg. **POWDER, oral suspension:** 125 mg/5 mL (75 mL, 150 mL); 187 mg/5 mL (50 mL, 100 mL); 250 mg/5 mL (75 mL, 150 mL); 375 mg/5 mL (50 mL, 100 mL). **TAB, extended release** (Ceclor® CD): 375 mg, 500 mg

Cefadroxil (sef a DROKS il)
Related Information
Prevention of Bacterial Endocarditis *on page 1429*
U.S. Brand Names Duricef®
Synonyms Cefadroxil Monohydrate
Therapeutic Category Antibiotic, Cephalosporin (First Generation)
Use Treatment of susceptible bacterial infections, including those caused by group A beta-hemolytic *Streptococcus*; prophylaxis against bacterial endocarditis in patients who are allergic to penicillin and undergoing surgical or dental procedures
Pregnancy Risk Factor B
Contraindications Hypersensitivity to cefadroxil, other cephalosporins, or any component of the formulation
(Continued)

Cefadroxil *(Continued)*

Warnings/Precautions Modify dosage in patients with severe renal impairment; prolonged use may result in superinfection; use with caution in patients with a history of penicillin allergy especially IgE-mediated reactions (eg, anaphylaxis, urticaria). May cause antibiotic-associated colitis or colitis secondary to *C. difficile.*

Common Adverse Reactions

1% to 10%: Gastrointestinal: Diarrhea

Reactions reported with other cephalosporins include toxic epidermal necrolysis, abdominal pain, superinfection, renal dysfunction, toxic nephropathy, aplastic anemia, hemolytic anemia, hemorrhage, prolonged prothrombin time, increased BUN, increased creatinine, eosinophilia, pancytopenia, seizures

Drug Interactions

Increased Effect/Toxicity: Bleeding may occur when administered with anticoagulants. Probenecid may decrease cephalosporin elimination.

Mechanism of Action Inhibits bacterial cell wall synthesis by binding to one or more of the penicillin-binding proteins (PBPs) which in turn inhibits the final transpeptidation step of peptidoglycan synthesis in bacterial cell walls, thus inhibiting cell wall biosynthesis. Bacteria eventually lyse due to ongoing activity of cell wall autolytic enzymes (autolysins and murein hydrolases) while cell wall assembly is arrested.

Pharmacodynamics/Kinetics

Absorption: Rapid and well absorbed

Distribution: Widely throughout the body and reaches therapeutic concentrations in most tissues and body fluids, including synovial, pericardial, pleural, and peritoneal fluids; bile, sputum, and urine; bone, myocardium, gallbladder, skin and soft tissue; crosses placenta; enters breast milk

Protein binding: 20%

Half-life elimination: 1-2 hours; Renal failure: 20-24 hours

Time to peak, serum: 70-90 minutes

Excretion: Urine (>90% as unchanged drug)

Dosage Oral:

Children: 30 mg/kg/day divided twice daily up to a maximum of 2 g/day

Adults: 1-2 g/day in 2 divided doses

Prophylaxis against bacterial endocarditis:

Children: 50 mg/kg 1 hour prior to the procedure

Adults: 2 g 1 hour prior to the procedure

Dosing interval in renal impairment:

Cl_{cr} 10-25 mL/minute: Administer every 24 hours

Cl_{cr} <10 mL/minute: Administer every 36 hours

Administration Administer around-the-clock to promote less variation in peak and trough serum levels.

Monitoring Parameters Observe for signs and symptoms of anaphylaxis during first dose

Patient Information Report persistent diarrhea; entire course of medication (10-14 days) should be taken to ensure eradication of organism; may interfere with oral contraceptives; females should report symptoms of vaginitis

Dosage Forms CAP: 500 mg. **POWDER, oral suspension:** 250 mg/5 mL (50 mL, 100 mL); 500 mg/5 mL (75 mL). **TAB:** 1 g

◆ **Cefadroxil Monohydrate** *see* Cefadroxil *on page 229*

Cefamandole *(sef a MAN dole)*

U.S. Brand Names Mandol® [DSC]

Synonyms Cefamandole Nafate

Therapeutic Category Antibiotic, Cephalosporin (Second Generation)

Use Treatment of susceptible bacterial infection; mainly respiratory tract, skin and skin structure, bone and joint, urinary tract and gynecologic, septicemia; surgical prophylaxis. Active against methicillin-sensitive staphylococci, many streptococci, and various gram-negative bacilli including *E. coli,* some *Klebsiella, P. mirabilis, H. influenzae,* and *Moraxella.*

Pregnancy Risk Factor B

Contraindications Hypersensitivity to cefamandole, any component of the formulation, or other cephalosporins

Warnings/Precautions Modify dosage in patients with severe renal impairment; prolonged use may result in superinfection; although rare, cefamandole may interfere with hemostasis via destruction of vitamin K producing intestinal bacteria, prevention of activation of prothrombin by the attachment of a methyltetrazolethiol side chain, and by an immune-mediated thrombocytopenia. Use with caution in patients with a history of penicillin allergy especially IgE-mediated reactions (eg, anaphylaxis, urticaria). May cause antibiotic-associated colitis or colitis secondary to *C. difficile.*

Common Adverse Reactions Contains MTT side chain which may lead to increased risk of hypoprothrombinemia and bleeding.

1% to 10%:

Gastrointestinal: Diarrhea

Local: Thrombophlebitis

Reactions reported with other cephalosporins include toxic epidermal necrolysis, Stevens-Johnson syndrome, abdominal pain, superinfection, renal dysfunction, toxic nephropathy, aplastic anemia, hemolytic anemia, hemorrhage, pancytopenia, vaginitis, seizures

Drug Interactions

Increased Effect/Toxicity: Disulfiram-like reaction has been reported when taken within 72 hours of ethanol consumption. Increased cefamandole plasma levels when taken with probenecid. Aminoglycosides, furosemide when taken with cefamandole may increase nephrotoxicity. Increase in hypoprothrombinemic effect with warfarin or heparin and cefamandole.

Mechanism of Action Inhibits bacterial cell wall synthesis by binding to one or more of the penicillin-binding proteins (PBPs) which in turn inhibits the final transpeptidation step of peptidoglycan synthesis in bacterial cell walls, thus inhibiting cell wall biosynthesis. Bacteria eventually lyse due to ongoing activity of cell wall autolytic enzymes (autolysins and murein hydrolases) while cell wall assembly is arrested.

Pharmacodynamics/Kinetics

Distribution: Well throughout the body, except CSF; poor penetration even with inflamed meninges

Protein binding: 56% to 78%

Metabolism: Extensive enterohepatic recirculation

Half-life elimination: 30-60 minutes

Time to peak, serum: I.M.: 1-2 hours

Excretion: Primarily urine (as unchanged drug); feces (high concentrations)

Dosage I.M., I.V.:

Children: 50-150 mg/kg/day in divided doses every 4-8 hours

Adults: Usual dose: 500-1000 mg every 4-8 hours; in life-threatening infections: 2 g every 4 hours may be needed

Dosing interval in renal impairment:

Cl_{cr} 25-50 mL/minute: 1-2 g every 8 hours

Cl_{cr} 10-25 mL/minute: 1 g every 8 hours

Cl_{cr} <10 mL/minute: 1 g every 12 hours

Hemodialysis: Moderately dialyzable (20% to 50%)

Monitoring Parameters Monitor for signs of bruising or bleeding; observe for signs and symptoms of anaphylaxis during first dose

Dosage Forms INJ, powder for reconstitution: 1 g, 2 g

♦ **Cefamandole Nafate** *see* Cefamandole *on page 230*

Cefazolin (sef A zoe lin)

Related Information

Community-Acquired Pneumonia in Adults *on page 1457*

Prevention of Bacterial Endocarditis *on page 1429*

Prevention of Wound Infection & Sepsis in Surgical Patients *on page 1436*

U.S. Brand Names Ancef®; Kefzol® [DSC]

Synonyms Cefazolin Sodium

Therapeutic Category Antibiotic, Cephalosporin (First Generation)

Use Treatment of gram-positive bacilli and cocci (except enterococcus); some gram-negative bacilli including *E. coli*, *Proteus*, and *Klebsiella* may be susceptible

Pregnancy Risk Factor B

Contraindications Hypersensitivity to cefazolin sodium, any component of the formulation, or other cephalosporins

Warnings/Precautions Modify dosage in patients with severe renal impairment; prolonged use may result in superinfection; use with caution in patients with a history of penicillin allergy especially IgE-mediated reactions (eg, anaphylaxis, angioedema, urticaria). May cause antibiotic-associated colitis or colitis secondary to *C. difficile*.

Common Adverse Reactions

1% to 10%:

Gastrointestinal: Diarrhea

Local: Pain at injection site

Reactions reported with other cephalosporins include toxic epidermal necrolysis, abdominal pain, cholestasis, superinfection, renal dysfunction, toxic nephropathy, aplastic anemia, hemolytic anemia, hemorrhage, prolonged prothrombin time, pancytopenia

Drug Interactions

Increased Effect/Toxicity: High-dose probenecid decreases clearance and increases effect of cefazolin. Aminoglycosides increase nephrotoxic potential when taken with cefazolin.

Mechanism of Action Inhibits bacterial cell wall synthesis by binding to one or more of the penicillin-binding proteins (PBPs) which in turn inhibits the final transpeptidation step of peptidoglycan synthesis in bacterial cell walls, thus inhibiting cell wall biosynthesis. Bacteria eventually lyse due to ongoing activity of cell wall autolytic enzymes (autolysins and murein hydrolases) while cell wall assembly is arrested.

Pharmacodynamics/Kinetics

Distribution: Widely into most body tissues and fluids including gallbladder, liver, kidneys, bone, sputum, bile, pleural, and synovial; CSF penetration is poor; crosses placenta; enters breast milk

Protein binding: 74% to 86%

Metabolism: Minimally hepatic

Half-life elimination: 90-150 minutes; prolonged with renal impairment

Time to peak, serum: I.M.: 0.5-2 hours

Excretion: Urine (80% to 100% as unchanged drug)

(Continued)

Cefazolin (Continued)

Dosage I.M., I.V.:
Children >1 month: 25-100 mg/kg/day divided every 6-8 hours; maximum: 6 g/day
Adults: 250 mg to 2 g every 6-12 (usually 8) hours, depending on severity of infection; maximum dose: 12 g/day
Prophylaxis against bacterial endocarditis:
Infants and Children: 25 mg/kg 30 minutes before procedure; maximum dose: 1 g
Adults: 1 g 30 minutes before procedure
Dosing adjustment in renal impairment:
Cl_{cr} 10-30 mL/minute: Administer every 12 hours
Cl_{cr} <10 mL/minute: Administer every 24 hours
Hemodialysis: Moderately dialyzable (20% to 50%); administer dose postdialysis or administer supplemental dose of 0.5-1 g after dialysis
Peritoneal dialysis: Administer 0.5 g every 12 hours
Continuous arteriovenous or venovenous hemofiltration: Dose as for Cl_{cr} 10-30 mL/minute; removes 30 mg of cefazolin per liter of filtrate per day
Monitoring Parameters Renal function periodically when used in combination with other nephrotoxic drugs, hepatic function tests, CBC; monitor for signs of anaphylaxis during first dose
Dosage Forms INF [premixed in D_5W]: 500 mg (50 mL); 1 g (50 mL). **INJ, powder for reconstitution:** 500 mg, 1 g, 10 g, 20 g; (Ancef®, Kefzol® [DSC]): 1 g, 10 g

◆ **Cefazolin Sodium** *see* Cefazolin *on page 231*

Cefdinir (SEF di ner)

U.S. Brand Names Omnicef®
Synonyms CFDN
Therapeutic Category Antibiotic, Cephalosporin (Third Generation)
Use Treatment of community-acquired pneumonia, acute exacerbations of chronic bronchitis, acute bacterial otitis media, acute maxillary sinusitis, pharyngitis/tonsillitis, and uncomplicated skin and skin structure infections.
Pregnancy Risk Factor B
Contraindications Hypersensitivity to cefdinir, other cephalosporins, any component of the formulation, or related antibiotics
Warnings/Precautions Administer cautiously to penicillin-sensitive patients, especially IgE-mediated reactions (eg, anaphylaxis, urticaria). There is evidence of partial cross-allergenicity and cephalosporins cannot be assumed to be an absolutely safe alternative to penicillin in the penicillin-allergic patient. Serum sickness-like reactions have been reported. Signs and symptoms occur after a few days of therapy and resolve a few days after drug discontinuation with no serious sequelae. Pseudomembranous colitis occurs; consider its diagnosis in patients who develop diarrhea with antibiotic use.
Common Adverse Reactions
1% to 10%
Dermatologic: Cutaneous moniliasis (1%)
Gastrointestinal: Diarrhea (8%), rash (3%), vomiting (1%), increased GGT (1%)
Reactions reported with other cephalosporins include dizziness, fever, headache, encephalopathy, asterixis, neuromuscular excitability, seizures, aplastic anemia, interstitial nephritis, toxic nephropathy, angioedema, hemorrhage, prolonged PT, serum-sickness reactions, and superinfection
Drug Interactions
Increased Effect/Toxicity: Probenecid increases the effects of cephalosporins by decreasing the renal elimination in those which are secreted by tubular secretion. Anticoagulant effects may be increased when administered with cephalosporins.
Decreased Effect: Coadministration with iron or antacids reduces the rate and extent of cefdinir absorption.
Mechanism of Action Inhibits bacterial cell wall synthesis by binding to one or more of the penicillin-binding proteins (PBPs) which in turn inhibits the final transpeptidation step of peptidoglycan synthesis in bacterial cell walls, thus inhibiting cell wall biosynthesis. Bacteria eventually lyse due to ongoing activity of cell wall autolytic enzymes (autolysins and murein hydrolases) while cell wall assembly is arrested.
Pharmacodynamics/Kinetics
Protein binding: 60% to 70%
Metabolism: Minimally hepatic
Bioavailability: Capsule: 16% to 21%; suspension 25%
Half-life elimination: 100 minutes
Excretion: Primarily urine
Dosage Oral:
Children: 7 mg/kg/dose twice daily for 5-10 days or 14 mg/kg/dose once daily for 10 days (maximum: 600 mg/day)
Adolescents and Adults: 300 mg twice daily or 600 mg once daily for 10 days
Dosing adjustment in renal impairment: Cl_{cr} <30 mL/minute: 300 mg once daily
Hemodialysis removes cefdinir; recommended initial dose: 300 mg (or 7 mg/kg/dose) every other day. At the conclusion of each hemodialysis session, 300 mg (or 7 mg/kg/dose) should be given. Subsequent doses (300 mg or 7 mg/kg/dose) should be administered every other day.
Monitoring Parameters Observe for signs and symptoms of anaphylaxis during first dose
Dosage Forms CAP: 300 mg. **POWDER, oral suspension:** 125 mg/5 mL (60 mL, 100 mL)

Cefditoren (sef de TOR en)

U.S. Brand Names Spectracef™

Synonyms Cefditoren Pivoxil

Therapeutic Category Antibiotic, Cephalosporin (Third Generation)

Use Treatment of acute bacterial exacerbation of chronic bronchitis or community-acquired pneumonia (due to susceptible organisms including *Haemophilus influenzae*, *Haemophilus parainfluenzae*, *Streptococcus pneumoniae*-penicillin susceptible only, *Moraxella catarrhalis*); pharyngitis or tonsillitis (*Streptococcus pyogenes*); and uncomplicated skin and skin-structure infections (*Staphylococcus aureus*-not MRSA, *Streptococcus pyogenes*)

Pregnancy Risk Factor B

Contraindications Hypersensitivity to cefditoren, other cephalosporins, milk protein, or any component of the formulation; carnitine deficiency

Warnings/Precautions Use with caution in patients with a history of penicillin allergy, especially IgE-mediated reactions (eg, anaphylaxis, urticaria). May cause antibiotic-associated colitis or colitis secondary to *C. difficile*. Modify dosage in patients with severe renal impairment. Caution in individuals with seizure disorders. Prolonged use may result in superinfection. Use caution in patients with renal or hepatic impairment. Cefditoren causes renal excretion of carnitine, do not use in patients with carnitine deficiency; not for long-term therapy due to the possible development of carnitine deficiency over time. Cefditoren tablets contain sodium caseinate, which may cause hypersensitivity reactions in patients with milk protein hypersensitivity; this does not affect patients with lactose intolerance. Safety and efficacy have not been established in children <12 years of age.

Common Adverse Reactions

>10%: Gastrointestinal: Diarrhea (11% to 15%)

1% to 10%:

Central nervous system: Headache (2% to 3%)

Endocrine & metabolic: Glucose increased (1%)

Gastrointestinal: Nausea (4% to 6%), abdominal pain (2%), dyspepsia (1% to 2%), vomiting (1%)

Genitourinary: Vaginal moniliasis (3% to 6%)

Hematologic: Hematocrit decreased (2%)

Renal: Hematuria (3%), urinary white blood cells increased (2%)

Additional adverse effects seen with cephalosporin antibiotics: Anaphylaxis, aplastic anemia, cholestasis, erythema multiforme, hemorrhage, hemolytic anemia, renal dysfunction, reversible hyperactivity, serum sickness-like reaction, Stevens-Johnson syndrome, toxic epidermal necrolysis, toxic nephropathy

Drug Interactions

Increased Effect/Toxicity: Increased levels of cefditoren with probenecid.

Decreased Effect: Antacids and H_2 receptor antagonists decrease cefditoren levels.

Mechanism of Action Inhibits bacterial cell wall synthesis by binding to one or more of the penicillin binding proteins (PBPs); which in turn inhibits the final transpeptidation step of peptidoglycan synthesis in bacterial cell walls, thus inhibiting cell wall biosynthesis. Bacteria eventually lyse due to ongoing activity of cell wall autolytic enzymes (autolysins and murein hydrolases) while cell wall assembly is arrested.

Pharmacodynamics/Kinetics

Distribution: 9.3 ± 1.6 L

Protein binding: 88% (*in vitro*), primarily to albumin

Metabolism: Cefditoren pivoxil is hydrolyzed to cefditoren (active) and pivalate

Bioavailability: ~14% to 16%, increased by moderate to high-fat meal

Half-life elimination: 1.6 ± 0.4 hours

Time to peak: 1.5-3 hours

Excretion: Urine (as cefditoren and pivaloylcarnitine)

Dosage Oral: Children ≥12 years and Adults:

Acute bacterial exacerbation of chronic bronchitis: 400 mg twice daily for 10 days

Community-acquired pneumonia: 400 mg twice daily for 14 days

Pharyngitis, tonsillitis, uncomplicated skin and skin structure infections: 200 mg twice daily for 10 days

Elderly: Refer to adult dosing

Dosage adjustment in renal impairment:

Cl_{cr} 30-49 mL/minute: Maximum dose: 200 mg twice daily

Cl_{cr} <30 mL/minute: Maximum dose: 200 mg once daily

End-stage renal disease: Appropriate dosing not established

Dosage adjustment in hepatic impairment:

Mild or moderate impairment: Adjustment not required

Severe impairment (Child-Pugh Class C): Specific guidelines not available

Administration Should be administered with meals.

Monitoring Parameters Assess patient at beginning and throughout therapy for infection; monitor for signs of anaphylaxis during first dose.

Patient Information Complete full course of medication to ensure eradication of organism. Report persistent diarrhea. Females should report symptoms of vaginitis.

Dosage Forms TAB: 200 mg

♦ **Cefditoren Pivoxil** *see* Cefditoren *on page 233*

Cefepime (SEF e pim)

Related Information
Antimicrobial Drugs of Choice *on page 1440*
Community-Acquired Pneumonia in Adults *on page 1457*

U.S. Brand Names Maxipime®

Synonyms Cefepime Hydrochloride

Therapeutic Category Antibiotic, Cephalosporin (Fourth Generation)

Use Treatment of uncomplicated and complicated urinary tract infections, including pyelonephritis caused by typical urinary tract pathogens; monotherapy for febrile neutropenia; uncomplicated skin and skin structure infections caused by *Streptococcus pyogenes*; moderate to severe pneumonia caused by pneumococcus, *Pseudomonas aeruginosa*, and other gram-negative organisms; complicated intra-abdominal infections (in combination with metronidazole). Also active against methicillin-susceptible staphylococci, *Enterobacter* sp, and many other gram-negative bacilli.

Children 2 months to 16 years: Empiric therapy of febrile neutropenia patients, uncomplicated skin/soft tissue infections, pneumonia, and uncomplicated/complicated urinary tract infections.

Pregnancy Risk Factor B

Contraindications Hypersensitivity to cefepime, any component of the formulation, or other cephalosporins

Warnings/Precautions Modify dosage in patients with severe renal impairment; prolonged use may result in superinfection; use with caution in patients with a history of penicillin or cephalosporin allergy, especially IgE-mediated reactions (eg, anaphylaxis, urticaria). May cause antibiotic-associated colitis or colitis secondary to *C. difficile*.

Common Adverse Reactions
>10%: Hematologic: Positive Coombs' test without hemolysis
1% to 10%:
    Central nervous system: Fever (1%), headache (1%)
    Dermatologic: Rash, pruritus
    Gastrointestinal: Diarrhea, nausea, vomiting
    Local: Pain, erythema at injection site
Reactions reported with other cephalosporins include aplastic anemia, erythema multiforme, hemolytic anemia, hemorrhage, pancytopenia, prolonged PT, renal dysfunction, Stevens-Johnson syndrome, superinfection, toxic epidermal necrolysis, toxic nephropathy, vaginitis

Drug Interactions
Increased Effect/Toxicity: High-dose probenecid decreases clearance and increases effect of cefepime. Aminoglycosides increase nephrotoxic potential when taken with cefepime.

Mechanism of Action Inhibits bacterial cell wall synthesis by binding to one or more of the penicillin-binding proteins (PBPs) which in turn inhibits the final transpeptidation step of peptidoglycan synthesis in bacterial cell walls, thus inhibiting cell wall biosynthesis. Bacteria eventually lyse due to ongoing activity of cell wall autolytic enzymes (autolysis and murein hydrolases) while cell wall assembly is arrested.

Pharmacodynamics/Kinetics
Absorption: I.M.: Rapid and complete
Distribution: V_d: Adults: 14-20 L; penetrates into inflammatory fluid at concentrations ~80% of serum levels and into bronchial mucosa at levels ~60% of those reached in the plasma; crosses blood-brain barrier
Protein binding, plasma: 16% to 19%
Metabolism: Minimally hepatic
Half-life elimination: 2 hours
Time to peak: 0.5-1.5 hours
Excretion: Urine (85% as unchanged drug)

Dosage
Children:
    Febrile neutropenia: I.V.: 50 mg/kg every 8 hours for 7-10 days
    Uncomplicated skin/soft tissue infections, pneumonia, and complicated/uncomplicated UTI: I.V.: 50 mg/kg twice daily

Cefepime Hydrochloride

Creatinine Clearance (mL/minute)	Recommended Maintenance Schedule			
>60				
Normal recommended dosing schedule	500 mg every 12 hours	1 g every 12 hours	2 g every 12 hours	2 g every 8 hours
30-60	500 mg every 24 hours	1 g every 24 hours	2 g every 24 hours	2 g every 12 hours
11-29	500 mg every 24 hours	500 mg every 24 hours	1 g every 24 hours	2 g every 24 hours
<11	250 mg every 24 hours	250 mg every 24 hours	500 mg every 24 hours	1 g every 24 hours

Adults:

Most infections: I.V.: 1-2 g every 12 hours for 7-10 days; higher doses or more frequent administration may be required in pseudomonal infections

Urinary tract infections, mild to moderate: I.M., I.V.: 500-1000 mg every 12 hours

Monotherapy for febrile neutropenic patients: I.V.: 2 g every 8 hours for 7 days or until the neutropenia resolves

Dosing adjustment in renal impairment: Adults: Recommended maintenance schedule based on creatinine clearance (mL/minute), compared to normal dosing schedule: See table on previous page.

Hemodialysis: Initial: 1 g (single dose) on day 1. Maintenance: 500 mg once daily (1 g once daily in febrile neutropenic patients). Dosage should be administered after dialysis on dialysis days.

Peritoneal dialysis: Removed to a lesser extent than hemodialysis; administer 250 mg every 48 hours

Continuous arteriovenous or venovenous hemofiltration: Dose as normal Cl_{cr} (eg, >30 mL/minute)

Administration May be administered either I.M. or I.V.

Monitoring Parameters Obtain specimen for culture and sensitivity prior to the first dose; monitor for signs of anaphylaxis during first dose

Patient Information Report side effects such as diarrhea, dyspepsia, headache, blurred vision, and lightheadedness.

Dosage Forms INJ, powder for reconstitution: 500 mg, 1 g, 2 g

♦ Cefepime Hydrochloride *see Cefepime on page 234*

Cefixime (sef IKS eem)

Related Information

Antimicrobial Drugs of Choice *on page 1440*

U.S. Brand Names Suprax® [DSC]

Therapeutic Category Antibiotic, Cephalosporin (Third Generation)

Use Treatment of urinary tract infections, otitis media, respiratory infections due to susceptible organisms including *S. pneumoniae* and *S. pyogenes*, *H. influenzae* and many Enterobacteriaceae; documented poor compliance with other oral antimicrobials; outpatient therapy of serious soft tissue or skeletal infections due to susceptible organisms; single-dose oral treatment of uncomplicated cervical/urethral gonorrhea due to *N. gonorrhoeae*

Pregnancy Risk Factor B

Contraindications Hypersensitivity to cefixime, any component of the formulation, or other cephalosporins

Warnings/Precautions Prolonged use may result in superinfection; modify dosage in patients with renal impairment; use with caution in patients with a history of penicillin allergy especially IgE-mediated reactions (eg, anaphylaxis, urticaria). May cause antibiotic-associated colitis or colitis secondary to *C. difficile*.

Common Adverse Reactions

>10%: Gastrointestinal: Diarrhea (16%)

1% to 10%: Gastrointestinal: Abdominal pain, nausea, dyspepsia, flatulence

Reactions reported with other cephalosporins include anaphylaxis, seizures, toxic epidermal necrolysis, renal dysfunction, toxic nephropathy, interstitial nephritis, cholestasis, aplastic anemia, hemolytic anemia, hemorrhage, pancytopenia, neutropenia, agranulocytosis, colitis, superinfection

Drug Interactions

Increased Effect/Toxicity: Probenecid increases cefixime concentration. Cefixime may increase carbamazepine.

Mechanism of Action Inhibits bacterial cell wall synthesis by binding to one or more of the penicillin binding proteins (PBPs); which in turn inhibits the final transpeptidation step of peptidoglycan synthesis in bacterial cell walls, thus inhibiting cell wall biosynthesis. Bacteria eventually lyse due to ongoing activity of cell wall autolytic enzymes (autolysins and murein hydrolases) while cell wall assembly is arrested.

Pharmacodynamics/Kinetics

Absorption: 40% to 50%

Distribution: Widely throughout the body and reaches therapeutic concentration in most tissues and body fluids, including synovial, pericardial, pleural, peritoneal; bile, sputum, and urine; bone, myocardium, gallbladder, and skin and soft tissue

Protein binding: 65%

Half-life elimination: Normal renal function: 3-4 hours; Renal failure: Up to 11.5 hours

Time to peak, serum: 2-6 hours (15% to 50% higher for oral suspension vs tablets); delayed with food

Excretion: Urine (50% of absorbed dose as active drug); feces (10%)

Dosage Oral:

Children: 8 mg/kg/day divided every 12-24 hours

Adolescents and Adults: 400 mg/day divided every 12-24 hours

Uncomplicated cervical/urethral gonorrhea due to *N. gonorrhoeae*: 400 mg as a single dose

For *S. pyogenes* infections, treat for 10 days; use suspension for otitis media due to increased peak serum levels as compared to tablet form

Dosing adjustment in renal impairment:

Cl_{cr} 21-60 mL/minute or with renal hemodialysis: Administer 75% of the standard dose

Cl_{cr} <20 mL/minute or with CAPD: Administer 50% of the standard dose

Moderately dialyzable (10%)

(Continued)

Cefixime *(Continued)*

Administration Oral: May be administered with or without 'food; administer with food to decrease GI distress

Monitoring Parameters With prolonged therapy, monitor renal and hepatic function periodically; observe for signs and symptoms of anaphylaxis during first dose

Patient Information Report diarrhea promptly; entire course of medication (10-14 days) should be taken to ensure eradication of organism; may interfere with oral contraceptives, females should report symptoms of vaginitis

Dosage Forms POWDER, oral suspension [DSC]: 100 mg/5 mL (50 mL, 75 mL, 100 mL). **TAB, film coated** [DSC]: 400 mg

♦ **Cefizox**® *see* Ceftizoxime *on page 243*

♦ **Cefobid**® **[DSC]** *see* Cefoperazone *on page 236*

Cefoperazone *(sef oh PER a zone)*

U.S. Brand Names Cefobid® [DSC]

Synonyms Cefoperazone Sodium

Therapeutic Category Antibiotic, Cephalosporin (Third Generation)

Use Treatment of susceptible bacterial infection; mainly respiratory tract, skin and skin structure, bone and joint, urinary tract and gynecologic as well as septicemia. Active against a variety of gram-negative bacilli, some gram-positive cocci, and has some activity against *Pseudomonas aeruginosa*.

Pregnancy Risk Factor B

Contraindications Hypersensitivity to cefoperazone, any component of the formulation, or other cephalosporins

Warnings/Precautions Modify dosage in patients with severe renal or hepatic impairment; prolonged use may result in superinfection; although rare, cefoperazone may interfere with hemostasis via destruction of vitamin K-producing intestinal bacteria, prevention of activation of prothrombin by the attachment of a methyltetrazolethiol side chain, and by an immune-mediated thrombocytopenia; use with caution in patients with a history of penicillin allergy especially IgE-mediated reactions (eg, anaphylaxis, urticaria). May cause antibiotic-associated colitis or colitis secondary to *C. difficile*.

Common Adverse Reactions Contains MTT side chain which may lead to increased risk of hypoprothrombinemia and bleeding.

1% to 10%:
   Dermatologic: Rash (maculopapular or erythematous) (2%)
   Gastrointestinal: Diarrhea (3%)
   Hematologic: Decreased neutrophils (2%), decreased hemoglobin or hematocrit (5%), eosinophilia (10%)
   Hepatic: Increased transaminases (5% to 10%)
   Reactions reported with other cephalosporins include anaphylaxis, seizures, Stevens-Johnson syndrome, toxic epidermal necrolysis, renal dysfunction, toxic nephropathy, cholestasis, aplastic anemia, hemolytic anemia, pancytopenia, agranulocytosis, colitis, superinfection

Drug Interactions

Increased Effect/Toxicity: Probenecid may decrease cephalosporin elimination resulting in increased levels. Furosemide, aminoglycosides in combination with cefoperazone may result in additive nephrotoxicity.

Mechanism of Action Inhibits bacterial cell wall synthesis by binding to one or more of the penicillin-binding proteins (PBPs) which in turn inhibits the final transpeptidation step of peptidoglycan synthesis in bacterial cell walls, thus inhibiting cell wall biosynthesis. Bacteria eventually lyse due to ongoing activity of cell wall autolytic enzymes (autolysins and murein hydrolases) while cell wall assembly is arrested.

Pharmacodynamics/Kinetics

Distribution: Widely in most body tissues and fluids; highest concentrations in bile; low penetration in CSF; variable when meninges are inflamed; crosses placenta; small amounts enter breast milk

Half-life elimination: 2 hours; prolonged with hepatic disease or biliary obstruction

Time to peak, serum: I.M.: 1-2 hours

Excretion: Feces via the biliary tract (70% to 75%); urine (20% to 30% as unchanged drug)

Dosage I.M., I.V.:

Children (not approved): 100-150 mg/kg/day divided every 8-12 hours; up to 12 g/day

Adults: 2-4 g/day in divided doses every 12 hours; up to 12 g/day

Dosing adjustment in hepatic impairment: Reduce dose 50% in patients with advanced liver cirrhosis; maximum daily dose: 4 g

Administration

I.M.: Inject deep into large muscle mass.

I.V.: Inject direct I.V. over 3-5 minutes. Infuse intermittent infusion over 30 minutes.

Monitoring Parameters Monitor for coagulation abnormalities and diarrhea; observe for signs and symptoms of anaphylaxis during first dose

Dosage Forms INJ, powder for reconstitution: 10 g

♦ **Cefoperazone Sodium** *see* Cefoperazone *on page 236*

♦ **Cefotan**® *see* Cefotetan *on page 238*

Cefotaxime (sef oh TAKS eem)
Related Information
Antimicrobial Drugs of Choice *on page 1440*
Community-Acquired Pneumonia in Adults *on page 1457*
U.S. Brand Names Claforan®
Synonyms Cefotaxime Sodium
Therapeutic Category Antibiotic, Cephalosporin (Third Generation)
Use Treatment of susceptible infection in respiratory tract, skin and skin structure, bone and joint, urinary tract, gynecologic as well as septicemia, and documented or suspected meningitis. Active against most gram-negative bacilli (not *Pseudomonas*) and gram-positive cocci (not enterococcus). Active against many penicillin-resistant pneumococci.
Pregnancy Risk Factor B
Contraindications Hypersensitivity to cefotaxime, any component of the formulation, or other cephalosporins
Warnings/Precautions Modify dosage in patients with severe renal impairment; prolonged use may result in superinfection; a potentially life-threatening arrhythmia has been reported in patients who received a rapid bolus injection via central line. Use caution in patients with colitis; minimize tissue inflammation by changing infusion sites when needed. Use with caution in patients with a history of penicillin allergy especially IgE-mediated reactions (eg, anaphylaxis, urticaria). May cause antibiotic-associated colitis or colitis secondary to *C. difficile*.
Common Adverse Reactions
1% to 10%:
  Dermatologic: Rash, pruritus
  Gastrointestinal: Diarrhea, nausea, vomiting, colitis
  Local: Pain at injection site
  Reactions reported with other cephalosporins include agranulocytosis, aplastic anemia, cholestasis, hemolytic anemia, hemorrhage, nephropathy, pancytopenia, renal dysfunction, seizures, superinfection.
Drug Interactions
Increased Effect/Toxicity: Probenecid may decrease cephalosporin elimination resulting in increased levels. Furosemide, aminoglycosides in combination with cefotaxime may result in additive nephrotoxicity.
Mechanism of Action Inhibits bacterial cell wall synthesis by binding to one or more of the penicillin-binding proteins (PBPs) which in turn inhibits the final transpeptidation step of peptidoglycan synthesis in bacterial cell walls, thus inhibiting cell wall biosynthesis. Bacteria eventually lyse due to ongoing activity of cell wall autolytic enzymes (autolysins and murein hydrolases) while cell wall assembly is arrested.
Pharmacodynamics/Kinetics
Distribution: Widely to body tissues and fluids including aqueous humor, ascitic and prostatic fluids, bone; penetrates CSF best when meninges are inflamed; crosses placenta; enters breast milk
Metabolism: Partially hepatic to active metabolite, desacetylcefotaxime
Half-life elimination:
  Cefotaxime: Premature neonates <1 week: 5-6 hours; Full-term neonates <1 week: 2-3.4 hours; Adults: 1-1.5 hours; prolonged with renal and/or hepatic impairment
  Desacetylcefotaxime: 1.5-1.9 hours; prolonged with renal impairment
Time to peak, serum: I.M.: Within 30 minutes
Excretion: Urine (as unchanged drug and metabolites)
Dosage
Infants and Children 1 month to 12 years: I.M., I.V.: <50 kg: 50-180 mg/kg/day in divided doses every 4-6 hours
  Meningitis: 200 mg/kg/day in divided doses every 6 hours
Children >12 years and Adults:
  Uncomplicated infections: I.M., I.V.: 1 g every 12 hours
  Moderate/severe infections: I.M., I.V.: 1-2 g every 8 hours
  Infections commonly needing higher doses (eg, septicemia): I.V.: 2 g every 6-8 hours
  Life-threatening infections: I.V.: 2 g every 4 hours
  Preop: I.M., I.V.: 1 g 30-90 minutes before surgery
  C-section: 1 g as soon as the umbilical cord is clamped, then 1 g I.M., I.V. at 6- and 12-hour intervals
Dosing interval in renal impairment:
  Cl_{cr} 10-50 mL/minute: Administer every 8-12 hours
  Cl_{cr} <10 mL/minute: Administer every 24 hours
  Hemodialysis: Moderately dialyzable
Dosing adjustment in hepatic impairment: Moderate dosage reduction is recommended in severe liver disease
Continuous arteriovenous or venovenous hemodiafiltration effects: Administer 1 g every 12 hour
Administration Can be administered IVP over 3-5 minutes or I.V. intermittent infusion over 15-30 minutes
Monitoring Parameters Observe for signs and symptoms of anaphylaxis during first dose; CBC with differential (especially with long courses)
Dosage Forms INF [premixed in D_5W]: 1 g (50 mL); 2 g (50 mL). **INJ, powder for reconstitution:** 500 mg, 1 g, 2 g, 10 g

♦ **Cefotaxime Sodium** *see* Cefotaxime *on page 237*

Cefotetan (SEF oh tee tan)
Related Information
Antimicrobial Drugs of Choice *on page 1440*
Prevention of Wound Infection & Sepsis in Surgical Patients *on page 1436*
U.S. Brand Names Cefotan®
Synonyms Cefotetan Disodium
Therapeutic Category Antibiotic, Anaerobic; Antibiotic, Cephalosporin (Second Generation)
Use Less active against staphylococci and streptococci than first generation cephalosporins, but active against anaerobes including *Bacteroides fragilis*; active against gram-negative enteric bacilli including *E. coli, Klebsiella,* and *Proteus*; used predominantly for respiratory tract, skin and skin structure, bone and joint, urinary tract and gynecologic as well as septicemia; surgical prophylaxis; intra-abdominal infections and other mixed infections
Pregnancy Risk Factor B
Contraindications Hypersensitivity to cefotetan, any component of the formulation, or other cephalosporins
Warnings/Precautions Modify dosage in patients with severe renal impairment; prolonged use may result in superinfection; although cefotetan contains the methyltetrazolethiol side chain, bleeding has not been a significant problem; use with caution in patients with a history of penicillin allergy especially IgE-mediated reactions (eg, anaphylaxis, urticaria). Cefotetan has been associated with a higher risk of hemolytic anemia relative to other cephalosporins (approximately threefold). May cause antibiotic-associated colitis or colitis secondary to *C. difficile.*
Common Adverse Reactions Contains MTT side chain which may lead to increased risk of hypoprothrombinemia and bleeding.

1% to 10%:
 Gastrointestinal: Diarrhea (1.3%)
 Hepatic: Increased transaminases (1.2%)
 Miscellaneous: Hypersensitivity reactions (1.2%)
Reactions reported with other cephalosporins include seizures, Stevens-Johnson syndrome, toxic epidermal necrolysis, renal dysfunction, toxic nephropathy, cholestasis, aplastic anemia, hemolytic anemia, hemorrhage, pancytopenia, agranulocytosis, colitis, superinfection

Drug Interactions
Increased Effect/Toxicity: Probenecid may decrease cephalosporin elimination. Furosemide, aminoglycosides in combination with cefotetan may result in additive nephrotoxicity. May cause disulfiram-like reaction with concomitant ethanol use. Effects of warfarin may be enhanced by cefotetan (due to effects on gastrointestinal flora).
Mechanism of Action Inhibits bacterial cell wall synthesis by binding to one or more of the penicillin-binding proteins (PBPs) which in turn inhibits the final transpeptidation step of peptidoglycan synthesis in bacterial cell walls, thus inhibiting cell wall biosynthesis. Bacteria eventually lyse due to ongoing activity of cell wall autolytic enzymes (autolysins and murein hydrolases) while cell wall assembly is arrested.
Pharmacodynamics/Kinetics
Distribution: Widely to body tissues and fluids including bile, sputum, prostatic, peritoneal; low concentrations enter CSF; crosses placenta; enters breast milk
Protein binding: 76% to 90%
Half-life elimination: 3-5 hours
Time to peak, serum: I.M.: 1.5-3 hours
Excretion: Primarily urine (as unchanged drug); feces (20%)
Dosage I.M., I.V.:
Children: 20-40 mg/kg/dose every 12 hours
Adults: 1-6 g/day in divided doses every 12 hours; usual dose: 1-2 g every 12 hours for 5-10 days; 1-2 g may be given every 24 hours for urinary tract infection
Dosing interval in renal impairment:
Cl$_{cr}$ 10-30 mL/minute: Administer every 24 hours
Cl$_{cr}$ <10 mL/minute: Administer every 48 hours
Hemodialysis: Slightly dialyzable (5% to 20%); administer $^1/_4$ the usual dose every 24 hours on days between dialysis; administer $^1/_2$ the usual dose on the day of dialysis.
Continuous arteriovenous or venovenous hemodiafiltration effects: Administer 750 mg every 12 hours
Administration
I.M.: Inject deep I.M. into large muscle mass.
I.V.: Inject direct I.V. over 3-5 minutes. Infuse intermittent infusion over 30 minutes
Monitoring Parameters Observe for signs and symptoms of anaphylaxis during first dose
Dosage Forms INF [premixed iso-osmotic solution]: 1 g (50 mL); 2 g (50 mL). INJ, powder for reconstitution: 1 g, 2 g, 10 g

♦ Cefotetan Disodium *see* Cefotetan *on page 238*

Cefoxitin (se FOKS i tin)
Related Information
Antimicrobial Drugs of Choice *on page 1440*
Prevention of Wound Infection & Sepsis in Surgical Patients *on page 1436*
U.S. Brand Names Mefoxin®
Synonyms Cefoxitin Sodium
Therapeutic Category Antibiotic, Anaerobic; Antibiotic, Cephalosporin (Second Generation)

Use Less active against staphylococci and streptococci than first generation cephalosporins, but active against anaerobes including *Bacteroides fragilis*; active against gram-negative enteric bacilli including *E. coli*, *Klebsiella*, and *Proteus*; used predominantly for respiratory tract, skin and skin structure, bone and joint, urinary tract and gynecologic as well as septicemia; surgical prophylaxis; intra-abdominal infections and other mixed infections; indicated for bacterial *Eikenella corrodens* infections

Pregnancy Risk Factor B

Contraindications Hypersensitivity to cefoxitin, any component of the formulation, or other cephalosporins

Warnings/Precautions Use with caution in patients with history of colitis; cefoxitin may increase resistance of organisms by inducing beta-lactamase; modify dosage in patients with severe renal impairment; prolonged use may result in superinfection; use with caution in patients with a history of penicillin allergy especially IgE-mediated reactions (eg, anaphylaxis, urticaria). May cause antibiotic-associated colitis or colitis secondary to *C. difficile*.

Common Adverse Reactions

1% to 10%: Gastrointestinal: Diarrhea

Reactions reported with other cephalosporins include seizures, Stevens-Johnson syndrome, toxic epidermal necrolysis, erythema multiforme, urticaria, serum-sickness reactions, renal dysfunction, toxic nephropathy, cholestasis, aplastic anemia, hemolytic anemia, hemorrhage, pancytopenia, agranulocytosis, colitis, vaginitis, superinfection

Drug Interactions

Increased Effect/Toxicity: Probenecid may decrease cephalosporin elimination. Furosemide, aminoglycosides in combination with cefoxitin may result in additive nephrotoxicity.

Mechanism of Action Inhibits bacterial cell wall synthesis by binding to one or more of the penicillin-binding proteins (PBPs) which in turn inhibits the final transpeptidation step of peptidoglycan synthesis in bacterial cell walls, thus inhibiting cell wall biosynthesis. Bacteria eventually lyse due to ongoing activity of cell wall autolytic enzymes (autolysins and murein hydrolases) while cell wall assembly is arrested.

Pharmacodynamics/Kinetics

Distribution: Widely to body tissues and fluids including the pleural, synovial, ascitic, bile; poorly penetrates into CSF even with inflammation of the meninges; crosses placenta; small amounts enter breast milk

Protein binding: 65% to 79%

Half-life elimination: 45-60 minutes; significantly prolonged with renal impairment

Time to peak, serum: I.M.: 20-30 minutes

Excretion: Urine (85% as unchanged drug)

Dosage

Infants >3 months and Children: I.M., I.V.:

Mild to moderate infection: 80-100 mg/kg/day in divided doses every 4-6 hours

Severe infection: 100-160 mg/kg/day in divided doses every 4-6 hours; maximum dose: 12 g/day

Perioperative prophylaxis: 30-40 mg/kg 30-60 minutes prior to surgery followed by 30-40 mg/kg/dose every 6 hours for no more than 24 hours after surgery depending on the procedure

Adolescents and Adults: I.M., I.V.: Perioperative prophylaxis: 1-2 g 30-60 minutes prior to surgery followed by 1-2 g every 6-8 hours for no more than 24 hours after surgery depending on the procedure

Adults: I.M., I.V.: 1-2 g every 6-8 hours (I.M. injection is painful); up to 12 g/day

Pelvic inflammatory disease:

Inpatients: I.V.: 2 g every 6 hours **plus** doxycycline 100 mg I.V. or 100 mg orally every 12 hours until improved, followed by doxycycline 100 mg orally twice daily to complete 14 days

Outpatients: I.M.: 2 g **plus** probenecid 1 g orally as a single dose, followed by doxycycline 100 mg orally twice daily for 14 days

Dosing interval in renal impairment:

Cl_{cr} 30-50 mL/minute: Administer 1-2 g every 8-12 hours

Cl_{cr} 10-29 mL/minute: Administer 1-2 g every 12-24 hours

Cl_{cr} 5-9 mL/minute: Administer 0.5-1 g every 12-24 hours

Cl_{cr} <5 mL/minute: Administer 0.5-1 g every 24-48 hours

Hemodialysis: Moderately dialyzable (20% to 50%); administer a loading dose of 1-2 g after each hemodialysis; maintenance dose as noted above based on Cl_{cr}

Continuous arteriovenous or venovenous hemodiafiltration effects: Dose as for Cl_{cr} 10-50 mL/minute

Administration

I.M.: Inject deep I.M. into large muscle mass.

I.V.: Inject direct I.V. over 3-5 minutes. Infuse intermittent infusion over 30 minutes.

Monitoring Parameters Monitor renal function periodically when used in combination with other nephrotoxic drugs; observe for signs and symptoms of anaphylaxis during first dose

Dosage Forms INF [premixed in D_5W, frozen]: 1 g (50 mL); 2 g (50 mL). **INJ, powder for reconstitution:** 1 g, 2 g, 10 g

◆ **Cefoxitin Sodium** *see* Cefoxitin *on page 238*

Cefpodoxime *(sef pode OKS eem)*

Related Information

Antimicrobial Drugs of Choice *on page 1440*
Community-Acquired Pneumonia in Adults *on page 1457*

(Continued)

Cefpodoxime *(Continued)*

U.S. Brand Names Vantin®

Synonyms Cefpodoxime Proxetil

Therapeutic Category Antibiotic, Cephalosporin (Third Generation)

Use Treatment of susceptible acute, community-acquired pneumonia caused by *S. pneumoniae* or nonbeta-lactamase producing *H. influenzae*; acute uncomplicated gonorrhea caused by *N. gonorrhoeae*; uncomplicated skin and skin structure infections caused by *S. aureus* or *S. pyogenes*; acute otitis media caused by *S. pneumoniae, H. influenzae,* or *M. catarrhalis*; pharyngitis or tonsillitis; and uncomplicated urinary tract infections caused by *E. coli, Klebsiella,* and *Proteus*

Pregnancy Risk Factor B

Contraindications Hypersensitivity to cefpodoxime, any component of the formulation, or other cephalosporins

Warnings/Precautions Modify dosage in patients with severe renal impairment; prolonged use may result in superinfection. Use with caution in patients with a history of penicillin allergy especially IgE-mediated reactions (eg, anaphylaxis, urticaria).

Common Adverse Reactions

>10%:

  Dermatologic: Diaper rash (12%)

  Gastrointestinal: Diarrhea in infants and toddlers (15%)

1% to 10%:

  Central nervous system: Headache (1%)

  Dermatologic: Rash (1%)

  Gastrointestinal: Diarrhea (7%), nausea (4%), abdominal pain (2%), vomiting (1% to 2%)

  Genitourinary: Vaginal infections (3%)

Reactions reported with other cephalosporins include seizures, Stevens-Johnson syndrome, toxic epidermal necrolysis, erythema multiforme, urticaria, serum-sickness reactions, renal dysfunction, interstitial nephritis toxic nephropathy, cholestasis, aplastic anemia, hemolytic anemia, hemorrhage, pancytopenia, agranulocytosis, colitis, vaginitis, superinfection

Drug Interactions

  Increased Effect/Toxicity: Probenecid may decrease cephalosporin elimination. Furosemide, aminoglycosides in combination with cefpodoxime may result in additive nephrotoxicity.

  Decreased Effect: Antacids and H_2-receptor antagonists reduce absorption and serum concentration of cefpodoxime.

Mechanism of Action Inhibits bacterial cell wall synthesis by binding to one or more of the penicillin-binding proteins (PBPs) which in turn inhibits the final transpeptidation step of peptidoglycan synthesis in bacterial cell walls, thus inhibiting cell wall biosynthesis. Bacteria eventually lyse due to ongoing activity of cell wall autolytic enzymes (autolysins and murein hydrolases) while cell wall assembly is arrested.

Pharmacodynamics/Kinetics

  Absorption: Rapid and well absorbed (50%), acid stable; enhanced in the presence of food or low gastric pH

  Distribution: Good tissue penetration, including lung and tonsils; penetrates into pleural fluid

  Protein binding: 18% to 23%

  Metabolism: De-esterified in GI tract to active metabolite, cefpodoxime

  Half-life elimination: 2.2 hours; prolonged with renal impairment

  Time to peak: Within 1 hour

  Excretion: Urine (80% as unchanged drug) in 24 hours

Dosage Oral:

  Children 2 months to 12 years:

    Acute otitis media: 10 mg/kg/day divided every 12 hours (400 mg/day) for 5 days (maximum: 200 mg/dose)

    Acute maxillary sinusitis: 10 mg/kg/day divided every 12 hours for 10 days (maximum: 200 mg/dose)

    Pharyngitis/tonsillitis: 10 mg/kg/day in 2 divided doses for 5-10 days (maximum: 100 mg/dose)

  Children ≥12 years and Adults:

    Acute community-acquired pneumonia and bacterial exacerbations of chronic bronchitis: 200 mg every 12 hours for 14 days and 10 days, respectively

    Acute maxillary sinusitis: 200 mg every 12 hours for 10 days

    Skin and skin structure: 400 mg every 12 hours for 7-14 days

    Uncomplicated gonorrhea (male and female) and rectal gonococcal infections (female): 200 mg as a single dose

    Pharyngitis/tonsillitis: 100 mg every 12 hours for 5-10 days

    Uncomplicated urinary tract infection: 100 mg every 12 hours for 7 days

    Dosing adjustment in renal impairment: Cl_{cr} <30 mL/minute: Administer every 24 hours

    Hemodialysis: Administer dose 3 times/week following hemodialysis

Monitoring Parameters Observe for signs and symptoms of anaphylaxis during first dose

Patient Information Take with food; chilling improves flavor (do not freeze); report persistent diarrhea; entire course of medication (10-14 days) should be taken to ensure eradication of organism; may interfere with oral contraceptives; females should report symptoms of vaginitis

Dosage Forms GRAN, oral suspension: 50 mg/5 mL (50 mL, 100 mL); 100 mg/5 mL (50 mL, 75 mL, 100 mL). **TAB, film coated:** 100 mg, 200 mg

♦ **Cefpodoxime Proxetil** *see* Cefpodoxime *on page 239*

Cefprozil (sef PROE zil)

Related Information
Community-Acquired Pneumonia in Adults *on page 1457*

U.S. Brand Names Cefzil®

Therapeutic Category Antibiotic, Cephalosporin (Second Generation)

Use Treatment of otitis media and infections involving the respiratory tract and skin and skin structure; active against methicillin-sensitive staphylococci, many streptococci, and various gram-negative bacilli including *E. coli*, some *Klebsiella*, *P. mirabilis*, *H. influenzae*, and *Moraxella*.

Pregnancy Risk Factor B

Contraindications Hypersensitivity to cefprozil, any component of the formulation, or other cephalosporins

Warnings/Precautions Modify dosage in patients with severe renal impairment; prolonged use may result in superinfection; use with caution in patients with a history of penicillin allergy especially IgE-mediated reactions (eg, anaphylaxis, urticaria). May cause antibiotic-associated colitis or colitis secondary to *C. difficile.*

Common Adverse Reactions
1% to 10%:
    Central nervous system: Dizziness (1%)
    Dermatologic: Diaper rash (2%)
    Gastrointestinal: Diarrhea (3%), nausea (4%), vomiting (1%), abdominal pain (1%)
    Genitourinary: Vaginitis, genital pruritus (2%)
    Hepatic: Increased transaminases (2%)
    Miscellaneous: Superinfection
Reactions reported with other cephalosporins include seizures, toxic epidermal necrolysis, renal dysfunction, interstitial nephritis, toxic nephropathy, aplastic anemia, hemolytic anemia, hemorrhage, pancytopenia, agranulocytosis, colitis, vaginitis, superinfection

Drug Interactions
Increased Effect/Toxicity: Probenecid may decrease cephalosporin elimination. Furosemide, aminoglycosides in combination with cefprozil may result in additive nephrotoxicity.

Mechanism of Action Inhibits bacterial cell wall synthesis by binding to one or more of the penicillin-binding proteins (PBPs) which in turn inhibits the final transpeptidation step of peptidoglycan synthesis in bacterial cell walls, thus inhibiting cell wall biosynthesis. Bacteria eventually lyse due to ongoing activity of cell wall autolytic enzymes (autolysins and murein hydrolases) while cell wall assembly is arrested.

Pharmacodynamics/Kinetics
Absorption: Well absorbed (94%)
Distribution: Low amounts enter breast milk
Protein binding: 35% to 45%
Half-life elimination: Normal renal function: 1.3 hours
Time to peak, serum: Fasting: 1.5 hours
Excretion: Urine (61% as unchanged drug)

Dosage Oral:
Infants and Children >6 months to 12 years: Otitis media: 15 mg/kg every 12 hours for 10 days
Pharyngitis/tonsillitis:
    Children 2-12 years: 7.5 -15 mg/kg/day divided every 12 hours for 10 days (administer for >10 days if due to *S. pyogenes*); maximum: 1 g/day
    Children >13 years and Adults: 500 mg every 24 hours for 10 days
Uncomplicated skin and skin structure infections:
    Children 2-12 years: 20 mg/kg every 24 hours for 10 days; maximum: 1 g/day
    Children >13 years and Adults: 250 mg every 12 hours, or 500 mg every 12-24 hours for 10 days
Secondary bacterial infection of acute bronchitis or acute bacterial exacerbation of chronic bronchitis: 500 mg every 12 hours for 10 days
Dosing adjustment in renal impairment: Cl$_{cr}$ <30 mL/minute: Reduce dose by 50%
Hemodialysis: Reduced by hemodialysis; administer dose after the completion of hemodialysis

Administration Administer around-the-clock to promote less variation in peak and trough serum levels. Chilling the reconstituted oral suspension improves flavor (do not freeze).

Monitoring Parameters Assess patient at beginning and throughout therapy for infection; monitor for signs of anaphylaxis during first dose

Patient Information Chilling improves flavor (do not freeze); report persistent diarrhea; entire course of medication (10-14 days) should be taken to ensure eradication of organism; may interfere with oral contraceptives; females should report symptoms of vaginitis

Dosage Forms POWDER, oral suspension: 125 mg/5 mL (50 mL, 75 mL, 100 mL); 250 mg/5 mL (50 mL, 75 mL, 100 mL). **TAB:** 250 mg, 500 mg

Ceftazidime (SEF tay zi deem)

Related Information
Antimicrobial Drugs of Choice *on page 1440*

U.S. Brand Names Ceptaz® [DSC]; Fortaz®; Tazicef®; Tazidime®

Therapeutic Category Antibiotic, Cephalosporin (Third Generation)

Use Treatment of documented susceptible *Pseudomonas aeruginosa* infection and infections due to other susceptible aerobic gram-negative organisms; empiric therapy of a febrile, granulocytopenic patient

Pregnancy Risk Factor B
(Continued)

Ceftazidime *(Continued)*

Contraindications Hypersensitivity to ceftazidime, any component of the formulation, or other cephalosporins

Warnings/Precautions Modify dosage in patients with severe renal impairment; prolonged use may result in superinfection; use with caution in patients with a history of penicillin allergy especially IgE-mediated reactions (eg, anaphylaxis, urticaria). May cause antibiotic-associated colitis or colitis secondary to *C. difficile.*

Common Adverse Reactions
1% to 10%:
    Gastrointestinal: Diarrhea (1%)
    Local: Pain at injection site (1%)
    Miscellaneous: Hypersensitivity reactions (2%)
Reactions reported with other cephalosporins include seizures, urticaria, serum-sickness reactions, renal dysfunction, interstitial nephritis, toxic nephropathy, elevated BUN, elevated creatinine, cholestasis, aplastic anemia, hemolytic anemia, pancytopenia, agranulocytosis, colitis, prolonged PT, hemorrhage, superinfection

Drug Interactions
Increased Effect/Toxicity: Probenecid may decrease cephalosporin elimination. Aminoglycosides: *in vitro* studies indicate additive or synergistic effect against some strains of Enterobacteriaceae and *Pseudomonas aeruginosa*. Furosemide, aminoglycosides in combination with ceftazidime may result in additive nephrotoxicity.

Mechanism of Action Inhibits bacterial cell wall synthesis by binding to one or more of the penicillin-binding proteins (PBPs) which in turn inhibits the final transpeptidation step of peptidoglycan synthesis in bacterial cell walls, thus inhibiting cell wall biosynthesis. Bacteria eventually lyse due to ongoing activity of cell wall autolytic enzymes (autolysins and murein hydrolases) while cell wall assembly is arrested.

Pharmacodynamics/Kinetics
Distribution: Widely throughout the body including bone, bile, skin, CSF (higher concentrations achieved when meninges are inflamed), endometrium, heart, pleural and lymphatic fluids
Protein binding: 17%
Half-life elimination: 1-2 hours, prolonged with renal impairment; Neonates <23 days: 2.2-4.7 hours
Time to peak, serum: I.M.: ~1 hour
Excretion: Urine (80% to 90% as unchanged drug)

Dosage
Infants and Children 1 month to 12 years: I.V.: 30-50 mg/kg/dose every 8 hours; maximum dose: 6 g/day
Adults: I.M., I.V.: 500 mg to 2 g every 8-12 hours
    Urinary tract infections: 250-500 mg every 12 hours
Dosing interval in renal impairment:
    Cl_{cr} 30-50 mL/minute: Administer every 12 hours
    Cl_{cr} 10-30 mL/minute: Administer every 24 hours
    Cl_{cr} <10 mL/minute: Administer every 48-72 hours
Hemodialysis: Dialyzable (50% to 100%)
Continuous arteriovenous or venovenous hemodiafiltration effects: Dose as for Cl_{cr} 30-50 mL/minute

Administration Any carbon dioxide bubbles that may be present in the withdrawn solution should be expelled prior to injection; administer around-the-clock to promote less variation in peak and trough serum levels; ceftazidime can be administered deep I.M. into large mass muscle, IVP over 3-5 minutes, or I.V. intermittent infusion over 15-30 minutes; do not admix with aminoglycosides in same bottle/bag; final concentration for I.V. administration should not exceed 100 mg/mL

Monitoring Parameters Observe for signs and symptoms of anaphylaxis during first dose

Dosage Forms INF [premixed iso-osmotic solution] (Fortaz®): 1 g (50 mL); 2 g (50 mL). **INJ, powder for reconstitution:** (Ceptaz® [DSC]): 10 g; (Fortaz®): 500 mg, 1 g, 2 g, 6 g; (Tazicef®, Tazidime®): 1 g, 2 g, 6 g

Ceftibuten *(sef TYE byoo ten)*

U.S. Brand Names Cedax®

Therapeutic Category Antibiotic, Cephalosporin (Third Generation)

Use Oral cephalosporin for treatment of bronchitis, otitis media, and pharyngitis/tonsillitis due to *H. influenzae* and *M. catarrhalis*, both beta-lactamase-producing and nonproducing strains, as well as *S. pneumoniae* (weak) and *S. pyogenes*

Pregnancy Risk Factor B

Contraindications Hypersensitivity to ceftibuten, any component of the formulation, or other cephalosporins

Warnings/Precautions Modify dosage in patients with severe renal impairment, prolonged use may result in superinfection; use with caution in patients with a history of penicillin allergy, especially IgE-mediated reactions (eg, anaphylaxis, urticaria). May cause antibiotic-associated colitis or colitis secondary to *C. difficile.*

Common Adverse Reactions
1% to 10%:
    Central nervous system: Headache (3%), dizziness (1%)
    Gastrointestinal: Nausea (4%), diarrhea (3%), dyspepsia (2%), vomiting (1%), abdominal pain (1%)
    Hematologic: Increased eosinophils (3%), decreased hemoglobin (2%), thrombocytosis

Hepatic: Increased ALT (1%), increased bilirubin (1%)
Renal: Increased BUN (4%)

Reactions reported with other cephalosporins include anaphylaxis, fever, paresthesia, pruritus, Stevens-Johnson syndrome, toxic epidermal necrolysis, erythema multiforme, angioedema, pseudomembranous colitis, hemolytic anemia, candidiasis, vaginitis, encephalopathy, asterixis, neuromuscular excitability, seizures, serum-sickness reactions, renal dysfunction, interstitial nephritis, toxic nephropathy, cholestasis, aplastic anemia, hemolytic anemia, pancytopenia, agranulocytosis, colitis, prolonged PT, hemorrhage, superinfection

Drug Interactions
Increased Effect/Toxicity: High-dose probenecid decreases clearance. Aminoglycosides in combination with ceftibuten may increase nephrotoxic potential.

Mechanism of Action Inhibits bacterial cell wall synthesis by binding to one or more of the penicillin-binding proteins (PBPs) which in turn inhibits the final transpeptidation step of peptidoglycan synthesis in bacterial cell walls, thus inhibiting cell wall biosynthesis. Bacteria eventually lyse due to ongoing activity of cell wall autolytic enzymes (autolysins and murein hydrolases) while cell wall assembly is arrested.

Pharmacodynamics/Kinetics
Absorption: Rapid; food decreases peak concentrations, delays T_{max}, and lowers AUC
Distribution: V_d: Children: 0.5 L/kg; Adults: 0.21 L/kg
Half-life elimination: 2 hours
Time to peak: 2-3 hours
Excretion: Urine

Dosage Oral:
Children <12 years: 9 mg/kg/day for 10 days; maximum daily dose: 400 mg
Children ≥12 years and Adults: 400 mg once daily for 10 days; maximum: 400 mg
Dosage adjustment in renal impairment:
Cl_{cr} 30-49 mL/minute: Administer 4.5 mg/kg or 200 mg every 24 hours
Cl_{cr} <29 mL/minute: Administer 2.25 mg/kg or 100 mg every 24 hours

Administration Shake suspension well before use.

Monitoring Parameters Observe for signs and symptoms of anaphylaxis during first dose; with prolonged therapy, monitor renal, hepatic, and hematologic function periodically

Patient Information Must be administered at least 2 hours before meals or 1 hour after a meal; discard any unused portion after 14 days; report prolonged diarrhea; entire course of medication should be taken to ensure eradication of organism; take at the same time each day to maintain adequate blood levels; may interfere with oral contraceptive; females should report symptoms of vaginitis

Dosage Forms CAP: 400 mg. POWDER, oral suspension: 90 mg/5 mL (30 mL, 60 mL, 120 mL)

♦ **Ceftin®** see Cefuroxime on page 245

Ceftizoxime (sef ti ZOKS eem)

Related Information
Antimicrobial Drugs of Choice on page 1440

U.S. Brand Names Cefizox®

Synonyms Ceftizoxime Sodium

Therapeutic Category Antibiotic, Cephalosporin (Third Generation)

Use Treatment of susceptible bacterial infection, mainly respiratory tract, skin and skin structure, bone and joint, urinary tract and gynecologic, as well as septicemia; active against many gram-negative bacilli (not *Pseudomonas*), some gram-positive cocci (not *Enterococcus*), and some anaerobes

Pregnancy Risk Factor B

Contraindications Hypersensitivity to ceftizoxime, any component of the formulation, or other cephalosporins

Warnings/Precautions Modify dosage in patients with severe renal impairment, prolonged use may result in superinfection; use with caution in patients with a history of penicillin allergy, especially IgE-mediated reactions (eg, anaphylaxis, urticaria). May cause antibiotic-associated colitis or colitis secondary to *C. difficile*.

Common Adverse Reactions
1% to 10%:
Central nervous system: Fever
Dermatologic: Rash, pruritus
Hematologic: Eosinophilia, thrombocytosis
Hepatic: Elevated transaminases, alkaline phosphatase
Local: Pain, burning at injection site

Other reactions reported with cephalosporins include Stevens-Johnson syndrome, toxic epidermal necrolysis, erythema multiforme, pseudomembranous colitis, angioedema, hemolytic anemia, candidiasis, encephalopathy, asterixis, neuromuscular excitability, seizures, serum-sickness reactions, renal dysfunction, interstitial nephritis, toxic nephropathy, cholestasis, aplastic anemia, hemolytic anemia, pancytopenia, agranulocytosis, colitis, prolonged PT, hemorrhage, superinfection

Drug Interactions
Increased Effect/Toxicity: Probenecid may decrease cephalosporin elimination. Furosemide, aminoglycosides in combination with ceftizoxime may result in additive nephrotoxicity.
(Continued)

Ceftizoxime *(Continued)*

Mechanism of Action Inhibits bacterial cell wall synthesis by binding to one or more of the penicillin-binding proteins (PBPs) which in turn inhibits the final transpeptidation step of peptidoglycan synthesis in bacterial cell walls, thus inhibiting cell wall biosynthesis. Bacteria eventually lyse due to ongoing activity of cell wall autolytic enzymes (autolysins and murein hydrolases) while cell wall assembly is arrested.

Pharmacodynamics/Kinetics

Distribution: V_d: 0.35-0.5 L/kg; widely into most body tissues and fluids including gallbladder, liver, kidneys, bone, sputum, bile, pleural and synovial fluids; has good CSF penetration; crosses placenta; small amounts enter breast milk

Protein binding: 30%

Half-life elimination: 1.6 hours; Cl_{cr} <10 mL/minute: 25 hours

Time to peak, serum: I.M.: 0.5-1 hour

Excretion: Urine (as unchanged drug)

Dosage I.M., I.V.:

Children ≥6 months: 150-200 mg/kg/day divided every 6-8 hours (maximum of 12 g/24 hours)

Adults: 1-2 g every 8-12 hours, up to 2 g every 4 hours or 4 g every 8 hours for life-threatening infections

Dosing adjustment in renal impairment: Adults:

Cl_{cr} 10-30 mL/minute: Administer 1 g every 12 hours

Cl_{cr} <10 mL/minute: Administer 1 g every 24 hours

Moderately dialyzable (20% to 50%)

Continuous arteriovenous or venovenous hemodiafiltration effects: Dose as for Cl_{cr} 10-50 mL/minute

Monitoring Parameters Observe for signs and symptoms of anaphylaxis during first dose

Dosage Forms INJ [premixed iso-osmotic solution]: 1 g (50 mL); 2 g (50 mL). **INJ, powder for reconstitution:** 1 g, 2 g, 10 g

♦ **Ceftizoxime Sodium** *see* Ceftizoxime *on page 243*

Ceftriaxone *(sef trye AKS one)*

Related Information

Antimicrobial Drugs of Choice *on page 1440*

Community-Acquired Pneumonia in Adults *on page 1457*

U.S. Brand Names Rocephin®

Synonyms Ceftriaxone Sodium

Therapeutic Category Antibiotic, Cephalosporin (Third Generation)

Use Treatment of lower respiratory tract infections, skin and skin structure infections, bone and joint infections, intra-abdominal and urinary tract infections, sepsis and meningitis due to susceptible organisms; documented or suspected infection due to susceptible organisms in home care patients and patients without I.V. line access; treatment of documented or suspected gonococcal infection or chancroid; emergency room management of patients at high risk for bacteremia, periorbital or buccal cellulitis, salmonellosis or shigellosis, and pneumonia of unestablished etiology (<5 years of age); treatment of Lyme disease, depends on the stage of the disease (used in Stage II and Stage III, but not stage I; doxycycline is the drug of choice for Stage I)

Pregnancy Risk Factor B

Contraindications Hypersensitivity to ceftriaxone sodium, any component of the formulation, or other cephalosporins; **do not use in hyperbilirubinemic neonates**, particularly those who are premature since ceftriaxone is reported to displace bilirubin from albumin binding sites

Warnings/Precautions Modify dosage in patients with severe renal impairment, prolonged use may result in superinfection; use with caution in patients with a history of penicillin allergy, especially IgE-mediated reactions (eg, anaphylaxis, urticaria). May cause antibiotic-associated colitis or colitis secondary to *C. difficile.*

Common Adverse Reactions

1% to 10%:

Dermatologic: Rash (2%)

Gastrointestinal: Diarrhea (3%)

Hematologic: Eosinophilia (6%), thrombocytosis (5%), leukopenia (2%)

Hepatic: Elevated transaminases (3.1% to 3.3%)

Local: Pain, induration at injection site (I.V. 1%); warmth, tightness, induration (5% to 17%) following I.M. injection

Renal: Increased BUN (1%)

Drug Interactions

Increased Effect/Toxicity: Aminoglycosides may result in synergistic antibacterial activity. High-dose probenecid decreases clearance. Aminoglycosides increase nephrotoxic potential.

Mechanism of Action Inhibits bacterial cell wall synthesis by binding to one or more of the penicillin-binding proteins (PBPs) which in turn inhibits the final transpeptidation step of peptidoglycan synthesis in bacterial cell walls, thus inhibiting cell wall biosynthesis. Bacteria eventually lyse due to ongoing activity of cell wall autolytic enzymes (autolysins and murein hydrolases) while cell wall assembly is arrested.

Pharmacodynamics/Kinetics

Absorption: I.M.: Well absorbed

Distribution: Widely throughout the body including gallbladder, lungs, bone, bile, CSF (higher concentrations achieved when meninges are inflamed); crosses placenta; enters amniotic fluid and breast milk

Protein binding: 85% to 95%

Half-life elimination: Normal renal and hepatic function: 5-9 hours
Neonates: Postnatal: 1-4 days old: 16 hours; 9-30 days old: 9 hours

Time to peak, serum: I.M.: 1-2 hours

Excretion: Urine (33% to 65% as unchanged drug); feces

Dosage I.M., I.V.:

Neonates:

Postnatal age ≤7 days: 50 mg/kg/day given every 24 hours

Postnatal age >7 days:
≤2000 g: 50 mg/kg/day given every 24 hours
>2000 g: 50-75 mg/kg/day given every 24 hours

Gonococcal prophylaxis: 25-50 mg/kg as a single dose (dose not to exceed 125 mg)

Gonococcal infection: 25-50 mg/kg/day (maximum dose: 125 mg) given every 24 hours for 10-14 days

Infants and Children: 50-75 mg/kg/day in 1-2 divided doses every 12-24 hours; maximum: 2 g/24 hours

Meningitis: 100 mg/kg/day divided every 12-24 hours, up to a maximum of 4 g/24 hours; loading dose of 75 mg/kg/dose may be given at start of therapy

Otitis media: I.M.: 50 mg/kg as a single dose (maximum: 1 g)

Uncomplicated gonococcal infections, sexual assault, and STD prophylaxis: I.M.: 125 mg as a single dose plus doxycycline

Complicated gonococcal infections:

Infants: I.M., I.V.: 25-50 mg/kg/day in a single dose (maximum: 125 mg/dose); treat for 7 days for disseminated infection and 7-14 days for documented meningitis

<45 kg: 50 mg/kg/day once daily; maximum: 1 g/day; for ophthalmia, peritonitis, arthritis, or bacteremia: 50-100 mg/kg/day divided every 12-24 hours; maximum: 2 g/day for meningitis or endocarditis

>45 kg: 1 g/day once daily for disseminated gonococcal infections; 1-2 g dose every 12 hours for meningitis or endocarditis

Acute epididymitis: I.M.: 250 mg in a single dose

Adults: 1-2 g every 12-24 hours (depending on the type and severity of infection); maximum dose: 2 g every 12 hours for treatment of meningitis

Uncomplicated gonorrhea: I.M.: 250 mg as a single dose

Surgical prophylaxis: 1 g 30 minutes to 2 hours before surgery

Dosing adjustment in renal or hepatic impairment: No change necessary

Hemodialysis: Not dialyzable (0% to 5%); administer dose postdialysis

Peritoneal dialysis: Administer 750 mg every 12 hours

Continuous arteriovenous or venovenous hemofiltration: Removes 10 mg of ceftriaxone per liter of filtrate per day

Monitoring Parameters Observe for signs and symptoms of anaphylaxis

Dosage Forms INF [premixed in dextrose]: 1 g (50 mL); 2 g (50 mL). **INJ, powder for reconstitution:** 250 mg, 500 mg, 1 g, 2 g, 10 g

♦ **Ceftriaxone Sodium** *see* Ceftriaxone *on page 244*

Cefuroxime (se fyoor OKS eem)

Related Information

Antimicrobial Drugs of Choice *on page 1440*

Community-Acquired Pneumonia in Adults *on page 1457*

Prevention of Wound Infection & Sepsis in Surgical Patients *on page 1436*

U.S. Brand Names Ceftin®; Kefurox® [DSC]; Zinacef®

Synonyms Cefuroxime Axetil; Cefuroxime Sodium

Therapeutic Category Antibiotic, Cephalosporin (Second Generation)

Use Treatment of infections caused by staphylococci, group B streptococci, *H. influenzae* (type A and B), *E. coli, Enterobacter, Salmonella,* and *Klebsiella*; treatment of susceptible infections of the lower respiratory tract, otitis media, urinary tract, skin and soft tissue, bone and joint, sepsis and gonorrhea

Pregnancy Risk Factor B

Contraindications Hypersensitivity to cefuroxime, any component of the formulation, or other cephalosporins

Warnings/Precautions Modify dosage in patients with severe renal impairment, prolonged use may result in superinfection; use with caution in patients with a history of penicillin allergy, especially IgE-mediated reactions (eg, anaphylaxis, urticaria). May cause antibiotic-associated colitis or colitis secondary to *C. difficile.* May be associated with increased INR, especially in nutritionally-deficient patients, prolonged treatment, hepatic or renal disease. Tablets and oral suspension are not bioequivalent (do not substitute on a mg-per-mg basis).

Common Adverse Reactions

1% to 10%:

Hematologic: Eosinophilia (7%), decreased hemoglobin and hematocrit (10%)

Hepatic: Increased transaminases (4%), increased alkaline phosphatase (2%)

Local: Thrombophlebitis (2%)

Reactions reported with other cephalosporins include agranulocytosis, aplastic anemia, asterixis, encephalopathy, hemorrhage, neuromuscular excitability, serum-sickness reactions, superinfection, toxic nephropathy

(Continued)

245

Cefuroxime *(Continued)*

Drug Interactions
Increased Effect/Toxicity: High-dose probenecid decreases clearance. Aminoglycosides in combination with cefuroxime may result in additive nephrotoxicity.

Mechanism of Action Inhibits bacterial cell wall synthesis by binding to one or more of the penicillin-binding proteins (PBPs) which in turn inhibits the final transpeptidation step of peptidoglycan synthesis in bacterial cell walls, thus inhibiting cell wall biosynthesis. Bacteria eventually lyse due to ongoing activity of cell wall autolytic enzymes (autolysins and murein hydrolases) while cell wall assembly is arrested.

Pharmacodynamics/Kinetics
Absorption: Oral (cefuroxime axetil): Increases with food

Distribution: Widely to body tissues and fluids; crosses blood-brain barrier; therapeutic concentrations achieved in CSF even when meninges are not inflamed; crosses placenta; enters breast milk

Protein binding: 33% to 50%

Bioavailability: Tablet: Fasting: 37%; Following food: 52%

Half-life elimination:
Neonates: ≤3 days old : 5.1-5.8 hours; 6-14 days old: 2-4.2 hours; 3-4 weeks old: 1-1.5 hours
Adults: 1-2 hours; prolonged with renal impairment

Time to peak, serum: I.M.: ~15-60 minutes; I.V.: 2-3 minutes

Excretion: Urine (66% to 100% as unchanged drug)

Dosage Note: Cefuroxime axetil film-coated tablets and oral suspension are not bioequivalent and are not substitutable on a mg/mg basis

Children ≥3 months to 12 years:
Pharyngitis, tonsillitis: Oral:
Suspension: 20 mg/kg/day (maximum: 500 mg/day) in 2 divided doses for 10 days
Tablet: 125 mg every 12 hours for 10 days
Acute otitis media, impetigo: Oral:
Suspension: 30 mg/kg/day (maximum: 1 g/day) in 2 divided doses for 10 days
Tablet: 250 mg twice daily for 10 days
I.M., I.V.: 75-150 mg/kg/day divided every 8 hours; maximum dose: 6 g/day
Meningitis: Not recommended (doses of 200-240 mg/kg/day divided every 6-8 hours have been used); maximum dose: 9 g/day
Acute bacterial maxillary sinusitis:
Suspension: 30 mg/kg/day in 2 divided doses for 10 days; maximum dose: 1 g/day
Tablet: 250 mg twice daily for 10 days

Children ≥13 years and Adults:
Oral: 250-500 mg twice daily for 10 days (5 days in selected patients with acute bronchitis)
Uncomplicated urinary tract infection: 125-250 mg every 12 hours for 7-10 days
Uncomplicated gonorrhea: 1 g as a single dose
Early Lyme disease: 500 mg twice daily for 20 days
I.M., I.V.: 750 mg to 1.5 g/dose every 8 hours or 100-150 mg/kg/day in divided doses every 6-8 hours; maximum: 6 g/24 hours

Dosing adjustment in renal impairment:
Cl$_{cr}$ 10-20 mL/minute: Administer every 12 hours
Cl$_{cr}$ <10 mL/minute: Administer every 24 hours
Hemodialysis: Dialyzable (25%)
Continuous arteriovenous or venovenous hemodiafiltration effects: Dose as for Cl$_{cr}$ 10-20 mL/minute

Administration
Oral: Administer around-the-clock to promote less variation in peak and trough serum levels.
Oral suspension: Administer with food. Shake well before use.
I.M.: Inject deep I.M. into large muscle mass.
I.V.: Inject direct I.V. over 3-5 minutes. Infuse intermittent infusion over 15-30 minutes.

Monitoring Parameters Observe for signs and symptoms of anaphylaxis during first dose; with prolonged therapy, monitor renal, hepatic, and hematologic function periodically; monitor prothrombin time in patients at risk of prolongation during cephalosporin therapy (nutritionally-deficient, prolonged treatment, renal or hepatic disease)

Patient Information Report prolonged diarrhea; entire course of medication (10-14 days) should be taken to ensure eradication of organism; may interfere with oral contraceptives; females should report symptoms of vaginitis

Dosage Forms INF, as sodium [premixed iso-osmotic solution] (Zinacef®): 750 mg (50 mL); 1.5 g (50 mL). **INJ, powder for reconstitution, as sodium** (Kefurox® [DSC], Zinacef®): 750 mg, 1.5 g, 7.5 g. **POWDER, oral suspension, as axetil** (Ceftin®): 125 mg/5 mL (100 mL); 250 mg/5 mL (50 mL, 100 mL). **TAB, as axetil:** 250 mg, 500 mg; (Ceftin®): 125 mg [DSC], 250 mg, 500 mg

♦ **Cefuroxime Axetil** *see* Cefuroxime *on page 245*
♦ **Cefuroxime Sodium** *see* Cefuroxime *on page 245*
♦ **Cefzil®** *see* Cefprozil *on page 241*
♦ **Celebrex®** *see* Celecoxib *on page 246*

Celecoxib *(se le KOKS ib)*
Related Information
Nonsteroidal Anti-Inflammatory Agents Comparison *on page 1401*
Sulfonamide Derivatives *on page 1404*

U.S. Brand Names Celebrex®

Therapeutic Category Analgesic, Selective COX-II Inhibitor; Anti-inflammatory Agent; Nonsteroidal Anti-inflammatory Drug (NSAID), COX-2 Selective

Use Relief of the signs and symptoms of osteoarthritis; relief of the signs and symptoms of rheumatoid arthritis in adults; decreasing intestinal polyps in familial adenomatous polyposis (FAP); management of acute pain; treatment of primary dysmenorrhea

Pregnancy Risk Factor C/D (3rd trimester)

Contraindications Hypersensitivity to celecoxib, any component of the formulation, sulfonamides, aspirin, or other NSAIDs; pregnancy (3rd trimester)

Warnings/Precautions Gastrointestinal irritation, ulceration, bleeding, and perforation may occur with NSAIDs (it is unclear whether celecoxib is associated with rates of these events which are similar to nonselective NSAIDs). Use with caution in patients with a history of GI disease (bleeding or ulcers), decreased renal function, hepatic disease, CHF, hypertension, or asthma. Anaphylactoid reactions may occur, even with no prior exposure to celecoxib. Use caution in patients with known or suspected deficiency of CYP2C9 isoenzyme. Safety and efficacy have not been established in patients <18 years of age.

Common Adverse Reactions
>10%: Central nervous system: Headache (16%)
2% to 10%:
  Cardiovascular: Peripheral edema (2%)
  Central nervous system: Insomnia (2%), dizziness (2%)
  Dermatologic: Skin rash (2%)
  Gastrointestinal: Dyspepsia (9%), diarrhea (6%), abdominal pain (4%), nausea (4%), flatulence (2%)
  Neuromuscular & skeletal: Back pain (3%)
  Respiratory: Upper respiratory tract infection (8%), sinusitis (5%), pharyngitis (2%), rhinitis (2%)
  Miscellaneous: Accidental injury (3%)
0.1% to 2%:
  Cardiovascular: Hypertension (aggravated), chest pain, myocardial infarction, palpitation, tachycardia, facial edema
  Central nervous system: Migraine, vertigo, hypoesthesia, fatigue, fever, pain, hypotonia, anxiety, depression, nervousness, somnolence
  Dermatologic: Alopecia, dermatitis, photosensitivity, pruritus, rash (maculopapular), rash (erythematous), dry skin, urticaria
  Endocrine & metabolic: Hot flashes, diabetes mellitus, hyperglycemia, hypercholesterolemia, breast pain, dysmenorrhea, menstrual disturbances, hypokalemia
  Gastrointestinal: Constipation, tenesmus, diverticulitis, eructation, esophagitis, gastroenteritis, vomiting, gastroesophageal reflux, hemorrhoids, hiatal hernia, melena, stomatitis, anorexia, increased appetite, taste disturbance, dry mouth, tooth disorder, weight gain
  Genitourinary: Prostate disorder, vaginal bleeding, vaginitis, monilial vaginitis, dysuria, cystitis, urinary frequency, incontinence, urinary tract infection,
  Hematologic: Anemia, thrombocytopenia, ecchymosis
  Hepatic: Elevated transaminases, increased alkaline phosphatase
  Neuromuscular & skeletal: Leg cramps, increased CPK, neck stiffness, arthralgia, myalgia, bone disorder, fracture, synovitis, tendonitis, neuralgia, paresthesia, neuropathy, weakness
  Ocular: Glaucoma, blurred vision, cataract, conjunctivitis, eye pain
  Otic: Deafness, tinnitus, earache, otitis media
  Renal: Increased BUN, increased creatinine, albuminuria, hematuria, renal calculi
  Respiratory: Bronchitis, bronchospasm, cough, dyspnea, laryngitis, pneumonia, epistaxis
  Miscellaneous: Allergic reactions, flu-like syndrome, breast cancer, herpes infection, bacterial infection, moniliasis, viral infection, increased diaphoresis

Drug Interactions
Cytochrome P450 Effect: Substrate (minor) of CYP2C8/9, 3A4; **Inhibits** CYP2D6 (weak)
Increased Effect/Toxicity: Fluconazole increases celecoxib concentrations twofold. Other inhibitors of cytochrome P450 isoenzyme 2C9 (ie, amiodarone, fluoxetine, sulfonamides, ritonavir, zafirlukast) theoretically may result in significant increases in celecoxib concentrations. Lithium and methotrexate concentrations may be increased by celecoxib. Celecoxib may be used with low-dose aspirin, however, rates of gastrointestinal bleeding may be increased with coadministration. Celecoxib has been associated with increased prothrombin times and some bleeding episodes (predominantly in elderly patients) during warfarin therapy.
Decreased Effect: Efficacy of thiazide diuretics, loop diuretics (furosemide), or ACE inhibitors may be diminished by celecoxib.

Mechanism of Action Inhibits prostaglandin synthesis by decreasing the activity of the enzyme, cyclooxygenase-2 (COX-2), which results in decreased formation of prostaglandin precursors. Celecoxib does not inhibit cyclooxygenase-1 (COX-1) at therapeutic concentrations.

Pharmacodynamics/Kinetics
Distribution: V_d (apparent): 400 L
Protein binding: 97% to albumin
Metabolism: Hepatic via CYP2C9; forms inactive metabolites
Bioavailability: Absolute: Unknown
Half-life elimination: 11 hours
Time to peak: 3 hours
Excretion: Urine (as metabolites, <3% as unchanged drug)
(Continued)

Celecoxib *(Continued)*

Dosage Adults: Oral:

Acute pain or primary dysmenorrhea: Initial dose: 400 mg, followed by an additional 200 mg if needed on day 1; maintenance dose: 200 mg twice daily as needed

Familial adenomatous polyposis (FAP): 400 mg twice daily

Osteoarthritis: 200 mg/day as a single dose or in divided dose twice daily

Rheumatoid arthritis: 100-200 mg twice daily

Elderly: No specific adjustment is recommended. However, the AUC in elderly patients may be increased by 50% as compared to younger subjects. Use the lowest recommended dose in patients weighing <50 kg.

Dosing adjustment in renal impairment: No specific dosage adjustment is recommended; not recommended in patients with advanced renal disease

Dosing adjustment in hepatic impairment: Reduced dosage is recommended (AUC may be increased by 40% to 180%); decrease dose by 50% in patients with moderate hepatic impairment (Child-Pugh Class II)

Monitoring Parameters Periodic LFTs; in patients treated for FAP, continue routine endoscopic exams

Patient Information Patients should be informed of the signs and symptoms of gastrointestinal bleeding. Gastrointestinal bleeding may occur as well as ulceration and perforation; pain may or may not be present. If gastric upset occurs, take with food, milk, or antacid; if gastric upset persists, contact prescriber.

Dosage Forms CAP: 100 mg, 200 mg, 400 mg

♦ **Celestone®** *see* Betamethasone *on page 159*

♦ **Celestone® Phosphate** *see* Betamethasone *on page 159*

♦ **Celestone® Soluspan®** *see* Betamethasone *on page 159*

♦ **Celexa™** *see* Citalopram *on page 286*

♦ **CellCept®** *see* Mycophenolate *on page 869*

♦ **Celontin®** *see* Methsuximide *on page 820*

♦ **Cenestin®** *see* Estrogens (Conjugated A/Synthetic) *on page 465*

♦ **Centrum® [OTC]** *see* Vitamins (Multiple/Oral) *on page 1312*

♦ **Centrum® Performance™ [OTC]** *see* Vitamins (Multiple/Oral) *on page 1312*

♦ **Centrum® Silver® [OTC]** *see* Vitamins (Multiple/Oral) *on page 1312*

♦ **Cēpacol® Maximum Strength [OTC]** *see* Dyclonine *on page 419*

♦ **Cēpacol Viractin® [OTC]** *see* Tetracaine *on page 1206*

Cephalexin *(sef a LEKS in)*

Related Information

Prevention of Bacterial Endocarditis *on page 1429*

U.S. Brand Names Biocef; Keflex®

Synonyms Cephalexin Hydrochloride; Cephalexin Monohydrate

Therapeutic Category Antibiotic, Cephalosporin (First Generation)

Use Treatment of susceptible bacterial infections, including those caused by group A beta-hemolytic *Streptococcus, Staphylococcus, Klebsiella pneumoniae, E. coli, Proteus mirabilis,* and *Shigella;* predominantly used for lower respiratory tract, urinary tract, skin and soft tissue, and bone and joint; prophylaxis against bacterial endocarditis in high-risk patients undergoing surgical or dental procedures who are allergic to penicillin

Pregnancy Risk Factor B

Contraindications Hypersensitivity to cephalexin, any component of the formulation, or other cephalosporins

Warnings/Precautions Modify dosage in patients with severe renal impairment, prolonged use may result in superinfection; use with caution in patients with a history of penicillin allergy, especially IgE-mediated reactions (eg, anaphylaxis, urticaria). May cause antibiotic-associated colitis or colitis secondary to *C. difficile.*

Common Adverse Reactions

1% to 10%: Gastrointestinal: Diarrhea

Reactions reported with other cephalosporins include anaphylaxis, vomiting, agranulocytosis, colitis, pancytopenia, aplastic anemia, hemolytic anemia, hemorrhage, prolonged PT, encephalopathy, asterixis, neuromuscular excitability, seizures, superinfection

Drug Interactions

Increased Effect/Toxicity: High-dose probenecid may decrease clearance of cephalexin. Aminoglycosides in combination with cephalexin may result in additive nephrotoxicity.

Mechanism of Action Inhibits bacterial cell wall synthesis by binding to one or more of the penicillin-binding proteins (PBPs) which in turn inhibits the final transpeptidation step of peptidoglycan synthesis in bacterial cell walls, thus inhibiting cell wall biosynthesis. Bacteria eventually lyse due to ongoing activity of cell wall autolytic enzymes (autolysins and murein hydrolases) while cell wall assembly is arrested.

Pharmacodynamics/Kinetics

Absorption: Delayed in young children; may be decreased up to 50% in neonates

Distribution: Widely into most body tissues and fluids, including gallbladder, liver, kidneys, bone, sputum, bile, and pleural and synovial fluids; CSF penetration is poor; crosses placenta; enters breast milk

Protein binding: 6% to 15%

Half-life elimination: Neonates: 5 hours old; Children 3-12 months: 2.5 hours; Adults: 0.5-1.2 hours; prolonged with renal impairment

Time to peak, serum: ~1 hour
Excretion: Urine (80% to 100% as unchanged drug) within 8 hours

Dosage Oral:

Children: 25-50 mg/kg/day every 6 hours; severe infections: 50-100 mg/kg/day in divided doses every 6 hours; maximum: 3 g/24 hours

Adults: 250-1000 mg every 6 hours; maximum: 4 g/day

Prophylaxis of bacterial endocarditis (dental, oral, respiratory tract, or esophageal procedures):

Children: 50 mg/kg 1 hour prior to procedure

Adults: 2 g 1 hour prior to procedure

Dosing adjustment in renal impairment: Adults:

Cl$_{cr}$ 10-40 mL/minute: 250-500 mg every 8-12 hours

Cl$_{cr}$ <10 mL/minute: 250 mg every 12-24 hours

Hemodialysis: Moderately dialyzable (20% to 50%)

Administration Take without regard to food. If GI distress, take with food. Give around-the-clock to promote less variation in peak and trough serum levels.

Monitoring Parameters With prolonged therapy monitor renal, hepatic, and hematologic function periodically; monitor for signs of anaphylaxis during first dose

Patient Information Report prolonged diarrhea; entire course of medication (10-14 days) should be taken to ensure eradication of organism; may interfere with oral contraceptives; females should report symptoms of vaginitis

Dosage Forms CAP: 250 mg, 500 mg; (Biocef®): 500 mg; (Keflex®): 250 mg, 500 mg.
POWDER, oral suspension: 125 mg/5 mL (100 mL, 200 mL); 250 mg/5 mL (100 mL, 200 mL); (Biocef®): 125 mg/5 mL (100 mL); 250 mg/5 mL (200 mL)

♦ **Cephalexin Hydrochloride** *see* Cephalexin *on page 248*

♦ **Cephalexin Monohydrate** *see* Cephalexin *on page 248*

Cephalothin (sef A loe thin)

Synonyms Cephalothin Sodium

Therapeutic Category Antibiotic, Cephalosporin (First Generation)

Use Treatment of infections when caused by susceptible strains in respiratory, genitourinary, gastrointestinal, skin and soft tissue, bone and joint infections; septicemia; treatment of susceptible gram-positive bacilli and cocci (never enterococcus); some gram-negative bacilli including *E. coli*, *Proteus*, and *Klebsiella* may be susceptible

Pregnancy Risk Factor B

Dosage I.V.:

Neonates:

Postnatal age <7 days:

<2000 g: 20 mg every 12 hours

>2000 g: 20 mg every 8 hours

Postnatal age >7 days:

<2000 g: 20 mg every 8 hours

>2000 g: 20 mg every 6 hours

Children: 75-125 mg/kg/day divided every 4-6 hours; maximum dose: 10 g in a 24-hour period

Adults: 500 mg to 2 g every 4-6 hours

Dosing interval in renal impairment:

Cl$_{cr}$ 10-50 mL/minute: Administer every 6-8 hours

Cl$_{cr}$ <10 mL/minute: Administer every 12 hours

Continuous arteriovenous or venovenous hemodiafiltration effects: Administer 1 g every 8 hours

Dosage Forms INJ, for infusion [frozen]: 1 g (50 mL); 2 g (50 mL)

♦ **Cephalothin Sodium** *see* Cephalothin *on page 249*

Cephradine (SEF ra deen)

U.S. Brand Names Velosef®

Therapeutic Category Antibiotic, Cephalosporin (First Generation)

Use Treatment of infections when caused by susceptible strains in respiratory, genitourinary, gastrointestinal, skin and soft tissue, bone and joint infections; treatment of susceptible gram-positive bacilli and cocci (never enterococcus); some gram-negative bacilli including *E. coli*, *Proteus*, and *Klebsiella* may be susceptible

Pregnancy Risk Factor B

Contraindications Hypersensitivity to cephradine, any component of the formulation, or cephalosporins

Warnings/Precautions Use caution with renal impairment; dose adjustment required. Prolonged use may result in superinfection; use with caution in patients with a history of penicillin allergy, especially IgE-mediated reactions (eg, anaphylaxis, urticaria). May cause antibiotic-associated colitis or colitis secondary to *C. difficile*.

Common Adverse Reactions Frequency not defined.

Central nervous system: Dizziness

Dermatologic: Rash, pruritus

Gastrointestinal: Diarrhea, nausea, vomiting, pseudomembranous colitis

Hematologic: Leukopenia, neutropenia, eosinophilia

Neuromuscular & skeletal: Joint pain

Renal: BUN increased, creatinine increased

(Continued)

Cephradine *(Continued)*

Reactions reported with other cephalosporins include anaphylaxis, erythema multiforme, toxic epidermal necrolysis, Stevens-Johnson syndrome, fever, headache, encephalopathy, asterixis, neuromuscular excitability, seizures, agranulocytosis, pancytopenia, aplastic anemia, hemolytic anemia, interstitial nephritis, toxic nephropathy, vaginitis, angioedema, cholestasis, hemorrhage, prolonged PT, serum-sickness reactions, superinfection

Drug Interactions

Increased Effect/Toxicity: High-dose probenecid decreases clearance of cephradine. Aminoglycosides in combination with cephradine may result in additive nephrotoxicity.

Mechanism of Action Inhibits bacterial cell wall synthesis by binding to one or more of the penicillin-binding proteins (PBPs) which in turn inhibits the final transpeptidation step of peptidoglycan synthesis in bacterial cell walls, thus inhibiting cell wall biosynthesis. Bacteria eventually lyse due to ongoing activity of cell wall autolytic enzymes (autolysins and murein hydrolases) while cell wall assembly is arrested.

Pharmacodynamics/Kinetics

Absorption: Well absorbed

Distribution: Widely into most body tissues and fluids including gallbladder, liver, kidneys, bone, sputum, bile, and pleural and synovial fluids; CSF penetration is poor; crosses placenta; enters breast milk

Protein binding: 18% to 20%

Half-life elimination: 1-2 hours; prolonged with renal impairment

Time to peak, serum: 1-2 hours

Excretion: Urine (~80% to 90% as unchanged drug) within 6 hours

Dosage Oral:

Children ≥9 months: Usual dose: 25-50 mg/kg/day in divided doses every 6 hours

Otitis media: 75-100 mg/kg/day in divided doses every 6 or 12 hours (maximum: 4 g/day)

Adults: 250-500 mg every 6-12 hours

Dosing adjustment in renal impairment: Adults:

Cl_{cr} 10-50 mL/minute: 250 mg every 6 hours

Cl_{cr} <10 mL/minute: 125 mg every 6 hours

Administration Administer around-the-clock to promote less variation in peak and trough serum levels. Shake oral suspension well.

Monitoring Parameters Observe for signs and symptoms of anaphylaxis during first dose

Patient Information Take until gone, do not miss doses; report diarrhea promptly; entire course of medication (10-14 days) should be taken to ensure eradication of organism; may interfere with oral contraceptives; females should report symptoms of vaginitis

Dosage Forms CAP: 250 mg, 500 mg. **POWDER, oral suspension:** 250 mg/5 mL (100 mL, 200 mL)

- ♦ **Ceptaz® [DSC]** *see* Ceftazidime *on page 241*
- ♦ **Cerebyx®** *see* Fosphenytoin *on page 568*
- ♦ **Ceredase®** *see* Alglucerase *on page 55*
- ♦ **Cerezyme®** *see* Imiglucerase *on page 653*
- ♦ **Cerubidine®** *see* DAUNOrubicin Hydrochloride *on page 346*
- ♦ **Cerumenex®** *see* Triethanolamine Polypeptide Oleate-Condensate *on page 1266*
- ♦ **Cervidil®** *see* Dinoprostone *on page 382*
- ♦ **C.E.S.** *see* Estrogens (Conjugated/Equine) *on page 466*
- ♦ **Cetacaine®** *see* Benzocaine, Butyl Aminobenzoate, Tetracaine, and Benzalkonium Chloride *on page 154*
- ♦ **Cetacort®** *see* Hydrocortisone *on page 632*
- ♦ **Cetafen® [OTC]** *see* Acetaminophen *on page 24*
- ♦ **Cetafen Cold® [OTC]** *see* Acetaminophen and Pseudoephedrine *on page 26*
- ♦ **Cetafen Extra® [OTC]** *see* Acetaminophen *on page 24*
- ♦ **Ceta-Plus®** *see* Hydrocodone and Acetaminophen *on page 627*

Cetirizine *(se TI ra zeen)*

U.S. Brand Names Zyrtec®

Synonyms Cetirizine Hydrochloride; P-071; UCB-P071

Therapeutic Category Antihistamine; Antihistamine, Low-Sedating

Use Perennial and seasonal allergic rhinitis and other allergic symptoms including urticaria; chronic idiopathic urticaria

Pregnancy Risk Factor B

Contraindications Hypersensitivity to cetirizine, hydroxyzine, or any component of the formulation

Warnings/Precautions Cetirizine should be used cautiously in patients with hepatic or renal dysfunction, the elderly and in nursing mothers. May cause drowsiness, use caution performing tasks which require alertness (eg, operating machinery or driving). Safety and efficacy in pediatric patients <6 months have not been established.

Common Adverse Reactions

>10%: Central nervous system: Headache (children 11% to 14%, placebo 12%), somnolence (adults 14%, children 2% to 4%)

2% to 10%:

Central nervous system: Insomnia (children 9%, adults <2%), fatigue (adults 6%), malaise (4%), dizziness (Adults 2%)

Gastrointestinal: Abdominal pain (children 4% to 6%), dry mouth (adults 5%), diarrhea (children 2% to 3%), nausea (children 2% to 3%, placebo 2%), vomiting (children 2% to 3%)

Respiratory: Epistaxis (children 2% to 4%, placebo 3%), pharyngitis (children 3% to 6%, placebo 3%), bronchospasm (children 2% to 3%, placebo 3%)

Drug Interactions
Cytochrome P450 Effect: Substrate of CYP3A4 (minor)
Increased Effect/Toxicity: Increased toxicity with CNS depressants and anticholinergics.
Mechanism of Action Competes with histamine for H_1-receptor sites on effector cells in the gastrointestinal tract, blood vessels, and respiratory tract
Pharmacodynamics/Kinetics
Onset of action: 15-30 minutes
Absorption: Rapid
Protein binding, plasma: Mean: 93%
Metabolism: Limited hepatic
Half-life elimination: 8 hours
Time to peak, serum: 1 hour
Excretion: Urine (70%); feces (10%)
Dosage Oral:
Children:
6-12 months: Chronic urticaria, perennial allergic rhinitis: 2.5 mg once daily
12 months to <2 years: Chronic urticaria, perennial allergic rhinitis: 2.5 mg once daily; may increase to 2.5 mg every 12 hours if needed
2-5 years: Chronic urticaria, perennial or seasonal allergic rhinitis: Initial: 2.5 mg once daily; may be increased to 2.5 mg every 12 hours **or** 5 mg once daily
Children ≥6 years and Adults: Chronic urticaria, perennial or seasonal allergic rhinitis: 5-10 mg once daily, depending upon symptom severity
Elderly: Initial: 5 mg once daily; may increase to 10 mg/day; adjust for renal impairment
Dosage adjustment in renal/hepatic impairment:
Children <6 years: Cetirizine use not recommended
Children 6-11 years: <2.5 mg once daily
Children ≥12 and Adults:
Cl_{cr} 11-31 mL/minute, hemodialysis, or hepatic impairment: Administer 5 mg once daily
Cl_{cr} <11 mL/minute, not on dialysis: Cetirizine use not recommended
Administration May be administered with or without food.
Monitoring Parameters Relief of symptoms, sedation and anticholinergic effects
Dosage Forms SYR: 5 mg/5 mL (120 mL, 480 mL). **TAB:** 5 mg, 10 mg

♦ **Cetirizine Hydrochloride** *see* Cetirizine *on page 250*

Cetrorelix (set roe REL iks)
U.S. Brand Names Cetrotide™
Synonyms Cetrorelix Acetate
Therapeutic Category Antigonadotropic Agent
Use Inhibits premature luteinizing hormone (LH) surges in women undergoing controlled ovarian stimulation
Pregnancy Risk Factor X
Contraindications Hypersensitivity to cetrorelix or any component of the formulation; extrinsic peptide hormones, mannitol, gonadotropin releasing hormone (GnRH) or GnRH analogs; pregnancy
Warnings/Precautions Should only be prescribed by fertility specialists. Pregnancy should be excluded before treatment is begun.
Common Adverse Reactions
1% to 10%:
Central nervous system: Headache (1%)
Endocrine & metabolic: Ovarian hyperstimulation syndrome, WHO grade II or III (3%)
Gastrointestinal: Nausea (1%)
Hepatic: Increased ALT, AST, GGT, and alkaline phosphatase (1% to 2%)
Drug Interactions
Increased Effect/Toxicity: No formal studies have been performed.
Decreased Effect: No formal studies have been performed.
Mechanism of Action Competes with naturally occurring GnRH for binding on receptors of the pituitary. This delays luteinizing hormone surge, preventing ovulation until the follicles are of adequate size.
Pharmacodynamics/Kinetics
Onset of action: 0.25 mg dose: 2 hours; 3 mg dose: 1 hour
Duration: 3 mg dose (single dose): 4 days
Absorption: Rapid
Protein binding: 86%
Metabolism: Transformed by peptidases; cetrorelix and peptides (1-9), (1-7), (1-6), and (1-4) are found in the bile; peptide (1-4) is the predominant metabolite
Bioavailability: 85%
Half-life elimination: 0.25 mg dose: 5 hours; 0.25 mg multiple doses: 20.6 hours; 3 mg dose: 62.8 hours
Time to peak: 0.25 mg dose: 1 hour; 3 mg dose: 1.5 hours
Excretion: Feces (5% to 10% as unchanged drug and metabolites); urine (2% to 4% as unchanged drug); within 24 hours
(Continued)

Cetrorelix *(Continued)*

Dosage S.C.: Adults: Female: Used in conjunction with controlled ovarian stimulation therapy using gonadotropins (FSH, HMG):

Single-dose regimen: 3 mg given when serum estradiol levels show appropriate stimulation response, usually stimulation day 7 (range days 5-9). If hCG is not administered within 4 days, continue cetrorelix at 0.25 mg/day until hCG is administered

Multiple-dose regimen: 0.25 mg morning or evening of stimulation day 5, or morning of stimulation day 6; continue until hCG is administered.

Dosing adjustment in renal impairment: No specific guidelines are available.

Dosing adjustment in hepatic impairment: No specific guidelines are available.

Elderly: Not intended for use in women ≥65 years of age (Phase 2 and Phase 3 studies included women 19-40 years of age)

Administration Cetrorelix is administered by S.C. injection following proper aseptic technique procedures. Injections should be to the lower abdomen, preferably around the navel. The injection site should be rotated daily. The needle should be inserted completely into the skin at a 45-degree angle.

Monitoring Parameters Ultrasound to assess follicle size

Patient Information An instructional leaflet will be provided if you will be administering this medication to yourself. Instructions will be given on how to administer S.C. injections and proper disposal of syringes and needles. Give at a similar time each day as instructed by prescriber. Do not skip doses. Keep all ultrasound appointments. Report any sudden weight gain, abdominal discomfort, or shortness of breath to prescriber. Do not take if pregnant.

Dosage Forms INJ, powder for reconstitution: 0.25 mg, 3 mg

- **Cetrorelix Acetate** *see Cetrorelix on page 251*
- **Cetrotide™** *see Cetrorelix on page 251*

Cetylpyridinium and Benzocaine (SEE til peer i DI nee um & BEN zoe kane)

Synonyms Benzocaine and Cetylpyridinium Chloride; Cetylpyridinium Chloride and Benzocaine

Therapeutic Category Local Anesthetic

Use Symptomatic relief of sore throat

Pregnancy Risk Factor C

Dosage Antiseptic/anesthetic: Oral: Dissolve in mouth as needed for sore throat

- **Cetylpyridinium Chloride and Benzocaine** *see Cetylpyridinium and Benzocaine on page 252*
- **Cevi-Bid® [OTC]** *see Ascorbic Acid on page 117*

Cevimeline (se vi ME leen)

U.S. Brand Names Evoxac™

Synonyms Cevimeline Hydrochloride

Therapeutic Category Cholinergic Agent

Use Treatment of symptoms of dry mouth in patients with Sjögren's syndrome

Pregnancy Risk Factor C

Contraindications Hypersensitivity to cevimeline or any component of the formulation; uncontrolled asthma; narrow-angle glaucoma; acute iritis; other conditions where miosis is undesirable

Warnings/Precautions May alter cardiac conduction and/or heart rate; use caution in patients with significant cardiovascular disease, including angina, myocardial infarction, or conduction disturbances. Cevimeline has the potential to increase bronchial smooth muscle tone, airway resistance, and bronchial secretions; use with caution in patients with controlled asthma, COPD, or chronic bronchitis. May cause decreased visual acuity (particularly at night and in patients with central lens changes) and impaired depth perception. Patients should be cautioned about driving at night or performing hazardous activities in reduced lighting. May cause a variety of parasympathomimetic effects, which may be particularly dangerous in elderly patients; excessive sweating may lead to dehydration in some patients.

Use with caution in patients with a history of biliary stones or nephrolithiasis; cevimeline may induce smooth muscle spasms, precipitating cholangitis, cholecystitis, biliary obstruction, renal colic, or ureteral reflux in susceptible patients. Patients with a known or suspected deficiency of CYP2D6 may be at higher risk of adverse effects. Safety and efficacy has not been established in pediatric patients.

Common Adverse Reactions

>10%:

Central nervous system: Headache (14%; placebo 20%)

Gastrointestinal: Nausea (14%), diarrhea (10%)

Respiratory: Rhinitis (11%), sinusitis (12%), upper respiratory infection (11%)

Miscellaneous: Increased diaphoresis (19%)

1% to 10%:

Cardiovascular: Peripheral edema, chest pain, edema, palpitation

Central nervous system: Dizziness (4%), fatigue (3%), pain (3%), insomnia (2%), anxiety (1%), fever, depression, migraine, hypoesthesia, vertigo

Dermatologic: Rash (4%; placebo 6%), pruritus, skin disorder, erythematous rash

Endocrine & metabolic: Hot flashes (2%)

Gastrointestinal: Dyspepsia (8%; placebo 9%), abdominal pain (8%), vomiting (5%), excessive salivation (2%), constipation, salivary gland pain, dry mouth, sialoadenitis, gastroesophageal reflux, flatulence, ulcerative stomatitis, eructation, increased amylase, anorexia, tooth disorder

Genitourinary: Urinary tract infection (6%), vaginitis, cystitis

Hematologic: Anemia

Local: Abscess

Neuromuscular & skeletal: Back pain (5%), arthralgia (4%), skeletal pain (3%), rigors (1%), hypertonia, tremor, myalgia, hyporeflexia, leg cramps

Ocular: Conjunctivitis (4%), abnormal vision, eye pain, eye abnormality, xerophthalmia

Otic: Ear ache, otitis media

Respiratory: Coughing (6%), bronchitis (4%), pneumonia, epistaxis

Miscellaneous: Flu-like syndrome, infection, fungal infection, allergy, hiccups

Drug Interactions

Cytochrome P450 Effect: Substrate (minor) of CYP2D6, CYP3A4

Increased Effect/Toxicity: Drugs which inhibit CYP2D6 (including amiodarone, fluoxetine, paroxetine, quinidine, ritonavir) or CYP3A4 (including diltiazem, erythromycin, itraconazole, ketoconazole, verapamil) may increase levels of cevimeline. The effects of other cholinergic agents may be increased during concurrent administration with cevimeline. Concurrent use of cevimeline and beta-blockers may increase the potential for conduction disturbances.

Decreased Effect: Anticholinergic agents (atropine, TCAs, phenothiazines) may antagonize the effects of cevimeline.

Mechanism of Action Binds to muscarinic (cholinergic) receptors, causing an increase in secretion of exocrine glands (including salivary glands)

Pharmacodynamics/Kinetics

Distribution: V_d: 6 L/kg

Protein binding: <20%

Metabolism: Hepatic via CYP2D6 and CYP3A4

Half-life elimination: 5 hours

Time to peak: 1.5-2 hours

Excretion: Urine (as metabolites and unchanged drug)

Dosage Adults: Oral: 30 mg 3 times/day

Dosage adjustment in renal/hepatic impairment: Not studied; no specific dosage adjustment is recommended

Elderly: No specific dosage adjustment is recommended; however, use caution when initiating due to potential for increased sensitivity

Patient Information May be taken with or without food; take with food if medicine causes upset stomach. May cause decreased visual acuity (particularly at night and in patients with central lens changes) and impaired depth perception; patients should be cautioned about driving at night or performing hazardous activities in reduced lighting.

Dosage Forms CAP: 30 mg

- ♦ **Cevimeline Hydrochloride** see Cevimeline on page 252
- ♦ **CFDN** see Cefdinir on page 232
- ♦ **CG** see Chorionic Gonadotropin (Human) on page 272
- ♦ **CGP-42446** see Zoledronic Acid on page 1330
- ♦ **CGP 57148B** see Imatinib on page 651
- ♦ **C-Gram [OTC]** see Ascorbic Acid on page 117
- ♦ **CharcoAid G® [OTC]** see Charcoal on page 253

Charcoal (CHAR kole)

Related Information

Toxicology Information on page 1497

U.S. Brand Names Actidose-Aqua® [OTC]; Actidose® with Sorbitol [OTC]; CharcoAid G® [OTC]; Charcoal Plus® DS [OTC]; Charcocaps® [OTC]; EZ-Char™ [OTC]; Kerr Insta-Char® [OTC]; Liqui-Char® [OTC] [DSC]

Synonyms Activated Carbon; Activated Charcoal; Adsorbent Charcoal; Liquid Antidote; Medicinal Carbon; Medicinal Charcoal

Therapeutic Category Antidiarrheal; Antidote, Adsorbent; Antiflatulent

Use Emergency treatment in poisoning by drugs and chemicals; aids the elimination of certain drugs and improves decontamination of excessive ingestions of sustained -release products or in the presence of bezoars; repetitive doses have proven useful to enhance the elimination of certain drugs (eg, theophylline, phenobarbital, and aspirin); repetitive doses for gastric dialysis in uremia to adsorb various waste products; dietary supplement (digestive aid)

Pregnancy Risk Factor C

Contraindications Intestinal obstruction; GI tract not anatomically intact; patients at risk of hemorrhage or GI perforation; if use would increase risk and severity of aspiration; not effective for cyanide, mineral acids, caustic alkalis, organic solvents, iron, ethanol, methanol poisoning, lithium; do not use charcoal with sorbitol in patients with fructose intolerance; charcoal with sorbitol not recommended in children <1 year of age

Warnings/Precautions When using ipecac with charcoal, induce vomiting with ipecac before administering activated charcoal since charcoal adsorbs ipecac syrup; charcoal may cause vomiting which is hazardous in petroleum distillate and caustic ingestions; if charcoal in sorbitol is administered, doses should be limited to prevent excessive fluid and electrolyte losses. Use caution with decreased peristalsis. Most effective when administered within 1 hour of ingestion for most ingestions.

(Continued)

Charcoal *(Continued)*

Common Adverse Reactions Frequency not defined.

Endocrine & metabolic: Hypernatremia, hypokalemia, and hypermagnesemia may occur with coadministration of cathartics

Gastrointestinal: Vomiting (incidence may increase with sorbitol), diarrhea (with sorbitol), constipation, swelling of abdomen, bowel obstruction

Miscellaneous: Fecal discoloration (black)

Drug Interactions

Decreased Effect: Charcoal decreases the effect of ipecac syrup.

Mechanism of Action Adsorbs toxic substances or irritants, thus inhibiting GI absorption; adsorbs intestinal gas; the addition of sorbitol results in hyperosmotic laxative action causing catharsis

Pharmacodynamics/Kinetics Excretion: Feces (as charcoal)

Dosage Oral:

Acute poisoning: **Note:** ~10 g of activated charcoal for each 1 g of toxin is considered adequate; this may require multiple doses. If sorbitol is also used, sorbitol dose should not exceed 1.5 g/kg. When using multiple doses of charcoal, sorbitol should be given with every other dose (not to exceed 2 doses/day).

Children: 1 g/kg as a single dose; if multiple doses are needed, additional doses can be given as 0.25 g/kg every hour or equivalent (ie, 0.5 g/kg every 2 hours) **or**

>1 year-12 years: 25-50 g as a single dose; smaller doses (10-25 g) may be used in children 1-5 years due to smaller gut lumen capacity

Children >12 years and Adults: 25-100 g as a single dose; if multiple doses are needed, additional doses may be given as 12.5 g/hour or equivalent (ie, 25 g every 2 hours)

Dietary supplement: Adult: 500-520 mg after meals; may repeat in 2 hours if needed (maximum 10 g/day)

Administration Flavoring agents (eg, chocolate) and sorbitol can enhance charcoal's palatability. If treatment includes ipecac syrup, induce vomiting prior to administration of charcoal.

Patient Information Charcoal causes the stools to turn black. Do not use prior to calling a poison control center or a physician.

Dosage Forms CAP, activated 260 mg. **GRAN, activated:** 15 g (120 mL). **LIQ, activated:** 15 g (72 mL, 75 mL); 25 g (120 mL); 50 g (240 mL). **LIQ, activated** [with sorbitol]: 25 g (120 mL); 50 g (240 mL). **PELLETS, activated:** 25 g. **POWDER, suspension, activated:** 30 g, 240 g. **TAB, activated:** 250 mg

- ◆ **Charcoal Plus® DS [OTC]** *see* Charcoal *on page 253*
- ◆ **Charcocaps® [OTC]** *see* Charcoal *on page 253*
- ◆ **Chemet®** *see* Succimer *on page 1165*
- ◆ **Cheracol®** *see* Guaifenesin and Codeine *on page 604*
- ◆ **Cheracol® D [OTC]** *see* Guaifenesin and Dextromethorphan *on page 604*
- ◆ **Cheracol® Plus [OTC]** *see* Guaifenesin and Dextromethorphan *on page 604*
- ◆ **Cheratussin DAC** *see* Guaifenesin, Pseudoephedrine, and Codeine *on page 606*
- ◆ **CHG** *see* Chlorhexidine Gluconate *on page 259*
- ◆ **Chicken Pox Vaccine** *see* Varicella Virus Vaccine *on page 1296*
- ◆ **Chiggerex® [OTC]** *see* Benzocaine *on page 154*
- ◆ **Chiggertox® [OTC]** *see* Benzocaine *on page 154*
- ◆ **Children's Dimetapp® Elixir Cold & Allergy [OTC]** *see* Brompheniramine and Pseudoephedrine *on page 181*
- ◆ **Children's Kaopectate® (reformulation) [OTC]** *see* Bismuth *on page 168*
- ◆ **Children's Sudafed® Cough & Cold [OTC]** *see* Pseudoephedrine and Dextromethorphan *on page 1062*
- ◆ **Children's Tylenol® Plus Cold [OTC]** *see* Acetaminophen, Chlorpheniramine, and Pseudoephedrine *on page 28*
- ◆ **Chirocaine®** *see* Levobupivacaine *on page 729*
- ◆ **Chloral** *see* Chloral Hydrate *on page 254*

Chloral Hydrate *(KLOR al HYE drate)*

U.S. Brand Names Aquachloral® Supprettes®; Somnote™

Synonyms Chloral; Hydrated Chloral; Trichloroacetaldehyde Monohydrate

Therapeutic Category Hypnotic; Sedative

Use Short-term sedative and hypnotic (<2 weeks), sedative/hypnotic for diagnostic procedures; sedative prior to EEG evaluations

Restrictions C-IV

Pregnancy Risk Factor C

Contraindications Hypersensitivity to chloral hydrate or any component of the formulation; hepatic or renal impairment; gastritis or ulcers; severe cardiac disease

Warnings/Precautions Use with caution in patients with porphyria; use with caution in neonates, drug may accumulate with repeated use; prolonged use in neonates associated with hyperbilirubinemia; tolerance to hypnotic effect develops, therefore, not recommended for use >2 weeks; taper dosage to avoid withdrawal with prolonged use; trichloroethanol (TCE), a metabolite of chloral hydrate, is a carcinogen in mice; there is no data in humans. Chloral hydrate is considered a second line hypnotic agent in the elderly. Recent interpretive guidelines from the Centers for Medicare and Medicaid Services (CMS) discourage the use of chloral hydrate in residents of long-term care facilities.

Common Adverse Reactions Frequency not defined.

Central nervous system: Ataxia, disorientation, sedation, excitement (paradoxical), dizziness, fever, headache, confusion, lightheadedness, nightmares, hallucinations, drowsiness, "hangover" effect

Dermatologic: Rash, urticaria

Gastrointestinal: Gastric irritation, nausea, vomiting, diarrhea, flatulence

Hematologic: Leukopenia, eosinophilia, acute intermittent porphyria

Miscellaneous: Physical and psychological dependence may occur with prolonged use of large doses

Drug Interactions

Increased Effect/Toxicity: Chloral hydrate and ethanol (and other CNS depressants) have additive CNS depressant effects; monitor for CNS depression. Chloral hydrate's metabolite may displace warfarin from its protein binding sites resulting in an increase in the hypoprothrombinemic response to warfarin; warfarin dosages may need to be adjusted. Diaphoresis, flushing, and hypertension have occurred in patients who received I.V. furosemide within 24 hours after administration of chloral hydrate; consider using a benzodiazepine.

Mechanism of Action Central nervous system depressant effects are due to its active metabolite trichloroethanol, mechanism unknown

Pharmacodynamics/Kinetics

Onset of action: Peak effect: 0.5-1 hour

Duration: 4-8 hours

Absorption: Oral, rectal: Well absorbed

Distribution: Crosses placenta; negligible amounts enter breast milk

Metabolism: Rapidly hepatic to trichloroethanol (active metabolite); variable amounts hepatically and renally to trichloroacetic acid (inactive)

Half-life elimination: Active metabolite: 8-11 hours

Excretion: Urine (as metabolites); feces (small amounts)

Dosage

Children:

Sedation or anxiety: Oral, rectal: 5-15 mg/kg/dose every 8 hours (maximum: 500 mg/dose)

Prior to EEG: Oral, rectal: 20-25 mg/kg/dose, 30-60 minutes prior to EEG; may repeat in 30 minutes to maximum of 100 mg/kg or 2 g total

Hypnotic: Oral, rectal: 20-40 mg/kg/dose up to a maximum of 50 mg/kg/24 hours or 1 g/dose or 2 g/24 hours

Conscious sedation: Oral: 50-75 mg/kg/dose 30-60 minutes prior to procedure; may repeat 30 minutes after initial dose if needed, to a total maximum dose of 120 mg/kg or 1 g total

Adults: Oral, rectal:

Sedation, anxiety: 250 mg 3 times/day

Hypnotic: 500-1000 mg at bedtime or 30 minutes prior to procedure, not to exceed 2 g/24 hours

Dosing adjustment/comments in renal impairment: Cl_{cr} <50 mL/minute: Avoid use

Hemodialysis: Dialyzable (50% to 100%); supplemental dose is not necessary

Dosing adjustment/comments in hepatic impairment: Avoid use in patients with severe hepatic impairment

Administration Chilling the syrup may help to mask unpleasant taste. Do not crush capsule (contains drug in liquid form).

Monitoring Parameters Vital signs, O_2 saturation and blood pressure with doses used for conscious sedation

Patient Information Take capsule with a full glass of water or fruit juice; swallow capsules whole, do not chew; avoid alcohol and other CNS depressants; avoid activities requiring psychomotor coordination until CNS effects are known; drug may cause physical or psychological dependence; avoid abrupt discontinuation after prolonged use; if taking at home prior to a diagnostic procedure, have someone else transport

Dosage Forms CAP (Somnote™): 500 mg. **SUPP, rectal** (Aquachloral® Supprettes®): 325 mg, 650 mg. **SYR:** 500 mg/5 mL (480 mL)

Chlorambucil (klor AM byoo sil)

U.S. Brand Names Leukeran®

Synonyms CB-1348; Chlorambucilum; Chloraminophene; Chlorbutinum; NSC-3088; WR-139013

Therapeutic Category Antineoplastic Agent, Alkylating Agent

Use Management of chronic lymphocytic leukemia, Hodgkin's and non-Hodgkin's lymphoma; breast and ovarian carcinoma; Waldenström's macroglobulinemia, testicular carcinoma, thrombocythemia, choriocarcinoma

Pregnancy Risk Factor D

Contraindications Hypersensitivity to chlorambucil or any component of the formulation; pregnancy

Warnings/Precautions The U.S. Food and Drug Administration (FDA) currently recommends that procedures for proper handling and disposal of antineoplastic agents are considered. Use with caution in patients with seizure disorder and bone marrow suppression; reduce initial dosage if patient has received radiation therapy, myelosuppressive drugs or has a depressed baseline leukocyte or platelet count within the previous 4 weeks. Can severely suppress bone marrow function; affects human fertility; carcinogenic in humans and probably mutagenic and teratogenic as well; chromosomal damage has been documented; secondary AML may be associated with chronic therapy.

(Continued)

Chlorambucil *(Continued)*

Common Adverse Reactions

>10%:

Dermatologic: Skin rashes

Hematologic: Myelosuppression (common, dose-limiting)

Onset (days): 7

Nadir (days): 14

Recovery (days): 28; may be prolonged to 6-8 weeks in some patients

Hepatic: Transient elevations in liver enzymes

1% to 10%:

Endocrine & metabolic: Hyperuricemia, menstrual cramps

Gastrointestinal: Mild nausea or vomiting, diarrhea, stomatitis

Drug Interactions

Decreased Effect: Patients may experience impaired immune response to vaccines; possible infection after administration of live vaccines in patients receiving immunosuppressants.

Mechanism of Action Interferes with DNA replication and RNA transcription by alkylation and cross-linking the strands of DNA

Pharmacodynamics/Kinetics

Absorption: 70% to 80% with meals

Distribution: V_d: 0.14-0.24 L/kg

Protein binding: ~99%

Metabolism: Hepatic; active metabolite, phenylacetic acid mustard

Bioavailability: Reduced 10% to 20% with food

Half-life elimination: 1.5 hours; Phenylacetic acid mustard: 2.5 hours

Excretion: Urine (60% primarily as metabolites, <1% as unchanged drug)

Dosage Oral (refer to individual protocols):

Children:

General short courses: 0.1-0.2 mg/kg/day **OR** 4.5 mg/m^2/day for 3-6 weeks for remission induction (usual: 4-10 mg/day); maintenance therapy: 0.03-0.1 mg/kg/day (usual: 2-4 mg/day)

Nephrotic syndrome: 0.1-0.2 mg/kg/day every day for 5-15 weeks with low-dose prednisone

Chronic lymphocytic leukemia (CLL):

Biweekly regimen: Initial: 0.4 mg/kg/dose every 2 weeks; increase dose by 0.1 mg/kg every 2 weeks until a response occurs and/or myelosuppression occurs

Monthly regimen: Initial: 0.4 mg/kg, increase dose by 0.2 mg/kg every 4 weeks until a response occurs and/or myelosuppression occurs

Malignant lymphomas:

Non-Hodgkin's lymphoma: 0.1 mg/kg/day

Hodgkin's lymphoma: 0.2 mg/kg/day

Adults: 0.1-0.2 mg/kg/day **or**

3-6 mg/m^2/day for 3-6 weeks, then adjust dose on basis of blood counts **or**

0.4 mg/kg and increased by 0.1 mg/kg biweekly or monthly **or**

14 mg/m^2/day for 5 days, repeated every 21-28 days

Hemodialysis: Supplemental dosing is not necessary

Peritoneal dialysis: Supplemental dosing is not necessary

Administration Usually administered as a single dose; preferably on an empty stomach

Monitoring Parameters Liver function tests, CBC, platelets, serum uric acid

Patient Information Take as directed. Maintain adequate hydration (2-3 L/day of fluids unless instructed to restrict fluid intake). Avoid OTC medications unless approved by prescriber. Hair may be lost during treatment (reversible). You may experience menstrual irregularities and/or sterility. You will be more susceptible to infection; avoid crowds and exposure to infection. Frequent mouth care with a soft toothbrush or cotton swab may reduce occurrence of mouth sores. Report easy bruising or bleeding; fever or chills; numbness, pain, or tingling of extremities; muscle cramping or weakness; unusual swelling of extremities; menstrual irregularities; or any difficulty breathing. Contraceptive measures are recommended during therapy.

Dosage Forms TAB, film coated: 2 mg

♦ **Chlorambucilum** *see Chlorambucil on page 255*

♦ **Chloraminophene** *see Chlorambucil on page 255*

Chloramphenicol *(klor am FEN i kole)*

Related Information

Antimicrobial Drugs of Choice *on page 1440*

Community-Acquired Pneumonia in Adults *on page 1457*

U.S. Brand Names Chloromycetin® Sodium Succinate; Chloroptic® [DSC]

Therapeutic Category Antibiotic, Anaerobic; Antibiotic, Ophthalmic; Antibiotic, Otic; Antibiotic, Miscellaneous

Use Treatment of serious infections due to organisms resistant to other less toxic antibiotics or when its penetrability into the site of infection is clinically superior to other antibiotics to which the organism is sensitive; useful in infections caused by *Bacteroides*, *H. influenzae*, *Neisseria meningitidis*, *Salmonella*, and *Rickettsia*; active against many vancomycin-resistant enterococci

Pregnancy Risk Factor C

Contraindications Hypersensitivity to chloramphenicol or any component of the formulation

Warnings/Precautions Use with caution in patients with impaired renal or hepatic function and in neonates; reduce dose with impaired liver function; use with care in patients with glucose 6-phosphate dehydrogenase deficiency. Serious and fatal blood dyscrasias have occurred after both short-term and prolonged therapy, including reports associated with topical treatment; should not be used when less potentially toxic agents are effective; prolonged use may result in superinfection.

Common Adverse Reactions
Three (3) major toxicities associated with chloramphenicol include:
Aplastic anemia, an idiosyncratic reaction which can occur with any route of administration; usually occurs 3 weeks to 12 months after initial exposure to chloramphenicol

Bone marrow suppression is thought to be dose-related with serum concentrations >25 µg/ mL and reversible once chloramphenicol is discontinued; anemia and neutropenia may occur during the first week of therapy

Gray syndrome is characterized by circulatory collapse, cyanosis, acidosis, abdominal distention, myocardial depression, coma, and death; reaction appears to be associated with serum levels ≥50 µg/mL; may result from drug accumulation in patients with impaired hepatic or renal function

Additional adverse reactions, frequency not defined:
Central nervous system: Confusion, delirium, depression, fever, headache
Dermatologic: Angioedema, rash, urticaria
Gastrointestinal: Diarrhea, enterocolitis, glossitis, nausea, stomatitis, vomiting
Hematologic: Granulocytopenia, hypoplastic anemia, pancytopenia, thrombocytopenia
Ocular: Optic neuritis
Miscellaneous: Anaphylaxis, hypersensitivity reactions

Drug Interactions
Cytochrome P450 Effect: Inhibits CYP2C8/9 (weak), 3A4 (weak)
Increased Effect/Toxicity: Chloramphenicol increases serum concentrations of chlorprop-amide, phenytoin, and oral anticoagulants.
Decreased Effect: Phenobarbital and rifampin may decrease serum concentrations of chlor-amphenicol.

Mechanism of Action Reversibly binds to 50S ribosomal subunits of susceptible organisms preventing amino acids from being transferred to growing peptide chains thus inhibiting protein synthesis

Pharmacodynamics/Kinetics
Distribution: To most tissues and body fluids; readily crosses placenta; enters breast milk
CSF:blood level ratio: Normal meninges: 66%; Inflamed meninges: >66%
Protein binding: 60%
Metabolism: Extensively hepatic (90%) to inactive metabolites, principally by glucuronidation; chloramphenicol palmitate is hydrolyzed by lipases in GI tract to the active base; chloramphenicol sodium succinate is hydrolyzed by esterases to active base
Half-life elimination
Normal renal function: 1.6-3.3 hours
End-stage renal disease: 3-7 hours
Cirrhosis: 10-12 hours
Neonates: Postnatal: 1-2 days old: 24 hours; 10-16 days old: 10 hours
Time to peak: Oral: Within 0.5-3 hours
Excretion: Urine (5% to 15%); Neonates: Urine (6% to 80% as unchanged drug), feces (4%)

Dosage
Meningitis: I.V.: Infants >30 days and Children: 50-100 mg/kg/day divided every 6 hours
Other infections: I.V.:
Infants >30 days and Children: 50-75 mg/kg/day divided every 6 hours; maximum daily dose: 4 g/day
Adults: 50-100 mg/kg/day in divided doses every 6 hours; maximum daily dose: 4 g/day
Ophthalmic: Children and Adults: Instill 1-2 drops 4-6 times/day; increase interval between applications after 72 hours to 2-3 times/day; treatment should continue for ~7 days
Dosing adjustment/comments in hepatic impairment: Avoid use in severe liver impairment as increased toxicity may occur
Hemodialysis: Slightly dialyzable (5% to 20%) via hemo- and peritoneal dialysis; no supplemental doses needed in dialysis or continuous arteriovenous or veno-venous hemofiltration

Administration Do not administer I.M.

Monitoring Parameters CBC with reticulocyte and platelet counts, periodic liver and renal function tests, serum drug concentration

Reference Range
Therapeutic levels:
Meningitis:
Peak: 15-25 µg/mL; toxic concentration: >40 µg/mL
Trough: 5-15 µg/mL
Other infections:
Peak: 10-20 µg/mL
Trough: 5-10 µg/mL
Timing of serum samples: Draw levels 1.5 hours and 3 hours after completion of I.V. or oral dose; trough levels may be preferred; should be drawn ≤1 hour prior to dose

Dosage Forms INJ, powder for reconstitution (Chloromycetin® Sodium Succinate): 1 g.
SOLN, ophthalmic (Chloroptic®) [DSC]: 0.5% [5 mg/mL] (2.5 mL, 7.5 mL)

◆ **ChloraPrep® [OTC]** *see* Chlorhexidine Gluconate *on page 259*
◆ **Chlorbutinum** *see* Chlorambucil *on page 255*

Chlordiazepoxide (klor dye az e POKS ide)

Related Information
Benzodiazepines Comparison *on page 1366*

U.S. Brand Names Librium®

Synonyms Methaminodiazepoxide Hydrochloride

Therapeutic Category Benzodiazepine; Hypnotic; Sedative

Use Management of anxiety disorder or for the short-term relief of symptoms of anxiety; withdrawal symptoms of acute alcoholism; preoperative apprehension and anxiety

Restrictions C-IV

Pregnancy Risk Factor D

Contraindications Hypersensitivity to chlordiazepoxide or any component of the formulation (cross-sensitivity with other benzodiazepines may also exist); narrow-angle glaucoma; pregnancy

Warnings/Precautions Active metabolites with extended half-lives may lead to delayed accumulation and adverse effects. Use with caution in elderly or debilitated patients, pediatric patients, patients with hepatic disease (including alcoholics) or renal impairment, patients with respiratory disease or impaired gag reflex, patients with porphyria.

Parenteral administration should be avoided in comatose patients or shock. Adequate resuscitative equipment/personnel should be available, and appropriate monitoring should be conducted at the time of injection and for several hours following administration. The parenteral formulation should be diluted for I.M. administration with the supplied diluent only. This diluent should not be used when preparing the drug for intravenous administration.

Causes CNS depression (dose-related) resulting in sedation, dizziness, confusion, or ataxia which may impair physical and mental capabilities. Patients must be cautioned about performing tasks which require mental alertness (eg, operating machinery or driving). Use with caution in patients receiving other CNS depressants or psychoactive agents (lithium, phenothiazines). Effects with other sedative drugs or ethanol may be potentiated. Benzodiazepines have been associated with falls and traumatic injury and should be used with extreme caution in patients who are at risk of these events (especially the elderly).

Use caution in patients with depression, particularly if suicidal risk may be present. Use with caution in patients with a history of drug dependence. Benzodiazepines have been associated with dependence and acute withdrawal symptoms on discontinuation or reduction in dose. Acute withdrawal, including seizures, may be precipitated in patients after administration of flumazenil to patients receiving long-term benzodiazepine therapy.

Benzodiazepines have been associated with anterograde amnesia. Paradoxical reactions, including hyperactive or aggressive behavior have been reported with benzodiazepines, particularly in adolescent/pediatric or psychiatric patients. Does not have analgesic, antidepressant, or antipsychotic properties.

Common Adverse Reactions
>10%:
    Central nervous system: Drowsiness, fatigue, ataxia, lightheadedness, memory impairment, dysarthria, irritability
    Dermatologic: Rash
    Endocrine & metabolic: Decreased libido, menstrual disorders
    Gastrointestinal: Xerostomia, decreased salivation, increased or decreased appetite, weight gain/loss
    Genitourinary: Micturition difficulties
1% to 10%:
    Cardiovascular: Hypotension
    Central nervous system: Confusion, dizziness, disinhibition, akathisia, increased libido
    Dermatologic: Dermatitis
    Gastrointestinal: Increased salivation
    Genitourinary: Sexual dysfunction, incontinence
    Neuromuscular & skeletal: Rigidity, tremor, muscle cramps
    Otic: Tinnitus
    Respiratory: Nasal congestion

Drug Interactions
Cytochrome P450 Effect: Substrate of CYP3A4 (major)
Increased Effect/Toxicity: Chlordiazepoxide potentiates the CNS depressant effects of narcotic analgesics, barbiturates, phenothiazines, ethanol, antihistamines, MAO inhibitors, sedative-hypnotics, and cyclic antidepressants. CYP3A4 inhibitors may increase the levels/effects of chlordiazepoxide; example inhibitors include azole antifungals, ciprofloxacin, clarithromycin, diclofenac, doxycycline, erythromycin, imatinib, isoniazid, nefazodone, nicardipine, propofol, protease inhibitors, quinidine, and verapamil.
Decreased Effect: CYP3A4 inducers may decrease the levels/effects of chlordiazepoxide; example inducers include aminoglutethimide, carbamazepine, nafcillin, nevirapine, phenobarbital, phenytoin, and rifamycins.

Mechanism of Action Binds to stereospecific benzodiazepine receptors on the postsynaptic GABA neuron at several sites within the central nervous system, including the limbic system, reticular formation. Enhancement of the inhibitory effect of GABA on neuronal excitability results by increased neuronal membrane permeability to chloride ions. This shift in chloride ions results in hyperpolarization (a less excitable state) and stabilization.

Pharmacodynamics/Kinetics
Distribution: V_d: 3.3 L/kg; crosses placenta; enters breast milk

Protein binding: 90% to 98%

Metabolism: Extensively hepatic to desmethyldiazepam (active and long-acting)

Half-life elimination: 6.6-25 hours; End-stage renal disease: 5-30 hours; Cirrhosis: 30-63 hours

Time to peak, serum: Oral: Within 2 hours; I.M.: Results in lower peak plasma levels than oral

Excretion: Urine (minimal as unchanged drug)

Dosage

Children:

<6 years: Not recommended

>6 years: Anxiety: Oral, I.M.: 0.5 mg/kg/24 hours divided every 6-8 hours

Adults:

Anxiety:

Oral: 15-100 mg divided 3-4 times/day

I.M., I.V.: Initial: 50-100 mg followed by 25-50 mg 3-4 times/day as needed

Preoperative anxiety: I.M.: 50-100 mg prior to surgery

Ethanol withdrawal symptoms: Oral, I.V.: 50-100 mg to start, dose may be repeated in 2-4 hours as necessary to a maximum of 300 mg/24 hours

Note: Up to 300 mg may be given I.M. or I.V. during a 6-hour period, but not more than this in any 24-hour period.

Dosing adjustment in renal impairment: Cl_{cr} <10 mL/minute: Administer 50% of dose

Hemodialysis: Not dialyzable (0% to 5%)

Dosing adjustment/comments in hepatic impairment: Avoid use

Administration

I.M.: Administer by deep I.M. injection slowly into the upper outer quadrant of the gluteus muscle; use only the diluent provided for I.M. use; solutions made with SWFI or NS cause pain with I.M. administration

I.V.: Administer slowly over at least 1 minute; do not use the diluent provided for I.M. use; air bubbles form during reconstitution

Monitoring Parameters Respiratory and cardiovascular status, mental status, check for orthostasis

Reference Range Therapeutic: 0.1-3 µg/mL (SI: 0-10 µmol/L); Toxic: >23 µg/mL (SI: >77 µmol/L)

Patient Information Avoid alcohol and other CNS depressants; avoid activities requiring psychomotor coordination until CNS effects are known; drug may cause physical or psychological dependence; avoid abrupt discontinuation after prolonged use, may cause drowsiness, poor balance

Dosage Forms CAP: 5 mg, 10 mg, 25 mg. **INJ, powder for reconstitution:** 100 mg

♦ **Chlordiazepoxide and Amitriptyline** see Amitriptyline and Chlordiazepoxide on page 81

♦ **Chlordiazepoxide and Clidinium** see Clidinium and Chlordiazepoxide on page 291

♦ **Chlorethazine** see Mechlorethamine on page 778

♦ **Chlorethazine Mustard** see Mechlorethamine on page 778

Chlorhexidine Gluconate (klor HEKS i deen GLOO koe nate)

U.S. Brand Names Avagard™ [OTC]; BactoShield® CHG [OTC]; Betasept® [OTC]; ChloraPrep® [OTC]; Chlorostat® [OTC]; Dyna-Hex® [OTC]; Hibiclens® [OTC]; Hibistat® [OTC]; Operand® Chlorhexidine Gluconate [OTC]; Peridex®; PerioChip®; PerioGard®

Synonyms CHG; 3M™ Avagard™ [OTC]

Therapeutic Category Antibacterial, Oral Rinse; Antibacterial, Topical; Mouthwash

Use Skin cleanser for surgical scrub, cleanser for skin wounds, preoperative skin preparation, germicidal hand rinse, and as antibacterial dental rinse. Chlorhexidine is active against gram-positive and gram-negative organisms, facultative anaerobes, aerobes, and yeast.

Orphan drug: Peridex®: Oral mucositis with cytoreductive therapy when used for patients undergoing bone marrow transplant

Pregnancy Risk Factor B

Dosage Adults:

Oral rinse (Peridex®, PerioGard®):

Precede use of solution by flossing and brushing teeth; completely rinse toothpaste from mouth. Swish 15 mL undiluted oral rinse around in mouth for 30 seconds, then expectorate. Caution patient not to swallow the medicine. Avoid eating for 2-3 hours after treatment. (The cap on bottle of oral rinse is a measure for 15 mL.)

When used as a treatment of gingivitis, the regimen begins with oral prophylaxis. Patient treats mouth with 15 mL chlorhexidine, swishes for 30 seconds, then expectorates. This is repeated twice daily (morning and evening). Patient should have a re-evaluation followed by a dental prophylaxis every 6 months.

Cleanser:

Surgical scrub: Scrub 3 minutes and rinse thoroughly, wash for an additional 3 minutes

Hand sanitizer (Avagard™): Dispense 1 pumpful in palm of one hand; dip fingertips of opposite hand into solution and work it under nails. Spread remainder evenly over hand and just above elbow, covering all surfaces. Repeat on other hand. Dispense another pumpful in each hand and reapply to each hand up to the wrist. Allow to dry before gloving.

Hand wash: Wash for 15 seconds and rinse

Hand rinse: Rub 15 seconds and rinse

Periodontal chip: One chip is inserted into a periodontal pocket with a probing pocket depth ≥5 mm. Up to 8 chips may be inserted in a single visit. Treatment is recommended every 3 months in pockets with a remaining depth ≥5 mm. If dislodgment occurs 7 days or more after

(Continued)

Chlorhexidine Gluconate *(Continued)*

placement, the subject is considered to have had the full course of treatment. If dislodgment occurs within 48 hours, a new chip should be inserted.

Dosage Forms CHIP, periodontal pocket insertion (PerioChip®): 2.5 mg. **LIQ, topical** [surgical scrub] (Avagard™): 1% (500 mL); (BactoShield® CHG): 2% (120 mL, 480 mL, 750 mL, 1000 mL, 3800 mL); 4% (120 mL, 480 mL, 750 mL, 1000 mL, 3800 mL); (Betasept®): 4% (120 mL, 240 mL, 480 mL, 960 mL, 3840 mL); (ChloraPrep®): 2% (0.67 mL, 1.5 mL, 3 mL, 10.5 mL); (Chlorostat®): 2% (360 mL, 3840 mL); (Dyna-Hex): 2% (120 mL, 960 mL, 3840 mL); 4% (120 mL, 960 mL, 3840 mL); (Hibiclens®): 4% (15 mL, 120 mL, 240 mL, 480 mL, 960 mL, 3840 mL); (Operand®): 2% (120 mL); 4% (120 mL, 240 mL, 480 mL, 960 mL, 3840 mL). **LIQ, oral rinse**: 0.12% (480 mL); (Peridex®): 0.12% (480 mL); (PerioGard®): 0.12% (480 mL). **LIQ, topical** (Hibistat®): 0.5% (240 mL, 480 mL). **PAD** [prep pad] (Hibistat®): 0.5% (50s). **SPONGE/ BRUSH** (BactoShield® CHG, Hibiclens®): 4% per sponge/brush

♦ **Chlormeprazine** *see Prochlorperazine on page 1042*

♦ **2-Chlorodeoxyadenosine** *see Cladribine on page 287*

♦ **Chloromag®** *see Magnesium Chloride on page 768*

♦ **Chloromycetin® Sodium Succinate** *see Chloramphenicol on page 256*

Chloroprocaine *(klor oh PROE kane)*

U.S. Brand Names Nesacaine®; Nesacaine®-MPF

Synonyms Chloroprocaine Hydrochloride

Therapeutic Category Local Anesthetic, Injectable

Use Infiltration anesthesia and peripheral and epidural anesthesia

Pregnancy Risk Factor C

Contraindications Hypersensitivity to chloroprocaine, other ester type anesthetics, or any component of the formulation; myasthenia gravis; concurrent use of bupivacaine; do not use for subarachnoid administration

Warnings/Precautions Use with caution in patients with cardiac disease, renal disease, and hyperthyroidism; convulsions and cardiac arrest have been reported presumably due to intra-vascular injection

Drug Interactions

Increased Effect/Toxicity: Avoid concurrent use of bupivacaine due to safety and efficacy concerns.

Decreased Effect: The para-aminobenzoic acid metabolite of chloroprocaine may decrease the efficacy of sulfonamide antibiotics.

Mechanism of Action Chloroprocaine HCl is benzoic acid, 4-amino-2-chloro-2-(diethylamino) ethyl ester monohydrochloride. Chloroprocaine is an ester-type local anesthetic, which stabilizes the neuronal membranes and prevents initiation and transmission of nerve impulses thereby affecting local anesthetic actions. Local anesthetics including chloroprocaine, reversibly prevent generation and conduction of electrical impulses in neurons by decreasing the transient increase in permeability to sodium. The differential sensitivity generally depends on the size of the fiber; small fibers are more sensitive than larger fibers and require a longer period for recovery. Sensory pain fibers are usually blocked first, followed by fibers that transmit sensations of temperature, touch, and deep pressure. High concentrations block sympathetic somatic sensory and somatic motor fibers. The spread of anesthesia depends upon the distribution of the solution. This is primarily dependent on the volume of drug injected.

Pharmacodynamics/Kinetics

Onset of action: 6-12 minutes

Duration: 30-60 minutes

Metabolism: Plasma cholinesterases

Excretion: Urine

Dosage Dosage varies with anesthetic procedure, the area to be anesthetized, the vascularity of the tissues, depth of anesthesia required, degree of muscle relaxation required, and duration of anesthesia; range: 1.5-25 mL of 2% to 3% solution; single adult dose should not exceed 800 mg

Infiltration and peripheral nerve block: 1% to 2%

Infiltration, peripheral and central nerve block, including caudal and epidural block: 2% to 3%, without preservatives

Administration Before injecting, withdraw syringe plunger to ensure injection is not into vein or artery

Dosage Forms INJ, solution (Nesacaine®): 1% (30 mL); 2% (30 mL). **INJ, solution** [preservative free] (Nesacaine®-MPF): 2% (20 mL); 3% (20 mL)

♦ **Chloroprocaine Hydrochloride** *see Chloroprocaine on page 260*

♦ **Chloroptic® [DSC]** *see Chloramphenicol on page 256*

Chloroquine *(KLOR oh kwin)*

Related Information

Malaria Treatment *on page 1464*

U.S. Brand Names Aralen®

Synonyms Chloroquine Phosphate

Therapeutic Category Amebicide; Aminoquinoline, Antimalarial; Antimalarial Agent; Antirheumatic, Disease Modifying

Use Suppression or chemoprophylaxis of malaria; treatment of uncomplicated or mild to moderate malaria; extraintestinal amebiasis

Unlabeled/Investigational Use Rheumatoid arthritis; discoid lupus erythematosus

Pregnancy Risk Factor C

Contraindications Hypersensitivity to chloroquine or any component of the formulation; retinal or visual field changes

Warnings/Precautions Use with caution in patients with liver disease, G6PD deficiency, alcoholism or in conjunction with hepatotoxic drugs. May exacerbate psoriasis or porphyria. Retinopathy (irreversible) has occurred with long or high-dose therapy; discontinue drug if any abnormality in the visual field or if muscular weakness develops during treatment. Use caution in patients with pre-existing auditory damage; discontinue immediately if hearing defects are noted. Use caution in patients with seizure disorders.

Common Adverse Reactions Frequency not defined.

Cardiovascular: Hypotension (rare), ECG changes (rare; including T-wave inversion), cardiomyopathy

Central nervous system: Fatigue, personality changes, headache, psychosis, seizures, delirium, depression

Dermatologic: Pruritus, hair bleaching, pleomorphic skin eruptions, alopecia, lichen planus eruptions, alopecia, mucosal pigmentary changes (blue-black), photosensitivity

Gastrointestinal: Nausea, diarrhea, vomiting, anorexia, stomatitis, abdominal cramps

Hematologic: Aplastic anemia, agranulocytosis (reversible), neutropenia, thrombocytopenia

Neuromuscular & skeletal: Rare cases of myopathy, neuromyopathy, proximal muscle atrophy, and depression of deep tendon reflexes have been reported

Ocular: Retinopathy (including irreversible changes in some patients long-term or high-dose therapy), blurred vision

Otic: Nerve deafness, tinnitus, reduced hearing (risk increased in patients with pre-existing auditory damage)

Drug Interactions

Cytochrome P450 Effect: Substrate (major) of CYP2D6, 3A4; **Inhibits** CYP2D6 (moderate)

Increased Effect/Toxicity: CYP2D6 inhibitors may increase the levels/effects of chloroquine; example inhibitors include chlorpromazine, delavirdine, fluoxetine, miconazole, paroxetine, pergolide, quinidine, quinine, ritonavir, and ropinirole. Chloroquine serum concentrations may be elevated with concomitant cimetidine use. Chloroquine may increase cyclosporine concentrations. CYP3A4 inhibitors may increase the levels/effects of chloroquine; example inhibitors include azole antifungals, ciprofloxacin, clarithromycin, diclofenac, doxycycline, erythromycin, imatinib, isoniazid, nefazodone, nicardipine, propofol, protease inhibitors, quinidine, and verapamil.

Decreased Effect: Chloroquine levels may be decreased by antacids or kaolin. Chloroquine may decrease ampicillin and/or praziquantel levels. CYP3A4 inducers may decrease the levels/effects of chloroquine; example inducers include aminoglutethimide, carbamazepine, nafcillin, nevirapine, phenobarbital, phenytoin, and rifamycins.

Mechanism of Action Binds to and inhibits DNA and RNA polymerase; interferes with metabolism and hemoglobin utilization by parasites; inhibits prostaglandin effects; chloroquine concentrates within parasite acid vesicles and raises internal pH resulting in inhibition of parasite growth; may involve aggregates of ferriprotoporphyrin IX acting as chloroquine receptors causing membrane damage; may also interfere with nucleoprotein synthesis

Pharmacodynamics/Kinetics

Duration: Small amounts may be present in urine months following discontinuation of therapy

Absorption: Oral: Rapid (~89%)

Distribution: Widely in body tissues (eg, eyes, heart, kidneys, liver, lungs) where retention prolonged; crosses placenta; enters breast milk

Metabolism: Partially hepatic

Half-life elimination: 3-5 days

Time to peak, serum: 1-2 hours

Excretion: Urine (~70% as unchanged drug); acidification of urine increases elimination

Dosage

Suppression or prophylaxis of malaria: Oral:

Children: Administer 5 mg base/kg/week on the same day each week (not to exceed 300 mg base/dose); begin 1-2 weeks prior to exposure; continue for 4-6 weeks after leaving endemic area; if suppressive therapy is not begun prior to exposure, double the initial loading dose to 10 mg base/kg and administer in 2 divided doses 6 hours apart, followed by the usual dosage regimen

Adults: 500 mg/week (300 mg base) on the same day each week; begin 1-2 weeks prior to exposure; continue for 4-6 weeks after leaving endemic area; if suppressive therapy is not begun prior to exposure, double the initial loading dose to 1 g (600 mg base) and administer in 2 divided doses 6 hours apart, followed by the usual dosage regimen

Acute attack: Oral:

Children: 10 mg/kg (base) on day 1, followed by 5 mg/kg (base) 6 hours later and 5 mg/kg (base) on days 2 and 3

Adults: 1 g (600 mg base) on day 1, followed by 500 mg (300 mg base) 6 hours later, followed by 500 mg (300 mg base) on days 2 and 3

Extraintestinal amebiasis:

Children: Oral: 10 mg/kg (base) once daily for 2-3 weeks (up to 300 mg base/day)

Adults: Oral: 1 g/day (600 mg base) for 2 days followed by 500 mg/day (300 mg base) for at least 2-3 weeks

Rheumatoid arthritis, lupus erythematosus (unlabeled uses): Adults: 250 mg (150 mg base) once daily; reduce dosage following maximal response (taper to discontinue after response in lupus); generally requires 3-6 weeks

(Continued)

Chloroquine *(Continued)*

Note: Not considered first-line agent.

Dosing adjustment in renal impairment: Cl$_{cr}$ <10 mL/minute: Administer 50% of dose
Hemodialysis: Minimally removed by hemodialysis

Administration Chloroquine phosphate tablets have also been mixed with chocolate syrup or enclosed in gelatin capsules to mask the bitter taste.

Monitoring Parameters Periodic CBC, examination for muscular weakness, and ophthalmologic examination in patients receiving prolonged therapy

Patient Information Take with meals; report any visual disturbances or difficulty in hearing or ringing in the ears; tablets are bitter tasting; may cause diarrhea, loss of appetite, nausea, stomach pain; notify prescriber if these become severe

Dosage Forms TAB, as phosphate: 250 mg; (Aralen®): 500 mg

♦ **Chloroquine Phosphate** *see Chloroquine on page 260*

♦ **Chlorostat® [OTC]** *see Chlorhexidine Gluconate on page 259*

Chlorothiazide *(klor oh THYE a zide)*

Related Information
Sulfonamide Derivatives *on page 1404*

U.S. Brand Names Diuril®

Therapeutic Category Antihypertensive Agent; Diuretic, Thiazide

Use Management of mild to moderate hypertension; adjunctive treatment of edema

Pregnancy Risk Factor C (manufacturer); D (expert analysis)

Dosage Note: The manufacturer states that I.V. and oral dosing are equivalent. Some clinicians may use lower I.V. doses, however, because of chlorothiazide's poor oral absorption. I.V. dosing in infants and children has not been well established.

Infants <6 months:

Oral: 20-40 mg/kg/day in 2 divided doses (maximum dose: 375 mg/day)

I.V. (unlabeled): 2-8 mg/kg/day in 2 divided doses; doses up to 20 mg/kg/day have been used (anecdotal reports)

Infants >6 months and Children:

Oral: 10-20 mg/kg/day in 2 divided doses (maximum dose: 375 mg/day in children <2 years or 1 g/day in children 2-12 years)

I.V. (unlabeled): 4 mg/kg/day in 1-2 divided doses; doses up to 20 mg/kg/day have been used (anecdotal reports)

Adults:

Hypertension: Oral: 500 mg to 2 g/day divided in 1-2 doses (manufacturer labeling); doses of 125-500 mg/day have also been recommended

Edema: Oral, I.V.: 500 mg to 1 g once or twice daily. Intermittent treatment (ie, therapy on alternate days) may be appropriate for some patients.

Elderly: Oral: 500 mg once daily **or** 1 g 3 times/week

Dosage Forms INJ, powder for reconstitution, as sodium: 500 mg. **SUSP, oral:** 250 mg/5 mL (237 mL). **TAB:** 250 mg, 500 mg

♦ **Chlorpheniramine, Acetaminophen, and Pseudoephedrine** *see Acetaminophen, Chlorpheniramine, and Pseudoephedrine on page 28*

Chlorpheniramine and Acetaminophen

(klor fen IR a meen & a seet a MIN oh fen)

U.S. Brand Names Coricidin HBP® Cold and Flu [OTC]

Synonyms Acetaminophen and Chlorpheniramine

Therapeutic Category Antihistamine/Analgesic

Use Symptomatic relief of congestion, headache, aches and pains of colds and flu

Dosage Adults: Oral: 2 tablets every 4 hours

Dosage Forms TAB: Chlorpheniramine 2 mg and acetaminophen 325 mg

♦ **Chlorpheniramine and Hydrocodone** *see Hydrocodone and Chlorpheniramine on page 630*

Chlorpheniramine and Phenylephrine *(klor fen IR a meen & fen il EF rin)*

U.S. Brand Names Dallergy-JR®; Ed A-Hist®; Histatab® Plus [OTC]; Rynatan®; Rynatan® Pediatric Suspension

Synonyms Chlorpheniramine Maleate and Phenylephrine Hydrochloride; Chlorpheniramine Tannate and Phenylephrine Tannate; Phenylephrine and Chlorpheniramine

Therapeutic Category Antihistamine/Decongestant

Use Temporary relief of nasal congestion and eustachian tube congestion as well as runny nose, sneezing, itching of nose or throat, itchy and watery eyes

Pregnancy Risk Factor C

Dosage General dosing guidelines; consult specific product labeling. Antihistamine/decongestant: Oral:

Children:

2-6 years: Chlorpheniramine tannate 4.5 mg and phenylephrine tannate 5 mg per 5 mL: 2.5-5 mL every 12 hours

6-12 years:

Chlorpheniramine maleate 4 mg and phenylephrine hydrochloride 20 mg every 12 hours **or**

Chlorpheniramine tannate 4.5 mg and phenylephrine tannate 5 mg per 5 mL: 5-10 mL every 12 hours

≥12 years: Chlorpheniramine maleate 8 mg and phenylephrine hydrochloride 40 mg every 12 hours

Adults:

Chlorpheniramine maleate 8 mg and phenylephrine hydrochloride 40 mg every 12 hours **or** Chlorpheniramine tannate 9 mg and phenylephrine tannate 25 mg every 12 hours

Dosage Forms CAP, extended release (Dallergy-JR®): Chlorpheniramine maleate 4 mg and phenylephrine hydrochloride 20 mg. **LIQUID** (Ed A-Hist®): Chlorpheniramine maleate 4 mg and phenylephrine hydrochloride 10 mg per 5 mL (480 mL). **SUSP, oral** (Rynatan® Pediatric Suspension): Chlorpheniramine tannate 4.5 mg and phenylephrine tannate 5 mg per 5 mL (480 mL). **TAB:** (Histatab® Plus): Chlorpheniramine maleate 2 mg and phenylephrine hydrochloride 5 mg; (Rynatan®): Chlorpheniramine tannate 9 mg and phenylephrine tannate 25 mg

Chlorpheniramine and Pseudoephedrine
(klor fen IR a meen & soo doe e FED rin)

U.S. Brand Names Allerest® Maximum Strength Allergy and Hay Fever [OTC]; A.R.M® [OTC]; Chlor-Trimeton® Allergy D [OTC]; C-Phed Tannate; Deconamine®; Deconamine® SR; Genaphed Plus [OTC]; Hayfebrol® [OTC]; Histex™; Kronofed-A®; Kronofed-A®-Jr; PediaCare® Cold and Allergy [OTC]; Rhinosyn® [OTC]; Rhinosyn-PD® [OTC]; Ryna® [DSC]; Sudafed® Sinus & Allergy [OTC]; Tanafed®; Tanafed DP™; Triaminic® Cold and Allergy [OTC]

Synonyms Chlorpheniramine Maleate and Pseudoephedrine Hydrochloride; Chlorpheniramine Tannate and Pseudoephedrine Tannate; Dexchlorpheniramine Tannate and Pseudoephedrine Tannate; Pseudoephedrine and Chlorpheniramine

Therapeutic Category Antihistamine/Decongestant

Use Relief of nasal congestion associated with the common cold, hay fever, and other allergies, sinusitis, eustachian tube blockage, and vasomotor and allergic rhinitis

Pregnancy Risk Factor C

Dosage General dosing guidelines; consult specific product labeling. Rhinitis/decongestant:
Oral:
Children:
2-6 years:
Chlorpheniramine maleate 1 mg and pseudoephedrine hydrochloride 15 mg every 4-6 hours
Chlorpheniramine tannate 4.5 mg and pseudoephedrine tannate 75 mg (Tanafed®): 2.5-5 mL every 12 hours (maximum: 10 mL/24 hours)
Dexchlorpheniramine tannate 2.5 mg and pseudoephedrine tannate 75 mg (Tanafed DP™): 2.5-5 mL every 12 hours (maximum: 10 mL/24 hours)
6-12 years:
Chlorpheniramine maleate 2 mg and pseudoephedrine hydrochloride 30 mg every 4-6 hours
Chlorpheniramine tannate 4.5 mg and pseudoephedrine tannate 75 mg (Tanafed®): 5-10 mL every 12 hours (maximum: 20 mL/24 hours)
Dexchlorpheniramine tannate 2.5 mg and pseudoephedrine tannate 75 mg (Tanafed DP™): 5-10 mL every 12 hours (maximum: 20 mL/24 hours)
Children ≥12 years and Adults:
Chlorpheniramine maleate 4 mg and pseudoephedrine hydrochloride 60 mg every 4-6 hours (immediate release products) or every 12 hours (extended release products)
Chlorpheniramine tannate 4.5 mg and pseudoephedrine tannate 75 mg (Tanafed®): 10-20 mL every 12 hours (maximum: 40 mL/24 hours)
Dexchlorpheniramine tannate 2.5 mg and pseudoephedrine tannate 75 mg (Tanafed DP™): 5-10 mL every 12 hours: (maximum: 20 mL/24 hours)

Dosage Forms CAP, extended release: Chlorpheniramine maleate 8 mg and pseudoephedrine hydrochloride 120 mg. **CAP, sustained release:** Chlorpheniramine maleate 8 mg and pseudoephedrine hydrochloride 120 mg; chlorpheniramine maleate 4 mg and pseudoephedrine hydrochloride 60 mg. **CAPLET:** Chlorpheniramine maleate 4 mg and pseudoephedrine hydrochloride 60 mg. **LIQUID:** Chlorpheniramine maleate 1 mg and pseudoephedrine sulfate 15 mg per 5 mL (120 mL); chlorpheniramine maleate 2 mg and pseudoephedrine sulfate 30 mg per 5 mL (120 mL, 480 mL). **SUSP, oral:** Chlorpheniramine tannate 4.5 mg and pseudoephedrine tannate 75 mg per 5 mL (120 mL, 480 mL); dexchlorpheniramine tannate 2.5 mg and pseudoephedrine tannate 75 mg (120 mL, 480 mL). **TAB:** Chlorpheniramine maleate 2 mg and pseudoephedrine hydrochloride 30 mg; chlorpheniramine maleate 4 mg and pseudoephedrine hydrochloride 60 mg. **TAB, chewable:** Chlorpheniramine maleate 1 mg and pseudoephedrine sulfate 15 mg

Chlorpheniramine, Ephedrine, Phenylephrine, and Carbetapentane
(klor fen IR a meen, e FED rin, fen il EF rin, & kar bay ta PEN tane)

U.S. Brand Names Rynatuss®; Rynatuss® Pediatric; Tetra Tannate Pediatric

Synonyms Carbetapentane, Ephedrine, Phenylephrine, and Chlorpheniramine; Ephedrine, Chlorpheniramine, Phenylephrine, and Carbetapentane; Phenylephrine, Ephedrine, Chlorpheniramine, and Carbetapentane

Therapeutic Category Antihistamine/Decongestant/Antitussive

Use Symptomatic relief of cough with a decongestant and an antihistamine

Pregnancy Risk Factor C

(Continued)

263

Chlorpheniramine, Ephedrine, Phenylephrine, and Carbetapentane *(Continued)*

Dosage Oral:
Children:
<2 years: Titrate dose individually
2-6 years: 2.5-5 mL every 12 hours
>6 years: 5-10 mL every 12 hours
Adults: 1-2 tablets every 12 hours

Dosage Forms SUSP, oral (Rynatuss® Pediatric, Tetra Tannate Pediatric): Carbetapentane 30 mg, ephedrine 5 mg, phenylephrine 5 mg, and chlorpheniramine 4 mg per 5 mL (240 mgL. 480 mL). **TAB** (Rynatuss®): Carbetapentane 60 mg, ephedrine 10 mg, phenylephrine 10 mg, and chlorpheniramine 5 mg

♦ **Chlorpheniramine, Hydrocodone, Phenylephrine, Acetaminophen, and Caffeine** *see* Hydrocodone, Chlorpheniramine, Phenylephrine, Acetaminophen, and Caffeine *on page 632*
♦ **Chlorpheniramine Maleate and Phenylephrine Hydrochloride** *see* Chlorpheniramine and Phenylephrine *on page 262*
♦ **Chlorpheniramine Maleate and Pseudoephedrine Hydrochloride** *see* Chlorpheniramine and Pseudoephedrine *on page 263*
♦ **Chlorpheniramine Maleate, Pseudoephedrine Hydrochloride, and Dextromethorphan Hydrobromide** *see* Chlorpheniramine, Pseudoephedrine, and Dextromethorphan *on page 265*

Chlorpheniramine, Phenylephrine, and Dextromethorphan
(klor fen IR a meen, fen il EF rin, & deks troe meth OR fan)

U.S. Brand Names Alka-Seltzer Plus® Cold and Cough [OTC]

Synonyms Dextromethorphan, Chlorpheniramine, and Phenylephrine; Phenylephrine, Chlorpheniramine, and Dextromethorphan

Therapeutic Category Antihistamine/Decongestant/Antitussive

Use Temporary relief of cough due to minor throat and bronchial irritation; relieves nasal congestion, runny nose and sneezing

Dosage Oral: Children >12 years and Adults: 2 tablets dissolved in water every 4 hours (maximum: 8 tablets/24 hours)

Dosage Forms TAB, effervescent: Chlorpheniramine 2 mg, phenylephrine 5 mg, and dextromethorphan 10 mg

Chlorpheniramine, Phenylephrine, and Methscopolamine
(klor fen IR a meen, fen il EF rin, & meth skoe POL a meen)

U.S. Brand Names AH-Chew®; D.A.II™ [DSC]; Dallergy®; Dehistine; Drize®-R; Dura-Vent®/DA [DSC]; Extendryl; Extendryl JR; Extendryl SR; Hista-Vent® DA; Vanex Forte™-D

Synonyms Methscopolamine, Chlorpheniramine, and Phenylephrine; Phenylephrine, Chlorpheniramine, and Methscopolamine

Therapeutic Category Antihistamine/Decongestant/Anticholinergic

Use Treatment of upper respiratory symptoms such as respiratory congestion, allergic rhinitis, vasomotor rhinitis, sinusitis, and allergic skin reactions of urticaria and angioedema

Pregnancy Risk Factor C

Dosage
Children 6-11 years: Relief of respiratory symptoms: Oral:
D.A.II™: One tablet every 12 hours
D.A. Chewable®, Extendryl chewable tablet: One tablet every 4 hours; do not exceed 4 doses in 24 hours
Dallergy®: One-half caplet every 12 hours
Dura-Vent®/DA: One-half tablet every 12 hours
Extendryl JR: One capsule every 12 hours
Extendryl syrup: 2.5-5 mL, may repeat up to every 4 hours depending on age and body weight
Children ≥12 years and Adults: Relief of respiratory symptoms: Oral: **Note:** If disturbances in urination occur in patients without renal impairment, medication should be discontinued for 1-2 days and should then be restarted at a lower dose
D.A.II™: Two tablets every 12 hours
Dallergy®, Extendryl SR: 1 capsule every 12 hours
Dura-Vent®/DA: One tablet every 12 hours
D.A. Chewable®, Extendryl: 1-2 chewable tablets every 4 hours
Extendryl syrup: 5-10 mL every 3-4 hours (4 times/day)
Elderly: Use with caution, may have increased adverse reactions
Dosage adjustment in renal impairment: Use is not recommended

Dosage Forms CAP: Chlorpheniramine 4 mg, phenylephrine 10 mg, and methscopolamine 1.25 mg; chlorpheniramine 8 mg, phenylephrine 20 mg, and methscopolamine 2.5 mg. **CAPLET, extended release:** Chlorpheniramine 12 mg, phenylephrine 20 mg, and methscopolamine 2.5 mg. **SYR:** Chlorpheniramine 2 mg, phenylephrine 10 mg, and methscopolamine 0.625 mg per 5 mL (480 mL); chlorpheniramine 2 mg, phenylephrine 10 mg, and methscopolamine 1.25 mg per 5 mL (480 mL). **TAB:** Chlorpheniramine 4 mg, phenylephrine 10 mg, and methscopolamine 1.25 mg; chlorpheniramine 8 mg, phenylephrine 20 mg, and methscopolamine 2.5 mg. **TAB, chewable** Chlorpheniramine 2 mg, phenylephrine 10 mg, and methscopolamine 1.25 mg. **TAB, extended release:** Chlorpheniramine 8 mg, phenylephrine 20 mg, and methscopolamine 2.5 mg

Chlorpheniramine, Phenylephrine, and Phenyltoloxamine
(klor fen IR a meen, fen il EF rin, & fen il tole LOKS a meen)

U.S. Brand Names Comhist®; Nalex®-A

Synonyms Phenylephrine, Chlorpheniramine, and Phenyltoloxamine; Phenyltoloxamine, Chlorpheniramine, and Phenylephrine

Therapeutic Category Antihistamine/Decongestant

Use Symptomatic relief of rhinitis and nasal congestion due to colds or allergy

Pregnancy Risk Factor C

Dosage Oral:
Children:
2-6 years: Nalex®-A liquid: 1.25-2.5 mL every 4 hours
6-12 years:
Nalex®-A liquid: 5 mL every 4 hours
Nalex®-A tablet: 1/2 tablet 2-3 times/day
Children >12 years and Adults:
Nalex®-A liquid: 10 mL every 4 hours
Nalex®-A tablet: 1 tablet 2-3 times/day

Dosage Forms LIQ (Nalex®-A): Chlorpheniramine 2.5 mg, phenylephrine 5 mg, and phenyltoloxamine 7.5 mg per 5 mL (480 mL). **TAB:** (Comhist®): Chlorpheniramine 2 mg, phenylephrine 10 mg, and phenyltoloxamine 25 mg; (Nalex®-A): Chlorpheniramine 4 mg, phenylephrine 20 mg, and phenyltoloxamine 40 mg

Chlorpheniramine, Phenylephrine, Codeine, and Potassium
Iodide (klor fen IR a meen, fen il EF rin, KOE deen, & poe TASS ee um EYE oh dide)

U.S. Brand Names Pediacof®

Synonyms Codeine, Chlorpheniramine, Phenylephrine, and Potassium Iodide; Phenylephrine, Chlorpheniramine, Codeine, and Potassium Iodide; Potassium Iodide, Chlorpheniramine, Phenylephrine, and Codeine

Therapeutic Category Antihistamine/Decongestant/Antitussive/Expectorant

Use Symptomatic relief of rhinitis, nasal congestion and cough due to colds or allergy

Restrictions C-V

Dosage Children 6 months to 12 years: 1.25-10 mL every 4-6 hours

Dosage Forms LIQ: (Pediacof®): Chlorpheniramine 0.75 mg, phenylephrine 2.5 mg, and codeine 5 mg and potassium iodide 75 mg per 5 mL (480 mL)

◆ **Chlorpheniramine, Pseudoephedrine, and Acetaminophen** *see* Acetaminophen, Chlorpheniramine, and Pseudoephedrine *on page 28*

Chlorpheniramine, Pseudoephedrine, and Codeine
(klor fen IR a meen, soo doe e FED rin, & KOE deen)

U.S. Brand Names Dihistine® DH; Ryna-C® [DSC]

Synonyms Codeine, Chlorpheniramine, and Pseudoephedrine; Pseudoephedrine, Chlorpheniramine, and Codeine

Therapeutic Category Antihistamine/Decongestant/Antitussive

Use Temporary relief of cough associated with minor throat or bronchial irritation or nasal congestion due to common cold, allergic rhinitis, or sinusitis

Restrictions C-V

Pregnancy Risk Factor C

Dosage Oral:
Children:
25-50 lb: 1.25-2.50 mL every 4-6 hours, up to 4 doses in 24-hour period
50-90 lb: 2.5-5 mL every 4-6 hours, up to 4 doses in 24-hour period
Adults: 10 mL every 4-6 hours, up to 4 doses in 24-hour period

Dosage Forms ELIX: Chlorpheniramine 2 mg, pseudoephedrine 30 mg, and codeine 10 mg per 5 mL (120 mL, 480 mL); (Dihistine® DH): Chlorpheniramine 2 mg, pseudoephedrine 30 mg, and codeine 10 mg per 5 mL (120 mL, 240 mL, 480 mL); (Ryna-C® [DSC]): Chlorpheniramine 2 mg, pseudoephedrine 30 mg, and codeine 10 mg per 5 mL (120 mL, 480 mL)

Chlorpheniramine, Pseudoephedrine, and Dextromethorphan
(klor fen IR a meen, soo doe e FED rin, & deks troe meth OR fan)

U.S. Brand Names Kidkare Cough and Cold [OTC]; PediaCare® Multi-Symptom Cold [OTC]; PediaCare® NightRest Cough and Cold [OTC]; Robitussin® Pediatric Night Relief [OTC]; Tanafed DM™; Tanafed DMX™; Triaminic® Cold and Night Time Cough [OTC]; Vicks® Children's NyQuil® [OTC]; Vicks® Pediatric 44®m [OTC]

Synonyms Chlorpheniramine Maleate, Pseudoephedrine Hydrochloride, and Dextromethorphan Hydrobromide; Chlorpheniramine Tannate, Pseudoephedrine Tannate, and Dextromethorphan Tannate; Dexchlorpheniramine Tannate, Pseudoephedrine Tannate, and Dextromethorphan Tannate; Dextromethorphan, Chlorpheniramine, and Pseudoephedrine; Pseudoephedrine, Chlorpheniramine, and Dextromethorphan

Therapeutic Category Antihistamine/Decongestant/Antitussive

Use Temporarily relieves nasal congestion, runny nose, cough, and sneezing due to the common cold, hay fever, or allergic rhinitis

Pregnancy Risk Factor C

Dosage General dosing guidelines; consult specific product labeling. Relief of cold symptoms:
Oral:
(Continued)

Chlorpheniramine, Pseudoephedrine, and Dextromethorphan
(Continued)

Children:

2-6 years:

Chlorpheniramine tannate 4.5 mg, dextromethorphan tannate 25 mg, and pseudoephedrine tannate 75 mg (Tanafed DM™): 2.5-5 mL every 12 hours (maximum: 10 mL/24 hours)

Dexchlorpheniramine tannate 2.5 mg, dextromethorphan tannate 25 mg, and pseudoephedrine tannate 75 mg (Tanafed DMX™): 2.5-5 mL every 12 hours (maximum: 10 mL/24 hours)

6-12 years:

Chlorpheniramine maleate 1 mg, dextromethorphan hydrobromide 7.5 mg, and pseudoephedrine 15 mg per 5 mL: 10 mL every 6 hours

Chlorpheniramine tannate 4.5 mg, dextromethorphan tannate 25 mg, and pseudoephedrine tannate 75 mg (Tanafed DM™): 5-10 mL every 12 hours (maximum: 20 mL/24 hours)

Dexchlorpheniramine tannate 2.5 mg, dextromethorphan tannate 25 mg, and pseudoephedrine tannate 75 mg (Tanafed DMX™): 5-10 mL every 12 hours (maximum: 20 mL/24 hours)

>12 years: Refer to Adults dosing

Adults:

Chlorpheniramine maleate 1 mg, dextromethorphan hydrobromide 7.5 mg, and pseudoephedrine 15 mg per 5 mL: 20 mL every 6 hours

Chlorpheniramine tannate 4.5 mg, dextromethorphan tannate 25 mg, and pseudoephedrine tannate 75 mg (Tanafed DM™): 10-20 mL every 12 hours (maximum: 40 mL/24 hours)

Dexchlorpheniramine tannate 2.5 mg, dextromethorphan tannate 25 mg, and pseudoephedrine tannate 75 mg (Tanafed DMX™): 10-20 mL every 12 hours (maximum: 40 mL/24 hours)

Dosage Forms LIQ: Chlorpheniramine maleate 1 mg, pseudoephedrine hydrochloride 15 mg, and dextromethorphan hydrobromide 5 mg per 5 mL (120 mL); (Kidkare Cough and Cold, PediaCare® Multi-Symptom Cold): Chlorpheniramine maleate 1 mg, pseudoephedrine hydrochloride 15 mg, and dextromethorphan hydrobromide 5 mg per 5 mL (120 mL); (PediaCare® NightRest Cough and Cold, Triaminic® Cold and Night Time Cough): Chlorpheniramine maleate 1 mg, pseudoephedrine hydrochloride 15 mg, and dextromethorphan hydrobromide 7.5 mg per 5 mL (120 mL); (Vicks® Pediatric 44®m, Vicks® Children's NyQuil®): Chlorpheniramine maleate 2 mg, pseudoephedrine hydrochloride 30 mg, and dextromethorphan hydrobromide 15 mg per 5 mL (120 mL). **SUSP:** (Tanafed DM™): Chlorpheniramine tannate 4.5 mg, pseudoephedrine tannate 75 mg, and dextromethorphan tannate 25 mg (120 mL, 480 mL); (Tanafed DMX™): Dexchlorpheniramine tannate 2.5 mg, pseudoephedrine tannate 75 mg, and dextromethorphan tannate 25 mg (120 mL, 480 mL). **SYR** (Robitussin® Pediatric Night Relief): Chlorpheniramine maleate 1 mg, pseudoephedrine hydrochloride 15 mg, and dextromethorphan hydrobromide 7.5 mg per 5 mL (120 mL)

♦ **Chlorpheniramine Tannate and Phenylephrine Tannate** *see* Chlorpheniramine and Phenylephrine *on page 262*

♦ **Chlorpheniramine Tannate and Pseudoephedrine Tannate** *see* Chlorpheniramine and Pseudoephedrine *on page 263*

♦ **Chlorpheniramine Tannate, Pseudoephedrine Tannate, and Dextromethorphan Tannate** *see* Chlorpheniramine, Pseudoephedrine, and Dextromethorphan *on page 265*

ChlorproMAZINE (klor PROE ma zeen)

Related Information

Antipsychotic Agents Comparison *on page 1364*

U.S. Brand Names Thorazine® [DSC]

Synonyms Chlorpromazine Hydrochloride; CPZ

Therapeutic Category Antiemetic; Antipsychotic Agent, Phenothiazine; Antipsychotic Agent, Phenothiazine, Aliphatic; Phenothiazine Derivative

Use Control of mania; treatment of schizophrenia; control of nausea and vomiting; relief of restlessness and apprehension before surgery; acute intermittent porphyria; adjunct in the treatment of tetanus; intractable hiccups; combativeness and/or explosive hyperexcitable behavior in children 1-12 years of age and in short-term treatment of hyperactive children

Unlabeled/Investigational Use Management of psychotic disorders

Pregnancy Risk Factor C

Contraindications Hypersensitivity to chlorpromazine or any component of the formulation (cross-reactivity between phenothiazines may occur); severe CNS depression; coma

Warnings/Precautions Safety in children <6 months of age has not been established; use with caution in patients with seizures, bone marrow suppression, or severe liver disease

Significant hypotension may occur, especially when the drug is administered parenterally; injection contains benzyl alcohol; injection also contains sulfites which may cause allergic reaction

Tardive dyskinesia: Prevalence rate may be 40% in elderly; development of the syndrome and the irreversible nature are proportional to duration and total cumulative dose over time. May be reversible if diagnosed early in therapy.

Extrapyramidal reactions are more common in elderly with up to 50% developing these reactions after 60 years of age. Drug-induced **Parkinson's syndrome** occurs often. **Akathisia** is the most common extrapyramidal symptom in elderly.

Increased confusion, memory loss, psychotic behavior, and agitation frequently occur as a consequence of anticholinergic effects

Orthostatic hypotension is due to alpha-receptor blockade, the elderly are at greater risk for orthostatic hypotension

Antipsychotic associated sedation in nonpsychotic patients is extremely unpleasant due to feelings of depersonalization, derealization, and dysphoria

Life-threatening arrhythmias have occurred at therapeutic doses of antipsychotics

Common Adverse Reactions Frequency not defined.

Cardiovascular: Postural hypotension, tachycardia, dizziness, nonspecific QT changes

Central nervous system: Drowsiness, dystonias, akathisia, pseudoparkinsonism, tardive dyskinesia, neuroleptic malignant syndrome, seizures

Dermatologic: Photosensitivity, dermatitis, skin pigmentation (slate gray)

Endocrine & metabolic: Lactation, breast engorgement, false-positive pregnancy test, amenorrhea, gynecomastia, hyper- or hypoglycemia

Gastrointestinal: Xerostomia, constipation, nausea

Genitourinary: Urinary retention, ejaculatory disorder, impotence

Hematologic: Agranulocytosis, eosinophilia, leukopenia, hemolytic anemia, aplastic anemia, thrombocytopenic purpura

Hepatic: Jaundice

Ocular: Blurred vision, corneal and lenticular changes, epithelial keratopathy, pigmentary retinopathy

Drug Interactions

Cytochrome P450 Effect: Substrate of CYP1A2 (minor), 2D6 (major), 3A4 (minor); **Inhibits** CYP2D6 (strong), 2E1 (weak)

Increased Effect/Toxicity: CYP2D6 inhibitors may increase the levels/effects of chlorpromazine; example inhibitors include delavirdine, fluoxetine, miconazole, paroxetine, pergolide, quinidine, quinine, ritonavir, and ropinirole. Effects on CNS depression may be additive when chlorpromazine is combined with CNS depressants (narcotic analgesics, ethanol, barbiturates, cyclic antidepressants, antihistamines, or sedative-hypnotics). Chlorpromazine may increase the effects/toxicity of anticholinergics, antihypertensives, lithium (rare neurotoxicity), trazodone, or valproic acid. Concurrent use with TCA may produce increased toxicity or altered therapeutic response. Chloroquine and propranolol may increase chlorpromazine concentrations. Hypotension may occur when chlorpromazine is combined with epinephrine. May increase the risk of arrhythmia when combined with antiarrhythmics, cisapride, pimozide, sparfloxacin, or other drugs which prolong QT interval. Metoclopramide may increase risk of extrapyramidal symptoms (EPS).

Decreased Effect: Phenothiazines inhibit the ability of bromocriptine to lower serum prolactin concentrations. Benztropine (and other anticholinergics) may inhibit the therapeutic response to chlorpromazine and excess anticholinergic effects may occur. Cigarette smoking and barbiturates may enhance the hepatic metabolism of chlorpromazine. Antihypertensive effects of guanethidine and guanadrel may be inhibited by chlorpromazine. Chlorpromazine may inhibit the antiparkinsonian effect of levodopa. Chlorpromazine and possibly other low potency antipsychotics may reverse the pressor effects of epinephrine.

Mechanism of Action Blocks postsynaptic mesolimbic dopaminergic receptors in the brain; exhibits a strong alpha-adrenergic blocking effect and depresses the release of hypothalamic and hypophyseal hormones; believed to depress the reticular activating system, thus affecting basal metabolism, body temperature, wakefulness, vasomotor tone, and emesis

Pharmacodynamics/Kinetics

Onset of action: I.M.: 15 minutes; Oral: 30-60 minutes

Absorption: Rapid

Distribution: V_d: 20 L/kg; crosses the placenta; enters breast milk

Protein binding: 92% to 97%

Metabolism: Extensively hepatic to active and inactive metabolites

Bioavailability: 20%

Half-life, biphasic: Initial: 2 hours; Terminal: 30 hours

Excretion: Urine (<1% as unchanged drug) within 24 hours

Dosage

Children ≥6 months:

Schizophrenia/psychoses:

Oral: 0.5-1 mg/kg/dose every 4-6 hours; older children may require 200 mg/day or higher

I.M., I.V.: 0.5-1 mg/kg/dose every 6-8 hours

<5 years (22.7 kg): Maximum: 40 mg/day

5-12 years (22.7-45.5 kg): Maximum: 75 mg/day

Nausea and vomiting:

Oral: 0.5-1 mg/kg/dose every 4-6 hours as needed

I.M., I.V.: 0.5-1 mg/kg/dose every 6-8 hours

<5 years (22.7 kg): Maximum: 40 mg/day

5-12 years (22.7-45.5 kg): Maximum: 75 mg/day

Adults:

Schizophrenia/psychoses:

Oral: Range: 30-2000 mg/day in 1-4 divided doses, initiate at lower doses and titrate as needed; usual dose: 400-600 mg/day; some patients may require 1-2 g/day

I.M., I.V.: Initial: 25 mg, may repeat (25-50 mg) in 1-4 hours, gradually increase to a maximum of 400 mg/dose every 4-6 hours until patient is controlled; usual dose: 300-800 mg/day

Intractable hiccups: Oral, I.M.: 25-50 mg 3-4 times/day

(Continued)

ChlorproMAZINE *(Continued)*

Nausea and vomiting:
Oral: 10-25 mg every 4-6 hours
I.M., I.V.: 25-50 mg every 4-6 hours

Elderly: Behavioral symptoms associated with dementia: Initial: 10-25 mg 1-2 times/day; increase at 4- to 7-day intervals by 10-25 mg/day. Increase dose intervals (bid, tid, etc) as necessary to control behavior response or side effects; maximum daily dose: 800 mg; gradual increases (titration) may prevent some side effects or decrease their severity.

Dosing comments in renal impairment: Hemodialysis: Not dialyzable (0% to 5%)

Dosing adjustment/comments in hepatic impairment: Avoid use in severe hepatic dysfunction

Administration Note: Avoid skin contact with oral solution or injection solution; may cause contact dermatitis.

Oral: Dilute oral concentrate solution in juice before administration. Chlorpromazine concentrate is not compatible with carbamazepine suspension; schedule dosing at least 1-2 hours apart from each other.

I.V.: Direct of intermittent infusion: Infuse 1 mg or portion thereof over 1 minute.

Monitoring Parameters Vital signs; lipid profile, fasting blood glucose/Hgb A_{1c}; BMI; mental status; abnormal involuntary movement scale (AIMS); extrapyramidal symptoms (EPS)

Reference Range
Therapeutic: 50-300 ng/mL (SI: 157-942 nmol/L)
Toxic: >750 ng/mL (SI: >2355 nmol/L); serum concentrations poorly correlate with expected response

Patient Information Do not stop taking unless informed by your prescriber. Do not take antacid within 1 hour of taking drug. Avoid alcohol. Avoid excess sun exposure (use sun block). May cause drowsiness; rise slowly from recumbent position. Use of supportive stockings may help prevent orthostatic hypotension.

Dosage Forms INJ, solution, as hydrochloride: 25 mg/mL (1 mL, 2 mL, 10 mL); (Thorazine® [DSC]): 25 mg/mL (10 mL). **TAB, as hydrochloride:** 10 mg, 25 mg, 50 mg, 100 mg, 200 mg

♦ **Chlorpromazine Hydrochloride** *see* ChlorproMAZINE *on page 266*

ChlorproPAMIDE *(klor PROE pa mide)*

Related Information
Hypoglycemic Drugs & Thiazolidinedione Information *on page 1378*
Sulfonamide Derivatives *on page 1404*

U.S. Brand Names Diabinese®

Therapeutic Category Antidiabetic Agent, Sulfonylurea; Hypoglycemic Agent, Oral; Sulfonylurea Agent

Use Management of blood sugar in type 2 diabetes mellitus (noninsulin dependent, NIDDM)

Unlabeled/Investigational Use Neurogenic diabetes insipidus

Pregnancy Risk Factor C

Dosage Oral: The dosage of chlorpropamide is variable and should be individualized based upon the patient's response

Initial dose:
Adults: 250 mg/day in mild to moderate diabetes in middle-aged, stable diabetic
Elderly: 100-125 mg/day in older patients

Subsequent dosages may be increased or decreased by 50-125 mg/day at 3- to 5-day intervals

Maintenance dose: 100-250 mg/day; severe diabetics may require 500 mg/day; avoid doses >750 mg/day

Dosing adjustment/comments in renal impairment: Cl_{cr} <50 mL/minute: Avoid use
Hemodialysis: Removed with hemoperfusion
Peritoneal dialysis: Supplemental dose is not necessary

Dosing adjustment in hepatic impairment: Dosage reduction is recommended. Conservative initial and maintenance doses are recommended in patients with liver impairment because chlorpropamide undergoes extensive hepatic metabolism.

Dosage Forms TAB: 100 mg, 250 mg

Chlorthalidone *(klor THAL i done)*

Related Information
Sulfonamide Derivatives *on page 1404*

U.S. Brand Names Thalitone®

Synonyms Hygroton

Therapeutic Category Antihypertensive Agent; Diuretic, Miscellaneous

Use Management of mild to moderate hypertension when used alone or in combination with other agents; treatment of edema associated with congestive heart failure or nephrotic syndrome. Recent studies have found chlorthalidone effective in the treatment of isolated systolic hypertension in the elderly.

Pregnancy Risk Factor B (manufacturer); D (expert analysis)

Dosage Oral:
Children (nonapproved): 2 mg/kg/dose 3 times/week or 1-2 mg/kg/day
Adults: 25-100 mg/day or 100 mg 3 times/week; usual dosage range (JNC 7): 12.5-25 mg/day
Elderly: Initial: 12.5-25 mg/day or every other day; there is little advantage to using doses >25 mg/day

Dosage adjustment in renal impairment: Cl_{cr} <10 mL/minute: Administer every 48 hours

Dosage Forms TAB: 25 mg, 50 mg, 100 mg; (Thalitone®): 15 mg

♦ **Chlorthalidone and Atenolol** *see Atenolol and Chlorthalidone on page 127*

♦ **Chlorthalidone and Clonidine** *see Clonidine and Chlorthalidone on page 301*

♦ **Chlor-Trimeton® Allergy D [OTC]** *see Chlorpheniramine and Pseudoephedrine on page 263*

Chlorzoxazone (klor ZOKS a zone)

U.S. Brand Names Parafon Forte® DSC

Therapeutic Category Centrally Acting Muscle Relaxant; Skeletal Muscle Relaxant

Use Symptomatic treatment of muscle spasm and pain associated with acute musculoskeletal conditions

Pregnancy Risk Factor C

Contraindications Hypersensitivity to chlorzoxazone or any component of the formulation; impaired liver function

Common Adverse Reactions Frequency not defined.

Central nervous system: Dizziness, drowsiness lightheadedness, paradoxical stimulation, malaise

Dermatologic: Rash, petechiae, ecchymoses (rare), angioneurotic edema

Gastrointestinal: Nausea, vomiting, stomach cramps

Genitourinary: Urine discoloration

Hepatic: Liver dysfunction

Miscellaneous: Anaphylaxis (very rare)

Drug Interactions

Cytochrome P450 Effect: Substrate of CYP1A2 (minor), 2A6 (minor), 2D6 (minor), 2E1 (major), 3A4 (minor); **Inhibits** CYP2E1 (weak), 3A4 (weak)

Increased Effect/Toxicity: Increased effect/toxicity when taken with ethanol or CNS depressants.

Mechanism of Action Acts on the spinal cord and subcortical levels by depressing polysynaptic reflexes

Pharmacodynamics/Kinetics

Onset of action: ~1 hour

Duration: 6-12 hours

Absorption: Readily absorbed

Metabolism: Extensively hepatic via glucuronidation

Excretion: Urine (as conjugates)

Dosage Oral:

Children: 20 mg/kg/day or 600 mg/m^2/day in 3-4 divided doses

Adults: 250-500 mg 3-4 times/day up to 750 mg 3-4 times/day

Monitoring Parameters Periodic liver functions tests

Patient Information May cause drowsiness or dizziness; avoid alcohol and other CNS depressants

Dosage Forms CAPLET (Parafon Forte® DSC): 500 mg. **TAB:** 500 mg

♦ **Cholac®** *see Lactulose on page 712*

Cholestyramine Resin (koe LES teer a meen REZ in)

Related Information

Lipid-Lowering Agents *on page 1381*

U.S. Brand Names Prevalite®; Questran®; Questran® Light

Therapeutic Category Antilipemic Agent, Bile Acid Sequestrant

Use Adjunct in the management of primary hypercholesterolemia; pruritus associated with elevated levels of bile acids; diarrhea associated with excess fecal bile acids; binding toxicologic agents; pseudomembranous colitis

Pregnancy Risk Factor C

Contraindications Hypersensitivity to bile acid sequestering resins or any component of the formulation; complete biliary obstruction; bowel obstruction

Warnings/Precautions Use with caution in patients with constipation (GI dysfunction) and patients with phenylketonuria (Questran® Light contains aspartame). Overdose may result in GI obstruction. Not to be taken simultaneously with many other medicines (decreased absorption). Treat any diseases contributing to hypercholesterolemia first. May interfere with fat-soluble vitamins (A, D, E, K) and folic acid. Chronic use may be associated with bleeding problems (especially in high doses).

Common Adverse Reactions

>10%: Gastrointestinal: Constipation, heartburn, nausea, vomiting, stomach pain

1% to 10%:

Central nervous system: Headache

Gastrointestinal: Belching, bloating, diarrhea

Drug Interactions

Decreased Effect:

Cholestyramine can reduce the absorption of numerous medications when used concurrently. Give other medications 1 hour before or 4-6 hours after giving cholestyramine. Medications which may be affected include HMG-CoA reductase inhibitors, thiazide diuretics, propranolol (and potentially other beta-blockers), corticosteroids, thyroid hormones, digoxin, valproic acid, NSAIDs, loop diuretics, sulfonylureas, troglitazone (and potentially other agents in this class).

(Continued)

Cholestyramine Resin *(Continued)*

Warfarin and other oral anticoagulants: Hypoprothrombinemic effects may be reduced by cholestyramine. Separate administration times (as detailed above) and monitor INR closely when initiating or discontinuing.

Mechanism of Action Forms a nonabsorbable complex with bile acids in the intestine, releasing chloride ions in the process; inhibits enterohepatic reuptake of intestinal bile salts and thereby increases the fecal loss of bile salt-bound low density lipoprotein cholesterol

Pharmacodynamics/Kinetics

Onset of action: Peak effect: 21 days

Absorption: None

Excretion: Feces (as insoluble complex with bile acids)

Dosage Oral (dosages are expressed in terms of anhydrous resin):

Children: 240 mg/kg/day in 3 divided doses; need to titrate dose depending on indication

Adults: 4 g 1-2 times/day to a maximum of 24 g/day and 6 doses/day

Dialysis: Not removed by hemo- or peritoneal dialysis; supplemental doses not necessary with dialysis or continuous arteriovenous or venovenous hemofiltration

Administration Mix powder with water or other fluid prior to administration; not to be taken in dry form. Suspension should not be sipped or held in mouth for prolonged periods (may cause tooth discoloration or enamel decay).

Patient Information Do not administer the powder in its dry form, mix with fluid or with applesauce; drink plenty of fluids; take other medications 1 hour before or 4-6 hours after binding resin; GI adverse reactions may decrease over time with continued use; adhere to prescribed diet

Dosage Forms POWDER, oral suspension: 4 g of resin/5.7 g of powder (5.7 g packets, 240 g can); 4 g of resin/9 g of powder (9 g packets, 378 g can); (Prevalite®): 4 g of resin/5.5 g of powder (5.5 g packets, 231 g can); (Questran®): 4 g of resin/9 g of powder (9 g packets, 378 g can); (Questran® Light): 4 g of resin/5 g of powder (5 g packets, 210 g can)

Choline Magnesium Trisalicylate *(KOE leen mag NEE zhum trye sa LIS i late)*

Related Information

Salicylates *on page 1500*

U.S. Brand Names Trilisate®

Synonyms Tricosal

Therapeutic Category Analgesic, Salicylate; Anti-inflammatory Agent; Nonsteroidal Anti-inflammatory Drug (NSAID), Oral; Salicylate

Use Management of osteoarthritis, rheumatoid arthritis, and other arthritis; acute painful shoulder

Pregnancy Risk Factor C/D (3rd trimester)

Contraindications Hypersensitivity to salicylates, other nonacetylated salicylates, other NSAIDs, or any component of the formulation; bleeding disorders; pregnancy (3rd trimester)

Warnings/Precautions Salicylate salts may not inhibit platelet aggregation and, therefore, should not be substituted for aspirin in the prophylaxis of thrombosis. Use with caution in patients with impaired renal function, dehydration, erosive gastritis, asthma, or peptic ulcer. Discontinue use 1 week prior to surgical procedures. Children and teenagers who have or are recovering from chickenpox or flu-like symptoms should not use this product. Changes in behavior (along with nausea and vomiting) may be an early sign of Reye's syndrome; patients should be instructed to contact their healthcare provider if these occur.

Elderly are a high-risk population for adverse effects from NSAIDs. As many as 60% of elderly can develop peptic ulceration and/or hemorrhage asymptomatically. Use lowest effective dose for shortest period possible. Tinnitus or impaired hearing may indicate toxicity. Tinnitus may be a difficult and unreliable indication of toxicity due to age-related hearing loss or eighth cranial nerve damage. CNS adverse effects may be observed in the elderly at lower doses than younger adults.

Common Adverse Reactions

<20%:

Gastrointestinal: Nausea, vomiting, diarrhea, heartburn, dyspepsia, epigastric pain, constipation

Otic: Tinnitus

<2%:

Central nervous system: Headache, lightheadedness, dizziness, drowsiness, lethargy

Otic: Hearing impairment

Drug Interactions

Increased Effect/Toxicity: Choline magnesium trisalicylate may increase the hypoprothrombinemic effect of warfarin.

Decreased Effect: Antacids may decrease choline magnesium trisalicylate absorption/ salicylate concentrations.

Mechanism of Action Inhibits prostaglandin synthesis; acts on the hypothalamus heat-regulating center to reduce fever; blocks the generation of pain impulses

Pharmacodynamics/Kinetics

Onset of action: Peak effect: ~2 hours

Absorption: Stomach and small intestines

Distribution: Readily into most body fluids and tissues; crosses placenta; enters breast milk

Half-life elimination (dose dependent): Low dose: 2-3 hours; High dose: 30 hours

Time to peak, serum: ~2 hours

Dosage Oral (based on total salicylate content):

Children <37 kg: 50 mg/kg/day given in 2 divided doses; 2250 mg/day for heavier children

Adults: 500 mg to 1.5 g 2-3 times/day **or** 3 g at bedtime; usual maintenance dose: 1-4.5 g/day

Elderly: 750 mg 3 times/day

Dosing adjustment/comments in renal impairment: Avoid use in severe renal impairment

Administration Liquid may be mixed with fruit juice just before drinking. Do not administer with antacids. Take with a full glass of water and remain in an upright position for 15-30 minutes after administration.

Monitoring Parameters Serum magnesium with high dose therapy or in patients with impaired renal function; serum salicylate levels, renal function, hearing changes or tinnitus, abnormal bruising, weight gain and response (ie, pain)

Reference Range Salicylate blood levels for anti-inflammatory effect: 150-300 µg/mL; analgesia and antipyretic effect: 30-50 µg/mL

Patient Information Take with food; do not take with antacids; watch for bleeding gums or any signs of GI bleeding; take with food or milk to minimize GI distress; notify prescriber if ringing in ears or persistent GI pain occurs

Dosage Forms LIQ: 500 mg/5 mL (240 mL). **TAB:** 500 mg, 750 mg, 1000 mg

Choline Salicylate (KOE leen sa LIS i late)

Related Information

Salicylates *on page 1500*

U.S. Brand Names Arthropan® [OTC] [DSC]

Therapeutic Category Analgesic, Salicylate; Anti-inflammatory Agent; Nonsteroidal Anti-inflammatory Drug (NSAID), Oral; Salicylate

Use Temporary relief of pain of rheumatoid arthritis, rheumatic fever, osteoarthritis, and other conditions for which oral salicylates are recommended; useful in patients in which there is difficulty in administering doses in a tablet or capsule dosage form, because of the liquid dosage form

Pregnancy Risk Factor C/D (3rd trimester)

Contraindications Hypersensitivity to salicylates or any component or other nonacetylated salicylates; pregnancy (3rd trimester)

Warnings/Precautions Use with caution in patients with impaired renal function, dehydration, erosive gastritis, or peptic ulcer; avoid use in patients with suspected varicella or influenza (salicylates have been associated with Reye's syndrome in children <16 years of age when used to treat symptoms of chickenpox or the flu); tinnitus or impaired hearing may indicate toxicity

Common Adverse Reactions

>10%: Gastrointestinal: Nausea, heartburn, stomach pains, dyspepsia, epigastric discomfort

1% to 10%:

Central nervous system: Fatigue

Dermatologic: Rash

Gastrointestinal: Gastrointestinal ulceration

Hematologic: Hemolytic anemia

Neuromuscular & skeletal: Weakness

Respiratory: Dyspnea

Miscellaneous: Anaphylactic shock

Drug Interactions

Increased Effect/Toxicity: Effect of warfarin may be increased.

Decreased Effect: Decreased effect of salicylates with antacids. Effect of ACE inhibitors and diuretics may be decreased by concurrent therapy with NSAIDs.

Mechanism of Action Inhibits prostaglandin synthesis; acts on the hypothalamus heat-regulating center to reduce fever; blocks the generation of pain impulses

Pharmacodynamics/Kinetics

Absorption: Stomach and small intestines in ~2 hours

Distribution: Readily into most body fluids and tissues; crosses placenta; enters breast milk

Protein binding: 75% to 90%

Metabolism: Hepatically hydrolyzed to salicylate

Half-life elimination (dose dependent): Low dose: 2-3 hours; High dose: 30 hours

Time to peak, serum: 1-2 hours

Excretion: Urine

Dosage

Children >12 years and Adults: Oral: 5 mL (870 mg) every 3-4 hours, if necessary, but not more than 6 doses in 24 hours

Rheumatoid arthritis: 870-1740 mg (5-10 mL) up to 4 times/day

Dosing adjustment/comments in renal impairment: Avoid use in severe renal impairment

Patient Information Take with food; do not take with antacids; watch for bleeding gums or any signs of GI bleeding; take with food or milk to minimize GI distress; notify prescriber if ringing in ears or persistent GI pain occurs

Dosage Forms LIQ: 870 mg/5 mL (480 mL)

Chondroitin Sulfate and Sodium Hyaluronate

(kon DROY tin SUL fate & SOW de um hye al yoor ON ate)

U.S. Brand Names Viscoat®

Synonyms Sodium Hyaluronate-Chrondroitin Sulfate

Therapeutic Category Ophthalmic Agent, Viscoelastic

(Continued)

Chondroitin Sulfate and Sodium Hyaluronate *(Continued)*

Use Surgical aid in anterior segment procedures, protects corneal endothelium and coats intraocular lens thus protecting it

Pregnancy Risk Factor C

Contraindications Hypersensitivity to hyaluronate

Warnings/Precautions Product is extracted from avian tissues and contains minute amounts of protein, potential risks of hypersensitivity may exist. Intraocular pressure may be elevated as a result of pre-existing glaucoma, compromised outflow by operative procedures and sequelae, including coma, compromised outflow and by operative procedures and sequelae, including enzymatic zonulysis, absence of an iridectomy, trauma to filtration structures and by blood and lenticular remnants in the anterior chamber. Monitor IOP, especially during the immediate postoperative period.

Common Adverse Reactions 1% to 10%: Ocular: Increased intraocular pressure

Mechanism of Action Functions as a tissue lubricant and is thought to play an important role in modulating the interactions between adjacent tissues

Pharmacodynamics/Kinetics
Absorption: Intravitreous injection: Diffusion occurs slowly
Excretion: By Canal of Schlemm

Dosage Carefully introduce (using a 27-gauge needle or cannula) into anterior chamber after thoroughly cleaning the chamber with a balanced salt solution

Administration May inject prior to or following delivery of the crystalline lens. Instillation prior to lens delivery provides additional protection to corneal endothelium, protecting it from possible damage arising from surgical instrumentation. May also be used to coat intraocular lens and tips of surgical instruments prior to implantation surgery. May inject additional solution during anterior segment surgery to fully maintain the solution lost during surgery. At the end of surgery, remove solution by thoroughly irrigating with a balanced salt solution.

Dosage Forms SOLN, ophthalmic: Sodium chondroitin 4% and sodium hyaluronate 3% (0.5 mL)

♦ **Chooz® [OTC]** *see* Calcium Carbonate *on page 203*

♦ **Choriogonadotropin Alfa** *see* Chorionic Gonadotropin (Recombinant) *on page 273*

Chorionic Gonadotropin (Human)

(kor ee ON ik goe NAD oh troe pin, HYU man)

U.S. Brand Names Novarel™; Pregnyl®; Profasi® [DSC]

Synonyms CG; hCG

Therapeutic Category Gonadotropin; Ovulation Stimulator

Use Induces ovulation and pregnancy in anovulatory, infertile females; treatment of hypogonadotropic hypogonadism, prepubertal cryptorchidism; spermatogenesis induction with follitropin alfa or follitropin beta

Pregnancy Risk Factor C

Contraindications Hypersensitivity to chorionic gonadotropin or any component of the formulation; precocious puberty, prostatic carcinoma or similar neoplasms

Warnings/Precautions Use with caution in asthma, seizure disorders, migraine, cardiac or renal disease; **not** effective in the treatment of obesity

Common Adverse Reactions
1% to 10%:
Central nervous system: Mental depression, fatigue
Endocrine & metabolic: Pelvic pain, ovarian cysts, enlargement of breasts, precocious puberty
Local: Pain at the injection site
Neuromuscular & skeletal: Premature closure of epiphyses

Mechanism of Action Stimulates production of gonadal steroid hormones by causing production of androgen by the testis; as a substitute for luteinizing hormone (LH) to stimulate ovulation

Pharmacodynamics/Kinetics
Half-life elimination: Biphasic: Initial: 11 hours; Terminal: 23 hours
Excretion: Urine (as unchanged drug) within 3-4 days

Dosage I.M.:
Children:
Prepubertal cryptorchidism: 1000-2000 units/m²/dose 3 times/week for 3 weeks **or** 4000 units 3 times/week for 3 weeks **or** 5000 units every second day for 4 injections **or** 500 units 3 times/week for 4-6 weeks
Hypogonadotropic hypogonadism: 500-1000 units 3 times/week for 3 weeks, followed by the same dose twice weekly for 3 weeks **or** 1000-2000 units 3 times/week **or** 4000 units 3 times/week for 6-9 months; reduce dosage to 2000 units 3 times/week for additional 3 months
Adults:
Induction of ovulation: Female: 5000-10,000 units one day following last dose of menotropins
Spermatogenesis induction: Male: Initial: 1500 int. units twice weekly to normalize serum testosterone levels. If no response in 8 weeks, increase dose to 3000 int. units twice weekly. After normalization of testosterone levels, combine with follitropin beta (Follistim®). Continue hCG at same dose used to normalize testosterone levels. Treatment response was noted at up to 12 months.

Administration I.M. administration only

Reference Range Depends on application and methodology; <3 mIU/mL (SI: <3 units/L) usually normal (nonpregnant)

Patient Information Discontinue immediately if possibility of pregnancy

Dosage Forms INJ, powder for reconstitution: 10,000 units

Chorionic Gonadotropin (Recombinant)

(kor ee ON ik goe NAD oh troe pin ree KOM be nant)

U.S. Brand Names Ovidrel®

Synonyms Choriogonadotropin Alfa; r-hCG

Therapeutic Category Gonadotropin; Ovulation Stimulator

Use As part of an assisted reproductive technology (ART) program, induces ovulation in infertile females who have been pretreated with follicle stimulating hormones (FSH); induces ovulation and pregnancy in infertile females when the cause of infertility is functional

Pregnancy Risk Factor X

Contraindications Hypersensitivity to hCG preparations or any component of the formulation; primary ovarian failure; uncontrolled thyroid or adrenal dysfunction; uncontrolled organic intracranial lesion (ie, pituitary tumor); abnormal uterine bleeding, ovarian cyst or enlargement of undetermined origin; sex hormone dependent tumors; pregnancy

Warnings/Precautions For use by infertility specialists; may cause ovarian hyperstimulation syndrome (OHSS); if severe, treatment should be discontinued and patient should be hospitalized. OHSS results in a rapid (<24 hours to 7 days) accumulation of fluid in the peritoneal cavity, thorax, and possibly the pericardium, which may become more severe if pregnancy occurs; monitor for ovarian enlargement; use may lead to multiple births; risk of arterial thromboembolism with hCG products; safety and efficacy in pediatric and geriatric patients have not been established.

Common Adverse Reactions

2% to 10%:

Endocrine & metabolic: Ovarian cyst (3%), ovarian hyperstimulation (<2% to 3%)

Gastrointestinal: Abdominal pain (3% to 4%), nausea (3%), vomiting (3%)

Local: Injection site: Pain (8%), bruising (3% to 5%), reaction (<2% to 3%), inflammation (<2% to 2%)

Miscellaneous: Postoperative pain (5%)

<2%:

Cardiovascular: Cardiac arrhythmia, heart murmur

Central nervous system: Dizziness, emotional lability, fever, headache, insomnia, malaise

Dermatologic: Pruritus, rash

Endocrine & metabolic: Breast pain, hot flashes, hyperglycemia, intermenstrual bleeding, vaginal hemorrhage

Gastrointestinal: Abdominal enlargement, diarrhea, flatulence

Genitourinary: Cervical carcinoma, cervical lesion, dysuria, genital herpes, genital moniliasis, leukorrhea, urinary incontinence, urinary tract infection, vaginitis

Hematologic: Leukocytosis

Neuromuscular & skeletal: Back pain, paresthesias

Renal: Albuminuria

Respiratory: Cough, pharyngitis, upper respiratory tract infection

Miscellaneous: Ectopic pregnancy, hiccups

In addition, the following have been reported with menotropin therapy: Adnexal torsion, hemoperitoneum, mild to moderate ovarian enlargement, pulmonary and vascular complications. Ovarian neoplasms have also been reported (rare) with multiple drug regimens used for ovarian induction (relationship not established).

Drug Interactions

Increased Effect/Toxicity: Specific drug interaction studies have not been conducted.

Mechanism of Action Luteinizing hormone analogue produced by recombinant DNA techniques; stimulates rupture of the ovarian follicle once follicular development has occurred.

Pharmacodynamics/Kinetics

Distribution: V_d: 5.9 ± 1 L

Bioavailability: 40%

Half-life elimination: Initial: 4 hours; Terminal: 29 hours

Time to peak: 12-24 hours

Excretion: Urine (10% of dose)

Dosage S.C.:

Adults: Female:

Assisted reproductive technologies (ART) and ovulation induction: 250 mcg given 1 day following the last dose of follicle stimulating agent. Use only after adequate follicular development has been determined. Hold treatment when there is an excessive ovarian response.

Elderly: Safety and efficacy have not been established

Dosage adjustment in renal impairment: Safety and efficacy have not been established

Dosage adjustment in hepatic impairment: Safety and efficacy have not been established

Administration Prior to administration, mix vial with 1 mL sterile water for injection. Gently mix by rotating vial to dissolve powder; do not shake. Use only if solution is clear and colorless. For S.C. use only; inject into stomach area. Use immediately following reconstitution.

Monitoring Parameters Ultrasound and/or estradiol levels to assess follicle development; ultrasound to assess number and size of follicles; ovulation (basal body temperature, serum progestin level, menstruation, sonography)

(Continued)

Chorionic Gonadotropin (Recombinant) *(Continued)*

Patient Information Instructions will be given on how to administer S.C. injections and proper disposal of syringes and needles. Use exactly as instructed by prescriber. Keep all ultrasound appointments. Report sudden weight gain, severe pelvic pain, nausea, vomiting, or shortness of breath to prescriber. Do not use if pregnant. As with other hCG products, there is a risk of multiple births associated with treatment. Avoid strenuous exercise, especially those with pelvic involvement.

Dosage Forms INJ, powder for reconstitution: 285 mcg [delivers 250 mcg r-hCG following reconstitution]. **INJ, solution** [prefilled syringe]: 257.5 mcg/0.515 mL (0.515 mL) [delivers 250 mcg r-hCG/0.5 mL]

◆ **Cialis®** *see* Tadalafil *on page 1184*

Ciclopirox (sye kloe PEER oks)

U.S. Brand Names Loprox®; Penlac™

Synonyms Ciclopirox Olamine

Therapeutic Category Antifungal Agent, Topical

Use

Cream/lotion/suspension: Treatment of tinea pedis (athlete's foot), tinea cruris (jock itch), tinea corporis (ringworm), cutaneous candidiasis, and tinea versicolor (pityriasis)

Gel: Treatment of tinea pedis (athlete's foot), tinea corporis (ringworm); seborrheic dermatitis of the scalp

Lacquer: Topical treatment of mild to moderate onychomycosis of the fingernails and toenails

Shampoo: Treatment of seborrheic dermatitis of the scalp

Pregnancy Risk Factor B

Contraindications Hypersensitivity to ciclopirox or any component of the formulation; avoid occlusive wrappings or dressings

Warnings/Precautions For external use only; avoid contact with eyes; nail lacquer is for topical use only and has not been studied in conjunction with systemic therapy

Common Adverse Reactions

>10%: Local: Burning sensation (gel: 34%; ≤1% with other forms)

1% to 10%:

Central nervous system: Headache

Dermatologic: Pruritus, rash

Local: Irritation, redness, or pain

Mechanism of Action Inhibiting transport of essential elements in the fungal cell disrupting the synthesis of DNA, RNA, and protein

Pharmacodynamics/Kinetics

Absorption: Cream, lotion, solution: <2% through intact skin; increased with gel; <5% with lacquer

Distribution: Scalp application: To epidermis, corium (dermis), including hair, hair follicles, and sebaceous glands

Protein binding: 94% to 98%

Half-life elimination: Biologic: 1.7 hours (solution); elimination: 5.5 hours (gel)

Excretion: Urine (gel: 3% to 10%); feces (small amounts)

Dosage Topical:

Children >10 years and Adults: Tinea pedis, tinea cruris, tinea corporis, cutaneous candidiasis, and tinea versicolor: Cream/lotion/suspension: Apply twice daily, gently massage into affected areas; if no improvement after 4 weeks of treatment, re-evaluate the diagnosis

Children >16 years and Adults:

Tinea pedis, tinea corporis, seborrheic dermatitis of the scalp: Gel: Apply twice daily, gently massage into affected areas and surrounding skin; if no improvement after 4 weeks of treatment, re-evaluate diagnosis

Seborrheic dermatitis of the scalp: Shampoo: Apply to wet hair, lather, and leave in place ~3 minute; rinse. Repeat twice weekly for 4 weeks; allow a minimum of 3 days between applications.

Adults: Onychomycosis of the fingernails and toenails: Lacquer (solution): Apply to affected nails daily (as a part of a comprehensive management program for onychomycosis)

Administration Lacquer (solution): Apply evenly over nail at bedtime (or allow 8 hours before washing); apply daily over previous coat for 7 days; may remove after 7 days with alcohol, and continue cycle.

Patient Information Avoid contact with eyes; if sensitivity or irritation occurs, discontinue use

Dosage Forms CRM, as olamine (Loprox®): 0.77% (15 g, 30 g, 90 g). **GEL** (Loprox®): 0.77% (30 g, 45 g, 100 g); **LOTION, as olamine** (Loprox®) [DSC]: 0.77% (30 mL, 60 mL). **SHAMPOO** (Loprox®): 1% (120 mL). **SOLN, topical** [nail lacquer] (Penlac™): 8% (3.3 mL [DSC], 6.6 mL). **SUSP, topical, as olamine** (Loprox®): 0.77% (30 mL, 60 mL)

◆ **Ciclopirox Olamine** *see* Ciclopirox *on page 274*

◆ **Cidecin** *see* Daptomycin *on page 342*

Cidofovir (si DOF o veer)

U.S. Brand Names Vistide®

Therapeutic Category Antiviral Agent; Antiviral Agent, Parenteral

Use Treatment of cytomegalovirus (CMV) retinitis in patients with acquired immunodeficiency syndrome (AIDS). **Note:** Should be administered with probenecid.

Pregnancy Risk Factor C

Contraindications Patients with hypersensitivity to cidofovir and in patients with a history of clinically severe hypersensitivity to probenecid or other sulfa-containing medications

Warnings/Precautions Dose-dependent nephrotoxicity requires dose adjustment or discontinuation if changes in renal function occur during therapy (eg, proteinuria, glycosuria, decreased serum phosphate, uric acid or bicarbonate, and elevated creatinine); avoid use in patients with creatinine >1.5 mg/dL; Cl_{cr} <55 mL/minute; use great caution with elderly patients; neutropenia and ocular hypotony have also occurred; safety and efficacy have not been established in children; administration must be accompanied by oral probenecid and intravenous saline prehydration; prepare admixtures in a class two laminar flow hood, wearing protective gear; dispose of cidofovir as directed

Common Adverse Reactions

>10%:

Central nervous system: Infection, chills, fever, headache, amnesia, anxiety, confusion, seizures, insomnia

Dermatologic: Alopecia, rash, acne, skin discoloration

Gastrointestinal: Nausea, vomiting, diarrhea, anorexia, abdominal pain, constipation, dyspepsia, gastritis

Hematologic: Thrombocytopenia, neutropenia, anemia

Neuromuscular & skeletal: Weakness, paresthesia

Ocular: Amblyopia, conjunctivitis, ocular hypotony

Renal: Tubular damage, proteinuria, elevated creatinine

Respiratory: Asthma, bronchitis, coughing, dyspnea, pharyngitis

1% to 10%:

Cardiovascular: Hypotension, pallor, syncope, tachycardia

Central nervous system: Dizziness, hallucinations, depression, somnolence, malaise

Dermatologic: Pruritus, urticaria

Endocrine & metabolic: Hyperglycemia, hyperlipidemia, hypocalcemia, hypokalemia, dehydration

Gastrointestinal: Abnormal taste, stomatitis

Genitourinary: Glycosuria, urinary incontinence, urinary tract infections

Neuromuscular & skeletal: Skeletal pain

Ocular: Retinal detachment, iritis, uveitis, abnormal vision

Renal: Hematuria

Respiratory: Pneumonia, rhinitis, sinusitis

Miscellaneous: Diaphoresis, allergic reactions

Drug Interactions

Increased Effect/Toxicity: Drugs with nephrotoxic potential (eg, amphotericin B, aminoglycosides, foscarnet, and I.V. pentamidine) should be avoided during cidofovir therapy.

Mechanism of Action Cidofovir is converted to cidofovir diphosphate which is the active intracellular metabolite; cidofovir diphosphate suppresses CMV replication by selective inhibition of viral DNA synthesis. Incorporation of cidofovir into growing viral DNA chain results in reductions in the rate of viral DNA synthesis.

Pharmacodynamics/Kinetics The following pharmacokinetic data is based on a combination of cidofovir administered with probenecid:

Distribution: V_d: 0.54 L/kg; does not cross significantly into CSF

Protein binding: <6%

Metabolism: Minimal; phosphorylation occurs intracellularly

Half-life elimination, plasma: ~2.6 hours

Excretion: Urine

Dosage

Induction: 5 mg/kg I.V. over 1 hour once weekly for 2 consecutive weeks

Maintenance: 5 mg/kg over 1 hour once every other week

Administer with probenecid - 2 g orally 3 hours prior to each cidofovir dose and 1 g at 2 and 8 hours after completion of the infusion (total: 4 g)

Hydrate with 1 L of 0.9% NS I.V. prior to cidofovir infusion; a second liter may be administered over a 1- to 3-hour period immediately following infusion, if tolerated

Dosing adjustment in renal impairment:

Cl_{cr} 41-55 mL/minute: 2 mg/kg

Cl_{cr} 30-40 mL/minute: 1.5 mg/kg

Cl_{cr} 20-29 mL/minute: 1 mg/kg

Cl_{cr} <19 mL/minute: 0.5 mg/kg

If the creatinine increases by 0.3-0.4 mg/dL, reduce the cidofovir dose to 3 mg/kg; discontinue therapy for increases ≥0.5 mg/dL or development of ≥3+ proteinuria

Monitoring Parameters Renal function (Cr, BUN, UAs), LFTs, WBCs, intraocular pressure and visual acuity

Patient Information Cidofovir is not a cure for CMV retinitis; regular follow-up ophthalmologic exams and careful monitoring of renal function are necessary; probenecid must be administered concurrently with cidofovir; report rash immediately; avoid use during pregnancy; use contraception during and for 3 months following treatment

Dosage Forms INJ, solution [preservative free]: 75 mg/mL (5 mL)

Cilostazol (sil OH sta zol)

U.S. Brand Names Pletal®

Synonyms OPC-13013

Therapeutic Category Phosphodiesterase Enzyme Inhibitor; Platelet Aggregation Inhibitor

(Continued)

Cilostazol *(Continued)*

Use Symptomatic management of peripheral vascular disease, primarily intermittent claudication; currently being investigated for the treatment of acute coronary syndromes and for graft patency improvement in percutaneous coronary interventions with or without stenting

Unlabeled/Investigational Use Investigational: Treatment of acute coronary syndromes and for graft patency improvement in percutaneous coronary interventions with or without stenting

Pregnancy Risk Factor C

Contraindications Hypersensitivity to cilostazol or any component of the formulation; heart failure (of any severity)

Warnings/Precautions Use with caution in patients receiving platelet aggregation inhibitors (effects are unknown), hepatic impairment (not studied). Use with caution in patients receiving inhibitors of CYP3A4 (such as ketoconazole or erythromycin) or inhibitors of CYP2C19 (such as omeprazole); use with caution in severe underlying heart disease; use is not recommended in nursing mothers

Common Adverse Reactions
>10%:
 Central nervous system: Headache (27% to 34%)
 Gastrointestinal: Abnormal stools (12% to 15%), diarrhea (12% to 19%)
 Miscellaneous: Infection (10% to 14%)
2% to 10%:
 Cardiovascular: Peripheral edema (7% to 9%), palpitation (5% to 10%), tachycardia (4%)
 Central nervous system: Dizziness (9% to 10%)
 Gastrointestinal: Dyspepsia (6%), nausea (6% to 7%), abdominal pain (4% to 5%), flatulence (2% to 3%)
 Neuromuscular & skeletal: Back pain (6% to 7%), myalgia (2% to 3%)
 Respiratory: Rhinitis (7% to 12%), pharyngitis (7% to 10%), cough (3% to 4%)

Drug Interactions
 Cytochrome P450 Effect: Substrate (minor) of CYP1A2, 2C19, 2D6, 3A4
 Increased Effect/Toxicity: Cilostazol serum concentrations may be increased by erythromycin, diltiazem, and omeprazole. Increased concentrations of cilostazol may be anticipated during concurrent therapy with other inhibitors of CYP3A4 (ie, clarithromycin, ketoconazole, itraconazole, fluconazole, miconazole, fluvoxamine, fluoxetine, nefazodone, and sertraline) or inhibitors of CYP2C19. Aspirin-induced inhibition of platelet aggregation is potentiated by concurrent cilostazol. The effect on platelet aggregation with other antiplatelet drugs is unknown.

Mechanism of Action Cilostazol and its metabolites are inhibitors of phosphodiesterase III. As a result cyclic AMP is increased leading to inhibition of platelet aggregation and vasodilation. Other effects of phosphodiesterase III inhibition include increased cardiac contractility, accelerated AV nodal conduction, increased ventricular automaticity, heart rate, and coronary blood flow.

Pharmacodynamics/Kinetics
 Onset of action: 2-4 weeks; may require up to 12 weeks
 Protein binding: 97% to 98%
 Metabolism: Hepatic via CYP3A4 (primarily), 1A2, 2C19, and 2D6; at least one metabolite has significant activity
 Half-life elimination: 11-13 hours
 Excretion: Urine (74%) and feces (20%) as metabolites

Dosage Adults: Oral: 100 mg twice daily taken at least one-half hour before or 2 hours after breakfast and dinner; dosage should be reduced to 50 mg twice daily during concurrent therapy with inhibitors of CYP3A4 or CYP2C19 (see Drug Interactions)

Dosage Forms TAB: 50 mg, 100 mg

♦ **Ciloxan®** *see Ciprofloxacin on page 278*

Cimetidine *(sye MET i deen)*

U.S. Brand Names Tagamet®; Tagamet® HB 200 [OTC]

Therapeutic Category Antihistamine, H_2 Blocker; Histamine H_2 Antagonist

Use Short-term treatment of active duodenal ulcers and benign gastric ulcers; long-term prophylaxis of duodenal ulcer; gastric hypersecretory states; gastroesophageal reflux; prevention of upper GI bleeding in critically-ill patients; labeled for OTC use for prevention or relief of heartburn, acid indigestion, or sour stomach

Unlabeled/Investigational Use Part of a multidrug regimen for *H. pylori* eradication to reduce the risk of duodenal ulcer recurrence

Pregnancy Risk Factor B

Contraindications Hypersensitivity to cimetidine, any component of the formulation, or other H_2 antagonists

Warnings/Precautions Adjust dosages in renal/hepatic impairment or patients receiving drugs metabolized through the P450 system

Common Adverse Reactions 1% to 10%:
 Central nervous system: Dizziness, agitation, headache, drowsiness
 Gastrointestinal: Diarrhea, nausea, vomiting

Drug Interactions
 Cytochrome P450 Effect: Inhibits CYP1A2 (moderate), 2C8/9 (weak), 2C19 (moderate), 2D6 (moderate), 2E1 (weak), 3A4 (moderate)
 Increased Effect/Toxicity: Cimetidine increases warfarin's effect in a dose-related manner. Cimetidine may increase serum concentrations of alfentanil, amiodarone, benzodiazepines

(except lorazepam, oxazepam, temazepam), beta-blockers (except atenolol, betaxolol, bisoprolol, nadolol, penbutolol), calcium channel blockers, carbamazepine, cisapride (avoid concurrent use), citalopram, flecainide, lidocaine, melphalan, meperidine, metronidazole, moricizine, paroxetine, phenytoin, procainamide, propafenone, quinidine, quinolone antibiotics, tacrine, TCAs, theophylline, and triamterene. Cimetidine increases carmustine's myelotoxicity; avoid concurrent use.

Decreased Effect: Ketoconazole, fluconazole, itraconazole (especially capsule) decrease serum concentration; avoid concurrent use with H_2 antagonists. Delavirdine's absorption is decreased; avoid concurrent use with H_2 antagonists.

Mechanism of Action Competitive inhibition of histamine at H_2-receptors of the gastric parietal cells resulting in reduced gastric acid secretion, gastric volume and hydrogen ion concentration reduced

Pharmacodynamics/Kinetics
Onset of action: 1 hour
Duration: 6 hours
Distribution: Crosses placenta; enters breast milk
Protein binding: 20%
Metabolism: Partially hepatic
Bioavailability: 60% to 70%
Half-life elimination: Neonates: 3.6 hours; Children: 1.4 hours; Adults: Normal renal function: 2 hours
Time to peak, serum: Oral: 1-2 hours
Excretion: Primarily urine (as unchanged drug); feces (some)

Dosage
Children: Oral, I.M., I.V.: 20-40 mg/kg/day in divided doses every 6 hours
Children ≥12 years and Adults: Oral: Heartburn, acid indigestion, sour stomach (OTC labeling): 200 mg up to twice daily; may take 30 minutes prior to eating foods or beverages expected to cause heartburn or indigestion
Adults:
Short-term treatment of active ulcers:
Oral: 300 mg 4 times/day or 800 mg at bedtime or 400 mg twice daily for up to 8 weeks
I.M., I.V.: 300 mg every 6 hours or 37.5 mg/hour by continuous infusion; I.V. dosage should be adjusted to maintain an intragastric pH ≥5
Patients with an active bleed: Administer cimetidine as a continuous infusion (see above)
Duodenal ulcer prophylaxis: Oral: 400-800 mg at bedtime
Gastric hypersecretory conditions: Oral, I.M., I.V.: 300-600 mg every 6 hours; dosage not to exceed 2.4 g/day
Helicobacter pylori eradication (unlabeled use): 400 mg twice daily; requires combination therapy with antibiotics
Dosing adjustment/interval in renal impairment: Children and Adults:
Cl_{cr} 20-40 mL/minute: Administer every 8 hours or 75% of normal dose
Cl_{cr} 0-20 mL/minute: Administer every 12 hours or 50% of normal dose
Hemodialysis: Slightly dialyzable (5% to 20%)
Dosing adjustment/comments in hepatic impairment: Usual dose is safe in mild liver disease but use with caution and in reduced dosage in severe liver disease; increased risk of CNS toxicity in cirrhosis suggested by enhanced penetration of CNS

Administration
Oral: Administer with meals so that the drug's peak effect occurs at the proper time (peak inhibition of gastric acid secretion occurs at 1 and 3 hours after dosing in fasting subjects and approximately 2 hours in nonfasting subjects; this correlates well with the time food is no longer in the stomach offering a buffering effect)
Injection: May be administered as a slow I.V. push or preferably as an I.V. intermittent or I.V. continuous infusion. Administer each 300 mg (or fraction thereof) over a minimum of 5 minutes when giving I.V. push. Give intermittent infusion over 15-30 minutes for each 300 mg dose. Intermittent infusions are administered over 15-30 minutes at a final concentration not to exceed 6 mg/mL; for patients with an active bleed, preferred method of administration is continuous infusion.

Monitoring Parameters CBC, gastric pH, occult blood with GI bleeding; monitor renal function to correct dose.

Patient Information Take with or immediately after meals; take 1 hour before or 2 hours after antacids; may cause drowsiness, impaired judgment, or coordination; avoid excessive alcohol

Dosage Forms INF, as hydrochloride [premixed in NS]: 300 mg (50 mL). **INJ, solution, as hydrochloride:** 150 mg/mL (2 mL, 8 mL). **LIQ, oral, as hydrochloride:** 300 mg/5 mL (240 mL, 480 mL). **LIQ, oral** (Tagamet® HB 200): 200 mg/20 mL (355 mL). **TAB:** 200 mg [OTC], 300 mg, 400 mg, 800 mg; (Tagamet): 300 mg, 400 mg; (Tagamet® HB 200): 200 mg

♦ **Cinobac®** see Cinoxacin on page 277

Cinoxacin (sin OKS a sin)
U.S. Brand Names Cinobac®
Therapeutic Category Antibiotic, Quinolone
Use Treatment and prevention of urinary tract infections (UTIs)
Pregnancy Risk Factor C
Dosage Adults: Oral:
Treatment of UTI: 1 g/day in 2-4 doses for 7-14 days
Prophylaxis against recurrent UTI: 250 mg once daily at bedtime (has been used up to 5 months)
(Continued)

Cinoxacin *(Continued)*

Dosing adjustment in renal impairment:
Cl$_{cr}$ >50-80 mL/minute: 250 mg 3 times/day
Cl$_{cr}$ 20-50 mL/minute: 250 mg twice daily
Cl$_{cr}$ <20 mL/minute: 250 mg/day

Dosage Forms CAP: 500 mg

♦ **Cipro®** *see Ciprofloxacin on page 278*

♦ **Ciprodex®** *see Ciprofloxacin and Dexamethasone on page 280*

Ciprofloxacin *(sip roe FLOKS a sin)*

Related Information
Antimicrobial Drugs of Choice *on page 1440*
Prevention of Wound Infection & Sepsis in Surgical Patients *on page 1436*
Tuberculosis Treatment Guidelines *on page 1466*

U.S. Brand Names Ciloxan®; Cipro®; Cipro® XR

Synonyms Ciprofloxacin Hydrochloride

Therapeutic Category Antibiotic, Ophthalmic; Antibiotic, Otic; Antibiotic, Quinolone

Use Treatment of documented or suspected infections of the lower respiratory tract, sinuses, skin and skin structure, bone/joints, and urinary tract (including prostatitis) due to susceptible bacterial strains; especially indicated for pseudomonal infections and those due to multi-drug-resistant gram-negative organisms, chronic bacterial prostatitis, infectious diarrhea, complicated gram-negative and anaerobic intra-abdominal infections (with metronidazole) due to *E. coli* (enteropathic strains), *B. fragilis*, *P. mirabilis*, *K. pneumoniae*, *P. aeruginosa*, *Campylobacter jejuni* or *Shigella*; approved for acute sinusitis caused by *H. influenzae* or *M. catarrhalis*; also used in treatment of typhoid fever due to *Salmonella typhi* (although eradication of the chronic typhoid carrier state has not been proven), osteomyelitis when parenteral therapy is not feasible, acute uncomplicated cystitis in females, to reduce incidence or progression of disease following exposure to aerolized *Bacillus anthracis*, febrile neutropenia (with piperacillin), and sexually-transmitted diseases such as uncomplicated cervical and urethral gonorrhea due to *Neisseria gonorrhoeae*; used ophthalmologically for superficial ocular infections (corneal ulcers, conjunctivitis) due to susceptible strains

Pregnancy Risk Factor C

Contraindications Hypersensitivity to ciprofloxacin, any component of the formulation, or other quinolones

Warnings/Precautions Not recommended in children <18 years of age (exception - postexposure treatment of inhalational anthrax); has caused transient arthropathy in children; CNS stimulation may occur (tremor, restlessness, confusion, and very rarely hallucinations or seizures); use with caution in patients with known or suspected CNS disorder; green discoloration of teeth in newborns has been reported; prolonged use may result in superinfection. Tendon inflammation and/or rupture have been reported with ciprofloxacin and other quinolone antibiotics. Discontinue at first sign of tendon inflammation or pain. Quinolones may exacerbate myasthenia gravis.

Severe hypersensitivity reactions, including anaphylaxis, have occurred with quinolone therapy. If an allergic reaction occurs (itching, urticaria, dyspnea, facial edema, loss of consciousness, tingling, cardiovascular collapse), discontinue drug immediately.

Common Adverse Reactions 1% to 10%:
Central nervous system: Headache (1%), restlessness (1%)
Dermatologic: Rash (1%)
Gastrointestinal: Nausea (5%), diarrhea (2%), vomiting (2%), abdominal pain (2%)
Hepatic: ALT/AST increased (2%)
Renal: Serum creatinine increased (1%)

Drug Interactions

Cytochrome P450 Effect: Inhibits CYP1A2 (strong), 3A4 (weak)

Increased Effect/Toxicity: Ciprofloxacin increases the levels/effect of cyclosporine, caffeine, theophylline, and warfarin. The CNS-stimulating effect of some quinolones may be enhanced by NSAIDs, and foscarnet has been associated with an increased risk of seizures with some quinolones. Serum levels of some quinolones are increased by loop diuretics, probenecid, and cimetidine (and possibly other H$_2$-blockers) due to altered renal elimination. This effect may be more important for quinolones with high percentage of renal elimination than with ciprofloxacin. Concurrent use of corticosteroids may increase risk of tendon rupture.

Decreased Effect: Enteral feedings may decrease plasma concentrations of ciprofloxacin probably by >30% inhibition of absorption. Aluminum/magnesium products, didanosine, quinapril, and sucralfate may decrease absorption of ciprofloxacin by ≥90% if administered concurrently. (Administer ciprofloxacin at least 4 hours and preferably 6 hours after the dose of these agents.) Calcium, iron, zinc, and multivitamins with minerals products may decrease absorption of ciprofloxacin significantly if administered concurrently. (Administer ciprofloxacin 2 hours before dose or at least 6 hours after the dose of these agents.) Antineoplastic agents may decrease quinolone absorption. Intravenous ciprofloxacin may decrease serum phenytoin concentrations.

Mechanism of Action Inhibits DNA-gyrase in susceptible organisms; inhibits relaxation of supercoiled DNA and promotes breakage of double-stranded DNA

Pharmacodynamics/Kinetics
Absorption: Oral: Immediate release tablet: Rapid (~50% to 85%)

Distribution: V_d: 2.1-2.7 L/kg; tissue concentrations often exceed serum concentrations especially in kidneys, gallbladder, liver, lungs, gynecological tissue, and prostatic tissue; CSF concentrations: 10% of serum concentrations (noninflamed meninges), 14% to 37% (inflamed meninges); crosses placenta; enters breast milk

Protein binding: 20% to 40%

Metabolism: Partially hepatic; forms 4 metabolites (limited activity)

Half-life elimination: Children: 2.5 hours; Adults: Normal renal function: 3-5 hours

Time to peak: Oral: Immediate release tablet: 0.5-2 hours; Extended release tablet: 1-2.5 hours

Excretion: Urine (30% to 50% as unchanged drug); feces (20% to 40%)

Dosage

Children (see Warnings/Precautions):

Oral: Immediate release formulation: 20-30 mg/kg/day in 2 divided doses; maximum: 1.5 g/day

Cystic fibrosis: 20-40 mg/kg/day divided every 12 hours

Anthrax:

Inhalational (postexposure prophylaxis): 15 mg/kg/dose every 12 hours for 60 days; maximum: 500 mg/dose

Cutaneous (treatment): 10-15 mg/kg every 12 hours for 60 days; amoxicillin 80 mg/kg/day divided every 8 hours is an option for completion of treatment after clinical improvement. **Note:** In the presence of systemic involvement, extensive edema, lesions on head/neck, refer to I.V. dosing for treatment of inhalational/gastrointestinal/oropharyngeal anthrax

I.V.: 15-20 mg/kg/day divided every 12 hours

Cystic fibrosis: 15-30 mg/kg/day divided every 8-12 hours

Anthrax:

Inhalational (postexposure prophylaxis): 10 mg/kg/dose every 12 hours for 60 days; do **not** exceed 400 mg/dose (800 mg/day)

Inhalational/gastrointestinal/oropharyngeal (treatment): Initial: 10-15 mg/kg every 12 hours for 60 days (maximum: 500 mg/dose); switch to oral therapy when clinically appropriate; refer to Adults dosing for notes on combined therapy and duration

Adults: Oral: **Note:** Extended release tablets and immediate release formulations are not interchangeable:

Urinary tract infection:

Acute uncomplicated: Immediate release formulation: 100 mg or 250 mg every 12 hours for 3 days

Acute uncomplicated pyelonephritis: Extended release formulation: 1000 mg every 24 hours for 7-14 days

Uncomplicated/acute cystitis: Extended release formulation: 500 mg every 24 hours for 3 days

Mild/moderate: Immediate release formulation: 250 mg every 12 hours for 7-14 days

Severe/complicated:

Immediate release formulation: 500 mg every 12 hours for 7-14 days

Extended release formulation: 1000 mg every 24 hours for 7-14 days

Lower respiratory tract, skin/skin structure infections: 500-750 mg twice daily for 7-14 days depending on severity and susceptibility

Bone/joint infections: 500-750 mg twice daily for 4-6 weeks, depending on severity and susceptibility

Infectious diarrhea: 500 mg every 12 hours for 5-7 days

Intra-abdominal (in combination with metronidazole): 500 mg every 12 hours for 7-14 days

Typhoid fever: 500 mg every 12 hours for 10 days

Urethral/cervical gonococcal infections: 250-500 mg as a single dose (CDC recommends concomitant doxycycline or azithromycin due to developing resistance; avoid use in Asian or Western Pacific travelers)

Disseminated gonococcal infection: 500 mg twice daily to complete 7 days of therapy (initial treatment with ceftriaxone 1 g I.M./I.V. daily for 24-48 hours after improvement begins)

Chancroid: 500 mg twice daily for 3 days

Sinusitis (acute): 500 mg every 12 hours for 10 days

Chronic bacterial prostatitis: 500 mg every 12 hours for 28 days

Anthrax:

Inhalational (postexposure prophylaxis): 500 mg every 12 hours for 60 days

Cutaneous (treatment): Immediate release formulation: 500 mg every 12 hours for 60 days. **Note:** In the presence of systemic involvement, extensive edema, lesions on head/neck, refer to I.V. dosing for treatment of inhalational/gastrointestinal/oropharyngeal anthrax

Adults: I.V.:

Bone/joint infections:

Mild to moderate: 400 mg every 12 hours for 4-6 weeks

Severe or complicated: 400 mg every 8 hours for 4-6 weeks

Lower respiratory tract, skin/skin structure infections:

Mild to moderate: 400 mg every 12 hours for 7-14 days

Severe or complicated: 400 mg every 8 hours for 7-14 days

Nosocomial pneumonia (mild to moderate to severe): 400 mg every 8 hours for 10-14 days

Prostatitis (chronic, bacterial): 400 mg every 12 hours for 28 days

Sinusitis (acute): 400 mg every 12 hours for 10 days

Urinary tract infection:

Mild to moderate: 200 mg every 12 hours for 7-14 days

Severe or complicated: 400 mg every 12 hours for 7-14 days

(Continued)

Ciprofloxacin *(Continued)*

Febrile neutropenia (with piperacillin): 400 mg every 8 hours for 7-14 days

Intra-abdominal infection (with metronidazole): 400 mg every 12 hours for 7-14 days

Anthrax:

Inhalational (postexposure prophylaxis): 400 mg every 12 hours for 60 days

Inhalational/gastrointestinal/oropharyngeal (treatment): 400 mg every 12 hours. **Note:** Initial treatment should include two or more agents predicted to be effective (per CDC recommendations). Agents suggested for use in conjunction with ciprofloxacin or doxy-cycline include rifampin, vancomycin, imipenem, penicillin, ampicillin, chloramphenicol, clindamycin, and clarithromycin. May switch to oral antimicrobial therapy when clinically appropriate. Continue combined therapy for 60 days.

Elderly: No adjustment needed in patients with normal renal function

Ophthalmic:

Solution: Children >1 year and Adults: Instill 1-2 drops in eye(s) every 2 hours while awake for 2 days and 1-2 drops every 4 hours while awake for the next 5 days

Ointment: Children >2 years and Adults: Apply a ½" ribbon into the conjunctival sac 3 times/day for the first 2 days, followed by a ½" ribbon applied twice daily for the next 5 days

Dosing adjustment in renal impairment:

Cl_{cr} 30-50 mL/minute: Oral: 250-500 mg every 12 hours

Cl_{cr} <30 mL/minute: Acute uncomplicated pyelonephritis or complicated UTI: Oral: Extended release formulation: 500 mg every 24 hours

Cl_{cr} 5-29 mL/minute:

Oral: 250-500 mg every 18 hours

I.V.: 200-400 mg every 18-24 hours

Dialysis: Only small amounts of ciprofloxacin are removed by hemo- or peritoneal dialysis (<10%); usual dose: Oral: 250-500 mg every 24 hours following dialysis

Continuous arteriovenous or venovenous hemodiafiltration effects: Administer 200-400 mg I.V. every 12 hours

Administration

Oral: May administer with food to minimize GI upset; avoid antacid use; maintain proper hydration and urine output. Administer at least 2 hours before or 6 hours after antacids or other products containing calcium, iron, or zinc (including dairy products or calcium-fortified juices). Separate oral administration from drugs which may impair absorption (see Drug Interactions).

Oral suspension: Should not be administered through feeding tubes (due to its physical characteristics). Patients should avoid chewing on the microcapsules if the suspension is administered orally. Do not administer commercial 5% or 10% oral suspension via enteral feeding tubes (due to physical characteristics of the suspension).

Tablet, extended release: Do not crush, split, or chew. May be administered with meals containing dairy products (calcium content <800 mg), but not with dairy products alone.

Parenteral: Administer by slow I.V. infusion over 60 minutes to reduce the risk of venous irritation (burning, pain, erythema, and swelling); final concentration for administration should not exceed 2 mg/mL

Monitoring Parameters Patients receiving concurrent ciprofloxacin, theophylline, or cyclosporine should have serum levels monitored

Reference Range Therapeutic: 2.6-3 µg/mL; Toxic: >5 µg/mL

Patient Information Take as directed, preferably on an empty stomach, 2 hours after meals. Extended release tablet may be taken with meals containing dairy products, but not with dairy products alone; do not crush, split, or chew extended release tablet. Swallow oral suspension, do not chew microcapsules. Take entire prescription even if feeling better. Maintain adequate hydration (2-3 L/day of fluids unless instructed to restrict fluid intake) to avoid concentrated urine and crystal formation. You may experience nausea, vomiting, or anorexia (small frequent meals, frequent mouth care, sucking lozenges, or chewing gum may help). You may experience increased sensitivity to sunlight; use sunblock, wear protective clothing and dark glasses, or avoid direct exposure to sunlight. Report immediately any signs of skin rash, joint or back pain, or difficulty breathing. Report unusual fever or chills; vaginal itching or foul-smelling vaginal discharge; easy bruising or bleeding. Report immediately any pain, inflammation, or rupture of tendon.

Dosage Forms INF [premixed in D_5W] (Cipro®): 200 mg (100 mL); 400 mg (200 mL). **INJ, solution** (Cipro®): 200 mg (20 mL); 400 mg (40 mL). **OINT, ophthalmic, as hydrochloride** (Ciloxan®): 3.33 mg/g [0.3% base] (3.5 g). **SOLN, ophthalmic as hydrochloride** (Ciloxan®): 3.33 mg/g [0.3% base] (2.5 mL, 5 mL, 10 mL). **SUSP, oral** (Cipro®): 250 mg/5 mL (100 mL); 500 mg/5 mL (100 mL). **TAB, film coated:** 250 mg, 500 mg, 750 mg; (Cipro®): 100 mg, 250 mg, 500 mg, 750 mg. **TAB, extended release, film coated** (Cipro® XR): 500 mg, 1000 mg

Ciprofloxacin and Dexamethasone

(sip roe FLOKS a sin & deks a METH a sone)

U.S. Brand Names Ciprodex®

Synonyms Ciprofloxacin Hydrochloride and Dexamethasone; Dexamethasone and Ciprofloxacin

Therapeutic Category Antibiotic/Corticosteroid, Otic

Use Treatment of acute otitis media in pediatric patients with tympanostomy tubes or acute otitis externa in children and adults

Pregnancy Risk Factor C

Dosage Otic:

Children: Acute otitis media in patients with tympanostomy tubes or acute otitis externa: Instill 4 drops into affected ear(s) twice daily for 7 days

Adults: Acute otitis externa: Instill 4 drops into affected ear(s) twice daily for 7 days

Dosage Forms SUSP, otic; Ciprofloxacin 0.3% and dexamethasone 0.1% (5 mL, 7.5 mL)

Ciprofloxacin and Hydrocortisone

(sip roe FLOKS a sin & hye droe KOR ti sone)

U.S. Brand Names Cipro® HC

Synonyms Hydrocortisone and Ciprofloxacin

Therapeutic Category Antibiotic/Corticosteroid, Otic

Use Treatment of acute otitis externa, sometimes known as "swimmer's ear"

Dosage Children >1 year of age and Adults: Otic: The recommended dosage for all patients is three drops of the suspension in the affected ear twice daily for seven day; twice-daily dosing schedule is more convenient for patients than that of existing treatments with hydrocortisone, which are typically administered three or four times a day; a twice-daily dosage schedule may be especially helpful for parents and caregivers of young children

Dosage Forms SUSP, otic: Ciprofloxacin 0.2% and hydrocortisone 1% (10 mL)

♦ **Ciprofloxacin Hydrochloride** *see* Ciprofloxacin *on page 278*

♦ **Ciprofloxacin Hydrochloride and Dexamethasone** *see* Ciprofloxacin and Dexamethasone *on page 280*

♦ **Cipro® HC** *see* Ciprofloxacin and Hydrocortisone *on page 281*

♦ **Cipro® XR** *see* Ciprofloxacin *on page 278*

Cisapride (SIS a pride)

U.S. Brand Names Propulsid®

Therapeutic Category Cholinergic Agent; Gastroprokinetic Agent

Use Treatment of nocturnal symptoms of gastroesophageal reflux disease (GERD); has demonstrated effectiveness for gastroparesis, refractory constipation, and nonulcer dyspepsia

Restrictions In U.S., available via limited-access protocol only.

Pregnancy Risk Factor C

Contraindications

Hypersensitivity to cisapride or any component of the formulations; GI hemorrhage, mechanical obstruction, GI perforation, or other situations when GI motility stimulation is dangerous

Serious cardiac arrhythmias including ventricular tachycardia, ventricular fibrillation, torsade de pointes, and QT prolongation have been reported in patients taking cisapride with other drugs that inhibit CYP3A4. Some of these events have been fatal. Concomitant oral or intravenous administration of the following drugs with cisapride may lead to elevated cisapride blood levels and is contraindicated:

Antibiotics: Oral or I.V. erythromycin, clarithromycin, troleandomycin

Antidepressants: Nefazodone

Antifungals: Oral or I.V. fluconazole, itraconazole, miconazole, oral ketoconazole

Protease inhibitors: Indinavir, ritonavir, amprenavir, atazanavir

Cisapride is also contraindicated for patients with a prolonged electrocardiographic QT intervals (QT_c >450 msec), a history of QT_c prolongation, or known family history of congenital long QT syndrome; clinically significant bradycardia, renal failure, history of ventricular arrhythmias, ischemic heart disease, and congestive heart failure; uncorrected electrolyte disorders (hypokalemia, hypomagnesemia); respiratory failure; and concomitant medications known to prolong the QT interval and increase the risk of arrhythmia, such as certain antiarrhythmics, certain antipsychotics, certain antidepressants, astemizole, bepridil, sparfloxacin, and terodiline. The preceding lists of drugs are not comprehensive. Cisapride should not be used in patients with uncorrected hypokalemia or hypomagnesemia or who might experience rapid reduction of plasma potassium such as those administered potassium-wasting diuretics and/or insulin in acute settings.

Warnings/Precautions Safety and effectiveness in children have not been established.

On March 24, 2000 the FDA announced that the manufacturer of cisapride would voluntarily withdraw its product from the U.S. market on July 14, 2000. This decision was based on 341 reports of heart rhythm abnormalities including 80 reports of deaths. The company will continue to make the drug available to patients who meet specific clinical eligibility criteria for a limited-access protocol (contact 1-800-JANSSEN). Serious cardiac arrhythmias including ventricular tachycardia, ventricular fibrillation, torsade de pointes, and QT prolongation have been reported in patients taking this drug. Many of these patients also took drugs expected to increase cisapride blood levels by inhibiting the cytochrome P450 3A4 enzymes that metabolize cisapride. These drugs include clarithromycin, erythromycin, troleandomycin, nefazodone, fluconazole, itraconazole, ketoconazole, indinavir and ritonavir. Some of these events have been fatal. Cisapride is contraindicated in patients taking any of these drugs. **QT prolongation, torsade de pointes (sometimes with syncope), cardiac arrest and sudden death have been reported in patients taking cisapride without the above-mentioned contraindicated drugs.** Most patients had disorders that may have predisposed them to arrhythmias with cisapride. Cisapride is contraindicated for those patients with: history of prolonged electrocardiographic QT intervals; renal failure; history of ventricular arrhythmias, ischemic heart disease, and CHF; uncorrected electrolyte disorders (hypokalemia, hypomagnesemia); respiratory failure; and concomitant medications known to prolong the QT interval and increase the risk of arrhythmia, such as certain antiarrhythmics, including those of Class 1A (such as quinidine and procainamide) and Class

(Continued)

Cisapride (Continued)

III (such as sotalol); tricyclic antidepressants (such as amitriptyline); certain tetracyclic antidepressants (such as maprotiline); certain antipsychotic medications (such as certain phenothiazines and sertindole), protease inhibitors, astemizole, bepridil, sparfloxacin and terodiline. (The preceding lists of drugs are not comprehensive.) Recommended doses of cisapride should not be exceeded.

Patients should have a baseline ECG and an electrolyte panel (magnesium, calcium, potassium) prior to initiating cisapride (see Contraindications). Potential benefits should be weighed against risks prior administration of cisapride to patients who have or may develop prolongation of cardiac conduction intervals, particularly QT_c. These include patients with conditions that could predispose them to the development of serious arrhythmias, such as multiple organ failure, COPD, apnea and advanced cancer. Cisapride should not be used in patients with uncorrected hypokalemia or hypomagnesemia, such as those with severe dehydration, vomiting or malnutrition, or those taking potassium-wasting diuretics. Cisapride should not be used in patients who might experience rapid reduction of plasma potassium, such as those administered potassium-wasting diuretics and/or insulin in acute settings.

Common Adverse Reactions

>5%:
  Central nervous system: Headache
  Dermatologic: Rash
  Gastrointestinal: Diarrhea, GI cramping, dyspepsia, flatulence, nausea, xerostomia
  Respiratory: Rhinitis

<5%:
  Cardiovascular: Tachycardia
  Central nervous system: Extrapyramidal effects, somnolence, fatigue, seizures, insomnia, anxiety
  Hematologic: Thrombocytopenia, increased LFTs, pancytopenia, leukopenia, granulocytopenia, aplastic anemia
  Respiratory: Sinusitis, coughing, upper respiratory tract infection, increased incidence of viral infection

Drug Interactions

Cytochrome P450 Effect: **Substrate** of CYP1A2 (minor), 2A6 (minor), 2B6 (minor), 2C8/9 (minor), 2C19 (minor), 3A4 (major); **Inhibits** CYP2D6 (weak), 3A4 (weak)

Increased Effect/Toxicity: Cisapride may increase blood levels of warfarin, diazepam, cimetidine, ranitidine, and CNS depressants. The risk of cisapride-induced malignant arrhythmias may be increased by azole antifungals (fluconazole, itraconazole, ketoconazole, miconazole), antiarrhythmics (Class Ia; quinidine, procainamide, and Class III; amiodarone, sotalol), bepridil, cimetidine, maprotiline, macrolide antibiotics (erythromycin, clarithromycin, troleandomycin), molindone, nefazodone, protease inhibitors (amprenavir, atazanavir, indinavir, nelfinavir, ritonavir), phenothiazines (eg, prochlorperazine, promethazine), sertindole, tricyclic antidepressants (eg amitriptyline), and some quinolone antibiotics (sparfloxacin, gatifloxacin, moxifloxacin). Cardiovascular disease or electrolyte imbalances (potentially due to diuretic therapy) increase the risk of malignant arrhythmias.

Decreased Effect: Cisapride may decrease the effect of atropine and digoxin.

Mechanism of Action Enhances the release of acetylcholine at the myenteric plexus. *In vitro* studies have shown cisapride to have serotonin-4 receptor agonistic properties which may increase gastrointestinal motility and cardiac rate; increases lower esophageal sphincter pressure and lower esophageal peristalsis; accelerates gastric emptying of both liquids and solids.

Pharmacodynamics/Kinetics

Onset of action: 0.5-1 hour
Protein binding: 97.5% to 98%
Metabolism: Extensively hepatic to norcisapride
Bioavailability: 35% to 40%
Half-life elimination: 6-12 hours
Excretion: Urine and feces (<10%)

Dosage Oral:

Children: 0.15-0.3 mg/kg/dose 3-4 times/day; maximum: 10 mg/dose
Adults: Initial: 10 mg 4 times/day at least 15 minutes before meals and at bedtime; in some patients the dosage will need to be increased to 20 mg to obtain a satisfactory result

Dosage Forms SUSP, oral: 1 mg/mL (450 mL). **TAB** [scored]: 10 mg, 20 mg

Cisatracurium (sis a tra KYOO ree um)

Related Information

Neuromuscular Blocking Agents Comparison *on page 1397*

U.S. Brand Names Nimbex®

Synonyms Cisatracurium Besylate

Therapeutic Category Neuromuscular Blocker Agent, Nondepolarizing

Use Adjunct to general anesthesia to facilitate endotracheal intubation and to relax skeletal muscles during surgery; to facilitate mechanical ventilation in ICU patients; does not relieve pain or produce sedation

Pregnancy Risk Factor B

Contraindications Hypersensitivity to cisatracurium besylate or any component of the formulation

Warnings/Precautions Certain clinical conditions may result in potentiation or antagonism of neuromuscular blockade:

Potentiation: Electrolyte abnormalities, severe hyponatremia, severe hypocalcemia, severe hypokalemia, hypermagnesemia, neuromuscular diseases, acidosis, acute intermittent porphyria, renal failure, hepatic failure

Antagonism: Alkalosis, hypercalcemia, demyelinating lesions, peripheral neuropathies, diabetes mellitus

Increased sensitivity in patients with myasthenia gravis, Eaton-Lambert syndrome; resistance in burn patients (>30% of body) for period of 5-70 days postinjury; resistance in patients with muscle trauma, denervation, immobilization, infection. Cross-sensitivity with other neuromuscular-blocking agents may occur; use extreme caution in patients with previous anaphylactic reactions.

Drug Interactions

Increased Effect/Toxicity: Increased effects are possible with aminoglycosides, beta-blockers, clindamycin, calcium channel blockers, halogenated anesthetics, imipenem, ketamine, lidocaine, loop diuretics (furosemide), macrolides (case reports), magnesium sulfate, procainamide, quinidine, quinolones, tetracyclines, and vancomycin. May increase risk of myopathy when used with high-dose corticosteroids for extended periods.

Decreased Effect: Effect of nondepolarizing neuromuscular blockers may be reduced by carbamazepine (chronic use), corticosteroids (also associated with myopathy - see increased effect), phenytoin (chronic use), sympathomimetics, and theophylline.

Mechanism of Action
Blocks neural transmission at the myoneural junction by binding with cholinergic receptor sites

Pharmacodynamics/Kinetics

Onset of action: I.V.: 2-3 minutes

Peak effect: 3-5 minutes

Duration: Recovery begins in 20-35 minutes when anesthesia is balanced; recovery is attained in 90% of patients in 25-93 minutes

Metabolism: Undergoes rapid nonenzymatic degradation in the bloodstream (Hofman elimination), additional metabolism occurs via ester hydrolysis; some active metabolites

Half-life elimination: 22-29 minutes

Dosage I.V. (not to be used I.M.):

Operating room administration:

Children 2-12 years: Intubating doses: 0.1 mg over 5-15 seconds during either halothane or opioid anesthesia. (**Note:** When given during stable opioid/nitrous oxide/oxygen anesthesia, 0.1 mg/kg produces maximum neuromuscular block in an average of 2.8 minutes and clinically effective block for 28 minutes.)

Adults: Intubating doses: 0.15-0.2 mg/kg as component of propofol/nitrous oxide/oxygen induction-intubation technique. (**Note:** May produce generally good or excellent conditions for tracheal intubation in 1.5-2 minutes with clinically effective duration of action during propofol anesthesia of 55-61 minutes.); initial dose after succinylcholine for intubation: 0.1 mg/kg; maintenance dose: 0.03 mg/kg 40-60 minutes after initial dose, then at ~20-minute intervals based on clinical criteria

Children ≥2 years and Adults: Continuous infusion: After an initial bolus, a diluted solution can be given by continuous infusion for maintenance of neuromuscular blockade during extended surgery; adjust the rate of administration according to the patient's response as determined by peripheral nerve stimulation. An initial infusion rate of 3 mcg/kg/minute may be required to rapidly counteract the spontaneous recovery of neuromuscular function; thereafter, a rate of 1-2 mcg/kg/minute should be adequate to maintain continuous neuromuscular block in the 89% to 99% range in most pediatric and adult patients. Consider reduction of the infusion rate by 30% to 40% when administering during stable isoflurane, enflurane, sevoflurane, or desflurane anesthesia. Spontaneous recovery from neuromuscular blockade following discontinuation of infusion of cisatracurium may be expected to proceed at a rate comparable to that following single bolus administration.

Intensive care unit administration: Follow the principles for infusion in the operating room. At initial signs of recovery from bolus dose, begin the infusion at a dose of 3 mcg/kg/minute and adjust rates accordingly; dosage ranges of 0.5-10 mcg/kg/minute have been reported. If patient is allowed to recover from neuromuscular blockade, readministration of a bolus dose may be necessary to quickly re-establish neuromuscular block prior to reinstituting the infusion. See table.

Cisatracurium Besylate Infusion Chart

Drug Delivery Rate (mcg/kg/min)	Infusion Rate (mL/kg/min) 0.1 mg/mL (10 mg/100 mL)	Infusion Rate (mL/kg/min) 0.4 mg/mL (40 mg/100 mL)
1	0.01	0.0025
1.5	0.015	0.00375
2	0.02	0.005
3	0.03	0.0075
5	0.05	0.0125

Dosing adjustment in renal impairment: Because slower times to onset of complete neuromuscular block were observed in renal dysfunction patients, extending the interval between the administration of cisatracurium and intubation attempt may be required to achieve adequate intubation conditions.

(Continued)

Cisatracurium *(Continued)*

Administration Administer I.V. only; the use of a peripheral nerve stimulator will permit the most advantageous use of cisatracurium, minimize the possibility of overdosage or underdosage and assist in the evaluation of recovery

Give undiluted as a bolus injection; not for I.M. injection, too much tissue irritation; continuous administration requires the use of an infusion pump

Monitoring Parameters Vital signs (heart rate, blood pressure, respiratory rate)

Patient Information May be difficult to talk because of head and neck muscle blockade

Dosage Forms INJ, solution: 2 mg/mL (5 mL, 10 mL); 10 mg/mL (20 mL)

♦ **Cisatracurium Besylate** *see* Cisatracurium *on page 282*

Cisplatin (SIS pla tin)

U.S. Brand Names Platinol®-AQ

Synonyms CDDP

Therapeutic Category Antineoplastic Agent, Alkylating Agent; Antineoplastic Agent, Vesicant; Vesicant

Use Treatment of head and neck, breast, testicular, and ovarian cancer; Hodgkin's and non-Hodgkin's lymphoma; neuroblastoma; sarcomas, bladder, gastric, lung, esophageal, cervical, and prostate cancer; myeloma, melanoma, mesothelioma, small cell lung cancer, and osteosarcoma

Pregnancy Risk Factor D

Contraindications Hypersensitivity to cisplatin, other platinum-containing compounds, or any component of the formulation (anaphylactic-like reactions have been reported); pre-existing renal insufficiency; myelosuppression; hearing impairment; pregnancy

Warnings/Precautions The U.S. Food and Drug Administration (FDA) currently recommends that procedures for proper handling and disposal of antineoplastic agents be considered. All patients should receive adequate hydration prior to and for 24 hours after cisplatin administration, with or without mannitol and/or furosemide, to ensure good urine output and decrease the chance of nephrotoxicity; reduce dosage in renal impairment. Cumulative renal toxicity may be severe; dose-related toxicities include myelosuppression, nausea, and vomiting; cumulative ototoxicity, especially pronounced in children, is manifested by tinnitus or loss of high frequency hearing and occasionally, deafness. **Serum magnesium, as well as other electrolytes, should be monitored both before and within 48 hours after cisplatin therapy.** Patients who are magnesium depleted should receive replacement therapy before the cisplatin is administered. When administered as sequential infusions, taxane derivatives (docetaxel, paclitaxel) should be administered before platinum derivatives (carboplatin, cisplatin) to limit myelosuppression and to enhance efficacy.

Common Adverse Reactions

>10%:

Central nervous system: Neurotoxicity: Peripheral neuropathy is dose- and duration-dependent. The mechanism is through axonal degeneration with subsequent damage to the long sensory nerves. Toxicity can first be noted at cumulative doses of 200 mg/m^2, with measurable toxicity at cumulative doses >350 mg/m^2. This process is irreversible and progressive with continued therapy.

Dermatologic: Mild alopecia

Gastrointestinal: Cisplatin is one of the most emetogenic agents used in cancer chemotherapy; nausea and vomiting occur in 76% to 100% of patients and is dose-related. Prophylactic antiemetics should always be prescribed; nausea and vomiting may last up to 1 week after therapy.

Hematologic: Myelosuppressive: Mild with moderate doses, mild to moderate with high-dose therapy

WBC: Mild

Platelets: Mild

Onset: 10 days

Nadir: 14-23 days

Recovery: 21-39 days

Hepatic: Elevation of liver enzymes

Renal: Nephrotoxicity: Related to elimination, protein binding, and uptake of cisplatin. Two types of nephrotoxicity: Acute renal failure and chronic renal insufficiency.

Acute renal failure and azotemia is a dose-dependent process and can be minimized with proper administration and prophylaxis. Damage to the proximal tubules by unbound cisplatin is suspected to cause the toxicity. It is manifested as increased BUN/creatinine, oliguria, protein wasting, and potassium, calcium, and magnesium wasting.

Chronic renal dysfunction can develop in patients receiving multiple courses of cisplatin. Slow release of tissue-bound cisplatin may contribute to chronic nephrotoxicity. Manifestations of this toxicity are varied, and can include sodium and water wasting, nephropathy, hyperuricemia, decreased Cl$_{cr}$, and magnesium wasting.

Recommendations for minimizing nephrotoxicity include:

Prepare cisplatin in saline-containing vehicles

Infuse dose over 24 hours

Vigorous hydration (125-150 mL/hour) before, during, and after cisplatin administration

Simultaneous administration of either mannitol or furosemide

Pretreatment with amifostine

Avoid other nephrotoxic agents (aminoglycosides, amphotericin, etc)

Otic: Ototoxicity: Ototoxicity occurs in 10% to 30%, and is manifested as high frequency hearing loss. Baseline audiography should be performed. Ototoxicity is especially pronounced in children.

1% to 10%: Local: Extravasation: May cause thrombophlebitis and tissue damage if infiltrated; may use sodium thiosulfate as antidote, but consult hospital policy for guidelines.

Irritant chemotherapy

Drug Interactions

Increased Effect/Toxicity: Cisplatin and ethacrynic acid have resulted in severe ototoxicity in animals. Delayed bleomycin elimination with decreased glomerular filtration rate. When administered as sequential infusions, observational studies indicate a potential for increased toxicity when platinum derivatives (carboplatin, cisplatin) are administered before taxane derivatives (docetaxel, paclitaxel).

Decreased Effect: Sodium thiosulfate theoretically inactivates drug systemically; has been used clinically to reduce systemic toxicity with intraperitoneal administration of cisplatin.

Mechanism of Action Inhibits DNA synthesis by the formation of DNA cross-links; denatures the double helix; covalently binds to DNA bases and disrupts DNA function; may also bind to proteins; the *cis*-isomer is 14 times more cytotoxic than the *trans*-isomer; both forms cross-link DNA but cis-platinum is less easily recognized by cell enzymes and, therefore, not repaired. Cisplatin can also bind two adjacent guanines on the same strand of DNA producing intrastrand cross-linking and breakage.

Pharmacodynamics/Kinetics

Distribution: I.V.: Rapidly into tissue; high concentrations in kidneys, liver, ovaries, uterus, and lungs

Protein binding: >90%

Metabolism: Nonenzymatic; inactivated (in both cell and bloodstream) by sulfhydryl groups; covalently binds to glutathione and thiosulfate

Half-life elimination: Initial: 20-30 minutes; Beta: 60 minutes; Terminal: ~24 hours; Secondary half-life: 44-73 hours

Excretion: Urine (>90%); feces (10%)

Dosage I.V. (refer to individual protocols):

An estimated Cl_{cr} should be on all cisplatin chemotherapy orders along with other patient parameters (ie, patient's height, weight, and body surface area). Pharmacy and nursing staff should check the Cl_{cr} on the order and determine the appropriateness of cisplatin dosing. The manufacturer recommends that subsequent cycles should only be given when serum creatinine <1.5 mg/dL, WBC $\geq 4,000/mm^3$, platelets $\geq 100,000/mm^3$, and BUN <25.

It is recommended that a 24-hour urine creatinine clearance be checked prior to a patient's first dose of cisplatin and periodically thereafter (ie, after every 2-3 cycles of cisplatin)

Pretreatment hydration with 1-2 L of chloride-containing fluid is recommended prior to cisplatin administration; adequate hydration and urinary output (>100 mL/hour) should be maintained for 24 hours after administration

If the dose prescribed is a reduced dose, then this should be indicated on the chemotherapy order

Children: Various dosage schedules range from 30-100 mg/m^2 once every 2-3 weeks; may also dose similar to adult dosing

Recurrent brain tumors: 60 mg/m^2 once daily for 2 consecutive days every 3-4 weeks

Adults:

Advanced bladder cancer: 50-70 mg/m^2 every 3-4 weeks

Head and neck cancer: 100-120 mg/m^2 every 3-4 weeks

Testicular cancer: 10-20 mg/m^2/day for 5 days repeated every 3-4 weeks

Metastatic ovarian cancer: 75-100 mg/m^2 every 3 weeks

Intraperitoneal: cisplatin has been administered intraperitoneal with systemic sodium thiosulfate for ovarian cancer; doses up to 90-270 mg/m^2 have been administered and retained for 4 hours before draining

Dosing adjustment in renal impairment:

Cl_{cr} 10-50 mL/minute: Administer 50% of normal dose

Cl_{cr} <10 mL/minute: Do not administer

Hemodialysis: Partially cleared by hemodialysis; administer dose posthemodialysis

CAPD effects: Unknown

CAVH effects: Unknown

Administration Needles, syringes, catheters, or I.V. administration sets that contain aluminum parts should not be used for administration of drug. Pretreatment hydration with 1-2 L of fluid is recommended prior to cisplatin administration; adequate hydration and urinary output (>100 mL/hour) should be maintained for 24 hours after administration.

I.V.: Rate of administration has varied from a 15- to 120-minute infusion, 1 mg/minute infusion, 6- to 8-hour infusion, 24-hour infusion, or per protocol; maximum rate of infusion of 1 mg/minute in patients with CHF

Extravasation management: Large extravasations (>20 mL) of concentrated solutions (>0.5 mg/mL) produce tissue necrosis. **Treatment is not recommended unless a large amount of highly concentrated solution is extravasated.** Mix 4 mL of 10% sodium thiosulfate with 6 mL sterile water for injection: Inject 1-4 mL through existing I.V. line cannula. Administer 1 mL for each mL extravasated; inject S.C. if needle is removed.

Monitoring Parameters Renal function (serum creatinine, BUN, Cl_{cr}); electrolytes (particularly magnesium, calcium, potassium) before and within 48 hours after cisplatin therapy; hearing test, neurologic exam (with high dose); liver function tests periodically; CBC with differential and platelet count; urine output, urinalysis

(Continued)

Cisplatin *(Continued)*

Patient Information This drug can only be given I.V. and numerous adverse side effects can occur. Maintaining adequate hydration is extremely important to help avoid kidney damage (2-3 L/day of fluids unless instructed to restrict fluid intake). Nausea and vomiting can be severe and can be delayed for up to 48 hours after infusion and last for 1 week; consult prescriber immediately for appropriate antiemetic medication. May cause hair loss (reversible). You will be susceptible to infection; avoid crowds or infectious situations (do not have any vaccinations without consulting prescriber). Report all unusual symptoms promptly to prescriber. Contraceptive measures are recommended during therapy.

Dosage Forms INJ, solution: 1 mg/mL (50 mL, 100 mL, 200 mL); (Platinol®-AQ): 1 mg/mL (50 mL, 100 mL)

♦ **13-*cis*-Retinoic Acid** *see* Isotretinoin *on page 696*

Citalopram *(sye TAL oh pram)*

Related Information
Antidepressant Agents Comparison *on page 1359*
Selective Serotonin Reuptake Inhibitors (SSRIs) Pharmacokinetics *on page 1403*

U.S. Brand Names Celexa™

Synonyms Citalopram Hydrobromide; Nitalapram

Therapeutic Category Antidepressant, Selective Serotonin Reuptake Inhibitor (SSRI)

Use Treatment of depression

Unlabeled/Investigational Use Treatment of dementia, smoking cessation, ethanol abuse, obsessive-compulsive disorder (OCD) in children, diabetic neuropathy

Pregnancy Risk Factor C

Contraindications Hypersensitivity to citalopram or any component of the formulation; hypersensitivity or other adverse sequelae during therapy with other SSRIs; concomitant use with MAO inhibitors or within 2 weeks of discontinuing MAO inhibitors.

Warnings/Precautions As with all antidepressants, use with caution in patients with a history of mania (may activate hypomania/mania). Use with caution in patients with a history of seizures. The possibility of a suicide attempt is inherent in major depression and may persist until remission occurs. Use caution in high-risk patients during initiation of therapy. Prescriptions should be written for the smallest quantity consistent with good patient care. Has potential to impair cognitive/motor performance - should use caution operating hazardous machinery. Elderly and patients with hepatic insufficiency should receive lower dosages. Use with caution in renal insufficiency. May cause hyponatremia/SIADH.

Common Adverse Reactions
>10%:
    Central nervous system: Somnolence, insomnia
    Gastrointestinal: Nausea, xerostomia
    Miscellaneous: Diaphoresis
<10%:
    Central nervous system: Anxiety, anorexia, agitation, yawning
    Dermatologic: Rash, pruritus
    Endocrine & metabolic: Sexual dysfunction
    Gastrointestinal: Diarrhea, dyspepsia, vomiting, abdominal pain, weight gain
    Neuromuscular & skeletal: Tremor, arthralgia, myalgia
    Respiratory: Cough, rhinitis, sinusitis

Drug Interactions

Cytochrome P450 Effect: Substrate of CYP2C19 (major), 2D6 (minor), 3A4 (major); **Inhibits** CYP1A2 (weak), 2B6 (weak), 2C19 (weak), 2D6 (weak)

Increased Effect/Toxicity: Citalopram should not be used with nonselective MAO inhibitors (phenelzine, isocarboxazid) or other drugs with MAO inhibition (linezolid); fatal reactions have been reported. Wait 5 weeks after stopping citalopram before starting a nonselective MAO inhibitor and 2 weeks after stopping an MAO inhibitor before starting citalopram. Concurrent selegiline has been associated with mania, hypertension, or serotonin syndrome (risk may be reduced relative to nonselective MAO inhibitors).

CYP2C19 inhibitors may increase the levels/effects of citalopram; example inhibitors include delavirdine, fluconazole, fluvoxamine, gemfibrozil, isoniazid, omeprazole, and ticlopidine. CYP3A4 inhibitors may increase the levels/effects of citalopram; example inhibitors include azole antifungals, ciprofloxacin, clarithromycin, diclofenac, doxycycline, erythromycin, imatinib, isoniazid, nefazodone, nicardipine, propofol, protease inhibitors, quinidine, and verapamil.

Combined used of SSRIs and amphetamines, buspirone, meperidine, nefazodone, serotonin agonists (such as sumatriptan), sibutramine, other SSRIs, sympathomimetics, ritonavir, tramadol, and venlafaxine may increase the risk of serotonin syndrome. Risk of hyponatremia may increase with concurrent use of loop diuretics (bumetanide, furosemide, torsemide). Citalopram may increase the hypoprothrombinemic response to warfarin.

Combined use of sumatriptan (and other serotonin agonists) may result in toxicity; weakness, hyper-reflexia, and incoordination have been observed with sumatriptan and SSRIs. In addition, concurrent use may theoretically increase the risk of serotonin syndrome; includes sumatriptan, naratriptan, rizatriptan, and zolmitriptan.

Decreased Effect: CYP2C19 inducers may decrease the levels/effects of citalopram; example inducers include aminoglutethimide, carbamazepine, phenytoin, and rifampin. Cyproheptadine may inhibit the effects of serotonin reuptake inhibitors. CYP3A4 inducers may decrease the levels/effects of citalopram; example inducers include aminoglutethimide, carbamazepine, nafcillin, nevirapine, phenobarbital, phenytoin, and rifamycins.

Mechanism of Action A bicyclic phthalane derivative, citalopram selectively inhibits serotonin reuptake in the presynaptic neurons

Pharmacodynamics/Kinetics

Distribution: V_d: 12 L/kg

Protein binding, plasma: ~80%

Metabolism: Extensively hepatic, including CYP, to N-demethylated, N-oxide, and deaminated metabolites

Bioavailability: 80%

Half-life elimination: 24-48 hours; average 35 hours (doubled with hepatic impairment)

Time to peak, serum: 1-6 hours, average within 4 hours

Excretion: Urine (10% as unchanged drug)

Note: Clearance was decreased, while AUC and half-life were significantly increased in elderly patients and in patients with hepatic impairment. Mild to moderate renal impairment may reduce clearance (17%) and prolong half-life of citalopram. No pharmacokinetic information is available concerning patients with severe renal impairment.

Dosage Oral:

Children and Adolescents: OCD (unlabeled use): 10-40 mg/day

Adults: Depression: Initial: 20 mg/day, generally with an increase to 40 mg/day; doses of more than 40 mg are not usually necessary. Should a dose increase be necessary, it should occur in 20 mg increments at intervals of no less than 1 week. Maximum dose: 60 mg/day; reduce dosage in elderly or those with hepatic impairment.

Monitoring Parameters Monitor patient periodically for symptom resolution, heart rate, blood pressure, liver function tests, and CBC with continued therapy

Patient Information Citalopram does not impair psychomotor performance, nevertheless, patients receiving treatment may have an impaired ability to drive or operate machinery; they should be warned of this possibility and advised to avoid these tasks if so affected

Dosage Forms SOLN, oral: 10 mg/5 mL (240 mL). **TAB:** 10 mg, 20 mg, 40 mg

♦ **Citalopram Hydrobromide** *see* Citalopram *on page 286*

♦ **Citracal® [OTC]** *see* Calcium Citrate *on page 205*

♦ **Citracal® Liquitab [OTC]** *see* Calcium Citrate *on page 205*

♦ **Citrate of Magnesia** *see* Magnesium Citrate *on page 768*

♦ **Citric Acid and Potassium Citrate** *see* Potassium Citrate and Citric Acid *on page 1021*

Citric Acid, Sodium Citrate, and Potassium Citrate

(SIT rik AS id, SOW dee um SIT rate, & poe TASS ee um SIT rate)

U.S. Brand Names Cytra-3; Polycitra®; Polycitra®-LC

Synonyms Potassium Citrate, Citric Acid, and Sodium Citrate; Sodium Citrate, Citric Acid, and Potassium Citrate

Therapeutic Category Alkalinizing Agent, Oral

Use Conditions where long-term maintenance of an alkaline urine is desirable as in control and dissolution of uric acid and cystine calculi of the urinary tract

Pregnancy Risk Factor Not established

Dosage Oral:

Children: 5-15 mL diluted in water after meals and at bedtime

Adults: 15-30 mL diluted in water after meals and at bedtime

Dosage Forms Note: Equivalent to potassium 1 mEq/mL, sodium 1 mEq/mL, and bicarbonate 2 mEq/mL. **SOLN, oral** (Polycitra®-LC): Sodium citrate 500 mg, citric acid 334 mg, and potassium citrate 550 mg per 5 mL (480 mL). **SYR, oral** (Cytra-3, Polycitra®): Sodium citrate 500 mg, citric acid 334 mg, and potassium citrate 550 mg per 5 mL (480 mL)

♦ **Citrovorum Factor** *see* Leucovorin *on page 723*

♦ **CL-118,532** *see* Triptorelin *on page 1274*

♦ **Cl-719** *see* Gemfibrozil *on page 583*

♦ **CL-825** *see* Pentostatin *on page 980*

♦ **CL-184116** *see* Porfimer *on page 1016*

♦ **Cla** *see* Clarithromycin *on page 288*

Cladribine (KLA dri been)

U.S. Brand Names Leustatin®

Synonyms 2-CdA; 2-Chlorodeoxyadenosine

Therapeutic Category Antineoplastic Agent, Antimetabolite (Purine)

Use Treatment of hairy cell leukemia, chronic lymphocytic leukemia (CLL), chronic myelogenous leukemia (CML)

Unlabeled/Investigational Use Non-Hodgkin's lymphomas, progressive multiple sclerosis

Pregnancy Risk Factor D

Contraindications Hypersensitivity to cladribine or any component of the formulation; pregnancy

Warnings/Precautions The U.S. Food and Drug Administration (FDA) currently recommends that procedures for proper handling and disposal of antineoplastic agents be considered. Because of its myelosuppressive properties, cladribine should be used with caution in patients with pre-existing hematologic or immunologic abnormalities.

(Continued)

Cladribine *(Continued)*

Common Adverse Reactions

>10%:

Allergic: Fever (70%), chills (18%); skin reactions (erythema, itching) at the catheter site (18%)

Central nervous system: Fatigue (17%), headache (13%)

Dermatologic: Rash

Hematologic: Myelosuppression, common, dose-limiting; leukopenia (70%); anemia (37%); thrombocytopenia (12%)

Nadir: 5-10 days

Recovery: 4-8 weeks

1% to 10%:

Cardiovascular: Edema, tachycardia

Central nervous system: Dizziness; pains; chills; malaise; severe infections, possibly related to thrombocytopenia

Dermatologic: Pruritus, erythema

Gastrointestinal: Nausea, mild to moderate, usually not seen at doses <0.3 mg/kg/day; constipation; abdominal pain

Neuromuscular & skeletal: Myalgia, arthralgia, weakness

Renal: Renal failure at high (>0.3 mg/kg/day) doses

Miscellaneous: Diaphoresis, delayed herpes zoster infections, tumor lysis syndrome

Mechanism of Action A purine nucleoside analogue; prodrug which is activated via phosphorylation by deoxycytidine kinase to a 5'-triphosphate derivative. This active form incorporates into DNA to result in the breakage of DNA strand and shutdown of DNA synthesis. This also results in a depletion of nicotinamide adenine dinucleotide and adenosine triphosphate (ATP). Cladribine is cell-cycle nonspecific.

Pharmacodynamics/Kinetics

Absorption: Oral: 55%; S.C.: 100%; Rectal: 20%

Distribution: V_d: 4.52 ± 2.82 L/kg

Protein binding, plasma: 20%

Metabolism: Hepatic; 5'-triphosphate moiety-active

Half-life elimination: Biphasic: Alpha: 25 minutes; Beta: 6.7 hours; Terminal, mean: Normal renal function: 5.4 hours

Excretion: Urine (21% to 44%)

Clearance: Estimated systemic: 640 mL/hour/kg

Dosage I.V.: Refer to individual protocols.

Pediatrics: Acute leukemias: 6.2-7.5 mg/m²/day continuous infusion for days 1-5; maximum tolerated dose was 8.9 mg/m²/day.

Adults:

Hairy cell leukemia: Continuous infusion:

0.09-0.1 mg/kg/day days 1-7; may be repeated every 28-35 days **or**

3.4 mg/m²/day S.C. days 1-7

Chronic lymphocytic leukemia: Continuous infusion:

0.1 mg/kg/day days 1-7 **or**

0.028-0.14 mg/kg/day as a 2-hour infusion days 1-5

Chronic myelogenous leukemia: 15 mg/m²/day as a 1-hour infusion days 1-5; if no response increase dose to 20 mg/m²/day in the second course.

Administration I.V.: Administer as a 1- to 2-hour infusion or by continuous infusion

Monitoring Parameters Monitor periodic assessment of peripheral blood counts, particularly during the first 4-8 weeks post-treatment, is recommended to detect the development of anemia, neutropenia, and thrombocytopenia and for early detection of any potential sequelae (ie, infection or bleeding)

Dosage Forms INJ, solution [preservative free]: 1 mg/mL (10 mL)

- **Claforan®** *see* Cefotaxime *on page 237*
- **Claravis™** *see* Isotretinoin *on page 696*
- **Clarinex®** *see* Desloratadine *on page 354*
- **Claripel™** *see* Hydroquinone *on page 636*

Clarithromycin (kla RITH roe mye sin)

Related Information

Antimicrobial Drugs of Choice *on page 1440*

Community-Acquired Pneumonia in Adults *on page 1457*

Prevention of Bacterial Endocarditis *on page 1429*

U.S. Brand Names Biaxin®; Biaxin® XL

Synonyms Cla

Therapeutic Category Antibiotic, Macrolide

Use

Children:

Pharyngitis/tonsillitis, acute maxillary sinusitis, uncomplicated skin/skin structure infections, and mycobacterial infections due to the above organisms

Acute otitis media (*H. influenzae, M. catarrhalis,* or *S. pneumoniae*)

Prevention of disseminated mycobacterial infections due to MAC disease in patients with advanced HIV infection

Adults:

Pharyngitis/tonsillitis due to susceptible *S. pyogenes*

Acute maxillary sinusitis and acute exacerbation of chronic bronchitis due to susceptible *H. influenzae, M. catarrhalis,* or *S. pneumoniae*

Pneumonia due to susceptible *H. influenzae, Mycoplasma pneumoniae, S. pneumoniae,* or *Chlamydia pneumoniae* (TWAR);

Uncomplicated skin/skin structure infections due to susceptible *S. aureus, S. pyogenes*

Disseminated mycobacterial infections due to *M. avium* or *M. intracellulare*

Prevention of disseminated mycobacterial infections due to *M. avium* complex (MAC) disease (eg, patients with advanced HIV infection)

Duodenal ulcer disease due to *H. pylori* in regimens with other drugs including amoxicillin and lansoprazole or omeprazole, ranitidine bismuth citrate, bismuth subsalicylate, tetracycline, and/or an H_2 antagonist

Alternate antibiotic for prophylaxis of bacterial endocarditis in patients who are allergic to penicillin and undergoing surgical or dental procedures

Pregnancy Risk Factor C

Contraindications Hypersensitivity to clarithromycin, erythromycin, or any macrolide antibiotic; use with ergot derivatives, pimozide, astemizole, cisapride; combination with ranitidine bismuth citrate should not be used in patients with history of acute porphyria or Cl_{cr} <25 mL/minute

Warnings/Precautions Dosage adjustment required with severe renal impairment, decreased dosage or prolonged dosing interval may be appropriate; antibiotic-associated colitis has been reported with use of clarithromycin. Macrolides (including clarithromycin) have been associated with rare QT prolongation and ventricular arrhythmias, including torsade de pointes. Safety and efficacy in children <6 months of age have not been established.

Common Adverse Reactions

1% to 10%:

Central nervous system: Headache (adults and children 2%)

Dermatologic: Rash (children 3%)

Gastrointestinal: Diarrhea (adults 6%, children 6%); vomiting (children 6%); nausea (adults 3%); abnormal taste (adults 7%); heartburn (adults 2%); abdominal pain (adults 2%, children 3%)

Hepatic: Prothrombin time increased (1%)

Renal: BUN increased (4%)

Drug Interactions

Cytochrome P450 Effect: Substrate of CYP3A4 (major); **Inhibits** CYP1A2 (weak), 3A4 (strong)

Increased Effect/Toxicity: Avoid concomitant use of the following with clarithromycin due to increased risk of malignant arrhythmias: Astemizole, cisapride, gatifloxacin, moxifloxacin, pimozide, sparfloxacin, thioridazine. Other agents that prolong the QT_c interval, including type Ia (eg, quinidine) and type III antiarrhythmic agents, and selected antipsychotic agents (eg, mesoridazine, thioridazine) should be used with extreme caution.

Clarithromycin may increase the serum concentrations (and possibly the toxicity) of the following agents: Alfentanil (and possibly other narcotic analgesics), benzodiazepines (alprazolam, diazepam, midazolam, triazolam), buspirone, calcium channel blockers, dihydropyridine (felodipine), carbamazepine, cilostazol, clozapine, colchicine, cyclosporine, digoxin, disopyramide, ergot alkaloids (eg, bromocriptine), HMG-CoA reductase inhibitors (except fluvastatin, pravastatin), loratadine, methylprednisolone, rifabutin, tacrolimus, theophylline, valproate, vinblastine, vincristine, zopiclone. Sildenafil, tadalafil, and vardenafil serum levels may be increased by clarithromycin; do not exceed single sildenafil doses of 25 mg in 48 hours, a single tadalafil dose of 10 mg in 72 hours, or a single vardenafil dose of 2.5 mg in 24 hours.

The effects of neuromuscular-blocking agents and warfarin have been potentiated by clarithromycin. Clarithromycin serum concentrations may be increased by amprenavir (and possibly other protease inhibitors). Digoxin serum levels may be increased by clarithromycin; digoxin toxicity and potentially fatal arrhythmias have been reported; monitor digoxin levels. Fluconazole increases clarithromycin levels and AUC by ~25%. Peak levels (but not AUC) of zidovudine may be increased; other studies suggest levels may be decreased.

Decreased Effect: Clarithromycin may decrease the serum concentrations of zafirlukast. Clarithromycin may antagonize the therapeutic effects of clindamycin and lincomycin. Peak levels (but not AUC) of zidovudine may be increased; other studies suggest levels may be decreased. CYP3A4 inducers may decrease the levels/effects of clarithromycin; example inducers include aminoglutethimide, carbamazepine, nafcillin, nevirapine, phenobarbital, phenytoin, and rifamycins.

Mechanism of Action Exerts its antibacterial action by binding to 50S ribosomal subunit resulting in inhibition of protein synthesis. The 14-OH metabolite of clarithromycin is twice as active as the parent compound against certain organisms.

Pharmacodynamics/Kinetics

Absorption: Highly stable in presence of gastric acid (unlike erythromycin); food delays but does not affect extent of absorption

Distribution: Widely into most body tissues except CNS

Metabolism: Partially hepatic; converted to 14-OH clarithromycin (active metabolite)

Bioavailability: 50%

Half-life elimination: 5-7 hours

Time to peak: 2-4 hours

Excretion: Primarily urine

Clearance: Approximates normal GFR

Dosage Oral:

Children ≥6 months: 15 mg/kg/day divided every 12 hours for 10 days

(Continued)

Clarithromycin *(Continued)*

Mycobacterial infection (prevention and treatment): 7.5 mg/kg twice daily, up to 500 mg twice daily

Prophylaxis of bacterial endocarditis: 15 mg/kg 1 hour before procedure (maximum dose: 500 mg)

Adults:

Usual dose: 250-500 mg every 12 hours **or** 1000 mg (two 500 mg extended release tablets) once daily for for 7-14 days

Upper respiratory tract: 250-500 mg every 12 hours for 10-14 days

Pharyngitis/tonsillitis: 250 mg every 12 hours for 10 days

Acute maxillary sinusitis: 500 mg every 12 hours **or** 1000 mg (two 500 mg extended release tablets) once daily for 14 days

Lower respiratory tract: 250-500 mg every 12 hours for 7-14 days

Acute exacerbation of chronic bronchitis due to:

M. catarrhalis and *S. pneumoniae*: 250 mg every 12 hours **or** 1000 mg (two 500 mg extended release tablets) once daily for 7-14 days

H. influenzae: 500 mg every 12 hours for 7-14 days

Pneumonia due to:

C. pneumoniae, *M. pneumoniae*, and *S. pneumoniae*: 250 mg every 12 hours for 7-14 days **or** 1000 mg (two 500 mg extended release tablets) once daily for 7 days

H. influenzae: 250 mg every 12 hours for 7 days **or** 1000 mg (two 500 mg extended release tablets) once daily for 7 days

Mycobacterial infection (prevention and treatment): 500 mg twice daily (use with other antimycobacterial drugs, eg, ethambutol, clofazimine, or rifampin)

Prophylaxis of bacterial endocarditis: 500 mg 1 hour prior to procedure

Uncomplicated skin and skin structure: 250 mg every 12 hours for 7-14 days

Helicobacter pylori: Combination regimen with bismuth subsalicylate, tetracycline, clarithromycin, and an H_2-receptor antagonist; or combination of omeprazole and clarithromycin; 250 mg twice daily to 500 mg 3 times/day

Dosing adjustment in renal impairment:

Cl_{cr} <30 mL/minute: Half the normal dose or double the dosing interval

In combination with ritonavir:

Cl_{cr} 30-60 mL/minute: Decrease clarithromycin dose by 50%

Cl_{cr} <30 mL/minute: Decrease clarithromycin dose by 75%

Dosing adjustment in hepatic impairment: No dosing adjustment is needed as long as renal function is normal

Elderly: Pharmacokinetics are similar to those in younger adults; may have age-related reductions in renal function; monitor and adjust dose if necessary

Administration Clarithromycin may be given with or without meals. Give every 12 hours rather than twice daily to avoid peak and trough variation.

Biaxin® XL: Should be given with food. Do not crush or chew extended release tablet.

Patient Information May be taken with meals; finish all medication; do not skip doses; do not refrigerate oral suspension, more palatable when taken at room temperature; do not crush or chew extended-release tablets

Dosage Forms GRAN, oral suspension (Biaxin®): 125 mg/5 mL (50 mL, 100 mL); 250 mg/5 mL (50 mL, 100 mL). **TAB, film coated** (Biaxin®): 250 mg, 500 mg. **TAB extended release, film coated** (Biaxin® XL): 500 mg

♦ **Clarithromycin, Lansoprazole, and Amoxicillin** *see* Lansoprazole, Amoxicillin, and Clarithromycin *on page 717*

♦ **Claritin® [OTC]** *see* Loratadine *on page 759*

♦ **Claritin-D® 12-Hour [OTC]** *see* Loratadine and Pseudoephedrine *on page 760*

♦ **Claritin-D® 24-Hour [OTC]** *see* Loratadine and Pseudoephedrine *on page 760*

♦ **Clear Eyes® [OTC]** *see* Naphazoline *on page 881*

♦ **Clear Eyes® ACR [OTC]** *see* Naphazoline *on page 881*

Clemastine *(KLEM as teen)*

U.S. Brand Names Tavist® Allergy [OTC]

Synonyms Clemastine Fumarate

Therapeutic Category Antihistamine

Use Perennial and seasonal allergic rhinitis and other allergic symptoms including urticaria

Pregnancy Risk Factor B

Contraindications Hypersensitivity to clemastine or any component of the formulation; narrow-angle glaucoma

Warnings/Precautions Safety and efficacy have not been established in children <6 years of age. Use caution with bladder neck obstruction, symptomatic prostate hypertrophy, asthmatic attacks, stenosing peptic ulcer, increased intraocular pressure, hyperthyroidism, cardiovascular disease, hypertension, and in the elderly. May cause drowsiness; use caution in performing tasks which require alertness.

Common Adverse Reactions Frequency not defined.

Cardiovascular: Palpitations, hypotension, tachycardia

Central nervous system: Dyscoordination, sedation, slight to moderate somnolence, sleepiness, confusion, restlessness, nervousness, insomnia, irritability, fatigue, headache, increased dizziness

Dermatologic: Rash, photosensitivity

Gastrointestinal: Diarrhea, nausea, xerostomia, epigastric distress, vomiting, constipation

Genitourinary: Urinary frequency, difficult urination, urinary retention
Hematologic: Hemolytic anemia, thrombocytopenia, agranulocytosis
Ocular: Blurred vision
Otic: Tinnitus
Respiratory: Thickening of bronchial secretions
Miscellaneous: Anaphylaxis

Drug Interactions

Cytochrome P450 Effect: Inhibits CYP2D6 (weak), 3A4 (weak)

Increased Effect/Toxicity: CNS depressants may increase the degree of sedation and respiratory depression with antihistamines. May increase the absorption of digoxin. Central and/or peripheral anticholinergic syndrome can occur when administered with amantadine, rimantadine, narcotic analgesics, phenothiazines and other antipsychotics (especially with high anticholinergic activity), tricyclic antidepressants, quinidine, disopyramide, procainamide, and antihistamines.

Decreased Effect: May increase gastric degradation of levodopa and decrease the amount of levodopa absorbed by delaying gastric emptying. Therapeutic effects of cholinergic agents (tacrine, donepezil) may be antagonized and neuroleptics may be antagonized.

Mechanism of Action Competes with histamine for H_1-receptor sites on effector cells in the gastrointestinal tract, blood vessels, and respiratory tract

Pharmacodynamics/Kinetics

Onset of action: Peak effect: Therapeutic: 5-7 hours
Duration: 8-16 hours
Absorption: Almost complete
Metabolism: Hepatic
Excretion: Urine

Dosage Oral:

Infants and Children <6 years: 0.05 mg/kg/day as **clemastine base** or 0.335-0.67 mg/day clemastine fumarate (0.25-0.5 mg base/day) divided into 2 or 3 doses; maximum daily dosage: 1.34 mg (1 mg base)

Children 6-12 years: 0.67-1.34 mg clemastine fumarate (0.5-1 mg base) twice daily; do not exceed 4.02 mg/day (3 mg/day base)

Children ≥12 years and Adults:
1.34 mg clemastine fumarate (1 mg base) twice daily to 2.68 mg (2 mg base) 3 times/day; do not exceed 8.04 mg/day (6 mg base)
OTC labeling: 1.34 mg clemastine fumarate (1 mg base) twice daily; do not exceed 2 mg base/24 hours

Elderly: Lower doses should be considered in patients >60 years

Monitoring Parameters Look for a reduction of rhinitis, urticaria, eczema, pruritus, or other allergic symptoms

Patient Information Avoid alcohol; may cause drowsiness, may impair coordination or judgment

Dosage Forms SYR [prescription formulation]: 0.67 mg/5 mL (120 mL). **TAB:** 1.34 mg [1 mg base; OTC], 2.68 mg [2 mg base; prescription formulation]; (Tavist® Allergy): 1.34 mg [1 mg base]

♦ **Clemastine Fumarate** see Clemastine on page 290
♦ **Clenia™** see Sulfur and Sulfacetamide on page 1177
♦ **Cleocin®** see Clindamycin on page 291
♦ **Cleocin HCl®** see Clindamycin on page 291
♦ **Cleocin Pediatric®** see Clindamycin on page 291
♦ **Cleocin Phosphate®** see Clindamycin on page 291
♦ **Cleocin T®** see Clindamycin on page 291

Clidinium and Chlordiazepoxide (kli DI nee um & klor dye az e POKS ide)

U.S. Brand Names Librax®
Synonyms Chlordiazepoxide and Clidinium
Therapeutic Category Anticholinergic Agent; Antispasmodic Agent, Gastrointestinal
Use Adjunct treatment of peptic ulcer; treatment of irritable bowel syndrome
Pregnancy Risk Factor D
Dosage Oral: 1-2 capsules 3-4 times/day, before meals or food and at bedtime
Dosage Forms CAP: Clidinium 2.5 mg and chlordiazepoxide 5 mg

♦ **Climara®** see Estradiol on page 459
♦ **Clindagel™** see Clindamycin on page 291
♦ **Clindamax** see Clindamycin on page 291

Clindamycin (klin da MYE sin)

Related Information
Antimicrobial Drugs of Choice on page 1440
Community-Acquired Pneumonia in Adults on page 1457
Malaria Treatment on page 1464
Prevention of Bacterial Endocarditis on page 1429
Prevention of Wound Infection & Sepsis in Surgical Patients on page 1436

U.S. Brand Names Cleocin®; Cleocin HCl®; Cleocin Pediatric®; Cleocin Phosphate®; Cleocin T®; Clindagel™; Clindamax; Clindets®

Synonyms Clindamycin Hydrochloride; Clindamycin Phosphate
(Continued)

Clindamycin *(Continued)*

Therapeutic Category Acne Product; Antibiotic, Anaerobic; Antibiotic, Topical; Antibiotic, Vaginal

Use Treatment against aerobic and anaerobic streptococci (except enterococci), most staphylococci, *Bacteroides* sp and *Actinomyces*; pelvic inflammatory disease (I.V.); topically in treatment of severe acne; vaginally for *Gardnerella vaginalis*

Unlabeled/Investigational Use Bacterial vaginosis; prophylaxis in the prevention of bacterial endocarditis in high-risk patients undergoing surgical or dental procedures in patients allergic to penicillin; may be useful in PCP; alternate treatment for toxoplasmosis

Pregnancy Risk Factor B

Contraindications Hypersensitivity to clindamycin or any component of the formulation; previous pseudomembranous colitis; hepatic impairment

Warnings/Precautions Dosage adjustment may be necessary in patients with severe hepatic dysfunction; can cause severe and possibly fatal colitis; use with caution in patients with a history of pseudomembranous colitis; discontinue drug if significant diarrhea, abdominal cramps, or passage of blood and mucus occurs

Common Adverse Reactions

Systemic:

>10%: Gastrointestinal: Diarrhea, abdominal pain

1% to 10%:

Cardiovascular: Hypotension

Dermatologic: Urticaria, rashes, Stevens-Johnson syndrome

Gastrointestinal: Pseudomembranous colitis, nausea, vomiting

Local: Thrombophlebitis, sterile abscess at I.M. injection site

Miscellaneous: Fungal overgrowth, hypersensitivity

Topical: >10%: Dermatologic: Dryness, burning, itching, scaliness, erythema, or peeling of skin (lotion, solution); oiliness (gel, lotion)

Vaginal:

>10%: Genitourinary: Vaginitis or vulvovaginal pruritus (from *Candida albicans*), painful intercourse

1% to 10%:

Central nervous system: Dizziness, headache

Gastrointestinal: Diarrhea, nausea, vomiting, stomach cramps

Drug Interactions

Increased Effect/Toxicity: Increased duration of neuromuscular blockade when given in conjunction with tubocurarine and pancuronium.

Mechanism of Action Reversibly binds to 50S ribosomal subunits preventing peptide bond formation thus inhibiting bacterial protein synthesis; bacteriostatic or bactericidal depending on drug concentration, infection site, and organism

Pharmacodynamics/Kinetics

Absorption: Topical: ~10%; Oral: Rapid (90%)

Distribution: High concentrations in bone and urine; no significant levels in CSF, even with inflamed meninges; crosses placenta; enters breast milk

Metabolism: Hepatic

Bioavailability: Topical: <1%

Half-life elimination: Neonates: Premature: 8.7 hours; Full-term: 3.6 hours; Adults: 1.6-5.3 hours (average: 2-3 hours)

Time to peak, serum: Oral: Within 60 minutes; I.M.: 1-3 hours

Excretion: Urine (10%) and feces (~4%) as active drug and metabolites

Dosage Avoid in neonates (contains benzyl alcohol)

Infants and Children:

Oral: 8-20 mg/kg/day as hydrochloride; 8-25 mg/kg/day as palmitate in 3-4 divided doses; minimum dose of palmitate: 37.5 mg 3 times/day

I.M., I.V.:

<1 month: 15-20 mg/kg/day

>1 month: 20-40 mg/kg/day in 3-4 divided doses

Children: Prevention of bacterial endocarditis (unlabeled use): Oral: 20 mg/kg 1 hour before procedure with no follow-up dose needed; for patients allergic to penicillin and unable to take oral medications: 20 mg/kg I.V. within 30 minutes before procedure

Children ≥12 years and Adults: Topical: Apply a thin film twice daily

Adults:

Oral: 150-450 mg/dose every 6-8 hours; maximum dose: 1.8 g/day

Prevention of bacterial endocarditis in patients unable to take amoxicillin (unlabeled use): Oral: 600 mg 1 hour before procedure with no follow-up dose needed; for patients allergic to penicillin and unable to take oral medications: 600 mg I.V. within 30 minutes before procedure

I.M., I.V.: 1.2-1.8 g/day in 2-4 divided doses; maximum dose: 4.8 g/day

Pelvic inflammatory disease: I.V.: 900 mg every 8 hours with gentamicin 2 mg/kg, then 1.5 mg/kg every 8 hours; continue after discharge with doxycycline 100 mg twice daily to complete 14 days of total therapy

Pneumocystis carinii pneumonia (unlabeled use):

Oral: 300-450 mg 4 times/day with primaquine

I.M., I.V.: 1200-2400 mg/day with pyrimethamine

I.V.: 600 mg 4 times/day with primaquine

Bacterial vaginosis (unlabeled use):

Oral: 300 mg twice daily for 7 days

Intravaginal:
Suppositories: Insert one ovule (100 mg clindamycin) daily into vagina at bedtime for 3 days
Cream: One full applicator inserted intravaginally once daily before bedtime for 3 or 7 consecutive days

Dosing adjustment in hepatic impairment: Adjustment recommended in patients with severe hepatic disease

Administration Administer oral dosage form with a full glass of water to minimize esophageal ulceration.

Monitoring Parameters Observe for changes in bowel frequency, monitor for colitis and resolution of symptoms; during prolonged therapy monitor CBC, liver and renal function tests periodically

Patient Information Report any severe diarrhea immediately and do not take antidiarrheal medication; take each oral dose with a full glass of water; finish all medication; do not skip doses; should not engage in sexual intercourse during treatment with vaginal product; avoid contact of topical gel/solution with eyes, abraded skin, or mucous membranes

Dosage Forms CAP, as hydrochloride: 150 mg, 300 mg; (Cleocin HCl®): 75 mg, 150 mg, 300 mg. **CRM, vaginal, as phosphate** (Cleocin®): 2% (40 g) **GEL, topical, as phosphate** (Cleocin T®): 1% [10 mg/g] (30 g, 60 g); (Clindagel™): 1% [10 mg/g] (42 g, 77 g); (Clindamax): 1% (30 g, 60 g). **GRAN, oral solution, as palmitate** (Cleocin Pediatric®): 75 mg/5 mL (100 mL). **INF, as phosphate** [premixed in D₅W] (Cleocin Phosphate®): 300 mg (50 mL); 600 mg (50 mL); 900 mg (50 mL). **INJ, solution, as phosphate** (Cleocin Phosphate®): 150 mg/mL (2 mL, 4 mL, 6 mL, 60 mL). **LOTION, as phosphate** (Cleocin T®, Clindamax): 1% (60 mL). **PLEDGET, topical:** 1% (60s); (Clindets®): 1% (69s); (Cleocin T®): 1% (60s). **SOLN, topical, as phosphate** (Cleocin T®): 1% (30 mL, 60 mL). **SUPP, vaginal, as phosphate** (Cleocin®): 100 mg (3s)

♦ **Clindamycin Hydrochloride** *see Clindamycin on page 291*
♦ **Clindamycin Phosphate** *see Clindamycin on page 291*
♦ **Clindets®** *see Clindamycin on page 291*
♦ **Clinoril®** *see Sulindac on page 1177*

Clobetasol (kloe BAY ta sol)

Related Information
Corticosteroids Comparison *on page 1372*

U.S. Brand Names Clobex™; Cormax®; Embeline™ E; Olux®; Temovate®; Temovate E®

Synonyms Clobetasol Propionate

Therapeutic Category Anti-inflammatory Agent; Corticosteroid, Topical (Very High Potency)

Use Short-term relief of inflammation of moderate to severe corticosteroid-responsive dermatoses (very high potency topical corticosteroid)

Pregnancy Risk Factor C

Dosage Topical: Discontinue when control achieved; if improvement not seen within 2 weeks, reassessment of diagnosis may be necessary.
Children <12 years: Use is not recommended
Children ≥12 years and Adults:
Steroid-responsive dermatoses:
Cream, emollient cream, gel, lotion, ointment: Apply twice daily for up to 2 weeks (maximum dose: 50 g/week)
Foam, solution: Apply to affected scalp twice daily for up to 2 weeks (maximum dose: 50 g/week or 50 mL/week)
Mild to moderate plaque-type psoriasis of nonscalp areas: Foam: Apply to affected area twice daily for up to 2 weeks (maximum dose: 50 g/week); do not apply to face or intertriginous areas
Children ≥16 years and Adults: Moderate to severe plaque-type psoriasis: Emollient cream, lotion: Apply twice daily for up to 2 weeks, has been used for up to 4 weeks when application is <10% of body surface area; use with caution (maximum dose: 50 g/week)

Dosage Forms CRM, as propionate: 0.05% (15 g, 30 g, 45 g, 60 g); (Cormax®): 0.05% (15 g, 30 g, 45 g); (Temovate®): 0.05% (15 g, 30 g, 45 g, 60 g). **CRM, as propionate** [in emollient base]: 0.05% (15 g, 30 g, 60 g); (Embeline™ E, Temovate E®): 0.05% (15 g, 30 g, 60 g). **FOAM, topical, as propionate** [for scalp application] (Olux®): 0.05% (50 g, 100 g). **GEL, as propionate** (Temovate™): 0.05% (15 g, 30 g, 60 g). **LOT, as propionate** (Clobex™): 0.05% (30 mL, 59 mL, 118 mL). **OINT, as propionate** (Cormax®): 0.05% (15 g, 30 g, 45 g, 60 g); (Temovate®): 0.05% (15 g, 30 g, 45 g, 60 g). **SOLN, topical, as propionate** [for scalp application]: (Cormax®, Temovate®): 0.05% (25 mL, 50 mL)

♦ **Clobetasol Propionate** *see Clobetasol on page 293*
♦ **Clobex™** *see Clobetasol on page 293*

Clocortolone (kloe KOR toe lone)

Related Information
Corticosteroids Comparison *on page 1372*

U.S. Brand Names Cloderm®

Synonyms Clocortolone Pivalate

Therapeutic Category Corticosteroid, Topical (Medium Potency)

Use Inflammation of corticosteroid-responsive dermatoses (intermediate-potency topical corticosteroid)

Pregnancy Risk Factor C
(Continued)

Clocortolone *(Continued)*

Contraindications Hypersensitivity to clocortolone or any component of the formulation; viral, fungal, or tubercular skin lesions

Warnings/Precautions Adrenal suppression can occur if used for >14 days

Common Adverse Reactions

1% to 10%:

Dermatologic: Itching, erythema

Local: Burning, dryness, irritation, papular rashes

Mechanism of Action Stimulates the synthesis of enzymes needed to decrease inflammation, suppress mitotic activity, and cause vasoconstriction

Pharmacodynamics/Kinetics

Absorption: Percutaneous absorption is variable and dependent upon many factors including vehicle used, integrity of epidermis, dose, and use of occlusive dressings; small amounts enter circulatory system via skin

Metabolism: Hepatic

Excretion: Urine and feces

Dosage Adults: Apply sparingly and gently; rub into affected area from 1-4 times/day. Therapy should be discontinued when control is achieved; if no improvement is seen, reassessment of diagnosis may be necessary.

Patient Information A thin film of cream or ointment is effective; do not overuse; do not use tight-fitting diapers or plastic pants on children being treated in the diaper area; use only as prescribed, and for no longer than the period prescribed; apply sparingly in light film; rub in lightly; avoid contact with eyes; notify prescriber if condition being treated persists or worsens

Dosage Forms CRM: 0.1% (15 g, 45 g)

♦ **Clocortolone Pivalate** *see* Clocortolone *on page 293*

♦ **Clocream® [OTC]** *see* Vitamin A and Vitamin D *on page 1311*

♦ **Cloderm®** *see* Clocortolone *on page 293*

Clofazimine *(kloe FA zi meen)*

Related Information

Antimicrobial Drugs of Choice *on page 1440*

Tuberculosis Treatment Guidelines *on page 1466*

U.S. Brand Names Lamprene®

Synonyms Clofazimine Palmitate

Therapeutic Category Antibiotic, Miscellaneous; Leprostatic Agent

Use Treatment of lepromatous leprosy including dapsone-resistant leprosy and lepromatous leprosy with erythema nodosum leprosum; multibacillary leprosy

Note: Clofazimine use has been associated with an adverse outcome in the treatment of MAC disease and should not be used.

Pregnancy Risk Factor C

Contraindications Hypersensitivity to clofazimine or any component of the formulation

Warnings/Precautions Clofazimine may crystallize and deposit in tissues, including intestinal mucosa, liver, spleen and mesenteric lymph nodes. Severe abdominal symptoms may occur and include rare reports of splenic infarction, bowel obstruction and gastrointestinal bleeding. Use with caution in patients with GI problems (ie, abdominal pain, diarrhea). Adjust dose or discontinue if abdominal symptoms occur; dosages >100 mg/day should be used for as short a duration as possible.

Common Adverse Reactions

>10%:

Dermatologic: Dry skin

Gastrointestinal: Abdominal pain, nausea, vomiting, diarrhea

Miscellaneous: Pink to brownish-black discoloration of the skin

1% to 10%:

Dermatologic: Rash, pruritus

Endocrine & metabolic: Elevated blood sugar

Gastrointestinal: Fecal discoloration

Genitourinary: Discoloration of urine

Ocular: Discoloration of conjunctiva; irritation, burning, and itching of the eyes

Miscellaneous: Discoloration of sputum, sweat

Drug Interactions

Cytochrome P450 Effect: Inhibits CYP3A4 (weak)

Decreased Effect: Combined use may decrease effect with dapsone (unconfirmed).

Mechanism of Action Binds preferentially to mycobacterial DNA to inhibit mycobacterial growth; also has some anti-inflammatory activity through an unknown mechanism

Pharmacodynamics/Kinetics

Absorption: Variable (45% to 62%)

Distribution: Highly lipophilic; deposited primarily in fatty tissue and cells of the reticuloendothelial system; taken up by macrophages throughout the body; distributed to breast milk, mesenteric lymph nodes, adrenal glands, subcutaneous fat, liver, bile, gallbladder, spleen, small intestine, muscles, bones, and skin; does not appear to cross blood-brain barrier; remains in tissues for prolonged periods

Metabolism: Partially hepatic to two metabolites

Half-life elimination: Terminal: 8 days; Tissue: 70 days

Time to peak, serum: Chronic therapy: 1-6 hours

Excretion: Primarily feces; urine (negligible amounts as unchanged drug); sputum, saliva, and sweat (small amounts)

Dosage Oral:

Children: Leprosy: 1 mg/kg/day every 24 hours in combination with dapsone and rifampin

Adults:

Dapsone-resistant leprosy: 100 mg/day in combination with one or more antileprosy drugs for 3 years; then alone 100 mg/day

Dapsone-sensitive multibacillary leprosy: 100 mg/day in combination with two or more antileprosy drugs for at least 2 years and continue until negative skin smears are obtained, then institute single drug therapy with appropriate agent

Erythema nodosum leprosum: 100-200 mg/day for up to 3 months or longer then taper dose to 100 mg/day when possible

Dosing adjustment in hepatic impairment: Should be considered in severe hepatic dysfunction

Patient Information Drug may cause a pink to brownish-black discoloration of the skin, conjunctiva, tears, sweat, urine, feces, and nasal secretions; although reversible, may take months to years to disappear after therapy is complete; take with meals

Dosage Forms CAP: 50 mg

♦ **Clofazimine Palmitate** *see Clofazimine on page 294*

Clofibrate (kloe FYE brate)

Related Information

Lipid-Lowering Agents *on page 1381*

Therapeutic Category Antilipemic Agent, Fibric Acid

Use Adjunct to dietary therapy in the management of hyperlipidemias associated with high triglyceride levels (types III, IV, V); primarily lowers triglycerides and very low density lipoprotein

Restrictions Not available in U.S.

Pregnancy Risk Factor C

Contraindications Hypersensitivity to clofibrate or any component of the formulation; significant hepatic or renal dysfunction; primary biliary cirrhosis

Warnings/Precautions Clofibrate has been shown to be tumorigenic in animal studies; increased risk of cholelithiasis, cholecystitis; discontinue if lipid response is not obtained; no evidence substantiates a beneficial effect on cardiovascular mortality; anemia and leukopenia have been reported; elevations in serum transaminases can be seen; use with caution in peptic ulcer disease; flu-like symptoms may occur. Be careful in patient selection; this is not a first- or second-line choice; other agents may be more suitable.

Common Adverse Reactions Frequency not defined.

Common: Gastrointestinal: Nausea, diarrhea

Less common:

Central nervous system: Headache, dizziness, fatigue

Gastrointestinal: Vomiting, loose stools, heartburn, flatulence, abdominal distress, epigastric pain

Neuromuscular & skeletal: Muscle cramping, aching, weakness, myalgia

Frequency unknown:

Central nervous system: Fever

Cardiovascular: Chest pain, cardiac arrhythmias

Dermatologic: Rash, urticaria, pruritus, alopecia, toxic epidermal necrolysis, erythema multiforme, Stevens-Johnson syndrome; dry, brittle hair

Endocrine & metabolic: Polyphagia, gynecomastia, hyperkalemia

Gastrointestinal: Stomatitis, gallstones, pancreatitis, gastritis, peptic ulcer, weight gain

Genitourinary: Impotence, decreased libido

Hematologic: Leukopenia, anemia, eosinophilia, agranulocytosis, thrombocytopenic purpura

Hepatic: Increased liver function test, hepatomegaly, jaundice

Local: Thrombophlebitis

Neuromuscular & skeletal: Myalgia, myopathy, myositis, arthralgia, rhabdomyolysis, increased creatinine phosphokinase (CPK), rheumatoid arthritis, tremor

Ocular: Photophobic

Renal: Dysuria, hematuria, proteinuria, renal toxicity (allergic), rhabdomyolysis-induced renal failure

Miscellaneous: Flu-like syndrome, increased diaphoresis, systemic lupus erythematosus

Drug Interactions

Cytochrome P450 Effect: Substrate of CYP3A4 (minor); **Inhibits** CYP2A6 (weak); **Induces** CYP2B6 (weak), 2E1 (weak), 3A4 (weak)

Increased Effect/Toxicity: Clofibrate may increase effects of warfarin, insulin, and sulfonylureas. Clofibrate's levels may be increased with probenecid. HMG-CoA reductase inhibitors (atorvastatin, cerivastatin, fluvastatin, lovastatin, pravastatin, simvastatin) may increase the risk of myopathy and rhabdomyolysis. The manufacturer warns against the concomitant use. However, combination therapy with statins has been used in some patients with resistant hyperlipidemias (with great caution).

Decreased Effect: Rifampin (and potentially other inducers of CYP3A4) may reduce blood levels of clofibrate.

Mechanism of Action Mechanism is unclear but thought to reduce cholesterol synthesis and triglyceride hepatic-vascular transference

Pharmacodynamics/Kinetics

Absorption: Complete

(Continued)

Clofibrate *(Continued)*

Distribution: V_d: 5.5 L/kg; crosses placenta

Protein binding: 95%

Metabolism: Hepatic to an inactive glucuronide ester; intestinal transformation required to activate drug

Half-life elimination: 6-24 hours, significantly prolonged with renal impairment; Anuria: 110 hours

Time to peak, serum: 3-6 hours

Excretion: Urine (40% to 70%)

Dosage Adults: Oral: 500 mg 4 times/day; some patients may respond to lower doses

Dosing interval in renal impairment:

Cl_{cr} >50 mL/minute: Administer every 6-12 hours

Cl_{cr} 10-50 mL/minute: Administer every 12-18 hours

Cl_{cr} <10 mL/minute: Avoid use

Hemodialysis: Elimination is not enhanced via hemodialysis; supplemental dose is not necessary

Administration Administer with meals or milk if GI upset occurs.

Monitoring Parameters Serum lipids, cholesterol and triglycerides, LFTs, CBC

Patient Information If GI upset occurs, may be taken with food. Report chest pain, shortness of breath, irregular heartbeat, severe stomach pain with nausea and vomiting, persistent fever, sore throat, or unusual bleeding or bruising. Adhere to prescribed diet.

Dosage Forms CAP: 500 mg

♦ Clomid® *see* ClomiPHENE *on page 296*

ClomiPHENE *(KLOE mi feen)*

U.S. Brand Names Clomid®; Serophene®

Synonyms Clomiphene Citrate

Therapeutic Category Ovulation Stimulator

Use Treatment of ovulatory failure in patients desiring pregnancy

Unlabeled/Investigational Use Male infertility

Pregnancy Risk Factor X

Contraindications Hypersensitivity to clomiphene citrate or any of its components; liver disease; abnormal uterine bleeding; enlargement or development of ovarian cyst; uncontrolled thyroid or adrenal dysfunction in the presence of an organic intracranial lesion such as pituitary tumor; pregnancy

Warnings/Precautions Patients unusually sensitive to pituitary gonadotropins (eg, polycystic ovary disease); multiple pregnancies, blurring or other visual symptoms can occur, ovarian hyperstimulation syndrome, and abdominal pain

Common Adverse Reactions

>10%: Endocrine & metabolic: Hot flashes, ovarian enlargement

1% to 10%:

Cardiovascular: Thromboembolism

Central nervous system: Mental depression, headache

Endocrine & metabolic: Breast enlargement (males), breast discomfort (females), abnormal menstrual flow

Gastrointestinal: Distention, bloating, nausea, vomiting, hepatotoxicity

Ocular: Blurring of vision, diplopia, floaters, after-images, phosphenes, photophobia

Drug Interactions

Decreased Effect: Decreased response when used with danazol. Decreased estradiol response when used with clomiphene.

Mechanism of Action Induces ovulation by stimulating the release of pituitary gonadotropins

Pharmacodynamics/Kinetics

Metabolism: Undergoes enterohepatic recirculation

Half-life elimination: 5-7 days

Excretion: Primarily feces; urine (small amounts)

Dosage Adults: Oral:

Male (infertility): 25 mg/day for 25 days with 5 days rest, or 100 mg every Monday, Wednesday, Friday

Female (ovulatory failure): 50 mg/day for 5 days (first course); start the regimen on or about the fifth day of cycle. The dose should be increased only in those patients who do not ovulate in response to cyclic 50 mg Clomid®. A low dosage or duration of treatment course is particularly recommended if unusual sensitivity to pituitary gonadotropin is suspected, such as in patients with polycystic ovary syndrome.

If ovulation does not appear to occur after the first course of therapy, a second course of 100 mg/day (two 50 mg tablets given as a single daily dose) for 5 days should be given. This course may be started as early as 30 days after the previous one after precautions are taken to exclude the presence of pregnancy. Increasing the dosage or duration of therapy beyond 100 mg/day for 5 days is not recommended. The majority of patients who are going to ovulate will do so after the first course of therapy. If ovulation does not occur after 3 courses of therapy, further treatment is not recommended and the patient should be re-evaluated. If 3 ovulatory responses occur, but pregnancy has not been achieved, further treatment is not recommended. If menses does not occur after an ovulatory response, the patient should be re-evaluated. Long-term cyclic therapy is not recommended beyond a total of about 6 cycles.

Reference Range FSH and LH are expected to peak 5-9 days after completing clomiphene; ovulation assessed by basal body temperature or serum progesterone 2 weeks after last clomiphene dose

Patient Information May cause visual disturbances, dizziness, lightheadedness. If possibility of pregnancy, stop the drug and consult your prescriber.

Dosage Forms TAB: 50 mg

♦ **Clomiphene Citrate** *see* ClomiPHENE *on page 296*

ClomiPRAMINE (kloe MI pra meen)

Related Information
Antidepressant Agents Comparison *on page 1359*

U.S. Brand Names Anafranil®

Synonyms Clomipramine Hydrochloride

Therapeutic Category Antidepressant, Tricyclic (Tertiary Amine)

Use Treatment of obsessive-compulsive disorder (OCD)

Unlabeled/Investigational Use Depression, panic attacks, chronic pain

Pregnancy Risk Factor C

Contraindications Hypersensitivity to clomipramine, other tricyclic agents, or any component of the formulation; use of MAO inhibitors within 14 days; use in a patient during the acute recovery phase of MI

Warnings/Precautions Seizures are likely and are dose-related; can be additive when coadministered with other drugs that can lower the seizure threshold. Use with caution in patients with asthma, bladder outlet destruction, narrow-angle glaucoma. Has been associated with a high incidence of sexual dysfunction. Weight gain may occur. May cause sedation, resulting in impaired performance of tasks requiring alertness (eg, operating machinery or driving). Sedative effects may be additive with other CNS depressants and/or ethanol. The degree of sedation is very high relative to other antidepressants. May worsen psychosis in some patients or precipitate a shift to mania or hypomania in patients with bipolar disease. May increase the risks associated with electroconvulsive therapy. This agent should be discontinued, when possible, prior to elective surgery. Therapy should not be abruptly discontinued in patients receiving high doses for prolonged periods.

May cause orthostatic hypotension (risk is moderate-high relative to other antidepressants) - use with caution in patients at risk of hypotension or in patients where transient hypotensive episodes would be poorly tolerated (cardiovascular disease or cerebrovascular disease). The degree of anticholinergic blockade produced by this agent is very high relative to other cyclic antidepressants - use caution in patients with urinary retention, benign prostatic hyperplasia, narrow-angle glaucoma, xerostomia, visual problems, constipation, or history of bowel obstruction.

The possibility of a suicide attempt is inherent in major depression and may persist until remission occurs. Use caution in high-risk patients during initiation of therapy. Prescriptions should be written for the smallest quantity consistent with good patient care. Use with caution in patients with a history of cardiovascular disease (including previous MI, stroke, tachycardia, or conduction abnormalities). The risk conduction abnormalities with this agent is high relative to other antidepressants. Use with caution in hyperthyroid patients or those receiving thyroid supplementation. Use with caution in patients with hepatic or renal dysfunction and in elderly patients. Safety and efficacy in pediatric patients <10 years of age have not been established.

Common Adverse Reactions
>10%:
Central nervous system: Dizziness, drowsiness, headache, insomnia, nervousness
Endocrine & metabolic: Libido changes
Gastrointestinal: Xerostomia, constipation, increased appetite, nausea, weight gain, dyspepsia, anorexia, abdominal pain
Neuromuscular & skeletal: Fatigue, tremor, myoclonus
Miscellaneous: Increased diaphoresis
1% to 10%:
Cardiovascular: Hypotension, palpitations, tachycardia
Central nervous system: Confusion, hypertonia, sleep disorder, yawning, speech disorder, abnormal dreaming, paresthesia, memory impairment, anxiety, twitching, impaired coordination, agitation, migraine, depersonalization, emotional lability, flushing, fever
Dermatologic: Rash, pruritus, dermatitis
Gastrointestinal: Diarrhea, vomiting
Genitourinary: Difficult urination
Ocular: Blurred vision, eye pain

Drug Interactions
Cytochrome P450 Effect: Substrate of CYP1A2 (major), 2C19 (major), 2D6 (major), 3A4 (minor); **Inhibits** CYP2D6 (moderate)
Increased Effect/Toxicity: CYP1A2 inhibitors may increase the levels/effects of clomipramine; example inhibitors include amiodarone, ciprofloxacin, fluvoxamine, ketoconazole, lomefloxacin, ofloxacin, and rofecoxib. CYP2C19 inhibitors may increase the levels/effects of clomipramine; example inhibitors include delavirdine, fluconazole, fluvoxamine, gemfibrozil, isoniazid, omeprazole, and ticlopidine. CYP2D6 inhibitors may increase the levels/effects of clomipramine. Example inhibitors include chlorpromazine, delavirdine, fluoxetine, miconazole, paroxetine, pergolide, quinidine, quinine, ritonavir, and ropinirole. Clomipramine increases the effects of amphetamines, anticholinergics, lithium, other CNS depressants (sedatives, hypnotics, ethanol), chlorpropamide, tolazamide, phenothiazines, and warfarin.
(Continued)

ClomiPRAMINE *(Continued)*

When used with MAO inhibitors or other serotonergic drugs, serotonin syndrome may occur. Serotonin syndrome has also been reported with ritonavir (rare). Pressor response to I.V. epinephrine, norepinephrine, and phenylephrine may be enhanced in patients receiving TCAs (**Note:** Effect is unlikely with epinephrine or levonordefrin dosages typically administered as infiltration in combination with local anesthetics). Combined use of beta-agonists or drugs which prolong QT_c (including quinidine, procainamide, disopyramide, cisapride, sparfloxacin, gatifloxacin, moxifloxacin) with TCAs may predispose patients to cardiac arrhythmias.

Decreased Effect: CYP1A2 inducers may decrease the levels/effects of clomipramine; example inducers include aminoglutethimide, carbamazepine, phenobarbital, and rifampin. CYP2C19 inducers may decrease the levels/effects of clomipramine; example inducers include aminoglutethimide, carbamazepine, phenytoin, and rifampin. Clomipramine inhibits the antihypertensive response to bethanidine, clonidine, debrisoquin, guanadrel, guanethidine, guanabenz, and guanfacine. Cholestyramine and colestipol may decrease the absorption of clomipramine.

Mechanism of Action Clomipramine appears to affect serotonin uptake while its active metabolite, desmethylclomipramine, affects norepinephrine uptake

Pharmacodynamics/Kinetics

Absorption: Rapid

Metabolism: Hepatic to desmethylclomipramine (active); extensive first-pass effect

Half-life elimination: 20-30 hours

Dosage Oral: Initial:

Children:

<10 years: Safety and efficacy have not been established.

≥10 years: OCD: 25 mg/day; gradually increase, as tolerated, to a maximum of 3 mg/kg/day or 200 mg/day (whichever is smaller)

Adults: OCD: 25 mg/day and gradually increase, as tolerated, to 100 mg/day the first 2 weeks, may then be increased to a total of 250 mg/day maximum

Monitoring Parameters Pulse rate and blood pressure prior to and during therapy; ECG/cardiac status in older adults and patients with cardiac disease

Patient Information May cause seizures; caution should be used in activities that require alertness like driving, operating machinery, or swimming; effect of drug may take several weeks to appear

Dosage Forms CAP: 25 mg, 50 mg, 75 mg

♦ **Clomipramine Hydrochloride** *see* ClomiPRAMINE *on page 297*

Clonazepam *(kloe NA ze pam)*

Related Information

Anticonvulsants by Seizure Type *on page 1358*
Benzodiazepines Comparison *on page 1366*
Epilepsy *on page 1477*

U.S. Brand Names Klonopin®

Therapeutic Category Anticonvulsant, Benzodiazepine; Benzodiazepine

Use Alone or as an adjunct in the treatment of petit mal variant (Lennox-Gastaut), akinetic, and myoclonic seizures; petit mal (absence) seizures unresponsive to succimides; panic disorder with or without agoraphobia

Unlabeled/Investigational Use Restless legs syndrome; neuralgia; multifocal tic disorder; parkinsonian dysarthria; bipolar disorder; adjunct therapy for schizophrenia

Restrictions C-IV

Pregnancy Risk Factor D

Contraindications Hypersensitivity to clonazepam or any component of the formulation (cross-sensitivity with other benzodiazepines may exist); significant liver disease; narrow-angle glaucoma; pregnancy

Warnings/Precautions Use with caution in elderly or debilitated patients, patients with hepatic disease (including alcoholics), or renal impairment. Use with caution in patients with respiratory disease or impaired gag reflex or ability to protect the airway from secretions (salivation may be increased). Worsening of seizures may occur when added to patients with multiple seizure types. Concurrent use with valproic acid may result in absence status. Monitoring of CBC and liver function tests has been recommended during prolonged therapy.

Causes CNS depression (dose-related) resulting in sedation, dizziness, confusion, or ataxia which may impair physical and mental capabilities. Patients must be cautioned about performing tasks which require mental alertness (eg, operating machinery or driving). Use with caution in patients receiving other CNS depressants or psychoactive agents. Effects with other sedative drugs or ethanol may be potentiated. Benzodiazepines have been associated with falls and traumatic injury and should be used with extreme caution in patients who are at risk of these events (especially the elderly).

Use caution in patients with depression, particularly if suicidal risk may be present. Use with caution in patients with a history of drug dependence. Benzodiazepines have been associated with dependence and acute withdrawal symptoms, including seizures, on discontinuation or reduction in dose. Acute withdrawal, including seizures, may be precipitated in patients after administration of flumazenil to patients receiving long-term benzodiazepine therapy.

Benzodiazepines have been associated with anterograde amnesia. Paradoxical reactions, including hyperactive or aggressive behavior, have been reported with benzodiazepines, particularly in adolescent/pediatric or psychiatric patients. Does not have analgesic, antidepressant, or antipsychotic properties.

Common Adverse Reactions
>10%: Central nervous system: Drowsiness
1% to 10%:
Central nervous system: Dizziness, abnormal coordination, ataxia, dysarthria, depression, memory disturbance, fatigue
Dermatologic: Dermatitis, allergic reactions
Endocrine & metabolic: Decreased libido
Gastrointestinal: Anorexia, constipation, diarrhea, xerostomia
Respiratory: Upper respiratory tract infection, sinusitis, rhinitis, coughing

Drug Interactions
Cytochrome P450 Effect: Substrate of CYP3A4 (major)
Increased Effect/Toxicity: Combined use of clonazepam and valproic acid has been associated with absence seizures. Clonazepam potentiates the CNS depressant effects of narcotic analgesics, barbiturates, phenothiazines, ethanol, antihistamines, MAO inhibitors, sedative-hypnotics, and cyclic antidepressants. CYP3A4 inhibitors may increase the levels/effects of clonazepam; example inhibitors include azole antifungals, ciprofloxacin, clarithromycin, diclofenac, doxycycline, erythromycin, imatinib, isoniazid, nefazodone, nicardipine, propofol, protease inhibitors, quinidine, and verapamil.
Decreased Effect: The combined use of clonazepam and valproic acid has been associated with absence seizures. CYP3A4 inducers may decrease the levels/effects of clonazepam; example inducers include aminoglutethimide, carbamazepine, nafcillin, nevirapine, phenobarbital, phenytoin, and rifamycins.

Mechanism of Action The exact mechanism is unknown, but believed to be related to its ability to enhance the activity of GABA; suppresses the spike-and-wave discharge in absence seizures by depressing nerve transmission in the motor cortex

Pharmacodynamics/Kinetics
Onset of action: 20-60 minutes
Duration: Infants and young children: 6-8 hours; Adults: ≤12 hours
Absorption: Well absorbed
Distribution: Adults: V_d: 1.5-4.4 L/kg
Protein binding: 85%
Metabolism: Extensively hepatic via glucuronide and sulfate conjugation
Half-life elimination: Children: 22-33 hours; Adults: 19-50 hours
Time to peak, serum: 1-3 hours; Steady-state: 5-7 days
Excretion: Urine (<2% as unchanged drug); metabolites excreted as glucuronide or sulfate conjugates

Dosage Oral:
Children <10 years or 30 kg: Seizure disorders:
Initial daily dose: 0.01-0.03 mg/kg/day (maximum: 0.05 mg/kg/day) given in 2-3 divided doses; increase by no more than 0.5 mg every third day until seizures are controlled or adverse effects seen
Usual maintenance dose: 0.1-0.2 mg/kg/day divided 3 times/day, not to exceed 0.2 mg/kg/day
Adults:
Seizure disorders:
Initial daily dose not to exceed 1.5 mg given in 3 divided doses; may increase by 0.5-1 mg every third day until seizures are controlled or adverse effects seen (maximum: 20 mg/day)
Usual maintenance dose: 0.05-0.2 mg/kg; do not exceed 20 mg/day
Panic disorder: 0.25 mg twice daily; increase in increments of 0.125-0.25 mg twice daily every 3 days; target dose: 1 mg/day (maximum: 4 mg/day)
Elderly: Initiate with low doses and observe closely
Hemodialysis: Supplemental dose is not necessary

Monitoring Parameters CBC, liver function tests
Reference Range Relationship between serum concentration and seizure control is not well established
Timing of serum samples: Peak serum levels occur 1-3 hours after oral ingestion; the half-life is 20-40 hours; therefore, steady-state occurs in 5-7 days
Therapeutic levels: 20-80 ng/mL; Toxic concentration: >80 ng/mL
Patient Information Avoid alcohol and other CNS depressants; avoid activities needing good psychomotor coordination until CNS effects are known; drug may cause physical or psychological dependence; avoid abrupt discontinuation after prolonged use
Dosage Forms TAB: 0.5 mg, 1 mg, 2 mg

Clonidine (KLON i deen)

U.S. Brand Names Catapres®; Catapres-TTS®; Duraclon™
Synonyms Clonidine Hydrochloride
Therapeutic Category Alpha-Adrenergic Agonist; Antihypertensive Agent; Antimigraine Agent, Prophylaxis
Use Management of mild to moderate hypertension; either used alone or in combination with other antihypertensives
Orphan drug: Duraclon™: For continuous epidural administration as adjunctive therapy with intraspinal opiates for treatment of cancer pain in patients tolerant to or unresponsive to intraspinal opiates
(Continued)

Clonidine *(Continued)*

Unlabeled/Investigational Use Heroin or nicotine withdrawal; severe pain; dysmenorrhea; vasomotor symptoms associated with menopause; ethanol dependence; prophylaxis of migraines; glaucoma; diabetes-associated diarrhea; impulse control disorder, attention-deficit/hyperactivity disorder (ADHD), clozapine-induced sialorrhea

Pregnancy Risk Factor C

Contraindications Hypersensitivity to clonidine hydrochloride or any component of the formulation

Warnings/Precautions Gradual withdrawal is needed (over 1 week for oral, 2-4 days with epidural) if drug needs to be stopped. Patients should be instructed about abrupt discontinuation (causes rapid increase in BP and symptoms of sympathetic overactivity). In patients on both a beta-blocker and clonidine where withdrawal of clonidine is necessary, withdraw the beta-blocker first and several days before clonidine. Then slowly decrease clonidine.

Use with caution in patients with severe coronary insufficiency; conduction disturbances; recent MI, CVA, or chronic renal insufficiency. Caution in sinus node dysfunction. Discontinue within 4 hours of surgery then restart as soon as possible after. Clonidine injection should be administered via a continuous epidural infusion device. Epidural clonidine is not recommended for perioperative, obstetrical, or postpartum pain. It is not recommended for use in patients with severe cardiovascular disease or hemodynamic instability. In all cases, the epidural may lead to cardiovascular instability (hypotension, bradycardia). May cause significant CNS depression and xerostomia. Caution in patients with pre-existing CNS disease or depression. Elderly may be at greater risk for CNS depressive effects, favoring other agents in this population.

Common Adverse Reactions Incidence of adverse events is not always reported.

>10%:
  Central nervous system: Drowsiness (35% oral, 12% transdermal), dizziness (16% oral, 2% transdermal)
  Dermatologic: Transient localized skin reactions characterized by pruritus, and erythema (15% to 50% transdermal)
  Gastrointestinal: Dry mouth (40% oral, 25% transdermal)

1% to 10%:
  Cardiovascular: Orthostatic hypotension (3% oral)
  Central nervous system: Headache (1% oral, 5% transdermal), sedation (3% transdermal), fatigue (6% transdermal), lethargy (3% transdermal), insomnia (2% transdermal), nervousness (3% oral, 1% transdermal), mental depression (1% oral)
  Dermatologic: Rash (1% oral), allergic contact sensitivity (5% transdermal), localized vesiculation (7%), hyperpigmentation (5% at application site), edema (3%), excoriation (3%), burning (3%), throbbing, blanching (1%), papules (1%), and generalized macular rash (1%) has occurred in patients receiving transdermal clonidine.
  Endocrine & metabolic: Sodium and water retention, sexual dysfunction (3% oral, 2% transdermal), impotence (3% oral, 2% transdermal), weakness (10% transdermal)
  Gastrointestinal: Nausea (5% oral, 1% transdermal), vomiting (5% oral), anorexia and malaise (1% oral), constipation (10% oral, 1% transdermal), dry throat (2% transdermal), taste disturbance (1% transdermal), weight gain (1% oral)
  Genitourinary: Nocturia (1% oral)
  Hepatic: Liver function test (mild abnormalities, 1% oral)
  Miscellaneous: Withdrawal syndrome (1% oral)

Drug Interactions

Increased Effect/Toxicity: Concurrent use with antipsychotics (especially low potency), narcotic analgesics, or nitroprusside may produce additive hypotensive effects. Clonidine may decrease the symptoms of hypoglycemia with oral hypoglycemic agents or insulin. Alcohol, barbiturates, and other CNS depressants may have additive CNS effects when combined with clonidine. Epidural clonidine may prolong the sensory and motor blockade of local anesthetics. Clonidine may increase cyclosporine (and perhaps tacrolimus) serum concentrations. Beta-blockers may potentiate bradycardia in patients receiving clonidine and may increase the rebound hypertension of withdrawal. Tricyclic antidepressants may also enhance the hypertensive response associated with abrupt clonidine withdrawal.

Decreased Effect: Tricyclic antidepressants (TCAs) antagonize the hypotensive effects of clonidine.

Mechanism of Action Stimulates alpha$_2$-adrenoceptors in the brain stem, thus activating an inhibitory neuron, resulting in reduced sympathetic outflow from the CNS, producing a decrease in peripheral resistance, renal vascular resistance, heart rate, and blood pressure; epidural clonidine may produce pain relief at spinal presynaptic and postjunctional alpha$_2$-adrenoceptors by preventing pain signal transmission; pain relief occurs only for the body regions innervated by the spinal segments where analgesic concentrations of clonidine exist

Pharmacodynamics/Kinetics

Onset of action: Oral: 0.5-1 hour
Duration: 6-10 hours
Distribution: V$_d$: Adults: 2.1 L/kg; highly lipid soluble; distributes readily into extravascular sites
Protein binding: 20% to 40%
Metabolism: Extensively hepatic to inactive metabolites; undergoes enterohepatic recirculation
Bioavailability: 75% to 95%
Half-life elimination: Adults: Normal renal function: 6-20 hours; Renal impairment: 18-41 hours
Time to peak: 2-4 hours
Excretion: Urine (65%, 32% as unchanged drug); feces (22%)

Dosage
Children:
Oral:
Hypertension: Initial: 5-10 mcg/kg/day in divided doses every 8-12 hours; increase gradually at 5- to 7-day intervals to 25 mcg/kg/day in divided doses every 6 hours; maximum: 0.9 mg/day

Clonidine tolerance test (test of growth hormone release from pituitary): 0.15 mg/m^2 or 4 mcg/kg as single dose

ADHD (unlabeled use): Initial: 0.05 mg/day; increase every 3-7 days by 0.05 mg/day to 3-5 mcg/kg/day given in divided doses 3-4 times/day (maximum dose: 0.3-0.4 mg/day)

Epidural infusion: Pain management: Reserved for patients with severe intractable pain, unresponsive to other analgesics or epidural or spinal opiates: Initial: 0.5 mcg/kg/hour; adjust with caution, based on clinical effect

Adults:
Oral:
Acute hypertension (urgency): Initial 0.1-0.2 mg; may be followed by additional doses of 0.1 mg every hour, if necessary, to a maximum total dose of 0.6 mg

Hypertension: Initial dose: 0.1 mg twice daily, usual maintenance dose: 0.2-1.2 mg/day in 2-4 divided doses; maximum recommended dose: 2.4 mg/day

Nicotine withdrawal symptoms: 0.1 mg twice daily to maximum of 0.4 mg/day for 3-4 weeks

Transdermal: Hypertension: Apply once every 7 days; for initial therapy start with 0.1 mg and increase by 0.1 mg at 1- to 2-week intervals; dosages >0.6 mg do not improve efficacy

Epidural infusion: Pain management: Starting dose: 30 mcg/hour; titrate as required for relief of pain or presence of side effects; minimal experience with doses >40 mcg/hour; should be considered an adjunct to intraspinal opiate therapy

Elderly: Initial: 0.1 mg once daily at bedtime, increase gradually as needed

Dosing adjustment in renal impairment: Cl$_{cr}$ <10 mL/minute: Administer 50% to 75% of normal dose initially

Dialysis: Not dialyzable (0% to 5%) via hemo- or peritoneal dialysis; supplemental dose not necessary

Administration
Oral: Do not discontinue clonidine abruptly. if needed, gradually reduce dose over 2-4 days to avoid rebound hypertension

Transdermal patch: Patches should be applied weekly at bedtime to a clean, hairless area of the upper outer arm or chest. Rotate patch sites weekly. Redness under patch may be reduced if a topical corticosteroid spray is applied to the area before placement of the patch.

Monitoring Parameters Blood pressure, standing and sitting/supine, mental status, heart rate

Reference Range Therapeutic: 1-2 ng/mL (SI: 4.4-8.7 nmol/L)

Patient Information Do not discontinue drug except on instruction of prescriber; check daily to be sure patch is present; may cause drowsiness, impaired coordination, and judgment; use extreme caution while driving or operating machines

Dosage Forms INJ, epidural solution [preservative free] (Duraclon™): 100 mcg/mL (10 mL); 500 mcg/mL (10 mL). **PATCH, transdermal** [once-weekly patch]: (Catapres-TTS®-1): 0.1 mg/ 24 hours (4s); (Catapres-TTS®-2): 0.2 mg/24 hours (4s); (Catapres-TTS®-3): 0.3 mg/24 hours (4s). **TAB** (Catapres®): 0.1 mg, 0.2 mg, 0.3 mg

Clonidine and Chlorthalidone (KLON i deen & klor THAL i done)

U.S. Brand Names Clorpres®; Combipres® [DSC]
Synonyms Chlorthalidone and Clonidine
Therapeutic Category Antihypertensive Agent, Combination
Use Management of mild to moderate hypertension
Pregnancy Risk Factor C
Dosage Oral: 1 tablet 1-2 times/day; maximum: 0.6 mg clonidine and 30 mg chlorthalidone
Dosage Forms TAB: (0.1): Clonidine 0.1 mg and chlorthalidone 15 mg; (0.2): Clonidine 0.2 mg and chlorthalidone 15 mg; (0.3): Clonidine 0.3 mg and chlorthalidone 15 mg

♦ **Clonidine Hydrochloride** see Clonidine on page 299

Clopidogrel (kloh PID oh grel)

U.S. Brand Names Plavix®
Synonyms Clopidogrel Bisulfate
Therapeutic Category Antiplatelet Agent; Platelet Aggregation Inhibitor
Use Reduce atherosclerotic events (myocardial infarction, stroke, vascular deaths) in patients with atherosclerosis documented by recent myocardial infarction (MI), recent stroke, or established peripheral arterial disease; prevention of thrombotic complications after coronary stenting; acute coronary syndrome (unstable angina or non-Q-wave MI)
Unlabeled/Investigational Use In aspirin-allergic patients, prevention of coronary artery bypass graft closure (saphenous vein)
Pregnancy Risk Factor B
Contraindications Hypersensitivity to clopidogrel or any component of the formulation; active pathological bleeding such as PUD or intracranial hemorrhage; coagulation disorders
Warnings/Precautions Cases of thrombotic thrombocytopenic purpura (TTP) have been reported, usually within the first 2 weeks of therapy. Patients receiving anticoagulants or other antiplatelet drugs concurrently, liver disease, patients having a previous hypersensitivity or other untoward effects related to ticlopidine, hypertension, renal impairment, history of
(Continued)

Clopidogrel *(Continued)*

bleeding or hemostatic disorders or drug-related hematologic disorders, and in patients scheduled for major surgery consider discontinuing 5 days prior to that surgery

Common Adverse Reactions As with all drugs which may affect hemostasis, bleeding is associated with clopidogrel. Hemorrhage may occur at virtually any site. Risk is dependent on multiple variables, including the concurrent use of multiple agents which alter hemostasis and patient susceptibility.

>10%: Gastrointestinal: The overall incidence of gastrointestinal events (including abdominal pain, vomiting, dyspepsia, gastritis and constipation) has been documented to be 27% compared to 30% in patients receiving aspirin.

3% to 10%:
Cardiovascular: Chest pain (8%), edema (4%), hypertension (4%)
Central nervous system: Headache (3% to 8%), dizziness (2% to 6%), depression (4%), fatigue (3%), general pain (6%)
Dermatologic: Rash (4%), pruritus (3%)
Endocrine & metabolic: Hypercholesterolemia (4%)
Gastrointestinal: Abdominal pain (2% to 6%), dyspepsia (2% to 5%), diarrhea (2% to 5%), nausea (3%)
Genitourinary: Urinary tract infection (3%)
Hematologic: Purpura (5%), epistaxis (3%)
Hepatic: Liver function test abnormalities (<3%; discontinued in 0.11%)
Neuromuscular & skeletal: Arthralgia (6%), back pain (6%)
Respiratory: Dyspnea (5%), rhinitis (4%), bronchitis (4%), coughing (3%), upper respiratory infections (9%)
Miscellaneous: Flu-like syndrome (8%)

1% to 3%:
Cardiovascular: Atrial fibrillation, cardiac failure, palpitation, syncope
Central nervous system: Fever, insomnia, vertigo, anxiety
Dermatologic: Eczema
Endocrine & metabolic: Gout, hyperuricemia
Gastrointestinal: Constipation, GI hemorrhage, vomiting
Genitourinary: Cystitis
Hematologic: Hematoma, anemia
Neuromuscular & skeletal: Arthritis, leg cramps, neuralgia, paresthesia, weakness
Ocular: Cataract, conjunctivitis

Drug Interactions
Cytochrome P450 Effect: Substrate (minor) of CYP1A2, 3A4; **Inhibits** CYP2C8/9 (weak)
Increased Effect/Toxicity: At high concentrations, clopidogrel may interfere with the metabolism of amiodarone, cisapride, cyclosporine, diltiazem, fluvastatin, irbesartan, losartan, oral hypoglycemics, paclitaxel, phenytoin, quinidine, sildenafil, tamoxifen, torsemide, verapamil, and some NSAIDs which may result in toxicity. Clopidogrel and naproxen resulted in an increase of GI occult blood loss. Anticoagulants (warfarin, thrombolytics, drotrecogin alfa) or other antiplatelet agents may increase the risk of bleeding. Rifampin may increase the effects of clopidogrel (monitor).
Decreased Effect: Atorvastatin may attenuate the effects of clopidogrel; monitor. CYP3A4-inhibiting macrolide antibiotics may attenuate the effects of clopidogrel (including clarithromycin, erythromycin, and troleandomycin); monitor.

Mechanism of Action Blocks the ADP receptors, which prevent fibrinogen binding at that site and thereby reduce the possibility of platelet adhesion and aggregation

Pharmacodynamics/Kinetics
Onset of action: Inhibition of platelet aggregation detected: 2 hours after 300 mg administered; after second day of treatment with 50-100 mg/day
Peak effect: 50-100 mg/day: Bleeding time: 5-6 days; Platelet function: 3-7 days
Absorption: Well absorbed
Metabolism: Extensively hepatic via hydrolysis; biotransformation to carboxyl acid derivative (active metabolite that inhibits platelet aggregation)
Half-life elimination: ~8 hours
Time to peak, serum: ~1 hour
Excretion: Urine

Dosage Oral: Adults:
Recent MI, recent stroke, or established arterial disease: 75 mg once daily
Acute coronary syndrome: Initial: 300 mg loading dose, followed by 75 mg once daily (in combination with aspirin 75-325 mg once daily)
Prevention of coronary artery bypass graft closure (saphenous vein): Aspirin-allergic patients (unlabeled use): Loading dose: 300 mg 6 hours following procedure; maintenance: 50-100 mg/day
Dosing adjustment in renal impairment and elderly: None necessary

Monitoring Parameters Signs of bleeding; hemoglobin and hematocrit periodically

Patient Information Report any unusual or prolonged bleeding or fever; inform your prescriber before starting any new medications, changing your diet, or undergoing any procedures that may be associated with a risk of bleeding

Dosage Forms TAB, film coated: 75 mg

♦ **Clopidogrel Bisulfate** *see* Clopidogrel *on page 301*

Clorazepate (klor AZ e pate)

Related Information

Benzodiazepines Comparison *on page 1366*
Epilepsy *on page 1477*

U.S. Brand Names Tranxene®; Tranxene® SD™; Tranxene® SD™-Half Strength; T-Tab®

Synonyms Clorazepate Dipotassium; Tranxene T-Tab®

Therapeutic Category Anticonvulsant, Benzodiazepine; Benzodiazepine; Sedative

Use Treatment of generalized anxiety disorder; management of ethanol withdrawal; adjunct anticonvulsant in management of partial seizures

Restrictions C-IV

Pregnancy Risk Factor D

Contraindications Hypersensitivity to clorazepate or any component of the formulation (cross-sensitivity with other benzodiazepines may exist); narrow-angle glaucoma; pregnancy

Warnings/Precautions Not recommended for use in patients <9 years of age or patients with depressive or psychotic disorders. Use with caution in elderly or debilitated patients, patients with hepatic disease (including alcoholics), or renal impairment. Active metabolites with extended half-lives may lead to delayed accumulation and adverse effects. Use with caution in patients with respiratory disease or impaired gag reflex. Avoid use in patients with sleep apnea.

Causes CNS depression (dose-related) resulting in sedation, dizziness, confusion, or ataxia which may impair physical and mental capabilities. Patients must be cautioned about performing tasks which require mental alertness (eg, operating machinery or driving). Use with caution in patients receiving other CNS depressants or psychoactive agents. Effects with other sedative drugs or ethanol may be potentiated. Benzodiazepines have been associated with falls and traumatic injury and should be used with extreme caution in patients who are at risk of these events (especially the elderly).

Use caution in patients with depression, particularly if suicidal risk may be present. Use with caution in patients with a history of drug dependence. Benzodiazepines have been associated with dependence and acute withdrawal symptoms on discontinuation or reduction in dose. Acute withdrawal, including seizures, may be precipitated in patients after administration of flumazenil to patients receiving long-term benzodiazepine therapy.

Benzodiazepines have been associated with anterograde amnesia. Paradoxical reactions, including hyperactive or aggressive behavior, have been reported with benzodiazepines, particularly in adolescent/pediatric or psychiatric patients. Does not have analgesic, antidepressant, or antipsychotic properties.

Common Adverse Reactions Frequency not defined.

Cardiovascular: Hypotension

Central nervous system: Drowsiness, fatigue, ataxia, lightheadedness, memory impairment, insomnia, anxiety, headache, depression, slurred speech, confusion, nervousness, dizziness, irritability

Dermatologic: Rash

Endocrine & metabolic: Decreased libido

Gastrointestinal: Xerostomia, constipation, diarrhea, decreased salivation, nausea, vomiting, increased or decreased appetite

Neuromuscular & skeletal: Dysarthria, tremor

Ocular: Blurred vision, diplopia

Drug Interactions

Cytochrome P450 Effect: Substrate of CYP3A4 (major)

Increased Effect/Toxicity: Clorazepate potentiates the CNS depressant effects of narcotic analgesics, barbiturates, phenothiazines, ethanol, antihistamines, MAO inhibitors, sedative-hypnotics, and cyclic antidepressants. CYP3A4 inhibitors may increase the levels/effects of clorazepate; example inhibitors include azole antifungals, ciprofloxacin, clarithromycin, diclofenac, doxycycline, erythromycin, imatinib, isoniazid, nefazodone, nicardipine, propofol, protease inhibitors, quinidine, and verapamil.

Decreased Effect: CYP3A4 inducers may decrease the levels/effects of clorazepate; example inducers include aminoglutethimide, carbamazepine, nafcillin, nevirapine, phenobarbital, phenytoin, and rifamycins.

Mechanism of Action Binds to stereospecific benzodiazepine receptors on the postsynaptic GABA neuron at several sites within the central nervous system, including the limbic system, reticular formation. Enhancement of the inhibitory effect of GABA on neuronal excitability results by increased neuronal membrane permeability to chloride ions. This shift in chloride ions results in hyperpolarization (a less excitable state) and stabilization.

Pharmacodynamics/Kinetics

Onset of action: 1-2 hours

Duration: Variable, 8-24 hours

Distribution: Crosses placenta; appears in urine

Metabolism: Rapidly decarboxylated to desmethyldiazepam (active) in acidic stomach prior to absorption; hepatically to oxazepam (active)

Half-life elimination: Adults: Desmethyldiazepam: 48-96 hours; Oxazepam: 6-8 hours

Time to peak, serum: ~1 hour

Excretion: Primarily urine

Dosage Oral:

Children 9-12 years: Anticonvulsant: Initial: 3.75-7.5 mg/dose twice daily; increase dose by 3.75 mg at weekly intervals, not to exceed 60 mg/day in 2-3 divided doses

(Continued)

303

Clorazepate *(Continued)*

Children >12 years and Adults: Anticonvulsant: Initial: Up to 7.5 mg/dose 2-3 times/day; increase dose by 7.5 mg at weekly intervals, not to exceed 90 mg/day

Adults:

Anxiety:

Regular release tablets (Tranxene® T-Tab®): 7.5-15 mg 2-4 times/day

Sustained release (Tranxene®-SD): 11.25 or 22.5 mg once daily at bedtime

Ethanol withdrawal: Initial: 30 mg, then 15 mg 2-4 times/day on first day; maximum daily dose: 90 mg; gradually decrease dose over subsequent days

Monitoring Parameters Respiratory and cardiovascular status, excess CNS depression

Reference Range Therapeutic: 0.12-1 µg/mL (SI: 0.36-3.01 µmol/L)

Patient Information Avoid alcohol and other CNS depressants; avoid activities needing good psychomotor coordination until CNS effects are known; drug may cause physical or psychological dependence; avoid abrupt discontinuation after prolonged use

Dosage Forms TAB: 3.75 mg, 7.5 mg, 15 mg; (Tranxene®-SD™): 22.5 mg [once daily]; (Tranxene®-SD™ Half Strength): 11.25 mg [once daily]; (Tranxene® T-Tab®): 3.75 mg, 7.5 mg, 15 mg

♦ **Clorazepate Dipotassium** *see Clorazepate on page 303*

♦ **Clorpres®** *see Clonidine and Chlorthalidone on page 301*

Clotrimazole *(kloe TRIM a zole)*

U.S. Brand Names Cruex® Cream [OTC]; Gyne-Lotrimin® 3 [OTC]; Lotrimin® AF Athlete's Foot Cream [OTC]; Lotrimin® AF Athlete's Foot Solution [OTC]; Lotrimin® AF Jock Itch Cream [OTC]; Mycelex®; Mycelex®-7 [OTC]; Mycelex® Twin Pack [OTC]

Therapeutic Category Antifungal Agent, Oral Nonabsorbed; Antifungal Agent, Topical; Antifungal Agent, Vaginal

Use Treatment of susceptible fungal infections, including oropharyngeal candidiasis, dermatophytoses, superficial mycoses, and cutaneous candidiasis, as well as vulvovaginal candidiasis; limited data suggest that clotrimazole troches may be effective for prophylaxis against oropharyngeal candidiasis in neutropenic patients

Pregnancy Risk Factor B (topical); C (troches)

Contraindications Hypersensitivity to clotrimazole or any component of the formulation

Warnings/Precautions Clotrimazole should not be used for treatment of systemic fungal infection; safety and effectiveness of clotrimazole lozenges (troches) in children <3 years of age have not been established; when using topical formulation, avoid contact with eyes

Common Adverse Reactions

Oral:

>10%: Hepatic: Abnormal liver function tests

1% to 10%:

Gastrointestinal: Nausea and vomiting may occur in patients on clotrimazole troches

Local: Mild burning, irritation, stinging to skin or vaginal area

Vaginal:

1% to 10%: Genitourinary: Vulvar/vaginal burning

Drug Interactions

Cytochrome P450 Effect: Inhibits CYP1A2 (weak), 2A6 (weak), 2B6 (weak), 2C8/9 (weak), 2C19 (weak), 2D6 (weak), 2E1 (weak), 3A4 (moderate)

Mechanism of Action Binds to phospholipids in the fungal cell membrane altering cell wall permeability resulting in loss of essential intracellular elements

Pharmacodynamics/Kinetics

Absorption: Topical: Negligible through intact skin

Time to peak, serum:

Oral topical: Salivary levels occur within 3 hours following 30 minutes of dissolution time

Vaginal cream: High vaginal levels: 8-24 hours

Vaginal tablet: High vaginal levels: 1-2 days

Excretion: Feces (as metabolites)

Dosage

Children >3 years and Adults:

Oral:

Prophylaxis: 10 mg troche dissolved 3 times/day for the duration of chemotherapy or until steroids are reduced to maintenance levels

Treatment: 10 mg troche dissolved slowly 5 times/day for 14 consecutive days

Topical (cream, solution): Apply twice daily; if no improvement occurs after 4 weeks of therapy, re-evaluate diagnosis

Children >12 years and Adults:

Vaginal:

Cream:

1%: Insert 1 applicatorful vaginal cream daily (preferably at bedtime) for 7 consecutive days

2%: Insert 1 applicatorful vaginal cream daily (preferably at bedtime) for 3 consecutive days

Tablet: Insert 100 mg/day for 7 days or 500 mg single dose

Topical (cream, solution): Apply to affected area twice daily (morning and evening) for 7 consecutive days

Administration

Oral: Allow to dissolve slowly over 15-30 minutes.

Topical: Avoid contact with eyes. For external use only. Apply sparingly. Protect hands with latex gloves. Do not use occlusive dressings.

Monitoring Parameters Periodic liver function tests during oral therapy with clotrimazole lozenges

Patient Information Oral: Do not swallow oral medication whole; allow to dissolve slowly in mouth. You may experience nausea or vomiting (small frequent meals, frequent mouth care, chewing gum, or sucking lozenges may help). Report signs of opportunistic infection (eg, white plaques in mouth, fever, chills, perianal itching or vaginal discharge, fatigue, unhealed wounds or sores).

Topical: Wash hands before applying or wear gloves. Apply thin film to affected area. May apply porous dressing. Report persistent burning, swelling, itching, worsening of condition, or lack of response to therapy.

Vaginal: Wash hands before using. Insert full applicator into vagina gently and expel cream, or insert tablet into vagina, at bedtime. Wash applicator with soap and water following use. Remain lying down for 30 minutes following administration. Avoid intercourse during therapy (sexual partner may experience penile burning or itching). Report adverse reactions (eg, vulvar itching, frequent urination), worsening of condition, or lack of response to therapy. Contact prescriber if symptoms do not improve within 3 days or you do not feel well within 7 days. Do not use tampons until therapy is complete. Contact prescriber immediately if you experience abdominal pain, fever, or foul-smelling discharge.

Dosage Forms COMBO PACK (Mycelex®-7): Vaginal tablet 100 mg (7s) and vaginal cream 1% (7 g). **CRM, topical** 1% (15 g, 30 g, 45 g); (Cruex®): 1% (15 g); (Lotrimin® AF Athlete's Foot): 1% (12 g, 24 g); (Lotrimin® AF Jock Itch): 1% (12 g). **CRM, vaginal:** 2% (25 g); (Mycelex®-7): 1% (45 g). **SOLN, topical:** 1% (10 mL, 30 mL); (Lotrimin® AF Athlete's Foot): 1% (10 mL). **TAB, vaginal** (Gyne-Lotrimin® 3): 200 mg (3s). **TROCHE** (Mycelex®): 10 mg

♦ **Clotrimazole and Betamethasone** see Betamethasone and Clotrimazole on page 161

Cloxacillin (kloks a SIL in)
Synonyms Cloxacillin Sodium
Therapeutic Category Antibiotic, Penicillin
Use Treatment of susceptible bacterial infections, notably penicillinase-producing staphylococci causing respiratory tract, skin and skin structure, bone and joint, urinary tract infections
Restrictions Not available in U.S.
Pregnancy Risk Factor B
Dosage Oral:
　Children >1 month (<20 kg): 50-100 mg/kg/day in divided doses every 6 hours; up to a maximum of 4 g/day
　Children (>20 kg) and Adults: 250-500 mg every 6 hours
　Hemodialysis: Not dialyzable (0% to 5%)
Dosage Forms CAP: 250 mg, 500 mg. **POWDER, oral suspension:** 125 mg/5 mL (100 mL, 200 mL)

♦ **Cloxacillin Sodium** see Cloxacillin on page 305

Clozapine (KLOE za peen)
Related Information
　Antipsychotic Agents Comparison on page 1364
U.S. Brand Names Clozaril®
Therapeutic Category Antipsychotic Agent, Atypical; Antipsychotic Agent, Dibenzodiazepine
Use Treatment-refractory schizophrenia; to reduce risk of recurrent suicidal behavior in schizophrenia or schizoaffective disorder
Unlabeled/Investigational Use Schizoaffective disorder, bipolar disorder, childhood psychosis, severe obsessive-compulsive disorder
Restrictions Patient-specific registration is required to dispense clozapine. Monitoring systems for individual clozapine manufacturers are independent. If a patient is switched from one brand/manufacturer of clozapine to another, the patient must be entered into a new registry (must be completed by the prescriber and delivered to the dispensing pharmacy). Healthcare providers, including pharmacists dispensing clozapine, are encouraged to verify the patient's hematological status and qualification to receive clozapine with all existing registries.
Pregnancy Risk Factor B
Contraindications Hypersensitivity to clozapine or any component of the formulation; history of agranulocytosis or granulocytopenia with clozapine; uncontrolled epilepsy; severe central nervous system depression or comatose state; myeloproliferative disorders or use with other agents which have a well-known risk of agranulocytosis or bone marrow suppression

In patients with WBC ≤3500 cells/mm^3 before therapy; if WBC falls to <3000 cells/mm^3 during therapy the drug should be withheld until signs and symptoms of infection disappear and WBC rises to >3000 cells/mm^3

Warnings/Precautions Medication should not be stopped abruptly; taper off over 1-2 weeks. If conditions warrant abrupt discontinuation (leukopenia, myocarditis, cardiomyopathy), monitor patient for psychosis and cholinergic rebound (headache, nausea, vomiting, diarrhea). Elderly patients are more susceptible to adverse effects (including agranulocytosis, cardiovascular, anticholinergic, and tardive dyskinesia).

Significant risk of agranulocytosis, potentially life-threatening. WBC testing should occur weekly for the first 6 months of therapy; thereafter, if acceptable WBC counts are maintained (WBC ≥3000/mm^3, ANC ≥1500/mm^3) then WBC counts can be monitored every other week. (Continued)

Clozapine *(Continued)*

WBCs must be monitored weekly for the first 4 weeks after therapy discontinuation. Use with caution in patients receiving other marrow suppressive agents. Eosinophilia has been reported to occur with clozapine and may require temporary or permanent interruption of therapy.

Cognitive and/or motor impairment (sedation) is common with clozapine, resulting in impaired performance of tasks requiring alertness (eg, operating machinery or driving). Use with caution in patients at risk of seizures, including those with a history of seizures, head trauma, brain damage, alcoholism, or concurrent therapy with medications which may lower seizure threshold. Has been associated with benign, self-limiting fever (<100.4°F, usually within first 3 weeks). However, clozapine may also be associated with severe febrile reactions, including neuroleptic malignant syndrome (NMS). Clozapine's potential for extrapyramidal symptoms appears to be extremely low.

May cause anticholinergic effects; use with caution in patients with urinary retention, benign prostatic hyperplasia, narrow-angle glaucoma, xerostomia, visual problems, constipation, or history of bowel obstruction. May cause hyperglycemia; use with caution in patients with diabetes or other disorders of glucose regulation. Use with caution in patients with hepatic disease or impairment; hepatitis has been reported as a consequence of therapy.

May cause orthostatic hypotension and tachycardia; use with caution in patients at risk of hypotension or in patients where transient hypotensive episodes would be poorly tolerated (cardiovascular disease or cerebrovascular disease). Concurrent use of psychotropics and benzodiazepines may increase the risk of severe cardiopulmonary reactions.

Myocarditis, pericarditis, pericardial effusion, cardiomyopathy, and CHF have also been associated with clozapine. Fatalities due to myocarditis have been reported; highest risk in the first month of therapy, however, later cases also reported. Myocarditis or cardiomyopathy should be considered in patients who present with signs/symptoms of heart failure (dyspnea, fatigue, orthopnea, paroxysmal nocturnal dyspnea, peripheral edema), chest pain, palpitations, new electrocardiographic abnormalities (arrhythmias, ST-T wave abnormalities), or unexplained fever. Patients with tachycardia during the first month of therapy should be closely monitored for other signs of myocarditis. Discontinue clozapine if myocarditis is suspected; do not rechallenge in patients with clozapine-related myocarditis. The reported rate of cardiomyopathy in clozapine-treated patients is similar to that in the general population. The majority of patients were over 50 years of age and were taking clozapine for >6 months. Clozapine should be discontinued in patients with confirmed cardiomyopathy unless benefit clearly outweighs risk. Rare cases of thromboembolism, including pulmonary embolism and stroke resulting in fatalities, have been associated with clozapine.

Common Adverse Reactions

>10%:

Cardiovascular: Tachycardia

Central nervous system: Drowsiness, dizziness

Gastrointestinal: Constipation, weight gain, sialorrhea

Genitourinary: Urinary incontinence

1% to 10%:

Cardiovascular: Angina, ECG changes, hypertension, hypotension, syncope

Central nervous system: Akathisia, seizures, headache, nightmares, akinesia, confusion, insomnia, fatigue, myoclonic jerks, restlessness, agitation, lethargy, ataxia, slurred speech, depression, anxiety

Dermatologic: Rash

Gastrointestinal: Abdominal discomfort, anorexia, diarrhea, heartburn, xerostomia, nausea, vomiting

Hematologic: Eosinophilia, leukopenia, leukocytosis

Hepatic: Liver function tests abnormal

Neuromuscular & skeletal: Tremor, rigidity, hyperkinesia, weakness

Ocular: Visual disturbances

Respiratory: Rhinorrhea

Miscellaneous: Diaphoresis (increased), fever

Drug Interactions

Cytochrome P450 Effect: Substrate of CYP1A2 (major), 2A6 (minor), 2C8/9 (minor), 2C19 (minor), 2D6 (minor), 3A4 (minor); **Inhibits** CYP1A2 (weak), 2C8/9 (weak), 2C19 (weak), 2D6 (moderate), 2E1 (weak), 3A4 (weak)

Increased Effect/Toxicity: May potentiate anticholinergic and hypotensive effects of other drugs. Benzodiazepines in combination with clozapine may produce respiratory depression and hypotension, especially during the first few weeks of therapy. May potentiate effect/toxicity of risperidone. Clozapine serum concentrations may be increased by inhibitors of CYP1A2 (list of inhibitors is extensive, but includes amiodarone, ciprofloxacin, fluvoxamine, ketoconazole, lomefloxacin, ofloxacin, and rofecoxib). Metoclopramide may increase risk of extrapyramidal symptoms (EPS).

Decreased Effect: Carbamazepine, phenytoin, primidone, and valproic acid may increase the hepatic metabolism (decrease serum levels) of clozapine. Cigarette smoking (nicotine) may enhance the metabolism of clozapine. Clozapine may reverse the pressor effect of epinephrine (avoid in treatment of drug-induced hypotension).

Mechanism of Action Clozapine is a weak dopamine$_1$ and dopamine$_2$ receptor blocker, but blocks D_1-D_5 receptors; in addition, it blocks the serotonin$_2$, alpha-adrenergic, histamine H_1, and cholinergic receptors

Pharmacodynamics/Kinetics

Protein binding: 97% to serum proteins

Metabolism: Extensively hepatic

Bioavailability: 12% to 81%

Half-life elimination: 12 hours (range: 4-66 hours)

Time to peak: 2.5 hours

Excretion: Urine (~50%) and feces (30%) with trace amounts of unchanged drug

Dosage Oral: If dosing is interrupted for >48 hours, therapy must be reinitiated at 12.5-25 mg/day; may be increased more rapidly than with initial titration.

Children and Adolescents: Childhood psychosis (unlabeled use): Initial: 25 mg/day; increase to a target dose of 25-400 mg/day

Adults: Schizophrenia or to reduce risk of suicidal behavior: Initial: 12.5 mg once or twice daily; increased, as tolerated, in increments of 25-50 mg/day to a target dose of 300-450 mg/day after 2-4 weeks, may require doses as high as 600-900 mg/day for the treatment of schizophrenia; median dose to reduce risk of suicidal behavior is ~300 mg/day (range 12.5-900 mg)

Elderly: Schizophrenia: Dose selection and titration should be cautious

Note: In the event of planned termination of clozapine, gradual reduction in dose over a 1- to 2-week period is recommended. If conditions warrant abrupt discontinuation (leukopenia), monitor patient for psychosis and cholinergic rebound (headache, nausea, vomiting, diarrhea).

Monitoring Parameters Mental status, ECG, WBC, vital signs, lipid profile, fasting blood glucose/Hgb A_{1c}, BMI, abnormal involuntary movement scale (AIMS). WBC should be obtained at baseline and at least weekly for the first 6 months of continuous treatment. If WBC counts remain acceptable (WBC ≥3000/mm^3, ANC ≥1500/mm^3) during this time period, then WBC counts may be monitored every other week thereafter. If clozapine is discontinued, a weekly WBC should be completed for an additional 4 weeks. If clozapine therapy is interrupted, the 6-month time period for initiation of biweekly WBCs may need to be reset. This determination depends upon the treatment duration, the length of the break in therapy, and whether or not an abnormal blood event occurred. Consult full prescribing information for determination of appropriate WBC-monitoring interval.

Patient Information Report any lethargy, fever, sore throat, flu-like symptoms, or any other signs or symptoms of infection; may cause drowsiness; frequent blood samples must be taken; do not stop taking even if you think it is not working

Dosage Forms TAB: 25 mg, 100 mg

♦ **Clozaril**® see Clozapine on page 305

♦ **CMV-IGIV** see Cytomegalovirus Immune Globulin (Intravenous-Human) on page 331

♦ **Coagulant Complex Inhibitor** see Anti-inhibitor Coagulant Complex on page 106

♦ **Coagulation Factor VIIa** see Factor VIIa (Recombinant) on page 502

Cocaine (koe KANE)

Synonyms Cocaine Hydrochloride

Therapeutic Category Local Anesthetic, Ester Derivative; Local Anesthetic, Topical

Use Topical anesthesia for mucous membranes

Restrictions C-II

Pregnancy Risk Factor C/X (nonmedicinal use)

Contraindications Hypersensitivity to cocaine or any component of the topical solution; ophthalmologic anesthesia (causing sloughing of the corneal epithelium); pregnancy (nonmedicinal use)

Warnings/Precautions For topical use only. Limit to office and surgical procedures only. Resuscitative equipment and drugs should be immediately available when any local anesthetic is used. Debilitated, elderly patients, acutely ill patients, and children should be given reduced doses consistent with their age and physical status. Use caution in patients with severely traumatized mucosa and sepsis in the region of the proposed application. Use with caution in patients with cardiovascular disease or a history of cocaine abuse. In patients being treated for cardiovascular complication of cocaine abuse, avoid beta-blockers for treatment.

Common Adverse Reactions

>10%:

Central nervous system: CNS stimulation

Gastrointestinal: Loss of taste perception

Respiratory: Rhinitis, nasal congestion

Miscellaneous: Loss of smell

1% to 10%:

Cardiovascular: Heart rate (decreased) with low doses, tachycardia with moderate doses, hypertension, cardiomyopathy, cardiac arrhythmias, myocarditis, QRS prolongation, Raynaud's phenomenon, cerebral vasculitis, thrombosis, fibrillation (atrial), flutter (atrial), sinus bradycardia, CHF, pulmonary hypertension, sinus tachycardia, tachycardia (supraventricular), arrhythmias (ventricular), vasoconstriction

Central nervous system: Fever, nervousness, restlessness, euphoria, excitation, headache, psychosis, hallucinations, agitation, seizures, slurred speech, hyperthermia, dystonic reactions, cerebral vascular accident, vasculitis, clonic-tonic reactions, paranoia, sympathetic storm

Dermatologic: Skin infarction, pruritus, madarosis

Gastrointestinal: Nausea, anorexia, colonic ischemia, spontaneous bowel perforation

Genitourinary: Priapism, uterine rupture

Hematologic: Thrombocytopenia

Neuromuscular & skeletal: Chorea (extrapyramidal), paresthesia, tremors, fasciculations

Ocular: Mydriasis (peak effect at 45 minutes; may last up to 12 hours), sloughing of the corneal epithelium, ulceration of the cornea, iritis, mydriasis, chemosis

(Continued)

Cocaine *(Continued)*

Renal: Myoglobinuria, necrotizing vasculitis
Respiratory: Tachypnea, nasal mucosa damage (when snorting), hyposmia, bronchiolitis obliterans organizing pneumonia
Miscellaneous: "Washed-out" syndrome

Drug Interactions

Cytochrome P450 Effect: Substrate of CYP3A4 (major); **Inhibits** CYP2D6 (strong), 3A4 (weak)

Increased Effect/Toxicity: Increased toxicity with MAO inhibitors. Use with epinephrine may cause extreme hypertension and/or cardiac arrhythmias.

Mechanism of Action Ester local anesthetic blocks both the initiation and conduction of nerve impulses by decreasing the neuronal membrane's permeability to sodium ions, which results in inhibition of depolarization with resultant blockade of conduction; interferes with the uptake of norepinephrine by adrenergic nerve terminals producing vasoconstriction

Pharmacodynamics/Kinetics Following topical administration to mucosa:

Onset of action: ~1 minute
Peak effect: ~5 minutes
Duration (dose dependent): ≥30 minutes; cocaine metabolites may appear in urine of neonates up to 5 days after birth due to maternal cocaine use shortly before birth
Absorption: Well absorbed through mucous membranes; limited by drug-induced vasoconstriction; enhanced by inflammation
Distribution: Enters breast milk
Metabolism: Hepatic; major metabolites are ecgonine methyl ester and benzoyl ecgonine
Half-life elimination: 75 minutes
Excretion: Primarily urine (<10% as unchanged drug and metabolites)

Dosage Topical application (ear, nose, throat, bronchoscopy): Dosage depends on the area to be anesthetized, tissue vascularity, technique of anesthesia, and individual patient tolerance; the lowest dose necessary to produce adequate anesthesia should be used; concentrations of 1% to 10% are used (not to exceed 1 mg/kg). Use reduced dosages for children, elderly, or debilitated patients.

Administration Topical: Use only on mucous membranes of the oral, laryngeal, and nasal cavities. Do not use on extensive areas of broken skin.

Monitoring Parameters Vital signs

Reference Range Therapeutic: 100-500 ng/mL (SI: 330 nmol/L); Toxic: >1000 ng/mL (SI: >3300 nmol/L)

Dosage Forms POWDER: 5 g, 25 g. **SOLN, topical:** 4% [40 mg/mL] (4 mL, 10 mL); 10% [100 mg/mL] (4 mL, 10 mL)

♦ **Cocaine Hydrochloride** *see* Cocaine *on page 307*

♦ **Codafed® Expectorant** *see* Guaifenesin, Pseudoephedrine, and Codeine *on page 606*

♦ **Codafed® Pediatric Expectorant** *see* Guaifenesin, Pseudoephedrine, and Codeine *on page 606*

Codeine *(KOE deen)*

Related Information

Narcotic Agonists Comparison *on page 1395*

Synonyms Codeine Phosphate; Codeine Sulfate; Methylmorphine

Therapeutic Category Analgesic, Narcotic; Antitussive

Use Treatment of mild to moderate pain; antitussive in lower doses; dextromethorphan has equivalent antitussive activity but has much lower toxicity in accidental overdose

Restrictions C-II

Pregnancy Risk Factor C/D (prolonged use or high doses at term)

Contraindications Hypersensitivity to codeine or any component of the formulation; pregnancy (prolonged use or high doses at term)

Warnings/Precautions An opioid-containing analgesic regimen should be tailored to each patient's needs and based upon the type of pain being treated (acute versus chronic), the route of administration, degree of tolerance for opioids (naive versus chronic user), age, weight, and medical condition. The optimal analgesic dose varies widely among patients. Doses should be titrated to pain relief/prevention.

Use with caution in patients with hypersensitivity reactions to other phenanthrene derivative opioid agonists (morphine, hydrocodone, hydromorphone, levorphanol, oxycodone, oxymorphone); respiratory diseases including asthma, emphysema, COPD, or severe liver or renal insufficiency; some preparations contain sulfites which may cause allergic reactions; tolerance or drug dependence may result from extended use

Not recommended for use for cough control in patients with a productive cough; not recommended as an antitussive for children <2 years of age; the elderly may be particularly susceptible to the CNS depressant and confusion as well as constipating effects of narcotics

Not approved for I.V. administration (although this route has been used clinically). If given intravenously, must be given slowly and the patient should be lying down. Rapid intravenous administration of narcotics may increase the incidence of serious adverse effects, in part due to limited opportunity to assess response prior to administration of the full dose. Access to respiratory support should be immediately available.

Common Adverse Reactions

Frequency not defined: Increased AST, ALT

>10%:
  Central nervous system: Drowsiness
  Gastrointestinal: Constipation
1% to 10%:
  Cardiovascular: Tachycardia or bradycardia, hypotension
  Central nervous system: Dizziness, lightheadedness, false feeling of well being, malaise, headache, restlessness, paradoxical CNS stimulation, confusion
  Dermatologic: Rash, urticaria
  Gastrointestinal: Xerostomia, anorexia, nausea, vomiting
  Genitourinary: Decreased urination, ureteral spasm
  Hepatic: Increased LFTs
  Local: Burning at injection site
  Neuromuscular & skeletal: Weakness
  Ocular: Blurred vision
  Respiratory: Dyspnea
  Miscellaneous: Histamine release

Drug Interactions

Cytochrome P450 Effect: Substrate of CYP2D6 (major), 3A4 (minor); **Inhibits** CYP2D6 (weak)

Increased Effect/Toxicity: May cause severely increased toxicity of codeine when taken with CNS depressants, phenothiazines, tricyclic antidepressants, other narcotic analgesics, guanabenz, MAO inhibitors, and neuromuscular blockers.

Decreased Effect: CYP2D6 inhibitors may decrease the effects of codeine. Example inhibitors include chlorpromazine, delavirdine, fluoxetine, miconazole, paroxetine, pergolide, quinidine, quinine, ritonavir, and ropinirole. Decreased effect with cigarette smoking.

Mechanism of Action Binds to opiate receptors in the CNS, causing inhibition of ascending pain pathways, altering the perception of and response to pain; causes cough supression by direct central action in the medulla; produces generalized CNS depression

Pharmacodynamics/Kinetics
  Onset of action: Oral: 0.5-1 hour; I.M.: 10-30 minutes
    Peak effect: Oral: 1-1.5 hours; I.M.: 0.5-1 hour
  Duration: 4-6 hours
  Absorption: Oral: Adequate
  Distribution: Crosses placenta; enters breast milk
  Protein binding: 7%
  Metabolism: Hepatic to morphine (active)
  Half-life elimination: 2.5-3.5 hours
  Excretion: Urine (3% to 16% as unchanged drug, norcodeine, and free and conjugated morphine)

Dosage Note: These are guidelines and do not represent the maximum doses that may be required in all patients. Doses should be titrated to pain relief/prevention. Doses >1.5 mg/kg body weight are not recommended.
  Analgesic:
    Children: Oral, I.M., S.C.: 0.5-1 mg/kg/dose every 4-6 hours as needed; maximum: 60 mg/dose
    Adults:
      Oral: 30 mg every 4-6 hours as needed; patients with prior opiate exposure may require higher initial doses. Usual range: 15-120 mg every 4-6 hours as needed
      Oral, controlled release formulation (Codeine Contin®, not available in U.S.): 50-300 mg every 12 hours. **Note:** A patient's codeine requirement should be established using prompt release formulations; conversion to long acting products may be considered when chronic, continuous treatment is required. Higher dosages should be reserved for use only in opioid-tolerant patients.
      I.M., S.C.: 30 mg every 4-6 hours as needed; patients with prior opiate exposure may require higher initial doses. Usual range: 15-120 mg every 4-6 hours as needed; more frequent dosing may be needed
  Antitussive: Oral (for nonproductive cough):
    Children: 1-1.5 mg/kg/day in divided doses every 4-6 hours as needed: Alternative dose according to age:
      2-6 years: 2.5-5 mg every 4-6 hours as needed; maximum: 30 mg/day
      6-12 years: 5-10 mg every 4-6 hours as needed; maximum: 60 mg/day
    Adults: 10-20 mg/dose every 4-6 hours as needed; maximum: 120 mg/day

Dosing adjustment in renal impairment:
  Cl_{cr} 10-50 mL/minute: Administer 75% of dose
  Cl_{cr} <10 mL/minute: Administer 50% of dose

Dosing adjustment in hepatic impairment: Probably necessary in hepatic insufficiency

Administration Not approved for I.V. administration (although this route has been used clinically). If given intravenously, must be given slowly and the patient should be lying down. Rapid intravenous administration of narcotics may increase the incidence of serious adverse effects, in part due to limited opportunity to assess response prior to administration of the full dose. Access to respiratory support should be immediately available.

Monitoring Parameters Pain relief, respiratory and mental status, blood pressure, heart rate

Reference Range Therapeutic: Not established; Toxic: >1.1 µg/mL

Patient Information Avoid alcohol; may cause drowsiness, impaired judgment, or coordination; may cause physical and psychological dependence with prolonged use

Dosage Forms INJ, as phosphate: 15 mg/mL (2 mL); 30 mg/mL (2 mL). **SOLN, oral, as phosphate:** 15 mg/5 mL (5 mL, 500 mL). **TAB, controlled release:** (Codeine Contin®): 50 mg, 100 mg, 150 mg, 200 mg [not available in U.S.]. **TAB, as phosphate:** 30 mg, 60 mg. **TAB, as sulfate:** 15 mg, 30 mg, 60 mg.

- ◆ **Codeine and Acetaminophen** *see* Acetaminophen and Codeine *on page 25*
- ◆ **Codeine and Aspirin** *see* Aspirin and Codeine *on page 122*
- ◆ **Codeine and Guaifenesin** *see* Guaifenesin and Codeine *on page 604*
- ◆ **Codeine and Promethazine** *see* Promethazine and Codeine *on page 1048*
- ◆ **Codeine, Aspirin, and Carisoprodol** *see* Carisoprodol, Aspirin, and Codeine *on page 222*
- ◆ **Codeine, Chlorpheniramine, and Pseudoephedrine** *see* Chlorpheniramine, Pseudoephedrine, and Codeine *on page 265*
- ◆ **Codeine, Chlorpheniramine, Phenylephrine, and Potassium Iodide** *see* Chlorpheniramine, Phenylephrine, Codeine, and Potassium Iodide *on page 265*
- ◆ **Codeine, Guaifenesin, and Pseudoephedrine** *see* Guaifenesin, Pseudoephedrine, and Codeine *on page 606*
- ◆ **Codeine Phosphate** *see* Codeine *on page 308*
- ◆ **Codeine, Promethazine, and Phenylephrine** *see* Promethazine, Phenylephrine, and Codeine *on page 1048*
- ◆ **Codeine, Pseudoephedrine, and Triprolidine** *see* Triprolidine, Pseudoephedrine, and Codeine *on page 1274*
- ◆ **Codeine Sulfate** *see* Codeine *on page 308*
- ◆ **Codiclear® DH** *see* Hydrocodone and Guaifenesin *on page 630*
- ◆ **Cod Liver Oil** *see* Vitamin A and Vitamin D *on page 1311*
- ◆ **Cogentin®** *see* Benztropine *on page 155*
- ◆ **Co-Gesic®** *see* Hydrocodone and Acetaminophen *on page 627*
- ◆ **Cognex®** *see* Tacrine *on page 1180*
- ◆ **Colace® [OTC]** *see* Docusate *on page 398*
- ◆ **Colazal®** *see* Balsalazide *on page 145*
- ◆ **ColBenemid** *see* Colchicine and Probenecid *on page 311*

Colchicine (KOL chi seen)

Therapeutic Category Antigout Agent; Anti-inflammatory Agent

Use Treatment of acute gouty arthritis attacks and prevention of recurrences of such attacks

Unlabeled/Investigational Use Primary biliary cirrhosis; management of familial Mediterranean fever

Pregnancy Risk Factor C (oral); D (parenteral)

Contraindications Hypersensitivity to colchicine or any component of the formulation; serious renal, gastrointestinal, hepatic, or cardiac disorders; blood dyscrasias; pregnancy (parenteral)

Warnings/Precautions Severe local irritation can occur following S.C. or I.M. administration; use with caution in debilitated patients or elderly patients or patients with severe GI, renal, or liver disease

Common Adverse Reactions

>10%: Gastrointestinal: Nausea, vomiting, diarrhea, abdominal pain

1% to 10%:

Dermatologic: Alopecia

Gastrointestinal: Anorexia

Drug Interactions

Cytochrome P450 Effect: Substrate of CYP3A4 (major); **Induces** CYP2C8/9 (weak), 2E1 (weak), 3A4 (weak)

Increased Effect/Toxicity: Increased toxicity may be seen when taken with sympathomimetic agents or CNS depressant (effects are enhanced). Alkalizing agents potentiate effects of colchicine. CYP3A4 inhibitors may increase the levels/effects of colchicine; example inhibitors include azole antifungals, ciprofloxacin, clarithromycin, diclofenac, doxycycline, erythromycin, imatinib, isoniazid, nefazodone, nicardipine, propofol, protease inhibitors, quinidine, and verapamil.

Decreased Effect: Vitamin B_{12} absorption may be decreased with colchicine. Acidifying agents inhibit action of colchicine.

Mechanism of Action Decreases leukocyte motility, decreases phagocytosis in joints and lactic acid production, thereby reducing the deposition of urate crystals that perpetuates the inflammatory response

Pharmacodynamics/Kinetics

Onset of action: Oral: Pain relief: ~12 hours if adequately dosed

Distribution: Concentrates in leukocytes, kidney, spleen, and liver; does not distribute in heart, skeletal muscle, and brain

Protein binding: 10% to 31%

Metabolism: Partially hepatic via deacetylation

Half-life elimination: 12-30 minutes; End-stage renal disease: 45 minutes

Time to peak, serum: Oral: 0.5-2 hours, declining for the next 2 hours before increasing again due to enterohepatic recycling

Excretion: Primarily feces; urine (10% to 20%)

Dosage

Familial Mediterranean fever (unlabeled use): Prophylaxis: Oral:

Children:

≤5 years: 0.5 mg/day

>5 years: 1-1.5 mg/day in 2-3 divided doses

Adults: 1-2 mg daily in divided doses (occasionally reduced to 0.6 mg/day in patients with GI intolerance)

Gouty arthritis, acute attacks: Adults:

Oral: Initial: 0.6-1.2 mg, then 0.6 mg every 1-2 hours or 1.2 mg every 2 hours until relief or GI side effects (nausea, vomiting, or diarrhea) occur to a maximum total dose of 8 mg; wait 3 days before initiating another course of therapy

I.V.: Initial: 1-3 mg, then 0.5 mg every 6 hours until response, not to exceed total dose of 4 mg. If pain recurs, it may be necessary to administer additional daily doses; the amount of colchicine administered intravenously in an acute treatment period (generally ~1 week) should not exceed a total dose of 4 mg. Do not administer more colchicine by any route for at least 7 days after a full course of I.V. therapy (4 mg); transfer to oral colchicine in a dose similar to that being given I.V.

Gouty arthritis, prophylaxis of recurrent attacks: Adults: Oral: 0.6 mg/day or every other day; patients who are to undergo surgical procedures may receive 0.6 mg 3 times/day for 3 days before and 3 days after surgery

Primary biliary cirrhosis (unlabeled use): Adults: Oral: 0.6 mg twice daily

Dosing adjustment in renal impairment:

Cl_{cr} <50 mL/minute: Avoid chronic use or administration

Cl_{cr} <10 mL/minute: Decrease dose by 75% for treatment of acute attacks

Hemodialysis: Not dialyzable (0% to 5%); supplemental dose is not necessary

Peritoneal dialysis: Supplemental dose is not necessary

Administration

I.V.: Injection should be made over 2-5 minutes into tubing of free-flowing I.V. with compatible fluid. Do not administer I.M. or S.C.; severe local irritation can occur following S.C. or I.M. administration. Extravasation can cause tissue irritation.

Tablet: Administer orally with water and maintain adequate fluid intake.

Monitoring Parameters CBC and renal function test

Patient Information Avoid alcohol; discontinue if nausea or vomiting occurs; if taking for acute attack, discontinue as soon as pain resolves or if nausea, vomiting, or diarrhea occurs

Dosage Forms INJ, solution: 0.5 mg/mL (2 mL). **TAB:** 0.6 mg

Colchicine and Probenecid (KOL chi seen & proe BEN e sid)

Synonyms ColBenemid; Probenecid and Colchicine

Therapeutic Category Antigout Agent; Uricosuric Agent

Use Treatment of chronic gouty arthritis when complicated by frequent, recurrent acute attacks of gout

Pregnancy Risk Factor C

Dosage Adults: Oral: 1 tablet daily for 1 week, then 1 tablet twice daily thereafter

Dosage Forms TAB: Colchicine 0.5 mg and probenecid 0.5 g

♦ Cold-Eeze® [OTC] see Zinc Supplements on page 1327

Colesevelam (koh le SEV a lam)

Related Information

Lipid-Lowering Agents on page 1381

U.S. Brand Names WelChol®

Therapeutic Category Antilipemic Agent, Bile Acid Sequestrant

Use Adjunctive therapy to diet and exercise in the management of elevated LDL in primary hypercholesterolemia (Fredrickson type IIa) when used alone or in combination with an HMG-CoA reductase inhibitor

Pregnancy Risk Factor B

Contraindications Hypersensitivity to colesevelam or any component of the formulation; bowel obstruction

Warnings/Precautions Use caution in treating patients with serum triglyceride levels >300 mg/dL (excluded from trials). Safety and efficacy has not been established in pediatric patients. Use caution in dysphagia, swallowing disorders, severe GI motility disorders, major GI tract surgery, pregnancy, nursing mothers, and in patients susceptible to fat-soluble vitamin deficiencies (vitamins A,D,E and K). Minimal effects are seen on HDL-C and triglyceride levels. Secondary causes of hypercholesterolemia should be excluded before initiation.

Common Adverse Reactions

>10%: Gastrointestinal: Constipation (11%)

2% to 10%:

Gastrointestinal: Dyspepsia (8%)

Neuromuscular & skeletal: Weakness (4%), myalgia (2%)

Respiratory: Pharyngitis (3%)

Incidence less than or equal to placebo: Infection, headache, pain, back pain, abdominal pain, flu syndrome, flatulence, diarrhea, nausea, sinusitis, rhinitis, cough

Drug Interactions

Increased Effect/Toxicity: Refer to Decreased Effect.

Decreased Effect: Sustained-release verapamil AUC and C_{max} were reduced. Clinical significance unknown.

Digoxin, lovastatin, metoprolol, quinidine, valproic acid, or warfarin absorption was not significantly affected with concurrent administration.

Clinical effects of atorvastatin, lovastatin, and simvastatin were not changed by concurrent administration.

(Continued)

Colesevelam *(Continued)*

Mechanism of Action Colesevelam binds bile acids including glycocholic acid in the intestine, impeding their reabsorption. Increases the fecal loss of bile salt-bound LDL-C

Pharmacodynamics/Kinetics

Onset of action: Peak effect: Therapeutic: ~2 weeks

Absorption: Insignificant

Excretion: Urine (0.05%) after 1 month of chronic dosing

Dosage Adult: Oral:

Monotherapy: 3 tablets twice daily with meals or 6 tablets once daily with a meal; maximum dose: 7 tablets/day

Combination therapy with an HMG-CoA reductase inhibitor: 4-6 tablets daily; maximum dose: 6 tablets/day

Dosage adjustment in renal impairment: No recommendations made

Dosage adjustment in hepatic impairment: No recommendations made

Elderly: No recommendations made

Administration Administer with meal(s). Make sure patient understands dietary guidelines.

Monitoring Parameters Serum cholesterol, LDL, and triglyceride levels should be obtained before initiating treatment and periodically thereafter (in accordance with NCEP guidelines)

Patient Information Take with meals. Follow diet and exercise plan as recommended by prescriber.

Dosage Forms TAB, film coated: 625 mg

♦ **Colestid®** *see Colestipol on page 312*

Colestipol *(koe LES ti pole)*

Related Information

Lipid-Lowering Agents *on page 1381*

U.S. Brand Names Colestid®

Synonyms Colestipol Hydrochloride

Therapeutic Category Antilipemic Agent, Bile Acid Sequestrant

Use Adjunct in management of primary hypercholesterolemia; regression of arteriolosclerosis; relief of pruritus associated with elevated levels of bile acids; possibly used to decrease plasma half-life of digoxin in toxicity

Pregnancy Risk Factor C

Contraindications Hypersensitivity to bile acid sequestering resins or any component of the formulation; bowel obstruction

Warnings/Precautions Not to be taken simultaneously with many other medicines (decreased absorption). Avoid in patients with high triglycerides, GI dysfunction (constipation); fecal impaction may occur; hemorrhoids may be worsened. May be associated with increased bleeding tendency as a result of hypothrombinemia secondary to vitamin K deficiency; may cause depletion of vitamins A, D, and E, and folic acid.

Common Adverse Reactions

>10%: Gastrointestinal: Constipation

1% to 10%:

Central nervous system: Headache, dizziness, anxiety, vertigo, drowsiness, fatigue

Gastrointestinal: Abdominal pain and distention, belching, flatulence, nausea, vomiting, diarrhea

Drug Interactions

Decreased Effect: Colestipol can reduce the absorption of numerous medications when used concurrently. Give other medications 1 hour before or 4 hours after giving colestipol. Medications which may be affected include HMG-CoA reductase inhibitors, thiazide diuretics, propranolol (and potentially other beta-blockers), corticosteroids, thyroid hormones, digoxin, valproic acid, NSAIDs, loop diuretics, sulfonylureas, troglitazone (and potentially other agents in this class - pioglitazone and rosiglitazone).

Warfarin and other oral anticoagulants: Absorption is reduced by cholestyramine and may also be reduced by colestipol. Separate administration times (as detailed above).

Mechanism of Action Binds with bile acids to form an insoluble complex that is eliminated in feces; it thereby increases the fecal loss of bile acid-bound low density lipoprotein cholesterol

Pharmacodynamics/Kinetics

Absorption: None

Excretion: Feces

Dosage Adults: Oral:

Granules: 5-30 g/day given once or in divided doses 2-4 times/day; initial dose: 5 g 1-2 times/day; increase by 5 g at 1- to 2-month intervals

Tablets: 2-16 g/day; initial dose: 2 g 1-2 times/day; increase by 2 g at 1- to 2-month intervals

Administration Dry powder should be added to at least 90 mL of liquid and stirred until completely mixed; other drugs should be administered at least 1 hour before or 4 hours after colestipol

Patient Information Take granules in water or fruit juice (~90 mL) or sprinkled on food; swallow tablets whole with plenty of fluids; other drugs should not be taken at least 1 hour before or 4 hours after colestipol; rinse glass with small amount of liquid to ensure full dose is taken

Dosage Forms GRAN: 5 g/7.5 g (300 g, 450 g, 500 g); 5 g/7.5 g packet (60s). **TAB:** 1 g

♦ **Colestipol Hydrochloride** *see Colestipol on page 312*

Colistimethate (koe lis ti METH ate)

U.S. Brand Names Coly-Mycin® M

Synonyms Colistimethate Sodium

Therapeutic Category Antibiotic, Miscellaneous

Use Treatment of infections due to sensitive strains of certain gram-negative bacilli which are resistant to other antibacterials or in patients allergic to other antibacterials

Unlabeled/Investigational Use Used as inhalation in the prevention of *Pseudomonas aeruginosa* respiratory tract infections in immunocompromised patients, and used as inhalation adjunct agent for the treatment of *P. aeruginosa* infections in patients with cystic fibrosis and other seriously ill or chronically ill patients

Pregnancy Risk Factor C

Contraindications Hypersensitivity to colistimethate or any component of the formulation

Warnings/Precautions Use with caution in patients with pre-existing renal disease

Common Adverse Reactions 1% to 10%:

Central nervous system: Vertigo, slurring of speech

Dermatologic: Urticaria

Gastrointestinal: GI upset

Respiratory: Respiratory arrest

Renal: Nephrotoxicity

Drug Interactions

Increased Effect/Toxicity: Other nephrotoxic drugs, neuromuscular blocking agents.

Mechanism of Action Hydrolyzed to colistin, which acts as a cationic detergent which damages the bacterial cytoplasmic membrane causing leaking of intracellular substances and cell death

Pharmacodynamics/Kinetics

Distribution: Widely, except for CNS, synovial, pleural, and pericardial fluids

Half-life elimination: 1.5-8 hours; Anuria: ≤2-3 days

Time to peak: ~2 hours

Excretion: Primarily urine (as unchanged drug)

Dosage Children and Adults:

I.M., I.V.: 2.5-5 mg/kg/day in 2-4 divided doses

Inhalation: 50-75 mg in NS (3-4 mL total) via nebulizer 2-3 times/day

Dosing interval in renal impairment: Adults:

S_{cr} 0.7-1.2 mg/dL: 100-125 mg 2-4 times/day

S_{cr} 1.3-1.5 mg/dL: 75-115 mg twice daily

S_{cr} 1.6-2.5 mg/dL: 66-150 mg once or twice daily

S_{cr} 2.6-4 mg/dL: 100-150 mg every 36 hours

Administration

Parenteral: Reconstitute vial with 2 mL SWFI resulting in a concentration of 75 mg colistin/mL; swirl gently to avoid frothing. Administer by I.M., direct I.V. injection over 3-10 minutes, intermittent infusion over 30 minutes, or by continuous I.V. infusion. For continuous I.V. infusion, one-half of the total daily dose is administered by direct I.V. injection over 3-10 minutes followed 1-2 hours later by the remaining one-half of the total daily dose diluted in a compatible I.V. solution infused over 22-23 hours. The final concentration for administration should be based on the patient's fluid needs.

Inhalation: Further dilute dose to a total volume of 3-4 mL in NS and administer via nebulizer. If patient is on a ventilator, place medicine in a T-piece at the midinspiratory circuit of the ventilator.

Dosage Forms INJ, powder for reconstitution: 150 mg

♦ **Colistimethate Sodium** *see* Colistimethate *on page 313*

♦ **Colistin, Neomycin, Hydrocortisone, and Thonzonium** *see* Neomycin, Colistin, Hydrocortisone, and Thonzonium *on page 892*

♦ **Collagen** *see* Microfibrillar Collagen Hemostat *on page 836*

Collagenase (KOL la je nase)

U.S. Brand Names Santyl®

Therapeutic Category Enzyme, Topical Debridement

Use Promotes debridement of necrotic tissue in dermal ulcers and severe burns

Orphan drug: Injection: Treatment of Peyronie's disease; treatment of Dupytren's disease

Pregnancy Risk Factor C

Dosage Topical: Apply once daily (or more frequently if the dressing becomes soiled)

Dosage Forms OINT (Santyl®): 250 units/g (15 g, 30 g)

♦ **Colocort™** *see* Hydrocortisone *on page 632*

♦ **Colo-Fresh™ [OTC]** *see* Bismuth *on page 168*

♦ **Coly-Mycin® M** *see* Colistimethate *on page 313*

♦ **Coly-Mycin® S** *see* Neomycin, Colistin, Hydrocortisone, and Thonzonium *on page 892*

♦ **Colyte®** *see* Polyethylene Glycol-Electrolyte Solution *on page 1013*

♦ **CombiPatch®** *see* Estradiol and Norethindrone *on page 463*

♦ **Combipres® [DSC]** *see* Clonidine and Chlorthalidone *on page 301*

♦ **Combivent®** *see* Ipratropium and Albuterol *on page 686*

♦ **Combivir®** *see* Zidovudine and Lamivudine *on page 1326*

♦ **Comhist®** *see* Chlorpheniramine, Phenylephrine, and Phenyltoloxamine *on page 265*

♦ **Commit™ [OTC]** *see* Nicotine *on page 901*

♦ **Community-Acquired Pneumonia in Adults** *see page 1457*
♦ **Compazine**® *see Prochlorperazine on page 1042*
♦ **Compound E** *see Cortisone on page 314*
♦ **Compound F** *see Hydrocortisone on page 632*
♦ **Compound S** *see Zidovudine on page 1324*
♦ **Compound S, Abacavir, and Lamivudine** *see Abacavir, Lamivudine, and Zidovudine on page 19*
♦ **Compoz**® **Nighttime Sleep Aid [OTC]** *see DiphenhydrAMINE on page 383*
♦ **Compro**™ *see Prochlorperazine on page 1042*
♦ **Comtan**® *see Entacapone on page 435*
♦ **Comtrex**® **Maximum Strength Sinus and Nasal Decongestant [OTC]** *see Acetaminophen, Chlorpheniramine, and Pseudoephedrine on page 28*
♦ **Comtrex**® **Non-Drowsy Cold and Cough Relief [OTC]** *see Acetaminophen, Dextromethorphan, and Pseudoephedrine on page 28*
♦ **Comtrex**® **Sore Throat Maximum Strength [OTC]** *see Acetaminophen on page 24*
♦ **Comvax**® *see Haemophilus b Conjugate and Hepatitis B Vaccine on page 607*
♦ **Concerta**® *see Methylphenidate on page 822*
♦ **Congestac**® *see Guaifenesin and Pseudoephedrine on page 605*
♦ **Conjugated Estrogen and Methyltestosterone** *see Estrogens (Esterified) and Methyltestosterone on page 471*
♦ **Constilac**® *see Lactulose on page 712*
♦ **Constulose**® *see Lactulose on page 712*
♦ **Contac**® **Severe Cold and Flu/Non-Drowsy [OTC]** *see Acetaminophen, Dextromethorphan, and Pseudoephedrine on page 28*
♦ **Convulsive Status Epilepticus** *see page 1479*
♦ **Copaxone**® *see Glatiramer Acetate on page 589*
♦ **Copegus**™ *see Ribavirin on page 1091*
♦ **Copolymer-1** *see Glatiramer Acetate on page 589*
♦ **Cordarone**® *see Amiodarone on page 77*
♦ **Cordran**® *see Flurandrenolide on page 543*
♦ **Cordran**® **SP** *see Flurandrenolide on page 543*
♦ **Coreg**® *see Carvedilol on page 225*
♦ **Corgard**® *see Nadolol on page 873*
♦ **Coricidin HBP**® **Cold and Flu [OTC]** *see Chlorpheniramine and Acetaminophen on page 262*
♦ **Corlopam**® *see Fenoldopam on page 513*
♦ **Cormax**® *see Clobetasol on page 293*
♦ **CortaGel**® **Maximum Strength [OTC]** *see Hydrocortisone on page 632*
♦ **Cortaid**® **Intensive Therapy [OTC]** *see Hydrocortisone on page 632*
♦ **Cortaid**® **Maximum Strength [OTC]** *see Hydrocortisone on page 632*
♦ **Cortaid**® **Sensitive Skin With Aloe [OTC]** *see Hydrocortisone on page 632*
♦ **Cortef**® *see Hydrocortisone on page 632*
♦ **Corticool**® **[OTC]** *see Hydrocortisone on page 632*
♦ **Corticosteroids Comparison** *see page 1372*
♦ **Cortifoam**® *see Hydrocortisone on page 632*
♦ **Cortisol** *see Hydrocortisone on page 632*

Cortisone (KOR ti sone)

Related Information
Corticosteroids Comparison *on page 1372*

Synonyms Compound E; Cortisone Acetate

Therapeutic Category Anti-inflammatory Agent; Corticosteroid, Adrenal; Corticosteroid, Systemic; Diagnostic Agent, Adrenocortical Insufficiency; Glucocorticoid; Mineralocorticoid

Use Management of adrenocortical insufficiency

Pregnancy Risk Factor D

Contraindications Hypersensitivity to cortisone acetate or any component of the formulation; serious infections, except septic shock or tuberculous meningitis; administration of live virus vaccines; pregnancy

Warnings/Precautions Use with caution in patients with hypothyroidism, cirrhosis, hypertension, CHF, ulcerative colitis, thromboembolic disorders, osteoporosis, convulsive disorders, peptic ulcer, diabetes mellitus, myasthenia gravis; prolonged therapy (>5 days) of pharmacologic doses of corticosteroids may lead to hypothalamic-pituitary-adrenal suppression, the degree of adrenal suppression varies with the degree and duration of glucocorticoid therapy; this must be taken into consideration when taking patients off steroids

Common Adverse Reactions
>10%:
Central nervous system: Insomnia, nervousness
Gastrointestinal: Increased appetite, indigestion
1% to 10%:
Dermatologic: Hirsutism
Endocrine & metabolic: Diabetes mellitus
Neuromuscular & skeletal: Arthralgia

Ocular: Cataracts, glaucoma
Respiratory: Epistaxis

Drug Interactions

Increased Effect/Toxicity: Estrogens may increase cortisone effects. Cortisone may increase ulcerogenic potential of NSAIDs, and may increase potassium deletion due to diuretics.

Decreased Effect: Enzyme inducers (barbiturates, phenytoin, rifampin) may decrease cortisone effects. Effect of live virus vaccines may be decreased. Anticholinesterase agents may decrease effect of cortisone.

Cortisone may decrease effects of warfarin and salicylates.

Mechanism of Action Decreases inflammation by suppression of migration of polymorphonuclear leukocytes and reversal of increased capillary permeability

Pharmacodynamics/Kinetics

Onset of action: Peak effect: Oral: ~2 hours; I.M.: 20-48 hours
Duration: 30-36 hours
Absorption: Slow
Distribution: Muscles, liver, skin, intestines, and kidneys; crosses placenta; enters breast milk
Metabolism: Hepatic to inactive metabolites
Half-life elimination: 0.5-2 hours; End-stage renal disease: 3.5 hours
Excretion: Urine and feces

Dosage If possible, administer glucocorticoids before 9 AM to minimize adrenocortical suppression; dosing depends upon the condition being treated and the response of the patient; **Note:** Supplemental doses may be warranted during times of stress in the course of withdrawing therapy

Children:
Anti-inflammatory or immunosuppressive: Oral: 2.5-10 mg/kg/day **or** 20-300 mg/m^2/day in divided doses every 6-8 hours
Physiologic replacement: Oral: 0.5-0.75 mg/kg/day **or** 20-25 mg/m^2/day in divided doses every 8 hours

Adults:
Anti-inflammatory or immunosuppressive: Oral: 25-300 mg/day in divided doses every 12-24 hours
Physiologic replacement: Oral: 25-35 mg/day
Hemodialysis: Supplemental dose is not necessary
Peritoneal dialysis: Supplemental dose is not necessary

Administration Insoluble in water.

Patient Information Take with meals or take with food or milk. Do not discontinue drug without notifying prescriber.

Dosage Forms TAB: 25 mg

- ◆ **Cortisone Acetate** see Cortisone on page 314
- ◆ **Cortisporin® Cream** see Neomycin, Polymyxin B, and Hydrocortisone on page 892
- ◆ **Cortisporin® Ointment** see Bacitracin, Neomycin, Polymyxin B, and Hydrocortisone on page 144
- ◆ **Cortisporin® Ophthalmic** see Neomycin, Polymyxin B, and Hydrocortisone on page 892
- ◆ **Cortisporin® Otic** see Neomycin, Polymyxin B, and Hydrocortisone on page 892
- ◆ **Cortisporin®-TC** see Neomycin, Colistin, Hydrocortisone, and Thonzonium on page 892
- ◆ **Cortizone®-5 [OTC]** see Hydrocortisone on page 632
- ◆ **Cortizone®-10 Maximum Strength [OTC]** see Hydrocortisone on page 632
- ◆ **Cortizone®-10 Plus Maximum Strength [OTC]** see Hydrocortisone on page 632
- ◆ **Cortizone® 10 Quick Shot [OTC]** see Hydrocortisone on page 632
- ◆ **Cortizone® for Kids [OTC]** see Hydrocortisone on page 632
- ◆ **Cortrosyn** see Cosyntropin on page 315
- ◆ **Corvert®** see Ibutilide on page 647
- ◆ **Cosmegen®** see Dactinomycin on page 334
- ◆ **Cosopt®** see Dorzolamide and Timolol on page 404

Cosyntropin (koe sin TROE pin)

U.S. Brand Names Cortrosyn®

Synonyms Synacthen; Tetracosactide

Therapeutic Category Diagnostic Agent, Adrenocortical Insufficiency

Use Diagnostic test to differentiate primary adrenal from secondary (pituitary) adrenocortical insufficiency

Pregnancy Risk Factor C

Contraindications Hypersensitivity to cosyntropin or any component of the formulation

Warnings/Precautions Use with caution in patients with pre-existing allergic disease or a history of allergic reactions to corticotropin.

Common Adverse Reactions Frequency not defined.
Cardiovascular: Bradycardia, hypertension, peripheral edema, tachycardia
Dermatologic: Rash
Local: Whealing with redness at the injection site
Miscellaneous: Anaphylaxis, hypersensitivity reaction

Mechanism of Action Stimulates the adrenal cortex to secrete adrenal steroids (including hydrocortisone, cortisone), androgenic substances, and a small amount of aldosterone
(Continued)

Cosyntropin *(Continued)*

Pharmacodynamics/Kinetics Time to peak, serum: I.M., IVP: ~1 hour; plasma cortisol levels rise in healthy individuals within 5 minutes

Dosage

Adrenocortical insufficiency: I.M., I.V. (over 2 minutes): Peak plasma cortisol concentrations usually occur 45-60 minutes after cosyntropin administration

Children <2 years: 0.125 mg

Children >2 years and Adults: 0.25-0.75 mg

When greater cortisol stimulation is needed, an I.V. infusion may be used:

Children >2 years and Adults: 0.25 mg administered at 0.04 mg/hour over 6 hours

Administration Administer I.V. doses over 2 minutes

Reference Range Normal baseline cortisol; increase in serum cortisol after cosyntropin injection of >7 µg/dL or peak response >18 µg/dL; plasma cortisol concentrations should be measured immediately before and exactly 30 minutes after a dose

Dosage Forms INJ, powder for reconstitution: 0.25 mg

- ◆ **Co-Trimoxazole** *see* Sulfamethoxazole and Trimethoprim *on page 1173*
- ◆ **Coumadin**® *see* Warfarin *on page 1315*
- ◆ **Covera-HS**® *see* Verapamil *on page 1302*
- ◆ **Co-Vidarabine** *see* Pentostatin *on page 980*
- ◆ **Coviracil** *see* Emtricitabine *on page 428*
- ◆ **Cozaar**® *see* Losartan *on page 762*
- ◆ **CP-99,219-27** *see* Trovafloxacin *on page 1277*
- ◆ **C-Phed Tannate** *see* Chlorpheniramine and Pseudoephedrine *on page 263*
- ◆ **CPM** *see* Cyclophosphamide *on page 320*
- ◆ **CPT-11** *see* Irinotecan *on page 687*
- ◆ **CPZ** *see* ChlorproMAZINE *on page 266*
- ◆ **Creon**® *see* Pancrelipase *on page 953*
- ◆ **Crestor**® *see* Rosuvastatin *on page 1118*
- ◆ **Crinone**® *see* Progesterone *on page 1044*
- ◆ **Crixivan**® *see* Indinavir *on page 662*
- ◆ **Crolom**® *see* Cromolyn *on page 316*
- ◆ **Cromoglycic Acid** *see* Cromolyn *on page 316*

Cromolyn *(KROE moe lin)*

U.S. Brand Names Crolom®; Gastrocrom®; Intal®; Nasalcrom® [OTC]; Opticrom®

Synonyms Cromoglycic Acid; Cromolyn Sodium; Disodium Cromoglycate; DSCG

Therapeutic Category Antiallergic, Inhalation; Antiallergic, Ophthalmic

Use

Inhalation: May be used as an adjunct in the prophylaxis of allergic disorders, including asthma; prevention of exercise-induced bronchospasm

Nasal: Prevention and treatment of seasonal and perennial allergic rhinitis

Oral: Systemic mastocytosis

Ophthalmic: Treatment of vernal keratoconjunctivitis, vernal conjunctivitis, and vernal keratitis

Unlabeled/Investigational Use Oral: Food allergy, treatment of inflammatory bowel disease

Pregnancy Risk Factor B

Contraindications Hypersensitivity to cromolyn or any component of the formulation; acute asthma attacks

Warnings/Precautions Severe anaphylactic reactions may occur rarely; cromolyn is a prophylactic drug with no benefit for acute situations; caution should be used when withdrawing the drug or tapering the dose as symptoms may reoccur; use with caution in patients with a history of cardiac arrhythmias. Transient burning or stinging may occur with ophthalmic use. Dosage of oral product should be decreased with hepatic or renal dysfunction.

Common Adverse Reactions

Inhalation: >10%: Gastrointestinal: Unpleasant taste in mouth

Nasal:

>10%: Respiratory: Increase in sneezing, burning, stinging, or irritation inside of nose

1% to 10%:

Central nervous system: Headache

Gastrointestinal: Unpleasant taste

Respiratory: Hoarseness, coughing, postnasal drip

<1% (Limited to important or life-threatening): Anaphylactic reactions, epistaxis

Ophthalmic: Frequency not defined:

Ocular: Conjunctival injection, dryness around the eye, edema, eye irritation, immediate hypersensitivity reactions, itchy eyes, puffy eyes, styes, rash, watery eyes

Respiratory: Dyspnea

Systemic: Frequency not defined:

Cardiovascular: Angioedema, chest pain, edema, flushing, palpitations, premature ventricular contractions, tachycardia

Central nervous system: Anxiety, behavior changes, convulsions, depression, dizziness, fatigue, hallucinations, headache, irritability, insomnia, lethargy, migraine, nervousness, hypoesthesia, postprandial lightheadedness, psychosis

Dermatologic: Erythema, photosensitivity, pruritus, purpura, rash, urticaria

Gastrointestinal: Abdominal pain, constipation, diarrhea, dyspepsia, dysphagia, esophago-spasm, flatulence, glossitis, nausea, stomatitis, unpleasant taste, vomiting

Genitourinary: Dysuria, urinary frequency

Hematologic: Neutropenia, pancytopenia, polycythemia

Hepatic: Liver function test abnormal

Local: Burning

Neuromuscular & skeletal: Arthralgia, leg stiffness, leg weakness, myalgia, paresthesia

Otic: Tinnitus

Respiratory: Dyspnea, pharyngitis

Miscellaneous: Lupus erythematosus

Mechanism of Action Prevents the mast cell release of histamine, leukotrienes and slow-reacting substance of anaphylaxis by inhibiting degranulation after contact with antigens

Pharmacodynamics/Kinetics

Onset: Response to treatment:

Nasal spray: May occur at 1-2 weeks

Ophthalmic: May be seen within a few days; treatment for up to 6 weeks is often required

Oral: May occur within 2-6 weeks

Absorption:

Inhalation: ~8% reaches lungs upon inhalation; well absorbed

Oral: <1% of dose absorbed

Half-life elimination: 80-90 minutes

Time to peak, serum: Inhalation: ~15 minutes

Excretion: Urine and feces (equal amounts as unchanged drug); exhaled gases (small amounts)

Dosage

Oral:

Systemic mastocytosis:

Children 2-12 years: 100 mg 4 times/day; not to exceed 40 mg/kg/day; given $1/2$ hour prior to meals and at bedtime

Children >12 years and Adults: 200 mg 4 times/day; given $1/2$ hour prior to meals and at bedtime; if control of symptoms is not seen within 2-3 weeks, dose may be increased to a maximum 40 mg/kg/day

Food allergy and inflammatory bowel disease (unlabeled use):

Children <2 years: Not recommended

Children 2-12 years: Initial dose: 100 mg 4 times/day; may double the dose if effect is not satisfactory within 2-3 weeks; not to exceed 40 mg/kg/day

Children >12 years and Adults: Initial dose: 200 mg 4 times/day; may double the dose if effect is not satisfactory within 2-3 weeks; up to 400 mg 4 times/day

Note: Once desired effect is achieved, dose may be tapered to lowest effective dose

Inhalation:

For chronic control of asthma, taper frequency to the lowest effective dose (ie, 4 times/day to 3 times/day to twice daily):

Nebulization solution: Children >2 years and Adults: Initial: 20 mg 4 times/day; usual dose: 20 mg 3-4 times/day

Metered spray:

Children 5-12 years: Initial: 2 inhalations 4 times/day; usual dose: 1-2 inhalations 3-4 times/day

Children ≥12 years and Adults: Initial: 2 inhalations 4 times/day; usual dose: 2-4 inhalations 3-4 times/day

Prevention of allergen- or exercise-induced bronchospasm: Administer 10-15 minutes prior to exercise or allergen exposure but no longer than 1 hour before:

Nebulization solution: Children >2 years and Adults: Single dose of 20 mg

Metered spray: Children >5 years and Adults: Single dose of 2 inhalations

Ophthalmic: Children >4 years and Adults: 1-2 drops in each eye 4-6 times/day

Nasal: Allergic rhinitis (treatment and prophylaxis): Children ≥2 years and Adults: 1 spray into each nostril 3-4 times/day; may be increased to 6 times/day (symptomatic relief may require 2-4 weeks)

Dosage adjustment in renal/hepatic impairment: Specific guidelines not available; consider lower dose of oral product.

Administration

Oral concentrate: Open ampul and squeeze contents into glass of water; stir well; administer at least 30 minutes before meals and at bedtime

Oral inhalation: Shake canister gently before use; do not immerse canister in water.

Nasal inhalation: Clear nasal passages by blowing nose prior to use.

Monitoring Parameters Periodic pulmonary function tests

Patient Information Do not discontinue abruptly; not effective for acute relief of symptoms; must be taken on a regularly scheduled basis

Dosage Forms SOLN, nebulization (Intal®): 20 mg/2 mL (60s, 120s). **SOLN, ophthalmic** (Crolom®, Opticrom®): 4% (10 mL). **SOLN, oral** (Gastrocrom®): 100 mg/5 mL (96s). **SPRAY, intranasal:** (Nasalcrom®): 40 mg/mL (13 mL, 26 mL). **SPRAY, oral inhalation** (Intal®): 800 mcg/inhalation (8.1 g, 14.2 g)

♦ **Cromolyn Sodium** see Cromolyn on page 316

Crotamiton (kroe TAM i tonn)

U.S. Brand Names Eurax®

Therapeutic Category Scabicidal Agent

(Continued)

Crotamiton *(Continued)*

Use Treatment of scabies (*Sarcoptes scabiei*) and symptomatic treatment of pruritus

Pregnancy Risk Factor C

Contraindications Hypersensitivity to crotamiton or any component of the formulation; patients who manifest a primary irritation response to topical medications

Warnings/Precautions Avoid contact with face, eyes, mucous membranes, and urethral meatus; do not apply to acutely inflamed or raw skin; for external use only

Common Adverse Reactions Frequency not defined. Topical:
Dermatologic: Pruritus, contact dermatitis, rash
Local: Local irritation
Miscellaneous: Allergic sensitivity reactions, warm sensation

Mechanism of Action Crotamiton has scabicidal activity against *Sarcoptes scabiei*; mechanism of action unknown

Dosage Topical:
Scabicide: Children and Adults: Wash thoroughly and scrub away loose scales, then towel dry; apply a thin layer and massage drug onto skin of the entire body from the neck to the toes (with special attention to skin folds, creases, and interdigital spaces). Repeat application in 24 hours. Take a cleansing bath 48 hours after the final application. Treatment may be repeated after 7-10 days if live mites are still present.
Pruritus: Massage into affected areas until medication is completely absorbed; repeat as necessary

Patient Information For topical use only; all contaminated clothing and bed linens should be washed to avoid reinfestation

Dosage Forms CRM: 10% (60 g). LOTION: 10% (60 mL, 480 mL)

♦ **Cruex® Cream [OTC]** *see* Clotrimazole *on page 304*
♦ **Cryselle™** *see* Ethinyl Estradiol and Norgestrel *on page 492*
♦ **Crystalline Penicillin** *see* Penicillin G (Parenteral/Aqueous) *on page 973*
♦ **Crystal Violet** *see* Gentian Violet *on page 588*
♦ **CsA** *see* CycloSPORINE *on page 323*
♦ **CTX** *see* Cyclophosphamide *on page 320*
♦ **Cubicin™** *see* Daptomycin *on page 342*
♦ **Cuprimine®** *see* Penicillamine *on page 970*
♦ **Cutivate®** *see* Fluticasone *on page 547*
♦ **CyA** *see* CycloSPORINE *on page 323*

Cyanocobalamin *(sye an oh koe BAL a min)*

U.S. Brand Names Nascobal®

Synonyms Vitamin B$_{12}$

Therapeutic Category Vitamin, Water Soluble

Use Treatment of pernicious anemia; vitamin B$_{12}$ deficiency; increased B$_{12}$ requirements due to pregnancy, thyrotoxicosis, hemorrhage, malignancy, liver or kidney disease

Pregnancy Risk Factor A/C (dose exceeding RDA recommendation); C (nasal gel)

Contraindications Hypersensitivity to cyanocobalamin or any component of the formulation, cobalt; hereditary optic nerve atrophy, Leber's disease

Warnings/Precautions I.M. route used to treat pernicious anemia; vitamin B$_{12}$ deficiency for >3 months results in irreversible degenerative CNS lesions; treatment of vitamin B$_{12}$ megaloblastic anemia may result in severe hypokalemia, sometimes, fatal, when anemia corrects due to cellular potassium requirements. B$_{12}$ deficiency masks signs of polycythemia vera; vegetarian diets may result in B$_{12}$ deficiency; pernicious anemia occurs more often in gastric carcinoma than in general population. Patients with Leber's disease may suffer rapid optic atrophy when treated with vitamin B$_{12}$.

Common Adverse Reactions
1% to 10%:
Central nervous system: Headache (2% to 11%), anxiety, dizziness, pain, nervousness, hypoesthesia
Dermatologic: Itching
Gastrointestinal: Sore throat, nausea and vomiting, dyspepsia, diarrhea
Neuromuscular & skeletal: Weakness (1% to 4%), back pain, arthritis, myalgia, paresthesia, abnormal gait
Respiratory: Dyspnea, rhinitis

Drug Interactions
Decreased Effect: Ethanol decreases B$_{12}$ absorption. Chloramphenicol, cholestyramine, cimetidine, colchicine, neomycin, PAS, and potassium may reduce absorption and/or effect of cyanocobalamin.

Mechanism of Action Coenzyme for various metabolic functions, including fat and carbohydrate metabolism and protein synthesis, used in cell replication and hematopoiesis

Pharmacodynamics/Kinetics
Absorption: From the terminal ileum in presence of calcium; gastric "intrinsic factor" must be present to transport the compound across the intestinal mucosa
Distribution: Principally stored in the liver, also stored in the kidneys and adrenals
Protein binding: To transcobalamin II
Metabolism: Converted in tissues to active coenzymes, methylcobalamin and deoxyadenosylcobalamin

Dosage
Recommended daily allowance (RDA):
Children: 0.3-2 mcg
Adults: 2 mcg
Nutritional deficiency:
Intranasal gel: 500 mcg once weekly
Oral: 25-250 mcg/day
Anemias: I.M. or deep S.C. (oral is not generally recommended due to poor absorption and I.V. is not recommended due to more rapid elimination):
Pernicious anemia, congenital (if evidence of neurologic involvement): 1000 mcg/day for at least 2 weeks; maintenance: 50-100 mcg/month or 100 mcg for 6-7 days; if there is clinical improvement, give 100 mcg every other day for 7 doses, then every 3-4 days for 2-3 weeks; follow with 100 mcg/month for life. Administer with folic acid if needed.
Children: 30-50 mcg/day for 2 or more weeks (to a total dose of 1000-5000 mcg), then follow with 100 mcg/month as maintenance dosage
Adults: 100 mcg/day for 6-7 days; if improvement, administer same dose on alternate days for 7 doses; then every 3-4 days for 2-3 weeks; once hematologic values have returned to normal, maintenance dosage: 100 mcg/month. **Note:** Use only parenteral therapy as oral therapy is not dependable.
Hematologic remission (without evidence of nervous system involvement): Intranasal gel: 500 mcg once weekly
Vitamin B_{12} deficiency:
Children:
Neurologic signs: 100 mcg/day for 10-15 days (total dose of 1-1.5 mg), then once or twice weekly for several months; may taper to 60 mcg every month
Hematologic signs: 10-50 mcg/day for 5-10 days, followed by 100-250 mcg/dose every 2-4 weeks
Adults: Initial: 30 mcg/day for 5-10 days; maintenance: 100-200 mcg/month
Schilling test: I.M.: 1000 mcg
Administration I.M. or deep S.C. are preferred routes of administration
Monitoring Parameters Serum potassium, erythrocyte and reticulocyte count, hemoglobin, hematocrit
Reference Range Normal range of serum B_{12} is 150-750 pg/mL; this represents 0.1% of total body content. Metabolic requirements are 2-5 µg/day; years of deficiency required before hematologic and neurologic signs and symptoms are seen. Occasional patients with significant neuropsychiatric abnormalities may have no hematologic abnormalities and normal serum cobalamin levels, 200 pg/mL (SI: >150 pmol/L), or more commonly between 100-200 pg/mL (SI: 75-150 pmol/L). There exists evidence that people, particularly elderly whose serum cobalamin concentrations <300 pg/mL, should receive replacement parenteral therapy; this recommendation is based upon neuropsychiatric disorders and cardiovascular disorders associated with lower sodium cobalamin concentrations.
Patient Information Pernicious anemia may require monthly injections for life
Dosage Forms GEL, intranasal (Nascobal®): 500 mcg/0.1 mL (2.3 mL). **INJ, solution:** 1000 mcg/mL (1 mL, 10 mL, 30 mL). **LOZ [OTC]:** 100 mcg, 250 mcg, 500 mcg. **TAB [OTC]:** 50 mcg, 100 mcg, 250 mcg, 500 mcg, 1000 mcg. **TAB, extended release [OTC]:** 1500 mcg. **TAB, sublingual [OTC]:** 2500 mcg

♦ **Cyanocobalamin, Folic Acid, and Pyridoxine** see Folic Acid, Cyanocobalamin, and Pyridoxine on page 555
♦ **Cyclessa®** see Ethinyl Estradiol and Desogestrel on page 477

Cyclobenzaprine (sye kloe BEN za preen)
U.S. Brand Names Flexeril®
Synonyms Cyclobenzaprine Hydrochloride
Therapeutic Category Skeletal Muscle Relaxant
Use Treatment of muscle spasm associated with acute painful musculoskeletal conditions
Pregnancy Risk Factor B
Contraindications Hypersensitivity to cyclobenzaprine or any component of the formulation; do not use concomitantly or within 14 days of MAO inhibitors; hyperthyroidism; congestive heart failure; arrhythmias; acute recovery phase of MI
Warnings/Precautions Cyclobenzaprine shares the toxic potentials of the tricyclic antidepressants and the usual precautions of tricyclic antidepressant therapy should be observed; use with caution in patients with urinary hesitancy, angle-closure glaucoma, hepatic impairment, or in the elderly. Do not use concomitantly or within 14 days after MAO inhibitors; combination may cause hypertensive crisis, severe convulsions. Safety and efficacy have not been established in patients <15 years of age.
Common Adverse Reactions
>10%:
Central nervous system: Drowsiness (29% to 39%), dizziness (1% to 11%)
Gastrointestinal: Xerostomia (21% to 32%)
1% to 10%:
Central nervous system: Fatigue (1% to 6%), confusion (1% to 3%), headache (1% to 3%), irritability (1% to 3%), mental acuity decreased (1% to 3%), nervousness (1% to 3%)
Gastrointestinal: Abdominal pain (1% to 3%), constipation (1% to 3%), diarrhea (1% to 3%), dyspepsia (1% to 3%), nausea (1% to 3%)
Neuromuscular & skeletal: Muscle weakness (1% to 3%)
Ocular: Blurred vision (1% to 3%)
(Continued)

Cyclobenzaprine *(Continued)*

Respiratory: Pharyngitis (1% to 3%)

Drug Interactions

Cytochrome P450 Effect: Substrate of CYP1A2 (major), 2D6 (minor), 3A4 (minor)

Increased Effect/Toxicity: CYP1A2 inhibitors may increase the levels/effects of cyclobenzaprine; example inhibitors include amiodarone, ciprofloxacin, fluvoxamine, ketoconazole, lomefloxacin, ofloxacin, and rofecoxib. Because of cyclobenzaprine's similarities to the tricyclic antidepressants, there may be additive toxicities and side effects similar to tricyclic antidepressants. Cyclobenzaprine's toxicity may also be additive with other agents with anticholinergic properties. Cyclobenzaprine may enhance effects of CNS depressants. Do not use concomitantly or within 14 days of MAO inhibitors. Tramadol may increase risk of seizure; effect seen with tricyclic antidepressants and tramadol.

Decreased Effect: Cyclobenzaprine may decrease effect of guanethidine; effect seen with tricyclic antidepressants and guanethidine

Mechanism of Action Centrally-acting skeletal muscle relaxant pharmacologically related to tricyclic antidepressants; reduces tonic somatic motor activity influencing both alpha and gamma motor neurons

Pharmacodynamics/Kinetics

Onset of action: ~1 hour

Duration: 12-24 hours

Absorption: Complete

Metabolism: Hepatic via CYP3A4, 1A2, and 2D6; may undergo enterohepatic recirculation

Bioavailability: 33% to 55%

Half-life elimination: 18 hours (range: 8-37 hours)

Time to peak, serum: 3-8 hours

Excretion: Urine (as inactive metabolites); feces (as unchanged drug)

Dosage Oral: **Note:** Do not use longer than 2-3 weeks

Adults: Initial: 5 mg 3 times/day; may increase to 10 mg 3 times/day if needed

Elderly: 5 mg 3 times/day; plasma concentration and incidence of adverse effects are increased in the elderly; dose should be titrated slowly

Dosage adjustment in hepatic impairment:

Mild: 5 mg 3 times/day; use with caution and titrate slowly

Moderate to severe: Use not recommended

Patient Information Drug may impair ability to perform hazardous activities requiring mental alertness or physical coordination, such as operating machinery or driving a motor vehicle

Dosage Forms TAB: 10 mg; (Flexeril®) 5 mg, 10 mg

♦ **Cyclobenzaprine Hydrochloride** *see* Cyclobenzaprine *on page 319*

♦ **Cyclocort®** *see* Amcinonide *on page 70*

♦ **Cyclogyl®** *see* Cyclopentolate *on page 320*

♦ **Cyclomydril®** *see* Cyclopentolate and Phenylephrine *on page 320*

Cyclopentolate *(sye kloe PEN toe late)*

Related Information

Cycloplegic Mydriatics Comparison *on page 1375*

U.S. Brand Names AK-Pentolate®; Cyclogyl®; Cylate®

Synonyms Cyclopentolate Hydrochloride

Therapeutic Category Anticholinergic Agent, Ophthalmic

Use Diagnostic procedures requiring mydriasis and cycloplegia

Pregnancy Risk Factor C

Dosage Ophthalmic:

Neonates and Infants: **Note:** Cyclopentolate and phenylephrine combination formulation is the preferred agent for use in neonates and infants due to lower cyclopentolate concentration and reduced risk for systemic reactions

Children: Instill 1 drop of 0.5%, 1%, or 2% in eye followed by 1 drop of 0.5% or 1% in 5 minutes, if necessary

Adults: Instill 1 drop of 1% followed by another drop in 5 minutes; 2% solution in heavily pigmented iris

Dosage Forms SOLN, ophthalmic: 1% (2 mL, 15 mL); (AK-Pentolate®, Cylate®): 1% (2 mL, 15 mL); (Cyclogyl®): 0.5% (15 mL); 1% (2 mL, 5 mL, 15 mL); 2% (2 mL, 5 mL, 15 mL)

Cyclopentolate and Phenylephrine *(sye kloe PEN toe late & fen il EF rin)*

U.S. Brand Names Cyclomydril®

Synonyms Phenylephrine and Cyclopentolate

Therapeutic Category Anticholinergic/Adrenergic Agonist

Use Induce mydriasis greater than that produced with cyclopentolate HCl alone

Pregnancy Risk Factor C

Dosage Ophthalmic: Neonates, Infants, Children, and Adults: Instill 1 drop into the eye every 5-10 minutes, for up to 3 doses, approximately 40-50 minutes before the examination

Dosage Forms SOLN, ophthalmic: Cyclopentolate 0.2% and phenylephrine 1% (2 mL, 5 mL)

♦ **Cyclopentolate Hydrochloride** *see* Cyclopentolate *on page 320*

Cyclophosphamide *(sye kloe FOS fa mide)*

U.S. Brand Names Cytoxan®; Neosar®

Synonyms CPM; CTX; CYT; NSC-26271

Therapeutic Category Antineoplastic Agent, Alkylating Agent

Use

Oncologic: Treatment of Hodgkin's and non-Hodgkin's lymphoma, Burkitt's lymphoma, chronic lymphocytic leukemia (CLL), chronic myelocytic leukemia (CML), acute myelocytic leukemia (AML), acute lymphocytic leukemia (ALL), mycosis fungoides, multiple myeloma, neuroblastoma, retinoblastoma, rhabdomyosarcoma, Ewing's sarcoma; breast, testicular, endometrial, ovarian, and lung cancers, and in conditioning regimens for bone marrow transplantation

Nononcologic: Prophylaxis of rejection for kidney, heart, liver, and bone marrow transplants, severe rheumatoid disorders, nephrotic syndrome, Wegener's granulomatosis, idiopathic pulmonary hemosideroses, myasthenia gravis, multiple sclerosis, systemic lupus erythematosus, lupus nephritis, autoimmune hemolytic anemia, idiopathic thrombocytic purpura (ITP), macroglobulinemia, and antibody-induced pure red cell aplasia

Pregnancy Risk Factor D

Contraindications Hypersensitivity to cyclophosphamide or any component of the formulation; pregnancy

Warnings/Precautions The U.S. Food and Drug Administration (FDA) currently recommends that procedures for proper handling and disposal of antineoplastic agents be considered. Possible dosage adjustment needed for renal or hepatic failure; use with caution in patients with bone marrow suppression.

Common Adverse Reactions

>10%:

Dermatologic: Alopecia (40% to 60%) but hair will usually regrow although it may be a different color and/or texture. Hair loss usually begins 3-6 weeks after the start of therapy.

Endocrine & metabolic: Fertility: May cause sterility; interferes with oogenesis and spermatogenesis; may be irreversible in some patients; gonadal suppression (amenorrhea)

Gastrointestinal: Nausea and vomiting occur more frequently with larger doses, usually beginning 6-10 hours after administration; anorexia, diarrhea, mucositis, and stomatitis are also seen

Genitourinary: Severe, potentially fatal acute hemorrhagic cystitis, believed to be a result of chemical irritation of the bladder by acrolein, a cyclophosphamide metabolite, occurs in 7% to 12% of patients and has been reported in up to 40% of patients in some series. Patients should be encouraged to drink plenty of fluids during therapy (most adults will require at least 2 L/day), void frequently, and avoid taking the drug at night. With large I.V. doses, I.V. hydration is usually recommended. The use of mesna and/or continuous bladder irrigation is rarely needed for doses <2 g/m^2.

Hematologic: Thrombocytopenia and anemia are less common than leukopenia

Onset: 7 days

Nadir: 10-14 days

Recovery: 21 days

1% to 10%:

Cardiovascular: Facial flushing

Central nervous system: Headache

Dermatologic: Skin rash

Renal: SIADH may occur, usually with doses >50 mg/kg (or 1 g/m^2); renal tubular necrosis, which usually resolves with discontinuation of the drug, is also reported

Respiratory: Nasal congestion occurs when I.V. doses are administered too rapidly (large doses via 30-60 minute infusion); patients experience runny eyes, rhinorrhea, sinus congestion, and sneezing during or immediately after the infusion. If needed, a decongestant or decongestant/antihistamine (eg, pseudoephedrine or pseudoephedrine/triprolidine) can be used to prevent or relieve these symptoms.

Drug Interactions

Cytochrome P450 Effect: Substrate of CYP2A6 (minor), 2B6 (major), 2C8/9 (minor), 2C19 (minor), 3A4 (major); **Inhibits** CYP3A4 (weak); **Induces** CYP2B6 (weak), 2C8/9 (weak)

Increased Effect/Toxicity: Allopurinol may cause an increase in bone marrow depression and may result in significant elevations of cyclophosphamide cytotoxic metabolites.

Anesthetic agents: Cyclophosphamide reduces serum pseudocholinesterase concentrations and may prolong the neuromuscular blocking activity of succinylcholine. Use with caution with halothane, nitrous oxide, and succinylcholine.

Chloramphenicol causes prolonged cyclophosphamide half-life and increased toxicity.

CYP2B6 inducers: CYP2B6 inducers may increase the levels/effects of acrolein (the active metabolite of cyclophosphamide). Example inducers include carbamazepine, nevirapine, phenobarbital, phenytoin, and rifampin.

CYP3A4 inducers: CYP3A4 inducers may increase the levels/effects of acrolein (the active metabolite of cyclophosphamide). Example inducers include aminoglutethimide, carbamazepine, nafcillin, nevirapine, phenobarbital, phenytoin, and rifamycins.

Doxorubicin: Cyclophosphamide may enhance cardiac toxicity of anthracyclines.

Tetrahydrocannabinol results in enhanced immunosuppression in animal studies.

Thiazide diuretics: Leukopenia may be prolonged.

Decreased Effect: Cyclophosphamide may decrease digoxin serum levels. CYP2B6 inhibitors may decrease the levels/effects of acrolein (the active metabolite of cyclophosphamide); example inhibitors include desipramine, paroxetine, and sertraline. CYP3A4 inhibitors may decrease the levels/effects of acrolein (the active metabolite of cyclophosphamide); example inhibitors include azole antifungals, ciprofloxacin, clarithromycin, diclofenac, doxycycline, erythromycin, imatinib, isoniazid, nefazodone, nicardipine, propofol, protease inhibitors, quinidine, and verapamil.

(Continued)

Cyclophosphamide *(Continued)*

Mechanism of Action Cyclophosphamide is an alkylating agent that prevents cell division by cross-linking DNA strands and decreasing DNA synthesis. It is a cell cycle phase nonspecific agent. Cyclophosphamide also possesses potent immunosuppressive activity. Cyclophosphamide is a prodrug that must be metabolized to active metabolites in the liver.

Pharmacodynamics/Kinetics

Absorption: Oral: Well absorbed

Distribution: V_d: 0.48-0.71 L/kg; crosses placenta; crosses into CSF (not in high enough concentrations to treat meningeal leukemia)

Protein binding: 10% to 56%

Metabolism: Hepatic to active metabolites acrolein, 4-aldophosphamide, 4-hydroperoxycyclophosphamide, and nor-nitrogen mustard

Bioavailability: >75%

Half-life elimination: 4-8 hours

Time to peak, serum: Oral: ~1 hour

Excretion: Urine (<30% as unchanged drug, 85% to 90% as metabolites)

Dosage Refer to individual protocols

Patients who are heavily pretreated with cytotoxic radiation or chemotherapy, or who have compromised bone marrow function may require a 33% to 50% reduction in initial dose.

Children:

SLE: I.V.: 500-750 mg/m^2 every month; maximum dose: 1 g/m^2

JRA/vasculitis: I.V.: 10 mg/kg every 2 weeks

Children and Adults:

Oral: 50-100 mg/m^2/day as continuous therapy or 400-1000 mg/m^2 in divided doses over 4-5 days as intermittent therapy

I.V.:

Single doses: 400-1800 mg/m^2 (30-50 mg/kg) per treatment course (1-5 days) which can be repeated at 2-4 week intervals

Continuous daily doses: 60-120 mg/m^2 (1-2.5 mg/kg) per day

Autologous BMT: IVPB: 50 mg/kg/dose x 4 days or 60 mg/kg/dose for 2 days; total dose is usually divided over 2-4 days

Nephrotic syndrome: Oral: 2-3 mg/kg/day every day for up to 12 weeks when corticosteroids are unsuccessful

Dosing adjustment in renal impairment: A large fraction of cyclophosphamide is eliminated by hepatic metabolism

Some authors recommend no dose adjustment unless severe renal insufficiency (Cl_{cr} <20 mL/minute)

Cl_{cr} >10 mL/minute: Administer 100% of normal dose

Cl_{cr} <10 mL/minute: Administer 75% of normal dose

Hemodialysis: Moderately dialyzable (20% to 50%); administer dose posthemodialysis

CAPD effects: Unknown

CAVH effects: Unknown

Dosing adjustment in hepatic impairment: Some authors recommend dosage reductions (of up to 30%); however, the pharmacokinetics of cyclophosphamide are not significantly altered in the presence of hepatic insufficiency.

Administration May be administered I.P., intrapleurally, IVPB, or continuous I.V. infusion; may also be administered slow IVP in doses ≤1 g.

I.V. infusions may be administered over 1-24 hours

Doses >500 mg to approximately 2 g may be administered over 20-30 minutes

To minimize bladder toxicity, increase normal fluid intake during and for 1-2 days after cyclophosphamide dose. Most adult patients will require a fluid intake of at least 2 L/day. High-dose regimens should be accompanied by vigorous hydration with or without mesna therapy.

Tablets are not scored and should not be cut or crushed; should be administered during or after meals.

Monitoring Parameters CBC with differential and platelet count, BUN, UA, serum electrolytes, serum creatinine

Patient Information Tablets may be taken during or after meals to reduce GI effects. Maintain adequate fluid balance (2-3 L/day of fluids unless instructed to restrict fluid intake). Void frequently and report any difficulty or pain with urination. May cause hair loss (reversible after treatment), sterility, or amenorrhea (sometimes reversible). If you are diabetic, you will need to monitor serum glucose closely to avoid hypoglycemia. You may be more susceptible to infection; avoid crowds and unnecessary exposure to infection. Report unusual bleeding or bruising; persistent fever or sore throat; blood in urine, stool (black stool), or vomitus; delayed healing of any wounds; skin rash; yellowing of skin or eyes; or changes in color of urine or stool. Contraceptive measures are recommended during therapy.

Dosage Forms INJ, powder for reconstitution: 500 mg, 1 g, 2 g; (Cytoxan®): 500 mg, 1 g, 2 g; (Neosar®): 100 mg, 200 mg, 500 mg, 1 g, 2 g. **TAB** (Cytoxan®): 25 mg, 50 mg

♦ **Cycloplegic Mydriatics Comparison** *see page 1375*

CycloSERINE *(sye kloe SER een)*

Related Information

Antimicrobial Drugs of Choice *on page 1440*

Tuberculosis Treatment Guidelines *on page 1466*

U.S. Brand Names Seromycin® Pulvules®

Therapeutic Category Antibiotic, Miscellaneous; Antitubercular Agent

Use Adjunctive treatment in pulmonary or extrapulmonary tuberculosis

Unlabeled/Investigational Use Treatment of Gaucher's disease

Pregnancy Risk Factor C

Contraindications Hypersensitivity to cycloserine or any component of the formulation

Warnings/Precautions Epilepsy, depression, severe anxiety, psychosis, severe renal insufficiency, chronic alcoholism

Common Adverse Reactions Frequency not defined.

Cardiovascular: Cardiac arrhythmias

Central nervous system: Drowsiness, headache, dizziness, vertigo, seizures, confusion, psychosis, paresis, coma

Dermatologic: Rash

Endocrine & metabolic: Vitamin B_{12} deficiency

Hematologic: Folate deficiency

Hepatic: Liver enzymes increased

Neuromuscular & skeletal: Tremor

Drug Interactions

Increased Effect/Toxicity: Alcohol, isoniazid, and ethionamide increase toxicity of cycloserine. Cycloserine inhibits the hepatic metabolism of phenytoin and may increase risk of epileptic seizures.

Mechanism of Action Inhibits bacterial cell wall synthesis by competing with amino acid (D-alanine) for incorporation into the bacterial cell wall; bacteriostatic or bactericidal

Pharmacodynamics/Kinetics

Absorption: ~70% to 90%

Distribution: Widely to most body fluids and tissues including CSF, breast milk, bile, sputum, lymph tissue, lungs, and ascitic, pleural, and synovial fluids; crosses placenta

Half-life elimination: Normal renal function: 10 hours

Metabolism: Hepatic

Time to peak, serum: 3-4 hours

Excretion: Urine (60% to 70% as unchanged drug) within 72 hours; feces (small amounts); remainder metabolized

Dosage Some of the neurotoxic effects may be relieved or prevented by the concomitant administration of pyridoxine

Tuberculosis: Oral:

Children: 10-20 mg/kg/day in 2 divided doses up to 1000 mg/day for 18-24 months

Adults: Initial: 250 mg every 12 hours for 14 days, then administer 500 mg to 1 g/day in 2 divided doses for 18-24 months (maximum daily dose: 1 g)

Dosing interval in renal impairment:

Cl_{cr} 10-50 mL/minute: Administer every 24 hours

Cl_{cr} <10 mL/minute: Administer every 36-48 hours

Monitoring Parameters Periodic renal, hepatic, hematological tests, and plasma cycloserine concentrations

Reference Range Toxicity is greatly increased at levels >30 μg/mL

Patient Information May cause drowsiness; report skin rash, mental confusion, dizziness, headache, or tremors; do not skip doses; do not drink excessive amounts of alcoholic beverages

Dosage Forms CAP: 250 mg

♦ Cyclosporin A *see* CycloSPORINE *on page 323*

CycloSPORINE (SYE kloe spor een)

U.S. Brand Names Gengraf™; Neoral®; Restasis™; Sandimmune®

Synonyms CsA; CyA; Cyclosporin A

Therapeutic Category Immunosuppressant Agent

Use Prophylaxis of organ rejection in kidney, liver, and heart transplants, has been used with azathioprine and/or corticosteroids; severe, active rheumatoid arthritis (RA) not responsive to methotrexate alone; severe, recalcitrant plaque psoriasis in nonimmunocompromised adults unresponsive to or unable to tolerate other systemic therapy

Ophthalmic emulsion (Restasis™): Increase tear production when suppressed tear production is presumed to be due to keratoconjunctivitis sicca-associated ocular inflammation (in patients not already using topical anti-inflammatory drugs or punctal plugs)

Unlabeled/Investigational Use Short-term, high-dose cyclosporine as a modulator of multidrug resistance in cancer treatment; allogenic bone marrow transplants for prevention and treatment of graft-versus-host disease; also used in some cases of severe autoimmune disease (ie, SLE, myasthenia gravis) that are resistant to corticosteroids and other therapy; focal segmental glomerulosclerosis

Pregnancy Risk Factor C

Contraindications Hypersensitivity to cyclosporine or any component of the formulation. Rheumatoid arthritis and psoriasis: Abnormal renal function, uncontrolled hypertension, malignancies. Concomitant treatment with PUVA or UVB therapy, methotrexate, other immunosuppressive agents, coal tar, or radiation therapy are also contraindications for use in patients with psoriasis. Ophthalmic emulsion is contraindicated in patients with active ocular infections.

Warnings/Precautions Dose-related risk of nephrotoxicity and hepatotoxicity; monitor. Use caution with other potentially nephrotoxic drugs. Increased risk of lymphomas and other malignancies. Increased risk of infection. May cause hypertension. Use caution when changing dosage forms. Monitor cyclosporine concentrations closely following the addition, *(Continued)*

CycloSPORINE *(Continued)*

modification, or deletion of other medications; live, attenuated vaccines may be less effective; use should be avoided.

Transplant patients: May cause significant hyperkalemia and hyperuricemia, seizures (particularly if used with high dose corticosteroids), and encephalopathy. To avoid toxicity or possible organ rejection, make dose adjustments based on cyclosporine blood concentrations. Anaphylaxis has been reported with I.V. use; reserve for patients who cannot take oral form.

Psoriasis: Patients should avoid excessive sun exposure; safety and efficacy in children <18 have not been established

Rheumatoid arthritis: Safety and efficacy for use in juvenile rheumatoid arthritis have not been established. If receiving other immunosuppressive agents, radiation or UV therapy, concurrent use of cyclosporine is not recommended.

Ophthalmic emulsion: Has not been studied in patients with a history of herpes keratitis. Safety and efficacy have not been established in patients <16 years of age.

Products may contain corn oil, castor oil, ethanol, or propylene glycol; injection also contains Cremophor® EL (polyoxyethylated castor oil).

Common Adverse Reactions Note: Adverse reactions reported with kidney, liver, and heart transplantation, unless otherwise noted. Although percentage is reported for specific condition, reaction may occur in anyone taking cyclosporine. [Reactions reported for rheumatoid arthritis (RA) are based on cyclosporine (modified) 2.5 mg/kg/day versus placebo.]

>10%:
  Cardiovascular: Hypertension (13% to 53%; psoriasis 25% to 27%)
  Central nervous system: Headache (2% to 15%; RA 17%, psoriasis 14% to 16%)
  Dermatologic: Hirsutism (21% to 45%), hypertrichosis (RA 19%)
  Endocrine & metabolic: Increased triglycerides (psoriasis 15%), female reproductive disorder (psoriasis 8% to 11%)
  Gastrointestinal: Nausea (RA 23%), diarrhea (RA 12%), gum hyperplasia (4% to 16%), abdominal discomfort (RA 15%), dyspepsia (RA 12%)
  Neuromuscular & skeletal: Tremor (12% to 55%)
  Renal: Renal dysfunction/nephropathy (25% to 38%; RA 10%, psoriasis 21%), creatinine elevation ≥50% (RA 24%), increased creatinine (psoriasis 16% to 20%)
  Respiratory: Upper respiratory infection (psoriasis 8% to 11%)
  Miscellaneous: Infection (psoriasis 24% to 25%)

Kidney, liver, and heart transplant only (≤2% unless otherwise noted):
  Cardiovascular: Flushes (<1% to 4%), myocardial infarction
  Central nervous system: Convulsions (1% to 5%), anxiety, confusion, fever, lethargy
  Dermatologic: Acne (1% to 6%), brittle fingernails, hair breaking, pruritus
  Endocrine & metabolic: Gynecomastia (<1% to 4%), hyperglycemia
  Gastrointestinal: Nausea (2% to 10%), vomiting (2% to 10%), diarrhea (3% to 8%), abdominal discomfort (<1% to 7%), cramps (0% to 4%), anorexia, constipation, gastritis, mouth sores, pancreatitis, swallowing difficulty, upper GI bleed, weight loss
  Hematologic: Leukopenia (<1% to 6%), anemia, thrombocytopenia
  Hepatic: Hepatotoxicity (<1% to 7%)
  Neuromuscular & skeletal: Paresthesia (1% to 3%), joint pain, muscle pain, tingling, weakness
  Ocular: Conjunctivitis, visual disturbance
  Otic: Hearing loss, tinnitus
  Renal: Hematuria
  Respiratory: Sinusitis (<1% to 7%)
  Miscellaneous: Lymphoma (<1% to 6%), allergic reactions, hiccups, night sweats

Rheumatoid arthritis only (1% to <3% unless otherwise noted):
  Cardiovascular: Hypertension (8%), edema (5%), chest pain (4%), arrhythmia (2%), abnormal heart sounds, cardiac failure, myocardial infarction, peripheral ischemia
  Central nervous system: Dizziness (8%), pain (6%), insomnia (4%), depression (3%), migraine (2%), anxiety, hypoesthesia, emotional lability, impaired concentration, malaise, nervousness, paranoia, somnolence, vertigo
  Dermatologic: Purpura (3%), abnormal pigmentation, angioedema, cellulitis, dermatitis, dry skin, eczema, folliculitis, nail disorder, pruritus, skin disorder, urticaria
  Endocrine & metabolic: Menstrual disorder (3%), breast fibroadenosis, breast pain, diabetes mellitus, goiter, hot flashes, hyperkalemia, hyperuricemia, hypoglycemia, libido increased/decreased
  Gastrointestinal: Vomiting (9%), flatulence (5%), gingivitis (4%), gum hyperplasia (2%), constipation, dry mouth, dysphagia, enanthema, eructation, esophagitis, gastric ulcer, gastritis, gastroenteritis, gingival bleeding, glossitis, peptic ulcer, salivary gland enlargement, taste perversion, tongue disorder, tooth disorder, weight loss/gain
  Genitourinary: Leukorrhea (1%), abnormal urine, micturition urgency, nocturia, polyuria, pyelonephritis, urinary incontinence, uterine hemorrhage
  Hematologic: Anemia, leukopenia
  Hepatic: Bilirubinemia
  Neuromuscular & skeletal: Paresthesia (8%), tremor (8%), leg cramps/muscle contractions (2%), arthralgia, bone fracture, joint dislocation, myalgia, neuropathy, stiffness, synovial cyst, tendon disorder, weakness
  Ocular: Abnormal vision, cataract, conjunctivitis, eye pain

Otic: Tinnitus, deafness, vestibular disorder

Renal: Increased BUN, hematuria, renal abscess

Respiratory: Cough (5%), dyspnea (5%), sinusitis (4%), abnormal chest sounds, bronchospasm, epistaxis

Miscellaneous: Infection (9%), abscess, allergy, bacterial infection, carcinoma, fungal infection, herpes simplex, herpes zoster, lymphadenopathy, moniliasis, diaphoresis increased, tonsillitis, viral infection

Psoriasis only (1% to <3% unless otherwise noted):

Cardiovascular: Chest pain, flushes

Central nervous system: Psychiatric events (4% to 5%), pain (3% to 4%), dizziness, fever, insomnia, nervousness, vertigo

Dermatologic: Hypertrichosis (5% to 7%), acne, dry skin, folliculitis, keratosis, pruritus, rash, skin malignancies

Endocrine & metabolic: Hot flashes

Gastrointestinal: Nausea (5% to 6%), diarrhea (5% to 6%), gum hyperplasia (4% to 6%), abdominal discomfort (3% to 6%), dyspepsia (2% to 3%), abdominal distention, appetite increased, constipation, gingival bleeding

Genitourinary: Micturition increased

Hematologic: Bleeding disorder, clotting disorder, platelet disorder, red blood cell disorder

Hepatic: Hyperbilirubinemia

Neuromuscular & skeletal: Paresthesia (5% to 7%), arthralgia (1% to 6%)

Ocular: Abnormal vision

Respiratory: Bronchospasm (5%), cough (5%), dyspnea (5%), rhinitis (5%), respiratory infection

Miscellaneous: Flu-like symptoms (8% to 10%)

Ophthalmic emulsion (Restasis™):

>10%: Ocular: Burning (17%)

1% to 10%: Ocular: Hyperemia (conjunctival 5%), eye pain, pruritus, stinging

Drug Interactions

Cytochrome P450 Effect: Substrate of CYP3A4 (major); **Inhibits** CYP2C8/9 (weak), 3A4 (moderate)

Increased Effect/Toxicity: Drugs that increase cyclosporine concentrations include allopurinol, metoclopramide, nicardipine, octreotide. CYP3A4 inhibitors may increase the levels/effects of cyclosporine; example inhibitors include azole antifungals, ciprofloxacin, clarithromycin, diclofenac, doxycycline, erythromycin, imatinib, isoniazid, nefazodone, nicardipine, propofol, protease inhibitors, quinidine, and verapamil. Drugs that enhance nephrotoxicity of cyclosporine include aminoglycosides, amphotericin B, acyclovir, cimetidine, ketoconazole, lovastatin, melphalan, NSAIDs, ranitidine, trimethoprim and sulfamethoxazole, tacrolimus. Cyclosporine increases toxicity of digoxin, diuretics, methotrexate, nifedipine.

Decreased Effect: Isoniazid and ticlopidine decrease cyclosporine concentrations. CYP3A4 inducers may decrease the levels/effects of cyclosporine; example inducers include aminoglutethimide, carbamazepine, nafcillin, nevirapine, phenobarbital, phenytoin, and rifamycins. Orlistat may decrease absorption of cyclosporine; avoid concomitant use. Vaccination may be less effective; avoid use of live vaccines during therapy.

Mechanism of Action
Inhibition of production and release of interleukin II and inhibits interleukin II-induced activation of resting T-lymphocytes.

Pharmacodynamics/Kinetics

Absorption:

Ophthalmic emulsion: Serum concentrations not detectable.

Oral:

Cyclosporine (non-modified): Erratic and incomplete; dependent on presence of food, bile acids, and GI motility; larger oral doses are needed in pediatrics due to shorter bowel length and limited intestinal absorption

Cyclosporine (modified): Erratic and incomplete; increased absorption, up to 30% when compared to cyclosporine (non-modified); less dependent on food, bile acids, or GI motility when compared to cyclosporine (non-modified)

Distribution: Widely in tissues and body fluids including the liver, pancreas, and lungs; crosses placenta; enters breast milk

V_{dss}: 4-6 L/kg in renal, liver, and marrow transplant recipients (slightly lower values in cardiac transplant patients; children <10 years have higher values)

Protein binding: 90% to 98% to lipoproteins

Metabolism: Extensively hepatic via CYP; forms at least 25 metabolites; extensive first-pass effect following oral administration

Bioavailability: Oral:

Cyclosporine (non-modified): Dependent on patient population and transplant type (<10% in adult liver transplant patients and as high as 89% in renal transplant patients); bioavailability of Sandimmune® capsules and oral solution are equivalent; bioavailability of oral solution is ~30% of the I.V. solution

Children: 28% (range: 17% to 42%); gut dysfunction common in BMT patients and oral bioavailability is further reduced

Cyclosporine (modified): Bioavailability of Neoral® capsules and oral solution are equivalent:

Children: 43% (range: 30% to 68%)

Adults: 23% greater than with cyclosporine (non-modified) in renal transplant patients; 50% greater in liver transplant patients

Half-life elimination: Oral: May be prolonged in patients with hepatic impairment and shorter in pediatric patients due to the higher metabolism rate

(Continued)

CycloSPORINE *(Continued)*

Cyclosporine (non-modified): Biphasic: Alpha: 1.4 hours; Terminal: 19 hours (range: 10-27 hours)

Cyclosporine (modified): Biphasic: Terminal: 8.4 hours (range: 5-18 hours)

Time to peak, serum: Oral:

Cyclosporine (non-modified): 2-6 hours; some patients have a second peak at 5-6 hours

Cyclosporine (modified): Renal transplant: 1.5-2 hours

Excretion: Primarily feces; urine (6%, 0.1% as unchanged drug and metabolites)

Dosage Note: Neoral® and Sandimmune® are not bioequivalent and cannot be used interchangeably

Children: Transplant: Refer to adult dosing; children may require, and are able to tolerate, larger doses than adults.

Adults:

Newly-transplanted patients: Adjunct therapy with corticosteroids is recommended. Initial dose should be given 4-12 hours prior to transplant or may be given postoperatively; adjust initial dose to achieve desired plasma concentration

Oral: Dose is dependent upon type of transplant and formulation:

Cyclosporine (modified):

Renal: 9 ± 3 mg/kg/day, divided twice daily

Liver: 8 ± 4 mg/kg/day, divided twice daily

Heart: 7 ± 3 mg/kg/day, divided twice daily

Cyclosporine (non-modified): Initial dose: 15 mg/kg/day as a single dose (range 14-18 mg/kg); lower doses of 10-14 mg/kg/day have been used for renal transplants. Continue initial dose daily for 1-2 weeks; taper by 5% per week to a maintenance dose of 5-10 mg/kg/day; some renal transplant patients may be dosed as low as 3 mg/kg/day

When using the non-modified formulation, cyclosporine levels may increase in liver transplant patients when the T-tube is closed; dose may need decreased

I.V.: Cyclosporine (non-modified): Initial dose: 5-6 mg/kg/day as a single dose ($^1/_3$ the oral dose), infused over 2-6 hours; use should be limited to patients unable to take capsules or oral solution; patients should be switched to an oral dosage form as soon as possible

Conversion to cyclosporine (modified) from cyclosporine (non-modified): Start with daily dose previously used and adjust to obtain preconversion cyclosporine trough concentration. Plasma concentrations should be monitored every 4-7 days and dose adjusted as necessary, until desired trough level is obtained. When transferring patients with previously poor absorption of cyclosporine (non-modified), monitor trough levels at least twice weekly (especially if initial dose exceeds 10 mg/kg/day); high plasma levels are likely to occur.

Rheumatoid arthritis: Oral: Cyclosporine (modified): Initial dose: 2.5 mg/kg/day, divided twice daily; salicylates, NSAIDs, and oral glucocorticoids may be continued (refer to Drug Interactions); dose may be increased by 0.5-0.75 mg/kg/day if insufficient response is seen after 8 weeks of treatment; additional dosage increases may be made again at 12 weeks (maximum dose: 4 mg/kg/day). Discontinue if no benefit is seen by 16 weeks of therapy.

Note: Increase the frequency of blood pressure monitoring after each alteration in dosage of cyclosporine. Cyclosporine dosage should be decreased by 25% to 50% in patients with no history of hypertension who develop sustained hypertension during therapy and, if hypertension persists, treatment with cyclosporine should be discontinued.

Psoriasis: Oral: Cyclosporine (modified): Initial dose: 2.5 mg/kg/day, divided twice daily; dose may be increased by 0.5 mg/kg/day if insufficient response is seen after 4 weeks of treatment. Additional dosage increases may be made every 2 weeks if needed (maximum dose: 4 mg/kg/day). Discontinue if no benefit is seen by 6 weeks of therapy. Once patients are adequately controlled, the dose should be decreased to the lowest effective dose. Doses lower than 2.5 mg/kg/day may be effective. Treatment longer than 1 year is not recommended.

Note: Increase the frequency of blood pressure monitoring after each alteration in dosage of cyclosporine. Cyclosporine dosage should be decreased by 25% to 50% in patients with no history of hypertension who develop sustained hypertension during therapy and, if hypertension persists, treatment with cyclosporine should be discontinued.

Focal segmental glomerulosclerosis: Initial: 3 mg/kg/day divided every 12 hours

Autoimmune diseases: 1-3 mg/kg/day

Keratoconjunctivitis sicca: Ophthalmic: Children ≥16 years and Adults: Instill 1 drop in each eye every 12 hours

Dosage adjustment in renal impairment: For severe psoriasis:

Serum creatinine levels ≥25% above pretreatment levels: Take another sample within 2 weeks; if the level remains ≥25% above pretreatment levels, decrease dosage of cyclosporine (modified) by 25% to 50%. If two dosage adjustments do not reverse the increase in serum creatinine levels, treatment should be discontinued.

Serum creatinine levels ≥50% above pretreatment levels: Decrease cyclosporine dosage by 25% to 50%. If two dosage adjustments do not reverse the increase in serum creatinine levels, treatment should be discontinued.

Hemodialysis: Supplemental dose is not necessary.

Peritoneal dialysis: Supplemental dose is not necessary.

Dosage adjustment in hepatic impairment: Probably necessary; monitor levels closely

Administration

Oral solution: Do not administer liquid from plastic or styrofoam cup. May dilute Neoral® oral solution with orange juice or apple juice. May dilute Sandimmune® oral solution with milk, chocolate milk, or orange juice. Avoid changing diluents frequently. Mix thoroughly and drink at once. Use syringe provided to measure dose. Mix in a glass container and rinse container with more diluent to ensure total dose is taken. Do not rinse syringe before or after use (may cause dose variation).

I.V.: Following dilution, intravenous admixture should be administered over 2-6 hours. Discard solution after 24 hours. Anaphylaxis has been reported with I.V. use; reserve for patients who cannot take oral form. Patients should be under continuous observation for at least the first 30 minutes of the infusion, and should be monitored frequently thereafter. Maintain patent airway; other supportive measures and agents for treating anaphylaxis should be present when I.V. drug is given.

Ophthalmic emulsion: Prior to use, invert vial several times to obtain a uniform emulsion. Remove contact lenses prior to instillation of drops; may be reinserted 15 minutes after administration. May be used with artificial tears; allow 15 minute interval between products.

Monitoring Parameters Monitor blood pressure and serum creatinine after any cyclosporine dosage changes or addition, modification, or deletion of other medications. Monitor plasma concentrations periodically.

Transplant patients: Cyclosporine trough levels, serum electrolytes, renal function, hepatic function, blood pressure, lipid profile

Psoriasis therapy: Baseline blood pressure, serum creatinine (2 levels each), BUN, CBC, serum magnesium, potassium, uric acid, lipid profile. Biweekly monitoring of blood pressure, complete blood count, and levels of BUN, uric acid, potassium, lipids, and magnesium during the first 3 months of treatment for psoriasis. Monthly monitoring is recommended after this initial period. Also evaluate any atypical skin lesions prior to therapy. Increase the frequency of blood pressure monitoring after each alteration in dosage of cyclosporine. Cyclosporine dosage should be decreased by 25% to 50% in patients with no history of hypertension who develop sustained hypertension during therapy and, if hypertension persists, treatment with cyclosporine should be discontinued.

Rheumatoid arthritis: Baseline blood pressure, and serum creatinine (2 levels each); serum creatinine every 2 weeks for first 3 months, then monthly if patient is stable. Increase the frequency of blood pressure monitoring after each alteration in dosage of cyclosporine. Cyclosporine dosage should be decreased by 25% to 50% in patients with no history of hypertension who develop sustained hypertension during therapy and, if hypertension persists, treatment with cyclosporine should be discontinued.

Reference Range Reference ranges are method dependent and specimen dependent; use the same analytical method consistently

Method-dependent and specimen-dependent: Trough levels should be obtained:

Oral: 12-18 hours after dose (chronic usage)

I.V.: 12 hours after dose **or** immediately prior to next dose

Therapeutic range: Not absolutely defined, dependent on organ transplanted, time after transplant, organ function and CsA toxicity:

General range of 100-400 ng/mL

Toxic level: Not well defined, nephrotoxicity may occur at any level

Patient Information Use glass container for liquid solution (do not use plastic or styrofoam cup). Diluting oral solution improves flavor. May dilute Neoral® oral solution with orange juice or apple juice. May dilute Sandimmune® oral solution with milk, chocolate milk, or orange juice. Avoid changing what you mix with your cyclosporine. Mix thoroughly and drink at once. Use syringe provided to measure dose. Mix in a glass container and rinse container with more juice/milk to ensure total dose is taken. Do not rinse syringe before or after use (may cause dose variation). Take dose at the same time each day. You will be susceptible to infection; avoid crowds and exposure to any infectious diseases. Do not have any vaccinations without consulting prescriber. Practice good oral hygiene to reduce gum inflammation; see dentist regularly during treatment. Report severe headache; unusual hair growth or deepening of voice; mouth sores or swollen gums; persistent nausea, vomiting, or abdominal pain; muscle pain or cramping; unusual swelling of extremities, weight gain, or change in urination; or chest pain or rapid heartbeat. Increases in blood pressure or damage to the kidney are possible. Your prescriber will need to monitor closely. Do not change one brand of cyclosporine for another; any changes must be done by your prescriber. If you are taking this medication for psoriasis, your risk of cancer may be increased when taking additional medications.

Ophthalmic emulsion: Prior to use, invert vial several times to obtain a uniform emulsion. Remove contact lenses prior to instillation of drops; may be reinserted 15 minutes after administration. May be used with artificial tears; allow 15 minute interval between products.

Dosage Forms

Cyclosporine, modified: **CAP, soft gel:** 25 mg, 100 mg; (Gengraf™): 25 mg, 100 mg; (Neoral®): 25 mg, 100 mg. **SOLN, oral:** (Neoral®): 100 mg/mL (50 mL).

Cyclosporine, non-modified (Sandimmune®): **CAP, soft gel:** 25 mg, 100 mg. **INJ:** 50 mg/mL (5 mL). **SOLN, oral:** 100 mg/mL (50 mL)

EMULSION, ophthalmic [preservative free, single-use vial] (Restasis™): 0.05% (0.4 mL)

♦ **Cyklokapron**® *see Tranexamic Acid on page 1252*

♦ **Cylate**® *see Cyclopentolate on page 320*

♦ **Cylert**® *see Pemoline on page 969*

♦ **Cylex**® **[OTC]** *see Benzocaine on page 154*

Cyproheptadine (si proe HEP ta deen)

Synonyms Cyproheptadine Hydrochloride; Periactin

Therapeutic Category Antihistamine

Use Perennial and seasonal allergic rhinitis and other allergic symptoms including urticaria
(Continued)

Cyproheptadine *(Continued)*

Unlabeled/Investigational Use Appetite stimulation, blepharospasm, cluster headaches, migraine headaches, Nelson's syndrome, pruritus, schizophrenia, spinal cord damage associated spasticity, and tardive dyskinesia

Pregnancy Risk Factor B

Contraindications Hypersensitivity to cyproheptadine or any component of the formulation; narrow-angle glaucoma; bladder neck obstruction; acute asthmatic attack; stenosing peptic ulcer; GI tract obstruction; concurrent use of MAO inhibitors; avoid use in premature and term newborns due to potential association with SIDS

Warnings/Precautions Do not use in neonates, safety and efficacy have not been established in children <2 years of age; symptomatic prostate hypertrophy; antihistamines are more likely to cause dizziness, excessive sedation, syncope, toxic confusion states, and hypotension in the elderly. In case reports, cyproheptadine has promoted weight gain in anorexic adults, though it has not been specifically studied in the elderly. All cases of weight loss or decreased appetite should be adequately assessed.

Common Adverse Reactions
>10%:
  Central nervous system: Slight to moderate drowsiness
  Respiratory: Thickening of bronchial secretions
1% to 10%:
  Central nervous system: Headache, fatigue, nervousness, dizziness
  Gastrointestinal: Appetite stimulation, nausea, diarrhea, abdominal pain, xerostomia
  Neuromuscular & skeletal: Arthralgia
  Respiratory: Pharyngitis

Drug Interactions
  Increased Effect/Toxicity: Cyproheptadine may potentiate the effect of CNS depressants. MAO inhibitors may cause hallucinations when taken with cyproheptadine.

Mechanism of Action A potent antihistamine and serotonin antagonist, competes with histamine for H_1-receptor sites on effector cells in the gastrointestinal tract, blood vessels, and respiratory tract

Pharmacodynamics/Kinetics
  Absorption: Completely
  Metabolism: Almost completely hepatic
  Excretion: Urine (>50% primarily as metabolites); feces (~25%)

Dosage Oral:
  Children:
    Allergic conditions: 0.25 mg/kg/day or 8 mg/m^2/day in 2-3 divided doses **or**
      2-6 years: 2 mg every 8-12 hours (not to exceed 12 mg/day)
      7-14 years: 4 mg every 8-12 hours (not to exceed 16 mg/day)
    Migraine headaches: 4 mg 2-3 times/day
  Children ≥12 years and Adults: Spasticity associated with spinal cord damage: 4 mg at bedtime; increase by a 4 mg dose every 3-4 days; average daily dose: 16 mg in divided doses; not to exceed 36 mg/day
  Children >13 years and Adults: Appetite stimulation (anorexia nervosa): 2 mg 4 times/day; may be increased gradually over a 3-week period to 8 mg 4 times/day
  Adults:
    Allergic conditions: 4-20 mg/day divided every 8 hours (not to exceed 0.5 mg/kg/day)
    Cluster headaches: 4 mg 4 times/day
    Migraine headaches: 4-8 mg 3 times/day
  Dosage adjustment in hepatic impairment: Reduce dosage in patients with significant hepatic dysfunction

Patient Information May cause drowsiness; may stimulate appetite; avoid alcohol and other CNS depressants; may impair judgment and coordination

Dosage Forms SYR: 2 mg/5 mL (473 mL). **TAB:** 4 mg

♦ **Cyproheptadine Hydrochloride** *see* Cyproheptadine *on page 327*
♦ **Cystadane®** *see* Betaine Anhydrous *on page 159*
♦ **Cystagon®** *see* Cysteamine *on page 328*

Cysteamine *(sis TEE a meen)*

U.S. Brand Names Cystagon®

Synonyms Cysteamine Bitartrate

Therapeutic Category Anticystine Agent; Urinary Tract Agent

Use Orphan drug: Treatment of nephropathic cystinosis

Pregnancy Risk Factor C

Dosage Oral: Initiate therapy with $^1/_4$ to $^1/_8$ of maintenance dose; titrate slowly upward over 4-6 weeks
  Children <12 years: Maintenance: 1.3 g/m^2/day divided into 4 doses
  Children >12 years and Adults (>110 lb): 2 g/day in 4 divided doses; dosage may be increased to 1.95 g/m^2/day if cystine levels are <1 nmol/$^1/_2$ cystine/mg protein, although intolerance and incidence of adverse events may be increased

Dosage Forms CAP: 50 mg, 150 mg

♦ **Cysteamine Bitartrate** *see* Cysteamine *on page 328*
♦ **Cystospaz®** *see* Hyoscyamine *on page 641*
♦ **Cystospaz-M®** *see* Hyoscyamine *on page 641*

♦ **CYT** *see* Cyclophosphamide *on page 320*

♦ **Cytadren®** *see* Aminoglutethimide *on page 75*

Cytarabine (sye TARE a been)

U.S. Brand Names Cytosar-U®

Synonyms Arabinosylcytosine; Ara-C; Cytarabine Hydrochloride; Cytosine Arabinosine Hydrochloride; NSC-63878

Therapeutic Category Antineoplastic Agent, Antimetabolite (Purine)

Use Cytarabine is one of the most active agents in leukemia; also active against lymphoma, meningeal leukemia, and meningeal lymphoma; has little use in the treatment of solid tumors

Pregnancy Risk Factor D

Contraindications Hypersensitivity to cytarabine or any component of the formulation; pregnancy

Warnings/Precautions The U.S. Food and Drug Administration (FDA) currently recommends that procedures for proper handling and disposal of antineoplastic agents be considered. Use with caution in pregnant women or women of childbearing age and in infants.

Common Adverse Reactions

>10%:

Central nervous system: Fever (>80%)

Dermatologic: Alopecia

Gastrointestinal: Nausea, vomiting, diarrhea, and mucositis which subside quickly after discontinuing the drug; GI effects may be more pronounced with divided I.V. bolus doses than with continuous infusion

Hematologic: Myelosuppression; neutropenia and thrombocytopenia are severe, anemia may also occur

Onset: 4-7 days

Nadir: 14-18 days

Recovery: 21-28 days

Hepatic: Hepatic dysfunction, mild jaundice, and acute increases in transaminases can be produced

Ocular: Tearing, ocular pain, foreign body sensation, photophobia, and blurred vision may occur with high-dose therapy; ophthalmic corticosteroids usually prevent or relieve the condition

1% to 10%:

Cardiovascular: Thrombophlebitis, cardiomegaly

Central nervous system: Dizziness, headache, somnolence, confusion, malaise; a severe cerebellar toxicity occurs in about 8% of patients receiving a high dose (>36-48 g/m^2/cycle); it is irreversible or fatal in about 1%

Dermatologic: Skin freckling, itching, cellulitis at injection site; rash, pain, erythema, and skin sloughing of the palmar and plantar surfaces may occur with high-dose therapy. Prophylactic topical steroids and/or skin moisturizers may be useful.

Genitourinary: Urinary retention

Neuromuscular & skeletal: Myalgia, bone pain

Respiratory: Syndrome of sudden respiratory distress, including tachypnea, hypoxemia, interstitial and alveolar infiltrates progressing to pulmonary edema, pneumonia

Drug Interactions

Increased Effect/Toxicity: Alkylating agents and radiation, purine analogs, and methotrexate when coadministered with cytarabine result in increased toxic effects.

Decreased Effect: Decreased effect of gentamicin, flucytosine. Decreased digoxin oral tablet absorption.

Mechanism of Action Inhibition of DNA synthesis. Cytosine gains entry into cells by a carrier process, and then must be converted to its active compound, aracytidine triphosphate. Cytosine is a purine analog and is incorporated into DNA; however, the primary action is inhibition of DNA polymerase resulting in decreased DNA synthesis and repair. The degree of cytotoxicity correlates linearly with incorporation into DNA; therefore, incorporation into the DNA is responsible for drug activity and toxicity. Cytarabine is specific for the S phase of the cell cycle.

Pharmacodynamics/Kinetics

Distribution: V_d: Total body water; widely and rapidly since it enters the cells readily; crosses blood-brain barrier with CSF levels of 40% to 50% of plasma level

Metabolism: Primarily hepatic; aracytidine triphosphate is the active moiety; about 86% to 96% of dose is metabolized to inactive uracil arabinoside

Half-life elimination: Initial: 7-20 minutes; Terminal: 0.5-2.6 hours

Excretion: Urine (~80% as metabolites) within 24-36 hours

Dosage I.V. bolus, IVPB, and CIV doses of cytarabine are very different. Bolus doses are relatively well tolerated since the drug is rapidly metabolized; but are associated with greater neurotoxicity. Continuous infusion uniformly results in myelosuppression. Refer to individual protocols. Children and Adults:

Remission induction:

I.V.: 100-200 mg/m^2/day for 5-10 days; a second course, beginning 2-4 weeks after the initial therapy, may be required in some patients.

I.T.: 5-75 mg/m^2 every 2-7 days until CNS findings normalize; or age-based dosing:

<1 year: 20 mg

1-2 years: 30 mg

2-3 years: 50 mg

>3 years: 75 mg

Remission maintenance:

I.V.: 70-200 mg/m^2/day for 2-5 days at monthly intervals

(Continued)

Cytarabine *(Continued)*

I.M., S.C.: 1-1.5 mg/kg single dose for maintenance at 1- to 4-week intervals

High-dose therapies:

Doses as high as 1-3 g/m^2 have been used for refractory or secondary leukemias or refractory non-Hodgkin's lymphoma.

Doses of 1-3 g/m^2 every 12 hours for up to 12 doses have been used

Bone marrow transplant: 1.5 g/m^2 continuous infusion over 48 hours

Hemodialysis: Supplemental dose is not necessary.

Peritoneal dialysis: Supplemental dose is not necessary.

Dosage adjustment in hepatic impairment: Dose may need to be adjusted since cytarabine is partially detoxified in the liver.

Administration Can be administered I.M., I.V. infusion, I.T., or S.C. at a concentration not to exceed 100 mg/mL

I.V. may be administered either as a bolus, IVPB (high doses of >500 mg/m^2), or continuous intravenous infusion (doses of 100-200 mg/m^2)

I.V. doses of ≥1.5 g/m^2 may produce conjunctivitis which can be ameliorated with prophylactic use of corticosteroid (0.1% dexamethasone) eye drops. Dexamethasone eye drops should be administered at 1-2 drops every 6 hours during and for 2-7 days after cytarabine is done.

Monitoring Parameters Liver function tests, CBC with differential and platelet count, serum creatinine, BUN, serum uric acid

Patient Information This drug can only be given by infusion or injection. You will be more susceptible to infection; avoid crowds and exposure to infection. Do not have any vaccinations without consulting prescriber. Small frequent meals, frequent mouth care, sucking lozenges, or chewing gum may reduce incidence of nausea or vomiting or loss of appetite. If these measures are ineffective, consult prescriber for antiemetic medication. Report immediately any signs of CNS changes or change in gait, easy bruising or bleeding, yellowing of eyes or skin, change in color of urine or blackened stool, respiratory difficulty, or palpitations. Contraceptive measures are recommended during therapy.

Dosage Forms INJ, powder for reconstitution: 100 mg, 500 mg, 1 g, 2 g

♦ **Cytarabine Hydrochloride** *see Cytarabine on page 329*

Cytarabine (Liposomal) *(sye TARE a been lip po SOE mal)*

U.S. Brand Names DepoCyt™

Therapeutic Category Antineoplastic Agent, Antimetabolite (Purine)

Use Treatment of neoplastic (lymphomatous) meningitis

Pregnancy Risk Factor D

Contraindications Hypersensitivity to cytarabine or any component of the formulation; active meningeal infection; pregnancy

Warnings/Precautions The U.S. Food and Drug Administration (FDA) currently recommends that procedures for proper handling and disposal of antineoplastic agents be considered. The incidence and severity of chemical arachnoiditis is reduced by coadministration with dexamethasone. May cause neurotoxicity. Blockage to CSF flow may increase the risk of neurotoxicity. Safety and use in pediatric patients has not been established.

Common Adverse Reactions Chemical arachnoiditis is commonly observed, and may include neck pain, neck rigidity, headache, fever, nausea, vomiting, and back pain. It may occur in up to 100% of cycles without dexamethasone prophylaxis. The incidence is reduced to 33% when dexamethasone is used concurrently.

>10%:

Central nervous system: Headache (28%), confusion (14%), somnolence (12%), fever (11%), pain (11%)

Gastrointestinal: Vomiting (12%), nausea (11%)

1% to 10%:

Cardiovascular: Peripheral edema (7%)

Gastrointestinal: Constipation (7%)

Genitourinary: Incontinence (3%)

Hematologic: Neutropenia (9%), thrombocytopenia (8%), anemia (1%)

Neuromuscular & skeletal: Back pain (7%), weakness (19%), abnormal gait (4%)

Drug Interactions

Increased Effect/Toxicity: No formal studies of interactions with other medications have been conducted. The limited systemic exposure minimizes the potential for interaction between liposomal cytarabine and other medications.

Decreased Effect: No formal studies of interactions with other medications have been conducted. The limited systemic exposure minimizes the potential for interaction between liposomal cytarabine and other medications.

Mechanism of Action This is a sustained-release formulation of the active ingredient cytarabine, which acts through inhibition of DNA synthesis; cell cycle-specific for the S phase of cell division; cytosine gains entry into cells by a carrier process, and then must be converted to its active compound; cytosine acts as an analog and is incorporated into DNA; however, the primary action is inhibition of DNA polymerase resulting in decreased DNA synthesis and repair; degree of its cytotoxicity correlates linearly with its incorporation into DNA; therefore, incorporation into the DNA is responsible for drug activity and toxicity

Pharmacodynamics/Kinetics

Absorption: Systemic exposure following intrathecal administration is negligible since transfer rate from CSF to plasma is slow

Metabolism: In plasma to ara-U (inactive)

Half-life elimination, CSF: 100-263 hours

Time to peak, CSF: Intrathecal: ~5 hours

Excretion: Primarily urine (as metabolites - ara-U)

Dosage Adults:

Induction: 50 mg intrathecally every 14 days for a total of 2 doses (weeks 1 and 3)

Consolidation: 50 mg intrathecally every 14 days for 3 doses (weeks 5, 7, and 9), followed by an additional dose at week 13

Maintenance: 50 mg intrathecally every 28 days for 4 doses (weeks 17, 21, 25, and 29)

If drug-related neurotoxicity develops, the dose should be reduced to 25 mg. If toxicity persists, treatment with liposomal cytarabine should be discontinued.

Note: Patients should be started on dexamethasone 4 mg twice daily (oral or I.V.) for 5 days, beginning on the day of liposomal cytarabine injection

Administration For intrathecal use only. Dose should be removed from vial immediately before administration (must be administered within 4 hours of removal). An in-line filter should **not** be used. Vials are intended for a single use and contain no preservative. Administer directly into the CSF via an intraventricular reservoir or by direct injection into the lumbar sac. Injection should be made slowly (over 1-5 minutes). Patients should lie flat for 1 hour after lumbar puncture. Patients should be monitored closely for immediate toxic reactions.

Monitoring Parameters Monitor closely for signs of an immediate reaction

Patient Information Report fever, sore throat, bleeding, or bruising. Contraceptive measures are recommended during therapy.

Dosage Forms INJ, suspension [preservative free]: 10 mg/mL (5 mL)

♦ **Cytochrome P450 Enzymes: Substrates, Inhibitors, and Inducers** *see page 1405*

♦ **CytoGam®** *see Cytomegalovirus Immune Globulin (Intravenous-Human) on page 331*

Cytomegalovirus Immune Globulin (Intravenous-Human)

(sye toe meg a low VYE rus i MYUN GLOB yoo lin in tra VEE nus HYU man)

U.S. Brand Names CytoGam®

Synonyms CMV-IGIV

Therapeutic Category Immune Globulin

Use Prophylaxis of cytomegalovirus (CMV) disease associated with kidney, lung, liver, pancreas, and heart transplants; concomitant use with ganciclovir should be considered in organ transplants (other than kidney) from CMV seropositive donors to CMV seronegative recipients

Unlabeled/Investigational Use Adjunct therapy in the treatment of CMV disease in immuno-compromised patients

Pregnancy Risk Factor C

Contraindications Hypersensitivity to CMV-IGIV, other immunoglobulins, or any component of the formulation; immunoglobulin A deficiency

Warnings/Precautions Monitor for anaphylactic reactions during infusion. May theoretically transmit blood-borne viruses. Use with caution in patients with renal insufficiency, diabetes mellitus, patients >65 years of age, volume depletion, sepsis, paraproteinemia, or patients on concomitant nephrotoxic drugs. Stabilized with sucrose and albumin, contains no preservative.

Common Adverse Reactions <6%:

Cardiovascular: Flushing

Central nervous system: Fever, chills

Gastrointestinal: Nausea, vomiting

Neuromuscular & skeletal: Arthralgia, back pain, muscle cramps

Respiratory: Wheezing

Drug Interactions

Decreased Effect: Decreased effect of live vaccines may be seen if given within 3 months of IGIV administration. Defer vaccination or revaccinate.

Mechanism of Action CMV-IGIV is a preparation of immunoglobulin G derived from pooled healthy blood donors with a high titer of CMV antibodies; administration provides a passive source of antibodies against cytomegalovirus

Dosage I.V.: Adults:

Kidney transplant:

Initial dose (within 72 hours of transplant): 150 mg/kg/dose

2-, 4-, 6-, and 8 weeks after transplant: 100 mg/kg/dose

12 and 16 weeks after transplant: 50 mg/kg/dose

Liver, lung, pancreas, or heart transplant:

Initial dose (within 72 hours of transplant): 150 mg/kg/dose

2-, 4-, 6-, and 8 weeks after transplant: 150 mg/kg/dose

12 and 16 weeks after transplant: 100 mg/kg/dose

Severe CMV pneumonia: Various regimens have been used, including 400 mg/kg CMV-IGIV in combination with ganciclovir on days 1, 2, 7, or 8, followed by 200 mg/kg CMV-IGIV on days 14 and 21

Elderly: Use with caution in patients >65 years of age, may be at increased risk of renal insufficiency

Dosage adjustment in renal impairment: Use with caution; specific dosing adjustments are not available. Infusion rate should be the minimum practical; do not exceed 180 mg/kg/hour

Administration Administer through an I.V. line containing an in-line filter (pore size 15 micron) using an infusion pump. Do not mix with other infusions; do not use if turbid. Begin infusion within 6 hours of entering vial, complete infusion within 12 hours.

(Continued)

Cytomegalovirus Immune Globulin (Intravenous-Human)
(Continued)

Infuse at 15 mg/kg/hour. If no adverse reactions occur within 30 minutes, may increase rate to 30 mg/kg/hour. If no adverse reactions occur within the second 30 minutes, may increase rate to 60 mg/kg/hour; maximum rate of infusion: 75 mL/hour. When infusing subsequent doses, may decrease titration interval from 30 minutes to 15 minutes. If patient develops nausea, back pain, or flushing during infusion, slow the rate or temporarily stop the infusion. Discontinue if blood pressure drops or in case of anaphylactic reaction.

Monitoring Parameters Vital signs (throughout infusion), flushing, chills, muscle cramps, back pain, fever, nausea, vomiting, wheezing, decreased blood pressure, or anaphylaxis; renal function and urine output

Dosage Forms INJ, solution [preservative free]: 50 mg ± 10 mg/mL (20 mL, 50 mL)

- **Cytomel®** *see Liothyronine on page 749*
- **Cytosar-U®** *see Cytarabine on page 329*
- **Cytosine Arabinosine Hydrochloride** *see Cytarabine on page 329*
- **Cytotec®** *see Misoprostol on page 848*
- **Cytovene®** *see Ganciclovir on page 577*
- **Cytoxan®** *see Cyclophosphamide on page 320*
- **Cytra-2** *see Sodium Citrate and Citric Acid on page 1147*
- **Cytra-3** *see Citric Acid, Sodium Citrate, and Potassium Citrate on page 287*
- **Cytra-K** *see Potassium Citrate and Citric Acid on page 1021*
- **D2E7** *see Adalimumab on page 38*
- **D-3-Mercaptovaline** *see Penicillamine on page 970*
- **d4T** *see Stavudine on page 1160*

Dacarbazine (da KAR ba zeen)

U.S. Brand Names DTIC-Dome®

Synonyms DIC; Dimethyl Triazeno Imidazol Carboxamide; DTIC; Imidazol Carboxamide Dimethyltriazene; Imidazole Carboxamide; WR-139007

Therapeutic Category Antineoplastic Agent, Alkylating Agent; Antineoplastic Agent, Vesicant; Antineoplastic Agent, Miscellaneous; Vesicant

Use Treatment of malignant melanoma, Hodgkin's disease, soft-tissue sarcomas, fibrosarcomas, rhabdomyosarcoma, islet cell carcinoma, medullary carcinoma of the thyroid, and neuroblastoma

Pregnancy Risk Factor C

Contraindications Hypersensitivity to dacarbazine or any component of the formulation

Warnings/Precautions The U.S. Food and Drug Administration (FDA) currently recommends that procedures for proper handling and disposal of antineoplastic agents be considered. Use with caution in patients with bone marrow suppression; in patients with renal and/or hepatic impairment since dosage reduction may be necessary.

Common Adverse Reactions

>10%:

Gastrointestinal: Nausea and vomiting (>90%), can be severe and dose-limiting; nausea and vomiting decrease on successive days when dacarbazine is given daily for 5 days; diarrhea

Hematologic: Myelosuppression, leukopenia, thrombocytopenia - dose-limiting

Onset: 5-7 days

Nadir: 7-10 days

Recovery: 21-28 days

Local: Pain on infusion, may be minimized by administration through a central line, or by administration as a short infusion (eg, 1-2 hours as opposed to bolus injection)

1% to 10%:

Dermatologic: Alopecia, rash, photosensitivity

Gastrointestinal: Anorexia, metallic taste

Miscellaneous: Flu-like syndrome (fever, myalgias, malaise)

Drug Interactions

Cytochrome P450 Effect: Substrate (major) of CYP1A2, 2E1

Increased Effect/Toxicity: CYP1A2 inhibitors may increase the levels/effects of dacarbazine; example inhibitors include amiodarone, ciprofloxacin, fluvoxamine, ketoconazole, lomefloxacin, ofloxacin, and rofecoxib. CYP2E1 inhibitors may increase the levels/effects of dacarbazine; example inhibitors include disulfiram, isoniazid, and miconazole.

Decreased Effect: CYP1A2 inducers may decrease the levels/effects of dacarbazine; example inducers include aminoglutethimide, carbamazepine, phenobarbital, and rifampin. Patients may experience impaired immune response to vaccines; possible infection after administration of live vaccines in patients receiving immunosuppressants.

Mechanism of Action Alkylating agent which appears to form methylcarbonium ions that attack nucleophilic groups in DNA; cross-links strands of DNA resulting in the inhibition of DNA, RNA, and protein synthesis, the exact mechanism of action is still unclear.

Pharmacodynamics/Kinetics

Onset of action: I.V.: 18-24 days

Distribution: V_d: 0.6 L/kg, exceeding total body water; suggesting binding to some tissue (probably liver)

Protein binding: 5%

Metabolism: Extensively hepatic; hepatobiliary excretion is probably of some importance; metabolites may also have an antineoplastic effect

Half-life elimination: Biphasic: Initial: 20-40 minutes; Terminal: 5 hours

Excretion: Urine (~30% to 50% as unchanged drug)

Dosage Refer to individual protocols. Some dosage regimens include:

Intra-arterial: 50-400 mg/m^2 for 5-10 days

I.V.:

Hodgkin's disease, ABVD: 375 mg/m^2 days 1 and 15 every 4 weeks **or** 100 mg/m^2/day for 5 days

Metastatic melanoma (alone or in combination with other agents): 150-250 mg/m^2 days 1-5 every 3-4 weeks

Metastatic melanoma: 850 mg/m^2 every 3 weeks

High dose: Bone marrow/blood cell transplantation: I.V.: 1-3 g/m^2; maximum dose as a single agent: 3.38 g/m^2; generally combined with other high-dose chemotherapeutic drugs

Dosage adjustment in renal/hepatic impairment: No guidelines exist for adjustment

Administration Infuse over 30-60 minutes; rapid infusion may cause severe venous irritation.

Extravasation management: Local pain, burning sensation, and irritation at the injection site may be relieved by local application of hot packs. If extravasation occurs, apply cold packs. Protect exposed tissue from light following extravasation.

Monitoring Parameters CBC with differential, liver function

Patient Information Limit oral intake for 4-6 hours before therapy. Do not use alcohol, aspirin-containing products, and/or OTC medications without consulting prescriber. It is important to maintain adequate nutrition and hydration (2-3 L/day of fluids unless you are instructed to restrict fluid intake) during therapy; frequent small meals may help. You may experience nausea or vomiting (frequent small meals, frequent mouth care, sucking lozenges, or chewing gum may help). If this is ineffective, consult prescriber for antiemetic medication. You may experience loss of hair (reversible); you will be more susceptible to infection (avoid crowds and exposure to infection as much as possible); you will be more sensitive to sunlight; use sunblock, wear protective clothing and dark glasses, or avoid direct exposure to sunlight. Flu-like symptoms (eg, malaise, fever, myalgia) may occur 1 week after infusion and persist for 1-3 weeks; consult prescriber for severe symptoms. Report fever, chills, unusual bruising or bleeding, signs of infection, excessive fatigue, yellowing of eyes or skin, or change in color of urine or stool. Contraceptive measures are recommended during therapy.

Dosage Forms INJ, powder for reconstitution: 200 mg, 500 mg; (DTIC-Dome®): 100 mg, 200 mg

Daclizumab (dac KLYE zue mab)

U.S. Brand Names Zenapax®

Therapeutic Category Immunosuppressant Agent

Use Part of an immunosuppressive regimen (including cyclosporine and corticosteroids) for the prophylaxis of acute organ rejection in patients receiving renal transplant

Unlabeled/Investigational Use Graft-versus-host disease

Pregnancy Risk Factor C

Contraindications Hypersensitivity to daclizumab or any component of the formulation

Warnings/Precautions Only physicians experienced in immunosuppressive therapy and management of organ transplant patients should prescribe daclizumab. Manage patients receiving the drug in facilities equipped and staffed with adequate laboratory and supportive medical resources. Readministration of daclizumab after an initial course of therapy has not been studied in humans. The potential risks of such readministration, specifically those associated with immunosuppression or the occurrence of anaphylaxis/anaphylactoid reactions, are not known.

Common Adverse Reactions Although reported adverse events are frequent, when daclizumab is compared with placebo the incidence of adverse effects is similar between the two groups. Many of the adverse effects reported during clinical trials of daclizumab may be related to the patient population, transplant procedure, and concurrent transplant medications. Diarrhea, fever, postoperative pain, pruritus, respiratory tract infections, urinary tract infections, and vomiting occurred more often in children than adults.

≥5%:

Cardiovascular: Chest pain, edema, hypertension, hypotension, tachycardia, thrombosis

Central nervous system: Dizziness, fatigue, fever, headache, insomnia, pain, post-traumatic pain, tremor

Dermatologic: Acne, cellulitis, wound healing impaired

Gastrointestinal: Abdominal distention, abdominal pain, constipation, diarrhea, dyspepsia, epigastric pain, nausea, pyrosis, vomiting

Genitourinary: Dysuria

Hematologic: Bleeding

Neuromuscular & skeletal: Back pain, musculoskeletal pain

Renal: Oliguria, renal tubular necrosis

Respiratory: Cough, dyspnea, pulmonary edema,

Miscellaneous: Lymphocele, wound infection

≥2% to <5%:

Central nervous system: Anxiety, depression, shivering

Dermatologic: Hirsutism, pruritus, rash

Endocrine & metabolic: Dehydration, diabetes mellitus, fluid overload

Gastrointestinal: Flatulence, gastritis, hemorrhoids

Genitourinary: Urinary retention, urinary tract bleeding

(Continued)

Daclizumab *(Continued)*

Local: Application site reaction
Neuromuscular & skeletal: Arthralgia, leg cramps, myalgia, weakness
Ocular: Vision blurred
Renal: Hydronephrosis, renal damage, renal insufficiency
Respiratory: Atelectasis, congestion, hypoxia, pharyngitis, pleural effusion, rales, rhinitis
Miscellaneous: Night sweats, prickly sensation, diaphoresis

Drug Interactions
Increased Effect/Toxicity: The combined use of daclizumab, cyclosporine, mycophenolate mofetil, and corticosteroids has been associated with an increased mortality in a population of cardiac transplant recipients, particularly in patients who received antilymphocyte globulin and in patients with severe infections.

Mechanism of Action Daclizumab is a chimeric (90% human, 10% murine) monoclonal IgG antibody produced by recombinant DNA technology. Daclizumab inhibits immune reactions by binding and blocking the alpha-chain of the interleukin-2 receptor (CD25) located on the surface of activated lymphocytes.

Pharmacodynamics/Kinetics
Distribution: V_d:
Adults: Central compartment: 0.031 L/kg; Peripheral compartment: 0.043 L/kg
Children: Central compartment: 0.067 L/kg; Peripheral compartment: 0.047 L/kg
Half-life elimination (estimated): Adults: Terminal: 20 days; Children: 13 days

Dosage Daclizumab is used adjunctively with other immunosuppressants (eg, cyclosporine, corticosteroids, mycophenolate mofetil, and azathioprine): I.V.:
Children: Use same weight-based dose as adults
Adults:
Immunoprophylaxis against acute renal allograft rejection: 1 mg/kg infused over 15 minutes within 24 hours before transplantation (day 0), then every 14 days for 4 additional doses
Treatment of graft-versus-host disease (unlabeled use, limited data): 0.5-1.5 mg/kg, repeat same dosage for transient response. Repeat doses have been administered 11-48 days following the initial dose.
Dosage adjustment in renal impairment: No adjustment needed.
Dosage adjustment in hepatic impairment: No data available for patients with severe impairment.

Administration For I.V. administration following dilution. Daclizumab solution should be administered within 4 hours of preparation if stored at room temperature; infuse over a 15-minute period via a peripheral or central vein.

Patient Information This medication can only be given by I.V. infusion by a healthcare professional. May cause side effects similar to those caused by surgery as well as other medications that you may be taking.

Dosage Forms INJ, solution [preservative free]: 5 mg/mL (5 mL)

♦ **DACT** *see Dactinomycin on page 334*

Dactinomycin *(dak ti noe MYE sin)*

U.S. Brand Names Cosmegen®

Synonyms ACT; Act-D; Actinomycin; Actinomycin CI; Actinomycin D; DACT; NSC-3053

Therapeutic Category Antineoplastic Agent, Antibiotic; Antineoplastic Agent, Vesicant; Vesicant

Use Treatment of testicular tumors, melanoma, choriocarcinoma, Wilms' tumor, neuroblastoma, retinoblastoma, rhabdomyosarcoma, uterine sarcomas, Ewing's sarcoma, Kaposi's sarcoma, sarcoma botryoides, and soft tissue sarcoma

Pregnancy Risk Factor C

Contraindications Hypersensitivity to dactinomycin or any component of the formulation; patients with concurrent or recent chickenpox or herpes zoster; avoid in infants <6 months of age

Warnings/Precautions The U.S. Food and Drug Administration (FDA) currently recommends that procedures for proper handling and disposal of antineoplastic agents be considered. Drug is extremely irritating to tissues and must be administered I.V.; if extravasation occurs during I.V. use, severe damage to soft tissues will occur. Dosage is calculated in micrograms and must be calculated on the basis of body surface area (BSA) in obese or edematous patients. Use with caution in patients who have received radiation therapy or in the presence of hepatobiliary dysfunction; reduce dosage in patients who are receiving radiation therapy simultaneously.

Common Adverse Reactions
>10%:
Central nervous system: Fatigue, malaise, fever, lethargy
Dermatologic: Alopecia (reversible), skin eruptions, acne, increased pigmentation or sloughing of previously irradiated skin, maculopapular rash
Endocrine & metabolic: Hypocalcemia
Gastrointestinal: Severe nausea, vomiting, anorexia
Hematologic: Myelosuppression, anemia
Onset: 7 days
Nadir: 14-21 days
Recovery: 21-28 days
Local: Extravasation: An irritant and should be administered through a rapidly running I.V. line; extravasation can lead to tissue necrosis, pain, and ulceration
1% to 10%: Gastrointestinal: Mucositis, stomatitis, diarrhea, abdominal pain

Drug Interactions
Increased Effect/Toxicity: Dactinomycin potentiates the effects of radiation therapy.
Mechanism of Action Binds to the guanine portion of DNA intercalating between guanine and cytosine base pairs inhibiting DNA and RNA synthesis and protein synthesis
Pharmacodynamics/Kinetics
Distribution: High concentrations found in bone marrow and tumor cells, submaxillary gland, liver, and kidney; crosses placenta; poor CSF penetration
Metabolism: Hepatic, minimal
Half-life elimination: 36 hours
Time to peak, serum: I.V.: 2-5 minutes
Excretion: Bile (50%); feces (14%); urine (~10% as unchanged drug)
Dosage Refer to individual protocols: I.V.
Note: Medication orders for dactinomycin are commonly written in MICROgrams (eg, 150 mcg) although many regimens list the dose in MILLIgrams (eg, mg/kg or mg/m^2). One-time doses for >1000 mcg, or multiple-day doses for >500 mcg/day are not common. Some practitioners recommend calculation of the dosage for obese or edematous patients on the basis of body surface area in an effort to relate dosage to lean body mass.
Children >6 months: 15 mcg/kg/day **or** 400-600 mcg/m^2/day for 5 days every 3-6 weeks
Adults: 2.5 mg/m^2 in divided doses over 1 week, repeated every 2 weeks **or**
0.75-2 mg/m^2 every 1-4 weeks **or**
400-600 mcg/m^2/day for 5 days, repeated every 3-6 weeks
Dosing in renal impairment: No adjustment necessary
Administration Avoid extravasation. Extremely damaging to soft tissue and will cause a severe local reaction if extravasation occurs. Administer slow I.V. push over 10-15 minutes. An in-line cellulose membrane filter should not be used during administration of dactinomycin solutions. Do not give I.M. or S.C.

Extravasation management: Apply ice immediately for 30-60 minutes, then alternate off/on every 15 minutes for 1 day. Data is not currently available regarding potential antidotes for dactinomycin.
Monitoring Parameters CBC with differential and platelet count, liver function tests, and renal function tests
Patient Information Limit oral intake for 4-6 hours before therapy. It is important to maintain adequate nutrition and hydration (2-3 L/day of fluids unless instructed to restrict fluid intake) during therapy; frequent small meals may help. You may experience nausea or vomiting (frequent small meals, frequent mouth care, sucking lozenges, or chewing gum may help). If this is ineffective, consult prescriber for antiemetic medication. You may experience loss of hair (reversible); you will be more susceptible to infection (avoid crowds and exposure to infection as much as possible); you will be more sensitive to sunlight; use sunblock, wear protective clothing and dark glasses, or avoid direct exposure to sunlight. Flu-like symptoms (eg, malaise, fever, myalgia) may occur 1 week after infusion and persist for 1-3 weeks; consult prescriber for severe symptoms. Report fever, chills, unusual bruising or bleeding, signs of infection, excessive fatigue, yellowing of eyes or skin, or change in color of urine or stool. Contraceptive measures are recommended during therapy.
Dosage Forms INJ, powder for reconstitution: 0.5 mg

♦ **DAD** *see* Mitoxantrone *on page 851*
♦ **D.A.II™ [DSC]** *see* Chlorpheniramine, Phenylephrine, and Methscopolamine *on page 264*
♦ **Dakin's Solution** *see* Sodium Hypochlorite Solution *on page 1149*
♦ **Dallergy®** *see* Chlorpheniramine, Phenylephrine, and Methscopolamine *on page 264*
♦ **Dallergy-JR®** *see* Chlorpheniramine and Phenylephrine *on page 262*
♦ **Dalmane®** *see* Flurazepam *on page 544*
♦ **d-Alpha Tocopherol** *see* Vitamin E *on page 1311*

Dalteparin (dal TE pa rin)
Related Information
Anticoagulants, Injectable *on page 1357*
U.S. Brand Names Fragmin®
Therapeutic Category Anticoagulant, Low Molecular Weight Heparin; Low Molecular Weight Heparin
Use Prevention of deep vein thrombosis which may lead to pulmonary embolism, in patients requiring abdominal surgery who are at risk for thromboembolism complications (eg, patients >40 years of age, obesity, patients with malignancy, history of deep vein thrombosis or pulmonary embolism, and surgical procedures requiring general anesthesia and lasting >30 minutes); prevention of DVT in patients undergoing hip-replacement surgery; patients immobile during an acute illness; acute treatment of unstable angina or non-Q-wave myocardial infarction; prevention of ischemic complications in patients on concurrent aspirin therapy
Unlabeled/Investigational Use Active treatment of deep vein thrombosis
Pregnancy Risk Factor B
Contraindications Hypersensitivity to dalteparin or any component of the formulation; thrombocytopenia associated with a positive *in vitro* test for antiplatelet antibodies in the presence of dalteparin; hypersensitivity to heparin or pork products; patients with active major bleeding; patients with unstable angina or non-Q-wave MI undergoing regional anesthesia; not for I.M. or I.V. use
Warnings/Precautions Use with caution in patients with pre-existing thrombocytopenia, recent childbirth, subacute bacterial endocarditis, peptic ulcer disease, pericarditis or pericardial effusion, liver or renal function impairment, recent lumbar puncture, vasculitis, concurrent
(Continued)

Dalteparin *(Continued)*

use of aspirin (increased bleeding risk), previous hypersensitivity to heparin, heparin-associated thrombocytopenia. If thromboembolism develops despite dalteparin prophylaxis, dalteparin should be discontinued and appropriate treatment should be initiated.

Use with caution in patients with known hypersensitivity to methylparaben or propylparaben. Monitor patient closely for signs or symptoms of bleeding. Certain patients are at increased risk of bleeding. Risk factors include bacterial endocarditis; congenital or acquired bleeding disorders; active ulcerative or angiodysplastic GI diseases; severe uncontrolled hypertension; hemorrhagic stroke; or use shortly after brain, spinal, or ophthalmology surgery; in patient treated concomitantly with platelet inhibitors; recent GI bleeding; thrombocytopenia or platelet defects; severe liver disease; hypertensive or diabetic retinopathy; or in patients undergoing invasive procedures. Use with caution in patients with severe renal failure (has not been studied). Safety and efficacy in pediatric patients have not been established. Rare cases of thrombocytopenia with thrombosis have occurred. Multidose vials contain benzyl alcohol and should not be used in pregnant women. Heparin can cause hyperkalemia by affecting aldosterone. Similar reactions could occur with LMWHs. Monitor for hyperkalemia. Discontinue therapy if platelets are <100,000/mm³.

Patients with recent or anticipated neuraxial anesthesia (epidural or spinal anesthesia) are at risk of spinal or epidural hematoma and subsequent paralysis. Consider risk versus benefit prior to neuraxial anesthesia. Risk is increased by concomitant agents which may alter hemostasis, as well as traumatic or repeated epidural or spinal puncture. Patient should be observed closely for bleeding if dalteparin is administered during or immediately following diagnostic lumbar puncture, epidural anesthesia, or spinal anesthesia.

Common Adverse Reactions 1% to 10%
Hematologic: Bleeding (3% to 5%), wound hematoma (0.1% to 3%)
Local: Pain at injection site (up to 12%), injection site hematoma (0.2% to 7%)

Drug Interactions
Increased Effect/Toxicity: The risk of bleeding with dalteparin may be increased by drugs which affect platelet function (eg, aspirin, NSAIDs, dipyridamole, ticlopidine, clopidogrel), oral anticoagulants, and thrombolytic agents. Although the risk of bleeding may be increased during concurrent warfarin therapy, dalteparin is commonly continued during the initiation of warfarin therapy to assure anticoagulation and to protect against possible transient hypercoagulability.

Mechanism of Action
Low molecular weight heparin analog with a molecular weight of 4000-6000 daltons; the commercial product contains 3% to 15% heparin with a molecular weight <3000 daltons, 65% to 78% with a molecular weight of 3000-8000 daltons and 14% to 26% with a molecular weight >8000 daltons; while dalteparin has been shown to inhibit both factor Xa and factor IIa (thrombin), the antithrombotic effect of dalteparin is characterized by a higher ratio of antifactor Xa to antifactor IIa activity (ratio = 4)

Pharmacodynamics/Kinetics
Onset of action: 1-2 hours
Duration: >12 hours
Half-life elimination (route dependent): 2-5 hours
Time to peak, serum: 4 hours

Dosage Adults: S.C.:
Abdominal surgery:
Low-to-moderate DVT risk: 2500 int. units 1-2 hours prior to surgery, then once daily for 5-10 days postoperatively
High DVT risk: 5000 int. units 1-2 hours prior to surgery and then once daily for 5-10 days postoperatively

Patients undergoing total hip surgery: **Note:** Three treatment options are currently available. Dose is given for 5-10 days, although up to 14 days of treatment have been tolerated in clinical trials:
Postoperative start:
Initial: 2500 int. units 4-8 hours* after surgery
Maintenance: 5000 int. units once daily; start at least 6 hours after postsurgical dose
Preoperative (starting day of surgery):
Initial: 2500 int. units within 2 hours before surgery
Adjustment: 2500 int. units 4-8 hours* after surgery
Maintenance: 5000 int. units once daily; start at least 6 hours after postsurgical dose
Preoperative (starting evening prior to surgery):
Initial: 5000 int. units 10-14 hours before surgery
Adjustment: 5000 int. units 4-8 hours* after surgery
Maintenance: 5000 int. units once daily, allowing 24 hours between doses.
*Dose may be delayed if hemostasis is not yet achieved.

Unstable angina or non-Q-wave myocardial infarction: 120 int. units/kg body weight (maximum dose: 10,000 int. units) every 12 hours for 5-8 days with concurrent aspirin therapy. Discontinue dalteparin once patient is clinically stable.

Immobility during acute illness: 5000 int. units once daily

Dosing adjustment in renal impairment: Half-life is increased in patients with chronic renal failure, use with caution, accumulation can be expected; specific dosage adjustments have not been recommended
Dosing adjustment in hepatic impairment: Use with caution in patients with hepatic insufficiency; specific dosage adjustments have not been recommended

Administration For deep S.C. injection only. May be injected in a U-shape to the area surrounding the navel, the upper outer side of the thigh, or the upper outer quadrangle of the buttock. Vary injection site daily. Use thumb and forefinger to lift a fold of skin when injecting dalteparin to the navel area or thigh. Insert needle at a 45- to 90-degree angle. The entire length of needle should be inserted.

Administration once daily beginning prior to surgery and continuing 5-10 days after surgery prevents deep vein thrombosis in patients at risk for thromboembolic complications. For unstable angina or non-Q-wave myocardial infarction, dalteparin is administered every 12 hours until the patient is stable (5-8 days).

Monitoring Parameters Periodic CBC including platelet count; stool occult blood tests; monitoring of PT and PTT is not necessary

Dosage Forms INJ, solution [multidose vial]: Antifactor Xa 10,000 int. units per 1 mL (9.5 mL). **INJ, solution** [preservative free; prefilled syringe]: Antifactor Xa 2500 int. units per 0.2 mL (0.2 mL); antifactor Xa 5000 int. units per 0.2 mL (0.2 mL); antifactor Xa 7500 int. units per 0.3 mL (0.3 mL); antifactor Xa 10,000 int. units per 1 mL (1 mL)

♦ **Damason-P®** see Hydrocodone and Aspirin on page 628

Danaparoid (da NAP a roid)

Related Information
Anticoagulants, Injectable on page 1357
U.S. Brand Names Orgaran® [DSC]
Synonyms Danaparoid Sodium
Therapeutic Category Anticoagulant, Heparinoid; Heparinoid
Use Prevention of postoperative deep vein thrombosis following elective hip replacement surgery
Unlabeled/Investigational Use Systemic anticoagulation for patients with heparin-induced thrombocytopenia: factor Xa inhibition is used to monitor degree of anticoagulation if necessary
Pregnancy Risk Factor B
Contraindications Hypersensitivity to danaparoid or thrombocytopenia associated with a positive in vitro test for antiplatelet antibodies in the presence of danaparoid; hypersensitivity to pork products or to sulfites (contains metabisulfite); patients with active major bleeding; severe hemorrhagic diathesis (hemophilia, idiopathic thrombocytopenic purpura); not for I.M. or I.V. use
Warnings/Precautions Do not administer intramuscularly. Danaparoid shows a low cross-sensitivity with antiplatelet antibodies in individuals with type II heparin-induced thrombocytopenia. This product contains sodium sulfite which may cause allergic-type reactions, including anaphylactic symptoms and life-threatening asthmatic episodes in susceptible people; this is seen more frequently in asthmatics.

Carefully monitor patients receiving low molecular weight heparins or heparinoids. These drugs, when used concurrently with spinal or epidural anesthesia or spinal puncture, may cause bleeding or hematomas within the spinal column. Increased pressure on the spinal cord may result in permanent paralysis if not detected and treated immediately.

Use with caution in patients with known hypersensitivity to methylparaben or propylparaben. Use with caution in patients with history of heparin-induced thrombocytopenia. Monitor patient closely for signs or symptoms of bleeding. Certain patients are at increased risk of bleeding. Risk factors include bacterial endocarditis; congenital or acquired bleeding disorders; active ulcerative or angiodysplastic GI diseases; severe uncontrolled hypertension; hemorrhagic stroke; use shortly after brain, spinal, or ophthalmology surgery; patient treated concomitantly with platelet inhibitors; recent GI bleeding; thrombocytopenia or platelet defects; severe liver disease; hypertensive or diabetic retinopathy; or patients undergoing invasive procedures. Use with caution in patients with severe renal failure (has not been studied). Safety and efficacy in pediatric patients have not been established. Heparin can cause hyperkalemia by affecting aldosterone. A similar reaction could occur with danaparoid. Monitor for hyperkalemia. Discontinue therapy if platelets are <100,000/mm^3.

Note: Danaparoid is **not** effectively antagonized by protamine sulfate. No other antidote is available, so extreme caution is needed in monitoring dose given and resulting Xa inhibition effect.

Common Adverse Reactions As with all anticoagulants, bleeding is the major adverse effect of danaparoid. Hemorrhage may occur at virtually any site. Risk is dependent on multiple variables.

>10%:
  Central nervous system: Fever (22%)
  Gastrointestinal: Nausea (4% to 14%), constipation (4% to 11%)
1% to 10%:
  Cardiovascular: Peripheral edema (3%), edema (3%)
  Central nervous system: Insomnia (3%), headache (3%), asthenia (2%), dizziness (2%), pain (9%)
  Dermatologic: Rash (2% to 5%), pruritus (4%)
  Gastrointestinal: Vomiting (3%)
  Genitourinary: Urinary tract infection (3% to 4%), urinary retention (2%)
  Hematologic: Anemia (2%)
  Local: Injection site pain (8% to 14%), injection site hematoma (5%)
  Neuromuscular & skeletal: Joint disorder (3%)
(Continued)

Danaparoid *(Continued)*

Miscellaneous: Infection (2%)

Drug Interactions

Increased Effect/Toxicity: The risk of hemorrhage associated with danaparoid may be increased with thrombolytic agents, oral anticoagulants (warfarin) and drugs which affect platelet function (eg, aspirin, NSAIDs, dipyridamole, ticlopidine, clopidogrel).

Mechanism of Action Prevents fibrin formation in coagulation pathway via thrombin generation inhibition by anti-Xa and anti-IIa effects.

Pharmacodynamics/Kinetics

Onset of action: Peak effect: S.C.: Maximum antifactor Xa and antithrombin (antifactor IIa) activities occur in 2-5 hours

Half-life elimination, plasma: Mean: Terminal: ~24 hours

Excretion: Primarily urine

Adult Danaparoid Treatment Dosing Regimens
(not FDA approved)

	Body Weight (kg)	I.V. Bolus aFXaU	Long-Term Infusion aFXaU	Level of aFX-aU/mL	Monitoring
Deep Vein Thrombosis OR Acute Pulmonary Embolism	<55 55-90 >90	1250 2500 3750	400 units/h over 4 h, then 300 units/h over 4 h, then 150-200 units/h maintenance dose	0.5-0.8	Days 1-3 daily, then every alternate day
Deep Vein Thrombosis OR Pulmonary Embolism >5 d old	<90 >90	1250 1250	S.C.: 3 x 750/d S.C.: 3 x 1250/d	<0.5	Not necessary
Embolectomy	<90 >90 and high risk	2500 preoperatively 2500 preoperatively	S.C.: 2 x 1250/d post-operatively 150-200 units/hour I.V.; perioperative arterial irrigation, if necessary: 750 units/20 mL NaCl	<0.4 0.5-0.8	Not necessary Days 1-3 daily, then every alternate day
Peripheral Arterial Bypass		2500 preoperatively	150-200 units/h	0.5-0.8	Days 1-3 daily, then every alternate day
Cardiac Catheter	<90 >90	2500 preoperatively 3750 preoperatively			
Surgery (excluding vascular)			S.C.: 750, 1-4 h pre-operatively S.C.: 750, 2-5 h post-operatively, then 2 x 750/d	<0.35	Not necessary

Hemodialysis With Danaparoid Sodium

Dialysis on alternate days:	Dosage prior to dialysis in aFXaU (dosage for body wt <55 kg):	
First dialysis	3750 (<55 kg 2500)	
Second dialysis	3750 (<55 kg 2000)	
Further dialysis:		
aFXa level before dialysis (eg, day 5)	Bolus before next dialysis, aFXaU (eg, day 7)	aFXa level during dialysis
<0.3	3000 (<55 kg 2000)	0.5-0.8
0.3-0.35	2500 (<55 kg 2000)	
0.35-0.4	2000 (<55 kg 1500)	
>0.4	No bolus; if fibrin strands occur, 1500 aFXaU I.V.	
Monitoring: 30 minutes before dialysis and after 4 hours of dialysis		
Daily Dialysis		
First dialysis	3750 (<55 kg 2500)	
Second dialysis	2500 (<55 kg 2000)	
Further dialyses	See above	
As with "dialysis on alternate days", always take the aFXa activity preceding the previous dialysis as a basis for the current dosage.		

Dosage S.C.:

Children: Safety and effectiveness have not been established.

Adults:

Prevention of DVT following hip replacement: S.C.: 750 anti-Xa units twice daily; beginning 1-4 hours before surgery and then not sooner than 2 hours after surgery and every 12 hours until the risk of DVT has diminished. The average duration of therapy is 7-10 days.

Adults: Treatment (unlabeled uses): Based on diagnosis/indication: See table on previous page.

Dosing adjustment in elderly and severe renal impairment: Adjustment may be necessary. Patients with serum creatinine levels ≥2.0 mg/dL should be carefully monitored.

Hemodialysis: See table on previous page.

Monitoring Parameters Platelets, occult blood, and anti-Xa activity, if available; the monitoring of PT and/or PTT is not necessary

Dosage Forms INJ, solution [prefilled syringe or ampul]: 750 anti-Xa units/0.6 mL (0.6 mL)

♦ **Danaparoid Sodium** *see Danaparoid on page 337*

Danazol (DA na zole)

U.S. Brand Names Danocrine®

Therapeutic Category Androgen; Antigonadotropic Agent

Use Treatment of endometriosis, fibrocystic breast disease, and hereditary angioedema

Pregnancy Risk Factor X

Contraindications Hypersensitivity to danazol or any component of the formulation; undiagnosed genital bleeding; pregnancy; breast-feeding; porphyria; markedly impaired hepatic, renal, or cardiac function

Warnings/Precautions Use with caution in patients with seizure disorders, migraine, or conditions influenced by edema. Thromboembolism, thrombotic, and thrombophlebitic events have been reported (including life-threatening or fatal strokes). Peliosis hepatis and benign hepatic adenoma have been reported with long-term use. May cause benign intracranial hypertension. Breast cancer should be ruled out prior to treatment for fibrocystic breast disease. May increase risk of atherosclerosis and coronary artery disease. May cause nonreversible androgenic effects. Pregnancy must be ruled out prior to treatment. Safety and efficacy in pediatric patients have not been established.

Common Adverse Reactions Frequency not defined.

Cardiovascular: Benign intracranial hypertension (rare), edema, flushing, hypertension

Central nervous system: Anxiety (rare), chills (rare), convulsions (rare), depression, dizziness, emotional lability, fainting, fever (rare), Guillain-Barré syndrome, headache, nervousness, sleep disorders, tremor

Dermatologic: Acne, hair loss, mild hirsutism, maculopapular rash, papular rash, petechial rash, pruritus, purpuric rash, seborrhea, Stevens-Johnson syndrome (rare), photosensitivity (rare), urticaria, vesicular rash

Endocrine & metabolic: Amenorrhea (which may continue post therapy), breast size reduction, clitoris hypertrophy, glucose intolerance, HDL decreased, LDL increased, libido changes, nipple discharge, menstrual disturbances (spotting, altered timing of cycle), semen abnormalities (changes in volume, viscosity, sperm count/motility), spermatogenesis reduction

Gastrointestinal: Appetite changes (rare), bleeding gums (rare), constipation, gastroenteritis, nausea, pancreatitis (rare), vomiting, weight gain

Genitourinary: Vaginal dryness, vaginal irritation, pelvic pain

Hematologic: Eosinophilia, erythrocytosis (reversible), leukocytosis, leukopenia, platelet count increased, polycythemia, RBC increased, thrombocytopenia

Hepatic: Cholestatic jaundice, hepatic adenoma, jaundice, liver enzymes (elevated), malignant tumors (after prolonged use), peliosis hepatis

Neuromuscular & skeletal: Back pain, carpal tunnel syndrome (rare), extremity pain, joint lockup, joint pain, joint swelling, muscle cramps, neck pain, paresthesias, spasms, weakness

Ocular: Cataracts (rare), visual disturbances

Renal: Hematuria

Respiratory: Nasal congestion (rare)

Miscellaneous: Voice change (hoarseness, sore throat, instability, deepening of pitch), diaphoresis

Drug Interactions

Cytochrome P450 Effect: Inhibits CYP3A4 (weak)

Increased Effect/Toxicity: Danazol may increase serum levels of carbamazepine, cyclosporine, tacrolimus, and warfarin leading to toxicity; dosage adjustment may be needed; monitor. Concomitant use of danazol and HMG-CoA reductase inhibitors may lead to severe myopathy or rhabdomyolysis. Danazol may enhance the glucose-lowering effect of hypoglycemic agents.

Decreased Effect: Danazol may decrease effectiveness of hormonal contraceptives. Nonhormonal birth control methods are recommended.

Mechanism of Action Suppresses pituitary output of follicle-stimulating hormone and luteinizing hormone that causes regression and atrophy of normal and ectopic endometrial tissue; decreases rate of growth of abnormal breast tissue; reduces attacks associated with hereditary angioedema by increasing levels of C4 component of complement

Pharmacodynamics/Kinetics

Onset of action: Therapeutic: ~4 weeks

Metabolism: Extensively hepatic, primarily to 2-hydroxymethylethisterone

Half-life elimination: 4.5 hours (variable)

(Continued)

Danazol *(Continued)*

Time to peak, serum: Within 2 hours

Excretion: Urine

Dosage Adults: Oral:

Female: Endometriosis: Initial: 200-400 mg/day in 2 divided doses for mild disease; individualize dosage. Usual maintenance dose: 800 mg/day in 2 divided doses to achieve amenorrhea and rapid response to painful symptoms. Continue therapy uninterrupted for 3-6 months (up to 9 months).

Female: Fibrocystic breast disease: Range: 100-400 mg/day in 2 divided doses

Male/Female: Hereditary angioedema: Initial: 200 mg 2-3 times/day; after favorable response, decrease the dosage by 50% or less at intervals of 1-3 months or longer if the frequency of attacks dictates. If an attack occurs, increase the dosage by up to 200 mg/day.

Monitoring Parameters Signs and symptoms of intracranial hypertension (papilledema, headache, nausea, vomiting), lipoproteins, androgenic changes, hepatic function

Patient Information Notify prescriber if masculinity effects occur; virilization may occur in female patients. Report menstrual irregularities; male patients report persistent penile erections; all patients should report persistent GI distress, diarrhea, or jaundice.

Dosage Forms CAP: 50 mg, 100 mg, 200 mg

- **Danocrine**® *see Danazol on page 339*
- **Dantrium**® *see Dantrolene on page 340*

Dantrolene *(DAN troe leen)*

U.S. Brand Names Dantrium®

Synonyms Dantrolene Sodium

Therapeutic Category Antidote, Malignant Hyperthermia; Hyperthermia Treatment; Skeletal Muscle Relaxant

Use Treatment of spasticity associated with spinal cord injury, stroke, cerebral palsy, or multiple sclerosis; treatment of malignant hyperthermia

Unlabeled/Investigational Use Neuroleptic malignant syndrome (NMS)

Pregnancy Risk Factor C

Contraindications Active hepatic disease; should not be used where spasticity is used to maintain posture or balance

Warnings/Precautions Use with caution in patients with impaired cardiac function or impaired pulmonary function; has potential for hepatotoxicity; overt hepatitis has been most frequently observed between the third and twelfth month of therapy; hepatic injury appears to be greater in females and in patients >35 years of age

Common Adverse Reactions

>10%:

Central nervous system: Drowsiness, dizziness, lightheadedness, fatigue

Dermatologic: Rash

Gastrointestinal: Diarrhea (mild), nausea, vomiting

Neuromuscular & skeletal: Muscle weakness

1% to 10%:

Cardiovascular: Pleural effusion with pericarditis

Central nervous system: Chills, fever, headache, insomnia, nervousness, mental depression

Gastrointestinal: Diarrhea (severe), constipation, anorexia, stomach cramps

Ocular: Blurred vision

Respiratory: Respiratory depression

Drug Interactions

Cytochrome P450 Effect: Substrate of CYP3A4 (major)

Increased Effect/Toxicity: Increased toxicity with estrogens (hepatotoxicity), CNS depressants (sedation), MAO inhibitors, phenothiazines, clindamycin (increased neuromuscular blockade), verapamil (hyperkalemia and cardiac depression), warfarin, clofibrate, and tolbutamide. CYP3A4 inhibitors may increase the levels/effects of dantrolene; example inhibitors include azole antifungals, ciprofloxacin, clarithromycin, diclofenac, doxycycline, erythromycin, imatinib, isoniazid, nefazodone, nicardipine, propofol, protease inhibitors, quinidine, and verapamil.

Decreased Effect: CYP3A4 inducers may decrease the levels/effects of dantrolene; example inducers include aminoglutethimide, carbamazepine, nafcillin, nevirapine, phenobarbital, phenytoin, and rifamycins.

Mechanism of Action Acts directly on skeletal muscle by interfering with release of calcium ion from the sarcoplasmic reticulum; prevents or reduces the increase in myoplasmic calcium ion concentration that activates the acute catabolic processes associated with malignant hyperthermia

Pharmacodynamics/Kinetics

Absorption: Oral: Slow and incomplete

Metabolism: Hepatic

Half-life elimination: 8.7 hours

Excretion: Feces (45% to 50%); urine (25% as unchanged drug and metabolites)

Dosage

Spasticity: Oral:

Children: Initial: 0.5 mg/kg/dose twice daily, increase frequency to 3-4 times/day at 4- to 7-day intervals, then increase dose by 0.5 mg/kg to a maximum of 3 mg/kg/dose 2-4 times/day up to 400 mg/day

Adults: 25 mg/day to start, increase frequency to 2-4 times/day, then increase dose by 25 mg every 4-7 days to a maximum of 100 mg 2-4 times/day or 400 mg/day

Malignant hyperthermia: Children and Adults:
Preoperative prophylaxis:
Oral: 4-8 mg/kg/day in 4 divided doses, begin 1-2 days prior to surgery with last dose 3-4 hours prior to surgery
I.V.: 2.5 mg/kg ~1¼ hours prior to anesthesia and infused over 1 hour with additional doses as needed and individualized
Crisis: I.V.: 2.5 mg/kg; may repeat dose up to cumulative dose of 10 mg/kg; if physiologic and metabolic abnormalities reappear, repeat regimen
Postcrisis follow-up: Oral: 4-8 mg/kg/day in 4 divided doses for 1-3 days; I.V. dantrolene may be used when oral therapy is not practical; individualize dosage beginning with 1 mg/kg or more as the clinical situation dictates
Neuroleptic malignant syndrome (unlabeled use): I.V.: 1 mg/kg; may repeat dose up to maximum cumulative dose of 10 mg/kg, then switch to oral dosage

Administration I.V.: Therapeutic or emergency dose can be administered with rapid continuous I.V. push. Follow-up doses should be administered over 2-3 minutes.

Monitoring Parameters Motor performance should be monitored for therapeutic outcomes; nausea, vomiting, and liver function tests should be monitored for potential hepatotoxicity; intravenous administration requires cardiac monitor and blood pressure monitor

Patient Information Avoid unnecessary exposure to sunlight (or use sunscreen, protective clothing); avoid alcohol and other CNS depressants; use caution while driving or performing other tasks requiring alertness

Dosage Forms CAP: 25 mg, 50 mg, 100 mg. **INJ, powder for reconstitution:** 20 mg

♦ **Dantrolene Sodium** see Dantrolene on page 340
♦ **Dapcin** see Daptomycin on page 342

Dapiprazole (DA pi pray zole)
U.S. Brand Names Rēv-Eyes™
Synonyms Dapiprazole Hydrochloride
Therapeutic Category Alpha-Adrenergic Blocking Agent, Ophthalmic
Use Reverse dilation due to drugs (adrenergic or parasympathomimetic) after eye exams
Pregnancy Risk Factor B
Dosage Adults: Ophthalmic: Instill 2 drops followed 5 minutes later by an additional 2 drops into the conjunctiva of each eye; should not be used more frequently than once a week in the same patient
Dosage Forms POWDER, ophthalmic: 25 mg

♦ **Dapiprazole Hydrochloride** see Dapiprazole on page 341

Dapsone (DAP sone)
Related Information
Antimicrobial Drugs of Choice on page 1440
Synonyms Diaminodiphenylsulfone
Therapeutic Category Antibiotic, Sulfone; Leprostatic Agent
Use Treatment of leprosy and dermatitis herpetiformis (infections caused by Mycobacterium leprae)
Unlabeled/Investigational Use Prophylaxis of toxoplasmosis in severely-immunocompromised patients; alternative agent for Pneumocystis carinii pneumonia prophylaxis (monotherapy) and treatment (in combination with trimethoprim)
Pregnancy Risk Factor C
Contraindications Hypersensitivity to dapsone or any component of the formulation
Warnings/Precautions Use with caution in patients with severe anemia, G6PD, methemoglobin reductase or hemoglobin M deficiency; hypersensitivity to other sulfonamides; aplastic anemia, agranulocytosis and other severe blood dyscrasias have resulted in death; monitor carefully; serious dermatologic reactions (including toxic epidermal necrolysis) are rare but potential occurrences; sulfone reactions may also occur as potentially fatal hypersensitivity reactions; these, but not leprosy reactional states, require drug discontinuation
Common Adverse Reactions 1% to 10%: Hematologic: Hemolysis, methemoglobinemia
Drug Interactions
Cytochrome P450 Effect: Substrate of CYP2C8/9 (minor), 2C19 (minor), 2E1 (minor), 3A4 (major)
Increased Effect/Toxicity: Folic acid antagonists (methotrexate) may increase the risk of hematologic reactions of dapsone; probenecid decreases dapsone excretion; trimethoprim with dapsone may increase toxic effects of both drugs. CYP3A4 inhibitors may increase the levels/effects of dapsone; example inhibitors include azole antifungals, ciprofloxacin, clarithromycin, diclofenac, doxycycline, erythromycin, imatinib, isoniazid, nefazodone, nicardipine, propofol, protease inhibitors, quinidine, and verapamil.
Decreased Effect: Para-aminobenzoic acid and rifampin levels are decreased when given with dapsone. CYP3A4 inducers may decrease the levels/effects of dapsone; example inducers include aminoglutethimide, carbamazepine, nafcillin, nevirapine, phenobarbital, phenytoin, and rifamycins.
Mechanism of Action Competitive antagonist of para-aminobenzoic acid (PABA) and prevents normal bacterial utilization of PABA for the synthesis of folic acid
(Continued)

Dapsone *(Continued)*

Pharmacodynamics/Kinetics
Absorption: Well absorbed

Distribution: V_d: 1.5 L/kg; throughout total body water and present in all tissues, especially liver and kidney

Metabolism: Hepatic

Half-life elimination: 30 hours (range: 10-50 hours)

Excretion: Urine

Dosage Oral:
Leprosy:

Children: 1-2 mg/kg/24 hours, up to a maximum of 100 mg/day

Adults: 50-100 mg/day for 3-10 years

Dermatitis herpetiformis: Adults: Start at 50 mg/day, increase to 300 mg/day, or higher to achieve full control, reduce dosage to minimum level as soon as possible

Pneumocystis carinii pneumonia (unlabeled use):

Prophylaxis:

Children >1 month: 2 mg/kg/day once daily (maximum dose: 100 mg/day) or 4 mg/kg/ dose once weekly (maximum dose: 200 mg)

Adults: 100 mg/day

Treatment: Adults: 100 mg/day in combination with trimethoprim (15-20 mg/kg/day) for 21 days

Dosing in renal impairment: No specific guidelines are available

Monitoring Parameters Monitor patient for signs of jaundice and hemolysis; CBC weekly for first month, monthly for 6 months, and semiannually thereafter

Patient Information Frequent blood tests are required during early therapy. Discontinue if rash develops and report persistent sore throat, fever, malaise, or fatigue. May cause photosensitivity.

Dosage Forms TAB: 25 mg, 100 mg

♦ **Daptacel™** *see* Diphtheria, Tetanus Toxoids, and Acellular Pertussis Vaccine *on page 389*

Daptomycin *(DAP toe mye sin)*

U.S. Brand Names Cubicin™

Synonyms Cidecin; Dapcin; LY146032

Therapeutic Category Antibiotic, Miscellaneous

Use Treatment of complicated skin and skin structure infections caused by susceptible aerobic Gram-positive organisms

Pregnancy Risk Factor B

Contraindications Hypersensitivity to daptomycin or any component of the formulation

Warnings/Precautions May be associated with an increased incidence of myopathy; discontinue in patients with signs and symptoms of myopathy in conjunction with an increase in CPK (>5 times ULN or 1000 units/L) or in asymptomatic patients with a CPK ≥10 times ULN. Myopathy may occur more frequently at dose and/or frequency in excess of recommended dosages. Use caution in patients receiving other drugs associated with myopathy (HMG-CoA reductase inhibitors). Use caution in renal impairment (dosage adjustment required). Superinfection by resistant strains and/or pseudomembranous colitis may be associated with use. Safety and efficacy in pediatric patients have not been established.

Common Adverse Reactions
1% to 10%:

Cardiovascular: Hypotension (2%), hypertension (1%)

Central nervous system: Headache (5%), insomnia (5%), dizziness (2%), fever (2%)

Dermatologic: Rash (4%), pruritus (3%)

Gastrointestinal: Constipation (6%), nausea (6%), diarrhea (5%), vomiting (3%), dyspepsia (1%)

Genitourinary: Urinary tract infection (2%)

Hematologic: Anemia (2%)

Hepatic: Transaminases increased (3%)

Local: Injection site reaction (6%)

Neuromuscular & skeletal: CPK increased (3%), limb pain (2%), arthralgia (1%)

Renal: Renal failure (2%)

Respiratory: Dyspnea (2%)

Miscellaneous: Infection (fungal, 3%)

Drug Interactions
Increased Effect/Toxicity: No clinically-significant interactions have been identified. Theoretically, concurrent use of drugs which may cause myopathy may increase the risk of these reactions. Limited clinical studies with HMG-CoA reductase inhibitors have not demonstrated an increase in adverse effects.

Mechanism of Action Daptomycin binds to components of the cell membrane of susceptible organisms and causes rapid depolarization, inhibiting intracellular synthesis of DNA, RNA, and protein. Daptomycin is bactericidal and bacterial killing is concentration-dependent.

Pharmacodynamics/Kinetics
Distribution: 0.09 L/kg

Protein binding: 92%

Half-life elimination: 8-9 hours (up to 28 hours in renal impairment)

Excretion: Urine (78%; primarily as unchanged drug); feces (6%)

Dosage I.V.: Adults: 4 mg/kg once daily for 7-14 days

Dosage adjustment in renal impairment: Cl$_{cr}$ <30 mL/minute: 4 mg/kg every 48 hours
Hemodialysis (administer after hemodialysis) and/or CAPD: Dose as in Cl$_{cr}$ <30 mL/minute
Administration Infuse over 30 minutes.
Monitoring Parameters Monitor signs and symptoms of infection. CPK should be monitored at least weekly during therapy.
Reference Range Trough concentrations at steady-state (4 mg/kg once daily): 5.9 µg/mL
Dosage Forms INJ, powder for reconstitution: 250 mg, 500 mg

♦ **Daraprim®** *see* Pyrimethamine *on page 1068*

Darbepoetin Alfa (dar be POE e tin AL fa)

U.S. Brand Names Aranesp™
Synonyms Erythropoiesis Stimulating Protein
Therapeutic Category Colony-Stimulating Factor; Recombinant Human Erythropoietin
Use Treatment of anemia associated with chronic renal failure (CRF), including patients on dialysis (ESRD) and patients not on dialysis; anemia associated with chemotherapy for nonmyeloid malignancies
Pregnancy Risk Factor C
Contraindications Hypersensitivity to darbepoetin or any component of the formulation (including polysorbate 80 and/or albumin); uncontrolled hypertension
Warnings/Precautions Erythropoietic therapies may be associated with an increased risk of cardiovascular and/or neurologic events in chronic renal failure. Darbepoetin alfa should be managed carefully; avoid hemoglobin increases >1 g/dL in any 2-week period, and do not exceed a target level of 12 g/dL. Prior to and during therapy, iron stores must be evaluated. Supplemental iron is recommended if serum ferritin <100 mcg/mL or serum transferrin saturation <20%.

Use with caution in patients with hypertension or with a history of seizures. If hypertension is difficult to control, reduce or hold darbepoetin alpha. Not recommended for acute correction of severe anemia or as a substitute for transfusion. Consider discontinuing in patients who receive a renal transplant.

Prior to treatment, correct or exclude deficiencies of vitamin B$_{12}$ and/or folate, as well as other factors which may impair erythropoiesis (aluminum toxicity, inflammatory conditions, infections). Poor response should prompt evaluation of these potential factors, as well as possible malignant processes, occult blood loss, hemolysis, and/or bone marrow fibrosis. Pure red cell aplasia (PRCA) with associated neutralizing antibodies to erythropoietin has been reported, predominantly in patients with CRF. Patients with loss of response to darbepoetin alfa should be evaluated. Discontinue treatment in patients with PRCA secondary to neutralizing antibodies to erythropoietin.

Due to the delayed onset of erythropoiesis, darbepoetin is of no value in the acute treatment of anemia. Safety and efficacy in patients with underlying hematologic diseases have not been established, including porphyria, thalassemia, hemolytic anemia, and sickle cell disease. Risk of thrombosis, including pulmonary embolism, increased in cancer patients. Safety and efficacy in pediatric patients have not been established.

Common Adverse Reactions Note: Frequency of adverse events cited in patients with CRF or cancer and may be, in part, a reflection of population in which the drug is used and/or associated with dialysis procedures.

>10%:
  Cardiovascular: Hypertension (4% to 23%), hypotension (22%), edema (21%), peripheral edema (11%), arrhythmia (10%)
  Central nervous system: Fatigue (9% to 33%), fever (9% to 19%), headache (12% to 16%), dizziness (8% to 14%)
  Gastrointestinal: Diarrhea (16% to 22%), constipation (5% to 18%) vomiting (15%), nausea (14%), abdominal pain (12%)
  Neuromuscular & skeletal: Myalgia (21%), arthralgia (11% to 13%), limb pain (10%)
  Respiratory: Upper respiratory infection (14%), dyspnea (12%), cough (10%)
  Miscellaneous: Infection (27%)
1% to 10%:
  Cardiovascular: Angina/chest pain (6% to 8%), fluid overload (6%), CHF (6%), thrombosis (6%), MI (2%)
  Central nervous system: Seizure (<1% to 1%), stroke (1%), TIA (1%)
  Dermatologic: Pruritus (8%), rash (7%)
  Endocrine & metabolic: Dehydration (5%)
  Local: Injection site pain (7%)
  Neuromuscular & skeletal: Back pain (8%), weakness (5%)
  Respiratory: Bronchitis (6%), pulmonary embolism (1%)
  Miscellaneous: Vascular access thrombosis (8%, annualized rate 0.22 events per patient year), vascular access infection (6%), influenza-like symptoms (6%), vascular access hemorrhage (6%)
Mechanism of Action Induces erythropoiesis by stimulating the division and differentiation of committed erythroid progenitor cells; induces the release of reticulocytes from the bone marrow into the bloodstream, where they mature to erythrocytes. There is a dose response relationship with this effect. This results in an increase in reticulocyte counts followed by a rise in hematocrit and hemoglobin levels. When administered S.C. or I.V., darbepoetin's half-life is ~3 times that of epoetin alfa concentrations.
(Continued)

Darbepoetin Alfa *(Continued)*

Pharmacodynamics/Kinetics

Onset of action: Increased hemoglobin levels not generally observed until 2-6 weeks after initiating treatment

Absorption: S.C.: Slow

Distribution: V_d: 0.06 L/kg

Bioavailability: CRF: S.C.: ~37% (range: 30% to 50%)

Half-life elimination: CRF: Terminal: I.V.: 21 hours, S.C.: 49 hours; **Note:** Half-life is ~3 times as long as epoetin alfa

Time to peak: S.C.: CRF: 34 hours (range: 24-72 hours); Cancer: 90 hours (range: 71-123 hours)

Dosage

I.V., S.C.: Correction of anemia associated with CRF:

Initial: 0.45 mcg/kg once weekly; dosage should be titrated to limit increases in hemoglobin to <1 g/dL over any 2-week interval, with a target concentration of <12 g/dL.

Maintenance: Titrated to hematologic response. Some patients may require doses <0.45 mcg/kg once weekly. Selected patients may be managed by administering S.C. doses every 2 weeks.

Conversion from epoetin alfa to darbepoetin alfa: Initial: Estimate dosage based on weekly epoetin alfa dosage; see table:

Conversion From Epoetin Alfa to Darbepoetin Alfa

Previous Dosage of Epoetin Alfa (units/week)	Darbepoetin Alfa Dosage (mcg/week)
<2500	6.25
2500-4999	12.5
5000-10,999	25
11,000-17,999	40
18,000-33,999	60
34,000-89,999	100
≥90,000	200

Note: In patients receiving epoetin alfa 2-3 times per week, darbepoetin alfa is administered once weekly. In patients receiving epoetin alfa once weekly, darbepoetin alfa is administered once every 2 weeks.

Dosage adjustment: Goal: Dose should be adjusted to achieve and maintain a target hemoglobin not to exceed 12 g/dL.

Inadequate response: Hemoglobin increases <1 g/dL over 4 weeks and iron stores are adequate: Increase by ~25% of the previous dose; increases should not be made more frequently than once monthly.

Excessive response:

Hemoglobin increases >1 g/dL in any 2-week period: Decrease dose

Hemoglobin increases and approaches the target value of 12 g/dL: Decrease weekly dosage by ~25%. If hemoglobin continues to increase, hold dose temporarily until hemoglobin begins to decrease, then restart at a dose 25% below the previous dose.

S.C.: Correction of anemia associated with cancer patients receiving chemotherapy: Initial: 2.25 mcg/kg once weekly; adjust dose as follows to achieve and maintain a target hemoglobin:

Inadequate response: Hemoglobin increases <1 g/dL after 6 weeks of therapy: Increase dose to 4.5 mcg/kg

Excessive responses:

Hemoglobin increases >1 g/dL in a 2-week period **OR** if hemoglobin exceeds 12 g/dL: Reduce dose by 25%

Hemoglobin >13 g/dL: Withhold dose until hemoglobin falls to 12 g/dL, then reinitiate at 25% less than previous dose.

Dosage adjustment in renal impairment: Dosage requirements for patients with chronic renal failure who do not require dialysis may be lower than in dialysis patients. Monitor patients closely during the time period in which a dialysis regimen is initiated, dosage requirement may increase.

Administration May be administered by S.C. or I.V. injection. Do not shake; vigorous shaking may denature darbepoetin alfa, rendering it biologically inactive. Do not dilute or administer in conjunction with other drug solutions. Discard any unused portion of the vial; do not pool unused portions. Discontinue immediately if signs/symptoms of anaphylaxis occur.

Monitoring Parameters Hemoglobin (weekly until maintenance dose established and after dosage changes; monitor at regular intervals once hemoglobin is stabilized); iron stores (prior to and during therapy)

Patient Information You will require frequent blood tests to determine appropriate dosage. Do not take other medications, vitamin or iron supplements, or make significant changes in your diet without consulting prescriber. Report signs or symptoms of edema (eg, swollen extremities, difficulty breathing, rapid weight gain), onset of severe headache, acute back pain, chest pain, or muscular tremors or seizure activity. Be careful to check blood pressure regularly.

Dosage Forms INJ, solution, with human albumin 2.5 mg/mL [preservative free]: 25 mcg/mL (1 mL); 40 mcg/mL (1 mL); 60 mcg/mL (1 mL); 100 mcg/mL (1 mL); 150 mcg/0.75 mL (0.75 mL); 200 mcg/mL (1 mL); 300 mcg/mL (1 mL); 500 mcg/mL (1 mL)

- **Darvocet A500**™ *see Propoxyphene and Acetaminophen on page 1054*
- **Darvocet-N® 50** *see Propoxyphene and Acetaminophen on page 1054*
- **Darvocet-N® 100** *see Propoxyphene and Acetaminophen on page 1054*
- **Darvon®** *see Propoxyphene on page 1053*
- **Darvon® Compound** *see Propoxyphene, Aspirin, and Caffeine on page 1054*
- **Darvon-N®** *see Propoxyphene on page 1053*
- **Daunomycin** *see DAUNOrubicin Hydrochloride on page 346*

DAUNOrubicin Citrate (Liposomal)
(daw noe ROO bi sin SI trate lip po SOE mal)

U.S. Brand Names DaunoXome®

Therapeutic Category Antineoplastic Agent, Anthracycline

Use First-line cytotoxic therapy for advanced HIV-associated Kaposi's sarcoma

Pregnancy Risk Factor D

Contraindications Hypersensitivity to daunorubicin or any component of the formulation; pregnancy

Warnings/Precautions The U.S. Food and Drug Administration (FDA) currently recommends that procedures for proper handling and disposal of antineoplastic agents be considered. Daunorubicin is associated with a dose-related cardiac toxicity. The risk of similar toxicity with liposome-encapsulated daunorubicin is not certain. Use caution patients with previous therapy with high cumulative doses of anthracyclines, cyclophosphamide, or thoracic radiation, or who have pre-existing cardiac disease.

Common Adverse Reactions

>10%:
  Central nervous system: Fatigue (51%), headache (28%), neuropathy (13%)
  Hematologic: Myelosuppression, neutropenia (51%), thrombocytopenia, anemia
    Onset: 7 days
    Nadir: 14 days
    Recovery: 21 days
  Gastrointestinal: Abdominal pain, vomiting, anorexia (23%); diarrhea (38%); nausea (55%)
  Respiratory: Cough (28%), dyspnea (26%), rhinitis
  Miscellaneous: Allergic reactions (24%)

1% to 10%:
  Cardiovascular: Hypertension, palpitations, syncope, tachycardia, chest pain, edema
  Dermatologic: Alopecia (8%), pruritus (7%)
  Endocrine & metabolic: Hot flashes
  Gastrointestinal: Constipation (7%), stomatitis (10%)
  Neuromuscular & skeletal: Arthralgia (7%), myalgia (7%)
  Ocular: Conjunctivitis, eye pain (5%)
  Respiratory: Sinusitis

Drug Interactions

Decreased Effect: Patients may experience impaired immune response to vaccines; possible infection after administration of live vaccines in patients receiving immunosuppressants.

Mechanism of Action Liposomes have been shown to penetrate solid tumors more effectively, possibly because of their small size and longer circulation time. Once in tissues, daunorubicin is released. Daunorubicin inhibits DNA and RNA synthesis by intercalation between DNA base pairs and by steric obstruction; and intercalates at points of local uncoiling of the double helix. Although the exact mechanism is unclear, it appears that direct binding to DNA (intercalation) and inhibition of DNA repair (topoisomerase II inhibition) result in blockade of DNA and RNA synthesis and fragmentation of DNA.

Pharmacodynamics/Kinetics

Distribution: V_d: 3-6.4 L
Metabolism: Similar to daunorubicin, but metabolite plasma levels are low
Half-life elimination: Distribution: 4.4 hours; Terminal: 3-5 hours
Excretion: Primarily feces; some urine
  Clearance, plasma: 17.3 mL/minute

Dosage Refer to individual protocols. Adults: I.V.:
20-40 mg/m^2 every 2 weeks
100 mg/m^2 every 3 weeks

Dosing adjustment in renal impairment: Serum creatinine >3 mg/dL: Administer 50% of normal dose

Dosing adjustment in hepatic impairment:
Bilirubin 1.2-3 mg/dL: Administer 75% of normal dose
Bilirubin >3 mg/dL: Administer 50% of normal dose

Administration Infuse over 1 hour; do not mix with other drugs. **Extravasation management:** Infiltration can cause severe inflammation, tissue necrosis, and ulceration. If the drug is infiltrated, consult institutional policy, apply ice to the area, and elevate the limb.

Monitoring Parameters Observe patient closely and monitor chemical and laboratory tests extensively. Evaluate cardiac, renal, and hepatic function. Repeat blood counts prior to each dose and withhold if the absolute granulocyte count is <750 cells/mm^3. Monitor serum uric acid levels.

Dosage Forms INJ, solution: 2 mg/mL (25 mL)

DAUNOrubicin Hydrochloride (daw noe ROO bi sin hye droe KLOR ide)

U.S. Brand Names Cerubidine®

Synonyms Daunomycin; DNR; NSC-82151; Rubidomycin Hydrochloride

Therapeutic Category Antineoplastic Agent, Anthracycline; Antineoplastic Agent, Vesicant; Vesicant

Use Treatment of acute lymphocytic (ALL) and nonlymphocytic (ANLL) leukemias

Pregnancy Risk Factor D

Contraindications Hypersensitivity to daunorubicin or any component of the formulation; congestive heart failure or arrhythmias; previous therapy with high cumulative doses of daunorubicin and/or doxorubicin; pre-existing bone marrow suppression; pregnancy

Warnings/Precautions The U.S. Food and Drug Administration (FDA) currently recommends that procedures for proper handling and disposal of antineoplastic agents be considered. I.V. use only, severe local tissue necrosis will result if extravasation occurs; reduce dose in patients with impaired hepatic, renal, or biliary function; severe myelosuppression is possible when used in therapeutic doses. Total cumulative dose should take into account previous or concomitant treatment with cardiotoxic agents or irradiation of chest.

Irreversible myocardial toxicity may occur as total dosage approaches:

550 mg/m^2 in adults

400 mg/m^2 in patients receiving chest radiation

300 mg/m^2 in children >2 years of age

Common Adverse Reactions

>10%:

Cardiovascular: Transient ECG abnormalities (supraventricular tachycardia, S-T wave changes, atrial or ventricular extrasystoles); generally asymptomatic and self-limiting. Congestive heart failure, dose-related, may be delayed for 7-8 years after treatment. Cumulative dose, radiation therapy, age, and use of cyclophosphamide all increase the risk. Recommended maximum cumulative doses:

No risk factors: $550\text{-}600 \text{ mg/m}^2$

Concurrent radiation: 450 mg/m^2

Regardless of cumulative dose, if the left ventricular ejection fraction is <30% to 40%, the drug is usually not given

Dermatologic: Alopecia, radiation recall

Gastrointestinal: Mild nausea or vomiting, stomatitis

Genitourinary: Discoloration of urine (red)

Hematologic: Myelosuppression, primarily leukopenia; thrombocytopenia and anemia

Onset: 7 days

Nadir: 10-14 days

Recovery: 21-28 days

1% to 10%:

Dermatologic: Skin "flare" at injection site; discoloration of saliva, sweat, or tears

Endocrine & metabolic: Hyperuricemia

Gastrointestinal: GI ulceration, diarrhea

Drug Interactions

Decreased Effect: Patients may experience impaired immune response to vaccines; possible infection after administration of live vaccines in patients receiving immunosuppressants.

Mechanism of Action Inhibition of DNA and RNA synthesis by intercalation between DNA base pairs and by steric obstruction. Daunomycin intercalates at points of local uncoiling of the double helix. Although the exact mechanism is unclear, it appears that direct binding to DNA (intercalation) and inhibition of DNA repair (topoisomerase II inhibition) result in blockade of DNA and RNA synthesis and fragmentation of DNA.

Pharmacodynamics/Kinetics

Distribution: Many body tissues, particularly the liver, kidneys, lung, spleen, and heart; not into CNS; crosses placenta; V_d: 40 L/kg

Metabolism: Primarily hepatic to daunorubicinol (active), then to inactive aglycones, conjugated sulfates and glucuronides

Half-life elimination: Distribution: 2 minutes; Elimination: 14-20 hours; Terminal: 18.5 hours; Daunorubicinol plasma half-life: 24-48 hours

Excretion: Feces (40%); urine (~25% as unchanged drug and metabolites)

Dosage I.V. (refer to individual protocols):

Children:

ALL combination therapy: Remission induction: $25\text{-}45 \text{ mg/m}^2$ on day 1 every week for 4 cycles **or** $30\text{-}45 \text{ mg/m}^2$/day for 3 days

AML combination therapy: Induction: I.V. continuous infusion: $30\text{-}60 \text{ mg/m}^2$/day on days 1-3 of cycle

Note: In children <2 years or <0.5 m^2, daunorubicin should be based on weight - mg/kg: 1 mg/kg per protocol with frequency dependent on regimen employed

Cumulative dose should not exceed 300 mg/m^2 in children >2 years; maximum cumulative doses for younger children are unknown.

Adults:

Range: $30\text{-}60 \text{ mg/m}^2$/day for 3-5 days, repeat dose in 3-4 weeks

AML: Single agent induction: 60 mg/m^2/day for 3 days; repeat every 3-4 weeks

AML: Combination therapy induction: 45 mg/m^2/day for 3 days of the first course of induction therapy; subsequent courses: Every day for 2 days

ALL combination therapy: 45 mg/m^2/day for 3 days

Cumulative dose should not exceed 400-600 mg/m^2

Dosing adjustment in renal impairment:

Cl$_{cr}$ <10 mL/minute: Administer 75% of normal dose

S$_{cr}$ >3 mg/dL: Administer 50% of normal dose

Dosing adjustment in hepatic impairment:

Serum bilirubin 1.2-3 mg/dL or AST 60-180 int. units: Reduce dose to 75%

Serum bilirubin 3.1-5 mg/dL or AST >180 int. units: Reduce dose to 50%

Serum bilirubin >5 mg/dL: Omit use

Administration Not for I.M. or S.C. administration. Administer IVP over 1-5 minutes into the tubing of a rapidly infusing I.V. solution of D$_5$W or NS; daunorubicin has also been diluted in 100 mL of D$_5$W or NS and infused over 15-30 minutes.

Extravasation management: Apply ice immediately for 30-60 minutes; then alternate off/on every 15 minutes for 1 day. Topical cooling may be achieved using ice packs or cooling pad with circulating ice water. Cooling of site for 24 hours as tolerated by the patient. Elevate and rest extremities 24-48 hours, then resume normal activity as tolerated. Application of cold inhibits vesicant's cytotoxicity. Application of heat or sodium bicarbonate can be harmful and is contraindicated. If pain, erythema, and/or swelling persist beyond 48 hours, refer patient immediately to plastic surgeon for consultation and possible debridement.

Monitoring Parameters CBC with differential and platelet count, liver function test, ECG, ventricular ejection fraction, renal function test

Patient Information This medication can only be administered I.V. During therapy, do not use alcohol, aspirin-containing products, and/or OTC medications without consulting prescriber. It is important to maintain adequate nutrition and hydration (2-3 L/day of fluids unless instructed to restrict fluid intake) during therapy; frequent small meals may help. You may experience nausea or vomiting (frequent small meals, frequent mouth care, sucking lozenges, or chewing gum may help). You may experience loss of hair (reversible); you will be more susceptible to infection (avoid crowds and exposure to infection as much as possible). Urine may turn red (normal). Yogurt or buttermilk may help reduce diarrhea (if unresolved, contact prescriber). Report fever, chills, unusual bruising or bleeding, signs of infection, abdominal pain or blood in stools, excessive fatigue, yellowing of eyes or skin, swelling of extremities, difficulty breathing, or unresolved diarrhea. Contraceptive measures are recommended during therapy.

Dosage Forms INJ, powder for reconstitution: 20 mg. **INJ, solution:** 5 mg/mL (4 mL, 10 mL)

♦ **DaunoXome®** *see* DAUNOrubicin Citrate (Liposomal) *on page 345*

♦ **1-Day™ [OTC]** *see* Tioconazole *on page 1232*

♦ **Daypro®** *see* Oxaprozin *on page 938*

♦ **dCF** *see* Pentostatin *on page 980*

♦ **DDAVP®** *see* Desmopressin *on page 354*

♦ **ddC** *see* Zalcitabine *on page 1321*

♦ **ddI** *see* Didanosine *on page 370*

♦ **1-Deamino-8-D-Arginine Vasopressin** *see* Desmopressin *on page 354*

♦ **Debrox® [OTC]** *see* Carbamide Peroxide *on page 216*

♦ **Decadron®** *see* Dexamethasone *on page 356*

♦ **Decadron® Phosphate [DSC]** *see* Dexamethasone *on page 356*

♦ **Deca-Durabolin® [DSC]** *see* Nandrolone *on page 880*

♦ **Declomycin®** *see* Demeclocycline *on page 350*

♦ **Decofed® [OTC]** *see* Pseudoephedrine *on page 1061*

♦ **Deconamine®** *see* Chlorpheniramine and Pseudoephedrine *on page 263*

♦ **Deconamine® SR** *see* Chlorpheniramine and Pseudoephedrine *on page 263*

♦ **Deconsal® II** *see* Guaifenesin and Pseudoephedrine *on page 605*

♦ **Defen-LA®** *see* Guaifenesin and Pseudoephedrine *on page 605*

Deferoxamine (de fer OKS a meen)

U.S. Brand Names Desferal®

Synonyms Deferoxamine Mesylate

Therapeutic Category Antidote, Aluminum Toxicity; Antidote, Iron Toxicity; Chelating Agent, Parenteral

Use Acute iron intoxication when serum iron is >450-500 µg/dL or when clinical signs of significant iron toxicity exist; chronic iron overload secondary to multiple transfusions; iron overload secondary to congenital anemias; hemochromatosis

Unlabeled/Investigational Use Removal of corneal rust rings following surgical removal of foreign bodies; diagnostic test for iron and aluminum overload

Investigational: Treatment of aluminum accumulation in renal failure; treatment of aluminum-induced bone disease

Pregnancy Risk Factor C

Contraindications Hypersensitivity to deferoxamine or any component of the formulation; patients with anuria, primary hemochromatosis

Warnings/Precautions Use with caution in patients with severe renal disease, pyelonephritis; may increase susceptibility to *Yersinia enterocolitica*. Ocular and auditory disturbances, as (Continued)

Deferoxamine *(Continued)*

well as growth retardation (children only), have been reported following prolonged administration. Has been associated with adult respiratory distress syndrome (ARDS) following excessively high-dose treatment of acute intoxication.

Common Adverse Reactions Frequency not defined.

Cardiovascular: Flushing, hypotension, tachycardia, shock, edema

Central nervous system: Convulsions, fever, dizziness, neuropathy, paresthesia, seizures, exacerbation of aluminum-related encephalopathy (dialysis), headache, CNS depression, coma, aphasia, agitation

Dermatologic: Erythema, urticaria, pruritus, rash, cutaneous wheal formation

Endocrine & metabolic: Hypocalcemia

Gastrointestinal: Abdominal discomfort, diarrhea, nausea

Genitourinary: Dysuria

Hematologic: Thrombocytopenia, leukopenia

Local: Pain and induration at injection site

Neuromuscular & skeletal: Leg cramps

Ocular: Blurred vision, visual loss, scotoma, visual field defects, impaired vision, optic neuritis, cataracts, retinal pigmentary abnormalities

Otic: Hearing loss, tinnitus

Renal: Renal impairment, acute renal failure

Respiratory: Acute respiratory distress syndrome (with dyspnea, cyanosis)

Miscellaneous: Anaphylaxis

Drug Interactions

Increased Effect/Toxicity: May cause loss of consciousness when administered with prochlorperazine. Concomitant treatment with vitamin C (>500 mg/day) has been associated with cardiac impairment.

Mechanism of Action Complexes with trivalent ions (ferric ions) to form ferrioxamine, which are removed by the kidneys

Pharmacodynamics/Kinetics

Absorption: Oral: <15%

Metabolism: Hepatic to ferrioxamine

Half-life elimination: Parent drug: 6.1 hours; Ferrioxamine: 5.8 hours

Excretion: Urine (as unchanged drug and metabolites)

Dosage

Children and Adults:

Acute iron toxicity: I.V. route is used when severe toxicity is evidenced by systemic symptoms (coma, shock, metabolic acidosis, or severe gastrointestinal bleeding) or potentially severe intoxications (serum iron level >500 µg/dL). When severe symptoms are not present, the I.M. route may be preferred; however, the use of deferoxamine in situations where the serum iron concentration is <500 µg/dL or when severe toxicity is not evident is a subject of some clinical debate.

Dose: For the first 1000 mg, infuse at 15 mg/kg/hour (although rates up to 40-50 mg/kg/ hour have been given in patients with massive iron intoxication); may be followed by 500 mg every 4 hours for up to 2 doses; subsequent doses of 500 mg have been administered every 4-12 hours

Maximum recommended dose: 6 g/day (however, doses as high as 16-37 g have been administered)

Children:

Chronic iron overload: S.C.: 20-40 mg/kg/day over 8-12 hours (via a portable, controlled infusion device)

Aluminum-induced bone disease (unlabeled use): 20-40 mg/kg every hemodialysis treatment, frequency dependent on clinical status of the patient

Adults: Chronic iron overload:

I.M.: 500-1000 mg/day; in addition, 2000 mg should be given with each unit of blood transfused (administer separately from blood)

I.V.: 2 g after each unit of blood infusion at 15 mg/kg/hour

S.C.: 1-2 g every day over 8-24 hours

Dosing adjustment in renal impairment: Cl_{cr} <10 mL/minute: Administer 50% of dose

Has been used investigationally as a single 40 mg/kg I.V. dose over 2 hours, to promote mobilization of aluminum from tissue stores as an aid in the diagnosis of aluminum-associated osteodystrophy

Administration Administer I.M., slow S.C., or I.V. infusion

I.M.: I.M. administration is preferred in patients not in shock. Add 2 mL sterile water to 500 mg vial. For I.M. or S.C. administration, no further dilution is required.

I.V.: The manufacturer states that the I.M. route is preferred; however, the I.V. route is generally preferred in patients with severe toxicity (ie, patients in shock). Urticaria, hypotension, and shock have occurred following rapid I.V. administration; maximum I.V. rate: 15 mg/ kg/hour for first 1000 mg; subsequent dosing, if needed, should not exceed 125 mg/hour

Monitoring Parameters Serum iron, total iron-binding capacity; ophthalmologic exam (fundoscopy, slit-lamp exam) and audiometry with chronic therapy

Patient Information May turn urine pink; blood and urine tests are necessary to follow therapy

Dosage Forms INJ, powder for reconstitution: 500 mg, 2 g

Delavirdine (de la VIR deen)

Related Information
Antiretroviral Therapy for HIV Infection *on page 1448*
Management of Healthcare Worker Exposures to HBV, HCV, and HIV *on page 1421*
U.S. Brand Names Rescriptor®
Synonyms U-90152S
Therapeutic Category Antiretroviral Agent, Non-nucleoside Reverse Transcriptase Inhibitor (NNRTI)
Use Treatment of HIV-1 infection in combination with at least two additional antiretroviral agents
Pregnancy Risk Factor C
Contraindications Hypersensitivity to delavirdine or any component of the formulation; concurrent use of alprazolam, astemizole, cisapride, ergot alkaloids, midazolam, pimozide, or triazolam
Warnings/Precautions Avoid use with benzodiazepines, cisapride, clarithromycin, dapsone, enzyme-inducing anticonvulsants (carbamazepine, phenytoin, phenobarbital, rifampin, rifabutin, or St John's wort); may lead to loss of efficacy or development of resistance. Concurrent use of lovastatin or simvastatin should be avoided (use caution with other statins). Use caution with amphetamines, antacids, antiarrhythmics, benzodiazepines (alprazolam, midazolam, and triazolam are contraindicated), clarithromycin, dihydropyridine, calcium channel blockers, dapsone, immunosuppressants, methadone, oral contraceptives, or sildenafil.

Use with caution in patients with hepatic or renal dysfunction; due to rapid emergence of resistance, delavirdine should not be used as monotherapy; cross-resistance may be conferred to other non-nucleoside reverse transcriptase inhibitors. Long-term effects of delavirdine are not known. Safety and efficacy have not been established in children. Rash, which occurs frequently, may require discontinuation of therapy; usually occurs within 1-3 weeks and lasts <2 weeks. Most patients may resume therapy following a treatment interruption.

Common Adverse Reactions
>10%: Dermatologic: Rash (3.2% required discontinuation)
1% to 10%:
Central nervous system: Headache, fatigue
Dermatologic: Pruritus
Gastrointestinal: Nausea, diarrhea, vomiting
Metabolic: Increased ALT (SGPT), increased AST (SGOT)
Drug Interactions
Cytochrome P450 Effect: Substrate of CYP2D6 (minor), 3A4 (major); **Inhibits** CYP1A2 (weak), 2C8/9 (strong), 2C19 (strong), 2D6 (strong), 3A4 (weak)
Increased Effect/Toxicity: Delavirdine concentrations may be increased by clarithromycin, ketoconazole, and fluoxetine. Delavirdine increases plasma concentrations of alprazolam, amiodarone, amphetamines, amprenavir, astemizole, bepridil, calcium channel blockers (dihydropyridine-type), cisapride, clarithromycin, dapsone, dexamethasone, ergot alkaloids, flecainide, HMG-CoA reductase inhibitors, indinavir, methadone, midazolam, pimozide, propafenone, quinidine, rifabutin, saquinavir, sildenafil, triazolam, and warfarin.
Decreased Effect: CYP3A4 inducers may decrease the levels/effects of delavirdine; example inducers include aminoglutethimide, carbamazepine, nafcillin, nevirapine, phenobarbital, phenytoin, and rifamycins. Decreased plasma concentrations of delavirdine with amprenavir, dexamethasone, rifabutin, rifampin, didanosine, and saquinavir. Decreased absorption of delavirdine with antacids, histamine-2 receptor antagonists, proton pump inhibitors (omeprazole, lansoprazole), and didanosine. Delavirdine decreases plasma concentrations of didanosine.
Mechanism of Action Delavirdine binds directly to reverse transcriptase, blocking RNA-dependent and DNA-dependent DNA polymerase activities
Pharmacodynamics/Kinetics
Absorption: Rapid
Distribution: Low concentration in saliva and semen; CSF 0.4% concurrent plasma concentration
Protein binding: ~98%, primarily albumin
Metabolism: Hepatic via CYP3A4 and 2D6 (**Note:** May reduce CYP3A activity and inhibit its own metabolism.)
Bioavailability: 85%
Half-life elimination: 2-11 hours
Time to peak, plasma: 1 hour
Excretion: Urine (51%, <5% as unchanged drug); feces (44%); nonlinear kinetics exhibited
Dosage Adults: Oral: 400 mg 3 times/day
Administration Patients with achlorhydria should take the drug with an acidic beverage; antacids and delavirdine should be separated by 1 hour
Monitoring Parameters Liver function tests if administered with saquinavir
Patient Information Stay under the care of a physician when using delavirdine; report rash or symptoms of rash with fever, blistering, oral lesions, conjunctivitis, swelling, or muscle/joint pain. Consult pharmacist or physician prior to taking any other medications (including OTC medications and herbal products) due to the potential for drug interactions.
Dosage Forms TAB: 100 mg, 200 mg

♦ **Delestrogen®** *see* Estradiol *on page 459*
♦ **Delta-9-tetrahydro-cannabinol** *see* Dronabinol *on page 416*

♦ **Delta-9 THC** *see* Dronabinol *on page 416*
♦ **Deltacortisone** *see* PredniSONE *on page 1033*
♦ **Deltadehydrocortisone** *see* PredniSONE *on page 1033*
♦ **Deltahydrocortisone** *see* PrednisoLONE *on page 1031*
♦ **Deltasone®** *see* PredniSONE *on page 1033*
♦ **Demadex®** *see* Torsemide *on page 1246*

Demeclocycline (dem e kloe SYE kleen)

U.S. Brand Names Declomycin®
Synonyms Demeclocycline Hydrochloride; Demethylchlortetracycline
Therapeutic Category Antibiotic, Tetracycline Derivative
Use Treatment of susceptible bacterial infections (acne, gonorrhea, pertussis and urinary tract infections) caused by both gram-negative and gram-positive organisms
Unlabeled/Investigational Use Treatment of chronic syndrome of inappropriate secretion of antidiuretic hormone (SIADH)
Pregnancy Risk Factor D
Contraindications Hypersensitivity to demeclocycline, tetracyclines, or any component of the formulation; children <8 years of age; concomitant use with methoxyflurane; pregnancy
Warnings/Precautions Photosensitivity reactions occur frequently with this drug, avoid prolonged exposure to sunlight, do not use tanning equipment. Use of tetracyclines during tooth development may cause permanent discoloration of the teeth and enamel, hypoplasia and retardation of skeletal development and bone growth with risk being the greatest for children <4 years and those receiving high doses; use caution in patients with renal or hepatic impairment; dosage modification required in patients with renal impairment; may act as an anti-anabolic agent and increase BUN; pseudotumor cerebri has been reported with tetracycline use (usually resolves with discontinuation); outdated drug can cause nephropathy; superinfection possible
Common Adverse Reactions Frequency not defined.
  Cardiovascular: Pericarditis
  Central nervous system: Bulging fontanels (infants), dizziness, headache, pseudotumor cerebri (adults)
  Dermatologic: Angioneurotic edema, erythema multiforme, erythematous rash, maculopapular rash, photosensitivity, pigmentation of skin, Stevens-Johnson syndrome (rare), urticaria
  Endocrine & metabolic: Discoloration of thyroid gland (brown/black), nephrogenic diabetes insipidus
  Gastrointestinal: Anorexia, diarrhea, dysphagia, enterocolitis, esophageal ulcerations, glossitis, nausea, pancreatitis, vomiting
  Genitourinary: Balanitis
  Hematologic: Eosinophilia, neutropenia, hemolytic anemia, thrombocytopenia
  Hepatic: Hepatitis (rare), hepatotoxicity (rare), liver enzymes increased, liver failure (rare)
  Neuromuscular & skeletal: Myasthenic syndrome, polyarthralgia, tooth discoloration (children < 8 years, rarely in adults)
  Ocular: Visual disturbances
  Otic: Tinnitus
  Renal: Acute renal failure
  Respiratory: Pulmonary infiltrates
  Miscellaneous: Anaphylaxis, anaphylactoid purpura, lupus-like syndrome, systemic lupus erythematosus exacerbation
Drug Interactions
  Increased Effect/Toxicity: Methoxyflurane anesthesia may cause fatal nephrotoxicity; retinoic acid derivatives may increase adverse and toxic effects; warfarin may result in increased anticoagulation; methotrexate levels may be increased
  Decreased Effect: Antacid preparations containing calcium, magnesium, aluminum bismuth, or sodium bicarbonate may decrease tetracycline absorption; bile acid sequestrants, quinapril (magnesium-containing formulation), iron, or zinc may also decrease absorption; penicillin decrease therapeutic effect of tetracyclines. Although anecdotal reports suggest oral contraceptive efficacy could be reduced by tetracyclines, this has been refuted by more rigorous scientific and clinical data.
Mechanism of Action Inhibits protein synthesis by binding with the 30S and possibly the 50S ribosomal subunit(s) of susceptible bacteria; may also cause alterations in the cytoplasmic membrane; inhibits the action of ADH in patients with chronic SIADH
Pharmacodynamics/Kinetics
  Onset of action: SIADH: Several days
  Absorption: ~50% to 80%; reduced by food and dairy products
  Protein binding: 41% to 50%
  Metabolism: Hepatic (small amounts) to inactive metabolites; undergoes enterohepatic recirculation
  Half-life elimination: 10-17 hours
  Time to peak, serum: 3-6 hours
  Excretion: Urine (42% to 50% as unchanged drug)
Dosage Oral:
  Children ≥8 years: 8-12 mg/kg/day divided every 6-12 hours
  Adults: 150 mg 4 times/day or 300 mg twice daily
    SIADH (unlabeled use): 900-1200 mg/day or 13-15 mg/kg/day divided every 6-8 hours initially, then decrease to 600-900 mg/day

Dosing adjustment/comments in renal/hepatic impairment: Should be avoided in patients with renal/hepatic dysfunction

Administration Administer 1 hour before or 2 hours after food or milk with plenty of fluid

Monitoring Parameters CBC, renal and hepatic function

Patient Information Avoid prolonged exposure to sunlight or sunlamps; avoid taking antacids before tetracyclines

Dosage Forms TAB: 150 mg, 300 mg

♦ **Demeclocycline Hydrochloride** *see* Demeclocycline *on page 350*

♦ **Demerol®** *see* Meperidine *on page 791*

♦ **4-Demethoxydaunorubicin** *see* Idarubicin *on page 648*

♦ **Demethylchlortetracycline** *see* Demeclocycline *on page 350*

♦ **Demser®** *see* Metyrosine *on page 833*

♦ **Demulen®** *see* Ethinyl Estradiol and Ethynodiol Diacetate *on page 480*

♦ **Denavir®** *see* Penciclovir *on page 970*

Denileukin Diftitox (de ni LOO kin DIF ti toks)

U.S. Brand Names ONTAK®

Therapeutic Category Antineoplastic Agent, Miscellaneous

Use Treatment of persistent or recurrent cutaneous T-cell lymphoma whose malignant cells express the CD25 component of the IL-2 receptor

Pregnancy Risk Factor C

Contraindications Hypersensitivity to denileukin diftitox, diphtheria toxin, interleukin-2, or any component of the formulation

Warnings/Precautions Acute hypersensitivity reactions, including anaphylaxis, may occur; most events occur during or within 24 hours of the first dose of a treatment cycle. Has been associated with a delayed-onset vascular leak syndrome, which may be severe. The onset of symptoms of vascular leak syndrome usually occurred within the first 2 weeks of infusion and may persist or worsen after cessation of denileukin diftitox. Pre-existing low serum albumin levels may predict or predispose to vascular leak syndrome. Denileukin diftitox may impair immune function. Use with caution in patients with pre-existing cardiovascular disease and in patients >65 years of age.

Common Adverse Reactions

The occurrence of adverse events diminishes after the first two treatment courses. Infusion-related hypersensitivity reactions have been reported in 69% of patients. Reactions are variable, but may include hypotension, back pain, dyspnea, vasodilation, rash, chest pain, tachycardia, dysphagia, syncope or anaphylaxis. In addition, a flu-like syndrome, beginning several hours to days following infusion, occurred in 91% of patients.

In 27% of patients a vascular leak syndrome occurred, characterized by hypotension, edema, or hypoalbuminemia. The syndrome usually developed within the first 2 weeks of infusion. Six percent of patients who developed this syndrome required hospitalization. The symptoms may persist or even worsen despite cessation of denileukin diftitox.

Severe (Grade 3 and 4) reactions which occurred with an incidence over 10% included: Chills/fever (22%), asthenia (22%), infection (24%), pain (13%), nausea/vomiting (14%), hypoalbuminemia (14%), transaminase elevation (15%), edema (15%), dyspnea (14%), and rash (13%).

The following list of symptoms reported during treatment includes all levels of severity:

>10%:

Cardiovascular: Edema (47%), hypotension (36%), chest pain (24%), vasodilation (22%), tachycardia (12%)

Central nervous system: Fever/chills (81%), headache (26%), pain (48%), dizziness (22%), nervousness (11%)

Dermatologic: Rash (34%), pruritus (20%)

Endocrine & metabolic: Hypoalbuminemia (83%), hypocalcemia (17%), weight loss (14%)

Gastrointestinal: Nausea/vomiting (64%), anorexia (36%), diarrhea (29%)

Hematologic: Decreased lymphocyte count (34%), anemia (18%)

Hepatic: Increased transaminases (61%)

Neuromuscular & skeletal: Asthenia (66%), myalgia (17%)

Respiratory: Dyspnea (29%), increased cough (26%), pharyngitis (17%), rhinitis (13%)

Miscellaneous: Hypersensitivity (69%), infection (48%), vascular leak syndrome (27%), increased diaphoresis (10%), paresthesia (13%)

1% to 10%:

Cardiovascular: Hypertension (6%), arrhythmias (6%), myocardial infarction (1%)

Central nervous system: Insomnia (9%), confusion (8%)

Endocrine & metabolic: Dehydration (9%), hypokalemia (6%), hyperthyroidism (<5%), hypothyroidism (<5%)

Gastrointestinal: Constipation (9%), dyspepsia (7%), dysphagia (6%), pancreatitis (<5%)

Genitourinary: Hematuria (10%), albuminuria (10%), pyuria (10%)

Hematologic: Thrombotic events (7%), thrombocytopenia (8%), leukopenia (6%)

Local: Injection site reaction (8%), anaphylaxis (1%)

Neuromuscular & skeletal: Arthralgia (8%)

Renal: Increased creatinine (7%), acute renal insufficiency (<5%), microscopic hematuria (<5%)

Respiratory: Lung disorder (8%)

Mechanism of Action Denileukin diftitox is a fusion protein (a combination of amino acid sequences from diphtheria toxin and interleukin-2) which selectively delivers the cytotoxic
(Continued)

Denileukin Diftitox *(Continued)*

activity of diphtheria toxin to targeted cells. It interacts with the high-affinity IL-2 receptor on the surface of malignant cells to inhibit intracellular protein synthesis, rapidly leading to cell death.

Pharmacodynamics/Kinetics
Distribution: V_d: 0.06-0.08 L/kg
Metabolism: Hepatic via proteolytic degradation (animal studies)
Half-life elimination: Distribution: 2-5 minutes; Terminal: 70-80 minutes

Dosage Adults: I.V.: A treatment cycle consists of 9 or 18 mcg/kg/day for 5 consecutive days administered every 21 days. The optimal duration of therapy has not been determined. Only 2% of patients who failed to demonstrate a response (at least a 25% decrease in tumor burden) prior to the fourth cycle responded to subsequent treatment.

Administration For I.V. use only. Should be infused over at least 15 minutes. Should not be given as an I.V. bolus. Patients should be closely observed during the infusion for symptoms of hypersensitivity. If a patient experiences a reaction, the severity of the reaction should be evaluated, and a decision should be made to either reduce the rate or discontinue the infusion. Resuscitation equipment must be readily available. Delay therapy if serum albumin is <3 g/dL.

Monitoring Parameters The patient should have a CBC, blood chemistry panel, renal and hepatic function tests as well as a serum albumin level. These tests should be repeated at weekly intervals during therapy. During the infusion, the patient should be monitored for symptoms of an acute hypersensitivity reaction. After infusion, the patient should be monitored for the development of a delayed vascular leak syndrome (usually in the first 2 weeks), including careful monitoring of weight, blood pressure, and serum albumin.

Dosage Forms INJ, solution [frozen]: 150 mcg/mL (2 mL)

Desipramine *(des IP ra meen)*

Related Information
Antidepressant Agents Comparison *on page 1359*

U.S. Brand Names Norpramin®

Synonyms Desipramine Hydrochloride; Desmethylimipramine Hydrochloride

Therapeutic Category Antidepressant, Tricyclic (Secondary Amine)

Use Treatment of depression

Unlabeled/Investigational Use Analgesic adjunct in chronic pain; peripheral neuropathies; substance-related disorders; attention-deficit/hyperactivity disorder (ADHD)

Pregnancy Risk Factor C

Contraindications Hypersensitivity to desipramine, drugs of similar chemical class, or any component of the formulation; use of MAO inhibitors within 14 days; use in a patient during the acute recovery phase of MI

Warnings/Precautions May cause sedation, resulting in impaired performance of tasks requiring alertness (eg, operating machinery or driving). Sedative effects may be additive with other CNS depressants and/or ethanol. The degree of sedation is low-moderate relative to other antidepressants. May worsen psychosis in some patients or precipitate a shift to mania or hypomania in patients with bipolar disease. May cause hyponatremia/SIADH. May increase the risks associated with electroconvulsive therapy. This agent should be discontinued, when possible, prior to elective surgery. Therapy should not be abruptly discontinued in patients receiving high doses for prolonged periods.

May cause orthostatic hypotension (risk is moderate relative to other antidepressants) - use with caution in patients at risk of hypotension or in patients where transient hypotensive episodes would be poorly tolerated (cardiovascular disease or cerebrovascular disease). The degree of anticholinergic blockade produced by this agent is low relative to other cyclic antidepressants - however, caution should be used in patients with urinary retention, benign prostatic hyperplasia, narrow-angle glaucoma, xerostomia, visual problems, constipation, or a history of bowel obstruction.

The possibility of a suicide attempt is inherent in major depression and may persist until remission occurs. Use caution in high-risk patients during initiation of therapy. Prescriptions should be written for the smallest quantity consistent with good patient care. Use with caution in patients with a history of cardiovascular disease (including previous MI, stroke, tachycardia, or conduction abnormalities). The risk conduction abnormalities with this agent is moderate relative to other antidepressants. Use caution in patients with a previous seizure disorder or condition predisposing to seizures such as brain damage, alcoholism, or concurrent therapy with other drugs which lower the seizure threshold. Use with caution in hyperthyroid patients or those receiving thyroid supplementation. Use with caution in patients with hepatic or renal dysfunction and in elderly patients.

Common Adverse Reactions Frequency not defined.

Cardiovascular: Arrhythmias, hypotension, hypertension, palpitations, heart block, tachycardia

Central nervous system: Dizziness, drowsiness, headache, confusion, delirium, hallucinations, nervousness, restlessness, parkinsonian syndrome, insomnia, disorientation, anxiety, agitation, hypomania, exacerbation of psychosis, incoordination, seizures, extrapyramidal symptoms

Dermatologic: Alopecia, photosensitivity, skin rash, urticaria

Endocrine & metabolic: Breast enlargement, galactorrhea, SIADH

Gastrointestinal: Xerostomia, decreased lower esophageal sphincter tone may cause GE reflux, constipation, nausea, unpleasant taste, weight gain/loss, anorexia, abdominal cramps, diarrhea, heartburn

Genitourinary: Difficult urination, sexual dysfunction, testicular edema

Hematologic: Agranulocytosis, eosinophilia, purpura, thrombocytopenia

Hepatic: Cholestatic jaundice, increased liver enzyme

Neuromuscular & skeletal: Fine muscle tremors, weakness, numbness, tingling, paresthesia of extremities, ataxia

Ocular: Blurred vision, disturbances of accommodation, mydriasis, increased intraocular pressure

Miscellaneous: Diaphoresis (excessive), allergic reactions

Drug Interactions

Cytochrome P450 Effect: Substrate of CYP1A2 (minor), 2D6 (major); **Inhibits** CYP2A6 (moderate), 2B6 (moderate), 2D6 (moderate), 2E1 (weak), 3A4 (moderate)

Increased Effect/Toxicity: Desipramine increases the effects of amphetamines, anticholinergics, other CNS depressants (sedatives, hypnotics, or ethanol), chlorpropamide, tolazamide, and warfarin. When used with MAO inhibitors, serotonin syndrome may occur. Serotonin syndrome has also been reported with ritonavir (rare). CYP2D6 inhibitors may increase the levels/effects of desipramine; example inhibitors include chlorpromazine, delavirdine, fluoxetine, miconazole, paroxetine, pergolide, quinidine, quinine, ritonavir, and ropinirole. Cimetidine, grapefruit juice, indinavir, methylphenidate, diltiazem, and verapamil may increase the serum concentration of TCAs. Use of lithium with a TCA may increase the risk for neurotoxicity. Phenothiazines may increase concentration of some TCAs and TCAs may increase concentration of phenothiazines. Pressor response to I.V. epinephrine, norepinephrine, and phenylephrine may be enhanced in patients receiving TCAs (**Note:** Effect is unlikely with epinephrine or levonordefrin dosages typically administered as infiltration in combination with local anesthetics). Combined use of beta-agonists or drugs which prolong QT$_c$ (including quinidine, procainamide, disopyramide, cisapride, sparfloxacin, gatifloxacin, moxifloxacin) with TCAs may predispose patients to cardiac arrhythmias.

Decreased Effect: Desipramine's serum levels/effect may be decreased by carbamazepine, cholestyramine, colestipol, phenobarbital, and rifampin. Desipramine inhibits the antihypertensive effect of to bethanidine, clonidine, debrisoquin, guanadrel, guanethidine, guanabenz, or guanfacine.

Mechanism of Action Traditionally believed to increase the synaptic concentration of norepinephrine (and to a lesser extent, serotonin) in the central nervous system by inhibition of its reuptake by the presynaptic neuronal membrane. However, additional receptor effects have been found including desensitization of adenyl cyclase, down regulation of beta-adrenergic receptors, and down regulation of serotonin receptors.

Pharmacodynamics/Kinetics

Onset of action: 1-3 weeks; Maximum antidepressant effect: >2 weeks

Absorption: Well absorbed

Metabolism: Hepatic

Half-life elimination: Adults: 7-60 hours

Time to peak, plasma: 4-6 hours

Excretion: Urine (70%)

Dosage Oral (dose is generally administered at bedtime):

Children 6-12 years: Depression: 10-30 mg/day or 1-3 mg/kg/day in divided doses; do not exceed 5 mg/kg/day

Adolescents: Depression: Initial: 25-50 mg/day; gradually increase to 100 mg/day in single or divided doses (maximum: 150 mg/day)

Adults: Depression: Initial: 75 mg/day in divided doses; increase gradually to 150-200 mg/day in divided or single dose (maximum: 300 mg/day)

(Continued)

Desipramine *(Continued)*

Elderly: Depression: Initial dose: 10-25 mg/day; increase by 10-25 mg every 3 days for inpatients and every week for outpatients if tolerated; usual maintenance dose: 75-100 mg/day, but doses up to 150 mg/day may be necessary

Hemodialysis/peritoneal dialysis: Supplemental dose is not necessary

Monitoring Parameters Monitor blood pressure and pulse rate prior to and during initial therapy evaluate mental status; monitor weight; ECG in older adults and those patients with cardiac disease; blood levels are useful for therapeutic monitoring

Reference Range

Plasma levels do not always correlate with clinical effectiveness

Timing of serum samples: Draw trough just before next dose

Therapeutic: 50-300 ng/mL

In elderly patients the response rate is greatest with steady-state plasma concentrations >115 ng/mL

Possible toxicity: >300 ng/mL

Toxic: >1000 ng/mL

Patient Information Avoid alcohol; do not discontinue medication abruptly; may cause urine to turn blue-green; may cause drowsiness; avoid unnecessary exposure to sunlight; sugarless hard candy or gum can help with dry mouth; full effect may not occur for 3-4 weeks

Dosage Forms TAB: 10 mg, 25 mg, 50 mg, 75 mg, 100 mg, 150 mg

♦ **Desipramine Hydrochloride** *see* Desipramine *on page 352*

Desloratadine *(des lor AT a deen)*

U.S. Brand Names Clarinex®

Therapeutic Category Antihistamine; Antihistamine, Nonsedating

Use Relief of nasal and non-nasal symptoms of seasonal allergic rhinitis (SAR) and perennial allergic rhinitis (PAR); treatment of chronic idiopathic urticaria (CIU)

Pregnancy Risk Factor C

Contraindications Hypersensitivity to desloratadine, loratadine, or any component of the formulation

Warnings/Precautions Dose should be adjusted in patients with liver or renal impairment. Use with caution in patients known to be slow metabolizers of desloratadine (incidence of side effects may be increased). RediTabs® contain phenylalanine. Safety and efficacy have not been established for children <12 years of age.

Common Adverse Reactions

>10%: Central nervous system: Headache (14%)

1% to 10%:

Central nervous system: Fatigue (2% to 5%), somnolence (2%), dizziness (4%)

Endocrine & metabolic: Dysmenorrhea (2%)

Gastrointestinal: Xerostomia (3%), nausea (5%), dyspepsia (3%)

Neuromuscular & skeletal: Myalgia (3%)

Respiratory: Pharyngitis (3% to 4%)

Drug Interactions

Increased Effect/Toxicity: With concurrent use of desloratadine and erythromycin or ketoconazole, the C_{max} and AUC of desloratadine and its metabolite are increased; however, no clinically-significant changes in the safety profile of desloratadine were observed in clinical studies.

Mechanism of Action Desloratadine, a major metabolite of loratadine, is a long-acting tricyclic antihistamine with selective peripheral histamine H_1 receptor antagonistic activity and additional anti-inflammatory properties.

Pharmacodynamics/Kinetics

Protein binding: Desloratadine: 82% to 87%; 3-hydroxydesloratadine: 85% to 89%

Metabolism: Hepatic to active metabolite, 3-hydroxydesloratadine (specific enzymes not identified); undergoes glucuronidation. Decreased in slow metabolizers of desloratadine. Not expected to affect or be affected by medications metabolized by CYP with normal doses.

Half-life elimination: 27 hours

Time to peak: 3 hours

Excretion: Urine and feces (as metabolites)

Dosage Oral: Adults and Children ≥12 years: 5 mg once daily

Dosage adjustment in renal/hepatic impairment: 5 mg every other day

Administration May be taken with or without food.

RediTabs® should be placed on the tongue; tablet will disintegrate immediately. May be taken with or without water.

Patient Information May be taken with or without food. Do not increase dose or take more often than recommended by prescriber. Drowsiness, tiredness, headache, or dry mouth may occur. Notify prescriber for increased heart beat, rash, itching or shortness of breath. Notify prescriber if pregnant; breast-feeding is not recommended.

Dosage Forms TAB (Clarinex®): 5 mg. **TAB, orally-disintegrating** (Clarinex® RediTabs®): 5 mg

♦ **Desmethylimipramine Hydrochloride** *see* Desipramine *on page 352*

Desmopressin *(des moe PRES in)*

U.S. Brand Names DDAVP®; Stimate™

Synonyms 1-Deamino-8-D-Arginine Vasopressin; Desmopressin Acetate

Therapeutic Category Antihemophilic Agent; Hemostatic Agent; Vasopressin Analog, Synthetic

Use Treatment of diabetes insipidus; control of bleeding in hemophilia A, and mild-to-moderate classic von Willebrand disease (type I); primary nocturnal enuresis

Pregnancy Risk Factor B

Contraindications Hypersensitivity to desmopressin or any component of the formulation; hemophilia B, severe classic von Willebrand disease (type IIB); patients with ≤5% factor VIII activity level; factor VIII antibodies

Warnings/Precautions Avoid overhydration especially when drug is used for its hemostatic effect

Common Adverse Reactions Frequency not defined (may be dose or route related).
Cardiovascular: Acute cerebrovascular thrombosis, acute MI, blood pressure increased/decreased, chest pain, edema, facial flushing, palpitations
Central nervous system: Agitation, chills, coma, dizziness, headache, insomnia, somnolence
Endocrine & metabolic: Hyponatremia, water intoxication
Gastrointestinal: Abdominal cramps, dyspepsia, nausea, sore throat, vomiting
Genitourinary: Balanitis, vulval pain
Local: Injection: Burning pain, erythema, and swelling at the injection site
Respiratory: Cough, nasal congestion, epistaxis
Miscellaneous: Allergic reactions (rare), anaphylaxis (rare)

Drug Interactions
Increased Effect/Toxicity: Chlorpropamide, fludrocortisone may increase ADH response.
Decreased Effect: Demeclocycline and lithium may decrease ADH response.

Mechanism of Action Enhances reabsorption of water in the kidneys by increasing cellular permeability of the collecting ducts; possibly causes smooth muscle constriction with resultant vasoconstriction; raises plasma levels of von Willebrand factor and factor VIII

Pharmacodynamics/Kinetics
Intranasal administration: Onset of increased factor VIII activity: 30 minutes (dose related)
Peak effect 1.5 hours
I.V. infusion:
Onset of increased factor VIII activity: 30 minutes (dose related)
Peak effect: 1.5-2 hours
Half-life elimination: Terminal: 75 minutes
Oral tablets:
Onset of action: ADH: ~1 hour
Peak effect: 4-7 hours
Half-life elimination: 1.5-2.5 hours
Bioavailability: 5% compared to intranasal; 0.16% compared to I.V.

Dosage
Children:
Diabetes insipidus:
Intranasal (using 100 mcg/mL nasal solution): 3 months to 12 years: Initial: 5 mcg/day (0.05 mL/day) divided 1-2 times/day; range: 5-30 mcg/day (0.05-0.3 mL/day) divided 1-2 times/day; adjust morning and evening doses separately for an adequate diurnal rhythm of water turnover; doses <10 mcg should be administered using the rhinal tube system
Oral: ≥4 years: Initial: 0.05 mg twice daily; total daily dose should be increased or decreased as needed to obtain adequate antidiuresis (range: 0.1-1.2 mg divided 2-3 times/day)
Hemophilia A and von Willebrand disease (type I):
I.V.: >3 months: 0.3 mcg/kg by slow infusion; may repeat dose if needed; begin 30 minutes before procedure
Intranasal: ≥11 months: Refer to adult dosing.
Nocturnal enuresis:
Intranasal (using 100 mcg/mL nasal solution): ≥6 years: Initial: 20 mcg (0.2 mL) at bedtime; range: 10-40 mcg; it is recommended that ½ of the dose be given in each nostril
Oral: 0.2 mg at bedtime; dose may be titrated up to 0.6 mg to achieve desired response. Patients previously on intranasal therapy can begin oral tablets 24 hours after the last intranasal dose.
Children ≥12 years and Adults:
Diabetes insipidus:
I.V., S.C.: 2-4 mcg/day (0.5-1 mL) in 2 divided doses or ¹/₁₀ of the maintenance intranasal dose
Intranasal (using 100 mcg/mL nasal solution): 10-40 mcg/day (0.1-0.4 mL) divided 1-3 times/day; adjust morning and evening doses separately for an adequate diurnal rhythm of water turnover. **Note:** The nasal spray pump can only deliver doses of 10 mcg (0.1 mL) or multiples of 10 mcg (0.1 mL); if doses other than this are needed, the rhinal tube delivery system is preferred.
Oral: Initial: 0.05 mg twice daily; total daily dose should be increased or decreased as needed to obtain adequate antidiuresis (range: 0.1-1.2 mg divided 2-3 times/day)
Hemophilia A and mild to moderate von Willebrand disease (type I):
I.V.: 0.3 mcg/kg by slow infusion, begin 30 minutes before procedure
Intranasal: Using high concentration spray (1.5 mg/mL): <50 kg: 150 mcg (1 spray); >50 kg: 300 mcg (1 spray each nostril); repeat use is determined by the patient's clinical condition and laboratory work; if using preoperatively, administer 2 hours before surgery

(Continued)

Desmopressin *(Continued)*

Administration
I.V.: Dilute in 0.9% sodium chloride and infuse over 15-30 minutes; dose should be diluted in 10 mL NS for children ≤10 kg; 50 mL NS for adults and children >10 kg

Intranasal: DDAVP®: Nasal pump spray delivers 0.1 mL (10 mcg); for other doses which are not multiples, use rhinal tube. DDAVP® Nasal spray delivers fifty 10 mcg doses. Any solution remaining after 50 doses should be discarded. Pump must be primed prior to first use.

Monitoring Parameters Blood pressure and pulse should be monitored during I.V. infusion
Diabetes insipidus: Fluid intake, urine volume, specific gravity, plasma and urine osmolality, serum electrolytes
Hemophilia: Factor VIII antigen levels, aPTT, bleeding time (for von Willebrand disease and thrombocytopathies)

Patient Information Avoid overhydration. Report headache, shortness of breath, heartburn, nausea, abdominal cramps, or vulval pain.

Dosage Forms INJ, solution (DDAVP®): 4 mcg/mL (1 mL, 10 mL). **SOLN, intranasal** (DDAVP®): 100 mcg/mL (2.5 mL). **SOLN, intranasal spray** (DDAVP®): 100 mcg/mL (5 mL); (Stimate™): 1.5 mg/mL (2.5 mL). **TAB** (DDAVP®): 0.1 mg, 0.2 mg

♦ **Desmopressin Acetate** *see Desmopressin on page 354*

♦ **Desogen®** *see Ethinyl Estradiol and Desogestrel on page 477*

♦ **Desogestrel and Ethinyl Estradiol** *see Ethinyl Estradiol and Desogestrel on page 477*

Desonide *(DES oh nide)*

Related Information
Corticosteroids Comparison *on page 1372*

U.S. Brand Names DesOwen®; Tridesilon®

Therapeutic Category Anti-inflammatory Agent; Corticosteroid, Topical (Low Potency); Corticosteroid, Topical (Medium Potency)

Use Adjunctive therapy for inflammation in acute and chronic corticosteroid responsive dermatosis (low potency corticosteroid)

Pregnancy Risk Factor C

Dosage Corticosteroid responsive dermatoses: Topical: Apply 2-4 times/day sparingly. Therapy should be discontinued when control is achieved; if no improvement is seen, reassessment of diagnosis may be necessary.

Dosage Forms CRM, topical (DesOwen®, Tridesilon®): 0.05% (15 g, 60 g). **LOTION, topical** (DesOwen®): 0.05% (60 mL, 120 mL). **OINT, topical:** 0.05% (15 g, 60 g); (DesOwen®): 0.05% (15 g, 60 g); (Tridesilon®): 0.05% (15 g)

♦ **DesOwen®** *see Desonide on page 356*

Desoximetasone *(des oks i MET a sone)*

Related Information
Corticosteroids Comparison *on page 1372*

U.S. Brand Names Topicort®; Topicort®-LP

Therapeutic Category Corticosteroid, Topical (Medium Potency); Corticosteroid, Topical (High Potency)

Use Relieves inflammation and pruritic symptoms of corticosteroid-responsive dermatosis (intermediate- to high-potency topical corticosteroid)

Pregnancy Risk Factor C

Dosage Desoximetasone is a potent fluorinated topical corticosteroid. Therapy should be discontinued when control is achieved; if no improvement is seen, reassessment of diagnosis may be necessary.

Children: Apply sparingly in a very thin film to affected area 1-2 times/day
Adults: Apply sparingly to affected area in a thin film twice daily

Dosage Forms CRM, topical: 0.25% (15 g, 60 g); 0.05% (15 g, 60 g); (Topicort®): 0.25% (15 g, 60 g); (Topicort®-LP): 0.05% (15 g, 60 g). **GEL, topical** (Topicort®): 0.05% (15 g, 60 g). **OINT, topical:** 0.25% (15 g, 60 g); (Topicort®): 0.25% (60 g)

♦ **Desoxyephedrine Hydrochloride** *see Methamphetamine on page 810*

♦ **Desoxyn®** *see Methamphetamine on page 810*

♦ **Desoxyphenobarbital** *see Primidone on page 1036*

♦ **Desyrel®** *see Trazodone on page 1256*

♦ **Detane® [OTC]** *see Benzocaine on page 154*

♦ **Detrol®** *see Tolterodine on page 1241*

♦ **Detrol® LA** *see Tolterodine on page 1241*

♦ **Detussin®** *see Hydrocodone and Pseudoephedrine on page 631*

♦ **Devrom®** *see Bismuth on page 168*

♦ **Dexacidin®** *see Neomycin, Polymyxin B, and Dexamethasone on page 892*

♦ **Dexacine™** *see Neomycin, Polymyxin B, and Dexamethasone on page 892*

Dexamethasone *(deks a METH a sone)*

Related Information
Corticosteroids Comparison *on page 1372*

U.S. Brand Names Decadron®; Decadron® Phosphate [DSC]; Dexamethasone Intensol®; Dexasone®; Dexasone® L.A.; DexPak® TaperPak®; Maxidex®; Solurex®; Solurex L.A.®

Synonyms Dexamethasone Acetate; Dexamethasone Sodium Phosphate

Therapeutic Category Antiemetic; Anti-inflammatory Agent; Anti-inflammatory Agent, Inhalant; Anti-inflammatory Agent, Ophthalmic; Corticosteroid, Inhalant; Corticosteroid, Ophthalmic; Corticosteroid, Systemic; Corticosteroid, Topical (Low Potency); Glucocorticoid

Use Systemically and locally for chronic swelling; allergic, hematologic, neoplastic, and autoimmune diseases; may be used in management of cerebral edema, septic shock, as a diagnostic agent, antiemetic

Unlabeled/Investigational Use General indicator consistent with depression; diagnosis of Cushing's syndrome

Pregnancy Risk Factor C

Contraindications Hypersensitivity to dexamethasone or any component of the formulation; active untreated infections; ophthalmic use in viral, fungal, or tuberculosis diseases of the eye

Warnings/Precautions Use with caution in patients with hypothyroidism, cirrhosis, hypertension, CHF, ulcerative colitis, thromboembolic disorders. Corticosteroids should be used with caution in patients with diabetes, osteoporosis, peptic ulcer, glaucoma, cataracts, or tuberculosis. Use caution in hepatic impairment. Because of the risk of adverse effects, systemic corticosteroids should be used cautiously in the elderly in the smallest possible dose and for the shortest possible time.

May cause suppression of hypothalamic-pituitary-adrenal (HPA) axis, particularly in younger children or in patients receiving high doses for prolonged periods. Particular care is required when patients are transferred from systemic corticosteroids to inhaled products due to possible adrenal insufficiency or withdrawal from steroids, including an increase in allergic symptoms. Patients receiving 20 mg per day of prednisone (or equivalent) may be most susceptible. Fatalities have occurred due to adrenal insufficiency in asthmatic patients during and after transfer from systemic corticosteroids to aerosol steroids; aerosol steroids do **not** provide the systemic steroid needed to treat patients having trauma, surgery, or infections

Controlled clinical studies have shown that orally-inhaled and intranasal corticosteroids may cause a reduction in growth velocity in pediatric patients. (In studies of orally-inhaled corticosteroids, the mean reduction in growth velocity was approximately 1 centimeter per year [range 0.3-1.8 cm per year] and appears to be related to dose and duration of exposure.) The growth of pediatric patients receiving inhaled corticosteroids, should be monitored routinely (eg, via stadiometry). To minimize the systemic effects of orally-inhaled and intranasal corticosteroids, each patient should be titrated to the lowest effective dose.

May suppress the immune system, patients may be more susceptible to infection. Use with caution in patients with systemic infections or ocular herpes simplex. Avoid exposure to chickenpox and measles.

Common Adverse Reactions Systemic:
>10%:
Central nervous system: Insomnia, nervousness
Gastrointestinal: Increased appetite, indigestion
1% to 10%:
Dermatologic: Hirsutism
Endocrine & metabolic: Diabetes mellitus
Neuromuscular & skeletal: Arthralgia
Ocular: Cataracts
Respiratory: Epistaxis

Drug Interactions
Cytochrome P450 Effect: Substrate of CYP3A4 (minor); **Induces** CYP2A6 (weak), 2B6 (weak), 2C8/9 (weak), 3A4 (weak)
Decreased Effect: Barbiturates, phenytoin, and rifampin may cause decreased dexamethasone effects. Dexamethasone decreases effect of salicylates, vaccines, and toxoids.

Mechanism of Action Decreases inflammation by suppression of migration of polymorphonuclear leukocytes and reversal of increased capillary permeability; suppresses normal immune response. Dexamethasone's mechanism of antiemetic activity is unknown.

Pharmacodynamics/Kinetics
Onset of action: Acetate: Prompt
Duration of metabolic effect: 72 hours; acetate is a long-acting repository preparation
Metabolism: Hepatic
Half-life elimination: Normal renal function: 1.8-3.5 hours; Biological half-life: 36-54 hours
Time to peak, serum: Oral: 1-2 hours; I.M.: ~8 hours
Excretion: Urine and feces

Dosage
Children:
Antiemetic (prior to chemotherapy): I.V. (should be given as sodium phosphate): 5-20 mg given 15-30 minutes before treatment
Anti-inflammatory immunosuppressant: Oral, I.M., I.V. (injections should be given as sodium phosphate): 0.08-0.3 mg/kg/day or 2.5-10 mg/m^2/day in divided doses given every 6-12 hours
Extubation or airway edema: Oral, I.M., I.V. (injections should be given as sodium phosphate): 0.5-2 mg/kg/day in divided doses every 6 hours beginning 24 hours prior to extubation and continuing for 4-6 doses afterwards
Cerebral edema: I.V. (should be given as sodium phosphate): Loading dose: 1-2 mg/kg/dose as a single dose; maintenance: 1-1.5 mg/kg/day (maximum: 16 mg/day) in divided doses every 4-6 hours for 5 days then taper for 5 days, then discontinue
Bacterial meningitis in infants and children >2 months: I.V. (should be given as sodium phosphate): 0.6 mg/kg/day in 4 divided doses every 6 hours for the first 4 days of antibiotic treatment; start dexamethasone at the time of the first dose of antibiotic
(Continued)

Dexamethasone *(Continued)*

Physiologic replacement: Oral, I.M., I.V.: 0.03-0.15 mg/kg/day **or** 0.6-0.75 mg/m²/day in divided doses every 6-12 hours

Adults:

Antiemetic:

Prophylaxis: Oral, I.V.: 10-20 mg 15-30 minutes before treatment on each treatment day
Continuous infusion regimen: Oral or I.V.: 10 mg every 12 hours on each treatment day
Mildly emetogenic therapy: Oral, I.M., I.V.: 4 mg every 4-6 hours
Delayed nausea/vomiting: Oral: 4-10 mg 1-2 times/day for 2-4 days **or**
8 mg every 12 hours for 2 days; then
4 mg every 12 hours for 2 days **or**
20 mg 1 hour before chemotherapy; then
10 mg 12 hours after chemotherapy; then
8 mg every 12 hours for 4 doses; then
4 mg every 12 hours for 4 doses

Anti-inflammatory:

Oral, I.M., I.V. (injections should be given as sodium phosphate): 0.75-9 mg/day in divided doses every 6-12 hours
I.M. (as acetate): 8-16 mg; may repeat in 1-3 weeks
Intralesional (as acetate): 0.8-1.6 mg
Intra-articular/soft tissue (as acetate): 4-16 mg; may repeat in 1-3 weeks
Intra-articular, intralesional, or soft tissue (as sodium phosphate): 0.4-6 mg/day
Ophthalmic:
Ointment: Apply thin coating into conjunctival sac 3-4 times/day; gradually taper dose to discontinue
Suspension: Instill 2 drops into conjunctival sac every hour during the day and every other hour during the night; gradually reduce dose to every 3-4 hours, then to 3-4 times/day
Topical: Apply 1-4 times/day. Therapy should be discontinued when control is achieved; if no improvement is seen, reassessment of diagnosis may be necessary.

Chemotherapy: Oral, I.V.: 40 mg every day for 4 days, repeated every 4 weeks (VAD regimen)

Cerebral edema: I.V. 10 mg stat, 4 mg I.M./I.V. (should be given as sodium phosphate) every 6 hours until response is maximized, then switch to oral regimen, then taper off if appropriate; dosage may be reduced after 24 days and gradually discontinued over 5-7 days

Dexamethasone suppression test (depression indicator) or diagnosis for Cushing's syndrome (unlabeled uses): Oral: 1 mg at 11 PM, draw blood at 8 AM the following day for plasma cortisol determination

Physiological replacement: Oral, I.M., I.V. (should be given as sodium phosphate): 0.03-0.15 mg/kg/day **or** 0.6-0.75 mg/m²/day in divided doses every 6-12 hours

Treatment of shock:
Addisonian crisis/shock (ie, adrenal insufficiency/responsive to steroid therapy): I.V. (given as sodium phosphate): 4-10 mg as a single dose, which may be repeated if necessary
Unresponsive shock (ie, unresponsive to steroid therapy): I.V. (given as sodium phosphate): 1-6 mg/kg as a single I.V. dose or up to 40 mg initially followed by repeat doses every 2-6 hours while shock persists

Hemodialysis: Supplemental dose is not necessary
Peritoneal dialysis: Supplemental dose is not necessary

Administration

Oral: Administer with meals to decrease GI upset.
I.M.: Acetate injection is **not** for I.V. use.
I.V.: Administer as a 5-10 minute bolus; rapid injection is associated with a high incidence of perianal discomfort.
Topical: For external use. Do not use on open wounds. Apply sparingly to occlusive dressings. Should not be used in the presence of open or weeping lesions.

Monitoring Parameters Hemoglobin, occult blood loss, serum potassium, and glucose

Reference Range Dexamethasone suppression test, overnight: 8 AM cortisol <6 μg/100 mL (dexamethasone 1 mg); plasma cortisol determination should be made on the day after giving dose

Patient Information Notify prescriber of any signs of infection or injuries during therapy; inform physician or dentist before surgery if you are taking a corticosteroid; may cause GI upset, take with food; do not overuse; use only as prescribed and for no longer than the period prescribed; notify prescriber if condition being treated persists or worsens

Ophthalmic: For ophthalmic use only. Wash hands before using. Tilt head back and look upward. Put drops of suspension or apply thin ribbon of ointment inside lower eyelid. Close eye and roll eyeball in all directions. Do not blink for ½ minute. Apply gentle pressure to inner corner of eye for 30 seconds. Do not use any other eye preparation for at least 10 minutes. Do not let tip of applicator touch eye; do not contaminate tip of applicator (may cause eye infection, eye damage, or vision loss). Do not share medication with anyone else. Wear sunglasses when in sunlight; you may be more sensitive to bright light. Inform prescriber if condition worsens or fails to improve or if you experience eye pain, disturbances of vision, or other adverse eye response.

Topical: Thin film of cream or ointment is effective, do not overuse; do not use tight-fitting diapers or plastic pants on children being treated in the diaper area; use only as prescribed, and for no longer than the period prescribed; rub in lightly; avoid contact with eyes

Dosage Forms ELIXIR, as base: 0.5 mg/5 mL (100 mL, 240 mL). **INJ, suspension, as acetate** (Dexasone® LA, Solurex LA®): 8 mg/mL (5 mL). **INJ, solution, as sodium phosphate:** 4 mg/mL (1 mL, 5 mL, 10 mL, 25 mL, 30 mL); 10 mg/mL (1 mL, 10 mL); (Decadron® Phosphate): 4 mg/mL (5 mL, 25 mL); 24 mg/mL (5 mL) [DSC]; (Dexasone®): 4 mg/mL (5 mL); (Solurex®): 4 mg/mL (5 mL, 10 mL, 30 mL). **OINT, ophthalmic, as sodium phosphate:** 0.05% (3.5 g). **SOLN, oral:** 0.5 mg/5 mL (5 mL, 500 mL). **SOLN, oral concentrate** (Dexamethasone Intensol®): 1 mg/mL (30 mL). **SUSP, ophthalmic** (Maxidex®): 0.1% (5 mL, 15 mL). **TAB:** 0.25 mg, 0.5 mg, 0.75 mg, 1 mg, 1.5 mg, 2 mg, 4 mg, 6 mg; (Decadron®): 0.5 mg, 0.75 mg, 4 mg; (DexPak® TaperPak®): 1.5 mg

♦ **Dexamethasone Acetate** *see Dexamethasone on page 356*
♦ **Dexamethasone and Ciprofloxacin** *see Ciprofloxacin and Dexamethasone on page 280*
♦ **Dexamethasone and Neomycin** *see Neomycin and Dexamethasone on page 891*
♦ **Dexamethasone and Tobramycin** *see Tobramycin and Dexamethasone on page 1237*
♦ **Dexamethasone Intensol®** *see Dexamethasone on page 356*
♦ **Dexamethasone, Neomycin, and Polymyxin B** *see Neomycin, Polymyxin B, and Dexamethasone on page 892*
♦ **Dexamethasone Sodium Phosphate** *see Dexamethasone on page 356*
♦ **Dexasone®** *see Dexamethasone on page 356*
♦ **Dexasone® L.A.** *see Dexamethasone on page 356*

Dexbrompheniramine and Pseudoephedrine (deks brom fen EER a meen & soo doe e FED rin)

U.S. Brand Names Drixomed®; Drixoral® Cold & Allergy [OTC]
Synonyms Pseudoephedrine and Dexbrompheniramine
Therapeutic Category Antihistamine/Decongestant
Use Relief of symptoms of upper respiratory mucosal congestion in seasonal and perennial nasal allergies, acute rhinitis, rhinosinusitis and eustachian tube blockage
Pregnancy Risk Factor B
Dosage Children >12 years and Adults: Oral: 1 timed release tablet every 12 hours, may require 1 tablet every 8 hours
Dosage Forms TAB, sustained action (Drixomed®, Drixoral® Cold & Allergy): Dexbrompheniramine 6 mg and pseudoephedrine 120 mg

Dexchlorpheniramine (deks klor fen EER a meen)

U.S. Brand Names Polaramine® [DSC]
Synonyms Dexchlorpheniramine Maleate
Therapeutic Category Antihistamine
Use Perennial and seasonal allergic rhinitis and other allergic symptoms including urticaria
Pregnancy Risk Factor B
Dosage Oral:
  Children:
    2-5 years: 0.5 mg every 4-6 hours (do not use timed release)
    6-11 years: 1 mg every 4-6 hours or 4 mg timed release at bedtime
  Adults: 2 mg every 4-6 hours or 4-6 mg timed release at bedtime or every 8-10 hours
Dosage Forms SYR: 2 mg/5 mL (480 mL, 3840 mL). **TAB** (Polaramine® [DSC]): 2 mg. **TAB, sustained action:** 4 mg, 6 mg

♦ **Dexchlorpheniramine Maleate** *see Dexchlorpheniramine on page 359*
♦ **Dexchlorpheniramine Tannate and Pseudoephedrine Tannate** *see Chlorpheniramine and Pseudoephedrine on page 263*
♦ **Dexchlorpheniramine Tannate, Pseudoephedrine Tannate, and Dextromethorphan Tannate** *see Chlorpheniramine, Pseudoephedrine, and Dextromethorphan on page 265*
♦ **Dexedrine®** *see Dextroamphetamine on page 362*
♦ **Dexferrum®** *see Iron Dextran Complex on page 690*

Dexmedetomidine (deks MED e toe mi deen)

U.S. Brand Names Precedex™
Synonyms Dexmedetomidine Hydrochloride
Therapeutic Category Alpha-Adrenergic Agonist; Sedative
Use Sedation of initially intubated and mechanically ventilated patients during treatment in an intensive care setting; duration of infusion should not exceed 24 hours
Unlabeled/Investigational Use Unlabeled uses include premedication prior to anesthesia induction with thiopental; relief of pain and reduction of opioid dose following laparoscopic tubal ligation; as an adjunct anesthetic in ophthalmic surgery; treatment of shivering; premedication to attenuate the cardiostimulatory and postanesthetic delirium of ketamine
Pregnancy Risk Factor C
Contraindications Hypersensitivity to dexmedetomidine or any component of the formulation; use outside of an intensive care setting
Warnings/Precautions Should be administered only by persons skilled in management of patients in intensive care setting. Patients should be continuously monitored. Episodes of bradycardia, hypotension, and sinus arrest have been associated with dexmedetomidine. Use caution in patients with heart block, severe ventricular dysfunction, hypovolemia, diabetes, chronic hypertension, and elderly. Use with caution in patients receiving vasodilators or drugs which decrease heart rate. If medical intervention is required, treatment may include stopping or decreasing the infusion; increasing the rate of I.V. fluid administration, use of pressor
(Continued)

Dexmedetomidine *(Continued)*

agents, and elevation of the lower extremities. Transient hypertension has been primarily observed during the dose in association with the initial peripheral vasoconstrictive effects of dexmedetomidine. Treatment of this is not generally necessary; however, reduction of infusion rate may be desirable.

Common Adverse Reactions
>10%:
Cardiovascular: Hypotension (30%)
Gastrointestinal: Nausea (11%)
1% to 10%:
Cardiovascular: Bradycardia (8%), atrial fibrillation (7%)
Central nervous system: Pain (3%)
Hematologic: Anemia (3%), leukocytosis (2%)
Renal: Oliguria (2%)
Respiratory: Hypoxia (6%), pulmonary edema (2%), pleural effusion (3%)
Miscellaneous: Infection (2%), thirst (2%)

Drug Interactions
Cytochrome P450 Effect: Substrate of CYP2A6 (major); **Inhibits** CYP1A2 (weak), 2C8/9 (weak), 2D6 (strong), 3A4 (weak)
Increased Effect/Toxicity:
CYP2A6 inhibitors may increase the levels/effects of dexmedetomidine; example inhibitors include isoniazid, methoxsalen, and miconazole.
Possible enhanced effects and pharmacodynamic interaction with sedatives, hypnotics, opioids, and anesthetics; monitor and decrease the dose as necessary of each agent and/or dexmedetomidine. Enhanced effects may occur with sevoflurane, isoflurane, propofol, alfentanil, and midazolam.
Hypotension and/or bradycardia may be increased by vasodilators and heart rate-lowering agents.

Mechanism of Action Selective alpha$_2$-adrenoceptor agonist with sedative properties; alpha$_1$ activity was observed at high doses or after rapid infusions

Pharmacodynamics/Kinetics
Onset of action: Rapid
Distribution: V$_{ss}$: Approximately 118 L; rapid
Protein binding: 94%
Metabolism: Hepatic via glucuronidation and CYP2A6
Half-life elimination: 6 minutes; Terminal: 2 hours
Excretion: Urine (95%); feces (4%)

Dosage Individualized and titrated to desired clinical effect
Adults: I.V.: Solution must be diluted prior to administration. Initial: Loading infusion of 1 mcg/kg over 10 minutes, followed by a maintenance infusion of 0.2-0.7 mcg/kg/hour; not indicated for infusions lasting >24 hours
Elderly (>65 years of age): Dosage reduction may need to be considered. No specific guidelines available. Dose selections should be cautious, at the low end of dosage range; titration should be slower, allowing adequate time to evaluate response.

Dosage adjustment in hepatic impairment: Dosage reduction may need to be considered. No specific guidelines available.

Administration Administer using a controlled infusion device. Must be diluted in 0.9% sodium chloride solution to achieve the required concentration prior to administration. Advisable to use administration components made with synthetic or coated natural rubber gaskets. Parenteral products should be inspected visually for particulate matter and discoloration prior to administration.

Monitoring Parameters Level of sedation, heart rate, respiration, rhythm, blood pressure
Dosage Forms INJ, solution: 100 mcg/mL (2 mL)

♦ **Dexmedetomidine Hydrochloride** *see* Dexmedetomidine *on page 359*

Dexmethylphenidate *(dex meth il FEN i date)*
U.S. Brand Names Focalin™
Synonyms Dexmethylphenidate Hydrochloride
Therapeutic Category Central Nervous System Stimulant, Nonamphetamine
Use Treatment of attention-deficit/hyperactivity disorder (ADHD)
Restrictions C-II
Pregnancy Risk Factor C
Dosage Oral: Children ≥6 years and Adults: Treatment of ADHD: Initial: 2.5 mg twice daily in patients not currently taking methylphenidate; dosage may be adjusted in 2.5-5 mg increments at weekly intervals (maximum dose: 20 mg/day); doses should be taken at least 4 hours apart
When switching from methylphenidate to dexmethylphenidate, the starting dose of dexmethylphenidate should be half that of methylphenidate (maximum dose: 20 mg/day)
Safety and efficacy for long-term use of dexmethylphenidate have not yet been established. Patients should be re-evaluated at appropriate intervals to assess continued need of the medication.
Dose reductions and discontinuation: Reduce dose or discontinue in patients with paradoxical aggravation. Discontinue if no improvement is seen after one month of treatment.
Dosage Forms TAB: 2.5 mg, 5 mg, 10 mg

♦ **Dexmethylphenidate Hydrochloride** *see* Dexmethylphenidate *on page 360*

♦ **DexPak® TaperPak®** see Dexamethasone on page 356

Dexpanthenol (deks PAN the nole)
U.S. Brand Names Panthoderm® [OTC]
Synonyms Pantothenyl Alcohol
Therapeutic Category Gastrointestinal Agent, Stimulant; Topical Skin Product
Use Prophylactic use to minimize paralytic ileus; treatment of postoperative distention; topical to relieve itching and to aid healing of minor dermatoses
Pregnancy Risk Factor C
Dosage
  Children and Adults: Relief of itching and aid in skin healing: Topical: Apply to affected area 1-2 times/day
  Adults:
    Prevention of postoperative ileus: I.M.: 250-500 mg stat, repeat in 2 hours, followed by doses every 6 hours until danger passes
    Paralytic ileus: I.M.: 500 mg stat, repeat in 2 hours, followed by doses every 6 hours, if needed
Dosage Forms CRM, topical (Panthoderm®) 2% (30 g, 60 g). **INJ, solution:** 250 mg/mL (2 mL)

Dexrazoxane (deks ray ZOKS ane)
U.S. Brand Names Zinecard®
Synonyms ICRF-187
Therapeutic Category Cardioprotective Agent
Use Reduction of the incidence and severity of cardiomyopathy associated with doxorubicin administration in women with metastatic breast cancer who have received a cumulative doxorubicin dose of 300 mg/m^2 and who would benefit from continuing therapy with doxorubicin. It is not recommended for use with the initiation of doxorubicin therapy.
Pregnancy Risk Factor C
Contraindications Do not use with chemotherapy regimens that do not contain an anthracycline
Warnings/Precautions Dexrazoxane may add to the myelosuppression caused by chemotherapeutic agents. Dexrazoxane does not eliminate the potential for anthracycline-induced cardiac toxicity. Carefully monitor cardiac function.
Common Adverse Reactions Unless specified, frequency not defined.
  Dermatologic: Alopecia, urticaria, recall skin reaction, extravasation
  Endocrine & metabolic: Serum amylase increased, serum calcium decreased, serum triglycerides increased
  Gastrointestinal: Nausea, vomiting (mild)
  Hematologic: Myelosuppression, neutropenia (~12%), thrombocytopenia (~4%)
  Hepatic: AST/ALT increased, bilirubin increased
Mechanism of Action Derivative of EDTA; potent intracellular chelating agent. The mechanism of cardioprotectant activity is not fully understood. Appears to be converted intracellularly to a ring-opened chelating agent that interferes with iron-mediated oxygen free radical generation thought to be responsible, in part, for anthracycline-induced cardiomyopathy.
Pharmacodynamics/Kinetics
  Distribution: V$_d$: 22-22.4 L/m^2
  Protein binding: None
  Half-life elimination: 2.1-2.5 hours
  Excretion: Urine (42%)
  Clearance, renal: 3.35 L/hour/m^2; Plasma: 6.25-7.88 L/hour/m^2
Dosage Adults: I.V.: A 10:1 ratio of dexrazoxane:doxorubicin (500 mg/m^2 dexrazoxane: 50 mg/m^2 doxorubicin)
  Dosage adjustment in hepatic impairment: Since doxorubicin dosage is reduced in hyperbilirubinemia, a proportional reduction in dexrazoxane dosage is recommended (maintain ratio of 10:1).
Administration Administer by slow I.V. push or rapid (5-15 minutes) I.V. infusion from a bag. Administer doxorubicin within 30 minutes after beginning the infusion with dexrazoxane.
Monitoring Parameters Since dexrazoxane will always be used with cytotoxic drugs, and since it may add to the myelosuppressive effects of cytotoxic drugs, frequent complete blood counts are recommended
Dosage Forms INJ, powder for reconstitution: 250 mg, 500 mg

Dextran (DEKS tran)
U.S. Brand Names Gentran®; LMD®
Synonyms Dextran 40; Dextran 70; Dextran, High Molecular Weight; Dextran, Low Molecular Weight
Therapeutic Category Plasma Volume Expander, Colloid
Use Blood volume expander used in treatment of shock or impending shock when blood or blood products are not available; dextran 40 is also used as a priming fluid in cardiopulmonary bypass and for prophylaxis of venous thrombosis and pulmonary embolism in surgical procedures associated with a high risk of thromboembolic complications
Pregnancy Risk Factor C
Contraindications Hypersensitivity to dextran or any component of the formulation; marked hemostatic defects (thrombocytopenia, hypofibrinogenemia) of all types including those caused by drugs; marked cardiac decompensation; renal disease with severe oliguria or anuria
(Continued)

Dextran *(Continued)*

Warnings/Precautions Hypersensitivity reactions have been reported (dextran 40 rarely causes a reaction), usually early in the infusion. Monitor closely during infusion initiation for signs or symptoms of a hypersensitivity reaction. Dextran 1 is indicated for prophylaxis of serious anaphylactic reactions to dextran infusions. Administration can cause fluid or solute overload. Use caution in patients with fluid overload. Use with caution in patients with active hemorrhage. Use caution in patients receiving corticosteroids. Renal failure has been reported. Fluid status including urine output should be monitored closely. Exercise care to prevent a depression of hematocrit <30% (can cause hemodilution). Observe for signs of bleeding.

Mechanism of Action Produces plasma volume expansion by virtue of its highly colloidal starch structure, similar to albumin

Pharmacodynamics/Kinetics

Onset of action: Minutes to 1 hour (depending upon the molecular weight polysaccharide administered)

Excretion: Urine (~75%) within 24 hours

Dosage I.V. (requires an infusion pump): Dose and infusion rate are dependent upon the patient's fluid status and must be individualized:

Volume expansion/shock:

Children: Total dose should not exceed 20 mL/kg during first 24 hours

Adults: 500-1000 mL at a rate of 20-40 mL/minute; maximum daily dose: 20 mL/kg for first 24 hours; 10 mL/kg/day thereafter; therapy should not be continued beyond 5 days

Pump prime (Dextran 40): Varies with the volume of the pump oxygenator; generally, the 10% solution is added in a dose of 1-2 g/kg

Prophylaxis of venous thrombosis/pulmonary embolism (Dextran 40): Begin during surgical procedure and give 50-100 g on the day of surgery; an additional 50 g (500 mL) should be administered every 2-3 days during the period of risk (up to 2 weeks postoperatively); usual maximum infusion rate for nonemergency use: 4 mL/minute

Dosing in renal and/or hepatic impairment: Use with extreme caution

Administration For I.V. infusion only (use an infusion pump). Infuse initial 500 mL at a rate of 20-40 mL/minute if hypervolemic. Reduce rate for additional infusion to 4 mL/minute. **Observe patients closely for anaphylactic reaction.**

Monitoring Parameters Observe patient for signs of circulatory overload and/or monitor central venous pressure; observe patients closely during the first minute of infusion and have other means of maintaining circulation should dextran therapy result in an anaphylactoid reaction; monitor hemoglobin and hematocrit, electrolytes, serum protein

Dosage Forms INJ, solution, high molecular weight (Gentran®): 6% dextran 70 [in sodium chloride 0.9%] (500 mL). **INJ, solution, low molecular weight** (Gentran®, LMD®): 10% dextran 40 [in dextrose 5%] (500 mL); 10% dextran 40 [in sodium chloride 0.9%] (500 mL)

Dextran 1 (DEKS tran won)

U.S. Brand Names Promit®

Therapeutic Category Dextran Adjunct; Plasma Volume Expander, Colloid

Use Prophylaxis of serious anaphylactic reactions to I.V. infusion of dextran

Pregnancy Risk Factor C

Contraindications Hypersensitivity to dextrans or any component of the formulation; **dextran** contraindicated

Warnings/Precautions Severe hypotension and bradycardia can occur. If any reaction occurs, do not administer dextran. Mild dextran-induced anaphylactic reactions are not prevented.

Mechanism of Action Binds to dextran-reactive immunoglobulin without bridge formation and no formation of large immune complexes

Dosage I.V. (time between dextran 1 and dextran solution should not exceed 15 minutes):

Children: 0.3 mL/kg 1-2 minutes before I.V. infusion of dextran

Adults: 20 mL 1-2 minutes before I.V. infusion of dextran

Dosage Forms INJ, solution: 150 mg/mL (20 mL)

- ◆ **Dextran 40** *see Dextran on page 361*
- ◆ **Dextran 70** *see Dextran on page 361*
- ◆ **Dextran, High Molecular Weight** *see Dextran on page 361*
- ◆ **Dextran, Low Molecular Weight** *see Dextran on page 361*

Dextroamphetamine (deks troe am FET a meen)

U.S. Brand Names Dexedrine®; Dextrostat®

Synonyms Dextroamphetamine Sulfate

Therapeutic Category Amphetamine; Anorexiant; Central Nervous System Stimulant, Amphetamine

Use Narcolepsy; attention-deficit/hyperactivity disorder (ADHD)

Unlabeled/Investigational Use Exogenous obesity; depression; abnormal behavioral syndrome in children (minimal brain dysfunction)

Restrictions C-II

Pregnancy Risk Factor C

Dosage Oral:
Children:
Narcolepsy: 6-12 years: Initial: 5 mg/day; may increase at 5 mg increments in weekly intervals until side effects appear (maximum dose: 60 mg/day)
ADHD:
3-5 years: Initial: 2.5 mg/day given every morning; increase by 2.5 mg/day in weekly intervals until optimal response is obtained; usual range: 0.1-0.5 mg/kg/dose every morning with maximum of 40 mg/day
≥6 years: 5 mg once or twice daily; increase in increments of 5 mg/day at weekly intervals until optimal response is obtained; usual range: 0.1-0.5 mg/kg/dose every morning (5-20 mg/day) with maximum of 40 mg/day
Children >12 years and Adults:
Narcolepsy: Initial: 10 mg/day, may increase at 10 mg increments in weekly intervals until side effects appear; maximum: 60 mg/day
Exogenous obesity (unlabeled use): 5-30 mg/day in divided doses of 5-10 mg 30-60 minutes before meals
Dosage Forms CAP, sustained release: 5 mg, 10 mg, 15 mg; (Dexedrine® Spansule®): 5 mg, 10 mg, 15 mg. **TAB:** 5 mg, 10 mg; (Dexedrine®, Dextrostat®): 5 mg, 10 mg

Dextroamphetamine and Amphetamine
(deks troe am FET a meen & am FET a meen)
U.S. Brand Names Adderall®; Adderall XR™
Synonyms Amphetamine and Dextroamphetamine
Therapeutic Category Amphetamine; Central Nervous System Stimulant, Amphetamine
Use Attention-deficit/hyperactivity disorder (ADHD); narcolepsy
Restrictions C-II
Pregnancy Risk Factor C
Dosage Oral: **Note:** Use lowest effective individualized dose; administer first dose as soon as awake
ADHD:
Children: <3 years: Not recommended
Children: 3-5 years (Adderall®): Initial 2.5 mg/day given every morning; increase daily dose in 2.5 mg increments at weekly intervals until optimal response is obtained (maximum dose: 40 mg/day given in 1-3 divided doses); use intervals of 4-6 hours between additional doses
Children: ≥6 years:
Adderall®: Initial: 5 mg 1-2 times/day; increase daily dose in 5 mg at weekly intervals until optimal response is obtained (usual maximum dose: 40 mg/day given in 1-3 divided doses); use intervals of 4-6 hours between additional doses
Adderall XR™: 5-10 mg once daily in the morning; if needed, may increase daily dose in 5-10 mg increments at weekly intervals (maximum dose: 30 mg/day)
Narcolepsy: Adderall®:
Children: 6-12 years: Initial: 5 mg/day; increase daily dose in 5 mg at weekly intervals until optimal response is obtained (maximum dose: 60 mg/day given in 1-3 divided doses)
Children >12 years and Adults: Initial: 10 mg/day; increase daily dose in 10 mg increments at weekly intervals until optimal response is obtained (maximum dose: 60 mg/day given in 1-3 divided doses)
Dosage Forms CAP, extended release (Adderall XR™): 5 mg [dextroamphetamine sulfate 1.25 mg, dextroamphetamine saccharate 1.25 mg, amphetamine aspartate monohydrate 1.25 mg, amphetamine sulfate 1.25 mg] (equivalent to amphetamine base 3.1 mg); 10 mg [dextroamphetamine sulfate 2.5 mg, dextroamphetamine saccharate 2.5 mg, amphetamine aspartate monohydrate 2.5 mg, amphetamine sulfate 2.5 mg] (equivalent to amphetamine base 6.3 mg); 15 mg [dextroamphetamine sulfate 3.75 mg, dextroamphetamine saccharate 3.75 mg, amphetamine aspartate monohydrate 3.75 mg, amphetamine sulfate 3.75 mg] (equivalent to amphetamine base 9.4 mg); 20 mg [dextroamphetamine sulfate 5 mg, dextroamphetamine saccharate 5 mg, amphetamine aspartate monohydrate 5 mg, amphetamine sulfate 5 mg] (equivalent to amphetamine base 12.5 mg); 25 mg [dextroamphetamine sulfate 6.25 mg, dextroamphetamine saccharate 6.25 mg, amphetamine aspartate monohydrate 6.25 mg, amphetamine sulfate 6.25 mg] (equivalent to amphetamine base 15.6 mg); 30 mg [dextroamphetamine sulfate 7.5 mg, dextroamphetamine saccharate 7.5 mg, amphetamine aspartate monohydrate 7.5 mg, amphetamine sulfate 7.5 mg] (equivalent to amphetamine base 18.8 mg). **TAB** (Adderall®): 5 mg [dextroamphetamine sulfate 1.25 mg, dextroamphetamine saccharate 1.25 mg, amphetamine aspartate 1.25 mg, amphetamine sulfate 1.25 mg] (equivalent to amphetamine base 3.13 mg); 7.5 mg [dextroamphetamine 1.875 mg, dextroamphetamine saccharate 1.875 mg, amphetamine aspartate 1.875 mg, amphetamine sulfate 1.875 mg] (equivalent to amphetamine base 4.7 mg); 10 mg [dextroamphetamine sulfate 2.5 mg, dextroamphetamine saccharate 2.5 mg, amphetamine aspartate 2.5 mg, amphetamine sulfate 2.5 mg] (equivalent to amphetamine base 6.3 mg); 12.5 mg [dextroamphetamine sulfate 3.125 mg, dextroamphetamine saccharate 3.125 mg, amphetamine aspartate 3.125 mg, amphetamine sulfate 3.125 mg] (equivalent to amphetamine base 7.8 mg); 15 mg [dextroamphetamine sulfate 3.75 mg, dextroamphetamine saccharate 3.75 mg, amphetamine aspartate 3.75 mg, amphetamine sulfate 3.75 mg] (equivalent to amphetamine base 9.4 mg); 20 mg [dextroamphetamine sulfate 5 mg, dextroamphetamine saccharate 5 mg, amphetamine aspartate 5 mg, amphetamine sulfate 5 mg] (equivalent to amphetamine base 12.6 mg); 30 mg [dextroamphetamine sulfate 7.5 mg, dextroamphetamine saccharate 7.5 mg, amphetamine aspartate 7.5 mg, amphetamine sulfate 7.5 mg] (equivalent to amphetamine base 18.8 mg)

♦ **Dextroamphetamine Sulfate** see Dextroamphetamine on page 362

♦ **Dextromethorphan, Acetaminophen, and Pseudoephedrine** *see* Acetaminophen, Dextromethorphan, and Pseudoephedrine *on page 28*

♦ **Dextromethorphan and Guaifenesin** *see* Guaifenesin and Dextromethorphan *on page 604*

♦ **Dextromethorphan and Promethazine** *see* Promethazine and Dextromethorphan *on page 1048*

♦ **Dextromethorphan and Pseudoephedrine** *see* Pseudoephedrine and Dextromethorphan *on page 1062*

♦ **Dextromethorphan, Carbinoxamine, and Pseudoephedrine** *see* Carbinoxamine, Pseudoephedrine, and Dextromethorphan *on page 219*

♦ **Dextromethorphan, Chlorpheniramine, and Phenylephrine** *see* Chlorpheniramine, Phenylephrine, and Dextromethorphan *on page 264*

♦ **Dextromethorphan, Chlorpheniramine, and Pseudoephedrine** *see* Chlorpheniramine, Pseudoephedrine, and Dextromethorphan *on page 265*

♦ **Dextromethorphan, Guaifenesin, and Pseudoephedrine** *see* Guaifenesin, Pseudoephedrine, and Dextromethorphan *on page 606*

♦ **Dextromethorphan, Pseudoephedrine, and Carbinoxamine** *see* Carbinoxamine, Pseudoephedrine, and Dextromethorphan *on page 219*

♦ **Dextropropoxyphene** *see* Propoxyphene *on page 1053*

♦ **Dextrostat®** *see* Dextroamphetamine *on page 362*

♦ **DFMO** *see* Eflornithine *on page 426*

♦ **DHAD** *see* Mitoxantrone *on page 851*

♦ **DHAQ** *see* Mitoxantrone *on page 851*

♦ **DHE** *see* Dihydroergotamine *on page 378*

♦ **D.H.E. 45®** *see* Dihydroergotamine *on page 378*

♦ **DHPG Sodium** *see* Ganciclovir *on page 577*

♦ **DHT™** *see* Dihydrotachysterol *on page 379*

♦ **DHT™ Intensol™** *see* Dihydrotachysterol *on page 379*

♦ **Diaβeta®** *see* GlyBURIDE *on page 594*

♦ **Diabetic Tussin C®** *see* Guaifenesin and Codeine *on page 604*

♦ **Diabetic Tussin® DM [OTC]** *see* Guaifenesin and Dextromethorphan *on page 604*

♦ **Diabetic Tussin® DM Maximum Strength [OTC]** *see* Guaifenesin and Dextromethorphan *on page 604*

♦ **Diabetic Tussin® EX [OTC]** *see* Guaifenesin *on page 603*

♦ **Diabinese®** *see* ChlorproPAMIDE *on page 268*

♦ **Diaminocyclohexane Oxalatoplatinum** *see* Oxaliplatin *on page 936*

♦ **Diaminodiphenylsulfone** *see* Dapsone *on page 341*

♦ **Diamox® Sequels®** *see* AcetaZOLAMIDE *on page 29*

♦ **Diastat® Rectal Delivery System** *see* Diazepam *on page 364*

♦ **Diatx™** *see* Vitamin B Complex Combinations *on page 1311*

♦ **DiatxFe™** *see* Vitamin B Complex Combinations *on page 1311*

Diazepam (dye AZ e pam)

Related Information

Benzodiazepines Comparison *on page 1366*
Convulsive Status Epilepticus *on page 1479*
Febrile Seizures *on page 1478*

U.S. Brand Names Diastat® Rectal Delivery System; Diazepam Intensol®; Valium®

Therapeutic Category Antianxiety Agent; Anticonvulsant, Benzodiazepine; Benzodiazepine; Sedative

Use Management of anxiety disorders, ethanol withdrawal symptoms; skeletal muscle relaxant; treatment of convulsive disorders

Orphan drug: Viscous solution for rectal administration: Management of selected, refractory epilepsy patients on stable regimens of antiepileptic drugs (AEDs) requiring intermittent use of diazepam to control episodes of increased seizure activity

Unlabeled/Investigational Use Panic disorders; preoperative sedation, light anesthesia, amnesia

Restrictions C-IV

Pregnancy Risk Factor D

Contraindications Hypersensitivity to diazepam or any component of the formulation (cross-sensitivity with other benzodiazepines may exist); narrow-angle glaucoma; not for use in children <6 months of age (oral) or <30 days of age (parenteral); pregnancy

Warnings/Precautions Diazepam has been associated with increasing the frequency of grand mal seizures. Withdrawal has also been associated with an increase in the seizure frequency. Use with caution with drugs which may decrease diazepam metabolism. Use with caution in elderly or debilitated patients, patients with hepatic disease (including alcoholics), or renal impairment. Active metabolites with extended half-lives may lead to delayed accumulation and adverse effects. Use with caution in patients with respiratory disease or impaired gag reflex.

Acute hypotension, muscle weakness, apnea, and cardiac arrest have occurred with parenteral administration. Acute effects may be more prevalent in patients receiving concurrent barbiturates, narcotics, or ethanol. Appropriate resuscitative equipment and qualified personnel should be available during administration and monitoring. Avoid use of the injection in patients with shock, coma, or acute ethanol intoxication. Intra-arterial injection or extravasation of the parenteral formulation should be avoided. Parenteral formulation contains propylene glycol, which has been associated with toxicity when administered in high dosages.

Causes CNS depression (dose-related) resulting in sedation, dizziness, confusion, or ataxia which may impair physical and mental capabilities. Patients must be cautioned about performing tasks which require mental alertness (eg, operating machinery or driving). Use with caution in patients receiving other CNS depressants or psychoactive agents. Effects with other sedative drugs or ethanol may be potentiated. The dosage of narcotics should be reduced by approximately 1/3 when diazepam is added. Benzodiazepines have been associated with falls and traumatic injury and should be used with extreme caution in patients who are at risk of these events (especially the elderly).

Use caution in patients with depression, particularly if suicidal risk may be present. Use with caution in patients with a history of drug dependence. Benzodiazepines have been associated with dependence and acute withdrawal symptoms on discontinuation or reduction in dose. Acute withdrawal, including seizures, may be precipitated in patients after administration of flumazenil to patients receiving long-term benzodiazepine therapy.

Diazepam has been associated with anterograde amnesia. Paradoxical reactions, including hyperactive or aggressive behavior, have been reported with benzodiazepines, particularly in adolescent/pediatric or psychiatric patients. Does not have analgesic, antidepressant, or antipsychotic properties.

Common Adverse Reactions Frequency not defined.
Cardiovascular: Hypotension
Central nervous system: Drowsiness, ataxia, amnesia, slurred speech, paradoxical excitement or rage, fatigue, insomnia, memory impairment, headache, anxiety, depression, vertigo, confusion
Dermatologic: Rash
Endocrine & metabolic: Changes in libido
Gastrointestinal: Changes in salivation, constipation, nausea
Genitourinary: Incontinence, urinary retention
Hepatic: Jaundice
Local: Phlebitis, pain with injection
Neuromuscular & skeletal: Dysarthria, tremor
Ocular: Blurred vision, diplopia
Respiratory: Decrease in respiratory rate, apnea

Drug Interactions
Cytochrome P450 Effect: Substrate of CYP1A2 (minor), 2B6 (minor), 2C8/9 (minor), 2C19 (major), 3A4 (major); **Inhibits** CYP2C19 (weak), 3A4 (weak)
Increased Effect/Toxicity: CYP2C19 inhibitors may increase the levels/effects of diazepam; example inhibitors include delavirdine, fluconazole, fluvoxamine, gemfibrozil, isoniazid, omeprazole, and ticlopidine. Diazepam potentiates the CNS depressant effects of narcotic analgesics, barbiturates, phenothiazines, ethanol, antihistamines, MAO inhibitors, sedative-hypnotics, and cyclic antidepressants. CYP3A4 inhibitors may increase the levels/effects of diazepam; example inhibitors include azole antifungals, ciprofloxacin, clarithromycin, diclofenac, doxycycline, erythromycin, imatinib, isoniazid, nefazodone, nicardipine, propofol, protease inhibitors, quinidine, and verapamil.
Decreased Effect: CYP2C19 inducers may decrease the levels/effects of diazepam; example inducers include aminoglutethimide, carbamazepine, phenytoin, and rifampin. CYP3A4 inducers may decrease the levels/effects of diazepam; example inducers include aminoglutethimide, carbamazepine, nafcillin, nevirapine, phenobarbital, phenytoin, and rifamycins.

Mechanism of Action Binds to stereospecific benzodiazepine receptors on the postsynaptic GABA neuron at several sites within the central nervous system, including the limbic system, reticular formation. Enhancement of the inhibitory effect of GABA on neuronal excitability results by increased neuronal membrane permeability to chloride ions. This shift in chloride ions results in hyperpolarization (a less excitable state) and stabilization.

Pharmacodynamics/Kinetics
I.V.: Status epilepticus:
Onset of action: Almost immediate
Duration: 20-30 minutes
Absorption: Oral: 85% to 100%, more reliable than I.M.
Protein binding: 98%
Metabolism: Hepatic
Half-life elimination: Parent drug: Adults: 20-50 hours; increased half-life in neonates, elderly, and those with severe hepatic disorders; Active major metabolite (desmethyldiazepam): 50-100 hours; may be prolonged in neonates

Dosage Oral absorption is more reliable than I.M.
Children:
Conscious sedation for procedures: Oral: 0.2-0.3 mg/kg (maximum: 10 mg) 45-60 minutes prior to procedure
Sedation/muscle relaxant/anxiety:
Oral: 0.12-0.8 mg/kg/day in divided doses every 6-8 hours
I.M., I.V.: 0.04-0.3 mg/kg/dose every 2-4 hours to a maximum of 0.6 mg/kg within an 8-hour period if needed
(Continued)

Diazepam *(Continued)*

Status epilepticus:

Infants 30 days to 5 years: I.V.: 0.05-0.3 mg/kg/dose given over 2-3 minutes, every 15-30 minutes to a maximum total dose of 5 mg; repeat in 2-4 hours as needed **or** 0.2-0.5 mg/dose every 2-5 minutes to a maximum total dose of 5 mg

>5 years: I.V.: 0.05-0.3 mg/kg/dose given over 2-3 minutes every 15-30 minutes to a maximum total dose of 10 mg; repeat in 2-4 hours as needed **or** 1 mg/dose given over 2-3 minutes, every 2-5 minutes to a maximum total dose of 10 mg

Rectal: 0.5 mg/kg, then 0.25 mg/kg in 10 minutes if needed

Anticonvulsant (acute treatment): Rectal gel formulation:

Infants <6 months: Not recommended

Children <2 years: Safety and efficacy have not been studied

Children 2-5 years: 0.5 mg/kg

Children 6-11 years: 0.3 mg/kg

Children ≥12 years and Adults: 0.2 mg/kg

Note: Dosage should be rounded upward to the next available dose, 2.5, 5, 10, 15, and 20 mg/dose; dose may be repeated in 4-12 hours if needed; do not use more than 5 times per month or more than once every 5 days

Adolescents: Conscious sedation for procedures:

Oral: 10 mg

I.V.: 5 mg, may repeat with ¹/₂ dose if needed

Adults:

Anxiety/sedation/skeletal muscle relaxant:

Oral: 2-10 mg 2-4 times/day

I.M., I.V.: 2-10 mg, may repeat in 3-4 hours if needed

Sedation in the ICU patient: I.V.: 0.03-0.1 mg/kg every 30 minutes to 6 hours

Status epilepticus: I.V.: 5-10 mg every 10-20 minutes, up to 30 mg in an 8-hour period; may repeat in 2-4 hours if necessary

Rapid tranquilization of agitated patient (administer every 30-60 minutes): Oral: 5-10 mg; average total dose for tranquilization: 20-60 mg

Elderly: Oral: Initial:

Anxiety: 1-2 mg 1-2 times/day; increase gradually as needed, rarely need to use >10 mg/day (watch for hypotension and excessive sedation)

Skeletal muscle relaxant: 2-5 mg 2-4 times/day

Hemodialysis: Not dialyzable (0% to 5%); supplemental dose is not necessary

Dosing adjustment in hepatic impairment: Reduce dose by 50% in cirrhosis and avoid in severe/acute liver disease

Administration Intensol® should be diluted before use; diazepam does not have any analgesic effects

In children, do not exceed 1-2 mg/minute IVP; adults 5 mg/minute

Monitoring Parameters Respiratory, cardiovascular, and mental status; check for orthostasis

Reference Range Therapeutic: Diazepam: 0.2-1.5 µg/mL (SI: 0.7-5.3 µmol/L); N-desmethyldiazepam (nordiazepam): 0.1-0.5 µg/mL (SI: 0.35-1.8 µmol/L)

Patient Information Avoid alcohol and other CNS depressants; avoid activities needing good psychomotor coordination until CNS effects are known; drug may cause physical or psychological dependence; avoid abrupt discontinuation after prolonged use

Dosage Forms GEL, rectal delivery system (Diastat®): Adult rectal tip [6 cm]: 5 mg/mL (15 mg, 20 mg); pediatric rectal tip [4.4 cm]: 5 mg/mL (2.5 mg, 5 mg); universal rectal tip [pediatric/adult 4.4 cm]: 5 mg/mL (10 mg). **INJ, solution:** 5 mg/mL (2 mL, 10 mL). **SOLN, oral:** 5 mg/5 mL (5 mL, 10 mL, 500 mL). **SOLN, oral concentrate** (Diazepam Intensol®): 5 mg/mL (30 mL). **TAB** (Valium®): 2 mg, 5 mg, 10 mg

♦ **Diazepam Intensol®** *see* Diazepam *on page 364*

Diazoxide *(dye az OKS ide)*

U.S. Brand Names Hyperstat®; Proglycem®

Therapeutic Category Antihypertensive Agent; Antihypoglycemic Agent

Use

Oral: Hypoglycemia related to islet cell adenoma, carcinoma, hyperplasia, or adenomatosis, nesidioblastosis, leucine sensitivity, or extrapancreatic malignancy

I.V.: Severe hypertension

Pregnancy Risk Factor C

Dosage

Hypertension: Children and Adults: I.V.: 1-3 mg/kg up to a maximum of 150 mg in a single injection; repeat dose in 5-15 minutes until blood pressure adequately reduced; repeat administration at intervals of 4-24 hours; monitor the blood pressure closely; do not use longer than 10 days

Hyperinsulinemic hypoglycemia: Oral: **Note:** Use lower dose listed as initial dose

Newborns and Infants: 8-15 mg/kg/day in divided doses every 8-12 hours

Children and Adults: 3-8 mg/kg/day in divided doses every 8-12 hours

Dosing adjustment in renal impairment: None

Dialysis: Elimination is not enhanced via hemo- or peritoneal dialysis; supplemental dose is not necessary

Dosage Forms CAP (Proglycem®): 50 mg [not available in the U.S.]. **INJ, solution** (Hyperstat®): 15 mg/mL (20 mL). **SUSP, oral** (Proglycem®): 50 mg/mL (30 mL).

♦ **Dibenzyline®** *see* Phenoxybenzamine *on page 990*

+ **DIC** *see* Dacarbazine *on page 332*
+ **Dichloralphenazone, Acetaminophen, and Isometheptene** *see* Acetaminophen, Isomethep-tene, and Dichloralphenazone *on page 29*
+ **Dichloralphenazone, Isometheptene, and Acetaminophen** *see* Acetaminophen, Isomethep-tene, and Dichloralphenazone *on page 29*
+ **6,7-Dichloro-1,5-Dihydroimidazo [2,1b] quinazolin-2(3H)-one Monohydrochloride** *see* Anagrelide *on page 99*

Dichlorodifluoromethane and Trichloromonofluoromethane
(dye klor oh dye flor oh METH ane & tri klor oh mon oh flor oh METH ane)
U.S. Brand Names Fluori-Methane®
Synonyms Trichloromonofluoromethane and Dichlorodifluoromethane
Therapeutic Category Analgesic, Topical
Use Management of pain associated with injections
Dosage Invert bottle over treatment area approximately 12" away from site of application; open dispensea spring valve completely, allowing liquid to flow in a stream from the bottle. The rate of spraying is approximately 10 cm/second and should be continued until entire muscle has been covered.
Dosage Forms AERO, topical: Dichlorodifluoromethane 15% and trichloromonofluoro-methane 85% (103 mL)

+ **Dichysterol** *see* Dihydrotachysterol *on page 379*

Diclofenac (dye KLOE fen ak)
Related Information
Nonsteroidal Anti-Inflammatory Agents Comparison *on page 1401*
U.S. Brand Names Cataflam®; Solaraze™; Voltaren®; Voltaren Ophthalmic®; Voltaren®-XR
Synonyms Diclofenac Potassium; Diclofenac Sodium
Therapeutic Category Analgesic, Nonsteroidal Anti-inflammatory Drug; Anti-inflammatory Agent; Nonsteroidal Anti-inflammatory Drug (NSAID), Oral
Use
Immediate-release tablets: Acute treatment of mild to moderate pain; ankylosing spondylitis; primary dysmenorrhea; acute and chronic treatment of rheumatoid arthritis, osteoarthritis
Delayed-release tablets: Acute and chronic treatment of rheumatoid arthritis, osteoarthritis, ankylosing spondylitis
Extended-release tablets: Chronic treatment of osteoarthritis, rheumatoid arthritis
Ophthalmic solution: Postoperative inflammation following cataract extraction; temporary relief of pain and photophobia in patients undergoing corneal refractive surgery
Topical gel: Actinic keratosis (AK) in conjunction with sun avoidance
Unlabeled/Investigational Use Juvenile rheumatoid arthritis
Pregnancy Risk Factor B/D (3rd trimester)
Contraindications Hypersensitivity to diclofenac, any component of the formulation, aspirin or other NSAIDs, including patients who experience bronchospasm, asthma, rhinitis, or urticaria following NSAID or aspirin; porphyria; pregnancy (3rd trimester)
Warnings/Precautions Use with caution in patients with CHF, dehydration, hypertension, decreased renal or hepatic function, history of GI disease, active gastrointestinal ulceration or bleeding, or those receiving anticoagulants. Anaphylactoid reactions have been reported with NSAID use, even without prior exposure; may be more common in patients with the aspirin triad. Use with caution in patients with pre-existing asthma. Rare cases of severe hepatic reactions (including necrosis, jaundice, fulminant hepatitis) have been reported. Vision changes (including changes in color) have been rarely reported with oral diclofenac. Topical gel should not be applied to the eyes, open wounds, infected areas, or to exfoliative dermatitis. Monitor patients for 1 year following application of ophthalmic drops for corneal refractive procedures. Patients using ophthalmic drops should not wear soft contact lenses. Ophthalmic drops may slow/delay healing or prolong bleeding time following surgery. Elderly are at a high risk for adverse effects from NSAIDs. As many as 60% of elderly can develop peptic ulceration and/or hemorrhage asymptomatically.

Use lowest effective dose for shortest period possible. Use of NSAIDs can compromise existing renal function especially when Cl_{cr} is <30 mL/minute. CNS adverse effects such as confusion, agitation, and hallucination are generally seen in overdose or high-dose situations; however, elderly may demonstrate these adverse effects at lower doses than younger adults. Withhold for at least 4-6 half-lives prior to surgical or dental procedures.
Common Adverse Reactions
>10%:
Local: Application site reactions (gel): Pruritus (31% to 52%), rash (35% to 46%), contact dermatitis (19% to 33%), dry skin (25% to 27%), pain (15% to 26%), exfoliation (6% to 24%), paresthesia (8% to 20%)
Ocular: Ophthalmic drops (incidence may be dependent upon indication): Lacrimation (30%), keratitis (28%), elevated IOP (15%), transient burning/stinging (15%)
1% to 10%:
Central nervous system: Headache (7%), dizziness (3%)
Dermatologic: Pruritus (1% to 3%), rash (1% to 3%)
Endocrine & metabolic: Fluid retention (1% to 3%)
Gastrointestinal: Abdominal cramps (3% to 9%), abdominal pain (3% to 9%), constipation (3% to 9%), diarrhea (3% to 9%), flatulence (3% to 9%), indigestion (3% to 9%), nausea (3% to 9%), abdominal distention (1% to 3%), peptic ulcer/GI bleed (0.6% to 2%)
(Continued)

Diclofenac *(Continued)*

    Hepatic: Increased ALT/AST (2%)

    Local: Application site reactions (gel): Edema (4%)

    Ocular: Ophthalmic drops: Abnormal vision, acute elevated IOP, blurred vision, conjunctivitis, corneal deposits, corneal edema, corneal opacity, corneal lesions, discharge, eyelid swelling, injection, iritis, irritation, itching, lacrimation disorder, ocular allergy

    Otic: Tinnitus (1% to 3%)

Drug Interactions

    Cytochrome P450 Effect: Substrate (minor) of CYP1A2, 2B6, 2C8/9, 2C19, 2D6, 3A4; **Inhibits** CYP1A2 (moderate), 2C8/9 (weak), 2E1 (weak), 3A4 (strong)

    Increased Effect/Toxicity: Increased toxicity of digoxin, methotrexate, cyclosporine, lithium, insulin, sulfonylureas, potassium-sparing diuretics, warfarin, and aspirin.

    Decreased Effect: Decreased effect of diclofenac with aspirin. Decreased effect of thiazides, furosemide.

Mechanism of Action Inhibits prostaglandin synthesis by decreasing the activity of the enzyme, cyclooxygenase, which results in decreased formation of prostaglandin precursors. Mechanism of action for the treatment of AK has not been established.

Pharmacodynamics/Kinetics

    Onset of action: Cataflam® is more rapid than sodium salt (Voltaren®) because it dissolves in the stomach instead of the duodenum

    Absorption: Topical gel: 10%

    Protein binding: 99% to albumin

    Metabolism: Hepatic to several metabolites

    Half-life elimination: 2 hours

    Time to peak, serum: Cataflam®: ~1 hour; Voltaren®: ~2 hours

    Excretion: Urine (65%); feces (35%)

Dosage Adults:

    Oral:

        Analgesia/primary dysmenorrhea: Starting dose: 50 mg 3 times/day; maximum dose: 150 mg/day

        Rheumatoid arthritis: 150-200 mg/day in 2-4 divided doses (100 mg/day of sustained release product)

        Osteoarthritis: 100-150 mg/day in 2-3 divided doses (100-200 mg/day of sustained release product)

        Ankylosing spondylitis: 100-125 mg/day in 4-5 divided doses

    Ophthalmic:

        Cataract surgery: Instill 1 drop into affected eye 4 times/day beginning 24 hours after cataract surgery and continuing for 2 weeks

        Corneal refractive surgery: Instill 1-2 drops into affected eye within the hour prior to surgery, within 15 minutes following surgery, and then continue for 4 times/day, up to 3 days

    Topical: Apply gel to lesion area twice daily for 60-90 days

    Dosage adjustment in renal impairment: Monitor closely in patients with significant renal impairment

    Dosage adjustment in hepatic impairment: No specific dosing recommendations

    Elderly: No specific dosing recommendations; elderly may demonstrate adverse effects at lower doses than younger adults, and >60% may develop asymptomatic peptic ulceration with or without hemorrhage; monitor renal function

Administration

    Oral: Do not crush tablets. Administer with food or milk to avoid gastric distress. Take with full glass of water to enhance absorption.

    Ophthalmic: Wait at least 5 minutes before administering other types of eye drops.

Monitoring Parameters Monitor CBC, liver enzymes; monitor urine output and BUN/serum creatinine; occult blood loss, hemoglobin, hematocrit

Patient Information Oral: Serious gastrointestinal bleeding can occur as well as ulceration and perforation. Pain may or may not be present. Avoid aspirin and aspirin-containing products while taking this medication. If gastric upset occurs, take with food, milk, or antacid. If gastric adverse effects persist, contact prescriber. May cause drowsiness, dizziness, blurred vision, and confusion. Use caution when performing tasks that require alertness (eg, driving). Do not take for more than 3 days for fever or 10 days for pain without prescriber's advice.

    Ophthalmic: Apply gentle pressure to inner corner of eye for 30 seconds. Do not use any other eye preparation for at least 10 minutes. May cause sensitivity to bright light. Do not wear soft contact lenses.

    Topical gel: Avoid sun during therapy. Cover lesion with gel and smooth into skin gently. You may not notice complete healing until 30 days after therapy is completed. Do not cover lesion with occlusive dressings or apply sunscreens, cosmetics, or other medications to affected area.

Dosage Forms GEL, as sodium (Solaraze™): 30 mg/g (50 g). **SOLN, ophthalmic, as sodium** (Voltaren Ophthalmic®): 0.1% (2.5 mL, 5 mL). **TAB, as potassium** (Cataflam®): 50 mg. **TAB, delayed release, enteric coated, as sodium** (Voltaren®): 25 mg, 50 mg, 75 mg. **TAB, extended release, as sodium** (Voltaren®-XR): 100 mg

Diclofenac and Misoprostol *(dye KLOE fen ak & mye soe PROST ole)*

U.S. Brand Names Arthrotec®

Synonyms Misoprostol and Diclofenac

Therapeutic Category Analgesic, Nonsteroidal Anti-inflammatory Drug; Prostaglandin

Use The diclofenac component is indicated for the treatment of osteoarthritis and rheumatoid arthritis; the misoprostol component is indicated for the prophylaxis of NSAID-induced gastric and duodenal ulceration

Pregnancy Risk Factor X

Dosage Oral:
Adults:
Arthrotec® 50:
Osteoarthritis: 1 tablet 2-3 times/day
Rheumatoid arthritis: 1 tablet 3-4 times/day
For both regimens, if not tolerated by patient, the dose may be reduced to 1 tablet twice daily
Arthrotec® 75:
Patients who cannot tolerate full daily Arthrotec® 50 regimens: 1 tablet twice daily
Note: The use of these tablets may not be as effective at preventing GI ulceration
Elderly: No specific dosage adjustment is recommended; may require reduced dosage due to lower body weight; monitor renal function

Dosage Forms TAB: Diclofenac 50 mg and misoprostol 200 mcg; diclofenac 75 mg and misoprostol 200 mcg

- **Diclofenac Potassium** see Diclofenac on page 367
- **Diclofenac Sodium** see Diclofenac on page 367

Dicloxacillin (dye kloks a SIL in)

Synonyms Dicloxacillin Sodium

Therapeutic Category Antibiotic, Penicillin

Use Treatment of systemic infections such as pneumonia, skin and soft tissue infections, and osteomyelitis caused by penicillinase-producing staphylococci

Pregnancy Risk Factor B

Contraindications Hypersensitivity to dicloxacillin, penicillin, or any component of the formulation

Warnings/Precautions Monitor PT if patient concurrently on warfarin; elimination of drug is slow in neonates; use with caution in patients allergic to cephalosporins

Common Adverse Reactions 1% to 10%: Gastrointestinal: Nausea, diarrhea, abdominal pain

Drug Interactions
Cytochrome P450 Effect: Induces CYP3A4 (weak)
Increased Effect/Toxicity: Disulfiram, probenecid may increase penicillin levels. Penicillins may increase the exposure to methotrexate during concurrent therapy; monitor.
Decreased Effect: Although anecdotal reports suggest oral contraceptive efficacy could be reduced by penicillins, this has been refuted by more rigorous scientific and clinical data. Decreased effect of (warfarin) anticoagulants.

Mechanism of Action Inhibits bacterial cell wall synthesis by binding to one or more of the penicillin binding proteins (PBPs); which in turn inhibits the final transpeptidation step of peptidoglycan synthesis in bacterial cell walls, thus inhibiting cell wall biosynthesis. Bacteria eventually lyse due to ongoing activity of cell wall autolytic enzymes (autolysins and murein hydrolases) while cell wall assembly is arrested.

Pharmacodynamics/Kinetics
Absorption: 35% to 76%; rate and extent reduced by food
Distribution: Throughout body with highest concentrations in kidney and liver; CSF penetration is low; crosses placenta; enters breast milk
Protein binding: 96%
Half-life elimination: 0.6-0.8 hour; slightly prolonged with renal impairment
Time to peak, serum: 0.5-2 hours
Excretion: Feces; urine (56% to 70% as unchanged drug); prolonged in neonates

Dosage Oral:
Use in newborns not recommended
Children <40 kg: 12.5-25 mg/kg/day divided every 6 hours; doses of 50-100 mg/kg/day in divided doses every 6 hours have been used for therapy of osteomyelitis
Children >40 kg and Adults: 125-250 mg every 6 hours
Dosage adjustment in renal impairment: Not necessary
Hemodialysis: Not dialyzable (0% to 5%); supplemental dosage not necessary
Peritoneal dialysis: Supplemental dosage not necessary
Continuous arteriovenous or venovenous hemofiltration: Supplemental dosage not necessary

Monitoring Parameters Monitor prothrombin time if patient concurrently on warfarin; monitor for signs of anaphylaxis during first dose

Patient Information Take all medication; take 1 hour before or 2 hours after meals, do not skip doses

Dosage Forms CAP: 250 mg, 500 mg

- **Dicloxacillin Sodium** see Dicloxacillin on page 369

Dicyclomine (dye SYE kloe meen)

U.S. Brand Names Bentyl®

Synonyms Dicyclomine Hydrochloride; Dicycloverine Hydrochloride

Therapeutic Category Anticholinergic Agent; Antispasmodic Agent, Gastrointestinal

Use Treatment of functional disturbances of GI motility such as irritable bowel syndrome

Unlabeled/Investigational Use Urinary incontinence

(Continued)

Dicyclomine *(Continued)*

Pregnancy Risk Factor B
Dosage
Oral:
Infants >6 months: 5 mg/dose 3-4 times/day
Children: 10 mg/dose 3-4 times/day
Adults: Begin with 80 mg/day in 4 equally divided doses, then increase up to 160 mg/day
I.M. **(should not be used I.V.):** Adults: 80 mg/day in 4 divided doses (20 mg/dose)
Dosage Forms CAP: 10 mg. **INJ, solution:** 10 mg/mL (2 mL). **SYR:** 10 mg/5 mL (480 mL).
TAB: 20 mg

♦ **Dicyclomine Hydrochloride** *see Dicyclomine on page 369*
♦ **Dicycloverine Hydrochloride** *see Dicyclomine on page 369*

Didanosine *(dye DAN oh seen)*

Related Information
Antiretroviral Therapy for HIV Infection *on page 1448*
Management of Healthcare Worker Exposures to HBV, HCV, and HIV *on page 1421*
U.S. Brand Names Videx®; Videx® EC
Synonyms ddI; Dideoxyinosine
Therapeutic Category Antiretroviral Agent, Nucleoside Reverse Transcriptase Inhibitor
(NRTI) [Adenosine Analog]
Use Treatment of HIV infection; always to be used in combination with at least two other
antiretroviral agents
Pregnancy Risk Factor B
Contraindications Hypersensitivity to didanosine or any component of the formulation
Warnings/Precautions Pancreatitis (sometimes fatal) has been reported, incidence is dose
related. Risk factors for developing pancreatitis include a previous history of the condition,
concurrent cytomegalovirus or *Mycobacterium avium-intracellulare* infection, and concomitant
use of stavudine, pentamidine, or co-trimoxazole. Discontinue didanosine if clinical signs of
pancreatitis occur. Lactic acidosis, symptomatic hyperlactatemia, and severe hepatomegaly
with steatosis (sometimes fatal) have occurred with antiretroviral nucleoside analogues,
including didanosine. Hepatotoxicity may occur even in the absence of marked transaminase
elevations; suspend therapy in any patient developing clinical/laboratory findings which
suggest hepatotoxicity. Pregnant women may be at increased risk of lactic acidosis and liver
damage.

Peripheral neuropathy occurs in ~20% of patients receiving the drug. Retinal changes
(including retinal depigmentation) and optic neuritis have been reported in adults and children
using didanosine. Patients should undergo retinal examination every 6-12 months. Use with
caution in patients with decreased renal or hepatic function, phenylketonuria, sodium-restricted
diets, or with edema, CHF, or hyperuricemia. Twice-daily dosing is the preferred dosing
frequency for didanosine tablets. Didanosine sustained release capsules are indicated for
once-daily use.
Common Adverse Reactions As reported in monotherapy studies; risk of toxicity may
increase when combined with other agents.

>10%:
Gastrointestinal: Increased amylase (15% to 17%), abdominal pain (7% to 13%), diarrhea
(19% to 28%)
Neuromuscular & skeletal: Peripheral neuropathy (17% to 20%)
1% to 10%:
Dermatologic: Rash, pruritus
Endocrine & metabolic: Increased uric acid
Gastrointestinal: Pancreatitis; patients >65 years of age had a higher frequency of pancrea-
titis than younger patients
Hepatic: Increased SGOT, increased SGPT, increased alkaline phosphatase
Drug Interactions
Increased Effect/Toxicity: Concomitant administration of other drugs which have the
potential to cause peripheral neuropathy or pancreatitis may increase the risk of these
toxicities Allopurinol may increase didanosine concentration; avoid concurrent use.
Concomitant use of antacids with buffered tablet or pediatric didanosine solution may
potentiate adverse effects of aluminum- or magnesium-containing antacids. Ganciclovir may
increase didanosine concentration; monitor. Hydroxyurea may precipitate dida-
nosine-induced pancreatitis if added to therapy; concomitant use is not recommended.
Coadministration with ribavirin or tenofovir may increase exposure to didanosine and/or its
active metabolite increasing the risk or severity of didanosine toxicities, including pancreatitis, lactic acidosis, and peripheral neuropathy; monitor closely and suspend therapy if signs
or symptoms of toxicity are noted.
Decreased Effect: Didanosine buffered tablets and buffered pediatric solution may
decrease absorption of quinolones or tetracyclines (administer 2 hours prior to didanosine
buffered formulations). Didanosine should be held during PCP treatment with pentamidine.
Didanosine may decrease levels of indinavir. Drugs whose absorption depends on the level
of acidity in the stomach such as ketoconazole, itraconazole, and dapsone should be
administered at least 2 hours prior to the buffered formulations of didanosine (not affected
by sustained release capsules). Methadone may decrease didanosine concentrations.
Mechanism of Action Didanosine, a purine nucleoside (adenosine) analog and the deamination product of dideoxyadenosine (ddA), inhibits HIV replication *in vitro* in both T cells and

monocytes. Didanosine is converted within the cell to the mono-, di-, and triphosphates of ddA. These ddA triphosphates act as substrate and inhibitor of HIV reverse transcriptase substrate and inhibitor of HIV reverse transcriptase thereby blocking viral DNA synthesis and suppressing HIV replication.

Pharmacodynamics/Kinetics

Absorption: Subject to degradation by acidic pH of stomach; some formulations are buffered to resist acidic pH; ≤50% reduction in peak plasma concentration is observed in presence of food. Sustained release capsules contain enteric-coated beadlets which dissolve in the small intestine.

Distribution: V_d: Children: 35.6 L/m^2; Adults: 1.08 L/kg

Protein binding: <5%

Metabolism: Has not been evaluated in humans; studies conducted in dogs show extensive metabolism with allantoin, hypoxanthine, xanthine, and uric acid being the major metabolites found in urine

Bioavailability: 42%

Half-life elimination:

Children and Adolescents: 0.8 hour

Adults: Normal renal function: 1.5 hours; active metabolite, ddATP, has an intracellular half-life >12 hours *in vitro*; Renal impairment: 2.5-5 hours

Time to peak: Buffered tablets: 0.67 hours; Sustained release capsules: 2 hours

Excretion: Urine (~55% as unchanged drug)

Clearance: Total body: Averages 800 mL/minute

Dosage Treatment of HIV infection: Oral (administer on an empty stomach):

Children:

2 weeks to 8 months: 100 mg/m^2 twice daily

>8 months: 120 mg/m^2 twice daily

Children <1 year should receive 1 tablet per dose and children >1 year should receive 2-4 tablets per dose for adequate buffering and absorption; tablets should be chewed or dispersed

Adults: Dosing based on patient weight:

Note: Preferred dosing frequency is twice daily for didanosine tablets

Tablets:

<60 kg: 125 mg twice daily or 250 mg once daily

≥60 kg: 200 mg twice daily or 400 mg once daily

Note: Adults should receive 2-4 tablets per dose for adequate buffering and absorption; tablets should be chewed or dispersed; didanosine has also been used as 300 mg once daily

Buffered Powder:

<60 kg: 167 mg twice daily

≥60 kg: 250 mg twice daily

Sustained release capsule:

<60 kg: 250 mg once daily

≥60 kg: 400 mg once daily

Dosing adjustment with tenofovir (didanosine tablets or sustained-release capsules; based on tenofovir product labeling):

≤60 kg: No data available

>60 kg: 250 mg once daily

Dosage adjustment in renal impairment: Dosing based on patient weight, creatinine clearance, and dosage form: See table.

Recommended Dose (mg) of Didanosine by Body Weight

Creatinine Clearance (mL/min)	≥60 kg			<60 kg		
	Tablet[1] (mg)	Buffered Powder[2] (mg)	Sustained Release Capsule (mg)	Tablet[1] (mg)	Buffered Powder[2] (mg)	Sustained Release Capsule (mg)
≥60	400 qd or 200 bid	250 bid	400 qd	250 qd or 125 bid	167 bid	250 qd
30-59	200 qd or 100 bid	100 bid	200 qd	150 qd or 75 bid	100 bid	125 qd
10-29	150 qd	167 qd	125 qd	100 qd	100 qd	125 qd
<10	100 qd	100 qd	125 qd	75 qd	100 qd	See footnote 3.

[1]Chewable/dispersible buffered tablet; 2 tablets must be taken with each dose; different strengths of tablets may be combined to yield the recommended dose.

[2]Buffered powder for oral solution.

[3]Not suitable for use in patients <60 kg with Cl$_{cr}$ <10 mL/minute; use alternate formulation.

Hemodialysis: Removed by hemodialysis (40% to 60%)

Dosing adjustment in hepatic impairment: Should be considered; monitor for toxicity

Elderly patients have a higher frequency of pancreatitis (10% versus 5% in younger patients); monitor renal function and dose accordingly

Administration

Chewable/dispersible buffered tablets: At least 2 tablets, but no more than 4 tablets, should be taken together to allow adequate buffering. Tablets may be chewed or dispersed prior to (Continued)

Didanosine *(Continued)*

consumption. To disperse, dissolve in 1 oz water, stir until uniform dispersion is formed, and drink immediately. May also add 1 oz of clear apple juice to initial dispersion if additional flavor is needed. The apple juice dilution is stable for 1 hour at room temperature. Do not mix with other juices.

Buffered powder for oral solution: Pour contents of packet into 4 ounces of water. Mix until dissolved and drink immediately. Do not mix with fruit juice.

Pediatric powder for oral solution: Prior to dispensing, the powder should be mixed with purified water USP to an initial concentration of 20 mg/mL and then further diluted with an appropriate antacid suspension to a final mixture of 10 mg/mL. Shake well prior to use.

Monitoring Parameters Serum potassium, uric acid, creatinine; hemoglobin, CBC with neutrophil and platelet count, CD4 cells; viral load; liver function tests, amylase; weight gain; perform dilated retinal exam every 6 months

Patient Information Take as directed, 1 hour before or 2 hours after eating. You will be susceptible to infection; avoid crowds. Report numbness or tingling of fingers, toes, or feet; abdominal pain; or persistent nausea or vomiting. Should have a retinal exam every 6-12 months. Chew tablets thoroughly and/or dissolve in water. Pour powder into 4 oz of liquid, stir, and drink immediately; may add 1 oz of apple juice to the water for flavoring (do not mix with other fruit juice or acid-containing liquids). Sustained release capsules should be swallowed whole; do not chew, crush or open the capsule. Shake pediatric oral solution well before use; store in refrigerator; discard after 30 days.

Dosage Forms CAP, sustained release (Videx® EC): 125 mg, 200 mg, 250 mg, 400 mg. **POWDER, oral solution, buffered** (Videx® [DSC]): 100 mg, 167 mg, 250 mg. **POWDER, oral solution, pediatric** (Videx®): 2 g, 4 g. **TAB, buffered, chewable/dispersible** (Videx®): 25 mg, 50 mg, 100 mg, 150 mg, 200 mg

- ◆ **Dideoxycytidine** *see* Zalcitabine *on page 1321*
- ◆ **Dideoxyinosine** *see* Didanosine *on page 370*
- ◆ **Didronel®** *see* Etidronate Disodium *on page 495*

Diethylpropion *(dye eth il PROE pee on)*

Related Information
Obesity Treatment Guidelines for Adults *on page 1482*

U.S. Brand Names Tenuate®; Tenuate® Dospan®

Synonyms Amfepramone; Diethylpropion Hydrochloride

Therapeutic Category Anorexiant

Use Short-term adjunct in a regimen of weight reduction based on exercise, behavioral modification, and caloric reduction in the management of exogenous obesity for patients with an initial body mass index ≥30 kg/m^2 or ≥27 kg/m^2 in the presence of other risk factors (diabetes, hypertension)

Unlabeled/Investigational Use Migraine

Restrictions C-IV

Pregnancy Risk Factor B

Dosage Adults: Oral:
Tablet: 25 mg 3 times/day before meals or food
Tablet, controlled release: 75 mg at midmorning

Dosage Forms TAB (Tenuate®): 25 mg. **TAB, controlled release** (Tenuate® Dospan®): 75 mg

- ◆ **Diethylpropion Hydrochloride** *see* Diethylpropion *on page 372*

Difenoxin and Atropine *(dye fen OKS in & A troe peen)*

U.S. Brand Names Motofen®

Synonyms Atropine and Difenoxin

Therapeutic Category Antidiarrheal

Use Treatment of diarrhea

Restrictions C-IV

Pregnancy Risk Factor C

Dosage Adults: Oral: Initial: 2 tablets, then 1 tablet after each loose stool; 1 tablet every 3-4 hours, up to 8 tablets in a 24-hour period; if no improvement after 48 hours, continued administration is not indicated

Dosage Forms TAB: Difenoxin 1 mg and atropine 0.025 mg

- ◆ **Differin®** *see* Adapalene *on page 39*

Diflorasone *(dye FLOR a sone)*

Related Information
Corticosteroids Comparison *on page 1372*

U.S. Brand Names Maxiflor®; Psorcon®; Psorcon® e™

Synonyms Diflorasone Diacetate

Therapeutic Category Corticosteroid, Topical (High Potency); Corticosteroid, Topical (Very High Potency)

Use Relieves inflammation and pruritic symptoms of corticosteroid-responsive dermatosis (high to very high potency topical corticosteroid)

Maxiflor®: High potency topical corticosteroid
Psorcon™: Very high potency topical corticosteroid

Pregnancy Risk Factor C

Contraindications Hypersensitivity to diflorasone

Warnings/Precautions Use with caution in patients with impaired circulation; skin infections

Mechanism of Action Decreases inflammation by suppression of migration of polymorphonuclear leukocytes and reversal of increased capillary permeability

Pharmacodynamics/Kinetics

Absorption: Negligible, around 1% reaches dermal layers or systemic circulation; occlusive dressings increase absorption percutaneously

Metabolism: Primarily hepatic

Dosage Topical: Apply ointment sparingly 1-3 times/day; apply cream sparingly 2-4 times/day. Therapy should be discontinued when control is achieved; if no improvement is seen, reassessment of diagnosis may be necessary.

Patient Information A thin film of cream or ointment is effective; do not overuse; do not use tight-fitting diapers or plastic pants on children being treated in the diaper area; use only as prescribed, and for no longer than the period prescribed; apply sparingly in light film; rub in lightly; avoid contact with eyes; notify prescriber if condition being treated persists or worsens

Dosage Forms CRM: 0.05% (15 g, 30 g, 60 g); (Maxiflor®): 0.05% (30 g, 60 g); (Psorcon® [DSC]): 0.05% (60 g); (Psorcon® e™): 0.05% (15 g, 30 g, 60 g). **OINT:** 0.05% (15 g, 30 g, 60 g); (Maxiflor®): 0.05% (30 g, 60 g); (Psorcon®): 0.05% (60 g); (Psorcon® e™): 0.05% (15 g, 30 g, 60 g)

♦ **Diflorasone Diacetate** *see Diflorasone on page 372*

♦ **Diflucan®** *see Fluconazole on page 527*

Diflunisal (dye FLOO ni sal)

Related Information

Nonsteroidal Anti-Inflammatory Agents Comparison *on page 1401*

U.S. Brand Names Dolobid®

Therapeutic Category Analgesic, Nonsteroidal Anti-inflammatory Drug; Anti-inflammatory Agent; Nonsteroidal Anti-inflammatory Drug (NSAID), Oral

Use Management of inflammatory disorders usually including rheumatoid arthritis and osteoarthritis; can be used as an analgesic for treatment of mild to moderate pain

Pregnancy Risk Factor C (1st and 2nd trimesters); D (3rd trimester)

Contraindications Hypersensitivity to diflunisal or any component of the formulation; may be a cross-sensitivity with other NSAIDs including aspirin; should not be used in patients with active GI bleeding; pregnancy (3rd trimester)

Warnings/Precautions Peptic ulceration and GI bleeding have been reported; platelet function and bleeding time are inhibited; ophthalmologic effects; impaired renal function, use lower dosage; dehydration; peripheral edema; possibility of Reye's syndrome; elevation in liver tests. Withhold for at least 4-6 half-lives prior to surgical or dental procedures.

Common Adverse Reactions

>10%:

Central nervous system: Headache

Endocrine & metabolic: Fluid retention

1% to 10%:

Cardiovascular: Angina pectoris, arrhythmias

Central nervous system: Dizziness

Dermatologic: Rash

Gastrointestinal: GI ulceration

Genitourinary: Vaginal bleeding

Otic: Tinnitus

Drug Interactions

Increased Effect/Toxicity: May cause increased toxicity of cyclosporine, digoxin, methotrexate, anticoagulants, phenytoin, sulfonylureas, sulfonamides, lithium, indomethacin, hydrochlorothiazide, and acetaminophen (levels) when coadministered with diflunisal.

Decreased Effect: Decreased effect with antacids, aspirin.

Mechanism of Action Inhibits prostaglandin synthesis by decreasing the activity of the enzyme, cyclooxygenase, which results in decreased formation of prostaglandin precursors

Pharmacodynamics/Kinetics

Onset of action: Analgesic: ~1 hour

Duration: 8-12 hours

Absorption: Well absorbed

Distribution: Enters breast milk

Metabolism: Extensively hepatic

Half-life elimination: 8-12 hours; prolonged with renal impairment

Time to peak, serum: 2-3 hours

Excretion: Urine (~3% as unchanged drug, 90% as glucuronide conjugates) within 72-96 hours

Dosage Adults: Oral:

Pain: Initial: 500-1000 mg followed by 250-500 mg every 8-12 hours; maximum daily dose: 1.5 g

Inflammatory condition: 500-1000 mg/day in 2 divided doses; maximum daily dose: 1.5 g

Dosing adjustment in renal impairment: Cl_{cr} <50 mL/minute: Administer 50% of normal dose

Patient Information May cause GI upset, take with water, milk, or meals; do not take aspirin with diflunisal; swallow tablets whole, do not crush or chew

Dosage Forms TAB: 250 mg, 500 mg

♦ **Digibind**® *see* Digoxin Immune Fab *on page 376*

♦ **DigiFab**™ *see* Digoxin Immune Fab *on page 376*

♦ **Digitek**® *see* Digoxin *on page 374*

Digoxin (di JOKS in)

U.S. Brand Names Digitek®; Lanoxicaps®; Lanoxin®

Therapeutic Category Antiarrhythmic Agent, Class IV; Cardiac Glycoside

Use Treatment of congestive heart failure and to slow the ventricular rate in tachyarrhythmias such as atrial fibrillation, atrial flutter, and supraventricular tachycardia (paroxysmal atrial tachycardia); cardiogenic shock

Pregnancy Risk Factor C

Contraindications Hypersensitivity to digoxin or any component of the formulation; hypersensitivity to cardiac glycosides (another may be tried); history of toxicity; ventricular tachycardia or fibrillation; idiopathic hypertrophic subaortic stenosis; constrictive pericarditis; amyloid disease; second- or third-degree heart block (except in patients with a functioning artificial pacemaker); Wolff-Parkinson-White syndrome and atrial fibrillation concurrently

Warnings/Precautions Use with caution in patients with hypoxia, myxedema, hypothyroidism, acute myocarditis; patients with incomplete AV block (Stokes-Adams attack) may progress to complete block with digitalis drug administration; use with caution in patients with acute myocardial infarction, severe pulmonary disease, advanced heart failure, idiopathic hypertrophic subaortic stenosis, Wolff-Parkinson-White syndrome, sick-sinus syndrome (bradyarrhythmias), amyloid heart disease, and constrictive cardiomyopathies; adjust dose with renal impairment and when verapamil, quinidine or amiodarone are added to a patient on digoxin; elderly and neonates may develop exaggerated serum/tissue concentrations due to age-related alterations in clearance and pharmacodynamic differences; exercise will reduce serum concentrations of digoxin due to increased skeletal muscle uptake; recent studies indicate photopsia, chromatopsia and decreased visual acuity may occur even with therapeutic serum drug levels; reduce or hold dose 1-2 days before elective electrical cardioversion

Common Adverse Reactions Incidence of reactions are not always reported.

Cardiovascular: Heart block; first-, second- (Wenckebach), or third-degree heart block; asystole; atrial tachycardia with block; AV dissociation; accelerated junctional rhythm; ventricular tachycardia or ventricular fibrillation; PR prolongation; ST segment depression

Central nervous system: Visual disturbances (blurred or yellow vision), headache (3%), weakness, dizziness (5%), apathy, confusion, mental disturbances (4%), anxiety, depression, delirium, hallucinations, fever

Dermatologic: Maculopapular rash (2%), erythematous, scarlatiniform, papular, vesicular or bullous rashes, urticaria, pruritus, facial, angioneurotic or laryngeal edema, shedding of fingernails or toenails, alopecia

Gastrointestinal: Nausea (3%), vomiting (2%), diarrhea (3%), abdominal pain

Children are more likely to experience cardiac arrhythmias as a sign of excessive dosing. The most common are conduction disturbances or tachyarrhythmias (atrial tachycardia with or without block) and junctional tachycardia. Ventricular tachyarrhythmias are less common. In infants, sinus bradycardia may be a sign of digoxin toxicity. Any arrhythmia seen in a child on digoxin should be considered as digoxin toxicity. The gastrointestinal and central nervous system symptoms are not frequently seen in children.

Drug Interactions

Cytochrome P450 Effect: Substrate of CYP3A4 (minor)

Increased Effect/Toxicity: Beta-blocking agents (propranolol), verapamil, and diltiazem may have additive effects on heart rate. Carvedilol has additive effects on heart rate and inhibits the metabolism of digoxin. Digoxin levels may be increased by amiodarone (reduce digoxin dose 50%), bepridil, cyclosporine, diltiazem, indomethacin, itraconazole, some macrolides (erythromycin, clarithromycin), methimazole, nitrendipine, propafenone, propylthiouracil, quinidine (reduce digoxin dose 33% to 50% on initiation), tetracyclines, and verapamil. Moricizine may increase the toxicity of digoxin (mechanism undefined). Spironolactone may interfere with some digoxin assays, but may also increase blood levels directly. Succinylcholine administration to patients on digoxin has been associated with an increased risk of arrhythmias. Rare cases of acute digoxin toxicity have been associated with parenteral calcium (bolus) administration. The following medications have been associated with increased digoxin blood levels which appear to be of limited clinical significance: Famciclovir, flecainide, ibuprofen, fluoxetine, nefazodone, cimetidine, famotidine, ranitidine, omeprazole, trimethoprim.

Decreased Effect: Amiloride and spironolactone may reduce the inotropic response to digoxin. Cholestyramine, colestipol, kaolin-pectin, and metoclopramide may reduce digoxin absorption. Levothyroxine (and other thyroid supplements) may decrease digoxin blood levels. Penicillamine has been associated with reductions in digoxin blood levels The following reported interactions appear to be of limited clinical significance: Aminoglutethimide, aminosalicylic acid, aluminum-containing antacids, sucralfate, sulfasalazine, neomycin, ticlopidine.

Mechanism of Action

Congestive heart failure: Inhibition of the sodium/potassium ATPase pump which acts to increase the intracellular sodium-calcium exchange to increase intracellular calcium leading to increased contractility

Supraventricular arrhythmias: Direct suppression of the AV node conduction to increase effective refractory period and decrease conduction velocity - positive inotropic effect, enhanced vagal tone, and decreased ventricular rate to fast atrial arrhythmias. Atrial fibrillation may decrease sensitivity and increase tolerance to higher serum digoxin concentrations.

Pharmacodynamics/Kinetics

Onset of action: Oral: 1-2 hours; I.V.: 5-30 minutes

Peak effect: Oral: 2-8 hours; I.V.: 1-4 hours

Duration: Adults: 3-4 days both forms

Absorption: By passive nonsaturable diffusion in the upper small intestine; food may delay, but does not affect extent of absorption

Distribution:

Normal renal function: 6-7 L/kg

V_d: Extensive to peripheral tissues, with a distinct distribution phase which lasts 6-8 hours; concentrates in heart, liver, kidney, skeletal muscle, and intestines. Heart/serum concentration is 70:1. Pharmacologic effects are delayed and do not correlate well with serum concentrations during distribution phase.

Hyperthyroidism: Increased V_d

Hyperkalemia, hyponatremia: Decreased digoxin distribution to heart and muscle

Hypokalemia: Increased digoxin distribution to heart and muscles

Concomitant quinidine therapy: Decreased V_d

Chronic renal failure: 4-6 L/kg

Decreased sodium/potassium ATPase activity - decreased tissue binding

Neonates, full-term: 7.5-10 L/kg

Children: 16 L/kg

Adults: 7 L/kg, decreased with renal disease

Protein binding: 30%; in uremic patients, digoxin is displaced from plasma protein binding sites

Metabolism: Via sequential sugar hydrolysis in the stomach or by reduction of lactone ring by intestinal bacteria (in ~10% of population, gut bacteria may metabolize up to 40% of digoxin dose); metabolites may contribute to therapeutic and toxic effects of digoxin; metabolism is reduced with CHF

Bioavailability: Oral (formulation dependent): Elixir: 75% to 85%; Tablet: 70% to 80%

Half-life elimination (age, renal and cardiac function dependent):

Neonates: Premature: 61-170 hours; Full-term: 35-45 hours

Infants: 18-25 hours

Children: 35 hours

Adults: 38-48 hours

Adults, anephric: 4-6 days

Half-life elimination: Parent drug: 38 hours; Metabolites: Digoxigenin: 4 hours; Monodigitoxoside: 3-12 hours

Time to peak, serum: Oral: ~1 hour

Excretion: Urine (50% to 70% as unchanged drug)

Dosage When changing from oral (tablets or liquid) or I.M. to I.V. therapy, dosage should be reduced by 20% to 25%. Refer to the following: See table.

Dosage Recommendations for Digoxin

Age	Total Digitalizing Dose[2] (mcg/kg[1])		Daily Maintenance Dose[3] (mcg/kg[1])	
	P.O.	I.V. or I.M.	P.O.	I.V. or I.M.
Preterm infant[1]	20-30	15-25	5-7.5	4-6
Full-term infant[1]	25-35	20-30	6-10	5-8
1 mo - 2 y[1]	35-60	30-50	10-15	7.5-12
2-5 y[1]	30-40	25-35	7.5-10	6-9
5-10 y[1]	20-35	15-30	5-10	4-8
>10 y[1]	10-15	8-12	2.5-5	2-3
Adults	0.75-1.5 mg	0.5-1 mg	0.125-0.5 mg	0.1-0.4 mg

[1]Based on lean body weight and normal renal function for age. Decrease dose in patients with ↓ renal function; digitalizing dose often not recommended in infants and children.

[2]Give one-half of the total digitalizing dose (TDD) in the initial dose, then give one-quarter of the TDD in each of two subsequent doses at 8- to 12-hour intervals. Obtain EKG 6 hours after each dose to assess potential toxicity.

[3]Divided every 12 hours in infants and children <10 years of age. Given once daily to children >10 years of age and adults.

Dosing adjustment/interval in renal impairment:

Cl_{cr} 10-50 mL/minute: Administer 25% to 75% of dose or every 36 hours

Cl_{cr} <10 mL/minute: Administer 10% to 25% of dose or every 48 hours

Reduce loading dose by 50% in ESRD

Hemodialysis: Not dialyzable (0% to 5%)

Monitoring Parameters

When to draw serum digoxin concentrations: Digoxin serum concentrations are monitored because digoxin possesses a narrow therapeutic serum range; the therapeutic endpoint is difficult to quantify and digoxin toxicity may be life-threatening. Digoxin serum levels should be drawn **at least 4 hours after an intravenous dose** and **at least 6 hours after an oral dose (optimally 12-24 hours after a dose).**

(Continued)

Digoxin *(Continued)*

Initiation of therapy:

If a loading dose is given: Digoxin serum concentration may be drawn within 12-24 hours after the initial loading dose administration. Levels drawn this early may confirm the relationship of digoxin plasma levels and response but are of little value in determining maintenance doses.

If a loading dose is not given: Digoxin serum concentration should be obtained after 3-5 days of therapy

Maintenance therapy:

Trough concentrations should be followed just prior to the next dose or at a minimum of 4 hours after an I.V. dose and at least 6 hours after an oral dose

Digoxin serum concentrations should be obtained within 5-7 days (approximate time to steady-state) after any dosage changes. Continue to obtain digoxin serum concentrations 7-14 days after any change in maintenance dose. **Note:** In patients with end-stage renal disease, it may take 15-20 days to reach steady-state.

Additionally, patients who are receiving potassium-depleting medications such as diuretics, should be monitored for potassium, magnesium, and calcium levels

Digoxin serum concentrations should be obtained whenever any of the following conditions occur:

Questionable patient compliance or to evaluate clinical deterioration following an initial good response

Changing renal function

Suspected digoxin toxicity

Initiation or discontinuation of therapy with drugs (amiodarone, quinidine, verapamil) which potentially interact with digoxin; if quinidine therapy is started; digoxin levels should be drawn within the first 24 hours after starting quinidine therapy, then 7-14 days later or empirically skip one day's digoxin dose and decrease the daily dose by 50%

Any disease changes (hypothyroidism)

Heart rate and rhythm should be monitored along with periodic ECGs to assess both desired effects and signs of toxicity

Follow closely (especially in patients receiving diuretics or amphotericin) for decreased serum potassium and magnesium or increased calcium, all of which predispose to digoxin toxicity

Assess renal function

Be aware of drug interactions

Reference Range

Digoxin therapeutic serum concentrations:

Congestive heart failure: 0.8-2 ng/mL

Arrhythmias: 1.5-2.5 ng/mL

Adults: <0.5 ng/mL; probably indicates underdigitalization unless there are special circumstances

Toxic: >2.5 ng/mL; tachyarrhythmias commonly require levels >2 ng/mL

Digoxin-like immunoreactive substance (DLIS) may cross-react with digoxin immunoassay. DLIS has been found in patients with renal and liver disease, congestive heart failure, neonates, and pregnant women (3rd trimester).

Patient Information Do not discontinue medication without checking with prescriber. Report loss of appetite or vision changes.

Dosage Forms CAP (Lanoxicaps®): 50 mcg, 100 mcg, 200 mcg. **ELIX:** 50 mcg/mL (2.5 mL, 5 mL, 60 mL); (Lanoxin® [pediatric]): 50 mcg/mL (60 mL). **INJ:** 250 mcg/mL (1 mL, 2 mL); (Lanoxin®): 250 mcg/mL (2 mL). **INJ, pediatric:** 100 mcg/mL (1 mL). **TAB:** 125 mcg, 250 mcg, 500 mcg; (Digitek®, Lanoxin®): 125 mcg, 250 mcg

Digoxin Immune Fab *(di JOKS in i MYUN fab)*

U.S. Brand Names Digibind®; DigiFab™

Synonyms Antidigoxin Fab Fragments, Ovine

Therapeutic Category Antidote, Digoxin

Use Treatment of life-threatening or potentially life-threatening digoxin intoxication, including:

- acute digoxin ingestion (ie, >10 mg in adults or >4 mg in children)
- chronic ingestions leading to steady-state digoxin concentrations > 6 ng/mL in adults or >4 ng/mL in children
- manifestations of digoxin toxicity due to overdose (life-threatening ventricular arrhythmias, progressive bradycardia, second- or third-degree heart block not responsive to atropine, serum potassium >5 mEq/L in adults or >6 mEq in children)

Pregnancy Risk Factor C

Contraindications Hypersensitivity to sheep products or any component of the formulation

Warnings/Precautions Use with caution in renal or cardiac failure; allergic reactions possible (sheep product)-skin testing not routinely recommended; epinephrine should be immediately available, Fab fragments may be eliminated more slowly in patients with renal failure, heart failure may be exacerbated as digoxin level is reduced; total serum digoxin concentration may rise precipitously following administration of Digibind®, but this will be almost entirely bound to the Fab fragment and not able to react with receptors in the body; Digibind® will interfere with digitalis immunoassay measurements - this will result in clinically misleading serum digoxin concentrations until the Fab fragment is eliminated from the body (several days to >1 week after Digibind® administration). Hypokalemia has been reported to occur following reversal of digitalis intoxication as has exacerbation of underlying heart failure. Serum digoxin levels drawn prior to therapy may be difficult to evaluate if 6-8 hours have not elapsed after the last dose of digoxin (time to equilibration between serum and tissue); redigitalization should not be initiated until Fab fragments have been eliminated from the body, which may occur over several days or greater than a week in patients with impaired renal function.

Common Adverse Reactions Frequency not defined.

    Cardiovascular: Effects (due to withdrawal of digitalis) include exacerbation of low cardiac output states and CHF, rapid ventricular response in patients with atrial fibrillation; postural hypotension

    Endocrine & metabolic: Hypokalemia

    Local: Phlebitis

    Miscellaneous: Allergic reactions, serum sickness

Drug Interactions

    Increased Effect/Toxicity: Digoxin: Following administration of digoxin immune Fab, serum digoxin levels are markedly increased due to bound complexes (may be clinically misleading, since bound complex cannot interact with receptors).

Mechanism of Action Digoxin immune antigen-binding fragments (Fab) are specific anti-bodies for the treatment of digitalis intoxication in carefully selected patients; binds with molecules of digoxin or digitoxin and then is excreted by the kidneys and removed from the body

Pharmacodynamics/Kinetics

    Onset of action: I.V.: Improvement in 2-30 minutes for toxicity

    Half-life elimination: 15-20 hours; prolonged with renal impairment

    Excretion: Urine; undetectable amounts within 5-7 days

Dosage Each vial of Digibind® 38 mg or DigiFab™ 40 mg will bind ~0.5 mg of digoxin or digitoxin.

Estimation of the dose is based on the body burden of digitalis. This may be calculated if the amount ingested is known or the postdistribution serum drug level is known (round dose to the nearest whole vial). See table.

Digoxin Immune Fab

Tablets Ingested (0.25 mg)	Fab Dose (vials)
5	2
10	4
25	10
50	20
75	30
100	40
150	60
200	80

Fab dose based on serum drug level postdistribution:

    Digoxin: No. of vials = level (ng/mL) x body weight (kg) divided by 100

    Digitoxin: No. of vials = digitoxin (ng/mL) x body weight (kg) divided by 1000

If neither amount ingested nor drug level are known, dose empirically as follows:

    For acute toxicity: 20 vials, administered in 2 divided doses to decrease the possibility of a febrile reaction, and to avoid fluid overload in small children.

    For chronic toxicity: 6 vials; for infants and small children (≤20kg), a single vial may be sufficient

Administration Continuous I.V. infusion over ≥30 minutes is preferred. May give by bolus injection if cardiac arrest is imminent. Small doses (infants/small children) may be administered using tuberculin syringe. Stopping the infusion and restarting at a slower rate may help if infusion-related reactions occur.

Monitoring Parameters Serum potassium, serum digoxin concentration prior to first dose of digoxin immune Fab; **digoxin levels will greatly increase with digoxin immune Fab use and are not an accurate determination of body stores**; standard digoxin concentration measurements may be misleading until Fab fragments are eliminated from the body.

Patients with renal failure should be monitored for a prolonged period for re-intoxication with digoxin following the re-release of bound digoxin into the blood.

Dosage Forms INJ, powder for reconstitution: (Digibind®): 38 mg; (DigiFab™): 40 mg

◆ **Dihematoporphyrin Ether** *see* Porfimer *on page 1016*

◆ **Dihistine® DH** *see* Chlorpheniramine, Pseudoephedrine, and Codeine *on page 265*

◆ **Dihistine® Expectorant** *see* Guaifenesin, Pseudoephedrine, and Codeine *on page 606*

Dihydrocodeine, Aspirin, and Caffeine

(dye hye droe KOE deen, AS pir in, & KAF een)

U.S. Brand Names Synalgos®-DC

Synonyms Dihydrocodeine Compound

Therapeutic Category Analgesic Combination, Narcotic

Use Management of mild to moderate pain that requires relaxation

Restrictions C-III

Pregnancy Risk Factor B/D (prolonged use or high doses at term)

(Continued)

Dihydrocodeine, Aspirin, and Caffeine *(Continued)*

Contraindications Hypersensitivity to dihydrocodeine or any component of the formulation; pregnancy (prolonged use or high doses at term)

Warnings/Precautions Use with caution in patients with hypersensitivity reactions to other phenanthrene derivative opioid agonists (morphine, hydrocodone, hydromorphone, levorphanol, oxycodone, oxymorphone); respiratory diseases including asthma, emphysema, COPD, or severe liver or renal insufficiency; some preparations contain sulfites which may cause allergic reactions; dextromethorphan has equivalent antitussive activity but has much lower toxicity in accidental overdose; tolerance of drug dependence may result from extended use

Common Adverse Reactions

>10%:

Central nervous system: Lightheadedness, dizziness, drowsiness, sedation
Dermatologic: Pruritus, skin reactions
Gastrointestinal: Nausea, vomiting, constipation

1% to 10%:

Cardiovascular: Hypotension, palpitations, bradycardia, peripheral vasodilation
Central nervous system: Increased intracranial pressure
Endocrine & metabolic: Antidiuretic hormone release
Gastrointestinal: Biliary tract spasm
Genitourinary: Urinary tract spasm
Ocular: Miosis
Respiratory: Respiratory depression
Miscellaneous: Histamine release, physical and psychological dependence with prolonged use

Drug Interactions

Cytochrome P450 Effect: Substrate of CYP2D6 (major) based on dihydrocodeine
Increased Effect/Toxicity: MAO inhibitors may increase adverse symptoms.
Decreased Effect: CYP2D6 inhibitors may decrease the effects of dihydrocodeine; example inhibitors include chlorpromazine, delavirdine, fluoxetine, miconazole, paroxetine, pergolide, quinidine, quinine, ritonavir, and ropinirole.

Mechanism of Action Binds to opiate receptors in the CNS, causing inhibition of ascending pain pathways, altering the perception of and response to pain; causes cough suppression by direct central action in the medulla; produces generalized CNS depression

Pharmacodynamics/Kinetics

Onset of action: 10-30 minutes
Duration: 4-6 hours
Metabolism: Hepatic
Half-life elimination, serum: 3.8 hours
Time to peak, serum: 30-60 minutes

Dosage

Adults: Oral: 1-2 capsules every 4-6 hours as needed for pain
Elderly: Initial dosing should be cautious (low end of adult dosing range)

Patient Information Avoid alcohol; may cause drowsiness, impaired judgment or coordination; may cause physical and psychological dependence with prolonged use

Dosage Forms CAP (Synalgos®-DC): Dihydrocodeine 16 mg, aspirin 356.4 mg, and caffeine 30 mg

♦ **Dihydrocodeine Compound** *see* Dihydrocodeine, Aspirin, and Caffeine *on page 377*

Dihydroergotamine *(dye hye droe er GOT a meen)*

U.S. Brand Names D.H.E. 45®; Migranal®
Synonyms DHE; Dihydroergotamine Mesylate
Therapeutic Category Antimigraine Agent, Prophylaxis; Ergot Alkaloid and Derivative
Use Treatment of migraine headache with or without aura; injection also indicated for treatment of cluster headaches
Unlabeled/Investigational Use Adjunct for DVT prophylaxis for hip surgery, for orthostatic hypotension, xerostomia secondary to antidepressant use, and pelvic congestion with pain
Pregnancy Risk Factor X
Contraindications Hypersensitivity to dihydroergotamine or any component of the formulation; high-dose aspirin therapy; uncontrolled hypertension, ischemic heart disease, angina pectoris, history of MI, silent ischemia, or coronary artery vasospasm including Prinzmetal's angina; hemiplegic or basilar migraine; peripheral vascular disease; sepsis; severe hepatic or renal dysfunction; following vascular surgery; avoid use within 24 hours of sumatriptan, zolmitriptan, other serotonin agonists, or ergot-like agents; avoid during or within 2 weeks of discontinuing MAO inhibitors; ergot alkaloids are contraindicated with potent inhibitors of CYP3A4 (includes protease inhibitors, azole antifungals, and some macrolide antibiotics); pregnancy
Warnings/Precautions Do not give to patients with risk factors for CAD until a cardiovascular evaluation has been performed; if evaluation is satisfactory, the healthcare provider should administer the first dose and cardiovascular status should be periodically evaluated. May cause vasospastic reactions; persistent vasospasm may lead to gangrene or death in patients with compromised circulation. Discontinue if signs of vasoconstriction develop. Rare reports of increased blood pressure in patients without history of hypertension. Rare reports of adverse cardiac events (acute MI, life-threatening arrhythmias, death) have been reported following use of the injection. Cerebral hemorrhage, subarachnoid hemorrhage, and stroke have also occurred following use of the injection. Not for prolonged use. Pleural and peritoneal fibrosis

have been reported with prolonged daily use. Cardiac valvular fibrosis has also been associated with ergot alkaloids. Safety and efficacy in pediatric patients have not been established.

Common Adverse Reactions
>10%: Nasal spray: Respiratory: Rhinitis (26%)
1% to 10%: Nasal spray:
Central nervous system: Dizziness (4%), somnolence (3%)
Endocrine & metabolic: Hot flashes (1%)
Gastrointestinal: Nausea (10%), taste disturbance (8%), vomiting (4%), diarrhea (2%)
Local: Application site reaction (6%)
Neuromuscular & skeletal: Weakness (1%), stiffness (1%)
Respiratory: Pharyngitis (3%)

Drug Interactions
Cytochrome P450 Effect: Substrate of CYP3A4 (major); **Inhibits** CYP3A4 (weak)
Increased Effect/Toxicity: Effects of dihydroergotamine may be increased by antifungals (azole derivatives); CYP3A4 inhibitors (eg, amiodarone, cimetidine, erythromycin, ritonavir); macrolide antibiotics; nitroglycerin; protease inhibitors; MAO inhibitors; beta blockers (vasoconstriction); sumatriptan (vasospasm); vasoconstrictors. Dihydroergotamine may increase the effects of heparin (injection site hematoma), sibutramine, and other serotonin agonists (serotonin syndrome)
Decreased Effect: Effects of dihydroergotamine may be diminished by antipsychotics, metoclopramide.

Mechanism of Action Ergot alkaloid alpha-adrenergic blocker directly stimulates vascular smooth muscle to vasoconstrict peripheral and cerebral vessels; also has effects on serotonin receptors

Pharmacodynamics/Kinetics
Onset of action: 15-30 minutes
Duration: 3-4 hours
Distribution: V_d: 14.5 L/kg
Protein binding: 93%
Metabolism: Extensively hepatic
Half-life elimination: 1.3-3.9 hours
Time to peak, serum: I.M.: 15-30 minutes
Excretion: Primarily feces; urine (10% mostly as metabolites)

Dosage Adults:
I.M., S.C.: 1 mg at first sign of headache; repeat hourly to a maximum dose of 3 mg total; maximum dose: 6 mg/week
I.V.: 1 mg at first sign of headache; repeat hourly up to a maximum dose of 2 mg total; maximum dose: 6 mg/week
Intranasal: 1 spray (0.5 mg) of nasal spray should be administered into each nostril; if needed, repeat after 15 minutes, up to a total of 4 sprays. **Note:** Do not exceed 3 mg (6 sprays) in a 24-hour period and no more than 8 sprays in a week.

Elderly: Patients >65 years of age were not included in controlled clinical studies

Dosing adjustment in renal impairment: Contraindicated in severe renal impairment

Dosing adjustment in hepatic impairment: Dosage reductions are probably necessary but specific guidelines are not available; contraindicated in severe hepatic dysfunction

Administration Prior to administration of nasal spray, the nasal spray applicator must be primed (pumped 4 times); in order to let the drug be absorbed through the skin in the nose, patients should not inhale deeply through the nose while spraying or immediately after spraying; for best results, treatment should be initiated at the first symptom or sign of an attack; however, nasal spray can be used at any stage of a migraine attack

Reference Range Minimum concentration for vasoconstriction is reportedly 0.06 ng/mL

Patient Information Rare feelings of numbness or tingling of fingers, toes, or face may occur. Avoid using this medication if you are pregnant, have heart disease, hypertension, liver disease, infection, itching.

Nasal spray: Do not assemble sprayer until you are ready to use it; prime as instructed. Do not tilt head back or inhale through nose while spraying.

Dosage Forms INJ, solution (D.H.E. 45®): 1 mg/mL (1 mL). **SOLN, intranasal spray** (Migranal®): 4 mg/mL [0.5 mg/spray] (1 mL)

♦ **Dihydroergotamine Mesylate** *see Dihydroergotamine on page 378*
♦ **Dihydroergotoxine** *see Ergoloid Mesylates on page 449*
♦ **Dihydrogenated Ergot Alkaloids** *see Ergoloid Mesylates on page 449*
♦ **Dihydrohydroxycodeinone** *see Oxycodone on page 944*
♦ **Dihydromorphinone** *see Hydromorphone on page 635*

Dihydrotachysterol (dye hye droe tak ISS ter ole)
U.S. Brand Names DHT™; DHT™ Intensol™; Hytakerol®
Synonyms Dichysterol
Therapeutic Category Vitamin, Fat Soluble
Use Treatment of hypocalcemia associated with hypoparathyroidism; prophylaxis of hypocalcemic tetany following thyroid surgery
Pregnancy Risk Factor A/D (dose exceeding RDA recommendation)
Dosage Oral:
Hypoparathyroidism:
Infants and young Children: Initial: 1-5 mg/day for 4 days, then 0.1-0.5 mg/day
(Continued)

Dihydrotachysterol (Continued)

Older Children and Adults: Initial: 0.8-2.4 mg/day for several days followed by maintenance doses of 0.2-1 mg/day

Nutritional rickets: 0.5 mg as a single dose or 13-50 mcg/day until healing occurs

Renal osteodystrophy: Maintenance: 0.25-0.6 mg/24 hours adjusted as necessary to achieve normal serum calcium levels and promote bone healing

Dosage Forms CAP (Hytakerol®): 0.125 mg. **SOLN, oral concentrate** (DHT™ Intensol™): 0.2 mg/mL (30 mL). **TAB** (DHT™): 0.125 mg, 0.2 mg, 0.4 mg

◆ **Dihydroxyanthracenedione Dihydrochloride** *see* Mitoxantrone *on page 851*

◆ **1,25 Dihydroxycholecalciferol** *see* Calcitriol *on page 200*

◆ **Dihydroxydeoxynorvinkaleukoblastine** *see* Vinorelbine *on page 1307*

◆ **Diiodohydroxyquin** *see* Iodoquinol *on page 683*

◆ **Dilacor® XR** *see* Diltiazem *on page 380*

◆ **Dilantin®** *see* Phenytoin *on page 995*

◆ **Dilatrate®-SR** *see* Isosorbide Dinitrate *on page 694*

◆ **Dilaudid®** *see* Hydromorphone *on page 635*

◆ **Dilaudid-HP®** *see* Hydromorphone *on page 635*

Diloxanide Furoate (dye LOKS ah nide FYOOR oh ate)

U.S. Brand Names Furamide®

Therapeutic Category Amebicide

Use Treatment of amebiasis (asymptomatic cyst passers)

Restrictions Not commercially available in U.S.

◆ **Diltia XT®** *see* Diltiazem *on page 380*

Diltiazem (dil TYE a zem)

Related Information

Calcium Channel Blockers Comparison *on page 1371*

U.S. Brand Names Cardizem®; Cardizem® CD; Cardizem® LA; Cardizem® SR; Cartia XT™; Dilacor® XR; Diltia XT®; Taztia XT™; Tiazac®

Synonyms Diltiazem Hydrochloride

Therapeutic Category Antianginal Agent; Antiarrhythmic Agent, Class IV; Antihypertensive Agent; Calcium Channel Blocker

Use

Oral: Essential hypertension; chronic stable angina or angina from coronary artery spasm

Injection: Atrial fibrillation or atrial flutter; paroxysmal supraventricular tachycardia (PSVT)

Unlabeled/Investigational Use Investigational: Therapy of Duchenne muscular dystrophy

Pregnancy Risk Factor C

Contraindications Hypersensitivity to diltiazem or any component of the formulation; sick sinus syndrome; second- or third-degree AV block (except in patients with a functioning artificial pacemaker); hypotension (systolic <90 mm Hg); acute MI and pulmonary congestion

Warnings/Precautions Use with caution and titrate dosages for patients with hypotension or patients taking antihypertensives, impaired renal or hepatic function, or when treating patients with CHF. Use caution with concomitant therapy with beta-blockers or digoxin. Monitor LFTs during therapy since these enzymes may rarely be increased and symptoms of hepatic injury may occur; usually reverses with drug discontinuation; avoid abrupt withdrawal of calcium blockers since rebound angina is theoretically possible.

Common Adverse Reactions Frequencies represent ranges for various dosage forms.

>10%:

Cardiovascular: Edema (2% to 15%)

Central nervous system: Headache (5% to 12%)

2% to 10%:

Cardiovascular: AV block (first degree 2% to 8%), edema (lower limb 2% to 8%), pain (6%), bradycardia (<2% to 6%), hypotension (<2% to 4%), vasodilation (2% to 3%), extrasystoles (2%), flushing (1% to 2%), palpitations (1% to 2%)

Central nervous system: Dizziness (3% to 10%), nervousness (2%)

Dermatologic: Rash (1% to 4%)

Endocrine & metabolic: Gout (1% to 2%)

Gastrointestinal: Dyspepsia (1% to 6%), constipation (<2% to 4%), vomiting (2%), diarrhea (1% to 2%)

Local: Injection site reactions: Burning, itching (4%)

Neuromuscular & skeletal: Weakness (1% to 4%), myalgia (2%)

Respiratory: Rhinitis (<2% to 10%), pharyngitis (2% to 6%), dyspnea (1% to 6%), bronchitis (1% to 4%), sinus congestion (1% to 2%)

Drug Interactions

Cytochrome P450 Effect: Substrate of CYP2C8/9 (minor), 2D6 (minor), 3A4 (major); **Inhibits** CYP2C8/9 (weak), 2D6 (weak), 3A4 (moderate)

Increased Effect/Toxicity: Diltiazem effects may be additive with amiodarone, beta-blockers, or digoxin, which may lead to bradycardia, other conduction delays, and decreased cardiac output. CYP3A4 inhibitors may increase the levels/effects of diltiazem; example inhibitors include azole antifungals, ciprofloxacin, clarithromycin, diclofenac, doxycycline, erythromycin, imatinib, isoniazid, nefazodone, nicardipine, propofol, protease inhibitors, quinidine, and verapamil. Diltiazem may increase serum levels/toxicity of alfentanil (possibly fentanyl and sufentanil), some benzodiazepines (specifically midazolam and triazolam), buspirone, carbamazepine, cisapride (QT prolongation, arrhythmia), cyclosporine, digoxin, HMG-CoA reductase inhibitors (atorvastatin, lovastatin, simvastatin), lithium (neurotoxicity), midazolam, moricizine, quinidine, and tacrolimus. Blood pressure-lowering effects may be additive with sildenafil, tadalafil, and vardenafil (use caution).

Decreased Effect: CYP3A4 inducers may decrease the levels/effects of diltiazem; example inducers include aminoglutethimide, carbamazepine, nafcillin, nevirapine, phenobarbital, phenytoin, and rifamycins.

Mechanism of Action Inhibits calcium ion from entering the "slow channels" or select voltage-sensitive areas of vascular smooth muscle and myocardium during depolarization, producing a relaxation of coronary vascular smooth muscle and coronary vasodilation; increases myocardial oxygen delivery in patients with vasospastic angina

Pharmacodynamics/Kinetics

Onset of action: Oral: Immediate release tablet: 30-60 minutes

Absorption: 70% to 80%

Distribution: V_d: 3-13 L/kg; enters breast milk

Protein binding: 77% to 85%

Metabolism: Hepatic; extensive first-pass effect; following single I.V. injection, plasma concentrations of N-monodesmethyldiltiazem and desacetyldiltiazem are typically undetectable; however, these metabolites accumulate to detectable concentrations following 24-hour constant rate infusion. N-monodesmethyldiltiazem appears to have 20% of the potency of diltiazem; desacetyldiltiazem is about 50% as potent as the parent compound.

Bioavailability: Oral: ~40% to 60%

Half-life elimination: Immediate release tablet: 3-4.5 hours, may be prolonged with renal impairment

Time to peak, serum: Immediate release tablet: 2-3 hours

Excretion: Urine and feces (primarily as metabolites)

Dosage Adults:

Oral:

Angina:

Capsule, extended release (Cardizem® CD, Cartia XT™, Dilacor XR®, Diltia XT™, Tiazac®): Initial: 120-180 mg once daily (maximum dose: 480 mg/day)

Tablet, immediate release (Cardizem®): Usual starting dose: 30 mg 4 times/day; usual range: 180-360 mg/day

Hypertension:

Capsule, extended release (Cardizem® CD, Cartia XT™, Dilacor XR®, Diltia XT™, Tiazac®): Initial: 180-240 mg once daily; dose adjustment may be made after 14 days; usual range: 180-480 mg/day (maximum dose: 540 mg/day)

Capsule, sustained release (Cardizem® SR): Initial: 60-120 mg twice daily; dose adjustment may be made after 14 days; usual range: 240-360 mg/day

Tablet, extended release (Cardizem® LA): Initial: 180-240 mg once daily; dose adjustment may be made after 14 days; usual range: 180-480 mg/day (maximum dose: 540 mg/day)

Note: Elderly: Patients ≥60 years may respond to a lower initial dose (ie, 120 mg once daily using extended release capsule)

I.V.: Atrial fibrillation, atrial flutter, PSVT:

• Initial bolus dose: 0.25 mg/kg actual body weight over 2 minutes (average adult dose: 20 mg)

• Repeat bolus dose (may be administered after 15 minutes if the response is inadequate.): 0.35 mg/kg actual body weight over 2 minutes (average adult dose: 25 mg)

• Continuous infusion (requires an infusion pump; infusions >24 hours or infusion rates >15 mg/hour are not recommended.): Initial infusion rate of 10 mg/hour; rate may be increased in 5 mg/hour increments up to 15 mg/hour as needed; some patients may respond to an initial rate of 5 mg/hour.

If diltiazem injection is administered by continuous infusion for >24 hours, the possibility of decreased diltiazem clearance, prolonged elimination half-life, and increased diltiazem and/or diltiazem metabolite plasma concentrations should be considered.

Conversion from I.V. diltiazem to oral diltiazem: Start oral approximately 3 hours after bolus dose.

Oral dose (mg/day) is approximately equal to [rate (mg/hour) x 3 + 3] x 10.

3 mg/hour = 120 mg/day

5 mg/hour = 180 mg/day

7 mg/hour = 240 mg/day

11 mg/hour = 360 mg/day

Dosing comments in renal/hepatic impairment: Use with caution as extensively metabolized by the liver and excreted in the kidneys and bile.

Dialysis: Not removed by hemo- or peritoneal dialysis; supplemental dose is not necessary.

Administration

Oral: Do not crush long acting dosage forms.

Tiazac®: Capsules may be opened and sprinkled on a spoonful of applesauce. Applesauce should be swallowed without chewing, followed by drinking a glass of water.

I.V.: Bolus doses given over 2 minutes with continuous ECG and blood pressure monitoring. Continuous infusion should be via infusion pump.

Monitoring Parameters Liver function tests, blood pressure, ECG

Patient Information Sustained release products should be taken in the morning; do not crush or chew; limit caffeine intake; notify prescriber if angina pain is not reduced when taking this
(Continued)

Diltiazem *(Continued)*

drug; report irregular heartbeat, shortness of breath, swelling, dizziness, constipation, nausea, or hypotension; do not stop therapy without advice of prescriber

Dosage Forms CAP, extended release [once-daily dosing]: 120 mg, 180 mg, 240 mg, 300 mg; (Cardizem® CD, Taztia XT™): 120 mg, 180 mg, 240 mg, 300 mg, 360 mg; (Cartia XT™): 120 mg, 180 mg, 240 mg, 300 mg; (Dilacor® XR, Diltia XT®): 120 mg, 180 mg, 240 mg; (Tiazac®): 120 mg, 180 mg, 240 mg, 300 mg, 360 mg, 420 mg. **CAP, sustained release** [twice-daily dosing] (Cardizem® SR): 60 mg, 90 mg, 120 mg. **INJ, solution:** 5 mg/mL (5 mL, 10 mL, 25 mL); (Cardizem® [DSC]): 5 mg/mL (5 mL, 10 mL). **INJ, powder for reconstitution** (Cardizem®): 25 mg, 100 mg. **TAB** (Cardizem®): 30 mg, 60 mg, 90 mg, 120 mg **TAB, extended release** (Cardizem® LA): 120 mg, 180 mg, 240 mg, 300 mg, 360 mg, 420 mg

♦ **Diltiazem Hydrochloride** *see* Diltiazem *on page 380*

Dimercaprol *(dye mer KAP role)*

U.S. Brand Names BAL in Oil®

Synonyms BAL; British Anti-Lewisite; Dithioglycerol

Therapeutic Category Antidote, Arsenic Toxicity; Antidote, Gold Toxicity; Antidote, Lead Toxicity; Antidote, Mercury Toxicity; Chelating Agent, Parenteral

Use Antidote to gold, arsenic (except arsine), and mercury poisoning (except nonalkyl mercury); adjunct to edetate calcium disodium in lead poisoning; possibly effective for antimony, bismuth, chromium, copper, nickel, tungsten, or zinc

Pregnancy Risk Factor C

Contraindications Hepatic insufficiency (unless due to arsenic poisoning); do not use on iron, cadmium, or selenium poisoning

Warnings/Precautions Potentially a nephrotoxic drug, use with caution in patients with oliguria or glucose 6-phosphate dehydrogenase deficiency; keep urine alkaline to protect kidneys; administer all injections deep I.M. at different sites

Common Adverse Reactions

>10%:

Cardiovascular: Hypertension, tachycardia (dose-related)

Central nervous system: Headache

1% to 10%: Gastrointestinal: Nausea, vomiting

Drug Interactions

Increased Effect/Toxicity: Toxic complexes with iron, cadmium, selenium, or uranium.

Mechanism of Action Sulfhydryl group combines with ions of various heavy metals to form relatively stable, nontoxic, soluble chelates which are excreted in urine

Pharmacodynamics/Kinetics

Distribution: To all tissues including the brain

Metabolism: Rapidly hepatic to inactive metabolites

Time to peak, serum: 0.5-1 hour

Excretion: Urine

Dosage Children and Adults: Deep I.M.:

Arsenic, mercury, and gold poisoning: 3 mg/kg every 4-6 hours for 2 days, then every 12 hours for 7-10 days or until recovery (initial dose may be up to 5 mg if severe poisoning)

Lead poisoning (in conjunction with calcium EDTA): For symptomatic acute encephalopathy or blood level >100 mcg/dL: 4-5 mg/kg every 4 hours for 3-5 days

Administration Administer deep I.M. only; keep urine alkaline to protect renal function

Patient Information Frequent blood and urine tests may be required

Dosage Forms INJ, oil [contains peanut oil]: 100 mg/mL (3 mL)

♦ **Dimetapp® 12-Hour Non-Drowsy Extentabs® [OTC]** *see* Pseudoephedrine *on page 1061*

♦ **Dimetapp® Decongestant [OTC]** *see* Pseudoephedrine *on page 1061*

♦ **β,β-Dimethylcysteine** *see* Penicillamine *on page 970*

♦ **Dimethyl Triazeno Imidazol Carboxamide** *see* Dacarbazine *on page 332*

Dinoprostone *(dye noe PROST one)*

U.S. Brand Names Cervidil®; Prepidil®; Prostin E₂®

Synonyms PGE₂; Prostaglandin E₂

Therapeutic Category Abortifacient; Prostaglandin

Use

Gel: Promote cervical ripening prior to labor induction; usage for gel include any patient undergoing induction of labor with an unripe cervix, most commonly for pre-eclampsia, eclampsia, postdates, diabetes, intrauterine growth retardation, and chronic hypertension

Suppositories: Terminate pregnancy from 12th through 28th week of gestation; evacuate uterus in cases of missed abortion or intrauterine fetal death; manage benign hydatidiform mole

Vaginal insert: Initiation and/or cervical ripening in patients at or near term in whom there is a medical or obstetrical indication for the induction of labor

Pregnancy Risk Factor C

Contraindications

Vaginal insert: Hypersensitivity to prostaglandins; fetal distress (suspicion or clinical evidence unless delivery is imminent); unexplained vaginal bleeding during this pregnancy; strong suspicion of marked cephalopelvic disproportion; patients in whom oxytoxic drugs are contraindicated or when prolonged contraction of the uterus may be detrimental to fetal safety or uterine integrity (including previous cesarean section or major uterine surgery); greater than 6 previous term pregnancies; patients already receiving oxytocic drugs

Gel: Hypersensitivity to prostaglandins or any constituents of the cervical gel, history of asthma, contracted pelvis, malpresentation of the fetus

Gel: The following are "relative" contraindications and should only be considered by the physician under these circumstances: Patients in whom vaginal delivery is not indicated (ie, herpes genitalia with a lesion at the time of delivery), prior uterine surgery, breech presentation, multiple gestation, polyhydramnios, premature rupture of membranes

Suppository: Hypersensitivity to dinoprostone, acute pelvic inflammatory disease, uterine fibroids, cervical stenosis

Warnings/Precautions Dinoprostone should be used only by medically trained personnel in a hospital; caution in patients with cervicitis, infected endocervical lesions, acute vaginitis, compromised (scarred) uterus or history of asthma, hypertension or hypotension, epilepsy, diabetes mellitus, anemia, jaundice, or cardiovascular, renal, or hepatic disease. Oxytocin should not be used simultaneously with Prepidil® (>6 hours of the last dose of Prepidil®).

Common Adverse Reactions
>10%:
  Central nervous system: Headache
  Gastrointestinal: Vomiting, diarrhea, nausea
1% to 10%:
  Cardiovascular: Bradycardia
  Central nervous system: Fever
  Neuromuscular & skeletal: Back pain

Drug Interactions
Increased Effect/Toxicity: Increased effect of oxytocics.

Mechanism of Action A synthetic prostaglandin E_2 abortifacient that stimulates uterine contractions similar to those seen during natural labor

Pharmacodynamics/Kinetics
Onset of action (uterine contractions): Within 10 minutes
Duration: Up to 2-3 hours
Absorption: Vaginal: Slow
Metabolism: In many tissues including renal, pulmonary, and splenic systems
Excretion: Primarily urine; feces (small amounts)

Dosage
Abortifacient: Insert 1 suppository high in vagina, repeat at 3- to 5-hour intervals until abortion occurs up to 240 mg (maximum dose); continued administration for longer than 2 days is not advisable
Cervical ripening:
  Gel:
    Intracervical: 0.25-1 mg
    Intravaginal: 2.5 mg
  Suppositories: Intracervical: 2-3 mg
  Vaginal Insert (Cervidil®): 10 mg (to be removed at the onset of active labor or after 12 hours)

Administration
Vaginal insert: One vaginal insert is placed transversely in the posterior fornix of the vagina immediately after removal from its foil package. Patients should remain in the recumbent position for 2 hours after insertion, but thereafter may be ambulatory
Endocervical gel: Intracervically: For cervical ripening, patient should be supine in the dorsal position

Dosage Forms GEL, endocervical (Prepidil®): 0.5 mg/3 g syringe. **INSERT, vaginal** (Cervidil®): 10 mg. **SUPP, vaginal** (Prostin E_2®): 20 mg

DiphenhydrAMINE (dye fen HYE dra meen)

U.S. Brand Names Aler-Dryl [OTC]; AllerMax® [OTC]; Banophen® [OTC]; Benadryl® Allergy [OTC]; Benadryl® Dye-Free Allergy [OTC]; Benadryl® Gel [OTC]; Benadryl® Gel Extra Strength [OTC]; Benadryl® Injection; Compoz® Nighttime Sleep Aid [OTC]; Diphen® [OTC]; Diphen® AF [OTC]; Diphen® Cough [OTC]; Diphenhist [OTC]; Genahist® [OTC]; Hydramine® [OTC]; Hydramine® Cough [OTC]; Hyrexin-50®; Nytol® [OTC]; Nytol® Maximum Strength [OTC]; Siladryl® Allergy [OTC]; Silphen® [OTC]; Sleepinal® [OTC]; Sominex® [OTC]; Sominex® Maximum Strength [OTC]; Tusstat®; Twilite® [OTC]; Unisom® Maximum Strength SleepGels® [OTC]

Synonyms Diphenhydramine Hydrochloride

Therapeutic Category Antidote, Hypersensitivity Reactions; Antihistamine; Sedative
(Continued)

DiphenhydrAMINE *(Continued)*

Use Symptomatic relief of allergic symptoms caused by histamine release which include nasal allergies and allergic dermatosis; can be used for mild nighttime sedation; prevention of motion sickness and as an antitussive; has antinauseant and topical anesthetic properties; treatment of antipsychotic-induced extrapyramidal symptoms

Pregnancy Risk Factor B

Contraindications Hypersensitivity to diphenhydramine or any component of the formulation; acute asthma; not for use in neonates

Warnings/Precautions Causes sedation, caution must be used in performing tasks which require alertness (eg, operating machinery or driving). Sedative effects of CNS depressants or ethanol are potentiated. Use with caution in patients with angle-closure glaucoma, pyloroduodenal obstruction (including stenotic peptic ulcer), urinary tract obstruction (including bladder neck obstruction and symptomatic prostatic hypertrophy), hyperthyroidism, increased intraocular pressure, and cardiovascular disease (including hypertension and tachycardia). Diphenhydramine has high sedative and anticholinergic properties, so it may not be considered the antihistamine of choice for prolonged use in the elderly. May cause paradoxical excitation in pediatric patients, and can result in hallucinations, coma, and death in overdose. Some preparations contain sodium bisulfite; syrup formulations may contain alcohol.

Common Adverse Reactions Frequency not defined.

Cardiovascular: Hypotension, palpitations, tachycardia

Central nervous system: Sedation, sleepiness, dizziness, disturbed coordination, headache, fatigue, nervousness, paradoxical excitement, insomnia, euphoria, confusion

Dermatologic: Photosensitivity, rash, angioedema, urticaria

Gastrointestinal: Nausea, vomiting, diarrhea, abdominal pain, xerostomia, appetite increase, weight gain, dry mucous membranes, anorexia

Genitourinary: Urinary retention, urinary frequency, difficult urination

Hematologic: Hemolytic anemia, thrombocytopenia, agranulocytosis

Neuromuscular & skeletal: Tremor, paresthesia

Ocular: blurred vision

Respiratory: Thickening of bronchial secretions

Drug Interactions

Cytochrome P450 Effect: Inhibits CYP2D6 (moderate)

Increased Effect/Toxicity: CNS depressants may increase the degree of sedation and respiratory depression with diphenhydramine. May increase the absorption of digoxin. Central and/or peripheral anticholinergic syndrome can occur when administered with amantadine, rimantadine, narcotic analgesics, phenothiazines and other antipsychotics (especially with high anticholinergic activity), tricyclic antidepressants, quinidine, disopyramide, procainamide, and antihistamines. Syrup should not be given to patients taking drugs that can cause disulfiram reactions (ie, metronidazole, chlorpropamide) due to high alcohol content.

Decreased Effect: May increase gastric degradation of levodopa and decrease the amount of levodopa absorbed by delaying gastric emptying. Therapeutic effects of cholinergic agents (tacrine, donepezil) and neuroleptics may be antagonized.

Mechanism of Action Competes with histamine for H_1-receptor sites on effector cells in the gastrointestinal tract, blood vessels, and respiratory tract; anticholinergic and sedative effects are also seen

Pharmacodynamics/Kinetics

Onset of action: Maximum sedative effect: 1-3 hours

Duration: 4-7 hours

Protein binding: 78%

Metabolism: Extensively hepatic; smaller degrees in pulmonary and renal systems; significant first-pass effect

Bioavailability: Oral: 40% to 60%

Half-life elimination: 2-8 hours; Elderly: 13.5 hours

Time to peak, serum: 2-4 hours

Excretion: Urine (as unchanged drug)

Dosage

Children:

Oral, I.M., I.V.:

Treatment of moderate to severe allergic reactions: 5 mg/kg/day or 150 mg/m^2/day in divided doses every 6-8 hours, not to exceed 300 mg/day

Minor allergic rhinitis or motion sickness:

2 to <6 years: 6.25 mg every 4-6 hours; maximum: 37.5 mg/day

6 to <12 years: 12.5-25 mg every 4-6 hours; maximum: 150 mg/day

≥12 years: 25-50 mg every 4-6 hours; maximum: 300 mg/day

Night-time sleep aid: 30 minutes before bedtime:

2 to <12 years: 1 mg/kg/dose; maximum: 50 mg/dose

≥12 years: 50 mg

Oral: Antitussive:

2 to <6 years: 6.25 mg every 4 hours; maximum 37.5 mg/day

6 to <12 years: 12.5 mg every 4 hours; maximum 75 mg/day

≥12 years: 25 mg every 4 hours; maximum 150 mg/day

I.M., I.V.: Treatment of dystonic reactions: 0.5-1 mg/kg/dose

Adults:

Oral: 25-50 mg every 6-8 hours

    Minor allergic rhinitis or motion sickness: 25-50 mg every 4-6 hours; maximum: 300 mg/
       day

    Moderate to severe allergic reactions: 25-50 mg every 4 hours, not to exceed 400 mg/day

    Nighttime sleep aid: 50 mg at bedtime

  I.M., I.V.: 10-50 mg in a single dose every 2-4 hours, not to exceed 400 mg/day

    Dystonic reaction: 50 mg in a single dose; may repeat in 20-30 minutes if necessary

  Topical: For external application, not longer than 7 days

Monitoring Parameters Relief of symptoms, mental alertness

Reference Range

  Antihistamine effects at levels >25 ng/mL

  Drowsiness at levels 30-40 ng/mL

  Mental impairment at levels >60 ng/mL

  Therapeutic: Not established

  Toxic: >0.1 µg/mL

Patient Information May cause drowsiness; swallow whole, do not crush or chew sustained release product; avoid alcohol, may impair coordination and judgment

Dosage Forms CAP: 25 mg, 50 mg; (Banophen®, Diphen®, Diphenhist®, Genahist®): 25 mg; (Nytol® Maximum Strength, Sleepinal®): 50 mg. **ELIX:** 12.5 mg/5 mL (5 mL, 10 mL, 20 mL, 120 mL, 480 mL, 3780 mL); (Banophen®): 12.5 mg/5 mL (120 mL, 480 mL, 3840 mL); (Diphen AF): 12.5 mg/5 mL (120 mL, 240 mL, 480 mL, 3840 mL); (Genahist®, Hydramine®): 12.5 mg/5 mL (120 mL); (Benadryl®): 12.5 mg/5 mL (120 mL). **GEL, topical** (Benadryl®): 1% (120 mL); (Benadryl® Extra Strength): 2% (120 mL). **INJ, solution:** 10 mg/mL (30 mL); 50 mg/mL (1 mL, 10 mL); (Benadryl®): 50 mg/mL (1 mL, 10 mL); (Hyrexin®): 50 mg/mL (10 mL). **LIQ:** (Benadryl® Allergy): 12.5 mg/5 mL (120 mL, 240 mL); (Benadryl® Dye-Free Allergy): 12.5 mg/5 mL (120 mL). **SOFTGEL:** (Benadryl® Dye-Free Allergy): 25 mg; (Unisom® Maximum Strength SleepGels®): 50 mg. **SOLN, oral** (AllerMax®): 12.5 mg/5 mL (120 mL); (Diphenhist®): 12.5 mg/5 mL (120 mL, 480 mL). **SOLN, topical:** 1% (60 mL); 2% (60 mL). **SYR:** 12.5 mg/5 mL (120 mL, 240 mL, 480 mL); (Diphen® Cough, Siladryl® Allergy, Silphen® Cough): 12.5 mg/5 mL (120 mL, 240 mL, 480 mL); (Diphenhist®): 12.5 mg/5 mL (120 mL); (Hydramine® Cough): 12.5 mg/5 mL (120 mL); (Tusstat®): 12.5 mg/5 mL (120 mL, 240 mL, 3840 mL). **TAB:** 25 mg, 50 mg; (Aler-Dryl, AllerMax®, Compoz® Nighttime Sleep Aid, Sominex® Maximum Strength, Twilite®): 50 mg; (Banophen®, Benadryl® Allergy, Diphenhist®, Genahist®, Nytol®, Sominex®): 25 mg. **TAB, chewable** (Benadryl® Allergy): 12.5 mg

♦ **Diphenhydramine and Acetaminophen** *see Acetaminophen and Diphenhydramine on page 26*

Diphenhydramine and Pseudoephedrine

  (dye fen HYE dra meen & soo doe e FED rin)

U.S. Brand Names Benadryl® Allergy and Sinus Fastmelt™ [OTC]; Benadryl® Allergy/Decongestant [OTC]; Benadryl® Children's Allergy and Cold Fastmelt™ [OTC]; Benadryl® Children's Allergy and Sinus [OTC]

Synonyms Pseudoephedrine and Diphenhydramine

Therapeutic Category Antihistamine/Decongestant

Use Relief of symptoms of upper respiratory mucosal congestion in seasonal and perennial nasal allergies, acute rhinitis, rhinosinusitis, and eustachian tube blockage

Dosage Based on **pseudoephedrine** component:

  Adults: Oral: 60 mg every 4-6 hours, maximum: 240 mg/day

Dosage Forms LIQ (Benadryl® Children's Allergy and Sinus): Diphenhydramine hydrochloride 12.5 mg and pseudoephedrine hydrochloride 30 mg per 5 mL. **TAB** (Benadryl® Allergy/Decongestant): Diphenhydramine hydrochloride 25 mg and pseudoephedrine hydrochloride 60 mg. **TAB, quick-dissolving** (Benadryl® Children's Allergy and Cold Fastmelt™, Benadryl® Allergy and Sinus Fastmelt™): Diphenhydramine citrate 19 mg [equivalent to diphenhydramine hydrochloride 12.5 mg] and pseudoephedrine 30 mg

♦ **Diphenhydramine Hydrochloride** *see DiphenhydrAMINE on page 383*

Diphenoxylate and Atropine (dye fen OKS i late & A troe peen)

U.S. Brand Names Lomocot®; Lomotil®; Lonox®

Synonyms Atropine and Diphenoxylate

Therapeutic Category Antidiarrheal

Use Treatment of diarrhea

Restrictions C-V

Pregnancy Risk Factor C

Contraindications Hypersensitivity to diphenoxylate, atropine, or any component of the formulation; severe liver disease; jaundice; dehydration; narrow-angle glaucoma; not for use in children <2 years of age

Warnings/Precautions High doses may cause physical and psychological dependence with prolonged use; use with caution in patients with ulcerative colitis, dehydration, and hepatic dysfunction; reduction of intestinal motility may be deleterious in diarrhea resulting from *Shigella*, *Salmonella*, toxigenic strains of *E. coli*, and from pseudomembranous enterocolitis associated with broad spectrum antibiotics; children may develop signs of atropinism (dryness of skin and mucous membranes, thirst, hyperthermia, tachycardia, urinary retention, flushing) even at the recommended dosages; if there is no response with 48 hours, the drug is unlikely to be effective and should be discontinued; if chronic diarrhea is not improved symptomatically within 10 days at maximum dosage of 20 mg/day, control is unlikely with further use. (Continued)

Diphenoxylate and Atropine *(Continued)*

Common Adverse Reactions 1% to 10%:
Central nervous system: Nervousness, restlessness, dizziness, drowsiness, headache, mental depression
Gastrointestinal: Paralytic ileus, xerostomia
Genitourinary: Urinary retention and dysuria
Ocular: Blurred vision
Respiratory: Respiratory depression

Drug Interactions
Increased Effect/Toxicity: MAO inhibitors (hypertensive crisis), CNS depressants when taken with diphenoxylate may result in increased adverse effects, antimuscarinics (paralytic ileus). May prolong half-life of drugs metabolized in liver.

Mechanism of Action Diphenoxylate inhibits excessive GI motility and GI propulsion; commercial preparations contain a subtherapeutic amount of atropine to discourage abuse

Pharmacodynamics/Kinetics
Atropine: See Atropine monograph.
Diphenoxylate:
Onset of action: Antidiarrheal: 45-60 minutes
Peak effect: Antidiarrheal: ~2 hours
Duration: Antidiarrheal: 3-4 hours
Absorption: Well absorbed
Metabolism: Extensively hepatic to diphenoxylic acid (active)
Half-life elimination: 2.5 hours
Time to peak, serum: 2 hours
Excretion: Primarily feces (as metabolites); urine (~14%, <1% as unchanged drug)

Dosage Oral:
Children (use with caution in young children due to variable responses): Liquid: 0.3-0.4 mg of diphenoxylate/kg/day in 2-4 divided doses **or**
<2 years: Not recommended
2-5 years: 2 mg of diphenoxylate 3 times/day
5-8 years: 2 mg of diphenoxylate 4 times/day
8-12 years: 2 mg of diphenoxylate 5 times/day
Adults: 15-20 mg/day of diphenoxylate in 3-4 divided doses; maintenance: 5-15 mg/day in 2-3 divided doses

Monitoring Parameters Watch for signs of atropinism (dryness of skin and mucous membranes, tachycardia, thirst, flushing); monitor number and consistency of stools; observe for signs of toxicity, fluid and electrolyte loss, hypotension, and respiratory depression

Patient Information May cause drowsiness, dizziness, dry mouth; use caution while driving or performing hazardous tasks; avoid alcohol or other CNS depressants; do not exceed prescribed dose; report persistent diarrhea, fever, or palpitations

Dosage Forms SOLN, oral: Diphenoxylate 2.5 mg and atropine 0.025 mg per 5 mL (5 mL, 10 mL, 60 mL); (Lomotil®): Diphenoxylate 2.5 mg and atropine 0.025 mg per 5 mL (60 mL). **TAB** (Lomocot®, Lomotil®, Lonox®): Diphenoxylate 2.5 mg and atropine 0.025 mg

♦ **Diphenylhydantoin** *see Phenytoin on page 995*

Diphtheria and Tetanus Toxoid *(dif THEER ee a & TET a nus TOKS oyd)*

Synonyms DT; Td; Tetanus and Diphtheria Toxoid
Therapeutic Category Toxoid

Use
Diphtheria and tetanus toxoids adsorbed for pediatric use (DT): Infants and children through 6 years of age: Active immunity against diphtheria and tetanus when pertussis vaccine is contraindicated
Tetanus and diphtheria toxoids adsorbed for adult use (Td): Children and adults ≥7 years of age: Active immunity against diphtheria and tetanus; tetanus prophylaxis in wound management

Pregnancy Risk Factor C

Contraindications Hypersensitivity to diphtheria, tetanus toxoid, or any component of the formulation

Warnings/Precautions Do not confuse pediatric diphtheria and tetanus (DT) with adult tetanus and diphtheria (Td). Immediate treatment for anaphylactic/anaphylactoid reaction should be available during administration. Patients with a history of severe local reaction (Arthus-type) or temperature of >39.4°C (103°F) following a previous dose should not be given further routine or emergency doses of Td more frequently than every 10 years. Continue use with caution if Guillain-Barré syndrome occurs within 6 weeks of prior tetanus toxoid. For I.M. administration; use caution with history of bleeding disorders or anticoagulant therapy. Defer administration during moderate or severe illness (with or without fever) or during outbreaks of poliomyelitis. Immune response may be decreased in immunocompromised patients. Safety and efficacy of DT have not been established in children <6 weeks of age; Td should be administered to children ≥7 years of age and adults.

Common Adverse Reactions All serious adverse reactions must be reported to the U.S. Department of Health and Human Services (DHHS) Vaccine Adverse Event Reporting System (VAERS) 1-800-822-7967.
>10%: Local: Injection site (adolescents and adults): Pain (81% to 85%), redness (5% to 21%), swelling (10% to 16%)
Frequency not defined; reactions reported with adult and pediatric preparations
Cardiovascular: EEG disturbances

Central nervous system: Brachial neuritis, Guillain-Barré syndrome

Local: Injection site: Persistent nodules

Miscellaneous: Allergic/anaphylactic reactions, Arthus-type hypersensitivity reaction (severe local reaction starting 2-8 hours after injection)

Drug Interactions

Decreased Effect: The effect of the vaccine may be decreased by immunosuppressant medications or therapies (antimetabolites, alkylating agents, cytotoxic drugs, corticosteroids, irradiation); consider deferring vaccination for 3 months after immunosuppressant therapy is discontinued

Dosage I.M.:

Infants and Children ≤6 years (DT): Primary immunization:

6 weeks to 1 year: Three 0.5 mL doses at least 4 weeks apart; administer a reinforcing dose 6-12 months after the third injection

1-6 years: Two 0.5 mL doses at least 4 weeks apart; reinforcing dose 6-12 months after second injection; if final dose is given after seventh birthday, use adult preparation

4-6 years (booster immunization): 0.5 mL; not necessary if the fourth dose was given after fourth birthday; routinely administer booster doses at 10-year intervals with the adult preparation

Children ≥7 years and Adults:

Primary immunization: Patients previously not immunized should receive 2 primary doses of 0.5 mL each, given at an interval of 4-6 weeks; third (reinforcing) dose of 0.5 mL 6-12 months later

Booster immunization: 0.5 mL every 10 years; to be given to children 11-12 years of age if at least 5 years have elapsed since last dose of toxoid containing vaccine. Subsequent routine doses are not recommended more often than every 10 years.

Tetanus prophylaxis in wound management; use of tetanus toxoid (Td*) and/or tetanus immune globulin (TIG) depends upon the number of prior tetanus toxoid doses and type of wound: See table.

Tetanus Prophylaxis in Wound Management

Number of Prior Tetanus Toxoid Doses	Clean, Minor Wounds		All Other Wounds	
	Td[1]	TIG[2]	Td[1]	TIG[2]
Unknown or <3	Yes	No	Yes	Yes
≥3[3]	No[4]	No	No[5]	No

[1]Adult tetanus and diphtheria toxoids; use pediatric preparations (DT or DTP) if the patient is <7 years old.

[2]Tetanus immune globulin.

[3]If only three doses of fluid tetanus toxoid have been received, a fourth dose of toxoid, preferably an adsorbed toxoid, should be given.

[4]Yes, if >10 years since last dose.

[5]Yes, if >5 years since last dose.

Adapted from Report of the Committee on Infectious Diseases, American Academy of Pediatrics, Elk Grove Village, IL: American Academy of Pediatrics, 1986.

Administration For I.M. administration; prior to use, shake suspension well

Td: Administer in the deltoid muscle; do not inject in the gluteal area

DT: Administer in the anterolateral aspect of the thigh or the deltoid muscle; do not inject in the gluteal area

For patients at risk of hemorrhage following intramuscular injection, the ACIP recommends "it should be administered intramuscularly if, in the opinion of the physician familiar with the patients bleeding risk, the vaccine can be administered with reasonable safety by this route. If the patient receives antihemophilia or other similar therapy, intramuscular vaccination can be scheduled shortly after such therapy is administered. A fine needle (23 gauge or smaller) can be used for the vaccination and firm pressure applied to the site (without rubbing) for at least 2 minutes. The patient should be instructed concerning the risk of hematoma from the injection."

Patient Information DT, Td and T vaccines cause few problems (mild fever or soreness, swelling, and redness/knot at the injection site); these problems usually last 1-2 days, but this does not happen nearly as often as with DTP vaccine

Dosage Forms INJ, suspension, adult: Diphtheria 2 Lf units and tetanus 5 Lf units per 0.5 mL (0.5 mL, 5 mL). **INJ, suspension, pediatric:** Diphtheria 6.7 Lf units and tetanus 5 Lf units per 0.5 mL (0.5 mL, 5 mL)

♦ **Diphtheria and Tetanus Toxoids and Acellular Pertussis Adsorbed, Hepatitis B (Recombinant) and Inactivated Poliovirus Vaccine Combined** see Diphtheria, Tetanus Toxoids, Acellular Pertussis, Hepatitis B (Recombinant), and Poliovirus (Inactivated) Vaccine on page 387

♦ **Diphtheria CRM₁₉₇ Protein** see Pneumococcal Conjugate Vaccine (7-Valent) on page 1010

♦ **Diphtheria CRM₁₉₇ Protein Conjugate** see Haemophilus b Conjugate Vaccine on page 607

Diphtheria, Tetanus Toxoids, Acellular Pertussis, Hepatitis B (Recombinant), and Poliovirus (Inactivated) Vaccine

(dif THEER ee a, TET a nus TOKS oyds, ay CEL yoo lar per TUS sis, hep a TYE tis bee ree KOM be nant, & POE lee oh VYE rus vak SEEN, in ak ti VAY ted vak SEEN)

U.S. Brand Names Pediarix™

(Continued)

Diphtheria, Tetanus Toxoids, Acellular Pertussis, Hepatitis B (Recombinant), and Poliovirus (Inactivated) Vaccine (Continued)

Synonyms Diphtheria and Tetanus Toxoids and Acellular Pertussis Adsorbed, Hepatitis B (Recombinant) and Inactivated Poliovirus Vaccine Combined

Therapeutic Category Vaccine

Use Combination vaccine for the active immunization against diphtheria, tetanus, pertussis, hepatitis B virus (all known subtypes), and poliomyelitis (caused by poliovirus types 1, 2, and 3)

Pregnancy Risk Factor C

Contraindications Hypersensitivity to diphtheria and tetanus toxoids, pertussis, hepatitis B, poliovirus vaccine, yeast, neomycin, polymyxin B, or any component of the vaccine; encephalopathy occurring within 7 days of a previous pertussis vaccine not (not attributable to another identifiable cause); progressive neurologic disorders (including infantile spasms, uncontrolled epilepsy, or progressive encephalopathy)

Warnings/Precautions Immediate treatment for anaphylactic/anaphylactoid reaction should be available during vaccine use. Infants born of HBsAg-positive mothers should receive monovalent hepatitis B vaccine and hepatitis B immune globulin; infants born of HBsAg-unknown mothers should receive monovalent hepatitis B vaccine; use of combination product in these patients to complete the hepatitis B vaccination series has not been studied. Use caution if one or more has occurred within 48 hours of whole-cell DTP or a vaccine containing acellular pertussis: Temperature ≥40.5°C (≥105°F) within 48 hours not due to an identifiable cause; collapse or shock-like state within 48 hours; persistent, inconsolable crying that occurs within 48 hours and lasts ≥3 hours; seizures with or without fever that occur within 3 days. Use caution if Guillain-Barré syndrome occurs within 6 weeks of prior vaccination with tetanus toxoid. Defer administration during moderate or severe illness with or without fever. Antipyretics should be administered at the time of and for 24 hours following vaccination to patients at high risk for seizures. Use caution with bleeding disorders. Not for use as a booster dose following the 3-dose primary series. Safety and efficacy have not been established for use in children <6 weeks or adults and children ≥7 years of age.

Common Adverse Reactions All serious adverse reactions must be reported to the U.S. Department of Health and Human Services (DHHS) Vaccine Adverse Event Reporting System (VAERS) 1-800-822-7967.

As reported in a U.S. lot Consistency Study:

>10%:

Central nervous system:

Sleeping increased (28% to 47%, grade 3: <1% to 2%)

Restlessness (28% to 30%, grade 3: ≤1%)

Fever ≥100.4°F (26% to 31%); >103.1°F (<1%); incidence of fever is higher than reported with separately administered vaccines

Gastrointestinal: Appetite decreased (19% to 22%, grade 3: <1%)

Local: Injection site:

Redness (25% to 36%, >20 mm: ≤1%)

Pain (23% to 30%, grade 3: ≤1%)

Swelling (15% to 22%; >20 mm: 1%)

Miscellaneous: Fussiness (57% to 64%; grade 3: 2% to 3%)

Refer to individual product monographs for additional adverse reactions, including postmarketing and case reports.

Drug Interactions

Decreased Effect: Immunosuppressant medications or therapies (antimetabolites, alkylating agents, cytotoxic drugs, corticosteroids, irradiation) may decrease vaccine effectiveness, consider deferring vaccination for 3 months after immunosuppressant therapy is discontinued.

Mechanism of Action Promotes active immunity to diphtheria, tetanus, pertussis, hepatitis B and poliovirus (types 1, 2 and 3) by inducing production of specific antibodies and antitoxins.

Pharmacodynamics/Kinetics Onset of action: Immune response observed to all components 1 month following the 3-dose series

Dosage I.M.: Children:

Immunization: 0.5 mL; repeat in 6-8 week intervals (preferably 8-week intervals) for a total of 3 doses. Vaccination usually begins at 2 months, but may be started as early as 6 weeks of age.

Use in children previously vaccinated with one or more component, and who are also scheduled to receive all vaccine components:

Hepatitis B vaccine: Infants born of HBsAg-negative mothers who received 1 dose of hepatitis B vaccine at birth may be given Pediarix™ (safety data limited); use in infants who received more than 1 dose of hepatitis B vaccine has not been studied. Infants who received 1 or more doses of hepatitis B vaccine (recombinant) may be given Pediarix™ to complete the hepatitis B series (safety and efficacy not established).

Diphtheria and tetanus toxoids, and acellular pertussis vaccine (DTaP): Infants previously vaccinated with 1 or 2 doses of Infanrix® may use Pediarix™ to complete the first 3 doses of the series (safety and efficacy not established); use of Pediarix™ to complete DTaP vaccination started with products other than Infanrix® is not recommended.

Inactivated polio vaccine (IPV): Infants previously vaccinated with 1 or 2 doses of IPV may use Pediarix™ to complete the first 3 doses of the series (safety and efficacy not established).

Administration For I.M. use only; do not administer I.V. or S.C. Shake well prior to use; do not use unless a homogeneous, turbid, white suspension forms. Administer in the anterolateral aspects of the thigh or the deltoid muscle of the upper arm. Do not inject in the gluteal area (suboptimal hepatitis B immune response) or where there may be a major nerve trunk. Do not administer additional vaccines or immunoglobulins at the same site, or using the same syringe.

For patients at risk of hemorrhage following intramuscular injection, the ACIP recommends "it should be administered intramuscularly if, in the opinion of the physician familiar with the patients bleeding risk, the vaccine can be administered with reasonable safety by this route. If the patient receives antihemophilia or other similar therapy, intramuscular vaccination can be scheduled shortly after such therapy is administered. A fine needle (23 gauge or smaller) can be used for the vaccination and firm pressure applied to the site (without rubbing) for at least 2 minutes. The patient should be instructed concerning the risk of hematoma from the injection."

Federal law requires that the date of administration, name of the vaccine manufacturer, lot number of vaccine, and the administering person's name, title, and address be entered into the patient's permanent medical record.

Patient Information Mild reactions include redness or soreness at the injection site, fever, fussiness, decreased appetite, or feeling tired. Contact prescriber for any of the following less common reactions: Fever of 101.3°F or higher, seizures, or if your child becomes limp, pale, or less alert. It is important that each child receive all the recommended doses in the series in order to be fully immunized. This vaccine is not used in adults or children ≥7 years or <6 weeks of age.

Dosage Forms Injection, suspension [single-dose]: Diphtheria toxoid 25 Lf, tetanus toxoid 10 Lf, inactivated PT 25 mcg, FHA 25 mcg, pertactin 8 mcg, HBsAg 10 mcg, poliovirus type 1 40 DU, poliovirus type 2 8 DU, and poliovirus type 3 32 DU per 0.5 mL [contains neomycin sulfate ≤0.05 ng/0.5 mL, polymyxin B ≤0.01 ng/0.5 mL and yeast protein ≤5%; packaged in vials or prefilled syringes; the needleless prefilled syringes contain dry natural latex rubber in the tip cap and plunger]

Diphtheria, Tetanus Toxoids, and Acellular Pertussis Vaccine

(dif THEER ee a, TET a nus TOKS oyds & ay CEL yoo lar per TUS sis vak SEEN)

U.S. Brand Names Daptacel™; Infanrix®; Tripedia®

Synonyms DTaP

Therapeutic Category Toxoid and Vaccine; Vaccine

Use Active immunization against diphtheria, tetanus, and pertussis from age 6 weeks through seventh birthday

Pregnancy Risk Factor C

Contraindications Hypersensitivity to diphtheria and tetanus toxoids, pertussis, or any component of the formulation; children ≥7 years of age; moderate or severe febrile illness (postpone vaccine); immediate anaphylactic reaction following previous dose; history of any of the following effects from previous administration of pertussis vaccine - anaphylactic reaction, convulsions, focal neurologic signs, or encephalopathy

Warnings/Precautions Carefully consider use in patients with history of any of the following effects from previous administration of pertussis vaccine: >105°F fever (40.5°C) within 48 hours of unknown cause, convulsions with or without fever occurring within 3 days, screaming episodes lasting ≥3 hours and occurring within 48 hours, shock or collapse within 48 hours; use with caution in children with coagulation disorders (including thrombocytopenia) where intramuscular injections should not be used; patients who are immunocompromised may have reduced response; may be used in patients with HIV infection; defer immunization during outbreaks of poliomyelitis. Use caution in patients with history of seizure disorder, progressive neurologic disease, or conditions predisposing to seizures; ACIP and APP guidelines recommend deferring immunization until health status can be assessed and condition stabilized. Products may contain thimerosal; packaging may contain natural latex rubber; safety and efficacy in children <6 weeks of age have not been established

Common Adverse Reactions All serious adverse reactions must be reported to the U.S. Department of Health and Human Services (DHHS) Vaccine Adverse Event Reporting System (VAERS) 1-800-822-7967.

Incidence of erythema, swelling and fever increase with successive doses

>10%:

  Central nervous system: Drowsiness, irritability

  Gastrointestinal: Decreased appetite

  Local: Redness, swelling

1% to 10%:

  Central nervous system: Fever

  Gastrointestinal: Vomiting

  Local: Pain, redness ≥3 cm, swelling ≥3 cm, tenderness

  Miscellaneous: High-pitched/unusual crying

Drug Interactions

  Increased Effect/Toxicity: Increased bleeding/bruising with anticoagulants.

  Decreased Effect: Vaccine effect may be decreased with corticosteroids and immunosuppressant agents. Consider deferring vaccine for 1 month after agent is discontinued.

Mechanism of Action Promotes active immunity to diphtheria, tetanus, and pertussis by inducing production of specific antibodies and antitoxins.

(Continued)

Diphtheria, Tetanus Toxoids, and Acellular Pertussis Vaccine
(Continued)
Dosage
Children 6 weeks to <7 years: I.M.: 0.5 mL

Primary series: Three doses, usually given at 2-, 4-, and 6 months of age; may be given as early as 6 weeks of age and repeated every 4-8 weeks; use same product for all 3 doses

Booster series:

Fourth dose: Given at ~15-20 months of age, but at least 6 months after third dose

Fifth dose: Given at 5-6 years of age, prior to starting school or kindergarten; if the fourth dose is given at ≥4 years of age, the fifth dose may be omitted

Children ≥7 years and Adults: Tetanus and diphtheria toxoids for adult use (Td) preparation is the preferred agent

Administration
Administer only I.M. in anterolateral aspect of thigh or deltoid muscle of upper arm

For patients at risk of hemorrhage following intramuscular injection, the ACIP recommends "it should be administered intramuscularly if, in the opinion of the physician familiar with the patients bleeding risk, the vaccine can be administered with reasonable safety by this route. If the patient receives antihemophilia or other similar therapy, intramuscular vaccination can be scheduled shortly after such therapy is administered. A fine needle (23 gauge or smaller) can be used for the vaccination and firm pressure applied to the site (without rubbing) for at least 2 minutes. The patient should be instructed concerning the risk of hematoma from the injection."

Patient Information
A nodule may be palpable at the injection site for a few weeks. Reactions to the vaccine, if seen, usually occur within 3 days. Mild reactions include sore arm or leg, fever, fussiness, decreased appetite, tiredness, or vomiting. Contact prescriber for any of the following less common reactions: Nonstop crying for 3 hours or more, fever of 105°F or higher, seizures, or if your child becomes limp, pale, or less alert. Reactions to the DTaP vaccine are less likely to occur then those previously seen with the DTP vaccine. It is important that each child receive all the recommended doses in the series in order to be fully immunized. This vaccine is not used in adults or children >7 years of age.

Dosage Forms
INJ, suspension: (Daptacel™): Diphtheria 15 Lf units, tetanus 5 Lf units, and acellular pertussis vaccine 10 mcg per 0.5 mL (0.5 mL); (Infanrix®): Diphtheria 25 Lf units, tetanus 10 Lf units, and acellular pertussis vaccine 25 mcg per 0.5 mL (0.5 mL); (Tripedia®): Diphtheria 6.7 Lf units, tetanus 5 Lf units, and acellular pertussis vaccine 46.8 mcg per 0.5 mL (7.5 mL)

Diphtheria, Tetanus Toxoids, and Acellular Pertussis Vaccine and *Haemophilus influenzae* b Conjugate Vaccine
(dif THEER ee a, TET a nus TOKS oyds & ay CEL yoo lar per TUS sis vak SEEN & hem OF fi lus in floo EN za bee KON joo gate vak SEEN)

U.S. Brand Names TriHIBit®

Synonyms *Haemophilus influenzae* b Conjugate Vaccine and Diphtheria, Tetanus Toxoids, and Acellular Pertussis Vaccine

Therapeutic Category Toxoid and Vaccine; Vaccine, Inactivated Bacteria

Use Active immunization of children 15-18 months of age for prevention of diphtheria, tetanus, pertussis, and invasive disease caused by *H. influenzae* type b.

Dosage Children >15 months of age: I.M.: 0.5 mL (as part of a general vaccination schedule; see individual vaccines). Vaccine should be used within 30 minutes of reconstitution.

Dosage Forms INJ, suspension: 5 Lf units tetanus toxoid, 6.7 Lf units diphtheria toxoid, 46.8 mcg pertussis antigens, and 10 mcg *H. influenzae* type b purified capsular polysaccharide per 0.5 mL (0.5 mL) [The combination of Tripedia® vaccine used to reconstitute ActHIB® forms TriHIBit®]

♦ **Diphtheria Toxoid Conjugate** *see Haemophilus b Conjugate Vaccine on page 607*

♦ **Dipivalyl Epinephrine** *see Dipivefrin on page 390*

Dipivefrin *(dye PI ve frin)*
Related Information
Glaucoma Drug Therapy Comparison *on page 1481*

U.S. Brand Names Propine®

Synonyms Dipivalyl Epinephrine; Dipivefrin Hydrochloride; DPE

Therapeutic Category Adrenergic Agonist Agent, Ophthalmic; Alpha/Beta Agonist; Ophthalmic Agent, Vasoconstrictor

Use Reduces elevated intraocular pressure in chronic open-angle glaucoma; also used to treat ocular hypertension, low tension, and secondary glaucomas

Pregnancy Risk Factor B

Dosage Adults: Ophthalmic: Instill 1 drop every 12 hours into the eyes

Dosage Forms SOLN, ophthalmic: 0.1% (5 mL, 10 mL, 15 mL)

♦ **Dipivefrin Hydrochloride** *see Dipivefrin on page 390*

♦ **Diprivan®** *see Propofol on page 1051*

♦ **Diprolene®** *see Betamethasone on page 159*

♦ **Diprolene® AF** *see Betamethasone on page 159*

♦ **Dipropylacetic Acid** *see Valproic Acid and Derivatives on page 1288*

Dipyridamole (dye peer ID a mole)

U.S. Brand Names Persantine®

Therapeutic Category Antiplatelet Agent; Platelet Aggregation Inhibitor; Vasodilator, Coronary

Use Maintains patency after surgical grafting procedures including coronary artery bypass; used with warfarin to decrease thrombosis in patients after artificial heart valve replacement; used with aspirin to prevent coronary artery thrombosis; in combination with aspirin or warfarin to prevent other thromboembolic disorders. Dipyridamole may also be given 2 days prior to open heart surgery to prevent platelet activation by extracorporeal bypass pump and as a diagnostic agent in CAD.

Unlabeled/Investigational Use Treatment of proteinuria in pediatric renal disease

Pregnancy Risk Factor B

Contraindications Hypersensitivity to dipyridamole or any component of the formulation

Warnings/Precautions Use caution in patients with hypotension. Use caution in patients on other antiplatelet agents or anticoagulation. Severe adverse reactions have occurred rarely with I.V. administration. Use the I.V. form with caution in patients with bronchospastic disease or unstable angina. Have aminophylline ready in case of urgency or emergency with I.V. use.

Common Adverse Reactions

>10%:
   Cardiovascular: Exacerbation of angina pectoris (20% I.V.)
   Central nervous system: Dizziness (14% oral), headache (12% I.V.)
1% to 10%:
   Cardiovascular: Hypotension (5%), hypertension (2%), blood pressure lability (2%), ECG abnormalities (ST-T changes, extrasystoles), chest pain, tachycardia (3% I.V.)
   Central nervous system: Headache (2% I.V.), flushing (3% I.V.), fatigue (1% I.V.)
   Dermatologic: Rash (2% oral)
   Gastrointestinal: Abdominal distress (6% oral), nausea (5% I.V.)
   Neuromuscular & skeletal: Paresthesia (1% I.V.)
   Respiratory: Dyspnea (3% I.V.)

Drug Interactions

Increased Effect/Toxicity: Dipyridamole enhances the risk of bleeding with aspirin (and other antiplatelet agents), heparin, low-molecular weight heparins, and warfarin. Adenosine blood levels and pharmacologic effects are increased with dipyridamole; consider reduced doses of adenosine.

Decreased Effect: Decreased vasodilation from I.V. dipyridamole when given to patients taking theophylline. Theophylline may reduce the pharmacologic effects of dipyridamole (hold theophylline preparations for 36-48 hours before dipyridamole facilitated stress test).

Mechanism of Action Inhibits the activity of adenosine deaminase and phosphodiesterase, which causes an accumulation of adenosine, adenine nucleotides, and cyclic AMP; these mediators then inhibit platelet aggregation and may cause vasodilation; may also stimulate release of prostacyclin or PGD_2; causes coronary vasodilation

Pharmacodynamics/Kinetics

Absorption: Readily, but variable
Distribution: Adults: V_d: 2-3 L/kg
Protein binding: 91% to 99%
Metabolism: Hepatic
Half-life elimination: Terminal: 10-12 hours
Time to peak, serum: 2-2.5 hours
Excretion: Feces (as glucuronide conjugates and unchanged drug)

Dosage

Children: Oral: 3-6 mg/kg/day in 3 divided doses
   Doses of 4-10 mg/kg/day have been used investigationally to treat proteinuria in pediatric renal disease
   Mechanical prosthetic heart valves: Oral: 2-5 mg/kg/day (used in combination with an oral anticoagulant in children who have systemic embolism despite adequate oral anticoagulant therapy, and used in combination with low-dose oral anticoagulation (INR 2-3) plus aspirin in children in whom full-dose oral anticoagulation is contraindicated)
Adults:
   Oral: 75-400 mg/day in 3-4 divided doses
   Evaluation of coronary artery disease: I.V.: 0.14 mg/kg/minute for 4 minutes; maximum dose: 60 mg
Hemodialysis: Significant drug removal is unlikely based on physiochemical characteristics

Administration I.V.: Dilute in at least a 1:2 ratio with normal saline, 1/2NS, or D_5W; infusion of undiluted dipyridamole may cause local irritation

Patient Information Notify prescriber or pharmacist if taking other medications that affect bleeding, such as NSAIDs or warfarin

Dosage Forms INJ, solution: 5 mg/mL (2 mL, 10 mL). **TAB:** 25 mg, 50 mg, 75 mg

♦ Dipyridamole and Aspirin see Aspirin and Dipyridamole on page 122

Dirithromycin (dye RITH roe mye sin)

U.S. Brand Names Dynabac®

Therapeutic Category Antibiotic, Macrolide

Use Treatment of mild to moderate upper and lower respiratory tract infections due to *Moraxella catarrhalis*, *Streptococcus pneumoniae*, *Legionella pneumophila*, *H. influenzae*, or *S. pyogenes*, ie, acute exacerbation of chronic bronchitis, secondary bacterial infection of acute

(Continued)

Dirithromycin *(Continued)*

bronchitis, community-acquired pneumonia, pharyngitis/tonsillitis, and uncomplicated infections of the skin and skin structure due to *Staphylococcus aureus*

Pregnancy Risk Factor C

Dosage Adults: Oral: 500 mg once daily for 5-14 days (14 days required for treatment of community-acquired pneumonia due to *Legionella, Mycoplasma,* or *S. pneumoniae;* 10 days is recommended for treatment of *S. pyogenes* pharyngitis/tonsillitis)

Dosing adjustment in renal impairment: None necessary
Dosing adjustment in hepatic impairment: None needed in mild dysfunction; not studied in moderate to severe dysfunction

Dosage Forms TAB, enteric coated: 250 mg

- ◆ **Disalcid® [DSC]** *see* Salsalate *on page 1122*
- ◆ **Disalicylic Acid** *see* Salsalate *on page 1122*
- ◆ **Disodium Cromoglycate** *see* Cromolyn *on page 316*
- ◆ **Disodium Thiosulfate Pentahydrate** *see* Sodium Thiosulfate *on page 1152*
- ◆ **d-Isoephedrine Hydrochloride** *see* Pseudoephedrine *on page 1061*

Disopyramide *(dye soe PEER a mide)*

U.S. Brand Names Norpace®; Norpace® CR
Synonyms Disopyramide Phosphate
Therapeutic Category Antiarrhythmic Agent, Class I-A
Use Suppression and prevention of unifocal and multifocal atrial and premature, ventricular premature complexes, coupled ventricular tachycardia; effective in the conversion of atrial fibrillation, atrial flutter, and paroxysmal atrial tachycardia to normal sinus rhythm and prevention of the recurrence of these arrhythmias after conversion by other methods
Pregnancy Risk Factor C
Contraindications Hypersensitivity to disopyramide or any component of the formulation; cardiogenic shock; pre-existing second- or third-degree heart block (except in patients with a functioning artificial pacemaker); congenital QT syndrome; sick sinus syndrome
Warnings/Precautions Monitor closely for hypotension during the initiation of therapy. Avoid concurrent use with other medications with prolong QT interval or decrease myocardial contractility. Pre-existing urinary retention, family history, or existing angle-closure glaucoma, myasthenia gravis, CHF unless caused by an arrhythmias, widening of QRS complex during therapy or QT interval (>25% to 50% of baseline QRS complex or QT interval), sick-sinus syndrome or WPW may require decrease in dosage; disopyramide ineffective in hypokalemia and potentially toxic with hyperkalemia. Due to changes in total clearance (decreased) in elderly, monitor closely; the anticholinergic action may be intolerable and require discontinuation. May precipitate or exacerbate CHF. Due to significant anticholinergic effects, do not use in patients with urinary retention, BPH, glaucoma, or myasthenia gravis. Reduce dosage in renal or hepatic impairment. The extended release form is not recommended for Cl_{cr} <40 mL/minute. In patients with atrial fibrillation or flutter, block the AV node before initiating. Use caution in Wolff-Parkinson-White syndrome or bundle branch block.
Common Adverse Reactions The most common adverse effects are related to cholinergic blockade. The most serious adverse effects of disopyramide are hypotension and CHF.

>10%:
    Gastrointestinal: Xerostomia (32%), constipation (11%)
    Genitourinary: Urinary hesitancy (14% to 23%)
1% to 10%:
    Cardiovascular: Congestive heart failure, hypotension, cardiac conduction disturbance, edema, syncope, chest pain
    Central nervous system: Fatigue, headache, malaise, dizziness, nervousness
    Dermatologic: Rash, generalized dermatoses, pruritus
    Endocrine & metabolic: Hypokalemia, elevated cholesterol, elevated triglycerides
    Gastrointestinal: Dry throat, nausea, abdominal distension, flatulence, abdominal bloating, anorexia, diarrhea, vomiting, weight gain
    Genitourinary: Urinary retention, urinary frequency, urinary urgency, impotence (1% to 3%)
    Neuromuscular & skeletal: Muscle weakness, muscular pain
    Ocular: Blurred vision, dry eyes
    Respiratory: Dyspnea

Drug Interactions
Cytochrome P450 Effect: Substrate of CYP3A4 (major)
Increased Effect/Toxicity: Disopyramide may increase the effects/toxicity of anticholinergics, beta-blockers, flecainide, procainamide, quinidine, or propafenone. Digoxin and quinidine serum concentrations may be increased by disopyramide. Erythromycin and clarithromycin may increase disopyramide serum concentrations, increasing toxicity (widening QT interval).

Disopyramide effect/toxicity may be additive with drugs which may prolong the QT interval - amiodarone, amitriptyline, astemizole, bepridil, cisapride (use is contraindicated), disopyramide, erythromycin, haloperidol, imipramine, pimozide, quinidine, sotalol, and thioridazine. In addition concurrent use with sparfloxacin, gatifloxacin, and moxifloxacin may result in additional prolongation of the QT interval; concurrent use is contraindicated.
Decreased Effect: Hepatic microsomal enzyme inducing agents (eg, phenytoin, phenobarbital, rifampin) may increase metabolism of disopyramide leading to a decreased effect.

Anticoagulants may have decreased prothrombin times after discontinuation of disopyramide.

Mechanism of Action Class Ia antiarrhythmic: Decreases myocardial excitability and conduction velocity; reduces disparity in refractory between normal and infarcted myocardium; possesses anticholinergic, peripheral vasoconstrictive, and negative inotropic effects

Pharmacodynamics/Kinetics
Onset of action: 0.5-3.5 hours
Duration: 1.5-8.5 hours
Absorption: 60% to 83%
Protein binding (concentration dependent): 20% to 60%
Metabolism: Hepatic to inactive metabolites
Half-life elimination: Adults: 4-10 hours; prolonged with hepatic or renal impairment
Excretion: Urine (40% to 60% as unchanged drug); feces (10% to 15%)

Dosage Oral:
Children:
<1 year: 10-30 mg/kg/24 hours in 4 divided doses
1-4 years: 10-20 mg/kg/24 hours in 4 divided doses
4-12 years: 10-15 mg/kg/24 hours in 4 divided doses
12-18 years: 6-15 mg/kg/24 hours in 4 divided doses
Adults:
<50 kg: 100 mg every 6 hours or 200 mg every 12 hours (controlled release)
>50 kg: 150 mg every 6 hours or 300 mg every 12 hours (controlled release); if no response, increase to 200 mg every 6 hours. Maximum dose required for patients with severe refractory ventricular tachycardia is 400 mg every 6 hours.
Elderly: Dose with caution, starting at the lower end of dosing range
Dosing adjustment in renal impairment: 100 mg (nonsustained release) given at the following intervals, based on creatinine clearance (mL/minute):
Cl_{cr} 30-40 mL/minute: Administer every 8 hours
Cl_{cr} 15-30 mL/minute: Administer every 12 hours
Cl_{cr} <15 mL/minute: Administer every 24 hours
or alter the dose as follows:
Cl_{cr} 30-<40 mL/minute: Reduce dose 50%
Cl_{cr} 15-30 mL/minute: Reduce dose 75%
Dialysis: Not dialyzable (0% to 5%) by hemo- or peritoneal methods; supplemental dose is not necessary.
Dosing interval in hepatic impairment: 100 mg every 6 hours or 200 mg every 12 hours (controlled release)

Administration Administer around-the-clock rather than 4 times/day (ie, 12-6-12-6, not 9-1-5-9) to promote less variation in peak and trough serum levels

Monitoring Parameters ECG, blood pressure, urinary retention, CNS anticholinergic effects (confusion, agitation, hallucinations, etc)

Reference Range
Therapeutic concentration:
Atrial arrhythmias: 2.8-3.2 μg/mL
Ventricular arrhythmias 3.3-7.5 μg/mL
Toxic concentration: >7 μg/mL

Patient Information Notify prescriber of urinary retention or worsening CHF; do not break or chew sustained release capsules

Dosage Forms CAP (Norpace®): 100 mg, 150 mg. **CAP, controlled release** (Norpace® CR): 100 mg, 150 mg

♦ **Disopyramide Phosphate** *see* Disopyramide *on page 392*

♦ **DisperMox**™ *see* Amoxicillin *on page 86*

Disulfiram (dye SUL fi ram)

U.S. Brand Names Antabuse®
Therapeutic Category Aldehyde Dehydrogenase Inhibitor Agent; Antialcoholic Agent
Use Management of chronic alcoholism
Pregnancy Risk Factor C
Contraindications Hypersensitivity to disulfiram and related compounds or any component of the formulation; patients receiving or using ethanol, metronidazole, paraldehyde, or ethanol-containing preparations like cough syrup or tonics; psychosis; severe myocardial disease and coronary occlusion

Warnings/Precautions Use with caution in patients with diabetes, hypothyroidism, seizure disorders, nephritis (acute or chronic); hepatic cirrhosis or insufficiency; should never be administered to a patient when he/she is in a state of alcohol intoxication, or without his/her knowledge. Patient must receive appropriate counseling, including information on "disguised" forms of alcohol (tonics, mouthwashes, etc) and the duration of the drug's activity (up to 14 days). Severe (sometimes fatal) hepatitis and/or hepatic failure have been associated with disulfiram. May occur in patients with or without prior history of abnormal hepatic function.

Common Adverse Reactions Frequency not defined.
Central nervous system: Drowsiness, headache, fatigue, psychosis
Dermatologic: Rash, acneiform eruptions, allergic dermatitis
Gastrointestinal: Metallic or garlic-like aftertaste
Genitourinary: Impotence
Hepatic: Hepatitis (cholestatic and fulminant), hepatic failure (multiple case reports)
Neuromuscular & skeletal: Peripheral neuritis, polyneuritis, peripheral neuropathy
(Continued)

Disulfiram *(Continued)*

Ocular: Optic neuritis

Drug Interactions

Cytochrome P450 Effect: Substrate (minor) of CYP1A2, 2A6, 2B6, 2D6, 2E1, 3A4; **Inhibits** CYP1A2 (weak), 2A6 (weak), 2B6 (weak), 2C8/9 (weak), 2D6 (weak), 2E1 (strong), 3A4 (weak)

Increased Effect/Toxicity: Disulfiram may increase serum concentrations of benzodiazepines that undergo oxidative metabolism (all but oxazepam, lorazepam, temazepam). Disulfiram increases phenytoin and theophylline serum concentrations; toxicity may occur. Disulfiram inhibits the metabolism of warfarin resulting in an increased hypoprothrombinemic response. Disulfiram results in severe ethanol intolerance (disulfiram reaction) secondary to disulfiram's ability to inhibit aldehyde dehydrogenase; this combination should be avoided. Combined use with isoniazid, metronidazole, or MAO inhibitors may result in adverse CNS effects; this combination should be avoided. Some pharmaceutic dosage forms include ethanol, including elixirs and intravenous trimethoprim-sulfamethoxazole (contains 10% ethanol as a solubilizing agent); these may inadvertently provoke a disulfiram reaction.

Mechanism of Action Disulfiram is a thiuram derivative which interferes with aldehyde dehydrogenase. When taken concomitantly with alcohol, there is an increase in serum acetaldehyde levels. High acetaldehyde causes uncomfortable symptoms including flushing, nausea, thirst, palpitations, chest pain, vertigo, and hypotension. This reaction is the basis for disulfiram use in postwithdrawal long-term care of alcoholism.

Pharmacodynamics/Kinetics

Onset of action: Full effect: 12 hours

Duration: ~1-2 weeks after last dose

Absorption: Rapid

Metabolism: To diethylthiocarbamate

Excretion: Feces and exhaled gases (as metabolites)

Dosage Adults: Oral: Do not administer until the patient has abstained from ethanol for at least 12 hours

Initial: 500 mg/day as a single dose for 1-2 weeks; maximum daily dose is 500 mg

Average maintenance dose: 250 mg/day; range: 125-500 mg; duration of therapy is to continue until the patient is fully recovered socially and a basis for permanent self control has been established; maintenance therapy may be required for months or even years

Monitoring Parameters Hypokalemia; liver function tests at baseline and after 10-14 days of treatment; CBC, serum chemistries, liver function tests should be monitored during therapy

Patient Information Notify prescriber of any respiratory difficulty, weakness, nausea, vomiting, decreased appetite, yellowing of skin or eyes, or dark-colored urine. Avoid alcohol, including products containing ethanol (cough and cold syrups), or use ethanol-containing skin products for at least 3 days and preferably 14 days after stopping this medication or while taking this medication; not for treatment of alcohol intoxication; may cause drowsiness; tablets can be crushed or mixed with water

Dosage Forms TAB: 250 mg

DOBUTamine *(doe BYOO ta meen)*

Related Information

Hemodynamic Support, Intravenous *on page 1377*

U.S. Brand Names Dobutrex®

Synonyms Dobutamine Hydrochloride

Therapeutic Category Adrenergic Agonist Agent; Sympathomimetic Agent

Use Short-term management of patients with cardiac decompensation

Unlabeled/Investigational Use Positive inotropic agent for use in myocardial dysfunction of sepsis

Pregnancy Risk Factor B

Contraindications Hypersensitivity to dobutamine or sulfites (some contain sodium metabisulfate), or any component of the formulation; idiopathic hypertrophic subaortic stenosis (IHSS)

Warnings/Precautions May increase heart rate. Patients with atrial fibrillation may experience an increase in ventricular response. An increase in blood pressure is more common, but occasionally a patient may become hypotensive. May exacerbate ventricular ectopy. If needed, correct hypovolemia first to optimize hemodynamics. Ineffective in the presence of mechanical obstruction such as severe aortic stenosis. Use caution post-MI (can increase myocardial oxygen demand). Use cautiously in the elderly starting at lower end of the dosage range.

Common Adverse Reactions Incidence of adverse events is not always reported.

Cardiovascular: Increased heart rate, increased blood pressure, increased ventricular ectopic activity, hypotension, premature ventricular beats (5%, dose-related), anginal pain (1% to 3%), nonspecific chest pain (1% to 3%), palpitations (1% to 3%)

Central nervous system: Fever (1% to 3%), headache (1% to 3%), paresthesia

Endocrine & metabolic: Slight decrease in serum potassium

Gastrointestinal: Nausea (1% to 3%)

Hematologic: Thrombocytopenia (isolated cases)

Local: Phlebitis, local inflammatory changes and pain from infiltration, cutaneous necrosis (isolated cases)

Neuromuscular & skeletal: Mild leg cramps

Respiratory: Dyspnea (1% to 3%)

Drug Interactions

Increased Effect/Toxicity: General anesthetics (eg, halothane or cyclopropane) and usual doses of dobutamine have resulted in ventricular arrhythmias in animals. Bretylium and may potentiate dobutamine's effects. Beta-blockers (nonselective ones) may increase hypertensive effect; avoid concurrent use. Cocaine may cause malignant arrhythmias. Guanethidine, MAO inhibitors, methyldopa, reserpine, and tricyclic antidepressants can increase the pressor response to sympathomimetics.

Decreased Effect: Beta-adrenergic blockers may decrease effect of dobutamine and increase risk of severe hypotension.

Mechanism of Action Stimulates beta$_1$-adrenergic receptors, causing increased contractility and heart rate, with little effect on beta$_2$- or alpha-receptors

Pharmacodynamics/Kinetics

Onset of action: I.V.: 1-10 minutes

Peak effect: 10-20 minutes

Metabolism: In tissues and hepatically to inactive metabolites

Half-life elimination: 2 minutes

Excretion: Urine (as metabolites)

Dosage Administration requires the use of an infusion pump; I.V. infusion:

Neonates: 2-15 mcg/kg/minute, titrate to desired response

Children and Adults: 2.5-20 mcg/kg/minute; maximum: 40 mcg/kg/minute, titrate to desired response. See table.

Infusion Rates of Various Dilutions of Dobutamine

Desired Delivery Rate (mcg/kg/min)	Infusion Rate (mL/kg/min)	
	500 mcg/mL[1]	1000 mcg/mL[2]
2.5	0.005	0.0025
5.0	0.01	0.005
7.5	0.015	0.0075
10.0	0.02	0.01
12.5	0.025	0.0125
15.0	0.03	0.015

[1]500 mg per liter or 250 mg per 500 mL of diluent.

[2]1000 mg per liter or 250 mg per 250 mL of diluent.

Administration Use infusion device to control rate of flow; administer into large vein. Do not administer through same I.V. line as heparin, hydrocortisone sodium succinate, cefazolin, or penicillin.

To prepare for infusion:

$$\frac{6 \times weight\ (kg) \times desired\ dose\ (mcg/kg/min)}{I.V.\ infusion\ rate\ (mL/h)} = \begin{array}{l} mg\ of\ drug\ to\ be\ added\ to \\ 100\ mL\ of\ I.V.\ fluid \end{array}$$

Extravasation management: Phentolamine: Mix 5 mg with 9 mL of NS; inject a small amount of this dilution into extravasated area. Blanching should reverse immediately. Monitor site. If blanching should recur, additional injections of phentolamine may be needed.

Monitoring Parameters Blood pressure, ECG, heart rate, CVP, RAP, MAP, urine output; if pulmonary artery catheter is in place, monitor CI, PCWP, and SVR; also monitor serum potassium

Dosage Forms INF [premixed in dextrose]: 1 mg/mL (250 mL, 500 mL); 2 mg/mL (250 mL); 4 mg/mL (250 mL). INJ, solution: 12.5 mg/mL (20 mL, 40 mL, 100 mL)

♦ **Dobutamine Hydrochloride** *see* DOBUTamine *on page 394*

♦ **Dobutrex®** *see* DOBUTamine *on page 394*

Docetaxel (doe se TAKS el)

U.S. Brand Names Taxotere®

Synonyms NSC-628503; RP-6976

Therapeutic Category Antineoplastic Agent, Antimicrotubular; Antineoplastic Agent, Natural Source (Plant) Derivative

Use Treatment of locally-advanced or metastatic breast cancer, after failure of prior chemotherapy; treatment of locally-advanced or metastatic nonsmall cell lung cancer (NSCLC) after failure of prior platinum-based chemotherapy; in combination with cisplatin in treatment of patients who have not previously received chemotherapy for unresected NSCLC

Unlabeled/Investigational Use Investigational: Treatment of gastric, pancreatic, head and neck, and ovarian cancers, soft tissue sarcoma, and melanoma

Pregnancy Risk Factor D

Contraindications Hypersensitivity to docetaxel, Polysorbate 80®, or any component of the formulation; pre-existing bone marrow suppression (neutrophils <1500 cells/mm^3); pregnancy

Warnings/Precautions Use caution in hepatic disease; avoid use in patients with AST/ALT >1.5 times ULN in conjunction in conjunction with alkaline phosphatase >2.5 ULN. Early studies reported severe hypersensitivity reactions characterized by hypotension, bronchospasms, or minor reactions characterized by generalized rash/erythema. The overall incidence was 25% in patients who did not receive premedication. Incidence reduced to 2.2% in patients who receive premedication. Patients should be premedicated with a steroid to prevent hypersensitivity reactions and fluid retention. A common regimen is dexamethasone 4-8 mg orally twice daily for 3-5 days, starting the day before docetaxel administration.

Fluid retention syndrome characterized by pleural effusions, ascites, edema, and weight gain (2-15 kg) has also been reported. It has not been associated with cardiac, pulmonary, renal, hepatic, or endocrine dysfunction. The incidence and severity of the syndrome increase sharply at cumulative doses ≥400 mg/m^2.

Neutropenia was the dose-limiting toxicity; however, this rarely resulted in treatment delays and prophylactic colony stimulating factors have not been routinely used. Patients with increased liver function tests experienced more episodes of neutropenia with a greater number of severe infections. Patients with an absolute neutrophil count <1500 cells/mm^3 should not receive docetaxel.

Docetaxel preparation should be performed in a Class II laminar flow biologic safety cabinet. Personnel should be wearing surgical gloves and a closed front surgical gown with knit cuffs. Appropriate safety equipment is recommended for preparation, administration, and disposal of antineoplastics. If docetaxel contacts the skin, wash and flush thoroughly with water.

When administered as sequential infusions, taxane derivatives (docetaxel, paclitaxel) should be administered before platinum derivatives (carboplatin, cisplatin) to limit myelosuppression and to enhance efficacy.

Common Adverse Reactions Note: Frequencies cited for nonsmall cell lung cancer and breast cancer treatment. Exact frequency may vary based on tumor type, prior treatment, premedication, and dosage of docetaxel.

>10%:

Cardiovascular: Fluid retention, including peripheral edema, pleural effusions, and ascites (33% to 47%); may be more common at cumulative doses ≥400 mg/m^2. Up to 64% in breast cancer patients with dexamethasone premedication.

Dermatologic: Alopecia (56% to 76%); nail disorder (11% to 31%, banding, onycholysis, hypo- or hyperpigmentation)

Gastrointestinal: Mucositis/stomatitis (26% to 42%, severe in 6% to 7%), may be dose-limiting (premedication may reduce frequency and severity); nausea and vomiting (40% to 80%, severe in 1% to 5%); diarrhea (33% to 43%)

Hematologic: Myelosuppression, neutropenia (75% to 85%), thrombocytopenia, anemia
  Onset: 4-7 days
  Nadir: 5-9 days
  Recovery: 21 days

Hepatic: Transaminase levels increased (18%)

Neuromuscular & skeletal: Myalgia (3% to 21%); neurosensory changes (paresthesia, dysesthesia, pain) noted in 23% to 49% (severe in up to 6%). Motor neuropathy (including weakness) noted in as many as 16% of lung cancer patients (severe in up to 5%). Neuropathy may be more common at higher cumulative docetaxel dosages or with prior cisplatin therapy.

Miscellaneous: Hypersensitivity reactions (6% to 13%); angioedema, rash, flushing, fever, hypotension); frequency substantially reduced by premedication with dexamethasone starting one day prior to docetaxel administration.

1% to 10%:

Cardiovascular: Hypotension (3%)

Dermatologic: Rash and skin eruptions (6%)

Gastrointestinal: Taste perversion (6%)

Hepatic: Bilirubin increased (9%)

Neuromuscular & skeletal: Arthralgia (3% to 9%)

Miscellaneous: Infusion site reactions (up to 4%)

Drug Interactions

Cytochrome P450 Effect: Substrate of CYP3A4 (major); **Inhibits** CYP3A4 (weak)

Increased Effect/Toxicity: Increased toxicity with cytochrome P450 substrate agents. Possibility of an inhibition of metabolism of docetaxel in patients treated with ketoconazole, erythromycin, astemizole, or cyclosporine. When administered as sequential infusions, observational studies indicate a potential for increased toxicity when platinum derivatives (carboplatin, cisplatin) are administered before taxane derivatives (docetaxel, paclitaxel).

Mechanism of Action Docetaxel promotes the assembly of microtubules from tubulin dimers, and inhibits the depolymerization of tubulin which stabilizes microtubules in the cell. This results in inhibition of DNA, RNA, and protein synthesis. Most activity occurs during the M phase of the cell cycle.

Pharmacodynamics/Kinetics Exhibits linear pharmacokinetics at the recommended dosage range

Distribution: Extensive extravascular distribution and/or tissue binding; V_d: 80-90 L/m², V_{dss}: 113 L (mean steady state)

Protein binding: 94%, primarily to alpha$_1$-acid glycoprotein, albumin, and lipoproteins

Metabolism: Hepatic; oxidation via CYP3A4 to metabolites

Half-life elimination: Alpha, beta, gamma: 4 minutes, 36 minutes, and 10-18 hours, respectively

Excretion: Feces (75%); urine (6%); ~80% within 48 hours

Clearance: Total body: Mean: 21 L/hour/m²

Dosage Adults: I.V. infusion: Refer to individual protocols:

Breast cancer (locally-advanced or metastatic): 60-100 mg/m² over 1 hour every 3 weeks; patients initially started at 60 mg/m² who do not develop toxicity may tolerate higher doses

Nonsmall-cell lung cancer: I.V.: 75 mg/m² over 1 hour every 3 weeks

Dosing adjustment for toxicity:

Note: Toxicity includes febrile neutropenia, neutrophils ≤500/mm³ for >1 week, severe or cumulative cutaneous reactions; in nonsmall cell lung cancer, this may also include other grade 3/4 nonhematologic toxicities.

Breast cancer: Patients dosed initially at 100 mg/m²; reduce dose to 75 mg/m²; **Note:** If the patient continues to experience these adverse reactions, the dosage should be reduced to 55 mg/m² or therapy should be discontinued

Nonsmall cell lung cancer:

Monotherapy: Patients dosed initially at 75 mg/m² should have dose held until toxicity is resolved, then resume at 55 mg/m²; discontinue patients who develop ≥ grade 3 peripheral neuropathy.

Combination therapy: Patients dosed initially at 75 mg/m², in combination with cisplatin, should have the docetaxel dosage reduced to 65 mg/m² in subsequent cycles; if further adjustment is required, dosage may be reduced to 50 mg/m²

Dosing adjustment in hepatic impairment: Total bilirubin ≥ the upper limit of normal (ULN), or AST/ALT >1.5 times ULN concomitant with alkaline phosphatase >2.5 times ULN: Docetaxel **should not be administered**.

Administration

Anaphylactoid-like reactions have been reported: Premedication with dexamethasone (4-8 mg orally twice daily for 3 or 5 days starting 1 day prior to administration of docetaxel).

Prevention of fluid retention (eg, pleural effusion, ascites, peripheral edema): Patients receiving docetaxel should be treated with a steroid (eg, dexamethasone 8-10 mg orally twice daily) for 3-5 days, beginning the day before docetaxel administration.

Administer I.V. infusion over 1-hour through nonsorbing (nonpolyvinylchloride) tubing; in-line filter is not necessary. When administered as sequential infusions, taxane derivatives should be administered before platinum derivatives (cisplatin, carboplatin) to limit myelosuppression and to enhance efficacy.

Monitoring Parameters Monitor for hypersensitivity reactions and fluid retention

Patient Information This medication can only be administered intravenously. You may experience nausea or vomiting (frequent small meals, frequent mouth care, sucking lozenges, or chewing gum may help); you may experience loss of hair (reversible); you will be more susceptible to infection (avoid crowds and exposure to infection as much as possible). Yogurt or buttermilk may help reduce diarrhea (if unresolved, contact prescriber for medication relief). Report swelling of extremities, difficulty breathing, unusual weight gain, abdominal distention, fever, chills, unusual bruising or bleeding, signs of infection, excessive fatigue, or unresolved diarrhea. Contraceptive measures are recommended during therapy.

Dosage Forms INJ, solution [concentrate]: 20 mg/0.5 mL (0.5 mL, 2 mL)

Docosanol (doe KOE san ole)

U.S. Brand Names Abreva® [OTC]

Synonyms Behenyl Alcohol; n-Docosanol

Therapeutic Category Antiviral Agent; Antiviral Agent, Topical

Use Treatment of herpes simplex of the face or lips

Contraindications Hypersensitivity to docosanol or any component of the formulation

Warnings/Precautions For external use only. Do not apply to inside of mouth or around eyes. Not for use in children <12 years of age.

Common Adverse Reactions Limited information; headache reported (frequency similar to placebo)

Mechanism of Action Prevents viral entry and replication at the cellular level

Dosage Children ≥12 years and Adults: Topical: Apply 5 times/day to affected area of face or lips. Start at first sign of cold sore or fever blister and continue until healed.

Patient Information Wash hands before and after applying cream. Begin treatment at first tingle of cold sore or fever blister. Rub into area gently, but completely. Do not apply directly to inside of mouth or around eyes. Contact prescriber if sore gets worse or does not heal within 10 days. Do not share this product with others, may spread infection.

Dosage Forms CRM: 10% (2 g)

Docusate (DOK yoo sate)
Related Information
Laxatives, Classification and Properties *on page 1380*
U.S. Brand Names Colace® [OTC]; Diocto® [OTC]; Docusoft-S™ [OTC]; DOS® [OTC]; D-S-S® [OTC]; ex-lax® Stool Softener [OTC]; Fleet® Sof-Lax® [OTC]; Genasoft® [OTC]; Phillips'® Stool Softener Laxative [OTC]; Surfak® [OTC]
Synonyms Dioctyl Calcium Sulfosuccinate; Dioctyl Sodium Sulfosuccinate; Docusate Calcium; Docusate Potassium; Docusate Sodium; DOSS; DSS
Therapeutic Category Laxative, Surfactant; Stool Softener
Use Stool softener in patients who should avoid straining during defecation and constipation associated with hard, dry stools; prophylaxis for straining (Valsalva) following myocardial infarction. A safe agent to be used in elderly; some evidence that doses <200 mg are ineffective; stool softeners are unnecessary if stool is well hydrated or "mushy" and soft; shown to be ineffective used long-term.
Unlabeled/Investigational Use Ceruminolytic
Pregnancy Risk Factor C
Dosage Docusate salts are interchangeable; the amount of sodium or calcium per dosage unit is clinically insignificant

Infants and Children <3 years: Oral: 10-40 mg/day in 1-4 divided doses
Children: Oral:
3-6 years: 20-60 mg/day in 1-4 divided doses
6-12 years: 40-150 mg/day in 1-4 divided doses
Adolescents and Adults: Oral: 50-500 mg/day in 1-4 divided doses
Older Children and Adults: Rectal: Add 50-100 mg of docusate liquid to enema fluid (saline or water); administer as retention or flushing enema

Ceruminolytic (unlabeled use): Intra-aural: Administer 1 mL of docusate sodium in 2 mL syringes; if no clearance in 15 minutes, irrigate with 50-100 mL normal saline (this method is 80% effective)
Dosage Forms CAP, as calcium (Surfak®): 240 mg. **CAP, as sodium:** 100 mg, 250 mg; (Colace®): 50 mg, 100 mg; (Docusoft-S™, Fleet® Sof-Lax®,Genasoft®, Phillips'® Stool Softener Laxative): 100 mg; (DOS®, D-S-S®): 100 mg, 250 mg. **LIQ, as sodium:** 150 mg/15 mL (480 mL); (Colace®): 150 mg/15 mL (30 mL); (Diocto®): 150 mg/15 mL (480 mL). **SYR, as sodium:** 50 mg/15 mL (30 mL); 60 mg/15 mL (480 mL); (Colace®, Diocto®): 60 mg/15 mL (480 mL). **TAB, as sodium** (ex-lax® Stool Softener): 100 mg

Docusate and Senna (DOK yoo sate & SEN na)
Related Information
Laxatives, Classification and Properties *on page 1380*
U.S. Brand Names Peri-Colace® *(reformulation)* [OTC]; Senokot-S® [OTC]
Synonyms Senna and Docusate; Senna-S
Therapeutic Category Laxative, Stimulant; Stool Softener
Use Short-term treatment of constipation
Unlabeled/Investigational Use Evacuate the colon for bowel or rectal examinations; management/prevention of opiate-induced constipation
Dosage Oral: Constipation: OTC ranges:
Children:
2-6 years: Initial: 4.3 mg sennosides plus 25 mg docusate (1/2 tablet) once daily (maximum: 1 tablet twice daily)
6-12 years: Initial: 8.6 sennosides plus 50 mg docusate (1 tablet) once daily (maximum: 2 tablets twice daily)
Children ≥12 years and Adults: Initial: 2 tablets (17.2 mg sennosides plus 100 mg docusate) once daily (maximum: 4 tablets twice daily)
Elderly: Consider half the initial dose in older, debilitated patients
Dosage Forms TAB: Docusate 50 mg and sennosides 8.6 mg

- **Docusate Calcium** *see Docusate on page 398*
- **Docusate Potassium** *see Docusate on page 398*
- **Docusate Sodium** *see Docusate on page 398*
- **Docusoft-S™ [OTC]** *see Docusate on page 398*

Dofetilide (doe FET il ide)
U.S. Brand Names Tikosyn™
Therapeutic Category Antiarrhythmic Agent, Class III
Use Maintenance of normal sinus rhythm in patients with chronic atrial fibrillation/atrial flutter of longer than 1-week duration who have been converted to normal sinus rhythm; conversion of atrial fibrillation and atrial flutter to normal sinus rhythm
Pregnancy Risk Factor C
Contraindications Hypersensitivity to dofetilide or any component of the formulation; patients with paroxysmal atrial fibrillation; patients with congenital or acquired long QT syndromes, do not use if a baseline QT interval or QT_c is >440 msec (500 msec in patients with ventricular

conduction abnormalities); severe renal impairment (estimated Cl_{cr} <20 mL/minute); concurrent use with verapamil, cimetidine, trimethoprim (alone or in combination with sulfamethoxazole), ketoconazole, prochlorperazine, or megestrol; baseline heart rate <50 beats/minute; other drugs that prolong QT intervals (phenothiazines, cisapride, bepridil, tricyclic antidepressants, certain oral macrolides: sparfloxacin, gatifloxacin, moxifloxacin); hypokalemia or hypomagnesemia; concurrent amiodarone

Warnings/Precautions Note: Must be initiated (or reinitiated) in a setting with continuous monitoring and staff familiar with the recognition and treatment of life-threatening arrhythmias. Patients must be monitored with continuous ECG for a minimum of 3 days, or for a minimum of 12 hours after electrical or pharmacological cardioversion to normal sinus rhythm, whichever is greater. Patients should be readmitted for continuous monitoring if dosage is later increased.

Reserve for patients who are highly symptomatic with atrial fibrillation/atrial flutter; torsade de pointes significantly increases with doses >500 mcg twice daily; hold Class Ia or Class II antiarrhythmics for at least three half-lives prior to starting dofetilide; use in patients on amiodarone therapy only if serum amiodarone level is <0.3 mg/L or if amiodarone was stopped for >3 months previously; correct hypokalemia or hypomagnesemia before initiating dofetilide and maintain within normal limits during treatment.

Patients with sick sinus syndrome or with second or third-degree heart block should not receive dofetilide unless a functional pacemaker is in place. Defibrillation threshold is reduced in patients with ventricular tachycardia or ventricular fibrillation undergoing implantation of a cardioverter-defibrillator device. Safety and efficacy in children (<18 years old) have not been established. Use with caution in renal impairment; not recommended in patients receiving drugs which may compete for renal secretion via cationic transport. Use with caution in patients with severe hepatic impairment.

Common Adverse Reactions
Supraventricular arrhythmia patients (incidence > placebo)
>10%: Central nervous system: Headache (11%)

2% to 10%:
Central nervous system: Dizziness (8%), insomnia (4%)
Cardiovascular: Ventricular tachycardia (2.6% to 3.7%), chest pain (10%), torsade de pointes (3.3% in CHF patients and 0.9% in patients with a recent MI; up to 10.5% in patients receiving doses in excess of those recommended). Torsade de pointes occurs most frequently within the first 3 days of therapy.
Dermatologic: Rash (3%)
Gastrointestinal: Nausea (5%), diarrhea (3%), abdominal pain (3%)
Neuromuscular & skeletal: Back pain (3%)
Respiratory: Dyspnea (6%), respiratory tract infection (7%)
Miscellaneous: Flu syndrome (4%)

<2%:
Central nervous system: CVA, facial paralysis, flaccid paralysis, migraine, paralysis
Cardiovascular: AV block (0.4% to 1.5%), ventricular fibrillation (0% to 0.4%), bundle branch block, heart block, edema, heart arrest, myocardial infarct, sudden death, syncope
Dermatologic: Angioedema
Gastrointestinal: Liver damage
Neuromuscular & skeletal: Paresthesia
Respiratory: Cough

>2% (incidence ≤ placebo): Anxiety, pain, angina, atrial fibrillation, hypertension, palpitation, supraventricular tachycardia, peripheral edema, urinary tract infection, weakness, arthralgia, diaphoresis

Drug Interactions
Cytochrome P450 Effect: Substrate of CYP3A4 (minor)
Increased Effect/Toxicity: Dofetilide concentrations are increased by cimetidine, verapamil, ketoconazole, and trimethoprim (concurrent use of these agents is contraindicated). Dofetilide levels may also be increased by renal cationic transport inhibitors (including triamterene, metformin, amiloride, and megestrol) or inhibitors of cytochrome P450 isoenzyme 3A4 (including amiodarone, azole antifungal agents, clarithromycin, cannabinoids, diltiazem, erythromycin, nefazodone, norfloxacin, protease inhibitors, quinidine, serotonin reuptake inhibitors. verapamil, and zafirlukast). Diuretics and other drugs which may deplete potassium and/or magnesium (aminoglycoside antibiotics, amphotericin, cyclosporine) may increase dofetilide's toxicity (torsade de pointes).
Mechanism of Action Vaughan Williams Class III antiarrhythmic activity. Blockade of the cardiac ion channel carrying the rapid component of the delayed rectifier potassium current. Dofetilide has no effect on sodium channels, adrenergic alpha-receptors, or adrenergic beta-receptors. It increases the monophasic action potential duration due to delayed repolarization. The increase in the QT interval is a function of prolongation of both effective and functional refractory periods in the His-Purkinje system and the ventricles. Changes in cardiac conduction velocity and sinus node function have not been observed in patients with or without structural heart disease. PR and QRS width remain the same in patients with pre-existing heart block or sick sinus syndrome.

Pharmacodynamics/Kinetics
Absorption: >90%
Distribution: V_d: 3 L/kg
Protein binding: 60% to 70%
Metabolism: Hepatic via CYP3A4, but low affinity for it; metabolites formed by N-dealkylation and N-oxidation
Bioavailability: >90%
(Continued)

Dofetilide (Continued)

Half-life elimination: 10 hours
Time to peak: Fasting: 2-3 hours
Excretion: Urine (80%, 80% as unchanged drug, 20% as inactive or minimally active metabolites); renal elimination consists of glomerular filtration and active tubular secretion via cationic transport system

Dosage Adults: Oral:

Note: QT or QT_c must be determined prior to first dose. If QT_c >440 msec (>500 msec in patients with ventricular conduction abnormalities), dofetilide is contraindicated (see Contraindications and Warnings/Precautions).

Initial: 500 mcg orally twice daily. Initial dosage must be adjusted in patients with estimated Cl_{cr} <60 mL/minute (see Dosage Adjustment in Renal Impairment). Dofetilide may be initiated at lower doses than recommended based on physician discretion.

Modification of dosage in response to initial dose:
QT_c interval should be measured 2-3 hours after the initial dose. If the QT_c >15% of baseline, or if the QT_c is >500 msec (550 msec in patients with ventricular conduction abnormalities) dofetilide should be adjusted. If the starting dose is 500 mcg twice daily, then adjust to 250 mcg twice daily. If the starting dose was 250 mcg twice daily, then adjust to 125 mcg twice daily. If the starting dose was 125 mcg twice daily then adjust to 125 mcg every day.

Continued monitoring for doses 2-5:
QT_c interval must be determined 2-3 hours after each subsequent dose of dofetilide for in-hospital doses 2-5. If the measured QT_c is >500 msec (550 msec in patients with ventricular conduction abnormalities) at any time, dofetilide should be discontinued.

Chronic therapy (following the 5th dose):
QT or QT_c and creatinine clearance should be evaluated every 3 months. If QT_c >500 msec (>550 msec in patients with ventricular conduction abnormalities), dofetilide should be discontinued.

Dosage adjustment in renal impairment:
Cl_{cr} >60 mL/minute: Administer 500 mcg twice daily.
Cl_{cr} 40-60 mL/minute: Administer 250 mcg twice daily.
Cl_{cr} 20-39 mL/minute: Administer 125 mcg twice daily.
Cl_{cr} <20 mL/minute: Contraindicated in this group.

Dosage adjustment in hepatic impairment: No dosage adjustments required in Child-Pugh Class A and B. Patients with severe hepatic impairment were not studied.

Elderly: No specific dosage adjustments are recommended based on age, however, careful assessment of renal function is particularly important in this population.

Monitoring Parameters ECG monitoring with attention to QT_c and occurrence of ventricular arrhythmias, baseline serum creatinine and changes in serum creatinine. Check serum potassium and magnesium levels if on medications where these electrolyte disturbances can occur, or if patient has a history of hypokalemia or hypomagnesemia. QT or QT_c must be monitored at specific times prior to the first dose and during the first 3 days of therapy. Thereafter, QT or QT_c and creatinine clearance must be evaluated at 3-month intervals.

Patient Information Take with or without food; take exactly the way it was prescribed; do not stop this medicine without talking with your prescriber; never take an extra dose; if you miss a dose just take your normal amount at the next scheduled time. If you take more medicine than you should call your prescriber now. If you cannot reach your prescriber, go to the nearest emergency room (take your medicine with you). Tell your prescriber about any new medicines before taking them; not all medicines mix well with this one. Call your prescriber now if you faint, become dizzy, have fast heartbeats, severe diarrhea, unusual sweating, vomiting, no appetite, or more thirst than normal. You may feel tired, weak, or have numbness, tingling, muscle cramps, constipation, vomiting, or rapid heartbeats if you have a low potassium level.

Dosage Forms CAP: 125 mcg, 250 mcg, 500 mcg

Dolasetron (dol A se tron)

U.S. Brand Names Anzemet®
Synonyms Dolasetron Mesylate; MDL 73,147EF
Therapeutic Category Antiemetic, Serotonin Antagonist; 5-HT₃ Receptor Antagonist; Serotonin 5-HT₃ Receptor Antagonist
Use Prevention of nausea and vomiting associated with emetogenic cancer chemotherapy, including initial and repeat courses; prevention of postoperative nausea and vomiting and treatment of postoperative nausea and vomiting (injectable form only)

Generally **not** recommended for treatment of existing chemotherapy-induced emesis (CIE) or for prophylaxis of nausea from agents with a low emetogenic potential.

Pregnancy Risk Factor B
Contraindications Hypersensitivity to dolasetron or any component of the formulation
Warnings/Precautions Dolasetron should be administered with caution in patients who have or may develop prolongation of cardiac conduction intervals, particularly QT_c intervals. These include patients with hypokalemia or hypomagnesemia, patients taking diuretics with potential for inducing electrolyte abnormalities, patients with congenital QT syndrome, patients taking antiarrhythmic drugs or other drugs which lead to QT prolongation, and cumulative high-dose anthracycline therapy.

Common Adverse Reactions
>10%:
Central nervous system: Headache (31%), dizziness, lightheadedness (23%)

Gastrointestinal: Loose stools/diarrhea (50%); increased appetite (27%); taste alterations (12%)

1% to 10%:

Cardiovascular: Hypertension, hypotension (6%), ECG abnormalities, prolonged P-R, QRS, and QT_c intervals

Central nervous system: Sedation (8%), slow movement (3%), nervousness (3%), fatigue (2%), listlessness, grogginess

Gastrointestinal: Nausea (6%), constipation (3%), diarrhea, abdominal pain, flatulence

Hepatic: Mild elevations of serum aminotransferases (7%)

Local: Pain at injection site (1%)

Neuromuscular & skeletal: Paresthesia

Ocular: Visual disturbances (mostly blurred vision) (9%); photosensitivity (2%)

Drug Interactions

Cytochrome P450 Effect: Substrate (minor) of CYP2C8/9, 3A4; **Inhibits** CYP2D6 (weak)

Increased Effect/Toxicity: Increased blood levels of active metabolite may occur during concurrent administration of cimetidine and atenolol. Inhibitors of this isoenzyme may increase blood levels of active metabolite. Due to the potential to potentiate QT_c prolongation, drugs which may prolong QT interval directly (eg, antiarrhythmics) or by causing alterations in electrolytes (eg, diuretics) should be used with caution.

Decreased Effect: Blood levels of active metabolite are decreased during coadministration of rifampin.

Mechanism of Action Selective serotonin receptor (5-HT$_3$) antagonist, blocking serotonin both peripherally (primary site of action) and centrally at the chemoreceptor trigger zone

Pharmacodynamics/Kinetics

Metabolism: Hepatic to a reduced alcohol (active metabolite MDL 74,156)

Half-life elimination: Dolasetron: 10 minutes; MDL 74,156: 8 hours

Excretion: Urine (as unchanged drug)

Dosage

Children <2 years: Not recommended for use

Nausea and vomiting prophylaxis, chemotherapy-induced (including initial and repeat courses):

Children 2-16 years:

Oral: 1.8 mg/kg within 1 hour before chemotherapy; maximum: 100 mg/dose

I.V.: 1.8 mg/kg ~30 minutes before chemotherapy; maximum: 100 mg/dose

Adults:

Oral: 200 mg single dose

I.V.:

0.6-5 mg/kg as a single dose

50 mg 1-2 minute bolus

2.4-3 mg/kg 20-minute infusion

Prevention of postoperative nausea and vomiting:

Children 2-16 years:

Oral: 1.2 mg/kg within 2 hours before surgery; maximum: 100 mg/dose

I.V.: 0.35 mg/kg (maximum: 12.5 mg) ~15 minutes before stopping anesthesia

Adults:

Oral: 100 mg within 2 hours before surgery

I.V.: 12.5 mg ~15 minutes before stopping anesthesia

Treatment of postoperative nausea and vomiting: I.V. (only):

Children: 0.35 mg/kg (maximum: 12.5 mg) as soon as needed

Adults: 12.5 mg as soon as needed

Dosing adjustment for elderly, renal/hepatic impairment: No dosage adjustment is recommended

Administration I.V. injection may be given either undiluted IVP over 30 seconds or infused over 15 minutes. Dolasetron injection may be diluted in apple or apple-grape juice and taken orally.

Monitoring Parameters Liver function tests, blood pressure and pulse, and ECG in patients with cardiovascular disease

Dosage Forms INJ, solution: 20 mg/mL (0.625 mL, 5 mL, 25 mL). **TAB:** 50 mg, 100 mg

- ◆ **Dolasetron Mesylate** *see* Dolasetron *on page 400*
- ◆ **Dolobid**® *see* Diflunisal *on page 373*
- ◆ **Dolophine**® *see* Methadone *on page 808*
- ◆ **Domeboro® [OTC]** *see* Aluminum Sulfate and Calcium Acetate *on page 68*
- ◆ **Dome Paste Bandage** *see* Zinc Gelatin *on page 1327*

Donepezil (doh NEP e zil)

U.S. Brand Names Aricept®

Synonyms E2020

Therapeutic Category Acetylcholinesterase Inhibitor; Cholinergic Agent

Use Treatment of mild to moderate dementia of the Alzheimer's type

Unlabeled/Investigational Use Attention-deficit/hyperactivity disorder (ADHD), behavioral syndromes in dementia

Pregnancy Risk Factor C

Contraindications Hypersensitivity to donepezil, piperidine derivatives, or any component of the formulation

(Continued)

Donepezil *(Continued)*

Warnings/Precautions Cholinesterase inhibitors may have vagotonic effects. May cause bradycardia and/or heart block with or without a history of cardiac disease; syncopal episodes have been associated with donepezil. Use with caution in patients with sick sinus syndrome or other supraventricular cardiac conduction abnormalities, in patients with seizures, COPD, or asthma; avoid use in nursing mothers. Use with caution in patients at risk of ulcer disease (ie, previous history or NSAID use), or in patients with bladder outlet obstruction. May cause diarrhea, nausea, and/or vomiting, which may be dose-related.

Common Adverse Reactions
>10%:
  Central nervous system: Headache
  Gastrointestinal: Nausea, diarrhea
1% to 10%:
  Cardiovascular: Syncope, chest pain, hypertension, atrial fibrillation, hypotension, hot flashes
  Central nervous system: Abnormal dreams, depression, dizziness, fatigue, insomnia, somnolence
  Dermatologic: Bruising
  Gastrointestinal: Anorexia, vomiting, weight loss, fecal incontinence, GI bleeding, bloating, epigastric pain
  Genitourinary: Frequent urination
  Neuromuscular & skeletal: Muscle cramps, arthritis, body pain

Drug Interactions
Cytochrome P450 Effect: Substrate (minor) of CYP2D6, 3A4
Increased Effect/Toxicity: Ketoconazole and quinidine inhibit donepezil's metabolism *in vitro* and may increase toxicity. A synergistic effect may be seen with concurrent administration of succinylcholine or cholinergic agonists (bethanechol).
Decreased Effect: Donepezil levels may be decreased by enzyme inducers (phenytoin, carbamazepine, dexamethasone, rifampin, and phenobarbital). Anticholinergic agents (benztropine) may inhibit the effects of donepezil.

Mechanism of Action Alzheimer's disease is characterized by cholinergic deficiency in the cortex and basal forebrain, which contributes to cognitive deficits. Donepezil reversibly and noncompetitively inhibits centrally-active acetylcholinesterase, the enzyme responsible for hydrolysis of acetylcholine. This appears to result in increased concentrations of acetylcholine available for synaptic transmission in the central nervous system.

Pharmacodynamics/Kinetics
Absorption: Well absorbed
Protein binding: 96%, primarily to albumin (75%) and α_1-acid glycoprotein (21%)
Metabolism: Extensively to four major metabolites (two are active) via CYP2D6 and 3A4; undergoes glucuronidation
Bioavailability: 100%
Half-life elimination: 70 hours; time to steady-state: 15 days
Time to peak, plasma: 3-4 hours
Excretion: Urine (as unchanged drug)

Dosage Oral:
Children: ADHD (unlabeled use): 5 mg/day
Adults: Dementia of Alzheimer's type: Initial: 5 mg/day at bedtime; may increase to 10 mg/day at bedtime after 4-6 weeks

Monitoring Parameters Behavior, mood, bowel function

Dosage Forms TAB: 5 mg, 10 mg

♦ **Donnatal®** *see* Hyoscyamine, Atropine, Scopolamine, and Phenobarbital *on page 643*
♦ **Donnatal Extentabs®** *see* Hyoscyamine, Atropine, Scopolamine, and Phenobarbital *on page 643*

DOPamine *(DOE pa meen)*

Related Information
  Hemodynamic Support, Intravenous *on page 1377*
Synonyms Dopamine Hydrochloride; Intropin
Therapeutic Category Adrenergic Agonist Agent; Sympathomimetic Agent; Vesicant
Use Adjunct in the treatment of shock (eg, MI, open heart surgery, renal failure, cardiac decompensation, etc) which persists after adequate fluid volume replacement
Unlabeled/Investigational Use Symptomatic bradycardia or heart block unresponsive to atropine or pacing
Pregnancy Risk Factor C
Contraindications Hypersensitivity to sulfites (commercial preparation contains sodium bisulfite); pheochromocytoma; ventricular fibrillation
Warnings/Precautions Use with caution in patients with cardiovascular disease or cardiac arrhythmias or patients with occlusive vascular disease. Correct hypovolemia and electrolytes when used in hemodynamic support. May cause increases in HR and arrhythmia. Avoid infiltration - may cause severe tissue necrosis. Use with caution in post-MI patients.
Common Adverse Reactions Frequency not defined.
  Cardiovascular: Ectopic beats, tachycardia, anginal pain, palpitations, hypotension, vasoconstriction
  Central nervous system: Headache
  Gastrointestinal: Nausea and vomiting

Respiratory: Dyspnea

Drug Interactions

Increased Effect/Toxicity: Dopamine's effects are prolonged and intensified by MAO inhibitors, alpha- and beta-adrenergic blockers, cocaine, general anesthetics, methyldopa, phenytoin, reserpine, and TCAs.

Decreased Effect: Tricyclic antidepressants may have a decreased effect when coadministered with dopamine. Guanethidine's hypotensive effects may only be partially reversed; may need to use a direct-acting sympathomimetic.

Mechanism of Action Stimulates both adrenergic and dopaminergic receptors, lower doses are mainly dopaminergic stimulating and produce renal and mesenteric vasodilation, higher doses also are both dopaminergic and beta₁-adrenergic stimulating and produce cardiac stimulation and renal vasodilation; large doses stimulate alpha-adrenergic receptors

Pharmacodynamics/Kinetics

Children: Dopamine has exhibited nonlinear kinetics in children; with medication changes, may not achieve steady-state for ~1 hour rather than 20 minutes

Onset of action: Adults: 5 minutes

Duration: Adults: <10 minutes

Metabolism: Renal, hepatic, plasma; 75% to inactive metabolites by monoamine oxidase and 25% to norepinephrine

Half-life elimination: 2 minutes

Excretion: Urine (as metabolites)

Clearance: Neonates: Varies and appears to be age related; clearance is more prolonged with combined hepatic and renal dysfunction

Dosage I.V. infusion (administration requires the use of an infusion pump):

Neonates: 1-20 mcg/kg/minute continuous infusion, titrate to desired response.

Children: 1-20 mcg/kg/minute, maximum: 50 mcg/kg/minute continuous infusion, titrate to desired response.

Adults: 1-5 mcg/kg/minute up to 20 mcg/kg/minute, titrate to desired response. Infusion may be increased by 1-4 mcg/kg/minute at 10- to 30-minute intervals until optimal response is obtained.

If dosages >20-30 mcg/kg/minute are needed, a more direct-acting pressor may be more beneficial (ie, epinephrine, norepinephrine).

The hemodynamic effects of dopamine are dose dependent:

Low-dose: 1-3 mcg/kg/minute, increased renal blood flow and urine output

Intermediate-dose: 3-10 mcg/kg/minute, increased renal blood flow, heart rate, cardiac contractility, and cardiac output

High-dose: >10 mcg/kg/minute, alpha-adrenergic effects begin to predominate, vasoconstriction, increased blood pressure

Administration Administer into large vein to prevent the possibility of extravasation (central line administration); monitor continuously for free flow; use infusion device to control rate of flow; administration into an umbilical arterial catheter is not recommended; when discontinuing the infusion, gradually decrease the dose of dopamine (sudden discontinuation may cause hypotension).

To prepare for infusion:

$$\frac{6 \times weight\ (kg) \times desired\ dose\ (mcg/kg/min)}{I.V.\ infusion\ rate\ (mL/h)} = \frac{mg\ of\ drug\ to\ be\ added\ to}{100\ mL\ of\ I.V.\ fluid}$$

Extravasation management: Due to short half-life, withdrawal of drug is often only necessary treatment. Use phentolamine as antidote. Mix 5 mg with 9 mL of NS; inject a small amount of this dilution into extravasated area. Blanching should reverse immediately. Monitor site. If blanching should recur, additional injections of phentolamine may be needed.

Monitoring Parameters Blood pressure, ECG, heart rate, CVP, RAP, MAP, urine output; if pulmonary artery catheter is in place, monitor CI, PCWP, SVR, and PVR

Dosage Forms INF [premixed in D₅W]: 0.8 mg/mL (250 mL, 500 mL); 1.6 mg/mL (250 mL, 500 mL); 3.2 mg/mL (250 mL). **INJ, solution:** 40 mg/mL (5 mL, 10 mL); 80 mg/mL (5 mL); 160 mg/mL (5 mL)

♦ **Dopamine Hydrochloride** see DOPamine on page 402

♦ **Dopar**® see Levodopa on page 731

♦ **Dopram**® see Doxapram on page 405

♦ **Doral**® see Quazepam on page 1069

Dornase Alfa (DOOR nase AL fa)

U.S. Brand Names Pulmozyme®

Synonyms DNase; Recombinant Human Deoxyribonuclease

Therapeutic Category Enzyme

Use Management of cystic fibrosis patients to reduce the frequency of respiratory infections that require parenteral antibiotics, and to improve pulmonary function

Unlabeled/Investigational Use Treatment of chronic bronchitis

Pregnancy Risk Factor B

Contraindications Hypersensitivity to dornase alfa, Chinese hamster ovary cell products (eg, epoetin alfa), or any component of the formulation

Warnings/Precautions No clinical trials have been conducted to demonstrate safety and effectiveness of dornase in children <5 years of age, in patients with pulmonary function <40% (Continued)

Dornase Alfa *(Continued)*

of normal, or in patients for longer treatment periods >12 months; no data exists regarding safety during lactation

Common Adverse Reactions

>10%:

Respiratory: Pharyngitis

Miscellaneous: Voice alteration

1% to 10%:

Cardiovascular: Chest pain

Dermatologic: Rash

Ocular: Conjunctivitis

Respiratory: Laryngitis, cough, dyspnea, hemoptysis, rhinitis, hoarse throat, wheezing

Mechanism of Action The hallmark of cystic fibrosis lung disease is the presence of abundant, purulent airway secretions composed primarily of highly polymerized DNA. The principal source of this DNA is the nuclei of degenerating neutrophils, which is present in large concentrations in infected lung secretions. The presence of this DNA produces a viscous mucous that may contribute to the decreased mucociliary transport and persistent infections that are commonly seen in this population. Dornase alfa is a deoxyribonuclease (DNA) enzyme produced by recombinant gene technology. Dornase selectively cleaves DNA, thus reducing mucous viscosity and as a result, airflow in the lung is improved and the risk of bacterial infection may be decreased.

Pharmacodynamics/Kinetics

Onset of action: Nebulization: Enzyme levels are measured in sputum in ~15 minutes

Duration: Rapidly declines

Dosage Inhalation:

Children >3 months to Adults: 2.5 mg once daily through selected nebulizers; experience in children <5 years is limited

Patients unable to inhale or exhale orally throughout the entire treatment period may use Pari-Baby™ nebulizer. Some patients may benefit from twice daily administration.

Administration Nebulization: Should not be diluted or mixed with any other drugs in the nebulizer, this may inactivate the drug

Dosage Forms SOLN, nebulization: 1 mg/mL (2.5 mL)

♦ **Doryx®** *see Doxycycline on page 413*

Dorzolamide *(dor ZOLE a mide)*

Related Information

Glaucoma Drug Therapy Comparison *on page 1481*

U.S. Brand Names Trusopt®

Synonyms Dorzolamide Hydrochloride

Therapeutic Category Carbonic Anhydrase Inhibitor

Use Lowers intraocular pressure to treat glaucoma in patients with ocular hypertension or open-angle glaucoma

Pregnancy Risk Factor C

Dosage Adults: Glaucoma: Instill 1 drop in the affected eye(s) 3 times/day

Dosage Forms SOLN, ophthalmic: 2% (5 mL, 10 mL)

Dorzolamide and Timolol *(dor ZOLE a mide & TYE moe lole)*

U.S. Brand Names Cosopt®

Synonyms Timolol and Dorzolamide

Therapeutic Category Beta Blocker/Carbonic Anhydrase Inhibitor, Ophthalmic

Use Lowers intraocular pressure to treat glaucoma in patients with ocular hypertension or open-angle glaucoma

Dosage Adults: ophthalmic: One drop in eye(s) twice daily

Dosage Forms SOLN, ophthalmic: Dorzolamide 2% and timolol 0.5% (5 mL, 10 mL)

♦ **Dorzolamide Hydrochloride** *see Dorzolamide on page 404*

♦ **DOS® [OTC]** *see Docusate on page 398*

♦ **DOSS** *see Docusate on page 398*

♦ **Dostinex®** *see Cabergoline on page 197*

♦ **Dovonex®** *see Calcipotriene on page 200*

Doxacurium *(doks a KYOO ri um)*

Related Information

Neuromuscular Blocking Agents Comparison *on page 1397*

U.S. Brand Names Nuromax®

Synonyms Doxacurium Chloride

Therapeutic Category Neuromuscular Blocker Agent, Nondepolarizing

Use Adjunct to general anesthesia to facilitate endotracheal intubation and to relax skeletal muscles during surgery; to facilitate mechanical ventilation in ICU patients; does not relieve pain or produce sedation; the characteristics of this agent make it especially useful in procedures requiring careful maintenance of hemodynamic stability for prolonged periods

Pregnancy Risk Factor C

Contraindications Hypersensitivity to doxacurium or any component of the formulation

Warnings/Precautions Use with caution in the elderly, effects and duration are more variable; product contains benzyl alcohol, use with caution in newborns; use with caution in patients with renal or hepatic impairment; certain clinical conditions may result in potentiation or antagonism of neuromuscular blockade:

Potentiation: Electrolyte abnormalities, severe hyponatremia, severe hypocalcemia, severe hypokalemia, hypermagnesemia, neuromuscular diseases, acidosis, acute intermittent porphyria, renal failure, hepatic failure

Antagonism: Alkalosis, hypercalcemia, demyelinating lesions, peripheral neuropathies, diabetes mellitus

Increased sensitivity in patients with myasthenia gravis, Eaton-Lambert syndrome; resistance in burn patients (>30% of body) for period of 5-70 days postinjury; resistance in patients with muscle trauma, denervation, immobilization, infection; does not counteract bradycardia produced by anesthetics/vagal stimulation. Cross-sensitivity with other neuromuscular-blocking agents may occur; use extreme caution in patients with previous anaphylactic reactions.

Drug Interactions

Increased Effect/Toxicity: Increased effects are possible with aminoglycosides, beta-blockers, clindamycin, calcium channel blockers, halogenated anesthetics, imipenem, ketamine, lidocaine, loop diuretics (furosemide), macrolides (case reports), magnesium sulfate, procainamide, quinidine, quinolones, tetracyclines, and vancomycin. May increase risk of myopathy when used with high- dose corticosteroids for extended periods.

Decreased Effect: Effect of nondepolarizing neuromuscular blockers may be reduced by carbamazepine (chronic use), corticosteroids (also associated with myopathy - see increased effect), phenytoin (chronic use), sympathomimetics, and theophylline.

Mechanism of Action Prevents depolarization of muscle membrane and subsequent muscle contraction by acting as a competitive antagonist to acetylcholine at the alpha subunits of the nicotinic cholinergic receptors on the motor endplates in skeletal muscle, also interferes with the mobilization of acetylcholine presynaptically; the neuromuscular blockade can be pharmacologically reversed with an anticholinesterase agent (neostigmine, edrophonium, pyridostigmine)

Pharmacodynamics/Kinetics
Onset of action: 5-11 minutes
Duration: 30 minutes (range: 12-54 minutes)
Protein binding: 30%
Excretion: Primarily urine and feces (as unchanged drug); recovery time prolonged in elderly

Dosage Administer I.V.; dose to effect; doses will vary due to interpatient variability; use ideal body weight for obese patients

Surgery:
Children >2 years: Initial: 0.03-0.05 mg/kg followed by maintenance doses of 0.005-0.01 mg/kg after 30-45 minutes
Adults: 0.05-0.08 mg/kg with thiopental/narcotic or 0.025 mg/kg after initial dose of succinylcholine for intubation; initial maintenance dose of 0.005-0.01 mg/kg after 100-160 minutes followed by repeat doses every 30-45 minutes
Pretreatment/priming: 10% of intubating dose given 3-5 minutes before initial dose
ICU: 0.05 mg/kg bolus followed by 0.025 mg/kg every 2-3 hours or 0.25-0.75 mcg/kg/minute once initial recovery from bolus dose observed

Dosing adjustment in renal impairment: Reduce initial dose and titrate carefully as duration may be prolonged

Administration May be given rapid I.V. injection undiluted or via a continuous infusion using an infusion pump; use infusion solutions within 24 hours of preparation

Monitoring Parameters Blockade is monitored with a peripheral nerve stimulator, should also evaluate ECG, blood pressure, and heart rate
In the ICU setting, prolonged paralysis and generalized myopathy, following discontinuation of agent, may be minimized by appropriately monitoring degree of blockade.

Dosage Forms INJ, solution: 1 mg/mL (5 mL)

♦ **Doxacurium Chloride** see Doxacurium on page 404

Doxapram (DOKS a pram)
U.S. Brand Names Dopram®
Synonyms Doxapram Hydrochloride
Therapeutic Category Central Nervous System Stimulant, Nonamphetamine; Respiratory Stimulant
Use Respiratory and CNS stimulant for respiratory depression secondary to anesthesia, drug-induced CNS depression; acute hypercapnia secondary to COPD
Pregnancy Risk Factor B
Dosage Contains a significant amount of benzyl alcohol (0.9%); I.V.: Adults:
Respiratory depression following anesthesia:
Intermittent injection: Initial: 0.5-1 mg/kg; may repeat at 5-minute intervals (only in patients who demonstrate initial response); maximum total dose: 2 mg/kg
I.V. infusion: Initial: 5 mg/minute until adequate response or adverse effects seen; decrease to 1-3 mg/minute; maximum total dose: 4 mg/kg
Drug-induced CNS depression:
Intermittent injection: Initial: 1-2 mg/kg, repeat after 5 minutes; may repeat at 1-2 hour intervals (until sustained consciousness); maximum 3 g/day
(Continued)

Doxapram *(Continued)*

I.V. infusion: Initial: Bolus dose of 2 mg/kg, repeat after 5 minutes. If no response, wait 1-2 hours and repeat. If some stimulation is noted, initiate infusion at 1-3 mg/minute (depending on size of patient/depth of CNS depression); suspend infusion if patient begins to awaken. Infusion should not be continued for >2 hours. May reinstitute infusion as described above, including bolus, after rest interval of 30 minutes to 2 hours; maximum: 3 g/day

Acute hypercapnia secondary to COPD: I.V. infusion: Initial: Initiate infusion at 1-2 mg/minute (depending on size of patient/depth of CNS depression); may increase to maximum rate of 3 mg/minute; infusion should not be continued for >2 hours. Monitor arterial blood gases prior to initiation of infusion and at 30-minute intervals during the infusion (to identify possible development of acidosis/CO_2 retention). Additional infusions are not recommended (per manufacturer).

Hemodialysis: Not dialyzable

Dosage Forms INJ, solution: 20 mg/mL (20 mL)

♦ **Doxapram Hydrochloride** *see Doxapram on page 405*

Doxazosin *(doks AY zoe sin)*

U.S. Brand Names Cardura®

Therapeutic Category Alpha-Adrenergic Blocking Agent, Oral; Antihypertensive Agent

Use Treatment of hypertension alone or in conjunction with diuretics, cardiac glycosides, ACE inhibitors, or calcium antagonists (particularly appropriate for those with hypertension and other cardiovascular risk factors such as hypercholesterolemia and diabetes mellitus); treatment of urinary outflow obstruction and/or obstructive and irritative symptoms associated with benign prostatic hyperplasia (BPH), particularly useful in patients with troublesome symptoms who are unable or unwilling to undergo invasive procedures, but who require rapid symptomatic relief

Pregnancy Risk Factor C

Contraindications Hypersensitivity to quinazolines (prazosin, terazosin), doxazosin, or any component of the formulation; concurrent use with phosphodiesterase-5 (PDE-5) inhibitors including sildenafil (>25 mg), tadalafil, or vardenafil

Warnings/Precautions Use with caution in patients with renal impairment. Can cause marked hypotension and syncope with sudden loss of consciousness with the first dose. Prostate cancer should be ruled out before starting for BPH. Anticipate a similar effect if therapy is interrupted for a few days, if dosage is increased rapidly, or if another antihypertensive drug is introduced.

Common Adverse Reactions

>10%: Central nervous system: Dizziness (16% to 19%), headache (10% to 14%)

1% to 10%:

Cardiovascular: Orthostatic hypotension (dose-related; 0.3% up to 10%), edema (3% to 4%), hypotension (2%), palpitation (1% to 2%), chest pain (1% to 2%), arrhythmia (1%), syncope (2%), flushing (1%)

Central nervous system: Fatigue (8% to 12%), somnolence (3% to 5%), nervousness (2%), pain (2%), vertigo (2%), insomnia (1%), anxiety (1%), paresthesia (1%), movement disorder (1%), ataxia (1%), hypertonia (1%), depression (1%), weakness (1%)

Dermatologic: Rash (1%), pruritus (1%)

Endocrine & metabolic: Sexual dysfunction (2%)

Gastrointestinal: Abdominal pain (2%), diarrhea (2%), dyspepsia (1% to 2%), nausea (2% to 3%), xerostomia (1% to 2%), constipation (1%), flatulence (1%)

Genitourinary: Urinary tract infection (1%), impotence (1%), polyuria (2%), incontinence (1%)

Neuromuscular & skeletal: Back pain (2%), arthritis (1%), muscle weakness (1%), myalgia (1%), muscle cramps (1%)

Ocular: Abnormal vision (1% to 2%), conjunctivitis (1%)

Otic: Tinnitus (1%)

Respiratory: Rhinitis (3%), dyspnea (1% to 3%), respiratory disorder (1%), epistaxis (1%)

Miscellaneous: Flu-like syndrome (1%), increased diaphoresis (1%)

Drug Interactions

Increased Effect/Toxicity: Increased hypotensive effect with beta-blockers, diuretics, ACE inhibitors, calcium channel blockers, other antihypertensive medications, sildenafil (use with extreme caution at a dose ≤25 mg), tadalafil (contraindicated by the manufacturer), and vardenafil (contraindicated by the manufacturer).

Decreased Effect: Decreased hypotensive effect with NSAIDs.

Mechanism of Action Competitively inhibits postsynaptic alpha-adrenergic receptors which results in vasodilation of veins and arterioles and a decrease in total peripheral resistance and blood pressure; approximately 50% as potent on a weight by weight basis as prazosin

Pharmacodynamics/Kinetics Not significantly affected by increased age

Duration: >24 hours

Metabolism: Extensively hepatic

Half-life elimination: 22 hours

Time to peak, serum: 2-3 hours

Excretion: Feces (63%); urine (9%)

Dosage Oral:

Adults: 1 mg once daily in morning or evening; may be increased to 2 mg once daily. Thereafter titrate upwards, if needed, over several weeks, balancing therapeutic benefit with doxazosin-induced postural hypotension

    Hypertension: Maximum dose: 16 mg/day
     BPH: Maximum dose: 8 mg/day
    Elderly: Initial: 0.5 mg once daily
Administration Syncope may occur usually within 90 minutes of the initial dose.
Monitoring Parameters Blood pressure, standing and sitting/supine
Patient Information Rise from sitting/lying position carefully; may cause dizziness; report if painful persistent erection occurs; take the first dose at bedtime
Dosage Forms TAB: 1 mg, 2 mg, 4 mg, 8 mg

Doxepin (DOKS e pin)
Related Information
Antidepressant Agents Comparison *on page 1359*
U.S. Brand Names Prudoxin™; Sinequan®; Zonalon®
Synonyms Doxepin Hydrochloride
Therapeutic Category Antianxiety Agent; Antidepressant, Tricyclic (Tertiary Amine)
Use
    Oral: Depression
    Topical: Short-term (<8 days) management of moderate pruritus in adults with atopic dermatitis or lichen simplex chronicus
Unlabeled/Investigational Use Analgesic for certain chronic and neuropathic pain; anxiety
Pregnancy Risk Factor B (cream); C (all other forms)
Contraindications Hypersensitivity to doxepin, drugs from similar chemical class, or any component of the formulation; narrow-angle glaucoma; urinary retention; use of MAO inhibitors within 14 days; use in a patient during acute recovery phase of MI
Warnings/Precautions Often causes sedation, which may result in impaired performance of tasks requiring alertness (eg, operating machinery or driving). Sedative effects may be additive with other CNS depressants and/or ethanol. The degree of sedation is very high relative to other antidepressants. May worsen psychosis in some patients or precipitate a shift to mania or hypomania in patients with bipolar disease. May increase the risks associated with electroconvulsive therapy. This agent should be discontinued, when possible, prior to elective surgery. Therapy should not be abruptly discontinued in patients receiving high doses for prolonged periods.

May cause orthostatic hypotension (risk is moderate relative to other antidepressants) - use with caution in patients at risk of hypotension or in patients where transient hypotensive episodes would be poorly tolerated (cardiovascular disease or cerebrovascular disease). The degree of anticholinergic blockade produced by this agent is high relative to other cyclic antidepressants - use caution in patients with benign prostatic hypertrophy, xerostomia, visual problems, constipation, or history of bowel obstruction.

The possibility of a suicide attempt is inherent in major depression and may persist until remission occurs. Use caution in high-risk patients during initiation of therapy. Prescriptions should be written for the smallest quantity consistent with good patient care. Use with caution in patients with a history of cardiovascular disease (including previous MI, stroke, tachycardia, or conduction abnormalities). The risk conduction abnormalities with this agent is moderate relative to other antidepressants. Use caution in patients with a previous seizure disorder or condition predisposing to seizures such as brain damage, alcoholism, or concurrent therapy with other drugs which lower the seizure threshold. Use with caution in hyperthyroid patients or those receiving thyroid supplementation. Use with caution in patients with hepatic or renal dysfunction and in elderly patients. Use in children <12 years of age has not been established.

Cream formulation is for external use only (not for ophthalmic, vaginal, or oral use). Do not use occlusive dressings. Use for >8 days may increase risk of contact sensitization. Doxepin is significantly absorbed following topical administration; plasma levels may be similar to those achieved with oral administration.
Common Adverse Reactions
Oral: Frequency not defined.
    Cardiovascular: Hypotension, hypertension, tachycardia
    Central nervous system: Drowsiness, dizziness, headache, disorientation, ataxia, confusion, seizure
    Dermatologic: Alopecia, photosensitivity, rash, pruritus
    Endocrine & metabolic: Breast enlargement, galactorrhea, SIADH, increase or decrease in blood sugar, increased or decreased libido
    Gastrointestinal: Xerostomia, constipation, vomiting, indigestion, anorexia, aphthous stomatitis, nausea, unpleasant taste, weight gain, diarrhea, trouble with gums, decreased lower esophageal sphincter tone may cause GE reflux
    Genitourinary: Urinary retention, testicular edema
    Hematologic: Agranulocytosis, leukopenia, eosinophilia, thrombocytopenia, purpura
    Neuromuscular & skeletal: Weakness, tremors, numbness, paresthesia, extrapyramidal symptoms, tardive dyskinesia
    Ocular: Blurred vision
    Otic: Tinnitus
    Miscellaneous: Diaphoresis (excessive), allergic reactions

Topical:
>10%:
    Central nervous system: Drowsiness (22%)
    Dermatologic: Stinging/burning (23%)
(Continued)

Doxepin *(Continued)*

1% to 10%:
Cardiovascular: Edema: (1%)
Central nervous system: Dizziness (2%), emotional changes (2%)
Gastrointestinal: Xerostomia (10%), taste alteration (2%)

Drug Interactions

Cytochrome P450 Effect: Substrate (major) of CYP1A2, 2D6, 3A4

Increased Effect/Toxicity: Doxepin increases the effects of amphetamines, anticholinergics, other CNS depressants (sedatives, hypnotics, or ethanol), chlorpropamide, tolazamide, and warfarin. When used with MAO inhibitors, hyperpyrexia, hypertension, tachycardia, confusion, seizures, and **deaths have been reported** (serotonin syndrome). Serotonin syndrome has also been reported with ritonavir (rare). CYP1A2 inhibitors may increase the levels/effects of doxepin; example inhibitors include amiodarone, fluvoxamine, ketoconazole, quinolone antibiotics, and rofecoxib. CYP2D6 inhibitors may increase the levels/effects of doxepin; example inhibitors include chlorpromazine, delavirdine, fluoxetine, miconazole, paroxetine, pergolide, quinidine, quinine, ritonavir, and ropinirole. Cimetidine, grapefruit juice, indinavir, methylphenidate, diltiazem, and verapamil may increase the serum concentrations of TCAs. Use of lithium with a TCA may increase the risk for neurotoxicity. Phenothiazines may increase concentration of some TCAs and TCAs may increase concentration of phenothiazines. Pressor response to I.V. epinephrine, norepinephrine, and phenylephrine may be enhanced in patients receiving TCAs (**Note:** Effect is unlikely with epinephrine or levonordefrin dosages typically administered as infiltration in combination with local anesthetics). Combined use of beta-agonists or drugs which prolong QT$_c$ (including quinidine, procainamide, disopyramide, cisapride, sparfloxacin, gatifloxacin, moxifloxacin) with TCAs may predispose patients to cardiac arrhythmias.

Decreased Effect: CYP1A2 inducers may decrease the levels/effects of doxepin; example inducers include aminoglutethimide, carbamazepine, phenobarbital, and rifampin. Doxepin inhibits the antihypertensive response to bethanidine, clonidine, debrisoquin, guanadrel, guanethidine, guanabenz, and guanfacine. Cholestyramine and colestipol may bind TCAs and reduce their absorption.

Mechanism of Action
Increases the synaptic concentration of serotonin and norepinephrine in the central nervous system by inhibition of their reuptake by the presynaptic neuronal membrane

Pharmacodynamics/Kinetics

Onset of action: Peak effect: Antidepressant: Usually >2 weeks; Anxiolytic: may occur sooner
Absorption: Following topical application, plasma levels may be similar to those achieved with oral administration
Distribution: Crosses placenta; enters breast milk
Protein binding: 80% to 85%
Metabolism: Hepatic; metabolites include desmethyldoxepin (active)
Half-life elimination: Adults: 6-8 hours
Excretion: Urine

Dosage

Oral (entire daily dose may be given at bedtime): Depression or anxiety (unlabeled use):
Children: 1-3 mg/kg/day in single or divided doses
Adolescents: Initial: 25-50 mg/day in single or divided doses; gradually increase to 100 mg/day
Adults: Initial: 30-150 mg/day at bedtime or in 2-3 divided doses; may gradually increase up to 300 mg/day; single dose should not exceed 150 mg; select patients may respond to 25-50 mg/day
Elderly: Use a lower dose and adjust gradually
Dosing adjustment in hepatic impairment: Use a lower dose and adjust gradually

Topical: Pruritus: Adults and Elderly: Apply a thin film 4 times/day with at least 3- to 4-hour interval between applications; not recommended for use >8 days. **Note:** Low-dose (25-50 mg) oral administration has also been used to treat pruritus, but systemic effects are increased.

Administration

Oral: Do not mix oral concentrate with carbonated beverages (physically incompatible).
Topical: Apply thin film to affected area; use of occlusive dressings is not recommended.

Monitoring Parameters
Monitor blood pressure and pulse rate prior to and during initial therapy; monitor mental status, weight; ECG in older adults; adverse effects may be increased if topical formulation is applied to >10% of body surface area

Reference Range
Proposed therapeutic concentration (doxepin plus desmethyldoxepin): 110-250 ng/mL. Toxic concentration (doxepin plus desmethyldoxepin): >500 ng/mL. Utility of serum level monitoring is controversial.

Patient Information
Avoid unnecessary exposure to sunlight; avoid alcohol; do not discontinue medication abruptly; may cause urine to turn blue-green; may cause drowsiness; can use sugarless gum or hard candy for dry mouth; full effect may not occur for 4-6 weeks; do not use occlusive dressings with topical formulation

Dosage Forms
CAP (Sinequan®): 10 mg, 25 mg, 50 mg, 75 mg, 100 mg, 150 mg. **CRM** (Prudoxin™): 5% (45 g); (Zonalon®): 5% (30 g, 45 g). **SOLN, oral concentrate** (Sinequan®): 10 mg/mL (120 mL)

♦ **Doxepin Hydrochloride** *see* Doxepin *on page 407*

Doxercalciferol (doks er kal si fe FEER ole)

U.S. Brand Names Hectorol®

Therapeutic Category Vitamin D Analog

Use Reduction of elevated intact parathyroid hormone (iPTH) in the management of secondary hyperparathyroidism in patients on chronic hemodialysis

Pregnancy Risk Factor B

Contraindications History of hypercalcemia or evidence of vitamin D toxicity; hyperphosphatemia should be corrected before initiating therapy

Warnings/Precautions Other forms of vitamin D should be discontinued when doxercalciferol is started. Overdose from vitamin D is dangerous and needs to be avoided. Careful dosage titration and monitoring can minimize risk. Hyperphosphatemia exacerbates secondary hyperparathyroidism, diminishing the effect of doxercalciferol. Hyperphosphatemia needs to be corrected for best results. Use with caution in patients with hepatic impairment. Safety and efficacy have not been established in pediatrics.

Common Adverse Reactions Some of the signs and symptoms of hypercalcemia include anorexia, nausea, vomiting, constipation, polyuria, weakness, fatigue, confusion, stupor, and coma.

>10%:
- Cardiovascular: Edema (34.4%)
- Central nervous system: Headache (28%), malaise (28%), dizziness (11.5%)
- Gastrointestinal: Nausea/vomiting (34%)
- Respiratory: Dyspnea (11.5%)

1% to 10%:
- Cardiovascular: Bradycardia (6.6%)
- Central nervous system: Sleep disorder (3.3%)
- Dermatologic: Pruritus (8.2%)
- Gastrointestinal: Anorexia (4.9%), constipation (3.3%), dyspepsia (4.9%)
- Neuromuscular & skeletal: Arthralgia (4.9%)
- Miscellaneous: Abscess (3.3%)

Drug Interactions

Increased Effect/Toxicity: Doxercalciferol toxicity may be increased by concurrent use of other vitamin D supplements or magnesium-containing antacids and supplements.

Decreased Effect: Absorption of doxercalciferol is reduced with mineral oil and cholestyramine.

Mechanism of Action Doxercalciferol is metabolized to the active form of vitamin D. The active form of vitamin D controls the intestinal absorption of dietary calcium, the tubular reabsorption of calcium by the kidneys, and in conjunction with PTH, the mobilization of calcium from the skeleton.

Pharmacodynamics/Kinetics

Metabolism: Hepatic via CYP27

Half-life elimination: Active metabolite: 32-37 hours; up to 96 hours

Dosage

Oral:

If the iPTH >400 pg/mL, then the initial dose is 10 mcg 3 times/week at dialysis. The dose is adjusted at 8-week intervals based upon the iPTH levels.

If the iPTH level is decreased by 50% and >300 pg/mL, then the dose can be increased to 12.5 mcg 3 times/week for 8 more weeks. This titration process can continue at 8-week intervals up to a maximum dose of 20 mcg 3 times/week. Each increase should be by 2.5 mcg/dose.

If the iPTH is between 150-300 pg/mL, maintain the current dose.

If the iPTH is <100 pg/mL, then suspend the drug for 1 week; resume doxercalciferol at a reduced dose. Decrease each dose (not weekly dose) by at least 2.5 mcg.

I.V.:

If the iPTH >400 pg/mL, then the initial dose is 4 mcg 3 times/week after dialysis, administered as a bolus dose

If the iPTH level is decreased by 50% and >300 pg/mL, then the dose can be increased by 1-2 mcg at 8-week intervals as necessary

If the iPTH is between 150-300 pg/mL, maintain the current dose.

If the iPTH is <100 pg/mL, then suspend the drug for 1 week; resume doxercalciferol at a reduced dose (at least 1 mcg lower)

Monitoring Parameters Before initiating, check iPTH, serum calcium and phosphorus. Check weekly thereafter until stable. Serum iPTH, calcium, phosphorus, and alkaline phosphatase should be monitored.

Reference Range Serum calcium times phosphorus product should be less than 70

Patient Information Be clear on dose and directions for taking. Stop other vitamin D products. Do not miss doses. Avoid magnesium-containing antacids and supplements. Report headache, dizziness, weakness, sleepiness, severe nausea, vomiting, and difficulty thinking or concentrating to your prescriber. Do not take over-the-counter medicines or supplements without first consulting your prescriber. Follow diet and calcium supplements as directed by your prescriber.

Dosage Forms CAP: 2.5 mcg. **INJ, solution:** 2 mcg/mL (1 mL, 2 mL)

♦ **Doxil®** *see* DOXOrubicin (Liposomal) *on page 411*

DOXOrubicin (doks oh ROO bi sin)

U.S. Brand Names Adriamycin PFS®; Adriamycin RDF®; Rubex®

Synonyms ADR; Adria; Doxorubicin Hydrochloride; Hydroxydaunomycin Hydrochloride; Hydroxyldaunorubicin Hydrochloride; NSC-123127

Therapeutic Category Antineoplastic Agent, Anthracycline; Vesicant

Use Treatment of leukemias, lymphomas, multiple myeloma, osseous and nonosseous sarcomas, mesotheliomas, germ cell tumors of the ovary or testis, and carcinomas of the head and neck, thyroid, lung, breast, stomach, pancreas, liver, ovary, bladder, prostate, uterus, and neuroblastoma

Pregnancy Risk Factor D

Contraindications Hypersensitivity to doxorubicin or any component of the formulation; congestive heart failure or arrhythmias; previous therapy with high cumulative doses of doxorubicin and/or daunorubicin; pre-existing bone marrow suppression; pregnancy

Warnings/Precautions The U.S. Food and Drug Administration (FDA) currently recommends that procedures for proper handling and disposal of antineoplastic agents be considered. Total dose should not exceed 550 mg/m^2 or 450 mg/m^2 in patients with previous or concomitant treatment with daunorubicin, cyclophosphamide, or irradiation of the cardiac region; irreversible myocardial toxicity may occur as total dosage approaches 550 mg/m^2. A baseline cardiac evaluation (ECG, LVEF, +/- ECHO) is recommended, especially in patients with risk factors for increased cardiac toxicity and in pediatric patients. Pediatric patients are at increased risk for delayed cardiotoxicity. Reduce dose in patients with impaired hepatic function; severe myelosuppression is also possible. Secondary acute myelogenous leukemia may occur following treatment.

Common Adverse Reactions

>10%:
Dermatologic: Alopecia, radiation recall
Gastrointestinal: Nausea, vomiting, stomatitis, GI ulceration, anorexia, diarrhea
Genitourinary: Discoloration of urine, mild dysuria, urinary frequency, hematuria, bladder spasms, cystitis following bladder instillation
Hematologic: Myelosuppression, primarily leukopenia (75%); thrombocytopenia and anemia
Onset: 7 days
Nadir: 10-14 days
Recovery: 21-28 days

1% to 10%:
Cardiovascular: Transient ECG abnormalities (supraventricular tachycardia, S-T wave changes, atrial or ventricular extrasystoles); generally asymptomatic and self-limiting. Congestive heart failure, dose-related, may be delayed for 7-8 years after treatment. Cumulative dose, mediastinal/pericardial radiation therapy, cardiovascular disease, age, and use of cyclophosphamide (or other cardiotoxic agents) all increase the risk.
Recommended maximum cumulative doses:
No risk factors: 550 mg/m^2
Concurrent radiation: 450 mg/m^2
Note: Regardless of cumulative dose, if the left ventricular ejection fraction is <30% to 40%, the drug is usually not given.
Dermatologic: Skin "flare" at injection site; discoloration of saliva, sweat, or tears
Endocrine & metabolic: Hyperuricemia

Drug Interactions

Cytochrome P450 Effect: Substrate (major) of CYP2D6, 3A4; **Inhibits** CYP2B6 (moderate), 2D6 (weak), 3A4 (weak)

Increased Effect/Toxicity: Allopurinol may enhance the antitumor activity of doxorubicin (animal data only). Cyclosporine may increase doxorubicin levels, enhancing hematologic toxicity or may induce coma or seizures. Cyclophosphamide enhances the cardiac toxicity of doxorubicin by producing additional myocardial cell damage. Mercaptopurine increases doxorubicin toxicities. Streptozocin greatly enhances leukopenia and thrombocytopenia. Verapamil alters the cellular distribution of doxorubicin and may result in increased cell toxicity by inhibition of the P-glycoprotein pump. Paclitaxel reduces doxorubicin clearance and increases toxicity if administered prior to doxorubicin. High doses of progesterone enhance toxicity (neutropenia and thrombocytopenia). CYP2D6 inhibitors may increase the levels/effects of doxorubicin; example inhibitors include chlorpromazine, delavirdine, fluoxetine, miconazole, paroxetine, pergolide, quinidine, quinine, ritonavir, and ropinirole. Based on mouse studies, cardiotoxicity may be enhanced by verapamil. Concurrent therapy with actinomycin-D may result in recall pneumonitis following radiation.

Decreased Effect: Doxorubicin may decrease plasma levels and effectiveness of digoxin and phenytoin. Phenobarbital increases elimination (decreases effect) of doxorubicin. Doxorubicin may decrease the antiviral effect of zidovudine.

Mechanism of Action Inhibition of DNA and RNA synthesis by intercalation between DNA base pairs by inhibition of topoisomerase II and by steric obstruction. Doxorubicin intercalates at points of local uncoiling of the double helix. Although the exact mechanism is unclear, it appears that direct binding to DNA (intercalation) and inhibition of DNA repair (topoisomerase II inhibition) result in blockade of DNA and RNA synthesis and fragmentation of DNA. Doxorubicin is also a powerful iron chelator; the iron-doxorubicin complex can bind DNA and cell membranes and produce free radicals that immediately cleave the DNA and cell membranes.

Pharmacodynamics/Kinetics

Absorption: Oral: Poor (<50%)
Distribution: V_d: 25 L/kg; to many body tissues, particularly liver, spleen, kidney, lung, heart; does not distribute into the CNS; crosses placenta

Protein binding, plasma: 70%

Metabolism: Primarily hepatic to doxorubicinol (active), then to inactive aglycones, conjugated sulfates, and glucuronides

Half-life elimination:

Distribution: 10 minutes

Elimination: Doxorubicin: 1-3 hours; Metabolites: 3-3.5 hours

Terminal: 17-30 hours

Male: 54 hours; Female: 35 hours

Excretion: Feces (~40% to 50% as unchanged drug); urine (~3% to 10% as metabolites, 1% doxorubicinol, <1% adrimycine aglycones, and unchanged drug)

Clearance: Male: 113 L/hour; Female: 44 L/hour

Dosage Refer to individual protocols. I.V.:

Children:

35-75 mg/m^2 as a single dose, repeat every 21 days **or**

20-30 mg/m^2 once weekly **or**

60-90 mg/m^2 given as a continuous infusion over 96 hours every 3-4 weeks

Adults: Usual or typical dose: 60-75 mg/m^2 as a single dose, repeat every 21 days **or** other dosage regimens like 20-30 mg/m^2/day for 2-3 days, repeat in 4 weeks **or** 20 mg/m^2 once weekly

The lower dose regimen should be given to patients with decreased bone marrow reserve, prior therapy or marrow infiltration with malignant cells

Dosing adjustment in renal impairment:

Mild to moderate renal failure: Adjustment is not required

Cl$_{cr}$ <10 mL/minute: Administer 75% of normal dose

Hemodialysis: Supplemental dose is not necessary

Dosing adjustment in hepatic impairment:

Bilirubin 1.2-3 mg/dL: Administer 50% of dose

Bilirubin 3.1-5 mg/dL: Administer 25% of dose

Bilirubin >5 mg/dL: Do not administer drug

Administration Administer I.V. push over 1-2 minutes or IVPB. Continuous infusions may be administered via central line. Avoid extravasation associated with severe ulceration and soft tissue necrosis. Flush with 5-10 mL of I.V. solution before and after drug administration. Incompatible with heparin. Monitor for local erythematous streaking along vein and/or facial flushing (may indicate rapid infusion rate).

Extravasation management: Apply ice immediately for 30-60 minutes; then alternate off/on every 15 minutes for 1 day. Topical cooling may be achieved using ice packs or cooling pad with circulating ice water. Cooling of site for 24 hours as tolerated by the patient. Elevate and rest extremity 24-48 hours, then resume normal activity as tolerated. Application of cold inhibits vesicant's cytotoxicity. **Application of heat or sodium bicarbonate can be harmful and is contraindicated.** If pain, erythema, and/or swelling persist beyond 48 hours, refer patient immediately to plastic surgeon for consultation and possible debridement.

Monitoring Parameters CBC with differential and platelet count, cardiac and liver function tests

Patient Information This medication can only be administered intravenously. During therapy, do not use aspirin-containing products, and/or OTC medications without consulting prescriber. It is important to maintain adequate nutrition during therapy; frequent small meals may help. You may experience nausea or vomiting (frequent small meals, frequent mouth care, sucking lozenges, or chewing gum may help). You may experience loss of hair (reversible); you will be more susceptible to infection (avoid crowds and exposure to infection as much as possible). Urine may turn darker yellow. Yogurt or buttermilk may help reduce diarrhea (if unresolved, contact prescriber for medication relief). Frequent mouth care and use of a soft toothbrush or cotton swabs may reduce mouth sores. Report fever, chills, unusual bruising or bleeding, signs of infection, abdominal pain or blood in stools, excessive fatigue, yellowing of eyes or skin, swelling of extremities, difficulty breathing, or unresolved diarrhea. Contraceptive measures are recommended during therapy.

Dosage Forms INJ, powder for reconstitution: 10 mg, 20 mg, 50 mg; (Adriamycin RDF®): 10 mg, 20 mg, 50 mg, 150 mg; (Rubex®): 50 mg, 100 mg. **INJ, solution** [preservative free]: 2 mg/mL (5 mL, 10 mL, 25 mL, 100 mL); (Adriamycin PFS®): 2 mg/mL (5 mL, 10 mL, 25 mL, 37.5 mL, 100 mL)

♦ **Doxorubicin Hydrochloride** *see* DOXOrubicin *on page 410*

♦ **Doxorubicin Hydrochloride (Liposomal)** *see* DOXOrubicin (Liposomal) *on page 411*

DOXOrubicin (Liposomal) (doks oh ROO bi sin lip pah SOW mal)

U.S. Brand Names Doxil®

Synonyms Doxorubicin Hydrochloride (Liposomal)

Therapeutic Category Antineoplastic Agent, Anthracycline

Use Treatment of AIDS-related Kaposi's sarcoma, breast cancer, ovarian cancer, solid tumors

Pregnancy Risk Factor D

Contraindications Hypersensitivity to doxorubicin, other anthracyclines, or any component of the formulation; pre-existing bone marrow suppression; pregnancy

Warnings/Precautions The U.S. Food and Drug Administration (FDA) currently recommends that procedures for proper handling and disposal of antineoplastic agents be considered. Total dose should not exceed 550 mg/m^2 or 400 mg/m^2 in patients with previous or concomitant treatment (with daunorubicin, cyclophosphamide, or irradiation of the cardiac region); irreversible myocardial toxicity may occur as total dosage approaches 550 mg/m^2. I.V. use only, (Continued)

DOXOrubicin (Liposomal) *(Continued)*

severe local tissue necrosis will result if extravasation occurs; reduce dose in patients with impaired hepatic function; severe myelosuppression is also possible.

Common Adverse Reactions

>10%:

Gastrointestinal: Nausea (18%)

Hematologic: Myelosuppression, leukopenia (60% to 80%), thrombocytopenia (6% to 24%), anemia (6% to 53%)

Onset: 7 days

Nadir: 10-14 days

Recovery: 21-28 days

1% to 10%:

Cardiovascular: Arrhythmias, pericardial effusion, tachycardia, cardiomyopathy, CHF (1%)

Dermatologic: Hyperpigmentation of nail beds; erythematous streaking of vein; alopecia (9%)

Gastrointestinal: Vomiting (8%), mucositis (7%)

Miscellaneous: Infusion-related reactions (bronchospasm, chest tightness, chills, dyspnea, facial edema, flushing, headache, hypotension, pruritus) have occurred (up to 10%)

Drug Interactions

Cytochrome P450 Effect: **Substrate** (major) of CYP2D6, 3A4; **Inhibits** CYP2B6 (moderate), 2D6 (weak), 3A4 (weak)

Increased Effect/Toxicity: Allopurinol may enhance the antitumor activity of doxorubicin (animal data only). Cyclosporine may induce coma or seizures. Cyclophosphamide enhances the cardiac toxicity of doxorubicin by producing additional myocardial cell damage. Mercaptopurine increases toxicities. Streptozocin greatly enhances leukopenia and thrombocytopenia. Verapamil alters the cellular distribution of doxorubicin and may result in increased cell toxicity by inhibition of the P-glycoprotein pump. CYP2D6 inhibitors may increase the levels/effects of doxorubicin; example inhibitors include chlorpromazine, delavirdine, fluoxetine, miconazole, paroxetine, pergolide, quinidine, quinine, ritonavir, and ropinirole.

Decreased Effect: Doxorubicin may decrease plasma levels and effectiveness of digoxin and phenytoin. Phenobarbital increases elimination (decreases effect) of doxorubicin. Doxorubicin may decrease the antiviral activity of zidovudine.

Recommended Dose Modification Guidelines

Toxicity Grade	Dose Adjustment
PALMAR-PLANTAR ERYTHRODYSESTHESIA	
1 (Mild erythema, swelling, or desquamation not interfering with daily activities)	Redose unless patient has experienced previous Grade 3 or 4 toxicity. If so, delay up to 2 weeks and decrease dose by 25%; return to original dosing interval.
2 (Erythema, desquamation, or swelling interfering with, but not precluding, normal physical activities; small blisters or ulcerations <2 cm in diameter)	Delay dosing up to 2 weeks or until resolved to Grade 0-1. If after 2 weeks there is no resolution, liposomal doxorubicin should be discontinued.
3 (Blistering, ulceration, or swelling interfering with walking or normal daily activities; cannot wear regular clothing)	Delay dosing up to 2 weeks or until resolved to Grade 0-1. Decrease dose by 25% and return to original dosing interval; if after 2 weeks there is no resolution, liposomal doxorubicin should be discontinued.
4 (Diffuse or local process causing infectious complications, or a bedridden state or hospitalization)	Delay dosing up to 2 weeks or until resolved to Grade 0-1. Decrease dose by 25% and return to original dosing interval. If after 2 weeks there is no resolution, liposomal doxorubicin should be discontinued.
STOMATITIS	
1 (Painless ulcers, erythema, or mild soreness)	Redose unless patient has experienced previous Grade 3 or 4 toxicity. If so, delay up to 2 weeks and decrease by 25%. Return to original dosing interval.
2 (Painful erythema, edema, or ulcers, but can eat)	Delay dosing up to 2 weeks or until resolved to Grade 0-1. If after 2 weeks there is no resolution, liposomal doxorubicin should be discontinued.
3 (Painful erythema, edema, or ulcers, but cannot eat)	Delay dosing up to 2 weeks or until resolved to Grade 0-1. Decrease dose by 25% and return to original dosing interval. If after 2 weeks there is no resolution, liposomal doxorubicin should be discontinued.
4 (Requires parenteral or enteral support)	Delay dosing up to 2 weeks or until resolved to Grade 0-1. Decrease dose by 25% and return to original dosing interval. If after 2 weeks there is no resolution, liposomal doxorubicin should be discontinued.

Mechanism of Action Doxil® is doxorubicin hydrochloride encapsulated in long-circulating STEALTH® liposomes. Liposomes are microscopic vesicles composed of a phospholipid bilayer that are capable of encapsulating active drugs. Doxorubicin works through inhibition of topoisomerase-II at the point of DNA cleavage. A second mechanism of action is the production of free radicals (the hydroxy radical OH) by doxorubicin, which in turn can destroy DNA and cancerous cells. Doxorubicin is also a very powerful iron chelator, equal to deferoxamine. The iron-doxorubicin complex can bind DNA and cell membranes rapidly and produce free radicals that immediately cleave the DNA and cell membranes. Inhibits DNA and RNA synthesis by intercalating between DNA base pairs and by steric obstruction; active throughout entire cell cycle.

Pharmacodynamics/Kinetics
Distribution: V_{dss}: Confined mostly to the vascular fluid volume
Protein binding, plasma: Doxorubicin: 70%
Metabolism: Hepatic and in plasma to both active and inactive metabolites
Excretion: Urine (5% as doxorubicin or doxorubicinol)
Clearance: Mean: 0.041 L/hour/m^2

Dosage Refer to individual protocols
I.V.: 20 mg/m^2 over 30 minutes, once every 3 weeks, for as long as patients respond satisfactorily and tolerate treatment.
AIDS-KS patients: I.V.: 20 mg/m^2/dose over 30 minutes once every 3 weeks for as long as patients respond satisfactorily and tolerate treatment
Breast cancer: I.V.: 20-80 mg/m^2/dose has been studied in a limited number of phase I/II trials
Ovarian cancer: I.V.: 50 mg/m^2/dose repeated every 4 weeks (minimum of 4 courses is recommended)
Solid tumors: I.V.: 50-60 mg/m^2/dose repeated every 3-4 weeks has been studied in a limited number of phase I/II trials

See table on previous page.

Dosing adjustment in hepatic impairment:
Bilirubin 1.2-3 mg/dL or AST 60-180 units/L: Administer 50% of dose
Bilirubin >3 mg/dL: Administer 25% of dose

See table below.

Hematological Toxicity

Grade	ANC	Platelets	Modification
1	1500-1900	75,000-150,000	Resume treatment with no dose reduction.
2	1000-<1500	50,000-<75,000	Wait until ANC ≥1500 and platelets ≥75,000; redose with no dose reduction.
3	500-999	25,000-<50,000	Wait until ANC ≥1500 and platelets ≥75,000; redose with no dose reduction.
4	<500	<25,000	Wait until ANC ≥1500 and platelets ≥75,000; redose at 25% dose reduction or continue full dose with cytokine support.

Administration Administer IVPB over 30 minutes; administer at initial rate of 1 mg/minute to minimize risk of infusion reactions; further dilute in D$_5$W; do not administer as a bolus injection or undiluted solution. **Do not administer I.M. or S.C. Do not use with in-line filters.** Avoid extravasation associated with severe ulceration and soft tissue necrosis. Flush with 5-10 mL of D$_5$W solution before and after drug administration. Incompatible with heparin. Monitor for local erythematous streaking along vein and/or facial flushing (may indicate rapid infusion rate).

Extravasation management: Apply ice immediately for 30-60 minutes; then alternate off/on every 15 minutes for 1 day. Topical cooling may be achieved using ice packs or cooling pad with circulating ice water. Cooling of site for 24 hours as tolerated by the patient. Elevate and rest extremity 24-48 hours, then resume normal activity as tolerated. Application of cold inhibits vesicant's cytotoxicity. **Application of heat or sodium bicarbonate can be harmful and is contraindicated.** If pain, erythema, and/or swelling persist beyond 48 hours, refer patient immediately to plastic surgeon for consultation and possible debridement.

Monitoring Parameters CBC with differential and platelet count, echocardiogram, liver function tests

Patient Information This medication can only be administered I.V. During therapy, do not use alcohol, aspirin-containing products, and/or OTC medications without consulting prescriber. It is important to maintain adequate nutrition and hydration (2-3 L/day of fluids unless instructed to restrict fluid intake) during therapy; frequent small meals may help. You may experience nausea or vomiting (frequent small meals, frequent mouth care, sucking lozenges, or chewing gum may help). You may experience loss of hair (reversible); you will be more susceptible to infection (avoid crowds and exposure to infection as much as possible). Urine may turn red-brown (normal). Yogurt or buttermilk may help reduce diarrhea (if unresolved, contact prescriber for medication relief). Frequent mouth care and use of a soft toothbrush or cotton swabs may reduce mouth sores. Report fever, chills, unusual bruising or bleeding, signs of infection, abdominal pain or blood in stools, excessive fatigue, yellowing of eyes or skin, darkening in color of urine or pale colored stools, swelling of extremities, difficulty breathing, or unresolved diarrhea. Contraceptive measures are recommended during therapy

Dosage Forms INJ, solution: 2 mg/mL (10 mL, 25 mL)

♦ **Doxy-100**® *see* Doxycycline *on page 413*

Doxycycline (doks i SYE kleen)
Related Information
Antimicrobial Drugs of Choice *on page 1440*
(Continued)

Doxycycline *(Continued)*

Community-Acquired Pneumonia in Adults *on page 1457*
Malaria Treatment *on page 1464*
Prevention of Wound Infection & Sepsis in Surgical Patients *on page 1436*

U.S. Brand Names Adoxa™; Doryx®; Doxy-100®; Monodox®; Periostat®; Vibramycin®; Vibra-Tabs®

Synonyms Doxycycline Calcium; Doxycycline Hyclate; Doxycycline Monohydrate

Therapeutic Category Antibiotic, Tetracycline Derivative

Use Principally in the treatment of infections caused by susceptible *Rickettsia*, *Chlamydia*, and *Mycoplasma*; alternative to mefloquine for malaria prophylaxis; treatment for syphilis, uncomplicated *Neisseria gonorrhoeae*, *Listeria*, *Actinomyces israelii*, and *Clostridium* infections in penicillin-allergic patients; used for community-acquired pneumonia and other common infections due to susceptible organisms; anthrax due to *Bacillus anthracis*, including inhalational anthrax (postexposure); treatment of infections caused by uncommon susceptible gram-negative and gram-positive organisms including *Borrelia recurrentis*, *Ureaplasma urealyticum*, *Haemophilus ducreyi*, *Yersinia pestis*, *Francisella tularensis*, *Vibrio cholerae*, *Campylobacter fetus*, *Brucella* spp, *Bartonella bacilliformis*, and *Calymmatobacterium granulomatis*

Unlabeled/Investigational Use Sclerosing agent for pleural effusion injection; vancomycin-resistant enterococci (VRE)

Pregnancy Risk Factor D

Contraindications Hypersensitivity to doxycycline, tetracycline or any component of the formulation; children <8 years of age, except in treatment of anthrax (including inhalational anthrax postexposure prophylaxis); severe hepatic dysfunction; pregnancy

Warnings/Precautions Do not use during pregnancy - use of tetracyclines during tooth development may cause permanent discoloration of the teeth and enamel hypoplasia; prolonged use may result in superinfection, including oral or vaginal candidiasis; photosensitivity reaction may occur with this drug; avoid prolonged exposure to sunlight or tanning equipment. Avoid in children ≤8 years of age.

Additional specific warnings for Periostat®: Effectiveness has not been established in patients with coexistent oral candidiasis; use with caution in patients with a history or predisposition to oral candidiasis

Common Adverse Reactions Frequency not defined.

Cardiovascular: Intracranial hypertension, pericarditis
Dermatologic: Angioneurotic edema, exfoliative dermatitis (rare), photosensitivity, rash, urticaria
Endocrine & metabolic: Brown/black discoloration of thyroid gland (no dysfunction reported)
Gastrointestinal: Anorexia, diarrhea, dysphagia, enterocolitis, esophagitis (rare), esophageal ulcerations (rare), glossitis, inflammatory lesions in anogenital region, tooth discoloration (children)
Hematologic: Eosinophilia, hemolytic anemia, neutropenia, thrombocytopenia
Renal: Increased BUN
Miscellaneous: Anaphylactoid purpura, anaphylaxis, bulging fontanels (infants), SLE exacerbation

Note: Adverse effects in clinical trials with Periostat® occurring at a frequency more than 1% greater than placebo included nausea, dyspepsia, joint pain, diarrhea, menstrual cramp, and pain.

Drug Interactions

Cytochrome P450 Effect: Substrate of CYP3A4 (major); **Inhibits** CYP3A4 (strong)

Increased Effect/Toxicity: Increased digoxin toxicity when taken with digoxin. Increased prothrombin time with warfarin.

Decreased Effect: Decreased levels of doxycycline may occur when taken with antacids containing aluminum, calcium, or magnesium. Decreased levels when taken with iron, bismuth subsalicylate, barbiturates, phenytoin, sucralfate, didanosine, quinapril, and carbamazepine. Concurrent use of tetracycline and Penthrane® has been reported to result in fatal renal toxicity. Although anecdotal reports suggest oral contraceptive efficacy could be reduced by tetracyclines, this has been refuted by more rigorous scientific and clinical data.

Mechanism of Action Inhibits protein synthesis by binding with the 30S and possibly the 50S ribosomal subunit(s) of susceptible bacteria; may also cause alterations in the cytoplasmic membrane

Periostat® capsules (proposed mechanism): Has been shown to inhibit collagenase activity *in vitro*. Also has been noted to reduce elevated collagenase activity in the gingival crevicular fluid of patients with periodontal disease. Systemic levels do not reach inhibitory concentrations against bacteria.

Pharmacodynamics/Kinetics

Absorption: Oral: Almost complete; reduced by food or milk by 20%
Distribution: Widely into body tissues and fluids including synovial, pleural, prostatic, seminal fluids, and bronchial secretions; saliva, aqueous humor, and CSF penetration is poor; readily crosses placenta; enters breast milk
Protein binding: 90%
Metabolism: Not hepatic; partially inactivated in GI tract by chelate formation
Half-life elimination: 12-15 hours (usually increases to 22-24 hours with multiple doses); End-stage renal disease: 18-25 hours
Time to peak, serum: 1.5-4 hours
Excretion: Feces (30%); urine (23%)

Dosage

Children:

Anthrax: Doxycycline should be used in children if antibiotic susceptibility testing, exhaustion of drug supplies, or allergic reaction preclude use of penicillin or ciprofloxacin. For treatment, the consensus recommendation does not include a loading dose for doxycycline.

Inhalational (postexposure prophylaxis) (*MMWR*, 2001, 50:889-893): Oral, I.V. (use oral route when possible):

≤8 years: 2.2 mg/kg every 12 hours for 60 days

>8 years and ≤45 kg: 2.2 mg/kg every 12 hours for 60 days

>8 years and >45 kg: 100 mg every 12 hours for 60 days

Cutaneous (treatment): Oral: See dosing for "Inhalational (postexposure prophylaxis)"
Note: In the presence of systemic involvement, extensive edema, and/or lesions on head/neck, doxycycline should initially be administered I.V.

Inhalational/gastrointestinal/oropharyngeal (treatment): I.V.: Refer to dosing for inhalational anthrax (postexposure prophylaxis); switch to oral therapy when clinically appropriate; refer to Adults dosing for "Note" on combined therapy and duration

Children ≥8 years (<45 kg): Susceptible infections: Oral, I.V.: 2-5 mg/kg/day in 1-2 divided doses, not to exceed 200 mg/day

Children >8 years (>45 kg) and Adults: Susceptible infections: Oral, I.V.: 100-200 mg/day in 1-2 divided doses

Acute gonococcal infection (PID) in combination with another antibiotic: 100 mg every 12 hours until improved, followed by 100 mg orally twice daily to complete 14 days

Community-acquired pneumonia: 100 mg twice daily

Lyme disease: Oral: 100 mg twice daily for 14-21 days

Early syphilis: 200 mg/day in divided doses for 14 days

Late syphilis: 200 mg/day in divided doses for 28 days

Uncomplicated chlamydial infections: 100 mg twice daily for ≥7 days

Endometritis, salpingitis, parametritis, or peritonitis: 100 mg I.V. twice daily with cefoxitin 2 g every 6 hours for 4 days and for ≥48 hours after patient improves; then continue with oral therapy 100 mg twice daily to complete a 10- to 14-day course of therapy

Sclerosing agent for pleural effusion injection (unlabeled use): 500 mg as a single dose in 30-50 mL of NS or SWI

Periodontitis: Oral (Periostat®): 20 mg twice daily as an adjunct following scaling and root planing; may be administered for up to 9 months. Safety beyond 12 months of treatment and efficacy beyond 9 months of treatment have not been established.

Adults:

Anthrax:

Inhalational (postexposure prophylaxis): Oral, I.V. (use oral route when possible): 100 mg every 12 hours for 60 days (*MMWR*, 2001, 50:889-93); **Note:** Preliminary recommendation, FDA review and update is anticipated.

Cutaneous (treatment): Oral: 100 mg every 12 hours for 60 days. **Note:** In the presence of systemic involvement, extensive edema, lesions on head/neck, refer to I.V. dosing for treatment of inhalational/gastrointestinal/oropharyngeal anthrax

Inhalational/gastrointestinal/oropharyngeal (treatment): I.V.: Initial: 100 mg every 12 hours; switch to oral therapy when clinically appropriate; some recommend initial loading dose of 200 mg, followed by 100 mg every 8-12 hours (*JAMA*, 1997, 278:399-411). **Note:** Initial treatment should include two or more agents predicted to be effective (per CDC recommendations). Agents suggested for use in conjunction with doxycycline or ciprofloxacin include rifampin, vancomycin, imipenem, penicillin, ampicillin, chloramphenicol, clindamycin, and clarithromycin. May switch to oral antimicrobial therapy when clinically appropriate. Continue combined therapy for 60 days

Dosing adjustment in renal impairment: No adjustment necessary

Dialysis: Not dialyzable; 0% to 5% by hemo- and peritoneal methods or by continuous arteriovenous or venovenous hemofiltration: No supplemental dosage necessary

Administration

Oral: Administer with adequate fluid to reduce risk of esophageal irritation and ulceration; may administer with meals to decrease GI upset

I.V.: Infuse I.V. doxycycline over 1-4 hours

Patient Information Avoid unnecessary exposure to sunlight; finish all medication; do not skip doses. Consult prescriber if you are pregnant.

Dosage Forms CAP, as hyclate: 50 mg, 100 mg; (Vibramycin®): 100 mg. **CAP, as monohydrate** (Monodox®): 50 mg, 100 mg. **CAP, coated pellets, as hyclate** (Doryx®): 75 mg, 100 mg. **INJ, powder for reconstitution, as hyclate** (Doxy-100®): 100 mg. **POWDER, oral suspension, as monohydrate** (Vibramycin®): 25 mg/5 mL (60 mL). **SYR, as calcium** (Vibramycin®): 50 mg/5 mL (480 mL). **TAB, as hyclate:** 100 mg; (Periostat®): 20 mg; (Vibra-Tabs®): 100 mg. **TAB, as monohydrate** (Adoxa™): 50 mg, 75 mg, 100 mg

- **Dried Smallpox Vaccine** *see Smallpox Vaccine on page 1142*
- **Drisdol**® *see Ergocalciferol on page 449*
- **Dristan**® **Sinus [OTC]** *see Pseudoephedrine and Ibuprofen on page 1062*
- **Drithocreme**® *see Anthralin on page 101*
- **Dritho-Scalp**® *see Anthralin on page 101*
- **Drixomed**® *see Dexbrompheniramine and Pseudoephedrine on page 359*
- **Drixoral**® **Cold & Allergy [OTC]** *see Dexbrompheniramine and Pseudoephedrine on page 359*
- **Drize**®**-R** *see Chlorpheniramine, Phenylephrine, and Methscopolamine on page 264*

Dronabinol (droe NAB i nol)

U.S. Brand Names Marinol®
Synonyms Delta-9-tetrahydro-cannabinol; Delta-9 THC; Tetrahydrocannabinol; THC
Therapeutic Category Antiemetic
Use Chemotherapy-associated nausea and vomiting refractory to other antiemetic; AIDS- and cancer-related anorexia
Restrictions C-III
Pregnancy Risk Factor C
Contraindications Hypersensitivity to dronabinol or any component of the formulation, or marijuana; should be avoided in patients with a history of schizophrenia
Warnings/Precautions Use with caution in patients with heart disease, hepatic disease, or seizure disorders. Reduce dosage in patients with severe hepatic impairment. May have potential for abuse; drug is psychoactive substance in marijuana. Monitor for possible psychotic reaction with first dose.
Common Adverse Reactions
>10%:
Central nervous system: Drowsiness (48%), sedation (53%), confusion (30%), dizziness (21%), detachment, anxiety, difficulty concentrating, mood change
Gastrointestinal: Appetite increased (when used as an antiemetic), xerostomia (38% to 50%)
1% to 10%:
Cardiovascular: Orthostatic hypotension, tachycardia
Central nervous system: Ataxia (4%), depression (7%), headache, vertigo, hallucinations (5%), memory lapse (4%)
Neuromuscular & skeletal: Paresthesia, weakness
Drug Interactions
Increased Effect/Toxicity: Increased toxicity (drowsiness) with alcohol, barbiturates, and benzodiazepines.
Mechanism of Action Unknown, may inhibit endorphins in the emetic center, suppress prostaglandin synthesis, and/or inhibit medullary activity through an unspecified cortical action
Pharmacodynamics/Kinetics
Onset of action: Within 1 hour
Absorption: Oral: 90% to 95%; ~5% to 10% of dose gets into systemic circulation
Distribution: V_d: 2.5-6.4 L; tetrahydrocannabinol is highly lipophilic and distributes to adipose tissue
Protein binding: 97% to 99%
Metabolism: Hepatic to at least 50 metabolites, some of which are active; 11-hydroxytetrahydrocannabinol (11-OH-THC) is the major metabolite; extensive first-pass effect
Half-life elimination: THC: 19-24 hours; THC metabolites: 49-53 hours
Time to peak, serum: 2-3 hours
Excretion: Feces (35% as unconjugated metabolites); urine (10% to 15% as acid metabolites and conjugates)
Dosage Refer to individual protocols. Oral:
Antiemetic:
Children: 5 mg/m² starting 6-8 hours before chemotherapy and every 4-6 hours after to be continued for 12 hours after chemotherapy is discontinued
Adults: 5 mg/m² 1-3 hours before chemotherapy, then 5 mg/m²/dose every 2-4 hours after chemotherapy for a total of 4-6 doses/day; increase doses in increments of 2.5 mg/m² to a maximum of 15 mg/m²/dose.
Appetite stimulant: Initial: 2.5 mg twice daily (before lunch and dinner); titrate up to a maximum of 20 mg/day.
Monitoring Parameters CNS effects, heart rate, blood pressure
Reference Range Antinauseant effects: 5-10 ng/mL
Patient Information Avoid activities such as driving which require motor coordination, avoid alcohol and other CNS depressants; may impair coordination and judgment
Dosage Forms CAP, gelatin: 2.5 mg, 5 mg, 10 mg

Droperidol (droe PER i dole)

U.S. Brand Names Inapsine®
Synonyms Dehydrobenzperidol
Therapeutic Category Antiemetic; Antipsychotic Agent, Butyrophenone
Use Antiemetic in surgical and diagnostic procedures; preoperative medication in patients when other treatments are ineffective or inappropriate
Pregnancy Risk Factor C

Contraindications Hypersensitivity to droperidol or any component of the formulation; known or suspected QT prolongation, including congenital long QT syndrome (prolonged QT_c is defined as >440 msec in males or >450 msec in females)

Warnings/Precautions May alter cardiac conduction. Cases of QT prolongation and torsade de pointes, including some fatal cases, have been reported. Use extreme caution in patients with bradycardia (<50 bpm), cardiac disease, concurrent MAOI therapy, Class I and Class III antiarrhythmics or other drugs known to prolong QT interval, and electrolyte disturbances (hypokalemia or hypomagnesemia), including concomitant drugs which may alter electrolytes (diuretics).

Use with caution in patients with seizures, bone marrow suppression, or severe liver disease. May be sedating, use with caution in disorders where CNS depression is a feature. Caution in patients with hemodynamic instability, predisposition to seizures, subcortical brain damage, renal or respiratory disease. Esophageal dysmotility and aspiration have been associated with antipsychotic use - use with caution in patients at risk of pneumonia (ie, Alzheimer's disease). Caution in breast cancer or other prolactin-dependent tumors (may elevate prolactin levels). May alter temperature regulation or mask toxicity of other drugs due to antiemetic effects. May cause orthostatic hypotension - use with caution in patients at risk of this effect or those who would tolerate transient hypotensive episodes (cerebrovascular disease, cardiovascular disease, or other medications which may predispose). Significant hypotension may occur; injection contains benzyl alcohol; injection also contains sulfites which may cause allergic reaction.

May cause anticholinergic effects (confusion, agitation, constipation, xerostomia, blurred vision, urinary retention). Therefore, they should be used with caution in patients with decreased gastrointestinal motility, urinary retention, BPH, xerostomia, or visual problems. Conditions which also may be exacerbated by cholinergic blockade include narrow-angle glaucoma (screening is recommended) and worsening of myasthenia gravis. Relative to other neuroleptics, droperidol has a low potency of cholinergic blockade.

May cause extrapyramidal symptoms, including pseudoparkinsonism, acute dystonic reactions, akathisia, and tardive dyskinesia (risk of these reactions is high relative to other neuroleptics). May be associated with neuroleptic malignant syndrome (NMS) or pigmentary retinopathy. Safety in children <6 months of age has not been established.

Common Adverse Reactions
>10%:
  Cardiovascular: QT_c prolongation (dose dependent)
  Central nervous system: Restlessness, anxiety, extrapyramidal symptoms, dystonic reactions, pseudoparkinsonian signs and symptoms, tardive dyskinesia, seizures, altered central temperature regulation, sedation, drowsiness
  Endocrine & metabolic: Swelling of breasts
  Gastrointestinal: Weight gain, constipation
1% to 10%:
  Cardiovascular: Hypotension (especially orthostatic), tachycardia, abnormal T waves with prolonged ventricular repolarization, hypertension
  Central nervous system: Hallucinations, persistent tardive dyskinesia, akathisia
  Gastrointestinal: Nausea, vomiting
  Genitourinary: Dysuria

Drug Interactions
Increased Effect/Toxicity: Droperidol in combination with certain forms of conduction anesthesia may produce peripheral vasodilitation and hypotension. Droperidol and CNS depressants will likely have additive CNS effects. Droperidol and cyclobenzaprine may have an additive effect on prolonging the QT interval. Use caution with other agents known to prolong QT interval (Class I or Class III antiarrhythmics, some quinolone antibiotics, cisapride, some phenothiazines, pimozide, tricyclic antidepressants). Potassium- or magnesium-depleting agents (diuretics, aminoglycosides, amphotericin B, cyclosporine) may increase risk of arrhythmias. Metoclopramide may increase risk of extrapyramidal symptoms (EPS).

Mechanism of Action Antiemetic effect is a result of blockade of dopamine stimulation of the chemoreceptor trigger zone. Other effects include alpha-adrenergic blockade, peripheral vascular dilation, and reduction of the pressor effect of epinephrine resulting in hypotension and decreased peripheral vascular resistance; may also reduce pulmonary artery pressure

Pharmacodynamics/Kinetics
Onset of action: Peak effect: Parenteral: ~30 minutes
Duration: Parenteral: 2-4 hours, may extend to 12 hours
Absorption: I.M.: Rapid
Distribution: Crosses blood-brain barrier and placenta
  V_d: Children: ~0.25-0.9 L/kg; Adults: ~2 L/kg
Protein binding: Extensive
Metabolism: Hepatic to p-fluorophenylacetic acid, benzimidazolone, p-hydroxypiperidine
Half-life elimination: Adults: 2.3 hours
Excretion: Urine (75%, <1% as unchanged drug); feces (22%, 11% to 50% as unchanged drug)

Dosage Titrate carefully to desired effect
Children 2-12 years: Nausea and vomiting: I.M., I.V.: 0.05-0.06 mg/kg (maximum initial dose: 0.1 mg/kg); additional doses may be repeated to achieve effect; administer additional doses with caution
Adults: Nausea and vomiting: I.M., I.V.: Initial: 2.5 mg; additional doses of 1.25 mg may be administered to achieve desired effect; administer additional doses with caution
(Continued)

Droperidol *(Continued)*

Administration Administer I.M. or I.V.; I.V. should be administered as a rapid IVP (over 30-60 seconds); for I.V. infusion, dilute in 50-100 mL NS or D_5W. ECG monitoring for 2-3 hours after administration is recommended.

Monitoring Parameters To identify QT prolongation, a 12-lead ECG prior to use is recommended; continued ECG monitoring for 2-3 hours following administration is recommended. Vital signs; lipid profile, fasting blood glucose/Hgb A_{1c}, serum magnesium and potassium; BMI; mental status, abnormal involuntary movement scale (AIMS); observe for dystonias, extrapyramidal side effects, and temperature changes

Dosage Forms INJ, solution: 2.5 mg/mL (1 mL, 2 mL)

♦ **Drospirenone and Ethinyl Estradiol** *see* Ethinyl Estradiol and Drospirenone *on page 478*

Drotrecogin Alfa (dro TRE coe jin AL fa)

U.S. Brand Names Xigris®

Synonyms Activated Protein C, Human, Recombinant; Drotrecogin Alfa, Activated; Protein C (Activated), Human, Recombinant

Therapeutic Category Protein C, Activated

Use Reduction of mortality from severe sepsis (associated with organ dysfunction) in adults at high risk of death (eg, APACHE II score ≥25)

Pregnancy Risk Factor C

Contraindications Hypersensitivity to drotrecogin alfa or any component of the formulation; active internal bleeding; recent hemorrhagic stroke (within 3 months); recent head trauma (within 2 months); recent intracranial or intraspinal surgery (within 2 months); intracranial neoplasm or mass lesion; evidence of cerebral herniation; presence of an epidural catheter; trauma with an increased risk of life-threatening bleeding

Warnings/Precautions Increases risk of bleeding; careful evaluation of risks and benefit is required prior to initiation (see Contraindications). Bleeding risk is increased in patients receiving concurrent therapeutic heparin, oral anticoagulants, glycoprotein IIb/IIIa antagonists, platelet aggregation inhibitors, or aspirin at a dosage of >650 mg/day (within 7 days). In addition, an increased bleeding risk is associated with prolonged INR (>3.0), gastrointestinal bleeding (within 6 weeks), decreased platelet count (<30,000/mm³), thrombolytic therapy (within 3 days), recent ischemic stroke (within 3 months), intracranial AV malformation or aneurysm, known bleeding diathesis, severe hepatic disease (chronic), or other condition where bleeding is a significant hazard or difficult to manage due to its location. Discontinue if significant bleeding occurs (may consider continued use after stabilization). Treatment interruption required for invasive procedures. APTT cannot be used to assess coagulopathy during treatment (PT/INR not affected).

Efficacy not established in adult patients at a low risk of death. Patients with pre-existing nonsepsis-related medical conditions with a poor prognosis (anticipated survival <28 days), HIV-infected patients with a CD4 count ≤50 cells/mm³, chronic dialysis patients, pre-existing hypercoagulable conditions, and patients who had received bone marrow, liver, lung, pancreas, or small bowel transplants were excluded from the clinical trial which established benefit. In addition, patients with a high body weight (>135 kg) were not evaluated. Safety and efficacy have not been established in pediatric patients.

Common Adverse Reactions As with all drugs which may affect hemostasis, bleeding is the major adverse effect associated with drotrecogin alfa. Hemorrhage may occur at virtually any site. Risk is dependent on multiple variables, including the dosage administered, concurrent use of multiple agents which alter hemostasis, and patient predisposition.

>10%

Dermatologic: Bruising

Gastrointestinal: Gastrointestinal bleeding

1% to 10%: Hematologic: Bleeding (serious 2.4% during infusion vs 3.5% during 28-day study period; individual events listed as <1%)

Drug Interactions

Increased Effect/Toxicity: Concurrent use of antiplatelet agents, including aspirin (>650 mg/day, recent use within 7 days), cilostazol, clopidogrel, dipyridamole, ticlopidine, NSAIDs, or glycoprotein IIb/IIIa antagonists (recent use within 7 days) may increase risk of bleeding. Concurrent use of low molecular weight heparins or heparin at therapeutic rates of infusion may increase the risk of bleeding. However, the use of low-dose prophylactic heparin does not appear to affect safety. Recent use of thrombolytic agents (within 3 days) may increase the risk of bleeding. Recent use of warfarin (within 7 days or elevation of INR ≥3) may increase the risk of bleeding. Other drugs which interfere with coagulation may increase risk of bleeding (including antithrombin III, danaparoid, direct thrombin inhibitors)

Mechanism of Action Inhibits factors Va and VIIIa, limiting thrombotic effects. Additional *in vitro* data suggest inhibition of plasminogen activator inhibitor-1 (PAF-1) resulting in profibrinolytic activity, inhibition of macrophage production of tumor necrosis factor, blocking of leukocyte adhesion, and limitation of thrombin-induced inflammatory responses. Relative contribution of effects on the reduction of mortality from sepsis is not completely understood.

Pharmacodynamics/Kinetics

Duration: Plasma nondetectable within 2 hours of discontinuation

Metabolism: Inactivated by endogenous plasma protease inhibitors; mean clearance: 40 L/hour; increased with severe sepsis (~50%)

Half-life elimination: 1.6 hours

Dosage I.V.: Adults: 24 mcg/kg/hour for a total of 96 hours; stop infusion **immediately** if clinically-important bleeding is identified

Dosage adjustment in renal impairment: No specific adjustment recommended.

Administration Infuse separately from all other medications. Only dextrose, normal saline, dextrose/saline combinations, and lactated Ringer's solution may be infused through the same line. May administer via infusion pump or syringe pump. Administration of prepared solution must be completed within 12 hours of preparation. Suspend administration for 2 hours prior to invasive procedures or other procedure with significant bleeding risk; may continue treatment immediately following uncomplicated, minimally-invasive procedures, but delay for 12 hours after major invasive procedures/surgery.

Monitoring Parameters Monitor for signs and symptoms of bleeding, hemoglobin/hematocrit, PT/INR, platelet count

Dosage Forms INJ, powder for reconstitution [preservative free]: 5 mg, 20 mg

◆ **Drotrecogin Alfa, Activated** *see* Drotrecogin Alfa *on page 418*
◆ **Droxia**™ *see* Hydroxyurea *on page 638*
◆ **Dryvax**® *see* Smallpox Vaccine *on page 1142*
◆ **DSCG** *see* Cromolyn *on page 316*
◆ **D-Ser(Bu¹)⁶,Azgly¹⁰-LHRH** *see* Goserelin *on page 599*
◆ **D-S-S**® **[OTC]** *see* Docusate *on page 398*
◆ **DT** *see* Diphtheria and Tetanus Toxoid *on page 386*
◆ **DTaP** *see* Diphtheria, Tetanus Toxoids, and Acellular Pertussis Vaccine *on page 389*
◆ **DTIC** *see* Dacarbazine *on page 332*
◆ **DTIC-Dome**® *see* Dacarbazine *on page 332*
◆ **DTO** *see* Opium Tincture *on page 931*
◆ **D-Trp(6)-LHRH** *see* Triptorelin *on page 1274*
◆ **Dulcolax**® **Milk of Magnesia [OTC]** *see* Magnesium Hydroxide *on page 769*
◆ **Dull-C**® **[OTC]** *see* Ascorbic Acid *on page 117*
◆ **Duocaine**™ *see* Lidocaine and Bupivacaine *on page 744*
◆ **DuoNeb**™ *see* Ipratropium and Albuterol *on page 686*
◆ **DuP 753** *see* Losartan *on page 762*
◆ **Duraclon**™ *see* Clonidine *on page 299*
◆ **Duragesic**® *see* Fentanyl *on page 514*
◆ **Duramorph**® *see* Morphine Sulfate *on page 861*
◆ **Duranest**® **[DSC]** *see* Etidocaine *on page 495*
◆ **Duratuss**™ *see* Guaifenesin and Pseudoephedrine *on page 605*
◆ **Duratuss**® **DM** *see* Guaifenesin and Dextromethorphan *on page 604*
◆ **Duratuss-G**® *see* Guaifenesin *on page 603*
◆ **Duratuss**™ **GP** *see* Guaifenesin and Pseudoephedrine *on page 605*
◆ **Dura-Vent**®**/DA [DSC]** *see* Chlorpheniramine, Phenylephrine, and Methscopolamine *on page 264*
◆ **Duricef**® *see* Cefadroxil *on page 229*

Dutasteride *(doo TAS teer ide)*

U.S. Brand Names Avodart™
Therapeutic Category 5 Alpha-Reductase Inhibitor
Use Treatment of symptomatic benign prostatic hyperplasia (BPH)
Unlabeled/Investigational Use Treatment of male patterned baldness
Pregnancy Risk Factor X
Dosage Oral: Adults: Male: 0.5 mg once daily
  Dosage adjustment in renal impairment: No adjustment required
  Dosage adjustment in hepatic impairment: Use caution; no specific adjustments recommended
Dosage Forms CAP: 0.5 mg

◆ **DW286** *see* Gemifloxacin *on page 584*
◆ **Dyazide**® *see* Hydrochlorothiazide and Triamterene *on page 627*

Dyclonine *(DYE kloe neen)*

U.S. Brand Names Cēpacol® Maximum Strength [OTC]; Sucrets® [OTC]
Synonyms Dyclonine Hydrochloride
Therapeutic Category Local Anesthetic, Mucous Membrane; Local Anesthetic, Oral
Use Local anesthetic prior to laryngoscopy, bronchoscopy, or endotracheal intubation; use topically for temporary relief of pain associated with oral mucosa or anogenital lesions
Pregnancy Risk Factor C
Dosage Use the lowest dose needed to provide effective anesthesia
  Children and Adults:
    Topical solution:
      Mouth sores: 5-10 mL of 0.5% or 1% to oral mucosa (swab or swish and then spit) 3-4 times/day as needed; maximum single dose: 200 mg (40 mL of 0.5% solution or 20 mL of 1% solution)
      Bronchoscopy: Use 2 mL of the 1% solution or 4 mL of the 0.5% solution sprayed onto the larynx and trachea every 5 minutes until the reflex has been abolished
  Children >2 years and Adults: Lozenge: Slowly dissolve 1 lozenge in mouth every 2 hours as needed
Dosage Forms LOZ (Sucrets®): 1.2 mg, 2 mg, 3 mg. **SPRAY, oral** (Cēpacol® Maximum Strength): 0.1% (120 mL)

- **Dyclonine Hydrochloride** *see* Dyclonine *on page 419*
- **Dymelor [DSC]** *see* AcetoHEXAMIDE *on page 31*
- **Dynabac®** *see* Dirithromycin *on page 391*
- **Dynacin®** *see* Minocycline *on page 844*
- **DynaCirc®** *see* Isradipine *on page 698*
- **DynaCirc® CR** *see* Isradipine *on page 698*
- **Dyna-Hex® [OTC]** *see* Chlorhexidine Gluconate *on page 259*
- **Dyrenium®** *see* Triamterene *on page 1264*
- **E₂C and MPA** *see* Estradiol and Medroxyprogesterone *on page 462*
- **7E3** *see* Abciximab *on page 20*
- **E2020** *see* Donepezil *on page 401*
- **EarSol® HC** *see* Hydrocortisone *on page 632*
- **Easprin®** *see* Aspirin *on page 120*

Echothiophate Iodide (ek oh THYE oh fate EYE oh dide)
Related Information
Glaucoma Drug Therapy Comparison *on page 1481*
U.S. Brand Names Phospholine Iodide®
Synonyms Ecostigmine Iodide
Therapeutic Category Ophthalmic Agent, Miotic
Use Used as miotic in treatment of open-angle glaucoma; may be useful in specific case of narrow-angle glaucoma; accommodative esotropia
Pregnancy Risk Factor C
Dosage Adults:
Ophthalmic: Glaucoma: Instill 1 drop twice daily into eyes with 1 dose just prior to bedtime; some patients have been treated with 1 dose daily or every other day
Accommodative esotropia:
Diagnosis: Instill 1 drop of 0.125% once daily into both eyes at bedtime for 2-3 weeks
Treatment: Use lowest concentration and frequency which gives satisfactory response, with a maximum dose of 0.125% once daily, although more intensive therapy may be used for short periods of time
Dosage Forms POWDER for reconstitution, ophthalmic: 6.25 mg [0.125%]

- **EC-Naprosyn®** *see* Naproxen *on page 882*
- **E. coli Asparaginase** *see* Asparaginase *on page 118*

Econazole (e KONE a zole)
U.S. Brand Names Spectazole®
Synonyms Econazole Nitrate
Therapeutic Category Antifungal Agent, Topical
Use Topical treatment of tinea pedis (athlete's foot), tinea cruris (jock itch), tinea corporis (ringworm), tinea versicolor, and cutaneous candidiasis
Pregnancy Risk Factor C
Contraindications Hypersensitivity to econazole or any component of the formulation
Warnings/Precautions Discontinue drug if sensitivity or chemical irritation occurs; not for ophthalmic or intravaginal use
Common Adverse Reactions 1% to 10%: Genitourinary: Vulvar/vaginal burning
Drug Interactions
Cytochrome P450 Effect: Inhibits CYP2E1 (weak)
Mechanism of Action Alters fungal cell wall membrane permeability; may interfere with RNA and protein synthesis, and lipid metabolism
Pharmacodynamics/Kinetics
Absorption: <10%
Metabolism: Hepatic to more than 20 metabolites
Excretion: Urine; feces (<1%)
Dosage Children and Adults: Topical:
Tinea pedis, tinea cruris, tinea corporis, tinea versicolor: Apply sufficient amount to cover affected areas once daily
Cutaneous candidiasis: Apply sufficient quantity twice daily (morning and evening)
Duration of treatment: Candidal infections and tinea cruris, versicolor, and corporis should be treated for 2 weeks and tinea pedis for 1 month; occasionally, longer treatment periods may be required
Patient Information For external use only; avoid eye contact; report if condition worsens or persists, or irritation occurs
Dosage Forms CRM, topical: 1% (15 g, 30 g, 85 g)

- **Econazole Nitrate** *see* Econazole *on page 420*
- **Econopred®** *see* PrednisoLONE *on page 1031*
- **Econopred® Plus** *see* PrednisoLONE *on page 1031*
- **Ecostigmine Iodide** *see* Echothiophate Iodide *on page 420*

+ **Ecotrin® [OTC]** *see* Aspirin *on page 120*
+ **Ecotrin® Low Adult Strength [OTC]** *see* Aspirin *on page 120*
+ **Ecotrin® Maximum Strength [OTC]** *see* Aspirin *on page 120*
+ **Ed A-Hist®** *see* Chlorpheniramine and Phenylephrine *on page 262*
+ **Edathamil Disodium** *see* Edetate Disodium *on page 422*
+ **Edecrin®** *see* Ethacrynic Acid *on page 474*

Edetate Calcium Disodium (ED e tate KAL see um dye SOW dee um)

U.S. Brand Names Calcium Disodium Versenate®

Synonyms Calcium Disodium Edetate; Calcium EDTA

Therapeutic Category Antidote, Lead Toxicity; Chelating Agent, Parenteral

Use Treatment of symptomatic acute and chronic lead poisoning or for symptomatic patients with high blood lead levels; used as an aid in the diagnosis of lead poisoning; possibly useful in poisoning by zinc, manganese, and certain heavy radioisotopes

Pregnancy Risk Factor B

Contraindications Severe renal disease, anuria

Warnings/Precautions Potentially nephrotoxic; renal tubular acidosis and fatal nephrosis may occur, especially with high doses; ECG changes may occur during therapy; do not exceed recommended daily dose; avoid rapid I.V. infusion in the management of lead encephalopathy, may increase intracranial pressure to lethal levels. If anuria, increasing proteinuria, or hematuria occurs during therapy, discontinue calcium EDTA. Minimize nephrotoxicity by adequate hydration, establishment of good urine output, avoidance of excessive doses, and limitation of continuous administration to ≤5 days.

Common Adverse Reactions Frequency not defined.
Cardiovascular: Arrhythmias, ECG changes, hypotension
Central nervous system: Chills, fever, headache
Dermatologic: Cheilosis, skin lesions
Endocrine & metabolic: Hypercalcemia
Gastrointestinal: Anorexia, GI upset, nausea, vomiting
Hematologic: Anemia, bone marrow suppression (transient)
Hepatic: Liver function test increased (mild)
Local: Thrombophlebitis following I.V. infusion (when concentration >5 mg/mL), pain at injection site following I.M. injection
Neuromuscular & skeletal: Arthralgia, numbness, tremor, paresthesia
Ocular: Lacrimation
Renal: Renal tubular necrosis, microscopic hematuria, proteinuria
Respiratory: Nasal congestion, sneezing
Miscellaneous: Zinc deficiency

Drug Interactions
Decreased Effect: Do not use simultaneously with zinc insulin preparations; do not mix in the same syringe with dimercaprol.

Mechanism of Action Calcium is displaced by divalent and trivalent heavy metals, forming a nonionizing soluble complex that is excreted in urine

Pharmacodynamics/Kinetics
Onset of action: Chelation of lead: I.V.: 1 hour
Absorption: I.M., S.C.: Well absorbed
Distribution: Into extracellular fluid; minimal CSF penetration
Half-life elimination, plasma: I.M.: 1.5 hours; I.V.: 20 minutes
Excretion: Urine (as metal chelates or unchanged drug); decreased GFR decreases elimination

Dosage Several regimens have been recommended:
Diagnosis of lead poisoning: Mobilization test (not recommended by AAP guidelines): I.M., I.V.:
Children: 500 mg/m^2/dose (maximum dose: 1 g) as a single dose or divided into 2 doses
Adults: 500 mg/m^2/dose
Note: Urine is collected for 24 hours after first EDTA dose and analyzed for lead content; if the ratio of mcg of lead in urine to mg calcium EDTA given is >1, then test is considered positive; for convenience, an 8-hour urine collection may be done after a single 50 mg/kg I.M. (maximum dose: 1 g) or 500 mg/m^2 I.V. dose; a positive test occurs if the ratio of lead excretion to mg calcium EDTA >0.5-0.6.
Treatment of lead poisoning: Children and Adults (each regimen is specific for route):
Symptoms of lead encephalopathy and/or blood lead level >70 mcg/dL: Treat 5 days; give in conjunction with dimercaprol; wait a minimum of 2 days with no treatment before considering a repeat course:
I.M.: 250 mg/m^2/dose every 4 hours
I.V.: 50 mg/kg/day as 24-hour continuous I.V. infusion **or** 1-1.5 g/m^2 I.V. as either an 8- to 24-hour infusion or divided into 2 doses every 12 hours
Symptomatic lead poisoning **without** encephalopathy **or** asymptomatic with blood lead level >70 mcg/dL: Treat 3-5 days; treatment with dimercaprol is recommended until the blood lead level concentration <50 mcg/dL:
I.M.: 167 mg/m^2 every 4 hours
I.V.: 1 g/m^2 as an 8- to 24-hour infusion or divided every 12 hours
Asymptomatic **children** with blood lead level 45-69 mcg/dL: I.V.: 25 mg/kg/day for 5 days as an 8- to 24-hour infusion or divided into 2 doses every 12 hours
Depending upon the blood lead level, additional courses may be necessary; repeat at least 2-4 days and preferably 2-4 weeks apart

(Continued)

Edetate Calcium Disodium *(Continued)*

Adults with lead nephropathy: An alternative dosing regimen reflecting the reduction in renal clearance is based upon the serum creatinine. Refer to the following:

Dose of Ca EDTA based on serum creatinine:
$S_{cr} \leq 2$ mg/dL: 1 g/m²/day for 5 days*
S_{cr} 2-3 mg/dL: 500 mg/m²/day for 5 days*
S_{cr} 3-4 mg/dL: 500 mg/m²/dose every 48 hours for 3 doses*
$S_{cr} >4$ mg/dL: 500 mg/m²/week*
*Repeat these regimens monthly until lead excretion is reduced toward normal.

Administration For intermittent I.V. infusion, administer the dose I.V. over at least 1 hour in asymptomatic patients, 2 hours in symptomatic patients; for I.V. continuous infusion, dilute to 2-4 mg/mL in D_5W or NS and infuse over at least 8 hours, usually over 12-24 hours; for I.M. injection, 1 mL of 1% procaine hydrochloride may be added to each mL of EDTA calcium to minimize pain at injection site

Monitoring Parameters BUN, creatinine, urinalysis, I & O, and ECG during therapy; intravenous administration requires a cardiac monitor, blood and urine lead concentrations

Dosage Forms INJ, solution: 200 mg/mL (5 mL)

Edetate Disodium *(ED e tate dye SOW dee um)*

U.S. Brand Names Endrate®

Synonyms Edathamil Disodium; EDTA; Sodium Edetate

Therapeutic Category Antidote, Hypercalcemia; Chelating Agent, Parenteral

Use Emergency treatment of hypercalcemia; control digitalis-induced cardiac dysrhythmias (ventricular arrhythmias)

Pregnancy Risk Factor C

Contraindications Severe renal failure or anuria

Warnings/Precautions Use of this drug is recommended only when the severity of the clinical condition justifies the aggressive measures associated with this type of therapy; use with caution in patients with renal dysfunction, intracranial lesions, seizure disorders, coronary or peripheral vascular disease

Common Adverse Reactions Rapid I.V. administration or excessive doses may cause a sudden drop in serum calcium concentration which may lead to hypocalcemic tetany, seizures, arrhythmias, and death from respiratory arrest. Do **not** exceed recommended dosage and rate of administration.

1% to 10%: Gastrointestinal: Nausea, vomiting, abdominal cramps, diarrhea

Drug Interactions

Increased Effect/Toxicity: Increased effect of insulin (edetate disodium may decrease blood glucose concentrations and reduce insulin requirements in diabetic patients treated with insulin).

Mechanism of Action Chelates with divalent or trivalent metals to form a soluble complex that is then eliminated in urine

Pharmacodynamics/Kinetics

Metabolism: None
Half-life elimination: 20-60 minutes
Time to peak: I.V.: 24-48 hours
Excretion: Following chelation: Urine (95%); chelates within 24-48 hours

Dosage Hypercalcemia: I.V.:

Children: 40-70 mg/kg/day slow infusion over 3-4 hours or more to a maximum of 3 g/24 hours; administer for 5 days and allow 5 days between courses of therapy

Adults: 50 mg/kg/day over 3 or more hours to a maximum of 3 g/24 hours; a suggested regimen of 5 days followed by 2 days without drug and repeated courses up to 15 total doses

Digitalis-induced arrhythmias: Children and Adults: 15 mg/kg/hour (maximum dose: 60 mg/kg/day) as continuous infusion

Administration Parenteral: I.V.: Must be diluted before I.V. use in D_5W or NS to a maximum concentration of 30 mg/mL (3%) and infused over at least 3 hours; avoid extravasation; not for I.M. use

Monitoring Parameters Cardiac function (ECG monitoring); blood pressure during infusion; renal function should be assessed before and during therapy; monitor calcium, magnesium, and potassium levels; cardiac monitor required

Dosage Forms INJ, solution: 150 mg/mL (20 mL)

♦ **Edex**® *see Alprostadil on page 61*

Edrophonium *(ed roe FOE nee um)*

U.S. Brand Names Enlon®; Reversol®

Synonyms Edrophonium Chloride

Therapeutic Category Antidote, Neuromuscular Blocking Agent; Cholinergic Agent; Diagnostic Agent, Myasthenia Gravis

Use Diagnosis of myasthenia gravis; differentiation of cholinergic crises from myasthenia crises; reversal of nondepolarizing neuromuscular blockers; adjunct treatment of respiratory depression caused by curare overdose

Pregnancy Risk Factor C

Contraindications Hypersensitivity to edrophonium, sulfites, or any component of the formulation; GI or GU obstruction

Warnings/Precautions Use with caution in patients with bronchial asthma and those receiving a cardiac glycoside; atropine sulfate should always be readily available as an antagonist. Overdosage can cause cholinergic crisis which may be fatal. I.V. atropine should be readily available for treatment of cholinergic reactions.

Common Adverse Reactions Frequency not defined.

Cardiovascular: Arrhythmias (especially bradycardia), hypotension, decreased carbon monoxide, tachycardia, AV block, nodal rhythm, nonspecific ECG changes, cardiac arrest, syncope, flushing

Central nervous system: Convulsions, dysarthria, dysphonia, dizziness, loss of consciousness, drowsiness, headache

Dermatologic: Skin rash, thrombophlebitis (I.V.), urticaria

Gastrointestinal: Hyperperistalsis, nausea, vomiting, salivation, diarrhea, stomach cramps, dysphagia, flatulence

Genitourinary: Urinary urgency

Neuromuscular & skeletal: Weakness, fasciculations, muscle cramps, spasms, arthralgias

Ocular: Small pupils, lacrimation

Respiratory: Increased bronchial secretions, laryngospasm, bronchiolar constriction, respiratory muscle paralysis, dyspnea, respiratory depression, respiratory arrest, bronchospasm

Miscellaneous: Diaphoresis (increased), anaphylaxis, allergic reactions

Drug Interactions

Increased Effect/Toxicity: Digoxin may enhance bradycardia potential of edrophonium. Effects of succinylcholine, decamethonium, nondepolarizing muscle relaxants (eg, pancuronium, vecuronium) are prolonged by edrophonium. I.V. acetazolamide, neostigmine, physostigmine, and acute muscle weakness may increase the effects of edrophonium.

Decreased Effect: Atropine, nondepolarizing muscle relaxants, procainamide, and quinidine may antagonize the effects of edrophonium.

Mechanism of Action Inhibits destruction of acetylcholine by acetylcholinesterase. This facilitates transmission of impulses across myoneural junction and results in increased cholinergic responses such as miosis, increased tonus of intestinal and skeletal muscles, bronchial and ureteral constriction, bradycardia, and increased salivary and sweat gland secretions.

Pharmacodynamics/Kinetics

Onset of action: I.M.: 2-10 minutes; I.V.: 30-60 seconds

Duration: I.M.: 5-30 minutes; I.V.: 10 minutes

Distribution: V_d: 1.1 L/kg

Half-life elimination: 1.8 hours

Dosage Usually administered I.V., however, if not possible, I.M. or S.C. may be used:

Infants:

I.M.: 0.5-1 mg

I.V.: Initial: 0.1 mg, followed by 0.4 mg if no response; total dose = 0.5 mg

Children:

Diagnosis: Initial: 0.04 mg/kg over 1 minute followed by 0.16 mg/kg if no response, to a maximum total dose of 5 mg for children <34 kg, or 10 mg for children >34 kg **or**

Alternative dosing (manufacturer's recommendation):

≤34 kg: 1 mg; if no response after 45 seconds, repeat dosage in 1 mg increments every 30-45 seconds, up to a total of 5 mg

>34 kg: 2 mg; if no response after 45 seconds, repeat dosage in 1 mg increments every 30-45 seconds, up to a total of 10 mg

I.M.:

<34 kg: 1 mg

>34 kg: 5 mg

Titration of oral anticholinesterase therapy: 0.04 mg/kg once given 1 hour after oral intake of the drug being used in treatment; if strength improves, an increase in neostigmine or pyridostigmine dose is indicated

Adults:

Diagnosis:

I.V.: 2 mg test dose administered over 15-30 seconds; 8 mg given 45 seconds later if no response is seen; test dose may be repeated after 30 minutes

I.M.: Initial: 10 mg; if no cholinergic reaction occurs, administer 2 mg 30 minutes later to rule out false-negative reaction

Titration of oral anticholinesterase therapy: 1-2 mg given 1 hour after oral dose of anticholinesterase; if strength improves, an increase in neostigmine or pyridostigmine dose is indicated

Reversal of nondepolarizing neuromuscular blocking agents (neostigmine with atropine usually preferred): I.V.: 10 mg over 30-45 seconds; may repeat every 5-10 minutes up to 40 mg

Termination of paroxysmal atrial tachycardia: I.V. rapid injection: 5-10 mg

Differentiation of cholinergic from myasthenic crisis: I.V.: 1 mg; may repeat after 1 minute. **Note:** Intubation and controlled ventilation may be required if patient has cholinergic crisis

Dosing adjustment in renal impairment: Dose may need to be reduced in patients with chronic renal failure

Administration Edrophonium is administered by direct I.V. injection; see Dosage

Dosage Forms INJ, solution: 10 mg/mL (15 mL); (Enlon®): 10 mg/mL (15 mL); (Reversol®): 10 mg/mL (10 mL)

Efalizumab (e fa li ZOO mab)

U.S. Brand Names Raptiva™

Synonyms Anti-CD11a; hu1124

Therapeutic Category Immunosuppressant Agent; Monoclonal Antibody

Use Treatment of chronic moderate-to-severe plaque psoriasis in patients who are candidates for systemic therapy or phototherapy

Pregnancy Risk Factor C

Contraindications Hypersensitivity to efalizumab or any component of the formulation

Warnings/Precautions May result in increased susceptibility to infections; use caution with chronic infections, history of recurrent infection, or the elderly. Discontinue therapy if serious infection develops. Use caution in patients at high risk for malignancy or history of malignancy; effects of efalizumab on the development of malignancies is unknown. Psoriasis may worsen with efalizumab treatment or following discontinuation (rare). First-dose reactions have been reported; a lower, conditioning dose is recommended to reduce the incidence and severity of reactions. Concomitant use with other immunosuppressant agents is not recommended. Produced in a Chinese hamster cell medium. Safety and efficacy in pediatric patients or patients with renal or hepatic impairment have not been established.

Common Adverse Reactions

>10%:
  Central nervous system: Headache (32%), chills (13%)
  Gastrointestinal: Nausea (11%)
  Hematologic: Lymphocytosis (40%), leukocytosis (26%)
  Miscellaneous: First-dose reaction (29%, described as chills, fever, headache, myalgia, and nausea occurring within 2 days of the first injection; percent reported in patients receiving a 1 mg/kg dose; severity decreased with 0.7 mg/kg dose); infection (29%, serious infection <1%)

1% to 10%:
  Cardiovascular: Peripheral edema (1% to 2%)
  Central nervous system: Pain (10%), fever (7%)
  Dermatologic: Acne (4%), psoriasis (1% to 2%), urticaria (1%)
  Hepatic: Alkaline phosphatase elevated (4%)
  Neuromuscular & skeletal: Myalgia (8%), back pain (4%), arthralgia (1% to 2%), weakness (1% to 2%)
  Miscellaneous: Antibodies to efalizumab (6%), hypersensitivity reaction (8%), flu-like syndrome (7%)

Drug Interactions

Decreased Effect: Note: Formal drug interaction studies have not been conducted. Acellular, live, and live-attenuated vaccines should not be administered during therapy.

Mechanism of Action Efalizumab is a recombinant monoclonal antibody which binds to CD11a, a subunit of leukocyte function antigen-1 (LFA-1) found on leukocytes. By binding to CD11a, efalizumab blocks multiple T-cell mediated responses involved in the pathogenesis of psoriatic plaques.

Pharmacodynamics/Kinetics

Onset: Reduction of CD11a expression and free CD11a-binding sites seen 1-2 days after the first dose; time to steady state serum concentration: 4 weeks
  Response to therapy (75% reduction from baseline of PASI score): Observed after 12 weeks
Duration: CD11a expression was ~74% of baseline at 5-13 weeks after discontinuing dose; free CD11a binding sites were at ~85% of baseline at 8-13 weeks following discontinuation; response to therapy (75% reduction from baseline PASI score) continued 1-2 months after discontinuation
Bioavailability: S.C.: 50%
Excretion: Time to eliminate (at steady state): 25 days

Dosage S.C.: Adults: Psoriasis: Initial: 0.7 mg/kg, followed by weekly dose of 1 mg/kg (maximum: 200 mg/dose)

Administration For S.C. injection in the abdomen, buttocks, thigh, or upper arm

Monitoring Parameters Platelet counts (at least monthly at the start of treatment, every 3 months as therapy continues); signs of infection; worsening of psoriasis

Dosage Forms INJ, powder for reconstitution: 150 mg [delivers 125 mg/1.25 mL; packaged with prefilled syringe containing SWFI]

Efavirenz (e FAV e renz)

Related Information

Antiretroviral Therapy for HIV Infection *on page 1448*
Management of Healthcare Worker Exposures to HBV, HCV, and HIV *on page 1421*

U.S. Brand Names Sustiva®

Therapeutic Category Antiretroviral Agent, Non-nucleoside Reverse Transcriptase Inhibitor (NNRTI)

Use Treatment of HIV-1 infections in combination with at least two other antiretroviral agents

Pregnancy Risk Factor C

Contraindications Clinically-significant hypersensitivity to efavirenz or any component of the formulation; concurrent use of astemizole, cisapride, midazolam, triazolam, or ergot alkaloids (includes dihydroergotamine, ergotamine, ergonovine, methylergonovine)

Warnings/Precautions Do not use as single-agent therapy; avoid pregnancy; women of childbearing potential should undergo pregnancy testing prior to initiation of therapy; use caution with other agents metabolized by cytochrome P450 isoenzyme 3A4 (see Contraindications); use caution with history of mental illness/drug abuse (predisposition to psychological reactions); may cause CNS and psychiatric symptoms, which include impaired concentration, dizziness or drowsiness (avoid potentially hazardous tasks such as driving or operating machinery if these effects are noted); serious psychiatric side effects have been associated with efavirenz, including severe depression, suicide, paranoia, and mania; discontinue if severe rash (involving blistering, desquamation, mucosal involvement or fever) develops. Children are more susceptible to development of rash; prophylactic antihistamines may be used. Caution in patients with known or suspected hepatitis B or C infection (monitoring of liver function is recommended); hepatic impairment. Persistent elevations of serum transaminases >5 times the upper limit of normal should prompt evaluation - benefit of continued therapy should be weighed against possible risk of hepatotoxicity. Concomitant use with St John's wort is not recommended.

Common Adverse Reactions

>10%:
Central nervous system: Dizziness* (2% to 28%), depression (1% to 16%), insomnia (6% to 16%), anxiety (1% to 11%), pain* (1% to 13%)

Dermatologic: Rash* (NCI grade 1: 9% to 11%, NCI grade 2: 15% to 32%, NCI grade 3 or 4: <1%); 26% experienced new rash vs 17% in control groups; up to 46% of pediatric patients experience rash (median onset: 8 days)

Endocrine & metabolic: HDL increased (25% to 35%), total cholesterol increased (20% to 40%)

Gastrointestinal: Diarrhea* (3% to 14%), nausea* (2% to 12%)

1% to 10%:
Central nervous system: Impaired concentration (2% to 8%), headache* (2% to 7%), somnolence (2% to 7%), fatigue (2% to 7%), abnormal dreams (1% to 6%), nervousness (2% to 6%), severe depression (2%), hallucinations (1%)

Dermatologic: Pruritus (1% to 9%), diaphoresis increased (1% to 2%)

Gastrointestinal: Vomiting* (6% to 7%), dyspepsia (3%), abdominal pain (1% to 3%), anorexia (1% to 2%)

*Adverse effect reported in ≥10% of patients 3-16 years of age

Drug Interactions

Cytochrome P450 Effect: Substrate (major) of CYP2B6, 3A4; **Inhibits** CYP2C8/9 (weak), 2C19 (weak), 3A4 (weak); **Induces** CYP2B6 (weak), 3A4 (weak)

Increased Effect/Toxicity: Coadministration with medications metabolized by these enzymes may lead to increased concentration-related effects. Cisapride, midazolam, triazolam, and ergot alkaloids may result in life-threatening toxicities; concurrent use is contraindicated. The AUC of nelfinavir is increased (20%); AUC of both ritonavir and efavirenz are increased by 20% during concurrent therapy. The AUC of ethinyl estradiol is increased 37% by efavirenz (clinical significance unknown). May increase (or decrease) effect of warfarin.

Decreased Effect: CYP2B6 inducers may decrease the levels/effects of efavirenz; example inducers include carbamazepine, nevirapine, phenobarbital, phenytoin, and rifampin. St John's wort may decrease serum concentrations of efavirenz. Concentrations of indinavir may be reduced; dosage increase to 1000 mg 3 times/day is recommended. Concentration of lopinavir are decreased; increase dosage of lopinavir/ritonavir to 533 mg/133 mg twice daily. Concentrations of saquinavir may be decreased (use as sole protease inhibitor is not recommended). The AUC of amprenavir may be decreased (36%). Plasma concentrations of clarithromycin are decreased (clinical significance unknown). Serum concentrations of methadone are decreased; monitor for withdrawal. May decrease (or increase) effect of warfarin. Serum concentrations of sertraline may be decreased by efavirenz.

Mechanism of Action As a non-nucleoside reverse transcriptase inhibitor, efavirenz has activity against HIV-1 by binding to reverse transcriptase. It consequently blocks the RNA-dependent and DNA-dependent DNA polymerase activities including HIV-1 replication. It does not require intracellular phosphorylation for antiviral activity.

Pharmacodynamics/Kinetics

Absorption: Increased by fatty meals

Distribution: CSF concentrations exceed free fraction in serum

Protein binding: >99%, primarily to albumin

Metabolism: Hepatic via CYP3A4 and 2B6; may induce its own metabolism

Half-life elimination: Single dose: 52-76 hours; Multiple doses: 40-55 hours

Time to peak: 3-8 hours

Excretion: Feces (16% to 41% primarily as unchanged drug); urine (14% to 34% as metabolites)

Dosage Oral: Dosing at bedtime is recommended to limit central nervous system effects; should not be used as single-agent therapy

Children: Dosage is based on body weight
10 kg to <15 kg: 200 mg once daily
15 kg to <20 kg: 250 mg once daily
20 kg to <25 kg: 300 mg once daily
25 kg to <32.5 kg: 350 mg once daily
32.5 kg to <40 kg: 400 mg once daily
≥40 kg: 600 mg once daily
Adults: 600 mg once daily

Dosing adjustment in renal impairment: None recommended

Dosing comments in hepatic impairment: Limited clinical experience, use with caution

Administration Administer on an empty stomach. ,

(Continued)

Efavirenz *(Continued)*

Monitoring Parameters Serum transaminases (discontinuation of treatment should be considered for persistent elevations greater than five times the upper limit of normal), cholesterol, triglycerides, signs and symptoms of infection

Patient Information Take efavirenz exactly as prescribed; report all side effects; do not alter dose or discontinue without consulting prescriber; many medications (OTC, herbals/supplements, prescription products) cannot be taken with efavirenz; may cause dizziness, drowsiness, impaired concentration, delusions or depression; taking at bedtime may minimize these effects; caution in performing potentially hazardous tasks such as operating machinery or driving; do not get pregnant; avoid high-fat meals

Dosage Forms CAP: 50 mg, 100 mg, 200 mg. **TAB:** 600 mg

♦ **Effer-K**™ *see* Potassium Bicarbonate and Potassium Citrate *on page 1019*

♦ **Effexor**® *see* Venlafaxine *on page 1300*

♦ **Effexor**® **XR** *see* Venlafaxine *on page 1300*

♦ **Eflone**® *see* Fluorometholone *on page 536*

Eflornithine *(ee FLOR ni theen)*

U.S. Brand Names Vaniqa™

Synonyms DFMO; Eflornithine Hydrochloride

Therapeutic Category Antiprotozoal; Topical Skin Product

Use Cream: Females ≥12 years: Reduce unwanted hair from face and adjacent areas under the chin

Orphan status: Injection: Treatment of meningoencephalitic stage of *Trypanosoma brucei gambiense* infection (sleeping sickness)

Pregnancy Risk Factor C

Contraindications Hypersensitivity to eflornithine or any component of the formulation

Warnings/Precautions

Injection: Must be diluted before use; frequent monitoring for myelosuppression should be done; use with caution in patients with a history of seizures and in patients with renal impairment; serial audiograms should be obtained; due to the potential for relapse, patients should be followed up for at least 24 months

Cream: For topical use by females only; discontinue if hypersensitivity occurs; safety and efficacy in children <12 years has not been studied

Common Adverse Reactions

Injection:

>10%: Hematologic (reversible): Anemia (55%), leukopenia (37%), thrombocytopenia (14%)

1% to 10%:

Central nervous system: Seizures (may be due to the disease) (8%), dizziness

Dermatologic: Alopecia

Gastrointestinal: Vomiting, diarrhea

Hematologic: Eosinophilia

Otic: Hearing impairment

Topical:

>10%: Dermatologic: Acne (11% to 21%), pseudofolliculitis barbae (5% to 15%)

1% to 10%:

Central nervous system: Headache (4% to 5%), dizziness (1%), vertigo (0.3% to 1%)

Dermatologic: Pruritus (3% to 4%), burning skin (2% to 4%), tingling skin (1% to 4%), dry skin (2% to 3%), rash (1% to 3%), facial edema (0.3% to 3%), alopecia (1% to 2%), skin irritation (1% to 2%), erythema (0% to 2%), ingrown hair (0.3% to 2%), folliculitis (0% to 1%)

Gastrointestinal: Dyspepsia (2%), anorexia (0.7% to 2%)

Drug Interactions

Increased Effect/Toxicity: Cream: Possible interactions with other topical products have not been studied.

Decreased Effect: Cream: Possible interactions with other topical products have not been studied.

Mechanism of Action Eflornithine exerts antitumor and antiprotozoal effects through specific, irreversible ("suicide") inhibition of the enzyme ornithine decarboxylase (ODC). ODC is the rate-limiting enzyme in the biosynthesis of putrescine, spermine, and spermidine, the major polyamines in nucleated cells. Polyamines are necessary for the synthesis of DNA, RNA, and proteins and are, therefore, necessary for cell growth and differentiation. Although many microorganisms and higher plants are able to produce polyamines from alternate biochemical pathways, all mammalian cells depend on ornithine decarboxylase to produce polyamines. Eflornithine inhibits ODC and rapidly depletes animal cells of putrescine and spermidine; the concentration of spermine remains the same or may even increase. Rapidly dividing cells appear to be most susceptible to the effects of eflornithine. Topically, the inhibition of ODC in the skin leads to a decreased rate of hair growth.

Pharmacodynamics/Kinetics

Absorption: Topical: <1%

Half-life elimination: I.V.: 3-3.5 hours; Topical: 8 hours

Excretion: Primarily urine (as unchanged drug)

Dosage

Children ≥12 years and Adults: Females: Topical: Apply thin layer of cream to affected areas of face and adjacent chin twice daily, at least 8 hours apart

Adults: I.V. infusion: 100 mg/kg/dose given every 6 hours (over at least 45 minutes) for 14 days

Dosing adjustment in renal impairment: Injection: Dose should be adjusted although no specific guidelines are available

Administration Cream: Apply thin layer of eflornithine cream to affected areas of face and adjacent chin area twice daily, at least 8 hours apart. Rub in thoroughly. Hair removal techniques must still be continued; wait at least 5 minutes after removing hair to apply cream. Do not wash affected area for at least 8 hours following application.

Monitoring Parameters CBC with platelet counts

Patient Information

Injection: Report any persistent or unusual fever, sore throat, fatigue, bleeding, or bruising; frequent blood tests are needed during therapy.

Cream: For topical use only. This product will not prevent hair growth, but will decrease the rate of growth. You will still need to use hair removal techniques, such as shaving and plucking, while using eflornithine cream. Wait at least 5 minutes after removing hair to apply cream. Improvement can be seen within 4-8 weeks of use. Following discontinuation of use, pretreatment hair growth will be seen in about 8 weeks. Contact prescriber if skin irritation or intolerance develop. Do not wash affected area for at least 8 hours following application. You may apply cosmetics or make-up over the affected area once the cream has dried.

Dosage Forms CRM, topical: 13.9% (30 g). **INJ, solution:** 200 mg/mL (100 mL)

- **Eflornithine Hydrochloride** *see* Eflornithine *on page 426*
- **Efudex®** *see* Fluorouracil *on page 536*
- **E-Gems® [OTC]** *see* Vitamin E *on page 1311*
- **EHDP** *see* Etidronate Disodium *on page 495*
- **Elavil® [DSC]** *see* Amitriptyline *on page 79*
- **Eldepryl®** *see* Selegiline *on page 1128*
- **Eldopaque® [OTC]** *see* Hydroquinone *on page 636*
- **Eldopaque Forte®** *see* Hydroquinone *on page 636*
- **Eldoquin® [OTC]** *see* Hydroquinone *on page 636*
- **Eldoquin Forte®** *see* Hydroquinone *on page 636*
- **Electrolyte Lavage Solution** *see* Polyethylene Glycol-Electrolyte Solution *on page 1013*
- **Elestat™** *see* Epinastine *on page 437*

Eletriptan (el e TRIP tan)

Related Information
Antimigraine Drugs Comparison *on page 1363*

U.S. Brand Names Relpax®

Synonyms Eletriptan Hydrobromide

Therapeutic Category Serotonin 5-HT$_{1B, 1D}$ Receptor Agonist

Use Acute treatment of migraine, with or without aura

Pregnancy Risk Factor C

Contraindications Hypersensitivity to eletriptan or any component of the formulation; ischemic heart disease or signs or symptoms of ischemic heart disease (including Prinzmetal's angina, angina pectoris, MI, silent myocardial ischemia); cerebrovascular syndromes (including strokes, transient ischemic attacks); peripheral vascular syndromes (including ischemic bowel disease); uncontrolled hypertension; use within 24 hours of ergotamine derivatives; use within 24 hours of another 5-HT$_1$ agonist; use within 72 hours of potent CYP3A4 inhibitors; management of hemiplegic or basilar migraine; prophylactic treatment of migraine; severe hepatic impairment

Warnings/Precautions Eletriptan is indicated only in patients ≥18 years of age with a clear diagnosis of migraine headache. If a patient does not respond to the first dose, the diagnosis of migraine should be reconsidered. Do not give to patients with risk factors for CAD until a cardiovascular evaluation has been performed; if evaluation is satisfactory, the healthcare provider should administer the first dose and cardiovascular status should be periodically evaluated. Cardiac events (coronary artery vasospasm, transient ischemia, MI, ventricular tachycardia/fibrillation, cardiac arrest, and death), cerebral/subarachnoid hemorrhage, stroke, peripheral vascular ischemia, and colonic ischemia have been reported with 5-HT$_1$ agonist administration. Significant elevation in blood pressure, including hypertensive crisis, has also been reported on rare occasions in patients with and without a history of hypertension. Use with caution in renal or mild to moderate hepatic impairment. Safety and efficacy in pediatric patients have not been established.

Common Adverse Reactions 1% to 10%:
Cardiovascular: Chest pain/tightness (1% to 4%; placebo 1%), palpitation
Central nervous system: Dizziness (3% to 7%; placebo 3%), somnolence (3% to 7%; placebo 4%), headache (3% to 4%; placebo 3%), chills, pain, vertigo
Gastrointestinal: Nausea (4% to 8%; placebo 5%), xerostomia (2% to 4%; placebo 2%), dysphagia (1% to 2%), abdominal pain/discomfort (1% to 2%; placebo 1%), dyspepsia (1% to 2%; placebo 1%)
Neuromuscular & skeletal: Weakness (4% to 10%), paresthesia (3% to 4%), back pain, hypertonia, hypesthesia
Respiratory: Pharyngitis
Miscellaneous: Diaphoresis
(Continued)

Eletriptan *(Continued)*

Drug Interactions
Cytochrome P450 Effect: Substrate of CYP3A4 (major)

Increased Effect/Toxicity: CYP3A4 inhibitors increase serum concentration and half-life of eletriptan; do not use eletriptan within 72 hours of potent CYP3A4 inhibitors (ie, erythromycin, fluconazole, ketoconazole, and verapamil). Ergot-containing drugs prolong vasospastic reactions; do not use within 24 hours of eletriptan.

Mechanism of Action Selective agonist for serotonin (5-HT$_{1B}$, 5-HT$_{1D}$, 5-HT$_{1F}$ receptors) in cranial arteries; causes vasoconstriction and reduce sterile inflammation associated with antidromic neuronal transmission correlating with relief of migraine

Pharmacodynamics/Kinetics
Absorption: Well absorbed

Distribution: V$_d$: 138 L

Protein binding: ~85%

Metabolism: Hepatic via CYP3A4; forms one metabolite (active)

Bioavailability: ~50%, increased with high-fat meal

Half-life elimination: 4 hours (Elderly: 4.4-5.7 hours); Metabolite: ~13 hours

Time to peak, plasma: 1.5-2 hours

Dosage Oral: Adults: Acute migraine: 20-40 mg; if the headache improves but returns, dose may be repeated after 2 hours have elapsed since first dose; maximum 80 mg/day.

Note: If the first dose is ineffective, diagnosis needs to be re-evaluated. Safety of treating >3 headaches/month has not been established.

Dosage adjustment in renal impairment: No dosing adjustment needed; monitor for increased blood pressure

Dosage adjustment in hepatic impairment:
Mild to moderate impairment: No adjustment necessary
Severe impairment: Use is contraindicated

Patient Information Inform prescriber of all prescriptions, OTC medications, or herbal products you are taking, and any allergies you have. This drug is to be used to reduce your migraine, not to prevent or reduce the number of attacks. Follow exact instructions for use. Do not use more than two doses in 24 hours and do not take within 24 hours of any other migraine medication without consulting prescriber. May cause dizziness, fatigue, or drowsiness (use caution when driving or engaging in tasks requiring alertness until response to drug is known). Report immediately any chest pain, palpitations, or throbbing; feelings of tightness or pressure in jaw or throat; acute headache or dizziness; muscle cramping, pain, or tremors; skin rash; hallucinations, anxiety, panic; or other adverse reactions.

Dosage Forms TAB [film-coated]: 20 mg, 40 mg (as base)

Emtricitabine *(em trye SYE ta been)*

Related Information
Antiretroviral Therapy for HIV Infection *on page 1448*

U.S. Brand Names Emtriva™

Synonyms BW524W91; Coviracil; FTC

Therapeutic Category Antiretroviral Agent, Nucleoside Reverse Transcriptase Inhibitor (NRTI) [Cytosine Analog]

Use Treatment of HIV infection in combination with at least two other antiretroviral agents

Unlabeled/Investigational Use Investigational: Hepatitis B

Pregnancy Risk Factor B

Contraindications Hypersensitivity to emtricitabine or any component of the formulation

Warnings/Precautions Lactic acidosis, severe hepatomegaly, and hepatic failure have occurred rarely with emtricitabine (similar to other nucleoside analogues). Some cases have been fatal; stop treatment if lactic acidosis or hepatotoxicity occur. Prior liver disease, obesity, extended duration of therapy, and female gender may represent risk factors for severe hepatic reactions. Testing for hepatitis B is recommended prior to the initiation of therapy; hepatitis B may be exacerbated following discontinuation of emtricitabine. Use caution in patients with renal impairment (dosage adjustment required).

Common Adverse Reactions Clinical trials were conducted in patients receiving other antiretroviral agents, and it is not possible to correlate frequency of adverse events with emtricitabine alone. The range of frequencies of adverse events is generally comparable to comparator groups, with the exception of hyperpigmentation, which occurred more frequently in patients receiving emtricitabine.

>10%:

Central nervous system: Headache (13% to 22%), dizziness (4% to 25%), insomnia (7% to 16%)

Dermatologic: Rash (17% to 30%; includes rash, pruritus, maculopapular rash, vesiculobullous rash, pustular rash, and allergic reaction)

Gastrointestinal: Diarrhea (23%), nausea (13% to 18%), abdominal pain (8% to 14%)

Neuromuscular & skeletal: Weakness (12% to 16%), CPK increased (11% to 12%)

Respiratory: Cough (14%), rhinitis (12% to 18%)

1% to 10%:

Central nervous system: Abnormal dreams (2% to 11%), depression (6% to 9%), neuropathy/neuritis (4%)

Dermatologic: Hyperpigmentation (2% to 6%; primarily of palms and/or soles but may include tongue, arms, lip and nails; generally mild and nonprogressive without associated local reactions such as pruritus or rash)

Endocrine & metabolic: Serum triglycerides increased (9% to 10%), disordered glucose homeostasis (2% to 3%), serum amylase increased (2% to 5%)

Gastrointestinal: Dyspepsia (4% to 8%), vomiting (9%)

Hepatic: Transaminases increased (2% to 6%), bilirubin increased (1%)

Neuromuscular & skeletal: Myalgia (4% to 6%), arthralgia (3% to 5%), paresthesia (5% to 6%)

Drug Interactions

Increased Effect/Toxicity: Concomitant use of ribavirin and nucleoside analogues may increase the risk of developing lactic acidosis.

Mechanism of Action Nucleoside reverse transcriptase inhibitor; emtricitabine is a cytosine analogue which is phosphorylated intracellularly to emtricitabine 5'-triphosphate which interferes with HIV viral RNA dependent DNA polymerase resulting in inhibition of viral replication.

Pharmacodynamics/Kinetics

Absorption: Rapid, extensive

Protein binding: <4%

Metabolism: Limited, via oxidation and conjugation (not via CYP isoenzymes)

Bioavailability: 93%

Half-life elimination: Normal renal function: 10 hours

Time to peak, plasma: 1-2 hours

Excretion: Urine (86% primarily as unchanged drug, 13% as metabolites); feces (14%)

Dosage Oral: Adults: 200 mg once daily

Dosage adjustment in renal impairment:

Cl_{cr} 30-49 mL/minute: 200 mg every 48 hours

Cl_{cr} 15-29 mL/minute: 200 mg every 72 hours

Cl_{cr} <15 mL/minute (including hemodialysis patients): 200 mg every 96 hours

Dosage adjustment in hepatic impairment: No adjustment required.

Administration May be administered with or without food.

Monitoring Parameters Viral load, CD4, liver function tests; hepatitis B testing is recommended prior to initiation of therapy

Patient Information Not a cure for HIV and does not reduce transmission of HIV. May cause headache, dizziness (use caution when driving or engaging in potentially hazardous tasks until response to drug is known); nausea, vomiting, (small, frequent meals, frequent mouth care, chewing gum, or sucking lozenges may help). May cause changes in skin pigmentation, especially on soles and palms. Report muscle weakness or pain; tingling, numbness, or pain in toes or fingers; weakness of extremities; chest pain, palpitations, or rapid heartbeat; swelling of extremities; weight gain or loss >5 lb/week; signs of infection (eg, fever, chills, sore throat, burning urination, fatigue); unusual bleeding (eg, tarry stools, easy bruising, or blood in stool, urine, or mouth); skin rash or irritation.

Dosage Forms CAP: 200 mg

♦ **Emtriva™** *see Emtricitabine on page 428*

♦ **ENA 713** *see Rivastigmine on page 1107*

Enalapril (e NAL a pril)

Related Information

Angiotensin Agents Comparison *on page 1353*

U.S. Brand Names Vasotec®; Vasotec® I.V.

Synonyms Enalaprilat; Enalapril Maleate

Therapeutic Category Angiotensin-Converting Enzyme (ACE) Inhibitor; Antihypertensive Agent

Use Management of mild to severe hypertension; treatment of congestive heart failure, left ventricular dysfunction after myocardial infarction

(Continued)

Enalapril *(Continued)*

Unlabeled/Investigational Use

Unlabeled: Hypertensive crisis, diabetic nephropathy, rheumatoid arthritis, diagnosis of anatomic renal artery stenosis, hypertension secondary to scleroderma renal crisis, diagnosis of aldosteronism, idiopathic edema, Bartter's syndrome, postmyocardial infarction for prevention of ventricular failure

Investigational: Severe congestive heart failure in infants, neonatal hypertension, acute pulmonary edema

Pregnancy Risk Factor C/D (2nd and 3rd trimesters)

Contraindications
Hypersensitivity to enalapril or enalaprilat; angioedema related to previous treatment with an ACE inhibitor; patients with idiopathic or hereditary angioedema; bilateral renal artery stenosis; pregnancy (2nd and 3rd trimesters)

Warnings/Precautions
Anaphylactic reactions can occur. Angioedema can occur at any time during treatment (especially following first dose). Angioedema may involve head and neck (potentially affecting the airway) or the intestine (presenting with abdominal pain). Careful blood pressure monitoring with first dose (hypotension can occur especially in volume depleted patients). Dosage adjustment needed in renal impairment. Use with caution in hypovolemia; collagen vascular diseases; valvular stenosis (particularly aortic stenosis); hyperkalemia; or before, during, or immediately after anesthesia. Avoid rapid dosage escalation which may lead to renal insufficiency. Hypersensitivity reactions may be seen during hemodialysis with high-flux dialysis membranes (eg, AN69). Hyperkalemia may rarely occur. Neutropenia/agranulocytosis with myeloid hyperplasia can rarely occur. If patient has renal impairment then a baseline WBC with differential and serum creatinine should be evaluated and monitored closely during the first 3 months of therapy. Use with caution in unilateral renal artery stenosis and pre-existing renal insufficiency. Experience in children is limited.

Common Adverse Reactions Note:
Frequency ranges include data from hypertension and heart failure trials. Higher rates of adverse reactions have generally been noted in patients with CHF. However, the frequency of adverse effects associated with placebo is also increased in this population.

1% to 10%:

Cardiovascular: Hypotension (0.9% to 7%), chest pain (2%), syncope (0.5% to 2%), orthostasis (2%), orthostatic hypotension (2%)

Central nervous system: Headache (2% to 5%), dizziness (4% to 8%), fatigue (2% to 3%), weakness (2%)

Dermatologic: Rash (2%)

Gastrointestinal: Abnormal taste, abdominal pain, vomiting, nausea, diarrhea, anorexia, constipation

Neuromuscular & skeletal: Weakness

Renal: Increased serum creatinine (0.2% to 20%), worsening of renal function (in patients with bilateral renal artery stenosis or hypovolemia)

Respiratory (1% to 2%): Bronchitis, cough, dyspnea

Drug Interactions

Cytochrome P450 Effect: Substrate of CYP3A4 (major)

Increased Effect/Toxicity: Potassium supplements, co-trimoxazole (high dose), angiotensin II receptor antagonists (candesartan, losartan, irbesartan, etc), or potassium-sparing diuretics (amiloride, spironolactone, triamterene) may result in elevated serum potassium levels when combined with enalapril. ACE inhibitor effects may be increased by phenothiazines or probenecid (increases levels of captopril). ACE inhibitors may increase serum concentrations/effects of digoxin, lithium, and sulfonlyureas.

Diuretics have additive hypotensive effects with ACE inhibitors, and hypovolemia increases the potential for adverse renal effects of ACE inhibitors. In patients with compromised renal function, coadministration with NSAIDs may result in further deterioration of renal function. Allopurinol and ACE inhibitors may cause a higher risk of hypersensitivity reaction when taken concurrently.

Decreased Effect: Aspirin (high dose) may reduce the therapeutic effects of ACE inhibitors; at low dosages this does not appear to be significant. Rifampin may decrease the effect of ACE inhibitors. Antacids may decrease the bioavailability of ACE inhibitors (may be more likely to occur with captopril); separate administration times by 1-2 hours. NSAIDs may reduce the hypotensive effects of ACE inhibitors. More likely to occur in low renin or volume dependent hypertensive patients.

Mechanism of Action
Competitive inhibitor of angiotensin-converting enzyme (ACE); prevents conversion of angiotensin I to angiotensin II, a potent vasoconstrictor; results in lower levels of angiotensin II which causes an increase in plasma renin activity and a reduction in aldosterone secretion

Pharmacodynamics/Kinetics

Onset of action: Oral: ~1 hour

Duration: Oral: 12-24 hours

Absorption: Oral: 55% to 75%

Protein binding: 50% to 60%

Metabolism: Prodrug, undergoes hepatic biotransformation to enalaprilat

Half-life elimination:

Enalapril: Adults: Healthy: 2 hours; Congestive heart failure: 3.4-5.8 hours

Enalaprilat: Infants 6 weeks to 8 months old: 6-10 hours; Adults: 35-38 hours

Time to peak, serum: Oral: Enalapril: 0.5-1.5 hours; Enalaprilat (active): 3-4.5 hours

Excretion: Urine (60% to 80%); some feces

Dosage Use lower listed initial dose in patients with hyponatremia, hypovolemia, severe congestive heart failure, decreased renal function, or in those receiving diuretics.

Oral: **Enalapril:** Children 1 month to 16 years: Hypertension: Initial: 0.08 mg/kg (up to 5 mg) once daily; adjust dosage based on patient response; doses >0.58 mg/kg (40 mg) have not been evaluated in pediatric patients

Investigational: Congestive heart failure: Initial oral doses of **enalapril**: 0.1 mg/kg/day increasing as needed over 2 weeks to 0.5 mg/kg/day have been used in infants

Investigational: Neonatal hypertension: I.V. doses of **enalaprilat**: 5-10 mcg/kg/dose administered every 8-24 hours have been used; monitor patients carefully; select patients may require higher doses

Adults:

Oral: **Enalapril:**

Hypertension: 2.5-5 mg/day then increase as required, usual therapeutic dose for hypertension: 10-40 mg/day in 1-2 divided doses. **Note:** Initiate with 2.5 mg if patient is taking a diuretic which cannot be discontinued. May add a diuretic if blood pressure cannot be controlled with enalapril alone.

Heart failure: As standard therapy alone or with diuretics, beta-blockers, and digoxin, initiate with 2.5 mg once or twice daily (usual range: 5-20 mg/day in 2 divided doses; target: 40 mg)

Asymptomatic left ventricular dysfunction: 2.5 mg twice daily, titrated as tolerated to 20 mg/day

I.V.: **Enalaprilat:**

Hypertension: 1.25 mg/dose, given over 5 minutes every 6 hours; doses as high as 5 mg/dose every 6 hours have been tolerated for up to 36 hours. **Note:** If patients are concomitantly receiving diuretic therapy, begin with 0.625 mg I.V. over 5 minutes; if the effect is not adequate after 1 hour, repeat the dose and administer 1.25 mg at 6-hour intervals thereafter; if adequate, administer 0.625 mg I.V. every 6 hours.

Heart failure: Avoid I.V. administration in patients with unstable heart failure or those suffering acute myocardial infarction.

Conversion from I.V. to oral therapy if not concurrently on diuretics: 5 mg once daily; subsequent titration as needed; if concurrently receiving diuretics and responding to 0.625 mg I.V. every 6 hours, initiate with 2.5 mg/day.

Dosing adjustment in renal impairment:

Oral: Enalapril:

Cl_{cr} 30-80 mL/minute: Administer 5 mg/day titrated upwards to maximum of 40 mg.

Cl_{cr} <30 mL/minute: Administer 2.5 mg day; titrated upward until blood pressure is controlled.

For heart failure patients with sodium <130 mEq/L or serum creatinine >1.6 mg/dL, initiate dosage with 2.5 mg/day, increasing to twice daily as needed. Increase further in increments of 2.5 mg/dose at >4-day intervals to a maximum daily dose of 40 mg.

I.V.: Enalaprilat:

Cl_{cr} >30 mL/minute: Initiate with 1.25 mg every 6 hours and increase dose based on response.

Cl_{cr} <30 mL/minute: Initiate with 0.625 mg every 6 hours and increase dose based on response.

Hemodialysis: Moderately dialyzable (20% to 50%); administer dose postdialysis (eg, 0.625 mg I.V. every 6 hours) or administer 20% to 25% supplemental dose following dialysis; Clearance: 62 mL/minute.

Peritoneal dialysis: Supplemental dose is not necessary, although some removal of drug occurs.

Dosing adjustment in hepatic impairment: Hydrolysis of enalapril to enalaprilat may be delayed and/or impaired in patients with severe hepatic impairment, but the pharmacodynamic effects of the drug do not appear to be significantly altered; no dosage adjustment.

Administration Administer direct IVP over at least 5 minutes or dilute up to 50 mL and infuse; discontinue diuretic, if possible, for 2-3 days before beginning enalapril therapy

Monitoring Parameters Blood pressure, renal function, WBC, serum potassium; blood pressure monitor required during intravenous administration

Patient Information Report vomiting, diarrhea, excessive perspiration, or dehydration; also if swelling of face, lips, tongue, or difficulty in breathing occurs or if persistent cough develops.

Dosage Forms INJ, solution, as enalaprilat (Vasotec® I.V.): 1.25 mg/mL (1 mL, 2 mL). **TAB, as maleate** (Vasotec®): 2.5 mg, 5 mg, 10 mg, 20 mg

Enalapril and Felodipine (e NAL a pril & fe LOE di peen)

U.S. Brand Names Lexxel®

Synonyms Felodipine and Enalapril

Therapeutic Category Angiotensin-Converting Enzyme (ACE) Inhibitor/Calcium Channel Blocker Combination; Antihypertensive Agent, Combination

Use Treatment of hypertension, however, not indicated for initial treatment of hypertension; replacement therapy in patients receiving separate dosage forms (for patient convenience); when monotherapy with one component fails to achieve desired antihypertensive effect, or when dose-limiting adverse effects limit upward titration of monotherapy

Pregnancy Risk Factor C/D (2nd and 3rd trimesters)

Dosage Adults: Oral: 1 tablet daily

Dosage Forms TAB, extended release: Enalapril 5 mg and felodipine 2.5 mg; enalapril 5 mg and felodipine 5 mg

Enalapril and Hydrochlorothiazide
(e NAL a pril & hye droe klor oh THYE a zide)
U.S. Brand Names Vaseretic®
Synonyms Hydrochlorothiazide and Enalapril
Therapeutic Category Angiotensin-Converting Enzyme (ACE) Inhibitor/Thiazide Diuretic; Antihypertensive Agent, Combination
Use Treatment of hypertension
Pregnancy Risk Factor C/D (2nd and 3rd trimesters)
Dosage Oral: Dose is individualized
Dosage Forms TAB: 5-12.5: Enalapril 5 mg and hydrochlorothiazide 12.5 mg; 10-25: Enalapril 10 mg and hydrochlorothiazide 25 mg

Enfuvirtide (en FYOO vir tide)
Related Information
Antiretroviral Therapy for HIV Infection *on page 1448*
U.S. Brand Names Fuzeon™
Synonyms T-20
Therapeutic Category Antiretroviral Agent, Fusion Protein Inhibitor
Use Treatment of HIV-1 infection in combination with other antiretroviral agents in treatment-experienced patients with evidence of HIV-1 replication despite ongoing antiretroviral therapy
Restrictions Initial supplies of Fuzeon™ are available through a progressive distribution program. This program is set up to ensure that patients started on treatment will receive an uninterrupted supply until full distribution is available. During this period, all medication will be dispensed by a specialty pharmacy. To access the program, call 866-694-6670.
Pregnancy Risk Factor B
Contraindications Hypersensitivity to enfuvirtide or any component of the formulation
Warnings/Precautions Monitor closely for signs/symptoms of pneumonia; associated with an increased incidence during clinical trials, particularly in patients with a low CD4 cell count, high initial viral load, I.V. drug use, smoking, or a history of lung disease. May cause hypersensitivity reactions (symptoms may include rash, fever, nausea, vomiting, hypotension, and elevated transaminases). In addition, local injection site reactions may occur. Safety and efficacy have not been established in children <6 years of age.
Common Adverse Reactions
>10%:
Central nervous system: Insomnia (11%)
Local: Injection site reactions (98%; may include pain, erythema, induration, pruritus, ecchymosis, nodule or cyst formation)
1% to 10%:
Central nervous system: Depression (9%), anxiety (6%)
Dermatologic: Pruritus (5%)
Endocrine & metabolic: Weight loss (7%), anorexia (3%)
Gastrointestinal: Triglycerides increased (9%), appetite decreased (6%), constipation (4%), abdominal pain (3%), pancreatitis (2%), taste disturbance (2%), serum amylase increased (6%)
Hematologic: Eosinophilia (8%), anemia (2%)
Hepatic: Serum transaminases increased (4%)
Local: Injection site infection (1%)
Neuromuscular & skeletal: Neuropathy (9%), weakness (6%), myalgia (5%)
Ocular: Conjunctivitis (2%)
Respiratory: Cough (7%), pneumonia (4.7 events per 100 patient years vs 0.61 events per 100 patient years in control group), sinusitis (6%)
Miscellaneous: Infections (4% to 6%), flu-like symptoms (2%), lymphadenopathy (2%)
Drug Interactions
Increased Effect/Toxicity: No significant interactions identified.
Decreased Effect: No significant interactions identified.
Mechanism of Action Binds to the first heptad-repeat (HR1) in the gp41 subunit of the viral envelope glycoprotein. Inhibits the fusion of HIV-1 virus with CD4 cells by blocking the conformational change in gp41 required for membrane fusion and entry into CD4 cells
Pharmacodynamics/Kinetics
Distribution: V_d: 5.5 L
Protein binding: 92%
Metabolism : Proteolytic hydrolysis (CYP isoenzymes do not appear to contribute to metabolism); clearance: 24.8 mL/hour/kg

Half-life elimination: 3.8 hours
Time to peak: 8 hours

Dosage S.C.:
Children ≥6 years: 2 mg/kg twice daily (maximum dose: 90 mg twice daily)
Adults: 90 mg twice daily
Dosage adjustment in renal impairment: No dosage adjustment required

Administration Inject subcutaneously into upper arm, abdomen, or anterior thigh. Do not inject into moles, scar tissue, bruises, or the navel. Rotate injection site, give injections at a site different from the preceding injection site; do not inject into any site where an injection site reaction is evident.

Patient Information Report any signs/symptoms of hypersensitivity or infection, including pneumonia (risk may be increased during therapy). Follow injection instructions closely. Rotate injection site, give injections at a site different from the preceding injection site; do not inject into any site where an injection site reaction is evident. Inject subcutaneously into upper arm, abdomen, or anterior thigh. Do not inject into moles, scar tissue, bruises, or the navel.

Dosage Forms INJ, powder for reconstitution [single-use vial]: 108 mg [90 mg/mL following reconstitution] (60s)

♦ **Engerix-B®** see Hepatitis B Vaccine *on page 617*
♦ **Engerix-B® and Havrix®** see Hepatitis A Inactivated and Hepatitis B (Recombinant) Vaccine *on page 615*
♦ **Enhanced-potency Inactivated Poliovirus Vaccine** see Poliovirus Vaccine (Inactivated) *on page 1013*
♦ **Enlon®** see Edrophonium *on page 422*

Enoxaparin (ee noks a PA rin)

Related Information
Anticoagulants, Injectable *on page 1357*
U.S. Brand Names Lovenox®
Synonyms Enoxaparin Sodium
Therapeutic Category Anticoagulant, Low Molecular Weight Heparin; Low Molecular Weight Heparin

Use
Prevention of deep vein thrombosis following hip or knee replacement surgery or abdominal surgery in patients at risk for thromboembolic complications (high-risk patients include those with one or more of the following risk factors: >40 years of age, obese, general anesthesia lasting >30 minutes, malignancy, history of deep vein thrombosis or pulmonary embolism)
Prevention of deep vein thrombosis in medical patients at risk for thromboembolic complications due to severely restricted mobility during acute illness
Inpatient treatment of acute deep vein thrombosis with and without pulmonary embolism when administered in conjunction with warfarin sodium
Outpatient treatment of acute deep vein thrombosis without pulmonary embolism when administered in conjunction with warfarin sodium
Prevention of ischemic complications of unstable angina and non-Q wave myocardial infarction (when administered with aspirin)

Unlabeled/Investigational Use Prophylaxis and treatment of thromboembolism in children
Pregnancy Risk Factor B
Contraindications Hypersensitivity to enoxaparin, heparin, or any component of the formulation; thrombocytopenia associated with a positive *in vitro* test for antiplatelet antibodies in the presence of enoxaparin; hypersensitivity to pork products; active major bleeding; not for I.M. or I.V. use

Warnings/Precautions Do not administer intramuscularly. **Patients with recent or anticipated neuraxial anesthesia (epidural or spinal anesthesia) are at risk of spinal or epidural hematoma and subsequent paralysis.** Consider risk versus benefit prior to neuraxial anesthesia; risk is increased by concomitant agents which may alter hemostasis, as well as traumatic or repeated epidural or spinal puncture. Patient should be observed closely for bleeding if enoxaparin is administered during or immediately following diagnostic lumbar puncture, epidural anesthesia, or spinal anesthesia.

Not recommended for thromboprophylaxis in patients with prosthetic heart valves (especially pregnant women). Not to be used interchangeably (unit for unit) with heparin or any other low molecular weight heparins. Use caution in patients with history of heparin-induced thrombocytopenia. Monitor patient closely for signs or symptoms of bleeding. Certain patients are at increased risk of bleeding. Risk factors include bacterial endocarditis; congenital or acquired bleeding disorders; active ulcerative or angiodysplastic GI diseases; severe uncontrolled hypertension; hemorrhagic stroke; use shortly after brain, spinal, or ophthalmology surgery; patients treated concomitantly with platelet inhibitors; recent GI bleeding; thrombocytopenia or platelet defects; severe liver disease; hypertensive or diabetic retinopathy; or in patients undergoing invasive procedures. Use caution in patients with renal failure; dosage adjustment needed if Cl_{cr} <30 mL/minute. Safety and efficacy in pediatric patients have not been established. Use with caution in the elderly (delayed elimination may occur). Heparin can cause hyperkalemia by affecting aldosterone. Similar reactions could occur with LMWHs. Monitor for hyperkalemia. Discontinue therapy if platelets are <100,000/mm³. Multiple-dose vials contain benzyl alcohol (use caution in pregnant women).

Common Adverse Reactions As with all anticoagulants, bleeding is the major adverse effect of enoxaparin. Hemorrhage may occur at virtually any site. Risk is dependent on multiple variables. At the recommended doses, single injections of enoxaparin do not significantly influence platelet aggregation or affect global clotting time (ie, PT or aPTT).
(Continued)

Enoxaparin *(Continued)*

1% to 10%:

Central nervous system: Fever (5% to 8%), confusion, pain

Dermatologic: Erythema, bruising

Gastrointestinal: Nausea (3%), diarrhea

Hematologic: Hemorrhage (5% to 13%), thrombocytopenia (2%), hypochromic anemia (2%)

Hepatic: Increased ALT/AST

Local: Injection site hematoma (9%), local reactions (irritation, pain, ecchymosis, erythema)

Thrombocytopenia with thrombosis: Cases of heparin-induced thrombocytopenia (some complicated by organ infarction, limb ischemia, or death) have been reported.

Drug Interactions

Increased Effect/Toxicity: Risk of bleeding with enoxaparin may be increased with thrombolytic agents, oral anticoagulants (warfarin), drugs which affect platelet function (eg, aspirin, NSAIDs, dipyridamole, ticlopidine, clopidogrel, and IIb/IIIa antagonists). Although the risk of bleeding may be increased during concurrent therapy with warfarin, enoxaparin is commonly continued during the initiation of warfarin therapy to assure anticoagulation and to protect against possible transient hypercoagulability. Some cephalosporins and penicillins may block platelet aggregation, theoretically increasing the risk of bleeding.

Mechanism of Action Standard heparin consists of components with molecular weights ranging from 4000-30,000 daltons with a mean of 16,000 daltons. Heparin acts as an anticoagulant by enhancing the inhibition rate of clotting proteases by antithrombin III impairing normal hemostasis and inhibition of factor Xa. Low molecular weight heparins have a small effect on the activated partial thromboplastin time and strongly inhibit factor Xa. Enoxaparin is derived from porcine heparin that undergoes benzylation followed by alkaline depolymerization. The average molecular weight of enoxaparin is 4500 daltons which is distributed as ($\leq$20%) 2000 daltons ($\geq$68%) 2000-8000 daltons, and ($\leq$15%) >8000 daltons. Enoxaparin has a higher ratio of antifactor Xa to antifactor IIa activity than unfractionated heparin.

Pharmacodynamics/Kinetics

Onset of action: Peak effect: S.C.: Antifactor Xa and antithrombin (antifactor IIa): 3-5 hours

Duration: 40 mg dose: Antifactor Xa activity: ~12 hours

Protein binding: Does not bind to heparin binding proteins

Half-life elimination, plasma: 2-4 times longer than standard heparin, independent of dose

Excretion: Urine

Dosage S.C.:

Infants and Children (unlabeled use):

Infants <2 months: Initial:

Prophylaxis: 0.75 mg/kg every 12 hours

Treatment: 1.5 mg/kg every 12 hours

Infants >2 months and Children $\leq$18 years: Initial:

Prophylaxis: 0.5 mg/kg every 12 hours

Treatment: 1 mg/kg every 12 hours

Maintenance: See **Dosage Titration** table:

Enoxaparin Dosage Titration

Antifactor Xa	Dose Titration	Time to Repeat Antifactor Xa Level
<0.35 units/mL	Increase dose by 25%	4 h after next dose
0.35-0.49 units/mL	Increase dose by 10%	4 h after next dose
0.5-1 unit/mL	Keep same dosage	Next day, then 1 wk later, then monthly (4 h after dose)
1.1-1.5 units/mL	Decrease dose by 20%	Before next dose
1.6-2 units/mL	Hold dose for 3 h and decrease dose by 30%	Before next dose, then 4 h after next dose
>2 units/mL	Hold all doses until antifactor Xa is 0.5 units/mL, then decrease dose by 40%	Before next dose and every 12 h until antifactor Xa <0.5 units/mL

Modified from Monagle P, Michelson AD, Bovill E, et al, "Antithrombotic Therapy in Children," *Chest*, 2001, 119:344S-70S.

Adults:

DVT prophylaxis in hip replacement:

30 mg twice daily: First dose within 12-24 hours after surgery and every 12 hours until risk of deep vein thrombosis has diminished or the patient is adequately anticoagulated on warfarin. Average duration of therapy: 7-10 days.

40 mg once daily: First dose within 9-15 hours before surgery and daily until risk of deep vein thrombosis has diminished and the patient is adequately anticoagulated on warfarin. Average duration of therapy: 7-10 days unless warfarin is not given concurrently, then 40 mg S.C. once daily should be continued for 3 more weeks (4 weeks total).

DVT prophylaxis in knee replacement: 30 mg twice daily: First dose within 12-24 hours after surgery and every 12 hours until risk of deep vein thrombosis has diminished. Average duration of therapy: 7-10 days; maximum course: 14 days.

DVT prophylaxis in high-risk patients undergoing abdominal surgery: 40 mg once daily, with initial dose given 2 hours prior to surgery; usual duration: 7-10 days and up to 12 days has been tolerated in clinical trials.

DVT prophylaxis in medical patients with severely restricted mobility during acute illness: 40 mg once daily; usual duration: 6-11 days; up to 14 days was used in clinical trial

Treatment of acute proximal DVT: Start warfarin within 72 hours and continue enoxaparin until INR is between 2.0 and 3.0 (usually 7 days).

Inpatient treatment of DVT with or without pulmonary embolism: 1 mg/kg/dose every 12 hours or 1.5 mg/kg once daily.

Outpatient treatment of DVT without pulmonary embolism: 1 mg/kg/dose every 12 hours.

Prevention of ischemic complications with unstable angina or non-Q-wave myocardial infarction: 1 mg/kg twice daily in conjunction with oral aspirin therapy (100-325 mg once daily); treatment should be continued for a minimum of 2 days and continued until clinical stabilization (usually 2-8 days).

Elderly: Increased incidence of bleeding with doses of 1.5 mg/kg/day or 1 mg/kg every 12 hours; injection-associated bleeding and serious adverse reactions are also increased in the elderly. Careful attention should be paid to elderly patients <45 kg.

Dosing adjustment in renal impairment: S.C.:

Cl_{cr} ≥30 mL/minute: No specific adjustment recommended (per manufacturer); monitor closely for bleeding

Cl_{cr} <30 mL/minute:

DVT prophylaxis in abdominal surgery, hip replacement, knee replacement, or in medical patients during acute illness: 30 mg once daily

DVT treatment (inpatient or outpatient treatment in conjunction with warfarin): 1 mg/kg once daily

Unstable angina, non-Q-wave MI (with ASA): 1 mg/kg once daily

Hemodialysis: Supplemental dose is not necessary.

Peritoneal dialysis: Significant drug removal is unlikely based on physiochemical characteristics.

Administration Should be administered by deep S.C. injection to the left or right anterolateral and left or right posterolateral abdominal wall. To avoid loss of drug from the 30 mg and 40 mg syringes, do not expel the air bubble from the syringe prior to injection. In order to minimize bruising, do not rub injection site. An automatic injector (Lovenox EasyInjector™) is available with the 30 mg and 40 mg syringes to aid the patient with self-injections. **Note:** Enoxaparin is available in 100 mg/mL and 150 mg/mL concentrations.

Monitoring Parameters Platelets, occult blood, and anti-Xa activity, if available; the monitoring of PT and/or PTT is not necessary

Dosage Forms INJ, solution [ampul; preservative free]: 30 mg/0.3 mL (0.3 mL) [DSC]. **INJ, solution** [graduated prefilled syringe; preservative free]: 60 mg/0.6 mL (0.6 mL), 80 mg/0.8 mL (0.8 mL), 100 mg/mL (1 mL), 120 mg/0.8 mL (0.8 mL), 150 mg/mL (1 mL). **INJ, solution** [multidose vial]: 100 mg/mL (3 mL). **INJ, solution** [prefilled syringe; preservative free]: 30 mg/0.3 mL (0.3 mL), 40 mg/0.4 mL (0.4 mL).

♦ **Enoxaparin Sodium** *see* Enoxaparin *on page 433*

♦ **Enpresse**™ *see* Ethinyl Estradiol and Levonorgestrel *on page 484*

Entacapone (en TA ka pone)

Related Information
Parkinson's Agents Comparison *on page 1402*

U.S. Brand Names Comtan®

Therapeutic Category Anti-Parkinson's Agent, COMT Inhibitor; Reverse COMT Inhibitor

Use Adjunct to levodopa/carbidopa therapy in patients with idiopathic Parkinson's disease who experience "wearing-off" symptoms at the end of a dosing interval

Pregnancy Risk Factor C

Contraindications Hypersensitivity to entacapone or any of component of the formulation

Warnings/Precautions Patient should not be treated concomitantly with entacapone and a nonselective MAO inhibitor. Orthostatic hypotension may be increased in patients on dopaminergic therapy in Parkinson's disease.

Common Adverse Reactions

>10%:

Gastrointestinal: Nausea (14%)

Neuromuscular & skeletal: Dyskinesia (25%), placebo (15%)

1% to 10%:

Cardiovascular: Orthostatic hypotension (4%), syncope (1%)

Central nervous system: Dizziness (8%), fatigue (6%), hallucinations (4%), anxiety (2%), somnolence (2%), agitation (1%)

Dermatologic: Purpura (2%)

Gastrointestinal: Diarrhea (10%), abdominal pain (8%), constipation (6%), vomiting (4%), dry mouth (3%), dyspepsia (2%), flatulence (2%), gastritis (1%), taste perversion (1%)

Genitourinary: Brown-orange urine discoloration (10%)

Neuromuscular & skeletal: Hyperkinesia (10%), hypokinesia (9%), back pain (4%), weakness (2%)

Respiratory: Dyspnea (3%)

Miscellaneous: Increased diaphoresis (2%), bacterial infection (1%)

Drug Interactions

Cytochrome P450 Effect: Inhibits CYP1A2 (weak), 2A6 (weak), 2C8/9 (weak), 2C19 (weak), 2D6 (weak), 2E1 (weak), 3A4 (weak)

(Continued)

Entacapone *(Continued)*

Increased Effect/Toxicity: Cardiac effects with drugs metabolized by COMT (eg, epinephrine, isoproterenol, dopamine, apomorphine, bitolterol, dobutamine, methyldopa) increased other CNS depressants; nonselective MAO inhibitors are not recommended; chelates iron. Caution with drugs that interfere with glucuronidation, intestinal, biliary excretion, intestinal beta-glucuronidase (eg, probenecid, cholestyramine, erythromycin, chloramphenicol, rifampicin, ampicillin).

Decreased Effect: Entacapone is an iron chelator and an iron supplement should not be administered concurrently with this medicine.

Mechanism of Action Entacapone is a reversible and selective inhibitor of catechol-O-methyltransferase (COMT). When entacapone is taken with levodopa, the pharmacokinetics are altered, resulting in more sustained levodopa serum levels compared to levodopa taken alone. The resulting levels of levodopa provide for increased concentrations available for absorption across the blood-brain barrier, thereby providing for increased CNS levels of dopamine, the active metabolite of levodopa.

Pharmacodynamics/Kinetics
Onset of action: Rapid
  Peak effect: 1 hour
Absorption: Rapid
Distribution: I.V.: V_{dss}: 20 L
Protein binding: 98%, primarily to albumin
Metabolism: Isomerization to the *cis*-isomer, followed by direct glucuronidation of the parent and *cis*-isomer
Bioavailability: 35%
Half-life elimination: B phase: 0.4-0.7 hours; Y phase: 2.4 hours
Time to peak, serum: 1 hour
Excretion: Feces (90%); urine (10%)

Dosage Oral: Adults: 200 mg with each dose of levodopa/carbidopa, up to a maximum of 8 times/day (maximum daily dose: 1600 mg/day). To optimize therapy, the dosage of levodopa may need reduced or the dosing interval may need extended. Patients taking levodopa ≥800mg/day or who had moderate-to-severe dyskinesias prior to therapy required an average decrease of 25% in the daily levodopa dose.

Dosage adjustment in hepatic impairment: Treat with caution and monitor carefully; AUC and C_{max} can be possibly doubled

Administration Always administer in association with levodopa/carbidopa; can be combined with both the immediate and sustained release formulations of levodopa/carbidopa. Can be taken with or without food. Should not be abruptly withdrawn from patient's therapy due to significant worsening of symptoms.

Monitoring Parameters Signs and symptoms of Parkinson's disease; liver function tests, blood pressure, patient's mental status

Patient Information Take only as prescribed; can be taken with or without food. Possible nausea, hallucinations, and change in color of urine (not clinically relevant) may occur. Do not drive a car or operate other complex machinery until there is sufficient experience with entacapone. Do not withdraw medication unless advised by healthcare professional.

Dosage Forms TAB: 200 mg

- **Entacapone, Carbidopa, and Levodopa** *see* Levodopa, Carbidopa, and Entacapone *on page 733*
- **Entex® LA** *see* Guaifenesin and Phenylephrine *on page 605*
- **Entex® PSE** *see* Guaifenesin and Pseudoephedrine *on page 605*
- **Entocort™ EC** *see* Budesonide *on page 182*
- **Entsol® [OTC]** *see* Sodium Chloride *on page 1146*
- **Enulose®** *see* Lactulose *on page 712*
- **Enzone®** *see* Pramoxine and Hydrocortisone *on page 1028*

Ephedrine *(e FED rin)*

U.S. Brand Names Pretz-D® [OTC]

Synonyms Ephedrine Sulfate

Therapeutic Category Adrenergic Agonist Agent; Alpha/Beta Agonist; Bronchodilator; Sympathomimetic Agent

Use Treatment of bronchial asthma, nasal congestion, acute bronchospasm, idiopathic orthostatic hypotension

Pregnancy Risk Factor C

Contraindications Hypersensitivity to ephedrine or any component of the formulation; cardiac arrhythmias; angle-closure glaucoma; concurrent use of other sympathomimetic agents

Warnings/Precautions Blood volume depletion should be corrected before ephedrine therapy is instituted; use caution in patients with unstable vasomotor symptoms, diabetes, hyperthyroidism, prostatic hyperplasia, a history of seizures or those on other sympathomimetic agents; also use caution in the elderly and those patients with cardiovascular disorders such as coronary artery disease, arrhythmias, and hypertension. Ephedrine may cause hypertension resulting in intracranial hemorrhage. Long-term use may cause anxiety and symptoms of paranoid schizophrenia. Avoid as a bronchodilator; generally not used as a bronchodilator since new beta₂ agents are less toxic. Use with caution in the elderly, since it crosses the blood-brain barrier and may cause confusion.

Common Adverse Reactions Frequency not defined.

Cardiovascular: Hypertension, tachycardia, palpitations, elevation or depression of blood pressure, unusual pallor, chest pain, arrhythmias

Central nervous system: CNS stimulating effects, nervousness, anxiety, apprehension, fear, tension, agitation, excitation, restlessness, irritability, insomnia, hyperactivity, dizziness, headache

Gastrointestinal: Xerostomia, nausea, anorexia, GI upset, vomiting

Genitourinary: Painful urination

Neuromuscular & skeletal: Trembling, tremor (more common in the elderly), weakness

Respiratory: Dyspnea

Miscellaneous: Diaphoresis (increased)

Drug Interactions

Increased Effect/Toxicity: Increased (toxic) cardiac stimulation with other sympathomimetic agents, theophylline, cardiac glycosides, or general anesthetics. Increased blood pressure with atropine or MAO inhibitors.

Decreased Effect: Alpha- and beta-adrenergic blocking agents decrease ephedrine vasopressor effects.

Mechanism of Action Releases tissue stores of epinephrine and thereby produces an alpha- and beta-adrenergic stimulation; longer-acting and less potent than epinephrine

Pharmacodynamics/Kinetics

Onset of action: Oral: Bronchodilation: 0.25-1 hour

Duration: Oral: 3-6 hours

Distribution: Crosses placenta; enters breast milk

Metabolism: Minimally hepatic

Half-life elimination: 2.5-3.6 hours

Excretion: Urine (60% to 77% as unchanged drug) within 24 hours

Dosage

Children:

Oral, S.C.: 3 mg/kg/day or 25-100 mg/m^2/day in 4-6 divided doses every 4-6 hours

I.M., slow I.V. push: 0.2-0.3 mg/kg/dose every 4-6 hours

Adults:

Oral: 25-50 mg every 3-4 hours as needed

I.M., S.C.: 25-50 mg, parenteral adult dose should not exceed 150 mg in 24 hours

I.V.: 5-25 mg/dose slow I.V. push repeated after 5-10 minutes as needed, then every 3-4 hours not to exceed 150 mg/24 hours

Nasal spray:

Children 6-12 years: 1-2 sprays into each nostril, not more frequently than every 4 hours

Children ≥12 years and Adults: 2-3 sprays into each nostril, not more frequently than every 4 hours

Monitoring Parameters Blood pressure, pulse, urinary output, mental status; cardiac monitor and blood pressure monitor required

Patient Information May cause wakefulness or nervousness; take last dose 4-6 hours before bedtime

Dosage Forms CAP: 25 mg. **INJ, solution:** 50 mg/mL (1 mL). **SOLN, intranasal spray** (Pretz-D®): 0.25% (50 mL)

♦ **Ephedrine, Chlorpheniramine, Phenylephrine, and Carbetapentane** *see* Chlorpheniramine, Ephedrine, Phenylephrine, and Carbetapentane *on page 263*

♦ **Ephedrine Sulfate** *see* Ephedrine *on page 436*

♦ **Epidermal Thymocyte Activating Factor** *see* Aldesleukin *on page 47*

♦ **Epifoam®** *see* Pramoxine and Hydrocortisone *on page 1028*

♦ **Epifrin®** *see* Epinephrine *on page 438*

♦ **Epilepsy** *see page 1477*

Epinastine (ep i NAS teen)

U.S. Brand Names Elestat™

Synonyms Epinastine Hydrochloride

Therapeutic Category Antihistamine, H$_1$ Blocker, Ophthalmic

Use Treatment of allergic conjunctivitis

Pregnancy Risk Factor C

Contraindications Hypersensitivity to epinastine or any component of the formulation

Warnings/Precautions Contains benzalkonium chloride; contact lenses should be removed prior to use. Not for the treatment of contact lens irritation. Safety and efficacy in children <3 years of age have not been established.

Common Adverse Reactions 1% to 10%:

Central nervous system: Headache (1% to 3%)

Ocular: Burning sensation, folliculosis, hyperemia, pruritus

Respiratory: Cough (1% to 3%), pharyngitis (1% to 3%), rhinitis (1% to 3%), sinusitis (1% to 3%)

Miscellaneous: Infection (10%; defined as cold symptoms and upper respiratory infections)

Mechanism of Action Selective H$_1$-receptor antagonist; inhibits release of histamine from the mast cell

Pharmacodynamics/Kinetics

Onset: 3-5 minutes

Duration: 8 hours

Absorption: Low systemic absorption following topical application

Distribution: Does not cross blood-brain barrier

(Continued)

Epinastine *(Continued)*

Protein binding: 64%
Metabolism: <10% metabolized
Half-life elimination: 12 hours
Excretion: I.V.: Urine (55%); feces (30%)

Dosage Ophthalmic: Allergic conjunctivitis: Children ≥3 years and Adults: Instill 1 drop into each eye twice daily; continue throughout period of exposure, even in the absence of symptoms

Administration For ophthalmic use only; avoid touching tip of applicator to eye or other surfaces. Contact lenses should be removed prior to application, may be reinserted after 10 minutes. Do not wear contact lenses if eyes are red.

Patient Information For use in the eye only; do not touch tip of applicator with eye, fingers or other surfaces. Contact lenses should be removed prior to application, may be reinserted after 10 minutes. Do not wear contact lenses if eyes are red. Store bottle tightly closed.

Dosage Forms SOLN, ophthalmic: 0.05% (5 mL, 10 mL)

♦ **Epinastine Hydrochloride** *see Epinastine on page 437*

Epinephrine *(ep i NEF rin)*

Related Information
Bronchodilators, Comparison of Inhaled Sympathomimetics *on page 1370*
Glaucoma Drug Therapy Comparison *on page 1481*
Hemodynamic Support, Intravenous *on page 1377*

U.S. Brand Names Adrenalin®; Epifrin®; EpiPen®; EpiPen® Jr; Primatene® Mist [OTC]

Synonyms Adrenaline; Epinephrine Bitartrate; Epinephrine Hydrochloride

Therapeutic Category Alpha/Beta Agonist

Use Treatment of bronchospasms, anaphylactic reactions, cardiac arrest, management of open-angle (chronic simple) glaucoma; added to local anesthetics to decrease systemic absorption, increase duration of action, and decrease toxicity of the local anesthetic

Unlabeled/Investigational Use ACLS guidelines: Ventricular fibrillation (VF) or pulseless ventricular tachycardia (VT) unresponsive to initial defibrillatory shocks; pulseless electrical activity, asystole, hypotension unresponsive to volume resuscitation; symptomatic bradycardia or heart block unresponsive to atropine or pacing

Pregnancy Risk Factor C

Contraindications Hypersensitivity to epinephrine or any component of the formulation; cardiac arrhythmias; angle-closure glaucoma

Warnings/Precautions Use with caution in elderly patients, patients with diabetes mellitus, cardiovascular diseases (angina, tachycardia, myocardial infarction), thyroid disease, or cerebral arteriosclerosis, Parkinson's; some products contain sulfites as preservatives. Rapid I.V. infusion may cause death from cerebrovascular hemorrhage or cardiac arrhythmias. Oral inhalation of epinephrine is **not** the preferred route of administration.

Common Adverse Reactions Frequency not defined.
Cardiovascular: Tachycardia (parenteral), pounding heartbeat, flushing, hypertension, pallor, chest pain, increased myocardial oxygen consumption, cardiac arrhythmias, sudden death, angina, vasoconstriction
Central nervous system: Nervousness, anxiety, restlessness, headache, dizziness, lightheadedness, insomnia
Gastrointestinal: Nausea, vomiting, xerostomia,dry throat
Genitourinary: Acute urinary retention in patients with bladder outflow obstruction
Neuromuscular & skeletal: Weakness, trembling
Ocular: Precipitation or or exacerbation of narrow-angle glaucoma, transient stinging, burning, eye pain, allergic lid reaction, ocular irritation
Renal: Decreased renal and splanchnic blood flow
Respiratory: Wheezing, dyspnea
Miscellaneous: Diaphoresis (increased)

Drug Interactions
Increased Effect/Toxicity: Increased cardiac irritability if administered concurrently with halogenated inhalation anesthetics, beta-blocking agents, or alpha-blocking agents.
Decreased Effect: Decreased bronchodilation with β-blockers. Decreases antihypertensive effects of methyldopa or guanethidine.

Mechanism of Action Stimulates alpha-, beta$_1$-, and beta$_2$-adrenergic receptors resulting in relaxation of smooth muscle of the bronchial tree, cardiac stimulation, and dilation of skeletal muscle vasculature; small doses can cause vasodilation via beta$_2$-vascular receptors; large doses may produce constriction of skeletal and vascular smooth muscle; decreases production of aqueous humor and increases aqueous outflow; dilates the pupil by contracting the dilator muscle

Pharmacodynamics/Kinetics
Onset of action: Bronchodilation: S.C.: ~5-10 minutes; Inhalation: ~1 minute; Conjunctival instillation: IOP declines ~1 hour
Peak effect: Conjunctival instillation: 4-8 hours
Duration: Conjunctival instillation: Ocular effect: 12-24 hours
Distribution: Crosses placenta; enters breast milk
Metabolism: Taken up into the adrenergic neuron and metabolized by monoamine oxidase and catechol-o-methyltransferase; circulating drug hepatically metabolized
Excretion: Urine (as inactive metabolites, metanephrine, and sulfate and hydroxy derivatives of mandelic acid, small amounts as unchanged drug)

Dosage

Neonates: Cardiac arrest: I.V.: Intratracheal: 0.01-0.03 mg/kg (0.1-0.3 mL/kg of **1:10,000** solution) every 3-5 minutes as needed; dilute intratracheal doses to 1-2 mL with normal saline

Infants and Children:

Bronchodilator: S.C.: 10 mcg/kg (0.01 mL/kg of **1:1000**) (single doses not to exceed 0.5 mg) **or** suspension (1:200): 0.005 mL/kg/dose (0.025 mg/kg/dose) to a maximum of 0.15 mL (0.75 mg for single dose) every 8-12 hours

Bradycardia:

I.V.: 0.01 mg/kg (0.1 mL/kg of **1:10,000** solution) every 3-5 minutes as needed (maximum: 1 mg/10 mL)

Intratracheal: 0.1 mg/kg (0.1 mL/kg of **1:1000** solution) every 3-5 minutes; doses as high as 0.2 mg/kg may be effective

Asystole or pulseless arrest:

I.V. or intraosseous: **First dose**: 0.01 mg/kg (0.1 mL/kg of a **1:10,000** solution); **subsequent doses**: 0.1 mg/kg (0.1 mL/kg of a **1:1000** solution); doses as high as 0.2 mg/kg may be effective; repeat every 3-5 minutes

Intratracheal: 0.1 mg/kg (0.1 mL/kg of a **1:1000** solution); doses as high as 0.2 mg/kg may be effective

Hypersensitivity reaction: S.C.: 0.01 mg/kg every 15 minutes for 2 doses then every 4 hours as needed (single doses not to exceed 0.5 mg)

Refractory hypotension (refractory to dopamine/dobutamine): Continuous I.V. infusions of 0.1-1 mcg/kg/minute; titrate dosage to desired effect

Nebulization: 0.25-0.5 mL of 2.25% **racemic epinephrine** solution diluted in 3 mL normal saline, or L-epinephrine at an equivalent dose; racemic epinephrine 10 mg = 5 mg L-epinephrine; use lower end of dosing range for younger infants

Intranasal: Children ≥6 years and Adults: Apply locally as drops or spray or with sterile swab

Adults:

Asystole:

I.V.: 1 mg every 3-5 minutes; if this approach fails, alternative regimens include:

Intermediate: 2-5 mg every 3-5 minutes

Escalating: 1 mg, 3 mg, 5 mg at 3-minute intervals

High: 0.1 mg/kg every 3-5 minutes

Intratracheal: 1 mg (although optimal dose is unknown, doses of 2-2.5 times the I.V. dose may be needed)

Bronchodilator: I.M., S.C. (**1:1000**): 0.1-0.5 mg every 10-15 minutes to 4 hours

Hypersensitivity reaction: I.M., S.C.: 0.3-0.5 mg every 15-20 minutes if condition requires; if hypotension is present: 0.1 mg I.V. slowly over 5-10 minutes followed by continuous infusion 1-10 mcg/minute

Symptomatic bradycardia or heart block (not responsive to atropine or pacing): I.V. infusion: 1-10 mcg/minute; titrate to desired effect

Refractory hypotension (refractory to dopamine/dobutamine): Continuous I.V. infusion 1 mcg/minute (range: 1-10 mcg/minute); titrate dosage to desired effect; severe cardiac dysfunction may require doses >10 mcg/minute (up to 0.1 mcg/kg/minute)

Nebulization: Instill 8-15 drops into nebulizer reservoirs; administer 1-3 inhalations 4-6 times/day

Ophthalmic: Instill 1-2 drops in eye(s) once or twice daily; when treating open-angle glaucoma, the concentration and dosage must be adjusted to the response of the patient

Administration Central line administration only; intravenous infusions require an infusion pump

Endotracheal: Doses (2-2.5 times the I.V. dose) should be diluted to 10 mL with NS or distilled water prior to administration

Epinephrine can be administered S.C., I.M., I.V., or intracardiac injection

I.M. administration into the buttocks should be avoided

Desired pediatric intravenous infusion solution preparation: "RULE OF 6"

Simplified equation: 0.6 x weight (kg) = amount (mg) of drug to be added to 100 mL of I.V. fluid
When infused at 1 mL/hour, then it will deliver the drug at a rate of 0.1 mcg/kg/minute

Complex equation: 6 x desired dose (mcg/minute) x body weight (kg) divided by desired rate (mL/hour) is the amount (mg) added to make 100 mL of solution

Preparation of adult I.V. infusion: Dilute 1 mg in 250 mL of D_5W or NS (4 mcg/mL); administer at an initial rate of 1 mcg/minute and increase to desired effects; at 20 mcg/minute pure alpha effects occur

1 mcg/minute: 15 mL/hour

2 mcg/minute: 30 mL/hour

3 mcg/minute: 45 mL/hour, etc

Extravasation management: Use phentolamine as antidote. Mix 5 mg with 9 mL of NS. Inject a small amount of this dilution into extravasated area. Blanching should reverse immediately. Monitor site. If blanching should recur, additional injections of phentolamine may be needed.

Monitoring Parameters Pulmonary function, heart rate, blood pressure, site of infusion for blanching; extravasation; cardiac monitor and blood pressure monitor required

Reference Range Therapeutic: 31-95 pg/mL (SI: 170-520 pmol/L)

Dosage Forms AERO, for oral inhalation (Primatene® Mist): 0.22 mg/inhalation (15 mL, 22.5 mL). **INJ, solution** [prefilled auto injector]: (EpiPen®): 0.3 mg/0.3 mL [1:1000] (2 mL); (EpiPen® Jr): 0.15 mg/0.3 mL [1:2000] (2 mL). **INJ, solution:** 0.1 mg/mL [1:10,000] (10 mL); 1 mg/mL [1:1000] (1 mL); (Adrenalin®): 1 mg/mL [1:1000] (1 mL, 30 mL). **SOLN, for oral inhalation** (Adrenalin®): 1% [10 mg/mL, 1:100] (7.5 mL). **SOLN, ophthalmic** (Epifrin®): 0.5% (15 mL); 1% (15 mL); 2% (15 mL)

♦ **Epinephrine and Lidocaine** *see* Lidocaine and Epinephrine *on page 745*

♦ **Epinephrine Bitartrate** *see* Epinephrine *on page 438*

♦ **Epinephrine Hydrochloride** *see* Epinephrine *on page 438*

♦ **EpiPen®** *see* Epinephrine *on page 438*

♦ **EpiPen® Jr** *see* Epinephrine *on page 438*

♦ **Epipodophyllotoxin** *see* Etoposide *on page 497*

♦ **EpiQuin™ Micro** *see* Hydroquinone *on page 636*

Epirubicin (ep i ROO bi sin)

U.S. Brand Names Ellence®
Synonyms Pidorubicin; Pidorubicin Hydrochloride
Therapeutic Category Antineoplastic Agent, Anthracycline
Use Adjuvant therapy for primary breast cancer
Pregnancy Risk Factor D
Contraindications Hypersensitivity to epirubicin, other anthracyclines, or anthracenediones; severe myocardial insufficiency, severe arrhythmias; recent myocardial infarction; severe hepatic dysfunction; baseline neutrophil count 1500 cells/mm³; previous anthracycline treatment up to maximum cumulative dose; pregnancy

Warnings/Precautions The U.S. Food and Drug Administration (FDA) currently recommends that procedures for proper handling and disposal of antineoplastic agents be considered. The primary toxicity is myelosuppression, especially of the granulocytic series, with less marked effects on platelets and erythroid series.

Potential cardiotoxicity, particularly in patients who have received prior anthracyclines or who have pre-existing cardiac disease, may occur. Acute toxicity (primarily arrhythmias) and delayed toxicity (CHF) have been described. Delayed toxicity usually develops late in the course of therapy or within 2-3 months after completion, however, events with an onset of several months to years after termination of treatment have been described. The risk of delayed cardiotoxicity increases more steeply at dosages above 900 mg/m², and this dose should be exceeded only with extreme caution. Toxicity may be additive with other anthracyclines or anthracenediones.

Reduce dosage and use with caution in mild to moderate hepatic impairment or in severe renal dysfunction (serum creatinine >5 mg/dL). May cause tumor lysis syndrome or radiation recall. Treatment with anthracyclines may increase the risk of secondary leukemias. For I.V. administration only, severe local tissue necrosis will result if extravasation occurs. Epirubicin is emetogenic.

Common Adverse Reactions

>10%:
  Central nervous system: Lethargy (1% to 46%)
  Dermatologic: Alopecia (69% to 95%)
  Endocrine & metabolic: Amenorrhea (69% to 72%), hot flashes (5% to 39%)
  Gastrointestinal: Nausea, vomiting (83% to 92%), mucositis (9% to 59%), diarrhea (7% to 25%)
  Hematologic: Leukopenia (49% to 80%; Grade 3 and 4: 1.5% to 58.6%), neutropenia (54% to 80%), anemia (13% to 72%), thrombocytopenia (5% to 49%)
  Local: Injection site reactions (3% to 20%)
  Ocular: Conjunctivitis (1% to 15%)
  Miscellaneous: Infection (15% to 21%)
1% to 10%:
  Cardiovascular: Congestive heart failure (0.4% to 1.5%), decreased LVEF (asymptomatic) (1.4% to 1.8%); recommended maximum cumulative dose: 900 mg/m²
  Central nervous system: Fever (1% to 5%)
  Dermatologic: Rash (1% to 9%), skin changes (0.7% to 5%)
  Gastrointestinal: Anorexia (2% to 3%)
Other reactions (percentage not specified): Acute myelogenous leukemia (0.2% at 3 years), acute lymphoid leukemia, increased transaminases, radiation recall, skin and nail hyperpigmentation, photosensitivity reaction, hypersensitivity, anaphylaxis, urticaria, premature menopause in women

Drug Interactions
  Increased Effect/Toxicity: Cimetidine increased the blood levels of epirubicin (AUC increased by 50%).

Mechanism of Action Epirubicin is an anthracycline antibiotic. Epirubicin is known to inhibit DNA and RNA synthesis by steric obstruction after intercalating between DNA base pairs; active throughout entire cell cycle. Intercalation triggers DNA cleavage by topoisomerase II, resulting in cytocidal activity. Epirubicin also inhibits DNA helicase, and generates cytotoxic free radicals.

Pharmacodynamics/Kinetics
  Distribution: V_{ss} 21-27 L/kg
  Protein binding: 77% to albumin
  Metabolism: Extensively via hepatic and extrahepatic (including RBCs) routes
  Half-life elimination: Triphasic; Mean terminal: 33 hours
  Excretion: Feces; urine (lesser extent)

Dosage Adults: I.V.: 100-120 mg/m^2 once weekly every 3-4 weeks **or** 50-60 mg/m^2 days 1 and 8 every 3-4 weeks
Breast cancer:
    CEF-120: 60 mg/m^2 on days 1 and 8 every 28 days for 6 cycles
    FEC-100: 100 mg/m^2 on day 1 every 21 days for 6 cycles

Dosage adjustment in renal impairment: Severe renal impairment (serum creatinine >5 mg/dL): Lower doses should be considered

Dosage adjustment in hepatic impairment:
    Bilirubin 1.2-3 mg/dL or AST 2-4 times the upper limit of normal: 50% of recommended starting dose
    Bilirubin >3 mg/dL or AST >4 times the upper limit of normal: 25% of recommended starting dose

Elderly: Plasma clearance of epirubicin in elderly female patients was noted to be reduced by 35%. Although no initial dosage reduction is specifically recommended, particular care should be exercised in monitoring toxicity and adjusting subsequent dosage in elderly patients (particularly females >70 years).

Administration Administer I.V. into the tubing of a freely-flowing intravenous infusion (0.9% sodium chloride or 5% glucose solution) over 3-5 minutes.

Monitoring Parameters Monitor injection site during infusion for possible extravasation or local reactions; CBC with differential and platelet count, liver function tests, renal function, ECG, and left ventricular ejection fraction

Patient Information Report any stinging or change in sensation during the infusion. This medication can only be administered I.V. During therapy, do not use alcohol, aspirin-containing products, and OTC medications without consulting prescriber. It is important to maintain adequate nutrition and hydration (2-3 L/day of fluids unless instructed to restrict fluid intake) during therapy; frequent small meals may help. You may experience nausea or vomiting (frequent small meals, frequent mouth care, sucking lozenges, or chewing gum may help). You may experience loss of hair (reversible); you will be more susceptible to infection (avoid crowds and exposure to infection as much as possible). Yogurt or buttermilk may help reduce diarrhea (if unresolved, contact prescriber for medication relief). Frequent mouth care and use of a soft toothbrush or cotton swabs may reduce mouth sores. May discolor urine (red/pink). Report fever, chills, unusual bruising or bleeding, signs of infection, abdominal pain or blood in stools, excessive fatigue, yellowing of eyes or skin, swelling of extremities, difficulty breathing, or unresolved diarrhea. Barrier contraceptive measures are recommended for both males and females while receiving this drug and for at least one month following administration. Risks of treatment include irreversible heart damage, treatment-related leukemia, and premature menopause in women.

Dosage Forms INJ, solution [preservative free]: 2 mg/mL (25 mL, 100 mL)

♦ **Epitol**® *see* Carbamazepine *on page 214*

♦ **Epivir**® *see* Lamivudine *on page 712*

♦ **Epivir-HBV**® *see* Lamivudine *on page 712*

Eplerenone (e PLER en one)

U.S. Brand Names Inspra™

Therapeutic Category Antihypertensive Agent; Selective Aldosterone Blocker

Use Treatment of hypertension (may be used alone or in combination with other antihypertensive agents); treatment of CHF following acute MI

Pregnancy Risk Factor B

Contraindications Hypersensitivity to eplerenone or any component of the formulation; serum potassium >5.5 mEq/L; Cl$_{cr}$ ≤30 mL/minute; concomitant use of strong CYP3A4 inhibitors (see Drug Interactions for details)

The following additional contraindications apply to patients with hypertension: Type 2 diabetes mellitus (noninsulin dependent, NIDDM) with microalbuminuria; serum creatinine >2.0 mg/dL in males or >1.8 mg/dL in females; Cl$_{cr}$ <50 mL/minute; concomitant use with potassium supplements or potassium-sparing diuretics

Warnings/Precautions Dosage adjustment needed for patients on moderate CYP3A4 inhibitors (see drug interactions for details). Monitor closely for hyperkalemia; increases in serum potassium were dose related during clinical trials and rates of hyperkalemia also increased with declining renal function. Safety and efficacy have not been established in pediatric patients or in patients with severe hepatic impairment. Use with caution in CHF patients post-MI with diabetes.

Common Adverse Reactions
>10%: Endocrine & metabolic: Hypertriglyceridemia (1% to 15%, dose related); hypokalemia (16% in CHF)
1% to 10%:
    Central nervous system: Dizziness (3%), fatigue (2%)
    Endocrine & metabolic: Breast pain (males <1% to 1%), serum creatinine increased (6% in CHF), gynecomastia (males <1% to 1%), hyponatremia (2%, dose related), hypercholesterolemia (<1% to 1%); hyperkalemia (dose related, <1%; 6% in left ventricular dysfunction)
    Gastrointestinal: Diarrhea (2%), abdominal pain (1%)
    Genitourinary: Abnormal vaginal bleeding (<1% to 2%)
    Renal: Albuminuria (1%)
    Respiratory: Cough (2%)
(Continued)

Eplerenone *(Continued)*

Miscellaneous: Flu-like syndrome (2%)

Drug Interactions

Cytochrome P450 Effect: Substrate of **CYP3A4**

Increased Effect/Toxicity: ACE inhibitors, angiotensin II receptor antagonists, NSAIDs, potassium supplements, and potassium-sparing diuretics increase the risk of hyperkalemia; concomitant use with potassium supplements and potassium-sparing diuretics is contraindicated; monitor potassium levels with ACE inhibitors and angiotensin II receptor antagonists. Potent CYP3A4 inhibitors (eg, itraconazole, ketoconazole) lead to fivefold increase in eplerenone; concurrent use is contraindicated. Less potent CYP3A4 inhibitors (eg, erythromycin, fluconazole, saquinavir, verapamil) lead to approximately twofold increase in eplerenone; starting dose should be decreased to 25 mg/day. Although interaction studies have not been conducted, monitoring of lithium levels is recommended.

Decreased Effect: NSAIDs may decrease the antihypertensive effects of eplerenone.

Mechanism of Action Aldosterone increases blood pressure primarily by inducing sodium reabsorption. Eplerenone reduces blood pressure by blocking aldosterone binding at mineralocorticoid receptors found in the kidney, heart, blood vessels and brain.

Pharmacodynamics/Kinetics

Distribution: V_d: 43-90 L

Protein binding: ~50%; primarily to alpha$_1$-acid glycoproteins

Metabolism: Primarily hepatic via CYP3A4; metabolites inactive

Half-life elimination: 4-6 hours

Time to peak, plasma: 1.5 hours; may take up to 4 weeks for full therapeutic effect

Excretion: Urine (67%; <5% as unchanged drug), feces (32%)

Dosage Oral: Adults:

Hypertension: Initial: 50 mg once daily; may increase to 50 mg twice daily if response is not adequate; may take up to 4 weeks for full therapeutic response. Doses >100 mg/day are associated with increased risk of hyperkalemia and no greater therapeutic effect.

Concurrent use with moderate CYP3A4 inhibitors: Initial: 25 mg once daily

Congestive heart failure (post-MI): Initial: 25 mg once daily; dosage goal: titrate to 50 mg once daily within 4 weeks, as tolerated

Dosage adjustment per serum potassium concentrations for CHF:

<5.0 mEq/L:

Increase dose from 25 mg every other day to 25 mg daily **or**

Increase dose from 25 mg daily to 50 mg daily

5.0-5.4 mEq/L: No adjustment needed

5.5-5.9 mEq/L:

Decrease dose from 50 mg daily to 25 mg daily **or**

Decrease dose from 25 mg daily to 25 mg every other day **or**

Decrease does from 25 mg every other day to withhold medication

≥6.0 mEq/L: Withhold medication until potassium <5.5 mEq/L, then restart at 25 mg every other day

Dosage adjustment in renal impairment:

Patients with hypertension with Cl_{cr} <50 mL/minute or serum creatinine >2.0 mg/dL in males or >1.8 mg/dL in females: Use is contraindicated; risk of hyperkalemia increases with declining renal function

Patients with CHF post-MI: Use with caution

Dosage adjustment in hepatic impairment: No dosage adjustment needed for mild-to-moderate impairment; safety and efficacy not established for severe impairment

Administration May be administered with or without food.

Monitoring Parameters Blood pressure; serum potassium (levels monitored every 2 weeks for the first 1-2 months, then monthly in clinical trials); renal function

Patient Information Take exact dose prescribed; do not change dosage without consulting prescriber. Take with or without regard to meals. Avoid excessive potassium intake (eg, salt substitutes, low-salt foods, bananas, nuts). May cause fatigue, dizziness, or postural hypotension; use caution when changing position from lying or sitting to standing, when driving, or when climbing stairs until response to medication is known. May cause diarrhea.

Dosage Forms Tab, film-coated: 25 mg, 50 mg

♦ **EPO** *see* Epoetin Alfa *on page 442*

Epoetin Alfa (e POE e tin AL fa)

U.S. Brand Names Epogen®; Procrit®

Synonyms EPO; Erythropoietin; rHuEPO-α

Therapeutic Category Colony-Stimulating Factor; Recombinant Human Erythropoietin

Use

Treatment of anemia related to zidovudine therapy in HIV-infected patients; in patients when the endogenous erythropoietin level is ≤500 mU/mL and the dose of zidovudine is ≤4200 mg/week

Treatment of anemia associated with chronic renal failure (CRF) including dialysis (end-stage renal disease, ESRD) and nondialysis patients. Prior to therapy, serum ferritin should be >100 ng/dL and transferrin saturation (serum iron/iron binding capacity x 100) of 20% to 30%; nondialysis patients should have a hematocrit <30%

Treatment of anemia in cancer patients on chemotherapy; in patients with nonmyeloid malignancies where anemia is caused by the effect of the concomitantly administered chemotherapy; to decrease the need for transfusions in patients who will be receiving chemotherapy for a minimum of 2 months

Reduction of allogeneic blood transfusion in surgery patients (with hemoglobin >10 g/dL up to 13 g/dL) scheduled to undergo elective, noncardiac, nonvascular surgery

Unlabeled/Investigational Use Anemia associated with rheumatic disease; hypogenerative anemia of Rh hemolytic disease; sickle cell anemia; acute renal failure; Gaucher's disease; Castleman's disease; paroxysmal nocturnal hemoglobinuria; anemia of critical illness (limited documentation); anemia of prematurity

Pregnancy Risk Factor C

Contraindications Hypersensitivity to albumin (human) or mammalian cell-derived products; uncontrolled hypertension

Warnings/Precautions Use caution with history of seizures or hypertension; blood pressure should be controlled prior to start of therapy and monitored closely throughout treatment. Excessive rate of rise of hematocrit may be possibly associated with the exacerbation of hypertension or seizures; decrease the epoetin dose if the hematocrit increase exceeds 4 points in any 2-week period. Use caution in patients at risk for thrombosis or with history of cardiovascular disease. Increased mortality has occurred when aggressive dosing is used in CHF or anginal patients undergoing hemodialysis. An Amgen-funded study determined that when patients were targeted for a hematocrit of 42% versus a less aggressive 30%, mortality was higher (35% versus 29%).

Pure red cell aplasia (PRCA) with neutralizing antibodies to erythropoietin has been reported in limited patients treated with recombinant products; may occur more in patients with CRF. Patients should be evaluated for any loss of effect to therapy and treatment discontinued with evidence of PRCA. Response to therapy may be limited by multiple factors; refer to Additional Information for details.

Prior to and during therapy iron stores must be evaluated. Iron supplementation should be given during therapy to provide for increased requirements during expansion of the red cell mass secondary to marrow stimulation by EPO unless iron stores are already in excess.

Use caution with porphyria. Not recommended for acute correction of severe anemia or as a substitute for transfusion. For patients receiving renal transplant, consider discontinuing at transplant or within 2 weeks of successful engraftment.

For patients with endogenous serum EPO levels which are inappropriately low for hemoglobin level, documentation of the serum EPO level will help indicate which patients may benefit from EPO therapy. Serum EPO levels can be ordered routinely from Clinical Chemistry (red top serum separator tube). Refer to "Reference Range" for information on interpretation of EPO levels.

Common Adverse Reactions
>10%:
  Cardiovascular: Hypertension
  Central nervous system: Headache, fever
  Gastrointestinal: Nausea
  Neuromuscular & skeletal: Arthralgias
1% to 10%:
  Cardiovascular: Edema, chest pain
  Central nervous system: Fatigue, seizures
  Gastrointestinal: Vomiting, diarrhea
  Hematologic: Clotted access
  Neuromuscular & skeletal: Asthenia

Mechanism of Action Induces erythropoiesis by stimulating the division and differentiation of committed erythroid progenitor cells; induces the release of reticulocytes from the bone marrow into the bloodstream, where they mature to erythrocytes. There is a dose response relationship with this effect. This results in an increase in reticulocyte counts followed by a rise in hematocrit and hemoglobin levels.

Pharmacodynamics/Kinetics
Onset of action: Several days
  Peak effect: 2-3 weeks
Distribution: V_d: 9 L; rapid in the plasma compartment; concentrated in liver, kidneys, and bone marrow
Metabolism: Some degradation does occur
Bioavailability: S.C.: ~21% to 31%; intraperitoneal epoetin: 3% (a few patients)
Half-life elimination: Circulating: Chronic renal failure: 4-13 hours; Healthy volunteers: 20% shorter
Time to peak, serum: S.C.: Chronic renal failure: 5-24 hours
Excretion: Feces (majority); urine (small amounts, 10% unchanged in normal volunteers)

Dosage
Chronic renal failure patients: I.V., S.C.:
  Children: Initial dose: 50 units/kg 3 times/week
  Adults: Initial dose: 50-100 units/kg 3 times/week
  Reduce dose when
    1) hematocrit approaches 36% **or**
    2) when hematocrit increases >4 points in any 2-week period
  Increase dose if hematocrit does not increase by 5-6 points after 8 weeks of therapy and hematocrit is below suggested target range
  Suggested target hematocrit range: 30% to 36%
  Maintenance dose: Individualize to target range
    Dialysis patients: Median dose:
      Children: 167 units/kg/week **or** 76 units/kg 2-3 times/week
      Adults: 75 units/kg 3 times/week
(Continued)

Epoetin Alfa *(Continued)*

Nondialysis patients:
Children: Dosing range: 50-250 units/kg 1-3 times/week
Adults: Median dose: 75-150 units/kg

Zidovudine-treated, HIV-infected patients (patients with erythropoietin levels >500 mU/mL are **unlikely** to respond): I.V., S.C.:
Children: Initial dose: Reported dosing range: 50-400 units/kg 2-3 times/week
Adults: 100 units/kg 3 times/week for 8 weeks
Increase dose by 50-100 units/kg 3 times/week if response is not satisfactory in terms of reducing transfusion requirements or increasing hematocrit after 8 weeks of therapy
Evaluate response every 4-8 weeks thereafter and adjust the dose accordingly by 50-100 units/kg increments 3 times/week
If patients have not responded satisfactorily to a 300 unit/kg dose 3 times/week, it is unlikely that they will respond to higher doses
Stop dose if hematocrit exceeds 40% and resume treatment at a 25% dose reduction when hematocrit drops to 36%

Cancer patients on chemotherapy: Treatment of patients with erythropoietin levels >200 mU/mL is **not recommended**
Children: I.V., S.C.: Dosing range: 25-300 units/kg 3-7 times/week; commonly reported initial does: 150 units/kg
Adults: Initial dose: S.C.: 150 units/kg 3 times/week; commonly used doses range from 10,000 units 3 times/week to 40,000-60,000 units once weekly.
Dose adjustment: If response is not satisfactory in terms of reducing transfusion requirement or increasing hematocrit after 8 weeks of therapy, the dose may be increased up to 300 units/kg 3 times/week. If patients do not respond, it is unlikely that they will respond to higher doses.
If hematocrit exceeds 40%, hold the dose until it falls to 36% and reduce the dose by 25% when treatment is resumed

Surgery patients: Prior to initiating treatment, obtain a hemoglobin to establish that is >10 mg/dL or ≤13 mg/dL: Adults: S.C.: Initial dose: 300 units/kg/day for 10 days before surgery, on the day of surgery, and for 4 days after surgery
Alternative dose: 600 units/kg in once weekly doses (21, 14, and 7 days before surgery) plus a fourth dose on the day of surgery

Anemia of critical illness (unlabeled use): Adults: S.C.: 40,000 units once weekly

Anemia of prematurity (unlabeled use): Infants: I.V., S.C.: Dosing range: 500-1250 units/kg/week; commonly used dose: 250 units/kg 3 times/week; supplement with oral iron therapy 3-8 mg/kg/day

Dosage adjustment in renal impairment:
Dialysis patient: Usually administered as I.V. bolus 3 times/week. While administration is independent of the dialysis procedure, it may be administered into the venous line at the end of the dialysis procedure to obviate the need for additional venous access.
Chronic renal failure patients not on dialysis: May be given either as an I.V. or S.C. injection.
Hemodialysis: Supplemental dose is not necessary.
Peritoneal dialysis: Supplemental dose is not necessary.

Administration
Patients with CRF on dialysis: May be administered I.V. bolus into the venous line after dialysis.
Patients with CRF not on dialysis: May be administered I.V. or S.C.

Monitoring Parameters
Careful monitoring of blood pressure is indicated; problems with hypertension have been noted especially in renal failure patients treated with rHuEPO. Other patients are less likely to develop this complication.

Suggested tests to be monitored and their frequency: See table.

Test	Initial Phase Frequency	Maintenance Phase Frequency
Hematocrit/hemoglobin	2 x/week	2-4 x/month
Blood pressure	3 x/week	3 x/week
Serum ferritin	Monthly	Quarterly
Transferrin saturation	Monthly	Quarterly
Serum chemistries including CBC with differential, creatinine, blood urea nitrogen, potassium, phosphorous	Regularly per routine	Regularly per routine

Hematocrit should be determined twice weekly until stabilization within the target range (30% to 36%), and twice weekly for at least 2-6 weeks after a dose increase.

Reference Range Guidelines should be based on the following figure or published literature
Guidelines for estimating appropriateness of endogenous EPO levels for varying levels of anemia via the EIA assay method: See figure. The reference range for erythropoietin in serum, for subjects with normal hemoglobin and hematocrit, is 4.1-22.2 mU/mL by the EIA method. Erythropoietin levels are typically inversely related to hemoglobin (and hematocrit) levels in anemias not attributed to impaired erythropoietin production.
Zidovudine-treated HIV patients: Available evidence indicates patients with endogenous serum erythropoietin levels >500 mU/mL are unlikely to respond

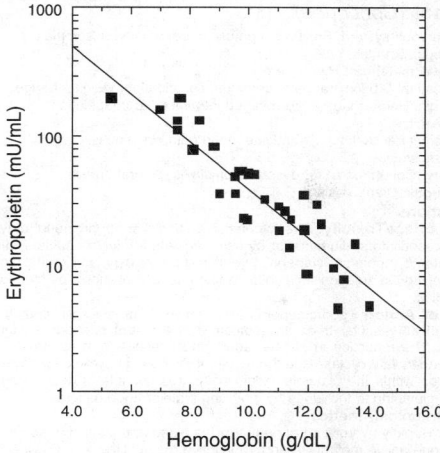

Cancer chemotherapy patients: Treatment of patients with endogenous serum erythropoietin levels >200 mU/mL is not recommended

Patient Information You will require frequent blood tests to determine appropriate dosage. Do not take other medications, vitamin or iron supplements, or make significant changes in your diet without consulting prescriber. Report signs or symptoms of edema (eg, swollen extremities, difficulty breathing, rapid weight gain), onset of severe headache, acute back pain, chest pain, muscular tremors, or seizure activity.

Dosage Forms INJ, solution [preservative free]: 2000 units/mL (1 mL); 3000 units/mL (1 mL); 4000 units/mL (1 mL); 10,000 units/mL (1 mL); 40,000 units/mL (1 mL). **INJ, solution:** 10,000 units/mL (2 mL); 20,000 units/mL (1 mL)

♦ **Epogen®** *see Epoetin Alfa on page 442*

Epoprostenol (e poe PROST en ole)

U.S. Brand Names Flolan®

Synonyms Epoprostenol Sodium; PGI₂; PGX; Prostacyclin

Therapeutic Category Prostaglandin

Use Orphan drug: Treatment of primary pulmonary hypertension; treatment of secondary pulmonary hypertension due to intrinsic precapillary pulmonary vascular disease

Unlabeled/Investigational Use Other potential uses include pulmonary hypertension associated with ARDS, SLE, or CHF; neonatal pulmonary hypertension; cardiopulmonary bypass surgery; hemodialysis; atherosclerosis; peripheral vascular disorders; and neonatal purpura fulminans

Restrictions Orders for epoprostenol are distributed by two sources in the United States. Information on orders or reimbursement assistance may be obtained from either Accredo Health, Inc (1-800-935-6526) or TheraCom, Inc (1-877-356-5264).

Pregnancy Risk Factor B

Contraindications Hypersensitivity to epoprostenol or to structurally-related compounds; chronic use in patients with CHF due to severe left ventricular systolic dysfunction

Warnings/Precautions Abrupt interruptions or large sudden reductions in dosage may result in rebound pulmonary hypertension; some patients with primary pulmonary hypertension have developed pulmonary edema during dose ranging, which may be associated with pulmonary veno-occlusive disease; during chronic use, unless contraindicated, anticoagulants should be coadministered to reduce the risk of thromboembolism. Clinical studies of epoprostenol in pulmonary hypertension did not include sufficient numbers of patients ≥65 years of age to substantiate its safety and efficacy in the geriatric population. As a result, in general, dose selection for an elderly patient should be cautious usually starting at the low end of the dosing range.

Common Adverse Reactions

>10%:
  Cardiovascular: Flushing, tachycardia, shock, syncope, heart failure
  Central nervous system: Fever, chills, anxiety, nervousness, dizziness, headache, hyperesthesia, pain
  Gastrointestinal: Diarrhea, nausea, vomiting
  Neuromuscular & skeletal: Jaw pain, myalgia, tremor, paresthesia
  Respiratory: Hypoxia
  Miscellaneous: Sepsis, flu-like symptoms

1% to 10%:
  Cardiovascular: Bradycardia, hypotension, angina pectoris, edema, arrhythmias, pallor, cyanosis, palpitations, cerebrovascular accident, myocardial ischemia, chest pain

(Continued)

Epoprostenol *(Continued)*

    Central nervous system: Seizures, confusion, depression, insomnia
    Dermatologic: Pruritus, rash
    Endocrine & metabolic: Hypokalemia
    Gastrointestinal: Abdominal pain, anorexia, constipation, weight change
    Hematologic: Hemorrhage, disseminated intravascular coagulation
    Hepatic: Ascites
    Neuromuscular & skeletal: Arthralgias, bone pain, weakness
    Ocular: Amblyopia
    Respiratory: Cough increase, dyspnea, epistaxis, pleural effusion
    Miscellaneous: Diaphoresis

Drug Interactions

Increased Effect/Toxicity: The hypotensive effects of epoprostenol may be exacerbated by other vasodilators, diuretics, or by using acetate in dialysis fluids. Patients treated with anticoagulants (heparins, warfarin, thrombin inhibitors) or antiplatelet agents (ticlopidine, clopidogrel, IIb/IIIa antagonists, aspirin) and epoprostenol should be monitored for increased bleeding risk.

Mechanism of Action Epoprostenol is also known as prostacyclin and PGI_2. It is a strong vasodilator of all vascular beds. In addition, it is a potent endogenous inhibitor of platelet aggregation. The reduction in platelet aggregation results from epoprostenol's activation of intracellular adenylate cyclase and the resultant increase in cyclic adenosine monophosphate concentrations within the platelets. Additionally, it is capable of decreasing thrombogenesis and platelet clumping in the lungs by inhibiting platelet aggregation.

Pharmacodynamics/Kinetics

    Metabolism: Rapidly hydrolyzed at neutral pH in blood and subject to some enzymatic degradation to one active metabolite and 13 inactive metabolites
    Half-life elimination: 2.7-6 minutes; Continuous infusion: ~15 minutes
    Excretion: Urine (12% as unchanged drug)

Dosage I.V.: The drug is administered by continuous intravenous infusion via a central venous catheter using an ambulatory infusion pump; during dose ranging it may be administered peripherally

Acute dose ranging: The initial infusion rate should be 2 ng/kg/minute by continuous I.V. and increased in increments of 2 ng/kg/minute every 15 minutes or longer until dose-limiting effects are elicited (such as chest pain, anxiety, dizziness, changes in heart rate, dyspnea, nausea, vomiting, headache, hypotension and/or flushing)

Continuous chronic infusion: Initial: 4 ng/kg/minute **less** than the maximum-tolerated infusion rate determined during acute dose ranging

    If maximum-tolerated infusion rate is <5 ng/kg/minute, the chronic infusion rate should be $\frac{1}{2}$ the maximum-tolerated acute infusion rate

Dosage adjustments: Dose adjustments in the chronic infusion rate should be based on persistence, recurrence, or worsening of patient symptoms of pulmonary hypertension

    If symptoms persist or recur after improving, the infusion rate should be increased by 1-2 ng/kg/minute increments, every 15 minutes or greater; following establishment of a new chronic infusion rate, the patient should be observed and vital signs monitored.

Administration

Using an ambulatory infusion pump, administer a chronic continuous infusion of epoprostenol through a central venous catheter. A peripheral intravenous catheter may be used during acute dose-ranging until central access is established. Consider a multilumen catheter if other intravenous therapies are routinely administered. During extended use at ambient temperatures exceeding 25°C (77°F), cold pouches with frozen gel packs were used during clinical trials.

The ambulatory infusion pump should be small and lightweight, be able to adjust infusion rates in 2 ng/kg/minute increments, have occlusion, end of infusion, and low battery alarms, have ± 6% accuracy of the programmed rate, and have positive continuous or pulsatile pressure with intervals ≤3 minutes between pulses. The reservoir should be made of polyvinyl chloride, polypropylene, or glass. The infusion pumps used in clinical trials were CADD-1 HFX 5100 (Pharmacia Deltec), Walk-Med 410 C (Medfusion, Inc) and the Auto Syringe AS2F (Baxter HealthCare).

Monitoring Parameters Monitor for improvements in pulmonary function, decreased exertional dyspnea, fatigue, syncope and chest pain, pulmonary vascular resistance, pulmonary arterial pressure and quality of life. In addition, the pump device and catheters should be monitored frequently to avoid "system" related failure.

Patient Information Therapy with this drug requires commitment to drug reconstitution, administration, and care of the permanent central venous catheter. The decision to receive epoprostenol should be based upon the understanding that there is a high likelihood that therapy will be needed for prolonged periods, possibly for life, and that the care of the catheter and infusion pump will be required and should be carefully considered. Promptly report any adverse drug reactions with epoprostenol, this may require dosage adjustments.

Dosage Forms INJ, powder for reconstitution: 0.5 mg, 1.5 mg

♦ **Epoprostenol Sodium** *see* Epoprostenol *on page 445*

Eprosartan *(ep roe SAR tan)*

Related Information

    Angiotensin Agents Comparison *on page 1353*

U.S. Brand Names Teveten®

Therapeutic Category Angiotensin II Receptor Antagonist (ARB); Antihypertensive Agent

Use Treatment of hypertension; may be used alone or in combination with other antihypertensives

Pregnancy Risk Factor C (1st trimester); D (2nd and 3rd trimesters)

Contraindications Hypersensitivity to eprosartan or any component of the formulation; sensitivity to other A-II receptor antagonists; bilateral renal artery stenosis; pregnancy (2nd and 3rd trimesters)

Warnings/Precautions Avoid use or use a smaller dose in patients who are volume depleted; correct depletion first. Deterioration in renal function can occur with initiation. Use with caution in unilateral renal artery stenosis and pre-existing renal insufficiency; significant aortic/mitral stenosis. Safety and efficacy not established in pediatric patients.

Common Adverse Reactions 1% to 10%:
Central nervous system: Fatigue (2%), depression (1%)
Endocrine & metabolic: Hypertriglyceridemia (1%)
Gastrointestinal: Abdominal pain (2%)
Genitourinary: Urinary tract infection (1%)
Respiratory: Upper respiratory tract infection (8%), rhinitis (4%), pharyngitis (4%), cough (4%)
Miscellaneous: Viral infection (2%), injury (2%)

Drug Interactions
Cytochrome P450 Effect: Inhibits CYP2C8/9 (weak)
Increased Effect/Toxicity: Eprosartan may increase risk of lithium toxicity. May increase risk of hyperkalemia with potassium-sparing diuretics (eg, amiloride, potassium, spironolactone, triamterene), potassium supplements, or high doses of trimethoprim.

Mechanism of Action Angiotensin II is formed from angiotensin I in a reaction catalyzed by angiotensin-converting enzyme (ACE, kininase II). Angiotensin II is the principal pressor agent of the renin-angiotensin system, with effects that include vasoconstriction, stimulation of synthesis and release of aldosterone, cardiac stimulation, and renal reabsorption of sodium. Eprosartan blocks the vasoconstrictor and aldosterone-secreting effects of angiotensin II by selectively blocking the binding of angiotensin II to the AT1 receptor in many tissues, such as vascular smooth muscle and the adrenal gland. Its action is therefore independent of the pathways for angiotensin II synthesis. Blockade of the renin-angiotensin system with ACE inhibitors, which inhibit the biosynthesis of angiotensin II from angiotensin I, is widely used in the treatment of hypertension. ACE inhibitors also inhibit the degradation of bradykinin, a reaction also catalyzed by ACE. Because eprosartan does not inhibit ACE (kininase II), it does not affect the response to bradykinin. Whether this difference has clinical relevance is not yet known. Eprosartan does not bind to or block other hormone receptors or ion channels known to be important in cardiovascular regulation.

Pharmacodynamics/Kinetics
Protein binding: 98%
Metabolism: Minimally hepatic
Bioavailability: 300 mg dose: 13%
Half-life elimination: Terminal: 5-9 hours
Time to peak, serum: Fasting: 1-2 hours
Excretion: Feces (90%); urine (7%, mostly as unchanged drug)
Clearance: 7.9 L/hour

Dosage Adults: Oral: Dosage must be individualized; can administer once or twice daily with total daily doses of 400-800 mg. Usual starting dose is 600 mg once daily as monotherapy in patients who are euvolemic. Limited clinical experience with doses >800 mg.
Dosage adjustment in renal impairment: No starting dosage adjustment is necessary; however, carefully monitor the patient
Dosage adjustment in hepatic impairment: No starting dosage adjustment is necessary; however, carefully monitor the patient

Elderly: No starting dosage adjustment is necessary; however, carefully monitor the patient

Patient Information May be taken with or without food; female patients should be counseled regarding appropriate birth control methods and to report any signs and symptoms of pregnancy. Monitor blood pressure regularly. Do not stop taking this medication without advising your healthcare professional. Take each dose at the same time each day. Take a missed dose as soon as possible, but do not double-up doses.

Dosage Forms TAB: 400 mg, 600 mg

♦ **Eprosartan and HCTZ** see Eprosartan and Hydrochlorothiazide on page 447

Eprosartan and Hydrochlorothiazide
(ep roe SAR tan & hye droe klor oh THYE a zide)

U.S. Brand Names Teveten® HCT

Synonyms Eprosartan and HCTZ; Eprosartan Mesylate and Hydrochlorothiazide; Hydrochlorothiazide and Eprosartan

Therapeutic Category Angiotensin II Antagonist/Thiazide Diuretic Combination; Antihypertensive Agent, Combination

Use Treatment of hypertension (not indicated for initial treatment)

Pregnancy Risk Factor C/D (2nd and 3rd trimesters)

Dosage Oral: Adults: Dose is individualized (combination substituted for individual components)
Usual recommended dose: Eprosartan 600 mg/hydrochlorothiazide 12.5 mg once daily (maximum dose: Eprosartan 600 mg/hydrochlorothiazide 25 mg once daily)
Dosage adjustment in renal impairment: Initial dose adjustments not recommended by manufacturer; carefully monitor patient. Hydrochlorothiazide is ineffective in patients with Cl_{cr} <30 mL/minute.
(Continued)

Eprosartan and Hydrochlorothiazide *(Continued)*

Dosage adjustment in hepatic impairment: Initial dose adjustments not recommended by manufacturer; carefully monitor patient.

Dosage Forms TAB: (600 mg/12.5 mg): Eprosartan mesylate 600 mg and hydrochlorothiazide 12.5 mg; (600 mg/25 mg): Eprosartan mesylate 600 mg and hydrochlorothiazide 25 mg

◆ **Eprosartan Mesylate and Hydrochlorothiazide** *see* Eprosartan and Hydrochlorothiazide *on page 447*

◆ **Epsom Salts** *see* Magnesium Sulfate *on page 772*

◆ **EPT** *see* Teniposide *on page 1195*

◆ **Eptacog Alfa (Activated)** *see* Factor VIIa (Recombinant) *on page 502*

Eptifibatide *(ep TIF i ba tide)*

Related Information
Glycoprotein Antagonists *on page 1376*

U.S. Brand Names Integrilin®

Synonyms Intrifiban

Therapeutic Category Antiplatelet Agent, Glycoprotein IIb/IIIa Inhibitor; Glycoprotein IIb/IIIa Inhibitor; Platelet Aggregation Inhibitor

Use Treatment of patients with acute coronary syndrome (UA/NQMI), including patients who are to be managed medically and those undergoing percutaneous coronary intervention (PCI including PTCA; intracoronary stenting)

Pregnancy Risk Factor B

Contraindications Hypersensitivity to eptifibatide or any component of the product; active abnormal bleeding or a history of bleeding diathesis within the previous 30 days; history of CVA within 30 days or a history of hemorrhagic stroke; severe hypertension (systolic blood pressure >200 mm Hg or diastolic blood pressure >110 mm Hg) not adequately controlled by antihypertensive therapy; major surgery within the preceding 6 weeks; current or planned administration of another parenteral GP IIb/IIIa inhibitor; thrombocytopenia; dependency on renal dialysis

Warnings/Precautions Bleeding is the most common complication. Most major bleeding occurs at the arterial access site where the cardiac catheterization was done. When bleeding can not be controlled with pressure, discontinue infusion and heparin. Use caution in patients with hemorrhagic retinopathy or with other drugs that affect hemostasis. Concurrent use with thrombolytics has not been established as safe. Minimize other procedures including arterial and venous punctures, I.M. injections, nasogastric tubes, etc. Prior to sheath removal, the aPTT or ACT should be checked (do not remove unless aPTT is <45 seconds or the ACT <150 seconds).

Common Adverse Reactions Bleeding is the major drug-related adverse effect. Major bleeding was reported in 4.4% to 10.8%; minor bleeding was reported in 10.5% to 14.2%; requirement for transfusion was reported in 5.5% to 12.8%. Incidence of bleeding is also related to heparin intensity (aPTT goal 50-70 seconds). Patients weighing <70 kg may have an increased risk of major bleeding.

Cardiovascular: Hypotension
Local: Injection site reaction
Neuromuscular & skeletal: Back pain

1% to 10%: Hematologic: Thrombocytopenia (1.2% to 3.2%)

Drug Interactions

Increased Effect/Toxicity: Eptifibatide effect may be increased by other drugs which affect hemostasis include thrombolytics, oral anticoagulants, NSAIDs, dipyridamole, heparin, low molecular weight heparins, ticlopidine, and clopidogrel. Avoid concomitant use of other IIb/IIIa inhibitors. Cephalosporins which contain the MTT side chain may theoretically increase the risk of hemorrhage. Use with aspirin and heparin may increase bleeding over aspirin and heparin alone. However, aspirin and heparin were used concurrently in the majority of patients in the major clinical studies of eptifibatide.

Mechanism of Action Eptifibatide is a cyclic heptapeptide which blocks the platelet glycoprotein IIb/IIIa receptor, the binding site for fibrinogen, von Willebrand factor, and other ligands. Inhibition of binding at this final common receptor reversibly blocks platelet aggregation and prevents thrombosis.

Pharmacodynamics/Kinetics

Onset of action: Within 1 hour
Duration: Platelet function restored ~4 hours following discontinuation
Protein binding: ~25%
Half-life elimination: 2.5 hours
Excretion: Primarily urine (as eptifibatide and metabolites); significant renal impairment may alter disposition of this compound
Clearance: Total body: 55-58 mL/kg/hour; Renal: ~50% of total in healthy subjects

Dosage I.V.: Adults:

Acute coronary syndrome: Bolus of 180 mcg/kg (maximum: 22.6 mg) over 1-2 minutes, begun as soon as possible following diagnosis, followed by a continuous infusion of 2 mcg/kg/minute (maximum: 15 mg/hour) until hospital discharge or initiation of CABG surgery, up to 72 hours. Concurrent aspirin (160-325 mg initially and daily thereafter) and heparin therapy (target aPTT 50-70 seconds) are recommended.

Percutaneous coronary intervention (PCI) with or without stenting: Bolus of 180 mcg/kg (maximum: 22.6 mg) administered immediately before the initiation of PCI, followed by a continuous infusion of 2 mcg/kg/minute (maximum: 15 mg/hour). A second 180 mcg/kg bolus (maximum: 22.6 mg) should be administered 10 minutes after the first bolus. Infusion should be continued until hospital discharge or for up to 18-24 hours, whichever comes first; minimum of 12 hours of infusion is recommended. Concurrent aspirin (160-325 mg 1-24 hours before PCI and daily thereafter) and heparin therapy (ACT 200-300 seconds during PCI) are recommended. Heparin infusion after PCI is discouraged. In patients who undergo coronary artery bypass graft surgery, discontinue infusion prior to surgery.

Dosing adjustment in renal impairment: Dialysis is a contraindication to use.

Acute coronary syndrome: Cl_{cr} <50 mL/minute or S_{cr} >2 mg/dL: Use 180 mcg/kg bolus (maximum: 22.6 mg) and 1 mcg/kg/minute infusion (maximum: 7.5 mg/hour)

Percutaneous coronary intervention (PCI) with or without stenting: Cl_{cr} <50 mL/minute or S_{cr} >2 mg/dL: Use 180 mcg/kg bolus (maximum: 22.6 mg) administered immediately before the initiation of PCI and followed by a continuous infusion of 1 mcg/kg/minute (maximum: 7.5 mg/hour). A second 180 mcg/kg (maximum: 22.6 mg) bolus should be administered 10 minutes after the first bolus.

Administration Visually inspect for discoloration or particulate matter prior to administration. The bolus dose should be withdrawn from the 10 mL vial into a syringe and administered by I.V. push over 1-2 minutes. Begin continuous infusion immediately following bolus administration, administered directly from the 100 mL vial. The 100 mL vial should be spiked with a vented infusion set.

Monitoring Parameters Coagulation parameters, signs/symptoms of excessive bleeding. Laboratory tests at baseline and monitoring during therapy: hematocrit and hemoglobin, platelet count, serum creatinine, PT/aPTT (maintain aPTT between 50-70 seconds unless PCI is to be performed), and ACT with PCI (maintain ACT between 200-300 seconds during PCI).

Dosage Forms INJ, solution: 0.75 mg/mL (100 mL); 2 mg/mL (10 mL, 100 mL)

♦ **Equagesic®** see Aspirin and Meprobamate *on page 123*

♦ **Equanil** see Meprobamate *on page 794*

♦ **Ergamisol®** see Levamisole *on page 727*

Ergocalciferol (er goe kal SIF e role)

U.S. Brand Names Calciferol™; Drisdol®

Synonyms Activated Ergosterol; Viosterol; Vitamin D_2

Therapeutic Category Vitamin, Fat Soluble

Use Treatment of refractory rickets, hypophosphatemia, hypoparathyroidism; dietary supplement

Pregnancy Risk Factor A/C (dose exceeding RDA recommendation)

Dosage Oral dosing is preferred; I.M. therapy required with GI, liver, or biliary disease associated with malabsorption

Dietary supplementation (each mcg = 40 USP units):
  Infants and Children: 5 mcg/day (200 units/day)
  Adults:
    18-50 years: 5 mcg/day (200 units/day)
    51-70 years: 10 mcg/day (400 units/day)
  Elderly >70 years: 15 mcg/day (600 units/day)
Renal failure:
  Children: 100-1000 mcg/day (4000-40,000 units)
  Adults: 500 mcg/day (20,000 units)
Hypoparathyroidism:
  Children: 1.25-5 mg/day (50,000-200,000 units) and calcium supplements
  Adults: 625 mcg to 5 mg/day (25,000-200,000 units) and calcium supplements
Vitamin D-dependent rickets:
  Children: 75-125 mcg/day (3000-5000 units); maximum: 1500 mcg/day
  Adults: 250 mcg to 1.5 mg/day (10,000-60,000 units)
Nutritional rickets and osteomalacia:
  Children and Adults (with normal absorption): 25-125 mcg/day (1000-5000 units)
  Children with malabsorption: 250-625 mcg/day (10,000-25,000 units)
  Adults with malabsorption: 250-7500 mcg (10,000-300,000 units)
Vitamin D-resistant rickets:
  Children: Initial: 1000-2000 mcg/day (40,000-80,000 units) with phosphate supplements; daily dosage is increased at 3- to 4-month intervals in 250-500 mcg (10,000-20,000 units) increments
  Adults: 250-1500 mcg/day (10,000-60,000 units) with phosphate supplements
Familial hypophosphatemia: 10,000-80,000 units daily plus 1-2 g/day elemental phosphorus
Osteoporosis prophylaxis: Adults:
  51-70 years: 400 units/day
  >70 years: 600 units/day
  Maximum daily dose: 2000 units/day

Dosage Forms CAP (Drisdol®): 50,000 units [1.25 mg]. **INJ, solution** (Calciferol™): 500,000 units/mL [12.5 mg/mL] (1 mL). **LIQ, drops** (Calciferol™, Drisdol®): 8000 units/mL [200 mcg/mL] (60 mL)

Ergoloid Mesylates (ER goe loid MES i lates)

Synonyms Dihydroergotoxine; Dihydrogenated Ergot Alkaloids; Hydergine [DSC]

Therapeutic Category Ergot Alkaloid and Derivative

Use Treatment of cerebrovascular insufficiency in primary progressive dementia, Alzheimer's dementia, and senile onset

(Continued)

Ergoloid Mesylates (Continued)

Pregnancy Risk Factor C

Dosage Adults: Oral: 1 mg 3 times/day up to 4.5-12 mg/day; up to 6 months of therapy may be necessary

Dosage Forms TAB: 1 mg. **TAB, sublingual:** 1 mg

♦ **Ergomar®** see Ergotamine on page 450

♦ **Ergometrine Maleate** see Ergonovine on page 450

Ergonovine (er goe NOE veen)

Synonyms Ergometrine Maleate; Ergonovine Maleate

Therapeutic Category Antimigraine Agent, Prophylaxis; Ergot Alkaloid and Derivative

Use Prevention and treatment of postpartum and postabortion hemorrhage caused by uterine atony or subinvolution

Unlabeled/Investigational Use Migraine headaches, diagnostically to identify Prinzmetal's angina

Pregnancy Risk Factor X

Contraindications Hypersensitivity to ergonovine or any component of the formulation; ergot alkaloids are contraindicated with potent inhibitors of CYP3A4 (includes protease inhibitors, azole antifungals, and some macrolide antibiotics); induction of labor, threatened spontaneous abortion, pregnancy

Warnings/Precautions Use with caution in patients with sepsis, heart disease, hypertension, or with hepatic or renal impairment; restore uterine responsiveness in calcium-deficient patients who do not respond to ergonovine by I.V. calcium administration; avoid prolonged use; discontinue if ergotism develops. Pleural and peritoneal fibrosis have been reported with prolonged daily use. Cardiac valvular fibrosis has also been associated with ergot alkaloids.

Common Adverse Reactions 1% to 10%: Gastrointestinal: Nausea, vomiting

Drug Interactions

Cytochrome P450 Effect: Substrate of CYP3A4 (major)

Increased Effect/Toxicity: Effects of ergonovine may be increased by antifungals (azole derivatives); CYP3A4 inhibitors (eg, amiodarone, cimetidine, erythromycin, ritonavir); macrolide antibiotics; protease inhibitors; MAO inhibitors; beta blockers (vasoconstriction); sumatriptan (vasospasm); vasoconstrictors. Ergonovine may increase the effects of sibutramine and other serotonin agonists (serotonin syndrome).

Decreased Effect: Effects of ergonovine may be diminished by antipsychotics, metoclopramide.

Mechanism of Action Ergot alkaloid alpha-adrenergic agonist directly stimulates vascular smooth muscle to vasoconstrict peripheral and cerebral vessels; may also have antagonist effects on serotonin

Pharmacodynamics/Kinetics

Onset of action: I.M.: ~2-5 minutes

Duration: I.M.: Uterine effect: 3 hours; I.V.: ~45 minutes

Metabolism: Hepatic

Excretion: Primarily feces; urine

Dosage Adults: I.M., I.V. (I.V. should be reserved for emergency use only): 0.2 mg, repeat dose in 2-4 hours as needed

Administration I.V. doses should be administered over a period of not <1 minute; dilute in NS to 5 mL for I.V. administration

Patient Information May cause nausea, vomiting, dizziness, increased blood pressure, headache, ringing in the ears, chest pain, or shortness of breath

Dosage Forms INJ: 0.2 mg/mL (1 mL)

♦ **Ergonovine Maleate** see Ergonovine on page 450

Ergotamine (er GOT a meen)

U.S. Brand Names Cafergot®; Ergomar®; Wigraine®

Synonyms Ergotamine Tartrate; Ergotamine Tartrate and Caffeine

Therapeutic Category Antimigraine Agent, Prophylaxis; Ergot Alkaloid and Derivative

Use Abort or prevent vascular headaches, such as migraine, migraine variants, or so-called "histaminic cephalalgia"

Pregnancy Risk Factor X

Contraindications Hypersensitivity to ergotamine, caffeine, or any component of the formulation; peripheral vascular disease; hepatic or renal disease; coronary artery disease; hypertension; sepsis; ergot alkaloids are contraindicated with potent inhibitors of CYP3A4 (includes protease inhibitors, azole antifungals, and some macrolide antibiotics); pregnancy

Warnings/Precautions Avoid prolonged administration or excessive dosage because of the danger of ergotism (intense vasoconstriction), gangrene, cardiac valvular fibrosis, retroperitoneal and/or pleuropulmonary fibrosis. Patients who take ergotamine for extended periods of time may experience withdrawal symptoms and rebound headache when ergotamine is discontinued. May be harmful due to reduction in cerebral blood flow; may precipitate angina, myocardial infarction, or aggravate intermittent claudication; therefore, not considered a drug of choice in the elderly.

Concomitant use with medications considered to be "potent" CYP3A4 inhibitors has been associated with acute ergot toxicity; use caution with medications considered "less potent" inhibitors of CYP3A4 enzymes.

Common Adverse Reactions Frequency not defined.

Cardiovascular: Absence of pulse, bradycardia, cardiac valvular fibrosis, cyanosis, edema, ECG changes, gangrene, hypertension, ischemia, precordial distress and pain, tachycardia, vasospasm

Central nervous system: Vertigo

Dermatologic: Itching

Gastrointestinal: Anal or rectal ulcer (with overuse of suppository), nausea, vomiting

Genitourinary: Retroperitoneal fibrosis

Neuromuscular & skeletal: Muscle pain, numbness, paresthesias, weakness

Respiratory: Pleuropulmonary fibrosis

Miscellaneous: Cold extremities

Drug Interactions

Cytochrome P450 Effect:

Ergotamine: **Substrate** of CYP3A4 (major); Inhibits CYP3A4 (weak)

Caffeine: **Substrate** of CYP1A2 (major), 2C8/9 (minor), 2D6 (minor), 2E1 (minor), 3A4 (minor); Inhibits CYP1A2 (weak), 3A4 (moderate)

Increased Effect/Toxicity: Effects of ergotamine may be increased by antifungals (azole derivatives); CYP3A4 inhibitors (eg, amiodarone, cimetidine, erythromycin, ritonavir); macrolide antibiotics; protease inhibitors; MAO inhibitors; beta blockers (vasoconstriction); sumatriptan (vasospasm); vasoconstrictors. Ergotamine may increase the effects of sibutramine and other serotonin agonists (serotonin syndrome). Effects of caffeine may be increased by quinolone antibiotics, CYP1A2 inhibitors (eg, cimetidine, fluvoxamine, ticlopidine); the effects of CYP1A2 substrates (eg, clozapine, doxepin, theophylline) may be increased by caffeine.

Decreased Effect: Effects of ergotamine may be diminished by antipsychotics, metoclopramide.

Mechanism of Action Has partial agonist and/or antagonist activity against tryptaminergic, dopaminergic and alpha-adrenergic receptors depending upon their site; is a highly active uterine stimulant; it causes constriction of peripheral and cranial blood vessels and produces depression of central vasomotor centers

Pharmacodynamics/Kinetics

Absorption: Ergotamine: Oral, rectal: Erratic; enhanced by caffeine coadministration

Metabolism: Extensively hepatic

Time to peak, serum: Ergotamine: 0.5-3 hours

Half-life elimination: 2 hours

Excretion: Feces (90% as metabolites)

Dosage

Oral (Cafergot®, Wigraine®): 2 tablets at onset of attack; then 1 tablet every 30 minutes as needed; maximum: 6 tablets per attack; do not exceed 10 tablets/week.

Sublingual (Ergomar®): 1 tablet under tongue at first sign, then 1 tablet every 30 minutes if needed; maximum dose: 3 tablets/24 hours, 5 tablets/week

Rectal (Cafergot®): 1 suppository rectally at first sign of an attack; follow with second dose after 1 hour, if needed; maximum: 2 per attack; do not exceed 5/week.

Administration Do not crush sublingual tablets.

Patient Information Report any symptoms such as nausea, vomiting, numbness or tingling, and chest, muscle, or abdominal pain. Initiate therapy at first sign of attack. Do **not** exceed recommended dosage.

Dosage Forms SUPP, rectal (Cafergot®): Ergotamine 2 mg and caffeine 100 mg (12s). **TAB** (Cafergot®, Wigraine®): Ergotamine 1 mg and caffeine 100 mg. **TAB, sublingual** (Ergomar®): Ergotamine 2 mg

- ◆ **Ergotamine Tartrate** *see Ergotamine on page 450*
- ◆ **Ergotamine Tartrate and Caffeine** *see Ergotamine on page 450*
- ◆ **Ergotamine Tartrate, Belladonna, and Phenobarbital** *see Belladonna, Phenobarbital, and Ergotamine on page 151*
- ◆ **E•R•O [OTC]** *see Carbamide Peroxide on page 216*

Ertapenem (er ta PEN em)

U.S. Brand Names Invanz®

Synonyms Ertapenem Sodium; L-749,345; MK0826

Therapeutic Category Antibiotic, Anaerobic; Antibiotic, Carbapenem

Use Treatment of moderate-severe, complicated intra-abdominal infections, skin and skin structure infections, pyelonephritis, acute pelvic infections, and community-acquired pneumonia. Antibacterial coverage includes aerobic gram-positive organisms, aerobic gram-negative organisms, anaerobic organisms.

Methicillin-resistant *Staphylococcus*, *Enterococcus* spp, penicillin-resistant strains of *Streptococcus pneumoniae*, beta-lactamase-positive strains of *Haemophilus influenzae* are **resistant** to ertapenem, as are most *Pseudomonas aeruginosa*.

Pregnancy Risk Factor B

Contraindications Hypersensitivity to ertapenem or any other component of the formulation; anaphylactic reactions to beta-lactam antibiotics. If using intramuscularly, known hypersensitivity to local anesthetics of the amide type (lidocaine is the diluent).

Warnings/Precautions Dosage adjustment required with impaired renal function; prolonged use may result in superinfection; use with caution in patients with CNS disorder (eg, brain lesions, history of seizures), compromised renal function, hypersensitivity to beta-lactams, the elderly; safety and efficacy in patients <18 years of age have not been established. (Continued)

Ertapenem *(Continued)*

Common Adverse Reactions

1% to 10%:

Cardiovascular: Swelling/edema (3%), chest pain (1%), hypertension (0.7% to 2%), hypotension (1% to 2%), tachycardia (1% to 2%)

Central nervous system: Headache (6% to 7%), altered mental status (ie, agitation, confusion, disorientation, decreased mental acuity, changed mental status, somnolence, stupor) (3% to 5%), fever (2% to 5%), insomnia (3%), dizziness (2%), fatigue (1%), anxiety (0.8% to 1%)

Dermatologic: Rash (2% to 3%), pruritus (1% to 2%), erythema (1% to 2%)

Gastrointestinal: Diarrhea (9% to 10%), nausea (6% to 9%), abdominal pain (4%), vomiting (4%), constipation (3% to 4%), acid regurgitation (1% to 2%), dyspepsia (1%), oral candidiasis (0.1% to 1%)

Genitourinary: Vaginitis (1% to 3%)

Hematologic: Platelet count increased (4% to 7%), eosinophils increased (1% to 2%)

Hepatic: Hepatic enzyme elevations (7% to 9%), alkaline phosphatase increase (4% to 7%)

Local: Infused vein complications (5% to 7%), phlebitis/thrombophlebitis (1.5% to 2%), extravasation (0.7% to 2%)

Neuromuscular & skeletal: Leg pain (0.4% to 1%)

Respiratory: Dyspnea (1% to 3%), cough (1% to 2%), pharyngitis (0.7% to 1%), rales/rhonchi (0.5% to 1%), respiratory distress (0.2% to 1%)

Drug Interactions

Increased Effect/Toxicity: Probenecid decreases the renal clearance of ertapenem.

Mechanism of Action Inhibits bacterial cell wall synthesis by binding to one or more of the penicillin binding proteins; which in turn inhibits the final transpeptidation step of peptidoglycan synthesis in bacterial cell walls, thus inhibiting cell wall biosynthesis. Bacteria eventually lyse due to ongoing activity of cell wall autolytic enzymes (autolysins and murein hydrolases) while cell wall assembly is arrested.

Pharmacodynamics/Kinetics

Absorption: I.M.: Almost complete

Distribution: V_{dss}: 8.2 L

Protein binding (concentration dependent): 85% at 300 mcg/mL, 95% at <100 mcg/mL

Metabolism: Hydrolysis to inactive metabolite

Bioavailability: I.M.: 90%

Half-life elimination: 4 hours

Time to peak: I.M.: 2.3 hours

Excretion: Urine (80% as unchanged drug and metabolite); feces (10%)

Dosage Adults: I.V., I.M.: **Note:** I.V. therapy may be administered for up to 14 days; I.M. for up to 7 days

Intra-abdominal infection: 1 g/day for 5-14 days

Skin and skin structure infections: 1 g/day for 7-14 days

Community-acquired pneumonia: 1 g/day; duration of total antibiotic treatment: 10-14 days

Urinary tract infections/pyelonephritis: 1 g/day; duration of total antibiotic treatment: 10-14 days

Acute pelvic infections: 1 g/day for 3-10 days

Elderly: Refer to adult dosing.

Dosage adjustment in renal impairment: Cl_{cr} <30 mL/minute: 500 mg/day

Hemodialysis: When the daily dose is given within 6 hours prior to hemodialysis, a supplementary dose of 150 mg is required following hemodialysis.

Dosage adjustment in hepatic impairment: Adjustments cannot be recommended (lack of experience and research in this patient population).

Administration

I.M.: Avoid injection into a blood vessel. Make sure patient does not have an allergy to lidocaine or another anesthetic of the amide type. Administer by deep I.M. injection into a large muscle mass (eg, gluteal muscle or lateral part of the thigh). Do not administer I.M. preparation or drug reconstituted for I.M. administration intravenously.

I.V.: Infuse over 30 minutes

Monitoring Parameters Periodic renal, hepatic, and hematopoietic assessment during prolonged therapy; neurological assessment

Patient Information Report warmth, swelling, irritation at infusion or injection site. Report unresolved nausea or vomiting (small, frequent meals may help). Report feelings of excessive dizziness, palpitations, visual disturbances, headache, diarrhea, and CNS changes. Report chills, unusual discharge, or foul-smelling urine.

Dosage Forms INJ, powder for reconstitution: 1 g

Erythromycin (er ith roe MYE sin)

Related Information
Antimicrobial Drugs of Choice *on page 1440*
Community-Acquired Pneumonia in Adults *on page 1457*
Prevention of Wound Infection & Sepsis in Surgical Patients *on page 1436*

U.S. Brand Names Akne-Mycin®; A/T/S®; E.E.S.®; Emgel®; Eryc®; Erycette®; Eryderm®; Erygel®; EryPed®; Ery-Tab®; Erythra-Derm™; Erythrocin®; PCE®; Romycin®; Staticin®; Theramycin Z®; T-Stat®

Synonyms Erythromycin Base; Erythromycin Estolate; Erythromycin Ethylsuccinate; Erythromycin Gluceptate; Erythromycin Lactobionate; Erythromycin Stearate

Therapeutic Category Antibiotic, Macrolide; Antibiotic, Ophthalmic; Antibiotic, Topical

Use
Systemic: Treatment of susceptible bacterial infections including *S. pyogenes*, some *S. pneumoniae*, some *S. aureus*, *M. pneumoniae*, *Legionella pneumophila*, diphtheria, pertussis, chancroid, *Chlamydia*, erythrasma, *N. gonorrhoeae*, *E. histolytica*, syphilis and nongonococcal urethritis, and *Campylobacter* gastroenteritis; used in conjunction with neomycin for decontaminating the bowel
Ophthalmic: Treatment of superficial eye infections involving the conjunctiva or cornea; neonatal ophthalmia
Topical: Treatment of acne vulgaris

Unlabeled/Investigational Use Systemic: Treatment of gastroparesis

Pregnancy Risk Factor B

Contraindications Hypersensitivity to erythromycin or any component of the formulation
Systemic: Pre-existing liver disease (erythromycin estolate); concomitant use with ergot derivatives, pimozide, astemizole, or cisapride; hepatic impairment

Warnings/Precautions Systemic: Hepatic impairment with or without jaundice has occurred, it may be accompanied by malaise, nausea, vomiting, abdominal colic, and fever; discontinue use if these occur; avoid using erythromycin lactobionate in neonates since formulations may contain benzyl alcohol which is associated with toxicity in neonates; observe for superinfections. Use in infants has been associated with infantile hypertrophic pyloric stenosis (IHPS). Macrolides have been associated with rare QT_c prolongation and ventricular arrhythmias, including torsade de pointes.

Common Adverse Reactions
Systemic:
Cardiovascular: Ventricular arrhythmias, QT_c prolongation, torsade de pointes (rare), ventricular tachycardia (rare)
Central nervous system: Headache (8%), pain (2%), fever, seizures
Dermatitis: Rash (3%), pruritus (1%)
Gastrointestinal: Abdominal pain (8%), cramping, nausea (8%), oral candidiasis, vomiting (3%), diarrhea (7%), dyspepsia (2%), flatulence (2%), anorexia, pseudomembranous colitis, hypertrophic pyloric stenosis (including cases in infants or IHPS), pancreatitis
Hematologic: Eosinophilia (1%)
Hepatic: Cholestatic jaundice (most common with estolate), increased liver function tests (2%)
Local: Phlebitis at the injection site, thrombophlebitis
Neuromuscular & skeletal: Weakness (2%)
Respiratory: Dyspnea (1%), cough (3%)
Miscellaneous: Hypersensitivity reactions, allergic reactions
Topical: 1% to 10%: Dermatologic: Erythema, desquamation, dryness, pruritus

Drug Interactions
Cytochrome P450 Effect: Substrate of CYP2B6 (minor), 3A4 (major); **Inhibits** CYP1A2 (weak), 3A4 (moderate)

Increased Effect/Toxicity: Avoid concomitant use of the following with erythromycin due to increased risk of malignant arrhythmias: Astemizole, cisapride, gatifloxacin, moxifloxacin, pimozide, sparfloxacin, thioridazine. Other agents that prolong the QT_c interval, including type Ia (eg, quinidine) and type III antiarrhythmic agents, and selected antipsychotic agents (eg, mesoridazine, thioridazine) should be used with extreme caution.

Erythromycin may increase the serum concentrations (and possibly the toxicity) of the following agents: Alfentanil (and possibly other narcotic analgesics), benzodiazepines (alprazolam, diazepam, midazolam, triazolam), buspirone, calcium channel blockers, dihydropyridine (felodipine), carbamazepine, cilostazol, clozapine, colchicine, cyclosporine, digoxin, disopyramide, ergot alkaloids (eg, bromocriptine), HMG-CoA reductase inhibitors (except fluvastatin, pravastatin), loratadine, methylprednisolone, rifabutin, tacrolimus, theophylline, valproate, vinblastine, vincristine, zopiclone. Sildenafil, tadalafil, and vardenafil serum concentrations may be substantially increased by erythromycin; do not exceed single sildenafil doses of 25 mg in 48 hours, a single tadalafil dose of 10 mg in 72 hours, or a single vardenafil dose of 2.5 mg in 24 hours.

The effects of neuromuscular-blocking agents and warfarin have been potentiated by erythromycin. Erythromycin serum concentrations may be increased by amprenavir (and possibly other protease inhibitors).

Decreased Effect: Erythromycin may decrease the serum concentrations of zafirlukast. Erythromycin may antagonize the therapeutic effects of clindamycin and lincomycin.

Mechanism of Action Inhibits RNA-dependent protein synthesis at the chain elongation step; binds to the 50S ribosomal subunit resulting in blockage of transpeptidation
(Continued)

Erythromycin *(Continued)*

Pharmacodynamics/Kinetics

Absorption: Oral: Variable but better with salt forms than with base form; 18% to 45%; ethylsuccinate may be better absorbed with food

Distribution: Crosses placenta; enters breast milk

Relative diffusion from blood into CSF: Minimal even with inflammation

CSF:blood level ratio: Normal meninges: 1% to 12%; Inflamed meninges: 7% to 25%

Protein binding: 75% to 90%

Metabolism: Hepatic via demethylation

Half-life elimination: Peak: 1.5-2 hours; End-stage renal disease: 5-6 hours

Time to peak, serum: Base: 4 hours; Ethylsuccinate: 0.5-2.5 hours; delayed with food due to differences in absorption

Excretion: Primarily feces; urine (2% to 15% as unchanged drug)

Dosage

Neonates: Ophthalmic: Prophylaxis of neonatal gonococcal or chlamydial conjunctivitis: 0.5-1 cm ribbon of ointment should be instilled into each conjunctival sac

Infants and Children (**Note:** 400 mg ethylsuccinate = 250 mg base, stearate, or estolate salts):

Oral: 30-50 mg/kg/day divided every 6-8 hours; may double doses in severe infections

Preop bowel preparation: 20 mg/kg erythromycin base at 1, 2, and 11 PM on the day before surgery combined with mechanical cleansing of the large intestine and oral neomycin

I.V.: Lactobionate: 20-40 mg/kg/day divided every 6 hours

Adults:

Oral:

Base: 250-500 mg every 6-12 hours

Ethylsuccinate: 400-800 mg every 6-12 hours

Preop bowel preparation: Oral: 1 g erythromycin base at 1, 2, and 11 PM on the day before surgery combined with mechanical cleansing of the large intestine and oral neomycin

I.V.: Lactobionate: 15-20 mg/kg/day divided every 6 hours or 500 mg to 1 g every 6 hours, or given as a continuous infusion over 24 hours (maximum: 4 g/24 hours)

Children and Adults:

Ophthalmic: Instill ½" (1.25 cm) 2-6 times/day depending on the severity of the infection

Topical: Apply over the affected area twice daily after the skin has been thoroughly washed and patted dry

Dialysis: Slightly dialyzable (5% to 20%); no supplemental dosage necessary in hemo or peritoneal dialysis or in continuous arteriovenous or venovenous hemofiltration

Gastrointestinal prokinetic (unlabeled use): Adults: I.V., Oral: Erythromycin has been used as a prokinetic agent to improve gastric emptying time and intestinal motility. In adults, 200 mg was infused I.V. initially followed by 250 mg orally 3 times/day 30 minutes before meals. Lower dosages have been used in some trials.

Administration

Oral: Do not crush enteric coated drug product. GI upset, including diarrhea, is common. May be administered with food to decrease GI upset. Do not give with milk or acidic beverages.

I.V.: Infuse 1 g over 20-60 minutes. I.V. infusion may be very irritating to the vein. If phlebitis/pain occurs with used dilution, consider diluting further (eg, 1:5) if fluid status of the patient will tolerate, or consider administering in larger available vein. The addition of lidocaine or bicarbonate does not decrease the irritation of erythromycin infusions.

Ophthalmic: Avoid contact of tip of ophthalmic ointment tube with affected eye

Patient Information Refrigerate after reconstitution, take until gone, do not skip doses; chewable tablets should not be swallowed whole; report if persistent diarrhea occurs; discard any unused portion after 10 days; absorption of estolate, ethylsuccinate, and base in a delayed release form are unaffected by food; take stearate salt and nondelayed release base preparations 2 hours before or after meals

Dosage Forms CAP, delayed release, enteric-coated pellets, as base (Eryc®): 250 mg. **GEL, topical:** 2% (30 g, 60 g); (A/T/S®): 2% (30 g); (Emgel®): 2% (27 g, 50 g); (Erygel®): 2% (30 g, 60 g). **GRAN, for oral suspension, as ethylsuccinate** (E.E.S.®): 200 mg/5 mL (100 mL, 200 mL). **INJ, powder for reconstitution, as lactobionate** (Erythrocin®): 500 mg, 1 g. **OINT, ophthalmic:** 0.5% [5 mg/g] (1 g, 3.5 g); (Romycin®): 0.5% [5 mg/g] (3.5 g). **OINT, topical** (Akne-Mycin®): 2% (25 g). **POWDER, for oral suspension, as ethylsuccinate** (Ery-Ped®): 200 mg/5 mL (5 mL, 100 mL, 200 mL); 400 mg/5 mL (5 mL, 60 mL, 100 mL, 200 mL). **POWDER, for oral suspension, as ethylsuccinate** [drops] (Ery-Ped®): 100 mg/2.5 mL (50 mL). **SOLN, topical:** 1.5% (60 mL); 2% (60 mL); (A/T/S/®, Eryderm®, Erythra-Derm™, T-Stat®, Theramycin™ Z): 2% (60 mL); (Staticin®): 1.5% (60 mL). **SUSP, oral, as estolate:** 125 mg/5 mL (480 mL); 250 mg/5 mL (480 mL). **SUSP, oral, as ethylsuccinate:** 200 mg/5 mL (480 mL); 400 mg/5 mL (480 mL); (E.E.S.®): 200 mg/5 mL (100 mL, 480 mL); 400 mg/5 mL (100 mL, 480 mL). **SWAB** (Erycette®, T-Stat®): 2% (60s). **TAB, chewable, as ethylsuccinate** (EryPed®): 200 mg. **TAB, delayed release, enteric coated, as base** (Ery-Tab®): 250 mg, 333 mg, 500 mg. **TAB, film coated, as base:** 250 mg, 500 mg. **TAB,** film coated, as ethylsuccinate (E.E.S.®): 400 mg. **TAB, film coated, as stearate** (Erythrocin®): 250 mg, 500 mg. **TAB, polymer-coated particles, as base** (PCE®): 333 mg, 500 mg

Erythromycin and Benzoyl Peroxide

(er ith roe MYE sin & BEN zoe il per OKS ide)

U.S. Brand Names Benzamycin®; Benzamycin® Pak

Synonyms Benzoyl Peroxide and Erythromycin

Therapeutic Category Acne Product

Use Topical control of acne vulgaris

Pregnancy Risk Factor C

Dosage Apply twice daily, morning and evening

Dosage Forms GEL, topical: (Benzamycin®): Erythromycin 30 mg and benzoyl peroxide 50 mg per g (47 g); (Benzamycin® Pak): Erythromycin 30 mg and benzoyl peroxide 50 mg per 0.8 g packet (60s)

Erythromycin and Sulfisoxazole (er ith roe MYE sin & sul fi SOKS a zole)

U.S. Brand Names Eryzole®; Pediazole®

Synonyms Sulfisoxazole and Erythromycin

Therapeutic Category Antibiotic, Macrolide Combination; Antibiotic, Sulfonamide Derivative

Use Treatment of susceptible bacterial infections of the upper and lower respiratory tract, otitis media in children caused by susceptible strains of *Haemophilus influenzae*, and many other infections in patients allergic to penicillin

Pregnancy Risk Factor C

Dosage Oral (dosage recommendation is based on the product's erythromycin content):

Children ≥2 months: 50 mg/kg/day erythromycin and 150 mg/kg/day sulfisoxazole in divided doses every 6 hours; not to exceed 2 g erythromycin/day or 6 g sulfisoxazole/day for 10 days

Adults >45 kg: 400 mg erythromycin and 1200 mg sulfisoxazole every 6 hours

Dosing adjustment in renal impairment (sulfisoxazole must be adjusted in renal impairment):

Cl_{cr} 10-50 mL/minute: Administer every 8-12 hours

Cl_{cr} <10 mL/minute: Administer every 12-24 hours

Dosage Forms SUSP, oral: Erythromycin ethylsuccinate 200 mg and sulfisoxazole acetyl 600 mg per 5 mL (100 mL, 150 mL, 200 mL)

♦ **Erythromycin Base** *see* Erythromycin *on page 453*

♦ **Erythromycin Estolate** *see* Erythromycin *on page 453*

♦ **Erythromycin Ethylsuccinate** *see* Erythromycin *on page 453*

♦ **Erythromycin Gluceptate** *see* Erythromycin *on page 453*

♦ **Erythromycin Lactobionate** *see* Erythromycin *on page 453*

♦ **Erythromycin Stearate** *see* Erythromycin *on page 453*

♦ **Erythropoiesis Stimulating Protein** *see* Darbepoetin Alfa *on page 343*

♦ **Erythropoietin** *see* Epoetin Alfa *on page 442*

♦ **Eryzole®** *see* Erythromycin and Sulfisoxazole *on page 455*

Escitalopram (es sye TAL oh pram)

Related Information

Antidepressant Agents Comparison *on page 1359*

Selective Serotonin Reuptake Inhibitors (SSRIs) Pharmacokinetics *on page 1403*

U.S. Brand Names Lexapro™

Synonyms Escitalopram Oxalate; Lu-26-054; S-Citalopram

Therapeutic Category Antidepressant, Selective Serotonin Reuptake Inhibitor (SSRI)

Use Treatment of major depressive disorder; generalized anxiety disorders (GAD)

Pregnancy Risk Factor C

Contraindications Hypersensitivity to escitalopram, citalopram, or any component of the formulation; concomitant use or within 2 weeks of MAO inhibitors

Warnings/Precautions Potential for severe reaction when used with MAO inhibitors; serotonin syndrome (hyperthermia, muscular rigidity, mental status changes/agitation, autonomic instability) may occur. May precipitate a shift to mania or hypomania in patients with bipolar disease. Has a low potential to impair cognitive or motor performance; caution operating hazardous machinery or driving. The possibility of a suicide attempt is inherent in major depression and may persist until remission occurs. Use caution in high-risk patients during initiation of therapy. Prescriptions should be written for the smallest quantity consistent with good patient care. Use caution with a previous seizure disorder or condition predisposing to seizures such as brain damage, alcoholism, or concurrent therapy with other drugs which lower the seizure threshold. May cause hyponatremia/SIADH. Use caution with renal or liver impairment; concomitant CNS depressants; pregnancy (high doses of citalopram has been associated with teratogenicity in animals). Use caution with concomitant use of NSAIDs, ASA, or other drugs that affect coagulation; the risk of bleeding is potentiated. Adverse effects may occur with abrupt discontinuation of therapy, a gradual decrease in dose is recommended. Safety and efficacy in pediatric patients have not been established.

Common Adverse Reactions

>10%:

Central nervous system: Headache (24%), somnolence (6% to 13%), insomnia (9% to 12%)

Gastrointestinal: Nausea (15%)

Genitourinary: Ejaculation disorder (9% to 14%)

1% to 10%:

Cardiovascular: Chest pain, hypertension, palpitation

Central nervous system: Dizziness (5%), fatigue (5% to 8%), dreaming abnormal, concentration impaired, fever, irritability, lethargy, lightheadedness, migraine, vertigo, yawning

Dermatologic: Rash

Endocrine & metabolic: Libido decreased (3% to 7%), anorgasmia (2% to 6%), hot flashes, menstrual cramps, menstrual disorder

Gastrointestinal: Diarrhea (8%), xerostomia (6% to 9%), appetite decreased (3%), constipation (3% to 5%), indigestion (3%), abdominal pain (2%), abdominal cramps, appetite

(Continued)

· Escitalopram *(Continued)*

increased, flatulence, gastroenteritis, gastroesophageal reflux, heartburn, toothache, vomiting, weight gain/loss

Genitourinary: Impotence (3%), urinary tract infection, urinary frequency

Neuromuscular & skeletal: Arthralgia, limb pain, muscle cramp, myalgia, neck/shoulder pain, paresthesia, tremor

Ocular: Blurred vision

Otic: Earache, tinnitus

Respiratory: Rhinitis (5%), sinusitis (3%), bronchitis, coughing, nasal or sinus congestion, sinus headache

Miscellaneous: Diaphoresis (4% to 5%), flu-like syndrome (5%), allergy

Drug Interactions

Cytochrome P450 Effect: Substrate (major) of CYP2C19, 3A4; **Inhibits** CYP2D6 (weak)

Increased Effect/Toxicity: Escitalopram should not be used with nonselective MAO inhibitors (phenelzine, isocarboxazid) or other drugs with MAO inhibition (linezolid); fatal reactions have been reported. Wait 5 weeks after stopping escitalopram before starting a nonselective MAO inhibitor and 2 weeks after stopping an MAO inhibitor before starting escitalopram. Concurrent selegiline has been associated with mania, hypertension, or serotonin syndrome (risk may be reduced relative to nonselective MAO inhibitors).

CYP2C19 inhibitors may increase the levels/effects of imipramine; example inhibitors include delavirdine, fluconazole, fluvoxamine, gemfibrozil, isoniazid, omeprazole, and ticlopidine.

Combined used of SSRIs and buspirone, meperidine, moclobemide, nefazodone, other SSRIs, tramadol, trazodone, and venlafaxine may increase the risk of serotonin syndrome. Escitalopram increases serum levels/effects of CYP2D6 substrates (tricyclic antidepressants). Escitalopram may increase desipramine levels.

Combined use of sumatriptan (and other serotonin agonists) may result in toxicity; weakness, hyper-reflexia, and incoordination have been observed with sumatriptan and SSRIs. In addition, concurrent use may theoretically increase the risk of serotonin syndrome; includes sumatriptan, naratriptan, rizatriptan, and zolmitriptan.

Combined use with aspirin, NSAIDs, or warfarin may increase risk of bleeding; use caution.

Decreased Effect: CYP2C19 inducers may decrease the levels/effects of imipramine; example inducers include aminoglutethimide, carbamazepine, phenytoin, and rifampin.

Mechanism of Action Escitalopram is the S-enantiomer of the racemic derivative citalopram, which selectively inhibits the reuptake of serotonin with little to no effect on norepinephrine or dopamine reuptake. It has no or very low affinity for 5-HT$_{1-7}$, alpha- and beta-andrenergic, D$_{1-5}$, H$_{1-3}$, M$_{1-5}$, and benzodiazepine receptors. Escitalopram does not bind or has low affinity for Na$^+$, K$^+$, Cl$^-$, and Ca^{++} ion channels.

Pharmacodynamics/Kinetics

Protein binding: 56% to plasma proteins

Metabolism: Hepatic via CYP2C19 and 3A4 to an active metabolite, S-desmethylcitalopram (S-DCT; 1/7 the activity); S-DCT is metabolized to S-didesmethylcitalopram (S-DDCT; active; 1/27 the activity) via CYP2D6

Half-life elimination: Escitalopram: 27-32 hours; S-desmethylcitalopram: 59 hours

Time to peak: Escitalopram: 5 ± 1.5 hours; S-desmethylcitalopram: 14 hours

Excretion: Urine (Escitalopram: 8%; S-DCT: 10%)

Clearance: Total body: 37-40 L/hour; Renal: Escitalopram: 2.7 L/hour; S-desmethylcitalopram: 6.9 L/hour

Dosage Oral:

Adults: Depression, GAD: Initial: 10 mg/day; dose may be increased to 20 mg/day after at least 1 week

Elderly: 10 mg/day; bioavailability and half-life are increased by 50% in the elderly

Dosage adjustment in renal impairment:

Mild to moderate impairment: No dosage adjustment needed

Severe impairment: Cl$_{cr}$ <20 mL/minute: Use caution

Dosage adjustment in hepatic impairment: 10 mg/day

Administration Administer once daily (morning or evening), with or without food.

Monitoring Parameters Depression, suicidal ideation, anxiety, social functioning

Patient Information The full effects of this medication may take up to 3 weeks to occur. Take as directed; do not alter dose or frequency without consulting prescriber. May be taken with or without food. Avoid alcohol, caffeine, and CNS stimulants. You may experience sexual dysfunction (reversible). May cause dizziness, anxiety, or blurred vision (rise slowly from sitting or lying position and use caution when driving or engaging in tasks requiring alertness until response to drug is known); nausea or dry mouth (frequent small meals, frequent mouth care, chewing gum, or sucking lozenges may help). Report confusion or impaired concentration, severe headache, palpitations, rash, insomnia or nightmares, changes in personality, muscle weakness or tremors, altered gait pattern, signs and symptoms of respiratory infection, or excessive perspiration.

Dosage Forms SOLN, oral: 1 mg/mL (240 mL). **TAB:** 5 mg, 10 mg, 20 mg

♦ **Escitalopram Oxalate** *see* Escitalopram *on page 455*

♦ **Esclim**® *see* Estradiol *on page 459*

♦ **Eserine Salicylate** *see* Physostigmine *on page 999*

♦ **Esgic**® *see* Butalbital, Acetaminophen, and Caffeine *on page 194*

♦ **Esgic-Plus™** *see Butalbital, Acetaminophen, and Caffeine on page 194*

♦ **Eskalith®** *see Lithium on page 751*

♦ **Eskalith CR®** *see Lithium on page 751*

Esmolol (ES moe lol)

Related Information
Beta-Blockers Comparison *on page 1368*

U.S. Brand Names Brevibloc®

Synonyms Esmolol Hydrochloride

Therapeutic Category Antiarrhythmic Agent, Class II; Antihypertensive Agent; Beta Blocker, Beta₁ Selective

Use Treatment of supraventricular tachycardia and atrial fibrillation/flutter (primarily to control ventricular rate); treatment of tachycardia and/or hypertension (especially intraoperative or postoperative)

Pregnancy Risk Factor C (manufacturer); D (2nd and 3rd trimesters - expert analysis)

Contraindications Hypersensitivity to esmolol or any component of the formulation; sinus bradycardia; heart block greater than first degree (except in patients with a functioning artificial pacemaker); cardiogenic shock; bronchial asthma; uncompensated cardiac failure; hypotension; pregnancy (2nd and 3rd trimesters)

Warnings/Precautions Hypotension is common; patients need close blood pressure monitoring. Administer cautiously in compensated heart failure and monitor for a worsening of the condition. Use caution in patients with PVD (can aggravate arterial insufficiency). Use caution with concurrent use of beta-blockers and either verapamil or diltiazem; bradycardia or heart block can occur. Avoid concurrent I.V. use of both agents. In general, beta-blockers should be avoided in patients with bronchospastic disease. Esmolol, a beta-1 selective beta-blocker, can be cautiously used in patients with bronchospastic disease. Monitor pulmonary status closely. Use cautiously in diabetics because it can mask prominent hypoglycemic symptoms. Can mask signs of thyrotoxicosis. Can cause fetal bradycardia when administered in the third trimester of pregnancy or at delivery. Use caution in patients with renal dysfunction (active metabolite retained). Do not use in the treatment of hypertension associated with vasoconstriction related to hypothermia. Concentrations >10 mcg/mL or infusion into small veins or through a butterfly catheter should be avoided (can cause thrombophlebitis). Extravasation can lead to skin necrosis and sloughing.

Common Adverse Reactions
>10%:
Cardiovascular: Asymptomatic hypotension (25%), symptomatic hypotension (12%)
Miscellaneous: Diaphoresis (10%)
1% to 10%:
Cardiovascular: Peripheral ischemia (1%)
Central nervous system: Dizziness (3%), somnolence (3%), confusion (2%), headache (2%), agitation (2%), fatigue (1%)
Gastrointestinal: Nausea (7%), vomiting (1%)
Local: Pain on injection (8%)

Drug Interactions
Increased Effect/Toxicity: Esmolol may increase the effect/toxicity of verapamil, and may increase potential for hypertensive crisis after or during withdrawal of either agent when combined with clonidine. Esmolol may extend the effect of neuromuscular blocking agents (succinylcholine). Esmolol may increase digoxin serum levels by 10% to 20% and may increase theophylline concentrations. Morphine may increase esmolol blood concentrations.

Decreased Effect: Decreased effect of beta-blockers with aluminum salts, barbiturates, calcium salts, cholestyramine, colestipol, NSAIDs, penicillins (ampicillin), rifampin, salicylates, and sulfinpyrazone due to decreased bioavailability and plasma levels. Beta-blockers may decrease the effect of sulfonylureas. Xanthines (eg, theophylline, caffeine) may decrease effects of esmolol.

Mechanism of Action Class II antiarrhythmic: Competitively blocks response to beta₁-adrenergic stimulation with little or no effect of beta₂-receptors except at high doses, no intrinsic sympathomimetic activity, no membrane stabilizing activity

Pharmacodynamics/Kinetics
Onset of action: Beta-blockade: I.V.: 2-10 minutes (quickest when loading doses are administered)
Duration: 10-30 minutes; prolonged following higher cumulative doses, extended duration of use
Protein binding: 55%
Metabolism: In blood by esterases
Half-life elimination: Adults: 9 minutes
Excretion: Urine (~69% as metabolites, 2% unchanged drug)

Dosage I.V. infusion requires an infusion pump (must be adjusted to individual response and tolerance):

Children: A limited amount of information regarding esmolol use in pediatric patients is currently available. Some centers have utilized doses of 100-500 mcg/kg given over 1 minute for control of supraventricular tachycardias.
Loading doses of 500 mcg/kg/minute over 1 minute with maximal doses of 50-250 mcg/kg/minute (mean = 173) have been used in addition to nitroprusside to treat postoperative hypertension after coarctation of aorta repair.
(Continued)

Esmolol *(Continued)*

Adults:

Intraoperative tachycardia and/or hypertension (immediate control): Initial bolus: 80 mg (~1 mg/kg) over 30 seconds, followed by a 150 mcg/kg/minute infusion, if necessary. Adjust infusion rate as needed to maintain desired heart rate and/or blood pressure, up to 300 mcg/kg/minute.

Supraventricular tachycardia or gradual control of postoperative tachycardia/hypertension: Loading dose: 500 mcg/kg over 1 minute; follow with a 50 mcg/kg/minute infusion for 4 minutes; response to this initial infusion rate may be a rough indication of the responsiveness of the ventricular rate.

Infusion may be continued at 50 mcg/kg/minute or, if the response is inadequate, titrated upward in 50 mcg/kg/minute increments (increased no more frequently than every 4 minutes) to a maximum of 200 mcg/kg/minute.

To achieve more rapid response, following the initial loading dose and 50 mcg/kg/minute infusion, rebolus with a second 500 mcg/kg loading dose over 1 minute, and increase the maintenance infusion to 100 mcg/kg/minute for 4 minutes. If necessary, a third (and final) 500 mcg/kg loading dose may be administered, prior to increasing to an infusion rate of 150 mcg/kg/minute. After 4 minutes of the 150 mcg/kg/minute infusion, the infusion rate may be increased to a maximum rate of 200 mcg/kg/minute (without a bolus dose).

Usual dosage range (SVT): 50-200 mcg/kg/minute with average dose of 100 mcg/kg/minute. For control of postoperative hypertension, as many as one-third of patients may require higher doses (250-300 mcg/kg/minute) to control blood pressure; the safety of doses >300 mcg/kg/minute has not been studied.

Esmolol: Hemodynamic effects of beta-blockade return to baseline within 20-30 minutes after discontinuing esmolol infusions.

Guidelines for withdrawal of therapy:

Transfer to alternative antiarrhythmic drug (propranolol, digoxin, verapamil).

Infusion should be reduced by 50% 30 minutes following the first dose of the alternative agent.

Following the second dose of the alternative drug, patient's response should be monitored and if control is adequate for the first hours, esmolol may be discontinued.

Dialysis: Not removed by hemo- or peritoneal dialysis; supplemental dose is not necessary.

Administration Infusions must be administered with an infusion pump. The concentrate (250 mg/mL ampul) is **not** for direct I.V. injection, but rather must first be diluted to a final concentration of 10 mg/mL (ie, 2.5 g in 250 mL or 5 g in 500 mL). Concentrations >10 mg/mL or infusion into small veins or through a butterfly catheter should be avoided (can cause thrombophlebitis). Decrease or discontinue infusion if hypotension or congestive heart failure occur. Medication port of premixed bags should be used to withdraw only the initial bolus, if necessary (not to be used for withdrawal of additional bolus doses).

Monitoring Parameters Blood pressure, heart rate, MAP, ECG, respiratory rate, I.V. site; cardiac monitor and blood pressure monitor required

Dosage Forms INF [premixed in sodium chloride; preservative free]: 10 mg/mL (250 mL). **INJ, solution:** 10 mg/mL (10 mL); 250 mg/mL (10 mL)

♦ **Esmolol Hydrochloride** *see Esmolol on page 457*

Esomeprazole *(es oh ME pray zol)*

U.S. Brand Names Nexium®

Synonyms Esomeprazole Magnesium

Therapeutic Category Gastric Acid Secretion Inhibitor; Proton Pump Inhibitor

Use Short-term (4-8 weeks) treatment of erosive esophagitis; maintaining symptom resolution and healing of erosive esophagitis; treatment of symptomatic gastroesophageal reflux disease; as part of a multidrug regimen for *Helicobacter pylori* eradication in patients with duodenal ulcer disease (active or history of within the past 5 years)

Pregnancy Risk Factor B

Contraindications Hypersensitivity to esomeprazole, lansoprazole, omeprazole, rabeprazole, or any component of the formulation

Warnings/Precautions Relief of symptoms does not preclude the presence of a gastric malignancy. Atrophic gastritis (by biopsy) has been noted with long-term omeprazole therapy; this may also occur with esomeprazole. No reports of enterochromaffin-like (ECL) cell carcinoids, dysplasia, or neoplasia has occurred. Safety and efficacy in pediatric patients have not been established.

Common Adverse Reactions 1% to 10%:

Central nervous system: Headache (4% to 6%)

Gastrointestinal: Diarrhea (4%), nausea, flatulence, abdominal pain (4%), constipation, xerostomia

Drug Interactions

Cytochrome P450 Effect: Substrate of CYP2C19 (major), 3A4 (minor)

Increased Effect/Toxicity: Esomeprazole and omeprazole may increase the levels of benzodiazepines metabolized by oxidation (eg, diazepam, midazolam, triazolam) and carbamazepine.

Decreased Effect: CYP2C19 inducers may decrease the levels/effects of esomeprazole; example inducers include aminoglutethimide, carbamazepine, phenytoin, and rifampin. Proton pump inhibitors may decrease the absorption of atazanavir, indinavir, iron salts, itraconazole, and ketoconazole.

Mechanism of Action Proton pump inhibitor suppresses gastric acid secretion by inhibition of the H^+/K^+-ATPase in the gastric parietal cell

Pharmacodynamics/Kinetics
Distribution: V_{dss}: 16 L
Protein binding: 97%
Metabolism: Hepatic via CYP2C19 and 3A4 enzymes to hydroxy, desmethyl, and sulfone metabolites (all inactive)
Bioavailability: 90% with repeat dosing
Half-life elimination: 1-1.5 hours
Time to peak: 1.5 hours
Excretion: Urine (80%); feces (20%)

Dosage Note: Delayed-release capsules should be swallowed whole and taken at least 1 hour before eating
Children: Safety and efficacy have not been established in pediatric patients
Adults: Oral:
Erosive esophagitis (healing): 20-40 mg once daily for 4-8 weeks; maintenance: 20 mg once daily
Symptomatic GERD: 20 mg once daily for 4 weeks
Helicobacter pylori eradication: 40 mg once daily; requires combination therapy
Elderly: No dosage adjustment needed

Dosage adjustment in renal impairment: No dosage adjustment needed

Dosage adjustment in hepatic impairment:
Mild to moderate liver impairment (Child-Pugh Class A or B): No dosage adjustment needed
Severe liver impairment (Child-Pugh Class C): Dose should not exceed 20 mg/day

Administration Capsule should be swallowed whole and taken at least 1 hour before eating (best if taken before breakfast). For patients with difficulty swallowing, open capsule and mix contents with 1 tablespoon of applesauce. Swallow immediately; mixture should not be chewed. The mixture should not be stored for future use.

Monitoring Parameters Susceptibility testing recommended in patients who fail *H. pylori* eradication regimen (esomeprazole, clarithromycin, and amoxicillin)

Patient Information Take on an empty stomach. Take 1 hour before meals. Swallow capsule whole. Do not chew, break, or crush. Take at a similar time everyday. For patients who have difficulty swallowing, put 1 tablespoon of applesauce in a bowl. Open esomeprazole capsule and sprinkle contents over applesauce. Mix and swallow now. The applesauce should not be hot and should be soft enough to swallow without chewing. Do not chew the mixture. It should not be stored for later use. Common side effects include headache, diarrhea, and abdominal pain. Notify prescriber if you have blood in the stool or toilet bowl, are vomiting blood, or have severe abdominal pain.

Dosage Forms CAP, delayed release: 20 mg, 40 mg

♦ **Esomeprazole Magnesium** *see Esomeprazole on page 458*
♦ **Esoterica® Regular [OTC]** *see Hydroquinone on page 636*

Estazolam (es TA zoe lam)

Related Information
Benzodiazepines Comparison *on page 1366*
U.S. Brand Names ProSom®
Therapeutic Category Benzodiazepine; Hypnotic; Sedative
Use Short-term management of insomnia
Restrictions C-IV
Pregnancy Risk Factor X
Dosage Adults: Oral: 1 mg at bedtime, some patients may require 2 mg; start at doses of 0.5 mg in debilitated or small elderly patients

Dosing adjustment in hepatic impairment: May be necessary
Dosage Forms TAB: 1 mg, 2 mg

♦ **Esterified Estrogen and Methyltestosterone** *see* Estrogens (Esterified) and Methyltestosterone *on page 471*
♦ **Esterified Estrogens** *see* Estrogens (Esterified) *on page 469*
♦ **Estinyl®** *see* Ethinyl Estradiol *on page 475*
♦ **Estrace®** *see* Estradiol *on page 459*
♦ **Estraderm®** *see* Estradiol *on page 459*

Estradiol (es tra DYE ole)

U.S. Brand Names Alora®; Climara®; Delestrogen®; Depo®-Estradiol; Esclim®; Estrace®; Estraderm®; Estrasorb™; Estring®; Femring™; Gynodiol®; Vagifem®; Vivelle®; Vivelle-Dot®
Synonyms Estradiol Acetate; Estradiol Cypionate; Estradiol Hemihydrate; Estradiol Transdermal; Estradiol Valerate
Therapeutic Category Contraceptive, Topical Patch; Contraceptive, Vaginal; Estrogen Derivative, Intramuscular; Estrogen Derivative, Oral; Estrogen Derivative, Topical; Estrogen Derivative, Vaginal
Use Treatment of moderate-to-severe vasomotor symptoms associated with menopause; treatment of vulvar and vaginal atrophy; hypoestrogenism (due to hypogonadism, castration, or primary ovarian failure); prostatic cancer (palliation), breast cancer (palliation), osteoporosis (prophylaxis); abnormal uterine bleeding due to hormonal imbalance; postmenopausal urogenital symptoms of the lower urinary tract (urinary urgency, dysuria)
Pregnancy Risk Factor X
(Continued)

Estradiol *(Continued)*

Contraindications Hypersensitivity to estradiol or any component of the formulation; undiagnosed abnormal vaginal bleeding; history of or current thrombophlebitis or thromboembolic disorders; carcinoma of the breast, except in appropriately selected patients being treated for metastatic disease; estrogen-dependent tumor; porphyria; pregnancy

Warnings/Precautions Should not be used to prevent coronary heart disease. May increase the risks of myocardial infarction, stroke, pulmonary emboli, and deep vein thrombosis; incidence of these effects was shown to be significantly increased in postmenopausal women using conjugated equine estrogens (CEE) in combination with medroxyprogesterone acetate (MPA). Unopposed estrogens may increase the risk of endometrial carcinoma in postmenopausal women. Estrogens may increase the risk of breast cancer (controversial/currently under study; increased risk of invasive breast cancer observed in postmenopausal women using CEE in combination with MPA).

Use with caution in patients with diseases which may be exacerbated by fluid retention, including asthma, epilepsy, migraine, diabetes, cardiac or renal dysfunction. Use with caution in patients with a history of hypercalcemia, cardiovascular disease, and gallbladder disease. May increase blood pressure. Use with caution in patients with hepatic disease. Estrogen compounds are generally associated with lipid effects such as increased HDL-cholesterol and decreased LDL-cholesterol. Triglycerides may also be increased; use with caution in patients with familial defects of lipoprotein metabolism. Estrogens may cause premature closure of the epiphyses in young individuals. Safety and efficacy in pediatric patients have not been established. May increase size of pre-existing uterine leiomyomata. May increase the risk of benign hepatic adenoma, which may cause significant consequences in the event of rupture. When used solely for prevention of osteoporosis in women at significant risk, nonestrogen treatment options should be considered.

When used solely for the treatment of vulvar and vaginal atrophy, topical vaginal products should be considered. Use caution applying topical products to severely atrophic vaginal mucosa. Absorption of topical emulsion is increased by application of sunscreen; do not apply both products within close proximity of each other.

Before prescribing estrogen therapy to postmenopausal women, the risks and benefits must be weighed for each patient. Women should be informed of these risks and benefits, as well as possible effects of progestin when added to estrogen therapy.

Common Adverse Reactions Frequency not defined.

Cardiovascular: Edema, hypertension, MI, venous thromboembolism

Central nervous system: Dizziness, epilepsy exacerbation, headache, irritability, mental depression, migraine, mood disturbances

Dermatologic: Chloasma, erythema multiforme, erythema nodosum, hemorrhagic eruption, hirsutism, loss of scalp hair, melasma

Endocrine & metabolic: Breast enlargement, breast tenderness, changes in libido, increased thyroid-binding globulin, increased total thyroid hormone (T_4), increased serum triglycerides/phospholipids, increased HDL-cholesterol, decreased LDL-cholesterol, impaired glucose tolerance, hypercalcemia

Gastrointestinal: Abdominal cramps, bloating, cholecystitis, cholelithiasis, gallbladder disease, nausea, pancreatitis, vomiting, weight gain/loss

Genitourinary: Alterations in frequency and flow of menses, changes in cervical secretions, endometrial cancer, increased size of uterine leiomyomata, vaginal candidiasis

Vaginal: Trauma from applicator insertion may occur in women with severely atrophic vaginal mucosa

Hematologic: Aggravation of porphyria, antithrombin III and antifactor Xa decreased, levels of fibrinogen increased, platelet aggregability increased and platelet count; increased prothrombin and factors VII, VIII, IX, X

Hepatic: Cholestatic jaundice

Local: Transdermal patch: Burning, erythema, irritation, pruritus, rash, thrombophlebitis

Neuromuscular & skeletal: Chorea

Ocular: Intolerance to contact lenses, steeping of corneal curvature

Respiratory: Pulmonary thromboembolism

Miscellaneous: Anaphylactoid/anaphylactic reactions, carbohydrate intolerance

Drug Interactions

Cytochrome P450 Effect: Substrate of CYP1A2 (major), 2A6 (minor), 2B6 (minor), 2C8/9 (minor), 2C19 (minor), 2D6 (minor), 2E1 (minor), 3A4 (major); **Inhibits** CYP1A2 (weak); **Induces** CYP3A4 (weak)

Increased Effect/Toxicity: Estradiol with hydrocortisone increases corticosteroid toxic potential. Anticoagulants and estradiol increase the potential for thromboembolic events.

Decreased Effect: CYP1A2 inducers may decrease the levels/effects of estradiol; example inducers include aminoglutethimide, carbamazepine, phenobarbital, and rifampin.

Mechanism of Action Estrogens are responsible for the development and maintenance of the female reproductive system and secondary sexual characteristics. Estradiol is the principle intracellular human estrogen and is more potent than estrone and estriol at the receptor level; it is the primary estrogen secreted prior to menopause. Following menopause, estrone and estrone sulfate are more highly produced. Estrogens modulate the pituitary secretion of gonadotropins, luteinizing hormone, and follicle-stimulating hormone through a negative feedback system; estrogen replacement reduces elevated levels of these hormones in postmenopausal women.

Pharmacodynamics/Kinetics

Absorption: Oral, topical: Well absorbed

Distribution: Crosses placenta; enters breast milk

Protein binding: 37% to sex hormone-binding globulin; 61% to albumin

Metabolism: Hepatic via oxidation and conjugation in GI tract; hydroxylated via CYP3A4 to metabolites; first-pass effect; enterohepatic recirculation; reversibly converted to estrone and estriol

Excretion: Primarily urine (as metabolites estrone and estriol); feces (small amounts)

Dosage All dosage needs to be adjusted based upon the patient's response

Oral:

Prostate cancer (androgen-dependent, inoperable, progressing): 10 mg 3 times/day for at least 3 months

Breast cancer (inoperable, progressing in appropriately selected patients): 10 mg 3 times/day for at least 3 months

Osteoporosis prophylaxis in postmenopausal females: 0.5 mg/day in a cyclic regimen (3 weeks on and 1 week off)

Female hypoestrogenism (due to hypogonadism, castration, or primary ovarian failure): 1-2 mg/day; titrate as necessary to control symptoms using minimal effective dose for maintenance therapy

Moderate to severe vasomotor symptoms associated with menopause: 1-2 mg/day, adjusted as necessary to limit symptoms; administration should be cyclic (3 weeks on, 1 week off). Patients should be re-evaluated at 3- to 6-month intervals to determine if treatment is still necessary.

I.M.

Prostate cancer: Valerate: ≥30 mg or more every 1-2 weeks

Moderate to severe vasomotor symptoms associated with menopause:

Cypionate: 1-5 mg every 3-4 weeks

Valerate: 10-20 mg every 4 weeks

Female hypoestrogenism (due to hypogonadism):

Cypionate: 1.5-2 mg monthly

Valerate: 10-20 mg every 4 weeks

Topical:

Emulsion: Moderate-to-severe vasomotor symptoms associated with menopause: 3.84 g applied once daily in the morning

Transdermal: Indicated dose may be used continuously in patients without an intact uterus. May be given continuously or cyclically (3 weeks on, 1 week off) in patients with an intact uterus. When changing patients from oral to transdermal therapy, start transdermal patch 1 week after discontinuing oral hormone (may begin sooner if symptoms reappear within 1 week):

Once-weekly patch:

Moderate to severe vasomotor symptoms associated with menopause (Climara®): Apply 0.025 mg/day patch once weekly. Adjust dose as necessary to control symptoms. Patients should be re-evaluated at 3- to 6-month intervals to determine if treatment is still necessary.

Osteoporosis prophylaxis in postmenopausal women (Climara®): Apply patch once weekly; minimum effective dose 0.025 mg/day; adjust response to therapy by biochemical markers and bone mineral density

Twice-weekly patch:

Moderate to severe vasomotor symptoms associated with menopause, vulvar/vaginal atrophy, female hypogonadism: Titrate to lowest dose possible to control symptoms, adjusting initial dose after the first month of therapy; re-evaluate therapy at 3- to 6-month intervals to taper or discontinue medication:

Alora®, Esclim®, Estraderm®, Vivelle-Dot®: Apply 0.05 mg patch twice weekly

Vivelle®: Apply 0.0375 mg patch twice weekly

Prevention of osteoporosis in postmenopausal women:

Alora®, Vivelle®, Vivelle-Dot®: Apply 0.025 mg patch twice weekly, increase dose as necessary

Estraderm®: Apply 0.05 mg patch twice weekly

Vaginal cream: Vulvar and vaginal atrophy: Insert 2-4 g/day intravaginally for 2 weeks, then gradually reduce to 1/2 the initial dose for 2 weeks, followed by a maintenance dose of 1 g 1-3 times/week

Vaginal ring:

Postmenopausal vaginal atrophy, urogenital symptoms: Estring®: 2 mg intravaginally; following insertion, ring should remain in place for 90 days

Moderate to severe vasomotor symptoms associated with menopause; vulvar/vaginal atrophy: Femring™: 0.05 mg intravaginally; following insertion, ring should remain in place for 3 months; dose may be increased to 0.1 mg if needed

Vaginal tablets: Atrophic vaginitis: Vagifem®: Initial: Insert 1 tablet once daily for 2 weeks; maintenance: Insert 1 tablet twice weekly; attempts to discontinue or taper medication should be made at 3- to 6-month intervals

Dosing adjustment in hepatic impairment:

Mild to moderate liver impairment: Dosage reduction of estrogens is recommended

Severe liver impairment: **Not recommended**

Administration

Injection formulation: Intramuscular use only

Emulsion: Apply to clean, dry skin while in a sitting position. Contents of two pouches (total 3.48 g) are to be applied individually, once daily in the morning. Apply contents of first pouch to left thigh; massage into skin of left thigh and calf until thoroughly absorbed (~3 minutes). (Continued)

Estradiol *(Continued)*

Apply excess from both hands to the buttocks. Apply contents of second pouch to the right thigh; massage into skin of right thigh and calf until thoroughly absorbed (~3 minutes). Apply excess from both hands to buttocks. Wash hands with soap and water. Allow skin to dry before covering legs with clothing. Do not apply to other areas of body. Do not apply to red or irritated skin.

Transdermal patch: Aerosol topical corticosteroids applied under the patch may reduce allergic reactions. Do not apply transdermal system to breasts, but place on trunk of body (preferably abdomen). Rotate application sites.

Vaginal ring: Exact positioning is not critical for efficacy, however, patient should not feel anything once inserted. In case of discomfort, ring should be pushed further into vagina. If ring is expelled prior to 90 days, it may be rinsed off and reinserted.

Monitoring Parameters Yearly physical examination that includes blood pressure and Papanicolaou smear, breast exam, mammogram. Monitor for signs of endometrial cancer in female patients with uterus; rule out malignancy if unexplained vaginal bleeding occurs

Reference Range

Children: <10 pg/mL (SI: <37 pmol/L)

Male: 10-50 pg/mL (SI: 37-184 pmol/L)

Female:

Premenopausal: 30-400 pg/mL (SI: 110-1468 pmol/L)

Postmenopausal: 0-30 pg/mL (SI: 0-110 pmol/L)

Patient Information Report signs or symptoms of any of the following: Thromboembolic or thrombotic disorders including sudden severe headache or vomiting, disturbance of vision or speech, loss of vision, numbness or weakness in an extremity, sharp or crushing chest pain, calf pain, shortness of breath, severe abdominal pain or mass, mental depression, or unusual bleeding. Patients should discontinue taking the medication if they suspect they are pregnant or become pregnant. Report if area under dermal patch becomes irritated or a rash develops. Patient package insert is available with product; insert vaginal product high into the vagina.

Dosage Forms CRM, vaginal (Estrace®): 0.1 mg/g (12 g); 0.1 mg/g (42.5 g). **EMULS, topical, as hemihydrate** (Estrasorb™): 2.5 g/g (56s) [each pouch contains estradiol 1.74 g; contents of two pouches delivers estradiol 0.05 mg/day]. **INJ, oil, as cypionate** (Depo®-Estradiol): 5 mg/mL (5 mL). **INJ, oil, as valerate** (Delestrogen®): 10 mg/mL (5 mL), 20 mg/mL (5 mL), 40 mg/mL (5 mL). **RING, vaginal, as base** (Estring®): 2 mg (1s). **RING, vaginal, as acetate** (Femring™): 0.05 mg (1s); 0.1 mg (1s). **TAB, oral**, micronized: 0.5 mg, 1 mg, 2 mg; (Estrace®): 0.5 mg, 1 mg, 2 mg; (Gynodiol®): 0.5 mg, 1 mg, 1.5 mg, 2 mg. **TAB, vaginal, as base** (Vagifem®): 25 mcg. **TRANSDERMAL SYSTEM:** 0.05 mg/24 hours (4s); 0.1 mg/24 hours (4s); (Alora®): 0.025 mg/24 hours [9 cm^2, total estradiol 0.77 mg] (8s); 0.05 mg/24 hours [18 cm^2, total estradiol 1.5 mg] (8s, 24s); 0.075 mg/24 hours [27 cm^2, total estradiol 2.3 mg] (8s); 0.1 mg/24 hours [36 cm^2, total estradiol 3 mg] (8s); (Climara®): 0.025 mg/24 hours [6.5 cm^2, total estradiol 2.04 mg] (4s); 0.0375 mg/24 hours [9.375 cm^2, total estradiol 2.85 mg] (4s); 0.05 mg/24 hours [12.5 cm^2, total estradiol 3.8 mg] (4s); 0.06 mg/24 hours [15 cm^2, total estradiol 4.55 mg] (4s); 0.075 mg/24 hours [18.75 cm^2, total estradiol 5.7 mg] (4s); 0.1 mg/24 hours [25 cm^2, total estradiol 7.6 mg] (4s); **Esclim**): 0.025 mg/24 hours [11 cm^2, total estradiol 5 mg] (8s); 0.0375 mg/day [16.5 cm^2, total estradiol 7.5 mg] (8s); 0.05 mg/day [22 cm^2, total estradiol 10 mg] (8s); 0.075 mg/day [33 cm^2, total estradiol 15 mg] (8s); 0.1 mg/day [44 cm^2, total estradiol 20 mg] (8s); (Estraderm®): 0.05 mg/24 hours [10 cm^2, total estradiol 4 mg] (8s); 0.1 mg/24 hours [20 cm^2, total estradiol 8 mg] (8s); (Vivelle®): 0.025 mg/24 hours [7.25 cm^2, total estradiol 2.17 mg] (8s); 0.0375 mg/24 hours [11 cm^2, total estradiol 3.28 mg] (8s); 0.05 mg/24 hours [14.5 cm^2, total estradiol 4.33 mg] (8s); 0.075 mg/24 hours [22 cm^2, total estradiol 6.57 mg] (8s); 0.1 mg/24 hours [29 cm^2, total estradiol 8.66 mg] (8s); (Vivelle-Dot®): 0.0375 mg/day [3.75 cm^2, total estradiol 0.585 mg] (8s); 0.05 mg/day [5 cm^2, total estradiol 0.78 mg] (8s); 0.075 mg/day [7.5 cm^2, total estradiol 1.17 mg] (8s); 0.1 mg/day [10 cm^2, total estradiol 1.56 mg] (8s)

♦ **Estradiol Acetate** *see* Estradiol *on page 459*

Estradiol and Medroxyprogesterone

(es tra DYE ole & me DROKS ee proe JES te rone)

U.S. Brand Names Lunelle™

Synonyms E$_2$C and MPA; Medroxyprogesterone Acetate and Estradiol Cypionate

Therapeutic Category Contraceptive, Parenteral (Estrogen/Progestin)

Use Prevention of pregnancy

Pregnancy Risk Factor X

Dosage Adults: Female: I.M.: 0.5 mL

First dose: Within first 5 days of menstrual period or within 5 days of a complete 1st trimester abortion; do not administer <4 weeks postpartum **if not breast-feeding** or <6 weeks postpartum **if breast-feeding**

Maintenance dose: Monthly, every 28-30 days following previous injection; do not exceed 33 days; pregnancy must be ruled out if >33 days have past between injections; bleeding episodes cannot be used to guide injection schedule; shortening schedule may lead to menstrual pattern changes

Switching from other forms of contraception: First injection should be given within 7 days of last active oral contraceptive pill; when switching from other methods, timing of injection should ensure continuous contraceptive coverage

Elderly: Not for postmenopausal use

Dosage adjustment in renal impairment: Studies have not been conducted; however, dosage adjustment is not anticipated due to hepatic metabolism

Dosage adjustment in hepatic impairment: Contraindicated in hepatic dysfunction

Dosage Forms INJ, suspension: Estradiol 5 mg and medroxyprogesterone 25 mg per 0.5 mL (0.5 mL)

Estradiol and Norethindrone (es tra DYE ole & nor eth IN drone)

U.S. Brand Names Activella™; CombiPatch®

Synonyms Norethindrone and Estradiol

Therapeutic Category Estrogen and Progestin Combination

Use Women with an intact uterus:

Tablet: Treatment of moderate-to-severe vasomotor symptoms associated with menopause; treatment of vulvar and vaginal atrophy; prophylaxis for postmenopausal osteoporosis

Transdermal patch: Treatment of moderate-to-severe vasomotor symptoms associated with menopause; treatment of vulvar and vaginal atrophy; treatment of hypoestrogenism due to hypogonadism, castration, or primary ovarian failure

Pregnancy Risk Factor X

Contraindications Hypersensitivity to estrogens, progestins, or any components; carcinoma of the breast; estrogen-dependent tumor; undiagnosed abnormal vaginal bleeding; thrombophlebitis, thromboembolic disorders, or stroke; hysterectomy; pregnancy

Warnings/Precautions For use only in women with an intact uterus. Use with caution in patients with diseases that may be exacerbated by fluid retention, including asthma, epilepsy, migraine, diabetes, cardiac or renal dysfunction. Use with caution in patients with a history of hypercalcemia, cardiovascular disease, or gallbladder disease. May increase blood pressure. Use with caution in patients with liver dysfunction or disease. May increase risk of venous thromboembolism. Unopposed estrogens may increase the risk of endometrial carcinoma in postmenopausal women (incidence is less likely with the addition of progesterone). Estrogens may increase the risk of breast cancer; estrogen compounds are generally associated with lipid effects such as increased HDL-cholesterol, and decreased LDL-cholesterol; triglycerides may also be increased. Use with caution in patients with familial defects of lipoprotein metabolism. Safety and efficacy in children have not been established. May cause visual abnormalities. Discontinue if papilledema or renal vascular lesions develop.

Common Adverse Reactions Frequency not defined.

Cardiovascular: Altered blood pressure, cardiovascular accident, edema, venous thromboembolism

Central nervous system: Dizziness, fatigue, headache, insomnia, mental depression, migraine, nervousness

Dermatologic: Chloasma, erythema multiforme, erythema nodosum, hemorrhagic eruption, hirsutism, itching, loss of scalp hair, melasma, pruritus, skin rash

Endocrine & metabolic: Breast enlargement, breast tenderness, breast pain, changes in libido

Gastrointestinal: Abdominal pain, bloating, changes in appetite, flatulence, gallbladder disease, nausea, pancreatitis, vomiting, weight gain/loss

Genitourinary: Alterations in frequency and flow of menses, changes in cervical secretions, cystitis-like syndrome, increased size of uterine leiomyomata, premenstrual-like syndrome, vaginal candidiasis, vaginitis

Hematologic: Aggravation of porphyria

Hepatic: Cholestatic jaundice

Local: Application site reaction (transdermal patch)

Neuromuscular & skeletal: Arthralgia, back pain, chorea, myalgia, weakness

Ocular: Intolerance to contact lenses, steeping of corneal curvature

Respiratory: Pharyngitis, pulmonary thromboembolism, rhinitis

Miscellaneous: Allergic reactions, carbohydrate intolerance, flu-like syndrome

Drug Interactions

Cytochrome P450 Effect:

Estradiol: **Substrate** of CYP1A2 (major), 2A6 (minor), 2B6 (minor), 2C8/9 (minor), 2C19 (minor), 2D6 (minor), 2E1 (minor), 3A4 (major); **Inhibits** CYP1A2 (weak); **Induces** CYP3A4 (weak)

Norethindrone: **Substrate** of CYP3A4 (major); **Induces** CYP2C19 (weak)

Pharmacodynamics/Kinetics

Activella™:

Bioavailability: Estradiol: 50%; Norethindrone: 100%

Half-life elimination: Estradiol: 12-14 hours; Norethindrone: 8-11 hours

Time to peak: Estradiol: 5-8 hours

See individual agents.

Dosage Adults:

Oral: 1 tablet daily

Transdermal patch:

Continuous combined regimen: Apply one patch twice weekly

Continuous sequential regimen: Apply estradiol-only patch for first 14 days of cycle, followed by one CombiPatch™ applied twice weekly for the remaining 14 days of a 28-day cycle

Administration Transdermal patch: Apply to clean dry skin. Do not apply transdermal patch to breasts; apply to lower abdomen, avoiding waistline. Rotate application sites.

Dosage Forms TAB (Activella™): Estradiol 1 mg and norethindrone 0.5 mg (28s). **TRANSDERMAL SYSTEM** (CombiPatch®): 0.05/0.14: Estradiol 0.05 mg and norethindrone 0.14 mg per day (8s) [9 sq cm]; 0.05/0.25: Estradiol 0.05 mg and norethindrone 0.25 mg per day (8s) [16 sq cm]

Estradiol and Testosterone (es tra DYE ole & tes TOS ter one)
U.S. Brand Names Depo-Testadiol® [DSC]
Synonyms Estradiol Cypionate and Testosterone Cypionate; Estradiol Valerate and Testosterone Enanthate; Testosterone and Estradiol
Therapeutic Category Estrogen and Androgen Combination
Use Vasomotor symptoms associated with menopause
Pregnancy Risk Factor X
Dosage Adults: All dosage needs to be adjusted based upon the patient's response
Dosage Forms INJ, oil: Estradiol 2 mg and testosterone 50 mg per mL (10 mL)

- **Estradiol Cypionate** see Estradiol on page 459
- **Estradiol Cypionate and Testosterone Cypionate** see Estradiol and Testosterone on page 464
- **Estradiol Hemihydrate** see Estradiol on page 459
- **Estradiol Transdermal** see Estradiol on page 459
- **Estradiol Valerate** see Estradiol on page 459
- **Estradiol Valerate and Testosterone Enanthate** see Estradiol and Testosterone on page 464

Estramustine (es tra MUS teen)
U.S. Brand Names Emcyt®
Synonyms Estramustine Phosphate Sodium; NSC-89199
Therapeutic Category Antineoplastic Agent, Alkylating Agent; Antineoplastic Agent, Hormone
Use Palliative treatment of prostatic carcinoma (progressive or metastatic)
Pregnancy Risk Factor C
Contraindications Hypersensitivity to estramustine or any component, estradiol or nitrogen mustard; active thrombophlebitis or thromboembolic disorders
Warnings/Precautions The U.S. Food and Drug Administration (FDA) currently recommends that procedures for proper handling and disposal of antineoplastic agents be considered. Glucose tolerance may be decreased; elevated blood pressure may occur; exacerbation of peripheral edema or congestive heart disease may occur; use with caution in patients with impaired liver function, renal insufficiency, metabolic bone diseases, or history of cardiovascular disease (eg, thrombophlebitis, thrombosis, or thromboembolic disease). Use caution in patients with prostate cancer and osteoblastic metastases due to increased risk of hypocalcemia.
Common Adverse Reactions
>10%:
  Cardiovascular: Impaired arterial circulation; ischemic heart disease; venous thromboembolism; cardiac decompensation (58%), about 50% of complications occur within the first 2 months of therapy, 85% occur within the first year; edema
  Endocrine & metabolic: Sodium and water retention, gynecomastia, breast tenderness, libido decreased
  Gastrointestinal: Nausea, vomiting, may be dose-limiting
  Hematologic: Thrombocytopenia
  Local: Thrombophlebitis (nearly 100% with I.V. administration)
  Respiratory: Dyspnea
1% to 10%:
  Cardiovascular: Myocardial infarction
  Central nervous system: Insomnia, lethargy
  Gastrointestinal: Diarrhea, anorexia, flatulence
  Hematologic: Leukopenia
  Hepatic: Serum transaminases increased, jaundice
  Neuromuscular & skeletal: Leg cramps
  Respiratory: Pulmonary embolism
Drug Interactions
  Decreased Effect: Milk products and calcium-rich foods/drugs may impair the oral absorption of estramustine phosphate sodium.
Mechanism of Action Mechanism is not completely clear. It appears to bind to microtubule proteins, preventing normal tubulin function. The antitumor effect may be due solely to an estrogenic effect. Estramustine causes a marked decrease in plasma testosterone and an increase in estrogen levels.
Pharmacodynamics/Kinetics
  Absorption: Oral: 75%
  Metabolism:
    GI tract: Initial dephosphorylation
    Hepatic: Oxidation and hydrolysis; metabolites include estramustine, estrone, estradiol, nitrogen mustard
  Half-life elimination: Terminal: 20-24 hours
  Time to peak, serum: 2-3 hours
  Excretion: Feces (2.9% to 4.8% as unchanged drug)
Dosage Refer to individual protocols.
  Oral: 10-16 mg/kg/day (14 mg/kg is most common) or 140 mg 4 times/day (some patients have been maintained for >3 years on therapy)
Monitoring Parameters Serum calcium, liver function tests

Patient Information It may take several weeks to manifest effects of this medication. Store capsules in refrigerator. Do not take with milk or milk products. Preferable to take on empty stomach (1 hour before or 2 hours after meals). Small frequent meals and frequent mouth care may reduce incidence of nausea or vomiting. You may experience flatulence, diarrhea, decreased libido (reversible), breast tenderness or enlargement. Report sudden acute pain or cramping in legs or calves, chest pain, shortness of breath, weakness or numbness of arms or legs, difficulty breathing, or edema (increased weight, swelling of legs or feet); contraceptive measures are recommended during therapy.

Dosage Forms CAP: 140 mg

- ♦ **Estramustine Phosphate Sodium**   *see* Estramustine *on page 464*
- ♦ **Estrasorb™**   *see* Estradiol *on page 459*
- ♦ **Estratest®**   *see* Estrogens (Esterified) and Methyltestosterone *on page 471*
- ♦ **Estratest® H.S.**   *see* Estrogens (Esterified) and Methyltestosterone *on page 471*
- ♦ **Estring®**   *see* Estradiol *on page 459*
- ♦ **Estrogenic Substances, Conjugated**   *see* Estrogens (Conjugated/Equine) *on page 466*

Estrogens (Conjugated A/Synthetic)

(ES troe jenz, KON joo gate ed, aye, sin THET ik)

U.S. Brand Names Cenestin®

Therapeutic Category Estrogen Derivative

Use Treatment of moderate to severe vasomotor symptoms of menopause; treatment of vulvar and vaginal atrophy

Pregnancy Risk Factor X

Contraindications Hypersensitivity to estrogens or any component of the formulation; undiagnosed abnormal vaginal bleeding; history of or current thrombophlebitis or thromboembolic disorders; liver disease; carcinoma of the breast; estrogen dependent tumor; pregnancy

Warnings/Precautions Should not be used to prevent coronary heart disease. May increase the risks of myocardial infarction, stroke, pulmonary emboli, and deep vein thrombosis; incidence of these effects was shown to be significantly increased in postmenopausal women using conjugated equine estrogens (CEE) in combination with medroxyprogesterone acetate (MPA). Unopposed estrogens may increase the risk of endometrial carcinoma in postmenopausal women. Estrogens may increase the risk of breast cancer (controversial/currently under study; increased risk of invasive breast cancer observed in postmenopausal women using CEE in combination with MPA). Use with caution in patients with diseases which may be exacerbated by fluid retention, including asthma, epilepsy, migraine, diabetes, cardiac or renal dysfunction. Use with caution in patients with a history of hypercalcemia, cardiovascular disease, and gallbladder disease. May increase blood pressure. Use with caution in patients with hepatic disease. May increase risk of venous thromboembolism.. Estrogen compounds are generally associated with lipid effects such as increased HDL-cholesterol and decreased LDL-cholesterol. Triglycerides may also be increased; use with caution in patients with familial defects of lipoprotein metabolism. May exacerbate endometriosis. Before prescribing estrogen therapy to postmenopausal women, the risks and benefits must be weighed for each patient. Women should be informed of these risks and benefits, as well as possible effects of progestin when added to estrogen therapy. Use for shortest duration possible consistent with treatment goals. Conduct periodic risk:benefit assessments. When used solely for the treatment of vulvar and vaginal atrophy, topical vaginal products should be considered. Safety and efficacy in pediatric patients have not been established.

Common Adverse Reactions Adverse effects associated with estrogen therapy; frequency not defined

Cardiovascular: Edema, hypertension, venous thromboembolism

Central nervous system: Dizziness, headache, mental depression, migraine

Dermatologic: Chloasma, erythema multiforme, erythema nodosum, hemorrhagic eruption, hirsutism, loss of scalp hair, melasma

Endocrine & metabolic: Breast enlargement, breast tenderness, changes in libido, thyroid-binding globulin increased, total thyroid hormone (T_4) increased, serum triglycerides/phospholipids increased, HDL-cholesterol increased, LDL-cholesterol decreased, impaired glucose tolerance, hypercalcemia

Gastrointestinal: Abdominal cramps, bloating, cholecystitis, cholelithiasis, gallbladder disease, nausea, pancreatitis, vomiting, weight gain/loss

Genitourinary: Alterations in frequency and flow of menses, changes in cervical secretions, endometrial cancer, increased size of uterine leiomyomata, vaginal candidiasis

Hematologic: Aggravation of porphyria, antithrombin III and antifactor Xa decreased, levels of fibrinogen decreased, platelet aggregability and platelet count increased; prothrombin and factors VII, VIII, IX, X increased

Hepatic: Cholestatic jaundice

Neuromuscular & skeletal: Chorea

Ocular: Intolerance to contact lenses, steeping of corneal curvature

Respiratory: Pulmonary thromboembolism

Miscellaneous: Carbohydrate intolerance

Drug Interactions

Cytochrome P450 Effect:

Based on estradiol and estrone **Substrate** of CYP1A2 (major), 2A6 (minor), 2B6 (minor), 2C8/9 (minor), 2C19 (minor), 2D6 (minor), 2E1 (minor), 3A4 (major); **Inhibits** CYP1A2 (weak); **Induces** CYP3A4 (weak)

Increased Effect/Toxicity: CYP3A4 enzyme inhibitors may increase estrogen plasma concentrations leading to increased incidence of adverse effects; examples of CYP3A4 *(Continued)*

Estrogens (Conjugated A/Synthetic) *(Continued)*

enzyme inhibitors include clarithromycin, erythromycin, itraconazole, ketoconazole, and ritonavir. Anticoagulants increase the potential for thromboembolic events Estrogens may enhance the effects of hydrocortisone and prednisone

Decreased Effect: CYP1A2 inducers may decrease the levels/effects of estrogens; example inducers include aminoglutethimide, carbamazepine, phenobarbital, and rifampin.

Mechanism of Action Conjugated A/synthetic estrogens contain a mixture of 9 synthetic estrogen substances, including sodium estrone sulfate, sodium equilin sulfate, sodium 17 alpha-dihydroequilin, sodium 17 alpha-estradiol and sodium 17 beta-dihydroequilin. Estrogens are responsible for the development and maintenance of the female reproductive system and secondary sexual characteristics. Estradiol is the principle intracellular human estrogen and is more potent than estrone and estriol at the receptor level; it is the primary estrogen secreted prior to menopause. Following menopause, estrone and estrone sulfate are more highly produced. Estrogens modulate the pituitary secretion of gonadotropins, luteinizing hormone, and follicle-stimulating hormone through a negative feedback system; estrogen replacement reduces elevated levels of these hormones in postmenopausal women.

Pharmacodynamics/Kinetics
Absorption: Readily absorbed
Protein-binding: Sex hormone-binding globulin (SHBG) and albumin
Metabolism: Hepatic to metabolites
Time to peak: 4-16 hours
Excretion: Urine

Dosage The lowest dose that will control symptoms should be used; medication should be discontinued as soon as possible. Oral:
Adults:
Moderate to severe vasomotor symptoms: 0.625 mg/day; may be titrated up to 1.25 mg/day. Attempts to discontinue medication should be made at 3- to 6-month intervals.
Vulvar and vaginal atrophy: 0.3 mg/day
Elderly: Refer to Adults dosing. A higher incidence of stroke and invasive breast cancer were observed in women >75 years in a WHI substudy using conjugated equine estrogen.

Monitoring Parameters Yearly physical examination that includes blood pressure and Papanicolaou smear, breast exam, mammogram. Monitor for signs of endometrial cancer in female patients with uterus; rule out malignancy if unexplained vaginal bleeding occurs

Patient Information Report signs or symptoms of any of the following: Thromboembolic or thrombotic disorders including sudden severe headache or vomiting, disturbance of vision or speech, loss of vision, numbness or weakness in an extremity, sharp or crushing chest pain, calf pain, shortness of breath, severe abdominal pain or mass, mental depression, or unusual bleeding

Dosage Forms TAB: 0.3 mg, 0.625 mg, 0.9 mg, 1.25 mg

Estrogens (Conjugated/Equine) (ES troe jenz KON joo gate ed, EE kwine)

U.S. Brand Names Premarin®

Synonyms CEE; C.E.S.; Estrogenic Substances, Conjugated

Therapeutic Category Estrogen Derivative; Estrogen Derivative, Intramuscular; Estrogen Derivative, Oral; Estrogen Derivative, Parenteral; Estrogen Derivative, Vaginal

Use Treatment of moderate to severe vasomotor symptoms associated with menopause; treatment of vulvar and vaginal atrophy; hypoestrogenism (due to hypogonadism, castration, or primary ovarian failure); prostatic cancer (palliation); breast cancer (palliation); osteoporosis (prophylaxis, postmenopausal women at significant risk only); abnormal uterine bleeding

Unlabeled/Investigational Use Uremic bleeding

Pregnancy Risk Factor X

Contraindications Hypersensitivity to estrogens or any component of the formulation; undiagnosed abnormal vaginal bleeding; history of or current thrombophlebitis or thromboembolic disorders; carcinoma of the breast (except in appropriately selected patients being treated for metastatic disease); estrogen-dependent tumor; pregnancy

Warnings/Precautions Should not be used to prevent coronary heart disease. May increase the risks of myocardial infarction, stroke, pulmonary emboli, and deep vein thrombosis; incidence of these effects was shown to be significantly increased in postmenopausal women using conjugated equine estrogens (CEE) in combination with medroxyprogesterone acetate (MPA). If possible, discontinue 4-6 weeks prior to surgery associated with high risk of thromboembolism or during periods of immobilization. Unopposed estrogens may increase the risk of endometrial carcinoma in postmenopausal women. Estrogens may increase the risk of breast cancer (controversial/currently under study; increased risk of invasive breast cancer observed in postmenopausal women using CEE in combination with MPA). Use with caution in patients with diseases which may be exacerbated by fluid retention, including asthma, epilepsy, migraine, diabetes, cardiac or renal dysfunction. Use with caution in patients with a history of hypercalcemia, hypocalcemia, hypothyroidism, cardiovascular disease, and gallbladder disease. May increase blood pressure. Use with caution in patients with hepatic disease. Estrogen compounds are generally associated with lipid effects such as increased HDL-cholesterol and decreased LDL-cholesterol. Triglycerides may also be increased; use with caution in patients with familial defects of lipoprotein metabolism. May increase size of pre-existing uterine leiomyomata. Before prescribing estrogen therapy to postmenopausal women, the risks and benefits must be weighed for each patient. Women should be informed of these risks and benefits, as well as possible effects of progestin when added to estrogen therapy. Use for shortest duration possible consistent with treatment goals. Conduct periodic risk:benefit assessments. When used solely for the treatment of vulvar and vaginal atrophy, topical vaginal products should be considered. When used solely for prevention of osteoporosis in women at significant risk, nonestrogen treatment options should be considered. Prior to puberty, estrogens may cause premature closure of the epiphyses, premature breast development in girls or gynecomastia in boys. Vaginal bleeding and vaginal cornification may also be induced in girls. Safety and efficacy in pediatric patients have not been established.

Common Adverse Reactions

Note: Percentages reported in postmenopausal women.

>10%:

Central nervous system: Headache (26% to 32%; placebo 28%)
Endocrine & metabolic: Breast pain (7% to 12%; placebo 9%)
Gastrointestinal: Abdominal pain (15% to 17%)
Genitourinary: Vaginal hemorrhage (2% to 14%)
Neuromuscular & skeletal: Back pain (13% to 14%)

1% to 10%:

Central nervous system: Nervousness (2% to 5%)
Endocrine & metabolic: Leukorrhea (4% to 7%)
Gastrointestinal: Flatulence (6% to 7%)
Genitourinary: Vaginitis (5% to 7%), vaginal moniliasis (5% to 6%)
Neuromuscular & skeletal: Weakness (7% to 8%), leg cramps (3% to 7%)

In addition, the following have been reported with estrogen and/or progestin therapy:

Cardiovascular: Edema, hypertension, myocardial infarction, stroke, venous thromboembolism
Central nervous system: Dizziness, epilepsy exacerbation, headache, irritability, mental depression, migraine, mood disturbances, nervousness
Dermatologic: Angioedema, chloasma, erythema multiforme, erythema nodosum, hemorrhagic eruption, hirsutism, loss of scalp hair, melasma, pruritus, rash, urticaria
Endocrine & metabolic: Breast cancer, breast enlargement, breast tenderness, changes in libido, increased thyroid-binding globulin, increased total thyroid hormone (T_4), increased serum triglycerides/phospholipids, increased HDL-cholesterol, decreased LDL-cholesterol, impaired glucose tolerance, hypercalcemia, hypocalcemia
Gastrointestinal: Abdominal cramps, bloating, cholecystitis, cholelithiasis, gallbladder disease, nausea, pancreatitis, vomiting, weight gain/loss
Genitourinary: Alterations in frequency and flow of menses, changes in cervical secretions, endometrial cancer, endometrial hyperplasia, increased size of uterine leiomyomata, vaginal candidiasis
Hematologic: Aggravation of porphyria, decreased antithrombin III and antifactor Xa, increased levels of fibrinogen, increased platelet aggregability and platelet count; increased prothrombin and factors VII, VIII, IX, X
Hepatic: Cholestatic jaundice, hepatic hemangiomas enlarged
Neuromuscular & skeletal: Arthralgias, chorea, leg cramps
Local: Thrombophlebitis
Ocular: Intolerance to contact lenses, retinal vascular thrombosis, steeping of corneal curvature
Respiratory: Asthma exacerbation, pulmonary thromboembolism
Miscellaneous: Anaphylactoid/anaphylactic reactions, carbohydrate intolerance

Drug Interactions

Cytochrome P450 Effect:

Based on estradiol and estrone: **Substrate** of CYP1A2 (major), 2A6 (minor), 2B6 (minor), 2C8/9 (minor), 2C19 (minor), 2D6 (minor), 2E1 (minor), 3A4 (major); Inhibits CYP1A2 (weak); Induces CYP3A4 (weak)

Increased Effect/Toxicity: Hydrocortisone taken with estrogen may cause corticosteroid-induced toxicity. Increased potential for thromboembolic events with anticoagulants.

Decreased Effect: CYP1A2 inducers may decrease the levels/effects of estrogens; example inducers include aminoglutethimide, carbamazepine, phenobarbital, and rifampin.

Mechanism of Action Conjugated estrogens contain a mixture of estrone sulfate, equilin sulfate, 17 alpha-dihydroequilin, 17 alpha-estradiol and 17 beta-dihydroequilin. Estrogens are responsible for the development and maintenance of the female reproductive system and secondary sexual characteristics. Estradiol is the principle intracellular human estrogen and is more potent than estrone and estriol at the receptor level; it is the primary estrogen secreted prior to menopause. Following menopause, estrone and estrone sulfate are more highly produced. Estrogens modulate the pituitary secretion of gonadotropins, luteinizing hormone, and follicle-stimulating hormone through a negative feedback system; estrogen replacement reduces elevated levels of these hormones in postmenopausal women.

Pharmacodynamics/Kinetics

Absorption: Well absorbed
Metabolism: Hepatic via CYP3A4; estradiol is converted to estrone and estriol; also undergoes enterohepatic recirculation; estrone sulfite is the main metabolite in postmenopausal women
Excretion: Urine (primarily estrone, also as estradiol, estriol and conjugates)

Dosage Adults:

Male: Androgen-dependent prostate cancer: Oral: 1.25-2.5 mg 3 times/day

Female:

Prevention of osteoporosis in postmenopausal women: Oral: Initial: 0.3 mg/day cyclically* or daily, depending on medical assessment of patient. Dose may be adjusted based on bone mineral density and clinical response. The lowest effective dose should be used.
Moderate to severe vasomotor symptoms associated with menopause: Oral: Initial: 0.3 mg/day, cyclically* or daily, depending on medical assessment of patient. The lowest dose

(Continued)

Estrogens (Conjugated/Equine) *(Continued)*

that will control symptoms should be used. Medication should be discontinued as soon as possible.

Vulvar and vaginal atrophy:

Oral: Initial: 0.3 mg/day; the lowest dose that will control symptoms should be used. May be given cyclically* or daily, depending on medical assessment of patient. Medication should be discontinued as soon as possible.

Vaginal cream: Intravaginal: $\frac{1}{2}$ to 2 g/day given cyclically*

Abnormal uterine bleeding:

Acute/heavy bleeding:

Oral (unlabeled route): 1.25 mg, may repeat every 4 hours for 24 hours, followed by 1.25 mg once daily for 7-10 days

I.V.: 25 mg, may repeat in 6-12 hours if needed

Note: Oral/I.V.: Treatment should be followed by a low-dose oral contraceptive; medroxyprogesterone acetate along with or following estrogen therapy can also be given

Nonacute/lesser bleeding: Oral (unlabeled route): 1.25 mg once daily for 7-10 days

Female hypogonadism: Oral: 0.3-0.625 mg/day given cyclically*; dose may be titrated in 6- to 12-month intervals; progestin treatment should be added to maintain bone mineral density once skeletal maturity is achieved.

Female castration, primary ovarian failure: Oral: 1.25 mg/day given cyclically*; adjust according to severity of symptoms and patient response. For maintenance, adjust to the lowest effective dose.

*Cyclic administration: Either 3 weeks on, 1 week off **or** 25 days on, 5 days off

Male and Female:

Breast cancer palliation, metastatic disease in selected patients: Oral: 10 mg 3 times/day for at least 3 months

Uremic bleeding (unlabeled use): I.V.: 0.6 mg/kg/day for 5 days

Elderly: Refer to Adults dosing; a higher incidence of stroke and invasive breast cancer was observed in women >75 years in a WHI substudy.

Administration

Injection: May also be administered intramuscularly; when administered I.V., drug should be administered slowly to avoid the occurrence of a flushing reaction

Oral tablet, vaginal cream: Administer at bedtime to minimize adverse effects.

Monitoring Parameters Yearly physical examination that includes blood pressure and Papanicolaou smear, breast exam, mammogram. Monitor for signs of endometrial cancer in female patients with uterus; rule out malignancy if unexplained vaginal bleeding occurs

Reference Range

Children: <10 µg/24 hours (SI: <35 µmol/day) (values at Mayo Medical Laboratories)

Adults:

Male: 15-40 µg/24 hours (SI: 52-139 µmol/day)

Female:

Menstruating: 15-80 µg/24 hours (SI: 52-277 µmol/day)

Postmenopausal: <20 µg/24 hours (SI: <69 µmol/day)

Patient Information It is important to maintain schedule. Estrogens have been shown to increase the risk of endometrial cancer. Annual gynecologic and breast exams are important. You may experience nausea or vomiting (small frequent meals may help); abdominal pain; difficult/painful menstrual cycles; dizziness or mental depression; headaches; rash; breast pain; or increased/decreased libido. Report significant swelling of extremities, sudden acute pain in legs or calves, chest or abdomen; shortness of breath; severe headache or vomiting; weakness or numbness of arms or legs; or unusual vaginal bleeding. You may become intolerant to wearing contact lenses, notify prescriber if this occurs. If taking for prevention of osteoporosis, ask prescriber about calcium and vitamin D intake, and weight-bearing exercises.

Dosage Forms CRM, vaginal: 0.625 mg/g (42.5 g). **INJ, powder for reconstitution:** 25 mg. **TAB:** 0.3 mg, 0.45 mg, 0.625 mg, 0.9 mg, 1.25 mg, 2.5 mg

Estrogens (Conjugated/Equine) and Medroxyprogesterone

(ES troe jenz KON joo gate ed/EE kwine & me DROKS ee proe JES te rone)

U.S. Brand Names Premphase®; Prempro™

Synonyms Medroxyprogesterone and Estrogens (Conjugated); MPA and Estrogens (Conjugated)

Therapeutic Category Estrogen and Progestin Combination

Use Women with an intact uterus: Treatment of moderate to severe vasomotor symptoms associated with menopause; treatment of atrophic vaginitis; osteoporosis (prophylaxis)

Pregnancy Risk Factor X

Dosage Oral: Adults:

Treatment of moderate to severe vasomotor symptoms associated with menopause or treatment of atrophic vaginitis in females with an intact uterus. (The lowest dose that will control symptoms should be used; medication should be discontinued as soon as possible):

Premphase®: One maroon conjugated estrogen 0.625 mg tablet daily on days 1 through 14 and one light blue conjugated estrogen 0.625 mg/MPA 5 mg tablet daily on days 15 through 28; re-evaluate patients at 3- and 6-month intervals to determine if treatment is still necessary; monitor patients for signs of endometrial cancer; rule out malignancy if unexplained vaginal bleeding occurs

Prempro™: One conjugated estrogen 0.3 mg/MPA 1.5 mg tablet daily; re-evaluate at 3-and 6-month intervals to determine if therapy is still needed; dose may be increased to a maximum of one conjugated estrogen 0.625 mg/MPA 5 mg tablet daily in patients with bleeding or spotting, once malignancy has been ruled out

Osteoporosis prophylaxis in females with an intact uterus:

Premphase®: One maroon conjugated estrogen 0.625 tablet daily on days 1 through 14 and one light blue conjugated estrogen 0.625 mg/MPA 5 mg tablet daily on days 15 through 28; monitor patients for signs of endometrial cancer; rule out malignancy if unexplained vaginal bleeding occurs

Prempro™: One conjugated estrogen 0.3 mg/MPA 1.5 mg tablet daily; dose may be increased to one conjugated estrogen 0.625 mg/MPA 5 mg tablet daily; in patients with bleeding or spotting, once malignancy has been ruled out

Elderly: Refer to Adults dosing; a higher incidence of stroke and invasive breast cancer was observed in women >75 years in a WHI substudy.

Dosage Forms TAB: (Premphase®): Conjugated estrogens 0.625 mg and conjugated estrogen 0.625 mg/medroxyprogesterone acetate 5 mg (28s); (Prempro™): 0.3/1.5: Conjugated estrogens 0.3 mg and medroxyprogesterone acetate 1.5 mg (28s); 0.45/1.5: Conjugated estrogens 0.45 mg and medroxyprogesterone acetate 1.5 mg (28s); 0.625/2.5: Conjugated estrogens 0.625 mg and medroxyprogesterone acetate 2.5 mg (28s); 0.625/5: Conjugated estrogens 0.625 mg and medroxyprogesterone acetate 5 mg (28s)

Estrogens (Esterified) (ES troe jenz, es TER i fied)

U.S. Brand Names Menest®

Synonyms Esterified Estrogens

Therapeutic Category Estrogen Derivative; Estrogen Derivative, Oral

Use Treatment of moderate to severe vasomotor symptoms associated with menopause; treatment of vulvar and vaginal atrophy; hypoestrogenism (due to hypogonadism, castration, or primary ovarian failure); prostatic cancer (palliation); breast cancer (palliation); osteoporosis (prophylaxis, in women at significant risk only)

Pregnancy Risk Factor X

Contraindications Hypersensitivity to estrogens or any component of the formulation; undiagnosed abnormal vaginal bleeding; history of or current thrombophlebitis or thromboembolic disorders; carcinoma of the breast, except in appropriately selected patients being treated for metastatic disease; estrogen-dependent tumor; pregnancy

Warnings/Precautions Should not be used to prevent coronary heart disease. May increase the risks of myocardial infarction, stroke, pulmonary emboli, and deep vein thrombosis; incidence of these effects was shown to be significantly increased in postmenopausal women using conjugated equine estrogens (CEE) in combination with medroxyprogesterone acetate (MPA). Unopposed estrogens may increase the risk of endometrial carcinoma in postmenopausal women. Estrogens may increase the risk of breast cancer (controversial/currently under study; increased risk of invasive breast cancer observed in postmenopausal women using CEE in combination with MPA). Use with caution in patients with diseases which may be exacerbated by fluid retention, including asthma, epilepsy, migraine, diabetes, cardiac or renal dysfunction. Use with caution in patients with a history of hypercalcemia, cardiovascular disease, and gallbladder disease. May increase blood pressure. Use with caution in patients with hepatic disease. May increase risk of venous thromboembolism. Estrogen compounds are generally associated with lipid effects such as increased HDL-cholesterol, and decreased LDL-cholesterol. Triglycerides may also be increased; use with caution in patients with familial defects of lipoprotein metabolism. May increase size of pre-existing uterine leiomyomata. Before prescribing estrogen therapy to postmenopausal women, the risks and benefits must be weighed for each patient. Women should be informed of these risks and benefits, as well as possible effects of progestin when added to estrogen therapy. Use for shortest duration possible consistent with treatment goals. Conduct periodic risk:benefit assessments. When used solely for the treatment of vulvar and vaginal atrophy, topical vaginal products should be considered. When used solely for prevention of osteoporosis in women at significant risk, nonestrogen treatment options should be considered. Estrogens may cause premature closure of the epiphyses in young individuals. Safety and efficacy in pediatric patients have not been established.

Common Adverse Reactions Frequency not defined.

Cardiovascular: Edema, hypertension, venous thromboembolism

Central nervous system: Dizziness, headache, mental depression, migraine

Dermatologic: Chloasma, erythema multiforme, erythema nodosum, hemorrhagic eruption, hirsutism, loss of scalp hair, melasma

Endocrine & metabolic: Breast enlargement, breast tenderness, changes in libido, increased thyroid-binding globulin, increased total thyroid hormone (T_4), increased serum triglycerides/phospholipids, increased HDL-cholesterol, decreased LDL-cholesterol, impaired glucose tolerance, hypercalcemia

Gastrointestinal: Abdominal cramps, bloating, cholecystitis, cholelithiasis, gallbladder disease, nausea, pancreatitis, vomiting, weight gain/loss

Genitourinary: Alterations in frequency and flow of menses, changes in cervical secretions, endometrial cancer, increased size of uterine leiomyomata, vaginal candidiasis

Hematologic: Aggravation of porphyria, decreased antithrombin III and antifactor Xa, increased levels of fibrinogen, increased platelet aggregability and platelet count; increased prothrombin and factors VII, VIII, IX, X

Hepatic: Cholestatic jaundice

Neuromuscular & skeletal: Chorea

Ocular: Intolerance to contact lenses, steeping of corneal curvature

(Continued)

Estrogens (Esterified) *(Continued)*

Respiratory: Pulmonary thromboembolism

Miscellaneous: Carbohydrate intolerance

Drug Interactions

Cytochrome P450 Effect: Based on estrone: **Substrate** of CYP1A2 (major), 2B6 (minor), 2C8/9 (minor), 2E1 (minor), 3A4 (major)

Increased Effect/Toxicity: Hydrocortisone taken with estrogen may cause corticosteroid-induced toxicity. Increased potential for thromboembolic events with anticoagulants.

Decreased Effect: CYP1A2 inducers may decrease the levels/effects of estrogens; example inducers include aminoglutethimide, carbamazepine, phenobarbital, and rifampin.

Mechanism of Action Esterified estrogens contain a mixture of estrogenic substances; the principle component is estrone. Preparations contain 75% to 85% sodium estrone sulfate and 6% to 15% sodium equilin sulfate such that the total is not <90%. Estrogens are responsible for the development and maintenance of the female reproductive system and secondary sexual characteristics. Estradiol is the principle intracellular human estrogen and is more potent than estrone and estriol at the receptor level; it is the primary estrogen secreted prior to menopause. In males and following menopause in females, estrone and estrone sulfate are more highly produced. Estrogens modulate the pituitary secretion of gonadotropins, luteinizing hormone, and follicle-stimulating hormone through a negative feedback system; estrogen replacement reduces elevated levels of these hormones.

Pharmacodynamics/Kinetics

Absorption: Readily

Metabolism: Rapidly hepatic to estrone sulfate, conjugated and unconjugated metabolites; first-pass effect

Excretion: Urine (as unchanged drug and as glucuronide and sulfate conjugates)

Dosage Oral: Adults:

Prostate cancer (palliation): 1.25-2.5 mg 3 times/day

Female hypogonadism: 2.5-7.5 mg of estrogen daily for 20 days followed by a 10-day rest period. Administer cyclically (3 weeks on and 1 week off). If bleeding does not occur by the end of the 10-day period, repeat the same dosing schedule; the number of courses is dependent upon the responsiveness of the endometrium. If bleeding occurs before the end of the 10-day period, begin an estrogen-progestin cyclic regimen of 2.5-7.5 mg esterified estrogens daily for 20 days. During the last 5 days of estrogen therapy, give an oral progestin. If bleeding occurs before regimen is concluded, discontinue therapy and resume on the fifth day of bleeding.

Moderate to severe vasomotor symptoms associated with menopause: 1.25 mg/day administered cyclically (3 weeks on and 1 week off). If patient has not menstruated within the last 2 months or more, cyclic administration is started arbitrary. If the patient is menstruating, cyclical administration is started on day 5 of the bleeding. For short-term use only and should be discontinued as soon as possible. Re-evaluate at 3- to 6-month intervals for tapering or discontinuation of therapy.

Atopic vaginitis and kraurosis vulvae: 0.3 to ≥1.25 mg/day, depending on the tissue response of the individual patient. Administer cyclically. For short-term use only and should be discontinued as soon as possible. Re-evaluate at 3- to 6-month intervals for tapering or discontinuation of therapy.

Breast cancer (palliation): 10 mg 3 times/day for at least 3 months

Osteoporosis in postmenopausal women: Initial: 0.3 mg/day and increase to a maximum daily dose of 1.25 mg/day; initiate therapy as soon as possible after menopause; cyclically or daily, depending on medical assessment of patient. Monitor patients with an intact uterus for signs of endometrial cancer; rule out malignancy if unexplained vaginal bleeding occurs

Female castration and primary ovarian failure: 1.25 mg/day, cyclically. Adjust dosage upward or downward, according to the severity of symptoms and patient response. For maintenance, adjust dosage to lowest level that will provide effective control.

Elderly: Refer to Adults dosing. A higher incidence of stroke and invasive breast cancer were observed in women >75 years in a WHI substudy using conjugated equine estrogen.

Dosing adjustment in hepatic impairment:

Mild to moderate liver impairment: Dosage reduction of estrogens is recommended

Severe liver impairment: **Not recommended**

Monitoring Parameters Yearly physical examination that includes blood pressure, Papanicolaou smear, breast exam, and mammogram. Monitor for signs of endometrial cancer in female patients with uterus; rule out malignancy if unexplained vaginal bleeding occurs.

Patient Information It is important to maintain schedule. Estrogens have been shown to increase the risk of endometrial cancer. Annual gynecologic and breast exams are important. You may experience nausea or vomiting (small frequent meals may help); abdominal pain; difficult/painful menstrual cycles; dizziness or mental depression; headaches; rash; breast pain; or increased/decreased libido. Report significant swelling of extremities, sudden acute pain in legs or calves, chest or abdomen; shortness of breath; severe headache or vomiting; weakness or numbness of arms or legs; or unusual vaginal bleeding. You may become intolerant to wearing contact lenses, notify prescriber if this occurs. If taking for prevention of osteoporosis, ask prescriber about calcium and vitamin D intake, and weight-bearing exercises.

Dosage Forms TAB: 0.3 mg, 0.625 mg, 1.25 mg, 2.5 mg

Estrogens (Esterified) and Methyltestosterone
(ES troe jenz es TER i fied & meth il tes TOS te rone)

U.S. Brand Names Estratest®; Estratest® H.S.

Synonyms Conjugated Estrogen and Methyltestosterone; Esterified Estrogen and Methyltestosterone

Therapeutic Category Estrogen and Androgen Combination

Use Vasomotor symptoms of menopause

Pregnancy Risk Factor X

Dosage Adults: Female: Oral: Lowest dose that will control symptoms should be chosen, normally given 3 weeks on and 1 week off

Dosage Forms TAB: (Estratest®): Esterified estrogen 1.25 mg and methyltestosterone 2.5 mg; (Estratest® H.S.): Esterified estrogen 0.625 mg and methyltestosterone 1.25 mg

Estropipate (ES troe pih pate)
U.S. Brand Names Ogen®; Ortho-Est®

Synonyms Ortho Est; Piperazine Estrone Sulfate

Therapeutic Category Estrogen Derivative; Estrogen Derivative, Oral; Estrogen Derivative, Vaginal

Use Treatment of moderate to severe vasomotor symptoms associated with menopause; treatment of vulvar and vaginal atrophy; hypoestrogenism (due to hypogonadism, castration, or primary ovarian failure); osteoporosis (prophylaxis, in women at significant risk only)

Pregnancy Risk Factor X

Contraindications Hypersensitivity to estrogens or any component of the formulation; undiagnosed abnormal vaginal bleeding; history of or current thrombophlebitis or thromboembolic disorders; carcinoma of the breast, except in appropriately selected patients being treated for metastatic disease; estrogen-dependent tumor; pregnancy

Warnings/Precautions Estrogens should not be used to prevent coronary heart disease. May increase the risks of myocardial infarction, stroke, pulmonary emboli, and deep vein thrombosis; incidence of these effects was shown to be significantly increased in postmenopausal women using conjugated equine estrogens (CEE) in combination with medroxyprogesterone acetate (MPA). Unopposed estrogens may increase the risk of endometrial carcinoma in postmenopausal women. Estrogens may increase the risk of breast cancer (controversial/currently under study; increased risk of invasive breast cancer observed in postmenopausal women using CEE in combination with MPA). Use with caution in patients with diseases which may be exacerbated by fluid retention, including asthma, epilepsy, migraine, diabetes, cardiac or renal dysfunction. Use with caution in patients with a history of hypercalcemia, cardiovascular disease, and gallbladder disease. May increase blood pressure. Use with caution in patients with hepatic dysfunction. May increase risk of venous thromboembolism. Estrogen compounds are generally associated with lipid effects such as increased HDL-cholesterol and decreased LDL-cholesterol. Triglycerides may also be increased; use with caution in patients with familial defects of lipoprotein metabolism. Estrogens may cause premature closure of the epiphyses in young individuals. May increase size of pre-existing uterine leiomyomata. Before prescribing estrogen therapy to postmenopausal women, the risks and benefits must be weighed for each patient. Women should be informed of these risks and benefits, as well as possible effects of progestin when added to estrogen therapy. Use for shortest duration possible consistent with treatment goals. Conduct periodic risk:benefit assessments. When used solely for the treatment of vulvar and vaginal atrophy, topical vaginal products should be considered. When used solely for prevention of osteoporosis in women at significant risk, nonestrogen treatment options should be considered. Safety and efficacy in pediatric patients have not been established.

Common Adverse Reactions Frequency not defined.
Cardiovascular: Edema, hypertension, venous thromboembolism
Central nervous system: Dizziness, headache, mental depression, migraine
Dermatologic: Chloasma, erythema multiforme, erythema nodosum, hemorrhagic eruption, hirsutism, loss of scalp hair, melasma
Endocrine & metabolic: Breast enlargement, breast tenderness, changes in libido, increased thyroid-binding globulin, increased total thyroid hormone (T_4), increased serum triglycerides/phospholipids, increased HDL-cholesterol, decreased LDL-cholesterol, impaired glucose tolerance, hypercalcemia
Gastrointestinal: Abdominal cramps, bloating, cholecystitis, cholelithiasis, gallbladder disease, nausea, pancreatitis, vomiting, weight gain/loss
Genitourinary: Alterations in frequency and flow of menses, changes in cervical secretions, endometrial cancer, increased size of uterine leiomyomata, vaginal candidiasis
Hematologic: Aggravation of porphyria, decreased antithrombin III and antifactor Xa, increased levels of fibrinogen, increased platelet aggregability and platelet count; increased prothrombin and factors VII, VIII, IX, X
Hepatic: Cholestatic jaundice
Neuromuscular & skeletal: Chorea
Ocular: Intolerance to contact lenses, steeping of corneal curvature
Respiratory: Pulmonary thromboembolism
Miscellaneous: Carbohydrate intolerance

Drug Interactions
Cytochrome P450 Effect: Based on estrone: **Substrate** of CYP1A2 (major), 2B6 (minor), 2C8/9 (minor), 2E1 (minor), 3A4 (major)
(Continued)

Estropipate *(Continued)*

Increased Effect/Toxicity: Hydrocortisone taken with estrogen may cause corticosteroid-induced toxicity. Increased potential for thromboembolic events with anticoagulants.

Decreased Effect: CYP1A2 inducers may decrease the levels/effects of estrogens; example inducers include aminoglutethimide, carbamazepine, phenobarbital, and rifampin.

Mechanism of Action Estrogens are responsible for the development and maintenance of the female reproductive system and secondary sexual characteristics. Estradiol is the principle intracellular human estrogen and is more potent than estrone and estriol at the receptor level; it is the primary estrogen secreted prior to menopause. In males and following menopause in females, estrone and estrone sulfate are more highly produced. Estrogens modulate the pituitary secretion of gonadotropins, luteinizing hormone, and follicle-stimulating hormone through a negative feedback system; estrogen replacement reduces elevated levels of these hormones. Estropipate is prepared from purified crystalline estrone that has been solubilized as the sulfate and stabilized with piperazine.

Pharmacodynamics/Kinetics

Absorption: Well absorbed

Metabolism: Hepatic and in target tissues; first-pass effect

Dosage Adults:

Oral:

Moderate to severe vasomotor symptoms associated with menopause: Usual dosage range: 0.75-6 mg estropipate daily; use the lowest dose and regimen that will control symptoms, and discontinue as soon as possible. Attempt to discontinue or taper medication at 3- to 6-month intervals. If a patient with vasomotor symptoms has not menstruated within the last ≥2 months, start the cyclic administration arbitrarily. If the patient has menstruated, start cyclic administration on day 5 of bleeding.

Female hypogonadism: 1.5-9 mg estropipate daily for the first 3 weeks, followed by a rest period of 8-10 days; use the lowest dose and regimen that will control symptoms. Repeat if bleeding does not occur by the end of the rest period. The duration of therapy necessary to product the withdrawal bleeding will vary according to the responsiveness of the endometrium. If satisfactory withdrawal bleeding does not occur, give an oral progestin in addition to estrogen during the third week of the cycle.

Female castration or primary ovarian failure: 1.5-9 mg estropipate daily for the first 3 weeks of a theoretical cycle, followed by a rest period of 8-10 days; use the lowest dose and regimen that will control symptoms

Osteoporosis prophylaxis: 0.75 mg estropipate daily for 25 days of a 31-day cycle

Atrophic vaginitis or kraurosis vulvae: 0.75-6 mg estropipate daily; administer cyclically. Use the lowest dose and regimen that will control symptoms; discontinue as soon as possible.

Intravaginal: Atrophic vaginitis or kraurosis vulvae: Instill 2-4 g/day intravaginally; use the lowest dose and regimen that will control symptoms; attempt to discontinue or taper medication at 3- to 6-month intervals

Elderly: Refer to Adults dosing. A higher incidence of stroke and invasive breast cancer were observed in women >75 years in a WHI substudy using conjugated equine estrogen.

Dosing adjustment in hepatic impairment:

Mild to moderate liver impairment: Dosage reduction of estrogens is recommended

Severe liver impairment: **Not recommended**

Monitoring Parameters Yearly physical examination that includes blood pressure and Papanicolaou smear, breast exam, mammogram. Monitor for signs of endometrial cancer in female patients with uterus; rule out malignancy if unexplained vaginal bleeding occurs

Patient Information It is important to maintain schedule. Estrogens have been shown to increase the risk of endometrial cancer. Annual gynecologic and breast exams are important. You may experience nausea or vomiting (small frequent meals may help); abdominal pain; difficult/painful menstrual cycles; dizziness or mental depression; headaches; rash; breast pain; or increased/decreased libido. Report significant swelling of extremities, sudden acute pain in legs or calves, chest or abdomen; shortness of breath; severe headache or vomiting; weakness or numbness of arms or legs; or unusual vaginal bleeding. You may become intolerant to wearing contact lenses, notify prescriber if this occurs. If taking for prevention of osteoporosis, ask prescriber about calcium and vitamin D intake, and weight-bearing exercises.

Intravaginal cream: Insert high in vagina; wash hands and applicator before and after application

Dosage Forms CRM, vaginal (Ogen®): 1.5 mg/g (42.5 g tube). **TAB** (Ogen®, Ortho-Est®): 0.625 mg [estropipate 0.75 mg]; 1.25 mg [estropipate 1.5 mg]; 2.5 mg [estropipate 3 mg]

♦ **Estrostep® Fe** *see* Ethinyl Estradiol and Norethindrone *on page 487*

♦ **ETAF** *see* Aldesleukin *on page 47*

Etanercept *(et a NER sept)*

U.S. Brand Names Enbrel®

Therapeutic Category Antirheumatic, Disease Modifying

Use Reduction in signs and symptoms of moderately to severely active rheumatoid arthritis, moderately to severely active polyarticular juvenile arthritis, or psoriatic arthritis in patients who have had an inadequate response to one or more disease-modifying antirheumatic drugs (DMARDs); reduction in signs and symptoms of active ankylosing spondylitis (AS)

Unlabeled/Investigational Use Crohn's disease

Pregnancy Risk Factor B

Contraindications Hypersensitivity to etanercept or any component of the formulation; patients with sepsis (mortality may be increased); active infections (including chronic or local infection)

Warnings/Precautions Etanercept may affect defenses against infections and malignancies. Safety and efficacy in patients with immunosuppression or chronic infections have not been evaluated. Discontinue administration if patient develops a serious infection. Do not start drug administration in patients with an active infection. Use caution in patients predisposed to infection, such as poorly-controlled diabetes.

Use caution in patients with pre-existing or recent-onset demyelinating CNS disorders. Use caution in patients with CHF. Use caution in patients with a history of significant hematologic abnormalities; has been associated with pancytopenia and aplastic anemia (rare). Discontinue if significant hematologic abnormalities are confirmed.

Treatment may result in the formation of autoimmune antibodies; cases of autoimmune disease have not been described. More cases of lymphoma were reported in patients receiving anti-TNF therapy (relative to controls).

Patients should be brought up to date with all immunizations before initiating therapy. Live vaccines should not be given concurrently. Patients with a significant exposure to varicella virus should temporarily discontinue etanercept. Treatment with varicella zoster immune globulin should be considered.

Common Adverse Reactions Events reported include those >3% with incidence higher than placebo.

>10%:
  Central nervous system: Headache (17%)
  Local: Injection site reaction (37%)
  Respiratory: Respiratory tract infection (38%), upper respiratory tract infection (29%), rhinitis (12%)
  Miscellaneous: Infection (35%), positive ANA (11%), positive antidouble-stranded DNA antibodies (15% by RIA, 3% by *Crithidia luciliae* assay)
≥3% to 10%:
  Central nervous system: Dizziness (7%)
  Dermatologic: Rash (5%)
  Gastrointestinal: Abdominal pain (5%), dyspepsia (4%), nausea (9%), vomiting (3%)
  Neuromuscular & skeletal: Weakness (5%)
  Respiratory: Pharyngitis (7%), respiratory disorder (5%), sinusitis (3%), cough (6%)
Pediatric patients (JRA): The percentages of patients reporting abdominal pain (17%) and vomiting (13%) were higher than in adult RA. Two patients developed varicella infection associated with aseptic meningitis which resolved without complications (see Warnings/Precautions).

Drug Interactions
  Increased Effect/Toxicity: Specific drug interaction studies have not been conducted with etanercept. An increased rate of serious infections has been noted with concurrent anakinra therapy, without additional improvement in American College of Rheumatology (ACR) response criteria.
  Decreased Effect: Specific drug interaction studies have not been conducted with etanercept. Live vaccines should not be given during therapy.

Mechanism of Action Etanercept is a recombinant DNA-derived protein composed of tumor necrosis factor receptor (TNFR) linked to the Fc portion of human IgG1. Etanercept binds tumor necrosis factor (TNF) and blocks its interaction with cell surface receptors. TNF plays an important role in the inflammatory processes of rheumatoid arthritis (RA) and the resulting joint pathology.

Pharmacodynamics/Kinetics
  Onset of action: ~2-3 weeks
  Half-life elimination: 115 hours (range: 98-300 hours)
  Time to peak: 72 hours (range: 48-96 hours)
  Excretion: Clearance: Children: 45.9 mL/hour/m^2; Adults: 89 mL/hour (52 mL/hour/m^2)

Dosage S.C.:
  Children 4-17 years: Juvenile rheumatoid arthritis:
    Once-weekly dosing: 0.8 mg/kg (maximum 50 mg per dose) once weekly; maximum amount in any single injection site should be no more than 25 mg
    Twice-weekly dosing: 0.4 mg/kg (maximum: 25 mg per dose) twice weekly (individual doses should be separated by 72-96 hours)
  Adults: Rheumatoid arthritis, psoriatic arthritis, ankylosing spondylitis:
    Once-weekly dosing: 50 mg once weekly; the maximum amount in any single injection site should be no more than 25 mg
    Twice weekly dosing: 25 mg given twice weekly (individual doses should be separated by 72-96 hours)
    Note: If the physician determines that it is appropriate, patients may self-inject after proper training in injection technique.
  Elderly: Although greater sensitivity of some elderly patients cannot be ruled out, no overall differences in safety or effectiveness were observed.

Administration Follow package instructions carefully for reconstitution. **Note:** The needle cover of the diluent syringe may contain dry natural rubber (latex) which should not be handled by persons sensitive to this substance. Injection sites should be rotated. The maximum amount injected at any single site is 25 mg. New injections should be given at least one inch from an old site and never into areas where the skin is tender, bruised, red, or hard. (Continued)

Etanercept *(Continued)*

Patient Information If self-injecting, follow instructions for injection and disposal of needles exactly. If redness, swelling, or irritation appears at the injection site, contact prescriber. Do not have any vaccinations while using this medication without consulting prescriber first. You may experience headache or dizziness (use caution when driving or engaging in tasks requiring alertness until response to drug is known). If stomach pain or cramping, unusual bleeding or bruising, persistent fever, paleness, blood in vomitus, stool, or urine occurs, stop taking medication and contact prescriber **immediately**. Also immediately report skin rash, unusual muscle or bone weakness, or signs of respiratory flu or other infection (eg, chills, fever, sore throat, easy bruising or bleeding, mouth sores, unhealed sores).

Dosage Forms INJ, powder for reconstitution: 25 mg

♦ **Ethacrynate Sodium** *see Ethacrynic Acid on page 474*

Ethacrynic Acid (eth a KRIN ik AS id)

U.S. Brand Names Edecrin®

Synonyms Ethacrynate Sodium

Therapeutic Category Diuretic, Loop

Use Management of edema associated with congestive heart failure; hepatic cirrhosis or renal disease; short-term management of ascites due to malignancy, idiopathic edema, and lymphedema

Pregnancy Risk Factor B

Dosage I.V. formulation should be diluted in D_5W or NS (1 mg/mL) and infused over several minutes.

Children: Oral: 1 mg/kg/dose once daily; increase at intervals of 2-3 days as needed, to a maximum of 3 mg/kg/day.

Adults:

Oral: 50-200 mg/day in 1-2 divided doses; may increase in increments of 25-50 mg at intervals of several days; doses up to 200 mg twice daily may be required with severe, refractory edema.

I.V.: 0.5-1 mg/kg/dose (maximum: 100 mg/dose); repeat doses not routinely recommended; however, if indicated, repeat doses every 8-12 hours.

Dosing adjustment/comments in renal impairment: Cl_{cr} <10 mL/minute: Avoid use.

Dialysis: Not removed by hemo- or peritoneal dialysis; supplemental dose is not necessary.

Dosage Forms INJ, powder for reconstitution: 50 mg. **TAB:** 25 mg

Ethambutol (e THAM byoo tole)

Related Information

Antimicrobial Drugs of Choice *on page 1440*

Tuberculosis Prophylaxis *on page 1438*

Tuberculosis Treatment Guidelines *on page 1466*

U.S. Brand Names Myambutol®

Synonyms Ethambutol Hydrochloride

Therapeutic Category Antitubercular Agent

Use Treatment of tuberculosis and other mycobacterial diseases in conjunction with other antituberculosis agents

Pregnancy Risk Factor C

Contraindications Hypersensitivity to ethambutol or any component of the formulation; optic neuritis

Warnings/Precautions May cause optic neuritis, resulting in decreased visual acuity or other vision changes. Discontinue promptly in patients with changes in vision, color blindness, or visual defects (effects normally reversible, but reversal may require up to a year). Use only in children whose visual acuity can accurately be determined and monitored (not recommended for use in children <13 years of age unless the benefit outweighs the risk); dosage modification required in patients with renal insufficiency

Common Adverse Reactions Frequency not defined.

Central nervous system: Headache, confusion, disorientation, malaise, mental confusion, fever, dizziness, hallucinations

Dermatologic: Rash, pruritus

Endocrine & metabolic: Acute gout or hyperuricemia

Gastrointestinal: Abdominal pain, anorexia, nausea, vomiting

Hematologic: Leukopenia, thrombocytopenia, eosinophilia

Hepatic: Abnormal LFTs

Neuromuscular & skeletal: Peripheral neuritis

Ocular: Optic neuritis; symptoms may include decreased acuity, scotoma, color blindness, or visual defects (usually reversible with discontinuation, irreversible blindness has been described)

Miscellaneous: Anaphylaxis

Drug Interactions

Decreased Effect: Ethambutol absorption is decreased when taken with aluminum salts.

Mechanism of Action Suppresses mycobacteria multiplication by interfering with RNA synthesis

Pharmacodynamics/Kinetics

Absorption: ~80%

Distribution: Widely throughout body; concentrated in kidneys, lungs, saliva, and red blood cells

Relative diffusion from blood into CSF: Adequate with or without inflammation (exceeds usual MICs)
CSF:blood level ratio: Normal meninges: 0%; Inflamed meninges: 25%
Protein binding: 20% to 30%
Metabolism: Hepatic (20%) to inactive metabolite
Half-life elimination: 2.5-3.6 hours; End-stage renal disease: 7-15 hours
Time to peak, serum: 2-4 hours
Excretion: Urine (~50%) and feces (20%) as unchanged drug

Dosage Oral:

Ethambutol is generally not recommended in children whose visual acuity cannot be monitored. However, ethambutol should be considered for all children with organisms resistant to other drugs, when susceptibility to ethambutol has been demonstrated, or susceptibility is likely.

Note: A four-drug regimen (isoniazid, rifampin, pyrazinamide, and either streptomycin or ethambutol) is preferred for the initial, empiric treatment of TB. When the drug susceptibility results are available, the regimen should be altered as appropriate.

Children and Adults:
Daily therapy: 15-25 mg/kg/day (maximum: 2.5 g/day)
Directly observed therapy (DOT): Twice weekly: 50 mg/kg (maximum: 2.5 g)
DOT: 3 times/week: 25-30 mg/kg (maximum: 2.5 g)
Adults: Treatment of disseminated *Mycobacterium avium* complex (MAC) in patients with advanced HIV infection: 15 mg/kg ethambutol in combination with azithromycin 600 mg daily

Dosing interval in renal impairment:
Cl_{cr} 10-50 mL/minute: Administer every 24-36 hours
Cl_{cr} <10 mL/minute: Administer every 48 hours
Hemodialysis: Slightly dialyzable (5% to 20%); Administer dose postdialysis
Peritoneal dialysis: Dose for Cl_{cr} <10 mL/minute
Continuous arteriovenous or venovenous hemofiltration: Administer every 24-36 hours

Monitoring Parameters Periodic visual testing in patients receiving >15 mg/kg/day; periodic renal, hepatic, and hematopoietic tests

Patient Information Report any visual changes or rash; may cause stomach upset, take with food; do not take within 2 hours of aluminum-containing antacids

Dosage Forms TAB: 100 mg, 400 mg

♦ **Ethambutol Hydrochloride** *see Ethambutol on page 474*
♦ **Ethamolin®** *see Ethanolamine Oleate on page 475*
♦ **Ethanoic Acid** *see Acetic Acid on page 31*

Ethanolamine Oleate (ETH a nol a meen OH lee ate)

U.S. Brand Names Ethamolin®
Synonyms Monoethanolamine
Therapeutic Category Sclerosing Agent
Use Orphan drug: Sclerosing agent used for bleeding esophageal varices
Pregnancy Risk Factor C
Contraindications Hypersensitivity to agent or oleic acid
Warnings/Precautions Fatal anaphylactic shock has been reported following administration; use with caution and decrease doses in patients with significant liver dysfunction (child class C), with concomitant cardiorespiratory disease, or in the elderly or critically-ill
Common Adverse Reactions 1% to 10%:
Central nervous system: Pyrexia (1.8%)
Gastrointestinal: Esophageal ulcer (2%), esophageal stricture (1.3%)
Respiratory: Pleural effusion (2%), pneumonia (1.2%)
Miscellaneous: Retrosternal pain (1.6%)
Mechanism of Action Derived from oleic acid and similar in physical properties to sodium morrhuate; however, the exact mechanism of the hemostatic effect used in endoscopic injection sclerotherapy is not known. Intravenously injected ethanolamine oleate produces a sterile inflammatory response resulting in fibrosis and occlusion of the vein; a dose-related extravascular inflammatory reaction occurs when the drug diffuses through the venous wall. Autopsy results indicate that variceal obliteration occurs secondary to mural necrosis and fibrosis. Thrombosis appears to be a transient reaction.
Dosage Adults: 1.5-5 mL per varix, up to 20 mL total or 0.4 mL/kg for a 50 kg patient; doses should be decreased in patients with severe hepatic dysfunction and should receive less than recommended maximum dose
Administration Use care to use acceptable technique to avoid necrosis
Dosage Forms INJ, solution: 5% [50 mg/mL] (2 mL)

Ethinyl Estradiol (ETH in il es tra DYE ole)

U.S. Brand Names Estinyl®
Therapeutic Category Estrogen Derivative; Estrogen Derivative, Oral
Use Treatment of moderate to severe vasomotor symptoms associated with menopause; hypogonadism; prostatic cancer (palliation); breast cancer (palliation)
Pregnancy Risk Factor X
Contraindications Hypersensitivity to estrogens or any component of the formulation; undiagnosed abnormal vaginal bleeding; history of or current thrombophlebitis or thromboembolic disorders; carcinoma of the breast, except in appropriately selected patients being treated for metastatic disease; estrogen-dependent tumor; pregnancy
(Continued)

Ethinyl Estradiol *(Continued)*

Warnings/Precautions Unopposed estrogens may increase the risk of endometrial carcinoma in postmenopausal women. Use with caution in patients with diseases which may be exacerbated by fluid retention, including asthma, epilepsy, migraine, diabetes, cardiac or renal dysfunction. Use with caution in patients with a history of hypercalcemia, cardiovascular disease, and gallbladder disease. May increase blood pressure. Use with caution in patients with hepatic disease. May increase risk of venous thromboembolism. Estrogens may increase the risk of breast cancer (controversial/currently under study). Estrogen compounds are generally associated with lipid effects such as increased HDL-cholesterol, and decreased LDL-cholesterol; triglycerides may also be increased. Use with caution in patients with familial defects of lipoprotein metabolism. May increase size of pre-existing uterine leiomyomata. Patients with a history of depression should be monitored, discontinue if depression recurs to a serious degree. Before prescribing estrogen therapy to postmenopausal women, the risks and benefits must be weighed for each patient. Women should be informed of these risks and benefits, as well as possible effects of progestin when added to estrogen therapy. Estrogens may cause premature closure of the epiphyses in young individuals. Safety and efficacy in pediatric patients have not been established. Some tablet formulations contain tartrazine.

Common Adverse Reactions Frequency not defined.

Cardiovascular: Edema, hypertension, venous thromboembolism

Central nervous system: Dizziness, headache, mental depression, migraine

Dermatologic: Chloasma, erythema multiforme, erythema nodosum, hemorrhagic eruption, hirsutism, loss of scalp hair, melasma

Endocrine & metabolic: Breast enlargement, breast tenderness, changes in libido, increased thyroid-binding globulin, increased total thyroid hormone (T_4), increased serum triglycerides/phospholipids, increased HDL-cholesterol, decreased LDL-cholesterol, impaired glucose tolerance, hypercalcemia

Gastrointestinal: Abdominal cramps, bloating, cholecystitis, cholelithiasis, gallbladder disease, nausea, pancreatitis, vomiting, weight gain/loss

Genitourinary: Alterations in frequency and flow of menses, changes in cervical secretions, endometrial cancer, increased size of uterine leiomyomata, vaginal candidiasis

Hematologic: Aggravation of porphyria, decreased antithrombin III and antifactor Xa, increased levels of fibrinogen, increased platelet aggregability and platelet count; increased prothrombin and factors VII, VIII, IX, X

Hepatic: Cholestatic jaundice

Neuromuscular & skeletal: Chorea

Ocular: Intolerance to contact lenses, steeping of corneal curvature

Respiratory: Pulmonary thromboembolism

Miscellaneous: Carbohydrate intolerance

Drug Interactions

Cytochrome P450 Effect: Substrate of CYP3A4 (major), 3A5-7 (minor); **Inhibits** CYP1A2 (weak), 2B6 (weak), 2C19 (weak), 3A4 (weak)

Increased Effect/Toxicity: Hydrocortisone taken with estrogen may cause corticosteroid-induced toxicity. Increased potential for thromboembolic events with anticoagulants.

Decreased Effect: Rifampin, nelfinavir, and ritonavir decrease estradiol serum concentrations. Anticonvulsants which are enzyme inducers (barbiturates, carbamazepine, phenobarbital, phenytoin, primidone) may potentially decrease estrogen levels.

Mechanism of Action Estrogens are responsible for the development and maintenance of the female reproductive system and secondary sexual characteristics. Estradiol is the principle intracellular human estrogen and is more potent than estrone and estriol at the receptor level; it is the primary estrogen secreted prior to menopause. In males and following menopause in females, estrone and estrone sulfate are more highly produced. Estrogens modulate the pituitary secretion of gonadotropins, luteinizing hormone, and follicle-stimulating hormone through a negative feedback system; estrogen replacement reduces elevated levels of these hormones. Ethinyl estradiol is a synthetic derivative of estradiol. The addition of the ethinyl group prevents rapid degradation by the liver.

Pharmacodynamics/Kinetics

Absorption: Oral: Rapid and complete

Distribution: V_d: 2-4 L/kg

Protein binding: 50% to 97%, primarily to albumin

Metabolism: Primarily hepatic via CYP3A4; less first-pass effect than with estradiol; extensive enterohepatic recirculation; converted to estrone and estriol

Bioavailability: 38% to 55%

Half-life elimination: ~8-25 hours

Time to peak: Initial: 2-3 hours; Secondary: 12 hours

Excretion: Urine and feces (as metabolites)

Dosage Oral: Adults:

Prostatic cancer (palliation): 0.15-2 mg/day

Female hypogonadism: 0.05 mg 1-3 times/day during the first 2 weeks of a theoretical menstrual cycle; follow with a progesterone during the last half of the arbitrary cycle; continue for 3-6 months. The patient should not be treated for the following 2 months to determine if additional therapy is needed.

Vasomotor symptoms associated with menopause: Usual dosage range: 0.02-0.05 mg/day; give cyclically for short-term use only and use the lowest dose that will control symptoms. Discontinue as soon as possible and administer cyclically (3 weeks on and 1 week off). Attempt to discontinue or taper medication at 3- to 6-month intervals. In severe cases (due to surgery or roentgenologic castration), doses of 0.05 mg 3 times/day may be needed initially; clinical improvement may be seen within a few weeks, decrease to lowest dose which will control symptoms

Breast cancer (palliation in appropriately selected postmenopausal women): 1 mg 3 times/ day

Dosing adjustment in hepatic impairment:
Mild to moderate liver impairment: Dosage reduction of estrogens is recommended
Severe liver impairment: **Not recommended**

Monitoring Parameters Yearly physical examination that includes blood pressure, Papanicolaou smear, breast exam, and mammogram. Monitor for signs of endometrial cancer in female patients with uterus; rule out malignancy if unexplained vaginal bleeding occurs.

Patient Information It is important to maintain schedule. Estrogens have been shown to increase the risk of endometrial cancer. Annual gynecologic and breast exams are important. You may experience nausea or vomiting (small frequent meals may help); abdominal pain; difficult/painful menstrual cycles; dizziness or mental depression; headaches; rash; breast pain; or increased/decreased libido. Report significant swelling of extremities, sudden acute pain in legs or calves, chest or abdomen; shortness of breath; severe headache or vomiting; weakness or numbness of arms or legs; or unusual vaginal bleeding. You may become intolerant to wearing contact lenses, notify prescriber if this occurs. If taking for prevention of osteoporosis, ask prescriber about calcium and vitamin D intake, and weight-bearing exercises.

Dosage Forms TAB: 0.02 mg, 0.05 mg

Ethinyl Estradiol and Desogestrel (ETH in il es tra DYE ole & des oh JES trel)

U.S. Brand Names Apri®; Cyclessa®; Desogen®; Kariva™; Mircette®; Ortho-Cept®
Synonyms Desogestrel and Ethinyl Estradiol; Ortho Cept
Therapeutic Category Contraceptive, Oral; Estrogen and Progestin Combination
Use Prevention of pregnancy
Pregnancy Risk Factor X
Dosage Oral: Adults: Female: Contraception:

Schedule 1 (Sunday starter): Dose begins on first Sunday after onset of menstruation; if the menstrual period starts on Sunday, take first tablet that very same day. **With a Sunday start, an additional method of contraception should be used until after the first 7 days of consecutive administration.**

For 21-tablet package: Dosage is 1 tablet daily for 21 consecutive days, followed by 7 days off of the medication; a new course begins on the 8th day after the last tablet is taken.
For 28-tablet package: Dosage is 1 tablet daily without interruption.

Schedule 2 (Day 1 starter): Dose starts on first day of menstrual cycle taking 1 tablet daily.
For 21-tablet package: Dosage is 1 tablet daily for 21 consecutive days, followed by 7 days off of the medication; a new course begins on the 8th day after the last tablet is taken.
For 28-tablet package: Dosage is 1 tablet daily without interruption.

If all doses have been taken on schedule and one menstrual period is missed, continue dosing cycle. If two consecutive menstrual periods are missed, pregnancy test is required before new dosing cycle is started.

Missed doses **monophasic formulations** (refer to package insert for complete information):
One dose missed: Take as soon as remembered or take 2 tablets next day
Two consecutive doses missed in the first 2 weeks: Take 2 tablets as soon as remembered or 2 tablets next 2 days. **An additional method of contraception should be used for 7 days after missed dose.**
Two consecutive doses missed in week 3 or three consecutive doses missed at any time:
Schedule 1 (Sunday starter): Continue to take 1 tablet daily until Sunday, then discard the rest of the pack, and a new pack is started that same day.
Schedule 2 (Day 1 starter): Current pack should be discarded, and a new pack started that same day. **An additional method of contraception should be used for 7 days after missed dose.**

Missed doses **biphasic/triphasic formulations** (refer to package insert for complete information):
One dose missed: Take as soon as remembered or take 2 tablets next day.
Two consecutive doses missed in week 1 or week 2 of the pack: Take 2 tablets as soon as remembered and 2 tablets the next day. Resume taking 1 tablet daily until the pack is empty. **An additional method of contraception should be used for 7 days after a missed dose.**
Two consecutive doses missed in week 3 of the pack; **an additional method of contraception must be used for 7 days after a missed dose:**
Schedule 1 (Sunday starter): Take 1 tablet every day until Sunday. Discard the remaining pack and start a new pack of pills on the same day.
Schedule 2 (Day 1 starter): Discard the remaining pack and start a new pack the same day.
Three or more consecutive doses missed; **an additional method of contraception must be used for 7 days after a missed dose:**
Schedule 1 (Sunday starter): Take 1 tablet every day until Sunday; on Sunday, discard the pack and start a new pack.
Schedule 2 (Day 1 starter): Discard the remaining pack and begin new pack of tablets starting on the same day.

Dosage adjustment in renal impairment: Specific guidelines not available; Use with caution
Dosage adjustment in hepatic impairment: Contraindicated in patients with hepatic impairment
(Continued)

Ethinyl Estradiol and Desogestrel *(Continued)*

Dosage Forms TAB, low-dose (Kariva™, Mircette®): Day 1-21: Ethinyl estradiol 0.02 mg and desogestrel 0.15 mg, Day 22-23: Inactive, Day 24-28: Ethinyl estradiol 0.01 mg (28s). **TAB, monophasic:** (Apri® 28): Ethinyl estradiol 0.03 mg and desogestrel 0.15 mg (28s); (Desogen®): Ethinyl estradiol 0.03 mg and desogestrel 0.15 mg (28s); (Ortho-Cept® 28): Ethinyl estradiol 0.03 mg and desogestrel 0.15 mg (28s). **TAB, triphasic** (Cyclessa®): Day 1-7: Ethinyl estradiol 0.025 mg and desogestrel 0.1 mg, Day 8-14: Ethinyl estradiol 0.025 mg and desogestrel 0.125 mg, Day 14-21: Ethinyl estradiol 0.025 mg and desogestrel 0.15 mg, Day 21-28: Inactive (28s)

Ethinyl Estradiol and Drospirenone

(ETH in il es tra DYE ole & droh SPYE re none)

U.S. Brand Names Yasmin®

Synonyms Drospirenone and Ethinyl Estradiol

Therapeutic Category Contraceptive, Oral

Use Prevention of pregnancy

Pregnancy Risk Factor X

Contraindications Hypersensitivity to ethinyl estradiol, drospirenone, or to any component of the formulation; thrombophlebitis or thromboembolic disorders (current or history of), cerebral vascular disease, coronary artery disease, severe hypertension; diabetes with vascular involvement; headache with focal neurological symptoms; known or suspected breast carcinoma, endometrial cancer, estrogen-dependent neoplasms, undiagnosed abnormal genital bleeding; renal insufficiency, hepatic dysfunction or tumor, adrenal insufficiency, cholestatic jaundice of pregnancy, jaundice with prior oral contraceptive use; heavy smoking (≥15 cigarettes/day) in patients >35 years of age; pregnancy

Warnings/Precautions Oral contraceptives do not protect against HIV infection or other sexually-transmitted diseases. The risk of cardiovascular side effects increases in women who smoke cigarettes, especially those who are >35 years of age; women who use oral contraceptives should be strongly advised not to smoke. Oral contraceptives may lead to increased risk of myocardial infarction, use with caution in patients with risk factors for coronary artery disease. May increase the risk of thromboembolism. Oral contraceptives may have a dose-related risk of vascular disease (decreases HDL), hypertension, and gallbladder disease; a preparation with the lowest effective estrogen/progesterone combination should be used. Women with high blood pressure should be encouraged to use another form of contraception. Oral contraceptives may cause glucose intolerance. Retinal thrombosis has been reported (rarely) with oral contraceptive use. Use with caution in patients with conditions that may be aggravated by fluid retention, depression, or patients with history of migraine. Not for use prior to menarche.

Drospirenone has antimineralocorticoid activity that may lead to hyperkalemia in patients with renal insufficiency, hepatic dysfunction, or adrenal insufficiency. Use caution with medications that may increase serum potassium.

Common Adverse Reactions

>1%:

Central nervous system: Depression, dizziness, emotional lability, headache, migraine, nervousness

Dermatologic: Acne, pruritus, rash

Endocrine & metabolic: Amenorrhea, dysmenorrhea, intermenstrual bleeding, menstrual irregularities

Gastrointestinal: Abdominal pain, diarrhea, gastroenteritis, nausea, vomiting

Genitourinary: Cystitis, leukorrhea, vaginal moniliasis, vaginitis

Neuromuscular & skeletal: Back pain, weakness

Respiratory: Bronchitis, pharyngitis, sinusitis, upper respiratory infection

Miscellaneous: Allergic reaction, flu-like syndrome, infection

Adverse reactions reported with other oral contraceptives: Appetite changes, antithrombin III decreased, arterial thromboembolism, benign liver tumors, breast changes, Budd-Chiari syndrome, carbohydrate intolerance, cataracts, cerebral hemorrhage, cerebral thrombosis, cervical changes, change in corneal curvature (steepening), cholestatic jaundice, colitis, contact lens intolerance, decreased lactation (postpartum), deep vein thrombosis, diplopia, edema, erythema multiforme, erythema nodosum; factors VII, VIII, IX, X increased; folate serum concentrations decreased, gallbladder disease, glucose intolerance, hemorrhagic eruption, hemolytic uremic syndrome, hepatic adenomas, hirsutism, hypercalcemia, hypertension, hyperglycemia, libido changes, melasma, mesenteric thrombosis, myocardial infarction, papilledema, platelet aggregability increased, porphyria, premenstrual syndrome, proptosis, prothrombin increased, pulmonary thromboembolism, renal function impairment, retinal thrombosis, sex hormone-binding globulin increased, thrombophlebitis, thyroid-binding globulin increased, total thyroid hormone (T_4) increased, triglycerides/phospholipids increased, vaginal candidiasis, weight changes

Drug Interactions

Cytochrome P450 Effect:

Ethinyl estradiol: **Substrate** of CYP3A4 (major), 3A5-7 (minor); **Inhibits** CYP1A2 (weak), 2B6 (weak), 2C19 (weak), 3A4 (weak)

Drospirenone: **Substrate** of CYP3A4 (minor); **Inhibits** CYP1A2 (weak), 2C8/9 (weak), 2C19 (weak), 3A4 (weak)

Increased Effect/Toxicity: ACE inhibitors, aldosterone antagonists, angiotensin II receptor antagonists, heparin, NSAIDs (when taken daily, long term), and potassium-sparing diuretics increase risk of hyperkalemia with concomitant use. Acetaminophen, ascorbic acid, and atorvastatin may increase plasma concentrations of oral contraceptives. Ethinyl estradiol may increase plasma concentrations of cyclosporine, prednisolone, selegiline, and theophylline. Oral contraceptives may increase (or decrease) the effects of coumarin derivatives.

Decreased Effect: Oral contraceptives may decrease the plasma concentration of acetaminophen, clofibric acid, morphine, salicylic acid, and temazepam. Aminoglutethimide, anticonvulsants (carbamazepine, felbamate, phenobarbital, phenytoin, topiramate), phenylbutazone, rifampin, and ritonavir may increase metabolism leading to decreased effect of oral contraceptives. Oral contraceptives may decrease (or increase) the effects of coumarin derivatives.

Mechanism of Action Combination oral contraceptives inhibit ovulation via a negative feedback mechanism on the hypothalamus, which alters the normal pattern of gonadotropin secretion of a follicle-stimulating hormone (FSH) and luteinizing hormone by the anterior pituitary. The follicular phase FSH and midcycle surge of gonadotropins are inhibited. In addition, oral contraceptives produce alterations in the genital tract, including changes in the cervical mucus, rendering it unfavorable for sperm penetration even if ovulation occurs. Changes in the endometrium may also occur, producing an unfavorable environment for nidation. Oral contraceptive drugs may alter the tubal transport of the ova through the fallopian tubes. Progestational agents may also alter sperm fertility. Drospirenone is a spironolactone analogue with antimineralocorticoid and antiandrogenic activity.

Pharmacodynamics/Kinetics

Ethinyl Estradiol: See Ethinyl Estradiol monograph.

Drospirenone:
Distribution: 4 L/kg
Protein binding: Serum proteins (excluding sex hormone-binding globulin and corticosteroid binding globulin): 97%
Metabolism: To inactive metabolites; minor metabolism hepatically via CYP3A4
Bioavailability: 76%
Half-life elimination: 30 hours
Time to peak: 1-3 hours
Excretion: Urine and feces

Dosage Oral: Adults: Female: Contraception: Dosage is 1 tablet daily for 28 consecutive days. Dose should be taken at the same time each day, either after the evening meal or at bedtime. Dosing may be started on the first day of menstrual period (Day 1 starter) or on the first Sunday after the onset of the menstrual period (Sunday starter).

Day 1 starter: Dose starts on first day of menstrual cycle taking 1 tablet daily.
Sunday starter: Dose begins on first Sunday after onset of menstruation; if the menstrual period starts on Sunday, take first tablet that very same day. **With a Sunday start, an additional method of contraception should be used until after the first 7 days of consecutive administration.**

If all doses have been taken on schedule and one menstrual period is missed, continue dosing cycle. If two consecutive menstrual periods are missed, pregnancy test is required before new dosing cycle is started.

If doses have been missed during the first 3 weeks and the menstrual period is missed, pregnancy should be ruled out prior to continuing treatment.

Missed doses (monophasic formulations) (refer to package insert for complete information):
One dose missed: Take as soon as remembered or take 2 tablets next day
Two consecutive doses missed in the first 2 weeks: Take 2 tablets as soon as remembered or 2 tablets next 2 days. **An additional method of contraception should be used for 7 days after missed dose.**
Two consecutive doses missed in week 3 or three consecutive doses missed at any time: **An additional method of contraception must be used for 7 days after a missed dose.**
Day 1 starter: Current pack should be discarded, and a new pack should be started that same day.
Sunday starter: Continue dose of 1 tablet daily until Sunday, then discard the rest of the pack, and a new pack should be started that same day.
Any number of doses missed in week 4: Continue taking one pill each day until pack is empty; no back-up method of contraception is needed

Dosage adjustment in renal impairment: Contraindicated in patients with renal dysfunction ($Cl_{cr} \leq 50$ mL/minute)

Dosage adjustment in hepatic impairment: Contraindicated in patients with hepatic dysfunction

Administration To be taken at the same time each day, either after the evening meal or at bedtime

Monitoring Parameters Blood pressure, pregnancy, serum potassium in high-risk patients and those on medications with potassium-retaining properties

Patient Information Take exactly as directed by prescriber (see package insert). An additional form of contraception should be used until after the first 7 consecutive days of administration. You are at risk of becoming pregnant if doses are missed. If you miss a dose, take as soon as possible or double the dose the next day. If two or more consecutive doses are missed, contact prescriber for restarting directions. Detailed and complete information on dosing and missed doses can be found in the package insert. If any number of doses are missed in week 4, continue taking one pill each day until pack is empty; no back-up method of contraception is needed. Be aware that some medications may reduce the effectiveness of oral contraceptives; (Continued)

Ethinyl Estradiol and Drospirenone *(Continued)*

an alternate form of contraception may be needed (see Drug Interactions). It is important that you check your blood pressure monthly (on same day each month) and report any increased blood pressure to prescriber. Have an annual physical assessment, Pap smear, and vision exam while taking this medication. Avoid smoking while taking this medication; smoking increases risk or adverse effects, including thromboembolic events and heart attacks. You may experience loss of appetite (small frequent meals will help); constipation (increased fluids, exercise, and dietary fiber, or stool softeners may help). If you are diabetic you should use accurate serum glucose testing to identify any changes in glucose tolerance; notify prescriber of significant changes so antidiabetic medication can be adjusted if necessary. Report immediately pain or muscle soreness; swelling, heat, or redness in calves; shortness of breath; sudden loss of vision; unresolved leg or foot swelling or weight gain (>5 lb); change in menstrual pattern (unusual bleeding, amenorrhea, breakthrough spotting); breast tenderness that does not go away; acute abdominal cramping; signs of vaginal infection (drainage, pain, itching); changes in CNS (blurred vision, confusion, acute anxiety, or unresolved depression); or other persistent adverse effects.

Dosage Forms TAB: Ethinyl estradiol 0.03 mg and drospirenone 3 mg (28s)

Ethinyl Estradiol and Ethynodiol Diacetate

(ETH in il es tra DYE ole & e thye noe DYE ole dye AS e tate)

U.S. Brand Names Demulen®; Zovia™

Synonyms Ethynodiol Diacetate and Ethinyl Estradiol

Therapeutic Category Contraceptive, Oral (Intermediate Potency Estrogen, Intermediate Potency Progestin); Contraceptive, Oral (Low Potency Estrogen, Intermediate Potency Progestin); Contraceptive, Oral (Monophasic); Estrogen and Progestin Combination

Use Prevention of pregnancy

Unlabeled/Investigational Use Treatment of hypermenorrhea, endometriosis, female hypogonadism

Pregnancy Risk Factor X

Contraindications Hypersensitivity to ethinyl estradiol, ethynodiol diacetate, or any component of the formulation; thrombophlebitis or thromboembolic disorders (current or history of), cerebral vascular disease, coronary artery disease, valvular heart disease with complications, severe hypertension; diabetes mellitus with vascular involvement; severe headache with focal neurological symptoms; known or suspected breast carcinoma, endometrial cancer, estrogen-dependent neoplasms, undiagnosed abnormal genital bleeding; hepatic dysfunction or tumor, cholestatic jaundice of pregnancy, jaundice with prior combination hormonal contraceptive use; major surgery with prolonged immobilization; heavy smoking (≥15 cigarettes/day) in patients >35 years of age; pregnancy

Warnings/Precautions Combination hormonal contraceptives do not protect against HIV infection or other sexually-transmitted diseases. The risk of cardiovascular side effects increases in women who smoke cigarettes, especially those who are >35 years of age; women who use combination hormonal contraceptives should be strongly advised not to smoke. Combination hormonal contraceptives may lead to increased risk of myocardial infarction, use with caution in patients with risk factors for coronary artery disease. May increase the risk of thromboembolism. Combination hormonal contraceptives may have a dose-related risk of vascular disease, hypertension, and gallbladder disease. Women with hypertension should be encouraged to use a nonhormonal form of contraception. The use of combination hormonal contraceptives has been associated with a slight increase in frequency of breast cancer, however, studies are not consistent. Combination hormonal contraceptives may cause glucose intolerance. Retinal thrombosis has been reported (rarely). Use with caution in patients with renal disease, conditions that may be aggravated by fluid retention, depression, or history of migraine. Not for use prior to menarche.

The minimum dosage combination of estrogen/progestin that will effectively treat the individual patient should be used. New patients should be started on products containing <50 mcg of estrogen per tablet.

Common Adverse Reactions Frequency not defined.

Cardiovascular: Arterial thromboembolism, cerebral hemorrhage, cerebral thrombosis, edema, hypertension, mesenteric thrombosis, myocardial infarction

Central nervous system: Depression, dizziness, headache, migraine, nervousness, premenstrual syndrome, stroke

Dermatologic: Acne, erythema multiforme, erythema nodosum, hirsutism, loss of scalp hair, melasma (may persist), rash (allergic)

Endocrine & metabolic: Amenorrhea, breakthrough bleeding, breast enlargement, breast secretion, breast tenderness, carbohydrate intolerance, lactation decreased (postpartum), glucose tolerance decreased, libido changes, menstrual flow changes, sex hormone-binding globulins (SHBG) increased, spotting, temporary infertility (following discontinuation), thyroid-binding globulin increased, triglycerides increased

Gastrointestinal: Abdominal cramps, appetite changes, bloating, cholestasis, colitis, gallbladder disease, jaundice, nausea, vomiting, weight gain/loss

Genitourinary: Cervical erosion changes, cervical secretion changes, cystitis-like syndrome, vaginal candidiasis, vaginitis

Hematologic: Antithrombin III decreased, folate levels decreased, hemolytic uremic syndrome, norepinephrine induced platelet aggregability increased, porphyria, prothrombin increased; factors VII, VIII, IX, and X increased

Hepatic: Benign liver tumors, Budd-Chiari syndrome, cholestatic jaundice, hepatic adenomas

Local: Thrombophlebitis

Ocular: Cataracts, change in corneal curvature (steepening), contact lens intolerance, optic neuritis, retinal thrombosis

Renal: Impaired renal function

Respiratory: Pulmonary thromboembolism

Miscellaneous: Hemorrhagic eruption

Drug Interactions

Cytochrome P450 Effect: Ethinyl estradiol: **Substrate** of CYP3A4 (major), 3A5-7 (minor); **Inhibits** CYP1A2 (weak), 2B6 (weak), 2C19 (weak), 3A4 (weak)

Increased Effect/Toxicity: Acetaminophen and ascorbic acid may increase plasma levels of estrogen component. Atorvastatin and indinavir increase plasma levels of combination hormonal contraceptives. Combination hormonal contraceptives increase the plasma levels of alprazolam, chlordiazepoxide, cyclosporine, diazepam, prednisolone, selegiline, theophylline, tricyclic antidepressants. Combination hormonal contraceptives may increase (or decrease) the effects of coumarin derivatives.

Decreased Effect: Combination hormonal contraceptives may decrease plasma levels of acetaminophen, clofibric acid, lorazepam, morphine, oxazepam, salicylic acid, temazepam. Contraceptive effect decreased by acitretin, aminoglutethimide, amprenavir, anticonvulsants, griseofulvin, lopinavir, nelfinavir, nevirapine, penicillins (effect not consistent), rifampin, ritonavir, tetracyclines (effect not consistent). Combination hormonal contraceptives may decrease (or increase) the effects of coumarin derivatives.

Mechanism of Action Combination hormonal contraceptives inhibit ovulation via a negative feedback mechanism on the hypothalamus, which alters the normal pattern of gonadotropin secretion of a follicle-stimulating hormone (FSH) and luteinizing hormone by the anterior pituitary. The follicular phase FSH and midcycle surge of gonadotropins are inhibited. In addition, combination hormonal contraceptives produce alterations in the genital tract, including changes in the cervical mucus, rendering it unfavorable for sperm penetration even if ovulation occurs. Changes in the endometrium may also occur, producing an unfavorable environment for nidation. Combination hormonal contraceptive drugs may alter the tubal transport of the ova through the fallopian tubes. Progestational agents may also alter sperm fertility.

Pharmacodynamics/Kinetics

Ethinyl Estradiol: See Ethinyl Estradiol monograph.

Ethynodiol diacetate (converted to norethindrone)

Metabolism: Hepatic conjugation

Half-life elimination: Terminal: 5-14 hours

See Norethindrone monograph.

Dosage Oral: Adults: Female: Contraception:

Schedule 1 (Sunday starter): Dose begins on first Sunday after onset of menstruation; if the menstrual period starts on Sunday, take first tablet that very same day. **With a Sunday start, an additional method of contraception should be used until after the first 7 days of consecutive administration.**

For 21-tablet package: 1 tablet/day for 21 consecutive days, followed by 7 days off of the medication; a new course begins on the 8th day after the last tablet is taken.

For 28-tablet package: 1 tablet/day without interruption.

Schedule 2 (Day 1 starter): Dose starts on first day of menstrual cycle taking 1 tablet daily.

For 21-tablet package: 1 tablet/day for 21 consecutive days, followed by 7 days off of the medication; a new course begins on the 8th day after the last tablet is taken.

For 28-tablet package: 1 tablet/day without interruption.

If all doses have been taken on schedule and one menstrual period is missed, continue dosing cycle. If two consecutive menstrual periods are missed, pregnancy test is required before new dosing cycle is started.

Missed doses **monophasic formulations** (refer to package insert for complete information):

One dose missed: Take as soon as remembered or take 2 tablets next day

Two consecutive doses missed in the first 2 weeks: Take 2 tablets as soon as remembered or 2 tablets next 2 days. **An additional method of contraception should be used for 7 days after missed dose.**

Two consecutive doses missed in week 3 or three consecutive doses missed at any time: **An additional method of contraception should be used for 7 days after missed dose:**

Schedule 1 (Sunday starter): Continue dose of 1 tablet daily until Sunday, then discard the rest of the pack, and a new pack should be started that same day.

Schedule 2 (Day 1 starter): Current package should be discarded, and a new pack should be started that same day.

Dosage adjustment in renal impairment: Specific guidelines not available; use with caution

Dosage adjustment in hepatic impairment: Contraindicated in patients with hepatic impairment

Administration Administer at the same time each day.

Monitoring Parameters Blood pressure, breast exam, Pap smear, and pregnancy; lipid profiles in patients being treated for hyperlipidemias

Patient Information Report signs or symptoms of any of the following: Thromboembolic or thrombotic disorders including sudden severe headache or vomiting, disturbance of vision or speech, loss of vision, numbness or weakness in an extremity, sharp or crushing chest pain, calf pain, shortness of breath, severe abdominal pain or mass, mental depression or unusual bleeding. Discontinue taking the medication if you suspect you are pregnant or become pregnant

Dosage Forms TAB, monophasic: (Demulen® 1/35-21) [DSC]: Ethinyl estradiol 0.035 mg and ethynodiol 1 mg (21s); (Demulen® 1/35-28): Ethinyl estradiol 0.035 mg and ethynodiol 1 mg (28s); (Demulen® 1/50-21): Ethinyl estradiol 0.05 mg and ethynodiol 1 mg (21s); (Demulen® 1/
(Continued)

Ethinyl Estradiol and Ethynodiol Diacetate *(Continued)*

50-28): Ethinyl estradiol 0.05 mg and ethynodiol 1 mg (28s); (Zovia™ 1/35-21): Ethinyl estradiol 0.035 mg and ethynodiol 1 mg (21s); (Zovia™ 1/35-28): Ethinyl estradiol 0.035 mg and ethynodiol 1 mg (28s); (Zovia™ 1/50-21): Ethinyl estradiol 0.05 mg and ethynodiol 1 mg (21s); (Zovia™ 1/50-28): Ethinyl estradiol 0.05 mg and ethynodiol 1 mg (28s)

Ethinyl Estradiol and Etonogestrel

(ETH in il es tra DYE ole & et oh noe JES trel)

U.S. Brand Names NuvaRing®

Synonyms Etonogestrel and Ethinyl Estradiol

Therapeutic Category Contraceptive, Vaginal; Estrogen and Progestin Combination

Use Prevention of pregnancy

Restrictions Initially, this product will be available only through physicians' offices.

Pregnancy Risk Factor X

Contraindications Hypersensitivity to ethinyl estradiol, etonogestrel, or any component of the formulation; thrombophlebitis or thromboembolic disorders (current or history of), major surgery with prolonged immobilization, cerebral vascular disease, coronary artery disease, valvular heart disease with complications, severe hypertension; diabetes mellitus with vascular involvement; severe headache with focal neurological symptoms; known or suspected breast carcinoma, endometrial cancer, estrogen-dependent neoplasms, undiagnosed abnormal genital bleeding; hepatic dysfunction or tumor, cholestatic jaundice of pregnancy, jaundice with prior combination hormonal contraceptive use; heavy smoking (≥15 cigarettes/day) in patients >35 years of age; conditions which make the vagina susceptible to irritation or ulceration; pregnancy

Warnings/Precautions Combination hormonal contraceptive agents do not protect against HIV infection or other sexually-transmitted diseases. The risk of cardiovascular side effects increases in women who smoke cigarettes, especially those who are >35 years of age; women who use combination hormonal contraceptives should be strongly advised not to smoke. May lead to increased risk of myocardial infarction, use with caution in patients with risk factors for coronary artery disease. May increase the risk of thromboembolism. May have a dose-related risk of vascular disease, hypertension, and gallbladder disease. Women with hypertension should be encouraged to use another form of contraception. May cause glucose intolerance. Retinal thrombosis has been reported (rarely). Use with caution in patients with renal disease, conditions that may be aggravated by fluid retention, depression, or history of migraine. Not for use prior to menarche.

Vaginally-administered combination hormonal contraceptive agents may have a similar adverse effects associated with oral contraceptive products. In order to reduce some of the possible risks, the minimum dosage combination of estrogen/progestin that will effectively treat the individual patient should be used.

Common Adverse Reactions Adverse reactions associated with oral combination hormonal contraceptive agents are also likely to appear with vaginally-administered products (frequency difficult to anticipate). Refer to oral contraceptive monographs for additional information.

5% to 14%:
Central nervous system: Headache
Gastrointestinal: Nausea, weight gain
Genitourinary: Leukorrhea, vaginitis
Respiratory: Sinusitis, upper respiratory tract infection

Frequency not defined:
Central nervous system: Emotional lability
Genitourinary: Coital problems, device expulsion, foreign body sensation, vaginal discomfort

Drug Interactions

Cytochrome P450 Effect:
Ethinyl estradiol: **Substrate** of CYP3A4 (major), 3A5-7 (minor); **Inhibits** CYP1A2 (weak), 2B6 (weak), 2C19 (weak), 3A4 (weak)
Etonogestrel: **Substrate** of CYP3A4 (minor)

Increased Effect/Toxicity: Acetaminophen and ascorbic acid may increase plasma levels of estrogen component. Atorvastatin and indinavir increase plasma levels of combination hormonal contraceptives. Combination hormonal contraceptives increase the plasma levels of alprazolam, chlordiazepoxide, cyclosporine, diazepam, prednisolone, selegiline, theophylline, tricyclic antidepressants. Combination hormonal contraceptives may increase (or decrease) the effects of coumarin derivatives.

Decreased Effect: Combination hormonal contraceptives may decrease plasma levels of acetaminophen, clofibric acid, lorazepam, morphine, oxazepam, salicylic acid, temazepam. Contraceptive effect decreased by acitretin, aminoglutethimide, amprenavir, anticonvulsants, griseofulvin, lopinavir, nelfinavir, nevirapine, penicillins (effect not consistent), rifampin, ritonavir, tetracyclines (effect not consistent). Combination hormonal contraceptives may decrease (or increase) the effects of coumarin derivatives.

Mechanism of Action Combination hormonal contraceptives inhibit ovulation via a negative feedback mechanism on the hypothalamus, which alters the normal pattern of gonadotropin secretion of a follicle-stimulating hormone (FSH) and luteinizing hormone by the anterior pituitary. The follicular phase FSH and midcycle surge of gonadotropins are inhibited. In addition, combination hormonal contraceptives produce alterations in the genital tract, including changes in the cervical mucus, rendering it unfavorable for sperm penetration even if ovulation occurs. Changes in the endometrium may also occur, producing an unfavorable environment for nidation. Combination hormonal contraceptive drugs may alter the tubal transport of the ova through the fallopian tubes. Progestational agents may also alter sperm fertility.

Pharmacodynamics/Kinetics

NuvaRing®:

Duration: Serum levels (contraceptive effectiveness) decrease after 3 weeks of continuous use

Absorption: Rapid

Bioavailability: Ethinyl estradiol: ~56% Etonogestrel: 100%

Half-life elimination: Ethinyl estradiol: 44.7 hours; Etonogestrel: 29.3 hours

Etonogestrel:

Absorption: Rapid

Protein binding: 32% to sex hormone-binding globulin (SHBG) and 66% to albumin; SHBG capacity is affected by plasma ethinyl estradiol levels

Metabolism: Hepatic via CYP3A4; forms metabolites (activity not known)

Bioavailability: 100%

Half-life elimination: 29.3 hours

Excretion: Urine, bile, and feces

Ethinyl Estradiol: See Ethinyl Estradiol monograph.

Dosage Vaginal: Adults: Female: Contraception: One ring, inserted vaginally and left in place for 3 consecutive weeks, then removed for 1 week. A new ring is inserted 7 days after the last was removed (even if bleeding is not complete) and should be inserted at approximately the same time of day the ring was removed the previous week.

Initial treatment should begin as follows (pregnancy should always be ruled out first):

No hormonal contraceptive use in the past month: Using the first day of menstruation as "Day 1," insert the ring on or prior to "Day 5," even if bleeding is not complete. **An additional form of contraception should be used for the following 7 days.***

Switching from combination oral contraceptive: Ring should be inserted within 7 days after the last active tablet was taken and no later than the first day a new cycle of tablets would begin. Additional forms of contraception are not needed.

Switching from progestin-only contraceptive: **An additional form of contraception should be used for the following 7 days with any of the following.***

If previously using a progestin-only mini-pill, insert the ring on any day of the month; do not skip days between the last pill and insertion of the ring.

If previously using an implant, insert the ring on the same day of implant removal.

If previously using a progestin-containing IUD, insert the ring on day of IUD removal.

If previously using a progestin injection, insert the ring on the day the next injection would be given.

Following complete 1st trimester abortion: Insert ring within the first five days of abortion. If not inserted within five days, follow instructions for "No hormonal contraceptive use in the past month" and instruct patient to use a nonhormonal contraceptive in the interim.

Following delivery or 2nd trimester abortion: Insert ring 4 weeks postpartum (in women who are not breast-feeding) or following 2nd trimester abortion. **An additional form of contraception should be used for the following 7 days.***

If the ring is accidentally removed from the vagina at anytime during the 3-week period of use, it may be rinsed with cool or lukewarm water (not hot) and reinserted as soon as possible. If the ring is not reinserted within three hours, contraceptive effectiveness will be decreased. **An additional form of contraception should be used until the ring has been inserted for 7 continuous days.***

If the ring has been removed for longer than 1 week, pregnancy must be ruled out prior to restarting therapy. **An additional form of contraception should be used for the following 7 days.***

If the ring has been left in place for >3 weeks, a new ring should be inserted following a 1-week (ring-free) interval. Pregnancy must be ruled out prior to insertion and **an additional form of contraception should be used for the following 7 days.***

*Note: Diaphragms may interfere with proper ring placement, and therefore, are not recommended for use as an additional form of contraception.

Dosage adjustment in renal impairment: Specific guidelines not available; use with caution.

Dosage adjustment in hepatic impairment: Contraindicated in patients with hepatic impairment

Administration Vaginal: Wash hands and remove ring from protective pouch (keep pouch for later ring disposal). Press sides of ring together between thumb and index finger and insert folded ring into vagina. Specific placement is not required for ring to be effective, but ring should be inserted far enough into the vagina as to be comfortable. To remove, hook index finger around rim and pull out. Vaginal ring **cannot** be disposed of in the toilet. New rings should be inserted at approximately the same time of day the ring was removed the previous week. If the ring accidentally falls out, it may be rinsed with cool or warm (not hot) water and replaced. However, it must be replaced within 3 hours. Refer to dosing if ring is out of place for >3 hours.

Monitoring Parameters Blood pressure, breast exam, Pap smear, and pregnancy; lipid profiles in patients being treated for hyperlipidemias

Patient Information Combination hormonal contraceptives do not protect against HIV or other sexually-transmitted diseases. Use exactly as directed by prescriber (also see package insert). You are at risk of becoming pregnant if schedule is not followed. Detailed and complete information can be found in the package insert. Be aware that some medications may reduce the effectiveness of combination hormonal contraceptives; an alternate form of contraception may be needed (diaphragms should not be used). Check all medicines (prescription and over-the-counter), herbal, and alternative products with prescriber. It is important that you check your blood pressure monthly (on same day each month) and that you have an annual physical assessment, Pap smear, and vision assessment while using this medication. Avoid (Continued)

Ethinyl Estradiol and Etonogestrel *(Continued)*

smoking; smoking increases risk or adverse effects, including thromboembolic events and heart attacks. You may experience loss of appetite (small frequent meals will help); constipation (increased fluids, exercise, and dietary fiber, or stool softeners may help). Diabetics should use accurate serum glucose testing to identify any changes in glucose tolerance; notify prescriber of significant changes so antidiabetic medication can be adjusted if necessary. Report immediately pain or muscle soreness; swelling, heat, or redness in calves; shortness of breath; sudden loss of vision; unresolved leg or foot swelling; change in menstrual pattern (unusual bleeding, amenorrhea, breakthrough spotting); breast tenderness that does not go away; acute abdominal cramping; signs of vaginal infection (drainage, pain, itching); changes in CNS (blurred vision, confusion, acute anxiety, or unresolved depression); or significant weight gain (>5 lb/week). Notify prescriber for changes in contact lens tolerance. This medication should not be used during pregnancy. If you suspect you may be pregnant, contact prescriber immediately. Breast-feeding is not recommended.

Although rare, it is possible for the ring to slip out of the vagina. This may occur if not inserted properly, while removing a tampon, during bowel movements, straining or severe constipation, or in women with a prolapsed (dropped) uterus. If the ring accidentally falls out, it may be rinsed with cool or warm (not hot) water and replaced. However, it must be replaced within 3 hours. Refer to patient leaflet or contact prescriber for additional instructions if ring is out of place for >3 hours.

Dosage Forms RING, intravaginal [3-week duration]: Ethinyl estradiol 0.015 mg/day and etonogestrel 0.12 mg/day (1s, 3s)

Ethinyl Estradiol and Levonorgestrel

(ETH in il es tra DYE ole & LEE voe nor jes trel)

U.S. Brand Names Alesse®; Aviane™; Enpresse™; Lessina™; Levlen®; Levlite™; Levora®; Nordette®; Portia™; PREVEN®; Seasonale®; Tri-Levlen®; Triphasil®; Trivora®

Synonyms Levonorgestrel and Ethinyl Estradiol

Therapeutic Category Contraceptive, Emergency; Contraceptive, Oral (Intermediate Potency Estrogen, Low Potency Progestin); Contraceptive, Oral (Low Potency Estrogen, Low Potency Progestin); Contraceptive, Oral (Monophasic); Contraceptive, Oral (Triphasic); Emergency Contraception Estrogen Derivative; Oral Progestin

Use Prevention of pregnancy; postcoital contraception

Unlabeled/Investigational Use Treatment of hypermenorrhea, endometriosis, female hypogonadism

Pregnancy Risk Factor X

Contraindications Hypersensitivity to ethinyl estradiol, levonorgestrel, or any component of the formulation; thrombophlebitis or thromboembolic disorders (current or history of); cerebral vascular disease, coronary artery disease, valvular heart disease with complications, severe hypertension; diabetes mellitus with vascular involvement; severe headache with focal neurological symptoms; known or suspected breast carcinoma, endometrial cancer, estrogen-dependent neoplasms, undiagnosed abnormal genital bleeding; hepatic dysfunction or tumor, cholestatic jaundice of pregnancy, jaundice with prior combination hormonal contraceptive use; major surgery with prolonged immobilization; heavy smoking (≥15 cigarettes/day) in patients >35 years of age; pregnancy

Warnings/Precautions Combination hormonal contraceptives do not protect against HIV infection or other sexually-transmitted diseases. The risk of cardiovascular side effects increases in women who smoke cigarettes, especially those who are >35 years of age; women who use combination hormonal contraceptives should be strongly advised not to smoke. Combination hormonal contraceptives may lead to increased risk of myocardial infarction, use with caution in patients with risk factors for coronary artery disease. May increase the risk of thromboembolism. Combination hormonal contraceptives may have a dose-related risk of vascular disease, hypertension, and gallbladder disease. Women with hypertension should be encouraged to use another form of contraception. The use of combination hormonal contraceptives has been associated with a slight increase in frequency of breast cancer, however, studies are not consistent. Combination hormonal contraceptives may cause glucose intolerance. Retinal thrombosis has been reported (rarely). Use with caution in patients with renal disease, conditions that may be aggravated by fluid retention, depression, or history of migraine. Not for use prior to menarche.

The minimum dosage combination of estrogen/progestin that will effectively treat the individual patient should be used. New patients should be started on products containing <50 mcg of estrogen per tablet.

Common Adverse Reactions Frequency not defined.

Cardiovascular: Arterial thromboembolism, cerebral hemorrhage, cerebral thrombosis, edema, hypertension, mesenteric thrombosis, myocardial infarction

Central nervous system: Depression, dizziness, headache, migraine, nervousness, premenstrual syndrome, stroke

Dermatologic: Acne, erythema multiforme, erythema nodosum, hirsutism, loss of scalp hair, melasma (may persist), rash (allergic)

Endocrine & metabolic: Amenorrhea, breakthrough bleeding, breast enlargement, breast secretion, breast tenderness, carbohydrate intolerance, lactation decreased (postpartum), glucose tolerance decreased, libido changes, menstrual flow changes, sex hormone-binding globulins (SHBG) increased, spotting, temporary infertility (following discontinuation), thyroid-binding globulin increased, triglycerides increased

Gastrointestinal: Abdominal cramps, appetite changes, bloating, cholestasis, colitis, gallbladder disease, jaundice, nausea, vomiting, weight gain/loss

Genitourinary: Cervical erosion changes, cervical secretion changes, cystitis-like syndrome, vaginal candidiasis, vaginitis

Hematologic: Antithrombin III decreased, folate levels decreased, hemolytic uremic syndrome, norepinephrine induced platelet aggregability increased, porphyria, prothrombin increased; factors VII, VIII, IX, and X increased

Hepatic: Benign liver tumors, Budd-Chiari syndrome, cholestatic jaundice, hepatic adenomas

Local: Thrombophlebitis

Ocular: Cataracts, change in corneal curvature (steepening), contact lens intolerance, optic neuritis, retinal thrombosis

Renal: Impaired renal function

Respiratory: Pulmonary thromboembolism

Miscellaneous: Hemorrhagic eruption

Drug Interactions

Cytochrome P450 Effect:

Ethinyl estradiol: **Substrate** of CYP3A4 (major), 3A5-7 (minor); **Inhibits** CYP1A2 (weak), 2B6 (weak), 2C19 (weak), 3A4 (weak)

Levonorgestrel: **Substrate** of CYP3A4 (major)

Increased Effect/Toxicity: Acetaminophen and ascorbic acid may increase plasma levels of estrogen component. Atorvastatin and indinavir increase plasma levels of combination hormonal contraceptives. Combination hormonal contraceptives increase the plasma levels of alprazolam, chlordiazepoxide, cyclosporine, diazepam, prednisolone, selegiline, theophylline, tricyclic antidepressants. Combination hormonal contraceptives may increase (or decrease) the effects of coumarin derivatives.

Decreased Effect: Combination hormonal contraceptives may decrease plasma levels of acetaminophen, clofibric acid, lorazepam, morphine, oxazepam, salicylic acid, temazepam. Contraceptive effect decreased by acitretin, aminoglutethimide, amprenavir, anticonvulsants, griseofulvin, lopinavir, nelfinavir, nevirapine, penicillins (effect not consistent), rifampin, ritonavir, tetracyclines (effect not consistent). Combination hormonal contraceptives may decrease (or increase) the effects of coumarin derivatives.

Mechanism of Action Combination hormonal contraceptives inhibit ovulation via a negative feedback mechanism on the hypothalamus, which alters the normal pattern of gonadotropin secretion of a follicle-stimulating hormone (FSH) and luteinizing hormone by the anterior pituitary. The follicular phase FSH and midcycle surge of gonadotropins are inhibited. In addition, combination hormonal contraceptives produce alterations in the genital tract, including changes in the cervical mucus, rendering it unfavorable for sperm penetration even if ovulation occurs. Changes in the endometrium may also occur, producing an unfavorable environment for nidation. Combination hormonal contraceptive drugs may alter the tubal transport of the ova through the fallopian tubes. Progestational agents may also alter sperm fertility.

Pharmacodynamics/Kinetics See individual agents.

Dosage Oral: Adults: Female:

Contraception, 28-day cycle:

Schedule 1 (Sunday starter): Dose begins on first Sunday after onset of menstruation; if the menstrual period starts on Sunday, take first tablet that very same day. With a Sunday start, an additional method of contraception should be used until after the first 7 days of consecutive administration:

For 21-tablet package: 1 tablet/day for 21 consecutive days, followed by 7 days off of the medication; a new course begins on the 8th day after the last tablet is taken

For 28-tablet package: 1 tablet/day without interruption

Schedule 2 (Day 1 starter): Dose starts on first day of menstrual cycle taking 1 tablet/day:

For 21-tablet package: 1 tablet/day for 21 consecutive days, followed by 7 days off of the medication; a new course begins on the 8th day after the last tablet is taken

For 28-tablet package: 1 tablet/day without interruption

If all doses have been taken on schedule and one menstrual period is missed, continue dosing cycle. If two consecutive menstrual periods are missed, pregnancy test is required before new dosing cycle is started.

Missed doses **monophasic formulations** (refer to package insert for complete information):

One dose missed: Take as soon as remembered or take 2 tablets next day

Two consecutive doses missed in the first 2 weeks: Take 2 tablets as soon as remembered or 2 tablets next 2 days. An additional method of contraception should be used for 7 days after missed dose.

Two consecutive doses missed in week 3 or three consecutive doses missed at any time: An additional method of contraception must be used for 7 days after a missed dose:

Schedule 1 (Sunday starter): Continue dose of 1 tablet daily until Sunday, then discard the rest of the pack, and a new pack should be started that same day.

Schedule 2 (Day 1 starter): Current pack should be discarded, and a new pack should be started that same day.

Missed doses **biphasic/triphasic formulations** (refer to package insert for complete information):

One dose missed: Take as soon as remembered or take 2 tablets next day.

Two consecutive doses missed in week 1 or week 2 of the pack: Take 2 tablets as soon as remembered and 2 tablets the next day. Resume taking 1 tablet daily until the pack is empty. An additional method of contraception should be used for 7 days after a missed dose.

Two consecutive doses missed in week 3 of the pack: An additional method of contraception must be used for 7 days after a missed dose.

Schedule 1 (Sunday starter): Take 1 tablet every day until Sunday. Discard the remaining pack and start a new pack of pills on the same day.

(Continued)

Ethinyl Estradiol and Levonorgestrel *(Continued)*

Schedule 2 (Day 1 starter): Discard the remaining pack and start a new pack the same day.

Three or more consecutive doses missed: An additional method of contraception must be used for 7 days after a missed dose.

Schedule 1 (Sunday starter): Take 1 tablet every day until Sunday; on Sunday, discard the pack and start a new pack.

Schedule 2 (Day 1 starter): Discard the remaining pack and begin new pack of tablets starting on the same day.

Contraception, 91-day cycle (Seasonale®): One active tablet/day for 84 consecutive days, followed by 1 inactive tablet/day for 7 days; if all doses have been taken on schedule and one menstrual period is missed, pregnancy should be ruled out prior to continuing therapy. Missed doses:

One dose missed: Take as soon as remembered or take 2 tablets the next day

Two consecutive doses missed: Take 2 tablets as soon as remembered or 2 tablets the next 2 days. An additional nonhormonal method of contraception should be used for 7 consecutive days after the missed dose.

Three or more consecutive doses missed: Do not take the missed doses; continue taking 1 tablet/day until pack is complete. Bleeding may occur during the following week. An additional nonhormonal method of contraception should be used for 7 consecutive days after the missed dose.

Emergency contraception (PREVEN®): Initial: 2 tablets as soon as possible (but within 72 hours of unprotected intercourse), followed by a second dose of 2 tablets 12 hours later. Repeat dose or use antiemetic if vomiting occurs within 1 hour of dose.

Dosage adjustment in renal impairment: Specific guidelines not available; use with caution

Dosage adjustment in hepatic impairment: Contraindicated in patients with hepatic impairment

Administration Administer at the same time each day.

Monitoring Parameters Blood pressure, breast exam, Pap smear, and pregnancy; lipid profiles in patients being treated for hyperlipidemias

Patient Information Report signs or symptoms of any of the following: Thromboembolic or thrombotic disorders including sudden severe headache or vomiting, disturbance of vision or speech, loss of vision, numbness or weakness in an extremity, sharp or crushing chest pain, calf pain, shortness of breath, severe abdominal pain or mass, mental depression or unusual bleeding. If any doses are missed, alternative contraceptive methods should be used for the next 2 days or until 2 days into the new cycle. Discontinue taking the medication if you suspect you are pregnant or become pregnant.

Emergency contraceptive kit (PREVEN®) is **not** recommended for ongoing pregnancy protection or as a routine form of contraception. PREVEN® emergency contraceptive kit contains a pregnancy test. This test can be used to verify an existing pregnancy resulting from intercourse that occurred earlier in the concurrent menstrual cycle or the previous cycle. If a positive pregnancy result is obtained, the patient should **not** take the pills in the PREVEN® kit. The patient should be instructed that if she vomits within 1 hour of taking either dose of the medication, she should contact her healthcare professional to discuss whether to repeat that dose or to take an antinausea medication.

Dosage Forms KIT [4 tablets and a pregnancy test] (PREVEN®): Ethinyl estradiol 0.05 mg and levonorgestrel 0.25 mg (4s). **TAB** (PREVEN®): Ethinyl estradiol 0.05 mg and levonorgestrel 0.25 mg (4s). **TAB, low-dose:** (Alesse®, Lessina™): Ethinyl estradiol 0.02 mg and levonorgestrel 0.1 mg (21s); (Alesse®, Lessina™, Levlite™): Ethinyl estradiol 0.02 mg and levonorgestrel 0.1 mg (28s); (Aviane™ 28): Ethinyl estradiol 0.02 mg and levonorgestrel 0.1 mg. **TAB, monophasic:** (Levlen®, Nordette®, Portia™): Ethinyl estradiol 0.03 mg and levonorgestrel 0.15 mg (21s, 28s); (Seasonale®): Ethinyl estradiol 0.03 mg and levonorgestrel 0.15 mg (91s). **TAB, triphasic:** (Enpresse™): Day 1-6: Ethinyl estradiol 0.03 mg and levonorgestrel 0.05, Day 7-11: Ethinyl estradiol 0.04 mg and levonorgestrel 0.075, Day 12-21: Ethinyl estradiol 0.03 mg and levonorgestrel 0.125; (Tri-Levlen® 21, Triphasil® 21): Day 1-6: Ethinyl estradiol 0.03 mg and levonorgestrel 0.05 mg, Day 7-11: Ethinyl estradiol 0.04 mg and levonorgestrel 0.075 mg, Day 12-21: Ethinyl estradiol 0.03 mg and levonorgestrel 0.125 mg (21s); (Tri-Levlen® 28, Triphasil® 28): Day 1-6: Ethinyl estradiol 0.03 mg and levonorgestrel 0.05 mg, Day 7-11: Ethinyl estradiol 0.04 mg and levonorgestrel 0.075 mg, Day 12-21: Ethinyl estradiol 0.03 mg and levonorgestrel 0.125 mg, Day 22-28: Inactive (28s); (Trivora® 28): Day 1-6: Ethinyl estradiol 0.03 mg and levonorgestrel 0.05 mg, Day 7-11: Ethinyl estradiol 0.04 mg and levonorgestrel 0.075 mg, Day 12-21: Ethinyl estradiol 0.03 mg and levonorgestrel 0.125 mg, Day 22-28: Inactive (28s)

♦ **Ethinyl Estradiol and NGM** *see* Ethinyl Estradiol and Norgestimate *on page 490*

Ethinyl Estradiol and Norelgestromin

(ETH in il es tra DYE ole & nor el JES troe min)

U.S. Brand Names Ortho Evra™

Synonyms Norelgestromin and Ethinyl Estradiol; Ortho-Evra

Therapeutic Category Contraceptive, Topical Patch; Estrogen and Progestin Combination

Use Prevention of pregnancy

Pregnancy Risk Factor X

Dosage Topical: Adults: Female:

Contraception: Apply one patch each week for 3 weeks (21 total days); followed by one week that is patch-free. Each patch should be applied on the same day each week ("patch change day") and only one patch should be worn at a time. No more than 7 days should pass during the patch-free interval.

Schedule 1 (Sunday starter): Dose begins on first Sunday after onset of menstruation; if the menstrual period starts on Sunday, apply one patch that very same day. **With a Sunday start, an additional method of contraception (nonhormonal) should be used until after the first 7 days of consecutive administration.** Each patch change will then occur on Sunday.

Schedule 2 (Day 1 starter): Dose starts on first day of menstrual cycle, applying one patch during the first 24 hours of menstrual cycle. No back-up method of contraception is needed as long as the patch is applied on the first day of cycle. Each patch change will then occur on that same day of the week.

Additional dosing considerations:

No bleeding during patch-free week/missed menstrual period: If patch has been applied as directed, continue treatment on usual "patch change day". If used correctly, no bleeding during patch-free week does not necessarily indicate pregnancy. However, if no withdrawal bleeding occurs for 2 consecutive cycles, pregnancy should be ruled out. If patch has not been applied as directed, and one menstrual period is missed, pregnancy should be ruled out prior to continuing treatment.

If a patch becomes partially or completely detached for <24 hours: Try to reapply to same place, or replace with a new patch immediately. Do not reapply if patch is no longer sticky, if it is sticking to itself or another surface, or if it has material sticking to it.

If a patch becomes partially or completely detached for >24 hours (or time period is unknown): Apply a new patch and use this day of the week as the new "patch change day" from this point on. **An additional method of contraception (nonhormonal) should be used until after the first 7 days of consecutive administration.**

Switching from oral contraceptives: Apply first patch on the first day of withdrawal bleeding. If there is no bleeding within 5 days of taking the last active tablet, pregnancy must first be ruled out. If patch is applied later than the first day of bleeding, **an additional method of contraception (nonhormonal) should be used until after the first 7 days of consecutive administration**

Use after childbirth: Therapy should not be started <4 weeks after childbirth. Pregnancy should be ruled out prior to treatment if menstrual periods have not restarted. **An additional method of contraception (nonhormonal) should be used until after the first 7 days of consecutive administration.**

Use after abortion or miscarriage: Therapy may be started immediately if abortion/miscarriage occur within the first trimester. If therapy is not started within 5 days, follow instructions for first time use. If abortion/miscarriage occur during the second trimester, therapy should not be started for at least 4 weeks. Follow directions for use after childbirth.

Dosage adjustment in renal impairment: Specific guidelines not available; use with caution

Dosage adjustment in hepatic impairment: Contraindicated in patients with hepatic impairment

Dosage Forms PATCH, transdermal: Ethinyl estradiol 0.75 mg and norelgestromin 6 mg (1s, 3s)

Ethinyl Estradiol and Norethindrone

(ETH in il es tra DYE ole & nor eth IN drone)

U.S. Brand Names Brevicon®; Estrostep® Fe; femhrt®; Junel™; Loestrin®; Loestrin® Fe; Microgestin™ Fe; Modicon®; Necon® 0.5/35; Necon® 1/35; Necon® 7/7/7; Necon® 10/11; Norinyl® 1+35; Nortrel™; Nortrel™ 7/7/7; Ortho-Novum®; Ovcon®; Tri-Norinyl®

Synonyms Norethindrone Acetate and Ethinyl Estradiol; Ortho Novum

Therapeutic Category Contraceptive, Oral (Biphasic); Contraceptive, Oral (Intermediate Potency Estrogen, Intermediate Potency Progestin); Contraceptive, Oral (Intermediate Potency Estrogen, Low Potency Progestin); Contraceptive, Oral (Low Potency Estrogen, Low Potency Progestin); Contraceptive, Oral (Monophasic); Contraceptive, Oral (Triphasic)

Use Prevention of pregnancy; treatment of acne; moderate to severe vasomotor symptoms associated with menopause; prevention of osteoporosis (in women at significant risk only)

Unlabeled/Investigational Use Treatment of hypermenorrhea, endometriosis, female hypogonadism

Pregnancy Risk Factor X

Contraindications Hypersensitivity to ethinyl estradiol, norethindrone, norethindrone acetate, or any component of the formulation; thrombophlebitis or thromboembolic disorders (current or history of), cerebral vascular disease, coronary artery disease, severe hypertension; diabetes mellitus with vascular involvement; severe headache with focal neurological symptoms; known or suspected breast carcinoma; endometrial cancer, estrogen-dependent neoplasms, undiagnosed abnormal genital bleeding; hepatic dysfunction or tumor, cholestatic jaundice of pregnancy, jaundice with prior combination hormonal contraceptive use; major surgery with prolonged immobilization; heavy smoking (≥15 cigarettes/day) in patients >35 years of age; pregnancy

Warnings/Precautions Combination hormonal contraceptives do not protect against HIV infection or other sexually-transmitted diseases. The risk of cardiovascular side effects increases in women who smoke cigarettes, especially those who are >35 years of age; women who use combination hormonal contraceptives should be strongly advised not to smoke. Combination hormonal contraceptives may lead to increased risk of myocardial infarction, use with caution in patients with risk factors for coronary artery disease. May increase the risk of thromboembolism. Combination hormonal contraceptives may have a dose-related risk of vascular disease, hypertension, and gallbladder disease. Women with hypertension should be (Continued)

487

Ethinyl Estradiol and Norethindrone *(Continued)*

encouraged to use another form of contraception. The use of combination hormonal contraceptives has been associated with a slight increase in frequency of breast cancer, however, studies are not consistent. Combination hormonal contraceptives may cause glucose intolerance. Retinal thrombosis has been reported (rarely). Use with caution in patients with renal disease, conditions that may be aggravated by fluid retention, depression, or history of migraine. Not for use prior to menarche.

The minimum dosage combination of estrogen/progestin that will effectively treat the individual patient should be used. New patients should be started on products containing <50 mcg of estrogen per tablet.

Acne: For use only in females ≥15 years, who also desire combination hormonal contraceptive therapy, are unresponsive to topical treatments, and have no contraindications to combination hormonal contraceptive use; treatment must continue for at least 6 months.

Vasomotor symptoms associated with menopause and prevention of osteoporosis: For use only in postmenopausal women with an intact uterus. Use for shortest duration possible consistent with treatment goals. Conduct periodic risk:benefit assessments. When used for the prevention of osteoporosis, estrogen/progestin products should be reserved for use in women at significant risk only; nonestrogen therapies should be considered.

Common Adverse Reactions As reported with oral contraceptive agents. Frequency not defined.

Cardiovascular: Arterial thromboembolism, cerebral hemorrhage, cerebral thrombosis, edema, hypertension, mesenteric thrombosis, myocardial infarction

Central nervous system: Depression, dizziness, headache, migraine, nervousness, premenstrual syndrome, stroke

Dermatologic: Acne, erythema multiforme, erythema nodosum, hirsutism, loss of scalp hair, melasma (may persist), rash (allergic)

Endocrine & metabolic: Amenorrhea, breakthrough bleeding, breast enlargement, breast secretion, breast tenderness, carbohydrate intolerance, lactation decreased (postpartum), glucose tolerance decreased, libido changes, menstrual flow changes, sex hormone-binding globulins (SHBG) increased, spotting, temporary infertility (following discontinuation), thyroid-binding globulin increased, triglycerides increased

Gastrointestinal: Abdominal cramps, appetite changes, bloating, cholestasis, colitis, gallbladder disease, jaundice, nausea, vomiting, weight gain/loss

Genitourinary: Cervical erosion changes, cervical secretion changes, cystitis-like syndrome, vaginal candidiasis, vaginitis

Hematologic: Antithrombin III decreased, folate levels decreased, hemolytic uremic syndrome, norepinephrine induced platelet aggregability increased, porphyria, prothrombin increased; factors VII, VIII, IX, and X

Hepatic: Benign liver tumors, Budd-Chiari syndrome, cholestatic jaundice, hepatic adenomas

Local: Thrombophlebitis

Ocular: Cataracts, change in corneal curvature (steepening), contact lens intolerance, optic neuritis, retinal thrombosis

Renal: Impaired renal function

Respiratory: Pulmonary thromboembolism

Miscellaneous: Hemorrhagic eruption

Drug Interactions

Cytochrome P450 Effect:

Ethinyl estradiol: **Substrate** of CYP3A4 (major), 3A5-7 (minor); **Inhibits** CYP1A2 (weak), 2B6 (weak), 2C19 (weak), 3A4 (weak)

Norethindrone: **Substrate** of CYP3A4 (major); Induces CYP2C19 (weak)

Increased Effect/Toxicity: Acetaminophen and ascorbic acid may increase plasma levels of estrogen component. Atorvastatin and indinavir increase plasma levels of combination hormonal contraceptives. Combination hormonal contraceptives increase the plasma levels of alprazolam, chlordiazepoxide, cyclosporine, diazepam, prednisolone, selegiline, theophylline, tricyclic antidepressants. Combination hormonal contraceptives may increase (or decrease) the effects of coumarin derivatives.

Decreased Effect: Combination hormonal contraceptives may decrease plasma levels of acetaminophen, clofibric acid, lorazepam, morphine, oxazepam, salicylic acid, temazepam. Contraceptive effect decreased by acitretin, aminoglutethimide, amprenavir, anticonvulsants, griseofulvin, lopinavir, nelfinavir, nevirapine, penicillins (effect not consistent), rifampin, ritonavir, tetracyclines (effect not consistent), troglitazone. Oral contraceptives may decrease (or increase) the effects of coumarin derivatives.

Mechanism of Action Combination oral contraceptives inhibit ovulation via a negative feedback mechanism on the hypothalamus, which alters the normal pattern of gonadotropin secretion of a follicle-stimulating hormone (FSH) and luteinizing hormone by the anterior pituitary. The follicular phase FSH and midcycle surge of gonadotropins are inhibited. In addition, combination hormonal contraceptives produce alterations in the genital tract, including changes in the cervical mucus, rendering it unfavorable for sperm penetration even if ovulation occurs. Changes in the endometrium may also occur, producing an unfavorable environment for nidation. Combination hormonal contraceptive drugs may alter the tubal transport of the ova through the fallopian tubes. Progestational agents may also alter sperm fertility.

In postmenopausal women, exogenous estrogen is used to replace decreased endogenous production. The addition of progestin reduces the incidence of endometrial hyperplasia and risk of adenocarcinoma in women with an intact uterus.

Pharmacodynamics/Kinetics See individual agents.

Dosage Oral:

Adolescents ≥15 years and Adults: Female: Acne: Estrostep®: Refer to dosing for contraception

Adults: Female:

Moderate to severe vasomotor symptoms associated with menopause: femhrt® 1/5: 1 tablet daily; patients should be re-evaluated at 3- to 6-month intervals to determine if treatment is still necessary

Prevention of osteoporosis: femhrt® 1/5: 1 tablet daily

Contraception:

Schedule 1 (Sunday starter): Dose begins on first Sunday after onset of menstruation; if the menstrual period starts on Sunday, take first tablet that very same day. With a Sunday start, an additional method of contraception should be used until after the first 7 days of consecutive administration.

For 21-tablet package: Dosage is 1 tablet daily for 21 consecutive days, followed by 7 days off of the medication; a new course begins on the 8th day after the last tablet is taken.

For 28-tablet package: Dosage is 1 tablet daily without interruption.

Schedule 2 (Day 1 starter): Dose starts on first day of menstrual cycle taking 1 tablet daily.

For 21-tablet package: Dosage is 1 tablet daily for 21 consecutive days, followed by 7 days off of the medication; a new course begins on the 8th day after the last tablet is taken.

For 28-tablet package: Dosage is 1 tablet daily without interruption.

If all doses have been taken on schedule and one menstrual period is missed, continue dosing cycle. If two consecutive menstrual periods are missed, pregnancy test is required before new dosing cycle is started.

Missed doses **monophasic formulations** (refer to package insert for complete information):

One dose missed: Take as soon as remembered or take 2 tablets next day Two consecutive doses missed in the first 2 weeks: Take 2 tablets as soon as remembered or 2 tablets next 2 days. An additional method of contraception should be used for 7 days after missed dose.

Two consecutive doses missed in week 3 or three consecutive doses missed at any time: An additional method of contraception must be used for 7 days after a missed dose.

Schedule 1 (Sunday starter): Continue dose of 1 tablet daily until Sunday, then discard the rest of the pack, and a new pack should be started that same day.

Schedule 2 (Day 1 starter): Current pack should be discarded, and a new pack should be started that same day.

Missed doses **biphasic/triphasic formulations** (refer to package insert for complete information):

One dose missed: Take as soon as remembered or take 2 tablets next day.

Two consecutive doses missed in week 1 or week 2 of the pack: Take 2 tablets as soon as remembered and 2 tablets the next day. Resume taking 1 tablet daily until the pack is empty. An additional method of contraception should be used for 7 days after a missed dose.

Two consecutive doses missed in week 3 of the pack: An additional method of contraception must be used for 7 days after a missed dose.

Schedule 1 (Sunday Starter): Take 1 tablet every day until Sunday. Discard the remaining pack and start a new pack of pills on the same day.

Schedule 2 (Day 1 starter): Discard the remaining pack and start a new pack the same day.

Three or more consecutive doses missed: An additional method of contraception must be used for 7 days after a missed dose.

Schedule 1 (Sunday Starter): Take 1 tablet every day until Sunday; on Sunday, discard the pack and start a new pack.

Schedule 2 (Day 1 Starter): Discard the remaining pack and begin new pack of tablets starting on the same day.

Dosage adjustment in renal impairment: Specific guidelines not available; use with caution.

Dosage adjustment in hepatic impairment: Contraindicated in patients with hepatic impairment.

Administration Administer at the same time each day. Chewable tablets may be swallowed whole or chewed; if chewed, drink 8 ounces of liquid immediately after swallowing.

Monitoring Parameters Blood pressure, breast exam, Pap smear, and pregnancy; lipid profiles in patients being treated for hyperlipidemias

Patient Information Take exactly as directed; use additional method of birth control during first week of administration of first cycle; photosensitivity may occur. Women should report signs or symptoms of any of the following: Thromboembolic or thrombotic disorders including sudden severe headache or vomiting, disturbance of vision or speech, loss of vision, numbness or weakness in an extremity, sharp or crushing chest pain, calf pain, shortness of breath, severe abdominal pain or mass, mental depression, or unusual bleeding. When any doses are missed, alternative contraceptive methods should be used for the next 2 days or until 2 days into the new cycle. Discontinue medication if you suspect you are pregnant or become pregnant.

Dosage Forms TAB (femhrt® 1/5): Ethinyl estradiol 0.005 mg and norethindrone 1 mg. **TAB, monophasic** (Brevicon®): Ethinyl estradiol 0.035 mg and norethindrone 0.5 mg (28s); (Junel™ 21 1/20, Loestrin® 21 1/20): Ethinyl estradiol 0.02 mg and norethindrone 1 mg (21s); (Junel™ 21 1.5/30, Loestrin® 21 1.5/30): Ethinyl estradiol 0.03 mg and norethindrone 1.5 mg (21s); (Junel™ Fe 1/20, Loestrin® Fe 1/20, Microgestin™ Fe 1/20): Ethinyl estradiol 0.02 mg and norethindrone 1 mg and ferrous fumarate 75 mg (28s); (Junel™ Fe 1.5/30, Loestrin® Fe 1.5/30, (Continued)

Ethinyl Estradiol and Norethindrone *(Continued)*

Microgestin™ Fe 1.5/30): Ethinyl estradiol 0.03 mg and norethindrone 1.5 mg and ferrous fumarate 75 mg (28s); (Modicon® 21): Ethinyl estradiol 0.035 mg and norethindrone 0.5 mg (21s); (Modicon® 28): Ethinyl estradiol 0.035 mg and norethindrone 0.5 mg (28s); (Necon® 0.5/35-21): Ethinyl estradiol 0.035 mg and norethindrone 0.5 mg (21s); (Necon® 0.5/35-28): Ethinyl estradiol 0.035 mg and norethindrone 0.5 mg (28s); (Necon® 1/35-21): Ethinyl estradiol 0.035 mg and norethindrone 1 mg (21s); (Necon® 1/35-28): Ethinyl estradiol 0.035 mg and norethindrone 1 mg (28s); (Norinyl® 1+35): Ethinyl estradiol 0.035 mg and norethindrone 1 mg (28s); (Nortrel™ 0.5/35 mg): Ethinyl estradiol 0.035 mg and norethindrone 0.5 mg (21s); Ethinyl estradiol 0.035 mg and norethindrone 0.5 mg (28s); (Nortrel™ 1/35 mg): Ethinyl estradiol 0.035 mg and norethindrone 1 mg (21s); Ethinyl estradiol 0.035 mg and norethindrone 1 mg (28s); (Ortho-Novum® 1/35 21): Ethinyl estradiol 0.035 mg and norethindrone 1 mg (21s); (Ortho-Novum® 1/35 28): Ethinyl estradiol 0.035 mg and norethindrone 1 mg (28s); (Ovcon® 35 21-day): Ethinyl estradiol 0.035 mg and norethindrone 0.4 mg (21s); (Ovcon® 35 28-day): Ethinyl estradiol 0.035 mg and norethindrone 0.4 mg (28s); (Ovcon® 50): Ethinyl estradiol 0.05 mg and norethindrone 1 mg (28s). **TAB, biphasic** (Necon® 10/11-21): Day 1-10: Ethinyl estradiol 0.035 mg and norethindrone 0.5 mg, Day 11-21: Ethinyl estradiol 0.035 mg and norethindrone 1 mg (21s); (Necon® 10/11-28): Day 1-10: Ethinyl estradiol 0.035 mg and norethindrone 0.5 mg, Day 11-21: Ethinyl estradiol 0.035 mg and norethindrone 1 mg, Day 22-28: Inactive (28s); (Ortho-Novum® 10/11-21): Day 1-10: Ethinyl estradiol 0.035 mg and norethindrone 0.5 mg, Day 11-21: Ethinyl estradiol 0.035 mg and norethindrone 1 mg (21s); (Ortho-Novum® 10/11-28): Day 1-10: Ethinyl estradiol 0.035 mg and norethindrone 0.5 mg, Day 11-21: Ethinyl estradiol 0.035 mg and norethindrone 1 mg, Day 22-28: Inactive (28s). **TAB, triphasic** (Estrostep® Fe): Day 1-5: Ethinyl estradiol 0.02 mg and norethindrone acetate 1 mg, Day 6-12: Ethinyl estradiol 0.03 mg and norethindrone acetate 1 mg, Day 13-21: Ethinyl estradiol 0.035 mg and norethindrone acetate 1 mg, Day 22-28: Ferrous fumarate 75 mg (28s); (Necon® 7/7/7, Ortho-Novum® 7/7/7 28): Day 1-7: Ethinyl estradiol 0.035 mg and norethindrone 0.5 mg, Day 8-14: Ethinyl estradiol 0.035 mg and norethindrone 0.75 mg, Day 15-21: Ethinyl estradiol 0.035 mg and norethindrone 1 mg, Day 22-28: Inactive (28s); (Nortrel™ 7/7/7 21): Day 1-7: Ethinyl estradiol 0.035 mg and norethindrone 0.5 mg; Day 8-14: Ethinyl estradiol 0.035 mg and norethindrone 0.75 mg; Day 15-21: Ethinyl estradiol 0.035 mg and norethindrone 1 mg (21s); (Nortrel™ 7/7/7 28): Day 1-7: Ethinyl estradiol 0.035 mg and norethindrone 0.5 mg; Day 8-14: Ethinyl estradiol 0.035 mg and norethindrone 0.75 mg; Day 15-21: Ethinyl estradiol 0.035 mg and norethindrone 1 mg; Day 22-28: Inactive (28s); (Ortho-Novum® 7/7/7 21): Day 1-7: Ethinyl estradiol 0.035 mg and norethindrone 0.5 mg, Day 8-14: Ethinyl estradiol 0.035 mg and norethindrone 0.75 mg, Day 15-21: Ethinyl estradiol 0.035 mg and norethindrone 1 mg (21s); (Tri-Norinyl® 28): Day 1-7: Ethinyl estradiol 0.035 mg and norethindrone 0.5 mg, Day 8-16: Ethinyl estradiol 0.035 mg and norethindrone 1 mg, Day 17-21: Ethinyl estradiol 0.035 mg and norethindrone 0.5 mg, Day 22-28: Inactive (28s). **TAB, chewable, monophasic** (Ovcon® 35 28-day): Ethinyl estradiol 0.035 mg and norethindrone 0.4 mg

Ethinyl Estradiol and Norgestimate

(ETH in il es tra DYE ole & nor JES ti mate)

U.S. Brand Names MonoNessa™; Ortho-Cyclen®; Ortho Tri-Cyclen®; Ortho Tri-Cyclen® Lo; Sprintec™

Synonyms Ethinyl Estradiol and NGM; Norgestimate and Ethinyl Estradiol; Ortho Cyclen; Ortho Tri Cyclen

Therapeutic Category Contraceptive, Oral

Use Prevention of pregnancy; treatment of acne

Pregnancy Risk Factor X

Contraindications Hypersensitivity to ethinyl estradiol, norgestimate, or any component of the formulation; thrombophlebitis or thromboembolic disorders (current or history of), cerebral vascular disease, coronary artery disease, valvular heart disease with complications, severe hypertension; severe headache with focal neurological symptoms; known or suspected breast carcinoma, endometrial cancer, estrogen-dependent neoplasms, undiagnosed abnormal genital bleeding; hepatic dysfunction or tumor, cholestatic jaundice of pregnancy, jaundice with prior combination hormonal contraceptive use; heavy smoking (≥15 cigarettes/day) in patients >35 years of age; pregnancy

Warnings/Precautions Combination hormonal contraceptives do not protect against HIV infection or other sexually-transmitted diseases. The risk of cardiovascular side effects increases in women who smoke cigarettes, especially those who are >35 years of age; women who use combination hormonal contraceptives should be strongly advised not to smoke. Combination hormonal contraceptives may lead to increased risk of myocardial infarction, use with caution in patients with risk factors for coronary artery disease. May increase the risk of thromboembolism. Combination hormonal contraceptives may have a dose-related risk of vascular disease, hypertension, and gallbladder disease. Women with hypertension should be encouraged to use a nonhormonal form of contraception. The use of combination hormonal contraceptives has been associated with a slight increase in frequency of breast cancer, however, studies are not consistent. Combination hormonal contraceptives may cause glucose intolerance. Retinal thrombosis has been reported (rarely). Use with caution in patients with renal disease, conditions that may be aggravated by fluid retention, depression, or history of migraine. Not for use prior to menarche.

The minimum dosage combination of estrogen/progestin that will effectively treat the individual patient should be used. New patients should be started on products containing <50 mcg of estrogen per tablet.

Acne: For use only in females ≥15 years, who also desire combination hormonal contraceptive therapy, are unresponsive to topical treatments, and have no contraindications to combination hormonal contraceptive use; treatment must continue for at least 6 months.

Common Adverse Reactions Frequency not defined.

Cardiovascular: Arterial thromboembolism, cerebral hemorrhage, cerebral thrombosis, edema, hypertension, mesenteric thrombosis, myocardial infarction

Central nervous system: Depression, dizziness, headache, migraine, nervousness, premenstrual syndrome, stroke

Dermatologic: Acne, erythema multiforme, erythema nodosum, hirsutism, loss of scalp hair, melasma (may persist), rash (allergic)

Endocrine & metabolic: Amenorrhea, breakthrough bleeding, breast enlargement, breast secretion, breast tenderness, carbohydrate intolerance, lactation decreased (postpartum), glucose tolerance decreased, libido changes, menstrual flow changes, sex hormone-binding globulins (SHBG) increased, spotting, temporary infertility (following discontinuation), thyroid-binding globulin increased, triglycerides increased

Gastrointestinal: Abdominal cramps, appetite changes, bloating, cholestasis, colitis, gallbladder disease, jaundice, nausea, vomiting, weight gain/loss

Genitourinary: Cervical erosion changes, cervical secretion changes, cystitis-like syndrome, vaginal candidiasis, vaginitis

Hematologic: Antithrombin III decreased, folate levels decreased, hemolytic uremic syndrome, norepinephrine induced platelet aggregability increased, porphyria, prothrombin increased; factors VII, VIII, IX, and X increased

Hepatic: Benign liver tumors, Budd-Chiari syndrome, cholestatic jaundice, hepatic adenomas

Local: Thrombophlebitis

Ocular: Cataracts, change in corneal curvature (steepening), contact lens intolerance, optic neuritis, retinal thrombosis

Renal: Impaired renal function

Respiratory: Pulmonary thromboembolism

Miscellaneous: Hemorrhagic eruption

Drug Interactions

Cytochrome P450 Effect: Ethinyl estradiol: **Substrate** of CYP3A4 (major), 3A5-7 (minor); **Inhibits** CYP1A2 (weak), 2B6 (weak), 2C19 (weak), 3A4 (weak)

Increased Effect/Toxicity: Acetaminophen and ascorbic acid may increase plasma levels of estrogen component. Atorvastatin and indinavir increase plasma levels of combination hormonal contraceptives. Combination hormonal contraceptives increase the plasma levels of alprazolam, chlordiazepoxide, cyclosporine, diazepam, prednisolone, selegiline, theophylline, tricyclic antidepressants. Combination hormonal contraceptives may increase (or decrease) the effects of coumarin derivatives.

Decreased Effect: Combination hormonal contraceptives may decrease plasma levels of acetaminophen, clofibric acid, lorazepam, morphine, oxazepam, salicylic acid, temazepam. Contraceptive effect decreased by acitretin, aminoglutethimide, amprenavir, anticonvulsants, griseofulvin, lopinavir, nelfinavir, nevirapine, penicillins (effect not consistent), rifampin, ritonavir, tetracyclines (effect not consistent). Combination hormonal contraceptives may decrease (or increase) the effects of coumarin derivatives.

Mechanism of Action Combination hormonal contraceptives inhibit ovulation via a negative feedback mechanism on the hypothalamus, which alters the normal pattern of gonadotropin secretion of a follicle-stimulating hormone (FSH) and luteinizing hormone by the anterior pituitary. The follicular phase FSH and midcycle surge of gonadotropins are inhibited. In addition, combination hormonal contraceptives produce alterations in the genital tract, including changes in the cervical mucus, rendering it unfavorable for sperm penetration even if ovulation occurs. Changes in the endometrium may also occur, producing an unfavorable environment for nidation. Combination hormonal contraceptive drugs may alter the tubal transport of the ova through the fallopian tubes. Progestational agents may also alter sperm fertility.

Pharmacodynamics/Kinetics

Ethinyl estradiol: See Ethinyl Estradiol monograph.

Norgestimate:

Absorption: Well absorbed

Protein binding: To albumin and sex hormone-binding globulin (SHBG); SHBG capacity is affected by plasma ethinyl estradiol levels

Metabolism: Hepatic; forms 17-deacetylnorgestimate (major active metabolite) and other metabolites

Half-life elimination: 17-deacetylnorgestimate: 12-30 hours

Excretion: Urine and feces

Dosage Oral:

Children ≥15 years and Adults: Female: Acne (Ortho Tri-Cyclen®): Refer to dosing for contraception

Adults: Female:

Contraception:

Schedule 1 (Sunday starter): Dose begins on first Sunday after onset of menstruation; if the menstrual period starts on Sunday, take first tablet that very same day. **With a Sunday start, an additional method of contraception should be used until after the first 7 days of consecutive administration.**

For 21-tablet package: Dosage is 1 tablet daily for 21 consecutive days, followed by 7 days off of the medication; a new course begins on the 8th day after the last tablet is taken.

For 28-tablet package: Dosage is 1 tablet daily without interruption.

Schedule 2 (Day 1 starter): Dose starts on first day of menstrual cycle taking 1 tablet daily. (Continued)

Ethinyl Estradiol and Norgestimate *(Continued)*

For 21-tablet package: Dosage is 1 tablet daily for 21 consecutive days, followed by 7 days off of the medication; a new course begins on the 8th day after the last tablet is taken.

For 28-tablet package: Dosage is 1 tablet daily without interruption.

If all doses have been taken on schedule and one menstrual period is missed, continue dosing cycle. If two consecutive menstrual periods are missed, pregnancy test is required before new dosing cycle is started.

Missed doses **monophasic formulations** (refer to package insert for complete information):

One dose missed: Take as soon as remembered or take 2 tablets next day

Two consecutive doses missed in the first 2 weeks: Take 2 tablets as soon as remembered or 2 tablets next 2 days. **An additional method of contraception should be used for 7 days after missed dose.**

Two consecutive doses missed in week 3 or three consecutive doses missed at any time: **An additional method of contraception must be used for 7 days after a missed dose:**

Schedule 1 (Sunday starter): Continue dose of 1 tablet daily until Sunday, then discard the rest of the pack, and a new pack should be started that same day.

Schedule 2 (Day 1 starter): Current pack should be discarded, and a new pack should be started that same day.

Missed doses **biphasic/triphasic formulations** (refer to package insert for complete information):

One dose missed: Take as soon as remembered or take 2 tablets next day.

Two consecutive doses missed in week 1 or week 2 of the pack: Take 2 tablets as soon as remembered and 2 tablets the next day. Resume taking 1 tablet daily until the pack is empty. **An additional method of contraception must be used for 7 days after a missed dose.**

Two consecutive doses missed in week 3 of the pack. **An additional method of contraception must be used for 7 days after a missed dose.**

Schedule 1 (Sunday starter): Take 1 tablet every day until Sunday. Discard the remaining pack and start a new pack of pills on the same day.

Schedule 2 (Day 1 starter): Discard the remaining pack and start a new pack the same day.

Three or more consecutive doses missed. **An additional method of contraception must be used for 7 days after a missed dose.**

Schedule 1 (Sunday starter): Take 1 tablet every day until Sunday; on Sunday, discard the pack and start a new pack.

Schedule 2 (Day 1 starter): Discard the remaining pack and begin new pack of tablets starting on the same day.

Dosage adjustment in renal impairment: Specific guidelines not available; use with caution.

Dosage adjustment in hepatic impairment: Contraindicated in patients with hepatic impairment.

Administration Administer at the same time each day.

Monitoring Parameters Blood pressure, breast exam, Pap smear, and pregnancy; lipid profiles in patients being treated for hyperlipidemias

Patient Information Report signs or symptoms of any of the following: Thromboembolic or thrombotic disorders including sudden severe headache or vomiting, disturbance of vision or speech, loss of vision, numbness or weakness in an extremity, sharp or crushing chest pain, calf pain, shortness of breath, severe abdominal pain or mass, mental depression or unusual bleeding. Women should be advised that when any doses are missed, alternative contraceptive methods should be used for the next 2 days or until 2 days into the new cycle; women should discontinue taking the medication if they suspect they are pregnant or become pregnant.

Dosage Forms TAB, monophasic (MonoNessa™, Ortho-Cyclen®, Sprintec™): Ethinyl estradiol 0.035 mg and norgestimate 0.25 mg (28s). **TAB, triphasic** (Ortho Tri-Cyclen®): Day 1-7: Ethinyl estradiol 0.035 mg and norgestimate 0.18 mg, Day 8-14: Ethinyl estradiol 0.035 mg and norgestimate 0.215 mg, Day 15-21: Ethinyl estradiol 0.035 mg and norgestimate 0.25 mg, Day 22-28: Inactive (28s); (Ortho Tri-Cyclen® Lo): Day 1-7: Ethinyl estradiol 0.025 mg and norgestimate 0.18 mg, Day 8-14: Ethinyl estradiol 0.025 mg and norgestimate 0.215 mg, Day 8-14: Ethinyl estradiol 0.025 and norgestimate 0.215 mg, Day 15-21: Ethinyl estradiol 0.025 mg and norgestimate 0.25 mg, Day 22-28: Inactive (28s)

Ethinyl Estradiol and Norgestrel *(ETH in il es tra DYE ole & nor JES trel)*

U.S. Brand Names Cryselle™; Lo/Ovral®; Low-Ogestrel®; Ogestrel®; Ovral®

Synonyms Morning After Pill; Norgestrel and Ethinyl Estradiol

Therapeutic Category Contraceptive, Emergency; Contraceptive, Oral (Intermediate Potency Estrogen, High Potency Progestin); Contraceptive, Oral (Low Potency Estrogen, Intermediate Potency Progestin); Contraceptive, Oral (Monophasic); Estrogen and Progestin Combination

Use Prevention of pregnancy; postcoital contraceptive or "morning after" pill

Unlabeled/Investigational Use Treatment of hypermenorrhea, endometriosis, female hypogonadism

Pregnancy Risk Factor X

Contraindications Hypersensitivity to ethinyl estradiol, norgestrel, or any component of the formulation; thrombophlebitis or thromboembolic disorders (current or history of), cerebral vascular disease, coronary artery disease, valvular heart disease with complications, severe hypertension; diabetes mellitus with vascular involvement; severe headache with focal neurological symptoms; known or suspected breast carcinoma, endometrial cancer, estrogen-dependent neoplasms, undiagnosed abnormal genital bleeding; hepatic dysfunction or tumor, cholestatic jaundice of pregnancy, jaundice with prior combination hormonal contraceptive use; major surgery with prolonged immobilization; heavy smoking (≥15 cigarettes/day) in patients >35 years of age; pregnancy

Warnings/Precautions Combination hormonal contraceptives do not protect against HIV infection or other sexually-transmitted diseases. The risk of cardiovascular side effects increases in women who smoke cigarettes, especially those who are >35 years of age; women who use combination hormonal contraceptives should be strongly advised not to smoke. Combination hormonal contraceptives may lead to increased risk of myocardial infarction, use with caution in patients with risk factors for coronary artery disease. May increase the risk of thromboembolism. Combination hormonal contraceptives may have a dose-related risk of vascular disease, hypertension, and gallbladder disease. Women with hypertension should be encouraged to use another form of contraception. The use of combination hormonal contraceptives has been associated with a slight increase in frequency of breast cancer, however, studies are not consistent. Combination hormonal contraceptives may cause glucose intolerance. Retinal thrombosis has been reported (rarely). Use with caution in patients with renal disease, conditions that may be aggravated by fluid retention, depression, or history of migraine. Not for use prior to menarche.

The minimum dosage combination of estrogen/progestin that will effectively treat the individual patient should be used. New patients should be started on products containing <50 mcg of estrogen per tablet.

Common Adverse Reactions Frequency not defined.

Cardiovascular: Arterial thromboembolism, cerebral hemorrhage, cerebral thrombosis, edema, hypertension, mesenteric thrombosis, myocardial infarction

Central nervous system: Depression, dizziness, headache, migraine, nervousness, premenstrual syndrome, stroke

Dermatologic: Acne, erythema multiforme, erythema nodosum, hirsutism, loss of scalp hair, melasma (may persist), rash (allergic)

Endocrine & metabolic: Amenorrhea, breakthrough bleeding, breast enlargement, breast secretion, breast tenderness, carbohydrate intolerance, lactation decreased (postpartum), glucose tolerance decreased, libido changes, menstrual flow changes, sex hormone-binding globulins (SHBG) increased, spotting, temporary infertility (following discontinuation), thyroid-binding globulin increased, triglycerides increased

Gastrointestinal: Abdominal cramps, appetite changes, bloating, cholestasis, colitis, gallbladder disease, jaundice, nausea, vomiting, weight gain/loss

Genitourinary: Cervical erosion changes, cervical secretion changes, cystitis-like syndrome, vaginal candidiasis, vaginitis

Hematologic: Antithrombin III decreased, folate levels decreased, hemolytic uremic syndrome, norepinephrine induced platelet aggregability increased, porphyria, prothrombin increased; factors VII, VIII, IX, and X

Hepatic: Benign liver tumors, Budd-Chiari syndrome, cholestatic jaundice, hepatic adenomas

Local: Thrombophlebitis

Ocular: Cataracts, change in corneal curvature (steepening), contact lens intolerance, optic neuritis, retinal thrombosis

Renal: Impaired renal function

Respiratory: Pulmonary thromboembolism

Miscellaneous: Hemorrhagic eruption

Drug Interactions

Cytochrome P450 Effect:

Ethinyl estradiol: **Substrate** of CYP3A4 (major), 3A5-7 (minor); **Inhibits** CYP1A2 (weak), 2B6 (weak), 2C19 (weak), 3A4 (weak)

Norgestrel: **Substrate** of CYP3A4 (major)

Increased Effect/Toxicity: Acetaminophen and ascorbic acid may increase plasma levels of estrogen component. Atorvastatin and indinavir increase plasma levels of combination hormonal contraceptives. Combination hormonal contraceptives increase the plasma levels of alprazolam, chlordiazepoxide, cyclosporine, diazepam, prednisolone, selegiline, theophylline, tricyclic antidepressants. Combination hormonal contraceptives may increase (or decrease) the effects of coumarin derivatives.

Decreased Effect: Combination hormonal contraceptives may decrease plasma levels of acetaminophen, clofibric acid, lorazepam, morphine, oxazepam, salicylic acid, temazepam. Contraceptive effect decreased by acitretin, aminoglutethimide, amprenavir, anticonvulsants, griseofulvin, lopinavir, nelfinavir, nevirapine, penicillins (effect not consistent), rifampin, ritonavir, tetracyclines (effect not consistent). Combination hormonal contraceptives may decrease (or increase) the effects of coumarin derivatives.

Mechanism of Action Combination hormonal contraceptives inhibit ovulation via a negative feedback mechanism on the hypothalamus, which alters the normal pattern of gonadotropin secretion of a follicle-stimulating hormone (FSH) and luteinizing hormone by the anterior pituitary. The follicular phase FSH and midcycle surge of gonadotropins are inhibited. In addition, combination hormonal contraceptives produce alterations in the genital tract, including changes in the cervical mucus, rendering it unfavorable for sperm penetration even if ovulation occurs. Changes in the endometrium may also occur, producing an unfavorable environment for nidation. Combination hormonal contraceptive drugs may alter the tubal transport of the ova through the fallopian tubes. Progestational agents may also alter sperm fertility.

Pharmacodynamics/Kinetics See individual agents.

(Continued)

Ethinyl Estradiol and Norgestrel *(Continued)*

Dosage Oral: Adults: Female:

Contraception:

Schedule 1 (Sunday starter): Dose begins on first Sunday after onset of menstruation; if the menstrual period starts on Sunday, take first tablet that very same day. **With a Sunday start, an additional method of contraception should be used until after the first 7 days of consecutive administration.**

For 21-tablet package: Dosage is 1 tablet daily for 21 consecutive days, followed by 7 days off the medication; a new course begins on the 8th day after the last tablet is taken.

For 28-tablet package: Dosage is 1 tablet daily without interruption.

Schedule 2 (Day 1 starter): Dose starts on first day of menstrual cycle taking 1 tablet daily.

For 21-tablet package: Dosage is 1 tablet daily for 21 consecutive days, followed by 7 days off the medication; a new course begins on the 8th day after the last tablet is taken.

For 28-tablet package: Dosage is 1 tablet daily without interruption.

If all doses have been taken on schedule and one menstrual period is missed, continue dosing cycle. If two consecutive menstrual periods are missed, pregnancy test is required before new dosing cycle is started.

Missed doses **monophasic formulations** (refer to package insert for complete information):

One dose missed: Take as soon as remembered or take 2 tablets next day

Two consecutive doses missed in the first 2 weeks: Take 2 tablets as soon as remembered or 2 tablets next 2 days. **An additional method of contraception should be used for 7 days after missed dose.**

Two consecutive doses missed in week 3 or three consecutive doses missed at any time:

Schedule 1 (Sunday starter): Continue to take 1 tablet daily until Sunday, then discard the rest of the pack, and a new pack is started that same day.

Schedule 2 (Day 1 starter): Current pack should be discarded, and a new pack started that same day. **An additional method of contraception should be used for 7 days after missed dose.**

Postcoital contraception:

Ethinyl estradiol 0.03 mg and norgestrel 0.3 mg formulation: 4 tablets within 72 hours of unprotected intercourse and 4 tablets 12 hours after first dose

Ethinyl estradiol 0.05 mg and norgestrel 0.5 mg formulation: 2 tablets within 72 hours of unprotected intercourse and 2 tablets 12 hours after first dose

Dosage adjustment in renal impairment: Specific guidelines not available; use with caution.

Dosage adjustment in hepatic impairment: Contraindicated in patients with hepatic impairment.

Administration Administer at the same time each day.

Monitoring Parameters Blood pressure, breast exam, Pap smear, and pregnancy; lipid profiles in patients being treated for hyperlipidemias

Patient Information Take exactly as directed; use additional method of birth control during first week of administration of first cycle; photosensitivity may occur. Women should report signs or symptoms of any of the following: Thromboembolic or thrombotic disorders including sudden severe headache or vomiting, disturbance of vision or speech, loss of vision, numbness or weakness in an extremity, sharp or crushing chest pain, calf pain, shortness of breath, severe abdominal pain or mass, mental depression or unusual bleeding. Women should be advised that when any doses are missed, alternative contraceptive methods should be used for the next 2 days or until 2 days into the new cycle Women should discontinue taking the medication if they suspect they are pregnant or become pregnant.

Dosage Forms TAB, monophasic: (Cryselle™): Ethinyl estradiol 0.03 mg and norgestrel 0.3 mg (28s); (Lo/Ovral®, Low-Ogestrel® 21): Ethinyl estradiol 0.03 mg and norgestrel 0.3 mg (21s); (Low-Ogestrel® 28): Ethinyl estradiol 0.03 mg and norgestrel 0.3 mg (28s); (Lo/Ovral® 28): Ethinyl estradiol 0.03 mg and norgestrel 0.3 mg (28s); (Ogestrel® 21, Ovral® 21): Ethinyl estradiol 0.05 mg and norgestrel 0.5 mg (21s); (Ogestrel® 28, Ovral® 28): Ethinyl estradiol 0.05 mg and norgestrel 0.5 mg (28s)

◆ **Ethiofos** *see* Amifostine *on page 70*

Ethionamide (e thye on AM ide)

Related Information

Antimicrobial Drugs of Choice *on page 1440*

Tuberculosis Treatment Guidelines *on page 1466*

U.S. Brand Names Trecator®-SC

Therapeutic Category Antitubercular Agent

Use Treatment of tuberculosis and other mycobacterial diseases, in conjunction with other antituberculosis agents, when first-line agents have failed or resistance has been demonstrated

Pregnancy Risk Factor C

Contraindications Hypersensitivity to ethionamide or any component of the formulation; severe hepatic impairment

Warnings/Precautions Use with caution in patients receiving cycloserine or isoniazid, in diabetics

Common Adverse Reactions Frequency not defined.

Cardiovascular: Postural hypotension

Central nervous system: Psychiatric disturbances, drowsiness, dizziness, seizures, headache

Dermatologic: Rash, alopecia

Endocrine & metabolic: Hypothyroidism or goiter, hypoglycemia, gynecomastia

Gastrointestinal: Metallic taste, diarrhea, anorexia, nausea, vomiting, stomatitis, abdominal pain

Hematologic: Thrombocytopenia

Hepatic: Hepatitis (5%), jaundice

Neuromuscular & skeletal: Peripheral neuritis, weakness (common)

Ocular: Optic neuritis, blurred vision

Respiratory: Olfactory disturbances

Drug Interactions

Increased Effect/Toxicity: Cycloserine and isoniazid; increased hepatotoxicity with rifampin

Mechanism of Action Inhibits peptide synthesis

Pharmacodynamics/Kinetics

Absorption: Rapid

Distribution: Crosses placenta

Protein binding: 10%

Metabolism: Extensively hepatic

Bioavailability: 80%

Half-life elimination: 2-3 hours

Time to peak, serum: ~3 hours

Excretion: Urine (as unchanged drug and active and inactive metabolites)

Dosage Oral:

Children: 15-20 mg/kg/day in 2 divided doses, not to exceed 1 g/day

Adults: 500-1000 mg/day in 1-3 divided doses

Dosing adjustment in renal impairment: Cl_{cr} <50 mL/minute: Administer 50% of dose

Monitoring Parameters Initial and periodic serum ALT and AST

Patient Information Take with meals; report persistent or severe stomach upset, loss of appetite, or metallic taste; frequent blood tests are needed for monitoring; increase dietary intake of pyridoxine

Dosage Forms TAB, sugar coated: 250 mg

◆ **Ethmozine**® *see Moricizine on page 860*

Ethosuximide *(eth oh SUKS i mide)*

Related Information

Anticonvulsants by Seizure Type *on page 1358*

Epilepsy *on page 1477*

U.S. Brand Names Zarontin®

Therapeutic Category Anticonvulsant, Succinimide

Use Management of absence (petit mal) seizures

Pregnancy Risk Factor C

Dosage Oral:

Children 3-6 years: Initial: 250 mg/day (or 15 mg/kg/day) in 2 divided doses; increase every 4-7 days; usual maintenance dose: 15-40 mg/kg/day in 2 divided doses

Children >6 years and Adults: Initial: 250 mg twice daily; increase by 250 mg as needed every 4-7 days, up to 1.5 g/day in 2 divided doses; usual maintenance dose: 20-40 mg/kg/day in 2 divided doses

Dosing comment in renal/hepatic dysfunction: Use with caution.

Dosage Forms CAP: 250 mg. **SYR:** 250 mg/5 mL (473 mL)

◆ **Ethoxynaphthamido Penicillin Sodium** *see Nafcillin on page 875*

◆ **Ethyl Aminobenzoate** *see Benzocaine on page 154*

◆ **Ethynodiol Diacetate and Ethinyl Estradiol** *see Ethinyl Estradiol and Ethynodiol Diacetate on page 480*

◆ **Ethyol**® *see Amifostine on page 70*

Etidocaine *(e TI doe kane)*

U.S. Brand Names Duranest® [DSC]

Synonyms Etidocaine Hydrochloride

Therapeutic Category Local Anesthetic, Injectable

Use Infiltration anesthesia; peripheral nerve blocks; central neural blocks

Pregnancy Risk Factor B

Dosage Varies with procedure; use 1% for peripheral nerve block, central nerve block, lumbar peridural caudal; use 1.5% for maxillary infiltration or inferior alveolar nerve block; use 1% or 1.5% for intra-abdominal or pelvic surgery, lower limb surgery, or caesarean section

Dosage Forms INJ, solution: 1% [10 mg/mL] (30 mL). **INJ, solution**, with epinephrine 1:200,000: 1% [10 mg/mL] (30 mL); 1.5% [15 mg/mL] (1.8 mL, 20 mL)

◆ **Etidocaine Hydrochloride** *see Etidocaine on page 495*

Etidronate Disodium *(e ti DROE nate dye SOW dee um)*

U.S. Brand Names Didronel®

Synonyms EHDP; Sodium Etidronate

Therapeutic Category Antidote, Hypercalcemia; Bisphosphonate Derivative

Use Symptomatic treatment of Paget's disease and heterotopic ossification due to spinal cord injury or after total hip replacement, hypercalcemia associated with malignancy

Pregnancy Risk Factor B (oral); C (parenteral)

(Continued)

Etidronate Disodium *(Continued)*

Dosage Adults: Oral formulation should be taken on an empty stomach 2 hours before any meal.

Paget's disease: Oral

Initial: 5-10 mg/kg/day (not to exceed 6 months) or 11-20 mg/kg/day (not to exceed 3 months). Doses >10 mg/kg/day are **not** recommended.

Retreatment: Initiate only after etidronate-free period ≥90 days. Monitor patients every 3-6 months. Retreatment regimens are the same as for initial treatment.

Heterotopic ossification: Oral:

Caused by spinal cord injury: 20 mg/kg/day for 2 weeks, then 10 mg/kg/day for 10 weeks; total treatment period: 12 weeks

Complicating total hip replacement: 20 mg/kg/day for 1 month preoperatively then 20 mg/kg/day for 3 months postoperatively; total treatment period is 4 months

Hypercalcemia associated with malignancy:

I.V. (dilute dose in at least 250 mL NS): 7.5 mg/kg/day for 3 days; there should be at least 7 days between courses of treatment

Oral: Start 20 mg/kg/day on the last day of infusion and continue for 30-90 days

Dosing adjustment in renal impairment:

S_{cr} 2.5-5 mg/dL: Use with caution

S_{cr} >5 mg/dL: **Not recommended**

Dosage Forms INJ, solution: 50 mg/mL (6 mL). **TAB:** 200 mg, 400 mg

Etodolac *(ee toe DOE lak)*

Related Information

Nonsteroidal Anti-Inflammatory Agents Comparison *on page 1401*

U.S. Brand Names Lodine®; Lodine® XL

Synonyms Etodolic Acid

Therapeutic Category Analgesic, Nonsteroidal Anti-inflammatory Drug; Anti-inflammatory Agent; Nonsteroidal Anti-inflammatory Drug (NSAID), Oral

Use Acute and long-term use in the management of signs and symptoms of osteoarthritis and management of pain; rheumatoid arthritis

Pregnancy Risk Factor C/D (3rd trimester)

Contraindications Hypersensitivity to etodolac, aspirin, other NSAIDs, or any component of the formulation; active gastric/duodenal ulcer disease; pregnancy (3rd trimester)

Warnings/Precautions Use with caution in patients with CHF, hypertension, dehydration, decreased renal or hepatic function, history of GI disease (bleeding or ulcers), or those receiving anticoagulants. Elderly are at a high risk for adverse effects from NSAIDs. As many as 60% of elderly can develop peptic ulceration and/or hemorrhage asymptomatically.

Use lowest effective dose for shortest period possible. Use of NSAIDs can compromise existing renal function especially when Cl_{cr} is <30 mL/minute. CNS adverse effects such as confusion, agitation, and hallucination are generally seen in overdose or high-dose situations; however, elderly may demonstrate these adverse effects at lower doses than younger adults. Withhold for at least 4-6 half-lives prior to surgical or dental procedures.

Common Adverse Reactions 1% to 10%:

Central nervous system: Depression (1% to 3%)

Dermatologic: Rash (1% to 3%), pruritus (1% to 3%)

Gastrointestinal: Abdominal cramps (3% to 9%), nausea (3% to 9%), vomiting (1% to 3%), dyspepsia (10%), diarrhea (3% to 9%), constipation (1% to 3%), flatulence (3% to 9%), melena (1% to 3%), gastritis (1% to 3%)

Genitourinary: Polyuria (1% to 3%)

Neuromuscular & skeletal: Weakness (3% to 9%)

Ocular: Blurred vision (1% to 3%)

Otic: Tinnitus (1% to 3%)

Drug Interactions

Increased Effect/Toxicity: Etodolac may increase effect/toxicity of aspirin (GI irritation), lithium, methotrexate, digoxin, cyclosporine (nephrotoxicity), and warfarin (bleeding).

Decreased Effect: Decreased effect with aspirin. May reduce effect of some diuretics and antihypertensive effect of β-blockers.

Mechanism of Action Inhibits prostaglandin synthesis by decreasing the activity of the enzyme, cyclooxygenase, which results in decreased formation of prostaglandin precursors

Pharmacodynamics/Kinetics

Onset of action: Analgesic: 2-4 hours; Maximum anti-inflammatory effect: A few days

Absorption: Well absorbed

Distribution: V_d: 0.4 L/kg

Protein binding: High

Metabolism: Hepatic

Half-life elimination: 7 hours

Time to peak, serum: 1 hour

Excretion: Urine

Dosage Single dose of 76-100 mg is comparable to the analgesic effect of aspirin 650 mg; in patients ≥65 years, no substantial differences in the pharmacokinetics or side-effects profile were seen compared with the general population

Adults: Oral:

Acute pain: 200-400 mg every 6-8 hours, as needed, not to exceed total daily doses of 1200 mg; for patients weighing <60 kg, total daily dose should not exceed 20 mg/kg/day

Osteoarthritis: Initial: 800-1200 mg/day given in divided doses: 400 mg 2 or 3 times/day; 300 mg 2, 3, or 4 times/day; 200 mg 3 or 4 times/day; total daily dose should not exceed 1200 mg; for patients weighing <60 kg, total daily dose should not exceed 20 mg/kg/day Lodine® XL: 400-1000 mg once daily

Monitoring Parameters Monitor CBC, liver enzymes; in patients receiving diuretics, monitor urine output and BUN/serum creatinine

Patient Information Do not crush tablets; take with food, milk, or water; report any signs of blood in stool

Dosage Forms CAP (Lodine®): 200 mg, 300 mg. **TAB** (Lodine®): 400 mg, 500 mg. **TAB, extended release** (Lodine® XL): 400 mg, 500 mg, 600 mg

♦ **Etodolic Acid** see Etodolac on page 496

Etomidate (e TOM i date)

U.S. Brand Names Amidate®
Therapeutic Category General Anesthetic
Use Induction and maintenance of general anesthesia
Unlabeled/Investigational Use Sedation for diagnosis of seizure foci
Pregnancy Risk Factor C
Contraindications Hypersensitivity to etomidate or any component of the formulation
Warnings/Precautions Consider exogenous corticosteroid replacement in patients undergoing severe stress
Common Adverse Reactions
>10%:
Endocrine & metabolic: Adrenal suppression
Gastrointestinal: Nausea, vomiting on emergence from anesthesia
Local: Pain at injection site (30% to 80%)
Neuromuscular & skeletal: Myoclonus (33%), transient skeletal movements, uncontrolled eye movements
1% to 10%: Hiccups
Drug Interactions
Increased Effect/Toxicity: Fentanyl decreases etomidate elimination. Verapamil may increase the anesthetic and respiratory depressant effects of etomidate.
Mechanism of Action Ultrashort-acting nonbarbiturate hypnotic (benzylimidazole) used for the induction of anesthesia; chemically, it is a carboxylated imidazole which produces a rapid induction of anesthesia with minimal cardiovascular effects; produces EEG burst suppression at high doses
Pharmacodynamics/Kinetics
Onset of action: 30-60 seconds
Peak effect: 1 minute
Duration: 3-5 minutes; terminated by redistribution
Distribution: V_d: 2-4.5 L/kg
Protein binding: 76%;
Metabolism: Hepatic and plasma esterases
Half-life elimination: Terminal: 2.6 hours
Dosage Children >10 years and Adults: I.V.: Initial: 0.2-0.6 mg/kg over 30-60 seconds for induction of anesthesia; maintenance: 5-20 mcg/kg/minute
Monitoring Parameters Cardiac monitoring and blood pressure required
Dosage Forms INJ, solution: 2 mg/mL (10 mL, 20 mL)

♦ **Etonogestrel and Ethinyl Estradiol** see Ethinyl Estradiol and Etonogestrel on page 482
♦ **Etopophos®** see Etoposide Phosphate on page 499

Etoposide (e toe POE side)

U.S. Brand Names Toposar®; VePesid®
Synonyms Epipodophyllotoxin; VP-16; VP-16-213
Therapeutic Category Antineoplastic Agent, Podophyllotoxin Derivative
Use Treatment of lymphomas, ANLL, lung, testicular, bladder, and prostate carcinoma, hepatoma, rhabdomyosarcoma, uterine carcinoma, neuroblastoma, mycosis fungoides, Kaposi's sarcoma, histiocytosis, gestational trophoblastic disease, Ewing's sarcoma, Wilms' tumor, and brain tumors
Pregnancy Risk Factor D
Contraindications Hypersensitivity to etoposide or any component of the formulation; **intrathecal administration**; pregnancy
Warnings/Precautions The U.S. Food and Drug Administration (FDA) currently recommends that procedures for proper handling and disposal of antineoplastic agents be considered. Severe myelosuppression with resulting infection or bleeding may occur.

Dosage should be adjusted in patients with hepatic or renal impairment
Common Adverse Reactions
>10%:
Cardiovascular: Hypotension if the drug is infused too fast
Dermatologic: Alopecia (22% to 93%)
Endocrine & metabolic: Ovarian failure (38%), amenorrhea
Gastrointestinal: Mild to moderate nausea and vomiting; mucositis, especially at high doses; anorexia (10% to 13%)
Hematologic: Myelosuppression, leukopenia (91%), thrombocytopenia (41%), anemia
(Continued)

Etoposide *(Continued)*

    Onset: 5-7 days
    Nadir: 7-14 days
    Recovery: 21-28 days
  1% to 10%:
    Gastrointestinal: Stomatitis (1% to 6%), diarrhea (1% to 13%), abdominal pain
    Neuromuscular & skeletal: Peripheral neuropathies (0.7% to 2%)

Drug Interactions
  Cytochrome P450 Effect: Substrate of CYP1A2 (minor), 2E1 (minor), 3A4 (major); **Inhibits** CYP2C8/9 (weak), 3A4 (weak)
  Increased Effect/Toxicity: The effects of etoposide may be increased by calcium antagonists (increased effects noted *in vitro*). Cyclosporine may increase the levels of etoposide. Etoposide may increase the effects/toxicity of methotrexate and warfarin. There have been reports of frequent hepatic dysfunction with hyperbilirubinemia, ascites, and thrombocytopenia when etoposide is combined with carmustine.

Mechanism of Action Etoposide does not inhibit microtubular assembly. It has been shown to delay transit of cells through the S phase and arrest cells in late S or early G_2 phase. The drug may inhibit mitochondrial transport at the NADH dehydrogenase level or inhibit uptake of nucleosides into HeLa cells. Etoposide is a topoisomerase II inhibitor and appears to cause DNA strand breaks.

Pharmacodynamics/Kinetics
  Absorption: Oral: 25% to 75%; significant inter- and intrapatient variation
  Distribution: Average V_d: 3-36 L/m^2; poor penetration across the blood-brain barrier; CSF concentrations <10% of plasma concentrations
  Protein binding: 94% to 97%
  Metabolism: Hepatic to hydroxy acid and cislactone metabolites
  Half-life elimination: Terminal: 4-15 hours; Children: Normal renal/hepatic function: 6-8 hours
  Time to peak, serum: Oral: 1-1.5 hours
  Excretion:
    Children: Urine (≤55% as unchanged drug)
    Adults: Urine (42% to 67%; 8% to 35% as unchanged drug) within 24 hours; feces (up to 16%)

Dosage Refer to individual protocols:
  Children: I.V.: 60-120 $mg/m^2/day$ for 3-5 days every 3-6 weeks
    AML:
      Remission induction: 150 $mg/m^2/day$ for 2-3 days for 2-3 cycles
      Intensification or consolidation: 250 $mg/m^2/day$ for 3 days, courses 2-5
    Brain tumor: 150 $mg/m^2/day$ on days 2 and 3 of treatment course
    Neuroblastoma: 100 $mg/m^2/day$ over 1 hour on days 1-5 of cycle; repeat cycle every 4 weeks
    BMT conditioning regimen used in patients with rhabdomyosarcoma or neuroblastoma: I.V. continuous infusion: 160 $mg/m^2/day$ for 4 days
    Conditioning regimen for allogenic BMT: 60 mg/kg/dose as a single dose
  Adults:
    Small cell lung cancer:
      Oral: Twice the I.V. dose rounded to the nearest 50 mg given once daily if total dose ≤400 mg or in divided doses if >400 mg
      I.V.: 35 $mg/m^2/day$ for 4 days or 50 $mg/m^2/day$ for 5 days every 3-4 weeks total dose ≤400 mg/day or in divided doses if >400 mg/day
      IVPB: 60-100 $mg/m^2/day$ for 3 days (with cisplatin)
      CIV: 500 mg/m^2 over 24 hours every 3 weeks
    Testicular cancer:
      IVPB: 50-100 $mg/m^2/day$ for 5 days repeated every 3-4 weeks
      I.V.: 100 mg/m^2 every other day for 3 doses repeated every 3-4 weeks
    BMT/relapsed leukemia: I.V.: 2.4-3.5 g/m^2 or 25-70 mg/kg administered over 4-36 hours

  Dosing adjustment in renal impairment:
    Cl_{cr} 10-50 mL/minute: Administer 75% of normal dose
    Cl_{cr} <10 mL minute: Administer 50% of normal dose
  Hemodialysis: Supplemental dose is not necessary
  Peritoneal dialysis: Supplemental dose is not necessary
  CAPD effects: Unknown
  CAVH effects: Unknown

  Dosing adjustment in hepatic impairment:
    Bilirubin 1.5-3 mg/dL or AST 60-180 units: Reduce dose by 50%
    Bilirubin 3-5 mg/dL or AST >180 units: Reduce by 75%
    Bilirubin >5 mg/dL: Do not administer

Administration
  Oral: Doses should be rounded to the nearest 50 mg; doses ≤400 mg/day should be given as a single daily dose. Doses ≥400 mg/day should be given in 2-4 divided doses.
  I.V.: As a bolus or 24-hour continuous infusion; bolus infusions are usually administered over at least 45-60 minutes. Infusion of doses in ≤30 minutes greatly increases the risk of hypotension.

  Extravasation management: Inject 150-900 units of hyaluronidase S.C. clockwise into the infiltrated area using a 25-gauge needle. Change the needle with each injection. Apply heat immediately for 1 hour, repeat 4 times/day for 3-5 days. **Application of cold or hydrocortisone is contraindicated.**

Monitoring Parameters CBC with differential, platelet count, and hemoglobin, vital signs (blood pressure), bilirubin, and renal function tests

Patient Information During therapy, do not use alcohol, aspirin-containing products, and/or OTC medications without consulting prescriber. It is important to maintain adequate nutrition and hydration (2-3 L/day of fluids unless instructed to restrict fluid intake) during therapy; frequent small meals may help. You may experience mild nausea or vomiting (frequent small meals, frequent mouth care, sucking lozenges, or chewing gum may help). You may experience loss of hair (reversible); you will be more susceptible to infection (avoid crowds and exposure to infection as much as possible). Yogurt or buttermilk may help reduce diarrhea. Frequent mouth care and use of a soft toothbrush or cotton swabs may help prevent mouth sores. This drug may cause sterility or birth defects. Report extreme fatigue, pain or numbness in extremities, severe GI upset or diarrhea, bleeding or bruising, fever, chills, sore throat, vaginal discharge, difficulty breathing, yellowing of eyes or skin, and any changes in color of urine or stool. Contraceptive measures are recommended during therapy. The drug may be excreted in breast milk, therefore, an alternative form of feeding your baby should be used.

Dosage Forms CAP (VePesid®): 50 mg. **INJ, solution:** 20 mg/mL (5 mL, 25 mL, 50 mL); (Toposar®): 20 mg/mL (5 mL, 10 mL, 25 mL); (VePesid®): 20 mg/mL (5 mL, 7.5 mg, 25 mL, 50 mL)

Etoposide Phosphate (e toe POE side FOS fate)

U.S. Brand Names Etopophos®

Therapeutic Category Antineoplastic Agent, Irritant; Antineoplastic Agent, Podophyllotoxin Derivative; Vesicant

Use Treatment of refractory testicular tumors and small cell lung cancer

Pregnancy Risk Factor D

Contraindications Hypersensitivity to etoposide, etoposide phosphate, or any component of the formulation; **intrathecal administration;** pregnancy

Warnings/Precautions The U.S. Food and Drug Administration (FDA) currently recommends that procedures for proper handling and disposal of antineoplastic agents be considered. Severe myelosuppression with resulting infection or bleeding may occur. Dosage should be adjusted in patients with hepatic or renal impairment. Use caution in elderly patients (may be more likely to develop severe myelosuppression, GI effects, and/or alopecia).

Common Adverse Reactions Based on **etoposide:**

>10%:

Cardiovascular: Hypotension if the drug is infused too fast

Dermatologic: Alopecia (22% to 93%)

Endocrine & metabolic: Ovarian failure (38%), amenorrhea

Gastrointestinal: Mild to moderate nausea and vomiting; mucositis, especially at high doses; anorexia (10% to 13%)

Hematologic: Myelosuppression, leukopenia (91%), thrombocytopenia (41%), anemia
Onset: 5-7 days
Nadir: 7-14 days
Recovery: 21-28 days

1% to 10%:

Gastrointestinal: Stomatitis (1% to 6%), diarrhea (1% to 13%), abdominal pain

Neuromuscular & skeletal: Peripheral neuropathies (0.7% to 2%)

Drug Interactions

Cytochrome P450 Effect: Substrate of CYP1A2 (minor), 2E1 (minor), 3A4 (major); **Inhibits** CYP2C8/9 (weak), 3A4 (weak)

Increased Effect/Toxicity: Etoposide taken with warfarin may result in prolongation of bleeding times. Alteration of methotrexate transport has been found as a slow efflux of methotrexate and its polyglutamated form out of the cell, leading to intercellular accumulation of methotrexate. Calcium antagonists increase the rate of VP-16-induced DNA damage and cytotoxicity *in vitro*. Use with carmustine has shown reports of frequent hepatic dysfunction with hyperbilirubinemia, ascites, and thrombocytopenia. Cyclosporine may cause additive cytotoxic effects on tumor cells.

Mechanism of Action Etoposide phosphate is converted *in vivo* to the active moiety, etoposide, by dephosphorylation. Etoposide inhibits mitotic activity; inhibits cells from entering prophase; inhibits DNA synthesis. Initially thought to be mitotic inhibitors similar to podophyllotoxin, but actually have no effect on microtubule assembly. However, later shown to induce DNA strand breakage and inhibition of topoisomerase II (an enzyme which breaks and repairs DNA); etoposide acts in late S or early G2 phases.

Pharmacodynamics/Kinetics

Distribution: Average V_d: 3-36 L/m²; poor penetration across blood-brain barrier; concentrations in CSF being <10% that of plasma

Protein binding: 94% to 97%

Metabolism: Hepatic (with a biphasic decay)

Half-life elimination: Terminal: 4-15 hours; Children: Normal renal/hepatic function: 6-8 hours

Excretion: Urine (as unchanged drug and metabolites), feces (2% to 16%); Children: I.V.: Urine (≤55% as unchanged drug)

Dosage Refer to individual protocols. Adults:

Small cell lung cancer: I.V. (in combination with other approved chemotherapeutic drugs): **Equivalent doses of etoposide phosphate to an etoposide dosage** range of 35 mg/m²/day for 4 days to 50 mg/m²/day for 5 days. Courses are repeated at 3- to 4-week intervals after adequate recovery from any toxicity.

Testicular cancer: I.V. (in combination with other approved chemotherapeutic agents): **Equivalent dose of etoposide phosphate to etoposide dosage** range of 50-100 mg/m²/day on (Continued)

Etoposide Phosphate *(Continued)*

days 1-5 to 100 mg/m^2/day on days 1, 3, and 5. Courses are repeated at 3- to 4-week intervals after adequate recovery from any toxicity.

Dosage adjustment in renal impairment:

Cl$_{cr}$ 15-50 mL/minute: Administer 75% of normal dose

Cl$_{cr}$ <15 mL minute: Data are not available and further dose reduction should be considered in these patients.

Hemodialysis: Supplemental dose is not necessary

Peritoneal dialysis: Supplemental dose is not necessary

CAPD effects: Unknown

CAVH effects: Unknown

Dosage adjustment in hepatic impairment:

Bilirubin 1.5-3 mg/dL or AST 60-180 units: Reduce dose by 50%

Bilirubin 3-5 mg/dL or AST >180 units: Reduce by 75%

Bilirubin >5 mg/dL: Do not administer

Administration I.V. infusion, usually over 5-210 minutes, infusions over 10-12 hours are reported. Unlike etoposide, etoposide phosphate may be administered rapidly without causing hypotension or anaphylactoid reactions.

Monitoring Parameters CBC with differential, platelet count, and hemoglobin, vital signs (blood pressure), bilirubin, and renal function tests

Patient Information This drug can only be administered by infusion. During therapy, do not use alcohol, aspirin-containing products, and/or OTC medications without consulting prescriber. It is important to maintain adequate nutrition and hydration (2-3 L/day of fluids unless instructed to restrict fluid intake) during therapy; frequent small meals may help. You may experience mild nausea or vomiting (frequent small meals, frequent mouth care, sucking lozenges, or chewing gum may help). You may experience loss of hair (reversible); you will be more susceptible to infection (avoid crowds and exposure to infection as much as possible). Yogurt or buttermilk may help reduce diarrhea. Frequent mouth care and use of a soft toothbrush or cotton swabs may help prevent mouth sores. This drug may cause sterility or birth defects. Report extreme fatigue, pain or numbness in extremities, severe GI upset or diarrhea, bleeding or bruising, fever, chills, sore throat, vaginal discharge, difficulty breathing, yellowing of eyes or skin, and any changes in color of urine or stool. Contraceptive measures should be used during therapy. The drug may cause permanent sterility and may cause birth defects. The drug may be excreted in breast milk, therefore, an alternative form of feeding your baby should be used.

Dosage Forms INJ, powder for reconstitution, as base: 100 mg

- ◆ **Eudal®-SR** *see Guaifenesin and Pseudoephedrine on page 605*
- ◆ **Eulexin®** *see Flutamide on page 546*
- ◆ **Eurax®** *see Crotamiton on page 317*
- ◆ **Evista®** *see Raloxifene on page 1079*
- ◆ **Evoxac™** *see Cevimeline on page 252*
- ◆ **Excedrin® Extra Strength [OTC]** *see Acetaminophen, Aspirin, and Caffeine on page 27*
- ◆ **Excedrin® Migraine [OTC]** *see Acetaminophen, Aspirin, and Caffeine on page 27*
- ◆ **Excedrin® P.M. [OTC]** *see Acetaminophen and Diphenhydramine on page 26*
- ◆ **Exelderm®** *see Sulconazole on page 1168*
- ◆ **Exelon®** *see Rivastigmine on page 1107*

Exemestane *(ex e MES tane)*

U.S. Brand Names Aromasin®

Therapeutic Category Antineoplastic Agent, Aromatase Inactivator

Use Treatment of advanced breast cancer in postmenopausal women whose disease has progressed following tamoxifen therapy

Pregnancy Risk Factor D

Contraindications Hypersensitivity to exemestane or any component of the formulation; pregnancy

Warnings/Precautions Exemestane has been associated with prolonged gestation, abnormal or difficult labor, increased resorption, reduced number of live fetuses, decreased fetal weight, and retarded ossification in rats. Patients who are exposed to exemestane during pregnancy should be apprised of the possible hazard to the fetus and risk for loss of the pregnancy. Exemestane should not be administered concurrently with estrogen-containing drugs; and is not recommended for use in premenopausal women.

Common Adverse Reactions

>10%:

Central nervous system: Fatigue (22%), pain (13%), depression (13%), insomnia (11%), anxiety (10%)

Endocrine & metabolic: Hot flashes (13%)

Gastrointestinal: Nausea (18%)

1% to 10%:

Cardiovascular: Edema (7%), hypertension (5%), chest pain

Central nervous system: Dizziness (8%), headache (8%), fever (5%), hypoesthesia, confusion

Dermatologic: Rash, itching, alopecia

Gastrointestinal: Vomiting (7%), abdominal pain (6%), anorexia (6%), constipation (5%), diarrhea (4%), increased appetite (3%), dyspepsia

Genitourinary: Urinary tract infection

Neuromuscular & skeletal: Weakness, paresthesia, pathological fracture, arthralgia
Respiratory: Dyspnea (10%), cough (6%), bronchitis, sinusitis, pharyngitis, rhinitis
Miscellaneous: Influenza-like symptoms (6%), diaphoresis (6%), lymphedema, infection
A dose-dependent decrease in sex hormone-binding globulin has been observed with daily doses of 25 mg or more. Serum luteinizing hormone and follicle-stimulating hormone levels have increased with this medicine.

Drug Interactions
Cytochrome P450 Effect: Substrate of CYP3A4 (minor)
Increased Effect/Toxicity: Although exemestane is a CYP3A4 substrate, ketoconazole, a CYP3A4 inhibitor, did not change the pharmacokinetics of exemestane. No other potential drug interactions have been evaluated.

Mechanism of Action Exemestane is an irreversible, steroidal aromatase inactivator. It prevents conversion of androgens to estrogens by tying up the enzyme aromatase. In breast cancers where growth is estrogen-dependent, this medicine will lower circulating estrogens.

Pharmacodynamics/Kinetics
Absorption: Rapid and moderate (~42%) following oral administration; absorption increases ~40% following high-fat meal
Distribution: Extensive
Protein binding: 90%, primarily to albumin and α_1-acid glycoprotein
Metabolism: Extensively hepatic; oxidation (CYP3A4) of methylene group, reduction of 17-keto group with formation of many secondary metabolites; metabolites are inactive
Half-life elimination: 24 hours
Time to peak: Women with breast cancer: 1.2 hours
Excretion: Urine (<1% as unchanged drug, 39% to 45% as metabolites); feces (36% to 48%)

Dosage Adults: Oral: 25 mg once daily after a meal
Dosing adjustment in renal/hepatic impairment: Safety of chronic doses has not been studied

Patient Information Take after a meal; use caution if you have uncontrolled high blood pressure. Do not use in pregnancy or lactation. Avoid driving or doing other tasks or hobbies that require alertness until you know how this medicine affects you. Take at approximately the same time every day.

Dosage Forms TAB: 25 mg

- ◆ **ex-lax® Stool Softener [OTC]** *see* Docusate *on page 398*
- ◆ **Exsel® [DSC]** *see* Selenium Sulfide *on page 1129*
- ◆ **Extendryl** *see* Chlorpheniramine, Phenylephrine, and Methscopolamine *on page 264*
- ◆ **Extendryl JR** *see* Chlorpheniramine, Phenylephrine, and Methscopolamine *on page 264*
- ◆ **Extendryl SR** *see* Chlorpheniramine, Phenylephrine, and Methscopolamine *on page 264*
- ◆ **Eye-Sed® [OTC]** *see* Zinc Supplements *on page 1327*
- ◆ **EZ-Char™ [OTC]** *see* Charcoal *on page 253*

Ezetimibe (ez ET i mibe)

Related Information
Lipid-Lowering Agents *on page 1381*
U.S. Brand Names Zetia™
Therapeutic Category Antilipemic Agent, 2-Azetidinone
Use Use in combination with dietary therapy for the treatment of primary hypercholesterolemia (as monotherapy or in combination with HMG-CoA reductase inhibitors); homozygous sitosterolemia; homozygous familial hypercholesterolemia (in combination with atorvastatin or simvastatin)
Pregnancy Risk Factor C
Contraindications Hypersensitivity to ezetimibe or any component of the formulation
Warnings/Precautions Secondary causes of hyperlipidemia should be ruled out prior to therapy. Use caution with renal or mild hepatic impairment; not recommended for use with moderate or severe hepatic impairment. Safety and efficacy have not been established in patients <10 years of age.
Common Adverse Reactions 1% to 10%:
Cardiovascular: Chest pain (3%), dizziness (3%), fatigue (2%)
Central nervous system: Headache (8%)
Gastrointestinal: Diarrhea (3% to 4%), abdominal pain (3%)
Neuromuscular & skeletal: Arthralgia (4%)
Respiratory: Sinusitis (4% to 5%), pharyngitis (2% to 3%, placebo 2%)
Drug Interactions
Increased Effect/Toxicity: Cyclosporine may increase plasma levels of ezetimibe. Fibric acid derivatives may increase bioavailability of ezetimibe (safety and efficacy of concomitant use not established).
Decreased Effect: Bile acid sequestrants may decrease ezetimibe bioavailability; administer ezetimibe ≥2 hours before or ≥4 hours after bile acid sequestrants.
Mechanism of Action Inhibits absorption of cholesterol at the brush border of the small intestine, leading to a decreased delivery of cholesterol to the liver, reduction of hepatic cholesterol stores and an increased clearance of cholesterol from the blood; decreases total C, LDL-cholesterol (LDL-C), ApoB, and triglycerides (TG) while increasing HDL-cholesterol (HDL-C).
Pharmacodynamics/Kinetics
Protein binding: >90% to plasma proteins
(Continued)

Ezetimibe *(Continued)*

Metabolism: Undergoes conjugation in the small intestine and liver; forms metabolite (active); may undergo enterohepatic recycling

Bioavailability: Variable

Half-life: 22 hours (ezetimibe and metabolite)

Time to peak, plasma: 4-12 hours

Excretion: Feces (78%, 69% as ezetimibe); urine (11%, 9% as metabolite)

Dosage Oral:

Hyperlipidemias: Children ≥10 years and Adults: 10 mg/day

Sitosterolemia: Adults: 10 mg/day

Elderly: Refer to Adults dosing

Dosage adjustment in renal impairment: Bioavailability increased with severe impairment; no dosing adjustment recommended

Dosage adjustment in hepatic impairment: Bioavailability increased with hepatic impairment

Mild impairment (Child-Pugh score 5-6): No dosing adjustment necessary

Moderate to severe impairment (Child-Pugh score 7-15): Use of ezetimibe not recommended

Administration May be administered without regard to meals. May be taken at the same time as HMG-CoA reductase inhibitors. Administer ≥2 hours before or ≥4 hours after bile acid sequestrants.

Monitoring Parameters Total cholesterol profile prior to therapy, and when clinically indicated and/or periodically thereafter

Patient Information Take with or without food. Maintain diet and exercise program as prescribed. You may experience stomach pain or tiredness; notify prescriber if severe.

Dosage Forms TAB: 10 mg

- ♦ **F₃T** *see Trifluridine on page 1268*
- ♦ **Fabrazyme**® *see Agalsidase Beta on page 41*
- ♦ **Factive**® *see Gemifloxacin on page 584*

Factor VIIa (Recombinant) (FAK ter SEV en ree KOM be nant)

U.S. Brand Names Novo-Seven®

Synonyms Coagulation Factor VIIa; Eptacog Alfa (Activated); rFVIIa

Therapeutic Category Antihemophilic Agent; Blood Product Derivative

Use Treatment of bleeding episodes in patients with hemophilia A or B when inhibitors to factor VIII or factor IX are present

Pregnancy Risk Factor C

Contraindications Hypersensitivity to factor VII or any component of the formulation; hypersensitivity to mouse, hamster, or bovine proteins

Warnings/Precautions Patients should be monitored for signs and symptoms of activation of the coagulation system or thrombosis. Thrombotic events may be increased in patients with disseminated intravascular coagulation (DIC), advanced atherosclerotic disease, sepsis or crush injury. Decreased dosage or discontinuation is warranted in confirmed DIC. Efficacy with prolonged infusions and data evaluating this agent's long-term adverse effects are limited.

Common Adverse Reactions 1% to 10%:

Cardiovascular: Hypertension

Hematologic: Hemorrhage, decreased plasma fibrinogen

Musculoskeletal: Hemarthrosis

Mechanism of Action Recombinant factor VIIa, a vitamin K-dependent glycoprotein, promotes hemostasis by activating the extrinsic pathway of the coagulation cascade. It replaces deficient activated coagulation factor VII, which complexes with tissue factor and may activate coagulation factor X to Xa and factor IX to IXa. When complexed with other factors, coagulation factor Xa converts prothrombin to thrombin, a key step in the formation of a fibrin-platelet hemostatic plug.

Pharmacodynamics/Kinetics

Distribution: V_d: 103 mL/kg (78-139)

Half-life elimination: 2.3 hours (1.7-2.7)

Excretion: Clearance: 33 mL/kg/hour (27-49)

Dosage Children and Adults: I.V. administration only: 90 mcg/kg every 2 hours until hemostasis is achieved or until the treatment is judged ineffective. The dose and interval may be adjusted based upon the severity of bleeding and the degree of hemostasis achieved. The duration of therapy following hemostasis has not been fully established; for patients experiencing severe bleeds, dosing should be continued at 3-6 hour intervals after hemostasis has been achieved and the duration of dosing should be minimized.

In clinical trials, dosages have ranged from 35-120 mcg/kg and a decision on the final therapeutic dosages was reached within 8 hours in the majority of patients

Administration I.V. administration only; reconstitute only with the specified volume of sterile water for injection, USP; administer within 3 hours after reconstitution

Monitoring Parameters Monitor for evidence of hemostasis; although the prothrombin time, aPTT, and factor VII clotting activity have no correlation with achieving hemostasis, these parameters may be useful as adjunct tests to evaluate efficacy and guide dose or interval adjustments

Dosage Forms INJ, powder for reconstitution: 1.2 mg, 2.4 mg, 4.8 mg

Factor IX (FAK ter nyne)

U.S. Brand Names AlphaNine® SD; BeneFix®; Mononine®
Therapeutic Category Antihemophilic Agent; Blood Product Derivative
Use Control bleeding in patients with factor IX deficiency (hemophilia B or Christmas disease)
Pregnancy Risk Factor C
Contraindications Hypersensitivity to mouse protein (Mononine®), hamster protein (BeneFix®), or any component of the formulation
Warnings/Precautions Use with caution in patients with liver dysfunction; some products prepared from pooled human plasma - the risk of viral transmission is not totally eradicated; monitor patients who receive repeated doses twice daily with PTT and level of factor being replaced (eg, IX). Observe closely for signs or symptoms of intravascular coagulation or thrombosis. Caution should be exercised when administering to patients with liver disease, postoperatively, neonates, or patients at risk of thromboembolic phenomena or disseminated intravascular coagulation because of the potential risk of thromboembolic complications.

AlphaNine® SD, Mononine® contain **nondetectable levels of factors II, VII, and X** (<0.0025 units per factor IX unit using standard coagulation assays) and are, therefore, **NOT INDICATED** for replacement therapy of any of these clotting factors.

BeneFix®, Mononine® are **NOT INDICATED** in the treatment or reversal of coumarin-induced anticoagulation or in a hemorrhagic state caused by hepatitis-induced lack of production of liver dependent coagulation factors.

Common Adverse Reactions Frequency not defined.
Cardiovascular: Angioedema, cyanosis, flushing, hypotension, tightness in chest, tightness in neck, (thrombosis following high dosages because of presence of activated clotting factors)
Central nervous system: Fever, headache, chills, somnolence, dizziness, drowsiness, light-headedness
Dermatologic: Urticaria, rash
Gastrointestinal: Nausea, vomiting, abnormal taste
Hematologic: Disseminated intravascular coagulation (DIC)
Local: Injection site discomfort
Neuromuscular & skeletal: Tingling
Respiratory: Dyspnea, laryngeal edema, allergic rhinitis
Miscellaneous: Transient fever (following rapid administration), anaphylaxis, burning sensation in jaw/skull

Drug Interactions
Increased Effect/Toxicity: Do not coadminister with aminocaproic acid; may increase risk for thrombosis.

Mechanism of Action Replaces deficient clotting factor IX; concentrate of factor IX; hemophilia B, or Christmas disease, is an X-linked inherited disorder of blood coagulation characterized by insufficient or abnormal synthesis of the clotting protein factor IX. Factor IX is a vitamin K-dependent coagulation factor which is synthesized in the liver. Factor IX is activated by factor XIa in the intrinsic coagulation pathway. Activated factor IX (IXa), in combination with factor VII:C activates factor X to Xa, resulting ultimately in the conversion of prothrombin to thrombin and the formation of a fibrin clot. The infusion of exogenous factor IX to replace the deficiency present in hemophilia B temporarily restores hemostasis. Depending upon the patient's level of biologically active factor IX, clinical symptoms range from moderate skin bruising or excessive hemorrhage after trauma or surgery to spontaneous hemorrhage into joints, muscles, or internal organs including the brain. Severe or recurring hemorrhages can produce death, organ dysfunction, or orthopedic deformity.

Pharmacodynamics/Kinetics Half-life elimination: IX component: 23-31 hours
Dosage Dosage is expressed in units of factor IX activity and must be individualized. I.V. only:

Formula for units required to raise blood level %:
AlphaNine® SD, Mononine®: Children and Adults:
Number of Factor IX Units Required = body weight (in kg) x desired Factor IX level increase (% normal) x 1 unit/kg
For example, for a 100% level a patient who has an actual level of 20%: Number of Factor IX Units needed = 70 kg x 80% x 1 Unit/kg = 5600 Units
BeneFix®:
Children <15 years:
Number of Factor IX Units Required = body weight (in kg) x desired Factor IX level increase (% normal) x 1.4 units/kg
Adults:
Number of Factor IX Units Required = body weight (in kg) x desired Factor IX level increase (% normal) x 1.2 units/kg

Guidelines: As a general rule, the level of factor IX required for treatment of different conditions is listed below:
Minor spontaneous hemorrhage, prophylaxis:
Desired levels of factor IX for hemostasis: 15% to 25%
Initial loading dose to achieve desired level: 20-30 units/kg
Frequency of dosing: Every 12-24 hours if necessary
Duration of treatment: 1-2 days
Moderate hemorrhage:
Desired levels of factor IX for hemostasis: 25% to 50%
Initial loading dose to achieve desired level: 25-50 units/kg
(Continued)

Factor IX *(Continued)*

Frequency of dosing: Every 12-24 hours
Duration of treatment: 2-7 days
Major hemorrhage:
    Desired levels of factor IX for hemostasis: >50%
    Initial loading dose to achieve desired level: 30-50 units/kg
    Frequency of dosing: Every 12-24 hours, depending on half-life and measured factor IX levels (after 3-5 days, maintain at least 20% activity)
    Duration of treatment: 7-10 days, depending upon nature of insult
Surgery:
    Desired levels of factor IX for hemostasis: 50% to 100%
    Initial loading dose to achieve desired level: 50-100 units/kg
    Frequency of dosing: Every 12-24 hours, depending on half-life and measured factor IX levels
    Duration of treatment: 7-10 days, depending upon nature of insult

Administration Solution should be infused at room temperature
    I.V. administration only: Should be infused **slowly**: The rate of administration should be determined by the response and comfort of the patient.
    Mononine®: Intravenous dosage administration rates of up to 225 units/minute (~2 mL/minute) have been regularly tolerated without incident. **Infuse at a rate not exceeding 2 mL/minute.**

Monitoring Parameters Levels of factors IX, PTT

Reference Range Average normal factor IX levels are 50% to 150%; patients with severe hemophilia will have levels <1%, often undetectable. Moderate forms of the disease have levels of 1% to 10% while some mild cases may have 11% to 49% of normal factor IX.

Maintain factor IX plasma level at least 20% until hemostasis achieved after acute joint or muscle bleeding
In preparation for and following surgery:
    Level to prevent spontaneous hemorrhage: 5%
    Minimum level for hemostasis following trauma and surgery: 30% to 50%
    Severe hemorrhage: >60%
    Major surgery: ≥50% prior to procedure, 30% to 50% for several days after surgery, and >20% for 10-14 days thereafter

Patient Information Early signs of hypersensitivity reactions including hives, generalized urticaria, tightness of the chest, wheezing, hypotension, and anaphylaxis indicate discontinuation of use of the concentrate and prescriber should be contacted if these symptoms occur

Dosage Forms (**Note:** Exact potency labeled on each vial): **INJ, powder for reconstitution:** (AlphaNine® SD) [human derived; solvent detergent treated, virus filtered; contains nondetectable levels of factors II, VII, X; supplied with diluent]; (BeneFix®) [recombinant formulation; supplied with diluent]; (Mononine®) [human derived; monoclonal antibody purified; contains nondetectable levels of factors II, VII, X; supplied with diluent]

Factor IX Complex (Human) *(FAK ter nyne KOM pleks HYU man)*

U.S. Brand Names Bebulin® VH; Profilnine® SD; Proplex® T

Synonyms Prothrombin Complex Concentrate

Therapeutic Category Antihemophilic Agent; Blood Product Derivative

Use

Control bleeding in patients with factor IX deficiency (hemophilia B or Christmas disease)
    Note: Factor IX concentrate containing **only** factor IX is also available and preferable for this indication.
Prevention/control of bleeding in hemophilia A patients with inhibitors to factor VIII
Prevention/control of bleeding in patients with factor VII deficiency
Emergency correction of the coagulopathy of warfarin excess in critical situations.

Pregnancy Risk Factor C

Contraindications Liver disease with signs of intravascular coagulation or fibrinolysis, not for use in factor VII deficiencies, patients undergoing elective surgery

Warnings/Precautions Use with caution in patients with liver dysfunction; prepared from pooled human plasma - the risk of viral transmission is not totally eradicated; monitor patients who receive repeated doses twice daily with PTT and prothrombin time and level of factor being replaced (eg, usually VII or IX); if PT is <10 seconds, this may indicate risk of hypercoagulable complication

Common Adverse Reactions 1% to 10%:
Central nervous system: Fever, headache, chills
Neuromuscular & skeletal: Tingling
Miscellaneous: Following rapid administration: Transient fever

Drug Interactions
    Increased Effect/Toxicity: Do not coadminister with aminocaproic acid; may increase risk for thrombosis.

Mechanism of Action Replaces deficient clotting factor including factor X; hemophilia B, or Christmas disease, is an X-linked recessively inherited disorder of blood coagulation characterized by insufficient or abnormal synthesis of the clotting protein factor IX. Factor IX is a vitamin K-dependent coagulation factor which is synthesized in the liver. Factor IX is activated by factor XIa in the intrinsic coagulation pathway. Activated factor IX (IXa), in combination with factor VII:C activates factor X to Xa, resulting ultimately in the conversion of prothrombin to thrombin and the formation of a fibrin clot. The infusion of exogenous factor IX to replace the deficiency present in hemophilia B temporarily restores hemostasis.

Pharmacodynamics/Kinetics
Half-life elimination:
   VII component: Initial: 4-6 hours; Terminal: 22.5 hours
   IX component: 24 hours

Dosage Children and Adults: Dosage is expressed in units of factor IX activity and must be individualized. I.V. only:
   Formula for units required to raise blood level %:
     Total blood volume (mL blood/kg) = 70 mL/kg (adults), 80 mL/kg (children)
     Plasma volume = total blood volume (mL) x [1 - Hct (in decimals)]
       For example, for a 70 kg adult with a Hct = 40%: Plasma volume = [70 kg x 70 mL/kg] x [1 - 0.4] = 2940 mL
       To calculate number of units needed to increase level to desired range (highly individualized and dependent on patient's condition): Number of units = desired level increase [desired level - actual level] x plasma volume (in mL)
       For example, for a 100% level in the above patient who has an actual level of 20%: Number of units needed = [1 (for a 100% level) - 0.2] x 2940 mL = 2352 units
   As a general rule, the level of factor IX required for treatment of different conditions is listed below:

Minor Spontaneous Hemorrhage, Prophylaxis:
   Desired levels of factor IX for hemostasis: 15% to 25%
   Initial loading dose to achieve desired level: <20-30 units/kg
   Frequency of dosing: Once; repeated in 24 hours if necessary
   Duration of treatment: Once; repeated if necessary

Major Trauma or Surgery:
   Desired levels of factor IX for hemostasis: 25% to 50%
   Initial loading dose to achieve desired level: <75 units/kg
   Frequency of dosing: Every 18-30 hours, depending on half-life and measured factor IX levels
   Duration of treatment: Up to 10 days, depending upon nature of insult

   Factor VIII inhibitor patients: 75 units/kg/dose; may be given every 6-12 hours
   Anticoagulant overdosage: I.V.: 15 units/kg

Administration Solution should be infused at room temperature
   I.V. administration only: Should be infused **slowly**: Start infusion at a rate of 2-3 mL/minute. If headache, flushing, changes in pulse rate or blood pressure appear, the infusion rate should be decreased. Initially, stop the infusion until the symptoms disappear, then resume the infusion at a slower rate. **Infuse at a rate not exceeding 3 mL/minute.**

Monitoring Parameters Levels of factors being replaced (eg, VII or IX), PT, PTT

Reference Range Average normal factor VII and factor IX levels are 50% to 150%; patients with severe hemophilia will have levels <1%, often undetectable. Moderate forms of the disease have levels of 1% to 10% while some mild cases may have 11% to 49% of normal factor IX.

   Maintain factor IX plasma level at least 20% until hemostasis achieved after acute joint or muscle bleeding
   In preparation for and following surgery:
   Level to prevent spontaneous hemorrhage: 5%
   Minimum level for hemostasis following trauma and surgery: 30% to 50%
   Severe hemorrhage: >60%
   Major surgery: >60% prior to procedure, 30% to 50% for several days after surgery, and >20% for 7-10 days thereafter

Patient Information Early signs of hypersensitivity reactions including hives, generalized urticaria, tightness of the chest, wheezing, hypotension, and anaphylaxis indicate discontinuation of use of the concentrate and prescriber should be contacted if these symptoms occur

Dosage Forms (**Note:** Exact potency labeled on each vial): **INJ, powder for reconstitution:** (Bebulin® VH) [single-dose vial; vapor heated; supplied with sterile water for injection]; (Profilnine® SD) [single-dose vial; solvent detergent treated]; (Proplex® T) [single-dose vial; heat treated; supplied with sterile water for injection]

♦ **Factor VIII (Human)** *see* Antihemophilic Factor (Human) *on page 103*
♦ **Factor VIII (Porcine)** *see* Antihemophilic Factor (Porcine) *on page 104*
♦ **Factor VIII (Recombinant)** *see* Antihemophilic Factor (Recombinant) *on page 105*
♦ **Factrel®** *see* Gonadorelin *on page 599*

Famciclovir (fam SYE kloe veer)

U.S. Brand Names Famvir®
Therapeutic Category Antiviral Agent
Use Management of acute herpes zoster (shingles) and recurrent episodes of genital herpes; treatment of recurrent herpes simplex in immunocompetent patients
Pregnancy Risk Factor B
Contraindications Hypersensitivity to famciclovir or any component of the formulation
Warnings/Precautions Has not been studied in immunocompromised patients or patients with ophthalmic or disseminated zoster; dosage adjustment is required in patients with renal insufficiency (Cl_{cr} <60 mL/minute) and in patients with noncompensated hepatic disease; safety and efficacy have not been established in children <18 years of age; animal studies indicated increases in incidence of carcinomas, mutagenic changes, and decreases in fertility with extremely large doses
(Continued)

Famciclovir (Continued)

Common Adverse Reactions 1% to 10%:
Central nervous system: Fatigue (4% to 6%), fever (1% to 3%), dizziness (3% to 5%), somnolence (1% to 2%), headache
Dermatologic: Pruritus (1% to 4%)
Gastrointestinal: Diarrhea (4% to 8%), vomiting (1% to 5%), constipation (1% to 5%), anorexia (1% to 3%), abdominal pain (1% to 4%), nausea
Neuromuscular & skeletal: Paresthesia (1% to 3%)
Respiratory: Sinusitis/pharyngitis (2%)

Drug Interactions
Increased Effect/Toxicity:
Cimetidine: Penciclovir AUC may increase due to impaired metabolism.
Digoxin: C_{max} of digoxin increases by ~19%.
Probenecid: Penciclovir serum levels significantly increase.
Theophylline: Penciclovir AUC/C_{max} may increase and renal clearance decrease, although not clinically significant.

Mechanism of Action After undergoing rapid biotransformation to the active compound, penciclovir, famciclovir is phosphorylated by viral thymidine kinase in HSV-1, HSV-2, and VZV-infected cells to a monophosphate form; this is then converted to penciclovir triphosphate and competes with deoxyguanosine triphosphate to inhibit HSV-2 polymerase (ie, herpes viral DNA synthesis/replication is selectively inhibited)

Pharmacodynamics/Kinetics
Absorption: Food decreases maximum peak concentration and delays time to peak; AUC remains the same
Distribution: V_{dss}: 0.98-1.08 L/kg
Protein binding: 20%
Metabolism: Rapidly deacetylated and oxidized to penciclovir; not via CYP
Bioavailability: 77%
Half-life elimination: Penciclovir: 2-3 hours (10, 20, and 7 hours in HSV-1, HSV-2, and VZV-infected cells, respectively); prolonged with renal impairment
Time to peak: 0.9 hours; C_{max} and T_{max} are decreased and prolonged with noncompensated hepatic impairment
Excretion: Urine (>90% as unchanged drug)

Dosage Initiate therapy as soon as herpes zoster is diagnosed: Adults: Oral:
Acute herpes zoster: 500 mg every 8 hours for 7 days
Recurrent herpes simplex in immunocompetent patients: 125 mg twice daily for 5 days
Genital herpes:
First episode: 250 mg 3 times/day for 7-10 days
Recurrent episodes: 125 mg twice daily for 5 days
Prophylaxis: 250 mg twice daily
Severe (hospitalized patients): 250 mg twice daily
Dosing interval in renal impairment:
Herpes zoster:
Cl_{cr} ≥60 mL/minute: Administer 500 mg every 8 hours
Cl_{cr} 40-59 mL/minute: Administer 500 mg every 12 hours
Cl_{cr} 20-39 mL/minute: Administer 500 mg every 24 hours
Cl_{cr} <20 mL/minute: Administer 250 mg every 24 hours
Recurrent genital herpes:
Cl_{cr} ≥40 mL/minute: Administer 125 mg every 12 hours
Cl_{cr} 20-39 mL/minute: Administer 125 mg every 24 hours
Cl_{cr} <20 mL/minute: Administer 125 mg every 48 hours
Suppression of recurrent genital herpes:
Cl_{cr} ≥40 mL/minute: Administer 250 mg every 12 hours
Cl_{cr} 20-39 mL/minute: Administer 125 mg every 12 hours
Cl_{cr} <20 mL/minute: Administer 125 mg every 24 hours
Recurrent orolabial or genital herpes in HIV-infected patients:
Cl_{cr} ≥40 mL/minute: Administer 500 mg every 12 hours
Cl_{cr} 20-39 mL/minute: Administer 500 mg every 24 hours
Cl_{cr} <20 mL/minute: Administer 250 mg every 24 hours

Monitoring Parameters Periodic CBC during long-term therapy
Patient Information Initiate therapy as soon as herpes zoster is diagnosed; may take medication with food or on an empty stomach
Dosage Forms TAB: 125 mg, 250 mg, 500 mg

Famotidine (fa MOE ti deen)

U.S. Brand Names Pepcid®; Pepcid® AC [OTC]
Therapeutic Category Antihistamine, H_2 Blocker; Histamine H_2 Antagonist
Use Therapy and treatment of duodenal ulcer, gastric ulcer, control gastric pH in critically-ill patients, symptomatic relief in gastritis, gastroesophageal reflux, active benign ulcer, and pathological hypersecretory conditions
OTC labeling: Relief of heartburn, acid indigestion, and sour stomach
Unlabeled/Investigational Use Part of a multidrug regimen for *H. pylori* eradication to reduce the risk of duodenal ulcer recurrence
Pregnancy Risk Factor B
Contraindications Hypersensitivity to famotidine, other H_2 antagonists, or any component of the formulation

Warnings/Precautions Modify dose in patients with renal impairment; chewable tablets contain phenylalanine; multidose vials contain benzyl alcohol

Common Adverse Reactions

Note: Agitation and vomiting have been reported in up to 14% of pediatric patients <1 year of age.

1% to 10%:

Central nervous system: Dizziness (1%), headache (5%)

Gastrointestinal: Constipation (1%), diarrhea (2%)

Drug Interactions

Decreased Effect: Decreased serum levels of ketoconazole and itraconazole (reduced absorption).

Mechanism of Action Competitive inhibition of histamine at H_2 receptors of the gastric parietal cells, which inhibits gastric acid secretion

Pharmacodynamics/Kinetics

Onset of action: GI: Oral: Within 1-3 hour

Duration: 10-12 hours

Protein binding: 15% to 20%

Bioavailability: Oral: 40% to 50%

Half-life elimination: 2.5-3.5 hours; prolonged with renal impairment; Oliguria: 20 hours

Time to peak, serum: Oral: ~1-3 hours

Excretion: Urine (as unchanged drug)

Dosage

Children: Treatment duration and dose should be individualized

Peptic ulcer: 1-16 years:

Oral: 0.5 mg/kg/day at bedtime or divided twice daily (maximum dose: 40 mg/day); doses of up to 1 mg/kg/day have been used in clinical studies

I.V.: 0.25 mg/kg every 12 hours (maximum dose: 40 mg/day); doses of up to 0.5 mg/kg have been used in clinical studies

GERD: Oral:

<3 months: 0.5 mg/kg once daily

3-12 months: 0.5 mg/kg twice daily

1-16 years: 1 mg/kg/day divided twice daily (maximum dose: 40 mg twice daily); doses of up to 2 mg/kg/day have been used in clinical studies

Children ≥12 years and Adults: Heartburn, indigestion, sour stomach: OTC labeling: Oral: 10-20 mg every 12 hours; dose may be taken 15-60 minutes before eating foods known to cause heartburn

Adults:

Duodenal ulcer: Oral: Acute therapy: 40 mg/day at bedtime for 4-8 weeks; maintenance therapy: 20 mg/day at bedtime

Helicobacter pylori eradication (unlabeled use): 40 mg once daily; requires combination therapy with antibiotics

Gastric ulcer: Oral: Acute therapy: 40 mg/day at bedtime

Hypersecretory conditions: Oral: Initial: 20 mg every 6 hours, may increase in increments up to 160 mg every 6 hours

GERD: Oral: 20 mg twice daily for 6 weeks

Esophagitis and accompanying symptoms due to GERD: Oral: 20 mg or 40 mg twice daily for up to 12 weeks

Patients unable to take oral medication: I.V.: 20 mg every 12 hours

Dosing adjustment in renal impairment: Cl_{cr} <50 mL/minute: Manufacturer recommendation: Administer 50% of dose **or** increase the dosing interval to every 36-48 hours (to limit potential CNS adverse effects).

Administration

I.V. push: Inject over at least 2 minutes

Solution for infusion: Administer over 15-30 minutes

Patient Information

Oral suspension: Shake well before use

OTC: Do not use for more than 14 days unless recommended by prescriber

Dosage Forms GELCAP (Pepcid® AC): 10 mg. **INF** [premixed in NS] (Pepcid®): 20 mg (50 mL). **INJ, solution** 10 mg/mL (4 mL, 20 mL, 50 mL); (Pepcid®): 10 mg/mL (4 mL, 20 mL). **INJ, solution** [preservative free] (Pepcid®): 10 mg/mL (2 mL). **POWDER, oral suspension** (Pepcid®): 40 mg/5 mL (50 mL). **TAB, chewable** (Pepcid® AC): 10 mg. **TAB:** 10 mg [OTC], 20 mg, 40 mg; (Pepcid®): 20 mg, 40 mg; (Pepcid® AC): 10 mg, 20 mg

Famotidine, Calcium Carbonate, and Magnesium Hydroxide

(fa MOE ti deen, KAL see um KAR bun ate, & mag NEE zhum hye DROKS ide)

U.S. Brand Names Pepcid® Complete [OTC]

Synonyms Calcium Carbonate, Magnesium Hydroxide, and Famotidine; Magnesium Hydroxide, Famotidine, and Calcium Carbonate

Therapeutic Category Antacid; Histamine H_2 Antagonist

Use Relief of heartburn due to acid indigestion

Contraindications Hypersensitivity to famotidine or other H_2 antagonists, calcium carbonate, magnesium hydroxide, or any component of the formulation. See individual agents for additional information.

Warnings/Precautions See individual agents.

Common Adverse Reactions See individual agents.

(Continued)

Famotidine, Calcium Carbonate, and Magnesium Hydroxide
(Continued)

Drug Interactions
Increased Effect/Toxicity: See individual agents.
Decreased Effect: See individual agents.
Mechanism of Action
Famotidine: H₂ antagonist
Calcium carbonate: Antacid
Magnesium hydroxide: Antacid
Pharmacodynamics/Kinetics See individual agents.
Dosage Children ≥12 years and Adults: Relief of heartburn due to acid indigestion: Oral: Pepcid® Complete: 1 tablet as needed; no more than 2 tablets in 24 hours; do **not** swallow whole, chew tablet completely before swallowing; do not use for longer than 14 days (see Additional Information for dosing ranges for individual ingredients)
Patient Information Do **not** swallow tablet whole; chew completely before swallowing. Contact prescriber if your symptoms last for more than 14 days. Should not be used in combination with other products for acid indigestion (prescription or over the counter). Certain foods are more likely to cause acid indigestion in some patients, including foods that are rich, spicy, fatty, or fried; chocolate; caffeine; alcohol; some fruits or vegetables. Avoid meals close to bedtime, eat slowly and avoid big meals to help decrease symptoms. Avoid smoking. Notify prescriber if you are pregnant or breast-feeding.
Dosage Forms TAB, chewable (Pepcid® Complete): Famotidine 10 mg, calcium 800 mg, and magnesium 165 mg

♦ **Famvir®** *see* Famciclovir *on page 505*
♦ **Fansidar®** *see* Sulfadoxine and Pyrimethamine *on page 1172*
♦ **Fareston®** *see* Toremifene *on page 1245*
♦ **Faslodex®** *see* Fulvestrant *on page 571*

Fat Emulsion (fat e MUL shun)
U.S. Brand Names Intralipid®; Liposyn® III
Synonyms Intravenous Fat Emulsion
Therapeutic Category Caloric Agent
Use Source of calories and essential fatty acids for patients requiring parenteral nutrition of extended duration
Pregnancy Risk Factor B/C
Contraindications Hypersensitivity to fat emulsion or any component of the formulation; severe egg (soybean) allergies; pathologic hyperlipidemia, lipoid nephrosis pancreatitis with hyperlipemia
Warnings/Precautions Use caution in patients with severe liver damage, pulmonary disease, anemia, or blood coagulation disorder; use with caution in jaundiced, premature, and low birth weight children
Common Adverse Reactions Frequency not defined.
Cardiovascular: Cyanosis, flushing, chest pain
Central nervous system: Headache, dizziness
Endocrine & metabolic: Hyperlipemia
Gastrointestinal: Nausea, vomiting, diarrhea
Hematologic: Hypercoagulability, thrombocytopenia in neonates (rare)
Hepatic: Hepatomegaly
Local: Thrombophlebitis
Respiratory: Dyspnea
Miscellaneous: Sepsis, diaphoresis
Mechanism of Action Essential for normal structure and function of cell membranes
Pharmacodynamics/Kinetics
Metabolism: Undergoes lipolysis to free fatty acids which are utilized by reticuloendothelial cells
Half-life elimination: 0.5-1 hour
Dosage Fat emulsion should not exceed 60% of the total daily calories
Premature Infants: Initial dose: 0.25-0.5 g/kg/day, increase by 0.25-0.5 g/kg/day to a maximum of 3 g/kg/day depending on needs/nutritional goals; limit to 1 g/kg/day if on phototherapy; maximum rate of infusion: 0.15 g/kg/hour (0.75 mL/kg/hour of 20% solution)
Infants and Children: Initial dose: 0.5-1 g/kg/day, increase by 0.5 g/kg/day to a maximum of 3 g/kg/day depending on needs/nutritional goals; maximum rate of infusion: 0.25 g/kg/hour (1.25 mL/kg/hour of 20% solution)
Adolescents and Adults: Initial dose: 1 g/kg/day, increase by 0.5-1 g/kg/day to a maximum of 2.5 g/kg/day of 10% and 3 g/kg/day of 20% depending on needs/nutritional goals; maximum rate of infusion: 0.25 g/kg/hour (1.25 mL/kg/hour of 20% solution); do not exceed 50 mL/hour (20%) or 100 mL/hour (10%)
Prevention of essential fatty acid deficiency (8% to 10% of total caloric intake): 0.5-1 g/kg/24 hours
Children: 5-10 mL/kg/day at 0.1 mL/minute then up to 100 mL/hour
Adults: 500 mL (10%) twice weekly at rate of 1 mL/minute for 30 minutes, then increase to 42 mL/hour (500 mL over 12 hours)
Note: At the onset of therapy, the patient should be observed for any immediate allergic reactions such as dyspnea, cyanosis, and fever; slower initial rates of infusion may be used

for the first 10-15 minutes of the infusion (eg, 0.1 mL/minute of 10% or 0.05 mL/minute of 20% solution)

Administration May be simultaneously infused with amino acid dextrose mixtures by means of Y-connector located near infusion site. The 10% isotonic solution which has 1.1 cal/mL (10%) and may be administered peripherally; the 20% (2 cal/mL) is not recommended for use in low birth weight infants.

Monitoring Parameters Serum triglycerides; before initiation of therapy and at least weekly during therapy. Frequent (some advise daily) platelet counts should be performed in neonatal patients receiving parenteral lipids.

Dosage Forms INJ, emulsion (Intralipid®): 10% [100 mg/mL] (100 mL, 250 mL, 500 mL); 20% [200 mg/mL] (50 mL, 100 mL, 250 mL, 500 mL, 1000 mL); 30% [300 mg/mL] (500 mL); (Liposyn® III): 10% [100 mg/mL] (200 mL, 500 mL); 20% [200 mg/mL] (200 mL, 500 mL); 30% [300 mg/mL] (300 mL)

♦ **5-FC** see Flucytosine on page 528

♦ **FC1157a** see Toremifene on page 1245

♦ **Febrile Seizures** see page 1478

♦ **Feiba VH®** see Anti-inhibitor Coagulant Complex on page 106

Felbamate (FEL ba mate)

U.S. Brand Names Felbatol®

Therapeutic Category Anticonvulsant, Miscellaneous

Use Not as a first-line antiepileptic treatment; only in those patients who respond inadequately to alternative treatments and whose epilepsy is so severe that a substantial risk of aplastic anemia and/or liver failure is deemed acceptable in light of the benefits conferred by its use. Patient must be fully advised of risk and provide signed written informed consent. Felbamate can be used as either monotherapy or adjunctive therapy in the treatment of partial seizures (with and without generalization) and in adults with epilepsy.

Orphan drug: Adjunctive therapy in the treatment of partial and generalized seizures associated with Lennox-Gastaut syndrome in children

Restrictions A patient "informed consent" form should be completed and signed by the patient and physician. Copies are available from Wallace Pharmaceuticals by calling 609-655-6147.

Pregnancy Risk Factor C

Contraindications Hypersensitivity to felbamate or any component of the formulation; use with caution in those patients who have demonstrated hypersensitivity reactions to other carbamates

Warnings/Precautions Use with caution in patients allergic to other carbamates (eg, meprobamate); antiepileptic drugs should not be suddenly discontinued because of the possibility of increasing seizure frequency; **ten cases of aplastic anemia reported in the U.S. after 2½ to 6 months of therapy**; Carter Wallace and the FDA recommended the use of this agent be suspended unless withdrawal of the product would place a patient at greater risk as compared to the frequently fatal form of anemia. Felbamate has also been associated with rare cases of hepatic failure (estimated >6 cases per 75,000 patients per year). Use caution in renal impairment (dose adjustment recommended). "Informed consent" (concerning hematological/hepatic risks) should be documented prior to initiation of therapy.

Common Adverse Reactions

>10%:
Central nervous system: Somnolence, headache, fatigue, dizziness
Gastrointestinal: Nausea, anorexia, vomiting, constipation

1% to 10%:
Cardiovascular: Chest pain, palpitations, tachycardia
Central nervous system: Depression or behavior changes, nervousness, anxiety, ataxia, stupor, malaise, agitation, psychological disturbances, aggressive reaction
Dermatologic: Skin rash, acne, pruritus
Gastrointestinal: Xerostomia, diarrhea, abdominal pain, weight gain, taste perversion
Neuromuscular & skeletal: Tremor, abnormal gait, paresthesia, myalgia
Ocular: Diplopia, abnormal vision
Respiratory: Sinusitis, pharyngitis
Miscellaneous: ALT increase

Drug Interactions

Cytochrome P450 Effect: Substrate of CYP2E1 (minor), 3A4 (major); **Inhibits** CYP2C19 (weak); **Induces** CYP3A4 (weak)

Increased Effect/Toxicity: Felbamate increases serum phenytoin, phenobarbital, and valproic acid concentrations which may result in toxicity; consider decreasing phenytoin or phenobarbital dosage by 25%. A decrease in valproic acid dosage may also be necessary.

Decreased Effect: Carbamazepine, phenytoin may decrease serum felbamate concentrations. Felbamate may decrease carbamazepine levels and increase levels of the active metabolite of carbamazepine (10,11-epoxide) resulting in carbamazepine toxicity; monitor for signs of carbamazepine toxicity (dizziness, ataxia, nystagmus, drowsiness).

Mechanism of Action Mechanism of action is unknown but has properties in common with other marketed anticonvulsants; has weak inhibitory effects on GABA-receptor binding, benzodiazepine receptor binding, and is devoid of activity at the MK-801 receptor binding site of the NMDA receptor-ionophore complex.

Pharmacodynamics/Kinetics

Absorption: Rapid and almost complete; food has no effect upon the tablet's absorption
Distribution: V_d: 0.7-1 L/kg
Protein binding: 22% to 25%, primarily to albumin
(Continued)

Felbamate *(Continued)*

Half-life elimination: 20-23 hours (average); prolonged in renal dysfunction
Time to peak, serum: ~3 hours
Excretion: Urine (40% to 50% as unchanged drug, 40% as inactive metabolites)

Dosage Anticonvulsant:

Monotherapy: Children >14 years and Adults:

Initial: 1200 mg/day in divided doses 3 or 4 times/day; titrate previously untreated patients under close clinical supervision, increasing the dosage in 600 mg increments every 2 weeks to 2400 mg/day based on clinical response and thereafter to 3600 mg/day as clinically indicated

Conversion to monotherapy: Initiate at 1200 mg/day in divided doses 3 or 4 times/day, reduce the dosage of the concomitant anticonvulsant(s) by 20% to 33% at the initiation of felbamate therapy; at week 2, increase the felbamate dosage to 2400 mg/day while reducing the dosage of the other anticonvulsant(s) up to an additional 33% of their original dosage; at week 3, increase the felbamate dosage up to 3600 mg/day and continue to reduce the dosage of the other anticonvulsant(s) as clinically indicated

Adjunctive therapy: Children with Lennox-Gastaut and ages 2-14 years:

Week 1:

Felbamate: 15 mg/kg/day divided 3-4 times/day
Concomitant anticonvulsant(s): Reduce original dosage by 20% to 30%

Week 2:

Felbamate: 30 mg/kg/day divided 3-4 times/day
Concomitant anticonvulsant(s): Reduce original dosage up to an additional 33%

Week 3:

Felbamate: 45 mg/kg/day divided 3-4 times/day
Concomitant anticonvulsant(s): Reduce dosage as clinically indicated

Adjunctive therapy: Children >14 years and Adults:

Week 1:

Felbamate: 1200 mg/day initial dose
Concomitant anticonvulsant(s): Reduce original dosage by 20% to 33%

Week 2:

Felbamate: 2400 mg/day (therapeutic range)
Concomitant anticonvulsant(s): Reduce original dosage by up to an additional 33%

Week 3:

Felbamate: 3600 mg/day (therapeutic range)
Concomitant anticonvulsant(s): Reduce original dosage as clinically indicated

Dosage adjustment in renal impairment: Use caution; reduce initial and maintenance doses by 50% (half-life prolonged by 9-15 hours)

Administration Administer on an empty stomach for best absorption.

Monitoring Parameters Monitor serum levels of concomitant anticonvulsant therapy; monitor AST, ALT, and bilirubin weekly. Hematologic evaluations before therapy begins, frequently during therapy, and for a significant period after discontinuation.

Reference Range Not necessary to routinely monitor serum drug levels, since dose should be titrated to clinical response

Patient Information Take exactly as directed (do not increase dose or frequency or discontinue without consulting prescriber). While using this medication, do not use alcohol and other prescription or OTC medications (especially pain medications, sedatives, antihistamines, or hypnotics) without consulting prescriber. Maintain adequate hydration (2-3 L/day of fluids unless instructed to restrict fluid intake). You may experience drowsiness, dizziness, or blurred vision (use caution when driving or engaging in tasks requiring alertness until response to drug is known); nausea, vomiting, loss of appetite, or dry mouth (small frequent meals, frequent mouth care, chewing gum, or sucking lozenges may help). Wear identification of epileptic status and medications. Report CNS changes, mentation changes, or changes in cognition; muscle cramping, weakness, tremors, changes in gait; persistent GI symptoms (cramping, constipation, vomiting, anorexia); rash or skin irritations; unusual bruising or bleeding (mouth, urine, stool); cough, runny nose, sore throat, or difficulty breathing; worsening of seizure activity, or loss of seizure control.

Dosage Forms SUSP, oral: 600 mg/5 mL (240 mL, 960 mL). **TAB:** 400 mg, 600 mg

♦ **Felbatol®** *see Felbamate on page 509*
♦ **Feldene®** *see Piroxicam on page 1008*

Felodipine *(fe LOE di peen)*

Related Information

Calcium Channel Blockers Comparison *on page 1371*

U.S. Brand Names Plendil®

Therapeutic Category Antihypertensive Agent; Calcium Channel Blocker

Use Treatment of hypertension, congestive heart failure

Pregnancy Risk Factor C

Contraindications Hypersensitivity to felodipine, any component of the formulation, or other calcium channel blocker

Warnings/Precautions Use with caution and titrate dosages for patients with impaired renal or hepatic function; use caution when treating patients with CHF, sick-sinus syndrome, severe left ventricular dysfunction, hypertrophic cardiomyopathy (especially obstructive), concomitant therapy with beta-blockers or digoxin, edema, or increased intracranial pressure with cranial tumors; do not abruptly withdraw (may cause chest pain); elderly may experience hypotension and constipation more readily. Safety and efficacy in children have not been established. Dosage titration should occur after 14 days on a given dose.

Common Adverse Reactions
>10%: Central nervous system: Headache (11% to 15%)
2% to 10%: Cardiovascular: Peripheral edema (2% to 17%), tachycardia (0.4% to 2.5%), flushing (4% to 7%)

Drug Interactions
  Cytochrome P450 Effect: Substrate of CYP3A4 (major); **Inhibits** CYP2C8/9 (weak), 2D6 (weak), 3A4 (weak)
  Increased Effect/Toxicity: Inhibitors of CYP3A4, including azole antifungals (ketoconazole, itraconazole) and erythromycin, may inhibit calcium channel blocker metabolism, increasing the effects of felodipine. Beta-blockers may have increased pharmacokinetic or pharmacodynamic interactions with felodipine. Cyclosporine increases felodipine's serum concentration. Ethanol increases felodipine's absorption; watch for a greater hypotensive effect. Blood pressure-lowering effects may be additive with sildenafil, tadalafil, and vardenafil (use caution).
  Decreased Effect: Felodipine may decrease pharmacologic actions of theophylline. Calcium may reduce the calcium channel blocker's effects, particularly hypotension. Carbamazepine significantly reduces felodipine's bioavailability; avoid this combination. Nafcillin decreases plasma concentration of felodipine; avoid this combination. Rifampin increases the metabolism of felodipine. Felodipine may decrease pharmacologic actions of theophylline.

Mechanism of Action Inhibits calcium ions from entering the "slow channels" or select voltage-sensitive areas of vascular smooth muscle and myocardium during depolarization, producing a relaxation of coronary vascular smooth muscle and coronary vasodilation; increases myocardial oxygen delivery in patients with vasospastic angina

Pharmacodynamics/Kinetics
  Onset of action: 2-5 hours
  Duration: 16-24 hours
  Absorption: 100%; Absolute: 20% due to first-pass effect
  Protein binding: >99%
  Metabolism: Hepatic; extensive first-pass effect
  Half-life elimination: 11-16 hours
  Excretion: Urine (as metabolites)

Dosage
  Adults: Oral: 2.5-10 mg once daily; usual initial dose: 5 mg; increase by 5 mg at 2-week intervals, as needed; maximum: 10 mg
  Elderly: Begin with 2.5 mg/day
  Dosing adjustment/comments in hepatic impairment: May require lower dosages (initial: 2.5 mg/day); monitor blood pressure

Administration Do not crush or chew extended release tablets; swallow whole.

Patient Information Do not crush or chew tablets; do not discontinue abruptly; report any dizziness, shortness of breath, palpitations or edema occurs

Dosage Forms TAB, extended release: 2.5 mg, 5 mg, 10 mg

♦ **Felodipine and Enalapril** *see* Enalapril and Felodipine *on page 431*

♦ **Femara®** *see* Letrozole *on page 722*

♦ **femhrt®** *see* Ethinyl Estradiol and Norethindrone *on page 487*

♦ **Femiron® [OTC]** *see* Ferrous Fumarate *on page 519*

♦ **Femizol-M™ [OTC]** *see* Miconazole *on page 834*

♦ **Fem-Prin® [OTC]** *see* Acetaminophen, Aspirin, and Caffeine *on page 27*

♦ **Femring™** *see* Estradiol *on page 459*

♦ **Fenesin™ [DSC]** *see* Guaifenesin *on page 603*

♦ **Fenesin™ DM** *see* Guaifenesin and Dextromethorphan *on page 604*

Fenofibrate (fen oh FYE brate)

Related Information
  Lipid-Lowering Agents *on page 1381*
U.S. Brand Names Lofibra™; TriCor®
Synonyms Procetofene; Proctofene
Therapeutic Category Antilipemic Agent, Fibric Acid
Use Adjunct to dietary therapy for the treatment of adults with very high elevations of serum triglyceride levels (types IV and V hyperlipidemia) who are at risk of pancreatitis and who do not respond adequately to a determined dietary effort; adjunct to dietary therapy for the reduction of low density lipoprotein cholesterol (LDL-C), total cholesterol (total-C), triglycerides, and apolipoprotein B (apo B) in adult patients with primary hypercholesterolemia or mixed dyslipidemia (Fredrickson types IIa and IIb)
Pregnancy Risk Factor C
Contraindications Hypersensitivity to fenofibrate or any component of the formulation; hepatic or severe renal dysfunction including primary biliary cirrhosis and unexplained persistent liver function abnormalities; pre-existing gallbladder disease
Warnings/Precautions The hypoprothrombinemic effect of anticoagulants is significantly increased with concomitant fenofibrate administration. Use with caution in patients with severe renal dysfunction. Hepatic transaminases can significantly elevate (dose-related). Regular monitoring of liver function tests is required. May cause cholelithiasis. Adjustments in warfarin therapy may be required with concurrent use. Use caution when combining fenofibrate with HMG-CoA reductase inhibitors (may lead to myopathy, rhabdomyolysis). The effect of CAD (Continued)

Fenofibrate *(Continued)*

morbidity and mortality has not been established. Therapy should be withdrawn if an adequate response is not obtained after 2 months of therapy at the maximal daily dose (201 mg). Rare hypersensitivity reactions may occur. Dose adjustment is required for renal impairment and elderly patients. Safety and efficacy in children have not been established.

Common Adverse Reactions

1% to 10%:

Gastrointestinal: Abdominal pain (5%), constipation (2%)

Hepatic: Abnormal liver function test (7%), creatine phosphokinase increased (3%), ALT increased (3%), AST increased (3%)

Neuromuscular & skeletal: Back pain (3%)

Respiratory: Respiratory disorder (6%), rhinitis (2%)

Frequency not defined:

Cardiovascular: Angina pectoris, arrhythmias, atrial fibrillation, cardiovascular disorder, chest pain, coronary artery disorder, edema, electrocardiogram abnormality, extrasystoles, hypertension, hypotension, migraine, myocardial infarction, palpitations, peripheral edema, peripheral vascular disorder, phlebitis, tachycardia, varicose veins, vasodilatation

Central nervous system: Anxiety, depression, dizziness, fever, insomnia, malaise, nervousness, neuralgia, pain, somnolence, vertigo

Dermatologic: Acne, alopecia, bruising, contact dermatitis, eczema, fungal dermatitis, maculopapular rash, nail disorder, photosensitivity reaction, pruritus, skin disorder, skin ulcer, urticaria

Endocrine & metabolic: Diabetes mellitus, gout, gynecomastia, hypoglycemia, hyperuricemia

Gastrointestinal: Anorexia, appetite increased, colitis, diarrhea, dry mouth, duodenal ulcer, dyspepsia, eructation, esophagitis, flatulence, gastroenteritis, gastritis, gastrointestinal disorder, nausea, peptic ulcer, rectal disorder, rectal hemorrhage, tooth disorder, vomiting, weight gain/loss

Genitourinary: Cystitis, dysuria, prostatic disorder, libido decreased, pregnancy (unintended), urinary frequency, urolithiasis, vaginal moniliasis

Hematologic: Anemia, eosinophilia, leukopenia, lymphadenopathy, thrombocytopenia

Hepatic: Cholelithiasis, cholecystitis, fatty liver deposits

Neuromuscular & skeletal: Arthralgia, arthritis, arthrosis, bursitis, hypertonia, joint disorder, leg cramps, myalgia, myasthenia, myositis, paresthesia, tenosynovitis

Ocular: Abnormal vision, amblyopia, cataract, conjunctivitis, eye disorder, refraction disorder

Otic: Ear pain, otitis media

Renal: Creatinine increased, kidney function abnormality

Respiratory: Asthma, bronchitis, cough increased, dyspnea, laryngitis, pharyngitis, pneumonia, sinusitis

Miscellaneous: Accidental injury, allergic reaction, cyst, diaphoresis, herpes simplex, herpes zoster, infection

Drug Interactions

Cytochrome P450 Effect: Substrate of CYP3A4 (minor)

Increased Effect/Toxicity: The hypolipidemic effect of fenofibrate is increased when used with cholestyramine or colestipol. Fenofibrate may increase the effect of chlorpropamide and warfarin. Concurrent use of fenofibrate with HMG-CoA reductase inhibitors (atorvastatin, cerivastatin, fluvastatin, lovastatin, pravastatin, simvastatin) may increase the risk of myopathy and rhabdomyolysis. The manufacturer warns against concomitant use. However, combination therapy with statins has been used in some patients with resistant hyperlipidemias (with great caution).

Decreased Effect: Rifampin (and potentially other enzyme inducers) may decrease levels of fenofibrate.

Mechanism of Action Fenofibric acid is believed to increase VLDL catabolism by enhancing the synthesis of lipoprotein lipase; as a result of a decrease in VLDL levels, total plasma triglycerides are reduced by 30% to 60%; modest increase in HDL occurs in some hypertriglyceridemic patients

Pharmacodynamics/Kinetics

Absorption: Increased when taken with meals

Distribution: Widely to most tissues

Protein binding: >99%

Metabolism: Tissue and plasma via esterases to active form, fenofibric acid; undergoes inactivation by glucuronidation hepatically or renally

Half-life elimination: 20 hours

Time to peak: 6-8 hours

Excretion: Urine (60% as metabolites); feces (25%); hemodialysis has no effect on removal of fenofibric acid from plasma

Dosage Oral:

Adults:

Hypertriglyceridemia: Initial:

Capsule: 67 mg/day with meals, up to 200 mg/day

Tablet: 54 mg/day with meals, up to 160 mg/day

Hypercholesterolemia or mixed hyperlipidemia: Initial:

Capsule: 200 mg/day with meals

Tablet: 160 mg/day with meals

Elderly: Initial: 67 mg/day (capsule) or 54 mg/day (tablet)

Dosage adjustment in renal impairment: Decrease dose or increase dosing interval for patients with renal failure: Initial: 67 mg/day (capsule) or 54 mg/day (tablet)
Hemodialysis has no effect on removal of fenofibric acid from the plasma.

Administration 6-8 weeks of therapy is required to determine efficacy.

Monitoring Parameters Total serum cholesterol and triglyceride concentration and CLDL, LDL, and HDL levels should be measured periodically; if only marginal changes are noted in 6-8 weeks, the drug should be discontinued; serum transaminases should be measured every 3 months; if ALT values increase >100 units/L, therapy should be discontinued. Monitor LFTs prior to initiation, at 6 and 12 weeks after initiation of first dose, then periodically thereafter.

Patient Information Take with food. Do not change dosage or dosage form without consulting prescriber. Maintain diet and exercise program as prescribed. You may experience mild GI disturbances (eg, gas, diarrhea, constipation, nausea); inform prescriber if these are severe. Report skin rash or irritation, insomnia, unusual muscle pain or tremors, or persistent dizziness.

Dosage Forms CAP [micronized] (Lofibra™): 67 mg, 134 mg, 200 mg. **TAB** (TriCor®): 54 mg, 160 mg

Fenoldopam (fe NOL doe pam)

U.S. Brand Names Corlopam®

Synonyms Fenoldopam Mesylate

Therapeutic Category Antihypertensive Agent

Use Treatment of severe hypertension particularly I.V. and in patients with renal compromise; potential use for congestive heart failure

Contraindications Hypersensitivity of fenoldopam or any component of the formulation; hypersensitivity to sulfites (contains sodium metabisulfite)

Warnings/Precautions Use with caution in patients with cirrhosis, portal hypertension (due to possible increases in portal venous pressure), unstable angina, or glaucoma

Common Adverse Reactions Frequency not defined.
Cardiovascular: Angina, asymptomatic T wave flattening on ECG, chest pain, edema, facial flushing, fibrillation (atrial), flutter (atrial), hypotension, tachycardia
Central nervous system: Dizziness, headache
Gastrointestinal: Diarrhea, nausea, vomiting, xerostomia
Ocular: Intraocular pressure (increased), blurred vision
Hepatic: Increases in portal pressure in cirrhotic patients

Drug Interactions
Increased Effect/Toxicity: Concurrent acetaminophen may increase fenoldopam levels (30% to 70%). Beta-blockers increase the risk of hypotension.

Mechanism of Action A selective postsynaptic dopamine agonist (D_1-receptors) which exerts hypotensive effects by decreasing peripheral vasculature resistance with increased renal blood flow, diuresis, and natriuresis; 6 times as potent as dopamine in producing renal vasodilitation; has minimal adrenergic effects

Pharmacodynamics/Kinetics
Onset of action: I.V.: 10 minutes
Duration: Oral: 2-4 hours; I.V.: 1 hour
Absorption: Oral: Good; peak serum levels at 1 hour
Distribution: V_d: 0.6 L/kg
Half-life elimination: I.V.: 9.8 minutes
Metabolism: Hepatic to multiple metabolites; the 8-sulfate metabolite may have some activity; extensive first-pass effect
Excretion: Urine (80%); feces (20%)

Dosage I.V.: Severe hypertension: Initial: 0.1 mcg/kg/minute; may be increased in increments of 0.05-0.2 mcg/kg/minute until target blood pressure is achieved; average rate: 0.25-0.5 mcg/kg/minute; usual length of treatment is 1-6 hours with tapering of 12% every 15-30 minutes

Dosing adjustment in renal impairment: None required
Dosing adjustment in hepatic impairment: None published

Monitoring Parameters Blood pressure, heart rate, ECG, renal/hepatic function tests

Reference Range Mean plasma fenoldopam levels after a 2 hour infusion (at 0.5 µg/kg/minute) and a 100 mg dose is approximately 13 ng/mL and 50 ng/mL

Dosage Forms INJ, solution: 10 mg/mL (1 mL, 2 mL)

♦ **Fenoldopam Mesylate** see Fenoldopam on page 513

Fenoprofen (fen oh PROE fen)

Related Information
Nonsteroidal Anti-Inflammatory Agents Comparison on page 1401

U.S. Brand Names Nalfon®

Synonyms Fenoprofen Calcium

Therapeutic Category Analgesic, Nonsteroidal Anti-inflammatory Drug; Anti-inflammatory Agent; Nonsteroidal Anti-inflammatory Drug (NSAID), Oral

Use Symptomatic treatment of acute and chronic rheumatoid arthritis and osteoarthritis; relief of mild to moderate pain

Pregnancy Risk Factor B/D (3rd trimester)

Contraindications Hypersensitivity to fenoprofen, aspirin, or other NSAIDs; pregnancy (3rd trimester)

Warnings/Precautions Use with caution in patients with CHF, hypertension, dehydration, decreased renal or hepatic function, history of GI disease (bleeding or ulcers), or those
(Continued)

Fenoprofen *(Continued)*

receiving anticoagulants. Elderly are at a high risk for adverse effects from NSAIDs. As many as 60% of elderly can develop peptic ulceration and/or hemorrhage asymptomatically.

Use lowest effective dose for shortest period possible. Use of NSAIDs can compromise existing renal function especially when Cl_{cr} is <30 mL/minute. CNS adverse effects such as confusion, agitation, and hallucination are generally seen in overdose or high-dose situations; however, elderly may demonstrate these adverse effects at lower doses than younger adults. Withhold for at least 4-6 half-lives prior to surgical or dental procedures.

Common Adverse Reactions
>10%:
Central nervous system: Dizziness (7% to 15%), somnolence (9% to 15%)
Gastrointestinal: Abdominal cramps (2% to 4%), heartburn, indigestion, nausea (8% to 14%), dyspepsia (10% to 14%), flatulence (14%), anorexia (14%), constipation (7% to 14%), occult blood in stool (14%), vomiting (3% to 14%), diarrhea (2% to 14%)
1% to 10%:
Central nervous system: Headache (9%)
Dermatologic: Itching
Endocrine & metabolic: Fluid retention

Drug Interactions
Increased Effect/Toxicity: Increased effect/toxicity of phenytoin, sulfonamides, sulfonylureas, salicylates, and oral anticoagulants. Serum concentration/toxicity of methotrexate may be increased.
Decreased Effect: Decreased effect with phenobarbital.

Mechanism of Action Inhibits prostaglandin synthesis by decreasing the activity of the enzyme, cyclooxygenase, which results in decreased formation of prostaglandin precursors

Pharmacodynamics/Kinetics
Onset of action: A few days
Absorption: Rapid, 80%
Distribution: Does not cross the placenta
Protein binding: 99%
Metabolism: Extensively hepatic
Half-life elimination: 2.5-3 hours
Time to peak, serum: ~2 hours
Excretion: Urine (2% to 5% as unchanged drug); feces (small amounts)

Dosage Adults: Oral:
Rheumatoid arthritis: 300-600 mg 3-4 times/day up to 3.2 g/day
Mild to moderate pain: 200 mg every 4-6 hours as needed

Monitoring Parameters Monitor CBC, liver enzymes; monitor urine output and BUN/serum creatinine in patients receiving diuretics

Reference Range Therapeutic: 20-65 µg/mL (SI: 82-268 µmol/L)

Patient Information Do not crush tablets; take with food, milk, or water; report any signs of blood in stool

Dosage Forms CAP (Nalfon®): 200 mg, 300 mg. **TAB:** 600 mg

♦ **Fenoprofen Calcium** *see Fenoprofen on page 513*

Fentanyl *(FEN ta nil)*

Related Information
Narcotic Agonists Comparison *on page 1395*

U.S. Brand Names Actiq®; Duragesic®; Sublimaze®

Synonyms Fentanyl Citrate

Therapeutic Category Analgesic, Narcotic

Use Sedation, relief of pain, preoperative medication, adjunct to general or regional anesthesia, management of chronic pain (transdermal product)

Actiq® is indicated only for management of breakthrough cancer pain in patients who are tolerant to and currently receiving opioid therapy for persistent cancer pain.

Restrictions C-II

Pregnancy Risk Factor C/D (prolonged use or high doses at term)

Contraindications Hypersensitivity to fentanyl or any component of the formulation; increased intracranial pressure; severe respiratory depression; severe liver or renal insufficiency; pregnancy (prolonged use or high doses near term)

Actiq® must not be used in patients who are intolerant to opioids. Patients are considered opioid-tolerant if they are taking at least 60 mg morphine/day, 50 mcg transdermal fentanyl/hour, or an equivalent dose of another opioid for ≥1 week.

Warnings/Precautions An opioid-containing analgesic regimen should be tailored to each patient's needs and based upon the type of pain being treated (acute versus chronic), the route of administration, degree of tolerance for opioids (naive versus chronic user), age, weight, and medical condition. The optimal analgesic dose varies widely among patients. Doses should be titrated to pain relief/prevention. Fentanyl shares the toxic potentials of opiate agonists, and precautions of opiate agonist therapy should be observed; use with caution in patients with bradycardia; rapid I.V. infusion may result in skeletal muscle and chest wall rigidity, impaired ventilation, respiratory distress, apnea, bronchoconstriction, laryngospasm; inject slowly over 3-5 minutes; nondepolarizing skeletal muscle relaxant may be required. Tolerance of drug dependence may result from extended use.

Actiq® should be used only for the care of cancer patients and is intended for use by specialists who are knowledgeable in treating cancer pain. Actiq® preparations contain an amount of medication that can be fatal to children. Keep all units out of the reach of children and discard any open units properly. Patients and caregivers should be counseled on the dangers to children including the risk of exposure to partially-consumed units. Safety and efficacy have not been established in children <16 years of age.

Topical patches: Serum fentanyl concentrations may increase approximately one-third for patients with a body temperature of 40°C secondary to a temperature-dependent increase in fentanyl release from the system and increased skin permeability. Patients who experience adverse reactions should be monitored for at least 12 hours after removal of the patch. Safety and efficacy of transdermal system have been limited to children >2 years of age who are opioid tolerant.

The elderly may be particularly susceptible to the CNS depressant and constipating effects of narcotics.

Common Adverse Reactions
>10%:
    Cardiovascular: Hypotension, bradycardia
    Central nervous system: CNS depression, drowsiness, sedation
    Gastrointestinal: Nausea, vomiting, constipation
    Neuromuscular & skeletal: Chest wall rigidity (high dose I.V.)
    Respiratory: Respiratory depression
1% to 10%:
    Cardiovascular: Cardiac arrhythmias, orthostatic hypotension
    Central nervous system: Confusion
    Gastrointestinal: Biliary tract spasm
    Ocular: Miosis

Drug Interactions
Cytochrome P450 Effect: Substrate of CYP3A4 (major); **Inhibits** CYP3A4 (weak)
Increased Effect/Toxicity: Increased sedation with CNS depressants, phenothiazines. Tricyclic antidepressants may potentiate fentanyl's adverse effects. Potential for serotonin syndrome if combined with other serotonergic drugs. CYP3A4 inhibitors (including erythromycin, clarithromycin, ketoconazole, itraconazole, and protease inhibitors) may increase serum concentration of fentanyl.
Decreased Effect: CYP3A4 inducers (including carbamazepine, phenytoin, phenobarbital, rifampin) may decrease serum levels of fentanyl by increasing metabolism.

Mechanism of Action Binds with stereospecific receptors at many sites within the CNS, increases pain threshold, alters pain reception, inhibits ascending pain pathways

Pharmacodynamics/Kinetics
Onset of action: Analgesic: I.M.: 7-15 minutes; I.V.: Almost immediate; Transmucosal: 5-15 minutes
Peak effect: Transmucosal: Analgesic: 20-30 minutes
Duration: I.M.: 1-2 hours; I.V.: 0.5-1 hour; Transmucosal: Related to blood level; respiratory depressant effect may last longer than analgesic effect
Absorption: Transmucosal: Rapid, ~25% from the buccal mucosa; 75% swallowed with saliva and slowly absorbed from GI tract
Distribution: Highly lipophilic, redistributes into muscle and fat
Metabolism: Hepatic
Bioavailability: Transmucosal: ~50% (range: 36% to 71%)
Half-life elimination: 2-4 hours; Transmucosal: 6.6 hours (range: 5-15 hours)
Excretion: Urine (primarily as metabolites, 10% as unchanged drug)

Dosage Note: These are guidelines and do not represent the maximum doses that may be required in all patients. Doses should be titrated to pain relief/prevention. Monitor vital signs routinely. Single I.M. doses have a duration of 1-2 hours, single I.V. doses last 0.5-1 hour.
Children 1-12 years:
    Sedation for minor procedures/analgesia: I.M., I.V.: 1-2 mcg/kg/dose; may repeat at 30- to 60-minute intervals. **Note:** Children 18-36 months of age may require 2-3 mcg/kg/dose
    Continuous sedation/analgesia: Initial I.V. bolus: 1-2 mcg/kg then 1 mcg/kg/hour; titrate upward; usual: 1-3 mcg/kg/hour
    Pain control: Transdermal (limited to children >2 years who are opioid tolerant): Initial dose: 25 mcg/hour system (higher doses have been used based on equianalgesic conversion)
Children >12 years and Adults: Sedation for minor procedures/analgesia: I.M., I.V.: 0.5-1 mcg/kg/dose; higher doses are used for major procedures
Adults:
    Premedication: I.M., slow I.V.: 50-100 mcg/dose 30-60 minutes prior to surgery
    Adjunct to regional anesthesia: I.M., slow I.V.: 50-100 mcg/dose; if I.V. used, give over 1-2 minutes
    Severe pain: I.M.: 50-100 mcg/dose every 1-2 hours as needed; patients with prior opiate exposure may tolerate higher initial doses
    Adjunct to general anesthesia: Slow I.V.:
        Low dose: Initial: 2 mcg/kg/dose; Maintenance: Additional doses infrequently needed
        Moderate dose: Initial: 2-20 mcg/kg/dose; Maintenance: 25-100 mcg/dose may be given slow I.V. or I.M. as needed
        High dose: Initial: 20-50 mcg/kg/dose; Maintenance: 25 mcg to one-half the initial loading dose may be given as needed
    General anesthesia without additional anesthetic agents: Slow I.V.: 50-100 mcg/kg with O$_2$ and skeletal muscle relaxant

(Continued)

Fentanyl *(Continued)*

Mechanically-ventilated patients (based on 70 kg patient): Slow I.V.: 0.35-1.5 mcg/kg every 30-60 minutes as needed; infusion: 0.7-10 mcg/kg/hour

Patient-controlled analgesia (PCA): I.V.: Usual concentration: 50 mcg/mL

Demand dose: Usual: 10 mcg; range: 10-50 mcg

Lockout interval: 5-8 minutes

Breakthrough cancer pain: Adults: Transmucosal: Actiq® dosing should be individually titrated to provide adequate analgesia with minimal side effects. It is indicated only for management of breakthrough cancer pain in patients who are tolerant to and currently receiving opioid therapy for persistent cancer pain. An initial starting dose of 200 mcg should be used for the treatment of breakthrough cancer pain. Patients should be monitored closely in order to determine the proper dose. If redosing for the same episode is necessary, the second dose may be started 15 minutes after completion of the first dose. Dosing should be titrated so that the patient's pain can be treated with one single dose. Generally, 1-2 days is required to determine the proper dose of analgesia with limited side effects. Once the dose has been determined, consumption should be limited to 4 units/day or less. Patients needing more than 4 units/day should have the dose of their long-term opioid re-evaluated. If signs of excessive opioid effects occur before a dose is complete, the unit should be removed from the patient's mouth immediately, and subsequent doses decreased.

Pain control: Adults: Transdermal: Initial: 25 mcg/hour system; if currently receiving opiates, convert to fentanyl equivalent and administer equianalgesic dosage titrated to minimize the adverse effects and provide analgesia. To convert patients from oral or parenteral opioids to Duragesic®, the previous 24-hour analgesic requirement should be calculated. This analgesic requirement should be converted to the equianalgesic oral morphine dose.

See tables.

Equianalgesic Doses of Opioid Agonists

Drug	Equianalgesic Dose (mg)	
	I.M.	P.O.
Codeine	75	130
Hydromorphone	1.5	7.5
Levorphanol	2 (acute)	4 (acute)
Meperidine	75	300
Methadone	10 (acute)	20 (acute)
Morphine	10	30
Oxycodone	—	20
Oxymorphone	1	10 (PR)

From "Principles of Analgesic Use," *Am Pain Soc*, 1999.

Corresponding Doses of Oral/Intramuscular Morphine and Duragesic™

P.O. 24-Hour Morphine (mg/d)	I.M. 24-Hour Morphine (mg/d)	Duragesic™ Dose (mcg/h)
45-134	8-22	25
135-224	28-37	50
225-314	38-52	75
315-404	53-67	100
405-494	68-82	125
495-584	83-97	150
585-674	98-112	175
675-764	113-127	200
765-854	128-142	225
855-944	143-157	250
945-1034	158-172	275
1035-1124	173-187	300

Product information, Duragesic™ — Janssen Pharmaceutica, January, 1991.

The dosage should not be titrated more frequently than every 3 days after the initial dose or every 6 days thereafter. The majority of patients are controlled on every 72-hour administration, however, a small number of patients require every 48-hour administration.

Elderly >65 years: Transmucosal: Actiq®: Dose should be reduced to 2.5-5 mcg/kg; elderly have been found to be twice as sensitive as younger patients to the effects of fentanyl. Patients in this age group generally require smaller doses of Actiq® than younger patients

Dosing adjustment in renal impairment:

Cl_{cr} 10-50 mL/minute: Administer at 75% of normal dose

Cl_{cr} <10 mL/minute: Administer at 50% of normal dose

Dosing adjustment in renal/hepatic impairment: Actiq®: Although fentanyl kinetics may be altered in renal/hepatic disease, Actiq® can be used successfully in the management of breakthrough cancer pain. Doses should be titrated to reach clinical effect with careful monitoring of patients with severe renal/hepatic disease.

Administration

I.V.: Muscular rigidity may occur with rapid I.V. administration. During prolonged administration, dosage requirements may decrease.

Transdermal: Apply to nonirritated and nonirradiated skin, such as chest, back, flank, or upper arm. Upper back is preferred location in children. Do not shave skin; hair at application site should be clipped. Prior to application, clean site with clear water and allow to dry completely. Do not cut patch. Apply patch immediately after removing from package. Firmly press in place and hold for 20 seconds. Keep transdermal product (both used and unused) out of the reach of children. Do **not** use soap, alcohol, or other solvents to remove transdermal gel if it accidentally touches skin, as they may increase transdermal absorption; use copious amounts of water. Avoid exposing application site to external heat sources (eg, heating pad, electric blanket, heat lamp, hot tub).

Transmucosal: Foil overwrap should be removed just prior to administration. Once removed, patient should place the unit in mouth and allow it to dissolve. Do **not** chew. Actiq® units may be occasionally moved from one side of the mouth to the other. The unit should be consumed over a period of 15 minutes. Unit should be removed after it is consumed or if patient has achieved an adequate response and/or shows signs of respiratory depression. For patients who have received transmucosal product within 6-12 hours, it is recommended that if other narcotics are required, they should be started at starting doses $1/4$ to $1/3$ those usually recommended.

Monitoring Parameters Respiratory and cardiovascular status, blood pressure, heart rate

Patient Information Actiq® preparations contain an amount of medication that can be fatal to children. Keep all units out of the reach of children and discard any open units properly. Actiq® Welcome Kits are available which contain educational materials, safe storage and disposal instructions.

Dosage Forms INJ, solution [preservative free]: 0.05 mg/mL (2 mL, 5 mL, 10 mL, 20 mL, 30 mL, 50 mL); (Sublimaze®): 0.05 mg/mL (2 mL, 5 mL, 10 mL, 20 mL). **LOZ, oral transmucosal** (Actiq®): 200 mcg, 400 mcg, 600 mcg, 800 mcg, 1200 mcg, 1600 mcg. **Transdermal system** (Duragesic®): 25 mcg/hour [10 cm^2] (5s); 50 mcg/hour [20 cm^2] (5s); 75 mcg/hour [30 cm^2]; 100 mcg/hour [40 cm^2] (5s)

- ◆ **Fentanyl Citrate** *see* Fentanyl *on page 514*
- ◆ **Feostat® [OTC]** *see* Ferrous Fumarate *on page 519*
- ◆ **Feratab® [OTC]** *see* Ferrous Sulfate *on page 520*
- ◆ **Fer-Gen-Sol [OTC]** *see* Ferrous Sulfate *on page 520*
- ◆ **Fergon® [OTC]** *see* Ferrous Gluconate *on page 520*
- ◆ **Fer-In-Sol® [OTC]** *see* Ferrous Sulfate *on page 520*
- ◆ **Fer-Iron® [OTC]** *see* Ferrous Sulfate *on page 520*
- ◆ **Fero-Grad 500® [OTC]** *see* Ferrous Sulfate and Ascorbic Acid *on page 521*
- ◆ **Ferretts [OTC]** *see* Ferrous Fumarate *on page 519*

Ferric Gluconate (FER ik GLOO koe nate)

U.S. Brand Names Ferrlecit®

Synonyms Sodium Ferric Gluconate

Therapeutic Category Iron Salt

Use Repletion of total body iron content in patients with iron-deficiency anemia who are undergoing hemodialysis in conjunction with erythropoietin therapy

Pregnancy Risk Factor B

Contraindications Hypersensitivity to ferric gluconate or any component of the formulation; use in any anemia not caused by iron deficiency; heart failure (of any severity); iron overload

Warnings/Precautions Potentially serious hypersensitivity reactions may occur. Fatal immediate hypersensitivity reactions have occurred with other iron carbohydrate complexes. Avoid rapid administration. Flushing and transient hypotension may occur. May augment hemodialysis-induced hypotension. Use with caution in elderly patients. Safety and efficacy in pediatric patients have not been established. Contains benzyl alcohol; do not use in neonates. Administration rate should not exceed 2.1 mg/minute.

Common Adverse Reactions Major adverse reactions include hypotension and hypersensitivity reactions. Hypersensitivity reactions have included pruritus, chest pain, hypotension, nausea, abdominal pain, flank pain, fatigue and rash.

Cardiovascular: Hypotension (serious hypotension in 1%), chest pain, hypertension, syncope, tachycardia, angina, myocardial infarction, pulmonary edema, hypovolemia, peripheral edema

Central nervous system: Headache, fatigue, fever, malaise, dizziness, paresthesia, insomnia, agitation, somnolence, pain

Dermatologic: Pruritus, rash

Endocrine & metabolic: Hyperkalemia, hypoglycemia, hypokalemia

Gastrointestinal: Abdominal pain, nausea, vomiting, diarrhea, rectal disorder, dyspepsia, flatulence, melena, epigastric pain

Genitourinary: Urinary tract infection

Hematologic: Anemia, abnormal erythrocytes, lymphadenopathy

Local: Injection site reactions, pain

(Continued)

Ferric Gluconate *(Continued)*

Neuromuscular & skeletal: Weakness, back pain, leg cramps, myalgia, arthralgia, paresthesia, groin pain

Ocular: Blurred vision, conjunctivitis

Respiratory: Dyspnea, cough, rhinitis, upper respiratory infection, pneumonia

Miscellaneous: Hypersensitivity reactions, infection, rigors, chills, flu-like syndrome, sepsis, carcinoma, increased diaphoresis

Drug Interactions

Decreased Effect: Chloramphenicol may decrease effect of ferric gluconate injection; ferric gluconate injection may decrease the absorption of oral iron

Mechanism of Action Supplies a source to elemental iron necessary to the function of hemoglobin, myoglobin and specific enzyme systems; allows transport of oxygen via hemoglobin

Pharmacodynamics/Kinetics Half-life elimination: Bound: 1 hour

Dosage Adults: A test dose of 2 mL diluted in 50 mL 0.9% sodium chloride over 60 minutes was previously recommended (not in current manufacturer labeling).

Repletion of iron in hemodialysis patients: I.V.: 125 mg elemental iron per 10 mL (either by I.V. infusion or slow I.V. injection). Most patients will require a cumulative dose of 1 g elemental iron over approximately 8 sequential dialysis treatments to achieve a favorable response.

Administration May be diluted prior to administration; avoid rapid administration. Infusion rate should not exceed 2.1 mg/minute. If administered undiluted, infuse slowly at a rate of up to 12.5 mg/minute. Monitor patient for hypotension or hypersensitivity reactions during infusion.

Monitoring Parameters Hemoglobin and hematocrit, serum ferritin, iron saturation; vital signs

Dosage Forms INJ, solution: Elemental iron 12.5 mg/mL (5 mL)

Ferric Hexacyanoferrate *(FER ik hex a SYE an oh fer ate)*

U.S. Brand Names Radiogardase™

Synonyms Ferric (III) Hexacyanoferrate (II); Insoluble Prussian Blue; Prussian Blue

Therapeutic Category Antidote

Use Treatment of known or suspected internal contamination with radioactive cesium and/or radioactive or nonradioactive thallium

Pregnancy Risk Factor C

Contraindications None known

Warnings/Precautions Ferric hexacyanoferrate increases the rate of elimination of thallium and cesium; it does not treat complications of radiation exposure. Supportive treatment for radiation toxicity should be given concomitantly. Use caution with decreased gastric motility; constipation should be avoided to prevent increased radiation absorption from the gastrointestinal tract. Use caution with pre-existing cardiac arrhythmias or electrolyte imbalances. Patients should be instructed to minimize radiation exposure to others. Additional decontamination and/or treatment may be needed if exposure to other radioactive isotopes is known or suspected.

Common Adverse Reactions

>10%: Gastrointestinal: Constipation (24%)

1% to 10%: Endocrine & metabolic: Hypokalemia (7%)

Frequency not defined: Gastrointestinal: Gastric distress, fecal discoloration (blue)

Mechanism of Action Binds to cesium and thallium isotopes in the gastrointestinal tract following their ingestion or excretion in the bile; reduces their gastrointestinal reabsorption (enterohepatic circulation)

Pharmacodynamics/Kinetics

Absorption: Ferric hexacyanoferrate: Oral: none

Half-life elimination:

Cesium-137: Effective: Adults: 80 days, decreased by 69% with ferric hexacyanoferrate; adolescents: 62 days, decreased by 46% with ferric hexacyanoferrate; children: 42 days, decreased by 43% with ferric hexacyanoferrate

Nonradioactive thallium: Biological: 8-10 days; with ferric hexacyanoferrate: 3 days

Excretion:

Cesium-137: Without ferric hexacyanoferrate: Urine (~80%); feces (~20%)

Thallium: Without ferric hexacyanoferrate: Fecal to urine excretion ration: 2:1

Ferric hexacyanoferrate: Feces (99%, unchanged)

Dosage Oral: Internal contamination with radioactive cesium and/or radioactive or nonradioactive thallium:

Children 2-12 years: 1 g 3 times/day; treatment should begin as soon as possible following exposure, but is also effective if therapy is delayed

Children >12 years and Adults: 3 g 3 times/day; treatment should begin as soon as possible following exposure, but is also effective if therapy is delayed

Note: Cesium exposure: Once internal radioactivity is substantially decreased, dosage may be reduced to 1-2 g 3 times/day to improve gastrointestinal tolerance

Elderly: Refer to Adults dosing

Dosage adjustment in renal impairment: Studies have not been conducted; however, ferric hexacyanoferrate is not renally eliminated.

Dosage adjustment in hepatic impairment: Studies have not been conducted; however, effectiveness may be decreased due to decreased bile excretion of cesium and thallium.

Administration Capsules may be opened and mixed with bland food or liquid (instruct patients that mouth and teeth may become blue). Administer with food to stimulate excretion of cesium or thallium. Increase dietary fiber or take with fiber laxative to decrease constipation.

Monitoring Parameters

Bowel movements; CBC and electrolytes weekly

Baseline cesium and/or thallium exposure (whole body counting and/or bioassay, feces or urine sample); urine and fecal cesium and/or thallium weekly during therapy; residual whole body radioactivity after 30 days of treatment

Patient Information Cesium is excreted in the urine and feces. To decrease radiation exposure to others, use of toilet is preferred over urinal. Toilet should be flushed several times after each use. Immediately clean any spilled urine, feces, or blood; wash hands thoroughly after cleaning up spill; exposed clothing should be washed separately. Adults should use caution when handling pediatric urine or feces to avoid re-exposure to the adult and child. Ferric hexacyanoferrate may turn feces blue. Capsules may be opened and mixed with a bland food or liquid; however, mouth and teeth may turn blue. Fiber laxatives and/or high-fiber diets are recommended during therapy to avoid constipation.

Dosage Forms CAP: 0.5 g

◆ **Ferric (III) Hexacyanoferrate (II)** *see Ferric Hexacyanoferrate on page 518*

◆ **Ferrlecit®** *see Ferric Gluconate on page 517*

◆ **Ferro-Sequels® [OTC]** *see Ferrous Fumarate on page 519*

Ferrous Fumarate (FER us FYOO ma rate)

U.S. Brand Names Femiron® [OTC]; Feostat® [OTC]; Ferretts [OTC]; Ferro-Sequels® [OTC]; Hemocyte® [OTC]; Ircon® [OTC]; Nephro-Fer® [OTC]

Synonyms Iron Fumarate

Therapeutic Category Iron Salt

Use Prevention and treatment of iron-deficiency anemias

Pregnancy Risk Factor A

Contraindications Hypersensitivity to iron salts or any component of the formulation; hemochromatosis, hemolytic anemia

Warnings/Precautions Avoid in patients with peptic ulcer, enteritis, or ulcerative colitis. Administration of iron for >6 months should be avoided except in patients with continuous bleeding or menorrhagia. Anemia in the elderly is often caused by "anemia of chronic disease" or associated with inflammation rather than blood loss. Iron stores are usually normal or increased, with a serum ferritin >50 ng/mL and a decreased total iron binding capacity. Hence, the "anemia of chronic disease" is not secondary to iron deficiency but the inability of the reticuloendothelial system to reclaim available iron stores. Avoid in patients receiving frequent blood transfusions Avoid use in premature infants until the vitamin E stores, deficient at birth, are replenished.

Common Adverse Reactions

>10%: Gastrointestinal: Stomach cramping, constipation, nausea, vomiting, dark stools

1% to 10%:

Gastrointestinal: Heartburn, diarrhea, staining of teeth

Genitourinary: Discoloration of urine

Drug Interactions

Increased Effect/Toxicity: Concurrent administration of ≥200 mg vitamin C per 30 mg elemental iron increases absorption of oral iron.

Decreased Effect: Absorption of oral preparation of iron and tetracyclines are decreased when both of these drugs are given together. Absorption of fluoroquinolones, levodopa, methyldopa, and penicillamine may be decreased due to formation of a ferric ion-quinolone complex. Concurrent administration of antacids, H_2 blockers (cimetidine), or proton pump inhibitors may decrease iron absorption. Response to iron therapy may be delayed by chloramphenicol.

Mechanism of Action Replaces iron found in hemoglobin, myoglobin, and enzymes; allows the transportation of oxygen via hemoglobin

Pharmacodynamics/Kinetics

Onset of action: Hematologic response: Oral, parenteral iron salts: ~3-10 days

Peak effect: Reticulocytosis: 5-10 days; hemoglobin values increase within 2-4 weeks

Absorption: Iron is absorbed in the duodenum and upper jejunum; in persons with normal serum iron stores, 10% of an oral dose is absorbed, this is increased to 20% to 30% in persons with inadequate iron stores. Food and achlorhydria will decrease absorption.

Protein binding: To serum transferrin

Excretion: Urine, sweat, sloughing of intestinal mucosa, and menses

Dosage Oral (dose expressed in terms of elemental iron):

Children:

Severe iron-deficiency anemia: 4-6 mg Fe/kg/day in 3 divided doses

Mild to moderate iron deficiency anemia: 3 mg Fe/kg/day in 1-2 divided doses

Prophylaxis: 1-2 mg Fe/kg/day

Adults:

Iron deficiency: 60-100 mg twice daily up to 60 mg 2 times/day

Prophylaxis: 60-100 mg/day

To avoid GI upset, start with a single daily dose and increase by 1 tablet/day each week or as tolerated until desired daily dose is achieved

Elderly: 200 mg 3-4 times/day

Reference Range

Serum iron:

Male: 75-175 µg/dL (SI: 13.4-31.3 µmol/L)

Female: 65-165 µg/dL (SI: 11.6-29.5 µmol/L)

Total iron binding capacity: 230-430 µg/dL

(Continued)

Ferrous Fumarate *(Continued)*

Transferrin: 204-360 mg/dL

Percent transferrin saturation: 20% to 50%

Iron levels >300 μg/dL can be considered toxic, should be treated as an overdose

Patient Information May color stool black, take between meals for maximum absorption; may take with food if GI upset occurs, do not take with milk or antacids; keep out of reach of children

Dosage Forms SUSP, oral (Feostat®) [DSC]: 100 mg/5 mL (240 mL). **TAB:** 325 mg; (Femiron®): 63 mg; (Ferretts): 325 mg; (Hemocyte®): 324 mg; (Ircon®): 200 mg; (Nephro-Fer®): 350 mg. **TAB, chewable** (Feostat®): 100 mg. **TAB, timed release** (Ferro-Sequels®): 150 mg

Ferrous Gluconate *(FER us GLOO koe nate)*

U.S. Brand Names Fergon® [OTC]

Synonyms Iron Gluconate

Therapeutic Category Iron Salt

Use Prevention and treatment of iron-deficiency anemias

Pregnancy Risk Factor A

Contraindications Hypersensitivity to iron salts or any component of the formulation; hemochromatosis, hemolytic anemia

Warnings/Precautions Administration of iron for >6 months should be avoided except in patients with continued bleeding, menorrhagia, or repeated pregnancies; avoid in patients with peptic ulcer, enteritis, or ulcerative colitis. Anemia in the elderly is often caused by "anemia of chronic disease" or associated with inflammation rather than blood loss. Iron stores are usually normal or increased, with a serum ferritin >50 ng/mL and a decreased total iron binding capacity. Hence, the "anemia of chronic disease" is not secondary to iron deficiency but the inability of the reticuloendothelial system to reclaim available iron stores.

Common Adverse Reactions

>10%: Gastrointestinal: Stomach cramping, constipation, nausea, vomiting, dark stools

1% to 10%:

Gastrointestinal: Heartburn, diarrhea, staining of teeth

Genitourinary: Discoloration of urine

Drug Interactions

Increased Effect/Toxicity: Concurrent administration of ≥200 mg vitamin C per 30 mg elemental iron increases absorption of oral iron.

Decreased Effect: Absorption of oral preparation of iron and tetracyclines are decreased when both of these drugs are given together. Absorption of fluoroquinolones, levodopa, methyldopa, and penicillamine may be decreased due to formation of a ferric ion-quinolone complex. Concurrent administration of antacids, H₂ blockers (cimetidine), or proton pump inhibitors may decrease iron absorption. Response to iron therapy may be delayed by chloramphenicol.

Mechanism of Action Replaces iron found in hemoglobin, myoglobin, and enzymes; allows the transportation of oxygen via hemoglobin

Pharmacodynamics/Kinetics Onset of action: Hematologic response: Oral: 3-10 days; peak reticulocytosis occurs in 5-10 days, and hemoglobin values increase in ~2-4 weeks

Dosage Oral **(dose expressed in terms of elemental iron):**

Children:

Severe iron-deficiency anemia: 4-6 mg Fe/kg/day in 3 divided doses

Mild to moderate iron deficiency anemia: 3 mg Fe/kg/day in 1-2 divided doses

Prophylaxis: 1-2 mg Fe/kg/day

Adults:

Iron deficiency: 60 mg twice daily up to 60 mg 4 times/day

Prophylaxis: 60 mg/day

Administration Administration of iron preparations to premature infants with vitamin E deficiency may cause increased red cell hemolysis and hemolytic anemia, therefore, vitamin E deficiency should be corrected if possible

Reference Range Therapeutic: Male: 75-175 μg/dL (SI: 13.4-31.3 μmol/L); Female: 65-165 μg/dL (SI: 11.6-29.5 μmol/L); serum iron level >300 μg/dL usually requires treatment of overdose due to severe toxicity

Patient Information May color stool black, take between meals for maximum absorption; may take with food if GI upset occurs, do not take with milk or antacids; keep out of reach of children

Dosage Forms Elemental iron listed in brackets: **TAB:** 300 mg [34 mg]; 325 mg [36 mg]; (Fergon®): 240 mg [27 mg]

Ferrous Sulfate *(FER us SUL fate)*

U.S. Brand Names Feratab® [OTC]; Fer-Gen-Sol [OTC]; Fer-In-Sol® [OTC]; Fer-Iron® [OTC]; Slow FE® [OTC]

Synonyms FeSO₄; Iron Sulfate

Therapeutic Category Iron Salt

Use Prevention and treatment of iron-deficiency anemias

Pregnancy Risk Factor A

Contraindications Hypersensitivity to iron salts or any component of the formulation; hemochromatosis, hemolytic anemia

Warnings/Precautions Administration of iron for >6 months should be avoided except in patients with continued bleeding, menorrhagia, or repeated pregnancies; avoid in patients with peptic ulcer, enteritis, or ulcerative colitis. Anemia in the elderly is often caused by "anemia of chronic disease" or associated with inflammation rather than blood loss. Iron stores are usually normal or increased, with a serum ferritin >50 ng/mL and a decreased total iron binding capacity. Hence, the "anemia of chronic disease" is not secondary to iron deficiency but the inability of the reticuloendothelial system to reclaim available iron stores.

Common Adverse Reactions
>10%: Gastrointestinal: GI irritation, epigastric pain, nausea, dark stool, vomiting, stomach cramping, constipation
1% to 10%:
Gastrointestinal: Heartburn, diarrhea
Genitourinary: Discoloration of urine
Miscellaneous: Liquid preparations may temporarily stain the teeth

Drug Interactions
Increased Effect/Toxicity: Concurrent administration of ≥200 mg vitamin C per 30 mg elemental iron increases absorption of oral iron.
Decreased Effect: Absorption of oral preparation of iron and tetracyclines are decreased when both of these drugs are given together. Absorption of fluoroquinolones, levodopa, methyldopa, and penicillamine may be decreased due to formation of a ferric ion-quinolone complex. Concurrent administration of antacids, H_2 blockers (cimetidine), or proton pump inhibitors may decrease iron absorption. Response to iron therapy may be delayed by chloramphenicol.

Mechanism of Action Replaces iron, found in hemoglobin, myoglobin, and other enzymes; allows the transportation of oxygen via hemoglobin

Pharmacodynamics/Kinetics
Onset of action: Hematologic response: Oral: ~3-10 days
Peak effect: Reticulocytosis: 5-10 days; hemoglobin increases within 2-4 weeks
Absorption: Iron is absorbed in the duodenum and upper jejunum; in persons with normal serum iron stores, 10% of an oral dose is absorbed; this is increased to 20% to 30% in persons with inadequate iron stores. Food and achlorhydria will decrease absorption
Protein binding: To transferrin
Excretion: Urine, sweat, sloughing of the intestinal mucosa, and menses

Dosage Oral:
Children (**dose expressed in terms of elemental iron**):
Severe iron-deficiency anemia: 4-6 mg Fe/kg/day in 3 divided doses
Mild to moderate iron deficiency anemia: 3 mg Fe/kg/day in 1-2 divided doses
Prophylaxis: 1-2 mg Fe/kg/day up to a maximum of 15 mg/day
Adults (**dose expressed in terms of ferrous sulfate**):
Iron deficiency: 300 mg twice daily up to 300 mg 4 times/day or 250 mg (extended release) 1-2 times/day
Prophylaxis: 300 mg/day

Administration Administer ferrous sulfate 2 hours prior to, or 4 hours after antacids

Reference Range
Serum iron:
Male: 75-175 µg/dL (SI: 13.4-31.3 µmol/L)
Female: 65-165 µg/dL (SI: 11.6-29.5 µmol/L)
Total iron binding capacity: 230-430 µg/dL
Transferrin: 204-360 mg/dL
Percent transferrin saturation: 20% to 50%

Patient Information May color stool black, take between meals for maximum absorption; may take with food if GI upset occurs, do not take with milk or antacids; keep out of reach of children

Dosage Forms ELIX: 220 mg/5 mL (480 mL). **LIQ, oral drops:** 75 mg/0.6 mL (50 mL); (Fer-Gen-Sol, Fer-In-Sol®, Fer-Iron): 75 mg/0.6 mL (50 mL). **TAB:** 324 mg; (Feratab®): 300 mg. **TAB, exsiccated** (Feosol®): 200 mg. **TAB, exsiccated, timed release** (Slow FE®): 160 mg

Ferrous Sulfate and Ascorbic Acid (FER us SUL fate & a SKOR bik AS id)
U.S. Brand Names Fero-Grad 500® [OTC]; Vitelle™ Irospan® [OTC]
Synonyms Ascorbic Acid and Ferrous Sulfate; Iron Sulfate and Vitamin C
Therapeutic Category Iron Salt; Vitamin
Use Treatment of iron deficiency in nonpregnant adults; treatment and prevention of iron deficiency in pregnant adults
Dosage Adults: Oral: 1 tablet daily
Dosage Forms CAP, extended release (Vitelle™ Irospan®): Ferrous sulfate [elemental iron 65 mg] and ascorbic acid 150 mg. **TAB** (Fero-Grad 500®): Ferrous sulfate 525 mg [elemental iron 105 mg] and ascorbic acid 500 mg. **TAB, extended release** (Vitelle™ Irospan®): Ferrous sulfate [elemental iron 65 mg] and ascorbic acid 150 mg

◆ **Fertinex® [DSC]** *see* Follitropins *on page 555*
◆ **FeSO₄** *see* Ferrous Sulfate *on page 520*
◆ **Fe-Tinic™ 150 [OTC]** *see* Polysaccharide-Iron Complex *on page 1016*
◆ **Feverall® [OTC]** *see* Acetaminophen *on page 24*

Fexofenadine (feks oh FEN a deen)
U.S. Brand Names Allegra®
Synonyms Fexofenadine Hydrochloride
(Continued)

Fexofenadine *(Continued)*

Therapeutic Category Antihistamine; Antihistamine, Nonsedating

Use Relief of symptoms associated with seasonal allergic rhinitis; treatment of chronic idiopathic urticaria

Pregnancy Risk Factor C

Contraindications Hypersensitivity to fexofenadine or any component of the formulation

Warnings/Precautions Safety and efficacy in children <6 years of age have not been established.

Common Adverse Reactions

>10%: Central nervous system: Headache (7% to 11%)

1% to 10%:

Central nervous system: Fever (2%), dizziness (2%), pain (2%), drowsiness (1% to 2%), fatigue (1%)

Endocrine & metabolic: Dysmenorrhea (2%)

Gastrointestinal: Nausea (2%), dyspepsia (1%)

Neuromuscular & skeletal: Back pain (2% to 3%)

Otic: Otitis media (2%)

Respiratory: Cough (4%), upper respiratory tract infection (3% to 4%), sinusitis (2%)

Miscellaneous: Viral infection (3%)

Drug Interactions

Cytochrome P450 Effect: Substrate of CYP3A4 (minor); **Inhibits** CYP2D6 (weak)

Increased Effect/Toxicity: Erythromycin and ketoconazole increased the levels of fexofenadine; however, no increase in adverse events or QT_c intervals was noted. The effect of other macrolide agents or azoles has not been investigated.

Decreased Effect: Aluminum- and magnesium-containing antacids decrease plasma levels of fexofenadine; separate administration is recommended.

Mechanism of Action Fexofenadine is an active metabolite of terfenadine and like terfenadine it competes with histamine for H_1-receptor sites on effector cells in the gastrointestinal tract, blood vessels and respiratory tract; it appears that fexofenadine does not cross the blood brain barrier to any appreciable degree, resulting in a reduced potential for sedation

Pharmacodynamics/Kinetics

Onset of action: 60 minutes

Duration: Antihistaminic effect: ≥12 hours

Protein binding: 60% to 70%, primarily albumin and alpha$_1$-acid glycoprotein

Metabolism: ~5% mostly by gut flora; 0.5% to 1.5% by CYP

Half-life elimination: 14.4 hours

Time to peak, serum: ~2.6 hours

Excretion: Feces (~80%) and urine (~11%) as unchanged drug

Dosage Oral:

Children 6-11 years: 30 mg twice daily

Children ≥12 years and Adults:

Seasonal allergic rhinitis: 60 mg twice daily **or** 180 mg once daily

Chronic idiopathic urticaria: 60 mg twice daily

Dosing adjustment in renal impairment: Cl_{cr} <80 mL/minute:

Children 6-11 years: Initial: 30 mg once daily

Children ≥12 years and Adults: Initial: 60 mg once daily

Monitoring Parameters Relief of symptoms

Patient Information Although relatively uncommon, fexofenadine may cause drowsiness. Report drowsiness, upset stomach, increased pain or cramping during menstruation while taking this medication.

Dosage Forms TAB: 30 mg, 60 mg, 180 mg

Fexofenadine and Pseudoephedrine

(feks oh FEN a deen & soo doe e FED rin)

U.S. Brand Names Allegra-D®

Synonyms Pseudoephedrine and Fexofenadine

Therapeutic Category Antihistamine/Decongestant

Use Relief of symptoms associated with seasonal allergic rhinitis in adults and children ≥12 years of age

Pregnancy Risk Factor C

Dosage Oral: Children ≥12 years and Adults: One tablet twice daily; it is recommended that the administration with food should be avoided.

Dosage adjustment in renal impairment: Cl_{cr} <80 mL/minute (based on fexofenadine component): One tablet once daily

Dosage Forms TAB, extended release: Fexofenadine 60 mg and pseudoephedrine 120 mg

♦ **Fexofenadine Hydrochloride** *see* Fexofenadine *on page 521*

♦ **Fiberall®** *see* Psyllium *on page 1063*

Filgrastim *(fil GRA stim)*

Related Information

Sargramostim *on page 1124*

U.S. Brand Names Neupogen®

Synonyms G-CSF; Granulocyte Colony Stimulating Factor

Therapeutic Category Colony-Stimulating Factor

Use Stimulation of granulocyte production in patients with malignancies, including myeloid malignancies; receiving myelosuppressive therapy associated with a significant risk of neutropenia; severe chronic neutropenia (SCN); receiving bone marrow transplantation (BMT); undergoing peripheral blood progenitor cell (PBPC) collection

Pregnancy Risk Factor C

Contraindications Hypersensitivity to filgrastim, *E. coli*-derived proteins, or any component of the formulation; concurrent myelosuppressive chemotherapy or radiation therapy

Warnings/Precautions Complete blood count and platelet count should be obtained prior to chemotherapy. Do not use G-CSF in the period 12-24 hours before to 24 hours after administration of cytotoxic chemotherapy because of the potential sensitivity of rapidly dividing myeloid cells to cytotoxic chemotherapy. Precaution should be exercised in the usage of G-CSF in any malignancy with myeloid characteristics. G-CSF can potentially act as a growth factor for any tumor type, particularly myeloid malignancies. Tumors of nonhematopoietic origin may have surface receptors for G-CSF.

Allergic-type reactions have occurred in patients receiving G-CSF with first or later doses. Reactions tended to occur more frequently with intravenous administration and within 30 minutes of infusion. Most cases resolved rapidly with antihistamines, steroids, bronchodilators, and/or epinephrine. Symptoms recurred in >50% of patients on rechallenge.

Common Adverse Reactions
>10%:
- Cardiovascular: Chest pain
- Central nervous system: Fever
- Dermatologic: Alopecia
- Endocrine & metabolic: Fluid retention
- Gastrointestinal: Nausea, vomiting, diarrhea, mucositis; splenomegaly - up to 33% of patients with cyclic neutropenia/congenital agranulocytosis receiving filgrastim for ≥14 days; rare in other patients
- Neuromuscular & skeletal: Bone pain (24%), commonly in the lower back, posterior iliac crest, and sternum

1% to 10%:
- Cardiovascular: S-T segment depression (3%)
- Central nervous system: Headache
- Dermatologic: Rash
- Gastrointestinal: Anorexia, constipation, sore throat
- Hematologic: Leukocytosis
- Local: Pain at injection site
- Neuromuscular & skeletal: Weakness
- Respiratory: Dyspnea, cough

Drug Interactions
Increased Effect/Toxicity: Drugs which may potentiate the release of neutrophils (eg, lithium) should be used with caution.

Mechanism of Action Stimulates the production, maturation, and activation of neutrophils, G-CSF activates neutrophils to increase both their migration and cytotoxicity. See table.

Comparative Effects — G-CSF vs GM-CSF

Proliferation/Differentiation	G-CSF (Filgrastim)	GM-CSF (Sargramostim)
Neutrophils	Yes	Yes
Eosinophils	No	Yes
Macrophages	No	Yes
Neutrophil migration	Enhanced	Inhibited

Pharmacodynamics/Kinetics
Onset of action: ~24 hours; plateaus in 3-5 days
Duration: ANC decreases by 50% within 2 days after discontinuing G-CSF; white counts return to the normal range in 4-7 days; peak plasma levels can be maintained for up to 12 hours
Absorption: S.C.: 100%
Distribution: V_d: 150 mL/kg; no evidence of drug accumulation over a 11- to 20-day period
Metabolism: Systemically degraded
Half-life elimination: 1.8-3.5 hours
Time to peak, serum: S.C.: 2-6 hours

Dosage Refer to individual protocols.
Dosing, even in morbidly obese patients, should be based on actual body weight. Rounding doses to the nearest vial size often enhances patient convenience and reduces costs without compromising clinical response.
Myelosuppressive therapy: 5 mcg/kg/day - doses may be increased by 5 mcg/kg according to the duration and severity of the neutropenia.
Bone marrow transplantation: 5-10 mcg/kg/day - doses may be increased by 5 mcg/kg according to the duration and severity of neutropenia; recommended steps based on neutrophil response:
When ANC >1000/mm³ for 3 consecutive days: Reduce filgrastim dose to 5 mcg/kg/day
If ANC remains >1000/mm³ for 3 more consecutive days: Discontinue filgrastim
If ANC decreases to <1000/mm³: Resume at 5 mcg/kg/day
If ANC decreases <1000/mm³ during the 5 mcg/kg/day dose, increase filgrastim to 10 mcg/kg/day and follow the above steps
(Continued)

Filgrastim *(Continued)*

Peripheral blood progenitor cell (PBPC) collection: 10 mcg/kg/day **or** 5-8 mcg/kg twice daily in donors. The optimal timing and duration of growth factor stimulation has not been determined.

Severe chronic neutropenia:
Congenital: 6 mcg/kg twice daily
Idiopathic/cyclic: 5 mcg/kg/day
Not removed by hemodialysis

Administration May be administered undiluted by S.C. or by I.V. infusion over 15-60 minutes in D$_5$W; **incompatible** with sodium chloride solutions

Monitoring Parameters CBC and platelet count should be obtained twice weekly. Leukocytosis (white blood cell counts ≥100,000/mm^3) has been observed in ~2% of patients receiving G-CSF at doses >5 mcg/kg/day. Monitor platelets and hematocrit regularly.

Reference Range No clinical benefit seen with ANC >10,000/mm^3

Patient Information Follow directions for proper storage and administration of S.C. medication. Never reuse syringes or needles. You may experience bone pain (request analgesic); nausea or vomiting (small frequent meals may help); hair loss (reversible); or sore mouth (frequent mouth care with a soft toothbrush or cotton swab may help). Report unusual fever or chills; unhealed sores; severe bone pain; pain, redness, or swelling at injection site; unusual swelling of extremities or difficulty breathing; or chest pain and palpitations.

Dosage Forms INJ, solution [preservative free; vial]: 300 mcg/mL (1 mL, 1.6 mL). **INJ, solution** [preservative free; prefilled Singleject® syringe]: 600 mcg/mL (0.5 mL, 0.8 mL)

♦ Finacea™ *see* Azelaic Acid *on page 138*

Finasteride *(fi NAS teer ide)*

U.S. Brand Names Propecia®; Proscar®

Therapeutic Category Antiandrogen

Use
Propecia®: Treatment of male pattern hair loss in **men only**. Safety and efficacy were demonstrated in men between 18-41 years of age.
Proscar®: Treatment of symptomatic benign prostatic hyperplasia (BPH)

Unlabeled/Investigational Use Adjuvant monotherapy after radical prostatectomy in the treatment of prostatic cancer; female hirsutism

Pregnancy Risk Factor X

Contraindications Hypersensitivity to finasteride or any component of the formulation; pregnancy; not for use in children

Warnings/Precautions A minimum of 6 months of treatment may be necessary to determine whether an individual will respond to finasteride. Use with caution in those patients with liver function abnormalities. Carefully monitor patients with a large residual urinary volume or severely diminished urinary flow for obstructive uropathy. These patients may not be candidates for finasteride therapy.

Common Adverse Reactions
1% to 10%:
Endocrine & metabolic: Libido decreased
Genitourinary: <4% incidence of erectile dysfunction, decreased volume of ejaculate

Drug Interactions
Cytochrome P450 Effect: Substrate of CYP3A4 (minor)

Mechanism of Action Finasteride is a 4-azo analog of testosterone and is a competitive inhibitor of both tissue and hepatic 5-alpha reductase. This results in inhibition of the conversion of testosterone to dihydrotestosterone and markedly suppresses serum dihydrotestosterone levels; depending on dose and duration, serum testosterone concentrations may or may not increase. Testosterone-dependent processes such as fertility, muscle strength, potency, and libido are not affected by finasteride.

Pharmacodynamics/Kinetics
Onset of action: 3-6 months of ongoing therapy
Duration:
After a single oral dose as small as 0.5 mg: 65% depression of plasma dihydrotestosterone levels persists 5-7 days
After 6 months of treatment with 5 mg/day: Circulating dihydrotestosterone levels are reduced to castrate levels without significant effects on circulating testosterone; levels return to normal within 14 days of discontinuation of treatment
Absorption: May be reduced with food
Protein binding: 90%
Metabolism: Hepatic; two active metabolites identified
Bioavailability: Mean: 63%
Half-life elimination, serum: Parent drug: ~5-17 hours (mean: 1.9 fasting, 4.2 with breakfast); Elderly: 8 hours; Adults: 6 hours (3-16); rate decreased in elderly, but no dosage adjustment needed
Time to peak, serum: 2-6 hours
Excretion: Feces (57%) and urine (39%) as metabolites

Dosage Oral: Adults:
Male:
Benign prostatic hyperplasia (Proscar®): 5 mg/day as a single dose; clinical responses occur within 12 weeks to 6 months of initiation of therapy; long-term administration is recommended for maximal response

Male pattern baldness (Propecia®): 1 mg daily

Female hirsutism (unlabeled use): 5 mg/day

Dosing adjustment in renal impairment: No dosage adjustment is necessary

Dosing adjustment in hepatic impairment: Use with caution in patients with liver function abnormalities because finasteride is metabolized extensively in the liver

Administration Administration with food may delay the rate and reduce the extent of oral absorption. Childbearing age women should not touch or handle this medication.

Monitoring Parameters Objective and subjective signs of relief of benign prostatic hyperplasia, including improvement in urinary flow, reduction in symptoms of urgency, and relief of difficulty in micturition

Dosage Forms TAB, film coated: (Propecia®): 1 mg; (Proscar®): 5 mg

- ◆ **Finevin®** see Azelaic Acid on page 138
- ◆ **Fioricet®** see Butalbital, Acetaminophen, and Caffeine on page 194
- ◆ **Fiorinal®** see Butalbital, Aspirin, and Caffeine on page 195
- ◆ **Fisalamine** see Mesalamine on page 798
- ◆ **FK506** see Tacrolimus on page 1181
- ◆ **Flagyl®** see Metronidazole on page 831
- ◆ **Flagyl ER®** see Metronidazole on page 831
- ◆ **Flarex®** see Fluorometholone on page 536

Flavoxate (fla VOKS ate)

U.S. Brand Names Urispas®

Synonyms Flavoxate Hydrochloride

Therapeutic Category Antispasmodic Agent, Urinary

Use Antispasmodic to provide symptomatic relief of dysuria, nocturia, suprapubic pain, urgency, and incontinence due to detrusor instability and hyper-reflexia in elderly with cystitis, urethritis, urethrocystitis, urethrotrigonitis, and prostatitis

Pregnancy Risk Factor B

Dosage Children >12 years and Adults: Oral: 100-200 mg 3-4 times/day; reduce the dose when symptoms improve

Dosage Forms TAB, film coated: 100 mg

- ◆ **Flavoxate Hydrochloride** see Flavoxate on page 525
- ◆ **Flebogamma®** see Immune Globulin (Intravenous) on page 659

Flecainide (fle KAY nide)

U.S. Brand Names Tambocor™

Synonyms Flecainide Acetate

Therapeutic Category Antiarrhythmic Agent, Class I-C

Use Prevention and suppression of documented life-threatening ventricular arrhythmias (eg, sustained ventricular tachycardia); controlling symptomatic, disabling supraventricular tachycardias in patients without structural heart disease in whom other agents fail

Pregnancy Risk Factor C

Contraindications Hypersensitivity to flecainide or any component of the formulation; pre-existing second- or third-degree AV block or with right bundle branch block when associated with a left hemiblock (bifascicular block) (except in patients with a functioning artificial pacemaker); cardiogenic shock; coronary artery disease (based on CAST study results); concurrent use of ritonavir or amprenavir

Warnings/Precautions Pre-existing sinus node dysfunction, sick-sinus syndrome, history of CHF or myocardial dysfunction; increases in PR interval ≥300 MS, QRS ≥180 MS, QT_c interval increases, and/or new bundle-branch block; patients with pacemakers, renal impairment, and/ or hepatic impairment. Not recommended for patients with chronic atrial fibrillation.

The manufacturer and FDA recommend that this drug be reserved for life-threatening ventricular arrhythmias unresponsive to conventional therapy. Its use for symptomatic nonsustained ventricular tachycardia, frequent premature ventricular complexes (PVCs), uniform and multiform PVCs and/or coupled PVCs is no longer recommended. Flecainide can worsen or cause arrhythmias with an associated risk of death. Proarrhythmic effects range from an increased number of PVCs to more severe ventricular tachycardias (eg, tachycardias that are more sustained or more resistant to conversion to sinus rhythm).

Common Adverse Reactions

>10%:
  Central nervous system: Dizziness (19% to 30%)
  Ocular: Visual disturbances (16%)
  Respiratory: Dyspnea (~10%)

1% to 10%:
  Cardiovascular: Palpitations (6%), chest pain (5%), edema (3.5%), tachycardia (1% to 3%), proarrhythmic (4% to 12%), sinus node dysfunction (1.2%)
  Central nervous system: Headache (4% to 10%), fatigue (8%), nervousness (5%) additional symptoms occurring at a frequency between 1% and 3%: fever, malaise, hypoesthesia, paresis, ataxia, vertigo, syncope, somnolence, tinnitus, anxiety, insomnia, depression
  Dermatologic: Rash (1% to 3%)
  Gastrointestinal: Nausea (9%), constipation (1%), abdominal pain (3%), anorexia (1% to 3%), diarrhea (0.7% to 3%)
  Neuromuscular & skeletal: Tremor (5%), weakness (5%), paresthesias (1%)
  Ocular: Diplopia (1% to 3%), blurred vision

(Continued)

Flecainide *(Continued)*

Drug Interactions

Cytochrome P450 Effect: Substrate of CYP1A2 (minor), 2D6 (major); **Inhibits** CYP2D6 (weak)

Increased Effect/Toxicity: CYP2D6 inhibitors may increase the levels/effects of flecainide; example inhibitors include chlorpromazine, delavirdine, fluoxetine, miconazole, paroxetine, pergolide, quinidine, quinine, ritonavir, and ropinirole. Flecainide concentrations may be increased by amiodarone (reduce flecainide 25% to 33%), and propranolol. Beta-adrenergic blockers, disopyramide, verapamil may enhance flecainide's negative inotropic effects. Alkalinizing agents (ie, high-dose antacids, cimetidine, carbonic anhydrase inhibitors, sodium bicarbonate) may decrease flecainide clearance, potentially increasing toxicity. Propranolol blood levels are increased by flecainide.

Decreased Effect: Smoking and acid urine increase flecainide clearance.

Mechanism of Action Class Ic antiarrhythmic; slows conduction in cardiac tissue by altering transport of ions across cell membranes; causes slight prolongation of refractory periods; decreases the rate of rise of the action potential without affecting its duration; increases electrical stimulation threshold of ventricle, His-Purkinje system; possesses local anesthetic and moderate negative inotropic effects

Pharmacodynamics/Kinetics

Absorption: Oral: Rapid

Distribution: Adults: V_d: 5-13.4 L/kg

Protein binding: Alpha$_1$ glycoprotein: 40% to 50%

Metabolism: Hepatic

Bioavailability: 85% to 90%

Half-life elimination: Infants: 11-12 hours; Children: 8 hours; Adults: 7-22 hours, increased with congestive heart failure or renal dysfunction; End-stage renal disease: 19-26 hours

Time to peak, serum: ~1.5-3 hours

Excretion: Urine (80% to 90%, 10% to 50% as unchanged drug and metabolites)

Dosage Oral:

Children:

Initial: 3 mg/kg/day or 50-100 mg/m^2/day in 3 divided doses

Usual: 3-6 mg/kg/day or 100-150 mg/m^2/day in 3 divided doses; up to 11 mg/kg/day or 200 mg/m^2/day for uncontrolled patients with subtherapeutic levels

Adults:

Life-threatening ventricular arrhythmias:

Initial: 100 mg every 12 hours

Increase by 50-100 mg/day (given in 2 doses/day) every 4 days; maximum: 400 mg/day. Use of higher initial doses and more rapid dosage adjustments have resulted in an increased incidence of proarrhythmic events and congestive heart failure, particularly during the first few days. Do not use a loading dose. Use very cautiously in patients with history of congestive heart failure or myocardial infarction.

Prevention of paroxysmal supraventricular arrhythmias in patients with disabling symptoms but no structural heart disease:

Initial: 50 mg every 12 hours

Increase by 50 mg twice daily at 4-day intervals; maximum: 300 mg/day.

Dosing adjustment in severe renal impairment: Cl_{cr} <35 mL/minute: Decrease initial dose to 50 mg every 12 hours; increase doses at intervals >4 days monitoring ECG levels closely.

Dialysis: Not dialyzable (0% to 5%) via hemo- or peritoneal dialysis; no supplemental dose necessary.

Dosing adjustment/comments in hepatic impairment: Monitoring of plasma levels is recommended because of significantly increased half-life.

When transferring from another antiarrhythmic agent, allow for 2-4 half-lives of the agent to pass before initiating flecainide therapy.

Administration Administer around-the-clock to promote less variation in peak and trough serum levels

Monitoring Parameters ECG, blood pressure, pulse, periodic serum concentrations, especially in patients with renal or hepatic impairment

Reference Range Therapeutic: 0.2-1 µg/mL; pediatric patients may respond at the lower end of the recommended therapeutic range

Patient Information Report chest pain, faintness, or palpitations. Take only as directed.

Dosage Forms TAB: 50 mg, 100 mg, 150 mg

Fluconazole (floo KOE na zole)

Related Information
Antifungal Agents Comparison *on page 1362*

U.S. Brand Names Diflucan®

Therapeutic Category Antifungal Agent, Oral; Antifungal Agent, Parental; Antifungal Agent, Systemic

Use Treatment of oral or vaginal candidiasis unresponsive to nystatin or clotrimazole; nonlife-threatening *Candida* infections (eg, cystitis, esophagitis); treatment of hepatosplenic candidiasis; treatment of other *Candida* infections in persons unable to tolerate amphotericin B; treatment of cryptococcal infections; secondary prophylaxis for cryptococcal meningitis in persons with AIDS; antifungal prophylaxis in allogeneic bone marrow transplant recipients

Oral fluconazole should be used in persons able to tolerate oral medications; parenteral fluconazole should be reserved for patients who are both unable to take oral medications and are unable to tolerate amphotericin B (eg, due to hypersensitivity or renal insufficiency)

Pregnancy Risk Factor C

Contraindications Hypersensitivity to fluconazole, other azoles, or any component of the formulation; concomitant administration with cisapride or astemizole

Warnings/Precautions Should be used with caution in patients with renal and hepatic dysfunction or previous hepatotoxicity from other azole derivatives. Patients who develop abnormal liver function tests during fluconazole therapy should be monitored closely and discontinued if symptoms consistent with liver disease develop.

Common Adverse Reactions Frequency not always defined.
Cardiovascular: Pallor, angioedema
Central nervous system: Headache (2% to 13%), seizures, dizziness
Dermatologic: Rash (2%), alopecia, toxic epidermal necrolysis, Stevens-Johnson syndrome
Endocrine & metabolic: Hypertriglyceridemia, hypokalemia
Gastrointestinal: Nausea (4% to 7%), vomiting (2%), abdominal pain (2% to 6%), diarrhea (2% to 3%), taste perversion
Hematologic: Leukopenia, thrombocytopenia
Hepatic: Hepatic failure (rare), hepatitis, cholestasis, jaundice, increased ALT/AST, increased alkaline phosphatase
Respiratory: Dyspnea
Miscellaneous: Anaphylactic reactions (rare)

Drug Interactions
Cytochrome P450 Effect: Inhibits CYP1A2 (weak), 2C8/9 (strong), 2C19 (strong), 3A4 (moderate)

Increased Effect/Toxicity: Fluconazole may increase serum concentrations/effects of cyclosporine, phenytoin, rifabutin, tacrolimus, theophylline, rifabutin, sulfonylureas, warfarin, and zidovudine. Fluconazole may also increase cisapride or astemizole levels which has been associated with malignant arrhythmias. Hydrochlorothiazide may increase fluconazole levels.

Decreased Effect: Rifampin decreases concentrations of fluconazole.

Mechanism of Action Interferes with cytochrome P450 activity, decreasing ergosterol synthesis (principal sterol in fungal cell membrane) and inhibiting cell membrane formation

Pharmacodynamics/Kinetics
Distribution: Widely throughout body with good penetration into CSF, eye, peritoneal fluid, sputum, skin, and urine
Relative diffusion blood into CSF: Adequate with or without inflammation (exceeds usual MICs)
CSF:blood level ratio: Normal meninges: 70% to 80%; Inflamed meninges: >70% to 80%
Protein binding, plasma: 11% to 12%
Bioavailability: Oral: >90%
Half-life elimination: Normal renal function: 25-30 hours
Time to peak, serum: Oral: ~2-4 hours
Excretion: Urine (80% as unchanged drug)

Dosage The daily dose of fluconazole is the same for oral and I.V. administration

Neonates: First 2 weeks of life, especially premature neonates: Same dose as older children every 72 hours
Children: Once-daily dosing by indication: See table.

Fluconazole Once-Daily Dosing – Children

Indication	Day 1	Daily Therapy	Minimum Duration of Therapy
Oropharyngeal candidiasis	6 mg/kg	3 mg/kg	14 d
Esophageal candidiasis	6 mg/kg	3-12 mg/kg	21 d and for at least 2 wk following resolution of symptoms
Systemic candidiasis	—	6-12 mg/kg	28 d
Cryptococcal meningitis acute	12 mg/kg	6-12 mg/kg	10-12 wk after CSF culture becomes negative
relapse suppression	6 mg/kg	6 mg/kg	N/A

N/A = Not applicable.

(Continued)

Fluconazole *(Continued)*

Adults: Oral, I.V.: Once-daily dosing by indication: See table.

Fluconazole Once-Daily Dosing – Adults

Indication	Day 1	Daily Therapy	Minimum Duration of Therapy
Oropharyngeal candidiasis	200 mg	100 mg	14 d
Esophageal candidiasis	200 mg	100 mg	21 d and for at least 14 d following resolution of symptoms
Prevention of candidiasis in bone marrow transplant	400 mg	400 mg	3 d before neutropenia, 7 d after neutrophils >1000 cells/mm³
Candidiasis UTIs, peritonitis	50-200 mg	50-200 mg	N/A
Systemic candidiasis	400 mg	200 mg	28 d
Cryptococcal meningitis			10-12 wk after CSF culture becomes negative
acute	400 mg	200 mg	
relapse suppression	200 mg	200 mg	N/A
Vaginal candidiasis	150 mg	Single dose	N/A

N/A = Not applicable.

Dosing adjustment/interval in renal impairment:
No adjustment for vaginal candidiasis single-dose therapy
For multiple dosing, administer usual load then adjust daily doses
Cl$_{cr}$ 11-50 mL/minute: Administer 50% of recommended dose or administer every 48 hours
Hemodialysis: One dose after each dialysis
Continuous arteriovenous or venovenous hemodiafiltration effects: Dose as for Cl$_{cr}$ 10-50 mL/minute

Administration Parenteral fluconazole must be administered by I.V. infusion over approximately 1-2 hours; do not exceed 200 mg/hour when giving I.V. infusion; maximum rate of infusion: 200 mg/hour

Monitoring Parameters Periodic liver function tests (AST, ALT, alkaline phosphatase) and renal function tests, potassium

Patient Information May take with food; complete full course of therapy; report if side effects develop; consider using an alternative method of contraception if taking concurrently with birth control pills

Dosage Forms INF [premixed in sodium chloride or dextrose]: 2 mg/mL (100 mL, 200 mL). **POWDER, oral suspension:** 10 mg/mL (35 mL); 40 mg/mL (35 mL). **TAB:** 50 mg, 100 mg, 150 mg, 200 mg

Flucytosine *(floo SYE toe seen)*

Related Information
Antifungal Agents Comparison *on page 1362*

U.S. Brand Names Ancobon®

Synonyms 5-FC; 5-Flurocytosine

Therapeutic Category Antifungal Agent, Oral; Antifungal Agent, Systemic

Use Adjunctive treatment of susceptible fungal infections (usually *Candida* or *Cryptococcus*); synergy with amphotericin B for certain fungal infections (*Cryptococcus* spp., *Candida* spp.)

Pregnancy Risk Factor C

Contraindications Hypersensitivity to flucytosine or any component of the formulation

Warnings/Precautions Use with extreme caution in patients with renal dysfunction; dosage adjustment required. Avoid use as monotherapy; resistance rapidly develops. Use with caution in patients with bone marrow depression; patients with hematologic disease or who have been treated with radiation or drugs that suppress the bone marrow may be at greatest risk. Bone marrow toxicity can be irreversible.

Common Adverse Reactions Frequency not defined.
Cardiovascular: Cardiac arrest, myocardial toxicity, ventricular dysfunction, chest pain
Central nervous system: Confusion, headache, hallucinations, dizziness, drowsiness, psychosis, parkinsonism, ataxia, sedation, pyrexia, seizures, fatigue
Dermatologic: Rash, photosensitivity, pruritus, urticaria, Lyell's syndrome
Endocrine & metabolic: Temporary growth failure, hypoglycemia, hypokalemia
Gastrointestinal: Nausea, vomiting, diarrhea, abdominal pain, loss of appetite, dry mouth, hemorrhage, ulcerative colitis
Hematologic: Bone marrow suppression, anemia, leukopenia, thrombocytopenia, agranulocytosis, aplastic anemia, eosinophilia, pancytopenia
Hepatic: Liver enzymes increased, hepatitis, jaundice, azotemia, bilirubin increased
Neuromuscular & skeletal: Peripheral neuropathy, paresthesia, weakness
Otic: Hearing loss
Renal: BUN and serum creatinine increased, renal failure, azotemia, crystalluria
Respiratory: Respiratory arrest, dyspnea
Miscellaneous: Anaphylaxis, allergic reaction

Drug Interactions

Increased Effect/Toxicity: Increased effect with amphotericin B. Amphotericin B-induced renal dysfunction may predispose patient to flucytosine accumulation and myelosuppression.

Decreased Effect: Cytarabine may inactivate flucytosine activity.

Mechanism of Action Penetrates fungal cells and is converted to fluorouracil which competes with uracil interfering with fungal RNA and protein synthesis

Pharmacodynamics/Kinetics

Absorption: 75% to 90%

Distribution: Into CSF, aqueous humor, joints, peritoneal fluid, and bronchial secretions; V_d: 0.6 L/kg

Protein binding: 2% to 4%

Metabolism: Minimally hepatic; deaminated, possibly via gut bacteria, to 5-fluorouracil

Half-life elimination:

Normal renal function: 2-5 hours

Anuria: 85 hours (range: 30-250)

End stage renal disease: 75-200 hours

Time to peak, serum: ~2-6 hours

Excretion: Urine (>90% as unchanged drug)

Dosage Children and Adults: Oral: 50-150 mg/kg/day in divided doses every 6 hours

Dosing interval in renal impairment: Use lower initial dose:

Cl_{cr} 20-40 mL/minute: Administer every 12 hours

Cl_{cr} 10-20 mL/minute: Administer every 24 hours

Cl_{cr} <10 mL/minute: Administer every 24-48 hours

Hemodialysis: Dialyzable (50% to 100%); administer dose posthemodialysis

Peritoneal dialysis: Adults: Administer 0.5-1 g every 24 hours

Continuous arteriovenous or venovenous hemodiafiltration effects: Dose as for Cl_{cr} 10-50 mL/minute

Administration Administer around-the-clock to promote less variation in peak and trough serum levels. To avoid nausea and vomiting, administer a few capsules at a time over 15 minutes until full dose is taken.

Monitoring Parameters

Pretreatment: Electrolytes, CBC, BUN, renal function, blood culture

During treatment: CBC and LFTS frequently, serum flucytosine concentration, renal function

Reference Range

Therapeutic: 25-100 µg/mL (peak) (SI: 195-775 µmol/L); peak levels should not exceed 100-120 µg/mL to avoid toxic bone marrow depressive effects

Trough: Draw just prior to dose administration

Peak: Draw 2 hours after an oral dose administration

Patient Information Take capsules a few at a time with food over a 15-minute period to avoid nausea

Dosage Forms CAP: 250 mg, 500 mg

♦ **Fludara**® *see Fludarabine on page 529*

Fludarabine *(floo DARE a been)*

U.S. Brand Names Fludara®

Synonyms Fludarabine Phosphate

Therapeutic Category Antineoplastic Agent, Antimetabolite (Purine)

Use Treatment of chronic lymphocytic leukemia (CLL) (including refractory CLL); non-Hodgkin's lymphoma in adults

Unlabeled/Investigational Use Treatment of non-Hodgkin's lymphoma and acute leukemias in pediatric patients

Pregnancy Risk Factor D

Contraindications Hypersensitivity of fludarabine or any component of the formulation; pregnancy

Warnings/Precautions The U.S. Food and Drug Administration (FDA) currently recommends that procedures for proper handling and disposal of antineoplastic agents be considered. Use with caution with renal insufficiency, patients with a fever, documented infection, or pre-existing hematological disorders (particularly granulocytopenia) or in patients with pre-existing central nervous system disorder (epilepsy), spasticity, or peripheral neuropathy. Life-threatening and sometimes fatal autoimmune hemolytic anemia have occurred. Severe myelosuppression (trilineage bone marrow hypoplasia/aplasia) has been reported (rare); the duration of significant cytopenias in these cases may be prolonged (up to 1 year).

Common Adverse Reactions

>10%:

Cardiovascular: Edema

Central nervous system: Fatigue, somnolence (30%), chills, pain

Dermatologic: Rash

Hematologic: Myelosuppression, common, dose-limiting toxicity, primarily leukopenia and thrombocytopenia

Nadir: 10-14 days

Recovery: 5-7 weeks

Neuromuscular & skeletal: Paresthesia, myalgia, weakness

1% to 10%:

Cardiovascular: Congestive heart failure

Central nervous system: Malaise, headache

(Continued)

Fludarabine (Continued)

Dermatologic: Alopecia

Endocrine & metabolic: Hyperglycemia

Gastrointestinal: Anorexia, stomatitis (1.5%), diarrhea (1.8%), mild nausea/vomiting (3% to 10%)

Hematologic: Eosinophilia, hemolytic anemia, may be dose-limiting, possibly fatal in some patients

Drug Interactions

Increased Effect/Toxicity: Combined use with pentostatin may lead to severe, even fatal, pulmonary toxicity.

Mechanism of Action Fludarabine inhibits DNA synthesis by inhibition of DNA polymerase and ribonucleotide reductase.

Pharmacodynamics/Kinetics

Distribution: V_d: 38-96 L/m^2; widely with extensive tissue binding

Metabolism: I.V.: Fludarabine phosphate is rapidly dephosphorylated to 2-fluoro-vidarabine, which subsequently enters tumor cells and is phosphorylated to the active triphosphate derivative; rapidly dephosphorylated in the serum

Bioavailability: 75%

Half-life elimination: 2-fluoro-vidarabine: 9 hours

Excretion: Urine (60%, 23% as 2-fluoro-vidarabine) within 24 hours

Dosage I.V.:

Children (unlabeled use):

Acute leukemia: 10 mg/m^2 bolus over 15 minutes followed by continuous infusion of 30.5 mg/m^2/day for 5 days **or**

10.5 mg/m^2 bolus over 15 minutes followed by 30.5 mg/m^2/day for 48 hours

Solid tumors: 9 mg/m^2 bolus followed by 27 mg/m^2/day continuous infusion for 5 days

Adults:

Chronic lymphocytic leukemia: 25 mg/m^2/day for 5 days every 28 days

Non-Hodgkin's lymphoma: Loading dose: 20 mg/m^2 followed by 30 mg/m^2/day for 48 hours

Dosing in renal impairment:

Cl_{cr} 30-70 mL/minute: Reduce dose by 20%

Cl_{cr} <30 mL/minute: Not recommended

Administration Fludarabine is administered intravenously, usually as a 15- to 30-minute infusion; continuous infusions are occasionally used

Monitoring Parameters CBC with differential, platelet count, AST, ALT, creatinine, serum albumin, uric acid

Dosage Forms INJ, powder for reconstitution: 50 mg

♦ **Fludarabine Phosphate** see Fludarabine on page 529

Fludrocortisone (floo droe KOR ti sone)

Related Information

Corticosteroids Comparison on page 1372

U.S. Brand Names Florinef®

Synonyms Fludrocortisone Acetate; Fluohydrisone Acetate; Fluohydrocortisone Acetate; 9α-Fluorohydrocortisone Acetate

Therapeutic Category Mineralocorticoid

Use Partial replacement therapy for primary and secondary adrenocortical insufficiency in Addison's disease; treatment of salt-losing adrenogenital syndrome

Pregnancy Risk Factor C

Contraindications Hypersensitivity to fludrocortisone or any component of the formulation; systemic fungal infections

Warnings/Precautions Taper dose gradually when therapy is discontinued; use with caution with Addison's disease, sodium retention and potassium loss

Common Adverse Reactions Frequency not defined.

Cardiovascular: Hypertension, edema, CHF

Central nervous system: Convulsions, headache, dizziness

Dermatologic: Acne, rash, bruising

Endocrine & metabolic: Hypokalemic alkalosis, suppression of growth, hyperglycemia, HPA suppression

Gastrointestinal: Peptic ulcer

Neuromuscular & skeletal: Muscle weakness

Ocular: Cataracts

Miscellaneous: Diaphoresis, anaphylaxis (generalized)

Drug Interactions

Decreased Effect: Anticholinesterases effects are antagonized. Decreased corticosteroid effects by rifampin, barbiturates, and hydantoins. May decrease salicylate levels.

Mechanism of Action Promotes increased reabsorption of sodium and loss of potassium from renal distal tubules

Pharmacodynamics/Kinetics

Absorption: Rapid and complete

Protein binding: 42%

Metabolism: Hepatic

Half-life elimination, plasma: 30-35 minutes; Biological: 18-36 hours

Time to peak, serum: ~1.7 hours

Dosage Oral:

Infants and Children: 0.05-0.1 mg/day

Adults: 0.1-0.2 mg/day with ranges of 0.1 mg 3 times/week to 0.2 mg/day

Addison's disease: Initial: 0.1 mg/day; if transient hypertension develops, reduce the dose to 0.05 mg/day. Preferred administration with cortisone (10-37.5 mg/day) or hydrocortisone (10-30 mg/day).

Salt-losing adrenogenital syndrome: 0.1-0.2 mg/day

Administration Administration in conjunction with a glucocorticoid is preferable

Monitoring Parameters Monitor blood pressure and signs of edema when patient is on chronic therapy; very potent mineralocorticoid with high glucocorticoid activity; monitor serum electrolytes, serum renin activity, and blood pressure; monitor for evidence of infection

Patient Information Report dizziness, severe or continuing headaches, swelling of feet or lower legs, or unusual weight gain.

Dosage Forms TAB: 0.1 mg

♦ **Fludrocortisone Acetate** *see* Fludrocortisone *on page 530*

♦ **Flumadine®** *see* Rimantadine *on page 1099*

Flumazenil (FLOO may ze nil)

U.S. Brand Names Romazicon®

Therapeutic Category Antidote, Benzodiazepine

Use Benzodiazepine antagonist - reverses sedative effects of benzodiazepines used in general anesthesia; for management of benzodiazepine overdose; flumazenil does **not** antagonize the CNS effects of other GABA agonists (eg, ethanol, barbiturates, or general anesthetics), **does not** reverse narcotics

Pregnancy Risk Factor C

Contraindications Hypersensitivity to flumazenil, benzodiazepines, or any component of the formulation; patients given benzodiazepines for control of potentially life-threatening conditions (eg, control of intracranial pressure or status epilepticus); patients who are showing signs of serious cyclic-antidepressant overdosage

Warnings/Precautions

Risk of seizures = high-risk patients:

Patients on benzodiazepines for long-term sedation

Tricyclic antidepressant overdose patients

Concurrent major sedative-hypnotic drug withdrawal

Recent therapy with repeated doses of parenteral benzodiazepines

Myoclonic jerking or seizure activity prior to flumazenil administration

Hypoventilation: Does not reverse respiratory depression/hypoventilation or cardiac depression

Resedation: Occurs more frequently in patients where a large single dose or cumulative dose of a benzodiazepine is administered along with a neuromuscular blocking agent and multiple anesthetic agents

Flumazenil should be used with caution in the intensive care unit because of increased risk of unrecognized benzodiazepine dependence in such settings.

Does **not** antagonize the CNS effects of other GABA agonists (such as ethanol, barbiturates, or general anesthetics), nor does it reverse narcotics

Common Adverse Reactions

>10%: Gastrointestinal: Vomiting, nausea

1% to 10%:

Cardiovascular: Palpitations

Central nervous system: Headache, anxiety, nervousness, insomnia, abnormal crying, euphoria, depression, agitation, dizziness, emotional lability, ataxia, depersonalization, increased tears, dysphoria, paranoia

Endocrine & metabolic: Hot flashes

Gastrointestinal: Xerostomia

Local: Pain at injection site

Neuromuscular & skeletal: Tremor, weakness, paresthesia

Ocular: Abnormal vision, blurred vision

Respiratory: Dyspnea, hyperventilation

Miscellaneous: Diaphoresis

Drug Interactions

Increased Effect/Toxicity: Use with caution in overdosage involving mixed drug overdose. Toxic effects may emerge (especially with cyclic antidepressants) with the reversal of the benzodiazepine effect by flumazenil.

Mechanism of Action Competitively inhibits the activity at the benzodiazepine recognition site on the GABA/benzodiazepine receptor complex. Flumazenil does not antagonize the CNS effect of drugs affecting GABA-ergic neurons by means other than the benzodiazepine receptor (ethanol, barbiturates, general anesthetics) and does not reverse the effects of opioids

Pharmacodynamics/Kinetics

Onset of action: 1-3 minutes; 80% response within 3 minutes

Peak effect: 6-10 minutes

Duration: Resedation: ~1 hour; duration related to dose given and benzodiazepine plasma concentrations; reversal effects of flumazenil may wear off before effects of benzodiazepine

Distribution: Initial V_d: 0.5 L/kg; V_{dss} 0.77-1.6 L/kg

(Continued)

Flumazenil *(Continued)*

Protein binding: 40% to 50%

Metabolism: Hepatic; dependent upon hepatic blood flow

Half-life elimination: Adults: Alpha: 7-15 minutes; Terminal: 41-79 minutes

Excretion: Feces; urine (0.2% as unchanged drug)

Dosage

Children and Adults: I.V.: See table.

Flumazenil

Pediatric Dosage (further studies needed)	
Pediatric dosage for **reversal of conscious sedation:** Administer intravenously through a freely running intravenous infusion into a large vein to minimize pain at the injection site.	
Initial dose	0.01 mg/kg over 15 seconds (maximum: 0.2 mg)
Repeat doses	0.005-0.01 mg/kg (maximum: 0.2 mg) repeated at 1-minute intervals
Maximum total cumulative dose	1 mg
Pediatric dosage for **management of benzodiazepine overdose:** Administer intravenously through a freely running intravenous infusion into a large vein to minimize pain at the injection site.	
Initial dose	0.01 mg/kg (maximum: 0.2 mg)
Repeat doses	0.01 mg/kg (maximum: 0.2 mg) repeated at 1-minute intervals
Maximum total cumulative dose	1 mg
In place of repeat bolus doses, follow-up continuous infusions of 0.005-0.01 mg/kg/hour have been used; further studies are needed.	
Adult Dosage	
Adult dosage for **reversal of conscious sedation:** Administer intravenously through a freely running intravenous infusion into a large vein to minimize pain at the injection site.	
Initial dose	0.2 mg intravenously over 15 seconds
Repeat doses	If desired level of consciousness is not obtained, 0.2 mg may be repeated at 1-minute intervals.
Maximum total cumulative dose	1 mg (usual dose: 0.6-1 mg) **In the event of resedation:** Repeat doses may be given at 20-minute intervals with maximum of 1 mg/dose and 3 mg/hour.
Adult dosage for **suspected benzodiazepine overdose:** Administer intravenously through a freely running intravenous infusion into a large vein to minimize pain at the injection site.	
Initial dose	0.2 mg intravenously over 30 seconds
Repeat doses	0.5 mg over 30 seconds repeated at 1-minute intervals
Maximum total cumulative dose	3 mg (usual dose 1-3 mg) Patients with a partial response at 3 mg may require additional titration up to a total dose of 5 mg. If a patient has not responded 5 minutes after cumulative dose of 5 mg, the major cause of sedation is not likely due to benzodiazepines. **In the event of resedation:** May repeat doses at 20-minute intervals with maximum of 1 mg/dose and 3 mg/hour.

Resedation: Repeated doses may be given at 20-minute intervals as needed; repeat treatment doses of 1 mg (at a rate of 0.5 mg/minute) should be given at any time and no more than 3 mg should be given in any hour. After intoxication with high doses of benzodiazepines, the duration of a single dose of flumazenil is not expected to exceed 1 hour; if desired, the period of wakefulness may be prolonged with repeated low intravenous doses of flumazenil, or by an infusion of 0.1-0.4 mg/hour. Most patients with benzodiazepine overdose will respond to a cumulative dose of 1-3 mg and doses >3 mg do not reliably produce additional effects. Rarely, patients with a partial response at 3 mg may require additional titration up to a total dose of 5 mg. **If a patient has not responded 5 minutes after receiving a cumulative dose of 5 mg, the major cause of sedation is not likely to be due to benzodiazepines.**

Elderly: No differences in safety or efficacy have been reported. However, increased sensitivity may occur in some elderly patients.

Dosing in renal impairment: Not significantly affected by renal failure (Cl_{cr} <10 mL/minute) or hemodialysis beginning 1 hour after drug administration

Dosing in hepatic impairment: Initial dose of flumazenil used for initial reversal of benzodiazepine effects is not changed; however, subsequent doses in liver disease patients should be reduced in size or frequency

Monitoring Parameters Monitor patients for return of sedation or respiratory depression

Patient Information Flumazenil does not consistently reverse amnesia; do not engage in activities requiring alertness for 18-24 hours after discharge; resedation may occur in patients on long-acting benzodiazepines (such as diazepam)

Dosage Forms INJ, solution: 0.1 mg/mL (5 mL, 10 mL)

♦ FluMist™ *see* Influenza Virus Vaccine *on page 667*

Flunisolide (floo NISS oh lide)

U.S. Brand Names AeroBid®; AeroBid®-M; Nasalide®; Nasarel®
Therapeutic Category Anti-inflammatory Agent, Inhalant; Corticosteroid, Inhalant; Corticosteroid, Intranasal
Use Steroid-dependent asthma; nasal solution is used for seasonal or perennial rhinitis
Pregnancy Risk Factor C
Dosage
Children >6 years:
Oral inhalation: 2 inhalations twice daily (morning and evening) up to 4 inhalations/day
Nasal: 1 spray each nostril twice daily (morning and evening), not to exceed 4 sprays/day each nostril
Adults:
Oral inhalation: 2 inhalations twice daily (morning and evening) up to 8 inhalations/day maximum
Nasal: 2 sprays each nostril twice daily (morning and evening); maximum dose: 8 sprays/day in each nostril
Dosage Forms AERO, oral inhalation (AeroBid®): 250 mcg/actuation (7 g); (AeroBid-M®): 250 mcg/actuation (7 g). **SOLN, intranasal spray** (Nasalide®, Nasarel®): 25 mcg/actuation (25 mL)

Fluocinolone (floo oh SIN oh lone)

Related Information
Corticosteroids Comparison *on page 1372*
U.S. Brand Names Capex™; Derma-Smoothe/FS®; Synalar®
Synonyms Fluocinolone Acetonide
Therapeutic Category Anti-inflammatory Agent; Corticosteroid, Shampoo; Corticosteroid, Topical (Low Potency); Corticosteroid, Topical (Medium Potency); Corticosteroid, Topical (High Potency)
Use Relief of susceptible inflammatory dermatosis [low, medium, high potency topical corticosteroid]; psoriasis of the scalp; atopic dermatitis in children ≥2 years of age
Pregnancy Risk Factor C
Dosage Topical:
Children ≥2 years: Atopic dermatitis (Derma-Smoothe/FS®): Moisten skin; apply to affected area twice daily; do not use for longer than 4 weeks
Children and Adults: Corticosteroid-responsive dermatoses: Cream, ointment, solution: Apply a thin layer to affected area 2-4 times/day; may use occlusive dressings to manage psoriasis or recalcitrant conditions
Adults:
Atopic dermatitis (Derma-Smoothe/FS®): Apply thin film to affected area 3 times/day
Scalp psoriasis (Derma-Smoothe/FS®): Massage thoroughly into wet or dampened hair/scalp; cover with shower cap. Leave on overnight (or for at least 4 hours). Remove by washing hair with shampoo and rinsing thoroughly.
Seborrheic dermatitis of the scalp (Capex™): Apply no more than 1 ounce to scalp once daily; work into lather and allow to remain on scalp for ~5 minutes. Remove from hair and scalp by rinsing thoroughly with water.
Dosage Forms CRM: 0.01% (15 g, 60 g); 0.025% (15 g, 60 g); (Synalar®): 0.025% (15 g, 60 g). **OIL** (Derma-Smoothe/FS®): 0.01% (120 mL). **OINT** (Synalar®): 0.025% (15 g, 60 g). **SHAMP** (Capex™): 0.01% (120 mL). **SOLN:** 0.01% (60 mL); (Synalar®): 0.01% (20 mL, 60 mL)

♦ **Fluocinolone Acetonide** *see Fluocinolone on page 533*

Fluocinolone, Hydroquinone, and Tretinoin

(floo oh SIN oh lone, HYE droe kwin one, & TRET i noyn)
U.S. Brand Names Tri-Luma™
Synonyms Hydroquinone, Fluocinolone Acetonide, and Tretinoin; Tretinoin, Fluocinolone Acetonide, and Hydroquinone
Therapeutic Category Depigmenting Agent; Retinoic Acid Derivative
Use Short-term treatment of moderate to severe melasma of the face
Pregnancy Risk Factor C
Contraindications Hypersensitivity to fluocinolone, hydroquinone, tretinoin, or any component of the formulation; TB of skin, herpes (including varicella); sulfite allergy
Warnings/Precautions For external use only. Should only be used along with measures for sun avoidance. Local irritation, dryness, and pruritus may be expected following application. Avoid contact with abraded skin, mucous membranes, eyes, mouth, angles of the nose. Due to corticosteroid component, adverse systemic effects (including HPA axis suppression) may occur when used on large areas of the body, denuded areas, for prolonged periods of time, and/or with use of an occlusive dressing.

Hydroquinone may produce exogenous ochronosis (gradual blue/black darkening of skin); discontinuation is recommended. Has not been evaluated in skin types V and VI; excessive bleaching may occur in individuals with darker skin. Safety and efficacy have not been established in pediatric patients.
Common Adverse Reactions
>10%
Dermatologic: Erythema (41%), desquamation (38%), burning (18%), dry skin (14%), pruritus (11%)
1% to 10%
Cardiovascular: Telangiectasia (3%)
(Continued)

Fluocinolone, Hydroquinone, and Tretinoin *(Continued)*

Central nervous system: Paresthesia (3%), hyperesthesia (2%)

Dermatologic: Acne (5%), pigmentation change (2%), irritation (2%), papules (1%), rash (1%), rosacea (1%), vesicles (1%)

Gastrointestinal: Xerostomia (1%)

Drug Interactions

Cytochrome P450 Effect: Tretinoin: **Substrate** (minor) of CYP2A6, 2B6, 2C8/9; **Inhibits** CYP2C8/9 (weak); **Induces** CYP2E1 (weak)

Increased Effect/Toxicity: Avoid soaps/cosmetic preparations which are medicated, abrasive, irritating, or any product with strong drying effects (including alcohol, astringent, benzoyl peroxide, resorcinol, salicylic acid, sulfur). Drugs with photosensitizing effects should also be avoided (includes tetracyclines, thiazides, fluoroquinolones, phenothiazines, sulfonamides).

Mechanism of Action Not clearly defined. Hydroquinone may interrupt melanin synthesis (tyrosine-tyrosinase pathway); reduces hyperpigmentation.

Pharmacodynamics/Kinetics

Absorption: Minimal

Metabolism: Hepatic for the small amount absorbed

Excretion: Urine and feces

Dosage Topical: Adults: Melasma: Apply a thin film once daily to hyperpigmented areas of melasma (including 1/2 inch of normal-appearing surrounding skin). Apply 30 minutes prior to bedtime; not indicated for use beyond 8 weeks. Do not use occlusive dressings.

Administration Apply 30 minutes before bedtime. Wash face with mild cleanser; rinse and pat dry. Apply to lesion and 1/2 inch of normal-appearing skin surrounding each lesion. Rub lightly and uniformly into the skin. Do not use occlusive dressings.

Monitoring Parameters Signs/symptoms of HPA axis suppression

Patient Information For external use only. A thin film of cream is effective; do not overuse; use only as prescribed, and for no longer than the period prescribed. Prior to application, wash face with mild cleanser, rinse and pat dry. Apply sparingly in light film; rub lightly. Avoid contact with abraded skin, mucous membranes, eyes, mouth, angles of the nose. Avoid sunlight (wear sunscreen with SPF 30 and protective clothing). May use moisturizers and/or cosmetics during the day (avoid medicated preparations or agents with irritating or drying effects). May cause irritation and sensitivity to temperature changes; excessive bleaching of the skin may occur. Notify prescriber if condition being treated persists or worsens.

Dosage Forms CRM, topical: Hydroquinone 4%, tretinoin 0.05%, fluocinolone acetonide 0.01% (30 g)

Fluocinonide *(floo oh SIN oh nide)*

Related Information

Corticosteroids Comparison *on page 1372*

U.S. Brand Names Lidex®; Lidex-E®

Therapeutic Category Corticosteroid, Topical (High Potency)

Use Anti-inflammatory, antipruritic, relief of inflammatory and pruritic manifestations [high potency topical corticosteroid]

Pregnancy Risk Factor C

Dosage Children and Adults: Topical: Apply thin layer to affected area 2-4 times/day depending on the severity of the condition. Therapy should be discontinued when control is achieved; if no improvement is seen, reassessment of diagnosis may be necessary.

Dosage Forms CRM, anhydrous, emollient (Lidex®): 0.05% (15 g, 30 g, 60 g, 120 g). **CRM, aqueous, emollient** (Lidex-E®): 0.05% (15 g, 30 g, 60 g). **GEL** (Lidex®): 0.05% (15 g, 30 g, 60 g). **OINT** (Lidex®): 0.05% (15 g, 30 g, 60 g). **SOLN** (Lidex®): 0.05% (20 mL, 60 mL)

♦ **Fluohydrisone Acetate** *see* Fludrocortisone *on page 530*

♦ **Fluohydrocortisone Acetate** *see* Fludrocortisone *on page 530*

♦ **Fluoracaine®** *see* Proparacaine and Fluorescein *on page 1050*

♦ **Fluor-A-Day [OTC]** *see* Fluoride *on page 535*

♦ **Fluorescein and Proparacaine** *see* Proparacaine and Fluorescein *on page 1050*

Fluorescein Sodium *(FLURE e seen SOW dee um)*

U.S. Brand Names AK-Fluor; Angiscein®; Fluorescite®; Fluorets®; Fluor-I-Strip®; Fluor-I-Strip-AT®; Ful-Glo®

Synonyms Soluble Fluorescein

Therapeutic Category Diagnostic Agent, Ophthalmic Dye

Use Demonstrates defects of corneal epithelium; diagnostic aid in ophthalmic angiography

Pregnancy Risk Factor C (topical); X (parenteral)

Dosage

Ophthalmic:

Solution: Instill 1-2 drops of 2% solution and allow a few seconds for staining; wash out excess with sterile water or irrigating solution

Strips: Moisten strip with sterile water. Place moistened strip at the fornix into the lower cul-de-sac close to the punctum. For best results, patient should close lid tightly over strip until desired amount of staining is obtained. Patient should blink several times after application.

Removal of foreign bodies, sutures or tonometry (Fluress®): Instill 1 or 2 drops (single instillations) into each eye before operating

Deep ophthalmic anesthesia (Fluress®): Instill 2 drops into each eye every 90 seconds up to 3 doses

Injection: Prior to use, perform intradermal skin test; have epinephrine 1:1000, an antihistamine, and oxygen available

Children: 3.5 mg/lb (7.5 mg/kg) injected rapidly into antecubital vein

Adults: 500-750 mg injected rapidly into antecubital vein

Dosage Forms INJ, solution (AK-Fluor®, Fluorescite®): 10% (5 mL); 25% (2 mL); (Angiscein®): 10% (5 mL). **STRIP, ophthalmic** (Fluorets®, Fluor-I-Strip-AT®): 1 mg; (Fluor-I-Strip®): 9 mg; (Ful-Glo®): 0.6 mg

♦ **Fluorescite®** see Fluorescein Sodium on page 534

♦ **Fluorets®** see Fluorescein Sodium on page 534

Fluoride (FLOR ide)

U.S. Brand Names ACT® [OTC]; Fluor-A-Day [OTC]; Fluorigard® [OTC]; Fluorinse®; Flura-Drops®; Flura-Loz®; Gel-Kam® [OTC]; Gel-Kam® Rinse; Lozi-Flur™; Luride®; Luride® Lozi-Tab®; NeutraCare®; NeutraGard® [OTC]; Pediaflor®; Pharmaflur®; Pharmaflur® 1.1; Phos-Flur®; Phos-Flur® Rinse [OTC]; PreviDent®; PreviDent® 5000 Plus™; Stan-gard®; Stop®; Thera-Flur-N®

Synonyms Acidulated Phosphate Fluoride; Sodium Fluoride; Stannous Fluoride

Therapeutic Category Mineral, Oral; Mineral, Oral Topical

Use Used exclusively in dental applications (prevention of dental caries)

Pregnancy Risk Factor C

Contraindications Hypersensitivity to fluoride, tartrazine, or any component of the formulation; when fluoride content of drinking water exceeds 0.7 ppm; low sodium or sodium-free diets; do not use 1 mg tablets in children <3 years of age or when drinking water fluoride content is ≥0.3 ppm; do not use 1 mg/5 mL rinse (as supplement) in children <6 years of age

Warnings/Precautions Prolonged ingestion with excessive doses may result in dental fluorosis and osseous changes; do **not** exceed recommended dosage; some products contain tartrazine

Drug Interactions

Decreased Effect: Decreased effect/absorption with magnesium-, aluminum-, and calcium-containing products.

Mechanism of Action Promotes remineralization of decalcified enamel; inhibits the cariogenic microbial process in dental plaque; increases tooth resistance to acid dissolution

Pharmacodynamics/Kinetics

Absorption: Oral: Rapid and complete; sodium fluoride; other soluble fluoride salts; calcium, iron, or magnesium may delay absorption

Distribution: 50% of fluoride is deposited in teeth and bone after ingestion; topical application works superficially on enamel and plaque; crosses placenta; enters breast milk

Excretion: Urine and feces

Dosage Oral:

The recommended daily dose of oral fluoride supplement (mg), based on fluoride ion content (ppm) in drinking water (2.2 mg of sodium fluoride is equivalent to 1 mg of fluoride ion): See table.

Fluoride Ion

Fluoride Content of Drinking Water	Daily Dose, Oral (mg)
<0.3 ppm	
Birth - 6 mo	None
6 mo - 3 y	0.25
3-6 y	0.5
6-16 y	1
0.3-0.6 ppm	
Birth - 6 mo	None
6 mo - 3 y	None
3-6 y	0.25
6-16 y	0.5

Table from: Recommended dosage schedule of The American Dental Association, The American Academy of Pediatric Dentistry, and The American Academy of Pediatrics

Dental rinse or gel:

Children 6-12 years: 5-10 mL rinse or apply to teeth and spit daily after brushing

Adults: 10 mL rinse or apply to teeth and spit daily after brushing

PreviDent® rinse: Children >6 years and Adults: Once weekly, rinse 10 mL vigorously around and between teeth for 1 minute, then spit; this should be done preferably at bedtime, after thoroughly brushing teeth; for maximum benefit, do not eat, drink, or rinse mouth for at least 30 minutes after treatment; do not swallow

Fluorinse®: Children >6 years and Adults: Once weekly, vigorously swish 5-10 mL in mouth for 1 minute, then spit

Patient Information Take with food (but not milk) to eliminate GI upset; with dental rinse or dental gel do **not** swallow, do **not** eat or drink for 30 minutes after use

(Continued)

Fluoride (Continued)

Dosage Forms CRM, topical, as sodium (PreviDent® 5000 Plus™): 1.1% (51 g). **GEL-DROPS, as sodium fluoride** (Thera-Flur-N®): 1.1% (24 mL). **GEL, topical, as acidulated phosphate fluoride** (Phos-Flur®): 1.1% (60 g). **GEL, topical, as sodium fluoride** (NeutraCare®, PreviDent®): 1.1% (60 g). **GEL, topical, as stannous fluoride** (Gel-Kam®): 0.4% (129 g); (Stan-Gard®): 0.4% (122 g); (Stop®): 0.4% (120 g). **LOZ, as sodium** (Flura-Loz®, Fluor-A-Day): 2.2 mg; (Lozi-Flur™): 2.21 mg. **SOLN, oral drops, as sodium** (Flura-Drops®): 0.55 mg/drop (24 mL); (Luride®, Pediaflor®): 1.1 mg/mL (50 mL). **SOLN, oral rinse, as sodium** (ACT®): 0.05% (530 mL); (Fluorigard®, NeutraGard®): 0.05% (480 mL); (Fluorinse®): 0.2% (480 mL); (Phos-Flur®): 0.44% (500 mL); (PreviDent®): 0.2% (250 mL). **SOLN, oral rinse concentrate, as stannous fluoride** (Gel-Kam®): 0.63% (300 mL). **TAB, chewable, as sodium** (Fluor-A-Day): 0.56 mg, 1.1 mg, 2.21 mg; (Luride® Lozi-Tabs®): 0.55 mg, 1.1 mg, 2.2 mg; (Pharmaflur®): 2.2 mg; (Pharmaflur® 1.1): 1.1 mg

♦ **Fluorigard® [OTC]** see Fluoride on page 535

♦ **Fluori-Methane®** see Dichlorodifluoromethane and Trichloromonofluoromethane on page 367

♦ **Fluorinse®** see Fluoride on page 535

♦ **Fluor-I-Strip®** see Fluorescein Sodium on page 534

♦ **Fluor-I-Strip-AT®** see Fluorescein Sodium on page 534

♦ **9α-Fluorohydrocortisone Acetate** see Fludrocortisone on page 530

Fluorometholone (flure oh METH oh lone)

U.S. Brand Names Eflone®; Flarex®; Fluor-Op®; FML®; FML® Forte

Therapeutic Category Anti-inflammatory Agent; Corticosteroid, Ophthalmic; Corticosteroid, Topical (Low Potency)

Use Treatment of steroid-responsive inflammatory conditions of the eye

Pregnancy Risk Factor C

Contraindications Hypersensitivity to fluorometholone or any component of the formulation; viral diseases of the cornea and conjunctiva (including epithelial herpes simplex keratitis, vaccinia and varicella); mycobacterial or fungal infections of the eye; untreated eye infections which may be masked/enhanced by a steroid

Warnings/Precautions Not recommended in children <2 years of age; prolonged use may result in glaucoma, elevated intraocular pressure, or other ocular damage; may exacerbate severity of viral infections, use caution in patients with history of herpes simplex; re-evaluate after 2 days if symptoms have not improved; may delay healing following cataract surgery; some products contain sulfites

Common Adverse Reactions Frequency not defined.

Ocular: Anterior uveitis, burning upon application, cataract formation, conjunctival hyperemia, conjunctivitis, corneal ulcers, glaucoma with optic nerve damage, perforation of the globe, secondary ocular infection (bacterial, fungal, viral), intraocular pressure elevation, visual acuity and field defects, keratitis, mydriasis, stinging upon application, delayed wound healing

Miscellaneous: Systemic hypercorticoidism (rare) and taste perversion have also been reported

Mechanism of Action Decreases inflammation by suppression of migration of polymorphonuclear leukocytes and reversal of increased capillary permeability

Pharmacodynamics/Kinetics Absorption: Into aqueous humor with slight systemic absorption

Dosage Children >2 years and Adults: Ophthalmic: Re-evaluate therapy if improvement is not seen within 2 days; use care not to discontinue prematurely; in chronic conditions, gradually decrease dosing frequency prior to discontinuing treatment

Ointment: Apply small amount (~1/2 inch ribbon) to conjunctival sac every 4 hours in severe cases; 1-3 times/day in mild to moderate cases

Solution: Instill 1-2 drops into conjunctival sac every hour during day, every 2 hours at night until favorable response is obtained, then use 1 drop every 4 hours; for mild to moderate inflammation, instill 1-2 drops into conjunctival sac 2-4 times/day

Monitoring Parameters Intraocular pressure in patients with glaucoma or when used for ≥10 days; presence of secondary infections (including the development of fungal infections and exacerbation of viral infections)

Dosage Forms OINT, ophthalmic, as base: (FML®): 0.1% (3.5 g). **SUSP, ophthalmic, as base:** 5 mL, 10 mL, 15 mL; (Fluor-Op®): 0.1% (5 mL, 10 mL, 15 mL); (FML®): 0.1% (1 mL, 5 mL, 10 mL, 15 mL); (FML® Forte): 0.25% (2 mL, 5 mL, 10 mL, 15 mL). **SUSP, ophthalmic, as acetate** (Eflone®, Flarex®): 0.1% (5 mL, 10 mL)

♦ **Fluorometholone and Sulfacetamide** see Sulfacetamide Sodium and Fluorometholone on page 1170

♦ **Fluor-Op®** see Fluorometholone on page 536

♦ **Fluoroplex®** see Fluorouracil on page 536

Fluorouracil (flure oh YOOR a sil)

U.S. Brand Names Adrucil®; Carac™; Efudex®; Fluoroplex®

Synonyms 5-Fluorouracil; FU; 5-FU

Therapeutic Category Antineoplastic Agent, Antimetabolite (Pyrimidine)

Use Treatment of carcinomas of the breast, colon, head and neck, pancreas, rectum, or stomach; topically for the management of actinic or solar keratoses and superficial basal cell carcinomas

Pregnancy Risk Factor D (injection); X (topical)

Contraindications Hypersensitivity to fluorouracil or any component of the formulation; poor nutritional status; depressed bone marrow function; thrombocytopenia; potentially serious infections; major surgery within the previous month; dihydropyrimidine dehydrogenase (DPD) enzyme deficiency; pregnancy

Warnings/Precautions The U.S. Food and Drug Administration (FDA) currently recommends that procedures for proper handling and disposal of antineoplastic agents be considered. Use with caution in patients with impaired kidney or liver function. The drug should be discontinued if intractable vomiting or diarrhea, precipitous falls in leukocyte or platelet counts, stomatitis, hemorrhage, or myocardial ischemia occurs. Use with caution in patients who have had high-dose pelvic radiation or previous use of alkylating agents. Palmar-plantar erythrodysesthesia (hand-foot) syndrome has been associated with use. Safety and efficacy have not been established in pediatric patients. Systemic toxicity normally associated with parenteral administration (including neutropenia, neurotoxicity, and gastrointestinal toxicity) has been associated with topical use particularly in patients with a genetic deficiency of dihydropyrimidine dehydrogenase (DPD).

Common Adverse Reactions Toxicity depends on route and duration of treatment

I.V.:
Cardiovascular: Angina, myocardial ischemia, nail changes
Central nervous system: Acute cerebellar syndrome, confusion, disorientation, euphoria, headache, nystagmus
Dermatologic: Alopecia, dermatitis, dry skin, fissuring, palmar-plantar erythrodysesthesia syndrome, pruritic maculopapular rash, photosensitivity, vein pigmentations
Gastrointestinal: Anorexia, bleeding, diarrhea, esophagopharyngitis, nausea, sloughing, stomatitis, ulceration, vomiting
Hematologic: Agranulocytosis, anemia, leukopenia, pancytopenia, thrombocytopenia
Myelosuppression:
Onset: 7-10 days
Nadir: 9-14 days
Recovery: 21-28 days
Local: Thrombophlebitis
Ocular: Lacrimation, lacrimal duct stenosis, photophobia, visual changes
Respiratory: Epistaxis
Miscellaneous: Anaphylaxis, generalized allergic reactions, loss of nails

Topical: Note: Systemic toxicity normally associated with parenteral administration (including neutropenia, neurotoxicity, and gastrointestinal toxicity) has been associated with topical use particularly in patients with a genetic deficiency of dihydropyrimidine dehydrogenase (DPD).
Central nervous system: Headache, telangiectasia
Dermatologic: Photosensitivity, pruritus, rash, scarring
Hematologic: Leukocytosis
Local: Allergic contact dermatitis, burning, crusting, dryness, edema, erosion, erythema, hyperpigmentation, irritation, pain, soreness, ulceration
Ocular: Eye irritation (burning, watering, sensitivity, stinging, itching)
Miscellaneous: Birth defects, miscarriage

Drug Interactions
Increased Effect/Toxicity: Fluorouracil may increase effects of warfarin.

Mechanism of Action A pyrimidine antimetabolite that interferes with DNA synthesis by blocking the methylation of deoxyuridylic acid; fluorouracil inhibits thymidylate synthetase (TS), or is incorporated into RNA. The reduced folate cofactor is required for tight binding to occur between the 5-FdUMP and TS.

Pharmacodynamics/Kinetics
Duration: ~3 weeks
Distribution: V_d: ~22% of total body water; penetrates extracellular fluid, CSF, and third space fluids (eg, pleural fluids and ascitic fluid)
Metabolism: Hepatic (90%); via a dehydrogenase enzyme; FU must be metabolized to be active
Bioavailability: <75%, erratic and undependable
Half-life elimination: Biphasic: Initial: 6-20 minutes; two metabolites, FdUMP and FUTP, have prolonged half-lives depending on the type of tissue
Excretion: Lung (large amounts as CO_2); urine (5% as unchanged drug) in 6 hours

Dosage Adults:
Refer to individual protocols:
I.V. bolus: 500-600 mg/m^2 every 3-4 weeks **or** 425 mg/m^2 on days 1-5 every 4 weeks
Continuous I.V. infusion: 1000 mg/m^2/day for 4-5 days every 3-4 weeks **or**
2300-2600 mg/m^2 on day 1 every week **or**
300-400 mg/m^2/day **or**
225 mg/m^2/day for 5-8 weeks (with radiation therapy)
Actinic keratoses: Topical:
Carac™: Apply thin film to lesions once daily for up to 4 weeks, as tolerated
Efudex®: Apply to lesions twice daily for 2-4 weeks; complete healing may not be evident for 1-2 months following treatment
Fluoroplex®: Apply to lesions twice daily for 2-6 weeks
Basal cell carcinoma: Topical: Efudex®: Apply to affected lesions twice daily for 3-6 weeks; treatment may be continued for up to 10-12 weeks
(Continued)

Fluorouracil *(Continued)*

Dosage adjustment for renal impairment: Hemodialysis: Administer dose following hemodialysis.

Dosage adjustment for hepatic impairment: Bilirubin >5 mg/dL: Omit use.

Administration

I.V.: I.V. bolus as a slow push or short (5-15 minutes) bolus infusion, or as a continuous infusion. I.V. formulation may be given orally mixed in water, grape juice, or carbonated beverage. It is generally best to drink undiluted solution, then rinse the mouth. CocaCola® has been recommended as the "best chaser" for oral fluorouracil.

Topical: Apply 10 minutes after washing, rinsing, and drying the affected area. Apply using fingertip (wash hands immediately after application) or nonmetal applicator. Avoid eyes, nostrils, and mouth. Do not cover area with an occlusive dressing.

Monitoring Parameters CBC with differential and platelet count, renal function tests, liver function tests

Patient Information Avoid alcohol and all OTC drugs unless approved by your prescriber. Maintain adequate hydration (2-3 L/day of fluids unless instructed to restrict fluid intake) and nutrition (small frequent meals may help). You may experience sensitivity to sunlight (use sunblock, wear protective clothing, or avoid direct sunlight); susceptibility to infection (avoid crowds or infected persons or persons with contagious diseases); nausea, vomiting, diarrhea, or loss of appetite (frequent small meals may help - request medication); weakness, lethargy, dizziness, decreased vision (use caution when driving or engaging in tasks requiring alertness until response to drug is known); headache (request medication). Report signs and symptoms of infection (eg, fever, chills, sore throat, burning urination, vaginal itching or discharge, fatigue, mouth sores); bleeding (eg, black or tarry stools, easy bruising, unusual bleeding); vision changes; unremitting nausea, vomiting, or abdominal pain; CNS changes; respiratory difficulty; chest pain or palpitations; severe skin reactions to topical application; or any other adverse reactions. Contraceptive measures are recommended during therapy. The drug may be excreted in breast milk, therefore, an alternative form of feeding your baby should be used.

Topical: Use as directed; do not overuse. Wash hands thoroughly before and after applying medication; avoid contact with eyes and mouth; avoid occlusive dressings; use a porous dressing. May cause local reaction (pain, burning, or swelling); if severe, contact prescriber.

Dosage Forms CRM, topical: (Carac™): 0.5% (30 g); (Efudex®): 5% (25 g); (Fluoroplex®): 1% (30 g). **INJ, solution:** 50 mg/mL (10 mL, 20 mL, 50 mL, 100 mL); (Adrucil®): 50 mg/mL (10 mL, 50 mL, 100 mL). **SOLN, topical:** (Efudex®): 2% (10 mL); 5% (10 mL); (Fluoroplex®): 1% (30 mL)

♦ **5-Fluorouracil** *see* Fluorouracil *on page 536*

Fluoxetine *(floo OKS e teen)*

Related Information

Antidepressant Agents Comparison *on page 1359*
Selective Serotonin Reuptake Inhibitors (SSRIs) Pharmacokinetics *on page 1403*

U.S. Brand Names Prozac®; Prozac® Weekly™; Sarafem™

Synonyms Fluoxetine Hydrochloride

Therapeutic Category Antidepressant, Selective Serotonin Reuptake Inhibitor (SSRI)

Use Treatment of major depressive disorder; treatment of binge-eating and vomiting in patients with moderate-to-severe bulimia nervosa; obsessive-compulsive disorder (OCD); premenstrual dysphoric disorder (PMDD); panic disorder with or without agoraphobia

Unlabeled/Investigational Use Selective mutism

Pregnancy Risk Factor C

Contraindications Hypersensitivity to fluoxetine or any component of the formulation; patients currently receiving MAO inhibitors, thioridazine, or mesoridazine

Note: MAO inhibitor therapy must be stopped for 14 days before fluoxetine is initiated. Treatment with MAO inhibitors, thioridazine, or mesoridazine should not be initiated until 5 weeks after the discontinuation of fluoxetine.

Warnings/Precautions Potential for severe reaction when used with MAO inhibitors - serotonin syndrome (hyperthermia, muscular rigidity, mental status changes/agitation, autonomic instability) may occur. Fluoxetine may elevate plasma levels of thioridazine and increase the risk of QT_c interval prolongation. This may lead to serious ventricular arrhythmias such as torsade de pointes-type arrhythmias and sudden death.

Fluoxetine use has been associated with occurrences of significant rash and allergic events, including vasculitis, lupus-like syndrome, laryngospasm, anaphylactoid reactions, and pulmonary inflammatory disease.

May precipitate a shift to mania or hypomania in patients with bipolar disease. May cause insomnia, anxiety, nervousness, or anorexia. Use with caution in patients where weight loss is undesirable. May impair cognitive or motor performance; caution operating hazardous machinery or driving. The possibility of a suicide attempt is inherent in major depression and may persist until remission occurs. Use caution in high-risk patients during initiation of therapy. Prescriptions should be written for the smallest quantity consistent with good patient care. Use caution in patients with a previous seizure disorder or condition predisposing to seizures such as brain damage, alcoholism, or concurrent therapy with other drugs which lower the seizure threshold. Use caution in patients with suicidal risk.

Use with caution in patients with hepatic or renal dysfunction and in elderly patients. May cause hyponatremia/SIADH. May increase the risks associated with electroconvulsive treatment. Use with caution in patients at risk of bleeding or receiving concurrent anticoagulant therapy; may cause impairment in platelet function. May alter glycemic control in patients with diabetes. Due to the long half-life of fluoxetine and its metabolites, the effects and interactions noted may persist for prolonged periods following discontinuation. May cause or exacerbate sexual dysfunction.

Common Adverse Reactions Percentages listed for adverse effects as reported in placebo-controlled trials and were generally similar in adults and children; actual frequency may be dependent upon diagnosis and in some cases the range presented may be lower than or equal to placebo for a particular disorder.

>10%:
Central nervous system: Insomnia (10% to 33%), headache (21%), anxiety (6% to 15%), nervousness (8% to 14%), somnolence (5% to 17%)
Endocrine & metabolic: Libido decreased (1% to 11%)
Gastrointestinal: Nausea (12% to 29%), diarrhea (8% to 18%), anorexia (4% to 11%), xerostomia (4% to 12%)
Neuromuscular & skeletal: Weakness (7% to 21%), tremor (3% to 13%)
Respiratory: Pharyngitis (3% to 11%), yawn (<1% to 11%)

1% to 10%:
Cardiovascular: Vasodilation (1% to 5%), fever (2%), chest pain, hemorrhage, hypertension, palpitation
Central nervous system: Dizziness (9%), dream abnormality (1% to 5%), thinking abnormality (2%), agitation, amnesia, chills, confusion, emotional lability, sleep disorder
Dermatologic: Rash (2% to 6%), pruritus (4%)
Endocrine & metabolic: Ejaculation abnormal (<1% to 7%), impotence (<1% to 7%)
Gastrointestinal: Dyspepsia (6% to 10%), constipation (5%), flatulence (3%), vomiting (3%), weight loss (2%), appetite increased, taste perversion, weight gain
Genitourinary: Urinary frequency
Ocular: Vision abnormal (2%)
Otic: Ear pain, tinnitus
Respiratory: Sinusitis (1% to 6%)
Miscellaneous: Flu-like syndrome (3% to 10%), diaphoresis (2% to 8%)

Drug Interactions

Cytochrome P450 Effect: Substrate of CYP1A2 (minor), 2B6 (minor), 2C8/9 (major), 2C19 (minor), 2D6 (major), 2E1 (minor), 3A4 (minor); Inhibits CYP1A2 (moderate), 2B6 (weak), 2C8/9 (weak), 2C19 (moderate), 2D6 (strong), 3A4 (weak)

Increased Effect/Toxicity: Fluoxetine should not be used with nonselective MAO inhibitors (phenelzine, isocarboxazid) or other drugs with MAO inhibition (linezolid); fatal reactions have been reported. Wait 5 weeks after stopping fluoxetine before starting a nonselective MAO inhibitor and 2 weeks after stopping an MAO inhibitor before starting fluoxetine. Concurrent selegiline has been associated with mania, hypertension, or serotonin syndrome (risk may be reduced relative to nonselective MAO inhibitors).

Fluoxetine may inhibit the metabolism of thioridazine or mesoridazine, resulting in increased plasma levels and increasing the risk of QT_c interval prolongation. This may lead to serious ventricular arrhythmias, such as torsade de pointes-type arrhythmias and sudden death. Do not use together. Wait at least 5 weeks after discontinuing fluoxetine prior to starting thioridazine.

CYP2C8/9 inhibitors may increase the levels/effects of fluoxetine; example inhibitors include delavirdine, fluconazole, gemfibrozil, ketoconazole, nicardipine, NSAIDs, pioglitazone, and sulfonamides. CYP2D6 inhibitors may increase the levels/effects of fluoxetine; example inhibitors include chlorpromazine, delavirdine, miconazole, paroxetine, pergolide, quinidine, quinine, ritonavir, and ropinirole.

Combined used of SSRIs and amphetamines, buspirone, meperidine, nefazodone, serotonin agonists (such as sumatriptan), sibutramine, other SSRIs, sympathomimetics, ritonavir, tramadol, and venlafaxine may increase the risk of serotonin syndrome. Fluoxetine may increase serum levels/effects of benzodiazepines (alprazolam and diazepam), beta-blockers (except atenolol or nadolol), carbamazepine, carvedilol, clozapine, cyclosporine (and possibly tacrolimus), dextromethorphan, digoxin, haloperidol, HMG-CoA reductase inhibitors (lovastatin and simvastatin - increasing the risk of rhabdomyolysis), phenytoin, propafenone, trazodone, tricyclic antidepressants, and valproic acid. Concurrent lithium may increase risk of neurotoxicity, and lithium levels may be increased. Risk of hyponatremia may increase with concurrent use of loop diuretics (bumetanide, furosemide, torsemide). Fluoxetine may increase the hypoprothrombinemic response to warfarin.

Combined use of sumatriptan (and other serotonin agonists) may result in toxicity; weakness, hyper-reflexia, and incoordination have been observed with sumatriptan and SSRIs. In addition, concurrent use may theoretically increase the risk of serotonin syndrome.

Decreased Effect: CYP2C8/9 inducers may decrease the levels/effects of fluoxetine; example inducers include carbamazepine, phenobarbital, phenytoin, rifampin, rifapentine, and secobarbital. Cyproheptadine may inhibit the effects of serotonin reuptake inhibitors. Lithium levels may be decreased by fluoxetine (in addition to reports of increased lithium levels).

Mechanism of Action Inhibits CNS neuron serotonin reuptake; minimal or no effect on reuptake of norepinephrine or dopamine; does not significantly bind to alpha-adrenergic, histamine, or cholinergic receptors

Pharmacodynamics/Kinetics
Absorption: Well absorbed; delayed 1-2 hours with weekly formulation
Protein binding: 95%
Metabolism: Hepatic to norfluoxetine (active; equal to fluoxetine)
(Continued)

Fluoxetine *(Continued)*

Half-life elimination: Adults:
    Parent drug: 1-3 days (acute), 4-6 days (chronic), 7.6 days (cirrhosis)
    Metabolite (norfluoxetine): 9.3 days (range: 4-16 days), 12 days (cirrhosis)
    Due to long half-life, resolution of adverse reactions after discontinuation may be slow
Time to peak: 6-8 hours
Excretion: Urine (10% as norfluoxetine, 2.5% to 5% as fluoxetine)

Note: Weekly formulation results in greater fluctuations between peak and trough concentrations of fluoxetine and norfluoxetine compared to once-daily dosing (24% daily/164% weekly; 17% daily/43% weekly, respectively). Trough concentrations are 76% lower for fluoxetine and 47% lower for norfluoxetine than the concentrations maintained by 20 mg once-daily dosing. Steady-state fluoxetine concentrations are ~50% lower following the once-weekly regimen compared to 20 mg once daily. Average steady-state concentrations of once-daily dosing were highest in children ages 6 to <13 (fluoxetine 171 ng/mL; norfluoxetine 195 ng/mL), followed by adolescents ages 13 to <18 (fluoxetine 86 ng/mL; norfluoxetine 113 ng/mL); concentrations were considered to be within the ranges reported in adults (fluoxetine 91-302 ng/mL; norfluoxetine 72-258 ng/mL).

Dosage Oral:
Children:
    Depression: 8-18 years: 10-20 mg/day; lower-weight children can be started at 10 mg/day, may increase to 20 mg/day after 1 week if needed
    OCD: 7-18 years: Initial: 10 mg/day; in adolescents and higher-weight children, dose may be increased to 20 mg/day after 2 weeks. Range: 10-60 mg/day
    Selective mutism (unlabeled use):
        <5 years: No dosing information available
        5-18 years: Initial: 5-10 mg/day; titrate upwards as needed (usual maximum dose: 60 mg/day)
Adults: 20 mg/day in the morning; may increase after several weeks by 20 mg/day increments; maximum: 80 mg/day; doses >20 mg may be given once daily or divided twice daily. **Note:** Lower doses of 5-10 mg/day have been used for initial treatment.
    Usual dosage range:
        Bulimia nervosa: 60-80 mg/day
        Depression: 20-40 mg/day; patients maintained on Prozac® 20 mg/day may be changed to Prozac® Weekly™ 90 mg/week, starting dose 7 days after the last 20 mg/day dose
        OCD: 40-80 mg/day
        Panic disorder: Initial: 10 mg/day; after 1 week, increase to 20 mg/day; may increase after several weeks; doses >60 mg/day have not been evaluated
        PMDD (Sarafem™): 20 mg/day continuously, **or** 20 mg/day starting 14 days prior to menstruation and through first full day of menses (repeat with each cycle)
Elderly: Depression: Some patients may require an initial dose of 10 mg/day with dosage increases of 10 and 20 mg every several weeks as tolerated; should not be taken at night unless patient experiences sedation
Dosing adjustment in renal impairment:
    Single dose studies: Pharmacokinetics of fluoxetine and norfluoxetine were similar among subjects with all levels of impaired renal function, including anephric patients on chronic hemodialysis
    Chronic administration: Additional accumulation of fluoxetine or norfluoxetine may occur in patients with severely impaired renal function
    Hemodialysis: Not removed by hemodialysis; use of lower dose or less frequent dosing is not usually necessary.
Dosing adjustment in hepatic impairment: Elimination half-life of fluoxetine is prolonged in patients with hepatic impairment; a lower or less frequent dose of fluoxetine should be used in these patients
    Cirrhosis patients: Administer a lower dose or less frequent dosing interval
    Compensated cirrhosis without ascites: Administer 50% of normal dose
Monitoring Parameters Signs and symptoms of depression, anxiety, sleep
Reference Range Therapeutic levels have not been well established
    Therapeutic: Fluoxetine: 100-800 ng/mL (SI: 289-2314 nmol/L); Norfluoxetine: 100-600 ng/mL (SI: 289-1735 nmol/L)
    Toxic: Fluoxetine plus norfluoxetine: >2000 ng/mL
Patient Information Avoid alcohol; take in morning to avoid insomnia; fluoxetine's potential stimulating and anorexic effects may be bothersome to some patients. Use sugarless hard candy for dry mouth; may cause drowsiness, improvement may take several weeks; rise slowly to prevent dizziness. If you miss a dose, take it as soon as you remember. However, if it is time for your next dose, skip the missed dose and take only your regularly scheduled dose. Do not take more than the daily amount that has been prescribed.
Dosage Forms CAP: 10 mg, 20 mg, 40 mg; (Prozac®): 10 mg, 20 mg, 40 mg; (Sarafem™): 10 mg, 20 mg. **CAP, delayed release** (Prozac® Weekly™): 90 mg. **SOLN, oral** (Prozac®): 20 mg/5 mL (120 mL). **TAB:** 10 mg, 20 mg; (Prozac®) [scored]: 10 mg

◆ **Fluoxetine Hydrochloride** *see* Fluoxetine *on page 538*

Fluoxymesterone *(floo oks i MES te rone)*
U.S. Brand Names Halotestin®
Therapeutic Category Androgen
Use Replacement of endogenous testicular hormone; in females, used as palliative treatment of breast cancer

Unlabeled/Investigational Use Stimulation of erythropoiesis, angioneurotic edema

Restrictions C-III

Pregnancy Risk Factor X

Contraindications Hypersensitivity to fluoxymesterone or any component of the formulation; serious cardiac disease, liver or kidney disease; pregnancy

Warnings/Precautions May accelerate bone maturation without producing compensatory gain in linear growth in children; in prepubertal children perform radiographic examination of the hand and wrist every 6 months to determine the rate of bone maturation and to assess the effect of treatment on the epiphyseal centers

Common Adverse Reactions

>10%:

Male: Priapism

Female: Menstrual problems (amenorrhea), virilism, breast soreness

Cardiovascular: Edema

Dermatologic: Acne

1% to 10%:

Male: Prostatic carcinoma, hirsutism (increase in pubic hair growth), impotence, testicular atrophy

Cardiovascular: Edema

Gastrointestinal: GI irritation, nausea, vomiting

Genitourinary: Prostatic hyperplasia

Hepatic: Hepatic dysfunction

Drug Interactions

Increased Effect/Toxicity: Fluoxymesterone may suppress clotting factors II, V, VII, and X; therefore, bleeding may occur in patients on anticoagulant therapy May elevate cyclosporine serum levels. May enhance hypoglycemic effect of insulin therapy; may decrease blood glucose concentrations and insulin requirements in patients with diabetes. Lithium may potentiate EPS and other CNS effect. May potentiate the effects of narcotics including respiratory depression

Decreased Effect: May decrease barbiturate levels and fluphenazine effectiveness.

Mechanism of Action Synthetic androgenic anabolic hormone responsible for the normal growth and development of male sex hormones and development of male sex organs and maintenance of secondary sex characteristics; synthetic testosterone derivative with significant androgen activity; stimulates RNA polymerase activity resulting in an increase in protein production; increases bone development; halogenated derivative of testosterone with up to 5 times the activity of methyltestosterone

Pharmacodynamics/Kinetics

Absorption: Rapid

Protein binding: 98%

Metabolism: Hepatic; enterohepatic recirculation

Half-life elimination: 10-100 minutes

Excretion: Urine (90%)

Dosage Adults: Oral:

Male:

Hypogonadism: 5-20 mg/day

Delayed puberty: 2.5-20 mg/day for 4-6 months

Female: Inoperable breast carcinoma: 10-40 mg/day in divided doses for 1-3 months

Monitoring Parameters In prepubertal children, perform radiographic examination of the hand and wrist every 6 months

Patient Information Take as directed; do not discontinue without consulting prescriber. Diabetics should monitor serum glucose closely and notify prescriber of changes; this medication can alter hypoglycemic requirements. You may experience acne, growth of body hair, loss of libido, impotence, or menstrual irregularity (usually reversible); nausea or vomiting (small frequent meals, frequent mouth care, sucking lozenges, or chewing gum may help). Report changes in menstrual pattern; deepening of voice or unusual growth of body hair; fluid retention (swelling of ankles, feet, or hands, difficulty breathing, or sudden weight gain); change in color of urine or stool; yellowing of eyes or skin; unusual bruising or bleeding; or other adverse reactions.

Dosage Forms TAB: 10 mg; (Halotestin®): 2 mg; 5 mg; 10 mg [DSC]

Fluphenazine (floo FEN a zeen)

Related Information

Antipsychotic Agents Comparison on page 1364

U.S. Brand Names Prolixin®; Prolixin Decanoate®; Prolixin Enanthate® [DSC]

Synonyms Fluphenazine Decanoate; Fluphenazine Enanthate; Fluphenazine Hydrochloride

Therapeutic Category Antipsychotic Agent, Phenothiazine; Antipsychotic Agent, Phenothiazine, Piperazine; Phenothiazine Derivative

Use Management of manifestations of psychotic disorders and schizophrenia; depot formulation may offer improved outcome in individuals with psychosis who are nonadherent with oral antipsychotics

Unlabeled/Investigational Use Pervasive developmental disorder

Pregnancy Risk Factor C

Contraindications Hypersensitivity to fluphenazine or any component of the formulation (cross-reactivity between phenothiazines may occur); severe CNS depression; coma; subcortical brain damage; blood dyscrasias; hepatic disease

(Continued)

Fluphenazine *(Continued)*

Warnings/Precautions Safety in children <6 months of age has not been established. May be sedating, use with caution in disorders where CNS depression is a feature. Use with caution in Parkinson's disease. Caution in patients with hemodynamic instability; bone marrow suppression; predisposition to seizures; severe cardiac, renal, or respiratory disease. Esophageal dysmotility and aspiration have been associated with antipsychotic use - use with caution in patients at risk of pneumonia (ie, Alzheimer's disease). Caution in breast cancer or other prolactin-dependent tumors (may elevate prolactin levels). May alter temperature regulation or mask toxicity of other drugs due to antiemetic effects. May alter cardiac conduction; life-threatening arrhythmias have occurred with therapeutic doses of phenothiazines. Hypotension may occur, particularly with I.M. administration. May cause orthostatic hypotension - use with caution in patients at risk of this effect or those who would tolerate transient hypotensive episodes (cerebrovascular disease, cardiovascular disease, or other medications which may predispose). Adverse effects of depot injections may be prolonged.

Phenothiazines may cause anticholinergic effects (confusion, agitation, constipation, xerostomia, blurred vision, urinary retention). Therefore, they should be used with caution in patients with decreased gastrointestinal motility, urinary retention, BPH, xerostomia, or visual problems. Conditions which also may be exacerbated by cholinergic blockade include narrow-angle glaucoma (screening is recommended) and worsening of myasthenia gravis. Relative to other antipsychotics, fluphenazine has a low potency of cholinergic blockade.

May cause extrapyramidal reactions, including pseudoparkinsonism, acute dystonic reactions, akathisia and tardive dyskinesia (risk of these reactions is high relative to other antipsychotics). May be associated with neuroleptic malignant syndrome (NMS) or pigmentary retinopathy.

Common Adverse Reactions Frequency not defined.

Cardiovascular: Hypotension, tachycardia, fluctuations in blood pressure, hypertension, arrhythmias, edema

Central nervous system: Parkinsonian symptoms, akathisia, dystonias, tardive dyskinesia, dizziness, hyper-reflexia, headache, cerebral edema, drowsiness, lethargy, restlessness, excitement, bizarre dreams, EEG changes, depression, seizures, NMS, altered central temperature regulation

Dermatologic: Increased sensitivity to sun, rash, skin pigmentation, itching, erythema, urticaria, seborrhea, eczema, dermatitis

Endocrine & metabolic: Changes in menstrual cycle, breast pain, amenorrhea, galactorrhea, gynecomastia, changes in libido, elevated prolactin, SIADH

Gastrointestinal: Weight gain, loss of appetite, salivation, xerostomia, constipation, paralytic ileus, laryngeal edema

Genitourinary: Ejaculatory disturbances, impotence, polyuria, bladder paralysis, enuresis

Hematologic: Agranulocytosis, leukopenia, thrombocytopenia, nonthrombocytopenic purpura, eosinophilia, pancytopenia

Hepatic: Cholestatic jaundice, hepatotoxicity

Neuromuscular & skeletal: Trembling of fingers, SLE, facial hemispasm

Ocular: Pigmentary retinopathy, cornea and lens changes, blurred vision, glaucoma

Respiratory: Nasal congestion, asthma

Drug Interactions

Cytochrome P450 Effect: Substrate of CYP2D6 (major); **Inhibits** CYP1A2 (weak), 2C8/9 (weak), 2D6 (weak), 2E1 (weak)

Increased Effect/Toxicity: CYP2D6 inhibitors may increase the levels/effects of fluphenazine; example inhibitors include chlorpromazine, delavirdine, fluoxetine, miconazole, paroxetine, pergolide, quinidine, quinine, ritonavir, and ropinirole. Effects on CNS depression may be additive when fluphenazine is combined with CNS depressants (narcotic analgesics, ethanol, barbiturates, cyclic antidepressants, antihistamines, sedative-hypnotics). Fluphenazine may increase the effects/toxicity of anticholinergics, antihypertensives, lithium (rare neurotoxicity), trazodone, or valproic acid. Concurrent use with TCA may produce increased toxicity or altered therapeutic response. Chloroquine and propranolol may increase chlorpromazine concentrations. Hypotension may occur when fluphenazine is combined with epinephrine. May increase the risk of arrhythmia when combined with antiarrhythmics, cisapride, pimozide, sparfloxacin, or other drugs which prolong QT interval. Metoclopramide may increase risk of extrapyramidal symptoms (EPS).

Decreased Effect: Phenothiazines inhibit the activity of guanethidine, guanadrel, levodopa, and bromocriptine. Barbiturates and cigarette smoking may enhance the hepatic metabolism of fluphenazine. Fluphenazine and possibly other low potency antipsychotics may reverse the pressor effects of epinephrine.

Mechanism of Action Blocks postsynaptic mesolimbic dopaminergic D_1 and D_2 receptors in the brain; depresses the release of hypothalamic and hypophyseal hormones; believed to depress the reticular activating system thus affecting basal metabolism, body temperature, wakefulness, vasomotor tone, and emesis

Pharmacodynamics/Kinetics

Onset of action: I.M., S.C. (derivative dependent): Hydrochloride salt: ~1 hour

Peak effect: Neuroleptic: Decanoate: 48-96 hours

Duration: Hydrochloride salt: 6-8 hours; Decanoate (lasts the longest): 24-72 hours

Absorption: Oral: Erratic and variable

Distribution: Crosses placenta; enters breast milk

Protein binding: 91% and 99%

Metabolism: Hepatic

Half-life elimination (derivative dependent): Enanthate: 84-96 hours; Hydrochloride: 33 hours; Decanoate: 163-232 hours

Excretion: Urine (as metabolites)

Dosage

Children: Oral: Childhood-onset pervasive developmental disorder (unlabeled use): 0.04 mg/kg/day

Adults: Psychoses:

Oral: 0.5-10 mg/day in divided doses at 6- to 8-hour intervals; some patients may require up to 40 mg/day

I.M.: 2.5-10 mg/day in divided doses at 6- to 8-hour intervals (parenteral dose is $1/3$ to $1/2$ the oral dose for the hydrochloride salts)

I.M. (decanoate): 12.5 mg every 2 weeks

Conversion from hydrochloride to decanoate I.M. 0.5 mL (12.5 mg) decanoate every 3 weeks is approximately equivalent to 10 mg hydrochloride/day

I.M. (enanthate): 12.5-25 mg every 2 weeks

Hemodialysis: Not dialyzable (0% to 5%)

Administration Avoid contact of oral solution or injection with skin (contact dermatitis). Oral liquid should be diluted in the following **only**: Water, saline, homogenized milk, carbonated orange beverages, pineapple, apricot, prune, orange, tomato, and grapefruit juices. Do **not** dilute in beverages containing caffeine, tannics, or pectinate. Watch for hypotension when administering I.M.

Monitoring Parameters Vital signs; lipid profile, fasting blood glucose/Hgb A_{1c}; BMI; mental status, abnormal involuntary movement scale (AIMS), extrapyramidal symptoms (EPS)

Reference Range Therapeutic: 5-20 ng/mL; correlation of serum concentrations and efficacy is controversial; most often dosed to best response

Patient Information Avoid alcohol; may cause drowsiness; do not discontinue without consulting prescriber

Dosage Forms ELIX, as hydrochloride (Prolixin®): 2.5 mg/5 mL (60 mL). **INJ, as enanthate** (Prolixin Enanthate®): 25 mg/mL (5 mL) [DSC]. **INJ, oil, as decanoate:** 25 mg/mL (1 mL, 5 mL); (Prolixin Decanoate®): 25 mg/mL (1 mL, 5 mL). **INJ, solution, as hydrochloride** (Prolixin®): 2.5 mg/mL (10 mL). **SOLN, oral concentrate, as hydrochloride** (Prolixin®): 5 mg/mL (120 mL). **TAB, as hydrochloride:** 1 mg, 2.5 mg, 5 mg, 10 mg; (Prolixin®): 1 mg, 2.5 mg, 5 mg, 10 mg

♦ **Fluphenazine Decanoate**   see Fluphenazine on page 541

♦ **Fluphenazine Enanthate**   see Fluphenazine on page 541

♦ **Fluphenazine Hydrochloride**   see Fluphenazine on page 541

♦ **Flura-Drops®**   see Fluoride on page 535

♦ **Flura-Loz®**   see Fluoride on page 535

Flurandrenolide (flure an DREN oh lide)

Related Information

Corticosteroids Comparison on page 1372

U.S. Brand Names Cordran®; Cordran® SP

Synonyms Flurandrenolone

Therapeutic Category Anti-inflammatory Agent; Corticosteroid, Topical (Low Potency); Corticosteroid, Topical (Medium Potency)

Use Inflammation of corticosteroid-responsive dermatoses [medium potency topical corticosteroid]

Pregnancy Risk Factor C

Contraindications Hypersensitivity to flurandrenolide or any component of the formulation; viral, fungal, or tubercular skin lesions

Warnings/Precautions Adverse systemic effects may occur when used on large areas of the body, denuded areas, for prolonged periods of time, with an occlusive dressing, and/or in infants or small children

Common Adverse Reactions Frequency not defined.

Cardiovascular: Intracranial hypertension

Dermatologic: Itching, dry skin, folliculitis, hypertrichosis, acneiform eruptions, hyperpigmentation, perioral dermatitis, allergic contact dermatitis, skin atrophy, striae, miliaria, acne, maceration of the skin

Endocrine & metabolic: Cushing's syndrome, growth retardation, HPA suppression

Local: Burning, irritation

Miscellaneous: Secondary infection

Mechanism of Action Decreases inflammation by suppression of migration of polymorphonuclear leukocytes and reversal of increased capillary permeability

Pharmacodynamics/Kinetics

Absorption: Adequate with intact skin; repeated applications lead to depot effects on skin, potentially resulting in enhanced percutaneous absorption

Metabolism: Hepatic

Excretion: Urine; feces (small amounts)

Dosage Topical: Therapy should be discontinued when control is achieved; if no improvement is seen, reassessment of diagnosis may be necessary.

Children:

Ointment, cream: Apply sparingly 1-2 times/day

Tape: Apply once daily

Adults: Cream, lotion, ointment: Apply sparingly 2-3 times/day

(Continued)

Flurandrenolide *(Continued)*

Dosage Forms CRM, emulsified (Cordran® SP): 0.025% (30 g, 60 g); 0.05% (15 g, 30 g, 60 g). **LOTION** (Cordran®): 0.05% (15 mL, 60 mL). **OINT** (Cordran®): 0.025% (30 g, 60 g); 0.05% (15 g, 30 g, 60 g). **TAPE, topical** [roll] (Cordran®): 4 mcg/cm^2 (7.5 cm x 60 cm, 7.5 cm x 200 cm)

♦ **Flurandrenolone** *see* Flurandrenolide *on page 543*

Flurazepam *(flure AZ e pam)*

Related Information
Benzodiazepines Comparison *on page 1366*

U.S. Brand Names Dalmane®

Synonyms Flurazepam Hydrochloride

Therapeutic Category Benzodiazepine; Hypnotic; Sedative

Use Short-term treatment of insomnia

Restrictions C-IV

Pregnancy Risk Factor X

Contraindications Hypersensitivity to flurazepam or any component of the formulation (cross-sensitivity with other benzodiazepines may exist); narrow-angle glaucoma; pregnancy

Warnings/Precautions Use with caution in patients receiving other CNS depressants, patients with low albumin, hepatic dysfunction, and in the elderly; do not use in pregnant women; may cause drug dependency; safety and efficacy have not been established in children <15 years of age

Common Adverse Reactions Frequency not defined.
Cardiovascular: Palpitations, chest pain
Central nervous system: Drowsiness, ataxia, lightheadedness, memory impairment, depression, headache, hangover effect, confusion, nervousness, dizziness, falling, apprehension, irritability, euphoria, slurred speech, restlessness, hallucinations, paradoxical reactions, talkativeness
Dermatologic: Rash, pruritus
Gastrointestinal: Xerostomia, constipation, increased/excessive salivation, heartburn, upset stomach, nausea, vomiting, diarrhea, increased or decreased appetite, bitter taste, weight gain/loss
Hematologic: Granulocytopenia
Hepatic: Elevated AST/ALT, total bilirubin, alkaline phosphatase, cholestatic jaundice
Neuromuscular & skeletal: Dysarthria, body/joint pain, reflex slowing, weakness
Ocular: Blurred vision, burning eyes, difficulty focusing
Otic: Tinnitus
Respiratory: Apnea, dyspnea
Miscellaneous: Diaphoresis, drug dependence

Drug Interactions
Cytochrome P450 Effect: Substrate of CYP3A4 (major); **Inhibits** CYP2E1 (weak)
Increased Effect/Toxicity: Serum levels and response to flurazepam may be increased by amprenavir, cimetidine, ciprofloxacin, clarithromycin, clozapine, CNS depressants, diltiazem, disulfiram, digoxin, erythromycin, ethanol, fluconazole, fluoxetine, fluvoxamine, grapefruit juice, isoniazid, itraconazole, ketoconazole, labetalol, levodopa, loxapine, metoprolol, metronidazole, miconazole, nefazodone, nelfinavir, omeprazole, phenytoin, rifabutin, rifampin, ritonavir, troleandomycin, valproic acid, and verapamil.
Decreased Effect: Carbamazepine, rifampin, and rifabutin may enhance the metabolism of flurazepam and decrease its therapeutic effect; consider using an alternative sedative/hypnotic agent.

Mechanism of Action Binds to stereospecific benzodiazepine receptors on the postsynaptic GABA neuron at several sites within the central nervous system, including the limbic system, reticular formation. Enhancement of the inhibitory effect of GABA on neuronal excitability results by increased neuronal membrane permeability to chloride ions. This shift in chloride ions results in hyperpolarization (a less excitable state) and stabilization.

Pharmacodynamics/Kinetics
Onset of action: Hypnotic: 15-20 minutes
Peak effect: 3-6 hours
Duration: 7-8 hours
Metabolism: Hepatic to N-desalkylflurazepam (active)
Half-life elimination: Desalkylflurazepam:
Adults: Single dose: 74-90 hours; Multiple doses: 111-113 hours
Elderly (61-85 years): Single dose: 120-160 hours; Multiple doses: 126-158 hours

Dosage Oral:
Children: Insomnia:
≤15 years: Dose not established
>15 years: 15 mg at bedtime
Adults: Insomnia: 15-30 mg at bedtime
Elderly: Insomnia: Oral: 15 mg at bedtime; avoid use if possible

Monitoring Parameters Respiratory and cardiovascular status

Reference Range Therapeutic: 0-4 ng/mL (SI: 0-9 nmol/L); Metabolite N-desalkylflurazepam: 20-110 ng/mL (SI: 43-240 nmol/L); Toxic: >0.12 µg/mL

Patient Information Avoid alcohol and other CNS depressants; avoid activities needing good psychomotor coordination until CNS effects are known; drug may cause physical or psychological dependence; avoid abrupt discontinuation after prolonged use

Dosage Forms CAP: 15 mg, 30 mg

♦ **Flurazepam Hydrochloride** *see Flurazepam on page 544*

Flurbiprofen *(flure BI proe fen)*

Related Information
Nonsteroidal Anti-Inflammatory Agents Comparison *on page 1401*

U.S. Brand Names Ansaid®; Ocufen®

Synonyms Flurbiprofen Sodium

Therapeutic Category Analgesic, Nonsteroidal Anti-inflammatory Drug; Anti-inflammatory Agent; Nonsteroidal Anti-inflammatory Drug (NSAID), Ophthalmic; Nonsteroidal Anti-inflammatory Drug (NSAID), Oral

Use
Oral: Treatment of rheumatoid arthritis and osteoarthritis
Ophthalmic: Inhibition of intraoperative miosis

Pregnancy Risk Factor C/D (3rd trimester)

Contraindications Hypersensitivity to flurbiprofen or any component of the formulation; dendritic keratitis; pregnancy (3rd trimester); patients with "aspirin triad" (bronchial asthma, aspirin intolerance, rhinitis)

Warnings/Precautions Use with caution in patients with CHF, hypertension, dehydration, decreased renal or hepatic function, history of GI disease (bleeding or ulcers), or those receiving anticoagulants. Elderly are at a high risk for adverse effects from NSAIDs. As many as 60% of elderly can develop peptic ulceration and/or hemorrhage asymptomatically.

Use lowest effective dose for shortest period possible. Use of NSAIDs can compromise existing renal function especially when Cl_{cr} is <30 mL/minute. CNS adverse effects such as confusion, agitation, and hallucination are generally seen in overdose or high-dose situations; however, elderly may demonstrate these adverse effects at lower doses than younger adults. Withhold for at least 4-6 half-lives prior to surgical or dental procedures. Use of ophthalmic solution may increase bleeding of ocular tissue during ocular surgery.

Common Adverse Reactions
Ophthalmic: Frequency not defined: Ocular: Slowing of corneal wound healing, mild ocular stinging, itching and burning, ocular irritation, fibrosis, miosis, mydriasis, bleeding tendency increased

Oral:
>1%:
Cardiovascular: Edema
Central nervous system: Amnesia, anxiety, depression, dizziness, headache, insomnia, malaise, nervousness, somnolence
Dermatologic: Rash
Gastrointestinal: Abdominal pain, constipation, diarrhea, dyspepsia, flatulence, GI bleeding, nausea, vomiting, weight changes
Hepatic: Liver enzymes elevated
Neuromuscular & skeletal: Reflexes increased, tremor, vertigo, weakness
Ocular: Vision changes
Otic: Tinnitus
Respiratory: Rhinitis

Drug Interactions
Cytochrome P450 Effect: Substrate of CYP2C8/9 (minor); **Inhibits** CYP2C8/9 (strong)

Increased Effect/Toxicity: Flurbiprofen may increase cyclosporine, digoxin, lithium, and methotrexate serum concentrations. The renal adverse effects of ACE inhibitors may be potentiated by NSAIDs. Corticosteroids may increase the risk of GI ulceration.

Decreased Effect: Ophthalmic: When used with concurrent administration of flurbiprofen, acetylcholine chloride and carbachol have been shown to be ineffective. Reports of acetylcholine chloride and carbachol being ineffective when used with flurbiprofen.

Mechanism of Action Inhibits prostaglandin synthesis by decreasing the activity of the enzyme, cyclooxygenase, which results in decreased formation of prostaglandin precursors

Pharmacodynamics/Kinetics
Onset of action: ~1-2 hours
Distribution: V_d: 0.12 L/kg
Protein binding: 99%, primarily albumin
Metabolism: Hepatic via CYP2C9; forms metabolites
Half-life elimination: 5.7 hours
Time to peak: 1.5 hours
Excretion: Urine

Dosage
Oral: Rheumatoid arthritis and osteoarthritis: 200-300 mg/day in 2-, 3-, or 4 divided doses; do not administer more than 100 mg for any single dose; maximum: 300 mg/day
Ophthalmic: Instill 1 drop every 30 minutes, beginning 2 hours prior to surgery (total of 4 drops in each affected eye)

Administration Tablet: Take with a full glass of water.

Patient Information Take the oral formulation with food to decrease any abdominal complaints. Eye drops may cause mild burning or stinging, notify prescriber if this becomes severe or persistent; do not touch dropper to eye, visual acuity may be decreased after administration.

Dosage Forms SOLN, ophthalmic (Ocufen®): 0.03% (2.5 mL). **TAB** (Ansaid®): 50 mg, 100 mg

♦ **Flurbiprofen Sodium** *see Flurbiprofen on page 545*

♦ **5-Flurocytosine** *see Flucytosine on page 528*

Flutamide (FLOO ta mide)

U.S. Brand Names Eulexin®

Synonyms Niftolid; 4'-Nitro-3'-Trifluoromethylisobutyrantide; NSC-147834; SCH 13521

Therapeutic Category Antiandrogen; Antineoplastic Agent, Antiandrogen

Use Treatment of metastatic prostatic carcinoma in combination therapy with LHRH agonist analogues

Unlabeled/Investigational Use Female hirsutism

Pregnancy Risk Factor D

Contraindications Hypersensitivity to flutamide or any component of the formulation; severe hepatic impairment; pregnancy

Warnings/Precautions Hospitalization and, rarely, death due to liver failure has been reported in patients taking flutamide. Elevated serum transaminase levels, jaundice, hepatic encephalopathy, and acute hepatic failure have been reported. Product labeling states flutamide is not for use in women, particularly for nonlife-threatening conditions. In some patients, the toxicity reverses after discontinuation of therapy. About 50% of the cases occur within the first 3 months of treatment. Serum transaminase levels should be measured prior to starting treatment, monthly for 4 months, and periodically thereafter. Liver function tests should be obtained at the first suggestion of liver dysfunction (nausea, vomiting, abdominal pain, fatigue, anorexia, "flu-like" symptoms, hyperbilirubinuria, jaundice, or right upper quadrant tenderness). Flutamide should be immediately discontinued any time a patient has jaundice, and/or an ALT level greater than twice the upper limit of normal. Flutamide should not be used in patients whose ALT values are greater than twice the upper limit of normal.

Patients with glucose-6 phosphate dehydrogenase deficiency or hemoglobin M disease or smokers are at risk of toxicities associated with aniline exposure, including methemoglobinemia, hemolytic anemia, and cholestatic jaundice. Monitor methemoglobin levels.

Common Adverse Reactions
>10%:
    Endocrine & metabolic: Gynecomastia, hot flashes, breast tenderness, galactorrhea (9% to 42%); impotence; decreased libido; tumor flare
    Gastrointestinal: Nausea, vomiting (11% to 12%)
    Hepatic: Increased AST (SGOT) and LDH levels, transient, mild
1% to 10%:
    Cardiovascular: Hypertension (1%), edema
    Central nervous system: Drowsiness, confusion, depression, anxiety, nervousness, headache, dizziness, insomnia
    Dermatologic: Pruritus, ecchymosis, photosensitivity, herpes zoster
    Gastrointestinal: Anorexia, increased appetite, constipation, indigestion, upset stomach (4% to 6%); diarrhea
    Hematologic: Anemia (6%), leukopenia (3%), thrombocytopenia (1%)
    Neuromuscular & skeletal: Weakness (1%)

Drug Interactions
    Cytochrome P450 Effect: Substrate (major) of CYP1A2, 3A4; **Inhibits** CYP1A2 (weak)
    Increased Effect/Toxicity: CYP1A2 inhibitors may increase the levels/effects of flutamide; example inhibitors include amiodarone, ciprofloxacin, fluvoxamine, ketoconazole, lomeflox-acin, ofloxacin, and rofecoxib. Warfarin effects may be increased.
    Decreased Effect: CYP1A2 inducers may decrease the levels/effects of flutamide; example inducers include aminoglutethimide, carbamazepine, phenobarbital, and rifampin.

Mechanism of Action Nonsteroidal antiandrogen that inhibits androgen uptake or inhibits binding of androgen in target tissues

Pharmacodynamics/Kinetics
    Absorption: Oral: Rapid and complete
    Protein binding: Parent drug: 94% to 96%; 2-hydroxyflutamide: 92% to 94%
    Metabolism: Extensively hepatic to more than 10 metabolites, primarily 2-hydroxyflutamide (active)
    Half-life elimination: 5-6 hours (2-hydroxyflutamide)
    Excretion: Primarily urine (as metabolites)

Dosage Oral: Adults:
    Prostatic carcinoma: 250 mg 3 times/day **or** 1.5 g once daily
    Female hirsutism: 250 mg daily

Administration Usually administered orally in 3 divided doses; contents of capsule may be opened and mixed with applesauce, pudding, or other soft foods; mixing with a beverage is not recommended

Monitoring Parameters Serum transaminase levels should be measured prior to starting treatment and should be repeated monthly for the first 4 months of therapy, and periodically thereafter. LFTs should be checked at the first sign or symptom of liver dysfunction (eg, nausea, vomiting, abdominal pain, fatigue, anorexia, flu-like symptoms, hyperbilirubinuria, jaundice, or right upper quadrant tenderness). Other parameters include tumor reduction, testosterone/estrogen, and phosphatase serum levels.

Patient Information Take as directed; do not discontinue without consulting prescriber. You may experience decreased libido, impotence, swelling of breasts, or decreased appetite (small frequent meals may help). Report chest pain or palpitation; acute abdominal pain; pain, tingling, or numbness of extremities; swelling of extremities or unusual weight gain; difficulty breathing; or other persistent adverse effects.

Dosage Forms CAP: 125 mg

Fluticasone (floo TIK a sone)

Related Information
Corticosteroids Comparison *on page 1372*

U.S. Brand Names Cutivate®; Flonase®; Flovent®; Flovent® Rotadisk®

Synonyms Fluticasone Propionate

Therapeutic Category Corticosteroid, Inhalant; Corticosteroid, Topical (Medium Potency)

Use
Inhalation: Maintenance treatment of asthma as prophylactic therapy. It is also indicated for patients requiring oral corticosteroid therapy for asthma to assist in total discontinuation or reduction of total oral dose. NOT indicated for the relief of acute bronchospasm.

Intranasal: Management of seasonal and perennial allergic rhinitis and nonallergic rhinitis in patients ≥4 years of age

Topical: Relief of inflammation and pruritus associated with corticosteroid-responsive dermatoses in patients ≥3 months of age

Pregnancy Risk Factor C

Contraindications Hypersensitivity to fluticasone or any component of the formulation; primary treatment of status asthmaticus

Topical: Do not use if infection is present at treatment site, in the presence of skin atrophy, or for the treatment of rosacea or perioral dermatitis

Warnings/Precautions May cause hypercorticism or suppression of hypothalamic-pituitary-adrenal (HPA) axis, particularly in younger children or in patients receiving high doses for prolonged periods. HPA axis suppression may lead to adrenal crisis. Fluticasone may cause less HPA axis suppression than therapeutically equivalent oral doses of prednisone. Particular care is required when patients are transferred from systemic corticosteroids to inhaled products due to possible adrenal insufficiency or withdrawal from steroids, including an increase in allergic symptoms. Patients receiving 20 mg per day of prednisone (or equivalent) may be most susceptible.

Controlled clinical studies have shown that orally-inhaled and intranasal corticosteroids may cause a reduction in growth velocity in pediatric patients. (In studies of orally-inhaled corticosteroids, the mean reduction in growth velocity was approximately 1 centimeter per year [range 0.3-1.8 cm per year] and appears to be related to dose and duration of exposure.) To minimize the systemic effects of orally-inhaled and intranasal corticosteroids, each patient should be titrated to the lowest effective dose.

May suppress the immune system, patients may be more susceptible to infection. Use with caution, if at all, in patients with systemic infections, active or quiescent tuberculosis infection, or ocular herpes simplex. Avoid exposure to chickenpox and measles.

Supplemental steroids (oral or parenteral) may be needed during stress or severe asthma attacks. Rare cases of vasculitis (Churg-Strauss syndrome) or other eosinophilic conditions can occur. Flovent® aerosol contains chlorofluorocarbons (CFCs).

Inhalation: Not to be used in status asthmaticus or for the relief of acute bronchospasm. Flovent® Rotadisk® contains lactose; very rare anaphylactic reactions have been reported in patients with severe milk protein allergy.

Topical: May also cause suppression of HPA axis, especially when used on large areas of the body, denuded areas, for prolonged periods of time or with an occlusive dressing. Pediatric patients may be more susceptible to systemic toxicity. Safety and efficacy in pediatric patients <3 months of age have not been established.

Common Adverse Reactions
Oral inhalation: Frequency depends upon population studied and dosing used. Reactions reported are representative of multiple oral formulations.
>3%:
Central nervous system: Headache (2% to 22%), fever (1% to 7%)
Gastrointestinal: Nausea/vomiting (1% to 8%), viral GI infection (3% to 5%), diarrhea (1% to 4%), GI discomfort/pain (1% to 4%)
Neuromuscular & skeletal: Muscle injury (1% to 5%), musculoskeletal pain (1% to 5%), back problems (<1% to 4%)
Respiratory: Upper respiratory tract infection (14% to 22%), throat irritation (3% to 22%), nasal congestion (4% to 16%), pharyngitis (6% to 14%), oral candidiasis (<1% to 11%), sinusitis/sinus infection (3% to 10%), rhinitis (1% to 9%), influenza (3% to 8%), bronchitis (1% to 9%), dysphonia (<1% to 8%), upper respiratory inflammation (5%), allergic rhinitis (3% to 5%), cough (1% to 5%), nasal discharge (1% to 5%), viral respiratory infection (1% to 5%)
Miscellaneous: Viral infection (2% to 5%)
1% to 3%:
Cardiovascular: Chest symptoms, edema, palpitations, swelling
Central nervous system: Dizziness, fatigue, malaise, migraine, mood disorders, nervousness, paralysis of cranial nerves, pain, sleep disorders, giddiness
Dermatologic: Acne, dermatitis/dermatosis, eczema, folliculitis, fungal skin infection, photodermatitis, pruritus, skin rash, urticaria, viral skin infection
Endocrine & metabolic: Dysmenorrhea, fluid disturbances, goiter, uric acid metabolism disorder
Gastrointestinal: Abdominal discomfort/pain, appetite disturbances, colitis, dyspepsia, gastroenteritis, gastrointestinal infections, mouth/tongue disorder, oral erythema, oral rash, oral ulcerations, stomach disorder, viral gastroenteritis, weight gain
(Continued)

Fluticasone *(Continued)*

Genitourinary: Urinary tract infection

Hematologic: Hematoma

Hepatic: Cholecystitis

Local: Irritation from inhalant

Neuromuscular & skeletal: Arthralgia/articular rheumatism, limb pain, muscle cramps/spasms, musculoskeletal inflammation

Ocular: Blepharoconjunctivitis, conjunctivitis, irritation, keratitis

Otic: Earache, ear polyps, otitis

Respiratory: Chest congestion, dyspnea, epistaxis, laryngitis, lower respiratory infections, mouth irritation, nasal pain, nasopharyngitis, nose/throat polyps, oropharyngeal plaques, sneezing, throat constriction

Miscellaneous: Bacterial infections, burns, contusion, cysts, dental discomfort/pain, dental problems, fungal infections, lumps, masses, pressure-induced disorders, postoperative complications, soft tissue injury, tonsillitis, tooth decay, wounds/lacerations

Nasal inhalation:

>10%: Headache (7% to 16%), pharyngitis (6% to 8%)

1% to 10%:

Central nervous system: Dizziness (1% to 3%), fever (1% to 3%)

Gastrointestinal: Nausea/vomiting (3% to 5%), abdominal pain (1% to 3%), diarrhea (1% to 3%)

Respiratory: Epistaxis (6% to 7%), asthma symptoms (3% to 7%), cough (4%), blood in nasal mucous (1% to 3%), runny nose (1% to 3%), bronchitis (1% to 3%)

Miscellaneous: Aches and pains (1% to 3%), flu-like symptoms (1% to 3%)

Topical: Pruritus (3%), skin irritation (3%), exacerbation of eczema (2%), dryness (1%), numbness of fingers (1%)

Reported with other topical corticosteroids (in decreasing order of occurrence): Irritation, folliculitis, acneiform eruptions, hypopigmentation, perioral dermatitis, allergic contact dermatitis, secondary infection, skin atrophy, striae, miliaria, pustular psoriasis from chronic plaque psoriasis

Drug Interactions

Cytochrome P450 Effect: Substrate of CYP3A4 (minor)

Increased Effect/Toxicity:

CYP3A4 inhibitors: Serum level and/or toxicity of fluticasone may be increased; this effect was shown with ketoconazole, but not erythromycin. Other potential inhibitors include amiodarone, cimetidine, clarithromycin, delavirdine, diltiazem, dirithromycin, disulfiram, fluoxetine, fluvoxamine, grapefruit juice, indinavir, itraconazole, ketoconazole, nefazodone, nevirapine, propoxyphene, quinupristin-dalfopristin, ritonavir, saquinavir, verapamil, zafirlukast, zileuton.

Salmeterol: The addition of salmeterol has been demonstrated to improve response to inhaled corticosteroids (as compared to increasing steroid dosage).

Mechanism of Action Fluticasone belongs to a new group of corticosteroids which utilizes a fluorocarbothioate ester linkage at the 17 carbon position; extremely potent vasoconstrictive and anti-inflammatory activity; has a weak HPA inhibitory potency when applied topically, which gives the drug a high therapeutic index. The effectiveness of inhaled fluticasone is due to its direct local effect. The mechanism of action for all topical corticosteroids is believed to be a combination of three important properties: anti-inflammatory activity, immunosuppressive properties, and antiproliferative actions.

Pharmacodynamics/Kinetics

Absorption:

Cream: 5% (increased with inflammation)

Oral inhalation: Primarily via lungs, minimal GI absorption due to presystemic metabolism

Distribution: 4.2 L/kg

Protein binding: 91%

Metabolism: Hepatic via CYP3A4 to 17β-carboxylic acid (negligible activity)

Bioavailability: Oral inhalation: 14% to 30%

Excretion: Feces (as parent drug and metabolites); urine (<5% as metabolites)

Dosage

Children:

Asthma: Inhalation, oral:

Flovent®: Children ≥12 years: Refer to adult dosing.

Flovent® Diskus® and Rotadisk®: **Note:** Titrate to the lowest effective dose once asthma stability is achieved; children previously maintained on Flovent® Rotadisk® may require dosage adjustments when transferred to Flovent® Diskus®

Children ≥4-11 years: Dosing based on previous therapy

Bronchodilator alone: Recommended starting dose: 50 mcg twice daily; highest recommended dose: 100 mcg twice daily

Inhaled corticosteroids: Recommended starting dose: 50 mcg twice daily; highest recommended dose: 100 mcg twice daily; a higher starting dose may be considered in patients previously requiring higher doses of inhaled corticosteroids

Children ≥11 years: Refer to adult dosing.

Inflammation/pruritus associated with corticosteroid-responsive dermatoses: Topical:

Children ≥3 months: Apply sparingly in a thin film twice daily; therapy should be discontinued when control is achieved. If no improvement is seen within 2 weeks, reassessment of diagnosis may be necessary. Safety and efficacy for use in pediatric patients <3 months have not been established.

Rhinitis: Intranasal: Children ≥4 years and Adolescents: Initial: 1 spray (50 mcg/spray) per nostril once daily; patients not adequately responding or patients with more severe symptoms may use 2 sprays (100 mcg) per nostril. Depending on response, dosage may be reduced to 100 mcg daily. Total daily dosage should not exceed 2 sprays in each nostril (200 mcg)/day. Dosing should be at regular intervals.

Adults:

Asthma: Inhalation, oral: Note: Titrate to the lowest effective dose once asthma stability is achieved

Flovent®: Dosing based on previous therapy

Bronchodilator alone: Recommended starting dose: 88 mcg twice daily; highest recommended dose: 440 mcg twice daily

Inhaled corticosteroids: Recommended starting dose: 88-220 mcg twice daily; highest recommended dose: 440 mcg twice daily; a higher starting dose may be considered in patients previously requiring higher doses of inhaled corticosteroids

Oral corticosteroids: Recommended starting dose: 880 mcg twice daily; highest recommended dose: 880 mcg twice daily; starting dose is patient dependent. In patients on chronic oral corticosteroids therapy, reduce prednisone dose no faster than 2.5 mg/day on a weekly basis; begin taper after ≥1 week of fluticasone therapy

Flovent® Diskus® and Rotadisk®: Dosing based on previous therapy

Bronchodilator alone: Recommended starting dose 100 mcg twice daily; highest recommended dose: 500 mcg twice daily

Inhaled corticosteroids: 100-250 mcg twice daily; highest recommended dose: 500 mcg twice daily; a higher starting dose may be considered in patients previously requiring higher doses of inhaled corticosteroids

Oral corticosteroids: 500-1000 mcg twice daily; highest recommended dose: 1000 mcg twice daily; starting dose is patient dependent. In patients on chronic oral corticosteroids therapy, reduce prednisone dose no faster than 2.5 mg/day on a weekly basis; begin taper after ≥1 week of fluticasone therapy

Inflammation/pruritus associated with corticosteroid-responsive dermatoses: Topical: Apply sparingly in a thin film twice daily; therapy should be discontinued when control is achieved. If no improvement is seen within 2 weeks, reassessment of diagnosis may be necessary.

Rhinitis: Intranasal: Initial: 2 sprays (50 mcg/spray) per nostril once daily; may also be divided into 100 mcg twice a day. After the first few days, dosage may be reduced to 1 spray per nostril once daily for maintenance therapy. Dosing should be at regular intervals.

Dosage adjustment in hepatic impairment: Fluticasone is primarily cleared in the liver. Fluticasone plasma levels may be increased in patients with hepatic impairment, use with caution; monitor.

Elderly: No differences in safety have been observed in the elderly when compared to younger patients. Based on current data, no dosage adjustment is needed based on age.

Administration

Aerosol inhalation: Shake container thoroughly before using. Take 3-5 deep breaths. Use inhaler on inspiration. Allow 1 full minute between inhalations. Rinse mouth with water after use to reduce aftertaste and incidence of candidiasis.

Nasal spray: Shake bottle gently before using. Prime pump prior to first use (press 6 times until fine spray appears). Blow nose to clear nostrils. Insert applicator into nostril, keeping bottle upright, and close off the other nostril. Breathe in through nose. While inhaling, press pump to release spray. Nasal applicator may be removed and rinsed with warm water to clean.

Powder for oral inhalation: Flovent® Diskus®: Do not use with a spacer device. Do not exhale into Diskus®. Do not wash or take apart. Use in horizontal position.

Topical: Apply sparingly in a thin film of cream or ointment. Rub in lightly. Do not use for diaper dermatitis.

Monitoring Parameters Growth (adolescents and children); signs/symptoms of HPA axis suppression/adrenal insufficiency; possible eosinophilic conditions (including Churg-Strauss syndrome)

Patient Information Use as directed; do not overuse and use only for length of time prescribed.

Inhalation: Rinse mouth after use; avoid spraying in eyes

Powder for oral inhalation: Flovent® Diskus®: Do not attempt to take device apart. Do not use with a spacer device. Do not exhale into the Diskus®, use in a level horizontal position. Do not wash the mouthpiece. Use within 2 months of opening foil overwrap.

Nasal spray: Shake gently before use. Use at regular intervals, no more frequently than directed. Report unusual cough or spasm; persistent nasal bleeding, burning, or irritation; or worsening of condition.

Topical: For external use only. Apply thin film to affected area only; rub in lightly. Do not apply occlusive covering (including under diapers or plastic pants) unless advised by prescriber. Wash hand thoroughly after use; avoid contact with eyes. Notify prescriber if skin condition persists or worsens. Do not use for treatment of diaper dermatitis, or under diapers or plastic pants.

Dosage Forms AERO, oral inhalation (Flovent®): 44 mcg/inhalation (7.9 g, 13 g); 110 mcg/inhalation (7.9 g, 13 g); 220 mcg/inhalation (7.9 g, 13 g). **CRM** (Cutivate®): 0.05% (15 g, 30 g, 60 g). **OINT** (Cutivate®): 0.005% (15 g, 30 g, 60 g). **POWDER, oral inhalation** (Flovent® (Continued)

Fluticasone *(Continued)*

Rotadisk®): 50 mcg: 44 mcg/inhalation (60s); 100 mcg: 88 mcg/inhalation (60s); 250 mcg: 220 mcg/inhalation (60s). **SUSP, intranasal spray** (Flonase®): 50 mcg/inhalation (16 g)

Fluticasone and Salmeterol *(floo TIK a sone & sal ME te role)*

U.S. Brand Names Advair Diskus®

Synonyms Salmeterol and Fluticasone

Therapeutic Category Anti-inflammatory/Beta$_2$-Adrenergic Agonist

Use Maintenance treatment of asthma in adults and children ≥12 years; **not** for use for relief of acute bronchospasm; maintenance treatment of COPD associated with chronic bronchitis

Pregnancy Risk Factor C

Contraindications Hypersensitivity to fluticasone, salmeterol, or any component of the formulation; status asthmaticus; acute episodes of asthma

Warnings/Precautions Not indicated for treatment of acute symptoms of asthma. Not for use in patients with rapidly deteriorating or life-threatening episodes of asthma. Fatalities have been reported. Do not use in conjunction with other long-acting beta$_2$ agonist inhalers. Do not exceed recommended dosage; short-acting beta$_2$ agonist should be used for acute symptoms and symptoms occurring between treatments. Do not use to transfer patients from oral corticosteroid therapy. Immediate hypersensitivity reactions (urticaria, angioedema, rash, bronchospasm) have been reported. Rare cases of vasculitis (Churg-Strauss syndrome) have been reported with fluticasone use.

May cause hypercorticism or suppression of hypothalamic-pituitary-adrenal (HPA) axis, particularly in younger children or in patients receiving high doses for prolonged periods. HPA axis suppression may lead to adrenal crisis. Withdrawal and discontinuation of a corticosteroid should be done slowly and carefully. Particular care is required when patients are transferred from systemic corticosteroids to inhaled products due to possible adrenal insufficiency or withdrawal from steroids, including an increase in allergic symptoms. Patients receiving 20 mg per day of prednisone (or equivalent) may be most susceptible. Fatalities have occurred due to adrenal insufficiency in asthmatic patients during and after transfer from systemic corticosteroids to aerosol steroids; aerosol steroids do **not** provide the systemic steroid needed to treat patients having trauma, surgery, or infections. May suppress the immune system; use with caution in patients with systemic infections or ocular herpes simplex. Avoid exposure to chickenpox and measles.

Controlled clinical studies have shown that orally-inhaled and intranasal corticosteroids may cause a reduction in growth velocity in pediatric patients. (In studies of orally-inhaled corticosteroids, the mean reduction in growth velocity was ~1 cm per year [range 0.3-1.8 cm per year] and appears to be related to dose and duration of exposure.) To minimize the systemic effects of orally-inhaled and intranasal corticosteroids, each patient should be titrated to the lowest effective dose.

Beta agonists may cause elevation in blood pressure, heart rate, and result in CNS excitement. Use caution in patients with cardiovascular disease (arrhythmia or hypertension or CHF), convulsive disorders, diabetes, glaucoma, hyperthyroidism, or hypokalemia. May increase risk of arrhythmia and may increase serum glucose or decrease serum potassium concentrations. In a large, randomized clinical trial (SMART), salmeterol was associated with a small, but statistically significant increase in asthma-related deaths (when added to usual asthma therapy); risk may be greater in African-American patients versus Caucasians. The elderly may be at greater risk of cardiovascular side effects. Safety and efficacy have not been established in children <12 years of age.

Powder for oral inhalation contains lactose; very rare anaphylactic reactions have been reported in patients with severe milk protein allergy.

Common Adverse Reactions Percentages reported in patients with asthma

>10%:
Central nervous system: Headache (12% to 13%)
Endocrine & metabolic: Serum glucose increased, serum potassium decreased
Respiratory: Upper respiratory tract infection (21% to 27%), pharyngitis (10% to 13%)

>3% to 10%:
Gastrointestinal: Nausea/vomiting (4% to 6%), diarrhea (2% to 4%), GI pain/discomfort (1% to 4%), oral candidiasis (1% to 4%)
Neuromuscular & skeletal: Musculoskeletal pain (2% to 4%)
Respiratory: Bronchitis (2% to 8%), upper respiratory tract inflammation (6% to 7%), cough (3% to 6%), sinusitis (4% to 5%), hoarseness/dysphonia (2% to 5%), viral respiratory tract infections (4%)

1% to 3%:
Cardiovascular: Chest symptoms, fluid retention, palpitations
Central nervous system: Compressed nerve syndromes, hypnagogic effects, pain, sleep disorders, tremors
Dermatologic: Hives, skin flakiness/ichthyosis, urticaria, viral skin infections
Gastrointestinal: Appendicitis, constipation, dental discomfort/pain, gastrointestinal disorder, gastrointestinal infections, gastrointestinal signs and symptoms (nonspecified), oral discomfort/pain, oral erythema/rash, oral ulcerations, unusual taste, viral GI infections (0% to 3%)
Hematologic: Contusions/hematomas, lymphatic signs and symptoms (nonspecified)
Hepatic: Abnormal liver function tests
Neuromuscular & skeletal: Arthralgia, articular rheumatism, bone/cartilage disorders, fractures, muscle injuries, muscle stiffness, tightness/rigidity

Ocular: Conjunctivitis, eye redness, keratitis

Otic: Ear signs and symptoms (nonspecified)

Respiratory: Blood in nasal mucosa, congestion, ear/nose/throat infections, lower respiratory tract infections, lower respiratory signs and symptoms (nonspecified), nasal irritation, nasal signs and symptoms (nonspecified), nasal sinus disorders, pneumonia, rhinitis, rhinorrhea/post nasal drip, sneezing, wheezing

Miscellaneous: Allergies/allergic reactions, bacterial infections, burns, candidiasis (0% to 3%), sweat/sebum disorders, diaphoresis, viral infections, wounds and lacerations

Drug Interactions

Cytochrome P450 Effect: Fluticasone: **Substrate** of CYP3A4 (minor)

Increased Effect/Toxicity: Diuretics (loop, thiazide): Hypokalemia from diuretics may be worsened by beta-agonists (dose related); use with caution. CYP3A4 inhibitors may increase levels and/or effects of fluticasone; example inhibitors include azole antifungals, ciprofloxacin, clarithromycin, diclofenac, doxycycline, erythromycin, imatinib, isoniazid, nefazodone, nicardipine, propofol, protease inhibitors, quinidine, and verapamil. May cause increased cardiovascular toxicity with MAO inhibitors or tricyclic antidepressants; wait at least 2 weeks after discontinuing these agents to start fluticasone/salmeterol.

Decreased Effect: Beta-adrenergic blockers (eg, propranolol) may decreased the effect of salmeterol component and may cause bronchospasm in asthmatics; use with caution.

Mechanism of Action Combination of fluticasone (corticosteroid) and salmeterol (long-acting beta$_2$ agonist) designed to improve pulmonary function and control over what is produced by either agent when used alone. Because fluticasone and salmeterol act locally in the lung, plasma levels do not predict therapeutic effect.

Fluticasone: The mechanism of action for all topical corticosteroids is believed to be a combination of three important properties: Anti-inflammatory activity, immunosuppressive properties, and antiproliferative actions. Fluticasone has extremely potent vasoconstrictive and anti-inflammatory activity.

Salmeterol: Relaxes bronchial smooth muscle by selective action on beta$_2$-receptors with little effect on heart rate

Pharmacodynamics/Kinetics

Advair™ Diskus®:

Onset of action: 30-60 minutes

Peak effect: ≥1 week for full effect

Duration: 12 hours

See individual agents.

Dosage Oral inhalation: **Note:** Do not use to transfer patients from systemic corticosteroid therapy.

COPD: Adults: Fluticasone 250 mcg/salmeterol 50 mcg twice daily, 12 hours apart

Asthma: Children ≥12 and Adults: One inhalation twice daily, morning and evening, 12 hours apart

Advair™ Diskus® is available in 3 strengths, initial dose prescribed should be based upon previous asthma therapy. Dose should be increased after 2 weeks if adequate response is not achieved. Patients should be titrated to lowest effective dose once stable. (Because each strength contains salmeterol 50 mcg/inhalation, dose adjustments should be made by changing inhaler strength. No more than 1 inhalation of any strength should be taken more than twice a day). Maximum dose: Fluticasone 500 mcg/salmeterol 50 mcg, one inhalation twice daily.

Patients not currently on inhaled corticosteroids: Fluticasone 100 mcg/salmeterol 50 mcg

Patients currently using inhaled beclomethasone dipropionate:

≤420 mcg/day: Fluticasone 100 mcg/salmeterol 50 mcg

462-840 mcg/day: Fluticasone 250 mcg/salmeterol 50 mcg

Patients currently using inhaled budesonide:

≤400 mcg/day: Fluticasone 100 mcg/salmeterol 50 mcg

800-1200 mcg/day: Fluticasone 250 mcg/salmeterol 50 mcg

1600 mcg/day: Fluticasone 500 mcg/salmeterol 50 mcg

Patients currently using inhaled flunisolide:

≤1000 mcg/day: Fluticasone 100 mcg/salmeterol 50 mcg

1250-2000 mcg/day: Fluticasone 250 mcg/salmeterol 50 mcg

Patients currently using inhaled fluticasone propionate aerosol:

≤176 mcg/day: Fluticasone 100 mcg/salmeterol 50 mcg

440 mcg/day: Fluticasone 250 mcg/salmeterol 50 mcg

660-880 mcg/day: Fluticasone 500 mcg/salmeterol 50 mcg

Patients currently using inhaled fluticasone propionate powder:

≤200 mcg/day: Fluticasone 100 mcg/salmeterol 50 mcg

500 mcg/day: Fluticasone 250 mcg/salmeterol 50 mcg

1000 mcg/day: Fluticasone 500 mcg/salmeterol 50 mcg

Patients currently using inhaled triamcinolone acetonide:

≤1000 mcg/day: Fluticasone 100 mcg/salmeterol 50 mcg

1100-1600 mcg/day: Fluticasone 250 mcg/salmeterol 50 mcg

Elderly: No differences in safety or effectiveness have been seen in studies of patients ≥65 years of age. However, increased sensitivity may be seen in the elderly. Use with caution in patients with concomitant cardiovascular disease.

Dosage adjustment in renal impairment: Specific guidelines are not available

Dosage adjustment in hepatic impairment: Fluticasone is cleared by hepatic metabolism. No dosing adjustment suggested. Use with caution in patients with impaired liver function.

(Continued)

Fluticasone and Salmeterol *(Continued)*

Administration Not to be used with a spacer device. Do not wash the mouthpiece or other parts of the Diskus®; do not attempt to take device apart. Do not exhale into device.

Monitoring Parameters FEV$_1$, peak flow, and/or other pulmonary function tests; blood pressure, heart rate; CNS stimulation; serum glucose, serum potassium. Monitor for increased use of short-acting beta$_2$-agonist inhalers; may be marker of a deteriorating asthma condition. The growth of pediatric patients receiving inhaled corticosteroids should be monitored routinely (eg, via stadiometry).

Patient Information See individual agents.

Dosage Forms POWDER, oral inhalation: 100/50: Fluticasone 100 mcg and salmeterol 50 mcg (28s, 60s); 250/50: Fluticasone 250 mcg and salmeterol 50 mcg (28s, 60s); 500/50: Fluticasone 500 mcg and salmeterol 50 mcg (28s, 60s)

♦ **Fluticasone Propionate** *see Fluticasone on page 547*

Fluvastatin *(FLOO va sta tin)*

Related Information
Lipid-Lowering Agents *on page 1381*

U.S. Brand Names Lescol®; Lescol® XL

Therapeutic Category Antilipemic Agent, HMG-CoA Reductase Inhibitor; HMG-CoA Reductase Inhibitor

Use To be used as a component of multiple risk factor intervention in patients at risk for atherosclerosis vascular disease due to hypercholesterolemia

Adjunct to dietary therapy to reduce elevated total cholesterol (total-C), LDL-C, triglyceride, and apolipoprotein B (apo-B) levels and to increase HDL-C in primary hypercholesterolemia and mixed dyslipidemia (Fredrickson types IIa and IIb); to slow the progression of coronary atherosclerosis in patients with coronary heart disease; reduce risk of coronary revascularization procedures in patients with coronary heart disease

Pregnancy Risk Factor X

Contraindications Hypersensitivity to fluvastatin or any component of the formulation; active liver disease; unexplained persistent elevations of serum transaminases; pregnancy; breast-feeding

Warnings/Precautions Secondary causes of hyperlipidemia should be ruled out prior to therapy. Liver function must be monitored by periodic laboratory assessment. Rhabdomyolysis with acute renal failure has occurred with fluvastatin and other HMG-CoA reductase inhibitors. Risk may be increased with concurrent use of other drugs which may cause rhabdomyolysis (including gemfibrozil, fibric acid derivatives, or niacin at doses ≥1 g/day). Temporarily discontinue in any patient experiencing an acute or serious condition predisposing to renal failure secondary to rhabdomyolysis. Use caution in patients with previous liver disease or heavy ethanol use. Treatment in patients <18 years of age is not recommended.

Common Adverse Reactions As reported with fluvastatin capsules; in general, adverse reactions reported with fluvastatin extended release tablet were similar, but the incidence was less.

1% to 10%:
Central nervous system: Headache (9%), fatigue (3%), insomnia (3%)
Gastrointestinal: Dyspepsia (8%), diarrhea (5%), abdominal pain (5%), nausea (3%)
Genitourinary: Urinary tract infection (2%)
Neuromuscular & skeletal: Myalgia (5%)
Respiratory: Sinusitis (3%), bronchitis (2%)

Drug Interactions

Cytochrome P450 Effect: Substrate (minor) of CYP2C8/9, 2D6, 3A4; **Inhibits** CYP1A2 (weak), 2C8/9 (moderate), 2D6 (weak), 3A4 (weak)

Increased Effect/Toxicity: Cimetidine, omeprazole, ranitidine, and ritonavir may increase fluvastatin blood levels. Clofibrate, erythromycin, gemfibrozil, fenofibrate, and niacin may increase the risk of myopathy and rhabdomyolysis. Anticoagulant effect of warfarin may be increased by fluvastatin. Cholestyramine effect will be additive with fluvastatin if administration times are separated. Fluvastatin may increase C$_{max}$ and decrease clearance of digoxin.

Decreased Effect: Administration of cholestyramine at the same time with fluvastatin reduces absorption and clinical effect of fluvastatin. Separate administration times by at least 4 hours. Rifampin and rifabutin may decrease fluvastatin blood levels.

Mechanism of Action Acts by competitively inhibiting 3-hydroxyl-3-methylglutaryl-coenzyme A (HMG-CoA) reductase, the enzyme that catalyzes the reduction of HMG-CoA to mevalonate; this is an early rate-limiting step in cholesterol biosynthesis. HDL is increased while total, LDL and VLDL cholesterols, apolipoprotein B, and plasma triglycerides are decreased.

Pharmacodynamics/Kinetics

Distribution: V$_d$: 0.35 L/kg

Protein binding: >98%

Metabolism: To inactive and active metabolites [oxidative metabolism via CYP2C9 (75%), 2C8 (~5%), and 3A4 (~20%) isoenzymes]; active forms do not circulate systemically; extensive first-pass hepatic extraction

Bioavailability: Absolute: Capsule: 24%; Extended release tablet: 29%

Half-life elimination: Capsule: <3 hours; Extended release tablet: 9 hours

Excretion: Feces (90%): urine (5%)

Dosage Adults: Oral:

Patients requiring ≥25% decrease in LDL-C: 40 mg capsule or 80 mg extended release tablet once daily in the evening; may also use 40 mg capsule twice daily

Patients requiring <25% decrease in LDL-C: 20 mg capsule once daily in the evening

Note: Dosing range: 20-80 mg/day; adjust dose based on response to therapy; maximum response occurs within 4-6 weeks

Dosage adjustment in renal impairment: Less than 6% excreted renally; no dosage adjustment needed with mild to moderate renal impairment; use with caution in severe renal impairment

Dosage adjustment in hepatic impairment: Levels may accumulate in patients with liver disease (increased AUC and C_{max}); use caution with severe hepatic impairment or heavy ethanol ingestion; contraindicated in active liver disease or unexplained transaminase elevations; decrease dose and monitor effects carefully in patients with hepatic insufficiency

Elderly: No dosage adjustment necessary based on age

Administration Patient should be placed on a standard cholesterol-lowering diet before and during treatment; fluvastatin may be taken without regard to meals; adjust dosage as needed in response to periodic lipid determinations during the first 4 weeks after a dosage change; lipid-lowering effects are additive when fluvastatin is combined with a bile-acid binding resin or niacin, however, it must be administered at least 2 hours following these drugs.

Monitoring Parameters Obtain baseline LFTs and total cholesterol profile; repeat tests at 12 weeks after initiation of therapy or elevation in dose, and periodically thereafter. Monitor LDL-C at intervals no less than 4 weeks.

Patient Information Avoid prolonged exposure to the sun and other ultraviolet light; report unexplained muscle pain or weakness, especially if accompanied by fever or malaise

Dosage Forms CAP (Lescol®): 20 mg, 40 mg. **TAB, extended release** (Lescol® XL): 80 mg

♦ **Fluvirin®** *see* Influenza Virus Vaccine *on page 667*

Fluvoxamine (floo VOKS a meen)

Related Information

Antidepressant Agents Comparison *on page 1359*

Selective Serotonin Reuptake Inhibitors (SSRIs) Pharmacokinetics *on page 1403*

Synonyms Luvox

Therapeutic Category Antidepressant, Selective Serotonin Reuptake Inhibitor (SSRI)

Use Treatment of obsessive-compulsive disorder (OCD) in children ≥8 years of age and adults

Unlabeled/Investigational Use Treatment of major depression; panic disorder; anxiety disorders in children

Pregnancy Risk Factor C

Contraindications Hypersensitivity to fluvoxamine or any component of the formulation; concurrent use with astemizole, pimozide, thioridazine, mesoridazine, or cisapride; use of MAO inhibitors within 14 days

Warnings/Precautions Potential for severe reaction when used with MAO inhibitors - serotonin syndrome (hyperthermia, muscular rigidity, mental status changes/agitation, autonomic instability) may occur. May precipitate a shift to mania or hypomania in patients with bipolar disease. The possibility of a suicide attempt is inherent in major depression and may persist until remission occurs. Use caution in high-risk patients during initiation of therapy. Prescriptions should be written for the smallest quantity consistent with good patient care. Has a low potential to impair cognitive or motor performance - caution operating hazardous machinery or driving. Use caution in patients with a previous seizure disorder or condition predisposing to seizures such as brain damage, alcoholism, or concurrent therapy with other drugs which lower the seizure threshold. Use with caution in patients with hepatic or renal dysfunction and in elderly patients. May cause hyponatremia/SIADH. Use with caution in patients with renal insufficiency or other concurrent illness (cardiovascular disease). Use with caution in patients at risk of bleeding or receiving concurrent anticoagulant therapy, although not consistently noted, fluvoxamine may cause impairment in platelet function. May cause or exacerbate sexual dysfunction.

Common Adverse Reactions

>10%:

Central nervous system: Headache (22%), somnolence (22%), insomnia (21%), nervousness (12%), dizziness (11%)

Gastrointestinal: Nausea (40%), diarrhea (11%), xerostomia (14%)

Neuromuscular & skeletal: Weakness (14%)

1% to 10%:

Cardiovascular: Palpitations

Central nervous system: Somnolence, mania, hypomania, vertigo, abnormal thinking, agitation, anxiety, malaise, amnesia, yawning, hypertonia, CNS stimulation, depression

Endocrine & metabolic: Decreased libido

Gastrointestinal: Abdominal pain, vomiting, dyspepsia, constipation, abnormal taste, anorexia, flatulence, weight gain

Genitourinary: Delayed ejaculation, impotence, anorgasmia, urinary frequency, urinary retention

Neuromuscular & skeletal: Tremors

Ocular: Blurred vision

Respiratory: Dyspnea

Miscellaneous: Diaphoresis

Drug Interactions

Cytochrome P450 Effect: Substrate (major) of CYP1A2, 2D6; **Inhibits** CYP1A2 (strong), 2B6 (weak), 2C8/9 (weak), 2C19 (strong), 2D6 (weak), 3A4 (weak)

(Continued)

Fluvoxamine *(Continued)*

Increased Effect/Toxicity: Fluvoxamine should not be used with nonselective MAO inhibitors (phenelzine, isocarboxazid) and drugs with MAO inhibitor properties (linezolid); fatal reactions have been reported. Wait 5 weeks after stopping fluvoxamine before starting a nonselective MAO inhibitor and 2 weeks after stopping an MAO inhibitor before starting fluvoxamine. Concurrent selegiline has been associated with mania, hypertension, or serotonin syndrome (risk may be reduced relative to nonselective MAO inhibitors).

Phenothiazines: Fluvoxamine may inhibit the metabolism of thioridazine or mesoridazine, resulting in increased plasma levels and increasing the risk of QT_c interval prolongation. This may lead to serious ventricular arrhythmias, such as torsade de pointes-type arrhythmias and sudden death. Do not use together. Wait at least 5 weeks after discontinuing fluvoxamine prior to starting thioridazine.

CYP1A2 inhibitors may increase the levels/effects of fluvoxamine; example inhibitors include amiodarone, ciprofloxacin, fluvoxamine, ketoconazole, lomefloxacin, ofloxacin, and rofecoxib. CYP2D6 inhibitors may increase the levels/effects of fluvoxamine; example inhibitors include chlorpromazine, delavirdine, fluoxetine, miconazole, paroxetine, pergolide, quinidine, quinine, ritonavir, and ropinirole.

Combined used of SSRIs and amphetamines, buspirone, meperidine, nefazodone, serotonin agonists (such as sumatriptan), sibutramine, other SSRIs, sympathomimetics, ritonavir, tramadol, and venlafaxine may increase the risk of serotonin syndrome. Fluvoxamine may increase serum levels/effects of benzodiazepines (alprazolam and diazepam), beta-blockers (except atenolol or nadolol), carbamazepine, carvedilol, clozapine, cyclosporin (and possibly tacrolimus), dextromethorphan, digoxin, haloperidol, HMG-CoA reductase inhibitors (lovastatin and simvastatin - increasing the risk of rhabdomyolysis), mexiletine, phenytoin, propafenone, quinidine, tacrine, theophylline, trazodone, tricyclic antidepressants, and valproic acid. Concurrent lithium may increase risk of nephrotoxicity. Risk of hyponatremia may increase with concurrent use of loop diuretics (bumetanide, furosemide, torsemide). Fluvoxamine may increase the hypoprothrombinemic response to warfarin.

Combined used of sumatriptan (and other serotonin agonists) may result in toxicity; weakness, hyper-reflexia, and incoordination have been observed with sumatriptan and SSRIs. In addition, concurrent use may theoretically increase the risk of serotonin syndrome; includes sumatriptan, naratriptan, rizatriptan, and zolmitriptan.

Decreased Effect: CYP1A2 inducers may decrease the levels/effects of fluvoxamine; example inducers include aminoglutethimide, carbamazepine, phenobarbital, and rifampin. Cyproheptadine, a serotonin antagonist, may inhibit the effects of serotonin reuptake inhibitors (fluvoxamine); monitor for altered antidepressant response.

Mechanism of Action Inhibits CNS neuron serotonin uptake; minimal or no effect on reuptake of norepinephrine or dopamine; does not significantly bind to alpha-adrenergic, histamine or cholinergic receptors

Pharmacodynamics/Kinetics

Absorption: Steady-state plasma concentrations have been noted to be 2-3 times higher in children than those in adolescents; female children demonstrated a significantly higher AUC than males

Distribution: V_d: ~25 L/kg

Protein binding: ~80%, primarily to albumin

Metabolism: Hepatic

Bioavailability: 53%; not significantly affected by food

Half-life elimination: ~15 hours

Time to peak, plasma: 3-8 hours

Excretion: Urine

Dosage Oral: **Note:** When total daily dose exceeds 50 mg, the dose should be given in 2 divided doses:

Children 8-17 years: Initial: 25 mg at bedtime; adjust in 25 mg increments at 4- to 7-day intervals, as tolerated, to maximum therapeutic benefit: Range: 50-200 mg/day

Maximum: Children: 8-11 years: 200 mg/day, adolescents: 300 mg/day; lower doses may be effective in female versus male patients

Adults: Initial: 50 mg at bedtime; adjust in 50 mg increments at 4- to 7-day intervals; usual dose range: 100-300 mg/day; divide total daily dose into 2 doses; administer larger portion at bedtime

Elderly: Reduce dose, titrate slowly

Dosage adjustment in hepatic impairment: Reduce dose, titrate slowly

Monitoring Parameters Signs and symptoms of depression, anxiety, weight gain or loss, nutritional intake, sleep

Patient Information Its favorable side effect profile makes it a useful alternative to the traditional agents; use sugarless hard candy for dry mouth; avoid alcohol, may cause drowsiness; improvement may take several weeks; rise slowly to prevent dizziness. As with all psychoactive drugs, fluvoxamine may impair judgment, thinking, or motor skills, so use caution when operating hazardous machinery, including automobiles, especially early on into therapy. Inform your prescriber of any concurrent medications you may be taking.

Dosage Forms TAB: 25 mg, 50 mg, 100 mg

♦ **Fluzone**® *see* Influenza Virus Vaccine *on page 667*
♦ **FML**® *see* Fluorometholone *on page 536*
♦ **FML**® **Forte** *see* Fluorometholone *on page 536*

- **FML-S®** *see* Sulfacetamide Sodium and Fluorometholone *on page 1170*
- **Focalin™** *see* Dexmethylphenidate *on page 360*
- **Foille® [OTC]** *see* Benzocaine *on page 154*
- **Foille® Medicated First Aid [OTC]** *see* Benzocaine *on page 154*
- **Foille® Plus [OTC]** *see* Benzocaine *on page 154*
- **Folacin** *see* Folic Acid *on page 555*
- **Folacin, Vitamin B₁₂, and Vitamin B₆** *see* Folic Acid, Cyanocobalamin, and Pyridoxine *on page 555*
- **Folate** *see* Folic Acid *on page 555*
- **Folgard® [OTC]** *see* Folic Acid, Cyanocobalamin, and Pyridoxine *on page 555*

Folic Acid (FOE lik AS id)

Synonyms Folacin; Folate; Pteroylglutamic Acid
Therapeutic Category Vitamin, Water Soluble
Use Treatment of megaloblastic and macrocytic anemias due to folate deficiency; dietary supplement to prevent neural tube defects
Pregnancy Risk Factor A/C (dose exceeding RDA recommendation)
Contraindications Pernicious, aplastic, or normocytic anemias
Warnings/Precautions Doses >0.1 mg/day may obscure pernicious anemia with continuing irreversible nerve damage progression. Resistance to treatment may occur with depressed hematopoiesis, alcoholism, deficiencies of other vitamins. Injection contains benzyl alcohol (1.5%) as preservative (use care in administration to neonates).
Common Adverse Reactions Slight flushing, general malaise, pruritus, rash, bronchospasm, allergic reaction
Drug Interactions
    Decreased Effect: In folate-deficient patients, folic acid therapy may increase phenytoin metabolism which may lead to a decrease in the effect of phenytoin. Phenytoin, primidone, para-aminosalicylic acid, and sulfasalazine may decrease serum folate concentrations resulting in a folic acid deficiency. Concurrent administration of chloramphenicol and folic acid may result in antagonism of the hematopoietic response to folic acid.
Mechanism of Action Folic acid is necessary for formation of a number of coenzymes in many metabolic systems, particularly for purine and pyrimidine synthesis; required for nucleoprotein synthesis and maintenance in erythropoiesis; stimulates WBC and platelet production in folate deficiency anemia
Pharmacodynamics/Kinetics
    Onset of effect: Peak effect: Oral: 0.5-1 hour
    Absorption: Proximal part of small intestine
Dosage
    Infants: 0.1 mg/day
    Children <4 years: Up to 0.3 mg/day
    Children >4 years and Adults: 0.4 mg/day
    Pregnant and lactating women: 0.8 mg/day
    RDA:
        Adult male: 0.15-0.2 mg/day
        Adult female: 0.15-0.18 mg/day
Administration Oral preferred, but may also be administered by deep I.M., S.C., or I.V. injection; a diluted solution for oral or for parenteral administration may be prepared by diluting 1 mL of folic acid injection (5 mg/mL), with 49 mL sterile water for injection; resulting solution is 0.1 mg folic acid per 1 mL
Reference Range Therapeutic: 0.005-0.015 µg/mL
Patient Information Take folic acid replacement only under recommendation of prescriber.
Dosage Forms INJ, solution: 5 mg/mL (10 mL). **TAB:** 0.4 mg, 0.8 mg, 1 mg

Folic Acid, Cyanocobalamin, and Pyridoxine

(FOE lik AS id, sye an oh koe BAL a min, & peer i DOKS een)
U.S. Brand Names Folgard® [OTC]; Foltx®
Synonyms Cyanocobalamin, Folic Acid, and Pyridoxine; Folacin, Vitamin B₁₂, and Vitamin B₆; Pyridoxine, Folic Acid, and Cyanocobalamin
Therapeutic Category Vitamin
Use Nutritional supplement in end-stage renal failure, dialysis, hyperhomocysteinemia, homocystinuria, malabsorption syndromes, dietary deficiencies
Dosage Oral: Adults: 1 tablet daily
Dosage Forms TAB (Folgard®): Folic acid 0.8 mg, cyanocobalamin 115 mcg, and pyridoxine 10 mg; (Foltx®): Folic acid 2.5 mg, cyanocobalamin 1 mg, and pyridoxine 25 mg

- **Folinic Acid** *see* Leucovorin *on page 723*
- **Follistim®** *see* Follitropins *on page 555*
- **Follitropin Alfa** *see* Follitropins *on page 555*
- **Follitropin Alpha** *see* Follitropins *on page 555*
- **Follitropin Beta** *see* Follitropins *on page 555*

Follitropins (foe li TRO pins)

U.S. Brand Names Bravelle™; Fertinex® [DSC]; Follistim®; Gonal-F®
Synonyms Follitropin Alfa; Follitropin Alpha; Follitropin Beta; Recombinant Human Follicle Stimulating Hormone; rFSH-alpha; rFSH-beta; rhFSH-alpha; rhFSH-beta; Urofollitropin
(Continued)

Follitropins *(Continued)*

Therapeutic Category Ovulation Stimulator

Use

Urofollitropin:

Bravelle™: Ovulation induction in patients who previously received pituitary suppression; Assisted Reproductive Technologies (ART)

Fertinex®: Ovulation induction in patients with polycystic ovary syndrome and infertility who have not responded to clomiphene citrate therapy; ART

Follitropin alfa (Gonal-F®), Follitropin beta (Follistim®): Ovulation induction in patients in whom the cause of infertility is functional and not caused by primary ovarian failure; ART; spermatogenesis induction

Pregnancy Risk Factor X

Contraindications Hypersensitivity to follitropins or any component of the formulation; high levels of FSH indicating primary gonadal failure (ovarian or testicular); uncontrolled thyroid or adrenal dysfunction; the presence of any cause of infertility other than anovulation; tumor of the ovary, breast, uterus, hypothalamus, testis, or pituitary gland; abnormal vaginal bleeding of undetermined origin; ovarian cysts or enlargement not due to polycystic ovary syndrome; pregnancy

Warnings/Precautions These medications should only be used by physicians who are thoroughly familiar with infertility problems and their management. To minimize risks, use only at the lowest effective dose. Monitor ovarian response with serum estradiol and vaginal ultrasound on a regular basis.

Ovarian enlargement which may be accompanied by abdominal distention or abdominal pain, occurs in ~20% of those treated with urofollitropin and hCG, and generally regresses without treatment within 2-3 weeks. Ovarian hyperstimulation syndrome, characterized by severe ovarian enlargement, abdominal pain/distention, nausea, vomiting, diarrhea, dyspnea, and oliguria, and may be accompanied by ascites, pleural effusion, hypovolemia, electrolyte imbalance, hemoperitoneum, and thromboembolic events is reported in about 6% of patients. If hyperstimulation occurs, stop treatment and hospitalize patient. This syndrome develops rapidly within 24 hours to several days and generally occurs during the 7-10 days immediately following treatment. Hemoconcentration associated with fluid loss into the abdominal cavity has occurred and should be assessed by fluid intake & output, weight, hematocrit, serum & urinary electrolytes, urine specific gravity, BUN and creatinine, and abdominal girth. Determinations should be performed daily or more often if the need arises. Treatment is primarily symptomatic and consists of bed rest, fluid and electrolyte replacement and analgesics. The ascitic, pleural and pericardial fluids should never be removed because of the potential danger of injury.

Serious pulmonary conditions (atelectasis, acute respiratory distress syndrome and exacerbation of asthma) have been reported. Thromboembolic events, both in association with and separate from ovarian hyperstimulation syndrome, have been reported.

Multiple pregnancies have been associated with these medications, including triplet and quintuplet gestations. Advise patient of the potential risk of multiple births before starting the treatment.

Common Adverse Reactions Frequency varies by specific product and route of administration.

2% to 10%:

Central nervous system: Headache, dizziness, fever

Dermatologic: Acne (male), dermoid cyst (male), dry skin, body rash, hair loss, hives

Endocrine & metabolic: Ovarian hyperstimulation syndrome, adnexal torsion, mild to moderate ovarian enlargement, abdominal pain, ovarian cysts, breast tenderness, gynecomastia (male)

Gastrointestinal: Nausea, vomiting, diarrhea, abdominal cramps, bloating, flatulence, dyspepsia

Genitourinary: Urinary tract infection, menstrual disorder, intermenstrual bleeding, dysmenorrhea, cervical lesion

Local: Pain, rash, swelling, or irritation at the site of injection

Neuromuscular & skeletal: Back pain, varicose veins (male)

Respiratory: Exacerbation of asthma, sinusitis, pharyngitis

Miscellaneous: Febrile reactions accompanied by chills, musculoskeletal, joint pains, malaise, headache, and fatigue; flu-like symptoms

Mechanism of Action Urofollitropin is a preparation of highly purified follicle-stimulating hormone (FSH) extracted from the urine of postmenopausal women. Follitropin alfa and follitropin beta are human FSH preparations of recombinant DNA origin. Follitropins stimulate ovarian follicular growth in women who do not have primary ovarian failure, and stimulate spermatogenesis in men with hypogonadotrophic hypogonadism. FSH is required for normal follicular growth, maturation, gonadal steroid production, and spermatogenesis.

Pharmacodynamics/Kinetics

Onset of action: Peak effect: Spermatogenesis, median: 165 days (range: 25-327 days); Follicle development: Within cycle

Absorption: Rate limited: I.M., S.C.: Slower than elimination rate

Distribution: Mean V_d: Follitropin alfa: 10 L; Follitropin beta: 8 L

Metabolism: Total clearance of follitropin alfa was 0.6 L/hour following I.V. administration

Bioavailability: Ranges from ~66% to 82% depending on agent

Half-life elimination:

Mean: S.C.: Follitropin alfa: 24-32 hours; Follitropin beta: ~30 hours; Urofollitropin: 32-37 hours

Mean terminal: Multiple doses: I.M. follitropin alfa, S.C. follitropin beta: ~30 hours; I.M. urofollitropin: 15 hours, S.C. urofollitropin: 21 hours

Time to peak:

Follitropin alfa: S.C.: 16 hours; I.M.: 25 hours

Follitropin beta: I.M.: 27 hours

Urofollitropin: Single dose: S.C.: 15-20 hours, I.M.: 10-17 hours; Multiple doses: I.M., S.C.: 10 hours

Excretion: Clearance: Follitropin alfa: I.V.: 0.6 L/hour

Dosage Adults:

Note: Use the lowest dose consistent with the expectation of good results. Over the course of treatment, doses may vary depending on individual patient response. When used for ovulation induction, if response to follitropin is appropriate, hCG is given 1 day following the last dose. Withhold hCG if serum estradiol is >2000 pg/mL, if the ovaries are abnormally enlarged, or if abdominal pain occurs.

Urofollitropin: Female:

Bravelle™:

Ovulation induction: I.M., S.C.: Initial: 150 int. units daily for the first 5 days of treatment. Dose adjustments of ≤75-150 int. units can be made every ≥2 days; maximum daily dose: 450 int. units; treatment >12 days is not recommended

ART: S.C.: 225 int. units for the first 5 days; dose may be adjusted based on patient response, but adjustments should not be made more frequently than once every 2 days; maximum adjustment: 75-150 int. units; maximum daily dose: 450 int. units; maximum duration of treatment: 12 days

Fertinex®: S.C.:

Ovulation induction: Initial: 75 int. units/day; consider dose adjustment after 5-7 days. Do not increase more than twice in any cycle or by more than 75 int. units per adjustment; dosage range: 75-300 int. units/day

ART: Initiate therapy in the early follicular phase (cycle day 2 or day 3) at a dose of 150 int. units/day, until sufficient follicular development is attained; in most cases, therapy should not exceed 10 days

Follitropin alfa: Gonal-F®: S.C.:

Ovulation induction: Female: Initial: 75 int. units/day; consider dose adjustment after 5-7 days; additional dose adjustments of up to 37.5 int. units may be considered after 14 days; further dose increases of the same magnitude can be made, if necessary, every 7 days (maximum dose: 300 int. units)

ART: Female: Initiate therapy with follitropin alfa in the early follicular phase (cycle day 2 or day 3) at a dose of 150 int. units/day, until sufficient follicular development is attained. In most cases, therapy should not exceed 10 days. In patients whose endogenous gonadotropin levels are suppressed, initiate follitropin alfa at a dose of 225 int. units/day. Continue treatment until adequate follicular development is indicated as determined by ultrasound in combination with measurement of serum estradiol levels. Consider adjustments to dose after 5 days based on the patient's response; adjust subsequent dosage every 3-5 days by ≤75-150 int. units additionally at each adjustment. Doses >450 int. units/day are not recommended. Once adequate follicular development is evident, administer hCG (5000-10,000 units) to induce final follicular maturation in preparation for oocyte.

Spermatogenesis induction: Male: Therapy should begin with hCG pretreatment until serum testosterone is in normal range, then 150 int. units 3 times/week with hCG 3 times/week; continue with lowest dose needed to induce spermatogenesis (maximum dose: 300 int. units 3 times/week); may be given for up to 18 months

Follitropin beta: Follistim®:

Female: I.M., S.C.:

Ovulation induction: Stepwise approach: Initiate therapy with 75 int. units/day for up to 14 days. Increase by 37.5 int. units at weekly intervals until follicular growth or serum estradiol levels indicate an adequate response. The maximum, individualized, daily dose that has been safely used for ovulation induction in patients during clinical trials is 300 int. units.

ART: A starting dose of 150-225 int. units of follitropin beta is recommended for at least the first 4 days of treatment. The dose may be adjusted for the individual patient based upon their ovarian response. Daily maintenance doses ranging from 75-300 int. units for 6-12 days are usually sufficient, although longer treatment may be necessary. Maintenance doses of up to 375-600 int. units may be necessary according to individual response. The maximum daily dose used in clinical studies is 600 int. units. When a sufficient number of follicles of adequate size are present, the final maturation of the follicles is induced by administering hCG at a dose of 5000-10,000 int. units. Oocyte retrieval is performed 34-36 hours later. Withhold hCG in cases where the ovaries are abnormally enlarged on the last day of follitropin beta therapy.

Male: S.C.: Spermatogenesis induction: **Note:** Begin therapy with hCG pretreatment to normalize serum testosterone levels. Once normal levels are reached, follitropin beta therapy is initiated, and must be administered concurrently with hCG treatment.

450 int. units/week given as 225 int. units twice weekly or 150 int. units 3 times/week with hCG; treatment response was noted at up to 12 months

(Continued)

Follitropins *(Continued)*

Administration

Urofollitropin:

Bravelle™: Administer S.C. or I.M.; gently massage site after administration. For S.C. injection, administer on lower abdomen; thigh is not recommended unless abdomen cannot be used. For I.M. injection, administer in upper quadrant of buttock near hip.

Fertinex®: Administer S.C.

Follitropin alpha: Gonal-F®: Administer S.C.

Follitropin beta: Follistim®: Administer S.C. or I.M. to female patients; administer S.C. only to males. The most convenient sites for S.C. injection are either in the abdomen around the navel or in the upper thigh. The best site for I.M. injection is the upper outer quadrant of the buttock muscle.

Monitoring Parameters Monitor sufficient follicular maturation. This may be directly estimated by sonographic visualization of the ovaries and endometrial lining or measuring serum estradiol levels. The combination of both ultrasonography and measurement of estradiol levels is useful for monitoring for the growth and development of follicles and timing hCG administration.

The clinical evaluation of estrogenic activity (changes in vaginal cytology and changes in appearance and volume of cervical mucus) provides an indirect estimate of the estrogenic effect upon the target organs and, therefore, it should only be used adjunctively with more direct estimates of follicular development (ultrasonography and serum estradiol determinations).

The clinical confirmation of ovulation is obtained by direct and indirect indices of progesterone production. The indices most generally used are: rise in basal body temperature, increase in serum progesterone, and menstruation (unless the shift in basal body temperature.

Spermatogenesis: Monitor serum testosterone levels, sperm count

Patient Information Discontinue immediately if possibility of pregnancy. Prior to therapy, inform patients of the following: Duration of treatment and monitoring required; possible adverse reactions; risk of multiple births.

Dosage Forms INJ, powder for reconstitution: Follitropin alfa [rDNA origin, single-dose ampul] (Gonal-F®): 75 int. units, 150 int. units; Follitropin beta [rDNA origin] (Follistim®): 75 int. units; Urofollitropin [urine derived]: (Bravelle™): 75 int. units; (Fertinex® [DSC]): 75 int. units, 150 int. units

♦ **Foltx**® *see Folic Acid, Cyanocobalamin, and Pyridoxine on page 555*

Fomepizole *(foe ME pi zole)*

U.S. Brand Names Antizol®

Synonyms 4-Methylpyrazole; 4-MP

Therapeutic Category Antidote, Ethylene Glycol Toxicity; Antidote, Methanol Toxicity

Use Orphan drug: Treatment of methanol or ethylene glycol poisoning alone or in combination with hemodialysis

Unlabeled/Investigational Use Known or suspected propylene glycol toxicity

Pregnancy Risk Factor C

Contraindications Documented serious hypersensitivity reaction to fomepizole or other pyrazoles; hypersensitivity to any component of the formulation

Warnings/Precautions Should not be given undiluted or by bolus injection; fomepizole is metabolized in the liver and excreted in the urine, use caution with hepatic or renal impairment; hemodialysis should be used in patients with renal failure, significant or worsening metabolic acidosis, or ethylene glycol/methanol levels ≥50 mg/dL; monitor and manage adverse events of intoxication (respiratory distress syndrome, visual disturbances, hypocalcemia); safety and efficacy in pediatric patients have not been established

Common Adverse Reactions

>10%:

Central nervous system: Headache (14%)

Gastrointestinal: Nausea (11%)

1% to 10% (≤3% unless otherwise noted):

Cardiovascular: Bradycardia, facial flush, hypotension, phlebosclerosis, shock, tachycardia

Central nervous system: Dizziness (6%), increased drowsiness (6%), agitation, anxiety, lightheadedness, seizure, vertigo

Dermatologic: Rash

Gastrointestinal: Bad/metallic taste (6%), abdominal pain, decreased appetite, diarrhea, heartburn, vomiting

Hematologic: Anemia, disseminated intravascular coagulation, eosinophilia, lymphangitis

Hepatic: Increased liver function tests

Local: Application site reaction, inflammation at the injection site, pain during injection, phlebitis

Neuromuscular & skeletal: Backache

Ocular: Nystagmus, transient blurred vision, visual disturbances

Renal: Anuria

Respiratory: Abnormal smell, hiccups, pharyngitis

Miscellaneous: Multiorgan failure, speech disturbances

Mechanism of Action Fomepizole competitively inhibits alcohol dehydrogenase, an enzyme which catalyzes the metabolism of ethanol, ethylene glycol, and methanol to their toxic metabolites. Ethylene glycol is metabolized to glycoaldehyde, then oxidized to glycolate, glyoxylate, and oxalate. Glycolate and oxalate are responsible for metabolic acidosis and renal damage. Methanol is metabolized to formaldehyde, then oxidized to formic acid. Formic acid is responsible for metabolic acidosis and visual disturbances.

Pharmacodynamics/Kinetics
Onset of effect: Peak effect: Maximum: 1.5-2 hours
Absorption: Oral: Readily absorbed
Distribution: V_d: 0.6-1.02 L/kg; rapidly into total body water
Protein binding: Negligible
Metabolism: Hepatic to 4-carboxypyrazole (80% to 85% of dose), 4-hydroxymethylpyrazole, and their N-glucuronide conjugates; following multiple doses, induces its own metabolism via CYP oxidases after 30-40 hours
Half-life elimination: Has not been calculated; varies with dose
Excretion: Urine (1% to 3.5% as unchanged drug and metabolites)

Dosage Adults: Ethylene glycol and methanol toxicity: I.V.: A loading dose of 15 mg/kg should be administered, followed by doses of 10 mg/kg every 12 hours for 4 doses, then 15 mg/kg every 12 hours thereafter until ethylene glycol levels have been reduced <20 mg/dL and patient is asymptomatic with normal pH

Dosage adjustment in renal impairment: Fomepizole and its metabolites are excreted in the urine; dialysis should be considered in addition to fomepizole in the case of renal failure, significant or worsening metabolic acidosis, or a measured ethylene glycol level of ≥50 mg/dL. Patients should be dialyzed to correct metabolic abnormalities and to lower the ethylene glycol level <50 mg/dL; fomepizole is dialyzable and the frequency of dosing should be increased to every 4 hours during hemodialysis

Fomepizole is dialyzable and the frequency of dosing should be increased to every 4 hours during hemodialysis

Dose at the beginning of hemodialysis:
If <6 hours since last fomepizole dose: Do not administer dose
If ≥6 hours since last fomepizole dose: Administer next scheduled dose

Dosing during hemodialysis: Dose every 4 hours

Dosing at the time hemodialysis is complete, based on time between last dose and the end of hemodialysis:
<1 hour: Do not administer dose at the end of hemodialysis
1-3 hours: Administer 1/2 of next scheduled dose
>3 hours: Administer next scheduled dose

Maintenance dose when off hemodialysis: Give next scheduled dose 12 hours from last dose administered.

Dosage adjustment in hepatic impairment: Fomepizole is metabolized in the liver; specific dosage adjustments have not been determined in patients with hepatic impairment

Administration The appropriate dose of fomepizole should be drawn from the vial with a syringe and injected into at least 100 mL of sterile 0.9% sodium chloride injection or dextrose 5% injection. All doses should be administered as a slow intravenous infusion (IVPB) over 30 minutes.

Monitoring Parameters Fomepizole plasma levels should be monitored; response to fomepizole; monitor plasma/urinary ethylene glycol or methanol levels, plasma oxalate (ethylene glycol), plasma/urinary osmolality, renal/hepatic function, serum electrolytes, arterial blood gases; anion and osmolar gaps, resolution of clinical signs and symptoms of ethylene glycol or methanol intoxication

Reference Range
Fomepizole: Concentrations 100-300 μmol/L (8.2-24.6 mg/L) should result in enzyme inhibition of alcohol dehydrogenase
Ethylene glycol: Lethal dose is ~1.4 mL/kg
Methanol: Lethal dose is ~1-2 mL/kg

Patient Information This medication is given to treat antifreeze or windshield wiper fluid ingestion. It can only be given by injection. If not treated, serious side effects will occur from ingesting these agents including kidney and/or eye damage, seizures, coma, and possibly death. The most common side effects from this medicine are headache and nausea. Notify prescriber if pregnant or breast-feeding.

Dosage Forms INJ, solution [preservative free]: 1 g/mL (1.5 mL)

Fomivirsen (foe MI vir sen)

U.S. Brand Names Vitravene™
Synonyms Fomivirsen Sodium
Therapeutic Category Antiviral Agent; Antiviral Agent, Ophthalmic
Use Local treatment of cytomegalovirus (CMV) retinitis in patients with acquired immunodeficiency syndrome who are intolerant or insufficiently responsive to other treatments for CMV retinitis or when other treatments for CMV retinitis are contraindicated
Contraindications Hypersensitivity to fomivirsen or any component
Warnings/Precautions For ophthalmic use via intravitreal injection only. Uveitis occurs frequently, particularly during induction dosing. Do not use in patients who have received intravenous or intravitreal cidofovir within 2-4 weeks (risk of exaggerated inflammation is increased). Patients should be monitored for CMV disease in the contralateral eye and/or extraocular disease. Commonly increases intraocular pressure - monitoring is recommended.
Common Adverse Reactions
5% to 10%:
Central nervous system: Fever, headache
Gastrointestinal: Abdominal pain, diarrhea, nausea, vomiting
(Continued)

Fomivirsen *(Continued)*

Hematologic: Anemia

Neuromuscular & skeletal: Asthenia

Ocular: Uveitis, abnormal vision, anterior chamber inflammation, blurred vision, cataract, conjunctival hemorrhage, decreased visual acuity, loss of color vision, eye pain, increased intraocular pressure, photophobia, retinal detachment, retinal edema, retinal hemorrhage, retinal pigment changes, vitreitis

Respiratory: Pneumonia, sinusitis

Miscellaneous: Systemic CMV, sepsis, infection

2% to 5%:

Cardiovascular: Chest pain

Central nervous system: Confusion, depression, dizziness, neuropathy, pain

Endocrine & metabolic: Dehydration

Gastrointestinal: Abnormal LFTs, pancreatitis, anorexia, weight loss

Hematologic: Thrombocytopenia, lymphoma

Neuromuscular & skeletal: Back pain, cachexia

Ocular: Application site reaction, conjunctival hyperemia, conjunctivitis, corneal edema, decreased peripheral vision, eye irritation, keratic precipitates, optic neuritis, photopsia, retinal vascular disease, visual field defect, vitreous hemorrhage, vitreous opacity

Renal: Kidney failure

Respiratory: Bronchitis, dyspnea, cough

Miscellaneous: Allergic reaction, flu-like syndrome, diaphoresis (increased)

Mechanism of Action Inhibits synthesis of viral protein by binding to mRNA which blocks replication of cytomegalovirus through an antisense mechanism

Pharmacodynamics/Kinetics Pharmacokinetic studies have not been conducted in humans. In animal models, the drug is cleared from the eye after 7-10 days. It is metabolized by sequential nucleotide removal, with a small amount of the radioactivity from a dose appearing in the urine.

Dosage Adults: Intravitreal injection: Induction: 330 mcg (0.05 mL) every other week for 2 doses, followed by maintenance dose of 330 mcg (0.05 mL) every 4 weeks

If progression occurs during maintenance, a repeat of the induction regimen may be attempted to establish resumed control. Unacceptable inflammation during therapy may be managed by temporary interruption, provided response has been established. Topical corticosteroids have been used to reduce inflammation.

Administration Administered by intravitreal injection following application of standard topical and/or local anesthetics and antibiotics.

Monitoring Parameters Immediately after injection, light perception and optic nerve head perfusion should be monitored. Anterior chamber paracentesis may be necessary if perfusion is not complete within 7-10 minutes after injection. Subsequent patient evaluation should include monitoring for contralateral CMV infection or extraocular CMV disease, and intraocular pressure prior to each injection.

Dosage Forms INJ, solution, intravitreal: 6.6 mg/mL (0.25 mL)

♦ **Fomivirsen Sodium** *see* Fomivirsen *on page 559*

Fondaparinux *(fon da PARE i nuks)*

Related Information

Anticoagulants, Injectable *on page 1357*

U.S. Brand Names Arixtra®

Synonyms Fondaparinux Sodium

Therapeutic Category Anticoagulant, Polysaccharide; Factor Xa Inhibitor, Selective

Use Prophylaxis of deep vein thrombosis (DVT) in patients undergoing surgery for hip replacement, knee replacement, or hip fracture surgery (including extended prophylaxis following hip fracture surgery)

Unlabeled/Investigational Use Treatment of DVT

Pregnancy Risk Factor B

Contraindications Hypersensitivity to fondaparinux or any component of the formulation; severe renal impairment (Cl_{cr} <30 mL/minute); body weight <50 kg; active major bleeding; bacterial endocarditis; thrombocytopenia associated with a positive *in vitro* test for antiplatelet antibody in the presence of fondaparinux

Warnings/Precautions Patients with recent or anticipated neuraxial anesthesia (epidural or spinal anesthesia) are at risk of spinal or epidural hematoma and subsequent paralysis. Not to be used interchangeably (unit-for-unit) with heparin, low molecular weight heparins (LMWHs), or heparinoids. Use caution in patients with moderate renal dysfunction (Cl_{cr} 30-50 mL/minute). Discontinue if severe dysfunction or labile function develops.

Use caution in congenital or acquired bleeding disorders; active ulcerative or angiodysplastic gastrointestinal disease; hemorrhagic stroke; shortly after brain, spinal, or ophthalmologic surgery; or in patients taking platelet inhibitors. Risk of major bleeding may be increased if initial dose is administered earlier then recommended (initiation recommended at 6-8 hours following surgery). Discontinue agents that may enhance the risk of hemorrhage if possible. If thrombocytopenia occurs discontinue fondaparinux. Use caution in the elderly, patients with a history of heparin-induced thrombocytopenia, patients with a bleeding diathesis, uncontrolled hypertension, recent gastrointestinal ulceration, diabetic retinopathy, and hemorrhage. Safety and efficacy in pediatric patients have not been established.

Common Adverse Reactions As with all anticoagulants, bleeding is the major adverse effect. Hemorrhage may occur at any site. Risk appears increased by a number of factors including renal dysfunction, age (>75 years), and weight (<50 kg).

>10%:
  Central nervous system: Fever (14%)
  Gastrointestinal: Nausea (11%)
  Hematologic: Anemia (20%)

1% to 10%:
  Cardiovascular: Edema (9%), hypotension (4%), confusion (3%)
  Central nervous system: Insomnia (5%), dizziness (4%), headache (2%), pain (2%)
  Dermatologic: Rash (8%), purpura (4%), bullous eruption (3%)
  Endocrine & metabolic: Hypokalemia (4%)
  Gastrointestinal: Constipation (9%), vomiting (6%), diarrhea (3%), dyspepsia (2%)
  Genitourinary: Urinary tract infection (4%), urinary retention (3%)
  Hematologic: Moderate thrombocytopenia (50,000-100,000/mm^3: 3%), major bleeding (2% to 3%), minor bleeding (3% to 4%), hematoma (3%); risk of major bleeding increased as high as 5% in patients receiving initial dose <6 hours following surgery
  Hepatic: SGOT increased (2%), SGPT increased (3%)
  Local: Injection site reaction (bleeding, rash, pruritus)
  Miscellaneous: Wound drainage increased (5%)

Drug Interactions
  Increased Effect/Toxicity: Anticoagulants, antiplatelet agents, drotrecogin alfa, NSAIDs, salicylates, and thrombolytic agents may enhance the anticoagulant effect and/or increase the risk of bleeding.

Mechanism of Action Fondaparinux is a synthetic pentasaccharide that causes an antithrombin III-mediated selective inhibition of factor Xa. Neutralization of factor Xa interrupts the blood coagulation cascade and inhibits thrombin formation and thrombus development.

Pharmacodynamics/Kinetics
  Absorption: Rapid and complete
  Distribution: V_d: 7-11 L; mainly in blood
  Protein binding: ≥94% to antithrombin III
  Bioavailability: 100%
  Half-life elimination: 17-21 hours; prolonged with worsening renal impairment
  Time to peak: 2-3 hours
  Excretion: Urine (as unchanged drug)

Dosage S.C.:
  Adults: ≥50 kg: Usual dose: 2.5 mg once daily. **Note:** Initiate dose after hemostasis has been established, 6-8 hours postoperatively.
    Usual duration: 5-9 days (up to 11 days) following hip replacement or knee replacement; extended prophylaxis is recommended following hip fracture surgery (has been tolerated for up to 32 days)
  Elderly: Use caution, elimination may be prolonged; assess renal function before initiating therapy
  Dosage adjustment in renal impairment:
    Cl$_{cr}$ 30-50 mL/minute: Use caution
    Cl$_{cr}$ <30 mL/minute: Contraindicated

Administration Do not administer I.M.; for S.C. administration only. Do not mix with other injections or infusions. Administer according to recommended regimen; early initiation (before 6 hours after surgery) has been associated with increased bleeding.

Monitoring Parameters Periodic monitoring of CBC, serum creatinine, occult blood testing of stools recommended. Antifactor Xa activity of fondaparinux can be measured by the assay if fondaparinux is used as the calibrator. PT and aPTT are insensitive measures of fondaparinux activity.

Patient Information This drug can only be administered by injection. You may have a tendency to bleed easily while taking this drug; brush teeth with soft brush, floss with waxed floss, use electric razor, avoid scissors or sharp knives, and potentially harmful activities. Report unusual bleeding or bruising (bleeding gums, nosebleed, blood in urine, dark stool); any falls or accidents; new joint pain or swelling, dizziness, severe headache, shortness of breath, weakness, fainting or passing out.

Dosage Forms INJ, solution [prefilled syringe]: 2.5 mg/0.5 mL (0.5 mL)

♦ **Fondaparinux Sodium** *see* Fondaparinux *on page 560*

♦ **Foradil® Aerolizer™** *see* Formoterol *on page 561*

Formoterol (for MOH te rol)

Related Information
  Bronchodilators, Comparison of Inhaled Sympathomimetics *on page 1370*

U.S. Brand Names Foradil® Aerolizer™

Synonyms Formoterol Fumarate

Therapeutic Category Beta$_2$-Adrenergic Agonist

Use Maintenance treatment of asthma and prevention of bronchospasm in patients ≥5 years of age with reversible obstructive airway disease, including patients with symptoms of nocturnal asthma, who require regular treatment with inhaled, short-acting beta$_2$ agonists; maintenance treatment of bronchoconstriction in patients with COPD; prevention of exercise-induced bronchospasm in patients ≥5 years of age

Pregnancy Risk Factor C

(Continued)

Formoterol *(Continued)*

Contraindications Hypersensitivity to adrenergic amines, formoterol, or any component of the formulation; need for acute bronchodilation

Warnings/Precautions Formoterol is not meant to relieve acute asthmatic symptoms. Acute episodes should be treated with short-acting beta$_2$ agonist. Optimize anti-inflammatory treatment before initiating maintenance treatment with formoterol. Do not use as a component of chronic therapy without an anti-inflammatory agent. Patient must be instructed to seek medical attention in cases where acute symptoms are not relieved by short-acting beta-agonist (**not** formoterol) or a previous level of response is diminished. Treatment must not be delayed.

Use caution in patients with cardiovascular disease (arrhythmia or hypertension or CHF), convulsive disorders, diabetes, glaucoma, hyperthyroidism, or hypokalemia. Beta agonists may cause elevation in blood pressure, heart rate, and result in CNS stimulation/excitation. Beta$_2$ agonists may increase risk of arrhythmia, increase serum glucose, or decrease serum potassium.

Do not exceed recommended dose; serious adverse events including fatalities, have been associated with excessive use of inhaled sympathomimetics. Rarely, paradoxical broncho-spasm may occur with use of inhaled bronchodilating agents; this should be distinguished from inadequate response. Safety and efficacy have not been established in children <5 years of age.

Common Adverse Reactions Children are more likely to have infection, inflammation, abdominal pain, nausea, and dyspepsia.

>10%:
Endocrine & metabolic: Serum glucose increased, serum potassium decreased
Miscellaneous: Viral infection (17%)
1% to 10%:
Cardiovascular: Chest pain (2%)
Central nervous system: Tremor (2%), dizziness (2%), insomnia (2%), dysphonia (1%)
Dermatologic: Rash (1%)
Respiratory: Bronchitis (5%), infection (3%), dyspnea (2%), tonsillitis (1%)

Drug Interactions
Cytochrome P450 Effect: Substrate (minor) of CYP2A6, 2C8/9, 2C19, 2D6
Increased Effect/Toxicity: Adrenergic agonists, antidepressants (tricyclic), beta-blockers, corticosteroids, diuretics, drugs that prolong QT$_c$ interval, MAO inhibitors, theophylline derivatives

Mechanism of Action Relaxes bronchial smooth muscle by selective action on beta$_2$ receptors with little effect on heart rate. Formoterol has a long-acting effect.

Pharmacodynamics/Kinetics
Duration: Improvement in FEV$_1$ observed for 12 hours in most patients
Absorption: Rapidly into plasma
Protein binding: 61% to 64% *in vitro* at higher concentrations than achieved with usual dosing
Metabolism: Hepatic via direct glucuronidation and O-demethylation; CYP2D6, CYP2C8/9, CYP2C19, CYP2A6 involved in O-demethylation
Half-life elimination: ~10-14 hours
Time to peak: Maximum improvement in FEV$_1$ in 1-3 hours
Excretion:
Children 5-12 years: Urine (7% to 9% as direct glucuronide metabolites, 6% as unchanged drug)
Adults: Urine (15% to 18% as direct glucuronide metabolites, 10% as unchanged drug)

Dosage Inhalation:
Children ≥5 years and Adults:
Asthma maintenance: 12 mcg capsule every 12 hours
Exercise-induced bronchospasm: 12 mcg capsule at least 15 minutes before exercise on an "as needed" basis; additional doses should not be used for another 12 hours. **Note:** If already using for asthma maintenance then should not use additional doses for exercise-induced bronchospasm.
Adults: Maintenance treatment for COPD: 12 mcg capsule every 12 hours
Elderly: No specific dosing recommendations

Dosage adjustment in renal impairment: Not studied
Dosage adjustment in hepatic impairment: Not studied

Administration Remove capsule from foil blister **immediately** before use. Place capsule in the capsule-chamber in the base of the Aerolizer™ Inhaler. Must only use the Aerolizer™ Inhaler. Press both buttons **once only** and then release. Keep inhaler in a level, horizontal position. Exhale fully. Do not exhale into inhaler. Tilt head slightly back and inhale (rapidly, steadily, and deeply). Hold breath as long as possible. If any powder remains in capsule, exhale and inhale again. Repeat until capsule is empty. Throw away empty capsule; do not leave in inhaler. Do not use a spacer with the Aerolizer™ Inhaler. Always keep capsules and inhaler dry.

Monitoring Parameters FEV$_1$, peak flow, and/or other pulmonary function tests; blood pressure, heart rate; CNS stimulation; serum glucose, serum potassium

Patient Information Do not swallow this capsule. You will put the capsule in the Aerolizer™ Inhaler and inhale the contents of the capsule into your lungs. Only this inhaler can be used for this medicine. Do not use this inhaler to take any other medicines. Check inhaler use with prescriber at each visit. Using the inhaler the right way is very important. Do not use a space with this inhaler. Never wash inhaler; always keep it dry. Do not use more than 2 times per day. Separate doses by about 12 hours. Wear medical alert identification for asthma. To prevent exercise-induced wheezing, take at least 15 minutes before exercise. Do not take another dose for at least 12 hours. Common side effects include shakiness, fast heartbeats, headache, muscle cramps, pain, nervousness, and irritation of the mouth or throat. Notify prescriber if asthma is worsening, peak flow measurements decreasing, short-acting bronchodilator not working as well, chest pain or pressure, any rash, no improvement or feeling worse.

Dosage Forms POWDER, oral inhalation [capsule]: 12 mcg (12s, 60s)

- ◆ **Formoterol Fumarate** *see* Formoterol *on page 561*
- ◆ **Formulation R™ [OTC]** *see* Phenylephrine *on page 993*
- ◆ **5-Formyl Tetrahydrofolate** *see* Leucovorin *on page 723*
- ◆ **Fortaz®** *see* Ceftazidime *on page 241*
- ◆ **Forteo™** *see* Teriparatide *on page 1200*
- ◆ **Fortovase®** *see* Saquinavir *on page 1123*
- ◆ **Fosamax®** *see* Alendronate *on page 52*

Fosamprenavir (FOS am pren a veer)

U.S. Brand Names Lexiva™

Synonyms Fosamprenavir Calcium; GW433908G

Therapeutic Category Antiretroviral Agent, Protease Inhibitor

Use Treatment of HIV infections in combination with at least two other antiretroviral agents

Pregnancy Risk Factor C

Contraindications Hypersensitivity to amprenavir or any component of the formulation; concurrent therapy with cisapride, ergot derivatives, midazolam, pimozide, and triazolam; severe previous allergic reaction to sulfonamides

Warnings/Precautions Because of hepatic metabolism and effect on cytochrome P450 enzymes, amprenavir should be used with caution in combination with other agents metabolized by this system (see Contraindications and Drug Interactions). Avoid concurrent administration of lovastatin or simvastatin (may increase the risk of rhabdomyolysis). Avoid use of hormonal contraceptives, rifampin, and/or St John's wort (may lead to loss of virologic response and/or resistance). Use with caution in patients with diabetes mellitus, sulfonamide allergy, hepatic impairment, or hemophilia. Redistribution of fat may occur (eg, buffalo hump, peripheral wasting, cushingoid appearance). Dosage adjustment is required for combination therapies (ritonavir and/or efavirenz); in addition, the risk of hyperlipidemia may be increased during concurrent therapy. Discontinue therapy in severe or dermatologic reactions or when a moderate rash is accompanied by systemic symptoms.

Common Adverse Reactions

>10%:
  Central nervous system: Headache (19% to 21%), fatigue (10% to 18%)
  Dermatologic: Rash (17% to 35%; moderate to severe reactions 3% to 8%)
  Gastrointestinal: Nausea (37% to 39%), diarrhea (34% to 52%), vomiting (16% to 20%), abdominal pain (5% to 11%)
1% to 10%:
  Central nervous system: Depression (8%), fatigue, headache, paresthesia
  Dermatologic: Pruritus (3% to 8%)
  Endocrine & metabolic: Hypertriglyceridemia (0% to 11%), serum lipase increased (6% to 8%), hyperglycemia (<1% to 2%)
  Hematologic: Neutropenia (3%)
  Hepatic: Increased transaminases (4% to 8%)
  Miscellaneous: Perioral tingling/numbness (2% to 10%)

Drug Interactions

Cytochrome P450 Effect: As amprenavir: **Substrate** of CYP2C8/9 (minor), 3A4 (major); **Inhibits** CYP2C19 (weak), 3A4 (strong)

Increased Effect/Toxicity: Concurrent use of cisapride is contraindicated. Serum concentrations/effect of many benzodiazepines may be increased; concurrent use of midazolam or triazolam is contraindicated. Concurrent use of ergot alkaloids (dihydroergotamine, ergotamine, ergonovine, methylergonovine) with amprenavir is also contraindicated (may cause vasospasm and peripheral ischemia). Serum concentrations of amiodarone, bepridil, lidocaine, quinidine and other antiarrhythmics may be increased, potentially leading to toxicity; when amprenavir is coadministered with ritonavir, flecainide and propafenone are contraindicated.

HMG-CoA reductase inhibitors serum concentrations may be increased by amprenavir, increasing the risk of myopathy/rhabdomyolysis; lovastatin and simvastatin are not recommended; fluvastatin and pravastatin may be safer alternatives. Serum concentrations/effect of some calcium channel blockers, cyclosporine, itraconazole, ketoconazole, rifabutin, tacrolimus, tricyclic antidepressants may be increased. May increase warfarin's effects, monitor INR. Sildenafil and/or vardenafil serum concentrations may be increased by amprenavir. When used concurrently with sildenafil, do not exceed a maximum sildenafil dose of 25 mg in a 48-hour period. When used concurrently with vardenafil, do not exceed vardenafil dose of 2.5 mg in a 24-hour period (2.5 mg in a 72-hour period if used with ritonavir). Concurrent therapy with ritonavir may result in increased serum concentrations: dosage adjustment is recommended. Clarithromycin, indinavir, nelfinavir may increase serum concentrations of amprenavir.

Decreased Effect: Enzyme-inducing agents (rifampin, phenobarbital, phenytoin) may decrease serum concentrations/effect of amprenavir; rifampin is not recommended. Serum concentrations of oral contraceptives may be altered; use alternative (nonhormonal) forms of contraception. Dexamethasone may decrease the therapeutic effect of amprenavir. Serum concentrations of delavirdine may be decreased; may lead to loss of virologic

(Continued)

Fosamprenavir *(Continued)*

response and possible resistance to delavirdine; concomitant use is not recommended. Efavirenz and nevirapine may decrease serum concentrations of amprenavir (dosing for combinations not established). Avoid St John's wort (may lead to subtherapeutic concentrations of amprenavir). Effect of amprenavir may be diminished when administered with methadone (consider alternative antiretroviral); in addition, effect of methadone may be reduced (dosage increase may be required).

Mechanism of Action Fosamprenavir is rapidly and almost completely converted to amprenavir *in vivo*. Amprenavir binds to the protease activity site and inhibits the activity of the enzyme. HIV protease is required for the cleavage of viral polyprotein precursors into individual functional proteins found in infectious HIV. Inhibition prevents cleavage of these polyproteins, resulting in the formation of immature, noninfectious viral particles.

Pharmacodynamics/Kinetics

Absorption: 63%

Bioavailability: Not established; food does not have a significant effect on absorption

Protein-binding: 90%

Half-Life elimination: 7.7 hours

Time to peak, plasma: 1.5-4 hours

Metabolism: Fosamprenavir is rapidly and almost completely converted to amprenavir by cellular phosphatases; amprenavir is hepatically metabolized via CYP isoenzymes (primarily CYP3A4)

Excretion: Feces (75%); urine (14% as metabolites; <1% as unchanged drug)

Dosage Oral: Adults: HIV infection:

Therapy-naive patients: 1400 mg twice daily (without ritonavir)

Dosage adjustments when administered in combination therapy:

Concurrent therapy with ritonavir: Adjustments necessary for both agents:

Fosamprenavir 1400 mg plus ritonavir 200 mg once daily **or**

Fosamprenavir 700 mg plus ritonavir 100 mg twice daily

Concurrent therapy with efavirenz and ritonavir: Fosamprenavir 1400 mg daily plus ritonavir 300 mg once daily; no dosage adjustment recommended for twice-daily regimen

Protease inhibitor-experienced patients: Fosamprenavir 700 mg plus ritonavir 100 mg twice daily. **Note:** Once-daily administration is not recommended in protease inhibitor-experienced patients.

Dosage adjustment in renal impairment: No dosage adjustment required.

Dosage adjustment in hepatic impairment:

Mild-to-moderate impairment (Child-Pugh score 5-8): Reduce dosage of fosamprenavir to 700 mg twice daily (without concurrent ritonavir)

Severe impairment: Use is not recommended

Note: No recommendations are available for dosage adjustment in patients receiving ritonavir and fosamprenavir.

Dosage Forms TAB, as calcium: 700 mg

♦ **Fosamprenavir Calcium** *see* Fosamprenavir *on page 563*

Foscarnet *(fos KAR net)*

U.S. Brand Names Foscavir®

Synonyms PFA; Phosphonoformate; Phosphonoformic Acid

Therapeutic Category Antiviral Agent; Antiviral Agent, Parenteral

Use

Treatment of herpes virus infections suspected to be caused by acyclovir-resistant (HSV, VZV) or ganciclovir-resistant (CMV) strains; this occurs almost exclusively in immunocompromised persons (eg, with advanced AIDS) who have received prolonged treatment for a herpes virus infection

Treatment of CMV retinitis in persons with AIDS

Unlabeled/Investigational Use Other CMV infections in persons unable to tolerate ganciclovir; may be given in combination with ganciclovir in patients who relapse after monotherapy with either drug

Pregnancy Risk Factor C

Contraindications Hypersensitivity to foscarnet or any component of the formulation; Cl_{cr} <0.4 mL/minute/kg during therapy

Warnings/Precautions Renal impairment occurs to some degree in the majority of patients treated with foscarnet; renal impairment may occur at any time and is usually reversible within 1 week following dose adjustment or discontinuation of therapy, however, several patients have died with renal failure within 4 weeks of stopping foscarnet; therefore, renal function should be closely monitored. Foscarnet is deposited in teeth and bone of young, growing animals; it has adversely affected tooth enamel development in rats; safety and effectiveness in children have not been studied. Imbalance of serum electrolytes or minerals occurs in 6% to 18% of patients (hypocalcemia, low ionized calcium, hypo- or hyperphosphatemia, hypomagnesemia or hypokalemia).

Patients with a low ionized calcium may experience perioral tingling, numbness, paresthesias, tetany, and seizures. Seizures have been experienced by up to 10% of AIDS patients. Risk factors for seizures include a low baseline absolute neutrophil count (ANC), impaired baseline renal function and low total serum calcium. Some patients who have experienced seizures have died, while others have been able to continue or resume foscarnet treatment after their mineral or electrolyte abnormality has been corrected, their underlying disease state treated, or their dose decreased. Foscarnet has been shown to be mutagenic *in vitro* and in mice at very high doses. Information on the use of foscarnet is lacking in the elderly; dose adjustments and proper monitoring must be performed because of the decreased renal function common in older patients.

Common Adverse Reactions
>10%:
Central nervous system: Fever (65%), headache (26%), seizures (10%)
Gastrointestinal: Nausea (47%), diarrhea (30%), vomiting
Hematologic: Anemia (33%)
Renal: Abnormal renal function/decreased creatinine clearance (27%)
1% to 10%:
Central nervous system: Fatigue, malaise, dizziness, hypoesthesia, depression/confusion/anxiety (≥5%)
Dermatologic: Rash
Endocrine & metabolic: Electrolyte imbalance (especially potassium, calcium, magnesium, and phosphorus)
Gastrointestinal: Anorexia
Hematologic: Granulocytopenia, leukopenia (≥5%), thrombocytopenia, thrombosis
Local: Injection site pain
Neuromuscular & skeletal: Paresthesia, involuntary muscle contractions, rigors, neuropathy (peripheral), weakness
Ocular: Vision abnormalities
Respiratory: Coughing, dyspnea (≥5%)
Miscellaneous: Sepsis, diaphoresis (increased)

Drug Interactions
Increased Effect/Toxicity: Concurrent use with ciprofloxacin (or other fluoroquinolone) increases seizure potential. Acute renal failure (reversible) has been reported with cyclosporine due most likely to a synergistic toxic effect. Nephrotoxic drugs (amphotericin B, I.V. pentamidine, aminoglycosides, etc) should be avoided, if possible, to minimize additive renal risk with foscarnet. Concurrent use of pentamidine also increases the potential for hypocalcemia. Protease inhibitors (ritonavir, saquinavir) have been associated with an increased risk of renal impairment during concurrent use of foscarnet

Mechanism of Action Pyrophosphate analogue which acts as a noncompetitive inhibitor of many viral RNA and DNA polymerases as well as HIV reverse transcriptase. Similar to ganciclovir, foscarnet is a virostatic agent. Foscarnet does not require activation by thymidine kinase.

Pharmacodynamics/Kinetics
Distribution: Up to 28% of cumulative I.V. dose may be deposited in bone
Metabolism: Biotransformation does not occur
Half-life elimination: ~3 hours
Excretion: Urine (≤28% as unchanged drug)

Dosage
CMV retinitis: I.V.:
Induction treatment: 60 mg/kg/dose every 8 hours **or** 100 mg/kg every 12 hours for 14-21 days
Maintenance therapy: 90-120 mg/kg/day as a single infusion
Acyclovir-resistant HSV induction treatment: I.V.: 40 mg/kg/dose every 8-12 hours for 14-21 days

Dosage adjustment in renal impairment:
Induction and maintenance dosing schedules based on creatinine clearance (mL/minute/kg): See tables below and on next page.

Hemodialysis:
Foscarnet is highly removed by hemodialysis (30% in 4 hours HD)
Doses of 50 mg/kg/dose posthemodialysis have been found to produce similar serum concentrations as doses of 90 mg/kg twice daily in patients with normal renal function
Doses of 60-90 mg/kg/dose loading dose (posthemodialysis) followed by 45 mg/kg/dose posthemodialysis (3 times/week) with the monitoring of weekly plasma concentrations to maintain peak plasma concentrations in the range of 400-800 μMolar has been recommended by some clinicians
Continuous arteriovenous or venovenous hemodiafiltration effects: Dose as for Cl_{cr} 10-50 mL/minute

Maintenance Dosing of Foscarnet in Patients With Abnormal Renal Function

Cl_{cr} (mL/min/kg)	CMV Equivalent to 90 mg/kg q24h	CMV Equivalent to 120 mg/kg q24h
<0.4	Not recommended	Not recommended
≥0.4-0.5	50 mg/kg every 48 hours	65 mg/kg every 48 hours
>0.5-0.6	60 mg/kg every 48 hours	80 mg/kg every 48 hours
>0.6-0.8	80 mg/kg every 48 hours	105 mg/kg every 48 hours
>0.8-1.0	50 mg/kg every 24 hours	65 mg/kg every 24 hours
>1.0-1.4	70 mg/kg every 24 hours	90 mg/kg every 24 hours
>1.4	90 mg/kg every 24 hours	120 mg/kg every 24 hours

(Continued)

Foscarnet *(Continued)*

Induction Dosing of Foscarnet in Patients With Abnormal Renal Function

Cl_cr (mL/min/kg)	HSV Equivalent to 40 mg/kg q12h	HSV Equivalent to 40 mg/kg q8h	CMV Equivalent to 60 mg/kg q8h	CMV Equivalent to 90 mg/kg q12h
<0.4	Not recommended	Not recommended	Not recommended	Not recommended
≥0.4-0.5	20 mg/kg every 24 hours	35 mg/kg every 24 hours	50 mg/kg every 24 hours	50 mg/kg every 24 hours
>0.5-0.6	25 mg/kg every 24 hours	40 mg/kg every 24 hours	60 mg/kg every 24 hours	60 mg/kg every 24 hours
>0.6-0.8	35 mg/kg every 24 hours	25 mg/kg every 12 hours	40 mg/kg every 12 hours	80 mg/kg every 24 hours
>0.8-1.0	20 mg/kg every 12 hours	35 mg/kg every 12 hours	50 mg/kg every 12 hours	50 mg/kg every 12 hours
>1.0-1.4	30 mg/kg every 12 hours	30 mg/kg every 8 hours	45 mg/kg every 8 hours	70 mg/kg every 12 hours
>1.4	40 mg/kg every 12 hours	40 mg/kg every 8 hours	60 mg/kg every 8 hours	90 mg/kg every 12 hours

Administration Foscarnet is administered by intravenous infusion, using an infusion pump, at a rate not exceeding 1 mg/kg/minute. Undiluted (24 mg/mL) solution can be administered without further dilution when using a central venous catheter for infusion. For peripheral vein administration, the solution **must** be diluted to a final concentration **not to exceed** 12 mg/mL. The recommended dosage, frequency, and rate of infusion should not be exceeded.

Patient Information Close monitoring is important and any symptom of electrolyte abnormalities should be reported immediately; maintain adequate fluid intake and hydration; regular ophthalmic examinations are necessary. Foscarnet is not a cure; disease progression may occur during or following treatment. Report any numbness in the extremities, paresthesias, or perioral tingling.

Dosage Forms INJ, solution: 24 mg/mL (250 mL, 500 mL)

♦ Foscavir® *see Foscarnet on page 564*

Fosfomycin *(fos foe MYE sin)*

Related Information
Antimicrobial Drugs of Choice *on page 1440*

U.S. Brand Names Monurol™

Synonyms Fosfomycin Tromethamine

Therapeutic Category Antibiotic, Miscellaneous

Use A single oral dose in the treatment of uncomplicated urinary tract infections in women due to susceptible strains of *E. coli* and *Enterococcus*; multiple doses have been investigated for complicated urinary tract infections in men; may have an advantage over other agents since it maintains high concentration in the urine for up to 48 hours

Pregnancy Risk Factor B

Common Adverse Reactions >1%:
Central nervous system: Headache
Dermatologic: Rash
Gastrointestinal: Diarrhea (2% to 8%), nausea, vomiting, epigastric discomfort, anorexia

Drug Interactions
Decreased Effect: Antacids or calcium salts may cause precipitate formation and decrease fosfomycin absorption. Increased gastrointestinal motility due to metoclopramide may lower fosfomycin tromethamine serum concentrations and urinary excretion. This drug interaction possibly could be extrapolated to other medications which increase gastrointestinal motility.

Mechanism of Action As a phosphonic acid derivative, fosfomycin inhibits bacterial wall synthesis (bactericidal) by inactivating the enzyme, pyruvyl transferase, which is critical in the synthesis of cell walls by bacteria; the tromethamine salt is preferable to the calcium salt due to its superior absorption

Pharmacodynamics/Kinetics
Absorption: Well absorbed
Distribution: V_d: 2 L/kg; high concentrations in urine; well into other tissues; crosses maximally into CSF with inflamed meninges
Protein binding: <3%
Bioavailability: 34% to 58%
Half-life elimination: 4-8 hours; Cl_{cr} <10 mL/minute: 50 hours
Time to peak, serum: 2 hours
Excretion: Urine (as unchanged drug); high urinary levels (100 mcg/mL) persist for >48 hours

Dosage Adults: Urinary tract infections: Oral:
Female: Single dose of 3 g in 4 oz of water
Male: 3 g once daily for 2-3 days for complicated urinary tract infections
Dosing adjustment in renal impairment: Decrease dose; 80% removed by dialysis, repeat dose after dialysis
Dosing adjustment in hepatic impairment: No dosage decrease needed

Administration Always mix with water before ingesting; do not administer in its dry form; pour contents of envelope into 90-120 mL of water (not hot), stir to dissolve and take immediately

Monitoring Parameters Signs and symptoms of urinary tract infection

Patient Information May be taken with or without food; avoid use of antacids or calcium salts within 4 hours before or 2 hours after taking fosfomycin; report signs of allergy; if symptoms do not improve after 2-3 days, contact your prescriber

Dosage Forms POWDER: 3 g

♦ **Fosfomycin Tromethamine** *see Fosfomycin on page 566*

Fosinopril (foe SIN oh pril)

Related Information

Angiotensin Agents Comparison *on page 1353*

U.S. Brand Names Monopril®

Therapeutic Category Angiotensin-Converting Enzyme (ACE) Inhibitor; Antihypertensive Agent

Use Treatment of hypertension, either alone or in combination with other antihypertensive agents; treatment of congestive heart failure, left ventricular dysfunction after myocardial infarction

Pregnancy Risk Factor C/D (2nd and 3rd trimesters)

Contraindications Hypersensitivity to fosinopril or any component of the formulation; angioedema related to previous treatment with an ACE inhibitor; idiopathic or hereditary angioedema; bilateral renal artery stenosis; pregnancy (2nd and 3rd trimesters)

Warnings/Precautions Anaphylactic reactions can occur. Angioedema can occur at any time during treatment (especially following first dose). Angioedema may involve head and neck (potentially affecting the airway) or the intestine (presenting with abdominal pain). Careful blood pressure monitoring (hypotension can occur especially in volume depleted patients). Dosage adjustment needed in severe renal impairment (Cl_{cr} <10 mL/minute). Use with caution in hypovolemia; collagen vascular diseases; valvular stenosis (particularly aortic stenosis); hyperkalemia; or before, during, or immediately after anesthesia. Avoid rapid dosage escalation which may lead to renal insufficiency. Hypersensitivity reactions may be seen during hemodialysis with high-flux dialysis membranes (eg, AN69). Hyperkalemia may rarely occur. Neutropenia/agranulocytosis with myeloid hyperplasia can rarely occur. If patient has renal impairment, then a baseline WBC with differential and serum creatinine should be evaluated and monitored closely during initial therapy. Use with caution in unilateral renal artery stenosis and pre-existing renal insufficiency.

Common Adverse Reactions Note: Frequency ranges include data from hypertension and heart failure trials. Higher rates of adverse reactions have generally been noted in patients with CHF. However, the frequency of adverse effects associated with placebo is also increased in this population.

>10%: Central nervous system: Dizziness (2% to 12%)

1% to 10%:

Cardiovascular: Orthostatic hypotension (1% to 2%), palpitation (1%)

Central nervous system: Dizziness (1% to 2%; up to 12% in CHF patients), headache (3%), weakness (1%), fatigue (1% to 2%)

Endocrine & metabolic: Hyperkalemia (2.6%)

Gastrointestinal: Diarrhea (2%), nausea/vomiting (1.2% to 2.2%)

Hepatic: Increased transaminases

Neuromuscular & skeletal: Musculoskeletal pain (<1% to 3%), noncardiac chest pain (<1% to 2%)

Renal: Increased serum creatinine, worsening of renal function (in patients with bilateral renal artery stenosis or hypovolemia)

Respiratory: Cough (2% to 10%)

Miscellaneous: Upper respiratory infection (2%)

>1% but ≤ frequency in patients receiving placebo: Sexual dysfunction, fever, flu-like syndrome, dyspnea, rash, headache, insomnia

Other events reported with ACE inhibitors: Neutropenia, agranulocytosis, eosinophilic pneumonitis, cardiac arrest, pancytopenia, hemolytic anemia, anemia, aplastic anemia, thrombocytopenia, acute renal failure, hepatic failure, jaundice, symptomatic hyponatremia, bullous pemphigus, exfoliative dermatitis, Stevens-Johnson syndrome. In addition, a syndrome which may include fever, myalgia, arthralgia, interstitial nephritis, vasculitis, rash, eosinophilia and positive ANA, and elevated ESR has been reported for other ACE inhibitors.

Drug Interactions

Increased Effect/Toxicity: Potassium supplements, co-trimoxazole (high dose), angiotensin II receptor antagonists (candesartan, losartan, irbesartan, etc), or potassium-sparing diuretics (amiloride, spironolactone, triamterene) may result in elevated serum potassium levels when combined with fosinopril. ACE inhibitor effects may be increased by phenothiazines or probenecid (increases levels of captopril). ACE inhibitors may increase serum concentrations/effects of digoxin, lithium, and sulfonlyureas.

Diuretics have additive hypotensive effects with ACE inhibitors, and hypovolemia increases the potential for adverse renal effects of ACE inhibitors. In patients with compromised renal function, coadministration with NSAIDs may result in further deterioration of renal function. Allopurinol and ACE inhibitors may cause a higher risk of hypersensitivity reaction when taken concurrently.

Decreased Effect: Aspirin (high dose) may reduce the therapeutic effects of ACE inhibitors; at low dosages this does not appear to be significant. Rifampin may decrease the effect of ACE inhibitors. Antacids may decrease the bioavailability of ACE inhibitors (may be more (Continued)

Fosinopril *(Continued)*

likely to occur with captopril); separate administration times by 1-2 hours. NSAIDs, specifically indomethacin, may reduce the hypotensive effects of ACE inhibitors. More likely to occur in low renin or volume dependent hypertensive patients.

Mechanism of Action Competitive inhibitor of angiotensin-converting enzyme (ACE); prevents conversion of angiotensin I to angiotensin II, a potent vasoconstrictor; results in lower levels of angiotensin II which causes an increase in plasma renin activity and a reduction in aldosterone secretion; a CNS mechanism may also be involved in hypotensive effect as angiotensin II increases adrenergic outflow from CNS; vasoactive kallikreins may be decreased in conversion to active hormones by ACE inhibitors, thus reducing blood pressure

Pharmacodynamics/Kinetics

Onset of action: 1 hour

Duration: 24 hours

Absorption: 36%

Protein binding: 95%

Metabolism: Prodrug, hydrolyzed to its active metabolite fosinoprilat by intestinal wall and hepatic esterases

Bioavailability: 36%

Half-life elimination, serum (fosinoprilat): 12 hours

Time to peak, serum: ~3 hours

Excretion: Urine and feces (as fosinoprilat and other metabolites in roughly equal proportions, 45% to 50%)

Dosage Oral:

Children >50 kg: Hypertension: Initial: 5-10 mg once daily

Adults:

Hypertension: Initial: 10 mg/day; most patients are maintained on 20-40 mg/day. May need to divide the dose into two if trough effect is inadequate; discontinue the diuretic, if possible 2-3 days before initiation of therapy; resume diuretic therapy carefully, if needed.

Heart failure: Initial: 10 mg/day (5 mg if renal dysfunction present) and increase, as needed, to a maximum of 40 mg once daily over several weeks; usual dose: 20-40 mg/day. If hypotension, orthostasis, or azotemia occur during titration, consider decreasing concomitant diuretic dose, if any.

Dosing adjustment/comments in renal impairment: None needed since hepatobiliary elimination compensates adequately diminished renal elimination.

Hemodialysis: Moderately dialyzable (20% to 50%)

Monitoring Parameters Blood pressure (supervise for at least 2 hours after the initial dose or any increase for significant orthostasis); serum potassium, creatinine, BUN, WBC

Patient Information Report vomiting, diarrhea, excessive perspiration, or dehydration; also swelling of face, lips, tongue, or difficulty in breathing or persistent cough; may be taken with meals; do not stop therapy or add a potassium salt replacement without physician's advice

Dosage Forms TAB: 10 mg, 20 mg, 40 mg

Fosphenytoin *(FOS fen i toyn)*

Related Information

Fosphenytoin and Phenytoin, Parenteral Comparison *on page 1375*

U.S. Brand Names Cerebyx®

Synonyms Fosphenytoin Sodium

Therapeutic Category Anticonvulsant, Hydantoin

Use Indicated for short-term parenteral administration when other means of phenytoin administration are unavailable, inappropriate or deemed less advantageous; the safety and effectiveness of fosphenytoin in this use has not been systematically evaluated for more than 5 days; may be used for the control of generalized convulsive status epilepticus and prevention and treatment of seizures occurring during neurosurgery

Pregnancy Risk Factor D

Contraindications Hypersensitivity to phenytoin, other hydantoins, or any component of the formulation; patients with sinus bradycardia, sinoatrial block, second- and third-degree AV block, or Adams-Stokes syndrome; occurrence of rash during treatment (should not be resumed if rash is exfoliative, purpuric, or bullous); not recommended for use in children <4 years of age; pregnancy

Warnings/Precautions Use with caution in patients with severe cardiovascular, hepatic, renal disease or diabetes mellitus; avoid abrupt discontinuation; dosing should be slowly reduced to avoid precipitation of seizures; increased toxicity with nephrotic syndrome patient; may increase frequency of petit mal seizures; use with caution in patients with porphyria, fever, or hypothyroidism

Common Adverse Reactions

Percentage unknown: Pain on injection, sensory paresthesia (long-term treatment), nephrotic syndrome

>10%:

Central nervous system: Dizziness (31%), somnolence (21%), ataxia (11%)

Dermatologic: Pruritus (49%)

Ocular: Nystagmus (44%)

1% to 10%:

Cardiovascular: Hypotension (8%), vasodilation (>1%), tachycardia (2%)

Central nervous system: Stupor (8%), incoordination (4%), paresthesia (4%), choreoathetosis (4%), tremor (3%), agitation (3%)

Gastrointestinal: Nausea (>5%), vomiting (2%)

Ocular: Blurred vision (2%), diplopia (3%)

Drug Interactions

Cytochrome P450 Effect: As phenytoin: **Substrate** of CYP2C8/9 (major), 2C19 (major), 3A4 (minor); **Induces** CYP2B6 (strong), 2C8/9 (strong), 2C19 (strong), 3A4 (strong)

Increased Effect/Toxicity: Selected anticonvulsants (felbamate, gabapentin, and topiramate) have been reported to increase phenytoin levels/effects. In addition, serum phenytoin concentrations may be increased by allopurinol, amiodarone, calcium channel blockers (including diltiazem and nifedipine), cimetidine, disulfiram, methylphenidate, metronidazole, omeprazole, selective serotonin reuptake inhibitors (SSRIs), ticlopidine, tricyclic antidepressants, trazodone, and trimethoprim. Case reports indicate ciprofloxacin may increase or decrease serum phenytoin concentrations.

The sedative effects of phenytoin may be additive with other CNS depressants including ethanol, barbiturates, sedatives, antidepressants, narcotic analgesics, and benzodiazepines. Phenytoin enhances the conversion of primidone to phenobarbital resulting in elevated phenobarbital serum concentrations.

CYP2C8/9 inhibitors may increase the levels/effects of phenytoin. Example inhibitors include delavirdine, fluconazole, gemfibrozil, ketoconazole, nicardipine, NSAIDs, pioglitazone, and sulfonamides. CYP2C19 inhibitors may increase the levels/effects of phenytoin. Example inhibitors include delavirdine, fluconazole, fluvoxamine, gemfibrozil, isoniazid, omeprazole, and ticlopidine.

Concurrent use of acetazolamide with phenytoin may result in an increased risk of osteomalacia. Concurrent use of phenytoin and lithium has resulted in lithium intoxication. Valproic acid (and sulfisoxazole) may displace phenytoin from binding sites; valproic acid may increase, decrease, or have no effect on phenytoin serum concentrations. Phenytoin transiently increased the response to warfarin initially; this is followed by an inhibition of the hypoprothrombinemic response. Phenytoin may enhance the hepatotoxic potential of acetaminophen overdoses. Concurrent use of dopamine and intravenous phenytoin may lead to an increased risk of hypotension.

Decreased Effect: Phenytoin may enhance the metabolism of estrogen or oral contraceptives, decreasing their clinical effect; an alternative method of contraception should be considered. Phenytoin may increase the metabolism of anticonvulsants including barbiturates, carbamazepine, ethosuximide, felbamate, lamotrigine, tiagabine, topiramate, and zonisamide. Valproic acid may increase, decrease, or have no effect on phenytoin serum concentrations.

Phenytoin may decrease serum concentrations of immunosuppressants (including cyclosporine and tacrolimus) and corticosteroids. Phenytoin may also decrease the serum concentrations/effects of some antiarrhythmics (disopyramide, propafenone, and quinidine), calcium channel blockers, HMG-CoA reductase inhibitors, and beta-blockers (except for agents which are not hepatically metabolized). The serum concentrations/effects of hepatically metabolized benzodiazepines, selected antipsychotics (including quetiapine), and tricyclic antidepressants may be reduced by phenytoin. Phenytoin may enhance the metabolism of doxycycline, decreasing its clinical effect; higher dosages may be required. Phenytoin may increase the metabolism of chloramphenicol or itraconazole.

CYP2C8/9 inducers may decrease the levels/effects of phenytoin. Example inducers include carbamazepine, phenobarbital, rifampin, rifapentine, and secobarbital. CYP2C19 inducers may decrease the levels/effects of phenytoin. Example inducers include aminoglutethimide, carbamazepine, phenytoin, and rifampin. Clozapine and vigabatrin may reduce phenytoin serum concentrations. Case reports indicate ciprofloxacin may increase or decrease serum phenytoin concentrations. Dexamethasone may decrease serum phenytoin concentrations. Replacement of folic acid has been reported to increase the metabolism of phenytoin, decreasing its serum concentrations and/or increasing seizures.

Initially, phenytoin increases the response to warfarin; this is followed by a decrease in response to warfarin. Phenytoin may inhibit the anti-Parkinson effect of levodopa. The duration of neuromuscular blockade from neuromuscular-blocking agents may be decreased by phenytoin. Phenytoin may enhance the metabolism of methadone resulting in methadone withdrawal. Phenytoin may decrease serum levels/effects of digitalis glycosides, theophylline, and thyroid hormones.

Several chemotherapeutic agents have been associated with a decrease in serum phenytoin levels; includes cisplatin, bleomycin, carmustine, methotrexate, and vinblastine. Enzyme-inducing anticonvulsant therapy may reduce the effectiveness of some chemotherapy regimens (specifically in ALL). Teniposide and methotrexate may be cleared more rapidly in these patients.

Mechanism of Action Diphosphate ester salt of phenytoin which acts as a water soluble prodrug of phenytoin; after administration, plasma esterases convert fosphenytoin to phosphate, formaldehyde and phenytoin as the active moiety; phenytoin works by stabilizing neuronal membranes and decreasing seizure activity by increasing efflux or decreasing influx of sodium ions across cell membranes in the motor cortex during generation of nerve impulses

Pharmacodynamics/Kinetics

Onset of action: May be more rapid due to more rapid infusion

Protein binding: 95% to 99% to albumin; can displace phenytoin and increase free fraction (up to 30% unbound) during the period required for conversion of fosphenytoin to phenytoin

Metabolism: Converted via hydrolysis to phenytoin

Bioavailability: I.M.: 100%

Half-life elimination: Variable (mean: 12-29 hours); kinetics of phenytoin are saturable

(Continued)

Fosphenytoin *(Continued)*

Time to peak: Conversion to phenytoin: Following I.V. administration conversion half-life elimination is 15 minutes; following I.M. administration, peak phenytoin levels are reached in 3 hours

Excretion: Urine (as inactive metabolites)

See Phenytoin monograph for additional information.

Dosage The dose, concentration in solutions, and infusion rates for fosphenytoin are expressed as phenytoin sodium equivalents; fosphenytoin should always be prescribed and dispensed in phenytoin sodium equivalents

Children 5-18 years: I.V.: A limited number of children have been studied. Seven children received a single I.V. loading dose of fosphenytoin 10-20 mg **PE**/kg for the treatment of acute generalized convulsive status epilepticus (Pellock, 1996). Some centers are using the phenytoin dosing guidelines in children and dosing fosphenytoin using **PE** doses equal to the phenytoin doses (ie, phenytoin 1 mg = fosphenytoin 1 mg **PE**). Further pediatric studies are needed.

Adults:

Status epilepticus: I.V.: Loading dose: Phenytoin equivalent: 15-20 mg/kg I.V. administered at 100-150 mg/minute

Nonemergent loading and maintenance dosing: I.V. or I.M.:

Loading dose: Phenytoin equivalent: 10-20 mg/kg I.V. or I.M. (maximum I.V. rate: 150 mg/minute)

Initial daily maintenance dose: Phenytoin equivalent: 4-6 mg/kg/day I.V. or I.M.

I.M. or I.V. substitution for oral phenytoin therapy: May be substituted for oral phenytoin sodium at the same total daily dose, however, Dilantin® capsules are ~90% bioavailable by the oral route; phenytoin, supplied as fosphenytoin, is 100% bioavailable by both the I.M. and I.V. routes; for this reason, plasma phenytoin concentrations may increase when I.M. or I.V. fosphenytoin is substituted for oral phenytoin sodium therapy; in clinical trials I.M. fosphenytoin was administered as a single daily dose utilizing either 1 or 2 injection sites; some patients may require more frequent dosing

Dosing adjustments in renal/hepatic impairment: Phenytoin clearance may be substantially reduced in cirrhosis and plasma level monitoring with dose adjustment advisable; free phenytoin levels should be monitored closely in patients with renal or hepatic disease or in those with hypoalbuminemia; furthermore, fosphenytoin clearance to phenytoin may be increased without a similar increase in phenytoin in these patients leading to increase frequency and severity of adverse events

Administration Since there is no precipitation problem with fosphenytoin, no I.V. filter is required; I.V. administration rate should not exceed 150 mg/minute

Monitoring Parameters Blood pressure, vital signs (with I.V. use), plasma level monitoring, CBC, liver function tests

Reference Range

Therapeutic: 10-20 µg/mL (SI: 40-79 µmol/L); toxicity is measured clinically, and some patients require levels outside the suggested therapeutic range

Toxic: 30-50 µg/mL (SI: 120-200 µmol/L)

Lethal: >100 µg/mL (SI: >400 µmol/L)

Manifestations of toxicity:

Nystagmus: 20 µg/mL (SI: 79 µmol/L)

Ataxia: 30 µg/mL (SI: 118.9 µmol/L)

Decreased mental status: 40 µg/mL (SI: 159 µmol/L)

Coma: 50 µg/mL (SI: 200 µmol/L)

Peak serum phenytoin level after a 375 mg I.M. fosphenytoin dose in healthy males: 5.7 µg/mL

Peak serum fosphenytoin levels and phenytoin levels after a 1.2 g infusion (I.V.) in healthy subjects over 30 minutes were 129 µg/mL and 17.2 µg/mL respectively

Dosage Forms INJ, solution: 75 mg/mL [equivalent to phenytoin sodium 50 mg/mL] (2 mL, 10 mL)

♦ **Fosphenytoin and Phenytoin, Parenteral Comparison** *see page 1375*

♦ **Fosphenytoin Sodium** *see Fosphenytoin on page 568*

♦ **Fragmin®** *see Dalteparin on page 335*

♦ **Frova®** *see Frovatriptan on page 570*

Frovatriptan *(froe va TRIP tan)*

Related Information

Antimigraine Drugs Comparison *on page 1363*

U.S. Brand Names Frova®

Synonyms Frovatriptan Succinate

Therapeutic Category Antimigraine Agent, Serotonin 5-HT$_{1D}$ Agonist; Serotonin 5-HT$_{1B, 1D}$ Receptor Agonist

Use Acute treatment of migraine with or without aura in adults

Pregnancy Risk Factor C

Contraindications Hypersensitivity to frovatriptan or any component of the formulation; patients with ischemic heart disease or signs or symptoms of ischemic heart disease (including Prinzmetal's angina, angina pectoris, myocardial infarction, silent myocardial ischemia); cerebrovascular syndromes (including strokes, transient ischemic attacks); peripheral vascular syndromes (including ischemic bowel disease); uncontrolled hypertension; use within 24 hours of ergotamine derivatives; use within 24 hours of another 5-HT$_1$ agonist; management of hemiplegic or basilar migraine; prophylactic treatment of migraine; severe hepatic impairment

Warnings/Precautions Not intended for migraine prophylaxis, or treatment of cluster headaches, hemiplegic or basilar migraines. Cardiac events, cerebral/subarachnoid hemorrhage, and stroke have been reported with 5-HT$_1$ agonist administration. May cause vasospastic reactions resulting in colonic, peripheral, or coronary ischemia. Do not give to patients with risk factors for CAD until a cardiovascular evaluation has been performed; if evaluation is satisfactory, the healthcare provider should administer the first dose and cardiovascular status should be periodically evaluated. Significant elevation in blood pressure, including hypertensive crisis, has also been reported on rare occasions in patients using other 5-HT$_{1D}$ agonists with and without a history of hypertension. Use with caution in patients with history of seizure disorder. Safety and efficacy in pediatric patients have not been established

Common Adverse Reactions 1% to 10%:

Cardiovascular: Chest pain (2%), flushing (4%), palpitation (1%)

Central nervous system: Dizziness (8%), fatigue (5%), headache (4%), hot or cold sensation (3%), anxiety (1%), dysesthesia (1%), hypoesthesia (1%), insomnia (1%), pain (1%)

Gastrointestinal: Hyposalivation (3%), dyspepsia (2%), abdominal pain (1%), diarrhea (1%), vomiting (1%)

Neuromuscular & skeletal: Paresthesia (4%), skeletal pain (3%)

Ocular: Visual abnormalities (1%)

Otic: Tinnitus (1%)

Respiratory: Rhinitis (1%), sinusitis (1%)

Miscellaneous: Diaphoresis (1%)

Drug Interactions

Cytochrome P450 Effect: Substrate of CYP1A2 (minor)

Increased Effect/Toxicity: The effects of frovatriptan may be increased by CYP1A2 inhibitors (eg, cimetidine, ciprofloxacin, erythromycin), estrogen derivatives, propranolol. Ergot derivatives may increase the effects of frovatriptan (do not use within 24 hours of each other). SSRIs may exhibit additive toxicity with frovatriptan or other serotonin agonists (eg, antidepressants, dextromethorphan, tramadol) leading to serotonin syndrome.

Decreased Effect: The effects of frovatriptan may be decreased by CYP1A2 inducers (eg, carbamazepine, phenobarbital, phenytoin, ritonavir), ergotamine.

Mechanism of Action Selective agonist for serotonin (5-HT$_{1B}$ and 5-HT$_{1D}$ receptor) in cranial arteries to cause vasoconstriction and reduces sterile inflammation associated with antidromic neuronal transmission correlating with relief of migraine.

Pharmacodynamics/Kinetics

Distribution: Male: 4.2 L/kg; Female: 3.0 L/kg

Protein binding: 15%

Metabolism: Primarily hepatic via CYP1A2

Bioavailability: 20% to 30%

Half-life elimination: 26 hours

Time to peak: 2-4 hours

Excretion: Feces (62%); urine (32%)

Dosage Oral: Adults: Migraine: 2.5 mg; if headache recurs, a second dose may be given if first dose provided some relief and at least 2 hours have elapsed since the first dose (maximum daily dose: 7.5 mg)

Dosage adjustment in renal impairment: No adjustment necessary

Dosage adjustment in hepatic impairment: No adjustment necessary in mild to moderate hepatic impairment; use with caution in severe impairment

Administration Administer with fluids.

Patient Information Take at first sign of migraine attack. This drug is to be used to relieve your migraine, not to prevent or reduce number of attacks. If headache returns or is not fully resolved after first dose, the dose may be repeated after 2 hours. **Do not exceed 7.5 mg (3 tablets) in 24 hours.** Take tablet whole with fluids. **Do not take within 24 hours of any other migraine medication without first consulting prescriber.** You may experience some dizziness (use caution); hot flashes (cool room may help); nausea or vomiting (frequent small meals, frequent mouth care, sucking lozenges or chewing gum may help); or excess sweating (will resolve). Report chest tightness or pain; excessive drowsiness; acute abdominal pain; skin rash or burning sensation; muscle weakness, soreness, or numbness; or respiratory difficulty.

Dosage Forms TAB: 2.5 mg

♦ **Frovatriptan Succinate** *see Frovatriptan on page 570*

♦ **Frusemide** *see Furosemide on page 573*

♦ **FTC** *see Emtricitabine on page 428*

♦ **FU** *see Fluorouracil on page 536*

♦ **5-FU** *see Fluorouracil on page 536*

♦ **Ful-Glo®** *see Fluorescein Sodium on page 534*

Fulvestrant (fool VES trant)

U.S. Brand Names Faslodex®

Synonyms ICI 182,780; Zeneca 182,780; ZM-182,780

Therapeutic Category Antineoplastic Agent, Estrogen Receptor Antagonist

Use Treatment of hormone receptor positive metastatic breast cancer in postmenopausal women with disease progression following antiestrogen therapy.

Unlabeled/Investigational Use Endometriosis; uterine bleeding

(Continued)

Fulvestrant *(Continued)*

Pregnancy Risk Factor D

Contraindications Hypersensitivity to fulvestrant or any component of the formulation; contra-indications to I.M. injections (bleeding diatheses, thrombocytopenia, or therapeutic anticoagulation); pregnancy

Warnings/Precautions Use caution in hepatic impairment.

Common Adverse Reactions

>10%:

Cardiovascular: Vasodilation (18%)

Central nervous system: Pain (19%), headache (15%)

Endocrine & metabolic: Hot flushes (19% to 24%)

Gastrointestinal: Nausea (26%), vomiting (13%), constipation (13%), diarrhea (12%), abdominal pain (12%)

Local: Injection site reaction (11%)

Neuromuscular & skeletal: Weakness (23%), bone pain (16%), back pain (14%)

Respiratory: Pharyngitis (16%), dyspnea (15%)

1% to 10%:

Cardiovascular: Edema (9%), chest pain (7%)

Central nervous system: Dizziness (7%), insomnia (7%), paresthesia (6%), fever (6%), depression (6%), anxiety (5%)

Dermatologic: Rash (7%)

Gastrointestinal: Anorexia (9%), weight gain (1% to 2%)

Genitourinary: Pelvic pain (10%), urinary tract infection (6%), vaginitis (2% to 3%)

Hematologic: Anemia (5%)

Neuromuscular and skeletal: Arthritis (3%)

Respiratory: Cough (10%)

Miscellaneous: Diaphoresis increased (5%)

Drug Interactions

Cytochrome P450 Effect: Substrate of CYP3A4 (major)

Increased Effect/Toxicity: Serum level and/or toxicity of fulvestrant may be increased by CYP3A4 inhibitors; inhibitors include amiodarone, cimetidine, clarithromycin, erythromycin, delavirdine, diltiazem, dirithromycin, disulfiram, fluoxetine, fluvoxamine, grapefruit juice, indinavir, itraconazole, ketoconazole, nefazodone, nevirapine, propoxyphene, quinupristin-dalfopristin, ritonavir, saquinavir, verapamil, zafirlukast, zileuton

Decreased Effect: Serum level of fulvestrant may be increased by enzyme-inducing agents, decreasing its therapeutic effect; potential inducers include phenobarbital, phenytoin, carbamazepine, rifampin, and rifabutin. However, a clinical study with rifampin did not demonstrate an effect on fulvestrant pharmacokinetics.

Mechanism of Action Steroidal compound which competitively binds to estrogen receptors on tumors and other tissue targets, producing a nuclear complex that decreases DNA synthesis and inhibits estrogen effects. Fulvestrant has no estrogen-receptor agonist activity. Causes down-regulation of estrogen receptors and inhibits tumor growth.

Pharmacodynamics/Kinetics

Duration: I.M.: Plasma levels maintained for at least 1 month

Distribution: V_d: 3-5 L/kg

Protein binding: 99%

Metabolism: Hepatic via multiple pathways (CYP3A4 substrate, relative contribution to metabolism unknown)

Bioavailability: Oral: Poor

Half-life elimination: ~40 days

Time to peak, plasma: I.M.: 7-9 days

Excretion: Feces (>90%); urine (<1%)

Dosage I.M.: Adults (postmenopausal women): 250 mg at 1-month intervals

Dosage adjustment in renal impairment: No adjustment required.

Dosage adjustment in hepatic impairment: Use in moderate to severe hepatic impairment has not been evaluated; use caution.

Administration I.M. injection into a relatively large muscle (ie, buttock); do not administer I.V., S.C., or intra-arterially. May be administered as a single 5 mL injection or two concurrent 2.5 mL injections.

Dosage Forms INJ, solution [prefilled syringe]: 50 mg/mL (2.5 mL, 5 mL)

♦ **Fulvicin® P/G** *see* Griseofulvin *on page 602*

♦ **Fulvicin-U/F®** *see* Griseofulvin *on page 602*

♦ **Fungi-Guard [OTC]** *see* Tolnaftate *on page 1241*

♦ **Fungizone®** *see* Amphotericin B (Conventional) *on page 90*

♦ **Fungoid® Tincture [OTC]** *see* Miconazole *on page 834*

♦ **Furadantin®** *see* Nitrofurantoin *on page 908*

♦ **Furamide®** *see* Diloxanide Furoate *on page 380*

Furazolidone *(fyoor a ZOE li done)*

Synonyms Furoxone

Therapeutic Category Antibiotic, Topical; Antibiotic, Miscellaneous; Antiprotozoal

Use Treatment of bacterial or protozoal diarrhea and enteritis caused by susceptible organisms *Giardia lamblia* and *Vibrio cholerae*

Restrictions Not available in U.S.

Pregnancy Risk Factor C

Dosage Oral:
Children >1 month: 5-8 mg/kg/day in 4 divided doses for 7 days, not to exceed 400 mg/day or 8.8 mg/kg/day
Adults: 100 mg 4 times/day for 7 days
Dosage Forms LIQ: 50 mg/15 mL (60 mL, 473 mL). **TAB:** 100 mg

♦ **Furazosin** see Prazosin on page 1030

Furosemide (fyoor OH se mide)
Related Information
Hemodynamic Support, Intravenous on page 1377
Sulfonamide Derivatives on page 1404
U.S. Brand Names Lasix®
Synonyms Frusemide
Therapeutic Category Antihypertensive Agent; Diuretic, Loop
Use Management of edema associated with congestive heart failure and hepatic or renal disease; alone or in combination with antihypertensives in treatment of hypertension
Pregnancy Risk Factor C
Contraindications Hypersensitivity to furosemide, any component, or sulfonylureas; anuria; patients with hepatic coma or in states of severe electrolyte depletion until the condition improves or is corrected
Warnings/Precautions Loop diuretics are potent diuretics; close medical supervision and dose evaluation is required to prevent fluid and electrolyte imbalance; use caution with other nephrotoxic or ototoxic drugs; use caution in patients with known hypersensitivity to sulfonamides or thiazides (due to possible cross-sensitivity; avoid in history of severe reactions).

Chemical similarities are present among sulfonamides, sulfonylureas, carbonic anhydrase inhibitors, thiazides, and loop diuretics (except ethacrynic acid). Use in patients with sulfonylurea allergy is specifically contraindicated in product labeling, however, a risk of cross-reaction exists in patients with allergy to any of these compounds; avoid use when previous reaction has been severe.

Common Adverse Reactions Frequency not defined.
Cardiovascular: Orthostatic hypotension, necrotizing angiitis, thrombophlebitis, chronic aortitis, acute hypotension, sudden death from cardiac arrest (with I.V. or I.M. administration)
Central nervous system: Paresthesias, vertigo, dizziness, lightheadedness, headache, blurred vision, xanthopsia , fever, restlessness
Dermatologic: Exfoliative dermatitis, erythema multiforme, purpura, photosensitivity, urticaria, rash, pruritus, cutaneous vasculitis
Endocrine & metabolic: Hyperglycemia, hyperuricemia, hypokalemia, hypochloremia, metabolic alkalosis, hypocalcemia, hypomagnesemia, gout, hypernatremia
Gastrointestinal: Nausea, vomiting, anorexia, oral and gastric irritation, cramping, diarrhea, constipation, pancreatitis, intrahepatic cholestatic jaundice, ischemia hepatitis
Genitourinary: Urinary bladder spasm, urinary frequency
Hematological: Aplastic anemia (rare), thrombocytopenia, agranulocytosis (rare), hemolytic anemia, leukopenia, anemia, purpura
Neuromuscular & skeletal: Muscle spasm, weakness
Otic: Hearing impairment (reversible or permanent with rapid I.V. or I.M. administration), tinnitus, reversible deafness (with rapid I.V. or I.M. administration)
Renal: Vasculitis, allergic interstitial nephritis, glycosuria, fall in glomerular filtration rate and renal blood flow (due to overdiuresis), transient rise in BUN
Miscellaneous: Anaphylaxis (rare), exacerbate or activate systemic lupus erythematosus

Drug Interactions
Increased Effect/Toxicity: Furosemide-induced hypokalemia may predispose to digoxin toxicity and may increase the risk of arrhythmia with drugs which may prolong QT interval, including type Ia and type III antiarrhythmic agents, cisapride, and some quinolones (sparfloxacin, gatifloxacin, and moxifloxacin). The risk of toxicity from lithium and salicylates (high dose) may be increased by loop diuretics. Hypotensive effects and/or adverse renal effects of ACE inhibitors and NSAIDs are potentiated by furosemide-induced hypovolemia. The effects of peripheral adrenergic-blocking drugs or ganglionic blockers may be increased by furosemide.

Furosemide may increase the risk of ototoxicity with other ototoxic agents (aminoglycosides, cis-platinum), especially in patients with renal dysfunction. Synergistic diuretic effects occur with thiazide-type diuretics. Diuretics tend to be synergistic with other antihypertensive agents, and hypotension may occur.
Decreased Effect: Indomethacin, aspirin, phenobarbital, phenytoin, and NSAIDs may reduce natriuretic and hypotensive effects of furosemide. Colestipol, cholestyramine, and sucralfate may reduce the effect of furosemide; separate administration by 2 hours. Furosemide may antagonize the effect of skeletal muscle relaxants (tubocurarine). Glucose tolerance may be decreased by furosemide, requiring an adjustment in the dose of hypoglycemic agents. Metformin may decrease furosemide concentrations.
Mechanism of Action Inhibits reabsorption of sodium and chloride in the ascending loop of Henle and distal renal tubule, interfering with the chloride-binding cotransport system, thus causing increased excretion of water, sodium, chloride, magnesium, and calcium
Pharmacodynamics/Kinetics
Onset of action: Diuresis: Oral: 30-60 minutes; I.M.: 30 minutes; I.V.: ~5 minutes
Peak effect: Oral: 1-2 hours
Duration: Oral: 6-8 hours; I.V.: 2 hours
(Continued)

Furosemide *(Continued)*

Absorption: Oral: 60% to 67%

Protein binding: >98%

Metabolism: Minimally hepatic

Half-life elimination: Normal renal function: 0.5-1.1 hours; End-stage renal disease: 9 hours

Excretion: Urine (Oral: 50%, I.V.: 80%) within 24 hours; feces (as unchanged drug); nonrenal clearance prolonged in renal impairment

Dosage

Infants and Children:

Oral: 1-2 mg/kg/dose increased in increments of 1 mg/kg/dose with each succeeding dose until a satisfactory effect is achieved to a maximum of 6 mg/kg/dose no more frequently than 6 hours.

I.M., I.V.: 1 mg/kg/dose, increasing by each succeeding dose at 1 mg/kg/dose at intervals of 6-12 hours until a satisfactory response up to 6 mg/kg/dose.

Adults:

Oral: 20-80 mg/dose initially increased in increments of 20-40 mg/dose at intervals of 6-8 hours; usual maintenance dose interval is twice daily or every day; may be titrated up to 600 mg/day with severe edematous states.

I.M., I.V.: 20-40 mg/dose, may be repeated in 1-2 hours as needed and increased by 20 mg/dose until the desired effect has been obtained. Usual dosing interval: 6-12 hours; for acute pulmonary edema, the usual dose is 40 mg I.V. over 1-2 minutes. If not adequate, may increase dose to 80 mg.

Continuous I.V. infusion: Initial I.V. bolus dose of 0.1 mg/kg followed by continuous I.V. infusion doses of 0.1 mg/kg/hour doubled every 2 hours to a maximum of 0.4 mg/kg/hour if urine output is <1 mL/kg/hour have been found to be effective and result in a lower daily requirement of furosemide than with intermittent dosing. Other studies have used a rate of ≤4 mg/minute as a continuous I.V. infusion.

Elderly: Oral, I.M., I.V.: Initial: 20 mg/day; increase slowly to desired response.

Refractory heart failure: Oral, I.V.: Doses up to 8 g/day have been used.

Dosing adjustment/comments in renal impairment: Acute renal failure: High doses (up to 1-3 g/day - oral/I.V.) have been used to initiate desired response; avoid use in oliguric states.

Dialysis: Not removed by hemo- or peritoneal dialysis; supplemental dose is not necessary.

Dosing adjustment/comments in hepatic disease: Diminished natriuretic effect with increased sensitivity to hypokalemia and volume depletion in cirrhosis; monitor effects, particularly with high doses.

Administration I.V. injections should be given slowly over 1-2 minutes; maximum rate of administration for IVPB or infusion: 4 mg/minute; replace parenteral therapy with oral therapy as soon as possible

Monitoring Parameters Monitor weight and I & O daily; blood pressure, serum electrolytes, renal function; in high doses, monitor hearing

Patient Information May be taken with food or milk; rise slowly from a lying or sitting position to minimize dizziness, lightheadedness, or fainting; also use extra care when exercising, standing for long periods of time, and during hot weather; take last dose of day early in the evening to prevent nocturia

Dosage Forms INJ, solution: 10 mg/mL (2 mL, 4 mL, 8 mL, 10 mL). **SOLN, oral:** 10 mg/mL (60 mL, 120 mL); 40 mg/5 mL (5 mL, 500 mL). **TAB** (Lasix®): 20 mg, 40 mg, 80 mg

◆ **Furoxone** *see Furazolidone on page 572*

◆ **Fuzeon**™ *see Enfuvirtide on page 432*

Gabapentin *(GA ba pen tin)*

Related Information

Anticonvulsants by Seizure Type *on page 1358*

Epilepsy *on page 1477*

U.S. Brand Names Neurontin®

Therapeutic Category Anticonvulsant, Miscellaneous

Use Adjunct for treatment of partial seizures with and without secondary generalized seizures in patients >12 years of age with epilepsy; adjunct for treatment of partial seizures in pediatric patients 3-12 years of age; management of post-herpetic neuralgia (PHN) in adults

Unlabeled/Investigational Use Bipolar disorder, social phobia; chronic pain

Pregnancy Risk Factor C

Contraindications Hypersensitivity to gabapentin or any component of the formulation

Warnings/Precautions Avoid abrupt withdrawal; may precipitate seizures; may be associated with a slight incidence (0.6%) of status epilepticus and sudden deaths (0.0038 deaths/patient year); use cautiously in patients with severe renal dysfunction; rat studies demonstrated an association with pancreatic adenocarcinoma in male rats; clinical implication unknown. May cause CNS depression, which may impair physical or mental abilities. Patients must be cautioned about performing tasks which require mental alertness (eg, operating machinery or driving). Effects with other sedative drugs or ethanol may be potentiated. Pediatric patients (3-12 years of age) have shown increased incidence of CNS-related adverse effects, including emotional lability, hostility, thought disorder, and hyperkinesia. Safety and efficacy in children <3 years of age have not been established.

Common Adverse Reactions As reported in patients >12 years of age, unless otherwise noted

>10%:
 Central nervous system: Somnolence (20%), dizziness (17%), ataxia (12%), fatigue (11% in adults)
 Miscellaneous: Viral infection (11% in children 3-12 years)

1% to 10%:
 Cardiovascular: Peripheral edema (2%)
 Central nervous system: Fever (10% in children 3-12 years), hostility (8% in children 3-12 years), somnolence (8% in children 3-12 years), emotional lability (4% to 6% in children 3-12 years), fatigue (3% in children 3-12 years), abnormal thinking (2% in children and adults), amnesia (2%), depression (2%), dizziness (2% in children 3-12 years), dysarthria (2%), nervousness (2%), abnormal coordination (1%), twitching (1%)
 Dermatologic: Pruritus (1%)
 Gastrointestinal: Nausea/vomiting (8% in children 3-12 years), weight gain (3% in adults and children), dyspepsia (2%), dry throat (2%), xerostomia (2%), appetite stimulation (1%), constipation (1%), dental abnormalities (1%)
 Genitourinary: Impotence (1%)
 Hematologic: Leukopenia (1%), decreased WBC (1%)
 Neuromuscular & skeletal: Tremor (7%), hyperkinesia (3% to 5% in children 3-12 years), back pain (2%), myalgia (2%)
 Ocular: Nystagmus (8%), diplopia (6%), blurred vision (4%)
 Respiratory: Rhinitis (4%), bronchitis (3% in children 3-12 years), pharyngitis (3%), coughing (2%), respiratory infection (2% in children 3-12 years)

Drug Interactions
 Increased Effect/Toxicity: Cimetidine may increased gabapentin levels. Gabapentin may increase peak concentrations of norethindrone. Morphine may increase gabapentin serum concentrations.
 Decreased Effect: Gabapentin does not modify plasma concentrations of standard anticonvulsant medications (eg, valproic acid, carbamazepine, phenytoin, or phenobarbital). Antacids reduce the bioavailability of gabapentin by 20%.

Mechanism of Action Exact mechanism of action is not known, but does have properties in common with other anticonvulsants; although structurally related to GABA, it does not interact with GABA receptors

Pharmacodynamics/Kinetics
 Absorption: 50% to 60%
 Distribution: V_d: 0.6-0.8 L/kg
 Protein binding: 0%
 Bioavailability: As gabapentin dose increases, bioavailability decreases; it is absorbed from proximal small bowel into blood by L-amino transport system (which becomes saturated, therefore is a major contributor to lack of proportionality in plasma levels). Interpatient variability exists; standard gabapentin doses may result in different plasma concentrations in individual patients.
  900 mg divided 3 times/day: 60%
  1200 mg divided 3 times/day: 47%
  2400 mg divided 3 times/day: 34%
  3600 mg divided 3 times/day: 33%
  4800 mg divided 3 times/day: 27%
 Half-life elimination: 5-6 hours
 Excretion: Urine (56% to 80%)

Dosage Oral:
 Children: Anticonvulsant:
  3-12 years: Initial: 10-15 mg/kg/day in 3 divided doses; titrate to effective dose over ~3 days; dosages of up to 50 mg/kg/day have been tolerated in clinical studies
   3-4 years: Effective dose: 40 mg/kg/day in 3 divided doses
   ≥5-12 years: Effective dose: 25-35 mg/kg/day in 3 divided doses
   Note: If gabapentin is discontinued or if another anticonvulsant is added to therapy, it should be done slowly over a minimum of 1 week
 Children >12 years and Adults:
  Anticonvulsant: Initial: 300 mg 3 times/day; if necessary the dose may be increased using 300 mg or 400 mg capsules 3 times/day up to 1800 mg/day
   Dosage range: 900-1800 mg administered in 3 divided doses at 8-hour intervals
  Pain (unlabeled use): 300-1800 mg/day given in 3 divided doses has been the most common dosage range
  Bipolar disorder (unlabeled use): 300-3000 mg/day given in 3 divided doses; **Note:** Does not appear to be effective as an adjunctive treatment for bipolar disorder (Pande AC, 2000)
  Adults: Post-herpetic neuralgia: Day 1: 300 mg, Day 2: 300 mg twice daily, Day 3: 300 mg 3 times/day; dose may be titrated as needed for pain relief (range: 1800-3600 mg/day, daily doses >1800 mg do not generally show greater benefit)

 Elderly: Studies in elderly patients have shown a decrease in clearance as age increases. This is most likely due to age-related decreases in renal function; dose reductions may be needed.

 Dosing adjustment in renal impairment: Children ≥12 years and Adults: See table on next page.
Administration Maximum time interval between multiple daily doses should not exceed 12 hours; administer first dose on first day at bedtime to avoid somnolence and dizziness
Monitoring Parameters Monitor serum levels of concomitant anticonvulsant therapy
Reference Range Minimum effective serum concentration may be 2 µg/mL
 (Continued)

Gabapentin (Continued)

Neurontin® Dosing Adjustments in Renal Impairment

Creatinine Clearance (mL/min)	Total Daily Dose Range (mg/day)	Dosage Regimens Based on Renal Function (mg)				
≥60	900-3600	300 tid	400 tid	600 tid	800 tid	1200 tid
>30-59	400-1400	200 bid	300 bid	400 bid	500 bid	700 bid
>15-29	200-700	200 qd	300 qd	400 qd	500 qd	700 qd
15[1]	100-300	100 qd	125 qd	150 qd	200 qd	300 qd
Hemodialysis[2]		Posthemodialysis Supplemental Dose				
		125 mg	150 mg	200 mg	250 mg	350 mg

[1]Cl_{cr} <15 mL/minute: Reduce daily dose in proportion to creatinine clearance.

[2]Supplemental dose administered after each 4 hours of hemodialysis (maintenance doses based on renal function).

Patient Information Take only as prescribed; may cause dizziness, somnolence, and other symptoms and signs of CNS depression; do not operate machinery or drive a car until you have experience with the drug; may be administered without regard to meals. Do not stop making medication abruptly; may lead to an increased seizure activity.

Dosage Forms CAP: 100 mg, 300 mg, 400 mg. **SOLN, oral:** 250 mg/5 mL (480 mL). **TAB:** 600 mg, 800 mg

♦ **Gabitril**® see Tiagabine on page 1224

Galantamine (ga LAN ta meen)
U.S. Brand Names Reminyl®
Synonyms Galantamine Hydrobromide
Therapeutic Category Acetylcholinesterase Inhibitor
Use Treatment of mild to moderate dementia of Alzheimer's disease
Pregnancy Risk Factor B
Contraindications Hypersensitivity to galantamine or any component of the formulation; severe liver dysfunction (Child-Pugh score 10-15); severe renal dysfunction (Cl_{cr} <9 mL/minute)
Warnings/Precautions Use caution in patients with supraventricular conduction delays (without a functional pacemaker in place) or patients taking medicines that slow conduction through SA or AV node. Use caution in peptic ulcer disease(or in patients at risk); seizure disorder; asthma; COPD; mild to moderate liver dysfunction; moderate renal dysfunction. May cause bladder outflow obstruction. May exaggerate neuromuscular blockade effects of succinylcholine and like agents. Safety and efficacy in children have not been established.
Common Adverse Reactions
>10%: Gastrointestinal: Nausea (6% to 24%), vomiting (4% to 13%), diarrhea (6% to 12%)
1% to 10%:
Cardiovascular: Bradycardia (2% to 3%), syncope (0.4% to 2.2%: dose-related), chest pain (≥1%)
Central nervous system: Dizziness (9%), headache (8%), depression (7%), fatigue (5%), insomnia (5%), somnolence (4%), tremor (3%)
Gastrointestinal: Anorexia (7% to 9%), weight loss (5% to 7%), abdominal pain (5%), dyspepsia (5%), flatulence (≥1%)
Genitourinary: Urinary tract infection (8%), hematuria (<1% to 3%), incontinence (≥1%)
Hematologic: Anemia (3%)
Respiratory: Rhinitis (4%)
Drug Interactions
Cytochrome P450 Effect: Substrate (minor) of CYP2D6, 3A4
Increased Effect/Toxicity: Succinylcholine: increased neuromuscular blockade. Amiodarone, beta-blockers without ISA activity, diltiazem, verapamil may increase bradycardia. NSAIDs increase risk of peptic ulcer. Cimetidine, ketoconazole, paroxetine, other CYP3A4 inhibitors, other CYP2D6 inhibitors increase levels of galantamine. Concurrent cholinergic agents may have synergistic effects. Digoxin may lead to AV block.
Decreased Effect: Anticholinergic agents are antagonized by galantamine. CYP inducers may decrease galantamine levels.
Mechanism of Action Centrally-acting cholinesterase inhibitor (competitive and reversible). It elevates acetylcholine in cerebral cortex by slowing the degradation of acetylcholine. Modulates nicotinic acetylcholine receptor to increase acetylcholine from surviving presynaptic nerve terminals. May increase glutamate and serotonin levels.
Pharmacodynamics/Kinetics
Duration: 3 hours; maximum inhibition of erythrocyte acetylcholinesterase ~40% at 1 hour post 10 mg oral dose; levels return to baseline at 30 hours
Absorption: Rapid and complete
Distribution: 1.8-2.6 L/kg; levels in the brain are 2-3 times higher than in plasma
Protein binding: 18%
Metabolism: Hepatic; linear, CYP2D6 and 3A4; metabolized to epigalanthaminone and galanthaminone both of which have acetylcholinesterase inhibitory activity 130 times less than galantamine
Bioavailability: 80% to 100%
Half-life elimination: 6-8 hours
Time to peak: 1 hour

Excretion: Urine (25%)

Dosage Note: Take with breakfast and dinner. If therapy is interrupted for ≥3 days, restart at the lowest dose and increase to current dose.

Oral: Adults: Mild to moderate dementia of Alzheimer's: Initial: 4 mg twice a day for 4 weeks
  If 8 mg per day tolerated, increase to 8 mg twice daily for ≥4 weeks
  If 16 mg per day tolerated, increase to 12 mg twice daily
  Range: 16-24 mg/day in 2 divided doses
Elderly: No dosage adjustment needed

Dosage adjustment in renal impairment:
  Moderate renal impairment: Maximum dose: 16 mg/day.
  Severe renal dysfunction (Cl$_{cr}$ <9 mL/minute): Use is not recommended

Dosage adjustment in hepatic impairment:
  Moderate liver dysfunction (Child-Pugh score 7-9): Maximum dose: 16 mg/day
  Severe liver dysfunction (Child-Pugh score 10-15): Use is not recommended

Administration Take with breakfast and dinner. If therapy is interrupted for ≥3 days, restart at the lowest dose and increase to current dose. If using oral solution, mix dose with 3-4 ounces of any nonalcoholic beverage; mix well and drink immediately.

Monitoring Parameters Mental status

Patient Information This medication will not cure Alzheimer's disease, but may help reduce symptoms. Use exactly as directed; do not increase dose or discontinue without consulting prescriber. Maintain adequate hydration (2-3 L/day) unless instructed to restrict fluids. May cause dizziness, sedation, hypotension, or tremor (use caution when driving or engaging in hazardous tasks, rise slowly from sitting or lying position, and use caution when climbing stairs until response to drug is known); diarrhea (boiled milk, yogurt, or buttermilk may help); or nausea or vomiting (frequent small meals, good mouth care, sucking lozenges, or chewing gum may help). Report persistent gastrointestinal disturbances; significantly increased salivation, sweating, or tearing; excessive fatigue, insomnia, dizziness, or depression; increased muscle, joint, or body pain or spasms; vision changes; respiratory changes, wheezing, or signs of dyspnea; chest pain or palpitations; or other adverse reactions.

Dosage Forms SOLN, oral: 4 mg/mL (100 mL). **TAB:** 4 mg, 8 mg, 12 mg

♦ **Galantamine Hydrobromide** *see* Galantamine *on page 576*

♦ **Gamimune® N** *see* Immune Globulin (Intravenous) *on page 659*

♦ **Gamma Benzene Hexachloride** *see* Lindane *on page 746*

♦ **Gammagard® S/D** *see* Immune Globulin (Intravenous) *on page 659*

♦ **Gamma Globulin** *see* Immune Globulin (Intramuscular) *on page 658*

♦ **Gamma Hydroxybutyric Acid** *see* Sodium Oxybate *on page 1149*

♦ **Gammaphos** *see* Amifostine *on page 70*

♦ **Gammar®-P I.V.** *see* Immune Globulin (Intravenous) *on page 659*

♦ **Gamunex®** *see* Immune Globulin (Intravenous) *on page 659*

Ganciclovir (gan SYE kloe veer)

U.S. Brand Names Cytovene®; Vitrasert®
Synonyms DHPG Sodium; GCV Sodium; Nordeoxyguanosine
Therapeutic Category Antiviral Agent; Antiviral Agent, Parenteral
Use
Parenteral: Treatment of CMV retinitis in immunocompromised individuals, including patients with acquired immunodeficiency syndrome; prophylaxis of CMV infection in transplant patients
Oral: Alternative to the I.V. formulation for maintenance treatment of CMV retinitis in immunocompromised patients, including patients with AIDS, in whom retinitis is stable following appropriate induction therapy and for whom the risk of more rapid progression is balanced by the benefit associated with avoiding daily I.V. infusions.
Implant: Treatment of CMV retinitis

Unlabeled/Investigational Use May be given in combination with foscarnet in patients who relapse after monotherapy with either drug

Pregnancy Risk Factor C

Contraindications Hypersensitivity to ganciclovir, acyclovir, or any component of the formulation; absolute neutrophil count <500/mm³; platelet count <25,000/mm³

Warnings/Precautions Dosage adjustment or interruption of ganciclovir therapy may be necessary in patients with neutropenia and/or thrombocytopenia and patients with impaired renal function. Use with extreme caution in children since long-term safety has not been determined and due to ganciclovir's potential for long-term carcinogenic and adverse reproductive effects; ganciclovir may adversely affect spermatogenesis and fertility; due to its mutagenic potential, contraceptive precautions for female and male patients need to be followed during and for at least 90 days after therapy with the drug; take care to administer only into veins with good blood flow.

Common Adverse Reactions
>10%:
  Central nervous system: Fever (38% to 48%)
  Dermatologic: Rash (15% oral, 10% I.V.)
  Gastrointestinal: Abdominal pain (17% to 19%), diarrhea (40%), nausea (25%), anorexia (15%), vomiting (13%)
  Hematologic: Anemia (20% to 25%), leukopenia (30% to 40%)
1% to 10%:
  Central nervous system: Confusion, neuropathy (8% to 9%), headache (4%)
(Continued)

Ganciclovir *(Continued)*

Dermatologic: Pruritus (5%)

Hematologic: Thrombocytopenia (6%), neutropenia with ANC <500/mm^3 (5% oral, 14% I.V.)

Neuromuscular & skeletal: Paresthesia (6% to 10%), weakness (6%)

Ocular: Retinal detachment (8% oral, 11% I.V.; relationship to ganciclovir not established)

Miscellaneous: Sepsis (4% oral, 15% I.V.)

Drug Interactions

Increased Effect/Toxicity: Immunosuppressive agents may increase hematologic toxicity of ganciclovir. Imipenem/cilastatin may increase seizure potential. Oral ganciclovir increases blood levels of zidovudine, although zidovudine decreases steady-state levels of ganciclovir. Since both drugs have the potential to cause neutropenia and anemia, some patients may not tolerate concomitant therapy with these drugs at full dosage. Didanosine levels are increased with concurrent ganciclovir. Other nephrotoxic drugs (eg, amphotericin and cyclosporine) may have additive nephrotoxicity with ganciclovir.

Decreased Effect: A decrease in blood levels of ganciclovir AUC may occur when used with didanosine.

Mechanism of Action Ganciclovir is phosphorylated to a substrate which competitively inhibits the binding of deoxyguanosine triphosphate to DNA polymerase resulting in inhibition of viral DNA synthesis

Pharmacodynamics/Kinetics

Distribution: V$_d$: 15.26 L/1.73 m^2; widely to all tissues including CSF and ocular tissue

Protein binding: 1% to 2%

Bioavailability: Oral: Fasting: 5%; Following food: 6% to 9%; Following fatty meal: 28% to 31%

Half-life elimination: 1.7-5.8 hours; prolonged with renal impairment; End-stage renal disease: 5-28 hours

Excretion: Urine (80% to 99% as unchanged drug)

Dosage

CMV retinitis: Slow I.V. infusion (dosing is based on total body weight):

Children >3 months and Adults:

Induction therapy: 5 mg/kg/dose every 12 hours for 14-21 days followed by maintenance therapy

Maintenance therapy: 5 mg/kg/day as a single daily dose for 7 days/week or 6 mg/kg/day for 5 days/week

CMV retinitis: Oral: 1000 mg 3 times/day with food **or** 500 mg 6 times/day with food

Prevention of CMV disease in patients with advanced HIV infection and normal renal function: Oral: 1000 mg 3 times/day with food

Prevention of CMV disease in transplant patients: Same initial and maintenance dose as CMV retinitis except duration of initial course is 7-14 days, duration of maintenance therapy is dependent on clinical condition and degree of immunosuppression

Intravitreal implant: One implant for 5- to 8-month period; following depletion of ganciclovir, as evidenced by progression of retinitis, implant may be removed and replaced

Elderly: Refer to adult dosing; in general, dose selection should be cautious, reflecting greater frequency of organ impairment

Dosing adjustment in renal impairment:

I.V. (Induction):

Cl$_{cr}$ 50-69 mL/minute: Administer 2.5 mg/kg/dose every 12 hours

Cl$_{cr}$ 25-49 mL/minute: Administer 2.5 mg/kg/dose every 24 hours

Cl$_{cr}$ 10-24 mL/minute: Administer 1.25 mg/kg/dose every 24 hours

Cl$_{cr}$ <10 mL/minute: Administer 1.25 mg/kg/dose 3 times/week following hemodialysis

I.V. (Maintenance):

Cl$_{cr}$ 50-69 mL/minute: Administer 2.5 mg/kg/dose every 24 hours

Cl$_{cr}$ 25-49 mL/minute: Administer 1.25 mg/kg/dose every 24 hours

Cl$_{cr}$ 10-24 mL/minute: Administer 0.625 mg/kg/dose every 24 hours

Cl$_{cr}$ <10 mL/minute: Administer 0.625 mg/kg/dose 3 times/week following hemodialysis

Oral:

Cl$_{cr}$ 50-69 mL/minute: Administer 1500 mg/day or 500 mg 3 times/day

Cl$_{cr}$ 25-49 mL/minute: Administer 1000 mg/day or 500 mg twice daily

Cl$_{cr}$ 10-24 mL/minute: Administer 500 mg/day

Cl$_{cr}$ <10 mL/minute: Administer 500 mg 3 times/week following hemodialysis

Hemodialysis effects: Dialyzable (50%) following hemodialysis; administer dose postdialysis. During peritoneal dialysis, dose as for Cl$_{cr}$ <10 mL/minute. During continuous arteriovenous or venovenous hemofiltration, administer 2.5 mg/kg/dose every 24 hours.

Administration The same precautions utilized with antineoplastic agents should be followed with ganciclovir administration. Ganciclovir should not be administered by I.M., S.C., or rapid IVP administration; administer by slow I.V. infusion over at least 1 hour at a final concentration for administration not to exceed 10 mg/mL. Oral ganciclovir should be administered with food.

Monitoring Parameters CBC with differential and platelet count, serum creatinine, ophthalmologic exams

Patient Information Ganciclovir is not a cure for CMV retinitis; regular ophthalmologic examinations should be done; close monitoring of blood counts should be done while on therapy and dosage adjustments may need to be made; take with food to increase absorption

Dosage Forms CAP (Cytovene®): 250 mg, 500 mg. **IMPLANT, intravitreal** (Vitrasert®): 4.5 mg. **INJ, powder for reconstitution** (Cytovene®): 500 mg

Ganirelix (ga ni REL ix)

U.S. Brand Names Antagon®

Synonyms Ganirelix Acetate

Therapeutic Category Antigonadotropic Agent

Use Inhibits premature luteinizing hormone (LH) surges in women undergoing controlled ovarian hyperstimulation in fertility clinics.

Pregnancy Risk Factor X

Contraindications Hypersensitivity to ganirelix or any component of the formulation; hypersensitivity to gonadotropin-releasing hormone or any other analog; known or suspected pregnancy

Warnings/Precautions Should only be prescribed by fertility specialists. The packaging contains natural rubber latex (may cause allergic reactions). Pregnancy must be excluded before starting medication.

Common Adverse Reactions 1% to 10%:

Central nervous system: Headache (3%)

Endocrine & metabolic: Ovarian hyperstimulation syndrome (2%)

Gastrointestinal: Abdominal pain (5%), nausea (1%), and abdominal pain (1%)

Genitourinary: Vaginal bleeding (2%)

Local: Injection site reaction (1%)

Drug Interactions

Increased Effect/Toxicity: No formal studies have been performed.

Decreased Effect: No formal studies have been performed.

Mechanism of Action Competitively blocks the gonadotropin-release hormone receptors on the pituitary gonadotroph and transduction pathway. This suppresses gonadotropin secretion and luteinizing hormone secretion preventing ovulation until the follicles are of adequate size.

Pharmacodynamics/Kinetics

Absorption: S.C.: Rapid

Distribution: Mean V_d: 43.7 L

Protein binding: 81.9%

Metabolism: Hepatic to two primary metabolites (1-4 and 1-6 peptide)

Bioavailability: 91.1%

Half-life elimination: 16.2 hours

Time to peak: 1.1 hours

Excretion: Feces (75%) within 288 hours; urine (22%) within 24 hours

Dosage Adult: S.C.: 250 mcg/day during the mid-to-late phase after initiating follicle-stimulating hormone on day 2 or 3 of cycle. Treatment should be continued daily until the day of chorionic gonadotropin administration.

Monitoring Parameters Ultrasound to assess the follicle's size

Patient Information Nurse to teach how to administer S.C. injections. Give at a similar time daily as instructed by fertility clinic. Do not skip doses. Keep all ultrasound appointments. Report any sudden weight gain, abdominal discomfort, or shortness of breath to clinic. Do not take if pregnant.

Dosage Forms INJ, solution [prefilled glass syringe]: 250 mcg/0.5 mL

♦ **Ganirelix Acetate** *see Ganirelix on page 579*

♦ **Gani-Tuss® NR** *see Guaifenesin and Codeine on page 604*

♦ **Gantrisin®** *see SulfiSOXAZOLE on page 1176*

♦ **Garamycin® [DSC]** *see Gentamicin on page 587*

♦ **Gastrocrom®** *see Cromolyn on page 316*

Gatifloxacin (gat i FLOKS a sin)

Related Information

Antimicrobial Drugs of Choice *on page 1440*

Community-Acquired Pneumonia in Adults *on page 1457*

U.S. Brand Names Tequin®; Zymar™

Therapeutic Category Antibiotic, Quinolone

Use Treatment of the following infections when caused by susceptible bacteria: Acute bacterial exacerbation of chronic bronchitis; acute sinusitis; community-acquired pneumonia; uncomplicated skin and skin structure infection; uncomplicated urinary tract infections (cystitis); complicated urinary tract infections; pyelonephritis; uncomplicated urethral and cervical gonorrhea; acute, uncomplicated rectal infections in women; bacterial conjunctivitis

Pregnancy Risk Factor C

Contraindications Hypersensitivity to gatifloxacin, other quinolone antibiotics, or any component of the formulation

Warnings/Precautions Use with caution in patients with significant bradycardia or acute myocardial ischemia. May prolong QT interval (concentration related). Use caution in patients with known prolongation of QT interval, uncorrected hypokalemia, or concurrent administration of other medications known to prolong the QT interval (including Class Ia and Class III antiarrhythmics, cisapride, erythromycin, antipsychotics, and tricyclic antidepressants). May cause increased CNS stimulation, increased intracranial pressure, convulsions, or psychosis. Use with caution in individuals at risk of seizures. Discontinue in patients who experience significant CNS adverse effects. Use caution in renal dysfunction (dosage adjustment required) and in severe hepatic insufficiency (no data available). Serious disruptions in glucose regulation (including hyperglycemia and severe hypoglycemia) may occur, generally in patients with diabetes and typically within 1-3 days of initiation. Monitor closely and discontinue if hyper- or hypoglycemia occur. Tendon inflammation and/or rupture has been reported with

(Continued)

Gatifloxacin *(Continued)*

this and other quinolone antibiotics. Discontinue at first signs or symptoms of tendon or pain. Quinolones may exacerbate myasthenia gravis.

Severe hypersensitivity reactions, including anaphylaxis, have occurred with quinolone therapy. Prolonged use may result in superinfection; pseudomembranous colitis may occur and should be considered in all patients who present with diarrhea.

Safety and efficacy for ophthalmic use have not been established in children <1 year of age. Safety and efficacy for systemic use have not been established in patients <18 years of age.

Common Adverse Reactions

Systemic therapy:

3% to 10%:

Central nervous system: Headache (3%), dizziness (3%)

Gastrointestinal: Nausea (8%), diarrhea (4%)

Genitourinary: Vaginitis (6%)

Local: Injection site reactions (5%)

0.1% to 3%: Abdominal pain, abnormal dreams, abnormal vision, agitation, alkaline phosphatase increased, allergic reaction, anorexia, anxiety, arthralgia, back pain, chest pain, chills, confusion, constipation, diaphoresis, dry skin, dyspepsia, dyspnea, dysuria, facial edema, fever, flatulence, gastritis, glossitis, hematuria, hyperglycemia, hypertension, insomnia, leg cramps, mouth ulceration, nervousness, oral candidiasis, palpitation, paresthesia, peripheral edema, pharyngitis, pruritus, rash, serum amylase increased, serum bilirubin increased, serum transaminases increased, somnolence, stomatitis, taste perversion, thirst, tinnitus, tremor, weakness, vasodilation, vertigo, vomiting

Ophthalmic therapy:

5% to 10%: Ocular: Conjunctival irritation, keratitis, lacrimation increased, papillary conjunctivitis

1% to 4%:

Central nervous system: Headache

Gastrointestinal: Taste disturbance

Ocular: Chemosis, conjunctival hemorrhage, discharge, dry eye, edema, irritation, pain, visual acuity decreased

Drug Interactions

Increased Effect/Toxicity: Use caution with drugs which prolong QT interval (including Class Ia and Class III antiarrhythmics, erythromycin, cisapride, antipsychotics, and cyclic antidepressants). Drugs which may induce bradycardia (eg, beta-blockers, amiodarone) should be avoided. Gatifloxacin may alter glucose control in patients receiving hypoglycemic agents with or without insulin. Cases of severe disturbances (including symptomatic hypoglycemia) have been reported, typically within 1-3 days of gatifloxacin initiation. Probenecid, loop diuretics, and cimetidine (possibly other H_2 antagonists) may increase the serum concentrations of gatifloxacin (based on experience with other quinolones). Digoxin levels may be increased in some patients by gatifloxacin. NSAIDs and foscarnet have been associated with an increased risk of seizures with some quinolones (not reported with gatifloxacin). The hypoprothrombinemic effect of warfarin is enhanced by some quinolone antibiotics. Monitoring of the INR during concurrent therapy is recommended by the manufacturer. Concurrent use of corticosteroids may increase risk of tendon rupture.

Decreased Effect: Metal cations (magnesium, aluminum, iron, and zinc) inhibit intestinal absorption of gatifloxacin (by up to 98%). Antacids, electrolyte supplements, sucralfate, quinapril, and some didanosine formulations should be avoided. Gatifloxacin should be administered 4 hours before or 8 hours after these agents. Calcium carbonate was not found to alter the absorption of gatifloxacin. Antineoplastic agents, H_2 antagonists, and proton pump inhibitors may also decrease absorption of some quinolones. Gatifloxacin may alter glucose control in patients receiving hypoglycemic agents with or without insulin.

Mechanism of Action

Gatifloxacin is a DNA gyrase inhibitor, and also inhibits topoisomerase IV. DNA gyrase (topoisomerase II) is an essential bacterial enzyme that maintains the superhelical structure of DNA. DNA gyrase is required for DNA replication and transcription, DNA repair, recombination, and transposition; inhibition is bactericidal.

Pharmacodynamics/Kinetics

Absorption: Oral: Well absorbed; Ophthalmic: Not measurable

Distribution: V_d: 1.5-2.0 L/kg; concentrates in alveolar macrophages and lung parenchyma

Protein binding: 20%

Metabolism: Only 1%; no interaction with CYP

Bioavailability: 96%

Half-life elimination: 7.1-13.9 hours; ESRD/CAPD: 30-40 hours

Time to peak: Oral: 1 hour

Excretion: Urine (70% as unchanged drug, <1% as metabolites); feces (5%)

Dosage

Children ≥1 year and Adults: Ophthalmic: Bacterial conjunctivitis:

Days 1 and 2: Instill 1 drop into affected eye(s) every 2 hours while awake (maximum: 8 times/day)

Days 3-7: Instill 1 drop into affected eye(s) up to 4 times/day while awake

Adults: Oral, I.V.:

Acute bacterial exacerbation of chronic bronchitis: 400 mg every 24 hours for 5 days

Acute sinusitis: 400 mg every 24 hours for 10 days

Community-acquired pneumonia: 400 mg every 24 hours for 7-14 days

Uncomplicated skin/skin structure infections: 400 mg every 24 hours for 7-10 days

Uncomplicated urinary tract infections (cystitis): 400 mg single dose or 200 mg every 24 hours for 3 days

Complicated urinary tract infections: 400 mg every 24 hours for 7-10 days

Acute pyelonephritis: 400 mg every 24 hours for 7-10 days

Uncomplicated urethral gonorrhea in men, cervical or rectal gonorrhea in women: 400 mg single dose

Elderly: No dosage adjustment is required based on age, however, assessment of renal function is particularly important in this population.

Dosage adjustment in renal impairment: Creatinine clearance <40 mL/minute (or patients on hemodialysis/CAPD) should receive an initial dose of 400 mg, followed by a subsequent dose of 200 mg every 24 hours. Patients receiving single-dose or 3-day therapy for appropriate indications do not require dosage adjustment. Administer after hemodialysis.

Dosage adjustment in hepatic impairment: No dosage adjustment is required in mild-moderate hepatic disease. No data are available in severe hepatic impairment (Child-Pugh Class C).

Administration

Oral: May be administered with or without food, milk, or calcium supplements. Gatifloxacin should be taken 4 hours before supplements (including multivitamins) containing iron, zinc, or magnesium.

I.V.: For I.V. infusion only. Concentrated injection (10 mg/mL) must be diluted to 2 mg/mL prior to administration. No further dilution is required for premixed 100 mL and 200 mL solutions. Infuse over 60 minutes. Avoid rapid or bolus infusions.

Monitoring Parameters WBC, signs of infection

Patient Information Tablets may be taken with or without food. Drink plenty of fluids. Avoid exposure to direct sunlight during therapy and for several days following. Take gatifloxacin 4 hours before antacids or mineral supplements (iron, magnesium, or zinc). Report immediately signs of allergy or signs of tendon inflammation or pain. Do not discontinue therapy until your course has been completed. Take a missed dose as soon as possible, unless it is almost time for your next dose.

Dosage Forms INJ, infusion [premixed in D_5W]: (Tequin®): 200 mg (100 mL); 400 mg (200 mL). **INJ, solution** [preservative free]: (Tequin®): 10 mg/mL (40 mL). **SOLN, ophthalmic** (Zymar™): 0.3% (5 mL). **TAB** (Tequin®): 200 mg, 400 mg

♦ **Gaviscon® Extra Strength [OTC]** see Aluminum Hydroxide and Magnesium Carbonate on page 67

♦ **Gaviscon® Liquid [OTC]** see Aluminum Hydroxide and Magnesium Carbonate on page 67

♦ **Gaviscon® Tablet [OTC]** see Aluminum Hydroxide and Magnesium Trisilicate on page 67

♦ **G-CSF** see Filgrastim on page 522

♦ **G-CSF (PEG Conjugate)** see Pegfilgrastim on page 963

♦ **GCV Sodium** see Ganciclovir on page 577

Gefitinib (ge FI tye nib)

U.S. Brand Names Iressa™

Synonyms NSC-715055; ZD1839

Therapeutic Category Antineoplastic Agent, Tyrosine Kinase Inhibitor

Use Second-line treatment of nonsmall cell lung cancer

Unlabeled/Investigational Use Brain cancer, breast cancer, colon cancer, head and neck cancer, ovarian cancer

Pregnancy Risk Factor D

Contraindications Hypersensitivity to gefitinib or any component of the formulation; pregnancy

Warnings/Precautions Rare, sometimes fatal, pulmonary toxicity (alveolitis, interstitial pneumonia, pneumonitis) has occurred; use caution in hepatic or severe renal impairment; safety and efficacy in pediatric patients have not been established

Common Adverse Reactions Based on 250 mg/day:

>10%:

Dermatologic: Rash (43%), acne (25%), dry skin (13%)

Gastrointestinal: Diarrhea (48%), nausea (13%), vomiting (12%)

1% to 10%:

Cardiovascular: Peripheral edema (2%)

Dermatologic: Pruritus (8%)

Gastrointestinal: Anorexia (7%), weight loss (3%), mouth ulceration (1%)

Neuromuscular & skeletal: Weakness (6%)

Ocular: Amblyopia (2%), conjunctivitis (1%)

Respiratory: Dyspnea (2%), interstitial lung disease (1%)

Drug Interactions

Cytochrome P450 Effect: Substrate of CYP3A4 (major); **Inhibits** CYP2C19 (weak), 2D6 (weak)

Increased Effect/Toxicity: Gefinitib effects may be increased by the azole antifungals, CYP3A4 inhibitors (eg, amiodarone, cimetidine, clarithromycin, diltiazem, erythromycin, fluvoxamine, ketoconazole, ritonavir); gefitinib may increase the effects of warfarin

Decreased Effect: Gefitinib effects may be decreased by CYP3A4 inducers (eg, carbamazepine, phenytoin, nevirapine, phenobarbital, rifampin); H_2-receptor blockers; rifamycins; sodium bicarbonate

Mechanism of Action The mechanism of antineoplastic action is not fully understood. Gefitinib inhibits tyrosine kinases (TK) associated with transmembrane cell surface receptors found (Continued)

Gefitinib (Continued)

on both normal and cancer cells. One such receptor is epidermal growth factor receptor. TK activity appears to be vitally important to cell proliferation and survival.

Pharmacodynamics/Kinetics

Absorption: Oral: slow

Distribution: I.V.: 1400 L

Protein binding: 90%, albumin and alpha$_1$-acid glycoprotein

Metabolism: Hepatic, primarily via CYP3A4; forms metabolites

Bioavailability: 60%

Half-life elimination: I.V.: 48 hours

Time to peak, plasma: Oral: 3-7 hours

Excretion: Feces (86%); urine (<4%)

Dosage Oral: Adults: 250 mg/day; consider 500 mg/day in patients receiving effective CYP3A4 inducers (eg, rifampin, phenytoin)

Dosage adjustment in renal/hepatic impairment: No adjustment necessary

Dosage adjustment for toxicity: Patients experiencing poorly-tolerated diarrhea may benefit from a brief (up to 14 days) therapy interruption. Patients experiencing acute onset (or worsening) of pulmonary symptoms should have therapy interrupted and be evaluated for drug-induced interstitial lung disease. Patients experiencing new eye symptoms should consider therapy interruption until situation resolved.

Administration May administer with or without food.

Monitoring Parameters Periodic liver function tests (asymptomatic increases in liver enzymes have occurred)

Patient Information Contact prescriber if any of the following symptoms occur: Severe, persistent diarrhea; nausea or vomiting; breathing difficulties (shortness of breath, painful breathing, cough); eye irritation. Avoid becoming pregnant while on this medication.

Dosage Forms TAB: 250 mg

- **Gelatin, Benzocaine, Pectin, and Sodium Carboxymethylcellulose** *see* Benzocaine, Gelatin, Pectin, and Sodium Carboxymethylcellulose *on page 155*

Gelatin, Pectin, and Methylcellulose

(JEL a tin, PEK tin, & meth il SEL yoo lose)

Synonyms Methylcellulose, Gelatin, and Pectin; Pectin, Gelatin, and Methylcellulose

Therapeutic Category Topical Skin Product

Use Temporary relief from minor oral irritations

Dosage Press small dabs into place until the involved area is coated with a thin film; do not try to spread onto area; may be used as often as needed

- **Gel-Kam® [OTC]** *see* Fluoride *on page 535*
- **Gel-Kam® Rinse** *see* Fluoride *on page 535*
- **Gelucast®** *see* Zinc Gelatin *on page 1327*

Gemcitabine (jem SITE a been)

U.S. Brand Names Gemzar®

Synonyms Gemcitabine Hydrochloride

Therapeutic Category Antineoplastic Agent, Antimetabolite

Use Adenocarcinoma of the pancreas; first-line therapy for patients with locally advanced (nonresectable stage II or stage III) or metastatic (stage IV) adenocarcinoma of the pancreas (indicated for patients previously treated with fluorouracil)

Unlabeled/Investigational Use Nonsmall-cell lung cancer

Pregnancy Risk Factor D

Contraindications Hypersensitivity to gemcitabine or any component of the formulation; pregnancy

Warnings/Precautions The U.S. Food & Drug Administration (FDA) recommends that procedures for proper handling and disposal of antineoplastic agents be considered. Prolongation of the infusion time >60 minutes and more frequent than weekly dosing have been shown to increase toxicity. Gemcitabine can suppress bone marrow function manifested by leukopenia, thrombocytopenia and anemia, and myelosuppression is usually the dose-limiting toxicity. Gemcitabine may cause fever in the absence of clinical infection. Gemcitabine should be used with caution in patients with pre-existing renal impairment and hepatic impairment.

Common Adverse Reactions

>10%:

Central nervous system: Fatigue, fever (40%), lethargy, pain (10% to 48%), somnolence (5% to 11%)

Dermatologic: Alopecia (15%); mild to moderate rashes (5% to 32%; typically a macular or finely-granular maculopapular pruritic eruption of mild-to-moderate severity involving the trunk and extremities)

Gastrointestinal: Mild nausea, vomiting, anorexia (20% to 70%); stomatitis (10% to 14%)

Hematologic: Myelosuppression (20% to 30%), primarily leukopenia, may be dose-limiting

Hepatic: Transaminases increased (66%; generally mild and transient, severe hepatotoxic reactions reported rarely)

Neuromuscular & skeletal: Weakness (15% to 25%)

Renal: Proteinuria, hematuria (45%, generally proteinuria and hematuria were mild, however, hemolytic uremic syndrome has also been reported); BUN increased

Respiratory: Mild to moderate dyspnea (10% to 23%)

Miscellaneous: Flu-like syndrome (myalgia, fever, chills, fatigue) (20% to 100%), may be dose-limiting

1% to 10%:
Dermatologic: Pruritus (8%)
Gastrointestinal: Mild diarrhea (7%), constipation (6%)
Hematologic: Thrombocytopenia (~10%), anemia (6%)
Hepatic: Elevated bilirubin (10%)
Neuromuscular & skeletal: Paresthesia (2% to 10%), peripheral neuropathies (paresthesias, decreased tendon reflexes) (3.5%)
Respiratory: Severe dyspnea (3%)
Miscellaneous: Allergic reactions (4%), mild, usually edema, bronchospasm

Drug Interactions
Decreased Effect: No confirmed interactions have been reported. No specific drug interaction studies have been conducted.

Mechanism of Action A pyrimidine antimetabolite that inhibits DNA synthesis by inhibition of DNA polymerase and ribonucleotide reductase, specific for the S-phase of the cycle.

Pharmacodynamics/Kinetics
Distribution: V_d: Male: 15.6 mL mL/m²; Female: 11.3 L/m²
Protein binding: Low
Metabolism: Hepatic, metabolites: di- and triphosphates (active); uridine derivative (inactive)
Half-life elimination: Infusion time: ≤1 hour: 32-94 minutes; Infusion time: 3-4 hours: 4-10.5 hours
Time to peak: 30 minutes
Excretion: Urine (99%, 92% to 98% as intact drug or inactive uridine metabolite); feces (<1%)

Dosage Refer to individual protocols. **Note**: Prolongation of the infusion time >60 minutes has been shown to increase toxicity. I.V.:
Pancreatic cancer: 1000 mg/m² over 30 minutes weekly for 3 or 7 weeks followed by 1 week rest; repeat cycles 3 out of every 4 weeks.
Nonsmall cell lung cancer in combination with cisplatin (unlabeled use): 1000 mg/m² over 30 minutes on days 1, 8, 15; repeat every 28 days **or** 1250 mg/m² over 30 minutes on days 1, 8; repeat every 21 days.
Dosing adjustment in renal/hepatic impairment: Use with caution; gemcitabine has not been studied in patients with significant renal or hepatic dysfunction

Administration Administer over 30 minutes. **Note**: Prolongation of the infusion time >60 minutes has been shown to increase toxicity.

Monitoring Parameters Patients should be monitored prior to each dose with a complete blood count (CBC), including differential and platelet count. The diagnosis of hemolytic-uremic syndrome (HUS) should be considered if evidence of microangiopathic hemolysis is noted (elevation of bilirubin or LDH, reticulocytosis, severe thrombocytopenia, and/or renal failure). Hepatic and renal function should be performed prior to initiation of therapy and periodically, thereafter

Dosage Forms INJ, powder for reconstitution: 200 mg, 1 g

◆ **Gemcitabine Hydrochloride** *see* Gemcitabine *on page 582*

Gemfibrozil (jem FI broe zil)
Related Information
Lipid-Lowering Agents *on page 1381*
U.S. Brand Names Lopid®
Synonyms CI-719
Therapeutic Category Antilipemic Agent, Fibric Acid
Use Treatment of hypertriglyceridemia in types IV and V hyperlipidemia for patients who are at greater risk for pancreatitis and who have not responded to dietary intervention
Pregnancy Risk Factor C
Contraindications Hypersensitivity to gemfibrozil or any component of the formulation; significant hepatic or renal dysfunction; primary biliary cirrhosis; pre-existing gallbladder disease
Warnings/Precautions Abnormal elevation of AST, ALT, LDH, bilirubin, and alkaline phosphatase has occurred; if no appreciable triglyceride or cholesterol lowering effect occurs after 3 months, the drug should be discontinued; not useful for type I hyperlipidemia; myositis may be more common in patients with poor renal function

Common Adverse Reactions
>10% Gastrointestinal: Dyspepsia (20%)
1% to 10%:
Central nervous system: Fatigue (4%), vertigo (2%), headache (1%)
Dermatologic: Eczema (2%), rash (2%)
Gastrointestinal: Abdominal pain (10%), diarrhea (7%), nausea/vomiting (3%), constipation (1%)

Reports where causal relationship has not been established: Weight loss, extrasystoles, pancreatitis, hepatoma, colitis, confusion, seizures, syncope, retinal edema, decreased fertility (male), renal dysfunction, positive ANA, drug-induced lupus-like syndrome, thrombocytopenia, anaphylaxis, vasculitis, alopecia, photosensitivity

Drug Interactions
Cytochrome P450 Effect: Substrate of CYP3A4 (minor); **Inhibits** CYP1A2 (moderate), 2C8/9 (strong), 2C19 (strong)
Increased Effect/Toxicity: Gemfibrozil may potentiate the effects of bexarotene (avoid concurrent use), sulfonylureas (including glyburide, chlorpropamide), and warfarin. (Continued)

Gemfibrozil *(Continued)*

HMG-CoA reductase inhibitors (atorvastatin, fluvastatin, lovastatin, pravastatin, simvastatin) may increase the risk of myopathy and rhabdomyolysis. The manufacturer warns against the concurrent use of lovastatin (if unavoidable, limit lovastatin to <20 mg/day). Combination therapy with statins has been used in some patients with resistant hyperlipidemias (with great caution). Gemfibrozil may increase the serum concentration of repaglinide (resulting in severe, prolonged hypoglycemia).

Decreased Effect: Cyclosporine's blood levels may be reduced during concurrent therapy. Rifampin may decrease gemfibrozil blood levels.

Mechanism of Action The exact mechanism of action of gemfibrozil is unknown, however, several theories exist regarding the VLDL effect; it can inhibit lipolysis and decrease subsequent hepatic fatty acid uptake as well as inhibit hepatic secretion of VLDL; together these actions decrease serum VLDL levels; increases HDL-cholesterol; the mechanism behind HDL elevation is currently unknown

Pharmacodynamics/Kinetics

Onset of action: May require several days

Absorption: Well absorbed

Protein binding: 99%

Metabolism: Hepatic via oxidation to two inactive metabolites; undergoes enterohepatic recycling

Half-life elimination: 1.4 hours

Time to peak, serum: 1-2 hours

Excretion: Urine (70% primarily as unchanged drug)

Dosage Adults: Oral: 1200 mg/day in 2 divided doses, 30 minutes before breakfast and dinner

Hemodialysis: Not removed by hemodialysis; supplemental dose is not necessary

Monitoring Parameters Serum cholesterol, LFTs

Patient Information May cause dizziness or blurred vision, abdominal or epigastric pain, diarrhea, nausea, or vomiting; report if these become pronounced.

Dosage Forms TAB, film coated: 600 mg

Gemifloxacin *(je mi FLOKS a sin)*

U.S. Brand Names Factive®

Synonyms DW286; Gemifloxacin Mesylate; LA 20304a; SB-265805

Therapeutic Category Antibiotic, Quinolone

Use Treatment of acute exacerbation of chronic bronchitis; treatment of community-acquired pneumonia, including pneumonia caused by multidrug-resistant strains of *S. pneumoniae* (MDRSP)

Unlabeled/Investigational Use Acute sinusitis, uncomplicated urinary tract infection

Pregnancy Risk Factor C

Contraindications Hypersensitivity to gemifloxacin, other fluoroquinolones, or any component of the formulation

Warnings/Precautions May prolong QT_c interval; avoid use in patients with uncorrected hypokalemia, hypomagnesemia, or concurrent administration of other medications known to prolong the Q-T interval (including class Ia and class III antiarrhythmics, cisapride, erythromycin, antipsychotics, and tricyclic antidepressants). Use with caution in patients with significant bradycardia or acute myocardial ischemia. Use with caution in individuals at risk of seizures; discontinue in patients who experience significant CNS adverse effects. Use caution in renal dysfunction (dosage adjustment required).

Severe hypersensitivity reactions, including anaphylaxis, have occurred with quinolone therapy. Tendon inflammation and/or rupture has been reported with other quinolone antibiotics. Discontinue at first sign of tendon inflammation or pain. Experience with quinolones in immature animals has resulted in permanent arthropathy. Safety and effectiveness in pediatric patients (<18 years of age) have not been established.

Common Adverse Reactions

1% to 10%:

Central nervous system: Headache (1%), dizziness (1%)

Dermatologic: Rash (3%)

Gastrointestinal: Diarrhea (4%), nausea (3%), abdominal pain (1%), vomiting (1%)

Hepatic: Transaminases increased (1% to 2%)

Important adverse effects reported with other agents in this drug class include (not reported for gemifloxacin): Allergic reactions, CNS stimulation, hepatitis, jaundice, seizures, severe dermatologic reactions (toxic epidermal necrolysis, Stevens-Johnson syndrome), pneumonitis (eosinophilic); tendon rupture, torsade de pointes, vasculitis

Drug Interactions

Increased Effect/Toxicity: Gemifloxacin may prolong QT interval; avoid use with drugs which prolong QT interval (including class Ia and class III antiarrhythmics, erythromycin, cisapride, antipsychotics, and cyclic antidepressants). Concurrent use of corticosteroids may increase the risk of tendon rupture with quinolones, particularly in elderly patients (overall incidence rare). Probenecid may increase systemic exposure to gemifloxacin (blocks renal secretion). Loop diuretics and cimetidine have been shown to increase serum concentrations of some quinolones (due to decreased renal secretion). Foscarnet and NSAIDs have been associated with an increased risk of CNS effects with some quinolones. The effect of warfarin may be enhanced by some quinolone antibiotics.

Decreased Effect: Metal cations (magnesium, aluminum, iron, and zinc) bind quinolones in the gastrointestinal tract and inhibit absorption (by up to 98%). Antacids, electrolyte supplements, sucralfate, quinapril, and some didanosine formulations should be avoided. Gemifloxacin should be administered 3 hours before or 2 hours after these agents. Calcium carbonate did not result in significant changes in the absorption of gemifloxacin. Antineoplastic agents may also decrease the absorption of quinolones.

Mechanism of Action Gemifloxacin is a DNA gyrase inhibitor and also inhibits topoisomerase IV. DNA gyrase (topoisomerase IV) is an essential bacterial enzyme that maintains the superhelical structure of DNA. DNA gyrase is required for DNA replication and transcription, DNA repair, recombination, and transposition; bactericidal

Pharmacodynamics/Kinetics
Absorption: Well absorbed from the GI tract
Bioavailability: 71%
Metabolism: Hepatic (minor); forms metabolites (CYP isoenzymes are not involved)
Time to peak, plasma: 1-2 hours
Protein binding: 60% to 70%
Half-life elimination: 7 hours (range 4-12 hours)
Excretion: Urine (30% to 40%); feces (60%)

Dosage Oral: Adults: 320 mg once daily
Duration of therapy:
Acute exacerbations of chronic bronchitis: 5 days
Community-acquired pneumonia (mild to moderate severity): 7 days

Dosage adjustment in renal impairment: Cl_{cr} ≤40 mL/minute (or patients on hemodialysis/CAPD): 160 mg once daily (administer dose following hemodialysis)

Dosage adjustment in hepatic impairment: No adjustment required.

Administration May be administered with or without food, milk, or calcium supplements. Gemifloxacin should be taken 3 hours before or 2 hours after supplements (including multivitamins) containing iron, zinc, or magnesium.

Monitoring Parameters WBC, signs/symptoms of infection

Dosage Forms TAB, as mesylate: 320 mg

♦ **Gemifloxacin Mesylate** *see Gemifloxacin on page 584*

Gemtuzumab Ozogamicin (gem TOO zoo mab oh zog a MY sin)

U.S. Brand Names Mylotarg®

Therapeutic Category Antineoplastic Agent, Monoclonal Antibody

Use Treatment of acute myeloid leukemia (CD33 positive) in first relapse in patients who are ≥60 years of age and who are not considered candidates for cytotoxic chemotherapy.

Pregnancy Risk Factor D

Contraindications Hypersensitivity to gemtuzumab ozogamicin, calicheamicin derivatives, or any component of the formulation; patients with anti-CD33 antibody; pregnancy

Warnings/Precautions The U.S. Food and Drug Administration (FDA) currently recommends that procedures for proper handling and disposal of antineoplastic agents be considered. Safety and efficacy in patients with poor performance status and organ dysfunction have not been established.

Infusion-related events are common, generally reported to occur with the first dose at the end of the 2-hour intravenous infusion. These symptoms usually resolved after 2-4 hours with a supportive therapy of acetaminophen, diphenhydramine, and intravenous fluids. Fewer infusion-related events were observed after the second dose. Postinfusion reactions, which may include fever, chills, hypotension, or dyspnea, may occur during the first 24 hours after administration. **Infusion-related reactions may be severe (including anaphylaxis, pulmonary edema, or ARDS).** Symptomatic intrinsic lung disease or high peripheral blast counts may increase the risk of severe reactions. Consider discontinuation in patients who develop severe infusion-related reactions.

Severe myelosuppression occurs in all patients at recommended dosages. Use caution in patients with renal impairment (no clinical experience) and hepatic impairment (no clinical experience in patients with bilirubin >2 mg/dL). Tumor lysis syndrome may occur as a consequence of leukemia treatment, adequate hydration and prophylactic allopurinol must be instituted prior to use. Other methods to lower WBC <30,000 cells/mm^3 may be considered (hydroxyurea or leukapheresis) to minimize the risk of tumor lysis syndrome, and/or severe infusion reactions. Has been associated with severe veno-occlusive disease or hepatotoxicity (risk may be increased by combination chemotherapy, previous hepatic disease, or hematopoietic stem cell transplant).

Common Adverse Reactions Percentages established in adults >60 years of age.

>10%:
Cardiovascular: Peripheral edema (21%), hypertension (20%), hypotension (16%)
Central nervous system: Chills (66%), fever (80%), headache (26%), pain (25%), dizziness (11%), insomnia (18%)
Dermatologic: Rash (23%), petechiae (21%), ecchymosis (15%)
Endocrine & metabolic: Hypokalemia (30%)
Gastrointestinal: Nausea (64%), vomiting (55%), diarrhea (38%), anorexia (31%), abdominal pain (29%), constipation (28%), stomatitis/mucositis (25%), abdominal distention (11%), dyspepsia (11%)
Hematologic: Neutropenia (98%; median recovery 40.5 days), thrombocytopenia (99%; median recovery 39 days); anemia (47%), bleeding (15%), lymphopenia
(Continued)

Gemtuzumab Ozogamicin *(Continued)*

Hepatic: Hyperbilirubinemia (23%) increased LDH (18%), increased transaminases (9% to 17%)

Local: Local reaction (25%)

Neuromuscular & skeletal: Weakness (45%), back pain (18%)

Respiratory: Dyspnea (36%), epistaxis (29%; severe 3%), cough (19%), pharyngitis (14%)

Miscellaneous: Infection (28%), sepsis (24%), neutropenic fever (20%)

1% to 10%:

Cardiovascular: Tachycardia (10%)

Central nervous system: Depression (10%), cerebral hemorrhage (2%), intracranial hemorrhage (2%)

Endocrine & metabolic: Hypomagnesemia (4%), hyperglycemia (2%)

Genitourinary: Hematuria (10%; severe 1%), vaginal hemorrhage (7%)

Hematologic: Hemorrhage (8%), disseminated intravascular coagulation (DIC) (2%)

Hepatic: Elevated PT

Neuromuscular & skeletal: Arthralgia (10%)

Respiratory: Rhinitis (10%), hypoxia (6%), pneumonia (10%)

Drug Interactions

Increased Effect/Toxicity: No formal drug interaction studies have been conducted.

Decreased Effect: No formal drug interaction studies have been conducted.

Mechanism of Action Antibody to CD33 antigen, which is expressed on leukemic blasts in >80% of patients with acute myeloid leukemia (AML), as well as normal myeloid cells. Binding results in internalization of the antibody-antigen complex. Following internalization, the calicheamicin derivative is released inside the myeloid cell. The calicheamicin derivative binds to DNA resulting in double strand breaks and cell death. Pluripotent stem cells and nonhematopoietic cells are not affected.

Pharmacodynamics/Kinetics Half-life elimination: Calicheamicin: Total: Initial: 45 hours, Repeat dose: 60 hours; Unconjugated: 100 hours (no change noted in repeat dosing)

Dosage I.V.: Adults ≥60 years: 9 mg/m^2, infused over 2 hours. The patient should receive diphenhydramine 50 mg orally and acetaminophen 650-1000 mg orally 1 hour prior to administration of each dose. Acetaminophen dosage should be repeated as needed every 4 hours for two additional doses. A full treatment course is a total of two doses administered with 14 days between doses. Full hematologic recovery is not necessary for administration of the second dose. There has been only limited experience with repeat courses of gemtuzumab ozogamicin.

Dosage adjustment in renal impairment: No recommendation (not studied)

Dosage adjustment in hepatic impairment: No recommendation (not studied)

Administration Administer as infusion only, over at least 2 hours. Do not administer I.V. push (bolus). Infuse through a separate line equipped with a low protein-binding 1.2 micron terminal filter. May be infused peripherally or through a central line. Premedication with acetaminophen and diphenhydramine should be administered prior to each infusion.

Monitoring Parameters Monitor vital signs during the infusion and for 4 hours following the infusion. Monitor for signs/symptoms of postinfusion reaction. Monitor electrolytes, LFTs, CBC with differential, and platelet counts frequently. Monitor for signs and symptoms of hepatitis reaction (weight gain, right upper quadrant abdominal pain, hepatomegaly, ascites).

Patient Information This medication can only be administered I.V. During therapy do not use ethanol, aspirin-containing products, antiplatelet medications (ticlopidine, clopidogrel, or dipyridamole), OTC medications, or supplements/herbal products without consulting prescriber. It is important to maintain adequate nutrition and hydration. You may experience nausea and vomiting (small frequent meals, frequent mouth care, sucking lozenges or chewing gum may help). Frequent mouth care and use of a soft toothbrush or cotton swabs may reduce mouth sores. You will be susceptible to infection (avoid crowds and exposure to infection). Report fever, chills, unusual bruising or bleeding, signs of infection, dizziness, lightheadedness, difficulty breathing, or yellowing of the eyes or skin to prescriber. Keep all appointments and get required blood work done.

Dosage Forms INJ, powder for reconstitution: 5 mg

Gentamicin (jen ta MYE sin)

Related Information

Aminoglycoside Dosing and Monitoring *on page 1350*
Antimicrobial Drugs of Choice *on page 1440*
Community-Acquired Pneumonia in Adults *on page 1457*
Prevention of Bacterial Endocarditis *on page 1429*
Prevention of Wound Infection & Sepsis in Surgical Patients *on page 1436*

U.S. Brand Names Garamycin® [DSC]; Genoptic®; Gentacidin®; Gentak®

Synonyms Gentamicin Sulfate

Therapeutic Category Antibiotic, Aminoglycoside; Antibiotic, Ophthalmic; Antibiotic, Topical

Use Treatment of susceptible bacterial infections, normally gram-negative organisms including *Pseudomonas, Proteus, Serratia,* and gram-positive *Staphylococcus*; treatment of bone infections, respiratory tract infections, skin and soft tissue infections, as well as abdominal and urinary tract infections, endocarditis, and septicemia; used topically to treat superficial infections of the skin or ophthalmic infections caused by susceptible bacteria; prevention of bacterial endocarditis prior to dental or surgical procedures

Pregnancy Risk Factor C

Contraindications Hypersensitivity to gentamicin or other aminoglycosides

Warnings/Precautions Not intended for long-term therapy due to toxic hazards associated with extended administration; pre-existing renal insufficiency, vestibular or cochlear impairment, myasthenia gravis, hypocalcemia, conditions which depress neuromuscular transmission

Parenteral aminoglycosides have been associated with significant nephrotoxicity or ototoxicity; the ototoxicity may be directly proportional to the amount of drug given and the duration of treatment; tinnitus or vertigo are indications of vestibular injury and impending hearing loss; renal damage is usually reversible

Common Adverse Reactions

>10%:
    Central nervous system: Neurotoxicity (vertigo, ataxia)
    Neuromuscular & skeletal: Gait instability
    Otic: Ototoxicity (auditory), ototoxicity (vestibular)
    Renal: Nephrotoxicity, decreased creatinine clearance
1% to 10%:
    Cardiovascular: Edema
    Dermatologic: Skin itching, reddening of skin, rash

Drug Interactions

Increased Effect/Toxicity: Penicillins, cephalosporins, amphotericin B, loop diuretics may increase nephrotoxic potential. Aminoglycosides may potentiate the effects of neuromuscular blocking agents.

Mechanism of Action Interferes with bacterial protein synthesis by binding to 30S and 50S ribosomal subunits resulting in a defective bacterial cell membrane

Pharmacodynamics/Kinetics

Absorption: Oral: None
Distribution: Crosses placenta
    V_d: Increased by edema, ascites, fluid overload; decreased with dehydration
        Neonates: 0.4-0.6 L/kg
        Children: 0.3-0.35 L/kg
        Adults: 0.2-0.3 L/kg
    Relative diffusion from blood into CSF: Minimal even with inflammation
    CSF:blood level ratio: Normal meninges: Nil; Inflamed meninges: 10% to 30%
Protein binding: <30%
Half-life elimination
    Infants: <1 week old: 3-11.5 hours; 1 week to 6 months old: 3-3.5 hours
    Adults: 1.5-3 hours; End-stage renal disease: 36-70 hours
Time to peak, serum: I.M.: 30-90 minutes; I.V.: 30 minutes after 30-minute infusion
Excretion: Urine (as unchanged drug)
    Clearance: Directly related to renal function

Dosage Individualization is critical because of the low therapeutic index; refer to "Aminoglycoside Dosing and Monitoring" *on page 1350* in the Appendix

Use of ideal body weight (IBW) for determining the mg/kg/dose appears to be more accurate than dosing on the basis of total body weight (TBW).

In morbid obesity, dosage requirement may best be estimated using a dosing weight of IBW + 0.4 (TBW - IBW)

Initial and periodic peak and trough plasma drug levels should be determined, particularly in critically-ill patients with serious infections or in disease states known to significantly alter aminoglycoside pharmacokinetics (eg, cystic fibrosis, burns, or major surgery)

(Continued)

Gentamicin *(Continued)*

Newborns: Intrathecal: 1 mg every day
Infants >3 months: Intrathecal: 1-2 mg/day
Infants and Children <5 years: I.M., I.V.: 2.5 mg/kg/dose every 8 hours*
  Cystic fibrosis: 2.5 mg/kg/dose every 6 hours
Children >5 years: I.M., I.V.: 1.5-2.5 mg/kg/dose every 8 hours*
  Prevention of bacterial endocarditis: Dental, oral, upper respiratory procedures, GI/GU procedures: 2 mg/kg with ampicillin (50 mg/kg) 30 minutes prior to procedure
  *Some patients may require larger or more frequent doses (eg, every 6 hours) if serum levels document the need (ie, cystic fibrosis or febrile granulocytopenic patients)
Adults: I.M., I.V.:
  Severe life-threatening infections: 2-2.5 mg/kg/dose
  Urinary tract infections: 1.5 mg/kg/dose
  Synergy (for gram-positive infections): 1 mg/kg/dose
  Prevention of bacterial endocarditis:
    Dental, oral, or upper respiratory procedures: 1.5 mg/kg not to exceed 80 mg with ampicillin (1-2 g) 30 minutes prior to procedure
    GI/GU surgery: 1.5 mg/kg not to exceed 80 mg with ampicillin (2 g) 30 minutes prior to procedure
Some clinicians suggest a daily dose of 4-7 mg/kg for all patients with normal renal function. This dose is at least as efficacious with similar, if not less, toxicity than conventional dosing.
Children and Adults:
  Intrathecal: 4-8 mg/day
  Ophthalmic:
    Ointment: Instill ½" (1.25 cm) 2-3 times/day to every 3-4 hours
    Solution: Instill 1-2 drops every 2-4 hours, up to 2 drops every hour for severe infections
  Topical: Apply 3-4 times/day to affected area
Dosing interval in renal impairment:
  Cl_{cr} ≥60 mL/minute: Administer every 8 hours
  Cl_{cr} 40-60 mL/minute: Administer every 12 hours
  Cl_{cr} 20-40 mL/minute: Administer every 24 hours
  Cl_{cr} <20 mL/minute: Loading dose, then monitor levels
Hemodialysis: Dialyzable; removal by hemodialysis: 30% removal of aminoglycosides occurs during 4 hours of HD; administer dose after dialysis and follow levels
Removal by continuous ambulatory peritoneal dialysis (CAPD):
  Administration via CAPD fluid:
  Gram-negative infection: 4-8 mg/L (4-8 mcg/mL) of CAPD fluid
  Gram-positive infection (ie, synergy): 3-4 mg/L (3-4 mcg/mL) of CAPD fluid
  Administration via I.V., I.M. route during CAPD: Dose as for Cl_{cr} <10 mL/minute and follow levels
Removal via continuous arteriovenous or venovenous hemofiltration: Dose as for Cl_{cr} 10-40 mL/minute and follow levels
Dosing adjustment/comments in hepatic disease: Monitor plasma concentrations
Monitoring Parameters Urinalysis, urine output, BUN, serum creatinine; hearing should be tested before, during, and after treatment; particularly in those at risk for ototoxicity or who will be receiving prolonged therapy (>2 weeks)
Reference Range
Timing of serum samples: Draw peak 30 minutes after 30-minute infusion has been completed or 1 hour after I.M. injection; draw trough immediately before next dose
Sample size: 0.5-2 mL blood (red top tube) or 0.1-1 mL serum (separated)
Therapeutic levels:
  Peak:
    Serious infections: 6-8 µg/mL (12-17 µmol/L)
    Life-threatening infections: 8-10 µg/mL (17-21 µmol/L)
    Urinary tract infections: 4-6 µg/mL
    Synergy against gram-positive organisms: 3-5 µg/mL
  Trough:
    Serious infections: 0.5-1 µg/mL
    Life-threatening infections: 1-2 µg/mL
Obtain drug levels after the third dose unless renal dysfunction/toxicity suspected
Patient Information Report any dizziness or sensations of ringing or fullness in ears; do not touch ophthalmics to eye; use no other eye drops within 5-10 minutes of instilling ophthalmic
Dosage Forms CRM, topical: 0.1% (15 g, 30 g); (Garamycin®): 0.1% (15 g) [DSC]. **INF** [premixed in NS]: 40 mg (50 mL); 60 mg (50 mL, 100 mL); 70 mg (50 mL); 80 mg (50 mL, 100 mL); 90 mg (100 mL); 100 mg (50 mL, 100 mL); 120 mg (100 mL). **INJ, solution** [ADD-Vantage® vial]: 10 mg/mL (6 mL, 8 mL, 10 mL). **INJ, solution:** 40 mg/mL (2 mL, 20 mL); (Garamycin®): 40 mg/mL (2 mL) [DSC]. **INJ, solution, pediatric:** 10 mg/mL (2 mL). **INJ, solution, pediatric** [preservative free]: 10 mg/mL (2 mL). **OINT, ophthalmic** (Gentak®): 0.3% [3 mg/g] (3.5 g). **OINT, topical:** 0.1% (15 g, 30 g). **SOLN, ophthalmic:** 0.3% (5 mL, 15 mL); (Gentacidin®): 0.3% (5 mL); (Genoptic®): 0.3% (1 mL, 5 mL); (Gentak®): 0.3% (5 mL, 15 mL)

♦ **Gentamicin and Prednisolone** *see* Prednisolone and Gentamicin *on page 1033*
♦ **Gentamicin Sulfate** *see* Gentamicin *on page 587*

Gentian Violet *(JEN shun VYE oh let)*
Synonyms Crystal Violet; Methylrosaniline Chloride
Therapeutic Category Antibacterial, Topical; Antifungal Agent, Topical

Use Treatment of cutaneous or mucocutaneous infections caused by *Candida albicans* and other superficial skin infections

Pregnancy Risk Factor C

Contraindications Hypersensitivity to gentian violet or any component of the formulation; ulcerated areas; porphyria

Warnings/Precautions Infants should be turned face down after application to minimize amount of drug swallowed; may result in tattooing of the skin when applied to granulation tissue; solution is for external use only; avoid contact with eyes

Common Adverse Reactions Frequency not defined.

Dermatologic: Vesicle formation

Gastrointestinal: Esophagitis, ulceration of mucous membranes

Local: Burning, irritation

Respiratory: Laryngitis, laryngeal obstruction, tracheitis

Miscellaneous: Sensitivity reactions

Mechanism of Action Topical antiseptic/germicide effective against some vegetative gram-positive bacteria, particularly *Staphylococcus* sp, and some yeast; it is much less effective against gram-negative bacteria and is ineffective against acid-fast bacteria

Dosage Children and Adults: Topical: Apply 0.5% to 2% locally with cotton to lesion 2-3 times/ day for 3 days, do not swallow and avoid contact with eyes

Patient Information Drug stains skin and clothing purple; do not apply to an ulcerative lesion; may result in "tattooing" of the skin.

Dosage Forms SOLN, topical: 1% (30 mL); 2% (30 mL)

♦ **Gentran**® *see* Dextran *on page 361*

♦ **Geocillin**® *see* Carbenicillin *on page 217*

♦ **Geodon**® *see* Ziprasidone *on page 1328*

♦ **Geref**® **[DSC]** *see* Sermorelin Acetate *on page 1130*

♦ **Geref**® **Diagnostic** *see* Sermorelin Acetate *on page 1130*

♦ **Geritol**® **Tonic [OTC]** *see* Vitamins (Multiple/Oral) *on page 1312*

♦ **German Measles Vaccine** *see* Rubella Virus Vaccine (Live) *on page 1119*

♦ **Gevrabon**® **[OTC]** *see* Vitamin B Complex Combinations *on page 1311*

♦ **GF196960** *see* Tadalafil *on page 1184*

♦ **GG** *see* Guaifenesin *on page 603*

♦ **GHB** *see* Sodium Oxybate *on page 1149*

♦ **GI87084B** *see* Remifentanil *on page 1084*

Glatiramer Acetate (gla TIR a mer AS e tate)

U.S. Brand Names Copaxone®

Synonyms Copolymer-1

Therapeutic Category Biological, Miscellaneous

Use Treatment of relapsing-remitting type multiple sclerosis; studies indicate that it reduces the frequency of attacks and the severity of disability; appears to be most effective for patients with minimal disability

Pregnancy Risk Factor B

Contraindications Previous hypersensitivity to any component of the copolymer formulation, glatiramer acetate, or mannitol

Warnings/Precautions For S.C. use only, **not for I.V. administration**. Glatiramer acetate is antigenic, and may possibly lead to the induction of untoward host responses. Systemic postinjection reactions occur in a substantial percentage of patients (~10% in premarketing studies). Safety and efficacy have not been established in patients <18 years of age.

Common Adverse Reactions Reported in >2% of patients in placebo-controlled trials:

>10%:

Cardiovascular: Chest pain (21%), vasodilation (27%), palpitations (17%)

Central nervous system: Pain (28%), anxiety (23%)

Dermatologic: Pruritus (18%), rash (18%), diaphoresis (15%)

Gastrointestinal: Nausea (22%), diarrhea (12%)

Local: Injection site reactions: Pain (73%), erythema (66%), inflammation (49%), pruritus (40%), mass (27%), induration (13%), welt (11%)

Neuromuscular & skeletal: Weakness (41%), arthralgia (24%), hypertonia (22%), back pain (16%)

Respiratory: Dyspnea (19%), rhinitis (14%)

Miscellaneous: Infection (50%), flu-like syndrome (19%), lymphadenopathy (12%)

1% to 10%:

Cardiovascular: Peripheral edema (7%), facial edema (6%), edema (3%), tachycardia (5%)

Central nervous system: Fever (8%), vertigo (6%), migraine (5%), syncope (5%), agitation (4%), chills (4%), confusion (2%), nervousness (2%), speech disorder (2%)

Dermatologic: Bruising (8%), erythema (4%), urticaria (4%), skin nodule (2%)

Endocrine & metabolic: Dysmenorrhea (6%)

Gastrointestinal: Anorexia (8%), vomiting (6%), gastrointestinal disorder (5%), gastroenteritis (3%), weight gain (3%)

Genitourinary: Urinary urgency (10%), vaginal moniliasis (8%)

Local: Injection site reactions: Hemorrhage (5%), urticaria (5%)

Neuromuscular & skeletal: Tremor (7%), foot drop (3%)

Ocular: Eye disorder (4%), nystagmus (2%)

Otic: Ear pain (7%)

(Continued)

Glatiramer Acetate *(Continued)*

Respiratory: Bronchitis (9%), laryngismus (5%)

Miscellaneous: Neck pain (8%), bacterial infection (5%), herpes simplex (4%), cyst (2%)

Mechanism of Action Glatiramer is a mixture of random polymers of four amino acids; L-alanine, L-glutamic acid, L-lysine and L-tyrosine, the resulting mixture is antigenically similar to myelin basic protein, which is an important component of the myelin sheath of nerves; glatiramer is thought to suppress T-lymphocytes specific for a myelin antigen, it is also proposed that glatiramer interferes with the antigen-presenting function of certain immune cells opposing pathogenic T-cell function

Pharmacodynamics/Kinetics

Distribution: Small amounts of intact and partial hydrolyzed drug enter lymphatic circulation

Metabolism: S.C.: Large percentage hydrolyzed locally

Dosage Adults: S.C.: 20 mg daily

Administration If using glass prefilled syringe, **only** the auto*ject*® 2 *for glass syringe* device should be used (not the original Copaxone® autoject).

Patient Information It is essential to provide the patient with proper handling and reconstitution instruction, since they will most likely have to self-administer the drug for an extended period. Patients using prefilled glass syringe should use **only** the auto*ject*® 2 *for glass syringe* device (not the original Copaxone® autoject).

Dosage Forms INJ, powder for reconstitution: 20 mg

- Glaucoma Drug Therapy Comparison *see page 1481*
- Gleevec™ *see* Imatinib *on page 651*
- Gliadel® *see* Carmustine *on page 222*
- Glibenclamide *see* GlyBURIDE *on page 594*

Glimepiride *(GLYE me pye ride)*

Related Information

Hypoglycemic Drugs & Thiazolidinedione Information *on page 1378*

Sulfonamide Derivatives *on page 1404*

U.S. Brand Names Amaryl®

Therapeutic Category Antidiabetic Agent, Sulfonylurea; Hypoglycemic Agent, Oral; Sulfonylurea Agent

Use Management of type 2 diabetes mellitus (noninsulin dependent, NIDDM) as an adjunct to diet and exercise to lower blood glucose or in combination with metformin; use in combination with insulin to lower blood glucose in patients whose hyperglycemia cannot be controlled by diet and exercise in conjunction with an oral hypoglycemic agent

Pregnancy Risk Factor C

Contraindications Hypersensitivity to glimepiride, any component of the formulation, or sulfonamides; diabetic ketoacidosis (with or without coma)

Warnings/Precautions All sulfonylurea drugs are capable of producing severe hypoglycemia. Hypoglycemia is more likely to occur when caloric intake is deficient, after severe or prolonged exercise, when ethanol is ingested, or when more than one glucose-lowering drug is used.

Chemical similarities are present among sulfonamides, sulfonylureas, carbonic anhydrase inhibitors, thiazides, and loop diuretics (except ethacrynic acid). Use in patients with sulfonamide allergy is specifically contraindicated in product labeling, however, a risk of cross-reaction exists in patients with allergy to any of these compounds; avoid use when previous reaction has been severe.

Product labeling states oral hypoglycemic drugs may be associated with an increased cardiovascular mortality as compared to treatment with diet alone or diet plus insulin. Data to support this association are limited, and several studies, including a large prospective trial (UKPDS) have not supported an association.

Common Adverse Reactions 1% to 10%: Central nervous system: Headache

Drug Interactions

Cytochrome P450 Effect: Substrate of CYP2C8/9 (major)

Increased Effect/Toxicity: CYP2C8/9 inhibitors may increase the levels/effects of glimepiride; example inhibitors include delavirdine, ketoconazole, nicardipine, NSAIDs, and pioglitazone. Beta-blockers, chloramphenicol, cimetidine, clofibrate, fluconazole, gemfibrozil, pegvisomant, salicylates, sulfonamides, and tricyclic antidepressants may increase the hypoglycemic effects of glimepiride. Glimepiride may increase effects of coumarins and cyclosporine.

Decreased Effect: CYP2C8/9 inducers may decrease the levels/effects of glimepiride; example inducers include carbamazepine, phenobarbital, phenytoin, rifampin, rifapentine, and secobarbital. There may be a decreased effect of glimepiride with corticosteroids, estrogens, oral contraceptives, thiazide and other diuretics, phenothiazines, NSAIDs, thyroid products, nicotinic acid, isoniazid, sympathomimetics, urinary alkalinizers, and charcoal. **Note:** However, pooled data did **not** demonstrate drug interactions with calcium channel blockers, estrogens, NSAIDs, HMG-CoA reductase inhibitors, sulfonamides, or thyroid hormone.

Mechanism of Action Stimulates insulin release from the pancreatic beta cells; reduces glucose output from the liver; insulin sensitivity is increased at peripheral target sites

Pharmacodynamics/Kinetics

Onset of action: Peak effect: Blood glucose reductions: 2-3 hours

Duration: 24 hours

Absorption: 100%; delayed when given with food

Protein binding: >99.5%
Metabolism: Completely hepatic
Half-life elimination: 5-9 hours
Excretion: Urine and feces (as metabolites)

Dosage Oral (allow several days between dose titrations):

Adults: Initial: 1-2 mg once daily, administered with breakfast or the first main meal; usual maintenance dose: 1-4 mg once daily; after a dose of 2 mg once daily, increase in increments of 2 mg at 1- to 2-week intervals based upon the patient's blood glucose response to a maximum of 8 mg once daily

Combination with insulin therapy (fasting glucose level for instituting combination therapy is in the range of >150 mg/dL in plasma or serum depending on the patient): initial recommended dose: 8 mg once daily with the first main meal

After starting with low-dose insulin, upward adjustments of insulin can be done approximately weekly as guided by frequent measurements of fasting blood glucose. Once stable, combination-therapy patients should monitor their capillary blood glucose on an ongoing basis, preferably daily.

Dosing adjustment/comments in renal impairment: Cl_{cr} <22 mL/minute: Initial starting dose should be 1 mg and dosage increments should be based on fasting blood glucose levels
Dosing adjustment in hepatic impairment: No data available

Elderly: Initial: 1 mg/day; dose titration and maintenance dosing should be conservative to avoid hypoglycemia

Administration May be administered with a meal/food

Monitoring Parameters Urine for glucose and ketones; monitor for signs and symptoms of hypoglycemia (fatigue, excessive hunger, profuse sweating, numbness of extremities), fasting blood glucose, hemoglobin A_{1c}, fructosamine

Reference Range Target range: Adults:
Fasting blood glucose: <120 mg/dL
Glycosylated hemoglobin: <7%

Patient Information Patients must be counseled by someone experienced in diabetes education, signs and symptoms of hyper- and hypoglycemia, exercise and diet, blood glucose monitoring, and other related topics; eat regularly, do not skip meals; carry quick source of sugar; wear medical alert bracelet

Dosage Forms TAB: 1 mg, 2 mg, 4 mg

GlipiZIDE (GLIP i zide)

Related Information

Hypoglycemic Drugs & Thiazolidinedione Information on page 1378
Sulfonamide Derivatives on page 1404

U.S. Brand Names Glucotrol®; Glucotrol® XL

Synonyms Glydiazinamide

Therapeutic Category Antidiabetic Agent, Sulfonylurea; Hypoglycemic Agent, Oral; Sulfonylurea Agent

Use Management of type 2 diabetes mellitus (noninsulin dependent, NIDDM)

Pregnancy Risk Factor C

Contraindications Hypersensitivity to glipizide or any component of the formulation, other sulfonamides; type 1 diabetes mellitus (insulin dependent, IDDM)

Warnings/Precautions Use with caution in patients with severe hepatic disease.

Chemical similarities are present among sulfonamides, sulfonylureas, carbonic anhydrase inhibitors, thiazides, and loop diuretics (except ethacrynic acid). Use in patients with sulfonamide allergy is specifically contraindicated in product labeling, however, a risk of cross-reaction exists in patients with allergy to any of these compounds; avoid use when previous reaction has been severe.

Product labeling states oral hypoglycemic drugs may be associated with an increased cardiovascular mortality as compared to treatment with diet alone or diet plus insulin. Data to support this association are limited, and several studies, including a large prospective trial (UKPDS) have not supported an association.

At higher dosages, sulfonylureas may block the ATP-sensitive potassium channels, which have been suggested to increase the risk of cardiovascular events. In May, 2000, the National Diabetes Center (a patient advocacy group, not a government agency) issued a warning to avoid the use of sulfonylureas at higher dosages. The clinical data supporting an association is inconsistent, and there is no consensus within the medical community to support this assertion.

Common Adverse Reactions Frequency not defined.

Cardiovascular: Edema, syncope
Central nervous system: Anxiety, depression, dizziness, headache, insomnia, nervousness
Dermatologic: Rash, urticaria, photosensitivity, pruritus
Endocrine & metabolic: Hypoglycemia, hyponatremia, SIADH (rare)
Gastrointestinal: Anorexia, nausea, vomiting, diarrhea, epigastric fullness, constipation, heartburn, flatulence
Hematologic: Blood dyscrasias, aplastic anemia, hemolytic anemia, bone marrow suppression, thrombocytopenia, agranulocytosis
Hepatic: Cholestatic jaundice, hepatic porphyria
Neuromuscular & skeletal: Arthralgia, leg cramps, myalgia, tremor
Ocular: Blurred vision
(Continued)

GlipiZIDE *(Continued)*

Renal: Diuretic effect (minor)

Miscellaneous: Diaphoresis, disulfiram-like reaction

Drug Interactions

Cytochrome P450 Effect: Substrate of 2C8/9 (major)

Increased Effect/Toxicity: CYP2C8/9 inhibitors may increase the levels/effects of glipizide; example inhibitors include delavirdine, fluconazole, gemfibrozil, ketoconazole, nicardipine, NSAIDs, pioglitazone, and sulfonamides. Increased effects/hypoglycemic effects of glipizide with H_2 antagonists, anticoagulants, androgens, cimetidine, salicylates, tricyclic antidepressants, probenecid, MAO inhibitors, methyldopa, digitalis glycosides, and urinary acidifiers.

Decreased Effect: CYP2C8/9 inducers may decrease the levels/effects of glipizide; example inducers include carbamazepine, phenobarbital, phenytoin, rifampin, rifapentine, and secobarbital. Decreased effect of glipizide with beta-blockers, cholestyramine, hydantoins, thiazide diuretics, urinary alkalinizers, and charcoal.

Mechanism of Action Stimulates insulin release from the pancreatic beta cells; reduces glucose output from the liver; insulin sensitivity is increased at peripheral target sites

Pharmacodynamics/Kinetics

Onset of action: Peak effect: Blood glucose reductions: 1.5-2 hours

Duration: 12-24 hours

Absorption: Delayed with food

Protein binding: 92% to 99%

Metabolism: Hepatic with metabolites

Half-life elimination: 2-4 hours

Excretion: Urine (60% to 80%, 91% to 97% as metabolites); feces (11%)

Dosage Oral (allow several days between dose titrations): Adults: Initial: 5 mg/day; adjust dosage at 2.5-5 mg daily increments as determined by blood glucose response at intervals of several days.

Immediate release tablet: Maximum recommended once-daily dose: 15 mg; maximum recommended total daily dose: 40 mg

Extended release tablet (Glucotrol® XL): Maximum recommended dose: 20 mg

When transferring from insulin to glipizide:

Current insulin requirement ≤20 units: Discontinue insulin and initiate glipizide at usual dose

Current insulin requirement >20 units: Decrease insulin by 50% and initiate glipizide at usual dose; gradually decrease insulin dose based on patient response. Several days should elapse between dosage changes.

Elderly: Initial: 2.5 mg/day; increase by 2.5-5 mg/day at 1- to 2-week intervals

Dosing adjustment/comments in renal impairment: Cl_{cr} <10 mL/minute: Some investigators recommend not using

Dosing adjustment in hepatic impairment: Initial dosage should be 2.5 mg/day

Administration Administer immediate release tablets 30 minutes before a meal to achieve greatest reduction in postprandial hyperglycemia. Extended release tablets should be given with breakfast. Patients who are NPO may need to have their dose held to avoid hypoglycemia.

Monitoring Parameters Urine for glucose and ketones; monitor for signs and symptoms of hypoglycemia (fatigue, excessive hunger, profuse sweating, numbness of extremities), fasting blood glucose, hemoglobin A_{1c}, fructosamine

Reference Range Target range: Adults:

Fasting blood glucose: <120 mg/dL

Glycosylated hemoglobin: <7%

Patient Information Patients must be counseled by someone experienced in diabetes education, signs and symptoms of hyper- and hypoglycemia, exercise and diet, blood glucose monitoring, and other related topics; eat regularly, do not skip meals; carry quick source of sugar; wear medical alert bracelet

Dosage Forms TAB (Glucotrol®): 5 mg, 10 mg. **TAB, extended release** (Glucotrol® XL): 2.5 mg, 5 mg, 10 mg

Glipizide and Metformin *(GLIP i zide & met FOR min)*

U.S. Brand Names Metaglip™

Synonyms Glipizide and Metformin Hydrochloride; Metformin and Glipizide

Therapeutic Category Antidiabetic Agent, Combination

Use Initial therapy for management of type 2 diabetes mellitus (noninsulin dependent, NIDDM) when hyperglycemia cannot be managed with diet and exercise alone. Second-line therapy for management of type 2 diabetes (NIDDM) when hyperglycemia cannot be managed with a sulfonylurea or metformin along with diet and exercise.

Pregnancy Risk Factor C

Contraindications See individual agents.

Warnings/Precautions See individual agents.

Common Adverse Reactions Also see individual agents.

>10%:

Central nervous system: Headache (12%)

Endocrine & metabolic: Hypoglycemia (8% to 13%)

Gastrointestinal: Diarrhea (2% to 18%)

1% to 10%:

Cardiovascular: Hypertension (3%)

Central nervous system: Dizziness (2% to 5%)

Gastrointestinal: Nausea/vomiting (<1% to 8%), abdominal pain (6%)
Neuromuscular & skeletal: Musculoskeletal pain (8%)
Renal: Urinary tract infection (1%)
Respiratory: Upper respiratory tract infection (8% to 10%)

Drug Interactions
Cytochrome P450 Effect: Glipizide: **Substrate** of 2C8/9 (major)
Increased Effect/Toxicity: See individual agents.
Decreased Effect: See individual agents.

Mechanism of Action See individual agents.
The combination of glipizide and metformin is used to improve glycemic control in patients with type 2 diabetes mellitus (noninsulin dependent, NIDDM) by using two different, but complementary, mechanisms of action.

Pharmacodynamics/Kinetics See individual agents.

Dosage Oral:
Adults:
Type 2 diabetes, first-line therapy: Initial: Glipizide 2.5 mg/metformin 250 mg once daily with a meal. Dose adjustment: Increase dose by 1 tablet/day every 2 weeks, up to a maximum of glipizide 10 mg/metformin 1000 mg daily
Patients with fasting plasma glucose (FPG) 280-320 mg/dL: Consider glipizide 2.5 mg/metformin 500 mg twice daily. Dose adjustment: Increase dose by 1 tablet/day every 2 weeks, up to a maximum of glipizide 10 mg/metformin 2000 mg daily in divided doses
Type 2 diabetes, second-line therapy: Glipizide 2.5 mg/metformin 500 mg **or** glipizide 5 mg/metformin 500 mg twice daily with morning and evening meals; starting dose should not exceed current daily dose of glipizide (or sulfonylurea equivalent) or metformin. Dose adjustment: Titrate dose in increments of no more than glipizide 5 mg/metformin 500 mg, up to a maximum dose of glipizide 20 mg/metformin 2000 mg daily.
Elderly: Conservative doses are recommended in the elderly due to potentially decreased renal function; **do not titrate to maximum dose**; should not be used in patients ≥80 years unless renal function is verified as normal
Dosage adjustment in renal impairment: Risk of lactic acidosis increases with degree of renal impairment; contraindicated in renal disease or renal dysfunction (see Contraindications)
Dosage adjustment in hepatic impairment: Use should be avoided; liver disease is a risk factor for the development of lactic acidosis during metformin therapy.

Administration All doses should be administered with a meal. Twice-daily dosing should be administered with the morning and evening meals.

Monitoring Parameters Signs and symptoms of hypoglycemia, urine (glucose and ketones), FPG, Hb A_{1c}, and fructosamine. Initial and periodic monitoring of hematologic parameters (eg, hemoglobin/hematocrit and red blood cell indices) and renal function should be performed. Monitor at least annually once patient is on maintenance therapy. While megaloblastic anemia has been rarely seen with metformin, if suspected, vitamin B_{12} deficiency should be excluded.

Reference Range Target range: Adults: Fasting blood glucose: <120 mg/dL; glycosylated hemoglobin: <7%

Dosage Forms TAB, film coated: 2.5/250: Glipizide 2.5 mg and metformin 250 mg; 2.5/500: Glipizide 2.5 mg and metformin 500 mg; 5/500: Glipizide 5 mg and metformin 500 mg

♦ **Glipizide and Metformin Hydrochloride** *see* Glipizide and Metformin *on page 592*
♦ **Glivec** *see* Imatinib *on page 651*
♦ **GlucaGen®** *see* Glucagon *on page 593*
♦ **GlucaGen® Diagnostic Kit** *see* Glucagon *on page 593*

Glucagon (GLOO ka gon)

U.S. Brand Names GlucaGen®; GlucaGen® Diagnostic Kit; Glucagon Diagnostic Kit; Glucagon Emergency Kit
Therapeutic Category Antidote, Hypoglycemia; Diagnostic Agent, Gastrointestinal
Use Management of hypoglycemia; diagnostic aid in the radiologic examination of GI tract when a hypnotic state is needed
Unlabeled/Investigational Use Used with some success as a cardiac stimulant in management of severe cases of beta-adrenergic blocking agent overdosage
Pregnancy Risk Factor B
Contraindications Hypersensitivity to glucagon or any component of the formulation
Warnings/Precautions Use with caution in patients with a history of insulinoma and/or pheochromocytoma
Common Adverse Reactions Frequency not defined.
Gastrointestinal: Nausea, vomiting (high incidence with rapid administration of high doses)
Miscellaneous: Hypersensitivity reactions (hypotension, respiratory distress, urticaria)
Drug Interactions
Increased Effect/Toxicity: Glucagon and warfarin - hypoprothrombinemic effects may be increased, possibly with bleeding.
Mechanism of Action Stimulates adenylate cyclase to produce increased cyclic AMP, which promotes hepatic glycogenolysis and gluconeogenesis, causing a raise in blood glucose levels
Pharmacodynamics/Kinetics
Onset of action: Peak effect: Blood glucose levels: Parenteral: 5-20 minutes
Duration: 60-90 minutes
Metabolism: Primarily hepatic; some inactivation occurring renally and in plasma
Half-life elimination, plasma: 3-10 minutes
(Continued)

Glucagon (Continued)

Dosage

Hypoglycemia or insulin shock therapy: I.M., I.V., S.C.:

Children: 0.025-0.1 mg/kg/dose, not to exceed 1 mg/dose, repeated in 20 minutes as needed

Adults: 0.5-1 mg, may repeat in 20 minutes as needed

If patient fails to respond to glucagon, I.V. dextrose must be given

Beta-blocker overdose (unlabeled use): I.V.: 3-10 mg **or** initially 0.5-5 mg bolus followed by continuous infusion 1-5 mg/hour

Diagnostic aid: Adults: I.M., I.V.: 0.25-2 mg 10 minutes prior to procedure

Administration Reconstitute powder for injection by adding 1 or 10 mL of sterile diluent to a vial containing 1 or 10 units of the drug, respectively, to provide solutions containing 1 mg of glucagon/mL; if dose to be administered is <2 mg of the drug → use only the diluent provided by the manufacturer; if >2 mg → use sterile water for injection; use immediately after reconstitution

Monitoring Parameters Blood pressure, blood glucose

Patient Information Identify appropriate support person to administer glucagon if necessary. Follow prescribers instructions for administering glucagon. Review diet, insulin administration, and testing procedures with prescriber or diabetic educator.

Dosage Forms INJ, powder for reconstitution: (GlucaGen®, Glucagon): 1 mg [1 unit]; (GlucaGen® Diagnostic Kit, [with sterile water]): 1 mg [1 unit]; (Glucagon Diagnostic Kit, Glucagon Emergency Kit [with diluent of glycerin 12 mg/mL and water for injection]): 1 mg [1 unit]

GlyBURIDE (GLYE byoor ide)

Related Information

Hypoglycemic Drugs & Thiazolidinedione Information *on page 1378*

Sulfonamide Derivatives *on page 1404*

U.S. Brand Names Diaβeta®; Glynase® PresTab®; Micronase®

Synonyms Diabeta; Glibenclamide; Glybenclamide; Glybenzcyclamide

Therapeutic Category Antidiabetic Agent, Sulfonylurea; Hypoglycemic Agent, Oral; Sulfonylurea Agent

Use Management of type 2 diabetes mellitus (noninsulin dependent, NIDDM)

Unlabeled/Investigational Use Alternative to insulin in women for the treatment of gestational diabetes (11-33 weeks gestation)

Pregnancy Risk Factor C

Contraindications Hypersensitivity to glyburide, any component of the formulation, or other sulfonamides; type 1 diabetes mellitus (insulin dependent, IDDM), diabetic ketoacidosis with or without coma

Warnings/Precautions Elderly: Rapid and prolonged hypoglycemia (>12 hours) despite hypertonic glucose injections have been reported; age and hepatic and renal impairment are independent risk factors for hypoglycemia; dosage titration should be made at weekly intervals. Use with caution in patients with renal and hepatic impairment, malnourished or debilitated conditions, or adrenal or pituitary insufficiency.

Chemical similarities are present among sulfonamides, sulfonylureas, carbonic anhydrase inhibitors, thiazides, and loop diuretics (except ethacrynic acid). Use in patients with sulfonamide allergy is specifically contraindicated in product labeling, however, a risk of cross-reaction exists in patients with allergy to any of these compounds; avoid use when previous reaction has been severe.

Product labeling states oral hypoglycemic drugs may be associated with an increased cardiovascular mortality as compared to treatment with diet alone or diet plus insulin. Data to support this association are limited, and several studies, including a large prospective trial (UKPDS) have not supported an association.

Common Adverse Reactions Frequency not defined.

Central nervous system: Headache, dizziness

Dermatologic: Pruritus, rash, urticaria, photosensitivity reaction

Endocrine & metabolic: Hypoglycemia, hyponatremia (SIADH reported with other sulfonylureas)

Gastrointestinal: Nausea, epigastric fullness, heartburn, constipation, diarrhea, anorexia

Genitourinary: Nocturia

Hematologic: Leukopenia, thrombocytopenia, hemolytic anemia, aplastic anemia, bone marrow suppression, agranulocytosis

Hepatic: Cholestatic jaundice, hepatitis
Neuromuscular & skeletal: Arthralgia, paresthesia
Ocular: Blurred vision
Renal: Diuretic effect (minor)

Drug Interactions
Cytochrome P450 Effect: Inhibits CYP3A4 (weak)
Increased Effect/Toxicity: Increased hypoglycemic effects of glyburide may occur with oral anticoagulants (warfarin), phenytoin, other hydantoins, salicylates, NSAIDs, sulfonamides, and beta-blockers. Ethanol ingestion may cause disulfiram reactions.
Decreased Effect: Thiazides and other diuretics, corticosteroids may decrease effectiveness of glyburide.

Mechanism of Action Stimulates insulin release from the pancreatic beta cells; reduces glucose output from the liver; insulin sensitivity is increased at peripheral target sites

Pharmacodynamics/Kinetics
Onset of action: Serum insulin levels begin to increase 15-60 minutes after a single dose
Duration: ≤24 hours
Protein binding, plasma: >99%
Metabolism: To one moderately active and several inactive metabolites
Half-life elimination: 5-16 hours; may be prolonged with renal or hepatic impairment
Time to peak, serum: Adults: 2-4 hours
Excretion: Feces (50%) and urine (50%) as metabolites

Dosage Oral:
Adults:
Initial: 2.5-5 mg/day, administered with breakfast or the first main meal of the day. In patients who are more sensitive to hypoglycemic drugs, start at 1.25 mg/day.
Increase in increments of no more than 2.5 mg/day at weekly intervals based on the patient's blood glucose response
Maintenance: 1.25-20 mg/day given as single or divided doses; maximum: 20 mg/day
Elderly: Initial: 1.25-2.5 mg/day, increase by 1.25-2.5 mg/day every 1-3 weeks
Micronized tablets (Glynase™ PresTab™): Adults:
Initial: 1.5-3 mg/day, administered with breakfast or the first main meal of the day in patients who are more sensitive to hypoglycemic drugs, start at 0.75 mg/day. Increase in increments of no more than 1.5 mg/day in weekly intervals based on the patient's blood glucose response.
Maintenance: 0.75-12 mg/day given as a single dose or in divided doses. Some patients (especially those receiving >6 mg/day) may have a more satisfactory response with twice-daily dosing.

Dosing adjustment/comments in renal impairment: Cl_{cr} <50 mL/minute: **Not recommended**
Dosing adjustment in hepatic impairment: Use conservative initial and maintenance doses and avoid use in severe disease

Administration Administer with meals at the same time each day.

Monitoring Parameters Signs and symptoms of hypoglycemia, fasting blood glucose, hemoglobin A_{1c}

Reference Range Target range: Adults:
Fasting blood glucose: <120 mg/dL
Glycosylated hemoglobin: <7%

Patient Information Patients must be counseled by someone experienced in diabetes education, signs and symptoms of hyper- and hypoglycemia, exercise and diet, blood glucose monitoring, and other related topics; eat regularly, do not skip meals; carry quick source of sugar; wear medical alert bracelet

Dosage Forms TAB (Diaβeta®, Micronase®): 1.25 mg, 2.5 mg, 5 mg. **TAB, micronized** (Glynase® PresTab®): 1.5 mg, 3 mg, 6 mg

Glyburide and Metformin (GLYE byor ide & met FOR min)

U.S. Brand Names Glucovance®
Synonyms Glyburide and Metformin Hydrochloride; Metformin and Glyburide
Therapeutic Category Antidiabetic Agent, Combination
Use Initial therapy for management of type 2 diabetes mellitus (noninsulin dependent, NIDDM). Second-line therapy for management of type 2 diabetes (NIDDM) when hyperglycemia cannot be managed with a sulfonylurea or metformin; combination therapy with a thiazolidinedione may be required to achieve additional control.
Pregnancy Risk Factor B (manufacturer); C (expert analysis)
Contraindications Hypersensitivity to glyburide or other sulfonamides, metformin, or any component of the formulation; renal disease or renal dysfunction (serum creatinine ≥1.5 mg/dL in males or ≥1.4 mg/dL in females, or abnormal creatinine clearance which may also result from conditions such as cardiovascular collapse, acute myocardial infarction, and septicemia); acute or chronic metabolic acidosis with or without coma (including diabetic ketoacidosis); congestive heart failure requiring pharmacologic treatment

Note: Temporarily discontinue in patients undergoing radiologic studies in which intravascular iodinated contrast materials are utilized.

Warnings/Precautions Age, hepatic and renal impairment are independent risk factors for hypoglycemia. Use with caution in patients with hepatic impairment, malnourished or debilitated conditions, or adrenal or pituitary insufficiency. Use caution in patients with renal impairment. Lactic acidosis is a rare, but potentially severe consequence of therapy with metformin. Withhold therapy in hypoxemia, dehydration, or sepsis. The risk of lactic acidosis is increased
(Continued)

Glyburide and Metformin *(Continued)*

in any patient with CHF requiring pharmacologic management. This risk is particularly high during acute or unstable CHF because of the risk of hypoperfusion and hypoxemia.

Metformin is substantially excreted by the kidney. The risk of accumulation and lactic acidosis increases with the degree of impairment of renal function. Patients with renal function below the limit of normal for their age should not receive metformin. In elderly patients, renal function should be monitored regularly; should not be used in any patient ≥80 years of age unless measurement of creatinine clearance verifies normal renal function. Use of concomitant medications that may affect renal function (ie, affect tubular secretion) may also affect metformin disposition. Metformin should be suspended in patients with dehydration and/or prerenal azotemia. Therapy should be suspended for any surgical procedures (resume only after normal intake resumed and normal renal function is verified).Intravascular iodinated contrast materials used for radiologic studies are associated with alteration of renal function and may increase risk of lactic acidosis. Discontinue Glucovance® at the time of or prior to the procedure and withhold for 48 hours subsequent to the procedure; reinstitute only after renal function has been re-evaluated and found to be normal.

Chemical similarities are present among sulfonamides, sulfonylureas, carbonic anhydrase inhibitors, thiazides, and loop diuretics (except ethacrynic acid). Use in patients with sulfonamide allergy is specifically contraindicated in product labeling, however a risk of cross-reaction exists in patients with allergy to any of these compounds; avoid use when previous reaction has been severe.

Product labeling states oral hypoglycemic drugs may be associated with an increased cardiovascular mortality as compared to treatment with diet alone or diet plus insulin. Data to support this association are limited, and several studies, including a large prospective trial (UKPDS), have not supported an association.

Common Adverse Reactions (Also refer to individual agents)

>10%:

Endocrine & metabolic: Hypoglycemia (11% to 38%, effects higher when increased doses were used as initial therapy)

Gastrointestinal: Diarrhea (17%)

Respiratory: Upper respiratory infection (17%)

1% to 10%:

Central nervous system: Headache (9%), dizziness (6%)

Gastrointestinal: Nausea (8%), vomiting (8%), abdominal pain (7%) (combined GI effects increased to 38% in patients taking high doses as initial therapy)

Drug Interactions

Increased Effect/Toxicity: See individual agents.

Decreased Effect: See individual agents.

Mechanism of Action See individual agents.

The combination of glyburide and metformin is used to improve glycemic control in patients with type 2 diabetes mellitus by using two different, but complementary, mechanisms of action.

Pharmacodynamics/Kinetics

Glucovance®:

Bioavailability: 18% with 2.5 mg glyburide/500 mg metformin dose; 7% with 5 mg glyburide/500 mg metformin dose; bioavailability is greater than that of Micronase® brand of glyburide and therefore not bioequivalent

Time to peak: 2.75 hours when taken with food

Glyburide: See Glyburide monograph.

Metformin: This component of Glucovance® is bioequivalent to metformin coadministration with glyburide.

Dosage Note: Dose must be individualized. Dosages expressed as glyburide/metformin components.

Adults: Oral:

Initial therapy (no prior treatment with sulfonylurea or metformin): 1.25 mg/250 mg once daily with a meal; patients with Hb A_{1c} >9% or fasting plasma glucose (FPG) >200 mg/dL may start with 1.25 mg/250 mg twice daily

Dosage may be increased in increments of 1.25 mg/250 mg, at intervals of not less than 2 weeks; maximum daily dose: 10 mg/2000 mg (limited experience with higher doses)

Previously treated with a sulfonylurea or metformin alone: Initial: 2.5 mg/500 mg or 5 mg/500 mg twice daily; increase in increments no greater than 5 mg/500 mg; maximum daily dose: 20 mg/2000 mg

When switching patients previously on a sulfonylurea and metformin together, do not exceed the daily dose of glyburide (or glyburide equivalent) or metformin.

Note: May combine with a thiazolidinedione in patients with an inadequate response to glyburide/metformin therapy (risk of hypoglycemia may be increased).

Elderly: Oral: Conservative doses are recommended in the elderly due to potentially decreased renal function; **do not titrate to maximum dose**; should not be used in patients ≥80 years of age unless renal function is verified as normal

Dosage adjustment in renal impairment: Risk of lactic acidosis increases with degree of renal impairment; contraindicated in renal disease or renal dysfunction (see Contraindications)

Dosage adjustment in hepatic impairment: Use conservative initial and maintenance doses and avoid use in severe hepatic disease

Administration All doses should be administered with a meal. Twice-daily dosing should be administered with the morning and evening meals.

Monitoring Parameters Signs and symptoms of hypoglycemia, urine for glucose and ketones, FPG, Hb A$_{1c}$, and fructosamine. Initial and periodic monitoring of hematologic parameters (eg, hemoglobin/hematocrit and red blood cell indices) and renal function should be performed. Monitor at least annually once patient is on maintenance therapy. While megaloblastic anemia has been rarely seen with metformin, if suspected, vitamin B$_{12}$ deficiency should be excluded.

Reference Range Target range: Adults: Fasting blood glucose: <120 mg/dL; glycosylated hemoglobin: <7%

Patient Information See individual agents.

Dosage Forms TAB, film coated: 1.25 mg/250 mg: Glyburide 1.25 mg and metformin 250 mg; 2.5 mg/500 mg: Glyburide 2.5 mg and metformin 500 mg; 5 mg/500 mg: Glyburide 5 mg and metformin 500 mg

♦ **Glyburide and Metformin Hydrochloride** see Glyburide and Metformin on page 595
♦ **Glycerol Guaiacolate** see Guaifenesin on page 603
♦ **Glyceryl Trinitrate** see Nitroglycerin on page 910
♦ **Glycoprotein Antagonists** see page 1376

Glycopyrrolate (glye koe PYE roe late)

U.S. Brand Names Robinul®; Robinul® Forte

Synonyms Glycopyrronium Bromide

Therapeutic Category Anticholinergic Agent; Antispasmodic Agent, Gastrointestinal

Use Inhibit salivation and excessive secretions of the respiratory tract preoperatively; reversal of neuromuscular blockade; control of upper airway secretions; adjunct in treatment of peptic ulcer

Pregnancy Risk Factor B

Contraindications Hypersensitivity to glycopyrrolate or any component of the formulation; ulcerative colitis; narrow-angle glaucoma; acute hemorrhage; tachycardia; obstructive uropathy; paralytic ileus, obstructive disease of GI tract; myasthenia gravis

Warnings/Precautions Not recommended in children <12 years of age for the management of peptic ulcer; infants, patients with Down syndrome, and children with spastic paralysis or brain damage may be hypersensitive to antimuscarine effects. Use caution in elderly, patients with autonomic neuropathy, hepatic or renal disease, ulcerative colitis may predispose megacolon, hyperthyroidism, CAD, CHF, arrhythmias, tachycardia, BPH, hiatal hernia, with reflux.

Common Adverse Reactions

>10%:
  Dermatologic: Dry skin
  Gastrointestinal: Constipation, dry throat, xerostomia
  Local: Irritation at injection site
  Respiratory: Dry nose
  Miscellaneous: Diaphoresis (decreased)

1% to 10%:
  Dermatologic: Increased sensitivity to light
  Endocrine & metabolic: Decreased flow of breast milk
  Gastrointestinal: Dysphagia

Drug Interactions

Increased Effect/Toxicity: Increased toxicity with amantadine and cyclopropane. Effects of other anticholinergic agents may be increased by glycopyrrolate.

Decreased Effect: Decreased effect of levodopa.

Mechanism of Action Blocks the action of acetylcholine at parasympathetic sites in smooth muscle, secretory glands, and the CNS

Pharmacodynamics/Kinetics

Onset of action: Oral: 50 minutes; I.M.: 20-40 minutes; I.V.: ~1 minute
  Peak effect: Oral: ~1 hour
Duration: Vagal effect: 2-3 hours; Inhibition of salivation: Up to 7 hours; Anticholinergic: Oral: 8-12 hours
Absorption: Oral: Poor and erratic
Metabolism: Hepatic (minimal)
Bioavailability: ~10%
Half-life elimination: 20-40 minutes

Dosage

Children:
  Control of secretions:
    Oral: 40-100 mcg/kg/dose 3-4 times/day
    I.M., I.V.: 4-10 mcg/kg/dose every 3-4 hours; maximum: 0.2 mg/dose or 0.8 mg/24 hours
    Intraoperative: I.V.: 4 mcg/kg not to exceed 0.1 mg; repeat at 2- to 3-minute intervals as needed
  Preoperative: I.M.:
    <2 years: 4.4-8.8 mcg/kg 30-60 minutes before procedure
    >2 years: 4.4 mcg/kg 30-60 minutes before procedure
Children and Adults: Reverse neuromuscular blockade: I.V.: 0.2 mg for each 1 mg of neostigmine or 5 mg of pyridostigmine administered or 5-15 mcg/kg glycopyrrolate with 25-70 mcg/kg of neostigmine or 0.1-0.3 mg/kg of pyridostigmine (agents usually administered simultaneously, but glycopyrrolate may be administered first if bradycardia is present)
Adults:
  Intraoperative: I.V.: 0.1 mg repeated as needed at 2- to 3-minute intervals
(Continued)

Glycopyrrolate *(Continued)*

Preoperative: I.M.: 4.4 mcg/kg 30-60 minutes before procedure
Peptic ulcer:
Oral: 1-2 mg 2-3 times/day
I.M., I.V.: 0.1-0.2 mg 3-4 times/day

Administration For I.V. administration, glycopyrrolate may also be administered via the tubing of a running I.V. infusion of a compatible solution

Patient Information Maintain good oral hygiene habits, because lack of saliva may increase chance of cavities. Observe caution while driving or performing other tasks requiring alertness, as may cause drowsiness, dizziness, or blurred vision. Report skin rash, flushing, or eye pain; or if difficulty in urinating, constipation, or sensitivity to light becomes severe or persists.

Dosage Forms INJ, solution (Robinul®): 0.2 mg/mL (1 mL, 2 mL, 5 mL, 20 mL). **TAB:** (Robinul®): 1 mg; (Robinul® Forte): 2 mg

- ◆ **Glycopyrronium Bromide** *see* Glycopyrrolate *on page 597*
- ◆ **Glydiazinamide** *see* GlipiZIDE *on page 591*
- ◆ **Glynase® PresTab®** *see* GlyBURIDE *on page 594*
- ◆ **Gly-Oxide® [OTC]** *see* Carbamide Peroxide *on page 216*
- ◆ **Glyquin®** *see* Hydroquinone *on page 636*
- ◆ **Glyset®** *see* Miglitol *on page 841*
- ◆ **Glytuss® [OTC]** *see* Guaifenesin *on page 603*
- ◆ **GM-CSF** *see* Sargramostim *on page 1124*
- ◆ **GnRH** *see* Gonadorelin *on page 599*
- ◆ **Gold Bond® Antifungal [OTC]** *see* Tolnaftate *on page 1241*

Gold Sodium Thiomalate *(gold SOW dee um thye oh MAL ate)*

U.S. Brand Names Aurolate®
Therapeutic Category Antirheumatic, Disease Modifying; Gold Compound
Use Treatment of progressive rheumatoid arthritis
Pregnancy Risk Factor C
Contraindications Hypersensitivity to gold compounds or any component of the formulation; systemic lupus erythematosus; history of blood dyscrasias; congestive heart failure, exfoliative dermatitis, colitis
Warnings/Precautions Frequent monitoring of patients for signs and symptoms of toxicity will prevent serious adverse reactions; NSAIDs and corticosteroids may be discontinued after initiating gold therapy; must not be injected I.V.

Explain the possibility of adverse reactions before initiating therapy; signs of gold toxicity include decrease in hemoglobin, leukopenia, granulocytes and platelets; proteinuria, hematuria, pigmentation, pruritus, stomatitis or persistent diarrhea, rash, metallic taste; advise patient to report any symptoms of toxicity; use with caution in patients with liver or renal disease

Common Adverse Reactions
>10%:
Dermatologic: Itching, rash
Gastrointestinal: Stomatitis, gingivitis, glossitis
Ocular: Conjunctivitis
1% to 10%:
Dermatologic: Urticaria, alopecia
Hematologic: Eosinophilia, leukopenia, thrombocytopenia
Renal: Proteinuria, hematuria

Drug Interactions
Decreased Effect: Penicillamine and acetylcysteine may decrease effect of gold sodium thiomalate.

Mechanism of Action Unknown, may decrease prostaglandin synthesis or may alter cellular mechanisms by inhibiting sulfhydryl systems

Pharmacodynamics/Kinetics
Onset of action: Delayed; may require up to 3 months
Half-life elimination: 5 days; may be prolonged with multiple doses
Time to peak, serum: 4-6 hours
Excretion: Urine (60% to 90%); feces (10% to 40%)

Dosage I.M.:
Children: Initial: Test dose of 10 mg is recommended, followed by 1 mg/kg/week for 20 weeks; maintenance: 1 mg/kg/dose at 2- to 4-week intervals thereafter for as long as therapy is clinically beneficial and toxicity does not develop. Administration for 2-4 months is usually required before clinical improvement is observed.
Adults: 10 mg first week; 25 mg second week; then 25-50 mg/week until 1 g cumulative dose has been given; if improvement occurs without adverse reactions, administer 25-50 mg every 2-3 weeks for 2-20 weeks, then every 3-4 weeks indefinitely
Dosing adjustment in renal impairment:
Cl$_{cr}$ 50-80 mL/minute: Administer 50% of normal dose
Cl$_{cr}$ <50 mL/minute: Avoid use

Administration Deep I.M. injection into the upper outer quadrant of the gluteal region addition of 0.1 mL of 1% lidocaine to each injection may reduce the discomfort associated with I.M. administration

Monitoring Parameters Signs and symptoms of gold toxicity, CBC with differential and platelet count, urinalysis

Reference Range Gold: Normal: 0-0.1 μg/mL (SI: 0-0.0064 μmol/L); Therapeutic: 1-3 μg/mL (SI: 0.06-0.18 μmol/L); Urine: <0.1 μg/24 hour

Patient Information Minimize exposure to sunlight; benefits from drug therapy may take as long as 3 months to appear; report pruritus, rash, sore mouth; metallic taste may occur

Dosage Forms INJ, solution: 50 mg/mL (1 mL, 10 mL)

♦ **GoLYTELY®** see Polyethylene Glycol-Electrolyte Solution on page 1013

Gonadorelin (goe nad oh RELL in)

U.S. Brand Names Factrel®

Synonyms GnRH; Gonadorelin Acetate; Gonadorelin Hydrochloride; Gonadotropin Releasing Hormone; LHRH; LRH; Luteinizing Hormone Releasing Hormone

Therapeutic Category Diagnostic Agent, Gonadotrophic Hormone; Gonadotropin

Use Evaluation of functional capacity and response of gonadotrophic hormones; evaluate abnormal gonadotropin regulation as in precocious puberty and delayed puberty.

Orphan drug: Lutrepulse®: Induction of ovulation in females with hypothalamic amenorrhea

Pregnancy Risk Factor B

Contraindications Hypersensitivity to gonadorelin or any component of the formulation; women with any condition that could be exacerbated by pregnancy; patients who have ovarian cysts or causes of anovulation other than those of hypothalamic origin; any condition that may worsened by reproductive hormones

Warnings/Precautions Hypersensitivity and anaphylactic reactions have occurred following multiple-dose administration; multiple pregnancy is a possibility; use with caution in women in whom pregnancy could worsen pre-existing conditions (eg, pituitary prolactinemia). Multiple pregnancy is a possibility with Lutrepulse®.

Common Adverse Reactions 1% to 10%: Local: Pain at injection site

Drug Interactions

    Increased Effect/Toxicity: Increased levels/effect with androgens, estrogens, progestins, glucocorticoids, spironolactone, and levodopa.

    Decreased Effect: Decreased levels/effect with oral contraceptives, digoxin, phenothiazines, and dopamine antagonists.

Mechanism of Action Stimulates the release of luteinizing hormone (LH) from the anterior pituitary gland

Pharmacodynamics/Kinetics

    Onset of action: Peak effect: Maximal LH release: ~20 minutes

    Duration: 3-5 hours

    Half-life elimination: 4 minutes

Dosage

    Diagnostic test: Children >12 years and Female Adults: I.V., S.C. hydrochloride salt: 100 mcg administered in women during early phase of menstrual cycle (day 1-7)

    Primary hypothalamic amenorrhea: Female Adults: Acetate: I.V.: 5 mcg every 90 minutes via Lutrepulse® pump kit at treatment intervals of 21 days (pump will pulsate every 90 minutes for 7 days)

Administration

    Factrel®: Dilute in 3 mL of normal saline; administer I.V. push over 30 seconds

    Lutrepulse®: A presterilized reservoir bag with the infusion catheter set supplied with the kit should be filled with the reconstituted solution and administered I.V. using the Lutrepulse® pump. Set the pump to deliver 25-50 mL of solution, based upon the dose, over a pulse period of 1 minute and at a pulse frequency of 90 minutes.

Monitoring Parameters LH, FSH

Dosage Forms INJ, powder for reconstitution (Factrel®): 100 mcg

♦ **Gonadorelin Acetate** see Gonadorelin on page 599

♦ **Gonadorelin Hydrochloride** see Gonadorelin on page 599

♦ **Gonadotropin Releasing Hormone** see Gonadorelin on page 599

♦ **Gonal-F®** see Follitropin on page 555

♦ **Goody's® Extra Strength Headache Powder [OTC]** see Acetaminophen, Aspirin, and Caffeine on page 27

♦ **Goody's® Extra Strength Pain Relief [OTC]** see Acetaminophen, Aspirin, and Caffeine on page 27

♦ **Goody's PM® Powder** see Acetaminophen and Diphenhydramine on page 26

♦ **Gormel® [OTC]** see Urea on page 1282

Goserelin (GOE se rel in)

U.S. Brand Names Zoladex®

Synonyms D-Ser(Bu^t)^6,Azgly^{10}-LHRH; Goserelin Acetate; ICI-118630; NSC-606864

Therapeutic Category Antineoplastic Agent, Miscellaneous; Gonadotropin Releasing Hormone Analog; Luteinizing Hormone-Releasing Hormone Analog

Use Palliative treatment of advanced breast cancer and carcinoma of the prostate; treatment of endometriosis, including pain relief and reduction of endometriotic lesions; endometrial thinning agent as part of treatment for dysfunctional uterine bleeding

Pregnancy Risk Factor X (endometriosis, endometrial thinning); D (advanced breast cancer)

Contraindications Hypersensitivity to goserelin or any component of the formulation; pregnancy (or potential to become pregnant); breast-feeding

(Continued)

Goserelin *(Continued)*

Warnings/Precautions Transient worsening of signs and symptoms, usually manifested by an increase in cancer-related pain, may develop during the first few weeks of treatment. Urinary tract obstruction or spinal cord compression have been reported when used for prostate cancer; closely observe patients for weakness, paresthesias, and urinary tract obstruction in first few weeks of therapy. Decreased bone density has been reported in women and may be irreversible; use caution if other risk factors are present; evaluate and institute preventative treatment if necessary. Safety and efficacy have not been established in pediatric patients.

Common Adverse Reactions Percentages reported in males with prostatic carcinoma and females with endometriosis using the 1-month implant:

>10%:

Central nervous system: Headache (female 75%, male 1% to 5%), emotional lability (female 60%), depression (female 54%, male 1% to 5%), pain (female 17%, male 8%), insomnia (female 11%, male 5%)

Dermatologic: Diaphoresis (female 45%, male 6%)

Endocrine & metabolic: Hot flashes (female 96%, male 62%), sexual dysfunction (21%), erections decreased (18%), libido decreased (female 61%), breast enlargement (female 18%)

Genitourinary: Lower urinary symptoms (male 13%), vaginitis (75%), dyspareunia (female 14%)

Miscellaneous: Infection (female 13%)

1% to 10%:

Cardiovascular: CHF (male 5%), arrhythmia, cerebrovascular accident, hypertension, myocardial infarction, peripheral vascular disorder, chest pain, palpitations, tachycardia, edema

Central nervous system: Lethargy (male 8%), dizziness (female 6%, male 5%), abnormal thinking, anxiety, chills, fever, malaise, migraine, somnolence

Dermatologic: Rash (female >1%, male 6%), alopecia, bruising, dry skin, skin discoloration

Endocrine & metabolic: Breast pain (female 7%), breast swelling/tenderness (male 1% to 5%), dysmenorrhea, gout, hyperglycemia

Gastrointestinal: Anorexia (female >1%, male 5%), nausea (male 5%), constipation, diarrhea, flatulence, dyspepsia, ulcer, vomiting, weight increased, xerostomia

Genitourinary: Renal insufficiency, urinary frequency, urinary obstruction, urinary tract infection, vaginal hemorrhage

Hematologic: Anemia, hemorrhage

Neuromuscular & skeletal: Arthralgia, bone mineral density decreased (female; ~4% decrease in 6 months), joint disorder, paresthesia

Ocular: Amblyopia, dry eyes

Respiratory: Upper respiratory tract infection (male 7%), COPD (male 5%), pharyngitis (female 5%), bronchitis, cough, epistaxis, rhinitis, sinusitis

Miscellaneous: Allergic reaction

Mechanism of Action Goserelin is a synthetic analog of luteinizing-hormone-releasing hormone (LHRH). Following an initial increase in luteinizing hormone (LH) and follicle stimulating hormone (FSH), chronic administration of goserelin results in a sustained suppression of pituitary gonadotropins. Serum testosterone falls to levels comparable to surgical castration. The exact mechanism of this effect is unknown, but may be related to changes in the control of LH or down-regulation of LH receptors.

Pharmacodynamics/Kinetics Note: Data reported using the 1-month implant.

Absorption: S.C.: Rapid and can be detected in serum in 10 minutes

Distribution: V_d: Male: 44.1 L; Female: 20.3 L

Time to peak, serum: S.C.: Male: 12-15 days, Female: 8-22 days

Half-life elimination: S.C.: Male: ~4 hours, Female: ~2 hours; Renal impairment: Male: 12 hours

Excretion: Urine (90%)

Dosage S.C.: Adults:

Prostate cancer:

Monthly implant: 3.6 mg injected into upper abdomen every 28 days

3-month implant: 10.8 mg injected into the upper abdominal wall every 12 weeks

Note: Treatment should begin 8 weeks prior to radiotherapy in Stage B2-C prostate cancer; treatment may continue indefinitely

Breast cancer, endometriosis, endometrial thinning: Monthly implant: 3.6 mg injected into upper abdomen every 28 days

Note: For breast cancer, treatment may continue indefinitely; for endometriosis, it is recommended that duration of treatment not exceed 6 months. Only 1-2 doses are recommended for endometrial thinning.

Dosing adjustment in renal/hepatic impairment: No adjustment is necessary

Administration Subcutaneous implant: Insert the hypodermic needle into the subcutaneous fat. Do not try to aspirate with the goserelin syringe. If the needle is in a large vessel, blood will immediately appear in the syringe chamber. Change the direction of the needle so it parallels the abdominal wall. Push the needle in until the barrel hub touches the patient's skin. Fully depress the plunger to discharge. Withdraw needle and bandage the site. Confirm discharge by ensuring tip of the plunger is visible within the tip of the needle.

Patient Information This drug must be implanted under the skin of your abdomen every 28 days; it is important to maintain appointment schedule. You may experience systemic hot flashes (cool clothes and temperatures may help), headache (analgesic may help), constipation (increased bulk and water in diet or stool softener may help), sexual dysfunction (decreased libido, decreased erection). Symptoms may worsen temporarily during first weeks of therapy. Report unusual nausea or vomiting, any chest pain, respiratory difficulty, unresolved dizziness, or constipation. Females must use reliable contraception during therapy.

Dosage Forms INJ, solution, 1-month implant [disposable syringe; single-dose]: 3.6 mg. **INJ, solution,** 3-month implant [disposable syringe; single-dose]: 10.8 mg

♦ **Goserelin Acetate**   see Goserelin on page 599

♦ **GP 47680**   see Oxcarbazepine on page 940

♦ **G-Phed**   see Guaifenesin and Pseudoephedrine on page 605

♦ **G-Phed-PD**   see Guaifenesin and Pseudoephedrine on page 605

♦ **GR38032R**   see Ondansetron on page 929

♦ **Gramicidin, Neomycin, and Polymyxin B**   see Neomycin, Polymyxin B, and Gramicidin on page 892

Granisetron   (gra NI se tron)

U.S. Brand Names Kytril®

Synonyms BRL 43694

Therapeutic Category Antiemetic, Serotonin Antagonist; 5-HT$_3$ Receptor Antagonist; Serotonin 5-HT$_3$ Receptor Antagonist

Use Prophylaxis of chemotherapy-related emesis; prophylaxis of nausea and vomiting associated with radiation therapy, including total body irradiation and fractionated abdominal radiation; prophylaxis of postoperative nausea and vomiting (PONV)

Generally **not** recommended for treatment of existing chemotherapy-induced emesis (CIE) or for prophylaxis of nausea from agents with a low emetogenic potential.

Pregnancy Risk Factor B

Contraindications Previous hypersensitivity to granisetron, other 5-HT$_3$ receptor antagonists, or any component of the formulation

Warnings/Precautions Chemotherapy-related emesis: **Granisetron should be used on a scheduled basis, not on an "as needed" (PRN) basis**, since data support the use of this drug in the prevention of nausea and vomiting and not in the rescue of nausea and vomiting. Granisetron should be used only in the first 24-48 hours of receiving chemotherapy or radiation. Data do not support any increased efficacy of granisetron in delayed nausea and vomiting. May be prescribed for patients who are refractory to or have severe adverse reactions to standard antiemetic therapy or young patients (ie, <45 years of age who are more likely to develop extrapyramidal symptoms to high-dose metoclopramide) who are to receive highly emetogenic chemotherapeutic agents. Should not be prescribed for chemotherapeutic agents with a low emetogenic potential (eg, bleomycin, busulfan, etoposide, 5-fluorouracil, vinblastine, vincristine).

Routine prophylaxis for PONV is not recommended. In patients where nausea and vomiting must be avoided postoperatively, administer to all patients even when expected incidence of nausea and vomiting is low. Use caution following abdominal surgery or in chemotherapy-induced nausea and vomiting; may mask progressive ileus or gastric distention. Use caution in patients with liver disease or in pregnancy.

Common Adverse Reactions

>10%:

Central nervous system: Headache (8% to 21%)

Gastrointestinal: Constipation (3% to 18%)

1% to 10%:

Cardiovascular: Hypertension (1% to 2%)

Central nervous system: Dizziness, insomnia, anxiety, somnolence, fever (3% to 8%), pain (10%)

Gastrointestinal: Abdominal pain, diarrhea (1% to 9%), dyspepsia

Hepatic: Elevated liver enzymes (5% to 6%)

Neuromuscular & skeletal: Weakness (5% to 18%)

Drug Interactions

Cytochrome P450 Effect: Substrate of CYP3A4 (minor)

Mechanism of Action Selective 5-HT$_3$-receptor antagonist, blocking serotonin, both peripherally on vagal nerve terminals and centrally in the chemoreceptor trigger zone

Pharmacodynamics/Kinetics

Duration: Generally up to 24 hours

Distribution: V$_d$: 2-4 L/kg; widely throughout body

Protein binding: 65%

Metabolism: Hepatic via N-demethylation, oxidation, and conjugation; some metabolites may have 5-HT$_3$ antagonist activity

Half-life elimination: Cancer patients: 10-12 hours; Healthy volunteers: 4-5 hours; PONV: 9 hours

Excretion: Urine (12% as unchanged drug, 49% as metabolites); feces (34% as metabolites)

Dosage

Oral: Adults:

Prophylaxis of chemotherapy-related emesis: 2 mg once daily up to 1 hour before chemotherapy or 1 mg twice daily; the first 1 mg dose should be given up to 1 hour before chemotherapy.

Prophylaxis of radiation therapy-associated emesis: 2 mg once daily given 1 hour before radiation therapy.

(Continued)

Granisetron (Continued)

I.V.:

Children ≥2 years and Adults: Prophylaxis of chemotherapy-related emesis:

Within U.S.: 10 mcg/kg/dose (or 1 mg/dose) administered IVPB over 5 minutes given within 30 minutes of chemotherapy: for some drugs (eg, carboplatin, cyclophosphamide) with a later onset of emetic action, 10 mcg/kg every 12 hours may be necessary.

Outside U.S.: 40 mcg/kg/dose (or 3 mg/dose); maximum: 9 mg/24 hours

Breakthrough: Repeat the dose 2-3 times within the first 24 hours as necessary **(not based on controlled trials, or generally recommended)**

Adults: PONV:

Prevention: 1 mg given undiluted over 30 seconds; administer before induction of anesthesia or before reversal of anesthesia

Treatment: 1 mg given undiluted over 30 seconds

Dosing interval in renal impairment: No dosage adjustment required.

Dosing interval in hepatic impairment: Kinetic studies in patients with hepatic impairment showed that total clearance was approximately halved, however, standard doses were very well tolerated

Administration

Oral: Doses should be given up to 1 hour prior to initiation of chemotherapy/radiation

I.V.: Administer as rapid (30 second) I.V. push or a short (5-10 minutes) infusion

For prevention of PONV, administer before induction of anesthesia or before reversal of anesthesia.

For PONV, administer undiluted over 30 seconds.

Dosage Forms INJ, solution: 1 mg/mL (4 mL). **INJ, solution** [preservative free]: 1 mg/mL (1 mL). **TAB:** 1 mg

◆ **Granulex®** see Trypsin, Balsam Peru, and Castor Oil on page 1278

◆ **Granulocyte Colony Stimulating Factor** see Filgrastim on page 522

◆ **Granulocyte Colony Stimulating Factor (PEG Conjugate)** see Pegfilgrastim on page 963

◆ **Granulocyte-Macrophage Colony Stimulating Factor** see Sargramostim on page 1124

◆ **Grifulvin® V** see Griseofulvin on page 602

Griseofulvin (gri see oh FUL vin)

Related Information

Antifungal Agents Comparison on page 1362

U.S. Brand Names Fulvicin® P/G; Fulvicin-U/F®; Grifulvin® V; Gris-PEG®

Synonyms Griseofulvin Microsize; Griseofulvin Ultramicrosize

Therapeutic Category Antifungal Agent, Oral; Antifungal Agent, Systemic

Use Treatment of susceptible tinea infections of the skin, hair, and nails

Pregnancy Risk Factor C

Contraindications Hypersensitivity to griseofulvin or any component of the formulation; severe liver disease; porphyria (interferes with porphyrin metabolism)

Warnings/Precautions Safe use in children ≤2 years of age has not been established; during long-term therapy, periodic assessment of hepatic, renal, and hematopoietic functions should be performed; may cause fetal harm when administered to pregnant women; avoid exposure to intense sunlight to prevent photosensitivity reactions; hypersensitivity cross reaction between penicillins and griseofulvin is possible

Common Adverse Reactions Frequency not defined.

Central nervous system: Headache, fatigue, dizziness, insomnia, mental confusion

Dermatologic: Rash (most common), urticaria (most common), photosensitivity, erythema multiforme, angioneurotic edema (rare)

Gastrointestinal: Nausea, vomiting, epigastric distress, diarrhea, GI bleeding

Genitourinary: Menstrual irregularities (rare)

Hematologic: Leukopenia, granulocytopenia

Neuromuscular & skeletal: Paresthesia (rare)

Renal: Hepatotoxicity, proteinuria, nephrosis

Miscellaneous: Oral thrush, drug-induced lupus-like syndrome (rare)

Drug Interactions

Cytochrome P450 Effect: Induces CYP1A2 (weak), 2C8/9 (weak), 3A4 (weak)

Increased Effect/Toxicity: Increased toxicity with ethanol, may cause tachycardia and flushing.

Decreased Effect: Barbiturates may decrease levels. Decreased warfarin activity. Decreased oral contraceptive effectiveness.

Mechanism of Action Inhibits fungal cell mitosis at metaphase; binds to human keratin making it resistant to fungal invasion

Pharmacodynamics/Kinetics

Absorption: Ultramicrosize griseofulvin absorption is almost complete; absorption of microsize griseofulvin is variable (25% to 70% of an oral dose); enhanced by ingestion of a fatty meal (GI absorption of ultramicrosize is ~1.5 times that of microsize)

Distribution: Crosses placenta

Metabolism: Extensively hepatic

Half-life elimination: 9-22 hours

Excretion: Urine (<1% as unchanged drug); feces; perspiration

Dosage Oral:
Children >2 years:
Microsize: 10-20 mg/kg/day in single or 2 divided doses
Ultramicrosize: >2 years: 5-10 mg/kg/day in single or 2 divided doses
Adults:
Microsize: 500-1000 mg/day in single or divided doses
Ultramicrosize: 330-375 mg/day in single or divided doses; doses up to 750 mg/day have
been used for infections more difficult to eradicate such as tinea unguium
Duration of therapy depends on the site of infection:
Tinea corporis: 2-4 weeks
Tinea capitis: 4-6 weeks or longer
Tinea pedis: 4-8 weeks
Tinea unguium: 3-6 months or longer
Administration Oral: Administer with a fatty meal (peanuts or ice cream to increase absorption), or with food or milk to avoid GI upset
Monitoring Parameters Periodic renal, hepatic, and hematopoietic function tests
Patient Information Avoid exposure to sunlight, take with fatty meal; if patient gets headache, it usually goes away with continued therapy; may cause dizziness, drowsiness, and impair judgment; do not take if pregnant; if you become pregnant, discontinue immediately
Dosage Forms SUSP, oral, microsize (Grifulvin® V): 125 mg/5 mL (120 mL). **TAB, microsize** (Fulvicin-U/F®): 250 mg, 500 mg. **TAB, ultramicrosize:** 125 mg, 250 mg, 330 mg; (Fulvicin® P/G): 125 mg, 165 mg, 250 mg, 330 mg; (Gris-PEG®): 125 mg, 250 mg

♦ **Griseofulvin Microsize** *see Griseofulvin on page 602*
♦ **Griseofulvin Ultramicrosize** *see Griseofulvin on page 602*
♦ **Gris-PEG®** *see Griseofulvin on page 602*
♦ **Growth Hormone** *see Human Growth Hormone on page 620*
♦ **Guaifed® [OTC]** *see Guaifenesin and Pseudoephedrine on page 605*
♦ **Guaifed-PD®** *see Guaifenesin and Pseudoephedrine on page 605*

Guaifenesin (gwye FEN e sin)
U.S. Brand Names Amibid LA; Breonesin® [OTC] [DSC]; Diabetic Tussin® EX [OTC]; Duratuss-G®; Fenesin™ [DSC]; Glytuss® [OTC]; Guaifenex® G; Guaifenex® LA; Guiatuss® [OTC]; Humibid® L.A.; Humibid® Pediatric; Hytuss® [OTC]; Hytuss-2X® [OTC]; Liquibid®; Liquibid® 1200; Mucinex™ [OTC]; Organidin® NR; Phanasin [OTC]; Respa-GF®; Robitussin® [OTC]; Scot-Tussin® Sugar Free Expectorant [OTC]; Touro Ex®
Synonyms GG; Glycerol Guaiacolate
Therapeutic Category Expectorant
Use Temporary control of cough due to minor throat and bronchial irritation
Pregnancy Risk Factor C
Contraindications Hypersensitivity to guaifenesin or any component of the formulation
Warnings/Precautions Not for persistent cough such as occurs with smoking, asthma, or emphysema or cough accompanied by excessive secretions
Common Adverse Reactions Frequency not defined.
Central nervous system: Drowsiness, headache
Dermatologic: Rash
Gastrointestinal: Nausea, vomiting, stomach pain
Drug Interactions
Increased Effect/Toxicity: May increase toxicity/effect of disulfiram, MAO inhibitors, metronidazole, and procarbazine.
Mechanism of Action Thought to act as an expectorant by irritating the gastric mucosa and stimulating respiratory tract secretions, thereby increasing respiratory fluid volumes and decreasing phlegm viscosity
Pharmacodynamics/Kinetics
Absorption: Well absorbed
Metabolism: Hepatic (60%)
Half-life elimination: ~1 hour
Excretion: Urine (as unchanged drug and metabolites)
Dosage Oral:
Children:
<2 years: 12 mg/kg/day in 6 divided doses
2-5 years: 50-100 mg every 4 hours, not to exceed 600 mg/day
6-11 years: 100-200 mg every 4 hours, not to exceed 1.2 g/day
Children >12 years and Adults: 200-400 mg every 4 hours to a maximum of 2.4 g/day
Patient Information Take with a large quantity of fluid to ensure proper action; if cough persists for more than 1 week or is accompanied by fever, rash, or persistent headache, prescriber should be consulted
Dosage Forms CAP (Breonesin® [DSC], Hytuss-2X®): 200 mg. **CAP, sustained release** (Humibid® Pediatric): 300 mg. **CAPLET, sustained release** (Touro Ex®): 575 mg. **LIQ:** 100 mg/5 mL (120 mL, 240 mL, 480 mL); (Diabetic Tussin EX®): 100 mg/5 mL (120 mL); (Organidin NR®): 100 mg/5 mL (480 mL). **SYR:** 100 mg/5 mL (120 mL, 240 mL, 480 mL); (Guiatuss®): 100 mg/5 mL (120 mL, 240 mL, 480 mL, 3840 mL); (Phanasin): 100 mg/5 mL (120 mL, 240 mL); (Robitussin®): 100 mg/5 mL (5 mL, 10 mL, 15 mL, 30 mL, 120 mL, 240 mL, 480 mL); (Scot-Tussin® Sugar Free Expectorant): 100 mg/5 mL (120 mL). **TAB:** 200 mg; (Glytuss®, Organidin® NR): 200 mg; (Hytuss®): 100 mg. **TAB, extended release** (Mucinex™): 600 mg. **TAB, sustained release:** 600 mg, 1200 mg; (Amibid LA, Fenesin™ [DSC], Guaifenex® LA, (Continued)

Guaifenesin *(Continued)*

Humibid® LA, Liquibid®, Respa-GF®): 600 mg; (Duratuss G, Guaifenex® G, Liquibid® 1200): 1200 mg

Guaifenesin and Codeine *(gwye FEN e sin & KOE deen)*

U.S. Brand Names Brontex®; Cheracol®; Diabetic Tussin C®; Gani-Tuss® NR; Guaituss AC®; Halotussin AC; Mytussin® AC; Robafen® AC; Romilar® AC; Tussi-Organidin® NR; Tussi-Organidin® S-NR

Synonyms Codeine and Guaifenesin

Therapeutic Category Antitussive/Expectorant

Use Temporary control of cough due to minor throat and bronchial irritation

Restrictions C-V

Pregnancy Risk Factor C

Dosage Oral:

Children:

2-6 years: 1-1.5 mg/kg codeine/day divided into 4 doses administered every 4-6 hours (maximum: 30 mg/24 hours)

6-12 years: 5 mL every 4 hours, not to exceed 30 mL/24 hours

Children >12 years and Adults: 5-10 mL every 6 hours not to exceed 60 mL/24 hours

Dosage Forms LIQ: Guaifenesin 100 mg and codeine 10 mg per 5 mL (120 mL, 480 mL); (Brontex®): Guaifenesin 75 mg and codeine 2.5 mg per 5 mL (480 mL); (Gani-Tuss® NR, Tussi-Organidin® NR): Guaifenesin 100 mg and codeine 10 mg per 5 mL (480 mL); (Halotussin AC): Guaifenesin 100 mg and codeine 10 mg per 5 mL (120 mL, 480 mL, 3840); (Tussi-Organidin® S-NR): Guaifenesin 100 mg and codeine 10 mg per 5 mL (120 mL); (Diabetic Tussin C®): Guaifenesin 200 mg and codeine 10 mg per 5 mL (480 mL); **SYR:** Guaifenesin 100 mg and codeine 10 mg per 5 mL (120 mL, 480 mL); (Cheracol®): Guaifenesin 100 mg and codeine 10 mg per 5 mL (120 mL); (Guaituss AC®, Robafen® AC): Guaifenesin 100 mg and codeine 10 mg per 5 mL (120 mL, 480 mL); (Mytussin® AC): Guaifenesin 100 mg and codeine 10 mg per 5 mL (120 mL, 480 mL, 3840 mL); (Romilar® AC): Guaifenesin 100 mg and codeine 10 mg per 5 mL (480 mL). **TAB** (Brontex®): Guaifenesin 300 mg and codeine 10 mg

Guaifenesin and Dextromethorphan

(gwye FEN e sin & deks troe meth OR fan)

U.S. Brand Names Aquatab® DM; Benylin® Expectorant [OTC]; Cheracol® D [OTC]; Cheracol® Plus [OTC]; Diabetic Tussin® DM [OTC]; Diabetic Tussin® DM Maximum Strength [OTC]; Duratuss® DM; Fenesin™ DM; Genatuss DM® [OTC]; Guaifenex® DM; Guiatuss-DM® [OTC]; Humibid® DM; Hydro-Tussin™ DM; Kolephrin® GG/DM [OTC]; Mytussin® DM [OTC]; Respa-DM®; Robitussin® DM [OTC]; Robitussin® Sugar Free Cough [OTC]; Safe Tussin® 30 [OTC]; Silexin® [OTC]; Tolu-Sed® DM [OTC]; Touro® DM [OTC]; Tussi-Organidin® DM NR; Vicks® 44E [OTC]; Vicks® Pediatric Formula 44E [OTC]; Z-Cof LA

Synonyms Dextromethorphan and Guaifenesin

Therapeutic Category Antitussive/Expectorant

Use Temporary control of cough due to minor throat and bronchial irritation

Pregnancy Risk Factor C

Contraindications Hypersensitivity to guaifenesin, dextromethorphan, or any component of the formulation

Warnings/Precautions Should not be used for persistent or chronic cough such as that occurring with smoking, asthma, chronic bronchitis, or emphysema or for cough associated with excessive phlegm

Common Adverse Reactions Frequency not defined.

Central nervous system: Drowsiness, headache

Dermatologic: Rash

Gastrointestinal: Nausea, vomiting

Drug Interactions

Cytochrome P450 Effect: Dextromethorphan: **Substrate** of CYP2B6 (minor), 2C8/9 (minor), 2C19 (minor), 2D6 (major), 2E1 (minor), 3A4(minor); **Inhibits** CYP2D6 (weak)

Increased Effect/Toxicity: See individual agents.

Decreased Effect: See individual agents.

Mechanism of Action

Guaifenesin is thought to act as an expectorant by irritating the gastric mucosa and stimulating respiratory tract secretions, thereby increasing respiratory fluid volumes and decreasing phlegm viscosity

Dextromethorphan is a chemical relative of morphine lacking narcotic properties except in overdose; controls cough by depressing the medullary cough center

Pharmacodynamics/Kinetics

Onset of action: Oral: Antitussive: 15-30 minutes

See individual agents.

Dosage Oral: **Note:** Dosing based on dextromethorphan 10 mg/5 mL liquid/syrup or 30 mg tablet (adjust dose for alternate formulations).

Children:

2-6 years: 2.5 mL every 4 hours (maximum: 6 doses/24 hours)

6-12 years: 5 mL every 4 hours (maximum: 6 doses/24 hours) **or** 1 tablet every 12 hours (maximum: 2 tablets/24 hours)

≥12 years: See Adults dosing

Adults: 10 mL every 4 hours (maximum: 6 doses/24 hours) **or** 1-2 tablets every 12 hours (maximum: 4 tablets/24 hours)

Patient Information Take with a large quantity of fluid to ensure proper action; if cough persists for more than one week, is recumbent, or is accompanied by fever, rash or persistent headache, prescriber should be consulted

Dosage Forms LIQ: Guaifenesin 100 mg and dextromethorphan 10 mg per 5 mL (120 mL, 240 mL); (Tussi-Organidin® DM NR): Guaifenesin 100 mg and dextromethorphan 10 mg per 5 mL (120 mL, 240 mL); guaifenesin 100 mg and dextromethorphan 15 mg per 5 mL (120 mL); guaifenesin 200 mg and dextromethorphan 10 mg per 5 mL (120 mL); (Hydro-Tussin™ DM): Guaifenesin 200 mg and dextromethorphan 20 mg per 5 mL (120 mL, 235 mL, 480 mL, 3840 mL). **SYR**: Guaifenesin 100 mg and dextromethorphan 5 mg per 5 mL (120 mL); guaifenesin 100 mg and dextromethorphan 10 mg per 5 mL (5 mL, 45 mL, 120 mL, 240 mL, 360 mL, 480 mL, 3840 mL); guaifenesin 150 mg and dextromethorphan 10 mg per 5 mL (120 mL). **TAB** (Silexin®): **TAB, extended release**: Guaifenesin 600 mg and dextromethorphan 30 mg; (Aquatab® DM): Guaifenesin 1200 mg and dextromethorphan 60 mg; (Fenesin™ DM, Guaifenex® DM, Humibid® DM, Respa-DM®): Guaifenesin 600 mg and dextromethorphan 30 mg; (Touro® DM): Guaifenesin 575 mg and dextromethorphan 30 mg. **TAB, long acting** [scored]: (Z-Cof LA): Guaifenesin 650 mg and dextromethorphan 30 mg

♦ **Guaifenesin and Hydrocodone** *see* Hydrocodone and Guaifenesin *on page 630*

Guaifenesin and Phenylephrine (gwye FEN e sin & fen il EF rin)

U.S. Brand Names Endal®; Entex® LA; Liquibid-D; Prolex-D

Synonyms Phenylephrine and Guaifenesin

Therapeutic Category Decongestant/Expectorant

Use Symptomatic relief of those respiratory conditions where tenacious mucous plugs and congestion complicate the problem such as sinusitis, pharyngitis, bronchitis, asthma, and as an adjunctive therapy in serous otitis media

Dosage Oral: Adults: 1 or 2 every 12 hours

Product labeling: Adults: Endal®: 1-2 timed release tablets every 12 hours

Dosage Forms TAB, extended release: Guaifenesin 600 mg and phenylephrine 20 mg; (Endal®): Guaifenesin 300 mg and phenylephrine 20 mg; (Liquibid-D): Guaifenesin 600 mg and phenylephrine 40 mg. **TAB, sustained release** (Entex® LA): Guaifenesin 600 mg and phenylephrine 30 mg

Guaifenesin and Pseudoephedrine (gwye FEN e sin & soo doe e FED rin)

U.S. Brand Names Ami-Tex PSE; Anatuss LA; Aquatab®; Aquatab® D Dose Pack; Congestac® II; Deconsal® II; Defen-LA®; Duratuss™; Duratuss™ GP; Entex® PSE; Eudal®-SR; G-Phed; G-Phed-PD; Guaifed® [OTC]; Guaifed-PD®; Guaifenex® PSE; Guaifen PSE; Guai-Vent™/PSE; Maxifed®; Maxifed-G®; Miraphen PSE; PanMist® Jr.; PanMist®; PanMist® S; Pseudo GG TR; Pseudovent™; Pseudovent™-Ped; Respa-1st®; Respaire®-60 SR; Respaire®-120 SR; Robitussin-PE® [OTC]; Robitussin® Severe Congestion [OTC]; Touro LA®; V-Dec-M®; Versacaps®; Zephrex®; Zephrex LA®

Synonyms Pseudoephedrine and Guaifenesin

Therapeutic Category Decongestant/Expectorant

Use Enhance the output of respiratory tract fluid and reduce mucosal congestion and edema in the nasal passage

Pregnancy Risk Factor C

Dosage Oral:

Children:

2-6 years: 2.5 mL every 4 hours not to exceed 15 mL/24 hours

6-12 years: 5 mL every 4 hours not to exceed 30 mL/24 hours

Children >12 years and Adults: 10 mL every 4 hours not to exceed 60 mL/24 hours

Dosage Forms CAP: (Pseudovent™): Guaifenesin 250 mg and pseudoephedrine 120 mg; (Pseudovent™-Ped): Guaifenesin 300 mg and pseudoephedrine 60 mg; (Robitussin® Severe Congestion [Liqui-Gels®]): Guaifenesin 200 mg and pseudoephedrine 30 mg. **CAP, extended release**: (G-Phed, Guaifed®, Respaire®-120 SR): Guaifenesin 250 mg and pseudoephedrine 120 mg; (G-Phed-PD, Guaifed-PD®, Versacaps®): Guaifenesin 300 mg and pseudoephedrine 60 mg; (Respaire®-60 SR): Guaifenesin 200 mg and pseudoephedrine 60 mg. **CAPLET** (Congestac®): Guaifenesin 400 mg and pseudoephedrine 60 mg. **CAPLET, long acting** (Touro LA®): Guaifenesin 500 mg and pseudoephedrine 120 mg. **SYR**: (PanMist®-S): Guaifenesin 200 mg and pseudoephedrine 45 mg per 5 mL (480 mL) (Robitussin-PE®): Guaifenesin 100 mg and pseudoephedrine 30 mg per 5 mL (120 mL, 240 mL). **TAB** (Zephrex®): Guaifenesin 400 mg and pseudoephedrine 60 mg. **TAB, extended release:** Guaifenesin 600 mg and pseudoephedrine 60 mg; guaifenesin 600 mg and pseudoephedrine 120 mg; guaifenesin 1200 mg and pseudoephedrine 60 mg; guaifenesin 1200 mg and pseudoephedrine 120 mg; (Amitex PSE, Duratuss®, Entex® PSE, Guaifen PSE, Guaifenex PSE® 120, Guai-Vent™/PSE, Miraphen PSE, Zephrex LA®): Guaifenesin 600 mg and pseudoephedrine 120 mg; (Anatuss LA, Eudal®-SR): Guaifenesin 400 mg and pseudoephedrine 120 mg; (Aquatab® D Dose Pack, Deconsal® II, Defen-LA®, Guaifenex PSE® 60, Respa-1st®): Guaifenesin 600 mg and pseudoephedrine 60 mg; (Duratuss™ GP, Guaifenex® GP): Guaifenesin 1200 mg and pseudoephedrine 120 mg; (Maxifed®): Guaifenesin 700 mg and pseudoephedrine 80 mg; (Maxifed-G®): Guaifenesin 550 mg and pseudoephedrine 60 mg; (PanMist®-Jr, Pseudo GG TR): Guaifenesin 600 mg and pseudoephedrine 45 mg; (PanMist®-LA): Guaifenesin 800 mg and pseudoephedrine 80 mg; (V-Dec-M®): Guaifenesin 500 mg and pseudoephedrine 120 mg

♦ **Guaifenesin and Theophylline** *see* Theophylline and Guaifenesin *on page 1210*

Guaifenesin, Pseudoephedrine, and Codeine
(gwye FEN e sin, soo doe e FED rin, & KOE deen)

U.S. Brand Names Cheratussin DAC; Codafed® Expectorant; Codafed® Pediatric Expectorant; Dihistine® Expectorant; Guiatuss™ DAC®; Halotussin® DAC; Mytussin® DAC; Nucofed® Expectorant; Nucofed® Pediatric Expectorant; Nucotuss®; Robitussin®-DAC [DSC]

Synonyms Codeine, Guaifenesin, and Pseudoephedrine; Pseudoephedrine, Guaifenesin, and Codeine

Therapeutic Category Antitussive/Decongestant/Expectorant

Use Temporarily relieves nasal congestion and controls cough due to minor throat and bronchial irritation; helps loosen phlegm and thin bronchial secretions to make coughs more productive

Restrictions C-III; C-V

Pregnancy Risk Factor C

Dosage Oral:

Children 6-12 years: 5 mL every 4 hours, not to exceed 40 mL/24 hours

Children >12 years and Adults: 10 mL every 4 hours, not to exceed 40 mL/24 hours

Dosage Forms LIQ: (Cheratussin DAC, Halotussin DAC): Guaifenesin 100 mg, pseudoephedrine 30 mg, and codeine 10 mg per 5 mL (480 mL); (Dihistine® Expectorant): Guaifenesin 100 mg, pseudoephedrine 30 mg, and codeine 10 mg per 5 mL (120 mL). **SYR:** (Codafed Expectorant): Guaifenesin 200 mg, pseudoephedrine 60 mg, and codeine 20 mg per 5 mL (480 mL); (Codafed Pediatric Expectorant, Guiatuss™ DAC, Nucofed Pediatric Expectorant, Nucotuss Pediatric Expectorant): Guaifenesin 100 mg, pseudoephedrine 30 mg, and codeine 10 mg per 5 mL (480 mL); (Robitussin® DAC [DSC]): Guaifenesin 100 mg, pseudoephedrine 30 mg, and codeine 10 mg per 5 mL; (Mytussin DAC): Guaifenesin 100 mg, pseudoephedrine 30 mg, and codeine 10 mg per 5 mL (120 mL, 480 mL); (Nucofed® Expectorant, Nucotuss Expectorant): Guaifenesin 200 mg, pseudoephedrine 60 mg, and codeine 20 mg per 5 mL (480 mL)

Guaifenesin, Pseudoephedrine, and Dextromethorphan
(gwye FEN e sin, soo doe e FED rin, & deks troe meth OR fan)

U.S. Brand Names Aquatab® C; Guiatuss™ CF; Maxifed® DM; PanMist®-DM; Protuss®-DM; Pseudovent™ DM; Robitussin® CF [OTC]; Robitussin® Cold and Congestion [OTC]; Robitussin® Cough and Cold Infant [OTC]; Touro™ CC; Tri-Vent™ DM

Synonyms Dextromethorphan, Guaifenesin, and Pseudoephedrine; Pseudoephedrine, Dextromethorphan, and Guaifenesin

Therapeutic Category Antitussive/Decongestant/Expectorant

Use Temporarily relieves nasal congestion and controls cough due to minor throat and bronchial irritation; helps loosen phlegm and thin bronchial secretions to make coughs more productive

Dosage Adults: Oral: 2 capsules or 10 mL every 4 hours

Dosage Forms CAP (Robitussin® Cold and Congestion): Guaifenesin 200 mg, pseudoephedrine 30 mg, and dextromethorphan 10 mg. **CAPLET** (Robitussin® Cold and Congestion): Guaifenesin 200 mg, pseudoephedrine 30 mg, and dextromethorphan 10 mg. **CAPLET, sustained release** (Touro™ CC): Guaifenesin 575 mg, pseudoephedrine 60 mg, and dextromethorphan 30 mg. **LIQ, oral drops** (Robitussin® Cough and Cold Infant): Guaifenesin 100 mg, pseudoephedrine 15 mg, and dextromethorphan 5 mg per 2.5 mL (30 mL). **SYR:** Guaifenesin 100 mg, pseudoephedrine 45 mg, and dextromethorphan 15 mg per 5 mL (480 mL); (Guiatuss™ CF): Guaifenesin 100 mg, pseudoephedrine 30 mg, and dextromethorphan 10 mg per 5 mL (120 mL); (Robitussin® CF): Guaifenesin 100 mg, pseudoephedrine 30 mg, and dextromethorphan 10 mg per 5 mL (120 mL, 240 mL, 360 mL); (Tri-Vent™ DM): Guaifenesin 100 mg, pseudoephedrine 40 mg, and dextromethorphan 15 mg per 5 mL (480 mL); (PanMist®-DM): Guaifenesin 100 mg, pseudoephedrine 45 mg, and dextromethorphan 15 mg per 5 mL (480 mL). **TAB, extended release:** Guaifenesin 600 mg, pseudoephedrine 45 mg, and dextromethorphan 30 mg; Guaifenesin 800 mg, pseudoephedrine 45 mg, and dextromethorphan 30 mg; Guaifenesin 1200 mg, pseudoephedrine 60 mg, and dextromethorphan 60 mg; Guaifenesin 1200 mg, pseudoephedrine 120 mg, and dextromethorphan 60 mg; (Protuss®-DM): Guaifenesin 600 mg, pseudoephedrine 60 mg, and dextromethorphan 30 mg; (Aquatab® C): Guaifenesin 1200 mg, pseudoephedrine 60 mg, and dextromethorphan 60 mg; (PanMist®-DM, Pseudovent™ DM): Guaifenesin 595 mg, pseudoephedrine 48 mg, and dextromethorphan 32 mg. **TAB, sustained release** (Maxifed® DM): Guaifenesin 550 mg, pseudoephedrine 60 mg, and dextromethorphan 30 mg

♦ **Guaifenex® DM** see Guaifenesin and Dextromethorphan on page 604

♦ **Guaifenex® G** see Guaifenesin on page 603

♦ **Guaifenex® GP** see Guaifenesin and Pseudoephedrine on page 605

♦ **Guaifenex® LA** see Guaifenesin on page 603

♦ **Guaifenex® PSE** see Guaifenesin and Pseudoephedrine on page 605

♦ **Guaifen PSE** see Guaifenesin and Pseudoephedrine on page 605

♦ **Guaituss AC®** see Guaifenesin and Codeine on page 604

♦ **Guai-Vent™/PSE** see Guaifenesin and Pseudoephedrine on page 605

Guanabenz (GWAHN a benz)
U.S. Brand Names Wytensin® [DSC]

Synonyms Guanabenz Acetate

Therapeutic Category Alpha-Adrenergic Agonist; Antihypertensive Agent

Use Management of hypertension

Pregnancy Risk Factor C

Dosage Adults: Oral: Initial: 4 mg twice daily; increase in increments of 4-8 mg/day every 1-2 weeks to a maximum of 32 mg twice daily.
Dosing adjustment in hepatic impairment: Probably necessary
Dosage Forms TAB: 4 mg, 8 mg

♦ **Guanabenz Acetate** *see* Guanabenz *on page 606*

Guanadrel (GWAHN a drel)
U.S. Brand Names Hylorel®
Synonyms Guanadrel Sulfate
Therapeutic Category Adrenergic Blocking Agent, Peripherally Acting; Antihypertensive Agent
Use Considered a second line agent in the treatment of hypertension, usually with a diuretic
Pregnancy Risk Factor B
Dosage Oral:
Adults: Initial: 10 mg/day (5 mg twice daily); adjust dosage weekly or monthly until blood pressure is controlled, usual dosage: 20-75 mg/day, given twice daily. For larger dosage, 3-4 times/day dosing may be needed.
Elderly: Initial: 5 mg once daily
Dosing interval in renal impairment:
Cl$_{cr}$ 10-50 mL/minute: Administer every 12-24 hours.
Cl$_{cr}$ <10 mL/minute: Administer every 24-48 hours.
Dosage Forms TAB: 10 mg, 25 mg

♦ **Guanadrel Sulfate** *see* Guanadrel *on page 607*

Guanfacine (GWAHN fa seen)
U.S. Brand Names Tenex®
Synonyms Guanfacine Hydrochloride
Therapeutic Category Alpha-Adrenergic Agonist; Antihypertensive Agent
Use Management of hypertension
Pregnancy Risk Factor B
Dosage Adults: Oral: Hypertension: 1 mg usually at bedtime, may increase if needed at 3- to 4-week intervals; 1 mg/day is most common dose
Dosage Forms TAB: 1 mg, 2 mg

♦ **Guanfacine Hydrochloride** *see* Guanfacine *on page 607*
♦ **Guiatuss® [OTC]** *see* Guaifenesin *on page 603*
♦ **Guiatuss™ CF** *see* Guaifenesin, Pseudoephedrine, and Dextromethorphan *on page 606*
♦ **Guiatuss™ DAC®** *see* Guaifenesin, Pseudoephedrine, and Codeine *on page 606*
♦ **Guiatuss-DM® [OTC]** *see* Guaifenesin and Dextromethorphan *on page 604*
♦ **GW433908G** *see* Fosamprenavir *on page 563*
♦ **Gynazole-1™** *see* Butoconazole *on page 195*
♦ **Gyne-Lotrimin® 3 [OTC]** *see* Clotrimazole *on page 304*
♦ **Gynodiol®** *see* Estradiol *on page 459*
♦ **Habitrol®** *see* Nicotine *on page 901*

Haemophilus b Conjugate and Hepatitis B Vaccine
(he MOF i lus bee KON joo gate & hep a TYE tis bee vak SEEN)
U.S. Brand Names Comvax®
Synonyms *Haemophilus* b (meningococcal protein conjugate) Conjugate Vaccine; Hib
Therapeutic Category Vaccine
Use
Immunization against invasive disease caused by *H. influenzae* type b and against infection caused by all known subtypes of hepatitis B virus in infants 8 weeks to 15 months of age born of HB$_s$Ag-negative mothers
Infants born of HB$_s$Ag-positive mothers or mothers of unknown HB$_s$Ag status should receive hepatitis B immune globulin and hepatitis B vaccine (recombinant) at birth and should complete the hepatitis B vaccination series given according to a particular schedule
Pregnancy Risk Factor C
Dosage Infants (>8 weeks of age): I.M.: 0.5 mL at 2, 4, and 12-15 months of age (total of 3 doses)

If the recommended schedule cannot be followed, the interval between the first two doses should be at least 2 months and the interval between the second and third dose should be as close as possible to 8-11 months.
Modified Schedule: Children who receive one dose of hepatitis B vaccine at or shortly after birth may receive Comvax® on a schedule of 2, 4, and 12-15 months of age
Dosage Forms INJ, suspension [preservative free]: 7.5 mcg *Haemophilus* b PRP and 5 mcg HB$_s$Ag/0.5 mL (0.5 mL)

Haemophilus b Conjugate Vaccine
(he MOF fi lus bee KON joo gate vak SEEN)
U.S. Brand Names ActHIB®; HibTITER®; PedvaxHIB®
Synonyms Diphtheria CRM$_{197}$ Protein Conjugate; Diphtheria Toxoid Conjugate; *Haemophilus* b Oligosaccharide Conjugate Vaccine; *Haemophilus* b Polysaccharide Vaccine; HbCV; Hib Polysaccharide Conjugate; PRP-D
(Continued)

Haemophilus b Conjugate Vaccine *(Continued)*

Therapeutic Category Vaccine; Vaccine, Inactivated Bacteria

Use Routine immunization of children 2 months to 5 years of age against invasive disease caused by *H. influenzae*

Unimmunized children ≥5 years of age with a chronic illness known to be associated with increased risk of *Haemophilus influenzae* type b disease, specifically, persons with anatomic or functional asplenia or sickle cell anemia or those who have undergone splenectomy, should receive Hib vaccine.

Haemophilus b conjugate vaccines are not indicated for prevention of bronchitis or other infections due to *H. influenzae* in adults; adults with specific dysfunction or certain complement deficiencies who are at especially high risk of *H. influenzae* type b infection (HIV-infected adults); patients with Hodgkin's disease (vaccinated at least 2 weeks before the initiation of chemotherapy or 3 months after the end of chemotherapy)

Pregnancy Risk Factor C

Contraindications Children with any febrile illness or active infection, hypersensitivity to *Haemophilus* b polysaccharide vaccine (thimerosal), children who are immunosuppressed or receiving immunosuppressive therapy

Warnings/Precautions The carrier proteins used in HbOC (but not PRP-OMP) are chemically and immunologically related to toxoids contained in DTP vaccine. Earlier or simultaneous vaccination with diphtheria or tetanus toxoids may be required to elicit an optimal anti-PRP antibody response to HbOC. In contrast, the immunogenicity of PRP-OMP is not affected by vaccination with DTP. In infants in whom DTP or DT vaccination is deferred, PRP-OMP may be advantageous for *Haemophilus influenzae* type b vaccination.

Children with immunologic impairment: Children with chronic illness associated with increased risk of *Haemophilus influenzae* type b disease may have impaired anti-PRP antibody responses to conjugate vaccination. Examples include those with HIV infection, immunoglobulin deficiency, anatomic or functional asplenia, and sickle cell disease, as well as recipients of bone marrow transplants and recipients of chemotherapy for malignancy. Some children with immunologic impairment may benefit from more doses of conjugate vaccine than normally indicated.

Common Adverse Reactions When administered during the same visit that DTP vaccine is given, the rates of systemic reactions do not differ from those observed only when DTP vaccine is administered. **All serious adverse reactions must be reported to the U.S. Department of Health and Human Services (DHHS) Vaccine Adverse Event Reporting System (VAERS) 1-800-822-7967.**

25%:
    Cardiovascular: Edema
    Dermatologic: Local erythema
    Local: Increased risk of *Haemophilus* b infections in the week after vaccination
    Miscellaneous: Warmth
>10%: Acute febrile reactions
1% to 10%:
    Central nervous system: Fever (up to 102.2°F), irritability, lethargy
    Gastrointestinal: Anorexia, diarrhea
    Local: Irritation at injection site

Drug Interactions
    Decreased Effect: Decreased effect with immunosuppressive agents, immunoglobulins within 1 month may decrease antibody production.

Mechanism of Action Stimulates production of anticapsular antibodies and provides active immunity to *Haemophilus influenzae*

Pharmacodynamics/Kinetics Seroconversion following one dose of Hib vaccine for children 18 months or 24 months of age or older is 75% to 90% respectively.

Onset of action: Serum antibody response: 1-2 weeks
Duration: Immunity: 1.5 years

Vaccination Schedule for *Haemophilus* b Conjugate Vaccines

Age at 1st Dose (mo)	HibTITER®		PedvaxHIB®		ProHIBiT®	
	Primary Series	Booster	Primary Series	Booster	Primary Series	Booster
2-6[1]	3 doses, 2 months apart	15 mo[2]	2 doses, 2 months apart	12 mo[2]		
7-11	2 doses, 2 months apart	15 mo[2]	2 doses, 2 months apart	15 mo[2]		
12-14	1 dose	15 mo[2]	1 dose	15 mo[2]		
15-60	1 dose	—	1 dose	—	1 dose	—

[1]It is not currently recommended that the various *Haemophilus* b conjugate vaccines be interchanged (ie, the same brand should be used throughout the entire vaccination series). If the healthcare provider does not know which vaccine was previously used, it is prudent that an infant, 2-6 months of age, be given a primary series of three doses.

[2]At least 2 months after previous dose.

Dosage Children: I.M.: 0.5 mL as a single dose should be administered according to one of the following "brand-specific" schedules; do not inject I.V. (see table on previous page)

Administration For patients at risk of hemorrhage following intramuscular injection, the ACIP recommends "it should be administered intramuscularly if, in the opinion of the physician familiar with the patients bleeding risk, the vaccine can be administered with reasonable safety by this route. If the patient receives antihemophilia or other similar therapy, intramuscular vaccination can be scheduled shortly after such therapy is administered. A fine needle (23 gauge or smaller) can be used for the vaccination and firm pressure applied to the site (without rubbing) for at least 2 minutes. The patient should be instructed concerning the risk of hematoma from the injection."

Patient Information May use acetaminophen for postdose fever

Dosage Forms INJ, powder for reconstitution (ActHIB®) [preservative free]: *Haemophilus* b capsular polysaccharide 10 mcg and tetanus toxoid 24 mcg per dose [may be reconstituted with provided diluent (forms solution), AvP DTP vaccine, or TriHIBit® (forms suspension)]. **INJ, solution** (HibTITER®): *Haemophilus* b saccharide 10 mcg and diphtheria CRM 197 protein 25 mcg per 0.5 mL (0.5 mL [preservative free]), (5 mL [contains thimerosal]). **INJ, suspension** (PedvaxHIB®): *Haemophilus* b capsular polysaccharide 7.5 mcg and *Neisseria meningitidis* OMPC 125 mcg per 0.5 mL (0.5 mL)

♦ *Haemophilus* **b (meningococcal protein conjugate) Conjugate Vaccine** *see Haemophilus* b Conjugate and Hepatitis B Vaccine *on page 607*

♦ *Haemophilus* **b Oligosaccharide Conjugate Vaccine** *see Haemophilus* b Conjugate Vaccine *on page 607*

♦ *Haemophilus* **b Polysaccharide Vaccine** *see Haemophilus* b Conjugate Vaccine *on page 607*

♦ *Haemophilus* **influenzae b Conjugate Vaccine and Diphtheria, Tetanus Toxoids, and Acellular Pertussis Vaccine** *see Diphtheria, Tetanus Toxoids, and Acellular Pertussis Vaccine and Haemophilus influenzae* b Conjugate Vaccine *on page 390*

Halcinonide (hal SIN oh nide)

Related Information
Corticosteroids Comparison *on page 1372*

U.S. Brand Names Halog®; Halog®-E

Therapeutic Category Corticosteroid, Topical (Medium Potency); Corticosteroid, Topical (High Potency)

Use Inflammation of corticosteroid-responsive dermatoses [high potency topical corticosteroid]

Pregnancy Risk Factor C

Dosage Children and Adults: Topical: Steroid-responsive dermatoses: Apply sparingly 1-3 times/day, occlusive dressing may be used for severe or resistant dermatoses; a thin film is effective; do not overuse. Therapy should be discontinued when control is achieved; if no improvement is seen, reassessment of diagnosis may be necessary.

Dosage Forms CRM (Halog®): 0.1% (15 g, 30 g, 60 g, 240 g). **CRM emollient base** (Halog®-E) : 0.1% (30 g, 60 g). **OINT** (Halog®): 0.1% (15 g, 30 g, 60 g, 240 g). **SOLN, topical** (Halog®): 0.1% (20 mL, 60 mL)

♦ **Halcion®** *see Triazolam on page 1264*

♦ **Haldol®** *see Haloperidol on page 609*

♦ **Haldol® Decanoate** *see Haloperidol on page 609*

♦ **Haley's M-O** *see Magnesium Hydroxide and Mineral Oil on page 770*

♦ **Halfprin® [OTC]** *see Aspirin on page 120*

Halobetasol (hal oh BAY ta sol)

Related Information
Corticosteroids Comparison *on page 1372*

U.S. Brand Names Ultravate®

Synonyms Halobetasol Propionate

Therapeutic Category Corticosteroid, Topical (Very High Potency)

Use Relief of inflammatory and pruritic manifestations of corticosteroid-response dermatoses [super high potency topical corticosteroid]

Pregnancy Risk Factor C

Dosage Children ≥12 years and Adults: Topical: Steroid-responsive dermatoses: Apply sparingly to skin twice daily, rub in gently and completely; treatment should not exceed 2 consecutive weeks and total dosage should not exceed 50 g/week. Therapy should be discontinued when control is achieved; if no improvement is seen, reassessment of diagnosis may be necessary.

Dosage Forms CRM: 0.05% (15 g, 50 g). **OINT:** 0.05% (15 g, 50 g)

♦ **Halobetasol Propionate** *see Halobetasol on page 609*

♦ **Halog®** *see Halcinonide on page 609*

♦ **Halog®-E** *see Halcinonide on page 609*

Haloperidol (ha loe PER i dole)

Related Information
Antipsychotic Agents Comparison *on page 1364*

U.S. Brand Names Haldol®; Haldol® Decanoate

Synonyms Haloperidol Decanoate; Haloperidol Lactate

Therapeutic Category Antipsychotic Agent, Butyrophenone; Sedative

(Continued)

Haloperidol *(Continued)*

Use Management of schizophrenia; control of tics and vocal utterances of Tourette's disorder in children and adults; severe behavioral problems in children

Unlabeled/Investigational Use Treatment of psychosis; may be used for the emergency sedation of severely-agitated or delirious patients; adjunctive treatment of ethanol dependence; antiemetic

Pregnancy Risk Factor C

Contraindications Hypersensitivity to haloperidol or any component of the formulation; Parkinson's disease; severe CNS depression; bone marrow suppression; severe cardiac or hepatic disease; coma

Warnings/Precautions Safety and efficacy have not been established in children <3 years of age. Use caution in patients with CNS depression and severe liver or cardiac disease. Hypotension may occur, particularly with parenteral administration. Decanoate form should never be administered I.V. Avoid in thyrotoxicosis. May be sedating, use with caution in disorders where CNS depression is a feature. Caution in patients with hemodynamic instability, predisposition to seizures, subcortical brain damage, renal or respiratory disease. Esophageal dysmotility and aspiration have been associated with antipsychotic use - use with caution in patients at risk of pneumonia (ie, Alzheimer's disease). Caution in breast cancer or other prolactin-dependent tumors (may elevate prolactin levels). May alter temperature regulation or mask toxicity of other drugs due to antiemetic effects. May alter cardiac conduction - life-threatening arrhythmias have occurred with therapeutic doses of antipsychotics. Adverse effects of decanoate may be prolonged. May cause orthostatic hypotension - use with caution in patients at risk of this effect or those who would tolerate transient hypotensive episodes (cerebrovascular disease, cardiovascular disease, or other medications which may predispose). Some tablets contain tartrazine.

May cause anticholinergic effects (confusion, agitation, constipation, xerostomia, blurred vision, urinary retention). Therefore, they should be used with caution in patients with decreased gastrointestinal motility, urinary retention, BPH, xerostomia, or visual problems. Conditions which also may be exacerbated by cholinergic blockade include narrow-angle glaucoma (screening is recommended) and worsening of myasthenia gravis. Relative to other neuroleptics, haloperidol has a low potency of cholinergic blockade.

May cause extrapyramidal reactions, including pseudoparkinsonism, acute dystonic reactions, akathisia, and tardive dyskinesia (risk of these reactions is high relative to other neuroleptics). May be associated with neuroleptic malignant syndrome (NMS) or pigmentary retinopathy.

Common Adverse Reactions Frequency not defined.

Cardiovascular: Hypotension, hypertension, tachycardia, arrhythmias, abnormal T waves with prolonged ventricular repolarization, torsade de pointes (case-control study ~4%)

Central nervous system: Restlessness, anxiety, extrapyramidal symptoms, dystonic reactions, pseudoparkinsonian signs and symptoms, tardive dyskinesia, neuroleptic malignant syndrome (NMS), altered central temperature regulation, akathisia, tardive dystonia, insomnia, euphoria, agitation, drowsiness, depression, lethargy, headache, confusion, vertigo, seizures

Dermatologic: Hyperpigmentation, pruritus, rash, contact dermatitis, alopecia, photosensitivity (rare)

Endocrine & metabolic: Amenorrhea, galactorrhea, gynecomastia, sexual dysfunction, lactation, breast engorgement, mastalgia, menstrual irregularities, hyperglycemia, hypoglycemia, hyponatremia

Gastrointestinal: Nausea, vomiting, anorexia, constipation, diarrhea, hypersalivation, dyspepsia, xerostomia

Genitourinary: Urinary retention, priapism

Hematologic: Cholestatic jaundice, obstructive jaundice

Ocular: Blurred vision

Respiratory: Laryngospasm, bronchospasm

Miscellaneous: Heat stroke, diaphoresis

Drug Interactions

Cytochrome P450 Effect: Substrate of CYP1A2 (minor), 2D6 (major), 3A4 (major); **Inhibits** CYP2D6 (moderate), 3A4 (moderate)

Increased Effect/Toxicity: CYP2D6 inhibitors may increase the levels/effects of haloperidol; example inhibitors include chlorpromazine, delavirdine, fluoxetine, miconazole, paroxetine, pergolide, quinidine, quinine, ritonavir, and ropinirole. Haloperidol concentrations/effects may be increased by chloroquine, propranolol, and sulfadoxine-pyrimethamine. Haloperidol may increase the effects of antihypertensives, CNS depressants (ethanol, narcotics, sedative-hypnotics), lithium, trazodone, and TCAs. Haloperidol in combination with indomethacin may result in drowsiness, tiredness, and confusion. Metoclopramide may increase risk of extrapyramidal symptoms (EPS).

Decreased Effect: Haloperidol may inhibit the ability of bromocriptine to lower serum prolactin concentrations. Benztropine (and other anticholinergics) may inhibit the therapeutic response to haloperidol and excess anticholinergic effects may occur. Barbiturates, carbamazepine, and cigarette smoking may enhance the hepatic metabolism of haloperidol. Haloperidol may inhibit the antiparkinsonian effect of levodopa; avoid this combination.

Mechanism of Action Blocks postsynaptic mesolimbic dopaminergic D_1 and D_2 receptors in the brain; depresses the release of hypothalamic and hypophyseal hormones; believed to depress the reticular activating system thus affecting basal metabolism, body temperature, wakefulness, vasomotor tone, and emesis

Pharmacodynamics/Kinetics

Onset of action: Sedation: I.V.: ~1 hour

Duration: Decanoate: ~3 weeks

Distribution: Crosses placenta; enters breast milk

Protein binding: 90%

Metabolism: Hepatic to inactive compounds

Bioavailability: Oral: 60%

Half-life elimination: 20 hours

Time to peak, serum: 20 minutes

Excretion: Urine (33% to 40% as metabolites) within 5 days; feces (15%)

Dosage

Children: 3-12 years (15-40 kg): Oral:

Initial: 0.05 mg/kg/day or 0.25-0.5 mg/day given in 2-3 divided doses; increase by 0.25-0.5 mg every 5-7 days; maximum: 0.15 mg/kg/day

Usual maintenance:

Agitation or hyperkinesia: 0.01-0.03 mg/kg/day once daily

Nonpsychotic disorders: 0.05-0.075 mg/kg/day in 2-3 divided doses

Psychotic disorders: 0.05-0.15 mg/kg/day in 2-3 divided doses

Children 6-12 years: Sedation/psychotic disorders: I.M. (as lactate): 1-3 mg/dose every 4-8 hours to a maximum of 0.15 mg/kg/day; change over to oral therapy as soon as able

Adults:

Psychosis:

Oral: 0.5-5 mg 2-3 times/day; usual maximum: 30 mg/day

I.M. (as lactate): 2-5 mg every 4-8 hours as needed

I.M. (as decanoate): Initial: 10-20 times the daily oral dose administered at 4-week intervals

Maintenance dose: 10-15 times initial oral dose; used to stabilize psychiatric symptoms

Delirium in the intensive care unit (unlabeled use, unlabeled route):

I.V.: 2-10 mg; may repeat bolus doses every 20-30 minutes until calm achieved then administer 25% of the maximum dose every 6 hours; monitor ECG and QT_c interval

Intermittent I.V.: 0.03-0.15 mg/kg every 30 minutes to 6 hours

Oral: Agitation: 5-10 mg

Continuous intravenous infusion (100 mg/100 mL D_5W): Rates of 3-25 mg/hour have been used

Rapid tranquilization of severely-agitated patient (unlabeled use): Administer every 30-60 minutes:

Oral: 5-10 mg

I.M.: 5 mg

Average total dose (oral or I.M.) for tranquilization: 10-20 mg

Elderly: Initial: Oral: 0.25-0.5 mg 1-2 times/day; increase dose at 4- to 7-day intervals by 0.25-0.5 mg/day; increase dosing intervals (twice daily, 3 times/day, etc) as necessary to control response or side effects

Hemodialysis/peritoneal dialysis: Supplemental dose is not necessary

Administration The decanoate injectable formulation should be administered I.M. only, **do not administer decanoate I.V.** Dilute the oral concentrate with water or juice before administration. Avoid skin contact with oral suspension or solution; may cause contact dermatitis.

Monitoring Parameters Vital signs; lipid profile, fasting blood glucose/Hgb A_{1c}; BMI; mental status, abnormal involuntary movement scale (AIMS), extrapyramidal symptoms (EPS)

Reference Range

Therapeutic: 5-15 ng/mL (SI: 10-30 nmol/L) (psychotic disorders - less for Tourette's and mania)

Toxic: >42 ng/mL (SI: >84 nmol/L)

Patient Information May cause drowsiness, restlessness; avoid alcohol and other CNS depressants; rise slowly from recumbent position; use of supportive stockings may help prevent orthostatic hypotension; do not alter dosage or discontinue without consulting prescriber; oral concentrate must be diluted in 2-4 oz of liquid (water, fruit juice, carbonated drinks, milk, or pudding)

Dosage Forms INJ, oil, as decanoate (Haldol® Decanoate): 50 mg/mL (1 mL, 5 mL); 100 mg/mL (1 mL, 5 mL). **INJ, solution, as lactate** (Haldol®): 5 mg/mL (1 mL, 10 mL). **SOLN, oral concentrate, as lactate:** 2 mg/mL (15 mL, 120 mL). **TAB:** 0.5 mg, 1 mg, 2 mg, 5 mg, 10 mg, 20 mg

- **hCG** *see* Chorionic Gonadotropin (Human) *on page 272*
- **HCTZ** *see* Hydrochlorothiazide *on page 625*
- **HCTZ and Telmisartan** *see* Telmisartan and Hydrochlorothiazide *on page 1191*
- **HDA® Toothache [OTC]** *see* Benzocaine *on page 154*
- **HDCV** *see* Rabies Virus Vaccine *on page 1078*
- **Head & Shoulders® Intensive Treatment [OTC]** *see* Selenium Sulfide *on page 1129*
- **Healon®** *see* Sodium Hyaluronate *on page 1148*
- **Healon®5** *see* Sodium Hyaluronate *on page 1148*
- **Healon GV®** *see* Sodium Hyaluronate *on page 1148*
- **Hectorol®** *see* Doxercalciferol *on page 409*
- **Helidac®** *see* Bismuth Subsalicylate, Metronidazole, and Tetracycline *on page 169*
- **Helistat®** *see* Microfibrillar Collagen Hemostat *on page 836*
- **Helixate® FS** *see* Antihemophilic Factor (Recombinant) *on page 105*
- **Hemabate®** *see* Carboprost Tromethamine *on page 220*
- **Hemocyte® [OTC]** *see* Ferrous Fumarate *on page 519*
- **Hemodynamic Support, Intravenous** *see page 1377*
- **Hemofil® M** *see* Antihemophilic Factor (Human) *on page 103*
- **Hemril-HC®** *see* Hydrocortisone *on page 632*

Heparin (HEP a rin)

Related Information
Anticoagulants, Injectable *on page 1357*
U.S. Brand Names Hep-Lock®
Synonyms Heparin Calcium; Heparin Lock Flush; Heparin Sodium
Therapeutic Category Anticoagulant
Use Prophylaxis and treatment of thromboembolic disorders
Pregnancy Risk Factor C
Contraindications Hypersensitivity to heparin or any component of the formulation; severe thrombocytopenia; uncontrolled active bleeding except when due to DIC; suspected intracranial hemorrhage; not for I.M. use; not for use when appropriate monitoring parameters cannot be obtained
Warnings/Precautions Use cautiously in patients with a documented hypersensitivity reaction and only in life-threatening situations. Hemorrhage is the most common complication. Monitor for signs and symptoms of bleeding. Certain patients are at increased risk of bleeding. Risk factors include bacterial endocarditis; congenital or acquired bleeding disorders; active ulcerative or angiodysplastic GI diseases; severe uncontrolled hypertension; hemorrhagic stroke; or use shortly after brain, spinal, or ophthalmology surgery; patient treated concomitantly with platelet inhibitors; conditions associated with increased bleeding tendencies (hemophilia, vascular purpura); recent GI bleeding; thrombocytopenia or platelet defects; severe liver disease; hypertensive or diabetic retinopathy; or in patients undergoing invasive procedures. A higher incidence of bleeding has been reported in patients >60 years of age, particularly women. They are also more sensitive to the dose.

Patients who develop thrombocytopenia on heparin may be at risk of developing a new thrombus ("White-clot syndrome"). Hypersensitivity reactions can occur. Osteoporosis can occur following long-term use (>6 months). Monitor for hyperkalemia. Discontinue therapy and consider alternatives if platelets are <100,000/mm³. Patients >60 years of age may require lower doses of heparin.

Some preparations contain benzyl alcohol as a preservative. In neonates, large amounts of benzyl alcohol (>100 mg/kg/day) have been associated with fatal toxicity (gasping syndrome). The use of preservative-free heparin is, therefore, recommended in neonates. Some preparations contain sulfite which may cause allergic reactions.

Heparin does not possess fibrinolytic activity and, therefore, cannot lyse established thrombi; discontinue heparin if hemorrhage occurs; severe hemorrhage or overdosage may require protamine
Common Adverse Reactions Frequency not defined.
Cardiovascular: Chest pain, vasospasm (possibly related to thrombosis), hemorrhagic shock
Central nervous system: Fever, headache, chills
Dermatologic: Unexplained bruising, urticaria, alopecia, dysesthesia pedis, purpura, eczema, cutaneous necrosis (following deep S.C. injection), erythematous plaques (case reports)
Endocrine & metabolic: Hyperkalemia (supression of aldosterone), rebound hyperlipidemia on discontinuation
Gastrointestinal: Nausea, vomiting, constipation, hematemesis
Genitourinary: Frequent or persistent erection
Hematologic: Hemorrhage, blood in urine, bleeding from gums, epistaxis, adrenal hemorrhage, ovarian hemorrhage, retroperitoneal hemorrhage, thrombocytopenia (see note)
Hepatic: Elevated liver enzymes (AST/ALT)
Local: Irritation, ulceration, cutaneous necrosis have been rarely reported with deep S.C. injections, I.M. injection (not recommended) is associated with a high incidence of these effects
Neuromuscular & skeletal: Peripheral neuropathy, osteoporosis (chronic therapy effect)
Ocular: Conjunctivitis (allergic reaction)
Respiratory: Hemoptysis, pulmonary hemorrhage, asthma, rhinitis, bronchospasm (case reports)

Miscellaneous: Allergic reactions, anaphylactoid reactions

Note: Thrombocytopenia has been reported to occur at an incidence between 0% and 30%. It is often of no clinical significance. However, immunologically mediated heparin-induced thrombocytopenia has been estimated to occur in 1% to 2% of patients, and is marked by a progressive fall in platelet counts and, in some cases, thromboembolic complications (skin necrosis, pulmonary embolism, gangrene of the extremities, stroke or myocardial infarction); daily platelet counts for 5-7 days at initiation of therapy may help detect the onset of this complication.

Drug Interactions

Increased Effect/Toxicity: The risk of hemorrhage associated with heparin may be increased by oral anticoagulants (warfarin), thrombolytics, dextran, and drugs which affect platelet function (eg, aspirin, NSAIDs, dipyridamole, ticlopidine, clopidogrel, IIb/IIIa antagonists). However, heparin is often used in conjunction with thrombolytic therapy or during the initiation of warfarin therapy to assure anticoagulation and to protect against possible transient hypercoagulability. Cephalosporins which contain the MTT side chain and parenteral penicillins (may inhibit platelet aggregation) may increase the risk of hemorrhage. Other drugs reported to increase heparin's anticoagulant effect include antihistamines, tetracycline, quinine, nicotine, and cardiac glycosides (digoxin).

Decreased Effect: Nitroglycerin (I.V.) may decrease heparin's anticoagulant effect. This interaction has not been validated in some studies, and may only occur at high nitroglycerin dosages.

Mechanism of Action Potentiates the action of antithrombin III and thereby inactivates thrombin (as well as activated coagulation factors IX, X, XI, XII, and plasmin) and prevents the conversion of fibrinogen to fibrin; heparin also stimulates release of lipoprotein lipase (lipoprotein lipase hydrolyzes triglycerides to glycerol and free fatty acids)

Pharmacodynamics/Kinetics

Onset of action: Anticoagulation: I.V.: Immediate; S.C.: ~20-30 minutes

Absorption: Oral, rectal, I.M.: Erratic at best from all these routes of administration; S.C. absorption is also erratic, but considered acceptable for prophylactic use

Distribution: Does not cross placenta; does not enter breast milk

Metabolism: Hepatic; may be partially metabolized in the reticuloendothelial system

Half-life elimination: Mean: 1.5 hours; Range: 1-2 hours; affected by obesity, renal function, hepatic function, malignancy, presence of pulmonary embolism, and infections

Excretion: Urine (small amounts as unchanged drug)

Dosage

Children:

Intermittent I.V.: Initial: 50-100 units/kg, then 50-100 units/kg every 4 hours

I.V. infusion: Initial: 50 units/kg, then 15-25 units/kg/hour; increase dose by 2-4 units/kg/hour every 6-8 hours as required

Adults:

Prophylaxis (low-dose heparin): S.C.: 5000 units every 8-12 hours

Intermittent I.V.: Initial: 10,000 units, then 50-70 units/kg (5000-10,000 units) every 4-6 hours

I.V. infusion (weight-based dosing per institutional nomogram recommended):

Acute coronary syndromes: MI: Fibrinolytic therapy:

Alteplase or reteplase with first or second bolus: Concurrent bolus of 60 units/kg (maximum: 4000 units), then 12 units/kg/hour (maximum: 1000 units/hour) as continuous infusion. Check aPTT every 4-6 hours; adjust to target of 1.5-2 times the upper limit of control (50-70 seconds in clinical trials); usual range 10-30 units/kg/hour. Duration of heparin therapy depends on concurrent therapy and the specific patient risks for systemic or venous thromboembolism.

Streptokinase: Heparin use optional depending on concurrent therapy and specific patient risks for systemic or venous thromboembolism (anterior MI, CHF, previous embolus, atrial fibrillation, LV thrombus): If heparin is administered, start when aPTT <2 times the upper limit of control; do not use a bolus, but initiate infusion adjusted to a target aPTT of 1.5-2 times the upper limit of control (50-70 seconds in clinical trials). If heparin is not administered by infusion, 7500-12,500 units S.C. every 12 hours (when aPTT <2 times the upper limit of control) is recommended.

Percutaneous coronary intervention: Heparin bolus and infusion may be administered to an activated clotting time (ACT) of 300-350 seconds if no concurrent GPIIb/IIIa receptor antagonist is administered or 200-250 seconds if a GPIIb/IIIa receptor antagonist is administered.

Treatment of unstable angina (high-risk and some intermediate-risk patients): Initial bolus of 60-70 units/kg (maximum: 5000 units), followed by an initial infusion of 12-15 units/kg/hour (maximum: 1000 units/hour). The American College of Chest Physicians consensus conference has recommended dosage adjustments to correspond to a therapeutic range equivalent to heparin levels of 0.3-0.7 units/mL by antifactor Xa determinations, which correlates with aPTT values between 60 and 80 seconds

Treatment of venous thromboembolism (DVT/PE): 80 units/kg I.V. push followed by continuous infusion of 18 units/kg/hour

Line flushing: When using daily flushes of heparin to maintain patency of single and double lumen central catheters, 10 units/mL is commonly used for younger infants (eg, <10 kg) while 100 units/mL is used for older infants, children, and adults. Capped PVC catheters and peripheral heparin locks require flushing more frequently (eg, every 6-8 hours). Volume of heparin flush is usually similar to volume of catheter (or slightly greater). Additional flushes

(Continued)

Heparin *(Continued)*

should be given when stagnant blood is observed in catheter, after catheter is used for drug or blood administration, and after blood withdrawal from catheter.

Addition of heparin (0.5-1 unit/mL) to peripheral and central TPN has been shown to increase duration of line patency. The final concentration of heparin used for TPN solutions may need to be decreased to 0.5 units/mL in small infants receiving larger amounts of volume in order to avoid approaching therapeutic amounts. Arterial lines are heparinized with a final concentration of 1 unit/mL.

Using a standard heparin solution (25,000 units/500 mL D_5 W), the following infusion rates can be used to achieve the listed doses.

For a dose of:

400 units/hour: Infuse at 8 mL/hour
500 units/hour: Infuse at 10 mL/hour
600 units/hour: Infuse at 12 mL/hour
700 units/hour: Infuse at 14 mL/hour
800 units/hour: Infuse at 16 mL/hour
900 units/hour: Infuse at 18 mL/hour
1000 units/hour: Infuse at 20 mL/hour
1100 units/hour: Infuse at 22 mL/hour
1200 units/hour: Infuse at 24 mL/hour
1300 units/hour: Infuse at 26 mL/hour
1400 units/hour: Infuse at 28 mL/hour
1500 units/hour: Infuse at 30 mL/hour
1600 units/hour: Infuse at 32 mL/hour
1700 units/hour: Infuse at 34 mL/hour
1800 units/hour: Infuse at 36 mL/hour
1900 units/hour: Infuse at 38 mL/hour
2000 units/hour: Infuse at 40 mL/hour

Dosing adjustments in the elderly: Patients >60 years of age may have higher serum levels and clinical response (longer aPTTs) as compared to younger patients receiving similar dosages; lower dosages may be required

Administration Do not administer I.M. due to pain, irritation, and hematoma formation; central venous catheters must be flushed with heparin solution when newly inserted, daily (at the time of tubing change), after blood withdrawal or transfusion, and after an intermittent infusion through an injectable cap. A volume of at least 10 mL of blood should be removed and discarded from a heparinized line before blood samples are sent for coagulation testing.

Monitoring Parameters Platelet counts, aPTT, hemoglobin, hematocrit, signs of bleeding

For intermittent I.V. injections, aPTT is measured 3.5-4 hours after I.V. injection

Note: Continuous I.V. infusion is preferred over I.V. intermittent injections. For full-dose heparin (ie, nonlow-dose), the dose should be titrated according to aPTT results. For anticoagulation, an aPTT 1.5-2.5 times normal is usually desired. Because of variation among hospitals in the control aPTT values, nomograms should be established at each institution, designed to achieve aPTT values in the target range (eg, for a control aPTT of 30 seconds, the target range [1.5-2.5 times control] would be 45-75 seconds). Measurements should be made prior to heparin therapy, 6 hours after initiation, and 6 hours after any dosage change, and should be used to adjust the heparin infusion until the aPTT exhibits a therapeutic level. When two consecutive aPTT values are therapeutic, the measurements may be made every 24 hours, and if necessary, dose adjustment carried out. In addition, a significant change in the patient's clinical condition (eg, recurrent ischemia, bleeding, hypotension) should prompt an immediate aPTT determination, followed by dose adjustment if necessary. Increase or decrease infusion by 2-4 units/kg/hour dependent upon aPTT.

Heparin infusion dose adjustment:
aPTT >3x control: Decrease infusion rate 50%
aPTT 2-3x control: Decrease infusion rate 25%
aPTT 1.5-2x control: No change
aPTT <1.5x control: Increase rate of infusion 25%; max 2500 units/hour

Reference Range Heparin: 0.3-0.5 unit/mL; aPTT: 1.5-2.5 times **the patient's baseline**

Dosage Forms INF [premixed in NaCl 0.45%]: 12,500 units (250 mL); 25,000 units (250 mL, 500 mL). **INF** [preservative free; premixed in D_5W; porcine intestinal mucosa source]: 10,000 units (100 mL); 12,500 units (250 mL); 20,000 units (500 mL); 25,000 units (250 mL, 500 mL). **INF** [preservative free; premixed in NaCl 0.9%; porcine intestinal mucosa source]: 1000 units (500 mL); 2000 units (1000 mL). **INJ, solution** [beef lung source]: 1000 units/mL (10 mL, 30 mL); 5000 units/mL (10 mL); 10,000 units/mL (1 mL, 4 mL). **INJ, solution** [lock flush preparation; porcine intestinal mucosa source]: 10 units/mL (1 mL, 10 mL, 30 mL); 100 units/mL (1 mL, 5 mL). **INJ, solution** [lock flush preparation; porcine intestinal mucosa source]: 10 units/mL (10 mL, 30 mL); 100 units/mL (10 mL, 30 mL). **INJ, solution** [lock flush preparation; porcine intestinal mucosa source; prefilled syringe]: 10 units/mL (1 mL, 2 mL, 2.5 mL, 3 mL, 5 mL); 100 units/mL (1 mL, 2 mL, 2.5 mL, 3 mL, 5 mL). **INJ, solution** [preservative free; lock flush preparation; porcine intestinal mucosa source; prefilled syringe]: 10 units/mL (1 mL, 2 mL, 3 mL, 5 mL, 10 mL); 100 units/mL (1 mL, 2 mL, 3 mL, 5 mL, 10 mL). **INJ, solution** [porcine intestinal mucosa source]: 10,000 units/mL (5 mL). **INJ, solution** [porcine intestinal mucosa source; prefilled syringe]: 1000 units/mL (1 mL); 2500 units/mL (1 mL); 5000 units/mL (0.5 mL, 1 mL); 7500 units/mL (1 mL); 10,000 units/mL (1mL); 20,000 units/mL (1 mL). **INJ, solution** [preservative free; porcine intestinal mucosa source; prefilled syringe]: 10,000 units/mL (0.25

mL, 0.5 mL, 0.75 mL, 1 mL). **INJ, solution** [preservative free; porcine intestinal mucosa source]: 1000 units/mL (2 mL); 2000 units/mL (5 mL, 10 mL); 2500 units/mL (5 mL, 10 mL)

♦ **Heparin Calcium** *see* Heparin *on page 612*
♦ **Heparin Cofactor I** *see* Antithrombin III *on page 107*
♦ **Heparin Lock Flush** *see* Heparin *on page 612*
♦ **Heparin Sodium** *see* Heparin *on page 612*

Hepatitis A Inactivated and Hepatitis B (Recombinant) Vaccine
(hep a TYE tis aye in ak ti VAY ted & hep a TYE tis bee ree KOM be nant vak SEEN)

U.S. Brand Names Twinrix®
Synonyms Engerix-B® and Havrix®; Havrix® and Engerix-B®; Hepatitis B (Recombinant) and Hepatitis A Inactivated Vaccine
Therapeutic Category Vaccine
Use Active immunization against disease caused by hepatitis A virus and hepatitis B virus (all known subtypes) in populations desiring protection against or at high risk of exposure to these viruses.

Populations include travelers to areas of intermediate/high endemicity for **both** HAV and HBV; those at increased risk of HBV infection due to behavioral or occupational factors; patients with chronic liver disease; laboratory workers who handle live HAV and HBV; healthcare workers, police, and other personnel who render first-aid or medical assistance; workers who come in contact with sewage; employees of day care centers and correctional facilities; patients/staff of hemodialysis units; male homosexuals; patients frequently receiving blood products; military personnel; users of injectable illicit drugs; close household contacts of patients with hepatitis A and hepatitis B infection.

Pregnancy Risk Factor C
Dosage I.M.: Adults: Primary immunization: Three doses (1 mL each) given on a 0-, 1-, and 6-month schedule
Dosage Forms INJ, suspension [prefilled syringe]: Inactivated hepatitis A virus 720 ELISA units and hepatitis B surface antigen 20 mcg per mL (1 mL)

Hepatitis A Vaccine (hep a TYE tis aye vak SEEN)
U.S. Brand Names Havrix®; VAQTA®
Therapeutic Category Vaccine; Vaccine, Inactivated Virus
Use For populations desiring protection against hepatitis A or for populations at high risk of exposure to hepatitis A virus (travelers to developing countries, household and sexual contacts of persons infected with hepatitis A), child day care employees, patients with chronic liver disease, illicit drug users, male homosexuals, institutional workers (eg, institutions for the mentally and physically handicapped persons, prisons, etc), and healthcare workers who may be exposed to hepatitis A virus (eg, laboratory employees); protection lasts for approximately 15 years
Pregnancy Risk Factor C
Contraindications Hypersensitivity to hepatitis A vaccine or any component of the formulation
Warnings/Precautions Use caution in patients with serious active infection, cardiovascular disease, or pulmonary disorders; treatment for anaphylactic reactions should be immediately available
Common Adverse Reactions All serious adverse reactions must be reported to the U.S. Department of Health and Human Services (DHHS) Vaccine Adverse Event Reporting System (VAERS) 1-800-822-7967.
Percentage unknown: Fatigue, fever (rare), transient LFT abnormalities
>10%:
    Central nervous system: Headache
    Local: Pain, tenderness, and warmth
1% to 10%:
    Endocrine & metabolic: Pharyngitis (1%)
    Gastrointestinal: Abdominal pain (1%)
    Local: Cutaneous reactions at the injection site (soreness, edema, and redness)
Mechanism of Action As an inactivated virus vaccine, hepatitis A vaccine offers active immunization against hepatitis A virus infection at an effective immune response rate in up to 99% of subjects
Pharmacodynamics/Kinetics
Onset of action (protection): 3 weeks after a single dose
Duration: Neutralizing antibodies have persisted for >3 years; unconfirmed evidence indicates that antibody levels may persist for 5-10 years
Dosage I.M.:
Havrix®:
    Children 2-18 years: 720 ELISA units (administered as 2 injections of 360 ELISA units [0.5 mL]) 15-30 days prior to travel with a booster 6-12 months following primary immunization; the deltoid muscle should be used for I.M. injection
    Adults: 1440 ELISA units(1 mL) 15-30 days prior to travel with a booster 6-12 months following primary immunization; injection should be in the deltoid
VAQTA®:
    Children 2-17 years: 25 units (0.5 mL) with 25 units (0.5 mL) booster to be given 6-18 months after primary immunization
    Adults: 50 units (1 mL) with 50 units (1 mL) booster to be given 6 months after primary immunization
(Continued)

Hepatitis A Vaccine *(Continued)*

Administration For patients at risk of hemorrhage following intramuscular injection, the ACIP recommends "it should be administered intramuscularly if, in the opinion of the physician familiar with the patients bleeding risk, the vaccine can be administered with reasonable safety by this route. If the patient receives antihemophilia or other similar therapy, intramuscular vaccination can be scheduled shortly after such therapy is administered. A fine needle (23 gauge or smaller) can be used for the vaccination and firm pressure applied to the site (without rubbing) for at least 2 minutes. The patient should be instructed concerning the risk of hematoma from the injection."

Monitoring Parameters Liver function tests

Reference Range Seroconversion for Havrix®: Antibody >20 milli-international units/mL

Dosage Forms INJ, suspension, adult [prefilled syringe] (Havrix®): Viral antigen 1440 ELISA units/mL (1 mL); (VAQTA®): HAV protein 50 units/mL (1 mL). **INJ, suspension**, pediatric [prefilled syringe] (Havrix®): Viral antigen 720 ELISA units/0.5 mL (0.5 mL). **INJ, suspension**, pediatric/adolescent [prefilled syringe] (VAQTA®): HAV protein 25 units/0.5 mL (0.5 mL)

Hepatitis B Immune Globulin *(hep a TYE tis bee i MYUN GLOB yoo lin)*

U.S. Brand Names BayHep B™; Nabi-HB®

Synonyms HBIG

Therapeutic Category Immune Globulin

Use Provide prophylactic passive immunity to hepatitis B infection to those individuals exposed; newborns of mothers known to be hepatitis B surface antigen positive; hepatitis B immune globulin is not indicated for treatment of active hepatitis B infections and is ineffective in the treatment of chronic active hepatitis B infection

Pregnancy Risk Factor C

Contraindications Hypersensitivity to hepatitis B immune globulin or any component of the formulation; allergies to gamma globulin or anti-immunoglobulin antibodies; allergies to thimerosal; IgA deficiency

Warnings/Precautions Have epinephrine 1:1000 available for anaphylactic reactions. As a product of human plasma, this product may potentially transmit disease; screening of donors, as well as testing and/or inactivation of certain viruses reduces this risk. Use caution in patients with thrombocytopenia or coagulation disorders (I.M. injections may be contraindicated), in patients with isolated IgA deficiency, or in patients with previous systemic hypersensitivity to human immunoglobulins. Not for intravenous administration.

Common Adverse Reactions Frequency not defined.

Central nervous system: Dizziness, malaise, fever, lethargy, chills

Dermatologic: Urticaria, angioedema, rash, erythema

Gastrointestinal: Vomiting, nausea

Genitourinary: Nephrotic syndrome

Local: Pain, tenderness, and muscular stiffness at injection site

Neuromuscular & skeletal: Arthralgia, myalgia

Miscellaneous: Anaphylaxis

Mechanism of Action Hepatitis B immune globulin (HBIG) is a nonpyrogenic sterile solution containing 10% to 18% protein of which at least 80% is monomeric immunoglobulin G (IgG). HBIG differs from immune globulin in the amount of anti-HB$_s$. Immune globulin is prepared from plasma that is not preselected for anti-HB$_s$ content. HBIG is prepared from plasma preselected for high titer anti-HB$_s$. In the U.S., HBIG has an anti-HB$_s$ high titer >1:100,000 by IRA. There is no evidence that the causative agent of AIDS (HTLV-III/LAV) is transmitted by HBIG.

Pharmacodynamics/Kinetics

Absorption: Slow

Time to peak, serum: 1-6 days

Dosage I.M.:

Newborns: Hepatitis B: 0.5 mL as soon after birth as possible (within 12 hours); may repeat at 3 months in order for a higher rate of prevention of the carrier state to be achieved; at this time an active vaccination program with the vaccine may begin

Adults: Postexposure prophylaxis: 0.06 mL/kg as soon as possible after exposure (ie, within 24 hours of needlestick, ocular, or mucosal exposure or within 14 days of sexual exposure); usual dose: 3-5 mL; repeat at 28-30 days after exposure

Note: HBIG may be administered at the same time (but at a different site) or up to 1 month preceding hepatitis B vaccination without impairing the active immune response

Administration I.M. injection only in gluteal or deltoid region; to prevent injury from injection, care should be taken when giving to patients with thrombocytopenia or bleeding disorders; has been administered intravenously in hepatitis B-positive liver transplant patients

Dosage Forms INJ, solution, neonatal [preservative free] (BayHep B™): 0.5 mL. **INJ, solution** [preservative free] (BayHep B™, Nabi-HB®): 1 mL, 5 mL

- **Hepatitis B Inactivated Virus Vaccine (plasma derived)** *see* Hepatitis B Vaccine *on page 617*
- **Hepatitis B Inactivated Virus Vaccine (recombinant DNA)** *see* Hepatitis B Vaccine *on page 617*
- **Hepatitis B (Recombinant) and Hepatitis A Inactivated Vaccine** *see* Hepatitis A Inactivated and Hepatitis B (Recombinant) Vaccine *on page 615*

Hepatitis B Vaccine (hep a TYE tis bee vak SEEN)

Related Information

Management of Healthcare Worker Exposures to HBV, HCV, and HIV *on page 1421*

U.S. Brand Names Engerix-B®; Recombivax HB®

Synonyms Hepatitis B Inactivated Virus Vaccine (plasma derived); Hepatitis B Inactivated Virus Vaccine (recombinant DNA)

Therapeutic Category Vaccine; Vaccine, Inactivated Virus

Use Immunization against infection caused by all known subtypes of hepatitis B virus, in individuals considered at high risk of potential exposure to hepatitis B virus or HB$_s$Ag-positive materials: See table.

Pre-exposure Prophylaxis for Hepatitis B
Healthcare workers[1]
Special patient groups (eg, adolescents, infants born to HB$_s$Ag-positive mothers, children born after 11/21/91, military personnel, etc)
Hemodialysis patients[2] (see dosing recommendations)
Recipients of certain blood products[3]
Lifestyle factors
Homosexual and bisexual men
Intravenous drug abusers
Heterosexually-active persons with multiple sexual partners or recently acquired sexually-transmitted diseases
Environmental factors
Household and sexual contacts of HBV carriers
Prison inmates
Clients and staff of institutions for the mentally handicapped
Residents, immigrants, and refugees from areas with endemic HBV infection
International travelers at increased risk of acquiring HBV infection

[1]The risk of hepatitis B virus (HBV) infection for healthcare workers varies both between hospitals and within hospitals. Hepatitis B vaccination is recommended for all healthcare workers with blood exposure.

[2]Hemodialysis patients often respond poorly to hepatitis B vaccination; higher vaccine doses or increased number of doses are required. A special formulation of one vaccine is now available for such persons (Recombivax HB®, 40 mcg/mL). The anti-HB$_s$ (antibody to hepatitis B surface antigen) response of such persons should be tested after they are vaccinated, and those who have not responded should be revaccinated with 1-3 additional doses.

Patients with chronic renal disease should be vaccinated as early as possible, ideally before they require hemodialysis. In addition, their anti-HB$_s$ levels should be monitored at 6- to 12-month intervals to assess the need for revaccination.

[3]Patients with hemophilia should be immunized subcutaneously, not intramuscularly.

Pregnancy Risk Factor C

Contraindications Hypersensitivity to yeast, hepatitis B vaccine, or any component of the formulation

Warnings/Precautions Immediate treatment for anaphylactic/anaphylactoid reaction should be available during vaccine use; consider delaying vaccination during acute febrile illness; use caution with decreased cardiopulmonary function; unrecognized hepatitis B infection may be present, immunization may not prevent infection in these patients; patients >65 years may have lower response rates

Common Adverse Reactions All serious adverse reactions must be reported to the U.S. Department of Health and Human Services (DHHS) Vaccine Adverse Event Reporting System (VAERS) 1-800-822-7967.

Frequency not defined. The most common adverse effects reported with both products included injection site reactions (>10%).

Cardiovascular: Hypotension

Central nervous system: Agitation, chills, dizziness, fatigue, fever (≥37.5°C / 100°F), flushing, headache, insomnia, irritability, lightheadedness, malaise, vertigo

Dermatologic: Angioedema, petechiae, pruritus, rash, urticaria

Gastrointestinal: Abdominal pain, appetite decreased, cramps, diarrhea, dyspepsia, nausea, vomiting

Genitourinary: Dysuria

Local: Injection site reactions: Ecchymosis, erythema, induration, pain, nodule formation, soreness, swelling, tenderness, warmth

Neuromuscular & skeletal: Achiness, arthralgia, back pain, myalgia, neck pain, neck stiffness, paresthesia, shoulder pain, weakness

Otic: Earache

Respiratory: Cough, pharyngitis, rhinitis, upper respiratory tract infection

Miscellaneous: Lymphadenopathy, diaphoresis

Drug Interactions

Decreased Effect: Decreased effect: Immunosuppressive agents

Mechanism of Action Recombinant hepatitis B vaccine is a noninfectious subunit viral vaccine. The vaccine is derived from hepatitis B surface antigen (HB$_s$Ag) produced through recombinant DNA techniques from yeast cells. The portion of the hepatitis B gene which codes for HB$_s$Ag is cloned into yeast which is then cultured to produce hepatitis B vaccine. (Continued)

Hepatitis B Vaccine *(Continued)*

Pharmacodynamics/Kinetics Duration of action: Following a 3-dose series, immunity lasts ~5-7 years

Dosage I.M.:

Immunization regimen: Regimen consists of 3 doses (0, 1, and 6 months): First dose given on the elected date, second dose given 1 month later, third dose given 6 months after the first dose; see table.

Routine Immunization Regimen of Three I.M. Hepatitis B Vaccine Doses

Age	Initial		1 mo		6 mo	
	Recombivax HB® (mL)	Enger-ix-B® (mL)	Recombivax HB® (mL)	Enger-ix-B® (mL)	Recombivax HB® (mL)	Enger-ix-B® (mL)
Birth[1] to 19 y	0.5[2]	0.5[3]	0.5[2]	0.5[3]	0.5[2]	0.5[3]
≥20 y	1[4]	1[5]	1[4]	1[5]	1[4]	1[5]
Dialysis or immunocompromised patients[6]	1[7]	2[8]	1[7]	2[8]	1[7]	2[8]

[1]Infants born of HB$_s$Ag **negative** mothers.

[2]5 mcg/0.5 mL pediatric/adolescent formulation

[3]10 mcg/0.5 mL formulation

[4]10 mcg/mL adult formulation

[5]20 mcg/mL formulation

[6]Revaccinate if anti-HB$_s$ <10 mIU/mL ≥1-2 months after third dose.

[7]40 mcg/mL dialysis formulation

[8]Two 1 mL doses given at different sites using the 40 mcg/2 mL dialysis formulation

Alternative dosing schedule for **Recombivax HB®:** Children 11-15 years (10 mcg/mL adult formulation): First dose of 1 mL given on the elected date, second dose given 4-6 months later

Alternative dosing schedules for **Engerix-B®:**

Children ≤10 years (10 mcg/0.5 mL formulation): High-risk children: 0.5 mL at 0, 1, 2, and 12 months; lower-risk children ages 5-10 who are candidates for an extended administration schedule may receive an alternative regimen of 0.5 mL at 0, 12, and 24 months. If booster dose is needed, revaccinate with 0.5 mL.

Adolescents 11-19 years (20 mcg/mL formulation): 1 mL at 0, 1, and 6 months. High-risk adolescents: 1 mL at 0, 1, 2, and 12 months; lower-risk adolescents 11-16 years who are candidates for an extended administration schedule may receive an alternative regimen of 0.5 mL (using the 10 mcg/0.5 mL) formulation at 0, 12, and 24 months. If booster dose is needed, revaccinate with 20 mcg.

Adults ≥20 years: High-risk adults (20 mcg/mL formulation): 1 mL at 0, 1, 2, and 12 months. If booster dose is needed, revaccinate with 1 mL.

Postexposure prophylaxis: See table.

Postexposure Prophylaxis Recommended Dosage for Infants Born to HB$_s$Ag-Positive Mothers

Treatment	Birth	Within 7 d	1 mo	6 mo
Engerix-B® (pediatric formulation 10 mcg/0.5 mL)[1]	Note[2]	0.5 mL[2]	0.5 mL	0.5 mL
Recombivax HB® (pediatric/adolescent formulation 5 mcg/0.5 mL)	Note[2]	0.5 mL[2]	0.5 mL	0.5 mL
Hepatitis B immune globulin	0.5 mL	—	—	—

[1]An alternate regimen is administration of the vaccine at birth, within 7 days of birth, and 1, 2, and 12 months later.

[2]The first dose may be given at birth at the same time as HBIG, but give in the opposite anterolateral thigh. This may better ensure vaccine absorption.

Administration It is possible to interchange the vaccines for completion of a series or for booster doses; the antibody produced in response to each type of vaccine is comparable, however, the quantity of the vaccine will vary

I.M. injection only; in adults, the deltoid muscle is the preferred site; the anterolateral thigh is the recommended site in infants and young children. Not for gluteal administration. Shake well prior to withdrawal and use.

For patients at risk of hemorrhage following intramuscular injection, the ACIP recommends "it should be administered intramuscularly if, in the opinion of the physician familiar with the patients bleeding risk, the vaccine can be administered with reasonable safety by this route. If the patient receives antihemophilia or other similar therapy, intramuscular vaccination can be scheduled shortly after such therapy is administered. A fine needle (23 gauge or smaller) can be used for the vaccination and firm pressure applied to the site (without rubbing) for at least 2 minutes. The patient should be instructed concerning the risk of hematoma from the injection."

Federal law requires that the date of administration, the vaccine manufacturer, lot number of vaccine, and the administering person's name, title, and address be entered into the patient's permanent medical record.

Patient Information Must complete full course of injections for adequate immunization
Dosage Forms INJ, suspension [recombinant DNA]: (Engerix-B®): Adult: Hepatitis B surface antigen 20 mcg/mL (1 mL), Pediatric/adolescent: Hepatitis B surface antigen 10 mcg/0.5 mL (0.5 mL); (Recombivax HB®): Adult: Hepatitis B surface antigen 10 mcg/mL (1 mL, 3 mL), Dialysis: Hepatitis B surface antigen 40 mcg/mL (1 mL), Pediatric/adolescent: Hepatitis B surface antigen 5 mcg/0.5 mL (0.5 mL) Pediatric/adolescent [preservative free]: Hepatitis B surface antigen 5 mcg/0.5 mL (0.5 mL)

- **Hep-Lock®** *see* Heparin *on page 612*
- **Hepsera™** *see* Adefovir *on page 39*
- **Herceptin®** *see* Trastuzumab *on page 1254*
- **HES** *see* Hetastarch *on page 619*
- **Hespan®** *see* Hetastarch *on page 619*

Hetastarch (HET a starch)
U.S. Brand Names Hespan®; Hextend®
Synonyms HES; Hydroxyethyl Starch
Therapeutic Category Plasma Volume Expander, Colloid
Use Blood volume expander used in treatment of hypovolemia
  Hespan®: Adjunct in leukapheresis to improve harvesting and increasing the yield of granulo-cytes by centrifugal means
Unlabeled/Investigational Use Hextend®: Priming fluid in pump oxygenators during cardio-pulmonary bypass, and as a plasma volume expander during cardiopulmonary bypass
Pregnancy Risk Factor C
Dosage I.V. infusion (requires an infusion pump):
  Children: Safety and efficacy have not been established
  Plasma volume expansion:
    Adults: 500-1000 mL (up to 1500 mL/day) or 20 mL/kg/day (up to 1500 mL/day); larger volumes (15,000 mL/24 hours) have been used safely in small numbers of patients
  Leukapheresis: 250-700 mL; **Note:** Citrate anticoagulant is added before use.

  Dosing adjustment in renal impairment: Cl_{cr} <10 mL/minute: Initial dose is the same but subsequent doses should be reduced by 20% to 50% of normal
Dosage Forms INF [premixed in lactated electrolyte injection] (Hextend®): 6% (500 mL, 1000 mL). **INF, solution** [premixed in NaCl 0.9%]: 6% (500 mL)

- **Hexachlorocyclohexane** *see* Lindane *on page 746*

Hexachlorophene (heks a KLOR oh feen)
U.S. Brand Names pHisoHex®
Therapeutic Category Antibacterial, Topical; Soap
Use Surgical scrub and as a bacteriostatic skin cleanser; control an outbreak of gram-positive infection when other procedures have been unsuccessful
Pregnancy Risk Factor C
Dosage Children and Adults: Topical: Apply 5 mL cleanser and water to area to be cleansed; lather and rinse thoroughly under running water
Dosage Forms LIQ, topical (pHisoHex®): 3% (150 mL, 500 mL, 3840 mL)

- **Hexalen®** *see* Altretamine *on page 66*
- **Hexamethylenetetramine** *see* Methenamine *on page 811*
- **Hexamethylmelamine** *see* Altretamine *on page 66*
- **HEXM** *see* Altretamine *on page 66*
- **Hextend®** *see* Hetastarch *on page 619*
- **Hib** *see* Haemophilus b Conjugate and Hepatitis B Vaccine *on page 607*
- **Hibiclens® [OTC]** *see* Chlorhexidine Gluconate *on page 259*
- **Hibistat® [OTC]** *see* Chlorhexidine Gluconate *on page 259*
- **Hib Polysaccharide Conjugate** *see* Haemophilus b Conjugate Vaccine *on page 607*
- **HibTITER®** *see* Haemophilus b Conjugate Vaccine *on page 607*
- **Hiprex®** *see* Methenamine *on page 811*
- **Hirulog** *see* Bivalirudin *on page 170*
- **Histatab® Plus [OTC]** *see* Chlorpheniramine and Phenylephrine *on page 262*
- **Hista-Vent® DA** *see* Chlorpheniramine, Phenylephrine, and Methscopolamine *on page 264*
- **Histex™** *see* Chlorpheniramine and Pseudoephedrine *on page 263*
- **Histex™ CT** *see* Carbinoxamine *on page 218*
- **Histex™ HC** *see* Hydrocodone, Carbinoxamine, and Pseudoephedrine *on page 632*
- **Histex™ I/E** *see* Carbinoxamine *on page 218*
- **Histex™ PD** *see* Carbinoxamine *on page 218*
- **Histex™ SR** *see* Brompheniramine and Pseudoephedrine *on page 181*
- **Histussin D®** *see* Hydrocodone and Pseudoephedrine *on page 631*
- **Hivid®** *see* Zalcitabine *on page 1321*
- **HMM** *see* Altretamine *on page 66*
- **HMS Liquifilm®** *see* Medrysone *on page 782*
- **HN₂** *see* Mechlorethamine *on page 778*

Homatropine (hoe MA troe peen)
Related Information
Cycloplegic Mydriatics Comparison *on page 1375*
U.S. Brand Names Isopto® Homatropine
Synonyms Homatropine Hydrobromide
Therapeutic Category Anticholinergic Agent, Ophthalmic; Ophthalmic Agent, Mydriatic
Use Producing cycloplegia and mydriasis for refraction; treatment of acute inflammatory conditions of the uveal tract
Pregnancy Risk Factor C
Contraindications Hypersensitivity to the drug or any component of the formulation; narrow-angle glaucoma, acute hemorrhage
Warnings/Precautions Use with caution in patients with hypertension, cardiac disease, or increased intraocular pressure; safety and efficacy not established in infants and young children, therefore, use with extreme caution due to susceptibility of systemic effects; use with caution in obstructive uropathy, paralytic ileus, ulcerative colitis, unstable cardiovascular status in acute hemorrhage
Common Adverse Reactions
>10%: Ocular: Blurred vision, photophobia
1% to 10%:
  Local: Stinging, local irritation
  Ocular: Increased intraocular pressure
  Respiratory: Congestion
Mechanism of Action Blocks response of iris sphincter muscle and the accommodative muscle of the ciliary body to cholinergic stimulation resulting in dilation and loss of accommodation
Pharmacodynamics/Kinetics
Onset of action: Accommodation and pupil effect: Ophthalmic:
  Maximum mydriatic effect: Within 10-30 minutes
  Maximum cycloplegic effect: Within 30-90 minutes
Duration:
  Mydriasis: 6 hours to 4 days
  Cycloplegia: 10-48 hours
Dosage Ophthalmic:
Children:
  Mydriasis and cycloplegia for refraction: Instill 1 drop of 2% solution immediately before the procedure; repeat at 10-minute intervals as needed
  Uveitis: Instill 1 drop of 2% solution 2-3 times/day
Adults:
  Mydriasis and cycloplegia for refraction: Instill 1-2 drops of 2% solution or 1 drop of 5% solution before the procedure; repeat at 5- to 10-minute intervals as needed; maximum of 3 doses for refraction
  Uveitis: Instill 1-2 drops of 2% or 5% 2-3 times/day up to every 3-4 hours as needed
Administration Ophthalmic instillation: Finger pressure should be applied to lacrimal sac for 1-2 minutes after instillation to decrease risk of absorption and systemic reactions
Dosage Forms SOLN, ophthalmic: 2% (5 mL); 5% (5 mL, 15 mL)

♦ **Homatropine and Hydrocodone** *see* Hydrocodone and Homatropine *on page 630*
♦ **Homatropine Hydrobromide** *see* Homatropine *on page 620*
♦ **Horse Antihuman Thymocyte Gamma Globulin** *see* Antithymocyte Globulin (Equine) *on page 108*
♦ **HTF919** *see* Tegaserod *on page 1190*
♦ **hu1124** *see* Efalizumab *on page 424*
♦ **Humalog®** *see* Insulin Preparations *on page 669*
♦ **Humalog® Mix 75/25™** *see* Insulin Preparations *on page 669*
♦ **Human Antitumor Necrosis Factor-alpha** *see* Adalimumab *on page 38*
♦ **Human Diploid Cell Cultures Rabies Vaccine** *see* Rabies Virus Vaccine *on page 1078*

Human Growth Hormone (HYU man grothe HOR mone)
U.S. Brand Names Genotropin®; Genotropin Miniquick®; Humatrope®; Norditropin®; Norditropin® Cartridges; Nutropin®; Nutropin AQ®; Nutropin Depot®; Protropin®; Saizen®; Serostim®; Zorbtive™
Synonyms Growth Hormone; Somatrem; Somatropin
Therapeutic Category Growth Hormone
Use
Children:
  Long-term treatment of growth failure due to lack of adequate endogenous growth hormone secretion (Genotropin®, Humatrope®, Norditropin®, Nutropin®, Nutropin AQ®, Nutropin Depot®, Protropin®, Saizen®)
  Long-term treatment of short stature associated with Turner syndrome (Humatrope®, Nutropin®, Nutropin AQ®)
  Treatment of Prader-Willi syndrome (Genotropin®)
  Treatment of growth failure associated with chronic renal insufficiency (CRI) up until the time of renal transplantation (Nutropin®, Nutropin AQ®)
  Long-term treatment of growth failure in children born small for gestational age who fail to manifest catch-up growth by 2 years of age (Genotropin®)

Long-term treatment of idiopathic short stature (nongrowth hormone-deficient short stature) defined by height standard deviation score (SDS) less than or equal to -2.25 and growth rate not likely to attain normal adult height (Humatrope®)

Adults:

AIDS-wasting or cachexia with concomitant antiviral therapy (Serostim®)

Replacement of endogenous growth hormone in patients with adult growth hormone deficiency who meet both of the following criteria (Genotropin®, Humatrope®, Nutropin®, Nutropin AQ®):

Biochemical diagnosis of adult growth hormone deficiency by means of a subnormal response to a standard growth hormone stimulation test (peak growth hormone ≤5 μg/ L)

and

Adult-onset: Patients who have adult growth hormone deficiency whether alone or with multiple hormone deficiencies (hypopituitarism) as a result of pituitary disease, hypothalamic disease, surgery, radiation therapy, or trauma

or

Childhood-onset: Patients who were growth hormone deficient during childhood, confirmed as an adult before replacement therapy is initiated

Treatment of short-bowel syndrome (Zorbtive™)

Unlabeled/Investigational Use Investigational: Congestive heart failure; AIDS-wasting/ cachexia in children (Serostim®)

Pregnancy Risk Factor B/C (depending upon manufacturer)

Contraindications Hypersensitivity to growth hormone or any component of the formulation; growth promotion in pediatric patients with closed epiphyses; progression of any underlying intracranial lesion or actively growing intracranial tumor; acute critical illness due to complications following open heart or abdominal surgery; multiple accidental trauma or acute respiratory failure; evidence of active malignancy; use in patients with Prader-Willi syndrome who are severely obese or have severe respiratory impairment

Warnings/Precautions Use with caution in patients with diabetes or with risk factors for glucose intolerance; when administering to newborns, reconstitute with sterile water for injection; intracranial hypertension has been reported with growth hormone product, funduscopic examinations are recommended; progression of scoliosis may occur in children experiencing rapid growth; patients with growth hormone deficiency may develop slipped capital epiphyses more frequently, evaluate any child with new onset of a limp or with complaints of hip or knee pain; patients with Turner syndrome are at increased risk for otitis media and other ear/hearing disorders, cardiovascular disorders (including stroke, aortic aneurysm, hypertension), and thyroid disease, monitor carefully; products may contain benzyl alcohol, m-Cresol or glycerin, some products may be manufactured by recombinant DNA technology using *E. coli* as a precursor, consult specific product labeling. Not for I.V. injection.

Fatalities have been reported in pediatric patients with Prader-Willi syndrome following the use of growth hormone. The reported fatalities occurred in patients with one or more risk factors, including severe obesity, sleep apnea, respiratory impairment, or unidentified respiratory infection. In addition, male patients may be at increased risk. Treatment interruption is recommended in patients who show signs of upper airway obstruction, including the onset of, or increased, snoring. In addition, evaluation of and/or monitoring for sleep apnea and respiratory infections are recommended.

Common Adverse Reactions

Growth hormone deficiency: Antigrowth hormone antibodies, carpal tunnel syndrome (rare), fluid balance disturbances, glucosuria, gynocomastia (rare), headache, hematuria, hyperglycemia (mild), hypoglycemia, hypothyroidism, leukemia, lipoatrophy, muscle pain, increased growth of pre-existing nevi (rare), pain/ local reactions at the injection site, pancreatitis (rare), peripheral edema, exacerbation of psoriasis, seizures

Idiopathic short stature: Myalgia (24%), scoliosis (19%), otitis media (16%), arthralgia (11%), arthrosis (11%), hyperlipidemia (8%), gynecomastia (5%), hip pain (3%), hypertension (3%)

Prader-Willi syndrome: Aggressiveness, arthralgia, edema, hair loss, headache, benign intracranial hypertension, myalgia; fatalities associated with use in this population have been reported

Turner syndrome: Humatrope®: Surgical procedures (45%), otitis media (43%), ear disorders (18%), hypothyroidism (13%), increased nevi (11%), peripheral edema (7%)

Adult growth hormone replacement: Increased ALT, increased AST, arthralgia, back pain, carpal tunnel syndrome, diabetes mellitus, fatigue, flu-like syndrome, generalized edema, gastritis, gynocomastia (rare), headache, hypoesthesia, joint disorder, myalgia, increased growth of pre-existing nevi (rare), pain, pancreatitis (rare), paresthesia, peripheral edema, pharyngitis, rhinitis, stiffness in extremities, weakness

AIDS wasting or cachexia (limited): Serostim®: Musculoskeletal discomfort (54%), increased tissue turgor (27%), diarrhea (26%), neuropathy (26%), nausea (26%), fatigue (17%), albuminuria (15%), increased diaphoresis (14%), anorexia (12%), anemia (12%), increased AST (12%), insomnia (11%), tachycardia (11%), hyperglycemia (10%), increased ALT (10%)

Short-bowel syndrome: Peripheral edema (69% to 81%), edema (facial 44% to 50%; peripheral 13%), arthralgia (13% to 44%), injection site reaction (19% to 31%), flatulence (25%), abdominal pain (20% to 25%), vomiting (19%), malaise (13%), nausea (13%), diaphoresis increased (13%), rhinitis (7%), dizziness (6%)

Postmarketing and/or case reports: Carpal tunnel syndrome

Small for gestational age: Mild, transient hyperglycemia; benign intracranial hypertension (rare); central precocious puberty; jaw prominence (rare); aggravation of pre-existing scoliosis (rare); injection site reactions; progression of pigmented nevi

(Continued)

Human Growth Hormone (Continued)

Drug Interactions

Decreased Effect: Glucocorticoid therapy may inhibit growth-promoting effects. Growth hormone may induce insulin resistance in patients with diabetes mellitus; monitor glucose and adjust insulin dose as necessary.

Mechanism of Action Somatropin and somatrem are purified polypeptide hormones of recombinant DNA origin; somatropin contains the identical sequence of amino acids found in human growth hormone while somatrem's amino acid sequence is identical plus an additional amino acid, methionine; human growth hormone stimulates growth of linear bone, skeletal muscle, and organs; stimulates erythropoietin which increases red blood cell mass; exerts both insulin-like and diabetogenic effects; enhances the transmucosal transport of water, electrolytes, and nutrients across the gut

Pharmacodynamics/Kinetics Somatrem and somatropin have equivalent pharmacokinetic properties

Duration: Maintains supraphysiologic levels for 18-20 hours

Absorption: I.M., S.C.: Well absorbed

Metabolism: Hepatic and renal (~90%)

Half-life elimination: Preparation and route of administration dependent

Excretion: Urine

Dosage

Children (individualize dose):

Growth hormone deficiency:

Somatrem: Protropin®: I.M., S.C.: Weekly dosage: 0.3 mg/kg divided into daily doses

Somatropin:

Genotropin®: S.C.: Weekly dosage: 0.16-0.24 mg/kg divided into 6-7 doses

Humatrope®: I.M., S.C.: Weekly dosage: 0.18 mg/kg; maximum replacement dose: 0.3 mg/kg/week; dosing should be divided into equal doses given 3 times/week on alternating days, 6 times/week, or daily

Norditropin®: S.C.: Weekly dosage: 0.024-0.034 mg/kg administered in the evening, divided into doses 6-7 times/week; cartridge and vial formulations are bioequivalent; cartridge formulation does not need to be reconstituted prior to use; cartridges must be administered using the corresponding color-coded NordiPen® injection pen

Nutropin Depot®: S.C.:

Once-monthly injection: 1.5 mg/kg administered on the same day of each month; patients >15 kg will require more than 1 injection per dose

Twice-monthly injection: 0.75 mg/kg administered twice each month on the same days of each month (eg, days 1 and 15 of each month); patients >30 kg will require more than 1 injection per dose

Nutropin®, Nutropin® AQ: S.C.: Weekly dosage: 0.3 mg/kg divided into daily doses; pubertal patients: ≤0.7 mg/kg/week divided daily

Saizen®: I.M., S.C.: Weekly dosage: 0.06 mg/kg administered 3 times/week

Note: Therapy should be discontinued when patient has reached satisfactory adult height, when epiphyses have fused, or when the patient ceases to respond. Growth of 5 cm/year or more is expected, if growth rate does not exceed 2.5 cm in a 6-month period, double the dose for the next 6 months; if there is still no satisfactory response, discontinue therapy

Chronic renal insufficiency (CRI): Nutropin®, Nutropin® AQ: S.C.: Weekly dosage: 0.35 mg/kg divided into daily injections; continue until the time of renal transplantation

Dosage recommendations in patients treated for CRI who require dialysis:

Hemodialysis: Administer dose at night prior to bedtime or at least 3-4 hours after hemodialysis to prevent hematoma formation from heparin

CCPD: Administer dose in the morning following dialysis

CAPD: Administer dose in the evening at the time of overnight exchange

Turner syndrome: Humatrope®, Nutropin®, Nutropin® AQ: S.C.: Weekly dosage: ≤0.375 mg/kg divided into equal doses 3-7 times per week

Prader-Willi syndrome: Genotropin®: S.C.: Weekly dosage: 0.24 mg/kg divided into 6-7 doses

Small for gestational age: Genotropin®: S.C.: Weekly dosage: 0.48 mg/kg divided into 6-7 doses

Idiopathic short stature: Humatrope®: S.C.: 0.37 mg/kg divided into equal doses 6-7 times per week

AIDS-wasting or cachexia (unlabeled use): Serostim®: S.C.: Limited data; doses of 0.04 mg/kg/day were reported in five children, 6-17 years of age; doses of 0.07 mg/kg/day were reported in six children, 8-14 years of age

Adults:

Growth hormone deficiency: To minimize adverse events in older or overweight patients, reduced dosages may be necessary. During therapy, dosage should be decreased if required by the occurrence of side effects or excessive IGF-I levels.

Somatropin:

Nutropin®, Nutropin® AQ: S.C.: ≤0.006 mg/kg/day; dose may be increased according to individual requirements, up to a maximum of 0.025 mg/kg/day in patients <35 years of age, or up to a maximum of 0.0125 mg/kg/day in patients ≥35 years of age

Humatrope®: S.C.: ≤0.006 mg/kg/day; dose may be increased according to individual requirements, up to a maximum of 0.0125 mg/kg/day

Genotropin®: S.C.: Weekly dosage: ≤0.04 mg/kg divided into 6-7 doses; dose may be increased at 4- to 8-week intervals according to individual requirements, to a maximum of 0.08 mg/kg/week

AIDS wasting or cachexia:
Serostim®: S.C.: Dose should be given once daily at bedtime; patients who continue to lose weight after 2 weeks should be re-evaluated for opportunistic infections or other clinical events; rotate injection sites to avoid lipodystrophy

Daily dose based on body weight:
<35 kg: 0.1 mg/kg
35-45 kg: 4 mg
45-55 kg: 5 mg
>55 kg: 6 mg

Short-bowel syndrome: Zorbtive™: S.C.: 0.1 mg/kg once daily for 4 weeks (maximum: 8 mg/day)

Fluid retention (moderate) or arthralgias: Treat symptomatically or reduce dose by 50%

Severe toxicity: Discontinue therapy for up to 5 days; when symptoms resolve, restart at 50% of dose. If severe toxicity recurs or does not disappear within 5 days after discontinuation, permanently discontinue treatment.

Elderly: Patients ≥65 years of age may be more sensitive to the action of growth hormone and more prone to adverse effects; in general, dosing should be cautious, beginning at low end of dosing range

Dosage adjustment in renal impairment Reports indicate patients with chronic renal failure tend to have decreased clearance; specific dosing suggestions not available

Dosage adjustment in hepatic impairment: Clearance may be reduced in patients with severe hepatic dysfunction; specific dosing suggestions not available

Administration Do not shake; administer S.C. or I.M.; refer to product labeling; when administering to newborns, reconstitute with sterile water for injection

Monitoring Parameters Growth curve, periodic thyroid function tests, bone age (annually), periodical urine testing for glucose, somatomedin C (IGF-I) levels; funduscopic examinations at initiation of therapy and periodically during treatment; serum phosphorus, alkaline phosphatase and parathyroid hormone. If growth deceleration is observed in children treated for growth hormone deficiency, and not due to other causes, evaluate for presence of antibody formation. Strict blood glucose monitoring in diabetic patients.

Somatrem (Protropin®): Consider changing to somatropin if antibody binding capacity is >2 mg/L

Prader-Willi syndrome: Monitor for sleep apnea, respiratory infections, snoring (onset of or increased)

Patient Information This medication can only be given by injection. You will be instructed how to prepare and administer the medication. Use a small enough syringe so that the prescribed dose can be drawn from the vial with reasonable accuracy; for I.M. injections, use a needle of sufficient length (≥1") to ensure that the injection reaches the muscle layer. Rotate injection sites. Dispose of needles and syringes properly. Follow storage instructions. Report the development of a severe headache, acute visual changes, a limp, or complaints of hip or knee pain to your prescriber.

Dosage Forms INJ, powder for reconstitution [rDNA origin]: Somatrem: (Protropin®): 5 mg [~15 int. units]; 10 mg [~30 int. units]; Somatropin: (Genotropin®): 5.8 mg [15 int. units/mL], 13.8 mg [36 int. units/mL]; (Genotropin®) [preservative free]: 1.5 mg [4 int. units/mL]; (Genotropin Miniquick®) [preservative free]: 0.2 mg, 0.4 mg, 0.6 mg, 0.8 mg, 1 mg, 1.2 mg, 1.4 mg, 1.6 mg, 1.8 mg, 2 mg; (Humatrope®): 5 mg [~15 int. units], 6 mg [18 int. units], 12 mg [36 int. units], 24 mg [72 int. units]; (Norditropin®): 4 mg [~12 int. units], 8 mg [~24 int. units], (Nutropin®): 5 mg [~15 int. units], 10 mg [~30 int. units]; (Nutropin Depot®) [preservative free]: 13.5 mg, 18 mg, 22.5 mg; (Saizen®): 5 mg [~15 int. units], 8.8 mg [~26.4 int. units]; (Serostim®): 4 mg [12 int. units], 5 mg [15 int. units], 6 mg [18 int. units]; (Zorbtive™): 4 mg [~12 int. units], 5 mg [~15 int. units], 6 mg [~18 int. units], 8.8 mg [~26.4 int. units]. **INJ, solution** [rDNA origin]: Somatropin: (Norditropin®): 5 mg/1.5 mL (1.5 mL), 10 mg/1.5 mL (1.5 mL), 15 mg/1.5 mL (1.5 mL); (Nutropin AQ®): 5 mg/mL [~30 int. units/2 mL] (2 mL)

- **Hyaluronic Acid** *see* Sodium Hyaluronate *on page 1148*
- **Hyate:C®** *see* Antihemophilic Factor (Porcine) *on page 104*
- **Hycamptamine** *see* Topotecan *on page 1244*
- **Hycamtin®** *see* Topotecan *on page 1244*
- **Hycoclear Tuss** *see* Hydrocodone and Guaifenesin *on page 630*
- **Hycodan®** *see* Hydrocodone and Homatropine *on page 630*
- **Hycomine® Compound** *see* Hydrocodone, Chlorpheniramine, Phenylephrine, Acetaminophen, and Caffeine *on page 632*
- **Hycosin** *see* Hydrocodone and Guaifenesin *on page 630*
- **Hycotuss®** *see* Hydrocodone and Guaifenesin *on page 630*
- **Hydergine [DSC]** *see* Ergoloid Mesylates *on page 449*

HydrALAZINE (hye DRAL a zeen)

Synonyms Apresoline [DSC]; Hydralazine Hydrochloride

Therapeutic Category Antihypertensive Agent; Vasodilator

Use Management of moderate to severe hypertension, congestive heart failure, hypertension secondary to pre-eclampsia/eclampsia; treatment of primary pulmonary hypertension

Pregnancy Risk Factor C

Contraindications Hypersensitivity to hydralazine or any component of the formulation; mitral valve rheumatic heart disease

Warnings/Precautions May cause a drug-induced lupus-like syndrome (more likely on larger doses, longer duration). Discontinue hydralazine in patients who develop SLE-like syndrome or positive ANA. Use with caution in patients with severe renal disease or cerebral vascular accidents or with known or suspected coronary artery disease; monitor blood pressure closely with I.V. use. Slow acetylators, patients with decreased renal function, and patients receiving >200 mg/day (chronically) are at higher risk for SLE. Titrate dosage to patient's response. Usually administered with diuretic and a beta-blocker to counteract side effects of sodium and water retention and reflex tachycardia.

Adjust dose in severe renal dysfunction. Use with caution in CAD (increase in tachycardia may increase myocardial oxygen demand). Use with caution in pulmonary hypertension (may cause hypotension). Patients may be poorly compliant because of frequent dosing. Hydralazine-induced fluid and sodium retention may require addition or increased dosage of a diuretics.

Common Adverse Reactions Frequency not defined.

  Cardiovascular: Tachycardia, angina pectoris, orthostatic hypotension (rare), dizziness (rare), paradoxical hypertension, peripheral edema, vascular collapse (rare), flushing

  Central nervous system: Increased intracranial pressure (I.V., in patient with pre-existing increased intracranial pressure), fever (rare), chills (rare), anxiety*, disorientation*, depression*, coma*

  Dermatologic: Rash (rare), urticaria (rash), pruritus (rash)

  Gastrointestinal: Anorexia, nausea, vomiting, diarrhea, constipation, adynamic ileus

  Genitourinary: Difficulty in micturition, impotence

  Hematologic: Hemolytic anemia (rare), eosinophilia (rare), decreased hemoglobin concentration (rare), reduced erythrocyte count (rare), leukopenia (rare), agranulocytosis (rare), thrombocytopenia (rare)

  Neuromuscular & skeletal: Rheumatoid arthritis, muscle cramps, weakness, tremors, peripheral neuritis (rare)

  Ocular: Lacrimation, conjunctivitis

  Respiratory: Nasal congestion, dyspnea

  Miscellaneous: Drug-induced lupus-like syndrome (dose-related; fever, arthralgia, splenomegaly, lymphadenopathy, asthenia, myalgia, malaise, pleuritic chest pain, edema, positive ANA, positive LE cells, maculopapular facial rash, positive direct Coombs' test, pericarditis, pericardial tamponade), diaphoresis

  *Seen in uremic patients and severe hypertension where rapidly escalating doses may have caused hypotension leading to these effects.

Drug Interactions

  Cytochrome P450 Effect: Inhibits CYP3A4 (weak)

  Increased Effect/Toxicity: Hydralazine may increase levels of beta-blockers (metoprolol, propranolol). Some beta-blockers (acebutolol, atenolol, and nadolol) are unlikely to be affected due to limited hepatic metabolism. Concurrent use of hydralazine with MAO inhibitors may cause a significant decrease in blood pressure. Propranolol may increase hydralazine serum concentrations.

  Decreased Effect: NSAIDs (eg, indomethacin) may decrease the hemodynamic effects of hydralazine.

Mechanism of Action Direct vasodilation of arterioles (with little effect on veins) with decreased systemic resistance

Pharmacodynamics/Kinetics

  Onset of action: Oral: 20-30 minutes; I.V.: 5-20 minutes

  Duration: Oral: 2-4 hours; I.V.: 2-6 hours

  Distribution: Crosses placenta; enters breast milk

  Protein binding: 85% to 90%

  Metabolism: Hepatically acetylated; extensive first-pass effect (oral)

  Bioavailability: 30% to 50%; increased with food

  Half-life elimination: Normal renal function: 2-8 hours; End-stage renal disease: 7-16 hours

  Excretion: Urine (14% as unchanged drug)

Dosage
Children:
Oral: Initial: 0.75-1 mg/kg/day in 2-4 divided doses; increase over 3-4 weeks to maximum of 7.5 mg/kg/day in 2-4 divided doses; maximum daily dose: 200 mg/day
I.M., I.V.: 0.1-0.2 mg/kg/dose (not to exceed 20 mg) every 4-6 hours as needed, up to 1.7-3.5 mg/kg/day in 4-6 divided doses

Adults:
Oral: Hypertension:
Initial dose: 10 mg 4 times/day for first 2-4 days; increase to 25 mg 4 times/day for the balance of the first week
Increase by 10-25 mg/dose gradually to 50 mg 4 times/day; 300 mg/day may be required for some patients
Oral: Congestive heart failure:
Initial dose: 10-25 mg 3-4 times/day
Adjustment: Dosage must be adjusted based on individual response
Target dose: 75 mg 4 times/day in combination with isosorbide dinitrate (40 mg 4 times/day)
Range: Typically 200-600 mg daily in 2-4 divided doses; dosages as high as 3 g/day have been used in some patients for symptomatic and hemodynamic improvement. Hydralazine 75 mg 4 times/day combined with isosorbide dinitrate 40 mg 4 times/day were shown in clinical trials to provide a mortality benefit in the treatment of CHF. Higher doses may be used for symptomatic and hemodynamic improvement following optimization of standard therapy.
I.M., I.V.:
Hypertension: Initial: 10-20 mg/dose every 4-6 hours as needed, may increase to 40 mg/dose; change to oral therapy as soon as possible.
Pre-eclampsia/eclampsia: 5 mg/dose then 5-10 mg every 20-30 minutes as needed.
Elderly: Oral: Initial: 10 mg 2-3 times/day; increase by 10-25 mg/day every 2-5 days.
Dosing interval in renal impairment:
Cl$_{cr}$ 10-50 mL/minute: Administer every 8 hours.
Cl$_{cr}$ <10 mL/minute: Administer every 8-16 hours in fast acetylators and every 12-24 hours in slow acetylators.
Hemodialysis: Supplemental dose is not necessary.
Peritoneal dialysis: Supplemental dose is not necessary.
Administration Inject over 1 minute. Hypotensive effect may be delayed and unpredictable in some patients.
Monitoring Parameters Blood pressure (monitor closely with I.V. use), standing and sitting/supine, heart rate, ANA titer
Patient Information Report flu-like symptoms, rise slowly from sitting/lying position; take with meals
Dosage Forms INJ, solution: 20 mg/mL (1 mL). **TAB:** 10 mg, 25 mg, 50 mg, 100 mg

Hydralazine and Hydrochlorothiazide
(hye DRAL a zeen & hye droe klor oh THYE a zide)
Synonyms Apresazide [DSC]; Hydrochlorothiazide and Hydralazine
Therapeutic Category Antihypertensive Agent, Combination
Use Management of moderate to severe hypertension and treatment of congestive heart failure
Pregnancy Risk Factor C
Dosage Adults: Oral: Take as directed; not to exceed 50 mg hydrochlorothiazide per day
Dosage Forms CAP: 25/25: Hydralazine 25 mg and hydrochlorothiazide 25 mg; 50/50: Hydralazine 50 mg and hydrochlorothiazide 50 mg; 100/50: Hydralazine 100 mg and hydrochlorothiazide 50 mg

♦ **Hydralazine Hydrochloride** see HydrALAZINE on page 624

Hydralazine, Hydrochlorothiazide, and Reserpine
(hye DRAL a zeen, hye droe klor oh THYE a zide, & re SER peen)
Synonyms Hydrochlorothiazide, Hydralazine, and Reserpine; Reserpine, Hydralazine, and Hydrochlorothiazide; Ser-Ap-Es [DSC]
Therapeutic Category Antihypertensive Agent, Combination
Use Treatment of hypertensive disorders
Pregnancy Risk Factor C
Dosage Adults: Oral: 1-2 tablets 3 times/day
Dosage Forms TAB: Hydralazine 25 mg, hydrochlorothiazide 15 mg, and reserpine 0.1 mg

♦ **Hydramine® [OTC]** see DiphenhydrAMINE on page 383
♦ **Hydramine® Cough [OTC]** see DiphenhydrAMINE on page 383
♦ **Hydrated Chloral** see Chloral Hydrate on page 254
♦ **Hydrea®** see Hydroxyurea on page 638

Hydrochlorothiazide (hye droe klor oh THYE a zide)
Related Information
Sulfonamide Derivatives on page 1404
U.S. Brand Names Aquazide® H; Microzide™; Oretic®
Synonyms HCTZ
Therapeutic Category Antihypertensive Agent; Diuretic, Thiazide
(Continued)

Hydrochlorothiazide *(Continued)*

Use Management of mild to moderate hypertension; treatment of edema in congestive heart failure and nephrotic syndrome

Unlabeled/Investigational Use Treatment of lithium-induced diabetes insipidus

Pregnancy Risk Factor B (manufacturer); D (expert analysis)

Contraindications Hypersensitivity to hydrochlorothiazide or any component of the formulation, thiazides, or sulfonamide-derived drugs; anuria; renal decompensation; pregnancy

Warnings/Precautions Avoid in severe renal disease (ineffective). Electrolyte disturbances (hypokalemia, hypochloremic alkalosis, hyponatremia) can occur. Use with caution in severe hepatic dysfunction; hepatic encephalopathy can be caused by electrolyte disturbances. Gout can be precipitate in certain patients with a history of gout, a familial predisposition to gout, or chronic renal failure. Cautious use in diabetics; may see a change in glucose control. Hypersensitivity reactions can occur. Can cause SLE exacerbation or activation. Use with caution in patients with moderate or high cholesterol concentrations. Photosensitization may occur. Correct hypokalemia before initiating therapy.

Chemical similarities are present among sulfonamides, sulfonylureas, carbonic anhydrase inhibitors, thiazides, and loop diuretics (except ethacrynic acid). Use in patients with sulfonamide allergy is specifically contraindicated in product labeling, however, a risk of cross-reaction exists in patients with allergy to any of these compounds; avoid use when previous reaction has been severe.

Common Adverse Reactions

1% to 10%:
Cardiovascular: Orthostatic hypotension, hypotension
Dermatologic: Photosensitivity
Endocrine & metabolic: Hypokalemia
Gastrointestinal: Anorexia, epigastric distress

Drug Interactions

Increased Effect/Toxicity: Increased effect of hydrochlorothiazide with furosemide and other loop diuretics. Increased hypotension and/or renal adverse effects of ACE inhibitors may result in aggressively diuresed patients. Beta-blockers increase hyperglycemic effects of thiazides in type 2 diabetes mellitus. Cyclosporine and thiazides can increase the risk of gout or renal toxicity. Digoxin toxicity can be exacerbated if a thiazide induces hypokalemia or hypomagnesemia. Lithium toxicity can occur with thiazides due to reduced renal excretion of lithium. Thiazides may prolong the duration of action with neuromuscular blocking agents.

Decreased Effect: Effects of oral hypoglycemics may be decreased. Decreased absorption of hydrochlorothiazide with cholestyramine and colestipol. NSAIDs can decrease the efficacy of thiazides, reducing the diuretic and antihypertensive effects.

Mechanism of Action Inhibits sodium reabsorption in the distal tubules causing increased excretion of sodium and water as well as potassium and hydrogen ions

Pharmacodynamics/Kinetics
Onset of action: Diuresis: ~2 hours
Peak effect: 4-6 hours
Duration: 6-12 hours
Absorption: ~50% to 80%
Distribution: 3.6-7.8 L/kg
Protein binding: 68%
Metabolism: Not metabolized
Bioavailability: 50% to 80%
Half-life elimination: 5.6-14.8 hours
Time to peak: 1-2.5 hours
Excretion: Urine (as unchanged drug)

Dosage Oral (effect of drug may be decreased when used every day):
Children (in pediatric patients, chlorothiazide may be preferred over hydrochlorothiazide as there are more dosage formulations [eg, suspension] available):
<6 months: 2-3 mg/kg/day in 2 divided doses
>6 months: 2 mg/kg/day in 2 divided doses
Adults:
Edema: 25-100 mg/day in 1-2 doses; maximum: 200 mg/day
Hypertension: 12.5-50 mg/day; minimal increase in response and more electrolyte disturbances are seen with doses >50 mg/day
Elderly: 12.5-25 mg once daily

Dosing adjustment/comments in renal impairment: Cl_{cr} 25-50 mL/minute: Not effective

Monitoring Parameters Assess weight, I & O reports daily to determine fluid loss; blood pressure, serum electrolytes, BUN, creatinine

Patient Information May be taken with food or milk; take early in day to avoid nocturia; take the last dose of multiple doses no later than 6 PM unless instructed otherwise. A few people who take this medication become more sensitive to sunlight and may experience skin rash, redness, itching, or severe sunburn, especially if sun block SPF ≥15 is not used on exposed skin areas. May increase blood glucose levels in diabetics.

Dosage Forms CAP (Microzide™): 12.5 mg. **SOLN, oral** [DSC]: 50 mg/5 mL (500 mL). **TAB:** 25 mg, 50 mg; (Aquazide® H, Oretic®): 50 mg

♦ **Hydrochlorothiazide and Amiloride**   *see* Amiloride and Hydrochlorothiazide *on page 74*
♦ **Hydrochlorothiazide and Benazepril**   *see* Benazepril and Hydrochlorothiazide *on page 153*
♦ **Hydrochlorothiazide and Bisoprolol**   *see* Bisoprolol and Hydrochlorothiazide *on page 170*

- Hydrochlorothiazide and Captopril *see* Captopril and Hydrochlorothiazide *on page 214*
- Hydrochlorothiazide and Enalapril *see* Enalapril and Hydrochlorothiazide *on page 432*
- Hydrochlorothiazide and Eprosartan *see* Eprosartan and Hydrochlorothiazide *on page 447*
- Hydrochlorothiazide and Hydralazine *see* Hydralazine and Hydrochlorothiazide *on page 625*
- Hydrochlorothiazide and Irbesartan *see* Irbesartan and Hydrochlorothiazide *on page 687*
- Hydrochlorothiazide and Lisinopril *see* Lisinopril and Hydrochlorothiazide *on page 751*
- Hydrochlorothiazide and Losartan *see* Losartan and Hydrochlorothiazide *on page 763*
- Hydrochlorothiazide and Methyldopa *see* Methyldopa and Hydrochlorothiazide *on page 821*
- Hydrochlorothiazide and Moexipril *see* Moexipril and Hydrochlorothiazide *on page 856*
- Hydrochlorothiazide and Olmesartan Medoxomil *see* Olmesartan and Hydrochlorothiazide *on page 925*
- Hydrochlorothiazide and Propranolol *see* Propranolol and Hydrochlorothiazide *on page 1057*
- Hydrochlorothiazide and Quinapril *see* Quinapril and Hydrochlorothiazide *on page 1072*

Hydrochlorothiazide and Spironolactone

(hye droe klor oh THYE a zide & speer on oh LAK tone)

U.S. Brand Names Aldactazide®

Synonyms Spironolactone and Hydrochlorothiazide

Therapeutic Category Antihypertensive Agent, Combination

Use Management of mild to moderate hypertension; treatment of edema in congestive heart failure and nephrotic syndrome, and cirrhosis of the liver accompanied by edema and/or ascites

Pregnancy Risk Factor C

Dosage Oral:

Children: 1.66-3.3 mg/kg/day (of spironolactone) in 2-4 divided doses

Adults:

Hydrochlorothiazide 25 mg and spironolactone 25 mg: $^1/_2$-8 tablets daily

Hydrochlorothiazide 50 mg and spironolactone 50 mg: $^1/_2$-4 tablets daily in 1-2 doses

Dosage Forms TAB: Hydrochlorothiazide 25 mg and spironolactone 25 mg; (Aldactazide®): 25/25: Hydrochlorothiazide 25 mg and spironolactone 25 mg; 50/50: Hydrochlorothiazide 50 mg and spironolactone 50 mg

- Hydrochlorothiazide and Telmisartan *see* Telmisartan and Hydrochlorothiazide *on page 1191*

Hydrochlorothiazide and Triamterene

(hye droe klor oh THYE a zide & trye AM ter een)

U.S. Brand Names Dyazide®; Maxzide®; Maxzide®-25

Synonyms Triamterene and Hydrochlorothiazide

Therapeutic Category Antihypertensive Agent, Combination; Diuretic, Potassium-Sparing/ Thiazide

Use Management of mild to moderate hypertension; treatment of edema in congestive heart failure and nephrotic syndrome

Pregnancy Risk Factor C (per manufacturer)

Dosage Adults: Oral:

Hydrochlorothiazide 25 mg and triamterene 37.5 mg: 1-2 tablets/capsules once daily

Hydrochlorothiazide 50 mg and triamterene 75 mg: $^1/_2$-1 tablet daily

Dosage Forms CAP: (Dyazide®): Hydrochlorothiazide 25 mg and triamterene 37.5 mg. **TAB:** (Maxzide®): Hydrochlorothiazide 50 mg and triamterene 75 mg; (Maxzide®-25): Hydrochlorothiazide 25 mg and triamterene 37.5 mg

- Hydrochlorothiazide and Valsartan *see* Valsartan and Hydrochlorothiazide *on page 1293*
- Hydrochlorothiazide, Hydralazine, and Reserpine *see* Hydralazine, Hydrochlorothiazide, and Reserpine *on page 625*
- Hydrocil® [OTC] *see* Psyllium *on page 1063*

Hydrocodone and Acetaminophen

(hye droe KOE done & a seet a MIN oh fen)

U.S. Brand Names Anexsia®; Bancap HC®; Ceta-Plus®; Co-Gesic®; Lorcet® 10/650; Lorcet®-HD; Lorcet® Plus; Lortab®; Margesic® H; Maxidone™; Norco®; Stagesic®; Vicodin®; Vicodin® ES; Vicodin® HP; Zydone®

Synonyms Acetaminophen and Hydrocodone

Therapeutic Category Analgesic Combination, Narcotic

Use Relief of moderate to severe pain; antitussive (hydrocodone)

Restrictions C-III

Pregnancy Risk Factor C

Contraindications Hypersensitivity to hydrocodone, acetaminophen, or any component of the formulation; CNS depression; severe respiratory depression

Warnings/Precautions Use with caution in patients with hypersensitivity reactions to other phenanthrene derivative opioid agonists (morphine, hydrocodone, hydromorphone, levorphanol, oxycodone, oxymorphone); tablets contain metabisulfite which may cause allergic reactions; tolerance or drug dependence may result from extended use

(Continued)

627

Hydrocodone and Acetaminophen *(Continued)*

Drug Interactions

Cytochrome P450 Effect:

Hydrocodone: **Substrate** of CYP2D6 (major)

Acetaminophen: **Substrate** (minor) of CYP1A2, 2A6, 2C8/9, 2D6, 2E1, 3A4; **Inhibits** CYP3A4 (weak)

Increased Effect/Toxicity: Hydrocodone with other narcotic analgesics, CNS depressants, antianxiety agents, or antipsychotics may cause enhanced CNS depression. MAO inhibitors or tricyclic antidepressants with hydrocodone may increase the effect of either agent.

Decreased Effect: Decreased effect with phenothiazines

Pharmacodynamics/Kinetics

Acetaminophen: See Acetaminophen monograph.

Hydrocodone:

Onset of action: Narcotic analgesic: 10-20 minutes

Duration: 4-8 hours

Distribution: Crosses placenta

Metabolism: Hepatic; O-demethylation; N-demethylation and 6-ketosteroid reduction

Half-life elimination: 3.3-4.4 hours

Excretion: Urine

Dosage Oral (doses should be titrated to appropriate analgesic effect); for children ≥12 years of age and adults, the dosage of acetaminophen should be limited to ≤4 g/day (and possibly less in patients with hepatic impairment or ethanol use)

Children:

Antitussive (hydrocodone): 0.6 mg/kg/day in 3-4 divided doses; even though dosing by hydrocodone, make sure to keep within age-specific acetaminophen doses as well

A single dose should not exceed 10 mg in children >12 years, 5 mg in children 2-12 years, and 1.25 mg in children <2 years of age

Analgesic (acetaminophen): Refer to Acetaminophen monograph

Adults: Analgesic: 1-2 tablets or capsules every 4-6 hours or 5-10 mL solution every 4-6 hours as needed for pain; do not exceed 4 g/day of acetaminophen

Hydrocodone 2.5-5 mg and acetaminophen 400-500 mg; maximum: 8 tablets/capsules per day

Hydrocodone 7.5 mg and acetaminophen: 400-650 mg; maximum: 6 tablets/capsules per day

Hydrocodone 2.5 mg and acetaminophen: 167 mg/5 mL (elixir/solution); maximum: 6 Tbsp/day

Hydrocodone 7.5 mg and acetaminophen 750 mg; maximum: 5 tablets/capsules per day

Hydrocodone 10 mg and acetaminophen: 350-660 mg; maximum: 6 tablets/day per product labeling

Do not exceed 4 g/day of acetaminophen

Monitoring Parameters Pain relief, respiratory and mental status, blood pressure

Patient Information May cause drowsiness; do not exceed recommended dose; do not take for more than 10 days without prescriber's advice

Dosage Forms CAP (Bancap HC®, Ceta-Plus®, Lorcet®-HD, Margesic® H, Stagesic®): Hydrocodone 5 mg and acetaminophen 500 mg. **ELIX** (Lortab®): Hydrocodone 2.5 mg and acetaminophen 167 mg per 5 mL (480 mL). **TAB:** Hydrocodone 2.5 mg and acetaminophen 500 mg; hydrocodone 5 mg and acetaminophen 325 mg; hydrocodone 5 mg and acetaminophen 500 mg; hydrocodone 7.5 mg and acetaminophen 325 mg; hydrocodone 7.5 mg and acetaminophen 500 mg; hydrocodone 7.5 mg and acetaminophen 650 mg; hydrocodone 7.5 mg and acetaminophen 750 mg; hydrocodone 10 mg and acetaminophen 325 mg; hydrocodone 10 mg and acetaminophen 500 mg; hydrocodone 10 mg and acetaminophen 650 mg; hydrocodone 10 mg and acetaminophen 660 mg; (Anexsia®): 5/500: Hydrocodone 5 mg and acetaminophen 500 mg; 7.5/650: Hydrocodone 7.5 mg and acetaminophen 650 mg; (Co-Gesic® 5/500): Hydrocodone 5 mg and acetaminophen 500 mg; (Lorcet® 10/650): Hydrocodone 10 mg and acetaminophen 650 mg; (Lorcet® Plus): Hydrocodone 7.5 mg and acetaminophen 650 mg; (Lortab®): 2.5/500: Hydrocodone 2.5 mg and acetaminophen 500 mg; 5/500: Hydrocodone 5 mg and acetaminophen 500 mg; 7.5/500: Hydrocodone 7.5 mg and acetaminophen 500 mg; 10/500: Hydrocodone 10 mg and acetaminophen 500 mg; (Maxidone™): Hydrocodone 10 mg and acetaminophen 750 mg; (Norco®): Hydrocodone 5 mg and acetaminophen 325 mg; Hydrocodone 7.5 mg and acetaminophen 325 mg; Hydrocodone 10 mg and acetaminophen 325 mg; (Vicodin®): Hydrocodone 5 mg and acetaminophen 500 mg; (Vicodin® ES): Hydrocodone 7.5 mg and acetaminophen 750 mg; (Vicodin® HP): Hydrocodone 10 mg and acetaminophen 660 mg; (Zydone®): Hydrocodone 5 mg and acetaminophen 400 mg; Hydrocodone 7.5 mg and acetaminophen 400 mg; Hydrocodone 10 mg and acetaminophen 400 mg

Hydrocodone and Aspirin *(hye droe KOE done & AS pir in)*

U.S. Brand Names Damason-P®

Synonyms Aspirin and Hydrocodone

Therapeutic Category Analgesic Combination, Narcotic

Use Relief of moderate to moderately severe pain

Restrictions C-III

Pregnancy Risk Factor D

Contraindications

Based on **hydrocodone** component: Hypersensitivity to hydrocodone or any component of the formulation

Based on **aspirin** component: Hypersensitivity to salicylates, other NSAIDs, or any component of the formulation; asthma; rhinitis; nasal polyps; inherited or acquired bleeding disorders (including factor VII and factor IX deficiency); pregnancy (in 3rd trimester especially); do not use in children (<16 years) for viral infections (chickenpox or flu symptoms), with or without fever, due to a potential association with Reye's syndrome

Warnings/Precautions Use with caution in patients with impaired renal function, erosive gastritis, or peptic ulcer disease; children and teenagers should not use for chickenpox or flu symptoms before a physician is consulted about Reye's syndrome; tolerance or drug dependence may result from extended use

Based on **hydrocodone** component: Use with caution in patients with hypersensitivity reactions to other phenanthrene-derivative opioid agonists (morphine, codeine, hydromorphone, levorphanol, oxycodone, oxymorphone); should be used with caution in elderly or debilitated patients, and those with severe impairment of hepatic or renal function, prostatic hyperplasia, or urethral stricture.

Based on **aspirin** component: Use with caution in patients with platelet and bleeding disorders, renal dysfunction, dehydration, erosive gastritis, or peptic ulcer disease. Heavy ethanol use (>3 drinks/day) can increase bleeding risks. Avoid use in severe renal failure or in severe hepatic failure. Discontinue use if tinnitus or impaired hearing occurs. Caution in mild-moderate renal failure (only at high dosages). Patients with sensitivity to tartrazine dyes, nasal polyps and asthma may have an increased risk of salicylate sensitivity. Surgical patients should avoid ASA if possible, for 1-2 weeks prior to surgery, to reduce the risk of excessive bleeding.

Common Adverse Reactions

>10%:
    Cardiovascular: Hypotension
    Central nervous system: Lightheadedness, dizziness, sedation, drowsiness, fatigue
    Gastrointestinal: Nausea, heartburn, stomach pains, dyspepsia, epigastric discomfort
    Neuromuscular & skeletal: Weakness

1% to 10%:
    Cardiovascular: Bradycardia
    Central nervous system: Confusion
    Dermatologic: Rash
    Gastrointestinal: Vomiting, gastrointestinal ulceration
    Genitourinary: Decreased urination
    Hematologic: Hemolytic anemia
    Respiratory: Dyspnea
    Miscellaneous: Anaphylactic shock

Drug Interactions

Cytochrome P450 Effect:
Hydrocodone: **Substrate** of CYP2D6 (major)
Aspirin: **Substrate** of CYP2C8/9 (minor)

Increased Effect/Toxicity:
Based on **hydrocodone** component: CNS depressants, MAO inhibitors, general anesthetics, and tricyclic antidepressants may potentiate the effects of opiate agonists; dextroamphetamine may enhance the analgesic effect of opiate agonists.

Based on **aspirin** component: May increase methotrexate serum levels/toxicity and may displace valproic acid from binding sites which can result in toxicity. NSAIDs and aspirin increase GI adverse effects (ulceration). Aspirin with oral anticoagulants (warfarin), thrombolytic agents, heparin, low molecular weight heparins, and antiplatelet agents (ticlopidine, clopidogrel, dipyridamole, NSAIDs, and IIb/IIIa antagonists) may increase risk of bleeding. Bleeding times may be additionally prolonged with verapamil. The effects of older sulfonylurea agents (tolazamide, tolbutamide) may be potentiated due to displacement from plasma proteins. This effect does not appear to be clinically significant for newer sulfonylurea agents (glyburide, glipizide, glimepiride).

Decreased Effect:
Based on **aspirin** component: The effects of ACE inhibitors may be blunted by aspirin administration (may be significant only at higher aspirin dosages). Aspirin may decrease the effects of beta-blockers, loop diuretics (furosemide), thiazide diuretics, and probenecid. Aspirin may cause a decrease in NSAIDs serum concentration and decrease the effects of probenecid. Increased serum salicylate levels when taken with with urine acidifiers (ammonium chloride, methionine).

Mechanism of Action

Based on **hydrocodone** component: Binds to opiate receptors in the CNS, altering the perception of and response to pain; suppresses cough in medullary center; produces generalized CNS depression

Based on **aspirin** component: Inhibits prostaglandin synthesis, acts on the hypothalamus heat-regulating center to reduce fever, blocks prostaglandin synthetase action which prevents formation of the platelet-aggregating substance thromboxane A_2

Pharmacodynamics/Kinetics

Aspirin: See Aspirin monograph.

Hydrocodone:
    Onset of action: Narcotic analgesic: 10-20 minutes
    Duration: 4-8 hours
    Distribution: Crosses placenta
    Metabolism: Hepatic; O-demethylation; N-demethylation and 6-ketosteroid reduction
    Half-life elimination: 3.3-4.4 hours
    Excretion: Urine

(Continued)

Hydrocodone and Aspirin *(Continued)*

Dosage Adults: Oral: 1-2 tablets every 4-6 hours as needed for pain

Administration Administer with food or a full glass of water to minimize GI distress

Monitoring Parameters Observe patient for excessive sedation, respiratory depression

Patient Information May cause drowsiness; avoid alcohol; watch for bleeding gums or any signs of GI bleeding; take with food or milk to minimize GI distress; report ringing in ears or persistent GI pain

Dosage Forms TAB: Hydrocodone 5 mg and aspirin 500 mg

Hydrocodone and Chlorpheniramine

(hye droe KOE done & klor fen IR a meen)

U.S. Brand Names Tussionex®

Synonyms Chlorpheniramine and Hydrocodone

Therapeutic Category Antihistamine/Antitussive

Use Symptomatic relief of cough and allergy

Restrictions C-III

Pregnancy Risk Factor C

Dosage Oral:

Children 6-12 years: 2.5 mL every 12 hours; do not exceed 5 mL/24 hours

Adults: 5 mL every 12 hours; do not exceed 10 mL/24 hours

Dosage Forms SYR, extended release: Hydrocodone polistirex 10 mg and chlorpheniramine polistirex 8 mg per 5 mL (480 mL)

Hydrocodone and Guaifenesin (hye droe KOE done & gwye FEN e sin)

U.S. Brand Names Codiclear® DH; Hycosin; Hycotuss®; Kwelcof®; Pneumotussin®; Vicodin Tuss®; Vitussin

Synonyms Guaifenesin and Hydrocodone; Hycoclear Tuss

Therapeutic Category Antitussive/Expectorant

Use Symptomatic relief of nonproductive coughs associated with upper and lower respiratory tract congestion

Restrictions C-III

Pregnancy Risk Factor C

Dosage Oral:

Children:

<2 years: 0.3 mg/kg/day (hydrocodone) in 4 divided doses

2-12 years: 2.5 mL every 4 hours, after meals and at bedtime

>12 years: 5 mL every 4 hours, after meals and at bedtime

Adults: 5 mL every 4 hours, after meals and at bedtime, not >30 mL in a 24-hour period

Dosage Forms LIQ: Hydrocodone 5 mg and guaifenesin 100 mg per 5 mL (480 mL, 960 mL); (Codiclear® DH): Hydrocodone 5 mg and guaifenesin 100 mg per 5 mL (120 mL, 480 mL); (Hycosin, Hycotuss®, Kwelcof®, Vicodin Tuss®, Vitussin): Hydrocodone 5 mg and guaifenesin 100 mg per 5 mL (480 mL); (Pneumotussin®): Hydrocodone 2.5 mg and guaifenesin 200 mg per 5 mL (480 mL). **TAB** (Pneumotussin®): Hydrocodone 2.5 mg and guaifenesin 300 mg

Hydrocodone and Homatropine (hye droe KOE done & hoe MA troe peen)

U.S. Brand Names Hycodan®; Hydromet®; Hydropane®; Tussigon®

Synonyms Homatropine and Hydrocodone

Therapeutic Category Antitussive; Cough Preparation

Use Symptomatic relief of cough

Restrictions C-III

Pregnancy Risk Factor C

Dosage Oral (based on hydrocodone component):

Children: 0.6 mg/kg/day in 3-4 divided doses; do not administer more frequently than every 4 hours

A single dose should not exceed 1.25 mg in children <2 years of age, 5 mg in children 2-12 years, and 10 mg in children >12 years

Adults: 10 mg every 4-6 hours, a single dose should not exceed 15 mg; do not administer more frequently than every 4 hours

Dosage Forms SYR (Hycodan®, Hydromet®, Hydropane®): Hydrocodone 5 mg and homatropine 1.5 mg per 5 mL (480 mL). **TAB** (Hycodan®, Tussigon®): Hydrocodone 5 mg and homatropine 1.5 mg

Hydrocodone and Ibuprofen (hye droe KOE done & eye byoo PROE fen)

U.S. Brand Names Vicoprofen®

Synonyms Ibuprofen and Hydrocodone

Therapeutic Category Analgesic Combination, Narcotic

Use Short-term (generally <10 days) management of moderate to severe acute pain; is not indicated for treatment of such conditions as osteoarthritis or rheumatoid arthritis

Restrictions C-III

Pregnancy Risk Factor C/D (3rd trimester)

Contraindications Hypersensitivity to hydrocodone, ibuprofen, aspirin, other NSAIDs, or any component of the formulation; pregnancy (3rd trimester)

Warnings/Precautions As with any opioid analgesic agent, this agent should be used with caution in elderly or debilitated patients, and those with severe impairment of hepatic or renal function, hypothyroidism, Addison's disease, prostatic hyperplasia, or urethral stricture. The usual precautions should be observed and the possibility of respiratory depression should be kept in mind. Patients with head injury, increased intracranial pressure, acute abdomen, active peptic ulcer disease, history of upper GI disease, impaired thyroid function, asthma, hypertension, edema, heart failure, and any bleeding disorder should use this agent cautiously. Hydrocodone suppresses the cough reflex; as with opioids, caution should be exercised when this agent is used postoperatively and in patients with pulmonary disease.

Common Adverse Reactions
>10%:
    Central nervous system: Headache (27%), dizziness (14%), sedation (22%)
    Dermatologic: Rash, urticaria
    Gastrointestinal: Constipation (22%), nausea (21%), dyspepsia (12%)
1% to 10%:
    Cardiovascular: Bradycardia, palpitations (<3%), vasodilation (<3%), edema (3% to 9%)
    Central nervous system: Headache, nervousness, confusion, fever (<3%), pain (3% to 9%), anxiety (3% to 9%), thought abnormalities
    Dermatologic: Itching (3% to 9%)
    Endocrine & metabolic: Fluid retention
    Gastrointestinal: Vomiting (3% to 9%), anorexia, diarrhea (3% to 9%), xerostomia (3% to 9%), flatulence (3% to 9%), gastritis (<3%), melena (<3%), mouth ulcers (<3%)
    Genitourinary: Polyuria (<3%)
    Neuromuscular & skeletal: Weakness (3% to 9%)
    Otic: Tinnitus
    Respiratory: Dyspnea, hiccups, pharyngitis, rhinitis
    Miscellaneous: Flu syndrome (<3%), infection (3% to 9%)

Drug Interactions
  Cytochrome P450 Effect:
    Hydrocodone: **Substrate** of CYP2D6 (major)
    Ibuprofen: **Substrate** (minor) of CYP2C8/9, 2C19; **Inhibits** CYP2C8/9 (strong)
  Increased Effect/Toxicity: Anticholinergic agents taken with hydrocodone may cause paralytic ileus. Aspirin taken concomitantly may enhance adverse effects. Other CNS depressants (eg, antihistamines, alcohol, antipsychotics, etc) taken concomitantly may exhibit additive CNS toxicity. Warfarin taken with ibuprofen may result in additional risk of bleeding. Methotrexate taken with ibuprofen may enhance methotrexate toxicity. Furosemide taken with ibuprofen may reduce the effect of furosemide. Lithium taken with ibuprofen may elevate lithium serum levels.
  Decreased Effect: Based on **ibuprofen** component: Aspirin may decrease ibuprofen serum concentrations. Ibuprofen may decrease the effect of some antihypertensive agents (including ACE inhibitors and angiotensin antagonists) and diuretics.

Mechanism of Action
  Based on **hydrocodone** component: Binds to opiate receptors in the CNS, altering the perception of and response to pain; suppresses cough in medullary center; produces generalized CNS depression
  Based on **ibuprofen** component: Inhibits prostaglandin synthesis by decreasing the activity of the enzyme, cyclooxygenase, which results in decreased formation of prostaglandin precursors

Pharmacodynamics/Kinetics
  Ibuprofen: See Ibuprofen monograph.
  Hydrocodone:
    Onset of action: Narcotic analgesic: 10-20 minutes
    Duration: 4-8 hours
    Distribution: Crosses placenta
    Protein binding: 19% to 45%
    Metabolism: Hepatic; O-demethylation; N-demethylation and 6-ketosteroid reduction
    Half-life elimination: 3.3-4.4 hours
    Time to peak: 1.7 hours
    Excretion: Urine

Dosage Adults: Oral: 1-2 tablets every 4-6 hours as needed for pain; maximum: 5 tablets/day

Patient Information Hydrocodone and ibuprofen, like other opioid-containing analgesics, may impair mental and/or physical abilities required for the performance of potentially hazardous tasks such as driving a car or operating machinery; patients should be cautioned accordingly. Alcohol and other CNS depressants may produce an additive CNS depression, when taken with this combination product, and should be avoided. This agent may be habit-forming. Patients should take the drug only for as long as it is prescribed, in the amounts prescribed, and no more frequently than prescribed.

Dosage Forms TAB: Hydrocodone 7.5 mg and ibuprofen 200 mg

Hydrocodone and Pseudoephedrine
  (hye droe KOE done & soo doe e FED rin)
U.S. Brand Names Detussin®; Histussin D®; P-V Tussin
Synonyms Pseudoephedrine and Hydrocodone
Therapeutic Category Analgesic, Narcotic and Decongestant
Use Symptomatic relief of cough due to colds, nasal congestion, and cough
Restrictions C-III
Dosage Oral: Adults: 5 mL 4 times/day
Dosage Forms LIQ (Detussin®, Histussin D®): Hydrocodone 5 mg and pseudoephedrine 60 mg per 5 mL (480 mL). **TAB** (P-V Tussin): Hydrocodone 5 mg and pseudoephedrine 60 mg

♦ **Hydrocodone Bitartrate, Carbinoxamine Maleate, and Pseudoephedrine Hydrochloride**
see Hydrocodone, Carbinoxamine, and Pseudoephedrine *on page 632*

Hydrocodone, Carbinoxamine, and Pseudoephedrine
(hye droe KOE done, kar bi NOKS a meen, & soo doe e FED rin)

U.S. Brand Names Histex™ HC; Tri-Vent™ HC

Synonyms Carbinoxamine, Pseudoephedrine, and Hydrocodone; Hydrocodone Bitartrate, Carbinoxamine Maleate, and Pseudoephedrine Hydrochloride; Pseudoephedrine, Hydrocodone, and Carbinoxamine

Therapeutic Category Antihistamine/Decongestant/Antitussive

Use Symptomatic relief of cough, congestion, and rhinorrhea associated with the common cold, influenza, bronchitis, or sinusitis

Restrictions C-III

Pregnancy Risk Factor C

Dosage Oral: Relief of cough, congestion, and runny nose:
Children:
2-10 years: Dosing based on hydrocodone content: 0.6 mg/kg/day given in 4 divided doses.
Alternately, the following dosing may be used based on age:
2-4 years: 1.25 mL every 4-6 hours; maximum dose: 7.5 mL/24 hours
4-10 years: 2.5 mL every 4-6 hours; maximum dose: 15 mL/24 hours
>10 years: Refer to Adults dosing
Adults: 5-10 mL every 4-6 hours; maximum dose: 30 mL/24 hours

Dosage Forms LIQ: Hydrocodone 5 mg, carbinoxamine 2 mg, and pseudoephedrine 30 mg (480 mL); (Histex™ HC, Tri-Vent™ HC): Hydrocodone 5 mg, carbinoxamine 2 mg, and pseudoephedrine 30 mg (480 mL)

Hydrocodone, Chlorpheniramine, Phenylephrine, Acetaminophen, and Caffeine
(hye droe KOE done, klor fen IR a meen, fen il EF rin, a seet a MIN oh fen, & KAF een)

U.S. Brand Names Hycomine® Compound

Synonyms Acetaminophen, Caffeine, Hydrocodone, Chlorpheniramine, and Phenylephrine; Caffeine, Hydrocodone, Chlorpheniramine, Phenylephrine, and Acetaminophen; Chlorpheniramine, Hydrocodone, Phenylephrine, Acetaminophen, and Caffeine; Phenylephrine, Hydrocodone, Chlorpheniramine, Acetaminophen, and Caffeine

Therapeutic Category Antitussive/Decongestant

Use Symptomatic relief of cough and symptoms of upper respiratory infection

Restrictions C-III

Pregnancy Risk Factor C

Dosage Adults: Oral: 1 tablet every 4 hours, up to 4 times/day

Dosage Forms TAB: Hydrocodone 5 mg, chlorpheniramine 2 mg, phenylephrine 10 mg, acetaminophen 250 mg, and caffeine 30 mg

Hydrocortisone (hye droe KOR ti sone)
Related Information
Corticosteroids Comparison *on page 1372*

U.S. Brand Names A-hydroCort®; Anucort-HC®; Anusol-HC®; Anusol® HC-1 [OTC]; Aquanil™ HC [OTC]; CaldeCORT® [OTC]; Cetacort®; Colocort™; CortaGel® Maximum Strength [OTC]; Cortaid® Intensive Therapy [OTC]; Cortaid® Maximum Strength [OTC]; Cortaid® Sensitive Skin With Aloe [OTC]; Cortef®; Corticool® [OTC]; Cortifoam®; Cortizone®-5 [OTC]; Cortizone®-10 Maximum Strength [OTC]; Cortizone®-10 Plus Maximum Strength [OTC]; Cortizone® 10 Quick Shot [OTC]; Cortizone® for Kids [OTC]; Dermarest Dricort® [OTC]; Dermtex® HC [OTC]; EarSol® HC; Hemril-HC®; Hydrocortone®; Hydrocortone® Phosphate; Hytone®; Lacti-Care-HC®; Locoid®; Locoid Lipocream®; Nupercainal® Hydrocortisone Cream [OTC]; Nutracort®; Pandel®; Post Peel Healing Balm [OTC]; Preparation H® Hydrocortisone [OTC]; Proctocort®; ProctoCream® HC; Proctosol-HC®; Sarnol®-HC [OTC]; Solu-Cortef®; Summer's Eve® SpecialCare™ Medicated Anti-Itch Cream [OTC]; Texacort®; Theracort® [OTC]; Westcort®

Synonyms Compound F; Cortisol; Hydrocortisone Acetate; Hydrocortisone Buteprate; Hydrocortisone Butyrate; Hydrocortisone Cypionate; Hydrocortisone Sodium Phosphate; Hydrocortisone Sodium Succinate; Hydrocortisone Valerate

Therapeutic Category Anti-inflammatory Agent; Anti-inflammatory Agent, Rectal; Corticosteroid, Rectal; Corticosteroid, Systemic; Corticosteroid, Topical (Low Potency); Corticosteroid, Topical (Medium Potency); Glucocorticoid; Mineralocorticoid

Use Management of adrenocortical insufficiency; relief of inflammation of corticosteroid-responsive dermatoses (low and medium potency topical corticosteroid); adjunctive treatment of ulcerative colitis

Pregnancy Risk Factor C

Contraindications Hypersensitivity to hydrocortisone or any component of the formulation; serious infections, except septic shock or tuberculous meningitis; viral, fungal, or tubercular skin lesions

Warnings/Precautions
Use with caution in patients with hyperthyroidism, cirrhosis, nonspecific ulcerative colitis, hypertension, osteoporosis, thromboembolic tendencies, CHF, convulsive disorders, myasthenia gravis, thrombophlebitis, peptic ulcer, diabetes, glaucoma, cataracts, or tuberculosis. Use caution in hepatic impairment.

May cause HPA axis suppression. Acute adrenal insufficiency may occur with abrupt withdrawal after long-term therapy or with stress; young pediatric patients may be more susceptible to adrenal axis suppression from topical therapy. Avoid use of topical preparations with occlusive dressings or on weeping or exudative lesions.

Because of the risk of adverse effects, systemic corticosteroids should be used cautiously in the elderly, in the smallest possible dose, and for the shortest possible time

Common Adverse Reactions

Systemic:

>10%:
Central nervous system: Insomnia, nervousness
Gastrointestinal: Increased appetite, indigestion

1% to 10%:
Dermatologic: Hirsutism
Endocrine & metabolic: Diabetes mellitus
Neuromuscular & skeletal: Arthralgia
Ocular: Cataracts
Respiratory: Epistaxis

Topical:
>10%: Dermatologic: Eczema (12.5%)
1% to 10%: Dermatologic: Pruritus (6%), stinging (2%), dry skin (2%)

Drug Interactions

Cytochrome P450 Effect: Substrate of CYP3A4 (minor); **Induces** CYP3A4 (weak)

Increased Effect/Toxicity: Hydrocortisone in combination with oral anticoagulants may increase prothrombin time. Potassium-depleting diuretics increase risk of hypokalemia. Cardiac glycosides increase risk of arrhythmias or digitalis toxicity secondary to hypokalemia.

Decreased Effect: Hydrocortisone may decrease the hypoglycemic effect of insulin. Phenytoin, phenobarbital, ephedrine, and rifampin increase metabolism of hydrocortisone resulting in a decreased steroid blood level.

Mechanism of Action Decreases inflammation by suppression of migration of polymorphonuclear leukocytes and reversal of increased capillary permeability

Pharmacodynamics/Kinetics

Onset of action:
Hydrocortisone acetate: Slow
Hydrocortisone sodium phosphate (water soluble): Rapid
Hydrocortisone sodium succinate (water soluble): Rapid
Duration:
Hydrocortisone acetate: Long
Hydrocortisone sodium phosphate (water soluble): Short
Absorption: Rapid by all routes, except rectally
Metabolism: Hepatic
Half-life elimination: Biologic: 8-12 hours
Excretion: Urine (primarily as 17-hydroxysteroids and 17-ketosteroids)

Dosage Dose should be based on severity of disease and patient response

Acute adrenal insufficiency: I.M., I.V.:
Infants and young Children: Succinate: 1-2 mg/kg/dose bolus, then 25-150 mg/day in divided doses every 6-8 hours
Older Children: Succinate: 1-2 mg/kg bolus then 150-250 mg/day in divided doses every 6-8 hours
Adults: Succinate: 100 mg I.V. bolus, then 300 mg/day in divided doses every 8 hours or as a continuous infusion for 48 hours; once patient is stable change to oral, 50 mg every 8 hours for 6 doses, then taper to 30-50 mg/day in divided doses

Chronic adrenal corticoid insufficiency: Adults: Oral: 20-30 mg/day

Anti-inflammatory or immunosuppressive:
Infants and Children:
Oral: 2.5-10 mg/kg/day **or** 75-300 mg/m^2/day every 6-8 hours
I.M., I.V.: Succinate: 1-5 mg/kg/day **or** 30-150 mg/m^2/day divided every 12-24 hours
Adolescents and Adults: Oral, I.M., I.V.: Succinate: 15-240 mg every 12 hours

Congenital adrenal hyperplasia: Oral: Initial: 10-20 mg/m^2/day in 3 divided doses; a variety of dosing schedules have been used. **Note:** Inconsistencies have occurred with liquid formulations; tablets may provide more reliable levels. Doses must be individualized by monitoring growth, bone age, and hormonal levels. Mineralocorticoid and sodium supplementation may be required based upon electrolyte regulation and plasma renin activity.

Physiologic replacement: Children:
Oral: 0.5-0.75 mg/kg/day **or** 20-25 mg/m^2/day every 8 hours
I.M.: Succinate: 0.25-0.35 mg/kg/day **or** 12-15 mg/m^2/day once daily

Shock: I.M., I.V.: Succinate:
Children: Initial: 50 mg/kg, then repeated in 4 hours and/or every 24 hours as needed
Adolescents and Adults: 500 mg to 2 g every 2-6 hours

Status asthmaticus: Children and Adults: I.V.: Succinate: 1-2 mg/kg/dose every 6 hours for 24 hours, then maintenance of 0.5-1 mg/kg every 6 hours

Adults:
Rheumatic diseases:
Intralesional, intra-articular, soft tissue injection: Acetate:
Large joints: 25 mg (up to 37.5 mg)
Small joints: 10-25 mg
Tendon sheaths: 5-12.5 mg

(Continued)

Hydrocortisone *(Continued)*

Soft tissue infiltration: 25-50 mg (up to 75 mg)

Bursae: 25-37.5 mg

Ganglia: 12.5-25 mg

Stress dosing (surgery) in patients known to be adrenally-suppressed or on chronic systemic steroids: I.V.:

Minor stress (ie, inguinal herniorrhaphy): 25 mg/day for 1 day

Moderate stress (ie, joint replacement, cholecystectomy): 50-75 mg/day (25 mg every 8-12 hours) for 1-2 days

Major stress (pancreatoduodenectomy, esophagogastrectomy, cardiac surgery): 100-150 mg/day (50 mg every 8-12 hours) for 2-3 days

Dermatosis: Children >2 years and Adults: Topical: Apply to affected area 2-4 times/day (Buteprate: Apply once or twice daily). Therapy should be discontinued when control is achieved; if no improvement is seen, reassessment of diagnosis may be necessary.

Ulcerative colitis: Adults: Rectal: 10-100 mg 1-2 times/day for 2-3 weeks

Administration

Oral: Administer with food or milk to decrease GI upset

Parenteral: Hydrocortisone sodium succinate may be administered by I.M. or I.V. routes

I.V. bolus: Dilute to 50 mg/mL and administer over 30 seconds to several minutes (depending on the dose)

I.V. intermittent infusion: Dilute to 1 mg/mL and administer over 20-30 minutes

Topical: Apply a thin film to clean, dry skin and rub in gently

Monitoring Parameters Blood pressure, weight, serum glucose, and electrolytes

Reference Range Therapeutic: AM: 5-25 µg/dL (SI: 138-690 nmol/L), PM: 2-9 µg/dL (SI: 55-248 nmol/L) depending on test, assay

Patient Information Notify surgeon or dentist before surgical repair; oral formulation may cause GI upset, take with food; report if any sign of infection occurs; avoid abrupt withdrawal when on long-term therapy. Before applying, gently wash area to reduce risk of infection; apply a thin film to cleansed area and rub in gently and thoroughly until medication vanishes; avoid exposure to sunlight, severe sunburn may occur.

Dosage Forms AERO, rectal, as acetate (Cortifoam®): 10% (15 g). **AERO, topical spray, as base** (Cortizone® 10 Quick Shot): 1% (44 mL); (Dermtex® HC): 1% (52 mL). **CRM, rectal, as acetate** (Nupercainal® Hydrocortisone Cream): 1% (30 g). **CRM, rectal, as base**: (Cortizone®-10): 1% (30 g); (Preparation H® Hydrocortisone): 1% (27 g). **CRM, topical, as acetate**: 0.5% (30 g); 1% (30 g); (Cortaid® Maximum Strength): 1% (15 g, 30 g, 40 g); (Cortaid® Sensitive Skin With Aloe): 0.5% (15 g). **CRM, topical, as base**: 0.5% (30 g); 1% (1.5 g, 30 g, 454 g); 2.5% (20 g, 30 g, 454 g); (Anusol-HC®): 2.5% (30 g); (CaldeCORT®): 1% (15 g, 30 g); (Cortaid® Intensive Therapy): 1% (60 g); (Cortaid® Maximum Strength): 1% (15 g, 30 g, 40 g, 60 g); (Cortizone®-5): 0.5% (30 g, 60 g); (Cortizone®-10 Maximum Strength): 1% (15 g, 30 g, 60 g); (Cortizone®-10 Plus Maximum Strength): 1% (30 g, 60 g); (Cortizone® for Kids): 0.5% (30 g); (Dermarest® Dri-Cort): 1% (15 g, 30 g); (Hytone®): 2.5% (30 g, 60 g); (Post Peel Healing Balm): 1% (23 g); (ProctoCream® HC): 2.5% (30 g); (Proctocort®): 1% (30 g); (Proctosol-HC®): 2.5% (30 g); (Summer's Eve® SpecialCare™ Medicated Anti-Itch Cream): 1% (30 g). **CRM, topical, as butyrate** (Locoid®, Locoid Lipocream®): 0.1% (15 g, 45 g). **CRM, topical, as probutate** (Pandel®): 0.1% (15 g, 45 g, 80 g). **CRM, topical, as valerate** (Westcort®): 0.2% (15 g, 45 g, 60 g). **GEL, topical, as base** (Corticool®): 1% (45 g); (Cortagel® Maximum Strength): 1% (15 g, 30 g). **INJ, powder for reconstitution, as sodium succinate**: (A-Hydrocort®): 100 mg, 250 mg; (Solu-Cortef®): 100 mg, 250 mg, 500 mg, 1 g. **INJ, solution, as sodium phosphate** (Hydrocortone® Phosphate): 50 mg/mL (2 mL). **LOTION, topical, as base**: 1% (120 mL); 2.5% (60 mL); (Aquanil™ HC): 1% (120 mL); (Cetacort®, Sarnol®-HC): 1% (60 mL); (Hytone®): 1% (30 mL, 120 mL); 2.5% (60 mL); (Lacti-Care-HC®): 1% (120 mL); 2.5% (60 mL, 120 mL); (Nutracort®): 1% (60 mL, 120 mL); 2.5% (60 mL, 120 mL); (Theracort®): 1% (120 mL). **OINT, topical, as acetate**: 1% (30 g); (Anusol® HC-1): 1% (21 g); (Cortaid® Maximum Strength): 1% (15 g, 30 g). **OINT, topical, as base**: 0.5% (30 g); 1% (30 g, 454 g); 2.5% (20 g, 30 g, 454 g); (Cortizone®-5): 0.5% (30 g); (Cortizone®-10 Maximum Strength): 1% (30 g, 60 g); (Hytone®): 2.5% (30 g). **OINT, topical, as base** [in Orabase®]: 1% (25 g, 110 g, 454 g). **OINT, topical, as butyrate** (Locoid®): 0.1% (15 g, 45 g). **OINT, topical, as valerate** (Westcort®): 0.2% (15 g, 45 g, 60 g). **SOLN, otic, as base** (EarSol® HC): 1% (30 mL). **SOLN, rectal, as base** (Colocort™): 100 mg/60 mL (7s). **SOLN, topical, as base** (Texacort®): 1% (30 mL) [DSC]; 2.5% (30 mL). **SOLN, topical, as butyrate** (Locoid®): 0.1% (20 mL, 60 mL). **SUPP, rectal**: 25 mg (12s, 24s); (Anucort™ HC): 25 mg (12s, 24s, 100s); (Anusol-HC®, Proctosol-HC®): 25 mg (12s, 24s); (Hemril® HC): 25 mg (12s); (Proctocort®): 30 mg (12s, 24s). **SUSP, oral, as cypionate** (Cortef®): 10 mg/5 mL (120 mL) [DSC]. **TAB, as base**: 20 mg; (Cortef®): 5 mg, 10 mg, 20 mg; (Hydrocortone®): 10 mg

♦ **Hydrocortisone Acetate** *see* Hydrocortisone *on page 632*

♦ **Hydrocortisone, Acetic Acid, and Propylene Glycol Diacetate** *see* Acetic Acid, Propylene Glycol Diacetate, and Hydrocortisone *on page 31*

♦ **Hydrocortisone and Benzoyl Peroxide** *see* Benzoyl Peroxide and Hydrocortisone *on page 155*

♦ **Hydrocortisone and Ciprofloxacin** *see* Ciprofloxacin and Hydrocortisone *on page 281*

♦ **Hydrocortisone and Iodoquinol** *see* Iodoquinol and Hydrocortisone *on page 683*

♦ **Hydrocortisone and Pramoxine** *see* Pramoxine and Hydrocortisone *on page 1028*

♦ **Hydrocortisone and Urea** *see* Urea and Hydrocortisone *on page 1282*

♦ **Hydrocortisone, Bacitracin, Neomycin, and Polymyxin B** *see* Bacitracin, Polymyxin B, and Hydrocortisone *on page 144*

♦ **Hydrocortisone Buteprate** *see* Hydrocortisone *on page 632*
♦ **Hydrocortisone Butyrate** *see* Hydrocortisone *on page 632*
♦ **Hydrocortisone Cypionate** *see* Hydrocortisone *on page 632*
♦ **Hydrocortisone, Neomycin, and Polymyxin B** *see* Neomycin, Polymyxin B, and Hydrocortisone *on page 892*
♦ **Hydrocortisone, Neomycin, Colistin, and Thonzonium** *see* Neomycin, Colistin, Hydrocortisone, and Thonzonium *on page 892*
♦ **Hydrocortisone, Propylene Glycol Diacetate, and Acetic Acid** *see* Acetic Acid, Propylene Glycol Diacetate, and Hydrocortisone *on page 31*
♦ **Hydrocortisone Sodium Phosphate** *see* Hydrocortisone *on page 632*
♦ **Hydrocortisone Sodium Succinate** *see* Hydrocortisone *on page 632*
♦ **Hydrocortisone Valerate** *see* Hydrocortisone *on page 632*
♦ **Hydrocortone®** *see* Hydrocortisone *on page 632*
♦ **Hydrocortone® Phosphate** *see* Hydrocortisone *on page 632*
♦ **Hydromet®** *see* Hydrocodone and Homatropine *on page 630*

Hydromorphone (hye droe MOR fone)

Related Information
Narcotic Agonists Comparison *on page 1395*
U.S. Brand Names Dilaudid®; Dilaudid-HP®
Synonyms Dihydromorphinone; Hydromorphone Hydrochloride
Therapeutic Category Analgesic, Narcotic; Antitussive
Use Management of moderate to severe pain; antitussive at lower doses
Restrictions C-II
Pregnancy Risk Factor B/D (prolonged use or high doses at term)
Contraindications Hypersensitivity to hydromorphone, any component of the formulation, or other phenanthrene derivative; increased intracranial pressure; acute or severe asthma; severe respiratory depression (in absence of resuscitative equipment or ventilatory support); severe CNS depression; pregnancy (prolonged use or high doses at term)
Warnings/Precautions Tablet and cough syrup contain tartrazine which may cause allergic reactions; hydromorphone shares toxic potential of opiate agonists, and precaution of opiate agonist therapy should be observed; extreme caution should be taken to avoid confusing the highly concentrated injection with the less concentrated injectable product, injection contains benzyl alcohol; use with caution in patients with hypersensitivity to other phenanthrene opiates, in patients with respiratory disease, or severe liver or renal failure; tolerance or drug dependence may result from extended use.
Common Adverse Reactions Frequency not defined.
Cardiovascular: Palpitations, hypotension, peripheral vasodilation, tachycardia, bradycardia, flushing of face
Central nervous system: CNS depression, increased intracranial pressure, fatigue, headache, nervousness, restlessness, dizziness, lightheadedness, drowsiness, hallucinations, mental depression, seizures
Dermatologic: Pruritus, rash, urticaria
Endocrine & metabolic: Antidiuretic hormone release
Gastrointestinal: Nausea, vomiting, constipation, stomach cramps, xerostomia, anorexia, biliary tract spasm, paralytic ileus
Genitourinary: Decreased urination, ureteral spasm, urinary tract spasm
Hepatic: LFTs increased, AST increased, ALT increased
Local: Pain at injection site (I.M.)
Neuromuscular & skeletal: Trembling, weakness, myoclonus
Ocular: Miosis
Respiratory: Respiratory depression, dyspnea
Miscellaneous: Histamine release, physical and psychological dependence
Drug Interactions
Increased Effect/Toxicity: CNS depressants, phenothiazines, and tricyclic antidepressants may potentiate the adverse effects of hydromorphone.
Mechanism of Action Binds to opiate receptors in the CNS, causing inhibition of ascending pain pathways, altering the perception of and response to pain; causes cough supression by direct central action in the medulla; produces generalized CNS depression
Pharmacodynamics/Kinetics
Onset of action: Analgesic: Oral: 15-30 minutes
Peak effect: Oral: 30-60 minutes
Duration: 4-5 hours
Absorption: I.M.: Variable and delayed
Metabolism: Hepatic; no active metabolites
Bioavailability: 62%
Half-life elimination: 1-3 hours
Excretion: Urine (primarily as glucuronide conjugates)
Dosage
Acute pain (moderate to severe): **Note:** These are guidelines and do not represent the maximum doses that may be required in all patients. Doses should be titrated to pain relief/prevention.
Young Children ≥6 months and <50 kg:
Oral: 0.03-0.08 mg/kg/dose every 3-4 hours as needed
I.V.: 0.015 mg/kg/dose every 3-6 hours as needed
(Continued)

Hydromorphone *(Continued)*

Older Children >50 kg and Adults:
Oral: Initial: Opiate-naive: 2-4 mg every 3-4 hours as needed; patients with prior opiate exposure may require higher initial doses; usual dosage range: 2-8 mg every 3-4 hours as needed

I.V.: Initial: Opiate-naive: 0.2-0.6 mg every 2-3 hours as needed; patients with prior opiate exposure may tolerate higher initial doses

Note: More frequent dosing may be needed.

Mechanically-ventilated patients (based on 70 kg patient): 0.7-2 mg every 1-2 hours as needed; infusion (based on 70 kg patient): 0.5-1 mg/hour

Patient-controlled analgesia (PCA): (Opiate-naive: Consider lower end of dosing range)
Usual concentration: 0.2 mg/mL
Demand dose: Usual: 0.1-0.2 mg; range: 0.05-0.5 mg
Lockout interval: 5-15 minutes
4-hour limit: 4-6 mg

Epidural:
Bolus dose: 1-1.5 mg
Infusion concentration: 0.05-0.075 mg/mL
Infusion rate: 0.04-0.4 mg/hour
Demand dose: 0.15 mg
Lockout interval: 30 minutes

I.M., S.C.: **Note:** I.M. use may result in variable absorption and a lag time to peak effect.
Initial: Opiate-naive: 0.8-1 mg every 4-6 hours as needed; patients with prior opiate exposure may require higher initial doses; usual dosage range: 1-2 mg every 3-6 hours as needed

Rectal: 3 mg every 4-8 hours as needed

Chronic pain: Patients taking opioids chronically may become tolerant and require doses higher than the usual dosage range to maintain the desired effect. Tolerance can be managed by appropriate dose titration. There is no optimal or maximal dose for hydromorphone in chronic pain. The appropriate dose is one that relieves pain throughout its dosing interval without causing unmanageable side effects.

Adults: Oral, controlled release formulation (Hydromorph Contin®, not available in U.S.): 3-30 mg every 12 hours. **Note:** A patient's hydromorphone requirement should be established using prompt release formulations; conversion to long acting products may be considered when chronic, continuous treatment is required. Higher dosages should be reserved for use only in opioid-tolerant patients.

Antitussive: Oral:
Children 6-12 years: 0.5 mg every 3-4 hours as needed
Children >12 years and Adults: 1 mg every 3-4 hours as needed

Dosing adjustment in hepatic impairment: Should be considered
Administration
Parenteral: May be given S.C. or I.M.; for IVP, must be given slowly over 2-3 minutes (rapid IVP has been associated with an increase in side effects, especially respiratory depression and hypotension). Vial stopper contains latex.
Oral: Capsule should be swallowed whole; do not crush or chew; contents may be sprinkled on soft food and swallowed
Monitoring Parameters Pain relief, respiratory and mental status, blood pressure
Patient Information May cause drowsiness; avoid alcohol; take with food or milk to minimize GI distress
Dosage Forms CAP, controlled release (Hydromorph Contin®) [not available in U.S.]: 3 mg, 6 mg, 12 mg, 18 mg, 24 mg, 30 mg. **INJ, powder for reconstitution** (Dilaudid-HP®): 250 mg. **INJ, solution:** 1 mg/mL (1 mL); 2 mg/mL (1 mL, 20 mL); 4 mg/mL (1 mL); 10 mg/mL (1 mL, 5 mL, 10 mL); (Dilaudid®): 1 mg/mL (1 mL); 2 mg/mL (1 mL, 20 mL); 4 mg/mL (1 mL); (Dilaudid-HP®): 10 mg/mL (1 mL, 5 mL, 50 mL). **LIQ, oral** (Dilaudid®): 1 mg/mL (480 mL). **SUPP, rectal** (Dilaudid®): 3 mg (6s). **TAB** (Dilaudid®): 2 mg, 4 mg, 8 mg

♦ **Hydromorphone Hydrochloride** *see* Hydromorphone *on page 635*
♦ **Hydropane®** *see* Hydrocodone and Homatropine *on page 630*
♦ **Hydroquinol** *see* Hydroquinone *on page 636*

Hydroquinone *(HYE droe kwin one)*

U.S. Brand Names Alphaquin HP; Alustra™; Claripel™; Eldopaque® [OTC]; Eldopaque Forte®; Eldoquin® [OTC]; Eldoquin Forte®; EpiQuin™ Micro; Esoterica® Regular [OTC]; Glyquin®; Lustra®; Lustra-AF™; Melanex®; Melpaque HP®; Melquin-3®; Melquin HP®; NeoStrata AHA [OTC]; Nuquin HP®; Palmer's® Skin Success Fade Cream™ [OTC]; Solaquin® [OTC]; Solaquin Forte®
Synonyms Hydroquinol; Quinol
Therapeutic Category Depigmenting Agent
Use Gradual bleaching of hyperpigmented skin conditions
Pregnancy Risk Factor C
Contraindications Hypersensitivity to hydroquinone or any component of the formulation; sunburn, depilatory usage
Warnings/Precautions Limit application to area no larger than face and neck or hands and arms
Common Adverse Reactions Frequency not defined.

Dermatologic: Dermatitis, dryness, erythema, stinging, inflammatory reaction, sensitization
Local: Irritation

Mechanism of Action Produces reversible depigmentation of the skin by suppression of melanocyte metabolic processes, in particular the inhibition of the enzymatic oxidation of tyrosine to DOPA (3,4-dihydroxyphenylalanine); sun exposure reverses this effect and will cause repigmentation.

Pharmacodynamics/Kinetics Onset and duration of depigmentation produced by hydroquinone varies among individuals

Dosage Children >12 years and Adults: Topical: Apply thin layer and rub in twice daily

Patient Information Use sunscreens or clothing; do not use on irritated or denuded skin; stop using if rash or irritation develops; for external use only, avoid eye contact

Dosage Forms CRM, topical: 4% (30 g); (Alphaquin HP, Alustra™, Eldopaque Forte®, Eldoquin Forte®): 4% (30 g); (Eldopaque®): 2% (15 g, 30 g); (EpiQuin™ Micro): 4% (30 g); (Esoterica® Regular): 2% (85 g); (Lustra®): 4% (30 g, 60 g); (Melquin HP®): 4% (15 g, 30 g); (Nuquin HP): 4% (15 g, 30 g, 60 g); (Palmer's® Skin Success Fade Cream™): 2% (81 g, 132 g). **CRM, topical** [with sunscreen]: 4% (30 g); (Claripel™): 4% (45 g); (Glyquin®, Solaquin Forte®): 4% (30 g); (Solaquin®): 2% (30 g); (Lustra-AF™): 4% (30 g, 60 g); (Melpaque HP®): 4% (15 g, 30 g). **GEL, topical** (NeoStrata AHA): 2% (45 g). **GEL, topical** [with sunscreen] (Nuquin HP): 4% (15 g, 30 g). **SOLN, topical** (Melanex®, Melquin-3®): 3% (30 mL)

♦ **Hydroquinone, Fluocinolone Acetonide, and Tretinoin** *see* Fluocinolone, Hydroquinone, and Tretinoin *on page 533*

♦ **Hydro-Tussin™-CBX** *see* Carbinoxamine and Pseudoephedrine *on page 218*

♦ **Hydro-Tussin™ DM** *see* Guaifenesin and Dextromethorphan *on page 604*

Hydroxocobalamin (hye droks oh koe BAL a min)

Synonyms Vitamin B$_{12}$

Therapeutic Category Vitamin, Water Soluble

Use Treatment of pernicious anemia, vitamin B$_{12}$ deficiency, increased B$_{12}$ requirements due to pregnancy, thyrotoxicosis, hemorrhage, malignancy, liver or kidney disease

Unlabeled/Investigational Use Neuropathies, multiple sclerosis

Pregnancy Risk Factor A/C (dose exceeding RDA recommendation)

Contraindications Hypersensitivity to cyanocobalamin or any component of the formulation, cobalt; patients with hereditary optic nerve atrophy

Warnings/Precautions Some products contain benzoyl alcohol; avoid use in premature infants; an intradermal test dose should be performed for hypersensitivity; use only if oral supplementation not possible or when treating pernicious anemia

Common Adverse Reactions Frequency not defined.
Cardiovascular: Peripheral vascular thrombosis
Dermatologic: Itching, urticaria
Gastrointestinal: Diarrhea
Miscellaneous: Hypersensitivity reactions

Mechanism of Action Coenzyme for various metabolic functions, including fat and carbohydrate metabolism and protein synthesis, used in cell replication and hematopoiesis

Dosage Vitamin B$_{12}$ deficiency: I.M.:
Children: 1-5 mg given in single doses of 100 mcg over 2 or more weeks, followed by 30-50 mcg/month
Adults: 30 mcg/day for 5-10 days, followed by 100-200 mcg/month

Administration Administer I.M. only; may require coadministration of folic acid

Patient Information Therapy is required throughout life; do not take folic acid instead of B$_{12}$ to prevent anemia

Dosage Forms INJ, solution: 1000 mcg/mL (30 mL)

♦ **4-Hydroxybutyrate** *see* Sodium Oxybate *on page 1149*

♦ **Hydroxycarbamide** *see* Hydroxyurea *on page 638*

Hydroxychloroquine (hye droks ee KLOR oh kwin)

U.S. Brand Names Plaquenil®

Synonyms Hydroxychloroquine Sulfate

Therapeutic Category Aminoquinoline, Antimalarial; Antimalarial Agent; Antirheumatic

Use Suppression and treatment of acute attacks of malaria; treatment of systemic lupus erythematosus and rheumatoid arthritis

Unlabeled/Investigational Use Porphyria cutanea tarda, polymorphous light eruptions

Pregnancy Risk Factor C

Contraindications Hypersensitivity to hydroxychloroquine, 4-aminoquinoline derivatives, or any component of the formulation; retinal or visual field changes attributable to 4-aminoquinolines

Warnings/Precautions Use with caution in patients with hepatic disease, G6PD deficiency, psoriasis, and porphyria; long-term use in children is not recommended; perform baseline and periodic (6 months) ophthalmologic examinations; test periodically for muscle weakness

Common Adverse Reactions Frequency not defined.
Cardiovascular: Cardiomyopathy (rare, relationship to hydroxychloroquine unclear)
Central nervous system: Irritability, nervousness, emotional changes, nightmares, psychosis, headache, dizziness, vertigo, seizures, ataxia, lassitude
Dermatologic: Bleaching of hair, alopecia, pigmentation changes (skin and mucosal; black-blue color); rash (urticarial, morbilliform, lichenoid, maculopapular, purpuric, erythema (Continued)

Hydroxychloroquine *(Continued)*

annulare centrifugum, Stevens-Johnson syndrome, acute generalized exanthematous pustulosis, and exfoliative dermatitis)

Endocrine & metabolic: Weight loss

Gastrointestinal: Anorexia, nausea, vomiting, diarrhea, abdominal cramping

Hematologic: Aplastic anemia, agranulocytosis, leukopenia, thrombocytopenia, hemolysis (in patients with glucose-6-phosphate deficiency)

Hepatic: Abnormal liver function/hepatic failure (isolated cases)

Neuromuscular & skeletal: Myopathy, palsy, or neuromyopathy leading to progressive weakness and atrophy of proximal muscle groups (may be associated with mild sensory changes, loss of deep tendon reflexes, and abnormal nerve conduction)

Ocular: Disturbance in accommodation, keratopathy, corneal changes/deposits (visual disturbances, blurred vision, photophobia - reversible on discontinuation), macular edema, atrophy, abnormal pigmentation, retinopathy (early changes reversible - may progress despite discontinuation if advanced), optic disc pallor/atrophy, attenuation of retinal arterioles, pigmentary retinopathy, scotoma, decreased visual acuity, nystagmus

Otic: Tinnitus, deafness

Miscellaneous: Exacerbation of porphyria and nonlight sensitive psoriasis

Drug Interactions

Increased Effect/Toxicity: Cimetidine increases levels of chloroquine and probably other 4-aminoquinolones.

Decreased Effect: Chloroquine and other 4-aminoquinolones absorption may be decreased due to GI binding with kaolin or magnesium trisilicate.

Mechanism of Action Interferes with digestive vacuole function within sensitive malarial parasites by increasing the pH and interfering with lysosomal degradation of hemoglobin; inhibits locomotion of neutrophils and chemotaxis of eosinophils; impairs complement-dependent antigen-antibody reactions

Pharmacodynamics/Kinetics

Onset of action: Rheumatic disease: May require 4-6 weeks to respond

Absorption: Complete

Protein binding: 55%

Metabolism: Hepatic

Half-life elimination: 32-50 days

Time to peak: Rheumatic disease: Several months

Excretion: Urine (as metabolites and unchanged drug); may be enhanced by urinary acidification

Dosage Note: Hydroxychloroquine sulfate 200 mg is equivalent to 155 mg hydroxychloroquine base and 250 mg chloroquine phosphate. Oral:

Children:

Chemoprophylaxis of malaria: 5 mg/kg (base) once weekly; should not exceed the recommended adult dose; begin 2 weeks before exposure; continue for 4-6 weeks after leaving endemic area; if suppressive therapy is not begun prior to the exposure, double the initial dose and give in 2 doses, 6 hours apart

Acute attack: 10 mg/kg (base) initial dose; followed by 5 mg/kg at 6, 24, and 48 hours

JRA or SLE: 3-5 mg/kg/day divided 1-2 times/day; avoid exceeding 7 mg/kg/day

Adults:

Chemoprophylaxis of malaria: 310 mg base weekly on same day each week; begin 2 weeks before exposure; continue for 4-6 weeks after leaving endemic area; if suppressive therapy is not begun prior to the exposure, double the initial dose and give in 2 doses, 6 hours apart

Acute attack: 620 mg first dose day 1; 310 mg in 6 hours day 1; 310 mg in 1 dose day 2; and 310 mg in 1 dose on day 3

Rheumatoid arthritis: 310-465 mg/day to start taken with food or milk; increase dose until optimum response level is reached; usually after 4-12 weeks dose should be reduced by $1/_2$ and a maintenance dose of 155-310 mg/day given

Lupus erythematosus: 310 mg every day or twice daily for several weeks depending on response; 155-310 mg/day for prolonged maintenance therapy

Administration Administer with food or milk

Monitoring Parameters Ophthalmologic exam, CBC

Patient Information Take with food or milk; complete full course of therapy; wear sunglasses in bright sunlight; report blurring or other vision changes, ringing in the ears, or hearing loss

Dosage Forms TAB: 200 mg

♦ **Hydroxychloroquine Sulfate** *see* Hydroxychloroquine *on page 637*

♦ **25-Hydroxycholecalciferol** *see* Calcifediol *on page 199*

♦ **Hydroxydaunomycin Hydrochloride** *see* DOXOrubicin *on page 410*

♦ **Hydroxyethyl Starch** *see* Hetastarch *on page 619*

♦ **Hydroxyldaunorubicin Hydrochloride** *see* DOXOrubicin *on page 410*

Hydroxyurea *(hye droks ee yoor EE a)*

Related Information

Antiretroviral Therapy for HIV Infection *on page 1448*

U.S. Brand Names Droxia™; Hydrea®; Mylocel™

Synonyms Hydroxycarbamide

Therapeutic Category Antineoplastic Agent, Antimetabolite (Ribonucleotide Reductase Inhibitor)

Use CML in chronic phase; radiosensitizing agent in the treatment of primary brain tumors, head and neck tumors, uterine cervix and nonsmall cell lung cancer, and psoriasis; treatment of hematologic conditions such as essential thrombocythemia, polycythemia vera, hypereosinophilia, and hyperleukocytosis due to acute leukemia. Has shown activity against renal cell cancer, melanoma, ovarian cancer, head and neck cancer (excluding lip cancer), and prostate cancer.

Orphan drug: Droxia™: Sickle cell anemia: Specifically for patients >18 years of age who have had at least three "painful crises" in the previous year - to reduce frequency of these crises and the need for blood transfusions

Unlabeled/Investigational Use Treatment of HIV; treatment of psoriasis

Pregnancy Risk Factor D

Contraindications Hypersensitivity to hydroxyurea or any component of the formulation; severe anemia; severe bone marrow suppression; WBC <2500/mm^3 or platelet count <100,000/mm^3; pregnancy

Warnings/Precautions The U.S. Food and Drug Administration (FDA) currently recommends that procedures for proper handling and disposal of antineoplastic agents be considered. Use with caution in patients with renal impairment, in patients who have received prior irradiation therapy with exacerbation of postirradiation erythema, bone marrow suppression, erythrocytic abnormalities, mucositis, and in the elderly. May cause pancreatitis, neuropathy, or hepatotoxicity; risk is increased in HIV-infected patients receiving didanosine and/or stavudine. With long-term use (myeloproliferative disorders), secondary leukemias have been reported.

Common Adverse Reactions Frequency not defined.

Cardiovascular: Edema

Central nervous system: Drowsiness (with high doses), hallucinations, headache, dizziness, disorientation, seizures, fever, chills

Dermatologic: Erythema of the hands and face, maculopapular rash, pruritus, dry skin, dermatomyositis-like skin changes, hyperpigmentation, atrophy of skin and nails, scaling and violet papules (long-term use), nail banding, skin cancer

Endocrine & metabolic: Hyperuricemia

Gastrointestinal: Nausea, vomiting, stomatitis, anorexia, diarrhea, constipation, mucositis (potentiated in patients receiving radiation), pancreatitis, ulceration of buccal mucosa and GI epithelium (severe intoxication)

Emetic potential: Low (10% to 30%)

Genitourinary: Dysuria

Hematologic: Myelosuppression (primarily leukopenia); Dose-limiting toxicity, causes a rapid drop in leukocyte count (seen in 4-5 days in nonhematologic malignancy and more rapidly in leukemia); thrombocytopenia and anemia occur less often

Onset: 24-48 hours

Nadir: 10 days

Recovery: 7 days after stopping drug (reversal of WBC count occurs rapidly but the platelet count may take 7-10 days to recover)

Other hematologic effects include megaloblastic erythropoiesis, macrocytosis, hemolysis, decreased serum iron, persistent cytopenias, secondary leukemias (long-term use)

Hepatic: Elevation of hepatic enzymes, hepatotoxicity, hyperbilirubinemia (polycythemia vera)

Neuromuscular & skeletal: Weakness, peripheral neuropathy

Renal: Increased creatinine and BUN due to impairment of renal tubular function

Respiratory: Acute diffuse pulmonary infiltrates (rare), dyspnea, pulmonary fibrosis

Drug Interactions

Increased Effect/Toxicity: Zidovudine, zalcitabine, didanosine may increase synergy. The potential for neurotoxicity may increase with concomitant administration with fluorouracil. Hydroxyurea modulates the metabolism and cytotoxicity of cytarabine; dose reduction is recommended. Hydroxyurea may precipitate didanosine- or stavudine-induced pancreatitis, hepatotoxicity, or neuropathy; concomitant use is not recommended.

Mechanism of Action Thought to interfere (unsubstantiated hypothesis) with synthesis of DNA, during the S phase of cell division, without interfering with RNA synthesis; inhibits ribonucleoside diphosphate reductase, preventing conversion of ribonucleotides to deoxyribonucleotides; cell-cycle specific for the S phase and may hold other cells in the G_1 phase of the cell cycle.

Pharmacodynamics/Kinetics

Absorption: Readily (≥80%)

Distribution: Readily crosses blood-brain barrier; well into intestine, brain, lung, kidney tissues, effusions and ascites; enters breast milk

Metabolism: Hepatic and via GI tract; 50% degradation by enzymes of intestinal bacteria

Half-life elimination: 3-4 hours

Time to peak: ~2 hours

Excretion: Urine (80%, 50% as unchanged drug, 30% as urea); exhaled gases (as CO_2)

Dosage Oral (refer to individual protocols): All dosage should be based on ideal or actual body weight, whichever is less:

Children:

No FDA-approved dosage regimens have been established; dosages of 1500-3000 mg/m^2 as a single dose in combination with other agents every 4-6 weeks have been used in the treatment of pediatric astrocytoma, medulloblastoma, and primitive neuroectodermal tumors

CML: Initial: 10-20 mg/kg/day once daily; adjust dose according to hematologic response

Adults: Dose should always be titrated to patient response and WBC counts; usual oral doses range from 10-30 mg/kg/day or 500-3000 mg/day; if WBC count falls to <2500 cells/mm^3, or

(Continued)

Hydroxyurea *(Continued)*

the platelet count to <100,000/mm^3, therapy should be stopped for at least 3 days and resumed when values rise toward normal

Solid tumors:

Intermittent therapy: 80 mg/kg as a single dose every third day

Continuous therapy: 20-30 mg/kg/day given as a single dose/day

Concomitant therapy with irradiation: 80 mg/kg as a single dose every third day starting at least 7 days before initiation of irradiation

Resistant chronic myelocytic leukemia: Continuous therapy: 20-30 mg/kg as a single daily dose

HIV (unlabeled use; in combination with antiretroviral agents): 1000-1500 mg daily in a single dose or divided doses

Psoriasis (unlabeled use): 1000-1500 mg/day in a single dose or divided doses

Sickle cell anemia (moderate/severe disease): Initial: 15 mg/kg/day, increased by 5 mg/kg every 12 weeks if blood counts are in an acceptable range until the maximum tolerated dose of 35 mg/kg/day is achieved or the dose that does not produce toxic effects

Acceptable range:

Neutrophils ≥2500 cells/mm^3

Platelets ≥95,000/mm^3

Hemoglobin >5.3 g/dL, and

Reticulocytes ≥95,000/mm^3 if the hemoglobin concentration is <9 g/dL

Toxic range:

Neutrophils <2000 cells/mm^3

Platelets <80,000/mm^3

Hemoglobin <4.5 g/dL

Reticulocytes <80,000/mm^3 if the hemoglobin concentration is <9 g/dL

Monitor for toxicity every 2 weeks; if toxicity occurs, stop treatment until the bone marrow recovers; restart at 2.5 mg/kg/day less than the dose at which toxicity occurs; if no toxicity occurs over the next 12 weeks, then the subsequent dose should be increased by 2.5 mg/kg/day; reduced dosage of hydroxyurea alternating with erythropoietin may decrease myelotoxicity and increase levels of fetal hemoglobin in patients who have not been helped by hydroxyurea alone

Dosing adjustment in renal impairment:

Sickle cell anemia: Cl$_{cr}$ <60 mL/minute or ESRD: Reduce initial dose to 7.5 mg/kg; titrate to response/avoidance of toxicity (refer to usual dosing)

Other indications:

Cl$_{cr}$ 10-50 mL/minute: Administer 50% of normal dose

Cl$_{cr}$ <10 mL/minute: Administer 20% of normal dose

Hemodialysis: Supplemental dose is not necessary. Hydroxyurea is a low molecular weight compound with high aqueous solubility that may be freely dialyzable, however, clinical studies confirming this hypothesis have not been performed; peak serum concentrations are reached within 2 hours after oral administration and by 24 hours, the concentration in the serum is zero

CAPD effects: Unknown

CAVH effects: Dose for GFR 10-50 mL/minute

Administration Capsules may be opened and emptied into water (will not dissolve completely).

Monitoring Parameters CBC with differential, platelets, hemoglobin, renal function and liver function tests, serum uric acid

Patient Information Take capsules exactly on schedule directed by prescriber (dosage and timing will be specific to purpose of therapy). Contents of capsule may be emptied into a glass of water and taken immediately. You will require frequent monitoring and blood tests while taking this medication to assess effectiveness and monitor adverse reactions. You will be susceptible to infection; avoid crowds, infected persons, and persons with contagious diseases. You may experience nausea, vomiting, or loss of appetite (small frequent meals, frequent mouth care, sucking lozenges, or chewing gum may help); constipation (increased exercise, fluid, or dietary fiber may help); diarrhea (buttermilk, boiled milk, or yogurt may help); mouth sores (frequent mouth care will help). Report persistent vomiting, diarrhea, constipation, stomach pain, or mouth sores; skin rash, redness, irritation, or sores; painful or difficult urination; increased confusion, depression, hallucinations, lethargy, or seizures; persistent fever or chills, unusual fatigue, white plaques in mouth, vaginal discharge, or unhealed sores; unusual lassitude, weakness, or muscle tremors; easy bruising/bleeding; or blood in vomitus, stool, or urine. People not taking hydroxyurea should not be exposed to it; if powder from capsule is spilled, wipe up with damp, disposable towel immediately, and discard the towel in a closed container, such as a plastic bag; wash hands thoroughly. Contraceptive measures are recommended during therapy.

Dosage Forms CAP: 500 mg; (Droxia™): 200 mg, 300 mg, 400 mg; (Hydrea®): 500 mg. **TAB** (Mylocel™): 1000 mg

♦ **25-Hydroxyvitamin D$_3$** *see* Calcifediol *on page 199*

HydrOXYzine *(hye DROKS i zeen)*

U.S. Brand Names Atarax®; Vistaril®

Synonyms Hydroxyzine Hydrochloride; Hydroxyzine Pamoate

Therapeutic Category Antianxiety Agent; Antiemetic; Antihistamine; Sedative

Use Treatment of anxiety; preoperative sedative; antipruritic

Unlabeled/Investigational Use Antiemetic; ethanol withdrawal symptoms

Pregnancy Risk Factor C

Contraindications Hypersensitivity to hydroxyzine or any component of the formulation

Warnings/Precautions Causes sedation, caution must be used in performing tasks which require alertness (eg, operating machinery or driving). Sedative effects of CNS depressants or ethanol are potentiated. S.C., intra-arterial, and I.V. administration are not recommended since thrombosis and digital gangrene can occur; extravasation can result in sterile abscess and marked tissue induration; should be used with caution in patients with narrow-angle glaucoma, prostatic hypertrophy, and bladder neck obstruction; should also be used with caution in patients with asthma or COPD.

Anticholinergic effects are not well tolerated in the elderly. Hydroxyzine may be useful as a short-term antipruritic, but it is not recommended for use as a sedative or anxiolytic in the elderly.

Common Adverse Reactions Frequency not defined.
Central nervous system: Drowsiness, headache, fatigue, nervousness, dizziness
Gastrointestinal: Xerostomia
Neuromuscular & skeletal: Tremor, paresthesia, seizure
Ocular: Blurred vision
Respiratory: Thickening of bronchial secretions

Drug Interactions
Cytochrome P450 Effect: Inhibits CYP2D6 (weak)
Increased Effect/Toxicity: CNS depressants, anticholinergics, used in combination with hydroxyzine may result in additive effects.

Mechanism of Action Competes with histamine for H_1-receptor sites on effector cells in the gastrointestinal tract, blood vessels, and respiratory tract. Possesses skeletal muscle relaxing, bronchodilator, antihistamine, antiemetic, and analgesic properties.

Pharmacodynamics/Kinetics
Onset of action: 15-30 minutes
Duration: 4-6 hours
Absorption: Oral: Rapid
Metabolism: Exact fate unknown
Half-life elimination: 3-7 hours
Time to peak: ~2 hours

Dosage
Children:
Oral: 0.6 mg/kg/dose every 6 hours
I.M.: 0.5-1.1 mg/kg/dose every 4-6 hours as needed
Adults:
Antiemetic: I.M.: 25-100 mg/dose every 4-6 hours as needed
Anxiety: Oral: 25-100 mg 4 times/day; maximum dose: 600 mg/day
Preoperative sedation:
Oral: 50-100 mg
I.M.: 25-100 mg
Management of pruritus: Oral: 25 mg 3-4 times/day

Dosing interval in hepatic impairment: Change dosing interval to every 24 hours in patients with primary biliary cirrhosis

Administration For I.M. administration in children, injections should be made into the midlateral muscles of the thigh; S.C., intra-arterial, and I.V. administration **not** recommended since thrombosis and digital gangrene can occur

Monitoring Parameters Relief of symptoms, mental status, blood pressure

Patient Information Will cause drowsiness, avoid alcohol and other CNS depressants, avoid driving and other hazardous tasks until the CNS effects are known

Dosage Forms CAP, as pamoate (Vistaril®): 25 mg, 50 mg, 100 mg. **INJ, solution, as hydrochloride:** 25 mg/mL (1 mL); 50 mg/mL (1 mL, 2 mL, 10 mL); (Vistaril® [DSC]): 50 mg/mL (10 mL). **SUSP, oral, as pamoate** (Vistaril®): 25 mg/5 mL (120 mL, 480 mL). **SYR, as hydrochloride:** 10 mg/5 mL (120 mL, 480 mL); (Atarax®): 10 mg/5 mL (480 mL). **TAB, as hydrochloride:** 10 mg, 25 mg, 50 mg; (Atarax®): 10 mg, 25 mg, 50 mg, 100 mg

- ◆ **Hydroxyzine Hydrochloride** *see* HydrOXYzine *on page 640*
- ◆ **Hydroxyzine Pamoate** *see* HydrOXYzine *on page 640*
- ◆ **Hygroton** *see* Chlorthalidone *on page 268*
- ◆ **Hylorel®** *see* Guanadrel *on page 607*
- ◆ **Hyoscine** *see* Scopolamine *on page 1126*

Hyoscyamine (hye oh SYE a meen)

U.S. Brand Names Anaspaz®; Cystospaz®; Cystospaz-M®; Hyosine; Levbid®; Levsin®; Levsinex®; Levsin/SL®; NuLev™; Spacol; Spacol T/S; Symax SL; Symax SR

Synonyms Hyoscyamine Sulfate; *l*-Hyoscyamine Sulfate

Therapeutic Category Anticholinergic Agent; Antispasmodic Agent, Gastrointestinal

Use
Oral: Adjunctive therapy for peptic ulcers, irritable bowel, neurogenic bladder/bowel; treatment of infant colic, GI tract disorders caused by spasm; to reduce rigidity, tremors, sialorrhea, and hyperhidrosis associated with parkinsonism; as a drying agent in acute rhinitis
Injection: Preoperative antimuscarinic to reduce secretions and block cardiac vagal inhibitory reflexes; to improve radiologic visibility of the kidneys; symptomatic relief of biliary and renal colic; reduce GI motility to facilitate diagnostic procedures (ie, endoscopy, hypotonic duodenography); reduce pain and hypersecretion in pancreatitis, certain cases of partial heart block associated with vagal activity; reversal of neuromuscular blockade

(Continued)

Hyoscyamine *(Continued)*

Pregnancy Risk Factor C

Contraindications Hypersensitivity to belladonna alkaloids or any component of the formulation; glaucoma; obstructive uropathy; myasthenia gravis; obstructive GI tract disease, paralytic ileus, intestinal atony of elderly or debilitated patients, severe ulcerative colitis, toxic megacolon complicating ulcerative colitis; unstable cardiovascular status in acute hemorrhage, myocardial ischemia

Warnings/Precautions Heat prostration may occur in hot weather. Diarrhea may be a sign of incomplete intestinal obstruction, treatment should be discontinued if this occurs. May produce side effects as seen with other anticholinergic medications including drowsiness, dizziness, blurred vision, or psychosis. Children and the elderly may be more susceptible to these effects. Use with caution in children with spastic paralysis. Use with caution in patients with autonomic neuropathy, coronary heart disease, CHF, cardiac arrhythmias, prostatic hyperplasia, hyperthyroidism, hypertension, chronic lung disease, renal disease, and hiatal hernia associated with reflux esophagitis. Use with caution in the elderly, may precipitate undiagnosed glaucoma and/or severely impair memory function (especially in those patients with previous memory problems).

NuLev™: Contains phenylalanine

Common Adverse Reactions Frequency not defined.

Cardiovascular: Palpitations, tachycardia

Central nervous system: Ataxia, dizziness, drowsiness, headache, insomnia, mental confusion/excitement, nervousness, speech disorder, weakness

Dermatologic: Urticaria

Endocrine & metabolic: Lactation suppression

Gastrointestinal: Bloating, constipation, dry mouth, loss of taste, nausea, vomiting

Genitourinary: Impotence, urinary hesitancy, urinary retention

Ocular: Blurred vision, cycloplegia, increased ocular tension, mydriasis

Miscellaneous: Allergic reactions, sweating decreased

Drug Interactions

Increased Effect/Toxicity: Increased toxicity with amantadine, antihistamines, antimuscarinics, haloperidol, phenothiazines, tricyclic antidepressants, and MAO inhibitors.

Decreased Effect: Decreased effect with antacids.

Mechanism of Action Blocks the action of acetylcholine at parasympathetic sites in smooth muscle, secretory glands and the CNS; increases cardiac output, dries secretions, antagonizes histamine and serotonin

Pharmacodynamics/Kinetics

Onset of action: 2-3 minutes

Duration: 4-6 hours

Absorption: Well absorbed

Distribution: Crosses placenta; small amounts enter breast milk

Protein binding: 50%

Metabolism: Hepatic

Half-life elimination: 3-5 hours

Excretion: Urine

Dosage

Oral: Children: Gastrointestinal disorders: Dose as listed, based on age and weight (kg) using 0.125 mg/mL drops; repeat dose every 4 hours as needed:

Children <2 years:

3.4 kg: 4 drops; maximum: 24 drops/24 hours

5 kg: 5 drops; maximum: 30 drops/24 hours

7 kg: 6 drops; maximum: 36 drops/24 hours

10 kg: 8 drops; maximum: 48 drops/24 hours

Oral, S.L.:

Children 2-12 years: Gastrointestinal disorders: Dose as listed, based on age and weight (kg); repeat dose every 4 hours as needed:

10 kg: 0.031-0.033 mg; maximum: 0.75 mg/24 hours

20 kg: 0.0625 mg; maximum: 0.75 mg/24 hours

40 kg: 0.0938 mg; maximum: 0.75 mg/24 hours

50 kg: 0.125 mg; maximum: 0.75 mg/24 hours

Children >12 years and Adults: Gastrointestinal disorders: 0.125-0.25 mg every 4 hours or as needed (before meals or food); maximum: 1.5 mg/24 hours

Cystospaz®: 0.15-0.3 mg up to 4 times/day

Oral (timed release): Children >12 years and Adults: Gastrointestinal disorders: 0.375-0.75 mg every 12 hours; maximum: 1.5 mg/24 hours

I.M., I.V., S.C.: Children >12 years and Adults: Gastrointestinal disorders: 0.25-0.5 mg; may repeat as needed up to 4 times/day, at 4-hour intervals

I.V.: Children >2 year and Adults: I.V.: Preanesthesia: 5 mcg/kg given 30-60 minutes prior to induction of anesthesia or at the time preoperative narcotics or sedatives are administered

I.V.: Adults: Diagnostic procedures: 0.25-0.5 mg given 5-10 minutes prior to procedure

To reduce drug-induced bradycardia during surgery: 0.125 mg; repeat as needed

To reverse neuromuscular blockade: 0.2 mg for every 1 mg neostigmine (or the physostigmine/pyridostigmine equivalent)

Administration

Oral: Tablets should be administered before meals or food.

Levbid®: Tablets are scored and may be broken in half for dose titration; do not crush or chew.

Levsin/SL®: Tablets may be used sublingually, chewed, or swallowed whole.

NuLev™: Tablet is placed on tongue and allowed to disintegrate before swallowing; may take with or without water.

Symax SL: Tablets may be used sublingually or swallowed whole.

I.M.: May be administered without dilution.

Inject over at least 1 minute. May be administered without dilution.

Patient Information Maintain good oral hygiene habits, because lack of saliva may increase chance of cavities. Observe caution while driving or performing other tasks requiring alertness, as may cause drowsiness, dizziness, or blurred vision. Report skin rash, flushing, or eye pain occurs; or if difficulty in urinating, constipation or sensitivity to light becomes severe or persists.

Dosage Forms CAP, timed release (Cystospaz-M®, Levsinex®): 0.375 mg. **ELIX:** 0.125 mg/5 mL (480 mL); (Hyosine, Levsin®): 0.125 mg/5 mL (480 mL). **INJ, solution** (Levsin®): 0.5 mg/ mL (1 mL). **LIQ** (Spacol): 0.125 mg/5 mL (120 mL). **SOLN, oral drops:** 0.125 mg/mL (15 mL); (Hyosine, Levsin®): 0.125 mg/mL (15 mL). **TAB** (Cystospaz®): 0.15 mg. **TAB** (Anaspaz®, Levsin®, Spacol): 0.125 mg. **TAB, extended release** (Levbid®, Symax SR, Spacol T/S): 0.375 mg. **TAB, orally-disintegrating** (NuLev™): 0.125 mg. **TAB, sublingual:** 0.125 mg; (Levsin/ SL®, Symax SL): 0.125 mg

Hyoscyamine, Atropine, Scopolamine, and Phenobarbital

(hye oh SYE a meen, A troe peen, skoe POL a meen, & fee noe BAR bi tal)

U.S. Brand Names Donnatal®; Donnatal Extentabs®

Synonyms Atropine, Hyoscyamine, Scopolamine, and Phenobarbital; Phenobarbital, Hyoscyamine, Atropine, and Scopolamine; Scopolamine, Hyoscyamine, Atropine, and Phenobarbital

Therapeutic Category Anticholinergic Agent; Antispasmodic Agent, Gastrointestinal

Use Adjunct in treatment of irritable bowel syndrome, acute enterocolitis, duodenal ulcer

Pregnancy Risk Factor C

Dosage Oral:

Children: Donnatal® elixir: To be given every 4-6 hours; initial dose based on weight:

4.5 kg: 0.5 mL every 4 hours **or** 0.75 mL every 6 hours

10 kg: 1 mL every 4 hours **or** 1.5 mL every 6 hours

14 kg: 1.5 mL every 4 hours **or** 2 mL every 6 hours

23 kg: 2.5 mL every 4 hours **or** 3.8 mL every 6 hours

34 kg: 3.8 mL every 4 hours **or** 5 mL every 6 hours

≥45 kg: 5 mL every 4 hours **or** 7.5 mL every 6 hours

Adults:

Donnatal®: 1-2 tablets or 5-10 mL of elixir 3-4 times/day

Donnatal Extentabs®: 1 tablet every 12 hours; may increase to 1 tablet every 8 hours if needed

Dosage Forms ELIX (Donnatal®): Hyoscyamine 0.1037 mg, atropine 0.0194 mg, scopolamine 0.0065 mg, and phenobarbital 16.2 mg per 5 mL (120 mL, 480 mL, 4000 mL). **TAB** (Donnatal®): Hyoscyamine 0.1037 mg, atropine 0.0194 mg, scopolamine 0.0065 mg, and phenobarbital 16.2 mg. **TAB, extended release** (Donnatal Extentabs®): Hyoscyamine sulfate 0.3111 mg, atropine sulfate 0.0582 mg, scopolamine hydrobromide 0.0195 mg, and phenobarbital 48.6 mg

♦ **Hyoscyamine, Methenamine, Sodium Biphosphate, Phenyl Salicylate, and Methylene Blue** see Methenamine, Sodium Biphosphate, Phenyl Salicylate, Methylene Blue, and Hyoscyamine on page 812

♦ **Hyoscyamine Sulfate** see Hyoscyamine on page 641

♦ **Hyosine** see Hyoscyamine on page 641

♦ **Hyperstat®** see Diazoxide on page 366

♦ **Hypoglycemic Drugs & Thiazolidinedione Information** see page 1378

♦ **Hyrexin-50®** see DiphenhydrAMINE on page 383

♦ **Hytakerol®** see Dihydrotachysterol on page 379

♦ **Hytinic® [OTC]** see Polysaccharide-Iron Complex on page 1016

♦ **Hytone®** see Hydrocortisone on page 632

♦ **Hytrin®** see Terazosin on page 1197

♦ **Hytuss® [OTC]** see Guaifenesin on page 603

♦ **Hytuss-2X® [OTC]** see Guaifenesin on page 603

♦ **Hyzaar®** see Losartan and Hydrochlorothiazide on page 763

♦ **131 I Anti-B1 Antibody** see Tositumomab and Iodine I 131 Tositumomab on page 1248

♦ **131 I-Anti-B1 Monoclonal Antibody** see Tositumomab and Iodine I 131 Tositumomab on page 1248

♦ **Iberet® [OTC]** see Vitamins (Multiple/Oral) on page 1312

♦ **Iberet®-500 [OTC]** see Vitamins (Multiple/Oral) on page 1312

♦ **Iberet-Folic-500®** see Vitamins (Multiple/Oral) on page 1312

♦ **Ibidomide Hydrochloride** see Labetalol on page 710

Ibritumomab (ib ri TYOO mo mab)

U.S. Brand Names Zevalin™

Synonyms Ibritumomab Tiuxetan; In-111 Zevalin; Y-90 Zevalin

Therapeutic Category Antineoplastic Agent, Monoclonal Antibody; Radiopharmaceutical

Use Treatment of relapsed or refractory low-grade, follicular, or transformed B-cell non-Hodgkin's lymphoma (including rituximab-refractory follicular non-Hodgkin's lymphoma) (Continued)

Ibritumomab (Continued)

as part of a therapeutic regimen with rituximab (Zevalin™ therapeutic regimen); **not to be used as single-agent therapy**; must be radiolabeled prior to use

Pregnancy Risk Factor D

Contraindications Known type I hypersensitivity or anaphylactic reactions to murine proteins, rituximab, yttrium chloride, indium chloride, or any component of the formulation; ≥25% lymphoma marrow involvement; prior myeloablative therapies; platelet count <100,000 cells/mm³; neutrophil count <1500 cells/mm³; hypocellular bone marrow (≤15% cellularity of marked reduction in bone marrow precursors); history of failed stem cell collection; pregnancy; breast-feeding. Y-90 ibritumomab should not be administered to patients with altered In-111 ibritumomab biodistribution.

Warnings/Precautions To be used as part of the Zevalin™ therapeutic regimen (in combination with rituximab). The contents of the kit are not radioactive until radiolabeling occurs. During and after radiolabeling, adequate shielding should be used with this product, in accordance with institutional radiation safety practices.

Severe, potentially-fatal infusion reactions (angioedema, bronchospasm, hypotension, hypoxia) have been reported, typically during the first rituximab infusion (during infusion or within 30-120 minutes of infusion). Patients should be screened for human antimouse antibodies (HAMA); may be at increased risk of allergic or serious hypersensitivity reactions. Interrupt infusion for severe reactions. Consult additional warnings for rituximab. Therapy is associated with severe hematologic adverse events (thrombocytopenia, neutropenia), severe infections, and hemorrhage (including fatal cerebral hemorrhage). Do not administer to patients with impaired bone marrow reserve (see Contraindications).

Safety and efficacy of repeated courses of the therapeutic regimen have not been established. Safety and efficacy have not been established in pediatric patients.

Common Adverse Reactions Severe, potentially life-threatening allergic reactions have occurred in association with infusions. Also refer to Rituximab monograph.

>10%:

Central nervous system: Chills (24%), fever (17%), pain (13%), headache (12%)

Gastrointestinal: Nausea (31%), abdominal pain (16%), vomiting (12%)

Hematologic: Thrombocytopenia (95%), neutropenia (77%), anemia (61%)

  Myelosuppressive:

    WBC: Severe

    Platelets: Severe

    Nadir: 7-9 weeks

    Recovery: 22-35 days

Neuromuscular & skeletal: Weakness (43%)

Respiratory: Dyspnea (14%)

Miscellaneous: Infection (29%)

1% to 10%:

Cardiovascular: Peripheral edema (8%), hypotension (6%), flushing (6%), angioedema (5%)

Central nervous system: Dizziness (10%), insomnia (5%), anxiety (4%)

Dermatologic: Pruritus (9%), rash (8%), urticaria (4%), petechia (3%)

Gastrointestinal: Diarrhea (9%), anorexia (8%), abdominal distension (5%), constipation (5%), dyspepsia (4%), melena (2%; life threatening in 1%), gastrointestinal hemorrhage (1%)

Hematologic: Bruising (7%), pancytopenia (2%), secondary malignancies (2%)

Neuromuscular & skeletal: Back pain (8%), arthralgia (7%), myalgia (7%)

Respiratory: Cough (10%), throat irritation (10%), rhinitis (6%), bronchospasm (5%), epistaxis (3%), apnea (1%)

Miscellaneous: Diaphoresis (4%), allergic reaction (2%; life-threatening in 1%)

Drug Interactions

Increased Effect/Toxicity: Due to the high incidence of thrombocytopenia associated with ibritumomab, the use of agents which decrease platelet function may be associated with a higher risk of bleeding (includes aspirin, NSAIDs, glycoprotein IIb/IIIa antagonists, clopidogrel and ticlopidine). In addition, the risk of bleeding may be increased with anticoagulant agents, including heparin, low molecular weight heparins, thrombolytics, and warfarin. The safety of live viral vaccines has not been established.

Decreased Effect: Response to vaccination may be impaired.

Mechanism of Action Ibritumomab is a monoclonal antibody directed against the CD20 antigen found on B lymphocytes (normal and malignant). Ibritumomab binding induces apoptosis in B lymphocytes *in vitro*. It is combined with the chelator tiuxetan, which acts as a specific chelation site for either Indium-111 (In-111) or Yttrium-90 (Y-90). The monoclonal antibody acts as a delivery system to direct the radioactive isotope to the targeted cells, however, binding has been observed in lymphoid cells throughout the body and in lymphoid nodules in organs such as the large and small intestines. Indium-111 is a gamma-emitter used to assess biodistribution of ibritumomab, while Y-90 emits beta particles. Beta-emission induces cellular damage through the formation of free radicals (in both target cells and surrounding cells).

Pharmacodynamics/Kinetics

Duration: Beta cell recovery begins in ~12 weeks; generally in normal range within 9 months

Distribution: To lymphoid cells throughout the body and in lymphoid nodules in organs such as the large and small intestines, spleen, testes, and liver

Metabolism: Has not been characterized; the product of yttrium-90 radioactive decay is zirconium-90 (nonradioactive); Indium-111 decays to cadmium-111 (nonradioactive)

Half-life elimination: Y-90 ibritumomab: 30 hours; Indium-111 decays with a physical half-life of 67 hours; Yttrium-90 decays with a physical half-life of 64 hours

Excretion: A median of 7.2% of the radiolabeled activity was excreted in urine over 7 days

Dosage I.V.: Adults: Ibritumomab is administered **only** as part of the Zevalin™ therapeutic regimen (a combined treatment regimen with rituximab). The regimen consists of two steps:

Step 1:

Rituximab infusion: 250 mg/m^2 at an initial rate of 50 mg/hour. If hypersensitivity or infusion-related events do not occur, increase infusion in increments of 50 mg/hour every 30 minutes, to a maximum of 400 mg/hour. Infusions should be temporarily slowed or interrupted if hypersensitivity or infusion-related events occur. The infusion may be resumed at one-half the previous rate upon improvement of symptoms.

In-111 ibritumomab infusion: Within 4 hours of the completion of rituximab infusion, inject 5 mCi (1.6 mg total antibody dose) over 10 minutes.

Biodistribution of In-111 ibritumomab should be assessed by imaging at 2-24 hours and at 48-72 hours postinjection. An optional third imaging may be performed 90-120 hours following injection. If biodistribution is not acceptable, the patient should not proceed to Step 2.

Step 2 (initiated 7-9 days following Step 1):

Rituximab infusion: 250 mg/m^2 at an initial rate of 100 mg/hour (50 mg/hour if infusion-related events occurred with the first infusion). If hypersensitivity or infusion-related events do not occur, increase infusion in increments of 100 mg/hour every 30 minutes, to a maximum of 400 mg/hour, as tolerated.

Y-90 ibritumomab infusion: Within 4 hours of the completion of rituximab infusion:

Platelet count >150,000 cells/mm^3: Inject 4 mCi (14.8 MBq/kg actual body weight) over 10 minutes

Platelet count between 100,000-149,000 cells/mm^3: Inject 3 mCi (11.1 MBq/kg actual body weight) over 10 minutes

Platelet count <100,000 cells/mm^3: Do **not** administer

Maximum dose: The prescribed, measured, and administered dose of Y-90 ibritumomab must not exceed 32 mCi (1184 MBq), regardless of the patient's body weight

Administration

Rituximab: Administer the first infusion of rituximab at an initial rate of 50 mg/hour. If hypersensitivity or infusion-related events do not occur, escalate the infusion rate in 50 mg/hour increments every 30 minutes, to a maximum of 400 mg/hour. If hypersensitivity or an infusion-related event develops, temporarily slow or interrupt the infusion (discontinue if reaction is severe). The infusion can continue at one-half the previous rate upon improvement of patient symptoms. Subsequent rituximab infusion can be administered at an initial rate of 100 mg/hour and increased in 100 mg/hour increments at 30-minute intervals, to a maximum of 400 mg/hour as tolerated.

Ibritumomab: Inject slowly, over 10 minutes. Use syringe shield. Appropriate measures should be undertaken to minimize radiation exposure to patients and medical personnel.

Monitoring Parameters Human antimurine antibody (HAMA) prior to treatment (if positive, may have an allergic or hypersensitivity reaction when treated with this or other murine or chimeric monoclonal antibodies).

Patients must be monitored for infusion-related allergic reactions (typically within 30-120 minutes of administration). Obtain complete blood counts and platelet counts at regular intervals during rituximab therapy (at least weekly and more frequently in patients who develop cytopenia). Platelet count must be obtained prior to step 2. Monitor for up to 3 months after use.

Biodistribution of In-111 ibritumomab should be assessed by imaging at 2-24 hours and at 48-72 hours post injection. An optional third imaging may be performed 90-120 hours following injection. If biodistribution is not acceptable, the patient should not proceed to Step 2.

Dosage Forms Each kit contains 4 vials for preparation of either In-111 or Y-90 conjugate (as indicated on container label): **INJ, solution:** 1.6 mg/mL (2 mL) [supplied with sodium acetate solution, formulation buffer vial (includes albumin 750 mg), and an empty reaction vial]

♦ **Ibritumomab Tiuxetan** see Ibritumomab on page 643

♦ **Ibu-200 [OTC]** see Ibuprofen on page 645

Ibuprofen (eye byoo PROE fen)

Related Information

Narcotic Agonists Comparison on page 1395
Nonsteroidal Anti-Inflammatory Agents Comparison on page 1401

U.S. Brand Names Advil® [OTC]; Advil® Children's [OTC]; Advil® Infants' [OTC]; Advil® Junior [OTC]; Advil® Migraine [OTC]; Genpril® [OTC]; Haltran® [OTC] [DSC]; Ibu-200 [OTC]; I-Prin [OTC]; Menadol® [OTC]; Midol® Maximum Strength Cramp Formula [OTC]; Motrin®; Motrin® Children's [OTC]; Motrin® IB [OTC]; Motrin® Infants' [OTC]; Motrin® Junior Strength [OTC]; Motrin® Migraine Pain [OTC]; Proprinal [OTC]; Ultraprin [OTC]

Synonyms p-Isobutylhydratropic Acid

Therapeutic Category Analgesic, Nonsteroidal Anti-inflammatory Drug; Anti-inflammatory Agent; Antimigraine Agent, Prophylaxis; Antipyretic; Nonsteroidal Anti-inflammatory Drug (NSAID), Oral

Use Inflammatory diseases and rheumatoid disorders including juvenile rheumatoid arthritis, mild to moderate pain, fever, dysmenorrhea

Unlabeled/Investigational Use Cystic fibrosis, gout, ankylosing spondylitis, acute migraine headache

(Continued)

Ibuprofen *(Continued)*

Pregnancy Risk Factor B/D (3rd trimester)

Contraindications Hypersensitivity to ibuprofen, any component of the formulation, aspirin, or other NSAIDs; patients with "aspirin triad" (bronchial asthma, aspirin intolerance, rhinitis); pregnancy (3rd trimester)

Warnings/Precautions Use with caution in patients with CHF, hypertension, dehydration, decreased renal or hepatic function, history of GI disease (bleeding or ulcers), or those receiving anticoagulants. Consuming ≥3 alcoholic beverages/day may increase the risk of GI bleeding. Elderly are at a high risk for adverse effects from NSAIDs. As many as 60% of elderly can develop peptic ulceration and/or hemorrhage asymptomatically. Fatal asthmatic and anaphylactoid reactions have occurred in patients with "aspirin triad" (see Contraindications).

Use lowest effective dose for shortest period possible. Use of NSAIDs can compromise existing renal function especially when Cl_{cr} is <30 mL/minute. CNS adverse effects such as confusion, agitation, and hallucination are generally seen in overdose or high-dose situations; however, elderly may demonstrate these adverse effects at lower doses than younger adults. Do not exceed 3200 mg/day. Withhold for at least 4-6 half-lives prior to surgical or dental procedures.

OTC labeling: When used for self-medication, patients should be instructed to contact healthcare provider if used for fever lasting >3 days or for pain lasting >10 days in adults or >3 days in children.

Common Adverse Reactions

1% to 10%:

Cardiovascular: Edema (1% to 3%)

Central nervous system: Dizziness (3% to 9%), headache (1% to 3%), nervousness (1% to 3%)

Dermatologic: Itching (1% to 3%), rash (3% to 9%)

Endocrine & metabolic: Fluid retention (1% to 3%)

Gastrointestinal: Dyspepsia (1% to 3%), vomiting (1% to 3%), abdominal pain/cramps/distress (1% to 3%), heartburn (3% to 9%), nausea (3% to 9%), diarrhea (1% to 3%), constipation (1% to 3%), flatulence (1% to 3%), epigastric pain (3% to 9%), appetite decreased (1% to 3%)

Otic: Tinnitus (3% to 9%)

Drug Interactions

Cytochrome P450 Effect: Substrate (minor) of CYP2C8/9, 2C19; **Inhibits** CYP2C8/9 (strong)

Increased Effect/Toxicity: Ibuprofen may increase cyclosporine, digoxin, lithium, and methotrexate serum concentrations. The renal adverse effects of ACE inhibitors may be potentiated by NSAIDs. Corticosteroids may increase the risk of GI ulceration.

Decreased Effect: Aspirin may decrease ibuprofen serum concentrations. Ibuprofen may decrease the effect of some antihypertensive agents (including ACE inhibitors and angiotensin antagonists) and diuretics.

Mechanism of Action Inhibits prostaglandin synthesis by decreasing the activity of the enzyme, cyclooxygenase, which results in decreased formation of prostaglandin precursors

Pharmacodynamics/Kinetics

Onset of action: Analgesic: 30-60 minutes; Anti-inflammatory: ≤7 days

Peak effect: 1-2 weeks

Duration: 4-6 hours

Absorption: Oral: Rapid (85%)

Protein binding: 90% to 99%

Metabolism: Hepatic via oxidation

Half-life elimination: 2-4 hours; End-stage renal disease: Unchanged

Time to peak: ~1-2 hours

Excretion: Urine (1% as free drug); some feces

Dosage Oral:

Children:

Antipyretic: 6 months to 12 years: Temperature <102.5°F (39°C): 5 mg/kg/dose; temperature >102.5°F: 10 mg/kg/dose given every 6-8 hours (maximum daily dose: 40 mg/kg/day)

Juvenile rheumatoid arthritis: 30-50 mg/kg/24 hours divided every 8 hours; start at lower end of dosing range and titrate upward (maximum: 2.4 g/day)

Analgesic: 4-10 mg/kg/dose every 6-8 hours

Ibuprofen Dosing

Weight (lbs)	Age	Dosage (mg)
12-17	6-11 mo	50
18-23	12-23 mo	75
24-35	2-3 y	100
35-47	4-5 y	150
48-59	6-8 y	200
60-71	9-10 y	250
72-95	11 y	300

Cystic fibrosis (unlabeled use): Chronic (>4 years) twice daily dosing adjusted to maintain serum levels of 50-100 µg/mL has been associated with slowing of disease progression in younger patients with mild lung disease

OTC labeling (analgesic, antipyretic):

Children 6 months to 11 years: See table on previous page; use of weight to select dose is preferred; doses may be repeated every 6-8 hours (maximum: 4 doses/day)

Children ≥12 years: 200 mg every 4-6 hours as needed (maximum: 1200 mg/24 hours)

Adults:

Inflammatory disease: 400-800 mg/dose 3-4 times/day (maximum dose: 3.2 g/day)

Analgesia/pain/fever/dysmenorrhea: 200-400 mg/dose every 4-6 hours (maximum daily dose: 1.2 g, unless directed by physician)

OTC labeling (analgesic, antipyretic): 200 mg every 4-6 hours as needed (maximum: 1200 mg/24 hours)

Dosing adjustment/comments in severe hepatic impairment: Avoid use

Administration Administer with food

Monitoring Parameters CBC; occult blood loss and periodic liver function tests; monitor response (pain, range of motion, grip strength, mobility, ADL function), inflammation; observe for weight gain, edema; monitor renal function (urine output, serum BUN and creatinine); observe for bleeding, bruising; evaluate gastrointestinal effects (abdominal pain, bleeding, dyspepsia); mental confusion, disorientation; with long-term therapy, periodic ophthalmic exams

Reference Range Plasma concentrations >200 µg/mL may be associated with severe toxicity

Patient Information Serious gastrointestinal bleeding can occur as well as ulceration and perforation. Pain may or may not be present. Avoid aspirin and aspirin-containing products while taking this medication. If gastric upset occurs, take with food, milk, or antacid. If gastric adverse effects persist, contact prescriber. May cause drowsiness, dizziness, blurred vision, and confusion. Use caution when performing tasks that require alertness (eg, driving). Do not take for more than 3 days for fever or 10 days for pain without prescriber's advice.

Dosage Forms CAPLET 200 mg [OTC]; (Motrin® Junior Strength): 100 mg; (Advil®, Ibu-200, Menadol®, Motrin® IB, Motrin® Migraine Pain): 200 mg. **CAP, liqui-gel** (Advil®, Advil® Migraine): 200 mg. **GELCAP** (Advil®, Motrin® IB): 200 mg. **SUSP, oral:** 100 mg/5 mL (5 mL, 120 mL, 480 mL); (Advil® Children's, Motrin® Children's): 100 mg/5 mL (60 mL, 120 mL). **SUSP, oral drops:** 40 mg/mL (15 mL); (Advil® Infants', Motrin® Infants'): 40 mg/mL (15 mL, 30 mL). **TAB:** 200 mg [OTC], 400 mg, 600 mg, 800 mg; (Advil® Junior): 100 mg; (Advil®, Genpril®, Haltran® [DSC], I-Prin, Midol®, Maximum Strength Cramp Formula, Motrin® IB, Proprinal, Ultraprin): 200 mg; (Motrin®): 400 mg, 600 mg, 800 mg. **TAB, chewable** (Advil® Children's, Motrin® Children's): 50 mg; (Advil® Junior, Motrin® Junior Strength): 100 mg.

♦ **Ibuprofen and Hydrocodone** *see* Hydrocodone and Ibuprofen *on page 630*

♦ **Ibuprofen and Pseudoephedrine** *see* Pseudoephedrine and Ibuprofen *on page 1062*

Ibutilide (i BYOO ti lide)

U.S. Brand Names Corvert®

Synonyms Ibutilide Fumarate

Therapeutic Category Antiarrhythmic Agent, Class III

Use Acute termination of atrial fibrillation or flutter of recent onset; the effectiveness of ibutilide has not been determined in patients with arrhythmias >90 days in duration

Pregnancy Risk Factor C

Contraindications Hypersensitivity to ibutilide or any component of the formulation; QT_c >440 msec

Warnings/Precautions Potentially fatal arrhythmias (eg, polymorphic ventricular tachycardia) can occur with ibutilide, **usually** in association with torsade de pointes (QT prolongation). Studies indicate a 1.7% incidence of arrhythmias in treated patients. The drug should be given in a setting of continuous ECG monitoring and by personnel trained in treating arrhythmias particularly polymorphic ventricular tachycardia. Patients with chronic atrial fibrillation may not be the best candidates for ibutilide since they often revert after conversion and the risks of treatment may not be justified when compared to alternative management. Dosing adjustments are not required in patients with renal or hepatic dysfunction since a maximum of only two 10-minute infusions are utilized. Drug distribution, rather than administration, is one of the primary mechanisms responsible for termination of the pharmacologic effect. Safety and efficacy in children have not been established. Avoid any drug that can prolong QT interval. Correct hyperkalemia and hypomagnesemia before using. Monitor for heart block.

Common Adverse Reactions 1% to 10%:

Cardiovascular: Sustained polymorphic ventricular tachycardia (ie, torsade de pointes) (1.7%, often requiring cardioversion), nonsustained polymorphic ventricular tachycardia (2.7%), nonsustained monomorphic ventricular tachycardia (4.9%), ventricular extrasystoles (5.1%), nonsustained monomorphic VT (4.9%), tachycardia/supraventricular tachycardia (2.7%), hypotension (2%), bundle branch block (1.9%), AV block (1.5%), bradycardia (1.2%), QT segment prolongation, hypertension (1.2%), palpitations (1%)

Central nervous system: Headache (3.6%)

Gastrointestinal: Nausea (>1%)

Drug Interactions

Increased Effect/Toxicity: Class Ia antiarrhythmic drugs (disopyramide, quinidine, and procainamide) and other class III drugs such as amiodarone and sotalol should not be given concomitantly with ibutilide due to their potential to prolong refractoriness. Signs of digoxin toxicity may be masked when coadministered with ibutilide. Toxicity of ibutilide is potentiated by concurrent administration of other drugs which may prolong QT interval: phenothiazines, (Continued)

Ibutilide *(Continued)*

tricyclic and tetracyclic antidepressants, cisapride, sparfloxacin, gatifloxacin, moxifloxacin, erythromycin, and astemizole.

Mechanism of Action Exact mechanism of action is unknown; prolongs the action potential in cardiac tissue

Pharmacodynamics/Kinetics

Onset of action: ~90 minutes after start of infusion ($\frac{1}{2}$ of conversions to sinus rhythm occur during infusion)

Distribution: V_d: 11 L/kg

Protein binding: 40%

Metabolism: Extensively hepatic; oxidation

Half-life elimination: 2-12 hours (average: 6 hours)

Excretion: Urine (82%, 7% as unchanged drug and metabolites); feces (19%)

Dosage I.V.: Initial:

Adults:

<60 kg: 0.01 mg/kg over 10 minutes

≥60 kg: 1 mg over 10 minutes

If the arrhythmia does not terminate within 10 minutes after the end of the initial infusion, a second infusion of equal strength may be infused over a 10-minute period

Elderly: Dose selection should be cautious, usually starting at the lower end of the dosing range.

Administration May be administered undiluted or diluted in 50 mL diluent (0.9% NS or D_5W); infuse over 10 minutes

Monitoring Parameters Observe patient with continuous ECG monitoring for at least 4 hours following infusion or until QT_c has returned to baseline; skilled personnel and proper equipment should be available during administration of ibutilide and subsequent monitoring of the patient

Dosage Forms INJ, solution: 0.1 mg/mL (10 mL)

Idarubicin *(eye da ROO bi sin)*

U.S. Brand Names Idamycin PFS®

Synonyms 4-Demethoxydaunorubicin; 4-DMDR; Idarubicin Hydrochloride; IDR; IMI 30; NSC-256439; SC 33428

Therapeutic Category Antineoplastic Agent, Anthracycline; Vesicant

Use Treatment of acute leukemias (AML, ANLL, ALL), accelerated phase or blast crisis of chronic myelogenous leukemia (CML), breast cancer

Pregnancy Risk Factor D

Contraindications Hypersensitivity to idarubicin, other anthracyclines, or any component of the formulation; bilirubin >5 mg/dL; pregnancy

Warnings/Precautions The U.S. Food and Drug Administration (FDA) currently recommends that procedures for proper handling and disposal of antineoplastic agents be considered. Can cause myocardial toxicity and is more common in patients who have previously received anthracyclines or have pre-existing cardiac disease; reduce dose in patients with impaired hepatic function.

Common Adverse Reactions

>10%:

Cardiovascular: Transient ECG abnormalities (supraventricular tachycardia, S-T wave changes, atrial or ventricular extrasystoles); generally asymptomatic and self-limiting. Congestive heart failure, dose-related. The relative cardiotoxicity of idarubicin compared to doxorubicin is unclear. Some investigators report no increase in cardiac toxicity at cumulative oral idarubicin doses up to 540 mg/m^2; other reports suggest a maximum cumulative intravenous dose of 150 mg/m^2.

Central nervous system: Headache

Dermatologic: Alopecia (25% to 30%), radiation recall, skin rash (11%), urticaria

Gastrointestinal: Nausea, vomiting (30% to 60%); diarrhea (9% to 22%); stomatitis (11%); GI hemorrhage (30%)

Genitourinary: Discoloration of urine (darker yellow)

Hematologic: Myelosuppression, primarily leukopenia; thrombocytopenia and anemia. Effects are generally less severe with oral dosing.

Nadir: 10-15 days

Recovery: 21-28 days

Hepatic: Elevations of bilirubin and transaminases (44%)

1% to 10%:

Central nervous system: Seizures

Neuromuscular & skeletal: Peripheral neuropathy

Drug Interactions

Decreased Effect: Patients may experience impaired immune response to vaccines; possible infection after administration of live vaccines in patients receiving immunosuppressants.

Mechanism of Action Similar to doxorubicin and daunorubicin; inhibition of DNA and RNA synthesis by intercalation between DNA base pairs

Pharmacodynamics/Kinetics

Absorption: Oral: Variable (4% to 77%; mean: ~30%)

Distribution: V_d: 64 L/kg (some reports indicate 2250 L); extensive tissue binding; CSF

Protein binding: 94% to 97%

Metabolism: Hepatic to idarubicinol (pharmacologically active)

Half-life elimination: Oral: 14-35 hours; I.V.: 12-27 hours

Time to peak, serum: 1-5 hours

Excretion:

Oral: Urine (~5% of dose; 0.5% to 0.7% as unchanged drug, 4% as idarubicinol); hepatic (8%)

I.V.: Urine (13% as idarubicinol, 3% as unchanged drug); hepatic (17%)

Dosage Refer to individual protocols. I.V.:

Children:

Leukemia: 10-12 mg/m^2/day for 3 days every 3 weeks

Solid tumors: 5 mg/m^2/day for 3 days every 3 weeks

Adults:

Leukemia induction: 12 mg/m^2/day for 3 days

Leukemia consolidation: 10-12 mg/m^2/day for 2 days

Dosing adjustment in renal impairment: S_{cr}: ≥2 mg/dL: Administer 75% of dose

Hemodialysis: Significant drug removal is unlikely based on physiochemical characteristics

Peritoneal dialysis: Significant drug removal is unlikely based on physiochemical characteristics

Dosing adjustment/comments in hepatic impairment:

Bilirubin 1.5-5.0 mg/dL or AST 60-180 int. units/L: Administer 50% of normal dose

Bilirubin >5.0 mg/dL: Do not administer drug

Administration Do not administer I.M. or S.C.; administer as slow push over 3-5 minutes, preferably into the side of a freely-running saline or dextrose infusion **or** as intermittent infusion over 10-15 minutes into a free-flowing I.V. solution of NS or D$_5$W; also occasionally administered as a bladder lavage.

Extravasation management: Topical cooling may be achieved using ice packs or cooling pad with circulating ice water. Cooling of site for 24 hours as tolerated by the patient. Elevate and rest extremity 24-48 hours, then resume normal activity as tolerated. Application of cold inhibits vesicant's cytotoxicity. **Application of heat can be harmful and is contraindicated.** If pain, erythema, and/or swelling persist beyond 48 hours, refer patient immediately to plastic surgeon for consultation and possible debridement.

Monitoring Parameters CBC with differential, platelet count, cardiac function, serum electrolytes, creatinine, uric acid, ALT, AST, bilirubin, signs of extravasation

Patient Information This drug can only be administered I.V. Maintain adequate nutrition and hydration (2-3 L/day of fluids unless instructed to restrict fluid intake). May cause hair loss (will grow back); nausea or vomiting (consult prescriber for antiemetic medication); you will be susceptible to infection (avoid crowds and exposure to infection); or urine may turn darker (normal). Report immediately any pain, burning, or stinging at infusion site; difficulty breathing; or swelling of extremities. Contraceptive measures are recommended during therapy.

Dosage Forms INJ, solution [preservative free] (Idamycin PFS®): 1 mg/mL (5 mL, 10 mL, 20 mL)

- ◆ **Idarubicin Hydrochloride** *see Idarubicin on page 648*
- ◆ **IDEC-C2B8** *see Rituximab on page 1106*
- ◆ **IDR** *see Idarubicin on page 648*
- ◆ **Ifex®** *see Ifosfamide on page 649*
- ◆ **IFLrA** *see Interferon Alfa-2a on page 672*

Ifosfamide (eye FOSS fa mide)

U.S. Brand Names Ifex®

Synonyms Isophosphamide; NSC-109724; Z4942

Therapeutic Category Antineoplastic Agent, Alkylating Agent

Use Treatment of lung cancer, Hodgkin's and non-Hodgkin's lymphoma, breast cancer, acute and chronic lymphocytic leukemias, ovarian cancer, sarcomas, pancreatic and gastric carcinomas

Orphan drug: Treatment of testicular cancer

Pregnancy Risk Factor D

Contraindications Hypersensitivity to ifosfamide or any component of the formulation; patients with severely depressed bone marrow function; pregnancy

Warnings/Precautions The U.S. Food and Drug Administration (FDA) currently recommends that procedures for proper handling and disposal of antineoplastic agents be considered. Be aware of hemorrhagic cystitis and severe myelosuppression. Use with caution in patients with impaired renal function or those with compromised bone marrow reserve. (Continued)

Ifosfamide *(Continued)*

Common Adverse Reactions

>10%:

Central nervous system: Somnolence, confusion, hallucinations (12%)

Dermatologic: Alopecia (75% to 100%)

Endocrine & metabolic: Metabolic acidosis (31%)

Gastrointestinal: Nausea and vomiting (58%), may be more common with higher doses or bolus infusions; constipation

Genitourinary: Hemorrhagic cystitis (40% to 50%), patients should be vigorously hydrated (at least 2 L/day) and receive mesna

Hematologic: Myelosuppression, leukopenia (65% to 100%), thrombocytopenia (10%) - dose-related

Onset: 7-14 days

Nadir: 21-28 days

Recovery: 21-28 days

Renal: Hematuria (6% to 92%)

1% to 10%:

Central nervous system: Hallucinations, depressive psychoses, polyneuropathy

Dermatologic: Dermatitis, nail banding/ridging, hyperpigmentation

Endocrine & metabolic: SIADH, sterility, elevated transaminases (3%)

Hematologic: Anemia

Local: Phlebitis

Renal: Increased creatinine/BUN (6%)

Respiratory: Nasal stuffiness

Drug Interactions

Cytochrome P450 Effect: Substrate of CYP2A6 (minor), 2B6 (minor), 2C8/9 (minor), 2C19 (minor), 3A4 (major); **Inhibits** CYP3A4 (weak); **Induces** CYP2C8/9 (weak)

Increased Effect/Toxicity: CYP3A4 inducers may increase the levels/effects of acrolein (the active metabolite of ifosfamide); example inducers include aminoglutethimide, carbamazepine, nafcillin, nevirapine, phenobarbital, phenytoin, and rifamycins.

Decreased Effect: CYP3A4 inhibitors may decrease the levels/effects of acrolein (the active metabolite of ifosfamide); example inhibitors include azole antifungals, ciprofloxacin, clarithromycin, diclofenac, doxycycline, erythromycin, imatinib, isoniazid, nefazodone, nicardipine, propofol, protease inhibitors, quinidine, and verapamil.

Mechanism of Action Causes cross-linking of strands of DNA by binding with nucleic acids and other intracellular structures; inhibits protein synthesis and DNA synthesis

Pharmacodynamics/Kinetics Pharmacokinetics are dose dependent

Distribution: V_d: 5.7-49 L; does penetrate CNS, but not in therapeutic levels

Protein binding: Negligible

Metabolism: Hepatic to active metabolites phosphoramide mustard, acrolein, and inactive dichloroethylated and carboxy metabolites; acrolein is the agent implicated in development of hemorrhagic cystitis

Bioavailability: Estimated at 100%

Half-life elimination: Beta: High dose: 11-15 hours (3800-5000 mg/m^2); Lower dose: 4-7 hours (1800 mg/m^2)

Time to peak, plasma: Oral: Within 1 hour

Excretion: Urine (15% to 50% as unchanged drug, 41% as metabolites)

Dosage Refer to individual protocols. To prevent bladder toxicity, ifosfamide should be given with the urinary protector mesna and hydration of at least 2 L of oral or I.V. fluid per day. I.V.:

Children:

1200-1800 mg/m^2/day for 3-5 days every 21-28 days **or**

5 g/m^2 once every 21-28 days **or**

3 g/m^2/day for 2 days every 21-28 days

Adults:

50 mg/kg/day or 700-2000 mg/m^2 for 5 days every 3-4 weeks

Alternatives: 2400 mg/m^2/day for 3 days or 5000 mg/m^2 as a single dose every 3-4 weeks

Dosing adjustment in renal impairment:

S_{cr} 2.1-3.0 mg/dL: Reduce dose by 25% to 50%

S_{cr} >3.0 mg/dL: Withhold drug

Dosing adjustment in hepatic impairment: Although no specific guidelines are available, it is possible that adjusted doses are indicated in hepatic disease. Falkson G, et al (*Invest New Drugs*, 1992, 10:337-43) recommended the following dosage adjustments:

AST >300 or bilirubin >3.0 mg/dL: Decrease ifosfamide dose by 75%

Administration Administer slow I.V. push, IVPB over 30 minutes to several hours or continuous I.V. over 5 days

Monitoring Parameters CBC with differential, hemoglobin, and platelet count, urine output, urinalysis, liver function, and renal function tests

Patient Information This drug can only be administered I.V. Report immediately any pain, stinging, or burning at infusion site. It is vital to maintain adequate hydration (2-3 L/day of fluids unless instructed to restrict fluid intake) for 3 days prior to infusion and each day of therapy. May cause hair loss (will grow back); nausea or vomiting (consult prescriber for antiemetic medication); and you will be susceptible to infection (avoid crowds and exposure to infection). Report immediately pain or irritation on urination, severe diarrhea, CNS changes (eg, hallucinations, confusion, somnolence), signs of opportunistic infection (eg, fever, chills, easy bruising or unusual bleeding), difficulty breathing, swelling of extremities, or any other adverse effects. Contraceptive measures are recommended during therapy.

Dosage Forms INJ, powder for reconstitution: 1 g, 3 g

- **IG** *see* Immune Globulin (Intramuscular) *on page 658*
- **IGIM** *see* Immune Globulin (Intramuscular) *on page 658*
- **IL-1Ra** *see* Anakinra *on page 99*
- **IL-2** *see* Aldesleukin *on page 47*
- **IL-11** *see* Oprelvekin *on page 931*

Imatinib (eye MAT eh nib)

U.S. Brand Names Gleevec™

Synonyms CGP 57148B; Glivec; Imatinib Mesylate; STI571

Therapeutic Category Antineoplastic Agent, Tyrosine Kinase Inhibitor

Use Treatment of adult patients with Philadelphia chromosome-positive (Ph+) chronic myeloid leukemia (CML), including newly-diagnosed patients as well as patients in blast crisis, accelerated phase, or in chronic phase after failure of interferon-alpha therapy; treatment of pediatric patients with Ph+ CML (chronic phase) recurring following stem cell transplant or who are resistant to interferon-alpha therapy; treatment of Kit-positive (CD117) unresectable and/or (metastatic) malignant gastrointestinal stromal tumors (GIST)

Pregnancy Risk Factor D

Contraindications Hypersensitivity to imatinib or any component of the formulation; pregnancy

Warnings/Precautions Often associated with fluid retention, weight gain, and edema (probability increases with higher doses and age >65 years); occasionally leading to significant complications, including pleural effusion, pericardial effusion, pulmonary edema, and ascites. Use caution in patients where fluid accumulation may be poorly tolerated, such as in cardiovascular disease (CHF or hypertension) and pulmonary disease. Use with caution in renal impairment, hematologic impairment, or hepatic disease. May cause GI irritation, hepatotoxicity, or hematologic toxicity (neutropenia or thrombocytopenia). Median duration of neutropenia is 2-3 weeks; median duration of thrombocytopenia is 3-4 weeks. Hepatotoxic reactions may be severe. Has been associated with development of opportunistic infections. Use with caution in patients receiving concurrent therapy with drugs which alter cytochrome P450 activity or require metabolism by these isoenzymes. Review all medications, including OTC and herbal products, before initiating therapy. Safety and efficacy in patients <3 years of age have not been established. Long-term safety data is limited.

Common Adverse Reactions Adverse reactions listed were established in patients with a wide variation in level of illness or specific diagnosis. In many cases, other medications were used concurrently (relationship to imatinib not specific). Effects reported in children were similar to adults, except that musculoskeletal pain was less frequent and peripheral edema was not reported.

>10%:

Central nervous system: Fatigue (29% to 41%), pyrexia (5% to 41%), headache (25% to 35%), dizziness (11% to 13%), insomnia (10% to 13%)

Dermatologic: Rash (26% to 44%), pruritus (8% to 13%), bruising (2% to 11%)

Endocrine & metabolic: Fluid retention (3% to 22% includes aggravated edema, anasarca, ascites, pericardial effusion, pleural effusion, pulmonary edema, excludes GIST); hypokalemia (5% to 13%)

Gastrointestinal: Nausea (42% to 71%), diarrhea (30% to 60%), vomiting (15% to 56%), abdominal pain (23% to 37%), weight increased (3% to 30%), dyspepsia (11% to 24), flatulence (16% to 23%), anorexia (6% to 17%), constipation (6% to 15%), taste disturbance (1% to 14%)

Hematologic: Hemorrhage (18% to 52%), neutropenia (grade 3 or 4: 2% to 48%), thrombocytopenia (grade 3 or 4: <1% to 31%)

Neuromuscular & skeletal: Muscle cramps (27% to 55%), musculoskeletal pain (11% to 46%), arthralgia (25% to 36%), joint pain (27%), myalgia (8% to 25%), weakness (5% to 12%), back pain (10% to 11%), rigors (8% to 11%)

Ocular: Lacrimation (6% to 11%)

Respiratory: Cough (12% to 26%), dyspnea (9% to 20%), nasopharyngitis (8% to 19%), upper respiratory tract infection (3% to 15%), pharyngolaryngeal pain (14%), epistaxis (5% to 13%), pneumonia (3% to 12%), sore throat (8% to 11%)

Miscellaneous: Superficial edema (53% to 76%), night sweats (10% to 14%)

1% to 10%:

Central nervous system: Paresthesia (1% to 10%)

Hematologic: Anemia (grade 3 or 4: <1% to 4%)

Hepatic: Ascites or pleural effusion (GIST: 4% to 6%), alkaline phosphatase increased (grade 3 or 4: <1% to 5%), ALT increased (grade 3 or 4: <1% to 4%), bilirubin increased (grade 3 or 4: <1% to 4%), AST increased (grade 3 or 4: <1% to 3%)

Renal: Albumin decreased (grade 3 or 4: 3% to 4%), creatine increased (grade 3 or 4: <1% to 3%)

Miscellaneous: Flu-like syndrome (<1% to 10%)

Drug Interactions

Cytochrome P450 Effect: Substrate of CYP1A2 (minor), 2D6 (minor), 2C8/9 (minor), 2C19 (minor), 3A4 (major), **Inhibits** CYP2C8/9 (weak), 2D6 (weak), 3A4 (strong)

Increased Effect/Toxicity: Note: Drug interaction data are limited. Few clinical studies have been conducted. Many interactions listed below are derived by extrapolation from *in vitro* inhibition of cytochrome P450 isoenzymes.

Acetaminophen: Chronic use may increase potential for hepatotoxic reaction with imatinib (case report of hepatic failure with concurrent therapy).

(Continued)

Imatinib *(Continued)*

Due to potent CYP3A4 inhibition, imatinib should not be used with cisapride, pimozide, thioridazine, and/or mesoridazine, may result in potential life-threatening toxicities. Imatinib may also inhibit the metabolism of benzodiazepines (alprazolam, diazepam, and triazolam), some beta-blockers, carbamazepine, carvedilol, clozapine, dextromethorphan, haloperidol, HMG-CoA reductase inhibitors (except pravastatin and fluvastatin), immuno-suppressants (cyclosporine, sirolimus, and tacrolimus), methadone, nefazodone, phenothiazines (thioridazine and mesoridazine should be avoided), phenytoin, propafenone, quinidine, sibutramine, tramadol, SSRIs, tricyclic antidepressants, trazodone, vinca alkaloids (vincristine, vinblastine), and warfarin. Increased toxicity leading to liver failure has been reported with regular concomitant acetaminophen use (case report). Sildenafil, tadalafil, and vardenafil serum concentrations may be increased. Specific dosage adjustment guidelines not established. Recommendations for other strong CYP3A4 inhibitors include single sildenafil doses not to exceed 25 mg in 48 hours, a single tadalafil dose not to exceed 10 mg in 72 hours, or a single vardenafil dose not to exceed 2.5 mg in 24 hours.

Serum concentrations and/or toxicity of imatinib may be increased by drugs which inhibit CYP3A4. Established with ketoconazole; other inhibitors include amiodarone, cimetidine, clarithromycin, delavirdine, diltiazem, dirithromycin, disulfiram, erythromycin, fluoxetine, fluvoxamine, grapefruit juice, indinavir, itraconazole, nefazodone, nevirapine, propoxyphene, quinupristin-dalfopristin, ritonavir, saquinavir, verapamil, zafirlukast, and zileuton.

Decreased Effect: Metabolism of imatinib may be increased by CYP3A4 enzyme inducers, decreasing its therapeutic effect. An interaction has been established with phenytoin; other potential inducers include phenobarbital, carbamazepine, rifampin, and rifabutin. Dosage of imatinib should be increased by at least 50% (with careful monitoring) when used concurrently with a potent inducer.

Mechanism of Action Inhibits Bcr-Abl tyrosine kinase, the constitutive abnormal gene product of the Philadelphia chromosome in chronic myeloid leukemia (CML). Inhibition of this enzyme blocks proliferation and induces apoptosis in Bcr-Abl positive cell lines as well as in fresh leukemic cells in Philadelphia chromosome positive CML. Also inhibits tyrosine kinase for platelet-derived growth factor (PDGF), stem cell factor (SCF), c-kit, and events mediated by PDGF and SCF.

Pharmacodynamics/Kinetics

Protein binding: 95% to albumin and alpha$_1$-acid glycoprotein

Metabolism: Hepatic via CYP3A4 (minor metabolism via CYP1A2, CYP2D6, CYP2C9, CYP2C19); primary metabolite (active): N-demethylated piperazine derivative

Bioavailability: 98%

Half-life elimination: Parent drug: 18 hours; N-demethyl metabolite: 40 hours

Time to peak: 2-4 hours

Excretion: Feces (68% primarily as metabolites, 20% as unchanged drug); urine (13% primarily as metabolites, 5% as unchanged drug)

Clearance: Highly variable; Mean: 8-14 L/hour (for 50 kg and 100 kg male, respectively)

Dosage Oral:

Children ≥3 years: CML (chronic phase): 260 mg/m^2/day; may be increased to 340 mg/m^2/day in the event of disease progression, loss of previously achieved response, or failure to achieve response after at least 3 months of therapy and in the absence of severe adverse reaction. Dose may be given once daily or in 2 divided doses.

Adults:

CML:

Chronic phase: 400 mg once daily; may be increased to 600 mg daily in the event of disease progression, loss of previously achieved response, or failure to achieve response after at least 3 months of therapy and in the absence of severe adverse reaction

Accelerated phase or blast crisis: 600 mg once daily; may be increased to 800 mg daily (400 mg twice daily) in the event of disease progression, loss of previously achieved response, or failure to achieve response after at least 3 months of therapy and in the absence of severe adverse reaction

Gastrointestinal stromal tumors: 400-600 mg/day

Note: Dosage should be increased by at least 50% when used concurrently with a potent enzyme-inducing agent (ie, rifampin, phenytoin).

Dosage adjustment for hepatotoxicity or other nonhematologic adverse reactions: If elevations of bilirubin >3 times upper limit of normal (ULN) or transaminases (ALT/AST) >5 times ULN occur, withhold until bilirubin <1.5 times ULN or transaminases <2.5 times ULN. Resume treatment at a reduced dose:

Children:

If initial dose 260 mg/m^2/day, reduce dose to 200 mg/m^2/day

If initial dose 340 mg/m^2/day, reduce dose to 260 mg/m^2/day

Adults:

If initial dose 400 mg, reduce dose to 300 mg

If initial dose 600 mg, reduce dose to 400 mg

Dosage adjustment for hematologic adverse reactions:

Chronic phase (initial dose 400 mg/day in adults or 260 mg/m^2/day in children) or GIST (initial dose 400 mg or 600 mg): If ANC <1.0 x 10^9/L and/or platelets <50 x 10^9/L: Discontinue until ANC ≥1.5 x 10^9/L and platelets ≥75 x 10^9/L; resume treatment at original

initial dose of 400 or 600 mg/day (260 mg/m^2/day in children). If depression in neutrophils or platelets recurs, withhold until recovery, and reinstitute treatment at a reduced dose:
Children:
If initial dose 260 mg/m^2/day, reduce dose to 200 mg/m^2/day
If initial dose 340 mg/m^2/day, reduce dose to 260 mg/m^2/day
Adults:
If initial dose 400 mg, reduce dose to 300 mg
If initial dose 600 mg, reduce dose to 400 mg
Accelerated phase or blast crisis: Adults: Check to establish whether cytopenia is related to leukemia (bone marrow aspirate). If unrelated to leukemia, reduce dose of imatinib by 25%. If cytopenia persists for an additional 2 weeks, further reduce dose to 50% of original dose. If cytopenia persists for 4 weeks and is still unrelated to leukemia, stop treatment until ANC ≥1.0 x 10^9/L and platelets ≥20 x 10^9/L, resume treatment at 50% of original dose.

Administration Should be administered with food and a large glass of water. Tablets may be dispersed in water or apple juice, stir until dissolved and use immediately.

Monitoring Parameters CBC (weekly for first month, biweekly for second month, then periodically thereafter), liver function tests (at baseline and monthly or as clinically indicated), renal function, weight, and edema/fluid status.

Patient Information Take exactly as directed; do not alter or discontinue dose without consulting prescriber. Take with food and a large glass of water. Avoid alcohol, chronic use of acetaminophen or aspirin, OTC or prescription medications, or herbal products unless approved by prescriber. Maintain adequate hydration (2-3 L/day) unless instructed to restrict fluids. You will be required to have regularly scheduled laboratory tests while on this medication. You will be more susceptible to infection (avoid crowds or contagious persons, and do not receive any vaccination unless approved by prescriber). You may experience headache or fatigue (use caution when driving or engaged in tasks requiring alertness until response to drug in known); loss of appetite, nausea, vomiting, or mouth sores (small frequent meals, frequent mouth care, chewing gum, or sucking lozenges may help); constipation (increased dietary fiber and fluids, exercise may help); or diarrhea (buttermilk, boiled milk, or yogurt may reduce diarrhea). Report chest pain, palpitations, or swelling of extremities; cough, difficulty breathing, or wheezing; weight gain greater than 5 lb; skin rash; muscle or bone pain, tremors, or cramping; persistent fatigue or weakness; easy bruising or unusual bleeding (eg, tarry stools, blood in vomitus, stool, urine, or mouth); persistent gastrointestinal problems or pain; or other adverse effects.

Dosage Forms CAP [DSC]: 100 mg. **TAB:** 100 mg, 400 mg

♦ **Imatinib Mesylate** see Imatinib on page 651
♦ **Imdur®** see Isosorbide Mononitrate on page 695
♦ **IMI 30** see Idarubicin on page 648
♦ **Imidazol Carboxamide Dimethyltriazene** see Dacarbazine on page 332
♦ **Imidazole Carboxamide** see Dacarbazine on page 332

Imiglucerase (i mi GLOO ser ace)

U.S. Brand Names Cerezyme®
Therapeutic Category Enzyme, Glucocerebrosidase
Use Long-term enzyme replacement therapy for patients with Type 1 Gaucher's disease
Pregnancy Risk Factor C
Contraindications Hypersensitivity to imiglucerase or any component of the formulation
Warnings/Precautions Anaphylactoid reactions have been reported (<1%). Most patients have continued treatment with pretreatment (antihistamines and/or corticosteroids) and a slower rate of infusion. Safety and efficacy have not been established in pediatric patients <2 years of age (limited experience).
Common Adverse Reactions
1% to 10%: Miscellaneous: Hypersensitivity reaction (7%; symptoms may include pruritus, flushing, urticaria, angioedema, bronchospasm); anaphylactoid reaction (2%)
Individual frequency not defined, but <1.5%:
Cardiovascular: Hypotension, cyanosis
Central nervous system: Headache, dizziness
Dermatologic: Rash, pruritus
Gastrointestinal: Nausea, abdominal discomfort
Genitourinary: Urinary frequency decreased
Pharmacodynamics/Kinetics
Distribution: V_d: 0.09-0.15 L/kg
Half-life elimination: 3.6-10.4 minutes
Dosage I.V.: Children ≥2 years and Adults: 2.5 units/kg 3 times/week up to as much as 60 units/kg administered as frequently as once a week or as infrequently as every 4 weeks; 60 units/kg administered every 2 weeks is the most common dose
Administration I.V.: Infuse over 1-2 hours; may use an in-line, low protein-binding 0.2 micron filter during infusion
Dosage Forms INJ, powder for reconstitution [preservative free]: 200 units, 400 units

♦ **Imipemide** see Imipenem and Cilastatin on page 653

Imipenem and Cilastatin (i mi PEN em & sye la STAT in)

Related Information
Antimicrobial Drugs of Choice on page 1440
(Continued)

Imipenem and Cilastatin *(Continued)*

U.S. Brand Names Primaxin®

Synonyms Imipemide

Therapeutic Category Antibiotic, Anaerobic; Antibiotic, Carbapenem

Use Treatment of respiratory tract, urinary tract, intra-abdominal, gynecologic, bone and joint, skin structure, and polymicrobic infections as well as bacterial septicemia and endocarditis. Antibacterial activity includes resistant gram-negative bacilli (*Pseudomonas aeruginosa* and *Enterobacter* sp), gram-positive bacteria (methicillin-sensitive *Staphylococcus aureus* and *Streptococcus* sp) and anaerobes.

Note: I.M. administration is not intended for severe or life-threatening infections (eg, septicemia, endocarditis, shock)

Pregnancy Risk Factor C

Contraindications Hypersensitivity to imipenem/cilastatin or any component of the formulation; consult information on Lidocaine for contraindications associated with I.M. dosing

Warnings/Precautions Dosage adjustment required in patients with impaired renal function; prolonged use may result in superinfection; has been associated with CNS adverse effects, including confusional states and seizures; use with caution in patients with a history of seizures or hypersensitivity to beta-lactams (including penicillins and cephalosporins); serious hypersensitivity reactions, including anaphylaxis, have been reported (some without a history of previous allergic reactions to beta-lactams); elderly patients often require lower doses; not recommended in pediatric CNS infections; refer to Lidocaine monograph for warnings/precautions associated with I.M. dosing

Common Adverse Reactions 1% to 10%:

Gastrointestinal: Nausea/diarrhea/vomiting (1% to 2%)

Local: Phlebitis (3%), pain at I.M. injection site (1.2%)

Drug Interactions

Increased Effect/Toxicity: Beta-lactam antibiotics and probenecid may increase potential for toxicity.

Mechanism of Action Inhibits bacterial cell wall synthesis by binding to one or more of the penicillin binding proteins (PBPs); which in turn inhibits the final transpeptidation step of peptidoglycan synthesis in bacterial cell walls, thus inhibiting cell wall biosynthesis. Bacteria eventually lyse due to ongoing activity of cell wall autolytic enzymes (autolysins and murein hydrolases) while cell wall assembly is arrested. Cilastatin prevents renal metabolism of imipenem by competitive inhibition of dehydropeptidase along the brush border of the renal tubules.

Pharmacodynamics/Kinetics

Absorption: I.M.: Imipenem: 60% to 75%; cilastatin: 95% to 100%

Distribution: Rapidly and widely to most tissues and fluids including sputum, pleural fluid, peritoneal fluid, interstitial fluid, bile, aqueous humor, reproductive organs, and bone; highest concentrations in pleural fluid, interstitial fluid, peritoneal fluid, and reproductive organs; low concentrations in CSF; crosses placenta; enters breast milk

Metabolism: Renally by dehydropeptidase; activity is blocked by cilastatin; cilastatin is partially metabolized renally

Half-life elimination: Both drugs: 60 minutes; prolonged with renal impairment

Excretion: Both drugs: Urine (~70% as unchanged drug)

Dosage Dosage based on **imipenem** content:

Neonates: Non-CNS infections: I.V.:

<1 week: 25 mg/kg every 12 hours

1-4 weeks: 25 mg/kg every 8 hours

4 weeks to 3 months: 25 mg/kg every 6 hours

Children >3 months: Non-CNS infections: I.V.: 15-25 mg/kg every 6 hours

Maximum dosage: Susceptible infections: 2 g/day; moderately susceptible organisms: 4 g/day

Children: Cystic fibrosis: I.V.: Doses up to 90 mg/kg/day have been used

Adults:

Mild infections:

I.M.: 750 mg every 12 hours

I.V.:

Fully-susceptible organisms: 500 mg every 6-8 hours (1.5-2 g/day)

Moderately-susceptible organisms: 500 mg every 6 hours (2 g/day)

Moderate infections:

I.M.: 750 mg every 12 hours

I.V.:

Fully-susceptible organisms: 500 mg every 6-8 hours (1.5-2 g/day)

Moderately-susceptible organisms: 500 mg every 6 hours or 1 g every 8 hours (2-3 g/day)

Severe infections: I.V.: **Note:** I.M. administration is not intended for severe or life-threatening infections (eg, septicemia, endocarditis, shock):

Fully-susceptible organisms: 500 mg every 6 hours (2 g/day)

Moderately-susceptible organisms: 1 g every 6-8 hours (3-4 g/day)

Maximum daily dose should not exceed 50 mg/kg or 4 g/day, whichever is lower

Urinary tract infection, uncomplicated: I.V.: 250 mg every 6 hours (1 g/day)

Urinary tract infection, complicated: I.V.: 500 mg every 6 hours (2 g/day) Dosage based on **imipenem** content:

Neonates: Non-CNS infections: I.V.:

<1 week: 25 mg/kg every 12 hours

1-4 weeks: 25 mg/kg every 8 hours
4 weeks to 3 months: 25 mg/kg every 6 hours
Children: >3 months: Non-CNS infections: I.V.: 15-25 mg/kg every 6 hours
  Maximum dosage: Susceptible infections: 2 g/day; moderately susceptible organisms: 4 g/day
Children: Cystic fibrosis: I.V.: Doses up to 90 mg/kg/day have been used
Adults:
  Moderate infections:
    I.M.: 750 mg every 12 hours
    I.V.:
      Fully-susceptible organisms: 500 mg every 6-8 hours (1.5-2 g/day)
      Moderately-susceptible organisms: 500 mg every 6 hours or 1 g every 8 hours (2-3 g/day)
  Severe infections: I.V.: **Note:** I.M. administration is not intended for severe or life-threatening infections (eg, septicemia, endocarditis, shock):
    Fully-susceptible organisms: 500 mg every 6 hours (2 g/day)
    Moderately-susceptible organisms: 1 g every 6-8 hours (3-4 g/day)
    Maximum daily dose should not exceed 50 mg/kg or 4 g/day, whichever is lower
  Urinary tract infection, uncomplicated: I.V.: 250 mg every 6 hours (1 g/day)
  Urinary tract infection, complicated: I.V.: 500 mg every 6 hours (2 g/day)
  Mild infections: **Note:** Rarely a suitable option in mild infections; normally reserved for moderate-severe cases:
    I.M.: 500 mg every 12 hours; intra-abdominal infections: 750 mg every 12 hours
    I.V.:
      Fully-susceptible organisms: 250 mg every 6 hours (1g/day)
      Moderately-susceptible organisms: 500 mg every 6 hours (2 g/day)

Dosage adjustment in renal impairment: I.V.: **Note:** Adjustments have not been established for I.M. dosing: See table.

Imipenem/Cilastatin

Creatinine Clearance (mL/min/1.73 m²)	Frequency	Dose (mg)
30-70	q8h	500
20-30	q12h	500
5-20	q12h	250

Patients with a Cl_{cr} <5 mL/minute/1.73 m² should not receive imipenem/cilastatin unless hemodialysis is instituted within 48 hours.
Patients weighing <30 kg with impaired renal function should not receive imipenem/cilastatin.
Hemodialysis: Use the dosing recommendation for patients with a Cl_{cr} 6-20 mL/minute
Peritoneal dialysis: Dose as for Cl_{cr} <10 mL/minute
Continuous arteriovenous or venovenous hemofiltration: Dose as for Cl_{cr} 20-30 mL/minute; monitor for seizure activity; imipenem is well removed by CAVH but cilastatin is not; removes 20 mg of imipenem per liter of filtrate per day

Administration
  I.M.: Prepare 500 mg vial with 2 mL 1% lidocaine; prepare 750 mg vial with 3 mL 1% lidocaine **(do not use lidocaine with epinephrine)**. Administer by deep injection into a large muscle (gluteal or lateral thigh). Aspiration is necessary to avoid inadvertent injection into a blood vessel.
  I.V.: Not for direct infusion; vial contents must be transferred to 100 mL of infusion solution; final concentration should not exceed 5 mg/mL; infuse each 250-500 mg dose over 20-30 minutes; infuse each 1 g dose over 40-60 minutes; watch for convulsions. If nausea and/or vomiting occur during administration, decrease the rate of I.V. infusion; do not mix with or physically add to other antibiotics; however, may administer concomitantly

Monitoring Parameters Periodic renal, hepatic, and hematologic function tests; monitor for signs of anaphylaxis during first dose

Dosage Forms INJ, powder for reconstitution [I.M.]: Imipenem 500 mg and cilastatin 500 mg. **INJ, powder for reconstitution [I.V.]:** Imipenem 250 mg and cilastatin 250 mg; imipenem 500 mg and cilastatin 500 mg

Imipramine (im IP ra meen)

Related Information
  Antidepressant Agents Comparison *on page 1359*
U.S. Brand Names Tofranil®; Tofranil-PM®
Synonyms Imipramine Hydrochloride; Imipramine Pamoate
Therapeutic Category Antidepressant, Tricyclic (Tertiary Amine)
Use Treatment of depression
Unlabeled/Investigational Use Enuresis in children; analgesic for certain chronic and neuropathic pain; panic disorder; attention-deficit/hyperactivity disorder (ADHD)
Pregnancy Risk Factor D
Contraindications Hypersensitivity to imipramine (cross-reactivity with other dibenzodiazepines may occur) or any component of the formulation; concurrent use of MAO inhibitors (within 14 days); in a patient during acute recovery phase of MI; pregnancy
(Continued)

Imipramine *(Continued)*

Warnings/Precautions Use with caution in patients with cardiovascular disease, conduction disturbances, seizure disorders, urinary retention, hyperthyroidism or those receiving thyroid replacement. Do not discontinue abruptly in patients receiving long-term, high-dose therapy. Some oral preparations contain tartrazine and injection contains sulfites, both of which can cause allergic reactions. May cause sedation, resulting in impaired performance of tasks requiring alertness (eg, operating machinery or driving). Sedative effects may be additive with other CNS depressants and/or ethanol. The degree of sedation is high relative to other antidepressants. May worsen psychosis in some patients or precipitate a shift to mania or hypomania in patients with bipolar disease. The possibility of a suicide attempt is inherent in major depression and may persist until remission occurs. Use caution in high-risk patients during initiation of therapy. Prescriptions should be written for the smallest quantity consistent with good patient care. May increase the risks associated with electroconvulsive therapy. This agent should be discontinued, when possible, prior to elective surgery. Therapy should not be abruptly discontinued in patients receiving high doses for prolonged periods.

Orthostatic hypotension is a concern with this agent, especially in patients taking other medications that may affect blood pressure; may precipitate arrhythmias in predisposed patients; may aggravate seizures. The degree of anticholinergic blockade produced by this agent is high relative to other cyclic antidepressants - use caution in patients with urinary retention, benign prostatic hyperplasia, narrow-angle glaucoma, xerostomia, visual problems, constipation, or history of bowel obstruction. A less anticholinergic antidepressant may be a better choice.

Common Adverse Reactions Frequency not defined.

Cardiovascular: Orthostatic hypotension, arrhythmias, tachycardia, hypertension, palpitations, myocardial infarction, heart block, ECG changes, CHF, stroke

Central nervous system: Dizziness, drowsiness, headache, agitation, insomnia, nightmares, hypomania, psychosis, fatigue, confusion, hallucinations, disorientation, delusions, anxiety, restlessness, seizures

Endocrine & metabolic: Gynecomastia, breast enlargement, galactorrhea, increase or decrease in libido, increase or decrease in blood sugar, SIADH

Gastrointestinal: Nausea, unpleasant taste, weight gain, xerostomia, constipation, ileus, stomatitis, abdominal cramps, vomiting, anorexia, epigastric disorders, diarrhea, black tongue, weight loss

Genitourinary: Urinary retention, impotence

Neuromuscular & skeletal: Weakness, numbness, tingling, paresthesias, incoordination, ataxia, tremor, peripheral neuropathy, extrapyramidal symptoms

Ocular: Blurred vision, disturbances of accommodation, mydriasis

Otic: Tinnitus

Miscellaneous: Diaphoresis

Drug Interactions

Cytochrome P450 Effect: Substrate of CYP1A2 (minor), 2B6 (minor), 2C19 (major), 2D6 (major), 3A4 (minor); **Inhibits** CYP1A2 (weak), 2C19 (weak), 2D6 (moderate), 2E1 (weak)

Increased Effect/Toxicity: When used with MAO inhibitors, hyperpyrexia, hypertension, tachycardia, confusion, seizures, and **deaths have been reported** (serotonin syndrome). Serotonin syndrome has also been reported with ritonavir (rare). Use of lithium with a TCA may increase the risk for neurotoxicity.

CYP2C19 inhibitors may increase the levels/effects of imipramine; example inhibitors include delavirdine, fluconazole, fluvoxamine, gemfibrozil, isoniazid, omeprazole, and ticlopidine. Imipramine increases the effects of amphetamines, anticholinergics, other CNS depressants (sedatives, hypnotics, or ethanol), chlorpropamide, tolazamide, and warfarin. CYP2D6 inhibitors may increase the levels/effects of imipramine; example inhibitors include chlorpromazine, delavirdine, fluoxetine, miconazole, paroxetine, pergolide, quinidine, quinine, ritonavir, and ropinirole.

Phenothiazines may increase concentration of some TCAs and TCAs may increase concentration of phenothiazines. Pressor response to I.V. epinephrine, norepinephrine, and phenylephrine may be enhanced in patients receiving TCAs (**Note:** Effect is unlikely with epinephrine or levonordefrin dosages typically administered as infiltration in combination with local anesthetics).

Combined use of beta-agonists or drugs which prolong QT_c (including quinidine, procainamide, disopyramide, cisapride, sparfloxacin, gatifloxacin, moxifloxacin) with TCAs may predispose patients to cardiac arrhythmias.

Decreased Effect: CYP2C19 inducers may decrease the levels/effects of imipramine; example inducers include aminoglutethimide, carbamazepine, phenytoin, and rifampin. Imipramine inhibits the antihypertensive response to bethanidine, clonidine, debrisoquin, guanadrel, guanethidine, guanabenz, and guanfacine. Cholestyramine and colestipol may bind TCAs and reduce their absorption; monitor for altered response.

Mechanism of Action Traditionally believed to increase the synaptic concentration of serotonin and/or norepinephrine in the central nervous system by inhibition of their reuptake by the presynaptic neuronal membrane. However, additional receptor effects have been found including desensitization of adenyl cyclase, down regulation of beta-adrenergic receptors, and down regulation of serotonin receptors.

Pharmacodynamics/Kinetics

Onset of action: Peak antidepressant effect: Usually after ≥2 weeks

Absorption: Well absorbed

Distribution: Crosses placenta

Metabolism: Hepatic via CYP to desipramine (active) and other metabolites; significant first-pass effect

Half-life elimination: 6-18 hours

Excretion: Urine (as metabolites)

Dosage Oral:

Children:

Depression: 1.5 mg/kg/day with dosage increments of 1 mg/kg every 3-4 days to a maximum dose of 5 mg/kg/day in 1-4 divided doses; monitor carefully especially with doses ≥3.5 mg/kg/day

Enuresis: ≥6 years: Initial: 10-25 mg at bedtime, if inadequate response still seen after 1 week of therapy, increase by 25 mg/day; dose should not exceed 2.5 mg/kg/day or 50 mg at bedtime if 6-12 years of age or 75 mg at bedtime if ≥12 years of age

Adjunct in the treatment of cancer pain: Initial: 0.2-0.4 mg/kg at bedtime; dose may be increased by 50% every 2-3 days up to 1-3 mg/kg/dose at bedtime

Adolescents: Initial: 25-50 mg/day; increase gradually; maximum: 100 mg/day in single or divided doses

Adults: Initial: 25 mg 3-4 times/day, increase dose gradually, total dose may be given at bedtime; maximum: 300 mg/day

Elderly: Initial: 10-25 mg at bedtime; increase by 10-25 mg every 3 days for inpatients and weekly for outpatients if tolerated; average daily dose to achieve a therapeutic concentration: 100 mg/day; range: 50-150 mg/day

Monitoring Parameters Monitor blood pressure and pulse rate prior to and during initial therapy; ECG in older adults; evaluate mental status; blood levels are useful for therapeutic monitoring

Reference Range Therapeutic: Imipramine and desipramine: 150-250 ng/mL (SI: 530-890 nmol/L); desipramine: 150-300 ng/mL (SI: 560-1125 nmol/L); Toxic: >500 ng/mL (SI: 446-893 nmol/L); utility of serum level monitoring controversial

Patient Information May require 2-4 weeks to achieve desired effect; avoid alcohol; do not discontinue medication abruptly; may cause urine to turn blue-green; may cause drowsiness, avoid alcohol and other CNS depressants; dry mouth may be helped by sips of water, sugarless gum, or hard candy; rise slowly to avoid dizziness

Dosage Forms CAP, as pamoate (Tofranil-PM®): 75 mg, 100 mg, 125 mg, 150 mg. **TAB, as hydrochloride** (Tofranil®): 10 mg, 25 mg, 50 mg

♦ **Imipramine Hydrochloride** see Imipramine on page 655

♦ **Imipramine Pamoate** see Imipramine on page 655

Imiquimod (i mi KWI mod)

U.S. Brand Names Aldara™

Therapeutic Category Skin and Mucous Membrane Agent; Topical Skin Product

Use Treatment of external genital and perianal warts/condyloma acuminata in children ≥12 years of age and adults

Unlabeled/Investigational Use Treatment of common warts, basal cell carcinoma

Pregnancy Risk Factor B

Contraindications Hypersensitivity to imiquimod or any component of the formulation

Warnings/Precautions Imiquimod has not been evaluated for the treatment of urethral, intra-vaginal, cervical, rectal, or intra-anal human papilloma viral disease and is not recommended for these conditions. Topical imiquimod is not intended for ophthalmic use. Topical imiquimod administration is not recommended until genital/perianal tissue is healed from any previous drug or surgical treatment. Imiquimod has the potential to exacerbate inflammatory conditions of the skin.

Common Adverse Reactions

>10%: Local, mild/moderate: Erythema (54% to 61%), itching (22% to 32%), erosion (21% to 32%), burning (9% to 26%), excoriation/flaking (18% to 25%), edema (12% to 17%), scabbing (9% to 13%)

1% to 10%:

Central nervous system: Pain (2% to 8%), headache (4% to 5%)

Local, severe: Erythema (4%), erosion (1%), edema (1%)

Local, mild/moderate: Pain, induration, ulceration (5% to 7%), vesicles (2% to 3%), soreness (<1% to 3%)

Neuromuscular & skeletal: Myalgia (1%)

Miscellaneous: Influenza-like symptoms (1% to 3%), fungal infections (2% to 11%)

Drug Interactions

Cytochrome P450 Effect: Substrate (minor) of CYP1A2, 3A4

Mechanism of Action Mechanism of action is unknown; however, induces cytokines, including interferon-alpha and others

Pharmacodynamics/Kinetics

Absorption: Minimal

Excretion: Urine and feces (<0.9%)

Dosage Topical:

Children ≥12 years and Adults: Perianal warts/condyloma acuminata: Apply 3 times/week prior to normal sleeping hours and leave on the skin for 6-10 hours. Following treatment period, remove cream by washing the treated area with mild soap and water. Examples of 3 times/week application schedules are: Monday, Wednesday, Friday; or Tuesday, Thursday, Saturday. Continue imiquimod treatment until there is total clearance of the genital/perianal warts for ≤16 weeks. A rest period of several days may be taken if required by the patient's

(Continued)

Imiquimod *(Continued)*

discomfort or severity of the local skin reaction. Treatment may resume once the reaction subsides.

Adults:

Common warts (unlabeled use): Apply once daily prior to normal sleeping hours

Basal cell carcinoma (unlabeled use): Apply once daily prior to normal sleeping hours, 5-7 days/week

Administration Nonocclusive dressings such as cotton gauze or cotton underwear may be used in the management of skin reactions. Handwashing before and after cream application is recommended. Imiquimod is packaged in single-use packets that contain sufficient cream to cover a wart area of up to 20 cm^2; avoid use of excessive amounts of cream. Instruct patients to apply imiquimod to external or perianal warts; not for vaginal use. Apply a thin layer to the wart area and rub in until the cream is no longer visible. Do not occlude the application site.

Monitoring Parameters Reduction in wart size is indicative of a therapeutic response; patients should be monitored for signs and symptoms of hypersensitivity to imiquimod

Patient Information Imiquimod is not a cure; new warts may develop during therapy. Imiquimod may weaken condoms and vaginal diaphragms; therefore, concurrent use is not recommended. This medication is for external use only; avoid contact with eyes. Do not occlude the treatment area with bandages or other covers or wraps. Avoid sexual (genital, anal, oral) contact while the cream is on the skin. (Females: Do not apply in the vagina.) Wash the treatment area with mild soap and water 6-10 hours following application of imiquimod. Patients commonly experience local skin reactions such as erythema, erosion, excoriation/flaking, and edema at the site of application or surrounding areas. Most skin reactions are mild to moderate. Severe skin reactions can occur; promptly report severe reactions. Uncircumcised males treating warts under the foreskin should retract the foreskin and clean the area daily.

Dosage Forms CRM: 5% (12s)

♦ **Imitrex®** *see* Sumatriptan *on page 1178*

Immune Globulin (Intramuscular) (i MYUN GLOB yoo lin, IN tra MUS kyoo ler)

U.S. Brand Names BayGam®

Synonyms Gamma Globulin; IG; IGIM; Immune Serum Globulin; ISG

Therapeutic Category Immune Globulin

Use Household and sexual contacts of persons with hepatitis A, measles, varicella, and possibly rubella; travelers to high-risk areas outside tourist routes; staff, attendees, and parents of diapered attendees in day-care center outbreaks

For travelers, IG is not an alternative to careful selection of foods and water; immune globulin can interfere with the antibody response to parenterally administered live virus vaccines. Frequent travelers should be tested for hepatitis A antibody, immune hemolytic anemia, and neutropenia (with ITP, I.V. route is usually used).

Pregnancy Risk Factor C

Contraindications Hypersensitivity to immune globulin, thimerosal, or any component of the formulation; IgA deficiency; I.M. injections in patients with thrombocytopenia or coagulation disorders

Warnings/Precautions Skin testing should not be performed as local irritation can occur and be misinterpreted as a positive reaction; IG should **not** be used to control outbreaks of measles. As a product of human plasma, this product may potentially transmit disease; screening of donors, as well as testing and/or inactivation of certain viruses reduces this risk. Epidemiologic and laboratory data indicate current IMIG products do not have a discernible risk of transmitting HIV. Use caution in patients with thrombocytopenia or coagulation disorders (I.M. injections may be contraindicated). Not for I.V. administration.

Common Adverse Reactions Frequency not defined.

Cardiovascular: Flushing, angioedema

Central nervous system: Chills, lethargy, fever

Dermatologic: Urticaria, erythema

Gastrointestinal: Nausea, vomiting

Local: Pain, tenderness, muscle stiffness at I.M. site

Neuromuscular & skeletal: Myalgia

Miscellaneous: Hypersensitivity reactions

Drug Interactions

Increased Effect/Toxicity: Increased toxicity: Live virus, vaccines (measles, mumps, rubella); do not administer within 3 months after administration of these vaccines.

Mechanism of Action Provides passive immunity by increasing the antibody titer and antigen-antibody reaction potential

Pharmacodynamics/Kinetics

Duration: Immune effect: Usually 3-4 weeks

Half-life elimination: 23 days

Time to peak, serum: I.M.: ~24-48 hours

Dosage I.M.:

Hepatitis A:

Pre-exposure prophylaxis upon travel into endemic areas (hepatitis A vaccine preferred):

0.02 mL/kg for anticipated risk 1-3 months

0.06 mL/kg for anticipated risk >3 months

Repeat approximate dose every 4-6 months if exposure continues

Postexposure prophylaxis: 0.02 mL/kg given within 7 days of exposure

Measles:

Prophylaxis: 0.25 mL/kg/dose (maximum dose: 15 mL) given within 6 days of exposure followed by live attenuated measles vaccine in 3 months or at 15 months of age (whichever is later)

For patients with leukemia, lymphoma, immunodeficiency disorders, generalized malignancy, or receiving immunosuppressive therapy: 0.5 mL/kg (maximum dose: 15 mL)

Poliomyelitis: Prophylaxis: 0.3 mL/kg/dose as a single dose

Rubella: Prophylaxis: 0.55 mL/kg/dose within 72 hours of exposure

Varicella:: Prophylaxis: 0.6-1.2 mL/kg (varicella zoster immune globulin preferred) within 72 hours of exposure

IgG deficiency: 1.3 mL/kg, then 0.66 mL/kg in 3-4 weeks

Hepatitis B: Prophylaxis: 0.06 mL/kg/dose (HBIG preferred)

Administration Intramuscular injection only

Dosage Forms INJ, solution [preservative free]: 15% to 18% (2 mL, 10 mL)

Immune Globulin (Intravenous) (i MYUN GLOB yoo lin, IN tra VEE nus)

U.S. Brand Names Carimune™; Flebogamma®; Gamimune® N; Gammagard® S/D; Gammar®-P I.V.; Gamunex®; Iveegam EN; Panglobulin®; Polygam® S/D; Venoglobulin®-S

Synonyms IVIG

Therapeutic Category Immune Globulin

Use

Treatment of primary immunodeficiency syndromes (congenital agammaglobulinemia, severe combined immunodeficiency syndromes [SCIDS], common variable immunodeficiency, X-linked immunodeficiency, Wiskott-Aldrich syndrome); idiopathic thrombocytopenic purpura (ITP); Kawasaki disease (in combination with aspirin)

Prevention of bacterial infection in B-cell chronic lymphocytic leukemia (CLL); pediatric HIV infection; bone marrow transplant (BMT)

Unlabeled/Investigational Use Autoimmune diseases (myasthenia gravis, SLE, bullous pemphigoid, severe rheumatoid arthritis), Guillain-Barré syndrome; used in conjunction with appropriate anti-infective therapy to prevent or modify acute bacterial or viral infections in patients with iatrogenically-induced or disease-associated immunodepression; autoimmune hemolytic anemia or neutropenia, refractory dermatomyositis/polymyositis

Pregnancy Risk Factor C

Contraindications Hypersensitivity to immune globulin or any component of the formulation; selective IgA deficiency

Warnings/Precautions Anaphylactic hypersensitivity reactions can occur, especially in IgA-deficient patients; studies indicate that the currently available products have no discernible risk of transmitting HIV or hepatitis B; aseptic meningitis may occur with high doses (≥2 g/kg). Use with caution in the elderly, patients with renal disease, diabetes mellitus, volume depletion, sepsis, paraproteinemia, and nephrotoxic medications due to risk of renal dysfunction. Patients should be adequately hydrated prior to therapy. Acute renal dysfunction (increased serum creatinine, oliguria, acute renal failure) can rarely occur; usually within 7 days of use (more likely with products stabilized with sucrose). Use caution in patients with a history of thrombotic events or cardiovascular disease; there is clinical evidence of a possible association between thrombotic events and administration of intravenous immune globulin. For intravenous administration only.

Common Adverse Reactions Frequency not defined.

Cardiovascular: Flushing of the face, tachycardia, hypertension, hypotension, chest tightness, angioedema, lightheadedness, chest pain, myocardial infarction, CHF, pulmonary embolism

Central nervous system: Anxiety, chills, dizziness, drowsiness, fatigue, fever, headache, irritability, lethargy, malaise, aseptic meningitis syndrome

Dermatologic: Pruritus, rash, urticaria

Gastrointestinal: Abdominal cramps, nausea, vomiting

Hematologic: Autoimmune hemolytic anemia, mild hemolysis

Local: Pain or irritation at the infusion site

Neuromuscular & skeletal: Arthralgia, back or hip pain, myalgia, nuchal rigidity

Ocular: Photophobia, painful eye movements

Renal: Acute renal failure, acute tubular necrosis, anuria, BUN elevated, creatinine elevated, nephrotic syndrome, oliguria, proximal tubular nephropathy, osmotic nephrosis

Respiratory: Dyspnea, wheezing, infusion-related lung injury

Miscellaneous: Diaphoresis, hypersensitivity reactions, anaphylaxis

Drug Interactions

Decreased Effect: Decreased effect of live virus vaccines (measles, mumps, rubella); separate administration by at least 3 months

Mechanism of Action Replacement therapy for primary and secondary immunodeficiencies; interference with F_c receptors on the cells of the reticuloendothelial system for autoimmune cytopenias and ITP; possible role of contained antiviral-type antibodies

Pharmacodynamics/Kinetics

Onset of action: I.V.: Provides immediate antibody levels

Duration: Immune effect: 3-4 weeks (variable)

Distribution: V_d: 0.09-0.13 L/kg

Intravascular portion: Healthy subjects: 41% to 57%; Patients with congenital humoral immunodeficiencies: ~70%

Half-life elimination: IgG (variable among patients): Healthy subjects: 14-24 days; Patients with congenital humoral immunodeficiencies: 26-35 days; hypermetabolism associated with fever and infection have coincided with a shortened half-life

(Continued)

Immune Globulin (Intravenous) *(Continued)*

Dosage Approved doses and regimens may vary between brands; check manufacturer guidelines. **Note:** Some clinicians dose IVIG on ideal body weight or an adjusted ideal body weight in morbidly obese patients. The volume of distribution of IVIG preparations in healthy subjects is similar to that observed with endogenous IgG. IVIG remains primarily in the intravascular space. Patients with congenital humoral immunodeficiencies appear to have about 70% of the IVIG available in the intravascular space.

Infants and Children: Prevention of gastroenteritis (unlabeled use): Oral: 50 mg/kg/day divided every 6 hours

Children: I.V.:

Pediatric HIV: 400 mg/kg every 28 days

Severe systemic viral and bacterial infections (unlabeled use): 500-1000 mg/kg/week

Children and Adults: I.V.:

Primary immunodeficiency disorders: 200-400 mg/kg every 4 weeks or as per monitored serum IgG concentrations

Gamunex®, Flebogamma®: 300-600 mg/kg every 3-4 weeks; adjusted based on dosage and interval in conjunction with monitored serum IgG concentrations.

B-cell chronic lymphocytic leukemia (CLL): 400 mg/kg/dose every 3 weeks

Idiopathic thrombocytopenic purpura (ITP):

Acute: 400 mg/kg/day for 5 days or 1000 mg/kg/day for 1-2 days

Chronic: 400 mg/kg as needed to maintain platelet count >30,000/mm³; may increase dose to 800 mg/kg (1000 mg/kg if needed)

Kawasaki disease: Initiate therapy within 10 days of disease onset: 2 g/kg as a single dose administered over 10 hours, or 400 mg/kg/day for 4 days. **Note:** Must be used in combination with aspirin: 80-100 mg/kg/day in 4 divided doses for 14 days; when fever subsides, dose aspirin at 3-5 mg/kg once daily for ≥6-8 weeks

Acquired immunodeficiency syndrome (patients must be symptomatic) (unlabeled use): Various regimens have been used, including:

200-250 mg/kg/dose every 2 weeks

or

400-500 mg/kg/dose every month or every 4 weeks

Autoimmune hemolytic anemia and neutropenia (unlabeled use): 1000 mg/kg/dose for 2-3 days

Autoimmune diseases (unlabeled use): 400 mg/kg/day for 4 days

Bone marrow transplant: 500 mg/kg beginning on days 7 and 2 pretransplant, then 500 mg/kg/week for 90 days post-transplant

Adjuvant to severe cytomegalovirus infections (unlabeled use): 500 mg/kg/dose every other day for 7 doses

Guillain-Barré syndrome (unlabeled use): Various regimens have been used, including:

400 mg/kg/day for 4 days

or

1000 mg/kg/day for 2 days

or

2000 mg/kg/day for one day

Refractory dermatomyositis (unlabeled use): 2 g/kg/dose every month x 3-4 doses

Refractory polymyositis (unlabeled use): 1 g/kg/day x 2 days every month x 4 doses

Chronic inflammatory demyelinating polyneuropathy (unlabeled use): Various regimens have been used, including:

400 mg/kg/day for 5 doses once each month

or

800 mg/kg/day for 3 doses once each month

or

1000 mg/kg/day for 2 days once each month

Dosing adjustment/comments in renal impairment: Cl$_{cr}$ <10 mL/minute: Avoid use; in patients at risk of renal dysfunction, consider infusion at a rate less than maximum.

Administration I.V. use only; for initial treatment, a lower concentration and/or a slower rate of infusion should be used. Administer in separate infusion line from other medications; if using primary line, flush with saline prior administration (**Note:** Venoglobulin®-S: Flush with D₅W). Decrease dose, rate and/or concentration of infusion in patients who may be at risk of renal failure. Decreasing the rate or stopping the infusion may help relieve some adverse effects (flushing, changes in pulse rate, changes in blood pressure). Epinephrine should be available during administration. The lot numbers of vials used should be recorded.

Monitoring Parameters Renal function, infusion-related adverse reactions, anaphylaxis

Dosage Forms INJ, powder for reconstitution [preservative free] (Carimune™): 1 g, 3 g, 6 g, 12 g; (Gammar®-P I.V.): 1 g, 2.5 g, 5 g, 10 g; (Iveegam EN): 0.5 g, 1 g, 2.5 g, 5 g; (Panglobulin®): 1 g, 3 g, 6 g, 12 g. **INJ, powder for reconstitution** [preservative free, solvent detergent treated] (Gammagard® S/D, Polygam® S/D): 2.5 g, 5 g, 10 g. **SOLN, injection** [preservative free, solvent detergent-treated] (Gamimune® N): 10% [100 mg/mL] (10 mL, 50 mL, 100 mL, 200 mL); (Venoglobulin®-S): 5% [50 mg/mL] (50 mL, 100 mL, 200 mL); 10% [100 mg/mL] (50 mL, 100 mL, 200 mL). **SOLN, injection** [preservative free]: (Flebogamma®): 5% (10 mL, 50 mL, 100 mL, 200 mL) [PEG precipitated/chromatography purified]; (Gamunex®): 10% (10 mL, 25 mL, 50 mL, 100 mL, 200 mL) [caprylate/chromatography purified] .

◆ **Immune Serum Globulin** *see* Immune Globulin (Intramuscular) *on page 658*

◆ **Imodium® A-D [OTC]** *see* Loperamide *on page 756*

◆ **Imogam®** *see* Rabies Immune Globulin (Human) *on page 1077*

♦ **Imovax® Rabies** *see Rabies Virus Vaccine on page 1078*

♦ **Imuran®** *see Azathioprine on page 137*

♦ **In-111 Zevalin** *see Ibritumomab on page 643*

Inamrinone (eye NAM ri none)

Related Information
Hemodynamic Support, Intravenous *on page 1377*

Synonyms Amrinone Lactate

Therapeutic Category Phosphodiesterase Enzyme Inhibitor

Use Infrequently used as a last resort, short-term therapy in patients with intractable heart failure

Pregnancy Risk Factor C

Contraindications Hypersensitivity to inamrinone, any component of the formulation, or bisulfites (contains sodium metabisulfite); patients with severe aortic or pulmonic valvular disease

Warnings/Precautions Due to a slight effect on AV conduction, may increase ventricular response rate in atrial fibrillation/atrial flutter; prior treatment with digoxin is recommended. Monitor liver function. Discontinue therapy if alteration in LFTs and clinical symptoms of hepatotoxicity occur. Observe for arrhythmias in this very high-risk patient population. Not recommended in acute MI treatment. Monitor fluid status closely; patients may require adjustment of diuretic and electrolyte replacement therapy. Can cause thrombocytopenia (dose dependent). Correct hypokalemia before initiating therapy. Increase risk of hospitalization and death with long-term therapy.

Common Adverse Reactions
1% to 10%:
  Cardiovascular: Arrhythmias (3%, especially in high-risk patients), hypotension (1% to 2%), (may be infusion rate-related)
  Gastrointestinal: Nausea (1% to 2%)
  Hematologic: Thrombocytopenia (may be dose-related)

Drug Interactions
Increased Effect/Toxicity: Diuretics may cause significant hypovolemia and decrease filling pressure. Inotropic effects with digitalis are additive.

Mechanism of Action Inhibits myocardial cyclic adenosine monophosphate (cAMP) phosphodiesterase activity and increases cellular levels of cAMP resulting in a positive inotropic effect and increased cardiac output; also possesses systemic and pulmonary vasodilator effects resulting in pre- and afterload reduction; slightly increases atrioventricular conduction

Pharmacodynamics/Kinetics
Onset of action: I.V.: 2-5 minutes
  Peak effect: ~10 minutes
Duration (dose dependent): Low dose: ~30 minutes; Higher doses: ~2 hours
Half-life elimination, serum: Adults: Healthy volunteers: 3.6 hours, Congestive heart failure: 5.8 hours

Dosage Dosage is based on clinical response (**Note:** Dose should not exceed 10 mg/kg/24 hours).
Infants, Children, and Adults: 0.75 mg/kg I.V. bolus over 2-3 minutes followed by maintenance infusion of 5-10 mcg/kg/minute; I.V. bolus may need to be repeated in 30 minutes.
Dosing adjustment in renal failure: Cl_{cr} <10 mL/minute: Administer 50% to 75% of dose.

Administration May be administered undiluted for I.V. bolus doses. For continuous infusion: Dilute with 0.45% or 0.9% sodium chloride to final concentration of 1-3 mg/mL use within 24 hours.

Dosage Forms INJ, solution: 5 mg/mL (20 mL)

♦ **Inapsine®** *see Droperidol on page 416*

Indapamide (in DAP a mide)

Related Information
Sulfonamide Derivatives *on page 1404*

U.S. Brand Names Lozol®

Therapeutic Category Antihypertensive Agent; Diuretic, Miscellaneous

Use Management of mild to moderate hypertension; treatment of edema in congestive heart failure and nephrotic syndrome

Pregnancy Risk Factor B (manufacturer); D (expert analysis)

Contraindications Hypersensitivity to indapamide or any component of the formulation, thiazides, or sulfonamide-derived drugs; anuria; renal decompensation; pregnancy (based on expert analysis)

Warnings/Precautions Use with caution in severe renal disease. Electrolyte disturbances (hypokalemia, hypochloremic alkalosis, hyponatremia) can occur. Use with caution in severe hepatic dysfunction; hepatic encephalopathy can be caused by electrolyte disturbances. Gout can be precipitate in certain patients with a history of gout, a familial predisposition to gout, or chronic renal failure. Cautious use in diabetics; may see a change in glucose control. I.V. use is generally not recommended (but is available). Hypersensitivity reactions can occur. Can cause SLE exacerbation or activation. Use with caution in patients with moderate or high cholesterol concentrations. Photosensitization may occur. Correct hypokalemia before initiating therapy.

Chemical similarities are present among sulfonamides, sulfonylureas, carbonic anhydrase inhibitors, thiazides, and loop diuretics (except ethacrynic acid). Use in patients with thiazide or sulfonamide allergy is specifically contraindicated in product labeling, however, a risk of
(Continued)

Indapamide *(Continued)*

cross-reaction exists in patients with allergy to any of these compounds; avoid use when previous reaction has been severe.

Common Adverse Reactions 1% to 10%:

Cardiovascular: Orthostatic hypotension, palpitations (<5%), flushing

Central nervous system: Dizziness (<5%), lightheadedness (<5%), vertigo (<5%), headache (≥5%), restlessness (<5%), drowsiness (<5%), fatigue, lethargy, malaise, lassitude, anxiety, agitation, depression, nervousness (≥5%)

Dermatologic: Rash (<5%), pruritus (<5%), hives (<5%)

Endocrine & metabolic: Hyperglycemia (<5%), hyperuricemia (<5%)

Gastrointestinal: Anorexia, gastric irritation, nausea, vomiting, abdominal pain, cramping, bloating, diarrhea, constipation, dry mouth, weight loss

Genitourinary: Nocturia, frequent urination, polyuria, impotence (<5%), reduced libido (<5%), glycosuria (<5%)

Neuromuscular & skeletal: Muscle cramps, spasm, weakness (≥5%)

Ocular: Blurred vision (<5%)

Renal: Necrotizing angiitis, vasculitis, cutaneous vasculitis (<5%)

Respiratory: Rhinorrhea (<5%)

Drug Interactions

Increased Effect/Toxicity: The diuretic effect of indapamide is synergistic with furosemide and other loop diuretics. Increased hypotension and/or renal adverse effects of ACE inhibitors may result in aggressively diuresed patients. Cyclosporine and thiazide-type diuretics can increase the risk of gout or renal toxicity. Digoxin toxicity can be exacerbated if a diuretic induces hypokalemia or hypomagnesemia. Lithium toxicity can occur with thiazide-type diuretics due to reduced renal excretion of lithium. Thiazide-type diuretics may prolong the duration of action of neuromuscular blocking agents.

Decreased Effect: Effects of oral hypoglycemics may be decreased. Decreased absorption of indapamide with cholestyramine and colestipol. NSAIDs can decrease the efficacy of thiazide-type diuretics, reducing the diuretic and antihypertensive effects.

Mechanism of Action Diuretic effect is localized at the proximal segment of the distal tubule of the nephron; it does not appear to have significant effect on glomerular filtration rate nor renal blood flow; like other diuretics, it enhances sodium, chloride, and water excretion by interfering with the transport of sodium ions across the renal tubular epithelium

Pharmacodynamics/Kinetics

Onset of action: 1-2 hours

Duration: ≤36 hours

Absorption: Complete

Protein binding, plasma: 71% to 79%

Metabolism: Extensively hepatic

Half-life elimination: 14-18 hours

Time to peak: 2-2.5 hours

Excretion: Urine (~60%) within 48 hours; feces (~16% to 23%)

Dosage Adults: Oral:

Edema: 2.5-5 mg/day. **Note:** There is little therapeutic benefit to increasing the dose >5 mg/day; there is, however, an increased risk of electrolyte disturbances

Hypertension: 1.25 mg in the morning, may increase to 5 mg/day by increments of 1.25-2.5 mg; consider adding another antihypertensive and decreasing the dose if response is not adequate

Monitoring Parameters Blood pressure (both standing and sitting/supine), serum electrolytes, renal function, assess weight, I & O reports daily to determine fluid loss

Patient Information May be taken with food or milk; take early in day to avoid nocturia; take the last dose of multiple doses no later than 6 PM unless instructed otherwise. A few people who take this medication become more sensitive to sunlight and may experience skin rash, redness, itching, or severe sunburn, especially if sun block SPF ≥15 is not used on exposed skin areas.

Dosage Forms TAB: 1.25 mg, 2.5 mg; (Lozol®): 1.25 mg

♦ **Inderal®** *see* Propranolol *on page 1054*

♦ **Inderal® LA** *see* Propranolol *on page 1054*

♦ **Inderide®** *see* Propranolol and Hydrochlorothiazide *on page 1057*

Indinavir *(in DIN a veer)*

Related Information

Antiretroviral Therapy for HIV Infection *on page 1448*

Management of Healthcare Worker Exposures to HBV, HCV, and HIV *on page 1421*

U.S. Brand Names Crixivan®

Therapeutic Category Antiretroviral Agent, Protease Inhibitor; Protease Inhibitor

Use Treatment of HIV infection; should always be used as part of a multidrug regimen (at least three antiretroviral agents)

Pregnancy Risk Factor C

Contraindications Hypersensitivity to indinavir or any component of the formulation; concurrent use of astemizole, cisapride, triazolam, midazolam, pimozide, or ergot alkaloids

Warnings/Precautions Because indinavir may cause nephrolithiasis/urolithiasis the drug should be discontinued if signs and symptoms occur; risk is substantially higher in pediatric patients versus adults. May cause interstitial nephritis (rare); severe asymptomatic leukocyturia may warrant evaluation. Indinavir should not be administered concurrently with lovastatin or simvastatin (caution with atorvastatin and cerivastatin) because of competition for metabolism of these drugs through the CYP3A4 system, and potential serious or life-threatening events. Use caution with other drugs metabolized by this enzyme (particular caution with sildenafil). Avoid concurrent use of St John's wort (may lead to loss of virologic response and/or resistance). Patients with hepatic insufficiency due to cirrhosis should have dose reduction. Warn patients about fat redistribution that can occur. Indinavir has been associated with hemolytic anemia (discontinue if diagnosed), hepatitis, and hyperglycemia (exacerbation or new-onset diabetes).

Common Adverse Reactions Protease inhibitors cause dyslipidemia which includes elevated cholesterol and triglycerides and a redistribution of body fat centrally to cause increased abdominal girth, buffalo hump, facial atrophy, and breast enlargement. These agents also cause hyperglycemia (exacerbation or new-onset diabetes).

10%:

Gastrointestinal: Nausea (12%)

Hepatic: Hyperbilirubinemia (14%)

Renal: Nephrolithiasis/urolithiasis (29%, pediatric patients; 12% adult patients)

1% to 10%:

Central nervous system: Headache (6%), insomnia (3%)

Gastrointestinal: Abdominal pain (9%), diarrhea/vomiting (4% to 5%), taste perversion (3%)

Neuromuscular & skeletal: Weakness (4%), flank pain (3%)

Renal: Hematuria

Drug Interactions

Cytochrome P450 Effect: Substrate of CYP2D6 (minor), 3A4 (major); **Inhibits** CYP2C8/9 (weak), 2C19 (weak), 2D6, (weak) 3A4 (strong)

Increased Effect/Toxicity: Levels of indinavir are increased by delavirdine, itraconazole, ketoconazole, nelfinavir, sildenafil, and ritonavir. Concurrent administration with atazanavir may increase risk of hyperbilirubinemia and is not recommended. Cisapride, pimozide, and astemizole should be avoided with indinavir due to life-threatening cardiotoxicity. Concurrent use of indinavir with lovastatin and simvastatin may increase the risk of myopathy or rhabdomyolysis. Cautious use of atorvastatin and cerivastatin may be possible. Benzodiazepines with indinavir may result in prolonged sedation and respiratory depression (midazolam and triazolam are contraindicated). Concurrent use of ergot alkaloids is contraindicated. Amprenavir and rifabutin concentrations are increased during concurrent therapy with indinavir. Other medications metabolized by cytochrome P450 isoenzyme 3A4 (including calcium channel blockers) may be affected. Concurrent sildenafil is associated with increased risk of hypotension, visual changes, and priapism. Clarithromycin and quinidine may increase serum concentrations of indinavir. Serum concentrations of these drugs may also be increased. Other CYP3A4 inhibitors may have similar effects.

Decreased Effect: Concurrent use of efavirenz, rifampin, and rifabutin may decrease the effectiveness of indinavir (dosage increase of indinavir is recommended); concurrent use of rifampin is not recommended; dosage decrease of rifabutin is recommended. The efficacy of protease inhibitors may be decreased when given with nevirapine. Gastric pH is lowered and absorption may be decreased when didanosine and indinavir are taken <1 hour apart. Fluconazole may decrease serum concentration of indinavir.

Mechanism of Action Indinavir is a human immunodeficiency virus protease inhibitor, binding to the protease activity site and inhibiting the activity of this enzyme. HIV protease is an enzyme required for the cleavage of viral polyprotein precursors into individual functional proteins found in infectious HIV. Inhibition prevents cleavage of these polyproteins resulting in the formation of immature noninfectious viral particles.

Pharmacodynamics/Kinetics

Absorption: Administration with a high fat, high calorie diet resulted in a reduction in AUC and in maximum serum concentration (77% and 84% respectively); lighter meal resulted in little or no change in these parameters.

Protein binding, plasma: 60%

Metabolism: Hepatic via CYP3A4; seven metabolites of indinavir identified

Bioavailability: Good

Half-life elimination: 1.8 ± 0.4 hour

Time to peak: 0.8 ± 0.3 hour

Excretion: Urine and feces

Dosage

Children (investigational): 500 mg/m^2 every 8 hours (patients with smaller BSA may require lower doses of 300-400 mg/m^2 every 8 hours)

Adults: Oral: 800 mg every 8 hours

Note: Dosage adjustments for indinavir when administered in combination therapy:

Delavirdine, itraconazole, or ketoconazole: Reduce indinavir dose to 600 mg every 8 hours

Efavirenz: Increase indinavir dose to 1000 mg every 8 hours

Lopinavir and ritonavir (Kaletra™): Indinavir 600 mg twice daily

Nevirapine: Increase indinavir dose to 1000 mg every 8 hours

Rifabutin: Reduce rifabutin to $^{1}/_{2}$ the standard dose plus increase indinavir to 1000 mg every 8 hours

Ritonavir: Adjustments necessary for both agents:

Ritonavir 100-200 mg twice daily plus indinavir 800 mg twice daily **or**

Ritonavir 400 mg twice daily plus indinavir 400 mg twice daily

Dosage adjustment in hepatic impairment: Mild-moderate impairment due to cirrhosis: 600 mg every 8 hours or with ketoconazole coadministration

(Continued)

Indinavir *(Continued)*

Administration Drink at least 48 oz of water daily. Administer with water, 1 hour before or 2 hours after a meal. Administer around-the-clock to avoid significant fluctuation in serum levels.

Monitoring Parameters Monitor viral load, CD4 count, triglycerides, cholesterol, glucose, liver function tests, CBC

Patient Information Take with a full glass of water; any symptoms of kidney stones, including flank pain, dysuria, etc, indicates the drug should be discontinued and physician or pharmacist should be contacted. Drug should be administered on an empty stomach 1 hour before or 2 hours after a large meal. May take with a small, light meal. Do not take any prescription medications, over-the-counter products or herbal products, especially St John's wort, without consulting prescriber. Indinavir should be stored and used in the original container.

Dosage Forms CAP: 100 mg, 200 mg, 333 mg, 400 mg

♦ **Indocin®** *see Indomethacin on page 664*

♦ **Indocin® I.V.** *see Indomethacin on page 664*

♦ **Indocin® SR** *see Indomethacin on page 664*

♦ **Indometacin** *see Indomethacin on page 664*

Indomethacin *(in doe METH a sin)*

Related Information
Nonsteroidal Anti-Inflammatory Agents Comparison *on page 1401*

U.S. Brand Names Indocin®; Indocin® I.V.; Indocin® SR

Synonyms Indometacin; Indomethacin Sodium Trihydrate

Therapeutic Category Analgesic, Nonsteroidal Anti-inflammatory Drug; Antigout Agent; Anti-inflammatory Agent; Antipyretic; Nonsteroidal Anti-inflammatory Drug (NSAID), Oral; Nonsteroidal Anti-inflammatory Drug (NSAID), Parenteral

Use Management of inflammatory diseases and rheumatoid disorders; moderate pain; acute gouty arthritis, acute bursitis/tendonitis, moderate to severe osteoarthritis, rheumatoid arthritis, ankylosing spondylitis; I.V. form used as alternative to surgery for closure of patent ductus arteriosus in neonates

Pregnancy Risk Factor B/D (3rd trimester)

Contraindications Hypersensitivity to indomethacin, any component of the formulation, aspirin, or other NSAIDs; patients in whom asthma, urticaria, or rhinitis are precipitated by NSAIDs/aspirin; active GI bleeding or ulcer disease; premature neonates with necrotizing enterocolitis; impaired renal function; active bleeding; thrombocytopenia; pregnancy (3rd trimester)

Warnings/Precautions Use with caution in patients with CHF, hypertension, dehydration, decreased renal or hepatic function, history of GI disease (bleeding or ulcers), or those receiving anticoagulants. Elderly are at a high risk for adverse effects from NSAIDs. As many as 60% of elderly can develop peptic ulceration and/or hemorrhage asymptomatically.

Use lowest effective dose for shortest period possible. Use of NSAIDs can compromise existing renal function especially when Cl_{cr} is <30 mL/minute.

CNS adverse effects such as confusion, agitation, and hallucination are generally seen in overdose or high-dose situations; but elderly may demonstrate these adverse effects at lower doses than younger adults. Withhold for at least 4-6 half-lives prior to surgical or dental procedures.

Common Adverse Reactions
>10%: Central nervous system: Headache (12%)
1% to 10%:
Central nervous system: Dizziness (3% to 9%), drowsiness (<1%), fatigue (<3%), vertigo (<3%), depression (<3%), malaise (<3%), somnolence (<3%)
Gastrointestinal: Nausea (3% to 9%), epigastric pain (3% to 9%), abdominal pain/cramps/distress (<3%), anorexia (<1%), GI bleeding (<1%), ulcers (<1%), perforation (<1%), heartburn (3% to 9%), indigestion (3% to 9%), constipation (<3%), diarrhea (<3%), dyspepsia (3% to 9%)
Hematologic: Inhibition of platelet aggregation (3% to 9%)
Otic: Tinnitus (<3%)

Drug Interactions
Cytochrome P450 Effect: Substrate (minor) of CYP2C8/9, 2C19; **Inhibits** CYP2C8/9 (strong), 2C19 (weak)

Increased Effect/Toxicity: Indomethacin may increase serum potassium with potassium-sparing diuretics. Probenecid may increase indomethacin serum concentrations. Other NSAIDs may increase GI adverse effects. May increase nephrotoxicity of cyclosporine and increase renal adverse effects of ACE inhibitors. Indomethacin may increase serum concentrations of digoxin, methotrexate, lithium, and aminoglycosides (reported with I.V. use in neonates).

Decreased Effect: May decrease antihypertensive effects of beta-blockers, hydralazine, ACE inhibitors, and angiotensin II antagonists. Indomethacin may decrease the antihypertensive and diuretic effect of thiazides (hydrochlorothiazide, etc) and loop diuretics (furosemide, bumetanide).

Mechanism of Action Inhibits prostaglandin synthesis by decreasing the activity of the enzyme, cyclooxygenase, which results in decreased formation of prostaglandin precursors

Pharmacodynamics/Kinetics
Onset of action: ~30 minutes
Duration: 4-6 hours

Absorption: Prompt and extensive

Distribution: V_d: 0.34-1.57 L/kg; crosses placenta; enters breast milk

Protein binding: 90%

Metabolism: Hepatic; significant enterohepatic recirculation

Half-life elimination: 4.5 hours; prolonged in neonates

Time to peak: Oral: ~3-4 hours

Excretion: Urine (primarily as glucuronide conjugates)

Dosage

Patent ductus arteriosus:

Neonates: I.V.: Initial: 0.2 mg/kg, followed by 2 doses depending on postnatal age (PNA):

PNA **at time of first dose** <48 hours: 0.1 mg/kg at 12- to 24-hour intervals

PNA **at time of first dose** 2-7 days: 0.2 mg/kg at 12- to 24-hour intervals

PNA **at time of first dose** >7 days: 0.25 mg/kg at 12- to 24-hour intervals

In general, may use 12-hour dosing interval if urine output >1 mL/kg/hour after prior dose; use 24-hour dosing interval if urine output is <1 mL/kg/hour but >0.6 mL/kg/hour; doses should be withheld if patient has oliguria (urine output <0.6 mL/kg/hour) or anuria

Inflammatory/rheumatoid disorders: Oral:

Children: 1-2 mg/kg/day in 2-4 divided doses; maximum dose: 4 mg/kg/day; not to exceed 150-200 mg/day

Adults: 25-50 mg/dose 2-3 times/day; maximum dose: 200 mg/day; extended release capsule should be given on a 1-2 times/day schedule

Administration

Oral: Administer with food, milk, or antacids to decrease GI adverse effects; extended release capsules must be swallowed whole, do not crush

I.V.: Administer over 20-30 minutes at a concentration of 0.5-1 mg/mL in preservative-free sterile water for injection or normal saline. Reconstitute I.V. formulation just prior to administration; discard any unused portion; avoid I.V. bolus administration or infusion via an umbilical catheter into vessels near the superior mesenteric artery as these may cause vasoconstriction and can compromise blood flow to the intestines. Do not administer intra-arterially.

Monitoring Parameters Monitor response (pain, range of motion, grip strength, mobility, ADL function), inflammation; observe for weight gain, edema; monitor renal function (serum creatinine, BUN); observe for bleeding, bruising; evaluate gastrointestinal effects (abdominal pain, bleeding, dyspepsia); mental confusion, disorientation, CBC, liver function tests

Patient Information Take with food, milk, or with antacids; sustained release capsules must be swallowed whole/intact, can cause dizziness or drowsiness

Dosage Forms CAP (Indocin®): 25 mg, 50 mg. **CAP, sustained release** (Indocin® SR): 75 mg. **INJ, powder for reconstitution** (Indocin® I.V.): 1 mg. **SUSP, oral** (Indocin®): 25 mg/5 mL (237 mL)

♦ **Indomethacin Sodium Trihydrate** *see* Indomethacin *on page 664*

♦ **INF-alpha 2** *see* Interferon Alfa-2b *on page 673*

♦ **Infanrix®** *see* Diphtheria, Tetanus Toxoids, and Acellular Pertussis Vaccine *on page 389*

♦ **Infants' Tylenol® Cold Plus Cough Concentrated Drops [OTC]** *see* Acetaminophen, Dextromethorphan, and Pseudoephedrine *on page 28*

♦ **Infasurf®** *see* Calfactant *on page 207*

♦ **INFeD®** *see* Iron Dextran Complex *on page 690*

♦ **Infergen®** *see* Interferon Alfacon-1 *on page 677*

♦ **Inflamase® Forte** *see* PrednisoLONE *on page 1031*

♦ **Inflamase® Mild** *see* PrednisoLONE *on page 1031*

Infliximab (in FLIKS e mab)

U.S. Brand Names Remicade®

Synonyms Infliximab, Recombinant

Therapeutic Category Antirheumatic, Disease Modifying; Gastrointestinal Agent, Anti-TNF; Monoclonal Antibody

Use

Crohn's disease: Induction and maintenance of remission in patients with moderate to severe disease who have an inadequate response to conventional therapy; to reduce the number of draining enterocutaneous and rectovaginal fistulas and to maintain fistula closure

Rheumatoid arthritis: Inhibits the progression of structural damage and improves physical function in patients with moderate to severe disease; used with methotrexate in patients who have had an inadequate response to methotrexate alone

Pregnancy Risk Factor B (manufacturer)

Contraindications Hypersensitivity to murine proteins or any component of the formulation; moderate or severe congestive heart failure (NYHA Class III/IV)

Warnings/Precautions Serious infections, including sepsis and fatal infections, have been reported in patients receiving TNF-blocking agents. Many of the serious infections in patients treated with infliximab have occurred in patients on concomitant immunosuppressive therapy. Caution should be exercised when considering the use of infliximab in patients with a chronic infection or history of recurrent infection. Infliximab should not be given to patients with a clinically-important, active infection. Patients should be evaluated for latent tuberculosis infection with a tuberculin skin test prior to infliximab therapy. Treatment of latent tuberculosis should be initiated before infliximab is used. Tuberculosis (may be disseminated or extrapulmonary) has been reactivated in patients previously exposed to TB while on infliximab. Most (Continued)

Infliximab *(Continued)*

cases have been reported within the first 3-6 months of treatment. Other opportunistic infections (eg, invasive fungal infections, listeriosis, *Pneumocystis*) have occurred during therapy. The risk/benefit ratio should be weighed in patients who have resided in regions where histoplasmosis is endemic. Patients who develop a new infection while undergoing treatment with infliximab should be monitored closely. If a patient develops a serious infection or sepsis, infliximab should be discontinued.

Hypersensitivity reactions, including urticaria, dyspnea, and hypotension have occurred. Discontinue the drug if a reaction occurs. Medications for the treatment of hypersensitivity reactions should be available for immediate use. Autoimmune antibodies and a lupus-like syndrome have been reported. If antibodies to double-stranded DNA are confirmed in a patient with lupus-like symptoms, treatment should be discontinued. Rare cases of demyelinating disease have been reported, use with caution in patients with pre-existing or recent onset CNS demyelinating disorders. Treatment may lead to antibody development to infliximab. Chronic exposure to immunosuppressants in patients with Crohn's disease or rheumatoid arthritis has been associated with the increased risk of developing lymphomas; the effect of infliximab is not known. Use caution with mild CHF (NYHA Class I/II); discontinue if exacerbated or new symptoms occur.

Safety and efficacy for use in juvenile rheumatoid arthritis and in pediatric patients with Crohn's disease have not been established.

Common Adverse Reactions Note: Although profile is similar, frequency of effects may be different in specific populations (Crohn's disease vs rheumatoid arthritis). Percentages reported with rheumatoid arthritis:

>10%:
 Central nervous system: Headache (29%), fatigue (13%), fever (13%)
 Dermatologic: Rash (18%)
 Gastrointestinal: Nausea (24%), diarrhea (19%), abdominal pain (17%)
 Genitourinary: Urinary tract infection (14%)
 Local: Infusion reactions (20%)
 Neuromuscular & skeletal: Arthralgia (13%), back pain (13%)
 Respiratory: Upper respiratory tract infection (40%), cough (18%), sinusitis (20%), pharyngitis (17%)
 Miscellaneous: Development of antinuclear antibodies (52%), infections (35%), development of antibodies to double-stranded DNA (17%); Crohn's patients with fistulizing disease: Development of new abscess (15%)

2% to 10%:
 Cardiovascular: Chest pain (7%), hypertension (10%)
 Central nervous system: Depression (8%), insomnia (6%)
 Dermatologic: Pruritus (9%)
 Gastrointestinal: Dyspepsia (10%)
 Respiratory: Bronchitis, dyspnea (6%)
 Miscellaneous: Moniliasis (8%), abscess (6%)

Drug Interactions

Increased Effect/Toxicity: Specific drug interaction studies have not been conducted.
Decreased Effect: Specific drug interaction studies have not been conducted.

Decreased toxicity: Immunosuppressants: When used with infliximab, may decrease the risk of infusion related reactions, and may decrease development of anti-double-stranded DNA antibodies

Mechanism of Action Infliximab is a chimeric monoclonal antibody that binds to human tumor necrosis factor alpha (TNFα), thereby interfering with endogenous TNFα activity. Biological activities of TNFα include the induction of pro-inflammatory cytokines (interleukins), enhancement of leukocyte migration, activation of neutrophils and eosinophils, and the induction of acute phase reactants and tissue degrading enzymes. Animal models have shown TNFα expression causes polyarthritis, and infliximab can prevent disease as well as allow diseased joints to heal.

Pharmacodynamics/Kinetics

Onset of action: Crohn's disease: ~2 weeks
Half-life elimination: 8-9.5 days

Dosage I.V.: Adults:
 Crohn's disease:
  Induction regimen: 5 mg/kg at 0, 2, and 6 weeks, followed by maintenance regimen
  Maintenance regimen: 5 mg/kg every 8 weeks; dose may be increased to 10 mg/kg in patients who respond but then lose their response. If no response by week 14, consider discontinuing therapy.
 Rheumatoid arthritis (in combination with methotrexate therapy): 3 mg/kg followed by an additional 3 mg/kg at 2- and 6 weeks after the first dose; then repeat every 8 weeks thereafter; doses have ranged from 3-10 mg/kg intravenous infusion repeated at 4-week intervals or 8-week intervals

Dosage adjustment with CHF:
 NYHA Class I/II: Maximum dose: 5 mg/kg
 NYHA Class III/IV: Use not recommended

Dosage adjustment in renal impairment: No specific adjustment is recommended
Dosage adjustment in hepatic impairment: No specific adjustment is recommended

Administration Infuse over at least 2 hours; must use an infusion set with an in-line filter (pore size ≤1.2 µm); infusion should begin within 3 hours of preparation; do not infuse with other agents

Monitoring Parameters Improvement of symptoms; signs of infection; place and read PPD before initiation.

Dosage Forms INJ, powder for reconstitution [preservative free]: 100 mg

♦ **Infliximab, Recombinant** *see* Infliximab *on page 665*

Influenza Virus Vaccine (in floo EN za VYE rus vak SEEN)

U.S. Brand Names FluMist™; Fluvirin®; Fluzone®

Synonyms Influenza Virus Vaccine (Purified Surface Antigen); Influenza Virus Vaccine (Split-Virus); Influenza Virus Vaccine (Trivalent, Live)

Therapeutic Category Vaccine; Vaccine, Inactivated Virus; Vaccine, Live Virus

Use Provide active immunity to influenza virus strains contained in the vaccine

Groups at Increased Risk for Influenza-Related Complications:
- Persons ≥65 years of age
- Residents of nursing homes and other chronic-care facilities that house persons of any age with chronic medical conditions
- Adults and children with chronic disorders of the pulmonary or cardiovascular systems, including children with asthma
- Adults and children who have required regular medical follow-up or hospitalization during the preceding year because of chronic metabolic diseases (including diabetes mellitus), renal dysfunction, hemoglobinopathies, or immunosuppression (including immunosuppression caused by medications)
- Children and adolescents (6 months to 18 years of age) who are receiving long-term aspirin therapy and therefore, may be at risk for developing Reye's syndrome after influenza
- Women who will be in the 2nd or 3rd trimester of pregnancy during the influenza season

Otherwise healthy children aged 6-23 months, healthy persons who may transmit influenza to those at risk, and others who are interested in immunization to influenza virus should receive the vaccine as long as supply is available.

Pregnancy Risk Factor C

Contraindications Hypersensitivity to influenza virus vaccine, or any component of the formulation; presence of acute respiratory disease or other active infections or illnesses; delay immunization in a patient with an active neurological disorder

In addition, for nasal spray: Patients at increased risk for influenza-related complications (see Use); history of Guillain-Barré syndrome; history of asthma or reactive airway disease; children 5-17 years of age receiving aspirin therapy

Warnings/Precautions Antigenic response may not be as great as expected in patients requiring immunosuppressive drug; some products contain thimerosal or are manufactured with eggs and/or gentamicin; hypersensitivity reactions (presumably to egg proteins) may occur; because of potential for febrile reactions, risks and benefits must carefully be considered in patients with history of febrile convulsions; influenza vaccines from previous seasons must not be used.

Injection: For I.M. use only; use caution with thrombocytopenia or any coagulation disorder. Safety and efficacy for use in children <6 months of age have not been established. Use caution with history of Guillain-Barré syndrome (GBS).

Nasal spray: For intranasal use only. **Avoid contact with immunocompromised individuals for at least 21 days following vaccination.** Safety and efficacy for use in children <5 years or adults ≥50 years of age have not been established.

Common Adverse Reactions All serious adverse reactions must be reported to the U.S. Department of Health and Human Services (DHHS) Vaccine Adverse Event Reporting System (VAERS) 1-800-822-7967.

Injection: Frequency not defined:
Central nervous system: Fever and malaise (may start within 6-12 hours and last 1-2 days; incidence equal to placebo in adults; occurs more frequently than placebo in children); GBS (previously reported with older vaccine formulations; relationship to current formulations not known, however, patients with history of GBS have a greater likelihood of developing GBS than those without)
Dermatologic: Angioedema, urticaria
Local: Tenderness, redness, or induration at the site of injection (10% to 64%; may last up to 2 days)
Neuromuscular & skeletal: Myalgia (may start within 6-12 hours and last 1-2 days; incidence equal to placebo in adults; occurs more frequently than placebo in children)
Miscellaneous: Allergic or anaphylactoid reactions (most likely to residual egg protein; includes allergic asthma, angioedema, hives, systemic anaphylaxis)

Nasal spray: **Note:** Frequency of events reported within 10 days
>10%:
Central nervous system: Headache (children 18% after first dose, < placebo after second dose; adults 40%) irritability (children 10% to 19%)
Neuromuscular & skeletal: Tiredness/weakness (adults 26%), muscle aches (children 5% to 6%; adults 17%)
Respiratory: Cough, nasal congestion/ runny nose (children 46% to 48%; adults 9% to 45%), sore throat (children < placebo; adults 28%)
(Continued)

Influenza Virus Vaccine *(Continued)*

Miscellaneous: Activity decreased (children 14% after first dose, < placebo after second dose)

1% to 10%:

Central nervous system: Chills,

Gastrointestinal: Abdominal pain, diarrhea, vomiting

Otic: Otitis media

Drug Interactions

Increased Effect/Toxicity: Concomitant use of aspirin and the nasal spray formulation may increase the risk of Reye syndrome in patients 5-17 years; concomitant use in this age group is contraindicated.

Decreased Effect: Decreased effect with immunosuppressive agents; some manufacturers and clinicians recommend that the flu vaccine not be administered concomitantly with DTP due to the potential for increased febrile reactions (specifically whole-cell pertussis) and that one should wait at least 3 days. However, ACIP recommends that children at high risk for influenza may get the vaccine concomitantly with DTP. Safety and efficacy of nasal spray with other vaccines have not been established; do not give within 1 month of other live virus vaccines or within 2 weeks of inactivated or subunit vaccines.

Mechanism of Action Promotes immunity to influenza virus by inducing specific antibody production. Each year the formulation is standardized according to the U.S. Public Health Service. Preparations from previous seasons must not be used.

Pharmacodynamics/Kinetics

Onset: Protective antibody levels achieved ~2 weeks after vaccination

Duration: Protective antibody levels persist approximately ≥6 months

Dosage Optimal time to receive vaccine is October-November, prior to exposure to influenza; however, vaccination can continue into December and later as long as vaccine is available.

I.M.:

Fluzone®:

Children 6-35 months: 0.25 mL/dose (1 or 2 doses per season; see **Note**)

Children 3-8 years: 0.5 mL/dose (1 or 2 doses per season; see **Note**)

Children ≥9 years and Adults: 0.5 mL/dose (1 dose per season)

Fluvirin®:

Children 4-8 years: 0.5 mL/dose (1 or 2 doses per season; see **Note**)

Children ≥9 years and Adults: 0.5 mL/dose (1 dose per season)

Note: Previously unvaccinated children <9 years should receive 2 doses, given >1 month apart in order to achieve satisfactory antibody response.

Intranasal (FluMist™):

Children 5-8 years, previously **not vaccinated** with influenza vaccine: 0.5 mL/dose (2 doses per season given 60 days apart)

Children 5-8 years, previously **vaccinated** with influenza vaccine: 0.5 mL/dose (1 dose per season)

Children ≥9 years and Adults ≤49 years: 0.5 mL/dose (1 dose per season)

Administration

Injection: For I.M. administration only. Inspect for particulate matter and discoloration prior to administration. Adults and older children should be vaccinated in the deltoid muscle. Infants and young children should be vaccinated in the anterolateral aspect of the thigh. Suspensions should be shaken well prior to use. **Note:** For patients at risk of hemorrhage following intramuscular injection, the ACIP recommends "it should be administered intramuscularly if, in the opinion of the physician familiar with the patients bleeding risk, the vaccine can be administered with reasonable safety by this route. If the patient receives antihemophilia or other similar therapy, intramuscular vaccination can be scheduled shortly after such therapy is administered. A fine needle (23 gauge or smaller) can be used for the vaccination and firm pressure applied to the site (without rubbing) for at least 2 minutes. The patient should be instructed concerning the risk of hematoma from the injection."

Intranasal: Must be thawed prior to administration. May thaw in refrigerator and store at 2°C to 8°C (36°F to 46°F) ≤24 hours; must be used within 24 hours after removal from the freezer. May also be thawed by holding sprayer in the palm of the hand and supporting the plunger rod with thumb; use immediately. Half the dose (0.25 mL) is administered to each nostril; patient should be in upright position. A dose divider clip is provided.

Patient Information You may experience the following: Soreness or swelling in the area where the shot is given, fever, aches. Some effects may last 1-2 days. Notify your prescriber immediately if these effects continue or are severe, or for a high fever, seizures, or allergic reaction (difficulty breathing, hives, weakness, dizziness, fast heart beat). Prior to vaccination, notify prescriber if you are allergic to eggs (develop hives, swelling of lip and/or tongue, or if you having trouble breathing after eating eggs).

Dosage Forms INJ, solution, purified split-virus surface antigen [preservative free] (Fluvirin®): (0.5 mL) [contains thimerosal (trace amounts); manufactured using neomycin and polymyxin]. **INJ, suspension, purified split-virus:** (Fluzone®): (0.5 mL) [contains thimerosal], (5 mL) [contains thimerosal]; (Fluzone®) [preservative free]: (0.25 mL, 0.5 mL) [contains thimerosal (trace amount)]. **SOLN, nasal spray, trivalent, live virus** [preservative free] (FluMist™): (0.5 mL) [manufactured using eggs and gentamicin]

◆ **Influenza Virus Vaccine (Purified Surface Antigen)** *see* Influenza Virus Vaccine *on page 667*

◆ **Influenza Virus Vaccine (Split-Virus)** *see* Influenza Virus Vaccine *on page 667*

◆ **Influenza Virus Vaccine (Trivalent, Live)** *see* Influenza Virus Vaccine *on page 667*

◆ **Infumorph®** *see* Morphine Sulfate *on page 861*

♦ **INH** *see Isoniazid on page 692*
♦ **Innohep®** *see Tinzaparin on page 1230*
♦ **InnoPran XL™** *see Propranolol on page 1054*
♦ **Insoluble Prussian Blue** *see Ferric Hexacyanoferrate on page 518*
♦ **Inspra™** *see Eplerenone on page 441*

Insulin Preparations (IN su lin prep a RAY shuns)

U.S. Brand Names Humalog®; Humalog® Mix 75/25™; Humulin® 50/50; Humulin® 70/30; Humulin® L; Humulin® N; Humulin® R; Humulin® R (Concentrated) U-500; Humulin® U; Lantus®; Lente® Iletin® II [DSC]; Novolin® 70/30; Novolin® L [DSC]; Novolin® N; Novolin® R; NovoLog®; NovoLog® Mix 70/30; NPH Iletin® II; Regular Iletin® II; Velosulin® BR (Buffered) [DSC]

Therapeutic Category Antidiabetic Agent, Insulin; Antidiabetic Agent, Parenteral; Antidote, Hyperglycemia

Use Treatment of type 1 diabetes mellitus (insulin dependent, IDDM); type 2 diabetes mellitus (noninsulin dependent, NIDDM) unresponsive to treatment with diet and/or oral hypoglycemics; adjunct to parenteral nutrition

Unlabeled/Investigational Use Hyperkalemia (regular insulin only; use with glucose to shift potassium into cells to lower serum potassium levels)

Pregnancy Risk Factor B; C (insulin glargine [Lantus®]; insulin aspart [NovoLog®])

Warnings/Precautions Hypoglycemia is the most common adverse effect of insulin. The timing of hypoglycemia differs among various insulin formulations. Any change of insulin should be made cautiously; changing manufacturers, type and/or method of manufacture, may result in the need for a change of dosage; human insulin differs from animal-source insulin; regular insulin is the only insulin to be used I.V.; hypoglycemia may result from increased work or exercise without eating; use of long-acting insulin preparations (insulin glargine, Ultralente®, insulin U) may delay recovery from hypoglycemia

In type 1 diabetes, insulin lispro (Humalog®) should be used in combination with a long-acting insulin. However, in type 2 diabetes it may be used without a long-acting insulin when used in combination with a sulfonylurea.

Use with caution in renal or hepatic impairment

Insulin aspart (NovoLog®, NovoLog® Mix 70/30): Safety and efficacy of use in children has not been established

Common Adverse Reactions Frequency not defined.
Cardiovascular: Palpitation, tachycardia, pallor
Central nervous system: Fatigue, mental confusion, loss of consciousness, headache, hypothermia
Dermatologic: Urticaria, redness
Endocrine & metabolic: Hypoglycemia
Gastrointestinal: Hunger, nausea, numbness of mouth
Local: Itching, edema, stinging, pain or warmth at injection site; atrophy or hypertrophy of S.C. fat tissue
Neuromuscular & skeletal: Muscle weakness, paresthesia, tremors
Ocular: Transient presbyopia or blurred vision
Miscellaneous: Diaphoresis, anaphylaxis

Drug Interactions
Cytochrome P450 Effect: Induces CYP1A2 (weak)
Increased Effect/Toxicity: Increased hypoglycemic effect of insulin with alcohol, alpha-blockers, anabolic steroids, beta-blockers (nonselective beta-blockers may delay recovery from hypoglycemic episodes and mask signs/symptoms of hypoglycemia; cardioselective beta-blocker agents may be alternatives), clofibrate, guanethidine, MAO inhibitors, pentamidine, phenylbutazone, salicylates, sulfinpyrazone, and tetracyclines.

Insulin increases the risk of hypoglycemia associated with oral hypoglycemic agents (including sulfonylureas, metformin, pioglitazone, rosiglitazone, and troglitazone).
Decreased Effect: Decreased hypoglycemic effect of insulin with corticosteroids, dextrothyroxine, diltiazem, dobutamine, epinephrine, niacin, oral contraceptives, thiazide diuretics, thyroid hormone, and smoking.

Mechanism of Action The principal hormone required for proper glucose utilization in normal metabolic processes; it is obtained from beef or pork pancreas or a biosynthetic process converting pork insulin to human insulin; insulins are categorized into 3 groups related to promptness, duration, and intensity of action

Pharmacodynamics/Kinetics
Onset of action and duration: Biosynthetic NPH human insulin shows a more rapid onset and shorter duration of action than corresponding porcine insulins; human insulin and purified porcine regular insulin are similarly efficacious following S.C. administration. The duration of action of highly purified porcine insulins is shorter than that of conventional insulin equivalents. Duration depends on type of preparation and route of administration as well as patient-related variables. In general, the larger the dose of insulin, the longer the duration of activity.

Absorption: Biosynthetic regular human insulin is absorbed from the S.C. injection site more rapidly than insulins of animal origin (60-90 minutes peak vs 120-150 minutes peak respectively) and lowers the initial blood glucose level faster. Human Ultralente® insulin is absorbed about twice as quickly as its bovine equivalent, and bioavailability is also improved. Human Lente® insulin preparations are also absorbed more quickly than their animal equivalents. Insulin glargine (Lantus®) is designed to form microprecipitates when injected subcutaneously. Small amounts of insulin glargine are then released over a 24-hour

(Continued)

Insulin Preparations *(Continued)*

period, with no pronounced peak. Insulin glargine (Lantus®) for the treatment of type 1 diabetes (insulin dependent, IDDM) and type 2 diabetes mellitus (noninsulin dependent, NIDDM) in patients who require basal (long-acting) insulin.

Bioavailability: Medium-acting S.C. Lente®-type human insulins did not differ from the corresponding porcine insulins

Lispro (Humalog®):
  Onset: 0.25 hours; Peak effect: 0.5-1.5 hours; Duration: 6-8 hours

Insulin aspart (NovoLog®):
  Onset: 0.5 hours; Peak effect: 1-3 hours; Duration: 3-5 hours

Insulin, regular (Novolin® R):
  Onset: 0.5-1 hours; Peak effect: 2-3 hours; Duration: 8-12 hours

Isophane insulin suspension (NPH) (Novolin® N):
  Onset: 1-1.5 hours; Peak effect: 4-12 hours; Duration: 24 hours

Insulin zinc suspension (Lente®):
  Onset: 1-2.5 hours; Peak effect: 8-12 hours; Duration: 18-24 hours

Isophane insulin suspension and regular insulin injection (Novolin® 70/30):
  Onset: 0.5 hours; Peak effect: 2-12 hours; Duration: 24 hours

Extended insulin zinc suspension (Ultralente®):
  Onset: 4-8 hours; Peak effect: 16-18 hours; Duration: >36 hours

Insulin glargine (Lantus®):
  Duration: 24 hours

Dosage Dose requires continuous medical supervision; may administer I.V. (regular), I.M., S.C.

Diabetes mellitus: The number and size of daily doses, time of administration, and diet and exercise require continuous medical supervision. In addition, specific formulations may require distinct administration procedures (see Administration).
  Children and Adults: 0.5-1 unit/kg/day in divided doses
  Adolescents (growth spurts): 0.8-1.2 units/kg/day in divided doses
  Adjust dose to maintain premeal and bedtime blood glucose of 80-140 mg/dL (children <5 years: 100-200 mg/dL)
  Insulin glargine (Lantus®): S.C.:
    Type 2 diabetes (patient not already on insulin): 10 units once daily, adjusted according to patient response (range in clinical study 2-100 units/day)
    Patients already receiving insulin: In clinical studies, when changing to insulin glargine from once-daily NPH or Ultralente® insulin, the initial dose was not changed; when changing from twice-daily NPH to once-daily insulin glargine, the total daily dose was reduced by 20% and adjusted according to patient response
Hyperkalemia (unlabeled use): Administer calcium gluconate and NaHCO3 first then 50% dextrose at 0.5-1 mL/kg and insulin 1 unit for every 4-5 g dextrose given
Diabetic ketoacidosis: Children and Adults: Regular insulin: I.V. loading dose: 0.1 unit/kg, then maintenance continuous infusion: 0.1 unit/kg/hour (range: 0.05-0.2 units/kg/hour depending upon the rate of decrease of serum glucose - too rapid decrease of serum glucose may lead to cerebral edema).
  Optimum rate of decrease (serum glucose): 80-100 mg/dL/hour
  Note: Newly-diagnosed patients with IDDM presenting in DKA and patients with blood sugars <800 mg/dL may be relatively "sensitive" to insulin and should receive loading and initial maintenance doses approximately 1/2 of those indicated above.

Dosing adjustment in renal impairment (regular): Insulin requirements are reduced due to changes in insulin clearance or metabolism
  Cl_{cr} 10-50 mL/minute: Administer at 75% of normal dose
  Cl_{cr} <10 mL/minute: Administer at 25% to 50% of normal dose and monitor glucose closely
Hemodialysis: Because of a large molecular weight (6000 daltons), insulin is not significantly removed by either peritoneal or hemodialysis
  Supplemental dose is not necessary
Peritoneal dialysis: Supplemental dose is not necessary
Continuous arteriovenous or venovenous hemofiltration effects: Supplemental dose is not necessary

Administration

S.C. administration: Cold injections should be avoided. S.C. administration is usually made into the thighs, arms, buttocks, or abdomen, with sites rotated. When mixing regular insulin with other preparations of insulin, regular insulin should be drawn into syringe first. Buffered insulin (Velosulin® BR) should not be mixed with any other form of insulin.
  Insulin lispro (Humalog®): May be administered within 15 minutes before or immediately after a meal.
  Insulin aspart (NovoLog®): Should be administered immediately before a meal (within 5-10 minutes of the start of a meal). Can be infused S.C. by external insulin pump; do not dilute or mix with other insulins when used in an external pump for S.C. infusion; should replace insulin in reservoir every 48 hours.
  Human regular insulin: Should be administered within 30-60 minutes before a meal.
  Intermediate-acting insulins (such as NPH): May be administered 1-2 times/day.
  Long-acting insulins (such as Ultralente®, Lantus®): May be administered once daily.

Insulin glargine (Lantus®): Should be administered once daily, at any time of day, but should be administered at the same time each day. Cannot be diluted or mixed with any other insulin or solution.

Regular insulin may be administered by S.C., I.M., or I.V. routes

I.V. administration (requires use of an infusion pump): **Only regular insulin** may be administered I.V.

I.V. infusions: To minimize adsorption problems to I.V. solution bag:

If new tubing is **not** needed: Wait a minimum of 30 minutes between the preparation of the solution and the initiation of the infusion

If new tubing is needed: After receiving the insulin drip solution, the administration set should be attached to the I.V. container and the line should be flushed with the insulin solution. The nurse should then wait 30 minutes, then flush the line again with the insulin solution prior to initiating the infusion

If insulin is required prior to the availability of the insulin drip, regular insulin should be administered by I.V. push injection

Because of adsorption, the actual amount of insulin being administered could be substantially less than the apparent amount. Therefore, adjustment of the insulin drip rate should be based on effect and not solely on the apparent insulin dose. Furthermore, the apparent dose should not be used as the basis for determining the subsequent insulin dose upon discontinuing the insulin drip. Dose requires continuous medical supervision.

To be ordered as units/hour

Example: Standard diluent of regular insulin only: 100 units/100 mL NS (can be administered as a more diluted solution, ie, 100 units/250 mL NS)

Insulin rate of infusion (100 units regular/100 mL NS)

1 unit/hour: 1 mL/hour
2 units/hour: 2 mL/hour
3 units/hour: 3 mL/hour
4 units/hour: 4 mL/hour
5 units/hour: 5 mL/hour, etc

Monitoring Parameters Urine sugar and acetone, serum glucose, electrolytes, Hb A_{1c}, lipid profile

Reference Range

Therapeutic, serum insulin (fasting): 5-20 µlU/mL (SI: 35-145 pmol/L)

Glucose, fasting:

Newborns: 60-110 mg/dL
Adults: 60-110 mg/dL
Elderly: 100-180 mg/dL

Patient Information This medication is used to control diabetes; it is not a cure. Other components of treatment plan are important: follow prescribed diet, medication, and exercise regimen. Take exactly as directed. Do not change dose or discontinue unless so advised by prescriber. Inform prescriber of all other prescription or OTC medications you are taking; do not introduce new medication without consulting prescriber. If you experience hypoglycemic reaction, contact prescriber immediately. Maintain regular dietary intake and exercise routine and always carry quick source of sugar with you. Report adverse side effects, including chest pain or palpitations; persistent fatigue, confusion, headache; skin rash or redness; numbness of mouth, lips, or tongue; muscle weakness or tremors; changes in vision; difficulty breathing; or nausea, vomiting, or flu-like symptoms. With insulin aspart (NovoLog®), you must start eating within 5-10 minutes after injection.

Dosage Forms RAPID-ACTING: INJ, solution, aspart, human (NovoLog®): 100 units/mL (10 mL vial); (NovoLog® [PenFill®]): 100 units/mL (3 mL cartridge). **INJ, solution,lispro, human** (Humalog®): 100 units/mL (1.5 mL cartridge, 3 mL disposable pen, 10 mL vial). **SHORT-ACTING: INJ, solution, regular, human** (Humulin® R): 100 units/mL (10 mL vial); (Novolin® R): 100 units/mL (1.5 mL prefilled syringe, 10 mL vial); (Novolin® R [PenFill®]): 100 units/mL (1.5 mL cartridge, 3 mL cartridge). **INJ, solution, regular, human, buffered** (Velosulin® BR) [DSC]: 100 units/mL (10 mL vial). **INJ, solution, regular, human, concentrate** (Humulin® R U-500): 500 units/mL (20 mL vial). **INJ, solution, regular, purified pork** (Regular Iletin® II): 100 units/mL (10 mL vial). **INTERMEDIATE-ACTING: INJ, suspension, lente, human [zinc]** (Humulin® L, Novolin® L [DSC]): 100 units/mL (10 mL vial). **INJ, suspension, lente, purified pork [zinc]** (Lente® Iletin® II): 100 units/mL (10 mL vial) [DSC]. **INJ, suspension, NPH, human [isophane]** (Humulin® N): 100 units/mL (3 mL disposable pen, 10 mL vial); (Novolin® N): 100 units/mL (1.5 mL prefilled syringe, 10 mL vial); (Novolin® N [PenFill®]): 100 units/mL (1.5 mL cartridge, 3 mL cartridge). **INJ, suspension, NPH, purified pork [isophane]** (NPH Iletin® II): 100 units/mL (10 mL vial). **LONG-ACTING: INJ, suspension,human [zinc]** (Humulin U Ultralente®):100 units/mL (10 mL vial). **INJ, solution, glargine, human** (Lantus®): 100 unit/mL (10 mL vial). **COMBINATION, INTERMEDIATE-ACTING: INJ, aspart protamine human suspension 75% and rapid-acting aspart human solution 30%** (NovoLog® Mix 70/30): 100 units/mL (3 mL cartridge, 3 mL prefilled syringe). **INJ, lispro protamine human suspension 75% and rapid-acting lispro human solution 25%** (Humalog® Mix 75/25™): 100 units/mL (3 mL disposable pen, 10 mL vial). **INJ, NPH human insulin suspension 50% and short-acting regular human insulin solution 50%** (Humulin® 50/50): 100 units/mL (10 mL vial). **INJ, NPH human insulin suspension 70% and short-acting regular human insulin solution 30%** (Humulin® 70/30): 100 units/mL (3 mL disposable pen, 10 mL vial); (Novolin® 70/30): 100 units/mL (1.5 mL prefilled syringe, 10 mL vial); (Novolin® 70/30 [PenFill®]): 100 units/mL (1.5 mL cartridge, 3 mL cartridge)

♦ **Intal®** *see* Cromolyn *on page 316*

♦ **Integrilin®** *see* Eptifibatide *on page 448*

♦ α-2-interferon *see* Interferon Alfa-2b *on page 673*

Interferon Alfa-2a (in ter FEER on AL fa too aye)

U.S. Brand Names Roferon-A®

Synonyms IFLrA; rIFN-A

Therapeutic Category Biological Response Modulator; Interferon

Use

> Patients >18 years of age: Hairy cell leukemia, AIDS-related Kaposi's sarcoma, chronic hepatitis C
>
> Children and Adults: Chronic myelogenous leukemia (CML), Philadelphia chromosome positive, within 1 year of diagnosis (limited experience in children)

Unlabeled/Investigational Use Adjuvant therapy for malignant melanoma, AIDS-related thrombocytopenia, cutaneous ulcerations of Behçet's disease, brain tumors, metastatic ileal carcinoid tumors, cervical and colorectal cancers, genital warts, idiopathic mixed cryoglobulinemia, hemangioma, hepatitis D, hepatocellular carcinoma, idiopathic hypereosinophilic syndrome, mycosis fungoides, Sézary syndrome, low-grade non-Hodgkin's lymphoma, macular degeneration, multiple myeloma, renal cell carcinoma, basal and squamous cell skin cancer, essential thrombocythemia, cutaneous T-cell lymphoma

Pregnancy Risk Factor C

Contraindications Hypersensitivity to alfa interferon, benzyl alcohol, or any component of the formulation; autoimmune disorders, including autoimmune hepatitis; visceral AIDS-related Kaposi's sarcoma associated with rapidly-progressing or life-threatening disease

Warnings/Precautions Use with caution in patients with seizure disorders, brain metastases, compromised CNS, multiple sclerosis, and patients with pre-existing cardiac disease (ischemic or thromboembolic), arrhythmias, renal impairment (Cl_{cr} <50 mL/minute) or hepatic impairment, or myelosuppression; caution in transplant patients receiving therapeutic immunosuppression; may cause severe psychiatric adverse events (psychosis, mania, depression, suicidal behavior/ideation) in patients with and without previous psychiatric symptoms, avoid use in severe psychiatric disorders or in patients with a history of depression; careful neuropsychiatric monitoring is required during therapy. May cause thyroid dysfunction or hyperglycemia, use caution in patients with diabetes. Use caution in patients with pulmonary dysfunction. Treatment should be discontinued in patients with worsening or persistently severe signs/symptoms of autoimmune, infectious (including radiographic changes or worsening hepatic function), or neuropsychiatric disorders (including depression and/or suicidal thoughts/behavior). Safety and efficacy in children <18 years of age have not been established. Higher doses in the elderly or in malignancies other than hairy cell leukemia may result in severe obtundation. Ophthalmologic disorders (including retinal hemorrhages, cotton wool spots, and retinal artery or vein obstruction) have occurred in patients receiving alpha interferons. **Due to differences in dosage, patients should not change brands of interferons.** Injection solution contains benzyl alcohol, do not use in neonates or infants.

Common Adverse Reactions Note: A flu-like syndrome (fever, chills, tachycardia, malaise, myalgia, arthralgia, headache) occurs within 1-2 hours of administration; may last up to 24 hours and may be dose-limiting (symptoms in up to 92% of patients). For the listing below, the percentage of incidence noted generally corresponds to highest reported ranges. Incidence depends upon dosage and indication.

>10%:

> Cardiovascular: Chest pain (4% to 11%), edema (11%), hypertension (11%)
>
> Central nervous system: Psychiatric disturbances (including depression and suicidal behavior/ideation; reported incidence highly variable, generally >15%), fatigue (90%), headache (52%), dizziness (21%), irritability (15%), insomnia (14%), somnolence, lethargy, confusion, mental impairment, and motor weakness (most frequently seen at high doses [>100 million units], usually reverses within a few days); vertigo (19%); mental status changes (12%)
>
> Dermatologic: Rash (usually maculopapular) on the trunk and extremities (7% to 18%), alopecia (19% to 22%), pruritus (13%), dry skin
>
> Endocrine & metabolic: Hypocalcemia (10% to 51%), hyperglycemia (33% to 39%), elevation of transaminase levels (25% to 30%), elevation of alkaline phosphatase (48%)
>
> Gastrointestinal: Loss of taste, anorexia (30% to 70%), nausea (28% to 53%), vomiting (10% to 30%, usually mild), diarrhea (22% to 34%, may be severe), taste change (13%), dry throat, xerostomia, abdominal cramps, abdominal pain
>
> Hematologic: (often due to underlying disease): Myelosuppression; neutropenia (32% to 70%); thrombocytopenia (22% to 70%); anemia (24% to 65%, may be dose-limiting, usually seen only during the first 6 months of therapy)
>
> > Onset: 7-10 days
> >
> > Nadir: 14 days, may be delayed 20-40 days in hairy cell leukemia
> >
> > Recovery: 21 days
>
> Hepatic: Elevation of AST (SGOT) (77% to 80%), LDH (47%), bilirubin (31%)
>
> Local: Injection site reaction (29%)
>
> Neuromuscular & skeletal: Weakness (may be severe at doses >20,000,000 units/day); arthralgia and myalgia (5% to 73%, usually during the first 72 hours of treatment); rigors
>
> Renal: Proteinuria (15% to 25%)
>
> Respiratory: Cough (27%), irritation of oropharynx (14%)
>
> Miscellaneous: Flu-like syndrome (up to 92% of patients), diaphoresis (15%)

1% to 10%:

> Cardiovascular: Hypotension (6%), supraventricular tachyarrhythmias, palpitations (<3%), acute myocardial infarction (<1% to 1%)
>
> Central nervous system: Confusion (10%), delirium

Dermatologic: Erythema (diffuse), urticaria

Endocrine & metabolic: Hyperphosphatemia (2%)

Gastrointestinal: Stomatitis, pancreatitis (<5%), flatulence, liver pain

Genitourinary: Impotence (6%), menstrual irregularities

Neuromuscular & skeletal: Leg cramps; peripheral neuropathy, paresthesias (7%), and numbness (4%) are more common in patients previously treated with vinca alkaloids or receiving concurrent vinblastine

Ocular: Conjunctivitis (4%)

Respiratory: Dyspnea (7.5%), epistaxis (4%), rhinitis (3%)

Miscellaneous: Antibody production to interferon (10%)

Drug Interactions

Cytochrome P450 Effect: Inhibits CYP1A2 (weak)

Increased Effect/Toxicity: Theophylline clearance has been reported to be decreased in hepatitis patients receiving interferon. Interferons may increase the adverse/toxic effects of ACE inhibitors, specifically the development of granulocytopenia. Agranulocytosis has been reported with concurrent use of clozapine (case report). Interferons may increase the anticoagulant effects of warfarin, and interferons may increase serum levels of zidovudine.

Decreased Effect: Prednisone may decrease the therapeutic effects of interferon alpha. A decreased response to erythropoietin has been reported (case reports) in patients receiving interferons. Interferon alpha may decrease the serum concentrations of melphalan (may or may not decrease toxicity of melphalan).

Mechanism of Action Following activation, multiple effects can be detected including induction of gene transcription. Inhibits cellular growth, alters the state of cellular differentiation, interferes with oncogene expression, alters cell surface antigen expression, increases phagocytic activity of macrophages, and augments cytotoxicity of lymphocytes for target cells

Pharmacodynamics/Kinetics

Absorption: Filtered and absorbed at the renal tubule

Distribution: V_d: 0.223-0.748 L/kg

Metabolism: Primarily renal; filtered through glomeruli and undergoes rapid proteolytic degradation during tubular reabsorption

Bioavailability: I.M.: 83%; S.C.: 90%

Half-life elimination: I.V.: 3.7-8.5 hours (mean ~5 hours)

Time to peak, serum: I.M., S.C.: ~6-8 hours

Dosage Refer to individual protocols

Children (limited data):

Chronic myelogenous leukemia (CML): I.M.: 2.5-5 million units/m^2/day; **Note:** In juveniles, higher dosages (30 million units/m^2/day) have been associated with severe adverse events, including death

Adults:

Hairy cell leukemia: S.C., I.M.: 3 million units/day for 16-24 weeks, then 3 million units 3 times/week for up to 6-24 months

Chronic myelogenous leukemia (CML): S.C., I.M.: 9 million units/day, continue treatment until disease progression

AIDS-related Kaposi's sarcoma: S.C., I.M.: 36 million units/day for 10-12 weeks, then 36 million units 3 times/week; to minimize adverse reactions, can use escalating dose (3-, 9-, then 18 million units each day for 3 days, then 36 million units daily thereafter).

Hepatitis C: S.C., I.M.: 3 million units 3 times/week for 12 months

Dosage adjustment in renal impairment: Not removed by hemodialysis

Administration S.C. administration is suggested for those who are at risk for bleeding or are thrombocytopenic; rotate S.C. injection site; patient should be well hydrated

Monitoring Parameters

Chronic hepatitis C: Monitor ALT and HCV-RNA to assess response (particularly in first 3 months of therapy)

CML/hairy cell leukemia: Hematologic monitoring should be performed monthly

Patient Information Use as directed; do not change dosage or schedule of administration without consulting prescriber. Maintain adequate hydration (2-3 L/day of fluids unless instructed to restrict fluid intake). You may experience flu-like syndrome (acetaminophen may help); this syndrome subsides after several weeks of continuous dosing, but usually recurs during each cycle of intermittent therapy. You may also experience nausea, vomiting, dry mouth, or metallic taste (frequent small meals, frequent mouth care, sucking lozenges, or chewing gum may help); drowsiness, dizziness, agitation, abnormal thinking (use caution when driving or engaging in tasks requiring alertness until response to drug is known). Inform prescriber **immediately** if you feel depressed or have any thoughts of suicide. Report unusual bruising or bleeding; persistent abdominal disturbances; unusual fatigue; muscle pain or tremors; chest pain or palpitation; swelling of extremities or unusual weight gain; difficulty breathing; pain, swelling, or redness at injection site; or other unusual symptoms.

Dosage Forms INJ, solution: 6 million units/mL (3 mL) [DSC]. **INJ, solution:** 36 million units/mL (1 mL). **INJ, solution** [prefilled syringe; S.C. use only]: 3 million units/0.5 mL (0.5 mL); 6 million units/0.5 mL (0.5 mL); 9 million units/0.5 mL (0.5 mL) [DSC]

♦ **Interferon Alfa-2a (PEG Conjugate)** see Peginterferon Alfa-2a on page 964

Interferon Alfa-2b (in ter FEER on AL fa too bee)

U.S. Brand Names Intron® A

Synonyms INF-alpha 2; α-2-interferon; rLFN-α2

Therapeutic Category Antiviral Agent, Hepatitis; Biological Response Modulator; Interferon

(Continued)

Interferon Alfa-2b *(Continued)*

Use

Patients ≥1 year of age: Chronic hepatitis B

Patients ≥18 years of age: Condyloma acuminata, chronic hepatitis C, hairy cell leukemia, malignant melanoma, AIDS-related Kaposi's sarcoma, follicular non-Hodgkin's lymphoma

Unlabeled/Investigational Use AIDS-related thrombocytopenia, cutaneous ulcerations of Behçet's disease, carcinoid syndrome, cervical cancer, lymphomatoid granulomatosis, genital herpes, hepatitis D, chronic myelogenous leukemia (CML), non-Hodgkin's lymphomas (other than follicular lymphoma, see approved use), polycythemia vera, medullary thyroid carcinoma, multiple myeloma, renal cell carcinoma, basal and squamous cell skin cancers, essential thrombocytopenia, thrombocytopenic purpura

Investigational: West Nile virus

Pregnancy Risk Factor C

Contraindications Hypersensitivity to interferon alfa or any component of the formulation; patients with visceral AIDS-related Kaposi's sarcoma associated with rapidly-progressing or life-threatening disease; decompensated liver disease; autoimmune hepatitis; history of autoimmune disease

Warnings/Precautions Use with caution in patients with a history of seizures, brain metastases, multiple sclerosis, cardiac disease (ischemic or thromboembolic), arrhythmias, myelosuppression, hepatic impairment, or renal dysfunction. Use caution in patients with a history of pulmonary disease, coagulopathy, thyroid disease, hypertension, or diabetes mellitus (particularly if prone to DKA). Avoid use in patient with autoimmune disorders; worsening of psoriasis and/or development of autoimmune disorders has been associated with alpha interferons. Caution in immunocompromised or transplant patients. May cause severe psychiatric adverse events (psychosis, mania, depression, suicidal behavior/ideation) in patients with and without previous psychiatric symptoms, avoid use in severe psychiatric disorders or in patients with a history of depression; careful neuropsychiatric monitoring is required during therapy. Higher doses in elderly patients, or diseases other than hairy cell leukemia, may result in increased CNS toxicity. Ophthalmologic disorders (including retinal hemorrhages, cotton wool spots, and retinal artery or vein obstruction) have occurred in patients receiving alpha interferons.

A transient increase in SGOT (>2x baseline) is common in patients treated with interferon alfa-2b for chronic hepatitis. Therapy generally may continue, however, functional indicators (albumin, prothrombin time, bilirubin) should be monitored at 2-week intervals. Treatment should be discontinued in patients who develop severe pulmonary symptoms with chest x-ray changes, autoimmune disorders, worsening of hepatic function, psychiatric symptoms (including depression and/or suicidal thoughts/behaviors), severe or persistent infectious or ischemic disorders. Safety and efficacy in children <18 years of age have not been established (except in chronic hepatitis B). **Due to differences in dosage, patients should not change brands of interferons.**

Common Adverse Reactions Note: In a majority of patients, a flu-like syndrome (fever, chills, tachycardia, malaise, myalgia, headache), occurs within 1-2 hours of administration; may last up to 24 hours and may be dose-limiting.

>10%:

Cardiovascular: Chest pain (2% to 28%)

Central nervous system: Fatigue (8% to 96%), headache (21% to 62%), fever (34% to 94%), depression (4% to 40%), somnolence (1% to 33%), irritability (1% to 22%), paresthesia (1% to 21%, more common in patients previously treated with vinca alkaloids or receiving concurrent vinblastine), dizziness (7% to 23%), confusion (1% to 12%), malaise (3% to 14%), pain (3% to 15%), insomnia (1% to 12%), impaired concentration (1% to 14%, usually reverses within a few days), amnesia (1% to 14%), chills (45% to 54%),

Dermatologic: Alopecia (8% to 38%), rash (usually maculopapular) on the trunk and extremities (1% to 25%), pruritus (3% to 11%), dry skin (1% to 10%)

Endocrine & metabolic: Hypocalcemia (10% to 51%), hyperglycemia (33% to 39%), amenorrhea (up to 12% in lymphoma)

Gastrointestinal: Anorexia (1% to 69%), nausea (19% to 66%), vomiting (2% to 32%, usually mild), diarrhea (2% to 45%, may be severe), taste change (2% to 24%), xerostomia (1% to 28%), abdominal pain (2% to 23%), gingivitis (2% to 14%), constipation (1% to 14%)

Hematologic: Myelosuppression; neutropenia (30% to 66%); thrombocytopenia (5% to 15%); anemia (15% to 32%, may be dose-limiting, usually seen only during the first 6 months of therapy)

Onset: 7-10 days

Nadir: 14 days, may be delayed 20-40 days in hairy cell leukemia

Recovery: 21 days

Hepatic: Increased transaminases (increased SGOT in up to 63%), elevation of alkaline phosphatase (48%), right upper quadrant pain (15% in hepatitis C)

Local: Injection site reaction (1% to 20%)

Neuromuscular & skeletal: Weakness (5% to 63%) may be severe at doses >20,000,000 units/day; mild arthralgia and myalgia (5% to 75% - usually during the first 72 hours of treatment), rigors (2% to 42%), back pain (1% to 19%), musculoskeletal pain (1% to 21%), paresthesia (1% to 21%)

Renal: Urinary tract infection (up to 5% in hepatitis C)

Respiratory: Dyspnea (1% to 34%), cough (1% to 31%), pharyngitis (1% to 31%),

Miscellaneous: Loss of smell, flu-like symptoms (5% to 79%), diaphoresis (2% to 21%)

5% to 10%:

Cardiovascular: Hypertension (9% in hepatitis C)

Central nervous system: Anxiety (1% to 9%), nervousness (1% to 3%), vertigo (up to 8% in lymphoma)

Dermatologic: Dermatitis (1% to 8%)

Endocrine & metabolic: Decreased libido (1% to 5%)

Gastrointestinal: Loose stools (1% to 21%), dyspepsia (2% to 8%)

Neuromuscular & skeletal: Hypoesthesia (1% to 10%)

Respiratory: Nasal congestion (1% to 10%)

Drug Interactions

Cytochrome P450 Effect: Inhibits CYP1A2 (weak)

Increased Effect/Toxicity: Theophylline clearance has been reported to be decreased in hepatitis patients receiving interferon. Interferons may increase the adverse/toxic effects of ACE inhibitors, specifically the development of granulocytopenia. Agranulocytosis has been reported with concurrent use of clozapine (case report). Interferons may increase the anticoagulant effects of warfarin, and interferons may increase serum levels of zidovudine.

Mechanism of Action Following activation, multiple effects can be detected including induction of gene transcription. Inhibits cellular growth, alters the state of cellular differentiation, interferes with oncogene expression, alters cell surface antigen expression, increases phagocytic activity of macrophages, and augments cytotoxicity of lymphocytes for target cells

Pharmacodynamics/Kinetics

Distribution: V_d: 31 L; but has been noted to be much greater (370-720 L) in leukemia patients receiving continuous infusion IFN; IFN does not penetrate the CSF

Metabolism: Primarily renal

Bioavailability: I.M.: 83%; S.C.: 90%

Half-life elimination: I.M., I.V.: 2 hours; S.C.: 3 hours

Time to peak, serum: I.M., S.C.: ~3-12 hours

Dosage Refer to individual protocols

Children 1-17 years: Chronic hepatitis B: S.C.: 3 million units/m^2 3 times/week for 1 week; then 6 million units/m^2 3 times/week; maximum: 10 million units 3 times/week; total duration of therapy 16-24 weeks

Adults:

Hairy cell leukemia: I.M., S.C.: 2 million units/m^2 3 times/week for 2-6 months

Lymphoma (follicular): S.C.: 5 million units 3 times/week for up to 18 months

Malignant melanoma: 20 million units/m^2 I.V. for 5 consecutive days per week for 4 weeks, then 10 million units/m^2 S.C. 3 times/week for 48 weeks

AIDS-related Kaposi's sarcoma: I.M., S.C.: 30 million units/m^2 3 times/week

Chronic hepatitis B: I.M., S.C.: 5 million units/day or 10 million units 3 times/week for 16 weeks

Chronic hepatitis C: I.M., S.C.: 3 million units 3 times/week for 16 weeks. In patients with normalization of ALT at 16 weeks, continue treatment for 18-24 months; consider discontinuation if normalization does not occur at 16 weeks. **Note:** May be used in combination therapy with ribavirin in previously untreated patients or in patients who relapse following alpha interferon therapy; refer to Interferon Alfa-2b and Ribavirin Combination Pack monograph.

Condyloma acuminata: Intralesionally: 1 million units/lesion (maximum: 5 lesions/treatment) 3 times/week (on alternate days) for 3 weeks.

Dosage adjustment in renal impairment: Not removed by peritoneal or hemodialysis

Dosage adjustment for toxicity: Manufacturer-recommended adjustments, listed according to indication:

Follicular lymphoma:

Severe toxicity (neutrophils <1000 cells/mm^3 or platelets <50,000 cells/mm^3): Reduce dose by 50% or temporarily discontinue

AST/ALT >5 times ULN: Permanently discontinue

Hairy cell leukemia:

Severe toxicity: Reduce dose by 50% or temporarily discontinue; permanently discontinue if persistent or recurrent severe toxicity is noted

Hepatitis B or C:

WBC <1500 cells/mm^3, granulocytes <750 cells/mm^3, or platelet count <50,000 cells/mm^3: Reduce dose by 50%

WBC <1000 cells/mm^3, granulocytes <500 cells/mm^3, or platelet count <25,000 cells/mm^3: Permanently discontinue

Kaposi sarcoma: Severe toxicity: Reduce dose by 50% or temporarily discontinue

Malignant melanoma:

Severe toxicity (neutrophils <500 cells/mm^3 or AST/ALT >5 times ULN): Reduce dose by 50% or temporarily discontinue

Neutrophils <250 cells/mm^3 or AST/ALT >10 times ULN: Permanently discontinue

Administration

Injection: Do not use 3-, 5-, 18-, and 25 million unit strengths intralesionally, solutions are hypertonic; 50 million unit strength is not for use in condylomata, hairy cell leukemia, or chronic hepatitis. Patients with platelet count <50,000/mm^3 should receive doses S.C., not I.M.

Oral: Capsules should not be crushed, chewed, or opened.

Monitoring Parameters Baseline chest x-ray, ECG, CBC with differential, liver function tests, electrolytes, thyroid function tests, platelets, weight; patients with pre-existing cardiac abnormalities, or in advanced stages of cancer should have ECGs taken before and during treatment.

(Continued)

Interferon Alfa-2b *(Continued)*

Patient Information Without the advice of prescriber, do not change brands of interferon as changes in dosage may result; do not operate heavy machinery while on therapy since changes in mental status may occur; report any persistent or severe sore throat, fever, fatigue, unusual bleeding, or bruising. You may experience flu-like syndrome (acetaminophen may help); this syndrome subsides after several weeks of continuous dosing, but usually recurs during each cycle of intermittent therapy.

Dosage Forms See also Interferon Alfa-2b and Ribavirin Combination Pack monograph. **INJ, powder for reconstitution:** 3 million units; 5 million units; 10 million units; 18 million units; 25 million units; 50 million units. **INJ, solution:** 3 million units/0.5 mL (0.5 mL); 5 million units/0.5 mL (0.5 mL); (10 million units/mL); 10 million units/mL (1 mL). **INJ, solution:** 6 million units/mL (3 mL); 10 million units/mL (2.5 mL). **INJ, solution** [prefilled pens]: Delivers 3 million units/0.2 mL (1.5 mL) [delivers 6 doses; 18 million units]; delivers 5 million units/0.2 mL (1.5 mL) [delivers 6 doses; 30 million units]; delivers 10 million units/0.2 mL (1.5 mL) [delivers 6 doses; 60 million units]

Interferon Alfa-2b and Ribavirin

(in ter FEER on AL fa too bee & rye ba VYE rin)

U.S. Brand Names Rebetron®

Synonyms Interferon Alfa-2b and Ribavirin Combination Pack; Ribavirin and Interferon Alfa-2b Combination Pack

Therapeutic Category Antiviral Agent; Antiviral Agent, Hepatitis; Biological Response Modulator

Use Combination therapy for the treatment of chronic hepatitis C in patients with compensated liver disease previously untreated with alpha interferon or who have relapsed after alpha interferon therapy

Pregnancy Risk Factor X

Dosage

Children: Chronic hepatitis C: **Note:** Safety and efficacy have not been established; dosing based on pharmacokinetic profile: Recommended dosage of combination therapy (Intron® A with Rebetol®):

Intron® A: S.C.:

25-61 kg: 3 million int. units/m^2 3 times/week

>61 kg: Refer to adult dosing

Rebetol® capsule: Oral:

25-36 kg: 400 mg/day (200 mg twice daily)

37-49 kg: 600 mg/day (200 mg in morning and 400 mg in evening)

50-61 kg: 800 mg/day (400 mg twice daily)

>61 kg: Refer to adult dosing

Adults: Chronic hepatitis C: Recommended dosage of combination therapy:

Intron® A: S.C.: 3 million int. units 3 times/week **and**

Rebetol® capsule: Oral:

≤75 kg (165 lb): 1000 mg/day (two 200 mg capsules in the morning and three 200 mg capsules in the evening)

>75 kg: 1200 mg/day (three 200 mg capsules in the morning and three 200 mg capsules in the evening)

Treatment duration recommendations:

Following relapse after alpha interferon monotherapy: 24 weeks

Previously untreated: 24-48 weeks (individualized based on response, tolerance, and baseline characteristics)

Consider discontinuing therapy in any patient not achieving HCV-RNA below the limit of assay detection by 24 weeks.

Dosing adjustment for toxicity: Note: Recommendations (per manufacturer labeling):

Anemia (RBC depression):

Patient **without** cardiac history:

Hemoglobin <10 g/dL:

Children: Decrease dose by $^1/_2$

Adults: Decrease dose to 600 mg/day

Hemoglobin <8.5 g/dL: Permanently discontinue treatment

Patient **with** cardiac history:

Hemoglobin has ≥2 g/dL decrease during any 4-week period of treatment:

Children: Decrease ribavirin dose by $^1/_2$ **and** decrease interferon alfa-2b to 1.5 million int. units 3 times/week

Adults: Decrease dose to ribavirin to 600 mg/day **and** decrease interferon-alfa 2b dose to 1.5 million int. units 3 times/week

Hemoglobin <12 g/dL after 4 weeks of reduced dose: Permanently discontinue treatment

WBC, neutrophil, and platelet depression:

WBC <1500 cells/mm^3, neutrophils <750 cells/mm^3, or platelet count <50,000 cells/mm^3 (<80,000 cells/ mm^3 in children): Reduce interferon alfa-2b dose to 1.5 million int. units 3 times/week (50% reduction)

WBC <1000 cells/mm^3, neutrophils <500 cells/mm^3, or platelet count <25,000 cells/mm^3 (<50,000 cells/mm^3 in children): Permanently discontinue therapy

Dosage adjustment in renal impairment: Patients with Cl_{cr} <50 mL/minutes should not receive ribavirin.

Dosage Forms

Combination package for patients ≤75 kg:

Injection, solution: Interferon alfa-2b (Intron® A): 3 million int. units/0.5 mL (0.5 mL) [6 vials (3 million int. units/vial), 6 syringes and alcohol swabs]
Capsules: Ribavirin (Rebetol®): 200 mg (70s)

Injection, solution: Interferon alfa-2b (Intron® A): 3 million int. units/0.5 mL (3.8 mL) [1 multidose vial (18 million int. units/vial), 6 syringes and alcohol swabs]
Capsules: Ribavirin (Rebetol®): 200 mg (70s)

Injection, solution: Interferon alfa-2b (Intron® A): 3 million int. units/0.2 mL (1.5 mL) [1 multidose pen (18 million int. units/pen), 6 needles and alcohol swabs]
Capsules: Ribavirin (Rebetol®): 200 mg (70s)

Combination package for patients >75 kg:

Injection, solution: Interferon alfa-2b (Intron® A): 3 million int. units/0.5 mL (0.5 mL) [6 vials (3 million int. units/vial), 6 syringes and alcohol swabs]
Capsules: Ribavirin (Rebetol®): 200 mg (84s)

Injection, solution: Interferon alfa-2b (Intron® A): 3 million int. units/0.5 mL (3.8 mL) [1 multidose vial (18 million int. units/vial), 6 syringes and alcohol swabs]
Capsules: Ribavirin (Rebetol®): 200 mg (84s)

Injection, solution: Interferon alfa-2b (Intron® A): 3 million int. units/0.2 mL (1.5 mL) [1 multidose pen (18 million int. units/pen), 6 needles and alcohol swabs]
Capsules: Ribavirin (Rebetol®): 200 mg (84s)

Combination package for Rebetol® dose reduction:

Injection, solution: Interferon alfa-2b (Intron® A): 3 million int. units/0.5 mL (0.5 mL) [6 vials (3 million int. units/vial), 6 syringes and alcohol swabs]
Capsules: Ribavirin (Rebetol®): 200 mg (42s)

Injection, solution: Interferon alfa-2b (Intron® A): 3 million int. units/0.5 mL (3.8 mL) [1 multidose vial (18 million int. units/vial), 6 syringes and alcohol swabs]
Capsules: Ribavirin (Rebetol®): 200 mg (42s)

Injection, solution: Interferon alfa-2b (Intron® A): 3 million int. units/0.2 mL (1.5 mL) [1 multidose pen (18 million int. units/pen), 6 needles and alcohol swabs]
Capsules: Ribavirin (Rebetol®): 200 mg (42s)

◆ **Interferon Alfa-2b and Ribavirin Combination Pack** *see* Interferon Alfa-2b and Ribavirin *on page 676*

◆ **Interferon Alfa-2b (PEG Conjugate)** *see* Peginterferon Alfa-2b *on page 966*

Interferon Alfacon-1 (in ter FEER on AL fa con one)

U.S. Brand Names Infergen®

Therapeutic Category Antiviral Agent, Hepatitis; Biological Response Modulator; Interferon

Use Treatment of chronic hepatitis C virus (HCV) infection in patients ≥18 years of age with compensated liver disease and anti-HCV serum antibodies or HCV RNA.

Pregnancy Risk Factor C

Contraindications Hypersensitivity to interferon alfacon-1 or any component of the formulation, other alpha interferons, or *E. coli*-derived products

Warnings/Precautions Severe psychiatric adverse effects, including depression, suicidal ideation, and suicide attempt, may occur. Avoid use in severe psychiatric disorders. Use with caution in patients with a history of depression. Use with caution in patients with prior cardiac disease (ischemic or thromboembolic), arrhythmias, patients who are chronically immunosuppressed, and patients with endocrine disorders. Do not use in patients with hepatic decompensation. Ophthalmologic disorders (including retinal hemorrhages, cotton wool spots and retinal artery or vein obstruction) have occurred in patients using other alpha interferons. Prior to start of therapy, visual exams are recommended for patients with diabetes mellitus or hypertension. Treatment should be discontinued in patients with worsening or persistently severe signs/symptoms of autoimmune, infectious, ischemic (including radiographic changes or worsening hepatic function), or neuropsychiatric disorders (including depression and/or suicidal thoughts/behavior). Use caution in patients with autoimmune disorders; type-1 interferon therapy has been reported to exacerbate autoimmune diseases. Do not use interferon alfacon-1 in patients with autoimmune hepatitis. Use caution in patients with low peripheral blood counts or myelosuppression, including concurrent use of myelosuppressive therapy. Safety and efficacy have not been determined for patients <18 years of age.

Common Adverse Reactions Adverse reactions reported using 9 mcg/dose interferon alfacon-1 3 times/week. Reactions listed were reported in ≥5% of patients treated.

>10%:

Central nervous system: Headache (82%), fatigue (69%), fever (61%), insomnia (39%), nervousness (31%), depression (22%), dizziness (22%), anxiety (19%), noncardiac chest pain (13%), emotional lability (12%), malaise (11%)

Dermatologic: Alopecia (14%), pruritus (14%), rash (13%)

Endocrine & metabolic: Hot flashes (13%)

Gastrointestinal: Abdominal pain (41%), nausea (40%), diarrhea (29%), anorexia (24%), dyspepsia (21%), vomiting (12%)

Hematologic: Granulocytopenia (23%), thrombocytopenia (19%), leukopenia (15%)

(Continued)

Interferon Alfacon-1 *(Continued)*

Local: Injection site erythema (23%)

Neuromuscular & skeletal: Myalgia (58%), body pain (54%), arthralgia (51%), back pain (42%), limb pain (26%), neck pain (14%), skeletal pain (14%), paresthesia (13%)

Respiratory: Pharyngitis (34%), upper respiratory tract infection (31%), cough (22%), sinusitis (17%), rhinitis (13%), respiratory tract congestion (12%)

Miscellaneous: Flu-like syndrome (15%), increased diaphoresis (12%)

1% to 10%:

Cardiovascular: Peripheral edema (9%), hypertension (5%), tachycardia (4%), palpitations (3%)

Central nervous system: Amnesia (10%), hypoesthesia (10%), abnormal thinking (8%), agitation (6%), confusion (4%), somnolence (4%)

Dermatologic: Bruising (6%), erythema (6%), dry skin (6%), wound (4%)

Endocrine & metabolic: Thyroid test abnormalities (9%), dysmenorrhea (9%), increased triglycerides (6%), menstrual disorder (6%), decreased libido (5%), hypothyroidism (4%)

Gastrointestinal: Constipation (9%), flatulence (8%), toothache (7%), decreased salivation (6%), hemorrhoids (6%), weight loss (5%), taste perversion (3%)

Genitourinary: Vaginitis (8%), genital moniliasis (2%)

Hepatic: Hepatomegaly (5%), liver tenderness (5%), increased prothrombin time (3%)

Local: Injection site pain (9%), access pain (8%), injection site bruising (6%)

Neuromuscular & skeletal: Weakness (9%), hypertonia (7%), musculoskeletal disorder (4%)

Ocular: Conjunctivitis (8%), eye pain (5%), vision abnormalities (3%)

Otic: Tinnitus (6%), earache (5%), otitis (2%)

Respiratory: Upper respiratory tract congestion (10%), epistaxis (8%), dyspnea (7%), bronchitis (6%)

Miscellaneous: Allergic reaction (7%), lymphadenopathy (6%), lymphocytosis (5%), infection (3%)

Flu-like symptoms, which included headache, fatigue, fever, myalgia, rigors, arthralgia, and increased diaphoresis, were the most commonly reported adverse reaction. This was reported separately from flu-like syndrome. Most patients were treated symptomatically.

Other adverse reactions associated with interferon therapy include arrhythmia, autoimmune disorders, chest pain, hepatotoxic reactions, lupus erythematosus, myocardial infarction, neuropsychiatric disorders (including suicidal thoughts/behavior), pneumonia, pneumonitis, severe hypersensitivity reactions (rare), vasculitis

Drug Interactions

Increased Effect/Toxicity: Cimetidine may augment the antitumor effects of interferon in melanoma. Theophylline clearance has been reported to be decreased in hepatitis patients receiving interferon. Vinblastine enhances interferon toxicity in several patients; increased incidence of paresthesia has also been noted. Interferons may increase the adverse/toxic effects of ACE inhibitors, specifically the development of granulocytopenia. Agranulocytosis has been reported with concurrent use of clozapine (case report). Interferons may increase the anticoagulant effects of warfarin, and interferons may increase serum levels of zidovudine.

Decreased Effect: Prednisone may decrease the therapeutic effects of interferon alpha. A decreased response to erythropoietin has been reported (case reports) in patients receiving interferons. Interferon alpha may decrease the serum concentrations of melphalan (may or may not decrease toxicity of melphalan).

Mechanism of Action Alpha interferons are a family of proteins, produced by nucleated cells, that have antiviral, antiproliferative, and immune-regulating activity. There are at least 25 alpha interferons identified. Interferons interact with cells through high affinity cell surface receptors. Following activation, multiple effects can be detected. Interferons induce gene transcription, inhibit cellular growth, alter the state of cellular differentiation, interfere with oncogene expression, alter cell surface antigen expression, increase phagocytic activity of macrophages, and augment cytotoxicity of lymphocytes for target cells. Although all alpha interferons share similar properties, the actual biological effects vary between subtypes.

Pharmacodynamics/Kinetics Pharmacokinetic studies have not been conducted on patients with chronic hepatitis C.

Time to peak: Healthy volunteers: 24-36 hours

Dosage Adults ≥18 years: S.C.:

Chronic HCV infection: 9 mcg 3 times/week for 24 weeks; allow 48 hours between doses

Patients who have previously tolerated interferon therapy but did not respond or relapsed: 15 mcg 3 times/week for 6 months

Dose reduction for toxicity: Dose should be held in patients who experience a severe adverse reaction, and treatment should be stopped or decreased if the reaction does not become tolerable.

Doses were reduced from 9 mcg to 7.5 mcg in the pivotal study.

For patients receiving 15 mcg/dose, doses were reduced in 3 mcg increments. Efficacy is decreased with doses <7.5 mcg

Dosage adjustment in renal impairment: No information available.

Dosage adjustment in hepatic impairment: Avoid use in decompensated hepatic disease.

Elderly: No information available.

Administration Interferon alfacon-1 is administered by S.C. injection, 3 times/week, with at least 48 hours between doses

Monitoring Parameters

Hemoglobin and hematocrit; white blood cell count; platelets; triglycerides; thyroid function. Laboratory tests should be taken 2 weeks prior to therapy, after therapy has begun, and periodically during treatment. HCV RNA, ALT to determine success/response to therapy.

The following guidelines were used during the clinical studies as acceptable baseline values:

Platelet count ≥75 x 10^9/L

Hemoglobin ≥100 g/L

ANC ≥1500 x 10^6/L

S_{cr} <180 μmol/L (<2 mg/dL) or Cl_{cr} >0.83 mL/second (>50 mL/minute)

Serum albumin ≥25 g/L

Bilirubin WNL

TSH and T$_4$ WNL

Patients should also be monitored for signs of depression. Patients with pre-existing diabetes mellitus or hypertension should have an ophthalmologic exam prior to treatment.

Patient Information There are many different types of interferon products. Do not change brands or change your dose without consulting with your prescriber. Promptly report any adverse effects to your prescriber, including flu-like symptoms, signs of infection, signs of depression, suicidal thoughts, or visual complaints. Flu-like symptoms include fatigue, fever, rigors, headache, arthralgia, myalgia, and increased sweating. Your prescriber may instruct you to use this medication in the evening, or to take a non-narcotic analgesic to help prevent or decrease these symptoms. Because interferon alfacon-1 may have hazardous effects to a fetus, males and females using this medication should use effective contraception. You will need periodic laboratory tests while on this medication. If you have diabetes or hypertension you should also have an eye exam prior to starting therapy. If self-administering this medication at home, follow procedures for proper disposal of your syringes and needles.

Dosage Forms INJ, solution [prefilled syringe; preservative free]: 30 mcg/mL (0.3 mL, 0.5 mL)

Interferon Alfa-n3 (in ter FEER on AL fa en three)

U.S. Brand Names Alferon® N

Therapeutic Category Biological Response Modulator; Interferon

Use Patients ≥18 years of age: Intralesional treatment of refractory or recurring genital or venereal warts (condylomata acuminata)

Pregnancy Risk Factor C

Contraindications Hypersensitivity to alpha interferon or any component of the formulation; anaphylactic sensitivity to mouse immunoglobulin, egg protein, or neomycin

Warnings/Precautions Use with caution in patients with pre-existing cardiac disease, including unstable angina, uncontrolled CHF, or arrhythmias; severe pulmonary disease; diabetes with ketoacidosis; coagulation disorders (such as thrombophlebitis, pulmonary embolism, hemophilia); severe myelosuppression; or seizure disorder. **Due to differences in dosage, patients should not change brands of interferons.** Safety and efficacy in patients <18 years of age have not been established.

Common Adverse Reactions Note: Adverse reaction incidence noted below is specific to intralesional administration in patients with condylomata acuminata. Flu-like reactions, consisting of headache, fever, and/or myalgia, was reported in 30% of patients, and abated with repeated dosing.

>10%:

Central nervous system: Fever (40%), headache (31%), chills (14%), fatigue (14%)

Hematologic: Decreased WBC (11%)

Neuromuscular & skeletal: Myalgia (45%)

Miscellaneous: Flu-like syndrome (30%)

1% to 10%:

Central nervous system: Malaise (9%), dizziness (9%), depression (2%), insomnia (2%), thirst (1%)

Dermatologic: Pruritus (2%)

Gastrointestinal: Nausea (45), vomiting (3%), dyspepsia (3%), diarrhea (2%), tongue hyperesthesia (1%), taste disturbance (1%)

Genitourinary: Groin lymph node swelling (1%)

Neuromuscular & skeletal: Arthralgia (5%), back pain (4%), cramps (1%), paresthesia (1%)

Ocular: Visual disturbance (1%)

Respiratory: Rhinitis (2%), pharyngitis (1%), nosebleed (1%)

Miscellaneous: Increased diaphoresis (2%), vasovagal reaction (2%)

Drug Interactions

Increased Effect/Toxicity: Interferons may increase the adverse/toxic effects of ACE inhibitors, specifically the development of granulocytopenia. Risk: Monitor A case report of agranulocytosis has been reported with concurrent use of clozapine. Case reports of decreased hematopoietic effect with erythropoietin. Interferon alpha may decrease the P450 isoenzyme metabolism of theophylline. Interferons may increase the anticoagulant effects of warfarin. Interferons may decrease the metabolism of zidovudine.

Decreased Effect: Interferon alpha may decrease the serum concentrations of melphalan; this may or may not decrease the potential toxicity of melphalan. Prednisone may decrease the therapeutic effects of Interferon alpha.

Mechanism of Action Interferons interact with cells through high affinity cell surface receptors. Following activation, multiple effects can be detected including induction of gene transcription. Inhibits cellular growth, alters the state of cellular differentiation, interferes with oncogene expression, alters cell surface antigen expression, increases phagocytic activity of macrophages, and augments cytotoxicity of lymphocytes for target cells

(Continued)

Interferon Alfa-n3 *(Continued)*

Dosage Adults: Inject 250,000 units (0.05 mL) in each wart twice weekly for a maximum of 8 weeks; therapy should not be repeated for at least 3 months after the initial 8-week course of therapy

Administration Inject into base of wart with a small 30-gauge needle

Patient Information Warts are highly contagious until they completely disappear, abstain from sexual activity or use barrier protection; inform nurse or physician if allergy exists to eggs, neomycin, mouse immunoglobulin, or to human interferon alpha; acetaminophen can be used to treat flu-like symptoms

Dosage Forms INJ, solution: 5 million int. units (1 mL)

Interferon Beta-1a (in ter FEER on BAY ta won aye)

U.S. Brand Names Avonex®; Rebif®

Synonyms rIFN beta-1a

Therapeutic Category Biological Response Modulator; Interferon

Use Treatment of relapsing forms of multiple sclerosis (MS)

Pregnancy Risk Factor C

Contraindications Hypersensitivity to natural or recombinant interferons, human albumin, or any other component of the formulation

Warnings/Precautions Interferons have been associated with severe psychiatric adverse events (psychosis, mania, depression, suicidal behavior/ideation) in patients with and without previous psychiatric symptoms; avoid use in severe psychiatric disorders and use caution in patients with a history of depression; patients exhibiting depressive symptoms should be closely monitored and discontinuation of therapy should be considered.

Allergic reactions, including anaphylaxis, have been reported. Hematologic effects, including pancytopenia (rare) and thrombocytopenia, have been reported. Associated with a high incidence of flu-like adverse effects; use of analgesics and/or antipyretics on treatment days may be helpful. Use caution in patients with pre-existing cardiovascular disease, pulmonary disease, seizure disorders, myelosuppression, renal impairment or hepatic impairment. Suspend treatment if jaundice or symptoms of hepatic dysfunction occur. Safety and efficacy in patients <18 years of age have not been established.

Common Adverse Reactions

>10%:

Central nervous system: Headache (Avonex® 58%; Rebif® 65% to 70%), fatigue (Rebif® 33% to 41%), fever (Avonex® 20%; Rebif® 25% to 28%), pain (Avonex® 23%), chills (Avonex® 19%), depression (Avonex® 18%), dizziness (Avonex® 14%)

Gastrointestinal: Nausea (Avonex® 23%), abdominal pain (Avonex® 8%; Rebif® 20% to 22%)

Genitourinary: Urinary tract infection (Avonex® 17%)

Hematologic: Leukopenia (Rebif® 28% to 36%)

Hepatic: ALT increased (Rebif® 20% to 27%), AST increased (Rebif® 10% to 17%)

Local: Injection site reaction (Avonex® 3%; Rebif® 89% to 92%)

Neuromuscular & skeletal: Myalgia (Avonex® 29%; Rebif® 25%), back pain (Rebif® 23% to 25%), weakness (Avonex® 24%), skeletal pain (Rebif® 10% to 15%), rigors (Rebif® 6% to 13%)

Ocular: Vision abnormal (Rebif® 7% to 13%)

Respiratory: Sinusitis (Avonex® 14%), upper respiratory tract infection (Avonex® 14%)

Miscellaneous: Flu-like symptoms (Avonex® 49%; Rebif® 56% to 59%), neutralizing antibodies (significance not known; Avonex® 5%; Rebif® 24%), lymphadenopathy (Rebif® 11% to 12%)

1% to 10% (reported with one or both products):

Cardiovascular: Chest pain, vasodilation

Central nervous system: Convulsions, malaise, migraine, somnolence

Dermatologic: Alopecia, rash

Endocrine & metabolic: Thyroid disorder

Gastrointestinal: Toothache, xerostomia

Genitourinary: Micturition frequency, urinary incontinence

Hematologic: Anemia, thrombocytopenia

Hepatic: Bilirubinemia, hepatic function abnormal

Local: Injection site bruising, injection site inflammation, injection site necrosis, injection site pain

Neuromuscular & skeletal: Arthralgia, coordination abnormal, hypertonia

Ocular: Eye disorder, xerophthalmia

Respiratory: Bronchitis

Miscellaneous: Infection

Drug Interactions

Increased Effect/Toxicity: Interferons may increase the adverse/toxic effects of ACE inhibitors, specifically the development of granulocytopenia. Agranulocytosis has been reported with concurrent use of clozapine (case report). Interferons may increase the anticoagulant effects of warfarin, and interferons may increase serum levels of zidovudine.

Mechanism of Action Interferon beta differs from naturally occurring human protein by a single amino acid substitution and the lack of carbohydrate side chains; alters the expression and response to surface antigens and can enhance immune cell activities. Properties of interferon beta that modify biologic responses are mediated by cell surface receptor interactions; mechanism in the treatment of MS is unknown.

Pharmacodynamics/Kinetics Limited data due to small doses used

Half-life elimination: Avonex®: 10 hours; Rebif®: 69 hours

Time to peak, serum: Avonex® (I.M.): 3-15 hours; Rebif® (S.C.): 16 hours

Dosage Adults:

I.M. (Avonex®): 30 mcg once weekly

S.C. (Rebif®): Initial: 8.8 mcg 3 times/week, increasing over a 4-week period to the recommended dose of 44 mcg 3 times/week; doses should be separated by at least 48 hours

Dosage adjustment in hepatic impairment: Rebif®: If liver function tests increase or in case of leukopenia: Decrease dose 20% to 50% until toxicity resolves.

Administration

Avonex®: Must be administered by I.M. injection

Rebif®: Administer S.C. at the same time of day on the same 3 days each week (ie, late afternoon/evening Mon, Wed, Fri)

Monitoring Parameters Monitor for signs and symptoms of thyroid abnormalities, hematologic suppression, liver functions tests, symptoms of autoimmune disorders

Avonex®: Frequency of monitoring for patients receiving Avonex® has not been specifically defined; in clinical trials, monitoring was at 6-month intervals.

Rebif®: CBC and liver function testing at 1-, 3-, and 6 months, then periodically thereafter. Thyroid function every 6 months (in patients with pre-existing abnormalities and/or clinical indications)

Patient Information Flu-like symptoms are not uncommon following initiation of therapy. Acetaminophen may reduce these symptoms. Do not change the dosage or schedule of administration without medical consultation. If self-injecting and you miss a dose, take it as soon as you remember, but 2 injections should not be given within 48 hours of each other. Report depression or suicide ideation to physicians. Avoid prolonged exposure to sunlight or sunlamps. Inform prescriber **immediately** if you feel depressed or have any thoughts of suicide.

Dosage Forms INJ, powder for reconstitution (Avonex®): 33 mcg [6.6 million units]. **INJ, solution** [prefilled syringe] (Avonex®): 30 mcg/0.5 mL (0.5 mL). **INJ, solution** [prefilled syringe; preservative free] (Rebif®): 22 mcg/mL (0.5 mL); 44 mcg/mL (0.5 mL) (12s)

Interferon Beta-1b (in ter FEER on BAY ta won bee)

U.S. Brand Names Betaseron®

Synonyms rIFN beta-1b

Therapeutic Category Biological Response Modulator; Interferon

Use Treatment of relapsing forms of multiple sclerosis (MS)

Pregnancy Risk Factor C

Contraindications Hypersensitivity to *E. coli*-derived products, natural or recombinant interferon beta, albumin human or any other component of the formulation

Warnings/Precautions Interferons have been associated with severe psychiatric adverse events (psychosis, mania, depression, suicidal behavior/ideation) in patients with and without previous psychiatric symptoms, avoid use in severe psychiatric disorders and use caution in patients with a history of depression; patients exhibiting symptoms of depression should be closely monitored and discontinuation of therapy should be considered. Due to high incidence of flu-like adverse effects, use caution in patients with pre-existing cardiovascular disease, pulmonary disease, seizure disorders, myelosuppression, renal impairment or hepatic impairment. Severe injection site reactions (necrosis) may occur; patient and/or caregiver competency in injection technique should be confirmed and periodically re-evaluated. Safety and efficacy in patients <18 years of age have not been established.

Common Adverse Reactions Note: Flu-like symptoms (including at least two of the following - headache, fever, chills, malaise, diaphoresis, and myalgias) are reported in the majority of patients (60%) and decrease over time (average duration ~1 week).

>10%:

Cardiovascular: Peripheral edema (15%), chest pain (11%)

Central nervous system: Headache (57%), fever (36%), pain (51%), chills (25%), dizziness (24%), insomnia (24%)

Dermatologic: Rash (24%), skin disorder (12%)

Endocrine & metabolic: Metrorrhagia (11%)

Gastrointestinal: Nausea (27%), diarrhea (19%), abdominal pain (19%), constipation (20%), dyspepsia (14%)

Genitourinary: Urinary urgency (13%)

Hematologic: Lymphopenia (88%), neutropenia (14%), leukopenia (14%)

Local: Injection site reaction (85 %), inflammation (53%), pain (18%)

Neuromuscular & skeletal: Weakness (61%), myalgia (27%), hypertonia (50%), myasthenia (46%), arthralgia (31%), incoordination (21%)

Miscellaneous: Flu-like symptoms (60%)

1% to 10%:

Cardiovascular: Palpitation (4%), vasodilation (8%), hypertension (7%), tachycardia (4%), peripheral vascular disorder (6%)

Central nervous system: Anxiety (10%), malaise (8%), nervousness (7%)

Dermatologic: Alopecia (4%)

Endocrine & metabolic: Menorrhagia (8%), dysmenorrhea (7%)

Genitourinary: Impotence (9%), pelvic pain (6%), cystitis (8%), urinary frequency (7%), weight gain (7%), prostatic disorder (3%)

Hematologic: Lymphadenopathy (8%)

Hepatic: SGPT increased >5x baseline (10%), SGOT increased >5x baseline (3%)

Local: Injection site necrosis (5%), edema (3%), mass (2%)

(Continued)

Interferon Beta-1b *(Continued)*

Neuromuscular & skeletal: Leg cramps (4%)
Respiratory: Dyspnea (7%)
Miscellaneous: Diaphoresis (4%), hypersensitivity (3%)

Drug Interactions

Increased Effect/Toxicity: Interferons may increase the adverse/toxic effects of ACE inhibitors, specifically the development of granulocytopenia. Risk: Monitor A case report of agranulocytosis has been reported with concurrent use of clozapine. Case reports of decreased hematopoietic effect with erythropoietin. Interferon alpha may decrease the P450 isoenzyme metabolism of theophylline. Interferons may increase the anticoagulant effects of warfarin. Interferons may decrease the metabolism of zidovudine.

Mechanism of Action Interferon beta-1b differs from naturally occurring human protein by a single amino acid substitution and the lack of carbohydrate side chains; alters the expression and response to surface antigens and can enhance immune cell activities. Properties of interferon beta-1b that modify biologic responses are mediated by cell surface receptor interactions; mechanism in the treatment of MS is unknown.

Pharmacodynamics/Kinetics Limited data due to small doses used
Half-life elimination: 8 minutes to 4.3 hours
Time to peak, serum: 1-8 hours

Dosage S.C.:
Children <18 years: Not recommended
Adults: 0.25 mg (8 million units) every other day

Administration Withdraw 1 mL of reconstituted solution from the vial into a sterile syringe fitted with a 27-gauge needle and inject the solution subcutaneously; sites for self-injection include arms, abdomen, hips, and thighs

Monitoring Parameters Hemoglobin, liver function, and blood chemistries

Patient Information Instruct patients on self-injection technique and procedures. If possible, perform first injection under the supervision of an appropriately qualified healthcare professional. Injection site reactions may occur during therapy. They are usually transient and do not require discontinuation of therapy, but careful assessment of the nature and severity of all reported reactions. Flu-like symptoms are not uncommon following initiation of therapy. Acetaminophen may reduce these symptoms. Do not change the dosage or schedule of administration without medical consultation. Inform prescriber **immediately** if you feel depressed or have any thoughts of suicide. Report any broken skin or black-blue discoloration around the injection site. Avoid prolonged exposure to sunlight or sunlamps.

Dosage Forms INJ, powder for reconstitution: 0.3 mg [9.6 million units]

Interferon Gamma-1b (in ter FEER on GAM ah won bee)

U.S. Brand Names Actimmune®

Therapeutic Category Biological Response Modulator; Interferon

Use Reduce frequency and severity of serious infections associated with chronic granulomatous disease; delay time to disease progression in patients with severe, malignant osteopetrosis

Pregnancy Risk Factor C

Contraindications Hypersensitivity to interferon gamma, *E. coli* derived proteins, or any component of the formulation

Warnings/Precautions Patients with pre-existing cardiac disease, seizure disorders, CNS disturbances, or myelosuppression should be carefully monitored; long-term effects on growth and development are unknown; safety and efficacy in children <1 year of age have not been established.

Common Adverse Reactions Based on 50 mcg/m^2 dose administered 3 times weekly for chronic granulomatous disease
>10%:
Central nervous system: Fever (52%), headache (33%), chills (14%), fatigue (14%)
Dermatologic: Rash (17%)
Gastrointestinal: Diarrhea (14%), vomiting (13%)
Local: Injection site erythema or tenderness (14%)
1% to 10%:
Central nervous system: Depression (3%)
Gastrointestinal: Nausea (10%), abdominal pain (8%)
Neuromuscular & skeletal: Myalgia (6%), arthralgia (2%), back pain (2%)

Drug Interactions

Cytochrome P450 Effect: Inhibits CYP1A2 (weak), 2E1 (weak)

Increased Effect/Toxicity: Interferon gamma-1b may increase hepatic enzymes or enhance myelosuppression when taken with other myelosuppressive agents. May decrease cytochrome P450 concentrations leading to increased serum concentrations of drugs metabolized by this pathway.

Pharmacodynamics/Kinetics
Absorption: I.M., S.C.: Slowly
Half-life elimination: I.V.: 38 minutes; I.M., S.C.: 3-6 hours
Time to peak, plasma: I.M.: 4 hours (1.5 ng/mL); S.C.: 7 hours (0.6 ng/mL)

Dosage If severe reactions occur, modify dose (50% reduction) or therapy should be discontinued until adverse reactions abate.
Chronic granulomatous disease: Children >1 year and Adults: S.C.:
BSA ≤0.5 m^2: 1.5 mcg/kg/dose 3 times/week
BSA >0.5 m^2: 50 mcg/m^2 (1 million int. units/m^2) 3 times/week

Severe, malignant osteopetrosis: Children >1 year: S.C.:
  BSA ≤0.5 m^2: 1.5 mcg/kg/dose 3 times/week
  BSA >0.5 m^2: 50 mcg/m^2 (1 million int. units/m^2) 3 times/week

Note: Previously expressed as 1.5 million units/m^2; 50 mcg is equivalent to 1 million int. units/m^2.

Monitoring Parameters CBC with differential, platelets, LFTs, electrolytes, BUN, creatinine, and urinalysis prior to therapy and at 3-month intervals

Patient Information Use as directed; do not change the dosage or schedule of administration without consulting prescriber. Maintain adequate hydration (2-3 L/day of fluids unless instructed to restrict fluid intake). You may experience flu-like syndrome (acetaminophen may help or can administer dose at bedtime); nausea, vomiting, or loss of appetite (frequent small meals, frequent mouth care, sucking lozenges, or chewing gum may help); drowsiness, dizziness, agitation, or abnormal thinking (use caution when driving or engaging in tasks requiring alertness until response to drug is known). Report unusual bruising or bleeding; persistent abdominal disturbances; unusual fatigue; muscle pain or tremors; chest pain or palpitations; swelling of extremities; visual disturbances; pain, swelling, or redness at injection site; or other unusual symptoms.

Dosage Forms INJ, solution [preservative free]: 100 mcg [2 million int. units] (0.5 mL). *Previously, 100 mcg was expressed as 3 million units. This is equivalent to 2 million int. units.*

♦ **Interleukin-1 Receptor antagonist** *see Anakinra on page 99*
♦ **Interleukin-2** *see Aldesleukin on page 47*
♦ **Interleukin-11** *see Oprelvekin on page 931*
♦ **Intralipid**® *see Fat Emulsion on page 508*
♦ **Intravenous Fat Emulsion** *see Fat Emulsion on page 508*
♦ **Intrifiban** *see Eptifibatide on page 448*
♦ **Intron**® **A** *see Interferon Alfa-2b on page 673*
♦ **Intropin** *see DOPamine on page 402*
♦ **Invanz**® *see Ertapenem on page 451*
♦ **Inversine**® *see Mecamylamine on page 777*
♦ **Invirase**® *see Saquinavir on page 1123*
♦ **Iodine I 131 Tositumomab and Tositumomab** *see Tositumomab and Iodine I 131 Tositumomab on page 1248*

Iodoquinol (eye oh doe KWIN ole)

U.S. Brand Names Yodoxin®
Synonyms Diiodohydroxyquin
Therapeutic Category Amebicide
Use Treatment of acute and chronic intestinal amebiasis; asymptomatic cyst passers; *Blastocystis hominis* infections; ineffective for amebic hepatitis or hepatic abscess
Pregnancy Risk Factor C
Contraindications Hypersensitivity to iodine or iodoquinol or any component of the formulation; hepatic damage; pre-existing optic neuropathy
Warnings/Precautions Optic neuritis, optic atrophy, and peripheral neuropathy have occurred following prolonged use; avoid long-term therapy
Common Adverse Reactions Frequency not defined.
  Central nervous system: Fever, chills, agitation, retrograde amnesia, headache
  Dermatologic: Rash, urticaria, pruritus
  Endocrine & metabolic: Thyroid gland enlargement
  Gastrointestinal: Diarrhea, nausea, vomiting, stomach pain, abdominal cramps
  Neuromuscular & skeletal: Peripheral neuropathy, weakness
  Ocular: Optic neuritis, optic atrophy, visual impairment
  Miscellaneous: Itching of rectal area
Mechanism of Action Contact amebicide that works in the lumen of the intestine by an unknown mechanism
Pharmacodynamics/Kinetics
  Absorption: Poor and erratic
  Metabolism: Hepatic
  Excretion: Feces (high percentage)
Dosage Oral:
  Children: 30-40 mg/kg/day (maximum: 650 mg/dose) in 3 divided doses for 20 days; not to exceed 1.95 g/day
  Adults: 650 mg 3 times/day after meals for 20 days; not to exceed 1.95 g/day
Monitoring Parameters Ophthalmologic exam
Patient Information May take with food or milk to reduce stomach upset; complete full course of therapy
Dosage Forms POWDER: 25 g, 100 g. **TAB:** 210 mg, 650 mg

Iodoquinol and Hydrocortisone (eye oh doe KWIN ole & hye droe KOR ti sone)

U.S. Brand Names Dermazene®; Vytone®
Synonyms Hydrocortisone and Iodoquinol
Therapeutic Category Antifungal/Corticosteroid, Topical
Use Treatment of eczema; infectious dermatitis; chronic eczematoid otitis externa; mycotic dermatoses
Pregnancy Risk Factor C
(Continued)

Iodoquinol and Hydrocortisone *(Continued)*

Dosage Apply 3-4 times/day

Dosage Forms CRM: Iodoquinol 1% and hydrocortisone 1% (30 g); (Dermazene®): Iodoquinol 1% and hydrocortisone 1% (30 g, 45 g); (Vytone®): Iodoquinol 1% and hydrocortisone 1% (30 g)

♦ **Ionamin®** *see* Phentermine *on page 991*

♦ **Iopidine®** *see* Apraclonidine *on page 110*

♦ **Iosat™ [OTC]** *see* Potassium Iodide *on page 1022*

Ioxilan *(eye OKS ee lan)*

U.S. Brand Names Oxilan®

Therapeutic Category Radiopaque Agents

Use

Intra-arterial: Ioxilan 300 mgI/mL is indicated for cerebral arteriography. Ioxilan 350 mgI/mL is indicated for coronary arteriography and left ventriculography, visceral angiography, aortography, and peripheral arteriography

Intravenous: Both products are indicated for excretory urography and contrast enhanced computed tomographic (CECT) imaging of the head and body

Pregnancy Risk Factor B

Dosage Adults:

Intra-arterial: Coronary arteriography and left ventriculography: For visualization of coronary arteries and left ventricle, ioxilan injection with a concentration of 350 mg iodine/mL is recommended

Usual injection volumes:

Left and right coronary: 2-10 mL (0.7-3.5 g iodine)

Left ventricle: 25-50 mL (8.75-17.5 g iodine)

Total doses should not exceed 250 mL; the injection rate of ioxilan should approximate the flow rate in the vessel injected

Cerebral arteriography: For evaluation of arterial lesions of the brain, a concentration of 300 mg iodine/mL is indicated

Recommended doses: 8-12 mL (2.4-3.6 g iodine)

Total dose should not exceed 150 mL

Dosage Forms INJ, solution: (Oxilan® 300): 62% (50 mL, 100 mL, 150 mL, 200 mL); (Oxilan® 350): 73% (50 mL, 100 mL, 150 mL, 200 mL)

Ipecac Syrup *(IP e kak SIR up)*

Therapeutic Category Antidote, Emetic

Use Treatment of acute oral drug overdosage and in certain poisonings

Pregnancy Risk Factor C

Contraindications Hypersensitivity to ipecac or any component of the formulation; do not use in unconscious patients; patients with no gag reflex; following ingestion of strong bases, acids, or volatile oils; when seizures are likely

Warnings/Precautions Do not confuse ipecac syrup with ipecac fluid extract, which is 14 times more potent; use with caution in patients with cardiovascular disease and bulimics; may not be effective in antiemetic overdose

Common Adverse Reactions Frequency not defined.

Cardiovascular: Cardiotoxicity

Central nervous system: Lethargy

Gastrointestinal: Protracted vomiting, diarrhea

Neuromuscular & skeletal: Myopathy

Drug Interactions

Increased Effect/Toxicity: Phenothiazines (chlorpromazine has been associated with serious dystonic reactions).

Decreased Effect: Activated charcoal, milk, carbonated beverages decrease the effect of ipecac syrup.

Mechanism of Action Irritates the gastric mucosa and stimulates the medullary chemoreceptor trigger zone to induce vomiting

Pharmacodynamics/Kinetics

Onset of action: 15-30 minutes

Duration: 20-25 minutes; 60 minutes in some cases

Absorption: Significant amounts, mainly when it does not produce emesis

Excretion: Urine; emetine (alkaloid component) may be detected in urine 60 days after excess dose or chronic use

Dosage Oral:

Children:

6-12 months: 5-10 mL followed by 10-20 mL/kg of water; repeat dose one time if vomiting does not occur within 20 minutes

1-12 years: 15 mL followed by 10-20 mL/kg of water; repeat dose one time if vomiting does not occur within 20 minutes

If emesis does not occur within 30 minutes after second dose, ipecac must be removed from stomach by gastric lavage

Adults: 15-30 mL followed by 200-300 mL of water; repeat dose one time if vomiting does not occur within 20 minutes

Patient Information Call Poison Center before administering. Patients should be kept active and moving following administration of ipecac; follow dose with 8 oz of water following initial episode; if vomiting, no food or liquids should be ingested for 1 hour

Dosage Forms SYR: 70 mg/mL (30 mL)

♦ **IPM Wound Gel**™ **[OTC]** *see* Sodium Hyaluronate *on page 1148*

♦ **IPOL**® *see* Poliovirus Vaccine (Inactivated) *on page 1013*

Ipratropium (i pra TROE pee um)

U.S. Brand Names Atrovent®

Synonyms Ipratropium Bromide

Therapeutic Category Anticholinergic Agent; Bronchodilator

Use Anticholinergic bronchodilator used in bronchospasm associated with COPD, bronchitis, and emphysema; symptomatic relief of rhinorrhea associated with the common cold and allergic and nonallergic rhinitis

Pregnancy Risk Factor B

Contraindications Hypersensitivity to atropine, its derivatives, or any component of the formulation

Warnings/Precautions Not indicated for the initial treatment of acute episodes of bronchospasm; use with caution in patients with myasthenia gravis, narrow-angle glaucoma, prostatic hyperplasia, or bladder neck obstruction; ipratropium has not been specifically studied in the elderly, but it is poorly absorbed from the airways and appears to be safe in this population.

Common Adverse Reactions Note: Ipratropium is poorly absorbed from the lung, so systemic effects are rare.

Inhalation aerosol and inhalation solution:

<10%: Respiratory: Upper respiratory infection (13%), bronchitis (15%)

1% to 10%:

Cardiovascular: Palpitations (2%)

Central nervous system: Nervousness (3%), dizziness (2%), fatigue, headache (6%), pain (4%)

Dermatologic: Rash (1%)

Gastrointestinal: Nausea, xerostomia, stomach upset, dry mucous membranes

Respiratory: Nasal congestion, dyspnea (10%), increased sputum (1%), bronchospasm (2%), pharyngitis (3%), rhinitis (2%), sinusitis (5%)

Miscellaneous: Influenza-like symptoms

Nasal spray: Epistaxis (8%), nasal dryness (5%), nausea (2%)

Drug Interactions

Increased Effect/Toxicity: Increased therapeutic effect with albuterol. Increased toxicity with anticholinergics or drugs with anticholinergic properties and dronabinol.

Mechanism of Action Blocks the action of acetylcholine at parasympathetic sites in bronchial smooth muscle causing bronchodilation

Pharmacodynamics/Kinetics

Onset of action: Bronchodilation: 1-3 minutes

Peak effect: 1.5-2 hours

Duration: ≤4-6 hours

Absorption: Negligible

Distribution: Inhalation: 15% of dose reaches lower airways

Dosage

Nebulization:

Infants and Children ≤12 years: 125-250 mcg 3 times/day

Children >12 years and Adults: 500 mcg (one unit-dose vial) 3-4 times/day with doses 6-8 hours apart

Oral inhalation: MDI:

Children 3-12 years: 1-2 inhalations 3 times/day, up to 6 inhalations/24 hours

Children >12 years and Adults: 2 inhalations 4 times/day, up to 12 inhalations/24 hours

Intranasal: Nasal spray:

Symptomatic relief of rhinorrhea associated with the common cold (safety and efficacy of use beyond 4 days in patients with the common cold have not been established):

Children 5-11 years: 0.06%: 2 sprays in each nostril 3 times/day

Children ≥5 years and Adults: 0.06%: 2 sprays in each nostril 3-4 times/day

Symptomatic relief of rhinorrhea associated with allergic/nonallergic rhinitis: Children ≥6 years and Adults: 0.03%: 2 sprays in each nostril 2-3 times/day

Administration Shake inhaler before each use; rinsing mouth after each use decreases dry mouth side effect

Patient Information

Inhaler: Effects are enhanced by breath-holding 10 seconds after inhalation; temporary blurred vision may occur if sprayed into eyes; shake canister well before each use of the inhaler; follow instructions for use accompanying the product; close eyes when administering ipratropium; wait at least one full minute between inhalations

Nebulizer: Twist open the top of one unit dose vial and squeeze the contents into the nebulizer reservoir. Connect the nebulizer reservoir to the mouthpiece or face mask. Connect the nebulizer to the compressor. Sit in a comfortable, upright position; place the mouthpiece in your mouth or put on the face mask and turn on the compressor. If a face mask is used, care should be taken to avoid leakage around the mask as temporary blurring of vision, precipitation

(Continued)

Ipratropium *(Continued)*

or worsening of narrow-angle glaucoma, or eye pain may occur if the solution comes into direct contact with the eyes. Breathe as calmly, deeply, and evenly as possible until no more mist is formed in the nebulizer chamber (about 5-15 minutes). At this point, the treatment is finished. Clean the nebulizer.

Dosage Forms SOLN, nebulization: 0.02% (2.5 mL). **SOLN, oral inhalation:** 18 mcg/actuation (14 g). **SOLN, intranasal spray:** 0.03% (30 mL); 0.06% (15 mL)

Ipratropium and Albuterol (i pra TROE pee um & al BYOO ter ole)

U.S. Brand Names Combivent®; DuoNeb™

Synonyms Albuterol and Ipratropium

Therapeutic Category Bronchodilator

Use Treatment of COPD in those patients that are currently on a regular bronchodilator who continue to have bronchospasms and require a second bronchodilator

Pregnancy Risk Factor C

Dosage Adults:

Inhalation: 2 inhalations 4 times/day (maximum: 12 inhalations/24 hours)

Inhalation via nebulization: Initial: 3 mL every 6 hours (maximum: 3 mL every 4 hours)

Dosage Forms AERO, oral inhalation (Combivent®): Ipratropium 18 mcg and albuterol 103 mcg per actuation (14.7 g). **SOLN, oral inhalation** (DuoNeb™): Ipratropium 0.5 mg [0.017%] and albuterol base 2.5 mg [0.083%] per 3 mL vial (30s, 60s)

- ◆ **Ipratropium Bromide** *see* Ipratropium *on page 685*
- ◆ **I-Prin [OTC]** *see* Ibuprofen *on page 645*
- ◆ **Iproveratril Hydrochloride** *see* Verapamil *on page 1302*
- ◆ **IPV** *see* Poliovirus Vaccine (Inactivated) *on page 1013*

Irbesartan (ir be SAR tan)

Related Information

Angiotensin Agents Comparison *on page 1353*

U.S. Brand Names Avapro®

Therapeutic Category Angiotensin II Receptor Antagonist (ARB); Antihypertensive Agent

Use Treatment of hypertension alone or in combination with other antihypertensives; treatment of diabetic nephropathy in patients with type 2 diabetes mellitus (noninsulin dependent, NIDDM) and hypertension

Pregnancy Risk Factor C/D (2nd and 3rd trimesters)

Contraindications Hypersensitivity to irbesartan or any component of the formulation; hypersensitivity to other A-II receptor antagonists; bilateral renal artery stenosis; pregnancy (2nd and 3rd trimesters)

Warnings/Precautions Safety and efficacy have not been established in pediatric patients <6 years of age. Avoid use or use a much smaller dose in patients who are intravascularly volume-depleted; use caution in patients with unilateral or bilateral renal artery stenosis to avoid a decrease in renal function; AUCs of irbesartan (not the active metabolite) are about 50% greater in patients with Cl_{cr} <30 mL/minute and are doubled in hemodialysis patients

Common Adverse Reactions Unless otherwise indicated, percentage of incidence is reported for patients with hypertension.

>10%: Endocrine & metabolic: Hyperkalemia (19%, diabetic nephropathy)

1% to 10%:

Cardiovascular: Orthostatic hypotension (5%, diabetic nephropathy)

Central nervous system: Fatigue (4%), dizziness (10%, diabetic nephropathy)

Gastrointestinal: Diarrhea (3%), dyspepsia (2%)

Respiratory: Upper respiratory infection (9%), cough (2.8% versus 2.7% in placebo)

>1% but frequency ≤ placebo: Abdominal pain, anxiety, chest pain, edema, headache, influenza, musculoskeletal pain, nausea, nervousness, pharyngitis, rash, rhinitis, sinus abnormality, syncope, tachycardia, urinary tract infection, vertigo, vomiting

Drug Interactions

Cytochrome P450 Effect: Substrate of CYP2C8/9 (minor); **Inhibits** CYP2C8/9 (moderate), 2D6 (weak), 3A4 (weak)

Increased Effect/Toxicity: Potassium salts/supplements, co-trimoxazole (high dose), ACE inhibitors, and potassium-sparing diuretics (amiloride, spironolactone, triamterene) may increase the risk of hyperkalemia.

Mechanism of Action Irbesartan is an angiotensin receptor antagonist. Angiotensin II acts as a vasoconstrictor. In addition to causing direct vasoconstriction, angiotensin II also stimulates the release of aldosterone. Once aldosterone is released, sodium as well as water are reabsorbed. The end result is an elevation in blood pressure. Irbesartan binds to the AT1 angiotensin II receptor. This binding prevents angiotensin II from binding to the receptor thereby blocking the vasoconstriction and the aldosterone secreting effects of angiotensin II.

Pharmacodynamics/Kinetics

Onset of action: Peak effect: 1-2 hours

Duration: >24 hours

Distribution: V_d: 53-93 L

Protein binding, plasma: 90%

Metabolism: Hepatic, primarily CYP2C9

Bioavailability: 60% to 80%

Half-life elimination: Terminal: 11-15 hours

Time to peak, serum: 1.5-2 hours

Excretion: Feces (80%); urine (20%)

Dosage Oral:

Hypertension:

Children:

<6 years: Safety and efficacy have not been established.

≥6-12 years: Initial: 75 mg once daily; may be titrated to a maximum of 150 mg once daily

Children ≥13 years and Adults: 150 mg once daily; patients may be titrated to 300 mg once daily

Note: Starting dose in volume-depleted patients should be 75 mg

Nephropathy in patients with type 2 diabetes and hypertension: Adults: Target dose: 300 mg once daily

Dosage adjustment in renal impairment: No dosage adjustment necessary with mild to severe impairment unless the patient is also volume depleted.

Patient Information Patients of childbearing age should be informed about the consequences of 2nd and 3rd trimester exposure to drugs that act on the renin-angiotensin system, and that these consequences do not appear to have resulted from intrauterine drug exposure that has been limited to the 1st trimester. Patients should report pregnancy to their prescriber as soon as possible.

Dosage Forms TAB: 75 mg, 150 mg, 300 mg

Irbesartan and Hydrochlorothiazide
(ir be SAR tan & hye droe klor oh THYE a zide)

U.S. Brand Names Avalide®

Synonyms Avapro® HCT; Hydrochlorothiazide and Irbesartan

Therapeutic Category Angiotensin II Antagonist/Thiazide Diuretic Combination; Antihypertensive Agent, Combination

Use Combination therapy for the management of hypertension

Pregnancy Risk Factor C/D (2nd and 3rd trimesters)

Dosage Dose must be individualized. A patient who is not controlled with either agent alone may be switched to the combination product. Mean effect increases with the dose of each component. The lowest dosage available is irbesartan 150 mg/hydrochlorothiazide 12.5 mg. Dose increases should be made not more frequently than every 2-4 weeks.

Dosage Forms TAB: Irbesartan 150 mg and hydrochlorothiazide 12.5 mg; Irbesartan 300 mg and hydrochlorothiazide 12.5 mg

♦ **Ircon® [OTC]** see Ferrous Fumarate on page 519

♦ **Iressa™** see Gefitinib on page 581

Irinotecan (eye rye no TEE kan)

U.S. Brand Names Camptosar®

Synonyms Camptothecin-11; CPT-11; NSC-616348

Therapeutic Category Antineoplastic Agent, Natural Source (Plant) Derivative

Use Treatment of metastatic carcinoma of the colon or rectum

Unlabeled/Investigational Use Lung cancer (small cell and nonsmall cell), cervical cancer, gastric cancer, pancreatic cancer, leukemia, lymphoma, breast cancer

Pregnancy Risk Factor D

Contraindications Hypersensitivity to irinotecan or any component of the formulation; concurrent use of atazanavir; pregnancy

Warnings/Precautions The U.S. Food and Drug Administration (FDA) currently recommends that procedures for proper handling and disposal of antineoplastic agents be considered

Deaths due to sepsis following severe myelosuppression have been reported. Therapy should be discontinued if neutropenic fever occurs or if the absolute neutrophil count is <500/mm³. The dose of irinotecan should be reduced if there is a clinically significant decrease in the total WBC (<200/mm³), neutrophil count (<1000/mm³), hemoglobin (<8 g/dL), or platelet count (<100,000/mm³). Routine administration of a colony-stimulating factor is generally not necessary. Avoid extravasation.

Patients with even modest elevations in total serum bilirubin levels (1.0-2.0 mg/dL) have a significantly greater likelihood of experiencing first-course grade 3 or 4 neutropenia than those with bilirubin levels that were <1.0 mg/dL. Patients with abnormal glucuronidation of bilirubin, such as those with Gilbert's syndrome, may also be at greater risk of myelosuppression when receiving therapy with irinotecan.

Hold diuretics during dosing due to potential risk of dehydration secondary to vomiting and/or diarrhea induced by irinotecan.

Common Adverse Reactions

>10%:

Cardiovascular: Vasodilation

Central nervous system: Insomnia, dizziness, fever (45.4%)

Dermatologic: Alopecia (60.5%), rash

Gastrointestinal: Irinotecan therapy may induce two different forms of diarrhea. Onset, symptoms, proposed mechanisms and treatment are different. Overall, 56.9% of patients treated experience abdominal pain and/or cramping during therapy. Anorexia, constipation, flatulence, stomatitis, and dyspepsia have also been reported.

Diarrhea: Dose-limiting toxicity with weekly dosing regimen

Early diarrhea (50.7% incidence, grade 3/4 8%) usually occurs during or within 24 hours of administration. May be accompanied by symptoms of cramping, vomiting, flushing,

(Continued)

Irinotecan *(Continued)*

and diaphoresis. It is thought to be mediated by cholinergic effects which can be successfully managed with atropine (refer to Warnings/Precautions).

Late diarrhea (87.8% incidence) usually occurs >24 hours after treatment. National Cancer Institute (NCI) grade 3 or 4 diarrhea (31%) occurs in 30.6% of patients. Late diarrhea generally occurs with a median of 11 days after therapy and lasts approximately 3 days. Patients experiencing grade 3 or 4 diarrhea were noted to have symptoms a total of 7 days. Correlated with irinotecan or SN-38 levels in plasma and bile. Due to the duration, dehydration and electrolyte imbalances are significant clinical concerns. Loperamide therapy is recommended. The incidence of grade 3 or 4 late diarrhea is significantly higher in patients ≥65 years of age; close monitoring and prompt initiation of high-dose loperamide therapy is prudent (refer to Warnings/Precautions).

Emetic potential: Moderately high (86.2% incidence, however, only 12.5% grade 3 or 4 vomiting)

Hematologic: Myelosuppressive: Dose-limiting toxicity with 3 week dosing regimen

Grade 1-4 neutropenia occurred in 53.9% of patients. Patients who had previously received pelvic or abdominal radiation therapy were noted to have a significantly increased incidence of grade 3 or 4 neutropenia. White blood cell count nadir is 15 days after administration and is more frequent than thrombocytopenia. Recovery is usually within 24-28 days and cumulative toxicity has not been observed.

WBC: Mild to severe
Platelets: Mild
Onset (days): 10
Nadir (days): 14-16
Recovery (days): 21-28

Neuromuscular & skeletal: Weakness (75.7%)
Respiratory: Dyspnea (22%), coughing, rhinitis, decreased DLCO (in a few patients)
Miscellaneous: Diaphoresis

1% to 10%: **Irritant chemotherapy**; thrombophlebitis has been reported

Drug Interactions

Cytochrome P450 Effect: Substrate (major) of CYP2B6, 3A4

Increased Effect/Toxicity: CYP2B6 inhibitors may increase the levels/effects of irinotecan; example inhibitors include desipramine, paroxetine, and sertraline. CYP3A4 inhibitors may increase irinotecan efficacy.

Decreased Effect: CYP3A4 inducers may decrease the levels/effects of irinotecan; example inducers include carbamazepine, nevirapine, phenobarbital, phenytoin, and rifampin. CYP3A4 inducers may decrease irinotecan efficacy.

Mechanism of Action Irinotecan and its active metabolite (SN-38) bind reversibly to topoisomerase I and stabilize the cleavable complex so that religation of the cleaved DNA strand cannot occur. This results in the accumulation of cleavable complexes and single-strand DNA breaks. This interaction results in single-stranded DNA breaks and cell death consistent with S-phase cell cycle specificity.

Pharmacodynamics/Kinetics

Distribution: V_d: 33-150 L/m^2

Protein binding, plasma: Parent drug: 30% to 68%; SN-38 (active drug): 95%

Metabolism: Via intestinal mucosa, plasma, hepatic, and perhaps in some tumors; converted to SN-38 by carboxylesterase enzymes; undergoes glucuronidation, the metabolite having much less activity than SN-38. Enterohepatic recirculation results in a second peak in the concentration of SN-38. The lactones of both irinotecan and SN-38 undergo hydrolysis to inactive hydroxy acid forms.

Half-life elimination: Parent drug: Alpha: 0.2 hours, Beta: 2.5 hours, Gamma: 14.2 hours; SN-38: 3-23.9 hours.

Time to peak: SN-38: 30-minute infusion: ~1 hour

Excretion: Urine (~20% of dose) within 24 hours; SN-38 excretion in 24 hours accounted for 0.25% of administered dose

Dosage Refer to individual protocols.

Single-agent therapy:

Weekly regimen: 125 mg/m^2 over 90 minutes on days 1, 8, 15, and 22, followed by a 2-week rest

Adjusted dose level -1: 100 mg/m^2
Adjusted dose level -2: 75 mg/m^2

Once-every-3-week regimen: 350 mg/m^2 over 90 minutes, once every 3 weeks

Adjusted dose level -1: 300 mg/m^2
Adjusted dose level -2: 250 mg/m^2

A reduction in the starting dose by one dose level may be considered for patients ≥65 years of age, prior pelvic/abdominal radiotherapy, performance status of 2, or increased bilirubin (dosing for patients with a bilirubin >2 mg/dL cannot be recommended based on lack of data per manufacturer)

Depending on the patient's ability to tolerate therapy, doses should be adjusted in increments of 25-50 mg/m^2. Irinotecan doses may range 50-150 mg/m^2.

Combination therapy with fluorouracil and leucovorin: Six-week (42-day) cycle (next cycle beginning on day 45):

125 mg/m^2 over 90 minutes on days 1, 8, 15, and 22; to be given in combination with bolus leucovorin and fluorouracil (leucovorin administered immediately following irinotecan; fluorouracil immediately following leucovorin)

Adjusted dose level -1: 100 mg/m²
Adjusted dose level -2: 75 mg/m²
180 mg/m² over 90 minutes on days 1, 15, and 22; to be given in combination with infusional leucovorin and bolus/infusion fluorouracil (leucovorin administered immediately following irinotecan; fluorouracil immediately following leucovorin)
Adjusted dose level -1: 150 mg/m²
Adjusted dose level -2: 120 mg/m²

Note: For all regimens: It is recommended that new courses begin only after the granulocyte count recovers to ≥1500/mm³, the platelet count recovers to ≥100,000/mm³, and treatment-related diarrhea has fully resolved. Treatment should be delayed 1-2 weeks to allow for recovery from treatment-related toxicities. If the patient has not recovered after a 2-week delay, consideration should be given to discontinuing irinotecan.

Dosing adjustment in renal impairment: Effects have not been evaluated
Dosing adjustment in hepatic impairment:

AUC of irinotecan and SN-38 have been reported to be higher in patients with known hepatic tumor involvement. The manufacturer recommends that no change in dosage or administration be made for patients with liver metastases and normal hepatic function.

In patients with a combined history of prior pelvic/abdominal irradiation and modestly elevated total serum bilirubin levels (1.0-2.0 mg/dL) prior to treatment with irinotecan, there may be substantially increased likelihood of grade 3 or 4 neutropenia. Consideration may be given to starting irinotecan at a lower dose (eg, 100 mg/m²) in such patients. Definite recommendations regarding the most appropriate starting dose in patients who have pretreatment total serum bilirubin elevations >2.0 mg/dL are not available, but it is likely that lower starting doses will need to be considered in such patients.

Dosage adjustment for toxicities: It is recommended that new courses begin only after the granulocyte count recovers to ≥1500/mm³, the platelet counts recovers to ≥100,000/mm³, and treatment-related diarrhea has fully resolved. Depending on the patient's ability to tolerate therapy, doses should be adjusted in increments of 25-50 mg/m². Irinotecan doses may range 50-150 mg/m². Treatment should be delayed 1-2 weeks to allow for recovery from treatment-related toxicities. If the patient has not recovered after a 2-week delay, consideration should be given to discontinuing irinotecan. See tables below and on next page.

Combination Schedules: Recommended Dosage Modifications[1]

Toxicity NCI[2] Grade (Value)	During a Cycle of Therapy	At the Start of Subsequent Cycles of Therapy (After Adequate Recovery), Compared to the Starting Dose in the Previous Cycle[1]
No toxicity	Maintain dose level	Maintain dose level
Neutropenia		
1 (1500-1999/mm³)	Maintain dose level	Maintain dose level
2 (1000-1499/mm³)	↓ 1 dose level	Maintain dose level
3 (500-999/mm³)	Omit dose until resolved to ≤ grade 2, then ↓ 1 dose level	↓ 1 dose level
4 (<500/mm³)	Omit dose until resolved to ≤ grade 2, then ↓ 2 dose levels	↓ 2 dose levels
Neutropenic Fever (grade 4 neutropenia and ≥ grade 2 fever)	Omit dose until resolved, then ↓ 2 dose levels	
Other Hematologic Toxicities	Dose modifications for leukopenia or thrombocytopenia during a course of therapy and at the start of subsequent courses of therapy are also based on NCI toxicity criteria and are the same as recommended for neutropenia above.	
Diarrhea		
1 (2-3 stools/day > pretreatment)	Delay dose until resolved to baseline, then give same dose	Maintain dose level
2 (4-6 stools/day > pretreatment)	Omit dose until resolved to baseline, then ↓ 1 dose level	Maintain dose level
3 (7-9 stools/day > pretreatment)	Omit dose until resolved to baseline, then ↓ by 1 dose level	↓ 1 dose level
4 (≥10 stools/day > pretreatment)	Omit dose until resolved to baseline, then ↓ 2 dose levels	↓ 2 dose levels
Other Nonhematologic Toxicities[3]		
1	Maintain dose level	Maintain dose level
2	Omit dose until resolved to ≤ grade 1, then ↓ 1 dose level	Maintain dose level
3	Omit dose until resolved to ≤ grade 2, then ↓ 1 dose level	↓ 1 dose level
4	Omit dose until resolved to ≤ grade 2, then ↓ 2 dose levels	↓ 2 dose levels
Mucositis and/or stomatitis	Decrease only 5-FU, not irinotecan	Decrease only 5-FU, not irinotecan

[1]All dose modifications should be based on the worst preceding toxicity.

[2]National Cancer Institute Common Toxicity Criteria (version 1.0).

[3]Excludes alopecia, anorexia, asthenia.

Administration Administer by I.V. infusion, usually over 90 minutes.
Monitoring Parameters CBC with differential, platelet count, and hemoglobin with each dose
Patient Information Patients and patients' caregivers should be informed of the expected toxic effects of irinotecan, particularly of its gastrointestinal manifestations, such as nausea, (Continued)

689

Irinotecan *(Continued)*

vomiting, and diarrhea. Each patient should be instructed to have loperamide readily available and to begin treatment for late diarrhea (occurring >24 hours after administration of irinotecan) at the first episode of poorly formed or loose stools or the earliest onset of bowel movements more frequent than normally expected for the patient. Refer to Warnings/Precautions. The patient should also be instructed to notify the prescriber if diarrhea occurs. Premedication with loperamide is not recommended. The use of drugs with laxative properties should be avoided because of the potential for exacerbation of diarrhea. Patients should be advised to contact their prescriber to discuss any laxative use. Patients should consult their prescriber if vomiting occurs, fever or evidence of infection develops, or if symptoms of dehydration, such as fainting, lightheadedness, or dizziness, are noted following therapy.

Dosage Forms INJ, solution: 20 mg/mL (2 mL, 5 mL)

Single-Agent Schedule: Recommended Dosage Modifications[1]

Toxicity NCI Grade[2] (Value)	During a Cycle of Therapy	At the Start of Subsequent Cycles of Therapy (After Adequate Recovery), Compared to the Starting Dose in the Previous Cycle[1]	
	Weekly	Weekly	Once Every 3 Weeks
No toxicity	Maintain dose level	↑ 25 mg/m^2 up to a maximum dose of 150 mg/m^2	Maintain dose level
Neutropenia			
1 (1500-1999/mm^3)	Maintain dose level	Maintain dose level	Maintain dose level
2 (1000-1499/mm^3)	↓ 25 mg/m^2	Maintain dose level	Maintain dose level
3 (500-999/mm^3)	Omit dose until resolved to ≤ grade 2, then ↓ 25 mg/m^2	↓ 25 mg/m^2	↓ 50 mg/m^2
4 (<500/mm^3)	Omit dose until resolved to ≤ grade 2, then ↓ 50 mg/m^2	↓ 50 mg/m^2	↓ 50 mg/m^2
Neutropenic Fever (grade 4 neutropenia and ≥ grade 2 fever)	Omit dose until resolved, then ↓ 50 mg/m^2	↓ 50 mg/m^2	↓ 50 mg/m^2
Other Hematologic Toxicities	Dose modifications for leukopenia, thrombocytopenia, and anemia during a course of therapy and at the start of subsequent courses of therapy are also based on NCI toxicity criteria and are the same as recommended for neutropenia above.		
Diarrhea			
1 (2-3 stools/day > pretreatment)	Maintain dose level	Maintain dose level	Maintain dose level
2 (4-6 stools/day > pretreatment)	↓ 25 mg/m^2	Maintain dose level	Maintain dose level
3 (7-9 stools/day > pretreatment)	Omit dose until resolved to ≤ grade 2, then ↓ 25 mg/m^2	↓ 25 mg/m^2	↓ 50 mg/m^2
4 (≥10 stools/day > pretreatment)	Omit dose until resolved to ≤ grade 2, then ↓ 50 mg/m^2	↓ 50 mg/m^2	↓ 50 mg/m^2
Other Nonhematologic Toxicities[3]			
1	Maintain dose level	Maintain dose level	Maintain dose level
2	↓ 25 mg/m^2	↓ 25 mg/m^2	↓ 50 mg/m^2
3	Omit dose until resolved to ≤ grade 2, then ↓ 25 mg/m^2	↓ 25 mg/m^2	↓ 50 mg/m^2
4	Omit dose until resolved to ≤ grade 2, then ↓ 50 mg/m^2	↓ 50 mg/m^2	↓ 50 mg/m^2

[1]All dose modifications should be based on the worst preceding toxicity.

[2]National Cancer Institute Common Toxicity Criteria (version 1.0).

[3]Excludes alopecia, anorexia, asthenia.

Iron Dextran Complex (EYE ern DEKS tran KOM pleks)

U.S. Brand Names Dexferrum®; INFeD®

Therapeutic Category Iron Salt

Use Treatment of microcytic hypochromic anemia resulting from iron deficiency in patients in whom oral administration is infeasible or ineffective

Pregnancy Risk Factor C

Contraindications Hypersensitivity to iron dextran or any component of the formulation; all anemias that are not involved with iron deficiency; hemochromatosis; hemolytic anemia

Warnings/Precautions Use with caution in patients with history of asthma, hepatic impairment, rheumatoid arthritis; not recommended in children <4 months of age; deaths associated with parenteral administration following anaphylactic-type reactions have been reported; use only in patients where the iron deficient state is not amenable to oral iron therapy. A test dose of 0.5 mL I.V. or I.M. should be given to observe for adverse reactions. Anemia in the elderly is often caused by "anemia of chronic disease" or associated with inflammation rather than blood loss. Iron stores are usually normal or increased, with a serum ferritin >50 ng/mL and a decreased total iron binding capacity. I.V. administration of iron dextran is often preferred over I.M. in the elderly secondary to a decreased muscle mass and the need for daily injections.

Common Adverse Reactions

>10%:

Cardiovascular: Flushing

Central nervous system: Dizziness, fever, headache, pain
Gastrointestinal: Nausea, vomiting, metallic taste
Local: Staining of skin at the site of I.M. injection
Miscellaneous: Diaphoresis
1% to 10%:
Cardiovascular: Hypotension (1% to 2%)
Dermatologic: Urticaria (1% to 2%), phlebitis (1% to 2%)
Gastrointestinal: Diarrhea
Genitourinary: Discoloration of urine
Note: Diaphoresis, urticaria, arthralgia, fever, chills, dizziness, headache, and nausea may be delayed 24-48 hours after I.V. administration or 3-4 days after I.M. administration.
Anaphylactoid reactions: Respiratory difficulties and cardiovascular collapse have been reported and occur most frequently within the first several minutes of administration.

Drug Interactions
Decreased Effect: Decreased effect with chloramphenicol.

Mechanism of Action The released iron, from the plasma, eventually replenishes the depleted iron stores in the bone marrow where it is incorporated into hemoglobin

Pharmacodynamics/Kinetics
Absorption:
I.M.: 50% to 90% is promptly absorbed, balance is slowly absorbed over month
I.V.: Uptake of iron by the reticuloendothelial system appears to be constant at about 10-20 mg/hour
Excretion: Urine and feces via reticuloendothelial system

Dosage I.M. (Z-track method should be used for I.M. injection), I.V.:
A 0.5 mL test dose (0.25 mL in infants) should be given prior to starting iron dextran therapy; total dose should be divided into a daily schedule for I.M., total dose may be given as a single continuous infusion
Iron-deficiency anemia: Dose (mL) = 0.0476 x LBW (kg) x (normal hemoglobin - observed hemoglobin) + (1 mL/5 kg of LBW to maximum of 14 mL for iron stores)
LBW = Lean Body Weight
Iron replacement therapy for blood loss: Replacement iron (mg) = blood loss (mL) x hematocrit
Maximum daily dose (can administer total dose at one time I.V.):
Infants <5 kg: 25 mg iron (0.5 mL)
Children:
5-10 kg: 50 mg iron (1 mL)
10-50 kg: 100 mg iron (2 mL)
Adults >50 kg: 100 mg iron (2 mL)

Administration Use Z-track technique for I.M. administration (deep into the upper outer quadrant of buttock); may be administered I.V. bolus at rate ≤50 mg/minute or diluted in 250-1000 mL NS and infused over 1-6 hours; infuse initial 25 mL slowly, observe for allergic reactions; have epinephrine nearby

Monitoring Parameters Hemoglobin, hematocrit, reticulocyte count, serum ferritin, serum iron, TIBC

Reference Range
Hemoglobin: Adults:
Males: 13.5-16.5 g/dL
Females: 12.0-15.0 g/dL
Serum iron: 40-160 µg/dL
Total iron binding capacity: 230-430 µg/dL
Transferrin: 204-360 mg/dL
Percent transferrin saturation: 20% to 50%

Dosage Forms INJ, solution (Dexferrum®): 50 mg/mL (1 mL, 2 mL); (INFeD®): 50 mg/mL (2 mL)

♦ **Iron Fumarate** see Ferrous Fumarate on page 519
♦ **Iron Gluconate** see Ferrous Gluconate on page 520
♦ **Iron-Polysaccharide Complex** see Polysaccharide-Iron Complex on page 1016
♦ **Iron Sulfate** see Ferrous Sulfate on page 520
♦ **Iron Sulfate and Vitamin C** see Ferrous Sulfate and Ascorbic Acid on page 521
♦ **ISD** see Isosorbide Dinitrate on page 694
♦ **ISDN** see Isosorbide Dinitrate on page 694
♦ **ISG** see Immune Globulin (Intramuscular) on page 658
♦ **ISMN** see Isosorbide Mononitrate on page 695
♦ **Ismo®** see Isosorbide Mononitrate on page 695
♦ **Isoamyl Nitrite** see Amyl Nitrite on page 99
♦ **Isobamate** see Carisoprodol on page 221

Isoetharine (eye soe ETH a reen)

Related Information
Bronchodilators, Comparison of Inhaled Sympathomimetics on page 1370

Synonyms Isoetharine Hydrochloride; Isoetharine Mesylate

Therapeutic Category Adrenergic Agonist Agent; Bronchodilator; Sympathomimetic Agent

Use Bronchodilator in bronchial asthma and for reversible bronchospasm occurring with bronchitis and emphysema

Pregnancy Risk Factor C

Dosage Treatments are not usually repeated more than every 4 hours, except in severe cases
(Continued)

Isoetharine *(Continued)*

Nebulizer: Children: 0.01 mL/kg; minimum dose 0.1 mL; maximum dose: 0.5 mL diluted in 2-3 mL normal saline

Dosage Forms SOLN, oral inhalation: 1% (10 mL) [DSC]

♦ **Isoetharine Hydrochloride** *see Isoetharine on page 691*

♦ **Isoetharine Mesylate** *see Isoetharine on page 691*

♦ **Isometheptene, Acetaminophen, and Dichloralphenazone** *see Acetaminophen, Isometheptene, and Dichloralphenazone on page 29*

♦ **Isometheptene, Dichloralphenazone, and Acetaminophen** *see Acetaminophen, Isometheptene, and Dichloralphenazone on page 29*

Isoniazid *(eye soe NYE a zid)*

Related Information

Tuberculosis Prophylaxis *on page 1438*
Tuberculosis Treatment Guidelines *on page 1466*

U.S. Brand Names Nydrazid®

Synonyms INH; Isonicotinic Acid Hydrazide

Therapeutic Category Antitubercular Agent

Use Treatment of susceptible tuberculosis infections; prophylactically in those individuals exposed to tuberculosis

Pregnancy Risk Factor C

Contraindications Hypersensitivity to isoniazid or any component of the formulation; acute liver disease; previous history of hepatic damage during isoniazid therapy

Warnings/Precautions Use with caution in patients with renal impairment and chronic liver disease. Severe and sometimes fatal hepatitis may occur or develop even after many months of treatment; patients must report any prodromal symptoms of hepatitis, such as fatigue, weakness, malaise, anorexia, nausea, or vomiting. Children with low milk and low meat intake should receive concomitant pyridoxine therapy. Periodic ophthalmic examinations are recommended even when usual symptoms do not occur; pyridoxine (10-50 mg/day) is recommended in individuals likely to develop peripheral neuropathies.

Common Adverse Reactions

>10%:
Gastrointestinal: Loss of appetite, nausea, vomiting, stomach pain
Hepatic: Mild increased LFTs (10% to 20%)
Neuromuscular & skeletal: Weakness, peripheral neuropathy (dose-related incidence, 10% to 20% incidence with 10 mg/kg/day)

1% to 10%:
Central nervous system: Dizziness, slurred speech, lethargy
Hepatic: Progressive liver damage (increases with age; 2.3% in patients >50 years of age)
Neuromuscular & skeletal: Hyper-reflexia

Drug Interactions

Cytochrome P450 Effect: Substrate of CYP2E1 (major); **Inhibits** CYP1A2 (weak), 2A6 (moderate), 2C8/9 (moderate), 2C19 (strong), 2D6 (moderate), 2E1 (moderate), 3A4 (strong); **Induces** CYP2E1 (after discontinuation) (weak)

Increased Effect/Toxicity: Increased toxicity/levels of oral anticoagulants, carbamazepines, cycloserine, hydantoins, and hepatically metabolized benzodiazepines. Reaction with disulfiram.

Decreased Effect: Decreased effect/levels of isoniazid with aluminum salts.

Mechanism of Action Unknown, but may include the inhibition of myocolic acid synthesis resulting in disruption of the bacterial cell wall

Pharmacodynamics/Kinetics

Absorption: Rapid and complete; rate can be slowed with food
Distribution: All body tissues and fluids including CSF; crosses placenta; enters breast milk
Protein binding: 10% to 15%
Metabolism: Hepatic with decay rate determined genetically by acetylation phenotype
Half-life elimination: Fast acetylators: 30-100 minutes; Slow acetylators: 2-5 hours; may be prolonged with hepatic or severe renal impairment
Time to peak, serum: 1-2 hours
Excretion: Urine (75% to 95%); feces; saliva

Dosage Recommendations often change due to resistant strains and newly developed information; consult *MMWR* for current CDC recommendations: **Oral** (injectable is available for patients who are unable to either take or absorb oral therapy):

Note: A four-drug regimen (isoniazid, rifampin, pyrazinamide, and either streptomycin or ethambutol) is preferred for the initial, empiric treatment of TB. When the drug susceptibility results are available, the regimen should be altered as appropriate.

Infants and Children:
Prophylaxis: 10 mg/kg/day in 1-2 divided doses (maximum: 300 mg/day) 6 months in patients who do not have HIV infection and 12 months in patients who have HIV infection
Treatment:
Daily therapy: 10-20 mg/kg/day in 1-2 divided doses (maximum: 300 mg/day)
Directly observed therapy (DOT): Twice weekly therapy: 20-40 mg/kg (maximum: 900 mg/day); 3 times/week therapy: 20-40 mg/kg (maximum: 900 mg)

Adults:
Prophylaxis: 300 mg/day for 6 months in patients who do not have HIV infection and 12 months in patients who have HIV infection

Treatment:

Daily therapy: 5 mg/kg/day given daily (usual dose: 300 mg/day); 10 mg/kg/day in 1-2 divided doses in patients with disseminated disease

Directly observed therapy (DOT): Twice weekly therapy: 15 mg/kg (maximum: 900 mg); 3 times/week therapy: 15 mg/kg (maximum: 900 mg)

Note: Concomitant administration of 6-50 mg/day pyridoxine is recommended in malnourished patients or those prone to neuropathy (eg, alcoholics, diabetics)

Hemodialysis: Dialyzable (50% to 100%)

Administer dose postdialysis

Peritoneal dialysis effects: Dose for Cl_{cr} <10 mL/minute

Continuous arteriovenous or venovenous hemofiltration: Dose for Cl_{cr} <10 mL/minute

Dosing adjustment in hepatic impairment: Dose should be reduced in severe hepatic disease

Monitoring Parameters Periodic liver function tests; monitoring for prodromal signs of hepatitis

Reference Range Therapeutic: 1-7 µg/mL (SI: 7-51 µmol/L); Toxic: 20-710 µg/mL (SI: 146-5176 µmol/L)

Patient Information Report any symptoms of hepatitis (fatigue, weakness, nausea, vomiting, dark urine, or yellowing of eyes) or any burning, tingling, or numbness in the extremities

Dosage Forms INJ, solution (Nydrazid®): 100 mg/mL (10 mL). **SYR:** 50 mg/5 mL (473 mL). **TAB:** 100 mg, 300 mg

♦ **Isonicotinic Acid Hydrazide** *see Isoniazid on page 692*

♦ **Isonipecaine Hydrochloride** *see Meperidine on page 791*

♦ **Isophosphamide** *see Ifosfamide on page 649*

Isoproterenol (eye soe proe TER e nole)

Related Information

Bronchodilators, Comparison of Inhaled Sympathomimetics *on page 1370*

Hemodynamic Support, Intravenous *on page 1377*

U.S. Brand Names Isuprel®

Synonyms Isoproterenol Hydrochloride

Therapeutic Category Adrenergic Agonist Agent; Bronchodilator; Sympathomimetic Agent

Use Ventricular arrhythmias due to AV nodal block; hemodynamically compromised bradyarrhythmias or atropine- and dopamine-resistant bradyarrhythmias (when transcutaneous/venous pacing is not available); temporary use in third-degree AV block until pacemaker insertion

Unlabeled/Investigational Use Temporizing measure before transvenous pacing for torsade de pointes; diagnostic aid (vasovagal syncope)

Pregnancy Risk Factor C

Contraindications Hypersensitivity to sulfites or isoproterenol, any component of the formulation, or other sympathomimetic amines; angina, pre-existing cardiac arrhythmias (ventricular); tachycardia or AV block caused by cardiac glycoside intoxication

Warnings/Precautions Use with extreme caution; not currently a treatment of choice; use with caution in elderly patients, diabetics, renal or cardiovascular disease, seizure disorder, or hyperthyroidism; excessive or prolonged use may result in decreased effectiveness.

Common Adverse Reactions Frequency not defined.

Cardiovascular: Premature ventricular beats, bradycardia, hypertension, hypotension, chest pain, palpitations, tachycardia, ventricular arrhythmias, myocardial infarction size increased

Central nervous system: Headache, nervousness or restlessness

Endocrine & metabolic: Serum glucose increased, serum potassium decreased, hypokalemia

Gastrointestinal: Nausea, vomiting

Respiratory: Dyspnea

Drug Interactions

Increased Effect/Toxicity: Sympathomimetic agents may cause headaches and elevate blood pressure. General anesthetics may cause arrhythmias.

Mechanism of Action Stimulates beta$_1$- and beta$_2$-receptors resulting in relaxation of bronchial, GI, and uterine smooth muscle, increased heart rate and contractility, vasodilation of peripheral vasculature

Pharmacodynamics/Kinetics

Onset of action: Bronchodilation: I.V.: Immediate

Duration: I.V.: 10-15 minutes

Metabolism: Via conjugation in many tissues including hepatic and pulmonary

Half-life elimination: 2.5-5 minutes

Excretion: Urine (primarily as sulfate conjugates)

Dosage I.V.: Cardiac arrhythmias:

Children: Initial: 0.1 mcg/kg/minute (usual effective dose 0.2-2 mcg/kg/minute)

Adults: Initial: 2 mcg/minute; titrate to patient response (2-10 mcg/minute)

Administration I.V. infusion administration requires the use of an infusion pump. To prepare for infusion: 1 mg isoproterenol to 500 mL D$_5$W, final concentration 2 mcg/mL

Monitoring Parameters ECG, heart rate, respiratory rate, arterial blood gas, arterial blood pressure, CVP; serum glucose, serum potassium, serum magnesium

Patient Information Do not exceed recommended dosage; excessive use may lead to adverse effects or loss of effectiveness. Shake canister well before use. Administer pressurized inhalation during the second half of inspiration, as the airways are open wider and the aerosol distribution is more extensive. If more than one inhalation per dose is necessary, wait (Continued)

Isoproterenol *(Continued)*

at least 1 full minute between inhalations - second inhalation is best delivered after 10 minutes. May cause nervousness, restlessness, insomnia; if these effects continue after dosage reduction, notify prescriber. Report palpitations, tachycardia, chest pain, muscle tremors, dizziness, headache, flushing or if breathing difficulty persists.

Dosage Forms INJ, solution: 0.02 mg/mL (10 mL); 0.2 mg/mL (1:5000) (1 mL, 5 mL)

- ◆ **Isoproterenol Hydrochloride** *see Isoproterenol on page 693*
- ◆ **Isoptin® SR** *see Verapamil on page 1302*
- ◆ **Isopto® Atropine** *see Atropine on page 133*
- ◆ **Isopto® Carbachol** *see Carbachol on page 214*
- ◆ **Isopto® Carpine** *see Pilocarpine on page 1001*
- ◆ **Isopto® Homatropine** *see Homatropine on page 620*
- ◆ **Isopto® Hyoscine** *see Scopolamine on page 1126*
- ◆ **Isordil®** *see Isosorbide Dinitrate on page 694*

Isosorbide Dinitrate *(eye soe SOR bide dye NYE trate)*

Related Information
Nitrates Comparison *on page 1400*
U.S. Brand Names Dilatrate®-SR; Isordil®
Synonyms ISD; ISDN
Therapeutic Category Antianginal Agent; Nitrate; Vasodilator, Coronary
Use Prevention and treatment of angina pectoris; for congestive heart failure; to relieve pain, dysphagia, and spasm in esophageal spasm with GE reflux
Pregnancy Risk Factor C
Contraindications Hypersensitivity to isosorbide dinitrate or any component of the formulation; hypersensitivity to organic nitrates; concurrent use with phosphodiesterase-5 (PDE-5) inhibitors (sildenafil, tadalafil, or vardenafil); angle-closure glaucoma (intraocular pressure may be increased); head trauma or cerebral hemorrhage (increase intracranial pressure); severe anemia
Warnings/Precautions Use with caution in patients with increased intracranial pressure, hypotension, hypovolemia, glaucoma; sustained release products may be absorbed erratically in patients with GI hypermotility or malabsorption syndrome; do not crush or chew sublingual dosage form; abrupt withdrawal may result in angina; tolerance may develop (adjust dose or change agent). Avoid use with sildenafil.
Common Adverse Reactions Frequency not defined.
Cardiovascular: Hypotension (infrequent), postural hypotension, crescendo angina (uncommon), rebound hypertension (uncommon), pallor, cardiovascular collapse, tachycardia, shock, flushing, peripheral edema
Central nervous system: Headache (most common), lightheadedness (related to blood pressure changes), syncope (uncommon), dizziness, restlessness
Gastrointestinal: Nausea, vomiting, bowel incontinence, xerostomia
Genitourinary: Urinary incontinence
Hematologic: Methemoglobinemia (rare, overdose)
Neuromuscular & skeletal: Weakness
Ocular: Blurred vision
Miscellaneous: Cold sweat

The incidence of hypotension and adverse cardiovascular events may be increased when used in combination with sildenafil (Viagra®).
Drug Interactions
Cytochrome P450 Effect: Substrate of CYP3A4 (major)
Increased Effect/Toxicity: Significant reduction of systolic and diastolic blood pressure with concurrent use of sildenafil, tadalafil, or vardenafil (contraindicated). Do not administer sildenafil, tadalafil, or vardenafil within 24 hours of a nitrate preparation.
Mechanism of Action Stimulation of intracellular cyclic-GMP results in vascular smooth muscle relaxation of both arterial and venous vasculature. Increased venous pooling decreases left ventricular pressure (preload) and arterial dilatation decreases arterial resistance (afterload). Therefore, this reduces cardiac oxygen demand by decreasing left ventricular pressure and systemic vascular resistance by dilating arteries. Additionally, coronary artery dilation improves collateral flow to ischemic regions; esophageal smooth muscle is relaxed via the same mechanism.
Pharmacodynamics/Kinetics
Onset of action: Sublingual tablet: 2-10 minutes; Chewable tablet: 3 minutes; Oral tablet: 45-60 minutes
Duration: Sublingual tablet: 1-2 hours; Chewable tablet: 0.5-2 hours; Oral tablet: 4-6 hours
Metabolism: Extensively hepatic to conjugated metabolites, including isosorbide 5-mononitrate (active) and 2-mononitrate (active)
Half-life elimination: Parent drug: 1-4 hours; Metabolite (5-mononitrate): 4 hours
Excretion: Urine and feces
Dosage Adults (elderly should be given lowest recommended daily doses initially and titrate upward): Oral:
Angina: 5-40 mg 4 times/day or 40 mg every 8-12 hours in sustained-release dosage form
Congestive heart failure:
Initial dose: 10 mg 3 times/day
Target dose: 40 mg 3 times/day

Maximum dose: 80 mg 3 times/day
Sublingual: 2.5-10 mg every 4-6 hours
Chewable tablet: 5-10 mg every 2-3 hours

Tolerance to nitrate effects develops with chronic exposure
Dose escalation does not overcome this effect. Short periods (14 hours) of nitrate withdrawal help minimize tolerance.

Hemodialysis: During hemodialysis, administer dose postdialysis or administer supplemental 10-20 mg dose

Peritoneal dialysis: Supplemental dose is not necessary

Administration Do not administer around-the-clock; the first dose of nitrates should be administered in a physician's office to observe for maximal cardiovascular dynamic effects and adverse effects (orthostatic blood pressure drop, headache); when immediate release products are prescribed twice daily - recommend 7 AM and noon; for 3 times/day dosing - recommend 7 AM, noon, and 5 PM; when sustained-release products are indicated, suggest once a day in morning or via twice daily dosing at 8 AM and 2 PM

Monitoring Parameters Monitor for orthostasis

Patient Information Do not chew or crush sublingual or sustained release dosage form; do not change brands without consulting your pharmacist or prescriber; keep tablets or capsules in original container and keep container tightly closed; if no relief from sublingual tablets after 15 minutes, report to nearest emergency room or seek emergency help

Dosage Forms CAP, sustained release (Dilatrate®-SR): 40 mg. **TAB:** 5 mg, 10 mg, 20 mg, 30 mg; (Isordil®): 5 mg, 10 mg, 20 mg, 30 mg, 40 mg. **TAB, chewable:** 5 mg, 10 mg. **TAB, sublingual** (Isordil®): 2.5 mg, 5 mg, 10 mg

Isosorbide Mononitrate (eye soe SOR bide mon oh NYE trate)

Related Information
Nitrates Comparison *on page 1400*

U.S. Brand Names Imdur®; Ismo®; Monoket®

Synonyms ISMN

Therapeutic Category Antianginal Agent; Nitrate; Vasodilator, Coronary

Use Long-acting metabolite of the vasodilator isosorbide dinitrate used for the prophylactic treatment of angina pectoris

Pregnancy Risk Factor C

Contraindications Hypersensitivity to isosorbide or any component of the formulation; hypersensitivity to organic nitrates; concurrent use with phosphodiesterase-5 (PDE-5) inhibitors (sildenafil, tadalafil, or vardenafil); angle-closure glaucoma (intraocular pressure may be increased); head trauma or cerebral hemorrhage (increase intracranial pressure); severe anemia

Warnings/Precautions Postural hypotension, transient episodes of weakness, dizziness, or syncope may occur even with small doses; ethanol accentuates these effects; tolerance and cross-tolerance to nitrate antianginal and hemodynamic effects may occur during prolonged isosorbide mononitrate therapy; (minimized by using the smallest effective dose, by alternating coronary vasodilators or offering drug-free intervals of as little as 12 hours). Excessive doses may result in severe headache, blurred vision, or xerostomia; increased anginal symptoms may be a result of dosage increases. Avoid use with sildenafil.

Common Adverse Reactions
>10%: Central nervous system: Headache (19% to 38%)
1% to 10%:
Central nervous system: Dizziness (3% to 5%)
Gastrointestinal: Nausea/vomiting (2% to 4%)

The incidence of hypotension and adverse cardiovascular events may be increased when used in combination with sildenafil (Viagra®).

Drug Interactions
Cytochrome P450 Effect: Substrate of CYP3A4 (major)
Increased Effect/Toxicity: Significant reduction of systolic and diastolic blood pressure with concurrent use of sildenafil or vardenafil (contraindicated); do not administer sildenafil or vardenafil within 24 hours of a nitrate preparation. CYP3A4 inhibitors may increase hypotensive response.

Mechanism of Action Prevailing mechanism of action for nitroglycerin (and other nitrates) is systemic venodilation, decreasing preload as measured by pulmonary capillary wedge pressure and left ventricular end diastolic volume and pressure; the average reduction in left ventricular end diastolic volume is 25% at rest, with a corresponding increase in ejection fractions of 50% to 60%. This effect improves congestive symptoms in heart failure and improves the myocardial perfusion gradient in patients with coronary artery disease.

Pharmacodynamics/Kinetics
Onset of action: 30-60 minutes
Absorption: Nearly complete and low intersubject variability in its pharmacokinetic parameters and plasma concentrations
Metabolism: Hepatic
Half-life elimination: Mononitrate: ~4 hours
Excretion: Urine and feces

Dosage Adults and Geriatrics (start with lowest recommended dose): Oral:
Regular tablet: 5-10 mg twice daily with the two doses given 7 hours apart (eg, 8 AM and 3 PM) to decrease tolerance development; then titrate to 10 mg twice daily in first 2-3 days.
Extended release tablet: Initial: 30-60 mg given in morning as a single dose; titrate upward as needed, giving at least 3 days between increases; maximum daily single dose: 240 mg
(Continued)

Isosorbide Mononitrate *(Continued)*

Dosing adjustment in renal impairment: Not necessary for elderly or patients with altered renal or hepatic function.

Tolerance to nitrate effects develops with chronic exposure. Dose escalation does not overcome this effect. Tolerance can only be overcome by short periods of nitrate absence from the body. Short periods (10-12 hours) of nitrate withdrawal help minimize tolerance. Recommended dosage regimens incorporate this interval. General recommendations are to take the last dose of short-acting agents no later than 7 PM; administer 2 times/day rather than 4 times/day. Administer sustained release tablet once daily in the morning.

Administration Do not administer around-the-clock; Monoket® and Ismo® should be scheduled twice daily with doses 7 hours apart (8 AM and 3 PM); Imdur® may be administered once daily

Monitoring Parameters Monitor for orthostasis, increased hypotension

Patient Information Dispense drug in easy-to-open container; do not change brands without consulting pharmacist or prescriber; keep tablets or capsules tightly closed in original container; extended release tablets should not be chewed or crushed and should be swallowed together with a half-glassful of fluid; the antianginal efficacy of tablets (Ismo®, Monoket®) can be maintained by carefully following the prescribed schedule of dosing (2 doses taken 7 hours apart); the extended-release (Imdur®) tablet should be given once daily; headaches are sometimes a marker of the activity of the drug

Dosage Forms TAB: 10 mg, 20 mg; (Ismo®): 20 mg; (Monoket®): 10 mg, 20 mg. **TAB, extended release** (Imdur®): 30 mg, 60 mg, 120 mg

Isotretinoin *(eye soe TRET i noyn)*

U.S. Brand Names Accutane®; Amnesteem™; Claravis™; Sotret®

Synonyms 13-*cis*-Retinoic Acid

Therapeutic Category Acne Product; Retinoic Acid Derivative; Vitamin A Derivative

Use Treatment of severe recalcitrant nodular acne unresponsive to conventional therapy

Unlabeled/Investigational Use Investigational: Treatment of children with metastatic neuroblastoma or leukemia that does not respond to conventional therapy

Restrictions Prescriptions for isotretinoin may not be dispensed unless they are affixed with a yellow, self-adhesive qualification sticker filled out by the prescriber. Telephone, fax, or computer-generated prescriptions are no longer valid. Prescriptions may not be written for more than a 1-month supply and must be dispensed with a patient education guide every month. In addition, prescriptions for females must be filled within 7 days of the qualification date noted on the yellow sticker; prescriptions filled after 7 days of the noted date are considered to be expired and cannot be honored. Pharmacists may call the manufacturer to confirm the prescriber's authority to write for this medication, however, this is not mandatory.

Prescribers will be provided with qualification stickers after they have read the details of the program and have signed and mailed to the manufacturer their agreement to participate. Audits of pharmacies will be conducted to monitor program compliance.

Pregnancy Risk Factor X

Contraindications Hypersensitivity to isotretinoin or any component of the formulation; sensitivity to parabens, vitamin A, or other retinoids; pregnancy

Warnings/Precautions This medication should only be prescribed by prescribers competent in treating severe recalcitrant nodular acne, are experienced in the use of systemic retinoids and are participating in the pregnancy prevention programs authorized by the FDA and product manufacturer. Use with caution in patients with diabetes mellitus, hypertriglyceridemia; acute pancreatitis and fatal hemorrhagic pancreatitis (rare) have been reported. Not to be used in women of childbearing potential unless woman is capable of complying with effective contraceptive measures. Patients must select and commit to two forms of contraception (microdosed progestin preparations may be inadequate as a form of contraception with isotretinoin, although other hormonal contraceptives are highly effective). Therapy is begun after two negative pregnancy tests; effective contraception must be used for at least 1 month before beginning therapy, during therapy, and for 1 month after discontinuation of therapy. Prescriptions should be written for no more than a 1-month supply, and pregnancy testing and counseling should be repeated monthly. Because of the high likelihood of teratogenic effects (~20%), do not prescribe isotretinoin for women who are or who are likely to become pregnant while using the drug (see Additional Information for details). Male and female patients must be enrolled in the manufacturer sponsored and FDA approved monitoring programs.

Depression, psychosis, aggressive or violent behavior, and rarely suicidal thoughts and actions have been reported during isotretinoin usage. Discontinuation of treatment alone may not be sufficient, further evaluation may be necessary. Cases of pseudotumor cerebri (benign intracranial hypertension) have been reported, some with concomitant use of tetracycline (avoid using together). Patients with papilledema, headache, nausea, vomiting, and visual disturbances should be referred to a neurologist and treatment with isotretinoin discontinued. Hearing impairment, which can continue after therapy is discontinued, may occur. Clinical hepatitis, elevated liver enzymes, inflammatory bowel disease, skeletal hyperostosis, premature epiphyseal closure, vision impairment, corneal opacities, and decreased night vision have also been reported with the use of isotretinoin. Bone mineral density may decrease; use caution in patients with a genetic predisposition to bone disorders (ie osteoporosis, osteomalacia) and with disease states or concomitant medications that can induce bone disorders. Patients may be at risk when participating in activities with repetitive impact (such as sports). Safety of long-term use is not established and is not recommended.

Common Adverse Reactions Frequency not defined.

Cardiovascular: Palpitation, tachycardia, vascular thrombotic disease, stroke, chest pain, syncope, flushing

Central nervous system: Edema, fatigue, pseudotumor cerebri, dizziness, drowsiness, headache, insomnia, lethargy, malaise, nervousness, paresthesias, seizures, stroke, suicidal ideation, suicide attempts, suicide, depression, psychosis, aggressive or violent behavior, emotional instability

Dermatologic: Cutaneous allergic reactions, purpura, acne fulminans, alopecia, bruising, cheilitis, dry mouth, dry nose, dry skin, epistaxis, eruptive xanthomas, fragility of skin, hair abnormalities, hirsutism, hyperpigmentation, hypopigmentation, peeling of palms, peeling of soles, photoallergic reactions, photosensitizing reactions, pruritus, rash, dystrophy, paronychia, facial erythema, seborrhea, eczema, increased sunburn susceptibility, diaphoresis, urticaria, abnormal wound healing

Endocrine & metabolic: Increased triglycerides (25%), elevated blood glucose, increased HDL, increased cholesterol, abnormal menses

Gastrointestinal: Weight loss, inflammatory bowel disease, regional ileitis, pancreatitis, bleeding and inflammation of the gums, colitis, nausea, nonspecific gastrointestinal symptoms

Genitourinary: Nonspecific urogenital findings

Hematologic: Anemia, thrombocytopenia, neutropenia, agranulocytosis, pyogenic granuloma

Hepatic: Hepatitis

Neuromuscular & skeletal: Skeletal hyperostosis, calcification of tendons and ligaments, premature epiphyseal closure, arthralgia, CPK elevations, arthritis, tendonitis, bone abnormalities, weakness, back pain (29% in pediatric patients), rhabdomyolysis (rare), bone mineral density decreased

Ocular: Corneal opacities, decreased night vision, cataracts, color vision disorder, conjunctivitis, dry eyes, eyelid inflammation, keratitis, optic neuritis, photophobia, visual disturbances

Otic: Hearing impairment, tinnitus

Renal: Vasculitis, glomerulonephritis,

Respiratory: Bronchospasms, respiratory infection, voice alteration, Wegener's granulomatosis

Miscellaneous: Allergic reactions, anaphylactic reactions, lymphadenopathy, infection, disseminated herpes simplex, diaphoresis

Drug Interactions

Increased Effect/Toxicity: Increased toxicity: Corticosteroids may cause osteoporosis; interactive effect with isotretinoin unknown; use with caution. Phenytoin may cause osteomalacia; interactive effect with isotretinoin unknown; use with caution. Cases of pseudotumor cerebri have been reported in concurrent use with tetracycline; avoid combination.

Decreased Effect: Isotretinoin may increase clearance of carbamazepine resulting in reduced carbamazepine levels. Microdosed progesterone preparations ("mini-pills") may not be an adequate form of contraception.

Mechanism of Action Reduces sebaceous gland size and reduces sebum production; regulates cell proliferation and differentiation

Pharmacodynamics/Kinetics

Distribution: Crosses placenta

Protein binding: 99% to 100%; primarily albumin

Metabolism: Hepatic via CYP2B6, 2C8, 2C9, 2D6, 3A4; forms metabolites; major metabolite: 4-oxo-isotretinoin (active)

Half-life elimination: Terminal: Parent drug: 21 hours; Metabolite: 21-24 hours

Time to peak, serum: 3-5 hours

Excretion: Urine and feces (equal amounts)

Dosage Oral:

Children: Maintenance therapy for neuroblastoma (investigational): 100-250 mg/m^2/day in 2 divided doses

Children and Adults: Severe recalcitrant nodular acne: 0.5-2 mg/kg/day in 2 divided doses (dosages as low as 0.05 mg/kg/day have been reported to be beneficial) for 15-20 weeks or until the total cyst count decreases by 70%, whichever is sooner. A second course of therapy may be initiated after a period of ≥2 months off therapy.

Dosing adjustment in hepatic impairment: Dose reductions empirically are recommended in hepatitis disease

Administration Administer with food. Capsules can be swallowed, or chewed and swallowed. The capsule may be opened with a large needle and the contents placed on applesauce or ice cream for patients unable to swallow the capsule. Whole capsules should be swallowed with a full glass of liquid.

Monitoring Parameters CBC with differential and platelet count, baseline sedimentation rate, glucose, CPK

Pregnancy test (for all female patients of childbearing potential): Two negative tests with a sensitivity of at least 25 mIU/mL prior to beginning therapy (the second performed during the first five days of the menstrual period immediately preceding the start of therapy); monthly tests to rule out pregnancy prior to refilling prescription.

Lipids: Prior to treatment and at weekly or biweekly intervals until response to treatment is established. Test should not be performed <36 hours after consumption of ethanol.

Liver function tests: Prior to treatment and at weekly or biweekly intervals until response to treatment is established.

Patient Information Avoid pregnancy during therapy; effective contraceptive measures must be used since this drug may harm the fetus; there is information from manufacturers about this product that you should receive. Discontinue therapy if visual difficulties, abdominal pain, rectal

(Continued)

Isotretinoin *(Continued)*

bleeding, diarrhea; exacerbation of acne may occur during first weeks of therapy. Avoid use of other vitamin A products. Decreased tolerance to contact lenses may occur. Do not donate blood for at least 1 month following stopping of the drug. Loss of night vision may occur, avoid prolonged exposure to sunlight. Do not double next dose if dose is skipped. Isolated reports of depression, psychosis, aggressive or violent behavior, and rarely suicidal thoughts and actions have been reported during isotretinoin usage.

Dosage Forms CAP: (Accutane®, Amnesteem™, Claravis™): 10 mg, 20 mg, 40 mg; (Sotret®): 10 mg, 20 mg, 30 mg, 40 mg

Isoxsuprine *(eye SOKS syoo preen)*

U.S. Brand Names Vasodilan®

Synonyms Isoxsuprine Hydrochloride

Therapeutic Category Vasodilator

Use Treatment of peripheral vascular diseases, such as arteriosclerosis obliterans and Raynaud's disease

Pregnancy Risk Factor C

Dosage Oral: Adults: 10-20 mg 3-4 times/day; start with lower dose in elderly due to potential hypotension

Dosage Forms TAB: 10 mg, 20 mg

♦ **Isoxsuprine Hydrochloride** *see* Isoxsuprine *on page 698*

Isradipine *(iz RA di peen)*

Related Information
Calcium Channel Blockers Comparison *on page 1371*

U.S. Brand Names DynaCirc®; DynaCirc® CR

Therapeutic Category Antihypertensive Agent; Antimigraine Agent, Prophylaxis; Calcium Channel Blocker

Use Treatment of hypertension

Pregnancy Risk Factor C

Contraindications Hypersensitivity to isradipine or any component of the formulation; hypotension (<90 mm Hg systolic)

Warnings/Precautions Avoid use in hypotension, CHF, cardiac conduction defects, PVCs, idiopathic hypertrophic subaortic stenosis; may cause platelet inhibition; do not abruptly withdraw (chest pain); may cause hepatic dysfunction or increased angina; increased intracranial pressure with cranial tumors; elderly may have greater hypotensive effect

Common Adverse Reactions
>10%: Central nervous system: Headache (dose-related 2% to 22%)

1% to 10%:
Cardiovascular: Edema (dose-related 1% to 9%), palpitations (dose-related 1% to 5%), flushing (dose-related 1% to 5%), tachycardia (1% to 3%), chest pain (2% to 3%)
Central nervous system: Dizziness (2% to 8%), fatigue (dose-related 1% to 9%), flushing (9%)
Dermatologic: Rash (1.5% to 2%)
Gastrointestinal: Nausea (1% to 5%), abdominal discomfort (≤3%), vomiting (≤1%), diarrhea (≤3%)
Renal: Urinary frequency (1% to 3%)
Respiratory: Dyspnea (1% to 3%)

Drug Interactions
Cytochrome P450 Effect: Substrate of CYP3A4 (major); **Inhibits** CYP3A4 (weak)
Increased Effect/Toxicity: Isradipine may increase cardiovascular adverse effects of beta-blockers. Isradipine may minimally increase cyclosporine levels. Azole antifungals (and potentially other inhibitors of CYP3A4) may increase levels of isradipine; avoid this combination. Blood pressure-lowering effects may be additive with sildenafil, tadalafil, and vardenafil (use caution).
Decreased Effect: NSAIDs (diclofenac) may decrease the antihypertensive response of isradipine. Isradipine may cause a decrease in lovastatin effect. Rifampin may reduce blood levels and effects of isradipine due to enzyme induction (other enzyme inducers may share this effect).

Mechanism of Action Inhibits calcium ion from entering the "slow channels" or select voltage-sensitive areas of vascular smooth muscle and myocardium during depolarization, producing a relaxation of coronary vascular smooth muscle and coronary vasodilation; increases myocardial oxygen delivery in patients with vasospastic angina

Pharmacodynamics/Kinetics
Duration: 8-16 hours
Absorption: 90% to 95%
Protein binding: 95%
Metabolism: Hepatic; extensive first-pass effect
Bioavailability: 15% to 24%
Half-life elimination: 8 hours
Time to peak, serum: 1-1.5 hours
Excretion: Urine (as metabolites)

Dosage Oral: Adults: 2.5 mg twice daily; antihypertensive response occurs in 2-3 hours; maximal response in 2-4 weeks; increase dose at 2- to 4-week intervals at 2.5-5 mg increments; usual dose range: 5-20 mg/day. **Note:** Most patients show no improvement with doses >10 mg/day except adverse reaction rate increases

Administration May open capsule; avoid crushing contents

Patient Information Do not discontinue abruptly; report any dizziness, shortness of breath, palpitations, or edema

Dosage Forms CAP (DynaCirc®): 2.5 mg, 5 mg. **TAB, controlled release** (DynaCirc® CR): 5 mg, 10 mg

♦ **Isuprel**® *see* Isoproterenol *on page 693*

Itraconazole (i tra KOE na zole)

Related Information
Antifungal Agents Comparison *on page 1362*

U.S. Brand Names Sporanox®

Therapeutic Category Antifungal Agent, Imidazole Derivative; Antifungal Agent, Oral; Antifungal Agent, Parental; Antifungal Agent, Systemic

Use Treatment of susceptible fungal infections in immunocompromised and immunocompetent patients including blastomycosis and histoplasmosis; indicated for aspergillosis, and onychomycosis of the toenail; treatment of onychomycosis of the fingernail without concomitant toenail infection via a pulse-type dosing regimen; has activity against *Aspergillus, Candida, Coccidioides, Cryptococcus, Sporothrix,* tinea unguium

Oral: Useful in superficial mycoses including dermatophytoses (eg, tinea capitis), pityriasis versicolor, sebopsoriasis, vaginal and chronic mucocutaneous candidiases; systemic mycoses including candidiasis, meningeal and disseminated cryptococcal infections, paracoccidioidomycosis, coccidioidomycoses; miscellaneous mycoses such as sporotrichosis, chromomycosis, leishmaniasis, fungal keratitis, alternariosis, zygomycosis
Oral solution: Treatment of oral and esophageal candidiasis

Intravenous solution: Indicated in the treatment of blastomycosis, histoplasmosis (nonmeningeal), and aspergillosis (in patients intolerant or refractory to amphotericin B therapy); empiric therapy of febrile neutropenic fever

Pregnancy Risk Factor C

Contraindications Hypersensitivity to itraconazole, any component of the formulation, or to other azoles; concurrent administration with astemizole, cisapride, dofetilide, ergot derivatives, lovastatin, midazolam, pimozide, quinidine, simvastatin, or triazolam; treatment of onychomycosis in patients with evidence of left ventricular dysfunction, CHF, or a history of CHF

Warnings/Precautions Discontinue if signs or symptoms of CHF or neuropathy occur during treatment. Rare cases of serious cardiovascular adverse events (including death), ventricular tachycardia, and torsade de pointes have been observed due to increased cisapride concentrations induced by itraconazole. Use with caution in patients with left ventricular dysfunction or a history of CHF. Not recommended for use in patients with active liver disease, elevated liver enzymes, or prior hepatotoxic reactions to other drugs. Itraconazole has been associated with rare cases of serious hepatotoxicity (including fatal cases and cases within the first week of treatment); treatment should be discontinued in patients who develop clinical symptoms of liver dysfunction or abnormal liver function tests during itraconazole therapy except in cases where expected benefit exceeds risk. Large differences in itraconazole pharmacokinetic parameters have been observed in cystic fibrosis patients receiving the solution; if a patient with cystic fibrosis does not respond to therapy, alternate therapies should be considered. Due to differences in bioavailability, oral capsules and oral solution **cannot** be used interchangeably.

Common Adverse Reactions Listed incidences are for higher doses appropriate for systemic fungal infections.

>10%: Gastrointestinal: Nausea (11%)

1% to 10%:
Cardiovascular: Edema (4%), hypertension (3%)
Central nervous system: Headache (4%), fatigue (2% to 3%), malaise (1%), fever (3%), dizziness (2%)
Dermatologic: Rash (9%), pruritus (3%)
Endocrine & metabolic: Decreased libido (1%), hypertriglyceridemia, hypokalemia (2%)
Gastrointestinal: Abdominal pain (2%), anorexia (1%), vomiting (5%), diarrhea (3%)
Hepatic: Abnormal LFTs (3%), hepatitis
Renal: Albuminuria (1%)

Drug Interactions
Cytochrome P450 Effect: Substrate of CYP3A4 (major); **Inhibits** CYP3A4 (strong)

Increased Effect/Toxicity: Due to inhibition of hepatic CYP3A4, itraconazole use is contraindicated with astemizole, cisapride, dofetilide, ergot derivatives, lovastatin, midazolam, pimozide, quinidine, simvastatin, and triazolam due to large substantial increases in the toxicity of these agents. Itraconazole may also increase the levels of alfentanil, benzodiazepines (alprazolam, diazepam, and others), buspirone, busulfan, calcium channel blockers (felodipine, nifedipine, verapamil), carbamazepine, cyclosporine, digoxin, docetaxel, HMG-CoA reductase inhibitors (except fluvastatin, pravastatin), indinavir, oral hypoglycemics (sulfonylureas), methylprednisolone, phenytoin, rifabutin, ritonavir, saquinavir, sirolimus, tacrolimus, trimetrexate, vincristine, vinblastine, warfarin, and zolpidem. Other medications metabolized by CYP3A4 should be used with caution. Amprenavir, clarithromycin, erythromycin, indinavir, nelfinavir, ritonavir, and saquinavir may increase itraconazole concentrations. Sildenafil serum concentrations may be increased by
(Continued)

Itraconazole *(Continued)*

itraconazole; consider dosage reduction; a maximum sildenafil dose of 25 mg in 48 hours is recommended with other strong CYP3A4 inhibitors. Tadalafil serum concentrations may be increased by itraconazole; a maximum tadalafil dose of 10 mg in 72 hours is recommended with strong CYP3A4 inhibitors. Vardenafil serum concentrations may be increased by itraconazole; if itraconazole dose is 200 mg/day, limit vardenafil dose to a maximum of 5 mg/24 hours; if itraconazole dose is 400 mg/day, limit vardenafil dose to a maximum of 2.5 mg/24 hours.

Decreased Effect: Serum levels of itraconazole may be decreased with carbamazepine, didanosine (oral solution only), isoniazid, nevirapine, phenobarbital, phenytoin, rifabutin, and rifampin; do not administer concomitantly with rifampin. Absorption of itraconazole requires gastric acidity; therefore, antacids, H_2 antagonists (cimetidine, famotidine, nizatidine, and ranitidine), proton pump inhibitors (omeprazole, lansoprazole, rabeprazole), and sucralfate may significantly reduce bioavailability resulting in treatment failures and should not be administered concomitantly. Antacids may decrease serum concentration of itraconazole; administer antacids 1 hour before or 2 hours after itraconazole capsules. Oral contraceptive efficacy may be reduced (limited data).

Mechanism of Action Interferes with cytochrome P450 activity, decreasing ergosterol synthesis (principal sterol in fungal cell membrane) and inhibiting cell membrane formation

Pharmacodynamics/Kinetics

Absorption: Requires gastric acidity; capsule better absorbed with food, solution better absorbed on empty stomach; hypochlorhydria has been reported in HIV-infected patients; therefore, oral absorption in these patients may be decreased

Distribution: V_d (average): 796 ± 185 L or 10 L/kg; highly lipophilic and tissue concentrations are higher than plasma concentrations. The highest concentrations: adipose, omentum, endometrium, cervical and vaginal mucus, and skin/nails. Aqueous fluids (eg, CSF and urine) contain negligible amounts.

Protein binding, plasma: 99.9%; metabolite hydroxy-itraconazole: 99.5%

Metabolism: Extensively hepatic via CYP3A4 into >30 metabolites including hydroxy-itraconazole (major metabolite); appears to have *in vitro* antifungal activity. Main metabolic pathway is oxidation; may undergo saturation metabolism with multiple dosing.

Bioavailability: Variable, ~ 55% (oral solution) in 1 small study; **Note:** Oral solution has a higher degree of bioavailability (149% ± 68%) relative to oral capsules; should not be interchanged

Half-life elimination: Oral: After single 200 mg dose: 21 ± 5 hours; 64 hours at steady-state; I.V.: steady-state: 35 hours; steady-state concentrations are achieved in 13 days with multiple administration of itraconazole 100-400 mg/day.

Excretion: Feces (~3% to 18%); urine (~0.03% as parent drug, 40% as metabolites)

Dosage Note: Capsule: Absorption is best if taken with food, therefore, it is best to administer itraconazole after meals; Solution: Should be taken on an empty stomach.

Children: Efficacy and safety have not been established; a small number of patients 3-16 years of age have been treated with 100 mg/day for systemic fungal infections with no serious adverse effects reported. A dose of 5 mg/kg once daily was used in a pharmacokinetic study using the oral solution in patients 6 months-12 years; duration of study was 2 weeks.

Adults:

Oral:

Blastomycosis/histoplasmosis: 200 mg once daily, if no obvious improvement or there is evidence of progressive fungal disease, increase the dose in 100 mg increments to a maximum of 400 mg/day; doses >200 mg/day are given in 2 divided doses; length of therapy varies from 1 day to >6 months depending on the condition and mycological response

Aspergillosis: 200-400 mg/day

Onychomycosis: 200 mg once daily for 12 consecutive weeks

Life-threatening infections: Loading dose: 200 mg 3 times/day (600 mg/day) should be given for the first 3 days of therapy

Oropharyngeal candidiasis: Oral solution: 200 mg once daily for 1-2 weeks; in patients unresponsive or refractory to fluconazole: 100 mg twice daily (clinical response expected in 1-2 weeks)

Esophageal candidiasis: Oral solution: 100-200 mg once daily for a minimum of 3 weeks; continue dosing for 2 weeks after resolution of symptoms

I.V.: 200 mg twice daily for 4 doses, followed by 200 mg daily

Dosing adjustment in renal impairment: Not necessary; itraconazole injection is not recommended in patients with Cl_{cr} <30 mL/minute

Hemodialysis: Not dialyzable

Dosing adjustment in hepatic impairment: May be necessary, but specific guidelines are not available. Risk-to-benefit evaluation should be undertaken in patients who develop liver function abnormalities during treatment.

Administration

Oral: Doses >200 mg/day are given in 2 divided doses; do not administer with antacids. Capsule absorption is best if taken with food, therefore, it is best to administer itraconazole after meals; solution should be taken on an empty stomach. When treating oropharyngeal and esophageal candidiasis, solution should be swished vigorously in mouth, then swallowed.

I.V.: Using a flow control device, infuse 60 mL of the dilute solution (3.33 mg/mL = 200 mg itraconazole, pH ~4.8) intravenously over 60 minutes, using an extension line and the infusion set provided. After administration, flush the infusion set with 15-20 mL of 0.9%

sodium chloride over 30 seconds to 15 minutes, via the two-way stopcock. Do not use bacteriostatic sodium chloride injection, USP. The compatibility of Sporanox® injection with flush solutions other than 0.9% sodium chloride (normal saline) is not known. Discard the entire infusion line.

Monitoring Parameters Liver function in patients with pre-existing hepatic dysfunction, and in all patients being treated for longer than 1 month

Patient Information Take capsule with food; take solution on an empty stomach; stop therapy and report any signs and symptoms that may suggest liver dysfunction immediately so that the appropriate laboratory testing can be done; signs and symptoms may include unusual fatigue, anorexia, nausea and/or vomiting, jaundice, dark urine, or pale stool

Dosage Forms CAP: 100 mg. **INJ, solution:** 10 mg/mL (25 mL). **SOLN, oral:** 100 mg/10 mL (150 mL)

♦ **Iveegam EN** see Immune Globulin (Intravenous) on page 659

Ivermectin (eye ver MEK tin)

U.S. Brand Names Stromectol®

Therapeutic Category Anthelmintic

Use Treatment of the following infections: Strongyloidiasis of the intestinal tract due to the nematode parasite *Strongyloides stercoralis*. Onchocerciasis due to the nematode parasite *Onchocerca volvulus*. Ivermectin is only active against the immature form of *Onchocerca volvulus*, and the intestinal forms of *Strongyloides stercoralis*.

Unlabeled/Investigational Use Has been used for other parasitic infections including *Ascaris lumbricoides*, Bancroftian filariasis, *Brugia malayi*, scabies, *Enterobius vermicularis*, *Mansonella ozzardi*, *Trichuris trichiura*.

Pregnancy Risk Factor C

Contraindications Hypersensitivity to ivermectin or any component of the formulation

Warnings/Precautions Data have shown that antihelmintic drugs like ivermectin may cause cutaneous and/or systemic reactions (Mazzoti reaction) of varying severity including ophthalmological reactions in patients with onchocerciasis. These reactions are probably due to allergic and inflammatory responses to the death of microfilariae. Patients with hyper-reactive onchodermatitis may be more likely than others to experience severe adverse reactions, especially edema and aggravation of the onchodermatitis. Repeated treatment may be required in immunocompromised patients (eg, HIV); control of extraintestinal strongyloidiasis may necessitate suppressive (once monthly) therapy. Pretreatment assessment for *Loa loa* infection is recommended in any patient with significant exposure to endemic areas (West and Central Africa); serious and/or fatal encephalopathy has been reported during treatment in patients with loiasis. Safety and efficacy in children <15 kg have not been established.

Common Adverse Reactions Frequency not defined.

Cardiovascular: Hypotension, mild ECG changes, peripheral and facial edema, transient tachycardia

Central nervous system: Dizziness, headache, hyperthermia, insomnia, somnolence, vertigo

Dermatologic: Pruritus, rash, urticaria

Gastrointestinal: Abdominal pain, diarrhea, nausea, vomiting

Hematologic: Eosinophilia, leukopenia

Hepatic: ALT/AST increased

Neuromuscular & skeletal: Limbitis, myalgia, tremor, weakness

Ocular: Blurred vision, mild conjunctivitis, punctate opacity

Mazzotti reaction (with onchocerciasis): Edema, fever, lymphadenopathy, ocular damage, pruritus, rash

Drug Interactions

Cytochrome P450 Effect: Substrate of CYP3A4 (minor)

Mechanism of Action Ivermectin is a semisynthetic antihelminthic agent; it binds selectively and with strong affinity to glutamate-gated chloride ion channels which occur in invertebrate nerve and muscle cells. This leads to increased permeability of cell membranes to chloride ions then hyperpolarization of the nerve or muscle cell, and death of the parasite.

Pharmacodynamics/Kinetics

Onset of action: Peak effect: 3-6 months

Absorption: Well absorbed

Distribution: Does not cross blood-brain barrier

Half-life elimination: 16-35 hours

Metabolism: Hepatic (>97%)

Excretion: Urine (<1%); remainder in feces

Dosage Oral: Children ≥15 kg and Adults:

Strongyloidiasis: 200 mcg/kg as a single dose; follow-up stool examinations

Onchocerciasis: 150 mcg/kg as a single dose; retreatment may be required every 3-12 months until the adult worms die

Administration Medication should be taken with water.

Monitoring Parameters Skin and eye microfilarial counts, periodic ophthalmologic exams

Patient Information If infected with strongyloidiasis, repeated stool examinations are required to document clearance of the organisms; repeated follow-up and retreatment is usually required in the treatment of onchocerciasis

Dosage Forms TAB: 3 mg

♦ **IVIG** see Immune Globulin (Intravenous) on page 659

♦ **IvyBlock® [OTC]** see Bentoquatam on page 153

♦ **Jantoven™** see Warfarin on page 1315

Japanese Encephalitis Virus Vaccine (Inactivated)
(jap a NEESE en sef a LYE tis VYE rus vak SEEN, in ak ti VAY ted)

U.S. Brand Names JE-VAX®

Therapeutic Category Vaccine; Vaccine, Live Virus

Use Active immunization against Japanese encephalitis for persons 1 year of age and older who plan to spend 1 month or more in endemic areas in Asia, especially persons traveling during the transmission season or visiting rural areas; consider vaccination for shorter trips to epidemic areas or extensive outdoor activities in rural endemic areas; elderly (>55 years of age) individuals should be considered for vaccination, since they have increased risk of developing symptomatic illness after infection; those planning travel to or residence in endemic areas should consult the Travel Advisory Service (Central Campus) for specific advice

Pregnancy Risk Factor C

Contraindications Serious adverse reaction (generalized urticaria or angioedema) to a prior dose of this vaccine; proven or suspected hypersensitivity to proteins or rodent or neural origin; hypersensitivity to thimerosal (used as a preservative). *CDC recommends that the following should not generally receive the vaccine, unless benefit to the individual clearly outweighs the risk:*

- those acutely ill or with active infections
- persons with heart, kidney, or liver disorders
- persons with generalized malignancies such as leukemia or lymphoma
- persons with a history of multiple allergies or hypersensitivity to components of the vaccine
- pregnant women, unless there is a very high risk of Japanese encephalitis during the woman's stay in Asia

Warnings/Precautions Severe adverse reactions manifesting as generalized urticaria or angioedema may occur within minutes following vaccination, or up to 17 days later; most reactions occur within 10 days, with the majority within 48 hours; observe vaccinees for 30 minutes after vaccination; warn them of the possibility of delayed generalized urticaria and to remain where medical care is readily available for 10 days following any dose of the vaccine; because of the potential for severe adverse reactions, Japanese encephalitis vaccine is **not** recommended for all persons traveling to or residing in Asia; safety and efficacy in infants <1 year of age have not been established; therefore, immunization of infants should be deferred whenever possible; it is not known whether the vaccine is excreted in breast milk

Common Adverse Reactions Report allergic or unusual adverse reactions to the Vaccine Adverse Event Reporting System (VAERS) 1-800-822-7967.
Frequency not defined, common:
Cardiovascular: Hypotension
Central nervous system: Fever, headache, malaise, chills, dizziness
Dermatologic: Rash, urticaria, itching with or without accompanying rash
Gastrointestinal: Nausea, vomiting, abdominal pain
Local: Tenderness, redness, and swelling at injection site
Neuromuscular & skeletal: Myalgia
Frequency not defined, rare:
Cardiovascular: Angioedema
Central nervous system: Seizure, encephalitis, encephalopathy
Dermatologic: Erythema multiforme, erythema nodosum
Neuromuscular & skeletal: Peripheral neuropathy, joint swelling
Respiratory: Dyspnea
Miscellaneous: Anaphylactic reaction

Dosage U.S. recommended primary immunization schedule:
Children 1-3 years: S.C.: Three 0.5 mL doses given on days 0, 7, and 30; abbreviated schedules should be used only when necessary due to time constraints
Children >3 years and Adults: S.C.: Three 1 mL doses given on days 0, 7, and 30. Give third dose on day 14 when time does not permit waiting; 2 doses a week apart produce immunity in about 80% of recipients; the longest regimen yields highest titers after 6 months.
Booster dose: Give after 2 years, or according to current recommendation
Note: Travel should not commence for at least 10 days after the last dose of vaccine, to allow adequate antibody formation and recognition of any delayed adverse reaction
Advise concurrent use of other means to reduce the risk of mosquito exposure when possible, including bed nets, insect repellents, protective clothing, avoidance of travel in endemic areas, and avoidance of outdoor activity during twilight and evening periods

Administration The single-dose vial should only be reconstituted with the full 1.3 mL of diluent supplied; administer 1 mL of the resulting liquid as one standard adult dose; discard the unused portion

Patient Information Adverse reactions may occur shortly after vaccination or up to 17 days (usually within 10 days) after vaccination

Dosage Forms INJ, powder for reconstitution: 1 mL, 10 mL

Kanamycin (kan a MYE sin)

Related Information
Antimicrobial Drugs of Choice *on page 1440*
Tuberculosis Prophylaxis *on page 1438*
Tuberculosis Treatment Guidelines *on page 1466*

U.S. Brand Names Kantrex®

Synonyms Kanamycin Sulfate

Therapeutic Category Antibiotic, Aminoglycoside

Use Treatment of serious infections caused by susceptible strains of *E. coli, Proteus species, Enterobacter aerogenes, Klebsiella pneumoniae, Serratia marcescens,* and *Acinetobacter* species; second-line treatment of *Mycobacterium tuberculosis*

Pregnancy Risk Factor D

Dosage Note: Dosing should be based on ideal body weight
Children: Infections: I.M., I.V.: 15 mg/kg/day in divided doses every 8-12 hours
Adults:
Infections: I.M., I.V.: 5-7.5 mg/kg/dose in divided doses every 8-12 hours (<15 mg/kg/day)
Intraperitoneal: After contamination in surgery: 500 mg
Irrigating solution: 0.25%; maximum 1.5 g/day (via all administration routes)
Aerosol: 250 mg 2-4 times/day

Dosing adjustment/interval in renal impairment:
Cl_{cr} 50-80 mL/minute: Administer 60% to 90% of dose or administer every 8-12 hours
Cl_{cr} 10-50 mL/minute: Administer 30% to 70% of dose or administer every 12 hours
Cl_{cr} <10 mL/minute: Administer 20% to 30% of dose or administer every 24-48 hours

Dosage Forms INJ, solution: 1 g/3 mL (3 mL)

♦ **Kanamycin Sulfate** *see Kanamycin on page 703*
♦ **Kantrex®** *see Kanamycin on page 703*
♦ **Kaon-Cl-10®** *see Potassium Chloride on page 1020*
♦ **Kaon-Cl® 20** *see Potassium Chloride on page 1020*
♦ **Kaopectate® [OTC]** *see Bismuth on page 168*
♦ **Kaopectate® Extra Strength [OTC]** *see Bismuth on page 168*
♦ **Kariva™** *see Ethinyl Estradiol and Desogestrel on page 477*
♦ **Kay Ciel®** *see Potassium Chloride on page 1020*
♦ **Kayexalate®** *see Sodium Polystyrene Sulfonate on page 1151*
♦ **K+ Care®** *see Potassium Chloride on page 1020*
♦ **KCl** *see Potassium Chloride on page 1020*
♦ **K-Dur® 10** *see Potassium Chloride on page 1020*
♦ **K-Dur® 20** *see Potassium Chloride on page 1020*
♦ **Keflex®** *see Cephalexin on page 248*
♦ **Kefurox® [DSC]** *see Cefuroxime on page 245*
♦ **Kefzol® [DSC]** *see Cefazolin on page 231*
♦ **Kemadrin®** *see Procyclidine on page 1043*
♦ **Kenalog®** *see Triamcinolone on page 1261*
♦ **Kenalog-10®** *see Triamcinolone on page 1261*
♦ **Kenalog-40®** *see Triamcinolone on page 1261*
♦ **Kenalog® in Orabase®** *see Triamcinolone on page 1261*
♦ **Keoxifene Hydrochloride** *see Raloxifene on page 1079*
♦ **Keppra®** *see Levetiracetam on page 727*
♦ **Kerlone®** *see Betaxolol on page 161*
♦ **Kerr Insta-Char® [OTC]** *see Charcoal on page 253*
♦ **Ketalar®** *see Ketamine on page 703*

Ketamine (KEET a meen)

U.S. Brand Names Ketalar®

Synonyms Ketamine Hydrochloride

Therapeutic Category General Anesthetic

Use Induction and maintenance of general anesthesia, especially when cardiovascular depression must be avoided (ie, hypotension, hypovolemia, cardiomyopathy, constrictive pericarditis); sedation; analgesia

Restrictions C-III

Pregnancy Risk Factor D

Contraindications Hypersensitivity to ketamine or any component of the formulation; elevated intracranial pressure; hypertension, aneurysms, thyrotoxicosis, congestive heart failure, angina, psychotic disorders; pregnancy

Warnings/Precautions Postanesthetic emergence reactions which can manifest as vivid dreams, hallucinations and/or frank delirium occur in 12% of patients; these reactions are less common in patients >65 and when given I.M.; emergence reactions, confusion, or irrational behavior may occur up to 24 hours postoperatively and may be reduced by pretreatment with a benzodiazepine. May cause dependence (withdrawal symptoms on discontinuation) and tolerance with prolonged use.
(Continued)

Ketamine *(Continued)*

Common Adverse Reactions
>10%:
Cardiovascular: Hypertension, increased cardiac output, paradoxical direct myocardial depression, tachycardia
Central nervous system: Increased intracranial pressure, visual hallucinations, vivid dreams
Neuromuscular & skeletal: Tonic-clonic movements, tremors
Miscellaneous: Emergence reactions, vocalization
1% to 10%:
Cardiovascular: Bradycardia, hypotension
Dermatologic: Pain at injection site, skin rash
Gastrointestinal: Anorexia, nausea, vomiting
Ocular: Diplopia, nystagmus
Respiratory: Respiratory depression

Drug Interactions
Cytochrome P450 Effect: Substrate (major) of CYP2B6, 2C8/9, 3A4
Increased Effect/Toxicity: CYP2B6 inhibitors may increase the levels/effects of ketamine; example inhibitors include desipramine, paroxetine, and sertraline. CYP2C8/9 inhibitors may increase the levels/effects of ketamine; example inhibitors include delavirdine, fluconazole, gemfibrozil, ketoconazole, nicardipine, NSAIDs, pioglitazone, and sulfonamides. Barbiturates, narcotics, hydroxyzine increase prolonged recovery; nondepolarizing neuromuscular blockers may increase effects. Muscle relaxants, thyroid hormones may increase blood pressure and heart rate. Halothane may decrease BP.

Mechanism of Action Produces a cataleptic-like state in which the patient is dissociated from the surrounding environment by direct action on the cortex and limbic system. Releases endogenous catecholamines (epinephrine, norepinephrine) which maintain blood pressure and heart rate. Reduces polysynaptic spinal reflexes.

Pharmacodynamics/Kinetics
Onset of action:
I.V.: General anesthesia: 1-2 minutes; Sedation: 1-2 minutes
I.M.: General anesthesia: 3-8 minutes
Duration: I.V.: 5-15 minutes; I.M.: 12-25 minutes
Metabolism: Hepatic via hydroxylation and N-demethylation; the metabolite norketamine is 25% as potent as parent compound
Half-life elimination: 11-17 minutes; Elimination: 2.5-3.1 hours
Excretion: Clearance: 18 mL/kg/minute

Dosage Used in combination with anticholinergic agents to decrease hypersalivation
Children:
Oral: 6-10 mg/kg for 1 dose (mixed in 0.2-0.3 mL/kg of cola or other beverage) given 30 minutes before the procedure
I.M.: 3-7 mg/kg
I.V.: Range: 0.5-2 mg/kg, use smaller doses (0.5-1 mg/kg) for sedation for minor procedures; usual induction dosage: 1-2 mg/kg
Continuous I.V. infusion: Sedation: 5-20 mcg/kg/minute
Adults:
I.M.: 3-8 mg/kg
I.V.: Range: 1-4.5 mg/kg; usual induction dosage: 1-2 mg/kg
Children and Adults: Maintenance: Supplemental doses of $^1/_3$ to $^1/_2$ of initial dose

Administration
Oral: Use 100 mg/mL I.V. solution and mix the appropriate dose in 0.2-0.3 mL/kg of cola or other beverage
Parenteral: I.V.: Do not exceed 0.5 mg/kg/minute or administer faster than 60 seconds; do not exceed final concentration of 2 mg/mL; dilute for I.V. administration with normal saline, sterile water, or D_5W

Monitoring Parameters Cardiovascular effects, heart rate, blood pressure, respiratory rate, transcutaneous O_2 saturation

Dosage Forms INJ, solution: 10 mg/mL (20 mL, 25 mL, 50 mL); 50 mg/mL (10 mL); 100 mg/mL (5 mL)

♦ **Ketamine Hydrochloride** *see* Ketamine *on page 703*

Ketoconazole *(kee toe KOE na zole)*
Related Information
Antifungal Agents Comparison *on page 1362*
U.S. Brand Names Nizoral®; Nizoral® A-D [OTC]
Therapeutic Category Antifungal Agent, Imidazole Derivative; Antifungal Agent, Oral; Antifungal Agent, Systemic; Antifungal Agent, Topical
Use Treatment of susceptible fungal infections, including candidiasis, oral thrush, blastomycosis, histoplasmosis, paracoccidioidomycosis, coccidioidomycosis, chromomycosis, candiduria, chronic mucocutaneous candidiasis, as well as certain recalcitrant cutaneous dermatophytoses; used topically for treatment of tinea corporis, tinea cruris, tinea versicolor, and cutaneous candidiasis, seborrheic dermatitis
Pregnancy Risk Factor C
Contraindications Hypersensitivity to ketoconazole or any component of the formulation; CNS fungal infections (due to poor CNS penetration); coadministration with ergot derivatives, astemizole, or cisapride is contraindicated due to risk of potentially fatal cardiac arrhythmias

Warnings/Precautions Use with caution in patients with impaired hepatic function; has been associated with hepatotoxicity, including some fatalities; perform periodic liver function tests; high doses of ketoconazole may depress adrenocortical function.

Common Adverse Reactions

Oral: 1% to 10%:

Dermatologic: Pruritus (2%)

Gastrointestinal: Nausea/vomiting (3% to 10%), abdominal pain (1%)

Cream: Severe irritation, pruritus, stinging (~5%)

Shampoo: Increases in normal hair loss, irritation (<1%), abnormal hair texture, scalp pustules, mild dryness of skin, itching, oiliness/dryness of hair

Drug Interactions

Cytochrome P450 Effect: Substrate of CYP3A4 (major); **Inhibits** CYP1A2 (strong), 2A6 (moderate), 2B6 (weak), 2C8/9 (strong), 2C19 (moderate), 2D6 (moderate), 3A4 (strong)

Increased Effect/Toxicity: Due to inhibition of hepatic CYP3A4, ketoconazole use is contraindicated with astemizole, cisapride, lovastatin, midazolam, simvastatin, and triazolam due to large substantial increases in the toxicity of these agents. Ketoconazole may also increase the levels of benzodiazepines (alprazolam. diazepam, and others), buspirone, busulfan, calcium channel blockers (felodipine, nifedipine, verapamil), cyclosporine, digoxin, docetaxel, HMG-CoA reductase inhibitors (except fluvastatin, pravastatin), oral hypoglycemics (sulfonylureas), methylprednisolone, phenytoin, quinolone, sirolimus, tacrolimus, trimetrexate, vincristine, vinblastine, warfarin, and zolpidem. Other medications metabolized by CYP3A4 should be used with caution. Amprenavir (and possibly other protease inhibitors), clarithromycin, and erythromycin may increase ketoconazole concentrations. Sildenafil serum concentrations may be increased by ketoconazole; consider dosage reduction; a maximum sildenafil dose of 25 mg in 48 hours is recommended with other strong CYP3A4 inhibitors. Tadalafil serum concentrations may be increased by ketoconazole; a maximum tadalafil dose of 10 mg in 72 hours is recommended with strong CYP3A4 inhibitors. Vardenafil serum concentrations may be increased by ketoconazole; if ketoconazole dose is 200 mg/day, limit vardenafil to a maximum of 5 mg/24 hours; if ketoconazole dose is 400 mg/day, limit vardenafil dose to a maximum of 2.5 mg/24 hours.

Decreased Effect: Oral: Decreased serum levels with carbamazepine, didanosine (oral solution only), isoniazid, phenobarbital, phenytoin, rifabutin, and rifampin. **Should not be administered concomitantly with rifampin.** Absorption requires gastric acidity; therefore, antacids, H₂ antagonists (cimetidine, famotidine, nizatidine, and ranitidine), proton pump inhibitors (omeprazole, lansoprazole, rabeprazole), and sucralfate may significantly reduce bioavailability resulting in treatment failures and should not be administered concomitantly. Oral contraceptive efficacy may be reduced (limited data).

Mechanism of Action Alters the permeability of the cell wall by blocking fungal cytochrome P450; inhibits biosynthesis of triglycerides and phospholipids by fungi; inhibits several fungal enzymes that results in a build-up of toxic concentrations of hydrogen peroxide

Pharmacodynamics/Kinetics

Absorption: Oral: Rapid (~75%); Shampoo: None

Distribution: Well into inflamed joint fluid, saliva, bile, urine, breast milk, sebum, cerumen, feces, tendons, skin and soft tissues, and testes; crosses blood-brain barrier poorly; only negligible amounts reach CSF

Protein binding: 93% to 96%

Metabolism: Partially hepatic via CYP3A4 to inactive compounds

Bioavailability: Decreases as gastric pH increases

Half-life elimination: Biphasic: Initial: 2 hours; Terminal: 8 hours

Time to peak, serum: 1-2 hours

Excretion: Feces (57%); urine (13%)

Dosage

Oral:

Children ≥2 years: 3.3-6.6 mg/kg/day as a single dose for 1-2 weeks for candidiasis, for at least 4 weeks in recalcitrant dermatophyte infections, and for up to 6 months for other systemic mycoses

Adults: 200-400 mg/day as a single daily dose for durations as stated above

Shampoo: Apply twice weekly for 4 weeks with at least 3 days between each shampoo

Topical: Rub gently into the affected area once daily to twice daily

Dosing adjustment in hepatic impairment: Dose reductions should be considered in patients with severe liver disease

Hemodialysis: Not dialyzable (0% to 5%)

Monitoring Parameters Liver function tests

Patient Information Cream is for topical application to the skin only; avoid contact with the eye; avoid taking antacids at the same time as ketoconazole; may take with food; may cause drowsiness, impair judgment or coordination. Report unusual fatigue, anorexia, vomiting, dark urine, or pale stools.

Dosage Forms CRM, topical: 2% (15 g, 30 g, 60 g). **SHAMP, topical** (Nizoral® A-D): 1% (6 mL, 120 mL, 210 mL). **TAB** (Nizoral®): 200 mg

Ketoprofen (kee toe PROE fen)

Related Information

Nonsteroidal Anti-Inflammatory Agents Comparison *on page 1401*

U.S. Brand Names Orudis® KT [OTC]; Oruvail®

Therapeutic Category Analgesic, Nonsteroidal Anti-inflammatory Drug; Anti-inflammatory Agent; Nonsteroidal Anti-inflammatory Drug (NSAID), Oral

(Continued)

Ketoprofen (Continued)

Use Acute and long-term treatment of rheumatoid arthritis and osteoarthritis; primary dysmenorrhea; mild to moderate pain

Pregnancy Risk Factor B/D (3rd trimester)

Contraindications Hypersensitivity to ketoprofen, any component of the formulation, or other NSAIDs/aspirin; pregnancy (3rd trimester)

Warnings/Precautions Use with caution in patients with CHF, hypertension, dehydration, decreased renal or hepatic function, history of GI disease (bleeding or ulcers), or those receiving anticoagulants. Elderly are at a high risk for adverse effects from NSAIDs. As many as 60% of elderly can develop peptic ulceration and/or hemorrhage asymptomatically.

Use lowest effective dose for shortest period possible. Use of NSAIDs can compromise existing renal function especially when Cl_{cr} is <30 mL/minute. CNS adverse effects such as confusion, agitation, and hallucination are generally seen in overdose or high-dose situations; however, elderly may demonstrate these adverse effects at lower doses than younger adults. Withhold for at least 4-6 half-lives prior to surgical or dental procedures. Safety and efficacy in pediatric patients have not been established.

Common Adverse Reactions
>10%: Gastrointestinal: Dyspepsia (11%)

1% to 10%:
  Central nervous system: Headache (3% to 9%), nervousness, dizziness, somnolence, insomnia, malaise, depression
  Dermatologic: Rash, itching
  Endocrine & metabolic: Fluid retention
  Gastrointestinal: Vomiting (>1%), diarrhea (3% to 9%), nausea (3% to 9%), constipation (3% to 9%), abdominal distress/cramping/pain (3% to 9%), flatulence (3% to 9%), anorexia (>1%), stomatitis (>1%)
  Genitourinary: Urinary tract infection (>1%)
  Ocular: Visual disturbances
  Otic: Tinnitus
  Renal: Renal function impairment

Drug Interactions
  Cytochrome P450 Effect: Inhibits CYP2C8/9 (weak)
  Increased Effect/Toxicity: Increased effect/toxicity with antiplatelet agents, corticosteroids, cyclosporine, probenecid, lithium, anticoagulants, and methotrexate.
  Decreased Effect: Decreased effect of diuretics (loop and thiazides). May decrease effects of antihypertensives.

Mechanism of Action Inhibits prostaglandin synthesis by decreasing the activity of the enzyme, cyclooxygenase, which results in decreased formation of prostaglandin precursors

Pharmacodynamics/Kinetics
  Absorption: Almost complete
  Protein binding: >99%, primarily albumin
  Metabolism: Hepatic
  Half-life elimination: Capsule: 2.5 hours; Capsule, extended release: 5.4 hours
  Time to peak, serum: Capsule: 0.5-2 hours; Capsule, extended release: 6-7 hours
  Excretion: Urine (~80%, primarily as glucuronide conjugates)

Dosage Oral:
  Children ≥16 years and Adults:
    Rheumatoid arthritis or osteoarthritis:
      Capsule: 50-75 mg 3-4 times/day up to a maximum of 300 mg/day
      Capsule, extended release: 200 mg once daily
    Mild to moderate pain: Capsule: 25-50 mg every 6-8 hours up to a maximum of 300 mg/day
      OTC labeling: 12.5 mg every 4-6 hours, up to a maximum of 6 tablets/24 hours
  Elderly: Initial dose should be decreased in patients >75 years; use caution when dosage changes are made
  Dosage adjustment in renal impairment:
    Mild impairment: Maximum dose: 150 mg/day
    Severe impairment: Maximum dose: 100 mg/day
  Dosage adjustment in hepatic impairment and serum albumin <3.5 g/dL: Maximum dose: 100 mg/day

Administration May take with food to reduce GI upset. Do not crush or break extended release capsules.

Patient Information Take with food; may cause dizziness or drowsiness

Dosage Forms CAP: 50 mg, 75 mg. **CAP, extended release** (Oruvail®): 100 mg, 150 mg, 200 mg. **TAB** (Orudis® KT): 12.5 mg

Ketorolac (KEE toe role ak)

Related Information
  Nonsteroidal Anti-Inflammatory Agents Comparison on page 1401

U.S. Brand Names Acular®; Acular LS™; Acular® PF; Toradol®

Synonyms Ketorolac Tromethamine

Therapeutic Category Analgesic, Nonsteroidal Anti-inflammatory Drug; Anti-inflammatory Agent; Anti-inflammatory Agent, Ophthalmic; Nonsteroidal Anti-inflammatory Drug (NSAID), Oral; Nonsteroidal Anti-inflammatory Drug (NSAID), Parenteral

KETOROLAC

Use
Oral, injection: Short-term (≤5 days) management of moderately-severe acute pain requiring analgesia at the opioid level

Ophthalmic: Temporary relief of ocular itching due to seasonal allergic conjunctivitis; postoperative inflammation following cataract extraction; reduction of ocular pain and photophobia following incisional refractive surgery, reduction of ocular pain, burning and stinging following corneal refractive surgery

Pregnancy Risk Factor C/D (3rd trimester); ophthalmic: C

Contraindications Hypersensitivity to ketorolac, aspirin, other NSAIDs, or any component of the formulation; patients who have developed nasal polyps, angioedema, or bronchospastic reactions to other NSAIDs; active or history of peptic ulcer disease; recent or history of GI bleeding or perforation; patients with advanced renal disease or risk of renal failure; labor and delivery; nursing mothers; prophylaxis before major surgery; suspected or confirmed cerebrovascular bleeding; hemorrhagic diathesis; concurrent ASA or other NSAIDs; epidural or intrathecal administration; concomitant probenecid; pregnancy (3rd trimester)

Warnings/Precautions
Systemic: Treatment should be started with I.V./I.M. administration then changed to oral only as a continuation of treatment. Total therapy is not to exceed 5 days. Should not be used for minor or chronic pain. Hypersensitivity reactions have occurred flowing the first dose of ketorolac injection, including patients without prior exposure to ketorolac, aspirin, or other NSAIDs. Use extra caution and reduce dosages in the elderly because it is cleared renally somewhat slower, and the elderly are also more sensitive to the renal effects of NSAIDs and have a greater risk of GI perforation and bleeding; use with caution in patients with CHF, hypertension, dehydration, decreased renal or hepatic function, or those receiving anticoagulants. May prolong bleeding time; do not use when hemostasis is critical. Patients should be euvolemic prior to treatment. Low doses of narcotics may be needed for breakthrough pain. Withhold for at least 4-6 half-lives prior to surgical or dental procedures.

Ophthalmic: May increase bleeding time associated with ocular surgery. Use with caution in patients with known bleeding tendencies or those receiving anticoagulants. Healing time may be slowed or delayed. Corneal thinning, erosion, or ulceration have been reported with topical NSAIDs; discontinue if corneal epithelial breakdown occurs. Use caution with complicated ocular surgery, corneal denervation, corneal epithelial defects, diabetes, rheumatoid arthritis, ocular surface disease, or ocular surgeries repeated within short periods of time; risk of corneal epithelial breakdown may be increased. Use for >24 hours prior to or for >14 days following surgery also increases risk of corneal adverse effects. Do not administer while wearing soft contact lenses. Safety and efficacy in pediatric patients <3 years of age have not been established.

Common Adverse Reactions
Systemic:
>10%:
Central nervous system: Headache (17%)
Gastrointestinal: Gastrointestinal pain (13%), dyspepsia (12%), nausea (12%)
>1% to 10%:
Cardiovascular: Edema (4%), hypertension
Central nervous system: Dizziness (7%), drowsiness (6%)
Dermatologic: Pruritus, purpura, rash
Gastrointestinal: Diarrhea (7%), constipation, flatulence, gastrointestinal fullness, vomiting, stomatitis
Local: Injection site pain (2%)
Miscellaneous: Diaphoresis

Ophthalmic solution:
>10%: Ocular: Transient burning/stinging (Acular®: 40%; Acular® PF: 20%)
>1% to 10%:
Central nervous system: Headache
Ocular: Conjunctival hyperemia, corneal infiltrates, iritis, ocular edema, ocular inflammation, ocular irritation, ocular pain, superficial keratitis, superficial ocular infection
Miscellaneous: Allergic reactions

Drug Interactions
Increased Effect/Toxicity: Increased toxicity: Lithium, methotrexate, probenecid increased drug level; increased effect/toxicity with salicylates, probenecid, anticoagulants, nondepolarizing muscle relaxants, alprazolam, fluoxetine, thiothixene

Decreased Effect: Decreased effect: Decreased antihypertensive effect seen with ACE inhibitors and angiotensin II antagonists; decreased antiepileptic effect seen with carbamazepine, phenytoin

Mechanism of Action Inhibits prostaglandin synthesis by decreasing the activity of the enzyme, cyclooxygenase, which results in decreased formation of prostaglandin precursors

Pharmacodynamics/Kinetics
Onset of action: Analgesic: I.M.: ~10 minutes
Peak effect: Analgesic: 2-3 hours
Duration: Analgesic: 6-8 hours
Absorption: Oral: Well absorbed
Distribution: Poor penetration into CSF; crosses placenta; enters breast milk
Protein binding: 99%
Metabolism: Hepatic
Half-life elimination: 2-8 hours; prolonged 30% to 50% in elderly
Time to peak, serum: I.M.: 30-60 minutes
Excretion: Urine (61% as unchanged drug)
(Continued)

Ketorolac *(Continued)*

Dosage

Children 2-16 years: **Do not exceed adult doses**
Single-dose treatment:
I.M.: 1 mg/kg (maximum: 30 mg)
I.V.: 0.5 mg/kg (maximum: 15 mg)
Oral (unlabeled): 1 mg/kg as a single dose reported in one study
Multiple-dose treatment (unlabeled): Limited pediatric studies. The maximum combined duration of treatment (for parenteral and oral) is 5 days; do not increase dose or frequency; supplement with low-dose opioids if needed for breakthrough pain. For patients <50 kg and/or ≥65 years, see Elderly dosing.
I.V.: Initial dose: 0.5 mg/kg, followed by 0.25-1 mg/kg every 6 hours for up to 48 hours (maximum daily dose: 90 mg)
Oral: 0.25 mg/kg every 6 hours

Adults (pain relief usually begins within 10 minutes with parenteral forms): **Note:** The maximum combined duration of treatment (for parenteral and oral) is 5 days; do not increase dose or frequency; supplement with low-dose opioids if needed for breakthrough pain. For patients <50 and/or ≥65 years, see Elderly dosing.
I.M.: 60 mg as a single dose or 30 mg every 6 hours (maximum daily dose: 120 mg)
I.V.: 30 mg as a single dose or 30 mg every 6 hours (maximum daily dose: 120 mg)
Oral: 20 mg, followed by 10 mg every 4-6 hours; do not exceed 40 mg/day; oral dosing is intended to be a continuation of I.M. or I.V. therapy only
Ophthalmic: Children ≥3 years and Adults:
Allergic conjunctivitis (relief of ocular itching) (Acular®): Instill 1 drop (0.25 mg) 4 times/day for seasonal allergic conjunctivitis
Inflammation following cataract extraction (Acular®): Instill 1 drop (0.25 mg) to affected eye(s) 4 times/day beginning 24 hours after surgery; continue for 2 weeks
Pain and photophobia following incisional refractive surgery (Acular® PF): Instill 1 drop (0.25 mg) 4 times/day to affected eye for up to 3 days
Pain following corneal refractive surgery (Acular LS™): Instill 1 drop 4 times/day as needed to affected eye for up to 4 days

Elderly >65 years: Renal insufficiency or weight <50 kg: **Note:** Ketorolac has decreased clearance and increased half-life in the elderly. In addition, the elderly have reported increased incidence of GI bleeding, ulceration, and perforation. The maximum combined duration of treatment (for parenteral and oral) is 5 days.
I.M.: 30 mg as a single dose or 15 mg every 6 hours (maximum daily dose: 60 mg)
I.V.: 15 mg as a single dose or 15 mg every 6 hours (maximum daily dose: 60 mg)
Oral: 10 mg every 4-6 hours; do not exceed 40 mg/day; oral dosing is intended to be a continuation of I.M. or I.V. therapy only

Dosage adjustment in renal impairment: Do not use in patients with advanced renal impairment. Patients with moderately-elevated serum creatinine should use half the recommended dose, not to exceed 60 mg/day I.M./I.V.
Dosage adjustment in hepatic impairment: Use with caution, may cause elevation of liver enzymes

Administration

Oral: May take with food to reduce GI upset
I.M.: Administer slowly and deeply into the muscle. Analgesia begins in 30 minutes and maximum effect within 2 hours
I.V.: Administer I.V. bolus over a minimum of 15 seconds; onset within 30 minutes; peak analgesia within 2 hours
Ophthalmic solution: Contact lenses should be removed before instillation.

Monitoring Parameters Monitor response (pain, range of motion, grip strength, mobility, ADL function), inflammation; observe for weight gain, edema; monitor renal function (serum creatinine, BUN, urine output); observe for bleeding, bruising; evaluate gastrointestinal effects (abdominal pain, bleeding, dyspepsia); mental confusion, disorientation, CBC, liver function tests

Reference Range Serum concentration: Therapeutic: 0.3-5 µg/mL; Toxic: >5 µg/mL

Patient Information Serious gastrointestinal bleeding can occur as well as ulceration and perforation. Pain may or may not be present. Avoid aspirin and aspirin-containing products while taking this medication. If gastric adverse effects persist, contact prescriber. May cause drowsiness, dizziness, blurred vision, and confusion. Use caution when performing tasks which require alertness (eg, driving).

Ophthalmic: Do not wear soft contact lenses.

Dosage Forms INJ, solution: 15 mg/mL (1 mL); 30 mg/mL (1 mL, 2 mL). **SOLN, ophthalmic** (Acular®): 0.5% (3 mL, 5 mL, 10 mL); (Acular LS™): 0.4% (5 mL). **SOLN, ophthalmic** [preservative free] (Acular® PF): 0.5% (0.4 mL). **TAB** (Toradol®): 10 mg

♦ **Ketorolac Tromethamine** *see Ketorolac on page 706*

Ketotifen *(kee toe TYE fen)*

U.S. Brand Names Zaditor™
Synonyms Ketotifen Fumarate
Therapeutic Category Antihistamine, H$_1$ Blocker, Ophthalmic; Antihistamine, Ophthalmic
Use Temporary prevention of eye itching due to allergic conjunctivitis
Pregnancy Risk Factor C
Contraindications Hypersensitivity to ketotifen or any component of the formulation (the preservative is benzalkonium chloride)

Warnings/Precautions For topical ophthalmic use only. Not to treat contact lens-related irritation. After ketotifen use, soft contact lens wearers should wait at least 10 minutes before putting their lenses in. Do not wear contact lenses if eyes are red. Do not contaminate dropper tip or solution when placing drops in eyes. Safety and efficacy not established for children <3 years of age.

Common Adverse Reactions 1% to 10%:
Ocular: Allergic reactions, burning or stinging, conjunctivitis, discharge, dry eyes, eye pain, eyelid disorder, itching, keratitis, lacrimation disorder, mydriasis, photophobia, rash
Respiratory: Pharyngitis
Miscellaneous: Flu syndrome

Mechanism of Action Relatively selective, noncompetitive H_1-receptor antagonist and mast cell stabilizer, inhibiting the release of mediators from cells involved in hypersensitivity reactions

Pharmacodynamics/Kinetics
Onset of action: Minutes
Duration: 8-12 hours
Absorption: Minimally systemic

Dosage Children ≥3 years and Adults: Ophthalmic: Instill 1 drop into the affected eye(s) twice daily, every 8-12 hours

Patient Information For topical ophthalmic use only. Not to be used to treat contact lens-related irritation. After ketotifen's use, soft contact lens wearers should wait at least 10 minutes before putting their contact lenses in. Do not wear contact lenses if eyes are red. Do not contaminate dropper tip or solution when placing drops in eyes. Store at room temperature

Dosage Forms SOLN, ophthalmic: 0.025% (5 mL)

Labetalol (la BET a lole)

Related Information
Beta-Blockers Comparison *on page 1368*

U.S. Brand Names Normodyne®; Trandate®

Synonyms Ibidomide Hydrochloride; Labetalol Hydrochloride

Therapeutic Category Alpha-/Beta-Adrenergic Blocker; Antihypertensive Agent; Beta Blocker, Alpha-Blocker

Use Treatment of mild to severe hypertension; I.V. for hypertensive emergencies

Pregnancy Risk Factor C (manufacturer); D (2nd and 3rd trimesters - expert analysis)

Contraindications Hypersensitivity to labetalol or any component of the formulation; sinus bradycardia; heart block greater than first degree (except in patients with a functioning artificial pacemaker); cardiogenic shock; bronchial asthma; uncompensated cardiac failure; pregnancy (2nd and 3rd trimesters)

Warnings/Precautions Paradoxical increase in blood pressure has been reported with treatment of pheochromocytoma or clonidine withdrawal syndrome; orthostatic hypotension may occur with I.V. administration; patient should remain supine during and for up to 3 hours after I.V. administration; use with caution in impaired hepatic function (discontinue if signs of liver dysfunction occur); may mask the signs and symptoms of hypoglycemia; a lower hemodynamic response rate and higher incidence of toxicity may be observed with administration to elderly patients.

Use only with extreme caution in compensated heart failure and monitor for a worsening of the condition. Avoid abrupt discontinuation in patients with a history of CAD; slowly wean while monitoring for signs and symptoms of ischemia. Use caution with concurrent use of beta-blockers and either verapamil or diltiazem; bradycardia or heart block can occur. Patients with bronchospastic disease should not receive beta-blockers. Labetalol may be used with caution in patients with nonallergic bronchospasm (chronic bronchitis, emphysema). Use cautiously in diabetics because it can mask prominent hypoglycemic symptoms. Can mask signs of thyrotoxicosis. Can cause fetal harm when administered in pregnancy. Use caution when using I.V. labetalol and halothane concurrently (significant myocardial depression).

Common Adverse Reactions
>10%:
Central nervous system: Dizziness (1% to 16%)
Gastrointestinal: Nausea (0% to 19%)
1% to 10%:
Cardiovascular: Edema (0% to 2%), hypotension (1% to 5%); with IV use, hypotension may occur in up to 58%
Central nervous system: Fatigue (1% to 10%), paresthesia (1% to 5%), headache (2%), vertigo (2%), weakness (1%)
Dermatologic: Rash (1%), scalp tingling (1% to 5%)
Gastrointestinal: Vomiting (<1% to 3%), dyspepsia (1% to 4%)
Genitourinary: Ejaculatory failure (0% to 5%), impotence (1% to 4%)
Hepatic: Increased transaminases (4%)
Respiratory: Nasal congestion (1% to 6%), dyspnea (2%)
Miscellaneous: Taste disorder (1%), abnormal vision (1%)
Other adverse reactions noted with beta-adrenergic blocking agents include mental depression, catatonia, disorientation, short-term memory loss, emotional lability, clouded sensorium, intensification of pre-existing AV block, laryngospasm, respiratory distress, agranulocytosis, thrombocytopenic purpura, nonthrombocytopenic purpura, mesenteric artery thrombosis, and ischemic colitis.

Drug Interactions
Cytochrome P450 Effect: Substrate of CYP2D6 (major); **Inhibits** CYP2D6 (weak)

Increased Effect/Toxicity: CYP2D6 inhibitors may increase the levels/effects of labetalol; example inhibitors include chlorpromazine, delavirdine, fluoxetine, miconazole, paroxetine, pergolide, quinidine, quinine, ritonavir, and ropinirole. Cimetidine increases the bioavailability of labetalol. Labetalol has additive hypotensive effects with other antihypertensive agents. Concurrent use with alpha-blockers (prazosin, terazosin) and beta-blockers increases the risk of orthostasis. Concurrent use with diltiazem, verapamil, or digoxin may increase the risk of bradycardia with beta-blocking agents. Halothane, enflurane, isoflurane, and potentially other inhalation anesthetics may cause synergistic hypotension. Beta-blockers may affect the action or levels of ethanol, disopyramide, nondepolarizing muscle relaxants, and theophylline although the effects are difficult to predict.

Decreased Effect: Decreased effect of beta-blockers with aluminum salts, barbiturates, calcium salts, cholestyramine, colestipol, NSAIDs, penicillins (ampicillin), rifampin, salicylates, and sulfinpyrazone due to decreased bioavailability and plasma levels. Beta-blockers may decrease the effect of sulfonylureas.

Mechanism of Action Blocks alpha-, beta$_1$-, and beta$_2$-adrenergic receptor sites; elevated renins are reduced

Pharmacodynamics/Kinetics
Onset of action: Oral: 20 minutes to 2 hours; I.V.: 2-5 minutes
Peak effect: Oral: 1-4 hours; I.V.: 5-15 minutes
Duration: Oral: 8-24 hours (dose dependent); I.V.: 2-4 hours
Distribution: V$_d$: Adults: 3-16 L/kg; mean: <9.4 L/kg; moderately lipid soluble, therefore, can enter CNS; crosses placenta; small amounts enter breast milk
Protein binding: 50%
Metabolism: Hepatic, primarily via glucuronide conjugation; extensive first-pass effect
Bioavailability: Oral: 25%; increased with liver disease, elderly, and concurrent cimetidine

Half-life elimination: Normal renal function: 2.5-8 hours
Excretion: Urine (<5% as unchanged drug)
    Clearance: Possibly decreased in neonates/infants
Dosage Due to limited documentation of its use, labetalol should be initiated cautiously in pediatric patients with careful dosage adjustment and blood pressure monitoring.

Children:
    Oral: Limited information regarding labetalol use in pediatric patients is currently available in literature. Some centers recommend initial oral doses of 4 mg/kg/day in 2 divided doses. Reported oral doses have started at 3 mg/kg/day and 20 mg/kg/day and have increased up to 40 mg/kg/day.
    I.V., intermittent bolus doses of 0.3-1 mg/kg/dose have been reported.
    For treatment of pediatric hypertensive emergencies, initial continuous infusions of 0.4-1 mg/kg/hour with a maximum of 3 mg/kg/hour have been used. Administration requires the use of an infusion pump.
Adults:
    Oral: Initial: 100 mg twice daily, may increase as needed every 2-3 days by 100 mg until desired response is obtained; usual dose: 200-400 mg twice daily; may require up to 2.4 g/day.
    I.V.: 20 mg (0.25 mg/kg for an 80 kg patient) IVP over 2 minutes; may administer 40-80 mg at 10-minute intervals, up to 300 mg total dose.
    I.V. infusion: Initial: 2 mg/minute; titrate to response up to 300 mg total dose, if needed. Administration requires the use of an infusion pump.
    I.V. infusion (500 mg/250 mL D_5W) rates:
        1 mg/minute: 30 mL/hour
        2 mg/minute: 60 mL/hour
        3 mg/minute: 90 mL/hour
        4 mg/minute: 120 mL/hour
        5 mg/minute: 150 mL/hour
        6 mg/minute: 180 mL/hour
Dialysis: Not removed by hemo- or peritoneal dialysis; supplemental dose is not necessary.
Dosage adjustment in hepatic impairment: Dosage reduction may be necessary.
Monitoring Parameters Blood pressure, standing and sitting/supine, pulse, cardiac monitor and blood pressure monitor required for I.V. administration
Patient Information Do not stop medication without aid of prescriber. May mask signs and symptoms of diabetes.
Dosage Forms INJ, solution (Normodyne®): 5 mg/mL (20 mL, 40 mL). **INJ, solution** [prefilled syringe]: 5 mg/mL (4 mL); (Normodyne®): 5 mg/mL (4 mL, 8 mL). **TAB:** 100 mg, 200 mg, 300 mg; (Normodyne®, Trandate®): 100 mg, 200 mg, 300 mg

♦ **Labetalol Hydrochloride** *see* Labetalol *on page 710*
♦ **LactiCare-HC®** *see* Hydrocortisone *on page 632*
♦ **Lactinex® [OTC]** *see* Lactobacillus *on page 711*

Lactobacillus (lak toe ba SIL us)

U.S. Brand Names Bacid® [OTC]; Kala® [OTC]; Lactinex® [OTC]; Megadophilus® [OTC]; MoreDophilus® [OTC]; Probiotica® [OTC]; Superdophilus® [OTC]
Synonyms *Lactobacillus acidophilus*; *Lactobacillus acidophilus* and *Lactobacillus bulgaricus*; *Lactobacillus reuteri*
Therapeutic Category Antidiarrheal
Use Treatment of uncomplicated diarrhea particularly that caused by antibiotic therapy; re-establish normal physiologic and bacterial flora of the intestinal tract
Pregnancy Risk Factor Not available
Contraindications Allergy to milk or lactose
Warnings/Precautions Discontinue if high fever present; do not use in children <2 years of age
Common Adverse Reactions No data reported
Mechanism of Action Creates an environment unfavorable to potentially pathogenic fungi or bacteria through the production of lactic acid, and favors establishment of an aciduric flora, thereby suppressing the growth of pathogenic microorganisms; helps re-establish normal intestinal flora
Pharmacodynamics/Kinetics
    Absorption: Oral: None
    Distribution: Local, primarily colon
    Excretion: Feces
Dosage Children >2 years and Adults: Oral:
    Capsules: 2 capsules 2-4 times/day
    Granules: 1 packet added to or taken with cereal, food, milk, fruit juice, or water, 3-4 times/day
    Powder: 1 teaspoonful daily with liquid
    Tablet, chewable: 4 tablets 3-4 times/day; may follow each dose with a small amount of milk, fruit juice, or water
    Probiotica®: 1 tablet/day; chew thoroughly before swallowing
Administration Granules may be added to or administered with cereal, food, milk, fruit juice, or water
Patient Information Refrigerate; granules may be added to or taken with cereal, food, milk, fruit juice, or water
    (Continued)

Lactobacillus *(Continued)*

Dosage Forms CAP: *Lactobacillus acidophilus* 100 million units; (Bacid®): 500 million units; (Megadophilus®, Superdophilus®): 2 billion units. **GRAN** (Lactinex®): Mixed culture *L. acidophilus, L. bulgaricus* per 1 g packet (12s). **POWDER:** (Megadophilus®, Superdophilus®): 2 billion units per half teaspoon (49 g); (MoreDophilus®): 12.4 billion units per teaspoon (30 g, 120 g). **TAB** (Kala®): 200 million units. **TAB, chewable:** (Lactinex®): Mixed culture *L. acidophilus, L. bulgaricus*; (Probiotica®): 100 million units *L. reuteri* (30s, 60s)

- ◆ **Lactobacillus acidophilus**   *see Lactobacillus on page 711*
- ◆ **Lactobacillus acidophilus and Lactobacillus bulgaricus**   *see Lactobacillus on page 711*
- ◆ **Lactobacillus reuteri**   *see Lactobacillus on page 711*
- ◆ **Lactoflavin**   *see Riboflavin on page 1093*

Lactulose *(LAK tyoo lose)*

Related Information
Laxatives, Classification and Properties *on page 1380*

U.S. Brand Names Cholac®; Constilac®; Constulose®; Enulose®; Generlac; Kristalose™

Therapeutic Category Ammonium Detoxicant; Laxative, Miscellaneous

Use Adjunct in the prevention and treatment of portal-systemic encephalopathy; treatment of chronic constipation

Pregnancy Risk Factor B

Contraindications Hypersensitivity to lactulose or any component of the formulation; galactosemia (or patients requiring a low galactose diet)

Warnings/Precautions Use with caution in patients with diabetes mellitus; monitor periodically for electrolyte imbalance when lactulose is used >6 months or in patients predisposed to electrolyte abnormalities (eg, elderly); patients receiving lactulose and an oral anti-infective agent should be monitored for possible inadequate response to lactulose

Common Adverse Reactions Frequency not defined: Gastrointestinal: Flatulence, diarrhea (excessive dose), abdominal discomfort, nausea, vomiting, cramping

Drug Interactions
Decreased Effect: Oral neomycin, laxatives, antacids

Mechanism of Action The bacterial degradation of lactulose resulting in an acidic pH inhibits the diffusion of NH_3 into the blood by causing the conversion of NH_3 to NH_4+; also enhances the diffusion of NH_3 from the blood into the gut where conversion to NH_4+ occurs; produces an osmotic effect in the colon with resultant distention promoting peristalsis

Pharmacodynamics/Kinetics
Absorption: Not appreciable
Metabolism: Via colonic flora to lactic acid and acetic acid; requires colonic flora for drug activation
Excretion: Primarily feces and urine ($\sim$3%)

Dosage Diarrhea may indicate overdosage and responds to dose reduction
Prevention of portal systemic encephalopathy (PSE): Oral:
Infants: 2.5-10 mL/day divided 3-4 times/day; adjust dosage to produce 2-3 stools/day
Older Children: Daily dose of 40-90 mL divided 3-4 times/day; if initial dose causes diarrhea, then reduce it immediately; adjust dosage to produce 2-3 stools/day
Constipation: Oral:
Children: 5 g/day (7.5 mL) after breakfast
Adults: 15-30 mL/day increased to 60 mL/day if necessary
Acute PSE: Adults:
Oral: 20-30 g (30-45 mL) every 1-2 hours to induce rapid laxation; adjust dosage daily to produce 2-3 soft stools; doses of 30-45 mL may be given hourly to cause rapid laxation, then reduce to recommended dose; usual daily dose: 60-100 g (90-150 mL) daily
Rectal administration: 200 g (300 mL) diluted with 700 mL of H_2O or NS; administer rectally via rectal balloon catheter and retain 30-60 minutes every 4-6 hours

Monitoring Parameters Blood pressure, standing/supine; serum potassium; bowel movement patterns, fluid status; serum ammonia

Patient Information Lactulose can be taken "as is" or diluted with water, fruit juice or milk, or taken in a food; laxative results may not occur for 24-48 hours

Dosage Forms CRYST (Kristalose™): 10 g/packet (30s), 20 g/packet (30s). **SYR:** 10 g/15 mL (15 mL, 30 mL, 237 mL, 473 mL, 946 mL, 1000 mL, 1890 mL); (Cholac®, Constilac®): 10 g/15 mL (30 mL, 240 mL, 480 mL, 960 mL, 1920 mL, 3875 mL); (Constulose®): 10 g/15 mL (240 mL, 960 mL); (Enulose®): 10 g/15 mL (480 mL, 1900 mL); (Generlac): 10 g/15 mL (480 mL, 1920 mL)

- ◆ **L-AmB**   *see Amphotericin B (Liposomal) on page 93*
- ◆ **Lamictal®**   *see Lamotrigine on page 714*
- ◆ **Lamisil®**   *see Terbinafine on page 1197*
- ◆ **Lamisil® AT™ [OTC]**   *see Terbinafine on page 1197*

Lamivudine *(la MI vyoo deen)*

Related Information
Antiretroviral Therapy for HIV Infection *on page 1448*
Management of Healthcare Worker Exposures to HBV, HCV, and HIV *on page 1421*

U.S. Brand Names Epivir®; Epivir-HBV®

Synonyms 3TC

Therapeutic Category Antiretroviral Agent, Nucleoside Reverse Transcriptase Inhibitor (NRTI) [Cytosine Analog]; Antiviral Agent, Hepatitis

Use
Epivir®: Treatment of HIV infection when antiretroviral therapy is warranted; should always be used as part of a multidrug regimen (at least three antiretroviral agents)

Epivir-HBV®: Treatment of chronic hepatitis B associated with evidence of hepatitis B viral replication and active liver inflammation

Unlabeled/Investigational Use Prevention of HIV following needlesticks (with or without protease inhibitor)

Pregnancy Risk Factor C

Contraindications Hypersensitivity to lamivudine or any component of the formulation

Warnings/Precautions A decreased dosage is recommended in patients with renal dysfunction; use with extreme caution in children with history of pancreatitis or risk factors for development of pancreatitis. Do not use as monotherapy in treatment of HIV. Treatment of HBV in patients with unrecognized/untreated HIV may lead to rapid HIV resistance. Treatment of HIV in patients with unrecognized/untreated HBV may lead to rapid HBV resistance.

Lactic acidosis and severe hepatomegaly with steatosis have been reported, including fatal cases. Use caution in hepatic impairment. Pregnancy, obesity, and/or prolonged therapy may increase the risk of lactic acidosis and liver damage.

Common Adverse Reactions (As reported in adults treated for HIV infection)
>10%:
  Central nervous system: Headache, fatigue
  Gastrointestinal: Nausea, diarrhea, vomiting, pancreatitis (range: 0.5% to 18%; higher percentage in pediatric patients)
  Neuromuscular & skeletal: Peripheral neuropathy, paresthesia, musculoskeletal pain
1% to 10%:
  Central nervous system: Dizziness, depression, fever, chills, insomnia
  Dermatologic: Rash
  Gastrointestinal: Anorexia, abdominal pain, heartburn, elevated amylase
  Hematologic: Neutropenia
  Hepatic: Elevated AST, ALT
  Neuromuscular & skeletal: Myalgia, arthralgia
  Respiratory: Nasal signs and symptoms, cough

Drug Interactions
Increased Effect/Toxicity: Zidovudine concentrations increase significantly (~39%) with lamivudine coadministration. sulfamethoxazole/trimethoprim increases lamivudine's blood levels. Concomitant use of ribavirin and nucleoside analogues may increase the risk of developing lactic acidosis (includes adefovir, didanosine, lamivudine, stavudine, zalcitabine, zidovudine). Trimethoprim (and other drugs excreted by organic cation transport) may increase serum levels/effects of lamivudine.

Decreased Effect: Zalcitabine and lamivudine may inhibit the intracellular phosphorylation of each other; concomitant use should be avoided.

Mechanism of Action Lamivudine is a cytosine analog. After lamivudine is triphosphorylated, the principle mode of action is inhibition of HIV reverse transcription via viral DNA chain termination; inhibits RNA- and DNA-dependent DNA polymerase activities of reverse transcriptase. The monophosphate form of lamivudine is incorporated into the viral DNA by hepatitis B virus polymerase, resulting in DNA chain termination.

Pharmacodynamics/Kinetics
Absorption: Rapid
Distribution: V_d: 1.3 L/kg
Protein binding, plasma: <36%
Metabolism: 5.6% to trans-sulfoxide metabolite
Bioavailability: Absolute; Cp_{max} decreased with food although AUC not significantly affected
  Children: 66%
  Adults: 87%
Half-life elimination: Children: 2 hours; Adults: 5-7 hours
Excretion: Primarily urine (as unchanged drug)

Dosage Note: The formulation and dosage of Epivir-HBV® are not appropriate for patients infected with both HBV and HIV. Use with at least two other antiretroviral agents when treating HIV
Oral:
  Children 3 months to 16 years: HIV: 4 mg/kg twice daily (maximum: 150 mg twice daily)
  Children 2-17 years: Treatment of hepatitis B (Epivir-HBV®): 3 mg/kg once daily (maximum: 100 mg/day)
  Adolescents and Adults: Prevention of HIV following needlesticks (unlabeled use): 150 mg twice daily (with zidovudine with or without a protease inhibitor, depending on risk)
  Adults:
    HIV: 150 mg twice daily **or** 300 mg once daily; <50 kg: 2 mg/kg twice daily
    Treatment of hepatitis B (Epivir-HBV®): 100 mg/day
Dosing interval in renal impairment in pediatric patients: Insufficient data; however, dose reduction should be considered.
Dosing interval in renal impairment in patients >16 years for HIV:
  Cl_{cr} 30-49 mL/minute: Administer 150 mg once daily
  Cl_{cr} 15-29 mL/minute: Administer 150 mg first dose, then 100 mg once daily
  Cl_{cr} 5-14 mL/minute: Administer 150 mg first dose, then 50 mg once daily
  Cl_{cr} <5 mL/minute: Administer 50 mg first dose, then 25 mg once daily
(Continued)

Lamivudine (Continued)

Dosing interval in renal impairment in adult patients with hepatitis B:
Cl$_{cr}$ 30-49: Administer 100 mg first dose then 50 mg once daily
Cl$_{cr}$ 15-29: Administer 100 mg first dose then 25 mg once daily
Cl$_{cr}$ 5-14: Administer 35 mg first dose then 15 mg once daily
Cl$_{cr}$ <5: Administer 35 mg first dose then 10 mg once daily
Dialysis: No data available

Administration May be taken with or without food. Adjust dosage in renal failure.

Monitoring Parameters Amylase, bilirubin, liver enzymes, hematologic parameters, viral load, and CD4 count; signs and symptoms of pancreatitis

Patient Information Patients may still experience illnesses associated with HIV infection; lamivudine is not a cure for HIV infection nor has it been shown to reduce the risk of transmission to others; long-term effects are unknown; take exactly as prescribed; children should be monitored for symptoms of pancreatitis

Dosage Forms SOLN, oral: (Epivir®): 10 mg/mL (240 mL); (Epivir-HBV®): 5 mg/mL (240 mL).
TAB: (Epivir®): 150 mg, 300 mg; (Epivir-HBV®): 100 mg

+ **Lamivudine, Abacavir, and Zidovudine** *see Abacavir, Lamivudine, and Zidovudine on page 19*

+ **Lamivudine and Zidovudine** *see Zidovudine and Lamivudine on page 1326*

Lamotrigine (la MOE tri jeen)

Related Information
Anticonvulsants by Seizure Type *on page 1358*
Epilepsy *on page 1477*

U.S. Brand Names Lamictal®

Synonyms BW-430C; LTG

Therapeutic Category Anticonvulsant, Miscellaneous

Use Adjunctive therapy in the treatment of generalized seizures of Lennox-Gastaut syndrome and partial seizures in adults and children ≥2 years of age; conversion to monotherapy in adults with partial seizures who are receiving treatment with valproate or a single enzyme-inducing antiepileptic drug; maintenance treatment of bipolar disorder

Pregnancy Risk Factor C

Contraindications Hypersensitivity to lamotrigine or any component of the formulation

Warnings/Precautions Severe and potentially life-threatening skin rashes requiring hospitalization have been reported (children 0.8%, adults 0.3%); risk may be increased by coadministration with valproic acid, higher than recommended starting doses, and rapid dose titration. The majority of cases occur in the first 8 weeks; however, isolated cases may occur after prolonged treatment. Discontinue at first sign of rash unless rash is clearly not drug related. Use caution in patients with impaired renal, hepatic, or cardiac function. Avoid abrupt cessation, taper over at least 2 weeks if possible. May cause CNS depression, which may impair physical or mental abilities. Patients must be cautioned about performing tasks which require mental alertness (eg, operating machinery or driving). Effects with other sedative drugs or ethanol may be potentiated. Binds to melanin and may accumulate in the eye and other melanin-rich tissues; the clinical significance of this is not known. Safety and efficacy has not been established for use as initial monotherapy, conversion to monotherapy from nonenzyme-inducing antiepileptic drugs (AED) except valproate, or conversion to monotherapy from two or more AEDs. **Use caution in writing and/or interpreting prescriptions/orders; medication dispensing errors have occurred with similar-sounding medications (Lamisil®, Ludiomil®, lamivudine, labetalol, and Lomotil®).**

Common Adverse Reactions Percentages reported in adults receiving adjunctive therapy:
>10%:
Central nervous system: Headache (29%), dizziness (38%), ataxia (22%), somnolence (14%)
Gastrointestinal: Nausea (19%)
Ocular: Diplopia (28%), blurred vision (16%)
Respiratory: Rhinitis (14%)
1% to 10%:
Cardiovascular: Peripheral edema
Central nervous system: Depression (4%), anxiety (4%), irritability (3%), confusion, speech disorder (3%), difficulty concentrating (2%), malaise, seizures (includes exacerbations) (2% to 3%), incoordination (6%), insomnia (6%), pain, amnesia, hostility, memory decreased, nervousness, vertigo
Dermatologic: Hypersensitivity rash (10%; serious rash requiring hospitalization - adults 0.3%, children 0.8%), pruritus (3%)
Gastrointestinal: Abdominal pain (5%), vomiting (9%), diarrhea (6%), dyspepsia (5%), xerostomia, constipation (4%), anorexia (2%), tooth disorder (3%)
Genitourinary: Vaginitis (4%), dysmenorrhea (7%), amenorrhea (2%)
Neuromuscular & skeletal: Tremor (4%), arthralgia (2%), neck pain (2%)
Ocular: Nystagmus (2%), visual abnormality
Respiratory: Epistaxis, bronchitis, dyspnea
Miscellaneous: Flu syndrome (7%), fever (6%)

Drug Interactions
Increased Effect/Toxicity: Lamotrigine may increase the epoxide metabolite of carbamazepine resulting in toxicity. Valproic acid increases blood levels of lamotrigine. Valproic acid inhibits the clearance of lamotrigine, dosage adjustment required when adding or withdrawing valproic acid; inhibition appears maximal at valproic acid 250-500 mg/day; the

incidence of serious rash may be increased by valproic acid. Toxicity has been reported following addition of sertraline (limited documentation).

Decreased Effect: Acetaminophen (chronic administration), carbamazepine, oral contraceptives (estrogens), phenytoin, phenobarbital may decrease concentrations of lamotrigine; dosage adjustments may be needed when adding or withdrawing agent; monitor

Mechanism of Action A triazine derivative which inhibits release of glutamate (an excitatory amino acid) and inhibits voltage-sensitive sodium channels, which stabilizes neuronal membranes. Lamotrigine has weak inhibitory effect on the $5-HT_3$ receptor; *in vitro* inhibits dihydrofolate reductase.

Pharmacodynamics/Kinetics

Distribution: V_d: 1.1 L/kg

Protein binding: 55%

Metabolism: Hepatic and renal; metabolized by glucuronic acid conjugation to inactive metabolites

Bioavailability: 98%

Half-life elimination: Adults: 25-33 hours; Concomitant valproic acid therapy: 59-70 hours; Concomitant phenytoin or carbamazepine therapy: 13-14 hours

Time to peak, plasma: 1-4 hours

Excretion: Urine (94%, ~90% as glucuronide conjugates and ~10% unchanged); feces (2%)

Dosage Note: Only whole tablets should be used for dosing, round calculated dose down to the nearest whole tablet: Oral:

Children 2-12 years: Lennox-Gastaut (adjunctive) or partial seizures (adjunctive): **Note:** Children 2-6 years will likely require maintenance doses at the higher end of recommended range:

Patients receiving AED regimens containing valproic acid:

Weeks 1 and 2: 0.15 mg/kg/day in 1-2 divided doses; round dose down to the nearest whole tablet. For patients >6.7 kg and <14 kg, dosing should be 2 mg every other day.

Weeks 3 and 4: 0.3 mg/kg/day in 1-2 divided doses; round dose down to the nearest whole tablet; may use combinations of 2 mg and 5 mg tablets. For patients >6.7 kg and <14 kg, dosing should be 2 mg/day.

Maintenance dose: Titrate dose to effect; after week 4, increase dose every 1-2 weeks by a calculated increment; calculate increment as 0.3 mg/kg/day rounded down to the nearest whole tablet; add this amount to the previously administered daily dose; usual maintenance: 1-5 mg/kg/day in 1-2 divided doses; maximum: 200 mg/day given in 1-2 divided doses

Patients receiving enzyme-inducing AED regimens without valproic acid:

Weeks 1 and 2: 0.6 mg/kg/day in 2 divided doses; round dose down to the nearest whole tablet

Weeks 3 and 4: 1.2 mg/kg/day in 2 divided doses; round dose down to the nearest whole tablet

Maintenance dose: Titrate dose to effect; after week 4, increase dose every 1-2 weeks by a calculated increment; calculate increment as 1.2 mg/kg/day rounded down to the nearest whole tablet; add this amount to the previously administered daily dose; usual maintenance: 5-15 mg/kg/day in 2 divided doses; maximum: 400 mg/day

Children >12 years: Lennox-Gastaut (adjunctive) or partial seizures (adjunctive): Refer to Adults dosing

Children ≥16 years: Conversion from single enzyme-inducing AED regimen to monotherapy: Refer to Adults dosing

Adults:

Lennox-Gastaut (adjunctive) or treatment of partial seizures (adjunctive):

Patients receiving AED regimens containing valproic acid: Initial dose: 25 mg every other day for 2 weeks, then 25 mg every day for 2 weeks. Dose may be increased by 25-50 mg every day for 1-2 weeks in order to achieve maintenance dose. Maintenance dose: 100-400 mg/day in 1-2 divided doses (usual range 100-200 mg/day).

Patients receiving enzyme-inducing AED regimens without valproic acid: Initial dose: 50 mg/day for 2 weeks, then 100 mg in 2 doses for 2 weeks; thereafter, daily dose can be increased by 100 mg every 1-2 weeks to be given in 2 divided doses. Usual maintenance dose: 300-500 mg/day in 2 divided doses; doses as high as 700 mg/day have been reported

Conversion to monotherapy (partial seizures in patients ≥16 years of age):

Adjunctive therapy with valproate: Initiate and titrate as per recommendations to a lamotrigine dose of 200 mg/day. Then taper valproate dose in decrements of not more than 500 mg/day at intervals of one week (or longer) to a valproate dosage of 500 mg/day; this dosage should be maintained for one week. The lamotrigine dosage should then be increased to 300 mg/day while valproate is decreased to 250 mg/day; this dosage should be maintained for one week. Valproate may then be discontinued, while the lamotrigine dose is increased by 100 mg/day at weekly intervals to achieve a lamotrigine maintenance dose of 500 mg/day.

Adjunctive therapy with enzyme-inducing AED: Initiate and titrate as per recommendations to a lamotrigine dose of 500 mg/day. Concomitant enzyme-inducing AED should then be withdrawn by 20% decrements each week over a 4-week period. Patients should be monitored for rash.

Adjunctive therapy with non-enzyme inducing AED: No specific guidelines available

Bipolar disorder: 25 mg/day for 2 weeks, followed by 50 mg/day for 2 weeks, followed by 100 mg/day for 1 week; thereafter, daily dosage may be increased to 200 mg/day

Patients receiving valproic acid: Initial: 25 mg every other day for 2 weeks, followed by 25 mg/day for 2 weeks, followed by 50 mg/day for 1 week, followed by 100 mg/day (target

(Continued)

Lamotrigine *(Continued)*

dose) thereafter. **Note:** If valproate is discontinued, increase daily lamotrigine dose in 50 mg increments at weekly intervals until daily dosage of 200 mg is attained.

Patients receiving enzyme-inducing drugs (eg, carbamazepine): Initial: 50 mg/day for 2 weeks, followed by 100 mg/day (in divided doses) for 2 weeks, followed by 200 mg/day (in divided doses) for 1 week, followed by 300 mg/day (in divided doses) for 1 week. May increase to 400 mg/day (in divided doses) during week 7 and thereafter. **Note:** If carbamazepine (or other enzyme-inducing drug) is discontinued, decrease daily lamotrigine dose in 100 mg increments at weekly intervals until daily dosage of 200 mg is attained.

Discontinuing therapy: Children and Adults: Decrease dose by ~50% per week, over at least 2 weeks unless safety concerns require a more rapid withdrawal.

Restarting therapy after discontinuation: If lamotrigine has been withheld for >5 half-lives, consider restarting according to initial dosing recommendations.

Dosage adjustment in renal impairment: Decreased dosage may be effective in patients with significant renal impairment; use with caution

Dosage adjustment in hepatic impairment:
Child-Pugh Grade B: Reduce initial, escalation, and maintenance doses by 50%
Child-Pugh Grade C: Reduce initial, escalation, and maintenance doses by 75%

Administration Doses should be rounded down to the nearest whole tablet. Dispersible tablets may be chewed, dispersed in water, or swallowed whole. To disperse tablets, add to a small amount of liquid (just enough to cover tablet); let sit ~1 minute until dispersed; swirl solution and consume immediately. Do not administer partial amounts of liquid. If tablets are chewed, a small amount of water or diluted fruit juice should be used to aid in swallowing.

Monitoring Parameters Seizure, frequency and duration, serum levels of concurrent anticonvulsants, hypersensitivity reactions, especially rash

Reference Range Therapeutic range: 2-20 µg/mL; a serum concentration relationship has not been demonstrated.

Dosage Forms TAB: 25 mg, 100 mg, 150 mg, 200 mg. **TAB, dispersible/chewable:** 2 mg, 5 mg, 25 mg

- **Lamprene®** *see Clofazimine on page 294*
- **Lanacane® [OTC]** *see Benzocaine on page 154*
- **Lanaphilic® [OTC]** *see Urea on page 1282*
- **Lanoxicaps®** *see Digoxin on page 374*
- **Lanoxin®** *see Digoxin on page 374*

Lansoprazole *(lan SOE pra zole)*

U.S. Brand Names Prevacid®; Prevacid® SoluTab™

Therapeutic Category Gastric Acid Secretion Inhibitor; Proton Pump Inhibitor

Use Short-term treatment of active duodenal ulcers; maintenance treatment of healed duodenal ulcers; as part of a multidrug regimen for *H. pylori* eradication to reduce the risk of duodenal ulcer recurrence; short-term treatment of active benign gastric ulcer; treatment of NSAID-associated gastric ulcer; to reduce the risk of NSAID-associated gastric ulcer in patients with a history of gastric ulcer who require an NSAID; short-term treatment of symptomatic GERD; short-term treatment for all grades of erosive esophagitis; to maintain healing of erosive esophagitis; long-term treatment of pathological hypersecretory conditions, including Zollinger-Ellison syndrome

Pregnancy Risk Factor B

Contraindications Hypersensitivity to lansoprazole or any component of the formulation

Warnings/Precautions Severe liver dysfunction may require dosage reductions. Symptomatic response does not exclude malignancy. Safety and efficacy have not been established in children <1 year of age.

Common Adverse Reactions 1% to 10%: Gastrointestinal: Abdominal pain (2%), diarrhea (4%, more likely at doses of 60 mg/day), constipation (1%), nausea (1%)

Drug Interactions

Cytochrome P450 Effect: Substrate of CYP2C8/9 (minor), 2C19 (major), 3A4 (major); **Inhibits** CYP2C8/9 (weak), 2C19 (moderate), 2D6 (weak), 3A4 (weak); **Induces** CYP1A2 (weak)

Decreased Effect: CYP2C19 inducers may decrease the levels/effects of lansoprazole; example inducers include aminoglutethimide, carbamazepine, phenytoin, and rifampin. Proton pump inhibitors may decrease the absorption of atazanavir, indinavir, itraconazole, and ketoconazole.

Mechanism of Action A proton pump inhibitor which decreases acid secretion in gastric parietal cells

Pharmacodynamics/Kinetics
Duration: >1 day
Absorption: Rapid
Protein binding: 97%
Metabolism: Hepatic via CYP2C19 and 3A4, and in parietal cells to two inactive metabolites
Bioavailability: 80%; decreased 50% to 70% if given 30 minutes after food
Half-life elimination: 2 hours; Elderly: 2-3 hours; Hepatic impairment: ≤7 hours
Time to peak, plasma: 1.7 hours
Excretion: Feces (67%); urine (33%)

Dosage Oral:

Children 1-11 years: GERD, erosive esophagitis:
≤30 kg: 15 mg once daily
>30 kg: 30 mg once daily

Adults:

Duodenal ulcer: Short-term treatment: 15 mg once daily for 4 weeks; maintenance therapy: 15 mg once daily

Gastric ulcer: Short-term treatment: 30 mg once daily for up to 8 weeks

NSAID-associated gastric ulcer (healing): 30 mg once daily for 8 weeks; controlled studies did not extend past 8 weeks of therapy

NSAID-associated gastric ulcer (to reduce risk): Oral: 15 mg once daily for up to 12 weeks; controlled studies did not extend past 12 weeks of therapy

Symptomatic GERD: Short-term treatment: 15 mg once daily for up to 8 weeks

Erosive esophagitis: Short-term treatment: 30 mg once daily for up to 8 weeks; continued treatment for an additional 8 weeks may be considered for recurrence or for patients that do not heal after the first 8 weeks of therapy; maintenance therapy: 15 mg once daily

Hypersecretory conditions: Initial: 60 mg once daily; adjust dose based upon patient response and to reduce acid secretion to <10 mEq/hour (5 mEq/hour in patients with prior gastric surgery); doses of 90 mg twice daily have been used; administer doses >120 mg/day in divided doses

Helicobacter pylori eradication: Currently accepted recommendations (may differ from product labeling): Dose varies with regimen: 30 mg once daily or 60 mg/day in 2 divided doses; requires combination therapy with antibiotics

Elderly: No dosage adjustment is needed in elderly patients with normal hepatic function

Dosage adjustment in renal impairment: No dosage adjustment is needed
Dosing adjustment in hepatic impairment: Dose reduction is necessary for severe hepatic impairment

Administration

Oral: Administer before food; best if taken before breakfast. The intact granules should not be chewed or crushed; however, in addition to oral suspension, several options are available for those patients unable to swallow capsules:

Capsules may be opened and the intact granules sprinkled on 1 tablespoon of applesauce, Ensure® pudding, cottage cheese, yogurt, or strained pears. The granules should then be swallowed immediately.

Capsules may be opened and emptied into ~60 mL orange juice, apple juice, or tomato juice; mix and swallow immediately. Rinse the glass with additional juice and swallow to assure complete delivery of the dose.

Capsule granules may be mixed with apple, cranberry, grape, orange, pineapple, prune, tomato and V-8® juice and stored for up to 30 minutes.

Delayed release oral suspension granules should be mixed with 2 tablespoonfuls (30 mL) of water; no other liquid should be used; should not be administered through enteral administration tubes

Orally-disintegrating tablets: Should not be swallowed whole or chewed. Place tablet on tongue; allow to dissolve (with or without water) until particles can be swallowed.

Nasogastric tube administration: Capsules can be opened, the granules mixed (not crushed) with 40 mL of apple juice and then injected through the NG tube into the stomach, then flush tube with additional apple juice.

Monitoring Parameters Patients with Zollinger-Ellison syndrome should be monitored for gastric acid output, which should be maintained at ≤10 mEq/hour during the last hour before the next lansoprazole dose; lab monitoring should include CBC, liver function, renal function, and serum gastrin levels

Patient Information Take before eating; do not crush or chew capsules or granules for oral suspension

Dosage Forms CAP, delayed release (Prevacid®): 15 mg, 30 mg. **GRAN, for oral suspension, delayed release** (Prevacid®): 15 mg/packet (30s), 30 mg/packet (30s). **TAB, orally-disintegrating** (Prevacid® SoluTab™): 15 mg, 30 mg

Lansoprazole, Amoxicillin, and Clarithromycin

(lan SOE pra zole, a moks i SIL in, & kla RITH roe mye sin)

U.S. Brand Names Prevpac®

Synonyms Amoxicillin, Lansoprazole, and Clarithromycin; Clarithromycin, Lansoprazole, and Amoxicillin

Therapeutic Category Antibiotic, Macrolide Combination; Antibiotic, Penicillin; Gastrointestinal Agent, *H. pylori*

Use Eradication of *H. pylori* to reduce the risk of recurrent duodenal ulcer

Pregnancy Risk Factor C (clarithromycin)

Dosage Oral: Lansoprazole 30 mg, amoxicillin 1 g, and clarithromycin 500 mg taken together twice daily for 10 or 14 days

Dosage Forms Combination package (Prevpac®) [each administration card contains]: **CAP** (Trimox®): Amoxicillin 500 mg (4 capsules/day); **CAP, delayed release** (Prevacid®): Lansoprazole 30 mg (2 capsules/day); **TAB** (Biaxin®): Clarithromycin 500 mg (2 tablets/day)

♦ **Lantus®** *see* Insulin Preparations *on page 669*
♦ **Lariam®** *see* Mefloquine *on page 783*
♦ **Larodopa®** *see* Levodopa *on page 731*

Laronidase (lair OH ni days)

U.S. Brand Names Aldurazyme®

Synonyms Recombinant α-L-Iduronidase (Glycosaminoglycan α-L-Iduronohydrolase)

Therapeutic Category Enzyme

Use Treatment of Hurler and Hurler-Scheie forms of mucopolysaccharidosis I (MPS I); treatment of Scheie form of MPS I in patients with moderate to severe symptoms

Pregnancy Risk Factor B

Contraindications No known contraindications

Warnings/Precautions Infusion-related hypersensitivity reactions have been reported, may be severe; use caution with pre-existing airway obstruction. Reactions tend to occur within 3 hours of the drug administration. Antipyretics and or antihistamines should be administered prior to infusion to reduce the incidence/severity of headache, fever, and/or flushing. In case of reaction, decrease the rate of infusion, temporarily discontinue the infusion, and/or administer additional antipyretics/antihistamines. Risks and benefits should be carefully considered prior to readministering following a severe hypersensitivity reaction. In the case of anaphylaxis, caution should be used if epinephrine is being considered; many patients with MPS I have pre-existing heart disease. Prepared infusions contain human albumin. Laronidase has not been studied in patients with mild symptoms of the Scheie form of MPS I. Not indicated for the CNS manifestations of the disorder. Safety and efficacy in patients <5 years were not established in clinical trials. A patient registry has been established and all patients are encouraged to participate. Registry information may be obtained at www.MPSIregistry.com or by calling 800-745-4447.

Common Adverse Reactions

>10%:

Cardiovascular: Vein disorder (14%)

Dermatologic: Rash (36%)

Local: Infusion reactions [31%; may be severe; includes flushing (23%), fever, and headache; frequency decreased over time during open-label extension period], injection site reaction (18%)

Neuromuscular & skeletal: Hyper-reflexia (14%), paresthesia (14%)

Respiratory: Upper respiratory tract infection (32%)

Miscellaneous: Antibody development to laronidase (91%; significance unknown)

1% to 10%:

Cardiovascular: Chest pain (9%), edema (9%), facial edema (9%), hypotension (9%)

Hematologic: Thrombocytopenia (9%)

Hepatic: Bilirubinemia

Local: Abscess (9%), injection site pain (9%)

Ocular: Corneal opacity (9%)

Mechanism of Action Laronidase is a recombinant (replacement) form of α-L-iduronidase derived from Chinese hamster cells. α-L-iduronidase is an enzyme needed to break down endogenous glycosaminoglycans (GAGs) within lysosomes. A deficiency of α-L-iduronidase leads to an accumulation of GAGs, causing cellular, tissue, and organ dysfunction as seen in MPS I. Improved pulmonary function and walking capacity have been demonstrated with the administration of laronidase to patients with Hurler, Hurler-Scheie, or Scheie (with moderate to severe symptoms) forms of MPS.

Pharmacodynamics/Kinetics

Distribution: V_d: 0.24-0.6 L/kg

Half-life elimination: 1.5-3.6 hours

Excretion: Clearance: 1.7 to 2.7 mL/minute/kg; during the first 12 weeks of therapy the clearance of laronidase increases proportionally to the amount of antibodies a given patient develops against the enzyme. However, with long-term use (≥26 weeks) antibody titers have no effect on laronidase clearance.

Dosage I.V.: Children ≥5 years and Adults: 0.58 mg/kg once weekly; dose should be rounded up to the nearest whole vial

Administration Administer using PVC container and PVC infusion set with in-line, low protein-binding 0.2 micrometer filter. Antipyretics and or antihistamines should be administered prior to infusion. Administration schedule is based on body weight. Vital signs should be monitored every 15 minutes, if stable; rate may be increased as follows:

≤20 kg: Total infusion volume: 100 mL

2 mL/hour for 15 minutes

4 mL/hour for 15 minutes

8 mL/hour for 15 minutes

16 mL/hour for 15 minutes

32 mL/hour for remainder of infusion

>20 kg: Total infusion volume: 250 mL

5 mL/hour for 15 minutes

10 mL/hour for 15 minutes

20 mL/hour for 15 minutes

40 mL/hour for 15 minutes

80 mL/hour for remainder of infusion

Note: In case of infusion-related reaction, decrease the rate of infusion, temporarily discontinue the infusion, and/or administer additional antipyretics/antihistamines.

Monitoring Parameters Vital signs; injection site reactions

Patient Information This medication can only be given intravenously. Rash and injection related disorders are common; medication will be given to prevent them and their frequency may decrease over time. Notify prescriber immediately if having trouble breathing.

Dosage Forms INJ, solution [preservative free]: 2.9 mg/5 mL (5 mL)

♦ **Lasix®** *see Furosemide on page 573*
♦ **L-asparaginase** *see Asparaginase on page 118*

Latanoprost (la TA noe prost)
Related Information
Glaucoma Drug Therapy Comparison *on page 1481*
U.S. Brand Names Xalatan®
Therapeutic Category Ophthalmic Agent, Prostaglandin Derivative; Prostaglandin, Ophthalmic
Use Reduction of elevated intraocular pressure in patients with open-angle glaucoma or ocular hypertension
Pregnancy Risk Factor C
Dosage Adults: Ophthalmic: 1 drop (1.5 mcg) in the affected eye(s) once daily in the evening; do not exceed the once daily dosage because it has been shown that more frequent administration may decrease the IOP lowering effect
Note: A medication delivery device (Xal-Ease™) is available for use with Xalatan®.
Dosage Forms SOLN, ophthalmic: 0.005% (2.5 mL)

♦ **Laxatives, Classification and Properties** *see page 1380*
♦ *l*-**Bunolol Hydrochloride** *see Levobunolol on page 729*
♦ **L-Carnitine** *see Levocarnitine on page 730*
♦ **LCR** *see VinCRIStine on page 1306*
♦ **L-Deprenyl** *see Selegiline on page 1128*
♦ *L*-**Dopa** *see Levodopa on page 731*
♦ **LDP-341** *see Bortezomib on page 173*

Leflunomide (le FLOO noh mide)
U.S. Brand Names Arava®
Therapeutic Category Antimetabolite; Antirheumatic, Disease Modifying
Use Treatment of active rheumatoid arthritis; indicated to reduce signs and symptoms, and to retard structural damage and improve physical function
Pregnancy Risk Factor X
Contraindications Hypersensitivity to leflunomide or any component of the formulation; pregnancy
Warnings/Precautions Leflunomide has been associated with rare reports of hepatotoxicity, hepatic failure, and death. Hepatic disease (including seropositive hepatitis B or C patients) and/or concurrent exposure to other hepatotoxins may increase the risk of hepatotoxicity. Monitoring of hepatic function is required.

Not recommended for patients with severe immune deficiency, bone marrow dysplasia, or uncontrolled infection. Has been associated with rare pancytopenia, agranulocytosis, and thrombocytopenia, particularly when given in combination with methotrexate or other immunosuppressive agents. Monitoring of hematologic function is required. Use with caution in patients with a prior history of significant hematologic abnormalities. Discontinue if evidence of bone marrow suppression occurs, and begin procedure to accelerate elimination (cholestyramine or activated charcoal, see Overdosage/Toxicology). Consider interruption of therapy and accelerated elimination in patients who develop serious infections while receiving leflunomide. The use of live vaccines is not recommended.

Women of childbearing potential should not receive leflunomide until pregnancy has been excluded; patients have been counseled concerning fetal risk and reliable contraceptive measures have been confirmed. Caution in renal impairment. Leflunomide will increase uric acid excretion. Immunosuppression may increase the risk of lymphoproliferative disorders or other malignancies.
Common Adverse Reactions
>10%:
Gastrointestinal: Diarrhea (17%)
Respiratory: Respiratory tract infection (15%)
1% to 10%:
Cardiovascular: Hypertension (10%), chest pain (2%), palpitation, tachycardia, vasculitis, vasodilation, varicose vein, edema (peripheral)
Central nervous system: Headache (7%), dizziness (4%), pain (2%), fever, malaise, migraine, anxiety, depression, insomnia, sleep disorder
Dermatologic: Alopecia (10%), rash (10%), pruritus (4%), dry skin (2%), eczema (2%), acne, dermatitis, hair discoloration, hematoma, herpes infection, nail disorder, subcutaneous nodule, skin disorder/discoloration, skin ulcer, bruising
Endocrine & metabolic: Hypokalemia (1%), diabetes mellitus, hyperglycemia, hyperlipidemia, hyperthyroidism, menstrual disorder
Gastrointestinal: Nausea (9%), abdominal pain (5%), dyspepsia (5%), weight loss (4%), anorexia (3%), gastroenteritis (3%), stomatitis (3%), vomiting (3%), cholelithiasis, colitis, constipation, esophagitis, flatulence, gastritis, gingivitis, melena, candidiasis (oral), enlarged salivary gland, tooth disorder, xerostomia, taste disturbance
Genitourinary: Urinary tract infection (5%), albuminuria, cystitis, dysuria, hematuria, vaginal candidiasis, prostate disorder, urinary frequency
Hematologic: Anemia
Hepatic: Abnormal LFTs (5%)
(Continued)

Leflunomide *(Continued)*

Neuromuscular & skeletal: Back pain (5%), joint disorder (4%), weakness (3%), tenosynovitis (3%), synovitis (2%), arthralgia (1%), paresthesia (2%), muscle cramps (1%), neck pain, pelvic pain, increased CPK, arthrosis, bursitis, myalgia, bone necrosis, bone pain, tendon rupture, neuralgia, neuritis

Ocular: Blurred vision, cataract, conjunctivitis, eye disorder

Respiratory: Bronchitis (7%), cough (3%), pharyngitis (3%), pneumonia (2%), rhinitis (2%), sinusitis (2%), asthma, dyspnea, epistaxis

Miscellaneous: Infection (4%), accidental injury (5%), allergic reactions (2%), diaphoresis

Drug Interactions

Cytochrome P450 Effect: Inhibits CYP2C8/9 (weak)

Increased Effect/Toxicity: Theoretically, concomitant use of drugs metabolized by this enzyme, including many NSAIDs, may result in increased serum concentrations and possible toxic effects. Coadministration with methotrexate increases the risk of hepatotoxicity. Leflunomide may also enhance the hepatotoxicity of other drugs. Tolbutamide free fraction may be increased. Rifampin may increase serum concentrations of leflunomide. Leflunomide has uricosuric activity and may enhance activity of other uricosuric agents.

Decreased Effect: Administration of cholestyramine and activated charcoal enhance the elimination of leflunomide's active metabolite.

Mechanism of Action Inhibits pyrimidine synthesis, resulting in antiproliferative and anti-inflammatory effects

Pharmacodynamics/Kinetics

Distribution: V_d: 0.13 L/kg

Metabolism: Hepatic to A77 1726 (MI) which accounts for nearly all pharmacologic activity; further metabolism to multiple inactive metabolites; undergoes enterohepatic recirculation

Bioavailability: 80%

Half-life elimination: Mean: 14-15 days; enterohepatic recycling appears to contribute to the long half-life of this agent, since activated charcoal and cholestyramine substantially reduce plasma half-life

Time to peak: 6-12 hours

Excretion: Feces (48%); urine (43%)

Dosage Oral:

Adults: Initial: 100 mg/day for 3 days, followed by 20 mg/day; dosage may be decreased to 10 mg/day in patients who have difficulty tolerating the 20 mg dose. Due to the long half-life of the active metabolite, plasma levels may require a prolonged period to decline after dosage reduction.

Elderly: Although hepatic function may decline with age, no specific dosage adjustment is recommended. Patients should be monitored closely for adverse effects which may require dosage adjustment.

Dosing adjustment in renal impairment: No specific dosage adjustment is recommended. There is no clinical experience in the use of leflunomide in patients with renal impairment. The free fraction of MI is doubled in dialysis patients. Patients should be monitored closely for adverse effects requiring dosage adjustment.

Dosing adjustment in hepatic impairment: No specific dosage adjustment is recommended. Since the liver is involved in metabolic activation and subsequent metabolism/elimination of leflunomide, patients with hepatic impairment should be monitored closely for adverse effects requiring dosage adjustment.

Dosing adjustment in hepatic toxicity: Guidelines for dosage adjustment or discontinuation based on the severity and persistence of ALT elevation secondary to leflunomide have been developed. If ALT elevations >2 times but ≤3 times ULN are noted, reduce dose to 10 mg/day, and monitor closely. If elevations persist or if elevations >3 times ULN are observed, discontinue leflunomide and initiate protocol to accelerate elimination. Cholestyramine (8 g 3 times/day for 1-3 days) or activated charcoal (50 g every 6 hours for 24 hours) may be administered to decrease leflunomide concentrations rapidly. If elevations >3 times ULN persist additional cholestyramine and/or activated charcoal may be required.

Monitoring Parameters A complete blood count (WBC, hemoglobin, hematocrit, and platelet count) as well as serum transaminase determinations should be monitored at baseline and monthly during the initial 6 months of treatment; if stable, monitoring frequency may be decreased to every 6-8 weeks thereafter (continue monthly when used in combination with other immunosuppressive agents). In addition, monitor for signs/symptoms of severe infection, abnormalities in hepatic function tests, or symptoms of hepatotoxicity.

Patient Information Do not take leflunomide if pregnant

Dosage Forms TAB: 10 mg, 20 mg

◆ **Legatrin PM®** **[OTC]** *see* Acetaminophen and Diphenhydramine *on page 26*

◆ **Lente® Iletin® II [DSC]** *see* Insulin Preparations *on page 669*

Lepirudin *(leh puh ROO din)*

U.S. Brand Names Refludan®

Synonyms Lepirudin (rDNA); Recombinant Hirudin

Therapeutic Category Anticoagulant, Thrombin Inhibitor

Use Indicated for anticoagulation in patients with heparin-induced thrombocytopenia (HIT) and associated thromboembolic disease in order to prevent further thromboembolic complications

Unlabeled/Investigational Use Investigational: Prevention or reduction of ischemic complications associated with unstable angina

Pregnancy Risk Factor B

Contraindications Hypersensitivity to hirudins or any component of the formulation

Warnings/Precautions

Hemorrhagic events: Intracranial bleeding following concomitant thrombolytic therapy with rt-PA or streptokinase may be life threatening. For patients with an increased risk of bleeding, a careful assessment weighing the risk of lepirudin administration versus its anticipated benefit has to be made by the treating physician. In particular, this includes the following conditions:

Recent puncture of large vessels or organ biopsy

Anomaly of vessels or organs

Recent cerebrovascular accident, stroke, intracerebral surgery, or other neuroaxial procedures

Severe uncontrolled hypertension

Bacterial endocarditis

Advanced renal impairment

Hemorrhagic diathesis

Recent major surgery

Recent major bleeding (eg, intracranial, gastrointestinal, intraocular, or pulmonary bleeding)

With renal impairment, relative overdose might occur even with standard dosage regimen. The bolus dose and rate of infusion must be reduced in patients with known or suspected renal insufficiency.

Formation of antihirudin antibodies was observed in ~40% of HIT patients treated with lepirudin. This may increase the anticoagulant effect of lepirudin possibly due to delayed renal elimination of active lepirudin-antihirudin complexes. Therefore, strict monitoring of aPTT is necessary also during prolonged therapy. No evidence of neutralization of lepirudin or of allergic reactions associated with positive antibody test results was found.

Serious liver injury (eg, liver cirrhosis) may enhance the anticoagulant effect of lepirudin due to coagulation defects secondary to reduced generation of vitamin K-dependent clotting factors

Clinical trials have provided limited information to support any recommendations for re-exposure to lepirudin (anaphylaxis has been reported).

Common Adverse Reactions As with all anticoagulants, bleeding is the most common adverse event associated with lepirudin. Hemorrhage may occur at virtually any site. Risk is dependent on multiple variables.

HIT patients:

>10%: Hematologic: Anemia (12%), bleeding from puncture sites (11%), hematoma (11%)

1% to 10%:

Cardiovascular: Heart failure (3%), pericardial effusion (1%), ventricular fibrillation (1%)

Central nervous system: Fever (7%)

Dermatologic: Eczema (3%), maculopapular rash (4%)

Gastrointestinal: GI bleeding/rectal bleeding (5%)

Genitourinary: Vaginal bleeding (2%)

Hepatic: Increased transaminases (6%)

Renal: Hematuria (4%)

Respiratory: Epistaxis (4%)

Non-HIT populations (including those receiving thrombolytics and/or contrast media):

1% to 10%: Respiratory: Bronchospasm/stridor/dyspnea/cough

Drug Interactions

Increased Effect/Toxicity: Thrombolytics may enhance anticoagulant properties of lepirudin on aPTT and can increase the risk of bleeding complications. Bleeding risk may also be increased by oral anticoagulants (warfarin) and platelet function inhibitors (NSAIDs, dipyridamole, ticlopidine, clopidogrel, IIb/IIIa antagonists, and aspirin).

Mechanism of Action Lepirudin is a highly specific direct inhibitor of thrombin; lepirudin is a recombinant hirudin derived from yeast cells

Pharmacodynamics/Kinetics

Distribution: Two-compartment model; confined to extracellular fluids.

Metabolism: Via release of amino acids via catabolic hydrolysis of parent drug

Half-life elimination: Initial: ~10 minutes; Terminal: Healthy volunteers: 1.3 hours; Marked renal impairment (Cl_{cr} <15 mL/minute and on hemodialysis): ≤2 days

Excretion: Urine (~48%, 35% as unchanged drug and unchanged drug fragments of parent drug); systemic clearance is proportional to glomerular filtration rate or creatinine clearance

Dosage Adults: Maximum dose: Do not exceed 0.21 mg/kg/hour unless an evaluation of coagulation abnormalities limiting response has been completed. **Dosing is weight-based, however, patients weighing >110 kg should not receive doses greater than the recommended dose for a patient weighing 110 kg (44 mg bolus and initial maximal infusion rate of 16.5 mg/hour).**

Heparin-induced thrombocytopenia: Bolus dose: 0.4 mg/kg IVP (over 15-20 seconds), followed by continuous infusion at 0.15 mg/kg/hour; bolus and infusion must be reduced in renal insufficiency

Concomitant use with thrombolytic therapy: Bolus dose: 0.2 mg/kg IVP (over 15-20 seconds), followed by continuous infusion at 0.1 mg/kg/hour

Dosing adjustments during infusions: Monitor first aPTT 4 hours after the start of the infusion. Subsequent determinations of aPTT should be obtained at least once daily during treatment. More frequent monitoring is recommended in renally impaired patients. Any aPTT ratio measurement out of range (1.5-2.5) should be confirmed prior to adjusting dose, unless a clinical need for immediate reaction exists. If the aPTT is below target range, increase

(Continued)

Lepirudin (Continued)

infusion by 20%. If the aPTT is in excess of the target range, decrease infusion rate by 50%. A repeat aPTT should be obtained 4 hours after any dosing change.

Use in patients scheduled for switch to oral anticoagulants: Reduce lepirudin dose gradually to reach aPTT ratio just above 1.5 before starting warfarin therapy; as soon as INR reaches 2.0, lepirudin therapy should be discontinued.

Dosing adjustment in renal impairment: All patients with a creatinine clearance of <60 mL/minute or a serum creatinine of >1.5 mg/dL should receive a reduction in lepirudin dosage; there is only limited information on the therapeutic use of lepirudin in HIT patients with significant renal impairment; the following dosage recommendations are mainly based on single-dose studies in a small number of patients with renal impairment.

Initial: Bolus dose: 0.2 mg/kg IVP (over 15-20 seconds), followed by adjusted infusion based on renal function; refer to the following infusion rate adjustments based on creatinine clearance (mL/minute) and serum creatinine (mg/dL):

Lepirudin infusion rates in patients with renal impairment: See table.

Lepirudin Infusion Rates in Patients With Renal Impairment

Creatinine Clearance (mL/min)	Serum Creatinine (mg/dL)	Adjusted Infusion Rate	
		% of Standard Initial Infusion Rate	mg/kg/h
45-60	1.6-2.0	50%	0.075
30-44	2.1-3.0	30%	0.045
15-29	3.1-6.0	15%	0.0225
<15	>6.0	Avoid or STOP infusion	

Note: Acute renal failure or hemodialysis: Infusion is to be avoided or stopped. Following the bolus dose, additional bolus doses of 0.1 mg/kg may be administered every other day (only if aPTT falls below lower therapeutic limit).

Administration Administer **only** intravenously; administer I.V. bolus over 15-20 seconds

Monitoring Parameters aPTT levels

Reference Range aPTT 1.5 to 2.5 times the control value

Dosage Forms INJ, powder for reconstitution: 50 mg

♦ **Lepirudin (rDNA)** see Lepirudin on page 720

♦ **Lescol**® see Fluvastatin on page 552

♦ **Lescol**® **XL** see Fluvastatin on page 552

♦ **Lessina**™ see Ethinyl Estradiol and Levonorgestrel on page 484

Letrozole (LET roe zole)

U.S. Brand Names Femara®

Therapeutic Category Antineoplastic Agent, Aromatase Inactivator; Aromatase Inhibitor

Use First-line treatment of hormone receptor positive or hormone receptor unknown, locally advanced, or metastatic breast cancer in postmenopausal women; treatment of advanced breast cancer in postmenopausal women with disease progression following antiestrogen therapy

Pregnancy Risk Factor D

Contraindications Hypersensitivity to letrozole or any component of the formulation; pregnancy

Warnings/Precautions Dose-related effects on hematologic or chemistry parameters have not been observed. Increases in transaminases ≥5 times the upper limit of normal and of bilirubin ≥1.5 times the upper limit of normal were most often, but not always, associated with metastatic liver disease. Safety and efficacy have not been established in pediatric patients.

Common Adverse Reactions

>10%:

Cardiovascular: Hot flushes (5% to 19%)

Central nervous system: Headache (8% to 12%), fatigue (6% to 13%)

Gastrointestinal: Nausea (13% to 17%)

Neuromuscular & skeletal: Musculoskeletal pain, bone pain (22%), back pain (18%), arthralgia (8% to 16%)

Respiratory: Dyspnea (7% to 18%), cough (5% to 13%)

2% to 10%:

Cardiovascular: Chest pain (3% to 8%), peripheral edema (5%), hypertension (5% to 8%)

Central nervous system: Pain (5%), insomnia (7%), dizziness (3% to 5%), somnolence (2% to 3%), depression (<5%), anxiety (<5%), vertigo (<5%)

Dermatologic: Rash (4% to 5%), alopecia (<5%), pruritus (1% to 2%)

Endocrine & metabolic: Breast pain (7%), hypercholesterolemia (3%), hypercalcemia (<5%)

Gastrointestinal: Vomiting (7%), constipation (6% to 10%), diarrhea (5% to 8%), abdominal pain (5% to 6%), anorexia (3% to 5%), dyspepsia (3% to 4%), weight loss (7%), weight gain (2%)

Neuromuscular & skeletal: Weakness (4% to 6%)

Miscellaneous: Flu (6%)

<2%: Angina, cardiac ischemia, coronary artery disease, hemiparesis, hemorrhagic stroke, bilirubin increased, transaminases increased, lymphopenia, MI, portal vein thrombosis, pulmonary embolism, thrombocytopenia, thrombophlebitis, thrombotic stroke, transient ischemic attack, vaginal bleeding, venous thrombosis

Drug Interactions

Cytochrome P450 Effect: Substrate (minor) of CYP2A6, 3A4; **Inhibits** CYP2A6 (weak), 2C19 (weak)

Increased Effect/Toxicity: Inhibitors of this enzyme may, in theory, increase letrozole blood levels. Letrozole inhibits cytochrome P450 isoenzyme 2A6 and 2C19 *in vitro* and may increase blood levels of drugs metabolized by these enzymes. Specific drug interaction studies have not been reported.

Mechanism of Action Competitive inhibitor of the aromatase enzyme system which binds to the heme group of aromatase, a cytochrome P450 enzyme which catalyzes conversion of androgens to estrogens (specifically, androstenedione to estrone and testosterone to estradiol). This leads to inhibition of the enzyme and a significant reduction in plasma estrogen levels. Does not affect synthesis of adrenal or thyroid hormones, aldosterone, or androgens.

Pharmacodynamics/Kinetics

Absorption: Well absorbed; not affected by food

Distribution: V_d: ~1.9 L/kg

Protein binding, plasma: Weak

Metabolism: Hepatic via CYP3A4 and CYP2A6 to an inactive carbinol metabolite

Half-life elimination: Terminal: ~2 days

Time to steady state, plasma: 2-6 weeks

Excretion: Urine (6% as unchanged drug, 75% as glucuronide carbinol metabolite)

Dosage Oral (refer to individual protocols): Adults: Breast cancer: 2.5 mg once daily

Elderly: No dosage adjustments required

Dosage adjustment in renal impairment: No dosage adjustment is required in patients with renal impairment if Cl_{cr} ≥10 mL/minute

Dosage adjustment in hepatic impairment: No dosage adjustment is recommended for patients with mild-to-moderate hepatic impairment. Patients with severe impairment of liver function have not been studied.

Monitoring Parameters Monitor periodically during therapy: complete blood counts, thyroid function tests, serum electrolytes, serum transaminases, and serum creatinine.

Patient Information May experience nausea, vomiting, hot flashes, or loss of appetite; musculoskeletal pain or headache; sleepiness, fatigue, or dizziness (use caution when driving, climbing stairs, or engaging in tasks that require alertness until response to drug is known); constipation; diarrhea; or loss of hair. Report chest pain, pressure, palpitations, or swollen extremities; weakness, severe headache, numbness, or loss of strength in any part of the body; difficulty speaking; vaginal bleeding; unusual signs of bleeding or bruising; difficulty breathing; severe nausea, or muscle pain; or skin rash.

Dosage Forms TAB: 2.5 mg

Leucovorin (loo koe VOR in)

Synonyms Calcium Leucovorin; Citrovorum Factor; Folinic Acid; 5-Formyl Tetrahydrofolate; Leucovorin Calcium

Therapeutic Category Antidote, Methotrexate; Folic Acid Derivative

Use Antidote for folic acid antagonists (methotrexate, trimethoprim, pyrimethamine); treatment of megaloblastic anemias when folate is deficient as in infancy, sprue, pregnancy, and nutritional deficiency when oral folate therapy is not possible; in combination with fluorouracil in the treatment of colon cancer

Pregnancy Risk Factor C

Contraindications Hypersensitivity to leucovorin or any component of the formulation; pernicious anemia or vitamin B_{12} deficient megaloblastic anemias; should **NOT** be administered intrathecally/intraventricularly

Common Adverse Reactions Frequency not defined.

Dermatologic: Rash, pruritus, erythema, urticaria

Hematologic: Thrombocytosis

Respiratory: Wheezing

Miscellaneous: Anaphylactoid reactions

Drug Interactions

Decreased Effect: May decrease efficacy of co-trimoxazole against *Pneumocystis carinii* pneumonitis

Mechanism of Action A reduced form of folic acid, leucovorin supplies the necessary cofactor blocked by methotrexate, enters the cells via the same active transport system as methotrexate. Stabilizes the binding of 5-dUMP and thrymidylate synthetase, enhancing the activity of fluorouracil.

Pharmacodynamics/Kinetics

Onset of action: Oral: ~30 minutes; I.V.: ~5 minutes

Absorption: Oral, I.M.: Rapid and well absorbed

Metabolism: Intestinal mucosa and hepatically to 5-methyl-tetrahydrofolate (5MTHF; active)

Bioavailability: 31% following 200 mg dose; 98% following doses ≤25 mg

Half-life elimination: Leucovorin: 15 minutes; 5MTHF: 33-35 minutes

Excretion: Urine (80% to 90%); feces (5% to 8%)

Dosage Note: This drug should be given parenterally instead of orally in patients with GI toxicity, nausea, vomiting, and when individual doses are >25 mg.

(Continued)

Leucovorin (Continued)

Children and Adults:

Treatment of folic acid antagonist overdosage: Oral: 2-15 mg/day for 3 days or until blood counts are normal, **or** 5 mg every 3 days; doses of 6 mg/day are needed for patients with platelet counts <100,000/mm³

Folate-deficient megaloblastic anemia: I.M.: 1 mg/day

Megaloblastic anemia secondary to congenital deficiency of dihydrofolate reductase: I.M.: 3-6 mg/day

Rescue dose: Initial: I.V.: 10 mg/m², then:

Oral, I.M., I.V., S.C.: 10-15 10 mg/m² every 6 hours until methotrexate level <0.05 μmol/mL; if methotrexate level remains >5 μmol/mL at 48-72 hours after the end of the methotrexate infusion, increase to 20-100 mg/m² every 6 hours until methotrexate level <0.05 μmol/mL

Investigational: Post I.T. methotrexate: Oral, I.V.: 12 mg/m² as a single dose

Administration Refer to individual protocols. Leucovorin calcium should be administered I.M. or I.V. I.V. infusion should not exceed 160 mg/minute of leucovorin. Leucovorin should not be administered concurrently with methotrexate. It is commonly initiated 24 hours after the start of methotrexate. Toxicity to normal tissues may be irreversible if leucovorin is not initiated by ~40 hours after the start of methotrexate.

As a rescue after folate antagonists: Leucovorin may be administered by I.V. bolus injection, I.M. injection, or orally. Doses >25 mg should be administered parenterally.

In combination with fluorouracil: When leucovorin is used to modulate fluorouracil activity, the fluorouracil is usually given after, or at the midpoint, of the leucovorin infusion. Leucovorin is usually administered by I.V. bolus injection or short (10-15 minutes) I.V. infusion. Other administration schedules have been used; refer to individual protocols.

Monitoring Parameters Plasma methotrexate concentration as a therapeutic guide to high-dose methotrexate therapy with leucovorin factor rescue. Leucovorin is continued until the plasma methotrexate level <0.05 μmol/mL.

With 4- to 6-hour high-dose methotrexate infusions, plasma drug values in excess of 50 and 1 μmol at 24 and 48 hours after starting the infusion, respectively, are often predictive of delayed methotrexate clearance

Patient Information Contact prescriber immediately if you have an allergic reaction after taking leucovorin calcium (trouble breathing, wheezing, fainting, skin rash, or hives). Inform prescriber if you are pregnant or are trying to get pregnant before taking leucovorin calcium. Leucovorin calcium can be taken with or without food. Take as directed, at evenly spaced intervals around-the-clock. Maintain hydration (2-3 L of water/day while taking for rescue therapy). For folic acid deficiency, eat foods high in folic acid (eg, meat proteins, bran, dried beans, asparagus, green leafy vegetables).

Dosage Forms INJ, powder for reconstitution: 50 mg, 100 mg, 200 mg, 350 mg. **INJ, solution:** 10 mg/mL (50 mL). **TAB:** 5 mg, 10 mg, 15 mg, 25 mg

◆ **Leucovorin Calcium** see Leucovorin on page 723
◆ **Leukeran®** see Chlorambucil on page 255
◆ **Leukine®** see Sargramostim on page 1124

Leuprolide (loo PROE lide)

U.S. Brand Names Eligard™; Lupron®; Lupron Depot®; Lupron Depot-Ped®; Viadur®

Synonyms Abbott-43818; Leuprolide Acetate; Leuprorelin Acetate; NSC-377526; TAP-144

Therapeutic Category Antineoplastic Agent, Miscellaneous; Gonadotropin Releasing Hormone Analog

Use Palliative treatment of advanced prostate carcinoma; management of endometriosis as initial treatment and/or treatment of recurrent symptoms; preoperative treatment of anemia caused by uterine leiomyomata (fibroids); central precocious puberty

Unlabeled/Investigational Use Treatment of breast, ovarian, and endometrial cancer; infertility; prostatic hyperplasia

Pregnancy Risk Factor X

Contraindications Hypersensitivity to leuprolide, GnRH, GnRH-agonist analogs, or any component of the formulation; spinal cord compression (orchiectomy suggested); undiagnosed abnormal vaginal bleeding; pregnancy; breast-feeding

Warnings/Precautions Transient increases in testosterone serum levels occur at the start of treatment. Tumor flare, bone pain, urinary tract obstruction or spinal cord compression have been reported when used for prostate cancer; closely observe patients for weakness, paresthesias, and urinary tract obstruction in first few weeks of therapy. Observe patients with metastatic vertebral lesions or urinary obstruction closely. Exacerbation of endometriosis or uterine leiomyomata may occur initially. Decreased bone density has been reported when used for ≥6 months. Use caution in patients with a history of psychiatric illness; alteration in mood, memory impairment, and depression have been associated with use.

Common Adverse Reactions

Children: 1% to 10%

Central nervous system: Pain (2%)

Dermatologic: Acne (2%), rash (2%), seborrhea (2%)

Genitourinary: Vaginitis (2%), vaginal bleeding (2%), vaginal discharge (2%)

Local: Injection site reaction (5%)

Adults (frequency dependent upon formulation and indication):

Cardiovascular: Angina, atrial fibrillation, CHF, deep vein thrombosis, edema, hot flashes, hypertension, MI, tachycardia

Central nervous system: Abnormal thinking, agitation, amnesia, confusion, convulsion, dementia, depression, dizziness, fever, headache, insomnia, pain, vertigo

Dermatologic: Alopecia, bruising, cellulitis

Endocrine & metabolic: Breast enlargement, breast tenderness, dehydration, hyperglycemia, hyperlipidemia, hyperphosphatemia, libido decreased, menstrual disorders, potassium decreased

Gastrointestinal: Anorexia, appetite increased, diarrhea, dysphagia, eructation, GI hemorrhage, gingivitis, gum hemorrhage, intestinal obstruction, nausea, peptic ulcer

Genitourinary: Balanitis, impotence, testicular atrophy, urinary disorder, vaginitis

Hematologic: Platelets decreased, PT prolonged, WBC increased

Hepatic: Hepatomegaly, liver function tests abnormal

Local: Abscess, injection site reaction

Neuromuscular & skeletal: Leg cramps, myalgia, paresthesia, weakness

Renal: BUN increased

Respiratory: Allergic reaction, emphysema, hemoptysis, hypoxia, lung edema, pulmonary embolism

Miscellaneous: Body odor, flu-like syndrome, neoplasm, voice alteration

Mechanism of Action Potent inhibitor of gonadotropin secretion; continuous daily administration results in suppression of ovarian and testicular steroidogenesis due to decreased levels of LH and FSH with subsequent decrease in testosterone (male) and estrogen (female) levels. Leuprolide may also have a direct inhibitory effect on the testes, and act by a different mechanism not directly related to reduction in serum testosterone.

Pharmacodynamics/Kinetics

Onset of action: Following transient increase, testosterone suppression occurs in ~2-4 weeks of continued therapy

Distribution: Males: V_d: 27 L

Protein binding: 43% to 49%

Metabolism: Not well defined; forms smaller, inactive peptides and metabolites

Bioavailability: Oral: None; S.C.: 94%

Half-life elimination: 3 hours

Excretion: Urine (<5% as parent and major metabolite)

Dosage

Children: Precocious puberty (consider discontinuing by age 11 for females and by age 12 for males):

S.C. (Lupron®): 20-45 mcg/kg/day; titrate dose upward by 10 mcg/kg/day if down-regulation is not achieved

I.M. (Lupron Depot-Ped®): 0.3 mg/kg/dose given every 28 days (minimum dose: 7.5 mg)

≤25 kg: 7.5 mg

>25-37.5 kg: 11.25 mg

>37.5 kg: 15 mg

Titrate dose upward in 3.75 mg every 4 weeks if down-regulation is not achieved.

Adults:

Advanced prostatic carcinoma:

S.C.:

Eligard™: 7.5 mg monthly **or** 22.5 mg every 3 months **or** 30 mg every 4 months

Lupron®: 1 mg/day

Viadur®: 65 mg implanted subcutaneously every 12 months

I.M.:

Lupron Depot®: 7.5 mg/dose given monthly (every 28-33 days) **or**

Lupron Depot-3®: 22.5 mg every 3 months **or**

Lupron Depot-4®: 30 mg every 4 months

Endometriosis: I.M.: Initial therapy may be with leuprolide alone or in combination with norethindrone; if retreatment for an additional 6 months is necessary, norethindrone should be used. Retreatment is not recommended for longer than one additional 6-month course.

Lupron Depot®: 3.75 mg/month for up to 6 months **or**

Lupron Depot-3®: 11.25 mg every 3 months for up to 2 doses (6 months total duration of treatment)

Uterine leiomyomata (fibroids): I.M. (in combination with iron):

Lupron Depot®: 3.75 mg/month for up to 3 months **or**

Lupron Depot-3®: 11.25 mg as a single injection

Administration

Eligard™: Packaged in two syringes; one contains the Atrigel® polymer system, and the second contains leuprolide acetate powder; follow instructions for mixing; must be administered within 30 minutes of mixing

Lupron Depot®: Do not use needles smaller than 22 gauge; reconstitute only with diluent provided

Viadur® implant: Requires surgical implantation and removal at 12-month intervals

Monitoring Parameters Bone mineral density

Precocious puberty: GnRH testing (blood LH and FSH levels), measurement of bone age every 6-12 months, testosterone in males and estradiol in females; Tanner staging

Prostatic cancer: LH and FSH levels, serum testosterone (2-4 weeks after initiation of therapy), PSA; weakness, paresthesias, and urinary tract obstruction in first few weeks of therapy

Patient Information Do not discontinue medication without prescriber's advice. May cause depression; report changes in mood or memory immediately.

Dosage Forms IMPLANT (Viadur®): 65 mg. **INJ, solution** (Lupron®): 5 mg/mL (2.8 mL). **INJ, powder for reconstitution** [depot formulation]: (Eligard™): 7.5 mg, 22.5 mg, 30 mg; (Lupron (Continued)

Leuprolide (Continued)

Depot®): 3.75 mg, 7.5 mg; (Lupron Depot®-3 Month): 11.25 mg, 22.5 mg; (Lupron Depot®-4 Month): 30 mg; (Lupron Depot-Ped®): 7.5 mg, 11.25 mg, 15 mg

♦ **Leuprolide Acetate** see Leuprolide on page 724
♦ **Leuprorelin Acetate** see Leuprolide on page 724
♦ **Leurocristine Sulfate** see VinCRIStine on page 1306
♦ **Leustatin®** see Cladribine on page 287

Levalbuterol (leve al BYOO ter ole)

Related Information
Bronchodilators, Comparison of Inhaled Sympathomimetics on page 1370

U.S. Brand Names Xopenex®

Synonyms R-albuterol

Therapeutic Category Beta$_2$-Adrenergic Agonist

Use Treatment or prevention of bronchospasm in adults and adolescents ≥6 years of age with reversible obstructive airway disease

Pregnancy Risk Factor C

Contraindications Hypersensitivity to levalbuterol, albuterol, or any component of the formulation

Warnings/Precautions Optimize anti-inflammatory treatment before initiating maintenance treatment with levalbuterol. Do not use as a component of chronic therapy without an anti-inflammatory agent. Only the mildest form of asthma (Step 1 and/or exercise-induced) would not require concurrent use based upon asthma guidelines. Patient must be instructed to seek medical attention in cases where acute symptoms are not relieved or a previous level of response is diminished. The need to increase frequency of use may indicate deterioration of asthma, and treatment must not be delayed.

Use caution in patients with cardiovascular disease (arrhythmia or hypertension or CHF), convulsive disorders, diabetes, glaucoma, hyperthyroidism, or hypokalemia. Beta agonists may cause elevation in blood pressure, heart rate, and result in CNS stimulation/excitation. Beta$_2$ agonists may increase risk of arrhythmia, increase serum glucose, or decrease serum potassium.

Do not exceed recommended dose; serious adverse events including fatalities, have been associated with excessive use of inhaled sympathomimetics. Rarely, paradoxical bronchospasm may occur with use of inhaled bronchodilating agents; this should be distinguished from inadequate response. Use with caution during labor and delivery. All patients should utilize a spacer device when using a metered-dose inhaler. Safety and efficacy have not been established in patients <6 years of age.

Common Adverse Reactions Events reported include those ≥2% with incidence higher than placebo in patients ≥12 years of age.

>10%:
Endocrine & metabolic: Serum glucose increased, serum potassium decreased
Respiratory: Viral infection (7% to 12%), rhinitis (3% to 11%)
>2% to 10%:
Central nervous system: Nervousness (3% to 10%), tremor (≤7%), anxiety (≤3%), dizziness (1% to 3%), migraine (≤3%), pain (1% to 3%)
Cardiovascular: Tachycardia (~3%)
Gastrointestinal: Dyspepsia (1% to 3%)
Neuromuscular & skeletal: Leg cramps (≤3%)
Respiratory: Cough (1% to 4%), nasal edema (1% to 3%), sinusitis (1% to 4%)
Miscellaneous: Flu-like syndrome (1% to 4%), accidental injury (≤3%)

Drug Interactions
Increased Effect/Toxicity: May add to effects of medications which deplete potassium (eg, loop or thiazide diuretics). Cardiac effects of levalbuterol may be potentiated in patients receiving MAO inhibitors, tricyclic antidepressants, sympathomimetics (eg, amphetamine, dobutamine), or inhaled anesthetics (eg, enflurane).
Decreased Effect: Beta-blockers (particularly nonselective agents) block the effect of levalbuterol. Digoxin levels may be decreased.

Mechanism of Action Relaxes bronchial smooth muscle by action on beta-2 receptors with little effect on heart rate

Pharmacodynamics/Kinetics
Onset of action: 10-17 minutes (measured as a 15% increase in FEV$_1$)
Peak effect: 1.5 hours
Duration: 5-6 hours (up to 8 hours in some patients)
Absorption: A portion of inhaled dose is absorbed to systemic circulation
Half-life elimination: 3.3-4 hours
Time to peak, serum: 0.2 hours

Dosage
Children 6-11 years: 0.31 mg 3 times/day via nebulization (maximum dose: 0.63 mg 3 times/day)
Children >12 years and Adults: Inhalation: 0.63 mg 3 times/day at intervals of 6-8 hours, via nebulization. Dosage may be increased to 1.25 mg 3 times/day with close monitoring for adverse effects. Most patients gain optimal benefit from regular use

Elderly: Only a small number of patients have been studied. Although greater sensitivity of some elderly patients cannot be ruled out, no overall differences in safety or effectiveness were observed. An initial dose of 0.63 mg should be used in all patients >65 years of age.

Administration Administered ONLY via nebulization. Safety and efficacy were established when administered with the following nebulizers: PARI LC Jet™, PARI LC Plus™, as well as the following compressors: PARI Master®, Dura-Neb® 2000, and Dura-Neb® 3000.

Monitoring Parameters Asthma symptoms; FEV$_1$, peak flow, and/or other pulmonary function tests; heart rate, blood pressure, CNS stimulation; arterial blood gases (if condition warrants); serum potassium, serum glucose (in selected patients)

Patient Information Use only when necessary or as prescribed; tolerance may develop with overuse. First dose should not be used when you are alone. Avoid OTC medications without consulting prescriber. Maintain adequate hydration (unless instructed to restrict fluid intake). Stress or excessive exercising may exacerbate wheezing or bronchospasm. If diabetic, you will need to monitor serum glucose levels closely until response is known. You may experience tremor, anxiety, dizziness (use caution when driving or engaging in hazardous activities until response to drug is known). Paradoxical bronchospasm can occur; stop drug immediately and notify prescriber if any of the following occur: chest pain or tightness, palpitations; severe headache; difficulty breathing; increased nervousness, restlessness, or trembling; muscle cramps or weakness; seizures.

Dosage Forms SOLN, nebulization: 0.31 mg/3 mL (24s); 0.63 mg/3 mL (24s); 1.25 mg/3 mL (24s)

Levamisole (lee VAM i sole)
U.S. Brand Names Ergamisol®
Synonyms Levamisole Hydrochloride
Therapeutic Category Immune Modulator
Use Adjuvant treatment with fluorouracil in Dukes stage C colon cancer
Pregnancy Risk Factor C
Contraindications Hypersensitivity to levamisole or any component of the formulation
Warnings/Precautions Agranulocytosis can occur asymptomatically and flu-like symptoms can occur without hematologic adverse effects; frequent hematologic monitoring is necessary
Common Adverse Reactions
>10%: Gastrointestinal: Nausea, diarrhea
1% to 10%:
Cardiovascular: Edema
Central nervous system: Fatigue, fever, dizziness, headache, somnolence, depression, nervousness, insomnia
Dermatologic: Dermatitis, alopecia
Gastrointestinal: Stomatitis, vomiting, anorexia, abdominal pain, constipation, taste perversion
Hematologic: Leukopenia
Neuromuscular & skeletal: Rigors, arthralgia, myalgia, paresthesia
Miscellaneous: Infection
Drug Interactions
Increased Effect/Toxicity: Increased toxicity/serum levels of phenytoin. Disulfiram-like reaction with alcohol.
Mechanism of Action Clinically, combined therapy with levamisole and 5-fluorouracil has been effective in treating colon cancer patients, whereas demonstrable activity has been demonstrated. Due to the broad range of pharmacologic activities of levamisole, it has been suggested that the drug may act as a biochemical modulator (of fluorouracil, for example, in colon cancer), an effect entirely independent of immune modulation. Further studies are needed to evaluate the mechanisms of action of the drug in cancer patients.
Pharmacodynamics/Kinetics
Absorption: Well absorbed
Metabolism: Hepatic (>70%)
Half-life elimination: 2-6 hours
Time to peak, serum: 1-2 hours
Excretion: Urine and feces within 48 hours
Dosage Adults: Oral: Initial: 50 mg every 8 hours for 3 days, then 50 mg every 8 hours for 3 days every 2 weeks (fluorouracil is always given concomitantly)

Dosing adjustment in hepatic impairment: May be necessary in patients with liver disease, but no specific guidelines are available
Monitoring Parameters CBC with platelet count prior to therapy and weekly prior to treatment; LFTs every 3 months
Patient Information Report immediately if flu-like symptoms appear; may cause dizziness, drowsiness, impair judgment or coordination.
Dosage Forms TAB: 50 mg

♦ **Levamisole Hydrochloride** see Levamisole on page 727
♦ **Levaquin®** see Levofloxacin on page 734
♦ **Levarterenol Bitartrate** see Norepinephrine on page 913
♦ **Levbid®** see Hyoscyamine on page 641

Levetiracetam (lee va tye RA se tam)
Related Information
Anticonvulsants by Seizure Type on page 1358
(Continued)

Levetiracetam *(Continued)*

U.S. Brand Names Keppra®

Therapeutic Category Anticonvulsant, Miscellaneous

Use Indicated as adjunctive therapy in the treatment of partial onset seizures in adults with epilepsy

Unlabeled/Investigational Use Bipolar disorder; partial onset seizures in children with epilepsy

Pregnancy Risk Factor C

Contraindications Hypersensitivity to levetiracetam or any component of the formulation

Warnings/Precautions Associated with the occurrence of central nervous system adverse events; somnolence and fatigue, which were treated by discontinuation, reduction, or hospitalization; coordination difficulty was treated by reduction, and only one patient was hospitalized. Behavioral abnormalities, such as psychosis, hallucinations, psychotic depression and other behavioral symptoms (agitation, hostility, anxiety, apathy, emotional lability, depersonalization, and depression) were treated by reduction of dose and in some cases hospitalization. Levetiracetam should be withdrawn gradually to minimize the potential of increased seizure frequency. There is a potential for dispensing errors between Keppra® and Kaletra™ (lopinavir/ritonavir); use caution when prescribing, dispensing, or administering. Use caution with renal impairment (dosage adjustment may be necessary).

Common Adverse Reactions

>10%:

Central nervous system: Somnolence (15%), headache (14%)

Neuromuscular & skeletal: Weakness (15%)

Miscellaneous: Infection (13%)

<10%:

Cardiovascular: Chest pain

Central nervous system: Pain (7%), psychotic symptoms (1%), amnesia (2%), ataxia (3%), depression (4%), dizziness (9%), emotional lability (2%), nervousness (4%), vertigo (3%), agitation, anger, aggression, irritability, hostility (2%), anxiety (2%), apathy, depersonalization, confusion, convulsion, fever, insomnia, thinking abnormal

Dermatologic: Bruising, rash

Gastrointestinal: Anorexia (3%), abdominal pain, constipation, diarrhea, dyspepsia, gastroenteritis, gingivitis, nausea, vomiting, weight gain

Hematologic: Decreased erythrocyte counts (3%), decreased leukocytes (2% to 3%)

Neuromuscular & skeletal: Ataxia and other coordination difficulties (3%), paresthesia (2%), arthralgia, back pain, tremor

Ocular: Diplopia (2%), amblyopia, otitis media

Respiratory: Pharyngitis (6%), rhinitis (4%), cough (2%), sinusitis (2%), bronchitis

Miscellaneous: Flu-like symptoms

Drug Interactions

Increased Effect/Toxicity: No interaction was observed in pharmacokinetic trials with other anticonvulsants, including phenytoin, carbamazepine, valproic acid, phenobarbital, lamotrigine, gabapentin, and primidone.

Mechanism of Action The precise mechanism by which levetiracetam exerts its antiepileptic effect is unknown and does not appear to derive from any interaction with known mechanisms involved in inhibitory and excitatory neurotransmission

Pharmacodynamics/Kinetics

Onset of action: Peak effect: 1 hour

Absorption: Rapid and complete

Protein binding: <10%

Metabolism: Not extensive; primarily by enzymatic hydrolysis; forms metabolites (inactive)

Bioavailability: 100%

Half-life elimination: 6-8 hours

Excretion: Urine (66%)

Dialyzable: ~50% of pooled levetiracetam removed during standard 4-hour hemodialysis

Dosage Oral:

Children 4-16 years: Partial onset seizures (unlabeled use): 10-20 mg/kg/day in 2 divided doses; may increase weekly by 10-20 mg/kg, up to a maximum of 60 mg/kg

Children ≥16 years and Adults:

Partial onset seizure: Initial: 500 mg twice daily; additional dosing increments may be given (1000 mg/day additional every 2 weeks) to a maximum recommended daily dose of 3000 mg

Bipolar disorder (unlabeled use): Initial: 500 mg twice daily; if tolerated, increase to 500 mg twice daily; dose may be increased every 3 days until target dose of 3000 mg/day is reached; maximum: 4000 mg/day

Dosing adjustment in renal impairment:

Cl_cr >80 mL/minute: 500-1500 mg every 12 hours

Cl_cr 50-80 mL/minute: 500-1000 mg every 12 hours

Cl_cr 30-50 mL/minute: 250-750 mg every 12 hours

Cl_cr <30 mL/minute: 250-500 mg every 12 hours

End-stage renal disease patients using dialysis: 500-1000 mg every 24 hours; a supplemental dose of 250-500 mg following dialysis is recommended hours

Administration Tablets may be crushed and placed in food if unable to swallow whole (bitter taste may be expected).

Patient Information Notify your prescriber and/or pharmacist if you become pregnant during therapy with levetiracetam; be advised that levetiracetam may cause dizziness and somnolence and accordingly, you should not drive or operate machinery or engage in other hazardous activities until sufficient experience has been gained on levetiracetam to gauge whether it adversely affects your performance of these activities
Dosage Forms SOLN, oral: 100 mg/mL (480 mL). **TAB:** 250 mg, 500 mg, 750 mg

♦ **Levitra®** *see Vardenafil on page 1295*
♦ **Levlen®** *see Ethinyl Estradiol and Levonorgestrel on page 484*
♦ **Levlite™** *see Ethinyl Estradiol and Levonorgestrel on page 484*

Levobetaxolol (lee voe be TAX oh lol)
Related Information
Glaucoma Drug Therapy Comparison *on page 1481*
U.S. Brand Names Betaxon®
Therapeutic Category Beta Blocker, Beta₁ Selective; Beta-Adrenergic Blocker, Ophthalmic
Use Lowering of intraocular pressure in patients with chronic open-angle glaucoma or ocular hypertension
Pregnancy Risk Factor C
Dosage Adults: Ophthalmic: Instill 1 drop in affected eye(s) twice daily
Dosage Forms SOLN, ophthalmic: 0.5% (5 mL, 10 mL, 15 mL)

Levobunolol (lee voe BYOO noe lole)
Related Information
Glaucoma Drug Therapy Comparison *on page 1481*
U.S. Brand Names Betagan®
Synonyms l-Bunolol Hydrochloride; Levobunolol Hydrochloride
Therapeutic Category Beta Blocker, Nonselective; Beta-Adrenergic Blocker, Ophthalmic
Use To lower intraocular pressure in chronic open-angle glaucoma or ocular hypertension
Pregnancy Risk Factor C
Dosage Adults: Ophthalmic: Instill 1 drop in the affected eye(s) 1-2 times/day
Dosage Forms SOLN, ophthalmic: 0.25% (5 mL, 10 mL); 0.5% (5 mL, 10 mL, 15 mL); (Betagan®): 0.25% (5 mL, 10 mL); 0.5% (2 mL, 5 mL, 10 mL, 15 mL)

♦ **Levobunolol Hydrochloride** *see Levobunolol on page 729*

Levobupivacaine (LEE voe byoo PIV a kane)
U.S. Brand Names Chirocaine®
Therapeutic Category Local Anesthetic, Injectable
Use Production of local or regional anesthesia for surgery and obstetrics, and for postoperative pain management
Pregnancy Risk Factor B
Dosage Adults: **Note:** Rapid injection of a large volume of local anesthetic solution should be avoided. Fractional (incremental) doses are recommended.
Guidelines (individual response varies): See table.

	Concentration	Volume	Dose	Motor Block
Surgical Anesthesia				
Epidural for surgery	0.5%-0.75%	10-20 mL	50-150 mg	Moderate to complete
Epidural for C-section	0.5%	20-30 mL	100-150 mg	Moderate to complete
Peripheral nerve	0.25%-0.5%	0.4 mL/kg (30 mL)	1-2 mg/kg (75-150 mg)	Moderate to complete
Ophthalmic	0.75%	5-15 mL	37.5-112.5 mg	Moderate to complete
Local infiltration	0.25%	60 mL	150 mg	Not applicable
Pain Management				
Levobupivacaine can be used epidurally with fentanyl or clonidine; dilutions for epidural administration should be made with preservative free 0.9% saline according to standard hospital procedures for sterility				
Labor analgesia (epidural bolus)	0.25%	10-20 mL	25-50 mg	Minimal to moderate
Postoperative pain (epidural infusion)	0.125%¹-0.25%	4-10 mL/h	5-25 mg/h	Minimal to moderate

¹0.125%: Adjunct therapy with fentanyl or clonidine.

Maximum dosage: Epidural doses up to 375 mg have been administered incrementally to patients during a surgical procedure.
Intraoperative block and postoperative pain: 695 mg in 24 hours
Postoperative epidural infusion over 24 hours: 570 mg
Single-fractionated injection for brachial plexus block: 300 mg
Dosage Forms INJ, solution [preservative free]: 2.5 mg/mL (10 mL, 30 mL); 5 mg/mL (10 mL, 30 mL); 7.5 mg/mL (10 mL, 30 mL)

Levocabastine (LEE voe kab as teen)
U.S. Brand Names Livostin®
Synonyms Levocabastine Hydrochloride
Therapeutic Category Antiallergic, Ophthalmic; Antihistamine; Antihistamine, H₁ Blocker, Ophthalmic; Antihistamine, Ophthalmic
(Continued)

Levocabastine *(Continued)*

Use Treatment of allergic conjunctivitis

Pregnancy Risk Factor C

Dosage Children ≥12 years and Adults: Instill 1 drop in affected eye(s) 4 times/day for up to 2 weeks

Dosage Forms SUSP, ophthalmic: 0.05% (5 mL, 10 mL)

♦ **Levocabastine Hydrochloride** *see* Levocabastine *on page 729*

Levocarnitine *(lee voe KAR ni teen)*

U.S. Brand Names Carnitor®

Synonyms L-Carnitine

Therapeutic Category Nutritional Supplement

Use Orphan drug:

Oral: Primary systemic carnitine deficiency; acute and chronic treatment of patients with an inborn error of metabolism which results in secondary carnitine deficiency

I.V.: Acute and chronic treatment of patients with an inborn error of metabolism which results in secondary carnitine deficiency; prevention and treatment of carnitine deficiency in patients with end-stage renal disease (ESRD) who are undergoing hemodialysis.

Pregnancy Risk Factor B

Warnings/Precautions Caution in patients with seizure disorders or in those at risk of seizures (CNS mass or medications which may lower seizure threshold). Both new-onset seizure activity as well as an increased frequency of seizures has been observed.

Common Adverse Reactions Frequencies noted with I.V. therapy (hemodialysis patients):

Cardiovascular: Hypertension (18% to 21%), peripheral edema (3% to 6%)

Central nervous system: Dizziness (10% to 18%), fever (5% to 12%), paresthesia (3% to 12%), depression (5% to 6%)

Endocrine & metabolic: Hypercalcemia (6% to 15%)

Gastrointestinal: Diarrhea (9% to 35%), abdominal pain (5% to 21%), vomiting (9% to 21%), nausea (5% to 12%)

Neuromuscular & skeletal: Weakness (9% to 12%)

Miscellaneous: Allergic reaction (2% to 6%)

Mechanism of Action Carnitine is a naturally occurring metabolic compound which functions as a carrier molecule for long-chain fatty acids within the mitochondria, facilitating energy production. Carnitine deficiency is associated with accumulation of excess acyl CoA esters and disruption of intermediary metabolism. Carnitine supplementation increases carnitine plasma concentrations. The effects on specific metabolic alterations have not been evaluated. ESRD patients on maintenance HD may have low plasma carnitine levels because of reduced intake of meat and dairy products, reduced renal synthesis, and dialytic losses. Certain clinical conditions (malaise, muscle weakness, cardiomyopathy and arrhythmias) in HD patients may be related to carnitine deficiency.

Pharmacodynamics/Kinetics

Metabolism: Hepatic (limited with moderate renal impairment), to trimethylamine (TMA) and trimethylamine N-oxide (TMAO)

Bioavailability: Tablet/solution: 15% to 16%

Half-life elimination: 17.4 hours

Time to peak: Tablet/solution: 3.3 hours

Excretion: Urine (4% to 9% as unchanged drug); metabolites also eliminated in urine

Dosage

Oral:

Infants/Children: Initial: 50 mg/kg/day; titrate to 50-100 mg/kg/day in divided doses with a maximum dose of 3 g/day

Adults: 990 mg (oral tablets) 2-3 times/day or 1-3 g/day (oral solution)

I.V.:

Metabolic disorders: 50 mg/kg as a slow 2- to 3-minute I.V. bolus or by I.V. infusion

Severe metabolic crisis:

A loading dose of 50 mg/kg over 2-3 minutes followed by an equivalent dose over the following 24 hours administered as every 3 hours or every 4 hours (never less than every 6 hours either by infusion or by intravenous injection)

All subsequent daily doses are recommended to be in the range of 50 mg/kg or as therapy may require

The highest dose administered has been 300 mg/kg

It is recommended that a plasma carnitine concentration be obtained prior to beginning parenteral therapy accompanied by weekly and monthly monitoring

ESRD patients on hemodialysis:

Predialysis levocarnitine concentrations below normal (40-50 μmol/L): 10-20 mg/kg dry body weight as a slow 2- to 3-minute bolus after each dialysis session

Dosage adjustments should be guided by predialysis trough levocarnitine concentrations and downward dose adjustments (to 5 mg/kg after dialysis) may be made as early as every 3rd or 4th week of therapy

Note: Safety and efficacy of oral carnitine have not been established in ESRD. Chronic administration of high oral doses to patients with severely compromised renal function or ESRD patients on dialysis may result in accumulation of metabolites.

Administration

Oral: Solution may be dissolved in either drink or liquid food, and should be consumed slowly. Doses should be spaced every 3 to 4 hours throughout the day, preferably during or following meals.

I.V.: Hemodialysis patients: Injection should be administered over 2-3 minutes into the venous return line after each dialysis session.

Monitoring Parameters Plasma concentrations should be obtained prior to beginning parenteral therapy, and should be monitored weekly to monthly. In metabolic disorders: monitor blood chemistry, vital signs, and plasma carnitine levels (maintain between 35-60 µmol/L). In ESRD patients on dialysis: Plasma levels below the normal range should prompt initiation of therapy. Monitor predialysis (trough) plasma carnitine levels.

Reference Range Normal carnitine levels are 40-50 µmol/L; levels should be maintained on therapy between 35-60 µmol/L

Patient Information The oral solution should be consumed slowly and spaced evenly throughout the day to improve tolerance

Dosage Forms CAP: 250 mg. **INJ, solution** (Carnitor®): 200 mg/mL (5 mL). **SOLN, oral** (Carnitor®): 100 mg/mL (118 mL). **TAB:** 500 mg; (Carnitor®): 330 mg

Levodopa (lee voe DOE pa)

U.S. Brand Names Dopar®; Larodopa®

Synonyms L-3-Hydroxytyrosine; L-Dopa

Therapeutic Category Anti-Parkinson's Agent, Dopamine Agonist; Dopaminergic Agent, Antiparkinson's

Use Treatment of Parkinson's disease

Unlabeled/Investigational Use Diagnostic agent for growth hormone deficiency

Pregnancy Risk Factor C

Contraindications Hypersensitivity to levodopa or any component of the formulation; narrow-angle glaucoma; use of MAO inhibitors within prior 14 days (however, may be administered concomitantly with the manufacturer's recommended dose of an MAO inhibitor with selectivity for MAO type B); history of melanoma or any undiagnosed skin lesions

Warnings/Precautions Use with caution in patients with history of cardiovascular disease (including myocardial infarction and arrhythmias); pulmonary diseases such as asthma, psychosis, wide-angle glaucoma, peptic ulcer disease; as well as in renal, hepatic, or endocrine disease. Sudden discontinuation of levodopa may cause a worsening of Parkinson's disease. Elderly may be more sensitive to CNS effects of levodopa. May cause or exacerbate dyskinesias. May cause orthostatic hypotension; Parkinson's disease patients appear to have an impaired capacity to respond to a postural challenge. Use with caution in patients at risk of hypotension (such as those receiving antihypertensive drugs) or where transient hypotensive episodes would be poorly tolerated (cardiovascular disease or cerebrovascular disease). Observe patients closely for development of depression with concomitant suicidal tendencies. Safety and effectiveness in pediatric patients have not been established. Some products may contain tartrazine. Dopaminergic agents have been associated with a syndrome resembling neuroleptic malignant syndrome on withdrawal or significant dosage reduction after long-term use. Pyridoxine may reverse effects of levodopa. Toxic reactions have occurred with dextromethorphan.

Common Adverse Reactions Frequency not defined.

Cardiovascular: Orthostatic hypotension, arrhythmias, chest pain, hypertension, syncope, palpitations, phlebitis

Central nervous system: Dizziness, anxiety, confusion, nightmares, headache, hallucinations, on-off phenomenon, decreased mental acuity, memory impairment, disorientation, delusions, euphoria, agitation, somnolence, insomnia, gait abnormalities, nervousness, ataxia, EPS, falling

Gastrointestinal: Anorexia, nausea, vomiting, constipation, GI bleeding, duodenal ulcer, diarrhea, dyspepsia, taste alterations, sialorrhea, heartburn

Genitourinary: Discoloration of urine, urinary frequency

Hematologic: Hemolytic anemia, agranulocytosis, thrombocytopenia, leukopenia, decreased hemoglobin and hematocrit, abnormalities in AST and ALT, LDH, bilirubin, BUN, Coombs' test

Neuromuscular & skeletal: Choreiform and involuntary movements, paresthesia, bone pain, shoulder pain, muscle cramps, weakness

Ocular: Blepharospasm

Renal: Difficult urination

Respiratory: Dyspnea, cough

Miscellaneous: Hiccups, discoloration of sweat

Drug Interactions

Increased Effect/Toxicity: Concurrent use of levodopa with nonselective MAO inhibitors may result in hypertensive reactions via an increased storage and release of dopamine, norepinephrine, or both. Use with carbidopa to minimize reactions if combination is necessary; otherwise avoid combination.

Decreased Effect: Antipsychotics, benzodiazepines, L-methionine, phenytoin, pyridoxine, spiramycin, and tacrine may inhibit the antiparkinsonian effects of levodopa; monitor for reduced effect. Antipsychotics may inhibit the antiparkinsonian effects of levodopa via dopamine receptor blockade. Use antipsychotics with low dopamine blockade (clozapine, olanzapine, quetiapine). High-protein diets may inhibit levodopa's efficacy; avoid high protein foods. Iron binds levodopa and reduces its bioavailability; separate doses of iron and levodopa.

Mechanism of Action Increases dopamine levels in the brain, then stimulates dopaminergic receptors in the basal ganglia to improve the balance between cholinergic and dopaminergic activity

Pharmacodynamics/Kinetics

Duration: Variable, usually 6-12 hours

(Continued)

Levodopa *(Continued)*

Absorption: May be reduced with a high-protein meal

Metabolism: Peripheral decarboxylation to dopamine; small amounts reach brain and are decarboxylated to active dopamine

Half-life elimination: 1.2-2.3 hours

Time to peak, serum: 1-2 hours

Excretion: Urine (80% as dopamine, norepinephrine, and homovanillic acid)

Dosage Oral:

Children (administer as a single dose to evaluate growth hormone deficiency [unlabeled use]): 0.5 g/m^2 **or**

    <30 lb: 125 mg

    30-70 lb: 250 mg

    >70 lb: 500 mg

Adults: Parkinson's disease: 500-1000 mg/day in divided doses every 6-12 hours; increase by 100-750 mg/day every 3-7 days until response or total dose of 8000 mg is reached

A significant therapeutic response may not be obtained for 6 months

Administration Administer with meals to decrease GI upset

Monitoring Parameters Serum growth hormone concentration

Patient Information Avoid vitamins with B$_6$ (pyridoxine); can take with food to prevent GI upset; do not stop taking this drug even if you do not think it is working; dizziness, lightheadedness, fainting may occur when you get up from a sitting or lying position.

Dosage Forms CAP: 100 mg, 250 mg, 500 mg. **TAB:** 100 mg, 250 mg, 500 mg

Levodopa and Carbidopa *(lee voe DOE pa & kar bi DOE pa)*

Related Information

Parkinson's Agents Comparison *on page 1402*

U.S. Brand Names Sinemet®; Sinemet® CR

Synonyms Carbidopa and Levodopa

Therapeutic Category Anti-Parkinson's Agent, Dopamine Agonist; Dopaminergic Agent, Antiparkinson's

Use Idiopathic Parkinson's disease; postencephalitic parkinsonism; symptomatic parkinsonism

Unlabeled/Investigational Use Restless leg syndrome

Pregnancy Risk Factor C

Contraindications Hypersensitivity to levodopa, carbidopa, or any component of the formulation; narrow-angle glaucoma; use of MAO inhibitors within prior 14 days (however, may be administered concomitantly with the manufacturer's recommended dose of an MAO inhibitor with selectivity for MAO type B); history of melanoma or undiagnosed skin lesions

Warnings/Precautions Use with caution in patients with history of cardiovascular disease (including myocardial infarction and arrhythmias); pulmonary diseases such as asthma, psychosis, wide-angle glaucoma, peptic ulcer disease; as well as in renal, hepatic, or endocrine disease. Sudden discontinuation of levodopa may cause a worsening of Parkinson's disease. Elderly may be more sensitive to CNS effects of levodopa. May cause or exacerbate dyskinesias. May cause orthostatic hypotension; Parkinson's disease patients appear to have an impaired capacity to respond to a postural challenge; use with caution in patients at risk of hypotension (such as those receiving antihypertensive drugs) or where transient hypotensive episodes would be poorly tolerated (cardiovascular disease or cerebrovascular disease). Observe patients closely for development of depression with concomitant suicidal tendencies. Some products may contain tartrazine. Has been associated with a syndrome resembling neuroleptic malignant syndrome on withdrawal or significant dosage reduction after long-term use. Toxic reactions have occurred with dextromethorphan. Protein in the diet should be distributed throughout the day to avoid fluctuations in levodopa absorption.

Common Adverse Reactions Frequency not defined.

Cardiovascular: Orthostatic hypotension, arrhythmias, chest pain, hypertension, syncope, palpitations, phlebitis

Central nervous system: Dizziness, anxiety, confusion, nightmares, headache, hallucinations, on-off phenomenon, decreased mental acuity, memory impairment, disorientation, delusions, euphoria, agitation, somnolence, insomnia, gait abnormalities, nervousness, ataxia, EPS, falling, psychosis, peripheral neuropathy, seizures (causal relationship not established)

Dermatologic: Rash, alopecia, malignant melanoma, hypersensitivity (angioedema, urticaria, pruritus, bullous lesions, Henoch-Schönlein purpura)

Endocrine & metabolic: Increased libido

Gastrointestinal: Anorexia, nausea, vomiting, constipation, GI bleeding, duodenal ulcer, diarrhea, dyspepsia, taste alterations, sialorrhea, heartburn

Genitourinary: Discoloration of urine, urinary frequency

Hematologic: Hemolytic anemia, agranulocytosis, thrombocytopenia, leukopenia; decreased hemoglobin and hematocrit; abnormalities in AST and ALT, LDH, bilirubin, BUN, Coombs' test

Neuromuscular & skeletal: Choreiform and involuntary movements, paresthesia, bone pain, shoulder pain, muscle cramps, weakness

Ocular: Blepharospasm, oculogyric crises (may be associated with acute dystonic reactions)

Renal: Difficult urination

Respiratory: Dyspnea, cough

Miscellaneous: Hiccups, discoloration of sweat, diaphoresis (increased)

Drug Interactions

Increased Effect/Toxicity: Concurrent use of levodopa with nonselective MAO inhibitors may result in hypertensive reactions via an increased storage and release of dopamine, norepinephrine, or both. Use with carbidopa to minimize reactions if combination is necessary; otherwise avoid combination.

Decreased Effect: Antipsychotics, benzodiazepines, L-methionine, phenytoin, pyridoxine, spiramycin, and tacrine may inhibit the antiparkinsonian effects of levodopa; monitor for reduced effect. Antipsychotics may inhibit the antiparkinsonian effects of levodopa via dopamine receptor blockade. Use antipsychotics with low dopamine blockade (clozapine, olanzapine, quetiapine). High-protein diets may inhibit levodopa's efficacy; avoid high protein foods. Iron binds levodopa and reduces its bioavailability; separate doses of iron and levodopa.

Mechanism of Action Parkinson's symptoms are due to a lack of striatal dopamine; levodopa circulates in the plasma to the blood-brain-barrier (BBB), where it crosses, to be converted by striatal enzymes to dopamine; carbidopa inhibits the peripheral plasma breakdown of levodopa by inhibiting its decarboxylation, and thereby increases available levodopa at the BBB

Pharmacodynamics/Kinetics

Duration: Variable, 6-12 hours; longer with sustained release forms

See individual agents.

Dosage Oral:

Adults: Initial: Carbidopa 25 mg/levodopa 100 mg 2-4 times/day, increase as necessary to a maximum of carbidopa 200 mg/levodopa 2000 mg per day

Restless leg syndrome (unlabeled use): Carbidopa 25 mg/levodopa 100 mg given 30-60 minutes before bedtime; may repeat dose once

Elderly: Initial: Carbidopa 25 mg/levodopa 100 mg twice daily, increase as necessary

Conversion from Sinemet® to Sinemet® CR (50/200): (Sinemet® [total daily dose of levodopa] / Sinemet® CR)

300-400 mg / 1 tablet twice daily

500-600 mg / 1½ tablets twice daily or one 3 times/day

700-800 mg / 4 tablets in 3 or more divided doses

900-1000 mg / 5 tablets in 3 or more divided doses

Intervals between doses of Sinemet® CR should be 4-8 hours while awake

Administration Administer with meals to decrease GI upset

Monitoring Parameters Blood pressure, standing and sitting/supine; symptoms of parkinsonism, dyskinesias, mental status

Patient Information Do not stop taking this drug even if you do not think it is working; take on an empty stomach if possible; if GI distress occurs, take with meals; rise carefully from lying or sitting position as dizziness, lightheadedness, or fainting may occur; do not crush or chew sustained release product

Dosage Forms TAB (Sinemet®): 10/100: Carbidopa 10 mg and levodopa 100 mg; 25/100: Carbidopa 25 mg and levodopa 100 mg; 25/250: Carbidopa 25 mg and levodopa 250 mg. **TAB, sustained release** (Sinemet® CR): Carbidopa 25 mg and levodopa 100 mg; carbidopa 50 mg and levodopa 200 mg

Levodopa, Carbidopa, and Entacapone

(lee voe DOE pa, kar bi DOE pa, & en TA ka pone)

U.S. Brand Names Stalevo™

Synonyms Carbidopa, Levodopa, and Entacapone; Entacapone, Carbidopa, and Levodopa

Therapeutic Category Anti-Parkinson's Agent, COMT Inhibitor; Anti-Parkinson's Agent, Dopamine Agonist

Use Treatment of idiopathic Parkinson's disease

Pregnancy Risk Factor C

Dosage Oral: Adults: Parkinson's disease:

Note: All strengths of Stalevo™ contain a carbidopa/levodopa ratio of 1:4 plus entacapone 200 mg.

Dose should be individualized based on therapeutic response; doses may be adjusted by changing strength or adjusting interval. Fractionated doses are not recommended and only 1 tablet should be given at each dosing interval; maximum dose: 8 tablets/day (equivalent to entacapone 1600 mg/day)

Patients previously treated with carbidopa/levodopa immediate release tablets (ratio of 1:4):

With current entacapone therapy: May switch directly to corresponding strength of combination tablet. No data available on transferring patients from controlled release preparations or products with a 1:10 ratio of carbidopa/levodopa.

Without entacapone therapy:

If current levodopa dose is >600 mg/day: Levodopa dose reduction may be required when adding entacapone to therapy; therefore, titrate dose using individual products first (carbidopa/levodopa immediate release with a ratio of 1:4 plus entacapone 200 mg); then transfer to combination product once stabilized.

If current levodopa dose is <600 mg without dyskinesias: May transfer to corresponding dose of combination product; monitor, dose reduction of levodopa may be required.

Dosage adjustment in renal impairment: Use caution with severe renal impairment; specific dosing recommendations not available

Dosage adjustment in hepatic impairment: Use with caution; specific dosing recommendations not available

(Continued)

Levodopa, Carbidopa, and Entacapone *(Continued)*

Dosage Forms TAB, film coated: (50): Carbidopa 12.5 mg, levodopa 50 mg, and entacapone 200 mg; (100): Carbidopa 25 mg, levodopa 100 mg, and entacapone 200 mg; (150): Carbidopa 37.5 mg, levodopa 150 mg, and entacapone 200 mg

♦ **Levo-Dromoran®** *see Levorphanol on page 739*

Levofloxacin *(lee voe FLOKS a sin)*
Related Information
Antimicrobial Drugs of Choice *on page 1440*
Community-Acquired Pneumonia in Adults *on page 1457*
Tuberculosis Treatment Guidelines *on page 1466*

U.S. Brand Names Levaquin®; Quixin™

Therapeutic Category Antibiotic, Ophthalmic; Antibiotic, Quinolone

Use
Systemic: Treatment of mild, moderate, or severe infections caused by susceptible organisms. Includes the treatment of community-acquired pneumonia (including penicillin-resistant strains of *S. pneumoniae*); nosocomial pneumonia; chronic bronchitis (acute bacterial exacerbation); acute maxillary sinusitis; urinary tract infection (uncomplicated or complicated), including acute pyelonephritis caused by *E. coli* ; prostatitis (chronic bacterial); skin or skin structure infections (uncomplicated or complicated)

Ophthalmic: Treatment of bacterial conjunctivitis caused by susceptible organisms

Pregnancy Risk Factor C

Contraindications Hypersensitivity to levofloxacin, any component of the formulation, or other quinolones

Warnings/Precautions
Systemic: Not recommended in children <18 years of age; CNS stimulation may occur (tremor, restlessness, confusion, and very rarely hallucinations or seizures); use with caution in patients with known or suspected CNS disorders or renal dysfunction; use caution to avoid possible photosensitivity reactions during and for several days following fluoroquinolone therapy

Rare cases of torsade de pointes have been reported in patients receiving levofloxacin. Use caution in patients with bradycardia, hypokalemia, hypomagnesemia, or in those receiving concurrent therapy with Class Ia or Class III antiarrhythmics.

Severe hypersensitivity reactions, including anaphylaxis, have occurred with quinolone therapy. If an allergic reaction occurs (itching, urticaria, dyspnea or facial edema, loss of consciousness, tingling, cardiovascular collapse), discontinue drug immediately. Prolonged use may result in superinfection; pseudomembranous colitis may occur and should be considered in all patients who present with diarrhea. Tendon inflammation and/or rupture has been reported; discontinue at first sign of tendon inflammation or pain. Quinolones may exacerbate myasthenia gravis.

Ophthalmic solution: For topical use only. Do not inject subconjunctivally or introduce into anterior chamber of the eye. Contact lenses should not be worn during treatment for bacterial conjunctivitis. Safety and efficacy in children <1 year of age have not been established.

Common Adverse Reactions 1% to 10%:
Central nervous system: Dizziness, fever, headache, insomnia
Gastrointestinal: Nausea, vomiting, diarrhea, constipation
Ocular (with ophthalmic solution use): Decreased vision (transient), foreign body sensation, transient ocular burning, ocular pain or discomfort, photophobia
Respiratory: Pharyngitis

Drug Interactions
Increased Effect/Toxicity: Quinolones may cause increased levels of azlocillin, cyclosporine, and caffeine/theophylline (effect of levofloxacin on theophylline metabolism appears limited). Azlocillin, cimetidine, loop diuretics (furosemide, torsemide), and probenecid increase quinolone levels (decreased renal secretion). An increased incidence of seizures may occur with foscarnet or NSAIDs. The hypoprothrombinemic effect of warfarin is enhanced by some quinolone antibiotics. QT$_c$-prolonging agents (including Class Ia and Class III antiarrhythmics, erythromycin, cisapride, antipsychotics, and cyclic antidepressants) should be avoided with levofloxacin. Levofloxacin does not alter warfarin levels, but may alter the gastrointestinal flora. Monitor INR closely during therapy. Concurrent use of corticosteroids may increase risk of tendon rupture.

Decreased Effect: Metal cations (magnesium, aluminum, iron, and zinc) bind quinolones in the gastrointestinal tract and inhibit absorption (by up to 98%). Due to electrolyte content, antacids, electrolyte supplements, sucralfate, quinapril, and some didanosine formulations should be avoided. Levofloxacin should be administered 2 hours before or 2 hours after these agents. Antineoplastic agents may decrease the absorption of quinolones.

Mechanism of Action As the S (-) enantiomer of the fluoroquinolone, ofloxacin, levofloxacin, inhibits DNA-gyrase in susceptible organisms thereby inhibits relaxation of supercoiled DNA and promotes breakage of DNA strands. DNA gyrase (topoisomerase II), is an essential bacterial enzyme that maintains the superhelical structure of DNA and is required for DNA replication and transcription, DNA repair, recombination, and transposition.

Pharmacodynamics/Kinetics
Absorption: Rapid and complete
Distribution: V$_d$: 1.25 L/kg; CSF concentrations ~15% of serum levels; high concentrations are achieved in prostate and gynecological tissues, sinus, breast milk, and saliva
Protein binding: 50%

Metabolism: Minimally hepatic
Bioavailability: 100%
Half-life elimination: 6 hours
Time to peak, serum: 1 hour
Excretion: Primarily urine (as unchanged drug)

Dosage

Oral, I.V. (infuse I.V. solution over 60 minutes): Adults:
  Chronic bronchitis (acute bacterial exacerbation): 500 mg every 24 hours for at least 7 days
  Maxillary sinusitis (acute): 500 mg every 24 hours for 10-14 days
  Pneumonia:
    Community-acquired: 500 mg every 24 hours for 7-14 days or 750 mg every 24 hours for 5 days
    Nosocomial: 750 mg every 24 hours for 7-14 days
  Prostatitis (chronic bacterial): 500 mg every 24 hours for 28 days
  Skin infections:
    Uncomplicated: 500 mg every 24 hours for 7-10 days
    Complicated: 750 mg every 24 hours for 7-14 days
  Urinary tract infections:
    Uncomplicated: 250 mg once daily for 3 days
    Complicated, including acute pyelonephritis: 250 mg every 24 hours for 10 days
Ophthalmic: Children ≥1 year and Adults:
  Treatment day 1 and day 2: Instill 1-2 drops into affected eye(s) every 2 hours while awake, up to 8 times/day
  Treatment day 3 through day 7: Instill 1-2 drops into affected eye(s) every 4 hours while awake, up to 4 times/day

Dosing adjustment in renal impairment:

Chronic bronchitis, acute maxillary sinusitis, uncomplicated skin infection, community-acquired pneumonia, chronic bacterial prostatitis, complicated UTI, or acute pyelonephritis: First dose as indicated in patients with normal renal function (250 mg or 500 mg), followed by:
  Cl_{cr} 20-49 mL/minute: 250 mg every 24 hours
  Cl_{cr} 10-19 mL/minute: 250 mg every 48 hours
  Uncomplicated UTI: No dosage adjustment required
Complicated skin infection, community-acquired pneumonia, or nosocomial pneumonia:
  Cl_{cr} 20-49 mL/minute: Administer 750 mg every 48 hours
  Cl_{cr} 10-19 mL/minute: Administer 500 mg every 48 hours (initial: 750 mg)
Hemodialysis/CAPD: 250 mg every 48 hours (initial: 500 mg for most infections; initial: 750 mg for complicated skin/soft tissue infections followed by 500 mg every 48 hours)

Administration

Oral: May be administered without regard to meals.
I.V.: Infuse I.V. solution over 60 minutes. Too rapid of infusion can lead to hypotension. Avoid administration through an intravenous line with a solution containing multivalent cations (ie, magnesium, calcium).

Monitoring Parameters Evaluation of organ system functions (renal, hepatic, ophthalmologic, and hematopoietic) is recommended periodically during therapy; the possibility of crystalluria should be assessed; WBC and signs of infection

Patient Information

Oral: Take per recommended schedule, preferably on an empty stomach (1 hour before or 2 hours after meals). Maintain adequate hydration (2-3 L/day of fluids unless instructed to restrict fluid intake). Take complete prescription; do not skip doses. Do not take with antacids; separate by 2 hours. You may experience dizziness, lightheadedness, or confusion; use caution when driving or engaging in tasks that require alertness until response to drug is known. Small frequent meals and frequent mouth care may reduce nausea or vomiting. You may experience photosensitivity; use sunscreen, wear protective clothing and eyewear, and avoid direct sunlight. Report palpitations or chest pain, persistent diarrhea, GI disturbances or abdominal pain, muscle tremor or pain, yellowing of eyes or skin, easy bruising or bleeding, unusual fatigue, fever, chills, signs of infection, or worsening of condition. Report immediately any rash, itching, unusual CNS changes, or any facial swelling. Report immediately any pain, inflammation, or rupture of tendon.

Ophthalmic: Wash hands before instilling solution. Sit or lie down to instill. Open eye, look at ceiling, and instill prescribed amount of solution. Close eye and roll eye in all directions, and apply gentle pressure to inner corner of eye. Do not let tip of applicator touch eye or contaminate tip of applicator. Temporary stinging or blurred vision may occur. Report persistent pain, burning, vision disturbances, swelling, itching, or worsening of condition. Discontinue medication and contact prescriber immediately if you develop a rash or allergic reaction. Do not wear contact lenses.

Dosage Forms INF [premixed in D_5W] (Levaquin®): 5 mg/mL (50 mL, 100 mL, 150 mL). **INJ, solution** [preservative free] (Levaquin®): 25 mg/mL (20 mL, 30 mL). **SOLN, ophthalmic** (Quixin™): 0.5% (5 mL). **TAB** (Levaquin®): 250 mg, 500 mg, 750 mg

Levomethadyl Acetate Hydrochloride

(lee voe METH a dil AS e tate hye droe KLOR ide)

U.S. Brand Names ORLAAM® [DSC]

Therapeutic Category Analgesic, Narcotic

(Continued)

Levomethadyl Acetate Hydrochloride *(Continued)*

Use Management of opiate dependence; should be reserved for use in treatment of opiate-addicted patients who fail to show an acceptable response to other adequate treatments for addiction

Restrictions C-II; must be dispensed in a designated clinic setting only

Pregnancy Risk Factor C

Contraindications Hypersensitivity to levomethadyl or any component of the formulation; known or suspected QT_c prolongation (male: 430 msec, female: 450 msec); bradycardia (<50 bpm); significant cardiac disease; concurrent treatment with drugs known to prolong QT interval, including class I and III antiarrhythmics; concurrent treatment with MAO inhibitors; hypokalemia or hypomagnesemia

Warnings/Precautions May cause QT prolongation. Use of levomethadyl has been associated with rare, but serious cardiac arrhythmias. Perform ECG prior to treatment, 12-14 days after initiation, and periodically thereafter. Not recommended for use outside of the treatment of opiate addiction; shall be dispensed only by treatment programs approved by FDA, DEA, and the designated state authority. Approved treatment programs shall dispense and use levomethadyl in oral form only and according to the treatment requirements stipulated in federal regulations. Failure to abide by these requirements may result in injunction precluding operation of the program, seizure of the drug supply, revocation of the program approval, and possible criminal prosecution.

Use with **extreme caution** in patients with head injury or increased intracranial pressure (ICP). Use with caution in patients with respiratory disease or asthma. Has been studied only in 3 times/week or every-other-day dosing; daily administration may lead to accumulation/risk of overdose. Use caution in the elderly and in patients with hepatic or renal dysfunctions. Safety and efficacy in pediatric patients have not been established.

Common Adverse Reactions

>10%:
  Central nervous system: Malaise
  Miscellaneous: Flu syndrome
1% to 10%:
  Central nervous system: CNS depression, sedation, chills, abnormal dreams, anxiety, euphoria, headache, insomnia, nervousness, hypesthesia
  Endocrine & metabolic: Hot flashes (males 2:1)
  Gastrointestinal: Abdominal pain, constipation, diarrhea, xerostomia, nausea, vomiting
  Genitourinary: Urinary tract spasm, difficult ejaculation, impotence, decreased sex drive
  Neuromuscular & skeletal: Arthralgia, back pain, weakness
  Ocular: Miosis, blurred vision

Drug Interactions

Cytochrome P450 Effect: Substrate of CYP2B6 (minor), 3A4 (major)

Increased Effect/Toxicity: CNS depressants, including sedatives, tranquilizers, propoxyphene, antidepressants, benzodiazepines, and ethanol may result in serious overdose when used with levomethadyl. Enzyme inducers (carbamazepine, phenobarbital, rifampin, phenytoin) may enhance the metabolism of levomethadyl leading to an increase in levomethadyl peak effect (however, duration of action is shortened). Enzyme inhibitors such as erythromycin, cimetidine, and ketoconazole may increase the risk of arrhythmia (including torsade de pointes) or may increase the duration of action of levomethadyl. Concurrent use of QT_c-prolonging agents is contraindicated (includes class I and III antiarrhythmics, cisapride, erythromycin, select quinolones, mesoridazine, thioridazine, zonisamide). Concurrent use of MAO inhibitors is contraindicated (per manufacturer), or drugs with MAO-blocking activity (linezolid). Safety of selegiline (selective MAO type B inhibitor) not established.

Decreased Effect: Levomethadyl used in combination with naloxone, naltrexone, pentazocine, nalbuphine, butorphanol, and buprenorphine may result in withdrawal symptoms. The effect of meperidine may be decreased by levomethadyl. Enzyme inducers (carbamazepine, phenobarbital, rifampin, phenytoin) may shorten levomethadyl's duration of action. Enzyme inhibitors, such as erythromycin, cimetidine, and ketoconazole may slow the onset, lower the activity levomethadyl (may also increase duration of action).

Mechanism of Action A synthetic opioid agonist with actions similar to morphine; principal actions are analgesia and sedation. Its clinical effects in the treatment of opiate abuse occur through two mechanisms: 1) cross-sensitivity for opiates of the morphine type, suppressing symptoms of withdrawal in opiate-dependent persons; 2) with chronic oral administration, can produce sufficient tolerance to block the subjective high of usual doses of parenterally administered opiates

Pharmacodynamics/Kinetics

Protein binding: 80%
Metabolism: Hepatic to L-alpha-noracetylmethadol and L-alpha-dinoracetylmethadol (active metabolites)
Half-life elimination: 35-60 hours
Time to peak, serum: 1.5-6 hours
Excretion: Urine (as methadol and normethadol)

Dosage Adults: Oral: 20-40 mg at 48- or 72-hour intervals, with ranges of 10 mg to as high as 140 mg 3 times/week; adjust dose in increments of 5-10 mg (too rapid induction may lead to overdose); always dilute before administration and mix with diluent prior to dispensing

Monitoring Parameters Patient adherence with regimen and avoidance of illicit substances; random drug testing is recommended; ECG prior to treatment, 12-14 days after initiation, and periodically thereafter

Dosage Forms SOLN, oral: 10 mg/mL (474 mL) [DSC]

Levonorgestrel (LEE voe nor jes trel)

U.S. Brand Names Mirena®; Norplant® Implant [DSC]; Plan B®

Synonyms LNg 20

Therapeutic Category Contraceptive, Emergency; Contraceptive, Implant (Progestin); Contraceptive, Intrauterine

Use Prevention of pregnancy

Pregnancy Risk Factor X

Contraindications Hypersensitivity to levonorgestrel or any component of the formulation; undiagnosed abnormal uterine bleeding, active hepatic disease or malignant tumors, active thrombophlebitis, or thromboembolic disorders (current or history of), known or suspected carcinoma of the breast; history of intracranial hypertension; renal impairment; pregnancy

Additional product-specific contraindications: Intrauterine system: Congenital or acquired uterine anomaly, acute pelvic inflammatory disease, history of pelvic inflammatory disease (unless there has been a subsequent intrauterine pregnancy), postpartum endometritis, infected abortion within past 3 months, known or suspected uterine or cervical neoplasia, unresolved/abnormal Pap smear, untreated acute cervicitis or vaginitis, patient or partner with multiple sexual partners, conditions which increase susceptibility to infections (ie, leukemia, AIDS, I.V. drug abuse), unremoved IUD, history of ectopic pregnancy, conditions which predispose to ectopic pregnancy

Warnings/Precautions Menstrual bleeding patterns may be altered, missed menstrual periods should not be used to identify early pregnancy. These products do not protect against HIV infection or other sexually-transmitted diseases. Patients presenting with lower abdominal pain should be evaluated for follicular atresia and ectopic pregnancy. Patients receiving enzyme-inducing medications should be evaluated for an alternative method of contraception. Levonorgestrel may affect glucose tolerance, monitor serum glucose in patients with diabetes. Safety and efficacy for use in renal or hepatic impairment have not been established. Use with caution in conditions that may be aggravated by fluid retention, depression, or history of migraine. Only for use in women of reproductive age.

Use of combination hormonal contraceptives increases the risk of cardiovascular side effects in women who smoke cigarettes, especially those who are >35 years of age; although this may be an estrogen-related effect, the risk with progestin-only contraceptives is not known and women should be strongly advised not to smoke. Combination hormonal contraceptives may lead to increased risk of myocardial infarction and should be used with caution in patients with risk factors for coronary artery disease; the actual risk with progestin-only contraceptives is not known, however, there have been postmarketing reports of myocardial infarction in women using levonorgestrel-only contraception. May increase the risk of thromboembolism; discontinue therapy if this occurs. Combination hormonal contraceptives may have a dose-related risk of vascular disease and hypertension; strokes have also been reported with postmarketing use of levonorgestrel-only contraception. Women with hypertension should be encouraged to use a nonhormonal form of contraception. The use of combination hormonal contraceptives has been associated with a slight increase in frequency of breast cancer (studies are not consistent); studies with progestin only contraceptives have been similar. Retinal thrombosis has been reported (rarely) with combination hormonal contraceptives and may be related to the estrogen component, however, progestin-only therapy should also be discontinued with unexplained partial or complete loss of vision.

Additional formulation-specific warnings:

Intrauterine system: Increased incidence of group A streptococcal sepsis and pelvic inflammatory disease (may be asymptomatic); may perforate uterus or cervix; risk of perforation is increased in lactating women; partial penetration or embedment in the myometrium may decrease effectiveness and lead to difficult removal; postpartum insertion should be delayed until uterine involution is complete; use caution in patients with coagulopathy or receiving anticoagulants

Oral tablet: Not intended to be used for routine contraception and will not terminate an existing pregnancy

Subdermal capsules: Insertion-related complications may occur; expulsion of capsules, capsule displacement, thrombophlebitis, and superficial phlebitis have been reported. Insertion and removal are surgical procedures. To decrease risk of thromboembolic disease, consider removing capsules with prolonged immobilization. Idiopathic intracranial hypertension has been reported and may be more likely to occur in obese females.

Common Adverse Reactions

Intrauterine system:

>5%:

Cardiovascular: Hypertension

Central nervous system: Headache, depression, nervousness

Dermatologic: Acne

Endocrine & metabolic: Breast pain, dysmenorrhea, decreased libido, abnormal Pap smear, amenorrhea (20% at 1 year), enlarged follicles (12%)

Gastrointestinal: Abdominal pain, nausea, weight gain

Genitourinary: Leukorrhea, vaginitis

Neuromuscular & skeletal: Back pain

Respiratory: Upper respiratory tract infection, sinusitis

<3% and postmarketing reports: Alopecia, anemia, cervicitis, dyspareunia, eczema, failed insertion, migraine, sepsis, vomiting

(Continued)

Levonorgestrel *(Continued)*

Oral tablets:
>10%:
  Central nervous system: Fatigue (17%), headache (17%), dizziness (11%)
  Endocrine & metabolic: Heavier menstrual bleeding (14%), lighter menstrual bleeding (12%), breast tenderness (11%)
  Gastrointestinal: Nausea (23%), abdominal pain (18%),
1% to 10%: Gastrointestinal: Vomiting (6%), diarrhea (5%)

Subdermal capsules:
>10%: Endocrine & metabolic: Increased/prolonged bleeding (28%), spotting (17%)
1% to 10%:
  Endocrine & metabolic: Breast discharge (≥5%), menstrual irregularities
  Gastrointestinal: Abdominal discomfort (≥5%)
  Genitourinary: Cervicitis (≥5%), leukorrhea (≥5%), vaginitis (≥5%)
  Local: Pain/itching at implant site (4%, usually transient)
  Neuromuscular & skeletal: Musculoskeletal pain (≥5%)
  Miscellaneous: Removal difficulties (6%); these may include multiple incisions, remaining capsule fragments, pain, multiple visits, deep placement, lengthy procedure

Drug Interactions
Cytochrome P450 Effect: Substrate of CYP3A4 (major)
Decreased Effect: Enzyme inducers: May increase the metabolism of levonorgestrel resulting in decreased effect; includes carbamazepine, phenobarbital, phenytoin, and rifampin; additional contraceptive measures may be needed with use of enzyme inducers or following their withdrawal

Mechanism of Action Pregnancy may be prevented through several mechanisms: Thickening of cervical mucus, which inhibits sperm passage through the uterus and sperm survival; inhibition of ovulation, from a negative feedback mechanism on the hypothalamus, leading to reduced secretion of follicle stimulating hormone (FSH) and luteinizing hormone (LH); inhibition of implantation. Levonorgestrel is not effective once the implantation process has begun.

Pharmacodynamics/Kinetics
Duration: Subdermal capsules and intrauterine system: Up to 5 years
Absorption: Rapid and complete
Protein binding: Highly bound to albumin and sex hormone-binding globulin
Metabolism: To inactive metabolites
Bioavailability: 100%
Half-life elimination: Oral tablet: ~24 hours
Excretion: Primarily urine

Dosage Adults:
Long-term prevention of pregnancy:
  Subdermal capsules: Total administration doses (implanted): 216 mg in 6 capsules which should be implanted during the first 7 days of onset of menses subdermally in the upper arm; each Norplant® silastic capsule releases 80 mcg of levonorgestrel/day for 6-18 months, following which a rate of release of 25-30 mcg/day is maintained for ≤5 years; capsules should be removed by end of 5th year
  Intrauterine system: To be inserted into uterine cavity; should be inserted within 7 days of onset of menstruation or immediately after 1st trimester abortion; releases 20 mcg levonorgestrel/day over 5 years. May be removed and replaced with a new unit at anytime during menstrual cycle; do not leave any one system in place for >5 years
Emergency contraception: Oral tablet: One 0.75 mg tablet as soon as possible within 72 hours of unprotected sexual intercourse; a second 0.75 mg tablet should be taken 12 hours after the first dose; may be used at any time during menstrual cycle

Dosage adjustment in renal impairment: Safety and efficacy have not been established
Dosage adjustment in hepatic impairment: Safety and efficacy have not been established

Elderly: Not intended for use in postmenopausal women

Administration
Intrauterine system: Inserted in the uterine cavity, to a depth of 6-9 cm, with the provided insertion device; should not be forced into the uterus
Subdermal capsules: Six capsules are subdermally inserted to the medial aspect of the upper arm (under local anesthetic). Capsules are inserted in a fan-like manner, ~8-10 cm above the elbow crease, with the instruments provided. Prior to removal, palpate the area to locate all 6 capsules. The removal may take more time and may be more painful than the insertion.

Monitoring Parameters Monitor for prolonged menstrual bleeding, amenorrhea, irregularity of menses, Pap smear, blood pressure, serum glucose in patients with diabetes, LDL levels in patients with hyperlipidemias

Reference Range Contraceptive protection usually with plasma levonorgestrel concentrations of 0.29-0.35 ng/mL. Due to variability in individual responses, blood levels alone are not predictive of pregnancy risk.

Patient Information This does not protect against HIV infection or other sexually-transmitted diseases. Cigarette smoking is not recommended. You may experience cramping, headache, abdominal discomfort, hair loss, weight changes, or unusual menses (breakthrough bleeding, irregularity, excessive bleeding). Report sudden acute headache or visual disturbance, unusual nausea or vomiting, any loss of feeling in arms or legs, or lower abdominal pain.

Intrauterine system: This method provides up to 5 years of birth control from a T-shaped device inserted into the uterus. It will be inserted and removed by your prescriber. Notify your prescriber if the system comes out by itself, if you have long-lasting or heavy bleeding, unusual vaginal discharge, low abdominal pain, painful sexual intercourse, chills or fever. There is an increased risk of ectopic pregnancy with this product. Thread placement should be checked following each menstrual cycle; do not pull thread.

Oral tablet: This method provides emergency contraception. It is used after your normal form of birth control has failed, or following unprotected sexual intercourse. It should be used within 72 hours. Contact prescriber if you vomit within 1 hour of taking either dose.

Subdermal capsules: This method consists of 6 capsules, which will be placed under the skin, on the inside of your upper arm. They can provide up to 5 years of birth control. The capsules must be inserted and removed by your prescriber, do not attempt to remove implants yourself. Following insertion, keep area dry and avoid heavy lifting for 2-3 days. Report irritation at insertion site.

Dosage Forms IMPLANT, subdermal capsule (Norplant® [DSC]): 36 mg (6s). **IUD** (Mirena®): 52 mg levonorgestrel/unit. **TAB** (Plan B®): 0.75 mg

♦ **Levonorgestrel and Ethinyl Estradiol** *see* Ethinyl Estradiol and Levonorgestrel *on page 484*

♦ **Levophed®** *see* Norepinephrine *on page 913*

♦ **Levora®** *see* Ethinyl Estradiol and Levonorgestrel *on page 484*

Levorphanol (lee VOR fa nole)
Related Information
Narcotic Agonists Comparison *on page 1395*
U.S. Brand Names Levo-Dromoran®
Synonyms Levorphanol Tartrate; Levorphan Tartrate
Therapeutic Category Analgesic, Narcotic
Use Relief of moderate to severe pain; also used parenterally for preoperative sedation and an adjunct to nitrous oxide/oxygen anesthesia; 2 mg levorphanol produces analgesia comparable to that produced by 10 mg of morphine
Restrictions C-II
Pregnancy Risk Factor B/D (prolonged use or high doses at term)
Contraindications Hypersensitivity to levorphanol or any component of the formulation; pregnancy (prolonged use or high doses at term)
Warnings/Precautions An opioid-containing analgesic regimen should be tailored to each patient's needs and based upon the type of pain being treated (acute versus chronic), the route of administration, degree of tolerance for opioids (naive versus chronic user), age, weight, and medical condition. The optimal analgesic dose varies widely among patients. Doses should be titrated to pain relief/prevention.

Use with caution in patients with hypersensitivity reactions to other phenanthrene derivative opioid agonists (morphine, hydrocodone, hydromorphone, levorphanol, oxycodone, oxymorphone); respiratory diseases including asthma, emphysema, COPD or severe liver or renal insufficiency; some preparations contain sulfites which may cause allergic reactions; tolerance or dependence may result from extended use; dextromethorphan has equivalent antitussive activity but has much lower toxicity in accidental overdose. Elderly may be particularly susceptible to the CNS depressant and constipating effects of narcotics.
Common Adverse Reactions Frequency not defined.
Cardiovascular: Palpitations, hypotension, bradycardia, peripheral vasodilation, cardiac arrest, shock, tachycardia
Central nervous system: CNS depression, fatigue, drowsiness, dizziness, nervousness, headache, restlessness, anorexia, malaise, confusion, coma, convulsion, insomnia, amnesia, mental depression, hallucinations, paradoxical CNS stimulation, intracranial pressure (increased)
Dermatologic: Pruritus, urticaria, rash
Endocrine & metabolic: Antidiuretic hormone release
Gastrointestinal: Nausea, vomiting, dyspepsia, stomach cramps, xerostomia, constipation, abdominal pain, dry mouth, biliary tract spasm, paralytic ileus
Genitourinary: Decreased urination, urinary tract spasm, urinary retention
Local: Pain at injection site
Neuromuscular & skeletal: Weakness
Ocular: Miosis, diplopia
Respiratory: Respiratory depression, apnea, hypoventilation, cyanosis
Miscellaneous: Histamine release, physical and psychological dependence
Drug Interactions
Increased Effect/Toxicity: CNS depression is enhanced with coadministration of other CNS depressants.
Mechanism of Action Levorphanol tartrate is a synthetic opioid agonist that is classified as a morphinan derivative. Opioids interact with stereospecific opioid receptors in various parts of the central nervous system and other tissues. Analgesic potency parallels the affinity for these binding sites. These drugs do not alter the threshold or responsiveness to pain, but the perception of pain.
Pharmacodynamics/Kinetics
Onset of action: Oral: 10-60 minutes
Duration: 4-8 hours
Metabolism: Hepatic
Half-life elimination: 11-16 hours
Excretion: Urine (as inactive metabolite)
(Continued)

Levorphanol *(Continued)*

Dosage Adults: **Note:** These are guidelines and do not represent the maximum doses that may be required in all patients. Doses should be titrated to pain relief/prevention.

Acute pain (moderate to severe):

Oral: Initial: Opiate-naive: 2 mg every 6-8 hours as needed; patients with prior opiate exposure may require higher initial doses; usual dosage range: 2-4 mg every 6-8 hours as needed

I.M., S.C.: Initial: Opiate-naive: 1 mg every 6-8 hours as needed; patients with prior opiate exposure may require higher initial doses; usual dosage range: 1-2 mg every 6-8 hours as needed

Slow I.V.: Initial: Opiate-naive: Up to 1 mg/dose every 3-6 hours as needed; patients with prior opiate exposure may require higher initial doses

Chronic pain: Patients taking opioids chronically may become tolerant and require doses higher than the usual dosage range to maintain the desired effect. Tolerance can be managed by appropriate dose titration. There is no optimal or maximal dose for levorphanol in chronic pain. The appropriate dose is one that relieves pain throughout its dosing interval without causing unmanageable side effects.

Premedication: I.M., S.C.: 1-2 mg/dose 60-90 minutes prior to surgery; older or debilitated patients usually require less drug

Dosing adjustment in hepatic disease: Reduction is necessary in patients with liver disease

Monitoring Parameters Pain relief, respiratory and mental status, blood pressure

Patient Information Avoid alcohol, may cause drowsiness, impaired judgment or coordination; may cause physical and psychological dependence with prolonged use

Dosage Forms INJ, solution: 2 mg/mL (1 mL, 10 mL). **TAB:** 2 mg

- ◆ **Levorphanol Tartrate** *see* Levorphanol *on page 739*
- ◆ **Levorphan Tartrate** *see* Levorphanol *on page 739*
- ◆ **Levothroid**® *see* Levothyroxine *on page 740*

Levothyroxine *(lee voe thye ROKS een)*

U.S. Brand Names Levothroid®; Levoxyl®; Novothyrox; Synthroid®; Unithroid®

Synonyms Levothyroxine Sodium; *L*-Thyroxine Sodium; T_4

Therapeutic Category Thyroid Product

Use Replacement or supplemental therapy in hypothyroidism; pituitary TSH suppression

Pregnancy Risk Factor A

Contraindications Hypersensitivity to levothyroxine sodium or any component of the formulation; recent MI or thyrotoxicosis; uncorrected adrenal insufficiency

Warnings/Precautions Ineffective and potentially toxic for weight reduction; high doses may produce serious or even life-threatening toxic effects particularly when used with some anorectic drugs. Use with caution and reduce dosage in patients with angina pectoris or other cardiovascular disease; use cautiously in elderly since they may be more likely to have compromised cardiovascular functions. Patients with adrenal insufficiency, myxedema, diabetes mellitus and insipidus may have symptoms exaggerated or aggravated; thyroid replacement requires periodic assessment of thyroid status. Chronic hypothyroidism predisposes patients to coronary artery disease.

Common Adverse Reactions Frequency not defined.

Cardiovascular: Angina, arrhythmias, blood pressure increased, cardiac arrest, flushing, heart failure, MI, palpitations, pulse increased, tachycardia

Central nervous system: Anxiety, emotional lability, fatigue, fever, headache, hyperactivity, insomnia, irritability, nervousness, pseudotumor cerebri (children), seizures (rare)

Dermatologic: Alopecia

Endocrine & metabolic: Fertility impaired, menstrual irregularities

Gastrointestinal: Abdominal cramps, appetite increased, diarrhea, vomiting, weight loss

Hepatic: Liver function tests increased

Neuromuscular & skeletal: Bone mineral density decreased, muscle weakness, tremors, slipped capital femoral epiphysis (children)

Respiratory: Dyspnea

Miscellaneous: Diaphoresis, heat intolerance, hypersensitivity (to inactive ingredients, symptoms include urticaria, pruritus, rash, flushing, angioedema, GI symptoms, fever, arthralgia, serum sickness, wheezing)

Drug Interactions

Increased Effect/Toxicity: Also refer to Additional Information. Levothyroxine may potentiate the hypoprothrombinemic effect of warfarin (and other oral anticoagulants). Tricyclic antidepressants (TCAs) coadministered with levothyroxine may increase potential for toxicity of both drugs. Coadministration with ketamine may lead to hypertension and tachycardia.

Decreased Effect: Also refer to Additional Information. Some medications may decrease absorption of levothyroxine: Cholestyramine, colestipol (separate administration by at least 2 hours); aluminum- and magnesium-containing antacids, iron preparations, sucralfate, Kayexalate® (separate administration by at least 4 hours). Enzyme inducers (phenytoin, phenobarbital, carbamazepine, and rifampin/rifabutin) may decrease levothyroxine levels. Levothyroxine may decrease effect of oral sulfonylureas. Serum levels of digoxin and theophylline may be altered by thyroid function. Estrogens may decrease serum free-thyroxine concentrations.

Mechanism of Action Exact mechanism of action is unknown; however, it is believed the thyroid hormone exerts its many metabolic effects through control of DNA transcription and protein synthesis; involved in normal metabolism, growth, and development; promotes gluconeogenesis, increases utilization and mobilization of glycogen stores, and stimulates protein synthesis, increases basal metabolic rate

Pharmacodynamics/Kinetics

Onset of action: Therapeutic: Oral: 3-5 days; I.V. 6-8 hours

Peak effect: I.V.: ~24 hours

Absorption: Oral: Erratic (40% to 80%); decreases with age

Protein binding: >99%

Metabolism: Hepatic to triiodothyronine (active)

Time to peak, serum: 2-4 hours

Half-life elimination: Euthyroid: 6-7 days; Hypothyroid: 9-10 days; Hyperthyroid: 3-4 days

Excretion: Urine and feces; decreases with age

Dosage Doses should be adjusted based on clinical response and laboratory parameters.

Oral:

Children: Hypothyroidism:

Newborns: Initial: 10-15 mcg/kg/day. Lower doses of 25 mcg/day should be considered in newborns at risk for cardiac failure. Newborns with T_4 levels <5 mcg/dL should be started at 50 mcg/day. Adjust dose at 4- to 6-week intervals.

Infants and Children: Dose based on body weight and age as listed below. Children with severe or chronic hypothyroidism should be started at 25 mcg/day; adjust dose by 25 mcg every 2-4 weeks. In older children, hyperactivity may be decreased by starting with $1/4$ of the recommended dose and increasing by $1/4$ dose each week until the full replacement dose is reached. Refer to adult dosing once growth and puberty are complete.

0-3 months: 10-15 mcg/kg/day

3-6 months: 8-10 mcg/kg/day

6-12 months: 6-8 mcg/kg/day

1-5 years: 5-6 mcg/kg/day

6-12 years: 4-5 mcg/kg/day

>12 years: 2-3 mcg/kg/day

Adults:

Hypothyroidism: 1.7 mcg/kg/day in otherwise healthy adults <50 years old, children in whom growth and puberty are complete, and older adults who have been recently treated for hyperthyroidism or who have been hypothyroid for only a few months. Titrate dose every 6 weeks. Average starting dose ~100 mcg; usual doses are ≤200 mcg/day; doses ≥300 mcg/day are rare (consider poor compliance, malabsorption, and/or drug interactions). **Note:** For patients >50 years or patients with cardiac disease, refer to Elderly dosing.

Severe hypothyroidism: Initial: 12.5-25 mcg/day; adjust dose by 25 mcg/day every 2-4 weeks as appropriate; **Note:** Oral agents are not recommended for myxedema (see I.V. dosing).

Subclinical hypothyroidism (if treated): 1 mcg/kg/day

TSH suppression:

Well-differentiated thyroid cancer: Highly individualized; Doses >2 mcg/kg/day may be needed to suppress TSH to <0.1 mU/L.

Benign nodules and nontoxic multinodular goiter: Goal TSH suppression: 0.1-0.3 mU/L

Elderly: Hypothyroidism:

>50 years without cardiac disease **or** <50 years with cardiac disease: Initial: 25-50 mcg/day; adjust dose at 6- to 8-week intervals as needed

>50 years with cardiac disease: Initial: 12.5-25 mcg/day; adjust dose by 12.5-25 mcg increments at 4- to 6-week intervals

Note: Elderly patients may require <1 mcg/kg/day

I.M., I.V.: Children, Adults, Elderly: Hypothyroidism: 50% of the oral dose

I.V.:

Adults: Myxedema coma or stupor: 200-500 mcg, then 100-300 mcg the next day if necessary; smaller doses should be considered in patients with cardiovascular disease

Elderly: Myxedema coma: Refer to Adults dosing; lower doses may be needed

Administration

Oral: Administer in the morning on an empty stomach, at least 30 minutes before food. Tablets may be crushed and suspended in 1-2 teaspoonfuls of water; suspension should be used immediately.

Parenteral: Dilute vial with 5 mL normal saline; use immediately after reconstitution; should not be admixed with other solutions

Monitoring Parameters Thyroid function test (serum thyroxine, thyrotropin concentrations), resin triiodothyronine uptake (rT_3U), free thyroxine index (FTI), T_4, TSH, heart rate, blood pressure, clinical signs of hypo- and hyperthyroidism; TSH is the most reliable guide for evaluating adequacy of thyroid replacement dosage. TSH may be elevated during the first few months of thyroid replacement despite patients being clinically euthyroid. In cases where T_4 remains low and TSH is within normal limits, an evaluation of "free" (unbound) T_4 is needed to evaluate further increase in dosage

Infants: Monitor closely for cardiac overload, arrhythmias, and aspiration from avid suckling

Infants/children: Monitor closely for under/overtreatment. Undertreatment may decrease intellectual development and linear growth, and lead to poor school performance due to impaired concentration and slowed mentation. Overtreatment may adversely affect brain maturation, accelerate bone age (leading to premature closure of the epiphyses and reduced adult height); craniosynostosis has been reported in infants. Treated children may experience a period of catch-up growth. Monitor TSH and total or free T_4 at 2 and 4 weeks after starting treatment; (Continued)

Levothyroxine *(Continued)*

every 1-2 months for first year of life; every 2-3 months during years 1-3; every 3-12 months until growth completed.

Adults: Monitor TSH every 6-8 weeks until normalized; 8-12 weeks after dosage changes; every 6-12 months throughout therapy

Reference Range Pediatrics: Cord T_4 and values in the first few weeks are much higher, falling over the first months and years. ≥10 years: ~5.8-11 µg/dL (SI: 75-142 nmol/L). Borderline low: ≤4.5-5.7 µg/dL (SI: 58-73 nmol/L); low: ≤4.4 µg/dL (SI: 57 nmol/L); results <2.5 µg/dL (SI: <32 nmol/L) are strong evidence for hypothyroidism.

Approximate adult normal range: 4-12 µg/dL (SI: 51-154 nmol/L). Borderline high: 11.1-13 µg/dL (SI: 143-167 nmol/L); high: ≥13.1 µg/dL (SI: 169 nmol/L). Normal range is increased in women on birth control pills (5.5-12 µg/dL); normal range in pregnancy: ~5.5-16 µg/dL (SI: ~71-206 nmol/L). TSH: 0.4-10 (for those ≥80 years) mIU/L; T_4: 4-12 µg/dL (SI: 51-154 nmol/L); T_3 (RIA) (total T_3): 80-230 ng/dL (SI: 1.2-3.5 nmol/L); T_4 free (free T_4): 0.7-1.8 ng/dL (SI: 9-23 pmol/L).

Patient Information Do not change brands without prescriber's knowledge; report immediately any chest pain, increased pulse, palpitations, heat intolerances, excessive sweating; do not discontinue without notifying prescriber

Dosage Forms INJ, powder for reconstitution (Synthroid®): 0.2 mg, 0.5 mg. **TAB:** (Levothroid®, Levoxyl®, Novothyrox, Synthroid®): 25 mcg, 50 mcg, 75 mcg, 88 mcg, 100 mcg, 112 mcg, 125 mcg, 137 mcg, 150 mcg, 175 mcg, 200 mcg, 300 mcg; (Unithroid®): 25 mcg, 50 mcg, 75 mcg, 88 mcg, 100 mcg, 112 mcg, 125 mcg, 150 mcg, 175 mcg, 200 mcg, 300 mcg

- ♦ **Levothyroxine Sodium** *see Levothyroxine on page 740*
- ♦ **Levoxyl®** *see Levothyroxine on page 740*
- ♦ **Levsin®** *see Hyoscyamine on page 641*
- ♦ **Levsinex®** *see Hyoscyamine on page 641*
- ♦ **Levsin/SL®** *see Hyoscyamine on page 641*
- ♦ **Levulan® Kerastick®** *see Aminolevulinic Acid on page 75*
- ♦ **Lexapro™** *see Escitalopram on page 455*
- ♦ **Lexiva™** *see Fosamprenavir on page 563*
- ♦ **Lexxel®** *see Enalapril and Felodipine on page 431*
- ♦ **LFA-3/IgG(1) Fusion Protein, Human** *see Alefacept on page 49*
- ♦ **LHRH** *see Gonadorelin on page 599*
- ♦ **l-Hyoscyamine Sulfate** *see Hyoscyamine on page 641*
- ♦ **Librax®** *see Clidinium and Chlordiazepoxide on page 291*
- ♦ **Librium®** *see Chlordiazepoxide on page 258*
- ♦ **LidaMantle®** *see Lidocaine on page 742*
- ♦ **Lidex®** *see Fluocinonide on page 534*
- ♦ **Lidex-E®** *see Fluocinonide on page 534*

Lidocaine *(LYE doe kane)*

U.S. Brand Names Anestacon®; Band-Aid® Hurt-Free™ Antiseptic Wash [OTC]; Burnamycin [OTC]; Burn Jel [OTC]; Burn-O-Jel [OTC]; LidaMantle®; Lidoderm®; L-M-X™ 4 [OTC]; L-M-X™ 5 [OTC]; Premjact® [OTC]; Solarcaine® Aloe Extra Burn Relief [OTC]; Topicaine® [OTC]; Xylocaine®; Xylocaine® MPF; Xylocaine® Viscous; Zilactin-L® [OTC]

Synonyms Lidocaine Hydrochloride; Lignocaine Hydrochloride

Therapeutic Category Antiarrhythmic Agent, Class I-B; Local Anesthetic, Injectable; Local Anesthetic, Topical

Use Local anesthetic and acute treatment of ventricular arrhythmias from myocardial infarction, cardiac manipulation, digitalis intoxication; drug of choice for ventricular ectopy, ventricular tachycardia (VT), ventricular fibrillation (VF); for pulseless VT or VF preferably administer **after** defibrillation and epinephrine; control of premature ventricular contractions, wide-complex paroxysmal supraventricular tachycardia (PSVT); control of hemodynamically compromising PVCs; hemodynamically stable VT

Rectal: Temporary relief of pain and itching due to anorectal disorders

Topical: Local anesthetic for use in laser, cosmetic, and outpatient surgeries; minor burns, cuts, and abrasions of the skin

Orphan drug: Lidoderm® Patch: Relief of allodynia (painful hypersensitivity) and chronic pain in postherpetic neuralgia

Pregnancy Risk Factor B (manufacturer); C (expert analysis)

Contraindications Hypersensitivity to lidocaine or any component of the formulation; hypersensitivity to another local anesthetic of the amide type; Adam-Stokes syndrome; severe degrees of SA, AV, or intraventricular heart block (except in patients with a functioning artificial pacemaker)

Warnings/Precautions

Intravenous: Constant ECG monitoring is necessary during I.V. administration. Use cautiously in hepatic impairment, any degree of heart block, Wolff-Parkinson-White syndrome, CHF, marked hypoxia, severe respiratory depression, hypovolemia, history of malignant hyperthermia, or shock. Increased ventricular rate may be seen when administered to a patient with atrial fibrillation. Correct any underlying causes of ventricular arrhythmias. Monitor closely for signs and symptoms of CNS toxicity. The elderly may be prone to increased CNS and cardiovascular side effects. Reduce dose in hepatic dysfunction and CHF.

Injectable anesthetic: Follow appropriate administration techniques so as not to administer any intravascularly. Solutions containing antimicrobial preservatives should not be used for epidural or spinal anesthesia. Some solutions contain a bisulfite; avoid in patients who are allergic to bisulfite. Resuscitative equipment, medicine and oxygen should be available in case of emergency. Use products containing epinephrine cautiously in patients with significant vascular disease, compromised blood flow, or during or following general anesthesia (increased risk of arrhythmias). Adjust the dose for the elderly, pediatric, acutely ill, and debilitated patients.

Topical: L-M-X™ 4 cream: Do not leave on large body areas for >2 hours. Observe young children closely to prevent accidental ingestion. Not for use ophthalmic use or for use on mucous membranes.

Common Adverse Reactions Effects vary with route of administration. Many effects are dose-related.

Frequency not defined:

Cardiovascular: Bradycardia, hypotension, heart block, arrhythmias, cardiovascular collapse, sinus node supression, increase defibrillator threshold, vascular insufficiency (periarticular injections), arterial spasms

Central nervous system: Drowsiness after administration is usually a sign of a high blood level. Other effects may include lightheadedness, dizziness, tinnitus, blurred vision, vomiting, twitching, tremors, lethargy, coma, agitation, slurred speech, seizures, anxiety, euphoria, hallucinations, paresthesia, psychosis

Dermatologic: Itching, rash, edema of the skin, contact dermatitis

Gastrointestinal: Nausea, vomiting, taste disorder

Local: Thrombophlebitis

Neuromuscular & skeletal: Transient radicular pain (subarachnoid administration; up to 1.9%)

Ocular: Blurred vision, diplopia

Respiratory: Dyspnea, respiratory depression or arrest, bronchospasm

Miscellaneous: Allergic reactions, urticaria, edema, anaphylactoid reaction

Following spinal anesthesia positional headache (3%), shivering (2%) nausea, peripheral nerve symptoms, respiratory inadequacy and double vision

Drug Interactions

Cytochrome P450 Effect: Substrate of CYP1A2 (minor), 2A6 (minor), 2B6 (minor), 2C8/9 (minor), 2D6 (major), 3A4 (major); **Inhibits** CYP1A2 (strong), 2D6 (moderate), 3A4 (moderate)

Increased Effect/Toxicity: CYP2D6 inhibitors may increase the levels/effects of lidocaine; example inhibitors include chlorpromazine, delavirdine, fluoxetine, miconazole, paroxetine, pergolide, quinidine, quinine, ritonavir, and ropinirole. Concomitant cimetidine or propranolol may result in increased serum concentrations of lidocaine resulting in toxicity. Serum concentrations/toxicity of lidocaine may be increased by inhibitors of CYP3A4, including amprenavir, cimetidine, ciprofloxacin, clarithromycin, clozapine, diltiazem, disulfiram, digoxin, erythromycin, ethanol, fluconazole, fluoxetine, fluvoxamine, grapefruit juice, isoniazid, itraconazole, ketoconazole, labetalol, levodopa, loxapine, metoprolol, metronidazole, miconazole, nefazodone, nelfinavir, omeprazole, phenytoin, rifabutin, rifampin, ritonavir, troleandomycin, valproic acid, and verapamil. Effect of succinylcholine may be enhanced by lidocaine.

Mechanism of Action Class Ib antiarrhythmic; suppresses automaticity of conduction tissue, by increasing electrical stimulation threshold of ventricle, His-Purkinje system, and spontaneous depolarization of the ventricles during diastole by a direct action on the tissues; blocks both the initiation and conduction of nerve impulses by decreasing the neuronal membrane's permeability to sodium ions, which results in inhibition of depolarization with resultant blockade of conduction

Pharmacodynamics/Kinetics

Onset of action: Single bolus dose: 45-90 seconds

Duration: 10-20 minutes

Distribution: V_d: 1.1-2.1 L/kg; alterable by many patient factors; decreased in CHF and liver disease; crosses blood-brain barrier

Protein binding: 60% to 80% to alpha$_1$ acid glycoprotein

Metabolism: 90% hepatic; active metabolites monoethylglycinexylidide (MEGX) and glycinexylidide (GX) can accumulate and may cause CNS toxicity

Half-life elimination: Biphasic: Prolonged with congestive heart failure, liver disease, shock, severe renal disease; Initial: 7-30 minutes; Terminal: Infants, premature: 3.2 hours, Adults: 1.5-2 hours

Dosage

Topical: Apply to affected area as needed; maximum: 3 mg/kg/dose; do not repeat within 2 hours.

L-M-X™ 4 cream: Apply ¼ inch thick layer to intact skin. Leave on until adequate anesthetic effect is obtained. Remove cream and cleanse area before beginning procedure.

Rectal: Relief of pain and itching (L-M-X™ 5): Children ≥12 years and Adults: Apply topically to clean, dry area or using applicator insert rectally, up to 6 times/day

Injectable local anesthetic: Varies with procedure, degree of anesthesia needed, vascularity of tissue, duration of anesthesia required, and physical condition of patient; maximum: 4.5 mg/kg/dose; do not repeat within 2 hours.

Patch: Postherpetic neuralgia: Apply patch to most painful area. Up to 3 patches may be applied in a single application. Patch may remain in place for up to 12 hours in any 24-hour period.

(Continued)

Lidocaine *(Continued)*

Antiarrhythmic:

I.V.: 1-1.5 mg/kg bolus over 2-3 minutes; may repeat doses of 0.5-0.75 mg/kg in 5-10 minutes up to a total of 3 mg/kg; continuous infusion: 1-4 mg/minute

I.V. (2 g/250 mL D$_5$W) infusion rates (infusion pump should be used for I.V. infusion administration):

1 mg/minute: 7.5 mL/hour

2 mg/minute: 15 mL/hour

3 mg/minute: 22.5 mL/hour

4 mg/minute: 30 mL/hour

Ventricular fibrillation (after defibrillation and epinephrine): Initial: 1-1.5 mg/kg. Repeat 0.5-0.75 mg/kg bolus may be given 3-5 minutes after initial dose. Total dose should not exceed 200-300 mg during a 1-hour period or 3 mg/kg total dose. Follow with continuous infusion after return of perfusion.

Endotracheal: 2-2.5 times the I.V. dose (2-4 mg/kg diluted with NS to a total volume of 10 mL)

Decrease dose in patients with CHF, shock, or hepatic disease.

Dosage adjustment in renal impairment: Not dialyzable (0% to 5%) by hemo- or peritoneal dialysis; supplemental dose is not necessary.

Dosage adjustment in hepatic impairment: Reduce dose in acute hepatitis and decompensated cirrhosis by 50%.

Administration

Endotracheal doses should be diluted to 10 mL with normal saline prior to E.T. administration

I.V.: Use microdrip (60 gtt/mL) or infusion pump to administer an accurate dose

Buffered lidocaine for injectable local anesthetic: Add 2 mL of sodium bicarbonate 8.4% to 18 mL of lidocaine 1%

Topical: Patch may be cut to appropriate size; remove immediately if burning sensation occurs; wash hands after application

Reference Range

Therapeutic: 1.5-5.0 µg/mL (SI: 6-21 µmol/L)

Potentially toxic: >6 µg/mL (SI: >26 µmol/L)

Toxic: >9 µg/mL (SI: >38 µmol/L)

Dosage Forms CRM, rectal (L-M-X™ 5): 5% (30 g). **CRM, topical** (L-M-X™ 4): 4% (5 g, 30 g). **CRM, topical, as hydrochloride** (LidaMantle®): 3% (30 g, 85 g). **GEL, topical:** (Burn-O-Jel): 0.5% (90 g); (Topicaine®): 4% (1 g, 10 g, 30 g, 113 g). **GEL, topical, as hydrochloride:** 2% (30 g); (Burn Jel): 2% (3.5 g, 120 g); (Solarcaine® Aloe Extra Burn Relief): 0.5% (226 g). **INF** [premixed in D$_5$W]: 0.4% [4 mg/mL] (250 mL, 500 mL); 0.8% [8 mg/mL] (250 mL, 500 mL). **INJ, solution:** 0.5% [5 mg/mL] (50 mL); 1% [10 mg/mL] (5 mL, 20 mL, 30 mL, 50 mL); 1.5% [15 mg/mL] (20 mL); 2% [20 mg/mL] (2 mL, 5 mL, 20 mL, 30 mL, 50 mL); (Xylocaine®): 0.5% [5 mg/mL] (50 mL); 1% [10 mg/mL] (10 mL, 20 mL, 50 mL); 2% [20 mg/mL] (1.8 mL, 10 mL, 20 mL, 50 mL); 4% [40 mg/mL] (5 mL). **INJ, solution, as hydrochloride** [preservative free]: 0.5% [5 mg/mL] (50 mL); 1% [10 mg/mL] (2 mL, 5 mL, 30 mL); 1.5% [15 mg/mL] (20 mL); 2% [20 mg/mL] (5 mL, 10 mL); 4% [40 mg/mL] (5 mL); 10% [100 mg/mL] (10 mL); 20% [200 mg/mL] (10 mL); (Xylocaine® MPF): 0.5% [5 mg/mL] (50 mL); 1% [10 mg/mL] (2 mL, 5 mL, 10 mL, 20 mL, 30 mL); 1.5% [15 mg/mL] (10 mL, 20 mL); 2% [2 mg/mL] (2 mL, 5 mL, 10 mL); 4% [40 mg/mL] (5 mL). **INJ, solution** [premixed in D$_{7.5}$W; preservative free]: 5% (2 mL); (Xylocaine®-MPF): 1.5% (2 mL). **JELLY, topical:** (Anestacon®): 2% (15 mL, 240 mL); (Xylocaine®): 2% (5 mL, 10 mL, 20 mL, 30 mL). **LIQ, topical** (Zilactin®-L): 2.5% (7.5 mL). **OINT, topical:** 5% (37 g); (Xylocaine®): 2.5% (35 g) [OTC]; 5% (3.5 g, 35 g). **PATCH, transdermal** (Lidoderm®): 5% (30s). **SOLN, topical:** 2% [20 mg/mL] (15 mL, 240 mL); 4% [40 mg/mL] (50 mL); (Band-Aid® Hurt-Free™ Antiseptic Wash): 2% (180 mL); (Xylocaine®): 4% [40 mg/mL] (50 mL). **SOLN, viscous:** 2% [20 mg/mL] (20 mL, 100 mL); (Xylocaine® Viscous): 2% [20 mg/mL] (20 mL, 100 mL, 450 mL). **SPRAY, topical:** (Burnamycin): 0.5% (60 mL); (Premjact®): 9.6% (13 mL); (Solarcaine® Aloe Extra Burn Relief): 0.5% (127 g)

Lidocaine and Bupivacaine *(LYE doe kane & byoo PIV a kane)*

U.S. Brand Names Duocaine™

Synonyms Bupivacaine and Lidocaine; Lidocaine Hydrochloride and Bupivacaine Hydrochloride

Therapeutic Category Local Anesthetic

Use Local or regional anesthesia in ophthalmologic surgery by peripheral nerve block techniques such as peribulbar, retrobulbar, and facial blocks; may be used with or without epinephrine

Pregnancy Risk Factor C

Dosage Adults: **Note:** Use lowest effective dose to limit toxic effects. Dosing based on lidocaine 1% and bupivacaine 0.375%

Retrobulbar injection: 2-5 mL; a portion of dose is injected retrobulbarly and remainder may be used to block the facial nerve

Peribulbar block: 6-12 mL

Maximum dose: 0.18 mL/kg or 12 mL; if used with epinephrine, the dose should not exceed 0.28 mL/kg or 20 mL

Dosage adjustment in renal impairment: Lidocaine: Accumulation of metabolites may increase with renal impairment

Dosage adjustment in hepatic impairment:

Lidocaine: Half-life of lidocaine is increased twofold with hepatic impairment

Bupivacaine: Toxicities may be increased with hepatic impairment

Dosage Forms INJ, solution [preservative free] (Duocaine™): Lidocaine hydrochloride 1% and bupivacaine hydrochloride 0.375% (10 mL)

Lidocaine and Epinephrine (LYE doe kane & ep i NEF rin)
U.S. Brand Names Xylocaine® MPF With Epinephrine; Xylocaine® With Epinephrine
Synonyms Epinephrine and Lidocaine
Therapeutic Category Local Anesthetic, Injectable
Use Local infiltration anesthesia; AVS for nerve block
Pregnancy Risk Factor B
Dosage
Children: Use lidocaine concentrations of 0.5% to 1% (or even more diluted) to decrease possibility of toxicity; lidocaine dose should not exceed 7 mg/kg/dose; do not repeat within 2 hours
Adults: Dosage varies with the anesthetic procedure, degree of anesthesia needed, vascularity of tissue, duration of anesthesia required, and physical condition of patient
Dosage Forms INJ, solution, with epinephrine 1:50,000 (Xylocaine® with Epinephrine): Lidocaine 2% [20 mg/mL] (1.8 mL). **INJ, solution**, with epinephrine 1:100,000: Lidocaine 1% [10 mg/mL] (20 mL, 30 mL, 50 mL); Lidocaine 2% (20 mL, 30 mL, 50 mL); (Xylocaine® with Epinephrine): Lidocaine 1% [10 mg/mL] (10 mL 20 mL, 50 mL); Lidocaine 2% (1.8 mL, 10 mL, 20 mL, 50 mL). **INJ, solution**, with epinephrine 1:200,000: Lidocaine 0.5% [5 mg/mL] (50 mL); (Xylocaine® with Epinephrine): Lidocaine 0.5% [5 mg/mL] (50 mL). **INJ, solution**, with epinephrine 1:200,000 [methylparaben free]: Lidocaine 1% [10 mg/mL] (30 mL); Lidocaine 1.5% (5 mL, 30 mL); Lidocaine 2% (20 mL); (Xylocaine® MPF with Epinephrine): Lidocaine 1% [10 mg/mL] (5 mL, 10 mL, 30 mL); 1.5% [15 mg/mL] (5 mL, 10 mL, 30 mL); Lidocaine 2% [20 mg/mL] (5 mL, 10 mL, 20 mL)

Lidocaine and Prilocaine (LYE doe kane & PRIL oh kane)
U.S. Brand Names EMLA®
Synonyms Prilocaine and Lidocaine
Therapeutic Category Analgesic, Topical; Anesthetic, Topical; Local Anesthetic, Topical
Use Topical anesthetic for use on normal intact skin to provide local analgesia for minor procedures such as I.V. cannulation or venipuncture; has also been used for painful procedures such as lumbar puncture and skin graft harvesting; for superficial minor surgery of genital mucous membranes and as an adjunct for local infiltration anesthesia in genital mucous membranes.
Pregnancy Risk Factor B
Contraindications
Hypersensitivity to amide type anesthetic agents [ie, lidocaine, prilocaine, dibucaine, mepivacaine, bupivacaine, etidocaine]; hypersensitivity to any component of the formulation selected; application on mucous membranes or broken or inflamed skin; infants <1 month of age if gestational age is <37 weeks; infants <12 months of age receiving therapy with methemoglobin-inducing agents; children with congenital or idiopathic methemoglobinemia, or in children who are receiving medications associated with drug-induced methemoglobinemia [ie, acetaminophen (overdosage), benzocaine, chloroquine, dapsone, nitrofurantoin, nitroglycerin, nitroprusside, phenazopyridine, phenelzine, phenobarbital, phenytoin, quinine, sulfonamides]
Warnings/Precautions Use with caution in patients receiving class I antiarrhythmic drugs, since systemic absorption occurs and synergistic toxicity is possible. Although the incidence of systemic adverse reactions with EMLA® is very low, caution should be exercised, particularly when applying over large areas and leaving on for longer than 2 hours.
Common Adverse Reactions Frequency not defined.
Cardiovascular: Hypotension, angioedema
Central nervous system: Shock
Dermatologic: Hyperpigmentation, erythema, itching, rash, burning, urticaria
Genitourinary: Blistering of foreskin (rare)
Local: Burning, stinging, edema
Respiratory: Bronchospasm
Miscellaneous: Alteration in temperature sensation, hypersensitivity reactions
Drug Interactions
Cytochrome P450 Effect: Lidocaine: **Substrate** of CYP1A2 (minor), 2A6 (minor), 2B6 (minor), 2C8/9 (minor), 2D6 (major), 3A4 (major); **Inhibits** CYP1A2 (strong), 2D6 (strong), 3A4 (moderate)
Increased Effect/Toxicity: Class I antiarrhythmic drugs (tocainide, mexiletine): Effects are additive and potentially synergistic. Prilocaine may enhance the effect of other drugs known to induce methemoglobinemia.
Mechanism of Action Local anesthetic action occurs by stabilization of neuronal membranes and inhibiting the ionic fluxes required for the initiation and conduction of impulses
Pharmacodynamics/Kinetics
EMLA®:
Onset of action: 1 hour
Peak effect: 2-3 hours
Duration: 1-2 hours after removal
Absorption: Related to duration of application and area where applied
3-hour application: 3.6% lidocaine and 6.1% prilocaine
24-hour application: 16.2% lidocaine and 33.5% prilocaine
See individual agents.
(Continued)

Lidocaine and Prilocaine (Continued)

Dosage Although the incidence of systemic adverse effects with EMLA® is very low, caution should be exercised, particularly when applying over large areas and leaving on for >2 hours

Children (intact skin): EMLA® should **not** be used in neonates with a gestation age <37 weeks nor in infants <12 months of age who are receiving treatment with methemoglobin-inducing agents

Dosing is based on child's age and weight:

Age 0-3 months or <5 kg: Apply a maximum of 1 g over no more than 10 cm^2 of skin; leave on for no longer than 1 hour

Age 3 months to 12 months and >5 kg: Apply no more than a maximum 2 g total over no more than 20 cm^2 of skin; leave on for no longer than 4 hours

Age 1-6 years and >10 kg: Apply no more than a maximum of 10 g total over no more than 100 cm^2 of skin; leave on for no longer than 4 hours.

Age 7-12 years and >20 kg: Apply no more than a maximum 20 g total over no more than 200 cm^2 of skin; leave on for no longer than 4 hours.

Note: If a patient greater than 3 months old does not meet the minimum weight requirement, the maximum total dose should be restricted to the corresponding maximum based on patient weight.

Adults (intact skin):

EMLA® cream and EMLA® anesthetic disc: A thick layer of EMLA® cream is applied to intact skin and covered with an occlusive dressing, or alternatively, an EMLA® anesthetic disc is applied to intact skin

Minor dermal procedures (eg, I.V. cannulation or venipuncture): Apply 2.5 g of cream (1/2 of the 5 g tube) over 20-25 cm of skin surface area, or 1 anesthetic disc (1 g over 10 cm^2) for at least 1 hour. **Note:** In clinical trials, 2 sites were usually prepared in case there was a technical problem with cannulation or venipuncture at the first site.

Major dermal procedures (eg, more painful dermatological procedures involving a larger skin area such as split thickness skin graft harvesting): Apply 2 g of cream per 10 cm^2 of skin and allow to remain in contact with the skin for at least 2 hours.

Adult male genital skin (eg, pretreatment prior to local anesthetic infiltration): Apply a thick layer of cream (1 g/10 cm^2) to the skin surface for 15 minutes. Local anesthetic infiltration should be performed immediately after removal of EMLA® cream.

Note: Dermal analgesia can be expected to increase for up to 3 hours under occlusive dressing and persist for 1-2 hours after removal of the cream

Adult females: Genital mucous membranes: Minor procedures (eg, removal of condylomata acuminata, pretreatment for local anesthetic infiltration): Apply 5-10 g (thick layer) of cream for 5-10 minutes

Patient Information Not for ophthalmic use; for external use only. EMLA® may block sensation in the treated area.

Dosage Forms CRM, topical: Lidocaine 2.5% and prilocaine 2.5% (30 g); (EMLA®): Lidocaine 2.5% and prilocaine 2.5% (5 g, 30 g). **DISC, topical:** 1 g (2s, 10s)

◆ **Lidocaine Hydrochloride** see Lidocaine on page 742

◆ **Lidocaine Hydrochloride and Bupivacaine Hydrochloride** see Lidocaine and Bupivacaine on page 744

◆ **Lidocaine, Neomycin, Bacitracin, and Polymyxin B** see Bacitracin, Neomycin, Polymyxin B, and Lidocaine on page 144

◆ **Lidoderm®** see Lidocaine on page 742

◆ **Lignocaine Hydrochloride** see Lidocaine on page 742

◆ **Limbitrol®** see Amitriptyline and Chlordiazepoxide on page 81

◆ **Limbitrol® DS** see Amitriptyline and Chlordiazepoxide on page 81

Lindane (LIN dane)

Synonyms Benzene Hexachloride; Gamma Benzene Hexachloride; Hexachlorocyclohexane

Therapeutic Category Antiparasitic Agent, Topical; Pediculocide; Scabicidal Agent; Shampoo

Use Treatment of Sarcoptes scabiei (scabies), Pediculus capitis (head lice), and Pthirus pubis (crab lice); FDA recommends reserving lindane as a second-line agent or with inadequate response to other therapies

Pregnancy Risk Factor C

Contraindications Hypersensitivity to lindane or any component of the formulation; uncontrolled seizure disorders; crusted (Norwegian) scabies, acutely-inflamed skin or raw, weeping surfaces or other skin conditions which may increase systemic absorption

Warnings/Precautions Not considered a drug of first choice; seizures and death have been reported with use; use with caution in infants, small children, patients <50 kg, or patients with a history of seizures; use caution with conditions which may increase risk of seizures or medications which decrease seizure threshold; use caution with hepatic impairment; avoid contact with face, eyes, mucous membranes, and urethral meatus. Because of the potential for systemic absorption and CNS side effects, lindane should be used with caution; consider permethrin or crotamiton agent first. Oil-based hair dressing may increase toxic potential. A lindane medication use guide must be given to all patients along with instructions for proper use. Should be used as a part of an overall lice management program.

Common Adverse Reactions Frequency not defined (includes postmarketing and/or case reports).

Cardiovascular: Cardiac arrhythmia

Central nervous system: Ataxia, dizziness, headache, restlessness, seizures, pain

Dermatologic: Alopecia, contact dermatitis, skin and adipose tissue may act as repositories, eczematous eruptions, pruritus, urticaria

Gastrointestinal: Nausea, vomiting

Hematologic: Aplastic anemia

Hepatic: Hepatitis

Local: Burning and stinging

Neuromuscular & skeletal: Paresthesias

Renal: Hematuria

Respiratory: Pulmonary edema

Drug Interactions

Increased Effect/Toxicity: Increased toxicity: Drugs which lower seizure threshold

Mechanism of Action Directly absorbed by parasites and ova through the exoskeleton; stimulates the nervous system resulting in seizures and death of parasitic arthropods

Pharmacodynamics/Kinetics

Absorption: ≤13% systemically

Distribution: Stored in body fat; accumulates in brain; skin and adipose tissue may act as repositories

Metabolism: Hepatic

Half-life elimination: Children: 17-22 hours

Time to peak, serum: Children: 6 hours

Excretion: Urine and feces

Dosage Children and Adults: Topical:

Scabies: Apply a thin layer of lotion and massage it on skin from the neck to the toes; after 8-12 hours, bathe and remove the drug

Head lice, crab lice: Apply shampoo to dry hair and massage into hair for 4 minutes; add small quantities of water to hair until lather forms, then rinse hair thoroughly and comb with a fine tooth comb to remove nits. Amount of shampoo needed is based on length and density of hair; most patients will require 30 mL (maximum: 60 mL).

Administration For topical use only; never administer orally. Caregivers should apply with gloves (avoid natural latex, may be permeable to lindane). Rinse off with warm (not hot) water.

Lotion: Apply to dry, cool skin; do not apply to face or eyes. Wait at least 1 hour after bathing or showering (wet or warm skin increases absorption). Skin should be clean and free of any other lotions, creams, or oil prior to lindane application.

Shampoo: Apply to clean, dry hair. Wait at least 1 hour after washing hair before applying lindane shampoo. Hair should be washed with a shampoo not containing a conditioner; hair and skin of head and neck should be free of any lotions, oils, or creams prior to lindane application.

Patient Information Topical use only, do not apply to face, avoid getting in eyes; do **not** apply lotion immediately after a hot, soapy bath. For scabies, Apply from neck to toes. Bathe to remove drug after 8-12 hours. For head lice or crab lice, massage into dry hair for 4 minutes; add water to hair to form lather, then rinse thoroughly. Clothing and bedding should be washed in hot water or by dry cleaning to kill the scabies mite. Combs and brushes may be washed with lindane shampoo then thoroughly rinsed with water. Notify prescriber if condition worsens; treat sexual contact simultaneously.

Dosage Forms LOTION, topical: 1% (60 mL, 473 mL). **SHAMP, topical:** 1% (60 mL, 473 mL)

Linezolid (li NE zoh lid)

Related Information

Antimicrobial Drugs of Choice *on page 1440*

Community-Acquired Pneumonia in Adults *on page 1457*

U.S. Brand Names Zyvox™

Therapeutic Category Antibiotic, Oxazolidinone

Use Treatment of vancomycin-resistant *Enterococcus faecium* (VRE) infections, nosocomial pneumonia caused by *Staphylococcus aureus* including MRSA or *Streptococcus pneumoniae* (penicillin-susceptible strains only), complicated and uncomplicated skin and skin structure infections (including diabetic foot infections without concomitant osteomyelitis), and community-acquired pneumonia caused by susceptible gram-positive organisms.

Pregnancy Risk Factor C

Contraindications Hypersensitivity to linezolid or any other component of the formulation

Warnings/Precautions Myelosuppression has been reported and may be dependent on duration of therapy (generally >2 weeks of treatment); use with caution in patients with pre-existing myelosuppression, in patients receiving other drugs which may cause bone marrow suppression, or in chronic infection (previous or concurrent antibiotic therapy). Weekly CBC monitoring is recommended. Discontinue linezolid in patients developing myelosuppression (or in whom myelosuppression worsens during treatment).

Linezolid has mild MAO inhibitor properties and has the potential to have the same interactions as other MAO inhibitors; use with caution in uncontrolled hypertension, pheochromocytoma, carcinoid syndrome, or untreated hyperthyroidism; avoid use with serotonergic agents such as TCAs, venlafaxine, trazodone, sibutramine, meperidine, dextromethorphan, and SSRIs; consider alternatives before initiating outpatient treatment (unnecessary use may lead the development of resistance to linezolid)

Common Adverse Reactions Percentages as reported in adults; frequency similar in pediatric patients

1% to 10%:

Cardiovascular: Hypertension (1% to 3%)

(Continued)

Linezolid *(Continued)*

Central nervous system: Headache (0.5% to 11%), insomnia (3%), dizziness (0.4% to 2%), fever (2%)

Dermatologic: Rash (2%)

Gastrointestinal: Nausea (3% to 10%), diarrhea (3% to 11%), vomiting (1% to 4%), constipation (2%), taste alteration (1% to 2%), tongue discoloration (0.2% to 1%), oral moniliasis (0.4% to 1%), pancreatitis

Genitourinary: Vaginal moniliasis (1% to 2%)

Hematologic: Thrombocytopenia (0.3% to 10%), anemia, leukopenia, neutropenia; **Note:** Myelosuppression (including anemia, leukopenia, pancytopenia, and thrombocytopenia; may be more common in patients receiving linezolid for >2 weeks)

Hepatic: Abnormal LFTs (0.4% to 1%)

Miscellaneous: Fungal infections (0.1% to 0.4%)

Drug Interactions

Increased Effect/Toxicity: Linezolid is a reversible, nonselective inhibitor of MAO. Serotonergic agents (eg, TCAs, venlafaxine, trazodone, sibutramine, meperidine, dextromethorphan, and SSRIs) may cause a serotonin syndrome (eg, hyperpyrexia, cognitive dysfunction) when used concomitantly. Adrenergic agents (eg, phenylpropanolamine, pseudoephedrine, sympathomimetic agents, vasopressor or dopaminergic agents) may cause hypertension. Tramadol may increase the risk of seizures when used concurrently with linezolid. Myelosuppressive medications may increase risk of myelosuppression when used concurrently with linezolid.

Mechanism of Action Inhibits bacterial protein synthesis by binding to bacterial 23S ribosomal RNA of the 50S subunit. This prevents the formation of a functional 70S initiation complex that is essential for the bacterial translation process. Linezolid is bacteriostatic against enterococci and staphylococci and bactericidal against most strains of streptococci.

Pharmacodynamics/Kinetics

Absorption: Rapid and extensive

Distribution: V_{dss}: Adults: 40-50 L

Protein binding: Adults: 31%

Metabolism: Hepatic via oxidation of the morpholine ring, resulting in two inactive metabolites (aminoethoxyacetic acid, hydroxyethyl glycine); does not involve CYP

Bioavailability: 100%

Half-life elimination: Children ≥1 week (full-term) to 11 years: 1.5-3 hours; Adults: 4-5 hours

Time to peak: Adults: Oral: 1-2 hours

Excretion: Urine (30% as parent drug, 50% as metabolites); feces (9% as metabolites)

Nonrenal clearance: 65%; increased in children ≥1 week to 11 years

Dosage

VRE infections: Oral, I.V.:

Infants (excluding preterm neonates <1 week) and Children ≤11 years: 10 mg/kg every 8 hours for 14-28 days

Children ≥12 years and Adults: 600 mg every 12 hours for 14-28 days

Nosocomial pneumonia, complicated skin and skin structure infections, community acquired pneumonia including concurrent bacteremia: Oral, I.V.:

Infants (excluding preterm neonates <1 week) and Children ≤11 years: 10 mg/kg every 8 hours for 10-14 days

Children ≥12 years and Adults: 600 mg every 12 hours for 10-14 days

Uncomplicated skin and skin structure infections: Oral:

Infants (excluding preterm neonates <1 week) and Children <5 years: 10 mg/kg every 8 hours for 10-14 days

Children 5-11 years: 10 mg/kg every 12 hours for 10-14 days

Children ≥12-18 years: 600 mg every 12 hours for 10-14 days

Adults: 400 mg every 12 hours for 10-14 days

Elderly: No dosage adjustment required

Dosage adjustment in hepatic impairment: No dosage adjustment required for mild to moderate hepatic insufficiency (Child-Pugh Class A or B). Use in severe hepatic insufficiency has not been adequately evaluated.

Administration

I.V.: Administer intravenous infusion over 30-120 minutes. Do not mix or infuse with other medications. When the same intravenous line is used for sequential infusion of other medications, flush line with D_5W, NS, or LR before and after infusing linezolid. The yellow color of the injection may intensify over time without affecting potency.

Oral suspension: Invert gently to mix prior to administration, do not shake.

Monitoring Parameters Weekly CBC and platelet counts, particularly in patients at increased risk of bleeding, with pre-existing myelosuppression, on concomitant medications that cause bone marrow suppression, in those who require >2 weeks of therapy, or in those with chronic infection who have received previous or concomitant antibiotic therapy.

Patient Information Take with or without food. Take with food if medicine causes stomach upset. Tell your prescriber if you have hypertension or are taking any cold remedy or decongestant. Limit quantities of tyramine-containing foods. Gently mix suspension. Store at room temperature. Notify your prescriber if you feel very weak, have any bleeding problems, bruising, new signs/symptoms of infection, shortness of breath, rapid heartbeats, or weight loss.

Dosage Forms INF [premixed]: 200 mg (100 mL); 400 mg (200 mL); 600 mg (300 mL). **POWDER, oral suspension:** 20 mg/mL (150 mL). **TAB:** 400 mg, 600 mg

♦ **Lioresal®** *see* Baclofen *on page 144*

Liothyronine (lye oh THYE roe neen)
U.S. Brand Names Cytomel®; Triostat®
Synonyms Liothyronine Sodium; Sodium *L*-Triiodothyronine; T_3 Sodium
Therapeutic Category Thyroid Product
Use
    Oral: Replacement or supplemental therapy in hypothyroidism; management of nontoxic goiter; a diagnostic aid
    I.V.: Treatment of myxedema coma/precoma
Pregnancy Risk Factor A
Dosage Doses should be adjusted based on clinical response and laboratory parameters.
    Children: Congenital hypothyroidism: Oral: 5 mcg/day increase by 5 mcg every 3-4 days until the desired response is achieved. Usual maintenance dose: 20 mcg/day for infants, 50 mcg/day for children 1-3 years of age, and adult dose for children >3 years.
    Adults:
        Hypothyroidism: Oral: 25 mcg/day increase by increments of 12.5-25 mcg/day every 1-2 weeks to a maximum of 100 mcg/day; usual maintenance dose: 25-75 mcg/day.
        Patients with cardiovascular disease: Refer to Elderly dosing.
        T_3 suppression test: Oral: 75-100 mcg/day for 7 days; use lowest dose for elderly
        Myxedema: Oral: Initial: 5 mcg/day; increase in increments of 5-10 mcg/day every 1-2 weeks. When 25 mcg/day is reached, dosage may be increased at intervals of 5-25 mcg/day every 1-2 weeks. Usual maintenance dose: 50-100 mcg/day.
        Myxedema coma: I.V.: 25-50 mcg
        Patients with known or suspected cardiovascular disease: 10-20 mcg
        Note: Normally, at least 4 hours should be allowed between doses to adequately assess therapeutic response and no more than 12 hours should elapse between doses to avoid fluctuations in hormone levels. Oral therapy should be resumed as soon as the clinical situation has been stabilized and the patient is able to take oral medication. If levothyroxine rather than liothyronine sodium is used in initiating oral therapy, the physician should bear in mind that there is a delay of several days in the onset of levothyroxine activity and that I.V. therapy should be discontinued gradually.
        Simple (nontoxic) goiter: Oral: Initial: 5 mcg/day; increase by 5-10 mcg every 1-2 weeks; after 25 mcg/day is reached, may increase dose by 12.5-25 mcg. Usual maintenance dose: 75 mcg/day
    Elderly: Oral: 5 mcg/day; increase by 5 mcg/day every 2 weeks
Dosage Forms INJ, solution: (Triostar®) 10 mcg/mL (1 mL). **TAB:** (Cytomel®) 5 mcg, 25 mcg, 50 mcg

♦ **Liothyronine Sodium** *see Liothyronine on page 749*

Liotrix (LYE oh triks)
U.S. Brand Names Thyrolar®
Synonyms T_3/T_4 Liotrix
Therapeutic Category Thyroid Product
Use Replacement or supplemental therapy in hypothyroidism (uniform mixture of T_4:T_3 in 4:1 ratio by weight); little advantage to this product exists and cost is not justified
Pregnancy Risk Factor A
Dosage Oral:
    Congenital hypothyroidism:
        Children (dose of T_4 or levothyroxine/day):
            0-6 months: 8-10 mcg/kg or 25-50 mcg/day
            6-12 months: 6-8 mcg/kg or 50-75 mcg/day
            1-5 years: 5-6 mcg/kg or 75-100 mcg/day
            6-12 years: 4-5 mcg/kg or 100-150 mcg/day
            >12 years: 2-3 mcg/kg or >150 mcg/day
    Hypothyroidism (dose of thyroid equivalent):
        Adults: 30 mg/day (15 mg/day if cardiovascular impairment), increasing by increments of 15 mg/day at 2- to 3-week intervals to a maximum of 180 mg/day (usual maintenance dose: 60-120 mg/day)
        Elderly: Initial: 15 mg, adjust dose at 2- to 4-week intervals by increments of 15 mg
Dosage Forms TAB (in mg of thyroid equivalent): 15 mg [levothyroxine 12.5 mcg and liothyronine 3.1 mcg]; 30 mg [levothyroxine 25 mcg and liothyronine 6.25 mcg]; 60 mg [levothyroxine 50 mcg and liothyronine 12.5 mcg]; 120 mg [levothyroxine 100 mcg and liothyronine 25 mcg]; 180 mg [levothyroxine 150 mcg and liothyronine 37.5 mcg]

♦ **Lipancreatin** *see Pancrelipase on page 953*
♦ **Lipid-Lowering Agents** *see page 1381*
♦ **Lipitor®** *see Atorvastatin on page 129*
♦ **Liposyn® III** *see Fat Emulsion on page 508*
♦ **Lipram 4500** *see Pancrelipase on page 953*
♦ **Lipram-CR** *see Pancrelipase on page 953*
♦ **Lipram-PN** *see Pancrelipase on page 953*
♦ **Lipram-UL** *see Pancrelipase on page 953*
♦ **Liquibid®** *see Guaifenesin on page 603*
♦ **Liquibid® 1200** *see Guaifenesin on page 603*
♦ **Liquibid-D** *see Guaifenesin and Phenylephrine on page 605*
♦ **Liqui-Char® [OTC] [DSC]** *see Charcoal on page 253*

◆ **Liquid Antidote** *see* Charcoal *on page 253*

Lisinopril (lyse IN oh pril)
Related Information
Angiotensin Agents Comparison *on page 1353*
U.S. Brand Names Prinivil®; Zestril®
Therapeutic Category Angiotensin-Converting Enzyme (ACE) Inhibitor; Antihypertensive Agent
Use Treatment of hypertension, either alone or in combination with other antihypertensive agents; adjunctive therapy in treatment of CHF (afterload reduction); treatment of hemodynamically stable patients within 24 hours of acute myocardial infarction, to improve survival; treatment of acute myocardial infarction within 24 hours in hemodynamically stable patients to improve survival; treatment of left ventricular dysfunction after myocardial infarction
Pregnancy Risk Factor C/D (2nd and 3rd trimesters)
Contraindications Hypersensitivity to lisinopril or any component of the formulation; angioedema related to previous treatment with an ACE inhibitor; bilateral renal artery stenosis; pregnancy (2nd and 3rd trimesters)
Warnings/Precautions Anaphylactic reactions can occur. Angioedema can occur at any time during treatment (especially following first dose). Angioedema may involve head and neck (potentially affecting the airway) or the intestine (presenting with abdominal pain). Careful blood pressure monitoring with first dose (hypotension can occur especially in volume depleted patients). Dosage adjustment needed in renal impairment. Use with caution in hypovolemia; collagen vascular diseases; valvular stenosis (particularly aortic stenosis); hyperkalemia; or before, during, or immediately after anesthesia. Avoid rapid dosage escalation, which may lead to renal insufficiency. Neutropenia/agranulocytosis with myeloid hyperplasia can rarely occur. If patient has renal impairment then a baseline WBC with differential and serum creatinine should be evaluated and monitored closely during the first 3 months of therapy. Hypersensitivity reactions may be seen during hemodialysis with high-flux dialysis membranes (eg, AN69). Deterioration in renal function can occur with initiation. Use with caution in unilateral renal artery stenosis and pre-existing renal insufficiency. Safety and efficacy have not been established in children <6 years of age.
Common Adverse Reactions Note: Frequency ranges include data from hypertension and heart failure trials. Higher rates of adverse reactions have generally been noted in patients with CHF. However, the frequency of adverse effects associated with placebo is also increased in this population.

1% to 10%:
Cardiovascular: Orthostatic effects (1%), hypotension (1% to 4%)
Central nervous system: Headache (4% to 6%), dizziness (5% to 12%), fatigue (3%), weakness (1%)
Dermatologic: Rash (1% to 2%)
Endocrine & metabolic: Hyperkalemia (2% to 5%)
Gastrointestinal: Diarrhea (3% to 4%), nausea (2%), vomiting (1%), abdominal pain (2%)
Genitourinary: Impotence (1%)
Hematologic: Decreased hemoglobin (small)
Neuromuscular & skeletal: Chest pain (3%)
Renal: Increased serum creatinine (often transient), increased BUN (2%); deterioration in renal function (in patients with bilateral renal artery stenosis or hypovolemia)
Respiratory: Cough (4% to 9%), upper respiratory infection (2% to 2%)

Drug Interactions
Increased Effect/Toxicity: Potassium supplements, co-trimoxazole (high dose), angiotensin II receptor antagonists (candesartan, losartan, irbesartan, etc), or potassium-sparing diuretics (amiloride, spironolactone, triamterene) may result in elevated serum potassium levels when combined with lisinopril. ACE inhibitor effects may be increased by phenothiazines or probenecid (increases levels of captopril). ACE inhibitors may increase serum concentrations/effects of digoxin, lithium, and sulfonlyureas.

Diuretics have additive hypotensive effects with ACE inhibitors, and hypovolemia increases the potential for adverse renal effects of ACE inhibitors. In patients with compromised renal function, coadministration with NSAIDs may result in further deterioration of renal function. Allopurinol and ACE inhibitors may cause a higher risk of hypersensitivity reaction when taken concurrently.
Decreased Effect: Aspirin (high dose) may reduce the therapeutic effects of ACE inhibitors; at low dosages this does not appear to be significant. Rifampin may decrease the effect of ACE inhibitors. Antacids may decrease the bioavailability of ACE inhibitors (may be more likely to occur with captopril); separate administration times by 1-2 hours. NSAIDs, specifically indomethacin, may reduce the hypotensive effects of ACE inhibitors. More likely to occur in low renin or volume dependent hypertensive patients.
Mechanism of Action Competitive inhibitor of angiotensin-converting enzyme (ACE); prevents conversion of angiotensin I to angiotensin II, a potent vasoconstrictor; results in lower levels of angiotensin II which causes an increase in plasma renin activity and a reduction in aldosterone secretion; a CNS mechanism may also be involved in hypotensive effect as angiotensin II increases adrenergic outflow from CNS; vasoactive kallikreins may be decreased in conversion to active hormones by ACE inhibitors, thus reducing blood pressure
Pharmacodynamics/Kinetics
Onset of action: 1 hour
Peak effect: Hypotensive: Oral: ~6 hours
Duration: 24 hours

Absorption: Well absorbed; unaffected by food
Protein binding: 25%
Half-life elimination: 11-12 hours
Excretion: Primarily urine (as unchanged drug)
Dosage Oral:
Hypertension:
Children ≥6 years: Initial: 0.07 mg/kg once daily (up to 5 mg); increase dose at 1- to 2-week intervals; doses >0.61 mg/kg or >40 mg have not been evaluated.
Adults: Initial: 10 mg/day; increase doses 5-10 mg/day at 1- to 2-week intervals; maximum daily dose: 40 mg
Elderly: Initial: 2.5-5 mg/day; increase doses 2.5-5 mg/day at 1- to 2-week intervals; maximum daily dose: 40 mg
Patients taking diuretics should have them discontinued 2-3 days prior to initiating lisinopril if possible. Restart diuretic after blood pressure is stable if needed. If diuretic cannot be discontinued prior to therapy, begin with 5 mg with close supervision until stable blood pressure. In patients with hyponatremia (<130 mEq/L), start dose at 2.5 mg/day,
Congestive heart failure: Adults: Initial: 5 mg; then increase by no more than 10 mg increments at intervals no less than 2 weeks to a maximum daily dose of 40 mg. Usual maintenance: 5-40 mg/day as a single dose. Patients should start/continue standard therapy, including diuretics, beta-blockers, and digoxin, as indicated.
Acute myocardial infarction (within 24 hours in hemodynamically stable patients): Oral: 5 mg immediately, then 5 mg at 24 hours, 10 mg at 48 hours, and 10 mg every day thereafter for 6 weeks. Patients should continue to receive standard treatments such as thrombolytics, aspirin, and beta-blockers.

Dosing adjustment in renal impairment:
Adults: Initial doses should be modified and upward titration should be cautious, based on response (maximum: 40 mg/day)
Cl_{cr} >30 mL/minute: Initial: 10 mg/day
Cl_{cr} 10-30 mL/minute: Initial: 5 mg/day
Hemodialysis: Initial: 2.5 mg/day; dialyzable (50%)
Children: Use in not recommended in pediatric patients with GFR <30 mL/minute/1.73 m^2
Administration Watch for hypotensive effects within 1-3 hours of first dose or new higher dose.
Monitoring Parameters BUN, serum creatinine, renal function, WBC, and potassium
Patient Information Report vomiting, diarrhea, excessive perspiration, or dehydration; also if swelling of face, lips, tongue or difficulty in breathing occurs or if persistent cough develops. Do not stop therapy without the advise of the prescriber; do not add a salt substitute (potassium) without prescriber advice.
Dosage Forms TAB: 2.5 mg, 5 mg, 10 mg, 20 mg, 30 mg, 40 mg

Lisinopril and Hydrochlorothiazide
(lyse IN oh pril & hye droe klor oh THYE a zide)
U.S. Brand Names Prinzide®; Zestoretic®
Synonyms Hydrochlorothiazide and Lisinopril
Therapeutic Category Angiotensin-Converting Enzyme (ACE) Inhibitor/Thiazide Diuretic; Antihypertensive Agent, Combination
Use Treatment of hypertension
Pregnancy Risk Factor C/D (2nd and 3rd trimesters)
Dosage Adults: Oral: Dosage is individualized; see each component for appropriate dosing suggestions; doses >80 mg/day lisinopril or >50 mg/day hydrochlorothiazide are not recommended.
Dosage Forms TAB: Lisinopril 10 mg and hydrochlorothiazide 12.5 mg; lisinopril 20 mg and hydrochlorothiazide 12.5 mg; lisinopril 20 mg and hydrochlorothiazide 25 mg

Lithium (LITH ee um)
U.S. Brand Names Eskalith®; Eskalith CR®; Lithobid®
Synonyms Lithium Carbonate; Lithium Citrate
Therapeutic Category Antimanic Agent
Use Management of bipolar disorders; treatment of mania in individuals with bipolar disorder (maintenance treatment prevents or diminishes intensity of subsequent episodes)
Unlabeled/Investigational Use Potential augmenting agent for antidepressants; aggression, post-traumatic stress disorder, conduct disorder in children
Pregnancy Risk Factor D
Contraindications Hypersensitivity to lithium or any component of the formulation; avoid use in patients with severe cardiovascular or renal disease, or with severe debilitation, dehydration, or sodium depletion; pregnancy
Warnings/Precautions Lithium toxicity is closely related to serum levels and can occur at therapeutic doses; serum lithium determinations are required to monitor therapy. Use with caution in patients with thyroid disease, mild-moderate renal impairment, or mild-moderate cardiovascular disease. Use caution in patients receiving medications which alter sodium excretion (eg, diuretics, ACE inhibitors, NSAIDs), or in patients with significant fluid loss (protracted sweating, diarrhea, or prolonged fever); temporary reduction or cessation of therapy may be warranted. Some elderly patients may be extremely sensitive to the effects of lithium, see Dosage and Reference Range. Chronic therapy results in diminished renal concentrating ability (nephrogenic DI); this is usually reversible when lithium is discontinued. Changes in renal function should be monitored, and re-evaluation of treatment may be necessary. Use caution in patients at risk of suicide (suicidal thoughts or behavior).
(Continued)

Lithium *(Continued)*

Use with caution in patients receiving neuroleptic medications - a syndrome resembling NMS has been associated with concurrent therapy. Lithium may impair the patient's alertness, affecting the ability to operate machinery or driving a vehicle. Neuromuscular-blocking agents should be administered with caution; the response may be prolonged.

Higher serum concentrations may be required and tolerated during an acute manic phase; however, the tolerance decreases when symptoms subside. Normal fluid and salt intake must be maintained during therapy.

Safety and efficacy have not been established in children <12 years of age.

Common Adverse Reactions Frequency not defined.

Cardiovascular: Cardiac arrhythmias, hypotension, sinus node dysfunction, flattened or inverted T waves (reversible), edema, bradycardia, syncope

Central nervous system: Dizziness, vertigo, slurred speech, blackout spells, seizures, sedation, restlessness, confusion, psychomotor retardation, stupor, coma, dystonia, fatigue, lethargy, headache, pseudotumor cerebri, slowed intellectual functioning, tics

Dermatologic: Dry or thinning of hair, folliculitis, alopecia, exacerbation of psoriasis, rash

Endocrine & metabolic: Euthyroid goiter and/or hypothyroidism, hyperthyroidism, hyperglycemia, diabetes insipidus

Gastrointestinal: Polydipsia, anorexia, nausea, vomiting, diarrhea, xerostomia, metallic taste, weight gain, salivary gland swelling, excessive salivation

Genitourinary: Incontinence, polyuria, glycosuria, oliguria, albuminuria

Hematologic: Leukocytosis

Neuromuscular & skeletal: Tremor, muscle hyperirritability, ataxia, choreoathetoid movements, hyperactive deep tendon reflexes, myasthenia gravis (rare)

Ocular: Nystagmus, blurred vision, transient scotoma

Miscellaneous: Coldness and painful discoloration of fingers and toes

Drug Interactions

Increased Effect/Toxicity: Concurrent use of lithium with carbamazepine, diltiazem, SSRIs (fluoxetine, fluvoxamine), haloperidol, methyldopa, metronidazole (rare), phenothiazines, phenytoin, TCAs, and verapamil may increase the risk for neurotoxicity. A rare encephalopathic syndrome has been reported in association with haloperidol (causal relationship not established). Lithium concentrations/toxicity may be increased by diuretics, NSAIDs (sulindac and aspirin may be exceptions), ACE inhibitors, angiotensin receptor antagonists (losartan), tetracyclines, or COX-2 inhibitors (celecoxib).

Lithium and MAO inhibitors should generally be avoided due to use reports of fatal malignant hyperpyrexia; risk with selective MAO type B inhibitors (selegiline) appears to be lower. Potassium iodide may enhance the hypothyroid effects of lithium. Combined use of lithium with tricyclic antidepressants or sibutramine may increase the risk of serotonin syndrome; this combination is best avoided. Lithium may potentiate effect of neuromuscular blockers.

Decreased Effect: Combined use of lithium and chlorpromazine may lower serum concentrations of both drugs. Lithium may blunt the pressor response to sympathomimetics (epinephrine, norepinephrine). Caffeine (xanthine derivatives) may lower lithium serum concentrations by increasing urinary lithium excretion (monitor).

Mechanism of Action Alters cation transport across cell membrane in nerve and muscle cells and influences reuptake of serotonin and/or norepinephrine; second messenger systems involving the phosphatidylinositol cycle are inhibited; postsynaptic D2 receptor supersensitivity is inhibited

Pharmacodynamics/Kinetics

Absorption: Rapid and complete

Distribution: V_d: Initial: 0.3-0.4 L/kg; V_{dss}: 0.7-1 L/kg; crosses placenta; enters breast milk at 35% to 50% the concentrations in serum; distribution is complete in 6-10 hours

CSF, liver concentrations: $1/3$ to $1/2$ of serum concentration

Erythrocyte concentration: $\sim 1/2$ of serum concentration

Heart, lung, kidney, muscle concentrations: Equivalent to serum concentration

Saliva concentration: 2-3 times serum concentration

Thyroid, bone, brain tissue concentrations: Increase 50% over serum concentrations

Protein binding: Not protein bound

Metabolism: Not metabolized

Bioavailability: Not affected by food; Capsule, immediate release tablet: 95% to 100%; Extended release tablet: 60% to 90%; Syrup: 100%

Half-life elimination: 18-24 hours; can increase to more than 36 hours in elderly or with renal impairment

Time to peak, serum: Nonsustained release: ~0.5-2 hours; slow release: 4-12 hours; syrup: 15-60 minutes

Excretion: Urine (90% to 98% as unchanged drug); sweat (4% to 5%); feces (1%)

Clearance: 80% of filtered lithium is reabsorbed in the proximal convoluted tubules; therefore, clearance approximates 20% of GFR or 20-40 mL/minute

Dosage Oral: Monitor serum concentrations and clinical response (efficacy and toxicity) to determine proper dose

Children 6-12 years:

Bipolar disorder: 15-60 mg/kg/day in 3-4 divided doses; dose not to exceed usual adult dosage

Conduct disorder (unlabeled use): 15-30 mg/kg/day in 3-4 divided doses; dose not to exceed usual adult dosage

Adults: Bipolar disorder: 900-2400 mg/day in 3-4 divided doses or 900-1800 mg/day (sustained release) in 2 divided doses

Elderly: Bipolar disorder: Initial dose: 300 mg once or twice daily; increase weekly in increments of 300 mg/day, monitoring levels; rarely need >900-1200 mg/day

Dosing adjustment in renal impairment:

Cl_{cr} 10-50 mL/minute: Administer 50% to 75% of normal dose

Cl_{cr} <10 mL/minute: Administer 25% to 50% of normal dose

Hemodialysis: Dialyzable (50% to 100%); 4-7 times more efficient than peritoneal dialysis

Administration Administer with meals to decrease GI upset. Slow release tablets must be swallowed whole; do not crush or chew.

Monitoring Parameters Serum lithium every 4-5 days during initial therapy; draw lithium serum concentrations 8-12 hours postdose; renal, thyroid, and cardiovascular function; fluid status; serum electrolytes; CBC with differential, urinalysis; monitor for signs of toxicity; b-HCG pregnancy test for all females not known to be sterile

Reference Range Levels should be obtained twice weekly until both patient's clinical status and levels are stable then levels may be obtained every 1-3 months

Timing of serum samples: Draw trough just before next dose (8-12 hours after previous dose)

Therapeutic levels:

Acute mania: 0.6-1.2 mEq/L (SI: 0.6-1.2 mmol/L)

Protection against future episodes in most patients with bipolar disorder: 0.8-1 mEq/L (SI: 0.8-1.0 mmol/L); a higher rate of relapse is described in subjects who are maintained at <0.4 mEq/L (SI: 0.4 mmol/L)

Elderly patients can usually be maintained at lower end of therapeutic range (0.6-0.8 mEq/L)

Toxic concentration: >1.5 mEq/L (SI: >2 mmol/L)

Adverse effect levels:

GI complaints/tremor: 1.5-2 mEq/L

Confusion/somnolence: 2-2.5 mEq/L

Seizures/death: >2.5 mEq/L

Patient Information Avoid tasks requiring psychomotor coordination until the CNS effects are known, blood level monitoring is required to determine the proper dose; maintain a steady salt and fluid intake especially during the summer months; do not crush or chew slow or extended release dosage form, swallow whole

Dosage Forms CAP, as carbonate: 150 mg, 300 mg, 600 mg; (Eskalith®): 300 mg. **SYR, as citrate:** 300 mg/5 mL (5 mL, 10 mL, 480 mL). **TAB, as carbonate:** 300 mg. **TAB, controlled release, as carbonate** (Eskalith CR®): 450 mg. **TAB, slow release, as carbonate** (Lithobid®): 300 mg

♦ **Lithium Carbonate** *see* Lithium *on page 751*
♦ **Lithium Citrate** *see* Lithium *on page 751*
♦ **Lithobid®** *see* Lithium *on page 751*
♦ **Livostin®** *see* Levocabastine *on page 729*
♦ **LMD®** *see* Dextran *on page 361*
♦ **L-M-X™ 4 [OTC]** *see* Lidocaine *on page 742*
♦ **L-M-X™ 5 [OTC]** *see* Lidocaine *on page 742*
♦ **LNg 20** *see* Levonorgestrel *on page 737*
♦ **Locoid®** *see* Hydrocortisone *on page 632*
♦ **Locoid Lipocream®** *see* Hydrocortisone *on page 632*
♦ **Lodine®** *see* Etodolac *on page 496*
♦ **Lodine® XL** *see* Etodolac *on page 496*
♦ **Lodosyn®** *see* Carbidopa *on page 218*

Lodoxamide (loe DOKS a mide)

U.S. Brand Names Alomide®

Synonyms Lodoxamide Tromethamine

Therapeutic Category Antiallergic, Ophthalmic

Use Treatment of vernal keratoconjunctivitis, vernal conjunctivitis, and vernal keratitis

Pregnancy Risk Factor B

Dosage Ophthalmic: Children ≥2 years and Adults: Instill 1-2 drops in eye(s) 4 times/day for up to 3 months

Dosage Forms SOLN, ophthalmic: 0.1% (10 mL)

♦ **Lodoxamide Tromethamine** *see* Lodoxamide *on page 753*
♦ **Lodrane®** *see* Brompheniramine and Pseudoephedrine *on page 181*
♦ **Lodrane® LD** *see* Brompheniramine and Pseudoephedrine *on page 181*
♦ **Loestrin®** *see* Ethinyl Estradiol and Norethindrone *on page 487*
♦ **Loestrin® Fe** *see* Ethinyl Estradiol and Norethindrone *on page 487*
♦ **Lofibra™** *see* Fenofibrate *on page 511*
♦ **L-OHP** *see* Oxaliplatin *on page 936*

Lomefloxacin (loe me FLOKS a sin)

U.S. Brand Names Maxaquin®

Synonyms Lomefloxacin Hydrochloride

Therapeutic Category Antibiotic, Quinolone

Use Lower respiratory infections, acute bacterial exacerbation of chronic bronchitis, and urinary tract infections caused by *E. coli, K. pneumoniae, P. mirabilis, P. aeruginosa*; also has
(Continued)

Lomefloxacin *(Continued)*

gram-positive activity including *S. pneumoniae* and some staphylococci; surgical prophylaxis (transrectal prostate biopsy or transurethral procedures)

Pregnancy Risk Factor C

Contraindications Hypersensitivity to lomefloxacin, any component of the formulation, or other members of the quinolone group (such as, nalidixic acid, oxolinic acid, cinoxacin, norfloxacin, and ciprofloxacin); avoid use in children <18 years of age due to association of other quinolones with transient arthropathies

Warnings/Precautions Not recommended in children <18 years of age; CNS stimulation may occur (tremor, restlessness, confusion, and very rarely hallucinations or seizures); use with caution in patients with known or suspected CNS disorders or renal dysfunction; use caution to avoid possible photosensitivity reactions during and for several days following fluoroquinolone therapy

Severe hypersensitivity reactions, including anaphylaxis, have occurred with quinolone therapy. If an allergic reaction occurs (itching, urticaria, dyspnea or facial edema, loss of consciousness, tingling, cardiovascular collapse), discontinue drug immediately. Prolonged use may result in superinfection; pseudomembranous colitis may occur and should be considered in all patients who present with diarrhea. Tendon inflammation and/or rupture has been reported; discontinue at first sign of tendon inflammation or pain. Quinolones may exacerbate myasthenia gravis, use with caution (rare, potentially life-threatening weakness of respiratory muscles may occur).

Common Adverse Reactions 1% to 10%:

Central nervous system: Headache (3%), dizziness (2%)

Dermatologic: Photosensitivity (2%)

Gastrointestinal: Nausea (4%)

Drug Interactions

Cytochrome P450 Effect: Inhibits CYP1A2 (strong)

Increased Effect/Toxicity: Quinolones can cause elevated levels of caffeine, warfarin, cyclosporine, and theophylline. Azlocillin, imipenem, cimetidine, loop diuretics, and probenecid may increase lomefloxacin serum levels. Increased CNS stimulation may occur with caffeine, theophylline, NSAIDs. Foscarnet has been associated with seizures in patients receiving quinolones. Concurrent use of corticosteroids may increase risk of tendon rupture.

Decreased Effect: Decreased absorption with antacids containing aluminum, magnesium, and/or calcium (by up to 98% if given at the same time). Antineoplastic agents may decrease quinolone absorption.

Mechanism of Action Inhibits DNA-gyrase in susceptible organisms thereby inhibits relaxation of supercoiled DNA and promotes breakage of DNA strands. DNA gyrase (topoisomerase II), is an essential bacterial enzyme that maintains the superhelical structure of DNA and is required for DNA replication and transcription, DNA repair, recombination, and transposition.

Pharmacodynamics/Kinetics

Absorption: Well absorbed

Distribution: V_d: 2.4-3.5 L/kg; into bronchus, prostatic tissue, and urine

Protein binding: 20%

Half-life elimination: 5-7.5 hours

Excretion: Primarily urine (as unchanged drug)

Dosage Oral: Adults:

Lower respiratory and urinary tract infections (UTI): 400 mg once daily for 10-14 days

Urinary tract infection (UTI) due to susceptible organisms:

Females:

Uncomplicated cystitis caused by *Escherichia coli*: 400 mg once daily for 3 successive days

Uncomplicated cystitis caused by *Klebsiella pneumoniae*, *Proteus mirabilis*, or *Staphylococcus saprophyticus*: 400 mg once daily for 10 successive days

Complicated UTI caused by *Escherichia coli*, *Klebsiella pneumoniae*, *Proteus mirabilis*, or *Pseudomonas aeruginosa*: 400 mg once daily for 14 successive days

Surgical prophylaxis: 400 mg 2-6 hours before surgery

Elderly: No dosage adjustment is needed for elderly patients with normal renal function

Dosing adjustment in renal impairment:

Cl_{cr} 11-39 mL/minute: Loading dose: 400 mg, then 200 mg every day

Hemodialysis: Same as above

Dosage Forms TAB: 400 mg

♦ **Lomefloxacin Hydrochloride** *see* Lomefloxacin *on page 753*

♦ **Lomocot®** *see* Diphenoxylate and Atropine *on page 385*

♦ **Lomotil®** *see* Diphenoxylate and Atropine *on page 385*

Lomustine *(loe MUS teen)*

U.S. Brand Names CeeNU®

Synonyms CCNU

Therapeutic Category Antineoplastic Agent, Alkylating Agent (Nitrosourea)

Use Treatment of brain tumors and Hodgkin's disease, non-Hodgkin's lymphoma, melanoma, renal carcinoma, lung cancer, colon cancer

Pregnancy Risk Factor D

Contraindications Hypersensitivity to lomustine, any component of the formulation, or other nitrosoureas; pregnancy

Warnings/Precautions The U.S. Food and Drug Administration (FDA) currently recommends that procedures for proper handling and disposal for antineoplastic agents be considered. Bone marrow suppression, notably thrombocytopenia and leukopenia, may lead to bleeding and overwhelming infections in an already compromised patient; will last for at least 6 weeks after a dose, do not administer courses more frequently than every 6 weeks because the toxicity is cumulative. Use with caution in patients with depressed platelet, leukocyte or erythrocyte counts, renal or hepatic impairment.

Common Adverse Reactions

> 10%:

Gastrointestinal: Nausea and vomiting, usually within 3-6 hours after oral administration. Administration of the dose at bedtime, with an antiemetic, significantly reduces both the incidence and severity of nausea.

Hematologic: Myelosuppression, common, dose-limiting, may be cumulative and irreversible

Onset: 10-14 days

Nadir: Leukopenia: 6 weeks

Thrombocytopenia: 4 weeks

Recovery: 6-8 weeks

1% to 10%:

Dermatologic: Rash

Gastrointestinal: Anorexia, stomatitis, diarrhea

Genitourinary: Progressive azotemia, renal failure, decrease in kidney size

Hematologic: Anemia

Hepatic: Elevated liver enzymes, transient, reversible

Drug Interactions

Cytochrome P450 Effect: Substrate of CYP2D6 (major); **Inhibits** CYP2D6 (weak), 3A4 (weak)

Increased Effect/Toxicity: CYP2D6 inhibitors may increase the levels/effects of lomustine; example inhibitors include chlorpromazine, delavirdine, fluoxetine, miconazole, paroxetine, pergolide, quinidine, quinine, ritonavir, and ropinirole. Increased toxicity with cimetidine, reported to cause bone marrow depression or to potentiate the myelosuppressive effects of lomustine.

Decreased Effect: Decreased effect with phenobarbital, resulting in reduced efficacy of both drugs.

Mechanism of Action Inhibits DNA and RNA synthesis via carbamylation of DNA polymerase, alkylation of DNA, and alteration of RNA, proteins, and enzymes

Pharmacodynamics/Kinetics

Duration: Marrow recovery: ≤6 weeks

Absorption: Complete; appears in plasma within 3 minutes after administration

Distribution: Crosses blood-brain barrier to a greater degree than BCNU; CNS concentrations are equal to that of plasma

Protein binding: 50%

Metabolism: Rapidly hepatic via hydroxylation producing at least two active metabolites; enterohepatically recycled

Half-life elimination: Parent drug: 16-72 hours; Active metabolite: Terminal: 1.3-2 days

Time to peak, serum: Active metabolite: ~3 hours

Excretion: Urine; feces (<5%); expired air (<10%)

Dosage Oral (refer to individual protocols):

Children: 75-150 mg/m² as a single dose every 6 weeks; subsequent doses are readjusted after initial treatment according to platelet and leukocyte counts

Adults: 100-130 mg/m² as a single dose every 6 weeks; readjust after initial treatment according to platelet and leukocyte counts

With compromised marrow function: Initial dose: 100 mg/m² as a single dose every 6 weeks

Repeat courses should only be administered after adequate recovery: WBC >4000 and platelet counts >100,000

Subsequent dosing adjustment based on nadir:

Leukocytes 2000-2900/mm³, platelets 25,000-74,999/mm³: Administer 70% of prior dose

Leukocytes <2000/mm³, platelets <25,000/mm³: Administer 50% of prior dose

Dosage adjustment in renal impairment:

Cl_{cr} 10-50 mL/minute: Administer 75% of normal dose

Cl_{cr} <10 mL/minute: Administer 50% of normal dose

Hemodialysis: Supplemental dose is not necessary

Peritoneal dialysis: Significant drug removal is unlikely based on physiochemical characteristics

Monitoring Parameters CBC with differential and platelet count, hepatic and renal function tests, pulmonary function tests

Patient Information Take with fluids on an empty stomach; do not eat or drink for 2 hours following administration. Do not use alcohol, aspirin, or aspirin-containing medications and/or OTC medications without consulting prescriber. Maintain adequate fluid balance (2-3 L/day of fluids unless instructed to restrict fluid intake). May cause hair loss (reversible); easy bleeding or bruising (use soft toothbrush or cotton swabs and frequent mouth care, use electric razor, avoid sharp knives or scissors); increased susceptibility to infection (avoid crowds or exposure to infection - do not have any vaccinations unless approved by prescriber). Report unusual bleeding or bruising or persistent fever or sore throat; blood in urine, stool, or vomitus; delayed healing of any wounds; skin rash; yellowing of skin or eyes; changes in color of urine of stool. Contraceptive measures are recommended during therapy.

Dosage Forms CAP: 10 mg, 40 mg, 100 mg. **CAP** [dose pack]: 10 mg (2s); 40 mg (2s); 100 mg (2s)

LOPERAMIDE

- **Loniten®** *see Minoxidil on page 845*
- **Lonox®** *see Diphenoxylate and Atropine on page 385*
- **Lo/Ovral®** *see Ethinyl Estradiol and Norgestrel on page 492*

Loperamide (loe PER a mide)

U.S. Brand Names Imodium® A-D [OTC]
Synonyms Loperamide Hydrochloride
Therapeutic Category Antidiarrheal
Use Treatment of acute diarrhea and chronic diarrhea associated with inflammatory bowel disease; chronic functional diarrhea (idiopathic); chronic diarrhea caused by bowel resection or organic lesions; to decrease the volume of ileostomy discharge
Unlabeled/Investigational Use Treatment of traveler's diarrhea in combination with trimethoprim-sulfamethoxazole (co-trimoxazole) (3-day therapy)
Pregnancy Risk Factor B
Contraindications Hypersensitivity to loperamide or any component of the formulation; bloody diarrhea; patients who must avoid constipation; diarrhea resulting from some infections; pseudomembranous colitis
Warnings/Precautions Large first-pass metabolism, use with caution in hepatic dysfunction; should not be used if diarrhea accompanied by high fever, blood in stool; use with caution in patients with a history of penicillin allergy, especially IgE-mediated reactions (eg, anaphylaxis, urticaria)
Common Adverse Reactions Frequency not defined.
Cardiovascular: Shock
Central nervous system: Dizziness, drowsiness, fatigue, sedation
Dermatologic: Rash, toxic epidermal necrolysis
Gastrointestinal: Abdominal cramping, abdominal distention, constipation, dry mouth, nausea, paralytic ileus, vomiting
Miscellaneous: Anaphylaxis
Drug Interactions
  Increased Effect/Toxicity: Loperamide may potentiate the adverse effects of CNS depressants, phenothiazines, tricyclic antidepressants.
Mechanism of Action Acts directly on intestinal muscles to inhibit peristalsis and prolongs transit time enhancing fluid and electrolyte movement through intestinal mucosa; reduces fecal volume, increases viscosity, and diminishes fluid and electrolyte loss; demonstrates antisecretory activity; exhibits peripheral action
Pharmacodynamics/Kinetics
Onset of action: 0.5-1 hour
Absorption: <40%
Distribution: Low amounts enter breast milk
Protein binding: 97%
Metabolism: Hepatic (>50%) to inactive compounds
Half-life elimination: 7-14 hours
Excretion: Urine and feces (1% as metabolites, 30% to 40% as unchanged drug)
Dosage Oral:
Children:
Acute diarrhea: Initial doses (in first 24 hours):
2-6 years: 1 mg 3 times/day
6-8 years: 2 mg twice daily
8-12 years: 2 mg 3 times/day
Maintenance: After initial dosing, 0.1 mg/kg doses after each loose stool, but not exceeding initial dosage
Chronic diarrhea: 0.08-0.24 mg/kg/day divided 2-3 times/day, maximum: 2 mg/dose
Adults:
Acute diarrhea: Initial: 4 mg (2 capsules), followed by 2 mg after each loose stool, up to 16 mg/day (8 capsules)
Chronic diarrhea: Initial: Follow acute diarrhea; maintenance dose should be slowly titrated downward to minimum required to control symptoms (typically, 4-8 mg/day in divided doses)
Traveler's diarrhea: Treat for no more than 2 days
6-8 years: 1 mg after first loose stool followed by 1 mg after each subsequent stool; maximum dose: 4 mg/day
9-11 years: 2 mg after first loose stool followed by 1 mg after each subsequent stool; maximum dose: 6 mg/day
12 years to Adults: 4 mg after first loose stool followed by 2 mg after each subsequent stool; maximum dose: 8 mg/day
Patient Information Do not take more than 8 capsules or 80 mL in 24 hours; may cause drowsiness; if acute diarrhea lasts longer than 48 hours, consult prescriber
Dosage Forms CAP: 2 mg. **CAPLET** (Imodium® A-D): 2 mg. **LIQ, oral:** 1 mg/5 mL (5 mL, 10 mL, 120 mL); (Imodium® A-D): 1 mg/5 mL (60 mL, 120 mL). **TAB:** 2 mg

- **Loperamide Hydrochloride** *see Loperamide on page 756*
- **Lopid®** *see Gemfibrozil on page 583*

Lopinavir and Ritonavir (loe PIN a veer & rit ON uh veer)
Related Information
Antiretroviral Therapy for HIV Infection *on page 1448*
Management of Healthcare Worker Exposures to HBV, HCV, and HIV *on page 1421*

U.S. Brand Names Kaletra™

Synonyms Ritonavir and Lopinavir

Therapeutic Category Antiretroviral Agent, Protease Inhibitor; Protease Inhibitor

Use Treatment of HIV infection in combination with other antiretroviral agents

Pregnancy Risk Factor C

Contraindications Hypersensitivity to lopinavir, ritonavir, or any component of the formulation; administration with medications highly dependent upon CYP3A or CYP2D6 for clearance for which increased levels are associated with serious and/or life-threatening events. Ritonavir is contraindicated with astemizole, cisapride, dihydroergotamine, ergonovine, ergotamine, methylergonovine, micazolam, pimozide, triazolam.

Warnings/Precautions Associated with many potential drug interactions; concurrent use of azole antifungals (high dose), lovastatin, rifampin, and simvastatin is not recommended (per manufacturer). Avoid concurrent use of St John's wort (may lead to loss of virologic response and/or resistance). Cases of pancreatitis, some fatal, have been associated with lopinavir/ritonavir; use caution in patients with a history of pancreatitis. Patients with signs or symptoms of pancreatitis should be evaluated and therapy suspended as clinically appropriate. Diabetes mellitus and exacerbation of diabetes mellitus have been reported in patients taking protease inhibitors. Use caution in patients with hepatic impairment; patients with hepatitis or elevations in transaminases prior to the start of therapy may be at increased risk for further increases in transaminases or hepatic dysfunction (rare fatalities reported in postmarketing). Large increases in total cholesterol and triglycerides have been reported; screening should be done prior to therapy and periodically throughout treatment. Hemophilia type A and type B have been reported with protease inhibitor use. Redistribution or accumulation of body fat has been observed in patients using antiretroviral therapy. The potential for cross-resistance with other protease inhibitors is currently under study. Safety and efficacy have not been established for children <6 months of age.

Common Adverse Reactions Protease inhibitors cause dyslipidemia which includes elevated cholesterol and triglycerides and a redistribution of body fat centrally to cause increased abdominal girth, buffalo hump, facial atrophy, and breast enlargement. These agents also cause hyperglycemia.

>10%:

  Endocrine & metabolic: Hypercholesterolemia (9% to 28%), triglycerides increased (9% to 28%)

  Gastrointestinal: Diarrhea (16% to 24%), nausea (3% to 15%)

  Hepatic: GGT increased (4% to 25%)

2% to 10%:

  Central nervous system: Headache (2% to 7%), pain (0% to 2%), insomnia (1% to 2%)

  Dermatologic: Rash (1% to 4%)

  Endocrine & metabolic: Hyperglycemia (1% to 4%), hyperuricemia (up to 4%), sodium decreased (3% children), organic phosphorus decreased (up to 2%), amylase increased (2% to 10%)

  Gastrointestinal: Abnormal stools (up to 6%), abdominal pain (2% to 4%), vomiting (2% to 5%), dyspepsia (0.5% to 2%)

  Hematologic: Platelets decreased (4% children), neutrophils decreased (1% to 3%)

  Hepatic: AST increased (2% to 9%), ALT increased (4% to 8%), bilirubin increased (children 3%)

  Neuromuscular & skeletal: Weakness (4% to 7%)

Drug Interactions

Cytochrome P450 Effect:

  Lopinavir: **Substrate** of 3A4 (minor)

  Ritonavir: **Substrate** of CYP1A2 (minor), 2B6 (minor), 2D6 (major), 3A4 (major); **Inhibits** CYP2C8/9 (weak), 2C19 (weak), 2D6 (strong), 2E1 (weak), 3A4 (strong); **Induces** CYP1A2 (weak), 2C8/9 (weak), 3A4 (weak)

Increased Effect/Toxicity:

  Contraindicated drugs: Life-threatening arrhythmias may result from concurrent use of flecainide or propafenone. Concurrent use is contraindicated. Concurrent use of cisapride, pimozide, astemizole is also contraindicated. Some benzodiazepines (midazolam and triazolam) are contraindicated, due to the potential for increased response/respiratory depression. Concurrent use of ergot alkaloids is contraindicated, due to potential toxicity.

  Serum levels of other antiarrhythmics, including amiodarone, bepridil, lidocaine (systemic), and quinidine may be increased with concurrent use. Serum levels of calcium channel blockers (including felodipine, nicardipine, and nifedipine), clarithromycin, immunosuppressants (cyclosporin, tacrolimus, sirolimus), HMG-CoA reductase inhibitors (lovastatin and simvastatin are not recommended, atorvastatin and cerivastatin should be used at lowest possible dose), itraconazole, ketoconazole, methadone, and rifabutin (decreased dose recommended) may be increased. Serum levels of protease inhibitors may be altered during concurrent therapy. Ritonavir may increase serum concentrations of amprenavir, indinavir, or saquinavir. Sildenafil, tadalafil, and vardenafil serum concentrations may be increased by lopinavir/ritonavir; use with caution at decreased dose of sildenafil (25 mg every 48 hours) and monitor; recommended maximum tadalafil dose is 10 mg in 72 hours; recommended maximum vardenafil dose with ritonavir is 2.5 mg in 72 hours. Warfarin serum levels may also be increased.

  Delavirdine increases levels of lopinavir; dosing recommendations are not yet established.

  Lopinavir/ritonavir solution contains alcohol, concurrent use with disulfiram or metronidazole should be avoided. May cause disulfiram-like reaction.

(Continued)

Lopinavir and Ritonavir *(Continued)*

Decreased Effect: Carbamazepine, dexamethasone, phenobarbital, phenytoin, and rifampin may decrease levels of lopinavir; concurrent use of rifampin is not recommended. Non-nucleoside reverse transcriptase inhibitors: Efavirenz, nevirapine may decrease levels of lopinavir. To avoid incompatibility with didanosine, administer didanosine 1 hour before or 2 hours after lopinavir/ritonavir. Decreased levels of ethinyl estradiol may result from concurrent use. Lopinavir/ritonavir may decrease levels of abacavir, atovaquone, or zidovudine.

Mechanism of Action A coformulation of lopinavir and ritonavir. The lopinavir component is the active inhibitor of HIV protease. Lopinavir inhibits HIV protease and renders the enzyme incapable of processing polyprotein precursor which leads to production of noninfectious immature HIV particles. The ritonavir component inhibits the CYP3A metabolism of lopinavir, allowing increased plasma levels of lopinavir.

Pharmacodynamics/Kinetics

Ritonavir: See Ritonavir monograph.

Lopinavir:
Protein binding: 98% to 99%
Metabolism: Hepatic via CYP3A; 13 metabolites identified
Half-life elimination: 5-6 hours
Excretion: Feces (83%, 20% as unchanged drug); urine (2%)

Dosage Oral (take with food):
Children 6 months to 12 years: Dosage based on weight, presented based on mg of lopinavir (maximum dose: Lopinavir 400 mg/ritonavir 100 mg)
7-<15 kg: 12 mg/kg twice daily
15-40 kg: 10 mg/kg twice daily
>40 kg: Refer to adult dosing
Children >12 years and Adults: Lopinavir 400 mg/ritonavir 100 mg twice daily

Dosage adjustment when taken with amprenavir, efavirenz, nelfinavir, or nevirapine:
Children 6 months to 12 years:
7-<15 kg: 13 mg/kg twice daily
15-45 kg: 11 mg/kg twice daily
>45 kg: Refer to adult dosing
Note: In the USHHS guidelines, the cutoff for adult dosing is 50 kg. (Pediatric Guidelines - December 14, 2001, are available at http://www.aidsinfo.nih.gov, last accessed January 22, 2003.)
Children >12 years and Adults: Lopinavir 533 mg/ritonavir 133 mg twice daily
Elderly: Initial studies did not include enough elderly patients to determine effects based on age. Use with caution due to possible decreased hepatic, renal, and cardiac function.

Dosage adjustment in renal impairment: Has not been studied in patients with renal impairment; however, a decrease in clearance is not expected

Dosage adjustment in hepatic impairment: Plasma levels may be increased in patients with hepatic impairment.

Administration Take with food; if using didanosine, take didanosine 1 hour before or 2 hours after lopinavir/ritonavir

Monitoring Parameters Triglycerides, cholesterol, LFTs, electrolytes, basic HIV monitoring, viral load and CD4 count, glucose

Patient Information This medication will be used with other medications to treat HIV infection. Take medication daily as prescribed. Take with food. Do not change doses or discontinue without contacting prescriber. It is important to find out what other medications cannot be taken with this medication. Do not take any prescription medications, over-the-counter products or herbal products, especially St John's wort, without consulting prescriber. May interfere with certain oral contraceptives; alternate contraceptive measures may be needed.

Dosage Forms CAP: Lopinavir 133.3 mg and ritonavir 33.3 mg. **SOLN, oral:** Lopinavir 80 mg and ritonavir 20 mg per mL (160 mL)

♦ **Lopressor**® *see* Metoprolol *on page 829*

♦ **Loprox**® *see* Ciclopirox *on page 274*

♦ **Lorabid**® *see* Loracarbef *on page 758*

Loracarbef *(lor a KAR bef)*

U.S. Brand Names Lorabid®

Therapeutic Category Antibiotic, Carbacephem

Use Infections caused by susceptible organisms involving the respiratory tract, acute otitis media, sinusitis, skin and skin structure, bone and joint, and urinary tract and gynecologic

Pregnancy Risk Factor B

Contraindications Hypersensitivity to loracarbef, any component of the formulation, or cephalosporins

Warnings/Precautions Modify dosage in patients with severe renal impairment; prolonged use may result in superinfection; use with caution in patients with a previous history of hypersensitivity to other beta-lactam antibiotics (eg, penicillins, cephalosporins)

Common Adverse Reactions ≥1%:
Central nervous system: Headache (1% to 3%), somnolence (<2%)
Dermatologic: Rash (1% to 3%)
Gastrointestinal: Diarrhea (4% to 6%), nausea (2%), vomiting (1% to 3%), anorexia (<2%), abdominal pain (1%)
Genitourinary: Vaginitis (1%)
Respiratory: Rhinitis (2% to 6%)

Drug Interactions

Increased Effect/Toxicity: Loracarbef serum levels are increased with coadministered probenecid.

Mechanism of Action Inhibits bacterial cell wall synthesis by binding to one or more of the penicillin binding proteins (PBPs); inhibits the final transpeptidation step of peptidoglycan synthesis in bacterial cell walls, thus inhibiting cell wall biosynthesis. It is thought that beta-lactam antibiotics inactivate transpeptidase via acylation of the enzyme with cleavage of the CO-N bond of the beta-lactam ring. Upon exposure to beta-lactam antibiotics, bacteria eventually lyse due to ongoing activity of cell wall autolytic enzymes (autolysins and murein hydrolases) while cell wall assembly is arrested.

Pharmacodynamics/Kinetics

Absorption: Rapid

Half-life elimination: ~1 hour

Time to peak, serum: ~1 hour

Excretion: Clearance: Plasma: ~200-300 mL/minute

Dosage Oral:

Children:

Acute otitis media: 15 mg/kg twice daily for 10 days

Pharyngitis and impetigo: 7.5-15 mg/kg twice daily for 10 days

Adults:

Uncomplicated urinary tract infections: 200 mg once daily for 7 days

Skin and soft tissue: 200-400 mg every 12-24 hours

Uncomplicated pyelonephritis: 400 mg every 12 hours for 14 days

Upper/lower respiratory tract infection: 200-400 mg every 12-24 hours for 7-14 days

Dosing comments in renal impairment:

Cl_{cr} 10-49 mL/minute: 50% of usual dose at usual interval or usual dose given half as often

Cl_{cr} <10 mL/minute: Administer usual dose every 3-5 days

Hemodialysis: Doses should be administered after dialysis sessions

Administration Take on an empty stomach at least 1 hour before or 2 hours after meals. Finish all medication. Shake suspension well before using.

Patient Information Take as directed, preferably on an empty stomach (1 hour before or 2 hours after meals). Take entire prescription even if feeling better. Shake suspension well before using. Maintain adequate hydration (2-3 L/day of fluids unless instructed to restrict fluid intake). Report immediately any signs of skin rash, joint or back pain, or difficulty breathing. Report unusual fever, chills, vaginal itching or foul-smelling vaginal discharge, or easy bruising or bleeding.

Dosage Forms CAP: 200 mg, 400 mg. **POWDER, oral suspension:** 100 mg/5 mL (100 mL); 200 mg/5 mL (100 mL).

Loratadine (lor AT a deen)

U.S. Brand Names Alavert™ [OTC]; Claritin® [OTC]

Therapeutic Category Antihistamine; Antihistamine, Nonsedating

Use Relief of nasal and non-nasal symptoms of seasonal allergic rhinitis; treatment of chronic idiopathic urticaria

Pregnancy Risk Factor B

Contraindications Hypersensitivity to loratadine or any component of the formulation

Warnings/Precautions Use with caution and modify dose in patients with liver or renal impairment; safety and efficacy in children <2 years of age have not been established

Common Adverse Reactions

Adults:

Central nervous system: Headache (12%), somnolence (8%), fatigue (4%)

Gastrointestinal: Xerostomia (3%)

Children:

Central nervous system: Nervousness (4% ages 6-12 years), fatigue (3% ages 6-12 years, 2% to 3% ages 2-5 years), malaise (2% ages 6-12 years)

Dermatologic: Rash (2% to 3% ages 2-5 years)

Gastrointestinal: Abdominal pain (2% ages 6-12 years), stomatitis (2% to 3% ages 2-5 years)

Neuromuscular & skeletal: Hyperkinesia (3% ages 6-12 years)

Ocular: Conjunctivitis (2% ages 6-12 years)

Respiratory: Wheezing (4% ages 6-12 years), dysphonia (2% ages 6-12 years), upper respiratory infection (2% ages 6-12 years), epistaxis (2% to 3% ages 2-5 years), pharyngitis (2% to 3% ages 2-5 years), flu-like symptoms (2% to 3% ages 2-5 years)

Miscellaneous: Viral infection (2% to 3% ages 2-5 years)

Drug Interactions

Cytochrome P450 Effect: Substrate (minor) of CYP2D6, 3A4; **Inhibits** CYP2C19 (moderate), 2D6 (weak)

Increased Effect/Toxicity: Increased plasma concentrations of loratadine and its active metabolite with ketoconazole and erythromycin, however, no change in QT_c interval was seen. Increased toxicity with procarbazine, other antihistamines, alcohol. Protease inhibitors (amprenavir, ritonavir, nelfinavir) may increase the serum levels of loratadine.

Mechanism of Action Long-acting tricyclic antihistamine with selective peripheral histamine H_1-receptor antagonistic properties

Pharmacodynamics/Kinetics

Onset of action: 1-3 hours

Peak effect: 8-12 hours

Duration: >24 hours

(Continued)

Loratadine *(Continued)*

Absorption: Rapid
Distribution: Significant amounts enter breast milk
Metabolism: Extensively hepatic via CYP2D6 and 3A4 to active metabolite
Half-life elimination: 12-15 hours
Excretion: Urine (40%) and feces (40%) as metabolites

Dosage Oral: Seasonal allergic rhinitis, chronic idiopathic urticaria:
Children 2-5 years: 5 mg once daily
Children ≥6 years and Adults: 10 mg once daily
Elderly: Peak plasma levels are increased; elimination half-life is slightly increased; specific dosing adjustments are not available

Dosage adjustment in renal impairment: Cl_{cr} ≤30 mL/minute:
Children 2-5 years: 5 mg every other day
Children ≥6 years and Adults: 10 mg every other day

Dosage adjustment in hepatic impairment: Elimination half-life increases with severity of disease
Children 2-5 years: 5 mg every other day
Children ≥6 years and Adults: 10 mg every other day

Patient Information Drink plenty of water; may cause dry mouth, sedation, drowsiness, and can impair judgment and coordination. Notify prescriber if pregnant.

Rapidly-disintegrating tablets: Place tablet on tongue; it dissolves rapidly. May be used with or without water. Use within 6 months of opening foil pouch, and immediately after opening individual tablet blister.

Dosage Forms SYR (Claritin®): 1 mg/mL (120 mL). **TAB** (Claritin®): 10 mg. **TAB, rapidly-disintegrating** (Alavert™, Claritin® RediTabs®): 10 mg

Loratadine and Pseudoephedrine *(lor AT a deen & soo doe e FED rin)*

U.S. Brand Names Claritin-D® 12-Hour [OTC]; Claritin-D® 24-Hour [OTC]
Synonyms Pseudoephedrine and Loratadine
Therapeutic Category Antihistamine/Decongestant
Use Temporary relief of symptoms of seasonal allergic rhinitis and nasal congestion
Pregnancy Risk Factor B
Dosage Children ≥12 years and Adults: Oral:
Claritin-D® 12-Hour: 1 tablet every 12 hours
Claritin-D® 24-Hour: 1 tablet daily

Dosage adjustment in renal impairment:
Claritin-D® 12-Hour: 1 tablet daily
Claritin-D® 24-Hour: 1 tablet every other day

Dosage Forms TAB, extended release: (Claritin-D® 12-hour): Loratadine 5 mg and pseudoephedrine 120 mg; (Claritin-D® 24-hour): Loratadine 10 mg and pseudoephedrine 240 mg

Lorazepam *(lor A ze pam)*

Related Information
Benzodiazepines Comparison *on page 1366*
Convulsive Status Epilepticus *on page 1479*
U.S. Brand Names Ativan®; Lorazepam Intensol®
Therapeutic Category Antianxiety Agent; Anticonvulsant, Benzodiazepine; Antiemetic; Benzodiazepine; Sedative
Use
Oral: Management of anxiety disorders or short-term relief of the symptoms of anxiety or anxiety associated with depressive symptoms
I.V.: Status epilepticus, preanesthesia for desired amnesia, antiemetic adjunct
Unlabeled/Investigational Use Ethanol detoxification; insomnia; psychogenic catatonia; partial complex seizures; agitation (I.V.)
Restrictions C-IV
Pregnancy Risk Factor D
Contraindications Hypersensitivity to lorazepam or any component of the formulation (cross-sensitivity with other benzodiazepines may exist); acute narrow-angle glaucoma; sleep apnea (parenteral); intra-arterial injection of parenteral formulation; severe respiratory insufficiency (except during mechanical ventilation); pregnancy
Warnings/Precautions Use with caution in elderly or debilitated patients, patients with hepatic disease (including alcoholics) or renal impairment. Use with caution in patients with respiratory disease or impaired gag reflex. Initial doses in elderly or debilitated patients should not exceed 2 mg. Prolonged lorazepam use may have a possible relationship to GI disease, including esophageal dilation.

The parenteral formulation of lorazepam contains polyethylene glycol and propylene glycol. Each agent has been associated with specific toxicities when administered in prolonged infusions at high dosages. Also contains benzyl alcohol - avoid rapid injection in neonates or prolonged infusions. Intra-arterial injection or extravasation should be avoided. Concurrent administration with scopolamine results in an increased risk of hallucinations, sedation, and irrational behavior.

Causes CNS depression (dose-related) resulting in sedation, dizziness, confusion, or ataxia which may impair physical and mental capabilities. Patients must be cautioned about performing tasks which require mental alertness (eg, operating machinery or driving). Use with caution in patients receiving other CNS depressants or psychoactive agents. Effects with other sedative drugs or ethanol may be potentiated. Benzodiazepines have been associated with falls and traumatic injury and should be used with extreme caution in patients who are at risk of these events (especially the elderly).

Lorazepam may cause anterograde amnesia. Paradoxical reactions, including hyperactive or aggressive behavior have been reported with benzodiazepines, particularly in adolescent/ pediatric or psychiatric patients. Does not have analgesic, antidepressant, or antipsychotic properties.

Use caution in patients with depression, particularly if suicidal risk may be present. Use with caution in patients with a history of drug dependence. Benzodiazepines have been associated with dependence and acute withdrawal symptoms on discontinuation or reduction in dose. Acute withdrawal, including seizures, may be precipitated after administration of flumazenil to patients receiving long-term benzodiazepine therapy.

As a hypnotic agent, should be used only after evaluation of potential causes of sleep disturbance. Failure of sleep disturbance to resolve after 7-10 days may indicate psychiatric or medical illness. A worsening of insomnia or the emergence of new abnormalities of thought or behavior may represent unrecognized psychiatric or medical illness and requires immediate and careful evaluation.

Common Adverse Reactions

>10%:
Central nervous system: Sedation
Respiratory: Respiratory depression
1% to 10%:
Cardiovascular: Hypotension
Central nervous system: Confusion, dizziness, akathisia, unsteadiness, headache, depression, disorientation, amnesia
Dermatologic: Dermatitis, rash
Gastrointestinal: Weight gain/loss, nausea, changes in appetite
Neuromuscular & skeletal: Weakness
Respiratory: Nasal congestion, hyperventilation, apnea

Drug Interactions

Increased Effect/Toxicity: Ethanol and other CNS depressants may increase the CNS effects of lorazepam. Scopolamine in combination with parenteral lorazepam may increase the incidence of sedation, hallucinations, and irrational behavior. There are rare reports of significant respiratory depression, stupor, and/or hypotension with concomitant use of loxapine and lorazepam. Use caution if concomitant administration of loxapine and CNS drugs is required.

Decreased Effect: Oral contraceptives may increase the clearance of lorazepam. Lorazepam may decrease the antiparkinsonian efficacy of levodopa. Theophylline and other CNS stimulants may antagonize the sedative effects of lorazepam.

Mechanism of Action Binds to stereospecific benzodiazepine receptors on the postsynaptic GABA neuron at several sites within the central nervous system, including the limbic system, reticular formation. Enhancement of the inhibitory effect of GABA on neuronal excitability results by increased neuronal membrane permeability to chloride ions. This shift in chloride ions results in hyperpolarization (a less excitable state) and stabilization.

Pharmacodynamics/Kinetics

Onset of action:
Hypnosis: I.M.: 20-30 minutes
Sedation: I.V.: 5-20 minutes
Anticonvulsant: I.V.: 5 minutes, oral: 30-60 minutes
Duration: 6-8 hours
Absorption: Oral, I.M.: Prompt
Distribution:
V_d: Neonates: 3.76 L/kg; Adults: 1.3 L/kg; crosses placenta; enters breast milk
Protein binding: 85%; free fraction may be significantly higher in elderly
Metabolism: Hepatic to inactive compounds
Half-life elimination: Neonates: 40.2 hours; Older children: 10.5 hours; Adults: 12.9 hours; Elderly: 15.9 hours; End-stage renal disease: 32-70 hours
Excretion: Urine; feces (minimal)

Dosage

Antiemetic:
Children 2-15 years: I.V.: 0.05 mg/kg (up to 2 mg/dose) prior to chemotherapy
Adults: Oral, I.V. (**Note:** May be administered sublingually; not a labeled route): 0.5-2 mg every 4-6 hours as needed
Anxiety and sedation:
Infants and Children: Oral, I.M., I.V.: Usual: 0.05 mg/kg/dose (range: 0.02-0.09 mg/kg) every 4-8 hours
I.V.: May use smaller doses (eg, 0.01-0.03 mg/kg) and repeat every 20 minutes, as needed to titrate to effect
Adults: Oral: 1-10 mg/day in 2-3 divided doses; usual dose: 2-6 mg/day in divided doses
Elderly: 0.5-4 mg/day; initial dose not to exceed 2 mg
Insomnia: Adults: Oral: 2-4 mg at bedtime
Preoperative: Adults:
I.M.: 0.05 mg/kg administered 2 hours before surgery (maximum: 4 mg/dose)
I.V.: 0.044 mg/kg 15-20 minutes before surgery (usual maximum: 2 mg/dose)
Operative amnesia: Adults: I.V.: Up to 0.05 mg/kg (maximum: 4 mg/dose)
(Continued)

Lorazepam *(Continued)*

Sedation (preprocedure): Infants and Children:

Oral, I.M., I.V.: Usual: 0.05 mg/kg (range: 0.02-0.09 mg/kg);

I.V.: May use smaller doses (eg, 0.01-0.03 mg/kg) and repeat every 20 minutes, as needed to titrate to effect

Status epilepticus: I.V.:

Infants and Children: 0.1 mg/kg slow I.V. over 2-5 minutes; do not exceed 4 mg/single dose; may repeat second dose of 0.05 mg/kg slow I.V. in 10-15 minutes if needed

Adolescents: 0.07 mg/kg slow I.V. over 2-5 minutes; maximum: 4 mg/dose; may repeat in 10-15 minutes

Adults: 4 mg/dose slow I.V. over 2-5 minutes; may repeat in 10-15 minutes; usual maximum dose: 8 mg

Rapid tranquilization of agitated patient (administer every 30-60 minutes):

Oral: 1-2 mg

I.M.: 0.5-1 mg

Average total dose for tranquilization: Oral, I.M.: 4-8 mg

Agitation in the ICU patient (unlabeled):

I.V.: 0.02-0.06 mg/kg every 2-6 hours

I.V. infusion: 0.01-0.1 mg/kg/hour

Administration

Lorazepam may be administered by I.M. or I.V.

I.M.: Should be administered deep into the muscle mass

I.V.: Do not exceed 2 mg/minute or 0.05 mg/kg over 2-5 minutes

Dilute I.V. dose with equal volume of compatible diluent (D_5W, NS, SWI)

Injection must be made slowly with repeated aspiration to make sure the injection is not intra-arterial and that perivascular extravasation has not occurred

Monitoring Parameters Respiratory and cardiovascular status, blood pressure, heart rate, symptoms of anxiety

Reference Range Therapeutic: 50-240 ng/mL (SI: 156-746 nmol/L)

Patient Information Advise patient of potential for physical and psychological dependence with chronic use; advise patient of possible retrograde amnesia after I.V. or I.M. use; will cause drowsiness, impairment of judgment or coordination

Dosage Forms INJ, solution (Ativan®): 2 mg/mL (1 mL, 10 mL); 4 mg/mL (1 mL, 10 mL). **SOLN, oral concentrate** (Lorazepam Intensol®): 2 mg/mL (30 mL). **TAB** (Ativan®): 0.5 mg, 1 mg, 2 mg

♦ **Lorazepam Intensol®** *see* Lorazepam *on page 760*

♦ **Lorcet® 10/650** *see* Hydrocodone and Acetaminophen *on page 627*

♦ **Lorcet®-HD** *see* Hydrocodone and Acetaminophen *on page 627*

♦ **Lorcet® Plus** *see* Hydrocodone and Acetaminophen *on page 627*

♦ **Lortab®** *see* Hydrocodone and Acetaminophen *on page 627*

Losartan (loe SAR tan)

Related Information

Angiotensin Agents Comparison *on page 1353*

U.S. Brand Names Cozaar®

Synonyms DuP 753; Losartan Potassium; MK594

Therapeutic Category Angiotensin II Receptor Antagonist (ARB); Antihypertensive Agent

Use Treatment of hypertension (HTN); treatment of diabetic nephropathy in patients with type 2 diabetes mellitus (noninsulin dependent, NIDDM) and a history of hypertension; stroke risk reduction in patients with HTN and left ventricular hypertrophy (LVH)

Pregnancy Risk Factor C/D (2nd and 3rd trimesters)

Contraindications Hypersensitivity to losartan or any component of the formulation; hypersensitivity to other A-II receptor antagonists; bilateral renal artery stenosis; pregnancy (2nd and 3rd trimesters)

Warnings/Precautions Avoid use or use a much smaller dose in patients who are volume-depleted; correct depletion first. Use with caution in patients with pre-existing renal insufficiency or significant aortic/mitral stenosis. Use caution in patients with unilateral or bilateral renal artery stenosis to avoid a decrease in renal function. AUCs of losartan (not the active metabolite) are about 50% greater in patients with Cl_{cr} <30 mL/minute and are doubled in hemodialysis patients. When used to reduce the risk of stroke in patients with HTN and LVH, may not be effective in African-American population. Use caution with hepatic dysfunction, dose adjustment may be needed. Safety and efficacy in pediatric patients have not been established.

Common Adverse Reactions

>10%:

Cardiovascular: Chest pain (12% diabetic nephropathy)

Central nervous system: Fatigue (14% diabetic nephropathy)

Endocrine: Hypoglycemia (14% diabetic nephropathy)

Gastrointestinal: Diarrhea (2% hypertension to 15% diabetic nephropathy)

Genitourinary: Urinary tract infection (13% diabetic nephropathy)

Hematologic: Anemia (14% diabetic nephropathy)

Neuromuscular & skeletal: Weakness (14% diabetic nephropathy), back pain (2% hypertension to 12% diabetic nephropathy)

Respiratory: Cough (11% diabetic nephropathy; 17% to 29% hypertension but similar to that associated with hydrochlorothiazide or placebo therapy)

1% to 10%:
  Cardiovascular: Hypotension (7% diabetic nephropathy), orthostatic hypotension (4% hypertension to 4% diabetic nephropathy), first-dose hypotension (dose-related: <1% with 50 mg, 2% with 100 mg)
  Central nervous system: Dizziness (4%), hypoesthesia (5% diabetic nephropathy), fever (4% diabetic nephropathy), insomnia (1%)
  Dermatology: Cellulitis (7% diabetic nephropathy)
  Endocrine: Hyperkalemia (<1% hypertension to 7% diabetic nephropathy)
  Gastrointestinal: Gastritis (5% diabetic nephropathy), weight gain (4% diabetic nephropathy), dyspepsia (1% to 4%), abdominal pain (2%), nausea (2%)
  Neuromuscular & skeletal: Muscular weakness (7% diabetic nephropathy), knee pain (5% diabetic nephropathy), leg pain (1% to 5%), muscle cramps (1%), myalgia (1%)
  Respiratory: Bronchitis (10% diabetic nephropathy), upper respiratory infection (8%), nasal congestion (2%), sinusitis (1% hypertension to 6% diabetic nephropathy)
  Miscellaneous: Infection (5% diabetic nephropathy), flu-like syndrome (10% diabetic nephropathy)

Drug Interactions
  Cytochrome P450 Effect: Substrate (major) of CYP2C8/9, 3A4; **Inhibits** CYP1A2 (weak), 2C8/9 (moderate), 2C19 (weak), 3A4 (weak)
  Increased Effect/Toxicity: Cimetidine may increase the absorption of losartan by 18% (clinical effect is unknown). Potassium salts/supplements, co-trimoxazole (high dose), ACE inhibitors, and potassium-sparing diuretics (amiloride, spironolactone, triamterene) may increase the risk of hyperkalemia. Risk of lithium toxicity may be increased by losartan.
  Decreased Effect: CYP2C8/9 inducers may decrease the levels/effects of losartan; example inducers include carbamazepine, phenobarbital, phenytoin, rifampin, rifapentine, and secobarbital. NSAIDs may decrease the efficacy of losartan.

Mechanism of Action As a selective and competitive, nonpeptide angiotensin II receptor antagonist, losartan blocks the vasoconstrictor and aldosterone-secreting effects of angiotensin II; losartan interacts reversibly at the AT1 and AT2 receptors of many tissues and has slow dissociation kinetics; its affinity for the AT1 receptor is 1000 times greater than the AT2 receptor. Angiotensin II receptor antagonists may induce a more complete inhibition of the renin-angiotensin system than ACE inhibitors, they do not affect the response to bradykinin, and are less likely to be associated with nonrenin-angiotensin effects (eg, cough and angioedema). Losartan increases urinary flow rate and in addition to being natriuretic and kaliuretic, increases excretion of chloride, magnesium, uric acid, calcium, and phosphate.

Pharmacodynamics/Kinetics
  Onset of action: 6 hours
  Distribution: V_d: Losartan: 34 L; E-3174: 12 L; does not cross blood brain barrier
  Protein binding, plasma: High
  Metabolism: Hepatic (14%) via CYP2C9 and 3A4 to active metabolite, E-3174 (40 times more potent than losartan); extensive first-pass effect
  Bioavailability: 25% to 33%; AUC of E-3174 is four times greater than that of losartan
  Half-life elimination: Losartan: 1.5-2 hours; E-3174: 6-9 hours
  Time to peak, serum: Losartan: 1 hour; E-3174: 3-4 hours
  Excretion: Urine (4% as unchanged drug, 6% as active metabolite)
  Clearance: Plasma: Losartan: 600 mL/minute; Active metabolite: 50 mL/minute

Dosage Oral: Adults:
  Hypertension: The usual starting dose is 50 mg once daily. Can be administered once or twice daily with total daily doses ranging from 25-100 mg.
    Usual initial doses in patients receiving diuretics or those with intravascular volume depletion: 25 mg
  Nephropathy in patients with type 2 diabetes and hypertension: Initial: 50 mg once daily; can be increased to 100 mg once daily based on blood pressure response
  Stroke reduction (HTN with LVH): 50 mg once daily (maximum daily dose: 100 mg); may be used in combination with a thiazide diuretic
  Dosing adjustment in renal impairment: None necessary
  Dosing adjustment in hepatic impairment: Reduce the initial dose to 25 mg/day; divide dosage intervals into two.
  Not removed via hemodialysis

Administration May be administered with or without food.

Monitoring Parameters Supine blood pressure, electrolytes, serum creatinine, BUN, urinalysis, symptomatic hypotension and tachycardia, CBC

Patient Information Use caution standing or rising abruptly following a dosage increase; report any symptoms of difficulty breathing, swallowing, swelling of face, lips, extremities, or tongue immediately, as well as symptoms of fever or sore throat; do not use if pregnant

Dosage Forms TAB, film coated: 25 mg, 50 mg, 100 mg

Losartan and Hydrochlorothiazide
(loe SAR tan & hye droe klor oh THYE a zide)

U.S. Brand Names Hyzaar®

Synonyms Hydrochlorothiazide and Losartan

Therapeutic Category Angiotensin II Antagonist/Thiazide Diuretic Combination; Antihypertensive Agent, Combination

Use Treatment of hypertension

Pregnancy Risk Factor C/D (2nd and 3rd trimesters)

Dosage Oral (dosage must be individualized): Adults: 1 tablet daily
  (Continued)

Losartan and Hydrochlorothiazide *(Continued)*

Dosage Forms TAB, film coated: 50-12.5: Losartan potassium 50 mg and hydrochlorothiazide 12.5 mg; 100-25: Losartan potassium 100 mg and hydrochlorothiazide 25 mg

♦ **Losartan Potassium** *see Losartan on page 762*
♦ **Lotemax®** *see Loteprednol on page 764*
♦ **Lotensin®** *see Benazepril on page 152*
♦ **Lotensin® HCT** *see Benazepril and Hydrochlorothiazide on page 153*

Loteprednol *(loe te PRED nol)*

U.S. Brand Names Alrex®; Lotemax®
Synonyms Loteprednol Etabonate
Therapeutic Category Corticosteroid, Ophthalmic
Use
Suspension, 0.2% (Alrex™): Temporary relief of signs and symptoms of seasonal allergic conjunctivitis
Suspension, 0.5% (Lotemax™): Inflammatory conditions (treatment of steroid-responsive inflammatory conditions of the palpebral and bulbar conjunctiva, cornea, and anterior segment of the globe such as allergic conjunctivitis, acne rosacea, superficial punctate keratitis, herpes zoster keratitis, iritis, cyclitis, selected infective conjunctivitis, when the inherent hazard of steroid use is accepted to obtain an advisable diminution in edema and inflammation) and treatment of postoperative inflammation following ocular surgery
Pregnancy Risk Factor C
Dosage Adults: Ophthalmic:
Suspension, 0.2% (Alrex™): Instill 1 drop into affected eye(s) 4 times/day
Suspension, 0.5% (Lotemax™):
Inflammatory conditions: Apply 1-2 drops into the conjunctival sac of the affected eye(s) 4 times/day. During the initial treatment within the first week, the dosing may be increased up to 1 drop every hour. Advise patients not to discontinue therapy prematurely. If signs and symptoms fail to improve after 2 days, re-evaluate the patient.
Postoperative inflammation: Apply 1-2 drops into the conjunctival sac of the operated eye(s) 4 times/day beginning 24 hours after surgery and continuing throughout the first 2 weeks of the postoperative period
Dosage Forms SUSP, ophthalmic: (Alrex®): 0.2% (5 mL, 10 mL); (Lotemax®): 0.5% (2.5 mL, 5 mL, 10 mL, 15 mL)

♦ **Loteprednol Etabonate** *see Loteprednol on page 764*
♦ **Lotrel®** *see Amlodipine and Benazepril on page 83*
♦ **Lotrimin® AF Athlete's Foot Cream [OTC]** *see Clotrimazole on page 304*
♦ **Lotrimin® AF Athlete's Foot Solution [OTC]** *see Clotrimazole on page 304*
♦ **Lotrimin® AF Jock Itch Cream [OTC]** *see Clotrimazole on page 304*
♦ **Lotrimin® AF Powder/Spray [OTC]** *see Miconazole on page 834*
♦ **Lotrimin® Ultra™ [OTC]** *see Butenafine on page 195*
♦ **Lotrisone®** *see Betamethasone and Clotrimazole on page 161*

Lovastatin *(LOE va sta tin)*

Related Information
Lipid-Lowering Agents *on page 1381*
U.S. Brand Names Altocor™; Mevacor®
Synonyms Mevinolin; Monacolin K
Therapeutic Category Antilipemic Agent, HMG-CoA Reductase Inhibitor; HMG-CoA Reductase Inhibitor
Use
Adjunct to dietary therapy to decrease elevated serum total and LDL-cholesterol concentrations in primary hypercholesterolemia
Primary prevention of coronary artery disease (patients without symptomatic disease with average to moderately elevated total and LDL-cholesterol and below average HDL-cholesterol); slow progression of coronary atherosclerosis in patients with coronary heart disease
Adjunct to dietary therapy in adolescent patients (10-17 years of age, females >1 year postmenarche) with heterozygous familial hypercholesterolemia having LDL >189 mg/dL, **or** LDL >160 mg/dL with positive family history of premature cardiovascular disease (CVD), **or** LDL >160 mg/dL with the presence of at least two other CVD risk factors
Pregnancy Risk Factor X
Contraindications Hypersensitivity to lovastatin or any component of the formulation; active liver disease; unexplained persistent elevations of serum transaminases; pregnancy; breast-feeding
Warnings/Precautions May elevate aminotransferases; LFTs should be performed before and every 4- 6 weeks during the first 12-15 months of therapy and periodically thereafter. Can also cause myalgia and rhabdomyolysis. Rhabdomyolysis with acute renal failure has occurred. Risk is increased with concurrent use of clarithromycin, danazol, diltiazem, fluvoxamine, indinavir, nefazodone, nelfinavir, ritonavir, verapamil, troleandomycin, cyclosporine, fibric acid derivatives, erythromycin, niacin, azole antifungals, or large quantities of grapefruit juice. Weigh the risk versus benefit when combining any of these drugs with lovastatin. Temporarily discontinue in any patient experiencing an acute or serious condition predisposing to renal failure secondary to rhabdomyolysis. Use with caution in patients who consume large

amounts of alcohol or have a history of liver disease. Safety and efficacy of the immediate release tablet have not been evaluated in prepubertal patients, patients <10 years of age, or doses >40 mg/day in appropriately-selected adolescents; extended release tablets have not been studied in patients <20 years of age.

Common Adverse Reactions Percentages as reported with immediate release tablets; similar adverse reactions seen with extended release tablets.

>10%: Neuromuscular & skeletal: Increased CPK (>2x normal) (11%)

1% to 10%:

Central nervous system: Headache (2% to 3%), dizziness (0.5% to 1%)

Dermatologic: Rash (0.8% to 1%)

Gastrointestinal: Abdominal pain (2% to 3%), constipation (2% to 4%), diarrhea (2% to 3%), dyspepsia (1% to 2%), flatulence (4% to 5%), nausea (2% to 3%)

Neuromuscular & skeletal: Myalgia (2% to 3%), weakness (1% to 2%), muscle cramps (0.6% to 1%)

Ocular: Blurred vision (0.8% to 1%)

Drug Interactions

Cytochrome P450 Effect: Substrate of CYP3A4 (major); **Inhibits** CYP2C8/9 (weak), 2D6 (weak), 3A4 (weak)

Increased Effect/Toxicity: Inhibitors of CYP3A4 (amiodarone, amprenavir, atazanavir, clarithromycin, cyclosporine, diltiazem, fluvoxamine, erythromycin, fluconazole, indinavir, itraconazole, ketoconazole, miconazole, nefazodone, nelfinavir, ritonavir, troleandomycin, and verapamil) increase lovastatin blood levels and may increase the risk of myopathy and rhabdomyolysis. Limit dose to ≤40 mg with amiodarone or verapamil. Suspend lovastatin therapy during concurrent clarithromycin, erythromycin, itraconazole, or ketoconazole therapy. Cyclosporine, clofibrate, fenofibrate, gemfibrozil, and niacin also may increase the risk of myopathy and rhabdomyolysis. Limit dose to ≤20 mg with concurrent gemfibrozil. The effect/toxicity of warfarin (elevated PT) and levothyroxine may be increased by lovastatin. Digoxin, norethindrone, and ethinyl estradiol levels may be increased. Effects are additive with other lipid-lowering therapies.

Decreased Effect: Cholestyramine taken with lovastatin reduces lovastatin absorption and effect.

Mechanism of Action Lovastatin acts by competitively inhibiting 3-hydroxyl-3-methylglutaryl-coenzyme A (HMG-CoA) reductase, the enzyme that catalyzes the rate-limiting step in cholesterol biosynthesis

Pharmacodynamics/Kinetics

Onset of action: LDL-cholesterol reductions: 3 days

Absorption: 30%; increased with extended release tablets

Protein binding: 95%

Metabolism: Hepatic extensive first-pass effect; hydrolyzed to B-hydroxy acid (active)

Bioavailability: Increased with extended release tablets

Half-life elimination: 1.1-1.7 hours

Time to peak, serum: 2-4 hours

Excretion: Feces (~80% to 85%); urine (10%)

Dosage Oral:

Adolescents 10-17 years: Immediate release tablet:

LDL reduction <20%: Initial: 10 mg/day with evening meal

LDL reduction ≥20%: Initial: 20 mg/day with evening meal

Usual range: 10-40 mg with evening meal, then adjust dose at 4-week intervals

Adults: Initial: 20 mg with evening meal, then adjust at 4-week intervals; maximum dose: 80 mg/day immediate release tablet **or** 60 mg/day extended release tablet; before initiation of therapy, patients should be placed on a standard cholesterol-lowering diet for 3-6 months and the diet should be continued during drug therapy. Patients receiving immunosuppressant drugs should start at 10 mg/day and not exceed 20 mg/day. Patients receiving concurrent therapy with fibrates should not exceed 20 mg lovastatin. Patients receiving amiodarone, niacin, or verapamil should not exceed 40 mg lovastatin daily.

Administration Administer with meals. Do not crush or chew extended release tablets.

Monitoring Parameters Obtain baseline LFTs and total cholesterol profile. LFTs should be performed before initiation of therapy, at 6- and 12 weeks after initiation or first dose, and periodically thereafter.

Reference Range NCEP classification of pediatric patients with familial history of hypercholesterolemia or premature CVD: Acceptable total cholesterol: <170 mg/dL, LDL: <110 mg/dL

Patient Information Promptly report any unexplained muscle pain, tenderness or weakness, especially if accompanied by malaise or fever; do not interrupt, increase, or decrease dose without advice of prescriber; take with meals

Dosage Forms TAB: (Mevacor®) 10 mg, 20 mg, 40 mg. **TAB, extended release:** (Altocor™) 10 mg, 20 mg, 40 mg, 60 mg

♦ **Lovastatin and Niacin** see Niacin and Lovastatin on page 899

♦ **Lovenox®** see Enoxaparin on page 433

♦ **Low-Ogestrel®** see Ethinyl Estradiol and Norgestrel on page 492

Loxapine (LOKS a peen)

Related Information

Antipsychotic Agents Comparison on page 1364

U.S. Brand Names Loxitane®; Loxitane® C

Synonyms Loxapine Hydrochloride; Loxapine Succinate; Oxilapine Succinate

Therapeutic Category Antipsychotic Agent, Dibenzoxazepine

(Continued)

Loxapine *(Continued)*

Use Management of psychotic disorders

Pregnancy Risk Factor C

Contraindications Hypersensitivity to loxapine or any component of the formulation; severe CNS depression; coma

Warnings/Precautions Watch for hypotension when administering I.M.; should not be given I.V. Safety in children <6 months of age has not been established. Moderately sedating, use with caution in disorders where CNS depression is a feature. Use with caution in Parkinson's disease. Caution in patients with hemodynamic instability; bone marrow suppression; predisposition to seizures; subcortical brain damage; severe cardiac, hepatic, renal or respiratory disease. Esophageal dysmotility and aspiration have been associated with antipsychotic use - use with caution in patients at risk of pneumonia (ie, Alzheimer's disease). Caution in breast cancer or other prolactin-dependent tumors (may elevate prolactin levels). May alter temperature regulation or mask toxicity of other drugs due to antiemetic effects. May alter cardiac conduction; life-threatening arrhythmias have occurred with therapeutic doses of phenothiazines. May cause orthostatic hypotension - use with caution in patients at risk of this effect or those who would tolerate transient hypotensive episodes (cerebrovascular disease, cardiovascular disease, or other medications which may predispose). Safety and effectiveness of loxapine in pediatric patients have not been established.

Phenothiazines may cause anticholinergic effects (confusion, agitation, constipation, xerostomia, blurred vision, urinary retention); therefore, they should be used with caution in patients with decreased gastrointestinal motility, urinary retention, BPH, xerostomia, or visual problems. Conditions which also may be exacerbated by cholinergic blockade include narrow-angle glaucoma (screening is recommended) and worsening of myasthenia gravis. Relative to other antipsychotics, loxapine has a low potency of cholinergic blockade.

May cause extrapyramidal reactions, including pseudoparkinsonism, acute dystonic reactions, akathisia, and tardive dyskinesia (risk of these reactions is moderate-high relative to other neuroleptics). May be associated with neuroleptic malignant syndrome (NMS) or pigmentary retinopathy.

Common Adverse Reactions Frequency not defined.

Cardiovascular: Orthostatic hypotension, tachycardia, arrhythmias, abnormal T-waves with prolonged ventricular repolarization, hypertension, hypotension, lightheadedness, syncope

Central nervous system: Drowsiness, extrapyramidal symptoms (dystonia, akathisia, pseudoparkinsonism, tardive dyskinesia, akinesia), dizziness, faintness, ataxia, insomnia, agitation, tension, seizures, slurred speech, confusion, headache, neuroleptic malignant syndrome (NMS), altered central temperature regulation

Dermatologic: Rash, pruritus, photosensitivity, dermatitis, alopecia, seborrhea

Endocrine & metabolic: Enlargement of breasts, galactorrhea, amenorrhea, gynecomastia, menstrual irregularity

Gastrointestinal: Xerostomia, constipation, nausea, vomiting, weight gain/loss, adynamic ileus, polydipsia

Genitourinary: Urinary retention, sexual dysfunction

Hematologic: Agranulocytosis, leukopenia, thrombocytopenia

Neuromuscular & skeletal: Weakness

Ocular: Blurred vision

Respiratory: Nasal congestion

Drug Interactions

Increased Effect/Toxicity: Loxapine concentrations may be increased by chloroquine, propranolol, sulfadoxine-pyrimethamine. Loxapine may increased the effect and/or toxicity of antihypertensives, lithium, TCAs, CNS depressants (ethanol, narcotics), and trazodone. There are rare reports of significant respiratory depression, stupor, and/or hypotension with the concomitant use of loxapine and lorazepam. Use caution if the concomitant administration of loxapine and CNS drugs is required. Metoclopramide may increase risk of extrapyramidal symptoms (EPS).

Decreased Effect: Antipsychotics inhibit the activity of bromocriptine and levodopa. Benztropine (and other anticholinergics) may inhibit the therapeutic response to loxapine and excess anticholinergic effects may occur. Barbiturates and cigarette smoking may enhance the hepatic metabolism of loxapine. Loxapine and possibly other low potency antipsychotic may reverse the pressor effects of epinephrine.

Mechanism of Action Blocks postsynaptic mesolimbic D_1 and D_2 receptors in the brain, and also possesses serotonin 5-HT_2 blocking activity

Pharmacodynamics/Kinetics

Onset of action: Neuroleptic: Oral: 20-30 minutes

Peak effect: 1.5-3 hours

Duration: ~12 hours

Metabolism: Hepatic to glucuronide conjugates

Half-life elimination: Biphasic: Initial: 5 hours; Terminal: 12-19 hours

Excretion: Urine; feces (small amounts)

Dosage Oral:

Adults: 10 mg twice daily, increase dose until psychotic symptoms are controlled; usual dose range: 20-100 mg/day in divided doses 2-4 times/day; dosages >250 mg/day are not recommended

Elderly: 20-60 mg/day

Administration Dilute the oral concentrate with water or juice before administration; avoid skin contact with solution; may cause contact dermatitis.

Monitoring Parameters Vital signs; lipid profile, fasting blood glucose/Hgb A_{1c}; BMI; mental status, abnormal involuntary movement scale (AIMS), extrapyramidal symptoms (EPS)

Patient Information May cause drowsiness; avoid alcohol; may impair judgment or coordination; may cause photosensitivity; avoid excessive sunlight; do not stop taking without consulting prescriber

Dosage Forms CAP, as succinate (Loxitane®): 5 mg, 10 mg, 25 mg, 50 mg. **SOLN, oral concentrate, as hydrochloride** (Loxitane® C): 25 mg/mL (120 mL)

- **Loxapine Hydrochloride** see Loxapine on page 765
- **Loxapine Succinate** see Loxapine on page 765
- **Loxitane®** see Loxapine on page 765
- **Loxitane® C** see Loxapine on page 765
- **Lozi-Flur™** see Fluoride on page 535
- **Lozol®** see Indapamide on page 661
- **L-PAM** see Melphalan on page 786
- **LRH** see Gonadorelin on page 599
- **L-Sarcolysin** see Melphalan on page 786
- **LTG** see Lamotrigine on page 714
- **L-Thyroxine Sodium** see Levothyroxine on page 740
- **Lu-26-054** see Escitalopram on page 455
- **Ludiomil** see Maprotiline on page 775
- **Lugol's Solution** see Potassium Iodide on page 1022
- **Lumigan®** see Bimatoprost on page 167
- **Luminal® Sodium** see Phenobarbital on page 988
- **Lumitene™** see Beta-Carotene on page 159
- **Lunelle™** see Estradiol and Medroxyprogesterone on page 462
- **Lupron®** see Leuprolide on page 724
- **Lupron Depot®** see Leuprolide on page 724
- **Lupron Depot-Ped®** see Leuprolide on page 724
- **Luride®** see Fluoride on page 535
- **Luride® Lozi-Tab®** see Fluoride on page 535
- **Lustra®** see Hydroquinone on page 636
- **Lustra-AF™** see Hydroquinone on page 636
- **Luteinizing Hormone Releasing Hormone** see Gonadorelin on page 599
- **Luvox** see Fluvoxamine on page 553
- **Luxiq™** see Betamethasone on page 159
- **LY139603** see Atomoxetine on page 127
- **LY146032** see Daptomycin on page 342
- **LY170053** see Olanzapine on page 923
- **Lymphocyte Immune Globulin** see Antithymocyte Globulin (Equine) on page 108
- **Lymphocyte Mitogenic Factor** see Aldesleukin on page 47
- **Lysodren®** see Mitotane on page 850
- **Maalox® [OTC] [DSC]** see Aluminum Hydroxide and Magnesium Hydroxide on page 67
- **Maalox® [OTC]** see Aluminum Hydroxide, Magnesium Hydroxide, and Simethicone on page 68
- **Maalox® Max [OTC]** see Aluminum Hydroxide, Magnesium Hydroxide, and Simethicone on page 68
- **Maalox® TC (Therapeutic Concentrate) [OTC] [DSC]** see Aluminum Hydroxide and Magnesium Hydroxide on page 67
- **Macrobid®** see Nitrofurantoin on page 908
- **Macrodantin®** see Nitrofurantoin on page 908

Mafenide (MA fe nide)

Related Information
Sulfonamide Derivatives on page 1404

U.S. Brand Names Sulfamylon®

Synonyms Mafenide Acetate

Therapeutic Category Antibacterial, Topical; Antibiotic, Topical

Use Adjunct in the treatment of second- and third-degree burns to prevent septicemia caused by susceptible organisms such as *Pseudomonas aeruginosa*

Orphan drug: Prevention of graft loss of meshed autografts on excised burn wounds

Pregnancy Risk Factor C

Contraindications Hypersensitivity to mafenide, sulfites, or any component of the formulation

Warnings/Precautions Use with caution in patients with renal impairment and in patients with G6PD deficiency; prolonged use may result in superinfection

Common Adverse Reactions Frequency not defined.
Cardiovascular: Facial edema
Central nervous system: Pain
Dermatologic: Rash, erythema
Endocrine & metabolic: Hyperchloremia, metabolic acidosis
Hematologic: Porphyria, bone marrow suppression, hemolytic anemia, bleeding
Local: Burning sensation, excoriation
(Continued)

Mafenide (Continued)

Respiratory: Hyperventilation, tachypnea, dyspnea
Miscellaneous: Hypersensitivity

Mechanism of Action Interferes with bacterial folic acid synthesis through competitive inhibition of para-aminobenzoic acid

Pharmacodynamics/Kinetics
Absorption: Diffuses through devascularized areas and is rapidly absorbed from burned surface
Metabolism: To para-carboxybenzene sulfonamide, a carbonic anhydrase inhibitor
Time to peak, serum: 2-4 hours
Excretion: Urine (as metabolites)

Dosage Children and Adults: Topical: Apply once or twice daily with a sterile gloved hand; apply to a thickness of approximately 16 mm; the burned area should be covered with cream at all times

Monitoring Parameters Acid base balance

Patient Information Discontinue and report immediately if rash, blisters, or swelling appear while using cream; discontinue if condition persists or worsens while using this product; for external use only

Dosage Forms CRM, topical: 85 mg/g (60 g, 120 g, 454 g). **POWDER for topical solution:** 5% (5s) [50 g/packet]

♦ **Mafenide Acetate** *see Mafenide on page 767*

Magaldrate and Simethicone (MAG al drate & sye METH i kone)

U.S. Brand Names Riopan Plus® [OTC]; Riopan Plus® Double Strength [OTC]
Synonyms Simethicone and Magaldrate
Therapeutic Category Antacid; Antiflatulent
Use Relief of hyperacidity associated with peptic ulcer, gastritis, peptic esophagitis and hiatal hernia which are accompanied by symptoms of gas
Pregnancy Risk Factor C
Dosage Adults: Oral: 540-1080 mg magaldrate between meals and at bedtime
Dosage Forms SUSP, oral (Riopan Plus®): Magaldrate 540 mg and simethicone 20 mg per 5 mL (360 mL); (Riopan Plus® Double Strength): Magaldrate 1080 mg and simethicone 40 mg per 5 mL (360 mL)

♦ **Mag Delay® [OTC]** *see Magnesium Chloride on page 768*
♦ **Mag G® [OTC]** *see Magnesium Gluconate on page 769*
♦ **Maginex™ [OTC]** *see Magnesium L-aspartate Hydrochloride on page 770*
♦ **Maginex™ DS [OTC]** *see Magnesium L-aspartate Hydrochloride on page 770*
♦ **Magnesia Magma** *see Magnesium Hydroxide on page 769*
♦ **Magnesium Carbonate and Aluminum Hydroxide** *see Aluminum Hydroxide and Magnesium Carbonate on page 67*

Magnesium Chloride (mag NEE zhum KLOR ide)

U.S. Brand Names Chloromag®; Mag Delay® [OTC]; Mag-SR® [OTC]; Slow-Mag® [OTC]
Therapeutic Category Electrolyte Supplement, Oral
Use Correction or prevention of hypomagnesemia
Pregnancy Risk Factor D
Dosage Dietary supplement:
Oral: Adults: 54-483 mg/day in divided doses; refer to product labeling. The recommended dietary allowance (RDA) of magnesium is 4.5 mg/kg which is a total daily allowance of 350-400 mg for adult men and 280-300 mg for adult women. During pregnancy the RDA is 300 mg and during lactation the RDA is 355 mg.
I.V. in TPN:
Children: 2-10 mEq/day
The usual recommended pediatric maintenance intake of magnesium ranges from 0.2-0.6 mEq/kg/day. The dose of magnesium may also be based on the caloric intake; on that basis, 3-10 mEq/day of magnesium are needed; maximum maintenance dose: 8-16 mEq/day
Adults: 8-24 mEq/day
Dosage Forms INJ, solution (Chloromag®): 200 mg/mL [1.97 mEq/mL] (50 mL). **TAB** [enteric coated] (Slo-Mag®): Elemental magnesium 64 mg. **TAB, extended release** (Mag Delay®, Mag-SR®): Magnesium chloride hexahydrate 535 mg

Magnesium Citrate (mag NEE zhum SIT rate)

Related Information
Laxatives, Classification and Properties *on page 1380*
Synonyms Citrate of Magnesia
Therapeutic Category Laxative, Saline; Magnesium Salt
Use Evacuation of bowel prior to certain surgical and diagnostic procedures or overdose situations
Pregnancy Risk Factor B
Contraindications Renal failure, appendicitis, abdominal pain, intestinal impaction, obstruction or perforation, diabetes mellitus, complications in gastrointestinal tract, patients with colostomy or ileostomy, ulcerative colitis or diverticulitis

Warnings/Precautions Use with caution in patients with impaired renal function, especially if Cl_{cr} <30 mL/minute (accumulation of magnesium which may lead to magnesium intoxication); use with caution in digitalized patients (may alter cardiac conduction leading to heart block); use with caution in patients with lithium administration; use with caution with neuromuscular blocking agents, CNS depressants

Common Adverse Reactions 1% to 10%:
Cardiovascular: Hypotension
Endocrine & metabolic: Hypermagnesemia
Gastrointestinal: Abdominal cramps, diarrhea, gas formation
Respiratory: Respiratory depression

Mechanism of Action Promotes bowel evacuation by causing osmotic retention of fluid which distends the colon with increased peristaltic activity

Pharmacodynamics/Kinetics
Absorption: Oral: 15% to 30%
Excretion: Urine

Dosage Cathartic: Oral:
Children:
<6 years: 0.5 mL/kg up to a maximum of 200 mL repeated every 4-6 hours until stools are clear
6-12 years: 100-150 mL
Children ≥12 years and Adults: $1/2$ to 1 full bottle (120-300 mL)

Reference Range Serum magnesium:
Children: 1.5-1.9 mg/dL ~1.2-1.6 mEq/L
Adults: 2.2-2.8 mg/dL ~1.8-2.3 mEq/L

Patient Information Take with a glass of water, fruit juice, or citrus flavored carbonated beverage to improve taste, chill before using; report severe abdominal pain

Dosage Forms SOLN, oral: 290 mg/5 mL (300 mL). **TAB:** 100 mg

Magnesium Gluconate (mag NEE zhum GLOO koe nate)

U.S. Brand Names Almora® [OTC]; Mag G® [OTC]; Magonate® [OTC]; Magonate® Sport [OTC]; Magtrate® [OTC]

Therapeutic Category Electrolyte Supplement, Oral

Use Dietary supplement for treatment of magnesium deficiencies

Dosage The recommended dietary allowance (RDA) of magnesium is 4.5 mg/kg which is a total daily allowance of 350-400 mg for adult men and 280-300 mg for adult women. During pregnancy the RDA is 300 mg and during lactation the RDA is 355 mg.

Dietary supplement: Oral:
Children: 3-6 mg/kg/day in divided doses 3-4 times/day; maximum: 400 mg/day
Adults: 54-483 mg/day in divided doses; refer to product labeling

Dosing in renal impairment: Patients in severe renal failure should not receive magnesium due to toxicity from accumulation. Patients with a Cl_{cr} <25 mL/minute receiving magnesium should be monitored by serum magnesium levels.

Dosage Forms SOLN (Magonate®): 1000 mg/5 mL (480 mL); (Magonate® Sport): 1000 mg/5 mL (30 mL). **TAB** (Almora®, Mag G®, Magonate®, Magtrate®): 500 mg

Magnesium Hydroxide (mag NEE zhum hye DROKS ide)

Related Information
Laxatives, Classification and Properties on page 1380

U.S. Brand Names Dulcolax® Milk of Magnesia [OTC]; Phillips'® Milk of Magnesia [OTC]

Synonyms Magnesia Magma; Milk of Magnesia; MOM

Therapeutic Category Antacid; Laxative, Saline; Magnesium Salt

Use Short-term treatment of occasional constipation and symptoms of hyperacidity, magnesium replacement therapy

Pregnancy Risk Factor B

Contraindications Hypersensitivity to any component of the formulation; patients with colostomy or an ileostomy, intestinal obstruction, fecal impaction, renal failure, appendicitis

Warnings/Precautions Use with caution in patients with severe renal impairment (especially when doses are >50 mEq magnesium/day); hypermagnesemia and toxicity may occur due to decreased renal clearance of absorbed magnesium. Decreased renal function (Cl_{cr} <30 mL/minute) may result in toxicity; monitor for toxicity.

Common Adverse Reactions Frequency not defined.
Cardiovascular: Hypotension
Endocrine & metabolic: Hypermagnesemia
Gastrointestinal: Diarrhea, abdominal cramps
Neuromuscular & skeletal: Muscle weakness
Respiratory: Respiratory depression

Drug Interactions
Decreased Effect: Absorption of tetracyclines, digoxin, iron salts, isoniazid, or quinolones may be decreased.

Mechanism of Action Promotes bowel evacuation by causing osmotic retention of fluid which distends the colon with increased peristaltic activity; reacts with hydrochloric acid in stomach to form magnesium chloride

Pharmacodynamics/Kinetics
Onset of action: Laxative: 4-8 hours
Excretion: Urine (up to 30% as absorbed magnesium ions); feces (as unabsorbed drug)
(Continued)

Magnesium Hydroxide *(Continued)*

Dosage Oral:

Average daily intakes of dietary magnesium have declined in recent years due to processing of food; the latest estimate of the average American dietary intake was 349 mg/day

Laxative:

Liquid:

Children

<2 years: 0.5 mL/kg/dose

2-5 years: 5-15 mL/day (2.5-7.5 mL/day of liquid concentrate) or in divided doses

6-12 years: 15-30 mL/day (7.5-15 mL/day of liquid concentrate) or in divided doses

Children ≥12 years and Adults: 30-60 mL/day (15-30 mL/day of liquid concentrate) or in divided doses

Tablet:

Children:

2-5 years: 1-2 tablets before bedtime

6-11 years: 3-4 tablets before bedtime

Children ≥12 years and Adults: 6-8 tablets before bedtime

Antacid:

Liquid:

Children: 2.5-5 mL as needed up to 4 times/day

Adults: 5-15 mL (2.5-7.5 mL of liquid concentrate) as needed up to 4 times/day

Tablet:

Children 7-14 years: 1 tablet up to 4 times/day

Adults: 2-4 tablets up to 4 times/day

Dosing in renal impairment: Patients in severe renal failure should not receive magnesium due to toxicity from accumulation. Patients with a Cl_{cr} <25 mL/minute receiving magnesium should be monitored by serum magnesium levels.

Administration Liquid doses may be diluted with a small amount of water prior to administration. All doses should be followed by 8 ounces of water.

Reference Range Serum magnesium:

Children: 1.5-1.9 mg/dL (1.2-1.6 mEq/L)

Adults: 1.5-2.5 mg/dL (1.2-2.0 mEq/L)

Dosage Forms LIQ, oral: 400 mg/5 mL (360 mL, 480 mL, 960 mL, 3780 mL); (Dulcolax® Milk of Magnesia): 400 mg/5 mL (360 mL, 780 mL); (Phillips'® Milk of Magnesia): 400 mg/5 mL (120 mL, 360 mL, 780 mL). **LIQ, oral concentrate:** 800 mg/5 mL (100 mL, 400 mL); (Phillips'® Milk of Magnesia): 800 mg/5 mL (240 mL). **TAB, chewable** (Phillips'® Milk of Magnesia): 311 mg

♦ **Magnesium Hydroxide, Aluminum Hydroxide, and Simethicone** *see* Aluminum Hydroxide, Magnesium Hydroxide, and Simethicone *on page 68*

♦ **Magnesium Hydroxide and Aluminum Hydroxide** *see* Aluminum Hydroxide and Magnesium Hydroxide *on page 67*

♦ **Magnesium Hydroxide and Calcium Carbonate** *see* Calcium Carbonate and Magnesium Hydroxide *on page 204*

Magnesium Hydroxide and Mineral Oil

(mag NEE zhum hye DROKS ide & MIN er al oyl)

U.S. Brand Names Phillips' M-O® [OTC]

Synonyms Haley's M-O; MOM/Mineral Oil Emulsion

Therapeutic Category Laxative

Use Short-term treatment of occasional constipation

Pregnancy Risk Factor B

Dosage

Children 6-11 years: 5-15 mL at bedtime or upon rising

Children ≥12 years and Adults: 30-60 mL at bedtime or upon rising

Dosage adjustment in renal impairment: Patients in severe renal failure should not receive magnesium due to toxicity from accumulation. Patients with a Cl_{cr} <25 mL/minute should be monitored by serum magnesium levels.

Dosage Forms SUSP, oral: Magnesium hydroxide 300 mg and mineral oil 1.25 mL per 5 mL (360 mL, 780 mL)

♦ **Magnesium Hydroxide, Famotidine, and Calcium Carbonate** *see* Famotidine, Calcium Carbonate, and Magnesium Hydroxide *on page 507*

Magnesium L-aspartate Hydrochloride

(mag NEE zhum el as PAR tate hye droe KLOR ide)

U.S. Brand Names Maginex™ [OTC]; Maginex™ DS [OTC]

Synonyms MAH™

Therapeutic Category Electrolyte Supplement, Oral

Use Dietary supplement

Contraindications Hypersensitivity to any component of the formulation

Warnings/Precautions Hypermagnesemia and toxicity may occur due to decreased renal clearance (Cl_{cr}<30 mL/minute) of absorbed magnesium; use with caution in digitalized patients (may alter cardiac conduction leading heart block); use with caution in patients with lithium administration; elderly, due to disease or drug therapy, may be predisposed to diarrhea; diarrhea may result in electrolyte imbalance; monitor for toxicity.

Common Adverse Reactions Frequency not defined: Gastrointestinal: Diarrhea, loose stools

Dosage Adults:

Recommended dietary allowance (RDA) of magnesium:

Male: 400-420 mg

Female: 310-320 mg

During pregnancy: 360 mg

During lactation: 320 mg

Dietary supplement: Oral: Magnesium-L-aspartate 1230 mg (magnesium 122 mg) up to 3 times/day

Dosage adjustment in renal impairment: Patients with severe renal failure should not receive magnesium due to toxicity from accumulation.

Administration

Granules: Mix each packet in 4 ounces of water or juice prior to administration

Tablet, enteric coated: Do not crush or chew

Patient Information Not for use in patients with kidney/renal disease.

Dosage Forms GRAN (Maginex™ DS): 1230 mg. **TAB** (Maginex™): 615 mg

Magnesium Oxide (mag NEE zhum OKS ide)

U.S. Brand Names Mag-Ox® 400 [OTC]; Uro-Mag® [OTC]

Therapeutic Category Antacid; Electrolyte Supplement, Oral; Laxative, Saline; Magnesium Salt

Use Electrolyte replacement

Pregnancy Risk Factor B

Contraindications Patients with colostomy or an ileostomy, appendicitis, ulcerative colitis, diverticulitis, heart block, myocardial damage, serious renal impairment, hepatitis, Addison's disease, hypersensitivity to any component

Warnings/Precautions Hypermagnesemia and toxicity may occur due to decreased renal clearance (Cl_{cr} <30 mL/minute) of absorbed magnesium; monitor serum magnesium level, respiratory rate, deep tendon reflex, renal function when $MgSO_4$ is administered parenterally; use with caution in digitalized patients (may alter cardiac conduction leading heart block); use with caution in patients with lithium administration; elderly, due to disease or drug therapy, may be predisposed to diarrhea; diarrhea may result in electrolyte imbalance; monitor for toxicity

Common Adverse Reactions

>10%: Gastrointestinal: Diarrhea

1% to 10%:

Cardiovascular: Hypotension, ECG changes

Central nervous system: Mental depression, coma

Gastrointestinal: Nausea, vomiting

Respiratory: Respiratory depression

Drug Interactions

Increased Effect/Toxicity: Nondepolarizing neuromuscular blockers

Decreased Effect: Decreased absorption of aminoquinolones, digoxin, nitrofurantoin, penicillamine, and tetracyclines may occur with magnesium salts

Pharmacodynamics/Kinetics

Onset of action: Laxative: 4-8 hours

Excretion: Urine (up to 30% as absorbed magnesium ions); feces (as unabsorbed drug)

Dosage The recommended dietary allowance (RDA) of magnesium is 4.5 mg/kg which is a total daily allowance of 350-400 mg for adult men and 280-300 mg for adult women. During pregnancy the RDA is 300 mg and during lactation the RDA is 355 mg.

Adults: Oral: Dietary supplement: 20-40 mEq (1-2 tablets) 2-3 times

Product labeling:

Mag-Ox 400®: 1-2 tablets daily with food

Uro-Mag®: 1-2 tablets 3 times/day with food

Dosing in renal impairment: Patients in severe renal failure should not receive magnesium due to toxicity from accumulation. Patients with a Cl_{cr} <25 mL/minute should be monitored by serum magnesium levels.

Note: Oral magnesium is not generally adequate for repletion in patients with serum magnesium concentrations <1.5 mEq/L

Reference Range Serum magnesium:

Children: 1.5-1.9 mg/dL (1.2-1.6 mEq/L)

Adults: 1.5-2.5 mg/dL (1.2-2.0 mEq/L)

Patient Information Chew tablets before swallowing; take with full glass of water; report if relief is not obtained or if any signs of bleeding occur (black tarry stools, "coffee ground" vomit)

Dosage Forms CAP (Uro-Mag®): 140 mg. **TAB** (Mag-Ox 400®): 400 mg

Magnesium Salicylate (mag NEE zhum sa LIS i late)

U.S. Brand Names Doan's® [OTC]; Doan's® Extra Strength [OTC]; Mobidin® [DSC]; Momentum® [OTC]

Therapeutic Category Nonsteroidal Anti-inflammatory Drug (NSAID), Oral

Use Mild to moderate pain, fever, various inflammatory conditions

Dosage Oral: Adults: 650 mg 4 times daily or 1090 mg 3 times daily; may increase to 3.6-4.8 mg/day in 3 or 4 divided doses

Dosage Forms CAPLET, as anhydrous magnesium salicylate: 467 mg; (Doan's®): 304 mg; (Doan's® Extra Strength, Momentum®): 467 mg; (Mobidin® [DSC]): 600 mg

Magnesium Sulfate (mag NEE zhum SUL fate)

Synonyms Epsom Salts

Therapeutic Category Antacid; Electrolyte Supplement, Parenteral; Laxative, Saline; Magnesium Salt

Use Treatment and prevention of hypomagnesemia; seizure prevention in severe pre-eclampsia or eclampsia, pediatric acute nephritis; short-term treatment torsade de pointes; treatment of cardiac arrhythmias (VT/VF) caused by hypomagnesemia; short-term treatment of constipation or soaking aid

Pregnancy Risk Factor B

Contraindications Heart block, serious renal impairment, myocardial damage, hepatitis, Addison's disease

Warnings/Precautions Use with caution in patients with impaired renal function (accumulation of magnesium which may lead to magnesium intoxication); use with caution in digitalized patients (may alter cardiac conduction leading to heart block); monitor serum magnesium level, respiratory rate, deep tendon reflex, renal function when $MgSO_4$ is administered parenterally

Common Adverse Reactions Hypotension and asystole may occur with rapid administration.
Serum magnesium levels >3 mg/dL:
  Central nervous system: Depressed CNS
  Gastrointestinal: Diarrhea
  Neuromuscular & skeletal: Blocked peripheral neuromuscular transmission leading to anti-convulsant effects
Serum magnesium levels >5 mg/dL:
  Cardiovascular: Flushing
  Central nervous system: Somnolence
Serum magnesium levels >12.5 mg/dL:
  Cardiovascular: Complete heart block, cardiac conduction affected
  Respiratory: Respiratory paralysis

Mechanism of Action Promotes bowel evacuation by causing osmotic retention of fluid which distends the colon with increased peristaltic activity when taken orally; parenterally, decreases acetylcholine in motor nerve terminals and acts on myocardium by slowing rate of S-A node impulse formation and prolonging conduction time

Pharmacodynamics/Kinetics
Onset of action: Oral: Cathartic: 1-2 hours; I.M.: 1 hour; I.V.: Immediate
Duration: I.M.: 3-4 hours; I.V.: 30 minutes
Excretion: Urine (as magnesium)

Dosage The recommended dietary allowance (RDA) of magnesium is 4.5 mg/kg which is a total daily allowance of 350-400 mg for adult men and 280-300 mg for adult women. During pregnancy the RDA is 300 mg and during lactation the RDA is 355 mg. Average daily intakes of dietary magnesium have declined in recent years due to processing of food. The latest estimate of the average American dietary intake was 349 mg/day. Dose represented as $MgSO_4$ unless stated otherwise.

Note: Serum magnesium is poor reflection of repletional status as the majority of magnesium is intracellular; serum levels may be transiently normal for a few hours after a dose is given, therefore, aim for consistently high normal serum levels in patients with normal renal function for most efficient repletion

Hypomagnesemia:
  Neonates: I.V.: 25-50 mg/kg/dose (0.2-0.4 mEq/kg/dose) every 8-12 hours for 2-3 doses
  Children: I.M., I.V.: 25-50 mg/kg/dose (0.2-0.4 mEq/kg/dose) every 4-6 hours for 3-4 doses, maximum single dose: 2000 mg (16 mEq), may repeat if hypomagnesemia persists (higher dosage up to 100 mg/kg/dose $MgSO_4$ I.V. has been used); maintenance: I.V.: 30-60 mg/kg/day (0.25-0.5 mEq/kg/day)
  Adults:
    Oral: 3 g every 6 hours for 4 doses as needed
    I.M., I.V.: 1 g every 6 hours for 4 doses; for severe hypomagnesemia: 8-12 g $MgSO_4$/day in divided doses has been used
Management of seizures and hypertension: Children: I.M., I.V.: 20-100 mg/kg/dose every 4-6 hours as needed; in severe cases doses as high as 200 mg/kg/dose have been used
Eclampsia, pre-eclampsia: Adults:
  I.M.: 1-4 g every 4 hours
  I.V.: Initial: 4 g, then switch to I.M. or 1-4 g/hour by continuous infusion
  Note: Maximum dose not to exceed 30-40 g/day; maximum rate of infusion: 1-2 g/hour
Life-threatening arrhythmia: I.V.: 1-2 g (8-16 mEq) in 100 mL D_5W, administered over 5-60 minutes followed by an infusion of 0.5-1 g/hour, **or**
  1-6 g administered over several minutes, followed by (in some cases) I.V. infusion of 3-20 mg/minute for 5-48 hours (depending on patient response and serum magnesium levels)
Maintenance electrolyte requirements:
  Daily requirements: 0.2-0.5 mEq/kg/24 hours or 3-10 mEq/1000 kcal/24 hours
  Maximum: 8-16 mEq/24 hours
Cathartic: Oral:
  Children:
    2-5 years: 2.5-5 g/kg/day in a single or divided doses
    6-11 years: 5-10 g/day in a single or divided doses
  Children ≥12 years and Adults: 10-30 g/day in a single or divided doses
Soaking aid: Topical: Adults: Dissolve 2 capfuls of powder per gallon of warm water

Dosing adjustment/comments in renal impairment: Cl_{cr} <25 mL/minute: Do not administer or monitor serum magnesium levels carefully

Administration Magnesium sulfate injection may be administered I.M. or I.V.

I.M.: A 25% or 50% concentration may be used for adults and a 20% solution is recommended for children

I.V.: Magnesium may be administered IVP, IVPB or I.V. infusion in an auxiliary medication infusion solution (eg, TPN); when giving I.V. push, must dilute first and should not be given any faster than 150 mg/minute

Maximal rate of infusion: 2 g/hour to avoid hypotension; doses of 4 g/hour have been given in emergencies (eclampsia, seizures); optimally, should add magnesium to I.V. fluids or to IVH, but bolus doses are also effective

For I.V., a concentration <20% (200 mg/mL) should be used and the rate of injection should not exceed 1.5 mL of a 10% solution (or equivalent) per minute (150 mg/minute)

Monitoring Parameters Monitor blood pressure when administering $MgSO_4$ I.V.; serum magnesium levels should be monitored to avoid overdose; monitor for diarrhea; monitor for arrhythmias, hypotension, respiratory and CNS depression during rapid I.V. administration

Reference Range Serum magnesium:
Children: 1.5-1.9 mg/dL (1.2-1.6 mEq/L)
Adults: 1.5-2.5 mg/dL (1.2-2.0 mEq/L)

Note: Serum magnesium is poor reflection of repletional status as the majority of magnesium is intracellular; serum levels may be transiently normal for a few hours after a dose is given, therefore, aim for consistently high normal serum levels in patients with normal renal function for most efficient repletion

Dosage Forms INF [premixed in D_5W]: 10 mg/mL (100 mL); 20 mg/mL (500 mL, 1000 mL). **INF** [premixed in water for injection]: 40 mg/mL (100 mL, 500 mL, 1000 mL); 80 mg/mL (50 mL). **INJ, solution:** 125 mg/mL (8 mL); 500 mg/mL (2 mL, 5 mL, 10 mL, 20 mL, 50 mL). **POWDER:** Magnesium sulfate USP (480 g, 1810 g, 1920 g)

♦ **Magnesium Trisilicate and Aluminum Hydroxide** see Aluminum Hydroxide and Magnesium Trisilicate on page 67

♦ **Magonate® [OTC]** see Magnesium Gluconate on page 769

♦ **Magonate® Sport [OTC]** see Magnesium Gluconate on page 769

♦ **Mag-Ox® 400 [OTC]** see Magnesium Oxide on page 771

♦ **Mag-SR® [OTC]** see Magnesium Chloride on page 768

♦ **Magtrate® [OTC]** see Magnesium Gluconate on page 769

♦ **MAH™** see Magnesium L-aspartate Hydrochloride on page 770

♦ **Malaria Treatment** see page 1464

♦ **Malarone™** see Atovaquone and Proguanil on page 131

Malathion (mal a THYE on)

U.S. Brand Names Ovide®

Therapeutic Category Antiparasitic Agent, Topical; Pediculocide; Scabicidal Agent

Use Treatment of head lice and their ova

Pregnancy Risk Factor B

Contraindications Hypersensitivity to malathion or any component of the formulation; use in neonates and/or infants

Warnings/Precautions For topical use only; avoid contact with eyes. Lotion is flammable; do not expose to open flames; patients should avoid electric heat sources (eg, hair dryers, curling irons). Safety and efficacy in children <6 years of age have not been established.

Common Adverse Reactions Frequency not defined.
Dermatologic: Skin/scalp irritation
Ocular: Conjunctivitis (following contact with eyes)

Dosage Sprinkle Ovide™ lotion on dry hair and rub gently until the scalp is thoroughly moistened; pay special attention to the back of the head and neck. Allow to dry naturally - use no heat and leave uncovered. After 8-12 hours, the hair should be washed with a nonmedicated shampoo; rinse and use a fine-toothed comb to remove dead lice and eggs. If required, repeat with second application in 7-9 days. Further treatment is generally not necessary. Other family members should be evaluated to determine if infested and if so, receive treatment.

Administration Refer to Dosing.

Patient Information For topical use only; avoid contact with eyes. Lotion is flammable; do not expose to open flames; patients should avoid electric heat sources (eg, hair dryers, curling irons).

Dosage Forms LOTION: 0.5% (59 mL)

♦ **Management of Healthcare Worker Exposures to HBV, HCV, and HIV** see page 1421

♦ **Management of Overdosages** see page 1485

♦ **Mandelamine®** see Methenamine on page 811

♦ **Mandol® [DSC]** see Cefamandole on page 230

♦ **Mandrake** see Podophyllum Resin on page 1012

Manganese (MAN ga nees)

Synonyms Manganese Chloride; Manganese Sulfate

Therapeutic Category Trace Element; Trace Element, Parenteral

Use Trace element added to total parenteral nutrition (TPN) solution to prevent manganese deficiency; orally as a dietary supplement
(Continued)

Manganese *(Continued)*

Pregnancy Risk Factor C

Contraindications High manganese levels; severe liver dysfunction or cholestasis (conjugated bilirubin >2 mg/dL) due to reduced biliary excretion

Warnings/Precautions Manganese chloride solution for injection contains aluminum; use caution with impaired renal function and in premature infants. Use caution with hepatic impairment.

Mechanism of Action Cofactor in many enzyme systems, stimulates synthesis of cholesterol and fatty acids in liver, and influences mucopolysaccharide synthesis

Pharmacodynamics/Kinetics

Absorption: Oral: Poor (3% to 4%)

Distribution: Concentrated in mitochondria of pituitary gland, pancreas, liver, kidney, and bone

Excretion: Bile (primarily); urine (negligible)

Dosage

Oral: Adequate intake:

0-6 months: 0.003 mg/day

7-12 months: 0.6 mg/day

1-3 years: 1.2 mg/day

4-8 years: 1.5 mg/day

9 years to Adults, Male: 1.9-2.3 mg/day

9 years to Adults, Female: 1.6-1.8 mg/day

Pregnancy: 2 mg/day

Lactation: 2.6 mg/day

I.V.:

Children: 2-10 mcg/kg/day usually administered in TPN solutions

Note: Use caution in premature neonates; manganese chloride solution for injection contains aluminum

Adults: 150-800 mcg/day usually administered in TPN solutions

Dosage adjustment in renal impairment: Use caution; manganese chloride solution for injection contains aluminum

Dosage adjustment in hepatic impairment: Use caution; dose may need to be decreased or withheld

Administration Solution for injection: Do not administer I.M. or by direct I.V. injection; acidic pH of the solution may cause tissue irritations and it is hypotonic

Monitoring Parameters Periodic manganese plasma level

Reference Range Plasma: 0.6-2 ng/mL

Dosage Forms INJ, solution, as chloride [preservative free]: 0.1 mg/mL (10 mL). **INJ, solution, as sulfate:** 0.1 mg/mL (10 mL). **TAB, elemental:** 50 mg, 100 mg

♦ **Manganese Chloride** *see* Manganese *on page 773*

♦ **Manganese Sulfate** *see* Manganese *on page 773*

Mannitol *(MAN i tole)*

U.S. Brand Names Osmitrol®; Resectisol®

Synonyms D-Mannitol

Therapeutic Category Diuretic, Osmotic

Use Reduction of increased intracranial pressure associated with cerebral edema; promotion of diuresis in the prevention and/or treatment of oliguria or anuria due to acute renal failure; reduction of increased intraocular pressure; promoting urinary excretion of toxic substances; genitourinary irrigant in transurethral prostatic resection or other transurethral surgical procedures

Pregnancy Risk Factor C

Contraindications Hypersensitivity to mannitol or any component or the formulation; severe renal disease (anuria); dehydration; active intracranial bleeding; severe pulmonary edema or congestion

Warnings/Precautions Should not be administered until adequacy of renal function and urine flow is established; cardiovascular status should also be evaluated; do not administer electrolyte-free mannitol solutions with blood

Common Adverse Reactions Frequency not defined.

Cardiovascular: Circulatory overload, CHF

Central nervous system: Headache, convulsions, headache, chills, dizziness

Dermatologic: Rash

Endocrine & metabolic: Fluid and electrolyte imbalance, water intoxication, dehydration and hypovolemia secondary to rapid diuresis, hyponatremia

Gastrointestinal: Nausea, vomiting, xerostomia

Genitourinary: Polyuria, dysuria

Local: Tissue necrosis

Ocular: Blurred vision

Respiratory: Pulmonary edema

Miscellaneous: Allergic reactions

Drug Interactions

Increased Effect/Toxicity: Lithium toxicity (with diuretic-induced hyponatremia).

Mechanism of Action Increases the osmotic pressure of glomerular filtrate, which inhibits tubular reabsorption of water and electrolytes and increases urinary output

Pharmacodynamics/Kinetics

Onset of action: Diuresis: Injection: 1-3 hours; Reduction in intracerebral pressure: ~15 minutes

Duration: Reduction in intracerebral pressure: 3-6 hours

Distribution: Remains confined to extracellular space (except in extreme concentrations); does not penetrate the blood-brain barrier

Metabolism: Minimally hepatic to glycogen

Half-life elimination: 1.1-1.6 hours

Excretion: Primarily urine (as unchanged drug)

Dosage I.V.:

Children:

Test dose (to assess adequate renal function): 200 mg/kg over 3-5 minutes to produce a urine flow of at least 1 mL/kg for 1-3 hours

Initial: 0.5-1 g/kg

Maintenance: 0.25-0.5 g/kg given every 4-6 hours

Adults:

Test dose (to assess adequate renal function): 12.5 g (200 mg/kg) over 3-5 minutes to produce a urine flow of at least 30-50 mL of urine per hour over the next 2-3 hours

Initial: 0.5-1 g/kg

Maintenance: 0.25-0.5 g/kg every 4-6 hours; usual adult dose: 20-200 g/24 hours

Intracranial pressure: Cerebral edema: 1.5-2 g/kg/dose I.V. as a 15% to 20% solution over ≥30 minutes; maintain serum osmolality 310-320 mOsm/kg

Preoperative for neurosurgery: 1.5-2 g/kg administered 1-1.5 hours prior to surgery

Transurethral irrigation: Use urogenital solution as required for irrigation

Administration In-line 5-micron filter set should always be used for mannitol infusion with concentrations ≥23%; administer test dose (for oliguria) I.V. push over 3-5 minutes; for cerebral edema or elevated ICP, administer over 20-30 minutes

Monitoring Parameters Renal function, daily fluid I & O, serum electrolytes, serum and urine osmolality; for treatment of elevated intracranial pressure, maintain serum osmolality 310-320 mOsm/kg

Dosage Forms INJ, solution: 5% [50 mg/mL] (1000 mL); 10% [100 mg/mL] (500 mL, 1000 mL); 15% [150 mg/mL] (500 mL); 20% [200 mg/mL] (150 mL, 250 mL, 500 mL); 25% [250 mg/mL] (50 mL); (Osmitrol®): 5% [50 mg/mL] (1000 mL); 10% [100 mg/mL] (500 mL, 1000 mL); 15% [150 mg/mL] (500 mL); 20% [200 mg/mL] (250 mL, 500 mL). **SOLN, urogenital** (Resectisol®): 5% [50 mg/mL] (2000 mL, 4000 mL)

- ◆ **Mantoux** see Tuberculin Tests on page 1279
- ◆ **Mapap® [OTC]** see Acetaminophen on page 24
- ◆ **Mapap® Arthritis [OTC]** see Acetaminophen on page 24
- ◆ **Mapap® Children's [OTC]** see Acetaminophen on page 24
- ◆ **Mapap® Extra Strength [OTC]** see Acetaminophen on page 24
- ◆ **Mapap® Infants [OTC]** see Acetaminophen on page 24
- ◆ **Mapap Sinus Maximum Strength [OTC]** see Acetaminophen and Pseudoephedrine on page 26

Maprotiline (ma PROE ti leen)

Related Information

Antidepressant Agents Comparison on page 1359

Synonyms Ludiomil; Maprotiline Hydrochloride

Therapeutic Category Antidepressant, Tetracyclic

Use Treatment of depression and anxiety associated with depression

Unlabeled/Investigational Use Bulimia; duodenal ulcers; enuresis; urinary symptoms of multiple sclerosis pain; panic attacks; tension headache; cocaine withdrawal

Pregnancy Risk Factor B

Dosage Oral:

Children 6-14 years: Depression/anxiety: 10 mg/day; increase to a maximum daily dose of 75 mg

Adults: Depression/anxiety: 75 mg/day to start, increase by 25 mg every 2 weeks up to 150-225 mg/day; given in 3 divided doses or in a single daily dose

Elderly: Depression/anxiety: Initial: 25 mg at bedtime, increase by 25 mg every 3 days for inpatients and weekly for outpatients if tolerated; usual maintenance dose: 50-75 mg/day, higher doses may be necessary in nonresponders

Dosage Forms TAB: 25 mg, 50 mg, 75 mg

- ◆ **Maprotiline Hydrochloride** see Maprotiline on page 775
- ◆ **Marcaine®** see Bupivacaine on page 186
- ◆ **Marcaine® Spinal** see Bupivacaine on page 186
- ◆ **Margesic® H** see Hydrocodone and Acetaminophen on page 627
- ◆ **Marinol®** see Dronabinol on page 416
- ◆ **Matulane®** see Procarbazine on page 1040
- ◆ **3M™ Avagard™ [OTC]** see Chlorhexidine Gluconate on page 259
- ◆ **Mavik®** see Trandolapril on page 1251
- ◆ **Maxair™ Autohaler™** see Pirbuterol on page 1007
- ◆ **Maxalt®** see Rizatriptan on page 1108
- ◆ **Maxalt-MLT®** see Rizatriptan on page 1108
- ◆ **Maxaquin®** see Lomefloxacin on page 753

- **Maxidex**® *see* Dexamethasone *on page 356*
- **Maxidone**™ *see* Hydrocodone and Acetaminophen *on page 627*
- **Maxifed**® *see* Guaifenesin and Pseudoephedrine *on page 605*
- **Maxifed**® **DM** *see* Guaifenesin, Pseudoephedrine, and Dextromethorphan *on page 606*
- **Maxifed-G**® *see* Guaifenesin and Pseudoephedrine *on page 605*
- **Maxiflor**® *see* Diflorasone *on page 372*
- **Maxipime**® *see* Cefepime *on page 234*
- **Maxitrol**® *see* Neomycin, Polymyxin B, and Dexamethasone *on page 892*
- **Maxivate**® *see* Betamethasone *on page 159*
- **Maxzide**® *see* Hydrochlorothiazide and Triamterene *on page 627*
- **Maxzide**®**-25** *see* Hydrochlorothiazide and Triamterene *on page 627*
- **May Apple** *see* Podophyllum Resin *on page 1012*
- **MCH** *see* Microfibrillar Collagen Hemostat *on page 836*
- **MDL 73,147EF** *see* Dolasetron *on page 400*

Measles, Mumps, and Rubella Vaccines (Combined)
(MEE zels, mumpz & roo BEL a vak SEENS, kom BINED)

U.S. Brand Names M-M-R® II

Synonyms MMR; Mumps, Measles and Rubella Vaccines, Combined; Rubella, Measles and Mumps Vaccines, Combined

Therapeutic Category Vaccine; Vaccine, Live Virus

Use Measles, mumps, and rubella prophylaxis

Pregnancy Risk Factor C

Dosage S.C.:

Infants <12 months: If there is risk of exposure to measles, single-antigen measles vaccine should be administered at 6-11 months of age with a second dose (of MMR) at >12 months of age.

Children ≥12 months: 0.5 mL at 12 months and then repeated at 4-6 years of age. If the second dose was not received, the schedule should be completed by the 11- to 12-year old visit. Administer in outer aspect of the upper arm. Recommended age of primary immunization is 12-15 months; revaccination is recommended prior to elementary school.

Dosage Forms INJ, powder for reconstitution [preservative free]: Measles virus 1000 $TCID_{50}$, rubella virus 1000 $TCID_{50}$, and mumps virus 20,000 $TCID_{50}$

Measles Virus Vaccine (Live) (MEE zels VYE rus vak SEEN, live)

U.S. Brand Names Attenuvax®

Synonyms More Attenuated Enders Strain; Rubeola Vaccine

Therapeutic Category Vaccine; Vaccine, Live Virus

Use Adults born before 1957 are generally considered to be immune. All those born in or after 1957 without documentation of live vaccine on or after first birthday, physician-diagnosed measles, or laboratory evidence of immunity should be vaccinated, ideally with two doses of vaccine separated by no less than 1 month. For those previously vaccinated with one dose of measles vaccine, revaccination is recommended for students entering colleges and other institutions of higher education, for healthcare workers at the time of employment, and for international travelers who visit endemic areas.

MMR is the vaccine of choice if recipients are likely to be susceptible to rubella and/or mumps as well as to measles. Persons vaccinated between 1963 and 1967 with a killed measles vaccine, followed by live vaccine within 3 months, or with a vaccine of unknown type should be revaccinated with live measles virus vaccine.

Pregnancy Risk Factor X

Contraindications Hypersensitivity to neomycin or any component of the formulation; acute respiratory infections, activated tuberculosis, immunosuppressed patients; pregnancy; known anaphylactoid reaction to eggs

Warnings/Precautions Avoid use in immunocompromised patients; defer administration in presence of acute respiratory or other active infections or inactive, untreated tuberculosis; avoid pregnancy for 3 months following vaccination; history of febrile seizures, hypersensitivity reactions may occur

Common Adverse Reactions All serious adverse reactions must be reported to the U.S. Department of Health and Human Services (DHHS) Vaccine Adverse Event Reporting System (VAERS) 1-800-822-7967.

>10%:
  Cardiovascular: Edema
  Central nervous system: Fever (<100°F)
  Local: Burning or stinging, induration

1% to 10%:
  Central nervous system: Fever between 100°F and 103°F usually between 5th and 12th days postvaccination
  Dermatologic: Rash (rarely generalized)

Mechanism of Action Promotes active immunity to measles virus by inducing specific measles IgG and IgM antibodies.

Dosage Children ≥15 months and Adults: S.C.: 0.5 mL in outer aspect of the upper arm, no routine boosters

Administration Vaccine should not be administered I.V.; S.C. injection preferred

Patient Information Parents should monitor children closely for fever for 5-11 days after vaccination; females should not become pregnant within 3 months of vaccination

Dosage Forms INJ, powder for reconstitution [preservative free]: 1000 $TCID_{50}$

♦ **Mebaral**® *see* Mephobarbital *on page 792*

Mebendazole (me BEN da zole)

U.S. Brand Names Vermox®

Therapeutic Category Anthelmintic

Use Treatment of pinworms (*Enterobius vermicularis*), whipworms (*Trichuris trichiura*), round-worms (*Ascaris lumbricoides*), and hookworms (*Ancylostoma duodenale*)

Pregnancy Risk Factor C

Contraindications Hypersensitivity to mebendazole or any component of the formulation

Warnings/Precautions Pregnancy and children <2 years of age are relative contraindications since safety has not been established; not effective for hydatid disease

Common Adverse Reactions Frequency not defined.

Cardiovascular: Angioedema

Central nervous system: Fever, dizziness, headache, seizures

Dermatologic: Rash, itching, alopecia (with high doses)

Gastrointestinal: Abdominal pain, diarrhea, nausea, vomiting

Hematologic: Neutropenia (sore throat, unusual fatigue)

Neuromuscular & skeletal: Unusual weakness

Drug Interactions

Decreased Effect: Anticonvulsants such as carbamazepine and phenytoin may increase metabolism of mebendazole

Mechanism of Action Selectively and irreversibly blocks glucose uptake and other nutrients in susceptible adult intestine-dwelling helminths

Pharmacodynamics/Kinetics

Absorption: 2% to 10%

Distribution: To serum, cyst fluid, liver, omental fat, and pelvic, pulmonary, and hepatic cysts; highest concentrations found in liver; relatively high concentrations found in muscle-encysted *Trichinella spiralis* larvae; crosses placenta

Protein binding: 95%

Metabolism: Extensively hepatic

Half-life elimination: 1-11.5 hours

Time to peak, serum: 2-4 hours

Excretion: Primarily feces; urine (5% to 10%)

Dosage Children and Adults: Oral:

Pinworms: 100 mg as a single dose; may need to repeat after 2 weeks; treatment should include family members in close contact with patient

Whipworms, roundworms, hookworms: One tablet twice daily, morning and evening on 3 consecutive days; if patient is not cured within 3-4 weeks, a second course of treatment may be administered

Capillariasis: 200 mg twice daily for 20 days

Dosing adjustment in hepatic impairment: Dosage reduction may be necessary in patients with liver dysfunction

Hemodialysis: Not dialyzable (0% to 5%)

Monitoring Parameters Check for helminth ova in feces within 3-4 weeks following the initial therapy

Patient Information Tablets may be chewed, swallowed whole, or crushed and mixed with food; hygienic precautions should be taken to prevent reinfection such as wearing shoes and washing hands

Dosage Forms TAB, chewable: 100 mg

Mecamylamine (mek a MIL a meen)

U.S. Brand Names Inversine®

Synonyms Mecamylamine Hydrochloride

Therapeutic Category Antihypertensive Agent; Ganglionic Blocking Agent

Use Treatment of moderately severe to severe hypertension and in uncomplicated malignant hypertension

Unlabeled/Investigational Use Tourette's syndrome

Pregnancy Risk Factor C

Contraindications Coronary insufficiency, pyloric stenosis, glaucoma, uremia, recent myocar-dial infarction, unreliable, uncooperative patients

Warnings/Precautions Use with caution in patients receiving sulfonamides or antibiotics that cause neuromuscular blockade; use with caution in patients with impaired renal function, previous CNS abnormalities, prostatic hyperplasia, bladder obstruction, or urethral strictive; do not abruptly discontinue

Common Adverse Reactions Frequency not defined.

Cardiovascular: Postural hypotension

Central nervous system: Drowsiness, convulsions, confusion, mental depression

Endocrine & metabolic: Sexual ability decreased

Gastrointestinal: Xerostomia, loss of appetite, nausea, vomiting, bloating; frequent stools followed by severe constipation

Genitourinary: Dysuria

Neuromuscular & skeletal: Uncontrolled movements of hands, arms, legs, or face; trembling

Ocular: Blurred vision; enlarged pupils

(Continued)

Mecamylamine (Continued)

Respiratory: Dyspnea

Drug Interactions

Increased Effect/Toxicity: Sulfonamides and antibiotics that cause neuromuscular blockade may increase effect of mecamylamine. The action of mecamylamine may be increased by anesthesia, other antihypertensives, and alcohol.

Mechanism of Action Mecamylamine is a ganglionic blocker. This agent inhibits acetylcholine at the autonomic ganglia, causing a decrease in blood pressure. Mecamylamine also blocks central nicotinic cholinergic receptors, which inhibits the effects of nicotine and may suppress the desire to smoke.

Dosage Adults: Oral: 2.5 mg twice daily after meals for 2 days; increased by increments of 2.5 mg at intervals ≥2 days until desired blood pressure response is achieved; average daily dose: 25 mg (usually in 3 divided doses)

Note: Reduce dosage of other antihypertensives when combined with mecamylamine with exception of thiazide diuretics which may be maintained at usual dose while decreasing mecamylamine by 50%

Dosing adjustment/comments in renal impairment: Use with caution, if at all, although no specific guidelines are available

Patient Information Take after meals at the same time each day; report immediately if frequent loose bowel movements occur; rise slowly from sitting or lying for prolonged periods; do not restrict salt intake

Dosage Forms TAB: 2.5 mg

♦ **Mecamylamine Hydrochloride** see Mecamylamine on page 777

Mechlorethamine (me klor ETH a meen)

U.S. Brand Names Mustargen®

Synonyms Chlorethazine; Chlorethazine Mustard; HN₂; Mechlorethamine Hydrochloride; Mustine; Nitrogen Mustard; NSC-762

Therapeutic Category Antineoplastic Agent, Alkylating Agent; Antineoplastic Agent, Nitrogen Mustard; Vesicant

Use Combination therapy of Hodgkin's disease and malignant lymphomas; non-Hodgkin's lymphoma; may be used by intracavitary injection for treatment of metastatic tumors; pleural and other malignant effusions; topical treatment of mycosis fungoides

Pregnancy Risk Factor D

Contraindications Hypersensitivity to mechlorethamine or any component of the formulation; pre-existing profound myelosuppression or infection; pregnancy

Warnings/Precautions The U.S. Food and Drug Administration (FDA) currently recommends that procedures for proper handling and disposal of antineoplastic agents be considered. Mechlorethamine is a potent vesicant; if extravasation occurs, severe tissue damage (leading to ulceration and necrosis) and pain may occur. Patients with lymphomas should receive prophylactic allopurinol 2-3 days prior to therapy to prevent complications resulting from tumor lysis.

Common Adverse Reactions

>10%:

Dermatologic: Alopecia; hyperpigmentation of veins; contact and allergic dermatitis (50% with topical use)

Endocrine & metabolic: Chromosomal abnormalities, delayed menses, oligomenorrhea, amenorrhea, impaired spermatogenesis

Gastrointestinal: Nausea and vomiting (almost 100%), onset may be within minutes of drug administration

Genitourinary: Azoospermia

Hematologic: Myelosuppression, leukopenia, and thrombocytopenia

Onset: 4-7 days

Nadir: 14 days

Recovery: 21 days

1% to 10%:

Central nervous system: Fever

Gastrointestinal: Diarrhea, anorexia, metallic taste

Otic: Tinnitus

Drug Interactions

Decreased Effect: Patients may experience impaired immune response to vaccines; possible infection after administration of live vaccines in patients receiving immunosuppressants.

Mechanism of Action Bifunctional alkylating agent that inhibits DNA and RNA synthesis via formation of carbonium ions; cross-links strands of DNA, causing miscoding, breakage, and failure of replication; produces interstrand and intrastrand cross-links in DNA resulting in miscoding, breakage, and failure of replication. Although not cell phase-specific *per se*, mechlorethamine effect is most pronounced in the S phase, and cell proliferation is arrested in the G_2 phase.

Pharmacodynamics/Kinetics

Duration: Unchanged drug is undetectable in blood within a few minutes

Absorption: Intracavitary administration: Incomplete secondary to rapid deactivation by body fluids

Metabolism: Rapid hydrolysis and demethylation, possibly in plasma

Half-life elimination: <1 minute

Excretion: Urine (50% as metabolites, <0.01% as unchanged drug)

Dosage Refer to individual protocols.

Children and Adults: I.V.: 6 mg/m^2 on days 1 and 8 of a 28-day cycle (MOPP regimen)

Adults:

I.V.: 0.4 mg/kg **or** 12-16 mg/m^2 for one dose **or** divided into 0.1 mg/kg/day for 4 days, repeated at 4- to 6-week intervals

Intracavitary: 0.2-0.4 mg/kg (10-20 mg) as a single dose; may be repeated if fluid continues to accumulate.

Intrapericardially: 0.2-0.4 mg/kg as a single dose; may be repeated if fluid continues to accumulate.

Topical: 0.01% to 0.02% solution, lotion, or ointment

Hemodialysis: Not removed; supplemental dosing is not required.

Peritoneal dialysis: Not removed; supplemental dosing is not required.

Administration I.V. as a slow push through the side of a freely-flowing saline or dextrose solution. Due to the limited stability of the drug, and the increased risk of phlebitis and venous irritation and blistering with increased contact time, infusions of the drug are not recommended.

Mechlorethamine may cause extravasation. Use within 1 hour of preparation. Avoid extravasation since mechlorethamine is a potent vesicant. **Extravasation management:** Sodium thiosulfate $^1/_6$ molar solution is the specific antidote for nitrogen mustard extravasations and should be used as follows: Mix 4 mL of 10% sodium thiosulfate with 6 mL of sterile water for injection. Inject 5-6 mL of this solution into the existing I.V. line. Remove the needle. Inject 2-3 mL of the solution S.C. clockwise into the infiltrated area using a 25-gauge needle. Change the needle with each new injection. Apply ice immediately for 6-12 hours.

Monitoring Parameters CBC with differential, hemoglobin, and platelet count

Patient Information This medication can only be given by infusion, usually in cycles of therapy. You will need frequent laboratory and medical monitoring during treatment. Do not use alcohol, aspirin or aspirin-containing medications, and/or OTC medications without consulting prescriber. Maintain adequate fluid balance (2-3 L/day of fluids unless instructed to restrict fluid intake) and adequate nutrition (small frequent meals, frequent mouth care, sucking lozenges, or chewing gum may reduce anorexia and nausea). May cause discoloration (brown color) of veins used for infusion, hair loss (reversible); easy bleeding or bruising (use soft toothbrush or cotton swabs and frequent mouth care, use electric razor, avoid sharp knives or scissors); increased susceptibility to infection (avoid crowds or exposure to infection - do not have any vaccinations unless approved by prescriber). This drug may cause menstrual irregularities, permanent sterility, and birth defects. Report changes in auditory or visual acuity; unusual bleeding or bruising or persistent fever or sore throat; blood in urine, stool, or vomitus; delayed healing of any wounds; skin rash; yellowing of skin or eyes; changes in color of urine or stool; acute or unresolved nausea or vomiting; diarrhea; or loss of appetite. The drug may be excreted in breast milk, therefore, an alternative form of feeding your baby should be used. Contraceptive measures are recommended during pregnancy.

Dosage Forms INJ, powder for reconstitution: 10 mg

♦ **Mechlorethamine Hydrochloride** see Mechlorethamine on page 778

Meclizine (MEK li zeen)

U.S. Brand Names Antivert®; Bonine® [OTC]; Dramamine® Less Drowsy Formula [OTC]

Synonyms Meclizine Hydrochloride; Meclozine Hydrochloride

Therapeutic Category Antiemetic; Antihistamine

Use Prevention and treatment of symptoms of motion sickness; management of vertigo with diseases affecting the vestibular system

Pregnancy Risk Factor B

Contraindications Hypersensitivity to meclizine or any component of the formulation

Warnings/Precautions Use with caution in patients with angle-closure glaucoma, prostatic hyperplasia, pyloric or duodenal obstruction, or bladder neck obstruction; use with caution in hot weather, and during exercise; elderly may be at risk for anticholinergic side effects such as glaucoma, prostatic hyperplasia, constipation, gastrointestinal obstructive disease; if vertigo does not respond in 1-2 weeks, it is advised to discontinue use

Common Adverse Reactions

>10%:

Central nervous system: Slight to moderate drowsiness

Respiratory: Thickening of bronchial secretions

1% to 10%:

Central nervous system: Headache, fatigue, nervousness, dizziness

Gastrointestinal: Appetite increase, weight gain, nausea, diarrhea, abdominal pain, xerostomia

Neuromuscular & skeletal: Arthralgia

Respiratory: Pharyngitis

Drug Interactions

Increased Effect/Toxicity: Increased toxicity with CNS depressants, neuroleptics, and anticholinergics.

Mechanism of Action Has central anticholinergic action by blocking chemoreceptor trigger zone; decreases excitability of the middle ear labyrinth and blocks conduction in the middle ear vestibular-cerebellar pathways

Pharmacodynamics/Kinetics

Onset of action: ~1 hour

Duration: 8-24 hours

(Continued)

Meclizine *(Continued)*

Metabolism: Hepatic
Half-life elimination: 6 hours
Excretion: Urine (as metabolites); feces (as unchanged drug)

Dosage Children >12 years and Adults: Oral:
Motion sickness: 12.5-25 mg 1 hour before travel, repeat dose every 12-24 hours if needed; doses up to 50 mg may be needed
Vertigo: 25-100 mg/day in divided doses

Patient Information Take after meals; do not discontinue drug abruptly; report adverse GI effects, fever, or heat intolerance; may cause drowsiness; avoid alcohol; adequate fluid intake, sugar free gum, or hard candy may help dry mouth; adequate fluid and exercise may help constipation; may impair ability to perform hazardous tasks

Dosage Forms TAB: 12.5 mg, 25 mg; (Antivert®): 12.5 mg, 25 mg, 50 mg; (Dramamine® Less Drowsy Formula): 25 mg. **TAB, chewable** (Bonine®): 25 mg

♦ **Meclizine Hydrochloride** *see* Meclizine *on page 779*

Meclofenamate (me kloe fen AM ate)

Related Information
Nonsteroidal Anti-Inflammatory Agents Comparison *on page 1401*

Synonyms Meclofenamate Sodium

Therapeutic Category Analgesic, Nonsteroidal Anti-inflammatory Drug; Anti-inflammatory Agent; Nonsteroidal Anti-inflammatory Drug (NSAID), Oral

Use Treatment of inflammatory disorders, arthritis, mild to moderate pain, dysmenorrhea

Pregnancy Risk Factor B/D (3rd trimester)

Contraindications Hypersensitivity to NSAIDs including aspirin, meclofenamate, or any component of the formulation; active GI bleeding, ulcer disease; pregnancy (3rd trimester)

Warnings/Precautions Use with caution in patients with CHF, hypertension, dehydration, decreased renal or hepatic function, history of GI disease (bleeding or ulcers), or those receiving anticoagulants. Elderly are at a high risk for adverse effects from NSAIDs. As many as 60% of elderly can develop peptic ulceration and/or hemorrhage asymptomatically.

Use lowest effective dose for shortest period possible. Use of NSAIDs can compromise existing renal function especially when Cl_{cr} is <30 mL/minute. CNS adverse effects such as confusion, agitation, and hallucination are generally seen in overdose or high-dose situations; however, elderly may demonstrate these adverse effects at lower doses than younger adults. Withhold for at least 4-6 half-lives prior to surgical or dental procedures. May have adverse effects on fetus. Use with caution with dehydration. Use in children is not recommended.

Common Adverse Reactions
>10%:
Central nervous system: Dizziness
Dermatologic: Rash
Gastrointestinal: Abdominal cramps, heartburn, indigestion, nausea
1% to 10%:
Central nervous system: Headache, nervousness
Dermatologic: Itching
Endocrine & metabolic: Fluid retention
Gastrointestinal: Vomiting
Otic: Tinnitus

Drug Interactions
Increased Effect/Toxicity: Anticoagulants (warfarin, heparin, LMWHs) in combination with NSAIDs can cause increased risk of bleeding. Other antiplatelet drugs (ticlopidine, clopidogrel, aspirin, abciximab, dipyridamole, eptifibatide, tirofiban) can cause an increased risk of bleeding. NSAIDs may increase serum creatinine, potassium, blood pressure, and cyclosporine levels during concurrent therapy; monitor cyclosporine levels and renal function carefully. Lithium levels can be increased; avoid concurrent use if possible or monitor lithium levels and adjust dose. Sulindac may have the least effect. When NSAID is stopped, lithium will need adjustment again. Corticosteroids may increase the risk of GI ulceration; avoid concurrent use. Serum concentration/toxicity of methotrexate may be increased.
Decreased Effect: Antihypertensive effects of ACE inhibitors, angiotensin antagonists, diuretics, and hydralazine may be decreased by concurrent therapy with NSAIDs; monitor blood pressure. Cholestyramine and colestipol reduce the bioavailability of diclofenac; separate administration times.

Mechanism of Action Inhibits prostaglandin synthesis by decreasing the activity of the enzyme, cyclooxygenase, which results in decreased formation of prostaglandin precursors

Pharmacodynamics/Kinetics
Duration: 2-4 hours
Distribution: Crosses placenta
Protein binding: 99%
Half-life elimination: 2-3.3 hours
Time to peak, serum: 0.5-1.5 hours
Excretion: Primarily urine and feces (as metabolites)

Dosage Children >14 years and Adults: Oral:
Mild to moderate pain: 50 mg every 4-6 hours, not to exceed 400 mg/day
Rheumatoid arthritis/osteoarthritis: 200-400 mg/day in 3-4 equal doses

Patient Information Take with food, milk, or antacids

Dosage Forms CAP: 50 mg, 100 mg

- ♦ **Meclofenamate Sodium** *see Meclofenamate on page 780*
- ♦ **Meclozine Hydrochloride** *see Meclizine on page 779*
- ♦ **Medicinal Carbon** *see Charcoal on page 253*
- ♦ **Medicinal Charcoal** *see Charcoal on page 253*
- ♦ **Medicone® [OTC]** *see Phenylephrine on page 993*
- ♦ **Medi-Synal [OTC]** *see Acetaminophen and Pseudoephedrine on page 26*
- ♦ **Medrol®** *see MethylPREDNISolone on page 824*

MedroxyPROGESTERone (me DROKS ee proe JES te rone)

U.S. Brand Names Depo-Provera®; Depo-Provera® Contraceptive; Provera®

Synonyms Acetoxymethylprogesterone; Medroxyprogesterone Acetate; Methylacetoxyprogesterone

Therapeutic Category Contraceptive, Parenteral (Estrogen/Progestin); Progestin

Use Endometrial carcinoma or renal carcinoma as well as secondary amenorrhea or abnormal uterine bleeding due to hormonal imbalance; reduction of endometrial hyperplasia in postmenopausal women receiving 0.625 mg conjugated estrogens for 12-14 consecutive days per month; Depo-Provera® injection is used for the prevention of pregnancy

Unlabeled/Investigational Use Hypoventilation disorders, advanced breast cancer

Pregnancy Risk Factor X

Contraindications Hypersensitivity to medroxyprogesterone or any component of the formulation; cerebral apoplexy, undiagnosed vaginal bleeding, liver dysfunction; thrombophlebitis; pregnancy

Warnings/Precautions Use with caution in patients with depression, diabetes, epilepsy, asthma, migraines, renal or cardiac dysfunction; pretreatment exams should include PAP smear, physical exam of breasts and pelvic areas. May increase serum cholesterol, LDL, decrease HDL and triglycerides; use of any progestin during the first 4 months of pregnancy is not recommended; monitor patient closely for loss of vision, sudden onset of proptosis, diplopia, migraine, and signs and symptoms of thromboembolic disorders.

Common Adverse Reactions Frequency not defined.

Cardiovascular: Edema, embolism, central thrombosis

Central nervous system: Mental depression, fever, insomnia, somnolence, headache (rare), dizziness

Dermatologic: Melasma or chloasma, allergic rash with or without pruritus, acne, hirsutism, angioneurotic edema

Endocrine & metabolic: Breakthrough bleeding, spotting, changes in menstrual flow, amenorrhea, increased breast tenderness, changes in cervical erosion and secretions

Gastrointestinal: Weight gain/loss, anorexia, nausea

Hepatic: Cholestatic jaundice

Local: Pain at injection site, sterile abscess, thrombophlebitis

Neuromuscular & skeletal: Weakness

Respiratory: Pulmonary embolism

Miscellaneous: Anaphylaxis

Drug Interactions

Cytochrome P450 Effect: Substrate of CYP3A4 (major); **Induces** CYP3A4 (weak)

Decreased Effect: Aminoglutethimide may decrease effects by increasing hepatic metabolism.

Mechanism of Action Inhibits secretion of pituitary gonadotropins, which prevents follicular maturation and ovulation; stimulates growth of mammary tissue

Pharmacodynamics/Kinetics

Absorption: Oral: Well absorbed; I.M.: Slow

Protein binding: 90% primarily to albumin; not to sex hormone-binding globulin

Metabolism: Oral: Hepatic via hydroxylated and conjugated

Bioavailability: 0.6% to 10%

Time to peak: Oral: 2-4 hours

Half-life elimination: Oral: 38-46 hours; I.M.: Acetate: 50 days

Excretion: Oral: Urine and feces

Dosage

Adolescents and Adults: Oral:

Amenorrhea: 5-10 mg/day for 5-10 days or 2.5 mg/day

Abnormal uterine bleeding: 5-10 mg for 5-10 days starting on day 16 or 21 of cycle

Accompanying cyclic estrogen therapy, postmenopausal: 2.5-10 mg the last 10-13 days of estrogen dosing each month

Hypoventilation syndromes (unlabeled use): 20 mg 3 times/day

Adults: I.M.:

Endometrial or renal carcinoma: 400-1000 mg/week

Contraception: 150 mg every 3 months

Dosing adjustment in hepatic impairment: Dose needs to be lowered in patients with alcoholic cirrhosis

Monitoring Parameters Monitor patient closely for loss of vision, sudden onset of proptosis, diplopia, migraine, and signs and symptoms of thromboembolic disorders

Patient Information Follow dosage schedule and do not take more than prescribed. You may experience sensitivity to sunlight (use sunblock, wear protective clothing and eyewear, and avoid extensive exposure to direct sunlight); dizziness, anxiety, depression (use caution when driving or engaging in tasks that require alertness until response to drug is known); changes in

(Continued)

MedroxyPROGESTERone *(Continued)*

appetite (maintain adequate hydration and diet - 2-3 L/day of fluids unless instructed to restrict fluid intake); decreased libido or increased body hair (reversible when drug is discontinued); hot flashes (cool clothes and environment may help). May cause discoloration of stool (green). Report swelling of face, lips, or mouth; absent or altered menses; abdominal pain; vaginal itching, irritation, or discharge; heat, warmth, redness, or swelling of extremities; or sudden change in vision.

Dosage Forms INJ, suspension (Depot-Provera®): 400 mg/mL (2.5 mL, 10 mL); **INJ, suspension** [prefilled syringe or vial] (Depot-Provera® Contraceptive): 150 mg/mL (1 mL). **TAB** (Provera®): 2.5 mg, 5 mg, 10 mg

♦ **Medroxyprogesterone Acetate** *see* MedroxyPROGESTERone *on page 781*

♦ **Medroxyprogesterone Acetate and Estradiol Cypionate** *see* Estradiol and Medroxyprogesterone *on page 462*

♦ **Medroxyprogesterone and Estrogens (Conjugated)** *see* Estrogens (Conjugated/Equine) and Medroxyprogesterone *on page 468*

Medrysone (ME dri sone)

U.S. Brand Names HMS Liquifilm®

Therapeutic Category Anti-inflammatory Agent, Ophthalmic; Corticosteroid, Ophthalmic

Use Treatment of allergic conjunctivitis, vernal conjunctivitis, episcleritis, ophthalmic epinephrine sensitivity reaction

Pregnancy Risk Factor C

Contraindications Hypersensitivity to medrysone or any component of the formulation; fungal, viral, or untreated pus-forming bacterial ocular infections; not for use in iritis and uveitis

Warnings/Precautions Prolonged use has been associated with the development of corneal or scleral perforation and posterior subcapsular cataracts; may mask or enhance the establishment of acute purulent untreated infections of the eye; use caution in patients with glaucoma. Medrysone is a synthetic corticosteroid; structurally related to progesterone; if no improvement after several days of treatment, discontinue medrysone and institute other therapy; duration of therapy: 3-4 days to several weeks dependent on type and severity of disease; taper dose to avoid disease exacerbation. Safety and efficacy have not been established in children <3 years of age.

Common Adverse Reactions Frequency not defined: Ocular: Acute anterior uveitis, allergic reactions, blurred vision (mild, temporary), burning, cataracts, conjunctivitis, corneal thinning, corneal ulcers, delayed wound healing, foreign body sensation, glaucoma, IOP increased, keratitis, mydriasis, optic nerve damage, ptosis, secondary ocular infection stinging, visual activity defects

Mechanism of Action Decreases inflammation by suppression of migration of polymorphonuclear leukocytes and reversal of increased capillary permeability

Pharmacodynamics/Kinetics
Absorption: Through aqueous humor
Metabolism: Hepatic if absorbed
Excretion: Urine and feces

Dosage Children ≥3 years and Adults: Ophthalmic: Instill 1 drop in conjunctival sac 2-4 times/day up to every 4 hours; may use every 1-2 hours during first 1-2 days

Administration Ophthalmic: Shake well before using. Do not touch dropper to the eye.

Monitoring Parameters Intraocular pressure (if duration of therapy is >10 days); periodic examination of lens (with prolonged use)

Patient Information Shake well before using. Do not touch dropper to the eye.

Dosage Forms SOLN, ophthalmic: 1% (5 mL, 10 mL)

Mefenamic Acid (me fe NAM ik AS id)

Related Information
Nonsteroidal Anti-Inflammatory Agents Comparison *on page 1401*

U.S. Brand Names Ponstel®

Therapeutic Category Analgesic, Nonsteroidal Anti-inflammatory Drug; Anti-inflammatory Agent; Nonsteroidal Anti-inflammatory Drug (NSAID), Oral

Use Short-term relief of mild to moderate pain including primary dysmenorrhea

Pregnancy Risk Factor C/D (3rd trimester)

Contraindications Hypersensitivity to NSAIDs including aspirin or any component of the formulation; pregnancy (3rd trimester)

Warnings/Precautions May have adverse effects on fetus. Withhold for at least 4-6 half-lives prior to surgical or dental procedures.

Common Adverse Reactions 1% to 10%:
Central nervous system: Headache, nervousness, dizziness (3% to 9%)
Dermatologic: Itching, rash
Endocrine & metabolic: Fluid retention
Gastrointestinal: Abdominal cramps, heartburn, indigestion, nausea (1% to 10%), vomiting (1% to 10%), diarrhea (1% to 10%), constipation (1% to 10%), abdominal distress/cramping/pain (1% to 10%), dyspepsia (1% to 10%), flatulence (1% to 10%), gastric or duodenal ulcer with bleeding or perforation (1% to 10%), gastritis (1% to 10%)
Hematologic: Bleeding (1% to 10%)
Hepatic: Elevated LFTs (1% to 10%)
Otic: Tinnitus (1% to 10%)

Drug Interactions

Cytochrome P450 Effect: Substrate of CYP2C8/9 (minor); **Inhibits** CYP2C8/9 (strong)

Increased Effect/Toxicity: Anticoagulants (warfarin, heparin, LMWHs) in combination with NSAIDs can cause increased risk of bleeding. Other antiplatelet drugs (ticlopidine, clopidogrel, aspirin, abciximab, dipyridamole, eptifibatide, tirofiban) can cause an increased risk of bleeding. NSAIDs may increase serum creatinine, potassium, blood pressure, and cyclosporine levels during concurrent therapy; monitor cyclosporine levels and renal function carefully. Lithium levels can be increased; avoid concurrent use if possible or monitor lithium levels and adjust dose. Sulindac may have the least effect. When NSAID is stopped, lithium will need adjustment again. Corticosteroids may increase the risk of GI ulceration; avoid concurrent use. Serum concentration/toxicity of methotrexate may be increased.

Decreased Effect: Antihypertensive effects of ACE inhibitors, angiotensin antagonists, diuretics, and hydralazine may be decreased by concurrent therapy with NSAIDs; monitor blood pressure. Cholestyramine and colestipol reduce the bioavailability of diclofenac; separate administration times.

Mechanism of Action Inhibits prostaglandin synthesis by decreasing the activity of the enzyme, cyclooxygenase, which results in decreased formation of prostaglandin precursors

Pharmacodynamics/Kinetics

Onset of action: Peak effect: 2-4 hours

Duration: ≤6 hours

Protein binding: High

Metabolism: Conjugated hepatically

Half-life elimination: 3.5 hours

Excretion: Urine (50%) and feces as unchanged drug and metabolites

Dosage Children >14 years and Adults: Oral: 500 mg to start then 250 mg every 4 hours as needed; maximum therapy: 1 week

Dosing adjustment/comments in renal impairment: Not recommended for use

Patient Information Take with food, milk, or antacids; extended release capsules must be swallowed intact

Dosage Forms CAP: 250 mg

Mefloquine (ME floe kwin)

Related Information

Malaria Treatment *on page 1464*

U.S. Brand Names Lariam®

Synonyms Mefloquine Hydrochloride

Therapeutic Category Antimalarial Agent

Use Treatment of acute malarial infections and prevention of malaria

Restrictions A medication guide must be provided to all patients when mefloquine is dispensed.

Pregnancy Risk Factor C

Contraindications Hypersensitivity mefloquine, related compounds (such as quinine and quinidine), or any component of the formulation; history of convulsions; cardiac conduction abnormalities; severe psychiatric disorder (including active or recent history of depression, generalized anxiety disorder, psychosis, or schizophrenia); use with halofantrine

Warnings/Precautions Use with caution in patients with a previous history of depression (see Contraindications regarding severe psychiatric illness, including active/recent depression). May cause a range of psychiatric symptoms (anxiety, paranoia, depression, hallucinations and psychosis). Occasionally, symptoms have been reported to persist long after mefloquine has been discontinued. Rare cases of suicidal ideation and suicide have been reported (no causal relationship established). The appearance of psychiatric symptoms such as acute anxiety, depression, restlessness or confusion may be considered a prodrome to more serious events. When used as prophylaxis, substitute an alternative medication. Discontinue if unexplained neuropsychiatric disturbances occur. Use caution in patients with significant cardiac disease. If mefloquine is to be used for a prolonged period, periodic evaluations including liver function tests and ophthalmic examinations should be performed. (Retinal abnormalities have not been observed with mefloquine in humans; however, it has with long-term administration to rats.) In cases of life-threatening, serious, or overwhelming malaria infections due to *Plasmodium falciparum*, patients should be treated with intravenous antimalarial drug. Mefloquine may be given orally to complete the course. Dizziness, loss of balance, and other CNS disorders have been reported; due to long half-life, effects may persist after mefloquine is discontinued. Use caution in activities requiring alertness and fine motor coordination (driving, piloting planes, operating machinery, deep sea diving, etc).

Common Adverse Reactions

Frequency not defined: Neuropsychiatric events

1% to 10%:

Central nervous system: Headache, fever, chills, fatigue

Dermatologic: Rash

Gastrointestinal: Vomiting (3%), diarrhea, stomach pain, nausea, appetite decreased

Neuromuscular & skeletal: Myalgia

Otic: Tinnitus

Drug Interactions

Cytochrome P450 Effect: Substrate of CYP3A4 (major); **Inhibits** CYP2D6 (weak), 3A4 (weak)

(Continued)

Mefloquine *(Continued)*

Increased Effect/Toxicity: Use caution with drugs that alter cardiac conduction; increased toxicity with chloroquine, quinine, and quinidine (hold treatment until at least 12 hours after these later drugs); increased toxicity with halofantrine (concurrent use is contraindicated)

Decreased Effect: Mefloquine may decrease the effect of valproic acid, carbamazepine, phenobarbital, and phenytoin.

Mechanism of Action Mefloquine is a quinoline-methanol compound structurally similar to quinine; mefloquine's effectiveness in the treatment and prophylaxis of malaria is due to the destruction of the asexual blood forms of the malarial pathogens that affect humans, *Plasmodium falciparum, P. vivax, P. malariae, P. ovale*

Pharmacodynamics/Kinetics

Absorption: Well absorbed

Distribution: V_d: 19 L/kg; blood, urine, CSF, tissues; enters breast milk

Protein binding: 98%

Metabolism: Extensively hepatic; main metabolite is inactive

Bioavailability: Increased by food

Half-life elimination: 21-22 days

Time to peak, plasma: 6-24 hours (median: ~17 hours)

Excretion: Primarily bile and feces; urine (9% as unchanged drug, 4% as primary metabolite)

Dosage Oral (dose expressed as mg of mefloquine hydrochloride):

Children ≥6 months and >5 kg:

Malaria treatment: 20-25 mg/kg in 2 divided doses, taken 6-8 hours apart (maximum: 1250 mg) Take with food and an ample amount of water. If clinical improvement is not seen within 48-72 hours, an alternative therapy should be used for retreatment.

Malaria prophylaxis: 5 mg/kg/once weekly (maximum dose: 250 mg) starting 1 week before, arrival in endemic area, continuing weekly during travel and for 4 weeks after leaving endemic area. Take with food and an ample amount of water.

Adults:

Malaria treatment (mild to moderate infection): 5 tablets (1250 mg) as a single dose. Take with food and at least 8 oz of water. If clinical improvement is not seen within 48-72 hours, an alternative therapy should be used for retreatment.

Malaria prophylaxis: 1 tablet (250 mg) weekly starting 1 week before, arrival in endemic area, continuing weekly during travel and for 4 weeks after leaving endemic area. Take with food and at least 8 oz of water.

Dosage adjustment in renal impairment: No dosage adjustment needed in patients with renal impairment or on dialysis.

Dosage adjustment in hepatic impairment: Half-life may be prolonged and plasma levels may be higher.

Administration Administer with food and with at least 8 oz of water. When used for malaria prophylaxis, dose should be taken once weekly on the same day each week. If vomiting occurs within 30-60 minutes after dose, an additional half-dose should be given. Tablets may be crushed and suspended in a small amount of water, milk, or another beverage for persons unable to swallow tablets.

Monitoring Parameters LFTS; ocular examination

Patient Information Begin therapy before trip and continue after; do not take drug on empty stomach; take with food and at least 8 oz of water; women of childbearing age should use reliable contraception during prophylaxis treatment and for 2 months after the last dose; be aware of signs and symptoms of malaria when traveling to an endemic area. Caution should be exercised with regard to driving, piloting airplanes, and operating machines since dizziness, disturbed sense of balance, or neuropsychiatric reactions have been reported with mefloquine. Report any symptoms of anxiety, confusion, depression, or restlessness immediately; if mefloquine is being used as malaria prophylaxis, drug should be discontinued (alternative therapy substituted).

Dosage Forms TAB: 250 mg

♦ **Mefloquine Hydrochloride** *see Mefloquine on page 783*

♦ **Mefoxin®** *see Cefoxitin on page 238*

♦ **Megace®** *see Megestrol on page 784*

♦ **Megadophilus® [OTC]** *see Lactobacillus on page 711*

Megestrol *(me JES trole)*

U.S. Brand Names Megace®

Synonyms 5071-1DL(6); Megestrol Acetate; NSC-10363

Therapeutic Category Antineoplastic Agent, Hormone; Progestin

Use Palliative treatment of breast and endometrial carcinoma

Orphan drug: Treatment of anorexia, cachexia, or significant weight loss (≥10% baseline body weight) and confirmed diagnosis of AIDS

Unlabeled/Investigational Use Uterine bleeding

Pregnancy Risk Factor X

Contraindications Hypersensitivity to megestrol or any component of the formulation; pregnancy

Warnings/Precautions Use during the first few months of pregnancy is not recommended. Use with caution in patients with a history of thrombophlebitis. Elderly females may have vaginal bleeding or discharge.

Common Adverse Reactions

Cardiovascular: Edema, hypertension (≤8%), cardiomyopathy, palpitations

Central nervous system: Insomnia, fever (2% to 6%), headache (≤10%), pain (≤6%, similar to placebo), confusion (1% to 3%), convulsions (1% to 3%), depression (1% to 3%)

Dermatologic: Allergic rash (2% to 12%) with or without pruritus, alopecia

Endocrine & metabolic: Breakthrough bleeding and amenorrhea, spotting, changes in menstrual flow, changes in cervical erosion and secretions, increased breast tenderness, changes in vaginal bleeding pattern, edema, fluid retention, hyperglycemia (≤6%), diabetes, HPA axis suppression, adrenal insufficiency, Cushing's syndrome

Gastrointestinal: Weight gain (not attributed to edema or fluid retention), nausea, vomiting (7%), diarrhea (8% to 15%, similar to placebo), flatulence (≤10%), constipation (1% to 3%)

Genitourinary: Impotence (4% to 14%), decreased libido (≤5%)

Hepatic: Cholestatic jaundice, hepatotoxicity, hepatomegaly (1% to 3%)

Local: Thrombophlebitis

Neuromuscular & skeletal: Carpal tunnel syndrome, weakness, paresthesia (1% to 3%)

Respiratory: Hyperpnea, dyspnea (1% to 3%), cough (1% to 3%)

Miscellaneous: Diaphoresis

Mechanism of Action A synthetic progestin with antiestrogenic properties which disrupt the estrogen receptor cycle. Megestrol interferes with the normal estrogen cycle and results in a lower LH titer. May also have a direct effect on the endometrium. Megestrol is an antineoplastic progestin thought to act through an antileutenizing effect mediated via the pituitary.

Pharmacodynamics/Kinetics

Absorption: Well absorbed orally

Metabolism: Completely hepatic to free steroids and glucuronide conjugates

Time to peak, serum: 1-3 hours

Half-life elimination: 15-100 hours

Excretion: Urine (57% to 78% as steroid metabolites and inactive compound); feces (8% to 30%)

Dosage Adults: Oral (refer to individual protocols):

Female:

Breast carcinoma: 40 mg 4 times/day

Endometrial carcinoma: 40-320 mg/day in divided doses; use for 2 months to determine efficacy; maximum doses used have been up to 800 mg/day

Uterine bleeding (unlabeled use): 40 mg 2-4 times/day

Male/Female: HIV-related cachexia: Initial dose: 800 mg/day; daily doses of 400 and 800 mg/day were found to be clinically effective

Dosing adjustment in renal impairment: No data available; however, the urinary excretion of megestrol acetate administered in doses of 4-90 mg ranged from 56% to 78% within 10 days

Hemodialysis: Megestrol acetate has not been tested for dialyzability; however, due to its low solubility, it is postulated that dialysis would not be an effective means of treating an overdose

Administration Megestrol acetate (Megace®) oral suspension is compatible with water, orange juice, apple juice, or Sustacal H.C. for immediate consumption.

Monitoring Parameters Observe for signs of thromboembolic phenomena

Patient Information Follow dosage schedule and do not take more than prescribed. You may experience sensitivity to sunlight (use sunblock, wear protective clothing, and avoid extended exposure to direct sunlight); dizziness, anxiety, depression (use caution when driving or engaging in tasks that require alertness until response to drug is known); change in appetite (maintain adequate hydration and diet - 2-3 L/day of fluids unless instructed to restrict fluid intake); decreased libido or increased body hair (reversible when drug is discontinued); hot flashes (cool clothes and environment may help). Report swelling of face, lips, or mouth; absence or altered menses; abdominal pain; vaginal itching, irritation, or discharge; heat, warmth, redness, or swelling of extremities; or sudden onset change in vision.

Dosage Forms SUSP, oral: 40 mg/mL (240 mL). **TAB:** 20 mg, 40 mg

♦ **Megestrol Acetate** *see* Megestrol *on page 784*

♦ **Melanex®** *see* Hydroquinone *on page 636*

♦ **Mellaril® [DSC]** *see* Thioridazine *on page 1217*

Meloxicam (mel OKS i kam)

Related Information

Nonsteroidal Anti-Inflammatory Agents Comparison *on page 1401*

U.S. Brand Names MOBIC®

Therapeutic Category Analgesic, Nonsteroidal Anti-inflammatory Drug; Anti-inflammatory Agent; Nonsteroidal Anti-Inflammatory Drug (NSAID), Oral

Use Relief of signs and symptoms of osteoarthritis

Pregnancy Risk Factor C/D (3rd trimester)

Contraindications Hypersensitivity to meloxicam or any component of the formulation, aspirin, or other NSAIDs; pregnancy C/D (3rd trimester)

Warnings/Precautions Use the lowest effective dose for the shortest period possible. Gastrointestinal irritation, ulceration, bleeding, and perforation may occur with NSAIDs. Use with caution in patients with a history of GI disease (bleeding or ulcers), decreased renal function, hepatic disease, CHF, dehydration, hypertension, or asthma. Use with caution in elderly patients. Use in advanced renal disease is not recommended. May alter platelet function. Withhold for at least 4-6 half-lives prior to surgical or dental procedures.

Common Adverse Reactions 2% to 10%:

Cardiovascular: Edema (2% to 5%)

(Continued)

Meloxicam *(Continued)*

Central nervous system: Headache and dizziness occurred in 2% to 8% of patients, but occurred less frequently than placebo in controlled trials

Dermatologic: Rash (1% to 3%)

Gastrointestinal: Diarrhea (3% to 8%), dyspepsia (5%), nausea (4%), flatulence (3%), abdominal pain (2% to 3%)

Respiratory: Upper respiratory infection (2% to 3%), pharyngitis (1% to 3%)

Miscellaneous: Flu-like symptoms (5% to 6%), falls (3%)

Drug Interactions

Cytochrome P450 Effect: Substrate (minor) of CYP2C8/9, 3A4; **Inhibits** CYP2C8/9 (weak)

Increased Effect/Toxicity: Anticoagulants (warfarin, heparin, LMWHs) in combination with NSAIDs can cause increased risk of bleeding. Antiplatelet drugs (ticlopidine, clopidogrel, aspirin, abciximab, dipyridamole, eptifibatide, tirofiban) can cause an increased risk of bleeding. Aspirin increases serum concentrations (AUC) of meloxicam (in addition to potential for additive adverse effects); concurrent use is not recommended. Corticosteroids may increase the risk of GI ulceration; avoid concurrent use. NSAIDs may increase serum creatinine, potassium, blood pressure, and cyclosporine levels; monitor cyclosporine levels and renal function carefully. Lithium levels can be increased; avoid concurrent use if possible or monitor lithium levels and adjust dose. When NSAID is stopped, lithium will need adjustment again. Serum concentration/toxicity of methotrexate may be increased. Warfarin INRs may be increased by meloxicam. Monitor INR closely, particularly during initiation or change in dose. May increase risk of bleeding. Use lowest possible dose for shortest duration possible.

Decreased Effect: Cholestyramine (and possibly colestipol) increases the clearance of meloxicam. Hydralazine's antihypertensive effect is decreased; avoid concurrent use. Loop diuretic efficacy (diuretic and antihypertensive effect) may be reduced by NSAIDs. Antihypertensive effects of thiazide diuretics are decreased; avoid concurrent use.

Mechanism of Action Inhibits prostaglandin synthesis by decreasing the activity of the enzyme, cyclooxygenase, which results in decreased formation of prostaglandin precursors

Pharmacodynamics/Kinetics

Distribution: 10 L

Protein binding: 99.4%

Metabolism: Hepatic via CYP2C9 and CYP3A4 (minor)

Bioavailability: 89%

Half-life elimination: 15-20 hours

Time to peak: 5-10 hours

Excretion: Urine and feces (as inactive metabolites)

Dosage Adult: Oral: Initial: 7.5 mg once daily; some patients may receive additional benefit from an increased dose of 15 mg once daily; maximum dose: 15 mg/day

Elderly: Increased concentrations may occur in elderly patients (particularly in females); however, no specific dosage adjustment is recommended

Dosage adjustment in renal impairment:

Mild to moderate impairment: No specific dosage recommendations

Significant impairment (Cl_{cr} ≤15 mL/minute): Avoid use

Dosage adjustment in hepatic impairment:

Mild (Child-Pugh class A) to moderate (Child-Pugh class B) hepatic dysfunction: No dosage adjustment is necessary

Severe hepatic impairment: Patients with severe hepatic impairment have not been adequately studied

Monitoring Parameters CBC, periodic liver function, renal function (serum BUN, and creatinine)

Patient Information If self-administered, use exactly as directed (do not increase dose or frequency); adverse reactions can occur with overuse. Take with food or milk. While using this medication, do not use alcohol, excessive amounts of vitamin C, or salicylate-containing foods (curry powder, prunes, raisins, tea, or licorice), other prescription or OTC medications containing aspirin or salicylate, or other NSAIDs without consulting prescriber. Maintain adequate hydration (2-3 L/day of fluids unless instructed to restrict fluid intake). You may experience nausea, vomiting, gastric discomfort (frequent mouth care, small frequent meals, chewing gum, sucking lozenges may help). GI bleeding, ulceration, or perforation can occur with or without pain. Stop taking medication and report ringing in ears; persistent cramping or pain in stomach; unresolved nausea or vomiting; difficulty breathing or shortness of breath; unusual bruising or bleeding (mouth, urine, stool); skin rash; unusual swelling of extremities; chest pain; or palpitations.

Dosage Forms TAB: 7.5 mg, 15 mg

♦ **Melpaque HP®** *see Hydroquinone on page 636*

Melphalan *(MEL fa lan)*

U.S. Brand Names Alkeran®

Synonyms L-PAM; L-Sarcolysin; Phenylalanine Mustard

Therapeutic Category Antineoplastic Agent, Alkylating Agent

Use Palliative treatment of multiple myeloma and nonresectable epithelial ovarian carcinoma; neuroblastoma, rhabdomyosarcoma, breast cancer

Pregnancy Risk Factor D

Contraindications Hypersensitivity to melphalan or any component of the formulation; severe bone marrow suppression; patients whose disease was resistant to prior therapy; pregnancy

Warnings/Precautions The U.S. Food and Drug Administration (FDA) currently recommends that procedures for proper handling and disposal for antineoplastic agents be considered. Is potentially mutagenic, carcinogenic, and teratogenic; produces amenorrhea. Reduce dosage or discontinue therapy if leukocyte count <3000/mm³ or platelet count <100,000/mm³; use with caution in patients with bone marrow suppression, impaired renal function, or who have received prior chemotherapy or irradiation; will cause amenorrhea. Toxicity to immunosuppressives is increased in elderly. Start with lowest recommended adult doses. Signs of infection, such as fever and WBC rise, may not occur. Lethargy and confusion may be more prominent signs of infection.

Common Adverse Reactions

>10%: Hematologic: Myelosuppressive: Leukopenia and thrombocytopenia are the most common effects of melphalan; irreversible bone marrow failure has been reported

WBC: Moderate

Platelets: Moderate

Onset: 7 days

Nadir: 8-10 days and 27-32 days

Recovery: 42-50 days

1% to 10%:

Cardiovascular: Vasculitis

Dermatologic: Vesiculation of skin, alopecia, pruritus, rash

Endocrine & metabolic: SIADH, sterility, amenorrhea

Gastrointestinal Nausea and vomiting are mild; stomatitis and diarrhea are infrequent

Genitourinary: Hemorrhagic cystitis, bladder irritation

Hematologic: Anemia, agranulocytosis, hemolytic anemia

Hepatic: Transaminases increased (hepatitis, jaundice have been reported)

Respiratory: Pulmonary fibrosis, interstitial pneumonitis

Miscellaneous: Hypersensitivity, secondary malignancy

Drug Interactions

Increased Effect/Toxicity: Cyclosporine: Risk of nephrotoxicity is increased by melphalan.

Decreased Effect: Cimetidine and other H_2 antagonists: The reduction in gastric pH has been reported to decrease bioavailability of melphalan by 30%.

Mechanism of Action Alkylating agent which is a derivative of mechlorethamine that inhibits DNA and RNA synthesis via formation of carbonium ions; cross-links strands of DNA

Pharmacodynamics/Kinetics

Absorption: Oral: Variable and incomplete

Distribution: V_d: 0.5-0.6 L/kg throughout total body water

Bioavailability: Unpredictable, decreasing from 85% to 58% with repeated doses

Half-life elimination Terminal: 1.5 hours

Time to peak, serum: ~2 hours

Excretion: Oral: Feces (20% to 50%); urine (10% to 30% as unchanged drug)

Dosage Refer to individual protocols.

Oral: Dose should always be adjusted to patient response and weekly blood counts:

Children: 4-20 mg/m²/day for 1-21 days

Adults:

Multiple myeloma: 6 mg/day initially adjusted as indicated **or** 0.15 mg/kg/day for 7 days **or** 0.25 mg/kg/day for 4 days; repeat at 4- to 6-week intervals.

Ovarian carcinoma: 0.2 mg/kg/day for 5 days, repeat every 4-5 weeks.

I.V.:

Children:

Pediatric rhabdomyosarcoma: 10-35 mg/m²/dose every 21-28 days

High-dose melphalan with bone marrow transplantation for neuroblastoma: I.V.: 100-220 mg/m² as a single dose or divided into 2-5 daily doses. Infuse over 20-60 minutes.

Adults: Multiple myeloma: 16 mg/m² administered at 2-week intervals for 4 doses, then repeat monthly as per protocol for multiple myeloma.

Dosing adjustment in renal impairment:

Cl_{cr} 10-50 mL/minute: Administer at 75% of normal dose

Cl_{cr} <10 mL/minute: Administer at 50% of normal dose

or

BUN >30 mg/dL: Reduce dose by 50%

Serum creatinine >1.5 mg/dL: Reduce dose by 50%

Hemodialysis: Unknown

CAPD effects: Unknown

CAVH effects: Dose for GFR 10-50 mL/minute

Dosing adjustment in hepatic impairment: BUN >30 mg/dL: Reduce dose by 50%

Administration

Oral: Administer on an empty stomach (1 hour prior to or 2 hours after meals)

Parenteral: Due to limited stability, complete administration of I.V. dose should occur within 60 minutes of reconstitution

I.V. infusion: I.V. dose is FDA-approved for administration as a single infusion over 15-20 minutes

I.V. bolus: I.V. may be administered via central line and via peripheral vein as a rapid I.V. bolus; there have not been any unexpected or serious adverse events specifically related to rapid I.V. bolus administration; the most common adverse events were transient mild symptoms of hot flush and tingling sensation over the body

(Continued)

Melphalan (Continued)

Central line: I.V. bolus doses of 17-200 mg/m^2 (reconstituted and not diluted) have been infused over 2-20 minutes

Peripheral line: I.V. bolus doses of 2-23 mg/m^2 (reconstituted and not diluted) have been infused over 1-4 minutes

Monitoring Parameters CBC with differential and platelet count, serum electrolytes, serum uric acid

Patient Information

Do not take alcohol, aspirin or aspirin-containing medications, and/or OTC medications without consulting prescriber. Inform prescriber of all prescription medication you are taking. Maintain adequate fluid balance (2-3 L/day of fluids unless instructed to restrict fluid intake). May cause hair loss (reversible); easy bleeding or bruising (use a soft toothbrush or cotton swabs and frequent mouth care, use electric razor, avoid sharp knives or scissors); increased suscepti-bility to infection (avoid crowds or exposure to infection - do not have any vaccinations unless approved by prescriber). Report unusual bleeding or bruising or persistent fever or sore throat; blood in urine, stool, or vomitus; delayed healing of any wounds; skin rash; yellowing of skin or eyes; changes in color of urine or black stool; pain or burning on urination; respiratory difficulty; or other severe adverse reactions. Contraceptive measures should be used during therapy. The drug may be excreted in breast milk, therefore, an alternative form of feeding your baby should be used.

I.V.: Report promptly any pain, irritation, or redness at infusion site.

Oral: Preferable to take on an empty stomach, 1 hour prior to or 2 hours after meals.

Dosage Forms INJ, powder for reconstitution: 50 mg. **TAB:** 2 mg

♦ **Melquin-3**® see Hydroquinone on page 636
♦ **Melquin HP**® see Hydroquinone on page 636

Memantine (me MAN teen)

U.S. Brand Names Namenda™

Synonyms Memantine Hydrochloride

Therapeutic Category N-Methyl-D-Aspartate Receptor Antagonist

Use Treatment of moderate-to-severe dementia of the Alzheimer's type

Pregnancy Risk Factor B

Contraindications Hypersensitivity to memantine or any component of the formulation

Warnings/Precautions Use caution with seizure disorders, hepatic impairment, or mild-to-moderate renal impairment. Use with severe renal impairment is not recommended. Clearance is significantly reduced by alkaline urine; use caution with medications, dietary changes, or patient conditions which may alter urine pH.

Common Adverse Reactions

1% to 10%:

Cardiovascular: Hypertension (4%), cardiac failure, syncope, cerebrovascular accident, transient ischemic attack

Central nervous system: Dizziness (7%), confusion (6%), headache (6%), hallucinations (3%), pain (3%), somnolence (3%), fatigue (2%), aggressive reaction, ataxia, vertigo

Dermatologic: Rash

Gastrointestinal: Constipation (5%), vomiting (3%), weight loss

Genitourinary: Micturition

Hematologic: Anemia

Hepatic: Alkaline phosphatase increased

Neuromuscular & skeletal: Back pain (3%), hypokinesia

Ocular: Cataract, conjunctivitis

Respiratory: Cough (4%), dyspnea (2%), pneumonia

Drug Interactions

Increased Effect/Toxicity: Clearance of memantine is decreased 80% at urinary pH 8; use caution with medications (carbonic anhydrase inhibitors, sodium bicarbonate) which may increase urinary pH.

Mechanism of Action Memantine reduces the decline in function in Alzheimer's disease by binding to N-methyl-D-aspartate (NMDA) receptors and blocking the actions of glutamate. Glutamate is an amino acid which may contribute to the pathogenesis of Alzheimer's disease by over-stimulating the NMDA receptor. Memantine does not prevent or slow neurodegenera-tion associated with Alzheimer's disease.

Pharmacodynamics/Kinetics

Distribution: 9-11 L/kg

Protein binding: 45%

Metabolism: Forms three metabolites (minimal activity)

Half-life elimination: Terminal: 60-80 hours

Time to peak, serum: 3-7 hours

Excretion: Urine (57% to 82% unchanged); excretion affected by urine pH

Dosage Oral: Adults: Alzheimer's disease: Initial: 5 mg/day; increase dose by 5 mg/day to a target dose of 20 mg/day; wait at least 1 week between dosage changes. Doses >5 mg/day should be given in 2 divided doses.

Suggested titration: 5 mg/day for ≥1 week; 5 mg twice daily for ≥1 week; 15 mg/day given in 5 mg and 10 mg separated doses for ≥1 week; then 10 mg twice daily

Dosage adjustment in renal impairment:

Moderate impairment: Consider dose reduction; specific recommendations are not available

Severe impairment: Use is not recommended

Patient Information Take as directed, do not adjust dose more often than prescribed. May cause dizziness. May take with or without food.

Dosage Forms TAB (Namenda™): 5 mg, 10 mg. **TAB, combination package** [titration pack contains 2 separate tablet formulations]: Memantine 5 mg (28s) and memantine 10 mg (21s)

♦ **Memantine Hydrochloride** *see Memantine on page 788*

♦ **Menadol® [OTC]** *see Ibuprofen on page 645*

♦ **Menest®** *see Estrogens (Esterified) on page 469*

Meningococcal Polysaccharide Vaccine (Groups A / C / Y and W-135)

(me NIN joe kok al pol i SAK a ride vak SEEN groops aye, see, why & dubl yoo won thur tee fyve)

U.S. Brand Names Menomune®-A/C/Y/W-135

Therapeutic Category Vaccine; Vaccine, Inactivated Bacteria

Use Provide active immunity to meningococcal serogroups contained in the vaccine; prevention and control of outbreaks of serogroup C meningococcal disease; recommended for use in:

Immunization of persons ≥2 years of age in epidemic or endemic areas as might be determined in a population delineated by neighborhood, school, dormitory, or other reasonable boundary. The prevalent serogroup in such a situation should match a serogroup in the vaccine. Individuals at particular high-risk include persons with terminal component complement deficiencies and those with anatomic or functional asplenia.

Travelers visiting areas of a country that are recognized as having hyperendemic or epidemic meningococcal disease

Vaccinations should be considered for household or institutional contacts of persons with meningococcal disease as an adjunct to appropriate antibiotic chemoprophylaxis as well as medical and laboratory personnel at risk of exposure to meningococcal disease

Pregnancy Risk Factor C

Contraindications Hypersensitivity to any component of the formulation; defer immunization during acute illness; children <2 years of age

Warnings/Precautions Patients who undergo splenectomy secondary to trauma or nonlymphoid tumors respond well; however, those asplenic patients with lymphoid tumors who receive either chemotherapy or irradiation respond poorly; pregnancy, unless there is substantial risk of infection. Response may not be as great as desired in patients requiring immunosuppressive therapy. Safety and efficacy in pediatric patients <2 years of age have not been established. Use with caution in patients with latex sensitivity; the stopper to the vial contains dry, natural latex rubber. Some dosage forms contain thimerosal.

Common Adverse Reactions All serious adverse reactions must be reported to the U.S. Department of Health and Human Services (DHHS) Vaccine Adverse Event Reporting System (VAERS) 1-800-822-7967. Incidence of erythema, swelling, or tenderness may be higher in children

>10%: Local: Tenderness (9% to 36% as reported in adults)

1% to 10%:

Central nervous system: Headache (2% to 5%), malaise (2%), fever (100°F to 106°F: 3%), chills (2%)

Local: Pain at injection site (2% to 3%), erythema (1% to 4%), induration (1% to 4%)

Drug Interactions

Increased Effect/Toxicity: Should not be administered with whole-cell pertussis or whole-cell typhoid vaccines due to combined endotoxin content.

Decreased Effect: Decreased effect with administration of immunoglobulin within 1 month.

Mechanism of Action Induces the formation of bactericidal antibodies to meningococcal antigens; the presence of these antibodies is strongly correlated with immunity to meningococcal disease caused by *Neisseria meningitidis* groups A, C, Y and W-135.

Pharmacodynamics/Kinetics

Onset of action: Antibody levels: 7-10 days

Duration: Antibodies against group A and C polysaccharides decline markedly (to prevaccination levels) over the first 3 years following a single dose of vaccine, especially in children <4 years of age

Dosage S.C.: Children ≥2 years and Adults: 0.5 mL; the need for booster is unknown, but may be considered in high-risk individuals, particularly children first vaccinated at <4 years of age. **Note:** Individuals who are sensitive to thimerosal should receive single-dose pack (reconstituted with 0.78 mL vial without preservative).

Administration Administer by S.C. injection; do not administer intradermally, I.M., or I.V.

Dosage Forms INJ, powder for reconstitution: 50 mcg each of polysaccharide antigen groups A, C, Y, and W-135

♦ **Menomune®-A/C/Y/W-135** *see Meningococcal Polysaccharide Vaccine (Groups A / C / Y and W-135) on page 789*

Menotropins (men oh TROE pins)

U.S. Brand Names Pergonal®; Repronex®

Therapeutic Category Gonadotropin; Ovulation Stimulator

Use Sequentially with hCG to induce ovulation and pregnancy in the infertile woman with functional anovulation or in patients who have previously received pituitary suppression; stimulation of multiple follicle development in ovulatory patients as part of an *in vitro* fertilization

(Continued)

Menotropins *(Continued)*

program; used with hCG in men to stimulate spermatogenesis in those with primary hypogonadotropic hypogonadism

Pregnancy Risk Factor X

Contraindications Hypersensitivity to menotropins or any component of the formulation; primary ovarian failure as indicated by a high follicle-stimulating hormone (FSH) level; uncontrolled thyroid and adrenal dysfunction; abnormal bleeding of undetermined origin; intracranial lesion (ie, pituitary tumor); ovarian cyst or enlargement not due to polycystic ovary syndrome; infertility due to any cause other than anovulation (except candidates for *in vitro* fertilization); men with normal urinary gonadotropin concentrations, elevated gonadotropin levels indicating primary testicular failure; pregnancy

Warnings/Precautions For use by infertility specialists. Advise patient of frequency and potential hazards of multiple pregnancy. May cause ovarian hyperstimulation syndrome (OHSS); if severe, treatment should be discontinued and patient should be hospitalized (may become more severe if pregnancy occurs). Monitor for ovarian enlargement; to minimize the hazard of abnormal ovarian enlargement, use the lowest possible dose. Serious pulmonary conditions (atelectasis, acute respiratory distress syndrome) and arterial thromboembolism have been reported. Safety and efficacy in pediatric and geriatric patients have not been established.

Common Adverse Reactions

Male:

>10%: Endocrine & metabolic: Gynecomastia

1% to 10%: Erythrocytosis (dyspnea, dizziness, anorexia, syncope, epistaxis)

Female:

1% to 10%:

Central nervous system: Headache

Endocrine & metabolic: Breast tenderness

Gastrointestinal: Abdominal cramping, abdominal pain, diarrhea, enlarged abdomen, nausea, vomiting

Genitourinary: Ectopic pregnancy, OHSS (% is dose related), ovarian disease, vaginal hemorrhage

Local: Injection site edema/reaction

Miscellaneous: Infection, pelvic pain

Percentage not reported:

Cardiovascular: Stroke, tachycardia, thrombosis (venous or arterial)

Central nervous system: Dizziness

Dermatologic: Angioedema, urticaria

Genitourinary: Adnexal torsion, hemoperitoneum, ovarian enlargement

Neuromuscular & skeletal: Limb necrosis

Respiratory: Acute respiratory distress syndrome, atelectasis, dyspnea, embolism, laryngeal edema pulmonary infarction tachypnea

Miscellaneous: Allergic reactions, anaphylaxis, rash

Drug Interactions

Increased Effect/Toxicity: Clomiphene may decrease the amount of human menopausal gonadotropin (HMG) needed to induce ovulation (Gonadorelin, Factrel®); should not be used with drugs that stimulate ovulation.

Mechanism of Action Actions occur as a result of both follicle stimulating hormone (FSH) effects and luteinizing hormone (LH) effects; menotropins stimulate the development and maturation of the ovarian follicle (FSH), cause ovulation (LH), and stimulate the development of the corpus luteum (LH); in males it stimulates spermatogenesis (LH)

Pharmacodynamics/Kinetics Excretion: Urine (~10% as unchanged drug)

Dosage Adults: I.M.:

Spermatogenesis (Male): Following pretreatment with hCG, 1 ampul 3 times/week and hCG 2000 units twice weekly until sperm is detected in the ejaculate (4-6 months) then may be increased to 2 ampuls of menotropins (150 units FSH/150 units LH) 3 times/week

Induction of ovulation (Female): 1 ampul/day (75 units of FSH and LH) for 9-12 days followed by 10,000 units hCG 1 day after the last dose; repeated at least twice at same level before increasing dosage to 2 ampuls (150 units FSH/150 units LH)

Repronex®: I.M., S.C.:

Infertile patients with oligo-anovulation: Initial: 150 int. units daily for the first 5 days of treatment. Adjustments should not be made more frequently than once every 2 days and should not exceed 75-150 int. units per adjustment. Maximum daily dose should not exceed 450 int. units and dosing beyond 12 days is not recommended. If patient's response to Repronex® is appropriate, hCG 5000-10,000 units should be given one day following the last dose of Repronex®. Hold dose if serum estradiol is >2000 pg/mL, if the ovaries are abnormally enlarged, or if abdominal pain occurs; the patient should also be advised to refrain from intercourse.

Assisted reproductive technologies: Initial (in patients who have received GnRH agonist or antagonist pituitary suppression): 225 int. units; adjustments in dose should not be made more frequently than once every 2 days and should not exceed more than 75-50 int. units per adjustment. The maximum daily doses of Repronex® given should not exceed 450 int. units and dosing beyond 12 days is not recommended. Once adequate follicular development is evident, hCG (5000-10,000 units) should be administered to induce final follicular maturation in preparation for oocyte retrieval. Withhold treatment when ovaries are abnormally enlarged on last day of therapy (to reduce chance of developing OHSS).

Administration I.M. or S.C. (Repronex® ONLY) administration. The lower abdomen (alternating sides) should be used for subcutaneous administration.

Monitoring Parameters hCG levels; serum estradiol; vaginal ultrasound; in cases of suspected OHSS, monitor fluid intake and output, weight, hematocrit, serum and urinary electrolytes, urine specific gravity, BUN and creatinine, and abdominal girth

Patient Information Multiple ovulations resulting in plural gestations have been reported

Dosage Forms INJ, powder for reconstitution (Pergonal®): Follicle stimulating hormone activity 75 int. units and luteinizing hormone activity 75 int. units; (Repronex®): Follicle stimulating hormone activity 75 int. units and luteinizing hormone activity 75 int. units; follicle stimulating hormone activity 150 int. units and luteinizing hormone activity 150 int. units

◆ **Mentax**® see Butenafine on page 195

◆ **Mepergan** see Meperidine and Promethazine on page 792

Meperidine (me PER i deen)

Related Information
Narcotic Agonists Comparison on page 1395

U.S. Brand Names Demerol®; Meperitab®

Synonyms Isonipecaine Hydrochloride; Meperidine Hydrochloride; Pethidine Hydrochloride

Therapeutic Category Analgesic, Narcotic

Use Management of moderate to severe pain; adjunct to anesthesia and preoperative sedation

Restrictions C-II

Pregnancy Risk Factor C/D (prolonged use or high doses at term)

Contraindications Hypersensitivity to meperidine or any component of the formulation; patients receiving MAO inhibitors presently or in the past 14 days; pregnancy (prolonged use or high doses near term)

Warnings/Precautions An opioid-containing analgesic regimen should be tailored to each patient's needs and based upon the type of pain being treated (acute versus chronic), the route of administration, degree of tolerance for opioids (naive versus chronic user), age, weight, and medical condition. The optimal analgesic dose varies widely among patients. Doses should be titrated to pain relief/prevention. Use for chronic pain management not recommended. Oral meperidine not recommended for acute pain management.

Use with caution in patients with pulmonary, hepatic, renal disorders, or increased intracranial pressure; use with caution in patients with renal failure or seizure disorders or those receiving high-dose meperidine; normeperidine (an active metabolite and CNS stimulant) may accumulate and precipitate twitches, tremors, or seizures; some preparations contain sulfites which may cause allergic reaction; not recommended as a drug of first choice for the treatment of chronic pain in the elderly due to the accumulation of normeperidine; for acute pain, its use should be limited to 1-2 doses; tolerance or drug dependence may result from extended use. Use only with extreme caution **(if at all)** in patients with head injury or increased intracranial pressure (ICP); potential to elevate ICP may be greatly exaggerated in these patients.

Common Adverse Reactions Frequency not defined.
Cardiovascular: Hypotension
Central nervous system: Fatigue, drowsiness, dizziness, nervousness, headache, restlessness, malaise, confusion, mental depression, hallucinations, paradoxical CNS stimulation, increased intracranial pressure, seizures (associated with metabolite accumulation)
Dermatologic: Rash, urticaria
Gastrointestinal: Nausea, vomiting, constipation, anorexia, stomach cramps, xerostomia, biliary spasm, paralytic ileus
Genitourinary: Ureteral spasms, decreased urination
Local: Pain at injection site
Neuromuscular & skeletal: Weakness
Respiratory: Dyspnea
Miscellaneous: Histamine release, physical and psychological dependence

Drug Interactions
Increased Effect/Toxicity: MAO inhibitors greatly potentiate the effects of meperidine; acute opioid overdosage symptoms can be seen, including severe toxic reactions. Concurrent use within 14 days of an MAO inhibitor is contraindicated. CNS depressants may potentiate the sedative effects of meperidine or increase respiratory depression. Phenothiazines may potentiate the sedative effects of meperidine and may increase the incidence of hypotension. Serotonin agonists, serotonin reuptake inhibitors, and tricyclic antidepressants may potentiate the effects of meperidine. In addition, concurrent therapy with these drugs potentially may increase the risk of serotonin syndrome. A number of drugs may increase meperidine metabolite concentrations (including acyclovir, cimetidine, and ritonavir).

Decreased Effect: Barbiturates may decrease the analgesic efficacy and increase the sedative effects of meperidine. Phenytoin may decrease the analgesic effects of meperidine.

Mechanism of Action Binds to opiate receptors in the CNS, causing inhibition of ascending pain pathways, altering the perception of and response to pain; produces generalized CNS depression

Pharmacodynamics/Kinetics
Onset of action: Analgesic: Oral, S.C., I.M.: 10-15 minutes; I.V.: ~5 minutes
Peak effect: Oral S.C., I.M.: ~1 hour
Duration: Oral, S.C., I.M.: 2-4 hours
Distribution: Crosses placenta; enters breast milk
Protein binding: 65% to 75%
(Continued)

Meperidine *(Continued)*

Metabolism: Hepatic; active metabolite (normeperidine)

Bioavailability: ~50% to 60%; increased with liver disease

Half-life elimination:

Parent drug: Terminal phase: Neonates: 23 hours (range: 12-39 hours); Adults: 2.5-4 hours, Liver disease: 7-11 hours

Normeperidine (active metabolite): 15-30 hours; can accumulate with high doses or with decreased renal function

Dosage Note: Doses should be titrated to necessary analgesic effect. When changing route of administration, note that oral doses are about half as effective as parenteral dose. Oral route not recommended for chronic pain. These are guidelines and do not represent the maximum doses that may be required in all patients.

Children: Pain: Oral, I.M., I.V., S.C.: 1-1.5 mg/kg/dose every 3-4 hours as needed; 1-2 mg/kg as a single dose preoperative medication may be used; maximum 100 mg/dose

Adults: Pain:

Oral: Initial: Opiate-naive: 50 mg every 3-4 hours as needed; usual dosage range: 50-150 mg every 2-4 hours as needed

I.M., S.C.: Initial: Opiate-naive: 50-75 mg every 3-4 hours as needed; patients with prior opiate exposure may require higher initial doses; usual dosage range: 50-150 mg every 2-4 hours as needed

Preoperatively: 50-100 mg given 30-90 minutes before the beginning of anesthesia

Slow I.V.: Initial: 5-10 mg every 5 minutes as needed

Patient-controlled analgesia (PCA): Usual concentration: 10 mg/mL

Initial dose: 10 mg

Demand dose: 1-5 mg (manufacturer recommendations); range 5-25 mg (American Pain Society, 1999).

Lockout interval: 5-10 minutes

Elderly:

Oral: 50 mg every 4 hours

I.M.: 25 mg every 4 hours

Dosing adjustment in renal impairment: Avoid repeated administration of meperidine in renal dysfunction:

Cl_{cr} 10-50 mL/minute: Administer at 75% of normal dose

Cl_{cr} <10 mL/minute: Administer at 50% of normal dose

Dosing adjustment/comments in hepatic disease: Increased narcotic effect in cirrhosis; reduction in dose more important for oral than I.V. route

Administration

Meperidine may be administered I.M. (preferably), S.C., or I.V.

I.V. push should be administered slowly, use of a 10 mg/mL concentration has been recommended

Monitoring Parameters Pain relief, respiratory and mental status, blood pressure; observe patient for excessive sedation, CNS depression, seizures, respiratory depression

Reference Range Therapeutic: 70-500 ng/mL (SI: 283-2020 nmol/L); Toxic: >1000 ng/mL (SI: >4043 nmol/L)

Patient Information Avoid alcohol; may cause drowsiness

Dosage Forms INJ, solution [ampul]: 50 mg/mL (1.5 mL, 2 mL); [prefilled syringe]: 25 mg/mL (1 mL); 50 mg/mL (1 mL); 75 mg/mL (1 mL); 100 mg/mL (1 mL); [prefilled syringe for PCA pump]: 10 mg/mL (50 mL); [vial]: 50 mg/mL (1 mL, 30 mL); 100 mg/mL (20 mL). **SYR:** 50 mg/5 mL (5 mL, 500 mL); (Demerol®): 50 mg/5 mL (480 mL). **TAB** (Demerol®, Meperitab®): 50 mg, 100 mg

Meperidine and Promethazine *(me PER i deen & proe METH a zeen)*

Synonyms Mepergan; Promethazine and Meperidine

Therapeutic Category Analgesic Combination, Narcotic

Use Management of moderate to severe pain

Restrictions C-II

Pregnancy Risk Factor B/D (prolonged use or high doses at term)

Dosage Adults: Oral: One (1) capsule every 4-6 hours as needed

Dosage Forms CAP: Meperidine 50 mg and promethazine 25 mg

♦ **Meperidine Hydrochloride** *see Meperidine on page 791*

♦ **Meperitab®** *see Meperidine on page 791*

Mephobarbital *(me foe BAR bi tal)*

U.S. Brand Names Mebaral®

Synonyms Methylphenobarbital

Therapeutic Category Anticonvulsant, Barbiturate; Barbiturate; Sedative

Use Sedative; treatment of grand mal and petit mal epilepsy

Restrictions C-IV

Pregnancy Risk Factor D

Contraindications Hypersensitivity to mephobarbital, other barbiturates, or any component of the formulation; pre-existing CNS depression; respiratory depression; severe uncontrolled pain; history of porphyria; pregnancy

Common Adverse Reactions

>10%: Central nervous system: Dizziness, lightheadedness, drowsiness, "hangover" effect

1% to 10%:

Central nervous system: Confusion, mental depression, unusual excitement, nervousness, faint feeling, headache, insomnia, nightmares

Gastrointestinal: Constipation, nausea, vomiting

Drug Interactions

Cytochrome P450 Effect: Substrate of CYP2B6 (minor), 2C8/9 (minor), 2C19 (major); **Inhibits** CYP2C19 (weak); **Induces** CYP2A6 (weak)

Increased Effect/Toxicity: When combined with other CNS depressants, ethanol, narcotic analgesics, antidepressants, or benzodiazepines, additive respiratory and CNS depression may occur. Barbiturates may enhance the hepatotoxic potential of acetaminophen overdoses. Chloramphenicol, MAO inhibitors, valproic acid, and felbamate may inhibit barbiturate metabolism. Barbiturates may impair the absorption of griseofulvin, and may enhance the nephrotoxic effects of methoxyflurane. Concurrent use of phenobarbital with meperidine may result in increased CNS depression. CYP2C19 inhibitors may increase the levels/effects of mephobarbital; example inhibitors include delavirdine, fluconazole, fluvoxamine, gemfibrozil, isoniazid, omeprazole, and ticlopidine.

Decreased Effect: Barbiturates are hepatic enzyme inducers, and may increase the metabolism of antipsychotics, some beta-blockers (unlikely with atenolol and nadolol), calcium channel blockers, chloramphenicol, cimetidine, corticosteroids, cyclosporine, disopyramide, doxycycline, ethosuximide, felbamate, furosemide, griseofulvin, lamotrigine, phenytoin, propafenone quinidine, tacrolimus, TCAs, and theophylline. Barbiturates may increase the metabolism of estrogens and reduce the efficacy of oral contraceptives; an alternative method of contraception should be considered. Barbiturates inhibit the hypoprothrombinemic effects of oral anticoagulants via increased metabolism. Barbiturates may enhance the metabolism of methadone resulting in methadone withdrawal. CYP2C19 inducers may decrease the levels/effects of mephobarbital; example inducers include aminoglutethimide, carbamazepine, phenytoin, and rifampin.

Mechanism of Action Increases seizure threshold in the motor cortex; depresses monosynaptic and polysynaptic transmission in the CNS

Pharmacodynamics/Kinetics

Onset of action: 20-60 minutes

Duration: 6-8 hours

Absorption: ~50%

Half-life elimination, serum: 34 hours

Dosage Oral:

Epilepsy:

Children: 6-12 mg/kg/day in 2-4 divided doses

Adults: 200-600 mg/day in 2-4 divided doses

Sedation:

Children:

<5 years: 16-32 mg 3-4 times/day

>5 years: 32-64 mg 3-4 times/day

Adults: 32-100 mg 3-4 times/day

Dosing adjustment in renal or hepatic impairment: Use with caution and reduce dosages

Dosage Forms TAB: 32 mg, 50 mg, 100 mg

♦ **Mephyton®** see Phytonadione on page 1000

Mepivacaine (me PIV a kane)

U.S. Brand Names Carbocaine® [DSC]; Polocaine®; Polocaine® MPF

Synonyms Mepivacaine Hydrochloride

Therapeutic Category Local Anesthetic, Injectable

Use Local anesthesia by nerve block; **not** for use in spinal anesthesia

Pregnancy Risk Factor C

Contraindications Hypersensitivity to mepivacaine, any component of the formulation, or other amide anesthetics; allergy to sodium bisulfate

Warnings/Precautions Use with caution in patients with cardiac disease, renal disease, and hyperthyroidism; convulsions due to systemic toxicity leading to cardiac arrest have been reported presumably due to intravascular injection

Common Adverse Reactions Degree of adverse effects in the CNS and cardiovascular system are directly related to the blood levels of mepivacaine. The effects below are more likely to occur after systemic administration rather than infiltration.

Cardiovascular: Bradycardia, cardiovascular collapse, edema, heart block, hypotension, myocardial depression, ventricular arrhythmias, angioneurotic edema

Central nervous system: High blood levels result in anxiety, restlessness, disorientation, confusion, dizziness, and seizures. This is followed by depression of CNS resulting in somnolence, unconsciousness, and possible respiratory arrest. In some cases, symptoms of CNS stimulation may be absent and the primary CNS effects are somnolence and unconsciousness.

Dermatologic: Cutaneous lesions, urticaria

Gastrointestinal: Nausea, vomiting

Local: Transient stinging or burning at injection site

Ophthalmic: Blurred vision

Otic: Tinnitus

Respiratory: Respiratory arrest

Miscellaneous: Anaphylactoid reactions

(Continued)

Mepivacaine *(Continued)*

Drug Interactions
Increased Effect/Toxicity: Beta-blockers could theoretically decrease clearance.

Mechanism of Action Mepivacaine is an amino amide local anesthetic similar to lidocaine; like all local anesthetics, mepivacaine acts by preventing the generation and conduction of nerve impulses

Pharmacodynamics/Kinetics
Onset of action: Epidural: 7-15 minutes
Duration: 2-2.5 hours; similar onset and duration following infiltration
Protein binding: 70% to 85%
Metabolism: Primarily hepatic via N-demethylation, hydroxylation, and glucuronidation
Half-life elimination: 1.9 hours
Excretion: Urine (95% as metabolites)

Dosage Children and Adults: Injectable local anesthetic: Varies with procedure, degree of anesthesia needed, vascularity of tissue, duration of anesthesia required, and physical condition of patient

Administration Before injecting, withdraw syringe plunger to ensure injection is not into vein or artery

Dosage Forms INJ, solution (Carbocaine® [DSC]): 1% (30 mL, 50 mL); 2% (20 mL, 50 mL); (Polocaine®): 1% (50 mL); 2% (50 mL); (Polocaine® MPF): 1% (30 mL); 1.5% (30 mL); 3% (20 mL)

♦ **Mepivacaine Hydrochloride** *see* Mepivacaine *on page 793*

Meprobamate *(me proe BA mate)*
U.S. Brand Names Miltown®
Synonyms Equanil
Therapeutic Category Antianxiety Agent
Use Management of anxiety disorders
Unlabeled/Investigational Use Demonstrated value for muscle contraction, headache, premenstrual tension, external sphincter spasticity, muscle rigidity, opisthotonos-associated with tetanus
Restrictions C-IV
Pregnancy Risk Factor D
Contraindications Hypersensitivity to meprobamate, related compounds (including carisoprodol), or any component of the formulation; acute intermittent porphyria; pre-existing CNS depression; narrow-angle glaucoma; severe uncontrolled pain; pregnancy
Warnings/Precautions Physical and psychological dependence and abuse may occur; abrupt cessation may precipitate withdrawal. Use with caution in patients with depression or suicidal tendencies, or in patients with a history of drug abuse. May cause CNS depression, which may impair physical or mental abilities. Patients must be cautioned about performing tasks which require mental alertness (eg, operating machinery or driving). Effects with other sedative drugs or ethanol may be potentiated. Not recommended in children <6 years of age; allergic reaction may occur in patients with history of dermatological condition (usually by fourth dose). Use with caution in patients with renal or hepatic impairment, or with a history of seizures. Use caution in the elderly as it may cause confusion, cognitive impairment, or excessive sedation.
Common Adverse Reactions Frequency not defined.
Cardiovascular: Syncope, peripheral edema, palpitations, tachycardia, arrhythmia
Central nervous system: Drowsiness, ataxia, dizziness, paradoxical excitement, confusion, slurred speech, headache, euphoria, chills, vertigo, paresthesia, overstimulation
Dermatologic: Rashes, purpura, dermatitis, Stevens-Johnson syndrome, petechiae, ecchymosis
Gastrointestinal: Diarrhea, vomiting, nausea
Hematologic: Leukopenia, eosinophilia, agranulocytosis, aplastic anemia
Neuromuscular & skeletal: Weakness
Ocular: Blurred vision, impairment of accommodation
Renal: Renal failure
Respiratory: Wheezing, dyspnea, bronchospasm, angioneurotic edema
Drug Interactions
Increased Effect/Toxicity: CNS depressants (ethanol) may increase CNS depression.
Mechanism of Action Affects the thalamus and limbic system; also appears to inhibit multineuronal spinal reflexes
Pharmacodynamics/Kinetics
Onset of action: Sedation: ~1 hour
Distribution: Crosses placenta; enters breast milk
Metabolism: Hepatic
Half-life elimination: 10 hours
Excretion: Urine (8% to 20% as unchanged drug); feces (10% as metabolites)
Dosage Oral:
Children 6-12 years: Anxiety: 100-200 mg 2-3 times/day
Adults: Anxiety: 400 mg 3-4 times/day, up to 2400 mg/day
Dosing interval in renal impairment:
Cl_{cr} 10-50 mL/minute: Administer every 9-12 hours
Cl_{cr} <10 mL/minute: Administer every 12-18 hours
Hemodialysis: Moderately dialyzable (20% to 50%)
Dosing adjustment in hepatic impairment: Probably necessary in patients with liver disease

Monitoring Parameters Mental status

Reference Range Therapeutic: 6-12 µg/mL (SI: 28-55 µmol/L); Toxic: >60 µg/mL (SI: >275 µmol/L)

Patient Information May cause drowsiness; avoid alcohol

Dosage Forms TAB: 200 mg, 400 mg

♦ **Meprobamate and Aspirin** *see Aspirin and Meprobamate on page 123*

♦ **Mepron®** *see Atovaquone on page 130*

Mequinol and Tretinoin (ME kwi nole & TRET i noyn)

U.S. Brand Names Solagé™

Synonyms Tretinoin and Mequinol

Therapeutic Category Retinoic Acid Derivative; Vitamin A Derivative

Use Treatment of solar lentigines; the efficacy of using Solagé™ daily for >24 weeks has not been established. The local cutaneous safety of Solagé™ in non-Caucasians has not been adequately established.

Pregnancy Risk Factor X

Contraindications Hypersensitivity to mequinol, tretinoin, or any component of the formulation; pregnancy, women of childbearing potential

Warnings/Precautions Discontinue if hypersensitivity is noted. Use extreme caution in eczematous skin conditions. Safety and efficacy have not been established in moderately or heavily pigmented skin. Not to be taken with photosensitizing drugs (eg, thiazides, tetracyclines, fluoroquinolones, phenothiazines, sulfonamides). Avoid sun (including sun lamps) or use protective clothing. Do not use in sunburned patients until they have fully recovered. Use extreme caution in patients who have significant exposure to the sun through their occupation. Use caution in patient with history or family history of vitiligo. For external use only. Weather extremes (wind, cold) may be irritating to users of Solagé™. Do not use in pediatric patients. No bathing or showering for at least 6 hours after application. Effects of chronic use (>52 weeks) are unknown.

Common Adverse Reactions

>10%: Dermatologic: Erythema (49%), burning, stinging or tingling (26%), desquamation (14%), pruritus (12%),

1% to 10%: Dermatologic: Skin irritation (5%), hypopigmentation (5%), halo hypopigmentation (7%), rash (3%), dry skin (3%), crusting (3%), vesicular bullae rash (2%), contact allergic reaction (1%)

Drug Interactions

Cytochrome P450 Effect: Tretinoin: **Substrate** (minor) of CYP2A6, 2B6, 2C8/9; **Inhibits** CYP2C8/9 (weak); **Induces** CYP2E1 (weak)

Increased Effect/Toxicity:

Topical products with skin drying effects (eg, those containing alcohol, astringents, spices, or lime; medicated soaps or shampoos; permanent wave solutions; hair depilatories or waxes; and others) may increase skin irritation. Avoid concurrent use.

Photosensitizing drugs (eg, thiazides, tetracyclines, fluoroquinolones, phenothiazines, sulfonamides) can further increase sun sensitivity. Avoid concurrent use.

Mechanism of Action Solar lentigines are localized, pigmented, macular lesions of the skin on areas of the body chronically exposed to the sun. Mequinol is a substrate for the enzyme tyrosinase and acts as a competitive inhibitor of the formation of melanin precursors. The mechanisms of depigmentation for both drugs is unknown.

Pharmacodynamics/Kinetics

Absorption: Percutaneous absorption was 4.4% of tretinoin when applied as 0.8 mL of Solagé™ to a 400 cm² area of the back

Time to peak: Mequinol: 2 hours

Dosage Solar lentigines: Topical: Apply twice daily to solar lentigines using the applicator tip while avoiding application to the surrounding skin. Separate application by at least 8 hours or as directed by physician.

Administration Avoid eyes, mouth, paranasal creases, and mucous membranes when applying

Patient Information No bathing or showering for at least 6 hours after application. Avoid eyes, mouth, paranasal creases, and mucous membranes when applying. Application of larger amounts or more frequently will not result in more rapid or better results. Follow application directions closely. Wait 30 minutes after use before applying cosmetics. Avoid sun exposure (including sun lamps) or use protective clothing. Some reappearance of freckles may occur after discontinuation. After application, short-term stinging, burning, or irritation may occur.

Dosage Forms LIQ, topical: Mequinol 2% and tretinoin 0.01% (30 mL)

Mercaptopurine (mer kap toe PYOOR een)

U.S. Brand Names Purinethol®

Synonyms 6-Mercaptopurine; 6-MP; NSC-755

Therapeutic Category Antineoplastic Agent, Antimetabolite (Purine)

Use Maintenance therapy in acute lymphoblastic leukemia (ALL); other (less common) uses include chronic granulocytic leukemia, induction therapy in ALL, and treatment of non-Hodgkin's lymphomas

Restrictions Note: I.V. formulation is not commercially available in the U.S.

Pregnancy Risk Factor D

(Continued)

Mercaptopurine *(Continued)*

Contraindications Hypersensitivity to mercaptopurine or any component of the formulation; patients whose disease showed prior resistance to mercaptopurine or thioguanine; severe liver disease, severe bone marrow suppression; pregnancy

Warnings/Precautions The U.S. Food and Drug Administration (FDA) currently recommends that procedures for proper handling and disposal of antineoplastic agents are considered. Mercaptopurine may cause birth defects; potentially carcinogenic; adjust dosage in patients with renal impairment or hepatic failure; use with caution in patients with prior bone marrow suppression; patients may be at risk for pancreatitis. Toxicity to immunosuppressives is increased in elderly. Start with lowest recommended adult doses. Signs of infection, such as fever and WBC rise, may not occur. Lethargy and confusion may be more prominent signs of infection.

To avoid potentially serious dosage errors, the terms "6-mercaptopurine" or "6-MP" should be avoided; use of these terms has been associated with sixfold overdosages.

Common Adverse Reactions

>10%:

Hematologic: Myelosuppression; leukopenia, thrombocytopenia, anemia

Onset: 7-10 days

Nadir: 14-16 days

Recovery: 21-28 days

Hepatic: Intrahepatic cholestasis and focal centralobular necrosis (40%), characterized by hyperbilirubinemia, increased alkaline phosphatase and AST, jaundice, ascites, encephalopathy; more common at doses >2.5 mg/kg/day. Usually occurs within 2 months of therapy but may occur within 1 week, or be delayed up to 8 years.

1% to 10%:

Central nervous system: Drug fever

Dermatologic: Hyperpigmentation, rash

Endocrine & metabolic: Hyperuricemia

Gastrointestinal: Nausea, vomiting, diarrhea, stomatitis, anorexia, stomach pain, mucositis

Renal: Renal toxicity

Drug Interactions

Increased Effect/Toxicity:

Allopurinol can cause increased levels of mercaptopurine by inhibition of xanthine oxidase. Decrease dose of mercaptopurine by 75% when both drugs are used concomitantly. Seen only with oral mercaptopurine usage, not with I.V. May potentiate effect of bone marrow suppression (reduce mercaptopurine to 25% of dose).

Doxorubicin: Synergistic liver toxicity with mercaptopurine in >50% of patients, which resolved with discontinuation of the mercaptopurine.

Hepatotoxic drugs: Any agent which could potentially alter the metabolic function of the liver could produce higher drug levels and greater toxicities from either mercaptopurine or thioguanine (6-TG).

Aminosalicylates (olsalazine, mesalamine, sulfasalazine): May inhibit TPMT, increasing toxicity/myelosuppression of mercaptopurine.

Decreased Effect: mercaptopurine inhibits the anticoagulation effect of warfarin by an unknown mechanism.

Mechanism of Action Purine antagonist which inhibits DNA and RNA synthesis; acts as false metabolite and is incorporated into DNA and RNA, eventually inhibiting their synthesis; specific for the S phase of the cell cycle

Pharmacodynamics/Kinetics

Absorption: Variable and incomplete (16% to 50%)

Distribution: V_d = total body water; CNS penetration is poor

Protein binding: 30%

Metabolism: Hepatic and in GI mucosa; hepatically via xanthine oxidase and methylation to sulfate conjugates, 6-thiouric acid, and other inactive compounds; first-pass effect

Half-life elimination (age dependent): Children: 21 minutes; Adults: 47 minutes

Time to peak, serum: ~2 hours

Excretion: Urine; following high (1 g/m^2) I.V. doses, 20% to 40% excreted unchanged; at lower doses renal elimination minor

Dosage Oral (refer to individual protocols):

Children:

Induction: 2.5-5 mg/kg/day **or** 70-100 mg/m^2/day given once daily

Maintenance: 1.5-2.5 mg/kg/day **or** 50-75 mg/m^2/day given once daily

Adults:

Induction: 2.5-5 mg/kg/day (100-200 mg)

Maintenance: 1.5-2.5 mg/kg/day **or** 80-100 mg/m^2/day given once daily

Elderly: Due to renal decline with age, start with lower recommended doses for adults

Note: In ALL, administration in the evening (vs morning administration) may lower the risk of relapse.

Dosing adjustment in renal or hepatic impairment: Dose should be reduced to avoid accumulation, but specific guidelines are not available.

Hemodialysis: Removed; supplemental dose is usually required

Administration Administer by slow I.V. continuous infusion.

Monitoring Parameters CBC with differential and platelet count, liver function tests, uric acid, urinalysis

Patient Information Take daily dose at the same time each day. Preferable to take an on empty stomach (1 hour before or 2 hours after meals). Maintain adequate hydration (2-3 L/day of fluids unless instructed to restrict fluid intake). You may experience nausea and vomiting, diarrhea, or loss of appetite (frequent small meals may help/request medication) or weakness or lethargy (use caution when driving or engaging in tasks that require alertness until response to drug is known). Use good oral care to reduce incidence of mouth sores. You may be more susceptible to infection (avoid crowds or exposure to infection). May cause headache (request medication). Report signs of opportunistic infection (eg, fever, chills, sore throat, burning urination, fatigue); bleeding (eg, tarry stools, easy bruising); unresolved mouth sores, nausea, or vomiting; swelling of extremities, difficulty breathing, or unusual weight gain. The drug may be excreted in breast milk, therefore, an alternative form of feeding your baby should be used. Contraceptive measures are recommended during therapy.

Dosage Forms TAB [scored]: 50 mg

♦ **6-Mercaptopurine** *see* Mercaptopurine *on page 795*

♦ **Mercapturic Acid** *see* Acetylcysteine *on page 32*

♦ **Meridia®** *see* Sibutramine *on page 1134*

Meropenem (mer oh PEN em)

Related Information
Antimicrobial Drugs of Choice *on page 1440*
Community-Acquired Pneumonia in Adults *on page 1457*

U.S. Brand Names Merrem® I.V.

Therapeutic Category Antibiotic, Anaerobic; Antibiotic, Carbapenem

Use Intra-abdominal infections (complicated appendicitis and peritonitis) caused by viridans group streptococci, *E. coli*, *K. pneumoniae*, *P. aeruginosa*, *B. fragilis*, *B. thetaiotaomicron*, and *Peptostreptococcus* sp; also indicated for bacterial meningitis in pediatric patients >3 months of age caused by *S. pneumoniae*, *H. influenzae*, and *N. meningitidis*; meropenem has also been used to treat soft tissue infections, febrile neutropenia, and urinary tract infections

Pregnancy Risk Factor B

Contraindications Hypersensitivity to meropenem, any component of the formulation, or other carbapenems (eg, imipenem); patients who have experienced anaphylactic reactions to other beta-lactams

Warnings/Precautions Pseudomembranous colitis and hypersensitivity reactions have occurred and often require immediate drug discontinuation; thrombocytopenia has been reported in patients with significant renal dysfunction; seizures have occurred in patients with underlying neurologic disorders (less frequent than with imipenem and cilastatin); safety and efficacy have not been established for children <3 months of age; superinfection possible with long courses of therapy

Common Adverse Reactions 1% to 10%:
Central nervous system: Headache (2%)
Dermatologic: Rash (2% to 3%, includes diaper-area moniliasis in pediatrics), pruritus (1%)
Gastrointestinal: Diarrhea (4% to 5%), nausea/vomiting (1% to 4%), constipation (1%), oral moniliasis (up to 2% in pediatric patients), glossitis
Local: Inflammation at the injection site (2%), phlebitis/thrombophlebitis (1%), injection site reaction (1%)
Respiratory: Apnea (1%)
Miscellaneous: Sepsis (2%), septic shock (1%)

Drug Interactions
Increased Effect/Toxicity: Probenecid interferes with renal excretion of meropenem.
Decreased Effect: Serum concentrations of valproic acid may be reduced during meropenem therapy (potentially to subtherapeutic levels).

Mechanism of Action Inhibits bacterial cell wall synthesis by binding to several of the penicillin-binding proteins, which in turn inhibit the final transpeptidation step of peptidoglycan synthesis in bacterial cell walls, thus inhibiting cell wall biosynthesis; bacteria eventually lyse due to ongoing activity of cell wall autolytic enzymes (autolysins and murein hydrolases) while cell wall assembly is arrested

Pharmacodynamics/Kinetics
Distribution: V_d: Adults: ~0.3 L/kg, Children: 0.4-0.5 L/kg; penetrates well into most body fluids and tissues; CSF concentrations approximate those of the plasma
Protein binding: 2%
Metabolism: Hepatic; metabolized to open beta-lactam form (inactive)
Half-life elimination:
Normal renal function: 1-1.5 hours
Cl_{cr} 30-80 mL/minute: 1.9-3.3 hours
Cl_{cr} 2-30 mL/minute: 3.82-5.7 hours
Time to peak, tissue: 1 hour following infusion
Excretion: Urine (~25% as inactive metabolites)

Dosage I.V.:
Neonates:
Preterm: 20 mg/kg/dose every 12 hours (may be increased to 40 mg/kg/dose if treating a highly resistant organism such as *Pseudomonas aeruginosa*)
Full-term (<3 months of age): 20 mg/kg/dose every 8 hours (may be increased to 40 mg/kg/dose if treating a highly resistant organism such as *Pseudomonas aeruginosa*)
Children >3 months (<50 kg):
Intra-abdominal infections: 20 mg/kg every 8 hours (maximum dose: 1 g every 8 hours)
Meningitis 40 mg/kg every 8 hours (maximum dose: 2 g every 8 hours)
Children >50 kg:
Intra-abdominal infections: 1 g every 8 hours
(Continued)

Meropenem *(Continued)*

Meningitis: 2 g every 8 hours

Adults: 1 g every 8 hours

Elderly: No differences in safety or efficacy have been reported. However, increased sensitivity may occur in some elderly patients; adjust dose based on renal function; see Warnings/Precautions

Dosing adjustment in renal impairment: Adults:

Cl_{cr} 26-50 mL/minute: Administer 1 g every 12 hours

Cl_{cr} 10-25 mL/minute: Administer 500 mg every 12 hours

Cl_{cr} <10 mL/minute: Administer 500 mg every 24 hours

Dialysis: Meropenem and its metabolites are readily dialyzable

Continuous arteriovenous or venovenous hemodiafiltration effects: Dose as Cl_{cr} 10-50 mL/minute

Administration Administer I.V. infusion over 15-30 minutes; I.V. bolus injection over 3-5 minutes

Monitoring Parameters Monitor for signs of anaphylaxis during first dose

Dosage Forms INJ, powder for reconstitution: 500 mg, 1 g

♦ **Merrem® I.V.** *see* Meropenem *on page 797*

♦ **Meruvax® II** *see* Rubella Virus Vaccine (Live) *on page 1119*

Mesalamine *(me SAL a meen)*

U.S. Brand Names Asacol®; Canasa™; Pentasa®; Rowasa®

Synonyms 5-Aminosalicylic Acid; 5-ASA; Fisalamine; Mesalazine

Therapeutic Category 5-Aminosalicylic Acid Derivative; Anti-inflammatory Agent; Anti-inflammatory Agent, Rectal

Use

Oral: Treatment and maintenance of remission of mildly to moderately active ulcerative colitis

Rectal: Treatment of active mild to moderate distal ulcerative colitis, proctosigmoiditis, or proctitis

Pregnancy Risk Factor B

Contraindications Hypersensitivity to mesalamine, sulfasalazine, salicylates, or any component of the formulation

Warnings/Precautions May cause an acute intolerance syndrome (cramping, acute abdominal pain, bloody diarrhea; sometimes fever, headache, rash); discontinue if this occurs. Patients with pyloric stenosis may have prolonged gastric retention of tablets, delaying the release of mesalamine in the colon. Pericarditis should be considered in patients with chest pain; pancreatitis should be considered in patients with new abdominal complaints. Use caution in patients with impaired renal or hepatic function. Renal impairment (including minimal change nephropathy and acute/chronic interstitial nephritis) has been reported; use caution with other medications converted to mesalamine. Postmarketing reports suggest an increased incidence of blood dyscrasias in patients >65 years of age. In addition, elderly may have difficulty administering and retaining rectal suppositories and decreased renal function; use with caution and monitor. Safety and efficacy in pediatric patients have not been established.

Rowasa® enema: Contains potassium metabisulfite; may cause severe hypersensitivity reactions (ie, anaphylaxis) in patients with sulfite allergies.

Common Adverse Reactions Adverse effects vary depending upon dosage form. Effects as reported with tablets, unless otherwise noted:

>10%:

Central nervous system: Pain (14%)

Gastrointestinal: Abdominal pain (18%; enema: 8%)

Genitourinary: Eructation (16%)

Respiratory: Pharyngitis (11%)

1% to 10%:

Cardiovascular: Chest pain (3%), peripheral edema (3%)

Central nervous system: Chills (3%), dizziness (suppository: 3%), fever (enema: 3%; suppository: 1%), insomnia (2%), malaise (2%)

Dermatologic: Rash (6%; suppository: 1%), pruritus (3%; enema: 1%), acne (2%; suppository: 1%)

Gastrointestinal: Dyspepsia (6%), constipation (5%), vomiting (5%), colitis exacerbation (3%; suppository: 1%), nausea (capsule: 3%), flatulence (enema: 6%), hemorrhoids (enema: 1%), nausea and vomiting (capsule: 1%), rectal pain (enema: 1%; suppository: 2%)

Local: Pain on insertion of enema tip (enema: 1%)

Neuromuscular & skeletal: Back pain (7%; enema: 1%), arthralgia (5%), hypertonia (5%), myalgia (3%), arthritis (2%), leg/joint pain (enema: 2%),

Ocular: Conjunctivitis (2%)

Respiratory: Flu-like syndrome (3%; enema: 5%), diaphoresis (3%), cough increased (2%)

Drug Interactions

Increased Effect/Toxicity: Mesalamine may increase the risk of myelosuppression from azathioprine, mercaptopurine, and thioguanine.

Decreased Effect: Decreased digoxin bioavailability.

Mechanism of Action Mesalamine (5-aminosalicylic acid) is the active component of sulfasalazine; the specific mechanism of action of mesalamine is unknown; however, it is thought that it modulates local chemical mediators of the inflammatory response, especially leukotrienes; action appears topical rather than systemic

Pharmacodynamics/Kinetics

Absorption: Rectal: Variable and dependent upon retention time, underlying GI disease, and colonic pH; Oral: Tablet: ~28%, Capsule: ~20% to 30%

Metabolism: Hepatic and via GI tract to acetyl-5-aminosalicylic acid

Half-life elimination: 5-ASA: 0.5-1.5 hours; acetyl-5-ASA: 5-10 hours

Time to peak, serum: 4-7 hours

Excretion: Urine (as metabolites); feces (<2%)

Dosage

Adults (usual course of therapy is 3-8 weeks):

Oral:

Treatment of ulcerative colitis:

Capsule: 1 g 4 times/day

Tablet: Initial: 800 mg (2 tablets) 3 times/day for 6 weeks

Maintenance of remission of ulcerative colitis:

Capsule: 1 g 4 times/day

Tablet: 1.6 g/day in divided doses

Rectal:

Retention enema: 60 mL (4 g) at bedtime, retained overnight, approximately 8 hours

Rectal suppository: Insert 1 suppository in rectum twice daily; retain suppositories for at least 1-3 hours to achieve maximum benefit

Canasa™: May increase to 3 times/day if inadequate response is seen after 2 weeks.

Note: Some patients may require rectal and oral therapy concurrently.

Elderly: See adult dosing; use with caution

Administration

Oral: Swallow capsules or tablets whole, do not chew or crush.

Rectal enema: Shake bottle well. Retain enemas for 8 hours or as long as practical.

Suppository: Remove foil wrapper; avoid excessive handling. Should be retained for at least 1-3 hours to achieve maximum benefit.

Monitoring Parameters CBC and renal function, particularly in elderly patients

Patient Information Retain enemas for 8 hours or as long as practical; shake bottle well; do not chew or break oral tablets; for suppositories, remove foil wrapper, avoid excessive handling

Dosage Forms CAP, controlled release (Pentasa®): 250 mg. **SUPP, rectal** (Canasa™): 500 mg. **SUSP, rectal** (Rowasa®): 4 g/60 mL (7s). **TAB, delayed release** [enteric coated] (Asacol®): 400 mg

♦ **Mesalazine** see Mesalamine on page 798

Mesna (MES na)

U.S. Brand Names Mesnex®

Synonyms Sodium 2-Mercaptoethane Sulfonate

Therapeutic Category Antidote, Cyclophosphamide-induced Hemorrhagic Cystitis; Antidote, Ifosfamide-induced Hemorrhagic Cystitis

Use Orphan drug: Prevention of hemorrhagic cystitis induced by ifosfamide

Unlabeled/Investigational Use Prevention of hemorrhagic cystitis induced by cyclophosphamide

Pregnancy Risk Factor B

Contraindications Hypersensitivity to mesna or other thiol compounds, or any component of the formulation

Warnings/Precautions Examine morning urine specimen for hematuria prior to ifosfamide or cyclophosphamide treatment; if hematuria (>50 RBC/HPF) develops, reduce the ifosfamide/cyclophosphamide dose or discontinue the drug; will not prevent or alleviate other toxicities associated with ifosfamide or cyclophosphamide and will not prevent hemorrhagic cystitis in all patients. Allergic reactions have been reported; patients with autoimmune disorders may be at increased risk. Symptoms ranged from mild hypersensitivity to systemic anaphylactic reactions. I.V. formulation contains benzyl alcohol; do not use in neonates or infants.

Common Adverse Reactions It is difficult to distinguish reactions from those caused by concomitant chemotherapy.

>10%: Gastrointestinal: Bad taste in mouth with oral administration (100%), vomiting (secondary to the bad taste after oral administration, or with high I.V. doses)

Drug Interactions

Decreased Effect: Warfarin: Questionable alterations in coagulation control.

Mechanism of Action In blood, mesna is oxidized to dimesna which in turn is reduced in the kidney back to mesna, supplying a free thiol group which binds to and inactivates acrolein, the urotoxic metabolite of ifosfamide and cyclophosphamide

Pharmacodynamics/Kinetics

Distribution: No tissue penetration

Protein binding: 69% to 75%

Metabolism: Rapidly oxidized intravascularly to mesna disulfide; mesna disulfide is reduced in renal tubules back to mesna following glomerular filtration.

Bioavailability: Oral: 45% to 79%

Half-life elimination: Parent drug: 24 minutes; Mesna disulfide: 72 minutes

Time to peak, plasma: 2-3 hours

Excretion: Urine; as unchanged drug (18% to 26%) and metabolites

Dosage Children and Adults (refer to individual protocols):

I.V.: Recommended dose is 60% of the ifosfamide dose given in 3 divided doses (0, 4, and 8 hours after the start of ifosfamide)

(Continued)

Mesna *(Continued)*

Alternative I.V. regimens include 80% of the ifosfamide dose given in 4 divided doses (0, 3, 6, and 9 hours after the start of ifosfamide) and continuous infusions

Oral: 20% of the ifosfamide dose hour 0, followed by 40% of the ifosfamide dose given 4 and 8 hours (or 3, 6, and 9 hours) after start of ifosfamide

Administration

Oral: Administer orally in tablet formulation or parenteral solution diluted in water, milk, juice, or carbonated beverages; patients who vomit within 2 hours of taking oral mesna should repeat the dose or receive I.V. mesna

I.V.: Administer by short (15-30 minutes) infusion or continuous (24 hour) infusion

Monitoring Parameters Urinalysis

Dosage Forms INJ, solution: 100 mg/mL (10 mL). **TAB:** 400 mg

♦ **Mesnex**® *see Mesna on page 799*

Mesoridazine *(mez oh RID a zeen)*

Related Information

Antipsychotic Agents Comparison *on page 1364*

U.S. Brand Names Serentil®

Synonyms Mesoridazine Besylate

Therapeutic Category Antipsychotic Agent, Phenothiazine; Antipsychotic Agent, Phenothiazine, Piperidine; Phenothiazine Derivative

Use Management of schizophrenic patients who fail to respond adequately to treatment with other antipsychotic drugs, either because of insufficient effectiveness or the inability to achieve an effective dose due to intolerable adverse effects from these drugs

Unlabeled/Investigational Use Psychosis

Pregnancy Risk Factor C

Contraindications Hypersensitivity to mesoridazine or any component of the formulation (cross-reactivity between phenothiazines may occur); severe CNS depression and coma; prolonged QT interval (>450 msec), including prolongation due to congenital causes; history of arrhythmias; concurrent use of medications which prolong QT_c (including type Ia and type III antiarrhythmics, cyclic antidepressants, some fluoroquinolones, cisapride)

Warnings/Precautions Safety in children <6 months of age has not been established; use with caution in patients with cardiovascular disease or seizures; benefits of therapy must be weighed against risks of therapy; doses >1 g/day frequently cause pigmentary retinopathy; some products contain sulfites and/or tartrazine; use with caution in patients with narrow-angle glaucoma, bone marrow suppression, severe liver disease.

Has been shown to prolong QT_c interval in a dose-dependent manner (associated with an increased risk of torsade de pointes). Patients should have a baseline ECG prior to initiation, and should not receive mesoridazine if baseline QT_c >450 msec. Mesoridazine should be discontinued in patients with a QT_c interval >500 msec. Potassium levels must be evaluated and normalized prior to and throughout treatment.

May cause hypotension, particularly with I.M. administration. Highly sedating, use with caution in disorders where CNS depression is a feature. Use with caution in Parkinson's disease. Caution in patients with hemodynamic instability; bone marrow suppression; predisposition to seizures; subcortical brain damage; severe cardiac, hepatic, renal, or respiratory disease. Esophageal dysmotility and aspiration have been associated with antipsychotic use; use with caution in patients at risk of pneumonia (ie, Alzheimer's disease). Caution in breast cancer or other prolactin-dependent tumors (may elevate prolactin levels). May alter temperature regulation or mask toxicity of other drugs due to antiemetic effects. May cause orthostatic hypotension - use with caution in patients at risk of this effect or those who would tolerate transient hypotensive episodes (cerebrovascular disease, cardiovascular disease, or other medications which may predispose).

Phenothiazines may cause anticholinergic effects (confusion, agitation, constipation, xerostomia, blurred vision, urinary retention). Therefore, they should be used with caution in patients with decreased gastrointestinal motility, urinary retention, BPH, xerostomia, or visual problems. Conditions which also may be exacerbated by cholinergic blockade include narrow-angle glaucoma (screening is recommended) and worsening of myasthenia gravis. Relative to other antipsychotics, mesoridazine has a high potency of cholinergic blockade.

May cause extrapyramidal reactions, including pseudoparkinsonism, acute dystonic reactions, akathisia, and tardive dyskinesia (risk of these reactions is low relative to other neuroleptics). May be associated with neuroleptic malignant syndrome (NMS) or pigmentary retinopathy (particularly at doses >1 g/day).

Common Adverse Reactions Frequency not defined.

Cardiovascular: Hypotension, orthostatic hypotension, tachycardia, QT prolongation (dose dependent, up to 100% of patients at higher dosages), syncope, edema

Central nervous system: Pseudoparkinsonism, akathisia, dystonias, tardive dyskinesia, dizziness, drowsiness, restlessness, ataxia, slurred speech, neuroleptic malignant syndrome (NMS), impairment of temperature regulation, lowering of seizure threshold

Dermatologic: Increased sensitivity to sun, rash, itching, angioneurotic edema, dermatitis, discoloration of skin (blue-gray)

Endocrine & metabolic: Changes in menstrual cycle, changes in libido, gynecomastia, lactation, galactorrhea

Gastrointestinal: Constipation, xerostomia, weight gain, nausea, vomiting, stomach pain

Genitourinary: Difficulty in urination, ejaculatory disturbances, impotence, enuresis, incontinence, priapism, urinary retention

Hematologic: Agranulocytosis, leukopenia, eosinophilia, thrombocytopenia, anemia, aplastic anemia

Hepatic: Cholestatic jaundice, hepatotoxicity

Neuromuscular & skeletal: Weakness, tremor, rigidity

Ocular: Pigmentary retinopathy, photophobia, blurred vision, cornea and lens changes

Respiratory: Nasal congestion

Miscellaneous: Diaphoresis (decreased), lupus-like syndrome

Drug Interactions

Increased Effect/Toxicity: Use of mesoridazine with other agents known to prolong QT_c may increase the risk of malignant arrhythmias; concurrent use is contraindicated - includes type I and type III antiarrhythmics, TCAs, and some quinolone antibiotics (sparfloxacin, moxifloxacin, gatifloxacin). Mesoridazine may increase the effect and/or toxicity of antihypertensives, anticholinergics, lithium, CNS depressants (ethanol, narcotics), and trazodone. Metoclopramide may increase risk of extrapyramidal symptoms (EPS).

Decreased Effect: Mesoridazine may inhibit the activity of bromocriptine and levodopa. Benztropine (and other anticholinergics) may inhibit the therapeutic response to mesoridazine and excess anticholinergic effects may occur. Mesoridazine and possibly other low potency antipsychotic may reverse the pressor effects of epinephrine.

Mechanism of Action Blockade of postsynaptic CNS dopamine$_2$ receptors in the mesolimbic and mesocortical areas

Pharmacodynamics/Kinetics

Duration: 4-6 hours

Absorption: Tablet: Erratic; Liquid: More dependable

Protein binding: 91% to 99%

Half-life elimination: 24-48 hours

Time to peak, serum: 2-4 hours; Steady-state serum: 4-7 days

Excretion: Urine

Dosage Concentrate may be diluted just prior to administration with distilled water, acidified tap water, orange or grape juice; do not prepare and store bulk dilutions

Adults: Schizophrenia/psychoses:

Oral: 25-50 mg 3 times/day; maximum: 100-400 mg/day

I.M.: Initial: 25 mg, repeat in 30-60 minutes as needed; optimal dosage range: 25-200 mg/day

Elderly: Behavioral symptoms associated with dementia:

Oral: Initial: 10 mg 1-2 times/day; if <10 mg/day is desired, consider administering 10 mg every other day (qod). Increase dose at 4- to 7-day intervals by 10-25 mg/day; increase dose intervals (bid, tid, etc) as necessary to control response or side effects. Maximum daily dose: 250 mg. Gradual increases (titration) may prevent some side effects or decrease their severity.

I.M.: Initial: 25 mg; repeat doses in 30-60 minutes if necessary. Dose range: 25-200 mg/day. Elderly usually require less than maximal daily dose.

Hemodialysis: Not dialyzable (0% to 5%)

Administration When administering I.M. or I.V., watch for hypotension. Dilute oral concentrate just prior to administration with distilled water, acidified tap water, orange or grape juice. Do not prepare and store bulk dilutions. Do not mix oral solutions of mesoridazine and lithium, these oral liquids are incompatible when mixed. **Note:** Avoid skin contact with oral medication; may cause contact dermatitis.

Monitoring Parameters Vital signs, orthostatic blood pressures; lipid profile, fasting blood glucose/Hgb A_{1c}, baseline (and periodic) serum potassium; BMI; mental status, abnormal involuntary movement scale (AIMS); tremors, gait changes, abnormal movement in trunk, neck, buccal area or extremities; monitor target behaviors for which the agent is given; monitor hepatic function (especially if fever with flu-like symptoms); baseline ECG, do not initiate if QT_c >450 msec (discontinue in any patient with a QT_c >500 msec)

Patient Information May cause drowsiness or restlessness, avoid alcohol and other CNS depressants; do not alter dosage or discontinue without consulting prescriber; avoid excessive sunlight, yearly ophthalmic examinations are necessary

Dosage Forms INJ, solution: 25 mg/mL (1 mL). **LIQ,** oral: 25 mg/mL (118 mL). **TAB:** 10 mg, 25 mg, 50 mg, 100 mg

- **Mesoridazine Besylate** see Mesoridazine on page 800
- **Mestinon®** see Pyridostigmine on page 1066
- **Mestinon® Timespan®** see Pyridostigmine on page 1066

Mestranol and Norethindrone (MES tra nole & nor eth IN drone)

U.S. Brand Names Necon® 1/50; Norinyl® 1+50; Ortho-Novum® 1/50

Synonyms Norethindrone and Mestranol; Ortho Novum 1/50

Therapeutic Category Contraceptive, Oral (Low Potency Estrogen, Low Potency Progestin); Contraceptive, Oral (Monophasic); Estrogen and Progestin Combination; Progestin

Use Prevention of pregnancy

Unlabeled/Investigational Use Treatment of hypermenorrhea, endometriosis, female hypogonadism

Pregnancy Risk Factor X

Contraindications Hypersensitivity to mestranol, norethindrone, or any component of the formulation; thrombophlebitis or thromboembolic disorders (current or history of), cerebral (Continued)

Mestranol and Norethindrone *(Continued)*

vascular disease, coronary artery disease, valvular heart disease with complications, severe hypertension; diabetes mellitus with vascular involvement; severe headache with focal neurological symptoms; known or suspected breast carcinoma, endometrial cancer, estrogen-dependent neoplasms, undiagnosed abnormal genital bleeding; hepatic dysfunction or tumor, cholestatic jaundice of pregnancy, jaundice with prior combination hormonal contraceptive use; major surgery with prolonged immobilization; heavy smoking (≥15 cigarettes/day) in patients >35 years of age; pregnancy

Warnings/Precautions Combination hormonal contraceptives do not protect against HIV infection or other sexually-transmitted diseases. The risk of cardiovascular side effects increases in women who smoke cigarettes, especially those who are >35 years of age; women who use combination hormonal contraceptives should be strongly advised not to smoke. Combination hormonal contraceptives may lead to increased risk of myocardial infarction, use with caution in patients with risk factors for coronary artery disease. May increase the risk of thromboembolism. Combination hormonal contraceptives may have a dose-related risk of vascular disease, hypertension, and gallbladder disease. Women with hypertension should be encouraged to use a nonhormonal form of contraception. The use of combination hormonal contraceptives has been associated with a slight increase in frequency of breast cancer, however, studies are not consistent. Combination hormonal contraceptives may cause glucose intolerance. Retinal thrombosis has been reported (rarely). Use with caution in patients with renal disease, conditions that may be aggravated by fluid retention, depression, or history of migraine. Not for use prior to menarche.

The minimum dosage combination of estrogen/progestin that will effectively treat the individual patient should be used. New patients should be started on products containing <50 mcg of estrogen per tablet.

Common Adverse Reactions Frequency not defined.

Cardiovascular: Arterial thromboembolism, cerebral hemorrhage, cerebral thrombosis, edema, hypertension, mesenteric thrombosis, myocardial infarction

Central nervous system: Depression, dizziness, headache, migraine, nervousness, premenstrual syndrome, stroke

Dermatologic: Acne, erythema multiforme, erythema nodosum, hirsutism, loss of scalp hair, melasma (may persist), rash (allergic)

Endocrine & metabolic: Amenorrhea, breakthrough bleeding, breast enlargement, breast secretion, breast tenderness, carbohydrate intolerance, lactation decreased (postpartum), glucose tolerance decreased, libido changes, menstrual flow changes, sex hormone-binding globulins (SHBG) increased, spotting, temporary infertility (following discontinuation), thyroid-binding globulin increased, triglycerides increased

Gastrointestinal: Abdominal cramps, appetite changes, bloating, cholestasis, colitis, gallbladder disease, jaundice, nausea, vomiting, weight gain/loss

Genitourinary: Cervical erosion changes, cervical secretion changes, cystitis-like syndrome, vaginal candidiasis, vaginitis

Hematologic: Antithrombin III decreased, folate levels decreased, hemolytic uremic syndrome, norepinephrine induced platelet aggregability increased, porphyria, prothrombin increased; factors VII, VIII, IX, and X increased

Hepatic: Benign liver tumors, Budd-Chiari syndrome, cholestatic jaundice, hepatic adenomas

Local: Thrombophlebitis

Ocular: Cataracts, change in corneal curvature (steepening), contact lens intolerance, optic neuritis, retinal thrombosis

Renal: Impaired renal function

Respiratory: Pulmonary thromboembolism

Miscellaneous: Hemorrhagic eruption

Drug Interactions

Cytochrome P450 Effect:

Mestranol: **Substrate** of CYP2C19 (major); Based on active metabolite ethinyl estradiol: **Substrate** of CYP3A4 (major), 3A5-7 (minor); **Inhibits** CYP1A2 (weak), 2B6 (weak), 2C19 (weak), 3A4 (weak)

Norethindrone: **Substrate** of CYP3A4 (major); **Induces** CYP2C19 (weak)

Increased Effect/Toxicity: CYP2C8/9 inhibitors may increase the levels of ethinyl estradiol (active metabolite of mestranol); example inhibitors include delavirdine, fluconazole, gemfibrozil, ketoconazole, nicardipine, NSAIDs, pioglitazone, and sulfonamides. Acetaminophen and ascorbic acid may increase plasma levels of estrogen component. Atorvastatin and indinavir increase plasma levels of combination hormonal contraceptives. Combination hormonal contraceptives increase the plasma levels of alprazolam, chlordiazepoxide, cyclosporine, diazepam, prednisolone, selegiline, theophylline, tricyclic antidepressants. Combination hormonal contraceptives may increase (or decrease) the effects of coumarin derivatives.

Decreased Effect: CYP3A4 inducers may decrease the levels of ethinyl estradiol (active metabolite of mestranol); example inducers include aminoglutethimide, carbamazepine, nafcillin, nevirapine, phenobarbital, phenytoin, and rifamycins. Combination hormonal contraceptives may decrease plasma levels of acetaminophen, clofibric acid, lorazepam, morphine, oxazepam, salicylic acid, temazepam. Contraceptive effect decreased by acitretin, aminoglutethimide, amprenavir, griseofulvin, lopinavir, nelfinavir, nevirapine, penicillins (effect not consistent), ritonavir, tetracyclines (effect not consistent) troglitazone. Combination hormonal contraceptives may decrease (or increase) the effects of coumarin derivatives.

Mechanism of Action Combination oral contraceptives inhibit ovulation via a negative feedback mechanism on the hypothalamus, which alters the normal pattern of gonadotropin secretion of a follicle-stimulating hormone (FSH) and luteinizing hormone by the anterior pituitary. The follicular phase FSH and midcycle surge of gonadotropins are inhibited. In addition, combination hormonal contraceptives produce alterations in the genital tract, including changes in the cervical mucus, rendering it unfavorable for sperm penetration even if ovulation occurs. Changes in the endometrium may also occur, producing an unfavorable environment for nidation. Combination hormonal contraceptive drugs may alter the tubal transport of the ova through the fallopian tubes. Progestational agents may also alter sperm fertility.

Pharmacodynamics/Kinetics
  Mestranol: Metabolism: Hepatic via demethylation to ethinyl estradiol
  Norethindrone: See Norethindrone monograph and Ethinyl Estradiol monograph for additional information.

Dosage Oral: Adults: Female: Contraception:
  Schedule 1 (Sunday starter): Dose begins on first Sunday after onset of menstruation; if the menstrual period starts on Sunday, take first tablet that very same day. **With a Sunday start, an additional method of contraception should be used until after the first 7 days of consecutive administration.**
    For 21-tablet package: Dosage is 1 tablet daily for 21 consecutive days, followed by 7 days off of the medication; a new course begins on the 8th day after the last tablet is taken.
    For 28-tablet package: Dosage is 1 tablet daily without interruption.
  Schedule 2 (Day 1 starter): Dose starts on first day of menstrual cycle taking 1 tablet daily.
    For 21-tablet package: Dosage is 1 tablet daily for 21 consecutive days, followed by 7 days off of the medication; a new course begins on the 8th day after the last tablet is taken.
    For 28-tablet package: Dosage is 1 tablet daily without interruption.
  If all doses have been taken on schedule and one menstrual period is missed, continue dosing cycle. If two consecutive menstrual periods are missed, pregnancy test is required before new dosing cycle is started.
  Missed doses **monophasic formulations** (refer to package insert for complete information):
    One dose missed: Take as soon as remembered or take 2 tablets next day
    Two consecutive doses missed in the first 2 weeks: Take 2 tablets as soon as remembered or 2 tablets next 2 days. **An additional method of contraception should be used for 7 days after missed dose.**
    Two consecutive doses missed in week 3 or three consecutive doses missed at any time: **An additional method of contraception must be used for 7 days after a missed dose:**
      Schedule 1 (Sunday starter): Continue dose of 1 tablet daily until Sunday, then discard the rest of the pack, and a new pack should be started that same day.
      Schedule 2 (Day 1 starter): Current pack should be discarded, and a new pack should be started that same day.
  Dosage adjustment in renal impairment: Specific guidelines not available; use with caution
  Dosage adjustment in hepatic impairment: Contraindicated in patients with hepatic impairment

Administration Administer at the same time each day.

Monitoring Parameters Blood pressure, breast exam, Pap smear, and pregnancy; lipid profiles in patients being treated for hyperlipidemias

Patient Information Take exactly as directed; use additional method of birth control during first week of administration of first cycle. Report signs or symptoms of any of the following: Thromboembolic or thrombotic disorders including sudden severe headache or vomiting, disturbance of vision or speech, loss of vision, numbness or weakness in an extremity, sharp or crushing chest pain, calf pain, shortness of breath, severe abdominal pain or mass, mental depression or unusual bleeding. Discontinue taking the medication if you suspect you are pregnant or become pregnant.

Dosage Forms TAB, monophasic (Necon® 1/50-21): Norethindrone 1 mg and mestranol 0.05 mg (21s); (Necon® 1/50-28, Norinyl® 1+50, Ortho-Novum® 1/50): Norethindrone 1 mg and mestranol 0.05 mg (28s)

♦ **Metacortandralone** see PrednisoLONE on page 1031
♦ **Metadate® CD** see Methylphenidate on page 822
♦ **Metadate™ ER** see Methylphenidate on page 822
♦ **Metaglip™** see Glipizide and Metformin on page 592
♦ **Metamucil® [OTC]** see Psyllium on page 1063
♦ **Metamucil® Smooth Texture [OTC]** see Psyllium on page 1063

Metaproterenol (met a proe TER e nol)

Related Information
  Bronchodilators, Comparison of Inhaled Sympathomimetics on page 1370

U.S. Brand Names Alupent®

Synonyms Metaproterenol Sulfate; Orciprenaline Sulfate

Therapeutic Category Beta₂-Adrenergic Agonist; Bronchodilator; Sympathomimetic Agent

Use Bronchodilator in reversible airway obstruction due to asthma or COPD; because of its delayed onset of action (1 hour) and prolonged effect (4 or more hours), this may not be the drug of choice for assessing response to a bronchodilator

Pregnancy Risk Factor C

Contraindications Hypersensitivity to metaproterenol or any component of the formulation; pre-existing cardiac arrhythmias associated with tachycardia
(Continued)

Metaproterenol *(Continued)*

Warnings/Precautions Optimize anti-inflammatory treatment before initiating maintenance treatment with metaproterenol. Do not use as a component of chronic therapy without an anti-inflammatory agent. Only the mildest form of asthma (Step 1 and/or exercise-induced) would not require concurrent use based upon asthma guidelines. Patient must be instructed to seek medical attention in cases where acute symptoms are not relieved or a previous level of response is diminished. The need to increase frequency of use may indicate deterioration of asthma, and treatment must not be delayed.

Use caution in patients with cardiovascular disease (arrhythmia or hypertension or CHF), convulsive disorders, diabetes, glaucoma, hyperthyroidism, or hypokalemia. Beta agonists may cause elevation in blood pressure, heart rate, and result in CNS stimulation/excitation. Beta$_2$ agonists may increase risk of arrhythmia, increase serum glucose, or decrease serum potassium.

Do not exceed recommended dose; serious adverse events including fatalities, have been associated with excessive use of inhaled sympathomimetics. Rarely, paradoxical broncho-spasm may occur with use of inhaled bronchodilating agents; this should be distinguished from inadequate response. All patients should utilize a spacer device when using a metered-dose inhaler; additionally, a face mask should be used in children <4 years of age.

Metaproterenol has more beta$_1$ activity than beta$_2$-selective agents such as albuterol and, therefore, may no longer be the beta agonist of first choice. Oral use should be avoided due to the increased incidence of adverse effects.

Common Adverse Reactions
>10%:
  Cardiovascular: Tachycardia (<17%)
  Central nervous system: Nervousness (3% to 14%)
  Endocrine & metabolic: Serum glucose increased, serum potassium decreased
  Neuromuscular & skeletal: Tremor (1% to 33%)
1% to 10%:
  Cardiovascular: Palpitations (<4%)
  Central nervous system: Headache (<4%), dizziness (1% to 4%), insomnia (2%)
  Gastrointestinal: Nausea, vomiting, bad taste, heartburn (≥4%), xerostomia
  Neuromuscular & skeletal: Trembling, muscle cramps, weakness (1%)
  Respiratory: Coughing, pharyngitis (≤4%)
  Miscellaneous: Diaphoresis (increased) (≤4%)

Drug Interactions
Increased Effect/Toxicity: Sympathomimetics, TCAs, MAO inhibitors taken with metapro-terenol may result in toxicity. Inhaled ipratropium may increase duration of bronchodilation. Halothane may increase risk of malignant arrhythmias; avoid concurrent use.
Decreased Effect: Decreased effect of beta-blockers.

Mechanism of Action
Relaxes bronchial smooth muscle by action on beta$_2$-receptors with very little effect on heart rate

Pharmacodynamics/Kinetics
Onset of action: Bronchodilation: Oral: ~15 minutes; Inhalation: ~60 seconds
  Peak effect: Oral: ~1 hour
Duration: ~1-5 hours

Dosage
Oral:
  Children:
    <2 years: 0.4 mg/kg/dose given 3-4 times/day; in infants, the dose can be given every 8-12 hours
    2-6 years: 1-2.6 mg/kg/day divided every 6 hours
    6-9 years: 10 mg/dose 3-4 times/day
  Children >9 years and Adults: 20 mg 3-4 times/day
  Elderly: Initial: 10 mg 3-4 times/day, increasing as necessary up to 20 mg 3-4 times/day
Inhalation: Children >12 years and Adults: 2-3 inhalations every 3-4 hours, up to 12 inhalations in 24 hours
Nebulizer:
  Infants and Children: 0.01-0.02 mL/kg of 5% solution; minimum dose: 0.1 mL; maximum dose: 0.3 mL diluted in 2-3 mL normal saline every 4-6 hours (may be given more frequently according to need)
  Adolescents and Adults: 5-20 breaths of full strength 5% metaproterenol **or** 0.2 to 0.3 mL 5% metaproterenol in 2.5-3 mL normal saline until nebulized every 4-6 hours (can be given more frequently according to need)

Administration
Inhalation: Do not use solutions for nebulization if they are brown or contain a precipitate. Shake inhaler well before using.
Oral: Administer around-the-clock to promote less variation in peak and trough serum levels

Monitoring Parameters Assess lung sounds, heart rate, and blood pressure before administration and during peak of medication; observe patient for wheezing after administration, if this occurs, call physician; monitor respiratory rate, arterial or capillary blood gases if applicable; FEV$_1$, peak flow, and/or other pulmonary function tests; CNS stimulation; serum glucose, serum potassium

Patient Information Do not exceed recommended dosage; excessive use may lead to adverse effects or loss of effectiveness. Shake canister well before use. Administer pressurized inhalation during the second half of inspiration, as the airways are open wider and the aerosol distribution is more extensive. If more than one inhalation per dose is necessary, wait at least 1 full minute between inhalations - second inhalation is best delivered after 10 minutes for Alupent®. May cause nervousness, restlessness, insomnia - if these effects continue after dosage reduction, notify prescriber. Also report palpitations, tachycardia, chest pain, muscle tremors, dizziness, headache, flushing, or if breathing difficulty persists.

Dosage Forms AERO, oral inhalation (Alupent®): 0.65 mg/inhalation (14 g). **SOLN, oral inhalation** [preservative free]: 0.4% [4 mg/mL] (2.5 mL); 0.6% [6 mg/mL] (2.5 mL); 5% [50 mg/mL] (10 mL, 30 mL). **SYR:** 10 mg/5 mL (480 mL). **TAB:** 10 mg, 20 mg

♦ **Metaproterenol Sulfate** *see* Metaproterenol *on page 803*

Metaraminol (met a RAM i nole)

Related Information
Hemodynamic Support, Intravenous *on page 1377*

U.S. Brand Names Aramine® [DSC]

Synonyms Metaraminol Bitartrate

Therapeutic Category Adrenergic Agonist Agent; Sympathomimetic Agent

Use Acute hypotensive crisis in the treatment of shock

Pregnancy Risk Factor D

Contraindications Hypersensitivity to metaraminol or any component of the formulation; cyclopropane or halothane anesthesia, or MAO inhibitors; pregnancy

Warnings/Precautions Can cause cardiac arrhythmias; use with caution in patients with a previous myocardial infarction, hypertension, hyperthyroidism; prolonged use may produce cumulative effects

Common Adverse Reactions Frequency not defined.
Cardiovascular: Tachycardia, hypertension, cardiac arrhythmias, flushing, palpitations, hypotension, angina
Central nervous system: Tremors, nervousness, headache, dizziness, weakness
Dermatologic: Sloughing of tissue
Gastrointestinal: Nausea
Local: Blanching of skin, abscess formation
Miscellaneous: Diaphoresis

Drug Interactions
Increased Effect/Toxicity: Increased toxicity with cyclopropane, halothane, MAO inhibitors (hypertensive crisis), digoxin, oxytocin, rauwolfia alkaloids, reserpine
Decreased Effect: Effect may be decreased by TCAs

Mechanism of Action Stimulates alpha-adrenergic receptors to cause vasoconstriction, reflex bradycardia, inhibits GI smooth muscle and vascular smooth muscle supplying skeletal muscle, increases heart rate and force of heart muscle contraction

Pharmacodynamics/Kinetics
Onset of action: Pressor effect: I.M.: ~10 minutes; I.V.: 1-2 minutes; S.C.: 5-20 minutes
Excretion: Not yet fully elucidated

Dosage
Children:
I.M.: 0.01 mg/kg as a single dose
I.V.: 0.01 mg/kg as a single dose or intravenous infusion of 5 mcg/kg/minute
Adults:
Prevention of hypotension: I.M., S.C.: 2-10 mg
Adjunctive treatment of hypotension: I.V.: 15-100 mg in 250-500 mL NS or 5% dextrose in water
Severe shock: I.V.: 0.5-5 mg direct I.V. injection followed by intravenous infusion of 15-100 mg in 250-500 mL NS or D₅W; may also be administered endotracheally

Administration May be administered I.M., I.V., S.C.; however, I.V. is the preferred route because extravasation or local injection can cause necrosis; to prevent necrosis infiltrate area with 10-15 mL of saline containing 5-10 mg of phentolamine

Monitoring Parameters Blood pressure, ECG, PCWP, CVP, pulse, and urine output

Dosage Forms INJ, solution [DSC]: 10 mg/mL (10 mL)

♦ **Metaraminol Bitartrate** *see* Metaraminol *on page 805*

♦ **Metastron®** *see* Strontium-89 *on page 1164*

Metaxalone (me TAKS a lone)

U.S. Brand Names Skelaxin®

Therapeutic Category Skeletal Muscle Relaxant

Use Relief of discomfort associated with acute, painful musculoskeletal conditions

Pregnancy Risk Factor C

Contraindications Hypersensitivity to metaxalone or any component of the formulation; impaired hepatic or renal function, history of drug-induced hemolytic anemias or other anemias

Warnings/Precautions Use with caution in patients with impaired hepatic function

Common Adverse Reactions Frequency not defined.
Central nervous system: Paradoxical stimulation, headache, drowsiness, dizziness, irritability
Dermatologic: Allergic dermatitis
Gastrointestinal: Nausea, vomiting, stomach cramps
Hematologic: Leukopenia, hemolytic anemia
Hepatic: Hepatotoxicity
Miscellaneous: Anaphylaxis
(Continued)

Metaxalone *(Continued)*

Drug Interactions
Increased Effect/Toxicity: Additive effects with ethanol or CNS depressants

Mechanism of Action Does not have a direct effect on skeletal muscle; most of its therapeutic effect comes from actions on the central nervous system

Pharmacodynamics/Kinetics
Onset of action: ~1 hour
Duration: ~4-6 hours
Metabolism: Hepatic
Bioavailability: Not established; food may increase
Half-life elimination: 9 hours
Time to peak: T_{max}: 3 hours
Excretion: Urine (as metabolites)

Dosage Children >12 years and Adults: Oral: 800 mg 3-4 times/day

Administration May be administered with or without food. However, serum concentrations may be increased when administered with food; clinical significance has not been established. Patients should be monitored.

Patient Information Avoid alcohol and other CNS depressants; may cause drowsiness, impairment of judgment, or coordination; report dark urine, pale stools, yellowing of eyes, severe nausea, vomiting, or abdominal pain

Dosage Forms TAB: 400 mg, 800 mg

Metformin *(met FOR min)*

Related Information
Hypoglycemic Drugs & Thiazolidinedione Information *on page 1378*

U.S. Brand Names Glucophage®; Glucophage® XR; Riomet™

Synonyms Metformin Hydrochloride

Therapeutic Category Antidiabetic Agent, Biguanide; Hypoglycemic Agent, Oral

Use Management of type 2 diabetes mellitus (noninsulin dependent, NIDDM) as monotherapy when hyperglycemia cannot be managed on diet alone. May be used concomitantly with a sulfonylurea or insulin to improve glycemic control.

Unlabeled/Investigational Use Treatment of HIV lipodystrophy syndrome

Pregnancy Risk Factor B

Contraindications Hypersensitivity to metformin or any component of the formulation; renal disease or renal dysfunction (serum creatinine ≥1.5 mg/dL in males or ≥1.4 mg/dL in females or abnormal creatinine clearance from any cause, including shock, acute myocardial infarction, or septicemia); congestive heart failure requiring pharmacological management; acute or chronic metabolic acidosis with or without coma (including diabetic ketoacidosis)

Note: Temporarily discontinue in patients undergoing radiologic studies in which intravascular iodinated contrast materials are utilized.

Warnings/Precautions Lactic acidosis is a rare, but potentially severe consequence of therapy with metformin. Lactic acidosis should be suspected in any diabetic patient receiving metformin who has evidence of acidosis when evidence of ketoacidosis is lacking. Discontinue metformin in clinical situations predisposing to hypoxemia, including conditions such as cardiovascular collapse, respiratory failure, acute myocardial infarction, acute congestive heart failure, and septicemia.

Metformin is substantially excreted by the kidney. The risk of accumulation and lactic acidosis increases with the degree of impairment of renal function. Patients with renal function below the limit of normal for their age should not receive metformin. In elderly patients, renal function should be monitored regularly; should not be used in any patient ≥80 years of age unless measurement of creatinine clearance verifies normal renal function. Use of concomitant medications that may affect renal function (ie, affect tubular secretion) may also affect metformin disposition. Metformin should be suspended in patients with dehydration and/or prerenal azotemia. Therapy should be suspended for any surgical procedures (resume only after normal intake resumed and normal renal function is verified). Metformin should also be temporarily discontinued for 48 hours in patients undergoing radiologic studies involving the intravascular administration of iodinated contrast materials (potential for acute alteration in renal function).

Avoid use in patients with impaired liver function. Patient must be instructed to avoid excessive acute or chronic ethanol use. Administration of oral antidiabetic drugs has been reported to be associated with increased cardiovascular mortality; metformin does not appear to share this risk. Safety and efficacy of metformin have been established for use in children ≥10 years of age; the extended release preparation is for use in patients ≥17 years of age.

Common Adverse Reactions
>10%:
Gastrointestinal: Nausea/vomiting (6% to 25%), diarrhea (10% to 53%), flatulence (12%)
Neuromuscular & skeletal: Weakness (9%)
1% to 10%:
Cardiovascular: Chest discomfort, flushing, palpitation
Central nervous system: Headache (6%), chills, dizziness, lightheadedness
Dermatologic: Rash
Endocrine & metabolic: Hypoglycemia
Gastrointestinal: Indigestion (7%), abdominal discomfort (6%), abdominal distention, abnormal stools, constipation, dyspepsia/ heartburn, taste disorder
Neuromuscular & skeletal: Myalgia

Respiratory: Dyspnea, upper respiratory tract infection

Miscellaneous: Decreased vitamin B_{12} levels (7%), increased diaphoresis, flu-like syndrome, nail disorder

Drug Interactions

Increased Effect/Toxicity: Furosemide and cimetidine may increase metformin blood levels. Cationic drugs (eg, amiloride, digoxin, morphine, procainamide, quinidine, quinine, ranitidine, triamterene, trimethoprim, and vancomycin) which are eliminated by renal tubular secretion have the potential to increase metformin levels by competing for common renal tubular transport systems. Contrast agents may increase the risk of metformin-induced lactic acidosis; discontinue metformin prior to exposure and withhold for 48 hours.

Decreased Effect: Drugs which tend to produce hyperglycemia (eg, diuretics, corticosteroids, phenothiazines, thyroid products, estrogens, oral contraceptives, phenytoin, nicotinic acid, sympathomimetics, calcium channel blocking drugs, isoniazid) may lead to a loss of glucose control.

Mechanism of Action Decreases hepatic glucose production, decreasing intestinal absorption of glucose and improves insulin sensitivity (increases peripheral glucose uptake and utilization)

Pharmacodynamics/Kinetics

Onset of action: Within days; maximum effects up to 2 weeks

Distribution: V_d: 654 ± 358 L

Protein binding: 92% to 99%; Plasma: negligible

Bioavailability: Absolute: Fasting: 50% to 60%

Half-life elimination, plasma: 6.2 hours

Excretion: Urine (90% as unchanged drug)

Dosage Note: Allow 1-2 weeks between dose titrations: Generally, clinically significant responses are not seen at doses <1500 mg daily; however, a lower recommended starting dose and gradual increased dosage is recommended to minimize gastrointestinal symptoms

Children 10-16 years: Management of type 2 diabetes mellitus: Oral (500 mg tablet or oral solution): Initial: 500 mg twice daily (given with the morning and evening meals); increases in daily dosage should be made in increments of 500 mg at weekly intervals, given in divided doses, up to a maximum of 2000 mg/day

Adults ≥17 years: Management of type 2 diabetes mellitus: Oral:

Immediate release tablet or oral solution: Initial: 500 mg twice daily (give with the morning and evening meals) **or** 850 mg once daily; increase dosage incrementally.

Incremental dosing recommendations based on dosage form:

500 mg tablet: One tablet/day at weekly intervals

850 mg tablet: One tablet/day every other week

Oral solution: 500 mg twice daily every other week

Doses of up to 2000 mg/day may be given twice daily. If a dose > 2000 mg/day is required, it may be better tolerated in three divided doses. Maximum recommended dose 2550 mg/day.

Extended release tablet: Initial: 500 mg once daily (with the evening meal); dosage may be increased by 500 mg weekly; maximum dose: 2000 mg once daily. If glycemic control is not achieved at maximum dose, may divide dose to 1000 mg twice daily. If doses >2000 mg/day are needed, switch to regular release tablets and titrate to maximum dose of 2550 mg/day.

Elderly: The initial and maintenance dosing should be conservative, due to the potential for decreased renal function. Generally, elderly patients should not be titrated to the maximum dose of metformin. Do not use in patients ≥80 years of age unless normal renal function has been established.

Transfer from other antidiabetic agents: No transition period is generally necessary except when transferring from chlorpropamide. When transferring from chlorpropamide, care should be exercised during the first 2 weeks because of the prolonged retention of chlorpropamide in the body, leading to overlapping drug effects and possible hypoglycemia.

Concomitant metformin and oral sulfonylurea therapy: If patients have not responded to 4 weeks of the maximum dose of metformin monotherapy, consider a gradual addition of an oral sulfonylurea, even if prior primary or secondary failure to a sulfonylurea has occurred. Continue metformin at the maximum dose.

Failed sulfonylurea therapy: Patients with prior failure on glyburide may be treated by gradual addition of metformin. Initiate glyburide 20 mg and metformin 500 mg daily. Metformin dosage may be increased by 500 mg/day at weekly intervals, up to a maximum of 2500 mg/day (dosage of glyburide maintained at 20 mg/day).

Concomitant metformin and insulin therapy: Initial: 500 mg metformin once daily, continue current insulin dose; increase by 500 mg metformin weekly until adequate glycemic control is achieved

Maximum dose: 2500 mg metformin; 2000 mg metformin extended release

Decrease insulin dose 10% to 25% when FPG <120 mg/dL; monitor and make further adjustments as needed

Dosing adjustment/comments in renal impairment: The plasma and blood half-life of metformin is prolonged and the renal clearance is decreased in proportion to the decrease in creatinine clearance. Per the manufacturer, metformin is contraindicated in the presence of renal dysfunction defined as a serum creatinine >1.5 mg/dL in males, or >1.4 mg/dL in females and in patients with abnormal clearance. Clinically, it has been recommended that metformin be avoided in patients with Cl_{cr} <60-70 mL/minute (DeFronzo, 1999).

Dosing adjustment in hepatic impairment: Avoid metformin; liver disease is a risk factor for the development of lactic acidosis during metformin therapy.

(Continued)

Metformin *(Continued)*

Administration Extended release dosage form should be swallowed whole; do not crush, break, or chew

Monitoring Parameters Urine for glucose and ketones, fasting blood glucose, and hemoglobin A_{1c}. Initial and periodic monitoring of hematologic parameters (eg, hemoglobin/hematocrit and red blood cell indices) and renal function should be performed, at least annually. Check vitamin B_{12} and folate if anemia is present.

Reference Range Target range: Adults:
Fasting blood glucose: <120 mg/dL
Glycosylated hemoglobin: <7%

Patient Information Patients must be counseled by someone experienced in diabetes education, signs and symptoms of hyper- and hypoglycemia, exercise and diet, blood glucose monitoring, and other related topics; eat regularly, do not skip meals; carry quick source of sugar; medical alert bracelet. Patients should be counselled against excessive alcohol intake while receiving metformin. Metformin alone does not usually cause hypoglycemia, although it may occur in conjunction with oral sulfonylureas.

Dosage Forms SOLN, oral (Riomet™): 100 mg/mL (118 mL, 473 mL). **TAB** (Glucophage®): 500 mg, 850 mg, 1000 mg. **TAB, extended release** (Glucophage® XR): 500 mg, 750 mg

- **Metformin and Glipizide** *see Glipizide and Metformin on page 592*
- **Metformin and Glyburide** *see Glyburide and Metformin on page 595*
- **Metformin and Rosiglitazone** *see Rosiglitazone and Metformin on page 1117*
- **Metformin Hydrochloride** *see Metformin on page 806*
- **Metformin Hydrochloride and Rosiglitazone Maleate** *see Rosiglitazone and Metformin on page 1117*

Methacholine (meth a KOLE leen)

U.S. Brand Names Provocholine®

Synonyms Methacholine Chloride

Therapeutic Category Cholinergic Agent; Diagnostic Agent, Bronchial Airway Hyperactivity

Use Diagnosis of bronchial airway hyperactivity

Pregnancy Risk Factor C

Dosage Before inhalation challenge, perform baseline pulmonary function tests; the patient must have a FEV_1 of at least 70% of the predicted value. The following is a suggested schedule for administration of methacholine challenge. Calculate cumulative units by multiplying number of breaths by concentration given. Total cumulative units is the sum of cumulative units for each concentration given. See table.

Methacholine

Vial	Serial Concentration (mg/mL)	No. of Breaths	Cumulative Units per Concentration	Total Cumulative Units
E	0.025	5	0.125	0.125
D	0.25	5	1.25	1.375
C	2.5	5	12.5	13.88
B	10	5	50	63.88
A	25	5	125	188.88

Determine FEV_1 within 5 minutes of challenge, a positive challenge is a 20% reduction in FEV_1

Dosage Forms POWDER, oral inhalation: 100 mg

- **Methacholine Chloride** *see Methacholine on page 808*

Methadone (METH a done)

Related Information
Narcotic Agonists Comparison *on page 1395*

U.S. Brand Names Dolophine®; Methadone Intensol™; Methadose®

Synonyms Methadone Hydrochloride

Therapeutic Category Analgesic, Narcotic

Use Management of severe pain; detoxification and maintenance treatment of narcotic addiction (if used for detoxification and maintenance treatment of narcotic addiction, it must be part of an FDA-approved program)

Restrictions C-II

Pregnancy Risk Factor B/D (prolonged use or high doses at term)

Contraindications Hypersensitivity to methadone or any component of the formulation; pregnancy (prolonged use or high doses near term)

Warnings/Precautions An opioid-containing analgesic regimen should be tailored to each patient's needs and based upon the type of pain being treated (acute versus chronic), the route of administration, degree of tolerance for opioids (naive versus chronic user), age, weight, and medical condition. The optimal analgesic dose varies widely among patients. Doses should be titrated to pain relief/prevention.

Tablets are to be used only for oral administration and **must not** be used for injection; use with caution in patients with respiratory diseases including asthma, emphysema, or COPD and in patients with severe liver disease; because methadone's effects on respiration last much longer than its analgesic effects, the dose must be titrated slowly; because of its long half-life and risk of accumulation, it is not considered a drug of first choice in the elderly, who may be particularly susceptible to its CNS depressant and constipating effects; tolerance or drug dependence may result from extended use.

Common Adverse Reactions Frequency not defined.

Cardiovascular: Bradycardia, peripheral vasodilation, cardiac arrest, syncope, faintness

Central nervous system: Euphoria, dysphoria, headache, insomnia, agitation, disorientation, drowsiness, dizziness, lightheadedness, sedation

Dermatologic: Pruritus, urticaria, rash

Endocrine & metabolic: Decreased libido

Gastrointestinal: Nausea, vomiting, constipation, anorexia, stomach cramps, xerostomia, biliary tract spasm

Genitourinary: Urinary retention or hesitancy, antidiuretic effect, impotence

Neuromuscular & skeletal: Weakness

Ocular: Miosis, visual disturbances

Respiratory: Respiratory depression, respiratory arrest

Miscellaneous: Physical and psychological dependence

Drug Interactions

Cytochrome P450 Effect: Substrate of CYP2C8/9 (minor), 2C19 (minor), 2D6 (minor), 3A4 (major); **Inhibits** CYP2D6 (moderate), 3A4 (weak)

Increased Effect/Toxicity: Fluconazole, itraconazole, and ketoconazole increase serum methadone concentrations via CYP3A4 inhibition; an increased narcotic effect may be experienced. Similar effects may be seen with ritonavir, nelfinavir, amiodarone, erythromycin, clarithromycin, diltiazem, verapamil, paroxetine, fluoxetine, and other inhibitors of CYP2D6 or CYP3A4.

Decreased Effect: Barbiturates, carbamazepine, nevirapine, phenytoin, primidone, rifampin and ritonavir may decrease serum methadone concentrations via enhanced hepatic metabolism; monitor for methadone withdrawal. Larger doses of methadone may be required.

Mechanism of Action Binds to opiate receptors in the CNS, causing inhibition of ascending pain pathways, altering the perception of and response to pain; produces generalized CNS depression

Pharmacodynamics/Kinetics

Onset of action: Oral: Analgesic: 0.5-1 hour; Parenteral: 10-20 minutes

Peak effect: Parenteral: 1-2 hours

Duration: Oral: 6-8 hours, increases to 22-48 hours with repeated doses

Distribution: Crosses placenta; enters breast milk

Protein binding: 80% to 85%

Metabolism: Hepatic via N-demethylation

Half-life elimination: 15-29 hours; may be prolonged with alkaline pH

Excretion: Urine (<10% as unchanged drug); increased with urine pH <6

Dosage Note: These are guidelines and do not represent the maximum doses that may be required in all patients Methadone accumulates with repeated doses and dosage may need reduction after 3-5 days to prevent CNS depressant effects. Some patients may benefit from every 8-12 hour dosing interval for chronic pain management. Doses should be titrated to appropriate effects.

Children:

Pain (analgesia):

Oral, I.M., S.C.: 0.7 mg/kg/24 hours divided every 4-6 hours as needed or 0.1-0.2 mg/kg every 4-12 hours as needed; maximum: 10 mg/dose

I.V.: 0.1 mg/kg every 4 hours initially for 2-3 doses, then every 6-12 hours as needed; maximum: 10 mg/dose

Iatrogenic narcotic dependency: Oral: General guidelines: Initial: 0.05-0.1 mg/kg/dose every 6 hours; increase by 0.05 mg/kg/dose until withdrawal symptoms are controlled; after 24-48 hours, the dosing interval can be lengthened to every 12-24 hours; to taper dose, wean by 0.05 mg/kg/day; if withdrawal symptoms recur, taper at a slower rate

Adults:

Pain (analgesia):

Oral: Initial: 2.5-5 mg every 3-8 hours as needed; patients with prior opiate exposure may require higher initial doses; usual dosage range: 2.5-20 mg every 3-8 hours as needed

I.M., S.C.: 2.5-10 mg every 6-8 hours as needed; patients with prior opiate exposure may require higher initial doses

Detoxification: Oral: 15-40 mg/day

Maintenance treatment of opiate dependence: Oral: 20-120 mg/day

Dosing adjustment in renal impairment: Cl_{cr} <10 mL/minute: Administer at 50% to 75% of normal dose

Dosing adjustment/comments in hepatic disease: Avoid in severe liver disease

Monitoring Parameters Pain relief, respiratory and mental status, blood pressure

Reference Range Therapeutic: 100-400 ng/mL (SI: 0.32-1.29 µmol/L); Toxic: >2 µg/mL (SI: >6.46 µmol/L)

Patient Information May cause drowsiness, avoid alcohol and other CNS depressants

Dosage Forms INJ, as solution (Dolophine®): 10 mg/mL (20 mL). **SOLN, oral:** 5 mg/5 mL (500 mL); 10 mg/5 mL (500 mL). **SOLN, oral concentrate:** (Methadone Intensol™, Methadose®): 10 mg/mL (30 mL). **TAB** (Dolophine®, Methadose®): 5 mg, 10 mg. **TAB, dispersible** (Methadose®): 40 mg

♦ **Methadone Hydrochloride** *see* Methadone *on page 808*

♦ **Methadone Intensol™** *see* Methadone *on page 808*

♦ **Methadose®** *see* Methadone *on page 808*

♦ **Methaminodiazepoxide Hydrochloride** *see* Chlordiazepoxide *on page 258*

Methamphetamine (meth am FET a meen)

Related Information
Obesity Treatment Guidelines for Adults *on page 1482*

U.S. Brand Names Desoxyn®

Synonyms Desoxyephedrine Hydrochloride; Methamphetamine Hydrochloride

Therapeutic Category Amphetamine; Central Nervous System Stimulant, Amphetamine

Use Treatment of attention-deficit/hyperactivity disorder (ADHD); exogenous obesity (short-term adjunct)

Unlabeled/Investigational Use Narcolepsy

Restrictions C-II

Pregnancy Risk Factor C

Contraindications Hypersensitivity or idiosyncrasy to amphetamines or other sympathomimetic amines; patients with advanced arteriosclerosis, symptomatic cardiovascular disease, moderate to severe hypertension (stage II or III), hyperthyroidism, glaucoma, agitated states; patients with a history of drug abuse; use during or within 14 days following MAO inhibitor therapy; stimulant medications are contraindicated for use in children with attention-deficit/ hyperactivity disorders and concomitant Tourette's syndrome or tics

Warnings/Precautions Use with caution in patients with bipolar disorder, diabetes mellitus, cardiovascular disease, seizure disorders, insomnia, porphyria, or mild hypertension (stage I). May exacerbate symptoms of behavior and thought disorder in psychotic patients. Potential for drug dependency exists - avoid abrupt discontinuation in patients who have received for prolonged periods. Use in weight reduction programs only when alternative therapy has been ineffective. Stimulant use in children has been associated with growth suppression. Stimulants may unmask tics in individuals with coexisting Tourette's syndrome.

Common Adverse Reactions Frequency not defined.
Cardiovascular: Hypertension, tachycardia, palpitations
Central nervous system: Restlessness, headache, exacerbation of motor and phonic tics and Tourette's syndrome, dizziness, psychosis, dysphoria, overstimulation, euphoria, insomnia
Dermatologic: Rash, urticaria
Endocrine & metabolic: Change in libido
Gastrointestinal: Diarrhea, nausea, vomiting, stomach cramps, constipation, anorexia, weight loss, xerostomia, unpleasant taste
Genitourinary: Impotence
Neuromuscular & skeletal: Tremor
Miscellaneous: Suppression of growth in children, tolerance and withdrawal with prolonged use

Drug Interactions
Cytochrome P450 Effect: Substrate of CYP2D6 (major)

Increased Effect/Toxicity: Amphetamines may precipitate hypertensive crisis or serotonin syndrome in patients receiving MAO inhibitors (selegiline >10 mg/day, isocarboxazid, phenelzine, tranylcypromine, furazolidone). Serotonin syndrome has also been associated with combinations of amphetamines and SSRIs; these combinations should be avoided. TCAs may enhance the effects of amphetamines, potentially leading to hypertensive crisis. CYP2D6 inhibitors may increase the levels/effects of methamphetamine; example inhibitors include chlorpromazine, delavirdine, fluoxetine, miconazole, paroxetine, pergolide, quinidine, quinine, ritonavir, and ropinirole. Large doses of antacids or urinary alkalinizers increase the half-life and duration of action of amphetamines. May precipitate arrhythmias in patients receiving general anesthetics. Inhibitors of CYP2D6 may increase the effects of amphetamines (includes amiodarone, cimetidine, delavirdine, fluoxetine, paroxetine, propafenone, quinidine, and ritonavir).

Decreased Effect: Amphetamines inhibit the antihypertensive response to guanethidine and guanadrel. Urinary acidifiers decrease the half-life and duration of action of amphetamines. Enzyme inducers (barbiturates, carbamazepine, phenytoin, and rifampin) may decrease serum concentrations of amphetamines.

Mechanism of Action A sympathomimetic amine related to ephedrine and amphetamine with CNS stimulant activity; peripheral actions include elevation of systolic and diastolic blood pressure and weak bronchodilator and respiratory stimulant action

Pharmacodynamics/Kinetics
Absorption: Rapid from GI tract
Metabolism: Hepatic
Half-Life elimination: 4-5 hours
Excretion: Urine primarily (dependent on urine pH)

Dosage Oral:
Children >6 years and Adults: ADHD: 2.5-5 mg 1-2 times/day; may increase by 5 mg increments at weekly intervals until optimum response is achieved, usually 20-25 mg/day
Children >12 years and Adults: Exogenous obesity: 5 mg 30 minutes before each meal; treatment duration should not exceed a few weeks

Monitoring Parameters Heart rate, respiratory rate, blood pressure, and CNS activity

Patient Information Take during day to avoid insomnia; do not discontinue abruptly, may cause physical and psychological dependence with prolonged use

Dosage Forms TAB: 5 mg

♦ **Methamphetamine Hydrochloride** *see* Methamphetamine *on page 810*

Methazolamide (meth a ZOE la mide)
Related Information
Glaucoma Drug Therapy Comparison *on page 1481*
Sulfonamide Derivatives *on page 1404*
U.S. Brand Names Neptazane® [DSC]
Therapeutic Category Carbonic Anhydrase Inhibitor; Diuretic, Carbonic Anhydrase Inhibitor
Use Adjunctive treatment of open-angle or secondary glaucoma; short-term therapy of narrow-angle glaucoma when delay of surgery is desired
Pregnancy Risk Factor C
Contraindications Hypersensitivity to methazolamide or any component of the formulation; marked kidney or liver dysfunction; severe pulmonary obstruction
Warnings/Precautions Sulfonamide-type reactions, melena, anorexia, nausea, vomiting, constipation, hematuria, glycosuria, urinary frequency, renal colic, renal calculi, crystalluria, polyuria, hepatic insufficiency, various CNS effects, transient myopia, bone marrow suppression, thrombocytopenia/purpura, hemolytic anemia, leukopenia, pancytopenia, agranulocytosis, urticaria, pruritus, rash, Stevens-Johnson syndrome, weight loss, fever, acidosis; use with caution in patients with respiratory acidosis and diabetes mellitus; impairment of mental alertness and/or physical coordination. Malaise and complaints of tiredness and myalgia are signs of excessive dosing and acidosis in the elderly.

Chemical similarities are present among sulfonamides, sulfonylureas, carbonic anhydrase inhibitors, thiazides, and loop diuretics (except ethacrynic acid). In patients with allergy to one of these compounds, a risk of cross-reaction exists; avoid use when previous reaction has been severe.
Common Adverse Reactions Frequency not defined.
Central nervous system: Malaise, fever, mental depression, drowsiness, dizziness, nervousness, headache, confusion, seizures, fatigue, trembling, unsteadiness
Dermatologic: Urticaria, pruritus, photosensitivity, rash, Stevens-Johnson syndrome
Endocrine & metabolic: Hyperchloremic metabolic acidosis, hypokalemia, hyperglycemia
Gastrointestinal: Metallic taste, anorexia, nausea, vomiting, diarrhea, constipation, weight loss, GI irritation, xerostomia, black tarry stools
Genitourinary: Polyuria, crystalluria, hematuria, polyuria, renal calculi, impotence
Hematologic: Bone marrow depression, thrombocytopenia, thrombocytopenic purpura, hemolytic anemia, leukopenia, pancytopenia, agranulocytosis
Hepatic: Hepatic insufficiency
Neuromuscular & skeletal: Weakness, ataxia, paresthesias
Miscellaneous: Hypersensitivity
Drug Interactions
Increased Effect/Toxicity: Methazolamide may induce hypokalemia which would sensitize a patient to digitalis toxicity. Hypokalemia may be compounded with concurrent diuretic use or steroids. Methazolamide may increase the potential for salicylate toxicity. Primidone absorption may be delayed.
Decreased Effect: Increased lithium excretion and altered excretion of other drugs by alkalinization of the urine, such as amphetamines, quinidine, procainamide, methenamine, phenobarbital, and salicylates.
Mechanism of Action Noncompetitive inhibition of the enzyme carbonic anhydrase; thought that carbonic anhydrase is located at the luminal border of cells of the proximal tubule. When the enzyme is inhibited there is an increase in urine volume and a change to an alkaline pH with a subsequent decrease in the excretion of titratable acid and ammonia.
Pharmacodynamics/Kinetics
Onset of action: Slow in comparison with acetazolamide (2-4 hours)
Peak effect: 6-8 hours
Duration: 10-18 hours
Absorption: Slow
Distribution: Well into tissue
Protein binding: ~55%
Metabolism: Slowly from GI tract
Half-life elimination: ~14 hours
Excretion: Urine (~25% as unchanged drug)
Dosage Adults: Oral: 50-100 mg 2-3 times/day
Patient Information Take with food; report any numbness or tingling in extremities; may cause drowsiness, impaired judgment or coordination
Dosage Forms TAB: 25 mg, 50 mg

Methenamine (meth EN a meen)
U.S. Brand Names Hiprex®; Mandelamine®; Urex®
Synonyms Hexamethylenetetramine; Methenamine Hippurate; Methenamine Mandelate
Therapeutic Category Antibiotic, Miscellaneous
Use Prophylaxis or suppression of recurrent urinary tract infections; urinary tract discomfort secondary to hypermotility
Pregnancy Risk Factor C
Contraindications Hypersensitivity to methenamine or any component of the formulation; severe dehydration, renal insufficiency, hepatic insufficiency in patients receiving hippurate salt; patients receiving sulfonamides
Warnings/Precautions Use with caution in patients with hepatic disease, gout, and the elderly; doses of 8 g/day for 3-4 weeks may cause bladder irritation; methenamine should not
(Continued)

Methenamine *(Continued)*

be used to treat infections outside of the lower urinary tract. Use care to maintain an acid pH of the urine, especially when treating infections due to urea splitting organisms (eg, *Proteus* and strains of *Pseudomonas*); reversible increases in LFTs have occurred during therapy especially in patients with hepatic dysfunction. Hiprex® contains tartrazine dye.

Common Adverse Reactions 1% to 10%:
Dermatologic: Rash (4%)
Gastrointestinal: Nausea, dyspepsia (4%)
Genitourinary: Dysuria (4%)

Drug Interactions
Increased Effect/Toxicity: Sulfonamides may precipitate in the urine.
Decreased Effect: Sodium bicarbonate and acetazolamide will decrease effect secondary to alkalinization of urine.

Mechanism of Action Methenamine is hydrolyzed to formaldehyde and ammonia in acidic urine; formaldehyde has nonspecific bactericidal action

Pharmacodynamics/Kinetics
Absorption: Readily
Metabolism: Gastric juices: Hydrolyze 10% to 30% unless protected via enteric coating; Hepatic: ~10% to 25%
Half-life elimination: 3-6 hours
Excretion: Urine (~70% to 90% as unchanged drug) within 24 hours

Dosage Oral:
Children:
<6 years: 0.25 g/30 lb 4 times/day
6-12 years:
Hippurate: 25-50 mg/kg/day divided every 12 hours or 0.5-1 g twice daily
Mandelate: 50-75 mg/kg/day divided every 6 hours or 0.5 g 4 times/day
Children >12 years and Adults:
Hippurate: 1 g twice daily
Mandelate: 1 g 4 times/day after meals and at bedtime
Dosing adjustment/comments in renal impairment: Cl$_{cr}$ <50 mL/minute: Avoid use

Monitoring Parameters Urinalysis, periodic liver function tests in patients

Patient Information Take with food to minimize GI upset; take with ascorbic acid to acidify urine; drink sufficient fluids to ensure adequate urine flow. Avoid excessive intake of alkalinizing foods (citrus fruits and milk products) or medication (bicarbonate, acetazolamide); report skin rash, painful urination or excessive abdominal pain.

Dosage Forms TAB, as hippurate (Hiprex®, Urex®): 1 g. **TAB, enteric coated, as mandelate** (Mandelamine®): 500 mg, 1 g

♦ **Methenamine Hippurate** *see* Methenamine *on page 811*
♦ **Methenamine Mandelate** *see* Methenamine *on page 811*

Methenamine, Sodium Biphosphate, Phenyl Salicylate, Methylene Blue, and Hyoscyamine

(meth EN a meen, SOW dee um bye FOS fate, fen nil sa LIS i late, METH i leen bloo, & hye oh SYE a meen)

U.S. Brand Names Urimar-T; Urimax®

Synonyms Hyoscyamine, Methenamine, Sodium Biphosphate, Phenyl Salicylate, and Methylene Blue; Methylene Blue, Methenamine, Sodium Biphosphate, Phenyl Salicylate, and Hyoscyamine; Phenyl Salicylate, Methenamine, Methylene Blue, Sodium Biphosphate, and Hyoscyamine; Sodium Biphosphate, Methenamine, Methylene Blue, Phenyl Salicylate, and Hyoscyamine

Therapeutic Category Antibiotic, Miscellaneous

Use Treatment of symptoms of irritative voiding; relief of local symptoms associated with urinary tract infections; relief of urinary tract symptoms caused by diagnostic procedures

Pregnancy Risk Factor C

Contraindications Hypersensitivity to methenamine, hyoscyamine, methylene blue, or any component of the formulation

Warnings/Precautions Use caution in patients with a history of intolerance to belladonna alkaloids or salicylates. Use caution in patients with cardiovascular disease (cardiac arrhythmias, CHF, coronary heart disease, mitral stenosis), gastrointestinal tract obstruction, glaucoma, myasthenia gravis, or obstructive uropathy (bladder neck obstruction or prostatic hypertrophy). Discontinue use immediately if tachycardia, dizziness, or blurred vision occur. Elderly may be more sensitive to anticholinergic effects of hyoscyamine; use caution. May cause urinary discoloration (blue). Safety and efficacy have not been established in children ≤6 years of age.

Common Adverse Reactions Frequency not defined.
Cardiovascular: Tachycardia, flushing
Central nervous system: Dizziness
Gastrointestinal: Xerostomia, nausea, vomiting
Genitourinary: Urinary retention (acute), micturition difficulty, discoloration of urine (blue)
Ocular: Blurred vision
Respiratory: Dyspnea, shortness of breath

Drug Interactions
Increased Effect/Toxicity: Refer to individual monographs for Hyoscyamine and Methenamine.

Decreased Effect: Refer to individual monographs for Hyoscyamine and Methenamine.

Dosage Oral:
Children >6 years: Dosage must be individualized
Adults: One tablet 4 times daily (followed by liberal fluid intake)

Dosage Forms TAB, delayed release [film coated] (Urimax®): Methenamine 81.6 mg, sodium biphosphate 40 8 mg, phenyl salicylate 36.2 mg, methylene blue 10.8 mg, hyoscyamine sulfate 0.12 mg. **TAB** [sugar coated] (Urimar-T): Methenamine 81.6 mg, sodium biphosphate 40.8 mg, phenyl salicylate 36.2 mg, methylene blue 10.8 mg, hyoscyamine sulfate 0.12 mg

♦ **Methergine®** see Methylergonovine on page 821

Methimazole (meth IM a zole)
U.S. Brand Names Tapazole®

Synonyms Thiamazole

Therapeutic Category Antithyroid Agent

Use Palliative treatment of hyperthyroidism, return the hyperthyroid patient to a normal metabolic state prior to thyroidectomy, and to control thyrotoxic crisis that may accompany thyroidectomy. The use of antithyroid thioamides is as effective in elderly as they are in younger adults; however, the expense, potential adverse effects, and inconvenience (compliance, monitoring) make them undesirable. The use of radioiodine due to ease of administration and less concern for long-term side effects and reproduction problems (some older males) makes it a more appropriate therapy.

Pregnancy Risk Factor D

Contraindications Hypersensitivity to methimazole or any component of the formulation; nursing mothers (per manufacturer; however, expert analysis and the AAP state this drug may be used with caution in nursing mothers); pregnancy

Warnings/Precautions Use with extreme caution in patients receiving other drugs known to cause myelosuppression particularly agranulocytosis, patients >40 years of age; avoid doses >40 mg/day (↑ myelosuppression); may cause acneiform eruptions or worsen the condition of the thyroid

Common Adverse Reactions Frequency not defined.
Cardiovascular: Edema
Central nervous system: Headache, vertigo, drowsiness, CNS stimulation, depression
Dermatologic: Skin rash, urticaria, pruritus, erythema nodosum, skin pigmentation, exfoliative dermatitis, alopecia
Endocrine & metabolic: Goiter
Gastrointestinal: Nausea, vomiting, stomach pain, abnormal taste, constipation, weight gain, salivary gland swelling
Hematologic: Leukopenia, agranulocytosis, granulocytopenia, thrombocytopenia, aplastic anemia, hypoprothrombinemia
Hepatic: Cholestatic jaundice, jaundice, hepatitis
Neuromuscular & skeletal: Arthralgia, paresthesia
Renal: Nephrotic syndrome
Miscellaneous: SLE-like syndrome

Drug Interactions
Cytochrome P450 Effect: Inhibits CYP1A2 (weak), 2A6 (weak), 2B6 (weak), 2C8/9 (weak), 2C19 (weak), 2D6 (moderate), 2E1 (weak), 3A4 (weak)

Increased Effect/Toxicity: Increased toxicity with lithium or potassium iodide. Anticoagulant effect of warfarin may be increased. Dosage of some drugs (including beta-blockers, digoxin, and theophylline) require adjustment during treatment of hyperthyroidism.

Mechanism of Action Inhibits the synthesis of thyroid hormones by blocking the oxidation of iodine in the thyroid gland, blocking iodine's ability to combine with tyrosine to form thyroxine and triiodothyronine (T_3), does not inactivate circulating T_4 and T_3

Pharmacodynamics/Kinetics
Onset of action: Antithyroid: Oral: 12-18 hours
Duration: 36-72 hours
Distribution: Concentrated in thyroid gland; crosses placenta; enters breast milk (1:1)
Protein binding, plasma: None
Metabolism: Hepatic
Bioavailability: 80% to 95%
Half-life elimination: 4-13 hours
Excretion: Urine (80%)

Dosage Oral: Administer in 3 equally divided doses at approximately 8-hour intervals
Children: Initial: 0.4 mg/kg/day in 3 divided doses; maintenance: 0.2 mg/kg/day in 3 divided doses up to 30 mg/24 hours maximum
Alternatively: Initial: 0.5-0.7 mg/kg/day **or** 15-20 mg/m²/day in 3 divided doses
Maintenance: $\frac{1}{3}$ to $\frac{2}{3}$ of the initial dose beginning when the patient is euthyroid
Maximum: 30 mg/24 hours
Adults: Initial: 15 mg/day for mild hyperthyroidism; 30-40 mg/day in moderately severe hyperthyroidism; 60 mg/day in severe hyperthyroidism; maintenance: 5-15 mg/day
Adjust dosage as required to achieve and maintain serum T_3, T_4, and TSH levels in the normal range. An elevated T_3 may be the sole indicator of inadequate treatment. An elevated TSH indicates excessive antithyroid treatment.
Dosing adjustment in renal impairment: Adjustment is not necessary
(Continued)

Methimazole *(Continued)*

Monitoring Parameters Monitor for signs of hypothyroidism, hyperthyroidism, T_4, T_3; CBC with differential, liver function (baseline and as needed), serum thyroxine, free thyroxine index

Patient Information Take with meals, take at regular intervals around-the-clock; report persistent fever, sore throat, fatigue, unusual bleeding or bruising

Dosage Forms TAB: 5 mg, 10 mg

♦ **Methitest®** *see* MethylTESTOSTERone *on page 826*

Methocarbamol *(meth oh KAR ba mole)*

U.S. Brand Names Robaxin®

Therapeutic Category Skeletal Muscle Relaxant

Use Treatment of muscle spasm associated with acute painful musculoskeletal conditions, supportive therapy in tetanus

Pregnancy Risk Factor C

Contraindications Hypersensitivity to methocarbamol or any component of the formulation; renal impairment (injection formulation)

Warnings/Precautions

Oral: Use caution with renal or hepatic impairment.

Injection: Rate of injection should not exceed 3 mL/minute; solution is hypertonic; avoid extravasation. Use with caution in patients with a history of seizures. Use caution with hepatic impairment.

Common Adverse Reactions Frequency not defined.

Cardiovascular: Flushing of face, bradycardia, hypotension, syncope

Central nervous system: Drowsiness, dizziness, lightheadedness, convulsion, vertigo, headache, fever, amnesia, confusion, insomnia, sedation, coordination impaired (mild)

Dermatologic: Allergic dermatitis, urticaria, pruritus, rash, angioneurotic edema

Gastrointestinal: Nausea, vomiting, metallic taste, dyspepsia

Hematologic: Leukopenia

Hepatic: Jaundice

Local: Pain at injection site, thrombophlebitis

Ocular: Nystagmus, blurred vision, diplopia, conjunctivitis

Renal: Renal impairment

Respiratory: Nasal congestion

Miscellaneous: Allergic manifestations, anaphylactic reaction

Drug Interactions

Increased Effect/Toxicity: Increased effect/toxicity with CNS depressants.

Mechanism of Action Causes skeletal muscle relaxation by general CNS depression

Pharmacodynamics/Kinetics

Onset of action: Muscle relaxation: Oral: ~30 minutes

Protein binding: 46% to 50%

Metabolism: Hepatic

Half-life elimination: 1-2 hours

Time to peak, serum: ~2 hours

Excretion: Urine (as metabolites)

Dosage

Tetanus: I.V.:

Children: Recommended **only** for use in tetanus: 15 mg/kg/dose or 500 mg/m²/dose, may repeat every 6 hours if needed; maximum dose: 1.8 g/m²/day for 3 days only

Adults: Initial dose: 1-3 g; may repeat dose every 6 hours until oral dosing is possible; injection should not be used for more than 3 consecutive days

Muscle spasm: Children ≥16 years and Adults:

Oral: 1.5 g 4 times/day for 2-3 days, then decrease to 4-4.5 g/day in 3-6 divided doses

I.M., I.V.: 1 g every 8 hours if oral not possible; injection should not be used for more than 3 consecutive days

Elderly: Specific dosing guidelines are not available; refer to Adults dosing; half-life is slightly prolonged and protein binding is slightly decreased

Dosing adjustment/comments in renal impairment: Do not administer parenteral formulation to patients with renal dysfunction.

Dosing adjustment in hepatic impairment: Specific dosing guidelines are not available; plasma protein binding and clearance are decreased; half-life is increased

Administration

Injection: Maximum rate: 3 mL/minute; should not be used for more than 3 consecutive days; may be administered undiluted

Tablet: May be crushed and mixed with food or liquid if needed. Avoid alcohol.

Patient Information May cause drowsiness, impair judgment or coordination; avoid alcohol or other CNS depressants; report rash, itching, or nasal congestion

Dosage Forms INJ, solution: 100 mg/mL (10 mL). **TAB:** 500 mg, 750 mg

Methohexital *(meth oh HEKS i tal)*

U.S. Brand Names Brevital® Sodium

Synonyms Methohexital Sodium

Therapeutic Category Barbiturate; General Anesthetic

Use Induction and maintenance of general anesthesia for short procedures

Can be used in pediatric patients ≥1 month of age as follows: For rectal or intramuscular induction of anesthesia prior to the use of other general anesthetic agents, as an adjunct to subpotent inhalational anesthetic agents for short surgical procedures, or for short surgical, diagnostic, or therapeutic procedures associated with minimal painful stimuli

Unlabeled/Investigational Use Wada test

Restrictions C-IV

Pregnancy Risk Factor C

Dosage Doses must be titrated to effect

Manufacturer's recommendations:

Infants <1 month: Safety and efficacy not established

Infants ≥1 month and Children:

I.M.: Induction: 6.6-10 mg/kg of a 5% solution

Rectal: Induction: Usual: 25 mg/kg of a 1% solution

Alternative pediatric dosing:

Children 3-12 years:

I.M.: Preoperative: 5-10 mg/kg/dose

I.V.: Induction: 1-2 mg/kg/dose

Rectal: Preoperative/induction: 20-35 mg/kg/dose; usual: 25 mg/kg/dose; maximum dose: 500 mg/dose; give as 10% aqueous solution

Adults: I.V.:

Induction: 50-120 mg to start; 20-40 mg every 4-7 minutes

Wada test (unlabeled): 3-4 mg over 3 second; following signs of recovery, administer a second dose of 2 mg over 2 seconds

Dosing adjustment/comments in hepatic impairment: Lower dosage and monitor closely

Dosage Forms INJ, powder for reconstitution: 500 mg, 2.5 g, 5 g

♦ **Methohexital Sodium** *see Methohexital on page 814*

Methotrexate (meth oh TREKS ate)

U.S. Brand Names Rheumatrex®; Trexall™

Synonyms Amethopterin; Methotrexate Sodium; MTX; NSC-740

Therapeutic Category Antineoplastic Agent, Antimetabolite; Antineoplastic Agent, Folate Antagonist; Antineoplastic Agent, Irritant; Immunosuppressant Agent

Use Treatment of trophoblastic neoplasms; leukemias; psoriasis; rheumatoid arthritis (RA), including polyarticular-course juvenile rheumatoid arthritis (JRA); breast, head and neck, and lung carcinomas; osteosarcoma; soft-tissue sarcomas; carcinoma of gastrointestinal tract, esophagus, testes; lymphomas

Pregnancy Risk Factor X (psoriasis, rheumatoid arthritis)

Contraindications Hypersensitivity to methotrexate or any component of the formulation; severe renal or hepatic impairment; pre-existing profound bone marrow suppression in patients with psoriasis or rheumatoid arthritis, alcoholic liver disease, AIDS, pre-existing blood dyscrasias; pregnancy (in patients with psoriasis or rheumatoid arthritis); breast-feeding

Warnings/Precautions The U.S. Food and Drug Administration (FDA) currently recommends that procedures for proper handling and disposal of antineoplastic agents be considered

Bone and soft tissue necrosis may occur following radiation treatment. Painful plaque erosions may occur with psoriasis treatment.

May cause photosensitivity-type reaction. Reduce dosage in patients with renal or hepatic impairment. Methotrexate penetrates slowly into 3rd space fluids, such as pleural effusions or ascites, and exits slowly from these compartments (slower than from plasma). Drain ascites and pleural effusions prior to treatment. Use with caution in patients with peptic ulcer disease, ulcerative colitis, pre-existing bone marrow suppression. May cause pneumonitis (at any dosage); monitor closely for pulmonary symptoms.

Because of the possibility of severe toxic reactions, fully inform patient of the risks involved. Do not use in women of childbearing age unless benefit outweighs risks; may cause hepatotoxicity, fibrosis and cirrhosis, renal failure, or bone marrow depression. Death from intestinal perforation may occur.

Severe bone marrow suppression, aplastic anemia, and GI toxicity have occurred during concomitant administration with NSAIDs.

Patients should receive 1-2 L of I.V. fluid prior to initiation of high-dose methotrexate. Patients should receive sodium bicarbonate to alkalinize their urine during and after high-dose methotrexate (urine SG <1.010 and pH >7 should be maintained for at least 24 hours after infusion).

Toxicity to methotrexate or any immunosuppressive is increased in elderly; must monitor carefully. For rheumatoid arthritis and psoriasis, immunosuppressive therapy should only be used when disease is active and less toxic, traditional therapy is ineffective. Recommended doses should be reduced when initiating therapy in elderly due to possible decreased metabolism, reduced renal function, and presence of interacting diseases and drugs. Methotrexate formulations and/or diluents containing preservatives should not be used for intrathecal or high-dose therapy. Methotrexate injection may contain benzyl alcohol and should not be used in neonates.

Use extreme caution in pregnancy (see Contraindications). Safety and efficacy in pediatric patients have been established only in cancer chemotherapy and polyarticular-course JRA.

Common Adverse Reactions Note: Adverse reactions vary by route and dosage. Hematologic and/or gastrointestinal toxicities may be common at dosages used in chemotherapy; these reactions are much less frequent when used at typical dosages for rheumatic diseases. >10%:

Cardiovascular: Vasculitis

(Continued)

Methotrexate *(Continued)*

Central nervous system (with I.T. administration or very high-dose therapy):

Arachnoiditis: Acute reaction manifested as severe headache, nuchal rigidity, vomiting, and fever; may be alleviated by reducing the dose

Subacute toxicity: 10% of patients treated with 12-15 mg/m² of I.T. methotrexate may develop this in the second or third week of therapy; consists of motor paralysis of extremities, cranial nerve palsy, seizures, or coma. This has also been seen in pediatric cases receiving very high-dose I.V. methotrexate (when enough methotrexate can get across into the CSF).

Demyelinating encephalopathy: Seen months or years after receiving methotrexate; usually in association with cranial irradiation or other systemic chemotherapy

Dermatologic: Reddening of skin

Endocrine & metabolic: Hyperuricemia, defective oogenesis or spermatogenesis

Gastrointestinal: Ulcerative stomatitis, glossitis, gingivitis, nausea, vomiting, diarrhea, anorexia, intestinal perforation, mucositis (dose dependent; appears in 3-7 days after therapy, resolving within 2 weeks)

Emetic potential:

<100 mg: Moderately low (10% to 30%)

≥100 mg or <250 mg: Moderate (30% to 60%)

≥250 mg: Moderately high (60% to 90%)

Hematologic: Leukopenia, thrombocytopenia

Renal: Renal failure, azotemia, nephropathy

Respiratory: Pharyngitis

1% to 10%:

Central nervous system: Dizziness, malaise, encephalopathy, seizures, fever, chills

Dermatologic: Alopecia, rash, photosensitivity, depigmentation or hyperpigmentation of skin

Endocrine & metabolic: Diabetes

Genitourinary: Cystitis

Hematologic: Hemorrhage

Myelosuppressive: This is the primary dose-limiting factor (along with mucositis) of methotrexate; occurs about 5-7 days after methotrexate therapy, and should resolve within 2 weeks

WBC: Mild

Platelets: Moderate

Onset: 7 days

Nadir: 10 days

Recovery: 21 days

Hepatic: Cirrhosis and portal fibrosis have been associated with chronic methotrexate therapy; acute elevation of liver enzymes are common after high-dose methotrexate, and usually resolve within 10 days.

Neuromuscular & skeletal: Arthralgia

Ocular: Blurred vision

Renal: Renal dysfunction: Manifested by an abrupt rise in serum creatinine and BUN and a fall in urine output; more common with high-dose methotrexate, and may be due to precipitation of the drug. The best treatment is prevention: Aggressively hydrate with 3 L/m²/day starting 12 hours before therapy and continue for 24-36 hours; alkalinize the urine by adding 50 mEq of bicarbonate to each liter of fluid; keep urine flow over 100 mL/hour and urine pH >7.

Respiratory: Pneumonitis: Associated with fever, cough, and interstitial pulmonary infiltrates; treatment is to withhold methotrexate during the acute reaction; interstitial pneumonitis has been reported to occur with an incidence of 1% in patients with RA (dose 7.5-15 mg/week)

Drug Interactions

Increased Effect/Toxicity:

Organic acids: Salicylates, sulfonamides, probenecid, and high doses of penicillins may reduce renal tubular secretion of methotrexate.

Cytarabine: Increased formation of the cytarabine nucleotide can occur when methotrexate precedes cytarabine, thus promoting the action of cytarabine.

Cyclosporine: Concomitant administration with methotrexate may increase levels and toxicity of each.

Live virus vaccines: Concurrent use with methotrexate may result in vaccinia infections.

Nonsteroidal anti-inflammatory drugs (NSAIDs): Severe bone marrow suppression, aplastic anemia, and GI toxicity have been reported with concomitant therapy. Should not be used during moderate or high-dose methotrexate due to increased and prolonged methotrexate levels (may increase toxicity). NSAID use during treatment of rheumatoid arthritis has not been fully explored, but continuation of prior regimen has been allowed in some circumstances, with cautious monitoring.

Patients receiving concomitant therapy with methotrexate and other potential hepatotoxins (eg, azathioprine, retinoids, sulfasalazine) should be closely monitored for possible increased risk of hepatotoxicity.

Decreased Effect: Corticosteroids have been reported to decrease methotrexate entry into leukemia cells. Administration should be separated by 12 hours. Dexamethasone has been reported to not affect methotrexate entry. May decrease phenytoin and fluorouracil activity.

Mechanism of Action Methotrexate is a folate antimetabolite that inhibits DNA synthesis. Methotrexate irreversibly binds to dihydrofolate reductase, inhibiting the formation of reduced folates, and thymidylate synthetase, resulting in inhibition of purine and thymidylic acid synthesis. Methotrexate is cell cycle specific for the S phase of the cycle.

The MOA in the treatment of rheumatoid arthritis is unknown, but may affect immune function. In psoriasis, methotrexate is thought to target rapidly proliferating epithelial cells in the skin.

Pharmacodynamics/Kinetics

Onset of action: Antirheumatic: 3-6 weeks; additional improvement may continue longer than 12 weeks

Absorption: Oral: Rapid; well absorbed at low doses (<30 mg/m^2), incomplete after large doses; I.M.: Complete

Distribution: Penetrates slowly into 3rd space fluids (eg, pleural effusions, ascites), exits slowly from these compartments (slower than from plasma); crosses placenta; small amounts enter breast milk; sustained concentrations retained in kidney and liver

Protein binding: 50%

Metabolism: <10%; degraded by intestinal flora to DAMPA by carboxypeptidase; hepatic aldehyde oxidase converts methotrexate to 7-OH methotrexate; polyglutamates are produced intracellularly and are just as potent as methotrexate; their production is dose- and duration-dependent and they are slowly eliminated by the cell once formed

Half-life elimination: Low dose: 3-10 hours; High dose: 8-12 hours

Time to peak, serum: Oral: 1-2 hours; I.M.: 30-60 minutes

Excretion: Urine (44% to 100%); feces (small amounts)

Dosage Refer to individual protocols.

Note: Doses between 100-500 mg/m^2 **may require** leucovorin rescue. Doses >500 mg/m^2 **require** leucovorin rescue.

Children:

Dermatomyositis: Oral: 15-20 mg/m^2/week as a single dose once weekly **or** 0.3-1 mg/kg/ dose once weekly

Juvenile rheumatoid arthritis: Oral, I.M.: 10 mg/m^2 once weekly, then 5-15 mg/m^2/week as a single dose **or** as 3 divided doses given 12 hours apart

Antineoplastic dosage range:

Oral, I.M.: 7.5-30 mg/m^2/week **or** every 2 weeks

I.V.: 10-18,000 mg/m^2 bolus dosing **or** continuous infusion over 6-42 hours

For dosing schedules, see table:

Methotrexate Dosing Schedules

Dose	Route	Frequency
Conventional		
15-20 mg/m^2	P.O.	Twice weekly
30-50 mg/m^2	P.O., I.V.	Weekly
15 mg/day for 5 days	P.O., I.M.	Every 2-3 weeks
Intermediate		
50-150 mg/m^{2*}	I.V. push	Every 2-3 weeks
240 mg/m^{2*}	I.V. infusion	Every 4-7 days
0.5-1 g/m^{2**}	I.V. infusion	Every 2-3 weeks
High		
1-25 g/m^{2*}	I.V. infusion	Every 1-3 weeks

*Doses between 100-500 mg/m^2 may require leucovorin rescue in some patients.

**Followed with leucovorin rescue - refer to Leucovorin monograph for details.

Pediatric solid tumors (high-dose): I.V.:

<12 years: 12-25 g/m^2

≥12 years: 8 g/m^2

Acute lymphocytic leukemia (intermediate-dose): I.V.: Loading: 100 mg/m^2 bolus dose, followed by 900 mg/m^2/day infusion over 23-41 hours.

Meningeal leukemia: I.T.: 10-15 mg/m^2 (maximum dose: 15 mg) **or** an age-based dosing regimen; one possible system is:

≤3 months: 3 mg/dose

4-11 months: 6 mg/dose

1 year: 8 mg/dose

2 years: 10 mg/dose

≥3 years: 12 mg/dose

Adults: I.V.: Range is wide from 30-40 mg/m^2/week to 100-12,000 mg/m^2 with leucovorin rescue

Trophoblastic neoplasms:

Oral, I.M.: 15-30 mg/day for 5 days; repeat in 7 days for 3-5 courses

I.V.: 11 mg/m^2 days 1 through 5 every 3 weeks

Head and neck cancer: Oral, I.M., I.V.: 25-50 mg/m^2 once weekly

Mycosis fungoides (cutaneous T-cell lymphoma): Oral, I.M.: Initial (early stages):

5-50 mg once weekly **or**

15-37.5 mg twice weekly

Bladder cancer: I.V.:

30 mg/m^2 day 1 and 8 every 3 weeks **or**

30 mg/m^2 day 1, 15, and 22 every 4 weeks

Breast cancer: I.V.: 30-60 mg/m^2 days 1 and 8 every 3-4 weeks

Gastric cancer: I.V.: 1500 mg/m^2 every 4 weeks

(Continued)

Methotrexate *(Continued)*

Lymphoma, non-Hodgkin's: I.V.:
30 mg/m² days 3 and 10 every 3 weeks **or**
120 mg/m² day 8 and 15 every 3-4 weeks **or**
200 mg/m² day 8 and 15 every 3 weeks **or**
400 mg/m² every 4 weeks for 3 cycles **or**
1 g/m² every 3 weeks **or**
1.5 g/m² every 4 weeks
Sarcoma: I.V.: 8-12 g/m² weekly for 2-4 weeks
Rheumatoid arthritis: Oral: 7.5 mg once weekly **or** 2.5 mg every 12 hours for 3 doses/week, not to exceed 20 mg/week
Psoriasis:
Oral: 2.5-5 mg/dose every 12 hours for 3 doses given weekly **or**
Oral, I.M.: 10-25 mg/dose given once weekly
Ectopic pregnancy: I.M., I.V.: 50 mg/m² as a single dose

Elderly: Rheumatoid arthritis/psoriasis: Oral: Initial: 5-7.5 mg/week, not to exceed 20 mg/week
Dosing adjustment in renal impairment:
Cl$_{cr}$ 61-80 mL/minute: Reduce dose to 75% of usual dose
Cl$_{cr}$ 51-60 mL/minute: Reduce dose to 70% of usual dose
Cl$_{cr}$ 10-50 mL/minute: Reduce dose to 30% to 50% of usual dose
Cl$_{cr}$ <10 mL/minute: Avoid use
Hemodialysis: Not dialyzable (0% to 5%); supplemental dose is not necessary
Peritoneal dialysis: Supplemental dose is not necessary
Dosage adjustment in hepatic impairment:
Bilirubin 3.1-5 mg/dL **or** AST >180 units: Administer 75% of usual dose
Bilirubin >5 mg/dL: Do not use

Administration Methotrexate may be administered I.M., I.V., or I.T.; I.V. administration may be as slow push, short bolus infusion, or 24- to 42-hour continuous infusion

Specific dosing schemes vary, but high dose should be followed by leucovorin calcium to prevent toxicity; refer to Leucovorin monograph *on page 723*

Monitoring Parameters For prolonged use (especially rheumatoid arthritis, psoriasis) a baseline liver biopsy, repeated at each 1-1.5 g cumulative dose interval, should be performed; WBC and platelet counts every 4 weeks; CBC and creatinine, LFTs every 3-4 months; chest x-ray

Reference Range Therapeutic levels: Variable; Toxic concentration: Variable; therapeutic range is dependent upon therapeutic approach.

High-dose regimens produce drug levels that are between 10⁻⁶ Molar and 10⁻⁷ Molar 24-72 hours after drug infusion
10⁻⁶ Molar unit = 1 microMolar unit
Toxic: Low-dose therapy: >9.1 ng/mL; high-dose therapy: >454 ng/mL

Patient Information Avoid alcohol to prevent serious side effects. Avoid intake of extra dietary folic acid, maintain adequate hydration (2-3 L/day of fluids unless instructed to restrict fluid intake) and adequate nutrition (frequent small meals may help). You may experience nausea and vomiting (small frequent meals may help or request antiemetic from prescriber); drowsiness, tingling, numbness, or blurred vision (avoid driving or engaging in tasks that require alertness until response to drug is known); mouth sores (frequent oral care is necessary); loss of hair; skin rash; photosensitivity (use sunscreen, wear protective clothing and eyewear, and avoid direct sunlight). Report black or tarry stools, fever, chills, unusual bleeding or bruising, shortness of breath or difficulty breathing, yellowing of skin or eyes, dark or bloody urine, or acute joint pain or other side effects you may experience. The drug may cause permanent sterility and may cause birth defects; contraceptive measures are recommended during therapy. Pregnancy should be avoided for a minimum of 3 months after completion of therapy in male patients, and at least one ovulatory cycle in female patients. The drug is excreted in breast milk, therefore, an alternative form of feeding your baby should be used.

Dosage Forms INJ, powder for reconstitution [preservative free]: 20 mg, 1 g. **INJ, solution:** 25 mg/mL (2 mL, 10 mL). **INJ, solution** [preservative free]: 25 mg/mL (2 mL, 4 mL, 8 mL, 10 mL). **TAB:** 2.5 mg; (Rheumatrex®): 2.5 mg; (Trexall™): 5 mg, 7.5 mg, 10 mg, 15 mg. **TAB** [dose pack] (Rheumatrex® Dose Pack): 2.5 mg (4 cards with 2, 3, 4, 5, or 6 tablets each)

♦ **Methotrexate Sodium** *see* Methotrexate *on page 815*

Methoxsalen *(meth OKS a len)*

U.S. Brand Names 8-MOP®; Oxsoralen®; Oxsoralen-Ultra®; Uvadex®
Synonyms Methoxypsoralen; 8-Methoxypsoralen; 8-MOP
Therapeutic Category Psoralen
Use
Oral: Symptomatic control of severe, recalcitrant disabling psoriasis; repigmentation of idiopathic vitiligo; palliative treatment of skin manifestations of cutaneous T-cell lymphoma (CTCL)
Topical: Repigmentation of idiopathic vitiligo
Extracorporeal: Palliative treatment of skin manifestations of CTCL
Pregnancy Risk Factor C/D (Uvadex®)
Contraindications Hypersensitivity to methoxsalen (psoralens) or any component of the formulation; diseases associated with photosensitivity; cataract; invasive squamous cell cancer; aphakia; melanoma; pregnancy (Uvadex®)

Warnings/Precautions Serious burns may occur from ultraviolet radiation or sunlight even if exposed through glass if dose and/or exposure schedule is not maintained. Therapy may lead to increased risk of melanoma; this risk may be increased with fair skin or prior exposure to prolonged tar and UVB treatment, ionizing radiation, or arsenic. Methoxsalen concentrates in the lens; eyes should be shielded from light for 24 hours to prevent possible formation of cataracts. Soft-gelatin capsules and hard-gelatin capsule are not interchangeable. Use caution with basal cell carcinoma, hepatic, kidney, cardiac disease, or in the elderly. Use caution with other agents that may cause photosensitivity.

CTCL: For use only if inadequate response to other forms of therapy. Used in conjunction with long wave radiation of white blood cells using the UVAR® photopheresis system. Safety and efficacy in pediatric patients have not been established.

Psoriasis: For use only if inadequate response to other therapies when the diagnosis is biopsy proven. Administer only in conjunction with scheduled controlled doses of long wave ultraviolet (UVA) radiation (combination referred to as PUVA). Safety and efficacy in pediatric patients have not been established.

Vitiligo: Used in conjunction with controlled doses of long wave ultraviolet radiation or sunlight. Lotion should only be applied under direct supervision of prescriber and should not be dispensed to the patient. Safety and efficacy in children <12 years of age have not been established.

Common Adverse Reactions Frequency not always defined.
Cardiovascular: Severe edema, hypotension
Central nervous system: Nervousness, vertigo, depression, dizziness, headache, malaise
Dermatologic: Painful blistering, burning, and peeling of skin; pruritus (10%), freckling, hypopigmentation, rash, cheilitis, erythema, itching, urticaria
Gastrointestinal: Nausea (10%)
Neuromuscular & skeletal: Loss of muscle coordination, leg cramps
Miscellaneous: Miliaria

Drug Interactions
Cytochrome P450 Effect: Substrate of CYP2A6 (minor); **Inhibits** CYP1A2 (strong), 2A6 (strong), 2C8/9 (weak), 2C19 (weak), 2D6 (weak), 2E1 (weak), 3A4 (weak)
Increased Effect/Toxicity: Concomitant therapy with other photosensitizing agents such as anthralin, coal tar, griseofulvin, phenothiazines, nalidixic acid, fluoroquinolones, sulfanilamides, tetracyclines, and thiazide diuretics.

Mechanism of Action Bonds covalently to pyrimidine bases in DNA, inhibits the synthesis of DNA, and suppresses cell division. The augmented sunburn reaction involves excitation of the methoxsalen molecule by radiation in the long-wave ultraviolet light (UVA), resulting in transference of energy to the methoxsalen molecule producing an excited state ("triplet electronic state"). The molecule, in this "triplet state", then reacts with cutaneous DNA.

Pharmacodynamics/Kinetics
Protein binding: Reversibly bound to albumin
Metabolism: Hepatic; forms metabolites
Bioavailability: Bioavailability increased with soft-gelatin capsules compared to hard-gelatin capsules; exposure using UVAR® system is ~200 times less than with oral administration
Time to peak, serum:
Hard-gelatin capsules: 1.5-6 hours (peak photosensitivity: ~4 hours)
Soft-gelatin capsules: 0.5-4 hours (peak photosensitivity: 1.5-2 hours)
Half-life elimination: ~2 hours
Excretion: Urine (~95% as metabolites)

Dosage Note: Refer to treatment protocols for UVA exposure guidelines.
Children >12 years and Adults: Vitiligo: Topical: Apply lotion 1-2 hours before exposure to UVA light, no more than once weekly
Adults:
Psoriasis: Oral: 10-70 mg 11/2-2 hours before exposure to UVA light; dose may be repeated 2-3 times per week, based on UVA exposure; doses must be given at least 48 hours apart; dosage is based upon patient's body weight and skin type:
<30 kg: 10 mg
30-50 kg: 20 mg
51-65 kg: 30 mg
66-80 kg: 40 mg
81-90 kg: 50 mg
91-115 kg: 60 mg
>115 kg: 70 mg
Vitiligo: (8-MCP®): Oral: 20 mg 2-4 hours before exposure to UVA light; dose may be repeated based on erythema and tenderness of skin; do not give on 2 consecutive days
CTCL: Extracorporeal (Uvadex®): 200 mcg injected into the photoactivation bag during the collection cycle using the UVAR® photopheresis system (consult user's guide). Treatment schedule: Two consecutive days every 4 weeks for a minimum of 7 treatment cycles

Administration Topical: Hands and fingers of person applying the lotion should be protected to prevent possible photosensitization and/or burns.

Patient Information To reduce nausea, oral drug can be taken with food or milk or in 2 divided doses 30 minutes apart. If burning or blistering or intractable pruritus occurs, discontinue therapy until effects subside. Do not sunbathe for at least 24 hours prior to therapy or 48 hours after PUVA therapy. Avoid direct and indirect sunlight for 8 hours after oral and 12-48 hours after topical therapy. **If sunlight cannot be avoided, protective clothing and/or sunscreens must be worn.** Following oral therapy, wraparound sunglasses with UVA-absorbing properties (Continued)

Methoxsalen *(Continued)*

must be worn for 24 hours. Avoid furocoumarin-containing foods (limes, figs, parsley, celery, cloves, lemon, mustard, carrots); do not exceed prescribed dose or exposure times.

Dosage Forms CAP (8-MOP®): 10 mg; (Oxsoralen-Ultra®): 10 mg. **LOTION** (Oxsoralen®): 1% (30 mL). **SOLN, for extracorporeal administration only** (Uvadex®): 20 mcg/mL (10 mL)

♦ **Methoxypsoralen** *see* Methoxsalen *on page 818*

♦ **8-Methoxypsoralen** *see* Methoxsalen *on page 818*

♦ **Methscopolamine, Chlorpheniramine, and Phenylephrine** *see* Chlorpheniramine, Phenylephrine, and Methscopolamine *on page 264*

Methsuximide *(meth SUKS i mide)*
Related Information
Epilepsy *on page 1477*
U.S. Brand Names Celontin®
Therapeutic Category Anticonvulsant, Succinimide
Use Control of absence (petit mal) seizures that are refractory to other drugs
Unlabeled/Investigational Use Partial complex (psychomotor) seizures
Pregnancy Risk Factor C
Dosage Oral:
Children: Anticonvulsant: Initial: 10-15 mg/kg/day in 3-4 divided doses; increase weekly up to maximum of 30 mg/kg/day
Adults: Anticonvulsant: 300 mg/day for the first week; may increase by 300 mg/day at weekly intervals up to 1.2 g/day in 2-4 divided doses/day
Dosage Forms CAP: 150 mg, 300 mg

Methyclothiazide *(meth i kloe THYE a zide)*
Related Information
Sulfonamide Derivatives *on page 1404*
U.S. Brand Names Aquatensen®; Enduron®
Therapeutic Category Antihypertensive Agent; Diuretic, Thiazide
Use Management of mild to moderate hypertension; treatment of edema in congestive heart failure and nephrotic syndrome
Pregnancy Risk Factor B
Dosage Adults: Oral:
Edema: 2.5-10 mg/day
Hypertension: 2.5-5 mg/day; may add another antihypertensive if 5 mg is not adequate after a trial of 8-12 weeks of therapy
Dosage Forms TAB: 5 mg

Methyclothiazide and Deserpidine
(meth i kloe THYE a zide & de SER pi deen)
U.S. Brand Names Enduronyl®; Enduronyl® Forte
Synonyms Deserpidine and Methyclothiazide
Therapeutic Category Antihypertensive Agent, Combination
Use Management of mild to moderately severe hypertension
Pregnancy Risk Factor C
Dosage Oral: Individualized, normally 1-4 tablets/day
Dosage Forms TAB (Enduronyl®): Methyclothiazide 5 mg and deserpidine 0.25 mg; (Enduronyl® Forte): Methyclothiazide 5 mg and deserpidine 0.5 mg

♦ **Methylacetoxyprogesterone** *see* MedroxyPROGESTERone *on page 781*

♦ **Methylcellulose, Gelatin, and Pectin** *see* Gelatin, Pectin, and Methylcellulose *on page 582*

Methyldopa *(meth il DOE pa)*
Synonyms Aldomet; Methyldopate Hydrochloride
Therapeutic Category Alpha-Adrenergic Agonist; Antihypertensive Agent
Use Management of moderate to severe hypertension
Pregnancy Risk Factor B
Dosage
Children:
Oral: Initial: 10 mg/kg/day in 2-4 divided doses; increase every 2 days as needed to maximum dose of 65 mg/kg/day; do not exceed 3 g/day.
I.V.: 5-10 mg/kg/dose every 6-8 hours up to a total dose of 65 mg/kg/24 hours or 3 g/24 hours
Adults:
Oral: Initial: 250 mg 2-3 times/day; increase every 2 days as needed; usual dose 1-1.5 g/day in 2-4 divided doses; maximum dose: 3 g/day.
I.V.: 250-500 mg every 6-8 hours; maximum dose: 1 g every 6 hours
Dosing interval in renal impairment:
Cl_{cr} >50 mL/minute: Administer every 8 hours.
Cl_{cr} 10-50 mL/minute: Administer every 8-12 hours.
Cl_{cr} <10 mL/minute: Administer every 12-24 hours.
Hemodialysis: Slightly dialyzable (5% to 20%)
Dosage Forms INJ, solution: 50 mg/mL (5 mL). **TAB:** 250 mg, 500 mg

Methyldopa and Hydrochlorothiazide
(meth il DOE pa & hye droe klor oh THYE a zide)

U.S. Brand Names Aldoril®; Aldoril® D

Synonyms Hydrochlorothiazide and Methyldopa

Therapeutic Category Antihypertensive Agent, Combination

Use Management of moderate to severe hypertension

Pregnancy Risk Factor C

Dosage Oral: Dosage titrated on individual components, then switch to combination product; no more than methyldopa 3 g/day and/or hydrochlorothiazide 50 mg/day; maintain initial dose for first 48 hours, then decrease or increase at intervals of not less than 2 days until an adequate response is achieved

Methyldopa 250 mg and hydrochlorothiazide 15 mg: 2-3 times/day

Methyldopa 250 mg and hydrochlorothiazide 25 mg: Twice daily

Methyldopa 500 mg and hydrochlorothiazide 30 mg: Once daily

Dosage Forms TAB: Methyldopa 250 mg and hydrochlorothiazide 15 mg; methyldopa 250 mg and hydrochlorothiazide 25 mg; (Aldoril® 15): Methyldopa 250 mg and hydrochlorothiazide 15 mg; (Aldoril® 25): Methyldopa 250 mg and hydrochlorothiazide 25 mg; (Aldoril® D30): Methyldopa 500 mg and hydrochlorothiazide 30 mg

♦ **Methyldopate Hydrochloride** see Methyldopa on page 820

Methylene Blue (METH i leen bloo)

U.S. Brand Names Urolene Blue®

Therapeutic Category Antidote, Cyanide; Antidote, Drug-induced Methemoglobinemia

Use Antidote for cyanide poisoning and drug-induced methemoglobinemia, indicator dye

Unlabeled/Investigational Use Has been used topically (0.1% solutions) in conjunction with polychromatic light to photoinactivate viruses such as herpes simplex; has been used alone or in combination with vitamin C for the management of chronic urolithiasis

Pregnancy Risk Factor C/D (injected intra-amniotically)

Contraindications Hypersensitivity to methylene blue or any component of the formulation; intraspinal injection; renal insufficiency; pregnancy (injected intra-amniotically)

Warnings/Precautions Do not inject S.C. or intrathecally; use with caution in young patients and in patients with G6PD deficiency; continued use can cause profound anemia

Common Adverse Reactions Frequency not defined.

Cardiovascular: Hypertension, precordial pain

Central nervous system: Dizziness, mental confusion, headache, fever

Dermatologic: Staining of skin

Gastrointestinal: Fecal discoloration (blue-green), nausea, vomiting, abdominal pain

Genitourinary: Discoloration of urine (blue-green), bladder irritation

Hematologic: Anemia

Miscellaneous: Diaphoresis

Mechanism of Action Weak germicide in low concentrations, hastens the conversion of methemoglobin to hemoglobin; has opposite effect at high concentrations by converting ferrous ion of reduced hemoglobin to ferric ion to form methemoglobin; in cyanide toxicity, it combines with cyanide to form cyanmethemoglobin preventing the interference of cyanide with the cytochrome system

Pharmacodynamics/Kinetics

Absorption: Oral: 53% to 97%

Excretion: Urine and feces

Dosage

Children: NADPH-methemoglobin reductase deficiency: Oral: 1-1.5 mg/kg/day (maximum: 300 mg/day) given with 5-8 mg/kg/day of ascorbic acid

Children and Adults: Methemoglobinemia: I.V.: 1-2 mg/kg or 25-50 mg/m^2 over several minutes; may be repeated in 1 hour if necessary

Adults: Genitourinary antiseptic: Oral: 65-130 mg 3 times/day with a full glass of water (maximum: 390 mg/day)

Administration Administer I.V. undiluted by direct I.V. injection over several minutes

Patient Information May discolor urine and feces blue-green; take oral formulation after meals with a glass of water; skin stains may be removed using a hypochlorite solution

Dosage Forms INJ, solution: 10 mg/mL (1 mL, 10 mL). **TAB** (Urolene Blue®): 65 mg

♦ **Methylene Blue, Methenamine, Sodium Biphosphate, Phenyl Salicylate, and Hyoscyamine** see Methenamine, Sodium Biphosphate, Phenyl Salicylate, Methylene Blue, and Hyoscyamine on page 812

♦ **Methylergometrine Maleate** see Methylergonovine on page 821

Methylergonovine (meth il er goe NOE veen)

U.S. Brand Names Methergine®

Synonyms Methylergometrine Maleate; Methylergonovine Maleate

Therapeutic Category Ergot Alkaloid and Derivative

Use Prevention and treatment of postpartum and postabortion hemorrhage caused by uterine atony or subinvolution

Pregnancy Risk Factor C

(Continued)

Methylergonovine *(Continued)*

Contraindications Hypersensitivity to methylergonovine or any component of the formulation; ergot alkaloids are contraindicated with potent inhibitors of CYP3A4 (includes protease inhibitors, azole antifungals, and some macrolide antibiotics); hypertension; induction of labor, threatened spontaneous abortion, toxemia

Warnings/Precautions Use caution in patients with sepsis, obliterative vascular disease, hepatic, or renal involvement, hypertension; administer with extreme caution if using intravenously. Pleural and peritoneal fibrosis have been reported with prolonged daily use. Cardiac valvular fibrosis has also been associated with ergot alkaloids.

Common Adverse Reactions Frequency not defined.

Cardiovascular: Hypertension, temporary chest pain, palpitations

Central nervous system: Hallucinations, dizziness, seizures, headache

Endocrine & metabolic: Water intoxication

Gastrointestinal: Nausea, vomiting, diarrhea, foul taste

Local: Thrombophlebitis

Neuromuscular & skeletal: Leg cramps

Otic: Tinnitus

Renal: Hematuria

Respiratory: Dyspnea, nasal congestion

Miscellaneous: Diaphoresis

Drug Interactions

Cytochrome P450 Effect: Substrate of CYP3A4 (major)

Increased Effect/Toxicity: Effects of methylergonovine may be increased by antifungals (azole derivatives); CYP3A4 inhibitors (eg, amiodarone, cimetidine, erythromycin, ritonavir); macrolide antibiotics; protease inhibitors; MAO inhibitors; beta blockers (vasoconstriction); sumatriptan (vasospasm); vasoconstrictors. Methylergonovine may increase the effects of sibutramine and other serotonin agonists (serotonin syndrome).

Decreased Effect: Effects of methylergonovine may be diminished by antipsychotics, metoclopramide/

Mechanism of Action Similar smooth muscle actions as seen with ergotamine; however, it affects primarily uterine smooth muscles producing sustained contractions and thereby shortens the third stage of labor

Pharmacodynamics/Kinetics

Onset of action: Oxytocic: Oral: 5-10 minutes; I.M.: 2-5 minutes; I.V.: Immediately

Duration: Oral: ~3 hours; I.M.: ~3 hours; I.V.: 45 minutes

Absorption: Rapid

Distribution: Rapid; primarily to plasma and extracellular fluid following I.V. administration; tissues

Metabolism: Hepatic

Half-life elimination: Biphasic: Initial: 1-5 minutes; Terminal: 0.5-2 hours

Time to peak, serum: 0.5-3 hours

Excretion: Urine and feces

Dosage Adults:

Oral: 0.2 mg 3-4 times/day for 2-7 days

I.M.: 0.2 mg after delivery of anterior shoulder, after delivery of placenta, or during puerperium; may be repeated as required at intervals of 2-4 hours

I.V.: Same dose as I.M., but should not be routinely administered I.V. because of possibility of inducing sudden hypertension and cerebrovascular accident

Administration Administer over no less than 60 seconds

Patient Information May cause nausea, vomiting, dizziness, increased blood pressure, headache, ringing in the ears, chest pain, or shortness of breath

Dosage Forms INJ, solution: 0.2 mg/mL (1 mL). **TAB:** 0.2 mg

♦ **Methylergonovine Maleate** *see* Methylergonovine *on page 821*

♦ **Methylin™** *see* Methylphenidate *on page 822*

♦ **Methylin™ ER** *see* Methylphenidate *on page 822*

♦ **Methylmorphine** *see* Codeine *on page 308*

Methylphenidate *(meth il FEN i date)*

U.S. Brand Names Concerta®; Metadate® CD; Metadate™ ER; Methylin™; Methylin™ ER; Ritalin®; Ritalin® LA; Ritalin-SR®

Synonyms Methylphenidate Hydrochloride

Therapeutic Category Central Nervous System Stimulant, Nonamphetamine

Use Treatment of attention-deficit/hyperactivity disorder (ADHD); symptomatic management of narcolepsy

Unlabeled/Investigational Use Depression (especially elderly or medically ill)

Restrictions C-II

Pregnancy Risk Factor C

Contraindications Hypersensitivity to methylphenidate, any component of the formulation, or idiosyncrasy to sympathomimetic amines; marked anxiety, tension, and agitation; glaucoma; use during or within 14 days following MAO inhibitor therapy; Tourette's syndrome or tics

Warnings/Precautions Methylphenidate has a high potential for abuse; avoid abrupt discontinuation in patients who have received for prolonged periods. Has demonstrated value as part of a comprehensive treatment program for ADHD. May have value in selected patients as an antidepressant.

Safety and efficacy in children <6 years of age not established. Use with caution in patients with bipolar disorder, diabetes mellitus, cardiovascular disease, seizure disorders, insomnia, porphyria, or mild hypertension (stage I). May exacerbate symptoms of behavior and thought disorder in psychotic patients. Do not use to treat severe depression or fatigue states. Stimulant use has been associated with growth suppression. Concerta® should not be used in patients with pre-existing severe gastrointestinal narrowing (small bowel disease, short gut syndrome, history of peritonitis, cystic fibrosis, chronic intestinal pseudo-obstruction, Meckel's diverticulum)

Common Adverse Reactions Frequency not defined.

Cardiovascular: Angina, cardiac arrhythmias, cerebral arteritis, cerebral occlusion, hypertension, hypotension, palpitations, pulse increase/decrease, tachycardia

Central nervous system: Depression, dizziness, drowsiness, fever, headache, insomnia, nervousness, neuroleptic malignant syndrome (NMS), Tourette's syndrome, toxic psychosis

Dermatologic: Erythema multiforme, exfoliative dermatitis, hair loss, rash, urticaria

Endocrine & metabolic: Growth retardation

Gastrointestinal: Abdominal pain, anorexia, nausea, vomiting, weight loss

Hematologic: Anemia, leukopenia, thrombocytopenic purpura

Hepatic: Abnormal liver function tests, hepatic coma, transaminase elevation

Neuromuscular & skeletal: Arthralgia, dyskinesia

Ocular: Blurred vision

Renal: Necrotizing vasculitis

Respiratory: Cough increased, pharyngitis, sinusitis, upper respiratory tract infection

Miscellaneous: Hypersensitivity reactions

Drug Interactions

Cytochrome P450 Effect: Substrate of CYP2D6 (major); **Inhibits** CYP2D6 (weak)

Increased Effect/Toxicity: Methylphenidate may cause hypertensive effects when used in combination with MAO inhibitors or drugs with MAO-inhibiting activity (linezolid). Risk may be less with selegiline (MAO type B selective at low doses); it is best to avoid this combination. CYP2D6 inhibitors may increase the levels/effects of methylphenidate; example inhibitors include chlorpromazine, delavirdine, fluoxetine, miconazole, paroxetine, pergolide, quinidine, quinine, ritonavir, and ropinirole. NMS has been reported in a patient receiving methylphenidate and venlafaxine. Methylphenidate may increase levels of phenytoin, phenobarbital, TCAs, and warfarin. Increased toxicity with clonidine and sibutramine.

Decreased Effect: Effectiveness of antihypertensive agents may be decreased. Carbamazepine may decrease the effect of methylphenidate.

Mechanism of Action Mild CNS stimulant; blocks the reuptake mechanism of dopaminergic neurons; appears to stimulate the cerebral cortex and subcortical structures similar to amphetamines

Pharmacodynamics/Kinetics

Onset of action: Peak effect:

Immediate release tablet: Cerebral stimulation: ~2 hours

Extended release capsule (Metadate® CD): Biphasic; initial peak similar to immediate release product, followed by second rising portion (corresponding to extended release portion)

Sustained release tablet: 4-7 hours

Osmotic release tablet (Concerta®): Initial: 1-2 hours

Duration: Immediate release tablet: 3-6 hours; Sustained release tablet: 8 hours

Absorption: Readily

Metabolism: Hepatic via de-esterification to active metabolite

Half-life elimination: 2-4 hours

Time to peak: C_{max}: 6-8 hours

Excretion: Urine (90% as metabolites and unchanged drug)

Dosage Oral (discontinue periodically to re-evaluate or if no improvement occurs within 1 month):

Children ≥6 years: ADHD: Initial: 0.3 mg/kg/dose or 2.5-5 mg/dose given before breakfast and lunch; increase by 0.1 mg/kg/dose or by 5-10 mg/day at weekly intervals; usual dose: 0.5-1 mg/kg/day; maximum dose: 2 mg/kg/day or 90 mg/day

Extended release products:

Metadate™ ER, Methylin™ ER, Ritalin® SR: Duration of action is 8 hours. May be given in place of regular tablets, once the daily dose is titrated using the regular tablets and the titrated 8-hour dosage corresponds to sustained release tablet size.

Metadate® CD, Ritalin® LA: Initial: 20 mg once daily; may be adjusted in 10-20 mg increments at weekly intervals; maximum: 60 mg/day

Concerta®: Duration of action is 12 hours:

Children not currently taking methylphenidate:

Initial: 18 mg once daily in the morning

Adjustment: May increase to maximum of 54 mg/day in increments of 18 mg/day; dose may be adjusted at weekly intervals

Children currently taking methylphenidate: **Note:** Dosing based on current regimen and clinical judgment; suggested dosing listed below:

Patients taking methylphenidate 5 mg 2-3 times/day or 20 mg/day sustained release formulation: Initial dose: 18 mg once every morning (maximum: 54 mg/day)

Patients taking methylphenidate 10 mg 2-3 times/day or 40 mg/day sustained release formulation: Initial dose: 36 mg once every morning (maximum: 54 mg/day)

Patients taking methylphenidate 15 mg 2-3 times/day or 60 mg/day sustained release formulation: Initial dose: 54 mg once every morning (maximum: 54 mg/day)

(Continued)

Methylphenidate *(Continued)*

Note: A 27 mg dosage strength is available for situations in which a dosage between 18 mg and 36 mg is desired.

Adults:

Narcolepsy: 10 mg 2-3 times/day, up to 60 mg/day

Depression (unlabeled use): Initial: 2.5 mg every morning before 9 AM; dosage may be increased by 2.5-5 mg every 2-3 days as tolerated to a maximum of 20 mg/day; may be divided (ie, 7 AM and 12 noon), but should not be given after noon; do not use sustained release product

Administration Do not crush or allow patient to chew sustained release dosage form. To effectively avoid insomnia, dosing should be completed by noon.

Concerta®: Administer dose once daily in the morning. May be taken with or without food, but must be taken with water, milk, or juice.

Metadate® CD, Ritalin® LA: Capsules may be opened and the contents sprinkled onto a small amount (equal to 1 tablespoon) of applesauce. Swallow applesauce without chewing. Do not crush or chew capsule contents.

Monitoring Parameters Blood pressure, heart rate, signs and symptoms of depression, CBC, differential and platelet counts, growth rate in children, signs of central nervous system stimulation

Patient Information Take exactly as directed; do not change dosage or discontinue without consulting prescriber. Response may take some time. Do not crush or chew sustained release dosage forms. Tablets and sustained release tablets should be taken 30-45 minutes before meals. Concerta® may be taken with or without food, but must be taken with water, milk, or juice. Metadate® CD and Ritalin® LA capsules may be opened and the contents sprinkled onto a small amount (equal to 1 tablespoon) of applesauce. Swallow applesauce without chewing. Do not crush or chew capsule contents. Avoid alcohol, caffeine, or other stimulants. Maintain adequate fluid intake (2-3 L/day of fluids unless instructed to restrict fluid intake). You may experience decreased appetite or weight loss (small frequent meals may help maintain adequate nutrition); restlessness, impaired judgment, or dizziness, especially during early therapy (use caution when driving or engaging in tasks requiring alertness until response to drug is known). Report unresolved rapid heartbeat; excessive agitation, nervousness, insomnia, tremors, or dizziness; blackened stool; skin rash or irritation; or altered gait or movement. Concerta™ tablet shell may appear intact in stool; this is normal.

Dosage Forms CAP, extended release (Metadate® CD): 10 mg, 20 mg, 30 mg; (Ritalin® LA): 20 mg, 30 mg, 40 mg. **TAB** (Methylin™, Ritalin®): 5 mg, 10 mg, 20 mg. **TAB, extended release:** 20 mg; (Concerta®): 18 mg, 27 mg, 36 mg, 54 mg; (Metadate™ ER, Methylin™ ER): 10 mg, 20 mg. **TAB, sustained release** (Ritalin-SR®): 20 mg

♦ **Methylphenidate Hydrochloride** *see* Methylphenidate *on page 822*

♦ **Methylphenobarbital** *see* Mephobarbital *on page 792*

♦ **Methylphenoxy-Benzene Propanamine** *see* Atomoxetine *on page 127*

♦ **Methylphenyl Isoxazolyl Penicillin** *see* Oxacillin *on page 935*

♦ **Methylphytyl Napthoquinone** *see* Phytonadione *on page 1000*

MethylPREDNISolone *(meth il pred NIS oh lone)*

Related Information

Corticosteroids Comparison *on page 1372*

U.S. Brand Names A-Methapred®; Depo-Medrol®; Medrol®; Solu-Medrol®

Synonyms 6-α-Methylprednisolone; Methylprednisolone Acetate; Methylprednisolone Sodium Succinate

Therapeutic Category Anti-inflammatory Agent; Corticosteroid, Systemic; Glucocorticoid

Use Primarily as an anti-inflammatory or immunosuppressant agent in the treatment of a variety of diseases including those of hematologic, allergic, inflammatory, neoplastic, and autoimmune origin. Prevention and treatment of graft-versus-host disease following allogeneic bone marrow transplantation.

Unlabeled/Investigational Use Treatment of fibrosing-alveolitis phase of adult respiratory distress syndrome (ARDS)

Pregnancy Risk Factor C

Contraindications Hypersensitivity to methylprednisolone or any component of the formulation; viral, fungal, or tubercular skin lesions; administration of live virus vaccines; serious infections, except septic shock or tuberculous meningitis. Methylprednisolone formulations containing benzyl alcohol preservative are contraindicated in infants.

Warnings/Precautions Use with caution in patients with hyperthyroidism, cirrhosis, nonspecific ulcerative colitis, hypertension, osteoporosis, thromboembolic tendencies, CHF, convulsive disorders, myasthenia gravis, thrombophlebitis, peptic ulcer, diabetes, glaucoma, cataracts, or tuberculosis. Use caution in hepatic impairment. Because of the risk of adverse effects, systemic corticosteroids should be used cautiously in the elderly, in the smallest possible dose, and for the shortest possible time

Acute adrenal insufficiency may occur with abrupt withdrawal after long-term therapy or with stress; young pediatric patients may be more susceptible to adrenal axis suppression from topical therapy

Common Adverse Reactions Frequency not defined.

Cardiovascular: Edema, hypertension, arrhythmias

Central nervous system: Insomnia, nervousness, vertigo, seizures, psychoses, pseudotumor cerebri, headache, mood swings, delirium, hallucinations, euphoria

Dermatologic: Hirsutism, acne, skin atrophy, bruising, hyperpigmentation

Endocrine & metabolic: Diabetes mellitus, adrenal suppression, hyperlipidemia, Cushing's syndrome, pituitary-adrenal axis suppression, growth suppression, glucose intolerance, hypokalemia, alkalosis, amenorrhea, sodium and water retention, hyperglycemia

Gastrointestinal: Increased appetite, indigestion, peptic ulcer, nausea, vomiting, abdominal distention, ulcerative esophagitis, pancreatitis

Hematologic: Transient leukocytosis

Neuromuscular & skeletal: Arthralgia, muscle weakness, osteoporosis, fractures

Ocular: Cataracts, glaucoma

Miscellaneous: Infections, hypersensitivity reactions, avascular necrosis, secondary malignancy, intractable hiccups

Drug Interactions

Cytochrome P450 Effect: Substrate of CYP3A4 (minor); **Inhibits** CYP3A4 (weak)

Increased Effect/Toxicity: Methylprednisolone may increase circulating glucose levels; may need adjustments of insulin or oral hypoglycemics. Methylprednisolone increases cyclosporine and tacrolimus blood levels. Itraconazole increases corticosteroid levels.

Decreased Effect: Phenytoin, phenobarbital, rifampin increase clearance of methylprednisolone. Potassium-depleting diuretics enhance potassium depletion. Skin test antigens, immunizations decrease antibody response and increase potential infections.

Mechanism of Action In a tissue-specific manner, corticosteroids regulate gene expression subsequent to binding specific intracellular receptors and translocation into the nucleus. Corticosteroids exert a wide array of physiologic effects including modulation of carbohydrate, protein, and lipid metabolism and maintenance of fluid and electrolyte homeostasis. Moreover cardiovascular, immunologic, musculoskeletal, endocrine, and neurologic physiology are influenced by corticosteroids. Decreases inflammation by suppression of migration of polymorphonuclear leukocytes and reversal of increased capillary permeability.

Pharmacodynamics/Kinetics

Onset of action: Peak effect (route dependent): Oral: 1-2 hours; I.M.: 4-8 days; Intra-articular: 1 week; methylprednisolone sodium succinate is highly soluble and has a rapid effect by I.M. and I.V. routes

Duration (route dependent): Oral: 30-36 hours; I.M.: 1-4 weeks; Intra-articular: 1-5 weeks; methylprednisolone acetate has a low solubility and has a sustained I.M. effect

Distribution: V_d: 0.7-1.5 L/kg

Half-life elimination: 3-3.5 hours; reduced in obese

Excretion: Clearance: Reduced in obese

Dosage Dosing should be based on the lesser of ideal body weight or actual body weight

Only sodium succinate may be given I.V.; methylprednisolone sodium succinate is highly soluble and has a rapid effect by I.M. and I.V. routes. Methylprednisolone acetate has a low solubility and has a sustained I.M. effect.

Children:

Anti-inflammatory or immunosuppressive: Oral, I.M., I.V. (sodium succinate): 0.5-1.7 mg/kg/day **or** 5-25 mg/m²/day in divided doses every 6-12 hours; "Pulse" therapy: 15-30 mg/kg/dose over ≥30 minutes given once daily for 3 days

Status asthmaticus: I.V. (sodium succinate): Loading dose: 2 mg/kg/dose, then 0.5-1 mg/kg/dose every 6 hours for up to 5 days

Acute spinal cord injury: I.V. (sodium succinate): 30 mg/kg over 15 minutes, followed in 45 minutes by a continuous infusion of 5.4 mg/kg/hour for 23 hours

Lupus nephritis: I.V. (sodium succinate): 30 mg/kg over ≥30 minutes every other day for 6 doses

Adults: **Only sodium succinate may be given I.V.;** methylprednisolone sodium succinate is highly soluble and has a rapid effect by I.M. and I.V. routes. Methylprednisolone acetate has a low solubility and has a sustained I.M. effect.

Acute spinal cord injury: I.V. (sodium succinate): 30 mg/kg over 15 minutes, followed in 45 minutes by a continuous infusion of 5.4 mg/kg/hour for 23 hours

Anti-inflammatory or immunosuppressive:

Oral: 2-60 mg/day in 1-4 divided doses to start, followed by gradual reduction in dosage to the lowest possible level consistent with maintaining an adequate clinical response.

I.M. (sodium succinate): 10-80 mg/day once daily

I.M. (acetate): 10-80 mg every 1-2 weeks

I.V. (sodium succinate): 10-40 mg over a period of several minutes and repeated I.V. or I.M. at intervals depending on clinical response; when high dosages are needed, give 30 mg/kg over a period ≥30 minutes and may be repeated every 4-6 hours for 48 hours.

Status asthmaticus: I.V. (sodium succinate): Loading dose: 2 mg/kg/dose, then 0.5-1 mg/kg/dose every 6 hours for up to 5 days

High-dose therapy for acute spinal cord injury: I.V. bolus: 30 mg/kg over 15 minutes, followed 45 minutes later by an infusion of 5.4 mg/kg/hour for 23 hours

Lupus nephritis: High-dose "pulse" therapy: I.V. (sodium succinate): 1 g/day for 3 days

Aplastic anemia: I.V. (sodium succinate): 1 mg/kg/day or 40 mg/day (whichever dose is higher), for 4 days. After 4 days, change to oral and continue until day 10 or until symptoms of serum sickness resolve, then rapidly reduce over approximately 2 weeks.

Pneumocystis pneumonia in AIDs patients: I.V.: 40-60 mg every 6 hours for 7-10 days

Intra-articular (acetate): Administer every 1-5 weeks.

Large joints: 20-80 mg

Small joints: 4-10 mg

Intralesional (acetate): 20-60 mg every 1-5 weeks

Administration

Oral: Administer after meals or with food or milk

(Continued)

MethylPREDNISolone *(Continued)*

Parenteral: Methylprednisolone sodium succinate may be administered I.M. or I.V.; I.V. administration may be IVP over one to several minutes or IVPB or continuous I.V. infusion

I.V.: Succinate:
Low dose: ≤1.8 mg/kg or ≤125 mg/dose: I.V. push over 3-15 minutes
Moderate dose: ≥2 mg/kg or 250 mg/dose: I.V. over 15-30 minutes
High dose: 15 mg/kg or ≥500 mg/dose: I.V. over ≥30 minutes
Doses >15 mg/kg or ≥1 g: Administer over 1 hour
Do **not** administer high-dose I.V. push; hypotension, cardiac arrhythmia, and sudden death have been reported in patients given high-dose methylprednisolone I.V. push over <20 minutes; intermittent infusion over 15-60 minutes; maximum concentration: I.V. push 125 mg/mL

Monitoring Parameters Blood pressure, blood glucose, electrolytes

Patient Information Do not discontinue or decrease the drug without contacting your prescriber; carry an identification card or bracelet advising that you are on steroids; may take with meals to decrease GI upset

Dosage Forms INJ, powder for reconstitution, as sodium succinate: 40 mg, 125 mg, 500 mg; (A-Methapred®): 40 mg, 125 mg, 500 mg, 1000 mg; (Solu-Medrol®): 40 mg, 125 mg, 500 mg, 1 g, 2 g; (Solu-Medrol®): 500 mg, 1 g. **INJ, suspension, as acetate** (Depo-Medrol®): 20 mg/mL (5 mL); 40 mg/mL (5 mL); 80 mg/mL (5 mL). **INJ, suspension, as acetate** [single-dose vial] (Depo-Medrol®): 40 mg/mL (1 mL); 80 mg/mL (1 mL). **TAB:** 4 mg; (Medrol®): 2 mg, 4 mg, 8 mg, 16 mg, 32 mg. **TAB** [dose-pack]: 4 mg (21s)

♦ **6-α-Methylprednisolone** *see* MethylPREDNISolone *on page 824*
♦ **Methylprednisolone Acetate** *see* MethylPREDNISolone *on page 824*
♦ **Methylprednisolone Sodium Succinate** *see* MethylPREDNISolone *on page 824*
♦ **4-Methylpyrazole** *see* Fomepizole *on page 558*
♦ **Methylrosaniline Chloride** *see* Gentian Violet *on page 588*

MethylTESTOSTERone *(meth il tes TOS te rone)*

U.S. Brand Names Android®; Methitest®; Testred®; Virilon®
Therapeutic Category Androgen
Use
Male: Hypogonadism; delayed puberty; impotence and climacteric symptoms
Female: Palliative treatment of metastatic breast cancer
Restrictions C-III
Pregnancy Risk Factor X
Contraindications Hypersensitivity to methyltestosterone or any component of the formulation; in males, known or suspected carcinoma of the breast or the prostate; pregnancy
Warnings/Precautions Use with extreme caution in patients with liver or kidney disease or serious heart disease; may accelerate bone maturation without producing compensatory gain in linear growth
Common Adverse Reactions Frequency not defined.
Male: Virilism, priapism, prostatic hyperplasia, prostatic carcinoma, impotence, testicular atrophy, gynecomastia
Female: Virilism, menstrual problems (amenorrhea), breast soreness, hirsutism (increase in pubic hair growth) atrophy
Cardiovascular: Edema
Central nervous system: Headache, anxiety, depression
Dermatologic: Acne, "male pattern" baldness, seborrhea
Endocrine & metabolic: Hypercalcemia, hypercholesterolemia
Gastrointestinal: GI irritation, nausea, vomiting
Hematologic: Leukopenia, polycythemia
Hepatic: Hepatic dysfunction, hepatic necrosis, cholestatic hepatitis
Miscellaneous: Hypersensitivity reactions
Drug Interactions
Increased Effect/Toxicity: Effects of oral anticoagulants and hypoglycemic agents may be increased. Toxicity may occur with cyclosporine; avoid concurrent use.
Decreased Effect: Decreased oral anticoagulant effect
Mechanism of Action Stimulates receptors in organs and tissues to promote growth and development of male sex organs and maintains secondary sex characteristics in androgen-deficient males
Pharmacodynamics/Kinetics
Metabolism: Hepatic
Excretion: Urine
Dosage Adults (buccal absorption produces twice the androgenic activity of oral tablets):
Male:
Hypogonadism, male climacteric and impotence: Oral: 10-40 mg/day
Androgen deficiency:
Oral: 10-50 mg/day
Buccal: 5-25 mg/day
Postpubertal cryptorchidism: Oral: 30 mg/day
Female:
Breast pain/engorgement:
Oral: 80 mg/day for 3-5 days
Buccal: 40 mg/day for 3-5 days

Breast cancer:
Oral: 50-200 mg/day
Buccal: 25-100 mg/day
Patient Information Men should report overly frequent or persistent penile erections; women should report menstrual irregularities; all patients should report persistent GI distress, diarrhea, or jaundice; buccal tablet should not be chewed or swallowed
Dosage Forms CAP (Android®, Testred®, Virilon®): 10 mg. **TAB** (Methitest®): 10 mg

Methysergide (meth i SER jide)
U.S. Brand Names Sansert® [DSC]
Synonyms Methysergide Maleate
Therapeutic Category Ergot Alkaloid and Derivative
Use Prophylaxis of vascular headache
Pregnancy Risk Factor X
Dosage Adults: Oral: 4-8 mg/day with meals; if no improvement is noted after 3 weeks, drug is unlikely to be beneficial; must not be given continuously for longer than 6 months, and a drug-free interval of 3-4 weeks must follow each 6-month course
Dosage Forms TAB: 2 mg

♦ **Methysergide Maleate** *see* Methysergide *on page 827*

Metipranolol (met i PRAN oh lol)
Related Information
Glaucoma Drug Therapy Comparison *on page 1481*
U.S. Brand Names OptiPranolol®
Synonyms Metipranolol Hydrochloride
Therapeutic Category Beta Blocker, Nonselective; Beta-Adrenergic Blocker, Ophthalmic
Use Agent for lowering intraocular pressure in patients with chronic open-angle glaucoma
Pregnancy Risk Factor C
Dosage Ophthalmic: Adults: Instill 1 drop in the affected eye(s) twice daily
Dosage Forms SOLN, ophthalmic: 0.3% (5 mL, 10 mL)

♦ **Metipranolol Hydrochloride** *see* Metipranolol *on page 827*

Metoclopramide (met oh kloe PRA mide)
U.S. Brand Names Reglan®
Therapeutic Category Antiemetic; Dopamine Antagonist; Gastroprokinetic Agent
Use Prevention and/or treatment of nausea and vomiting associated with chemotherapy, radiation therapy, or postsurgery; symptomatic treatment of diabetic gastric stasis; gastroesophageal reflux; facilitation of intubation of the small intestine
Pregnancy Risk Factor B
Contraindications Hypersensitivity to metoclopramide or any component of the formulation; GI obstruction, perforation or hemorrhage; pheochromocytoma; history of seizure disorder
Warnings/Precautions Use with caution in patients with Parkinson's disease and in patients with a history of mental illness; has been associated with extrapyramidal symptoms and depression; may exacerbate seizures; neuroleptic malignant syndrome (NMS) has rarely been reported. Use lowest recommended doses initially; may cause transient increase in serum aldosterone; use caution in patients who are at risk of fluid overload (CHF, cirrhosis); dosage and/or frequency of administration should be modified in response to degree of renal impairment.
Common Adverse Reactions Adverse reactions are more common/severe at dosages used for prophylaxis of chemotherapy-induced emesis.
>10%:
Central nervous system: Restlessness, drowsiness, extrapyramidal symptoms (high-dose, up to 34%)
Gastrointestinal: Diarrhea (may be dose-limiting)
Neuromuscular & skeletal: Weakness
1% to 10%:
Central nervous system: Insomnia, depression
Dermatologic: Rash
Endocrine & metabolic: Breast tenderness, prolactin stimulation
Gastrointestinal: Nausea, xerostomia
Drug Interactions
Cytochrome P450 Effect: Substrate (minor) of CYP1A2, 2D6; **Inhibits** CYP2D6 (weak)
Increased Effect/Toxicity: Opiate analgesics may increase CNS depression. Metoclopramide may increase extrapyramidal symptoms (EPS) or risk when used concurrently with antipsychotic agents.
Decreased Effect: Anticholinergic agents antagonize metoclopramide's actions.
Mechanism of Action Blocks dopamine receptors and (when given in higher doses) also blocks serotonin receptors in chemoreceptor trigger zone of the CNS; enhances the response to acetylcholine of tissue in upper GI tract causing enhanced motility and accelerated gastric emptying without stimulating gastric, biliary, or pancreatic secretions
Pharmacodynamics/Kinetics
Onset of action: Oral: 0.5-1 hour; I.V.: 1-3 minutes
Duration: Therapeutic: 1-2 hours, regardless of route
Distribution: V_d: 2-4 L/kg; Crosses placenta; enters breast milk
Protein binding: 30% to 40%, primarily to α_1-acid glycoprotein
(Continued)

Metoclopramide *(Continued)*

Half-life elimination: Normal renal function: 4-7 hours (may be dose dependent)

Time to peak, serum: Oral: 1-3 hours; I.M.: 2-3 hours; I.V.: Within 5 minutes; Rectal: 1-8 hours

Excretion: Urine (70% to 85%, ~19% as unchanged drug); feces (2% to 3%)

Dosage

Children:

Gastroesophageal reflux: Oral: 0.1-0.2 mg/kg/dose up to 4 times/day; efficacy of continuing metoclopramide beyond 12 weeks in reflux has not been determined; total daily dose should not exceed 0.5 mg/kg/day

Gastrointestinal hypomotility (gastroparesis): Oral, I.M., I.V.: 0.1 mg/kg/dose up to 4 times/day, not to exceed 0.5 mg/kg/day

Antiemetic (chemotherapy-induced emesis): I.V.: 1-2 mg/kg 30 minutes before chemotherapy and every 2-4 hours, for a total of 5 doses (5-10 mg/kg) daily

Facilitate intubation: I.V.:

<6 years: 0.1 mg/kg

6-14 years: 2.5-5 mg

Adults:

Gastroesophageal reflux: Oral: 10-15 mg/dose up to 4 times/day 30 minutes before meals or food and at bedtime; single doses of 20 mg are occasionally needed for provoking situations; efficacy of continuing metoclopramide beyond 12 weeks in reflux has not been determined

Gastrointestinal hypomotility (gastroparesis):

Oral: 10 mg 30 minutes before each meal and at bedtime for 2-8 weeks

I.V. (for severe symptoms): 10 mg over 1-2 minutes; 10 days of I.V. therapy may be necessary for best response

Antiemetic (chemotherapy-induced emesis): I.V.: 1-2 mg/kg 30 minutes before chemotherapy and every 2-4 hours, for a total of 5 doses (5-10 mg/kg) daily

Postoperative nausea and vomiting: I.M.: 10 mg near end of surgery; 20 mg doses may be used

Facilitate intubation: I.V.: 10 mg

Elderly:

Gastroesophageal reflux: Oral: 5 mg 4 times/day (30 minutes before meals and at bedtime); increase dose to 10 mg 4 times/day if no response at lower dose

Gastrointestinal hypomotility:

Oral: Initial: 5 mg 30 minutes before meals and at bedtime for 2-8 weeks; increase if necessary to 10 mg doses

I.V.: Initiate at 5 mg over 1-2 minutes; increase to 10 mg if necessary

Postoperative nausea and vomiting: I.M.: 5 mg near end of surgery; may repeat dose if necessary

Dosing adjustment in renal impairment:

Cl_{cr} 10-40 mL/minute: Administer at 50% of normal dose

Cl_{cr} <10 mL/minute: Administer at 25% of normal dose

Hemodialysis: Not dialyzable (0% to 5%); supplemental dose is not necessary

Administration Injection solution may be given I.M., direct I.V. push, short infusion (15-30 minutes), or continuous infusion; lower doses (≤10 mg) of metoclopramide can be given I.V. push undiluted over 1-2 minutes; higher doses to be given IVPB over at least 15 minutes; continuous S.C. infusion and rectal administration have been reported

Monitoring Parameters Periodic renal function test; monitor for dystonic reactions; monitor for signs of hypoglycemia in patients using insulin and those being treated for gastroparesis; monitor for agitation and irritable confusion

Patient Information May impair mental alertness or physical coordination; avoid alcohol, barbiturates or other CNS depressants; take 30 minutes before meals; report if involuntary movements occur

Dosage Forms INJ, solution (Reglan®): 5 mg/mL (2 mL, 10 mL, 30 mL). **SYR:** 5 mg/5 mL (10 mL, 480 mL). **TAB** (Reglan®): 5 mg, 10 mg

Metolazone *(me TOLE a zone)*

Related Information

Sulfonamide Derivatives *on page 1404*

U.S. Brand Names Mykrox® [DSC]; Zaroxolyn®

Therapeutic Category Antihypertensive Agent; Diuretic, Miscellaneous

Use Management of mild to moderate hypertension; treatment of edema in congestive heart failure and nephrotic syndrome, impaired renal function

Pregnancy Risk Factor B (manufacturer); D (expert analysis)

Contraindications Hypersensitivity to metolazone, any component of the formulation, other thiazides, and sulfonamide derivatives; anuria; hepatic coma; pregnancy (expert analysis)

Warnings/Precautions Use with caution in renal disease, hepatic disease, gout, lupus erythematosus, diabetes mellitus; some products may contain tartrazine. **Mykrox® is not bioequivalent to Zaroxolyn® and should not be interchanged for one another.** Electrolyte disturbances (hypokalemia, hypochloremic alkalosis, hyponatremia) can occur. Orthostatic hypotension may occur (potentiated by alcohol, barbiturates, narcotics, other antihypertensive drugs).

Chemical similarities are present among sulfonamides, sulfonylureas, carbonic anhydrase inhibitors, thiazides, and loop diuretics (except ethacrynic acid). Use in patients with thiazide or sulfonamide allergy is specifically contraindicated in product labeling, however, a risk of cross-reaction exists in patients with allergy to any of these compounds; avoid use when previous reaction has been severe.

Common Adverse Reactions

>10%: Central nervous system: Dizziness

1% to 10%:

Cardiovascular: Orthostatic hypotension, palpitations, chest pain, cold extremities (rapidly acting), edema (rapidly acting), venous thrombosis (slow acting), syncope (slow acting)

Central nervous system: Headache, fatigue, lethargy, malaise, lassitude, anxiety, depression, nervousness, "weird" feeling (rapidly acting), chills (slow acting)

Dermatologic: Rash, pruritus, dry skin (rapidly acting)

Endocrine & metabolic: Hypokalemia, impotence, reduced libido, excessive volume depletion (slow acting), hemoconcentration (slow acting), acute gouty attach (slow acting), weakness

Gastrointestinal: Nausea, vomiting, abdominal pain, cramping, bloating, diarrhea or constipation, dry mouth

Genitourinary: Nocturia

Neuromuscular & skeletal: Muscle cramps, spasm

Ocular: Eye itching (rapidly acting)

Otic: Tinnitus (rapidly acting)

Respiratory: Cough (rapidly acting), epistaxis (rapidly acting), sinus congestion (rapidly acting), sore throat (rapidly acting)

Drug Interactions

Increased Effect/Toxicity: Increased diuretic effect of metolazone with furosemide and other loop diuretics. Increased hypotension and/or renal adverse effects of ACE inhibitors may result in aggressively diuresed patients. Cyclosporine and thiazide-type diuretics can increase the risk of gout or renal toxicity. Digoxin toxicity can be exacerbated if a diuretic induces hypokalemia or hypomagnesemia. Lithium toxicity can occur with thiazide-type diuretics due to reduced renal excretion of lithium. Thiazide-type diuretics may prolong the duration of action of neuromuscular blocking agents.

Decreased Effect: Decreased absorption of metolazone with cholestyramine and colestipol. NSAIDs can decrease the efficacy of thiazide-type diuretics, reducing the diuretic and antihypertensive effects.

Mechanism of Action Inhibits sodium reabsorption in the distal tubules causing increased excretion of sodium and water, as well as, potassium and hydrogen ions

Pharmacodynamics/Kinetics

Onset of action: Diuresis: ~60 minutes

Duration: 12-24 hours

Absorption: Incomplete

Distribution: Crosses placenta; enters breast milk

Protein binding: 95%

Metabolism: Undergoes enterohepatic recirculation

Bioavailability: Mykrox® reportedly has highest

Half-life elimination (renal function dependent): 6-20 hours

Excretion: Urine (80% to 95%)

Dosage Adults: Oral:

Edema: 5-20 mg/dose every 24 hours

Hypertension (Zaroxolyn®): 2.5-5 mg/dose every 24 hours

Hypertension (Mykrox®): 0.5 mg/day; if response is not adequate, increase dose to maximum of 1 mg/day

Dialysis: Not dialyzable (0% to 5%) via hemo- or peritoneal dialysis; supplemental dose is not necessary

Administration May be taken with food or milk. Take early in day to avoid nocturia. Take the last dose of multiple doses no later than 6 PM unless instructed otherwise.

Monitoring Parameters Serum electrolytes (potassium, sodium, chloride, bicarbonate), renal function, blood pressure (standing, sitting/supine)

Patient Information May be taken with food or milk; take early in day to avoid nocturia; take the last dose of multiple doses no later than 6 PM unless instructed otherwise. A few people who take this medication become more sensitive to sunlight and may experience skin rash, redness, itching, or severe sunburn, especially if sun block SPF ≥15 is not used on exposed skin areas.

Dosage Forms TAB, rapid acting (Mykrox®): 0.5 mg [DSC]. **TAB, slow acting:** 2.5 mg; (Zaroxolyn®): 2.5 mg, 5 mg, 10 mg

Metoprolol (me toe PROE lole)

Related Information

Beta-Blockers Comparison on page 1368

U.S. Brand Names Lopressor®; Toprol-XL®

Synonyms Metoprolol Tartrate

Therapeutic Category Antihypertensive Agent; Beta Blocker, Beta₁ Selective

Use Treatment of hypertension and angina pectoris; prevention of myocardial infarction, atrial fibrillation, flutter, symptomatic treatment of hypertrophic subaortic stenosis; to reduce mortality/hospitalization in patients with congestive heart failure (stable NYHA Class II or III) in patients already receiving ACE inhibitors, diuretics, and/or digoxin (sustained-release only)

Unlabeled/Investigational Use Treatment of ventricular arrhythmias, atrial ectopy, migraine prophylaxis, essential tremor, aggressive behavior

Pregnancy Risk Factor C (manufacturer); D (2nd and 3rd trimesters - expert analysis) (Continued)

Metoprolol *(Continued)*

Contraindications Hypersensitivity to metoprolol or any component of the formulation; sinus bradycardia; heart block greater than first degree (except in patients with a functioning artificial pacemaker); cardiogenic shock; uncompensated cardiac failure; pregnancy (2nd and 3rd trimesters)

Warnings/Precautions Abrupt withdrawal of the drug should be avoided (may result in an exaggerated cardiac beta-adrenergic response, tachycardia, hypertension, ischemia, angina, myocardial infarction, and sudden death), drug should be discontinued over 1-2 weeks. Must use care in compensated heart failure and monitor closely for a worsening of the condition (efficacy has not been established for metoprolol). Avoid abrupt discontinuation in patients with a history of CAD; slowly wean while monitoring for signs and symptoms of ischemia. Use caution in patients with PVD (can aggravate arterial insufficiency). Use caution with concurrent use of beta-blockers and either verapamil or diltiazem; bradycardia or heart block can occur. Avoid concurrent I.V. use of both agents. In general, beta-blockers should be avoided in patients with bronchospastic disease. Metoprolol, with B1 selectivity, should be used cautiously in bronchospastic disease with close monitoring, since selectivity can be lost with higher doses. Beta-blockers may increase the risk of anaphylaxis (in predisposed patients) and blunt response to epinephrine. Use cautiously in diabetics because it can mask prominent hypoglycemic symptoms. Can mask signs of thyrotoxicosis. Can cause fetal harm when administered in pregnancy. Use cautiously in the hepatically impaired. Use care with anesthetic agents which decrease myocardial function.

Common Adverse Reactions

>10%:

Central nervous system: Drowsiness, insomnia

Endocrine & metabolic: Decreased sexual ability

1% to 10%:

Cardiovascular: Bradycardia, palpitations, edema, CHF, reduced peripheral circulation

Central nervous system: Mental depression

Gastrointestinal: Diarrhea or constipation, nausea, stomach discomfort

Respiratory: Bronchospasm

Miscellaneous: Cold extremities

Drug Interactions

Cytochrome P450 Effect: Substrate of CYP2C19 (minor), 2D6 (major); **Inhibits** CYP2D6 (weak)

Increased Effect/Toxicity: CYP2D6 inhibitors may increase the levels/effects of metoprolol; example inhibitors include chlorpromazine, delavirdine, fluoxetine, miconazole, paroxetine, pergolide, quinidine, quinine, ritonavir, and ropinirole. Metoprolol may increase the effects of other drugs which slow AV conduction (digoxin, verapamil, diltiazem), alpha-blockers (prazosin, terazosin), and alpha-adrenergic stimulants (epinephrine, phenylephrine). Metoprolol may mask the tachycardia from hypoglycemia caused by insulin and oral hypoglycemics. In patients receiving concurrent therapy, the risk of hypertensive crisis is increased when either clonidine or the beta-blocker is withdrawn. Reserpine has been shown to enhance the effect of beta-blockers. Beta-blockers may increase the action or levels of ethanol, disopyramide, nondepolarizing muscle relaxants, and theophylline although the effects are difficult to predict.

Decreased Effect: Decreased effect of beta-blockers with aluminum salts, barbiturates, calcium salts, cholestyramine, colestipol, NSAIDs, penicillins (ampicillin), rifampin, salicylates, and sulfinpyrazone due to decreased bioavailability and plasma levels. Beta-blockers may decrease the effect of sulfonylureas.

Mechanism of Action Selective inhibitor of beta$_1$-adrenergic receptors; competitively blocks beta$_1$-receptors, with little or no effect on beta$_2$-receptors at doses <100 mg; does not exhibit any membrane stabilizing or intrinsic sympathomimetic activity

Pharmacodynamics/Kinetics

Onset of action: Peak effect: Antihypertensive: Oral: 1.5-4 hours

Duration: 10-20 hours

Absorption: 95%

Protein binding: 8%

Metabolism: Extensively hepatic; significant first-pass effect

Bioavailability: Oral: 40% to 50%

Half-life elimination: 3-4 hours; End-stage renal disease: 2.5-4.5 hours

Excretion: Urine (3% to 10% as unchanged drug)

Dosage

Children: Oral: 1-5 mg/kg/24 hours divided twice daily; allow 3 days between dose adjustments

Adults:

Hypertension: Oral: 100-450 mg/day in 2-3 divided doses, begin with 50 mg twice daily and increase doses at weekly intervals to desired effect; usual dosage range (JNC 7): 50-100 mg/day

Extended release: Same daily dose administered as a single dose

Angina, SVT, MI prophylaxis: Oral: 100-450 mg/day in 2-3 divided doses, begin with 50 mg twice daily and increase doses at weekly intervals to desired effect

Extended release: Same daily dose administered as a single dose

Hypertension/ventricular rate control: I.V. (in patients having nonfunctioning GI tract): Initial: 1.25-5 mg every 6-12 hours; titrate initial dose to response. Initially, low doses may be appropriate to establish response; however, up to 15 mg every 3-6 hours has been employed.

Congestive heart failure: Oral (extended release): Initial: 25 mg once daily (reduce to 12.5 mg once daily in NYHA class higher than class II); may double dosage every 2 weeks as tolerated, up to 200 mg/day

Myocardial infarction (acute): I.V.: 5 mg every 2 minutes for 3 doses in early treatment of myocardial infarction; thereafter give 50 mg orally every 6 hours 15 minutes after last I.V. dose and continue for 48 hours; then administer a maintenance dose of 100 mg twice daily.

Elderly: Oral: Initial: 25 mg/day; usual range: 25-300 mg/day

Extended release: 25-50 mg/day initially as a single dose; increase at 1- to 2-week intervals.

Hemodialysis: Administer dose posthemodialysis or administer 50 mg supplemental dose; supplemental dose is not necessary following peritoneal dialysis

Dosing adjustment/comments in hepatic disease: Reduced dose probably necessary

Administration

Oral: Do not crush or chew extended release tablets.

I.V.: When administered acutely for cardiac treatment, monitor ECG and blood pressure. May administer by rapid infusion (I.V. push) over 1 minute or by slow infusion (ie, 5-10 mg of metoprolol in 50 mL of fluid) over ~30 minutes. Necessary monitoring for surgical patients who are unable to take oral beta-blockers (prolonged ileus) has not been defined. Some institutions require monitoring of baseline and postinfusion heart rate and blood pressure when a patient's response to beta-blockade has not been characterized (ie, the patient's initial dose or following a change in dose). Consult individual institutional policies and procedures.

Monitoring Parameters Acute cardiac treatment: Monitor ECG and blood pressure with I.V. administration; Heart rate and blood pressure with oral administration

Patient Information Do not discontinue medication abruptly, sudden stopping of medication may precipitate or cause angina; consult pharmacist or prescriber before taking with other adrenergic drugs (eg, cold medications); use with caution while driving or performing tasks requiring alertness; may mask signs of hypoglycemia in diabetics; regular tablets may be taken with food; extended release tablets may be taken without regard to meals

Dosage Forms INJ, solution, as tartrate (Lopressor®): 1 mg/mL (5 mL). **TAB, as tartrate** (Lopressor®): 50 mg, 100 mg. **TAB, extended release, as succinate** (Toprol XL®): 25 mg, 50 mg, 100 mg, 200 mg

- ◆ **Metoprolol Tartrate** see Metoprolol on page 829
- ◆ **MetroCream®** see Metronidazole on page 831
- ◆ **MetroGel®** see Metronidazole on page 831
- ◆ **MetroGel-Vaginal®** see Metronidazole on page 831
- ◆ **MetroLotion®** see Metronidazole on page 831

Metronidazole (me troe NI da zole)

Related Information

Antimicrobial Drugs of Choice on page 1440
Community-Acquired Pneumonia in Adults on page 1457
Prevention of Wound Infection & Sepsis in Surgical Patients on page 1436

U.S. Brand Names Flagyl®; Flagyl ER®; MetroCream®; MetroGel®; MetroGel-Vaginal®; MetroLotion®; Noritate®

Synonyms Metronidazole Hydrochloride

Therapeutic Category Amebicide; Antibiotic, Anaerobic; Antibiotic, Topical; Antibiotic, Vaginal; Antiprotozoal

Use Treatment of susceptible anaerobic bacterial and protozoal infections in the following conditions: Amebiasis, symptomatic and asymptomatic trichomoniasis; skin and skin structure infections; CNS infections; intra-abdominal infections (as part of combination regimen); systemic anaerobic infections; treatment of antibiotic-associated pseudomembranous colitis (AAPC), bacterial vaginosis; as part of a multidrug regimen for *H. pylori* eradication to reduce the risk of duodenal ulcer recurrence

Topical: Treatment of inflammatory lesions and erythema of rosacea

Unlabeled/Investigational Use Crohn's disease

Pregnancy Risk Factor B (may be contraindicated in 1st trimester)

Contraindications Hypersensitivity to metronidazole or any component of the formulation; pregnancy (1st trimester - found to be carcinogenic in rats)

Warnings/Precautions Use with caution in patients with liver impairment due to potential accumulation, blood dyscrasias; history of seizures, CHF, or other sodium retaining states; reduce dosage in patients with severe liver impairment, CNS disease, and severe renal failure; seizures and neuropathies have been reported especially with increased doses and chronic treatment; if this occurs, discontinue therapy

Common Adverse Reactions

Systemic: Frequency not defined:

Cardiovascular: Flattening of the T-wave, flushing

Central nervous system: Ataxia, confusion, coordination impaired, dizziness, fever, headache, insomnia, irritability, seizures, vertigo

Dermatologic: Erythematous rash, urticaria

Endocrine & metabolic: Disulfiram-like reaction, dysmenorrhea, libido decreased

Gastrointestinal: Nausea (~12%), anorexia, abdominal cramping, constipation, diarrhea, furry tongue, glossitis, proctitis, stomatitis, unusual/metallic taste, vomiting, xerostomia

Genitourinary: Cystitis, darkened urine (rare), dysuria, incontinence, polyuria, vaginitis

Hematologic: Neutropenia (reversible), thrombocytopenia (reversible, rare)

Neuromuscular & skeletal: Peripheral neuropathy, weakness

(Continued)

Metronidazole *(Continued)*

Respiratory: Nasal congestion, rhinitis, sinusitis, pharyngitis
Miscellaneous: Flu-like syndrome, moniliasis

Topical: Frequency not defined:
Central nervous system: Headache
Dermatologic: Burning, contact dermatitis, dryness, erythema, irritation, pruritus, rash
Gastrointestinal: Unusual/metallic taste, nausea, constipation
Local: Local allergic reaction
Neuromuscular & skeletal: Tingling/numbness of extremities
Ocular: Eye irritation

Vaginal:
>10%: Genitourinary: Vaginal discharge (12%)
1% to 10%:
Central nervous system: Headache (5%), dizziness (2%)
Gastrointestinal: Gastrointestinal discomfort (7%), nausea and/or vomiting (4%), unusual/
metallic taste (2%), diarrhea (1%)
Genitourinary: Vaginitis (10%), vulva/vaginal irritation (9%), pelvic discomfort (3%)
Hematologic: WBC increased (2%)

Drug Interactions
Cytochrome P450 Effect: Inhibits CYP2C8/9 (weak), 3A4 (moderate)
Increased Effect/Toxicity: Ethanol may cause a disulfiram-like reaction. Warfarin and
metronidazole may increase bleeding times (PT) which may result in bleeding. Cimetidine
may increase metronidazole levels. Metronidazole may inhibit metabolism of cisapride,
causing potential arrhythmias; avoid concurrent use. Metronidazole may increase lithium
levels/toxicity.
Decreased Effect: Phenytoin, phenobarbital (potentially other enzyme inducers) may
decrease metronidazole half-life and effects.
Mechanism of Action Reduced to a product which interacts with DNA to cause a loss of
helical DNA structure and strand breakage resulting in inhibition of protein synthesis and cell
death in susceptible organisms

Pharmacodynamics/Kinetics
Absorption: Oral: Well absorbed; Topical: Concentrations achieved systemically after applica-
tion of 1 g topically are 10 times less than those obtained after a 250 mg oral dose
Distribution: To saliva, bile, seminal fluid, breast milk, bone, liver, and liver abscesses, lung
and vaginal secretions; crosses placenta and blood-brain barrier
CSF:blood level ratio: Normal meninges: 16% to 43%; Inflamed meninges: 100%
Protein binding: <20%
Metabolism: Hepatic (30% to 60%)
Half-life elimination: Neonates: 25-75 hours; Others: 6-8 hours, prolonged with hepatic impair-
ment; End-stage renal disease: 21 hours
Time to peak, serum: Oral: Immediate release: 1-2 hours
Excretion: Urine (20% to 40% as unchanged drug); feces (6% to 15%)

Dosage
Infants and Children:
Amebiasis: Oral: 35-50 mg/kg/day in divided doses every 8 hours for 10 days
Trichomoniasis: Oral: 15-30 mg/kg/day in divided doses every 8 hours for 7 days
Anaerobic infections:
Oral: 15-35 mg/kg/day in divided doses every 8 hours
I.V.: 30 mg/kg/day in divided doses every 6 hours
Clostridium difficile (antibiotic-associated colitis): Oral: 20 mg/kg/day divided every 6 hours
Maximum dose: 2 g/day
Adults:
Amebiasis: Oral: 500-750 mg every 8 hours for 5-10 days
Trichomoniasis: Oral: 250 mg every 8 hours for 7 days **or** 375 mg twice daily for 7 days **or** 2
g as a single dose
Anaerobic infections: Oral, I.V.: 500 mg every 6-8 hours, not to exceed 4 g/day
Antibiotic-associated pseudomembranous colitis: Oral: 250-500 mg 3-4 times/day for 10-14
days
Helicobacter pylori eradication: Oral: 250-500 mg with meals and at bedtime for 14 days;
requires combination therapy with at least one other antibiotic and an acid-suppressing
agent (proton pump inhibitor or H_2 blocker)
Bacterial vaginosis:
Oral: 750 mg (extended release tablet) once daily for 7 days
Vaginal: 1 applicatorful (~37.5 mg metronidazole) intravaginally once or twice daily for 5
days; apply once in morning and evening if using twice daily, if daily, use at bedtime
Acne rosacea: Topical:
0.75%: Apply and rub a thin film twice daily, morning and evening, to entire affected areas
after washing. Significant therapeutic results should be noticed within 3 weeks. Clinical
studies have demonstrated continuing improvement through 9 weeks of therapy.
1%: Apply thin film to affected area once daily
Elderly: Use lower end of dosing recommendations for adults, do not administer as a single
dose

Dosing adjustment in renal impairment: Cl_{cr} <10 mL/minute: Administer 50% of dose or
every 12 hours

Hemodialysis: Extensively removed by hemodialysis and peritoneal dialysis (50% to 100%); administer dose posthemodialysis

Peritoneal dialysis: Dose as for Cl$_{cr}$ <10 mL/minute

Continuous arteriovenous or venovenous hemofiltration: Administer usual dose

Dosing adjustment/comments in hepatic disease: Unchanged in mild liver disease; reduce dosage in severe liver disease

Administration

Oral: May be taken with food to minimize stomach upset. Extended release tablets should be taken on an empty stomach (1 hour before or 2 hours after meals).

I.V.: Avoid contact between the drug and aluminum in the infusion set.

Topical: No disulfiram-like reactions have been reported after **topical** application, although metronidazole can be detected in the blood. Apply to clean, dry skin. Cosmetics may be used after application (wait at least 5 minutes after using lotion).

Patient Information Urine may be discolored to a dark or reddish-brown; do not take alcohol for at least 24 hours after the last dose; avoid beverage alcohol or any topical products containing alcohol during therapy; may cause metallic taste; may be taken with food to minimize stomach upset; report numbness or tingling in extremities; avoid contact of the topical product with the eyes; cleanse areas to be treated well before application

Dosage Forms CAP (Flagyl®): 375 mg. **CRM, topical** (MetroCream®): 0.75% (45 g); (Noritate®): 1% (30 g). **GEL, topical** (MetroGel®): 0.75% [7.5 mg/mL] (30 g, 45 g). **GEL, vaginal** (MetroGel-Vaginal®): 0.75% (70 g). **INF** [premixed iso-osmotic sodium chloride solution]: 500 mg (100 mL). **INJ, powder for reconstitution** (Flagyl®): 500 mg. **LOTION** (MetroLotion®): 0.75% (60 mL). **TAB** (Flagyl®): 250 mg, 500 mg. **TAB, extended release** (Flagyl® ER): 750 mg

♦ **Metronidazole, Bismuth Subsalicylate, and Tetracycline** see Bismuth Subsalicylate, Metronidazole, and Tetracycline on page 169

♦ **Metronidazole Hydrochloride** see Metronidazole on page 831

♦ **Metronidazole, Tetracycline, and Bismuth Subsalicylate** see Bismuth Subsalicylate, Metronidazole, and Tetracycline on page 169

Metyrosine (me TYE roe seen)

U.S. Brand Names Demser®

Synonyms AMPT; OGMT

Therapeutic Category Tyrosine Hydroxylase Inhibitor

Use Short-term management of pheochromocytoma before surgery, long-term management when surgery is contraindicated or when chronic malignant pheochromocytoma exists

Pregnancy Risk Factor C

Dosage Children >12 years and Adults: Oral: Initial: 250 mg 4 times/day, increased by 250-500 mg/day up to 4 g/day; maintenance: 2-3 g/day in 4 divided doses; for preoperative preparation, administer optimum effective dosage for 5-7 days

Dosing adjustment in renal impairment: Adjustment should be considered

Dosage Forms CAP: 250 mg

♦ **Mevacor®** see Lovastatin on page 764

♦ **Mevinolin** see Lovastatin on page 764

Mexiletine (MEKS i le teen)

U.S. Brand Names Mexitil®

Therapeutic Category Antiarrhythmic Agent, Class I-B

Use Management of serious ventricular arrhythmias; suppression of PVCs

Unlabeled/Investigational Use Diabetic neuropathy

Pregnancy Risk Factor C

Contraindications Hypersensitivity to mexiletine or any component of the formulation; cardiogenic shock; second- or third-degree AV block (except in patients with a functioning artificial pacemaker)

Warnings/Precautions Exercise extreme caution in patients with pre-existing sinus node dysfunction; mexiletine can worsen CHF, bradycardias, and other arrhythmias; mexiletine, like other antiarrhythmic agents, is proarrhythmic; CAST study indicates a trend toward increased mortality with antiarrhythmics in the face of cardiac disease (myocardial infarction); leukopenia, agranulocytopenia, and thrombocytopenia; seizures; alterations in urinary pH may change urinary excretion; may cause acute hepatic injury; use caution in patients with significant hepatic dysfunction; electrolyte disturbances alter response; rare hepatic toxicity may occur; electrolyte abnormalities should be corrected before initiating therapy (can worsen CHF)

Common Adverse Reactions

>10%:

Central nervous system: Lightheadedness (11% to 25%), dizziness (20% to 25%), nervousness (5% to 10%), incoordination (10%)

Gastrointestinal: GI distress (41%), nausea/vomiting (40%)

Neuromuscular & skeletal: Trembling, unsteady gait, tremor (13%), ataxia (10% to 20%)

1% to 10%:

Cardiovascular: Chest pain (3% to 8%), premature ventricular contractions (1% to 2%), palpitations (4% to 8%), angina (2%), proarrhythmic (10% to 15% in patients with malignant arrhythmias)

Central nervous system: Confusion, headache, insomnia (5% to 7%), depression (2%)

Dermatologic: Rash (4%)

(Continued)

Mexiletine *(Continued)*

Gastrointestinal: Constipation or diarrhea (4% to 5%), xerostomia (3%), abdominal pain (1%)

Neuromuscular & skeletal: Weakness (5%), numbness of fingers or toes (2% to 4%), paresthesias (2%), arthralgias (1%)

Ocular: Blurred vision (5% to 7%), nystagmus (6%)

Otic: Tinnitus (2% to 3%)

Respiratory: Dyspnea (3%)

Drug Interactions

Cytochrome P450 Effect: Substrate (major) of CYP1A2, 2D6; **Inhibits** CYP1A2 (strong)

Increased Effect/Toxicity: CYP1A2 inhibitors may increase the levels/effects of mexiletine; example inhibitors include amiodarone, ciprofloxacin, fluvoxamine, ketoconazole, lomeflox-acin, ofloxacin, and rofecoxib. CYP2D6 inhibitors may increase the levels/effects of mexile-tine; example inhibitors include chlorpromazine, delavirdine, fluoxetine, miconazole, paroxetine, pergolide, quinidine, quinine, ritonavir, and ropinirole. Mexiletine and caffeine or theophylline may result in elevated levels of theophylline and caffeine. Quinidine and urinary alkalinizers (antacids, sodium bicarbonate, acetazolamide) may increase mexiletine blood levels.

Decreased Effect: CYP1A2 inducers may decrease the levels/effects of mexiletine; example inducers include aminoglutethimide, carbamazepine, phenobarbital, and rifampin. Urinary acidifying agents may decrease mexiletine levels.

Mechanism of Action Class IB antiarrhythmic, structurally related to lidocaine, which inhibits inward sodium current, decreases rate of rise of phase 0, increases effective refractory period/ action potential duration ratio

Pharmacodynamics/Kinetics

Absorption: Elderly have a slightly slower rate, but extent of absorption is the same as young adults

Distribution: V_d: 5-7 L/kg

Protein binding: 50% to 70%

Metabolism: Hepatic; low first-pass effect

Half-life elimination: Adults: 10-14 hours (average: elderly: 14.4 hours, younger adults: 12 hours); prolonged with hepatic impairment or heart failure

Time to peak: 2-3 hours

Excretion: Urine (10% to 15% as unchanged drug); urinary acidification increases excretion, alkalinization decreases excretion

Dosage Adults: Oral: Initial: 200 mg every 8 hours (may load with 400 mg if necessary); adjust dose every 2-3 days; usual dose: 200-300 mg every 8 hours; maximum dose: 1.2 g/day (some patients respond to every 12-hour dosing). When switching from another antiarrhythmic, initiate a 200 mg dose 6-12 hours after stopping former agents, 3-6 hours after stopping procainamide.

Dosage adjustment in hepatic impairment: Reduce dose to 25% to 30% of usual dose

Administration Administer around-the-clock rather than 3 times/day to promote less variation in peak and trough serum levels; administer with food

Reference Range Therapeutic range: 0.5-2 µg/mL; potentially toxic: >2 µg/mL

Patient Information Take with food or antacid; report severe or persistent abdominal pain, nausea, vomiting, yellowing of eyes or skin, pale stools, dark urine, or persistent fever, sore throat, bleeding, or bruising

Dosage Forms CAP: 150 mg, 200 mg, 250 mg

♦ **Mexitil®** *see* Mexiletine *on page 833*

♦ **Miacalcin®** *see* Calcitonin *on page 200*

♦ **Micaderm®** **[OTC]** *see* Miconazole *on page 834*

♦ **Micardis®** *see* Telmisartan *on page 1191*

♦ **Micardis® HCT** *see* Telmisartan and Hydrochlorothiazide *on page 1191*

♦ **Micatin®** **[OTC]** *see* Miconazole *on page 834*

Miconazole *(mi KON a zole)*

Related Information

Antifungal Agents Comparison *on page 1362*

U.S. Brand Names Aloe Vesta® 2-n-1 Antifungal [OTC]; Baza® Antifungal [OTC]; Carrington Antifungal [OTC]; Femizol-M™ [OTC]; Fungoid® Tincture [OTC]; Lotrimin® AF Powder/Spray [OTC]; Micaderm® [OTC]; Micatin® [OTC]; Micro-Guard® [OTC]; Mitrazol™ [OTC]; Monistat® 1 Combination Pack [OTC]; Monistat® 3 [OTC]; Monistat® 7 [OTC]; Monistat-Derm®; Triple Care® Antifungal [OTC]; Zeasorb®-AF [OTC]

Synonyms Miconazole Nitrate

Therapeutic Category Antifungal Agent, Imidazole Derivative; Antifungal Agent, Parental; Antifungal Agent, Topical; Antifungal Agent, Vaginal

Use Treatment of vulvovaginal candidiasis and a variety of skin and mucous membrane fungal infections

Pregnancy Risk Factor C

Contraindications Hypersensitivity to miconazole or any component of the formulation

Warnings/Precautions For external use only; discontinue if sensitivity or irritation develop. Petrolatum-based vaginal products may damage rubber or latex condoms or diaphragms. Separate use by 3 days.

Common Adverse Reactions Frequency not defined.

Topical: Allergic contact dermatitis, burning, maceration

Vaginal: Abdominal cramps, burning, irritation, itching

Drug Interactions

Cytochrome P450 Effect: Substrate of CYP3A4 (major); **Inhibits** CYP1A2 (moderate), 2A6 (strong), 2B6 (weak), 2C8/9 (strong), 2C19 (strong), 2D6 (strong), 2E1 (moderate), 3A4 (strong)

Increased Effect/Toxicity: Note: The majority of reported drug interactions were observed following intravenous miconazole administration. Although systemic absorption following topical and/or vaginal administration is low, potential interactions due to CYP isoenzyme inhibition may occur (rarely). This may be particularly true in situations where topical absorption may be increased (ie, inflamed tissue).

Miconazole coadministered with warfarin has increased the anticoagulant effect of warfarin (including reports associated with vaginal miconazole therapy of as little as 3 days). Phenytoin levels may be increased. Miconazole may inhibit the metabolism of oral sulfonylureas. Concurrent administration of cisapride is contraindicated due to an increased risk of card otoxicity.

Decreased Effect: Amphotericin B may decrease antifungal effect of both agents.

Mechanism of Action Inhibits biosynthesis of ergosterol, damaging the fungal cell wall membrane, which increases permeability causing leaking of nutrients

Pharmacodynamics/Kinetics

Absorption: Topical: Negligible

Distribution: Widely to body tissues; penetrates well into inflamed joints, vitreous humor of eye, and peritoneal cavity, but poorly into saliva and sputum; crosses blood-brain barrier but only to a small extent

Protein binding: 91% to 93%

Metabolism: Hepatic

Half-life elimination: Multiphasic: Initial: 40 minutes; Secondary: 126 minutes; Terminal: 24 hours

Excretion: Feces (~50%); urine (<1% as unchanged drug)

Dosage

Topical: Children and Adults: **Note:** Not for OTC use in children <2 years:

Tinea pedis and tinea corporis: Apply twice daily for 4 weeks

Tinea cruris: Apply twice daily for 2 weeks

Vaginal: Adults: Vulvovaginal candidiasis:

Cream, 2%: Insert 1 applicatorful at bedtime for 7 days

Cream, 4%: Insert 1 applicatorful at bedtime for 3 days

Suppository, 100 mg: Insert 1 suppository at bedtime for 7 days

Suppository, 200 mg: Insert 1 suppository at bedtime for 3 days

Suppository, 1200 mg: Insert 1 suppository at bedtime (a one-time dose)

Note: Many products are available as a combination pack, with a suppository for vaginal instillation and cream to relieve external symptoms.

Patient Information Take full course of therapy as directed; do not discontinue without consulting prescriber. Some infections may require long periods of therapy. Practice good hygiene measures to prevent reinfection. If you are diabetic, you should test serum glucose regularly at the same time of day. You may experience nausea and vomiting (small, frequent meals may help) or headache, dizziness (use caution when driving). Report unresolved headache, rash, burning, itching, anorexia, unusual fatigue, diarrhea, nausea, or vomiting.

Topical: Wash and dry area before applying medication; apply thinly. Do not get in or near eyes.

Vaginal: Insert high in vagina. Refrain from intercourse during treatment. OTC products, even if administered topically, may not mix well with certain prescription medications (which may lead to drug interactions). Consult with your prescriber.

Dosage Forms COMBO PACK: Miconazole vaginal suppository 200 mg (3s) and miconazole external cream 2%; Miconazole vaginal suppository 100 mg (7s) and miconazole external cream 2%; (Monistat® 1 Combination Pack): Miconazole vaginal insert 1200 mg (1) and miconazole external cream 2% (5 g) [Note: Do not confuse with 1-Day™ (formerly Monistat® 1) which contains tioconazole]; (Monistat® 3 Combination Pack): Miconazole vaginal suppository 200 mg (3s) and miconazole external cream 2%; (Monistat® 3 Cream Combination Pack): Miconazole vaginal cream 4% and miconazole external cream 2%; (Monistat® 7 Combination Pack): Miconazole vaginal suppository 100 mg (7s) and miconazole external cream 2%; Miconazole vaginal cream 2% (7 prefilled applicators) and miconazole external cream 2%. **CRM, topical** 2% (15 g, 30 g, 45 g); (Baza® Antifungal): 2% (4 g, 57 g, 142 g); (Carrington Antifungal): 2% (150 g); (Micaderm®): 2% (30 g); (Micatin®): 2% (15 g); (Micro-Guard®, Mitrazol™): 2% (60 g); (Monistat-Derm®): 2% (15 g, 30 g, 85 g); (Triple Care® Antifungal): 2% (60 g, 98 g). **CRM, vaginal** [available in prefilled or single refillable applicator]: 2% (45 g); (Femizol-M™): 2% (47 g); (Monistat® 3): 4% (15 g, 25 g); (Monistat® 7): 2% (45 g). **LOTION, powder** (Zeasorb®-AF): 2% (56 g). **OINT, topical** (Aloe Vesta® 2-n-1 Antifungal): 2% (60 g, 150 g). **POWDER, topical** (Lotrimin® AF, Micatin®, Micro-Guard®): 2% (90 g); (Mitrazol™): 2% (30 g); (Zeasorb®-AF): 2% (70 g). **SPRAY, liquid** (Micatin®): 2% (90 mL, 105 mL). **SPRAY, powder, topical** (Lotrimin® AF): 2% (100 g). **SUPP, vaginal:** 100 mg (7s); 200 mg (3s); (Monistat® 3): 200 mg (3s); (Monistat® 7): 100 mg (7s). **TINCT, topical** (Fungoid®): 2% (30 mL, 473 mL).

♦ **Miconazole Nitrate** *see* Miconazole *on page 834*

♦ **MICRhoGAM®** *see* Rh₀(D) Immune Globulin *on page 1089*

Microfibrillar Collagen Hemostat (mye kro FI bri lar KOL la jen HEE moe stat)
U.S. Brand Names Avitene®; Helistat®
Synonyms Collagen; MCH
Therapeutic Category Hemostatic Agent
Use Adjunct to hemostasis when control of bleeding by ligature is ineffective or impractical
Pregnancy Risk Factor C
Dosage Apply dry directly to source of bleeding
Dosage Forms SPONGE (Avitene®): 2 cm x 6.25 cm x 7 mm (12s); 8 cm x 6.25 cm x 1 cm (6s); 8 cm x 12.5 cm x 1 cm (6s); 8 cm x 12.5 cm x 3 mm (6s); 8 cm x 25 cm x1 cm (6s); (Helistat®): 0.5 inch x 1 inch x 7 mm (18s)

♦ **Microgestin™ Fe** *see Ethinyl Estradiol and Norethindrone on page 487*
♦ **Micro-Guard® [OTC]** *see Miconazole on page 834*
♦ **microK®** *see Potassium Chloride on page 1020*
♦ **microK® 10** *see Potassium Chloride on page 1020*
♦ **Micronase®** *see GlyBURIDE on page 594*
♦ **Microzide™** *see Hydrochlorothiazide on page 625*
♦ **Midamor® [DSC]** *see Amiloride on page 73*

Midazolam (MID aye zoe lam)
Related Information
  Benzodiazepines Comparison *on page 1366*
U.S. Brand Names Versed® [DSC]
Synonyms Midazolam Hydrochloride
Therapeutic Category Benzodiazepine; Hypnotic; Sedative
Use Preoperative sedation and provides conscious sedation prior to diagnostic or radiographic procedures; ICU sedation (continuous infusion); intravenous anesthesia (induction); intravenous anesthesia (maintenance)
Unlabeled/Investigational Use Anxiety, status epilepticus
Restrictions C-IV
Pregnancy Risk Factor D
Contraindications Hypersensitivity to midazolam or any component of the formulation, including benzyl alcohol (cross-sensitivity with other benzodiazepines may exist); parenteral form is not for intrathecal or epidural injection; narrow-angle glaucoma; concurrent use of potent inhibitors of CYP3A4 (amprenavir, atazanavir, or ritonavir); pregnancy
Warnings/Precautions May cause severe respiratory depression, respiratory arrest, or apnea. Use with extreme caution, particularly in noncritical care settings. Appropriate resuscitative equipment and qualified personnel must be available for administration and monitoring. Initial dosing must be cautiously titrated and individualized, particularly in elderly or debilitated patients, patients with hepatic impairment (including alcoholics), or in renal impairment, particularly if other CNS depressants (including opiates) are used concurrently. Initial doses in elderly or debilitated patients should not exceed 2.5 mg. Use with caution in patients with respiratory disease or impaired gag reflex. Use during upper airway procedures may increase risk of hypoventilation. Prolonged responses have been noted following extended administration by continuous infusion (possibly due to metabolite accumulation) or in the presence of drugs which inhibit midazolam metabolism.

May cause hypotension - hemodynamic events are more common in pediatric patients or patients with hemodynamic instability. Hypotension and/or respiratory depression may occur more frequently in patients who have received narcotic analgesics. Use with caution in obese patients, chronic renal failure, and CHF. Parenteral form contains benzyl alcohol - avoid rapid injection in neonates or prolonged infusions. Does not protect against increases in heart rate or blood pressure during intubation. Should not be used in shock, coma, or acute alcohol intoxication. Avoid intra-arterial administration or extravasation of parenteral formulation.

Causes CNS depression (dose-related) resulting in sedation, dizziness, confusion, or ataxia which may impair physical and mental capabilities. Patients must be cautioned about performing tasks which require mental alertness (eg, operating machinery or driving). A minimum of 1 day should elapse after midazolam administration before attempting these tasks. Use with caution in patients receiving other CNS depressants or psychoactive agents. Effects with other sedative drugs or ethanol may be potentiated. Benzodiazepines have been associated with falls and traumatic injury and should be used with extreme caution in patients who are at risk of these events (especially the elderly).

Midazolam causes anterograde amnesia. Paradoxical reactions, including hyperactive or aggressive behavior have been reported with benzodiazepines, particularly in adolescent/ pediatric or psychiatric patients. Does not have analgesic, antidepressant, or antipsychotic properties.

Benzodiazepines have been associated with dependence and acute withdrawal symptoms on discontinuation or reduction in dose. Acute withdrawal, including seizures, may be precipitated after administration of flumazenil in patients receiving long-term benzodiazepine therapy.
Common Adverse Reactions As reported in adults unless otherwise noted:
  >10%: Respiratory: Decreased tidal volume and/or respiratory rate decrease, apnea (3% children)
  1% to 10%:
    Cardiovascular: Hypotension (3% children)

Central nervous system: Drowsiness (1%), oversedation, headache (1%), seizure-like activity (1% children)

Gastrointestinal: Nausea (3%), vomiting (3%)

Local: Pain and local reactions at injection site (4% I.M., 5% I.V.; severity less than diazepam)

Ocular: Nystagmus (1% children)

Respiratory: Cough (1%)

Miscellaneous: Physical and psychological dependence with prolonged use, hiccups (4%, 1% children), paradoxical reaction (2% children)

Drug Interactions

Cytochrome P450 Effect: Substrate of CYP2B6 (minor), 3A4 (major); **Inhibits** CYP2C8/9 (weak), 3A4 (weak)

Increased Effect/Toxicity: Midazolam levels/effects may be increased by inhibitors of CYP3A4, including delavirdine, indinavir, saquinavir, quinupristin-dalfopristin, zafirlukast, zileuton, verapamil, troleandomycin, miconazole, itraconazole, nifedipine, grapefruit juice, diltiazem, fluconazole, ketoconazole, clarithromycin, and erythromycin. Use is contraindicated with amprenavir, atazanavir, and ritonavir. **If narcotics or other CNS depressants are administered concomitantly, the midazolam dose should be reduced by 30% if <65 years of age, or by at least 50% if >65 years of age.**

Decreased Effect: Carbamazepine, phenytoin, and rifampin may reduce the effects of midazolam.

Mechanism of Action

Binds to stereospecific benzodiazepine receptors on the postsynaptic GABA neuron at several sites within the central nervous system, including the limbic system, reticular formation. Enhancement of the inhibitory effect of GABA on neuronal excitability results by increased neuronal membrane permeability to chloride ions. This shift in chloride ions results in hyperpolarization (a less excitable state) and stabilization.

Pharmacodynamics/Kinetics

Onset of action: I.M.: Sedation: ~15 minutes; I.V.: 1-5 minutes

Peak effect: I.M.: 0.5-1 hour

Duration: I.M.: Up to 6 hours; Mean: 2 hours

Absorption: Oral: Rapid

Distribution: V_d: 0.8-2.5 L/kg; increased with congestive heart failure (CHF) and chronic renal failure

Protein binding: 95%

Metabolism: Extensively hepatic via CYP3A4

Bioavailability: Mean: 45%

Half-life elimination: 1-4 hours; prolonged with cirrhosis, congestive heart failure, obesity, and elderly

Excretion: Urine (as glucuronide conjugated metabolites); feces (~2% to 10%)

Dosage

The dose of midazolam needs to be individualized based on the patient's age, underlying diseases, and concurrent medications. Decrease dose (by ~30%) if narcotics or other CNS depressants are administered concomitantly. **Personnel and equipment needed for standard respiratory resuscitation should be immediately available during midazolam administration.**

Children <6 years may require higher doses and closer monitoring than older children; calculate dose on ideal body weight

Conscious sedation for procedures or preoperative sedation:

Oral: 0.25-0.5 mg/kg as a single dose preprocedure, up to a maximum of 20 mg; administer 30-45 minutes prior to procedure. Children <6 years or less cooperative patients may require as much as 1 mg/kg as a single dose; 0.25 mg/kg may suffice for children 6-16 years of age.

Intranasal (not an approved route): 0.2 mg/kg (up to 0.4 mg/kg in some studies), to a maximum of 15 mg; may be administered 30-45 minutes prior to procedure

I.M.: 0.1-0.15 mg/kg 30-60 minutes before surgery or procedure; range 0.05-0.15 mg/kg; doses up to 0.5 mg/kg have been used in more anxious patients; maximum total dose: 10 mg

I.V.:

Infants <6 months: Limited information is available in nonintubated infants; dosing recommendations not clear; infants <6 months are at higher risk for airway obstruction and hypoventilation; titrate dose in small increments to desired effect; monitor carefully

Infants 6 months to Children 5 years: Initial: 0.05-0.1 mg/kg; titrate dose carefully; total dose of 0.6 mg/kg may be required; usual maximum total dose: 6 mg

Children 6-12 years: Initial: 0.025-0.05 mg/kg; titrate dose carefully; total doses of 0.4 mg/kg may be required; usual maximum total dose: 10 mg

Children 12-16 years: Dose as adults; usual maximum total dose: 10 mg

Conscious sedation during mechanical ventilation: Children: Loading dose: 0.05-0.2 mg/kg, followed by initial continuous infusion: 0.06-0.12 mg/kg/hour (1-2 mcg/kg/minute); titrate to the desired effect; usual range: 0.4-6 mcg/kg/minute

Status epilepticus refractory to standard therapy (unlabeled use): Infants >2 months and Children: Loading dose: 0.15 mg/kg followed by a continuous infusion of 1 mcg/kg/minute; titrate dose upward every 5 minutes until clinical seizure activity is controlled; mean infusion rate required in 24 children was 2.3 mcg/kg/minute with a range of 1-18 mcg/kg/minute

(Continued)

Midazolam (Continued)

Adults:

Preoperative sedation:

I.M.: 0.07-0.08 mg/kg 30-60 minutes prior to surgery/procedure; usual dose: 5 mg; **Note:** Reduce dose in patients with COPD, high-risk patients, patients ≥60 years of age, and patients receiving other narcotics or CNS depressants

I.V.: 0.02-0.04 mg/kg; repeat every 5 minutes as needed to desired effect or up to 0.1-0.2 mg/kg

Intranasal (not an approved route): 0.2 mg/kg (up to 0.4 mg/kg in some studies); administer 30-45 minutes prior to surgery/procedure

Conscious sedation: I.V.: Initial: 0.5-2 mg slow I.V. over at least 2 minutes; slowly titrate to effect by repeating doses every 2-3 minutes if needed; usual total dose: 2.5-5 mg; use decreased doses in elderly

Healthy Adults <60 years: Some patients respond to doses as low as 1 mg; no more than 2.5 mg should be administered over a period of 2 minutes. Additional doses of midazolam may be administered after a 2-minute waiting period and evaluation of sedation after each dose increment. A total dose >5 mg is generally not needed. If narcotics or other CNS depressants are administered concomitantly, the midazolam dose should be reduced by 30%.

Anesthesia: I.V.:

Induction:

Unpremedicated patients: 0.3-0.35 mg/kg (up to 0.6 mg/kg in resistant cases)

Premedicated patients: 0.15-0.35 mg/kg

Maintenance: 0.05-0.3 mg/kg as needed, or continuous infusion 0.25-1.5 mcg/kg/minute

Sedation in mechanically-ventilated patients: I.V. continuous infusion: 100 mg in 250 mL D_5W or NS (if patient is fluid-restricted, may concentrate up to a maximum of 0.5 mg/mL); initial dose: 0.02-0.08 mg/kg (~1 mg to 5 mg in 70 kg adult) initially and either repeated at 5-15 minute intervals until adequate sedation is achieved or continuous infusion rates of 0.04-0.2 mg/kg/hour and titrate to reach desired level of sedation

Elderly: I.V.: Conscious sedation: Initial: 0.5 mg slow I.V.; give no more than 1.5 mg in a 2-minute period; if additional titration is needed, give no more than 1 mg over 2 minutes, waiting another 2 or more minutes to evaluate sedative effect; a total dose of >3.5 mg is rarely necessary

Dosage adjustment in renal impairment:

Hemodialysis: Supplemental dose is not necessary

Peritoneal dialysis: Significant drug removal is unlikely based on physiochemical characteristics

Administration

Intranasal: Administer using a 1 mL needleless syringe into the nares over 15 seconds; use the 5 mg/mL injection; $1/_2$ of the dose may be administered to each nare

Oral: Do not mix with any liquid (such as grapefruit juice) prior to administration

Parenteral:

I.M.: Administer deep I.M. into large muscle.

I.V.: Administer by slow I.V. injection over at least 2-5 minutes at a concentration of 1-5 mg/mL or by I.V. infusion. Continuous infusions should be administered via an infusion pump.

Monitoring Parameters Respiratory and cardiovascular status, blood pressure, blood pressure monitor required during I.V. administration

Dosage Forms INJ, solution (Versed® [DSC]): 1 mg/mL (2 mL, 5 mL, 10 mL); 5 mg/mL (1 mL, 2 mL, 5 mL, 10 mL). **INJ, solution** [preservative free]: 1 mg/mL (2 mL, 5 mL); 5 mg/mL (1 mL, 2 mL). **SYR** (Versed® [DSC]): 2 mg/mL (118 mL)

♦ **Midazolam Hydrochloride** see Midazolam on page 836

Midodrine (MI doe dreen)

U.S. Brand Names ProAmatine®

Synonyms Midodrine Hydrochloride

Therapeutic Category Alpha-Adrenergic Agonist

Use Orphan drug: Treatment of symptomatic orthostatic hypotension

Unlabeled/Investigational Use Investigational: Management of urinary incontinence

Pregnancy Risk Factor C

Contraindications Hypersensitivity to midodrine or any component of the formulation; severe organic heart disease; urinary retention; pheochromocytoma; thyrotoxicosis; persistent and significant supine hypertension; concurrent use of fludrocortisone

Warnings/Precautions Only indicated for patients for whom orthostatic hypotension significantly impairs their daily life. Use is not recommended with supine hypertension and caution should be exercised in patients with diabetes, visual problems, urinary retention (reduce initial dose) or hepatic dysfunction; monitor renal and hepatic function prior to and periodically during therapy; safety and efficacy has not been established in children; discontinue and re-evaluate therapy if signs of bradycardia occur.

Common Adverse Reactions

>10%:

Dermatologic: Piloerection (13%), pruritus (12%)

Genitourinary: Urinary urgency, retention, or polyuria, dysuria (up to 13%)

Neuromuscular & skeletal: Paresthesia (18.3%)

1% to 10%:

Cardiovascular: Supine hypertension (7%), facial flushing

Central nervous system: Confusion, anxiety, dizziness, chills (5%)
Dermatologic: Rash, dry skin (2%)
Gastrointestinal: Xerostomia, nausea, abdominal pain
Neuromuscular & skeletal: Pain (5%)

Drug Interactions
Increased Effect/Toxicity: Concomitant fludrocortisone results in hypernatremia or an increase in intraocular pressure and glaucoma. Bradycardia may be accentuated with concomitant administration of cardiac glycosides, psychotherapeutics, and beta-blockers. Alpha agonists may increase the pressure effects and alpha antagonists may negate the effects of midodrine.

Mechanism of Action Midodrine forms an active metabolite, desglymidodrine, that is an alpha$_1$-agonist. This agent increases arteriolar and venous tone resulting in a rise in standing, sitting, and supine systolic and diastolic blood pressure in patients with orthostatic hypotension. See table.

Causes of Orthostatic Hypotension

Primary Autonomic Causes
Pure autonomic failure (Bradbury-Eggleston syndrome, idiopathic orthostatic hypotension)
Autonomic failure with multiple system atrophy (Shy-Drager syndrome)
Familial dysautonomia (Riley-Day syndrome)
Dopamine beta-hydroxylase deficiency
Secondary Autonomic Causes
Chronic alcoholism
Parkinson's disease
Diabetes mellitus
Porphyria
Amyloidosis
Various carcinomas
Vitamin B_1 or B_{12} deficiency
Nonautonomic Causes
Hypovolemia (such as associated with hemorrhage, burns, or hemodialysis) and dehydration
Diminished homeostatic regulation (such as associated with aging, pregnancy, fever, or prolonged bedrest)
Medications (eg, antihypertensives, insulin, tricyclic antidepressants)

Pharmacodynamics/Kinetics
Onset of action: ~1 hour
Duration: 2-3 hours
Absorption: Rapid
Distribution: V_d (desglymidodrine): <1.6 L/kg; poorly across membrane (eg, blood brain barrier)
Protein binding: Minimal
Metabolism: Hepatic; rapid deglycination to desglymidodrine occurs in many tissues and plasma
Bioavailability: Absolute: 93%
Half-life elimination: Active drug: ~3-4 hours; Prodrug: 25 minutes
Time to peak, serum: Active drug: 1-2 hours; Prodrug: 30 minutes
Excretion: Urine (2% to 4%)
Clearance: Desglymidodrine: 385 mL/minute (predominantly by renal secretion)

Dosage Adults: Oral: 10 mg 3 times/day during daytime hours (every 3-4 hours) when patient is upright (maximum: 40 mg/day)

Dosing adjustment in renal impairment: 2.5 mg 3 times/day, gradually increasing as tolerated

Monitoring Parameters Blood pressure, renal and hepatic parameters

Patient Information Use caution with over-the-counter medications which may affect blood pressure (cough and cold, diet, stay-awake medications); avoid taking a particular dose if you are to be supine for any length of time; take your last daily dose 3-4 hours before bedtime to minimize nighttime supine hypertension

Dosage Forms TAB: 2.5 mg, 5 mg, 10 mg

◆ **Midodrine Hydrochloride** *see* Midodrine *on page 838*
◆ **Midol® Maximum Strength Cramp Formula [OTC]** *see* Ibuprofen *on page 645*
◆ **Midrin®** *see* Acetaminophen, Isometheptene, and Dichloralphenazone *on page 29*
◆ **Mifeprex®** *see* Mifepristone *on page 839*

Mifepristone *(mi FE pris tone)*
U.S. Brand Names Mifeprex®
Synonyms RU-486; RU-38486
Therapeutic Category Abortifacient; Antiprogestin
Use Medical termination of intrauterine pregnancy, through day 49 of pregnancy. Patients may need treatment with misoprostol and possibly surgery to complete therapy
Unlabeled/Investigational Use Treatment of unresectable meningioma; has been studied in the treatment of breast cancer, ovarian cancer, and adrenal cortical carcinoma
(Continued)

Mifepristone *(Continued)*

Restrictions There are currently no clinical trials with mifepristone in oncology open in the U.S.; investigators wishing to obtain the agent for use in oncology patients must apply for a patient-specific IND from the FDA. Mifepristone will be supplied only to licensed physicians who sign and return a "Prescriber's Agreement." Distribution of mifepristone will be subject to specific requirements imposed by the distributor. Mifepristone will **not** be available to the public through licensed pharmacies.

Pregnancy Risk Factor X

Contraindications Hypersensitivity to mifepristone, misoprostol, other prostaglandins, or any component of the formulation; chronic adrenal failure; porphyrias; hemorrhagic disorder or concurrent anticoagulant therapy; pregnancy termination >49 days; intrauterine device (IUD) in place; ectopic pregnancy or undiagnosed adnexal mass; concurrent long-term corticosteroid therapy; inadequate or lack of access to emergency medical services; inability to understand effects and/or comply with treatment

Warnings/Precautions Patient must be instructed of the treatment procedure and expected effects. A signed agreement form must be kept in the patient's file. Physicians may obtain patient agreement forms, physician enrollment forms, and medical consultation directly from Danco Laboratories at 1-877-432-7596. Adverse effects (including blood transfusions, hospitalization, ongoing pregnancy, and other major complications) must be reported in writing to the medication distributor. To be administered only by physicians who can date pregnancy, diagnose ectopic pregnancies, provide access to surgical abortion (if needed), and can provide access to emergency care. Medication will be distributed directly to these physicians following signed agreement with the distributor. Must be administered under supervision by the qualified physician. Pregnancy is dated from day 1 of last menstrual period (presuming a 28-day cycle, ovulation occurring mid-cycle). Pregnancy duration can be determined using menstrual history and clinical examination. Ultrasound should be used if an ectopic pregnancy is suspected or if duration of pregnancy is uncertain. Bleeding occurs and should be expected (average 9-16 days, may be ≥30 days). Bleeding may require blood transfusion (rare), curettage, saline infusions, and/or vasoconstrictors. Use caution in patients with severe anemia. Confirmation of pregnancy termination by clinical exam or ultrasound must be made 14 days following treatment. Manufacturer recommends surgical termination of pregnancy when medical termination fails or is not complete. Prescriber should determine in advance whether they will provide such care themselves or through other providers. Preventative measures to prevent rhesus immunization must be taken prior to surgical abortion. Prescriber should also give the patient clear instructions on whom to call and what to do in the event of an emergency following administration of mifepristone.

Safety and efficacy have not been established for use in women with chronic cardiovascular, hypertensive, respiratory, or renal disease, diabetes mellitus, severe anemia, or heavy smokers. Women >35 years of age and smokers (>10 cigarettes/day) were excluded from clinical trials. Safety and efficacy in pediatric patients have not been established.

Common Adverse Reactions Vaginal bleeding and uterine cramping are expected to occur when this medication is used to terminate a pregnancy; 90% of women using this medication for this purpose also report adverse reactions

>10%:
Central nervous system: Headache (2% to 31%), dizziness (1% to 12%)
Gastrointestinal: Abdominal pain (cramping) (96%), nausea (43% to 61%), vomiting (18% to 26%), diarrhea (12% to 20%)
Genitourinary: Uterine cramping (83%)
1% to 10%:
Cardiovascular: Syncope (1%)
Central nervous system: Fatigue (10%), fever (4%), insomnia (3%), anxiety (2%), fainting (2%)
Gastrointestinal: Dyspepsia (3%)
Genitourinary: Uterine hemorrhage (5%), vaginitis (3%), pelvic pain (2%)
Hematologic: Decreased hemoglobin >2 g/dL (6%), anemia (2%), leukorrhea (2%)
Neuromuscular & skeletal: Back pain (9%), rigors (3%), leg pain (2%), weakness (2%)
Respiratory: Sinusitis (2%)
Miscellaneous: Viral infection (4%)

Drug Interactions

Cytochrome P450 Effect: Substrate of CYP3A4 (minor); **Inhibits** CYP2D6 (weak), 3A4 (weak)

Increased Effect/Toxicity: There are no reported interactions. It might be anticipated that the effects of one or both agents would be minimized if mifepristone were administered concurrently with a progestin (exogenous). During concurrent use of CYP3A4 inhibitors, serum level and/or toxicity of mifepristone may be increased; inhibitors include amiodarone, cimetidine, clarithromycin, erythromycin, delavirdine, diltiazem, dirithromycin, disulfiram, fluoxetine, fluvoxamine, grapefruit juice, indinavir, itraconazole, ketoconazole, nefazodone, nevirapine, propoxyphene, quinupristin-dalfopristin, ritonavir, saquinavir, verapamil, zafirlukast, zileuton; monitor for altered response

Decreased Effect: Enzyme inducers may increase the metabolism of mifepristone resulting in decreased effect; includes carbamazepine, dexamethasone, phenobarbital, phenytoin, and rifampin. St John's wort may induce mifepristone metabolism, leading to decreased levels.

Mechanism of Action Mifepristone, a synthetic steroid, competitively binds to the intracellular progesterone receptor, blocking the effects of progesterone. When used for the termination of pregnancy, this leads to contraction-inducing activity in the myometrium. In the absence of progesterone, mifepristone acts as a partial progesterone agonist. Mifepristone also has weak antiglucocorticoid and antiandrogenic properties; it blocks the feedback effect of cortisol on corticotropin secretion.

Pharmacodynamics/Kinetics

Protein binding: 98% to albumin and α_1-acid glycoprotein

Metabolism: Hepatic via CYP3A4 to three metabolites (may possess some antiprogestin and antiglucocorticoid activity)

Bioavailability: 69%

Half-life elimination: Terminal: 18 hours following a slower phase where 50% eliminated between 12-72 hours

Time to peak: 90 minutes

Excretion: Feces (83%); urine (9%)

Dosage Oral:

Adults: Termination of pregnancy: Treatment consists of three office visits by the patient; the patient must read medication guide and sign patient agreement prior to treatment:

Day 1: 600 mg (three 200 mg tablets) taken as a single dose under physician supervision

Day 3: Patient must return to the healthcare provider 2 days following administration of mifepristone; if termination of pregnancy cannot be confirmed using ultrasound or clinical examination: 400 mcg (two 200 mcg tablets) of misoprostol; patient may need treatment for cramps or gastrointestinal symptoms at this time

Day 14: Patient must return to the healthcare provider ~14 days after administration of mifepristone; confirm complete termination of pregnancy by ultrasound or clinical exam. Surgical termination is recommended to manage treatment failures.

Elderly: Safety and efficacy have not been established

Dosage adjustment in renal impairment: Safety and efficacy have not been established

Dosage adjustment in hepatic impairment: Safety and efficacy have not been established; use with caution due to CYP3A4 metabolism

Unlabeled use: Refer to individual protocols. The dose used in meningioma is usually 200 mg/day, continued based on toxicity and response.

Monitoring Parameters Clinical exam and/or ultrasound to confirm complete termination of pregnancy; hemoglobin, hematocrit, and red blood cell count in cases of heavy bleeding

Patient Information This medication is used to terminate pregnancy. It is not to be used for pregnancies >49 days (7 weeks). Vaginal bleeding and cramping are expected to occur and may require medical treatment if severe. Most women report that this is heavier bleeding than experienced during a heavy menstrual period. Other side effects that may be expected include abdominal pain, nausea, vomiting, and diarrhea. Follow-up with prescriber at approximately 3 days and 14 days following initial treatment. Surgical termination of pregnancy may be required if medication fails. There is a risk of fetal malformation if treatment fails. Your prescriber will give you a phone number to call for problems, questions, or emergencies; you should not use this medication if you do not have access to emergency care. It is possible to become pregnant again before following treatment with this medication but before your next period starts. Contraception should be started once the pregnancy's end has been proven and before resuming sexual intercourse. You will be given a medication guide to help you understand this medication and its effects. It is important to review this carefully. Ask any questions you may have. You will also be required to sign a form saying that you understand the effects of this treatment and are able to return to the prescriber for follow-up appointments. Do not breast feed while using this medication.

Dosage Forms TAB: 200 mg

Miglitol (MIG li tol)

Related Information

Hypoglycemic Drugs & Thiazolidinedione Information *on page 1378*

U.S. Brand Names Glyset®

Therapeutic Category Alpha-Glucosidase Inhibitor; Antidiabetic Agent, Alpha-glucosidase Inhibitor; Hypoglycemic Agent, Oral

Use Type 2 diabetes mellitus (noninsulin-dependent, NIDDM):

Monotherapy adjunct to diet to improve glycemic control in patients with type 2 diabetes mellitus (non insulin-dependent, NIDDM) whose hyperglycemia cannot be managed with diet alone

Combination therapy with a sulfonylurea when diet plus either miglitol or a sulfonylurea alone do not result in adequate glycemic control. The effect of miglitol to enhance glycemic control is additive to that of sulfonylureas when used in combination.

Pregnancy Risk Factor B

Contraindications Hypersensitivity to miglitol or any of component of the formulation; diabetic ketoacidosis; inflammatory bowel disease; colonic ulceration; partial intestinal obstruction or predisposition to intestinal obstruction; chronic intestinal diseases associated with marked disorders of digestion or absorption or with conditions that may deteriorate as a result of increased gas formation in the intestine

Warnings/Precautions GI symptoms are the most common reactions. The incidence of abdominal pain and diarrhea tend to diminish considerably with continued treatment. Long-term clinical trials in diabetic patients with significant renal dysfunction (serum creatinine >2 mg/dL) have not been conducted. Treatment of these patients is not recommended. Because of its mechanism of action, miglitol administered alone should not cause hypoglycemia in the fasting of postprandial state. In combination with a sulfonylurea will cause a further lowering of blood glucose and may increase the hypoglycemic potential of the sulfonylurea.

(Continued)

Miglitol *(Continued)*

Common Adverse Reactions
>10%: Gastrointestinal: Flatulence (42%), diarrhea (29%), abdominal pain (12%)
1% to 10%: Dermatologic: Rash

Drug Interactions
Decreased Effect: Miglitol may decrease the absorption and bioavailability of digoxin, propranolol, and ranitidine. Digestive enzymes (amylase, pancreatin, charcoal) may reduce the effect of miglitol and should **not** be taken concomitantly.

Mechanism of Action In contrast to sulfonylureas, miglitol does not enhance insulin secretion; the antihyperglycemic action of miglitol results from a reversible inhibition of membrane-bound intestinal alpha-glucosidases which hydrolyze oligosaccharides and disaccharides to glucose and other monosaccharides in the brush border of the small intestine; in diabetic patients, this enzyme inhibition results in delayed glucose absorption and lowering of postprandial hyperglycemia

Pharmacodynamics/Kinetics
Absorption: Saturable at high doses: 25 mg dose: Completely absorbed; 100 mg dose: 50% to 70% absorbed
Distribution: V_d: 0.18 L/kg
Protein binding: <4%
Metabolism: None
Half-life elimination: ~2 hours
Time to peak: 2-3 hours
Excretion: Urine (as unchanged drug)

Dosage Adults: Oral: 25 mg 3 times/day with the first bite of food at each meal; the dose may be increased to 50 mg 3 times/day after 4-8 weeks; maximum recommended dose: 100 mg 3 times/day

Dosing adjustment in renal impairment: Miglitol is primarily excreted by the kidneys; there is little information of miglitol in patients with a Cl_{cr} <25 mL/minute
Dosing adjustment in hepatic impairment: No adjustment necessary
Administration Should be taken orally at the start (with the first bite) of each main meal
Monitoring Parameters Monitor therapeutic response by periodic blood glucose tests; measurement of glycosylated hemoglobin is recommended for the monitoring of long-term glycemic control

Reference Range Target range: Adults:
Fasting blood glucose: <120 mg/dL
Glycosylated hemoglobin: <7%

Patient Information Take orally 3 times/day with the first bite of each main meal. It is important to continue to adhere to dietary instructions, a regular exercise program, and regular testing of urine or blood glucose. If side effects occur, they usually develop during the first few weeks of therapy. They are most commonly mild-to-moderate dose-related GI effects, such as flatulence, soft stools, diarrhea, or abdominal discomfort, and they generally diminish in frequency and intensity with time. Discontinuation of drug usually results in rapid resolution of these GI symptoms.

Dosage Forms TAB: 25 mg, 50 mg, 100 mg

Miglustat *(MIG loo stat)*

U.S. Brand Names Zavesca®

Synonyms OGT-918

Therapeutic Category Enzyme Inhibitor

Use Treatment of mild-to-moderate type 1 Gaucher disease when enzyme replacement therapy is not a therapeutic option

Pregnancy Risk Factor X

Contraindications Hypersensitivity to miglustat or any component of the formulation; pregnancy

Warnings/Precautions Peripheral neuropathy has been reported with use and neurologic monitoring is required. Tremor or exacerbations of existing tremor may occur; may resolve over time or respond to dosage reduction. Weigh risk versus benefit of therapy if patient develops numbness and tingling. Use caution in renal impairment. Safety and efficacy in severe type 1 Gaucher disease have not been established. Safety and efficacy in patients <18 or >65 years of age have not been established.

Common Adverse Reactions Percentages reported from open-label, uncontrolled monotherapy trials.
>10%:
Central nervous system: Headache (21% to 22%), dizziness (up to 11%)
Gastrointestinal: Diarrhea (89%; up to 100% in other studies), weight loss (39% to 67%), abdominal pain (18% to 50%), flatulence (29% to 44%), nausea (14% to 22%), vomiting (4% to 11%), cramps (up to 11%)
Neuromuscular & skeletal: Tremor (11%; up to 30% in other studies), leg cramps (4% to 11%),
Ocular: visual disturbances (up to 17%)
1% to 10%:
Central nervous system: headache (up to 6%)
Endocrine & metabolic: Menstrual disorder (up to 6%)
Gastrointestinal: Anorexia (up to 7%), dyspepsia (up to 7%), epigastric pain (up to 6%)
Hematologic: Thrombocytopenia (6% to 7%)

Neuromuscular & skeletal: Paresthesia (up to 7%)

Drug Interactions
    Decreased Effect: Miglustat increases the clearance of imiglucerase; combination therapy is not indicated.

Mechanism of Action Miglustat inhibits the enzyme needed to produce glycosphingolipids and decreases the rate of glycosphingolipid glucosylceramide formation. Glucosylceramide accumulates in type 1 Gaucher disease, causing complications specific to this disease.

Pharmacodynamics/Kinetics
    Distribution: V_d: 83-105 L
    Protein binding No binding to plasma proteins
    Bioavailability: 97%
    Half-life elimination: 6-7 hours
    Time to peak, plasma: 2-2.5 hours
    Excretion: Urine (as unchanged drug)

Dosage Oral: Adults: Type 1 Gaucher disease: 100 mg 3 times/day; dose may be reduced to 100 mg 1-2 times/day in patients with adverse effects (ie, tremor, GI distress)
    Dosage adjustment in renal impairment:
        Cl_{cr} 50-75 mL/minute: 100 mg twice daily
        Cl_{cr} 30-50 mL/minute: 100 mg once daily
        Cl_{cr} <30 mL/minute: Not recommended

Administration Capsules should be swallowed whole and taken at the same time each day. May be taken with or without food.

Monitoring Parameters Neurologic evaluations baseline and repeated every 6 months; adverse effects; weight

Patient Information Diarrhea and weight loss are very common side effects of this medication. Tremors may occur or worsen at the beginning of treatment. Notify prescriber immediately for numbness and tingling in hands, arms, legs or feet. Pregnancy and/or breast-feeding are not recommended while taking this medication. Men and women should use an effective form of contraception during treatment. Men should continue contraceptive use for at least 3 months after therapy is complete.

Dosage Forms CAP: 100 mg

♦ **Migranal**® *see* Dihydroergotamine *on page 378*

♦ **Migrin-A** *see* Acetaminophen, Isometheptene, and Dichloralphenazone *on page 29*

♦ **Milk of Magnesia** *see* Magnesium Hydroxide *on page 769*

Milrinone (MIL ri none)

Related Information
    Hemodynamic Support, Intravenous *on page 1377*

U.S. Brand Names Primacor®

Synonyms Milrinone Lactate

Therapeutic Category Phosphodiesterase Enzyme Inhibitor

Use Short-term I.V. therapy of congestive heart failure; calcium antagonist intoxication

Pregnancy Risk Factor C

Contraindications Hypersensitivity to milrinone, inamrinone, or any component of the formulation; concurrent use of inamrinone

Warnings/Precautions Avoid in severe obstructive aortic or pulmonic valvular disease, history of ventricular arrhythmias; atrial fibrillation, flutter. Life-threatening arrhythmias were infrequent and have been associated with pre-existing arrhythmias, metabolic abnormalities, abnormal digoxin levels, and catheter insertion. It may aggravate outflow tract obstruction in hypertrophic subaortic stenosis. Monitor closely during the infusion. Ensure that ventricular rate controlled in atrial fibrillation/flutter before initiating. Not recommended for use in acute MI patients. Monitor and correct fluid and electrolyte problems. Adjust dose in renal dysfunction.

Common Adverse Reactions
    >10%: Cardiovascular: Ventricular arrhythmia (ectopy 9%, NSVT 3%, sustained ventricular tachycardia 1%, ventricular fibrillation <1%); life-threatening arrhythmias are infrequent, often associated with underlying factors (eg, pre-existing arrhythmia, electrolyte disturbances, catheter insertion)
    1% to 10%:
        Cardiovascular: Supraventricular arrhythmia (4%), hypotension
        Central nervous system: Headache

Mechanism of Action Phosphodiesterase inhibitor resulting in vasodilation

Pharmacodynamics/Kinetics
    Onset of action: I.V.: 5-15 minutes
    Serum level: I.V.: Following a 125 mcg/kg dose, peak plasma concentrations ~1000 ng/mL were observed at 2 minutes postinjection, decreasing to <100 ng/mL in 2 hours
    Drug concentration levels:
        Therapeutic
            Serum levels of 166 ng/mL, achieved during I.V. infusions of 0.25-1 mcg/kg/minute, were associated with sustained hemodynamic benefit in severe congestive heart failure patients over a 24-hour period
            Maximum beneficial effects on cardiac output and pulmonary capillary wedge pressure following I.V. infusion have been associated with plasma milrinone concentrations of 150-250 ng/mL
        Toxic: Serum concentrations >250-300 ng/mL have been associated with marked reductions in mean arterial pressure and tachycardia; however, more studies are required to determine the toxic serum levels for milrinone

(Continued)

Milrinone *(Continued)*

Distribution: V_{dss}: 0.32 L/kg; Severe congestive heart failure (CHF): V_d: 0.33-0.47 L/kg; not significantly bound to tissues; excretion in breast milk unknown

Protein binding, plasma: ~70%

Metabolism: Hepatic (12%)

Half-life elimination: I.V.: 136 minutes in patients with CHF; patients with severe CHF have a more prolonged half-life, with values ranging from 1.7-2.7 hours. Patients with CHF have a reduction in the systemic clearance of milrinone, resulting in a prolonged elimination half-life. Alternatively, one study reported that 1 month of therapy with milrinone did not change the pharmacokinetic parameters for patients with CHF despite improvement in cardiac function.

Excretion: I.V.: Urine (85% as unchanged drug) within 24 hours; active tubular secretion is a major elimination pathway for milrinone

Clearance: I.V. bolus: 25.9 ± 5.7 L/hour (0.37 L/hour/kg); Severe congestive heart failure: 0.11-0.13 L/hour/kg. The reduction in clearance may be a result of reduced renal function. Creatinine clearance values were ½ those reported for healthy adults in patients with severe congestive heart failure (52 vs 119 mL/minute).

Dosage Adults: I.V.: Loading dose: 50 mcg/kg administered over 10 minutes followed by a maintenance dose titrated according to the hemodynamic and clinical response; see following table:

Maintenance Dosage	Dose Rate (mcg/kg/min)	Total Dose (mg/kg/24 h)
Minimum	0.375	0.59
Standard	0.500	0.77
Maximum	0.750	1.13

Dosing adjustment in renal impairment:

Cl_{cr} 50 mL/minute/1.73 m²: Administer 0.43 mcg/kg/minute.

Cl_{cr} 40 mL/minute/1.73 m²: Administer 0.38 mcg/kg/minute.

Cl_{cr} 30 mL/minute/1.73 m²: Administer 0.33 mcg/kg/minute.

Cl_{cr} 20 mL/minute/1.73 m²: Administer 0.28 mcg/kg/minute.

Cl_{cr} 10 mL/minute/1.73 m²: Administer 0.23 mcg/kg/minute.

Cl_{cr} 5 mL/minute/1.73 m²: Administer 0.2 mcg/kg/minute.

Administration Requires an infusion pump; continuous I.V. infusion; 20 mg/100 mL 0.9% sodium chloride or D_5W (0.2 mg/mL); see table.

Dose (mcg/kg/min)	Rate (mL/kg/h)
0.375	0.11
0.400	0.12
0.500	0.15
0.600	0.18
0.700	0.21
0.750	0.22

Monitoring Parameters Cardiac monitor and blood pressure monitor required; serum potassium

Therapeutic: Patients should be monitored for improvement in the clinical signs and symptoms of congestive heart failure

Toxic: Patients should be monitored for ventricular arrhythmias and exacerbation of anginal symptoms; during I.V. therapy with milrinone, blood pressure and heart rate should be monitored

Dosage Forms INF [premixed in D_5W] (Primacor®): 200 mcg/mL (100 mL, 200 mL). **INJ, solution:** 1 mg/mL (10 mL, 20 mL, 50 mL); (Primacor®): 1 mg/mL (5 mL, 10 mL, 20 mL, 50 mL)

♦ **Milrinone Lactate** *see Milrinone on page 843*

♦ **Miltown®** *see Meprobamate on page 794*

♦ **Minidyne® [OTC]** *see Povidone-Iodine on page 1025*

♦ **Minipress®** *see Prazosin on page 1030*

♦ **Minitran™** *see Nitroglycerin on page 910*

♦ **Minizide®** *see Prazosin and Polythiazide on page 1031*

♦ **Minocin®** *see Minocycline on page 844*

Minocycline *(mi noe SYE kleen)*

Related Information

Antimicrobial Drugs of Choice *on page 1440*

Community-Acquired Pneumonia in Adults *on page 1457*

U.S. Brand Names Dynacin®; Minocin®

Synonyms Minocycline Hydrochloride

Therapeutic Category Acne Product; Antibiotic, Tetracycline Derivative

Use Treatment of susceptible bacterial infections of both gram-negative and gram-positive organisms; treatment of anthrax (inhalational, cutaneous, and gastrointestinal); acne; meningococcal carrier state; Rickettsial diseases (including Rocky Mountain spotted fever, Q fever); nongonococcal urethritis, gonorrhea; acute intestinal amebiasis

Pregnancy Risk Factor D

Contraindications Hypersensitivity to minocycline, other tetracyclines, or any component of the formulation; pregnancy

Warnings/Precautions Avoid use during tooth development (children ≤8 years of age) unless other drugs are not likely to be effective or are contraindicated. May be associated with increases in BUN secondary to anti-anabolic effects. Avoid in renal insufficiency (associated with hepatotoxicity). CNS effects (lightheadedness, vertigo) may occur, potentially affecting a patient's ability to drive or operate heavy machinery. Has been associated (rarely) with pseudotumor cerebri. May cause photosensitivity.

Common Adverse Reactions
>10%: Miscellaneous: Discoloration of teeth (in children)
1% to 10%:
 Central nervous system: Lightheadedness, vertigo
 Dermatologic: Photosensitivity
 Gastrointestinal: Nausea, diarrhea

Drug Interactions
Increased Effect/Toxicity: Minocycline may increase the effect of warfarin.

Decreased Effect: Decreased effect with antacids (aluminum, calcium, zinc, or magnesium), bismuth salts, sodium bicarbonate, barbiturates, carbamazepine, hydantoins. Although anecdotal reports suggest oral contraceptive efficacy could be reduced by tetracyclines, this has been refuted by more rigorous scientific and clinical data.

Mechanism of Action Inhibits bacterial protein synthesis by binding with the 30S and possibly the 50S ribosomal subunit(s) of susceptible bacteria; cell wall synthesis is not affected

Pharmacodynamics/Kinetics
Absorption: Well absorbed
Distribution: Majority deposits for extended periods in fat; crosses placenta; enters breast milk
Protein binding: 70% to 75%
Half-life elimination: 15 hours
Excretion: Urine

Dosage
Children >8 years: Oral, I.V.: Initial: 4 mg/kg followed by 2 mg/kg/dose every 12 hours
Adults:
 Infection: Oral, I.V.: 200 mg stat, 100 mg every 12 hours not to exceed 400 mg/24 hours
 Acne: Oral: 50 mg 1-3 times/day
Dosage adjustment in renal impairment: Consider decreasing dose or increasing dosing interval with renal impairment.

Administration
Oral: May be taken with food or milk. Administer with adequate fluid to decrease the risk of esophageal irritation and ulceration.
I.V.: Infuse slowly, usually over a 4- to 6-hour period.

Patient Information Avoid unnecessary exposure to sunlight; do not take with antacids or iron products; finish all medication; do not skip doses; take 1 hour before or 2 hours after meals; take with adequate fluids to decrease risk of irritation

Dosage Forms CAP: 50 mg, 75 mg, 100 mg; (Dynacin®): 50 mg, 75 mg, 100 mg. **CAP, pellet-filled** (Minocin®): 50 mg, 100 mg. **INJ, powder for reconstitution** (Minocin®): 100 mg. **TAB, as hydrochloride** (Dynacin®): 50 mg, 75 mg, 100 mg

♦ **Minocycline Hydrochloride** see Minocycline on page 844

Minoxidil (mi NOKS i dil)

U.S. Brand Names Loniten®; Rogaine® Extra Strength for Men [OTC]; Rogaine® for Men [OTC]; Rogaine® for Women [OTC]

Therapeutic Category Antihypertensive Agent; Vasodilator

Use Management of severe hypertension (usually in combination with a diuretic and beta-blocker); treatment (topical formulation) of alopecia androgenetica in males and females

Pregnancy Risk Factor C

Contraindications Hypersensitivity to minoxidil or any component of the formulation; pheochromocytoma; acute MI; dissecting aortic aneurysm

Warnings/Precautions Note: Minoxidil can cause pericardial effusion, occasionally progressing to tamponade and it can exacerbate angina pectoris; use with caution in patients with pulmonary hypertension, significant renal failure, or CHF; use with caution in patients with coronary artery disease or recent myocardial infarction; renal failure or dialysis patients may require smaller doses; usually used with a beta-blocker (to treat minoxidil-induced tachycardia) and a diuretic (for treatment of water retention/edema); may take 1-6 months for hypertrichosis to totally reverse after minoxidil therapy is discontinued.

Common Adverse Reactions
Oral: Incidence of reactions not always reported.
 Cardiovascular: Peripheral edema (7%), sodium and water retention, CHF, tachycardia, angina pectoris, pericardial effusion with or without tamponade, pericarditis, ECG changes (T-wave changes, 60%), rebound hypertension (in children after a gradual withdrawal)
 Central nervous system: Headache (rare), fatigue
(Continued)

Minoxidil *(Continued)*

Dermatologic: Hypertrichosis (common, 80%), transient pruritus, changes in pigmentation (rare), serosanguineous bullae (rare), rash (rare), Stevens-Johnson syndrome

Hepatic: Increased alkaline phosphatase

Renal: Transient increase in serum BUN and creatinine

Respiratory: Pulmonary edema

Topical: Incidence of adverse events is not always reported.

Cardiovascular: Increased left ventricular end-diastolic volume, increased cardiac output, increased left ventricular mass, dizziness, tachycardia, edema, transient chest pain, palpitation, increase or decrease in blood pressure, increase or decrease in pulse rate (1.5%, placebo 1.6%)

Central nervous system: Headache, dizziness, weakness, taste alterations, faintness, light-headedness (3.4%, placebo 3.5%), vertigo (1.2%, placebo 1.2%), anxiety (rare), mental depression (rare), fatigue (rare 0.4%, placebo 1%)

Dermatologic: Local irritation, dryness, erythema, allergic contact dermatitis (7.4%, placebo 5.4%), pruritus, scaling/flaking, eczema, seborrhea, papular rash, folliculitis, local erythema, flushing, exacerbation of hair loss, alopecia, hypertrichosis, increased hair growth outside the area of application (face, beard, eyebrows, ear, arm)

Gastrointestinal: Diarrhea, nausea, vomiting (4.3%, placebo 6.6%), weight gain (1.2%, placebo 1.3%)

Neuromuscular & skeletal: Fractures, back pain, retrosternal chest pain of muscular origin, tendonitis (2.6%, placebo 2.2%)

Ocular: Conjunctivitis, visual disturbances, decreased visual acuity

Respiratory: Bronchitis, upper respiratory infections, sinusitis (7.2%, placebo 8.6%)

Drug Interactions

Increased Effect/Toxicity: Concurrent use of guanethidine can cause severe orthostasis; avoid concurrent use - discontinue 1-3 weeks prior to initiating minoxidil. Effects of other antihypertensives may be additive with minoxidil.

Mechanism of Action Produces vasodilation by directly relaxing arteriolar smooth muscle, with little effect on veins; effects may be mediated by cyclic AMP; stimulation of hair growth is secondary to vasodilation, increased cutaneous blood flow and stimulation of resting hair follicles

Pharmacodynamics/Kinetics

Onset of action: Hypotensive: Oral: ~30 minutes

Peak effect: 2-8 hours

Duration: 2-5 days

Protein binding: None

Metabolism: 88%, primarily via glucuronidation

Bioavailability: Oral: 90%

Half-life elimination: Adults: 3.5-4.2 hours

Excretion: Urine (12% as unchanged drug)

Dosage

Children <12 years: Hypertension: Oral: Initial: 0.1-0.2 mg/kg once daily; maximum: 5 mg/day; increase gradually every 3 days; usual dosage: 0.25-1 mg/kg/day in 1-2 divided doses; maximum: 50 mg/day

Children >12 years and Adults: Hypertension: Oral: Initial: 5 mg once daily, increase gradually every 3 days; usual dose: 10-40 mg/day in 1-2 divided doses; maximum: 100 mg/day

Adults: Alopecia: Topical: Apply twice daily; 4 months of therapy may be necessary for hair growth.

Elderly: Initial: 2.5 mg once daily; increase gradually.

Note: Dosage adjustment is needed when added to concomitant therapy.

Dialysis: Supplemental dose is not necessary via hemo- or peritoneal dialysis.

Monitoring Parameters Blood pressure, standing and sitting/supine; fluid and electrolyte balance and body weight should be monitored

Patient Information Topical product must be used every day. Concentrated topical solution (5%) may be flammable; keep away from fire or flame. Hair growth usually takes 4 months. Report any of the following: Heart rate ≥20 beats per minute over normal; rapid weight gain >5 lb (2 kg); unusual swelling of extremities, face, or abdomen; breathing difficulty, especially when lying down; rise slowly from prolonged lying or sitting; new or aggravated angina symptoms (chest, arm, or shoulder pain); severe indigestion; dizziness, lightheadedness, or fainting; nausea or vomiting may occur. Do not make up for missed doses.

Dosage Forms SOLN, topical: 2% (60 mL); 5% (60 mL); (Rogaine® for Men, Rogaine® for Women): 2% (60 mL); (Rogaine® Extra Strength for Men): 5% (60 mL). **TAB** (Loniten®): 2.5 mg, 10 mg

♦ **Mintezol®** *see* Thiabendazole *on page 1213*

♦ **Miochol-E®** *see* Acetylcholine *on page 32*

♦ **Miostat®** *see* Carbachol *on page 214*

♦ **MiraLax™** *see* Polyethylene Glycol-Electrolyte Solution *on page 1013*

♦ **Mirapex®** *see* Pramipexole *on page 1027*

♦ **Miraphen PSE** *see* Guaifenesin and Pseudoephedrine *on page 605*

♦ **Mircette®** *see* Ethinyl Estradiol and Desogestrel *on page 477*

♦ **Mirena®** *see* Levonorgestrel *on page 737*

Mirtazapine (mir TAZ a peen)

Related Information
Antidepressant Agents Comparison *on page 1359*

U.S. Brand Names Remeron®; Remeron SolTab®

Therapeutic Category Antidepressant, Alpha-2 Antagonist

Use Treatment of depression

Pregnancy Risk Factor C

Contraindications Hypersensitivity to mirtazapine or any component of the formulation; use of MAO inhibitors within 14 days

Warnings/Precautions Discontinue immediately if signs and symptoms of neutropenia/agranulocytosis occur. May cause sedation, resulting in impaired performance of tasks requiring alertness (eg, operating machinery or driving). Sedative effects may be additive with other CNS depressants and/or ethanol. The degree of sedation is moderate-high relative to other antidepressants. May worsen psychosis in some patients or precipitate a shift to mania or hypomania in patients with bipolar disease. The risks of orthostatic hypotension or anticholinergic effects are low relative to other antidepressants. The incidence of sexual dysfunction with mirtazapine is generally lower than with SSRIs.

May increase appetite and stimulate weight gain, may increase serum cholesterol and triglyceride levels. The possibility of a suicide attempt is inherent in major depression and may persist until remission occurs. Use caution in high-risk patients during initiation of therapy. Prescriptions should be written for the smallest quantity consistent with good patient care. Use caution in patients with a previous seizure disorder or condition predisposing to seizures such as brain damage, alcoholism, or concurrent therapy with other drugs which lower the seizure threshold. Use with caution in patients with hepatic or renal dysfunction and in elderly patients.

SolTab® formulation contains phenylalanine

Common Adverse Reactions
>10%:
Central nervous system: Somnolence (54%)
Endocrine & metabolic: Increased cholesterol
Gastrointestinal: Constipation (13%), xerostomia (25%), increased appetite (17%), weight gain (12% weight gain of >7% reported in 8% of adults, ≤49% of pediatric patients)
1% to 10%:
Cardiovascular: Hypertension, vasodilatation, peripheral edema (2%), edema (1%)
Central nervous system: Dizziness (7%), abnormal dreams (4%), abnormal thoughts (3%), confusion (2%), malaise
Endocrine & metabolic: Increased triglycerides
Gastrointestinal: Vomiting, anorexia, abdominal pain
Genitourinary: Urinary frequency (2%)
Neuromuscular & skeletal: Myalgia (2%), back pain (2%), arthralgias, tremor (2%), weakness (8%)
Respiratory: Dyspnea (1%)
Miscellaneous: Flu-like symptoms (5%), thirst

Drug Interactions
Cytochrome P450 Effect: Substrate of CYP1A2 (major), 2C8/9 (minor), 2D6 (major), 3A4 (major); **Inhibits** CYP1A2 (weak), 3A4 (weak)
Increased Effect/Toxicity: CYP1A2 inhibitors may increase the levels/effects of mirtazapine; example inhibitors include amiodarone, ciprofloxacin, fluvoxamine, ketoconazole, lomefloxacin, ofloxacin, and rofecoxib. CYP2D6 inhibitors may increase the levels/effects of mirtazapine; example inhibitors include chlorpromazine, delavirdine, fluoxetine, miconazole, paroxetine, pergolide, quinidine, quinine, ritonavir, and ropinirole. Increased sedative effect seen with CNS depressants, CYP3A4 inhibitors, linezolid, MAO inhibitors, selegiline, sibutramine.
Decreased Effect: CYP1A2 inducers may decrease the levels/effects of mirtazapine; example inducers include aminoglutethimide, carbamazepine, phenobarbital, and rifampin. Decreased effect seen with clonidine.

Mechanism of Action Mirtazapine is a tetracyclic antidepressant that works by its central presynaptic alpha₂-adrenergic antagonist effects, which results in increased release of norepinephrine and serotonin. It is also a potent antagonist of 5-HT₂ and 5-HT₃ serotonin receptors and H1 histamine receptors and a moderate peripheral alpha₁-adrenergic and muscarinic antagonist; it does not inhibit the reuptake of norepinephrine or serotonin.

Pharmacodynamics/Kinetics
Protein binding: 85%
Metabolism: Extensively hepatic via CYP1A2, 2C9, 2D6, 3A4 and via demethylation and hydroxylation
Bioavailability: 50%
Half-life elimination: 20-40 hours; hampered with renal or hepatic impairment
Time to peak, serum: 2 hours
Excretion: Urine (75%) and feces (15%) as metabolites

Dosage
Children: Safety and efficacy in children have not been established
Treatment of depression: Adults: Oral: Initial: 15 mg nightly, titrate up to 15-45 mg/day with dose increases made no more frequently than every 1-2 weeks; there is an inverse relationship between dose and sedation
Elderly: Decreased clearance seen (40% males, 10% females); no specific dosage adjustment recommended by manufacturer
(Continued)

Mirtazapine *(Continued)*

Dosage adjustment in renal impairment:
Cl$_{cr}$ 11-39 mL/minute: 30% decreased clearance
Cl$_{cr}$ <10 mL/minute: 50% decreased clearance

Dosage adjustment in hepatic impairment: Clearance decreased by 30%

Administration SolTab®: Open blister pack and place tablet on the tongue. Do not split tablet. Tablet is formulated to dissolve on the tongue without water.

Monitoring Parameters Patients should be monitored for signs of agranulocytosis or severe neutropenia such as sore throat, stomatitis or other signs of infection or a low WBC; monitor for improvement in clinical signs and symptoms of depression, improvement may be observed within 1-4 weeks after initiating therapy

Patient Information Be aware of the risk of developing agranulocytosis; contact prescriber if any indication of infection occurs (ie, fever, chills, sore throat, mucous membrane ulceration, and especially flu-like symptoms); may impair judgment, thinking, and particularly motor skills; may impair ability to drive, use machinery, or perform tasks that require you remain alert; avoid concurrent alcohol use

SolTab®: Open blister pack and place tablet on the tongue. Do not split tablet. Tablet is formulated to dissolve on the tongue without water.

Dosage Forms TAB (Remeron®): 15 mg, 30 mg, 45 mg. **TAB, orally-disintegrating** (Remeron SolTab®): 15 mg, 30 mg, 45 mg

Misoprostol *(mye soe PROST ole)*

U.S. Brand Names Cytotec®

Therapeutic Category Prostaglandin

Use Prevention of NSAID-induced gastric ulcers; medical termination of pregnancy of ≤49 days (in conjunction with mifepristone)

Unlabeled/Investigational Use Cervical ripening and labor induction; NSAID-induced nephropathy; fat malabsorption in cystic fibrosis

Pregnancy Risk Factor X

Contraindications Hypersensitivity to misoprostol, prostaglandins, or any component of the formulation; pregnancy (when used to reduce NSAID-induced ulcers)

Warnings/Precautions Safety and efficacy have not been established in children <18 years of age; use with caution in patients with renal impairment and the elderly; not to be used in pregnant women or women of childbearing potential unless woman is capable of complying with effective contraceptive measures; therapy is normally begun on the second or third day of next normal menstrual period. Uterine perforation and/or rupture have been reported in association with intravaginal use to induce labor or with combined oral/intravaginal use to induce abortion. Should not be used as a cervical-ripening agent for induction of labor. However, The American College of Obstetricians and Gynecologists (ACOG) continues to support this off-label use.

Common Adverse Reactions
>10%: Gastrointestinal: Diarrhea, abdominal pain
1% to 10%:
Central nervous system: Headache
Gastrointestinal: Constipation, flatulence, nausea, dyspepsia, vomiting

Drug Interactions
Decreased Effect: Antacids may diminish absorption (not clinically significant)

Mechanism of Action Misoprostol is a synthetic prostaglandin E$_1$ analog that replaces the protective prostaglandins consumed with prostaglandin-inhibiting therapies (eg, NSAIDs); has been shown to induce uterine contractions

Pharmacodynamics/Kinetics
Absorption: Rapid
Metabolism: Hepatic; rapidly de-esterified to misoprostol acid (active)
Half-life elimination: Metabolite: 20-40 minutes
Time to peak, serum: Active metabolite: Fasting: 15-30 minutes
Excretion: Urine (64% to 73%) and feces (15%) within 24 hours

Dosage
Oral:
Children 8-16 years: Fat absorption in cystic fibrosis (unlabeled use): 100 mcg 4 times/day
Adults:
Prevention of NSAID-induced gastric ulcers: 200 mcg 4 times/day with food; if not tolerated, may decrease dose to 100 mcg 4 times/day with food or 200 mcg twice daily with food; last dose of the day should be taken at bedtime
Medical termination of pregnancy: Refer to Mifepristone monograph.
Intravaginal: Adults: Labor induction or cervical ripening (unlabeled use): 25 mcg (¼ of 100 mcg tablet); may repeat at intervals no more frequent than every 3-6 hours. Do not use in patients with previous cesarean delivery or prior major uterine surgery.

Administration Incidence of diarrhea may be lessened by having patient take dose right after meals. Therapy is usually begun on the second or third day of the next normal menstrual period.

Patient Information May cause diarrhea when first being used; take after meals and at bedtime; avoid taking with magnesium-containing antacids

Dosage Forms TAB: 100 mcg, 200 mcg

◆ **Misoprostol and Diclofenac** *see* Diclofenac and Misoprostol *on page 368*

Mitomycin (mye toe MYE sin)

U.S. Brand Names Mutamycin®

Synonyms Mitomycin-C; Mitomycin-X; MTC; NSC-26980

Therapeutic Category Antineoplastic Agent, Antibiotic; Antineoplastic Agent, Vesicant; Vesicant

Use Treatment of adenocarcinoma of stomach or pancreas, bladder cancer, breast cancer, or colorectal cancer

Unlabeled/Investigational Use Prevention of excess scarring in glaucoma filtration procedures in patients at high risk of bleb failure

Pregnancy Risk Factor D

Contraindications Hypersensitivity to mitomycin or any component of the formulation; platelet counts <75,000/mm³; leukocyte counts <3000/mm³ or serum creatinine >1.7 mg/dL; thrombocytopenia; coagulation disorders, increased bleeding tendency; pregnancy

Warnings/Precautions The U.S. Food and Drug Administration (FDA) currently recommends that procedures for proper handling and disposal of antineoplastic agents be considered. Use with caution in patients who have received radiation therapy or in the presence of hepatobiliary dysfunction; reduce dosage in patients who are receiving radiation therapy simultaneously. Hemolytic-uremic syndrome, potentially fatal, occurs in some patients receiving long-term therapy. It is correlated with total dose (single doses ≥60 mg or cumulative doses ≥50 mg/m²) and total duration of therapy (>5-11 months). **Mitomycin is a potent vesicant, may cause ulceration, necrosis, cellulitis, and tissue sloughing if infiltrated.**

Common Adverse Reactions

>10%:

Cardiovascular: Congestive heart failure (3% to 15%) (doses >30 mg/m²)

Central nervous system: Fever (14%)

Dermatologic: Alopecia, nail banding/discoloration

Gastrointestinal: Nausea, vomiting and anorexia (14%)

Hematologic: Anemia (19% to 24%); myelosuppression, common, dose-limiting, delayed

Onset: 3 weeks

Nadir: 4-6 weeks

Recovery: 6-8 weeks

1% to 10%:

Dermatologic: Rash

Gastrointestinal: Stomatitis

Neuromuscular: Paresthesias

Renal: Creatinine increase (2%)

Respiratory: Interstitial pneumonitis, infiltrates, dyspnea, cough (7%)

Drug Interactions

Increased Effect/Toxicity: *Vinca* alkaloids or doxorubicin may enhance cardiac toxicity when coadministered with mitomycin.

Mechanism of Action Acts like an alkylating agent and produces DNA cross-linking (primarily with guanine and cytosine pairs); cell-cycle nonspecific; inhibits DNA and RNA synthesis; degrades preformed DNA, causes nuclear lysis and formation of giant cells. While not phase-specific *per se*, mitomycin has its maximum effect against cells in late G and early S phases.

Pharmacodynamics/Kinetics

Distribution: V_d: 22 L/m²; high drug concentrations found in kidney, tongue, muscle, heart, and lung tissue; probably not distributed into the CNS

Metabolism: Hepatic

Half-life elimination: 23-78 minutes; Terminal: 50 minutes

Excretion: Urine (<10% as unchanged drug), with elevated serum concentrations

Dosage Refer to individual protocols. Children and Adults:

Single agent therapy: I.V.: 20 mg/m² every 6-8 weeks

Combination therapy: I.V.: 10 mg/m² every 6-8 weeks

Bladder carcinoma: Intravesicular instillation (unapproved route): 20-40 mg/dose instilled into the bladder for 3 hours repeated up to 3 times/week for up to 20 procedures per course

Glaucoma surgery (unlabeled use): Dosages and techniques vary; 0.2-0.5 mg may be applied to a pledget (using a 0.2-0.5 mg/mL solution), and placed in contact with the surgical wound for 2-5 minutes; other protocols have been reported

Dosage adjustment in renal impairment: Varying approaches to dosing adjustments have been published; one representative recommendation: Cl_{cr} <10 mL/minute: Administer 75% of normal dose

Note: The manufacturers state that products should not be given to patients with serum creatinine >1.7 mg/dL.

Hemodialysis: Unknown

CAPD effects: Unknown

CAVH effects: Unknown

Dosage adjustment in hepatic impairment: Although some mitomycin may be excreted in the bile, no specific guidelines regarding dosage adjustment in hepatic impairment can be made.

Administration Administer slow I.V. push or by slow (15-30 minute) infusion via a freely-running dextrose or saline infusion. Consider using a central venous catheter. **Avoid extravasation**; severe local tissue necrosis occurs. Flush with 5-10 mL of I.V. solution before and after drug administration; IVPB infusions should be closely monitored for adequate vein patency.

(Continued)

Mitomycin *(Continued)*

Extravasation management: Care should be taken to avoid extravasation. If extravasation occurs, the site should be observed closely. These injuries frequently cause necrosis. A plastic surgery consult may be required. Few agents have been effective as antidotes, but there are reports in the literature of some benefit with dimethylsulfoxide (DSMO). Delayed dermal reactions with mitomycin are possible, even in patients who are asymptomatic at time of drug administration.

Monitoring Parameters Platelet count, CBC with differential, hemoglobin, prothrombin time, renal and pulmonary function tests

Patient Information This drug can only be given I.V. Make note of scheduled return dates. You may experience, rash, skin lesions, loss of hair, or permanent sterility. Small frequent meals may help if you experience nausea, vomiting, or loss of appetite. Frequent mouth care will help reduce the incidence of mouth sores. Use caution when driving or engaging in tasks that require alertness because you may experience dizziness, drowsiness, syncope, or blurred vision. Report difficulty breathing, swelling of extremities, or sudden weight gain; burning, pain, or redness at infusion site; unusual bruising or bleeding; pain on urination; or other adverse effects. The drug may be excreted in breast milk, therefore, an alternative form of feeding your baby should be used. Contraceptive measures are recommended during therapy.

Dosage Forms INJ, powder for reconstitution (Mutamycin®): 5 mg, 20 mg, 40 mg

- ♦ **Mitomycin-C** *see Mitomycin on page 849*
- ♦ **Mitomycin-X** *see Mitomycin on page 849*

Mitotane *(MYE toe tane)*

U.S. Brand Names Lysodren®

Synonyms NSC-38721; o,p'-DDD

Therapeutic Category Antiadrenal Agent; Antineoplastic Agent, Miscellaneous

Use Treatment of adrenocortical carcinoma

Unlabeled/Investigational Use Treatment of Cushing's syndrome

Pregnancy Risk Factor C

Contraindications Hypersensitivity to mitotane or any component of the formulation

Warnings/Precautions The U.S. Food and Drug Administration (FDA) currently recommends that procedures for proper handling and disposal of antineoplastic agents be considered. Discontinue temporarily following trauma or shock since the prime action of mitotane is adrenal suppression; exogenous steroids may be indicated since adrenal function may not start immediately. Administer with care to patients with severe hepatic impairment; observe patients for neurotoxicity with prolonged (2 years) use.

Common Adverse Reactions

>10%:
    Central nervous system: CNS depression (32%), dizziness (15%)
    Dermatologic: Skin rash (12%)
    Gastrointestinal: Anorexia (24%), nausea (39%), vomiting (37%), diarrhea (13%)
    Neuromuscular & skeletal: Weakness (12%)
1% to 10%:
    Central nervous system: Headache (5%), confusion (3%)
    Neuromuscular & skeletal: Muscle tremor (3%)

Drug Interactions

Increased Effect/Toxicity: CNS depressants taken with mitotane may enhance CNS depression.

Decreased Effect: Mitotane may enhance the clearance of barbiturates and warfarin by induction of the hepatic microsomal enzyme system resulting in a decreased effect. Coadministration of spironolactone has resulted in negation of mitotane's effect. Mitotane may increase clearance of phenytoin by microsomal enzyme stimulation.

Mechanism of Action Causes adrenal cortical atrophy; drug affects mitochondria in adrenal cortical cells and decreases production of cortisol; also alters the peripheral metabolism of steroids

Pharmacodynamics/Kinetics

Absorption: Oral: ~35% to 40%
Distribution: Stored mainly in fat tissue but is found in all body tissues
Metabolism: Hepatic and other tissues
Half-life elimination: 18-159 days
Time to peak, serum: 3-5 hours
Excretion: Urine and feces (as metabolites)

Dosage Oral:

Children: 0.1-0.5 mg/kg or 1-2 g/day in divided doses increasing gradually to a maximum of 5-7 g/day
Adults: Start at 1-6 g/day in divided doses, then increase incrementally to 8-10 g/day in 3-4 divided doses (maximum daily dose: 18 g)

Dosing adjustment in hepatic impairment: Dose may need to be decreased in patients with liver disease

Patient Information Desired effects of this drug may not be seen for 2-3 months. Wear identification that alerts medical personnel that you are taking this drug in event of shock or trauma. Maintain adequate hydration (2-3 L/day of fluids unless instructed to restrict fluid intake) and nutrition. May cause dizziness and vertigo (avoid driving or performing tasks requiring alertness until response to drug is known); nausea, vomiting, or loss of appetite (small frequent meals, frequent mouth care, sucking lozenges, or chewing gum may help);

orthostatic hypotension (use caution when rising from sitting or lying position or climbing stairs); muscle aches or pain (if severe, request medication from prescriber). Report severe vomiting or acute loss of appetite, muscular twitching, fever or infection, blood in urine or pain on urinating, or darkening of skin. Contraceptive measures are recommended during therapy.

Dosage Forms TAB [scored]: 500 mg

Mitoxantrone (mye toe ZAN trone)

U.S. Brand Names Novantrone®

Synonyms DAD; DHAD; DHAQ; Dihydroxyanthracenedione Dihydrochloride; Mitoxantrone Hydrochloride CL-232315; Mitozantrone; NSC-301739

Therapeutic Category Antineoplastic Agent, Anthracycline; Antineoplastic Agent, Irritant; Vesicant

Use Treatment of acute leukemias, lymphoma, breast cancer, pediatric sarcoma, progressive or relapsing-remitting multiple sclerosis, prostate cancer

Pregnancy Risk Factor D

Contraindications Hypersensitivity to mitoxantrone or any component of the formulation; multiple sclerosis with left ventricular ejection fraction (LVEF) <50% or clinically significant decrease in LVEF; pregnancy

Warnings/Precautions The FDA currently recommends that procedures for proper handling and disposal of antineoplastic agents be considered. Dosage should be reduced in patients with impaired hepatobiliary function; not for treatment of multiple sclerosis in patients with concurrent hepatic impairment. Treatment may lead to severe myelosuppression; use with caution in patients with pre-existing myelosuppression. Do not use if baseline neutrophil count <1500 cells/mm^3 (except for treatment of ANLL). May cause myocardial toxicity and potentially-fatal CHF; risk increases with cumulative dosing. Predisposing factors for mitoxantrone-induced cardiotoxicity include prior anthracycline therapy, prior cardiovascular disease, and mediastinal irradiation. Not for treatment of primary progressive multiple sclerosis. Has been associated with the development of secondary acute myelogenous leukemia and myelodysplasia when used in combination with other antineoplastic agents. For I.V. use only. May cause urine, saliva, tears, and sweat to turn blue-green for 24 hours postinfusion. Whites of eyes may have blue-green tinge (this is normal).

Common Adverse Reactions Reported with any indication; incidence varies based on treatment/dose

>10%:

Cardiovascular: Abnormal ECG, arrhythmia (3% to 18%), edema, nail bed changes

Central nervous system: Fatigue, fever, headache (6% to 13%)

Dermatologic: Alopecia (20% to 61%)

Endocrine & metabolic: Amenorrhea, menstrual disorder

Gastrointestinal: Abdominal pain, anorexia, nausea (29% to 76%), constipation, diarrhea (16% to 47%), GI bleeding, mucositis (10% to 29%), stomatitis, vomiting, weight gain/loss

Genitourinary: Abnormal urine, urinary tract infection

Hematologic: Decreased hemoglobin, leukopenia, lymphopenia, petechiae/bruising; myelosuppressive effects of chemotherapy:

WBC: Mild

Platelets: Mild

Onset: 7-10 days

Nadir: 14 days

Recovery: 21 days

Hepatic: Increased GGT

Neuromuscular & skeletal: Weakness (24%)

Respiratory: Cough, dyspnea, upper respiratory tract infection

Miscellaneous: Fungal infections, infection, sepsis

1% to 10%:

Cardiovascular: CHF (2% to 3%; risk is much lower with anthracyclines, some reports suggest cumulative doses >160 mg/mL cause CHF in ~10% of patients), ECG changes, hypotension, ischemia, LVEF decreased (≤5%)

Central nervous system: Chills, anxiety, depression, seizures

Dermatologic: Skin infection

Endocrine & metabolic: Hypocalcemia, hypokalemia, hyponatremia, hyperglycemia

Gastrointestinal: Dyspepsia, aphthosis

Genitourinary: Impotence, proteinuria, renal failure, sterility

Hematologic: Anemia, granulocytopenia, hemorrhage

Hepatic: Jaundice, increased SGOT, increased SGPT

Neuromuscular & skeletal: Back pain, myalgia, arthralgia

Ocular: Blurred vision, conjunctivitis

Renal: Hematuria

Respiratory: Pneumonia, rhinitis, sinusitis

Miscellaneous: Systemic infection, sweats, development of secondary leukemia

Drug Interactions

Cytochrome P450 Effect: Inhibits CYP3A4 (weak)

Decreased Effect: Patients may experience impaired immune response to vaccines; possible infection after administration of live vaccines in patients receiving immunosuppressants.

Mechanism of Action Analogue of the anthracyclines, mitoxantrone intercalates DNA; binds to nucleic acids and inhibits DNA and RNA synthesis by template disordering and steric obstruction; replication is decreased by binding to DNA topoisomerase II and seems to inhibit

(Continued)

Mitoxantrone *(Continued)*

the incorporation of uridine into RNA and thymidine into DNA; active throughout entire cell cycle

Pharmacodynamics/Kinetics

Absorption: Oral: Poor

Distribution: V_d: 14 L/kg; distributes into pleural fluid, kidney, thyroid, liver, heart, and red blood cells

Protein binding: >95%, 76% to albumin

Metabolism: Hepatic; pathway not determined

Half-life elimination: Terminal: 23-215 hours; may be prolonged with hepatic impairment

Excretion: Urine (6% to 11%) and feces as unchanged drug and metabolites

Dosage Refer to individual protocols. I.V. (dilute in D_5W or NS):

Acute leukemias:

Children ≤2 years: 0.4 mg/kg/day once daily for 3-5 days

Children >2 years and Adults: 8-12 mg/m²/day once daily for 4-5 days

Solid tumors:

Children: 18-20 mg/m² every 3-4 weeks **or** 5-8 mg/m² every week

Adults: 12-14 mg/m² every 3-4 weeks **or** 2-4 mg/m²/day for 5 days every 4 weeks

Hormone-refractory prostate cancer: Adults: 12-14 mg/m²

Multiple sclerosis: Adults: 12 mg/m²

Dosing adjustment in renal impairment: Safety and efficacy have not been established

Hemodialysis: Supplemental dose is not necessary

Peritoneal dialysis: Supplemental dose is not necessary

Elderly: Clearance is decreased in elderly patients; use with caution

Dosing adjustment in hepatic impairment: Official dosage adjustment recommendations have not been established.

Moderate dysfunction (bilirubin 1.5-3 mg/dL): Some clinicians recommend a 50% dosage reduction

Severe dysfunction (bilirubin >3.0 mg/dL) may require a dosage adjustment to 8 mg/m²; some clinicians recommend a dosage reduction to 25% of dose

Administration Administered as a short (15-30 minutes) I.V. infusion; continuous 24-hour infusions are occasionally used. Although not generally recommended, mitoxantrone has been given as a rapid bolus over 1-3 minutes. High doses for bone marrow transplant are usually given as 1- to 4-hour infusions.

Monitoring Parameters CBC, serum uric acid (for treatment of leukemia), liver function tests, signs and symptoms of CHF; evaluate LVEF prior to start of therapy and regularly during treatment. In addition, for the treatment of multiple sclerosis, monitor LVEF prior to all doses following cumulative dose of ≥100 mg/m².

Patient Information This drug can only be given I.V. Make note of scheduled return dates. Your urine may turn blue-green for 24 hours after infusion and the whites of your eyes may have a blue-green tinge; this is normal. Maintain adequate hydration (2-3 L/day of fluids unless instructed to restrict fluid intake) and nutrition. You may experience rash, skin lesions, or loss of hair. Small frequent meals may help if you experience nausea, vomiting, or loss of appetite. Frequent mouth care will help reduce the incidence of mouth sores. Use caution when driving or engaging in tasks that require alertness because you may experience dizziness, drowsiness, syncope, or blurred vision. Report chest pain or heart palpitations; difficulty breathing or constant cough; swelling of extremities or sudden weight gain; burning, pain, or redness at the I.V. infusion site; persistent fever or chills; unusual bruising or bleeding; twitching or tremors; or pain on urination. Contraceptive measures are recommended during therapy.

Dosage Forms INJ, solution: 2 mg base/mL (10 mL, 12.5 mL, 15 mL)

♦ **Mitoxantrone Hydrochloride CL-232315** *see Mitoxantrone on page 851*

♦ **Mitozantrone** *see Mitoxantrone on page 851*

♦ **Mitrazol™ [OTC]** *see Miconazole on page 834*

♦ **Mivacron®** *see Mivacurium on page 852*

Mivacurium *(mye va KYOO ree um)*

Related Information

Neuromuscular Blocking Agents Comparison *on page 1397*

U.S. Brand Names Mivacron®

Synonyms Mivacurium Chloride

Therapeutic Category Neuromuscular Blocker Agent, Nondepolarizing

Use Adjunct to general anesthesia to facilitate endotracheal intubation and to relax skeletal muscles during surgery; to facilitate mechanical ventilation in ICU patients; does not relieve pain or produce sedation

Pregnancy Risk Factor C

Contraindications Hypersensitivity to mivacurium chloride, any component of the formulation, or other benzylisoquinolinium agents; use of multidose vials in patients with allergy to benzyl alcohol; pre-existing tachycardia

Warnings/Precautions Ventilation must be supported during neuromuscular blockade; does not counteract bradycardia produced by anesthetics/vagal stimulation; prolonged neuromuscular block may be seen in patients with reduced or atypical plasma cholinesterase activity (eg, pregnancy, liver or kidney disease, infections, peptic ulcer, anemia); patients homozygous for the atypical plasma cholinesterase gene are extremely sensitive to the neuromuscular blocking effect of mivacurium (use extreme caution if at all in those patients); duration prolonged in patients with renal and/or hepatic impairment; reduce initial dosage and inject slowly (over 60 seconds) in patients in whom substantial histamine release would be potentially hazardous; certain clinical conditions may result in potentiation or antagonism of neuromuscular blockade:

Potentiation: Electrolyte abnormalities, severe hyponatremia, severe hypocalcemia, severe hypokalemia, hypermagnesemia, neuromuscular diseases, acidosis, acute intermittent porphyria, renal failure, hepatic failure

Antagonism: Alkalosis, hypercalcemia, demyelinating lesions, peripheral neuropathies, diabetes mellitus

Increased sensitivity in patients with myasthenia gravis, Eaton-Lambert syndrome, resistance in burn patients (>30% of body) for period of 5-70 days postinjury; resistance in patients with muscle trauma, denervation, immobilization, infection. Cross-sensitivity with other neuromuscular-blocking agents may occur; use extreme caution in patients with previous anaphylactic reactions.

Common Adverse Reactions
>10%: Cardiovascular: Flushing of face
1% to 10%: Cardiovascular: Hypotension

Drug Interactions
Increased Effect/Toxicity: Increased effects are possible with aminoglycosides, beta-blockers, clindamycin, calcium channel blockers, halogenated anesthetics, imipenem, ketamine, lidocaine, loop diuretics (furosemide), macrolides (case reports), magnesium sulfate, procainamide, quinidine, quinolones, tetracyclines, and vancomycin. May increase risk of myopathy when used with high-dose corticosteroids for extended periods. Drugs which inhibit acetylcholinesterase may prolong effect of mivacurium.

Decreased Effect: Effect of nondepolarizing neuromuscular blockers may be reduced by carbamazepine (chronic use), corticosteroids (also associated with myopathy - see increased effect), phenytoin (chronic use), sympathomimetics, and theophylline.

Mechanism of Action
Mivacurium is a short-acting, nondepolarizing, neuromuscular-blocking agent. Like other nondepolarizing drugs, mivacurium antagonizes acetylcholine by competitively binding to cholinergic sites on motor endplates in skeletal muscle. This inhibits contractile activity in skeletal muscle leading to muscle paralysis. This effect is reversible with cholinesterase inhibitors such as edrophonium, neostigmine, and physostigmine.

Pharmacodynamics/Kinetics
Onset of action: Neuromuscular blockade (dose dependent): I.V.: 1.5-3 minutes
Duration: Short: due to rapid hydrolysis by plasma cholinesterases; clinically effective block may last for 12-20 minutes; spontaneous recovery may be 95% complete in 25-30 minutes; duration shorter in children and may be slightly longer in elderly
Metabolism: Via plasma cholinesterase, inactive metabolites
Half-life elimination: 2 minutes (more active isomers only)
Excretion: Urine (<10%)

Dosage
Continuous infusion requires an infusion pump; dose to effect; doses will vary due to interpatient variability; use ideal body weight for obese patients

Children 2-12 years (duration of action is shorter and dosage requirements are higher): 0.2 mg/kg I.V. followed by average infusion rate of 14 mcg/kg/minute (range: 5-31 mcg/kg/minute) upon evidence of spontaneous recovery from initial dose

Adults: Initial: I.V.: 0.15-0.25 mg/kg bolus followed by maintenance doses of 0.1 mg/kg at approximately 15-minute intervals; for prolonged neuromuscular block, initial infusion of 9-10 mcg/kg/minute is used upon evidence of spontaneous recovery from initial dose, usual infusion rate of 6-7 mcg/kg/minute (1-15 mcg/kg/minute) under balanced anesthesia; initial dose after succinylcholine for intubation (balanced anesthesia): Adults: 0.1 mg/kg

Pretreatment/priming: 10% of intubating dose given 3-5 minutes before initial dose

Dosing adjustment in renal impairment: 0.15 mg/kg I.V. bolus; duration of action of blockade: 1.5 times longer in ESRD, may decrease infusion rates by as much as 50%, dependent on degree of renal impairment

Dosing adjustment in hepatic impairment: 0.15 mg/kg I.V. bolus; duration of blockade: 3 times longer in ESLD, may decrease rate of infusion by as much as 50% in ESLD, dependent on the degree of impairment

Administration
Children require higher neuromuscular infusion rates than adults; during opioid/nitrous oxide/oxygen anesthesia, the infusion rate required to maintain 89% to 99% neuromuscular block averages 14 mcg/kg/minute (range: 5-31). For adults and children, the amount of infusion solution required per hour depends upon the clinical requirements of the patient, the concentration of mivacurium in the infusion solution, and the patient's weight. The contribution of the infusion solution to the fluid requirements of the patient must be considered.

Dosage Forms INJ, solution [preservative free]: 2 mg/mL (5 mL, 10 mL). **INJ, solution:** 2 mg/mL (20 mL, 50 mL)

♦ **MOBIC®** *see Meloxicam on page 785*

♦ **Mobidin® [DSC]** *see Magnesium Salicylate on page 771*

Modafinil (moe DAF i nil)

U.S. Brand Names Provigil®

Therapeutic Category Central Nervous System Stimulant, Nonamphetamine

Use Improve wakefulness in patients with excessive daytime sleepiness associated with narcolepsy

Unlabeled/Investigational Use Attention-deficit/hyperactivity disorder (ADHD); treatment of fatigue in MS and other disorders

Restrictions C-IV

Pregnancy Risk Factor C

Contraindications Hypersensitivity to modafinil or any component of the formulation

Warnings/Precautions History of angina, ischemic ECG changes, left ventricular hypertrophy, or clinically significant mitral valve prolapse in association with CNS stimulant use; caution should be exercised when modafinil is given to patients with a history of psychosis, recent history of myocardial infarction, and because it has not yet been adequately studied in patients with hypertension, periodic monitoring of hypertensive patients receiving modafinil may be appropriate; caution is warranted when operating machinery or driving, although functional impairment has not been demonstrated with modafinil, all CNS-active agents may alter judgment, thinking and/or motor skills. Efficacy of oral contraceptives may be reduced, therefore, use of alternative contraception should be considered. Stimulants may unmask tics in individuals with coexisting Tourette's syndrome.

Common Adverse Reactions Limited to reports equal to or greater than placebo-related events.

<10%:

Cardiovascular: Chest pain (2%), hypertension (2%), hypotension (2%), vasodilation (1%), arrhythmia (1%), syncope (1%)

Central nervous system: Headache (50%, compared to 40% with placebo), nervousness (8%), dizziness (5%), depression (4%), anxiety (4%), cataplexy (3%), insomnia (3%), chills (2%), fever (1%), confusion (1%), amnesia (1%), emotional lability (1%), ataxia (1%)

Dermatologic: Dry skin (1%)

Endocrine & metabolic: Hyperglycemia (1%), albuminuria (1%)

Gastrointestinal: Diarrhea (8%), nausea (13%, compared to 4% with placebo), xerostomia (5%), anorexia (5%), vomiting (1%), mouth ulceration (1%), gingivitis (1%)

Genitourinary: Abnormal urine (1%), urinary retention (1%), ejaculatory disturbance (1%)

Hematologic: Eosinophilia (1%)

Hepatic: Abnormal LFTs (3%)

Neuromuscular & skeletal: Paresthesias (3%), dyskinesia (2%), neck pain (2%), hypertonia (2%), neck rigidity (1%), joint disorder (1%), tremor (1%)

Ocular: Amblyopia (2%), abnormal vision (2%)

Respiratory: Pharyngitis (6%), rhinitis (11%, compared to 8% with placebo), lung disorder (4%), dyspnea (2%), asthma (1%), epistaxis (1%)

Drug Interactions

Cytochrome P450 Effect: Substrate of CYP3A4 (major); **Inhibits** CYP1A2 (weak), 2A6 (weak), 2C8/9 (weak), 2C19 (strong), 2E1 (weak), 3A4 (weak); **Induces** CYP1A2 (weak), 2B6 (weak), 3A4 (weak)

Increased Effect/Toxicity: Modafinil may increase levels of diazepam, mephenytoin, phenytoin, propranolol, and warfarin. In populations deficient in the CYP2D6 isoenzyme, where CYP2C19 acts as a secondary metabolic pathway, concentrations of tricyclic antidepressants and selective serotonin reuptake inhibitors may be increased during coadministration.

Decreased Effect: Modafinil may decrease serum concentrations of oral contraceptives, cyclosporine, and to a lesser degree, theophylline. Agents that induce CYP3A4, including phenobarbital, carbamazepine, and rifampin may result in decreased modafinil levels. There is also evidence to suggest that modafinil may induce its own metabolism.

Mechanism of Action The exact mechanism of action is unclear, it does not appear to alter the release of dopamine or norepinephrine, it may exert its stimulant effects by decreasing GABA-mediated neurotransmission, although this theory has not yet been fully evaluated; several studies also suggest that an intact central alpha-adrenergic system is required for modafinil's activity; the drug increases high-frequency alpha waves while decreasing both delta and theta wave activity, and these effects are consistent with generalized increases in mental alertness

Pharmacodynamics/Kinetics Modafinil is a racemic compound (10% *d*-isomer and 90% *l*-isomer at steady state) whose enantiomers have different pharmacokinetics

Distribution: V_d: 0.9 L/kg

Protein binding: 60%, primarily to albumin

Metabolism: Hepatic; multiple pathways including CYP3A4

Half-life elimination: Effective half-life: 15 hours; Steady-state: 2-4 days

Time to peak, serum: 2-4 hours

Excretion: Urine (as metabolites, <10% as unchanged drug)

Dosage Oral:

Children: ADHD (unlabeled use): 50-100 mg once daily

Adults:

ADHD (unlabeled use): 100-300 mg once daily

Narcolepsy: Initial: 200 mg as a single daily dose in the morning

Doses of 400 mg/day, given as a single dose, have been well tolerated, but there is no consistent evidence that this dose confers additional benefit

Elderly: Elimination of modafinil and its metabolites may be reduced as a consequence of aging and as a result, lower doses should be considered.

Dosing adjustment in renal impairment: Inadequate data to determine safety and efficacy in severe renal impairment

Dosing adjustment in hepatic impairment: Dose should be reduced to one-half of that recommended for patients with normal liver function

Patient Information Take during the day to avoid insomnia; may cause dependence with prolonged use; patients should be reminded to notify their prescriber if they become pregnant, intend to become pregnant, or are breast-feeding an infant; patients should be advised that combined use with alcohol has not been studied and that it is prudent to avoid this combination. Patients should notify their prescriber and/or pharmacist of any concomitant medications they are taking, due to the drug interaction potential this might represent.

Dosage Forms TAB: 100 mg, 200 mg

♦ **Modane® Bulk [OTC]** *see* Psyllium *on page 1063*

♦ **Modicon®** *see* Ethinyl Estradiol and Norethindrone *on page 487*

♦ **Modified Dakin's Solution** *see* Sodium Hypochlorite Solution *on page 1149*

♦ **Modified Shohl's Solution** *see* Sodium Citrate and Citric Acid *on page 1147*

♦ **Moduretic® [DSC]** *see* Amiloride and Hydrochlorothiazide *on page 74*

Moexipril (mo EKS i pril)

Related Information
Angiotensin Agents Comparison *on page 1353*

U.S. Brand Names Univasc®

Synonyms Moexipril Hydrochloride

Therapeutic Category Angiotensin-Converting Enzyme (ACE) Inhibitor; Antihypertensive Agent

Use Treatment of hypertension, alone or in combination with thiazide diuretics; treatment of left ventricular dysfunction after myocardial infarction

Pregnancy Risk Factor C/D (2nd and 3rd trimesters)

Contraindications Hypersensitivity to moexipril, moexiprilat, or any component of the formulation; hypersensitivity or allergic reactions or angioedema related to previous treatment with an ACE inhibitor; pregnancy (2nd or 3rd trimester)

Warnings/Precautions Do not administer in pregnancy; use with caution and modify dosage in patients with renal impairment especially renal artery stenosis, severe CHF, or with coadministered diuretic therapy; experience in children is limited. Severe hypotension may occur in patients who are sodium and/or volume depleted; initiate lower doses and monitor closely when starting therapy in these patients; ACE inhibitors may be preferred agents in elderly patients with CHF and diabetes mellitus (diabetic proteinuria is reduced, minimal CNS effects, and enhanced insulin sensitivity), however, due to decreased renal function, tolerance must be carefully monitored; if possible, discontinue the diuretic 2-3 days prior to initiating moexipril in patients receiving them to reduce the risk of symptomatic hypotension.

Anaphylactic reactions can occur. Angioedema can occur at any time during treatment (especially following first dose). Angioedema may involve head and neck (potentially affecting the airway) or the intestine (presenting with abdominal pain). Use with caution in collagen vascular diseases; valvular stenosis (particularly aortic stenosis); hyperkalemia; or before, during, or immediately after anesthesia. Avoid rapid dosage escalation which may lead to renal insufficiency. Neutropenia/agranulocytosis with myeloid hyperplasia can rarely occur. If patient has renal impairment then a baseline WBC with differential and serum creatinine should be evaluated and monitored closely during the first 3 months of therapy. Hypersensitivity reactions may be seen during hemodialysis with high-flux dialysis membranes (eg, AN69). Deterioration in renal function can occur with initiation.

Common Adverse Reactions 1% to 10%:
Cardiovascular: Hypotension, peripheral edema
Central nervous system: Headache, dizziness, fatigue
Dermatologic: Rash, alopecia, flushing, rash
Endocrine & metabolic: Hyperkalemia, hyponatremia
Gastrointestinal: Diarrhea, nausea, heartburn
Genitourinary: Polyuria
Neuromuscular & skeletal: Myalgia
Renal: Reversible increases in creatinine or BUN
Respiratory: Cough, pharyngitis, upper respiratory infection, sinusitis

Drug Interactions

Increased Effect/Toxicity: Potassium supplements, co-trimoxazole (high dose), angiotensin II receptor antagonists (candesartan, losartan, irbesartan, etc), or potassium-sparing diuretics (amiloride, spironolactone, triamterene) may result in elevated serum potassium levels when combined with moexipril. ACE inhibitor effects may be increased by probenecid (increases levels of captopril). ACE inhibitors may increase serum concentrations/effects of digoxin, lithium, and sulfonlyureas.

Diuretics have additive hypotensive effects with ACE inhibitors, and hypovolemia increases the potential for adverse renal effects of ACE inhibitors. In patients with compromised renal function, coadministration with NSAIDs may result in further deterioration of renal function. Allopurinol and ACE inhibitors may cause a higher risk of hypersensitivity reaction when taken concurrently.

(Continued)

Moexipril *(Continued)*

Decreased Effect: Aspirin (high dose) may reduce the therapeutic effects of ACE inhibitors; at low dosages this does not appear to be significant. Rifampin may decrease the effect of ACE inhibitors. Antacids may decrease the bioavailability of ACE inhibitors (may be more likely to occur with captopril); separate administration times by 1-2 hours. NSAIDs, specifically indomethacin, may reduce the hypotensive effects of ACE inhibitors. More likely to occur in low renin or volume dependent hypertensive patients.

Mechanism of Action Competitive inhibitor of angiotensin-converting enzyme (ACE); prevents conversion of angiotensin I to angiotensin II, a potent vasoconstrictor; results in lower levels of angiotensin II which causes an increase in plasma renin activity and a reduction in aldosterone secretion

Pharmacodynamics/Kinetics
Onset of action: Peak effect: 1-2 hours
Duration: >24 hours
Distribution: V_d (moexiprilat): 180 L
Protein binding, plasma: Moexipril: 90%; Moexiprilat: 50% to 70%
Metabolism: Parent drug: Hepatic and via GI tract to moexiprilat, 1000 times more potent than parent
Bioavailability: Moexiprilat: 13%; reduced with food (AUC decreased by ~40%)
Half-life elimination: Moexipril: 1 hour; Moexiprilat: 2-9 hours
Time to peak: 1.5 hours
Excretion: Feces (50%)

Dosage Adults: Oral: Initial: 7.5 mg once daily (in patients **not** receiving diuretics), 1 hour prior to a meal **or** 3.75 mg once daily (when combined with thiazide diuretics); maintenance dose: 7.5-30 mg/day in 1 or 2 divided doses 1 hour before meals

Dosing adjustment in renal impairment: Cl_{cr} ≤40 mL/minute: Patients may be cautiously placed on 3.75 mg once daily, then upwardly titrated to a maximum of 15 mg/day.

Monitoring Parameters Blood pressure, heart rate, electrolytes, CBC, symptoms of hypotension

Patient Information Food may delay and reduce peak serum levels; take on an empty stomach, if possible. Report immediately any swelling of the face, mouth, or tongue, rash, or difficulty breathing; bothersome side effects such as cough, dizziness, diarrhea, tiredness, rash, headache, irregular heartbeat, anxiety, and flu-like symptoms should also be reported; avoid use of this medication if you are pregnant or have had a previous reaction to other ACE inhibitors.

Dosage Forms TAB, film coated, scored: 7.5 mg, 15 mg

Moexipril and Hydrochlorothiazide
(mo EKS i pril & hye droe klor oh THYE a zide)

U.S. Brand Names Uniretic®

Synonyms Hydrochlorothiazide and Moexipril

Therapeutic Category Angiotensin-Converting Enzyme (ACE) Inhibitor/Thiazide Diuretic; Antihypertensive Agent, Combination

Use Combination therapy for hypertension, however, not indicated for initial treatment of hypertension; replacement therapy in patients receiving separate dosage forms (for patient convenience); when monotherapy with one component fails to achieve desired antihypertensive effect, or when dose-limiting adverse effects limit upward titration of monotherapy

Pregnancy Risk Factor C/D (2nd and 3rd trimesters)

Dosage Adults: Oral: 7.5-30 mg of moexipril, taken either in a single or divided dose one hour before meals; hydrochlorothiazide dose should be ≤50 mg/day

Dosage Forms TAB [film coated, scored] (7.5/12.5): Moexipril 7.5 mg and hydrochlorothiazide 12.5 mg; (15/12.5): Moexipril 15 mg and hydrochlorothiazide 12.5 mg; (15/25): Moexipril 15 mg and hydrochlorothiazide 25 mg

♦ **Moexipril Hydrochloride** *see* Moexipril *on page 855*

Molindone *(moe LIN done)*

Related Information
Antipsychotic Agents Comparison *on page 1364*

U.S. Brand Names Moban®

Synonyms Molindone Hydrochloride

Therapeutic Category Antipsychotic Agent, Dihydroindolone

Use Management of schizophrenia

Unlabeled/Investigational Use Management of psychotic disorders

Pregnancy Risk Factor C

Contraindications Hypersensitivity to molindone or any component of the formulation (cross-reactivity between phenothiazines may occur); severe CNS depression; coma

Warnings/Precautions May be sedating, use with caution in disorders where CNS depression is a feature. Use with caution in Parkinson's disease. Caution in patients with hemodynamic instability; bone marrow suppression; predisposition to seizures; subcortical brain damage; severe cardiac, hepatic, renal, or respiratory disease. Esophageal dysmotility and aspiration have been associated with antipsychotic use - use with caution in patients at risk of pneumonia (ie, Alzheimer's disease). Caution in breast cancer or other prolactin-dependent tumors (may elevate prolactin levels). May alter temperature regulation or mask toxicity of other drugs due to antiemetic effects. May alter cardiac conduction; life-threatening arrhythmias have occurred with therapeutic doses of neuroleptics. May cause orthostatic hypotension - use with caution in patients at risk of this effect or those who would tolerate transient hypotensive episodes (cerebrovascular disease, cardiovascular disease, or other medications which may predispose).

May cause anticholinergic effects (confusion, agitation, constipation, xerostomia, blurred vision, urinary retention); therefore, they should be used with caution in patients with decreased gastrointestinal motility, urinary retention, BPH, xerostomia, or visual problems. Conditions which also may be exacerbated by cholinergic blockade include narrow-angle glaucoma (screening is recommended) and worsening of myasthenia gravis. Relative to other neuroleptics, molindone has a low potency of cholinergic blockade.

May cause extrapyramidal reactions, including pseudoparkinsonism, acute dystonic reactions, akathisia, and tardive dyskinesia (risk of these reactions is moderate-high relative to other neuroleptics). May be associated with neuroleptic malignant syndrome (NMS) or pigmentary retinopathy.

Common Adverse Reactions Frequency not defined.

Cardiovascular: Orthostatic hypotension, tachycardia, arrhythmias

Central nervous system: Extrapyramidal reactions (akathisia, pseudoparkinsonism, dystonia, tardive dyskinesia), mental depression, altered central temperature regulation, sedation, drowsiness, restlessness, anxiety, hyperactivity, euphoria, seizures, neuroleptic malignant syndrome (NMS)

Dermatologic: Pruritus, rash, photosensitivity

Endocrine & metabolic: Change in menstrual periods, edema of breasts, amenorrhea, galactorrhea, gynecomastia

Gastrointestinal: Constipation, xerostomia, nausea, salivation, weight gain (minimal compared to other antipsychotics), weight loss

Genitourinary: Urinary retention, priapism

Hematologic: Leukopenia, leukocytosis

Ocular: Blurred vision, retinal pigmentation

Miscellaneous: Diaphoresis (decreased)

Drug Interactions

Increased Effect/Toxicity: Molindone concentrations may be increased by chloroquine, propranolol, sulfadoxine-pyrimethamine. Molindone may increase the effect and/or toxicity of antihypertensives, lithium, TCAs, CNS depressants (ethanol, narcotics), and trazodone. Metoclopramide may increase risk of extrapyramidal symptoms (EPS).

Decreased Effect: Antipsychotics inhibit the activity of bromocriptine and levodopa. Benztropine (and other anticholinergics) may inhibit the therapeutic response to molindone and excess anticholinergic effects may occur. Barbiturates and cigarette smoking may enhance the hepatic metabolism of molindone. Molindone and possibly other low potency antipsychotic may reverse the pressor effects of epinephrine.

Mechanism of Action Mechanism of action mimics that of chlorpromazine; however, it produces more extrapyramidal symptoms and less sedation than chlorpromazine

Pharmacodynamics/Kinetics

Metabolism: Hepatic

Half-life elimination: 1.5 hours

Time to peak, serum: ~1.5 hours

Excretion: Urine and feces (90%) within 24 hours

Dosage Oral:

Children: Schizophrenia/psychoses:

3-5 years: 1-2.5 mg/day in 4 divided doses

5-12 years: 0.5-1 mg/kg/day in 4 divided doses

Adults: Schizophrenia/psychoses: 50-75 mg/day increase at 3- to 4-day intervals up to 225 mg/day

Elderly: Behavioral symptoms associated with dementia: Initial: 5-10 mg 1-2 times/day; increase at 4- to 7-day intervals by 5-10 mg/day; increase dosing intervals (bid, tid, etc) as necessary to control response or side effects.

Monitoring Parameters Vital signs; lipid profile, fasting blood glucose/Hgb A$_{1c}$; BMI; mental status, abnormal involuntary movement scale (AIMS), extrapyramidal symptoms (EPS)

Patient Information Dry mouth may be helped by sips of water, sugarless gum or hard candy; avoid alcohol; it is very important to maintain established dosage regimen; photosensitivity to sunlight can occur, do not discontinue abruptly; full effect may not occur for 3-4 weeks; full dosage may be taken at bedtime to avoid daytime sedation; report any involuntary movements or feelings of restlessness

Dosage Forms SOLN, oral concentrate: 20 mg/mL (120 mL). **TAB:** 5 mg, 10 mg, 25 mg, 50 mg, 100 mg

♦ **Molindone Hydrochloride** see Molindone on page 856

♦ **MOM** see Magnesium Hydroxide on page 769

♦ **Momentum® [OTC]** see Magnesium Salicylate on page 771

Mometasone Furoate (moe MET a sone FYOOR oh ate)

Related Information

Corticosteroids Comparison on page 1372

U.S. Brand Names Elocon®; Nasonex®

Therapeutic Category Corticosteroid, Topical (Medium Potency)

Use Relief of the inflammatory and pruritic manifestations of corticosteroid-responsive dermatoses (medium potency topical corticosteroid); treatment of nasal symptoms of seasonal and (Continued)

Mometasone Furoate *(Continued)*

perennial allergic rhinitis in adults and children ≥2 years of age; prevention of nasal symptoms associated with seasonal allergic rhinitis in children ≥12 years of age and adults

Pregnancy Risk Factor C

Contraindications Hypersensitivity to mometasone or any component of the formulation; fungal, viral, or tubercular skin lesions, herpes simplex or zoster

Warnings/Precautions

Nasal: Use caution if replacing systemic corticosteroid with nasal; may cause symptoms of withdrawal or acute adrenal insufficiency May cause suppression of hypothalamic-pituitary-adrenal (HPA) axis, particularly in younger children or in patients receiving high doses for prolonged periods. Controlled clinical studies have shown that intranasal corticosteroids may cause a reduction in growth velocity in pediatric patients; titrate to the lowest effective dose. May suppress the immune system, patients may be more susceptible to infection. Use with caution, if at all, in patients with systemic infections, active or quiescent tuberculosis infection, or ocular herpes simplex. Avoid exposure to chickenpox and measles.

Topical: May cause suppression of HPA axis, especially when used on large areas of the body, denuded areas, for prolonged periods of time or with an occlusive dressing. Pediatric patients may be more susceptible to systemic toxicity.

Common Adverse Reactions

Nasal:

>10%:

Central nervous system: Headache (17% to 26%)

Respiratory: Pharyngitis (10% to 12%), cough (7% to 13%), epistaxis (8% to 11%)

Miscellaneous: Viral infection (8% to 14%)

1% to 10%:

Cardiovascular: Chest pain

Endocrine & metabolic: Dysmenorrhea (1% to 5%)

Gastrointestinal: Vomiting (1% to 5%), diarrhea, dyspepsia, nausea

Neuromuscular & skeletal: Musculoskeletal pain (1% to 5%), arthralgia, myalgia

Ocular: Conjunctivitis

Otic: Earache, otitis media

Respiratory: Upper respiratory tract infection (5% to 6%), sinusitis (4% to 5%), asthma, bronchitis, nasal irritation, rhinitis, wheezing

Miscellaneous: Flu-like symptoms

Topical:

1% to 10%: Dermatologic: Bacterial skin infection, burning, furunculosis, pruritus, skin atrophy, tingling/stinging

Cataract formation, reduction in growth velocity, and HPA axis suppression have been reported with other corticosteroids

Drug Interactions

Cytochrome P450 Effect: Substrate of CYP3A4 (minor)

Mechanism of Action May depress the formation, release, and activity of endogenous chemical mediators of inflammation (kinins, histamine, liposomal enzymes, prostaglandins). Leukocytes and macrophages may have to be present for the initiation of responses mediated by the above substances. Inhibits the margination and subsequent cell migration to the area of injury, and also reverses the dilatation and increased vessel permeability in the area resulting in decreased access of cells to the sites of injury.

Pharmacodynamics/Kinetics

Absorption:

Nasal: Mometasone furoate monohydrate: Undetectable in plasma

Ointment: 0.7%; increased by occlusive dressings

Protein binding: Mometasone furoate: 98% to 99%

Metabolism: Mometasone furoate: Hepatic via CYP3A4; forms metabolite

Half-life elimination: I.V.: 5.8 hours

Excretion: Bile, urine

Dosage

Nasal spray:

Children 2-11 years: 1 spray (50 mcg) in each nostril daily

Children ≥12 years and Adults: 2 sprays (100 mcg) in each nostril daily; when used for the prevention of allergic rhinitis, treatment should begin 2-4 weeks prior to pollen season

Topical: Apply sparingly, do not use occlusive dressings. Therapy should be discontinued when control is achieved; if no improvement is seen in 2 weeks, reassessment of diagnosis may be necessary.

Cream, ointment: Children ≥2 years and Adults: Apply a thin film to affected area once daily; do not use in pediatric patients for longer than 3 weeks

Lotion: Children ≥12 years and Adults: Apply a few drops to affected area once daily

Administration

Nasal spray: Prior to first use, prime pump by actuating 10 times or until fine spray appears; may store for a maximum of 1 week without repriming. Spray should be administered once daily, at a regular interval. Shake well prior to use.

Topical: Apply sparingly; avoid eyes, face, underarms, and groin. Do not wrap or bandage affected area.

Monitoring Parameters HPA axis suppression

Patient Information

Nasal spray: Shake well before using. Prime pump prior to first use; may store for a maximum of 1 week without repriming. Protect from light

Topical: Before applying, gently wash area to reduce risk of infection; apply a thin film to cleansed area and rub in gently and thoroughly until medication vanishes; avoid exposure to sunlight, severe sunburn may occur.

Dosage Forms CRM, topical (Elocon®): 0.1% (15 g, 45 g). **LOTION, topical** (Elocon®): 0.1% (30 mL, 60 mL). **OINT, topical** (Elocon®): 0.1% (15 g, 45 g). **SUSP, intranasal spray** (Nasonex®): 50 mcg/spray (17 g)

♦ **MOM/Mineral Oil Emulsion** *see* Magnesium Hydroxide and Mineral Oil *on page 770*
♦ **Monacolin K** *see* Lovastatin *on page 764*
♦ **Monarc® M** *see* Antihemophilic Factor (Human) *on page 103*
♦ **Monistat® 1 Combination Pack [OTC]** *see* Miconazole *on page 834*
♦ **Monistat® 3 [OTC]** *see* Miconazole *on page 834*
♦ **Monistat® 7 [OTC]** *see* Miconazole *on page 834*
♦ **Monistat-Derm®** *see* Miconazole *on page 834*
♦ **Monoclate-P®** *see* Antihemophilic Factor (Human) *on page 103*
♦ **Monoclonal Antibody** *see* Muromonab-CD3 *on page 867*
♦ **Monodox®** *see* Doxycycline *on page 413*
♦ **Monoethanolamine** *see* Ethanolamine Oleate *on page 475*
♦ **Mono-Gesic®** *see* Salsalate *on page 1122*
♦ **Monoket®** *see* Isosorbide Mononitrate *on page 695*
♦ **MonoNessa™** *see* Ethinyl Estradiol and Norgestimate *on page 490*
♦ **Mononine®** *see* Factor IX *on page 503*
♦ **Monopril®** *see* Fosinopril *on page 567*

Montelukast (mon te LOO kast)

U.S. Brand Names Singulair®
Synonyms Montelukast Sodium
Therapeutic Category Leukotriene Receptor Antagonist
Use Prophylaxis and chronic treatment of asthma in adults and children ≥1 year of age; relief of symptoms of seasonal allergic rhinitis in adults and children ≥2 years of age
Pregnancy Risk Factor B
Contraindications Hypersensitivity to montelukast or any component of the formulation
Warnings/Precautions Montelukast is not indicated for use in the reversal of bronchospasm in acute asthma attacks, including status asthmaticus. Should not be used as monotherapy for the treatment and management of exercise-induced bronchospasm. Advise patients to have appropriate rescue medication available. Appropriate clinical monitoring and caution are recommended when systemic corticosteroid reduction is considered in patients receiving montelukast. Inform phenylketonuric patients that the chewable tablet contains phenylalanine. Safety and efficacy in children <1 year of age have not been established.

In rare cases, patients on therapy with montelukast may present with systemic eosinophilia, sometimes presenting with clinical features of vasculitis consistent with Churg-Strauss syndrome, a condition which is often treated with systemic corticosteroid therapy. Healthcare providers should be alert to eosinophilia, vasculitic rash, worsening pulmonary symptoms, cardiac complications, and/or neuropathy presenting in their patients. A causal association between montelukast and these underlying conditions has not been established.

Common Adverse Reactions (As reported in adults with asthma)
>10%: Central nervous system: Headache (18%)
1% to 10%:
  Central nervous system: Dizziness (2%), fatigue (2%), fever (2%)
  Dermatologic: Rash (2%)
  Gastrointestinal: Dyspepsia (2%), dental pain (2%), gastroenteritis (2%), abdominal pain (3%)
  Neuromuscular & skeletal: Weakness (2%)
  Respiratory: Cough (3%), nasal congestion (2%)
  Miscellaneous: Flu-like symptoms (4%), trauma (1%)
Drug Interactions
  Cytochrome P450 Effect: Substrate (major) of CYP2C8/9, 3A4; **Inhibits** CYP2C8/9 (weak)
  Decreased Effect: CYP2C8/9 inducers may decrease the levels/effects of montelukast; example inducers include carbamazepine, phenobarbital, phenytoin, rifampin, rifapentine, and secobarbital. No dosage adjustment is recommended when taking phenobarbital with montelukast.
Mechanism of Action Selective leukotriene receptor antagonist that inhibits the cysteinyl leukotriene receptor. Cysteinyl leukotrienes and leukotriene receptor occupation have been correlated with the pathophysiology of asthma, including airway edema, smooth muscle contraction, and altered cellular activity associated with the inflammatory process, which contribute to the signs and symptoms of asthma.
Pharmacodynamics/Kinetics
  Duration: >24 hours
  Absorption: Rapid
  Distribution: V_d: 8-11 L
  (Continued)

Montelukast *(Continued)*

Protein binding, plasma: >99%
Metabolism: Extensively hepatic via CYP3A4 and 2C8/9
Bioavailability: Tablet: 10 mg: Mean: 64%; 5 mg: 63% to 73%
Half-life elimination, plasma: Mean: 2.7-5.5 hours
Time to peak, serum: Tablet: 10 mg: 3-4 hours; 5 mg: 2-2.5 hours; 4 mg: 2 hours
Excretion: Feces (86%); urine (<0.2%)

Dosage Oral:
Children:
<1 year: Safety and efficacy have not been established
12-23 months: Asthma: 4 mg (oral granules) once daily, taken in the evening
2-5 years: Asthma or seasonal allergic rhinitis: 4 mg (chewable tablet or oral granules) once daily, taken in the evening
6-14 years: Asthma or seasonal allergic rhinitis: Chew one 5 mg chewable tablet/day, taken in the evening
Children ≥15 years and Adults: Asthma or seasonal allergic rhinitis: 10 mg/day, taken in the evening

Dosing adjustment in hepatic impairment: Mild to moderate: No adjustment necessary

Administration Take dose in the evening. Granules may be administered directly in the mouth or mixed with applesauce, carrots, rice, or ice cream. Administer within 15 minutes of opening packet. Do not mix in liquids.

Patient Information Advise patients to take montelukast daily as prescribed, even when they are symptomatic, as well as during periods of worsening asthma, and to contact prescriber if the asthma is not well controlled. Advise patients that oral tablets of montelukast are not for the treatment of acute asthma attacks. Patients should have appropriate short-acting inhaled beta-agonist medication available to treat asthma exacerbations. Advise patients using montelukast to seek medical attention if short-acting inhaled bronchodilators are needed more often than usual or if more than the maximum number of inhalations of short-acting bronchodilator treatment prescribed for a 24-hour period are needed. Instruct patients receiving montelukast not to decrease the dose or to stop taking any other antiasthma medications unless instructed by a physician. Instruct patients who have exacerbations of asthma after exercise to continue to use their usual regimen of inhaled beta-agonists as prophylaxis unless otherwise instructed by a physician. All patients should have a short-acting inhaled beta-agonist available for rescue. Chewable tablets contain phenylalanine.

Dosage Forms GRAN: 4 mg/packet. **TAB:** 10 mg. **TAB, chewable:** 4 mg, 5 mg

♦ **Montelukast Sodium** *see* Montelukast *on page 859*
♦ **Monurol™** *see* Fosfomycin *on page 566*
♦ **8-MOP®** *see* Methoxsalen *on page 818*
♦ **More Attenuated Enders Strain** *see* Measles Virus Vaccine (Live) *on page 776*
♦ **MoreDophilus® [OTC]** *see* Lactobacillus *on page 711*

Moricizine *(mor I siz een)*

U.S. Brand Names Ethmozine®
Synonyms Moricizine Hydrochloride
Therapeutic Category Antiarrhythmic Agent, Class I
Use Treatment of ventricular tachycardia and life-threatening ventricular arrhythmias
Unlabeled/Investigational Use PVCs, complete and nonsustained ventricular tachycardia, atrial arrhythmias
Pregnancy Risk Factor B
Contraindications Hypersensitivity to moricizine or any component of the formulation; pre-existing second- or third-degree AV block (except in patients with a functioning artificial pacemaker); right bundle branch block when associated with left hemiblock or bifascicular block (unless functional pacemaker in place); cardiogenic shock
Warnings/Precautions Considering the known proarrhythmic properties and lack of evidence of improved survival for any antiarrhythmic drug in patients without life-threatening arrhythmias, it is prudent to reserve the use for patients with life-threatening ventricular arrhythmias; CAST II trial demonstrated a trend towards decreased survival for patients treated with moricizine; proarrhythmic effects occur as with other antiarrhythmic agents; hypokalemia, hyperkalemia, hypomagnesemia may effect response to class I agents; use with caution in patients with sick-sinus syndrome, hepatic, and renal impairment; safety and efficacy have not been established in pediatric patients
Common Adverse Reactions
>10%: Central nervous system: Dizziness
1% to 10%:
Cardiovascular: Proarrhythmia, palpitations, cardiac death, ECG abnormalities, CHF
Central nervous system: Headache, fatigue, insomnia
Endocrine & metabolic: Decreased libido
Gastrointestinal: Nausea, diarrhea, ileus
Ocular: Blurred vision, periorbital edema
Respiratory: Dyspnea
Drug Interactions
Cytochrome P450 Effect: Substrate of CYP3A4 (major); **Induces** CYP1A2 (weak), 3A4 (weak)
Increased Effect/Toxicity: Moricizine levels may be increased by cimetidine and diltiazem. Digoxin may result in additive prolongation of the PR interval when combined with moricizine

(but not rate of second- and third-degree AV block). Drugs which may prolong QT interval (including cisapride, erythromycin, phenothiazines, cyclic antidepressants, and some quinolones) are contraindicated with type Ia antiarrhythmics. Moricizine has some type Ia activity, and caution should be used.

Decreased Effect: Moricizine may decrease levels of theophylline (50%) and diltiazem.

Mechanism of Action Class I antiarrhythmic agent; reduces the fast inward current carried by sodium ions, shortens Phase I and Phase II repolarization, resulting in decreased action potential duration and effective refractory period

Pharmacodynamics/Kinetics
Protein binding, plasma: 95%
Metabolism: Significant first-pass effect; some enterohepatic recycling
Bioavailability: 38%
Half-life elimination: Healthy volunteers: 3-4 hours; Cardiac disease: 6-13 hours
Excretion: Feces (56%); urine (39%)

Dosage Adults: Oral: 200-300 mg every 8 hours, adjust dosage at 150 mg/day at 3-day intervals.
Recommendations for transferring patients from other antiarrhythmic agents to Ethmozine®: See table.

Moricizine

Transferred From	Start Ethmozine®
Encainide, propafenone, tocainide, or mexiletine	8-12 hours after last dose
Flecainide	12-24 hours after last dose
Procainamide	3-6 hours after last dose
Quinidine, disopyramide	6-12 hours after last dose

Dosing interval in renal or hepatic impairment: Start at 600 mg/day or less.

Patient Information Take as directed; do not change dose except from advice of your prescriber; report any chest pain and irregular heartbeats

Dosage Forms TAB: 200 mg, 250 mg, 300 mg

♦ **Moricizine Hydrochloride** see Moricizine on page 860
♦ **Morning After Pill** see Ethinyl Estradiol and Norgestrel on page 492

Morphine Sulfate (MOR feen SUL fate)

Related Information
Narcotic Agonists Comparison on page 1395

U.S. Brand Names Astramorph/PF™; Avinza™; Duramorph®; Infumorph®; Kadian®; MS Contin®; MSIR®; Oramorph SR®; RMS®; Roxanol®; Roxanol 100®; Roxanol®-T

Synonyms MS

Therapeutic Category Analgesic, Narcotic

Use Relief of moderate to severe acute and chronic pain; relief of pain of myocardial infarction; relief of dyspnea of acute left ventricular failure and pulmonary edema; preanesthetic medication
Orphan drug: Infumorph™: Used in microinfusion devices for intraspinal administration in treatment of intractable chronic pain

Restrictions C-II

Pregnancy Risk Factor B/D (prolonged use or high doses at term)

Contraindications Hypersensitivity to morphine sulfate or any component of the formulation; increased intracranial pressure; severe respiratory depression (in absence of resuscitative equipment or ventilatory support); acute or severe asthma; known or suspected paralytic ileus (sustained release products only); sustained release products are not recommended in acute/postoperative pain; pregnancy (prolonged use or high doses at term)

Warnings/Precautions An opioid-containing analgesic regimen should be tailored to each patient's needs and based upon the type of pain being treated (acute versus chronic), the route of administration, degree of tolerance for opioids (naive versus chronic user), age, weight, and medical condition. The optimal analgesic dose varies widely among patients. Doses should be titrated to pain relief/prevention.

Some preparations contain sulfites which may cause allergic reactions; infants <3 months of age are more susceptible to respiratory depression, use with caution and generally in reduced doses in this age group; use with caution in patients with impaired respiratory function or severe hepatic dysfunction and in patients with hypersensitivity reactions to other phenanthrene derivative opioid agonists (codeine, hydrocodone, hydromorphone, levorphanol, oxycodone, oxymorphone). Morphine shares the toxic potential of opiate agonists and usual precautions of opiate agonist therapy should be observed; may cause hypotension in patients with acute myocardial infarction. Tolerance or drug dependence may result from extended use. MS Contin® 200 mg tablets are for use only in opioid-tolerant patients requiring >400 mg/day.

Elderly may be particularly susceptible to the CNS depressant and constipating effects of narcotics

Common Adverse Reactions Note: Percentages are based on a study in 19 chronic cancer pain patients (J Pain Symptom Manage, 1995, 10:416-22). Chronic use of various opioids in cancer pain is accompanied by similar adverse reactions; individual patient differences are unpredictable, and percentage may differ in acute pain (surgical) treatment.
(Continued)

Morphine Sulfate *(Continued)*

Frequency not defined: Flushing, CNS depression, sedation, antidiuretic hormone release, physical and psychological dependence, diaphoresis

>10%:

Cardiovascular: Palpitations, hypotension, bradycardia

Central nervous system: Drowsiness (48%, tolerance usually develops to drowsiness with regular dosing for 1-2 weeks); dizziness (20%); confusion

Dermatologic: Pruritus (may be secondary to histamine release)

Gastrointestinal: Nausea (28%, tolerance usually develops to nausea and vomiting with chronic use); vomiting (9%); constipation (40%, tolerance develops very slowly if at all); xerostomia (78%)

Genitourinary: Urinary retention (16%)

Local: Pain at injection site

Neuromuscular & skeletal: Weakness

Miscellaneous: Histamine release

1% to 10%:

Central nervous system: Restlessness, headache, false feeling of well being

Gastrointestinal: Anorexia, GI irritation, paralytic ileus

Genitourinary: Decreased urination

Neuromuscular & skeletal: Trembling

Ocular: Vision problems

Respiratory: Respiratory depression, dyspnea

Drug Interactions

Cytochrome P450 Effect: Substrate of CYP2D6 (minor)

Increased Effect/Toxicity: CNS depressants (phenothiazines, tranquilizers, anxiolytics, sedatives, hypnotics, or alcohol), tricyclic antidepressants may potentiate the effects of morphine and other opiate agonists. Dextroamphetamine may enhance the analgesic effect of morphine and other opiate agonists. Concurrent use of MAO inhibitors and meperidine has been associated with significant adverse effects. Use caution with morphine. Some manufacturers recommend avoiding use within 14 days of MAO inhibitors.

Decreased Effect: Diuretic effects may be decreased (due to antidiuretic hormone release).

Mechanism of Action Binds to opiate receptors in the CNS, causing inhibition of ascending pain pathways, altering the perception of and response to pain; produces generalized CNS depression

Pharmacodynamics/Kinetics

Onset of action: Oral: 1 hour; I.V.: 5-10 minutes

Duration: Pain relief (not sustained/controlled/extended release forms): 4 hours

Absorption: Variable

Distribution: Binds to opioid receptors in the CNS and periphery (eg, GI tract)

Metabolism: Hepatic via conjugation with glucuronic acid to morphine-3-glucuronide (inactive), morphine-6-glucuronide (active), and in lesser amounts, morphine-3-6-diglucuronide; other minor metabolites include normorphine (active) and the 3-ethereal sulfate

Bioavailability: Oral: 17% to 33% (first-pass effect limits oral bioavailability; oral:parenteral effectiveness reportedly varies from 1:6 in opioid naive patients to 1:3 with chronic use)

Half-life elimination: Adults: 2-4 hours (not sustained/controlled/extended release forms)

Excretion: Urine (primarily as morphine-3-glucuronide, ~2% to 12% excreted unchanged); feces (~7% to 10%). It has been suggested that accumulation of morphine-6-glucuronide might cause toxicity with renal insufficiency. All of the metabolites (ie, morphine-3-glucuronide, morphine-6-glucuronide, and normorphine) have been suggested as possible causes of neurotoxicity (eg, myoclonus).

Dosage Note: These are guidelines and do not represent the maximum doses that may be required in all patients. Doses should be titrated to pain relief/prevention.

Children >6 months and <50 kg: Acute pain (moderate to severe):

Oral (prompt release): 0.15-0.3 mg/kg every 3-4 hours as needed

I.M.: 0.1 mg/kg every 3-4 hours as needed

I.V.: 0.05-0.1 mg/kg every 3-4 hours as needed

I.V. infusion: Range: 10-30 mcg/kg/hour

Adolescents >12 years: Sedation/analgesia for procedures: I.V.: 3-4 mg and repeat in 5 minutes if necessary

Adults: Acute pain (moderate to severe):

Oral: Prompt release formulations: Opiate-naive: Initial: 10 mg every 3-4 hours as needed; patients with prior opiate exposure may require higher initial doses: usual dosage range: 10-30 mg every 3-4 hours as needed

Oral: Controlled-, extended-, or sustained-release formulations: **Note:** A patient's morphine requirement should be established using prompt-release formulations. Conversion to long-acting products may be considered when chronic, continuous treatment is required. Higher dosages should be reserved for use only in opioid-tolerant patients.

Capsules, extended release (Avinza™): Daily dose administered once daily (for best results, administer at same time each day)

Capsules, sustained release (Kadian®): Daily dose administered once daily or in 2 divided doses daily (every 12 hours)

Tablets, controlled release (MS Contin®), sustained release (Oramorph SR®), or extended release: Daily dose divided and administered every 8 or every 12 hours

I.V.: Initial: Opiate-naive: 2.5-5 mg every 3-4 hours; patients with prior opiate exposure may require higher initial doses. **Note:** Repeated doses (up to every 5 minutes if needed) in small increments (eg, 1-4 mg) may be preferred to larger and less frequent doses.

I.V., S.C. continuous infusion: 0.8-10 mg/hour; may increase depending on pain relief/ adverse effects: usual range: up to 80 mg/hour although higher doses may be required
Mechanically-ventilated patients (based on 70 kg patient): 0.7-10 mg every 1-2 hours as needed; infusion: 5-35 mg/hour
Patient-controlled analgesia (PCA): (Opiate-naive: Consider lower end of dosing range):
Usual concentration: 1 mg/mL
Demand dose: Usual: 1 mg; range: 0.5-2.5 mg
Lockout interval: 5-10 minutes
Epidural: **Note:** Administer with extreme caution and in reduced dosage to geriatric or debilitated patients.
Bolus dose: 1-6 mg
Infusion rate: 0.1-1 mg/hour
Maximum dose: 10 mg/24 hours
Intrathecal (IT): One-tenth of epidural dose; **Note:** Administer with extreme caution and in reduced dosage to geriatric or debilitated patients.
Opiate-naive: 0.2-1 mg/dose (may provide adequate relief for 24 hours); repeat doses **not** recommended except to establish initial IT dose.
I.M., S.C.: **Note:** Repeated S.C. administration causes local tissue irritation, pain, and induration.
Initial: Opiate-naive: 5-10 mg every 3-4 hours as needed; patients with prior opiate exposure may require higher initial doses; usual dosage range: 5-20 mg every 3-4 hours as needed
Rectal: 10-20 mg every 3- 4 hours
Chronic pain: Patients taking opioids chronically may become tolerant and require doses higher than the usual dosage range to maintain the desired effect. Tolerance can be managed by appropriate dose titration. There is no optimal or maximal dose for morphine in chronic pain. The appropriate dose is one that relieves pain throughout its dosing interval without causing unmanageable side effects.
Elderly or debilitated patients: Use with caution; may require dose reduction
Dosing adjustment in renal impairment:
Cl$_{cr}$ 10-50 mL/minute: Administer at 75% of normal dose
Cl$_{cr}$ <10 mL/minute: Administer at 50% of normal dose
Dosing adjustment/comments in hepatic disease: Unchanged in mild liver disease; substantial extrahepatic metabolism may occur; excessive sedation may occur in cirrhosis
Administration
Oral: Do not crush controlled release drug product, swallow whole. Kadian® can be opened and sprinkled on applesauce. Avinza™ can also be opened and sprinkled on applesauce; do not crush or chew the beads. Administration of oral morphine solution with food may increase bioavailability (not observed with Oramorph SR®).
I.V.: When giving morphine I.V. push, it is best to first dilute in 4-5 mL of sterile water, and then to administer slowly (eg, 15 mg over 3-5 minutes)
Epidural or intrathecal: Use preservative-free solutions
Monitoring Parameters Pain relief, respiratory and mental status, blood pressure
Reference Range Therapeutic: Surgical anesthesia: 65-80 ng/mL (SI: 227-280 nmol/L); Toxic: 200-5000 ng/mL (SI: 700-17,500 nmol/L)
Patient Information Avoid alcohol, may cause drowsiness, impaired judgment or coordination; may cause physical and psychological dependence with prolonged use
Dosage Forms CAP (MSIR®): 15 mg, 30 mg. **CAP, extended release** (Avinza™): 30 mg, 60 mg, 90 mg, 120 mg. **CAP, sustained release** (Kadian®): 20 mg, 30 mg, 50 mg, 60 mg, 100 mg. **INF** [premixed in D$_5$W]: 0.2 mg/mL (250 mL, 500 mL); 1 mg/mL (100 mL, 250 mL, 500 mL). **INJ, solution:** 2 mg/mL (1 mL); 4 mg/mL (1 mL); 5 mg/mL (1 mL); 8 mg/mL (1 mL); 10 mg/mL (1 mL, 2 mL, 10 mL); 15 mg/mL (1 mL, 20 mL); 25 mg/mL (4 mL, 10 mL, 20 mL, 40 mL). **INJ, solution** [epidural, intrathecal, or I.V. infusion; preservative free] (Astramorph/PF™): 0.5 mg/mL (2 mL, 10 mL); 1 mg/mL (2 mL, 10 mL); (Duramorph®): 0.5 mg/mL (10 mL); 1 mg/ mL (10 mL). **INJ, solution** [epidural or intrathecal infusion via microinfusion device; preservative free] (Infumorph®): 10 mg/mL (20 mL); 25 mg/mL (20 mL). **INJ, solution** [I.V. infusion via PCA pump]: 1 mg/mL (50 mL); 5 mg/mL (50 mL). **INJ, solution** [preservative free]: 0.5 mg/mL (10 mL); 1 mg/mL (10 mL, 30 mL); 10 mg/mL (10 mL); 15 mg/mL (20 mL); 25 mg/mL (4 mL, 10 mL, 20 mL); 50 mg/mL (10 mL, 20 mL, 50 mL). **SOLN, oral:** 10 mg/5 mL (5 mL, 10 mL, 100 mL, 500 mL); 20 mg/mL (30 mL, 120 mL, 240 mL); 20 mg/5 mL (100 mL, 500 mL); (MSIR®): 10 mg/5 mL (120 mL); 20 mg/mL (30 mL, 120 mL); 20 mg/5 mL (120 mL); (Roxanol®, Roxanol® T): 20 mg/mL (30 mL, 120 mL); (Roxanol 100®): 100 mg/5 mL (240 mL). **SUPP, rectal** (RMS®): 5 mg (12s), 10 mg (12s), 20 mg (12s), 30 mg (12s). **TAB** (MSIR®): 15 mg, 30 mg. **TAB, controlled release** (MS Contin®): 15 mg, 30 mg, 60 mg, 100 mg, 200 mg. **TAB, extended release:** 15 mg, 30 mg, 60 mg, 100 mg, 200 mg. **TAB, sustained release** (Oramorph SR®): 15 mg, 30 mg, 60 mg, 100 mg

Morrhuate Sodium (MOR yoo ate SOW dee um)

U.S. Brand Names Scleromate™
Therapeutic Category Sclerosing Agent
Use Treatment of small, uncomplicated varicose veins of the lower extremities
Pregnancy Risk Factor C
Contraindications Hypersensitivity to morrhuate sodium or any component of the formulation; arterial disease, thrombophlebitis
Warnings/Precautions Sloughing and necrosis of tissue may occur following extravasation; anaphylactoid and allergic reactions have occurred; this drug should only be administered by a
(Continued)

Morrhuate Sodium *(Continued)*

physician familiar with proper injection techniques; a test dose of 0.25-5 mL of a 5% injection should be given 24 hours before full-dose treatment

Common Adverse Reactions Frequency not defined.

Cardiovascular: Thrombosis, valvular incompetency, vascular collapse

Central nervous system: Drowsiness, headache, dizziness

Dermatologic: Urticaria

Gastrointestinal: Nausea, vomiting

Local: Burning at the site of injection, severe extravasation effects

Neuromuscular & skeletal: Weakness

Respiratory: Asthma

Miscellaneous: Anaphylaxis, hypersensitivity reactions

Mechanism of Action Both varicose veins and esophageal varices are treated by the thrombotic action of morrhuate sodium. By causing inflammation of the vein's intima, a thrombus is formed. Occlusion secondary to the fibrous tissue and the thrombus results in the obliteration of the vein.

Pharmacodynamics/Kinetics

Onset of action: ~5 minutes

Absorption: Most stays at site of injection

Distribution: Esophageal varices treatment: ~20% of dose to lungs

Dosage Adults: I.V.: 50-250 mg, repeated at 5- to 7-day intervals (50-100 mg for small veins, 150-250 mg for large veins)

Administration For I.V. use only

Dosage Forms INJ, solution: 50 mg/mL (30 mL)

- ◆ **Motofen®** *see* Difenoxin and Atropine *on page 372*
- ◆ **Motrin®** *see* Ibuprofen *on page 645*
- ◆ **Motrin® Children's [OTC]** *see* Ibuprofen *on page 645*
- ◆ **Motrin® Cold and Sinus [OTC]** *see* Pseudoephedrine and Ibuprofen *on page 1062*
- ◆ **Motrin® Cold, Children's [OTC]** *see* Pseudoephedrine and Ibuprofen *on page 1062*
- ◆ **Motrin® IB [OTC]** *see* Ibuprofen *on page 645*
- ◆ **Motrin® Infants' [OTC]** *see* Ibuprofen *on page 645*
- ◆ **Motrin® Junior Strength [OTC]** *see* Ibuprofen *on page 645*
- ◆ **Motrin® Migraine Pain [OTC]** *see* Ibuprofen *on page 645*

Moxifloxacin *(moxs i FLOKS a sin)*

Related Information

Antimicrobial Drugs of Choice *on page 1440*

Community-Acquired Pneumonia in Adults *on page 1457*

U.S. Brand Names Avelox®; Avelox® I.V.; Vigamox™

Synonyms Moxifloxacin Hydrochloride

Therapeutic Category Antibiotic, Quinolone

Use Treatment of mild to moderate community-acquired pneumonia, including penicillin-resistant *Streptococcus pneumoniae* (PRSP); acute bacterial exacerbation of chronic bronchitis; acute bacterial sinusitis; uncomplicated skin infections; bacterial conjunctivitis (ophthalmic formulation)

Pregnancy Risk Factor C

Contraindications Hypersensitivity to moxifloxacin, other quinolone antibiotics, or any component of the formulation

Warnings/Precautions Use with caution in patients with significant bradycardia or acute myocardial ischemia. Moxifloxacin causes a concentration-dependent QT prolongation. Do not exceed recommended dose or infusion rate. Coadministration of moxifloxacin with other drugs that also prolong the QT interval or induce bradycardia should be avoided. Use with caution in individuals at risk of seizures (CNS disorders or concurrent therapy with medications which may lower seizure threshold). Discontinue in patients who experience significant CNS adverse effects (dizziness, hallucinations, suicidal ideation or actions). Not recommended in patients with moderate to severe hepatic insufficiency. Use with caution in diabetes; glucose regulation may be altered. Tendon inflammation and/or rupture have been reported with quinolone antibiotics. Risk may be increased with concurrent corticosteroids, particularly in the elderly. Discontinue at first signs or symptoms of tendon pain.

Severe hypersensitivity reactions, including anaphylaxis, have occurred with quinolone therapy. If an allergic reaction occurs (itching, urticaria, dyspnea or facial edema, loss of consciousness, tingling, cardiovascular collapse) discontinue drug immediately. Prolonged use may result in superinfection; pseudomembranous colitis may occur and should be considered in all patients who present with diarrhea. Quinolones may exacerbate myasthenia gravis.

Ophthalmic: Eye drops should not be injected subconjunctivally or introduced directly into the anterior chamber of the eye. Contact lenses should not be worn during therapy.

Common Adverse Reactions

Systemic:

3% to 10%:

Central nervous system: Dizziness (3%)

Gastrointestinal: Nausea (7%), diarrhea (6%)

0.1% to 3%:

Cardiovascular: Chest pain, hypertension, palpitation, peripheral edema, QT prolongation, tachycardia

Central nervous system: Anxiety, chills, confusion, headache, insomnia, nervousness, pain, somnolence, tremor, vertigo

Dermatologic: Dry skin, pruritus, rash (maculopapular, purpuric, pustular)

Endocrine & metabolic: Serum chloride increased (≥2%), serum ionized calcium increased (≥2%), serum glucose decreased (≥2%)

Gastrointestinal: Abdominal pain, amylase increased, amylase decreased (≥2%), anorexia, constipation, dry mouth, dyspepsia, flatulence, glossitis, lactic dehydrogenase increased, stomatitis, taste perversion, vomiting

Hematologic: Eosinophilia, leukopenia, prothrombin time decreased, increased INR, thrombocythemia, thrombocytopenia

Increased serum levels of the following (≥2%): MCH, neutrophils, WBC

Decreased serum levels of the following (≥2%): Basophils, eosinophils, hemoglobin, RBC, neutrophils

Hepatic: Bilirubin decreased (≥2%), cholestatic jaundice, GGTP increased, liver function test abnormal

Local: Injection site reaction

Neuromuscular & skeletal: Arthralgia, back pain, leg pain, myalgia, paresthesia, malaise, weakness

Renal: Serum albumin increased (≥2%)

Respiratory: Dyspnea, pharyngitis, pneumonia, rhinitis, sinusitis, PO_2 increased (≥2%)

Miscellaneous: Allergic reaction, infection, moniliasis, diaphoresis

Additional reactions with **ophthalmic** preparation: 1% to 6%: Conjunctivitis, dry eye, ocular discomfort, ocular hyperemia, ocular pain, ocular pruritus, subconjunctival hemorrhage, tearing, visual acuity decreased

Drug Interactions

Increased Effect/Toxicity: Drugs which prolong QT interval (including Class Ia and Class III antiarrhythmics, erythromycin, cisapride, antipsychotics, and cyclic antidepressants) are contraindicated with moxifloxacin. Cimetidine and probenecid increase quinolone levels. An increased incidence of seizures may occur with foscarnet or NSAIDs. Serum levels of some quinolones are increased by loop diuretic administration. Digoxin levels may be increased in some patients by quinolones. The hypoprothrombinemic effect of warfarin is enhanced by some quinolone antibiotics. Although moxifloxacin has not been shown to alter warfarin disposition, monitoring of the INR during concurrent therapy is recommended by the manufacturer. Concurrent use of corticosteroids may increase risk of tendon rupture.

Decreased Effect: Metal cations (magnesium, aluminum, iron, and zinc) bind quinolones in the gastrointestinal tract and inhibit absorption (by up to 98%). Antacids, multivitamins with minerals, sucralfate, and some didanosine formulations should be avoided. Moxifloxacin should be administered 4 hours before or 8 hours (a minimum of 2 hours before and 2 hours after) after these agents. Antineoplastic agents may decrease the absorption of quinolones.

Mechanism of Action
Moxifloxacin is a DNA gyrase inhibitor, and also inhibits topoisomerase IV. DNA gyrase (topoisomerase II) is an essential bacterial enzyme that maintains the superhelical structure of DNA. DNA gyrase is required for DNA replication and transcription, DNA repair, recombination, and transposition; inhibition is bactericidal.

Pharmacodynamics/Kinetics

Absorption: Well absorbed; not affected by high fat meal or yogurt

Distribution: V_d: 1.7 to 2.7 L/kg; tissue concentrations often exceed plasma concentrations in respiratory tissues, alveolar macrophages, and sinus tissues

Protein binding: 50%

Metabolism: Hepatic (52% of dose) via glucuronide (14%) and sulfate (38%) conjugation

Bioavailability: 90%

Half-life elimination: Oral: 12 hours; I.V.: 15 hours

Excretion: Approximately 45% of a dose is excreted in feces (25%) and urine (20%) as unchanged drug

Metabolites: Sulfate conjugates in feces, glucuronide conjugates in urine

Dosage

Oral, I.V.: Adults:

Acute bacterial sinusitis: 400 mg every 24 hours for 10 days

Chronic bronchitis, acute bacterial exacerbation: 400 mg every 24 hours for 5 days

Note: Avelox® ABC Pack™ (Avelox® Bronchitis Course) contains five tablets of 400 mg each.

Community-acquired pneumonia: 400 mg every 24 hours for 7-14 days

Uncomplicated skin infections: 400 mg every 24 hours for 7 days

Elderly: No dosage adjustments are required based on age

Dosage adjustment in renal impairment: No dosage adjustment is required, including patients on hemodialysis or CAPD

Dosage adjustment in hepatic impairment: No dosage adjustment is required in mild to moderate hepatic insufficiency (Child-Pugh Class A and B). Not recommended in patients with severe hepatic insufficiency.

Ophthalmic: Children ≥1 year and Adults: Instill 1 drop into affected eye(s) 3 times/day for 7 days

Administration I.V.: Infuse over 60 minutes; do not infuse by rapid or bolus intravenous infusion

Monitoring Parameters WBC, signs of infection

(Continued)

Moxifloxacin (Continued)

Patient Information Tablet: May be taken with or without food; drink plenty of fluids; do not take antacids within 4 hours before or 8 hours after dosing. Contact your prescriber immediately if signs of allergy occur. Contact your prescriber immediately if signs of tendon inflammation or pain occur. Do not discontinue therapy until your course has been completed. Take a missed dose as soon as possible, unless it is almost time for your next dose.

Dosage Forms INF [premixed in sodium chloride 0.8%] (Avelox® I.V.): 400 mg (250 mL). **SOLN, ophthalmic, as hydrochloride** (Vigamox™): 0.5% (3 mL). **TAB, film coated** (Avelox®): 400 mg. **TAB, film coated, unit-dose pack** (Avelox® ABC Pack): 400 mg (5s)

- ◆ **Moxifloxacin Hydrochloride** *see* Moxifloxacin *on page 864*
- ◆ **Moxilin®** *see* Amoxicillin *on page 86*
- ◆ **4-MP** *see* Fomepizole *on page 558*
- ◆ **6-MP** *see* Mercaptopurine *on page 795*
- ◆ **MPA and Estrogens (Conjugated)** *see* Estrogens (Conjugated/Equine) and Medroxyprogesterone *on page 468*
- ◆ **MS** *see* Morphine Sulfate *on page 861*
- ◆ **MS Contin®** *see* Morphine Sulfate *on page 861*
- ◆ **MSIR®** *see* Morphine Sulfate *on page 861*
- ◆ **MTC** *see* Mitomycin *on page 849*
- ◆ **MTX** *see* Methotrexate *on page 815*
- ◆ **Mucinex™ [OTC]** *see* Guaifenesin *on page 603*
- ◆ **Mucomyst®** *see* Acetylcysteine *on page 32*
- ◆ **Mucosil™ [DSC]** *see* Acetylcysteine *on page 32*
- ◆ **Multiple Vitamins** *see* Vitamins (Multiple/Oral) *on page 1312*
- ◆ **Multitest CMI®** *see* Skin Test Antigens (Multiple) *on page 1142*
- ◆ **Multivitamin Products** *see page 1382*
- ◆ **Mumps, Measles, and Rubella Vaccines, Combined** *see* Measles, Mumps, and Rubella Vaccines (Combined) *on page 776*
- ◆ **Mumpsvax®** *see* Mumps Virus Vaccine (Live/Attenuated) *on page 866*

Mumps Virus Vaccine (Live/Attenuated)

(mumpz VYE rus vak SEEN, live, a ten YOO ate ed)

U.S. Brand Names Mumpsvax®

Therapeutic Category Vaccine; Vaccine, Live Virus

Use Mumps prophylaxis by promoting active immunity

Note: Trivalent measles-mumps-rubella (MMR) vaccine is the preferred agent for most children and many adults; persons born prior to 1957 are generally considered immune and need not be vaccinated

Pregnancy Risk Factor X

Warnings/Precautions Pregnancy, immunocompromised persons, history of anaphylactic reaction following egg ingestion or receipt of neomycin

Common Adverse Reactions All serious adverse reactions must be reported to the U.S. Department of Health and Human Services (DHHS) Vaccine Adverse Event Reporting System (VAERS) 1-800-822-7967.

>10%: Local: Burning or stinging at injection site

1% to 10%:
  Central nervous system: Fever (≤100°F)
  Dermatologic: Rash
  Endocrine & metabolic: Parotitis

Mechanism of Action Promotes active immunity to mumps virus by inducing specific antibodies.

Dosage Children ≥15 months and Adults: 0.5 mL S.C. in outer aspect of the upper arm, no booster

Administration Reconstitute only with diluent provided; administer only S.C. on outer aspect of upper arm

Patient Information Pregnancy should be avoided for 3 months following vaccination; a little swelling of the glands in the cheeks and under the jaw may occur that lasts for a few days; this could happen from 1-2 weeks after getting the mumps vaccine; this happens rarely

Dosage Forms INJ, powder for reconstitution: [preservative free] 20,000 TCID$_{50}$

Mupirocin (myoo PEER oh sin)

U.S. Brand Names Bactroban®; Bactroban® Nasal

Synonyms Mupirocin Calcium; Pseudomonic Acid A

Therapeutic Category Antibiotic, Topical

Use

Intranasal: Eradication of nasal colonization with MRSA in adult patients and healthcare workers

Topical treatment of impetigo due to *Staphylococcus aureus*, beta-hemolytic *Streptococcus*, and *S. pyogenes*

Unlabeled/Investigational Use Intranasal: Surgical prophylaxis to prevent wound infections

Pregnancy Risk Factor B

Contraindications Hypersensitivity to mupirocin, polyethylene glycol, or any component of the formulation

Warnings/Precautions Potentially toxic amounts of polyethylene glycol contained in the vehicle may be absorbed percutaneously in patients with extensive burns or open wounds; prolonged use may result in over growth of nonsusceptible organisms; for external use only; not for treatment of pressure sores

Common Adverse Reactions Frequency not defined.

Central nervous system: Dizziness, headache

Dermatologic: Pruritus, rash, erythema, dry skin, cellulitis, dermatitis

Gastrointestinal: Nausea, taste perversion

Local: Burning stinging, tenderness, edema, pain

Respiratory: Rhinitis, upper respiratory tract infection, pharyngitis, cough

Mechanism of Action Binds to bacterial isoleucyl transfer-RNA synthetase resulting in the inhibition of protein and RNA synthesis

Pharmacodynamics/Kinetics

Absorption: Topical: Penetrates outer layers of skin; systemic absorption minimal through intact skin

Protein binding: 95%

Metabolism: Skin: 3% to monic acid

Half-life elimination: 17-36 minutes

Excretion: Urine

Dosage

Children ≥12 years and Adults: Intranasal: Approximately one-half of the ointment from the single-use tube should be applied into one nostril and the other half into the other nostril twice daily for 5 days

Children ≥3 months and Adults: Topical: Apply small amount to affected area 2-5 times/day for 5-14 days

Patient Information For topical use only; do not apply into the eye; discontinue if rash, itching, or irritation occurs; improvement should be seen in 5 days

Dosage Forms CRM, topical (Bactroban®): 2% (15 g, 30 g). **OINT, intranasal, topical** (Bactroban® Nasal): 2% (1 g tube). **OINT, topical** (Bactroban®): 2% (22 g)

♦ **Mupirocin Calcium** *see Mupirocin on page 866*

♦ **Murine® Ear [OTC]** *see Carbamide Peroxide on page 216*

♦ **Muro 128® [OTC]** *see Sodium Chloride on page 1146*

♦ **Murocoll-2®** *see Phenylephrine and Scopolamine on page 994*

Muromonab-CD3 (myoo roe MOE nab see dee three)

U.S. Brand Names Orthoclone OKT® 3

Synonyms Monoclonal Antibody; OKT3

Therapeutic Category Immunosuppressant Agent

Use Treatment of acute allograft rejection in renal transplant patients; treatment of acute hepatic, kidney, and pancreas rejection episodes resistant to conventional treatment. Acute graft-versus-host disease following bone marrow transplantation resistant to conventional treatment.

Pregnancy Risk Factor C

Contraindications Hypersensitivity to OKT3 or any murine product; patients in fluid overload or those with >3% weight gain within 1 week prior to start of OKT3; mouse antibody titers >1:1000

Warnings/Precautions It is imperative, especially prior to the first few doses, that there be no clinical evidence of volume overload, uncontrolled hypertension, or uncompensated heart failure, including a clear chest x-ray and weight restriction of ≤3% above the patient's minimum weight during the week prior to injection.

May result in an increased susceptibility to infection; dosage of concomitant immunosuppressants should be reduced during OKT3 therapy; cyclosporine should be decreased to 50% usual maintenance dose and maintenance therapy resumed about 4 days before stopping OKT3.

Severe pulmonary edema has occurred in patients with fluid overload.

Suggested Prevention/Treatment of Muromonab-CD3 First-Dose Effects

Adverse Reaction	Effective Prevention or Palliation	Supportive Treatment
Severe pulmonary edema	Clear chest x-ray within 24 hours preinjection; weight restriction to ≤3% gain over 7 days preinjection	Prompt intubation and oxygenation; 24 hours close observation
Fever, chills	15 mg/kg methylprednisolone sodium succinate 1 hour preinjection; fever reduction to <37.8°C (100°F) 1 hour preinjection; acetaminophen (1 g orally) and diphenhydramine (50 mg orally) 1 hour preinjection	Cooling blanket Acetaminophen prn
Respiratory effects	100 mg hydrocortisone sodium succinate 30 minutes postinjection	Additional 100 mg hydrocortisone sodium succinate prn for wheezing; if respiratory distress, give epinephrine 1:1000 (0.3 mL S.C.)

(Continued)

Muromonab-CD3 *(Continued)*

First dose effect (flu-like symptoms, anaphylactic-type reaction): may occur within 30 minutes to 6 hours up to 24 hours after the first dose and may be minimized by using the recommended regimens. See table on previous page.

Cardiopulmonary resuscitation may be needed. If the patient's temperature is >37.8°C, reduce before administering OKT3

Common Adverse Reactions

>10%:

"First-dose" (cytokine release) effects: Onset: 1-3 hours after the dose; duration: 12-16 hours. Severity is mild to life-threatening. Signs and symptoms include fever, chilling, dyspnea, wheezing, chest pain, chest tightness, nausea, vomiting, and diarrhea. Hypervolemic pulmonary edema, nephrotoxicity, meningitis, and encephalopathy are possible. Reactions tend to decrease with repeated doses.

Cardiovascular: Tachycardia (including ventricular)

Central nervous system: Dizziness, faintness

Gastrointestinal: Diarrhea, nausea, vomiting

Hematologic: Transient lymphopenia

Neuromuscular & skeletal: Trembling

Respiratory: Dyspnea

1% to 10%:

Central nervous system: Headache

Neuromuscular & skeletal: Stiff neck

Ocular: Photophobia

Respiratory: Pulmonary edema

Drug Interactions

Increased Effect/Toxicity: Recommend decreasing dose of prednisone to 0.5 mg/kg, azathioprine to 0.5 mg/kg (approximate 50% decrease in dose), and discontinuing cyclosporine while patient is receiving OKT3.

Decreased Effect: Decreased effect with immunosuppressive drugs.

Mechanism of Action Reverses graft rejection by binding to T cells and interfering with their function by binding T-cell receptor-associated CD3 glycoprotein

Pharmacodynamics/Kinetics

Duration: 7 days after discontinuation

Time to peak: Steady-state: Trough: 3-14 days

Dosage I.V. (refer to individual protocols):

Children <30 kg: 2.5 mg/day once daily for 7-14 days

Children >30 kg: 5 mg/day once daily for 7-14 days

OR

Children <12 years: 0.1 mg/kg/day once daily for 10-14 days

Children ≥12 years and Adults: 5 mg/day once daily for 10-14 days

Hemodialysis: Molecular size of OKT3 is 150,000 daltons; not dialyzed by most standard dialyzers; however, may be dialyzed by high flux dialysis; OKT3 will be removed by plasmapheresis; administer following dialysis treatments

Peritoneal dialysis: Significant drug removal is unlikely based on physiochemical characteristics

Administration Filter each dose through a low protein-binding 0.22 micron filter (Millex GV) before administration; administer I.V. push over <1 minute at a final concentration of 1 mg/mL

Children and Adults:

Methylprednisolone sodium succinate 15 mg/kg I.V. administered prior to first muromonab-CD3 administration and I.V. hydrocortisone sodium succinate 50-100 mg given 30 minutes after administration are strongly recommended to decrease the incidence of reactions to the first dose

Patient temperature should not exceed 37.8°C (100°F) at time of administration

Monitoring Parameters Chest x-ray, weight gain, CBC with differential, temperature, vital signs (blood pressure, temperature, pulse, respiration); immunologic monitoring of T cells, serum levels of OKT3

Reference Range

OKT3 serum concentrations:

Serum level monitoring should be performed in conjunction with lymphocyte subset determinations; Trough concentration sampling best correlates with clinical outcome. Serial monitoring may provide a better early indicator of inadequate dosing during induction or rejection.

Mean serum trough levels rise during the first 3 days, then average 0.9 mcg/mL on days 3-14

Circulating levels ≥0.8 mcg/mL block the function of cytotoxic T cells *in vitro* and *in vivo*

Several recent analysis have suggested appropriate dosage adjustments of OKT3 induction course are better determined with OKT3 serum levels versus lymphocyte subset determination; however, no prospective controlled trials have been performed to validate the equivalency of these tests in predicting clinical outcome.

Lymphocyte subset monitoring: CD3+ cells: Trough sample measurement is preferable and reagent utilized defines reference range.

OKT3-FITC: <10-50 cells/mm³ or <3% to 5%

CD3(IgG1)-FITC: similar to OKT3-FITC

Leu-4a: Higher number of CD3+ cells appears acceptable

Dosage adjustments should be made in conjunction with clinical response and based upon trends over several consecutive days

Patient Information Inform patient of expected first dose effects which are markedly reduced with subsequent treatments

Dosage Forms INJ, solution: 1 mg/mL (5 mL)

Mycophenolate (mye koe FEN oh late)

U.S. Brand Names CellCept®

Synonyms Mycophenolate Mofetil

Therapeutic Category Immunosuppressant Agent

Use Prophylaxis of organ rejection concomitantly with cyclosporine and corticosteroids in patients receiving allogenic renal, cardiac, or hepatic transplants. Intravenous formulation is an alternative dosage form to oral capsules, suspension, and tablets.

Unlabeled/Investigational Use Treatment of rejection in liver transplant patients unable to tolerate tacrolimus or cyclosporine due to neurotoxicity; mild rejection in heart transplant patients; treatment of moderate-severe psoriasis

Pregnancy Risk Factor C (manufacturer)

Contraindications Hypersensitivity to mycophenolate mofetil, mycophenolic acid, or any component of the formulation; intravenous is contraindicated in patients who are allergic to polysorbate 80

Warnings/Precautions Increased risk for infection and development of lymphoproliferative disorders. Patients should be monitored appropriately and given supportive treatment should these conditions occur. Increased toxicity in patients with renal impairment. Should be used with caution in patients with active peptic ulcer disease.

Because mycophenolate mofetil has demonstrated teratogenic effects in rats and rabbits, tablets should not be crushed, and capsules should not be opened or crushed. Avoid inhalation or direct contact with skin or mucous membranes of the powder contained in the capsules and the powder for oral suspension. Caution should be exercised in the handling and preparation of solutions of intravenous mycophenolate. Avoid skin contact with the intravenous solution and reconstituted suspension. If such contact occurs, wash thoroughly with soap and water, rinse eyes with plain water.

Theoretically, use should be avoided in patients with the rare hereditary deficiency of hypoxanthine-guanine phosphoribosyltransferase (such as Lesch-Nyhan or Kelley-Seegmiller syndrome). Intravenous solutions should be given over at least 2 hours; **never** administer intravenous solution by rapid or bolus injection.

Common Adverse Reactions As reported in adults following oral dosing of mycophenolate alone in renal, cardiac, and hepatic allograft rejection studies. In general, lower doses used in renal rejection patients had less adverse effects than higher doses. Rates of adverse effects were similar for each indication, except for those unique to the specific organ involved. The type of adverse effects observed in pediatric patients was similar to those seen in adults; abdominal pain, anemia, diarrhea, fever, hypertension, infection, pharyngitis, respiratory tract infection, sepsis, and vomiting were seen in higher proportion; lymphoproliferative disorder was the only type of malignancy observed.

>20%:

Cardiovascular: Hypertension (28% to 77%), peripheral edema (27% to 64%), edema (27% to 28%), tachycardia (20% to 22%)

Central nervous system: Pain (31% to 76%), headache (16% to 54%), insomnia (41% to 52%), fever (21% to 52%), anxiety (28%)

Dermatologic: Rash (22%)

Endocrine & metabolic: Hypercholesterolemia (41%), hypokalemia (32% to 37%)

Gastrointestinal: Abdominal pain (25% to 62%), nausea (20% to 54%), diarrhea (31% to 52%), constipation (18% to 41%), vomiting (33% to 34%), anorexia (25%), dyspepsia (22%)

Genitourinary: Urinary tract infection (37%)

Hematologic: Leukopenia (23% to 46%), leukocytosis (22% to 40%), hypochromic anemia (25%)

Hepatic: Liver function tests abnormal (25%), ascites (24%)

Neuromuscular & skeletal: Back pain (35% to 47%), weakness (35% to 43%), tremor (24% to 34%), paresthesia (21%)

(Continued)

Mycophenolate *(Continued)*

Respiratory: Dyspnea (31% to 37%), respiratory tract infection (22% to 37%), cough (31%), lung disorder (22% to 30%)

Miscellaneous: Infection (18% to 27%), *Candida* (11% to 22%), herpes simplex (10% to 21%)

3% to <20%:

Cardiovascular: Angina, arrhythmia, arterial thrombosis, atrial fibrillation, atrial flutter, bradycardia, cardiac arrest, cardiac failure, CHF, extrasystole, facial edema, hypervolemia, hypotension, pallor, palpitation, pericardial effusion, peripheral vascular disorder, postural hypotension, supraventricular extrasystoles, supraventricular tachycardia, syncope, thrombosis, vasodilation, vasospasm, venous pressure increased, ventricular extrasystole, ventricular tachycardia

Central nervous system: Agitation, chills with fever, confusion, convulsion, delirium, depression, emotional lability, hallucinations, hypesthesia, malaise, nervousness, psychosis, somnolence, thinking abnormal, vertigo

Dermatologic: Acne, alopecia, bruising, cellulitis, hirsutism, pruritus, skin carcinoma, skin hypertrophy

Endocrine & metabolic: Acidosis, Cushing's syndrome, dehydration, diabetes mellitus, gout, hypercalcemia, hyperlipemia, hyperphosphatemia, hyperuricemia, hypothyroidism, parathyroid disorder

Gastrointestinal: Abdomen enlarged, dry mouth, dysphagia, esophagitis, flatulence, gastritis, gastroenteritis, gastrointestinal hemorrhage, gastrointestinal moniliasis, gingivitis, gum hyperplasia, melena, mouth ulceration, oral moniliasis, stomach disorder, stomatitis

Genitourinary: Impotence, pelvic pain, prostatic disorder, urinary frequency, urinary incontinence, urinary retention, urinary tract disorder

Hematologic: Coagulation disorder, hemorrhage, pancytopenia, polycythemia, prothrombin time increased, thromboplastin increased

Hepatic: Alkaline phosphatase increased, alkalosis, bilirubinemia, cholangitis, cholestatic jaundice, GGT increased, hepatitis, jaundice, liver damage

Local: Abscess, ALT increased, AST increased

Neuromuscular & skeletal: Arthralgia, hypertonia, joint disorder, leg cramps, myalgia, myasthenia, neck pain, neuropathy, osteoporosis

Ocular: Amblyopia, cataract, conjunctivitis, eye hemorrhage, lacrimation disorder, vision abnormal

Otic: Deafness, ear disorder, ear pain, tinnitus

Renal: Albuminuria, creatinine increased, dysuria, hematuria, hydronephrosis, kidney failure, kidney tubular necrosis, oliguria

Respiratory: Apnea, asthma, atelectasis, bronchitis, epistaxis, hemoptysis, hiccup, hyperventilation, hypoxia, respiratory acidosis, lung edema, pharyngitis, pleural effusion, pneumonia, pneumothorax, pulmonary hypertension, respiratory moniliasis, rhinitis, sinusitis, sputum increased, voice alteration

Miscellaneous: *Candida* (mucocutaneous 11% to 18%), CMV viremia/syndrome (12% to 14%), CMV tissue invasive disease (6% to 11%), herpes zoster cutaneous disease (4% to 10%), cyst, diaphoresis, flu-like syndrome, fungal dermatitis, healing abnormal, hernia, ileus infection, lactic dehydrogenase increased, peritonitis, pyelonephritis, scrotal edema, thirst

Drug Interactions

Increased Effect/Toxicity: Acyclovir and ganciclovir levels may increase due to competition for tubular secretion of these drugs. Probenecid may increase mycophenolate levels due to inhibition of tubular secretion. High doses of salicylates may increase free fraction of mycophenolic acid. Azathioprine's bone marrow suppression may be potentiated; do not administer together.

Decreased Effect: Antacids decrease serum levels (C_{max} and AUC); **do not administer together**. Cholestyramine resin decreases serum levels; **do not administer together**. Avoid use of live vaccines; vaccinations may be less effective. Influenza vaccine may be of value. During concurrent use of oral contraceptives, progesterone levels are not significantly affected, however, effect on estrogen component varies; an additional form of contraception should be used.

Mechanism of Action Inhibition of purine synthesis of human lymphocytes and proliferation of human lymphocytes

Pharmacodynamics/Kinetics

Onset of action: Peak effect: Correlation of toxicity or efficacy is still being developed, however, one study indicated that 12-hour AUCs >40 mcg/mL/hour were correlated with efficacy and decreased episodes of rejection

Absorption: AUC values for MPA are lower in the early post-transplant period versus later (>3 months) post-transplant period. The extent of absorption in pediatrics is similar to that seen in adults, although there was wide variability reported.

Distribution: Oral: 4 L/kg; I.V.: 3.6 L/kg

Protein binding: MPA: 97%, MPAG 82%

Metabolism: Hepatic and via GI tract; hydrolyzed to mycophenolic acid (MPA; active metabolite); enterohepatic recirculation of MPA may occur; MPA is glucuronidated to MPAG (inactive metabolite)

Bioavailability: Oral: 94%

Half-life elimination: Oral: 17 hours; I.V.: 18 hours

Excretion: MPAG: Urine and feces; MPA: Urine (87% as inactive MPAG)

Dosage

Children: Renal transplant: Oral:

Suspension: 600 mg/m²/dose twice daily; maximum dose: 1 g twice daily

Alternatively, may use solid dosage forms according to BSA as follows:

BSA 1.25-1.5 m²: 750 mg capsule twice daily

BSA >1.5 m²: 1 g capsule or tablet twice daily

Adults: The initial dose should be given as soon as possible following transplantation; intravenous solution may be given until the oral medication can be tolerated (up to 14 days)

Renal transplant:

Oral: 1 g twice daily. Although a dose of 1.5 g twice daily was used in clinical trials and shown to be effective, no efficacy advantage was established. Patients receiving 2 g/day demonstrated an overall better safety profile than patients receiving 3 g/day. Doses >2 g/day are not recommended in these patients because of the possibility for enhanced immunosuppression as well as toxicities.

I.V.: 1 g twice daily

Cardiac transplantation:

Oral: 1.5 g twice daily

I.V.: 1.5 g twice daily

Hepatic transplantation:

Oral: 1.5 g twice daily

I.V.: 1 g twice daily

Dosing adjustment in renal impairment:

Renal transplant: GFR <25 mL/minute in patients outside the immediate post-transplant period: Doses of >1 g administered twice daily should be avoided; patients should also be carefully observed; no dose adjustments are needed in renal transplant patients experiencing delayed graft function postoperatively

Cardiac or liver transplant: No data available; mycophenolate may be used in cardiac or hepatic transplant patients with severe chronic renal impairment if the potential benefit outweighs the potential risk

Hemodialysis: Not removed; supplemental dose is not necessary

Peritoneal dialysis: Supplemental dose is not necessary

Dosage adjustment in hepatic impairment: No dosage adjustment is recommended for renal patients with severe hepatic parenchymal disease; however, it is not currently known whether dosage adjustments are necessary for hepatic disease with other etiologies

Elderly: Dosage is the same as younger patients, however, dosing should be cautious due to possibility of increased hepatic, renal or cardiac dysfunction; elderly patients may be at an increased risk of certain infections, gastrointestinal hemorrhage, and pulmonary edema, as compared to younger patients

Dosing adjustment for toxicity (neutropenia): ANC <1.3 x 10³/µL: Dosing should be interrupted or the dose reduced, appropriate diagnostic tests performed and patients managed appropriately

Administration

Oral dosage formulations (tablet, capsule, suspension) should be administered as soon as possible following transplantation. Oral dosage forms should be administered on an empty stomach. The oral solution may be administered via a nasogastric tube (minimum 8 French, 1.7 mm interior diameter) and cannot be mixed with other medications.

Intravenous solutions should be administered over at least 2 hours (either peripheral or central vein); do **not** administer intravenous solution by rapid or bolus injection. Following reconstitution, dilute to a concentration of 6 mg/mL using D_5W; mycophenolate is not compatible with other solutions.

Monitoring Parameters Complete blood count

Patient Information Take as directed, preferably 1 hour before or 2 hours after meals. Do not take within 1 hour before or 2 hours after antacids or cholestyramine medications. Do not alter dose and do not discontinue without consulting prescriber. Maintain adequate hydration (2-3 L/day of fluids unless instructed to restrict fluid intake) during entire course of therapy. You will be susceptible to infection (avoid crowds and people with infections or contagious diseases). If you are diabetic, monitor glucose levels closely (may alter glucose levels). You may experience dizziness or trembling (use caution until response to medication is known); nausea or vomiting (frequent small meals, frequent mouth care may help); diarrhea (boiled milk, yogurt, or buttermilk may help); sores or white plaques in mouth (frequent rinsing of mouth and frequent mouth care may help); or muscle or back pain (mild analgesics may be recommended). Report chest pain; acute headache or dizziness; symptoms of respiratory infection, cough, or difficulty breathing; unresolved gastrointestinal effects; fatigue, chills, fever unhealed sores, white plaques in mouth; irritation in genital area or unusual discharge; unusual bruising or bleeding; or other unusual effects related to this medication. May be at increased risk for skin cancer; wear protective clothing and use sunscreen with high protective factor to help limit exposure to sunlight and UV light. Two reliable forms of contraception should be used prior to, during, and for 6 weeks after therapy.

Dosage Forms CAP: 250 mg. **INJ, powder for reconstitution:** 500 mg. **POWDER, oral suspension:** 200 mg/mL (225 mL). **TAB, film coated:** 500 mg

- ◆ **Mycophenolate Mofetil** see Mycophenolate on page 869
- ◆ **Mycostatin®** see Nystatin on page 919
- ◆ **Mydfrin®** see Phenylephrine on page 993
- ◆ **Mydriacyl®** see Tropicamide on page 1277
- ◆ **Mykrox® [DSC]** see Metolazone on page 828
- ◆ **Mylanta® Children's [OTC]** see Calcium Carbonate on page 203

Nabumetone (na BYOO me tone)

Related Information
Nonsteroidal Anti-Inflammatory Agents Comparison *on page 1401*

U.S. Brand Names Relafen®

Therapeutic Category Analgesic, Nonsteroidal Anti-inflammatory Drug; Anti-inflammatory Agent; Nonsteroidal Anti-inflammatory Drug (NSAID), Oral

Use Management of osteoarthritis and rheumatoid arthritis

Unlabeled/Investigational Use Sunburn, mild to moderate pain

Pregnancy Risk Factor C/D (3rd trimester)

Contraindications Hypersensitivity to NSAIDs including aspirin, or any component of the formulation; should not be administered to patients with active peptic ulceration and those with severe hepatic impairment or in patients in whom nabumetone, aspirin, or other NSAIDs have induced asthma, urticaria, or other allergic-type reactions; fatal asthmatic reactions have occurred following NSAID administration; pregnancy (3rd trimester)

Warnings/Precautions Elderly patients may sometimes require lower doses; patients with impaired renal function may need a dose reduction; use with caution in patients with severe hepatic impairment; dehydration. Withhold for at least 4-6 half-lives prior to surgical or dental procedures.

Common Adverse Reactions
>10%:
    Central nervous system: Dizziness
    Dermatologic: Rash
    Gastrointestinal: Abdominal cramps, abdominal pain (12%), diarrhea (14%), dyspepsia (13%), heartburn, indigestion, nausea
1% to 10%:
    Central nervous system: Headache, nervousness
    Dermatologic: Itching
    Endocrine & metabolic: Fluid retention
    Gastrointestinal: Vomiting
    Otic: Tinnitus

Drug Interactions
Increased Effect/Toxicity: NSAIDs may increase digoxin, methotrexate, and lithium serum concentrations. The renal adverse effects of ACE inhibitors may be potentiated by NSAIDs. Potential for bleeding may be increased with anticoagulants or antiplatelet agents. Concurrent use of corticosteroids may increase the risk of GI ulceration.

Decreased Effect: NSAIDs may decrease the effect of some antihypertensive agents, including ACE inhibitors, angiotensin receptor antagonists, and hydralazine. The efficacy of diuretics (loop and/or thiazide) may be decreased.

Mechanism of Action Nabumetone is a nonacidic NSAID that is rapidly metabolized after absorption to a major active metabolite, 6-methoxy-2-naphthylacetic acid. As found with previous NSAIDs, nabumetone's active metabolite inhibits the cyclooxygenase enzyme which is indirectly responsible for the production of inflammation and pain during arthritis by way of enhancing the production of endoperoxides and prostaglandins E_2 and I_2 (prostacyclin). The active metabolite of nabumetone is felt to be the compound primarily responsible for therapeutic effect. Comparatively, the parent drug is a poor inhibitor of prostaglandin synthesis.

Pharmacodynamics/Kinetics
Onset of action: Several days
Distribution: Diffusion occurs readily into synovial fluid
Protein binding: >99%
Metabolism: Prodrug, rapidly metabolized to an active metabolite (6-methoxy-2-naphthylacetic acid); extensive first-pass effect
Half-life elimination: Major metabolite: 24 hours
Time to peak, serum: Metabolite: Oral: 3-6 hours; Synovial fluid: 4-12 hours
Excretion: Urine (80%) and feces (10%) with little as unchanged drug

Dosage Adults: Oral: 1000 mg/day; an additional 500-1000 mg may be needed in some patients to obtain more symptomatic relief; may be administered once or twice daily

Dosing adjustment in renal impairment: None necessary; however, adverse effects due to accumulation of inactive metabolites of nabumetone that are renally excreted have not been studied and should be considered

Monitoring Parameters Patients with renal insufficiency: Baseline renal function followed by repeat test within weeks (to determine if renal function has deteriorated)

Patient Information Take this medication at meal times or with food or milk to minimize gastric irritation; report if you develop stomach disturbances, blurred vision, or other eye symptoms, rash, weight gain, or edema; report if you pass dark-colored or tarry stools; concomitant use of alcohol should be avoided, if possible, since it may add to the irritant action of nabumetone in the stomach; aspirin should be avoided

Dosage Forms TAB: 500 mg, 750 mg

- ◆ **NAC** see Acetylcysteine on page 32
- ◆ **N-Acetylcysteine** see Acetylcysteine on page 32
- ◆ **N-Acetyl-L-cysteine** see Acetylcysteine on page 32
- ◆ **N-Acetyl-P-Aminophenol** see Acetaminophen on page 24
- ◆ **NaCl** see Sodium Chloride on page 1146

Nadolol (nay DOE lole)

Related Information

Beta-Blockers Comparison on page 1368

U.S. Brand Names Corgard®

Therapeutic Category Antianginal Agent; Antihypertensive Agent; Antimigraine Agent, Prophylaxis; Beta Blocker, Nonselective

Use Treatment of hypertension and angina pectoris; prophylaxis of migraine headaches

Pregnancy Risk Factor C

Contraindications Hypersensitivity to nadolol or any component of the formulation; bronchial asthma; sinus bradycardia; sinus node dysfunction; heart block greater than first degree (except in patients with a functioning artificial pacemaker); cardiogenic shock; uncompensated cardiac failure

Warnings/Precautions Administer only with extreme caution in patients with compensated heart failure, monitor for a worsening of the condition. Efficacy in heart failure has not been established for nadolol. Beta-blocker therapy should not be withdrawn abruptly (particularly in patients with CAD), but gradually tapered to avoid acute tachycardia, hypertension, and/or ischemia. Use caution with concurrent use of beta-blockers and either verapamil or diltiazem; bradycardia or heart block can occur. In general, patients with bronchospastic disease should not receive beta-blockers. Nadolol, if used at all, should be used cautiously in bronchospastic disease with close monitoring. Use cautiously in diabetics because it can mask prominent hypoglycemic symptoms. Can mask signs of thyrotoxicosis. Can cause fetal harm when administered in pregnancy. Use cautiously in the renally impaired (dosage adjustments are required). Use care with anesthetic agents which decrease myocardial function.

Common Adverse Reactions

>10%:

Central nervous system: Drowsiness, insomnia

Endocrine & metabolic: Decreased sexual ability

1% to 10%:

Cardiovascular: Bradycardia, palpitations, edema, CHF, reduced peripheral circulation

Central nervous system: Mental depression

Gastrointestinal: Diarrhea or constipation, nausea, vomiting, stomach discomfort

Respiratory: Bronchospasm

Miscellaneous: Cold extremities

Drug Interactions

Increased Effect/Toxicity: The heart rate lowering effects of nadolol are additive with other drugs which slow AV conduction (digoxin, verapamil, diltiazem). Concurrent use of alpha-blockers (prazosin, terazosin) with beta-blockers may increase risk of orthostasis. Nadolol may mask the tachycardia from hypoglycemia caused by insulin and oral hypoglycemics. In patients receiving concurrent therapy, the risk of hypertensive crisis is increased when either clonidine or the beta-blocker is withdrawn. Reserpine has been shown to enhance the effect of beta-blockers. Avoid using with alpha-adrenergic stimulants (phenylephrine, epinephrine, etc) which may have exaggerated hypertensive responses. Beta-blockers may affect the action or levels of ethanol, disopyramide, nondepolarizing muscle relaxants, and theophylline although the effects are difficult to predict. The vasoconstrictive effects of ergot alkaloids may be enhanced.

Decreased Effect: Decreased effect of beta-blockers with aluminum salts, barbiturates, calcium salts, cholestyramine, colestipol, NSAIDs, penicillins (ampicillin), rifampin, salicylates, and sulfinpyrazone due to decreased bioavailability and plasma levels. Beta-blockers may decrease the effect of sulfonylureas (possibly hyperglycemia). Nonselective beta-blockers blunt the effect of beta-2 adrenergic agonists (albuterol).

Mechanism of Action Competitively blocks response to beta₁- and beta₂-adrenergic stimulation; does not exhibit any membrane stabilizing or intrinsic sympathomimetic activity

Pharmacodynamics/Kinetics

Duration: 17-24 hours

Absorption: 30% to 40%

Distribution: Concentration in human breast milk is 4.6 times higher than serum

Protein binding: 28%

Half-life elimination: Adults: 10-24 hours; prolonged with renal impairment; End-stage renal disease: 45 hours

(Continued)

Nadolol *(Continued)*

Time to peak, serum: 2-4 hours

Excretion: Urine (as unchanged drug)

Dosage Oral:

Adults: Initial: 40 mg/day, increase dosage gradually by 40-80 mg increments at 3- to 7-day intervals until optimum clinical response is obtained with profound slowing of heart rate; doses up to 160-240 mg/day in angina and 240-320 mg/day in hypertension may be necessary.

Elderly: Initial: 20 mg/day; increase doses by 20 mg increments at 3- to 7-day intervals; usual dosage range: 20-240 mg/day.

Dosing adjustment in renal impairment:

Cl_{cr} 31-40 mL/minute: Administer every 24-36 hours or administer 50% of normal dose.

Cl_{cr} 10-30 mL/minute: Administer every 24-48 hours or administer 50% of normal dose.

Cl_{cr} <10 mL/minute: Administer every 40-60 hours or administer 25% of normal dose.

Hemodialysis: Moderately dialyzable (20% to 50%); administer dose postdialysis or administer 40 mg supplemental dose.

Peritoneal dialysis: Supplemental dose is not necessary.

Dosing adjustment/comments in hepatic disease: Reduced dose probably necessary.

Patient Information Check pulse daily prior to taking medication. If pulse is <50, hold medication and consult prescriber. Do not adjust dosage without consulting prescriber. May cause dizziness, fatigue, blurred vision; change position slowly (lying/sitting to standing) and use caution when driving or engaging in tasks that require alertness until response to drug is known. Exercise and increasing bulk or fiber in diet may help resolve constipation. If diabetic, monitor serum glucose closely (the drug may mask symptoms of hypoglycemia). Report swelling in feet or legs, difficulty breathing or persistent cough, unresolved fatigue, unusual weight gain >5 lb/week, or unresolved constipation.

Dosage Forms TAB: 20 mg, 40 mg, 80 mg, 120 mg, 160 mg

Nafarelin *(NAF a re lin)*

U.S. Brand Names Synarel®

Synonyms Nafarelin Acetate

Therapeutic Category Hormone, Posterior Pituitary; Luteinizing Hormone-Releasing Hormone Analog

Use Treatment of endometriosis, including pain and reduction of lesions; treatment of central precocious puberty (gonadotropin-dependent precocious puberty) in children of both sexes

Pregnancy Risk Factor X

Contraindications Hypersensitivity to GnRH, GnRH-agonist analogs, or any component of the formulation; undiagnosed abnormal vaginal bleeding; pregnancy

Warnings/Precautions Use with caution in patients with risk factors for decreased bone mineral content, nafarelin therapy may pose an additional risk; hypersensitivity reactions occur in 0.2% of the patients; safety and efficacy in children have not been established

Common Adverse Reactions

>10%:

Central nervous system: Headache, emotional lability

Dermatologic: Acne

Endocrine & metabolic: Hot flashes, decreased libido, decreased breast size

Genitourinary: Vaginal dryness

Neuromuscular & skeletal: Myalgia

Respiratory: Nasal irritation

1% to 10%:

Cardiovascular: Edema, chest pain

Central nervous system: Insomnia

Dermatologic: Urticaria, rash, pruritus, seborrhea

Respiratory: Dyspnea

Mechanism of Action Potent synthetic decapeptide analogue of gonadotropin-releasing hormone (GnRH; LHRH) which is approximately 200 times more potent than GnRH in terms of pituitary release of luteinizing hormone (LH) and follicle-stimulating hormone (FSH). Effects on the pituitary gland and sex hormones are dependent upon its length of administration. After acute administration, an initial stimulation of the release of LH and FSH from the pituitary is observed; an increase in androgens and estrogens subsequently follows. Continued administration of nafarelin, however, suppresses gonadotrope responsiveness to endogenous GnRH resulting in reduced secretion of LH and FSH and, secondarily, decreased ovarian and testicular steroid production.

Pharmacodynamics/Kinetics

Protein binding, plasma: 80%

Time to peak, serum: 10-45 minutes

Dosage

Endometriosis: Adults: Female: 1 spray (200 mcg) in 1 nostril each morning and the other nostril each evening starting on days 2-4 of menstrual cycle for 6 months

Central precocious puberty: Children: Males/Females: 2 sprays (400 mcg) into each nostril in the morning 2 sprays (400 mcg) into each nostril in the evening. If inadequate suppression, may increase dose to 3 sprays (600 mcg) into alternating nostrils 3 times/day.

Patient Information Begin treatment between days 2 and 4 of menstrual cycle; usually menstruation will stop (as well as ovulation), but is not a reliable contraceptive, use of a nonhormonal contraceptive is suggested; full compliance with taking the medicine is very important; do not use nasal decongestant for at least 30 minutes after using nafarelin spray; report if regular menstruation persists

Dosage Forms SPRAY, intranasal: 2 mg/mL (8 mL)

♦ **Nafarelin Acetate** *see* Nafarelin *on page 874*

Nafcillin (naf SIL in)
Related Information
Community-Acquired Pneumonia in Adults *on page 1457*

Synonyms Ethoxynaphthamido Penicillin Sodium; Nafcillin Sodium; Nallpen; Sodium Nafcillin

Therapeutic Category Antibiotic, Penicillin

Use Treatment of infections such as osteomyelitis, septicemia, endocarditis, and CNS infections caused by susceptible strains of staphylococci species

Pregnancy Risk Factor B

Contraindications Hypersensitivity to nafcillin, or any component of the formulation, or penicillins

Warnings/Precautions Extravasation of I.V. infusions should be avoided; modification of dosage is necessary in patients with both severe renal and hepatic impairment; elimination rate will be slow in neonates; use with caution in patients with cephalosporin hypersensitivity

Common Adverse Reactions Frequency not defined.
Central nervous system: Pain, fever
Dermatologic: Rash
Gastrointestinal: Nausea, diarrhea
Hematologic: Agranulocytosis, bone marrow depression, neutropenia
Local: Pain, swelling, inflammation, phlebitis, skin sloughing, and thrombophlebitis at the injection site; oxacillin (less likely to cause phlebitis) is often preferred in pediatric patients
Renal: Interstitial nephritis (acute)
Miscellaneous: Hypersensitivity reactions

Drug Interactions
Cytochrome P450 Effect: Induces CYP3A4 (strong)
Increased Effect/Toxicity: Probenecid may cause an increase in nafcillin levels. Penicillins may increase the exposure to methotrexate during concurrent therapy; monitor.
Decreased Effect: Chloramphenicol may decrease nafcillin efficacy. If taken concomitantly with warfarin, nafcillin may inhibit the anticoagulant response to warfarin. This effect may persist for up to 30 days after nafcillin has been discontinued. Subtherapeutic cyclosporine levels may result when taken concomitantly with nafcillin. Although anecdotal reports suggest oral contraceptive efficacy could be reduced by penicillins, this has been refuted by more rigorous scientific and clinical data.

Mechanism of Action Interferes with bacterial cell wall synthesis during active multiplication, causing cell wall death and resultant bactericidal activity against susceptible bacteria

Pharmacodynamics/Kinetics
Distribution: Widely distributed; CSF penetration is poor but enhanced by meningeal inflammation; crosses placenta
Protein binding: 70% to 90%
Metabolism: Primarily hepatic; undergoes enterohepatic recirculation
Half-life elimination:
Neonates: <3 weeks: 2.2-5.5 hours; 4-9 weeks: 1.2-2.3 hours
Children 3 months to 14 years: 0.75-1.9 hours
Adults: 30 minutes to 1.5 hours with normal renal and hepatic function
Time to peak, serum: I.M.: 30-60 minutes
Excretion: Primarily feces; urine (10% to 30% as unchanged drug)

Dosage
Neonates:
<2000 g, <7 days: 50 mg/kg/day divided every 12 hours
<2000 g, >7 days: 75 mg/kg/day divided every 8 hours
>2000 g, <7 days: 50 mg/kg/day divided every 8 hours
>2000 g, >7 days: 75 mg/kg/day divided every 6 hours
Children:
I.M.: 25 mg/kg twice daily
I.V.:
Mild to moderate infections: 50-100 mg/kg/day in divided doses every 6 hours
Severe infections: 100-200 mg/kg/day in divided doses every 4-6 hours
Maximum dose: 12 g/day
Adults:
I.M.: 500 mg every 4-6 hours
I.V.: 500-2000 mg every 4-6 hours
Dosing adjustment in renal impairment: Not necessary
Dosing adjustment in hepatic impairment: In patients with both hepatic and renal impairment, modification of dosage may be necessary; no data available.
Dialysis: Not dialyzable (0% to 5%) via hemodialysis; supplemental dosage not necessary with hemo- or peritoneal dialysis or continuous arteriovenous or venovenous hemofiltration

Administration
I.M.: Rotate injection sites
I.V.: Vesicant. Administer around-the-clock to promote less variation in peak and trough serum levels; infuse over 30-60 minutes
(Continued)

875

Nafcillin *(Continued)*

Extravasation management: Use cold packs. Hyaluronidase (Wydase®): Add 1 mL NS to 150 unit vial to make 150 units/mL of concentration; mix 0.1 mL of above with 0.9 mL NS in 1 mL syringe to make final concentration = 15 units/mL.

Monitoring Parameters Periodic CBC, urinalysis, BUN, serum creatinine, AST and ALT; observe for signs and symptoms of anaphylaxis during first dose

Dosage Forms INF [premixed iso-osmotic dextrose solution]: 1 g (50 mL); 2 g (100 mL). **INJ, powder for reconstitution:** 1 g, 2 g, 10 g

♦ **Nafcillin Sodium** *see Nafcillin on page 875*

Naftifine *(NAF ti feen)*

U.S. Brand Names Naftin®
Synonyms Naftifine Hydrochloride
Therapeutic Category Antifungal Agent, Topical
Use Topical treatment of tinea cruris (jock itch), tinea corporis (ringworm), and tinea pedis (athlete's foot)
Pregnancy Risk Factor B
Contraindications Hypersensitivity to any component
Warnings/Precautions For external use only
Common Adverse Reactions
>10%: Local: Burning, stinging
1% to 10%:
Dermatologic: Erythema, itching
Local: Dryness, irritation
Mechanism of Action Synthetic, broad-spectrum antifungal agent in the allylamine class; appears to have both fungistatic and fungicidal activity. Exhibits antifungal activity by selectively inhibiting the enzyme squalene epoxidase in a dose-dependent manner which results in the primary sterol, ergosterol, within the fungal membrane not being synthesized.
Pharmacodynamics/Kinetics
Absorption: Systemic: Cream: 6%; Gel: ≤4%
Half-life elimination: 2-3 days
Excretion: Urine and feces (as metabolites)
Dosage Adults: Topical: Apply cream once daily and gel twice daily (morning and evening) for up to 4 weeks
Patient Information External use only; avoid eyes, mouth, and other mucous membranes; do not use occlusive dressings unless directed to do so; discontinue if irritation or sensitivity develops; wash hands after application
Dosage Forms CRM: 1% (15 g, 30 g, 60 g). **GEL:** 1% (20 g, 40 g, 60 g)

♦ **Naftifine Hydrochloride** *see Naftifine on page 876*

♦ **Naftin®** *see Naftifine on page 876*

♦ **NaHCO₃** *see Sodium Bicarbonate on page 1144*

Nalbuphine *(NAL byoo feen)*

Related Information
Narcotic Agonists Comparison *on page 1395*
U.S. Brand Names Nubain®
Synonyms Nalbuphine Hydrochloride
Therapeutic Category Analgesic, Narcotic
Use Relief of moderate to severe pain; preoperative analgesia, postoperative and surgical anesthesia, and obstetrical analgesia during labor and delivery
Pregnancy Risk Factor B/D (prolonged use or high doses at term)
Contraindications Hypersensitivity to nalbuphine or any component, including sulfites; pregnancy (prolonged use or high dosages at term)
Warnings/Precautions Use with caution in patients with recent myocardial infarction, biliary tract surgery, or sulfite sensitivity; may produce respiratory depression; use with caution in women delivering premature infants; use with caution in patients with a history of drug dependence, head trauma or increased intracranial pressure, decreased hepatic or renal function, or pregnancy; tolerance or drug dependence may result from extended use
Common Adverse Reactions
>10%:
Central nervous system: Fatigue, drowsiness
Miscellaneous: Histamine release
1% to 10%:
Cardiovascular: Hypotension
Central nervous system: Headache, nightmares, dizziness
Gastrointestinal: Anorexia, nausea, vomiting, dry mouth
Local: Pain at injection site
Neuromuscular & skeletal: Weakness
Drug Interactions
Increased Effect/Toxicity: Barbiturate anesthetics may increase CNS depression.
Mechanism of Action Binds to opiate receptors in the CNS, causing inhibition of ascending pain pathways, altering the perception of and response to pain; produces generalized CNS depression

Pharmacodynamics/Kinetics
Onset of action: Peak effect: I.M.: 30 minutes; I.V.: 1-3 minutes
Metabolism: Hepatic
Half-life elimination: 3.5-5 hours
Excretion: Feces; urine (~7% as metabolites)

Dosage I.M., I.V. S.C.:
Children 10 months to 14 years: Premedication: 0.2 mg/kg; maximum: 20 mg/dose
Adults: 10 mg/70 kg every 3-6 hours; maximum single dose: 20 mg; maximum daily dose: 160 mg

Dosing adjustment/comments in hepatic impairment: Use with caution and reduce dose

Administration Administer I.M., S.C., or I.V.

Monitoring Parameters Relief of pain, respiratory and mental status, blood pressure

Patient Information Avoid alcohol, may cause drowsiness, impaired judgment or coordination; may cause physical and psychological dependence with prolonged use; will cause withdrawal in patients currently dependent on narcotics

Dosage Forms INJ, solution: 10 mg/mL (1 mL, 10 mL); 20 mg/mL (1 mL, 10 mL)

- ◆ **Nalbuphine Hydrochloride** *see* Nalbuphine *on page 876*
- ◆ **Nalex®-A** *see* Chlorpheniramine, Phenylephrine, and Phenyltoloxamine *on page 265*
- ◆ **Nalfon®** *see* Fenoprofen *on page 513*

Nalidixic Acid (nal i DIKS ik AS id)

U.S. Brand Names NegGram®

Synonyms Nalidixinic Acid

Therapeutic Category Antibiotic, Quinolone

Use Treatment of urinary tract infections

Pregnancy Risk Factor B

Contraindications Hypersensitivity to nalidixic acid or any component of the formulation; infants <3 months of age

Warnings/Precautions Use with caution in patients with impaired hepatic or renal function and prepubertal children; has been shown to cause cartilage degeneration in immature animals; may induce hemolysis in patients with G6PD deficiency. Tendon inflammation and/or rupture have been reported with other quinolone antibiotics. Discontinue at first sign of tendon inflammation or pain. Quinolones may exacerbate myasthenia gravis.

Common Adverse Reactions Frequency not defined.
Central nervous system: Dizziness, drowsiness, headache, increased intracranial pressure, malaise, vertigo, confusion, toxic psychosis, convulsions, fever, chills
Dermatologic: Rash, urticaria, photosensitivity reactions
Endocrine & metabolic: Metabolic acidosis
Gastrointestinal: Nausea, vomiting
Hematologic: Leukopenia, thrombocytopenia
Hepatic: Hepatotoxicity
Ocular: Visual disturbances
Miscellaneous: Quinolones have been associated with tendonitis and tendon rupture

Drug Interactions
Cytochrome P450 Effect: Inhibits CYP1A2 (strong)

Increased Effect/Toxicity: Nalidixic acid increases the levels/effect of cyclosporine, caffeine, theophylline, and warfarin. The CNS-stimulating effect of some quinolones may be enhanced by NSAIDs, and foscarnet has been associated with an increased risk of seizures with some quinolones. Serum levels of some quinolones are increased by loop diuretics, probenecid, and cimetidine (and possibly other H_2-blockers) due to altered renal elimination. This effect may be more important for quinolones with high percentage of renal elimination than with nalidixic acid. Concurrent use of corticosteroids may increase risk of tendon rupture.

Decreased Effect: Enteral feedings may decrease plasma concentrations of nalidixic acid probably by >30% inhibition of absorption. Aluminum/magnesium products, didanosine, quinapril, and sucralfate may decrease absorption of nalidixic acid by ≥90% if administered concurrently. (Administer nalidixic acid at least 4 hours and preferably 6 hours after the dose of these agents.) Calcium, iron, zinc, and multivitamins with minerals products may decrease absorption of nalidixic acid significantly if administered concurrently. (Administer nalidixic acid 2 hours before dose or at least 2 hours after the dose of these agents). Antineoplastic agents may decrease quinolone absorption.

Mechanism of Action Inhibits DNA polymerization in late stages of chromosomal replication

Pharmacodynamics/Kinetics
Distribution: Achieves significant antibacterial concentrations only in the urinary tract; crosses placenta; enters breast milk
Protein binding: 90%
Metabolism: Partially hepatic
Half-life elimination: 6-7 hours; significantly prolonged with renal impairment
Time to peak, serum: 1-2 hours
Excretion: Urine (as unchanged drug, 80% as metabolites); feces (small amounts)

Dosage Oral:
Children 3 months to 12 years: 55 mg/kg/day divided every 6 hours; suppressive therapy is 33 mg/kg/day divided every 6 hours
Adults: 1 g 4 times/day for 2 weeks; then suppressive therapy of 500 mg 4 times/day
Dosing comments in renal impairment: Cl_{cr} <50 mL/minute: Avoid use
(Continued)

Nalidixic Acid *(Continued)*

Patient Information Avoid undue exposure to direct sunlight or use a sunscreen; take 1 hour before meals, but can take with food to decrease GI upset, finish all medication, do not skip doses; report persistent cough

Dosage Forms SUSP, oral: 250 mg/5 mL (473 mL). **TAB:** 250 mg, 500 mg, 1 g

◆ **Nalidixinic Acid** *see Nalidixic Acid on page 877*

◆ **Nallpen** *see Nafcillin on page 875*

◆ **N-allylnoroxymorphine Hydrochloride** *see Naloxone on page 879*

Nalmefene (NAL me feen)

U.S. Brand Names Revex®

Synonyms Nalmefene Hydrochloride

Therapeutic Category Antidote, Narcotic Agonist; Narcotic Antagonist

Use Complete or partial reversal of opioid drug effects, including respiratory depression induced by natural or synthetic opioids; reversal of postoperative opioid depression; management of known or suspected opioid overdose

Pregnancy Risk Factor B

Contraindications Hypersensitivity to nalmefene, naltrexone, or any component of the formulation

Warnings/Precautions May induce symptoms of acute withdrawal in opioid-dependent patients; recurrence of respiratory depression is possible if the opioid involved is long-acting; observe patients until there is no reasonable risk of recurrent respiratory depression. Safety and efficacy have not been established in children. Avoid abrupt reversal of opioid effects in patients of high cardiovascular risk or who have received potentially cardiotoxic drugs. Pulmonary edema and cardiovascular instability have been reported in association with abrupt reversal with other narcotic antagonists.

Common Adverse Reactions

>10%: Gastrointestinal: Nausea

1% to 10%:

Cardiovascular: Tachycardia, hypertension, hypotension, vasodilation

Central nervous system: Fever, dizziness, headache, chills

Gastrointestinal: Vomiting

Miscellaneous: Postoperative pain

Drug Interactions

Increased Effect/Toxicity: Potential increased risk of seizures may exist with use of flumazenil and nalmefene coadministration.

Mechanism of Action As a 6-methylene analog of naltrexone, nalmefene acts as a competitive antagonist at opioid receptor sites, preventing or reversing the respiratory depression, sedation, and hypotension induced by opiates; no pharmacologic activity of its own (eg, opioid agonist activity) has been demonstrated

Pharmacodynamics/Kinetics

Onset of action: I.M., S.C.: 5-15 minutes

Distribution: V_d: 8.6 L/kg; rapid

Protein binding: 45%

Metabolism: Hepatic via glucuronide conjugation to metabolites with little or no activity

Bioavailability: I.M., I.V., S.C.: 100%

Half-life elimination: 10.8 hours

Time to peak, serum: I.M.: 2.3 hours; I.V.: <2 minutes; S.C.: 1.5 hours

Excretion: Feces (17%); urine (<5% as unchanged drug)

Clearance: 0.8 L/hour/kg

Dosage

Reversal of postoperative opioid depression: Blue labeled product (100 mcg/mL): Titrate to reverse the undesired effects of opioids; initial dose for nonopioid dependent patients: 0.25 mcg/kg followed by 0.25 mcg/kg incremental doses at 2- to 5-minute intervals; after a total dose >1 mcg/kg, further therapeutic response is unlikely

Management of known/suspected opioid overdose: Green labeled product (1000 mcg/mL): Initial dose: 0.5 mg/70 kg; may repeat with 1 mg/70 kg in 2-5 minutes; further increase beyond a total dose of 1.5 mg/70 kg will not likely result in improved response and may result in cardiovascular stress and precipitated withdrawal syndrome. (If opioid dependency is suspected, administer a challenge dose of 0.1 mg/70 kg; if no withdrawal symptoms are observed in 2 minutes, the recommended doses can be administered.)

Note: If recurrence of respiratory depression is noted, dose may again be titrated to clinical effect using incremental doses.

Note: If I.V. access is lost or not readily obtainable, a single S.C. or I.M. dose of 1 mg may be effective in 5-15 minutes.

Dosing adjustment in renal or hepatic impairment: Not necessary with single uses, however, slow administration (over 60 seconds) of incremental doses is recommended to minimize hypertension and dizziness

Administration Dilute drug (1:1) with diluent and use smaller doses in patients known to be at increased cardiovascular risk; may be administered via I.M. or S.C. routes if I.V. access is not feasible

Dosage Forms INJ, solution: 100 mcg/mL (1 mL); 1000 mcg/mL (2 mL)

◆ **Nalmefene Hydrochloride** *see Nalmefene on page 878*

Naloxone (nal OKS one)

U.S. Brand Names Narcan®

Synonyms *N*-allylnoroxymorphine Hydrochloride; Naloxone Hydrochloride

Therapeutic Category Antidote, Narcotic Agonist; Narcotic Antagonist

Use

Complete or partial reversal of opioid depression, including respiratory depression, induced by natural and synthetic opioids, including propoxyphene, methadone, and certain mixed agonist-antagonist analgesics: nalbuphine, pentazocine, and butorphanol

Diagnosis of suspected opioid tolerance or acute opioid overdose

Adjunctive agent to increase blood pressure in the management of septic shock

Unlabeled/Investigational Use PCP and ethanol ingestion

Pregnancy Risk Factor C

Contraindications Hypersensitivity to naloxone or any component of the formulation

Warnings/Precautions Use with caution in patients with cardiovascular disease; excessive dosages should be avoided after use of opiates in surgery, because naloxone may cause an increase in blood pressure and reversal of anesthesia; may precipitate withdrawal symptoms in patients addicted to opiates, including pain, hypertension, sweating, agitation, irritability, shrill cry, failure to feed

Common Adverse Reactions Frequency not defined.

Cardiovascular: Hypertension, hypotension, tachycardia, ventricular arrhythmias, cardiac arrest

Central nervous system: Irritability, anxiety, narcotic withdrawal, restlessness, seizures

Gastrointestinal: Nausea, vomiting, diarrhea

Neuromuscular & skeletal: Tremulousness

Respiratory: Dyspnea, pulmonary edema, runny nose, sneezing

Miscellaneous: Diaphoresis

Drug Interactions

Decreased Effect: Decreased effect of narcotic analgesics.

Mechanism of Action Pure opioid antagonist that competes and displaces narcotics at opioid receptor sites

Pharmacodynamics/Kinetics

Onset of action: Endotracheal, I.M., S.C.: 2-5 minutes; I.V.: ~2 minutes

Duration: 20-60 minutes; since shorter than that of most opioids, repeated doses are usually needed

Distribution: Crosses placenta

Metabolism: Primarily hepatic via glucuronidation

Half-life elimination: Neonates: 1.2-3 hours; Adults: 1-1.5 hours

Excretion: Urine (as metabolites)

Dosage I.M., I.V (preferred), intratracheal, S.C.:

Postanesthesia narcotic reversal: Infants and Children: 0.01 mg/kg; may repeat every 2-3 minutes, as needed based on response

Opiate intoxication:

Children:

Birth (including premature infants) to 5 years or <20 kg: 0.1 mg/kg; repeat every 2-3 minutes if needed; may need to repeat doses every 20-60 minutes

>5 years or ≥20 kg: 2 mg/dose; if no response, repeat every 2-3 minutes; may need to repeat doses every 20-60 minutes

Children and Adults: Continuous infusion: I.V.: If continuous infusion is required, calculate dosage/hour based on effective intermittent dose used and duration of adequate response seen, titrate dose 0.04-0.16 mg/kg/hour for 2-5 days in children, adult dose typically 0.25-6.25 mg/hour (short-term infusions as high as 2.4 mg/kg/hour have been tolerated in adults during treatment for septic shock); alternatively, continuous infusion utilizes $^2/_3$ of the initial naloxone bolus on an hourly basis; add 10 times this dose to each liter of D_5W and infuse at a rate of 100 mL/hour; $^1/_2$ of the initial bolus dose should be readministered 15 minutes after initiation of the continuous infusion to prevent a drop in naloxone levels; increase infusion rate as needed to assure adequate ventilation

Narcotic overdose: Adults: I.V.: 0.4-2 mg every 2-3 minutes as needed; may need to repeat doses every 20-60 minutes; if no response is observed after 10 mg, question the diagnosis. **Note:** Use 0.1-0.2 mg increments in patients who are opioid dependent and in postoperative patients to avoid large cardiovascular changes.

Administration

Intratracheal: Dilute to 1-2 mL with normal saline

I.V. push: Administer over 30 seconds as undiluted preparation

I.V. continuous infusion: Dilute to 4 mcg/mL in D_5W or normal saline

Monitoring Parameters Respiratory rate, heart rate, blood pressure

Dosage Forms INJ, neonatal solution: 0.02 mg/mL (2 mL). **INJ, solution:** 0.4 mg/mL (1 mL, 2 mL, 10 mL); 1 mg/mL (2 mL, 10 mL)

- **Naloxone and Buprenorphine** *see* Buprenorphine and Naloxone *on page 189*
- **Naloxone Hydrochloride** *see* Naloxone *on page 879*
- **Naloxone Hydrochloride and Pentazocine Hydrochloride** *see* Pentazocine *on page 977*
- **Naloxone Hydrochloride Dihydrate and Buprenorphine Hydrochloride** *see* Buprenorphine and Naloxone *on page 189*

Naltrexone (nal TREKS one)

U.S. Brand Names ReVia®

Synonyms Naltrexone Hydrochloride

Therapeutic Category Antidote, Narcotic Agonist; Narcotic Antagonist

Use Treatment of ethanol dependence; blockade of the effects of exogenously administered opioids

Pregnancy Risk Factor C

Contraindications Hypersensitivity to naltrexone or any component of the formulation; narcotic dependence or current use of opioid analgesics; acute opioid withdrawal; failure to pass Narcan® challenge or positive urine screen for opioids; acute hepatitis; liver failure

Warnings/Precautions Dose-related hepatocellular injury is possible; the margin of separation between the apparent safe and hepatotoxic doses appear to be only fivefold or less

Common Adverse Reactions

>10%:

  Central nervous system: Insomnia, nervousness, headache, low energy

  Gastrointestinal: Abdominal cramping, nausea, vomiting

  Neuromuscular & skeletal: Arthralgia

1% to 10%:

  Central nervous system: Increased energy, feeling down, irritability, dizziness, anxiety, somnolence

  Dermatologic: Rash

  Endocrine & metabolic: Polydipsia

  Gastrointestinal: Diarrhea, constipation

  Genitourinary: Delayed ejaculation, impotence

Drug Interactions

  Increased Effect/Toxicity: Lethargy and somnolence have been reported with the combination of naltrexone and thioridazine.

  Decreased Effect: Naltrexone decreases effects of opioid-containing products.

Mechanism of Action Naltrexone (a pure opioid antagonist) is a cyclopropyl derivative of oxymorphone similar in structure to naloxone and nalorphine (a morphine derivative); it acts as a competitive antagonist at opioid receptor sites

Pharmacodynamics/Kinetics

Duration: 50 mg: 24 hours; 100 mg: 48 hours; 150 mg: 72 hours

Absorption: Almost complete

Distribution: V_d: 19 L/kg; widely throughout the body but considerable interindividual variation exists

Protein binding: 21%

Metabolism: Extensive first-pass effect to 6-β-naltrexol

Half-life elimination: 4 hours; 6-β-naltrexol: 13 hours

Time to peak, serum: ~60 minutes

Excretion: Primarily urine (as metabolites and unchanged drug)

Dosage Do not give until patient is opioid-free for 7-10 days as determined by urine analysis

Adults: Oral: 25 mg; if no withdrawal signs within 1 hour give another 25 mg; maintenance regimen is flexible, variable and individualized (50 mg/day to 100-150 mg 3 times/week for 12 weeks); up to 800 mg/day has been tolerated in adults without an adverse effect

  Dosing cautions in renal/hepatic impairment: Caution in patients with renal and hepatic impairment. An increase in naltrexone AUC of approximately five- and 10-fold in patients with compensated or decompensated liver cirrhosis respectively, compared with normal liver function has been reported.

Administration If there is any question of occult opioid dependence, perform a naloxone challenge test; do not attempt treatment until naloxone challenge is negative

Naltrexone is administered orally; to minimize adverse gastrointestinal effects, administer with food or antacids or after meals; advise patient not to self-administer opiates while receiving naltrexone therapy

Monitoring Parameters For narcotic withdrawal; liver function tests

Patient Information Will cause narcotic withdrawal; serious overdose can occur after attempts to overcome the blocking effect of naltrexone

Dosage Forms TAB: 50 mg

♦ **Naltrexone Hydrochloride** *see* Naltrexone *on page 880*

♦ **Namenda**™ *see* Memantine *on page 788*

Nandrolone (NAN droe lone)

U.S. Brand Names Deca-Durabolin® [DSC]

Synonyms Nandrolone Decanoate; Nandrolone Phenpropionate

Therapeutic Category Anabolic Steroid; Androgen

Use Control of metastatic breast cancer; management of anemia of renal insufficiency

Restrictions C-III

Pregnancy Risk Factor X

Contraindications Hypersensitivity to nandrolone or any component of the formulation; carcinoma of breast or prostate; nephrosis; pregnancy; not for use in infants

Warnings/Precautions Monitor diabetic patients carefully; anabolic steroids may cause peliosis hepatis, liver cell tumors, and blood lipid changes with increased risk of arteriosclerosis; use with caution in elderly patients, they may be at greater risk for prostatic hyperplasia; use with caution in patients with cardiac, renal, or hepatic disease or epilepsy

Common Adverse Reactions
Male:
Postpubertal:
>10%:
  Dermatologic: Acne
  Endocrine & metabolic: Gynecomastia
  Genitourinary: Bladder irritability, priapism
1% to 10%:
  Central nervous system: Insomnia, chills
  Endocrine & metabolic: Decreased libido, hepatic dysfunction
  Gastrointestinal: Nausea, diarrhea
  Genitourinary: Prostatic hyperplasia (elderly)
  Hematologic: Iron deficiency anemia, suppression of clotting factors
Prepubertal:
>10%:
  Dermatologic: Acne
  Endocrine & metabolic: Virilism
1% to 10%:
  Central nervous system: Chills, insomnia
  Dermatologic: Hyperpigmentation
  Gastrointestinal: Diarrhea, nausea
  Hematologic: Iron deficiency anemia, suppression of clotting
Female:
>10%: Endocrine & metabolic: Virilism
1% to 10%:
  Central nervous system: Chills, insomnia
  Endocrine & metabolic: Hypercalcemia
  Gastrointestinal: Nausea, diarrhea
  Hematologic: Iron deficiency anemia, suppression of clotting factors
  Hepatic: Hepatic dysfunction

Drug Interactions
Increased Effect/Toxicity: Nandrolone may increase the effect of oral anticoagulants, insulin, oral hypoglycemic agents, adrenal steroids, or ACTH when taken together.

Mechanism of Action Promotes tissue-building processes, increases production of erythropoietin, causes protein anabolism; increases hemoglobin and red blood cell volume

Pharmacodynamics/Kinetics
Onset of action: 3-6 months
Duration: Up to 30 days
Absorption: I.M.: 77%
Metabolism: Hepatic
Excretion: Urine

Dosage Deep I.M. (into gluteal muscle):
Children 2-13 years (decanoate): 25-50 mg every 3-4 weeks
Adults:
  Male:
    Breast cancer (phenpropionate): 50-100 mg/week
    Anemia of renal insufficiency (decanoate): 100-200 mg/week
  Female: 50-100 mg/week
    Breast cancer (phenpropionate): 50-100 mg/week
    Anemia of renal insufficiency (decanoate): 50-100 mg/week

Administration Inject deeply I.M., preferably into the gluteal muscle

Patient Information Virilization may occur in female patients; report menstrual irregularities; male patients report persistent penile erections; all patients should report persistent GI distress, diarrhea, dark urine, pale stools, yellow coloring of skin or sclera; diabetic patients should monitor glucose closely

Dosage Forms INJ, solution: 100 mg/mL (2 mL); 200 mg/mL (1 mL)

♦ **Nandrolone Decanoate** *see* Nandrolone *on page 880*
♦ **Nandrolone Phenpropionate** *see* Nandrolone *on page 880*

Naphazoline (naf AZ oh leen)
U.S. Brand Names AK-Con™; Albalon®; Allersol®; Clear Eyes® [OTC]; Clear Eyes® ACR [OTC]; Naphcon® [OTC]; Privine® [OTC]; VasoClear® [OTC]

Synonyms Naphazoline Hydrochloride

Therapeutic Category Adrenergic Agonist Agent, Ophthalmic; Decongestant, Nasal; Nasal Agent, Vasoconstrictor; Ophthalmic Agent, Vasoconstrictor

Use Topical ocular vasoconstrictor; will temporarily relieve congestion, itching, and minor irritation, and to control hyperemia in patients with superficial corneal vascularity; treatment of nasal congestion adjunct for sinusitis

Pregnancy Risk Factor C

Contraindications Hypersensitivity to naphazoline or any component of the formulation; narrow-angle glaucoma, prior to peripheral iridectomy (in patients susceptible to angle block)

Warnings/Precautions Rebound congestion may occur with extended use; use with caution in the presence of hypertension, diabetes, hyperthyroidism, heart disease, coronary artery disease, cerebral arteriosclerosis, or long-standing bronchial asthma

Common Adverse Reactions Frequency not defined.
Cardiovascular: Systemic cardiovascular stimulation
(Continued)

Naphazoline *(Continued)*

Central nervous system: Dizziness, headache, nervousness
Gastrointestinal: Nausea
Local: Transient stinging, nasal mucosa irritation, dryness, rebound congestion
Ocular: Mydriasis, increased intraocular pressure, blurring of vision
Respiratory: Sneezing

Mechanism of Action Stimulates alpha-adrenergic receptors in the arterioles of the conjunctiva and the nasal mucosa to produce vasoconstriction

Pharmacodynamics/Kinetics
Onset of action: Decongestant: Topical: ~10 minutes
Duration: 2-6 hours

Dosage
Nasal:
Children:
<6 years: Intranasal: Not recommended (especially infants) due to CNS depression
6-12 years: 1 spray of 0.05% into each nostril every 6 hours if necessary; therapy should not exceed 3-5 days
Children >12 years and Adults: 0.05%, instill 1-2 drops or sprays every 6 hours if needed; therapy should not exceed 3-5 days
Ophthalmic:
Children <6 years: Not recommended for use due to CNS depression (especially in infants)
Children >6 years and Adults: Instill 1-2 drops into conjunctival sac of affected eye(s) every 3-4 hours; therapy generally should not exceed 3-4 days

Patient Information Do not use discolored solutions; discontinue eye drops if visual changes or ocular pain occur; report insomnia, tremor, or irregular heartbeat; stinging, burning, or drying of the nasal mucosa may occur; do not use beyond 72 hours

Dosage Forms DROPS, intranasal (Privine®): 0.05% (25 mL). **SOLN, ophthalmic:** 0.1% (15 mL); (AK-Con™, Albalon®, Allersol®): 0.1% (15 mL); (Clear Eyes®): 0.012% (6 mL, 15 mL, 30 mL); (Clear Eyes® ACR): 0.012% (15 mL, 30 mL); (Naphcon®): 0.012% (15 mL); (VasoClear®): 0.02% (15 mL). **SPRAY, intranasal** (Privine®): 0.05% (20 mL, 480 mL)

Naphazoline and Antazoline *(naf AZ oh leen & an TAZ oh leen)*

U.S. Brand Names Vasocon-A® [OTC]
Synonyms Antazoline and Naphazoline
Therapeutic Category Ophthalmic Agent, Vasoconstrictor
Use Topical ocular congestion, irritation and itching
Pregnancy Risk Factor C
Dosage Ophthalmic: 1-2 drops every 3-4 hours
Dosage Forms SOLN, ophthalmic: Naphazoline 0.05% and antazoline 0.5% (15 mL)

Naphazoline and Pheniramine *(naf AZ oh leen & fen NIR a meen)*

U.S. Brand Names Naphcon-A® [OTC]; Opcon-A® [OTC]; Visine-A™ [OTC]
Synonyms Pheniramine and Naphazoline
Therapeutic Category Ophthalmic Agent, Vasoconstrictor
Use Treatment of ocular congestion, irritation, and itching
Pregnancy Risk Factor C
Dosage Ophthalmic: Children ≥6 years and Adults: 1-2 drops up to 4 times/day
Dosage Forms SOLN, ophthalmic: Naphazoline 0.025% and pheniramine 0.3% (15 mL)

♦ **Naphazoline Hydrochloride** *see Naphazoline on page 881*
♦ **Naphcon®** [OTC] *see Naphazoline on page 881*
♦ **Naphcon-A®** [OTC] *see Naphazoline and Pheniramine on page 882*
♦ **Naprelan®** *see Naproxen on page 882*
♦ **Naprosyn®** *see Naproxen on page 882*

Naproxen *(na PROKS en)*

Related Information
Nonsteroidal Anti-Inflammatory Agents Comparison *on page 1401*
U.S. Brand Names Aleve® [OTC]; Anaprox®; Anaprox® DS; EC-Naprosyn®; Naprelan®; Naprosyn®; Pamprin® Maximum Strength All Day Relief [OTC]
Synonyms Naproxen Sodium
Therapeutic Category Analgesic, Nonsteroidal Anti-inflammatory Drug; Anti-inflammatory Agent; Antimigraine Agent, Prophylaxis; Antipyretic; Nonsteroidal Anti-inflammatory Drug (NSAID), Oral
Use Management of inflammatory disease and rheumatoid disorders (including juvenile rheumatoid arthritis); acute gout; mild to moderate pain; dysmenorrhea; fever, migraine headache
Pregnancy Risk Factor B/D (3rd trimester)
Contraindications Hypersensitivity to naproxen, aspirin, other NSAIDs, or any component of the formulation; patients with "aspirin triad" (bronchial asthma, aspirin intolerance, rhinitis); pregnancy (3rd trimester)
Warnings/Precautions Use with caution in patients with GI disease (bleeding or ulcers), cardiovascular disease (CHF, hypertension), dehydration, renal or hepatic impairment, and patients receiving anticoagulants; perform ophthalmologic evaluation for those who develop eye complaints during therapy (blurred vision, diminished vision, changes in color vision, retinal changes); NSAIDs may mask signs/symptoms of infections; photosensitivity reported.

Consuming ≥3 alcoholic beverages per day may increase risk of GI bleeding. Elderly are at especially high-risk for adverse effects (including gastrointestinal and CNS adverse effects) from NSAIDs. As many as 60% of elderly can develop peptic ulceration and/or hemorrhage asymptomatically. Use lowest effective dose for shortest period possible. Use of NSAIDs can compromise existing renal function especially when Cl_{cr} is <30 mL/minute. Withhold for at least 4-6 half-lives prior to surgical or dental procedures.

OTC labeling: When used for self-medication, patients should be instructed to contact health-care provider if used for fever lasting >3 days or pain lasting >10 days.

Common Adverse Reactions

1% to 10%:

Central nervous system: Headache (11%), nervousness, malaise (<3%), somnolence (3% to 9%)

Dermatologic: Itching, pruritus, rash, ecchymosis (3% to 9%)

Endocrine & metabolic: Fluid retention (3% to 9%)

Gastrointestinal: Abdominal discomfort, nausea (3% to 9%), heartburn, constipation (3% to 9%), GI bleeding, ulcers, perforation, indigestion, diarrhea (<3%), abdominal distress/cramps/pain (3% to 9%), dyspepsia (<3%), stomatitis (<3%), heartburn (<3%)

Hematologic: Hemolysis (3% to 9%), ecchymosis (3% to 9%)

Otic: Tinnitus (3% to 9%)

Respiratory: Dyspnea (3% to 9%)

Drug Interactions

Cytochrome P450 Effect: Substrate (minor) of CYP1A2, 2C8/9

Increased Effect/Toxicity: Naproxen could displace other highly protein-bound drugs, increasing the effect of oral anticoagulants, hydantoins, salicylates, sulfonamides, and first-generation sulfonylureas. Naproxen and warfarin may cause a slight increase in free warfarin. Naproxen and probenecid may cause increased levels of naproxen. Naproxen and methotrexate may significantly increase and prolong blood methotrexate concentration, which may be severe or fatal. May increase lithium or cyclosporine levels. Corticosteroids may increase risk of GI ulceration.

Decreased Effect: NSAIDs may decrease the effect of some antihypertensive agents, including ACE inhibitors, angiotensin receptor antagonists, and hydralazine. The efficacy of diuretics (loop and/or thiazide) may be decreased.

Mechanism of Action Inhibits prostaglandin synthesis by decreasing the activity of the enzyme, cyclooxygenase, which results in decreased formation of prostaglandin precursors

Pharmacodynamics/Kinetics

Onset of action: Analgesic: 1 hour; Anti-inflammatory: ~2 weeks

Peak effect: Anti-inflammatory: 2-4 weeks

Duration: Analgesic: ≤7 hours; Anti-inflammatory: ≤12 hours

Absorption: Almost 100%

Protein binding: >90%; increased free fraction in elderly

Half-life elimination: Normal renal function: 12-15 hours; End-stage renal disease: Unchanged

Time to peak, serum: 1-2 hours

Excretion: Urine (95%)

Dosage Oral:

Children >2 years:

Fever: 2.5-10 mg/kg/dose; maximum: 10 mg/kg/day

Juvenile arthritis: 10 mg/kg/day in 2 divided doses

Adults:

Rheumatoid arthritis, osteoarthritis, and ankylosing spondylitis: 500-1000 mg/day in 2 divided doses; may increase to 1.5 g/day of naproxen base for limited time period

Mild to moderate pain or dysmenorrhea: Initial: 500 mg, then 250 mg every 6-8 hours; maximum: 1250 mg/day naproxen base

OTC labeling: Pain/fever:

Children ≥12 years and Adults ≤65 years: 200 mg naproxen base every 8-12 hours; if needed, may take 400 mg naproxen base for the initial dose; maximum: 600 mg naproxen base/24 hours

Adults >65 years: 200 mg naproxen base every 12 hours

Dosing adjustment in hepatic impairment: Reduce dose to 50%

Administration Administer with food, milk, or antacids to decrease GI adverse effects

Monitoring Parameters Occult blood loss, periodic liver function test, CBC, BUN, serum creatinine

Patient Information Serious gastrointestinal bleeding can occur as well as ulceration and perforation. Pain may or may not be present. Avoid aspirin and aspirin-containing products while taking this medication. If gastric upset occurs, take with food, milk, or antacid. If gastric adverse effects persist, contact prescriber. May cause drowsiness, dizziness, blurred vision, and confusion. Use caution when performing tasks which require alertness (eg, driving). Do not take for more than 3 days for fever or 10 days for pain without prescriber's advice.

Dosage Forms CAPLET (Aleve®, Pamprin® Maximum Strength All Day Relief): 220 mg. **GELCAP** (Aleve®): 220 mg. **SUSP, oral** (Naprosyn®): 125 mg/5 mL (480 mL). **TAB:** 220 mg, 275 mg, 550 mg; (Aleve®): 220 mg; (Anaprox®): 275 mg; (Anaprox® DS): 550 mg; (Naprosyn®): 250 mg, 375 mg, 500 mg. **TAB, controlled release:** 550 mg; (Naprelan®): 421.5 mg, 550 mg. **TAB, delayed release** (EC-Naprosyn®): 375 mg, 500 mg

- **Naproxen Sodium** *see* Naproxen *on page 882*
- **Naqua**® *see* Trichlormethiazide *on page 1265*

Naratriptan (NAR a trip tan)
Related Information
Antimigraine Drugs Comparison *on page 1363*
U.S. Brand Names Amerge®
Synonyms Naratriptan Hydrochloride
Therapeutic Category Antimigraine Agent, Serotonin 5-HT$_{1D}$ Agonist; Serotonin 5-HT$_4$ Receptor Agonist
Use Treatment of acute migraine headache with or without aura
Pregnancy Risk Factor C
Contraindications Hypersensitivity to naratriptan or any component of the formulation; cerebrovascular, peripheral vascular disease (ischemic bowel disease), ischemic heart disease (angina pectoris, history of myocardial infarction, or proven silent ischemia); or in patients with symptoms consistent with ischemic heart disease, coronary artery vasospasm, or Prinzmetal's angina; uncontrolled hypertension or patients who have received within 24 hours another 5-HT agonist (sumatriptan, zolmitriptan) or ergotamine-containing product; patients with known risk factors associated with coronary artery disease; patients with severe hepatic or renal disease (Cl$_{cr}$ <15 mL/minute); do not administer naratriptan to patients with hemiplegic or basilar migraine
Warnings/Precautions Use only if there is a clear diagnosis of migraine. May cause vasospastic reactions resulting in colonic, peripheral, or coronary ischemia. Monitor closely, especially after the first dose. Patients who are at risk of CAD (based on risk factor evaluation) but have had a satisfactory cardiovascular evaluation may receive naratriptan, but extreme caution should be used; administration of the first dose in a setting with medical staff and equipment (ie, in a physician's office) is recommended, and ECG monitoring after the first dose should be considered. Periodically re-evaluate risk factors for CAD in patients receiving long-term intermittent treatment. Blood pressure may increase with the administration of naratriptan. If the patient does not respond to the first dose, re-evaluate the diagnosis of migraine before trying a second dose.
Common Adverse Reactions 1% to 10%:
Central nervous system: Dizziness, drowsiness, malaise/fatigue
Gastrointestinal: Nausea, vomiting
Neuromuscular & skeletal: Paresthesias
Miscellaneous: Pain or pressure in throat or neck
Drug Interactions
Increased Effect/Toxicity: Ergot-containing drugs (dihydroergotamine or methysergide) may cause vasospastic reactions when taken with naratriptan. Avoid concomitant use with ergots; separate dose of naratriptan and ergots by at least 24 hours. Oral contraceptives taken with naratriptan reduced the clearance of naratriptan ~30% which may contribute to adverse effects. Selective serotonin reuptake inhibitors (SSRIs) (eg, fluoxetine, fluvoxamine, paroxetine, sertraline) may cause lack of coordination, hyper-reflexia, or weakness and should be avoided when taking naratriptan.
Decreased Effect: Smoking increases the clearance of naratriptan.
Mechanism of Action The therapeutic effect for migraine is due to serotonin agonist activity
Pharmacodynamics/Kinetics
Onset of action: 30 minutes
Absorption: Well absorbed
Protein binding, plasma: 28% to 31%
Metabolism: Hepatic via CYP
Bioavailability: 70%
Time to peak: 2-3 hours
Excretion: Urine
Dosage
Adults: Oral: 1-2.5 mg at the onset of headache; it is recommended to use the lowest possible dose to minimize adverse effects. If headache returns or does not fully resolve, the dose may be repeated after 4 hours; do not exceed 5 mg in 24 hours.
Elderly: Not recommended for use in the elderly
Dosing in renal impairment:
Cl$_{cr}$: 18-39 mL/minute: Initial: 1 mg; do not exceed 2.5 mg in 24 hours
Cl$_{cr}$: <15 mL/minute: Do not use
Dosing in hepatic impairment: Contraindicated in patients with severe liver failure; maximum dose: 2.5 mg in 24 hours for patients with mild or moderate liver failure; recommended starting dose: 1 mg
Patient Information Do not crush or chew tablet; swallow whole with water. This drug is to be used to reduce migraine, not to prevent or reduce the number of attacks. If headache returns or is not fully resolved, the dose may be repeated after 4 hours. If no relief with first dose, do not take a second dose without consulting prescriber. Do not exceed 5 mg in 24 hours. Do not take within 24 hours of any other migraine medication without first consulting prescriber. May experience some dizziness, fatigue, or drowsiness; use caution when driving or engaging in tasks that require alertness. Frequent mouth care and sucking on lozenges may relieve dry mouth. Report immediately any chest pain, heart throbbing, tightness in throat, skin rash or hives, hallucinations, anxiety, or panic.
Dosage Forms TAB: 1 mg, 2.5 mg

♦ **Naratriptan Hydrochloride** *see* Naratriptan *on page 884*
♦ **Narcan®** *see* Naloxone *on page 879*
♦ **Narcotic Agonists Comparison** *see page 1395*

- **Nardil®** *see* Phenelzine *on page 987*
- **Naropin®** *see* Ropivacaine *on page 1114*
- **Nasacort® [DSC]** *see* Triamcinolone *on page 1261*
- **Nasacort® AQ** *see* Triamcinolone *on page 1261*
- **NaSal™ [OTC]** *see* Sodium Chloride *on page 1146*
- **Nasalcrom® [OTC]** *see* Cromolyn *on page 316*
- **Nasalide®** *see* Flunisolide *on page 533*
- **Nasal Moist® [OTC]** *see* Sodium Chloride *on page 1146*
- **Nasarel®** *see* Flunsolide *on page 533*
- **Nascobal®** *see* Cyanocobalamin *on page 318*
- **Nasonex®** *see* Mometasone Furoate *on page 857*
- **Natacyn®** *see* Natamycin *on page 885*

Natamycin (na ta MYE sin)
U.S. Brand Names Natacyn®
Synonyms Pimaricin
Therapeutic Category Antifungal Agent, Ophthalmic
Use Treatment of blepharitis, conjunctivitis, and keratitis caused by susceptible fungi (*Aspergillus*, *Candida*), *Cephalosporium*, *Curvularia*, *Fusarium*, *Penicillium*, *Microsporum*, *Epidermophyton*, *Blastomyces dermatitidis*, *Coccidioides immitis*, *Cryptococcus neoformans*, *Histoplasma capsulatum*, *Sporothrix schenckii*, and *Trichomonas vaginalis*
Pregnancy Risk Factor C
Contraindications Hypersensitivity to natamycin or any component of the formulation
Warnings/Precautions Failure to improve (keratitis) after 7-10 days of administration suggests infection caused by a microorganism not susceptible to natamycin; inadequate as a single agent in fungal endophthalmitis
Common Adverse Reactions Frequency not defined: Ocular: Blurred vision, photophobia, eye pain, eye irritation not present before therapy
Drug Interactions
Increased Effect/Toxicity: Topical corticosteroids (concomitant use contraindicated).
Mechanism of Action Increases cell membrane permeability in susceptible fungi
Pharmacodynamics/Kinetics
Absorption: Ophthalmic: Systemic, <2%
Distribution: Adheres to cornea, retained in conjunctival fornices
Dosage Adults: Ophthalmic: Instill 1 drop in conjunctival sac every 1-2 hours, after 3-4 days reduce to one drop 6-8 times/day; usual course of therapy is 2-3 weeks.
Patient Information Shake well before using, do not touch dropper to eye; notify prescriber if condition worsens or does not improve after 3-4 days
Dosage Forms SUSP, ophthalmic: 5% (15 mL)

Nateglinide (na te GLYE nide)
Related Information
Hypoglycemic Drugs & Thiazolidinedione Information *on page 1378*
U.S. Brand Names Starlix®
Therapeutic Category Antidiabetic Agent, Secretogue; Meglitinide
Use Management of type 2 diabetes mellitus (noninsulin dependent, NIDDM) as monotherapy when hyperglycemia cannot be managed by diet and exercise alone; in combination with metformin or a thiazolidinedione to lower blood glucose in patients whose hyperglycemia cannot be controlled by exercise, diet, or a single agent alone
Pregnancy Risk Factor C
Contraindications Hypersensitivity to nateglinide or any component of the formulation; diabetic ketoacidosis, with or without coma (treat with insulin); type 1 diabetes mellitus (insulin dependent, IDDM)
Warnings/Precautions Use with caution in patients with moderate to severe hepatic impairment. All oral hypoglycemic agents are capable of producing hypoglycemia. Proper patient selection, dosage, and instructions to the patients are important to avoid hypoglycemic episodes. It may be necessary to discontinue nateglinide and administer insulin if the patient is exposed to stress (ie, fever, trauma, infection, surgery). Indicated for adjunctive therapy with metformin; not to be used as a substitute for metformin monotherapy. Combination treatment with sulfonylureas is not recommended (no additional benefit). Patients not adequately controlled on oral agents which stimulate insulin release (eg, glyburide) should not be switched to nateglinide or have nateglinide added to therapy. Safety and efficacy in pediatric patients have not been established.
Common Adverse Reactions As reported with nateglinide monotherapy:
1% to 10%:
Central nervous system: Dizziness (4%)
Endocrine & metabolic: Hypoglycemia (2%), increased uric acid
Gastrointestinal: Weight gain
Neuromuscular & skeletal: Arthropathy (3%)
Respiratory: Upper respiratory infection (10%)
Miscellaneous: Flu-like symptoms (4%)
Drug Interactions
Cytochrome P450 Effect: Substrate (major) of CYP2C8/9, 3A4; **Inhibits** CYP2C8/9 (weak)
(Continued)

Nateglinide *(Continued)*

Increased Effect/Toxicity: CYP2C8/9 inhibitors may increase the levels/effects of nateglinide; example inhibitors include delavirdine, fluconazole, gemfibrozil, ketoconazole, nicardipine, NSAIDs, pioglitazone, and sulfonamides. Possible increased hypoglycemic effect may be seen with salicylates, MAO inhibitors, and nonselective beta-adrenergic blocking agents; monitor glucose closely when agents are initiated, modified, or discontinued.

Decreased Effect: CYP2C8/9 inducers may decrease the levels/effects of nateglinide; example inducers include carbamazepine, phenobarbital, phenytoin, rifampin, rifapentine, and secobarbital. Possible decreased hypoglycemic effect may be seen with thiazides, corticosteroids, thyroid products, and sympathomimetic drugs; monitor glucose closely when agents are initiated, modified, or discontinued.

Mechanism of Action A phenylalanine derivative, nonsulfonylurea hypoglycemic agent used in the management of type 2 diabetes mellitus (noninsulin dependent, NIDDM); stimulates insulin release from the pancreatic beta cells to reduce postprandial hyperglycemia; amount of insulin release is dependent upon existing glucose levels

Pharmacodynamics/Kinetics

Onset of action: Insulin secretion: ~20 minutes

Peak effect: 1 hour

Duration: 4 hours

Absorption: Rapid

Distribution: 10 L

Protein binding: 98%, primarily to albumin

Metabolism: Hepatic via hydroxylation followed by glucuronide conjugation via CYP2C9 (70%) and CYP3A4 (30%) to metabolites

Bioavailability: 73%

Half-life elimination: 1.5 hours

Time to peak: ≤1 hour

Excretion: Urine (83%, 16% as unchanged drug); feces (10%)

Dosage

Children: Safety and efficacy have not been established

Adults: Management of type 2 diabetes mellitus: Oral: Initial and maintenance dose: 120 mg 3 times/day, 1-30 minutes before meals; may be given alone or in combination with metformin or a thiazolidinedione; patients close to Hb A_{1c} goal may be started at 60 mg 3 times/day

Elderly: No changes in safety and efficacy were seen in patients ≥65 years; however, some elderly patients may show increased sensitivity to dosing

Dosage adjustment in renal impairment: No specific dosage adjustment is recommended for patients with mild to severe renal disease; patients on dialysis showed reduced medication exposure and plasma protein binding

Dosage adjustment in hepatic impairment: Increased serum levels seen with mild hepatic insufficiency; no dosage adjustment is needed. Has not been studied in patients with moderate to severe liver disease; use with caution.

Monitoring Parameters Glucose and Hb A_{1c} levels, weight, lipid profile

Reference Range Target range: Adults:

Fasting blood glucose: <110 mg/dL

Glycosylated hemoglobin: <6%

Patient Information Take this medication exactly as directed, 3 times/day, 1-30 minutes prior to a meal. If you skip a meal, skip the dose for that meal. Do not change dosage or discontinue without first consulting prescriber. It is important to follow dietary and lifestyle recommendations of prescriber. You will be instructed in signs of hypo-/hyperglycemia by prescriber or diabetic educator; be alert for adverse hypoglycemia (tachycardia, profuse perspiration, tingling of lips and tongue, seizures, or change in sensorium) and follow prescriber's instructions for intervention. The risk of hypoglycemia may be increased by strenuous physical exercise, alcohol ingestion, or insufficient calorie intake. You may experience dizziness or joint pain; if these do not diminish, notify prescriber.

Dosage Forms TAB: 60 mg, 120 mg

◆ **Natrecor®** *see* Nesiritide *on page 894*

◆ **Natriuretic Peptide** *see* Nesiritide *on page 894*

◆ **Natural Lung Surfactant** *see* Beractant *on page 158*

◆ **Nature-Throid® NT** *see* Thyroid *on page 1222*

◆ **Navane®** *see* Thiothixene *on page 1221*

◆ **Navelbine®** *see* Vinorelbine *on page 1307*

◆ **Na-Zone® [OTC]** *see* Sodium Chloride *on page 1146*

◆ *n*-Docosanol *see* Docosanol *on page 397*

◆ **Nebcin®** *see* Tobramycin *on page 1235*

◆ **NebuPent®** *see* Pentamidine *on page 976*

◆ **Necon® 0.5/35** *see* Ethinyl Estradiol and Norethindrone *on page 487*

◆ **Necon® 1/35** *see* Ethinyl Estradiol and Norethindrone *on page 487*

◆ **Necon® 1/50** *see* Mestranol and Norethindrone *on page 801*

◆ **Necon® 7/7/7** *see* Ethinyl Estradiol and Norethindrone *on page 487*

◆ **Necon® 10/11** *see* Ethinyl Estradiol and Norethindrone *on page 487*

Nedocromil (ne doe KROE mil)

U.S. Brand Names Alocril™; Tilade®

Synonyms Nedocromil Sodium

Therapeutic Category Antiallergic, Inhalation; Antiallergic, Ophthalmic

Use

Aerosol: Maintenance therapy in patients with mild to moderate bronchial asthma

Ophthalmic: Treatment of itching associated with allergic conjunctivitis

Pregnancy Risk Factor B

Contraindications Hypersensitivity to nedocromil or any component of the formulation

Warnings/Precautions

Aerosol: Safety and efficacy in children <6 years of age have not been established; if systemic or inhaled steroid therapy is at all reduced, monitor patients carefully; nedocromil is **not** a bronchodilator and, therefore, should not be used for reversal of acute bronchospasm

Ophthalmic solution: Users of contact lenses should not wear them during periods of symptomatic allergic conjunctivitis

Common Adverse Reactions

Inhalation aerosol:

>10%: Gastrointestinal: Unpleasant taste

1% to 10%:

Cardiovascular: Chest pain

Central nervous system: Dizziness, dysphonia, headache, fatigue

Dermatologic: Rash

Gastrointestinal: Nausea, vomiting, dyspepsia, diarrhea, abdominal pain, xerostomia, unpleasant taste

Hepatic: Increased ALT

Neuromuscular & skeletal: Arthritis, tremor

Respiratory: Cough, pharyngitis, rhinitis, bronchitis, upper respiratory infection, bronchospasm, increased sputum production

Ophthalmic solution:

>10%:

Central nervous system: Headache (40%)

Gastrointestinal: Unpleasant taste

Ocular: Burning, irritation, stinging

Respiratory: Nasal congestion

1% to 10%:

Ocular: Conjunctivitis, eye redness, photophobia

Respiratory: Asthma, rhinitis

Mechanism of Action Inhibits the activation of and mediator release from a variety of inflammatory cell types associated with asthma including eosinophils, neutrophils, macrophages, mast cells, monocytes, and platelets; it inhibits the release of histamine, leukotrienes, and slow-reacting substance of anaphylaxis; it inhibits the development of early and late bronchoconstriction responses to inhaled antigen

Pharmacodynamics/Kinetics

Duration: Therapeutic effect: 2 hours

Protein binding, plasma: 89%

Bioavailability: 7% to 9%

Half-life elimination: 1.5-2 hours

Excretion: Urine (as unchanged drug)

Dosage

Inhalation: Children >6 years and Adults: 2 inhalations 4 times/day; may reduce dosage to 2-3 times/day once desired clinical response to initial dose is observed

Ophthalmic: 1-2 drops in each eye twice daily

Dosage Forms AERO, inhalation (Tilgade®): 1.75 mg/activation (16.2 g). **SOLN, ophthalmic** (Alocril™): 2% (5 mL)

♦ **Nedocromil Sodium** see Nedocromil on page 887

Nefazodone (nef AY zoe done)

Related Information

Antidepressant Agents Comparison on page 1359

U.S. Brand Names Serzone®

Synonyms Nefazodone Hydrochloride

Therapeutic Category Antidepressant, Serotonin Reuptake Inhibitor/Antagonist (SRIA)

Use Treatment of depression

Unlabeled/Investigational Use Post-traumatic stress disorder

Pregnancy Risk Factor C

Contraindications Hypersensitivity to nefazodone, related compounds (phenylpiperazines), or any component of the formulation; liver injury due to previous nefazodone treatment, active liver disease, or elevated serum transaminases; concurrent use or use of MAO inhibitors within previous 14 days; use in a patient during the acute recovery phase of MI; concurrent use with astemizole, carbamazepine, cisapride, or pimozide; concurrent therapy with triazolam or alprazolam is generally contraindicated (dosage must be reduced by 75% for triazolam and 50% for alprazolam; such reductions may not be possible with available dosage forms).

Warnings/Precautions Cases of life-threatening hepatic failure have been reported; discontinue if clinical signs or symptoms suggest liver failure. Safety and efficacy in children <18 (Continued)

Nefazodone *(Continued)*

years of age have not been established. May cause sedation, resulting in impaired performance of tasks requiring alertness (eg, operating machinery or driving). Sedative effects may be additive with other CNS depressants. Does not potentiate ethanol but use is not advised. The degree of sedation is low relative to other antidepressants. May worsen psychosis in some patients or precipitate a shift to mania or hypomania in patients with bipolar disease. May increase the risks associated with electroconvulsive therapy. This agent should be discontinued, when possible, prior to elective surgery. Therapy should not be abruptly discontinued in patients receiving high doses for prolonged periods. Rare reports of priapism have occurred. The incidence of sexual dysfunction with nefazodone is generally lower than with SSRIs.

Use with caution in patients at risk of hypotension or in patients where transient hypotensive episodes would be poorly tolerated (cardiovascular disease or cerebrovascular disease). The risk of postural hypotension is low relative to other antidepressants. Use with caution in patients with urinary retention, benign prostatic hypertrophy, narrow-angle glaucoma, xerostomia, visual problems, constipation, or history of bowel obstruction (due to anticholinergic effects). The degree of anticholinergic blockade produced by this agent is very low relative to other cyclic antidepressants.

The possibility of a suicide attempt is inherent in major depression and may persist until remission occurs. Use caution in high-risk patients during initiation of therapy. Prescriptions should be written for the smallest quantity consistent with good patient care. Use caution in patients with a previous seizure disorder or condition predisposing to seizures such as brain damage, alcoholism, or concurrent therapy with other drugs which lower the seizure threshold. Use with caution in patients with hepatic or renal dysfunction and in elderly patients. Use with caution in patients with a history of cardiovascular disease (including previous MI, stroke, tachycardia, or conduction abnormalities). However, the risk of conduction abnormalities with this agent is very low relative to other antidepressants.

Common Adverse Reactions

>10%:

Central nervous system: Headache, drowsiness, insomnia, agitation, dizziness

Gastrointestinal: Xerostomia, nausea, constipation

Neuromuscular & skeletal: Weakness

1% to 10%:

Cardiovascular: Bradycardia, hypotension, peripheral edema, postural hypotension, vasodilation

Central nervous system: Chills, fever, incoordination, lightheadedness, confusion, memory impairment, abnormal dreams, decreased concentration, ataxia, psychomotor retardation, tremor

Dermatologic: Pruritus, rash

Endocrine & metabolic: Breast pain, impotence, libido decreased

Gastrointestinal: Gastroenteritis, vomiting, dyspepsia, diarrhea, increased appetite, thirst, taste perversion

Genitourinary: Urinary frequency, urinary retention

Hematologic: Hematocrit decreased

Neuromuscular & skeletal: Arthralgia, hypertonia, paresthesia, neck rigidity, tremor

Ocular: Blurred vision (9%), abnormal vision (7%), eye pain, visual field defect

Otic: Tinnitus

Respiratory: Bronchitis, cough, dyspnea, pharyngitis

Miscellaneous: Flu syndrome, infection

Drug Interactions

Cytochrome P450 Effect: Substrate (major) of CYP2D6, 3A4; **Inhibits** CYP1A2 (weak), 2B6 (weak), 2D6 (weak), 3A4 (strong)

Increased Effect/Toxicity:

CYP3A4 substrates: Serum concentrations of drugs metabolized by CYP3A4 may be elevated by nefazodone; cisapride, pimozide, HMG-CoA reductase inhibitors (lovastatin, simvastatin), and triazolam are contraindicated. Nefazodone may increase the serum levels/effects of antiarrhythmics (amiodarone, lidocaine, propafenone, quinidine), some antipsychotics (clozapine, haloperidol, mesoridazine, quetiapine, and risperidone), some benzodiazepines (triazolam is contraindicated; decrease alprazolam dose by 50%), buspirone (limit buspirone dose to <2.5 mg/day), calcium channel blockers, cyclosporine, digoxin, donepezil, methadone, oral contraceptives, protease inhibitors (ritonavir, saquinavir), sibutramine, tacrolimus, tricyclic antidepressants, vinca alkaloids, and zolpidem. Serum concentrations of sildenafil, tadalafil, or vardenafil may be increased by nefazodone via inhibition of CYP3A4 (use caution); specific dosage adjustment guidelines have not been established; recommendations for other strong CYP3A4 inhibitors include single sildenafil sildenafil dose not to exceed 25 mg in a 48-hour period, a single tadalafil dose not to exceed 10 mg in a 72-hour period, or single vardenafil dose not to exceed 2.5 mg in a 24-hour period.

CYP3A4 inhibitors: Serum level and/or toxicity of nefazodone may be increased; inhibitors include amiodarone, cimetidine, clarithromycin, erythromycin, delavirdine, diltiazem, dirithromycin, disulfiram, fluoxetine, fluvoxamine, grapefruit juice, indinavir, itraconazole, ketoconazole, metronidazole, nevirapine, propoxyphene, quinupristin-dalfopristin, ritonavir, saquinavir, verapamil, zafirlukast, zileuton

CYP2D6 inhibitors may increase the levels/effects of nefazodone; example inhibitors include chlorpromazine, delavirdine, fluoxetine, miconazole, paroxetine, pergolide, quinidine, quinine, ritonavir, and ropinirole.

MAO inhibitors Concurrent use may lead to serotonin syndrome; avoid concurrent use or use within 14 days (includes phenelzine, isocarboxazid, and linezolid). Selegiline may increase the risk of serotonin syndrome, particularly at higher doses (>10 mg/day, where selectivity for MAO type B is decreased).

Theoretically, concurrent use of buspirone, meperidine, serotonin agonists (sumatriptan, rizatriptan), SSRIs, and venlafaxine may result in serotonin syndrome.

Decreased Effect: Carbamazepine may reduce serum concentrations of nefazodone - concurrent administration should be avoided.

Mechanism of Action Inhibits neuronal reuptake of serotonin and norepinephrine; also blocks $5-HT_2$ and alpha receptors; has no significant affinity for $alpha_2$, beta-adrenergic, $5-HT_{1A}$, cholinergic, dopaminergic, or benzodiazepine receptors

Pharmacodynamics/Kinetics
Onset of action: Therapeutic: Up to 6 weeks
Metabolism: Hepatic to three active metabolites: Triazoledione, hydroxynefazodone, and m-chloropheny piperazine (mCPP)
Bioavailability: 20% (variable)
Half-life elimination: Parent drug: 2-4 hours; active metabolites persist longer
Time to peak, serum: 1 hour, prolonged in presence of food
Excretion: Primarily urine (as metabolites); feces

Dosage Oral:
Children and Adolescents: Depression: Target dose: 300-400 mg/day (mean: 3.4 mg/kg)
Adults: Depression: 200 mg/day, administered in 2 divided doses initially, with a range of 300-600 mg/day in 2 divided doses thereafter

Administration Dosing after meals may decrease lightheadedness and postural hypotension, but may also decrease absorption and therefore effectiveness.

Monitoring Parameters If AST/ALT increase >3 times ULN, the drug should be discontinued and not reintroduced.

Reference Range Therapeutic plasma levels have not yet been defined

Patient Information Take shortly after a meal or light snack; can be given at bedtime if drowsiness occurs; optimum effect may take 2-4 weeks to be achieved; avoid alcohol; may cause painful erections (contact prescriber if this should occur); avoid sudden changes in position; report signs/symptoms of liver failure immediately (jaundice, gastrointestinal complaints, malaise)

Dosage Forms TAB: 100 mg, 150 mg, 200 mg, 250 mg; (Serzone®): 50 mg, 100 mg, 150 mg, 200 mg, 250 mg

♦ **Nefazodone Hydrochloride** *see* Nefazodone *on page 887*

♦ **NegGram®** *see* Nalidixic Acid *on page 877*

Nelfinavir (nel FIN a veer)

Related Information
Antiretroviral Therapy for HIV Infection *on page 1448*
Management of Healthcare Worker Exposures to HBV, HCV, and HIV *on page 1421*

U.S. Brand Names Viracept®

Therapeutic Category Antiretroviral Agent, Protease Inhibitor; Protease Inhibitor

Use In combination with other antiretroviral therapy in the treatment of HIV infection

Pregnancy Risk Factor B

Contraindications Hypersensitivity to nelfinavir or any component of the formulation; concurrent therapy with amiodarone, ergot derivatives, midazolam, pimozide, quinidine, triazolam; additional medications which should not be coadministered (per manufacturer) include lovastatin and simvastatin

Warnings/Precautions Nelfinavir is hepatically metabolized and has multiple drug interactions. A listing of medications that should not be used is available with each bottle and patients should be provided with this information. Use caution with hepatic impairment. Warn patients that redistribution of body fat can occur. New onset diabetes mellitus, exacerbation of diabetes, and hyperglycemia have been reported in HIV-infected patients receiving protease inhibitors. The oral powder contains phenylalanine; use caution in patients with phenylketonuria.

Common Adverse Reactions
>10%: Gastrointestinal: Diarrhea
2% to 10%:
Dermatologic: Rash
Gastrointestinal: Nausea, flatulence
Hematologic: Abnormal creatine kinase, hemoglobin, lymphocytes, neutrophils
Hepatic: Abnormal ALT, AST

Drug Interactions
Cytochrome P450 Effect: Substrate of CYP2C8/9 (minor), 2C19 (major), 2D6 (minor), 3A4 (major); **Inhibits** CYP1A2 (weak), 2B6 (weak), 2C8/9 (weak), 2C19 (weak), 2D6 (weak), 3A4 (strong)

Increased Effect/Toxicity: Nelfinavir effects may be increased by delavirdine, protease inhibitors; nelfinavir may increase the effects of amiodarone, benzodiazepines (metabolized by oxidation), cisapride, cyclosporine, CYP3A4 substrates, ergot alkaloids, HMG-CoA reductase inhibitors, pimozide, quinidine, rifabutin, sirolimus, tacrolimus; nelfinavir serum levels may be increased by azithromycin. Sildenafil serum concentration may be substantially increased (do not exceed single doses of 25 mg in 48 hours). Serum concentrations of vardenafil may be increased by nelfinavir; specific dosage adjustment guidelines have not been established; recommendations for other strong CYP3A4 inhibitors include vardenafil (Continued)

Nelfinavir *(Continued)*

dose not to exceed 2.5 mg in 24 hours. Serum concentrations of tadalafil may be increased by nelfinavir; maximum tadalafil dose of 10 mg in 72 hours is recommended with strong CYP3A4 inhibitors.

Decreased Effect: CYP2C19 inducers may decrease the levels/effects of nelfinavir; example inducers include aminoglutethimide, carbamazepine, phenytoin, and rifampin. Nelfinavir effects may be decreased by enzyme-inducing antiepileptic drugs, nevirapine, St John's wort. Nelfinavir may decrease the effects of delavirdine, methadone, and oral contraceptives

Mechanism of Action Inhibits the HIV-1 protease; inhibition of the viral protease prevents cleavage of the gag-pol polyprotein resulting in the production of immature, noninfectious virus

Pharmacodynamics/Kinetics

Absorption: Food increases plasma concentration-time curve (AUC) by two- to threefold

Distribution: V_d: 2-7 L/kg

Protein binding: 98%

Metabolism: Hepatic via CYP2C19 and 3A4; major metabolite has activity comparable to parent drug

Half-life elimination: 3.5-5 hours

Time to peak, serum: 2-4 hours

Excretion: Feces (98% to 99%, 78% as metabolites, 22% as unchanged drug); urine (1% to 2%)

Dosage Oral:

Children 2-13 years (labeled dose): 20-30 mg/kg 3 times/day with a meal or light snack; if tablets are unable to be taken, use oral powder in small amount of water, milk, formula, or dietary supplements; do not use acidic food/juice or store for >6 hours

Note: Clinically, dosages as high as 45 mg/kg every 8 hours are used; twice-daily dosages of 50-55 mg/kg are under investigation in older children (>6 years)

Adults: 750 mg 3 times/day with meals or 1250 mg twice daily with meals in combination with other antiretroviral therapies

Note: Dosage adjustments for nelfinavir when administered in combination with ritonavir: Nelfinavir 500-750 mg twice daily plus ritonavir 400 mg twice daily

Dosing adjustment in renal impairment: No adjustment needed

Dosing adjustment in hepatic impairment: Use caution

Administration Mix powder or tablets in a small amount of water, milk, formula, soy milk, soy formula, or dietary supplement. Be sure entire contents is consumed to receive full dose. Do not use acidic food/juice to dilute due to bitter taste. Do not store dilution for longer than 6 hours.

Monitoring Parameters Liver function tests, viral load, CD4 count, triglycerides, cholesterol, blood glucose, CBC with differential

Patient Information Nelfinavir should be taken with food to increase its absorption; it is not a cure for HIV infection and the long-term effects of the drug are unknown at this time; the drug has not demonstrated a reduction in the risk of transmitting HIV to others. Take the drug as prescribed; if you miss a dose, take it as soon as possible and then return to your usual schedule (never double a dose, however). If tablets are unable to be taken, use oral powder in small amount of water, milk, formula, or dietary supplement; do not use acidic food/juice or store dilution for >6 hours. Do not take any prescription medications, over-the-counter products or herbal products, especially St John's wort, without consulting prescriber. Nelfinavir has many drug interactions. A listing of medications that should not be used is available and should be reviewed with every prescription refill. Use an alternative method of contraception from birth control pills during nelfinavir therapy.

Dosage Forms POWDER, oral: 50 mg/g (144 g). **TAB, film coated:** 250 mg, 625 mg

♦ **Nembutal**® *see* Pentobarbital *on page 978*

♦ **NeoDecadron**® *see* Neomycin and Dexamethasone *on page 891*

♦ **Neo-Fradin**™ *see* Neomycin *on page 890*

Neomycin *(nee oh MYE sin)*

Related Information

Prevention of Wound Infection & Sepsis in Surgical Patients *on page 1436*

U.S. Brand Names Myciguent [OTC]; Neo-Fradin™; Neo-Rx

Synonyms Neomycin Sulfate

Therapeutic Category Ammonium Detoxicant; Antibiotic, Aminoglycoside; Antibiotic, Irrigation; Antibiotic, Topical

Use Orally to prepare GI tract for surgery; topically to treat minor skin infections; treatment of diarrhea caused by *E. coli*; adjunct in the treatment of hepatic encephalopathy; bladder irrigation; ocular infections

Pregnancy Risk Factor C

Contraindications Hypersensitivity to neomycin or any component of the formulation, or other aminoglycosides; intestinal obstruction

Warnings/Precautions Use with caution in patients with renal impairment, pre-existing hearing impairment, neuromuscular disorders; neomycin is more toxic than other aminoglycosides when given parenterally; **do not administer parenterally**; topical neomycin is a contact sensitizer with sensitivity occurring in 5% to 15% of patients treated with the drug; symptoms include itching, reddening, edema, and failure to heal; **do not use as peritoneal lavage** due to significant systemic adsorption of the drug

Common Adverse Reactions

Oral: >10%: Gastrointestinal: Nausea, diarrhea, vomiting, irritation or soreness of the mouth or rectal area

Topical: >10%: Dermatologic: Contact dermatitis

Drug Interactions

Increased Effect/Toxicity: Oral neomycin may potentiate the effects of oral anticoagulants. Neomycin may increase the adverse effects with other neurotoxic, ototoxic, or nephrotoxic drugs.

Decreased Effect: May decrease GI absorption of digoxin and methotrexate.

Mechanism of Action Interferes with bacterial protein synthesis by binding to 30S ribosomal subunits

Pharmacodynamics/Kinetics

Absorption: Oral, percutaneous: Poor (3%)

Distribution: V_d: 0.36 L/kg

Metabolism: Slightly hepatic

Half-life elimination (age and renal function dependent): 3 hours

Time to peak, serum: Oral: 1-4 hours; I.M.: ~2 hours

Excretion: Feces (97% of oral dose as unchanged drug); urine (30% to 50% of absorbed drug as unchanged drug)

Dosage

Children: Oral:

Preoperative intestinal antisepsis: 90 mg/kg/day divided every 4 hours for 2 days; or 25 mg/kg at 1 PM, 2 PM, and 11 PM on the day preceding surgery as an adjunct to mechanical cleansing of the intestine and in combination with erythromycin base

Hepatic encephalopathy: 50-100 mg/kg/day in divided doses every 6-8 hours or 2.5-7 g/m^2/day divided every 4-6 hours for 5-6 days not to exceed 12 g/day

Children and Adults: Topical: Apply ointment 1-4 times/day; topical solutions containing 0.1% to 1% neomycin have been used for irrigation

Adults: Oral:

Preoperative intestinal antisepsis: 1 g each hour for 4 doses then 1 g every 4 hours for 5 doses; or 1 g at 1 PM, 2 PM, and 11 PM on day preceding surgery as an adjunct to mechanical cleansing of the bowel and oral erythromycin; or 6 g/day divided every 4 hours for 2-3 days

Hepatic encephalopathy: 500-2000 mg every 6-8 hours or 4-12 g/day divided every 4-6 hours for 5-6 days

Chronic hepatic insufficiency: 4 g/day for an indefinite period

Monitoring Parameters Renal function tests, audiometry in symptomatic patients

Patient Information Report redness, burning, itching, ringing in the ears, hearing impairment, or dizziness or if condition does not improve in 3-4 days

Dosage Forms OINT (Myciguent): 3.5% (15 g, 30 g). **POWDER** (Neo-Rx): 10 g, 100 g. **SOLN, oral** (Neo-Fradin™): 125 mg/5 mL (480 mL). **TAB:** 500 mg

Neomycin and Dexamethasone (nee oh MYE sin & deks a METH a sone)

U.S. Brand Names NeoDecadron®

Synonyms Dexamethasone and Neomycin

Therapeutic Category Antibiotic/Corticosteroid, Ophthalmic

Use Treatment of steroid responsive inflammatory conditions of the palpebral and bulbar conjunctiva, lid, cornea, and anterior segment of the globe

Pregnancy Risk Factor C

Dosage Ophthalmic: Instill 1-2 drops in eye(s) every 3-4 hours

Dosage Forms SOLN, ophthalmic: Neomycin 0.35% [3.5 mg/mL] and dexamethasone 0.1% [1 mg/mL] (5 mL)

Neomycin and Polymyxin B (nee oh MYE sin & pol i MIKS in bee)

U.S. Brand Names Neosporin® G.U. Irrigant

Synonyms Polymyxin B and Neomycin

Therapeutic Category Antibiotic, Topical; Antibiotic, Urinary Irrigation

Use Short-term as a continuous irrigant or rinse in the urinary bladder to prevent bacteriuria and gram-negative rod septicemia associated with the use of indwelling catheters; to help prevent infection in minor cuts, scrapes, and burns

Pregnancy Risk Factor C/D (for G.U. irrigant)

Dosage Children and Adults: Bladder irrigation: **Not for injection**; add 1 mL irrigant to 1 liter isotonic saline solution and connect container to the inflow of lumen of 3-way catheter. Continuous irrigant or rinse in the urinary bladder for up to a maximum of 10 days with administration rate adjusted to patient's urine output; usually no more than 1 L of irrigant is used per day.

Dosage Forms SOLN, irrigant: Neomycin 40 mg and polymyxin B 200,000 units per mL (1 mL, 20 mL)

♦ **Neomycin, Bacitracin, and Polymyxin B** see Bacitracin, Neomycin, and Polymyxin B on page 143

♦ **Neomycin, Bacitracin, Polymyxin B, and Hydrocortisone** see Bacitracin, Neomycin, Polymyxin B, and Hydrocortisone on page 144

♦ **Neomycin, Bacitracin, Polymyxin B, and Lidocaine** see Bacitracin, Neomycin, Polymyxin B, and Lidocaine on page 144

Neomycin, Colistin, Hydrocortisone, and Thonzonium

(nee oh MYE sin, koe LIS tin, hye droe KOR ti sone, & thon ZOE nee um)

U.S. Brand Names Coly-Mycin® S; Cortisporin®-TC

Synonyms Colistin, Neomycin, Hydrocortisone, and Thonzonium; Hydrocortisone, Neomycin, Colistin, and Thonzonium; Thonzonium, Neomycin, Colistin, and Hydrocortisone

Therapeutic Category Antibiotic/Corticosteroid, Otic

Use Treatment of superficial and susceptible bacterial infections of the external auditory canal; for treatment of susceptible bacterial infections of mastoidectomy and fenestration cavities

Dosage Otic:

Calibrated dropper:

Children: 4 drops in affected ear 3-4 times/day

Adults: 5 drops in affected ear 3-4 times/day

Dropper bottle:

Children: 3 drops in affected ear 3-4 times/day

Adults: 4 drops in affected ear 3-4 times/day

Note: Alternatively, a cotton wick may be inserted in the ear canal and saturated with suspension every 4 hours; wick should be replaced at least every 24 hours

Dosage Forms SUSP, otic [drops] (Coly-Mycin® S): Colistin 0.3%, neomycin 0.33%, and hydrocortisone 1% (5 mL); (Cortisporin®-TC): Colistin 0.3%, neomycin 0.33%, and hydrocortisone 1% (10 mL)

Neomycin, Polymyxin B, and Dexamethasone

(nee oh MYE sin, pol i MIKS in bee, & deks a METH a sone)

U.S. Brand Names AK-Trol®; Dexacidin®; Dexacine™; Maxitrol®

Synonyms Dexamethasone, Neomycin, and Polymyxin B; Polymyxin B, Neomycin, and Dexamethasone

Therapeutic Category Antibiotic/Corticosteroid, Ophthalmic

Use Steroid-responsive inflammatory ocular conditions in which a corticosteroid is indicated and where bacterial infection or a risk of bacterial infection exists

Pregnancy Risk Factor C

Dosage Children and Adults: Ophthalmic:

Ointment: Place a small amount ($\sim 1/2$") in the affected eye 3-4 times/day or apply at bedtime as an adjunct with drops

Suspension: Instill 1-2 drops into affected eye(s) every 3-4 hours; in severe disease, drops may be used hourly and tapered to discontinuation

Dosage Forms OINT, ophthalmic (Dexacine™, Maxitrol®): Neomycin 3.5 mg, polymyxin B 10,000 units, and dexamethasone 0.1% per g (3.5 g). **SUSP, ophthalmic** (AK-Trol®, Dexacidin®, Maxitrol®): Neomycin 3.5 mg, polymyxin B 10,000 units, and dexamethasone 0.1% per mL (5 mL)

Neomycin, Polymyxin B, and Gramicidin

(nee oh MYE sin, pol i MIKS in bee, & gram i SYE din)

U.S. Brand Names Neosporin® Ophthalmic Solution

Synonyms Gramicidin, Neomycin, and Polymyxin B; Polymyxin B, Neomycin, and Gramicidin

Therapeutic Category Antibiotic, Ophthalmic

Use Treatment of superficial ocular infection

Pregnancy Risk Factor C

Contraindications Hypersensitivity to neomycin, polymyxin B, gramicidin or any component of the formulation

Warnings/Precautions Symptoms of neomycin sensitization include itching, reddening, edema, failure to heal; prolonged use may result in glaucoma, defects in visual acuity, posterior subcapsular cataract formation, and secondary ocular infections

Common Adverse Reactions Frequency not defined: Ocular: Transient irritation, burning, stinging, itching, inflammation, angioneurotic edema, urticaria, vesicular and maculopapular dermatitis

Drug Interactions

Increased Effect/Toxicity: See individual agents.

Decreased Effect: See individual agents.

Mechanism of Action Interferes with bacterial protein synthesis by binding to 30S ribosomal subunits; binds to phospholipids, alters permeability, and damages the bacterial cytoplasmic membrane permitting leakage of intracellular constituents

Dosage Children and Adults: Ophthalmic: Instill 1-2 drops 4-6 times/day or more frequently as required for severe infections

Patient Information Tilt head back, place medication in conjunctival sac, and close eyes; apply finger pressure on lacrimal sac for 1 minute following instillation

Dosage Forms SOLN, ophthalmic: Neomycin 1.75 mg, polymyxin B 10,000 units, and gramicidin 0.025 mg per mL (10 mL)

Neomycin, Polymyxin B, and Hydrocortisone

(nee oh MYE sin, pol i MIKS in bee, & hye droe KOR ti sone)

U.S. Brand Names AntibiOtic® Ear; Cortisporin® Cream; Cortisporin® Ophthalmic; Cortisporin® Otic; PediOtic®

Synonyms Hydrocortisone, Neomycin, and Polymyxin B; Polymyxin B, Neomycin, and Hydrocortisone

Therapeutic Category Antibiotic/Corticosteroid, Ophthalmic; Antibiotic/Corticosteroid, Otic; Antibiotic, Otic; Antibiotic, Topical

Use Steroid-responsive inflammatory condition for which a corticosteroid is indicated and where bacterial infection or a risk of bacterial infection exists

Pregnancy Risk Factor C

Dosage Duration of use should be limited to 10 days unless otherwise directed by the physician
Otic solution is used **only** for swimmer's ear (infections of external auditory canal)
Otic:
  Children: Instil 3 drops into affected ear 3-4 times/day
  Adults: Instill 4 drops 3-4 times/day; otic suspension is the preferred otic preparation
Children and Adults:
  Ophthalmic: Drops: Instill 1-2 drops 2-4 times/day, or more frequently as required for severe infections; in acute infections, instill 1-2 drops every 15-30 minutes gradually reducing the frequency of administration as the infection is controlled
  Topical: Apply a thin layer 1-4 times/day. Therapy should be discontinued when control is achieved; if no improvement is seen, reassessment of diagnosis may be necessary.

Dosage Forms CRM, topical (Cortisporin®): Neomycin 5 mg, polymyxin B 10,000 units, and hydrocortisone 5 mg per g (7.5 g). **SOLN, otic** (Antibiotic Ear, Cortisporin®): Neomycin 5 mg, polymyxin B 10,000 units, and hydrocortisone 10 mg per mL (10 mL). **SUSP, ophthalmic** (Cortisporin®): Neomycin 5 mg, polymyxin B 10,000 units, and hydrocortisone 10 mg per mL (7.5 mL). **SUSP, otic** (AntibiOtic ® Ear, Cortisporin®): Neomycin 5 mg, polymyxin B 10,000 units, and hydrocortisone 10 mg per mL (10 mL); (PediOtic®): Neomycin 5 mg, polymyxin B 10,000 units, and hydrocortisone 10 mg per mL (7.5 mL)

Neomycin, Polymyxin B, and Prednisolone
(nee oh MYE sin, pol i MIKS in bee, & pred NIS oh lone)

U.S. Brand Names Poly-Pred®

Synonyms Polymyxin B, Neomycin, and Prednisolone; Prednisolone, Neomycin, and Polymyxin B

Therapeutic Category Antibiotic/Corticosteroid, Ophthalmic

Use Steroid-responsive inflammatory ocular condition in which bacterial infection or a risk of bacterial ocular infection exists

Pregnancy Risk Factor C

Dosage Children and Adults: Ophthalmic: Instill 1-2 drops every 3-4 hours; acute infections may require every 30-minute instillation initially with frequency of administration reduced as the infection is brought under control. To treat the lids: Instill 1-2 drops every 3-4 hours, close the eye and rub the excess on the lids and lid margins.

Dosage Forms SUSP, ophthalmic: Neomycin 0.35%, polymyxin B 10,000 units, and prednisolone 0.5% per mL (5 mL, 10 mL)

- **Neomycin Sulfate** see Neomycin on page 890
- **Neoral®** see CycloSPORINE on page 323
- **Neo-Rx** see Neomycin on page 890
- **Neosar®** see Cyclophosphamide on page 320
- **Neosporin® G.U. Irrigant** see Neomycin and Polymyxin B on page 891
- **Neosporin® Ophthalmic Ointment** see Bacitracin, Neomycin, and Polymyxin B on page 143
- **Neosporin® Ophthalmic Solution** see Neomycin, Polymyxin B, and Gramicidin on page 892
- **Neosporin® Topical [OTC]** see Bacitracin, Neomycin, and Polymyxin B on page 143

Neostigmine (nee oh STIG meen)

U.S. Brand Names Prostigmin®

Synonyms Neostigmine Bromide; Neostigmine Methylsulfate

Therapeutic Category Acetylcholinesterase Inhibitor; Antidote, Neuromuscular Blocking Agent; Cholinergic Agent; Diagnostic Agent, Myasthenia Gravis

Use Diagnosis and treatment of myasthenia gravis; prevention and treatment of postoperative bladder distention and urinary retention; reversal of the effects of nondepolarizing neuromuscular-blocking agents after surgery

Pregnancy Risk Factor C

Contraindications Hypersensitivity to neostigmine, bromides, or any component of the formulation; GI or GU obstruction

Warnings/Precautions Does **not** antagonize and may prolong the phase I block of depolarizing muscle relaxants (eg, succinylcholine); use with caution in patients with epilepsy, asthma, bradycardia, hyperthyroidism, cardiac arrhythmias, or peptic ulcer; adequate facilities should be available for cardiopulmonary resuscitation when testing and adjusting dose for myasthenia gravis; have atropine and epinephrine ready to treat hypersensitivity reactions; overdosage may result in cholinergic crisis, this must be distinguished from myasthenic crisis; anticholinesterase insensitivity can develop for brief or prolonged periods

Common Adverse Reactions Frequency not defined.
  Cardiovascular: Arrhythmias (especially bradycardia), hypotension, decreased carbon monoxide, tachycardia, AV block, nodal rhythm, nonspecific ECG changes, cardiac arrest, syncope, flushing
  Central nervous system: Convulsions, dysarthria, dysphonia, dizziness, loss of consciousness, drowsiness, headache
  Dermatologic: Skin rash, thrombophlebitis (I.V.), urticaria
  Gastrointestinal: Hyperperistalsis, nausea, vomiting, salivation, diarrhea, stomach cramps, dysphagia, flatulence
(Continued)

Neostigmine *(Continued)*

Genitourinary: Urinary urgency
Neuromuscular & skeletal: Weakness, fasciculations, muscle cramps, spasms, arthralgias
Ocular: Small pupils, lacrimation
Respiratory: Increased bronchial secretions, laryngospasm, bronchiolar constriction, respiratory muscle paralysis, dyspnea, respiratory depression, respiratory arrest, bronchospasm
Miscellaneous: Diaphoresis (increased), anaphylaxis, allergic reactions

Drug Interactions
Increased Effect/Toxicity: Neuromuscular blocking agent effects are increased when combined with neostigmine.
Decreased Effect: Antagonizes effects of nondepolarizing muscle relaxants (eg, pancuronium, tubocurarine). Atropine antagonizes the muscarinic effects of neostigmine.

Mechanism of Action Inhibits destruction of acetylcholine by acetylcholinesterase which facilitates transmission of impulses across myoneural junction

Pharmacodynamics/Kinetics
Onset of action: I.M.: 20-30 minutes; I.V.: 1-20 minutes
Duration: I.M.: 2.5-4 hours; I.V.: 1-2 hours
Absorption: Oral: Poor, <2%
Metabolism: Hepatic
Half-life elimination: Normal renal function: 0.5-2.1 hours; End-stage renal disease: Prolonged
Excretion: Urine (50% as unchanged drug)

Dosage
Myasthenia gravis: Diagnosis: I.M.:
Children: 0.04 mg/kg as a single dose
Adults: 0.02 mg/kg as a single dose
Myasthenia gravis: Treatment:
Children:
Oral: 2 mg/kg/day divided every 3-4 hours
I.M., I.V., S.C.: 0.01-0.04 mg/kg every 2-4 hours
Adults:
Oral: 15 mg/dose every 3-4 hours up to 375 mg/day maximum
I.M., I.V., S.C.: 0.5-2.5 mg every 1-3 hours up to 10 mg/24 hours maximum
Reversal of nondepolarizing neuromuscular blockade after surgery in conjunction with atropine: I.V.:
Infants: 0.025-0.1 mg/kg/dose
Children: 0.025-0.08 mg/kg/dose
Adults: 0.5-2.5 mg; total dose not to exceed 5 mg
Bladder atony: Adults: I.M., S.C.:
Prevention: 0.25 mg every 4-6 hours for 2-3 days
Treatment: 0.5-1 mg every 3 hours for 5 doses after bladder has emptied
Dosing adjustment in renal impairment:
Cl_{cr} 10-50 mL/minute: Administer 50% of normal dose
Cl_{cr} <10 mL/minute: Administer 25% of normal dose

Administration May be administered undiluted by slow I.V. injection over several minutes
Patient Information Side effects are generally due to exaggerated pharmacologic effects; most common are salivation and muscle fasciculations; report nausea, vomiting, muscle weakness, severe abdominal pain, or difficulty breathing
Dosage Forms INJ, solution, as methysulfate: 0.5 mg/mL (1 mL, 10 mL); 1 mg/mL (10 mL).
TAB, as bromide: 15 mg

Nesiritide *(ni SIR i tide)*

Related Information
Hemodynamic Support, Intravenous *on page 1377*
U.S. Brand Names Natrecor®
Synonyms B-type Natriuretic Peptide (Human); hBNP; Natriuretic Peptide
Therapeutic Category Natriuretic Peptide, B-Type, Human; Vasodilator

Use Treatment of acutely decompensated congestive heart failure (CHF) in patients with dyspnea at rest or with minimal activity

Pregnancy Risk Factor C

Contraindications Hypersensitivity to natriuretic peptide or any component of the formulation; cardiogenic shock (when used as primary therapy); hypotension (systolic blood pressure <90 mm Hg)

Warnings/Precautions May cause hypotension; administer in clinical situations when blood pressure may be closely monitored. Use caution in patients with systolic blood pressure <100 mm Hg (contraindicated if <90 mm Hg); more likely to experience hypotension. Effects may be additive with other agents capable of causing hypotension. Hypotensive effects may last for several hours.

Should not be used in patients with low filling pressures, or in patients with conditions which depend on venous return including significant valvular stenosis, restrictive or obstructive cardiomyopathy, constrictive pericarditis, and pericardial tamponade. May be associated with development of azotemia; use caution in patients with renal impairment or in patients where renal perfusion is dependent on renin-angiotensin-aldosterone system.

Atrial natriuretic peptide (ANP), a related peptide, has been associated with increased vascular permeability and decreased intravascular volume. This has not been observed in clinical trials with nesiritide, however, patients should be monitored for this effect.

Monitor for allergic or anaphylactic reactions. Use caution with prolonged infusions; limited experience for infusions >48 hours. Safety and efficacy in pediatric patients have not been established.

Common Adverse Reactions Note: Frequencies cited below were recorded in VMAC trial at dosages similar to approved labeling. Higher frequencies have been observed in trials using higher dosages of nesiritide.

>10%:

Cardiovascular: Hypotension (total: 11%; symptomatic: 4% at recommended dose, up to 17% at higher doses)

Renal: Increased serum creatinine (28% with >0.5 mg/dL increase over baseline)

1% to 10%:

Cardiovascular: Ventricular tachycardia (3%)*, ventricular extrasystoles (3%)*, angina (2%)*, bradycardia (1%), tachycardia, atrial fibrillation, AV node conduction abnormalities

Central nervous system: Headache (8%)*, dizziness (3%)*, insomnia (2%), anxiety (3%), fever, confusion, paresthesia, somnolence, tremor

Dermatologic: Pruritus, rash

Gastrointestinal: Nausea (4%)*, abdominal pain (1%)*, vomiting (1%)*

Hematologic: Anemia

Local: Injection site reaction

Neuromuscular & skeletal: Back pain (4%), leg cramps

Ocular: Amblyopia

Respiratory: Cough (increased), hemoptysis, apnea

Miscellaneous: Increased diaphoresis

*Frequency less than or equal to placebo or other standard therapy

Drug Interactions

Increased Effect/Toxicity: An increased frequency of symptomatic hypotension was observed with concurrent administration of ACE inhibitors. Other hypotensive agents are likely to have additive effects on hypotension. In patients receiving diuretic therapy leading to depletion of intravascular volume, the risk of hypotension and/or renal impairment may be increased. Nesiritide should be avoided in patients with low filling pressures.

Mechanism of Action Binds to guanylate cyclase receptor on vascular smooth muscle and endothelial cells, increasing intracellular cyclic GMP, resulting in smooth muscle cell relaxation. Has been shown to produce dose-dependent reductions in pulmonary capillary wedge pressure (PCWP) and systemic arterial pressure.

Pharmacodynamics/Kinetics

Onset of action: 15 minutes (60% of 3-hour effect achieved)

Duration: >60 minutes (up to several hours) for systolic blood pressure; hemodynamic effects persist longer than serum half-life would predict

Distribution: V_{ss} 0.19 L/kg

Metabolism: Proteolytic cleavage by vascular endopeptidases and proteolysis following receptor binding and cellular internalization

Half-life elimination: Initial (distribution) 2 minutes; Terminal: 18 minutes

Time to peak: 1 hour

Excretion: Urine

Dosage Adults: I.V.: Initial: 2 mcg/kg (bolus); followed by continuous infusion at 0.01 mcg/kg/minute; **Note:** Should not be initiated at a dosage higher than initial recommended dose. At intervals of ≥3 hours, the dosage may be increased by 0.005 mcg/kg/minute (preceded by a bolus of 1 mcg/kg), up to a maximum of 0.03 mcg/kg/minute. Increases beyond the initial infusion rate should be limited to selected patients and accompanied by hemodynamic monitoring.

Patients experiencing hypotension during the infusion: Infusion should be interrupted. May attempt to restart at a lower dose (reduce initial infusion dose by 30% and omit bolus).

Dosage adjustment in renal impairment: No adjustment required

Administration Do not administer through a heparin-coated catheter (concurrent administration of heparin via a separate catheter is acceptable, per manufacturer).

(Continued)

Nesiritide *(Continued)*

Prime I.V. tubing with 25 mL of infusion prior to connection with vascular access port and prior to administering bolus or starting the infusion. Withdraw bolus from the prepared infusion bag and administer over 60 seconds. Begin infusion immediately following administration of the bolus. Using a standard 6 mcg/mL concentration, bolus volume in mL = patient weight in kg x 0.33.

Physically incompatible with heparin, insulin, ethacrynate sodium, bumetanide, enalaprilat, hydralazine, and furosemide. Do not administer through the same catheter. Do not administer with any solution containing sodium metabisulfite. Catheter must be flushed between administration of nesiritide and physically incompatible drugs.

Monitoring Parameters Blood pressure, hemodynamic responses (PCWP, RAP, CI)

Patient Information This medication can only be administered I.V. You will be closely monitored during and following infusion. Remain in bed until advised otherwise. Do not make sudden turns or changes in position; call for assistance to change position. Immediately report any acute headache, dizziness, chest pain or palpitations, abdominal pain or nausea, back pain, or increase in breathing difficulty.

Dosage Forms INJ, powder for reconstitution: 1.5 mg

- **Neulasta**™ *see Pegfilgrastim on page 963*
- **Neumega**® *see Oprelvekin on page 931*
- **Neupogen**® *see Filgrastim on page 522*
- **Neuromuscular Blocking Agents Comparison** *see page 1397*
- **Neurontin**® *see Gabapentin on page 574*
- **Neut**® *see Sodium Bicarbonate on page 1144*
- **NeutraCare**® *see Fluoride on page 535*
- **NeutraGard**® **[OTC]** *see Fluoride on page 535*
- **Neutra-Phos**® **[OTC]** *see Potassium Phosphate and Sodium Phosphate on page 1024*
- **Neutra-Phos**®**-K [OTC]** *see Potassium Phosphate on page 1023*
- **Neutrexin**® *see Trimetrexate Glucuronate on page 1271*

Nevirapine *(ne VYE ra peen)*

Related Information

Antiretroviral Therapy for HIV Infection *on page 1448*
Management of Healthcare Worker Exposures to HBV, HCV, and HIV *on page 1421*
Prevention of Perinatal HIV-1 Transmission *on page 1434*

U.S. Brand Names Viramune®

Synonyms NVP

Therapeutic Category Antiretroviral Agent, Non-nucleoside Reverse Transcriptase Inhibitor (NNRTI)

Use In combination therapy with other antiretroviral agents for the treatment of HIV-1

Pregnancy Risk Factor C

Contraindications Hypersensitivity to nevirapine or any component of the formulation

Warnings/Precautions Consider alteration of antiretroviral therapies if disease progression occurs while patients are receiving nevirapine. Safety and efficacy have not been established in neonates.

Severe life-threatening skin reactions (eg, Stevens-Johnson syndrome, toxic epidermal necrolysis, hypersensitivity reactions with rash and organ dysfunction) have occurred. Nevirapine must be initiated with a 14-day lead-in dosing period to decrease the incidence of adverse effects. Severe hepatotoxic reactions may also occur (fulminant and cholestatic hepatitis, hepatic necrosis), and in some cases have resulted in hepatic failure and death. Intensive monitoring is required during the initial 18 weeks of therapy to detect potentially life-threatening dermatologic, hypersensitivity, and hepatic reactions. The greatest risk of these reactions is within the initial 6 weeks of treatment. Patients with a history of chronic hepatitis (B or C) or increased baseline transaminase levels (AST or ALT) may be at increased risk of hepatotoxic reactions. Female gender and increased CD4$^+$ cell counts may be at substantially greater risk of rash-associated hepatic events.

If a severe dermatologic or hypersensitivity reaction occurs, or if signs and symptoms of hepatitis occur, nevirapine should be permanently discontinued. These may include a severe rash, or a rash associated with fever, blisters, oral lesions, conjunctivitis, facial edema, muscle or joint aches, general malaise, hepatitis, eosinophilia, granulocytopenia, lymphadenopathy or renal dysfunction.

Common Adverse Reactions

>10%:
Central nervous system: Headache (11%), fever (8% to 11%)
Dermatologic: Rash (15% to 20%)
Gastrointestinal: Diarrhea (15% to 20%)
Hematologic: Neutropenia (10% to 11%)

1% to 10%:
Gastrointestinal: Ulcerative stomatitis (4%), nausea, abdominal pain (2%)
Hematologic: Anemia
Hepatic: Hepatitis, increased LFTs (2% to 4%)
Neuromuscular & skeletal: Peripheral neuropathy, paresthesia (2%), myalgia

Hypersensitivity (frequency not defined): Symptoms of severe hypersensitivity/dermatologic reactions may include: Severe rash (or rash with fever), blisters, oral lesions, conjunctivitis, facial edema, muscle or joint aches, general malaise, hepatitis, eosinophilia, granulocytopenia, lymphadenopathy, or renal dysfunction. Nevirapine should be permanently discontinued.

Drug Interactions

Cytochrome P450 Effect: Substrate of CYP2B6 (minor), 2D6 (minor), 3A4 (major); **Inhibits** CYP1A2 (weak), 2D6 (weak), 3A4 (weak); **Induces** CYP2B6 (strong), 3A4 (strong)

Increased Effect/Toxicity: Cimetidine, itraconazole, ketoconazole, and some macrolide antibiotics may increase nevirapine plasma concentrations. Concurrent administration of prednisone for the initial 14 days of nevirapine therapy was associated with an increased incidence and severity of rash. Rifabutin concentrations are increased by nevirapine.

Decreased Effect: Rifampin and rifabutin may decrease nevirapine concentrations due to induction of CYP3A; avoid concurrent use. Nevirapine may decrease serum concentrations of some protease inhibitors (AUC of indinavir, lopinavir, nelfinavir, and saquinavir may be decreased, however, no effect noted with ritonavir); specific dosage adjustments have not been recommended; no adjustment recommended for ritonavir, unless combined with lopinavir (Kaletra™). Nevirapine may decrease serum levels of immunosuppressants, antiarrhythmics, anticonvulsants, clarithromycin, and cyclophosphamide. Nevirapine may decrease the effectiveness of oral contraceptives; suggest alternate method or additional form of birth control. Nevirapine also decreases the effect of ketoconazole and methadone.

Mechanism of Action As a non-nucleoside reverse transcriptase inhibitor, nevirapine has activity against HIV-1 by binding to reverse transcriptase. It consequently blocks the RNA-dependent and DNA-dependent DNA polymerase activities including HIV-1 replication. It does not require intracellular phosphorylation for antiviral activity.

Pharmacodynamics/Kinetics

Absorption: >90%

Distribution: Widely; V_d: 1.2-1.4 L/kg; crosses placenta; enters breast milk; CSF penetration approximates 50% of plasma

Protein binding, plasma: 50% to 60%

Metabolism: Extensively hepatic via CYP3A4 (hydroxylation to inactive compounds); may undergo enterohepatic recycling

Half-life elimination: Decreases over 2- to 4-week time with chronic dosing due to autoinduction (ie, half-life = 45 hours initially and decreases to 23 hours)

Time to peak, serum: 2-4 hours

Excretion: Urine (as metabolites, <3% as unchanged drug)

Dosage Oral:

Children 2 months to <8 years: Initial: 4 mg/kg/dose once daily for 14 days; increase dose to 7 mg/kg/dose every 12 hours if no rash or other adverse effects occur; maximum dose: 200 mg/dose every 12 hours

Children ≥8 years: Initial: 4 mg/kg/dose once daily for 14 days; increase dose to 4 mg/kg/dose every 12 hours if no rash or other adverse effects occur; maximum dose: 200 mg/dose every 12 hours

Note: Alternative pediatric dosing (unlabeled): 120-200 mg/m^2 every 12 hours; this dosing has been proposed due to the fact that dosing based on mg/kg may result in an abrupt decrease in dose at the 8th birthday, which may be inappropriate.

Adults: Initial: 200 mg once daily for 14 days; maintenance: 200 mg twice daily (in combination with an additional antiretroviral agent)

Note: If patient experiences a rash during the 14-day lead-in period, dose should not be increased until the rash has resolved. Discontinue if severe rash, or rash with constitutional symptoms, is noted. If therapy is interrupted for >7 days, restart with initial dose for 14 days

Dosage adjustment in renal impairment:

Cl_{cr} ≥20 mL/minute: No adjustment required

Hemodialysis: An additional 200 mg dose is recommended following dialysis.

Dosage adjustment in hepatic impairment: Do not administer to patients with severe hepatic impairment. Discontinue (and do not re-initiate) if clinical hepatitis occurs.

Administration Oral: May be administered with or without food; may be administered with an antacid or didanosine; shake suspension gently prior to administration

Monitoring Parameters Liver function tests should be monitored at baseline, and intensively during the first 18 weeks of therapy (optimal frequency not established, recommendations recommend more often than once a month, including prior to dose escalation, and at 2 weeks following dose escalation), then periodically throughout therapy; observe for CNS side effects. Discontinue if patient experiences severe rash, constitutional symptoms associated with rash, or clinical hepatitis.

Patient Information Report any right upper quadrant pain, jaundice, or rash immediately

Dosage Forms SUSP, oral: 50 mg/5 mL (240 mL). **TAB:** 200 mg

♦ **Nexium**® *see Esomeprazole on page 458*

Niacin (NYE a sin)

Related Information

Lipid-Lowering Agents *on page 1381*

U.S. Brand Names Niacor®; Niaspan®; Nicotinex [OTC]; Slo-Niacin® [OTC]

Synonyms Nicotinic Acid; Vitamin B$_3$

Therapeutic Category Antilipemic Agent, Miscellaneous; Vitamin, Water Soluble

Use Adjunctive treatment of dyslipidemias (alone or with lovastatin or bile acid sequestrant); peripheral vascular disease and circulatory disorders; treatment of pellagra; dietary supplement

(Continued)

Niacin *(Continued)*

Pregnancy Risk Factor A/C (dose exceeding RDA recommendation)

Contraindications Hypersensitivity to niacin, niacinamide, or any component of the formulation; hepatic disease; active peptic ulcer; severe hypotension; arterial hemorrhage

Warnings/Precautions Use caution in heavy ethanol users, unstable angina or MI, diabetes (interferes with glucose control), renal disease, active gallbladder disease (can exacerbate), gout, past history of hepatic disease, or allergies. Flushing is common and can be attenuated with a gradual increase in dose. Monitor liver function tests.

Common Adverse Reactions Frequency not defined.

Cardiovascular: Arrhythmias, atrial fibrillation, edema, flushing, hypotension, orthostasis, palpitations, syncope (rare), tachycardia

Central nervous system: Chills, dizziness, insomnia, migraine

Dermatologic: Acanthosis nigricans, dry skin, hyperpigmentation, maculopapular rash, pruritus, rash, urticaria

Endocrine & metabolic: Glucose tolerance decreased, gout, phosphorous levels decreased, uric acid level increased

Gastrointestinal: Abdominal pain, nausea, peptic ulcers, vomiting

Hepatic: Hepatic necrosis (rare), jaundice, liver enzymes elevated

Neuromuscular & skeletal: Myalgia, myopathy (with concurrent HMG-CoA reductase inhibitor), rhabdomyolysis (with concurrent HMG-CoA reductase inhibitor; rare), weakness

Ocular: Cystoid macular edema, toxic amblyopia

Respiratory: Dyspnea

Miscellaneous: Diaphoresis

Drug Interactions

Increased Effect/Toxicity: Use with adrenergic blocking agents may result in additive vasodilating effect and postural hypotension.

Decreased Effect: The effect of oral hypoglycemics may be decreased by niacin. Niacin may inhibit uricosuric effects of sulfinpyrazone and probenecid. Aspirin (or other NSAIDs) decreases niacin-induced flushing. Bile acid sequestrants decrease the absorption of niacin.

Mechanism of Action Component of two coenzymes which is necessary for tissue respiration, lipid metabolism, and glycogenolysis; inhibits the synthesis of very low density lipoproteins

Pharmacodynamics/Kinetics

Absorption: Rapid and extensive

Distribution: Mainly to hepatic, renal, and adipose tissue

Metabolism: Extensive first-pass effects; converted to nicotinamide (dose dependent); niacinamide (30%) hepatically metabolized

Half-life elimination: 45 minutes

Time to peak, serum: Immediate release formulation: ~45 minutes; extended release formulation: 4-5 hours

Excretion: Urine (unchanged drug and metabolites); with larger doses, greater percentage as unchanged drug

Dosage

Children: Oral:

Pellagra: 50-100 mg/dose 3 times/day

Recommended daily allowances:

0-0.5 years: 5 mg/day

0.5-1 year: 6 mg/day

1-3 years: 9 mg/day

4-6 years: 12 mg/day

7-10 years: 13 mg/day

Children and Adolescents: Recommended daily allowances:

Male:

11-14 years: 17 mg/day

15-18 years: 20 mg/day

19-24 years: 19 mg/day

Female: 11-24 years: 15 mg/day

Adults: Oral:

Recommended daily allowances:

Male: 25-50 years: 19 mg/day; >51 years: 15 mg/day

Female: 25-50 years: 15 mg/day; >51 years: 13 mg/day

Hyperlipidemia: Usual target dose: 1.5-6 g/day in 3 divided doses with or after meals using a dosage titration schedule; extended release: 375 mg to 2 g once daily at bedtime

Regular release formulation (Niacor®): Initial: 250 mg once daily (with evening meal); increase frequency and/or dose every 4-7 days to desired response or first-level therapeutic dose (1.5-2 g/day in 2-3 divided doses); after 2 months, may increase at 2- to 4-week intervals to 3 g/day in 3 divided doses

Extended release formulation (Niaspan®): 500 mg at bedtime for 4 weeks, then 1 g at bedtime for 4 weeks; adjust dose to response and tolerance; can increase to a maximum of 2 g/day, but only at bedtime and only at 4-week intervals

With lovastatin: Maximum lovastatin dose: 40 mg/day

Pellagra: 50-100 mg 3-4 times/day, maximum: 500 mg/day

Niacin deficiency: 10-20 mg/day, maximum: 100 mg/day

Dosage adjustment in renal impairment: Use with caution

Dosage adjustment in hepatic impairment: Not recommended for use in patients with significant or unexplained hepatic dysfunction

Dosage adjustment for toxicity: Transaminases rise to 3 times ULN: Discontinue therapy.

Administration Administer with food. Niaspan® tablet strengths are not interchangeable. When switching from immediate release tablet, initiate Niaspan® at lower dose and titrate. Long-acting forms should not be crushed, broken, or chewed. Do not substitute long-acting forms for immediate release ones.

Monitoring Parameters Blood glucose; liver function tests (dyslipidemia, high dose, prolonged therapy) pretreatment and every 6-12 weeks for first year then periodically; lipid profile; elevated uric acid levels have been reported

Patient Information Take exactly as directed; do not exceed recommended dosage. Take with food to reduce incidence of GI upset. Do not crush, break, or chew long-acting capsules or tablets. You may experience flushing, sensation of heat, or headache; these reactions may be decreased by increasing dose slowly or by taking aspirin (consult prescriber) 30 minutes prior to taking niacin. Avoid alcohol and hot drinks around the time of niacin dose. You may experience dizziness, lightheadedness (use caution when driving or engaging in tasks requiring alertness until response to drug is known). Report persistent GI disturbance or changes in color of urine or stool.

Dosage Forms CAP, extended release: 125 mg, 250 mg, 400 mg, 500 mg. **CAP, timed release:** 250 mg. **ELIX** (Nicotinex): 50 mg/5 mL (473 mL). **TAB:** 50 mg, 100 mg, 250 mg, 500 mg; (Niacor®): 500 mg. **TAB, controlled release** (Slo-Niacin®): 250 mg, 500 mg, 750 mg. **TAB, extended release** (Niaspan®): 500 mg, 750 mg, 1000 mg. **TAB, timed release:** 250 mg, 500 mg, 750 mg, 1000 mg

Niacinamide (nye a SIN a mide)

Synonyms Nicotinamide; Vitamin B_3

Therapeutic Category Vitamin, Water Soluble

Use Prophylaxis and treatment of pellagra

Pregnancy Risk Factor A/C (dose exceeding RDA recommendation)

Contraindications Hypersensitivity to niacin, niacinamide, or any component of the formulation; liver disease; active peptic ulcer; severe hypotension; arterial hemorrhage

Warnings/Precautions Large doses should be administered with caution to patients with gallbladder disease or diabetes; monitor blood glucose; may elevate uric acid levels; use with caution in patients predisposed to gout; some products may contain tartrazine

Common Adverse Reactions Frequency not defined.
Cardiovascular: Tachycardia
Dermatologic: Increased sebaceous gland activity, rash
Gastrointestinal: Bloating, flatulence, nausea
Neuromuscular & skeletal: Paresthesia in extremities
Ocular: Blurred vision
Respiratory: Wheezing

Mechanism of Action Used by the body as a source of niacin; is a component of two coenzymes which is necessary for tissue respiration, lipid metabolism, and glycogenolysis; inhibits the synthesis of very low density lipoproteins; does not have hypolipidemia or vasodilating effects

Pharmacodynamics/Kinetics
Absorption: Rapid
Metabolism: Hepatic
Half-life elimination: 45 minutes
Time to peak, serum: 20-70 minutes
Excretion: Urine

Dosage Oral:
Children: Pellagra: 100-300 mg/day in divided doses
Adults: 50 mg 3-10 times/day
Pellagra: 300-500 mg/day
Recommended daily allowance: 13-19 mg/day

Dosage Forms TAB: 100 mg, 250 mg, 500 mg

Niacin and Lovastatin (NYE a sin & LOE va sta tin)

U.S. Brand Names Advicor™

Synonyms Lovastatin and Niacin

Therapeutic Category Antilipemic Agent, HMG-CoA Reductase Inhibitor; Antilipemic Agent, Miscellaneous

Use Treatment of primary hypercholesterolemia (heterozygous familial and nonfamilial) and mixed dyslipidemia (Fredrickson types IIa and IIb) in patients previously treated with either agent alone (patients who require further lowering of triglycerides (TG) or increase in HDL-cholesterol (HDL-C) from addition of niacin or further lowering of LDL-cholesterol (LDL-C) from addition of lovastatin). Combination product; not intended for initial treatment.

Pregnancy Risk Factor X

Dosage Dosage forms are a fixed combination of niacin and lovastatin.
Oral: Adults: Lowest dose: Niacin 500 mg/lovastatin 20 mg; may increase by not more than 500 mg (niacin) at 4-week intervals (maximum dose: Niacin 2000 mg/lovastatin 40 mg daily); should be taken at bedtime with a low-fat snack
Not for use as initial therapy of dyslipidemias. May be substituted for equivalent dose of Niaspan®, however, manufacturer does not recommend direct substitution with other niacin products.

Dosage Forms TAB, extended release (niacin) and immediate release (lovastatin): Niacin 500 mg and lovastatin 20 mg; niacin 750 mg and lovastatin 20 mg; niacin 1000 mg and lovastatin 20 mg

♦ **Niacor®** *see Niacin on page 897*
♦ **Niaspan®** *see Niacin on page 897*

NiCARdipine (nye KAR de peen)

Related Information
   Calcium Channel Blockers Comparison *on page 1371*
U.S. Brand Names Cardene®; Cardene® I.V.; Cardene® SR
Synonyms Nicardipine Hydrochloride
Therapeutic Category Antianginal Agent; Antihypertensive Agent; Antimigraine Agent, Prophylaxis; Calcium Channel Blocker
Use Chronic stable angina (immediate-release product only); management of essential hypertension (immediate and sustained release; parenteral only for short time that oral treatment is not feasible)
Unlabeled/Investigational Use Congestive heart failure
Pregnancy Risk Factor C
Contraindications Hypersensitivity to nicardipine or any component of the formulation; advanced aortic stenosis; severe hypotension; cardiogenic shock; ventricular tachycardia
Warnings/Precautions Blood pressure lowering should be done at a rate appropriate for the patient's condition. Rapid drops in blood pressure can lead to arterial insufficiency. Use with caution in CAD (can cause increase in angina), CHF (can worsen heart failure symptoms), and pheochromocytoma (limited clinical experience). Peripheral infusion sites (for I.V. therapy) should be changed ever 12 hours. Titrate I.V. dose cautiously in patients with CHF, renal, or hepatic dysfunction. Use the I.V. form cautiously in patients with portal hypertension (can cause increase in hepatic pressure gradient). Safety and efficacy have not been demonstrated in pediatric patients. Abrupt withdrawal may cause rebound angina in patients with CAD.
Common Adverse Reactions
   1% to 10%:
       Cardiovascular: Flushing (6% to 10%), palpitations (3% to 4%), tachycardia (1% to 4%), peripheral edema (dose-related 7% to 8%), increased angina (dose-related 6%), hypotension (I.V. 6%), orthostasis (I.V. 1%)
       Central nervous system: Headache (6% to 15%), dizziness (4% to 7%), somnolence (4% to 6%), paresthesia (1%)
       Dermatologic: Rash (1%)
       Gastrointestinal: Nausea (2% to 5%), dry mouth (1%)
       Genitourinary: Polyuria (1%)
       Local: Injection site reaction (I.V. 1%)
       Neuromuscular & skeletal: Weakness (4% to 6%), myalgia (1%)
       Miscellaneous: Diaphoresis
Drug Interactions
   Cytochrome P450 Effect: Substrate of CYP1A2 (minor), 2C8/9 (minor), 2D6 (minor), 2E1 (minor), 3A4 (major); **Inhibits** CYP2C8/9 (strong), 2C19 (moderate), 2D6 (moderate), 3A4 (strong)
   Increased Effect/Toxicity: H_2 blockers (cimetidine) may increase the bioavailability of nicardipine. Serum concentrations/toxicity of nicardipine may be increased by inhibitors of CYP3A4, including amprenavir, cimetidine, ciprofloxacin, clarithromycin, clozapine, diltiazem, disulfiram, digoxin, erythromycin, ethanol, fluconazole, fluoxetine, fluvoxamine, grapefruit juice, isoniazid, itraconazole, ketoconazole, labetalol, levodopa, loxapine, metoprolol, metronidazole, miconazole, nefazodone, nelfinavir, omeprazole, phenytoin, propranolol, rifabutin, rifampin, ritonavir, troleandomycin, valproic acid, and verapamil. Calcium may reduce the calcium channel blocker's effects, particularly hypotension. Cyclosporine levels (and possibly tacrolimus) may be increased by nicardipine. May increase effect of vecuronium (reduce dose 25%) and increase serum levels of metoprolol. Blood pressure-lowering effects may be additive with sildenafil, tadalafil, and vardenafil (use caution).
   Decreased Effect: Rifampin (and potentially other enzyme inducers) increase the metabolism of calcium channel blockers.
Mechanism of Action Inhibits calcium ion from entering the "slow channels" or select voltage-sensitive areas of vascular smooth muscle and myocardium during depolarization, producing a relaxation of coronary vascular smooth muscle and coronary vasodilation; increases myocardial oxygen delivery in patients with vasospastic angina
Pharmacodynamics/Kinetics
   Onset of action: Oral: 1-2 hours; I.V.: 10 minutes; Hypotension: ~20 minutes
   Duration: 2-6 hours
   Absorption: Oral: ~100%
   Protein binding: 95%
   Metabolism: Hepatic; extensive first-pass effect
   Bioavailability: 35%
   Half-life elimination: 2-4 hours
   Time to peak, serum: 20-120 minutes
   Excretion: Urine (as metabolites)
Dosage Adults:
   Oral:
       Immediate release: Initial: 20 mg 3 times/day; usual: 20-40 mg 3 times/day (allow 3 days between dose increases)
       Sustained release: Initial: 30 mg twice daily, titrate up to 60 mg twice daily
       Note: The total daily dose of immediate-release product may not automatically be equivalent to the daily sustained-release dose; use caution in converting.

I.V. (dilute to 0.1 mg/mL):

Acute hypertension: Initial: 5 mg/hour increased by 2.5 mg/hour every 15 minutes to a maximum of 15 mg/hour; consider reduction to 3 mg/hour after response is achieved. Monitor and titrate to lowest dose necessary to maintain stable blood pressure.

Substitution for oral therapy (approximate equivalents):

20 mg every 8 hours oral, equivalent to 0.5 mg/hour I.V. infusion

30 mg every 8 hours oral, equivalent to 1.2 mg/hour I.V. infusion

40 mg every 8 hours oral, equivalent to 2.2 mg/hour I.V. infusion

Dosing adjustment in renal impairment: Titrate dose beginning with 20 mg 3 times/day (immediate release) or 30 mg twice daily (sustained release). Specific guidelines for adjustment of I.V. nicardipine are not available, but careful monitoring/adjustment is warranted.

Dosing adjustment in hepatic impairment: Starting dose: 20 mg twice daily (immediate release) with titration. Specific guidelines for adjustment of I.V. nicardipine are not available, but careful monitoring/adjustment is warranted.

Administration

Oral: The total daily dose of immediate-release product may not automatically be equivalent to the daily sustained-release dose; use caution in converting. Do not chew or crush the sustained release formulation, swallow whole. Do not open or cut capsules.

I.V.: Ampuls must be diluted before use. Administer as a slow continuous infusion.

Patient Information Sustained release products should be taken with food (not fatty meal); do not crush; limit caffeine intake; avoid alcohol; notify prescriber if angina pain is not reduced when taking this drug, irregular heartbeat, shortness of breath, swelling, dizziness, constipation, nausea, or hypotension occur; do not stop therapy without advice of prescriber

Dosage Forms CAP (Cardene®): 20 mg, 30 mg. **CAP, sustained release** (Cardene® SR): 30 mg, 45 mg, 60 mg. **INJ, solution** (Cardene® IV): 2.5 mg/mL (10 mL)

♦ **Nicardipine Hydrochloride** *see* NiCARDipine *on page 900*

♦ **NicoDerm® CQ® [OTC]** *see* Nicotine *on page 901*

♦ **Nicorette® [OTC]** *see* Nicotine *on page 901*

♦ **Nicotinamide** *see* Niacinamide *on page 899*

Nicotine (nik oh TEEN)

Related Information

Nicotine Products Comparison *on page 1399*

U.S. Brand Names Commit™ [OTC]; NicoDerm® CQ® [OTC]; Nicorette® [OTC]; Nicotrol® Inhaler; Nicotrol® NS; Nicotrol® Patch [OTC]

Synonyms Habitrol®

Therapeutic Category Smoking Deterrent

Use Treatment to aid smoking cessation for the relief of nicotine withdrawal symptoms (including nicotine craving)

Unlabeled/Investigational Use Management of ulcerative colitis (transdermal)

Pregnancy Risk Factor D (transdermal); X (chewing gum)

Contraindications Hypersensitivity to nicotine or any component of the formulation; patients who are smoking during the postmyocardial infarction period; patients with life-threatening arrhythmias, or severe or worsening angina pectoris; active temporomandibular joint disease (gum); pregnancy; not for use in nonsmokers

Warnings/Precautions Use with caution in oropharyngeal inflammation and in patients with history of esophagitis, peptic ulcer, coronary artery disease, vasospastic disease, angina, hypertension, hyperthyroidism, diabetes, and hepatic dysfunction; nicotine is known to be one of the most toxic of all poisons; while the gum is being used to help the patient overcome a health hazard, it also must be considered a hazardous drug vehicle.

Common Adverse Reactions

Chewing gum/lozenge:

>10%:

Cardiovascular: Tachycardia

Central nervous system: Headache (mild)

Gastrointestinal: Nausea, vomiting, indigestion, excessive salivation, belching, increased appetite

Miscellaneous: Mouth or throat soreness, jaw muscle ache, hiccups

1% to 10%:

Central nervous system: Insomnia, dizziness, nervousness

Endocrine & metabolic: Dysmenorrhea

Gastrointestinal: GI distress, eructation

Neuromuscular & skeletal: Muscle pain

Respiratory: Hoarseness

Miscellaneous: Hiccups

Transdermal systems:

>10%:

Central nervous system: Insomnia, abnormal dreams

Dermatologic: Pruritus, erythema

Local: Application site reaction

Respiratory: Rhinitis, cough, pharyngitis, sinusitis

1% to 10%:

Cardiovascular: Chest pain

Central nervous system: Dysphoria, anxiety, difficulty concentrating, dizziness, somnolence

Dermatologic: Rash

(Continued)

Nicotine *(Continued)*

Gastrointestinal: Diarrhea, dyspepsia, nausea, xerostomia, constipation, anorexia, abdominal pain

Neuromuscular & skeletal: Arthralgia, myalgia

Drug Interactions

Cytochrome P450 Effect: Substrate (minor) of CYP1A2, 2A6, 2B6, 2C8/9, 2C19, 2D6, 2E1, 3A4; **Inhibits** CYP2A6 (weak), 2E1 (weak)

Increased Effect/Toxicity: Nicotine increases the hemodynamic and AV blocking effects of adenosine; monitor. Cimetidine increases nicotine concentrations; therefore, may decrease amount of gum or patches needed. Monitor for treatment-emergent hypertension in patients treated with the combination of nicotine patch and bupropion.

Mechanism of Action Nicotine is one of two naturally-occurring alkaloids which exhibit their primary effects via autonomic ganglia stimulation. The other alkaloid is lobeline which has many actions similar to those of nicotine but is less potent. Nicotine is a potent ganglionic and central nervous system stimulant, the actions of which are mediated via nicotine-specific receptors. Biphasic actions are observed depending upon the dose administered. The main effect of nicotine in small doses is stimulation of all autonomic ganglia; with larger doses, initial stimulation is followed by blockade of transmission. Biphasic effects are also evident in the adrenal medulla; discharge of catecholamines occurs with small doses, whereas prevention of catecholamines release is seen with higher doses as a response to splanchnic nerve stimulation. Stimulation of the central nervous system (CNS) is characterized by tremors and respiratory excitation. However, convulsions may occur with higher doses, along with respiratory failure secondary to both central paralysis and peripheral blockade to respiratory muscles.

Pharmacodynamics/Kinetics

Onset of action: Intranasal: More closely approximate the time course of plasma nicotine levels observed after cigarette smoking than other dosage forms

Duration: Transdermal: 24 hours

Absorption: Transdermal: Slow

Metabolism: Hepatic, primarily to cotinine ($\frac{1}{5}$ as active)

Half-life elimination: 4 hours

Time to peak, serum: Transdermal: 8-9 hours

Excretion: Urine

Clearance: Renal: pH dependent

Dosage

Smoking deterrent: Patients should be advised to completely stop smoking upon initiation of therapy.

Gum: Chew 1 piece of gum when urge to smoke, up to 30 pieces/day; most patients require 10-12 pieces of gum/day

Inhaler: Usually 6 to 16 cartridges per day; best effect was achieved by frequent continuous puffing (20 minutes); recommended duration of treatment is 3 months, after which patients may be weaned from the inhaler by gradual reduction of the daily dose over 6-12 weeks

Lozenge: Patients who smoke their first cigarette within 30 minutes of waking should use the 4 mg strength; otherwise the 2 mg strength is recommended.

Weeks 1-6: One lozenge every 1-2 hours

Weeks 7-9: One lozenge every 2-4 hours

Weeks 10-12: One lozenge every 4-8 hours

Note: Use at least 9 lozenges/day during first 6 weeks to improve chances of quitting; do not use more than one lozenge at a time (maximum: 5 lozenges every 6 hours, 20 lozenges/day)

Transdermal patch: Apply new patch every 24 hours to nonhairy, clean, dry skin on the upper body or upper outer arm; each patch should be applied to a different site. **Note:** Adjustment may be required during initial treatment (move to higher dose if experiencing withdrawal symptoms; lower dose if side effects are experienced).

Habitrol®, NicoDerm CQ®:

Patients smoking ≥10 cigarettes/day: Begin with **step 1** (21 mg/day) for 4-6 weeks, followed by **step 2** (14 mg/day) for 2 weeks; finish with **step 3** (7 mg/day) for 2 weeks

Patients smoking <10 cigarettes/day: Begin with **step 2** (14 mg/day) for 6 weeks, followed by **step 3** (7 mg/day) for 2 weeks

Note: Initial starting dose for patients <100 pounds, history of cardiovascular disease: 14 mg/day for 4-6 weeks, followed by 7 mg/day for 2-4 weeks

Note: Patients receiving >600 mg/day of cimetidine: Decrease to the next lower patch size

Nicotrol®: One patch daily for 6 weeks

Note: Benefits of use of nicotine transdermal patches beyond 3 months have not been demonstrated.

Spray: 1-2 sprays/hour; do not exceed more than 5 doses (10 sprays) per hour; each dose (2 sprays) contains 1 mg of nicotine. **Warning:** A dose of 40 mg can cause fatalities.

Ulcerative colitis (unlabeled use): Transdermal: Titrated to 22-25 mg/day

Administration

Gum: Should be chewed slowly to avoid jaw ache and to maximize benefit.

Lozenge: Should not be chewed or swallowed.

Monitoring Parameters Heart rate and blood pressure periodically during therapy; discontinue therapy if signs of nicotine toxicity occur (eg, severe headache, dizziness, mental confusion, disturbed hearing and vision, abdominal pain; rapid, weak and irregular pulse; salivation, nausea, vomiting, diarrhea, cold sweat, weakness); therapy should be discontinued if rash develops; discontinuation may be considered if other adverse effects of patch occur such as myalgia, arthralgia, abnormal dreams, insomnia, nervousness, dry mouth, sweating

Patient Information Report persistent rash, itching, or burning; do not smoke

Dosage Forms GUM, chewing (Nicorette®): 2 mg/square (48s, 108s, 168s); 4 mg/square (48s, 108s, 168s). **LOZ** (Commit™): 2 mg, 4 mg. **Oral inhalation system** (Nicotrol® Inhaler): 10 mg cartridge (42s). **PATCH, transdermal:** 7 mg/24 hours (7s, 30s); 14 mg/24 hours (7s, 14s, 30s); 21 mg/24 hours (7s, 14s, 30s); Kit (Step 1): 21 mg/24 hours (28s); (Step 2): 14 mg/24 hours (14s); (Step 3): 7 mg/24 hours (14s); (NicoDerm® CQ®) [clear patch]: 7 mg/24 hours (14s); 14 mg/24 hours (14s); 21 mg/24 hours (14s); (NicoDerm® CQ®) [tan patch]: 7 mg/24 hours (14s); 14 mg/24 hours (14s); 21 mg/24 hours (7s, 14s); (Nicotrol®): 15 mg/16 hours (7s). **SPRAY, intranasal** (Nicotrol® NS): 10 mg/mL (10 mL)

- **Nicotine Products Comparison** *see page 1399*
- **Nicotinex [OTC]** *see Niacin on page 897*
- **Nicotinic Acid** *see Niacin on page 897*
- **Nicotrol® Inhaler** *see Nicotine on page 901*
- **Nicotrol® NS** *see Nicotine on page 901*
- **Nicotrol® Patch [OTC]** *see Nicotine on page 901*
- **Nifedical™ XL** *see NIFEdipine on page 903*

NIFEdipine (nye FED i peen)

Related Information

Calcium Channel Blockers Comparison *on page 1371*

U.S. Brand Names Adalat® CC; Nifedical™ XL; Procardia®; Procardia XL®

Therapeutic Category Antianginal Agent; Antihypertensive Agent; Antimigraine Agent, Prophylaxis; Calcium Channel Blocker

Use Angina and hypertension (sustained release only), pulmonary hypertension

Pregnancy Risk Factor C

Contraindications Hypersensitivity to nifedipine or any component of the formulation; immediate release preparation for treatment of urgent or emergent hypertension; acute MI

Warnings/Precautions The routine use of short-acting nifedipine capsules in hypertensive emergencies and pseudoemergencies is not recommended. **The use of sublingual short-acting nifedipine in hypertensive emergencies is neither safe or effective and SHOULD BE ABANDONED!** Serious adverse events (cerebrovascular ischemia, syncope, heart block, stroke, sinus arrest, severe hypotension, acute myocardial infarction, ECG changes, and fetal distress) have been reported in relation to the administration of short-acting nifedipine in hypertensive emergencies.

Increased angina may be seen upon starting or increasing doses; may increase frequency, duration, and severity of angina during initiation of therapy; use with caution in patients with CHF or aortic stenosis (especially with concomitant beta-adrenergic blocker); severe left ventricular dysfunction, hepatic or renal impairment, hypertrophic cardiomyopathy (especially obstructive), concomitant therapy with beta-blockers or digoxin, edema

Mild and transient elevations in liver function enzymes may be apparent within 8 weeks of therapy initiation

Therapeutic potential of sustained-release formulation (elementary osmotic pump, gastrointestinal therapeutic system [GITS]) may be decreased in patients with certain GI disorders that accelerate intestinal transit time (eg, short bowel syndrome, inflammatory bowel disease, severe diarrhea)

Note: Elderly patients may experience a greater hypotensive response and the use of the immediate release formulation in patients >71 years of age has been associated with a nearly fourfold increased risk for all-cause mortality when compared to beta-blockers, ACE inhibitors, or other classes of calcium channel blockers

Common Adverse Reactions

>10%:
Cardiovascular: Flushing (10% to 25%), peripheral edema (dose-related 7% to 10%; up to 50%)
Central nervous system: Dizziness/lightheadedness/giddiness (10% to 27%), headache (10% to 23%)
Gastrointestinal: Nausea/heartburn (10% to 11%)
Neuromuscular & skeletal: Weakness (10% to 12%)

≥1% to 10%:
Cardiovascular: Palpitations (≤2% to 7%), transient hypotension (dose-related 5%), CHF (2%)
Central nervous system: Nervousness/mood changes (≤2% to 7%), shakiness (≤2%), jitteriness (≤2%) sleep disturbances (≤2%), difficulties in balance (≤2%), fever (≤2%), chills (≤2%)
Dermatologic: Dermatitis (≤2%), pruritus (≤2%), urticaria (≤2%)
Endocrine & metabolic: Sexual difficulties (≤2%)
Gastrointestinal: Diarrhea (≤2%), constipation (≤2%), cramps (≤2%), flatulence (≤2%), gingival hyperplasia (≤10%)
Neuromuscular & skeletal: Muscle cramps/tremor (≤2% to 8%), weakness (10%), inflammation (≤2%), joint stiffness (≤2%)
Ocular: Blurred vision (≤2%)
Respiratory: Dyspnea/cough/wheezing (6%), nasal congestion/sore throat (≤2% to 6%), chest congestion (≤2%), dyspnea (≤2%)

(Continued)

NIFEdipine *(Continued)*

Miscellaneous: Diaphoresis (≤2%)

Drug Interactions

Cytochrome P450 Effect: Substrate of CYP2D6 (minor), 3A4 (major); **Inhibits** CYP1A2 (moderate), 2C8/9 (weak), 2D6 (weak), 3A4 (weak)

Increased Effect/Toxicity: H_2-blockers may increase bioavailability and serum concentrations of nifedipine. Serum concentrations/toxicity of nifedipine may be increased by inhibitors of CYP3A4, including amprenavir, cimetidine, ciprofloxacin, clarithromycin, clozapine, diltiazem, disulfiram, digoxin, erythromycin, ethanol, fluconazole, fluoxetine, fluvoxamine, grapefruit juice, isoniazid, itraconazole, ketoconazole, labetalol, levodopa, loxapine, metoprolol, metronidazole, miconazole, nefazodone, nelfinavir, omeprazole, phenytoin, rifabutin, rifampin, ritonavir, troleandomycin, valproic acid, and verapamil. Nifedipine may increase serum levels of digoxin, phenytoin, theophylline, and vincristine. Blood pressure-lowering effects may be additive with sildenafil, tadalafil, and vardenafil (use caution).

Decreased Effect: Phenobarbital and nifedipine may decrease nifedipine levels. Quinidine and nifedipine may decrease quinidine serum levels. Rifampin and nifedipine may decrease nifedipine serum levels. Calcium may reduce the hypotension from of calcium channel blockers.

Mechanism of Action Inhibits calcium ion from entering the "slow channels" or select voltage-sensitive areas of vascular smooth muscle and myocardium during depolarization, producing a relaxation of coronary vascular smooth muscle and coronary vasodilation; increases myocardial oxygen delivery in patients with vasospastic angina

Pharmacodynamics/Kinetics

Onset of action: ~20 minutes

Protein binding (concentration dependent): 92% to 98%

Metabolism: Hepatic to inactive metabolites

Bioavailability: Capsules: 45% to 75%; Sustained release: 65% to 86%

Half-life elimination: Adults: Healthy: 2-5 hours, Cirrhosis: 7 hours; Elderly: 6.7 hours

Excretion: Urine

Dosage Oral:

Children: Hypertrophic cardiomyopathy: 0.6-0.9 mg/kg/24 hours in 3-4 divided doses

Adolescents and Adults: (**Note:** When switching from immediate release to sustained release formulations, total daily dose will start the same)

Initial: 30 mg once daily as sustained release formulation, or if indicated, 10 mg 3 times/day as capsules

Usual dose: 10-30 mg 3 times/day as capsules or 30-60 mg once daily as sustained release

Maximum dose: 120-180 mg/day

Increase sustained release at 7- to 14-day intervals

Hemodialysis: Supplemental dose is not necessary.

Peritoneal dialysis effects: Supplemental dose is not necessary.

Dosing adjustment in hepatic impairment: Reduce oral dose by 50% to 60% in patients with cirrhosis.

Administration Extended release tablets should be swallowed whole; do not crush or chew.

Monitoring Parameters Heart rate, blood pressure, signs and symptoms of CHF, peripheral edema

Patient Information Sustained release products should not be crushed or chewed; Adalat® CC should be taken on an empty stomach; limit caffeine intake; avoid alcohol; notify prescriber if angina pain is not reduced when taking this drug, irregular heartbeat, shortness of breath, swelling, dizziness, constipation, nausea, or hypotension occurs; do not stop therapy without advice of prescriber; the shell of the sustained-release tablet may appear intact in the stool, this is no cause for concern

Dosage Forms CAP, liquid-filled (Procardia®): 10 mg, 20 mg. **TAB, extended release:** 30 mg, 60 mg, 90 mg; (Adalat® CC, Procardia XL®): 30 mg, 60 mg, 90 mg; (Nifedical™ XL): 30 mg, 60 mg

♦ **Niferex® [OTC]** *see* Polysaccharide-Iron Complex *on page 1016*

♦ **Niferex® 150 [OTC]** *see* Polysaccharide-Iron Complex *on page 1016*

♦ **Niftolid** *see* Flutamide *on page 546*

♦ **Nilandron®** *see* Nilutamide *on page 904*

Nilutamide *(ni LOO ta mide)*

U.S. Brand Names Nilandron®

Synonyms RU-23908

Therapeutic Category Antiandrogen; Antineoplastic Agent, Antiandrogen

Use Treatment of metastatic prostate cancer

Pregnancy Risk Factor C

Contraindications Hypersensitivity to nilutamide or any component of the formulation; severe hepatic impairment; severe respiratory insufficiency

Warnings/Precautions Interstitial pneumonitis has been reported in 2% of patients exposed to nilutamide. Patients typically experienced progressive exertional dyspnea, and possibly cough, chest pain and fever. X-rays showed interstitial or alveolo-interstitial changes. The suggestive signs of pneumonitis most often occurred within the first 3 months of nilutamide treatment.

Hepatitis or marked increases in liver enzymes leading to drug discontinuation occurred in 1% of nilutamide patients. Rare cases of elevated hepatic enzymes followed by death have been reported.

Foreign postmarketing surveillance has revealed isolated cases of aplastic anemia in which a causal relationship with nilutamide could not be ascertained.

13% to 57% of patients receiving nilutamide reported a delay in adaptation to the dark, ranging from seconds to a few minutes. This effect sometimes does not abate as drug treatment is continued. Caution patients who experience this effect about driving at night or through tunnels. This effect can be alleviated by wearing tinted glasses.

Common Adverse Reactions
>10%:
Central nervous system: Headache, insomnia
Endocrine & metabolic: Hot flashes (30% to 67%), gynecomastia (10%)
Gastrointestinal: Nausea (mild - 10% to 32%), abdominal pain (10%), constipation, anorexia
Genitourinary: Testicular atrophy (16%), libido decreased
Hepatic: Transient elevation in serum transaminases (8% to 13%)
Ocular: Impaired dark adaptation (13% to 57%), usually reversible with dose reduction, may require discontinuation of the drug in 1% to 2% of patients
Respiratory: Dyspnea (11%)
1% to 10%:
Cardiovascular: Chest pain, edema, heart failure, hypertension, syncope
Central nervous system: Dizziness, drowsiness, malaise, hypesthesia, depression
Dermatologic: Pruritus, alopecia, dry skin, rash
Endocrine & metabolic: Disulfiram-like reaction (hot flashes, rashes) (5%); Flu-like syndrome, fever
Gastrointestinal: Vomiting, diarrhea, dyspepsia, GI hemorrhage, melena, weight loss, xerostomia
Genitourinary: Hematuria, nocturia
Hematologic: Anemia
Hepatic: Hepatitis (1%)
Neuromuscular & skeletal: Arthritis, paresthesia
Ocular: Chromatopsia (9%), abnormal vision (6% to 7%), cataracts, photophobia
Respiratory: Interstitial pneumonitis (2% - typically exertional dyspnea, cough, chest pain, and fever; most often occurring within the first 3 months of treatment); rhinitis
Miscellaneous: Diaphoresis

Drug Interactions
Cytochrome P450 Effect: Substrate of CYP2C19 (major); **Inhibits** CYP2C19 (weak)
Increased Effect/Toxicity: CYP2C19 inhibitors may increase the levels/effects of nilutamide; example inhibitors include delavirdine, fluconazole, fluvoxamine, gemfibrozil, isoniazid, omeprazole, and ticlopidine.
Decreased Effect: CYP2C19 inducers may decrease the levels/effects of nilutamide; example inducers include aminoglutethimide, carbamazepine, phenytoin, and rifampin.
Mechanism of Action Nonsteroidal antiandrogen that inhibits androgen uptake or inhibits binding of androgen in target tissues. It specifically blocks the action of androgens by interacting with cytosolic androgen receptor F sites in target tissue

Pharmacodynamics/Kinetics
Absorption: Rapid and complete
Protein binding: 72% to 85%
Metabolism: Hepatic, forms active metabolites
Half-life elimination: Terminal: 23-87 hours; Metabolites: 35-137 hours
Excretion: Urine (up to 78% at 120 hours); <1% as unchanged drug); feces (1% to 7%)

Dosage Refer to individual protocols.
Adults: Oral: 300 mg daily for 30 days starting the same day or day after surgical castration, then 150 mg/day

Monitoring Parameters Obtain a chest x-ray if a patient reports dyspnea; if there are findings suggestive of interstitial pneumonitis, discontinue treatment with nilutamide. Measure serum hepatic enzyme levels at baseline and at regular intervals (3 months); if transaminases increase over 2-3 times the upper limit of normal, discontinue treatment. Perform appropriate laboratory testing at the first symptom/sign of liver injury (eg, jaundice, dark urine, fatigue, abdominal pain or unexplained GI symptoms).

Patient Information Take as prescribed; do not change dosing schedule or stop taking without consulting prescriber. May cause a severe reaction with alcohol. Use alcohol cautiously while taking this medication; if the reaction occurs, avoid alcohol. Periodic laboratory tests are necessary while taking this medication. You may experience dizziness, confusion, or blurred vision (avoid driving or engaging in tasks that require alertness until response to drug is known); loss of light accommodation (avoid night driving and use caution in poorly lighted or changing light situations); impotence; or loss of libido (discuss with prescriber). Report yellowing of skin or eyes; change in color of urine or stool; unusual bruising or bleeding; chest pain; difficulty or painful voiding. Report immediately any shortness of breath, difficulty breathing, or increased cough.

Dosage Forms TAB: 150 mg

♦ Nimbex® see Cisatracurium on page 282

Nimodipine (nye MOE di peen)
Related Information
Calcium Channel Blockers Comparison on page 1371
(Continued)

Nimodipine *(Continued)*

U.S. Brand Names Nimotop®

Therapeutic Category Calcium Channel Blocker

Use Spasm following subarachnoid hemorrhage from ruptured intracranial aneurysms regardless of the patients neurological condition postictus (Hunt and Hess grades I-V)

Pregnancy Risk Factor C

Contraindications Hypersensitivity to nimodipine or any component of the formulation

Warnings/Precautions Use with caution and titrate dosages for patients with impaired renal or hepatic function; use caution when treating patients with CHF, sick-sinus syndrome, PVCs, severe left ventricular dysfunction, hypertrophic cardiomyopathy (especially obstructive, IHSS), concomitant therapy with beta-blockers or digoxin, edema, or increased intracranial pressure with cranial tumors; do not abruptly withdraw (may cause chest pain); elderly may experience hypotension and constipation more readily; intestinal pseudo-obstruction and ileus have been reported during the use of nimodipine; use caution in patients with decreased GI motility of a history of bowel obstruction

Common Adverse Reactions 1% to 10%:
  Cardiovascular: Reductions in systemic blood pressure (1% to 8%)
  Central nervous system: Headache (1% to 4%)
  Dermatologic: Rash (1% to 2%)
  Gastrointestinal: Diarrhea (2% to 4%), abdominal discomfort (2%)

Drug Interactions

  Cytochrome P450 Effect: Substrate of CYP3A4 (major)

  Increased Effect/Toxicity: Calcium channel blockers and nimodipine may result in enhanced cardiovascular effects of other calcium channel blockers. Cimetidine, omeprazole, and valproic acid may increase serum nimodipine levels. The effects of antihypertensive agents may be increased by nimodipine. Azole antifungals (itraconazole, ketoconazole, fluconazole), erythromycin, protease inhibitors (amprenavir, nelfinavir, ritonavir) and other inhibitors of cytochrome P450 isoenzyme 3A4 may inhibit calcium channel blocker metabolism. Blood pressure-lowering effects may be additive with sildenafil, tadalafil, and vardenafil (use caution).

  Decreased Effect: Rifampin (and potentially other enzyme inducers) increase the metabolism of calcium channel blockers.

Mechanism of Action Nimodipine shares the pharmacology of other calcium channel blockers; animal studies indicate that nimodipine has a greater effect on cerebral arterials than other arterials; this increased specificity may be due to the drug's increased lipophilicity and cerebral distribution as compared to nifedipine; inhibits calcium ion from entering the "slow channels" or select voltage sensitive areas of vascular smooth muscle and myocardium during depolarization

Pharmacodynamics/Kinetics
  Protein binding: >95%
  Metabolism: Extensively hepatic
  Bioavailability: 13%
  Half-life elimination: 3 hours; prolonged with renal impairment
  Time to peak, serum: ~1 hour
  Excretion: Urine (50%) and feces (32%) within 4 days

Dosage Adults: Oral: 60 mg every 4 hours for 21 days, start therapy within 96 hours after subarachnoid hemorrhage.

  Dialysis: Not removed by hemo- or peritoneal dialysis; supplemental dose is not necessary.

  Dosing adjustment in hepatic impairment: Reduce dosage to 30 mg every 4 hours in patients with liver failure.

Administration If the capsules cannot be swallowed, the liquid may be removed by making a hole in each end of the capsule with an 18-gauge needle and extracting the contents into a syringe. If administered via NG tube, follow with a flush of 30 mL NS.

Dosage Forms CAP, liquid-filled: 30 mg

♦ **Nimotop**® *see* Nimodipine *on page 905*

♦ **Nipent**® *see* Pentostatin *on page 980*

Nisoldipine *(NYE sole di peen)*

Related Information
  Calcium Channel Blockers Comparison *on page 1371*

U.S. Brand Names Sular®

Therapeutic Category Antihypertensive Agent; Calcium Channel Blocker

Use Management of hypertension, alone or in combination with other antihypertensive agents

Pregnancy Risk Factor C

Contraindications Hypersensitivity to nisoldipine, any component of the formulation, or other dihydropyridine calcium channel blockers

Warnings/Precautions Increased angina and/or myocardial infarction in patients with coronary artery disease. Use with caution in patients with hypotension, CHF, and hepatic impairment. Blood pressure lowering must be done at a rate appropriate for the patient's condition.

Common Adverse Reactions
  >10%:
    Cardiovascular: Peripheral edema (dose-related 7% to 29%)
    Central nervous system: Headache (22%)

1% to 10%:
Cardiovascular: Chest pain (2%), palpitations (3%), vasodilation (4%)
Central nervous system: Dizziness (3% to 10%)
Dermatologic: Rash (2%)
Gastrointestinal: Nausea (2%)
Respiratory: Pharyngitis (5%), sinusitis (3%), dyspnea (3%), cough (5%)

Drug Interactions
Cytochrome P450 Effect: Substrate of CYP3A4 (major); **Inhibits** CYP1A2 (weak), 3A4 (weak)
Increased Effect/Toxicity: H$_2$-antagonists or omeprazole may cause an increase in the serum concentrations of nisoldipine. Digoxin and nisoldipine may increase digoxin effect. Azole antifungals (itraconazole, ketoconazole, fluconazole), erythromycin, and other inhibitors of cytochrome P450 isoenzyme 3A4 may inhibit calcium channel blocker metabolism. Calcium may reduce the calcium channel blocker's effects, particularly hypotension. Blood pressure-lowering effects may be additive with sildenafil, tadalafil, and vardenafil (use caution).
Decreased Effect: Rifampin, phenytoin, and potentially other enzyme inducers decrease the levels of nisoldipine. Calcium may decrease the hypotension from calcium channel blockers.

Mechanism of Action As a dihydropyridine calcium channel blocker, structurally similar to nifedipine, nisoldipine impedes the movement of calcium ions into vascular smooth muscle and cardiac muscle. Dihydropyridines are potent vasodilators and are not as likely to suppress cardiac contractility and slow cardiac conduction as other calcium antagonists such as verapamil and diltiazem; nisoldipine is 5-10 times as potent a vasodilator as nifedipine.

Pharmacodynamics/Kinetics
Duration: >24 hours
Absorption: Well absorbed
Metabolism: Extensively hepatic to inactive metabolites; first-pass effect
Bioavailability: 5%
Half-life elimination: 7-12 hours
Time to peak: 6-12 hours
Excretion: Urine

Dosage Adults: Oral: Initial: 20 mg once daily, then increase by 10 mg/week (or longer intervals) to attain adequate control of blood pressure; doses >60 mg once daily are not recommended. A starting dose not exceeding 10 mg/day is recommended for the elderly and those with hepatic impairment.

Administration Administer at the same time each day to ensure minimal fluctuation of serum levels. Avoid high-fat diet.

Patient Information Avoid grapefruit products before and after dosing; administration with a high fat meal can lead to excessive peak drug concentrations and should be avoided

Dosage Forms TAB, extended release: 10 mg, 20 mg, 30 mg, 40 mg

♦ **Nitalapram** see Citalopram on page 286

Nitazoxanide (nye ta ZOX a nide)

U.S. Brand Names Alinia™
Synonyms NTZ
Therapeutic Category Antiprotozoal
Use Treatment of diarrhea caused by Cryptosporidium parvum and Giardia lamblia in pediatric patients 1-11 years of age
Pregnancy Risk Factor B
Contraindications Hypersensitivity to nitazoxanide or any component of the formulation
Warnings/Precautions Use caution with renal or hepatic impairment. Safety and efficacy have not been established with HIV infection, immunodeficiency, children <1 year, children >11 years, or adults.
Common Adverse Reactions Rates of adverse effects were similar to those reported with placebo.
1% to 10%:
Central nervous system: Headache (1%)
Gastrointestinal: Abdominal pain (8%), diarrhea (2%), vomiting (1%)
Mechanism of Action Nitazoxanide is rapidly metabolized to the active metabolite tizoxanide in vivo. Activity may be due to interference with the pyruvate:ferredoxin oxidoreductase (PFOR) enzyme-dependent electron transfer reaction which is essential to anaerobic metabolism. In vitro, nitazoxanide and tizoxanide inhibit the growth of sporozoites and oocysts of Cryptosporidium parvum and trophozoites of Giardia lamblia.
Pharmacodynamics/Kinetics
Protein binding: Tizoxanide: >99%
Metabolism: Hepatic, to an active metabolite, tizoxanide. Tizoxanide undergoes conjugation to form tizoxanide glucuronide. Nitazoxanide is not detectable in the serum following oral administration.
Time to peak, plasma: Tizoxanide and tizoxanide glucuronide: 1-4 hours
Excretion: Tizoxanide: Urine, bile, and feces; Tizoxanide glucuronide: Urine and bile
Dosage Oral: Diarrhea: Children:
12-47 months: 100 mg every 12 hours for 3 days
4-11 years: 200 mg every 12 hours for 3 days
Dosage adjustment in renal/hepatic impairment: Specific recommendations are not available; use with caution
Administration Shake suspension well prior to administration. Administer with food.
(Continued)

Nitazoxanide *(Continued)*

Patient Information Shake suspension well prior to using; take with food. May discolor eyes or urine.

Dosage Forms POWDER for oral suspension: 100 mg/5 mL (60 mL)

Nitisinone *(ni TIS i known)*

U.S. Brand Names Orfadin®

Therapeutic Category 4-Hydroxyphenylpyruvate Dioxygenase Inhibitor

Use Treatment of hereditary tyrosinemia type 1 (HT-1); to be used with dietary restriction of tyrosine and phenylalanine

Restrictions Distributed by Rare Disease Therapeutics, Inc (contact 615-399-0700)

Pregnancy Risk Factor C

Contraindications Hypersensitivity to nitisinone or any component of the formulation

Warnings/Precautions For use by physicians experienced in treating HT-1. Must be used with dietary restriction of tyrosine and phenylalanine; inadequate restriction can result in toxic effects to the eyes, skin, and nervous system (nutritional consultation required). Patients should have slit-lamp examination of the eyes prior to beginning treatment. Careful monitoring of liver, platelet and white blood cell counts, plasma tyrosine levels and other recommended laboratory parameters are required.

Common Adverse Reactions 1% to 10%:
Dermatologic: Alopecia (1%), dry skin (1%), exfoliative dermatitis (1%), maculopapular rash (1%), pruritus (1%)
Hematologic: Thrombocytopenia (3%), leukopenia (3%), porphyria (1%), epistaxis (1%)
Hepatic: Hepatic neoplasm (8%), hepatic failure (7%)
Ocular: Conjunctivitis (2%), corneal opacity (2%), keratitis (2%), photophobia (2%), cataracts (1%), blepharitis (1%), eye pain (1%)

Mechanism of Action In patients with HT-1, tyrosine metabolism is interrupted due to a lack of the enzyme (fumarylacetoacetate hydrolase) needed in the last step of tyrosine degradation. Toxic metabolites of tyrosine accumulate and cause liver and kidney toxicity. Nitisinone competitively inhibits 4-hydroxyphenyl-pyruvate dioxygenase, an enzyme needed earlier in the tyrosine degradation pathway, and therefore prevents the build-up of the damaging metabolites.

Pharmacodynamics/Kinetics Limited pharmacokinetic studies in children or HT-1 patients.

Bioavailability: Animal studies: >90%
Half-life elimination: Terminal: Male: Healthy: 54 hours
Time to peak: 3 hours
Excretion (animal studies): Urine

Dosage Oral: **Note:** Must be used in conjunction with a low protein diet restricted in tyrosine and phenylalanine.
Infants: See dosing for Children and Adults; infants may require maximal dose once liver function has improved
Children and Adults: Initial: 1 mg/kg/day in divided doses, given in the morning and evening, 1 hour before meals; doses do not need to be divided evenly
Dose adjustment: If biochemical parameters (see Monitoring Parameters) are not normalized within in 1-month period, dose may be increased to 1.5 mg/kg/day (maximum dose: 2 mg/kg/day).

Administration Administer 1 hour prior to a meal. Capsules may be opened and contents suspended in a small quantity of water, formula, or apple sauce; use immediately.

Monitoring Parameters
Dietary tyrosine and phenylalanine
Liver: Ultrasound, computerized tomography, magnetic resonance imaging
Ophthalmic exam: Slit-lamp examination prior to treatment; repeat during therapy in patients with photophobia, eye pain, redness, swelling, or burning of the eyes.
Plasma tyrosine: Levels should be kept <500 µmol/L to avoid toxicity.
Plasma succinylacetone: May take up to 3 months to normalize after start of therapy
Platelets, white blood cell counts
Serum alpha-fetoprotein: To monitor effectiveness of treatment and potential liver neoplasia.
Serum phosphate in patients with renal dysfunction
Urine succinylacetone: Should not be detectable during treatment; dose should be increased if detectable after the first month of treatment.

Patient Information Must follow a low protein diet restricted in tyrosine and phenylalanine. Report immediately rash, excessive bleeding, eye pain, sensitivity to light, skin changes on feet or hands, yellowing of skin or eyes to prescriber.

Dosage Forms CAP: 2 mg, 5 mg, 10 mg

- **Nitrates Comparison** see page 1400
- **Nitrek®** see Nitroglycerin on page 910
- **4'-Nitro-3'-Trifluoromethylisobutyrantide** see Flutamide on page 546
- **Nitro-Bid®** see Nitroglycerin on page 910
- **Nitro-Dur®** see Nitroglycerin on page 910

Nitrofurantoin *(nye troe fyoor AN toyn)*

Related Information
Antimicrobial Drugs of Choice *on page 1440*

U.S. Brand Names Furadantin®; Macrobid®; Macrodantin®

Therapeutic Category Antibiotic, Miscellaneous

Use Prevention and treatment of urinary tract infections caused by susceptible gram-negative and some gram-positive organisms; *Pseudomonas, Serratia,* and most species of *Proteus* are generally resistant to nitrofurantoin

Pregnancy Risk Factor B (contraindicated at term)

Contraindications Hypersensitivity to nitrofurantoin or any component of the formulation; renal impairment (anuria, oliguria, significantly elevated serum creatinine, or Cl_{cr}< 60 mL/minute); infants <1 month (due to the possibility of hemolytic anemia); pregnancy at term (38-42 weeks gestation), during labor and delivery, or when the onset of labor is imminent

Warnings/Precautions Use with caution in patients with G6PD deficiency or in patients with anemia. Therapeutic concentrations of nitrofurantoin are not attained in urine of patients with Cl_{cr}<60 mL/minute. Use with caution if prolonged therapy is anticipated due to possible pulmonary toxicity. Acute, subacute, or chronic (usually after 6 months of therapy) pulmonary reactions have been observed in patients treated with nitrofurantoin; if these occur, discontinue therapy immediately; monitor closely for malaise, dyspnea, cough, fever, radiologic evidence of diffuse interstitial pneumonitis or fibrosis. Rare, but severe hepatic reactions have been associated with nitrofurantoin (onset may be insidious); discontinue immediately if hepatitis occurs. Has been associated with peripheral neuropathy (rare); risk may be increased by renal impairment, diabetes, vitamin B deficiency, or electrolyte imbalance; use caution.

Common Adverse Reactions Frequency not defined.

Cardiovascular: Chest pain, cyanosis, ECG changes (associated with pulmonary toxicity)

Central nervous system: Chills, depression, dizziness, drowsiness, fatigue, fever, headache, pseudotumor cerebri, psychotic reaction

Dermatologic: Alopecia, erythema multiforme, exfoliative dermatitis, pruritus, rash, Stevens-Johnson syndrome

Gastrointestinal: Abdominal pain, *C. difficile*-colitis, constipation, diarrhea, dyspepsia, loss of appetite, nausea (most common), pancreatitis, sore throat, vomiting

Hematologic: Agranulocytosis, aplastic anemia, eosinophilia, hemolytic anemia, methemoglobinemia, thrombocytopenia

Hepatic: Cholestasis, hepatitis, hepatic necrosis, serum transaminases increased, jaundice (cholestatic)

Neuromuscular & skeletal: Arthralgia, numbness, paresthesia, peripheral neuropathy, weakness

Ocular: Amblyopia, nystagmus, optic neuritis (rare)

Respiratory: Cough, dyspnea, pneumonitis, pulmonary fibrosis

Miscellaneous: Hypersensitivity (including acute pulmonary hypersensitivity), lupus-like syndrome

Drug Interactions

Increased Effect/Toxicity: Probenecid decreases renal excretion of nitrofurantoin.

Decreased Effect: Antacids decrease absorption of nitrofurantoin.

Mechanism of Action Inhibits several bacterial enzyme systems including acetyl coenzyme A interfering with metabolism and possibly cell wall synthesis

Pharmacodynamics/Kinetics

Absorption: Well absorbed; macrocrystalline form absorbed more slowly due to slower dissolution (causes less GI distress)

Distribution: V_d: 0.8 L/kg; crosses placenta; enters breast milk

Protein binding: ~40%

Metabolism: Body tissues (except plasma) metabolize 60% of drug to inactive metabolites

Bioavailability: Increased with food

Half-life elimination: 20-60 minutes; prolonged with renal impairment

Excretion:

Suspension: Urine (40%) and feces (small amounts) as metabolites and unchanged drug

Macrocrystals: Urine (20% to 25% as unchanged drug)

Dosage Oral:

Children >1 month: 5-7 mg/kg/day in divided doses every 6 hours; maximum: 400 mg/day

UTI prophylaxis (chronic): 1-2 mg/kg/day in divided doses every 12-24 hours; maximum: 100 mg/day

Adults: 50-100 mg/dose every 6 hours

Macrocrystal/monohydrate: 100 mg twice daily

UTI prophylaxis (chronic): 50-100 mg/dose at bedtime

Dosing adjustment in renal impairment: Cl_{cr} <60 mL/minute: Avoid use

Avoid use in hemo- and peritoneal dialysis and continuous arteriovenous or venovenous hemofiltration

Administration Administer with meals to slow the rate of absorption and decrease adverse effects; suspension may be mixed with water, milk, fruit juice, or infant formula

Monitoring Parameters Signs of pulmonary reaction, signs of numbness or tingling of the extremities, periodic liver function tests

Patient Information Take with food or milk; may discolor urine to a dark yellow or brown color; report fever, chest pain, persistent, nonproductive cough, or difficulty breathing; avoid alcohol

Dosage Forms CAP, macrocrystal: 50 mg, 100 mg; (Macrodantin®): 25 mg, 50 mg, 100 mg. **CAP, macrocrystal/monohydrate** (Macrobid®): 100 mg. **SUSP, oral** (Furadantin®): 25 mg/5 mL (60 mL, 470 mL).

♦ **Nitrogard®** *see Nitroglycerin on page 910*

♦ **Nitrogen Mustard** *see Mechlorethamine on page 778*

Nitroglycerin (nye troe GLI ser in)

Related Information

Hemodynamic Support, Intravenous *on page 1377*

Nitrates Comparison *on page 1400*

U.S. Brand Names Minitran™; Nitrek®; Nitro-Bid®; Nitro-Dur®; Nitrogard®; Nitrol® [DSC]; Nitrolingual®; NitroQuick®; Nitrostat®; Nitro-Tab®; NitroTime®

Synonyms Glyceryl Trinitrate; Nitroglycerol; NTG

Therapeutic Category Antianginal Agent; Antihypertensive Agent; Nitrate; Vasodilator; Vasodilator, Coronary

Use Treatment of angina pectoris; I.V. for congestive heart failure (especially when associated with acute myocardial infarction); pulmonary hypertension; hypertensive emergencies occurring perioperatively (especially during cardiovascular surgery)

Pregnancy Risk Factor C

Contraindications Hypersensitivity to organic nitrates; hypersensitivity to isosorbide, nitroglycerin, or any component of the formulation; concurrent use with phosphodiesterase-5 (PDE-5) inhibitors (sildenafil, tadalafil, or vardenafil); angle-closure glaucoma (intraocular pressure may be increased); head trauma or cerebral hemorrhage (increase intracranial pressure); severe anemia; allergy to adhesive (transdermal product)

I.V. product: Hypotension; uncorrected hypovolemia; inadequate cerebral circulation; increased intracranial pressure; constrictive pericarditis; pericardial tamponade

Warnings/Precautions Do not use extended release preparations in patients with GI hypermotility or malabsorptive syndrome; use with caution in patients with hepatic impairment, CHF, or acute myocardial infarction; available preparations of I.V. nitroglycerin differ in concentration or volume; pay attention to dilution and dosage; I.V. preparations contain alcohol and/or propylene glycol; avoid loss of nitroglycerin in standard PVC tubing; dosing instructions must be followed with care when the appropriate infusion sets are used

Hypotension may occur, use with caution in patients who are volume-depleted, are hypotensive, have inadequate circulation; nitrate therapy may aggravate angina caused by hypertrophic cardiomyopathy

Common Adverse Reactions

Spray or patch:

>10%: Central nervous system: Headache (patch 63%, spray 50%)

1% to 10%:

Cardiovascular: Hypotension (patch 4%), increased angina (patch 2%)

Central nervous system: Lightheadedness (patch 6%), syncope (patch 4%)

Topical, sublingual, intravenous: Frequency not defined:

Cardiovascular: Hypotension (infrequent), postural hypotension, crescendo angina (uncommon), rebound hypertension (uncommon), pallor, cardiovascular collapse, tachycardia, shock, flushing, peripheral edema

Central nervous system: Headache (most common), lightheadedness (related to blood pressure changes), syncope (uncommon), dizziness, restlessness

Gastrointestinal: Nausea, vomiting, bowel incontinence, xerostomia

Genitourinary: Urinary incontinence

Hematologic: Methemoglobinemia (rare, overdose)

Neuromuscular & skeletal: Weakness

Ocular: Blurred vision

Miscellaneous: Cold sweat

The incidence of hypotension and adverse cardiovascular events may be increased when used in combination with sildenafil (Viagra®).

Drug Interactions

Increased Effect/Toxicity: Significant reduction of systolic and diastolic blood pressure with concurrent use of sildenafil, tadalafil, or vardenafil (contraindicated); do not administer sildenafil, tadalafil, or vardenafil within 24 hours of a nitrate preparation. Ethanol can cause hypotension when nitrates are taken 1 hour or more after ethanol ingestion.

Decreased Effect: I.V. nitroglycerin may antagonize the anticoagulant effect of heparin (possibly only at high nitroglycerin dosages); monitor closely. May need to decrease heparin dosage when nitroglycerin is discontinued. Alteplase (tissue plasminogen activator) has a lesser effect when used with I.V. nitroglycerin; avoid concurrent use. Ergot alkaloids may cause an increase in blood pressure and decrease in antianginal effects; avoid concurrent use.

Mechanism of Action Reduces cardiac oxygen demand by decreasing left ventricular pressure and systemic vascular resistance; dilates coronary arteries and improves collateral flow to ischemic regions

Pharmacodynamics/Kinetics

Onset of action: Sublingual tablet: 1-3 minutes; Translingual spray: 2 minutes; Buccal tablet: 2-5 minutes; Sustained release: 20-45 minutes; Topical: 15-60 minutes; Transdermal: 40-60 minutes; I.V. drip: Immediate

Peak effect: Sublingual tablet: 4-8 minutes; Translingual spray: 4-10 minutes; Buccal tablet: 4-10 minutes; Sustained release: 45-120 minutes; Topical: 30-120 minutes; Transdermal: 60-180 minutes; I.V. drip: Immediate

Duration: Sublingual tablet: 30-60 minutes; Translingual spray: 30-60 minutes; Buccal tablet: 2 hours; Sustained release: 4-8 hours; Topical: 2-12 hours; Transdermal: 18-24 hours; I.V. drip: 3-5 minutes

Protein binding: 60%

Metabolism: Extensive first-pass effect

Half-life elimination: 1-4 minutes

Excretion: Urine (as inactive metabolites)

Dosage Note: Hemodynamic and antianginal tolerance often develop within 24-48 hours of continuous nitrate administration

Children: Pulmonary hypertension: Continuous infusion: Start 0.25-0.5 mcg/kg/minute and titrate by 1 mcg/kg/minute at 20- to 60-minute intervals to desired effect; usual dose: 1-3 mcg/kg/minute; maximum: 5 mcg/kg/minute

Adults:

Buccal: Initial: 1 mg every 3-5 hours while awake (3 times/day); titrate dosage upward if angina occurs with tablet in place

Oral: 2.5-9 mg 2-4 times/day (up to 26 mg 4 times/day)

I.V.: 5 mcg/minute, increase by 5 mcg/minute every 3-5 minutes to 20 mcg/minute; if no response at 20 mcg/minute increase by 10 mcg/minute every 3-5 minutes, up to 200 mcg/minute

Ointment: $^1/_2$" upon rising and $^1/_2$" 6 hours later; the dose may be doubled and even doubled again as needed

Patch, transdermal: Initial: 0.2-0.4 mg/hour, titrate to doses of 0.4-0.8 mg/hour; tolerance is minimized by using a patch-on period of 12-14 hours and patch-off period of 10-12 hours

Sublingual: 0.2-0.6 mg every 5 minutes for maximum of 3 doses in 15 minutes; may also use prophylactically 5-10 minutes prior to activities which may provoke an attack

Translingual: 1-2 sprays into mouth under tongue every 3-5 minutes for maximum of 3 doses in 15 minutes, may also be used 5-10 minutes prior to activities which may provoke an attack prophylactically

Hemodialysis: Supplemental dose is not necessary

Peritoneal dialysis: Supplemental dose is not necessary

May need to use nitrate-free interval (10-12 hours/day) to avoid tolerance development; gradually decrease dose in patients receiving NTG for prolonged period to avoid withdrawal reaction

Elderly: In general, dose selection should be cautious, usually starting at the low end of the dosing range

Monitoring Parameters Blood pressure, heart rate

Patient Information Go to hospital if no relief after 3 sublingual doses; do not swallow or chew sublingual form; do not change brands without notifying your prescriber or pharmacist; take oral nitrates on an empty stomach; keep tablets and capsules in original container; keep tightly closed; use spray only when lying down; highly flammable; do not inhale spray; do not chew sustained release products; a treatment-free interval of 8-12 hours is recommended each day; take 3 times/day rather than every 8 hours

Dosage Forms AERO, translingual (Nitrolingual® Pumpspray): 0.4 mg/metered spray (12 g). **CAP, extended release** (Nitro-Time®): 2.5 mg, 6.5 mg, 9 mg. **INF** [premixed in D_5W]: 0.1 mg/mL (250 mL, 500 mL); 0.2 mg/mL (250 mL); 0.4 mg/mL (250 mL, 500 mL). **INJ, solution:** 5 mg/mL (5 mL, 10 mL). **OINT, topical** (Nitro-Bid®, Nitrol® [DSC]): 2% [20 mg/g] (30 g, 60 g). **PATCH, transdermal:** Systems deliver 0.1 mg/hour (30s), 0.2 mg/hour (30s), 0.4 mg/hour (30s), 0.6 mg/hour (30s); (Minitran™): 0.1 mg/hour (30s), 0.2 mg/hour (30s), 0.4 mg/hour (30s), 0.6 mg/hour (30s); (Nitrek®): 0.2 mg/hour (30s), 0.4 mg/hour (30s), 0.6 mg/hour (30s); (Nitro-Dur®): 0.1 mg/hour (30s), 0.2 mg/hour (30s), 0.3 mg/hour (30s), 0.4 mg/hour (30s), 0.6 mg/hour (30s), 0.8 mg/hour (30s). **TAB, buccal, extended release** (Nitrogard®): 2 mg, 3 mg. **TAB, sublingual** (NitroQuick®, Nitrostat®, NitroTab®): 0.3 mg, 0.4 mg, 0.6 mg.

♦ **Nitroglycerol** see Nitroglycerin on page 910
♦ **Nitrol® [DSC]** see Nitroglycerin on page 910
♦ **Nitrolingual®** see Nitroglycerin on page 910
♦ **Nitropress®** see Nitroprusside on page 911

Nitroprusside (nye troe PRUS ide)

Related Information

Hemodynamic Support, Intravenous on page 1377

U.S. Brand Names Nitropress®

Synonyms Nitroprusside Sodium; Sodium Nitroferricyanide; Sodium Nitroprusside

Therapeutic Category Antihypertensive Agent; Vasodilator

Use Management of hypertensive crises; congestive heart failure; used for controlled hypotension to reduce bleeding during surgery

Pregnancy Risk Factor C

Contraindications Hypersensitivity to nitroprusside or any component of the formulation; treatment of compensatory hypertension (aortic coarctation, arteriovenous shunting); high output failure; congenital optic atrophy or tobacco amblyopia

Warnings/Precautions Use with caution in patients with increased intracranial pressure (head trauma, cerebral hemorrhage); severe renal impairment, hepatic failure, hypothyroidism; use only as an infusion with 5% dextrose in water; continuously monitor patient's blood pressure; excessive amounts of nitroprusside can cause cyanide toxicity (usually in patients with decreased liver function) or thiocyanate toxicity (usually in patients with decreased renal function, or in patients with normal renal function but prolonged nitroprusside use)

Common Adverse Reactions 1% to 10%:

Cardiovascular: Excessive hypotensive response, palpitations, substernal distress

Central nervous system: Disorientation, psychosis, headache, restlessness

Endocrine & metabolic: Thyroid suppression

Gastrointestinal: Nausea, vomiting

Neuromuscular & skeletal: Weakness, muscle spasm

Otic: Tinnitus

(Continued)

Nitroprusside *(Continued)*

Respiratory: Hypoxia

Miscellaneous: Diaphoresis, thiocyanate toxicity

Mechanism of Action Causes peripheral vasodilation by direct action on venous and arteriolar smooth muscle, thus reducing peripheral resistance; will increase cardiac output by decreasing afterload; reduces aortal and left ventricular impedance

Pharmacodynamics/Kinetics

Onset of action: BP reduction <2 minutes

Duration: 1-10 minutes

Metabolism: Nitroprusside is converted to cyanide ions in the bloodstream; decomposes to prussic acid which in the presence of sulfur donor is converted to thiocyanate (hepatic and renal rhodanase systems)

Half-life elimination: Parent drug: <10 minutes; Thiocyanate: 2.7-7 days

Excretion: Urine (as thiocyanate)

Dosage Administration requires the use of an infusion pump. Average dose: 5 mcg/kg/minute.

Children: Pulmonary hypertension: I.V.: Initial: 1 mcg/kg/minute by continuous I.V. infusion; increase in increments of 1 mcg/kg/minute at intervals of 20-60 minutes; titrating to the desired response; usual dose: 3 mcg/kg/minute, rarely need >4 mcg/kg/minute; maximum: 5 mcg/kg/minute.

Adults: I.V. Initial: 0.3-0.5 mcg/kg/minute; increase in increments of 0.5 mcg/kg/minute, titrating to the desired hemodynamic effect or the appearance of headache or nausea; usual dose: 3 mcg/kg/minute; rarely need >4 mcg/kg/minute; maximum: 10 mcg/kg/minute. When administered by prolonged infusion faster than 2 mcg/kg/minute, cyanide is generated faster than an unaided patient can handle.

Administration I.V. infusion only, not for direct injection

Monitoring Parameters Blood pressure, heart rate; monitor for cyanide and thiocyanate toxicity; monitor acid-base status as acidosis can be the earliest sign of cyanide toxicity; monitor thiocyanate levels if requiring prolonged infusion (>3 days) or dose ≥4 mcg/kg/minute or patient has renal dysfunction; monitor cyanide blood levels in patients with decreased hepatic function; cardiac monitor and blood pressure monitor required

Reference Range Monitor thiocyanate levels if requiring prolonged infusion (>4 days) or ≥4 µg/kg/minute; not to exceed 100 µg/mL (or 10 mg/dL) plasma thiocyanate

Thiocyanate:

Therapeutic: 6-29 µg/mL

Toxic: 35-100 µg/mL

Fatal: >200 µg/mL

Cyanide: Normal <0.2 µg/mL; normal (smoker): <0.4 µg/mL

Toxic: >2 µg/mL

Potentially lethal: >3 µg/mL

Dosage Forms INJ, powder for reconstitution: 50 mg [DSC]. **INJ, solution:** 25 mg/mL (2 mL)

- **Nitroprusside Sodium** *see Nitroprusside on page 911*
- **NitroQuick®** *see Nitroglycerin on page 910*
- **Nitrostat®** *see Nitroglycerin on page 910*
- **Nitro-Tab®** *see Nitroglycerin on page 910*
- **NitroTime®** *see Nitroglycerin on page 910*
- **Nix® [OTC]** *see Permethrin on page 984*

Nizatidine *(ni ZA ti deen)*

U.S. Brand Names Axid®; Axid® AR [OTC]

Therapeutic Category Antihistamine, H_2 Blocker; Histamine H_2 Antagonist

Use Treatment and maintenance of duodenal ulcer; treatment of benign gastric ulcer; treatment of gastroesophageal reflux disease (GERD); OTC tablet used for the prevention of meal-related heartburn, acid indigestion, and sour stomach

Unlabeled/Investigational Use Part of a multidrug regimen for *H. pylori* eradication to reduce the risk of duodenal ulcer recurrence

Pregnancy Risk Factor C

Contraindications Hypersensitivity to nizatidine or any component of the formulation; hypersensitivity to other H_2 antagonists (cross-sensitivity has been observed)

Warnings/Precautions Use with caution in children <12 years of age; use with caution in patients with liver and renal impairment; dosage modification required in patients with renal impairment

Common Adverse Reactions

>10%: Central nervous system: Headache (16%)

1% to 10%:

Central nervous system: Dizziness, insomnia, somnolence, nervousness, anxiety

Dermatologic: Rash, pruritus

Gastrointestinal: Abdominal pain, constipation, diarrhea, nausea, flatulence, vomiting, heartburn, dry mouth, anorexia

Drug Interactions

Cytochrome P450 Effect: Inhibits 3A4 (weak)

Decreased Effect: May decrease the absorption of itraconazole or ketoconazole.

Mechanism of Action Nizatidine is an H_2-receptor antagonist. In healthy volunteers, nizatidine has been effective in suppressing gastric acid secretion induced by pentagastrin infusion or food. Nizatidine reduces gastric acid secretion by 30% to 78%. This compares with a 60% reduction by cimetidine. Nizatidine 100 mg is reported to provide equivalent acid suppression as cimetidine 300 mg.

Pharmacodynamics/Kinetics
Distribution: V_d: 0.8-1.5 L/kg
Protein binding: 35% to α_1-acid glycoprotein
Metabolism: Partially hepatic
Bioavailability: >70%
Half-life elimination: 1-2 hours; prolonged with renal impairment
Time to peak, plasma: 0.5-3.0 hours
Excretion: Urine (~60% as unchanged drug); feces (<6%)

Dosage Adults: Oral:
Active duodenal ulcer:
Treatment: 300 mg at bedtime or 150 mg twice daily
Maintenance: 150 mg/day
Gastric ulcer: 150 mg twice daily or 300 mg at bedtime
GERD: 150 mg twice daily
Meal-induced heartburn, acid indigestion, and sour stomach: 75 mg tablet [OTC] twice daily, 30 to 60 minutes prior to consuming food or beverages
Helicobacter pylori eradication (unlabeled use): 150 mg twice daily; requires combination therapy

Dosing adjustment in renal impairment:
Cl_{cr} 50-80 mL/minute: Administer 75% of normal dose
Cl_{cr} 10-50 mL/minute: Administer 50% of normal dose or 150 mg/day for active treatment and 150 mg every other day for maintenance treatment
Cl_{cr} <10 mL/minute: Administer 25% of normal dose or 150 mg every other day for treatment and 150 mg every 3 days for maintenance treatment

Patient Information May take several days before medication begins to relieve stomach pain; antacids may be taken with nizatidine unless prescriber has instructed you not to use them; wait 30-60 minutes between taking the antacid and nizatidine; avoid aspirin, cough and cold preparations; avoid use of black pepper, caffeine, alcohol, and harsh spices; may cause drowsiness or impair coordination and judgment

Dosage Forms CAP (Axid®): 150 mg, 300 mg. **TAB** (Axid® AR): 75 mg

- ◆ **Nizoral®** *see* Ketoconazole *on page 704*
- ◆ **Nizoral® A-D [OTC]** *see* Ketoconazole *on page 704*
- ◆ **N-Methylhydrazine** *see* Procarbazine *on page 1040*
- ◆ **Nocosyn™** *see* Sulfur and Sulfacetamide *on page 1177*
- ◆ **Nolvadex®** *see* Tamoxifen *on page 1186*
- ◆ **Nonsteroidal Anti-Inflammatory Agents Comparison** *see page 1401*
- ◆ **Noradrenaline** *see* Norepinephrine *on page 913*
- ◆ **Noradrenaline Acid Tartrate** *see* Norepinephrine *on page 913*
- ◆ **Norco®** *see* Hydrocodone and Acetaminophen *on page 627*
- ◆ **Norcuron®** *see* Vecuronium *on page 1299*
- ◆ **Nordeoxyguanosine** *see* Ganciclovir *on page 577*
- ◆ **Nordette®** *see* Ethinyl Estradiol and Levonorgestrel *on page 484*
- ◆ **Norditropin®** *see* Human Growth Hormone *on page 620*
- ◆ **Norditropin® Cartridges** *see* Human Growth Hormone *on page 620*
- ◆ **Norelgestromin and Ethinyl Estradiol** *see* Ethinyl Estradiol and Norelgestromin *on page 486*

Norepinephrine (nor ep i NEF rin)
Related Information
Hemodynamic Support, Intravenous *on page 1377*
U.S. Brand Names Levophed®
Synonyms Levarterenol Bitartrate; Noradrenaline; Noradrenaline Acid Tartrate; Norepinephrine Bitartrate
Therapeutic Category Adrenergic Agonist Agent; Alpha/Beta Agonist; Sympathomimetic Agent
Use Treatment of shock which persists after adequate fluid volume replacement
Pregnancy Risk Factor C
Contraindications Hypersensitivity to norepinephrine, bisulfites (contains metabisulfite), or any component of the formulation; hypotension from hypovolemia except as an emergency measure to maintain coronary and cerebral perfusion until volume could be replaced; mesenteric or peripheral vascular thrombosis unless it is a lifesaving procedure; during anesthesia with cyclopropane or halothane anesthesia (risk of ventricular arrhythmias)
Warnings/Precautions Assure adequate circulatory volume to minimize need for vasoconstrictors. Avoid hypertension; monitor blood pressure closely and adjust infusion rate. Infuse into a large vein if possible. Avoid infusion into leg veins. Watch I.V. site closely. Avoid extravasation. Never use leg veins for infusion sites.
Common Adverse Reactions Frequency not defined.
Cardiovascular: Bradycardia, arrhythmias, peripheral (digital) ischemia
Central nervous system: Headache (transient), anxiety
Local: Skin necrosis (with extravasation)
Respiratory: Dyspnea, respiratory difficulty
(Continued)

Norepinephrine *(Continued)*

Drug Interactions

Increased Effect/Toxicity: The effects of norepinephrine may be increased by tricyclic antidepressants, MAO inhibitors, antihistamines (diphenhydramine, tripelennamine), beta-blockers (nonselective), guanethidine, ergot alkaloids, reserpine, and methyldopa. Atropine sulfate may block the reflex bradycardia caused by norepinephrine and enhances the vasopressor response.

Decreased Effect: Alpha-blockers may blunt response to norepinephrine.

Mechanism of Action Stimulates beta$_1$-adrenergic receptors and alpha-adrenergic receptors causing increased contractility and heart rate as well as vasoconstriction, thereby increasing systemic blood pressure and coronary blood flow; clinically alpha effects (vasoconstriction) are greater than beta effects (inotropic and chronotropic effects)

Pharmacodynamics/Kinetics

Onset of action: I.V.: Very rapid-acting

Duration: Limited

Metabolism: Via catechol-o-methyltransferase (COMT) and monoamine oxidase (MAO)

Excretion: Urine (84% to 96% as inactive metabolites)

Dosage Administration requires the use of an infusion pump!

Note: Norepinephrine dosage is stated in terms of norepinephrine base and intravenous formulation is norepinephrine bitartrate

Norepinephrine bitartrate 2 mg = Norepinephrine base 1 mg

Continuous I.V. infusion:

Children: Initial: 0.05-0.1 mcg/kg/minute; titrate to desired effect; maximum dose: 1-2 mcg/kg/minute

Adults: Initial: 0.5-1 mcg/minute and titrate to desired response; 8-30 mcg/minute is usual range; range used in clinical trials: 0.01-3 mcg/kg/minute; ACLS dosage range: 0.5-30 mcg/minute

Administration Administer into large vein to avoid the potential for extravasation; potent drug, must be diluted prior to use. Rate (mL/hour) = dose (mcg/kg/minute) x weight (kg) x 60 minutes/hour divided by concentration (mcg/mL)

To prepare for infusion:

$$\frac{6 \text{ x weight (kg) x desired dose (mcg/kg/min)}}{\text{I.V. infusion rate (mL/h)}} = \text{mg of drug to be added to 100 mL of I.V. fluid}$$

"Rule of 6" method for infusion preparation:

Simplified equation: 0.6 x weight (kg) = amount (mg) of drug to be added to 100 mL of I.V. fluid

When infused at 1 mL/hour, then it will deliver the drug at a rate of 0.1 mcg/kg/minute

Complex equation: 6 x desired dose (mcg/kg/minute) x body weight (kg) divided by desired rate (mL/hour) is the mg added to make 100 mL of solution

Dosage Forms INJ, solution: 1 mg/mL (4 mL)

◆ **Norepinephrine Bitartrate** *see* Norepinephrine *on page 913*

◆ **Norethindrone Acetate and Ethinyl Estradiol** *see* Ethinyl Estradiol and Norethindrone *on page 487*

◆ **Norethindrone and Estradiol** *see* Estradiol and Norethindrone *on page 463*

◆ **Norethindrone and Mestranol** *see* Mestranol and Norethindrone *on page 801*

◆ **Norflex™** *see* Orphenadrine *on page 933*

Norfloxacin *(nor FLOKS a sin)*

U.S. Brand Names Noroxin®

Therapeutic Category Antibiotic, Quinolone

Use Uncomplicated urinary tract infections and cystitis caused by susceptible gram-negative and gram-positive bacteria; sexually-transmitted disease (eg, uncomplicated urethral and cervical gonorrhea) caused by *N. gonorrhoeae*; prostatitis due to *E. coli*

Pregnancy Risk Factor C

Contraindications Hypersensitivity to norfloxacin, quinolones, or any component of the formulation

Warnings/Precautions Not recommended in children <18 years of age; other quinolones have caused transient arthropathy in children; CNS stimulation may occur which may lead to tremor, restlessness, confusion, and very rarely to hallucinations or convulsive seizures; use with caution in patients with known or suspected CNS disorders. Tendon inflammation and/or rupture have been reported with norfloxacin and other quinolone antibiotics. Discontinue at first sign of tendon inflammation or pain. Quinolones may exacerbate myasthenia gravis.

Severe hypersensitivity reactions, including anaphylaxis, have occurred with quinolone therapy. If an allergic reaction occurs (itching, urticaria, dyspnea, facial edema, loss of consciousness, tingling, cardiovascular collapse), discontinue drug immediately. Prolonged use may result in superinfection; pseudomembranous colitis may occur and should be considered in all patients who present with diarrhea. Use caution with renal impairment.

Common Adverse Reactions 1% to 10%:

Central nervous system: Headache (3%), dizziness (3%)

Gastrointestinal: Nausea (4%)

Neuromuscular & skeletal: Weakness (1%)

Drug Interactions

Cytochrome P450 Effect: Inhibits CYP1A2 (strong), 3A4 (moderate)

Increased Effect/Toxicity: Quinolones cause increased levels of caffeine, warfarin, cyclosporine, and theophylline. Cimetidine and probenecid may increase norfloxacin serum levels. Concurrent use of corticosteroids may increase risk of tendon rupture.

Decreased Effect: Decreased absorption with antacids containing aluminum, magnesium, and/or calcium (by up to 98% if given at the same time); decreased serum levels of fluoroquinolones by antineoplastics; nitrofurantoin may antagonize effects of norfloxacin; phenytoin serum levels may be decreased by fluoroquinolones; didanosine (chewable/buffered or pediatric powder) may decrease quinolone absorption

Mechanism of Action Norfloxacin is a DNA gyrase inhibitor. DNA gyrase is an essential bacterial enzyme that maintains the superhelical structure of DNA. DNA gyrase is required for DNA replication and transcription, DNA repair, recombination, and transposition; bactericidal

Pharmacodynamics/Kinetics

Absorption: Oral: Rapid, up to 40%

Distribution: Crosses placenta; small amounts enter breast milk

Protein binding: 15%

Metabolism: Hepatic

Half-life elimination: 3-4 hours; Renal impairment (Cl_{cr} ≤30 mL/minute): 6.5 hours; Elderly: 4 hours

Time to peak, serum: 1-2 hours

Excretion: Urine (26% to 36%); feces (30%)

Dosage Oral: Adults:

Urinary tract infections: 400 mg twice daily for 3-21 days depending on severity of infection or organism sensitivity; maximum: 800 mg/day

Uncomplicated gonorrhea: 800 mg as a single dose (CDC recommends as an alternative regimen to ciprofloxacin or ofloxacin)

Prostatitis: 400 mg every 12 hours for 4 weeks

Dosing interval in renal impairment: Cl_{cr} 10-30 mL/minute: Urinary tract infections: Administer 400 mg every 24 hours

Administration Hold antacids or sucralfate for 3-4 hours after giving norfloxacin; do not administer together. Best taken on an empty stomach with water (1 hour before or 2 hours after meals, milk, or other dairy products).

Patient Information Tablets should be taken at least 1 hour before or at least 2 hours after a meal with a glass of water; patients receiving norfloxacin should be well hydrated; take all the medication, do not skip doses; do not take with antacids; contact your prescriber immediately with inflammation or tendon pain

Dosage Forms TAB: 400 mg

- ♦ **Norgesic™** *see* Orphenadrine, Aspirin, and Caffeine *on page 933*
- ♦ **Norgesic™ Forte** *see* Orphenadrine, Aspirin, and Caffeine *on page 933*
- ♦ **Norgestimate and Ethinyl Estradiol** *see* Ethinyl Estradiol and Norgestimate *on page 490*

Norgestrel (nor JES trel)

U.S. Brand Names Ovrette®

Therapeutic Category Contraceptive, Emergency; Contraceptive, Oral (Progestin); Progestin

Use Prevention of pregnancy; **progestin only products have higher risk of failure in contraceptive use**

Pregnancy Risk Factor X

Contraindications Hypersensitivity to norgestrel or any component of the formulation; hypersensitivity to tartrazine; thromboembolic disorders; severe hepatic disease; breast cancer; undiagnosed vaginal bleeding; pregnancy

Warnings/Precautions Discontinue if sudden loss of vision or if diplopia or proptosis occur; use with caution in patients with a history of mental depression.

Common Adverse Reactions Frequency not defined.

Cardiovascular: Embolism, cerebral thrombosis, edema

Central nervous system: Mental depression, fever, insomnia

Dermatologic: Melasma or chloasma, allergic rash with or without pruritus

Endocrine & metabolic: Breakthrough bleeding, spotting, changes in menstrual flow, amenorrhea, changes in cervical erosion and secretions, increased breast tenderness

Gastrointestinal: Weight gain/loss, anorexia

Hepatic: Cholestatic jaundice

Local: Thrombophlebitis

Neuromuscular & skeletal: Weakness

Drug Interactions

Cytochrome P450 Effect: Substrate of CYP3A4 (major)

Increased Effect/Toxicity: Oral contraceptives may increase toxicity of acetaminophen, anticoagulants, benzodiazepines, caffeine, corticosteroids, metoprolol, theophylline, and tricyclic antidepressants.

Decreased Effect: Azole antifungals (ketoconazole, itraconazole, fluconazole), barbiturates, hydantoins (phenytoin), carbamazepine, and rifampin decrease oral contraceptive efficacy due to increased metabolism. Antibiotics (penicillins, tetracyclines, griseofulvin) may decrease efficacy of oral contraceptives.

Mechanism of Action Inhibits secretion of pituitary gonadotropin (LH) which prevents follicular maturation and ovulation

(Continued)

Norgestrel *(Continued)*

Pharmacodynamics/Kinetics

Absorption: Oral: Well absorbed

Protein binding: >97% to sex hormone-binding globulin

Metabolism: Primarily hepatic via reduction and conjugation

Half-life elimination: ~20 hours

Excretion: Urine (as metabolites)

Dosage Oral: Administer daily, starting the first day of menstruation, take 1 tablet at the same time each day, every day of the year. If one dose is missed, take as soon as remembered, then next tablet at regular time; if two doses are missed, take 1 tablet as soon as it is remembered, followed by an additional dose that same day at the usual time. When one or two doses are missed, additional contraceptive measures should be used until 14 consecutive tablets have been taken. If three doses are missed, discontinue norgestrel and use an additional form of birth control until menses or pregnancy is ruled out.

Patient Information Take this medicine only as directed; do not take more of it and do not take it for a longer period of time; if you suspect you may have become pregnant, stop taking this medicine; report any loss of vision or vision changes immediately; avoid excessive exposure to sunlight

Dosage Forms TAB: 0.075 mg

♦ **Norgestrel and Ethinyl Estradiol** *see* Ethinyl Estradiol and Norgestrel *on page 492*

♦ **Norinyl® 1+35** *see* Ethinyl Estradiol and Norethindrone *on page 487*

♦ **Norinyl® 1+50** *see* Mestranol and Norethindrone *on page 801*

♦ **Noritate®** *see* Metronidazole *on page 831*

♦ **Normal Human Serum Albumin** *see* Albumin *on page 44*

♦ **Normal Saline** *see* Sodium Chloride *on page 1146*

♦ **Normal Serum Albumin (Human)** *see* Albumin *on page 44*

♦ **Normodyne®** *see* Labetalol *on page 710*

♦ **Noroxin®** *see* Norfloxacin *on page 914*

♦ **Norpace®** *see* Disopyramide *on page 392*

♦ **Norpace® CR** *see* Disopyramide *on page 392*

♦ **Norplant® Implant [DSC]** *see* Levonorgestrel *on page 737*

♦ **Norpramin®** *see* Desipramine *on page 352*

♦ **Nortrel™** *see* Ethinyl Estradiol and Norethindrone *on page 487*

♦ **Nortrel™ 7/7/7** *see* Ethinyl Estradiol and Norethindrone *on page 487*

Nortriptyline *(nor TRIP ti leen)*

Related Information

Antidepressant Agents Comparison *on page 1359*

U.S. Brand Names Aventyl® HCl; Pamelor®

Synonyms Nortriptyline Hydrochloride

Therapeutic Category Antidepressant, Tricyclic (Secondary Amine)

Use Treatment of symptoms of depression

Unlabeled/Investigational Use Chronic pain, anxiety disorders, enuresis, attention-deficit/hyperactivity disorder (ADHD)

Pregnancy Risk Factor D

Contraindications Hypersensitivity to nortriptyline and similar chemical class, or any component of the formulation; use of MAO inhibitors within 14 days; use in a patient during the acute recovery phase of MI; pregnancy

Warnings/Precautions May cause sedation, resulting in impaired performance of tasks requiring alertness (eg, operating machinery or driving). Sedative effects may be additive with other CNS depressants and/or ethanol. The degree of sedation is low-moderate relative to other antidepressants. May worsen psychosis in some patients or precipitate a shift to mania or hypomania in patients with bipolar disease. May increase the risks associated with electroconvulsive therapy. This agent should be discontinued, when possible, prior to elective surgery. Therapy should not be abruptly discontinued in patients receiving high doses for prolonged periods. May alter glucose regulation - use caution in patients with diabetes.

May cause orthostatic hypotension (risk is low relative to other antidepressants) - use with caution in patients at risk of hypotension or in patients where transient hypotensive episodes would be poorly tolerated (cardiovascular disease or cerebrovascular disease). The degree of anticholinergic blockade produced by this agent is moderate relative to other cyclic antidepressants, however, caution should still be used in patients with urinary retention, benign prostatic hypertrophy, narrow-angle glaucoma, xerostomia, visual problems, constipation, or history of bowel obstruction.

The possibility of a suicide attempt is inherent in major depression and may persist until remission occurs. Use caution in high-risk patients during initiation of therapy. Prescriptions should be written for the smallest quantity consistent with good patient care. Use with caution in patients with a history of cardiovascular disease (including previous MI, stroke, tachycardia, or conduction abnormalities). The risk conduction abnormalities with this agent is moderate relative to other antidepressants. Use caution in patients with a previous seizure disorder or condition predisposing to seizures such as brain damage, alcoholism, or concurrent therapy with other drugs which lower the seizure threshold. Use with caution in hyperthyroid patients or those receiving thyroid supplementation. Use with caution in patients with hepatic or renal dysfunction and in elderly patients.

Common Adverse Reactions Frequency not defined.

Cardiovascular: Postural hypotension, arrhythmias, hypertension, heart block, tachycardia, palpitations, myocardial infarction

Central nervous system: Confusion, delirium, hallucinations, restlessness, insomnia, disorientation, delusions, anxiety, agitation, panic, nightmares, hypomania, exacerbation of psychosis, incoordination, ataxia, extrapyramidal symptoms, seizures

Dermatologic: Alopecia, photosensitivity, rash, petechiae, urticaria, itching

Endocrine & metabolic: Sexual dysfunction, gynecomastia, breast enlargement, galactorrhea, increase or decrease in libido, increase in blood sugar, SIADH

Gastrointestinal: Xerostomia, constipation, vomiting, anorexia, diarrhea, abdominal cramps, black tongue, nausea, unpleasant taste, weight gain/loss

Genitourinary: Urinary retention, delayed micturition, impotence, testicular edema

Hematologic: Rarely agranulocytosis, eosinophilia, purpura, thrombocytopenia

Hepatic: Increased liver enzymes, cholestatic jaundice

Neuromuscular & skeletal: Tremor, numbness, tingling, paresthesias, peripheral neuropathy

Ocular: Blurred vision, eye pain, disturbances in accommodation, mydriasis

Otic: Tinnitus

Miscellaneous: Diaphoresis (excessive), allergic reactions

Drug Interactions

Cytochrome P450 Effect: Substrate of CYP1A2 (minor), 2C19 (minor), 2D6 (major), 3A4 (minor); **Inhibits** CYP2D6 (weak), 2E1 (weak)

Increased Effect/Toxicity: Nortriptyline increases the effects of amphetamines, anticholinergics, other CNS depressants (sedatives, hypnotics, ethanol), chlorpropamide, tolazamide, and warfarin. When used with MAO inhibitors, hyperpyrexia, hypertension, tachycardia, confusion, seizures, and **deaths have been reported** (serotonin syndrome). Serotonin syndrome has also been reported with ritonavir (rare). CYP2D6 inhibitors may increase the levels/effects of nortriptyline; example inhibitors include chlorpromazine, delavirdine, fluoxetine, miconazole, paroxetine, pergolide, quinidine, quinine, ritonavir, and ropinirole. Cimetidine, grapefruit juice, indinavir, methylphenidate, diltiazem, and verapamil may increase the serum concentrations of TCAs. Use of lithium with a TCA may increase the risk for neurotoxicity. Phenothiazines may increase concentration of some TCAs and TCAs may increase concentration of phenothiazines. Pressor response to I.V. epinephrine, norepinephrine, and phenylephrine may be enhanced in patients receiving TCAs (**Note:** Effect is unlikely with epinephrine or levonordefrin dosages typically administered as infiltration in combination with local anesthetics). Combined use of beta-agonists or drugs which prolong QT_c (including quinidine, procainamide, disopyramide, cisapride, sparfloxacin, gatifloxacin, moxifloxacin) with TCAs may predispose patients to cardiac arrhythmias. Use with altretamine may cause orthostatic hypotension.

Decreased Effect: Carbamazepine, phenobarbital, and rifampin may increase the metabolism of nortriptyline resulting in decreased effect of nortriptyline. Nortriptyline inhibits the antihypertensive response to bethanidine, clonidine, debrisoquin, guanadrel, guanethidine, guanabenz, or guanfacine. Cholestyramine and colestipol may bind TCAs and reduce their absorption; monitor for altered response.

Mechanism of Action Traditionally believed to increase the synaptic concentration of serotonin and/or norepinephrine in the central nervous system by inhibition of their reuptake by the presynaptic neuronal membrane. However, additional receptor effects have been found including desensitization of adenyl cyclase, down regulation of beta-adrenergic receptors, and down regulation of serotonin receptors.

Pharmacodynamics/Kinetics

Onset of action: Therapeutic: 1-3 weeks

Distribution: V_d: 21 L/kg

Protein binding: 93% to 95%

Metabolism: Primarily hepatic; extensive first-pass effect

Half-life elimination: 28-31 hours

Time to peak, serum: 7-8.5 hours

Excretion: Urine (as metabolites and small amounts of unchanged drug); feces (small amounts)

Dosage Oral:

Nocturnal enuresis:

Children:

6-7 years (20-25 kg): 10 mg/day

8-11 years (25-35 kg): 10-20 mg/day

>11 years (35-54 kg): 25-35 mg/day

Depression or ADHD (unlabeled use):

Children 6-12 years: 1-3 mg/kg/day or 10-20 mg/day in 3-4 divided doses

Adolescents: 30-100 mg/day in divided doses

Depression:

Adults: 25 mg 3-4 times/day up to 150 mg/day

Elderly (**Note:** Nortriptyline is one of the best tolerated TCAs in the elderly)

Initial: 10-25 mg at bedtime

Dosage can be increased by 25 mg every 3 days for inpatients and weekly for outpatients if tolerated

Usual maintenance dose: 75 mg as a single bedtime dose or 2 divided doses; however, lower or higher doses may be required to stay within the therapeutic window

Dosing adjustment in hepatic impairment: Lower doses and slower titration dependent on individualization of dosage is recommended

(Continued)

Nortriptyline *(Continued)*

Monitoring Parameters Blood pressure and pulse rate (ECG, cardiac monitoring) prior to and during initial therapy in older adults; weight; blood levels are useful for therapeutic monitoring

Reference Range

Plasma levels do not always correlate with clinical effectiveness

Therapeutic: 50-150 ng/mL (SI: 190-570 nmol/L)

Toxic: >500 ng/mL (SI: >1900 nmol/L)

Patient Information Avoid alcohol; do not discontinue medication abruptly; may cause urine to turn blue-green; may cause drowsiness; full effect may not occur for 3-6 weeks; dry mouth may be helped by sips of water, sugarless gum, or hard candy

Dosage Forms CAP: 10 mg, 25 mg, 50 mg, 75 mg; (Aventyl® HCl): 10 mg, 25 mg; (Pamelor®): 10 mg, 25 mg, 50 mg, 75 mg. **SOLN** (Aventyl® HCl, Pamelor®): 10 mg/5 mL (473 mL)

◆ **NSC-706363** see Arsenic Trioxide on page 115
◆ **NSC-715055** see Gefitinib on page 581
◆ **NTG** see Nitroglycerin on page 910
◆ **N-trifluoroacetyladriamycin-14-valerate** see Valrubicin on page 1291
◆ **NTZ** see Nitazoxanide on page 907
◆ **Nubain®** see Nalbuphine on page 876
◆ **Nucofed® Expectorant** see Guaifenesin, Pseudoephedrine, and Codeine on page 606
◆ **Nucofed® Pediatric Expectorant** see Guaifenesin, Pseudoephedrine, and Codeine on page 606
◆ **Nucotuss®** see Guaifenesin, Pseudoephedrine, and Codeine on page 606
◆ **Nu-Iron® 150 [OTC]** see Polysaccharide-Iron Complex on page 1016
◆ **NuLev™** see Hyoscyamine on page 641
◆ **NuLytely®** see Polyethylene Glycol-Electrolyte Solution on page 1013
◆ **Numorphan®** see Oxymorphone on page 946
◆ **Nupercainal® Hydrocortisone Cream [OTC]** see Hydrocortisone on page 632
◆ **Nuquin HP®** see Hydroquinone on page 636
◆ **Nuromax®** see Doxacurium on page 404
◆ **Nutracort®** see Hydrocortisone on page 632
◆ **Nutraplus® [OTC]** see Urea on page 1282
◆ **Nutropin®** see Human Growth Hormone on page 620
◆ **Nutropin AQ®** see Human Growth Hormone on page 620
◆ **Nutropin Depot®** see Human Growth Hormone on page 620
◆ **NuvaRing®** see Ethinyl Estradiol and Etonogestrel on page 482
◆ **NVB** see Vinorelbine on page 1307
◆ **NVP** see Nevirapine on page 896
◆ **Nydrazid®** see Isoniazid on page 692

Nystatin (nye STAT in)

Related Information
Antifungal Agents Comparison on page 1362

U.S. Brand Names Bio-Statin®; Mycostatin®; Nystat-Rx®; Nystop®; Pedi-Dri®

Therapeutic Category Antifungal Agent, Oral Nonabsorbed; Antifungal Agent, Topical; Antifungal Agent, Vaginal

Use Treatment of susceptible cutaneous, mucocutaneous, and oral cavity fungal infections normally caused by the Candida species

Pregnancy Risk Factor B/C (oral)

Contraindications Hypersensitivity to nystatin or any component of the formulation

Common Adverse Reactions
Frequency not defined: Dermatologic: Contact dermatitis, Stevens-Johnson syndrome
1% to 10%: Gastrointestinal: Nausea, vomiting, diarrhea, stomach pain

Mechanism of Action Binds to sterols in fungal cell membrane, changing the cell wall permeability allowing for leakage of cellular contents

Pharmacodynamics/Kinetics
Onset of action: Symptomatic relief from candidiasis: 24-72 hours
Absorption: Topical: None through mucous membranes or intact skin; Oral: Poorly absorbed
Excretion: Feces (as unchanged drug)

Dosage
Oral candidiasis:
Suspension (swish and swallow orally):
Premature infants: 100,000 units 4 times/day
Infants: 200,000 units 4 times/day or 100,000 units to each side of mouth 4 times/day
Children and Adults: 400,000-600,000 units 4 times/day
Troche: Children and Adults: 200,000-400,000 units 4-5 times/day
Powder for compounding: Children and Adults: 1/8 teaspoon (500,000 units) to equal approximately 1/2 cup of water; give 4 times/day
Mucocutaneous infections: Children and Adults: Topical: Apply 2-3 times/day to affected areas; very moist topical lesions are treated best with powder
Intestinal infections: Adults: Oral: 500,000-1,000,000 units every 8 hours
Vaginal infections: Adults: Vaginal tablets: Insert 1 tablet/day at bedtime for 2 weeks

Patient Information The oral suspension should be swished about the mouth and retained in the mouth for as long as possible (several minutes) before swallowing. For neonates and infants, paint nystatin suspension into recesses of the mouth. Troches must be allowed to dissolve slowly and should not be chewed or swallowed whole. If topical irritation occurs, discontinue; for external use only; do not discontinue therapy even if symptoms are gone

Dosage Forms CAP (Bio-Statin®): 500,000 units, 1 million units. **CRM, topical:** 100,000 units/ g (15 g, 30 g); (Mycostatin®): 100,000 units/g (30 g). **LOZ** (Mycostatin®): 200,000 units [DSC]. **OINT, topical:** 100,000 units/g (15 g, 30 g). **POWDER, for prescription compounding:** 50 million units (10 g), 150 million units (30 g), 500 million units (100 g), 2 billion units (400 g); (Nystat-Rx®): 50 million units (10 g), 150 million units (30 g), 500 million units (100 g), 1 billion units (190 g), 2 billion units (350 g). **POWDER, topical** (Mycostatin®): 100,000 units/g (15 g); (Nystop®): 100,000 units (15 g, 30 g, 60 g); (Pedi-Dri®): 100,000 units/g (56.7 g). **SUSP, oral:** 100,000 units/mL (5 mL, 60 mL, 480 mL); (Mycostatin®): 100,000 units/mL (60 mL, 480 mL). **TAB:** 500,000 units. **TAB, vaginal:** 100,000 units (15s).

Nystatin and Triamcinolone (nye STAT in & trye am SIN oh lone)

U.S. Brand Names Mycolog®-II; Mytrex®

Synonyms Triamcinolone and Nystatin

Therapeutic Category Antifungal/Corticosteroid, Topical

Use Treatment of cutaneous candidiasis

Pregnancy Risk Factor C

Dosage Children and Adults: Topical: Apply sparingly 2-4 times/day. Therapy should be discontinued when control is achieved; if no improvement is seen, reassessment of diagnosis may be necessary.

Dosage Forms CRM (Mycolog®-II, Mytrex®): Nystatin 100,000 units and triamcinolone 0.1% (15 g, 30 g, 60 g). **OINT**: Nystatin 100,000 units and triamcinolone 0.1% (15 g, 30 g, 60 g); (Mycolog®-II): Nystatin 100,000 units and triamcinolone 0.1% (15 g, 30 g, 60 g); (Mytrex®): Nystatin 100,000 units and triamcinolone 0.1% (15 g, 30 g)

♦ **Nystat-Rx®** *see* Nystatin *on page 919*

♦ **Nystop®** *see* Nystatin *on page 919*

♦ **Nytol® [OTC]** *see* DiphenhydrAMINE *on page 383*

♦ **Nytol® Maximum Strength [OTC]** *see* DiphenhydrAMINE *on page 383*

♦ **Obesity Treatment Guidelines for Adults** *see page 1482*

♦ **OCBZ** *see* Oxcarbazepine *on page 940*

♦ **Ocean® [OTC]** *see* Sodium Chloride *on page 1146*

♦ **OCL® [DSC]** *see* Polyethylene Glycol-Electrolyte Solution *on page 1013*

Octreotide (ok TREE oh tide)

U.S. Brand Names Sandostatin®; Sandostatin LAR®

Synonyms Octreotide Acetate

Therapeutic Category Antidiarrheal; Antisecretory Agent; Somatostatin Analog

Use Control of symptoms in patients with metastatic carcinoid and vasoactive intestinal peptide-secreting tumors (VIPomas); pancreatic tumors, gastrinoma, secretory diarrhea, acromegaly

Unlabeled/Investigational Use AIDS-associated secretory diarrhea, control of bleeding of esophageal varices, breast cancer, cryptosporidiosis, Cushing's syndrome, insulinomas, small bowel fistulas, postgastrectomy dumping syndrome, chemotherapy-induced diarrhea, graft-versus-host disease (GVHD) induced diarrhea, Zollinger-Ellison syndrome, congenital hyperinsulinism

Pregnancy Risk Factor B

Contraindications Hypersensitivity to octreotide or any component of the formulation

Warnings/Precautions Dosage adjustment may be required to maintain symptomatic control; insulin requirements may be reduced as well as sulfonylurea requirements; monitor patients for cholelithiasis, hyper- or hypoglycemia; use with caution in patients with renal impairment

Common Adverse Reactions

>10%:
  Cardiovascular: Sinus bradycardia (19% to 25%)
  Endocrine & metabolic: Hyperglycemia (15% acromegaly, 27% carcinoid)
  Gastrointestinal: Diarrhea (36% to 58% acromegaly), abdominal pain (30% to 44% acromegaly), flatulence (13% to 26% acromegaly), constipation (9% to 19% acromegaly), nausea (10% to 30%)

1% to 10%:
  Cardiovascular: Flushing, edema, conduction abnormalities (9% to 10%), arrhythmias (3% to 9%)
  Central nervous system: Fatigue, headache, dizziness, vertigo, anorexia, depression
  Endocrine & metabolic: Hypoglycemia (2% acromegaly, 4% carcinoid), hyperglycemia (1%), hypothyroidism, galactorrhea
  Gastrointestinal: Nausea, vomiting, diarrhea, constipation, abdominal pain, cramping, discomfort, fat malabsorption, loose stools, flatulence, tenesmus
  Hepatic: Jaundice, hepatitis, increase LFTs, cholelithiasis has occurred, presumably by altering fat absorption and decreasing the motility of the gallbladder
  Local: Pain at injection site (dose-related)
  Neuromuscular & skeletal: Weakness

Drug Interactions

Increased Effect/Toxicity: Octreotide may increase the effect of insulin or sulfonylurea agents which may result in hypoglycemia.

Decreased Effect: Octreotide may lower cyclosporine serum levels (case report of a transplant rejection due to reduction of serum cyclosporine levels). Codeine effect may be reduced.

Mechanism of Action Mimics natural somatostatin by inhibiting serotonin release, and the secretion of gastrin, VIP, insulin, glucagon, secretin, motilin, and pancreatic polypeptide. Decreases growth hormone and IGF-1 in acromegaly.

Pharmacodynamics/Kinetics

Duration: S.C.: 6-12 hours
Absorption: S.C.: Rapid
Distribution: V_d: 14 L
Protein binding: 65% to lipoproteins
Metabolism: Extensively hepatic
Bioavailability: S.C.: 100%

Half-life elimination: 60-110 minutes

Excretion: Urine (32%)

Dosage

Infants and Children:

Diarrhea: I.V., S.C.: Doses of 1-10 mcg/kg every 12 hours have been used in children beginning at the low end of the range and increasing by 0.3 mcg/kg/dose at 3-day intervals. Suppression of growth hormone (animal data) is of concern when used as long-term therapy.

Congenital hyperinsulinism (unlabeled): S.C.: Doses of 3-40 mcg/kg/day have been used

Adults: S.C.: Initial: 50 mcg 1-2 times/day and titrate dose based on patient tolerance and response

Carcinoid: 100-600 mcg/day in 2-4 divided doses

VIPomas: 200-300 mcg/day in 2-4 divided doses

Diarrhea: Initial: I.V.: 50-100 mcg every 8 hours; increase by 100 mcg/dose at 48-hour intervals; maximum dose: 500 mcg every 8 hours

Esophageal varices bleeding: I.V. bolus: 25-50 mcg followed by continuous I.V. infusion of 25-50 mcg/hour

Acromegaly: Initial: S.C.: 50 mcg 3 times/day; titrate to achieve growth hormone levels <5 ng/mL or IGF-I (somatomedin C) levels <1.9 U/mL in males and <2.2 U/mL in females; usual effective dose 100 mcg 3 times/day; range 300-1500 mcg/day

Note: Should be withdrawn yearly for a 4-week interval in patients who have received irradiation. Resume if levels increase and signs/symptoms recur.

Acromegaly, carcinoid tumors, and VIPomas (depot injection): Patients must be stabilized on subcutaneous octreotide for at least 2 weeks before switching to the long-acting depot: Upon switch: 20 mg I.M. intragluteally every 4 weeks for 2-3 months, then the dose may be modified based upon response

Dosage adjustment for acromegaly: After 3 months of depot injections the dosage may be continued or modified as follows:

GH ≤2.5 ng/mL, IGF-1 is normal, symptoms controlled: Maintain octreotide LAR® at 20 mg I.M. every 4 weeks

GH >2.5 ng/mL, IGF-1 is elevated, and/or symptoms uncontrolled: Increase octreotide LAR® to 30 mg I.M. every 4 weeks

GH ≤1 ng/mL, IGF-1 is normal, symptoms controlled: Reduce octreotide LAR® to 10 mg I.M. every 4 weeks

Dosages >40 mg are not recommended

Dosage adjustment for carcinoid tumors and VIPomas: After 2 months of depot injections the dosage may be continued or modified as follows:

Increase to 30 mg I.M. every 4 weeks if symptoms are inadequately controlled

Decrease to 10 mg I.M. every 4 weeks, for a trial period, if initially responsive to 20 mg dose

Dosage >30 mg is not recommended

Administration

Regular injection formulation (do not use if solution contains particles or is discolored): Administer S.C. or I.V. I.V. administration may be IVP, IVPB, or continuous I.V. infusion:

IVP should be administered undiluted over 3 minutes

IVPB should be administered over 15-30 minutes

Continuous I.V. infusion rates have ranged from 25-50 mcg/hour for the treatment of esophageal variceal bleeding

Depot formulation: Administer I.M. intragluteal; must be administered immediately after mixing

Reference Range Vasoactive intestinal peptide: <75 ng/L; levels vary considerably between laboratories

Dosage Forms INJ, microspheres for suspension [depot formulation] (Sandostatin LAR®): 10 mg, 20 mg, 30 mg. **INJ, solution** (Sandostatin®): 0.05 mg/mL (1 mL); 0.1 mg/mL (1 mL); 0.2 mg/mL (5 mL); 0.5 mg/mL (1 mL); 1 mg/mL (5 mL)

♦ **Octreotide Acetate** see Octreotide on page 920

♦ **Ocufen®** see Flurbiprofen on page 545

♦ **Ocuflox®** see Ofloxacin on page 921

♦ **Ocupress®** see Carteolol on page 224

♦ **Ocusulf-10** see Sulfacetamide on page 1169

Ofloxacin (oh FLOKS a sin)

Related Information

Antimicrobial Drugs of Choice on page 1440

Prevention of Wound Infection & Sepsis in Surgical Patients on page 1436

Tuberculosis Treatment Guidelines on page 1466

U.S. Brand Names Foxin®; Ocuflox®

Therapeutic Category Antibiotic, Ophthalmic; Antibiotic, Otic; Antibiotic, Quinolone

Use Quinolone antibiotic for skin and skin structure, lower respiratory, and urinary tract infections and sexually-transmitted diseases. Active against many gram-positive and gram-negative aerobic bacteria.

Ophthalmic: Treatment of superficial ocular infections involving the conjunctiva or cornea due to strains of susceptible organisms

Otic: Otitis externa, chronic suppurative otitis media, acute otitis media

Pregnancy Risk Factor C

(Continued)

Ofloxacin *(Continued)*

Contraindications Hypersensitivity to ofloxacin or other members of the quinolone group such as nalidixic acid, oxolinic acid, cinoxacin, norfloxacin, and ciprofloxacin; hypersensitivity to any component of the formulation

Warnings/Precautions Use with caution in patients with epilepsy or other CNS diseases which could predispose seizures; use with caution in patients with renal impairment; failure to respond to an ophthalmic antibiotic after 2-3 days may indicate the presence of resistant organisms, or another causative agent; use caution with systemic preparation in children <18 years of age due to association of other quinolones with transient arthropathy. Tendon inflammation and/or rupture have been reported with other quinolone antibiotics. Discontinue at first sign of tendon inflammation or pain. Quinolones may exacerbate myasthenia gravis.

Severe hypersensitivity reactions, including anaphylaxis, have occurred with quinolone therapy. If an allergic reaction occurs (itching, urticaria, dyspnea, facial edema, loss of consciousness, tingling, cardiovascular collapse), discontinue drug immediately. Prolonged use may result in superinfection; pseudomembranous colitis may occur and should be considered in all patients who present with diarrhea.

Common Adverse Reactions

Systemic:

1% to 10%:

Cardiovascular: Chest pain (1% to 3%)

Central nervous system: Headache (1% to 9%), insomnia (3% to 7%), dizziness (1% to 5%), fatigue (1% to 3%), somnolence (1% to 3%), sleep disorders, nervousness (1% to 3%), pyrexia (1% to 3%), pain

Dermatologic: Rash/pruritus (1% to 3%)

Gastrointestinal: Diarrhea (1% to 4%), vomiting (1% to 3%), GI distress, cramps, abdominal cramps (1% to 3%), flatulence (1% to 3%), abnormal taste (1% to 3%), xerostomia (1% to 3%), decreased appetite, nausea (3% to 10%)

Genitourinary: Vaginitis (1% to 3%), external genital pruritus in women

Local: Pain at injection site

Ocular: Superinfection (ophthalmic), lacrimation, dry eyes, stinging, visual disturbances (1% to 3%)

Ophthalmic: Frequency not defined:

Central nervous system: Dizziness

Gastrointestinal: Nausea

Ocular: Blurred vision, burning, chemical conjunctivitis/keratitis, discomfort, dryness, edema, eye pain, foreign body sensation, itching, photophobia, redness, stinging, tearing

Otic: 1% to 10%:

Central nervous system: Dizziness (≤1%), transient neuropsychiatric disturbances (≤1%), vertigo (≤1%)

Dermatologic: Pruritus (1% to 4%), rash (1%)

Gastrointestinal: Taste perversion (7%)

Neuromuscular & skeletal: Paresthesia (1%)

Otic: Application site reactions (<1% to 3%), earache (≤1%)

Miscellaneous: Trunk pain

Drug Interactions

Cytochrome P450 Effect: Inhibits CYP1A2 (strong)

Increased Effect/Toxicity: Quinolones can cause increased caffeine, warfarin, cyclosporine, and theophylline levels (unlikely to occur with ofloxacin). Azlocillin, cimetidine, and probenecid may increase ofloxacin serum levels. Foscarnet and NSAIDs have been associated with an increased risk of seizures with some quinolones. Serum levels of some quinolones are increased by loop diuretic administration. The hypoprothrombinemic effect of warfarin is enhanced by some quinolone antibiotics. Ofloxacin does not alter warfarin levels, but may alter the gastrointestinal flora which may increase warfarin's effect. Concurrent use of corticosteroids may increase risk of tendon rupture.

Decreased Effect: Metal cations (magnesium, aluminum, iron, and zinc) bind quinolones in the gastrointestinal tract and inhibit absorption (as much as 98%). Antacids, electrolyte supplements, sucralfate, quinapril, and some didanosine formulations should be avoided. Ofloxacin should be administered 4 hours before or 8 hours after these agents. Antineoplastic agents may decrease the absorption of quinolones.

Mechanism of Action Ofloxacin is a DNA gyrase inhibitor. DNA gyrase is an essential bacterial enzyme that maintains the superhelical structure of DNA. DNA gyrase is required for DNA replication and transcription, DNA repair, recombination, and transposition; bactericidal

Pharmacodynamics/Kinetics

Absorption: Well absorbed; food causes only minor alterations

Distribution: V_d: 2.4-3.5 L/kg

Protein binding: 20%

Half-life elimination: 5-7.5 hours; prolonged with renal impairment

Excretion: Primarily urine (as unchanged drug)

Dosage

Oral, I.V.: Adults:

Lower respiratory tract infection: 400 mg every 12 hours for 10 days

Epididymitis (gonorrhea): 300 mg twice daily for 10 days

Cervicitis due to *C. trachomatis* and/or *N. gonorrhoeae*: 300 mg every 12 hours for 7 days

Skin/skin structure: 400 mg every 12 hours for 10 days

Urinary tract infection: 200-400 mg every 12 hours for 3-10 days

Prostatitis: 300 mg every 12 hours for 6 weeks

Ophthalmic: Children >1 year and Adults:

Conjunctivitis: Instill 1-2 drops in affected eye(s) every 2-4 hours for the first 2 days, then use 4 times/day for an additional 5 days

Corneal ulcer: Instill 1-2 drops every 30 minutes while awake and every 4-6 hours after retiring for the first 2 days; beginning on day 3, instill 1-2 drops every hour while awake for 4-6 additional days; thereafter, 1-2 drops 4 times/day until clinical cure.

Otic:

Acute otitis media with tympanostomy tubes: Children 1-12 years: Instill 5 drops into affected ear(s) twice daily for 10 days

Chronic suppurative otitis media with perforated tympanic membranes: Children >12 years and Adults: 10 drops into affected ear twice daily for 14 days

Otitis externa:

Children 6 months to 13 years: Instill 5 drops into affected ear(s) once daily for 7 days

Children ≥13 years and Adults: Instill 10 drops into affected ear(s) once daily for 7 days

Dosing adjustment/interval in renal impairment: Adults: I.V., Oral:

Cl_{cr} 10-50 mL/minute: Administer 200-400 mg every 24 hours

Cl_{cr} <10 mL/minute: Administer 100-200 mg every 24 hours

Continuous arteriovenous or venovenous hemodiafiltration effects: Administer 300 mg every 24 hours

Administration

I.V.: Administer over at least 60 minutes. Infuse separately. Do not infuse though lines containing solutions with magnesium or calcium.

Ophthalmic: For ophthalmic use only; avoid touching tip of applicator to eye or other surfaces.

Oral: Do not take within 2 hours of food or any antacids which contain zinc, magnesium, or aluminum.

Otic: Prior to use, warm solution by holding bottle in hands for 1-2 minutes. Patient should lie down with affected ear upward and medication instilled. Pump tragus 4 times to ensure penetration of medication. Patient should remain in this position for 5 minutes.

Patient Information Report any skin rash or other allergic reactions; avoid excessive sunlight; do not take with food; do not take within 2 hours of any products including antacids which contain calcium, magnesium, or aluminum; contact your prescriber immediately with signs of inflammation or tendon pain

Dosage Forms INF [premixed in D_5W] (Floxin®): 200 mg (50 mL); 400 mg (100 mL). **INJ, solution** (Floxin®): 40 mg/mL (10 mL). **SOLN, ophthalmic** (Ocuflox®): 0.3% (5 mL, 10 mL). **SOLN, otic** (Floxin®): 0.3% (5 mL, 10 mL). **TAB** (Floxin®): 200 mg, 300 mg, 400 mg

♦ **Ogen®** see Estropipate on page 471

♦ **Ogestrel®** see Ethinyl Estradiol and Norgestrel on page 492

♦ **OGMT** see Metyrosine on page 833

♦ **OGT-918** see Miglustat on page 842

♦ **OKT3** see Muromonab-CD3 on page 867

Olanzapine (oh LAN za peen)

Related Information

Antipsychotic Agents Comparison on page 1364

U.S. Brand Names Zyprexa®; Zyprexa® Zydis®

Synonyms LY170053; Zyprexa Zydis

Therapeutic Category Antipsychotic Agent, Atypical; Antipsychotic Agent, Thienobenzodiazepine

Use Treatment of the manifestations of schizophrenia; treatment of acute mania episodes associated with bipolar disorder (as monotherapy or in combination with lithium or valproate); maintenance treatment of bipolar disorder

Unlabeled/Investigational Use Treatment of psychotic symptoms; chronic pain

Pregnancy Risk Factor C

Contraindications Hypersensitivity to olanzapine or any component of the formulation

Warnings/Precautions Moderate to highly sedating, use with caution in disorders where CNS depression is a feature. Use with caution in Parkinson's disease and Alzheimer's disease. Caution in patients with hemodynamic instability; bone marrow suppression; predisposition to seizures; subcortical brain damage; severe cardiac, hepatic, renal, or respiratory disease. Esophageal dysmotility and aspiration have been associated with antipsychotic use - use with caution in patients at risk of pneumonia (ie, Alzheimer's disease). Caution in breast cancer or other prolactin-dependent tumors (may elevate prolactin levels). May alter temperature regulation or mask toxicity of other drugs due to antiemetic effects. Life-threatening arrhythmias have occurred with therapeutic doses of some neuroleptics. An increased incidence of cerebrovascular adverse events has been reported in elderly patients with dementia-related psychosis. Significant weight gain may occur.

May cause anticholinergic effects (constipation, xerostomia, blurred vision, urinary retention); therefore, they should be used with caution in patients with decreased gastrointestinal motility, urinary retention, BPH, xerostomia, or visual problems. Conditions which also may be exacerbated by cholinergic blockade include narrow-angle glaucoma (screening is recommended) and worsening of myasthenia gravis. Relative to other neuroleptics, olanzapine has a moderate potency of cholinergic blockade.

May cause extrapyramidal reactions, including pseudoparkinsonism, acute dystonic reactions, akathisia, and tardive dyskinesia (risk of these reactions is very low relative to other neuroleptics). May be associated with neuroleptic malignant syndrome (NMS).
(Continued)

Olanzapine *(Continued)*

Common Adverse Reactions

>10%:

Central nervous system: Headache, somnolence, insomnia, agitation, nervousness, hostility, dizziness

Gastrointestinal: Dyspepsia, constipation, weight gain (clinically and long term)

Neuromuscular & skeletal: Weakness

1% to 10%:

Cardiovascular: Postural hypotension, tachycardia, hypotension, peripheral edema, chest pain, hypertension

Central nervous system: Dystonic reactions, parkinsonian events, amnesia, euphoria, stuttering, akathisia, anxiety, personality changes, fever, abnormal dreams, speech disorder

Dermatologic: Rash, bruising

Endocrine & metabolic: Prolactin increased, amenorrhea

Gastrointestinal: Xerostomia, abdominal pain, appetite increased, vomiting, salivation increased

Genitourinary: Premenstrual syndrome, incontinence

Hematologic: Leukopenia

Neuromuscular & skeletal: Arthralgia, neck rigidity, twitching, hypertonia, tremor, back pain, abnormal gait, akathisia

Ocular: Amblyopia

Respiratory: Rhinitis, cough, pharyngitis, dyspnea

Miscellaneous: Diaphoresis

Drug Interactions

Cytochrome P450 Effect: Substrate (minor) of CYP1A2, 2D6; **Inhibits** CYP1A2 (weak), 2C8/9 (weak), 2C19 (weak), 2D6 (weak), 3A4 (weak)

Increased Effect/Toxicity: Olanzapine levels may be increased by CYP1A2 inhibitors such as cimetidine and fluvoxamine. Sedations from olanzapine is increased with ethanol or other CNS depressants. The risk of hypotension and orthostatic hypotension from olanzapine is increased by concurrent antihypertensives. Metoclopramide may increase risk of extrapyramidal symptoms (EPS).

Decreased Effect: Olanzapine levels may be decreased by cytochrome P450 enzyme inducers such as rifampin, omeprazole, and carbamazepine (also cigarette smoking). Olanzapine may antagonize the effects of levodopa and dopamine agonists.

Mechanism of Action Olanzapine is a thienobenzodiazepine neuroleptic; thought to work by antagonizing dopamine and serotonin activities. It is a selective monoaminergic antagonist with high affinity binding to serotonin 5-HT$_{2A}$ and 5-HT$_{2C}$, dopamine D$_{1-4}$, muscarinic M$_{1-5}$, histamine H$_1$- and alpha$_1$-adrenergic receptor sites. Olanzapine binds weakly to GABA-A, BZD, and beta-adrenergic receptors.

Pharmacodynamics/Kinetics

Absorption: Well absorbed; not affected by food; tablets and orally-disintegrating tablets are bioequivalent

Distribution: V$_d$: Extensive, 1000 L

Protein binding, plasma: 93% bound to albumin and alpha$_1$-glycoprotein

Metabolism: Highly metabolized via direct glucuronidation and cytochrome P450 mediated oxidation (CYP1A2, CYP2D6)

Bioavailability: >57%

Half-life elimination: 21-54 hours; ~1.5 times greater in elderly

Time to peak: ~6 hours

Excretion: 40% removed via first pass metabolism; urine (57%, 7% as unchanged drug); feces (30%)

Clearance: 40% increase in olanzapine clearance in smokers

Dosage Oral:

Children: Schizophrenia/bipolar disorder: Initial: 2.5 mg/day; titrate as necessary to 20 mg/day (0.12-0.29 mg/kg/day)

Adults:

Schizophrenia: Usual starting dose: 5-10 mg once daily; increase to 10 mg once daily within 5-7 days, thereafter adjust by 5-10 mg/day at 1-week intervals, up to a maximum of 20 mg/day; doses of 30-50 mg/day have been used; typical dosage range: 10-30 mg/day

Bipolar mania:

Monotherapy: Usual starting dose: 10-15 mg once daily; increase by 5 mg/day at intervals of not less than 24 hours; maintenance: 5-20 mg/day; maximum dose: 20 mg/day

Combination therapy (olanzapine in combination with lithium or valproate): Initial: 10 mg once daily; dosing range: 5-20 mg/day

Elderly: Schizophrenia: Usual starting dose: 2.5 mg/day, increase as clinically indicated and monitor blood pressure; typical dosage range: 2.5-10 mg/day

Dosage comment in renal impairment: Not removed by dialysis

Administration Orally-disintegrating tablets: Remove from foil blister by peeling back (do not push tablet through the foil); place tablet in mouth immediately upon removal; tablet dissolves rapidly in saliva and may be swallowed with or without liquid

Monitoring Parameters Vital signs; lipid profile, fasting blood glucose/Hgb A$_{1c}$; BMI; mental status, abnormal involuntary movement scale (AIMS), extrapyramidal symptoms (EPS)

Dosage Forms TAB (Zyprexa®): 2.5 mg, 5 mg, 7.5 mg, 10 mg, 15 mg, 20 mg. **TAB, orally-disintegrating** (Zyprexa® Zydis®): 5 mg, 10 mg, 15 mg, 20 mg

♦ **Oleovitamin A** *see* Vitamin A *on page 1309*

Olmesartan (ole me SAR tan)

Related Information
  Angiotensin Agents Comparison *on page 1353*
U.S. Brand Names Benicar™
Synonyms Olmesartan Medoxomil
Therapeutic Category Angiotensin II Receptor Antagonist (ARB); Antihypertensive Agent
Use Treatment of hypertension with or without concurrent use of other antihypertensive agents
Pregnancy Risk Factor C/D (2nd and 3rd trimesters)
Contraindications Hypersensitivity to olmesartan or any component of the formulation; hypersensitivity to other A-II receptor antagonists; bilateral renal artery stenosis; pregnancy (2nd and 3rd trimesters)
Warnings/Precautions Avoid use or use a smaller dose in patients who are volume depleted; correct depletion first. Deterioration in renal function can occur with initiation. Use with caution in unilateral renal artery stenosis and pre-existing renal insufficiency; significant aortic/mitral stenosis. Safety and efficacy in pediatric patients have not been established.
Common Adverse Reactions 1% to 10%:
  Central nervous system: Dizziness (3%), headache
  Endocrine & metabolic: Hyperglycemia, hypertriglyceridemia
  Gastrointestinal: Diarrhea
  Neuromuscular & skeletal: Back pain, CPK increased
  Renal: Hematuria
  Respiratory: Bronchitis, pharyngitis, rhinitis, sinusitis
  Miscellaneous: Flu-like syndrome
Drug Interactions
  Increased Effect/Toxicity: The risk of hyperkalemia may be increased during concomitant use with potassium-sparing diuretics, potassium supplements, and trimethoprim; may increase risk of lithium toxicity.
  Decreased Effect: NSAIDs may decrease the efficacy of olmesartan.
Mechanism of Action As a selective and competitive, nonpeptide angiotensin II receptor antagonist, olmesartan blocks the vasoconstrictor and aldosterone-secreting effects of angiotensin II; olmesartan interacts reversibly at the AT1 and AT2 receptors of many tissues and has slow dissociation kinetics; its affinity for the AT1 receptor is 12,500 times greater than the AT2 receptor. Angiotensin II receptor antagonists may induce a more complete inhibition of the renin-angiotensin system than ACE inhibitors, they do not affect the response to bradykinin, and are less likely to be associated with nonrenin-angiotensin effects (eg, cough and angioedema). Olmesartan increases urinary flow rate and, in addition to being natriuretic and kaliuretic, increases excretion of chloride, magnesium, uric acid, calcium, and phosphate.
Pharmacodynamics/Kinetics
  Distribution: 17 L; does not cross the blood-brain barrier (animal studies)
  Protein binding: 99%
  Metabolism: Olmesartan medoxomil is hydrolyzed in the GI tract to active olmesartan. No further metabolism occurs.
  Bioavailability: 26%
  Half-life elimination: Terminal: 13 hours
  Time to peak: 1-2 hours
  Excretion: All as unchanged drug: Feces (50% to 65%); urine (35% to 50%)
Dosage Oral:
  Adults: Initial: Usual starting dose is 20 mg once daily; if initial response is inadequate, may be increased to 40 mg once daily after 2 weeks. May administer with other antihypertensive agents if blood pressure inadequately controlled with olmesartan. Consider lower starting dose in patients with possible depletion of intravascular volume (eg, patients receiving diuretics).
  Elderly: No dosage adjustment necessary
  Dosage adjustment in renal impairment: No specific guidelines for dosage adjustment; patients undergoing hemodialysis have not been studied.
  Dosage adjustment in hepatic impairment: No adjustment necessary.
Administration May be administered with or without food.
Monitoring Parameters Blood pressure, serum potassium
Dosage Forms TAB, film coated: 5 mg, 20 mg, 40 mg

Olmesartan and Hydrochlorothiazide

(ole me SAR tan & hye droe klor oh THYE a zide)
U.S. Brand Names Benicar HCT™
Synonyms Hydrochlorothiazide and Olmesartan Medoxomil; Olmesartan Medoxomil and Hydrochlorothiazide
Therapeutic Category Angiotensin II Receptor Antagonist (ARB); Diuretic, Thiazide
Use Treatment of hypertension (not recommended for initial treatment)
Pregnancy Risk Factor C/D (2nd and 3rd trimesters)
Dosage Oral: Adults: One tablet daily; dosage must be individualized (see below). May be titrated at 2- to 4-week intervals.
  Replacement therapy: May be substituted for previously titrated dosages of the individual components.
  Patients not controlled with single-agent therapy: Initiate by adding the lowest available dose of the alternative component (hydrochlorothiazide 12.5 mg or olmesartan 20 mg). Titrate to effect (maximum daily hydrochlorothiazide dose: 25 mg; maximum daily olmesartan dose: 40 mg).
  (Continued)

Olmesartan and Hydrochlorothiazide *(Continued)*

Dosage adjustment in renal impairment: Not recommended in patients with Cl$_{cr}$ <30 mL/minute

Dosage Forms TAB: (20/125): Olmesartan 20 mg and hydrochlorothiazide 12.5 mg; (40/12.5): Olmesartan 40 mg and hydrochlorothiazide 12.5 mg; (40/25): Olmesartan 40 mg and hydrochlorothiazide 25 mg

♦ **Olmesartan Medoxomil** *see* Olmesartan *on page 925*

♦ **Olmesartan Medoxomil and Hydrochlorothiazide** *see* Olmesartan and Hydrochlorothiazide *on page 925*

Olopatadine (oh loe pa TA deen)

U.S. Brand Names Patanol®

Therapeutic Category Antihistamine; Ophthalmic Agent, Miscellaneous

Use Treatment of the signs and symptoms of allergic conjunctivitis

Pregnancy Risk Factor C

Contraindications Hypersensitivity to olopatadine hydrochloride or any component of the formulation

Common Adverse Reactions

>5%: Central nervous system: Headache (7%)

<5%:

Central nervous system: Weakness, cold syndrome

Gastrointestinal: Taste perversion

Ocular: Burning, stinging, dry eyes, foreign body sensation, hyperemia, keratitis, eyelid edema, itching

Respiratory: Pharyngitis, rhinitis, sinusitis

Dosage Adults: Ophthalmic: 1 to 2 drops in affected eye(s) twice daily every 6 to 8 hours; results from an environmental study demonstrated that olopatadine was effective when dosed twice daily for up to 6 weeks

Dosage Forms SOLN, ophthalmic: 0.1% (5 mL)

Olsalazine (ole SAL a zeen)

U.S. Brand Names Dipentum®

Synonyms Olsalazine Sodium

Therapeutic Category 5-Aminosalicylic Acid Derivative; Anti-inflammatory Agent

Use Maintenance of remission of ulcerative colitis in patients intolerant to sulfasalazine

Pregnancy Risk Factor C

Contraindications Hypersensitivity to olsalazine, salicylates, or any component of the formulation

Warnings/Precautions Diarrhea is a common adverse effect of olsalazine; use with caution in patients with hypersensitivity to salicylates, sulfasalazine, or mesalamine

Common Adverse Reactions

>10%: Gastrointestinal: Diarrhea, cramps, abdominal pain

1% to 10%:

Central nervous system: Headache, fatigue, depression

Dermatologic: Rash, itching

Gastrointestinal: Nausea, heartburn, bloating, anorexia

Neuromuscular & skeletal: Arthralgia

Drug Interactions

Increased Effect/Toxicity: Olsalazine has been reported to increase the prothrombin time in patients taking warfarin. Olsalazine may increase the risk of myelosuppression with azathioprine, mesalamine, or sulfasalazine.

Mechanism of Action The mechanism of action appears to be topical rather than systemic

Pharmacodynamics/Kinetics

Absorption: <3%; very little intact olsalazine is systemically absorbed

Protein binding, plasma: >99%

Metabolism: Primarily via colonic bacteria to active drug, 5-aminosalicylic acid

Half-life elimination: 56 minutes

Time to peak: ~1 hour

Excretion: Primarily feces

Dosage Adults: Oral: 1 g/day in 2 divided doses

Administration Take with food in evenly divided doses.

Patient Information Take with food in evenly divided doses; report any sign of allergic reaction including rash

Dosage Forms CAP: 250 mg

♦ **Olsalazine Sodium** *see* Olsalazine *on page 926*

♦ **Olux®** *see* Clobetasol *on page 293*

Omalizumab (oh mah lye ZOO mab)

U.S. Brand Names Xolair®

Synonyms rhuMAb-E25

Therapeutic Category Monoclonal Antibody, Anti-Asthmatic

Use Treatment of moderate-to-severe, persistent allergic asthma not adequately controlled with inhaled corticosteroids

Pregnancy Risk Factor B

Contraindications Hypersensitivity to omalizumab or any component of the formulation; acute bronchospasm, status asthmaticus

Warnings/Precautions For use in patients with a documented reactivity to a perennial aeroallergen and with symptoms uncontrolled using inhaled corticosteroids; not used to control acute asthma symptoms. Dosing is based on pretreatment IgE serum levels and body weight. IgE levels remain elevated up to 1 year following treatment, therefore, levels taken during treatment can not be used as a dosage guide. Corticosteroid therapy should be tapered gradually, do not discontinue abruptly. Anaphylactic reactions have been reported within 2 hours of initial dose; appropriate medications for the treatment of hypersensitivity reactions should be available. Malignant neoplasm have been reported with use (<1%) in short-term studies; impact of long-term use is not known. Safety and efficacy in children <12 years of age have not been established.

Common Adverse Reactions
>10%:
Central nervous system: Headache (15%)
Local: Injection site reaction (45%; placebo 43%), severe injection site reactions (12%; placebo 9%). Most reactions occurred within 1 hour, lasted <8 days, and decreased in frequency with additional dosing.
Respiratory: Upper respiratory tract infection (23%), sinusitis (16%), pharyngitis (11%)
Miscellaneous: Viral infection (23%)
1% to 10%:
Central nervous system: Pain (7%), fatigue (3%), dizziness (3%)
Dermatologic: Dermatitis (2%), pruritus (2%)
Neuromuscular & skeletal: Arthralgia (8%), leg pain (4%), arm pain (2%), fracture (2%)
Otic: Earache (2%)

Mechanism of Action Omalizumab is an IgG monoclonal antibody (recombinant DNA-derived) which inhibits IgE binding to the high-affinity IgE receptor on mast cells and basophils. By decreasing bound IgE, the activation and release of mediators in the allergic response (early and late phase) is limited. Serum free IgE levels and the number of high-affinity IgE receptors are decreased. Long-term treatment in patients with allergic asthma showed a decrease in asthma exacerbations and corticosteroid usage.

Pharmacodynamics/Kinetics
Absorption: Slow following S.C. injection
Distribution: V_d: 78 ± 32 mL/kg
Metabolism: Hepatic; IgG degradation by reticuloendothelial system and endothelial cells
Bioavailability: 62%
Half-life elimination: 26 days
Time to peak: 7-8 days
Excretion: Primarily via hepatic degradation; intact IgG may be secreted in bile

Dosage S.C.: Children ≥12 years and Adults: Asthma: Dose is based on pretreatment IgE serum levels and body weight. Dosing should not be adjusted based on IgE levels taken during treatment or <1 year following therapy; doses should be adjusted during treatment for significant changes in body weight
IgE ≥30-100 int. units/mL:
30-90 kg: 150 mg every 4 weeks
>90-150 kg: 300 mg every 4 weeks
IgE >100-200 int. units/mL:
30-90 kg: 300 mg every 4 weeks
>90-150 kg: 225 mg every 2 weeks
IgE >200-300 int. units/mL:
30-60 kg: 300 mg every 4 weeks
>60-90 kg: 225 mg every 2 weeks
>90-150 kg: 300 mg every 2 weeks
IgE >300-400 int. units/mL:
30-70 kg: 225 mg every 2 weeks
>70-90 kg: 300 mg every 2 weeks
>90 kg: Do not administer dose
IgE >400-500 int. units/mL:
30-70 kg: 300 mg every 2 weeks
>70-90 kg: 375 mg every 2 weeks
>90 kg: Do not administer dose
IgE >500-600 int. units/mL:
30-60 kg: 300 mg every 2 weeks
>60-70 kg: 375 mg every 2 weeks
>70 kg: Do not administer dose
IgE >600-700 int. units/mL:
30-60 kg: 375 mg every 2 weeks
>60 kg: Do not administer dose

Administration For S.C. injection only; doses >150 mg should divided over more than one site. Injections may take 5-10 seconds to administer.

Monitoring Parameters Baseline IgE; FEV₁, peak flow, and/or other pulmonary function tests

Patient Information This medication can only be given by injection and it may take several weeks to see its full effects. Do not change dosing of current asthma medications without consulting prescriber.

Dosage Forms INJ, powder for reconstitution [preservative free]: 150 mg

Omeprazole (oh ME pray zol)

Related Information
Antimicrobial Drugs of Choice *on page 1440*

U.S. Brand Names Prilosec®; Prilosec OTC™ [OTC]

Therapeutic Category Gastric Acid Secretion Inhibitor; Proton Pump Inhibitor

Use Short-term (4-8 weeks) treatment of active duodenal ulcer disease or active benign gastric ulcer; treatment of heartburn and other symptoms associated with gastroesophageal reflux disease (GERD); short-term (4-8 weeks) treatment of endoscopically-diagnosed erosive esophagitis; maintenance healing of erosive esophagitis; long-term treatment of pathological hypersecretory conditions; as part of a multidrug regimen for *H. pylori* eradication to reduce the risk of duodenal ulcer recurrence

OTC labeling: Short-term treatment of frequent, uncomplicated heartburn occurring ≥2 days/week

Unlabeled/Investigational Use Healing NSAID-induced ulcers; prevention of NSAID-induced ulcers

Pregnancy Risk Factor C

Contraindications Hypersensitivity to omeprazole or any component of the formulation

Warnings/Precautions In long-term (2-year) studies in rats, omeprazole produced a dose-related increase in gastric carcinoid tumors. While available endoscopic evaluations and histologic examinations of biopsy specimens from human stomachs have not detected a risk from short-term exposure to omeprazole, further human data on the effect of sustained hypochlorhydria and hypergastrinemia are needed to rule out the possibility of an increased risk for the development of tumors in humans receiving long-term therapy. Bioavailability may be increased in the elderly, Asian population, and with hepatic dysfunction. Safety and efficacy have not been established in children <2 years of age. When used for self-medication (OTC), do not use for >14 days; treatment should not be repeated more often than every 4 months; not approved for OTC use in children <18 years of age.

Common Adverse Reactions 1% to 10%:
Central nervous system: Headache (7%), dizziness (2%)
Dermatologic: Rash (2%)
Gastrointestinal: Diarrhea (3%), abdominal pain (2%), nausea (2%), vomiting (2%), constipation (1%), taste perversion (<1% to 15%)
Neuromuscular & skeletal: Weakness (1%), back pain (1%)
Respiratory: Upper respiratory infection (2%), cough (1%)

Drug Interactions
Cytochrome P450 Effect: Substrate of CYP2A6 (minor), 2C8/9 (minor), 2C19 (major), 2D6 (minor), 3A4 (minor); **Inhibits** CYP1A2 (weak), 2C8/9 (moderate), 2C19 (strong), 2D6 (weak), 3A4 (weak); **Induces** CYP1A2 (weak)
Increased Effect/Toxicity: Esomeprazole and omeprazole may increase the levels of benzodiazepines metabolized by oxidation (eg, diazepam, midazolam, triazolam) and carbamazepine. Elimination of phenytoin or warfarin may be prolonged when used concomitantly with omeprazole.
Decreased Effect: CYP2C19 inducers may decrease the levels/effects of omeprazole; example inducers include aminoglutethimide, carbamazepine, phenytoin, and rifampin. Proton pump inhibitors may decrease the absorption of atazanavir, indinavir, itraconazole, and ketoconazole.

Mechanism of Action Suppresses gastric acid secretion by inhibiting the parietal cell H+/K+ ATP pump

Pharmacodynamics/Kinetics
Onset of action: Antisecretory: ~1 hour
Peak effect: 2 hours
Duration: 72 hours
Protein binding: 95%
Metabolism: Extensively hepatic to inactive metabolites
Bioavailability: Oral: 30% to 40%; increased in Asian patients and with hepatic dysfunction
Half-life elimination: 0.5-1 hour
Excretion: Urine (77% as metabolites, very small amount as unchanged drug); feces

Dosage Oral:
Children ≥2 years: GERD or other acid-related disorders:
<20 kg: 10 mg once daily
≥20 kg: 20 mg once daily
Adults:
Active duodenal ulcer: 20 mg/day for 4-8 weeks
Gastric ulcers: 40 mg/day for 4-8 weeks
Symptomatic GERD: 20 mg/day for up to 4 weeks
Erosive esophagitis: 20 mg/day for 4-8 weeks
Helicobacter pylori eradication: Dose varies with regimen: 20 mg once daily **or** 40 mg/day as single dose or in 2 divided doses; requires combination therapy with antibiotics
Pathological hypersecretory conditions: Initial: 60 mg once daily; doses up to 120 mg 3 times/day have been administered; administer daily doses >80 mg in divided doses
Frequent heartburn (OTC labeling): 20 mg/day for 14 days; treatment may be repeated after 4 months if needed

Dosage adjustment in hepatic impairment: Specific guidelines are not available; bioavailability is increased with chronic liver disease

Administration Capsule should be swallowed whole. Do not chew, crush, or open. Best if taken before breakfast. May be opened and contents added to applesauce. Administration via NG tube should be in an acidic juice.

Patient Information Take before eating; do not chew, crush, or open capsule.

OTC product: Not for immediate relief of heartburn; may take 1-4 days to reach full effect. Do not use if heartburn has lasted >3 months or is accompanied by lightheadedness, dizziness, sweating, frequent chest pain, wheezing, nausea, vomiting, or stomach pain; contact prescriber first. Do not use more frequently than 14 days every 4 months.

Dosage Forms CAP, delayed release: 10 mg, 20 mg; (Prilosec®): 10 mg, 20 mg, 40 mg; (Prilosec OTC™): 20 mg

- ♦ **Omnicef®** see Cefdinir on page 232
- ♦ **Oncaspar®** see Pegaspargase on page 962
- ♦ **Oncovin® [DSC]** see VinCRIStine on page 1306

Ondansetron (on DAN se tron)

U.S. Brand Names Zofran®; Zofran® ODT

Synonyms GR38032R; Ondansetron Hydrochloride

Therapeutic Category Antiemetic, Serotonin Antagonist; 5-HT$_3$ Receptor Antagonist; Serotonin 5-HT$_3$ Receptor Antagonist

Use Prevention of nausea and vomiting associated with moderately- to highly-emetogenic cancer chemotherapy; radiotherapy in patients receiving total body irradiation or fractions to the abdomen; prevention and treatment of postoperative nausea and vomiting

Generally **not** recommended for treatment of existing chemotherapy-induced emesis (CIE) or for prophylaxis of agents from with a low emetogenic potential.

Unlabeled/Investigational Use Treatment of early-onset alcoholism

Pregnancy Risk Factor B

Contraindications Hypersensitivity to ondansetron, other selective 5-HT$_3$ antagonists, or any component of the formulation

Warnings/Precautions Ondansetron should be used on a scheduled basis, not on an "as needed" (PRN) basis, since data support the use of this drug only in the prevention of nausea and vomiting (due to antineoplastic therapy) and not in the rescue of nausea and vomiting. Ondansetron should only be used in the first 24-48 hours of chemotherapy. Data do not support any increased efficacy of ondansetron in delayed nausea and vomiting. Does not stimulate gastric or intestinal peristalsis; may mask progressive ileus and/or gastric distension. Orally-disintegrating tablets contain phenylalanine.

Common Adverse Reactions
>10%:
  Cardiovascular: Malaise/fatigue (9% to 13%)
  Central nervous system: Headache (9% to 27%)
1% to 10%:
  Central nervous system: Drowsiness (8%), fever (2% to 8%), dizziness (4% to 7%), anxiety (6%), cold sensation (2%)
  Dermatologic: Pruritus (2% to 5%), rash (1%)
  Gastrointestinal: Constipation (6% to 9%), diarrhea (3% to 7%)
  Genitourinary: Gynecological disorder (7%), urinary retention (5%)
  Hepatic: Increased ALT/AST (1% to 2%)
  Local: Injection site reaction (4%)
  Neuromuscular & skeletal: Paresthesia (2%)
  Respiratory: Hypoxia (9%)

Drug Interactions
  Cytochrome P450 Effect: Substrate of CYP1A2 (minor), 2C8/9 (minor), 2D6 (minor), 2E1 (minor), 3A4 (major); **Inhibits** CYP1A2 (weak), 2C8/9 (weak), 2D6 (weak)
  Increased Effect/Toxicity: Increased toxicity: CYP1A2, 2D6, 2E1, and 3A4 enzyme inhibitors (eg, cimetidine, allopurinol, and disulfiram) may change the clearance of ondansetron; monitor
  Decreased Effect: Decreased effect: CYP1A2, 2D6, 2E1, and 3A4 enzyme inducers (eg, barbiturates, carbamazepine, rifampin, phenytoin, and phenylbutazone) may change the clearance of ondansetron; monitor

Mechanism of Action Selective 5-HT$_3$-receptor antagonist, blocking serotonin, both peripherally on vagal nerve terminals and centrally in the chemoreceptor trigger zone

Pharmacodynamics/Kinetics
  Onset of action: ~30 minutes
  Distribution: V$_d$: 2.2-2.5 L/kg
  Protein binding, plasma: 70% to 76%
  Metabolism: Extensively hepatic via hydroxylation, followed by glucuronide or sulfate conjugation; CYP1A2, CYP2D6, and CYP3A4 substrate; some demethylation occurs
  Bioavailability: Oral: 56% to 71%; Rectal: 58% to 74%
  Half-life elimination: Children <15 years: 2-3 hours; Adults: 3-6 hours
  Time to peak: Oral: ~2 hours
  Excretion: Urine (44% to 60% as metabolites, 5% to 10% as unchanged drug); feces (~25%)
  (Continued)

Ondansetron *(Continued)*

Dosage

Children:

I.V.:

Chemotherapy-induced emesis: 4-18 years: 0.15 mg/kg/dose administered 30 minutes prior to chemotherapy, 4 and 8 hours after the first dose **or** 0.45 mg/kg/day as a single dose

Postoperative nausea and vomiting: 2-12 years:

≤40 kg: 0.1 mg/kg

>40 kg: 4 mg

Oral: Chemotherapy-induced emesis:

4-11 years: 4 mg 30 minutes before chemotherapy; repeat 4 and 8 hours after initial dose, then 4 mg every 8 hours for 1-2 days after chemotherapy completed

≥12 years: Refer to adult dosing.

Adults:

I.V.: Chemotherapy-induced emesis:

0.15 mg/kg 3 times/day beginning 30 minutes prior to chemotherapy **or**

0.45 mg/kg once daily **or**

8-10 mg 1-2 times/day **or**

24 mg or 32 mg once daily

I.M., I.V.: Postoperative nausea and vomiting: 4 mg as a single dose approximately 30 minutes before the end of anesthesia, or as treatment if vomiting occurs after surgery

Oral:

Chemotherapy-induced emesis:

Highly-emetogenic agents/single-day therapy: 24 mg given 30 minutes prior to the start of therapy

Moderately-emetogenic agents: 8 mg every 12 hours beginning 30 minutes before chemotherapy, continuously for 1-2 days after chemotherapy completed

Total body irradiation: 8 mg 1-2 hours before daily each fraction of radiotherapy

Single high-dose fraction radiotherapy to abdomen: 8 mg 1-2 hours before irradiation, then 8 mg every 8 hours after first dose for 1-2 days after completion of radiotherapy

Daily fractionated radiotherapy to abdomen: 8 mg 1-2 hours before irradiation, then 8 mg 8 hours after first dose for each day of radiotherapy

Postoperative nausea and vomiting: 16 mg given 1 hour prior to induction of anesthesia

Elderly: No dosing adjustment required

Dosage adjustment in renal impairment: No dosing adjustment required

Dosage adjustment in hepatic impairment: Maximum daily dose: 8 mg in patients with severe liver disease (Child-Pugh score ≥10)

Administration

Oral: Oral dosage forms should be administered 30 minutes prior to chemotherapy; 1-2 hours before radiotherapy; 1 hour prior to the induction of anesthesia

Orally-disintegrating tablets: Do not remove from blister until needed. Peel backing off the blister, do not push tablet through. Using dry hands, place tablet on tongue and allow to dissolve. Swallow with saliva.

I.M.: Should be administered undiluted

I.V.: Give first dose 30 minutes prior to beginning chemotherapy; the I.V. preparation has been successful when administered orally

IVPB: Infuse over 15-30 minutes; 24-hour continuous infusions have been reported, but are rarely used

Patient Information Orally-disintegrating tablets: Do not remove from blister until needed. Peel backing off the blister, do not push tablet through. Using dry hands, place tablet on tongue and allow to dissolve. Swallow with saliva. Contains <0.03 mg phenylalanine/tablet.

Dosage Forms INF [premixed in D_5W] (Zofran®): 32 mg (50 mL). **INJ, solution** (Zofran®): 2 mg/mL (2 mL, 20 mL). **SOLN** (Zofran®): 4 mg/5 mL (50 mL). **TAB** (Zofran®): 4 mg, 8 mg, 24 mg. **TAB, orally-disintegrating** (Zofran® ODT): 4 mg, 8 mg

Opium Tincture (OH pee um TING chur)
Synonyms DTO; Opium Tincture, Deodorized
Therapeutic Category Analgesic, Narcotic; Antidiarrheal
Use Treatment of diarrhea or relief of pain
Restrictions C-II
Pregnancy Risk Factor B/D (prolonged use or high doses at term)
Contraindications Hypersensitivity to morphine sulfate or any component of the formulation; increased intracranial pressure; severe respiratory depression; severe hepatic or renal insufficiency; pregnancy (prolonged use or high dosages near term)
Warnings/Precautions Opium shares the toxic potential of opiate agonists, and usual precautions of opiate agonist therapy should be observed; some preparations contain sulfites which may cause allergic reactions; infants <3 months of age are more susceptible to respiratory depression, use with caution and generally in reduced doses in this age group; this is **not** paregoric, dose accordingly
Common Adverse Reactions Frequency not defined.
Cardiovascular: Palpitations, hypotension, bradycardia, peripheral vasodilation
Central nervous system: Drowsiness, dizziness, restlessness, headache, malaise, CNS depression, increased intracranial pressure, insomnia, mental depression
Gastrointestinal: Nausea, vomiting, constipation, anorexia, stomach cramps, biliary tract spasm
Genitourinary: Decreased urination, urinary tract spasm
Neuromuscular & skeletal: Weakness
Ocular: Miosis
Respiratory: Respiratory depression
Miscellaneous: Histamine release, physical and psychological dependence
Drug Interactions
Increased Effect/Toxicity: Opium tincture and CNS depressants, MAO inhibitors, tricyclic antidepressants may potentiate the effects of opiate agonists (eg, codeine, morphine, etc). Dextroamphetamine may enhance the analgesic effect of opiate agonists.
Mechanism of Action Contains many narcotic alkaloids including morphine; its mechanism for gastric motility inhibition is primarily due to this morphine content; it results in a decrease in digestive secretions, an increase in GI muscle tone, and therefore a reduction in GI propulsion
Pharmacodynamics/Kinetics
Duration: 4-5 hours
Absorption: Variable
Metabolism: Hepatic
Excretion: Urine
Dosage Oral:
Children:
Diarrhea: 0.005-0.01 mL/kg/dose every 3-4 hours for a maximum of 6 doses/24 hours
Analgesia: 0.01-0.02 mL/kg/dose every 3-4 hours
Adults:
Diarrhea: 0.3-1 mL/dose every 2-6 hours to maximum of 6 mL/24 hours
Analgesia: 0.6-1.5 mL/dose every 3-4 hours
Monitoring Parameters Observe patient for excessive sedation, respiratory depression, implement safety measures, assist with ambulation
Patient Information Avoid alcohol, may cause drowsiness, impair judgment, or coordination; may cause physical and psychological dependence with prolonged use
Dosage Forms LIQ: 10% (120 mL, 480 mL)

♦ Opium Tincture, Deodorized see Opium Tincture on page 931

Oprelvekin (oh PREL ve kin)
U.S. Brand Names Neumega®
Synonyms IL-11; Interleukin-11; Recombinant Human Interleukin-11; Recombinant Interleukin-11; rhIL-11; rIL-11
Therapeutic Category Platelet Growth Factor
Use Prevention of severe thrombocytopenia and the reduction of the need for platelet transfusions following myelosuppressive chemotherapy
Pregnancy Risk Factor C
Contraindications Hypersensitivity to oprelvekin or any component of the formulation
Warnings/Precautions Oprelvekin should be used cautiously in patients with conditions where expansion of plasma volume should be avoided (eg, left ventricular dysfunction, CHF, hypertension); cardiac arrhythmias or conduction defects, respiratory disease; history of thromboembolic problems; hepatic or renal dysfunction; not indicated following myeloablative chemotherapy. Per the manufacturer, should not be used in children, particularly those <12 years of age, except as part of a controlled clinical trial.
Common Adverse Reactions
>10%:
Cardiovascular: Tachycardia (19% to 30%), palpitations (14% to 24%), atrial arrhythmias (12%), peripheral edema (60% to 75%), syncope (6% to 13%)
Central nervous system: Headache (41%), dizziness (38%), insomnia (33%), fatigue (30%), fever (36%)
Dermatologic: Rash (25%)
Endocrine & metabolic: Fluid retention
Gastrointestinal: Nausea (50% to 77%), vomiting, anorexia
(Continued)

Oprelvekin *(Continued)*

Hematologic: Anemia (100%), probably a dilutional phenomena; appears within 3 days of initiation of therapy, resolves in about 2 weeks after cessation of oprelvekin

Neuromuscular & skeletal: Arthralgia, myalgias

Respiratory: Dyspnea (48%), pleural effusions (10%)

1% to 10%: Gastrointestinal: Weight gain (5%)

Mechanism of Action Oprelvekin stimulates multiple stages of megakaryocytopoiesis and thrombopoiesis, resulting in proliferation of megakaryocyte progenitors and megakaryocyte maturation

Pharmacodynamics/Kinetics

Metabolism: Uncertain

Half-life elimination: Terminal: 5-8 hours

Time to peak, serum: 1-6 hours

Excretion: Urine (primarily as metabolites)

Dosage S.C.: **Note:** First dose should not be administered until 24-36 hours after the end of chemotherapy. Discontinue the drug at least 48 hours before beginning the next cycle of chemotherapy.

Children: 75-100 mcg/kg once daily for 10-21 days (until postnadir platelet count ≥50,000 cells/µL)

Note: The manufacturer states that, until efficacy/toxicity parameters are established, the use of oprelvekin in pediatric patients (particularly those <12 years of age) should be restricted to use in controlled clinical trials.

Adults: 50 mcg/kg once daily for 10-21 days (until postnadir platelet count ≥50,000 cells/µL)

Administration Subcutaneously in either the abdomen, thigh, or hip (or upper arm if not self-injected). Discontinue treatment with oprelvekin ≥2 days before starting the next planned cycle of chemotherapy.

Monitoring Parameters Monitor fluid balance during therapy Obtain a CBC at regular intervals during therapy. Monitor platelet counts until adequate recovery has occurred.

Patient Information Report any swelling in the arms or legs (peripheral edema), shortness of breath (congestive failure, anemia), irregular heartbeat, headaches

Dosage Forms INJ, powder for reconstitution: 5 mg

Orlistat *(OR li stat)*

Related Information

Obesity Treatment Guidelines for Adults *on page 1482*

U.S. Brand Names Xenical®

Therapeutic Category Lipase Inhibitor

Use Management of obesity, including weight loss and weight management when used in conjunction with a reduced-calorie diet; reduce the risk of weight regain after prior weight loss; indicated for obese patients with an initial body mass index (BMI) ≥30 kg/m² or ≥27 kg/m² in the presence of other risk factors

Pregnancy Risk Factor B

Contraindications Hypersensitivity to orlistat or any component of the formulation; chronic malabsorption syndrome or cholestasis

Warnings/Precautions Patients should be advised to adhere to dietary guidelines; gastrointestinal adverse events may increase if taken with a diet high in fat (>30% total daily calories from fat). The daily intake of fat should be distributed over three main meals. If taken with any one meal very high in fat, the possibility of gastrointestinal effects increases. Patients should be counseled to take a multivitamin supplement that contains fat-soluble vitamins to ensure adequate nutrition because orlistat has been shown to reduce the absorption of some fat-soluble vitamins and beta-carotene. Some patients may develop increased levels of urinary oxalate following treatment; caution should be exercised when prescribing it to patients with a history of hyperoxaluria or calcium oxalate nephrolithiasis. As with any weight-loss agent, the potential exists for misuse in appropriate patient populations (eg, patients with anorexia nervosa or bulimia). Write and fill prescriptions carefully; confusion has occurred between Xenical® and Xeloda®.

Common Adverse Reactions
>10%
Central nervous system: Headache (31%)
Gastrointestinal: Oily spotting (27%), abdominal pain/discomfort (26%), flatus with discharge (24%), fatty/oily stool (20%), fecal urgency (22%), oily evacuation (12%), increased defecation (11%)
Neuromuscular & skeletal: Back pain (14%)
Respiratory: Upper respiratory infection (38%)
1% to 10%
Central nervous system: Fatigue (7%), anxiety (5%), sleep disorder (4%)
Dermatologic: Dry skin (2%)
Endocrine & metabolic: Menstrual irregularities (10%)
Gastrointestinal: Fecal incontinence (8%), nausea (8%), infectious diarrhea (5%), rectal pain/discomfort (5%), vomiting (4%)
Neuromuscular & skeletal: Arthritis (5%), myalgia (4%)
Otic: Otitis (4%)

Drug Interactions
Decreased Effect: Orlistat may decrease amiodarone absorption (monitor). Coadministration with cyclosporine may decrease plasma levels of cyclosporine (administer cyclosporine 2 hours before or after orlistat and monitor). Orlistat does not alter the pharmacokinetics of warfarin, however, vitamin K absorption may be decreased during orlistat therapy (patients stabilized on warfarin should be monitored for changes in warfarin effects).

Mechanism of Action A reversible inhibitor of gastric and pancreatic lipases thus inhibiting absorption of dietary fats by 30% (at doses of 120 mg 3 times/day).

Pharmacodynamics/Kinetics
Absorption: Minimal
Metabolism: Metabolized within the gastrointestinal wall; forms inactive metabolites
Excretion: Feces (83% as unchanged drug)

Dosage Oral: Children ≥12 years and Adults: 120 mg 3 times/day with each main meal containing fat (during or up to 1 hour after the meal); omit dose if meal is occasionally missed or contains no fat.

Patient Information Patient should be on a nutritionally balanced, reduced-calorie diet that contains approximately 30% of calories from fat; daily intake of fat, carbohydrate, and protein should be distributed over the three main meals

Dosage Forms CAP: 120 mg

♦ **Ornex® [OTC]** *see* Acetaminophen and Pseudoephedrine *on page 26*
♦ **Ornex® Maximum Strength [OTC]** *see* Acetaminophen and Pseudoephedrine *on page 26*

Orphenadrine (or FEN a dreen)

U.S. Brand Names Norflex™
Synonyms Orphenadrine Citrate
Therapeutic Category Anti-Parkinson's Agent, Anticholinergic; Skeletal Muscle Relaxant
Use Treatment of muscle spasm associated with acute painful musculoskeletal conditions; supportive therapy in tetanus
Pregnancy Risk Factor C
Dosage Adults:
Oral: 100 mg twice daily
I.M., I.V.: 60 mg every 12 hours
Dosage Forms INJ, solution: 30 mg/mL (2 mL). **TAB, extended release:** 100 mg

Orphenadrine, Aspirin, and Caffeine (or FEN a dreen, AS pir in, & KAF een)

U.S. Brand Names Norgesic™; Norgesic™ Forte; Orphengesic; Orphengesic Forte
Synonyms Aspirin, Orphenadrine, and Caffeine; Caffeine, Orphenadrine, and Aspirin
Therapeutic Category Analgesic/Skeletal Muscle Relaxant
Use Relief of discomfort associated with skeletal muscular conditions
Pregnancy Risk Factor D
Dosage Oral: 1-2 tablets 3-4 times/day
Dosage Forms TAB: Orphenadrine citrate 25 mg, aspirin 385 mg, and caffeine 30 mg; orphenadrine citrate 50 mg, aspirin 770 mg, and caffeine 60 mg; (Norgesic™, Orphengesic): Orphenadrine citrate 25 mg, aspirin 385 mg, and caffeine 30 mg; (Norgesic™ Forte, Orphengesic Forte): Orphenadrine citrate 50 mg, aspirin 770 mg, and caffeine 60 mg

- ♦ **Orphenadrine Citrate** *see* Orphenadrine *on page 933*
- ♦ **Orphengesic** *see* Orphenadrine, Aspirin, and Caffeine *on page 933*
- ♦ **Orphengesic Forte** *see* Orphenadrine, Aspirin, and Caffeine *on page 933*
- ♦ **Ortho-Cept®** *see* Ethinyl Estradiol and Desogestrel *on page 477*
- ♦ **Orthoclone OKT® 3** *see* Muromonab-CD3 *on page 867*
- ♦ **Ortho-Cyclen®** *see* Ethinyl Estradiol and Norgestimate *on page 490*
- ♦ **Ortho-Est®** *see* Estropipate *on page 471*
- ♦ **Ortho Evra™** *see* Ethinyl Estradiol and Norelgestromin *on page 486*
- ♦ **Ortho-Novum®** *see* Ethinyl Estradiol and Norethindrone *on page 487*
- ♦ **Ortho-Novum® 1/50** *see* Mestranol and Norethindrone *on page 801*
- ♦ **Ortho Tri-Cyclen®** *see* Ethinyl Estradiol and Norgestimate *on page 490*
- ♦ **Ortho Tri-Cyclen® Lo** *see* Ethinyl Estradiol and Norgestimate *on page 490*
- ♦ **Orudis® KT [OTC]** *see* Ketoprofen *on page 705*
- ♦ **Oruvail®** *see* Ketoprofen *on page 705*
- ♦ **Os-Cal® 500 [OTC]** *see* Calcium Carbonate *on page 203*

Oseltamivir (oh sel TAM i vir)

U.S. Brand Names Tamiflu®

Therapeutic Category Antiviral Agent, Influenza; Neuraminidase Inhibitor

Use Treatment of uncomplicated acute illness due to influenza (A or B) infection in adults and children >1 year of age who have been symptomatic for no more than 2 days; prophylaxis against influenza (A or B) infection in adults and adolescents ≥13 years of age

Pregnancy Risk Factor C

Contraindications Hypersensitivity to oseltamivir or any component of the formulation

Warnings/Precautions Oseltamivir is not a substitute for the flu shot. Dosage adjustment is required for creatinine clearance between 10-30 mL/minute. Safety and efficacy in children (<1 year of age) have not been established for treatment regimens. Safety and efficacy have not been established for prophylactic use in patients <13 years of age. Also consider primary or concomitant bacterial infections. Safety and efficacy for treatment or prophylaxis in immunocompromised patients have not been established.

Common Adverse Reactions
As seen with **treatment** doses: 1% to 10%:
   Central nervous system: Insomnia (adults 1%), vertigo (adults 1%)
   Gastrointestinal: Nausea (adults 10%), vomiting (adults 9%, children 15%), abdominal pain (children 5%)
   Ocular: Conjunctivitis (children 1%)
   Otic: Ear disorder (children 2%)
   Respiratory: Epistaxis (children 3%)
Similar adverse effects were seen in **prophylactic** use, however, the incidence was generally less. The following reactions were seen more commonly with prophylactic use: Headache (20%), fatigue (8%), diarrhea (3%)

Drug Interactions
Increased Effect/Toxicity: Cimetidine and amoxicillin have no effect on plasma concentrations. Probenecid increases oseltamivir carboxylate serum concentration by twofold. Dosage adjustments are not required.

Mechanism of Action Oseltamivir, a prodrug, is hydrolyzed to the active form, oseltamivir carboxylate. It is thought to inhibit influenza virus neuraminidase, with the possibility of alteration of virus particle aggregation and release. In clinical studies of the influenza virus, 1.3% of post-treatment isolates had decreased neuraminidase susceptibility to oseltamivir carboxylate.

Pharmacodynamics/Kinetics
Absorption: Well absorbed
Distribution: V_d: 23-26 L (oseltamivir carboxylate)
Protein binding, plasma: Oseltamivir carboxylate: 3%; Oseltamivir: 42%
Metabolism: Hepatic (90%) to oseltamivir carboxylate; neither the parent drug nor active metabolite has any effect on CYP
Bioavailability: 75% reaches systemic circulation in active form
Half-life elimination: Oseltamivir carboxylate: 6-10 hours; similar in geriatrics (68-78 years)
Time to peak: C_{max}: Oseltamivir: 65 ng/mL; Oseltamivir carboxylate: 348 ng/mL
Excretion: Urine (as carboxylate metabolite)

Dosage Oral:
Treatment: Initiate treatment within 2 days of onset of symptoms; duration of treatment: 5 days:
   Children: 1-12 years:
      ≤15 kg: 30 mg twice daily
      >15 kg - ≤23 kg: 45 mg twice daily
      >23 kg - ≤40 kg: 60 mg twice daily
      >40 kg: 75 mg twice daily
   Adolescents and Adults: 75 mg twice daily
Prophylaxis: Adolescents and Adults: 75 mg once daily for at least 7 days; treatment should begin within 2 days of contact with an infected individual. During community outbreaks, dosing is 75 mg once daily. May be used for up to 6 weeks; duration of protection lasts for length of dosing period

Dosage adjustment in renal impairment:
Cl_{cr} 10-30 mL/minute:
   Treatment: Reduce dose to 75 mg once daily for 5 days

Prophylaxis: 75 mg every other day
Cl_{cr} <10 mL/minute: Has not been studied
Dosage adjustment in hepatic impairment: Has not been evaluated
Elderly: No adjustments required

Patient Information When used as treatment of influenza infection, take within 2 days of onset of flu symptoms (fever, cough, headache, fatigue, muscular weakness, and sore throat). When used as prevention of influenza infection, take every day during the "flu season" as instructed by your prescriber. This is not a substitute for the flu shot. Not recommended for pregnant or nursing women For best results, do not miss doses.

Suspension: Shake well before using; may be stored under refrigeration or at room temperature. Use the oral syringe provided to measure appropriate dose.

Dosage Forms CAP: 75 mg. **POWDER, for oral suspension:** 12 mg/mL (25 mL)

♦ **Osmitrol**® *see* Mannitol *on page 774*
♦ **Otic Domeboro**® *see* Aluminum Acetate and Acetic Acid *on page 66*
♦ **Ovace**™ *see* Sulfacetamide *on page 1169*
♦ **Ovcon**® *see* Ethinyl Estradiol and Norethindrone *on page 487*
♦ **Ovide**® *see* Malathion *on page 773*
♦ **Ovidrel**® *see* Chorionic Gonadotropin (Recombinant) *on page 273*
♦ **Ovral**® *see* Ethinyl Estradiol and Norgestrel *on page 492*
♦ **Ovrette**® *see* Norgestrel *on page 915*

Oxacillin (oks a SIL in)

Related Information
Community-Acquired Pneumonia in Adults *on page 1457*
Synonyms Methylphenyl Isoxazolyl Penicillin; Oxacillin Sodium
Therapeutic Category Antibiotic, Penicillin
Use Treatment of infections such as osteomyelitis, septicemia, endocarditis, and CNS infections caused by susceptible strains of *Staphylococcus*
Pregnancy Risk Factor B
Contraindications Hypersensitivity to oxacillin or other penicillins or any component of the formulation
Warnings/Precautions Elimination rate will be slow in neonates; modify dosage in patients with renal impairment and in the elderly; use with caution in patients with cephalosporin hypersensitivity
Common Adverse Reactions Frequency not defined.
Central nervous system: Fever
Dermatologic: Rash
Gastrointestinal: Nausea, diarrhea, vomiting
Hematologic: Eosinophilia, leukopenia, neutropenia, thrombocytopenia, agranulocytosis
Hepatic: Hepatotoxicity, AST increased
Renal: Acute interstitial nephritis, hematuria
Miscellaneous: Serum sickness-like reactions
Drug Interactions
Increased Effect/Toxicity: Probenecid increases penicillin levels. Penicillins and anticoagulants may increase the effect of anticoagulants. Penicillins may increase the exposure to methotrexate during concurrent therapy; monitor.
Decreased Effect: Although anecdotal reports suggest oral contraceptive efficacy could be reduced by penicillins, this has been refuted by more rigorous scientific and clinical data.
Mechanism of Action Inhibits bacterial cell wall synthesis by binding to one or more of the penicillin binding proteins (PBPs); which in turn inhibits the final transpeptidation step of peptidoglycan synthesis in bacterial cell walls, thus inhibiting cell wall biosynthesis. Bacteria eventually lyse due to ongoing activity of cell wall autolytic enzymes (autolysins and murein hydrolases) while cell wall assembly is arrested.
Pharmacodynamics/Kinetics
Distribution: Into bile, synovial and pleural fluids, bronchial secretions, peritoneal, and pericardial fluids; crosses placenta; enters breast milk; penetrates the blood-brain barrier only when meninges are inflamed
Protein binding: ~94%
Metabolism: Hepatic to active metabolites
Half-life elimination: Children 1 week to 2 years: 0.9-1.8 hours; Adults: 23-60 minutes; prolonged in neonates and with renal impairment
Time to peak, serum: I.M.: 30-60 minutes
Excretion: Urine and feces (small amounts as unchanged drug and metabolites)
Dosage I.M., I.V.:
Neonates:
Postnatal age <7 days:
<2000 g: 25 mg/kg/dose every 12 hours
>2000 g: 25 mg/kg/dose every 8 hours
Postnatal age >7 days:
<1200 g: 25 mg/kg/dose every 12 hours
1200-2000 g: 30 mg/kg/dose every 8 hours
>2000 g: 37.5 mg/kg/dose every 6 hours
Infants and Children: 150-200 mg/kg/day in divided doses every 6 hours; maximum dose: 12 g/day
Adults: 250 mg to 2 g/dose every 4-6 hours
(Continued)

Oxacillin (Continued)

Dosing adjustment in renal impairment: Cl_{cr} <10 mL/minute: Use lower range of the usual dosage

Hemodialysis: Not dialyzable (0% to 5%)

Administration Administer around-the-clock to promote less variation in peak and trough serum levels. Administer IVP over 10 minutes. Administer IVPB over 30 minutes.

Monitoring Parameters Observe for signs and symptoms of anaphylaxis during first dose

Dosage Forms INF [premixed iso-osmotic dextrose solution]: 1 g (50 mL); 2 g (50 mL). **INJ, powder for reconstitution:** 1 g, 2 g, 10 g

♦ **Oxacillin Sodium** *see* Oxacillin *on page 935*

Oxaliplatin (ox AL i pla tin)

U.S. Brand Names Eloxatin™

Synonyms Diaminocyclohexane Oxalatoplatinum; L-OHP; NSC-266046

Therapeutic Category Antineoplastic Agent, Alkylating Agent

Use Treatment of advanced colon or rectal carcinoma

Unlabeled/Investigational Use Head and neck cancer, nonsmall cell lung cancer, non-Hodgkin's lymphoma, ovarian cancer

Pregnancy Risk Factor D

Contraindications Hypersensitivity to oxaliplatin, other platinum-containing compounds, or any component of the formulation; pregnancy

Warnings/Precautions The U.S. Food and Drug Administration (FDA) currently recommends that procedures for proper handling and disposal of antineoplastic agents be considered. Anaphylactic-like reaction may occur within minutes of oxaliplatin administration. Two different types of neuropathy may occur: First, an acute (within first 2 days), reversible (resolves within 14 days), primarily peripheral symptoms that are often exacerbated by cold (may include pharyngolaryngeal dysesthesia); and secondly, a more persistent (>14 days) presentation that often interferes with daily activities (eg, writing, buttoning, swallowing), these symptoms may improve upon discontinuing treatment. May cause pulmonary fibrosis. Caution in renal dysfunction. Safety and efficacy in pediatric patients have not been established.

Common Adverse Reactions Based on clinical trial data using oxaliplatin alone. Some adverse effects may be increased when therapy is combined with fluorouracil/leucovorin.

>10%:

Central nervous system: Fatigue (61%), fever (25%), pain (14%), headache (13%), insomnia (11%)

Gastrointestinal: Nausea (64%), diarrhea (46%), vomiting (37%), abdominal pain (31%), constipation (31%), anorexia (20%), stomatitis (14%)

Hematologic: Anemia (64%), thrombocytopenia (30%), leukopenia (13%)

Hepatic: SGOT increased (54%), SGPT increased (36%); total bilirubin increased (13%)

Neuromuscular & skeletal: Neuropathy (may be dose-limiting), peripheral (acute 65%, persistent 43%), back pain (11%)

Respiratory: Dyspnea (13%), coughing (11%)

1% to 10%:

Cardiovascular: Edema (10%), chest pain (5%), flushing (3%), thrombosis (2% to 6%), thromboembolism (6% to 9%)

Central nervous system: Rigors (9%), dizziness (7%), hand-foot syndrome (1%)

Dermatologic: Rash (5%), alopecia (3%)

Endocrine & metabolic: Dehydration (5%), hypokalemia (3%)

Gastrointestinal: Dyspepsia (7%), taste perversion (5%), flatulence (3%), mucositis (2%), gastroesophageal reflux (1%), dysphagia (acute 1% to 2%)

Genitourinary: Dysuria (1%)

Hematologic: Neutropenia (7%)

Local: Injection site reaction (9%)

Neuromuscular & skeletal: Arthralgia (7%)

Ocular: Abnormal lacrimation (1%)

Renal: Serum creatinine increased (10%)

Respiratory: URI (7%), rhinitis (6%), epistaxis (2%), pharyngitis (2%), pharyngolaryngeal dysesthesia (1% to 2%)

Miscellaneous: Allergic reactions (3%), hiccup (2%)

Drug Interactions

Increased Effect/Toxicity: Taxane derivatives may increase oxaliplatin toxicity if administered before the platin as a sequential infusion; nephrotoxic agents (aminoglycosides) may increase oxaliplatin toxicity

Mechanism of Action Oxaliplatin is an alkylating agent. Following intracellular hydrolysis, the platinum compound binds to DNA, RNA, or proteins. Cytotoxicity is cell-cycle nonspecific.

Pharmacodynamics/Kinetics

Distribution: 400 L

Protein binding: >90% primarily albumin and gamma globulin (irreversible binding to platinum)

Metabolism: Nonenzymatic (rapid and extensive), forms active and inactive derivatives

Half-life elimination: 391 hours; Distribution: 0.4-16.8 hours

Excretion: Primarily urine

Dosage I.V.: Colorectal cancer (labeled dosing): Refer to individual protocols.

Adults:

85 mg/m^2 every 2 weeks **or**

20-25 mg/m^2 days 1-5 every 3 weeks **or**

100-130 mg/m^2 every 2-3 weeks

Elderly: No dosing adjustment recommended

Dosage adjustments for toxicity: Infusion may be prolonged (from 2 hours to 6 hours) to attempt to mitigate acute toxicities. In patients experiencing persistent neurosensory events (grade 2) which do not resolve, a dose reduction to 65 mg/m^2 may be considered. Grade 3 neurosensory events may prompt consideration to discontinue oxaliplatin (while fluorouracil/leucovorin are continued). After recovery from grade 3/4 gastrointestinal toxicity, grade 4 neutropenia, or grade 3/4 thrombocytopenia, dosage reduction to 65 mg/m^2 is recommended.

Dosage adjustment in renal impairment: Use with caution; specific guidelines not established

Administration Administer as I.V. infusion over 2-6 hours. Longer infusion (eg, 6 hours) may mitigate signs/symptoms of acute reactions. Flush infusion line with D_5W prior to administration of any concomitant medication.

Monitoring Parameters CBC, serum creatinine, liver function tests; signs of neuropathy, hypersensitivity, and/or respiratory effects; delay dosage until recover of neutrophils ≥1.5 x 10^9/L and platelets ≥75 x 10^9/L

Patient Information Maintain adequate nutrition (frequent small meals may help) and adequate hydration (2-3 L/day of fluids unless instructed to restrict fluid intake). Nausea and vomiting may be severe; request antiemetic. You will be susceptible to infection; avoid crowds or exposure to infection. Report sore throat, fever, chills, unusual fatigue or unusual bruising/bleeding, difficulty breathing, muscle cramps or twitching, tingling/numbness in arms, fingers, legs, or toes (may be increased by cold temperature). Inform prescriber if you are pregnant. Do not get pregnant during or for 1 month following therapy. Male: Do not cause a female to become pregnant. Male/female: Consult prescriber for instruction on appropriate barrier contraceptive measures. This drug may cause severe fetal defects. Do not breast-feed.

Dosage Forms INJ, powder for reconstitution: 50 mg, 100 mg

♦ Oxandrin® see Oxandrolone on page 937

Oxandrolone (oks AN droe lone)

U.S. Brand Names Oxandrin®

Therapeutic Category Androgen

Use Adjunctive therapy to promote weight gain after weight loss following extensive surgery, chronic infections, or severe trauma, and in some patients who, without definite pathophysiologic reasons, fail to gain or to maintain normal weight

Restrictions C-III

Pregnancy Risk Factor X

Contraindications Hypersensitivity to oxandrolone or any component of the formulation; nephrosis; carcinoma of breast or prostate; pregnancy

Warnings/Precautions May stunt bone growth in children; anabolic steroids may cause peliosis hepatis, liver cell tumors, and blood lipid changes with increased risk of arteriosclerosis; monitor diabetic patients carefully; use with caution in elderly patients, they may be at greater risk for prostatic hyperplasia; use with caution in patients with cardiac, renal, or hepatic disease or epilepsy

Common Adverse Reactions

Male:

Postpubertal:

>10%:

Dermatologic: Acne

Endocrine & metabolic: Gynecomastia

Genitourinary: Bladder irritability, priapism

1% to 10%:

Central nervous system: Insomnia, chills

Endocrine & metabolic: Decreased libido, hepatic dysfunction

Gastrointestinal: Nausea, diarrhea

Genitourinary: Prostatic hyperplasia (elderly)

Hematologic: Iron deficiency anemia, suppression of clotting factors

Prepubertal:

>10%:

Dermatologic: Acne

Endocrine & metabolic: Virilism

1% to 10%:

Central nervous system: Chills, insomnia

Dermatologic: Hyperpigmentation

Gastrointestinal: Diarrhea, nausea

Hematologic: Iron deficiency anemia, suppression of clotting factors

Female:

>10%: Endocrine & metabolic: Virilism

1% to 10%:

Central nervous system: Chills, insomnia

Endocrine & metabolic: Hypercalcemia

Gastrointestinal: Nausea, diarrhea

Hematologic: Iron deficiency anemia, suppression of clotting factors

Hepatic: Hepatic dysfunction

(Continued)

Oxandrolone *(Continued)*

Drug Interactions

Increased Effect/Toxicity: ACTH, adrenal steroids may increase risk of edema and acne. Stanozolol enhances the hypoprothrombinemic effects of oral anticoagulants, and enhances the hypoglycemic effects of insulin and sulfonylureas (oral hypoglycemics).

Mechanism of Action Synthetic testosterone derivative with similar androgenic and anabolic actions

Pharmacodynamics/Kinetics

Onset of action: 1 month

Absorption: High

Distribution: V_d: 0.578 L/kg

Protein binding, plasma: 94% to 97%

Metabolism: Hepatic

Excretion: Urine (60%); feces (3%)

Dosage

Children: Total daily dose: ≤0.1 mg/kg **or** ≤0.045 mg/lb

Adults: 2.5 mg 2-4 times/day; however, since the response of individuals to anabolic steroids varies, a daily dose of as little as 2.5 mg or as much as 20 mg may be required to achieve the desired response. A course of therapy of 2-4 weeks is usually adequate. This may be repeated intermittently as needed.

Dosing adjustment in renal impairment: Caution is recommended because of the propensity of oxandrolone to cause edema and water retention

Dosing adjustment in hepatic impairment: Caution is advised but there are not specific guidelines for dosage reduction

Patient Information High protein, high caloric diet is suggested, restrict salt intake; glucose tolerance may be altered in diabetics

Dosage Forms TAB: 2.5 mg, 10 mg

Oxaprozin *(oks a PROE zin)*

Related Information

Nonsteroidal Anti-Inflammatory Agents Comparison *on page 1401*

U.S. Brand Names Daypro®

Therapeutic Category Analgesic, Nonsteroidal Anti-inflammatory Drug; Anti-inflammatory Agent; Nonsteroidal Anti-inflammatory Drug (NSAID), Oral

Use Acute and long-term use in the management of signs and symptoms of osteoarthritis and rheumatoid arthritis; juvenile rheumatoid arthritis

Pregnancy Risk Factor C/D (3rd trimester)

Contraindications Hypersensitivity to oxaprozin, aspirin, other NSAIDs, or any component of the formulation; advanced kidney disease; pregnancy (3rd trimester)

Warnings/Precautions GI toxicity (bleeding, ulceration, perforation) may occur at any time without symptoms. Use caution with history of ulcer disease, gastrointestinal bleeding, elderly, or debilitated patients; use lowest effective dose for shortest period possible. Anaphylactoid reactions have been reported with NSAID use, even without prior exposure; may be more common in patients with the aspirin triad. Use caution in patients with pre-existing asthma. Use caution with decreased renal or hepatic function, congestive heart failure, dehydration, hypertension, coagulation disorders, anticoagulants. Rare cases of severe hepatic reactions (including necrosis, jaundice, fulminant hepatitis) have been reported. Use of NSAIDs can compromise existing renal function especially when Cl_{cr} is <30 mL/minute; renal toxicity, renal papillary necrosis may occur. May cause mild photosensitivity reactions. Elderly are at a high risk for adverse effects from NSAIDs. As much as 60% of elderly can develop peptic ulceration and/or hemorrhage asymptomatically. Withhold for at least 4-6 half-lives prior to surgical or dental procedures. Safety and efficacy have not been established in children <6 years of age.

Common Adverse Reactions

1% to 10%:

Cardiovascular: Edema

Central nervous system: Confusion, depression, dizziness, headache, sedation, sleep disturbance, somnolence

Dermatologic: Pruritus, rash

Gastrointestinal: Abdominal distress, abdominal pain, anorexia, constipation, diarrhea, flatulence, gastrointestinal ulcer, gross bleeding with perforation, heartburn, nausea, vomiting

Hematologic: Anemia, bleeding time increased

Hepatic: Liver enzyme elevation

Otic: Tinnitus

Renal: Dysuria, renal function abnormal, urinary frequency

Drug Interactions

Increased Effect/Toxicity: Oxaprozin may increase cyclosporine, digoxin, lithium, and methotrexate serum concentrations. The renal adverse effects of ACE inhibitors may be potentiated by NSAIDs. Corticosteroids may increase the risk of GI ulceration. The risk of bleeding with anticoagulants (warfarin, antiplatelet agents, low molecular weight heparins) may be increased.

Decreased Effect: Oxaprozin may decrease the effect of some antihypertensive agents (including ACE inhibitors and angiotensin antagonists) and diuretics.

Mechanism of Action Inhibits prostaglandin synthesis by decreasing the activity of the enzyme, cyclooxygenase, which results in decreased formation of prostaglandin precursors

Pharmacodynamics/Kinetics

Absorption: Almost complete

Protein binding: >99%

Metabolism: Hepatic via oxidation and glucuronidation; no active metabolites

Half-life elimination: 40-50 hours

Time to peak: 2-4 hours

Excretion: Urine (5% unchanged, 65% as metabolites); feces (35% as metabolites)

Dosage Oral (individualize dosage to lowest effective dose to minimize adverse effects):

Children 6-16 years: Juvenile rheumatoid arthritis:

22-31 kg: 600 mg once daily

32-54 kg: 900 mg once daily

≥55 kg: 1200 mg once daily

Adults:

Osteoarthritis: 1200 mg once daily; patients should be titrated to lowest dose possible; patients with low body weight should start with 600 mg daily

Rheumatoid arthritis: 1200 mg once daily; a one-time loading dose of up to 1800 mg/day or 26 mg/kg (whichever is lower) may be given

Maximum daily dose: 1800 mg or 26 mg/kg (whichever is lower) in divided doses

Dosing adjustment in renal impairment: 600 mg once daily; dose may be increased to 1200 mg with close monitoring

Dosing adjustment in hepatic impairment: Use caution in patients with severe dysfunction

Monitoring Parameters Monitor CBC; hepatic, renal, and ocular function

Dosage Forms TAB: 600 mg

Oxazepam (oks A ze pam)

Related Information

Benzodiazepines Comparison on page 1366

U.S. Brand Names Serax®

Therapeutic Category Antianxiety Agent; Anticonvulsant, Benzodiazepine; Benzodiazepine

Use Treatment of anxiety; management of ethanol withdrawal

Unlabeled/Investigational Use Anticonvulsant in management of simple partial seizures; hypnotic

Restrictions C-IV

Pregnancy Risk Factor D

Contraindications Hypersensitivity to oxazepam or any component of the formulation (cross-sensitivity with other benzodiazepines may exist); narrow-angle glaucoma (not in product labeling, however, benzodiazepines are contraindicated); not indicated for use in the treatment of psychosis; pregnancy

Warnings/Precautions May cause hypotension (rare) - use with caution in patients with cardiovascular or cerebrovascular disease, or in patients who would not tolerate transient decreases in blood pressure. Serax® 15 contains tartrazine; use is not recommended in pediatric patients <6 years of age; dose has not been established between 6-12 years of age.

Use with caution in elderly or debilitated patients, patients with hepatic disease (including alcoholics), or renal impairment. Use with caution in patients with respiratory disease or impaired gag reflex. Avoid use in patients with sleep apnea.

Causes CNS depression (dose-related) resulting in sedation, dizziness, confusion, or ataxia which may impair physical and mental capabilities. Patients must be cautioned about performing tasks which require mental alertness (eg, operating machinery or driving). Use with caution in patients receiving other CNS depressants or psychoactive agents. Effects with other sedative drugs or ethanol may be potentiated. Benzodiazepines have been associated with falls and traumatic injury and should be used with extreme caution in patients who are at risk of these events (especially the elderly).

Use caution in patients with suicidal risk. Use with caution in patients with a history of drug dependence. Benzodiazepines have been associated with dependence and acute withdrawal symptoms on discontinuation or reduction in dose. Acute withdrawal, including seizures, may be precipitated after administration of flumazenil to patients receiving long-term benzodiazepine therapy.

Benzodiazepines have been associated with anterograde amnesia. Paradoxical reactions, including hyperactive or aggressive behavior have been reported with benzodiazepines, particularly in adolescent/pediatric or psychiatric patients. Does not have analgesic, antidepressant, or antipsychotic properties.

Common Adverse Reactions Frequency not defined.

Cardiovascular: Syncope (rare), edema

Central nervous system: Drowsiness, ataxia, dizziness, vertigo, memory impairment, headache, paradoxical reactions (excitement, stimulation of effect), lethargy, amnesia, euphoria

Dermatologic: Rash

Endocrine & metabolic: Decreased libido, menstrual irregularities

Genitourinary: Incontinence

Hematologic: Leukopenia, blood dyscrasias

Hepatic: Jaundice

Neuromuscular & skeletal: Dysarthria, tremor, reflex slowing

Ocular: Blurred vision, diplopia

Miscellaneous: Drug dependence

Drug Interactions

Increased Effect/Toxicity: Ethanol and other CNS depressants may increase the CNS effects of oxazepam. Oxazepam may decrease the antiparkinsonian efficacy of levodopa.

(Continued)

Oxazepam *(Continued)*

Flumazenil may cause seizures if administered following long-term benzodiazepine treatment.

Decreased Effect: Oral contraceptives may increase the clearance of oxazepam. Theophylline and other CNS stimulants may antagonize the sedative effects of oxazepam. Phenytoin may increase the clearance of oxazepam.

Mechanism of Action Binds to stereospecific benzodiazepine receptors on the postsynaptic GABA neuron at several sites within the central nervous system, including the limbic system, reticular formation. Enhancement of the inhibitory effect of GABA on neuronal excitability results by increased neuronal membrane permeability to chloride ions. This shift in chloride ions results in hyperpolarization (a less excitable state) and stabilization.

Pharmacodynamics/Kinetics
Absorption: Almost complete
Protein binding: 86% to 99%
Metabolism: Hepatic to inactive compounds (primarily as glucuronides)
Half-life elimination: 2.8-5.7 hours
Time to peak, serum: 2-4 hours
Excretion: Urine (as unchanged drug (50%) and metabolites)

Dosage Oral:
Children: Anxiety: 1 mg/kg/day has been administered
Adults:
  Anxiety: 10-30 mg 3-4 times/day
  Ethanol withdrawal: 15-30 mg 3-4 times/day
  Hypnotic: 15-30 mg
Elderly: Oral: Anxiety: 10 mg 2-3 times/day; increase gradually as needed to a total of 30-45 mg/day. Dose titration should be slow to evaluate sensitivity.
Hemodialysis: Not dialyzable (0% to 5%)

Administration Administer orally in divided doses

Monitoring Parameters Respiratory and cardiovascular status

Reference Range Therapeutic: 0.2-1.4 µg/mL (SI: 0.7-4.9 µmol/L)

Patient Information Avoid alcohol and other CNS depressants; avoid activities needing good psychomotor coordination until CNS effects are known; drug may cause physical or psychological dependence; avoid abrupt discontinuation after prolonged use

Dosage Forms CAP: 10 mg, 15 mg, 30 mg. **TAB:** 15 mg

Oxcarbazepine *(ox car BAZ e peen)*

Related Information
Anticonvulsants by Seizure Type *on page 1358*
Epilepsy *on page 1477*

U.S. Brand Names Trileptal®

Synonyms GP 47680; OCBZ

Therapeutic Category Anticonvulsant, Miscellaneous

Use Monotherapy or adjunctive therapy in the treatment of partial seizures in adults and children (4-16 years of age) with epilepsy

Unlabeled/Investigational Use Bipolar disorder

Pregnancy Risk Factor C

Contraindications Hypersensitivity to oxcarbazepine or any component of the formulation

Warnings/Precautions Clinically-significant hyponatremia (sodium <125 mmol/L) can develop during oxcarbazepine use. As with all antiepileptic drugs, oxcarbazepine should be withdrawn gradually to minimize the potential of increased seizure frequency. Use of oxcarbazepine has been associated with CNS related adverse events, most significant of these were cognitive symptoms including psychomotor slowing, difficulty with concentration, and speech or language problems, somnolence or fatigue, and coordination abnormalities, including ataxia and gait disturbances. Use caution in patients with previous hypersensitivity to carbamazepine (cross-sensitivity occurs in 25% to 30%). May reduce the efficacy of oral contraceptives (nonhormonal contraceptive measures are recommended).

Common Adverse Reactions As reported in adults with doses of up to 2400 mg/day (includes patients on monotherapy, adjunctive therapy, and those not previously on AEDs); incidence in children was similar.

>10%:
Central nervous system: Dizziness (22% to 49%), somnolence (20% to 36%), headache (13% to 32%, placebo 23%), ataxia (5% to 31%), fatigue (12% to 15%), vertigo (6% to 15%)
Gastrointestinal: Vomiting (7% to 36%), nausea (15% to 29%), abdominal pain (10% to 13%)
Neuromuscular & skeletal: Abnormal gait (5% to 17%), tremor (3% to 16%)
Ocular: Diplopia (14% to 40%), nystagmus (7% to 26%), abnormal vision (4% to 14%)
1% to 10%:
Cardiovascular: Hypotension (1% to 2%), leg edema (1% to 2%, placebo 1%)
Central nervous system: Nervousness (2% to 5%, placebo 1% to 2%), amnesia (4%), abnormal thinking (2% to 4%), insomnia (2% to 4%), speech disorder (1% to 3%), EEG abnormalities (2%), abnormal feelings (1% to 2%), agitation (1% to 2%, placebo 1%), confusion (1% to 2%, placebo 1%)
Dermatologic: Rash (4%), acne (1% to 2%)
Endocrine & metabolic: Hyponatremia (1% to 3%, placebo 1%)

Gastrointestinal: Diarrhea (5% to 7%), dyspepsia (5% to 6%), constipation (2% to 6%, placebo 0% to 4%), gastritis (1% to 2%, placebo 1%), weight gain (1% to 2%, placebo 1%)

Neuromuscular & skeletal: Weakness (3% to 6%, placebo 5%), back pain (4%), falling down (4%), abnormal coordination (1% to 4%, placebo 1% to 2%), dysmetria (1% to 3%), sprains/strains (2%), muscle weakness (1% to 2%)

Ocular: Abnormal accommodation (2%)

Respiratory: Upper respiratory tract infection (7%), rhinitis (2% to 5%, placebo 4%), chest infection (4%), epistaxis (4%), sinusitis (4%)

Drug Interactions

Cytochrome P450 Effect: Inhibits CYP2C19 (weak); **Induces** CYP3A4 (strong)

Increased Effect/Toxicity: Serum concentrations of phenytoin and phenobarbital are increased by oxcarbazepine.

Decreased Effect: Oxcarbazepine serum concentrations may be reduced by carbamazepine, phenytoin, phenobarbital, valproic acid and verapamil (decreases levels of active oxcarbazepine metabolite). Oxcarbazepine reduces the serum concentrations of felodipine (similar effects may be anticipated with other dihydropyridines), oral contraceptives (use alternative contraceptive measures), and verapamil. Oxcarbazepine may decrease the levels of CYP3A4 substrates (include calcium channel blockers, benzodiazepines, cyclosporine, pimozide, protease inhibitors, quinidine, sirolimus and tacrolimus).

Mechanism of Action Pharmacological activity results from both oxcarbazepine and its monohydroxy metabolite (MHD). Precise mechanism of anticonvulsant effect has not been defined. Oxcarbazepine and MHD block voltage sensitive sodium channels, stabilizing hyperexcited neuronal membranes, inhibiting repetitive firing, and decreasing the propagation of synaptic impulses. These actions are believed to prevent the spread of seizures. Oxcarbazepine and MHD also increase potassium conductance and modulate the activity of high-voltage activated calcium channels.

Pharmacodynamics/Kinetics

Absorption: Complete; food has no affect on rate or extent

Distribution: MHD: V_d: 49 L

Protein binding, serum: MHD: 40%

Metabolism: Hepatic to 10-monohydroxy metabolite (MHC; active); MHD is further conjugated to DHD (inactive)

Bioavailability: Decreased in children <8 years; increased in elderly >60 years

Half-life elimination: Parent drug: 2 hours; MHD: 9 hours; renal impairment (Cl_{cr} 30 mL/minute): 19 hours

Time to peak, serum: 4.5 hours (3-13 hours)

Excretion: Urine (95%, <1% as unchanged oxcarbazepine, 27% as unchanged MHD, 49% as MHD glucuronides); feces (<4%)

Dosage Oral:

Children 4-16 years:

Adjunctive therapy: 8-10 mg/kg/day, not to exceed 600 mg/day, given in 2 divided daily doses. Maintenance dose should be achieved over 2 weeks, and is dependent upon patient weight, according to the following:

20-29 kg: 900 mg/day in 2 divided doses

29.1-39 kg: 1200 mg/day in 2 divided doses

>39 kg: 1800 mg/day in 2 divided doses

Conversion to monotherapy: Oxcarbazepine 8-10 mg/kg/day in twice daily divided doses, while simultaneously initiating the reduction of the dose of the concomitant antiepileptic drug; the concomitant drug should be withdrawn over 3-6 weeks. Oxcarbazepine dose may be increased by a maximum of 10 mg/kg/day at weekly intervals. See below for recommended total daily dose by weight.

Initiation of monotherapy: Oxcarbazepine should be initiated at 8-10 mg/kg/day in twice daily divided doses; doses may be titrated by 5 mg/kg/day every third day. See below for recommended total daily dose by weight.

Range of maintenance doses by weight during monotherapy:

20 kg: 600-900 mg/day

25-30 kg: 900-1200 mg/day

35-40 kg: 900-1500 mg/day

45 kg: 1200-1500 mg/day

50-55 kg: 1200-1800 mg/day

60-65 kg: 1200-2100 mg/day

70 kg: 1500-2100 mg/day

Adults:

Adjunctive therapy: Initial: 300 mg twice daily; dose may be increased by as much as 600 mg/day at weekly intervals; recommended daily dose: 1200 mg/day in 2 divided doses. Although daily doses >1200 mg/day demonstrated greater efficacy, most patients were unable to tolerate 2400 mg/day (due to CNS effects).

Conversion to monotherapy: Oxcarbazepine 600 mg/day in twice daily divided doses while simultaneously initiating the reduction of the dose of the concomitant antiepileptic drug. The concomitant dosage should be withdrawn over 3-6 weeks, while the maximum dose of oxcarbazepine should be reached in about 2-4 weeks. Recommended daily dose: 2400 mg/day.

Initiation of monotherapy: Oxcarbazepine should be initiated at a dose of 600 mg/day in twice daily divided doses; doses may be titrated upward by 300 mg/day every third day to a final dose of 1200 mg/day given in 2 divided doses

(Continued)

Oxcarbazepine *(Continued)*

Dosing adjustment in renal impairment: Therapy should be initiated at one-half the usual starting dose (300 mg/day) and increased slowly to achieve the desired clinical response

Dosing adjustment in hepatic impairment: Adjustment not needed for mild-to-moderate impairment

Administration Suspension: Prior to using for the first time, firmly insert the plastic adapter provided with the bottle. Cover adapter with child-resistant cap when not in use. Shake bottle for at least 10 seconds, remove child-resistant cap and insert the oral dosing syringe provided to withdraw appropriate dose. Dose may be taken directly from oral syringe or may be mixed in a small glass of water immediately prior to swallowing. Rinse syringe with warm water after use and allow to dry thoroughly. Discard any unused portion after 7 weeks of first opening bottle.

Monitoring Parameters Seizure frequency, serum sodium (particularly during first 3 months of therapy), symptoms of CNS depression (dizziness, headache, somnolence). Additional serum sodium monitoring recommended during maintenance treatment in patients receiving other medications known to decrease sodium levels, in patients with signs/symptoms of hyponatremia, and in patients with an increase in seizure frequency or severity.

Patient Information Hormonal contraceptives may be less effective when used with oxcarbazepine; caution should be exercised if alcohol is taken with oxcarbazepine, due to the possible additive sedative effects and that it may cause dizziness and somnolence; therefore, early in therapy be advised not to drive or operate machinery

Dosage Forms SUSP, oral: 300 mg/5 mL (250 mL). **TAB, film coated:** 150 mg, 300 mg, 600 mg

Oxiconazole *(oks i KON a zole)*

U.S. Brand Names Oxistat®

Synonyms Oxiconazole Nitrate

Therapeutic Category Antifungal Agent, Topical

Use Treatment of tinea pedis (athlete's foot), tinea cruris (jock itch), and tinea corporis (ringworm)

Pregnancy Risk Factor B

Contraindications Hypersensitivity to oxiconazole or any component of the formulation; not for ophthalmic use

Warnings/Precautions May cause irritation during therapy; if a sensitivity to oxiconazole occurs, therapy should be discontinued; avoid contact with eyes or vagina

Common Adverse Reactions 1% to 10%:

Dermatologic: Itching, erythema

Local: Transient burning, local irritation, stinging, dryness

Mechanism of Action The cytoplasmic membrane integrity of fungi is destroyed by oxiconazole which exerts a fungicidal activity through inhibition of ergosterol synthesis. Effective for treatment of tinea pedis, tinea cruris, and tinea corporis. Active against *Trichophyton rubrum*, *Trichophyton mentagrophytes*, *Trichophyton violaceum*, *Microsporum canis*, *Microsporum audouini*, *Microsporum gypseum*, *Epidermophyton floccosum*, *Candida albicans*, and *Malassezia furfur*.

Pharmacodynamics/Kinetics

Absorption: In each layer of the dermis; very little systemically after one topical dose

Distribution: To each layer of the dermis; enters breast milk

Excretion: Urine (<0.3%)

Dosage Children and Adults: Topical: Apply once to twice daily to affected areas for 2 weeks (tinea corporis/tinea cruris) to 1 month (tinea pedis)

Patient Information External use only; discontinue if sensitivity or chemical irritation occurs, contact prescriber if condition fails to improve in 3-4 days

Dosage Forms CRM, topical: 1% (15 g, 30 g, 60 g). **LOTION, topical:** 1% (30 mL)

♦ **Oxiconazole Nitrate** *see Oxiconazole on page 942*

♦ **Oxilan®** *see Ioxilan on page 684*

♦ **Oxilapine Succinate** *see Loxapine on page 765*

♦ **Oxistat®** *see Oxiconazole on page 942*

♦ **Oxpentifylline** *see Pentoxifylline on page 981*

♦ **Oxsoralen®** *see Methoxsalen on page 818*

♦ **Oxsoralen-Ultra®** *see Methoxsalen on page 818*

Oxybutynin *(oks i BYOO ti nin)*

U.S. Brand Names Ditropan®; Ditropan® XL; Oxytrol™

Synonyms Oxybutynin Chloride

Therapeutic Category Antispasmodic Agent, Urinary

Use Antispasmodic for neurogenic bladder (urgency, frequency, urge incontinence) and uninhibited bladder

Pregnancy Risk Factor B

Contraindications Hypersensitivity to oxybutynin or any component of the formulation; untreated glaucoma; partial or complete GI obstruction; GU obstruction; urinary retention; megacolon; toxic megacolon

Warnings/Precautions Use with caution in patients with urinary tract obstruction, angle-closure glaucoma (treated), hyperthyroidism, reflux esophagitis (including concurrent therapy with oral bisphosphonates or drugs which may increase the risk of esophagitis), heart disease, hepatic or renal disease, prostatic hyperplasia, autonomic neuropathy, ulcerative colitis (may cause ileus and toxic megacolon), hypertension, hiatal hernia, myasthenia gravis, ulcerative colitis, or intestinal atony. Caution should be used in elderly due to anticholinergic activity (eg, confusion, constipation, blurred vision, and tachycardia). May increase the risk of heat prostration.

Common Adverse Reactions

Oral:

>10%:

Central nervous system: Dizziness (6% to 16%), somnolence (12% to 13%)

Gastrointestinal: Xerostomia (61% to 71%), constipation (13%)

Genitourinary Urination impaired (11%)

1% to 10%:

Cardiovascular: Palpitation (2% to <5%), peripheral edema (2% to <5%), hypertension (2% to <5%), vasodilation (2% to <5%)

Central nervous system: Headache (6% to 10%), pain (7%), confusion (2% to <5%), insomnia (2% to <5%), nervousness (2% to <5%)

Dermatologic: Dry skin (2% to <5%), skin rash (2% to <5%)

Gastrointestinal: Nausea (9% to 10%), dyspepsia (7%), abdominal pain (2% to 6%), diarrhea (5% to 9%), flatulence (2% to <5%), gastrointestinal reflux (2% to <5%), taste perversion (2% to <5%)

Genitourinary: Post-void residuals increased (2% to 9%), urinary tract infection (5%)

Neuromuscular & skeletal: Weakness (2% to 7%)

Ocular: Blurred vision (8% to 9%), dry eyes (2% to 6%)

Respiratory: Rhinitis (6%), dry nasal and sinus membranes (2% to <5%)

Transdermal:

>10%: Local: Application site reaction (17%), pruritus (14%)

1% to 10%:

Gastrointestinal: Xerostomia (4% to 10%), diarrhea (3%), constipation (3%)

Genitourinary: Dysuria (2%)

Local: Erythema (6% to 8%), vesicles (3%), rash (3%)

Ocular: Vision changes (3%)

Drug Interactions

Cytochrome P450 Effect: Substrate of CYP3A4 (minor); **Inhibits** CYP2D6 (weak), 3A4 (weak)

Increased Effect/Toxicity: Additive sedation with CNS depressants and ethanol. Additive anticholinergic effects with antihistamines and anticholinergic agents. Effects of CYP2D6 substrates may be increased by concurrent therapy with beta-blockers, many phenothiazines, and tricyclic antidepressants. CYP3A4 inhibitors may increase effects of oxybutynin during concurrent therapy; inhibitors include amiodarone, ciprofloxacin, clarithromycin, diltiazem, erythromycin, itraconazole, ketoconazole, protease inhibitors, and verapamil.

Mechanism of Action Direct antispasmodic effect on smooth muscle, also inhibits the action of acetylcholine on smooth muscle (exhibits $1/5$ the anticholinergic activity of atropine, but is 4-10 times the antispasmodic activity); does not block effects at skeletal muscle or at autonomic ganglia; increases bladder capacity, decreases uninhibited contractions, and delays desire to void; therefore, decreases urgency and frequency

Pharmacodynamics/Kinetics

Onset of action: Oral: 30-60 minutes

Peak effect: 3-6 hours

Duration: 6-10 hours

Absorption: Oral: Rapid and well absorbed; Transdermal: High

Distribution: V_d: 193 L

Metabolism: Hepatic via CYP3A4; Oral: High first-pass metabolism; I.V.: Forms active and inactive metabolites

Half-life elimination I.V.: ~2 hours (parent drug), 7-8 hours (metabolites)

Time to peak, serum: Oral: ~60 minutes; Transdermal: 24-48 hours

Excretion: Urine (<0.1%)

Dosage

Oral:

Children:

1-5 years (unlabeled use): 0.2 mg/kg/dose 2-4 times/day

>5 years: 5 mg twice daily, up to 5 mg 3 times/day maximum

>6 years: Extended release: 5 mg once daily; maximum dose: 20 mg/day

Adults: 5 mg 2-3 times/day up to 5 mg 4 times/day maximum

Extended release: Initial: 5 mg once daily, may increase in 5-10 mg increments; maximum: 30 mg daily

Elderly: 2.5-5 mg 2-3 times/day

Transdermal: Adults: Apply one 3.9 mg/day patch twice weekly (every 3-4 days)

Note: Should be discontinued periodically to determine whether the patient can manage without the drug and to minimize resistance to the drug

Administration

Oral: Immediate release tablets and solution should be administered on an empty stomach with water. Extended release tablets may be taken with or without food and must be swallowed whole; do not crush, divide, or chew.

Transdermal: Apply to clean, dry skin on abdomen, hip, or buttock. Select a new site for each new system (avoid re-application to same site within 7 days).

Monitoring Parameters Incontinence episodes, postvoid residual (PVR)

(Continued)

Oxybutynin *(Continued)*

Patient Information May impair ability to perform activities requiring mental alertness or physical coordination; alcohol or other sedating drugs may enhance drowsiness. Take prescribed oral dose preferably on an empty stomach, 1 hour before or 2 hours after meals; swallow extended release tablets whole, do not crush, chew, or break. Apply transdermal patch to dry, intact skin on abdomen, hip, or buttock; do not apply to same site within 7 days.

Dosage Forms SYR (Ditropan®): 5 mg/5 mL (473 mL). **TAB** (Ditropan®): 5 mg. **TAB, extended release** (Ditropan® XL): 5 mg, 10 mg, 15 mg. **PATCH, transdermal** (Oxytrol™): 3.9 mg/day (8s, 24s)

♦ **Oxybutynin Chloride** *see* Oxybutynin *on page 942*

Oxycodone *(oks i KOE done)*

U.S. Brand Names OxyContin®; Oxydose™; OxyFast®; OxyIR®; Percolone® [DSC]; Roxicodone™; Roxicodone™ Intensol™

Synonyms Dihydrohydroxycodeinone; Oxycodone Hydrochloride

Therapeutic Category Analgesic, Narcotic

Use Management of moderate to severe pain, normally used in combination with non-narcotic analgesics

OxyContin® is indicated for around-the-clock management of moderate to severe pain when an analgesic is needed for an extended period of time. **Note:** OxyContin® is not intended for use as an "as needed" analgesic or for immediately-postoperative pain management (should be used postoperatively only if the patient has received it prior to surgery or if severe, persistent pain is anticipated).

Restrictions C-II

Pregnancy Risk Factor B/D (prolonged use or high doses at term)

Contraindications Hypersensitivity to oxycodone or any component of the formulation; significant respiratory depression; hypercarbia; acute or severe bronchial asthma; OxyContin® is also contraindicated in paralytic ileus (known or suspected); pregnancy (prolonged use or high doses at term)

Warnings/Precautions Use with caution in patients with hypersensitivity reactions to other phenanthrene derivative opioid agonists (morphine, hydrocodone, hydromorphone, levorphanol, oxycodone, oxymorphone); respiratory diseases including asthma, emphysema, COPD, or severe liver or renal insufficiency; some preparations contain sulfites which may cause allergic reactions; dextromethorphan has equivalent antitussive activity but has much lower toxicity in accidental overdose; tolerance or drug dependence may result from extended use.

Use with caution in the elderly, debilitated, severe hepatic or renal function, hypothyroidism, Addison's disease, prostatic hyperplasia, or urethral stricture. Respiratory depressant effects and capacity to elevate CSF pressure may be exaggerated in presence of head injury, other intracranial lesion, or pre-existing intracranial pressure. Tolerance or drug dependence may result from extended use. Healthcare provider should be alert to problems of abuse, misuse, and diversion. Do NOT crush controlled-release tablets.

Common Adverse Reactions
>10%:
  Central nervous system: Fatigue, drowsiness, dizziness, somnolence
  Dermatologic: Pruritus
  Gastrointestinal: Nausea, vomiting, constipation
  Neuromuscular & skeletal: Weakness
1% to 10%:
  Cardiovascular: Postural hypotension
  Central nervous system: Nervousness, headache, restlessness, malaise, confusion, anxiety, abnormal dreams, euphoria, thought abnormalities
  Dermatologic: Rash
  Gastrointestinal: Anorexia, stomach cramps, xerostomia, biliary spasm, abdominal pain, dyspepsia, gastritis
  Genitourinary: Ureteral spasms, decreased urination
  Local: Pain at injection site
  Respiratory: Dyspnea, hiccoughs
  Miscellaneous: Diaphoresis

Drug Interactions
Cytochrome P450 Effect: Substrate of CYP2D6 (major)
Increased Effect/Toxicity: MAO inhibitors may increase adverse symptoms. Cimetidine may increase narcotic analgesic serum levels resulting in toxicity. CNS depressants (barbiturates, ethanol) and TCAs may potentiate the sedative and respiratory depressive effects of morphine and other opiate agonists. Dextroamphetamine may enhance the analgesic effect of morphine and other opiate agonists.

Mechanism of Action Binds to opiate receptors in the CNS, causing inhibition of ascending pain pathways, altering the perception of and response to pain; produces generalized CNS depression

Pharmacodynamics/Kinetics
Onset of action: Pain relief: 10-15 minutes
  Peak effect: 0.5-1 hour
Duration: 3-6 hours; Controlled release: ≤12 hours
Metabolism: Hepatic
Half-life elimination: 2-3 hours

Excretion: Urine

Dosage Oral:

Immediate release:

Children:

6-12 years: 1.25 mg every 6 hours as needed

>12 years: 2.5 mg every 6 hours as needed

Adults: 5 mg every 6 hours as needed

Controlled release: Adults:

Opioid naive (not currently on opioid): 10 mg every 12 hours

Currently on opioid/ASA or acetaminophen or NSAID combination:

1-5 tablets: 10-20 mg every 12 hours

6-9 tablets: 20-30 mg every 12 hours

10-12 tablets: 30-40 mg every 12 hours

May continue the nonopioid as a separate drug.

Currently on opioids: Use standard conversion chart to convert daily dose to oxycodone equivalent. Divide daily dose in 2 (for every 12-hour dosing) and round down to nearest dosage form.

Note: 80 mg or 160 mg tablets are for use **only** in opioid-tolerant patients. Special safety considerations must be addressed when converting to OxyContin® doses ≥160 mg every 12 hours. Dietary caution must be taken when patients are initially titrated to 160 mg tablets.

Dosing adjustment in hepatic impairment: Reduce dosage in patients with severe liver disease

Administration Do not crush controlled-release tablets; 80 mg and 160 mg tablets are for use **only** in opioid-tolerant patients. Do not administer OxyContin® 160 mg tablet with a high-fat meal.

Monitoring Parameters Pain relief, respiratory and mental status, blood pressure

Reference Range Blood level of 5 mg/L associated with fatality

Patient Information Avoid alcohol; may cause drowsiness, impaired judgment or coordination; may be addicting if used for prolonged periods; do not crush or chew the controlled-release product

Dosage Forms CAP, immediate release (OxyIR®): 5 mg. **SOLN, oral** (Roxicodone™): 5 mg/mL (5 mL, 500 mL). **SOLN, oral concentrate:** (Oxydose™, OxyFast®, Roxicodone Intensol®): 20 mg/mL (30 mL). **TAB:** 5 mg; (Percolone® [DSC]): 5 mg; (Roxicodone™): 5 mg, 15 mg, 30 mg. **TAB, controlled release** (OxyContin®): 10 mg, 20 mg, 40 mg, 80 mg, 160 mg

Oxycodone and Acetaminophen (oks i KOE done & a seet a MIN oh fen)

U.S. Brand Names Endocet®; Percocet®; Roxicet™; Roxicet™ 5/500; Tylox®

Synonyms Acetaminophen and Oxycodone

Therapeutic Category Analgesic Combination, Narcotic

Use Management of moderate to severe pain

Restrictions C-II

Pregnancy Risk Factor C/D (prolonged periods or high doses at term)

Dosage Oral: Doses should be given every 4-6 hours as needed and titrated to appropriate analgesic effects. **Note:** Initial dose is based on the **oxycodone** content; however, the maximum daily dose is based on the **acetaminophen** content.

Children: Maximum acetaminophen dose: Children <45 kg: 90 mg/kg/day; children >45 kg: 4 g/day

Mild to moderate pain: Initial dose, **based on oxycodone content:** 0.05-0.1 mg/kg/dose

Severe pain: Initial dose, **based on oxycodone content:** 0.3 mg/kg/dose

Adults:

Mild to moderate pain: Initial dose, **based on oxycodone content:** 5 mg

Severe pain: Initial dose, **based on oxycodone content:** 15-30 mg. Do not exceed acetaminophen 4 g/day.

Elderly: Doses should be titrated to appropriate analgesic effects: Initial dose, **based on oxycodone content:** 2.5-5 mg every 6 hours. Do not exceed acetaminophen 4 g/day.

Dosage adjustment in hepatic impairment: Dose should be reduced in patients with severe liver disease.

Dosage Forms CAP (Tylox®): Oxycodone 5 mg and acetaminophen 500 mg. **CAPLET** (Roxicet® 5/500): Oxycodone 5 mg and acetaminophen 500 mg. **SOLN, oral** (Roxicet®): Oxycodone 5 mg and acetaminophen 325 mg per 5 mL (5 mL, 500 mL). **TAB:** Oxycodone hydrochloride 5 mg and acetaminophen 325 mg; oxycodone hydrochloride 7.5 mg and acetaminophen 325 mg; oxycodone hydrochloride 7.5 mg and acetaminophen 500 mg; oxycodone hydrochloride 10 mg and acetaminophen 325 mg; oxycodone hydrochloride 10 mg and acetaminophen 650 mg; (Endocet®, Percocet® 5/325): Oxycodone 5 mg and acetaminophen 325 mg; (Percocet® 2.5/325): Oxycodone 2.5 mg and acetaminophen 325 mg; (Percocet® 7.5/325): Oxycodone 7.5 mg and acetaminophen 325 mg; (Percocet® 7.5/500): Oxycodone 7.5 mg and acetaminophen 500 mg; (Percocet® 10/325): Oxycodone 10 mg and acetaminophen 325 mg; (Percocet® 10/650): Oxycodone 10 mg and acetaminophen 650 mg; (Roxicet®): Oxycodone 5 mg and acetaminophen 325 mg

Oxycodone and Aspirin (oks i KOE done & AS pir in)

U.S. Brand Names Endodan®; Percodan®; Percodan®-Demi [DSC]

Synonyms Aspirin and Oxycodone

Therapeutic Category Analgesic Combination, Narcotic

Use Management of moderate to severe pain

(Continued)

Oxycodone and Aspirin *(Continued)*

Restrictions C-II

Pregnancy Risk Factor D

Dosage Oral (based on oxycodone combined salts):

Children: 0.05-0.15 mg/kg/dose every 4-6 hours as needed; maximum: 5 mg/dose (1 tablet Percodan® or 2 tablets Percodan®-Demi/dose)

Adults: Percodan®: 1 tablet every 6 hours as needed for pain or Percodan®-Demi: 1-2 tablets every 6 hours as needed for pain

Dosing adjustment in hepatic impairment: Dose should be reduced in patients with severe liver disease

Dosage Forms TAB: Oxycodone 4.5 mg, oxycodone 0.38 mg, and aspirin 325 mg; (Endodan®, Percodan®): Oxycodone 4.5 mg, oxycodone 0.38 mg, and aspirin 325 mg; (Percodan®-Demi [DSC]): Oxycodone 2.25 mg, oxycodone 0.19 mg, and aspirin 325 mg

- ◆ **Oxycodone Hydrochloride** *see Oxycodone on page 944*
- ◆ **OxyContin®** *see Oxycodone on page 944*
- ◆ **Oxydose™** *see Oxycodone on page 944*
- ◆ **OxyFast®** *see Oxycodone on page 944*
- ◆ **OxyIR®** *see Oxycodone on page 944*

Oxymetholone *(oks i METH oh lone)*

U.S. Brand Names Anadrol®

Therapeutic Category Anabolic Steroid; Androgen

Use Anemias caused by the administration of myelotoxic drugs

Restrictions C-III

Pregnancy Risk Factor X

Dosage Adults: Erythropoietic effects: Oral: 1-5 mg/kg/day in one daily dose; usual effective dose: 1-2 mg/kg/day; give for a minimum trial of 3-6 months because response may be delayed

Dosing adjustment in hepatic impairment:

Mild to moderate hepatic impairment: Oxymetholone should be used with caution in patients with liver dysfunction because of its hepatotoxic potential

Severe hepatic impairment: Oxymetholone should **not** be used

Dosage Forms TAB: 50 mg

Oxymorphone *(oks i MOR fone)*

Related Information

Narcotic Agonists Comparison *on page 1395*

U.S. Brand Names Numorphan®

Synonyms Oxymorphone Hydrochloride

Therapeutic Category Analgesic, Narcotic

Use Management of moderate to severe pain and preoperatively as a sedative and a supplement to anesthesia

Restrictions C-II

Pregnancy Risk Factor B/D (prolonged use or high doses at term)

Contraindications Hypersensitivity to oxymorphone or any component of the formulation; increased intracranial pressure; severe respiratory depression; pregnancy (prolonged use or high doses at term)

Warnings/Precautions Some preparations contain sulfites which may cause allergic reactions; infants <3 months of age are more susceptible to respiratory depression, use with caution and generally in reduced doses in this age group; use with caution in patients with impaired respiratory function or severe hepatic dysfunction and in patients with hypersensitivity reactions to other phenanthrene derivative opioid agonists (codeine, hydrocodone, hydromorphone, levorphanol, oxycodone, oxymorphone); tolerance or drug dependence may result from extended use

Common Adverse Reactions

>10%:

Cardiovascular: Hypotension

Central nervous system: Fatigue, drowsiness, dizziness

Gastrointestinal: Nausea, vomiting, constipation

Neuromuscular & skeletal: Weakness

Miscellaneous: Histamine release

1% to 10%:

Central nervous system: Nervousness, headache, restlessness, malaise, confusion

Gastrointestinal: Anorexia, stomach cramps, xerostomia, biliary spasm

Genitourinary: Decreased urination, ureteral spasms

Local: Pain at injection site

Respiratory: Dyspnea

Drug Interactions

Increased Effect/Toxicity: Increased effect/toxicity with CNS depressants (phenothiazines, tranquilizers, anxiolytics, sedatives, hypnotics, alcohol), tricyclic antidepressants, and dextroamphetamine.

Decreased Effect: Decreased effect with phenothiazines.

Mechanism of Action Oxymorphone hydrochloride (Numorphan®) is a potent narcotic analgesic with uses similar to those of morphine. The drug is a semisynthetic derivative of morphine (phenanthrene derivative) and is closely related to hydromorphone chemically (Dilaudid®).

Pharmacodynamics/Kinetics
Onset of action: Analgesic: I.V., I.M., S.C.: 5-10 minutes; Rectal: 15-30 minutes
Duration: Analgesic: Parenteral, rectal: 3-4 hours
Metabolism: Hepatic via glucuronidation
Excretion: Urine

Dosage Adults: **Note:** More frequent dosing may be required.
I.M., S.C.: 0.5 mg initially, 1-1.5 mg every 4-6 hours as needed
I.V.: 0.5 mg initially
Rectal: 5 mg every 4-6 hours

Monitoring Parameters Respiratory rate, heart rate, blood pressure, CNS activity

Patient Information Avoid alcohol, may cause drowsiness, impaired judgment or coordination; may cause physical and psychological dependence with prolonged use

Dosage Forms INJ, solution: 1 mg (1 mL); 1.5 mg/mL (10 mL). **SUPP, rectal:** 5 mg

♦ Oxymorphone Hydrochloride *see* Oxymorphone *on page 946*

Oxytetracycline (oks i tet ra SYE kleen)

U.S. Brand Names Terramycin® I.M.
Synonyms Oxytetracycline Hydrochloride
Therapeutic Category Antibiotic, Tetracycline Derivative
Use Treatment of susceptible bacterial infections; both gram-positive and gram-negative, as well as, *Rickettsia* and *Mycoplasma* organisms
Pregnancy Risk Factor D
Contraindications Hypersensitivity to tetracycline or any component of the formulation
Warnings/Precautions Avoid in children ≤8 years of age, pregnant and nursing women; photosensitivity can occur with oxytetracycline
Common Adverse Reactions Frequency not defined; also refer to Tetracycline monograph
Cardiovascular: Pericarditis
Central nervous system: Bulging fontanels (infants), intracranial hypertension (adults)
Dermatologic: Angioneurotic edema, erythematous rash, exfoliative dermatitis (uncommon), maculopapular rash, photosensitivity, urticaria
Gastrointestinal: Anogenital inflammatory lesions, diarrhea, dysphagia, enamel hypoplasia, enterocolitis, glossitis, nausea, tooth discoloration, vomiting
Hematologic: Anemia, eosinophilia, neutropenia, thrombocytopenia
Local: Irritation
Renal: BUN increased
Miscellaneous: Anaphylactoid purpura, anaphylaxis, hypersensitivity reaction, SLE exacerbation

Drug Interactions
Increased Effect/Toxicity: Oral anticoagulant (warfarin) effects may be increased.
Decreased Effect: Barbiturates, phenytoin, and carbamazepine decrease serum levels of tetracyclines. Although anecdotal reports suggest oral contraceptive efficacy could be reduced by tetracyclines, this has been refuted by more rigorous scientific and clinical data.

Mechanism of Action Inhibits bacterial protein synthesis by binding with the 30S and possibly the 50S ribosomal subunit(s) of susceptible bacteria, cell wall synthesis is not affected

Pharmacodynamics/Kinetics
Absorption: Poor
Distribution: Crosses placenta
Metabolism: Hepatic (small amounts)
Half-life elimination: 8.5-9.6 hours; prolonged with renal impairment
Excretion: Urine; feces

Dosage I.M.:
Children >8 years: 15-25 mg/kg/day (maximum: 250 mg/dose) in divided doses every 8-12 hours
Adults: 250 mg every 24 hours or 300 mg/day divided every 8-12 hours
Dosing interval in renal impairment: Cl_{cr} <10 mL/minute: Administer every 24 hours or avoid use if possible
Dosing adjustment/comments in hepatic impairment: Avoid use in patients with severe liver disease

Administration Injection for intramuscular use only.
Patient Information Avoid unnecessary exposure to sunlight.
Dosage Forms INJ, solution: 5% [50 mg/mL] (10 mL)

Oxytetracycline and Polymyxin B (oks i tet ra SYE kleen & pol i MIKS in bee)

U.S. Brand Names Terramycin® w/Polymyxin B Ophthalmic
Synonyms Polymyxin B and Oxytetracycline
Therapeutic Category Antibiotic, Ophthalmic
Use Treatment of superficial ocular infections involving the conjunctiva and/or cornea
Pregnancy Risk Factor D
Dosage Topical: Apply ½" of ointment onto the lower lid of affected eye 2-4 times/day
Dosage Forms OINT, ophthalmic: Oxytetracycline 5 mg and polymyxin B 10,000 units per g (3.5 g)

♦ Oxytetracycline Hydrochloride *see* Oxytetracycline *on page 947*

Oxytocin (oks i TOE sin)

U.S. Brand Names Pitocin®

Synonyms Pit

Therapeutic Category Oxytocic Agent

Use Induction of labor at term; control of postpartum bleeding; adjunctive therapy in management of abortion

Pregnancy Risk Factor X

Contraindications Hypersensitivity to oxytocin or any component of the formulation; significant cephalopelvic disproportion; unfavorable fetal positions; fetal distress; hypertonic or hyperactive uterus; contraindicated vaginal delivery (invasive cervical cancer, active genital herpes, prolapse of the cord, cord presentation, total placenta previa, or vasa previa)

Warnings/Precautions To be used for medical rather than elective induction of labor; may produce antidiuretic effect (ie, water intoxication and excess uterine contractions); high doses or hypersensitivity to oxytocin may cause uterine hypertonicity, spasm, tetanic contraction, or rupture of the uterus; severe water intoxication with convulsions, coma, and death is associated with a slow oxytocin infusion over 24 hours

Common Adverse Reactions Frequency not defined.

Fetus or neonate:

Cardiovascular: Arrhythmias (including premature ventricular contractions), bradycardia

Central nervous system: Brain or CNS damage (permanent), neonatal seizures

Hepatic: Neonatal jaundice

Ocular: Neonatal retinal hemorrhage

Miscellaneous: Fetal death, low Apgar score (5 minute)

Mother:

Cardiovascular: Arrhythmias, hypertensive episodes, premature ventricular contractions

Gastrointestinal: Nausea, vomiting

Genitourinary: Pelvic hematoma, postpartum hemorrhage, uterine hypertonicity, tetanic contraction of the uterus, uterine rupture, uterine spasm

Hematologic: Afibrinogenemia (fatal)

Miscellaneous: Anaphylactic reaction, subarachnoid hemorrhage

Mechanism of Action Produces the rhythmic uterine contractions characteristic to delivery

Pharmacodynamics/Kinetics

Onset of action: Uterine contractions: I.M.: 3-5 minutes; I.V.: ~1 minute

Duration: I.M.: 2-3 hour; I.V.: 1 hour

Metabolism: Rapidly hepatic and via plasma (by oxytocinase) and to a smaller degree the mammary gland

Half-life elimination: 1-5 minutes

Excretion: Urine

Dosage I.V. administration requires the use of an infusion pump. Adults:

Induction of labor: I.V.: 0.5-1 milliunits/minute; gradually increase dose in increments of 1-2 milliunits/minute until desired contraction pattern is established; dose may be decreased after desired frequency of contractions is reached and labor has progressed to 5-6 cm dilation. Infusion rates of 6 milliunits/minute provide oxytocin levels similar to those at spontaneous labor; rates of >9-10 milliunits/minute are rarely required.

Postpartum bleeding:

I.M.: Total dose of 10 units after delivery

I.V.: 10-40 units by I.V. infusion in 1000 mL of intravenous fluid at a rate sufficient to control uterine atony

Adjunctive treatment of abortion: I.V.: 10-20 milliunits/minute; maximum total dose: 30 units/12 hours

Administration I.V.: Refer to Stability (reconstitution) for dilution information; an infusion pump is required for administration

Monitoring Parameters Fluid intake and output during administration; fetal monitoring

Dosage Forms INJ, solution: 10 units/mL (1 mL, 10 mL); (Pitocin®): 10 units/mL (1 mL)

- **Oxytrol™** see Oxybutynin on page 942
- **Oysco 500 [OTC]** see Calcium Carbonate on page 203
- **Oyst-Cal 500 [OTC]** see Calcium Carbonate on page 203
- **P-071** see Cetirizine on page 250
- **Pacerone®** see Amiodarone on page 77

Paclitaxel (PAK li taks el)

U.S. Brand Names Onxol™; Taxol®

Synonyms NSC-125973

Therapeutic Category Antineoplastic Agent, Antimicrotubular; Antineoplastic Agent, Natural Source (Plant) Derivative

Use Treatment of breast, lung (small cell and nonsmall cell), and ovarian cancers

Pregnancy Risk Factor D

Contraindications Hypersensitivity to paclitaxel, Cremophor® EL (polyoxyethylated castor oil), or any component of the formulation; pregnancy

Warnings/Precautions Severe hypersensitivity reactions have been reported; prolongation of the infusion (to ≥6 hours) plus premedication may minimize this effect. When administered as sequential infusions, taxane derivatives (docetaxel, paclitaxel) should be administered before platinum derivatives (carboplatin, cisplatin) to limit myelosuppression. Elderly patients have an increased risk of toxicity (neutropenia, neuropathy).

Common Adverse Reactions

>10%:

Allergic: Appear to be primarily nonimmunologically mediated release of histamine and other vasoactive substances; almost always seen within the first hour of an infusion (~75% occur within 10 minutes of starting the infusion); incidence is significantly reduced by premedication

Cardiovascular: Bradycardia (transient, 25%)

Dermatologic: Alopecia (87%), venous erythema, tenderness, discomfort

Hematologic: Myelosuppression, leukopenia, neutropenia (6% to 21%), thrombocytopenia

Hepatic: Mild increases in liver enzymes

Onset: 8-11 days

Nadir: 15-21 days

Recovery: 21 days

Neurotoxicity: Sensory and/or autonomic neuropathy (numbness, tingling, burning pain), myopathy or myopathic effects (25% to 55%), and central nervous system toxicity. May be cumulative and dose-limiting. **Note:** Motor neuropathy is uncommon at doses <250 mg/m^2; sensory neuropathy is almost universal at doses >250 mg/m^2; myopathic effects are common with doses >250 mg/m^2, generally occurring within 2-3 days of treatment, resolving over 5-6 days; pre-existing neuropathy may increase the risk of neuropathy.

Gastrointestinal: Severe, potentially dose-limiting mucositis, stomatitis (15%), most common at doses >390 mg/m^2

Neuromuscular & skeletal: Arthralgia, myalgia

1% to 10%:

Cardiovascular: Myocardial infarction

Dermatologic: Phlebitis (2%)

Gastrointestinal: Mild nausea and vomiting (5% to 6%), diarrhea (5% to 6%)

Hematologic: Anemia

Drug Interactions

Cytochrome P450 Effect: Substrate (major) of CYP2C8/9, 3A4; **Induces** CYP3A4 (weak)

Increased Effect/Toxicity: CYP2C8/9 inhibitors may increase the levels/effects of paclitaxel; example inhibitors include delavirdine, fluconazole, gemfibrozil, ketoconazole, nicardipine, NSAIDs, pioglitazone, and sulfonamides. In Phase I trials, myelosuppression was more profound when given after cisplatin than with alternative sequence. administered as sequential infusions, studies indicate a potential for increased toxicity when platinum derivatives (carboplatin, cisplatin) are administered before taxane derivatives (docetaxel, paclitaxel). Paclitaxel may increase doxorubicin levels/toxicity.

Decreased Effect: CYP2C8/9 inducers may decrease the levels/effects of paclitaxel; example inducers include carbamazepine, phenobarbital, phenytoin, rifampin, rifapentine, and secobarbital.

Mechanism of Action Paclitaxel promotes microtubule assembly by enhancing the action of tubulin dimers, stabilizing existing microtubules, and inhibiting their disassembly, interfering with the late G_2 mitotic phase, and inhibiting cell replication. In addition, the drug can distort mitotic spindles, resulting in the breakage of chromosomes. Paclitaxel may also suppress cell proliferation and modulate immune response.

Pharmacodynamics/Kinetics

Distribution:

V_d: Widely distributed into body fluids and tissues; affected by dose and duration of infusion

V_{dss}:

1- to 6-hour infusion: 67.1 L/m^2

24-hour infusion: 227-688 L/m^2

Protein binding: 89% to 98%

Metabolism: Hepatic via CYP2C8/9 and 3A4; forms metabolites

Half-life elimination:

1- to 6-hour infusion: Mean (beta): 6.4 hours

3-hour infusion: Mean (terminal): 13.1-20.2 hours

24-hour infusion: Mean (terminal): 15.7-52.7 hours

Excretion: Feces (~70%, 5% as unchanged drug); urine (14%)

Clearance: Mean Total body: After 1- and 6-hour infusions: 5.8-16.3 L/hour/m^2; After 24-hour infusions: 14.2-17.2 L/hour/m^2

Dosage Premedication with dexamethasone (20 mg orally or I.V. at 12 and 6 hours **or** 14 and 7 hours before the dose), diphenhydramine (50 mg I.V. 30-60 minutes prior to the dose), and cimetidine, famotidine or ranitidine (I.V. 30-60 minutes prior to the dose) is recommended

Adults: I.V.: Refer to individual protocols

Ovarian carcinoma: 135-175 mg/m^2 over 3 hours every 3 weeks **or**

50-80 mg/m^2 over 1-3 hours weekly **or**

1.4-4 mg/m^2/day continuous infusion for 14 days every 4 weeks

Metastatic breast cancer: 175-250 mg/m^2 over 3 hours every 3 weeks **or**

50-80 mg/m^2 weekly **or**

1.4-4 mg/m^2/day continuous infusion for 14 days every 4 weeks

Nonsmall cell lung carcinoma: 135 mg/m^2 over 24 hours every 3 weeks

AIDS-related Kaposi's sarcoma: 135 mg/m^2 over 3 hours every 3 weeks **or**

100 mg/m^2 over 3 hours every 2 weeks

Dosage modification for toxicity (solid tumors, including ovary, breast, and lung carcinoma): Courses of paclitaxel should not be repeated until the neutrophil count is ≥1500 cells/mm^3 and the platelet count is ≥100,000 cells/mm^3; reduce dosage by 20% for patients experiencing severe peripheral neuropathy or severe neutropenia (neutrophil <500 cells/mm^3 for a week or longer)

(Continued)

Paclitaxel (Continued)

Dosage modification for immunosuppression in advanced HIV disease: Paclitaxel should not be given to patients with HIV if the baseline or subsequent neutrophil count is <1000 cells/mm³. Additional modifications include: Reduce dosage of dexamethasone in premedication to 10 mg orally; reduce dosage by 20% in patients experiencing severe peripheral neuropathy or severe neutropenia (neutrophil <500 cells/mm³ for a week or longer); initiate concurrent hematopoietic growth factor (G-CSF) as clinically indicated

Dosage adjustment in hepatic impairment: Note: These recommendations are based upon the patient's first course of therapy where the usual dose would be 135 mg/m² dose over 24 hours or the 175 mg/m² dose over 3 hours in patients with normal hepatic function. Dosage in subsequent courses should be based upon individual tolerance. Adjustments for other regimens are not available.

24-hour infusion:

If transaminase levels <2 times upper limit of normal (ULN) and bilirubin level ≤1.5 mg/dL: 135 mg/m²

If transaminase levels 2-<10 times ULN and bilirubin level ≤1.5 mg/dL: 100 mg/m²

If transaminase levels <10 times ULN and bilirubin level 1.6-7.5 mg/dL: 50 mg/m²

If transaminase levels ≥10 times ULN and bilirubin level >7.5 mg/dL: Avoid use

3-hour infusion:

If transaminase levels <10 times ULN and bilirubin level ≤1.25 times ULN: 175 mg/m²

If transaminase levels <10 times ULN and bilirubin level 1.26-2 times ULN: 135 mg/m²

If transaminase levels <10 times ULN and bilirubin level 2.01-5 times ULN: 90 mg/m²

If transaminase levels ≥10 times ULN and bilirubin level >5 times ULN: Avoid use

Administration

Anaphylactoid-like reactions have been reported: Corticosteroids (dexamethasone), H_1-antagonists (diphenhydramine), and H_2-antagonists, should be administered prior to paclitaxel administration to minimize potential for anaphylaxis. The following regimen is suggested: Dexamethasone I.V. 10-20 mg, diphenhydramine I.V. 50 mg, and cimetidine I.V. 300 mg **or** ranitidine I.V. 50 mg, all given 30 minutes prior to paclitaxel administration.

Administer I.V. infusion over 1-24 hours; use of a 0.22 micron in-line filter and nonsorbing administration set is recommended during the infusion

Nonpolyvinyl (non-PVC) tubing (eg, polyethylene) should be used to minimize leaching. Formulated in a vehicle known as Cremophor® EL (polyoxyethylated castor oil). Cremophor® EL has been found to leach the plasticizer DEHP from polyvinyl chloride infusion bags or administration sets. Contact of the undiluted concentrate with plasticized polyvinyl chloride (PVC) equipment or devices is not recommended. Administer through I.V. tubing containing an in-line (NOT >0.22 μ) filter; administration through IVEX-2® filters (which incorporate short inlet and outlet polyvinyl chloride-coated tubing) has not resulted in significant leaching of DEHP.

Monitoring Parameters Monitor for hypersensitivity reactions

Reference Range Mean maximum serum concentrations: 435-802 ng/mL following 24-hour infusions of 200-275 mg/m² and were approximately 10% to 30% of those following 6-hour infusions of equivalent doses

Patient Information This medication can only be administered by I.V. infusion, usually on a cyclic basis. Maintain adequate hydration (2-3 L/day of fluids unless instructed to restrict fluid intake) and nutrition (small frequent meals will help). You will most likely lose your hair (will grow back after therapy); experience some nausea or vomiting (request antiemetic); feel weak or lethargic (use caution when driving or engaging in tasks that require alertness until response to drug is known). Use good oral care to reduce incidence of mouth sores. You will be more susceptible to infection; avoid crowds or exposure to infection. Report numbness or tingling in fingers or toes (use care to prevent injury); signs of infection (fever, chills, sore throat, burning urination, fatigue); unusual bleeding (tarry stools, easy bruising, or blood in stool, urine, or mouth); unresolved mouth sores; nausea or vomiting; or skin rash or itching. Contraceptive measures are recommended during therapy.

Dosage Forms INJ, solution: 6 mg/mL (5 mL, 16.7 mL, 50 mL); (Onxol™): 6 mg/mL (5 mL, 25 mL, 50 mL); (Taxol®): 6 mg/mL (5 mL, 16.7 mL, 50 mL)

♦ **Pain-Off [OTC]** *see* Acetaminophen, Aspirin, and Caffeine *on page 27*

♦ **Palgic®-D** *see* Carbinoxamine and Pseudoephedrine *on page 218*

♦ **Palgic®-DS** *see* Carbinoxamine and Pseudoephedrine *on page 218*

Palivizumab (pah li VIZ u mab)

U.S. Brand Names Synagis®

Therapeutic Category Antiviral Agent; Monoclonal Antibody

Use Prevention of serious lower respiratory tract disease caused by respiratory syncytial virus (RSV) in infants and children <2 years of age at high risk of RSV disease

Pregnancy Risk Factor C

Contraindications History of severe prior reaction to palivizumab or any component of the formulation

Warnings/Precautions Very rare cases of anaphylaxis have been observed following palivizumab. Rare cases of severe acute hypersensitivity reactions have also been reported. Safety and efficacy of palivizumab have not been demonstrated in the treatment of established RSV disease. Use with caution in patients with thrombocytopenia or any coagulation disorder.

Common Adverse Reactions The incidence of adverse events was similar between the palivizumab and placebo groups.

>1%:

Central nervous system: Nervousness, fever

Dermatologic: Fungal dermatitis, eczema, seborrhea, rash

Gastrointestinal: Diarrhea, vomiting, gastroenteritis

Hematologic: Anemia

Hepatic: ALT increase, abnormal LFTs

Local: Injection site reaction, erythema, induration

Ocular: Conjunctivitis

Otic: Otitis media

Respiratory: Cough, wheezing, bronchiolitis, pneumonia, bronchitis, asthma, croup, dyspnea, sinusitis, apnea, upper respiratory infection, rhinitis

Miscellaneous: Oral moniliasis, failure to thrive, viral infection, flu syndrome

Postmarketing and/or case reports: Hypersensitivity reactions, anaphylaxis (very rare)

Mechanism of Action Exhibits neutralizing and fusion-inhibitory activity against RSV; these activities inhibit RSV replication in laboratory and clinical studies

Pharmacodynamics/Kinetics

Half-life elimination: Children <24 months: 20 days; Adults: 18 days

Time to peak, serum: 48 hours

Dosage I.M.: Infants and Children: 15 mg/kg of body weight, monthly throughout RSV season (First dose administered prior to commencement of RSV season)

Administration Injection should (preferably) be in the anterolateral aspect of the thigh; gluteal muscle should not be used routinely; injection volume over 1 mL should be administered as divided doses

Dosage Forms INJ, powder for reconstitution: 50 mg, 100 mg

♦ **Palmer's® Skin Success Fade Cream™ [OTC]** *see Hydroquinone on page 636*

♦ **Palmitate-A® [OTC]** *see Vitamin A on page 1309*

Palonosetron (pal oh NOE se tron)

U.S. Brand Names Aloxi™

Synonyms Palonosetron Hydrochloride; RS-25259; RS-25259-197

Therapeutic Category Antiemetic; Serotonin 5-HT₃ Receptor Antagonist

Use Prevention of acute (within 24 hours) and delayed (2-5 days) chemotherapy-induced nausea and vomiting

Unlabeled/Investigational Use Prevention of postoperative vomiting

Pregnancy Risk Factor B

Contraindications Hypersensitivity to palonosetron or any component of the formulation

Warnings/Precautions Use caution in patients allergic to other 5-HT₃ receptor antagonists; cross-reactivity is possible. Caution in patients with congenital QT syndrome or other risk factors for QT prolongation (eg, drugs, electrolyte abnormalities). Safety and efficacy in pediatric patients (<18 years of age) have not been established.

Common Adverse Reactions

>10%: Dermatologic: Pruritus (8% to 22%)

1% to 10%:

Cardiovascular: Bradycardia (1%), hypotension (1%), tachycardia (nonsustained) (1%)

Central nervous system: Headache (6% to 9%), anxiety (1% to 5%), dizziness (1%)

Endocrine & metabolic: Hyperkalemia (1%)

Gastrointestinal: Constipation (5% to 10%), diarrhea (1%)

Neuromuscular & skeletal: Weakness (1%)

Drug Interactions

Cytochrome P450 Effect: Substrate (minor) of CYP1A2, 2D6, 3A4

Increased Effect/Toxicity: No drug interactions of concern have been identified.

Mechanism of Action Selective 5-HT₃ receptor antagonist, blocking serotonin, both peripherally on vagal nerve terminals and centrally in the chemoreceptor trigger zone

Pharmacodynamics/Kinetics

Distribution: V_d: 8.3 ± 2.5 L/kg

Protein binding: 62%

Metabolism: ~50% metabolized via CYP enzymes (and likely other pathways) to relatively inactive metabolites; CYP1A2, 2D6, and 3A4 contribute to its metabolism

Half-life elimination: Terminal: 40 hours

Excretion: Urine (80%, 40% as unchanged drug)

Dosage I.V.: Adults:

Chemotherapy-induced nausea and vomiting: 0.25 mg 30 minutes prior to chemotherapy administration, day 1 of each cycle (doses should not be given more than once weekly)

Postoperative vomiting (unlabeled use): 30 mcg/kg (used in hysterectomy, lower doses ineffective; no significant reduction in nausea at any dose)

Elderly: No dosage adjustment necessary

Dosage adjustment in renal/hepatic impairment: No dosage adjustment necessary

Administration I.V.: Infuse over 30 seconds; flush I.V. line with NS prior to and following administration.

Patient Information Inform prescriber of all prescriptions, OTC medications, or herbal products you are taking, and any allergies you have. Do not take anything new during treatment unless approved by prescriber. May cause drowsiness or dizziness (use caution when driving or engaging in tasks that require alertness until response to drug is known); or fatigue, diarrhea, constipation, or headache (request appropriate treatment from prescriber). Do not change position rapidly (rise slowly). Report persistent headache, excessive drowsiness, fever, numbness or tingling, or changes in elimination patterns (constipation or diarrhea); or chest pain or palpitations.

Dosage Forms INJ, solution, as hydrochloride: 0.05 mg/mL (5 mL)

♦ **Palonosetron Hydrochloride** *see* Palonosetron *on page 951*

♦ **2-PAM** *see* Pralidoxime *on page 1025*

♦ **Pamelor**® *see* Nortriptyline *on page 916*

Pamidronate (pa mi DROE nate)

U.S. Brand Names Aredia®

Synonyms Pamidronate Disodium

Therapeutic Category Antidote, Hypercalcemia; Bisphosphonate Derivative

Use Treatment of hypercalcemia associated with malignancy; treatment of osteolytic bone lesions associated with multiple myeloma or metastatic breast cancer; moderate to severe Paget's disease of bone

Pregnancy Risk Factor D

Contraindications Hypersensitivity to pamidronate, other biphosphonates, or any component of the formulation; pregnancy

Warnings/Precautions May cause deterioration in renal function. Use caution in patients with renal impairment and avoid in severe renal impairment. Assess serum creatinine prior to each dose; withhold dose in patients with bone metastases who experience deterioration in renal function. Leukopenia has been observed with oral pamidronate and monitoring of white blood cell counts is suggested. Vein irritation and thrombophlebitis may occur with infusions. In elderly patients, monitor serum electrolytes periodically since elderly are often receiving diuretics which can result in decreases in serum calcium, potassium, and magnesium.

Common Adverse Reactions As reported with hypercalcemia of malignancy; percentage of adverse effect varies upon dose and duration of infusion.

>10%:

Central nervous system: Fever (18% to 26%), fatigue (12%)

Endocrine & metabolic: Hypophosphatemia (9% to 18%), hypokalemia (4% to 18%), hypomagnesemia (4% to 12%), hypocalcemia (1% to 12%)

Gastrointestinal: Nausea (up to 18%), anorexia (1% to 12%)

Local: Infusion site reaction (up to 18%)

1% to 10%:

Cardiovascular: Atrial fibrillation (up to 6%), hypertension (up to 6%), syncope (up to 6%), tachycardia (up to 6%), atrial flutter (up to 1%), cardiac failure (up to 1%)

Central nervous system: Somnolence (1% to 6%), psychosis (up to 4%), insomnia (up to 1%)

Endocrine & metabolic: Hypothyroidism (6%)

Gastrointestinal: Constipation (4% to 6%), stomatitis (up to 1%)

Hematologic: Leukopenia (up to 4%), neutropenia (up to 1%), thrombocytopenia (up to 1%)

Neuromuscular & skeletal: Myalgia (up to 1%)

Renal: Uremia (up to 4%)

Respiratory: Rales (up to 6%), rhinitis (up to 6%), upper respiratory tract infection (up to 3%)

Mechanism of Action A biphosphonate which inhibits bone resorption via actions on osteoclasts or on osteoclast precursors. Does not appear to produce any significant effects on renal tubular calcium handling and is poorly absorbed following oral administration (high oral doses have been reported effective); therefore, I.V. therapy is preferred.

Pharmacodynamics/Kinetics

Onset of action: 24-48 hours

Peak effect: Maximum: 5-7 days

Absorption: Poor; pharmacokinetic studies lacking

Metabolism: Not metabolized

Half-life elimination: 21-35 hours; Bone: Terminal: ~300 days

Excretion: Biphasic; urine (~50% as unchanged drug) within 120 hours

Dosage Drug must be diluted properly before administration and infused intravenously slowly. Due to risk of nephrotoxicity, doses should not exceed 90 mg. I.V.: Adults:

Hypercalcemia of malignancy:

Moderate cancer-related hypercalcemia (corrected serum calcium: 12-13.5 mg/dL): 60-90 mg, as a single dose, given as a slow infusion over 2-24 hours; dose should be diluted in 1000 mL 0.45% NaCl, 0.9% NaCl, or D₅W

Severe cancer-related hypercalcemia (corrected serum calcium: >13.5 mg/dL): 90 mg, as a single dose, as a slow infusion over 2-24 hours; dose should be diluted in 1000 mL 0.45% NaCl, 0.9% NaCl, or D₅W

A period of 7 days should elapse before the use of second course; repeat infusions every 2-3 weeks have been suggested, however, could be administered every 2-3 months according to the degree and of severity of hypercalcemia and/or the type of malignancy.

Note: Some investigators have suggested a lack of a dose-response relationship. Courses of pamidronate for hypercalcemia may be repeated at varying intervals, depending on the duration of normocalcemia (median 2-3 weeks), but the manufacturer recommends a minimum interval between courses of 7 days. Oral etidronate at a dose of 20 mg/kg/day has been used to maintain the calcium lowering effect following I.V. bisphosphonates, although it is of limited effectiveness.

Osteolytic bone lesions with multiple myeloma: 90 mg in 500 mL D₅W, 0.45% NaCl or 0.9% NaCl administered over 4 hours on a monthly basis

Osteolytic bone lesions with metastatic breast cancer: 90 mg in 250 mL D₅W, 0.45% NaCl or 0.9% NaCl administered over 2 hours, repeated every 3-4 weeks

Paget's disease: 30 mg in 500 mL 0.45% NaCl, 0.9% NaCl or D₅W administered over 4 hours for 3 consecutive days

Dosing adjustment in renal impairment: Not recommended in severe renal impairment (patients with bone metastases)

Dosing adjustment in renal toxicity: In patients with bone metastases, treatment should be withheld in patients who experience deterioration in renal function (increase of serum creatinine ≥0.5 mg/dL in patients with normal baseline or ≥1.0 mg/dL in patients with abnormal baseline). Resumption of therapy may be considered when serum creatinine returns to within 10% of baseline.

Administration Drug must be properly diluted before administration and slowly infused intravenously (over at least 2 hours).

Monitoring Parameters Serum electrolytes, monitor for hypocalcemia for at least 2 weeks after therapy; serum calcium, phosphate, magnesium, potassium, CBC with differential; monitor serum creatinine prior to each dose

Reference Range Calcium (total): Adults: 9.0-11.0 mg/dL (SI: 2.05-2.54 mmol/L), may slightly decrease with aging; Phosphorus: 2.5-4.5 mg/dL (SI: 0.81-1.45 mmol/L)

Patient Information This medication can only be administered I.V. Avoid foods high in calcium, or vitamins with minerals, during infusion or for 2-3 hours after completion. You may experience nausea or vomiting (small frequent meals and good mouth care may help); or recurrent bone pain (consult prescriber for analgesic). Report unusual muscle twitching or spasms, severe diarrhea/constipation, or acute bone pain.

Dosage Forms INJ, powder for reconstitution: 30 mg, 90 mg. **INJ, solution:** 3 mg/mL (10 mL); 6 mg/mL (10 mL); 9 mg/mL (10 mL)

- **Pamidronate Disodium** *see Pamidronate on page 952*
- **p-Aminoclonidine** *see Apraclonidine on page 110*
- **Pamprin® Maximum Strength All Day Relief [OTC]** *see Naproxen on page 882*
- **Pan-B Antibody** *see Rituximab on page 1106*
- **Pancrease®** *see Pancrelipase on page 953*
- **Pancrease® MT** *see Pancrelipase on page 953*
- **Pancrecarb MS®** *see Pancrelipase on page 953*

Pancrelipase (pan kre LI pase)

U.S. Brand Names Creon®; Ku-Zyme® HP; Lipram 4500; Lipram-CR; Lipram-PN; Lipram-UL; Pancrease®; Pancrease® MT; Pancrecarb MS®; Pangestyme™ CN; Pangestyme™ EC; Pangestyme™ MT Pangestyme™ UL; Ultrase®; Ultrase® MT; Viokase®

Synonyms Lipancreatin

Therapeutic Category Enzyme, Pancreatic; Pancreatic Enzyme

Use Replacement therapy in symptomatic treatment of malabsorption syndrome caused by pancreatic insufficiency

Unlabeled/Investigational Use Treatment of occluded feeding tubes

Pregnancy Risk Factor B/C (product specific)

Contraindications Hypersensitivity to pork protein or any component of the formulation; acute pancreatitis or acute exacerbations of chronic pancreatic disease

Warnings/Precautions Pancrelipase is inactivated by acids; use microencapsulated products whenever possible, since these products permit better dissolution of enzymes in the duodenum and protect the enzyme preparations from acid degradation in the stomach. Fibrotic strictures in the colon, some requiring surgery, have been reported with high doses; use caution, especially in children with cystic fibrosis. Use caution when adjusting doses or changing brands. Avoid inhalation of powder, may cause nasal and respiratory tract irritation.

Common Adverse Reactions Frequency not defined; occurrence of events may be dose related.

Central nervous system: Pain

Dermatologic: Rash

Endocrine & metabolic: Hyperuricemia

Gastrointestinal: Nausea, cramps, constipation, diarrhea, perianal irritation/inflammation (large doses), irritation of the mouth, abdominal pain, intestinal obstruction, vomiting, flatulence, melena, weight loss, fibrotic strictures, greasy stools

Ocular: Lacrimation

Renal: Hyperuricosuria

Respiratory: Sneezing, dyspnea, bronchospasm

Miscellaneous: Allergic reactions

Mechanism of Action Pancrelipase is a natural product harvested from the hog pancreas. It contains a combination of lipase, amylase, and protease. Products are formulated to dissolve in the more basic pH of the duodenum so that they may act locally to break down fats, protein, and starch.

Pharmacodynamics/Kinetics

Absorption: None; acts locally in GI tract

Excretion: Feces

Dosage Oral:

Powder: Actual dose depends on the condition being treated and the digestive requirements of the patient

Children <1 year: Start with ⅛ teaspoonful with feedings

Adults: 0.7 g (¼ teaspoonful) with meals

Capsules/tablets: The following dosage recommendations are only an approximation for initial dosages. The actual dosage will depend on the condition being treated and the digestive

(Continued)

Pancrelipase *(Continued)*

requirements of the individual patient. Adjust dose based on body weight and stool fat content. Total daily dose reflects ~3 meals/day and 2-3 snacks/day, with half the mealtime dose given with a snack. Older patients may need less units/kg due to increased weight, but decreased ingestion of fat/kg. Maximum dose: 2500 units of lipase/kg/meal (10,000 units of lipase/kg/day)

Children:

<1 year: 2000 units of lipase with meals

1-6 years: 4000-8000 units of lipase with meals and 4000 units with snacks

7-12 years: 4000-12,000 units of lipase with meals and snacks

Adults: 4000-48,000 units of lipase with meals and with snacks

Occluded feeding tubes: One tablet of Viokase® crushed with one 325 mg tablet of sodium bicarbonate (to activate the Viokase®) in 5 mL of water can be instilled into the nasogastric tube and clamped for 5 minutes; then, flushed with 50 mL of tap water

Administration Oral: Administer with meals or snacks and swallow whole with a generous amount of liquid. Do not crush or chew; retention in the mouth before swallowing may cause mucosal irritation and stomatitis. Delayed-release capsules containing enteric-coated microspheres or microtablets may also be opened and the contents sprinkled on soft food with a low pH that does not require chewing, such as applesauce, gelatin; apricot, banana, or sweet potato baby food; baby formula. Dairy products such as milk, custard, or ice cream may have a high pH and should be avoided. Avoid inhalation of powder, may cause nasal and respiratory tract irritation.

Monitoring Parameters Abdominal symptoms, nutritional intake, growth (in children), stool character, fecal fat

Patient Information To be taken with a meal or a snack. Swallow tablets and capsules whole, do not chew, crush, or dissolve. Swallow with a generous amount of liquid; do not let dissolve in mouth. Capsules may also be opened and sprinkled on soft food with a low pH such as applesauce, gelatin; apricot, banana, or sweet potato baby food; baby formula. Do not sprinkle on dairy products such as milk, custard, or ice cream as they may have a high pH. Do not change brands, increase or decrease dosage without consulting prescriber. May experience nausea, vomiting, cramps, or constipation. Notify prescriber if experiencing abdominal pain, ongoing diarrhea or poor weight gain, especially if using large doses, are <12 years of age, or have cystic fibrosis.

Dosage Forms CAP (Ku-Zyme® HP): Lipase 8000 units, protease 30,000 units, amylase 30,000 units. **CAP, delayed release:** (Pangestyme™ CN-10): Lipase 10,000 units, protease 37,500 units, amylase 33,200 units; (Pangestyme™ CN-20): Lipase 20,000 units, protease 75,000 units, amylase 66,400 units. **CAP, delayed release, enteric coated microspheres:** (Creon® 5): Lipase 5000 units, protease 18,750 units, amylase 16,600 units; (Creon® 10): Lipase 10,000 units, protease 37,500 units, amylase 33,200 units; (Creon® 20): Lipase 20,000 units, protease 75,000 units, amylase 66,400 units; (Lipram 4500): Lipase 4500 units, protease 25,000 units, amylase 20,000 units; (Lipram-CR10): Lipase 10,000 units, protease 37,500 units, amylase 33,200 units; (Lipram-CR20): Lipase 20,000 units, protease 75,000 units, amylase 66,400 units; (Lipram-PN10): Lipase 10,000 units, protease 30,000 units, amylase 30,000 units; (Lipram-PN16): Lipase 16,000 units, protease 48,000 units, amylase 48,000 units; (Lipram-UL12): Lipase 12,000 units, protease 39,000 units, amylase 39,000 units; (Lipram-UL18): Lipase 18,000 units, protease 58,500 units, amylase 58,500 units; (Lipram-UL20): Lipase 20,000 units, protease 65,000 units, amylase 65,000 units; (Pancrecarb MS-4®): Lipase 4000 units, protease 25,000 units, amylase 25,000 units; (Pancrecarb MS-8®): Lipase 8000 units, protease 45,000 units, amylase 40,000 units. **CAP, enteric-coated microspheres:** (Pancrease®, Pangestyme™ EC, Ultrase®): Lipase 4500 units, protease 25,000 units, amylase 20,000 units. **CAP, enteric coated microtablets:** (Pancrease® MT 4): Lipase 4000 units, protease 12,000 units, amylase 12,000 units; (Pancrease® MT 10): Lipase 10,000 units, protease 30,000 units, amylase 30,000 units; (Pancrease® MT 16, Pangestyme™ MT 16): Lipase 16,000 units, protease 48,000 units, amylase 48,000 units; (Pancrease® MT 20): Lipase 20,000 units, protease 44,000 units, amylase 56,000 units; (Pangestyme™ UL 12): Lipase 12,000 units, protease 39,000 units, amylase 39,000 units; (Pangestyme™ UL 18): Lipase 18,000 units, protease 58,500 units, amylase 58,500 units; (Pangestyme™ UL 20): Lipase 20,000 units, protease 65,000 units, amylase 65,000 units. **CAP, enteric coated minitablets:** (Ultrase® MT12): Lipase 12,000 units, protease 39,000 units, amylase 39,000 units; (Ultrase® MT18): Lipase 18,000 units, protease 58,500 units, amylase 58,500 units; (Ultrase® MT20): Lipase 20,000 units, protease 65,000 units, amylase 65,000 units. **POWDER** (Viokase®): Lipase 16,800 units, protease 70,000 units, amylase 70,000 units per 0.7 g (227 g). **TAB:** (Viokase® 8): Lipase 8000 units, protease 30,000 units, amylase 30,000 units; (Viokase® 16): Lipase 16,000 units, protease 60,000 units, amylase 60,000 units

Pancuronium *(pan kyoo ROE nee um)*

Related Information

Neuromuscular Blocking Agents Comparison *on page 1397*

Synonyms Pancuronium Bromide; Pavulon [DSC]

Therapeutic Category Neuromuscular Blocker Agent, Nondepolarizing

Use Adjunct to general anesthesia to facilitate endotracheal intubation and to relax skeletal muscles during surgery; to facilitate mechanical ventilation in ICU patients; does not relieve pain or produce sedation

Drug of choice for neuromuscular blockade except in patients with renal failure, hepatic failure, or cardiovascular instability or in situations not suited for pancuronium's long duration of action

Pregnancy Risk Factor C

Contraindications Hypersensitivity to pancuronium, bromide, or any component of the formulation

Warnings/Precautions Ventilation must be supported during neuromuscular blockade; use with caution in patients with renal and/or hepatic impairment (adjust dose appropriately); certain clinical conditions may result in potentiation or antagonism of neuromuscular blockade:

Potentiation: Electrolyte abnormalities, severe hyponatremia, severe hypocalcemia, severe hypokalemia, hypermagnesemia, neuromuscular diseases, acidosis, acute intermittent porphyria, renal failure, hepatic failure

Antagonism: Alkalosis, hypercalcemia, demyelinating lesions, peripheral neuropathies, diabetes mellitus

Increased sensitivity in patients with myasthenia gravis, Eaton-Lambert syndrome; resistance in burn patients (>30% of body) for period of 5-70 days postinjury; resistance in patients with muscle trauma, denervation, immobilization, infection. Cross-sensitivity with other neuromuscular-blocking agents may occur; use extreme caution in patients with previous anaphylactic reactions.

Common Adverse Reactions Frequency not defined.

Cardiovascular: Elevation in pulse rate, elevated blood pressure and cardiac output, tachycardia, edema, skin flushing, circulatory collapse

Dermatologic: Rash, itching, erythema, burning sensation along the vein

Gastrointestinal: Excessive salivation

Neuromuscular & skeletal: Profound muscle weakness

Respiratory: Wheezing, bronchospasm

Miscellaneous: Hypersensitivity reaction

Causes of prolonged neuromuscular blockade: Excessive drug administration; cumulative drug effect, decreased metabolism/excretion (hepatic and/or renal impairment); accumulation of active metabolites; electrolyte imbalance (hypokalemia, hypocalcemia, hypermagnesemia, hypernatremia); hypothermia; drug interactions; increased sensitivity to muscle relaxants (eg, neuromuscular disorders such as myasthenia gravis or polymyositis)

Drug Interactions

Increased Effect/Toxicity: Increased effects are possible with aminoglycosides, beta-blockers, clindamycin, calcium channel blockers, halogenated anesthetics, imipenem, ketamine, lidocaine, loop diuretics (furosemide), macrolides (case reports), magnesium sulfate, procainamide, quinidine, quinolones, tetracyclines, and vancomycin. May increase risk of myopathy when used with high-dose corticosteroids for extended periods.

Decreased Effect: Effect of nondepolarizing neuromuscular blockers may be reduced by carbamazepine (chronic use), corticosteroids (also associated with myopathy - see increased effect), phenytoin (chronic use), sympathomimetics, and theophylline.

Mechanism of Action Blocks neural transmission at the myoneural junction by binding with cholinergic receptor sites

Pharmacodynamics/Kinetics

Onset of effect: Peak effect: I.V.: 2-3 minutes

Duration (dose dependent): 60-100 minutes

Metabolism: Hepatic (30% to 45%); active metabolite 3-hydroxypancuronium ($\frac{1}{3}$ to $\frac{1}{2}$ the activity of parent drug)

Half-life elimination: 110 minutes

Excretion: Urine (55% to 70% as unchanged drug)

Dosage Administer I.V.; dose to effect; doses will vary due to interpatient variability; use ideal body weight for obese patients

Surgery:

Neonates <1 month:

Test dose: 0.02 mg/kg to measure responsiveness

Initial: 0.03 mg/kg/dose repeated twice at 5- to 10-minute intervals as needed; maintenance: 0.03-0.09 mg/kg/dose every 30 minutes to 4 hours as needed

Infants >1 month, Children, and Adults: Initial: 0.06-0.1 mg/kg or 0.05 mg/kg after initial dose of succinylcholine for intubation; maintenance dose: 0.01 mg/kg 60-100 minutes after initial dose and then 0.01 mg/kg every 25-60 minutes

Pretreatment/priming: 10% of intubating dose given 3-5 minutes before initial dose

ICU: 0.05-0.1 mg/kg bolus followed by 0.8-1.7 mcg/kg/minute once initial recovery from bolus observed or 0.1-0.2 mg/kg every 1-3 hours

Dosing adjustment in renal impairment: Elimination half-life is doubled, plasma clearance is reduced and rate of recovery is sometimes much slower

Cl_{cr} 10-50 mL/minute: Administer 50% of normal dose

Cl_{cr} <10 mL/minute: Do not use

Dosing adjustment/comments in hepatic/biliary tract disease: Elimination half-life is doubled, plasma clearance is reduced, recovery time is prolonged, volume of distribution is increased (50%) and results in a slower onset, higher total initial dosage and prolongation of neuromuscular blockade

Administration May be administered undiluted by rapid I.V. injection

Monitoring Parameters Heart rate, blood pressure, assisted ventilation status; cardiac monitor, blood pressure monitor, and ventilator required

Dosage Forms INJ, solution: 1 mg/mL (10 mL); 2 mg/mL (2 mL, 5 mL)

♦ **Pancuronium Bromide** *see* Pancuronium *on page 954*

♦ **Pandel**® *see* Hydrocortisone *on page 632*

♦ **Pangestyme**™ **CN** *see* Pancrelipase *on page 953*

- ◆ Pangestyme™ EC *see Pancrelipase on page 953*
- ◆ Pangestyme™ MT *see Pancrelipase on page 953*
- ◆ Pangestyme™ UL *see Pancrelipase on page 953*
- ◆ Panglobulin® *see Immune Globulin (Intravenous) on page 659*
- ◆ PanMist®-DM *see Guaifenesin, Pseudoephedrine, and Dextromethorphan on page 606*
- ◆ PanMist® Jr. *see Guaifenesin and Pseudoephedrine on page 605*
- ◆ PanMist® LA *see Guaifenesin and Pseudoephedrine on page 605*
- ◆ PanMist® S *see Guaifenesin and Pseudoephedrine on page 605*
- ◆ Panretin® *see Alitretinoin on page 56*
- ◆ Panthoderm® [OTC] *see Dexpanthenol on page 361*

Pantoprazole (pan TOE pra zole)

U.S. Brand Names Protonix®

Therapeutic Category Gastric Acid Secretion Inhibitor; Proton Pump Inhibitor

Use

Oral: Treatment and maintenance of healing of erosive esophagitis associated with GERD; reduction in relapse rates of daytime and nighttime heartburn symptoms in GERD; hypersecretory disorders associated with Zollinger-Ellison syndrome or other neoplastic disorders

I.V.: As an alternative to oral therapy in patients unable to continue oral pantoprazole; hypersecretory disorders associated with Zollinger-Ellison syndrome or other neoplastic disorders

Unlabeled/Investigational Use Peptic ulcer disease, active ulcer bleeding with parenterally-administered pantoprazole; adjunct treatment with antibiotics for *Helicobacter pylori* eradication

Pregnancy Risk Factor B

Contraindications Hypersensitivity to pantoprazole or any component of the formulation

Warnings/Precautions Symptomatic response does not preclude gastric malignancy; not indicated for maintenance therapy; safety and efficacy for use beyond 16 weeks have not been established; safety and efficacy in pediatric patients have not been established

Common Adverse Reactions

1% to 10%:

Cardiovascular: Chest pain

Central nervous system: Pain, migraine, anxiety, dizziness

Endocrine & metabolic: Hyperglycemia (1%), hyperlipidemia

Gastrointestinal: Diarrhea (4%), constipation, dyspepsia, gastroenteritis, nausea, rectal disorder, vomiting

Genitourinary: Urinary frequency, urinary tract infection

Hepatic: Liver function test abnormality increased SGPT

Neuromuscular & skeletal: Weakness, back pain, neck pain, arthralgia, hypertonia

Respiratory: Bronchitis, increased cough, dyspnea, pharyngitis, rhinitis, sinusitis, upper respiratory tract infection

Miscellaneous: Flu syndrome, infection

Drug Interactions

Cytochrome P450 Effect: Substrate of CYP2C19 (major), 3A4 (minor); **Inhibits** 2C8/9 (moderate); **Induces** CYP1A2 (weak), 3A4 (weak)

Decreased Effect: CYP2C19 inducers may decrease the levels/effects of pantoprazole; example inducers include aminoglutethimide, carbamazepine, phenytoin, and rifampin. Proton pump inhibitors may decrease the absorption of atazanavir, indinavir, itraconazole, and ketoconazole.

Mechanism of Action Suppresses gastric acid secretin by inhibiting the parietal cell H^+/K^+ ATP pump

Pharmacodynamics/Kinetics

Absorption: Well absorbed

Distribution: V_d: 11-24 L

Protein binding: 98%, primarily to albumin

Metabolism: Extensively hepatic; CYP2C19 (demethylation), CYP3A4; no evidence that metabolites have pharmacologic activity

Bioavailability: 77%

Half-life elimination: 1 hour

Time to peak: Oral: 2.5 hours

Excretion: Urine (71%); feces (18%)

Dosage Adults:

Oral:

Erosive esophagitis associated with GERD:

Treatment: 40 mg once daily for up to 8 weeks; an additional 8 weeks may be used in patients who have not healed after an 8-week course

Maintenance of healing: 40 mg once daily

Note: Lower doses (20 mg once daily) have been used successfully in mild GERD treatment and maintenance of healing

Hypersecretory disorders (including Zollinger-Ellison): Initial: 40 mg twice daily; adjust dose based on patient needs; doses up to 240 mg/day have been administered

I.V.:

Erosive esophagitis associated with GERD: 40 mg once daily (infused over 15 minutes) for 7-10 days

Helicobacter pylori eradication (unlabeled use): Doses up to 40 mg twice daily have been used as part of combination therapy

Hypersecretory disorders: 80 mg twice daily; adjust dose based on acid output measurements; 160-240 mg/day in divided doses has been used for a limited period (up to 7 days)
Prevention of rebleeding in peptic ulcer bleed (unlabeled use): 80 mg, followed by 8 mg/hour infusion for 72 hours

Elderly: Dosage adjustment not required

Dosage adjustment in renal impairment: Not required; pantoprazole is not removed by hemodialysis

Dosage adjustment in hepatic impairment: Not required

Administration

I.V.:

2-minute infusion: The volume of reconstituted solution (4 mg/mL) to be injected may be administered intravenously over at least 2 minutes; use filter provided

15-minute infusion: Infuse over 15 minutes at a rate not to exceed 3 mg/minute; use in-line filter (positioned below Y-site if applicable)

Oral: Tablets should be swallowed whole, do not crush or chew. Best if taken before breakfast.

Monitoring Parameters Hypersecretory disorders: Acid output measurements, target level <10 mEq/hour (<5 mEq/hour if prior gastric acid-reducing surgery)

Patient Information Take with or without food. Do not split, chew or crush tablet. Take at a similar time every day.

Dosage Forms INJ, powder for reconstitution: 40 mg. **TAB, delayed release:** 20 mg, 40 mg

♦ **Pantothenyl Alcohol** *see* Dexpanthenol *on page 361*

Papaverine (pa PAV er een)

U.S. Brand Names Para-Time S.R.®

Synonyms Papaverine Hydrochloride; Pavabid [DSC]

Therapeutic Category Vasodilator

Use Oral: Relief of peripheral and cerebral ischemia associated with arterial spasm and myocardial ischemia complicated by arrhythmias

Unlabeled/Investigational Use Investigational: Parenteral: Various vascular spasms associated with muscle spasms as in myocardial infarction, angina, peripheral and pulmonary embolism, peripheral vascular disease, angiospastic states, and visceral spasm (ureteral, biliary, and GI colic); testing for impotence

Pregnancy Risk Factor C

Dosage

I.M., I.V.:

Children: 6 mg/kg/day in 4 divided doses

Adults: 30-65 mg (rarely up to 120 mg); may repeat every 3 hours

Oral, sustained release: Adults: 150-300 mg every 12 hours; in difficult cases: 150 mg every 8 hours

Dosage Forms CAP, sustained release (Para-Time SR®): 150 mg. **INJ, solution:** 30 mg/mL (2 mL, 10 mL)

♦ **Papaverine Hydrochloride** *see* Papaverine *on page 957*

♦ **Para-Aminosalicylate Sodium** *see* Aminosalicylic Acid *on page 76*

♦ **Paracetamol** *see* Acetaminophen *on page 24*

♦ **Parafon Forte® DSC** *see* Chlorzoxazone *on page 269*

♦ **Paraplatin®** *see* Carboplatin *on page 219*

♦ **Parathyroid Hormone (1-34)** *see* Teriparatide *on page 1200*

♦ **Para-Time S.R.®** *see* Papaverine *on page 957*

Paregoric (par e GOR ik)

Synonyms Camphorated Tincture of Opium

Therapeutic Category Analgesic, Narcotic; Antidiarrheal

Use Treatment of diarrhea or relief of pain; neonatal opiate withdrawal

Restrictions C-III

Pregnancy Risk Factor B/D (prolonged use or high doses)

Contraindications Hypersensitivity to opium or any component of the formulation; diarrhea caused by poisoning until the toxic material has been removed; pregnancy (prolonged use or high doses)

Warnings/Precautions Use with caution in patients with respiratory, hepatic or renal dysfunction, severe prostatic hyperplasia, or history of narcotic abuse; opium shares the toxic potential of opiate agonists, and usual precautions of opiate agonist therapy should be observed; some preparations contain sulfites which may cause allergic reactions; infants <3 months of age are more susceptible to respiratory depression, use with caution and generally in reduced doses in this age group; tolerance or drug dependence may result from extended use

Common Adverse Reactions Frequency not defined.

Cardiovascular: Hypotension, peripheral vasodilation

Central nervous system: Drowsiness, dizziness, insomnia, CNS depression, mental depression, increased intracranial pressure, restlessness, headache, malaise

Gastrointestinal: Constipation, anorexia, stomach cramps, nausea, vomiting, biliary tract spasm

Genitourinary: Ureteral spasms, decreased urination, urinary tract spasm

Hepatic: Increased liver function tests

Neuromuscular & skeletal: Weakness

Ocular: Miosis

(Continued)

Paregoric *(Continued)*

Respiratory: Respiratory depression

Miscellaneous: Physical and psychological dependence, histamine release

Drug Interactions

Increased Effect/Toxicity: Increased effect/toxicity with CNS depressants (eg, alcohol, narcotics, benzodiazepines, tricyclic antidepressants, MAO inhibitors, phenothiazine).

Mechanism of Action Increases smooth muscle tone in GI tract, decreases motility and peristalsis, diminishes digestive secretions

Pharmacodynamics/Kinetics In terms of opium:

Metabolism: Hepatic

Excretion: Urine (primarily as morphine glucuronide conjugates and unchanged drug - morphine, codeine, papaverine, etc)

Dosage Oral:

Neonatal opiate withdrawal: 3-6 drops every 3-6 hours as needed, or initially 0.2 mL every 3 hours; increase dosage by approximately 0.05 mL every 3 hours until withdrawal symptoms are controlled; it is rare to exceed 0.7 mL/dose. Stabilize withdrawal symptoms for 3-5 days, then gradually decrease dosage over a 2- to 4-week period.

Children: 0.25-0.5 mL/kg 1-4 times/day

Adults: 5-10 mL 1-4 times/day

Patient Information Avoid alcohol, may cause drowsiness, impaired judgment or coordination; may cause physical and psychological dependence with prolonged use

Dosage Forms LIQ: 2 mg morphine equivalent/5 mL (473 mL)

Paricalcitol *(pah ri KAL si tole)*

U.S. Brand Names Zemplar™

Therapeutic Category Vitamin D Analog

Use Prevention and treatment of secondary hyperparathyroidism associated with chronic renal failure. Has been evaluated only in hemodialysis patients.

Pregnancy Risk Factor C

Contraindications Hypersensitivity to paricalcitol or any component of the formulation; patients with evidence of vitamin D toxicity; hypercalcemia

Warnings/Precautions The most frequently reported adverse reactions with paricalcitol include nausea, vomiting, and edema. Chronic administration can place patients at risk of hypercalcemia, elevated calcium-phosphorus product and metastatic calcification; it should not be used in patients with evidence of hypercalcemia or vitamin D toxicity.

Common Adverse Reactions The three most frequently reported events in clinical studies were nausea, vomiting, and edema, which are commonly seen in hemodialysis patients.

>10%: Gastrointestinal: Nausea (13%)

1% to 10%:

Cardiovascular: Palpitations, peripheral edema (7%)

Central nervous system: Chills, malaise, fever, lightheadedness (5%)

Gastrointestinal: Vomiting (8%), GI bleeding (5%), xerostomia (3%)

Respiratory: Pneumonia (5%)

Miscellaneous: Flu-like symptoms, sepsis

Drug Interactions

Increased Effect/Toxicity: Phosphate or vitamin D-related compounds should not be taken concurrently. Digitalis toxicity is potentiated by hypercalcemia.

Mechanism of Action Synthetic vitamin D analog which has been shown to reduce PTH serum concentrations

Pharmacodynamics/Kinetics

Protein binding: >99%

Excretion: Feces (74%) in healthy subjects; urine (16%); 51% to 59% as metabolites

Dosage Adults: I.V.: 0.04-0.1 mcg/kg (2.8-7 mcg) given as a bolus dose no more frequently than every other day at any time during dialysis; doses as high as 0.24 mcg/kg (16.8 mcg) have been administered safely; usually start with 0.04 mcg/kg 3 times/week by I.V. bolus, increased by 0.04 mcg/kg every 2 weeks; the dose of paricalcitol should be adjusted based on serum PTH levels, as follows:

Same or increasing serum PTH level: Increase paricalcitol dose

Serum PTH level decreased by <30%: Increase paricalcitol dose

Serum PTH level decreased by >30% and <60%: Maintain paricalcitol dose

Serum PTH level decrease by >60%: Decrease paricalcitol dose

Serum PTH level 1.5-3 times upper limit of normal: Maintain paricalcitol dose

Monitoring Parameters Serum calcium and phosphorus should be monitored closely (eg, twice weekly) during dose titration; monitor for signs and symptoms of vitamin D intoxication; serum PTH; in trials, a mean PTH level reduction of 30% was achieved within 6 weeks

Patient Information To ensure effectiveness of therapy, it is important to adhere to a dietary regimen of calcium supplementation and phosphorous restriction; avoid excessive use of aluminum-containing compounds

Dosage Forms INJ, solution: 5 mcg/mL (1 mL, 2 mL)

♦ **Pariprazole** *see* Rabeprazole *on page 1077*
♦ **Parkinson's Agents Comparison** *see page 1402*
♦ **Parlodel®** *see* Bromocriptine *on page 180*
♦ **Parnate®** *see* Tranylcypromine *on page 1253*

Paromomycin (par oh moe MYE sin)

U.S. Brand Names Humatin®

Synonyms Paromomycin Sulfate

Therapeutic Category Amebicide

Use Treatment of acute and chronic intestinal amebiasis; hepatic coma

Unlabeled/Investigational Use Treatment of cryptosporidiosis

Pregnancy Risk Factor C

Contraindications Hypersensitivity to paromomycin or any component of the formulation; intestinal obstruction, renal failure

Warnings/Precautions Use with caution in patients with impaired renal function or possible or proven ulcerative bowel lesions

Common Adverse Reactions

1% to 10%: Gastrointestinal: Diarrhea, abdominal cramps, nausea, vomiting, heartburn

Mechanism of Action Acts directly on ameba; has antibacterial activity against normal and pathogenic organisms in the GI tract; interferes with bacterial protein synthesis by binding to 30S ribosomal subunits

Pharmacodynamics/Kinetics

Absorption: None

Excretion: Feces (100% as unchanged drug)

Dosage Oral:

Intestinal amebiasis: Children and Adults: 25-35 mg/kg/day in 3 divided doses for 5-10 days

Dientamoeba fragilis: Children and Adults: 25-30 mg/kg/day in 3 divided doses for 7 days

Cryptosporidium (unlabeled use): Adults with AIDS: 1.5-2.25 g/day in 3-6 divided doses for 10-14 days (occasionally courses of up to 4-8 weeks may be needed)

Tapeworm (fish, dog, bovine, porcine):

Children: 11 mg/kg every 15 minutes for 4 doses

Adults: 1 g every 15 minutes for 4 doses

Hepatic coma: Adults: 4 g/day in 2-4 divided doses for 5-6 days

Dwarf tapeworm: Children and Adults: 45 mg/kg/dose every day for 5-7 days

Patient Information Take full course of therapy; do not skip doses; report ringing in ears, hearing loss, or dizziness

Dosage Forms CAP: 250 mg

♦ **Paromomycin Sulfate** *see* Paromomycin *on page 959*

Paroxetine (pa ROKS e teen)

Related Information

Antidepressant Agents Comparison *on page 1359*

Selective Serotonin Reuptake Inhibitors (SSRIs) Pharmacokinetics *on page 1403*

U.S. Brand Names Paxil®; Paxil CR™

Therapeutic Category Antidepressant, Selective Serotonin Reuptake Inhibitor (SSRI)

Use Treatment of depression in adults; treatment of panic disorder with or without agoraphobia; obsessive-compulsive disorder (OCD) in adults; social anxiety disorder (social phobia); generalized anxiety disorder (GAD); post-traumatic stress disorder (PTSD)

Paxil CR™: Treatment of depression; panic disorder; premenstrual mood disorder; social anxiety disorder

Unlabeled/Investigational Use May be useful in eating disorders, impulse control disorders, self-injurious behavior; premenstrual disorders, vasomotor symptoms of menopause; treatment of depression and obsessive-compulsive disorder (OCD) in children

Pregnancy Risk Factor C

Contraindications Hypersensitivity to paroxetine or any component of the formulation; use of MAO inhibitors or within 14 days; concurrent use with thioridazine or mesoridazine

Warnings/Precautions Use cautiously in children or during breast-feeding in lactating women. Upon discontinuation of paroxetine therapy, gradually taper dose. If intolerable symptoms occur following a decrease in dosage or upon discontinuation of therapy, then resuming the previous dose with a more gradual taper should be considered. Potential for severe reaction when used with MAO inhibitors - serotonin syndrome (hyperthermia, muscular rigidity, mental status changes/agitation, autonomic instability) may occur. May precipitate a shift to mania or hypomania in patients with bipolar disease. The possibility of a suicide attempt is inherent in major depression and may persist until remission occurs. Use caution in high-risk patients during initiation of therapy. Prescriptions should be written for the smallest quantity consistent with good patient care. Has a low potential to impair cognitive or motor performance - caution operating hazardous machinery or driving. Low potential for sedation or anticholinergic effects relative to cyclic antidepressants. Use caution in patients with a previous seizure disorder or condition predisposing to seizures such as brain damage, alcoholism, or concurrent therapy with other drugs which lower the seizure threshold. Use with caution in patients with hepatic or dysfunction and in elderly patients. May cause hyponatremia/SIADH. Use with caution in patients at risk of bleeding or receiving anticoagulant therapy - may cause impairment in platelet aggregation. Use with caution in patients with renal insufficiency or other concurrent illness (due to limited experience). May cause or exacerbate sexual dysfunction.

Common Adverse Reactions

>10%:

Central nervous system: Headache, somnolence, dizziness, insomnia

Gastrointestinal: Nausea, xerostomia, constipation, diarrhea

Genitourinary: Ejaculatory disturbances

Neuromuscular & skeletal: Weakness

(Continued)

Paroxetine *(Continued)*

Miscellaneous: Diaphoresis

1% to 10%:
Cardiovascular: Palpitations, vasodilation, postural hypotension
Central nervous system: Nervousness, anxiety, yawning, abnormal dreams, dizziness
Dermatologic: Rash
Endocrine & metabolic: Decreased libido, delayed ejaculation
Gastrointestinal: Anorexia, flatulence, vomiting, dyspepsia, taste perversion, weight gain
Genitourinary: Urinary frequency, impotence
Neuromuscular & skeletal: Tremor, paresthesia, myopathy, myalgia

Drug Interactions

Cytochrome P450 Effect: Substrate of CYP2D6 (major); **Inhibits** CYP1A2 (weak), 2B6 (moderate), 2C8/9 (weak), 2C19 (weak), 2D6 (strong), 3A4 (weak)

Increased Effect/Toxicity: Paroxetine should not be used with nonselective MAO inhibitors (phenelzine, isocarboxazid) or other drugs with MAO inhibition (linezolid); fatal reactions have been reported. Wait 5 weeks after stopping fluoxetine before starting a nonselective MAO inhibitor and 2 weeks after stopping an MAO inhibitor before starting paroxetine. Concurrent selegiline has been associated with mania, hypertension, or serotonin syndrome (risk may be reduced relative to nonselective MAO inhibitors).

Phenothiazines: Paroxetine may inhibit the metabolism of thioridazine or mesoridazine, resulting in increased plasma levels and increasing the risk of QT_c interval prolongation. This may lead to serious ventricular arrhythmias, such as torsade de pointes-type arrhythmias and sudden death. Do not use together. Wait at least 5 weeks after discontinuing paroxetine prior to starting thioridazine.

CYP2D6 inhibitors may increase the levels/effects of paroxetine; example inhibitors include chlorpromazine, delavirdine, fluoxetine, miconazole, pergolide, quinidine, quinine, ritonavir, and ropinirole.

Combined used of SSRIs and amphetamines, buspirone, meperidine, nefazodone, serotonin agonists (such as sumatriptan), sibutramine, other SSRIs, sympathomimetics, ritonavir, tramadol, and venlafaxine may increase the risk of serotonin syndrome. Paroxetine may increase serum levels/effects of benzodiazepines (alprazolam and diazepam), carbamazepine, carvedilol, clozapine, cyclosporine (and possibly tacrolimus), dextromethorphan, digoxin, haloperidol, HMG-CoA reductase inhibitors (lovastatin and simvastatin - increasing the risk of rhabdomyolysis), phenytoin, propafenone, theophylline, trazodone, tricyclic antidepressants, and valproic acid. Concurrent lithium may increase risk of nephrotoxicity. Risk of hyponatremia may increase with concurrent use of loop diuretics (bumetanide, furosemide, torsemide). Paroxetine may increase the hypoprothrombinemic response to warfarin. Combined use of sumatriptan (and other serotonin agonists) may result in toxicity; weakness, hyper-reflexia, and incoordination have been observed with sumatriptan and SSRIs. In addition, concurrent use may theoretically increase the risk of serotonin syndrome; includes sumatriptan, naratriptan, rizatriptan, and zolmitriptan.

Decreased Effect: Cyproheptadine, a serotonin antagonist, may inhibit the effects of serotonin reuptake inhibitors (paroxetine).

Mechanism of Action Paroxetine is a selective serotonin reuptake inhibitor, chemically unrelated to tricyclic, tetracyclic, or other antidepressants; presumably, the inhibition of serotonin reuptake from brain synapse stimulated serotonin activity in the brain

Pharmacodynamics/Kinetics

Distribution: V_d: 8.7 L/kg (3-28 L/kg)

Protein binding: 93% to 95%

Metabolism: Extensively hepatic via CYP enzymes via oxidation and methylation; nonlinear pharmacokinetics may be seen with higher doses and longer duration of therapy

Half-life elimination: 21 hours (3-65 hours)

Time to peak, serum: Immediate release: 5.2 hours; controlled release: 6-10 hours

Excretion: As metabolites in urine and bile; 2% as unchanged drug in urine

Dosage Oral:

Children:
Depression (unlabeled use; not recommended by FDA): Initial: 10 mg/day and adjusted upward on an individual basis to 20 mg/day
OCD (unlabeled use): Initial: 10 mg/day and titrate up as necessary to 60 mg/day
Self-injurious behavior (unlabeled use): 20 mg/day
Social phobia (unlabeled use): 2.5-15 mg/day

Adults:
Depression: Initial: 20 mg once daily, preferably in the morning; increase if needed by 10 mg/day increments at intervals of at least 1 week; maximum dose: 50 mg/day
Paxil CR™: Initial: 25 mg once daily; increase if needed by 12.5 mg/day increments at intervals of at least 1 week; maximum dose: 62.5 mg/day
GAD: Initial: 20 mg once daily, preferably in the morning; doses of 20-50 mg/day were used in clinical trials, however, no greater benefit was seen with doses >20 mg. If dose is increased, adjust in increments of 10 mg/day at 1-week intervals.
OCD: Initial: 20 mg once daily, preferably in the morning; increase if needed by 10 mg/day increments at intervals of at least 1 week; recommended dose: 40 mg/day; range: 20-60 mg/day; maximum dose: 60 mg/day
Panic disorder: Initial: 10 mg once daily, preferably in the morning; increase if needed by 10 mg/day increments at intervals of at least 1 week; recommended dose: 40 mg/day; range: 10-60 mg/day; maximum dose: 60 mg/day

Paxil CR™: Initial: 12.5 mg once daily; increase if needed by 12.5 mg/day at intervals of at least 1 week; maximum dose: 75 mg/day

Premenstrual mood disorder (Paxil CR™): Initial: 12.5 mg once daily; may be increased to 25 mg/day; dosing changes should occur at intervals of at least 1 week

PTSD: Initial: 20 mg once daily, preferably in the morning; increase if needed by 10 mg/day increments at intervals of at least 1 week; range: 20-50 mg

Social anxiety disorder: Initial: 20 mg once daily, preferably in the morning; recommended dose: 20 mg/day; range: 20-60 mg/day; doses >20 mg may not have additional benefit

Paxil CR™: Initial: 12.5 mg once daily, preferably in the morning; may be increased by 12.5 mg/day at intervals of at least 1 week; maximum dose: 37.5 mg/day

Vasomotor symptoms of menopause (unlabeled use): Paxil CR™: 12.5-25 mg/day

Elderly: Initial: 10 mg/day; increase if needed by 10 mg/day increments at intervals of at least 1 week; maximum dose: 40 mg/day

Paxil CR™: Initial: 12.5 mg/day; increase if needed by 12.5 mg/day increments at intervals of at least 1 week; maximum dose: 50 mg/day

Note: Upon discontinuation of paroxetine therapy, gradually taper dose:

Paxil®: Taper-phase regimen used in PTSD/GAD clinical trials involved an incremental decrease in the daily dose by 10 mg/day at weekly intervals; when 20 mg/day dose was reached, this dose was continued for 1 week before treatment was discontinued.

Paxil CR™: Patients receiving 37.5 mg/day in clinical trials had their dose decreased by 12.5 mg/day to a dose of 25 mg/day and remained at a dose of 25 mg/day for 1 week before treatment was discontinued.

Dosage adjustment in severe renal/hepatic impairment: Adults: Initial: 10 mg/day; increase if needed by 10 mg/day increments at intervals of at least 1 week; maximum dose: 40 mg/day

Paxil CR™: Initial: 12.5 mg/day; increase if needed by 12.5 mg/day increments at intervals of at least 1 week; maximum dose: 50 mg/day

Administration May be administered with or without food. Do not crush, break, or chew controlled release tablets.

Monitoring Parameters Hepatic and renal function tests, blood pressure, heart rate

Dosage Forms SUSP, oral (Paxil®): 10 mg/5 mL (250 mL). **TAB** (Paxil®): 10 mg, 20 mg, 30 mg, 40 mg. **TAB, controlled release** (Paxil CR™): 12.5 mg, 25 mg, 37.5 mg

Pegademase Bovine (peg A de mase BOE vine)

U.S. Brand Names Adagen®

Therapeutic Category Enzyme, Replacement Therapy

Use Orphan drug: Enzyme replacement therapy for adenosine deaminase (ADA) deficiency in patients with severe combined immunodeficiency disease (SCID) who can not benefit from bone marrow transplant; not a cure for SCID, unlike bone marrow transplants, injections must be used the rest of the child's life, therefore is not really an alternative

Pregnancy Risk Factor C

Contraindications Hypersensitivity to pegademase bovine or any component of the formulation; not to be used as preparatory or support therapy for bone marrow transplantation

Warnings/Precautions Use with caution in patients with thrombocytopenia.

Mechanism of Action Adenosine deaminase is an enzyme that catalyzes the deamination of both adenosine and deoxyadenosine. Hereditary lack of adenosine deaminase activity results in severe combined immunodeficiency disease, a fatal disorder of infancy characterized by profound defects of both cellular and humoral immunity. It is estimated that 25% of patients with the autosomal recessive form of severe combined immunodeficiency lack adenosine deaminase.

Pharmacodynamics/Kinetics

Absorption: Rapid

Half-life elimination: 48-72 hours

Time to peak: Plasma adenosine deaminase activity: 2-3 weeks

Dosage Children: I.M.: Dose given every 7 days, 10 units/kg the first dose, 15 units/kg the second dose, and 20 units/kg the third dose; maintenance dose: 20 units/kg/week is recommended depending on patient's ADA level; maximum single dose: 30 units/kg

Patient Information Not a cure for SCID; unlike bone marrow transplants, injections must be used the rest of the child's life; frequent blood tests are necessary to monitor effect and adjust the dose as needed

Dosage Forms INJ, solution: 250 units/mL (1.5 mL)

Pegaspargase (peg AS par jase)

U.S. Brand Names Oncaspar®

Synonyms NSC-644954; PEG-L-asparaginase

Therapeutic Category Antineoplastic Agent, Protein Synthesis Inhibitor

Use Treatment of acute lymphocytic leukemia, blast crisis of chronic lymphocytic leukemia (CLL), salvage therapy of non-Hodgkin's lymphoma; may be used in some patients who have had hypersensitivity reactions to *E. coli* asparaginase

Pregnancy Risk Factor C

Contraindications Hypersensitivity to pegaspargase or any component of the formulation; pancreatitis or a history of pancreatitis; patients who have had significant hemorrhagic events associated with prior asparaginase therapy; previous serious allergic reactions, such as generalized urticaria, bronchospasm, laryngeal edema, hypotension, or other unacceptable adverse reactions to pegaspargase

Warnings/Precautions The U.S. Food and Drug Administration (FDA) currently recommends that procedures for proper handling and disposal of antineoplastic agents be considered.

Hypersensitivity reactions to pegaspargase, including life-threatening anaphylaxis, may occur during therapy, especially in patients with known hypersensitivity to the other forms of asparaginase. As a routine precaution, keep patients under observation for 1 hour with resuscitation equipment and other agents necessary to treat anaphylaxis (eg, epinephrine, oxygen, I.V. steroids) available. Use caution when treating patients with pegaspargase in combination with hepatotoxic agents, especially when liver dysfunction is present

Common Adverse Reactions In general, pegaspargase toxicities tend to be less frequent and appear somewhat later than comparable toxicities of asparaginase. Intramuscular rather than intravenous injection may decrease the incidence of coagulopathy; GI, hepatic, and renal toxicity.

>10%:

Cardiovascular: Edema

Central nervous system: Fatigue, disorientation (10%)

Gastrointestinal: Nausea, vomiting (50% to 60%), generally mild to moderate, but may be severe and protracted in some patients; anorexia (33%); abdominal pain (38%); diarrhea (28%); increased serum lipase and amylase

Hematologic: Hypofibrinogenemia and depression of clotting factors V and VII, variable decreases in factors VII and IX, severe protein C deficiency and decrease in antithrombin III - overt bleeding is uncommon, but may be dose-limiting, or fatal in some patients

Hypersensitivity: Acute allergic reactions, including fever, rash, urticaria, arthralgia, hypotension, angioedema, bronchospasm, anaphylaxis (10% to 30%) - dose-limiting in some patients

Neuromuscular & skeletal: Weakness (33%)

1% to 10%:

Cardiovascular: Hypotension, tachycardia, thrombosis

Dermatologic: Urticaria, erythema, lip edema

Endocrine & metabolic: Hyperglycemia (3%)

Gastrointestinal: Acute pancreatitis (1%)

Drug Interactions
Increased Effect/Toxicity:
Aspirin, dipyridamole, heparin, warfarin, NSAIDs: Imbalances in coagulation factors have been noted with the use of pegaspargase - use with caution.

Vincristine and prednisone: An increased toxicity has been noticed when asparaginase is administered with VCR and prednisone.

Cyclophosphamide (decreased metabolism)

Mercaptopurine (increased hepatotoxicity)

Vincristine (increased neuropathy)

Prednisone (hyperglycemia)

Decreased Effect: Asparaginase terminates methotrexate action by inhibition of protein synthesis and prevention of cell entry into the S Phase.

Mechanism of Action Pegaspargase is a modified version of asparaginase. Leukemic cells, especially lymphoblasts, require exogenous asparagine; normal cells can synthesize asparagine. Asparaginase contains L-asparaginase amidohydrolase type EC-2 which inhibits protein synthesis by deaminating asparagine to aspartic acid and ammonia in the plasma and extracellular fluid and therefore deprives tumor cells of the amino acid for protein synthesis. Asparaginase is cycle-specific for the G_1 phase of the cell cycle.

Pharmacodynamics/Kinetics
Duration: Asparaginase was measurable for at least 15 days following initial treatment with pegaspargase

Distribution: V_d: 4-5 L/kg; 70% to 80% of plasma volume; does not penetrate the CSF

Metabolism: Systemically degraded

Half-life elimination: 5.73 days; unaffected by age, renal or hepatic function

Excretion: Urine (trace amounts)

Dosage Refer to individual protocols.

I.M. administration is **preferred** over I.V. administration; I.M. administration may decrease the incidence of hepatotoxicity, coagulopathy, and GI and renal disorders

Children: I.M., I.V.:
Body surface area <0.6 m²: 82.5 international units/kg every 14 days
Body surface area ≥0.6 m²: 2500 international units/m² every 14 days

Adults: I.M., I.V.: 2500 international units/m² every 14 days

Hemodialysis: Significant drug removal is unlikely based on physiochemical characteristics

Peritoneal dialysis: Significant drug removal is unlikely based on physiochemical characteristics

Administration
I.M.: Must only be administered as a deep intramuscular injection into a large muscle

I.V.: May be administered as a 1- to 2-hour I.V. infusion; **do not administer I.V. push**. Some institutions recommend the following precautions for pegaspargase administration: Have parenteral epinephrine, diphenhydramine, and hydrocortisone available at the bedside; have a freely-running I.V. in place; have a physician readily accessible; monitor the patient closely for 30-60 minutes

Monitoring Parameters Vital signs during administration, coagulation factors, amylase, liver enzymes, prothrombin time, renal function tests, urine dipstick for glucose, blood glucose

Patient Information This drug can only be given I.M. or I.V. Inform prescriber if you are using any other medications that may increase risk of bleeding. Possibility of hypersensitivity reactions includes anaphylaxis. Maintain adequate hydration (2-3 L/day of fluids unless instructed to restrict fluid intake) and nutrition (small frequent meals may help if you experience nausea, vomiting, or loss of appetite). You may experience dizziness, drowsiness, syncope, or blurred vision (use caution when driving or engaging in tasks that require alertness until response to drug is known). You may experience increased sweating, decreased sexual drive, or cough. Report immediately chest pain or heart palpitations; difficulty breathing or constant cough; rash, hives, or swelling of lips or mouth; or abdominal pain. Report swelling of extremities or sudden weight gain; burning, pain, or redness at infusion site; persistent fever or chills; unusual bruising or bleeding; twitching or tremors; pain on urination; or persistent nausea or diarrhea.

Dosage Forms INJ [preservative free]: 750 units/mL

♦ **Pegasys**® see Peginterferon Alfa-2a on page 964

Pegfilgrastim (peg fil GRA stim)
U.S. Brand Names Neulasta™

Synonyms G-CSF (PEG Conjugate); Granulocyte Colony Stimulating Factor (PEG Conjugate)

Therapeutic Category Colony-Stimulating Factor

Use Decrease the incidence of infection, by stimulation of granulocyte production, in patients with nonmyeloid malignancies receiving myelosuppressive therapy associated with a significant risk of febrile neutropenia

Pregnancy Risk Factor C

Contraindications Hypersensitivity to pegfilgrastim, filgrastim, E. coli-derived proteins, or any component of the formulation; concurrent myelosuppressive, chemotherapy, or radiation therapy

Warnings/Precautions Complete blood count and platelet count should be obtained prior to chemotherapy. Do not use pegfilgrastim in the period 14 days before to 24 hours after administration of cytotoxic chemotherapy because of the potential sensitivity of rapidly dividing myeloid cells to cytotoxic chemotherapy. Pegfilgrastim can potentially act as a growth factor for any tumor type, particularly myeloid malignancies. Precaution should be exercised in the (Continued)

Pegfilgrastim *(Continued)*

usage of pegfilgrastim in any malignancy with myeloid characteristics. Tumors of nonhemato-poietic origin may have surface receptors for pegfilgrastim.

Allergic-type reactions have occurred in patients receiving the parent compound, filgrastim (G-CSF) with first or later doses. Reactions tended to occur more frequently with intravenous administration and within 30 minutes of infusion. Rare cases of splenic rupture or adult respiratory distress syndrome have been reported in association with filgrastim; patients must be instructed to report left upper quadrant pain or shoulder tip pain or respiratory distress. Use caution in patients with sickle cell diseases; sickle cell crises have been reported following filgrastim therapy. Safety and efficacy in pediatric patients have not been established; not for use in adolescents weighing <45 kg.

Common Adverse Reactions
>10%
Neuromuscular & skeletal: Bone pain (medullary, 26%)
Hepatic: Increased LDH (19%)
1% to 10%
Endocrine & metabolic: Uric acid increased (8%)
Hepatic: Alkaline phosphatase increased (9%)

Drug Interactions
Increased Effect/Toxicity: No formal drug interactions studies have been conducted. Lithium may potentiate release of neutrophils.

Mechanism of Action Stimulates the production, maturation, and activation of neutrophils, pegfilgrastim activates neutrophils to increase both their migration and cytotoxicity. Pegfil-grastim has a prolonged duration of effect relative to filgrastim and a reduced renal clearance.

Pharmacodynamics/Kinetics Half-life elimination: S.C.: 15-80 hours

Dosage S.C.: Adolescents >45 kg and Adults: 6 mg once per chemotherapy cycle; do not administer in the period between 14 days before and 24 hours after administration of cytotoxic chemotherapy; do not use in patients infants, children and smaller adolescents weighing <45 kg

Administration Do not use 6 mg fixed dose in infants, children, or adolescents <45 kg. Engage/activate needle guard following use to prevent accidental needlesticks.

Monitoring Parameters Complete blood count and platelet count should be obtained prior to chemotherapy. Leukocytosis (white blood cell counts 100,000/mm^3) has been observed in <1% of patients receiving pegfilgrastim. Monitor platelets and hematocrit regularly.

Reference Range No clinical benefit seen with ANC >10,000/mm^3.

Patient Information Follow directions for proper storage and administration of S.C. medica-tion. Never reuse syringes or needles. You may experience bone pain (request analgesic). Report unusual fever or chills; unhealed sores; severe bone pain; pain, redness, or swelling at injection site; pain in the upper abdomen or shoulder tip; unusual swelling of extremities or difficulty breathing; or chest pain and palpitations.

Dosage Forms INJ, solution [prefilled syringe; preservative free]: 10 mg/mL (0.6 mL)

Peginterferon Alfa-2a *(peg in ter FEER on AL fa too aye)*

U.S. Brand Names Pegasys®

Synonyms Interferon Alfa-2a (PEG Conjugate); Pegylated Interferon Alfa-2a

Therapeutic Category Biological Response Modulator; Interferon

Use Treatment of chronic hepatitis C, alone or in combination with ribavirin, in patients with compensated liver disease

Pregnancy Risk Factor C

Contraindications Hypersensitivity to polyethylene glycol (PEG), interferon alfa, or any component of the formulation; autoimmune hepatitis; decompensated liver disease; previous treatment with interferon; neonates and infants

Warnings/Precautions Severe psychiatric adverse effects (including depression, suicidal ideation, and suicide attempt) may occur. Avoid use in severe psychiatric disorders; use caution with history of depression. Use caution with prior cardiovascular disease, endocrine disorders, autoimmune disorders, and pulmonary dysfunction. Discontinue treatment with worsening or persistently severe signs/symptoms of autoimmune, infectious, ischemic (including radiographic changes or worsening hepatic function), or neuropsychiatric disorders (including depression and/or suicidal thoughts/behavior). Use caution with renal dysfunction (Cl$_{cr}$<50 mL/minute). Patients with renal dysfunction should be monitored for signs/symptoms of toxicity (dosage adjustment required if toxicity occurs). Ophthalmologic disorders (including retinal hemorrhages, cotton wool spots, and retinal artery or vein obstruction) have been reported. Prior to start of therapy, visual exams are recommended.

Use caution with baseline neutrophil count <1500/mm^3, platelet count <90,000/mm^3 or hemo-globin <10 g/dL. Discontinue therapy (at least temporarily) if ANC <500/mm^3 or platelet count <25,000/mm^3; colitis develops; known or suspected pancreatitis develops. Pancreatitis has occurred during alpha interferon and ribavirin treatment. Transient elevations in ALT have been reported; discontinue if ALT increase is progressive or accompanied by increased bili-rubin.

Use caution in geriatric patients. Safety and efficacy have not been established in patients who have failed other alpha interferon therapy, received organ transplants, have been infected with HIV or hepatitis B, or for treatment >48 weeks. Due to differences in dosage, patient should not change brands of interferon. Safety and efficacy have not been established in children.

Common Adverse Reactions Note: Percentages indicated as "with ribavirin" are those which have been seen with peginterferon alfa-2b/ribavirin combination therapy.

>10%:

Central nervous system: Headache (54%), fatigue (50%), pyrexia (36%), insomnia (19%; 30% with ribavirin), depression (1% to 18%), dizziness (16%), irritability (13%), irritability/ anxiety/nervousness (33% with ribavirin), pain (11%)

Dermatologic: Alopecia (23%), pruritus (12%; 19% with ribavirin), dermatitis (16% with ribavirin)

Gastrointestinal: Nausea (5% to 23%), anorexia (17%; 24% with ribavirin), diarrhea (16%), abdominal pain (15%)

Hematologic: Neutropenia (21%), lymphopenia (14% with ribavirin), anemia (11% with riba-virin)

Local: Injection site reaction (22%)

Neuromuscular & skeletal: Myalgia (37%), rigors (32%), arthralgia (28%)

Respiratory: Dyspnea (13% with ribavirin)

1% to 10%:

Central nervous system: Concentration impaired (8%), anxiety (6%), memory impaired (5%)

Dermatologic: Dermatitis (8%), rash (5%), eczema (5% with ribavirin)

Endocrine & metabolic: Hypothyroidism (4%), hyperthyroidism (1%)

Gastrointestinal: Xerostomia (6%), vomiting (5%)

Hematologic: Thrombocytopenia (5%), platelets decreased <50,000/mm^3 (5%)

Neuromuscular & skeletal: Back pain (9%), weakness (5%)

Miscellaneous: Diaphoresis (6%)

Drug Interactions

Cytochrome P450 Effect: Inhibits CYP1A2 (weak)

Increased Effect/Toxicity: Interferons may increase the risk of neutropenia when used with ACE inhibitors; fluorouracil concentrations doubled with interferon alpha-2b; interferon alpha may decrease the metabolism of theophylline and zidovudine; interferons may increase the anticoagulant effects of warfarin

Decreased Effect: Prednisone may decrease the therapeutic effects of interferon alpha; interferon alpha may decrease the serum concentrations of melphalan

Mechanism of Action Alpha interferons are a family of proteins, produced by nucleated cells, that have antiviral, antiproliferative, and immune-regulating activity. There are 16 known subtypes of alpha interferons. Interferons interact with cells through high affinity cell surface receptors. Following activation, multiple effects can be detected including induction of gene transcription. Inhibits cellular growth, alters the state of cellular differentiation, interferes with oncogene expression, alters cell surface antigen expression, increases phagocytic activity of macrophages, and augments cytotoxicity of lymphocytes for target cells.

Pharmacodynamics/Kinetics

Half-life elimination: Terminal: 80 hours; increased with renal dysfunction

Time to peak, serum: 72-96 hours

Dosage S.C.: Adults: Chronic hepatitis C:

Monotherapy: 180 mcg once weekly for 48 weeks

Combination therapy with ribavirin: Recommended dosage: 180 mcg once/week with ribavirin (Copegus™)

Note: Duration of therapy based on genotype:

Genotype 1,4: Treat for 48 weeks

Genotype 2,3: Treat for 24 weeks

Dose modification:

For moderate to severe adverse reactions: Initial: 135 mcg/week; may need decreased to 90 mcg/week in some cases

Based on hematologic parameters:

ANC <750/mm^3: 135 mcg/week

ANC <500/mm^3: Suspend therapy until >1000/mm^3, then restart at 90 mcg/week and monitor

Platelet count <50,000/mm^3: 90 mcg/week

Platelet count <25,000/mm^3: Discontinue therapy

Depression (severity based on DSM-IV criteria):

Mild depression: No dosage adjustment required; evaluate once weekly by visit/phone call. If depression remains stable, continue weekly visits. If depression improves, resume normal visit schedule

Moderate depression: Decrease interferon dose to 90-135 mcg once/week; evaluate once weekly with an office visit at least every other week. If depression remains stable, consider psychiatric evaluation and continue with reduced dosing. If symptoms improve and remain stable for 4 weeks, resume normal visit schedule; continue reduced dosing or return to normal dose.

Severe depression: Discontinue interferon permanently. Obtain immediate psychiatric consultation. Discontinue ribavirin if using concurrently.

Dosage adjustment in renal impairment: End-stage renal disease requiring hemodialysis: 135 mcg/week; monitor for toxicity

Dosage adjustment in hepatic impairment: ALT progressively rising above baseline: Decrease dose to 135 mcg/week. If ALT continues to rise or is accompanied by increased bilirubin or hepatic decompensation, discontinue therapy immediately.

Administration S.C.: Administer in the abdomen or thigh. Rotate injection site. Do not use if solution contains particulate matter or is discolored. Discard unused solution.

Monitoring Parameters Standard hematological tests should be performed prior to therapy, at week 2, and periodically. Standard biochemical tests should be performed prior to therapy, at (Continued)

Peginterferon Alfa-2a *(Continued)*

week 4, and periodically. Evaluate for depression and other psychiatric symptoms before and during therapy; baseline eye examination and periodically in patients with baseline disorders; baseline echocardiogram in patients with cardiac disease; serum HCV RNA levels after 12 weeks of treatment

Clinical studies tested as follows: CBC (including hemoglobin, WBC, and platelets) and chemistries (including liver function tests and uric acid) measured at weeks 1, 2, 4, 6, and 8, and then every 4 weeks; TSH measured every 12 weeks

In addition, the following baseline values were used as entrance criteria:
Platelet count ≥90,000/mm³ (as low as 75,000/mm³ in patients with cirrhosis or transition to cirrhosis)
ANC ≥1500/mm³
Serum creatinine <1.5 times ULN
TSH and T_4 within normal limits or adequately controlled

Consider discontinuing treatment if virologic tests indicate no response by week 12.

Patient Information You may be taught to give yourself the injection if you are willing and able to learn. Blood work will be done before the start of this medicine and during its use. Other tests may be needed depending on your medical history. An eye examination is recommended before starting treatment. Maintain adequate hydration (2-3 L/day of fluids unless instructed to restrict fluid intake). Avoid alcohol. You may experience flu-like syndrome (giving the medicine at bedtime or using acetaminophen may help), nausea and vomiting (frequent small meals, frequent mouth care, sucking lozenges, or chewing gum may help), feeling tired (use caution when driving or engaging in tasks requiring alertness until response to drug is known), or headache. Report persistent abdominal pain, bloody diarrhea, and fever; symptoms of depression, suicidal ideas; unusual bruising or bleeding, any signs or symptoms of infection, unusual fatigue, chest pain or palpitations, difficulty breathing, wheezing, severe nausea or vomiting.

Dosage Forms INJ, solution: 180 mcg/mL (1.2 mL); **INJ, solution** [prefilled syringe]: 180 mcg/mL (0.5 mL).

Peginterferon Alfa-2b (peg in ter FEER on AL fa too bee)

U.S. Brand Names PEG-Intron®

Synonyms Interferon Alfa-2b (PEG Conjugate); Pegylated Interferon Alfa-2b

Therapeutic Category Antiviral Agent, Hepatitis; Biological Response Modulator; Interferon

Use Treatment of chronic hepatitis C (as monotherapy or in combination with ribavirin) in adult patients who have never received interferon alpha and have compensated liver disease

Restrictions Patients must have an Access Assurance ID number (obtained by calling Schering-Plough at 1-888-437-2608). Pharmacists should receive the ID number from the patient, and must obtain an order authorization number from the manufacturer prior to placing an order with their wholesaler (effective October 22, 2001). The patient's authorization number will be retained throughout therapy. This number may be inactivated if the patient fails to fill the prescription over any 60-day period, and access will no longer be assured by the manufacturer.

Pregnancy Risk Factor C (manufacturer) as monotherapy; X in combination with ribavirin

Contraindications Hypersensitivity to polyethylene glycol (PEG), interferon alfa, or any component of the formulation; autoimmune hepatitis; decompensated liver disease; previous treatment with interferon; severe psychiatric disorder; pregnancy (in combination with ribavirin)

Warnings/Precautions Severe psychiatric adverse effects, including depression, suicidal ideation, and suicide attempt, may occur. Avoid use in severe psychiatric disorders. Use with caution in patients with a history of depression. Use caution in patients with cardiovascular disease, endocrine disorders, autoimmune disorders, and pulmonary dysfunction. Avoid use in renal dysfunction (Cl_{cr} <50 mL/minute). Use caution in geriatric patients, patients with chronic immunosuppression, low peripheral blood counts or myelosuppression, including concurrent use of myelosuppressive therapy. Discontinue therapy when significant decreases in neutrophil (<0.5 x 10^9/L) or platelet counts (<50,000/mm³); colitis develops; known or suspected pancreatitis develops. Treatment should be discontinued in patients with worsening or persistently severe signs/symptoms of autoimmune, infectious, ischemic (including radiographic changes or worsening hepatic function), or neuropsychiatric disorders (including depression and/or suicidal thoughts/behavior). Visual exams are recommended for patients with diabetes mellitus or hypertension. Safety and efficacy have not been established in children.

Common Adverse Reactions

>10% :
Central nervous system: Headache (56%), fatigue (52%), depression (16% to 29%), anxiety/emotional liability/irritability (28%), insomnia (23%), fever (22%), dizziness (12%), impaired concentration (5% to 12%), pain (12%)
Dermatologic: Alopecia (22%), pruritus (12%), dry skin (11%)
Gastrointestinal: Nausea (26%), anorexia (20%), diarrhea (18%), abdominal pain (15%), weight loss (11%)
Local: Injection site inflammation/reaction (47%),
Neuromuscular & skeletal: Musculoskeletal pain (56%), myalgia (38% to 42%), rigors (23% to 45%)
Respiratory: Epistaxis (14%), nasopharyngitis (11%)
Miscellaneous: Flu-like syndrome (46%), viral infection (11%)

>1% to 10%:
Cardiovascular: Flushing (6%)
Central nervous system: Malaise (8%)

Dermatologic: Rash (6%), dermatitis (7%)
Endocrine & metabolic: Hypothyroidism (5%)
Gastrointestinal: Vomiting (7%), dyspepsia (6%), taste perversion
Hematologic: Neutropenia, thrombocytopenia
Hepatic: Transient increase in transaminases (10%), hepatomegaly (6%)
Local: Injection site pain (2%)
Neuromuscular & skeletal: Hypertonia (5%)
Respiratory: Pharyngitis (10%), sinusitis (7%), cough (6%)
Miscellaneous: Diaphoresis (6%)

Drug Interactions
Cytochrome P450 Effect: Inhibits CYP1A2 (weak)
Increased Effect/Toxicity: ACE inhibitors, clozapine, erythropoietin may increase risk of bone marrow suppression. Fluorouracil, theophylline, zidovudine concentrations may increase. Warfarin's anticoagulant effect may increase.
Decreased Effect: Melphalan concentrations may decrease. Prednisone may decrease effects of interferon alpha.

Mechanism of Action Alpha interferons are a family of proteins, produced by nucleated cells, that have antiviral, antiproliferative, and immune-regulating activity. There are 16 known subtypes of alpha interferons. Interferons interact with cells through high affinity cell surface receptors. Following activation, multiple effects can be detected including induction of gene transcription. Inhibits cellular growth, alters the state of cellular differentiation, interferes with oncogene expression, alters cell surface antigen expression, increases phagocytic activity of macrophages, and augments cytotoxicity of lymphocytes for target cells.

Pharmacodynamics/Kinetics
Bioavailability: Increases with chronic dosing
Half-life elimination: 40 hours
Time to peak: 15-44 hours
Excretion: Urine (30%)

Dosage S.C.:
Children: Safety and efficacy have not been established
Adults: Chronic hepatitis C: Administer dose once weekly; **Note:** Usual duration is for 1 year; after 24 weeks of treatment, if serum HCV RNA is not below the limit of detection of the assay, consider discontinuation:
Monotherapy: Initial:
≤45 kg: 40 mcg
46-56 kg: 50 mcg
57-72 kg: 64 mcg
73-88 kg: 80 mcg
89-106 kg: 96 mcg
107-136 kg: 120 mcg
137-160 kg: 150 mcg
Combination therapy with ribavirin (400 mg twice daily): Initial: 1.5 mcg/kg/week
<40 kg: 50 mcg
40-50 kg: 64 mcg
51-60 kg: 80 mcg
61-75 kg: 96 mcg
76-85 kg: 120 mcg
>85 kg: 150 mcg
Elderly: May require dosage reduction based upon renal dysfunction, but no established guidelines are available.

Dosage adjustment if serious adverse event occurs: Depression (severity based upon DSM-IV criteria):
Mild depression: No dosage adjustment required; evaluate once weekly by visit/phone call. If depression remains stable, continue weekly visits. If depression improves, resume normal visit schedule.
Moderate depression: Decrease interferon dose by 50%; evaluate once weekly with an office visit at least every other week. If depression remains stable, consider psychiatric evaluation and continue with reduced dosing. If symptoms improve and remain stable for 4 weeks, resume normal visit schedule; continue reduced dosing or return to normal dose.
Severe depression: Discontinue interferon and ribavirin permanently. Obtain immediate psychiatric consultation.

Dosage adjustment in renal impairment: Monitor for signs and symptoms of toxicity and if toxicity occurs then adjust dose. Do not use patients with Cl_{cr} <50 mL/minute. Patients were excluded from the clinical trials if serum creatinine >1.5 times the upper limits of normal.
Dosage adjustment in hepatic impairment: Contraindicated in decompensated liver disease
Dosage adjustment in hematologic toxicity:
Hemoglobin:
Hemoglobin <10 g/dL: Continue current peginterferon alfa-2b dose; decrease ribavirin dose by 200 mg/day.
Hemoglobin <8.5 g/dL: Permanently discontinue peginterferon alfa-2b and ribavirin.
Hemoglobin decrease >2 g/dL in any 4-week period and stable cardiac disease: Decrease peginterferon alfa-2b dose by half; decrease ribavirin dose by 200 mg per day. Hemoglobin <12 g/dL after ribavirin dose is decreased: Permanently discontinue both peginterferon alfa-2b and ribavirin.
White blood cells:
WBC <1.5 x 10^9/L: Decrease peginterferon alfa-2b dose by half.
(Continued)

Peginterferon Alfa-2b *(Continued)*

WBC <1.0 x 10⁹/L: Permanently discontinue peginterferon alfa-2b and ribavirin.

Neutrophils:

Neutrophils <0.75 x 10⁹/L: Decrease peginterferon alfa-2b dose by half.

Neutrophils <0.5 x 10⁹/L: Permanently discontinue peginterferon alfa-2b and ribavirin.

Platelets:

Platelet count <80 x 10⁹/L: Decrease peginterferon alfa-2b dose by half.

Platelet count <50 x 10⁹/L: Permanently discontinue peginterferon alfa-2b and ribavirin.

Administration For S.C. administration; rotate injection site

Monitoring Parameters Baseline and periodic TSH, hematology (including CBC with differential, platelets), and chemistry (including LFTs) testing. Evaluate for depression and other psychiatric symptoms before and after initiation of therapy; baseline eye examination in diabetic and hypertensive patients; baseline echocardiogram in patients with cardiac disease; serum HCV RNA levels after 24 weeks of treatment

Patient Information Blood work will be done before the start of this medicine and during its use. Maintain adequate hydration (2-3 L/day of fluids unless instructed to restrict fluid intake). You may experience flu-like syndrome (giving the medicine at bedtime or using acetaminophen may help), nausea and vomiting (frequent small meals, frequent mouth care, sucking lozenges, or chewing gum may help), feeling tired (use caution when driving or engaging in tasks requiring alertness until response to drug is known), or headache. Report persistent abdominal pain, bloody diarrhea, and fever; symptoms of depression, suicidal ideas; unusual bruising or bleeding, any signs or symptoms of infection, unusual fatigue, chest pain or palpitations, difficulty breathing, wheezing, severe nausea or vomiting.

Dosage Forms INJ, powder for reconstitution: 50 mcg, 80 mcg, 120 mcg, 150 mcg

♦ **PEG-Intron®** *see* Peginterferon Alfa-2b *on page 966*

♦ **PEG-L-asparaginase** *see* Pegaspargase *on page 962*

Pegvisomant *(peg VI soe mant)*

U.S. Brand Names Somavert®

Synonyms B2036-PEG

Therapeutic Category Growth Hormone Receptor Antagonist

Use Treatment of acromegaly in patients resistant to or unable to tolerate other therapies

Pregnancy Risk Factor B

Contraindications Hypersensitivity to polyethylene glycol or any component of the formulation

Warnings/Precautions Use caution with hepatic or renal disease, or in the elderly. Growth hormone (GH)-secreting tumor size and liver function should be carefully monitored. Interferes with commercially available GH assays; IGF-I levels not GH levels, should be used to adjust therapy. The manufacturer recommends the initial dose be administered under the supervision of prescribing health care provider. Safety and efficacy in pediatric patients have not been established.

Common Adverse Reactions

>10:

Central nervous system: Pain (4% to 14%; placebo: 6%)

Gastrointestinal: Diarrhea (4% to 14%), nausea (8% to 14%)

Hepatic: Liver function tests abnormal (4% to 12%)

Local: Injection site reaction (4% to 11%)

Miscellaneous: Infection (23%), non-neutralizing anti-GH antibodies (17%; relevance unknown), flu-like syndrome (4% to 12%)

1% to 10%:

Cardiovascular: Hypertension (8%), chest pain (4% to 8%), peripheral edema (4% to 8%)

Central nervous system: Dizziness (4% to 8%; placebo: 6%)

Neuromuscular & skeletal: Back pain (4% to 8%), paresthesia (7%)

Respiratory: Sinusitis (4% to 8%)

Drug Interactions

Increased Effect/Toxicity: Increased doses of pegvisomant may be needed when used with opioids.

Decreased Effect: Pegvisomant may increase glucose tolerance; dose reduction of hypoglycemic agents may be needed.

Mechanism of Action An analogue of human growth hormone, pegvisomant selectively binds to growth hormone (GH) receptors, blocking the binding of endogenous GH, leading to decreased serum concentrations of insulin-like growth factor-I (IGF-I) and other GH-responsive proteins. Pegvisomant is made up of a recombinant DNA protein covalently bound to polyethylene glycol (PEG) polymers.

Pharmacodynamics/Kinetics

Absorption: 57%

Distribution: 7 L

Half-life elimination: 6 days

Time to peak, serum: 33-77 hours

Excretion: Urine (<1%)

Dosage S.C.: Adults: Initial loading dose: 40 mg; maintenance dose: 10 mg once daily; doses may be adjusted by 5 mg in 4- to 6-week intervals based on IGF-I concentrations (maximum dose: 30 mg/day)

Dosage adjustment in hepatic impairment:

Baseline liver function tests (LFT) >3 times ULN: Do not initiate treatment without comprehensive work-up to determine cause; monitor closely if treatment is started.

LFT ≥3 times but <5 times ULN: Continue treatment, but monitor weekly if no signs or symptoms of hepatitis or liver injury; perform comprehensive hepatic work-up

LFT ≥5 times ULN or transaminase >3 times ULN associated with any increase in total bilirubin: Discontinue immediately and perform comprehensive hepatic work-up. If LFTs return to normal, may cautiously consider restarting therapy with frequent monitoring.

Signs or symptoms of hepatitis or hepatic injury: Evaluate liver function tests; discontinue if liver injury is confirmed

Administration For S.C. administration only; rotate injection site daily; may administer in upper arm, upper thigh, abdomen, or buttocks; do not rub injection site. The manufacturer recommends the initial dose be administered under the supervision of prescribing healthcare provider.

Monitoring Parameters GH-secreting tumor size, serum glucose, signs and symptoms of growth hormone deficiency, serum IGF-I (every 4-6 weeks after initial dose and dosage change, every 6 months when normalized)

Liver function tests:
Normal at baseline: Monthly for first 6 months, quarterly for next 6 months, biannually for the next year
Elevated, but ≤3 times ULN: Monitor monthly for at least 1 year, then biannually the next year

Patient Information For S.C. injection only. When mixing dose, do not shake vial. May cause nausea, vomiting, tiredness, or pain. Notify prescriber if symptoms are severe.

Dosage Forms INJ, powder for reconstitution [preservative free]: 10 mg, 15 mg, 20 mg

♦ **Pegylated Interferon Alfa-2a** *see* Peginterferon Alfa-2a *on page 964*
♦ **Pegylated Interferon Alfa-2b** *see* Peginterferon Alfa-2b *on page 966*
♦ **PemADD®** *see* Pemoline *on page 969*
♦ **PemADD® CT** *see* Pemoline *on page 969*

Pemirolast (pe MIR oh last)

U.S. Brand Names Alamast™
Therapeutic Category Antiallergic, Ophthalmic
Use Prevention of itching of the eye due to allergic conjunctivitis
Pregnancy Risk Factor C
Dosage Children >3 years and Adults: 1-2 drops instilled in affected eye(s) 4 times/day
Dosage Forms SOLN, ophthalmic: 0.1% (10 mL)

Pemoline (PEM oh leen)

U.S. Brand Names Cylert®; PemADD®; PemADD® CT
Synonyms Phenylisohydantoin; PIO
Therapeutic Category Central Nervous System Stimulant, Nonamphetamine
Use Treatment of attention-deficit/hyperactivity disorder (ADHD) (not first-line)
Unlabeled/Investigational Use Narcolepsy
Restrictions C-IV
Pregnancy Risk Factor B
Contraindications Hypersensitivity to pemoline or any component of the formulation; hepatic impairment (including abnormalities on baseline liver function tests); children <6 years of age; Tourette's syndrome; psychosis

Warnings/Precautions Not considered first-line therapy for ADHD due to association with hepatic failure. The manufacturer has recommended that signed informed consent following a discussion of risks and benefits must or should be obtained prior to the initiation of therapy. Therapy should be discontinued if a response is not evident after 3 weeks of therapy. Pemoline should not be started in patients with abnormalities in baseline liver function tests, and should be discontinued if clinically significant liver function test abnormalities are revealed at any time during therapy. Use with caution in patients with renal dysfunction or psychosis. In general, stimulant medications should be used with caution in patients with bipolar disorder, diabetes mellitus, cardiovascular disease, seizure disorders, insomnia, porphyria, or hypertension (although pemoline has been demonstrated to have a low potential to elevated blood pressure relative to other stimulants). May exacerbate symptoms of behavior and thought disorder in psychotic patients. Potential for drug dependency exists - avoid abrupt discontinuation in patients who have received for prolonged periods. Stimulant use has been associated with growth suppression, and careful monitoring is recommended. Stimulants may unmask tics in individuals with coexisting Tourette's syndrome.

Common Adverse Reactions Frequency not defined.
Central nervous system: Insomnia, dizziness, drowsiness, mental depression, increased irritability, seizures, precipitation of Tourette's syndrome, hallucinations, headache, movement disorders
Dermatologic: Rash
Endocrine & metabolic: Suppression of growth in children
Gastrointestinal: Anorexia, weight loss, stomach pain, nausea
Hematologic: Aplastic anemia
Hepatic: Increased liver enzyme (usually reversible upon discontinuation), hepatitis, jaundice, hepatic failure

Drug Interactions
Increased Effect/Toxicity: Use caution when pemoline is used with other CNS-acting medications.
(Continued)

Pemoline *(Continued)*

Decreased Effect: Pemoline in combination with antiepileptic medications may decrease seizure threshold.

Mechanism of Action Blocks the reuptake mechanism of dopaminergic neurons, appears to act at the cerebral cortex and subcortical structures; CNS and respiratory stimulant with weak sympathomimetic effects; actions may be mediated via increase in CNS dopamine

Pharmacodynamics/Kinetics
Onset of action: Peak effect: 4 hours
Duration: 8 hours
Protein binding: 50%
Metabolism: Partially hepatic
Half-life elimination: Children: 7-8.6 hours; Adults: 12 hours
Time to peak, serum: 2-4 hours
Excretion: Urine; feces (negligible amounts)

Dosage Children ≥6 years: Oral: Initial: 37.5 mg given once daily in the morning, increase by 18.75 mg/day at weekly intervals; usual effective dose range: 56.25-75 mg/day; maximum: 112.5 mg/day; dosage range: 0.5-3 mg/kg/24 hours; significant benefit may not be evident until third or fourth week of administration

Dosing adjustment/comments in renal impairment: Cl_{cr} <50 mL/minute: Avoid use

Administration Administer medication in the morning.

Monitoring Parameters Liver enzymes (baseline and every 2 weeks)

Patient Information Avoid caffeine; avoid alcohol; last daily dose should be given several hours before retiring; do not abruptly discontinue; prolonged use may cause dependence

Dosage Forms TAB (Cylert®, PemADD®): 18.75 mg, 37.5 mg, 75 mg. **TAB, chewable** (Cylert®, PemADD® CT): 37.5 mg

Penciclovir *(pen SYE kloe veer)*

U.S. Brand Names Denavir®

Therapeutic Category Antiviral Agent; Antiviral Agent, Topical

Use Topical treatment of herpes simplex labialis (cold sores)

Pregnancy Risk Factor B

Contraindications Hypersensitivity to the penciclovir or any component of the formulation; previous and significant adverse reactions to famciclovir

Warnings/Precautions Penciclovir should only be used on herpes labialis on the lips and face; because no data are available, application to mucous membranes is not recommended. Avoid application in or near eyes since it may cause irritation. The effect of penciclovir has not been established in immunocompromised patients.

Common Adverse Reactions
>10%: Dermatologic: Erythema (mild) (50%)
1% to 10%: Central nervous system: Headache (5.3%)
<1% (Limited to important or life-threatening): Local anesthesia, application site reaction, local edema, urticaria, pain, pruritus, paresthesia, skin discoloration, erythematous rash, oropharyngeal edema, parosmia

Mechanism of Action In cells infected with HSV-1 or HSV-2, viral thymidine kinase phosphorylates penciclovir to a monophosphate form which, in turn, is converted to penciclovir triphosphate by cellular kinases. Penciclovir triphosphate inhibits HSV polymerase competitively with deoxyguanosine triphosphate. Consequently, herpes viral DNA synthesis and, therefore, replication are selectively inhibited

Pharmacodynamics/Kinetics Absorption: Topical: None

Dosage Children ≥12 years and Adults: Topical: Apply cream at the first sign or symptom of cold sore (eg, tingling, swelling); apply every 2 hours during waking hours for 4 days

Monitoring Parameters Reduction in virus shedding, negative cultures for herpes virus; resolution of pain and healing of cold sore lesion

Patient Information Report if you experience significant burning, itching, stinging, or redness when using this medication

Dosage Forms CRM: 1% (1.5 g)

Penicillamine *(pen i SIL a meen)*

U.S. Brand Names Cuprimine®; Depen®

Synonyms D-3-Mercaptovaline; β,β-Dimethylcysteine; D-Penicillamine

Therapeutic Category Antidote, Copper Toxicity; Antidote, Lead Toxicity; Chelating Agent, Oral

Use Treatment of Wilson's disease, cystinuria, adjunct in the treatment of rheumatoid arthritis

Unlabeled/Investigational Use Lead, mercury, copper, and possibly gold poisoning (**Note:** Oral succimer [DMSA] is preferable for lead or mercury poisoning)

Pregnancy Risk Factor D

Contraindications Hypersensitivity to penicillamine or any component of the formulation; renal insufficiency; patients with previous penicillamine-related aplastic anemia or agranulocytosis; concomitant administration with other hematopoietic-depressant drugs (eg, gold, immunosuppressants, antimalarials, phenylbutazone); pregnancy

Warnings/Precautions Cross-sensitivity with penicillin is possible; therefore, should be used cautiously in patients with a history of penicillin allergy. Patients on penicillamine for Wilson's disease or cystinuria should receive pyridoxine supplementation 25 mg/day; once instituted for Wilson's disease or cystinuria, continue treatment on a daily basis; interruptions of even a few days have been followed by hypersensitivity with reinstitution of therapy. Penicillamine has been associated with fatalities due to agranulocytosis, aplastic anemia, thrombocytopenia, Goodpasture's syndrome, and myasthenia gravis; patients should be warned to report promptly any symptoms suggesting toxicity; approximately 33% of patients will experience an allergic reaction; since toxicity may be dose related, it is recommended not to exceed 750 mg/day in elderly.

Common Adverse Reactions
>10%:
   Dermatologic: Rash, urticaria, itching (44% to 50%)
   Gastrointestinal: Hypogeusia (25% to 33%), diarrhea (17%)
   Neuromuscular & skeletal: Arthralgia
1% to 10%:
   Cardiovascular: Edema of the face, feet, or lower legs
   Central nervous system: Fever, chills
   Gastrointestinal: Weight gain, sore throat, anorexia, epigastric pain
   Genitourinary: Bloody or cloudy urine
   Hematologic: Aplastic or hemolytic anemia, leukopenia (2%), thrombocytopenia (4%)
   Renal: Proteinuria (6%)
   Miscellaneous: White spots on lips or mouth, positive ANA

Drug Interactions
   Increased Effect/Toxicity: Increased effect or toxicity of gold, antimalarials, immunosuppressants, and phenylbutazone (hematologic, renal toxicity).
   Decreased Effect: Decreased effect of penicillamine when taken with iron and zinc salts, antacids (magnesium, calcium, aluminum), and food. Digoxin levels may be decreased when taken with penicillamine.

Mechanism of Action Chelates with lead, copper, mercury and other heavy metals to form stable, soluble complexes that are excreted in urine; depresses circulating IgM rheumatoid factor, depresses T-cell but not B-cell activity; combines with cystine to form a compound which is more soluble, thus cystine calculi are prevented

Pharmacodynamics/Kinetics
Absorption: 40% to 70%
Protein binding: 80% to albumin
Metabolism: Hepatic (small amounts)
Half-life elimination: 1.7-3.2 hours
Time to peak, serum: ~2 hours
Excretion: Urine (30% to 60% as unchanged drug)

Dosage Oral:
Rheumatoid arthritis:
   Children: Initial: 3 mg/kg/day (≤250 mg/day) for 3 months, then 6 mg/kg/day (≤500 mg/day) in divided doses twice daily for 3 months to a maximum of 10 mg/kg/day in 3-4 divided doses
   Adults: 125-250 mg/day, may increase dose at 1- to 3-month intervals up to 1-1.5 g/day
Wilson's disease (doses titrated to maintain urinary copper excretion >1 mg/day):
   Infants <6 months: 250 mg/dose once daily
   Children <12 years: 250 mg/dose 2-3 times/day
   Adults: 250 mg 4 times/day
Cystinuria:
   Children: 30 mg/kg/day in 4 divided doses
   Adults: 1-4 g/day in divided doses every 6 hours
Lead poisoning (unlabeled use): In acute poisoning, continue until blood lead level is <15 µg/dL; may also be used in other heavy metal poisoning:
   Children: 25-35 mg/kg/day, administered in 3-4 divided doses; initiating treatment at 25% of this dose and gradually increasing to the full dose over 2-3 weeks may minimize adverse reactions
   Adults: 250-500 mg/dose every 8-12 hours
Primary biliary cirrhosis: 250 mg/day to start, increase by 250 mg every 2 weeks up to a maintenance dose of 1 g/day, usually given 250 mg 4 times/day
Arsenic poisoning: Children: 100 mg/kg/day in divided doses every 6 hours for 5 days; maximum: 1 g/day

Dosing adjustment/comments in renal impairment: Cl_cr <50 mL/minute: Avoid use

Administration Administer on an empty stomach (1 hour before meals and at bedtime). Patients unable to swallow capsules may mix contents of capsule with fruit juice or chilled pureed fruit.

Monitoring Parameters Urinalysis, CBC with differential, platelet count, liver function tests; weekly measurements of urinary and blood concentration of the intoxicating metal is indicated (3 months has been tolerated)

CBC: WBC <3500/mm^3, neutrophils <2000/mm^3 or monocytes >500/mm^3 indicate need to stop therapy immediately; quantitative 24-hour urine protein at 1- to 2-week intervals initially (first 2-3 months); urinalysis, LFTs occasionally; platelet counts <100,000/mm^3 indicate need to stop therapy until numbers of platelets increase

Patient Information Take at least 1 hour before a meal on an empty stomach; patients with cystinuria should drink copious amounts of water; report unusual bleeding or bruising, or persistent fever, sore throat, or fatigue; report any unexplained cough, shortness of breath, or rash; loss of taste may occur; do not skip or miss doses or discontinue without notifying prescriber

Dosage Forms CAP (Cuprimine®): 125 mg, 250 mg. **TAB** (Depen®): 250 mg

Penicillin G Benzathine (pen i SIL in jee BENZ a theen)

U.S. Brand Names Bicillin® L-A; Permapen® Isoject®

Synonyms Benzathine Benzylpenicillin; Benzathine Penicillin G; Benzylpenicillin Benzathine

Therapeutic Category Antibiotic, Penicillin

Use Active against some gram-positive organisms, few gram-negative organisms such as *Neisseria gonorrhoeae*, and some anaerobes and spirochetes; used in the treatment of syphilis; used only for the treatment of mild to moderately severe infections caused by organisms susceptible to low concentrations of penicillin G or for prophylaxis of infections caused by these organisms

Pregnancy Risk Factor B

Contraindications Hypersensitivity to penicillin or any component of the formulation

Warnings/Precautions Use with caution in patients with impaired renal function, seizure disorder, or history of hypersensitivity to other beta-lactams; CDC and AAP do not currently recommend the use of penicillin G benzathine to treat congenital syphilis or neurosyphilis due to reported treatment failures and lack of published clinical data on its efficacy

Common Adverse Reactions Frequency not defined.
Central nervous system: Convulsions, confusion, drowsiness, myoclonus, fever
Dermatologic: Rash
Endocrine & metabolic: Electrolyte imbalance
Hematologic: Positive Coombs' reaction, hemolytic anemia
Local: Pain, thrombophlebitis
Renal: Acute interstitial nephritis
Miscellaneous: Anaphylaxis, hypersensitivity reactions, Jarisch-Herxheimer reaction

Drug Interactions

Increased Effect/Toxicity: Probenecid increases penicillin levels. Aminoglycosides may lead to synergistic efficacy. Penicillins may increase the exposure to methotrexate during concurrent therapy; monitor.

Decreased Effect: Tetracyclines may decrease penicillin effectiveness. Although anecdotal reports suggest oral contraceptive efficacy could be reduced by penicillins, this has been refuted by more rigorous scientific and clinical data.

Mechanism of Action Interferes with bacterial cell wall synthesis during active multiplication, causing cell wall death and resultant bactericidal activity against susceptible bacteria

Pharmacodynamics/Kinetics
Duration: 1-4 weeks (dose dependent); larger doses result in more sustained levels
Absorption: I.M.: Slow
Time to peak, serum: 12-24 hours

Dosage I.M.: Administer undiluted injection; higher doses result in more sustained rather than higher levels. Use a penicillin G benzathine-penicillin G procaine combination to achieve early peak levels in acute infections.

Infants and Children:
Group A streptococcal upper respiratory infection: 25,000-50,000 units/kg as a single dose; maximum: 1.2 million units
Prophylaxis of recurrent rheumatic fever: 25,000-50,000 units/kg every 3-4 weeks; maximum: 1.2 million units/dose
Early syphilis: 50,000 units/kg as a single injection; maximum: 2.4 million units
Syphilis of more than 1-year duration: 50,000 units/kg every week for 3 doses; maximum: 2.4 million units/dose

Adults:
Group A streptococcal upper respiratory infection: 1.2 million units as a single dose
Prophylaxis of recurrent rheumatic fever: 1.2 million units every 3-4 weeks or 600,000 units twice monthly
Early syphilis: 2.4 million units as a single dose in 2 injection sites
Syphilis of more than 1-year duration: 2.4 million units in 2 injection sites once weekly for 3 doses
Not indicated as single drug therapy for neurosyphilis, but may be given 1 time/week for 3 weeks following I.V. treatment; refer to Penicillin G Parenteral/Aqueous monograph for dosing

Administration Administer by deep I.M. injection in the upper outer quadrant of the buttock do **not** administer I.V., intra-arterially, or S.C.; in children <2 years of age, I.M. injections should be made into the midlateral muscle of the thigh, not the gluteal region; when doses are repeated, rotate the injection site

Monitoring Parameters Observe for signs and symptoms of anaphylaxis during first dose

Patient Information Report any rash

Dosage Forms INJ, suspension [prefilled syringe]: (Bicillin® L-A): 600,000 units/mL (1 mL, 2 mL, 4 mL); (Permapen® Isoject®): 600,000 units/mL (2 mL)

Penicillin G Benzathine and Penicillin G Procaine
(pen i SIL in jee BENZ a theen & pen i SIL in jee PROE kane)

U.S. Brand Names Bicillin® C-R; Bicillin® C-R 900/300

Synonyms Penicillin G Procaine and Benzathine Combined

Therapeutic Category Antibiotic, Penicillin

Use May be used in specific situations in the treatment of streptococcal infections

Pregnancy Risk Factor B

Contraindications Hypersensitivity to penicillin or any component of the formulation

Warnings/Precautions Use with caution in patients with impaired renal function, impaired cardiac function or seizure disorder

Common Adverse Reactions Frequency not defined.

Central nervous system: CNS toxicity (convulsions, confusion, drowsiness, myoclonus)

Hematologic: Positive Coombs' reaction, hemolytic anemia

Renal: Interstitial nephritis

Miscellaneous: Hypersensitivity reactions, Jarisch-Herxheimer reaction

Drug Interactions

Increased Effect/Toxicity: Probenecid increases penicillin levels. Aminoglycosides may lead to synergistic efficacy. Warfarin effects may be increased. Penicillins may increase the exposure to methotrexate during concurrent therapy; monitor.

Decreased Effect: Tetracyclines may decrease penicillin effectiveness. Although anecdotal reports suggest oral contraceptive efficacy could be reduced by penicillins, this has been refuted by more rigorous scientific and clinical data.

Mechanism of Action Inhibits bacterial cell wall synthesis by binding to one or more of the penicillin binding proteins (PBPs); which in turn inhibits the final transpeptidation step of peptidoglycan synthesis in bacterial cell walls, thus inhibiting cell wall biosynthesis. Bacteria eventually lyse due to ongoing activity of cell wall autolytic enzymes (autolysins and murein hydrolases) while cell wall assembly is arrested.

Dosage I.M.:

Children:

<30 lb: 600,000 units in a single dose

30-60 lb: 900,000 units to 1.2 million units in a single dose

Children >60 lb and Adults: 2.4 million units in a single dose

Administration Administer by deep I.M. injection in the upper outer quadrant of the buttock; administered around-the-clock rather than 4 times/day, 3 times/day, etc (ie, 12-6-12-6, not 9-1-5-9) to promote less variation in peak and trough serum levels; do **not** administer I.V., intravascularly, or intra-arterially. In infants and children, I.M. injections should be made into the midlateral muscle of the thigh.

Monitoring Parameters Observe for signs and symptoms of anaphylaxis during first dose

Dosage Forms INJ, suspension [prefilled syringe]: (Bicillin® C-R 600,000 units): Penicillin G benzathine 300,000 units and penicillin G procaine 300,000 units per 1 mL (1 mL); (Bicillin® C-R 1,200,000 units): Penicillin G benzathine 600,000 units and penicillin G procaine 600,000 units per 2 mL (2 mL); (Bicillin® C-R 2,400,000 units): Penicillin G benzathine 1,200,000 units and penicillin G procaine 1,200,000 units per 4 mL (4 mL); (Bicillin® C-R 900/300): 1,200,000 units: Penicillin G benzathine 900,000 units and penicillin G procaine 300,000 units per 2 mL (2 mL)

Penicillin G (Parenteral/Aqueous)

(pen i SIL in jee, pa REN ter al, AYE kwee us)

Related Information

Antimicrobial Drugs of Choice *on page 1440*

U.S. Brand Names Pfizerpen®

Synonyms Benzylpenicillin Potassium; Benzylpenicillin Sodium; Crystalline Penicillin; Penicillin G Potassium; Penicillin G Sodium

Therapeutic Category Antibiotic, Penicillin

Use Active against some gram-positive organisms, generally not *Staphylococcus aureus*; some gram-negative organisms such as *Neisseria gonorrhoeae*, and some anaerobes and spirochetes

Pregnancy Risk Factor B

Contraindications Hypersensitivity to penicillin or any component of the formulation

Warnings/Precautions Avoid intra-arterial administration or injection into or near major peripheral nerves or blood vessels since such injections may cause severe and/or permanent neurovascular damage; use with caution in patients with renal impairment (dosage reduction required), pre-existing seizure disorders, or with a history of hypersensitivity to cephalosporins

Common Adverse Reactions Frequency not defined.

Central nervous system: Convulsions, confusion, drowsiness, myoclonus, fever

Dermatologic: Rash

Endocrine & metabolic: Electrolyte imbalance

Hematologic: Positive Coombs' reaction, hemolytic anemia

Local: Thrombophlebitis

Renal: Acute interstitial nephritis

Miscellaneous: Anaphylaxis, hypersensitivity reactions, Jarisch-Herxheimer reaction

Drug Interactions

Increased Effect/Toxicity: Probenecid increases penicillin levels. Aminoglycosides may lead to synergistic efficacy. Penicillins may increase the exposure to methotrexate during concurrent therapy; monitor.

Decreased Effect: Tetracyclines may decrease penicillin effectiveness. Although anecdotal reports suggest oral contraceptive efficacy could be reduced by penicillins, this has been refuted by more rigorous scientific and clinical data.

Mechanism of Action Interferes with bacterial cell wall synthesis during active multiplication, causing cell wall death and resultant bactericidal activity against susceptible bacteria

(Continued)

Penicillin G (Parenteral/Aqueous) *(Continued)*

Pharmacodynamics/Kinetics

Distribution: Poor penetration across blood-brain barrier, despite inflamed meninges; crosses placenta; enters breast milk

Relative diffusion from blood into CSF: Good only with inflammation (exceeds usual MICs)

CSF:blood level ratio: Normal meninges: <1%; Inflamed meninges: 3% to 5%

Protein binding: 65%

Metabolism: Hepatic (30%) to penicilloic acid

Half-life elimination:

Neonates: <6 days old: 3.2-3.4 hours; 7-13 days old: 1.2-2.2 hours; >14 days old: 0.9-1.9 hours

Children and Adults: Normal renal function: 20-50 minutes

End-stage renal disease: 3.3-5.1 hours

Time to peak, serum: I.M.: ~30 minutes; I.V. ~1 hour

Excretion: Urine

Dosage I.M., I.V.:

Infants:

<7 days, <2000 g: 50,000 units/kg/day in divided doses every 12 hours

<7 days, >2000 g: 50,000 units/kg/day in divided doses every 8 hours

>7 days, <2000 g: 75,000 units/kg/day in divided doses every 8 hours

>7 days, >2000 g: 100,000 units/kg/day in divided doses every 6 hours

Infants and Children (sodium salt is preferred in children): 100,000-250,000 units/kg/day in divided doses every 4 hours

Severe infections: Up to 400,000 units/kg/day in divided doses every 4 hours; maximum dose: 24 million units/day

Congenital syphilis:

Newborns: 50,000 units/kg/day I.V. every 8-12 hours for 10-14 days

Infants: 50,000 units/kg every 4-6 hours for 10-14 days

Disseminated gonococcal infections or gonococcus ophthalmia (if organism proven sensitive): 100,000 units/kg/day in 2 equal doses (4 equal doses/day for infants >1 week)

Gonococcal meningitis: 150,000 units/kg in 2 equal doses (4 doses/day for infants >1 week)

Adults: 2-24 million units/day in divided doses every 4 hours depending on sensitivity of the organism and severity of the infection

Neurosyphilis: 18-24 million units/day in divided doses every 3-4 hours for 10-14 days

Dosing interval in renal impairment:

Cl_{cr} 30-50 mL/minute: Administer every 6 hours

Cl_{cr} 10-30 mL/minute: Administer every 8 hours

Cl_{cr} <10 mL/minute: Administer every 12 hours

Hemodialysis: Moderately dialyzable (20% to 50%)

Continuous arteriovenous or venovenous hemodiafiltration effects: Dose as for Cl_{cr} 10-50 mL/minute

Administration Administer I.M. by deep injection in the upper outer quadrant of the buttock

Monitoring Parameters Observe for signs and symptoms of anaphylaxis during first dose

Patient Information Report any rash or shortness of breath

Dosage Forms INF, as potassium: 1 million units (50 mL), 2 million units (50 mL), 3 million units (50 mL). **INJ, powder for reconstitution, as potassium** (Pfizerpen®): 5 million units, 20 million units. **INJ, powder for reconstitution, as sodium:** 5 million units

♦ **Penicillin G Potassium** *see* Penicillin G (Parenteral/Aqueous) *on page 973*

Penicillin G Procaine *(pen i SIL in jee PROE kane)*

Synonyms APPG; Aqueous Procaine Penicillin G; Procaine Benzylpenicillin; Procaine Penicillin G; Wycillin [DSC]

Therapeutic Category Antibiotic, Penicillin

Use Moderately severe infections due to *Treponema pallidum* and other penicillin G-sensitive microorganisms that are susceptible to low, but prolonged serum penicillin concentrations; anthrax due to *Bacillus anthracis* (postexposure) to reduce the incidence or progression of disease following exposure to aerolized *Bacillus anthracis*

Pregnancy Risk Factor B

Contraindications Hypersensitivity to penicillin, procaine, or any component of the formulation

Warnings/Precautions May need to modify dosage in patients with severe renal impairment, seizure disorders, or history of hypersensitivity to cephalosporins; avoid I.V., intravascular, or intra-arterial administration of penicillin G procaine since severe and/or permanent neurovascular damage may occur; use of penicillin for longer than 2 weeks may be associated with an increased risk for some adverse reactions (neutropenia, serum sickness)

Common Adverse Reactions Frequency not defined.

Cardiovascular: Myocardial depression, vasodilation, conduction disturbances

Central nervous system: Confusion, drowsiness, myoclonus, CNS stimulation, seizures

Hematologic: Positive Coombs' reaction, hemolytic anemia, neutropenia

Local: Pain at injection site, thrombophlebitis, sterile abscess at injection site

Renal: Interstitial nephritis

Miscellaneous: Pseudoanaphylactic reactions, hypersensitivity reactions, Jarisch-Herxheimer reaction, serum sickness

Drug Interactions

Increased Effect/Toxicity: Probenecid increases penicillin levels. Aminoglycosides may lead to synergistic efficacy. Penicillins may increase the exposure to methotrexate during concurrent therapy; monitor.

Decreased Effect: Tetracyclines may decrease penicillin effectiveness. Although anecdotal reports suggest oral contraceptive efficacy could be reduced by penicillins, this has been refuted by more rigorous scientific and clinical data.

Mechanism of Action Inhibits bacterial cell wall synthesis by binding to one or more of the penicillin binding proteins (PBPs); which in turn inhibits the final transpeptidation step of peptidoglycan synthesis in bacterial cell walls, thus inhibiting cell wall biosynthesis. Bacteria eventually lyse due to ongoing activity of cell wall autolytic enzymes (autolysins and murein hydrolases) while cell wall assembly is arrested.

Pharmacodynamics/Kinetics
Duration: Therapeutic: 15-24 hours
Absorption: I.M.: Slow
Distribution: Penetration across the blood-brain barrier is poor, despite inflamed meninges; enters breast milk
Protein binding: 65%
Metabolism: ~30% hepatically inactivated
Time to peak, serum: 1-4 hours
Excretion: Urine (60% to 90% as unchanged drug)
Clearance: Renal: Delayed in neonates, young infants, and with impaired renal function

Dosage I.M.:
Children: 25,000-50,000 units/kg/day in divided doses 1-2 times/day; not to exceed 4.8 million units/24 hours
  Anthrax, inhalational (postexposure prophylaxis): 25,000 units/kg every 12 hours (maximum: 1,200,000 units every 12 hours); see "Note" in Adults dosing
  Congenital syphilis: 50,000 units/kg/day for 10-14 days
Adults: 0.6-4.8 million units/day in divided doses every 12-24 hours
  Anthrax:
    Inhalational (postexposure prophylaxis): 1,200,000 units every 12 hours
    Note: Overall treatment duration should be 60 days. Available safety data suggest continued administration of penicillin G procaine for longer than 2 weeks may incur additional risk for adverse reactions. Clinicians may consider switching to effective alternative treatment for completion of therapy beyond 2 weeks.
    Cutaneous (treatment): 600,000-1,200,000 units/day; alternative therapy is recommended in severe cutaneous or other forms of anthrax infection
  Endocarditis caused by susceptible viridans *Streptococcus* (when used in conjunction with an aminoglycoside): 1.2 million units every 6 hours for 2-4 weeks
  Neurosyphilis: I.M.: 2-4 million units/day with 500 mg probenecid by mouth 4 times/day for 10-14 days; **penicillin G aqueous I.V. is the preferred agent**
Hemodialysis: Moderately dializable (20% to 50%)

Administration Procaine suspension for deep I.M. injection only; rotate the injection site avoid I.V., intravascular, or intra-arterial administration of penicillin G procaine since severe and/or permanent neurovascular damage may occur

Monitoring Parameters Periodic renal and hematologic function tests with prolonged therapy; fever, mental status, WBC count

Patient Information Report skin rash, itching, hives, or severe diarrhea.

Dosage Forms INJ, suspension: 600,000 units/mL (1 mL, 2 mL)

◆ **Penicillin G Procaine and Benzathine Combined** *see* Penicillin G Benzathine and Penicillin G Procaine *on page 972*

◆ **Penicillin G Sodium** *see* Penicillin G (Parenteral/Aqueous) *on page 973*

Penicillin V Potassium (pen i SIL in vee poe TASS ee um)

Related Information
Antimicrobial Drugs of Choice *on page 1440*

U.S. Brand Names Veetids®

Synonyms Pen VK; Phenoxymethyl Penicillin

Therapeutic Category Antibiotic, Penicillin

Use Treatment of infections caused by susceptible organisms involving the respiratory tract, otitis media, sinusitis, skin, and urinary tract; prophylaxis in rheumatic fever

Pregnancy Risk Factor B

Contraindications Hypersensitivity to penicillin or any component of the formulation

Warnings/Precautions Use with caution in patients with severe renal impairment (modify dosage), history of seizures, or hypersensitivity to cephalosporins

Common Adverse Reactions >10%: Gastrointestinal: Mild diarrhea, vomiting, nausea, oral candidiasis

Drug Interactions
Increased Effect/Toxicity: Probenecid increases penicillin levels. Aminoglycosides may cause synergistic efficacy. Penicillins may increase the exposure to methotrexate during concurrent therapy; monitor.
Decreased Effect: Tetracyclines may decrease penicillin effectiveness. Although anecdotal reports suggest oral contraceptive efficacy could be reduced by penicillins, this has been refuted by more rigorous scientific and clinical data.

Mechanism of Action Inhibits bacterial cell wall synthesis by binding to one or more of the penicillin binding proteins (PBPs); which in turn inhibits the final transpeptidation step of peptidoglycan synthesis in bacterial cell walls, thus inhibiting cell wall biosynthesis. Bacteria eventually lyse due to ongoing activity of cell wall autolytic enzymes (autolysins and murein hydrolases) while cell wall assembly is arrested.
(Continued)

Penicillin V Potassium *(Continued)*

Pharmacodynamics/Kinetics
Absorption: 60% to 73%
Distribution: Enters breast milk
Protein binding, plasma: 80%
Half-life elimination: 30 minutes; prolonged with renal impairment
Time to peak, serum: 0.5-1 hour
Excretion: Urine (as unchanged drug and metabolites)

Dosage Oral:
Systemic infections:
Children <12 years: 25-50 mg/kg/day in divided doses every 6-8 hours; maximum dose: 3 g/day
Children ≥12 years and Adults: 125-500 mg every 6-8 hours
Prophylaxis of pneumococcal infections:
Children <5 years: 125 mg twice daily
Children ≥5 years and Adults: 250 mg twice daily
Prophylaxis of recurrent rheumatic fever:
Children <5 years: 125 mg twice daily
Children ≥5 years and Adults: 250 mg twice daily

Dosing interval in renal impairment: Cl_{cr} <10 mL/minute: Administer 250 mg every 6 hours

Administration Administer on an empty stomach to increase oral absorption

Monitoring Parameters Periodic renal and hematologic function tests during prolonged therapy; monitor for signs of anaphylaxis during first dose

Patient Information Take on an empty stomach 1 hour before or 2 hours after meals, take until gone, do not skip doses, report any rash or shortness of breath; shake liquid well before use

Dosage Forms 250 mg = 400,000 units
POWDER for oral solution: 125 mg/5 mL (100 mL, 200 mL); 250 mg/5 mL (100 mL, 200 mL).
TAB: 250 mg, 500 mg

♦ **Penicilloyl-polylysine** *see* Benzylpenicilloyl-polylysine *on page 156*
♦ **Penlac™** *see* Ciclopirox *on page 274*
♦ **Pentahydrate** *see* Sodium Thiosulfate *on page 1152*
♦ **Pentam-300®** *see* Pentamidine *on page 976*

Pentamidine *(pen TAM i deen)*

U.S. Brand Names NebuPent®; Pentam-300®
Synonyms Pentamidine Isethionate
Therapeutic Category Antibiotic, Miscellaneous
Use Treatment and prevention of pneumonia caused by *Pneumocystis carinii* (PCP)
Unlabeled/Investigational Use Treatment of trypanosomiasis and visceral leishmaniasis
Pregnancy Risk Factor C
Contraindications Hypersensitivity to pentamidine isethionate or any component of the formulation (inhalation and injection)
Warnings/Precautions Use with caution in patients with diabetes mellitus, renal or hepatic dysfunction; hypertension or hypotension; leukopenia, thrombocytopenia, asthma, hypo/hyperglycemia
Common Adverse Reactions Injection (I); Aerosol (A)
>10%:
Cardiovascular: Chest pain (I - 10% to 23%)
Central nervous system: Fatigue (A - 50% to 70%); dizziness (A - 31% to 47%)
Dermatologic: Rash (31% to 47%)
Endocrine & metabolic: Hyperkalemia
Gastrointestinal: Anorexia (A - 50% to 70%), nausea (A - 10% to 23%)
Local: Local reactions at injection site
Renal: Increased creatinine (I - 23%)
Respiratory: Wheezing (A - 10% to 23%), dyspnea (A - 50% to 70%), coughing (A - 31% to 47%), pharyngitis (10% to 23%)
1% to 10%:
Cardiovascular: Hypotension (I - 4%)
Central nervous system: Confusion/hallucinations (1% to 2%), headache (A - 1% to 5%)
Dermatologic: Rash (I - 3.3%)
Endocrine & metabolic: Hypoglycemia <25 mg/dL (I - 2.4%)
Gastrointestinal: Nausea/anorexia (I - 6%), diarrhea (A - 1% to 5%), vomiting
Hematologic: Severe leukopenia (I - 2.8%), thrombocytopenia <20,000/mm^3 (I - 1.7%), anemia (A - 1% to 5%)
Hepatic: Increased LFTs (I - 8.7%)

Drug Interactions
Cytochrome P450 Effect: Substrate of CYP2C19 (major); **Inhibits** CYP2C8/9 (weak), 2C19 (weak), 2D6 (weak), 3A4 (weak)
Increased Effect/Toxicity: CYP2C19 inhibitors may increase the levels/effects of pentamidine; example inhibitors include delavirdine, fluconazole, fluvoxamine, gemfibrozil, isoniazid, omeprazole, and ticlopidine. Pentamidine may potentiate the effect of other drugs which prolong QT interval (cisapride, sparfloxacin, gatifloxacin, moxifloxacin, pimozide, and type Ia and type III antiarrhythmics).
Decreased Effect: CYP2C19 inducers may decrease the levels/effects of pentamidine; example inducers include aminoglutethimide, carbamazepine, phenytoin, and rifampin.

Mechanism of Action Interferes with RNA/DNA, phospholipids and protein synthesis, through inhibition of oxidative phosphorylation and/or interference with incorporation of nucleotides and nucleic acids into RNA and DNA, in protozoa

Pharmacodynamics/Kinetics

Absorption: I.M.: Well absorbed; Inhalation: Limited systemic absorption

Half-life elimination: Terminal: 6.4-9.4 hours; may be prolonged with severe renal impairment

Excretion: Urine (33% to 66% as unchanged drug)

Dosage

Children:

Treatment of PCP pneumonia: I.M., I.V. (I.V. preferred): 4 mg/kg/day once daily for 10-14 days

Prevention of PCP pneumonia:

I.M., I.V.: 4 mg/kg monthly or every 2 weeks

Inhalation (aerosolized pentamidine in children ≥5 years): 300 mg/dose given every 3-4 weeks via Respirgard® II inhaler (8 mg/kg dose has also been used in children <5 years)

Treatment of trypanosomiasis (unlabeled use): I.V.: 4 mg/kg/day once daily for 10 days

Adults:

Treatment: I.M., I.V. (I.V. preferred): 4 mg/kg/day once daily for 14-21 days

Prevention: Inhalation: 300 mg every 4 weeks via Respirgard® II nebulizer

Dialysis: Not removed by hemo or peritoneal dialysis or continuous arteriovenous or venovenous hemofiltration; supplemental dosage is not necessary

Dosing adjustment in renal impairment: Adults: I.V.:

Cl_{cr} 10-50 mL/minute: Administer 4 mg/kg every 24-36 hours

Cl_{cr} <10 mL/minute: Administer 4 mg/kg every 48 hours

Administration Infuse I.V. slowly over a period of at least 60 minutes or administer deep I.M.; patients receiving I.V. or I.M. pentamidine should be lying down and blood pressure should be monitored closely during administration of drug and several times thereafter until it is stable

Monitoring Parameters Liver function tests, renal function tests, blood glucose, serum potassium and calcium, ECG, blood pressure

Patient Information PCP pneumonia may still occur despite pentamidine use; report fever, shortness of breath, or coughing up blood; maintain adequate fluid intake

Dosage Forms INJ, powder for reconstitution (Pentam® 300): 300 mg. **POWDER, nebulization** (NebuPent®): 300 mg

♦ **Pentamidine Isethionate** see Pentamidine on page 976

♦ **Pentasa®** see Mesalamine on page 798

Pentazocine (pen TAZ oh seen)

Related Information

Narcotic Agonists Comparison on page 1395

U.S. Brand Names Talwin®; Talwin® NX

Synonyms Naloxone Hydrochloride and Pentazocine Hydrochloride; Pentazocine Hydrochloride; Pentazocine Hydrochloride and Naloxone Hydrochloride; Pentazocine Lactate

Therapeutic Category Analgesic, Narcotic; Sedative

Use Relief of moderate to severe pain; has also been used as a sedative prior to surgery and as a supplement to surgical anesthesia

Restrictions C-IV

Pregnancy Risk Factor C/D (prolonged use or high doses at term)

Contraindications Hypersensitivity to pentazocine, naloxone, or any component of the formulation; increased intracranial pressure (unless the patient is mechanically ventilated); pregnancy (prolonged use or high doses at term)

Warnings/Precautions Use with caution in seizure-prone patients, acute myocardial infarction, patients undergoing biliary tract surgery, patients with renal and hepatic dysfunction, head trauma, increased intracranial pressure, and patients with a history of prior opioid dependence or abuse; pentazocine may precipitate opiate withdrawal symptoms in patients who have been receiving opiates regularly; injection contains sulfites which may cause allergic reaction; tolerance or drug dependence may result from extended use. Talwin® NX is intended for oral administration **only** - severe vascular reactions have resulted from misuse by injection.

Common Adverse Reactions Frequency not defined.

Cardiovascular: Hypotension, circulatory depression, shock, tachycardia, syncope, flushing

Central nervous system: Malaise, headache, nightmares, insomnia, CNS depression, sedation, hallucinations, confusion, disorientation, dizziness, euphoria, drowsiness, lightheadedness, irritability, chills, excitement

Dermatologic: Rash, pruritus, dermatitis, urticaria, Stevens-Johnson syndrome, toxic epidermal necrolysis, erythema multiforme

Gastrointestinal: Nausea, vomiting, xerostomia, constipation, anorexia, diarrhea, abdominal distress

Genitourinary: Urinary retention

Hematologic: WBCs decreased, eosinophilia

Local: Tissue damage and irritation with I.M./S.C. use

Neuromuscular & skeletal: Weakness, tremor, paresthesia

Ocular: Blurred vision, miosis

Otic: Tinnitus

Respiratory: Dyspnea, respiratory depression (rare)

Miscellaneous: Physical and psychological dependence, facial edema, diaphoresis, anaphylaxis

(Continued)

Pentazocine *(Continued)*

Drug Interactions

Increased Effect/Toxicity: Increased effect/toxicity with tripelennamine (can be lethal), CNS depressants (eg, phenothiazines, tranquilizers, anxiolytics, sedatives, hypnotics, alcohol).

Decreased Effect: May potentiate or reduce analgesic effect of opiate agonist (eg, morphine) depending on patients tolerance to opiates; can precipitate withdrawal in narcotic addicts.

Mechanism of Action Binds to opiate receptors in the CNS, causing inhibition of ascending pain pathways, altering the perception of and response to pain; produces generalized CNS depression; partial agonist-antagonist

Pharmacodynamics/Kinetics

Onset of action: Oral, I.M., S.C.: 15-30 minutes; I.V.: 2-3 minutes

Duration: Oral: 4-5 hours; Parenteral: 2-3 hours

Protein binding: 60%

Metabolism: Hepatic via oxidative and glucuronide conjugation pathways; extensive first-pass effect

Bioavailability: Oral: ~20%; increased to 60% to 70% with cirrhosis

Half-life elimination: 2-3 hours; prolonged with hepatic impairment

Excretion: Urine (small amounts as unchanged drug)

Dosage

Preoperative/pre-anesthetic: Children 1-16 years: I.M.: 0.5 mg/kg

Analgesia:

Children: I.M.:

5-8 years: 15 mg

8-14 years: 30 mg

Children >12 years and Adults: Oral: 50 mg every 3-4 hours; may increase to 100 mg/dose if needed, but should not exceed 600 mg/day

Adults:

I.M., S.C.: 30-60 mg every 3-4 hours, not to exceed total daily dose of 360 mg

I.V.: 30 mg every 3-4 hours (maximum: 360 mg/day)

Elderly: Elderly patients may be more sensitive to the analgesic and sedating effects. The elderly may also have impaired renal function. If needed, dosing should be started at the lower end of dosing range and adjust dose for renal function.

Dosing adjustment in renal impairment:

Cl_{cr} 10-50 mL/minute: Administer 75% of normal dose

Cl_{cr} <10 mL/minute: Administer 50% of normal dose

Dosing adjustment in hepatic impairment: Reduce dose or avoid use in patients with liver disease

Administration Rotate injection site for I.M., S.C. use; avoid intra-arterial injection; avoid S.C. use unless absolutely necessary (may cause tissue damage)

Monitoring Parameters Relief of pain, respiratory and mental status, blood pressure

Patient Information Avoid alcohol, may cause drowsiness, impaired judgment or coordination; may cause physical and psychological dependence with prolonged use; will cause withdrawal in patients currently dependent on narcotics

Dosage Forms INJ, solution (Talwin®): 30 mg/mL (1 mL, 2 mL, 10 mL). **TAB** (Talwin® NX): Pentazocine 50 mg and naloxone 0.5 mg

- ♦ **Pentazocine Hydrochloride** *see* Pentazocine *on page 977*
- ♦ **Pentazocine Hydrochloride and Naloxone Hydrochloride** *see* Pentazocine *on page 977*
- ♦ **Pentazocine Lactate** *see* Pentazocine *on page 977*

Pentobarbital *(pen toe BAR bi tal)*

U.S. Brand Names Nembutal®

Synonyms Pentobarbital Sodium

Therapeutic Category Anticonvulsant, Barbiturate; Barbiturate; Sedative

Use Sedative/hypnotic; preanesthetic; high-dose barbiturate coma for treatment of increased intracranial pressure or status epilepticus unresponsive to other therapy

Restrictions C-II

Pregnancy Risk Factor D

Contraindications Hypersensitivity to barbiturates or any component of the formulation; marked hepatic impairment; dyspnea or airway obstruction; porphyria; pregnancy

Warnings/Precautions Tolerance to hypnotic effect can occur; do not use for >2 weeks to treat insomnia. Potential for drug dependency exists, abrupt cessation may precipitate withdrawal, including status epilepticus in epileptic patients. Do not administer to patients in acute pain. Use caution in elderly, debilitated, renally impaired, hepatic dysfunction, or pediatric patients. May cause paradoxical responses, including agitation and hyperactivity, particularly in acute pain and pediatric patients. Use with caution in patients with depression or suicidal tendencies, or in patients with a history of drug abuse. Tolerance, psychological and physical dependence may occur with prolonged use.

May cause CNS depression, which may impair physical or mental abilities. Patients must be cautioned about performing tasks which require mental alertness (eg, operating machinery or driving). Effects with other sedative drugs or ethanol may be potentiated. Use of this agent as a hypnotic in the elderly is not recommended due to its long half-life and potential for physical and psychological dependence.

May cause respiratory depression or hypotension, particularly when administered intravenously. Use with caution in hemodynamically unstable patients or patients with respiratory disease. High doses (loading doses of 15-35 mg/kg given over 1-2 hours) have been utilized to induce pentobarbital coma, but these higher doses often cause hypotension requiring vasopressor therapy.

Common Adverse Reactions Frequency not defined.

Cardiovascular: Bradycardia, hypotension, syncope

Central nervous system: Drowsiness, lethargy, CNS excitation or depression, impaired judgment, "hangover" effect, confusion, somnolence, agitation, hyperkinesia, ataxia, nervousness, headache, insomnia, nightmares, hallucinations, anxiety, dizziness

Dermatologic: Rash, exfoliative dermatitis, Stevens-Johnson syndrome

Gastrointestinal: Nausea, vomiting, constipation

Hematologic: Agranulocytosis, thrombocytopenia, megaloblastic anemia

Local: Pain at injection site, thrombophlebitis with I.V. use

Renal: Oliguria

Respiratory: Laryngospasm, respiratory depression, apnea (especially with rapid I.V. use), hypoventilation, apnea

Miscellaneous: Gangrene with inadvertent intra-arterial injection

Drug Interactions

Cytochrome P450 Effect: Induces CYP2A6 (strong), 3A4 (strong)

Increased Effect/Toxicity: When combined with other CNS depressants, ethanol, narcotic analgesics, antidepressants, or benzodiazepines, additive respiratory and CNS depression may occur. Chronic use of barbiturates may enhance the hepatotoxic potential of acetaminophen overdoses. Chloramphenicol, MAO inhibitors, valproic acid, and felbamate may inhibit barbiturate metabolism. Barbiturates may impair the absorption of griseofulvin, and may enhance the nephrotoxic effects of methoxyflurane.

Decreased Effect: Barbiturates such as pentobarbital are hepatic enzyme inducers, and (only with chronic use) may increase the metabolism of antipsychotics, some beta-blockers (unlikely with atenolol and nadolol), calcium channel blockers, chloramphenicol, cimetidine, corticosteroids, cyclosporine, disopyramide, doxycycline, ethosuximide, felbamate, furosemide, griseofulvin, lamotrigine, phenytoin, propafenone, quinidine, tacrolimus, TCAs, and theophylline. Barbiturates may increase the metabolism of estrogens and reduce the efficacy of oral contraceptives; an alternative method of contraception should be considered. Barbiturates inhibit the hypoprothrombinemic effects of oral anticoagulants via increased metabolism. Barbiturates may enhance the metabolism of methadone resulting in methadone withdrawal.

Mechanism of Action Short-acting barbiturate with sedative, hypnotic, and anticonvulsant properties. Barbiturates depress the sensory cortex, decrease motor activity, alter cerebellar function, and produce drowsiness, sedation, and hypnosis. In high doses, barbiturates exhibit anticonvulsant activity; barbiturates produce dose-dependent respiratory depression.

Pharmacodynamics/Kinetics

Onset of action: I.M.: 10-15 minutes; I.V.: ~1 minute

Duration: I.V.: 15 minutes

Distribution: V_d: Children: 0.8 L/kg; Adults: 1 L/kg

Protein binding: 35% to 55%

Metabolism: Extensively hepatic via hydroxylation and oxidation pathways

Half-life elimination: Terminal: Children: 25 hours; Adults: Healthy: 22 hours (range: 15-50 hours)

Excretion: Urine (<1% as unchanged drug)

Dosage

Children:

Hypnotic: I.M.: 2-6 mg/kg; maximum: 100 mg/dose

Preoperative/preprocedure sedation: ≥6 months:

Note: Limited information is available for infants <6 months of age.

I.M.: 2-6 mg/kg; maximum: 100 mg/dose

I.V.: 1-3 mg/kg to a maximum of 100 mg until asleep

Conscious sedation prior to a procedure: Children 5-12 years: I.V.: 2 mg/kg 5-10 minutes before procedures, may repeat one time

Adolescents: Conscious sedation: I.V.: 100 mg prior to a procedure

Children and Adults: Barbiturate coma in head injury patients: I.V.: Loading dose: 5-10 mg/kg given slowly over 1-2 hours; monitor blood pressure and respiratory rate; Maintenance infusion: Initial: 1 mg/kg/hour; may increase to 2-3 mg/kg/hour; maintain burst suppression on EEG

Status epilepticus: I.V.: **Note:** Intubation required; monitor hemodynamics

Children: Loading dose: 5-15 mg/kg given slowly over 1-2 hours; maintenance infusion: 0.5-5 mg/kg/hour

Adults: Loading dose: 2-15 mg/kg given slowly over 1-2 hours; maintenance infusion: 0.5-3 mg/kg/hour

Adults:

Hypnotic:

I.M.: 150-200 mg

I.V.: Initial: 100 mg, may repeat every 1-3 minutes up to 200-500 mg total dose

Preoperative sedation: I.M.: 150-200 mg

Dosing adjustment in hepatic impairment: Reduce dosage in patients with severe liver dysfunction

Administration Pentobarbital may be administered by deep I.M. or slow I.V. injection.

(Continued)

Pentobarbital *(Continued)*

I.M.: No more than 5 mL (250 mg) should be injected at any one site because of possible tissue irritation.

I.V.: I.V. push doses can be given undiluted, but should be administered no faster than 50 mg/minute; parenteral solutions are highly alkaline; avoid extravasation; avoid rapid I.V. administration >50 mg/minute; avoid intra-arterial injection

Monitoring Parameters Respiratory status (for conscious sedation, includes pulse oximetry), cardiovascular status, CNS status; cardiac monitor and blood pressure monitor required

Reference Range

Therapeutic:
Hypnotic: 1-5 µg/mL (SI: 4-22 µmol/L)
Coma: 10-50 µg/mL (SI: 88-221 µmol/L)
Toxic: >10 µg/mL (SI: >44 µmol/L)

Patient Information Avoid alcohol and other CNS depressants; avoid driving and other hazardous tasks; avoid abrupt discontinuation; may cause physical and psychological dependence; do not alter dose without notifying prescriber

Dosage Forms INJ, solution: 50 mg/mL (20 mL, 50 mL)

♦ **Pentobarbital Sodium** *see Pentobarbital on page 978*

Pentosan Polysulfate Sodium *(PEN toe san pol i SUL fate SOW dee um)*

U.S. Brand Names Elmiron®

Synonyms PPS

Therapeutic Category Analgesic, Urinary

Use Orphan drug: Relief of bladder pain or discomfort due to interstitial cystitis

Pregnancy Risk Factor B

Dosage Adults: Oral: 100 mg 3 times/day taken with water 1 hour before or 2 hours after meals

Patients should be evaluated at 3 months and may be continued an additional 3 months if there has been no improvement and if there are no therapy-limiting side effects. **The risks and benefits of continued use beyond 6 months in patients who have not responded is not yet known.**

Dosage Forms CAP: 100 mg

Pentostatin *(PEN toe stat in)*

U.S. Brand Names Nipent®

Synonyms CL-825; Co-Vidarabine; dCF; Deoxycoformycin; 2'-Deoxycoformycin; NSC-218321

Therapeutic Category Antineoplastic Agent, Antimetabolite

Use Treatment of hairy cell leukemia; non-Hodgkin's lymphoma, cutaneous T-cell lymphoma

Pregnancy Risk Factor D

Contraindications Hypersensitivity to pentostatin or any component; pregnancy

Warnings/Precautions The FDA currently recommends that procedures for proper handling and disposal of antineoplastic agents be considered. Pregnant women or women of child-bearing age should be apprised of the potential risk to the fetus; use extreme caution in the presence of renal insufficiency; use with caution in patients with signs or symptoms of impaired hepatic function.

Common Adverse Reactions

>10%:
Central nervous system: Fever, chills, headache
Dermatologic: Skin rashes (25% to 30%), alopecia (10%)
Gastrointestinal: Mild to moderate nausea, vomiting (60%), stomatitis, diarrhea (13%), anorexia
Genitourinary: Acute renal failure (35%)
Hematologic: Thrombocytopenia (50%), dose-limiting in 25% of patients; anemia (40% to 45%), neutropenia, mild to moderate, not dose-limiting (11%)
Nadir: 7 days
Recovery: 10-14 days
Hepatic: Mild to moderate increases in transaminase levels (30%), usually transient; hepatitis (19%), usually reversible
Respiratory: Pulmonary edema (15%), may be exacerbated by fludarabine
Miscellaneous: Infection (57%; 35% severe, life-threatening)

1% to 10%:
Cardiovascular: Chest pain, arrhythmia, peripheral edema
Central nervous system: Opportunistic infections (8%); anxiety, confusion, depression, dizziness, insomnia, nervousness, somnolence, myalgias, malaise
Dermatologic: Dry skin, eczema, pruritus
Gastrointestinal: Constipation, flatulence, weight loss
Neuromuscular & skeletal: Paresthesia, weakness
Ocular: Moderate to severe keratoconjunctivitis, abnormal vision, eye pain
Otic: Ear pain
Respiratory: Dyspnea, pneumonia, bronchitis, pharyngitis, rhinitis, epistaxis, sinusitis (3% to 7%)

Drug Interactions

Increased Effect/Toxicity: Increased toxicity with vidarabine and allopurinol; combined use with fludarabine may lead to severe, even fatal, pulmonary toxicity

Mechanism of Action Pentostatin is a purine antimetabolite that inhibits adenosine deaminase, preventing the deamination of adenosine to inosine. Accumulation of deoxyadenosine (dAdo) and deoxyadenosine 5'-triphosphate (dATP) results in a reduction of purine metabolism and DNA synthesis and cell death.

Pharmacodynamics/Kinetics
Distribution: I.V.: V_d: 36.1 L (20.1 L/m^2); rapidly to body tissues
Half-life elimination: Distribution half-life: 30-85 minutes; Terminal: 5-15 hours
Excretion: Urine (~50% to 96%) within 24 hours (30% to 90% as unchanged drug)

Dosage Refractory hairy cell leukemia: Adults (refer to individual protocols):
4 mg/m^2 every other week **or**
4 mg/m^2 weekly for 3 weeks, then every 2 weeks **or**
5 mg/m^2 daily for 3 days every 3 weeks

Dosing interval in renal impairment:
Cl$_{cr}$ <60 mL/minute: Use extreme caution
Cl$_{cr}$ 50-60 mL/minute: 2 mg/m^2/dose

Administration Administer I.V. as a 15- to 30-minute infusion; continuous infusion regimens have been reported, but are not commonly used
I.V. bolus over ≥3-5 minutes in D$_5$W or NS at concentrations ≥2 mg/mL

Dosage Forms INJ, powder for reconstitution: 10 mg

♦ **Pentothal**® *see* Thiopental *on page 1216*

Pentoxifylline (pen toks I fi leen)

U.S. Brand Names Pentoxil®; Trental®

Synonyms Oxpentifylline

Therapeutic Category Blood Viscosity Reducer Agent; Hemorheologic Agent

Use Treatment of intermittent claudication on the basis of chronic occlusive arterial disease of the limbs; may improve function and symptoms, but not intended to replace more definitive therapy

Unlabeled/Investigational Use AIDS patients with increased TNF, CVA, cerebrovascular diseases, diabetic atherosclerosis, diabetic neuropathy, gangrene, hemodialysis shunt thrombosis, vascular impotence, cerebral malaria, septic shock, sickle cell syndromes, and vasculitis

Pregnancy Risk Factor C

Contraindications Hypersensitivity to pentoxifylline, xanthines, or any component of the formulation; recent cerebral and/or retinal hemorrhage

Warnings/Precautions Use with caution in patients with renal impairment

Common Adverse Reactions 1% to 10%:
Central nervous system: Dizziness, headache
Gastrointestinal: Dyspepsia, nausea, vomiting

Drug Interactions
Cytochrome P450 Effect: Inhibits CYP1A2 (weak)
Increased Effect/Toxicity: Pentoxifylline levels may be increased with cimetidine and other H$_2$ antagonists. May increase anticoagulation with warfarin. Pentoxifylline may increase the serum levels of theophylline.
Decreased Effect: Blood pressure changes (decreases) have been observed with the addition of pentoxifylline therapy in patients receiving antihypertensives.

Mechanism of Action Mechanism of action remains unclear; is thought to reduce blood viscosity and improve blood flow by altering the rheology of red blood cells

Pharmacodynamics/Kinetics
Absorption: Well absorbed
Metabolism: Hepatic and via erythrocytes; extensive first-pass effect
Half-life elimination: Parent drug: 24-48 minutes; Metabolites: 60-96 minutes
Time to peak, serum: 2-4 hours
Excretion: Primarily urine

Dosage Adults: Oral: 400 mg 3 times/day with meals; may reduce to 400 mg twice daily if GI or CNS side effects occur

Patient Information Take with food or meals; if GI or CNS side effects continue, contact prescriber; while effects may be seen in 2-4 weeks, continue treatment for at least 8 weeks

Dosage Forms TAB, controlled release (Trental®): 400 mg. **TAB, extended release** (Pentoxil®): 400 mg

♦ **Pentoxil**® *see* Pentoxifylline *on page 981*
♦ **Pen VK** *see* Penicillin V Potassium *on page 975*
♦ **Pepcid**® *see* Famotidine *on page 506*
♦ **Pepcid**® **AC [OTC]** *see* Famotidine *on page 506*
♦ **Pepcid**® **Complete [OTC]** *see* Famotidine, Calcium Carbonate, and Magnesium Hydroxide *on page 507*
♦ **Pepto-Bismol**® **[OTC]** *see* Bismuth *on page 168*
♦ **Pepto-Bismol**® **Maximum Strength [OTC]** *see* Bismuth *on page 168*
♦ **Percocet**® *see* Oxycodone and Acetaminophen *on page 945*
♦ **Percodan**® *see* Oxycodone and Aspirin *on page 945*
♦ **Percodan**®**-Demi [DSC]** *see* Oxycodone and Aspirin *on page 945*
♦ **Percogesic**® **[OTC]** *see* Acetaminophen and Phenyltoloxamine *on page 26*
♦ **Percogesic**® **Extra Strength [OTC]** *see* Acetaminophen and Diphenhydramine *on page 26*
♦ **Percolone**® **[DSC]** *see* Oxycodone *on page 944*
♦ **Perdiem**® **Fiber Therapy [OTC]** *see* Psyllium *on page 1063*

Pergolide (PER go lide)

Related Information
Parkinson's Agents Comparison *on page 1402*

U.S. Brand Names Permax®

Synonyms Pergolide Mesylate

Therapeutic Category Anti-Parkinson's Agent, Dopamine Agonist; Dopaminergic Agent, Antiparkinson's; Ergot Alkaloid and Derivative

Use Adjunctive treatment to levodopa/carbidopa in the management of Parkinson's disease

Unlabeled/Investigational Use Tourette's disorder, chronic motor or vocal tic disorder

Pregnancy Risk Factor B

Contraindications Hypersensitivity to pergolide mesylate, other ergot derivatives, or any component of the formulation; ergot alkaloids are contraindicated with potent inhibitors of CYP3A4 (includes protease inhibitors, azole antifungals, and some macrolide antibiotics)

Warnings/Precautions Symptomatic hypotension occurs in 10% of patients; use with caution in patients with a history of cardiac arrhythmias, hallucinations, or mental illness. Cardiac valvular, pleural, and peritoneal fibrosis have been reported with prolonged daily use. Avoid rapid dose reduction or abrupt discontinuation.

Pergolide has been associated with somnolence. Some patients have been reported to fall asleep during activities of daily living, including driving, while taking this medication. Not all patients exhibited somnolence prior to these events.

Common Adverse Reactions
>10%:
- Central nervous system: Dizziness (19%), hallucinations (14%), dystonia (12%), somnolence (10%), confusion (10%)
- Gastrointestinal: Nausea (24%), constipation (11%)
- Neuromuscular & skeletal: Dyskinesia (62%)
- Respiratory: Rhinitis (12%)

1% to 10%:
- Cardiovascular: Hypotension or postural hypotension (10%), peripheral edema (7%), chest pain (4%), vasodilation (3%), palpitation (2%), syncope (2%), arrhythmias (1%), hypertension (2%), MI (1%)
- Central nervous system: Insomnia (8%), pain (7%), anxiety (6%), psychosis (2%), EPS (2%), incoordination (2%), chills (1%)
- Dermatologic: Rash (3%)
- Gastrointestinal: Diarrhea (6%), dyspepsia (6%), abdominal pain (6%), anorexia (5%), xerostomia (4%), vomiting (3%), dysphagia (1%), nausea (1%)
- Hematologic: Anemia (1%)
- Neuromuscular & skeletal: Myalgia (1%), neuralgia (1%)
- Ocular: Abnormal vision (6%), diplopia (2%)
- Respiratory: Dyspnea (5%), epistaxis (2%)
- Miscellaneous: Flu syndrome (3%), hiccups (1%)

Drug Interactions
Cytochrome P450 Effect: Substrate of CYP3A4 (major); **Inhibits** CYP2D6 (strong), 3A4 (weak)

Increased Effect/Toxicity: Effects of pergolide may be increased by antifungals (azole derivatives); CYP3A4 inhibitors (eg, amiodarone, cimetidine, erythromycin, ritonavir); macrolide antibiotics; levodopa (hallucinations); protease inhibitors; MAO inhibitors. Pergolide may increase the effects of CYP2D6 substrates (eg, TCAs, fluoxetine, fluvoxamine, risperidone); sibutramine; and other serotonin agonists (serotonin syndrome).

Decreased Effect: Effects of pergolide may be diminished by antipsychotics, metoclopramide.

Mechanism of Action Pergolide is a semisynthetic ergot alkaloid similar to bromocriptine but stated to be more potent (10-1000 times) and longer-acting; it is a centrally-active dopamine agonist stimulating both D_1 and D_2 receptors. Pergolide is believed to exert its therapeutic effect by directly stimulating postsynaptic dopamine receptors in the nigrostriatal system.

Pharmacodynamics/Kinetics
- Absorption: Well absorbed
- Protein binding, plasma: 90%
- Metabolism: Extensively hepatic
- Half-life elimination: 27 hours
- Excretion: Urine (~50%); feces (50%)

Dosage When adding pergolide to levodopa/carbidopa, the dose of the latter can usually and should be decreased. Patients no longer responsive to bromocriptine may benefit by being switched to pergolide. Oral:
- Children and Adolescents: Tourette's disorder, chronic motor or vocal disorder (unlabeled uses): Up to 300 mcg/day
- Adults: Parkinson's disease: Start with 0.05 mg/day for 2 days, then increase dosage by 0.1 or 0.15 mg/day every 3 days over next 12 days, increase dose by 0.25 mg/day every 3 days until optimal therapeutic dose is achieved, up to 5 mg/day maximum; usual dosage range: 2-3 mg/day in 3 divided doses

Monitoring Parameters Blood pressure (both sitting/supine and standing), symptoms of parkinsonism, dyskinesias, mental status

Patient Information Take with food or milk; rise slowly from sitting or lying down; report any confusion or change in mental status. Patients should be advised of this issue and factors which may increase risk (sleep disorders or other sedating medications) and instructed to report daytime somnolence or any episode of falling asleep during activities to the prescriber.

Patients should use caution in performing activities which require alertness (driving or operating machinery), and to avoid other medications which may cause CNS depression, including ethanol.

Dosage Forms TAB: 0.05 mg, 0.25 mg, 1 mg

♦ **Pergolide Mesylate** *see Pergolide on page 982*

♦ **Pergonal®** *see Menotropins on page 789*

♦ **Periactin** *see Cyproheptadine on page 327*

♦ **Peri-Colace® *(reformulation)* [OTC]** *see Docusate and Senna on page 398*

♦ **Peridex®** *see Chlorhexidine Gluconate on page 259*

Perindopril Erbumine (per IN doe pril er BYOO meen)

Related Information
Angiotensin Agents Comparison *on page 1353*

U.S. Brand Names Aceon®

Therapeutic Category Angiotensin-Converting Enzyme (ACE) Inhibitor; Antihypertensive Agent

Use Treatment of stage I or II hypertension and congestive heart failure; treatment of left ventricular dysfunction after myocardial infarction

Pregnancy Risk Factor D (especially 2nd and 3rd trimesters)

Contraindications Hypersensitivity to perindopril or any component of the formulation; angioedema related to previous treatment with an ACE inhibitor; bilateral renal artery stenosis; pregnancy (2nd and 3rd trimesters)

Warnings/Precautions Anaphylactic reactions can occur. Angioedema can occur at any time during treatment (especially following first dose). Angioedema may involve head and neck (potentially affecting the airway) or the intestine (presenting with abdominal pain). Careful blood pressure monitoring with first dose (hypotension can occur especially in volume depleted patients). Dosage adjustment needed in renal impairment. Use with caution in hypovolemia; collagen vascular diseases; valvular stenosis (particularly aortic stenosis); hyperkalemia; or before, during, or immediately after anesthesia. Avoid rapid dosage escalation, which may lead to renal insufficiency. Neutropenia/agranulocytosis with myeloid hyperplasia can rarely occur. If patient has renal impairment then a baseline WBC with differential and serum creatinine should be evaluated and monitored closely during the first 3 months of treatment. Hypersensitivity reactions may be seen during hemodialysis with high-flux dialysis membranes (eg, AN69). Use with caution in unilateral renal artery stenosis and pre-existing renal insufficiency.

Common Adverse Reactions
>10% Central nervous system: Headache (23%)

1% to 10%:
Cardiovascular: edema (4%), chest pain (2%)
Central nervous system: Dizziness (8%), sleep disorders (3%), depression (2%), fever (2%), weakness (8%), nervousness (1%)
Dermatologic: Rash (2%)
Endocrine & metabolic: Hyperkalemia (1%), increased triglycerides (1%)
Gastrointestinal: Nausea (2%), diarrhea (4%), vomiting (2%), dyspepsia (2%), abdominal pain (3%), flatulence (1%)
Genitourinary: Sexual dysfunction (male: 1%)
Hepatic: Increased ALT (2%)
Neuromuscular & skeletal: Back pain (6%), upper extremity pain (3%), lower extremity pain (5%), paresthesia (2%), joint pain (1%), myalgia (1%), arthritis (1%)
Renal: Proteinuria (2%)
Respiratory: Cough (incidence is higher in women, 3:1) (12%), sinusitis (5%), rhinitis (5%), pharyngitis (3%)
Otic: Tinnitus (2%)
Miscellaneous: Viral infection (3%)

Note: Some reactions occurred at an incidence >1% but ≤ placebo.

Additional adverse effects associated with with **ACE inhibitors** include agranulocytosis (especially in patients with renal impairment or collagen vascular disease), neutropenia, decreases in creatinine clearance in some elderly hypertensive patients or those with chronic renal failure, and worsening of renal function in patients with bilateral renal artery stenosis or hypovolemic patients (diuretic therapy). In addition, a syndrome which may include fever, myalgia, arthralgia, interstitial nephritis, vasculitis, rash, eosinophilia and positive ANA, and elevated ESR has been reported with ACE inhibitors.

Drug Interactions
Increased Effect/Toxicity: Potassium supplements, co-trimoxazole (high dose), angiotensin II receptor antagonists (candesartan, losartan, irbesartan, etc), or potassium-sparing diuretics (amiloride, spironolactone, triamterene) may result in elevated serum potassium levels when combined with perindopril. ACE inhibitor effects may be increased by phenothiazines or probenecid (increases levels of captopril). ACE inhibitors may increase serum concentrations/effects of digoxin, lithium, and sulfonylureas.

Diuretics have additive hypotensive effects with ACE inhibitors, and hypovolemia increases the potential for adverse renal effects of ACE inhibitors. In patients with compromised renal function, coadministration with NSAIDs may result in further deterioration of renal function. Allopurinol and ACE inhibitors may cause a higher risk of hypersensitivity reaction when taken concurrently.

(Continued)

Perindopril Erbumine *(Continued)*

Decreased Effect: Aspirin (high dose) may reduce the therapeutic effects of ACE inhibitors; at low dosages this does not appear to be significant. Rifampin may decrease the effect of ACE inhibitors. Antacids may decrease the bioavailability of ACE inhibitors (may be more likely to occur with captopril); separate administration times by 1-2 hours. NSAIDs, specifically indomethacin, may reduce the hypotensive effects of ACE inhibitors. More likely to occur in low renin or volume dependent hypertensive patients.

Mechanism of Action Competitive inhibitor of angiotensin-converting enzyme (ACE); prevents conversion of angiotensin I to angiotensin II, a potent vasoconstrictor; results in lower levels of angiotensin II which, in turn, causes an increase in plasma renin activity and a reduction in aldosterone secretion

Pharmacodynamics/Kinetics
Onset of action: Peak effect: 1-2 hours
Distribution: Small amounts enter breast milk
Protein binding: Perindopril: 60%; Perindoprilat: 10% to 20%
Metabolism: Hepatically hydrolyzed to active metabolite, perindoprilat (~17% to 20% of a dose) and other inactive metabolites
Bioavailability: Perindopril: 65% to 95%
Half-life elimination: Parent drug: 1.5-3 hours; Metabolite: Effective: 3-10 hours, Terminal: 30-120 hours
Time to peak: Chronic therapy: Perindopril: 1 hour; Perindoprilat: 3-4 hours (maximum perindoprilat serum levels are 2-3 times higher and T_{max} is shorter following chronic therapy); CHF: Perindoprilat: 6 hours
Excretion: Urine (75%, 10% as unchanged drug)

Dosage Adults: Oral:
Congestive heart failure: 4 mg once daily
Hypertension: Initial: 4 mg/day but may be titrated to response; usual range: 4-8 mg/day, maximum: 16 mg/day

Dosing adjustment in renal impairment:
Cl_{cr} >60 mL/minute: Administer 4 mg/day.
Cl_{cr} 30-60 mL/minute: Administer 2 mg/day.
Cl_{cr} 15-29 mL/minute: Administer 2 mg every other day.
Cl_{cr} <15 mL/minute: Administer 2 mg on the day of dialysis.
Hemodialysis: Perindopril and its metabolites are dialyzable

Dosing adjustment in hepatic impairment: None needed

Dosing adjustment in geriatric patients: Due to greater bioavailability and lower renal clearance of the drug in elderly subjects, dose reduction of 50% is recommended.

Monitoring Parameters Serum creatinine, electrolytes, and WBC with differential initially and repeated at 2-week intervals for at least 90 days; urinalysis for protein

Patient Information This medication does not replace the to need to follow exercise and diet recommendations for hypertension. Take as directed; do not miss doses, alter dosage, or discontinue without consulting prescriber. Consult prescriber for appropriate diet. Change position slowly when rising from sitting or lying. May cause transient drowsiness; avoid driving or engaging in tasks that require alertness until response to drug is known. May be taken consistently either with or without food; however, small frequent meals may help reduce any nausea, vomiting, or epigastric pain. Notify prescriber of persistent cough or other side effects. Do not end therapy except under prescriber advice; especially in first week of therapy may experience dizziness, fainting, and lightheadedness. Have blood pressure monitored regularly.

Dosage Forms TAB: 2 mg, 4 mg, 8 mg

- **PerioChip®** *see* Chlorhexidine Gluconate *on page 259*
- **PerioGard®** *see* Chlorhexidine Gluconate *on page 259*
- **Periostat®** *see* Doxycycline *on page 413*
- **Permapen® Isoject®** *see* Penicillin G Benzathine *on page 972*
- **Permax®** *see* Pergolide *on page 982*

Permethrin *(per METH rin)*

U.S. Brand Names A200® Lice [OTC]; Acticin®; Elimite®; Nix® [OTC]; Rid® Spray [OTC]
Therapeutic Category Antiparasitic Agent, Topical; Scabicidal Agent; Shampoo
Use Single-application treatment of infestation with *Pediculus humanus capitis* (head louse) and its nits or *Sarcoptes scabiei* (scabies); indicated for prophylactic use during epidemics of lice
Pregnancy Risk Factor B
Contraindications Hypersensitivity to pyrethroid, pyrethrin, chrysanthemums, or any component of the formulation; lotion is contraindicated for use in infants <2 months of age
Warnings/Precautions Treatment may temporarily exacerbate the symptoms of itching, redness, swelling; for external use only; use during pregnancy only if clearly needed
Common Adverse Reactions 1% to 10%:
Dermatologic: Pruritus, erythema, rash of the scalp
Local: Burning, stinging, tingling, numbness or scalp discomfort, edema
Mechanism of Action Inhibits sodium ion influx through nerve cell membrane channels in parasites resulting in delayed repolarization and thus paralysis and death of the pest
Pharmacodynamics/Kinetics
Absorption: <2%
Metabolism: Hepatic via ester hydrolysis to inactive metabolites
Excretion: Urine

Dosage Topical:

Head lice: Children >2 months and Adults: After hair has been washed with shampoo, rinsed with water, and towel dried, apply a sufficient volume of topical liquid (lotion or cream rinse) to saturate the hair and scalp. Leave on hair for 10 minutes before rinsing off with water; remove remaining nits; may repeat in 1 week if lice or nits still present.

Scabies: Apply cream from head to toe; leave on for 8-14 hours before washing off with water; for infants, also apply on the hairline, neck, scalp, temple, and forehead; may reapply in 1 week if live mites appear

Permethrin 5% cream was shown to be safe and effective when applied to an infant <1 month of age with neonatal scabies; time of application was limited to 6 hours before rinsing with soap and water

Administration

Cream: Apply from neck to toes. Bathe to remove drug after 8-14 hours. Repeat in 7 days if lice or nits are still present. Report if condition persists or infection occurs.

Cream rinse/lotion: Apply immediately after hair is shampooed, rinsed, and towel-dried. Apply enough to saturate hair and scalp (especially behind ears and on nape of neck). Leave on hair for 10 minutes before rinsing with water. Remove nits with fine-tooth comb. May repeat in 1 week if lice or nits are still present.

Patient Information Avoid contact with eyes and mucous membranes during application; shake well before using; notify prescriber if irritation persists; clothing and bedding should be washed in hot water or dry cleaned to kill the scabies mite

Dosage Forms CRM, topical (Acticin®, Elimite®): 5% (60 g). **LIQ, topical** (Nix®): 1% (60 mL). **LOTION, topical:** 1% (59 mL). **SPRAY, solution:** (A200® Lice): 0.5% (180 mL); (Nix®): 0.25% (148 mL); (Rid®): 0.5% (150 mL)

Perphenazine (per FEN a zeen)

Related Information

Antipsychotic Agents Comparison *on page 1364*

U.S. Brand Names Trilafon® [DSC]

Therapeutic Category Antipsychotic Agent, Phenothiazine; Antipsychotic Agent, Phenothiazine, Piperazine; Phenothiazine Derivative

Use Treatment of schizophrenia; nausea and vomiting

Unlabeled/Investigational Use Ethanol withdrawal; dementia in elderly; Tourette's syndrome; Huntington's chorea; spasmodic torticollis; Reye's syndrome; psychosis

Pregnancy Risk Factor C

Contraindications Hypersensitivity to perphenazine or any component of the formulation (cross-reactivity between phenothiazines may occur); severe CNS depression; subcortical brain damage; bone marrow suppression; blood dyscrasias; coma

Warnings/Precautions Safety in children <6 months of age has not been established. May cause hypotension. May be sedating, use with caution in disorders where CNS depression is a feature. Use with caution in Parkinson's disease. Caution in patients with hemodynamic instability; predisposition to seizures; severe cardiac, hepatic, renal, or respiratory disease. Esophageal dysmotility and aspiration have been associated with antipsychotic use - use with caution in patients at risk of pneumonia (ie, Alzheimer's disease). Caution in breast cancer or other prolactin-dependent tumors (may elevate prolactin levels). May alter temperature regulation or mask toxicity of other drugs due to antiemetic effects. May alter cardiac conduction - life-threatening arrhythmias have occurred with therapeutic doses of phenothiazines. May cause orthostatic hypotension - use with caution in patients at risk of this effect or those who would tolerate transient hypotensive episodes (cerebrovascular disease, cardiovascular disease, or other medications which may predispose).

Phenothiazines may cause anticholinergic effects (confusion, agitation, constipation, xerostomia, blurred vision, urinary retention); therefore, they should be used with caution in patients with decreased gastrointestinal motility, urinary retention, BPH, xerostomia, or visual problems. Conditions which also may be exacerbated by cholinergic blockade include narrow-angle glaucoma (screening is recommended) and worsening of myasthenia gravis. Relative to other neuroleptics, perphenazine has a low potency of cholinergic blockade.

May cause extrapyramidal reactions, including pseudoparkinsonism, acute dystonic reactions, akathisia, and tardive dyskinesia (risk of these reactions is moderate-high relative to other neuroleptics). May be associated with neuroleptic malignant syndrome (NMS) or pigmentary retinopathy.

Common Adverse Reactions Frequency not defined.

Cardiovascular: Hypotension, orthostatic hypotension, hypertension, tachycardia, bradycardia, dizziness, cardiac arrest

Central nervous system: Extrapyramidal symptoms (pseudoparkinsonism, akathisia, dystonias, tardive dyskinesia), dizziness, cerebral edema, seizures, headache, drowsiness, paradoxical excitement, restlessness, hyperactivity, insomnia, neuroleptic malignant syndrome (NMS), impairment of temperature regulation

Dermatologic: Increased sensitivity to sun, rash, discoloration of skin (blue-gray)

Endocrine & metabolic: Hypoglycemia, hyperglycemia, galactorrhea, lactation, breast enlargement, gynecomastia, menstrual irregularity, amenorrhea, SIADH, changes in libido

Gastrointestinal: Constipation, weight gain, vomiting, stomach pain, nausea, xerostomia, salivation, diarrhea, anorexia, ileus

Genitourinary: Difficulty in urination, ejaculatory disturbances, incontinence, polyuria, ejaculating dysfunction, priapism

Hematologic: Agranulocytosis, leukopenia, eosinophilia, hemolytic anemia, thrombocytopenic purpura, pancytopenia

(Continued)

Perphenazine *(Continued)*

Hepatic: Cholestatic jaundice, hepatotoxicity
Neuromuscular & skeletal: Tremor
Ocular: Pigmentary retinopathy, blurred vision, cornea and lens changes
Respiratory: Nasal congestion
Miscellaneous: Diaphoresis

Drug Interactions

Cytochrome P450 Effect: Substrate of CYP1A2 (minor), 2C8/9 (minor), 2C19 (minor), 2D6 (major), 3A4 (minor); **Inhibits** CYP1A2 (weak), 2D6 (weak)

Increased Effect/Toxicity: CYP2D6 inhibitors may increase the levels/effects of perphenazine; example inhibitors include chlorpromazine, delavirdine, fluoxetine, miconazole, paroxetine, pergolide, quinidine, quinine, ritonavir, and ropinirole. Effects on CNS depression may be additive when perphenazine is combined with CNS depressants (narcotic analgesics, ethanol, barbiturates, cyclic antidepressants, antihistamines, or sedative-hypnotics). Perphenazine may increase the effects/toxicity of anticholinergics, antihypertensives, lithium (rare neurotoxicity), trazodone, or valproic acid. Concurrent use with TCA may produce increased toxicity or altered therapeutic response. Chloroquine and propranolol may increase perphenazine concentrations. Hypotension may occur when perphenazine is combined with epinephrine. May increase the risk of arrhythmia when combined with antiarrhythmics, cisapride, pimozide, sparfloxacin, or other drugs which prolong QT interval. Metoclopramide may increase risk of extrapyramidal symptoms (EPS).

Decreased Effect: Phenothiazines inhibit the ability of bromocriptine to lower serum prolactin concentrations. Benztropine (and other anticholinergics) may inhibit the therapeutic response to perphenazine and excess anticholinergic effects may occur. Cigarette smoking and barbiturates may enhance the hepatic metabolism of chlorpromazine. Antihypertensive effects of guanethidine and guanadrel may be inhibited by perphenazine. Perphenazine may inhibit the antiparkinsonian effect of levodopa. Perphenazine and possibly other low potency antipsychotics may reverse the pressor effects of epinephrine.

Mechanism of Action Blocks postsynaptic mesolimbic dopaminergic receptors in the brain; exhibits alpha-adrenergic blocking effect and depresses the release of hypothalamic and hypophyseal hormones

Pharmacodynamics/Kinetics

Absorption: Oral: Well absorbed

Distribution: Crosses placenta

Metabolism: Extensively hepatic to metabolites via sulfoxidation, hydroxylation, dealkylation, and glucuronidation

Half-life elimination: Perphenazine: 9-12 hours; 7-hydroxyperphenazine: 11.3 hours

Time to peak, serum: Perphenazine: 1-3 hours; 7-hydroxyperphenazine: 2-4 hours

Excretion: Urine and feces

Dosage Oral:

Children:

Schizophrenia/psychoses:

1-6 years: 4-6 mg/day in divided doses

6-12 years: 6 mg/day in divided doses

>12 years: 4-16 mg 2-4 times/day

Adults:

Schizophrenia/psychoses: 4-16 mg 2-4 times/day not to exceed 64 mg/day

Nausea/vomiting: 8-16 mg/day in divided doses up to 24 mg/day

Elderly: Behavioral symptoms associated with dementia: Initial: 2-4 mg 1-2 times/day; increase at 4- to 7-day intervals by 2-4 mg/day. Increase dose intervals (bid, tid, etc) as necessary to control behavior response or side effects. Maximum daily dose: 32 mg; gradual increase (titration) and bedtime administration may prevent some side effects or decrease their severity.

Hemodialysis: Not dialyzable (0% to 5%)

Dosing adjustment in hepatic impairment: Dosage reductions should be considered in patients with liver disease although no specific guidelines are available

Monitoring Parameters Vital signs; lipid profile, fasting blood glucose/Hgb A$_{1c}$; BMI; mental status, abnormal involuntary movement scale (AIMS), extrapyramidal symptoms (EPS)

Reference Range 2-6 nmol/L

Patient Information May cause drowsiness, impair judgment and coordination; report any feelings of restlessness or any involuntary movements; avoid alcohol and other CNS depressants; do not alter dose or discontinue without consulting prescriber

Dosage Forms TAB: 2 mg, 4 mg, 8 mg, 16 mg

- ♦ **Perphenazine and Amitriptyline** *see* Amitriptyline and Perphenazine *on page 81*
- ♦ **Persantine®** *see* Dipyridamole *on page 391*
- ♦ **Pethidine Hydrochloride** *see* Meperidine *on page 791*
- ♦ **PFA** *see* Foscarnet *on page 564*
- ♦ **Pfizerpen®** *see* Penicillin G (Parenteral/Aqueous) *on page 973*
- ♦ **PGE₁** *see* Alprostadil *on page 61*
- ♦ **PGE₂** *see* Dinoprostone *on page 382*
- ♦ **PGI₂** *see* Epoprostenol *on page 445*
- ♦ **PGX** *see* Epoprostenol *on page 445*
- ♦ **Phanasin [OTC]** *see* Guaifenesin *on page 603*

♦ **Pharmaflur**® *see Fluoride on page 535*
♦ **Pharmaflur**® **1.1** *see Fluoride on page 535*

Phenazopyridine (fen az oh PEER i deen)

U.S. Brand Names Azo-Gesic® [OTC]; Azo-Standard® [OTC]; Prodium® [OTC]; Pyridium®; ReAzo [OTC]; Uristat® [OTC]; UTI Relief® [OTC]
Synonyms Phenazopyridine Hydrochloride; Phenylazo Diamino Pyridine Hydrochloride
Therapeutic Category Analgesic, Urinary; Local Anesthetic, Urinary
Use Symptomatic relief of urinary burning, itching, frequency and urgency in association with urinary tract infection or following urologic procedures
Pregnancy Risk Factor B
Contraindications Hypersensitivity to phenazopyridine or any component of the formulation; kidney or liver disease; patients with a Cl_{cr} <50 mL/minute
Warnings/Precautions Does not treat infection, acts only as an analgesic; drug should be discontinued if skin or sclera develop a yellow color; use with caution in patients with renal impairment. Use of this agent in the elderly is limited since accumulation of phenazopyridine can occur in patients with renal insufficiency. Use is contraindicated in patients with a Cl_{cr} <50 mL/minute.
Common Adverse Reactions 1% to 10%:
Central nervous system: Headache, dizziness
Gastrointestinal: Stomach cramps
Mechanism of Action An azo dye which exerts local anesthetic or analgesic action on urinary tract mucosa through an unknown mechanism
Pharmacodynamics/Kinetics
Metabolism: Hepatic and via other tissues
Excretion: Urine (65% as unchanged drug)
Dosage Oral:
Children: 12 mg/kg/day in 3 divided doses administered after meals for 2 days
Adults: 100-200 mg 3 times/day after meals for 2 days when used concomitantly with an antibacterial agent
Dosing interval in renal impairment:
Cl_{cr} 50-80 mL/minute: Administer every 8-16 hours
Cl_{cr} <50 mL/minute: Avoid use
Patient Information Take after meals; tablets may color urine orange or red and may stain clothing
Dosage Forms TAB: 95 mg, 97 mg, 97.2 mg, 100 mg, 200 mg

♦ **Phenazopyridine Hydrochloride** *see Phenazopyridine on page 987*

Phenelzine (FEN el zeen)

Related Information
Antidepressant Agents Comparison *on page 1359*
U.S. Brand Names Nardil®
Synonyms Phenelzine Sulfate
Therapeutic Category Antidepressant, Monoamine Oxidase Inhibitor
Use Symptomatic treatment of atypical, nonendogenous, or neurotic depression
Unlabeled/Investigational Use Selective mutism
Pregnancy Risk Factor C
Contraindications Hypersensitivity to phenelzine or any component of the formulation; uncontrolled hypertension; pheochromocytoma; hepatic disease; congestive heart failure; concurrent use of sympathomimetics (and related compounds), CNS depressants, ethanol, meperidine, bupropion, buspirone, guanethidine, serotonergic drugs (including SSRIs) - do not use within 5 weeks of fluoxetine discontinuation or 2 weeks of other antidepressant discontinuation; general anesthesia, local vasoconstrictors; spinal anesthesia (hypotension may be exaggerated); foods with a high content of tyramine, tryptophan, or dopamine, chocolate, or caffeine (may cause hypertensive crisis)
Warnings/Precautions Safety in children <16 years of age has not been established; use with caution in patients who are hyperactive, hyperexcitable, or who have glaucoma. Hypertensive crisis may occur with tyramine.

Should not be used in combination with other antidepressants. Hypotensive effects of antihypertensives (beta-blockers, thiazides) may be exaggerated. May cause orthostatic hypotension - use with caution in patients with hypotension or patients who would not tolerate transient hypotensive episodes (cardiovascular or cerebrovascular disease) - effects may be additive with other agents which cause orthostasis. Has been associated with activation of hypomania and/or mania in bipolar patients. May worsen psychotic symptoms in some patients. The possibility of a suicide attempt is inherent in major depression and may persist until remission occurs. Use caution in high-risk patients during initiation of therapy. Prescriptions should be written for the smallest quantity consistent with good patient care. Use with caution in patients at risk of seizures, or in patients receiving other drugs which may lower seizure threshold. Toxic reactions have occurred with dextromethorphan. Discontinue at least 48 hours prior to myelography. Discontinue at least 10 days prior to elective surgery.

The MAO inhibitors are effective and generally well tolerated by older patients. It is the potential interactions with tyramine or tryptophan-containing foods and other drugs, and their effects on blood pressure that have limited their use.
Common Adverse Reactions Frequency not defined.
Cardiovascular: Orthostatic hypotension, edema
(Continued)

Phenelzine *(Continued)*

Central nervous system: Dizziness, headache, drowsiness, sleep disturbances, fatigue, hyper-reflexia, twitching, ataxia, mania

Dermatologic: Rash, pruritus

Endocrine & metabolic: Decreased sexual ability (anorgasmia, ejaculatory disturbances, impotence), hypernatremia, hypermetabolic syndrome

Gastrointestinal: Xerostomia, constipation, weight gain

Genitourinary: Urinary retention

Hematologic: Leukopenia

Hepatic: Hepatitis

Neuromuscular & skeletal: Weakness, tremor, myoclonus

Ocular: Blurred vision, glaucoma

Miscellaneous: Diaphoresis

Drug Interactions

Increased Effect/Toxicity: In general, the combined use of phenelzine with TCAs, venlafaxine, trazodone, dexfenfluramine, sibutramine, lithium, meperidine, fenfluramine, dextromethorphan, and SSRIs should be avoided due to the potential for severe adverse reactions (serotonin syndrome, death); avoid meperidine within 2 weeks of phenelzine use, allow 5 weeks between discontinuing fluoxetine and starting MAO inhibitors, allow at least 10 days after discontinuing MAO inhibitors and starting fluoxetine; concurrent use with dextromethorphan is contraindicated. MAO inhibitors (including phenelzine) may inhibit the metabolism of barbiturates and prolong their effect. Phenelzine in combination with amphetamines, other stimulants (methylphenidate), levodopa, metaraminol, reserpine, and decongestants (pseudoephedrine) may result in severe hypertensive reactions. Concurrent use with amphetamines, methylphenidate, metaraminol, and pseudoephedrine is contraindicated.

Foods (eg, cheese) and beverages (eg, ethanol) containing tyramine should be avoided; hypertensive crisis may result. Phenelzine may increase the pressor response of norepinephrine and may prolong neuromuscular blockade produced by succinylcholine. Tramadol may increase the risk of seizures and serotonin syndrome in patients receiving an MAO inhibitor. Phenelzine may produce additive hypoglycemic effect in patients receiving hypoglycemic agents and may produce delirium in patients receiving disulfiram. Concurrent use with bupropion is contraindicated; allow at least 14 days between discontinuing MAO inhibitors and starting bupropion. Concurrent use with buspirone may cause hypertension; wait at least 14 days between discontinuing one agent and starting the other.

Decreased Effect: Phenelzine (and other MAO inhibitors) inhibits the antihypertensive response to guanadrel or guanethidine; concurrent use is contraindicated.

Mechanism of Action Thought to act by increasing endogenous concentrations of norepinephrine, dopamine, and serotonin through inhibition of the enzyme (monoamine oxidase) responsible for the breakdown of these neurotransmitters

Pharmacodynamics/Kinetics

Onset of action: Therapeutic: 2-4 weeks

Duration: May continue to have a therapeutic effect and interactions 2 weeks after discontinuing therapy

Absorption: Well absorbed

Metabolism: Oxidized via monoamine oxidase (primary pathway) and acetylation (minor pathway)

Half-life elimination: 11 hours

Excretion: Urine (primarily as metabolites and unchanged drug)

Dosage Oral:

Children: Selective mutism (unlabeled use): 30-60 mg/day

Adults: Depression: 15 mg 3 times/day; may increase to 60-90 mg/day during early phase of treatment, then reduce dose for maintenance therapy slowly after maximum benefit is obtained; takes 2-4 weeks for a significant response to occur

Elderly: Depression: Initial: 7.5 mg/day; increase by 7.5-15 mg/day every 3-4 days as tolerated; usual therapeutic dose: 15-60 mg/day in 3-4 divided doses

Monitoring Parameters Blood pressure, heart rate, diet, weight, mood (if depressive symptoms)

Patient Information Avoid tyramine-containing foods: Red wine, cheese (except cottage, ricotta, and cream), smoked or pickled fish, beef or chicken liver, dried sausage, fava or broad bean pods, yeast vitamin supplements; do not begin any prescription or OTC medications without consulting your prescriber or pharmacist; may take as long as 3 weeks to see effects; report any severe headaches, irregular heartbeats, skin rash, insomnia, sedation, changes in strength; sensations of pain, burning, touch, or vibration; or any other unusual symptoms to your prescriber; avoid alcohol; get up slowly from chair or bed

Dosage Forms TAB: 15 mg

♦ **Phenelzine Sulfate** *see* Phenelzine *on page 987*

♦ **Phenergan®** *see* Promethazine *on page 1046*

♦ **Phenergan® With Codeine** *see* Promethazine and Codeine *on page 1048*

♦ **Pheniramine and Naphazoline** *see* Naphazoline and Pheniramine *on page 882*

Phenobarbital *(fee noe BAR bi tal)*

Related Information

Anticonvulsants by Seizure Type *on page 1358*

Convulsive Status Epilepticus *on page 1479*

Epilepsy *on page 1477*
Febrile Seizures *on page 1478*
U.S. Brand Names Luminal® Sodium
Synonyms Phenobarbital Sodium; Phenobarbitone; Phenylethylmalonylurea
Therapeutic Category Anticonvulsant, Barbiturate; Barbiturate; Hypnotic; Sedative
Use Management of generalized tonic-clonic (grand mal) and partial seizures; sedative
Unlabeled/Investigational Use Febrile seizures in children; may also be used for prevention and treatment of neonatal hyperbilirubinemia and lowering of bilirubin in chronic cholestasis; neonatal seizures; management of sedative/hypnotic withdrawal
Restrictions C-IV
Pregnancy Risk Factor D
Contraindications Hypersensitivity to barbiturates or any component of the formulation; marked hepatic impairment; dyspnea or airway obstruction; porphyria; pregnancy
Warnings/Precautions Use with caution in patients with hypovolemic shock, CHF, hepatic impairment, respiratory dysfunction or depression, previous addiction to the sedative/hypnotic group, chronic or acute pain, renal dysfunction, and the elderly, due to its long half-life and risk of dependence, phenobarbital is not recommended as a sedative in the elderly; tolerance or psychological and physical dependence may occur with prolonged use. Use with caution in patients with depression or suicidal tendencies, or in patients with a history of drug abuse. **Abrupt withdrawal in patients with epilepsy may precipitate status epilepticus.**
Common Adverse Reactions Frequency not defined.
Cardiovascular: Bradycardia, hypotension, syncope
Central nervous system: Drowsiness, lethargy, CNS excitation or depression, impaired judgment, "hangover" effect, confusion, somnolence, agitation, hyperkinesia, ataxia, nervousness, headache, insomnia, nightmares, hallucinations, anxiety, dizziness
Dermatologic: Rash, exfoliative dermatitis, Stevens-Johnson syndrome
Gastrointestinal: Nausea, vomiting, constipation
Hematologic: Agranulocytosis, thrombocytopenia, megaloblastic anemia
Local: Pain at injection site, thrombophlebitis with I.V. use
Renal: Oliguria
Respiratory: Laryngospasm, respiratory depression, apnea (especially with rapid I.V. use), hypoventilation
Miscellaneous: Gangrene with inadvertent intra-arterial injection
Drug Interactions
Cytochrome P450 Effect: Substrate of CYP2C8/9 (minor), 2C19 (major), 2E1 (minor); **Induces** CYP1A2 (strong), 2A6 (strong), 2B6 (strong), 2C8/9 (strong), 3A4 (strong)
Increased Effect/Toxicity: When combined with other CNS depressants, ethanol, narcotic analgesics, antidepressants, or benzodiazepines, additive respiratory and CNS depression may occur. Barbiturates may enhance the hepatotoxic potential of acetaminophen overdoses. Chloramphenicol, MAO inhibitors, valproic acid, and felbamate may inhibit barbiturate metabolism. Barbiturates may impair the absorption of griseofulvin, and may enhance the nephrotoxic effects of methoxyflurane. Concurrent use of phenobarbital with meperidine may result in increased CNS depression. Concurrent use of phenobarbital with primidone may result in elevated phenobarbital serum concentrations. CYP2C19 inhibitors may increase the levels/effects of phenobarbital; example inhibitors include delavirdine, fluconazole, fluvoxamine, gemfibrozil, isoniazid, omeprazole, and ticlopidine.
Decreased Effect: Barbiturates are hepatic enzyme inducers, and may increase the metabolism of antipsychotics, some beta-blockers (unlikely with atenolol and nadolol), calcium channel blockers, chloramphenicol, cimetidine, corticosteroids, cyclosporine, disopyramide, doxycycline, ethosuximide, felbamate, furosemide, griseofulvin, lamotrigine, phenytoin, propafenone, quinidine, tacrolimus, TCAs, and theophylline. Barbiturates may increase the metabolism of estrogens and reduce the efficacy of oral contraceptives; an alternative method of contraception should be considered. Barbiturates inhibit the hypoprothrombinemic effects of oral anticoagulants via increased metabolism. Barbiturates may enhance the metabolism of methadone resulting in methadone withdrawal. CYP2C19 inducers may decrease the levels/effects of phenobarbital; example inducers include aminoglutethimide, carbamazepine, phenytoin, and rifampin.
Mechanism of Action Short-acting barbiturate with sedative, hypnotic, and anticonvulsant properties. Barbiturates depress the sensory cortex, decrease motor activity, alter cerebellar function, and produce drowsiness, sedation, and hypnosis. In high doses, barbiturates exhibit anticonvulsant activity; barbiturates produce dose-dependent respiratory depression.
Pharmacodynamics/Kinetics
Onset of action: Oral: Hypnosis: 20-60 minutes; I.V.: ~5 minutes
  Peak effect: I.V.: ~30 minutes
Duration: Oral: 6-10 hours; I.V.: 4-10 hours
Absorption: Oral: 70% to 90%
Protein binding: 20% to 45%; decreased in neonates
Metabolism: Hepatic via hydroxylation and glucuronide conjugation
Half-life elimination: Neonates: 45-500 hours; Infants: 20-133 hours; Children: 37-73 hours; Adults: 53-140 hours
Time to peak, serum: Oral: 1-6 hours
Excretion: Urine (20% to 50% as unchanged drug)
Dosage
Children:
  Sedation: Oral: 2 mg/kg 3 times/day
  Hypnotic: I.M., I.V., S.C.: 3-5 mg/kg at bedtime
  Preoperative sedation: Oral, I.M., I.V.: 1-3 mg/kg 1-1.5 hours before procedure
(Continued)

Phenobarbital *(Continued)*

Adults:
  Sedation: Oral, I.M.: 30-120 mg/day in 2-3 divided doses
  Hypnotic: Oral, I.M., I.V., S.C.: 100-320 mg at bedtime
  Preoperative sedation: I.M.: 100-200 mg 1-1.5 hours before procedure

Anticonvulsant: Status epilepticus: **Loading dose:** I.V.:
  Infants and Children: 10-20 mg/kg in a single or divided dose; in select patients may administer additional 5 mg/kg/dose every 15-30 minutes until seizure is controlled or a total dose of 40 mg/kg is reached
  Adults: 300-800 mg initially followed by 120-240 mg/dose at 20-minute intervals until seizures are controlled or a total dose of 1-2 g
Anticonvulsant maintenance dose: Oral, I.V.:
  Infants: 5-8 mg/kg/day in 1-2 divided doses
  Children:
    1-5 years: 6-8 mg/kg/day in 1-2 divided doses
    5-12 years: 4-6 mg/kg/day in 1-2 divided doses
    Children >12 years and Adults: 1-3 mg/kg/day in divided doses or 50-100 mg 2-3 times/day
Sedative/hypnotic withdrawal (unlabeled use): Initial daily requirement is determined by substituting phenobarbital 30 mg for every 100 mg pentobarbital used during tolerance testing; then daily requirement is decreased by 10% of initial dose

Dosing interval in renal impairment: Cl$_{cr}$ <10 mL/minute: Administer every 12-16 hours
Hemodialysis: Moderately dialyzable (20% to 50%)
Dosing adjustment/comments in hepatic disease: Increased side effects may occur in severe liver disease; monitor plasma levels and adjust dose accordingly
Administration Avoid rapid I.V. administration >50 mg/minute; avoid intra-arterial injection
Monitoring Parameters Phenobarbital serum concentrations, mental status, CBC, LFTs, seizure activity
Reference Range
  Therapeutic:
    Infants and children: 15-30 µg/mL (SI: 65-129 µmol/L)
    Adults: 20-40 µg/mL (SI: 86-172 µmol/L)
  Toxic: >40 µg/mL (SI: >172 µmol/L)
  Toxic concentration: Slowness, ataxia, nystagmus: 35-80 µg/mL (SI: 150-344 µmol/L)
  Coma with reflexes: 65-117 µg/mL (SI: 279-502 µmol/L)
  Coma without reflexes: >100 µg/mL (SI: >430 µmol/L)
Patient Information Avoid alcohol and other CNS depressants; avoid driving and other hazardous tasks; avoid abrupt discontinuation; may cause physical and psychological dependence; do not alter dose without notifying prescriber
Dosage Forms ELIX: 20 mg/5 mL (5 mL, 7.5 mL, 15 mL, 473 mL, 946 mL, 4000 mL). **INJ, solution, as sodium:** 60 mg/mL (1 mL); 130 mg/mL (1 mL); (Luminal® Sodium): 60 mg/mL (1 mL); 130 mg/mL (1 mL). **TAB:** 15 mg, 30 mg, 32 mg, 60 mg, 65 mg, 100 mg

♦ **Phenobarbital, Belladonna, and Ergotamine Tartrate** *see* Belladonna, Phenobarbital, and Ergotamine *on page 151*

♦ **Phenobarbital, Hyoscyamine, Atropine, and Scopolamine** *see* Hyoscyamine, Atropine, Scopolamine, and Phenobarbital *on page 643*

♦ **Phenobarbital Sodium** *see* Phenobarbital *on page 988*

♦ **Phenobarbitone** *see* Phenobarbital *on page 988*

♦ **Phenoptic®** *see* Phenylephrine *on page 993*

Phenoxybenzamine *(fen oks ee BEN za meen)*
U.S. Brand Names Dibenzyline®
Synonyms Phenoxybenzamine Hydrochloride
Therapeutic Category Alpha-Adrenergic Blocking Agent, Oral; Antihypertensive Agent
Use Symptomatic management of pheochromocytoma; treatment of hypertensive crisis caused by sympathomimetic amines
Unlabeled/Investigational Use Micturition problems associated with neurogenic bladder, functional outlet obstruction, and partial prostate obstruction
Pregnancy Risk Factor C
Contraindications Hypersensitivity to phenoxybenzamine or any component of the formulation; conditions in which a fall in blood pressure would be undesirable (eg, shock); concurrent use with phosphodiesterase-5 (PDE-5) inhibitors including sildenafil (>25 mg), tadalafil, or vardenafil
Warnings/Precautions Use with caution in patients with renal impairment, cerebral, or coronary arteriosclerosis, can exacerbate symptoms of respiratory tract infections. Because of the risk of adverse effects, avoid the use of this medication in the elderly if possible.
Common Adverse Reactions Frequency not defined.
  Cardiovascular: Postural hypotension, tachycardia, syncope, shock
  Central nervous system: Lethargy, headache, confusion, fatigue
  Gastrointestinal: Vomiting, nausea, diarrhea, xerostomia
  Genitourinary: Inhibition of ejaculation
  Neuromuscular & skeletal: Weakness
  Ocular: Miosis
  Respiratory: Nasal congestion

Drug Interactions

Increased Effect/Toxicity: Beta-blockers may result in increased toxicity (hypotension, tachycardia). Blood pressure-lowering effects are additive with sildenafil (use with extreme caution at a dose ≤25 mg), tadalafil (use is contraindicated by the manufacturer), and vardenafil (use is contraindicated by the manufacturer).

Decreased Effect: Alpha adrenergic agonists decrease the effect of phenoxybenzamine.

Mechanism of Action Produces long-lasting noncompetitive alpha-adrenergic blockade of postganglionic synapses in exocrine glands and smooth muscle; relaxes urethra and increases opening of the bladder

Pharmacodynamics/Kinetics

Onset of action: ~2 hours

Peak effect: 4-6 hours

Duration: ≥4 days

Half-life elimination: 24 hours

Excretion: Primarily urine and feces

Dosage Oral:

Children: Initial: 0.2 mg/kg (maximum: 10 mg) once daily, increase by 0.2 mg/kg increments; usual maintenance dose: 0.4-1.2 mg/kg/day every 6-8 hours, higher doses may be necessary

Adults: Initial: 10 mg twice daily, increase by 10 mg every other day until optimum dose is achieved; usual range: 20-40 mg 2-3 times/day

Administration GI irritation may be reduced by giving in divided doses

Monitoring Parameters Blood pressure, pulse, urine output, orthostasis

Patient Information Avoid alcohol; if dizziness occurs, avoid sudden changes in posture; may cause nasal congestion and constricted pupils; may inhibit ejaculation; avoid cough, cold or allergy medications containing sympathomimetics

Dosage Forms CAP: 10 mg

♦ **Phenoxybenzamine Hydrochloride** see Phenoxybenzamine on page 990

♦ **Phenoxymethyl Penicillin** see Penicillin V Potassium on page 975

Phentermine (FEN ter meen)

Related Information

Obesity Treatment Guidelines for Adults on page 1482

U.S. Brand Names Adipex-P®; Ionamin®

Synonyms Phentermine Hydrochloride

Therapeutic Category Anorexiant

Use Short-term adjunct in a regimen of weight reduction based on exercise, behavioral modification, and caloric reduction in the management of exogenous obesity for patients with an initial body mass index ≥30 kg/m^2 or ≥27 kg/m^2 in the presence of other risk factors (diabetes, hypertension)

Restrictions C-IV

Pregnancy Risk Factor C

Contraindications Hypersensitivity or idiosyncrasy to sympathomimetic amines or any component of the formulation; patients with advanced arteriosclerosis, symptomatic cardiovascular disease, moderate to severe hypertension (stage II or III), hyperthyroidism, glaucoma, agitated states; patients with a history of drug abuse; use during or within 14 days following MAO inhibitor therapy; children <16 years of age (per manufacturer)

Warnings/Precautions Use with caution in patients with bipolar disorder, diabetes mellitus, cardiovascular disease, seizure disorders, insomnia, porphyria, or mild hypertension (stage I). May exacerbate symptoms of behavior and thought disorder in psychotic patients. Stimulants may unmask tics in individuals with coexisting Tourette's syndrome. Potential for drug dependency exists; avoid abrupt discontinuation in patients who have received for prolonged periods. Stimulant use has been associated with growth suppression, and careful monitoring is recommended.

Primary pulmonary hypertension (PPH), a rare and frequently fatal pulmonary disease, has been reported to occur in patients receiving a combination of phentermine and fenfluramine or dexfenfluramine. The possibility of an association between PPH and the use of phentermine alone cannot be ruled out.

Use in weight reduction programs only when alternative therapy has been ineffective. Serious, potentially life-threatening toxicities may occur when thyroid hormones (at dosages above usual daily hormonal requirements) are used in combination with sympathomimetic amines to induce weight loss. Treatment of obesity is not an approved use for thyroid hormone.

Common Adverse Reactions Frequency not defined.

Cardiovascular: Hypertension, palpitations, tachycardia, primary pulmonary hypertension and/or regurgitant cardiac valvular disease

Central nervous system: Euphoria, insomnia, overstimulation, dizziness, dysphoria, headache, restlessness, psychosis

Dermatologic: Urticaria

Endocrine & metabolic: Changes in libido, impotence

Gastrointestinal: Nausea, constipation, xerostomia, unpleasant taste, diarrhea

Hematologic: Blood dyscrasias

Neuromuscular & skeletal: Tremor

Ocular: Blurred vision

(Continued)

Phentermine *(Continued)*

Drug Interactions

Increased Effect/Toxicity: Dosage of hypoglycemic agents may need to be adjusted when phentermine is used in a diabetic receiving a special diet. Concurrent use of MAO inhibitors and drugs with MAO activity (furazolidone, linezolid) may be associated with hypertensive episodes. Concurrent use of SSRIs may be associated with a risk of serotonin syndrome.

Decreased Effect: Phentermine may decrease the effect of antihypertensive medications The efficacy of anorexiants may be decreased by antipsychotics; in addition, amphetamines or related compounds may induce an increase in psychotic symptoms in some patients. Amphetamines (and related compounds) inhibit the antihypertensive response to guanethidine; probably also may occur with guanadrel.

Mechanism of Action Phentermine is structurally similar to dextroamphetamine and is comparable to dextroamphetamine as an appetite suppressant, but is generally associated with a lower incidence and severity of CNS side effects. Phentermine, like other anorexiants, stimulates the hypothalamus to result in decreased appetite; anorexiant effects are most likely mediated via norepinephrine and dopamine metabolism. However, other CNS effects or metabolic effects may be involved.

Pharmacodynamics/Kinetics

Duration: Resin produces more prolonged clinical effects

Absorption: Well absorbed; resin absorbed slower

Half-life elimination: 20 hours

Excretion: Primarily urine (as unchanged drug)

Dosage Oral: Adults: Obesity: 8 mg 3 times/day 30 minutes before meals or food or 15-37.5 mg/day before breakfast or 10-14 hours before retiring

Monitoring Parameters CNS

Patient Information Take during day to avoid insomnia; do not discontinue abruptly, may cause physical and psychological dependence with prolonged use

Dosage Forms CAP: 15 mg, 30 mg; (Adipex-P®): 37.5 mg. **CAP, resin complex** (Ionamin®): 15 mg, 30 mg. **TAB** (Adipex-P®): 37.5 mg

♦ **Phentermine Hydrochloride** *see* Phentermine *on page 991*

Phentolamine *(fen TOLE a meen)*

Synonyms Phentolamine Mesylate; Regitine [DSC]

Therapeutic Category Alpha-Adrenergic Blocking Agent, Parenteral; Antidote, Extravasation; Antihypertensive Agent; Diagnostic Agent, Pheochromocytoma

Use Diagnosis of pheochromocytoma and treatment of hypertension associated with pheochromocytoma or other forms of hypertension caused by excess sympathomimetic amines; as treatment of dermal necrosis after extravasation of drugs with alpha-adrenergic effects (norepinephrine, dopamine, epinephrine, dobutamine)

Unlabeled/Investigational Use Treatment of pralidoxime-induced hypertension

Pregnancy Risk Factor C

Contraindications Hypersensitivity to phentolamine or any component of the formulation; renal impairment; coronary or cerebral arteriosclerosis; concurrent use with phosphodiesterase-5 (PDE-5) inhibitors including sildenafil (>25 mg), tadalafil, or vardenafil

Warnings/Precautions Myocardial infarction, cerebrovascular spasm and cerebrovascular occlusion have occurred following administration; use with caution in patients with gastritis or peptic ulcer, tachycardia, or a history of cardiac arrhythmias

Common Adverse Reactions Frequency not defined.

Cardiovascular: Hypotension, tachycardia, arrhythmia, flushing, orthostatic hypotension

Central nervous system: Weakness, dizziness

Gastrointestinal: Nausea, vomiting, diarrhea

Respiratory: Nasal congestion

Case report: Pulmonary hypertension

Drug Interactions

Increased Effect/Toxicity: Phentolamine's toxicity is increased with ethanol (disulfiram reaction). Blood pressure-lowering effects are additive with sildenafil (use with extreme caution at a dose ≤25 mg), tadalafil (use is contraindicated by the manufacturer), and vardenafil (use is contraindicated by the manufacturer).

Decreased Effect: Decreased effect of phentolamine with epinephrine and ephedrine.

Mechanism of Action Competitively blocks alpha-adrenergic receptors to produce brief antagonism of circulating epinephrine and norepinephrine to reduce hypertension caused by alpha effects of these catecholamines; also has a positive inotropic and chronotropic effect on the heart

Pharmacodynamics/Kinetics

Onset of action: I.M.: 15-20 minutes; I.V.: Immediate

Duration: I.M.: 30-45 minutes; I.V.: 15-30 minutes

Metabolism: Hepatic

Half-life elimination: 19 minutes

Excretion: Urine (10% as unchanged drug)

Dosage

Treatment of alpha-adrenergic drug extravasation: S.C.:

Children: 0.1-0.2 mg/kg diluted in 10 mL 0.9% sodium chloride infiltrated into area of extravasation within 12 hours

Adults: Infiltrate area with small amount of solution made by diluting 5-10 mg in 10 mL 0.9% sodium chloride within 12 hours of extravasation; do not exceed 0.1-0.2 mg/kg or 5 mg total

If dose is effective, normal skin color should return to the blanched area within 1 hour

Diagnosis of pheochromocytoma: I.M., I.V.:

Children: 0.05-0.1 mg/kg/dose, maximum single dose: 5 mg

Adults: 5 mg

Surgery for pheochromocytoma: Hypertension: I.M., I.V.:

Children: 0.05-0.1 mg/kg/dose given 1-2 hours before procedure; repeat as needed every 2-4 hours until hypertension is controlled; maximum single dose: 5 mg

Adults: 5 mg given 1-2 hours before procedure and repeated as needed every 2-4 hours

Hypertensive crisis: Adults: 5-20 mg

Treatment of pralidoxime-induced hypertension (unlabeled use): I.V.:

Children: 1 mg

Adults and Elderly: 5 mg

Administration Infiltrate the area of dopamine extravasation with multiple small injections using only 27- or 30-gauge needles and changing the needle between each skin entry; take care not to cause so much swelling of the extremity or digit that a compartment syndrome occurs

Monitoring Parameters Blood pressure, heart rate; area of infiltration

Dosage Forms INJ, powder for reconstitution: 5 mg

♦ **Phentolamine Mesylate** see Phentolamine on page 992

♦ **Phenylalanine Mustard** see Melphalan on page 786

♦ **Phenylazo Diamino Pyridine Hydrochloride** see Phenazopyridine on page 987

Phenylephrine (fen il EF rin)

Related Information

Hemodynamic Support, Intravenous on page 1377

U.S. Brand Names AK-Dilate®; AK-Nefrin®; Formulation R™ [OTC]; Medicone® [OTC]; Mydfrin®; Neo-Synephrine® Extra Strength [OTC]; Neo-Synephrine® Mild [OTC]; Neo-Synephrine® Ophthalmic; Neo-Synephrine® Regular Strength [OTC]; Nostril® [OTC]; Phenoptic®; Prefrin™ [DSC]; Relief® [OTC]; Vicks® Sinex® Nasal Spray [OTC]; Vicks® Sinex® UltraFine Mist [OTC]

Synonyms Phenylephrine Hydrochloride

Therapeutic Category Adrenergic Agonist Agent; Adrenergic Agonist Agent, Ophthalmic; Alpha-Adrenergic Agonist; Nasal Agent, Vasoconstrictor; Ophthalmic Agent, Mydriatic; Sympathomimetic Agent

Use Treatment of hypotension, vascular failure in shock; as a vasoconstrictor in regional analgesia; as a mydriatic in ophthalmic procedures and treatment of wide-angle glaucoma; supraventricular tachycardia

For OTC use as symptomatic relief of nasal and nasopharyngeal mucosal congestion, treatment of hemorrhoids, relief of redness of the eye due to irritation

Pregnancy Risk Factor C

Contraindications Hypersensitivity to phenylephrine, bisulfite (some products contain metabisulfite), or any component of the formulation; hypertension; ventricular tachycardia

Warnings/Precautions Use with caution in the elderly, patients with hyperthyroidism, bradycardia, partial heart block, myocardial disease, or severe CAD. Not a substitute for volume replacement. Avoid hypertension; monitor blood pressure closely and adjust infusion rate. Infuse into a large vein if possible. Watch I.V. site closely. Avoid extravasation. With intranasal formulation use, rebound congestion can occur when the drug is discontinued after chronic use.

Common Adverse Reactions Frequency not defined.

Cardiovascular: Reflex bradycardia, excitability, restlessness, arrhythmias (rare), precordial pain or discomfort, pallor, hypertension, severe peripheral and visceral vasoconstriction, decreased cardiac output

Central nervous system: Headache, anxiety, weakness, dizziness, tremor, paresthesia, restlessness

Endocrine & metabolic: Metabolic acidosis

Local: I.V.: Extravasation which may lead to necrosis and sloughing of surrounding tissue, blanching of skin

Neuromuscular & skeletal: Pilomotor response, weakness

Renal: Decreased renal perfusion, reduced urine output, reduced urine output

Respiratory: Respiratory distress

Drug Interactions

Increased Effect/Toxicity: Phenylephrine, taken with sympathomimetics, may induce tachycardia or arrhythmias. If taken with MAO inhibitors or oxytocic agents, actions may be potentiated.

Decreased Effect: Alpha- and beta-adrenergic blocking agents may have a decreased effect if taken with phenylephrine.

Mechanism of Action Potent, direct-acting alpha-adrenergic stimulator with weak beta-adrenergic activity; causes vasoconstriction of the arterioles of the nasal mucosa and conjunctiva; activates the dilator muscle of the pupil to cause contraction; produces vasoconstriction of arterioles in the body; produces systemic arterial vasoconstriction

Pharmacodynamics/Kinetics

Onset of action: I.M., S.C.: 10-15 minutes; I.V.: Immediate

(Continued)

Phenylephrine *(Continued)*

Duration: I.M.: 0.5-2 hours; I.V.: 15-30 minutes; S.C.: 1 hour

Metabolism: Hepatic, via intestinal monoamine oxidase to phenolic conjugates

Half-life elimination: 2.5 hours; prolonged after long-term infusion

Excretion: Urine (90%)

Dosage

Ocular procedures:

Infants <1 year: Instill 1 drop of 2.5% 15-30 minutes before procedures

Children and Adults: Instill 1 drop of 2.5% or 10% solution, may repeat in 10-60 minutes as needed

Ophthalmic irritation (OTC formulation for relief of eye redness): Adults: Instill 1-2 drops 0.12% solution into affected eye, up to 4 times/day; do not use for >72 hours

Nasal decongestant (therapy should not exceed 3 continuous days):

Children:

2-6 years: Instill 1 drop every 2-4 hours of 0.125% solution as needed

6-12 years: Instill 1-2 sprays or instill 1-2 drops every 4 hours of 0.25% solution as needed

Children >12 years and Adults: Instill 1-2 sprays or instill 1-2 drops every 4 hours of 0.25% to 0.5% solution as needed; 1% solution may be used in adult in cases of extreme nasal congestion; do not use nasal solutions more than 3 days

Hypotension/shock:

Children:

I.M., S.C.: 0.1 mg/kg/dose every 1-2 hours as needed (maximum: 5 mg)

I.V. bolus: 5-20 mcg/kg/dose every 10-15 minutes as needed

I.V. infusion: 0.1-0.5 mcg/kg/minute

Adults:

I.M., S.C.: 2-5 mg/dose every 1-2 hours as needed (initial dose should not exceed 5 mg)

I.V. bolus: 0.1-0.5 mg/dose every 10-15 minutes as needed (initial dose should not exceed 0.5 mg)

I.V. infusion: 10 mg in 250 mL D_5W or NS (1:25,000 dilution) (40 mcg/mL); start at 100-180 mcg/minute (2-5 mL/minute; 50-90 drops/minute) initially; when blood pressure is stabilized, maintenance rate: 40-60 mcg/minute (20-30 drops/minute); rates up to 360 mcg/minute have been reported; dosing range: 0.4-9.1 mcg/kg/minute

Note: Concentrations up to 100-500 mg in 250 mL have been used.

Paroxysmal supraventricular tachycardia: I.V.:

Children: 5-10 mcg/kg/dose over 20-30 seconds

Adults: 0.25-0.5 mg/dose over 20-30 seconds

Hemorrhoids: Children ≥12 years and Adults: Rectal:

Cream/ointment: Apply to clean dry area, up to 4 times/day; may be used externally or inserted rectally using applicator.

Suppository: Insert 1 suppository rectally, up to 4 times/day

Administration Concentration and rate of infusion can be calculated using the following formulas: Dilute 0.6 mg x weight (kg) to 100 mL; then the dose in mcg/kg/minute = 0.1 x the infusion rate in mL/hour

May cause necrosis or sloughing tissue if extravasation occurs during I.V. administration or S.C. administration.

Extravasation management: Use phentolamine as antidote; mix 5 mg with 9 mL of NS. Inject a small amount of this dilution into extravasated area. Blanching should reverse immediately. Monitor site. If blanching should recur, additional injections of phentolamine may be needed.

Monitoring Parameters Blood pressure, heart rate, arterial blood gases, central venous pressure

Patient Information Nasal decongestant should not be used for >3 days in a row, thereby reducing problems of rebound congestion; report insomnia, dizziness, tremor, or irregular heartbeat; if symptoms do not improve within 7 days or are accompanied by signs of infection, consult prescriber

Dosage Forms CRM, rectal (Formulation R™): 0.25% (30 g, 60 g). **INJ, solution:** 1% [10 mg/mL] (1 mL). **DROPS, intranasal:** (Neo-Synephrine® Regular Strength): 0.5% (15 mL); (Neo-Synephrine® Extra Strength): 1% (15 mL); **OINT, rectal** (Formulation R™): 0.25% (30 g, 60 g). **SPRAY, intranasal:** (Neo-Synephrine® Mild): 0.25% (15 mL); (Neo-Synephrine® Extra Strength): 1% (15 mL); (Neo-Synephrine® Regular Strength): 0.5% (15 mL); (Nostril®): 0.25% (15 mL), 0.5% (15 mL); (Vicks® Sinex®, Vicks® Sinex® UltraFine Mist): 0.5% (15 mL). **SOLN, ophthalmic:** 2.5% (2 mL, 3 mL, 5 mL, 15 mL); (AK-Dilate®): 2.5% (2 mL, 15 mL), 10% (5 mL); (AK-Nefrin®): 0.12% (15 mL); (Mydfrin®): 2.5% (3 mL, 5 mL); (Neo-Synephrine®): 2.5% (15 mL), 10% (5 mL); (Neo-Synephrine® Viscous): 10% (5 mL); (Phenoptic®): 2.5% (15 mL); (Prefrin™ [DSC], Relief®): 0.12% (15 mL). **SUPP, rectal:** 0.25% (12s); (Medicone®): 0.25% (18s, 24s)

◆ **Phenylephrine and Chlorpheniramine** *see* Chlorpheniramine and Phenylephrine *on page 262*

◆ **Phenylephrine and Cyclopentolate** *see* Cyclopentolate and Phenylephrine *on page 320*

◆ **Phenylephrine and Guaifenesin** *see* Guaifenesin and Phenylephrine *on page 605*

◆ **Phenylephrine and Promethazine** *see* Promethazine and Phenylephrine *on page 1048*

Phenylephrine and Scopolamine *(fen il EF rin & skoe POL a meen)*

U.S. Brand Names Murocoll-2®

Synonyms Scopolamine and Phenylephrine

Therapeutic Category Anticholinergic/Adrenergic Agonist

Use Mydriasis, cycloplegia, and to break posterior synechiae in iritis
Pregnancy Risk Factor C
Dosage Ophthalmic: Instill 1-2 drops into eye(s); repeat in 5 minutes
Dosage Forms SOLN, ophthalmic: Phenylephrine 10% and scopolamine 0.3% (5 mL)

Phenylephrine and Zinc Sulfate (fen il EF rin & zingk SUL fate)
U.S. Brand Names Zincfrin® [OTC]
Synonyms Zinc Sulfate and Phenylephrine
Therapeutic Category Adrenergic Agonist Agent
Use Soothe, moisturize, and remove redness due to minor eye irritation
Dosage Ophthalmic: Instill 1-2 drops in eye(s) 2-4 times/day as needed
Dosage Forms SOLN, ophthalmic: Phenylephrine 0.12% and zinc 0.25% (15 mL)

♦ **Phenylephrine, Chlorpheniramine, and Dextromethorphan** see Chlorpheniramine, Phenylephrine, and Dextromethorphan on page 264

♦ **Phenylephrine, Chlorpheniramine, and Methscopolamine** see Chlorpheniramine, Phenylephrine, and Methscopolamine on page 264

♦ **Phenylephrine, Chlorpheniramine, and Phenyltoloxamine** see Chlorpheniramine, Phenylephrine, and Phenyltoloxamine on page 265

♦ **Phenylephrine, Chlorpheniramine, Codeine, and Potassium Iodide** see Chlorpheniramine, Phenylephrine, Codeine, and Potassium Iodide on page 265

♦ **Phenylephrine, Ephedrine, Chlorpheniramine, and Carbetapentane** see Chlorpheniramine, Ephedrine, Phenylephrine, and Carbetapentane on page 263

♦ **Phenylephrine Hydrochloride** see Phenylephrine on page 993

♦ **Phenylephrine, Hydrocodone, Chlorpheniramine, Acetaminophen, and Caffeine** see Hydrocodone, Chlorpheniramine, Phenylephrine, Acetaminophen, and Caffeine on page 632

♦ **Phenylephrine, Promethazine, and Codeine** see Promethazine, Phenylephrine, and Codeine on page 1048

♦ **Phenylethylmalonylurea** see Phenobarbital on page 988

♦ **Phenylgesic®** [OTC] see Acetaminophen and Phenyltoloxamine on page 26

♦ **Phenylisohydantoin** see Pemoline on page 969

♦ **Phenyl Salicylate, Methenamine, Methylene Blue, Sodium Biphosphate, and Hyoscyamine** see Methenamine, Sodium Biphosphate, Phenyl Salicylate, Methylene Blue, and Hyoscyamine on page 812

♦ **Phenyltoloxamine and Acetaminophen** see Acetaminophen and Phenyltoloxamine on page 26

♦ **Phenyltoloxamine, Chlorpheniramine, and Phenylephrine** see Chlorpheniramine, Phenylephrine, and Phenyltoloxamine on page 265

♦ **Phenytek™** see Phenytoin on page 995

Phenytoin (FEN i toyn)
Related Information
    Anticonvulsants by Seizure Type on page 1358
    Convulsive Status Epilepticus on page 1479
    Epilepsy on page 1477
    Fosphenytoin and Phenytoin, Parenteral Comparison on page 1375
U.S. Brand Names Dilantin®; Phenytek™
Synonyms Diphenylhydantoin; DPH; Phenytoin Sodium; Phenytoin Sodium, Extended; Phenytoin Sodium, Prompt
Therapeutic Category Antiarrhythmic Agent, Class I-B; Anticonvulsant, Hydantoin
Use Management of generalized tonic-clonic (grand mal), complex partial seizures; prevention of seizures following head trauma/neurosurgery
Unlabeled/Investigational Use Ventricular arrhythmias, including those associated with digitalis intoxication, prolonged QT interval and surgical repair of congenital heart diseases in children; epidermolysis bullosa
Pregnancy Risk Factor D
Contraindications Hypersensitivity to phenytoin, other hydantoins, or any component of the formulation; pregnancy
Warnings/Precautions May increase frequency of petit mal seizures; I.V. form may cause hypotension, skin necrosis at I.V. site; avoid I.V. administration in small veins; use with caution in patients with porphyria; discontinue if rash or lymphadenopathy occurs; use with caution in patients with hepatic dysfunction, sinus bradycardia, S-A block, or A-V block; use with caution in elderly or debilitated patients, or in any condition associated with low serum albumin levels, which will increase the free fraction of phenytoin in the serum and, therefore, the pharmacologic response. Sedation, confusional states, or cerebellar dysfunction (loss of motor coordination) may occur at higher total serum concentrations, or at lower total serum concentrations when the free fraction of phenytoin is increased. Abrupt withdrawal may precipitate status epilepticus.
Common Adverse Reactions I.V. effects: Hypotension, bradycardia, cardiac arrhythmias, cardiovascular collapse (especially with rapid I.V. use), venous irritation and pain, thrombophlebitis

    Effects not related to plasma phenytoin concentrations: Hypertrichosis, gingival hypertrophy, thickening of facial features, carbohydrate intolerance, folic acid deficiency, peripheral neuropathy, vitamin D deficiency, osteomalacia, systemic lupus erythematosus
    (Continued)

Phenytoin *(Continued)*

Concentration-related effects: Nystagmus, blurred vision, diplopia, ataxia, slurred speech, dizziness, drowsiness, lethargy, coma, rash, fever, nausea, vomiting, gum tenderness, confusion, mood changes, folic acid depletion, osteomalacia, hyperglycemia

Related to elevated concentrations:

>20 mcg/mL: Far lateral nystagmus

>30 mcg/mL: 45° lateral gaze nystagmus and ataxia

>40 mcg/mL: Decreased mentation

>100 mcg/mL: Death

Cardiovascular: Hypotension, bradycardia, cardiac arrhythmias, cardiovascular collapse

Central nervous system: Psychiatric changes, slurred speech, dizziness, drowsiness, headache, insomnia

Dermatologic: Rash

Gastrointestinal: Constipation, nausea, vomiting, gingival hyperplasia, enlargement of lips

Hematologic: Leukopenia, thrombocytopenia, agranulocytosis

Hepatic: Hepatitis

Local: Thrombophlebitis

Neuromuscular & skeletal: Tremor, peripheral neuropathy, paresthesia

Ocular: Diplopia, nystagmus, blurred vision

Rarely seen effects: SLE-like syndrome, lymphadenopathy, hepatitis, Stevens-Johnson syndrome, blood dyscrasias, dyskinesias, pseudolymphoma, lymphoma, venous irritation and pain, coarsening of the facial features, hypertrichosis

Drug Interactions

Cytochrome P450 Effect: Substrate of CYP2C8/9 (major), 2C19 (major), 3A4 (minor); **Induces** CYP2B6 (strong), 2C8/9 (strong), 2C19 (strong), 3A4 (strong)

Increased Effect/Toxicity: Selected anticonvulsants (felbamate, gabapentin, and topiramate) have been reported to increase phenytoin levels/effects. In addition, serum phenytoin concentrations may be increased by allopurinol, amiodarone, calcium channel blockers (including diltiazem and nifedipine), cimetidine, disulfiram, methylphenidate, metronidazole, omeprazole, selective serotonin reuptake inhibitors (SSRIs), ticlopidine, tricyclic antidepressants, trazodone, and trimethoprim. Case reports indicate ciprofloxacin may increase or decrease serum phenytoin concentrations.

The sedative effects of phenytoin may be additive with other CNS depressants including ethanol, barbiturates, sedatives, antidepressants, narcotic analgesics, and benzodiazepines. Phenytoin enhances the conversion of primidone to phenobarbital resulting in elevated phenobarbital serum concentrations.

CYP2C8/9 inhibitors may increase the levels/effects of phenytoin. Example inhibitors include delavirdine, fluconazole, gemfibrozil, ketoconazole, nicardipine, NSAIDs, pioglitazone, and sulfonamides. CYP2C19 inhibitors may increase the levels/effects of phenytoin. Example inhibitors include delavirdine, fluconazole, fluvoxamine, gemfibrozil, isoniazid, omeprazole, and ticlopidine.

Concurrent use of acetazolamide with phenytoin may result in an increased risk of osteomalacia. Concurrent use of phenytoin and lithium has resulted in lithium intoxication. Valproic acid (and sulfisoxazole) may displace phenytoin from binding sites; valproic acid may increase, decrease, or have no effect on phenytoin serum concentrations. Phenytoin transiently increased the response to warfarin initially; this is followed by an inhibition of the hypoprothrombinemic response. Phenytoin may enhance the hepatotoxic potential of acetaminophen overdoses. Concurrent use of dopamine and intravenous phenytoin may lead to an increased risk of hypotension.

Decreased Effect: Phenytoin may enhance the metabolism of estrogen and/or oral contraceptives, decreasing their clinical effect; an alternative method of contraception should be considered. Phenytoin may increase the metabolism of anticonvulsants including barbiturates, carbamazepine, ethosuximide, felbamate, lamotrigine, tiagabine, topiramate, and zonisamide. Valproic acid may increase, decrease, or have no effect on phenytoin serum concentrations.

Phenytoin may decrease serum concentrations of immunosuppressants (including cyclosporine and tacrolimus) and corticosteroids. Phenytoin may also decrease the serum concentrations/effects of some antiarrhythmics (disopyramide, propafenone, and quinidine), calcium channel blockers, HMG-CoA reductase inhibitors, and beta-blockers (except for agents which are not hepatically metabolized). The serum concentrations/effects of hepatically metabolized benzodiazepines, selected antipsychotics (including quetiapine), and tricyclic antidepressants may be reduced by phenytoin. Phenytoin may enhance the metabolism of doxycycline, decreasing its clinical effect; higher dosages may be required. Phenytoin may increase the metabolism of chloramphenicol or itraconazole.

CYP2C8/9 inducers may decrease the levels/effects of phenytoin. Example inducers include carbamazepine, phenobarbital, rifampin, rifapentine, and secobarbital. CYP2C19 inducers may decrease the levels/effects of phenytoin. Example inducers include aminoglutethimide, carbamazepine, phenytoin, and rifampin. Clozapine and vigabatrin may reduce phenytoin serum concentrations. Case reports indicate ciprofloxacin may increase or decrease serum phenytoin concentrations. Antacids and/or sucralfate may decrease absorption of phenytoin; separate oral doses by several hours. Dexamethasone may decrease serum phenytoin concentrations. Replacement of folic acid has been reported to increase the metabolism of phenytoin, decreasing its serum concentrations and/or increasing seizures.

Initially, phenytoin increases the response to warfarin; this is followed by a decrease in response to warfarin. Phenytoin may inhibit the anti-Parkinson effect of levodopa. The duration of neuromuscular blockade from neuromuscular-blocking agents may be decreased by phenytoin. Phenytoin may enhance the metabolism of methadone resulting in methadone withdrawal. Phenytoin may decrease serum levels/effects of digitalis glycosides, theophylline, and thyroid hormones.

Several chemotherapeutic agents have been associated with a decrease in serum phenytoin levels; includes cisplatin, bleomycin, carmustine, methotrexate, and vinblastine. Enzyme-inducing anticonvulsant therapy may reduce the effectiveness of some chemotherapy regimens (specifically in ALL). Teniposide and methotrexate may be cleared more rapidly in these patients.

Mechanism of Action Stabilizes neuronal membranes and decreases seizure activity by increasing efflux or decreasing influx of sodium ions across cell membranes in the motor cortex during generation of nerve impulses; prolongs effective refractory period and suppresses ventricular pacemaker automaticity, shortens action potential in the heart

Pharmacodynamics/Kinetics
Onset of action: I.V.: ~0.5-1 hour
Absorption: Oral: Slow
Distribution: V_d:
 Neonates: Premature: 1-1.2 L/kg; Full-term: 0.8-0.9 L/kg
 Infants: 0.7-0.8 L/kg
 Children: 0.7 L/kg
 Adults: 0.6-0.7 L/kg
Protein binding:
 Neonates: ≥80% (≤20% free)
 Infants: ≥85% (≤15% free)
 Adults: 90% to 95%
 Others: Decreased protein binding
  Disease states resulting in a decrease in serum albumin concentration: Burns, hepatic cirrhosis, nephrotic syndrome, pregnancy, cystic fibrosis
  Disease states resulting in an apparent decrease in affinity of phenytoin for serum albumin: Renal failure, jaundice (severe), other drugs (displacers), hyperbilirubinemia (total bilirubin >15 mg/dL), Cl_{cr} <25 mL/minute (unbound fraction is increased two- to threefold in uremia)
Metabolism: Follows dose-dependent capacity-limited (Michaelis-Menten) pharmacokinetics with increased V_{max} in infants >6 months of age and children versus adults; major metabolite (via oxidation), HPPA, undergoes enterohepatic recirculation
Bioavailability: Form dependent
Half-life elimination: Oral: 22 hours (range: 7-42 hours)
Time to peak, serum (form dependent): Oral: Extended-release capsule: 4-12 hours; Immediate release preparation: 2-3 hours
Excretion: Urine (<5% as unchanged drug); as glucuronides
 Clearance: Highly variable, dependent upon intrinsic hepatic function and dose administered; increased clearance and decreased serum concentrations with febrile illness

Dosage
Status epilepticus: I.V.:
 Infants and Children: Loading dose: 15-20 mg/kg in a single or divided dose; maintenance dose: Initial: 5 mg/kg/day in 2 divided doses; usual doses:
  6 months to 3 years: 8-10 mg/kg/day
  4-6 years: 7.5-9 mg/kg/day
  7-9 years: 7-8 mg/kg/day
  10-16 years: 6-7 mg/kg/day, some patients may require every 8 hours dosing
 Adults: Loading dose: Manufacturer recommends 10-15 mg/kg, however, 15-25 mg/kg has been used clinically; maintenance dose: 300 mg/day or 5-6 mg/kg/day in 3 divided doses or 1-2 divided doses using extended release
Anticonvulsant: Children and Adults: Oral:
 Loading dose: 15-20 mg/kg; based on phenytoin serum concentrations and recent dosing history; administer oral loading dose in 3 divided doses given every 2-4 hours to decrease GI adverse effects and to ensure complete oral absorption; maintenance dose: same as I.V.
 Neurosurgery (prophylactic): 100-200 mg at approximately 4-hour intervals during surgery and during the immediate postoperative period

Dosing adjustment/comments in renal impairment or hepatic disease: Safe in usual doses in mild liver disease; clearance may be substantially reduced in cirrhosis and plasma level monitoring with dose adjustment advisable. Free phenytoin levels should be monitored closely.

Administration
Oral: Suspension: Shake well prior to use. Absorption is impaired when phenytoin suspension is given concurrently to patients who are receiving continuous nasogastric feedings. A method to resolve this interaction is to divide the daily dose of phenytoin and withhold the administration of nutritional supplements for 1-2 hours before and after each phenytoin dose.
I.M.: Although approved for I.M. use, I.M. administration is not recommended due to erratic absorption and pain on injection. Fosphenytoin may be considered.
I.V.: Vesicant. Fosphenytoin may be considered for loading in patients who are in status epilepticus, hemodynamically unstable, or develop hypotension/bradycardia with I.V. administration of phenytoin. Phenytoin may be administered by IVP or IVPB administration. The
(Continued)

Phenytoin *(Continued)*

maximum rate of I.V. administration is 50 mg/minute. Highly sensitive patients (eg, elderly, patients with pre-existing cardiovascular conditions) should receive phenytoin more slowly (eg, 20 mg/minute). An in-line 0.22-5 micron filter is recommended for IVPB solutions due to the high potential for precipitation of the solution. Avoid extravasation. Following I.V. administration, NS should be injected through the same needle or I.V. catheter to prevent irritation. pH: 10.0-12.3

S.C.: S.C. administration is not recommended because of the possibility of local tissue damage.

Monitoring Parameters Blood pressure, vital signs (with I.V. use), plasma phenytoin level, CBC, liver function tests

Reference Range Timing of serum samples: Because it is slowly absorbed, peak blood levels may occur 4-8 hours after ingestion of an oral dose. The serum half-life varies with the dosage and the drug follows Michaelis-Menten kinetics. The average adult half-life is about 24 hours. Steady-state concentrations are reached in 5-10 days.

Children and Adults: Toxicity is measured clinically, and some patients require levels outside the suggested therapeutic range

Therapeutic range:

Total phenytoin: 10-20 µg/mL (children and adults), 8-15 µg/mL (neonates)

Concentrations of 5-10 µg/mL may be therapeutic for some patients but concentrations <5 µg/mL are not likely to be effective

50% of patients show decreased frequency of seizures at concentrations >10 µg/mL

86% of patients show decreased frequency of seizures at concentrations >15 µg/mL

Add another anticonvulsant if satisfactory therapeutic response is not achieved with a phenytoin concentration of 20 µg/mL

Free phenytoin: 1-2.5 µg/mL

Toxic: <30-50 µg/mL (SI: <120-200 µmol/L)

Lethal: >100 µg/mL (SI: >400 µmol/L)

When to draw levels: This is dependent on the disease state being treated and the clinical condition of the patient

Key points:

Slow absorption of extended capsules and prolonged half-life minimize fluctuations between peak and trough concentrations, timing of sampling not crucial

Trough concentrations are generally recommended for routine monitoring. Daily levels are not necessary and may result in incorrect dosage adjustments. If it is determined essential to monitor free phenytoin concentrations, concomitant monitoring of total phenytoin concentrations is not necessary and expensive.

After a loading dose: Draw level within 48-96 hours

Rapid achievement: Draw within 2-3 days of therapy initiation to ensure that the patient's metabolism is not remarkably different from that which would be predicted by average literature-derived pharmacokinetic parameters; early levels should be used cautiously in design of new dosing regimens

Second concentration: Draw within 6-7 days with subsequent doses of phenytoin adjusted accordingly

If plasma concentrations have not changed over a 3- to 5-day period, monitoring interval may be increased to once weekly in the acute clinical setting

In stable patients requiring long-term therapy, generally monitor levels at 3- to 12-month intervals

Adjustment of serum concentration: See tables.

Adjustment of Serum Concentration in Patients With Low Serum Albumin

Measured Total Phenytoin Concentration (mcg/mL)	Patient's Serum Albumin (g/dL)			
	3.5	3	2.5	2
	Adjusted Total Phenytoin Concentration (mcg/mL)[1]			
5	6	7	8	10
10	13	14	17	20
15	19	21	25	30

[1]Adjusted concentration = measured total concentration divided by [(0.2 x albumin) + 0.1].

Adjustment of Serum Concentration in Patients With Renal Failure (Cl_{cr} ≤10 mL/min)

Measured Total Phenytoin Concentration (mcg/mL)	Patient's Serum Albumin (g/dL)				
	4	3.5	3	2.5	2
	Adjusted Total Phenytoin Concentration (mcg/mL)[1]				
5	10	11	13	14	17
10	20	22	25	29	33
15	30	33	38	43	50

[1]Adjusted concentration = measured total concentration divided by [(0.1 x albumin) + 0.1].

Patient Information Shake oral suspension well prior to each dose; do not change brand or dosage form without consulting prescriber; do not skip doses, may cause drowsiness, dizziness, ataxia, loss of coordination or judgment; take with food; maintain good oral hygiene; do not crush or open extended capsules

Dosage Forms CAP, extended release: (Dilantin®): 30 mg, 100 mg; (Phenytek™): 200 mg, 300 mg. **CAP, prompt release:** 100 mg. **INJ, solution:** 50 mg/mL (2 mL, 5 mL). **SUSP, oral** (Dilantin®): 125 mg/5 mL (240 mL). **TAB, chewable** (Dilantin®): 50 mg

Physostigmine (fye zoe STIG meen)

Related Information
Glaucoma Drug Therapy Comparison *on page 1481*

Synonyms Eserine Salicylate; Physostigmine Salicylate; Physostigmine Sulfate

Therapeutic Category Acetylcholinesterase Inhibitor; Antidote, Anticholinergic Agent; Antidote, Belladonna Alkaloids; Cholinergic Agent; Cholinergic Agent, Ophthalmic; Ophthalmic Agent, Miotic

Use Reverse toxic CNS effects caused by anticholinergic drugs

Pregnancy Risk Factor C

Contraindications Hypersensitivity to physostigmine or any component of the formulation; GI or GU obstruction; physostigmine therapy of drug intoxications should be used with extreme caution in patients with asthma, gangrene, severe cardiovascular disease, or mechanical obstruction of the GI tract or urogenital tract. In these patients, physostigmine should be used only to treat life-threatening conditions.

Warnings/Precautions Use with caution in patients with epilepsy, asthma, diabetes, gangrene, cardiovascular disease, bradycardia. Discontinue if excessive salivation or emesis, frequent urination or diarrhea occur. Reduce dosage if excessive sweating or nausea occurs. Administer I.V. slowly or at a controlled rate not faster than 1 mg/minute. Due to the possibility of hypersensitivity or overdose/cholinergic crisis, atropine should be readily available; not intended as a first-line agent for anticholinergic toxicity or Parkinson's disease.

Common Adverse Reactions Frequency not defined.
Cardiovascular: Palpitations, bradycardia
Central nervous system: Restlessness, nervousness, hallucinations, seizures
Gastrointestinal: Nausea, salivation, diarrhea, stomach pains
Genitourinary: Frequent urge to urinate
Neuromuscular & skeletal: Muscle twitching
Ocular: Lacrimation, miosis
Respiratory: Dyspnea, bronchospasm, respiratory paralysis, pulmonary edema
Miscellaneous: Diaphoresis

Drug Interactions
Increased Effect/Toxicity: Increased toxicity with bethanechol, methacholine. Succinylcholine may increase neuromuscular blockade with systemic administration.

Mechanism of Action Inhibits destruction of acetylcholine by acetylcholinesterase which facilitates transmission of impulses across myoneural junction and prolongs the central and peripheral effects of acetylcholine

Pharmacodynamics/Kinetics
Onset of action: ~5 minutes
Duration: 0.5-5 hours
Absorption: I.M., S.C.: Readily absorbed
Distribution: Crosses blood-brain barrier readily and reverses both central and peripheral anticholinergic effects
Metabolism: Hepatic and via hydrolysis by cholinesterases
Half-life elimination: 15-40 minutes
(Continued)

Physostigmine *(Continued)*

Dosage

Children: Anticholinergic drug overdose: Reserve for life-threatening situations only: I.V.: 0.01-0.03 mg/kg/dose (maximum: 0.5 mg/minute); may repeat after 5-10 minutes to a maximum total dose of 2 mg or until response occurs or adverse cholinergic effects occur

Adults: Anticholinergic drug overdose:

I.M., I.V., S.C.: 0.5-2 mg to start, repeat every 20 minutes until response occurs or adverse effect occurs

Repeat 1-4 mg every 30-60 minutes as life-threatening signs (arrhythmias, seizures, deep coma) recur; maximum I.V. rate: 1 mg/minute

Administration Injection: Infuse slowly I.V. at a maximum rate of 0.5 mg/minute in children or 1 mg/minute in adults. Too rapid administration (I.V. rate not to exceed 1 mg/minute) can cause bradycardia, hypersalivation leading to respiratory difficulties and seizures.

Patient Information Report abdominal cramps, sweating, salivation, or cramps

Dosage Forms INJ, solution: 1 mg/mL (2 mL)

♦ **Physostigmine Salicylate** *see Physostigmine on page 999*
♦ **Physostigmine Sulfate** *see Physostigmine on page 999*
♦ **Phytomenadione** *see Phytonadione on page 1000*

Phytonadione *(fye toe na DYE one)*

U.S. Brand Names AquaMEPHYTON® [DSC]; Mephyton®

Synonyms Methylphytyl Napthoquinone; Phylloquinone; Phytomenadione; Vitamin K_1

Therapeutic Category Vitamin, Fat Soluble

Use Prevention and treatment of hypoprothrombinemia caused by drug-induced or anticoagulant-induced vitamin K deficiency, hemorrhagic disease of the newborn; phytonadione is more effective and is preferred to other vitamin K preparations in the presence of impending hemorrhage; oral absorption depends on the presence of bile salts

Pregnancy Risk Factor C

Contraindications Hypersensitivity to phytonadione or any component of the formulation

Warnings/Precautions Severe reactions resembling anaphylaxis or hypersensitivity have occurred rarely during or immediately after I.V. administration (even with proper dilution and rate of administration), as well as I.M. administration; restrict I.V. administration for emergency use only; allergic reactions have also occurred with I.M. and S.C. injection; ineffective in hereditary hypoprothrombinemia, hypoprothrombinemia caused by severe liver disease; severe hemolytic anemia has been reported rarely in neonates following large doses (10-20 mg) of phytonadione

Drug Interactions

Decreased Effect: The anticoagulant effects of warfarin, dicumarol, anisindione are reversed by phytonadione.

Mechanism of Action Promotes liver synthesis of clotting factors (II, VII, IX, X); however, the exact mechanism as to this stimulation is unknown. Menadiol is a water soluble form of vitamin K; phytonadione has a more rapid and prolonged effect than menadione; menadiol sodium diphosphate (K_4) is half as potent as menadione (K_3).

Pharmacodynamics/Kinetics

Onset of action: Increased coagulation factors: Oral: 6-12 hours; Parenteral: 1-2 hours; prothrombin may become normal after 12-14 hours

Absorption: Oral: From intestines in presence of bile

Metabolism: Rapidly hepatic

Excretion: Urine and feces

Dosage S.C. is the preferred (per manufacturer) parenteral route; I.V. route should be restricted for emergency use only

Minimum daily requirement: Not well established

Infants: 1-5 mcg/kg/day

Adults: 0.03 mcg/kg/day

Hemorrhagic disease of the newborn:

Prophylaxis: I.M.: 0.5-1 mg within 1 hour of birth

Treatment: I.M., S.C.: 1-2 mg/dose/day

Oral anticoagulant overdose:

Infants and Children:

No bleeding, rapid reversal needed, patient **will require** further oral anticoagulant therapy: S.C., I.V.: 0.5-2 mg

No bleeding, rapid reversal needed, patient **will not require** further oral anticoagulant therapy: S.C., I.V.: 2-5 mg

Significant bleeding, not life-threatening: S.C., I.V.: 0.5-2 mg

Significant bleeding, life-threatening: I.V.: 5 mg over 10-20 minutes

Adults: Oral, I.V., S.C.: 1-10 mg/dose depending on degree of INR elevation

Serious bleeding or major overdose: 10 mg I.V. (slow infusion); may repeat every 12 hours (have required doses up to 25 mg)

Vitamin K deficiency: Due to drugs, malabsorption, or decreased synthesis of vitamin K

Infants and Children:

Oral: 2.5-5 mg/24 hours

I.M., I.V., S.C.: 1-2 mg/dose as a single dose

Adults:

Oral: 5-25 mg/24 hours

I.M., I.V., S.C.: 10 mg

Administration I.V. administration: Dilute in normal saline, D$_5$W or D$_5$NS and infuse slowly; rate of infusion should not exceed 1 mg/minute. **This route should be used only if administration by another route is not feasible.** The parenteral preparation has been administered orally to neonates. I.V. administration should not exceed 1 mg/minute; for I.V. infusion, dilute in PF (preservative free) D$_5$W or normal saline.

Monitoring Parameters PT

Dosage Forms INJ, aqueous colloidal: 2 mg/mL (0.5 mL), 10 mg/mL (1 mL); (AquaMEPH-YTON®): 2 mg/mL (0.5 mL), 10 mg/mL (1 mL). **TAB** (Mephyton®): 5 mg

♦ **Pidorubicin**   see Epirubicin on page 440
♦ **Pidorubicin Hydrochloride**   see Epirubicin on page 440
♦ **Pilocar®**   see Pilocarpine on page 1001

Pilocarpine (pye loe KAR peen)

Related Information
Glaucoma Drug Therapy Comparison on page 1481

U.S. Brand Names Isopto® Carpine; Pilocar®; Pilopine HS®; Piloptic®; Salagen®

Synonyms Pilocarpine Hydrochloride

Therapeutic Category Cholinergic Agent; Cholinergic Agent, Ophthalmic; Ophthalmic Agent, Miotic

Use
Ophthalmic: Management of chronic simple glaucoma, chronic and acute angle-closure glaucoma

Oral: Symptomatic treatment of xerostomia caused by salivary gland hypofunction resulting from radiotherapy for cancer of the head and neck or Sjögren's syndrome

Unlabeled/Investigational Use Counter effects of cycloplegics

Pregnancy Risk Factor C

Contraindications Hypersensitivity to pilocarpine or any component of the formulation; acute inflammatory disease of the anterior chamber of the eye; in addition, tablets are also contraindicated in patients with uncontrolled asthma, angle-closure glaucoma, severe hepatic impairment

Warnings/Precautions Use with caution in patients with corneal abrasion, CHF, asthma, peptic ulcer, urinary tract obstruction, Parkinson's disease, or narrow-angle glaucoma

Common Adverse Reactions
Ophthalmic: Frequency not defined:
Cardiovascular: Hypertension, tachycardia
Dermatologic: Diaphoresis
Gastrointestinal: Diarrhea, nausea, salivation, vomiting
Ocular: Burning, ciliary spasm, conjunctival vascular congestion, corneal granularity (gel 10%), lacrimation, lens opacity, myopia, retinal detachment, supraorbital or temporal headache, visual acuity decreased
Respiratory: Bronchial spasm, pulmonary edema

Oral (frequency varies by indication and dose):
>10%:
Cardiovascular: Flushing (8% to 13%)
Central nervous system: Chills (3% to 15%), dizziness (5% to 12%), headache (11%)
Dermatologic: Diaphoresis (29% to 68%)
Gastrointestinal: Nausea (6% to 15%)
Genitourinary: Urinary frequency (9% to 12%)
Neuromuscular & skeletal: Weakness (2% to 12%)
Respiratory: Rhinitis (5% to 14%)
1% to 10%:
Cardiovascular: Edema (<1% to 5%), facial edema, hypertension (3%), palpitation, tachycardia
Central nervous system: Pain (4%), fever, somnolence
Dermatologic: Pruritus, rash
Gastrointestinal: Diarrhea (4% to 7%), dyspepsia (7%), vomiting (3% to 4%), constipation, flatulence, glossitis, salivation increased, stomatitis, taste perversion
Genitourinary: Vaginitis, urinary incontinence
Neuromuscular & skeletal: Myalgias, tremor
Ocular: Lacrimation (6%), amblyopia (4%), abnormal vision, blurred vision, conjunctivitis
Otic: Tinnitus
Respiratory: Cough increased, dysphagia, epistaxis, sinusitis
Miscellaneous: Allergic reaction, voice alteration

Drug Interactions
Cytochrome P450 Effect: Inhibits CYP2A6 (weak), 2E1 (weak), 3A4 (weak)
Increased Effect/Toxicity: Concurrent use with beta-blockers may cause conduction disturbances.
Decreased Effect: May decrease effects of anticholinergic drugs (atropine, ipratropium).

Mechanism of Action Directly stimulates cholinergic receptors in the eye causing miosis (by contraction of the iris sphincter), loss of accommodation (by constriction of ciliary muscle), and lowering of intraocular pressure (with decreased resistance to aqueous humor outflow)

Pharmacodynamics/Kinetics
Onset of action:
Ophthalmic: Miosis: 10-30 minutes; Intraocular pressure reduction: 1 hour
Oral: 20 minutes
(Continued)

Pilocarpine *(Continued)*

Duration:
Ophthalmic: Miosis: 4-8 hours; Intraocular pressure reduction: 4-12 hours
Oral: 3-5 hours
Half-life elimination: Oral: 0.76-1.35 hours; increased with hepatic impairment
Excretion: Urine

Dosage Adults:
Ophthalmic:
Glaucoma:
Solution: Instill 1-2 drops up to 6 times/day; adjust the concentration and frequency as required to control elevated intraocular pressure
Gel: Instill 0.5" ribbon into lower conjunctival sac once daily at bedtime
To counteract the mydriatic effects of sympathomimetic agents (unlabeled use): Solution: Instill 1 drop of a 1% solution in the affected eye
Oral: Xerostomia:
Following head and neck cancer: 5 mg 3 times/day, titration up to 10 mg 3 times/day may be considered for patients who have not responded adequately; do not exceed 2 tablets/dose
Sjögren's syndrome: 5 mg 4 times/day
Dosage adjustment in hepatic impairment: Oral: Patients with moderate impairment: 5 mg 2 times/day regardless of indication; adjust dose based on response and tolerability. Do not use with severe impairment (Child-Pugh score 10-15).

Administration
Oral: Avoid administering with high-fat meal. Fat decreases the rate of absorption, maximum concentration, and increases the time it takes to reach maximum concentration.
Ophthalmic: If both solution and gel are used, the solution should be applied first, then the gel at least 5 minutes later. Following administration of the solution, finger pressure should be applied on the lacrimal sac for 1-2 minutes.

Monitoring Parameters Intraocular pressure, funduscopic exam, visual field testing

Patient Information Ophthalmic: May sting on instillation; report sweating, urinary retention; usually causes difficulty in dark adaptation; advise patients to use caution while night driving or performing hazardous tasks in poor illumination; after topical instillation, finger pressure should be applied to lacrimal sac to decrease drainage into the nose and throat and minimize possible systemic absorption

Dosage Forms GEL, ophthalmic (Pilopine HS®): 4% (3.5 g). **SOLN, ophthalmic:** 1% (15 mL), 2% (15 mL), 4% (15 mL), 6% (15 mL); (Isopto® Carpine): 1% (15 mL); 2% (15 mL, 30 mL); 4% (15 mL, 30 mL); 6% (15 mL); 8% (15 mL); (Pilocar®): 0.5% (15 mL); 1% (1 mL, 15 mL); 2% (1 mL, 15 mL); 3% (15 mL); 4% (1 mL, 15 mL); 6% (15 mL); (Piloptic®): 0.5% (15 mL); 1% (15 mL); 2% (15 mL); 3% (15 mL); 4% (15 mL); 6% (15 mL). **TAB** (Salagen®): 5 mg

♦ **Pilocarpine Hydrochloride** *see Pilocarpine on page 1001*

♦ **Pilopine HS®** *see Pilocarpine on page 1001*

♦ **Piloptic®** *see Pilocarpine on page 1001*

♦ **Pima®** *see Potassium Iodide on page 1022*

♦ **Pimaricin** *see Natamycin on page 885*

Pimecrolimus *(pim e KROE li mus)*

U.S. Brand Names Elidel®

Therapeutic Category Immunosuppressant Agent; Topical Skin Product

Use Short-term and intermittent long-term treatment of mild to moderate atopic dermatitis in patients not responsive to conventional therapy or when conventional therapy is not appropriate

Pregnancy Risk Factor C

Contraindications Hypersensitivity to pimecrolimus or any component of the formulation; Netherton's syndrome

Warnings/Precautions Do not apply to areas of active cutaneous viral infections. May be increased risk of varicella zoster, herpes simplex viral infections, or eczema herpeticum. Consider discontinuation if lymphadenopathy or worsening of skin papillomas occur. Minimize or avoid natural/artificial sunlight exposure. No data to support use in immunocompromised patients. Use caution with CYP3A4 inhibitors in patients with widespread and/or erythrodermic disease. Not recommended in children <2 years of age.

Common Adverse Reactions
>10% :
Central nervous system: Headache (7% to 25%), pyrexia (1% to 13%)
Local: Burning at application site (2% to 26%)
Respiratory: Nasopharyngitis (8% to 27%), cough (2% to 16%), upper respiratory tract infection (4% to 19%), bronchitis (0.4% to 11%)
Miscellaneous: Influenza (3% to 13%)
1% to 10%:
Dermatologic: Skin papilloma (warts) (up to 3%), molluscum contagiosum (0.7% to 2%), herpes simplex dermatitis (up to 2%)
Gastrointestinal: Diarrhea (0.6% to 8%), constipation (up to 4%)
Local: Irritation at application site (0.4% to 6%), erythema at application site (0.4% to 2%), pruritus at application site (0.6% to 6%)
Ocular: Eye infection (up to 1%)
Otic: Ear infection (0.6% to 6%)

Respiratory: Pharyngitis (0.7% to 8%), sinusitis (0.6% to 3%), nasal congestion (0.6% to 3%)

Miscellaneous: Viral infection (up to 7%), herpes simplex infections (0.4% to 4%), tonsillitis (0.4% to 6%)

Adverse events ≤ placebo: Abdominal pain, acne, arthralgias, asthma exacerbation, back pain, bacterial infection, conjunctivitis, dyspnea, dysmenorrhea, earache, epistaxis, folliculitis, hypersensitivity, impetigo, nausea, otitis media, pharyngitis (streptococcal), pneumonia, rhinorrhea, rhinitis, sinus congestion, skin infection, sore throat, Staphylococcal infection, toothache, urticaria, vomiting, wheezing

Drug Interactions

Cytochrome P450 Effect: Substrate of CYP3A4 (minor)

Increased Effect/Toxicity: CYP3A inhibitors may increase pimecrolimus levels in patients where increased absorption expected.

Mechanism of Action Penetrates inflamed epidermis to inhibit T cell activation by blocking transcription of proinflammatory cytokine genes such as interleukin-2, interferon gamma (Th1-type), interleukin-4, and interleukin-10 (Th2-type). Blocks catalytic function of calcineurin. Prevents release of inflammatory cytokines and mediators from mast cells *in vitro* after stimulation by antigen/IgE.

Pharmacodynamics/Kinetics Absorption: Poor when applied to 13% to 62% body surface area for up to a year

Dosage Children ≥2 years and Adults: Topical: Apply thin layer to affected area twice daily; rub in gently and completely. **Note:** Continue as long as signs and symptoms persist; discontinue if resolution occurs; re-evaluate if symptoms persist >6 weeks.

Administration Do not use with occlusive dressings. Continue as long as signs and symptoms persist; discontinue if resolution occurs; re-evaluate if symptoms persist >6 weeks.

Dosage Forms CRM, topical: 1% (15 g, 30 g, 60 g, 100 g)

Pimozide (PI moe zide)

Related Information

Antipsychotic Agents Comparison *on page 1364*

U.S. Brand Names Orap®

Therapeutic Category Antipsychotic Agent, Diphenylbutylpiperidine

Use Suppression of severe motor and phonic tics in patients with Tourette's disorder who have failed to respond satisfactorily to standard treatment

Unlabeled/Investigational Use Psychosis; reported use in individuals with delusions focused on physical symptoms (ie, preoccupation with parasitic infestation); Huntington's chorea

Pregnancy Risk Factor C

Dosage Oral: **Note:** An ECG should be performed baseline and periodically thereafter, especially during dosage adjustment:

Children ≤12 years: Tourette's disorder: Initial: 0.05 mg/kg preferably once at bedtime; may be increased every third day; usual range: 2-4 mg/day; do not exceed 10 mg/day (0.2 mg/kg/day)

Children >12 years and Adults: Tourette's disorder: Initial: 1-2 mg/day in divided doses, then increase dosage as needed every other day; range is usually 7-16 mg/day, maximum dose: 10 mg/day or 0.2 mg/kg/day are not generally recommended

Note: Sudden unexpected deaths have occurred in patients taking doses >10 mg. Therefore, dosages exceeding 10 mg/day are generally not recommended.

Dosing adjustment in hepatic impairment: Reduction of dose is necessary in patients with liver disease

Dosage Forms TAB: 1 mg, 2 mg

Pindolol (PIN doe lole)

Related Information

Beta-Blockers Comparison *on page 1368*

Therapeutic Category Antihypertensive Agent; Beta Blocker, Intrinsic Sympathomimetic Activity (ISA)

Use Management of hypertension

Unlabeled/Investigational Use Potential augmenting agent for antidepressants; ventricular arrhythmias/tachycardia, antipsychotic-induced akathisia, situational anxiety; aggressive behavior associated with dementia

Pregnancy Risk Factor B

Contraindications Hypersensitivity to pindolol, beta-blockers, or any component of the formulation; uncompensated congestive heart failure; cardiogenic shock; bradycardia, sinus node dysfunction, or heart block (2nd or 3rd degree) except in patients with a functioning artificial pacemaker; pulmonary edema; severe hyperactive airway disease (asthma or COPD); Raynaud's disease

Warnings/Precautions Use with caution in patients with inadequate myocardial function, undergoing anesthesia, bronchospastic disease, diabetes mellitus, hyperthyroidism, impaired hepatic function; abrupt withdrawal of the drug should be avoided (may exacerbate symptoms; discontinue over 1-2 weeks); do not use in pregnant or nursing women; may potentiate hypoglycemia in a diabetic patient and mask signs and symptoms; beta-blockers with intrinsic sympathomimetic activity (including pindolol) do not appear to be of benefit in CHF

Common Adverse Reactions 1% to 10%:

Cardiovascular: Chest pain (3%), edema (6%)

Central nervous system: Nightmares/vivid dreams (5%), dizziness (9%), insomnia (10%), fatigue (8%), nervousness (7%), anxiety (<2%)

(Continued)

Pindolol *(Continued)*

Dermatologic: Rash, itching (4%)

Gastrointestinal: Nausea (5%), abdominal discomfort (4%)

Neuromuscular & skeletal: Weakness (4%), paresthesia (3%), arthralgia (7%), muscle pain (10%)

Respiratory: Dyspnea (5%)

Drug Interactions

Cytochrome P450 Effect: Substrate of CYP2D6 (major); **Inhibits** CYP2D6 (weak)

Increased Effect/Toxicity: CYP2D6 inhibitors may increase the levels/effects of pindolol; example inhibitors include chlorpromazine, delavirdine, fluoxetine, miconazole, paroxetine, pergolide, quinidine, quinine, ritonavir, and ropinirole. Pindolol may increase the effects of other drugs which slow AV conduction (digoxin, verapamil, diltiazem), alpha-blockers (prazosin, terazosin), and alpha-adrenergic stimulants (epinephrine, phenylephrine). Pindolol may mask the tachycardia from hypoglycemia caused by insulin and oral hypoglycemics. In patients receiving concurrent therapy, the risk of hypertensive crisis is increased when either clonidine or the beta-blocker is withdrawn. Reserpine has been shown to enhance the effect of beta-blockers. Beta-blockers may increase the action or levels of ethanol, disopyramide, nondepolarizing muscle relaxants, and theophylline although the effects are difficult to predict.

Decreased Effect: Decreased levels/effect of pindolol with aluminum salts, barbiturates, calcium salts, cholestyramine, colestipol, NSAIDs, penicillins (ampicillin), rifampin, salicylates, and sulfinpyrazone due to decreased bioavailability and plasma levels. Beta-blockers may decrease the effect of sulfonylureas (possibly hyperglycemia). Nonselective beta-blockers blunt the effect of beta-2 adrenergic agonists (albuterol).

Mechanism of Action Blocks both beta$_1$- and beta$_2$-receptors and has mild intrinsic sympathomimetic activity; pindolol has negative inotropic and chronotropic effects and can significantly slow AV nodal conduction. Augmentive action of antidepressants thought to be mediated via a serotonin 1A autoreceptor antagonism.

Pharmacodynamics/Kinetics

Absorption: Rapid, 50% to 95%

Protein binding: 50%

Metabolism: Hepatic (60% to 65%) to conjugates

Half-life elimination: 2.5-4 hours; prolonged with renal impairment, age, and cirrhosis

Time to peak, serum: 1-2 hours

Excretion: Urine (35% to 50% as unchanged drug)

Dosage Oral:

Adults:

Hypertension: Initial: 5 mg twice daily, increase as necessary by 10 mg/day every 3-4 weeks; maximum daily dose: 60 mg

Antidepressant augmentation: 2.5 mg 3 times/day

Elderly: Initial: 5 mg once daily, increase as necessary by 5 mg/day every 3-4 weeks

Dosing adjustment in renal and hepatic impairment: Reduction is necessary in severely impaired

Monitoring Parameters Blood pressure, standing and sitting/supine, pulse, respiratory function

Patient Information Adhere to dosage regimen; watch for postural hypotension; abrupt withdrawal of the drug should be avoided; take at the same time each day; may mask diabetes symptoms; do not discontinue medication abruptly; consult pharmacist or prescriber before taking over-the-counter cold preparations

Dosage Forms TAB: 5 mg, 10 mg

♦ **Pink Bismuth** *see Bismuth on page 168*

♦ **Pin-X® [OTC]** *see Pyrantel Pamoate on page 1064*

♦ **PIO** *see Pemoline on page 969*

Pioglitazone *(pye oh GLI ta zone)*

Related Information

Hypoglycemic Drugs & Thiazolidinedione Information *on page 1378*

U.S. Brand Names Actos®

Therapeutic Category Antidiabetic Agent, Thiazolidinedione; Hypoglycemic Agent, Oral

Use

Type 2 diabetes mellitus (noninsulin dependent, NIDDM), monotherapy: Adjunct to diet and exercise, to improve glycemic control

Type 2 diabetes mellitus (noninsulin dependent, NIDDM), combination therapy with sulfonylurea, metformin, or insulin: When diet, exercise, and a single agent alone does not result in adequate glycemic control

Pregnancy Risk Factor C

Contraindications Hypersensitivity to pioglitazone or any component of the formulation; active liver disease (transaminases >2.5 times the upper limit of normal at baseline); patients who have experienced jaundice during troglitazone therapy

Warnings/Precautions Should not be used in diabetic ketoacidosis. Mechanism requires the presence of insulin, therefore use in type 1 diabetes is not recommended. May potentiate hypoglycemia when used in combination with sulfonylureas or insulin. Use with caution in premenopausal, anovulatory women - may result in a resumption of ovulation, increasing the risk of pregnancy. Use with caution in patients with anemia (may reduce hemoglobin and hematocrit). Use with caution in patients with edema; may increase plasma volume and/or increase cardiac hypertrophy. Monitor closely for signs and symptoms of heart failure (including weight gain, edema, or dyspnea). Avoid use in patients with NYHA Class III or IV heart failure. Discontinue if heart failure develops. Use with caution in patients with minor elevations in transaminases (AST or ALT) - see Contraindications and Monitoring Parameters. Idiosyncratic hepatotoxicity has been reported with another thiazolidinedione agent (troglitazone) and postmarketing case reports of hepatitis (with rare hepatic failure) have been received for pioglitazone. Monitoring should include periodic determinations of liver function. Not for use in children <18 years of age.

Common Adverse Reactions

>10%:
Endocrine & metabolic: Serum triglycerides decreased, HDL-cholesterol increased
Gastrointestinal: Weight gain
Respiratory: Upper respiratory tract infection (13%)

1% to 10%:
Cardiovascular: Edema (5%) (in combination trials with sulfonylureas or insulin, the incidence of edema was as high as 15%)
Central nervous system: Headache (9%), fatigue (4%)
Endocrine & metabolic: Aggravation of diabetes mellitus (5%), hypoglycemia (range 2% to 15% when used in combination with sulfonylureas or insulin)
Hematologic: Anemia (1%)
Neuromuscular & skeletal: Myalgia (5%)
Respiratory: Sinusitis (6%), pharyngitis (5%)

Drug Interactions

Cytochrome P450 Effect: Substrate (major) of CYP2C8/9, 3A4; **Inhibits** CYP2C8/9 (strong), 2C19 (weak), 2D6 (moderate); **Induces** CYP3A4 (weak)

Increased Effect/Toxicity: Concomitant use with thioridazine is contraindicated (may increase thioridazine levels). CYP2C8/9 inhibitors may increase the levels/effects of pioglitazone; example inhibitors include delavirdine, fluconazole, gemfibrozil, ketoconazole, nicardipine, NSAIDs, and sulfonamides. Ketoconazole (in vitro) inhibits metabolism of pioglitazone. Other inhibitors of CYP3A4, including itraconazole, are likely to decrease pioglitazone metabolism. Patients receiving inhibitors of CYP3A4 should have their glycemic control evaluated more frequently. Gemfibrozil may increase pioglitazone levels.

Decreased Effect: CYP2C8/9 inducers may decrease the levels/effects of pioglitazone; example inducers include carbamazepine, phenobarbital, phenytoin, rifampin, rifapentine, and secobarbital. Effects of oral contraceptives (hormonal) may be decreased, based on data from a related compound. This has not been specifically evaluated for pioglitazone. CYP3A4 inducers may decrease the therapeutic effect of pioglitazone. Bile acid sequestrants may decrease pioglitazone levels.

Mechanism of Action Thiazolidinedione antidiabetic agent that lowers blood glucose by improving target cell response to insulin, without increasing pancreatic insulin secretion. It has a mechanism of action that is dependent on the presence of insulin for activity. Pioglitazone is a potent and selective agonist for peroxisome proliferator-activated receptor-gamma (PPAR-gamma). Activation of nuclear PPARgamma receptors influences the production of a number of gene products involved in glucose and lipid metabolism.

Pharmacodynamics/Kinetics

Onset of action: Delayed
Peak effect: Glucose control: Several weeks
Distribution: V_{ss} (apparent): 0.63 L/kg
Protein binding: 99.8%
Metabolism: Hepatic (99%) via CYP2C8/9 and 3A4 to both active and inactive metabolites
Half-life elimination: Parent drug: 3-7 hours; Total: 16-24 hours
Time to peak: ~2 hours
Excretion: Urine (15% to 30%) and feces as metabolites

Dosage Adults: Oral:
Monotherapy: Initial: 15-30 mg once daily; if response is inadequate, the dosage may be increased in increments up to 45 mg once daily; maximum recommended dose: 45 mg once daily
Combination therapy (doses >30 mg/day have not been evaluated in combination regimens):
With sulfonylureas: Initial: 15-30 mg once daily; dose of sulfonylurea should be reduced if the patient reports hypoglycemia
With metformin: Initial: 15-30 mg once daily; it is unlikely that the dose of metformin will need to be reduced due to hypoglycemia
With insulin: Initial: 15-30 mg once daily; dose of insulin should be reduced by 10% to 25% if the patient reports hypoglycemia or if the plasma glucose falls to <100 mg/dL.
Elderly: No dosage adjustment is recommended in elderly patients.

Dosage adjustment in renal impairment: No dosage adjustment is required.

Dosage adjustment in hepatic impairment: Clearance is significantly lower in hepatic impairment. Therapy should not be initiated if the patient exhibits active liver disease or increased transaminases (>2.5 times the upper limit of normal) at baseline.

Administration May be administered without regard to meals

Monitoring Parameters Hemoglobin A_{1c}, liver enzymes (prior to initiation and every 2 months for the first year of treatment, then periodically). If the ALT is increased to >2.5 times the upper limit of normal, liver function testing should be performed more frequently until the levels return to normal or pretreatment values. Patients with an elevation in ALT >3 times the upper limit of normal should be rechecked as soon as possible. If the ALT levels remain >3 times the upper limit of normal, therapy with pioglitazone should be discontinued.
(Continued)

Pioglitazone *(Continued)*

Patient Information May be taken without regard to meals. Follow directions of prescriber. Monitor urine or serum glucose as recommended by prescriber. More frequent monitoring is required during periods of stress, trauma, surgery, pregnancy, increased activity or exercise. Avoid alcohol. Report chest pain, rapid heartbeat or palpitations, abdominal pain, fever, rash, hypoglycemia reactions, yellowing of skin or eyes, dark urine or light stool, unusual fatigue, or nausea/vomiting.

Dosage Forms TAB: 15 mg, 30 mg, 45 mg

Piperacillin (pi PER a sil in)

Related Information

Antimicrobial Drugs of Choice *on page 1440*

Community-Acquired Pneumonia in Adults *on page 1457*

U.S. Brand Names Pipracil® [DSC]

Synonyms Piperacillin Sodium

Therapeutic Category Antibiotic, Penicillin

Use Treatment of susceptible infections such as septicemia, acute and chronic respiratory tract infections, skin and soft tissue infections, and urinary tract infections due to susceptible strains of *Pseudomonas*, *Proteus*, and *Escherichia coli* and *Enterobacter*; active against some streptococci and some anaerobic bacteria; febrile neutropenia (as part of combination regimen)

Pregnancy Risk Factor B

Dosage

Neonates: 100 mg/kg every 12 hours

Infants and Children: I.M., I.V.: 200-300 mg/kg/day in divided doses every 4-6 hours

Higher doses have been used in cystic fibrosis: 350-500 mg/kg/day in divided doses every 4-6 hours

Adults: I.M., I.V.:

Moderate infections (urinary tract infections): 2-3 g/dose every 6-12 hours; maximum: 2 g I.M./site

Serious infections: 3-4 g/dose every 4-6 hours; maximum: 24 g/24 hours

Uncomplicated gonorrhea: 2 g I.M. in a single dose accompanied by 1 g probenecid 30 minutes prior to injection

Dosing adjustment in renal impairment: Adults: I.V.:

Cl_{cr} 20-40 mL/minute: Administer 3-4 g every 8 hours

Cl_{cr} <20 mL/minute: Administer 3-4 g every 12 hours

Moderately dialyzable (20% to 50%)

Continuous arteriovenous or venovenous hemodiafiltration effects: Dose as for Cl_{cr} 10-50 mL/minute

Dosage Forms INJ, powder for reconstitution: 2 g, 3 g, 4 g

Piperacillin and Tazobactam Sodium

(pi PER a sil in & ta zoe BAK tam SOW dee um)

Related Information

Antimicrobial Drugs of Choice *on page 1440*

Community-Acquired Pneumonia in Adults *on page 1457*

U.S. Brand Names Zosyn®

Synonyms Piperacillin Sodium and Tazobactam Sodium

Therapeutic Category Antibiotic, Anaerobic; Antibiotic, Penicillin & Beta-lactamase Inhibitor

Use Treatment of infections caused by susceptible organisms, including infections of the lower respiratory tract (community-acquired pneumonia, nosocomial pneumonia); urinary tract; skin and skin structures; gynecologic (endometritis, pelvic inflammatory disease); bone and joint infections; intra-abdominal infections (appendicitis with rupture/abscess, peritonitis); and septicemia. Tazobactam expands activity of piperacillin to include beta-lactamase producing strains of *S. aureus*, *H. influenzae*, *Bacteroides*, and other gram-negative bacteria.

Pregnancy Risk Factor B

Contraindications Hypersensitivity to penicillins, beta-lactamase inhibitors, or any component of the formulation

Warnings/Precautions Due to sodium load and to the adverse effects of high serum concentrations of penicillins, dosage modification is required in patients with impaired or underdeveloped renal function; use with caution in patients with seizures or in patients with history of beta-lactam allergy; safety and efficacy have not been established in children <12 years of age

Common Adverse Reactions

>10%: Gastrointestinal: Diarrhea (11%)

1% to 10%:

Cardiovascular: Hypertension (2%)

Central nervous system: Insomnia (7%), headache (7% to 8%), agitation (2%), fever (2%), dizziness (1%)

Dermatologic: Rash (4%), pruritus (3%)

Gastrointestinal: Constipation (7% to 8%), nausea (7%), vomiting/dyspepsia (3%)

Hepatic: Transaminases increased

Respiratory: Rhinitis/dyspnea (~1%)

Miscellaneous: Serum sickness-like reaction

Several laboratory abnormalities have rarely been associated with piperacillin/tazobactam including reversible eosinophilia, and neutropenia (associated most often with prolonged therapy), positive direct Coombs' test, prolonged PT and aPTT, transient elevations of LFT, increases in creatinine

Drug Interactions

Increased Effect/Toxicity: Probenecid may increase penicillin levels. Neuromuscular blockers may increase duration of blockade. Penicillins may increase methotrexate exposure; clinical significance has not been established.

Decreased Effect: Tetracyclines may decrease penicillin effectiveness. Aminoglycosides may cause physical inactivation of aminoglycosides in the presence of high concentrations of piperacillin and potential toxicity in patients with mild-moderate renal dysfunction. Although anecdotal reports suggest oral contraceptive efficacy could be reduced by penicillins, this has been refuted by more rigorous scientific and clinical data.

Mechanism of Action Inhibits bacterial cell wall synthesis by binding to one or more of the penicillin binding proteins (PBPs); which in turn inhibits the final transpeptidation step of peptidoglycan synthesis in bacterial cell walls, thus inhibiting cell wall biosynthesis. Bacteria eventually lyse due to ongoing activity of cell wall autolytic enzymes (autolysins and murein hydrolases) while cell wall assembly is arrested. Tazobactam inhibits many beta-lactamases, including staphylococcal penicillinase and Richmond and Sykes types II, III, IV, and V, including extended spectrum enzymes; it has only limited activity against class I beta-lactamases other than class Ic types.

Pharmacodynamics/Kinetics Both AUC and peak concentrations are dose proportional; hepatic impairment does not affect kinetics

Distribution: Well into lungs, intestinal mucosa, skin, muscle, uterus, ovary, prostate, gallbladder, and bile; penetration into CSF is low in subject with noninflamed meninges

Protein binding: Piperacillin: ~26% to 33%; Tazobactam: 31% to 32%

Metabolism: Piperacillin: 6% to 9%; Tazobactam: ~26%

Half-life elimination: Piperacillin: 1 hour; Metabolite: 1-1.5 hours; Tazobactam: 0.7-0.9 hour

Excretion: Both piperacillin and tazobactam are directly proportional to renal function

Piperacillin: Urine (50% to 70%); feces (10% to 20%)

Tazobactam: Urine (26% as inactive metabolite) within 24 hours

Dosage

Infants and Children ≥6 months: **Note:** Not FDA-approved for use in children <12 years of age:

I.V.: 240 mg of piperacillin component/kg/day in divided doses every 8 hours; higher doses have been used for serious pseudomonal infections: 300-400 mg of piperacillin component/kg/day in divided doses every 6 hours.

Children >12 years and Adults:

Nosocomial pneumonia: I.V.: Piperacillin/tazobactam 4/0.5 g every 6 hours for 7-14 days (when used empirically, combination with an aminoglycoside is recommended; consider discontinuation of aminoglycoside if *P. aeruginosa* is not isolated)

Severe infections: I.V.: Piperacillin/tazobactam 4/0.5 g every 8 hours or 3/0.375 g every 6 hours for 7-10 days

Moderate infections: I.M.: Piperacillin/tazobactam 2/0.25 g every 6-8 hours; treatment should be continued for ≥7-10 days depending on severity of disease (**Note:** I.M. route not FDA-approved)

Dosing interval in renal impairment:

Cl$_{cr}$ 20-40 mL/minute: Administer 2/0.25 g every 6 hours (3/0.375 g every 6 hours for nosocomial pneumonia)

Cl$_{cr}$ <20 mL/minute: Administer 2/0.25 g every 8 hours (2/0.25 g every 6 hours for nosocomial pneumonia)

Hemodialysis: Administer 2/0.25 g every 12 hours (every 8 hours for nosocomial pneumonia) with an additional dose of 0.75 g after each dialysis

Continuous arteriovenous or venovenous hemodiafiltration effects: Dose as for Cl$_{cr}$ 10-50 mL/minute

Administration Administer by I.V. infusion over 30 minutes; reconstitute with 5 mL of diluent per 1 g of piperacillin and then further dilute; **compatible** diluents include NS, SW, dextran 6%, D$_5$W, D$_5$W with potassium chloride 40 mEq, bacteriostatic saline and water; **incompatible** with lactated Ringer's solution; discontinue primary infusion, if possible, during infusion and administer aminoglycosides separately from Zosyn®.

Monitoring Parameters LFTs, creatinine, BUN, CBC with differential, serum electrolytes, urinalysis, PT, PTT; monitor for signs of anaphylaxis during first dose

Dosage Forms Note: 8:1 ratio of piperacillin sodium/tazobactam sodium: **INF:** Piperacillin 2 g and tazobactam sodium 0.25 g (50 mL), piperacillin 3 g and tazobactam sodium 0.375 g (50 mL), piperacillin 4 g and tazobactam sodium 0.5 g (50 mL). **INJ, powder for reconstitution:** Piperacillin 2 g and tazobactam sodium 0.25 g, piperacillin 3 g and tazobactam sodium 0.375 g, piperacillin 4 g and tazobactam sodium 0.5 g, piperacillin 36 g and tazobactam sodium 4.5 g

Pirbuterol (peer BYOO ter ole)

Related Information

Bronchodilators, Comparison of Inhaled Sympathomimetics *on page 1370*

U.S. Brand Names Maxair™ Autohaler™

Synonyms Pirbuterol Acetate

Therapeutic Category Beta$_2$-Adrenergic Agonist; Bronchodilator

Use Prevention and treatment of reversible bronchospasm including asthma

(Continued)

Pirbuterol *(Continued)*

Pregnancy Risk Factor C

Contraindications Hypersensitivity to pirbuterol, albuterol, or any component of the formulation

Warnings/Precautions Optimize anti-inflammatory treatment before initiating maintenance treatment with pirbuterol. Do not use as a component of chronic therapy without an anti-inflammatory agent. Only the mildest form of asthma (Step 1 and/or exercise-induced) would not require concurrent use based upon asthma guidelines. Patient must be instructed to seek medical attention in cases where acute symptoms are not relieved or a previous level of response is diminished. The need to increase frequency of use may indicate deterioration of asthma, and treatment must not be delayed.

Use caution in patients with cardiovascular disease (arrhythmia or hypertension or CHF), convulsive disorders, diabetes, glaucoma, hyperthyroidism, or hypokalemia. Beta agonists may cause elevation in blood pressure, heart rate, and result in CNS stimulation/excitation. Beta$_2$ agonists may increase risk of arrhythmia, increase serum glucose, or decrease serum potassium.

Do not exceed recommended dose; serious adverse events including fatalities, have been associated with excessive use of inhaled sympathomimetics. Rarely, paradoxical bronchospasm may occur with use of inhaled bronchodilating agents; this should be distinguished from inadequate response. All patients should utilize a spacer device when using a metered-dose inhaler. Safety and efficacy have not been established in children <12 years of age.

Common Adverse Reactions

>10%:

Central nervous system: Nervousness (7%)

Endocrine & metabolic: Serum glucose increased, serum potassium decreased

Neuromuscular & skeletal: Trembling (6%)

1% to 10%:

Cardiovascular: Palpitations (2%), tachycardia (1%)

Central nervous system: Headache (2%), dizziness (1%)

Gastrointestinal: Nausea (2%)

Respiratory: Cough (1%)

Drug Interactions

Increased Effect/Toxicity: Increased toxicity with other beta agonists, MAO inhibitors, tricyclic antidepressants.

Decreased Effect: Decreased effect with beta-blockers.

Mechanism of Action Pirbuterol is a beta$_2$-adrenergic agonist with a similar structure to albuterol, specifically a pyridine ring has been substituted for the benzene ring in albuterol. The increased beta$_2$ selectivity of pirbuterol results from the substitution of a tertiary butyl group on the nitrogen of the side chain, which additionally imparts resistance of pirbuterol to degradation by monoamine oxidase and provides a lengthened duration of action in comparison to the less selective previous beta-agonist agents.

Pharmacodynamics/Kinetics

Onset of action: Peak effect: Therapeutic: Oral: 2-3 hours with peak serum concentration of 6.2-9.8 mcg/L; Inhalation: 0.5-1 hour

Half-life elimination: 2-3 hours

Metabolism: Hepatic

Excretion: Urine (10% as unchanged drug)

Dosage Children ≥12 years and Adults: 2 inhalations every 4-6 hours for prevention; two inhalations at an interval of at least 1-3 minutes, followed by a third inhalation in treatment of bronchospasm, not to exceed 12 inhalations/day

Administration Inhalation: Shake inhaler well before use.

Monitoring Parameters Respiratory rate; FEV$_1$, peak flow, and/or other pulmonary function tests; blood pressure, heart rate; CNS stimulation; serum glucose, serum potassium

Patient Information Patient instructions are available with product. Do not exceed recommended dosage; rinse mouth with water following each inhalation to help with dry throat and mouth.

Dosage Forms AERO, for oral inhalation: (Maxair™ Autohaler™): 0.2 mg/inhalation (2.8 g) [80 inhalations], 14 g [400 inhalations]

♦ **Pirbuterol Acetate** *see Pirbuterol on page 1007*

Piroxicam *(peer OKS i kam)*

Related Information

Nonsteroidal Anti-Inflammatory Agents Comparison *on page 1401*

U.S. Brand Names Feldene®

Therapeutic Category Analgesic, Nonsteroidal Anti-inflammatory Drug; Anti-inflammatory Agent; Nonsteroidal Anti-inflammatory Drug (NSAID), Oral

Use Symptomatic treatment of acute and chronic rheumatoid arthritis and osteoarthritis

Unlabeled/Investigational Use Ankylosing spondylitis

Pregnancy Risk Factor B/D (3rd trimester or near term)

Contraindications Hypersensitivity to piroxicam, aspirin, other NSAIDs or any component of the formulation; active GI bleeding; pregnancy (3rd trimester or near term)

Warnings/Precautions Use with caution in patients with impaired cardiac function, dehydration, hypertension, impaired renal function, GI disease (bleeding or ulcers) and patients receiving anticoagulants; elderly have increased risk for adverse reactions to NSAIDs. As many as 60% of elderly can develop peptic ulceration and/or hemorrhage asymptomatically.

Use lowest effective dose for shortest period possible. Use of NSAIDs can compromise existing renal function especially when Cl_{cr} is <30 mL/minute. Withhold for at least 4-6 half-lives prior to surgical or dental procedures. May have adverse effects on fetus. Use with caution with dehydration. Use in children is not recommended.

Common Adverse Reactions
>10%:
Central nervous system: Dizziness
Dermatologic: Rash
Gastrointestinal: Abdominal cramps, heartburn, indigestion, nausea
1% to 10%:
Central nervous system: Headache, nervousness
Dermatologic: Itching
Endocrine & metabolic: Fluid retention
Gastrointestinal: Vomiting
Otic: Tinnitus

Drug Interactions
Cytochrome P450 Effect: Substrate of CYP2C8/9 (minor); **Inhibits** CYP2C8/9 (strong)
Increased Effect/Toxicity: Increased effect/toxicity of lithium, warfarin, and methotrexate (controversial).
Decreased Effect: Decreased effect of diuretics, beta-blockers. Decreased effect with aspirin, antacids, and cholestyramine.

Mechanism of Action Inhibits prostaglandin synthesis, acts on the hypothalamus heat-regulating center to reduce fever, blocks prostaglandin synthetase action which prevents formation of the platelet-aggregating substance thromboxane A_2; decreases pain receptor sensitivity. Other proposed mechanisms of action for salicylate anti-inflammatory action are lysosomal stabilization, kinin and leukotriene production, alteration of chemotactic factors, and inhibition of neutrophil activation. This latter mechanism may be the most significant pharmacologic action to reduce inflammation.

Pharmacodynamics/Kinetics
Onset of action: Analgesic: ~1 hour
  Peak effect: 3-5 hours
Protein binding: 99%
Metabolism: Hepatic
Half-life elimination: 45-50 hours
Excretion: Primarily urine and feces (small amounts) as unchanged drug (5%) and metabolites

Dosage Oral:
Children: 0.2-0.3 mg/kg/day once daily; maximum dose: 15 mg/day
Adults: 10-20 mg/day once daily; although associated with increase in GI adverse effects, doses >20 mg/day have been used (ie, 30-40 mg/day)
Dosing adjustment in hepatic impairment: Reduction of dosage is necessary
Monitoring Parameters Occult blood loss, hemoglobin, hematocrit, and periodic renal and hepatic function tests; periodic ophthalmologic exams with chronic use
Patient Information Take with food, may cause drowsiness or dizziness
Dosage Forms CAP: 10 mg, 20 mg

- *p*-Isobutylhydratropic Acid *see* Ibuprofen *on page 645*
- **Pit** *see* Oxytocin *on page 948*
- **Pitocin**® *see* Oxytocin *on page 948*
- **Pitressin**® *see* Vasopressin *on page 1298*

Plague Vaccine (plaig vak SEEN)
Therapeutic Category Vaccine; Vaccine, Inactivated Bacteria
Use Selected travelers to countries reporting cases for whom avoidance of rodents and fleas is impossible; all laboratory and field personnel working with *Yersinia pestis* organisms possibly resistant to antimicrobials; those engaged in *Yersinia pestis* aerosol experiments or in field operations in areas with enzootic plague where regular exposure to potentially infected wild rodents, rabbits, or their fleas cannot be prevented. Prophylactic antibiotics may be indicated following definite exposure, whether or not the exposed persons have been vaccinated.
Pregnancy Risk Factor C
Contraindications Hypersensitivity to any of the vaccine constituents (see manufacturer's label); patients who have had severe local or systemic reactions to a previous dose; defer immunization in patients with a febrile illness until resolved
Warnings/Precautions Pregnancy, unless there is substantial and unavoidable risk of exposure; the expected immune response may not be obtained if plague vaccine is administered to immunosuppressed persons or patients receiving immunosuppressive therapy; be prepared with epinephrine injection (1:1000) in cases of anaphylaxis
Common Adverse Reactions All serious adverse reactions must be reported to the U.S. Department of Health and Human Services (DHHS) Vaccine Adverse Event Reporting System (VAERS) 1-800-822-7967.
1% to 10%:
Central nervous system: Malaise (10%), fever, headache (7% to 20%)
Dermatologic: Tenderness (20% to 80%)
Mechanism of Action Promotes active immunity to plague in high-risk individuals.
(Continued)

Plague Vaccine *(Continued)*

Dosage Three I.M. doses: First dose 1 mL, second dose (0.2 mL) 1 month later, third dose (0.2 mL) 5 months after the second dose; booster doses (0.2 mL) at 1- to 2-year intervals if exposure continues

Administration For patients at risk of hemorrhage following intramuscular injection, the ACIP recommends "it should be administered intramuscularly if, in the opinion of the physician familiar with the patients bleeding risk, the vaccine can be administered with reasonable safety by this route. If the patient receives antihemophilia or other similar therapy, intramuscular vaccination can be scheduled shortly after such therapy is administered. A fine needle (23 gauge or smaller) can be used for the vaccination and firm pressure applied to the site (without rubbing) for at least 2 minutes. The patient should be instructed concerning the risk of hematoma from the injection."

Dosage Forms INJ: 2 mL, 20 mL

♦ **Plan B**® *see* Levonorgestrel *on page 737*
♦ **Plantago Seed** *see* Psyllium *on page 1063*
♦ **Plantain Seed** *see* Psyllium *on page 1063*
♦ **Plaquenil**® *see* Hydroxychloroquine *on page 637*
♦ **Plasbumin**® *see* Albumin *on page 44*
♦ **Platinol**®-**AQ** *see* Cisplatin *on page 284*
♦ **Plavix**® *see* Clopidogrel *on page 301*
♦ **Plenaxis**™ *see* Abarelix *on page 19*
♦ **Plendil**® *see* Felodipine *on page 510*
♦ **Pletal**® *see* Cilostazol *on page 275*
♦ **Plexion**® *see* Sulfur and Sulfacetamide *on page 1177*
♦ **Plexion SCT**™ *see* Sulfur and Sulfacetamide *on page 1177*
♦ **Plexion**™ **TS** *see* Sulfur and Sulfacetamide *on page 1177*
♦ **PMPA** *see* Tenofovir *on page 1195*
♦ **Pneumococcal 7-Valent Conjugate Vaccine** *see* Pneumococcal Conjugate Vaccine (7-Valent) *on page 1010*

Pneumococcal Conjugate Vaccine (7-Valent)

(noo moe KOK al KON ju gate vak SEEN, seven vay lent)

U.S. Brand Names Prevnar®

Synonyms Diphtheria CRM$_{197}$ Protein; PCV7; Pneumococcal 7-Valent Conjugate Vaccine

Therapeutic Category Vaccine; Vaccine, Inactivated Bacteria

Use Immunization of infants and toddlers against *Streptococcus pneumoniae* infection caused by serotypes included in the vaccine

Advisory Committee on Immunization Practices (ACIP) guidelines also recommend PCV7 for use in:

Children ≥2-59 months with cochlear implants

All children ≥23 months

Children ages 24-59 months with: Sickle cell disease (including other sickle cell hemoglobinopathies, asplenia, splenic dysfunction), HIV infection, immunocompromising conditions (congenital immunodeficiencies, renal failure, nephrotic syndrome, diseases associated with immunosuppressive or radiation therapy, solid organ transplant), chronic illnesses (cardiac disease, cerebrospinal fluid leaks, diabetes mellitus, pulmonary disease excluding asthma unless on high dose corticosteroids)

Consider use in all children 24-59 months with priority given to:

Children 24-35 months

Children 24-59 months who are of Alaska native, American Indian, or African-American descent

Children 24-59 months who attend group day care centers

Pregnancy Risk Factor C

Contraindications Hypersensitivity to pneumococcal vaccine or any component of the formulation, including diphtheria toxoid; current or recent severe or moderate febrile illness; thrombocytopenia; any contraindication to I.M. injection; not for I.V. use

Warnings/Precautions Caution in latex sensitivity. Children with impaired immune responsiveness may have a reduced response to active immunization. Safety and efficacy have not been established in children <6 weeks of age. Not for I.V. use.

Common Adverse Reactions All serious adverse reactions must be reported to the U.S. Department of Health and Human Services (DHHS) Vaccine Adverse Event Reporting System (VAERS) 1-800-822-7967.

>10%:

Central nervous system: Fever, irritability, drowsiness, restlessness

Dermatologic: Erythema

Gastrointestinal: Decreased appetite, vomiting, diarrhea

Local: Induration, tenderness, nodule

1% to 10%: Dermatologic: Rash (0.5% to 1.4%)

Mechanism of Action Contains saccharides of capsular antigens of serotypes 4, 6B, 9V, 18C, 19F, and 23F, individually conjugated to CRM197 protein

Dosage I.M.:

Infants: 2-6 months: 0.5 mL at approximately 2-month intervals for 3 consecutive doses, followed by a fourth dose of 0.5 mL at 12-15 months of age; first dose may be given as young as 6 weeks of age, but is typically given at 2 months of age. In case of a moderate shortage of vaccine, defer the fourth dose until shortage is resolved; in case of a severe shortage of vaccine, defer third and fourth doses until shortage is resolved.

Previously Unvaccinated Infants and Children:

7-11 months: 0.5 mL for a total of 3 doses; 2 doses at least 4 weeks apart, followed by a third dose after the 1-year birthday (12-15 months), separated from the second dose by at least 2 months. In case of a severe shortage of vaccine, defer the third dose until shortage is resolved.

12-23 months: 0.5 mL for a total of 2 doses, separated by at least 2 months. In case of a severe shortage of vaccine, defer the second dose until shortage is resolved.

24-59 months:

Healthy Children: 0.5 mL as a single dose. In case of a severe shortage of vaccine, defer dosing until shortage is resolved.

Children with sickle cell disease, asplenia, HIV infection, chronic illness or immunocompromising conditions (not including bone marrow transplants - results pending; use PPV23 [pneumococcal polysaccharide vaccine, polyvalent] at 12- and 24-months until studies are complete): 0.5 mL for a total of 2 doses, separated by 2 months

Previously Vaccinated Children with a lapse in vaccine administration:

7-11 months: Previously received 1 or 2 doses PCV7: 0.5 mL dose at 7-11 months of age, followed by a second dose ≥2 months later at 12-15 months of age

12-23 months:

Previously received 1 dose before 12 months of age: 0.5 mL dose, followed by a second dose ≥2 months later

Previously received 2 doses before age 12 months: 0.5 mL dose ≥2 months after the most recent dose

24-59 months: Any incomplete schedule: 0.5 mL as a single dose; **Note:** Patients with chronic diseases or immunosuppressing conditions should receive 2 doses ≥2 months apart

Administration Do not inject I.V.; avoid intradermal route; administer I.M. (deltoid muscle or lateral mid thigh)

For patients at risk of hemorrhage following intramuscular injection, the ACIP recommends "it should be administered intramuscularly if, in the opinion of the physician familiar with the patients bleeding risk, the vaccine can be administered with reasonable safety by this route. If the patient receives antihemophilia or other similar therapy, intramuscular vaccination can be scheduled shortly after such therapy is administered. A fine needle (23 gauge or smaller) can be used for the vaccination and firm pressure applied to the site (without rubbing) for at least 2 minutes. The patient should be instructed concerning the risk of hematoma from the injection."

Dosage Forms INJ, suspension: 2 mcg of each saccharide for serotypes 4, 9V, 14, 18C, 19F, and 23F, and 4 mcg of serotype 6B per 0.5 mL (0.5 mL)

Pneumococcal Polysaccharide Vaccine (Polyvalent)

(noo moe KOK al pol i SAK a ride vak SEEN, pol i VAY lent)

U.S. Brand Names Pneumovax® 23; Pnu-Imune® 23 [DSC]

Synonyms PPV23; 23PS; 23-Valent Pneumococcal Polysaccharide Vaccine

Therapeutic Category Vaccine; Vaccine, Inactivated Bacteria

Use Children >2 years of age and adults who are at increased risk of pneumococcal disease and its complications because of underlying health conditions (including patients with cochlear implants); older adults, including all those ≥65 years of age

Current Advisory Committee on Immunization Practices (ACIP) guidelines recommend **pneumococcal 7-valent conjugate vaccine (PCV7)** be used for children 2-23 months of age and, in certain situations, children up to 59 months of age

Pregnancy Risk Factor C

Contraindications Hypersensitivity to pneumococcal vaccine or any component of the formulation. **Note:** Epinephrine injection (1:1000) must be immediately available in the case of anaphylaxis.

Warnings/Precautions Use caution in patients with severe cardiovascular or pulmonary disease where a systemic reaction may pose a significant risk. Use caution and consider delay of vaccination in any active infection. Avoid use in pregnancy (unless potential benefit justifies possible risks). Use caution in individuals who have had episodes of pneumococcal infection within the preceding 3 years (pre-existing pneumococcal antibodies may result in increased reactions to vaccine); may cause relapse in patients with stable idiopathic thrombocytopenia purpura.

Patients who will be receiving immunosuppressive therapy (including Hodgkin's disease, cancer chemotherapy, or transplantation) should be vaccinated at least 2 weeks prior to the initiation of therapy. Immune responses may be impaired for several months following intensive immunosuppressive therapy (up to 2 years in Hodgkin's disease patients). Patients who will undergo splenectomy should also be vaccinated 2 weeks prior to surgery, if possible. Patients with HIV should be vaccinated as soon as possible (following confirmation of the diagnosis). Not recommended in children ≤2 years of age.

Common Adverse Reactions All serious adverse reactions must be reported to the U.S. Department of Health and Human Services (DHHS) Vaccine Adverse Event Reporting System (VAERS) 1-800-822-7967.

>10%: Local: Induration and soreness at the injection site (~72%) (2-3 days)

Mechanism of Action Although there are more than 80 known pneumococcal capsular types, pneumococcal disease is mainly caused by only a few types of pneumococci. Pneumococcal vaccine contains capsular polysaccharides of 23 pneumococcal types which represent at least

(Continued)

Pneumococcal Polysaccharide Vaccine (Polyvalent) *(Continued)*

98% of pneumococcal disease isolates in the United States and Europe. The pneumococcal vaccine with 23 pneumococcal capsular polysaccharide types became available in 1983. The 23 capsular pneumococcal vaccine contains purified capsular polysaccharides of pneumococcal types 1, 2, 3, 4, 5, 8, 9, 12, 14, 17, 19, 20, 22, 23, 26, 34, 43, 51, 56, 57, 67, 70 (American Classification). These are the main pneumococcal types associated with serious infections in the United States.

Dosage I.M., S.C.:

Children >2 years and Adults: 0.5 mL

Previously vaccinated with PCV7 vaccine: Children ≥2 years and Adults:

With sickle cell disease, asplenia, immunocompromised or HIV infection: 0.5 mL at ≥2 years of age and ≥2 months after last dose of PCV7; revaccination with PPV23 should be given ≥5 years for children >10 years of age and every 3-5 years for children ≤10 years of age; revaccination should not be administered <3 years after the previous PPV23 dose

With chronic illness: 0.5 mL at ≥2 years of age and ≥2 months after last dose of PCV7; revaccination with PPV23 is not recommended

Following bone marrow transplant (use of PCV7 under study): Administer one dose PPV23 at 12- and 24-months following BMT

Revaccination should be considered:

1. If ≥6 years since initial vaccination has elapsed, or
2. In patients who received 14-valent pneumococcal vaccine and are at highest risk (asplenic) for fatal infection or
3. At ≥6 years in patients with nephrotic syndrome, renal failure, or transplant recipients, or
4. 3-5 years in children with nephrotic syndrome, asplenia, or sickle cell disease

Administration Do not inject I.V., avoid intradermal, administer S.C. or I.M. (deltoid muscle or lateral midthigh)

For patients at risk of hemorrhage following intramuscular injection, the ACIP recommends "it should be administered intramuscularly if, in the opinion of the physician familiar with the patients bleeding risk, the vaccine can be administered with reasonable safety by this route. If the patient receives antihemophilia or other similar therapy, intramuscular vaccination can be scheduled shortly after such therapy is administered. A fine needle (23 gauge or smaller) can be used for the vaccination and firm pressure applied to the site (without rubbing) for at least 2 minutes. The patient should be instructed concerning the risk of hematoma from the injection."

Dosage Forms INJ, solution: 25 mcg each of 23 polysaccharide isolates/0.5 mL (0.5 mL)

♦ **Pneumotussin®** *see Hydrocodone and Guaifenesin on page 630*

♦ **Pneumovax® 23** *see Pneumococcal Polysaccharide Vaccine (Polyvalent) on page 1011*

♦ **Pnu-Imune® 23 [DSC]** *see Pneumococcal Polysaccharide Vaccine (Polyvalent) on page 1011*

♦ **Podocon-25®** *see Podophyllum Resin on page 1012*

♦ **Podophyllin** *see Podophyllum Resin on page 1012*

Podophyllum Resin *(po DOF fil um REZ in)*

U.S. Brand Names Podocon-25®

Synonyms Mandrake; May Apple; Podophyllin

Therapeutic Category Keratolytic Agent

Use Topical treatment of benign growths including external genital and perianal warts, papillomas, fibroids; compound benzoin tincture generally is used as the medium for topical application

Pregnancy Risk Factor X

Contraindications Not to be used on birthmarks, moles, or warts with hair growth; cervical, urethral, oral warts; not to be used by diabetic patient or patient with poor circulation; pregnancy

Warnings/Precautions Use of large amounts of drug should be avoided; avoid contact with the eyes as it can cause severe corneal damage; do not apply to moles, birthmarks, or unusual warts; to be applied by a physician only; for external use only; 25% solution should not be applied to or near mucous membranes

Common Adverse Reactions 1% to 10%:

Dermatologic: Pruritus

Gastrointestinal: Nausea, vomiting, abdominal pain, diarrhea

Mechanism of Action Directly affects epithelial cell metabolism by arresting mitosis through binding to a protein subunit of spindle microtubules (tubulin)

Dosage Topical:

Children and Adults: 10% to 25% solution in compound benzoin tincture; apply drug to dry surface, use 1 drop at a time allowing drying between drops until area is covered; total volume should be limited to <0.5 mL per treatment session

Condylomata acuminatum: 25% solution is applied daily; use a 10% solution when applied to or near mucous membranes

Verrucae: 25% solution is applied 3-5 times/day directly to the wart

Patient Information Notify prescriber if undue skin irritation develops; should be applied by a physician

Dosage Forms LIQ, topical: 25% (15 mL)

♦ **Polaramine® [DSC]** *see Dexchlorpheniramine on page 359*

Poliovirus Vaccine (Inactivated)
(POE lee oh VYE rus vak SEEN, in ak ti VAY ted)

U.S. Brand Names IPOL®

Synonyms Enhanced-potency Inactivated Poliovirus Vaccine; IPV; Salk Vaccine

Therapeutic Category Vaccine; Vaccine, Inactivated Virus

Use

As the global eradication of poliomyelitis continues, the risk for importation of wild-type poliovirus into the United States decreases dramatically. To eliminate the risk for vaccine-associated paralytic poliomyelitis (VAPP), an all-IPV schedule is recommended for routine childhood vaccination in the United States. All children should receive four doses of IPV (at age 2 months, age 4 months, between ages 6-18 months, and between ages 4-6 years). Oral poliovirus vaccine (OPV), if available, may be used only for the following special circumstances:

Mass vaccination campaigns to control outbreaks of paralytic polio

Unvaccinated children who will be traveling within 4 weeks to areas where polio is endemic or epidemic

Children of parents who do not accept the recommended number of vaccine injections; these children may receive OPV only for the third or fourth dose or both. In this situation, healthcare providers should administer OPV only after discussing the risk for VAPP with parents or caregivers.

OPV supplies are expected to be very limited in the United States after inventories are depleted. ACIP reaffirms its support for the global eradication initiative and use of OPV as the vaccine of choice to eradicate polio where it is endemic.

Pregnancy Risk Factor C

Contraindications Hypersensitivity to any component including neomycin, streptomycin, or polymyxin B; defer vaccination for persons with acute febrile illness until recovery

Warnings/Precautions Although there is no convincing evidence documenting adverse effects of either OPV or E-IPV on the pregnant woman or developing fetus, it is prudent on theoretical grounds to avoid vaccinating pregnant women. However, if immediate protection against poliomyelitis is needed, OPV is recommended. OPV should not be given to immunocompromised individuals or to persons with known or possibly immunocompromised family members; E-IPV is recommended in such situations.

Common Adverse Reactions All serious adverse reactions must be reported to the U.S. Department of Health and Human Services (DHHS) Vaccine Adverse Event Reporting System (VAERS) 1-800-822-7967.

1% to 10%:

Central nervous system: Fever (>101.3°F)

Dermatologic: Rash

Local: Tenderness or pain at injection site

Dosage S.C.: **Enhanced-potency inactivated poliovirus vaccine (E-IPV) is preferred for primary vaccination of adults**, two doses S.C. 4-8 weeks apart, a third dose 6-12 months after the second. For adults with a completed primary series and for whom a booster is indicated, either OPV or E-IPV can be given (E-IPV preferred). If immediate protection is needed, either OPV or E-IPV is recommended.

Administration Do not administer I.V.

Dosage Forms INJ, suspension: Type 1 poliovirus 40 D antigen units/0.5 mL, Type 2 poliovirus 8 D antigen units/0.5 mL, and Type 3 poliovirus 32 D antigen units/0.5 mL (0.5 mL, 5 mL)

♦ **Polocaine®** *see* Mepivacaine *on page 793*

♦ **Polocaine® MPF** *see* Mepivacaine *on page 793*

♦ **Polycitra®-K** *see* Potassium Citrate and Citric Acid *on page 1021*

♦ **Polycitra®** *see* Citric Acid, Sodium Citrate, and Potassium Citrate *on page 287*

♦ **Polycitra®-LC** *see* Citric Acid, Sodium Citrate, and Potassium Citrate *on page 287*

Polyethylene Glycol-Electrolyte Solution
(pol i ETH i leen GLY kol ee LEK troe lite soe LOO shun)

Related Information

Laxatives, Classification and Properties *on page 1380*

U.S. Brand Names Colyte®; GoLYTELY®; MiraLax™; NuLytely®; OCL® [DSC]

Synonyms Electrolyte Lavage Solution

Therapeutic Category Cathartic; Laxative, Bowel Evacuant

Use Bowel cleansing prior to GI examination or following toxic ingestion (electrolyte containing solutions only); treatment of occasional constipation (MiraLax™)

Pregnancy Risk Factor C

Contraindications Hypersensitivity to polyethylene glycol or any component of the formulation; gastrointestinal obstruction, gastric retention, bowel perforation, toxic colitis, megacolon

Warnings/Precautions Do not add flavorings as additional ingredients before use; observe unconscious or semiconscious patients with impaired gag reflex or those who are otherwise prone to regurgitation or aspiration during administration; use with caution in ulcerative colitis, caution against the use of hot loop polypectomy. Evaluate patients with symptoms of bowel obstruction (nausea, vomiting, abdominal pain or distension) prior to use. Do not use MiraLax™ for longer than 2 weeks.

Common Adverse Reactions Frequency not defined.

Dermatologic: Dermatitis, rash, urticaria

Gastrointestinal: Nausea, abdominal fullness, bloating, abdominal cramps, vomiting, anal irritation, diarrhea, flatulence

(Continued)

Polyethylene Glycol-Electrolyte Solution *(Continued)*

Drug Interactions

Decreased Effect: Oral medications should not be administered within 1 hour of start of therapy.

Mechanism of Action Induces catharsis by strong electrolyte and osmotic effects

Pharmacodynamics/Kinetics Onset of effect: Oral: Bowel cleansing: ~1-2 hours; Constipation: 48-96 hours

Dosage

Oral:

Children ≥6 months: Bowel cleansing prior to GI exam (solutions with electrolytes only): 25-40 mL/kg/hour for 4-10 hours (until rectal effluent is clear). Ideally, patients should fast for ~3-4 hours prior to administration; absolutely no solid food for at least 2 hours before the solution is given. The solution may be given via nasogastric tube to patients who are unwilling or unable to drink the solution. Patients <2 years should be monitored closely.

Adults:

Bowel cleansing prior to GI exam (solutions with electrolytes only): 240 mL (8 oz) every 10 minutes, until 4 L are consumed or the rectal effluent is clear; rapid drinking of each portion is preferred to drinking small amounts continuously. Ideally, patients should fast for ~3-4 hours prior to administration; absolutely no solid food for at least 2 hours before the solution is given. The solution may be given via nasogastric tube to patients who are unwilling or unable to drink the solution.

Occasional constipation (MiraLax™): 17 g of powder (~1 heaping tablespoon) dissolved in 8 oz of water; once daily; do not use for >2 weeks.

Nasogastric tube:

Children ≥6 months: Bowel cleansing prior to GI exam (solutions with electrolytes only): 25 mL/kg/hour until rectal effluent is clear. Ideally, patients should fast for ~3-4 hours prior to administration; absolutely no solid food for at least 2 hours before the solution is given.

Adults: Bowel cleansing prior to GI exam (solutions with electrolytes only): 20-30 mL/minute (1.2-1.8 L/hour); the first bowel movement should occur ~1 hour after the start of administration. Ideally, patients should fast for ~3-4 hours prior to administration; absolutely no solid food for at least 2 hours before the solution is given.

Administration Bowel cleansing prior to GI exam (solutions with electrolytes only): Oral: Rapid drinking of each portion is preferred to drinking small amounts continuously. Do not add flavorings as additional ingredients before use. Chilled solution often more palatable.

Monitoring Parameters Electrolytes, serum glucose, BUN, urine osmolality; children <2 years of age should be monitored for hypoglycemia, dehydration, hypokalemia

Patient Information Chilled solution is often more palatable

Dosage Forms POWDER for oral solution: (Colyte®): PEG 3350 240 g, sodium sulfate 22.72 g, sodium bicarbonate 6.72 g, sodium chloride 5.84 g, and potassium chloride 2.98 g (4000 mL); PEG 3350 227.1 g, sodium sulfate 21.5 g, sodium bicarbonate 6.36 g, sodium chloride 5.53 g, and potassium chloride 2.82 g (4000 mL); (GoLYTELY®): Disposable jug: PEG 3350 236 g, sodium sulfate 22.74 g, sodium bicarbonate 6.74 g, sodium chloride 5.86 g, and potassium chloride 2.97 g (4000 mL); Packets: PEG 3350 227.1 g, sodium sulfate 21.5 g, sodium bicarbonate 6.36 g, sodium chloride 5.53 g, and potassium chloride 2.82 g (4000 mL); (MiraLax™): PEG 3350 255 g (14 oz), PEG 3350 527 g (26 oz); (NuLytely®): PEG 3350 420 g, sodium bicarbonate 5.72 g, sodium chloride 11.2 g, and potassium chloride 1.48 (4000 mL).

SOLN, oral (OCL®): PEG 3350 6 g, sodium sulfate decahydrate 1.29 g, sodium bicarbonate 168 mg, potassium chloride 75 mg, and polysorbate 80 30 mg per 100 mL (1500 mL) [DSC]

♦ **Polygam® S/D** *see* Immune Globulin (Intravenous) *on page 659*

Polymyxin B *(pol i MIKS in bee)*

U.S. Brand Names Poly-Rx

Synonyms Polymyxin B Sulfate

Therapeutic Category Antibiotic, Irrigation; Antibiotic, Miscellaneous

Use Treatment of acute infections caused by susceptible strains of *Pseudomonas aeruginosa*; used occasionally for gut decontamination; parenteral use of polymyxin B has mainly been replaced by less toxic antibiotics, reserved for life-threatening infections caused by organisms resistant to the preferred drugs (eg, pseudomonal meningitis - intrathecal administration)

Pregnancy Risk Factor B (per expert opinion)

Contraindications Hypersensitivity to polymyxin B or any component of the formulation; concurrent use of neuromuscular blockers

Warnings/Precautions Use with caution in patients with impaired renal function (modify dosage); polymyxin B-induced nephrotoxicity may be manifested by albuminuria, cellular casts, and azotemia. Discontinue therapy with decreasing urinary output and increasing BUN; neurotoxic reactions are usually associated with high serum levels, often in patients with renal dysfunction. Avoid concurrent or sequential use of other nephrotoxic and neurotoxic drugs (eg, aminoglycosides). The drug's neurotoxicity can result in respiratory paralysis from neuromuscular blockade, especially when the drug is given soon after anesthesia or muscle relaxants. Polymyxin B sulfate is most toxic when given parenterally; avoid parenteral use whenever possible.

Common Adverse Reactions Frequency not defined.

Cardiovascular: Facial flushing

Central nervous system: Neurotoxicity (irritability, drowsiness, ataxia, perioral paresthesia, numbness of the extremities, and blurring of vision); dizziness, drug fever, meningeal irritation with intrathecal administration

Dermatologic: Urticarial rash

Endocrine & metabolic: Hypocalcemia, hyponatremia, hypokalemia, hypochloremia
Local: Pain at injection site
Neuromuscular & skeletal: Neuromuscular blockade, weakness
Renal: Nephrotoxicity
Respiratory: Respiratory arrest
Miscellaneous: Anaphylactoid reaction

Drug Interactions
Increased Effect/Toxicity: Increased/prolonged effect of neuromuscular blocking agents.

Mechanism of Action Binds to phospholipids, alters permeability, and damages the bacterial cytoplasmic membrane permitting leakage of intracellular constituents

Pharmacodynamics/Kinetics
Absorption: Well absorbed from peritoneum; minimal from GI tract (except in neonates) from mucous membranes or intact skin
Distribution: Minimal into CSF; does not cross placenta
Half-life elimination: 4.5-6 hours; prolonged with renal impairment
Time to peak, serum: I.M.: ~2 hours
Excretion: Urine (>60% primarily as unchanged drug)

Dosage
Otic (in combination with other drugs): 1-2 drops, 3-4 times/day; should be used sparingly to avoid accumulation of excess debris
Infants <2 years:
I.M.: Up to 40,000 units/kg/day divided every 6 hours (not routinely recommended due to pain at injection sites)
I.V.: Up to 40,000 units/kg/day divided every 12 hours
Intrathecal: 20,000 units/day for 3-4 days, then 25,000 units every other day for at least 2 weeks after CSF cultures are negative and CSF (glucose) has returned to within normal limits
Children ≥2 years and Adults:
I.M.: 25,000-30,000 units/kg/day divided every 4-6 hours (not routinely recommended due to pain at injection sites)
I.V.: 15,000-25,000 units/kg/day divided every 12 hours
Intrathecal: 50,000 units/day for 3-4 days, then every other day for at least 2 weeks after CSF cultures are negative and CSF (glucose) has returned to within normal limits
Total daily dose should not exceed 2,000,000 units/day
Bladder irrigation: Continuous irrigant or rinse in the urinary bladder for up to 10 days using 20 mg (equal to 200,000 units) added to 1 L of normal saline; usually no more than 1 L of irrigant is used per day unless urine flow rate is high; administration rate is adjusted to patient's urine output
Topical irrigation or topical solution: 500,000 units/L of normal saline; topical irrigation should not exceed 2 million units/day in adults
Gut sterilization: Oral: 15,000-25,000 units/kg/day in divided doses every 6 hours
Clostridium difficile enteritis: Oral: 25,000 units every 6 hours for 10 days
Ophthalmic: A concentration of 0.1% to 0.25% is administered as 1-3 drops every hour, then increasing the interval as response indicates to 1-2 drops 4-6 times/day
Dosing adjustment/interval in renal impairment:
Cl_{cr} 20-50 mL/minute: Administer 75% to 100% of normal dose every 12 hours
Cl_{cr} 5-20 mL/minute: Administer 50% of normal dose every 12 hours
Cl_{cr} <5 mL/minute: Administer 15% of normal dose every 12 hours

Administration Dissolve 500,000 units in 300-500 mL D_5W for continuous I.V. drip; dissolve 500,000 units in 2 mL water for injection, saline, or 1% procaine solution for I.M. injection; dissolve 500,000 units in 10 mL physiologic solution for intrathecal administration

Extravasation management: Monitor I.V. site closely; extravasation may cause serious injury with possible necrosis and tissue sloughing. Rotate infusion site frequently.

Monitoring Parameters Neurologic symptoms and signs of superinfection; renal function (decreasing urine output and increasing BUN may require discontinuance of therapy)

Reference Range Serum concentrations >5 μg/mL are toxic in adults

Patient Information Report any dizziness or sensations of ringing in the ear, loss of hearing, or any muscle weakness

Dosage Forms INJ, powder for reconstitution: 500,000 units. **POWDER** [for prescription compounding] (Poly-Rx): 100 million units (13 g)

♦ **Polymyxin B, Neomycin, and Prednisolone** *see* Neomycin, Polymyxin B, and Prednisolone *on page 893*

♦ **Polymyxin B, Neomycin, Bacitracin, and Lidocaine** *see* Bacitracin, Neomycin, Polymyxin B, and Lidocaine *on page 144*

♦ **Polymyxin B Sulfate** *see* Polymyxin B *on page 1014*

♦ **Poly-Pred®** *see* Neomycin, Polymyxin B, and Prednisolone *on page 893*

♦ **Poly-Rx** *see* Polymyxin B *on page 1014*

Polysaccharide-Iron Complex (pol i SAK a ride-EYE ern KOM pleks)

U.S. Brand Names Fe-Tinic™ 150 [OTC]; Hytinic® [OTC]; Niferex® [OTC]; Niferex® 150 [OTC]; Nu-Iron® 150 [OTC]

Synonyms Iron-Polysaccharide Complex

Therapeutic Category Iron Salt

Use Prevention and treatment of iron-deficiency anemias

Pregnancy Risk Factor A

Common Adverse Reactions
>10%: Gastrointestinal: Stomach cramping, constipation, nausea, vomiting, dark stools, GI irritation, epigastric pain, nausea

1% to 10%:
Gastrointestinal: Heartburn, diarrhea
Genitourinary: Discolored urine
Miscellaneous: Staining of teeth

Dosage
Children ≥6 years: Tablets/elixir: 50-100 mg/day; may be given in divided doses
Adults:
Tablets/elixir: 50-100 mg twice daily
Capsules: 150-300 mg/day

Patient Information May color stool black, take between meals for maximum absorption; may take with food if GI upset occurs, do not take with milk or antacids; keep out of reach of children

Dosage Forms CAP: Elemental iron 150 mg. **ELIX:** Elemental iron 100 mg/5 mL (240 mL). **TAB:** Elemental iron 50 mg

♦ **Polysporin® Ophthalmic** *see* Bacitracin and Polymyxin B *on page 143*

♦ **Polysporin® Topical [OTC]** *see* Bacitracin and Polymyxin B *on page 143*

Polythiazide (pol i THYE a zide)

Related Information
Sulfonamide Derivatives *on page 1404*

U.S. Brand Names Renese®

Therapeutic Category Antihypertensive Agent; Diuretic, Thiazide

Use Adjunctive therapy in treatment of edema and hypertension

Pregnancy Risk Factor D

Dosage Adults: Oral:
Edema: 1-4 mg/day
Hypertension: 2-4 mg/day

Dosage Forms TAB: 1 mg [DSC], 2 mg

♦ **Polythiazide and Prazosin** *see* Prazosin and Polythiazide *on page 1031*

♦ **Polytrim®** *see* Trimethoprim and Polymyxin B *on page 1270*

♦ **Ponstel®** *see* Mefenamic Acid *on page 782*

♦ **Pontocaine®** *see* Tetracaine *on page 1206*

Porfimer (POR fi mer)

U.S. Brand Names Photofrin®

Synonyms CL-184116; Dihematoporphyrin Ether; Porfimer Sodium

Therapeutic Category Antineoplastic Agent, Miscellaneous

Use Adjunct to laser light therapy for obstructing esophageal cancer, obstructing endobronchial nonsmall cell lung cancer (NSCLC), ablation of high-grade dysplasia in Barrett's esophagus

Unlabeled/Investigational Use Transitional cell carcinoma *in situ* of the urinary bladder; gastric and rectal cancers

Pregnancy Risk Factor C

Contraindications Hypersensitivity to porfimer, porphyrins, or any component of the formulation; porphyria; tracheoesophageal or bronchoesophageal fistula; tumors eroding into a major blood vessel

Warnings/Precautions The U.S. Food and Drug Administration (FDA) currently recommends that procedures for proper handling and disposal of antineoplastic agents be considered. Photosensitivity reactions are common is patients are exposed to direct sunlight or bright indoor light (eg fluorescent lights, unshaded light bulbs, examination/operating lights). Photosensitivity may last 30-90 days. Ocular discomfort has been reported; for at least 30 days, when outdoors, patients should wear dark sunglasses which have an average white light transmittance of <4%. When treating endobronchial tumors, use caution if treatment-induced inflammation may obstruct airway.

Common Adverse Reactions
>10%:
Cardiovascular: Atrial fibrillation (10%), chest pain (5% to 22%)

Central nervous system: Insomnia (14%), hyperthermia (31%)

Dermatologic: Photosensitivity reaction (10% to 80%, minor reactions may occur in up to 100%)

Gastrointestinal: Abdominal pain (20%), constipation (23%), dysphagia, nausea (24%), vomiting (17%)

Genitourinary: Urinary tract irritation including frequency, urgency, nocturia, painful urination, or bladder spasm (~100% of bladder cancer patients)

Hematologic: Anemia (26% of esophageal cancer patients)

Neuromuscular & skeletal: Back pain

Respiratory: Dyspnea (20%), pharyngitis (11%), pleural effusion (32% of esophageal cancer patients), pneumonia (18%), respiratory insufficiency

Miscellaneous: Mild-moderate allergic-type reactions (34% of lung cancer patients)

1% to 10%:

Cardiovascular: Hypertension (6% to 7%), hypotension (6% to 7%), edema, cardiac failure (6% to 7%), tachycardia (6%), chest pain (substernal)

Central nervous system: Anxiety (7%), confusion (8%)

Dermatologic: Increased hair growth, skin discoloration, skin wrinkles, skin nodules, increased skin fragility

Endocrine & metabolic: Dehydration

Gastrointestinal: Diarrhea (5%), dyspepsia (6%), eructation (5%), esophageal edema (8%), esophageal tumor bleeding, esophageal stricture, esophagitis, hematemesis, melena, weight loss, anorexia

Genitourinary: Urinary tract infection

Neuromuscular & skeletal: Weakness

Respiratory: Coughing, tracheoesophageal fistula

Miscellaneous: Moniliasis, surgical complication

Drug Interactions

Increased Effect/Toxicity: Concomitant administration of other photosensitizing agents (eg, tetracyclines, sulfonamides, phenothiazines, sulfonylureas, thiazide diuretics, griseofulvin) could increase the photosensitivity reaction.

Decreased Effect: Compounds that quench active oxygen species or scavenge radicals (eg, dimethyl sulfoxide, beta-carotene, ethanol, mannitol) would be expected to decrease photodynamic therapy (PDT) activity. Allopurinol, calcium channel blockers, and some prostaglandin synthesis inhibitors could interfere with porfimer. Drugs that decrease clotting, vasoconstriction, or platelet aggregation could decrease the efficacy of PDT. Glucocorticoid hormones may decrease the efficacy of the treatment.

Mechanism of Action Porfimer's cytotoxic activity is dependent on light and oxygen. Following administration, the drug is selectively retained in neoplastic tissues. Exposure of the drug to laser light at wavelengths >630 nm results in the production of oxygen free-radicals. Release of thromboxane A_2, leading to vascular occlusion and ischemic necrosis, may also occur.

Pharmacodynamics/Kinetics

Distribution: V_{dss}: 0.49 L/kg

Protein binding, plasma: 90%

Half-life elimination: Mean: 21.5 days (range: 11-28 days)

Time to peak, serum: ~2 hours

Excretion: Feces; Clearance: Plasma: Total: 0.051 mL/minute/kg

Dosage I.V. (refer to individual protocols):

Children: Safety and efficacy have not been established

Adults: 2 mg/kg, followed by exposure to the appropriate laser light

Administration Administer slow I.V. injection over 3-5 minutes. Wipe up spills with a damp cloth. Avoid skin and eye contact due to the potential for photosensitivity reactions upon exposure to light; use of rubber gloves and eye protection is recommended.

Patient Information This medication can only be administered I.V. and will be followed by laser light therapy. Avoid any exposure to sunlight or bright indoor light for 30 days following therapy (cover skin with protective clothing and wear dark sunglasses with light transmittance <4% when outdoors - severe blistering, burning, and skin/eye damage can result). After 30 days, test a small area of skin (not face) for remaining sensitivity. Retest sensitivity if traveling to a different geographic area with greater sunshine. Exposure to indoor normal light is beneficial since it will help dissipate photosensitivity gradually. Maintain adequate hydration (2-3 L/day of fluids unless instructed to restrict fluid intake); maintain good oral hygiene (use a soft toothbrush or cotton applicators several times a day and rinse mouth frequently). Small frequent meals, frequent mouth care, sucking lozenges, or chewing gum may reduce nausea or vomiting. Report rapid heart rate, chest pain or palpitations, difficulty breathing or air hunger, persistent fever or chills, foul-smelling urine or burning on urination, swelling of extremities, increased anxiety, confusion, or hallucination.

Dosage Forms INJ, powder for reconstitution: 75 mg

♦ **Porfimer Sodium** see Porfimer on page 1016

♦ **Portia™** see Ethinyl Estradiol and Levonorgestrel on page 484

♦ **Post Peel Healing Balm [OTC]** see Hydrocortisone on page 632

Potassium Acetate (poe TASS ee um AS e tate)

Therapeutic Category Electrolyte Supplement, Parenteral; Potassium Salt; Vesicant

Use Potassium deficiency; to avoid chloride when high concentration of potassium is needed, source of bicarbonate

Pregnancy Risk Factor C

Contraindications Severe renal impairment; hyperkalemia

(Continued)

Potassium Acetate *(Continued)*

Warnings/Precautions Use with caution in patients with renal disease, hyperkalemia, cardiac disease, metabolic alkalosis; must be administered in patients with adequate urine flow. Potassium acetate solution for injection contains aluminum; use caution with impaired renal function and in premature infants.

Common Adverse Reactions

1% to 10%:

Cardiovascular: Bradycardia

Endocrine & metabolic: Hyperkalemia

Neuromuscular & skeletal: Weakness

Respiratory: Dyspnea

Local: Local tissue necrosis with extravasation

Drug Interactions

Increased Effect/Toxicity: Potassium-sparing diuretics, salt substitutes, and ACE inhibitors

Mechanism of Action Potassium is the major cation of intracellular fluid and is essential for the conduction of nerve impulses in heart, brain, and skeletal muscle; contraction of cardiac, skeletal and smooth muscles; maintenance of normal renal function, acid-base balance, carbohydrate metabolism, and gastric secretion

Pharmacodynamics/Kinetics

Distribution: Enters cells via active transport from extracellular fluid

Excretion: Primarily urine; skin and feces (small amounts); most intestinal potassium reabsorbed

Dosage I.V. doses should be incorporated into the patient's maintenance I.V. fluids, intermittent I.V. potassium administration should be reserved for severe depletion situations and requires ECG monitoring; doses listed as mEq of potassium

Children:

Treatment of hypokalemia: I.V.: 2-5 mEq/kg/day

I.V. intermittent infusion (must be diluted prior to administration): 0.5-1 mEq/kg/dose (maximum: 30 mEq/dose) to infuse at 0.3-0.5 mEq/kg/hour (maximum: 1 mEq/kg/hour)

Note: Use caution in premature neonates; potassium acetate for injection contains aluminum.

Adults:

Treatment of hypokalemia: I.V.: 40-100 mEq/day

I.V. intermittent infusion (must be diluted prior to administration): 5-10 mEq/dose (maximum: 40 mEq/dose) to infuse over 2-3 hours (maximum: 40 mEq over 1 hour)

Note: Continuous cardiac monitor recommended for rates >0.5 mEq/hour

Potassium dosage/rate of infusion guidelines:

Serum potassium >2.5 mEq/L: Maximum infusion rate: 10 mEq/hour; maximum concentration: 40 mEq/L; maximum 24-hour dose: 200 mEq

Serum potassium <2.5 mEq/L: Maximum infusion rate: 40 mEq/hour; maximum concentration: 80 mEq/L; maximum 24-hour dose: 400 mEq

Dosage adjustment in renal impairment: Use caution; potassium acetate injection contains aluminum

Administration Potassium must be diluted prior to parenteral administration; maximum recommended concentration (peripheral line): 80 mEq/L; maximum recommended concentration (central line): 150 mEq/L or 15 mEq/100 mL; in severely fluid-restricted patients (with central lines): 200 mEq/L or 20 mEq/100 mL has been used; maximum rate of infusion, see Dosage, I.V. intermittent infusion

Dosage Forms INJ, solution: 2 mEq/mL (20 mL, 50 mL, 100 mL); 4 mEq/mL (50 mL)

Potassium Acetate, Potassium Bicarbonate, and Potassium Citrate

(poe TASS ee um AS e tate, poe TASS ee um bye KAR bun ate, & poe TASS ee um SIT rate)

U.S. Brand Names Tri-K®

Synonyms Potassium Acetate, Potassium Citrate, and Potassium Bicarbonate; Potassium Bicarbonate, Potassium Acetate, and Potassium Citrate; Potassium Bicarbonate, Potassium Citrate, and Potassium Acetate; Potassium Citrate, Potassium Acetate, and Potassium Bicarbonate; Potassium Citrate, Potassium Bicarbonate, and Potassium Acetate

Therapeutic Category Electrolyte Supplement, Oral

Use Treatment or prevention of hypokalemia

Pregnancy Risk Factor C

Dosage Oral:

Children: 1-4 mEq/kg/24 hours in divided doses as required to maintain normal serum potassium

Adults:

Prevention: 16-24 mEq/day in 2-4 divided doses

Treatment: 40-100 mEq/day in 2-4 divided doses

Dosage Forms SOLN, oral: Potassium 45 mEq/15 mL (480 mL) [from potassium acetate 1500 mg, potassium bicarbonate 1500 mg, and potassium citrate 1500 mg per 15 mL]

♦ **Potassium Acetate, Potassium Citrate, and Potassium Bicarbonate** *see* Potassium Acetate, Potassium Bicarbonate, and Potassium Citrate *on page 1018*

Potassium Acid Phosphate (poe TASS ee um AS id FOS fate)
U.S. Brand Names K-Phos® Original
Therapeutic Category Potassium Salt; Urinary Acidifying Agent
Use Acidifies urine and lowers urinary calcium concentration; reduces odor and rash caused by ammoniacal urine; increases the antibacterial activity of methenamine
Pregnancy Risk Factor C
Contraindications Severe renal impairment; hyperkalemia, hyperphosphatemia; infected magnesium ammonium phosphate stones
Warnings/Precautions Use with caution in patients receiving other potassium supplementation and in patients with renal insufficiency, or severe tissue breakdown (eg, chemotherapy or hemodialysis)
Common Adverse Reactions
>10%: Gastrointestinal: Diarrhea, nausea, stomach pain, flatulence, vomiting
1% to 10%:
Cardiovascular: Bradycardia
Endocrine & metabolic: Hyperkalemia
Local: Local tissue necrosis with extravasation
Neuromuscular & skeletal: Weakness
Respiratory: Dyspnea
Drug Interactions
Increased Effect/Toxicity: Potassium-sparing diuretics, salt substitutes, salicylates, and ACE inhibitors
Decreased Effect: Antacids containing magnesium, calcium or aluminum (bind phosphate and decreased its absorption)
Mechanism of Action The principal intracellular cation; involved in transmission of nerve impulses, muscle contractions, enzyme activity, and glucose utilization
Pharmacodynamics/Kinetics
Absorption: Well absorbed from upper GI tract
Distribution: Enters cells via active transport from extracellular fluid
Excretion: Primarily urine; skin and feces (small amounts); most intestinal potassium reabsorbed
Dosage Adults: Oral: 1000 mg dissolved in 6-8 oz of water 4 times/day with meals and at bedtime; for best results, soak tablets in water for 2-5 minutes, then stir and swallow
Monitoring Parameters Serum potassium, sodium, phosphate, calcium; serum salicylates (if taking salicylates)
Patient Information Dissolve tablets completely before drinking; avoid taking magnesium, calcium, or aluminum antacids at the same time; patients may pass old kidney stones when starting therapy; report nausea, vomiting, or abdominal pain
Dosage Forms TAB: 500 mg

Potassium Bicarbonate and Potassium Chloride
(poe TASS ee um bye KAR bun ate & poe TASS ee um KLOR ide)
U.S. Brand Names K-Lyte/Cl®; K-Lyte/Cl® 50
Synonyms Potassium Bicarbonate and Potassium Chloride (Effervescent)
Therapeutic Category Electrolyte Supplement, Oral
Use Treatment or prevention of hypokalemia
Pregnancy Risk Factor C
Dosage Oral:
Children: 1-4 mEq/kg/24 hours in divided doses as required to maintain normal serum potassium
Adults:
Prevention: 16-24 mEq/day in 2-4 divided doses
Treatment: 40-100 mEq/day in 2-4 divided doses
Dosage Forms TAB for oral solution, effervescent: (K-Lyte/Cl®): Potassium chloride 25 mEq; (K-Lyte/Cl® 50): Potassium chloride 50 mEq

♦ **Potassium Bicarbonate and Potassium Chloride (Effervescent)** see Potassium Bicarbonate and Potassium Chloride on page 1019

Potassium Bicarbonate and Potassium Citrate
(poe TASS ee um bye KAR bun ate & poe TASS ee um SIT rate)
U.S. Brand Names Effer-K™; Klor-Con®/EF; K-Lyte®; K-Lyte® DS
Synonyms Potassium Bicarbonate and Potassium Citrate (Effervescent)
Therapeutic Category Electrolyte Supplement, Oral; Potassium Salt
Use Treatment or prevention of hypokalemia
Pregnancy Risk Factor C
Dosage Oral:
Children: 1-4 mEq/kg/24 hours in divided doses as required to maintain normal serum potassium
Adults:
Prevention: 16-24 mEq/day in 2-4 divided doses
Treatment: 40-100 mEq/day in 2-4 divided doses
Dosage Forms TAB, effervescent: Potassium 25 mEq; (Effer-K™, Klor-Con®/EF, K-Lyte®): Potassium 25 mEq; (K-Lyte® DS): Potassium 50 mEq

♦ **Potassium Bicarbonate and Potassium Citrate (Effervescent)** see Potassium Bicarbonate and Potassium Citrate *on page 1019*

♦ **Potassium Bicarbonate, Potassium Acetate, and Potassium Citrate** see Potassium Acetate, Potassium Bicarbonate, and Potassium Citrate *on page 1018*

♦ **Potassium Bicarbonate, Potassium Citrate, and Potassium Acetate** see Potassium Acetate, Potassium Bicarbonate, and Potassium Citrate *on page 1018*

Potassium Chloride (poe TASS ee um KLOR ide)

U.S. Brand Names K+8; K+10; Kaon-Cl-10®; Kaon-Cl® 20; Kay Ciel®; K+ Care®; K-Dur® 10; K-Dur® 20; K-Lor™; Klor-Con®; Klor-Con® 8; Klor-Con® 10; Klor-Con®/25; Klor-Con® M; Klotrix®; K-Tab®; microK®; microK® 10; Rum-K®

Synonyms KCl

Therapeutic Category Electrolyte Supplement, Oral; Electrolyte Supplement, Parenteral; Potassium Salt; Vesicant

Use Treatment or prevention of hypokalemia

Pregnancy Risk Factor A

Contraindications Severe renal impairment, untreated Addison's disease, heat cramps, hyperkalemia, severe tissue trauma; solid oral dosage forms are contraindicated in patients in whom there is a structural, pathological, and/or pharmacologic cause for delay or arrest in passage through the GI tract; an oral liquid potassium preparation should be used in patients with esophageal compression or delayed gastric emptying time

Warnings/Precautions Use with caution in patients with cardiac disease, severe renal impairment, hyperkalemia

Common Adverse Reactions

>10%: Gastrointestinal: Diarrhea, nausea, stomach pain, flatulence, vomiting (oral)

1% to 10%:
    Cardiovascular: Bradycardia
    Endocrine & metabolic: Hyperkalemia
    Local: Local tissue necrosis with extravasation, pain at the site of injection
    Neuromuscular & skeletal: Weakness
    Respiratory: Dyspnea

Drug Interactions

Increased Effect/Toxicity: Potassium-sparing diuretics, salt substitutes, ACE inhibitors

Mechanism of Action Potassium is the major cation of intracellular fluid and is essential for the conduction of nerve impulses in heart, brain, and skeletal muscle; contraction of cardiac, skeletal and smooth muscles; maintenance of normal renal function, acid-base balance, carbohydrate metabolism, and gastric secretion

Pharmacodynamics/Kinetics

Absorption: Well absorbed from upper GI tract

Distribution: Enters cells via active transport from extracellular fluid

Excretion: Primarily urine; skin and feces (small amounts); most intestinal potassium reabsorbed

Dosage I.V. doses should be incorporated into the patient's maintenance I.V. fluids; intermittent I.V. potassium administration should be reserved for severe depletion situations in patients undergoing ECG monitoring.

Normal daily requirements: Oral, I.V.:
    Premature infants: 2-6 mEq/kg/24 hours
    Term infants 0-24 hours: 0-2 mEq/kg/24 hours
    Infants >24 hours: 1-2 mEq/kg/24 hours
    Children: 2-3 mEq/kg/day
    Adults: 40-80 mEq/day

Prevention during diuretic therapy: Oral:
    Children: 1-2 mEq/kg/day in 1-2 divided doses
    Adults: 20-40 mEq/day in 1-2 divided doses

Treatment of hypokalemia: Children:
    Oral: 1-2 mEq/kg initially, then as needed based on frequently obtained lab values. If deficits are severe or ongoing losses are great, I.V. route should be considered.
    I.V.: 1 mEq/kg over 1-2 hours initially, then repeated as needed based on frequently obtained lab values; severe depletion or ongoing losses may require >200% of normal limit needs
    I.V. intermittent infusion: Dose should not exceed 1 mEq/kg/hour, or 40 mEq/hour; if it exceeds 0.5 mEq/kg/hour, physician should be at bedside and patient should have continuous ECG monitoring; usual pediatric maximum: 3 mEq/kg/day or 40 mEq/m²/day

Treatment of hypokalemia: Adults:
    I.V. intermittent infusion: 5-10 mEq/hour (continuous cardiac monitor recommended for rates >5 mEq/hour), not to exceed 40 mEq/hour; usual adult maximum per 24 hours: 400 mEq/day.

    Potassium dosage/rate of infusion guidelines:
        Serum potassium >2.5 mEq/L: Maximum infusion rate: 10 mEq/hour; maximum concentration: 40 mEq/L; maximum 24-hour dose: 200 mEq
        Serum potassium <2.5 mEq/L: Maximum infusion rate: 40 mEq/hour; maximum concentration: 80 mEq/L; maximum 24-hour dose: 400 mEq

    Potassium >2.5 mEq/L:
    Oral: 60-80 mEq/day plus additional amounts if needed
    I.V.: 10 mEq over 1 hour with additional doses if needed

Potassium <2.5 mEq/L:

Oral: Up to 40-60 mEq initial dose, followed by further doses based on lab values

I.V.: Up to 40 mEq over 1 hour, with doses based on frequent lab monitoring; deficits at a plasma level of 2 mEq/L may be as high as 400-800 mEq of potassium

Administration Potassium must be diluted prior to parenteral administration; maximum recommended concentration (peripheral line): 80 mEq/L; maximum recommended concentration (central line): 150 mEq/L or 15 mEq/100 mL; in severely fluid-restricted patients (with central lines): 200 mEq/L or 20 mEq/100 mL has been used; maximum rate of infusion, see Dosage, I.V. intermittent infusion

Monitoring Parameters Serum potassium, glucose, chloride, pH, urine output (if indicated), cardiac monitor (if intermittent infusion or potassium infusion rates >0.25 mEq/kg/hour)

Patient Information Long acting and wax matrix tablets should be swallowed whole, do not crush or chew; powder must be dissolved in water before use; take with food; liquid can be diluted or dissolved in water or juice

Dosage Forms CAP, extended release: 10 mEq [800 mg]; (microK® [microencapsulated]): 8 mEq [600 mg]; (microK® 10 [microencapsulated]): 10 mEq [800 mg]. **INF** [premixed in D₅W]: 20 mEq (1000 mL), 30 mEq (1000 mL), 40 mEq (1000 mL). **INF** [premixed in D₅W and LR]: 20 mEq (1000 mL), 30 mEq (1000 mL). **INF** [premixed in D₅W and ¼NS]: 10 mEq (500 mL, 1000 mL), 20 mEq (1000 mL), 30 mEq (1000 mL), 40 mEq (1000 mL). **INF** [premixed in D₅W and ½NS]: 10 mEq (500 mL, 1000 mL), 20 mEq (1000 mL), 30 mEq (1000 mL), 40 mEq (1000 mL). **INF** [premixed in D₅W and NS]: 20 mEq (1000 mL), 40 mEq (1000 mL). **INF** [premixed in D₅W and sodium chloride 0.3%]: 10 mEq (500 mL), 20 mEq (1000 mL). **INF** [premixed in NS]: 20 mEq (1000 mL), 40 mEq (1000 mL). **INF** [premixed in SWFI]: 10 mEq (50 mL, 100 mL), 20 mEq (50 mL, 100 mL), 30 mEq (100 mL), 40 mEq (100 mL). **INJ, solution [concentrate]:** 2 mEq/mL (5 mL, 10 mL, 15 mL, 20 mL, 250 mL). **POWDER, for oral solution:** 20 mEq/packet (30s, 100s, 1000s); (K+ Care®): 20 mEq/packet (30s); (K-Lor®, Kay Ciel® 10%, Klor-Con®): 20 mEq/packet (30s, 100s); (Klor-Con®/25): 25 mEq/packet (30s, 100s). **SOLN, oral:** 20 mEq/15 mL (480 mL), 40 mEq/15 mL (480 mL); (Kaon-Cl® 20): 40 mEq/15 mL (480 mL); (Kay Ciel® 10%): 20 mEq/15 mL (120 mL, 480 mL); (Rum-K®): 20 mEq/10 mL (480 mL). **TAB, extended release:** 8 mEq [600 mg], 10 mEq [800 mg], 20 mEq [1500 mg]; (K+8, Klor-Con® 8): 8 mEq [600 mg]; (K+10, K-Tab®, Klor-Con® 10): 10 mEq [800 mg]; (K-Dur® 10, Klor-Con® M10) [microencapsulated]: 10 mEq [800 mg]; (Klor-Con® M15) [microencapsulated]: 15 mEq [1125 mg]; (K-Dur® 20, Klor-Con® M20) [microencapsulated]: 20 mEq [1500 mg]; (Kaon-Cl® 10) [film coated]: 10 mEq [800 mg]. **TAB, slow release** (Klotrix®) [film coated]: 10 mEq [800 mg]

Potassium Citrate and Citric Acid (poe TASS ee um SIT rate & SI trik AS id)

U.S. Brand Names Cytra-K; Polycitra®-K

Synonyms Citric Acid and Potassium Citrate

Therapeutic Category Alkalinizing Agent, Oral

Use Treatment of metabolic acidosis; alkalinizing agent in conditions where long-term maintenance of an alkaline urine is desirable

Pregnancy Risk Factor A

Dosage Urine alkalizing agent:

Children: Solution: 5-15 mL after meals and at bedtime; adjust dose based on urinary pH

Adults:

Powder: One packet dissolved in water after meals and at bedtime; adjust dose to urinary pH

Solution: 15-30 mL after meals and at bedtime; adjust dose based on urinary pH

Dosage Forms Equivalent to potassium 2 mEq/mL and bicarbonate 2 mEq/mL: **POWDER:** (Cytra-K, Polycitra®-K): Potassium citrate 3300 mg and citric acid 1002 mg per packet (100s). **SOLN:** (Cytra-K, Polycitra®-K): Potassium citrate 1100 mg and citric acid monohydrate 334 mg per 5 mL (480 mL)

♦ **Potassium Citrate, Citric Acid, and Sodium Citrate** see Citric Acid, Sodium Citrate, and Potassium Citrate on page 287

♦ **Potassium Citrate, Potassium Acetate, and Potassium Bicarbonate** see Potassium Acetate, Potassium Bicarbonate, and Potassium Citrate on page 1018

♦ **Potassium Citrate, Potassium Bicarbonate, and Potassium Acetate** see Potassium Acetate, Potassium Bicarbonate, and Potassium Citrate on page 1018

Potassium Gluconate (poe TASS ee um GLOO coe nate)

U.S. Brand Names Glu-K® [OTC]

Therapeutic Category Electrolyte Supplement, Oral; Potassium Salt

Use Treatment or prevention of hypokalemia

Pregnancy Risk Factor A

Contraindications Severe renal impairment, untreated Addison's disease, heat cramps, hyperkalemia, severe tissue trauma; solid oral dosage forms are contraindicated in patients in whom there is a structural, pathological, and/or pharmacologic cause for delay or arrest in passage through the GI tract

Warnings/Precautions Use with caution in patients with cardiac disease, severe renal impairment, hyperkalemia; patients must be on a cardiac monitor during intermittent infusions

Common Adverse Reactions

>10%: Gastrointestinal: Diarrhea, nausea, stomach pain, flatulence, vomiting (oral)

1% to 10%:

Cardiovascular: Bradycardia

Endocrine & metabolic: Hyperkalemia

Neuromuscular & skeletal: Weakness

(Continued)

Potassium Gluconate *(Continued)*

Respiratory: Dyspnea

Drug Interactions

Increased Effect/Toxicity: Potassium-sparing diuretics, salt substitutes, ACE inhibitors; increased effect of digitalis

Mechanism of Action Potassium is the major cation of intracellular fluid and is essential for the conduction of nerve impulses in heart, brain, and skeletal muscle; contraction of cardiac, skeletal and smooth muscles; maintenance of normal renal function, acid-base balance, carbohydrate metabolism, and gastric secretion

Pharmacodynamics/Kinetics

Absorption: Well absorbed from upper GI tract

Distribution: Enters cells via active transport from extracellular fluid

Excretion: Primarily urine; skin and feces (small amounts); most intestinal potassium reabsorbed

Dosage Oral (doses listed as mEq of potassium):

Normal daily requirement:

Children: 2-3 mEq/kg/day

Adults: 40-80 mEq/day

Prevention of hypokalemia during diuretic therapy:

Children: 1-2 mEq/kg/day in 1-2 divided doses

Adults: 16-24 mEq/day in 1-2 divided doses

Treatment of hypokalemia:

Children: 2-5 mEq/kg/day in 2-4 divided doses

Adults: 40-100 mEq/day in 2-4 divided doses

Monitoring Parameters Serum potassium, chloride, glucose, pH, urine output (if indicated)

Patient Information Take with food, water, or fruit juice; swallow tablets whole; do not crush or chew

Dosage Forms TAB: 500 mg, 610 mg; (Glu-K®): 486 mg. **TAB, timed release:** 595 mg

Potassium Iodide *(poe TASS ee um EYE oh dide)*

U.S. Brand Names Iosat™ [OTC]; Pima®; SSKI®

Synonyms KI; Lugol's Solution; Strong Iodine Solution

Therapeutic Category Antithyroid Agent; Expectorant

Use Expectorant for the symptomatic treatment of chronic pulmonary diseases complicated by mucous; reduce thyroid vascularity prior to thyroidectomy and management of thyrotoxic crisis; block thyroidal uptake of radioactive isotopes of iodine in a radiation emergency or other exposure to radioactive iodine

Unlabeled/Investigational Use Lymphocutaneous and cutaneous sporotrichosis

Pregnancy Risk Factor D

Contraindications Hypersensitivity to iodine or any component of the formulation; hyperkalemia; pulmonary edema; impaired renal function; hyperthyroidism; iodine-induced goiter; pregnancy

Warnings/Precautions Prolonged use can lead to hypothyroidism; cystic fibrosis patients have an exaggerated response; can cause acne flare-ups, can cause dermatitis; use with caution in patients with a history of thyroid disease, Addison's disease, cardiac disease, myotonia congenita, tuberculosis, acute bronchitis

Common Adverse Reactions Frequency not defined.

Cardiovascular: Irregular heart beat

Central nervous system: Confusion, tiredness, fever

Dermatologic: Skin rash

Endocrine & metabolic: Goiter, salivary gland swelling/tenderness, thyroid adenoma, swelling of neck/throat, myxedema, lymph node swelling

Gastrointestinal: Diarrhea, gastrointestinal bleeding, metallic taste, nausea, stomach pain, stomach upset, vomiting

Neuromuscular & skeletal: Numbness, tingling, weakness

Miscellaneous: Chronic iodine poisoning (with prolonged treatment/high doses); iodism, hypersensitivity reactions (angioedema, cutaneous and mucosal hemorrhage, serum sickness-like symptoms)

Drug Interactions

Increased Effect/Toxicity: Lithium may cause additive hypothyroid effects; ACE inhibitors, potassium-sparing diuretics, and potassium/potassium-containing products may lead to hyperkalemia, cardiac arrhythmias, or cardiac arrest

Mechanism of Action Reduces viscosity of mucus by increasing respiratory tract secretions; inhibits secretion of thyroid hormone, fosters colloid accumulation in thyroid follicles

Pharmacodynamics/Kinetics

Onset of action: 24-48 hours

Peak effect: 10-15 days after continuous therapy

Duration: May persist for up to 6 weeks

Excretion: Clearance: Euthyroid patient: Renal: 2 times that of thyroid

Dosage Oral:

Adults: RDA: 150 mcg (iodide)

Expectorant:

Children (Pima®):

<3 years: 162 mg 3 times day

>3 years: 325 mg 3 times/day

Adults:
Pima®: 325-650 mg 3 times/day
SSKI®: 300-600 mg 3-4 times/day
Preoperative thyroidectomy: Children and Adults: 50-250 mg (1-5 drops SSKI®) 3 times/day **or** 0.1-0.3 mL (3-5 drops) of strong iodine (Lugol's solution) 3 times/day; administer for 10 days before surgery
Radiation protectant to radioactive isotopes of iodine (Pima®):
Children:
Infants up to 1 year: 65 mg once daily for 10 days; start 24 hours prior to exposure
>1 year: 130 mg once daily for 10 days; start 24 hours prior to exposure
Adults: 195 mg once daily for 10 days; start 24 hours prior to exposure
To reduce risk of thyroid cancer following nuclear accident (dosing should continue until risk of exposure has passed or other measures are implemented):
Children (see adult dose for children >68 kg):
Infants <1 month: 16 mg once daily
1 month to 3 years: 32 mg once daily
3-18 years: 65 mg once daily
Children >68 kg and Adults (including pregnant/lactating women): 130 mg once daily
Thyrotoxic crisis:
Infants <1 year: 150-250 mg (3-5 drops SSKI®) 3 times/day
Children and Adults: 300-500 mg (6-10 drops SSKI®) 3 times/day or 1 mL strong iodine (Lugol's solution) 3 times/day
Sporotrichosis (cutaneous, lymphocutaneous): Adults: Oral: Initial: 5 drops (SSKI®) 3 times/day; increase to 40-50 drops (SSKI®) 3 times/day as tolerated for 3-6 months
Administration
Pima®: When used as an expectorant, take each dose with at least 4-6 ounces of water
SSKI®: Dilute in a glassful of water, fruit juice or milk. Take with food to decrease gastric irritation
Monitoring Parameters Thyroid function tests, signs/symptoms of hyperthyroidism
Patient Information SSKI®: Take after meals. Dilute in 6 oz of water, fruit juice, or milk. Do not exceed recommended dosage. You may experience a metallic taste. Discontinue use and report stomach pain, severe nausea or vomiting, black or tarry stools, or unresolved weakness.
Dosage Forms SOLN, oral: (SSKI®): 1 g/mL (30 mL, 240 mL); Lugol's solution, strong iodine: Potassium iodide 100 mg/mL and iodine 50 mg/mL (15 mL, 480 mL). **SYR** (Pima®): 325 mg/5 mL (473 mL). **TAB:** 65 mg; (Iosat™): 130 mg

♦ **Potassium Iodide, Chlorpheniramine, Phenylephrine, and Codeine** see Chlorpheniramine, Phenylephrine, Codeine, and Potassium Iodide *on page 265*

Potassium Phosphate (poe TASS ee um FOS fate)
U.S. Brand Names Neutra-Phos®-K [OTC]
Synonyms Phosphate, Potassium
Therapeutic Category Electrolyte Supplement, Oral; Electrolyte Supplement, Parenteral; Phosphate Salt; Potassium Salt; Vesicant
Use Treatment and prevention of hypophosphatemia or hypokalemia
Pregnancy Risk Factor C
Contraindications Hyperphosphatemia, hyperkalemia, hypocalcemia, hypomagnesemia, renal failure
Warnings/Precautions Use with caution in patients with renal insufficiency, cardiac disease, metabolic alkalosis; admixture of phosphate and calcium in I.V. fluids can result in calcium phosphate precipitation
Common Adverse Reactions
>10%: Gastrointestinal: Diarrhea, nausea, stomach pain, flatulence, vomiting
1% to 10%:
Cardiovascular: Bradycardia
Endocrine & metabolic: Hyperkalemia
Neuromuscular & skeletal: Weakness
Respiratory: Dyspnea
Drug Interactions
Increased Effect/Toxicity: Potassium-sparing diuretics, salt substitutes, or ACE inhibitors; increased effect of digitalis
Decreased Effect: Aluminum and magnesium-containing antacids or sucralfate can act as phosphate binders
Dosage I.V. doses should be incorporated into the patient's maintenance I.V. fluids; intermittent I.V. infusion should be reserved for severe depletion situations in patients undergoing continuous ECG monitoring. It is difficult to determine total body phosphorus deficit; the following dosages are empiric guidelines:

Normal requirements elemental phosphorus: Oral:
0-6 months: 240 mg
6-12 months: 360 mg
1-10 years: 800 mg
>10 years: 1200 mg
Pregnancy lactation: Additional 400 mg/day
Adults: 800 mg
Treatment: It is difficult to provide concrete guidelines for the treatment of severe hypophosphatemia because the extent of total body deficits and response to therapy are difficult to
(Continued)

Potassium Phosphate (Continued)

predict. Aggressive doses of phosphate may result in a transient serum elevation followed by redistribution into intracellular compartments or bone tissue. It is recommended that repletion of severe hypophosphatemia (<1 mg/dL in adults) be done I.V. because large doses of oral phosphate may cause diarrhea and intestinal absorption may be unreliable

Pediatric I.V. phosphate repletion:

Children: 0.25-0.5 mmol/kg **administer over 4-6 hours and repeat if symptomatic hypophosphatemia persists**; to assess the need for further phosphate administration, obtain serum inorganic phosphate after administration of the first dose and base further doses on serum levels and clinical status

Adult I.V. phosphate repletion:

Initial dose: 0.08 mmol/kg if recent uncomplicated hypophosphatemia

Initial dose: 0.16 mmol/kg if prolonged hypophosphatemia with presumed total body deficits; increase dose by 25% to 50% if patient symptomatic with severe hypophosphatemia

Do not exceed 0.24 mmol/kg/dose; administer over 6-12 hours by I.V. infusion. Some investigators have used more rapid infusions.

With orders for I.V. phosphate, there is considerable confusion associated with the use of millimoles (mmol) versus milliequivalents (mEq) to express the phosphate requirement. Because inorganic phosphate exists as monobasic and dibasic anions, with the mixture of valences dependent on pH, ordering by mEq amounts is unreliable and may lead to large dosing errors. In addition, I.V. phosphate is available in the sodium and potassium salt; therefore, the content of these cations must be considered when ordering phosphate. The most reliable method of ordering I.V. phosphate is by millimoles, then specifying the potassium or sodium salt. For example, an order for 15 mmol of phosphate as potassium phosphate in one liter of normal saline. The dosing of phosphate should be 0.2-0.3 mmol/kg with a usual daily requirement of 30-60 mmol/day or 15 mmol of phosphate per liter of TPN or 15 mmol phosphate per 1000 calories of dextrose. Would also provide 22 mEq of potassium.

Maintenance:

I.V. solutions:

Children: 0.5-1.5 mmol/kg/24 hours I.V. or 2-3 mmol/kg/24 hours orally in divided doses

Adults: 15-30 mmol/24 hours I.V. or 50-150 mmol/24 hours orally in divided doses

Oral:

Children <4 years: 1 capsule (250 mg phosphorus/8 mmol) 4 times/day; dilute as instructed

Children >4 years and Adults: 1-2 capsules (250-500 mg phosphorus/8-16 mmol) 4 times/day; dilute as instructed

Administration Injection must be diluted in appropriate I.V. solution and volume prior to administration and administered over a minimum of 4 hours

Monitoring Parameters Serum potassium, calcium, phosphate, sodium, cardiac monitor (when intermittent infusion or high-dose I.V. replacement needed)

Patient Information Do not swallow the capsule; empty contents of capsule into 3-4 oz of water before taking; take with food to reduce the risk of diarrhea

Dosage Forms INJ, solution: Phosphate 3 mmol and potassium 4.4 mEq per mL (5 mL, 15 mL, 50 mL). **POWDER for oral solution** (Neutra-Phos®-K): Monobasic potassium phosphate and dibasic potassium phosphate/packet (100s)

Potassium Phosphate and Sodium Phosphate

(poe TASS ee um FOS fate & SOW dee um FOS fate)

U.S. Brand Names K-Phos® MF; K-Phos® Neutral; K-Phos® No. 2; Neutra-Phos® [OTC]; Uro-KP-Neutral®

Synonyms Sodium Phosphate and Potassium Phosphate

Therapeutic Category Electrolyte Supplement, Oral; Phosphate Salt; Potassium Salt

Use Treatment of conditions associated with excessive renal phosphate loss or inadequate GI absorption of phosphate; to acidify the urine to lower calcium concentrations; to increase the antibacterial activity of methenamine; reduce odor and rash caused by ammonia in urine

Pregnancy Risk Factor C

Contraindications Addison's disease, hyperkalemia, hyperphosphatemia, infected urolithiasis or struvite stone formation, patients with severely impaired renal function

Warnings/Precautions Use with caution in patients with renal disease, cardiac disease, metabolic alkalosis, acute dehydration, hepatic impairment, hypernatremia, and hypotension. Products also contain potassium and sodium.

Common Adverse Reactions Frequency not defined.

Cardiovascular: Bradycardia, arrhythmia, chest pain, edema, tachycardia

Central nervous system: Mental confusion, tetany (with large doses of phosphate), headache, dizziness, seizures

Endocrine & metabolic: Hyperkalemia, alkalosis

Gastrointestinal: Diarrhea, nausea, stomach pain, flatulence, vomiting, throat pain, weight gain

Genitourinary: Urine output decreased

Local: Phlebitis

Neuromuscular & skeletal: Weakness, arthralgia, bone pain, paralysis, paresthesias, pain/weakness of extremities, muscle cramps

Renal: Acute renal failure

Respiratory: Dyspnea

Miscellaneous: Thirst

Drug Interactions
 Increased Effect/Toxicity: Potassium-sparing diuretics, salt substitutes, or ACE inhibitors; increased effect of digitalis
 Decreased Effect: Aluminum and magnesium-containing antacids or sucralfate can act as phosphate binders
Pharmacodynamics/Kinetics Excretion: Urine
Dosage All dosage forms to be mixed in 6-8 oz of water prior to administration
 Children ≥4 years: Elemental phosphorus 250 mg 4 times/day after meals and at bedtime
 Adults: Elemental phosphorus 250-500 mg 4 times/day after meals and at bedtime
Administration
 Powder: Following dilution of powder, solution may be chilled to increase palatability.
 Tablet: Should be taken with a full glass of water.
Monitoring Parameters Serum potassium, sodium, calcium, phosphate, ECG
Patient Information Powder packets are to be mixed in 6-8 oz of water; following dilution, solution may be chilled to increase palatability. Tablets should be taken with a full glass of water.
Dosage Forms POWDER, for oral suspension (Neutra-Phos®): Monobasic sodium, dibasic sodium, and potassium phosphate/packet (100s). **TAB:** (K-Phos® MF): Potassium acid phosphate 155 mg and sodium acid phosphate 250 mg; (K-Phos® Neutral): Dibasic sodium phosphate 852 mg, monobasic potassium phosphate 155 mg, and monobasic sodium phosphate 130 mg; (K-Phos® No. 2): Potassium acid phosphate 305 mg and sodium acid phosphate 700 mg; (Uro-KP-Neutral®): Sodium phosphate monobasic, dipotassium phosphate, and disodium phosphate

Povidone-Iodine (POE vi done EYE oh dyne)

U.S. Brand Names ACU-dyne® [OTC]; Betadine® [OTC]; Betadine® Ophthalmic; Minidyne® [OTC]; Operand® [OTC]; Summer's Eve® Medicated Douche [OTC]; Vagi-Gard® [OTC]
Therapeutic Category Antibacterial, Topical; Antibiotic, Vaginal; Antifungal Agent, Topical; Antiviral Agent, Topical; Shampoo; Topical Skin Product
Use External antiseptic with broad microbicidal spectrum against bacteria, fungi, viruses, protozoa, and yeasts
Pregnancy Risk Factor D
Contraindications Hypersensitivity to iodine or any component of the formulation; pregnancy
Warnings/Precautions Highly toxic if ingested; sodium thiosulfate is the most effective chemical antidote; avoid contact with eyes; use with caution in infants and nursing women
Common Adverse Reactions 1% to 10%:
 Dermatologic: Rash, pruritus
 Local: Local edema
Mechanism of Action Povidone-iodine is known to be a powerful broad spectrum germicidal agent effective against a wide range of bacteria, viruses, fungi, protozoa, and spores.
Pharmacodynamics/Kinetics Absorption: Topical: Healthy volunteers: Little systemic absorption; Vaginal: Rapid, serum concentrations of total iodine and inorganic iodide are increased significantly
Dosage
 Shampoo: Apply 2 teaspoons to hair and scalp, lather and rinse; repeat application 2 times/week until improvement is noted, then shampoo weekly
 Topical: Apply as needed for treatment and prevention of susceptible microbial infections
Patient Information Do not swallow; avoid contact with eyes
Dosage Forms GEL, topical: 10% (120 g). **LIQ, topical:** 7.5% (60 mL, 120 mL, 240 mL, 480 mL, 960 mL, 3840 mL). **LIQ, topical scrub:** 7.5% (120 mL, 480 mL, 960 mL, 3840 mL). **OINT, topical:** 10% (0.9 g, 1 g, 3.5 g, 3.7 g, 30 g). **PAD:** 10% (200s). **SOLN, ophthalmic** (Betadine®): 5% (50 mL). **SOLN, perineal:** 10% (240 mL). **SOLN, topical:** 10% (15 mL, 30 mL, 60 mL, 120 mL, 240 mL, 480 mL, 960 mL, 3840 mL). **SOLN, topical scrub:** 7.5% (60 mL, 120 mL, 240 mL, 480 mL, 960 mL, 3840 mL). **SOLN, vaginal douche:** 0.3% (135 mL), 10% (180 mL, 240 mL). **SOLN, whirlpool:** 1% (3840 mL), 10% (3840 mL). **SPRAY, topical:** 5% (90 mL). **SWABSTICKS:** 7.5% (25s, 50s); 10% (25s, 50s, 150s, 200s, 1000s)

♦ **PPD** see Tuberculin Tests on page 1279
♦ **PPL** see Benzylpenicilloyl-polylysine on page 156
♦ **PPS** see Pentosan Polysulfate Sodium on page 980
♦ **PPV23** see Pneumococcal Polysaccharide Vaccine (Polyvalent) on page 1011

Pralidoxime (pra li DOKS eem)

U.S. Brand Names Protopam®
Synonyms 2-PAM; Pralidoxime Chloride; 2-Pyridine Aldoxime Methochloride
Therapeutic Category Antidote, Ambenonium; Antidote, Anticholinesterase; Antidote, Neostigmine; Antidote, Organophosphate Poisoning; Antidote, Pyridostigmine
Use Reverse muscle paralysis caused by toxic exposure to organophosphate anticholinesterase pesticides and chemicals; control of overdose of anticholinesterase medications used to treat myasthenia gravis (ambenonium, neostigmine, pyridostigmine)
Unlabeled/Investigational Use Treatment of nerve agent toxicity (chemical warfare) in combination with atropine
Pregnancy Risk Factor C
 (Continued)

Pralidoxime *(Continued)*

Contraindications Hypersensitivity to pralidoxime or any component of the formulation; poisonings due to phosphorus, inorganic phosphates, or organic phosphates without anticholinesterase activity; poisonings due to pesticides or carbamate class (may increase toxicity of carbaryl)

Warnings/Precautions Use with caution in patients with myasthenia gravis; dosage modification required in patients with impaired renal function; use with caution in patients receiving theophylline, succinylcholine, phenothiazines, respiratory depressants (eg, narcotics, barbiturates)

Common Adverse Reactions Frequency not defined.
Cardiovascular: Tachycardia, hypertension
Central nervous system: Dizziness, headache, drowsiness
Dermatologic: Rash
Gastrointestinal: Nausea
Hepatic: Transient increases in ALT, AST
Local: Pain at injection site after I.M. administration
Neuromuscular & skeletal: Muscle rigidity, weakness
Ocular: Accommodation impaired, blurred vision, diplopia
Renal: Renal function decreased
Respiratory: Hyperventilation, laryngospasm

Drug Interactions

Increased Effect/Toxicity: Increased effect with barbiturates (potentiated). Use with aminophylline, morphine, theophylline, and succinylcholine is contraindicated. Use with reserpine and phenothiazines should be avoided in patients with organophosphate poisoning.

Decreased Effect: Atropine is often used concurrently with pralidoxime to blunt excessive cholinergic stimulation. However, the onset of atropine's effect may be unpredictable, and may occur earlier than anticipated, diminishing the therapeutic response to pralidoxime

Mechanism of Action Reactivates cholinesterase that had been inactivated by phosphorylation due to exposure to organophosphate pesticides by displacing the enzyme from its receptor sites; removes the phosphoryl group from the active site of the inactivated enzyme

Pharmacodynamics/Kinetics
Protein binding: None
Metabolism: Hepatic
Half-life elimination: 74-77 minutes
Time to peak, serum: I.V.: 5-15 minutes
Excretion: Urine (80% to 90% as metabolites and unchanged drug)

Dosage
Organic phosphorus poisoning (use in conjunction with atropine; atropine effects should be established before pralidoxime is administered): I.V. (may be given I.M. or S.C. if I.V. is not feasible):
Children: 20-50 mg/kg/dose; repeat in 1-2 hours if muscle weakness has not been relieved, then at 8- to 12-hour intervals if cholinergic signs recur
Adults: 1-2 g; repeat in 1 hour if muscle weakness has not been relieved, then at 8- to 12-hour intervals if cholinergic signs recur. When the poison has been ingested, continued absorption from the lower bowel may require additional doses; patients should be titrated as long as signs of poisoning recur; dosing may need repeated every 3-8 hours.
Treatment of acetylcholinesterase inhibitor toxicity: Adults: I.V.: Initial: 1-2 g followed by increments of 250 mg every 5 minutes until response is observed
Nerve agent toxicity management (unlabeled use): **Note:** Atropine is a component of the management of nerve agent toxicity; consult atropine monograph for specific route and dose. To be effective, pralidoxime must be administered within minutes to a few hours following exposure (depending on the nerve agent).
Infants and Children:
Prehospital ("in the field"): Mild-to-moderate symptoms: I.M.: 15 mg/kg; severe symptoms: 25 mg/kg
Hospital/emergency department: Mild-to-severe symptoms: I.V.: 15 mg/kg (up to 1 g)
Adults:
Prehospital ("in the field"): Mild-to-moderate symptoms: I.M.: 600 mg; severe symptoms: 1800 mg
Hospital/emergency department: Mild-to-severe symptoms: I.V.: 15 mg/kg (up to 1 g)
Frail patients, elderly:
Prehospital ("in the field"): Mild-to-moderate symptoms: I.M.: 10 mg/kg; severe symptoms: 25 mg/kg
Hospital/emergency department: Mild-to-severe symptoms: I.V.: 5-10 mg/kg
Elderly: Refer to Adults dosing; dosing should be cautious, considering possibility of decreased hepatic, renal, or cardiac function

Dosing adjustment in renal impairment: Dose should be reduced

Administration I.V.: Infuse over 15-30 minutes at a rate not to exceed 200 mg/minute; may administer I.M. or S.C. if I.V. is not accessible. If a more concentrated 5% solution is used, infuse over at least 5 minutes.

Monitoring Parameters Heart rate, respiratory rate, blood pressure, continuous ECG; cardiac monitor and blood pressure monitor required for I.V. administration

Reference Range Minimum therapeutic concentration: 4 mcg/mL

Dosage Forms INJ, powder for reconstitution: 1 g

♦ **Pralidoxime Chloride** *see* Pralidoxime *on page 1025*

Pramipexole (pra mi PEKS ole)

Related Information

Parkinson's Agents Comparison *on page 1402*

U.S. Brand Names Mirapex®

Therapeutic Category Anti-Parkinson's Agent, Dopamine Agonist; Dopaminergic Agent, Antiparkinson's

Use Treatment of the signs and symptoms of idiopathic Parkinson's disease

Unlabeled/Investigational Use Treatment of depression

Pregnancy Risk Factor C

Contraindications Hypersensitivity to pramipexole or any component of the formulation

Warnings/Precautions Caution should be taken in patients with renal insufficiency and in patients with pre-existing dyskinesias. May cause orthostatic hypotension; Parkinson's disease patients appear to have an impaired capacity to respond to a postural challenge. Use with caution in patients at risk of hypotension (such as those receiving antihypertensive drugs) or where transient hypotensive episodes would be poorly tolerated (cardiovascular disease or cerebrovascular disease). Parkinson's patients being treated with dopaminergic agonists ordinarily require careful monitoring for signs and symptoms of postural hypotension, especially during dose escalation, and should be informed of this risk. May cause hallucinations, particularly in older patients.

Although not reported for pramipexole, other dopaminergic agents have been associated with a syndrome resembling neuroleptic malignant syndrome on withdrawal or significant dosage reduction after long-term use. Dopaminergic agents from the ergot class have also been associated with fibrotic complications, such as retroperitoneum, lungs, and pleura.

Pramipexole has been associated with somnolence, particularly at higher dosages (>1.5 mg/day). In addition, patients have been reported to fall asleep during activities of daily living, including driving, while taking this medication. Whether these patients exhibited somnolence prior to these events is not clear. Patients should be advised of this issue and factors which may increase risk (sleep disorders, other sedating medications, or concomitant medications which increase pramipexole concentrations) and instructed to report daytime somnolence or sleepiness to the prescriber. Patients should use caution in performing activities which require alertness (driving or operating machinery), and to avoid other medications which may cause CNS depression, including ethanol.

Common Adverse Reactions

>10%:

Cardiovascular: Postural hypotension

Central nervous system: Asthenia, dizziness, somnolence, insomnia, hallucinations, abnormal dreams

Gastrointestinal: Nausea, constipation

Neuromuscular & skeletal: Weakness, dyskinesia, EPS

1% to 10%:

Cardiovascular: Edema, syncope, tachycardia, chest pain

Central nervous system: Malaise, confusion, amnesia, dystonias, akathisia, thinking abnormalities, myoclonus, hyperesthesia, paranoia, fever

Endocrine & metabolic: Decreased libido

Gastrointestinal: Anorexia, weight loss, xerostomia, dysphagia

Genitourinary: Urinary frequency, impotence, urinary incontinence

Neuromuscular & skeletal: Muscle twitching, leg cramps, arthritis, bursitis, myasthenia, gait abnormalities, hypertonia

Ocular: Vision abnormalities

Respiratory: Dyspnea, rhinitis

Drug Interactions

Increased Effect/Toxicity: Cimetidine in combination with pramipexole produced a 50% increase in AUC and a 40% increase in half-life. Drugs secreted by the cationic transport system (diltiazem, triamterene, verapamil, quinidine, quinine, ranitidine) decrease the clearance of pramipexole by ~20%.

Decreased Effect: Dopamine antagonists (antipsychotics, metoclopramide) may decrease the efficiency of pramipexole.

Mechanism of Action Pramipexole is a nonergot dopamine agonist with specificity for the D_2 subfamily dopamine receptor, and has also been shown to bind to D_3 and D_4 receptors. By binding to these receptors, it is thought that pramipexole can stimulate dopamine activity on the nerves of the striatum and substantia nigra.

Pharmacodynamics/Kinetics

Protein binding: 15%

Bioavailability: 90%

Half-life elimination: ~8 hours; Elderly: 12-14 hours

Time to peak, serum: ~2 hours

Excretion: Urine (90% as unchanged drug)

Dosage Adults: Oral: Initial: 0.375 mg/day given in 3 divided doses, increase gradually by 0.125 mg/dose every 5-7 days; range: 1.5-4.5 mg/day

Dosage adjustment in renal impairment:

Cl_{cr} 35-59 mL/minute: Initial: 0.125 mg twice daily (maximum dose: 1.5 mg twice daily)

Cl_{cr} 15-34 mL/minute: Initial: 0.125 mg once daily (maximum dose: 1.5 mg once daily)

Cl_{cr} <15 mL/minute (or hemodialysis patients): Not adequately studied

(Continued)

Pramipexole *(Continued)*

Administration Doses should be titrated gradually in all patients to avoid the onset of intolerable side effects. The dosage should be increased to achieve a maximum therapeutic effect, balanced against the side effects of dyskinesia, hallucinations, somnolence, and dry mouth.

Monitoring Parameters Monitor for improvement in symptoms of Parkinson's disease (eg, mentation, behavior, daily living activities, motor examinations), blood pressure, body weight changes, and heart rate

Patient Information Ask your prescriber or pharmacist before taking any other medicine, including over-the-counter products; especially important are other medicines that could make you sleepy such as sleeping pills, tranquilizers, some cold and allergy medicines, narcotic pain killers, or medicines that relax muscles. Avoid alcohol; use caution in performing activities that require alertness (driving or operating machinery); can cause significant drowsiness.

Dosage Forms TAB: 0.125 mg, 0.25 mg, 0.5 mg, 1 mg, 1.5 mg

♦ **Pramosone®** *see Pramoxine and Hydrocortisone on page 1028*

Pramoxine and Hydrocortisone (pra MOKS een & hye droe KOR ti sone)

U.S. Brand Names Analpram-HC®; Enzone®; Epifoam®; Pramosone®; ProctoFoam®-HC; Zone-A®; Zone-A Forte®

Synonyms Hydrocortisone and Pramoxine

Therapeutic Category Anesthetic/Corticosteroid, Topical

Use Relief of inflammatory and pruritic manifestations of corticosteroid-responsive dermatoses

Pregnancy Risk Factor C

Dosage Topical/rectal: Apply to affected areas 3-4 times/day

Dosage Forms CRM, rectal (Analpram-HC®): Pramoxine 1% and hydrocortisone acetate 1% (30 g), pramoxine 1% and hydrocortisone acetate 2.5% (30 g). **CRM, topical:** (Enzone®): Pramoxine 1% and hydrocortisone acetate 1% (30 g); (Pramosone®): Pramoxine 1% and hydrocortisone acetate 1% (30 g, 60 g), pramoxine 1% and hydrocortisone acetate 2.5% (30 g, 60 g). **FOAM, rectal** (ProctoFoam®-HC): Pramoxine 1% and hydrocortisone acetate 1% (10 g). **FOAM, topical:** (Epifoam®): Pramoxine 1% and hydrocortisone acetate 1% (10 g). **LOT, rectal** (Analpram-HC®): Pramoxine 1% and hydrocortisone 2.5% (60 mL). **LOT, topical:** (Pramosone®): Pramoxine 1% and hydrocortisone 1% (60 mL, 120 mL, 240 mL), pramoxine 1% and hydrocortisone 2.5% (60 mL, 120 mL); (Zone-A®): Pramoxine 1% and hydrocortisone 1% (60 mL); (Zone-A Forte®): Pramoxine 1% and hydrocortisone 2.5% (60 mL). **OINT, topical:** Pramoxine 1% and hydrocortisone 1% (30 g), pramoxine 1% and hydrocortisone 2.5% (30 g)

♦ **Prandin®** *see Repaglinide on page 1085*
♦ **Pravachol®** *see Pravastatin on page 1028*

Pravastatin (PRA va stat in)

Related Information
Lipid-Lowering Agents *on page 1381*

U.S. Brand Names Pravachol®

Synonyms Pravastatin Sodium

Therapeutic Category Antilipemic Agent, HMG-CoA Reductase Inhibitor; HMG-CoA Reductase Inhibitor

Use Use with dietary therapy for the following:

Primary prevention of coronary events: In hypercholesterolemic patients without established coronary heart disease to reduce cardiovascular morbidity (myocardial infarction, coronary revascularization procedures) and mortality.

Secondary prevention of cardiovascular events in patients with established coronary heart disease: To slow the progression of coronary atherosclerosis; to reduce cardiovascular morbidity (myocardial infarction, coronary vascular procedures) and to reduce mortality; to reduce the risk of stroke and transient ischemic attacks

Hyperlipidemias: Reduce elevations in total cholesterol, LDL-C, apolipoprotein B, and triglycerides (elevations of 1 or more components are present in Fredrickson type IIa, IIb, III, and IV hyperlipidemias)

Heterozygous familial hypercholesterolemia (HeFH): In pediatric patients, 8-18 years of age, with HeFH having LDL-C ≥190 mg/dL **or** LDL ≥160 mg/dL with positive family history of premature cardiovascular disease (CVD) or 2 or more CVD risk factors in the pediatric patient

Pregnancy Risk Factor X

Contraindications Hypersensitivity to pravastatin or any component of the formulation; active liver disease; unexplained persistent elevations of serum transaminases; pregnancy; breast-feeding

Warnings/Precautions Secondary causes of hyperlipidemia should be ruled out prior to therapy. Liver function must be monitored by periodic laboratory assessment. Rhabdomyolysis with acute renal failure has occurred. Risk may be increased with concurrent use of other drugs which may cause rhabdomyolysis (including gemfibrozil, fibric acid derivatives, or niacin at doses ≥1 g/day). Temporarily discontinue in any patient experiencing an acute or serious condition predisposing to renal failure secondary to rhabdomyolysis. Use caution in patients with previous liver disease or heavy ethanol use. Treatment in patients <8 years of age is not recommended.

Common Adverse Reactions As reported in short-term trials; safety and tolerability with long-term use were similar to placebo

1% to 10%:
   Cardiovascular: Chest pain (4%)
   Central nervous system: Headache (2% to 6%), fatigue (4%), dizziness (1% to 3%)
   Dermatologic: Rash (4%)
   Gastrointestinal: Nausea/vomiting (7%), diarrhea (6%), heartburn (3%)
   Hepatic: Increased transaminases (>3x normal on two occasions - 1%)
   Neuromuscular & skeletal: Myalgia (2%)
   Respiratory: Cough (3%)
   Miscellaneous: Influenza (2%)
Additional class-related events or case reports (not necessarily reported with pravastatin therapy): Angioedema, cataracts, depression, dyspnea, eosinophilia, erectile dysfunction, facial paresis, hypersensitivity reaction, impaired extraocular muscle movement, impotence, leukopenia, malaise, memory loss, ophthalmoplegia, paresthesia, peripheral neuropathy, photosensitivity, psychic disturbance, skin discoloration, thrombocytopenia, thyroid dysfunction, toxic epidermal necrolysis, transaminases increased, vomiting

Drug Interactions
   Cytochrome P450 Effect: Substrate of CYP3A4 (minor); **Inhibits** CYP2C8/9 (weak), 2D6 (weak), 3A4 (weak)
   Increased Effect/Toxicity: Clofibrate, fenofibrate, gemfibrozil, and niacin may increase the risk of myopathy and rhabdomyolysis. Imidazole antifungals (itraconazole, ketoconazole), P-glycoprotein inhibitors may increase pravastatin concentrations.
   Decreased Effect: Concurrent administration of cholestyramine or colestipol can decrease pravastatin absorption.

Mechanism of Action Pravastatin is a competitive inhibitor of 3-hydroxy-3-methylglutaryl coenzyme A (HMG-CoA) reductase, which is the rate-limiting enzyme involved in *de novo* cholesterol synthesis.

Pharmacodynamics/Kinetics
   Onset of action: Several days
   Peak effect: 4 weeks
   Absorption: Poor
   Protein binding: 50%
   Metabolism: Hepatic to at least two metabolites
   Bioavailability: 17%
   Half-life elimination: ~2-3 hours
   Time to peak, serum: 1-1.5 hours
   Excretion: Urine (≤20%, 8% as unchanged drug)

Dosage Oral: **Note:** Doses should be individualized according to the baseline LDL-cholesterol levels, the recommended goal of therapy, and patient response; adjustments should be made at intervals of 4 weeks or more; doses may need adjusted based on concomitant medications
   Children: HeFH:
      8-13 years: 20 mg/day
      14-18 years: 40 mg/day
      Dosage adjustment for pravastatin based on concomitant immunosuppressants (ie, cyclosporine): Refer to Adults dosing section
   Adults: Hyperlipidemias, primary prevention of coronary events, secondary prevention of cardiovascular events: Initial: 40 mg once daily; titrate dosage to response; usual range: 10-80 mg; (maximum dose: 80 mg once daily)
      Dosage adjustment for pravastatin based on concomitant immunosuppressants (ie, cyclosporine): Initial: 10 mg/day, titrate with caution (maximum dose: 20 mg/day)
   Elderly: No specific dosage recommendations. Clearance is reduced in the elderly, resulting in an increase in AUC between 25% to 50%. However, substantial accumulation is not expected.
   Dosing adjustment in renal impairment: Initial: 10 mg/day
   Dosing adjustment in hepatic impairment: Initial: 10 mg/day

Administration May be taken without regard to meals.

Monitoring Parameters Obtain baseline LFTs and total cholesterol profile; creatine phosphokinase due to possibility of myopathy. Repeat LFTs prior to elevation of dose. May be measured when clinically indicated and/or periodically thereafter.

Patient Information Promptly report any unexplained muscle pain, tenderness or weakness, especially if accompanied by malaise or fever

Dosage Forms TAB: 10 mg, 20 mg, 40 mg, 80 mg

♦ **Pravastatin and Aspirin** *see* Aspirin and Pravastatin *on page 124*
♦ **Pravastatin Sodium** *see* Pravastatin *on page 1028*
♦ **Pravigard™ PAC** *see* Aspirin and Pravastatin *on page 124*

Praziquantel (pray zi KWON tel)
   U.S. Brand Names Biltricide®
   Therapeutic Category Anthelmintic
   Use All stages of schistosomiasis caused by all *Schistosoma* species pathogenic to humans; clonorchiasis and opisthorchiasis
   Unlabeled/Investigational Use Cysticercosis and many intestinal tapeworms
   Pregnancy Risk Factor B
   Contraindications Hypersensitivity to praziquantel or any component of the formulation; ocular cysticercosis
   Warnings/Precautions Use caution in patients with severe hepatic disease; patients with cerebral cysticercosis require hospitalization
   (Continued)

Praziquantel *(Continued)*

Common Adverse Reactions 1% to 10%:
Central nervous system: Dizziness, drowsiness, headache, malaise, CSF reaction syndrome in patients being treated for neurocysticercosis
Gastrointestinal: Abdominal pain, loss of appetite, nausea, vomiting
Miscellaneous: Diaphoresis

Drug Interactions
Cytochrome P450 Effect: Inhibits CYP2D6 (weak)

Mechanism of Action Increases the cell permeability to calcium in schistosomes, causing strong contractions and paralysis of worm musculature leading to detachment of suckers from the blood vessel walls and to dislodgment

Pharmacodynamics/Kinetics
Absorption: Oral: ~80%
Distribution: CSF concentration is 14% to 20% of plasma concentration; enters breast milk
Protein binding: ~80%
Metabolism: Extensive first-pass effect
Half-life elimination: Parent drug: 0.8-1.5 hours; Metabolites: 4.5 hours
Time to peak, serum: 1-3 hours
Excretion: Urine (99% as metabolites)

Dosage Children >4 years and Adults: Oral:
Schistosomiasis: 20 mg/kg/dose 2-3 times/day for 1 day at 4- to 6-hour intervals
Flukes (unlabeled use): 25 mg/kg/dose every 8 hours for 1-2 days
Cysticercosis (unlabeled use): 50 mg/kg/day divided every 8 hours for 14 days
Tapeworms (unlabeled use): 10-20 mg/kg as a single dose (25 mg/kg for *Hymenolepis nana*)
Clonorchiasis/opisthorchiasis: 3 doses of 25 mg/kg as a 1-day treatment

Patient Information Do not chew tablets due to bitter taste; take with food; caution should be used when performing tasks requiring mental alertness, may impair judgment and coordination

Dosage Forms TAB: 600 mg

Prazosin *(PRA zoe sin)*

U.S. Brand Names Minipress®
Synonyms Furazosin; Prazosin Hydrochloride
Therapeutic Category Alpha-Adrenergic Blocking Agent, Oral; Antihypertensive Agent
Use Treatment of hypertension
Unlabeled/Investigational Use Benign prostatic hyperplasia; Raynaud's syndrome
Pregnancy Risk Factor C
Contraindications Hypersensitivity to quinazolines (doxazosin, prazosin, terazosin) or any component of the formulation; concurrent use with phosphodiesterase-5 (PDE-5) inhibitors including sildenafil (>25 mg), tadalafil, or vardenafil
Warnings/Precautions Marked orthostatic hypotension, syncope, and loss of consciousness may occur with first dose ("first dose phenomenon") occurs more often in patients receiving beta-blockers, diuretics, low sodium diets, or larger first doses (ie, >1 mg/dose in adults); avoid rapid increase in dose; use with caution in patients with renal impairment; use cautiously in patients with a known sensitivity to other quinazolines (eg, terazosin, doxazosin)

Common Adverse Reactions
>10%: Central nervous system: Dizziness (10%)
1% to 10%:
Cardiovascular: Palpitations (5%), edema, orthostatic hypotension, syncope (1%)
Central nervous system: Headache (8%), drowsiness (8%), weakness (7%), vertigo, depression, nervousness
Dermatologic: Rash (1% to 4%)
Endocrine & metabolic: Decreased energy (7%)
Gastrointestinal: Nausea (5%), vomiting, diarrhea, constipation
Genitourinary: Urinary frequency (1% to 5%)
Ocular: Blurred vision, reddened sclera, xerostomia
Respiratory: Dyspnea, epistaxis, nasal congestion

Drug Interactions
Increased Effect/Toxicity: Prazosin's hypotensive effect may be increased with beta-blockers, diuretics, ACE inhibitors, calcium channel blockers, other antihypertensive medications, sildenafil (use with extreme caution at a dose ≤25 mg), tadalafil (use is contraindicated by the manufacturer), and vardenafil (use is contraindicated or the manufacturer). Concurrent use with tricyclic antidepressants (TCAs) and low-potency antipsychotics may increase risk of orthostasis.
Decreased Effect: Decreased antihypertensive effect if taken with NSAIDs.

Mechanism of Action Competitively inhibits postsynaptic alpha-adrenergic receptors which results in vasodilation of veins and arterioles and a decrease in total peripheral resistance and blood pressure

Pharmacodynamics/Kinetics
Onset of action: BP reduction: ~2 hours
Maximum decrease: 2-4 hours
Duration: 10-24 hours
Distribution: Hypertensive adults: V_d: 0.5 L/kg
Protein binding: 92% to 97%
Metabolism: Extensively hepatic
Bioavailability: 43% to 82%
Half-life elimination: 2-4 hours; prolonged with congestive heart failure

Excretion: Urine (6% to 10% as unchanged drug)

Dosage Oral:

Children: Initial: 5 mcg/kg/dose (to assess hypotensive effects); usual dosing interval: every 6 hours; increase dosage gradually up to maximum of 25 mcg/kg/dose every 6 hours

Adults:

Hypertension: Initial: 1 mg/dose 2-3 times/day; usual maintenance dose: 3-15 mg/day in divided doses 2-4 times/day; maximum daily dose: 20 mg

Hypertensive urgency: 10-20 mg once, may repeat in 30 minutes

Raynaud's (unlabeled use): 0.5-3 mg twice daily

Benign prostatic hyperplasia (unlabeled use): 2 mg twice daily

Monitoring Parameters Blood pressure, standing and sitting/supine

Patient Information Rise from sitting/lying carefully; take first dose at bedtime; may cause dizziness; report if painful, persistent erection occurs; avoid alcohol

Dosage Forms CAP: 1 mg, 2 mg, 5 mg

Prazosin and Polythiazide (PRA zoe sin & pol i THYE a zide)

U.S. Brand Names Minizide®

Synonyms Polythiazide and Prazosin

Therapeutic Category Antihypertensive Agent, Combination

Use Management of mild to moderate hypertension

Pregnancy Risk Factor C

Dosage Adults: Oral: 1 capsule 2-3 times/day

Dosage Forms CAP: (Minizide® 1): Prazosin 1 mg and polythiazide 0.5 mg; (Minizide® 2): Prazosin 2 mg and polythiazide 0.5 mg; (Minizide® 5): Prazosin 5 mg and polythiazide 0.5 mg

♦ **Prazosin Hydrochloride** see Prazosin on page 1030

♦ **Precedex™** see Dexmedetomidine on page 359

♦ **Precose®** see Acarbose on page 21

♦ **Pred Forte®** see PrednisoLONE on page 1031

♦ **Pred-G®** see Prednisolone and Gentamicin on page 1033

♦ **Pred Mild®** see PrednisoLONE on page 1031

Prednicarbate (PRED ni kar bate)

Related Information

Corticosteroids Comparison on page 1372

U.S. Brand Names Dermatop® e™

Therapeutic Category Corticosteroid, Topical (Medium Potency)

Use Relief of the inflammatory and pruritic manifestations of corticosteroid-responsive dermatoses (medium potency topical corticosteroid)

Pregnancy Risk Factor C

Contraindications Hypersensitivity to prednicarbate or any component of the formulation; fungal, viral, or tubercular skin lesions, herpes simplex or zoster

Warnings/Precautions Systemic absorption of topical corticosteroids has produced reversible HPA axis suppression. This is more likely to occur when the preparation is used on large surface or denuded areas for prolonged periods of time or with an occlusive dressing.

Common Adverse Reactions 1% to 10%: Dermatologic: Skin atrophy, shininess, thinness, mild telangiectasia

Mechanism of Action Topical corticosteroids have anti-inflammatory, antipruritic, vasoconstrictive, and antiproliferative actions

Dosage Adults: Topical: Apply a thin film to affected area twice daily. Therapy should be discontinued when control is achieved; if no improvement is seen, reassessment of diagnosis may be necessary.

Monitoring Parameters Relief of symptoms

Patient Information Use only as prescribed and for no longer than the period prescribed; apply sparingly in a thin film and rub in lightly; avoid contact with eyes; do not apply to the face, underarms, or groin areas; notify prescriber if condition persists or worsens

Dosage Forms CRM: 0.1% (15 g, 60 g). **OINT:** 0.1% (15 g, 60 g)

PrednisoLONE (pred NISS oh lone)

Related Information

Corticosteroids Comparison on page 1372

U.S. Brand Names AK-Pred®; Econopred®; Econopred® Plus; Inflamase® Forte; Inflamase® Mild; Orapred®; Pediapred®; Pred Forte®; Pred Mild®; Prelone®

Synonyms Deltahydrocortisone; Metacortandralone; Prednisolone Acetate; Prednisolone Acetate, Ophthalmic; Prednisolone Sodium Phosphate; Prednisolone Sodium Phosphate, Ophthalmic

Therapeutic Category Anti-inflammatory Agent; Anti-inflammatory Agent, Ophthalmic; Corticosteroid, Ophthalmic; Corticosteroid, Systemic; Glucocorticoid

Use Treatment of palpebral and bulbar conjunctivitis; corneal injury from chemical, radiation, thermal burns, or foreign body penetration; endocrine disorders, rheumatic disorders, collagen diseases, dermatologic diseases, allergic states, ophthalmic diseases, respiratory diseases, hematologic disorders, neoplastic diseases, edematous states, and gastrointestinal diseases; useful in patients with inability to activate prednisone (liver disease)

Pregnancy Risk Factor C

(Continued)

PrednisoLONE *(Continued)*

Contraindications Hypersensitivity to prednisolone or any component of the formulation; acute superficial herpes simplex keratitis; systemic fungal infections; varicella

Warnings/Precautions Use with caution in patients with hyperthyroidism, cirrhosis, nonspecific ulcerative colitis, hypertension, osteoporosis, thromboembolic tendencies, CHF, convulsive disorders, myasthenia gravis, thrombophlebitis, peptic ulcer, diabetes; acute adrenal insufficiency may occur with abrupt withdrawal after long-term therapy or with stress; young pediatric patients may be more susceptible to adrenal axis suppression from topical therapy. Because of the risk of adverse effects, systemic corticosteroids should be used cautiously in the elderly, in the smallest possible dose, and for the shortest possible time.

Common Adverse Reactions
>10%:
Central nervous system: Insomnia, nervousness
Gastrointestinal: Increased appetite, indigestion
1% to 10%:
Dermatologic: Hirsutism
Endocrine & metabolic: Diabetes mellitus
Neuromuscular & skeletal: Arthralgia
Ocular: Cataracts, glaucoma
Respiratory: Epistaxis

Drug Interactions
Cytochrome P450 Effect: Substrate of CYP3A4 (minor); **Inhibits** CYP3A4 (weak)
Increased Effect/Toxicity: Systemic: The combined use of cyclosporine and prednisolone may result in elevated levels of both agents. Oral contraceptives may enhance the effect of prednisolone.
Decreased Effect: Systemic: Decreased effect or corticosteroids with barbiturates, aminoglutethimide, phenytoin, and rifampin. Decreased effect of salicylates, vaccines, and toxoids. Prednisolone may decrease the effect of isoniazid. Corticosteroids may decrease the effect of warfarin or IUD contraceptives.

Mechanism of Action Decreases inflammation by suppression of migration of polymorphonuclear leukocytes and reversal of increased capillary permeability; suppresses the immune system by reducing activity and volume of the lymphatic system

Pharmacodynamics/Kinetics
Duration: 18-36 hours
Protein binding (concentration dependent): 65% to 91%
Metabolism: Primarily hepatic, but also metabolized in most tissues, to inactive compounds
Half-life elimination: 3.6 hours; End-stage renal disease: 3-5 hours
Excretion: Primarily urine (as glucuronides, sulfates, and unconjugated metabolites)

Dosage Dose depends upon condition being treated and response of patient; dosage for infants and children should be based on severity of the disease and response of the patient rather than on strict adherence to dosage indicated by age, weight, or body surface area. Consider alternate day therapy for long-term therapy. Discontinuation of long-term therapy requires gradual withdrawal by tapering the dose.

Children: Oral:
Acute asthma: 1-2 mg/kg/day in divided doses 1-2 times/day for 3-5 days
Anti-inflammatory or immunosuppressive dose: 0.1-2 mg/kg/day in divided doses 1-4 times/day
Nephrotic syndrome:
Initial (first 3 episodes): 2 mg/kg/day **or** 60 mg/m^2/day (maximum: 80 mg/day) in divided doses 3-4 times/day until urine is protein free for 3 consecutive days (maximum: 28 days); followed by 1-1.5 mg/kg/dose **or** 40 mg/m^2/dose given every other day for 4 weeks
Maintenance (long-term maintenance dose for frequent relapses): 0.5-1 mg/kg/dose given every other day for 3-6 months
Adults: Oral:
Usual range: 5-60 mg/day
Multiple sclerosis: 200 mg/day for 1 week followed by 80 mg every other day for 1 month
Rheumatoid arthritis: Initial: 5-7.5 mg/day; adjust dose as necessary
Elderly: Use lowest effective dose
Dosing adjustment in hyperthyroidism: Prednisolone dose may need to be increased to achieve adequate therapeutic effects
Hemodialysis: Slightly dialyzable (5% to 20%); administer dose posthemodialysis
Peritoneal dialysis: Supplemental dose is not necessary
Ophthalmic suspension/solution: Children and Adults: Instill 1-2 drops into conjunctival sac every hour during day, every 2 hours at night until favorable response is obtained, then use 1 drop every 4 hours

Administration Administer oral formulation with food or milk to decrease GI effects

Monitoring Parameters Blood pressure, blood glucose, electrolytes

Patient Information Notify surgeon or dentist before surgical repair; may cause GI upset, take orally with food; notify prescriber if any sign of infection occurs; avoid abrupt withdrawal when on long-term therapy

Dosage Forms SOLN, ophthalmic, as sodium phosphate: 1% (5 mL, 10 mL, 15 mL); (AK-Pred®): 1% (5 mL, 15 mL); (Inflamase® Forte): 1% (5 mL, 10 mL, 15 mL); (Inflamase® Mild): 0.125% (5 mL, 10 mL). **SOLN, oral, as sodium phosphate:** Prednisolone base 5 mg/5 mL (120 mL); (Orapred®): 20 mg/5 mL (240 mL); (Pediapred®): 6.7 mg/5 mL (120 mL). **SUSP, ophthalmic, as acetate:** 1% (5 mL, 10 mL, 15 mL); (Econopred®): 0.125% (5 mL, 10 mL);

(Econopred® Plus): 1% (5 mL, 10 mL); (Pred Forte®): 1% (1 mL, 5 mL, 10 mL, 15 mL); (Pred Mild®): 0.12% (5 mL, 10 mL). **SYR, as base:** 5 mg/5 mL (120 mL), 15 mg/5 mL (240 mL, 480 mL); (Prelone®): 5 mg/5 mL (120 mL), 15 mg/5 mL (240 mL, 480 mL). **TAB, as base:** 5 mg

♦ **Prednisolone Acetate** see PrednisoLONE on page 1031
♦ **Prednisolone Acetate, Ophthalmic** see PrednisoLONE on page 1031

Prednisolone and Gentamicin (pred NIS oh lone & jen ta MYE sin)

U.S. Brand Names Pred-G®
Synonyms Gentamicin and Prednisolone
Therapeutic Category Antibiotic/Corticosteroid, Ophthalmic
Use Treatment of steroid responsive inflammatory conditions and superficial ocular infections due to microorganisms susceptible to gentamicin
Pregnancy Risk Factor C
Dosage Ophthalmic: Children and Adults:
 Ointment: Apply ½ inch ribbon in the conjunctival sac 1-3 times/day
 Suspension: 1 drop 2-4 times/day; during the initial 24-48 hours, the dosing frequency may be increased if necessary up to 1 drop every hour
Dosage Forms OINT, ophthalmic: Prednisolone 0.6% and gentamicin 0.3% (3.5 g). **SUSP, ophthalmic:** Prednisolone 1% and gentamicin 0.3% (2 mL, 5 mL, 10 mL)

♦ **Prednisolone and Sulfacetamide** see Sulfacetamide and Prednisolone on page 1170
♦ **Prednisolone, Neomycin, and Polymyxin B** see Neomycin, Polymyxin B, and Prednisolone on page 893
♦ **Prednisolone Sodium Phosphate** see PrednisoLONE on page 1031
♦ **Prednisolone Sodium Phosphate, Ophthalmic** see PrednisoLONE on page 1031

PredniSONE (PRED ni sone)

Related Information
 Corticosteroids Comparison on page 1372
U.S. Brand Names Deltasone®; Prednisone Intensol™; Sterapred®; Sterapred® DS
Synonyms Deltacortisone; Deltadehydrocortisone
Therapeutic Category Anti-inflammatory Agent; Corticosteroid, Systemic; Glucocorticoid
Use Treatment of a variety of diseases including adrenocortical insufficiency, hypercalcemia, rheumatic, and collagen disorders; dermatologic, ocular, respiratory, gastrointestinal, and neoplastic diseases; organ transplantation and a variety of diseases including those of hematologic, allergic, inflammatory, and autoimmune in origin; not available in injectable form, prednisolone must be used
Unlabeled/Investigational Use Investigational: Prevention of postherpetic neuralgia and relief of acute pain in the early stages
Pregnancy Risk Factor B
Contraindications Hypersensitivity to prednisone or any component of the formulation; serious infections, except tuberculous meningitis; systemic fungal infections; varicella
Warnings/Precautions Withdraw therapy with gradual tapering of dose, may retard bone growth. Use with caution in patients with hypothyroidism, cirrhosis, CHF, ulcerative colitis, thromboembollic disorders, and patients at increased risk for peptic ulcer disease. Corticosteroids should be used with caution in patients with diabetes, hypertension, osteoporosis, glaucoma, cataracts, or tuberculosis. Use caution in hepatic impairment. Because of the risk of adverse effects, systemic corticosteroids should be used cautiously in the elderly, in the smallest possible dose, and for the shortest possible time.
Common Adverse Reactions
 >10%:
  Central nervous system: Insomnia, nervousness
  Gastrointestinal: Increased appetite, indigestion
 1% to 10%:
  Dermatologic: Hirsutism
  Endocrine & metabolic: Diabetes mellitus, glucose intolerance, hyperglycemia
  Neuromuscular & skeletal: Arthralgia
  Ocular: Cataracts, glaucoma
  Respiratory: Epistaxis
Drug Interactions
 Cytochrome P450 Effect: Substrate of CYP3A4 (minor); **Induces** CYP2C19 (weak), 3A4 (weak)
 Increased Effect/Toxicity: Concurrent use with NSAIDs may increase the risk of GI ulceration.
 Decreased Effect: Decreased effect with barbiturates, phenytoin, rifampin; decreased effect of salicylates, vaccines, and toxoids.
Mechanism of Action Decreases inflammation by suppression of migration of polymorphonuclear leukocytes and reversal of increased capillary permeability; suppresses the immune system by reducing activity and volume of the lymphatic system; suppresses adrenal function at high doses. Antitumor effects may be related to inhibition of glucose transport, phosphorylation, or induction of cell death in immature lymphocytes. Antiemetic effects are thought to occur due to blockade of cerebral innervation of the emetic center via inhibition of prostaglandin synthesis.
Pharmacodynamics/Kinetics
 Protein binding (concentration dependent): 65% to 91%
 (Continued)

PredniSONE *(Continued)*

Metabolism: Hepatically converted from prednisone (inactive) to prednisolone (active); may be impaired with hepatic dysfunction

Half-life elimination: Normal renal function: 2.5-3.5 hours

See Prednisolone monograph for complete information.

Dosage Oral: Dose depends upon condition being treated and response of patient; dosage for infants and children should be based on severity of the disease and response of the patient rather than on strict adherence to dosage indicated by age, weight, or body surface area. Consider alternate day therapy for long-term therapy. Discontinuation of long-term therapy requires gradual withdrawal by tapering the dose.

Children:

Anti-inflammatory or immunosuppressive dose: 0.05-2 mg/kg/day divided 1-4 times/day

Acute asthma: 1-2 mg/kg/day in divided doses 1-2 times/day for 3-5 days

Alternatively (for 3- to 5-day "burst"):
<1 year: 10 mg every 12 hours
1-4 years: 20 mg every 12 hours
5-13 years: 30 mg every 12 hours
>13 years: 40 mg every 12 hours

Asthma long-term therapy (alternative dosing by age):
<1 year: 10 mg every other day
1-4 years: 20 mg every other day
5-13 years: 30 mg every other day
>13 years: 40 mg every other day

Nephrotic syndrome:
Initial (first 3 episodes): 2 mg/kg/day **or** 60 mg/m²/day (maximum: 80 mg/day) in divided doses 3-4 times/day until urine is protein free for 3 consecutive days (maximum: 28 days); followed by 1-1.5 mg/kg/dose **or** 40 mg/m²/dose given every other day for 4 weeks

Maintenance dose (long-term maintenance dose for frequent relapses): 0.5-1 mg/kg/dose given every other day for 3-6 months

Children and Adults: Physiologic replacement: 4-5 mg/m²/day

Children ≥5 years and Adults: Asthma:

Moderate persistent: Inhaled corticosteroid (medium dose) or inhaled corticosteroid (low-medium dose) with a long-acting bronchodilator

Severe persistent: Inhaled corticosteroid (high dose) and corticosteroid tablets or syrup long term: 2 mg/kg/day, generally not to exceed 60 mg/day

Adults:

Immunosuppression/chemotherapy adjunct: Range: 5-60 mg/day in divided doses 1-4 times/day

Allergic reaction (contact dermatitis):
Day 1: 30 mg divided as 10 mg before breakfast, 5 mg at lunch, 5 mg at dinner, 10 mg at bedtime
Day 2: 5 mg at breakfast, 5 mg at lunch, 5 mg at dinner, 10 mg at bedtime
Day 3: 5 mg 4 times/day (with meals and at bedtime)
Day 4: 5 mg 3 times/day (breakfast, lunch, bedtime)
Day 5: 5 mg 2 times/day (breakfast, bedtime)
Day 6: 5 mg before breakfast

Pneumocystis carinii pneumonia (PCP):
40 mg twice daily for 5 days **followed by**
40 mg once daily for 5 days **followed by**
20 mg once daily for 11 days or until antimicrobial regimen is completed

Thyrotoxicosis: Oral: 60 mg/day

Chemotherapy (refer to individual protocols): Oral: Range: 20 mg/day to 100 mg/m²/day

Rheumatoid arthritis: Oral: Use lowest possible daily dose (often ≤7.5 mg/day)

Idiopathic thrombocytopenia purpura (ITP): Oral: 60 mg daily for 4-6 weeks, gradually tapered over several weeks

Systemic lupus erythematosus (SLE): Oral:
Acute: 1-2 mg/kg/day in 2-3 divided doses
Maintenance: Reduce to lowest possible dose, usually <1 mg/kg/day as single dose (morning)

Elderly: Use the lowest effective dose

Dosing adjustment in hepatic impairment: Prednisone is inactive and must be metabolized by the liver to prednisolone. This conversion may be impaired in patients with liver disease, however, prednisolone levels are observed to be higher in patients with severe liver failure than in normal patients. Therefore, compensation for the inadequate conversion of prednisone to prednisolone occurs.

Dosing adjustment in hyperthyroidism: Prednisone dose may need to be increased to achieve adequate therapeutic effects

Hemodialysis: Supplemental dose is not necessary

Peritoneal dialysis: Supplemental dose is not necessary

Administration Administer with meals to decrease gastrointestinal upset

Monitoring Parameters Blood pressure, blood glucose, electrolytes

Patient Information Notify surgeon or dentist before surgical repair; may cause GI upset, take with food; notify prescriber if any sign of infection occurs; avoid abrupt withdrawal when on long-term therapy; do not discontinue or decrease drug without contacting physician, carry an identification card or bracelet advising that you are on steroids

Dosage Forms SOLN, oral: 1 mg/mL (5 mL, 120 mL, 500 mL). **SOLN, oral concentrate** (Prednisone Intensol™): 5 mg/mL (30 mL). **TAB:** 1 mg, 2.5 mg, 5 mg, 10 mg, 20 mg, 50 mg; (Deltasone®): 2.5 mg, 10 mg, 20 mg, 50 mg; (Sterapred®): 5 mg; (Sterapred® DS): 10 mg

Primaquine (PRIM a kween)

Related Information
Malaria Treatment on page 1464
Synonyms Primaquine Phosphate; Prymaccone
Therapeutic Category Aminoquinoline, Antimalarial; Antimalarial Agent
Use Treatment of malaria
Unlabeled/Investigational Use Prevention of malaria; treatment Pneumocystis carinii pneumonia
Pregnancy Risk Factor C
Contraindications Hypersensitivity to primaquine, similar alkaloids, or any component of the formulation; acutely ill patients who have a tendency to develop granulocytopenia (rheumatoid arthritis, SLE); patients receiving other drugs capable of depressing the bone marrow (eg, quinacrine and primaquine)
Warnings/Precautions Use with caution in patients with G6PD deficiency, NADH methemoglobin reductase deficiency; do not exceed recommended dosage
Common Adverse Reactions Frequency not defined.
Cardiovascular: Arrhythmias
Central nervous system: Headache
Dermatologic: Pruritus
Gastrointestinal: Abdominal pain, nausea, vomiting
Hematologic: Agranulocytosis, hemolytic anemia in G6PD deficiency, leukopenia, leukocytosis, methemoglobinemia in NADH-methemoglobin reductase-deficient individuals
Ocular: Interference with visual accommodation
Drug Interactions
Cytochrome P450 Effect: **Substrate** of CYP3A4 (major); **Inhibits** CYP1A2 (strong), 2D6 (weak), 3A4 (weak); **Induces** CYP1A2 (weak)
Increased Effect/Toxicity: Increased toxicity/levels with quinacrine.
Mechanism of Action Eliminates the primary tissue exoerythrocytic forms of P. falciparum; disrupts mitochondria and binds to DNA
Pharmacodynamics/Kinetics
Absorption: Well absorbed
Metabolism: Hepatic to carboxyprimaquine (active)
Half-life elimination: 3.7-9.6 hours
Time to peak, serum: 1-2 hours
Excretion: Urine (small amounts as unchanged drug)
Dosage Oral: Dosage expressed as mg of base (15 mg base = 26.3 mg primaquine phosphate) (Continued)

Primaquine *(Continued)*

Treatment of malaria (decrease risk of delayed primary attacks and prevent relapse):
  Children: 0.3 mg base/kg/day once daily for 14 days (not to exceed 15 mg/day) or 0.9 mg base/kg once weekly for 8 weeks not to exceed 45 mg base/week
  Adults: 15 mg/day (base) once daily for 14 days or 45 mg base once weekly for 8 weeks
  CDC treatment recommendations: Begin therapy during last 2 weeks of, or following a course of, suppression with chloroquine or a comparable drug
  Note: A second course (30 mg/day) for 14 days may be required in patients with relapse. Higher initial doses (30 mg/day) have also been used following exposure in S.E. Asia or Somalia.
Prevention of malaria (unlabeled use): Initiate prior to travel and continue for 7 days after departure from malaria-endemic area:
  Children: 0.5 mg/kg once daily
  Adults: 30 mg once daily
Pneumocystis carinii pneumonia (unlabeled use): Adults: 30 mg once daily for 21 days (in conjunction with clindamycin)
Administration Take with meals to decrease adverse GI effects. Drug has a bitter taste.
Monitoring Parameters Periodic CBC, visual color check of urine, glucose, electrolytes; if hemolysis suspected, monitor CBC, haptoglobin, peripheral smear, urinalysis dipstick for occult blood
Patient Information Take with meals to decrease adverse GI effects; drug has a bitter taste; report if darkening of urine occurs or if shortness of breath, weakness or skin discoloration (chocolate cyanosis) occurs; complete full course of therapy
Dosage Forms TAB: 26.3 mg

♦ **Primaquine Phosphate** *see Primaquine on page 1035*
♦ **Primatene® Mist [OTC]** *see Epinephrine on page 438*
♦ **Primaxin®** *see Imipenem and Cilastatin on page 653*

Primidone *(PRI mi done)*

Related Information
Anticonvulsants by Seizure Type *on page 1358*
Epilepsy *on page 1477*
U.S. Brand Names Mysoline®
Synonyms Desoxyphenobarbital; Primaclone
Therapeutic Category Anticonvulsant, Barbiturate; Barbiturate
Use Management of grand mal, psychomotor, and focal seizures
Unlabeled/Investigational Use Benign familial tremor (essential tremor)
Pregnancy Risk Factor D
Contraindications Hypersensitivity to primidone, phenobarbital, or any component of the formulation; porphyria; pregnancy
Warnings/Precautions Use with caution in patients with renal or hepatic impairment, pulmonary insufficiency; abrupt withdrawal may precipitate status epilepticus. Potential for drug dependency exists. Do not administer to patients in acute pain. Use caution in elderly, debilitated, or pediatric patients - may cause paradoxical responses. May cause CNS depression, which may impair physical or mental abilities. Patients must cautioned about performing tasks which require mental alertness (eg, operating machinery or driving). Effects with other sedative drugs or ethanol may be potentiated. Use with caution in patients with depression or suicidal tendencies, or in patients with a history of drug abuse. Tolerance or psychological and physical dependence may occur with prolonged use. Primidone's metabolite, phenobarbital, has been associated with cognitive deficits in children. Use with caution in patients with hypoadrenalism.
Common Adverse Reactions Frequency not defined.
  Central nervous system: Drowsiness, vertigo, ataxia, lethargy, behavior change, fatigue, hyperirritability
  Dermatologic: Rash
  Gastrointestinal: Nausea, vomiting, anorexia
  Genitourinary: Impotence
  Hematologic: Agranulocytopenia, agranulocytosis, anemia
  Ocular: Diplopia, nystagmus
Drug Interactions
  Cytochrome P450 Effect: Metabolized to phenobarbital; **Induces** CYP1A2 (strong), 2B6 (strong), 2C8/9 (strong), 3A4 (strong)
  Increased Effect/Toxicity: Central nervous system depression (and possible respiratory depression) may be increased when combined with other CNS depressants, benzodiazepines, valproic acid, chloramphenicol, or antidepressants. MAO inhibitors may prolong the effect of primidone.
  Decreased Effect: Primidone may induce the hepatic metabolism of many drugs due to enzyme induction, and may reduce the efficacy of beta-blockers, chloramphenicol, cimetidine, clozapine, corticosteroids, cyclosporine, disopyramide, doxycycline, ethosuximide, furosemide, griseofulvin, haloperidol, lamotrigine, methadone, nifedipine, oral contraceptives, phenothiazine, phenytoin, propafenone, quinidine, tacrolimus, TCAs, theophylline, warfarin, and verapamil.
Mechanism of Action Decreases neuron excitability, raises seizure threshold similar to phenobarbital; primidone has two active metabolites, phenobarbital and phenylethylmalonamide (PEMA); PEMA may enhance the activity of phenobarbital

Pharmacodynamics/Kinetics
Distribution: Adults: V_d: 2-3 L/kg
Protein binding: 99%
Metabolism: Hepatic to phenobarbital (active) and phenylethylmalonamide (PEMA)
Bioavailability: 60% to 80%
Half-life elimination (age dependent): Primidone: 10-12 hours; PEMA: 16 hours; Phenobarbital: 52-118 hours
Time to peak, serum: ~4 hours
Excretion: Urine (15% to 25% as unchanged drug and active metabolites)

Dosage Oral:
Children <8 years: Initial: 50-125 mg/day given at bedtime; increase by 50-125 mg/day increments every 3-7 days; usual dose: 10-25 mg/kg/day in divided doses 3-4 times/day
Children ≥8 years and Adults: Initial: 125-250 mg/day at bedtime; increase by 125-250 mg/day every 3-7 days; usual dose: 750-1500 mg/day in divided doses 3-4 times/day with maximum dosage of 2 g/day

Dosing interval in renal impairment:
Cl_{cr} 50-80 mL/minute: Administer every 8 hours
Cl_{cr} 10-50 mL/minute: Administer every 8-12 hours
Cl_{cr} <10 mL/minute: Administer every 12-24 hours
Hemodialysis: Moderately dialyzable (20% to 50%); administer dose postdialysis or administer supplemental 30% dose

Monitoring Parameters Serum primidone and phenobarbital concentration, CBC, neurological status. Due to CNS effects, monitor closely when initiating drug in elderly. Monitor CBC at 6-month intervals to compare with baseline obtained at start of therapy. Since elderly metabolize phenobarbital at a slower rate than younger adults, it is suggested to measure both primidone and phenobarbital levels together.

Reference Range Therapeutic: Children <5 years: 7-10 µg/mL (SI: 32-46 µmol/L); Adults: 5-12 µg/mL (SI: 23-55 µmol/L); toxic effects rarely present with levels <10 µg/mL (SI: 46 µmol/L) if phenobarbital concentrations are low. Dosage of primidone is adjusted with reference mostly to the phenobarbital level; Toxic: >15 µg/mL (SI: >69 µmol/L)

Patient Information May cause drowsiness, impair judgment and coordination; do not abruptly discontinue or change dosage without notifying prescriber; can take with food to avoid GI upset

Dosage Forms TAB: 50 mg, 250 mg

- ◆ **Primsol**® see Trimethoprim on page 1270
- ◆ **Principen**® see Ampicillin on page 95
- ◆ **Prinivil**® see Lisinopril on page 750
- ◆ **Prinzide**® see Lisinopril and Hydrochlorothiazide on page 751
- ◆ **Priscoline**® [DSC] see Tolazoline on page 1238
- ◆ **Privine**® [OTC] see Naphazoline on page 881
- ◆ **ProAmatine**® see Midodrine on page 838

Probenecid (proe BEN e sid)

Synonyms Benemid [DSC]

Therapeutic Category Uricosuric Agent

Use Prevention of gouty arthritis; hyperuricemia; prolongation of beta-lactam effect (ie, serum levels)

Pregnancy Risk Factor B

Contraindications Hypersensitivity to probenecid or any component of the formulation; high-dose aspirin therapy; moderate to severe renal impairment; children <2 years of age

Warnings/Precautions Use with caution in patients with peptic ulcer; use extreme caution in the use of probenecid with penicillin in patients with renal insufficiency; probenecid may not be effective in patients with a creatinine clearance <30-50 mL/minute; may cause exacerbation of acute gouty attack

Common Adverse Reactions Frequency not defined.
Cardiovascular: Flushing of face
Central nervous system: Headache, dizziness
Dermatologic: Rash, itching
Gastrointestinal: Anorexia, nausea, vomiting, sore gums
Genitourinary: Painful urination
Hematologic: Aplastic anemia, hemolytic anemia, leukopenia
Hepatic: Hepatic necrosis
Neuromuscular & skeletal: Gouty arthritis (acute)
Renal: Renal calculi, nephrotic syndrome, urate nephropathy
Miscellaneous: Anaphylaxis

Drug Interactions
Cytochrome P450 Effect: Inhibits CYP2C19 (weak)
Increased Effect/Toxicity: Increases methotrexate toxic potential. Probenecid increases the serum concentrations of quinolones and beta-lactams such as penicillins and cephalosporins. Also increases levels/toxicity of acyclovir, diflunisal, ketorolac, thiopental, benzodiazepines, dapsone, fluoroquinolones, methotrexate, NSAIDs, sulfonylureas, zidovudine.
Decreased Effect: Salicylates (high-dose) may decrease uricosuria. Decreased urinary levels of nitrofurantoin may decrease efficacy.

Mechanism of Action Competitively inhibits the reabsorption of uric acid at the proximal convoluted tubule, thereby promoting its excretion and reducing serum uric acid levels; (Continued)

Probenecid *(Continued)*

increases plasma levels of weak organic acids (penicillins, cephalosporins, or other beta-lactam antibiotics) by competitively inhibiting their renal tubular secretion

Pharmacodynamics/Kinetics

Onset of action: Effect on penicillin levels: 2 hours

Absorption: Rapid and complete

Metabolism: Hepatic

Half-life elimination (dose dependent): Normal renal function: 6-12 hours

Time to peak, serum: 2-4 hours

Excretion: Urine

Dosage Oral:

Children:

    <2 years: Not recommended

    2-14 years: Prolong penicillin serum levels: 25 mg/kg starting dose, then 40 mg/kg/day given 4 times/day

    Gonorrhea: <45 kg: 25 mg/kg x 1 (maximum: 1 g/dose) 30 minutes before penicillin, ampicillin or amoxicillin

Adults:

    Hyperuricemia with gout: 250 mg twice daily for one week; increase to 250-500 mg/day; may increase by 500 mg/month, if needed, to maximum of 2-3 g/day (dosages may be increased by 500 mg every 6 months if serum urate concentrations are controlled)

    Prolong penicillin serum levels: 500 mg 4 times/day

    Gonorrhea: 1 g 30 minutes before penicillin, ampicillin, procaine, or amoxicillin

    Pelvic inflammatory disease: Cefoxitin 2 g I.M. plus probenecid 1 g orally as a single dose

    Neurosyphilis: Aqueous procaine penicillin 2.4 million units/day I.M. plus probenecid 500 mg 4 times/day for 10-14 days

Dosing adjustment in renal impairment: Cl_{cr} <50 mL/minute: Avoid use

Administration Administer with food or antacids to minimize GI effects

Monitoring Parameters Uric acid, renal function, CBC

Patient Information Take with food or antacids; drink plenty of fluids to reduce the risk of uric acid stones; the frequency of acute gouty attacks may increase during the first 6-12 months of therapy; avoid taking large doses of aspirin or other salicylates

Dosage Forms TAB: 500 mg

♦ **Probenecid and Colchicine** *see Colchicine and Probenecid on page 311*

♦ **Probiotica® [OTC]** *see Lactobacillus on page 711*

Procainamide *(proe kane A mide)*

U.S. Brand Names Procanbid®; Pronestyl®; Pronestyl-SR®

Synonyms PCA; Procainamide Hydrochloride; Procaine Amide Hydrochloride

Therapeutic Category Antiarrhythmic Agent, Class I-A

Use Treatment of ventricular tachycardia (VT), premature ventricular contractions, paroxysmal atrial tachycardia (PSVT), and atrial fibrillation (AF); prevent recurrence of ventricular tachycardia, paroxysmal supraventricular tachycardia, atrial fibrillation or flutter

Unlabeled/Investigational Use ACLS guidelines:

Intermittent/recurrent VF or pulseless VT not responsive to earlier interventions

Monomorphic VT (EF >40%, no CHF)

Polymorphic VT with normal baseline QT interval

Wide complex tachycardia of unknown type (EF >40%, no CHF, patient stable)

Refractory paroxysmal SVT

Atrial fibrillation or flutter (EF >40%, no CHF) including pre-excitation syndrome

Pregnancy Risk Factor C

Contraindications Hypersensitivity to procaine, other ester-type local anesthetics, or any component of the formulation; complete heart block (except in patients with a functioning artificial pacemaker); second-degree AV block (without a functional pacemaker); various types of hemiblock (without a functional pacemaker); SLE; torsade de pointes; concurrent cisapride use; QT prolongation

Warnings/Precautions Use with caution in patients with marked AV conduction disturbances, myasthenia gravis, bundle-branch block, or severe cardiac glycoside intoxication, ventricular arrhythmias with impaired organic heart disease or coronary occlusion, CHF supraventricular tachyarrhythmias unless adequate measures are taken to prevent marked increases in ventricular rates; concurrent therapy with other class Ia drugs may accumulate in patients with renal or hepatic dysfunction; some tablets contain tartrazine; injection may contain bisulfite (allergens). Long-term administration leads to the development of a positive antinuclear antibody (ANA) test in 50% of patients which may result in a lupus erythematosus-like syndrome (in 20% to 30% of patients); discontinue procainamide with SLE symptoms and choose an alternative agent; elderly have reduced clearance and frequent drug interactions. Potentially fatal blood dyscrasias have occurred with therapeutic doses; close monitoring is recommended during the first 3 months of therapy.

Common Adverse Reactions >1%:

Cardiovascular: Hypotension (I.V., up to 5%)

Dermatologic: Rash

Gastrointestinal: Diarrhea (3% to 4%), nausea, vomiting, taste disorder, GI complaints (3% to 4%)

Drug Interactions
Cytochrome P450 Effect: Substrate of CYP2D6 (major)

Increased Effect/Toxicity: Amiodarone, cimetidine, ofloxacin (and potentially other renally eliminated quinolones), ranitidine, and trimethoprim increase procainamide and NAPA blood levels; consider reducing procainamide dosage by 25% with concurrent use. Cisapride and procainamide may increase the risk of malignant arrhythmia; concurrent use is contraindicated. Procainamide may potentiate neuromuscular blockade of neuromuscular-blocking agents. CYP2D6 inhibitors may increase the levels/effects of procainamide; example inhibitors include chlorpromazine, delavirdine, fluoxetine, miconazole, paroxetine, pergolide, quinidine, quinine, ritonavir, and ropinirole.

Drugs which may prolong the QT interval include amiodarone, amitriptyline, astemizole, bepridil, cisapride, disopyramide, erythromycin, haloperidol, imipramine, pimozide, quinidine, sotalol, mesoridazine, thioridazine, and some quinolone antibiotics (sparfloxacin, gatifloxacin, moxifloxacin); concurrent use may result in additional prolongation of the QT interval.

Mechanism of Action Decreases myocardial excitability and conduction velocity and may depress myocardial contractility, by increasing the electrical stimulation threshold of ventricle, His-Purkinje system and through direct cardiac effects

Pharmacodynamics/Kinetics
Onset of action: I.M. 10-30 minutes

Distribution: V_d: Children: 2.2 L/kg; Adults: 2 L/kg; Congestive heart failure or shock: Decreased V_d

Protein binding: 15% to 20%

Metabolism: Hepatic via acetylation to produce N-acetyl procainamide (NAPA) (active metabolite)

Bioavailability: Oral: 75% to 95%

Half-life elimination:
Procainamide (hepatic acetylator, phenotype, cardiac and renal function dependent):
Children: 1.7 hours; Adults: 2.5-4.7 hours; Anephric: 11 hours
NAPA (dependent upon renal function):
Children: 6 hours; Adults: 6-8 hours; Anephric: 42 hours

Time to peak, serum: Capsule: 45 minutes to 2.5 hours; I.M.: 15-60 minutes

Excretion: Urine (25% as NAPA)

Dosage Must be titrated to patient's response
Children:
Oral: 15-50 mg/kg/24 hours divided every 3-6 hours
I.M.: 50 mg/kg/24 hours divided into doses of $^1/_8$ to $^1/_4$ every 3-6 hours in divided doses until oral therapy is possible
I.V. (infusion requires use of an infusion pump):
Load: 3-6 mg/kg/dose over 5 minutes not to exceed 100 mg/dose; may repeat every 5-10 minutes to maximum of 15 mg/kg/load
Maintenance as continuous I.V. infusion: 20-80 mcg/kg/minute; maximum: 2 g/24 hours
Adults:
Oral: 250-500 mg/dose every 3-6 hours or 500 mg to 1 g every 6 hours extended release; usual dose: 50 mg/kg/24 hours; maximum: 4 g/24 hours (**Note:** Twice daily dosing approved for Procanbid®)
I.M.: 0.5-1 g every 4-8 hours until oral therapy is possible
I.V. (infusion requires use of an infusion pump): Loading dose: 15-18 mg/kg administered as slow infusion over 25-30 minutes or 100-200 mg/dose repeated every 5 minutes as needed to a total dose of 1 g; maintenance dose: 1-4 mg/minute by continuous infusion
Infusion rate: **2 g/250 mL** D_5W/NS (I.V. infusion requires use of an infusion pump):
1 mg/minute: 7.5 mL/hour
2 mg/minute: 15 mL/hour
3 mg/minute: 22.5 mL/hour
4 mg/minute: 30 mL/hour
5 mg/minute: 37.5 mL/hour
6 mg/minute: 45 mL/hour
Intermittent/recurrent VF or pulseless VT:
Initial: 20-30 mg/minute (maximum: 50 mg/minute if necessary), up to a total of 17 mg/kg. ACLS guidelines: I.V.: Infuse 20 mg/minute until arrhythmia is controlled, hypotension occurs, QRS complex widens by 50% of its original width, or total of 17 mg/kg is given. **Note:** Reduce to 12 mg/kg in setting of cardiac or renal dysfunction
I.V. maintenance infusion: 1-4 mg/minute; monitor levels and do not exceed 3 mg/minute for >24 hours in adults with renal failure.

Dosing interval in renal impairment:
Cl_{cr} 10-50 mL/minute: Administer every 6-12 hours.
Cl_{cr} <10 mL/minute: Administer every 8-24 hours.
Dialysis:
Procainamide: Moderately hemodialyzable (20% to 50%): 200 mg supplemental dose posthemodialysis is recommended.
N-acetylprocainamide: Not dialyzable (0% to 5%)
Procainamide/N-acetylprocainamide: Not peritoneal dialyzable (0% to 5%)
Procainamide/N-acetylprocainamide: Replace by blood level during continuous arteriovenous or venovenous hemofiltration

Dosing adjustment in hepatic impairment: Reduce dose by 50%.
(Continued)

Procainamide *(Continued)*

Administration Dilute I.V. with D₅W; maximum rate: 50 mg/minute; administer around-the-clock rather than 4 times/day to promote less variation in peak and trough serum levels. Do **not** crush or chew extended release drug products.

Monitoring Parameters ECG, blood pressure, CBC with differential, platelet count; cardiac monitor and blood pressure monitor required during I.V. administration; blood levels in patients with renal failure or receiving constant infusion >3 mg/minute for longer than 24 hours

Reference Range

Timing of serum samples: Draw trough just before next oral dose; draw 6-12 hours after I.V. infusion has started; half-life is 2.5-5 hours

Therapeutic levels: Procainamide: 4-10 µg/mL; NAPA 15-25 µg/mL; Combined: 10-30 µg/mL

Toxic concentration: Procainamide: >10-12 µg/mL

Patient Information Do not discontinue therapy unless instructed by prescriber; report soreness of mouth, throat or gums, unexplained fever, or symptoms of upper respiratory tract infection. Do not chew extended release tablets; some extended release tablets contain a wax core that slowly releases the drug; when this process is complete, the empty, nonabsorbable wax core is eliminated and may be visible in feces.

Dosage Forms CAP: 250 mg, 500 mg; (Pronestyl®): 250 mg. **INJ, solution:** 100 mg/mL (10 mL), 500 mg/mL (2 mL); (Pronestyl®): 100 mg/mL (10 mL). **TAB** (Pronestyl®): 250 mg, 375 mg, 500 mg. **TAB, extended release:** 750 mg, 1000 mg; (Procanbid®): 500 mg, 1000 mg; (Pronestyl-SR®): 500 mg

♦ **Procainamide Hydrochloride** *see Procainamide on page 1038*

Procaine *(PROE kane)*

U.S. Brand Names Novocain®

Synonyms Procaine Hydrochloride

Therapeutic Category Local Anesthetic, Injectable

Use Produces spinal anesthesia and epidural and peripheral nerve block by injection and infiltration methods

Pregnancy Risk Factor C

Contraindications Hypersensitivity to procaine, PABA, parabens, other ester local anesthetics, or any component of the formulation

Warnings/Precautions Patients with cardiac diseases, hyperthyroidism, or other endocrine diseases may be more susceptible to toxic effects of local anesthetics; some preparations contain metabisulfite

Common Adverse Reactions 1% to 10%: Local: Burning sensation at site of injection, tissue irritation, pain at injection site

Drug Interactions

Decreased Effect: Decreased effect of sulfonamides with the PABA metabolite of procaine, chloroprocaine, and tetracaine. Decreased/increased effect of vasopressors, ergot alkaloids, and MAO inhibitors on blood pressure when using anesthetic solutions with a vasoconstrictor.

Mechanism of Action Blocks both the initiation and conduction of nerve impulses by decreasing the neuronal membrane's permeability to sodium ions, which results in inhibition of depolarization with resultant blockade of conduction

Pharmacodynamics/Kinetics

Onset of action: 2-5 minutes

Duration (patient, type of block, concentration, and method of anesthesia dependent): 0.5-1.5 hours

Metabolism: Rapidly hydrolyzed by plasma enzymes to para-aminobenzoic acid and diethylaminoethanol (80% conjugated before elimination)

Half-life elimination: 7.7 minutes

Excretion: Urine (as metabolites and some unchanged drug)

Dosage Dose varies with procedure, desired depth, and duration of anesthesia, desired muscle relaxation, vascularity of tissues, physical condition, and age of patient

Dosage Forms INJ, solution: 1% (30 mL), 2% (30 mL); (Novocain®): 1% [10 mg/mL] (2 mL, 6 mL, 30 mL), 2% [20 mg/mL] (30 mL), 10% (2 mL)

♦ **Procaine Amide Hydrochloride** *see Procainamide on page 1038*
♦ **Procaine Benzylpenicillin** *see Penicillin G Procaine on page 974*
♦ **Procaine Hydrochloride** *see Procaine on page 1040*
♦ **Procaine Penicillin G** *see Penicillin G Procaine on page 974*
♦ **Procanbid®** *see Procainamide on page 1038*

Procarbazine *(proe KAR ba zeen)*

U.S. Brand Names Matulane®

Synonyms Benzmethyzin; N-Methylhydrazine; NSC-77213; Procarbazine Hydrochloride

Therapeutic Category Antineoplastic Agent, Alkylating Agent

Use Treatment of Hodgkin's disease

Unlabeled/Investigational Use Treatment of non-Hodgkin's lymphoma, brain tumors, melanoma, lung cancer, multiple myeloma

Pregnancy Risk Factor D

Contraindications Hypersensitivity to procarbazine or any component of the formulation; pre-existing bone marrow aplasia; ethanol ingestion; pregnancy

Warnings/Precautions The U.S. Food and Drug Administration (FDA) currently recommends that procedures for proper handling and disposal of antineoplastic agents be considered; use with caution in patients with pre-existing renal or hepatic impairment; procarbazine possesses MAO inhibitor activity. Procarbazine is a carcinogen which may cause acute leukemia; procarbazine may cause infertility.

Common Adverse Reactions Frequency not defined.

Central nervous system: Reports of neurotoxicity with procarbazine generally originate from early usage with single agent oral (continuous) or I.V. dosing; CNS depression is commonly reported to be additive with other CNS depressants

Hematologic: Myelosuppression, hemolysis in patients with G6PD deficiency

Gastrointestinal: Nausea and vomiting (60% to 90%); increasing the dose in a stepwise fashion over several days may minimize this

Genitourinary: Reproductive dysfunction >10% (in animals, hormone treatment has prevented azoospermia)

Respiratory: Pulmonary toxicity (<1%); the most commonly reported pulmonary toxicity is a hypersensitivity pneumonitis which responds to steroids and discontinuation of the drug. At least one report of persistent pulmonary fibrosis has been reported, however, a higher incidence (18%) of pulmonary toxicity (fibrosis) was reported when procarbazine was given prior to BCNU (BCNU alone does cause pulmonary fibrosis).

Miscellaneous: Second malignancies (cumulative incidence 2% to 15% reported with MOPP combination therapy)

Drug Interactions

Increased Effect/Toxicity: Procarbazine exhibits weak MAO inhibitor activity. Foods containing high amounts of tyramine should, therefore, be avoided. When an MAO inhibitor is given with food high in tyramine, hypertensive crisis, intracranial bleeding, and headache have been reported.

Sympathomimetic amines (epinephrine and amphetamines) and antidepressants (tricyclics) should be used cautiously with procarbazine. Barbiturates, narcotics, phenothiazines, and other CNS depressants can cause somnolence, ataxia, and other symptoms of CNS depression. Ethanol has caused a disulfiram-like reaction with procarbazine. May result in headache, respiratory difficulties, nausea, vomiting, sweating, thirst, hypotension, and flushing.

Mechanism of Action Mechanism of action is not clear, methylating of nucleic acids; inhibits DNA, RNA, and protein synthesis; may damage DNA directly and suppresses mitosis; metabolic activation required by host

Pharmacodynamics/Kinetics

Absorption: Rapid and complete

Distribution: Crosses blood-brain barrier; distributes into CSF

Metabolism: Hepatic and renal

Half-life elimination: 1 hour

Excretion: Urine and respiratory tract (<5% as unchanged drug, 70% as metabolites)

Dosage Refer to individual protocols. Dose based on patient's ideal weight if the patient is obese or has abnormal fluid retention. Oral (may be given as a single daily dose or in 2-3 divided doses):

Children:

BMT aplastic anemia conditioning regimen: 12.5 mg/kg/dose every other day for 4 doses

Hodgkin's disease: MOPP/IC-MOPP regimens: 100 mg/m²/day for 14 days and repeated every 4 weeks

Neuroblastoma and medulloblastoma: Doses as high as 100-200 mg/m²/day once daily have been used

Adults: Initial: 2-4 mg/kg/day in single or divided doses for 7 days then increase dose to 4-6 mg/kg/day until response is obtained or leukocyte count decreased <4000/mm³ or the platelet count decreased <100,000/mm³; maintenance: 1-2 mg/kg/day

Dosing in renal/hepatic impairment: Use with caution, may result in increased toxicity; decrease dose if serum creatinine >2 mg/dL or total bilirubin >3 mg/dL

Monitoring Parameters CBC with differential, platelet and reticulocyte count, urinalysis, liver function test, renal function test.

Patient Information Take as directed. Maintain adequate hydration (2-3 L/day of fluids unless instructed to restrict fluid intake). Avoid aspirin and aspirin-containing substances; use alcohol cautiously, may cause acute disulfiram-like reaction - flushing, headache, acute vomiting, chest and/or abdominal pain; avoid tyramine-containing foods (aged cheese, chocolate, pickles, aged meat, wine, etc). You may experience mental depression, nervousness, insomnia, nightmares, dizziness, confusion, or lethargy (use caution when driving or engaging in tasks that require alertness until response to drug is known); photosensitivity (use sunscreen, wear protective clothing and eyewear, and avoid direct sunlight). You may experience rash or hair loss (reversible), loss of libido, increased sensitivity to infection (avoid crowds and infected persons). Report persistent fever, chills, sore throat; unusual bleeding; blood in urine, stool (black stool), or vomitus; unresolved depression; mania; hallucinations; nightmares; disorientation; seizures; chest pain or palpitations; or difficulty breathing.

Dosage Forms CAP: 50 mg

♦ **Procarbazine Hydrochloride** *see* Procarbazine *on page 1040*

♦ **Procardia®** *see* NIFEdipine *on page 903*

♦ **Procardia XL®** *see* NIFEdipine *on page 903*

♦ **Procetofene** *see* Fenofibrate *on page 511*

♦ **Prochieve™** *see* Progesterone *on page 1044*

Prochlorperazine (proe klor PER a zeen)

U.S. Brand Names Compazine®; Compro™

Synonyms Chlormeprazine; Prochlorperazine Edisylate; Prochlorperazine Maleate

Therapeutic Category Antiemetic; Antipsychotic Agent, Phenothiazine; Antipsychotic Agent, Phenothiazine, Piperazine; Phenothiazine Derivative

Use Management of nausea and vomiting; psychosis; anxiety

Unlabeled/Investigational Use Behavioral syndromes in dementia

Pregnancy Risk Factor C

Contraindications Hypersensitivity to prochlorperazine or any component of the formulation (cross-reactivity between phenothiazines may occur); severe CNS depression; coma; should not be used in children <2 years of age or <10 kg

Warnings/Precautions Injection contains sulfites which may cause allergic reactions; may impair ability to perform hazardous tasks requiring mental alertness or physical coordination; some products contain tartrazine dye, avoid use in sensitive individuals

Tardive dyskinesia: Prevalence rate may be 40% in elderly; development of the syndrome and the irreversible nature are proportional to duration and total cumulative dose over time. May be reversible if diagnosed early in therapy.

High incidence of extrapyramidal symptoms, especially in children or the elderly, so reserve use in children <5 years of age to those who are unresponsive to other antiemetics; incidence of extrapyramidal symptoms is increased with acute illnesses such as chicken pox, measles, CNS infections, gastroenteritis, and dehydration

Drug-induced **Parkinson's syndrome** occurs often. **Akathisia** is the most common extrapyramidal symptom in elderly.

Increased confusion, memory loss, psychotic behavior, and agitation frequently occur as a consequence of anticholinergic effects

Lowers seizure threshold, use cautiously in patients with seizure history

Orthostatic hypotension is due to alpha-receptor blockade, the elderly are at greater risk for orthostatic hypotension

Antipsychotic associated sedation in nonpsychotic patients is extremely unpleasant due to feelings of depersonalization, derealization, and dysphoria

Life-threatening arrhythmias have occurred at therapeutic doses of antipsychotics

Some products contain tartrazine dye.

Common Adverse Reactions Frequency not defined.

Cardiovascular: Hypotension, orthostatic hypotension, hypertension, tachycardia, bradycardia, dizziness, cardiac arrest

Central nervous system: Extrapyramidal signs (pseudoparkinsonism, akathisia, dystonias, tardive dyskinesia), dizziness, cerebral edema, seizures, headache, drowsiness, paradoxical excitement, restlessness, hyperactivity, insomnia, neuroleptic malignant syndrome (NMS), impairment of temperature regulation

Dermatologic: Increased sensitivity to sun, rash, discoloration of skin (blue-gray)

Endocrine & metabolic: Hypoglycemia, hyperglycemia, galactorrhea, lactation, breast enlargement, gynecomastia, menstrual irregularity, amenorrhea, SIADH, changes in libido

Gastrointestinal: Constipation, weight gain, vomiting, stomach pain, nausea, xerostomia, salivation, diarrhea, anorexia, ileus

Genitourinary: Difficulty in urination, ejaculatory disturbances, incontinence, polyuria, ejaculating dysfunction, priapism

Hematologic: Agranulocytosis, leukopenia, eosinophilia, hemolytic anemia, thrombocytopenic purpura, pancytopenia

Hepatic: Cholestatic jaundice, hepatotoxicity

Neuromuscular & skeletal: Tremor

Ocular: Pigmentary retinopathy, blurred vision, cornea and lens changes

Respiratory: Nasal congestion

Miscellaneous: Diaphoresis

Drug Interactions

Increased Effect/Toxicity: Chloroquine, propranolol, and sulfadoxine-pyrimethamine may increase prochlorperazine concentrations. Concurrent use with TCA may produce increased toxicity or altered therapeutic response. Prochlorperazine plus lithium may rarely produce neurotoxicity. Prochlorperazine may produce additive CNS depressant effects with CNS depressants (ethanol, narcotics). Metoclopramide may increase risk of extrapyramidal symptoms (EPS).

Decreased Effect: Barbiturates and carbamazepine may increase the metabolism of prochlorperazine, lowering its serum levels. Benztropine (and other anticholinergics) may inhibit the therapeutic response to prochlorperazine. Antipsychotics such as prochlorperazine inhibit the ability of bromocriptine to lower serum prolactin concentrations. The antihypertensive effects of guanethidine and guanadrel may be inhibited by prochlorperazine. Prochlorperazine may inhibit the antiparkinsonian effect of levodopa. Prochlorperazine (and possibly other low potency antipsychotics) may reverse the pressor effects of epinephrine.

Mechanism of Action Blocks postsynaptic mesolimbic dopaminergic D_1 and D_2 receptors in the brain, including the medullary chemoreceptor trigger zone; exhibits a strong alpha-adrenergic and anticholinergic blocking effect and depresses the release of hypothalamic and hypophyseal hormones; believed to depress the reticular activating system, thus affecting basal metabolism, body temperature, wakefulness, vasomotor tone and emesis

Pharmacodynamics/Kinetics

Onset of action: Oral: 30-40 minutes; I.M.: 10-20 minutes; Rectal: ~60 minutes

Duration: I.M., oral extended-release: 12 hours; Rectal, immediate release: 3-4 hours

Distribution: V_d: 1400-1548 L; crosses placenta; enters breast milk

Metabolism: Primarily hepatic; N-desmethyl prochlorperazine (major active metabolite)
Bioavailability: Oral: 12.5%
Half-life elimination: Oral: 3-5 hours; I.V.: ~7 hours

Dosage
Antiemetic: Children (not recommended in children <10 kg or <2 years):
Oral, rectal: >10 kg: 0.4 mg/kg/24 hours in 3-4 divided doses; **or**
9-14 kg: 2.5 mg every 12-24 hours as needed; maximum: 7.5 mg/day
14-18 kg: 2.5 mg every 8-12 hours as needed; maximum: 10 mg/day
18-39 kg: 2.5 mg every 8 hours or 5 mg every 12 hours as needed; maximum: 15 mg/day
I.M.: 0.1-0.15 mg/kg/dose; usual: 0.13 mg/kg/dose; change to oral as soon as possible
Antiemetic: Adults:
Oral:
Tablet: 5-10 mg 3-4 times/day; usual maximum: 40 mg/day
Capsule, sustained action: 15 mg upon arising or 10 mg every 12 hours
I.M.: 5-10 mg every 3-4 hours; usual maximum: 40 mg/day
I.V.: 2.5-10 mg; maximum 10 mg/dose or 40 mg/day; may repeat dose every 3-4 hours as needed
Rectal: 25 mg twice daily
Surgical nausea/vomiting: Adults:
I.M.: 5-10 mg 1-2 hours before induction; may repeat once if necessary
I.V.: 5-10 mg 15-30 minutes before induction; may repeat once if necessary
Antipsychotic:
Children 2-12 years (not recommended in children <10 kg or <2 years):
Oral, rectal: 2.5 mg 2-3 times/day; increase dosage as needed to maximum daily dose of 20 mg for 2-5 years and 25 mg for 6-12 years
I.M.: 0.13 mg/kg/dose; change to oral as soon as possible
Adults:
Oral: 5-10 mg 3-4 times/day; doses up to 150 mg/day may be required in some patients for treatment of severe disturbances
I.M.: 10-20 mg every 4-6 hours may be required in some patients for treatment of severe disturbances; change to oral as soon as possible
Nonpsychotic anxiety: Oral: Adults: Usual dose: 15-20 mg/day in divided doses; do not give doses >20 mg/day or for longer than 12 weeks
Elderly: Behavioral symptoms associated with dementia (unlabeled use): Initial: 2.5-5 mg 1-2 times/day; increase dose at 4- to 7-day intervals by 2.5-5 mg/day; increase dosing intervals (twice daily, 3 times/day, etc) as necessary to control response or side effects; maximum daily dose should probably not exceed 75 mg in elderly; gradual increases (titration) may prevent some side effects or decrease their severity
Hemodialysis: Not dialyzable (0% to 5%)

Administration May be administered orally, I.M., or I.V.: I.V. doses should be given as a short (~30 minute) infusion or by slow (5-10 minutes) IVP to avoid orthostatic hypotension.

Monitoring Parameters Vital signs; lipid profile, fasting blood glucose/Hgb A_{1c}; BMI; mental status, abnormal involuntary movement scale (AIMS); periodic ophthalmic exams (if chronically used); extrapyramidal symptoms (EPS)

Patient Information May cause drowsiness, impair judgment and coordination; may cause photosensitivity; avoid excessive sunlight; report involuntary movements or feelings of restlessness

Dosage Forms CAP, sustained release, as maleate (Compazine®) [DSC]: 10 mg, 15 mg **INJ, solution, as edisylate:** 5 mg/mL (2 mL); (Compazine®): 5 mg/mL (2 mL, 10 mL). **SUPP, rectal:** 2.5 mg (12s), 5 mg (12s), 25 mg (12s); (Compazine®): 2.5 mg (12s), 5 mg (12s), 25 mg (12s); (Compro™): 25 mg (12s). **SYR, as edisylate** (Compazine®): 5 mg/5 mL (120 mL). **TAB, as maleate** (Compazine®): 5 mg, 10 mg

♦ **Prochlorperazine Edisylate** see Prochlorperazine on page 1042
♦ **Prochlorperazine Maleate** see Prochlorperazine on page 1042
♦ **Procrit®** see Epoetin Alfa on page 442
♦ **Proctocort®** see Hydrocortisone on page 632
♦ **ProctoCream® HC** see Hydrocortisone on page 632
♦ **Proctofene** see Fenofibrate on page 511
♦ **ProctoFoam®-HC** see Pramoxine and Hydrocortisone on page 1028
♦ **Proctosol-HC®** see Hydrocortisone on page 632

Procyclidine (proe SYE kli deen)
U.S. Brand Names Kemadrin®
Synonyms Procyclidine Hydrochloride
Therapeutic Category Anticholinergic Agent; Anti-Parkinson's Agent, Anticholinergic
Use Relieves symptoms of parkinsonian syndrome and drug-induced extrapyramidal symptoms
Pregnancy Risk Factor C
Contraindications Hypersensitivity to procyclidine or any component of the formulation; angle-closure glaucoma; myasthenia gravis; safe use in children not established
Warnings/Precautions Use with caution in hot weather or during exercise. Elderly patients frequently develop increased sensitivity and require strict dosage regulation - side effects may be more severe in elderly patients with atherosclerotic changes. Use with caution in patients with tachycardia, cardiac arrhythmias, hypertension, hypotension, prostatic hyperplasia (especially in the elderly) or any tendency toward urinary retention, liver or kidney disorders and (Continued)

Procyclidine (Continued)

obstructive disease of the GI or GU tract. When given in large doses or to susceptible patients, may cause weakness and inability to move particular muscle groups.

Common Adverse Reactions Frequency not defined.

Cardiovascular: Tachycardia, palpitations

Central nervous system: Confusion, drowsiness, headache, loss of memory, fatigue, ataxia, giddiness, lightheadedness

Dermatologic: Dry skin, increased sensitivity to light, rash

Gastrointestinal: Constipation, xerostomia, dry throat, nausea, vomiting, epigastric distress

Genitourinary: Difficult urination

Neuromuscular & skeletal: Weakness

Ocular: Increased intraocular pain, blurred vision, mydriasis

Respiratory: Dry nose

Miscellaneous: Diaphoresis (decreased)

Drug Interactions

Increased Effect/Toxicity: Central and/or peripheral anticholinergic syndrome can occur when administered with amantadine, rimantadine, narcotic analgesics, phenothiazines and other antipsychotics (especially with high anticholinergic activity), tricyclic antidepressants, quinidine and some other antiarrhythmics, and antihistamines.

Decreased Effect: May increase gastric degradation of levodopa and decrease the amount of levodopa absorbed by delaying gastric emptying; the opposite may be true for digoxin. Therapeutic effects of cholinergic agents (tacrine, donepezil) and neuroleptics may be antagonized.

Mechanism of Action Thought to act by blocking excess acetylcholine at cerebral synapses; many of its effects are due to its pharmacologic similarities with atropine; it exerts an antispasmodic effect on smooth muscle, is a potent mydriatic; inhibits salivation

Pharmacodynamics/Kinetics

Onset of action: 30-40 minutes

Duration: 4-6 hours

Dosage Adults: Oral: 2.5 mg 3 times/day after meals; if tolerated, gradually increase dose, maximum of 20 mg/day if necessary

Dosing adjustment in hepatic impairment: Decrease dose to a twice daily dosing regimen

Administration Should be administered after meals to minimize stomach upset.

Monitoring Parameters Symptoms of EPS or Parkinson's disease, pulse, anticholinergic effects (ie, CNS, bowel and bladder function)

Patient Information Take after meals; do not discontinue drug abruptly; report adverse GI effects, fever or heat intolerance; may cause drowsiness; avoid alcohol; adequate fluid intake or sugar free gum or hard candy may help dry mouth; adequate fluid and exercise may help constipation

Dosage Forms TAB: 5 mg

♦ **Procyclidine Hydrochloride** see Procyclidine on page 1043

♦ **Prodium®** [OTC] see Phenazopyridine on page 987

♦ **Profasi®** [DSC] see Chorionic Gonadotropin (Human) on page 272

♦ **Profilnine® SD** see Factor IX Complex (Human) on page 504

♦ **Progestasert®** see Progesterone on page 1044

Progesterone (proe JES ter one)

U.S. Brand Names Crinone®; Prochieve™; Progestasert®; Prometrium®

Synonyms Pregnenedione; Progestin

Therapeutic Category Progestin

Use

Oral: Prevention of endometrial hyperplasia in nonhysterectomized, postmenopausal women who are receiving conjugated estrogen tablets; secondary amenorrhea

I.M.: Amenorrhea; abnormal uterine bleeding due to hormonal imbalance

Intrauterine device (IUD): Contraception in women who have had at least one child, are in a stable and mutually-monogamous relationship, and have no history of pelvic inflammatory disease; amenorrhea; functional uterine bleeding

Intravaginal gel: Part of assisted reproductive technology (ART) for infertile women with progesterone deficiency; secondary amenorrhea

Pregnancy Risk Factor B (Prometrium®, per manufacturer); none established for gel (Crinone®), injection (contraindicated), or intrauterine device (contraindicated)

Contraindications Hypersensitivity to progesterone or any component of the formulation; thrombophlebitis; undiagnosed vaginal bleeding; carcinoma of the breast; cerebral apoplexy; severe liver dysfunction; missed abortion; diagnostic test for pregnancy; pregnancy (see Pregnancy Risk Factor)

Capsule: Contains peanut oil; contraindicated in patients with allergy to peanuts

IUD: Should also not be used in patients with current or history of ectopic pregnancy, pelvic inflammatory disease, sexually-transmitted disease, postpartum endometritis, incomplete involution of uterus; vaginitis or cervicitis, genital actinomycosis, uterus <6 cm or >10 cm, cervical cancer, or conditions associated with increased susceptibility to infection.

Warnings/Precautions Use with caution in patients with impaired liver function, depression, diabetes, and epilepsy. Except when used as indicated in ART, use of any progestin during the first 4 months of pregnancy is not recommended. Monitor closely for loss of vision, proptosis, diplopia, migraine, and signs or symptoms of embolic disorders. Not a progestin of choice in the elderly for hormonal cycling. May cause some degree of fluid retention, use with caution in conditions which may be aggravated by this factor, including CHF, renal dysfunction, epilepsy, migraine, or asthma. Patients should be warned that progesterone may cause transient dizziness or drowsiness during initial therapy.

Use of the IUD is associated with increased risk of ectopic pregnancy if pregnancy occurs. In addition, women should be informed that the IUD does not protect against HIV infection, pelvic inflammatory disease, or other sexually-transmitted diseases.

Common Adverse Reactions

Intrauterine device:
Cardiovascular: Bradycardia and syncope (secondary to insertion)

Central nervous system: Pain

Endocrine & metabolic: Amenorrhea, delayed menses, dysmenorrhea, ectopic pregnancy, endometritis, pregnancy, septic abortion, prolonged menstrual flow, spontaneous abortion, spotting

Genitourinary: Cervical erosion, dyspareunia, leukorrhea, pelvic infection, tubal damage, tubo-ovarian abscess, vaginitis

Hematologic: Anemia

Local: Embedment or fragmentation of the IUD, perforation of uterus and cervix

Neuromuscular & skeletal: Backache

Miscellaneous: Abscess formation and erosion of adjacent area, abdominal adhesions, complete or partial IUD expulsion, congenital anomalies, cramping, cystic masses in the pelvis, death, difficult removal, fetal damage, hormonal imbalance, intestinal penetration, intestinal obstruction, local inflammatory reaction, loss of fertility, peritonitis, septicemia

Injection (I.M.):
Cardiovascular: Edema

Central nervous system: Depression, fever, insomnia, somnolence

Dermatologic: Acne, allergic rash (rare), alopecia, hirsutism, pruritus, rash, urticaria

Endocrine & metabolic: Amenorrhea, breakthrough bleeding, breast tenderness, galactorrhea, menstrual flow changes, spotting

Gastrointestinal: Nausea, weight gain, weight loss

Genitourinary: Cervical erosion changes, cervical secretion changes

Hepatic: Cholestatic jaundice

Local: Pain at the injection site

Miscellaneous: Anaphylactoid reactions

Oral capsule:
>10%:
Central nervous system: Dizziness (16%)

Endocrine & metabolic: Breast pain (11%)

5% to 10%:
Central nervous system: Headache (10%), fatigue (7%), emotional lability (6%), irritability (5%)

Gastrointestinal: Abdominal pain (10%), abdominal distention (6%)

Neuromuscular & skeletal: Musculoskeletal pain (6%)

Respiratory: Upper respiratory tract infection (5%)

Miscellaneous: Viral infection (7%)

Drug Interactions

Cytochrome P450 Effect: Substrate of CYP1A2 (minor), 2A6 (minor), 2C8/9 (minor), 2C19 (major), 2D6 (minor), 3A4 (major); **Inhibits** CYP2C8/9 (weak), 2C19 (weak), 3A4 (weak)

Increased Effect/Toxicity: Ketoconazole may increase the bioavailability of progesterone. Progesterone may increase concentrations of estrogenic compounds during concurrent therapy with conjugated estrogens.

Decreased Effect: CYP2C19 inducers may decrease the levels/effects of progesterone; example inducers include aminoglutethimide, carbamazepine, phenytoin, and rifampin. Aminoglutethimide may decrease effect by increasing hepatic metabolism.

Mechanism of Action Natural steroid hormone that induces secretory changes in the endometrium, promotes mammary gland development, relaxes uterine smooth muscle, blocks follicular maturation and ovulation, and maintains pregnancy

Pharmacodynamics/Kinetics
Duration: 24 hours

Protein binding: 96% to 99%

Metabolism: Hepatic

Half-life elimination: 5 minutes

Time to peak: Oral: 1.5-2.3 hours

Excretion: Urine (50% to 60%); feces (~10%)

Dosage
I.M.: Adults: Female:

Amenorrhea: 5-10 mg/day for 6-8 consecutive days

Functional uterine bleeding: 5-10 mg/day for 6 doses

IUD: Adults: Female: Contraception: Insert a single system into the uterine cavity; contraceptive effectiveness is retained for 1 year and system must be replaced 1 year after insertion

Oral: Adults: Female:

Prevention of endometrial hyperplasia (in postmenopausal women with a uterus who are receiving daily conjugated estrogen tablets): 200 mg as a single daily dose every evening for 12 days sequentially per 28-day cycle

Amenorrhea: 400 mg every evening for 10 days

(Continued)

Progesterone *(Continued)*

Intravaginal gel: Adults: Female:
ART in women who require progesterone supplementation: 90 mg (8% gel) once daily; if pregnancy occurs, may continue treatment for up to 10-12 weeks
ART in women with partial or complete ovarian failure: 90 mg (8% gel) intravaginally twice daily; if pregnancy occurs, may continue up to 10-12 weeks
Secondary amenorrhea: 45 mg (4% gel) intravaginally every other day for up to 6 doses; women who fail to respond may be increased to 90 mg (8% gel) every other day for up to 6 doses

Administration
I.M.: Administer deep I.M. only
Intravaginal: Vaginal gel: (A small amount of gel will remain in the applicator following insertion): Administer into the vagina directly from sealed applicator. Remove applicator from wrapper; holding applicator by thickest end, shake down to move contents to thin end; while holding applicator by flat section of thick end, twist off tab; gently insert into vagina and squeeze thick end of applicator.
For use at altitudes above 2500 feet: Remove applicator from wrapper; hold applicator on both sides of bubble in the thick end; using a lancet, make a single puncture in the bubble to relieve air pressure; holding applicator by thickest end, shake down to move contents to thin end; while holding applicator by flat section of thick end, twist off tab; gently insert into vagina and squeeze thick end of applicator.

Monitoring Parameters Before starting therapy, a physical exam including the breasts and pelvis are recommended, also a Pap smear; signs or symptoms of depression, glucose in diabetics

Patient Information Notify prescriber if sudden loss of vision or migraine headache occur or if you suspect you may have become pregnant; may cause photosensitivity, wear protective clothing or sunscreen

Dosage Forms CAP (Prometrium®): 100 mg, 200 mg. **GEL, vaginal** (Crinone®, Prochieve™): 4% (45 mg); 8% (90 mg). **INJ, oil:** 50 mg/mL (10 mL). **INTRAUTERINE SYSTEM** (Progestasert®): 38 mg

+ **Progestin** *see Progesterone on page 1044*
+ **Proglycem®** *see Diazoxide on page 366*
+ **Prograf®** *see Tacrolimus on page 1181*
+ **Proguanil and Atovaquone** *see Atovaquone and Proguanil on page 131*
+ **Proleukin®** *see Aldesleukin on page 47*
+ **Prolex-D** *see Guaifenesin and Phenylephrine on page 605*
+ **Prolixin®** *see Fluphenazine on page 541*
+ **Prolixin Decanoate®** *see Fluphenazine on page 541*
+ **Prolixin Enanthate® [DSC]** *see Fluphenazine on page 541*
+ **Proloprim®** *see Trimethoprim on page 1270*

Promethazine *(proe METH a zeen)*

U.S. Brand Names Phenergan®
Synonyms Promethazine Hydrochloride
Therapeutic Category Antiemetic; Antihistamine; Phenothiazine Derivative; Sedative
Use Symptomatic treatment of various allergic conditions; antiemetic; motion sickness; sedative; postoperative pain (adjunctive therapy); anesthetic (adjunctive therapy); anaphylactic reactions (adjunctive therapy)
Pregnancy Risk Factor C
Contraindications Hypersensitivity to promethazine or any component of the formulation (cross-reactivity between phenothiazines may occur); severe CNS depression; coma; intra-arterial or subcutaneous injection
Warnings/Precautions Do not administer S.C. or intra-arterially, necrotic lesions may occur; injection may contain sulfites which may cause allergic reactions in some patients; use with caution in patients with cardiovascular disease, impaired liver function, asthma, sleep apnea; May lower seizure threshold; use caution in persons with seizure disorders or in persons using narcotics or local anesthetics which may also affect seizure threshold. Rapid I.V. administration may produce a transient fall in blood pressure, rate of administration should not exceed 25 mg/minute; slow I.V. administration may produce a slightly elevated blood pressure. Because promethazine is a phenothiazine (and can, therefore, cause side effects such as extrapyramidal symptoms), it is not considered an antihistamine of choice in the elderly.
Common Adverse Reactions Frequency not defined.
Cardiovascular: Bradycardia, hypertension, postural hypotension, tachycardia, nonspecific QT changes
Central nervous system: Catatonic states, confusion, disorientation, dizziness, drowsiness, dystonias, euphoria, excitation, extrapyramidal symptoms, fatigue, hallucinations, hysteria, insomnia, akathisia, pseudoparkinsonism, tardive dyskinesia, nervousness, neuroleptic malignant syndrome, sedation, seizures, somnolence
Dermatologic: Angioneurotic edema, photosensitivity, dermatitis, skin pigmentation (slate gray), urticaria
Endocrine & metabolic: Lactation, breast engorgement, amenorrhea, gynecomastia, hyper- or hypoglycemia
Gastrointestinal: Xerostomia, constipation, nausea, vomiting
Genitourinary: Urinary retention, ejaculatory disorder, impotence

Hematologic: Agranulocytosis, eosinophilia, leukopenia, hemolytic anemia, aplastic anemia, thrombocytopenia, thrombocytopenic purpura

Hepatic: Jaundice

Neuromuscular & skeletal: Incoordination, tremors

Ocular: Blurred vision, corneal and lenticular changes, diplopia, epithelial keratopathy, pigmentary retinopathy

Otic: Tinnitus

Respiratory: Apnea, respiratory depression

Drug Interactions

Cytochrome P450 Effect: Substrate (major) of CYP2B6, 2D6; **Inhibits** CYP2D6 (weak)

Increased Effect/Toxicity: CYP2B6 inhibitors may increase the levels/effects of promethazine; example inhibitors include desipramine, paroxetine, and sertraline. CYP2D6 inhibitors may increase the levels/effects of promethazine; example inhibitors include chlorpromazine, delavirdine, fluoxetine, miconazole, paroxetine, pergolide, quinidine, quinine, ritonavir, and ropinirole. Chloroquine, propranolol, and sulfadoxine-pyrimethamine also may increase promethazine concentrations. Concurrent use with TCA may produce increased toxicity or altered therapeutic response. Promethazine plus lithium may rarely produce neurotoxicity. Concurrent use of promethazine and CNS depressants (ethanol, narcotics) may produce additive depressant effects.

Decreased Effect: CYP2B6 inducers may decrease the levels/effects of promethazine; example inducers include carbamazepine, nevirapine, phenobarbital, phenytoin, and rifampin. Benztropine (and other anticholinergics) may inhibit the therapeutic response to promethazine. Promethazine may inhibit the ability of bromocriptine to lower serum prolactin concentrations. The antihypertensive effects of guanethidine and guanadrel may be inhibited by promethazine. Promethazine may inhibit the antiparkinsonian effect of levodopa. Promethazine (and possibly other low potency antipsychotics) may reverse the pressor effects of epinephrine.

Mechanism of Action Blocks postsynaptic mesolimbic dopaminergic receptors in the brain; exhibits a strong alpha-adrenergic blocking effect and depresses the release of hypothalamic and hypophyseal hormones; competes with histamine for the H_1-receptor; reduces stimuli to the brainstem reticular system

Pharmacodynamics/Kinetics

Onset of action: I.M.: ~20 minutes; I.V.: 3-5 minutes

Peak effect: C_{max}: 9.04 ng/mL (suppository); 19.3 ng/mL (syrup)

Duration: 2-6 hours

Absorption:

I.M.: Bioavailability may be greater than with oral or rectal administration

Oral: Rapid and complete; large first pass effect limits systemic bioavailability

Distribution: V_d: 171 L

Protein binding: 93%

Metabolism: Hepatic; primarily oxidation; forms metabolites

Half-life elimination: 9-16 hours

Time to maximum serum concentration: 4.4 hours (syrup); 6.7-8.6 hours (suppositories)

Excretion: Primarily urine and feces (as inactive metabolites)

Dosage

Children ≥2 years:

Allergic conditions: Oral, rectal: 0.1 mg/kg/dose (maximum: 12.5 mg) every 6 hours during the day and 0.5 mg/kg/dose (maximum: 25 mg) at bedtime as needed

Antiemetic: Oral, I.M., I.V., rectal: 0.25-1 mg/kg 4-6 times/day as needed (maximum: 25 mg/dose)

Motion sickness: Oral, rectal: 0.5 mg/kg/dose 30 minutes to 1 hour before departure, then every 12 hours as needed (maximum dose: 25 mg twice daily)

Sedation: Oral, I.M., I.V., rectal: 0.5-1 mg/kg/dose every 6 hours as needed (maximum: 50 mg/dose)

Adults:

Allergic conditions (including allergic reactions to blood or plasma):

Oral, rectal: 12.5 mg 3 times/day and 25 mg at bedtime

I.M., I.V.: 25 mg, may repeat in 2 hours when necessary; switch to oral route as soon as feasible

Antiemetic: Oral, I.M., I.V., rectal: 12.5-25 mg every 4-6 hours as needed

Motion sickness: Oral, rectal: 25 mg 30-60 minutes before departure, then every 12 hours as needed

Sedation: Oral, I.M., I.V., rectal: 12.5-50 mg/dose

Administration Formulations available for oral, rectal, I.M./I.V. administration; not for S.C. or intra-arterial administration. Administer I.M. into deep muscle (preferred route of administration). Due to the possibility of orthostatic hypotension, I.V. administration is **not** the preferred route. Solution for injection may be diluted in 25-100 mL NS or D_5W (maximum concentration of 25 mg/mL) and infused over 15-30 minutes at a rate ≤25 mg/minute.

Monitoring Parameters Relief of symptoms, mental status

Patient Information May cause drowsiness, impair judgment and coordination; may cause photosensitivity; avoid excessive sunlight; report involuntary movements or feelings of restlessness

Dosage Forms INJ, solution: 25 mg/mL (1 mL); 50 mg/mL (1 mL); (Phenergan®): 25 mg/mL (1 mL); 50 mg/mL (1 mL). **SUPP, rectal** (Phenergan®): 12.5 mg, 25 mg, 50 mg. **SYR:** 6.25 mg/5 mL (120 mL, 480 mL). **TAB:** 25 mg, 50 mg; (Phenergan®): 12.5 mg, 25 mg, 50 mg

Promethazine and Codeine (proe METH a zeen & KOE deen)
U.S. Brand Names Phenergan® With Codeine
Synonyms Codeine and Promethazine
Therapeutic Category Antihistamine/Antitussive
Use Temporary relief of coughs and upper respiratory symptoms associated with allergy or the common cold
Restrictions C-V
Pregnancy Risk Factor C
Dosage Oral (in terms of codeine):
  Children: 1-1.5 mg/kg/day every 4 hours as needed; maximum: 30 mg/day **or**
    2-6 years: 1.25-2.5 mL every 4-6 hours or 2.5-5 mg/dose every 4-6 hours as needed; maximum: 30 mg codeine/day
    6-12 years: 2.5-5 mL every 4-6 hours as needed or 5-10 mg/dose every 4-6 hours as needed; maximum: 60 mg codeine/day
  Adults: 10-20 mg/dose every 4-6 hours as needed; maximum: 120 mg codeine/day; or 5-10 mL every 4-6 hours as needed
Dosage Forms SYR: Promethazine 6.25 mg and codeine 10 mg per 5 mL (120 mL, 473 mL, 3840 mL); (Phenergan® with Codeine): Promethazine 6.25 mg and codeine 10 mg per 5 mL (120 mL)

Promethazine and Dextromethorphan
(proe METH a zeen & deks troe meth OR fan)
Synonyms Dextromethorphan and Promethazine
Therapeutic Category Antihistamine/Antitussive
Use Temporary relief of coughs and upper respiratory symptoms associated with allergy or the common cold
Pregnancy Risk Factor C
Dosage Oral:
  Children:
    2-6 years: 1.25-2.5 mL every 4-6 hours up to 10 mL in 24 hours
    6-12 years: 2.5-5 mL every 4-6 hours up to 20 mL in 24 hours
  Adults: 5 mL every 4-6 hours up to 30 mL in 24 hours
Dosage Forms SYR: Promethazine 6.25 mg and dextromethorphan 15 mg per 5 mL (120 mL, 480 mL, 4000 mL)

♦ **Promethazine and Meperidine** *see* Meperidine and Promethazine *on page 792*

Promethazine and Phenylephrine (proe METH a zeen & fen il EF rin)
Synonyms Phenylephrine and Promethazine
Therapeutic Category Antihistamine/Decongestant
Use Temporary relief of upper respiratory symptoms associated with allergy or the common cold
Pregnancy Risk Factor C
Dosage Oral:
  Children:
    2-6 years: 1.25 mL every 4-6 hours, not to exceed 7.5 mL in 24 hours
    6-12 years: 2.5 mL every 4-6 hours, not to exceed 15 mL in 24 hours
  Children >12 years and Adults: 5 mL every 4-6 hours, not to exceed 30 mL in 24 hours
Dosage Forms SYR: Promethazine 6.25 mg and phenylephrine 5 mg per 5 mL (120 mL, 473 mL, 3840 mL)

♦ **Promethazine Hydrochloride** *see* Promethazine *on page 1046*

Promethazine, Phenylephrine, and Codeine
(proe METH a zeen, fen il EF rin, & KOE deen)
Synonyms Codeine, Promethazine, and Phenylephrine; Phenylephrine, Promethazine, and Codeine
Therapeutic Category Antihistamine/Decongestant/Antitussive
Use Temporary relief of coughs and upper respiratory symptoms including nasal congestion
Restrictions C-V
Pregnancy Risk Factor C
Dosage Oral:
  Children (expressed in terms of codeine dosage): 1-1.5 mg/kg/day every 4 hours, maximum: 30 mg/day **or**
    <2 years: Not recommended
    2-6 years:
      Weight 25 lb: 1.25-2.5 mL every 4-6 hours, not to exceed 6 mL/24 hours
      Weight 30 lb: 1.25-2.5 mL every 4-6 hours, not to exceed 7 mL/24 hours
      Weight 35 lb: 1.25-2.5 mL every 4-6 hours, not to exceed 8 mL/24 hours
      Weight 40 lb: 1.25-2.5 mL every 4-6 hours, not to exceed 9 mL/24 hours
    6 to <12 years: 2.5-5 mL every 4-6 hours, not to exceed 15 mL/24 hours
  Adults: 5 mL every 4-6 hours, not to exceed 30 mL/24 hours
Dosage Forms SYR: Promethazine 6.25 mg, phenylephrine 5 mg, and codeine 10 mg per 5 mL (120 mL, 480 mL)

♦ **Prometrium®** *see* Progesterone *on page 1044*
♦ **Promit®** *see* Dextran 1 *on page 362*
♦ **Pronap-100®** *see* Propoxyphene and Acetaminophen *on page 1054*

♦ **Pronestyl**® *see Procainamide on page 1038*
♦ **Pronestyl-SR**® *see Procainamide on page 1038*
♦ **Pronto**® **[OTC]** *see Pyrethrins and Piperonyl Butoxide on page 1065*

Propafenone (proe pa FEEN one)

U.S. Brand Names Rythmol®; Rythmol® SR
Synonyms Propafenone Hydrochloride
Therapeutic Category Antiarrhythmic Agent, Class I-C
Use Treatment of life-threatening ventricular arrhythmias
  Rythmol® SR: Maintenance of normal sinus rhythm in patients with symptomatic atrial fibrilla-
  tion
Unlabeled/Investigational Use Supraventricular tachycardias, including those patients with
  Wolff-Parkinson-White syndrome
Pregnancy Risk Factor C
Contraindications Hypersensitivity to propafenone or any component of the formulation; sino-
  atrial, AV, and intraventricular disorders of impulse generation and/or conduction (except in
  patients with a functioning artificial pacemaker); sinus bradycardia; cardiogenic shock; uncompensated cardiac failure; hypotension; bronchospastic disorders; uncorrected electrolyte
  abnormalities; concurrent use of amprenavir, cimetidine, metoprolol, propranolol, quinidine,
  and ritonavir (see Drug Interactions)
Warnings/Precautions Until evidence to the contrary, propafenone should be considered
  acceptable only for the treatment of life-threatening arrhythmias; propafenone may cause new
  or worsened arrhythmias, worsen CHF, decrease AV conduction and alter pacemaker thresh-
  olds; use with caution in patients with recent myocardial infarction, CHF, hepatic or renal
  dysfunction; elderly may be at greater risk for toxicity
Common Adverse Reactions 1% to 10%:
  Cardiovascular: New or worsened arrhythmias (proarrhythmic effect) (2% to 10%), angina (2%
    to 5%), CHF (1% to 4%), ventricular tachycardia (1% to 3%), palpitations (1% to 3%), AV
    block (first-degree) (1% to 3%), syncope (1% to 2%), increased QRS interval (1% to 2%),
    chest pain (1% to 2%), PVCs (1% to 2%), bradycardia (1% to 2%), edema (0% to 1%),
    bundle branch block (0% to 1%), atrial fibrillation (1%), hypotension (0% to 1%), intraventric-
    ular conduction delay (0% to 1%)
  Central nervous system: Dizziness (4% to 15%), fatigue (2% to 6%), headache (2% to 5%),
    weakness (1% to 2%), ataxia (0% to 2%), insomnia (0% to 2%), anxiety (1% to 2%),
    drowsiness (1%)
  Dermatologic: Rash (1% to 3%)
  Gastrointestinal: Nausea/vomiting (2% to 11%), unusual taste (3% to 23%), constipation (2%
    to 7%), dyspepsia (1% to 3%), diarrhea (1% to 3%), xerostomia (1% to 2%), anorexia (1% to
    2%), abdominal pain (1% to 2%), flatulence (0% to 1%)
  Neuromuscular & skeletal: Tremor (0% to 1%), arthralgia (0% to 1%)
  Ocular: Blurred vision (1% to 6%)
  Respiratory: Dyspnea (2% to 5%)
  Miscellaneous: Diaphoresis (1%)
Drug Interactions
  Cytochrome P450 Effect: Substrate of CYP1A2 (minor), 2D6 (major), 3A4 (minor);
    Inhibits CYP1A2 (weak), 2C8/9 (weak), 2D6 (weak)
  Increased Effect/Toxicity: Amprenavir, cimetidine, metoprolol, propranolol, quinidine, and
    ritonavir may increase propafenone levels; concurrent use is contraindicated. CYP2D6
    inhibitors may increase the levels/effects of propafenone; example inhibitors include chlor-
    promazine, delavirdine, fluoxetine, miconazole, paroxetine, pergolide, quinidine, quinine,
    ritonavir, and ropinirole. Digoxin (reduce dose by 25%), cyclosporine, local anesthetics,
    theophylline, and warfarin blood levels are increased by propafenone.
  Decreased Effect: Enzyme inducers (phenobarbital, phenytoin, rifabutin, rifampin) may
    decrease propafenone blood levels.
Mechanism of Action Propafenone is a class 1c antiarrhythmic agent which possesses local
  anesthetic properties, blocks the fast inward sodium current, and slows the rate of increase of
  the action potential. Prolongs conduction and refractoriness in all areas of the myocardium,
  with a slightly more pronounced effect on intraventricular conduction; it prolongs effective
  refractory period, reduces spontaneous automaticity and exhibits some beta-blockade activity.
Pharmacodynamics/Kinetics
  Absorption: Well absorbed
  Metabolism: Hepatic; two genetically determined metabolism groups exist: fast or slow
    metabolizers; 10% of Caucasians are slow metabolizers; exhibits nonlinear pharmacoki-
    netics; when dose is increased from 300-900 mg/day, serum concentrations increase
    tenfold; this nonlinearity is thought to be due to saturable first-pass effect
  Bioavailability: 150 mg: 3.4%; 300 mg: 10.6%
  Half-life elimination: Single dose (100-300 mg): 2-8 hours; Chronic dosing: 10-32 hours
  Time to peak: 150 mg dose: 2 hours, 300 mg dose: 3 hours
Dosage Oral: Adults: **Note:** Patients who exhibit significant widening of QRS complex or
  second- or third-degree AV block may need dose reduction.
  Immediate release tablet: Initial: 150 mg every 8 hours, increase at 3- to 4-day intervals up to
    300 mg every 8 hours.
  Extended release capsule: Initial: 225 mg every 12 hours; dosage increase may be made at a
    minimum of 5-day intervals; may increase to 325 mg every 12 hours; if further increase is
    necessary, may increase to 425 mg every 12 hours
  (Continued)

Propafenone *(Continued)*

Dosing adjustment in hepatic impairment: Reduction is necessary; however, specific guidelines are not available.

Administration Capsules should be swallowed whole; do not crush or chew.

Monitoring Parameters ECG, blood pressure, pulse (particularly at initiation of therapy)

Patient Information Take dose the same way each day, either with or without food; do not double the next dose if present dose is missed; do not discontinue drug or change dose without advice of prescriber; report any severe or persistent fatigue, sore throat, or any unusual bleeding or bruising; may cause drowsiness and impair coordination and judgment

Dosage Forms CAP, extended release: 225 mg, 325 mg, 425 mg. **TAB:** 150 mg, 225 mg, 300 mg

♦ **Propafenone Hydrochloride** *see* Propafenone *on page 1049*

Propantheline *(proe PAN the leen)*

Synonyms Propantheline Bromide

Therapeutic Category Anticholinergic Agent; Antispasmodic Agent, Gastrointestinal

Use Adjunctive treatment of peptic ulcer, irritable bowel syndrome, pancreatitis, ureteral and urinary bladder spasm; reduce duodenal motility during diagnostic radiologic procedures

Pregnancy Risk Factor C

Dosage Oral:

Antisecretory:

Children: 1-2 mg/kg/day in 3-4 divided doses

Adults: 15 mg 3 times/day before meals or food and 30 mg at bedtime

Elderly: 7.5 mg 3 times/day before meals and at bedtime

Antispasmodic:

Children: 2-3 mg/kg/day in divided doses every 4-6 hours and at bedtime

Adults: 15 mg 3 times/day before meals or food and 30 mg at bedtime

Dosage Forms TAB: 15 mg

♦ **Propantheline Bromide** *see* Propantheline *on page 1050*

Proparacaine *(proe PAR a kane)*

U.S. Brand Names Alcaine®; Ophthetic®

Synonyms Proparacaine Hydrochloride; Proxymetacaine

Therapeutic Category Local Anesthetic, Ophthalmic

Use Anesthesia for tonometry, gonioscopy; suture removal from cornea; removal of corneal foreign body; cataract extraction, glaucoma surgery; short operative procedure involving the cornea and conjunctiva

Pregnancy Risk Factor C

Contraindications Hypersensitivity to proparacaine or any component of the formulation

Warnings/Precautions Use with caution in patients with cardiac disease, hyperthyroidism; for topical ophthalmic use only; prolonged use not recommended

Common Adverse Reactions 1% to 10%: Local: Burning, stinging, redness

Drug Interactions

Increased Effect/Toxicity: Effects of phenylephrine and tropicamide (ophthalmics) are increased

Mechanism of Action Prevents initiation and transmission of impulse at the nerve cell membrane by decreasing ion permeability through stabilizing

Pharmacodynamics/Kinetics

Onset of action: ~20 seconds

Duration: 15-20 minutes

Dosage Children and Adults:

Ophthalmic surgery: Instill 1 drop of 0.5% solution in eye every 5-10 minutes for 5-7 doses

Tonometry, gonioscopy, suture removal: Instill 1-2 drops of 0.5% solution in eye just prior to procedure

Patient Information May slow wound healing; use sparingly, avoid touching or rubbing the eye until anesthesia has worn off

Dosage Forms SOLN, ophthalmic: 0.5% (15 mL)

Proparacaine and Fluorescein *(proe PAR a kane & FLURE e seen)*

U.S. Brand Names Flucaine®; Fluoracaine®

Synonyms Fluorescein and Proparacaine

Therapeutic Category Diagnostic Agent, Ophthalmic Dye; Local Anesthetic, Ester Derivative (Ophthalmic); Local Anesthetic, Ophthalmic

Use Anesthesia for tonometry, gonioscopy; suture removal from cornea; removal of corneal foreign body; cataract extraction, glaucoma surgery

Pregnancy Risk Factor C

Dosage

Ophthalmic surgery: Children and Adults: Instill 1 drop in each eye every 5-10 minutes for 5-7 doses

Tonometry, gonioscopy, suture removal: Adults: Instill 1-2 drops in each eye just prior to procedure

Dosage Forms SOLN, ophthalmic: Proparacaine 0.5% and fluorescein sodium 0.25% (5 mL)

♦ **Proparacaine Hydrochloride** *see* Proparacaine *on page 1050*

♦ **Propecia®** *see Finasteride on page 524*
♦ **Propine®** *see Dipivefrin on page 390*
♦ **Proplex® T** *see Factor IX Complex (Human) on page 504*

Propofol (PROE po fole)

U.S. Brand Names Diprivan®

Therapeutic Category General Anesthetic; Sedative

Use Induction of anesthesia for inpatient or outpatient surgery in patients ≥3 years of age; maintenance of anesthesia for inpatient or outpatient surgery in patients >2 months of age; in adults, for the induction and maintenance of monitored anesthesia care sedation during diagnostic procedures; may be used (for patients >18 years of age who are intubated and mechanically ventilated) as an alternative to benzodiazepines for the treatment of agitation in the intensive care unit

Unlabeled/Investigational Use Postoperative antiemetic; refractory delirium tremens (case reports)

Pregnancy Risk Factor B

Contraindications

Absolute contraindications:

Patients with a hypersensitivity to propofol or any component of the formulation

Patients who are not intubated or mechanically ventilated

Patients who are pregnant

When general anesthesia or sedation is contraindicated

Relative contraindications:

Pediatric intensive care unit patients: Safety and efficacy of propofol are not established

Patients with severe cardiac disease (ejection fraction <50%) or respiratory disease - propofol may have more profound adverse cardiovascular responses

Patients with a history of epilepsy or seizures; risk of seizure during recovery phase

Patients with increased intracranial pressure or impaired cerebral circulation - substantial decreases in mean arterial pressure and subsequent decreases in cerebral perfusion pressure may occur

Patients with hyperlipidemia as evidenced by increased serum triglyceride levels or serum turbidity

Patients who are hypotensive, hypovolemic, hemodynamically unstable, or abnormally low vascular tone (eg, sepsis)

Warnings/Precautions Use slower rate of induction in the elderly; transient local pain may occur during I.V. injection; perioperative myoclonia has occurred; do not administer with blood or blood products through the same I.V. catheter; not for obstetrics, including cesarean section deliveries. Abrupt discontinuation prior to weaning or daily wake up assessments should be avoided. Abrupt discontinuation can result in rapid awakening, anxiety, agitation, and resistance to mechanical ventilation. Several deaths associated with severe metabolic acidosis have been reported in pediatric ICU patients on long-term propofol infusion. Propofol emulsion contains soybean oil, egg phosphatide, and glycerol.

Common Adverse Reactions

>10%:

Cardiovascular: Hypotension (3% to 26% adults, 17% children)

Central nervous system: Movement (17% children)

Local: Injection site burning, stinging, or pain (adults 18%, children 10%)

Respiratory: Apnea, lasting 30-60 seconds (24% adults, 10% children); Apnea, lasting >60 seconds (12% adults, 5% children)

3% to 10%:

Cardiovascular: Hypertension (8% children)

Central nervous system: Movement (adults)

Dermatologic: Pruritus (adults), rash

Endocrine & metabolic: Hyperlipidemia

Respiratory: Respiratory acidosis during weaning

1% to 3%:

Cardiovascular: Arrhythmia, bradycardia, decreased cardiac output, tachycardia

Dermatologic: Pruritus (children)

Drug Interactions

Cytochrome P450 Effect: Substrate of CYP1A2 (minor), 2A6 (minor), 2B6 (major), 2C8/9 (major), 2C19 (minor), 2D6 (minor), 2E1 (minor), 3A4 (minor); **Inhibits** CYP1A2 (moderate), 2C8/9 (weak), 2C19 (moderate), 2D6 (weak), 2E1 (weak), 3A4 (strong)

Increased Effect/Toxicity: CYP2B6 inhibitors may increase the levels/effects of propofol; example inhibitors include desipramine, paroxetine, and sertraline. CYP2C8/9 inhibitors may increase the levels/effects of propofol; example inhibitors include delavirdine, fluconazole, gemfibrozil, ketoconazole, nicardipine, NSAIDs, and sulfonamides. Propofol may potentiate the neuromuscular blockade of vecuronium (and possibly other neuromuscular-blocking agents). Additive CNS depression and respiratory depression may necessitate dosage reduction when used with anesthetics, benzodiazepines, opiates, ethanol, narcotics, phenothiazines.

Mechanism of Action Propofol is a hindered phenolic compound with intravenous general anesthetic properties. The drug is unrelated to any of the currently used barbiturate, opioid, benzodiazepine, arylcyclohexylamine, or imidazole intravenous anesthetic agents.

Pharmacodynamics/Kinetics

Onset of action: Anesthetic: Bolus infusion (dose dependent): 9-51 seconds (average 30 seconds)

Duration (dose and rate dependent): 3-10 minutes

(Continued)

Propofol (Continued)

Distribution: V_d: 2-10 L/kg; highly lipophilic

Protein binding: 97% to 99%

Metabolism: Hepatic to water-soluble sulfate and glucuronide conjugates

Half-life elimination: Biphasic: Initial: 40 minutes; Terminal: 4-7 hours (up to 1-3 days)

Excretion: Urine (~88% as metabolites, 40% as glucuronide metabolite); feces (<2%)

Clearance: 20-30 mL/kg/minute; total body clearance exceeds liver blood flow

Dosage Dosage must be individualized based on total body weight and titrated to the desired clinical effect; wait at least 3-5 minutes between dosage adjustments to clinically assess drug effects; smaller doses are required when used with narcotics; the following are general dosing guidelines:

General anesthesia:

Induction: I.V.:

Children 3-16 years, ASA I or II: 2.5-3.5 mg/kg over 20-30 seconds; use a lower dose for children ASA III or IV

Adults, ASA I or II, <55 years: 2-2.5 mg/kg (~40 mg every 10 seconds until onset of induction)

Elderly, debilitated, hypovolemic, or ASA III or IV: 1-1.5 mg/kg (~20 mg every 10 seconds until onset of induction)

Cardiac anesthesia: 0.5-1.5 mg/kg (~20 mg every 10 seconds until onset of induction)

Neurosurgical patients: 1-2 mg/kg (~20 mg every 10 seconds until onset of induction)

Maintenance: I.V. infusion:

Children 2 months to 16 years, ASA I or II: Initial: 200-300 mcg/kg/minute; decrease dose after 30 minutes if clinical signs of light anesthesia are absent; usual infusion rate: 125-150 mcg/kg/minute (range: 125-300 mcg/kg/minute; 7.5-18 mg/kg/hour); children ≤5 years may require larger infusion rates compared to older children

Adults, ASA I or II, <55 years: Initial: 150-200 mcg/kg/minute for 10-15 minutes; decrease by 30% to 50% during first 30 minutes of maintenance; usual infusion rate: 100-200 mcg/kg/minute (6-12 mg/kg/hour)

Elderly, debilitated, hypovolemic, ASA III or IV: 50-100 mcg/kg/minute (3-6 mg/kg/ hour)

Cardiac anesthesia:

Low-dose propofol with primary opioid: 50-100 mcg/kg/minute (see manufacturer's labeling)

Primary propofol with secondary opioid: 100-150 mcg/kg/minute

Neurosurgical patients: 100-200 mcg/kg/minute (6-12 mg/kg/hour)

Maintenance: I.V. intermittent bolus: Adults, ASA I or II, <55 years: 20-50 mg increments as needed

Monitored anesthesia care sedation:

Initiation:

Adults, ASA I or II, <55 years: Slow I.V. infusion: 100-150 mcg/kg/minute for 3-5 minutes **or** slow injection: 0.5 mg/kg over 3-5 minutes

Elderly, debilitated, neurosurgical, or ASA III or IV patients: Use similar doses to healthy adults; avoid rapid I.V. boluses

Maintenance:

Adults, ASA I or II, <55 years: I.V. infusion using variable rates (preferred over intermittent boluses): 25-75 mcg/kg/minute **or** incremental bolus doses: 10 mg or 20 mg

Elderly, debilitated, neurosurgical, or ASA III or IV patients: Use 80% of healthy adult dose; **do not** use rapid bolus doses (single or repeated)

ICU sedation in intubated mechanically-ventilated patients: Avoid rapid bolus injection; individualize dose and titrate to response

Adults: Continuous infusion: Initial: 0.3 mg/kg/hour; increase by 0.3-0.6 mg/kg/hour every 5-10 minutes until desired sedation level is achieved; usual maintenance: 0.3-3 mg/kg/ hour or higher; reduce dose by 80% in elderly, debilitated, and ASA III or IV patients; reduce dose after adequate sedation established and adjust to response (ie, evaluate frequently to use minimum dose for sedation). Some clinicians recommend daily interruption of infusion to perform clinical evaluation.

Administration To reduce pain associated with injection, use larger veins of forearm or antecubital fossa; lidocaine I.V. (1 mL of a 1% solution) may also be used prior to administration. Do not use filter with <5 micron for administration. Soybean fat emulsion is used as a vehicle for propofol. Strict aseptic technique must be maintained in handling although a preservative has been added. Do not administer through the same I.V. catheter with blood or plasma. The American College of Critical Care Medicine recommends the use of a central vein for administration in an ICU setting.

Monitoring Parameters Cardiac monitor, blood pressure monitor, and ventilator required; serum triglyceride levels should be obtained prior to initiation of therapy (ICU setting) and every 3-7 days thereafter; daily sedation levels using standardized scale

Vital signs: Blood pressure, heart rate, cardiac output, pulmonary capillary wedge pressure should be monitored

Monitor zinc levels in patients predisposed to deficiency (burns, diarrhea, major sepsis). In patients at risk for renal impairment, urinalysis and urine sediment should be monitored prior to treatment and every other day of sedation.

Dosage Forms INJ, emulsion: 10 mg/mL (20 mL, 50 mL, 100 mL); (Diprivan®): 10 mg/mL (20 mL, 50 mL, 100 mL)

Propoxyphene (proe POKS i feen)
Related Information
Narcotic Agonists Comparison *on page 1395*
U.S. Brand Names Darvon®; Darvon-N®
Synonyms Dextropropoxyphene; Propoxyphene Hydrochloride; Propoxyphene Napsylate
Therapeutic Category Analgesic, Narcotic
Use Management of mild to moderate pain
Restrictions C-IV
Pregnancy Risk Factor C/D (prolonged use)
Contraindications Hypersensitivity to propoxyphene or any component of the formulation
Warnings/Precautions When given in excessive doses, either alone or in combination with other CNS depressants, propoxyphene is a major cause of drug-related deaths; do not exceed recommended dosage; give with caution in patients dependent on opiates, substitution may result in acute opiate withdrawal symptoms. Avoid use in severely depressed or suicidal patients. Tolerance or drug dependence may result from extended use. Propoxyphene should be used with caution in patients with renal or hepatic dysfunction or in the elderly; consider dosing adjustment.
Common Adverse Reactions Frequency not defined.
Cardiovascular: Hypotension, bundle branch block
Central nervous system: Dizziness, lightheadedness, sedation, paradoxical excitement and insomnia, fatigue, drowsiness, mental depression, hallucinations, paradoxical CNS stimulation, increased intracranial pressure, nervousness, headache, restlessness, malaise, confusion, dysphoria, vertigo
Dermatologic: Rash, urticaria
Endocrine & metabolic: Hypoglycemia, urinary 17-OHCS decreased
Gastrointestinal: Anorexia, stomach cramps, xerostomia, biliary spasm, nausea, vomiting, constipation, paralytic ileus, abdominal pain
Genitourinary: Urination decreased, ureteral spasms
Neuromuscular & skeletal: Weakness
Hepatic: LFTs increased, jaundice
Ocular: Visual disturbances
Respiratory: Dyspnea
Miscellaneous: Psychologic and physical dependence with prolonged use, histamine release, hypersensitivity reaction
Drug Interactions
Cytochrome P450 Effect: Inhibits CYP2C8/9 (weak), 2D6 (weak), 3A4 (weak)
Increased Effect/Toxicity: CNS depressants (phenothiazines, tranquilizers, anxiolytics, sedatives, hypnotics, or alcohol) may potentiate pharmacologic effects. Propoxyphene may inhibit the metabolism and increase the serum concentrations of carbamazepine, phenobarbital, MAO inhibitors, tricyclic antidepressants, and warfarin.
Decreased Effect: Decreased effect with cigarette smoking.
Mechanism of Action Propoxyphene is a weak narcotic analgesic which acts through weak binding to opiate receptors to inhibit ascending pain pathways. Propoxyphene, as with other narcotic (opiate) analgesics, blocks pain perception in the cerebral cortex by binding to specific receptor molecules (opiate receptors) within the neuronal membranes of synapses. This binding results in a decreased synaptic chemical transmission throughout the CNS thus inhibiting the flow of pain sensations into the higher centers. Mu and kappa are the two subtypes of the opiate receptor which propoxyphene binds to to cause analgesia.
Pharmacodynamics/Kinetics
Onset of action: 0.5-1 hour
Duration: 4-6 hours
Metabolism: Hepatic to active metabolite (norpropoxyphene) and inactive metabolites; first-pass effect
Half-life elimination: Adults: Parent drug: 6-12 hours; Norpropoxyphene: 30-36 hours
Excretion: Urine (primarily as metabolites)
Dosage Oral:
Children: Doses for children are not well established; doses of the hydrochloride of 2-3 mg/kg/d divided every 6 hours have been used
Adults:
Hydrochloride: 65 mg every 3-4 hours as needed for pain; maximum: 390 mg/day
Napsylate: 100 mg every 4 hours as needed for pain; maximum: 600 mg/day
Elderly: Refer to Adults dosing; consider increasing dosing interval
Dosing adjustment in renal impairment: Serum concentrations of propoxyphene may be increased or elimination may be delayed. Avoid use in Cl$_{cr}$ <10 mL/minute. Specific dosing recommendations not available for less severe impairment.
Not dialyzable (0% to 5%)
Dosing adjustment in hepatic impairment: Serum concentrations of propoxyphene may be increased or elimination may be delayed; specific dosing recommendations not available.
Administration Should be administered with glass of water on an empty stomach. Food may decrease rate of absorption, but may slightly increase bioavailability.
Monitoring Parameters Pain relief, respiratory and mental status, blood pressure
Reference Range
Therapeutic: Ranges published vary between laboratories and may not correlate with clinical effect
Therapeutic concentration: 0.1-0.4 µg/mL (SI: 0.3-1.2 µmol/L)
Toxic: >0.5 µg/mL (SI: >1.5 µmol/L)
(Continued)

Propoxyphene *(Continued)*

Patient Information May cause drowsiness, dizziness, or blurring of vision; avoid alcohol and other sedatives; may take with food; can impair judgment and coordination

Dosage Forms CAP, as hydrochloride (Darvon®): 65 mg. **TAB, as napsylate** (Darvon®): 100 mg

Propoxyphene and Acetaminophen *(proe POKS i feen & a seet a MIN oh fen)*

U.S. Brand Names Darvocet A500™; Darvocet-N® 50; Darvocet-N® 100; Pronap-100®

Synonyms Propoxyphene Hydrochloride and Acetaminophen; Propoxyphene Napsylate and Acetaminophen

Therapeutic Category Analgesic Combination, Narcotic

Use Management of mild to moderate pain

Restrictions C-IV

Pregnancy Risk Factor C

Dosage Oral: Adults:

Darvocet A500™, Darvocet-N®: 1-2 tablets every 4 hours as needed; maximum: 600 mg propoxyphene napsylate/day

Darvocet-N® 100: 1 tablet every 4 hours as needed; maximum: 600 mg propoxyphene napsylate/day

Note: Dosage of acetaminophen should not exceed 4 g/day (6 tablets of Darvocet-N® 100); possibly less in patients with ethanol

Elderly: Refer to Adults dosing; consider increasing dosing interval

Dosing adjustment in renal/hepatic impairment: Serum concentrations of propoxyphene may be increased or elimination may be delayed; specific dosing recommendations not available.

Dosage Forms TAB: Propoxyphene hydrochloride 65 mg and acetaminophen 650 mg, propoxyphene napsylate 100 mg, and acetaminophen 650 mg; (Darvocet A500™): Propoxyphene napsylate 100 mg and acetaminophen 500 mg; (Darvocet-N® 50): Propoxyphene napsylate 50 mg and acetaminophen 325 mg; (Darvocet-N® 100, Pronap-100®): Propoxyphene napsylate 100 mg and acetaminophen 650 mg

Propoxyphene, Aspirin, and Caffeine

(proe POKS i feen, AS pir in, & KAF een)

U.S. Brand Names Darvon® Compound

Synonyms Aspirin, Caffeine, and Propoxyphene; Caffeine, Propoxyphene, and Aspirin; Propoxyphene Hydrochloride, Aspirin, and Caffeine

Therapeutic Category Analgesic Combination, Narcotic

Use Treatment of mild-to-moderate pain

Restrictions C-IV

Pregnancy Risk Factor C

Dosage Oral: Adults: Pain: One capsule (providing propoxyphene 32 mg or 65 mg) every 4 hours as needed; maximum propoxyphene 390 mg/day. This will also provide aspirin 389 mg and caffeine 32.4 mg per capsule.

Elderly: Refer to Adults dosing; consider increasing dosing interval

Dosage adjustment in renal impairment: Serum concentrations of propoxyphene may be increased or elimination may be delayed; specific dosing recommendations not available. Avoid use with Cl$_{cr}$ <10 mL/minute.

Dosage adjustment in hepatic impairment: Serum concentrations or propoxyphene may be increased or elimination may be delayed; specific dosing recommendations not available.

Dosage Forms CAP: (Darvon® Compound 32): Propoxyphene hydrochloride 32 mg, aspirin 389 mg, and caffeine 32.4 mg; (Darvon® Compound 65): Propoxyphene hydrochloride 65 mg, aspirin 389 mg, and caffeine 32.4 mg

♦ **Propoxyphene Hydrochloride** *see* Propoxyphene *on page 1053*

♦ **Propoxyphene Hydrochloride and Acetaminophen** *see* Propoxyphene and Acetaminophen *on page 1054*

♦ **Propoxyphene Hydrochloride, Aspirin, and Caffeine** *see* Propoxyphene, Aspirin, and Caffeine *on page 1054*

♦ **Propoxyphene Napsylate** *see* Propoxyphene *on page 1053*

♦ **Propoxyphene Napsylate and Acetaminophen** *see* Propoxyphene and Acetaminophen *on page 1054*

Propranolol *(proe PRAN oh lole)*

Related Information

Beta-Blockers Comparison *on page 1368*

U.S. Brand Names Inderal®; Inderal® LA; InnoPran XL™; Propranolol Intensol™

Synonyms Propranolol Hydrochloride

Therapeutic Category Antianginal Agent; Antiarrhythmic Agent, Class II; Antihypertensive Agent; Antimigraine Agent, Prophylaxis; Beta Blocker, Nonselective

Use Management of hypertension; angina pectoris; pheochromocytoma; essential tremor; tetralogy of Fallot cyanotic spells; arrhythmias (such as atrial fibrillation and flutter, AV nodal re-entrant tachycardias, and catecholamine-induced arrhythmias); prevention of myocardial infarction; migraine headache; symptomatic treatment of hypertrophic subaortic stenosis

Unlabeled/Investigational Use Tremor due to Parkinson's disease; ethanol withdrawal; aggressive behavior; antipsychotic-induced akathisia; prevention of bleeding esophageal varices; anxiety; schizophrenia; acute panic; gastric bleeding in portal hypertension; thyrotoxicosis

Pregnancy Risk Factor C (manufacturer); D (2nd and 3rd trimesters - expert analysis)

Contraindications Hypersensitivity to propranolol, beta-blockers, or any component of the formulation; uncompensated congestive heart failure (unless the failure is due to tachyarrhythmias being treated with propranolol), cardiogenic shock, bradycardia or heart block (2nd or 3rd degree), pulmonary edema, severe hyperactive airway disease (asthma or COPD), Raynaud's disease; pregnancy (2nd and 3rd trimesters)

Warnings/Precautions Administer cautiously in compensated heart failure and monitor for a worsening of the condition (efficacy of propranolol in CHF has not been demonstrated). Beta-blocker therapy should not be withdrawn abruptly (particularly in patients with CAD), but gradually tapered (over 2 weeks) to avoid acute tachycardia, hypertension, and/or ischemia. Use caution in patient with PVD. Use caution with concurrent use of beta-blockers and either verapamil or diltiazem; bradycardia or heart block can occur. Avoid concurrent I.V. use of both agents. Use cautiously in diabetics because it can mask prominent hypoglycemic symptoms. Can mask signs of thyrotoxicosis. Can cause fetal harm when administered in pregnancy. Use cautiously in hepatic dysfunction (dosage adjustment required). Use care with anesthetic agents which decrease myocardial function. Not indicated for hypertensive emergencies.

Common Adverse Reactions Frequency not defined.

Cardiovascular: Bradycardia, CHF, reduced peripheral circulation, chest pain, hypotension, impaired myocardial contractility, worsening of AV conduction disturbance, cardiogenic shock, Raynaud's syndrome, mesenteric thrombosis (rare)

Central nervous system: Mental depression, lightheadedness, amnesia, emotional lability, confusion, hallucinations, dizziness, insomnia, fatigue, vivid dreams, lethargy, cold extremities, vertigo, syncope, cognitive dysfunction, psychosis, hypersomnolence

Dermatologic: Rash, alopecia, exfoliative dermatitis, psoriasiform eruptions, eczematous eruptions, hyperkeratosis, nail changes, pruritus, urticaria, ulcerative lichenoid, contact dermatitis

Endocrine & metabolic: Hypoglycemia, hyperglycemia, hyperlipidemia, hyperkalemia

Gastrointestinal: Diarrhea, nausea, vomiting, stomach discomfort, constipation, anorexia

Genitourinary: Impotence, proteinuria (rare), oliguria (rare), interstitial nephritis (rare), Peyronie's disease

Hematologic: Agranulocytosis, thrombocytopenia, thrombocytopenic purpura

Neuromuscular & skeletal: Weakness, carpal tunnel syndrome (rare), paresthesias, myotonus, polyarthritis, arthropathy

Respiratory: Wheezing, pharyngitis, bronchospasm, pulmonary edema

Ocular: Hyperemia of the conjunctiva, decreased tear production, decreased visual acuity, mydriasis

Miscellaneous: Lupus-like syndrome (rare)

Drug Interactions

Cytochrome P450 Effect: Substrate of CYP1A2 (major), 2C19 (major), 2D6 (major), 3A4 (minor); **Inhibits** CYP1A2 (weak), 2D6 (weak)

Increased Effect/Toxicity: CYP1A2 inhibitors may increase the levels/effects of propranolol; example inhibitors include amiodarone, ciprofloxacin, fluvoxamine, ketoconazole, lomefloxacin, ofloxacin, and rofecoxib. CYP2C19 inhibitors may increase the levels/effects of propranolol; example inhibitors include delavirdine, fluconazole, fluvoxamine, gemfibrozil, isoniazid, omeprazole, and ticlopidine. CYP2D6 inhibitors may increase the levels/effects of propranolol; example inhibitors include chlorpromazine, delavirdine, fluoxetine, miconazole, paroxetine, pergolide, quinidine, quinine, ritonavir, and ropinirole. The heart rate-lowering effects of propranolol are additive with other drugs which slow AV conduction (digoxin, verapamil, diltiazem). Reserpine increases the effects of propranolol. Concurrent use of propranolol may increase the effects of alpha-blockers (prazosin, terazosin), alpha-adrenergic stimulants (epinephrine, phenylephrine), and the vasoconstrictive effects of ergot alkaloids. Propranolol may mask the tachycardia from hypoglycemia caused by insulin and oral hypoglycemics. In patients receiving concurrent therapy, the risk of hypertensive crisis is increased when either clonidine or the beta-blocker is withdrawn. Beta-blockers may increase the action or levels of ethanol, disopyramide, nondepolarizing muscle relaxants, and theophylline although the effects are difficult to predict. Propranolol may increase the bioavailability of serotonin 5-HT$_{1D}$ receptor agonists. Propranolol may decrease the metabolism of lidocaine.

Beta-blocker effects may be enhanced by oral contraceptives, flecainide, haloperidol (hypotensive effects), cimetidine, hydralazine, phenothiazines, propafenone, thyroid hormones (when hypothyroid patient is converted to euthyroid state). Beta-blockers may increase the effect/toxicity of flecainide, haloperidol (hypotensive effects), hydralazine, phenothiazines, acetaminophen, anticoagulants (warfarin), and benzodiazepines.

Decreased Effect: CYP1A2 inducers may decrease the levels/effects of propranolol; example inducers include aminoglutethimide, carbamazepine, phenobarbital, and rifampin. CYP2C19 inducers may decrease the levels/effects of propranolol; example inducers include aminoglutethimide, carbamazepine, phenytoin, and rifampin. Aluminum salts, calcium salts, cholestyramine, colestipol, NSAIDs, penicillins (ampicillin), salicylates, and sulfinpyrazone decrease effect of beta-blockers due to decreased bioavailability and plasma levels. Beta-blockers may decrease the effect of sulfonylureas. Ascorbic acid decreases propranolol Cp_{max} and AUC and increases the T_{max} significantly resulting in a greater decrease in the reduction of heart rate, possibly due to decreased absorption and first pass metabolism (n=5). Nefazodone decreased peak plasma levels and AUC of propranolol and increases time to reach steady-state; monitoring of clinical response is recommended. Nonselective beta-blockers blunt the response to beta-2 adrenergic agonists (albuterol).

(Continued)

Propranolol *(Continued)*

Mechanism of Action Nonselective beta-adrenergic blocker (class II antiarrhythmic); competitively blocks response to beta$_1$- and beta$_2$-adrenergic stimulation which results in decreases in heart rate, myocardial contractility, blood pressure, and myocardial oxygen demand

Pharmacodynamics/Kinetics

Onset of action: Beta-blockade: Oral: 1-2 hours

Duration: ~6 hours

Distribution: V_d: 3.9 L/kg in adults; crosses placenta; small amounts enter breast milk

Protein binding: Newborns: 68%; Adults: 93%

Metabolism: Hepatic to active and inactive compounds; extensive first-pass effect

Bioavailability: 30% to 40%; may be increased in Down syndrome

Half-life elimination: Neonates and Infants: Possible increased half-life; Children: 3.9-6.4 hours; Adults: 4-6 hours

Excretion: Urine (96% to 99%)

Dosage

Akathisia: Oral: Adults: 30-120 mg/day in 2-3 divided doses

Angina: Oral: Adults: 80-320 mg/day in doses divided 2-4 times/day

Long-acting formulation: Initial: 80 mg once daily; maximum dose: 320 mg once daily

Essential tremor: Oral: Adults: 20-40 mg twice daily initially; maintenance doses: usually 120-320 mg/day

Hypertension:

Oral:

Children: Initial: 0.5-1 mg/kg/day in divided doses every 6-12 hours; increase gradually every 5-7 days; maximum: 16 mg/kg/24 hours

Adults: Initial: 40 mg twice daily; increase dosage every 3-7 days; usual dose: ≤320 mg divided in 2-3 doses/day; maximum daily dose: 640 mg

Long-acting formulation: Initial: 80 mg once daily; usual maintenance: 120-160 mg once daily; maximum daily dose: 640 mg

I.V.: Children: 0.01-0.05 mg/kg over 1 hour; maximum dose: 10 mg

Hypertrophic subaortic stenosis: Oral: Adults: 20-40 mg 3-4 times/day

Long-acting formulation: 80-160 mg once daily

Migraine headache prophylaxis: Oral:

Children: Initial: 2-4 mg/kg/day **or**

≤35 kg: 10-20 mg 3 times/day

>35 kg: 20-40 mg 3 times/day

Adults: Initial: 80 mg/day divided every 6-8 hours; increase by 20-40 mg/dose every 3-4 weeks to a maximum of 160-240 mg/day given in divided doses every 6-8 hours; if satisfactory response not achieved within 6 weeks of starting therapy, drug should be withdrawn gradually over several weeks

Long-acting formulation: Initial: 80 mg once daily; effective dose range: 160-240 mg once daily

Myocardial infarction prophylaxis: Oral: Adults: 180-240 mg/day in 3-4 divided doses

Pheochromocytoma: Oral: Adults: 30-60 mg/day in divided doses

Tachyarrhythmias:

Oral:

Children: Initial: 0.5-1 mg/kg/day in divided doses every 6-8 hours; titrate dosage upward every 3-7 days; usual dose: 2-6 mg/kg/day; higher doses may be needed; do not exceed 16 mg/kg/day or 60 mg/day

Adults: 10-30 mg/dose every 6-8 hours

Elderly: Initial: 10 mg twice daily; increase dosage every 3-7 days; usual dosage range: 10-320 mg given in 2 divided doses

I.V.:

Children: 0.01-0.1 mg/kg/dose slow IVP over 10 minutes; maximum dose: 1 mg for infants; 3 mg for children

Adults (in patients having nonfunctional GI tract): 1 mg/dose slow IVP; repeat every 5 minutes up to a total of 5 mg; titrate initial dose to desired response

Tetralogy spells: Children:

Oral: Palliation: Initial: 1 mg/kg/day every 6 hours; if ineffective, may increase dose after 1 week by 1 mg/kg/day to a maximum of 5 mg/kg/day; if patient becomes refractory, may increase slowly to a maximum of 10-15 mg/kg/day. Allow 24 hours between dosing changes.

I.V.: 0.01-0.2 mg/kg/dose infused over 10 minutes; maximum initial dose: 1 mg

Thyrotoxicosis:

Oral:

Children: 2 mg/kg/day, divided every 6-8 hours, titrate to effective dose

Adolescents and Adults: Oral: 10-40 mg/dose every 6 hours

I.V.: Adults: 1-3 mg/dose slow IVP as a single dose

Dosing adjustment in renal impairment:

Cl$_{cr}$ 31-40 mL/minute: Administer every 24-36 hours or administer 50% of normal dose

Cl$_{cr}$ 10-30 mL/minute: Administer every 24-48 hours or administer 50% of normal dose

Cl$_{cr}$ <10 mL/minute: Administer every 40-60 hours or administer 25% of normal dose

Hemodialysis: Not dialyzable (0% to 5%); supplemental dose is not necessary

Peritoneal dialysis: Supplemental dose is not necessary

Dosing adjustment/comments in hepatic disease: Marked slowing of heart rate may occur in cirrhosis with conventional doses; low initial dose and regular heart rate monitoring

Administration I.V. dose is much smaller than oral dose. When administered acutely for cardiac treatment, monitor ECG and blood pressure. May administer by rapid infusion (I.V. push) at a rate of 1 mg/minute or by slow infusion over ~30 minutes. Necessary monitoring for surgical patients who are unable to take oral beta-blockers (prolonged ileus) has not been defined. Some institutions require monitoring of baseline and postinfusion heart rate and blood pressure when a patient's response to beta-blockade has not been characterized (ie, the patient's initial dose or following a change in dose). Consult individual institutional policies and procedures.

Monitoring Parameters
Acute cardiac treatment: Monitor ECG and blood pressure with I.V. administration; heart rate and blood pressure with oral administration
Tetralogy spells: Heart rate, heart size, cardiac contractility

Reference Range Therapeutic: 50-100 ng/mL (SI: 190-390 nmol/L) at end of dose interval

Patient Information Do not discontinue abruptly; notify prescriber if CHF symptoms become worse or side effects develop; take at the same time each day; may mask diabetes symptoms; consult pharmacist or prescriber before taking with other adrenergic drugs (eg, cold medications); use with caution while driving or performing tasks requiring alertness

Dosage Forms CAP, extended release (InnPran™): 80 mg, 120 mg. **CAP, sustained release** (Inderal® LA): 60 mg, 80 mg, 120 mg, 160 mg. **INJ, solution** (Inderal®): 1 mg/mL (1 mL). **SOLN, oral** (Inderal®): 4 mg/mL (5 mL, 500 mL); 8 mg/mL (500 mL). **SOLN, oral concentrate** (Propranolol Intensol™): 80 mg/mL (30 mL). **TAB** (Inderal®): 10 mg, 20 mg, 40 mg, 60 mg, 80 mg

Propranolol and Hydrochlorothiazide
(proe PRAN oh lole & hye droe klor oh THYE a zide)

U.S. Brand Names Inderide®

Synonyms Hydrochlorothiazide and Propranolol

Therapeutic Category Antihypertensive Agent, Combination

Use Management of hypertension

Pregnancy Risk Factor C

Dosage Oral: Adults: Hypertension: Dose is individualized; typical dosages of **hydrochlorothiazide**: 12.5-50 mg/day; initial dose of **propranolol**: 80 mg/day
Daily dose of tablet form should be divided into 2 daily doses; may be used to maximum dosage of up to 160 mg of propranolol; higher dosages would result in higher than optimal thiazide dosages.

Dosage Forms TAB (Inderide®): 40/25: Propranolol 40 mg and hydrochlorothiazide 25 mg; 80/25: Propranolol 80 mg and hydrochlorothiazide 25 mg

- ♦ **Propranolol Hydrochloride** see Propranolol on page 1054
- ♦ **Propranolol Intensol™** see Propranolol on page 1054
- ♦ **Proprinal [OTC]** see Ibuprofen on page 645
- ♦ **Propulsid®** see Cisapride on page 281
- ♦ **Propylene Glycol Diacetate, Acetic Acid, and Hydrocortisone** see Acetic Acid, Propylene Glycol Diacetate, and Hydrocortisone on page 31
- ♦ **Propylene Glycol Diacetate, Hydrocortisone, and Acetic Acid** see Acetic Acid, Propylene Glycol Diacetate, and Hydrocortisone on page 31
- ♦ **2-Propylpentanoic Acid** see Valproic Acid and Derivatives on page 1288

Propylthiouracil (proe pil thye oh YOOR a sil)

Synonyms PTU

Therapeutic Category Antithyroid Agent

Use Palliative treatment of hyperthyroidism as an adjunct to ameliorate hyperthyroidism in preparation for surgical treatment or radioactive iodine therapy; management of thyrotoxic crisis

Pregnancy Risk Factor D

Contraindications Hypersensitivity to propylthiouracil or any component of the formulation; pregnancy

Warnings/Precautions Use with caution in patients >40 years of age because PTU may cause hypoprothrombinemia and bleeding; use with extreme caution in patients receiving other drugs known to cause agranulocytosis; may cause agranulocytosis, thyroid hyperplasia, thyroid carcinoma (usage >1 year). Discontinue in the presence of agranulocytosis, aplastic anemia, ANCA-positive vasculitis, hepatitis, unexplained fever, or exfoliative dermatitis. Safety and efficacy have not been established in children <6 years of age.

Common Adverse Reactions Frequency not defined.
Cardiovascular: Edema, cutaneous vasculitis, leukocytoclastic vasculitis, ANCA-positive vasculitis
Central nervous system: Fever, drowsiness, vertigo, headache, drug fever, dizziness, neuritis
Dermatologic: Skin rash, urticaria, pruritus, exfoliative dermatitis, alopecia, erythema nodosum
Endocrine & metabolic: Goiter, weight gain, swollen salivary glands
Gastrointestinal: Nausea, vomiting, loss of taste perception, stomach pain, constipation
Hematologic: Leukopenia, agranulocytosis, thrombocytopenia, bleeding, aplastic anemia
Hepatic: Cholestatic jaundice, hepatitis
Neuromuscular & skeletal: Arthralgia, paresthesia
Renal: Nephritis, glomerulonephritis, acute renal failure
Respiratory: Interstitial pneumonitis, alveolar hemorrhage
Miscellaneous: SLE-like syndrome
(Continued)

Propylthiouracil *(Continued)*

Drug Interactions
Increased Effect/Toxicity: Propylthiouracil may increase the anticoagulant activity of warfarin.

Decreased Effect: Oral anticoagulant activity is increased only until metabolic effect stabilizes. Anticoagulants may be potentiated by antivitamin K effect of propylthiouracil. Correction of hyperthyroidism may alter disposition of beta-blockers, digoxin, and theophylline, necessitating a dose reduction of these agents.

Mechanism of Action Inhibits the synthesis of thyroid hormones by blocking the oxidation of iodine in the thyroid gland; blocks synthesis of thyroxine and triiodothyronine

Pharmacodynamics/Kinetics
Onset of action: Therapeutic: 24-36 hours
Peak effect: Remission: 4 months of continued therapy
Duration: 2-3 hours
Distribution: Concentrated in the thyroid gland
Protein binding: 75% to 80%
Metabolism: Hepatic
Bioavailability: 80% to 95%
Half-life elimination: 1.5-5 hours; End-stage renal disease: 8.5 hours
Time to peak, serum: ~1 hour
Excretion: Urine (35%)

Dosage Oral: Administer in 3 equally divided doses at approximately 8-hour intervals. Adjust dosage to maintain T_3, T_4, and TSH levels in normal range; elevated T_3 may be sole indicator of inadequate treatment. Elevated TSH indicates excessive antithyroid treatment.

Children: Initial: 5-7 mg/kg/day **or** 150-200 mg/m²/day in divided doses every 8 hours
  or
  6-10 years: 50-150 mg/day
  >10 years: 150-300 mg/day
  Maintenance: Determined by patient response **or** $1/3$ to $2/3$ of the initial dose in divided doses every 8-12 hours. This usually begins after 2 months on an effective initial dose.
Adults: Initial: 300 mg/day in divided doses every 8 hours. In patients with severe hyperthyroidism, very large goiters, or both, the initial dosage is usually 450 mg/day; an occasional patient will require 600-900 mg/day; maintenance: 100-150 mg/day in divided doses every 8-12 hours
Elderly: Use lower dose recommendations; Initial: 150-300 mg/day
Withdrawal of therapy: Therapy should be withdrawn gradually with evaluation of the patient every 4-6 weeks for the first 3 months then every 3 months for the first year after discontinuation of therapy to detect any reoccurrence of a hyperthyroid state.
Dosing adjustment in renal impairment: Adjustment is not necessary

Monitoring Parameters CBC with differential, prothrombin time, liver function tests, thyroid function tests (TSH, T_3, T_4); periodic blood counts are recommended chronic therapy

Reference Range Normal laboratory values:
Total T_4: 5-12 mcg/dL
Serum T_3: 90-185 ng/dL
Free thyroxine index (FT_4 I): 6-10.5
TSH: 0.5-4.0 microU/mL

Patient Information Do not exceed prescribed dosage; take at regular intervals around-the-clock; report fever, sore throat, unusual bleeding or bruising, headache, or general malaise

Dosage Forms TAB: 50 mg

◆ **2-Propylvaleric Acid** *see* Valproic Acid and Derivatives *on page 1288*
◆ **Proscar®** *see* Finasteride *on page 524*
◆ **ProSom®** *see* Estazolam *on page 459*
◆ **Prostacyclin** *see* Epoprostenol *on page 445*
◆ **Prostaglandin E₁** *see* Alprostadil *on page 61*
◆ **Prostaglandin E₂** *see* Dinoprostone *on page 382*
◆ **Prostigmin®** *see* Neostigmine *on page 893*
◆ **Prostin E₂®** *see* Dinoprostone *on page 382*
◆ **Prostin VR Pediatric®** *see* Alprostadil *on page 61*

Protamine Sulfate *(PROE ta meen SUL fate)*

Therapeutic Category Antidote, Heparin

Use Treatment of heparin overdosage; neutralize heparin during surgery or dialysis procedures

Unlabeled/Investigational Use Treatment of low molecular weight heparin (LMWH) overdose

Pregnancy Risk Factor C

Contraindications Hypersensitivity to protamine or any component of the formulation

Warnings/Precautions May not be totally effective in some patients following cardiac surgery despite adequate doses; may cause hypersensitivity reaction in patients with a history of allergy to fish (have epinephrine 1:1000 available) and in patients sensitized to protamine (via protamine zinc insulin); too rapid administration can cause severe hypotensive and anaphylactoid-like reactions. Heparin rebound associated with anticoagulation and bleeding has been reported to occur occasionally; symptoms typically occur 8-9 hours after protamine administration, but may occur as long as 18 hours later.

Common Adverse Reactions Frequency not defined.
Cardiovascular: Sudden fall in blood pressure, bradycardia, flushing, hypotension
Central nervous system: Lassitude
Gastrointestinal: Nausea, vomiting
Hematologic: Hemorrhage
Respiratory: Dyspnea, pulmonary hypertension
Miscellaneous: Hypersensitivity reactions

Mechanism of Action Combines with strongly acidic heparin to form a stable complex (salt) neutralizing the anticoagulant activity of both drugs

Pharmacodynamics/Kinetics Onset of action: I.V.: Heparin neutralization: ~5 minutes

Dosage
Heparin neutralization: I.V.: Protamine dosage is determined by the dosage of heparin; 1 mg of protamine neutralizes 90 USP units of heparin (lung) and 115 USP units of heparin (intestinal); maximum dose: 50 mg

Heparin overdosage, following intravenous administration: I.V.: Since blood heparin concentrations decrease rapidly **after** administration, adjust the protamine dosage depending upon the duration of time since heparin administration as follows: See table.

Time Elapsed	Dose of Protamine (mg) to Neutralize 100 units of Heparin
Immediate	1-1.5
30-60 min	0.5-0.75
>2 h	0.25-0.375

Heparin overdosage, following S.C. injection: I.V.: 1-1.5 mg protamine per 100 units heparin; this may be done by a portion of the dose (eg, 25-50 mg) given slowly I.V. followed by the remaining portion as a continuous infusion over 8-16 hours (the expected absorption time of the S.C. heparin dose)

LMWH overdose (unlabeled use): **Note:** Anti-factor Xa activity never completely neutralized (maximum: ~60% to 75%)

Enoxaparin: 1 mg protamine for each mg of enoxaparin; if PTT prolonged 2-4 hours after first dose, consider additional dose of 0.5 mg for each mg of enoxaparin.

Dalteparin or tinzaparin: 1 mg protamine for each 100 anti-Xa IU of dalteparin or tinzaparin; if PTT prolonged 2-4 hours after first dose, consider additional dose of 0.5 mg for each 100 anti-Xa IU of dalteparin or tinzaparin.

Note: Excessive protamine doses may worsen bleeding potential.

Administration For I.V. use only; **incompatible** with cephalosporins and penicillins; administer slow IVP (50 mg over 10 minutes); rapid I.V. infusion causes hypotension; reconstitute vial with 5 mL sterile water; if using protamine in neonates, reconstitute with preservative-free sterile water for injection; resulting solution equals 10 mg/mL; inject without further dilution over 1-3 minutes; maximum of 50 mg in any 10-minute period

Monitoring Parameters Coagulation test, aPTT or ACT, cardiac monitor and blood pressure monitor required during administration

Dosage Forms INJ, solution [preservative free]: 10 mg/mL (5 mL, 25 mL)

♦ **Protein C (Activated), Human, Recombinant** *see Drotrecogin Alfa on page 418*
♦ **Prothrombin Complex Concentrate** *see Factor IX Complex (Human) on page 504*
♦ **Protonix®** *see Pantoprazole on page 956*
♦ **Protopam®** *see Pralidoxime on page 1025*
♦ **Protopic®** *see Tacrolimus on page 1181*

Protriptyline (proe TRIP ti leen)

Related Information
Antidepressant Agents Comparison *on page 1359*

U.S. Brand Names Vivactil®

Synonyms Protriptyline Hydrochloride

Therapeutic Category Antidepressant, Tricyclic (Secondary Amine)

Use Treatment of depression

Pregnancy Risk Factor C

Contraindications Hypersensitivity to protriptyline (cross-reactivity to other cyclic antidepressants may occur) or any component of the formulation; use of MAO inhibitors within 14 days; use of cisapride; use in a patient during the acute recovery phase of MI

Warnings/Precautions May cause sedation, resulting in impaired performance of tasks requiring alertness (eg, operating machinery or driving). Sedative effects may be additive with other CNS depressants and/or ethanol. May worsen psychosis in some patients or precipitate a shift to mania or hypomania in patients with bipolar disease. May aggravate aggressive behavior. May increase the risks associated with electroconvulsive therapy. This agent should be discontinued, when possible, prior to elective surgery. Therapy should not be abruptly discontinued in patients receiving high doses for prolonged periods. May alter glucose regulation - use with caution in patients with diabetes.

May cause orthostatic hypotension (risk is moderate relative to other antidepressants) - use with caution in patients at risk of hypotension or in patients where transient hypotensive episodes would be poorly tolerated (cardiovascular disease or cerebrovascular disease). The degree of anticholinergic blockade produced by this agent is moderate relative to other cyclic antidepressants, however, caution should still be used in patients with urinary retention, benign

(Continued)

Protriptyline *(Continued)*

prostatic hypertrophy, narrow-angle glaucoma, xerostomia, visual problems, constipation, or history of bowel obstruction.

The possibility of a suicide attempt is inherent in major depression and may persist until remission occurs. Use caution in high-risk patients during initiation of therapy. Prescriptions should be written for the smallest quantity consistent with good patient care. Use with caution in patients with a history of cardiovascular disease (including previous MI, stroke, tachycardia, or conduction abnormalities). The risk of conduction abnormalities with this agent is moderate-high relative to other antidepressants. Use caution in patients with a previous seizure disorder or condition predisposing to seizures such as brain damage, alcoholism, or concurrent therapy with other drugs which lower the seizure threshold. Use with caution in hyperthyroid patients or those receiving thyroid supplementation. Use with caution in patients with hepatic or renal dysfunction and in elderly patients.

Common Adverse Reactions Frequency not defined.

Cardiovascular: Arrhythmias, hypotension, myocardial infarction, stroke, heart block, hypertension, tachycardia, palpitations

Central nervous system: Dizziness, drowsiness, headache, confusion, delirium, hallucinations, restlessness, insomnia, nightmares, fatigue, delusions, anxiety, agitation, hypomania, exacerbation of psychosis, panic, seizures, incoordination, ataxia, EPS

Dermatologic: Alopecia, photosensitivity, rash, petechiae, urticaria, itching

Endocrine & metabolic: Breast enlargement, galactorrhea, SIADH, gynecomastia, increased or decreased libido

Gastrointestinal: Xerostomia, constipation, unpleasant taste, weight gain/loss, increased appetite, nausea, diarrhea, heartburn, vomiting, anorexia, trouble with gums, decreased lower esophageal sphincter tone may cause GE reflux

Genitourinary: Difficult urination, impotence, testicular edema

Hematologic: Agranulocytosis, leukopenia, eosinophilia, thrombocytopenia, purpura

Hepatic: Cholestatic jaundice, increased liver enzymes

Neuromuscular & skeletal: Fine muscle tremors, weakness, tremor, numbness, tingling

Ocular: Blurred vision, eye pain, increased intraocular pressure

Otic: Tinnitus

Miscellaneous: Diaphoresis (excessive), allergic reactions

Drug Interactions

Increased Effect/Toxicity: Protriptyline increases the effects of amphetamines, anticholinergics, other CNS depressants (sedatives, hypnotics, or ethanol), chlorpropamide, tolazamide, and warfarin. When used with MAO inhibitors, hyperpyrexia, hypertension, tachycardia, confusion, seizures, and **deaths have been reported** (serotonin syndrome). The SSRIs (to varying degrees), cimetidine, grapefruit juice, indinavir, methylphenidate, ritonavir, quinidine, diltiazem, and verapamil inhibit the metabolism of TCAs. Use of lithium with a TCA may increase the risk for neurotoxicity. Phenothiazines may increase concentration of some TCAs and TCAs may increase concentration of phenothiazines. Pressor response to I.V. epinephrine, norepinephrine, and phenylephrine may be enhanced in patients receiving TCAs (**Note:** Effect is unlikely with epinephrine or levonordefrin dosages typically administered as infiltration in combination with local anesthetics). Combined use of beta-agonists or drugs which prolong QT_c (including quinidine, procainamide, disopyramide, cisapride, sparfloxacin, gatifloxacin, moxifloxacin) with TCAs may predispose patients to cardiac arrhythmias.

Decreased Effect: Carbamazepine, phenobarbital, and rifampin may increase the metabolism of protriptyline, decreasing its effects. Protriptyline inhibits the antihypertensive response to bethanidine, clonidine, debrisoquin, guanadrel, guanethidine, guanabenz, guanfacine. Cimetidine and methylphenidate may decrease the metabolism of protriptyline. Cholestyramine and colestipol may bind TCAs and reduce their absorption.

Mechanism of Action Increases the synaptic concentration of serotonin and/or norepinephrine in the central nervous system by inhibition of their reuptake by the presynaptic neuronal membrane

Pharmacodynamics/Kinetics

Distribution: Crosses placenta

Protein binding: 92%

Metabolism: Extensively hepatic via N-oxidation, hydroxylation, and glucuronidation; first-pass effect (10% to 25%)

Half-life elimination: 54-92 hours (average: 74 hours)

Time to peak, serum: 24-30 hours

Excretion: Urine

Dosage Oral:

Adolescents: 15-20 mg/day

Adults: 15-60 mg in 3-4 divided doses

Elderly: 15-20 mg/day

Administration Make any dosage increase in the morning dose

Monitoring Parameters Monitor for cardiac abnormalities in elderly patients receiving doses >20 mg

Reference Range Therapeutic: 70-250 ng/mL (SI: 266-950 nmol/L); Toxic: >500 ng/mL (SI: >1900 nmol/L)

Patient Information Avoid unnecessary exposure to sunlight; do not discontinue abruptly; take dose in morning to avoid insomnia

Dosage Forms TAB: 5 mg, 10 mg

Pseudoephedrine (soo doe e FED rin)

U.S. Brand Names Biofed [OTC]; Decofed® [OTC]; Dimetapp® 12-Hour Non-Drowsy Extentabs® [OTC]; Dimetapp® Decongestant [OTC]; Genaphed® [OTC]; Kidkare Decongestant [OTC]; Kodet SE [OTC]; Oranyl [OTC]; PediaCare® Decongestant Infants [OTC]; Silfedrine Children's [OTC]; Sudafed® [OTC]; Sudafed® 12 Hour [OTC]; Sudafed® 24 Hour [OTC]; Sudafed® Children's [OTC]; Sudodrin [OTC]; Triaminic® Allergy Congestion [OTC]

Synonyms d-Isoephedrine Hydrochloride; Pseudoephedrine Hydrochloride; Pseudoephedrine Sulfate

Therapeutic Category Adrenergic Agonist Agent; Alpha/Beta Agonist; Decongestant, Oral; Sympathomimetic Agent

Use Temporary symptomatic relief of nasal congestion due to common cold, upper respiratory allergies, and sinusitis; also promotes nasal or sinus drainage

Pregnancy Risk Factor C

Contraindications Hypersensitivity to pseudoephedrine or any component of the formulation; MAO inhibitor therapy

Warnings/Precautions Use with caution in patients >60 years of age; administer with caution to patients with hypertension, hyperthyroidism, diabetes mellitus, cardiovascular disease, ischemic heart disease, increased intraocular pressure, or prostatic hyperplasia. Elderly patients are more likely to experience adverse reactions to sympathomimetics. Overdosage may cause hallucinations, seizures, CNS depression, and death. Avoid prolonged use; generally limited to not more than 5 days.

Common Adverse Reactions Frequency not defined.
Cardiovascular: Tachycardia, palpitations, arrhythmias
Central nervous system: Nervousness, transient stimulation, insomnia, excitability, dizziness, drowsiness, convulsions, hallucinations, headache
Gastrointestinal: Nausea, vomiting
Genitourinary: Dysuria
Neuromuscular & skeletal: Weakness, tremor
Respiratory: Dyspnea
Miscellaneous: Diaphoresis

Drug Interactions
Increased Effect/Toxicity: MAO inhibitors may increase blood pressure effects of pseudoephedrine. Sympathomimetic agents may increase toxicity.
Decreased Effect: Decreased effect of methyldopa, reserpine.

Mechanism of Action Directly stimulates alpha-adrenergic receptors of respiratory mucosa causing vasoconstriction; directly stimulates beta-adrenergic receptors causing bronchial relaxation, increased heart rate and contractility

Pharmacodynamics/Kinetics
Onset of action: Decongestant: Oral: 15-30 minutes
Duration: Immediate release tablet: 4-6 hours; Extended release: ≤12 hours
Absorption: Rapid
Metabolism: Partially hepatic
Half-life elimination: 9-16 hours
Excretion: Urine (70% to 90% as unchanged drug, 1% to 6% as active norpseudoephedrine); dependent on urine pH and flow rate; alkaline urine decreases renal elimination of pseudoephedrine

Dosage Oral:
Children:
<2 years: 4 mg/kg/day in divided doses every 6 hours
2-5 years: 15 mg every 6 hours; maximum: 60 mg/24 hours
6-12 years: 30 mg every 6 hours; maximum: 120 mg/24 hours
Adults: 30-60 mg every 4-6 hours, sustained release: 120 mg every 12 hours; maximum: 240 mg/24 hours
(Continued)

Pseudoephedrine *(Continued)*

Dosing adjustment in renal impairment: Reduce dose

Patient Information Do not exceed recommended dosage and do not use for more than 3-5 days; may cause wakefulness or nervousness; take last dose 4-6 hours before bedtime; do not crush sustained release product; consult pharmacist or prescriber before using

Dosage Forms DROPS, oral: 7.5 mg/0.8 mL (15 mL, 30 mL). **GELCAP:** 30 mg. **LIQ:** 15 mg/5 mL (120 mL, 480 mL). **SYR:** 30 mg/5 mL (120 mL, 240 mL, 480 mL, 3840 mL). **TAB:** 30 mg, 60 mg. **TAB, chewable:** 15 mg. **TAB, extended release:** 120 mg, 240 mg

- ♦ **Pseudoephedrine, Acetaminophen, and Chlorpheniramine** *see* Acetaminophen, Chlorpheniramine, and Pseudoephedrine *on page 28*
- ♦ **Pseudoephedrine, Acetaminophen, and Dextromethorphan** *see* Acetaminophen, Dextromethorphan, and Pseudoephedrine *on page 28*
- ♦ **Pseudoephedrine and Acetaminophen** *see* Acetaminophen and Pseudoephedrine *on page 26*
- ♦ **Pseudoephedrine and Acrivastine** *see* Acrivastine and Pseudoephedrine *on page 35*
- ♦ **Pseudoephedrine and Brompheniramine** *see* Brompheniramine and Pseudoephedrine *on page 181*
- ♦ **Pseudoephedrine and Carbetapentane** *see* Carbetapentane and Pseudoephedrine *on page 217*
- ♦ **Pseudoephedrine and Carbinoxamine** *see* Carbinoxamine and Pseudoephedrine *on page 218*
- ♦ **Pseudoephedrine and Chlorpheniramine** *see* Chlorpheniramine and Pseudoephedrine *on page 263*
- ♦ **Pseudoephedrine and Dexbrompheniramine** *see* Dexbrompheniramine and Pseudoephedrine *on page 359*

Pseudoephedrine and Dextromethorphan

(soo doe e FED rin & deks troe meth OR fan)

U.S. Brand Names Children's Sudafed® Cough & Cold [OTC]; Pediacare® Decongestant Plus Cough [OTC]; Pediacare® Long Acting Cough Plus Cold [OTC]; Robitussin® Maximum Strength Cough & Cold [OTC]; Robitussin® Pediatric Cough & Cold [OTC]; Vicks® 44D Cough & Head Congestion [OTC]

Synonyms Dextromethorphan and Pseudoephedrine

Therapeutic Category Antitussive/Decongestant

Use Temporary symptomatic relief of nasal congestion due to common cold, upper respiratory allergies, and sinusitis; also promotes nasal or sinus drainage; symptomatic relief of coughs caused by minor viral upper respiratory tract infections or inhaled irritants; most effective for a chronic nonproductive cough

Dosage Oral:

Children: Dose should be based on pseudoephedrine component

Adults: 5-10 mL every 6 hours

Dosage Forms DROPS, oral: Pseudoephedrine 7.5 mg and dextromethorphan 2.5 mg per 0.8 mL (15 mL). **LIQ:** Pseudoephedrine 15 mg and dextromethorphan 5 mg per 5 mL (120 mL), pseudoephedrine 15 mg and dextromethorphan 7.5 mg per 5 mL (120 mL, 240 mL), pseudoephedrine 20 mg and dextromethorphan 10 mg per 5 mL (120 mL, 240 mL), pseudoephedrine 30 mg and dextromethorphan 15 mg per 5 mL (120 mL, 240 mL). **TAB, chewable:** Pseudoephedrine 7.5 mg and dextromethorphan 2.5 mg

- ♦ **Pseudoephedrine and Diphenhydramine** *see* Diphenhydramine and Pseudoephedrine *on page 385*
- ♦ **Pseudoephedrine and Fexofenadine** *see* Fexofenadine and Pseudoephedrine *on page 522*
- ♦ **Pseudoephedrine and Guaifenesin** *see* Guaifenesin and Pseudoephedrine *on page 605*
- ♦ **Pseudoephedrine and Hydrocodone** *see* Hydrocodone and Pseudoephedrine *on page 631*

Pseudoephedrine and Ibuprofen (soo doe e FED rin & eye byoo PROE fen)

U.S. Brand Names Advil® Cold, Children's [OTC]; Advil® Cold & Sinus [OTC]; Dristan® Sinus [OTC]; Motrin® Cold and Sinus [OTC]; Motrin® Cold, Children's [OTC]

Synonyms Ibuprofen and Pseudoephedrine

Therapeutic Category Analgesic, Non-narcotic and Decongestant

Use For temporary relief of cold, sinus and flu symptoms (including nasal congestion, headache, sore throat, minor body aches and pains, and fever)

Pregnancy Risk Factor Ibuprofen: B/D (3rd trimester)

Dosage OTC labeling: Oral:

Children: Ibuprofen 100 mg and pseudoephedrine 15 mg per 5 mL: May repeat dose every 6 hours (maximum: 4 doses/24 hours); dose should be based on weight when possible. Contact healthcare provider if symptoms have not improved within 3 days (2 days if treating sore throat accompanied by fever).

2-5 years or 11 to <22 kg (24-47 pounds): 5 mL

6-11 years or 22-43 kg (48-95 pounds): 10 mL

Children ≥12 years and Adults: Ibuprofen 200 mg and pseudoephedrine 30 mg per dose: One dose every 4-6 hours as needed; may increase to 2 doses if necessary (maximum: 6 doses/24 hours). Contact healthcare provider if symptoms have not improved within 7 days when treating cold symptoms or within 3 days when treating fever.

Dosage Forms CAP, liquid filled: Pseudoephedrine 30 mg and ibuprofen 200 mg. **CAPLET:** Pseudoephedrine 30 mg and ibuprofen 200 mg. **SUSP, oral:** Pseudoephedrine 15 mg and ibuprofen 100 mg per 5 mL (120 mL). **TAB:** Pseudoephedrine 30 mg and ibuprofen 200 mg

♦ **Pseudoephedrine and Loratadine** *see* Loratadine and Pseudoephedrine *on page 760*
♦ **Pseudoephedrine and Triprolidine** *see* Triprolidine and Pseudoephedrine *on page 1273*
♦ **Pseudoephedrine, Carbinoxamine, and Dextromethorphan** *see* Carbinoxamine, Pseudoephedrine, and Dextromethorphan *on page 219*
♦ **Pseudoephedrine, Chlorpheniramine, and Acetaminophen** *see* Acetaminophen, Chlorpheniramine, and Pseudoephedrine *on page 28*
♦ **Pseudoephedrine, Chlorpheniramine, and Codeine** *see* Chlorpheniramine, Pseudoephedrine, and Codeine *on page 265*
♦ **Pseudoephedrine, Chlorpheniramine, and Dextromethorphan** *see* Chlorpheniramine, Pseudoephedrine, and Dextromethorphan *on page 265*
♦ **Pseudoephedrine, Dextromethorphan, and Acetaminophen** *see* Acetaminophen, Dextromethorphan, and Pseudoephedrine *on page 28*
♦ **Pseudoephedrine, Dextromethorphan, and Carbinoxamine** *see* Carbinoxamine, Pseudoephedrine, and Dextromethorphan *on page 219*
♦ **Pseudoephedrine, Dextromethorphan, and Guaifenesin** *see* Guaifenesin, Pseudoephedrine, and Dextromethorphan *on page 606*
♦ **Pseudoephedrine, Guaifenesin, and Codeine** *see* Guaifenesin, Pseudoephedrine, and Codeine *on page 606*
♦ **Pseudoephedrine Hydrochloride** *see* Pseudoephedrine *on page 1061*
♦ **Pseudoephedrine, Hydrocodone, and Carbinoxamine** *see* Hydrocodone, Carbinoxamine, and Pseudoephedrine *on page 632*
♦ **Pseudoephedrine Sulfate** *see* Pseudoephedrine *on page 1061*
♦ **Pseudoephedrine, Triprolidine, and Codeine Pseudoephedrine, Codeine, and Triprolidine** *see* Triprolidine, Pseudoephedrine, and Codeine *on page 1274*
♦ **Pseudo GG TR** *see* Guaifenesin *on page 605*
♦ **Pseudomonic Acid A** *see* Mupirocin *on page 866*
♦ **Pseudovent™** *see* Guaifenesin and Pseudoephedrine *on page 605*
♦ **Pseudovent™ DM** *see* Guaifenesin, Pseudoephedrine, and Dextromethorphan *on page 606*
♦ **Pseudovent™-Ped** *see* Guaifenesin and Pseudoephedrine *on page 605*
♦ **Psorcon®** *see* Diflorasone *on page 372*
♦ **Psorcon® e™** *see* Diflorasone *on page 372*
♦ **Psoriatec™** *see* Anthralin *on page 101*

Psyllium (SIL i yum)
Related Information
Laxatives, Classification and Properties *on page 1380*
U.S. Brand Names Fiberall®; Genfiber® [OTC]; Hydrocil® [OTC]; Konsyl® [OTC]; Konsyl-D® [OTC]; Konsyl® Easy Mix [OTC]; Konsyl® Orange [OTC]; Metamucil® [OTC]; Metamucil® Smooth Texture [OTC]; Modane® Bulk [OTC]; Perdiem® Fiber Therapy [OTC]; Reguloid® [OTC]; Serutan® [OTC]
Synonyms Plantago Seed; Plantain Seed; Psyllium Hydrophilic Mucilloid
Therapeutic Category Antidiarrheal; Laxative, Bulk-Producing
Use Treatment of chronic atonic or spastic constipation and in constipation associated with rectal disorders; management of irritable bowel syndrome; labeled for OTC use as fiber supplement, treatment of constipation
Pregnancy Risk Factor B
Contraindications Hypersensitivity to psyllium or any component of the formulation; fecal impaction; GI obstruction
Warnings/Precautions Products must be taken with adequate fluid. Use with caution in patients with esophageal strictures, ulcers, stenosis, or intestinal adhesions; elderly may have insufficient fluid intake which may predispose them to fecal impaction and bowel obstruction.
Common Adverse Reactions Frequency not defined.
  Gastrointestinal: Esophageal or bowel obstruction, diarrhea, constipation, abdominal cramps
  Respiratory: Bronchospasm
  Miscellaneous: Anaphylaxis upon inhalation in susceptible individuals, rhinoconjunctivitis
Drug Interactions
  Decreased Effect: Decreased effect of warfarin, digitalis, potassium-sparing diuretics, salicylates, tetracyclines, nitrofurantoin when taken together. Separate administration times to reduce potential for drug-drug interaction.
Mechanism of Action Adsorbs water in the intestine to form a viscous liquid which promotes peristalsis and reduces transit time
Pharmacodynamics/Kinetics
  Onset of action: 12-24 hours
    Peak effect: 2-3 days
  Absorption: None; small amounts of grain extracts present in the preparation have been reportedly absorbed following colonic hydrolysis
Dosage Oral (administer at least 2 hours before or after other drugs):
  Children 6-11 years: Approximately ½ adult dosage
  Children ≥12 years and Adults: Take 1 dose up to 3 times/day; all doses should be followed with 8 oz of water or liquid
    Capsule: 4 capsules/dose (range: 2-6); swallow capsules one at a time
  (Continued)

Psyllium *(Continued)*

Powder: 1 rounded tablespoonful/dose (1 teaspoonful/dose for many sugar free or select concentrated products) mixed in 8 oz liquid
Tablet: 1 tablet/dose
Wafer: 2 wafers/dose

Administration Inhalation of psyllium dust may cause sensitivity to psyllium (eg, runny nose, watery eyes, wheezing). Drink a full glass of liquid with each dose. Powder must be mixed in a glass of water or juice. Separate dose from other drug therapies.

Patient Information Drink a full glass of liquid with each dose; powders must be mixed in a glass of water or juice; do not use for longer than 1 week without the advice of a physician

Dosage Forms CAP: 0.52 g. **GRAN:** 2.5 g/teaspoon (510 g), 4 g/teaspoon (250 g). **POWDER:** 3.4 g/dose (unit-dose packets, 6.5 g unit-dose packets, 12 g unit-dose packets, 300 g, 325 g, 390 g, 397 g, 425 g, 450 g, 500 g, 538 g, 570 g, 595 g, 609 g, 660 g, 699 g, 870 g, 912 g, 1254 g, 1368 g), 3.5 g/dose (300 g, 454 g), 6 g/dose (6 g unit-dose packets, 250 g, 300 g, 450 g). **WAFER:** 3.4 g/dose (24s)

- **Psyllium Hydrophilic Mucilloid** *see Psyllium on page 1063*
- **Pteroylglutamic Acid** *see Folic Acid on page 555*
- **PTU** *see Propylthiouracil on page 1057*
- **Pulmicort Respules®** *see Budesonide on page 182*
- **Pulmicort Turbuhaler®** *see Budesonide on page 182*
- **Pulmozyme®** *see Dornase Alfa on page 403*
- **Purified Chick Embryo Cell** *see Rabies Virus Vaccine on page 1078*
- **Purinethol®** *see Mercaptopurine on page 795*
- **P-V Tussin** *see Hydrocodone and Pseudoephedrine on page 631*

Pyrantel Pamoate *(pi RAN tel PAM oh ate)*

U.S. Brand Names Pin-X® [OTC]; Reese's® Pinworm Medicine [OTC]

Therapeutic Category Anthelmintic

Use Treatment of pinworms (*Enterobius vermicularis*) and roundworms (*Ascaris lumbricoides*)

Unlabeled/Investigational Use Treatment of whipworms (*Trichuris trichiura*) and hookworms (*Ancylostoma duodenale*)

Pregnancy Risk Factor C

Contraindications Hypersensitivity to pyrantel pamoate or any component of the formulation

Warnings/Precautions Use with caution in patients with liver impairment, anemia, malnutrition, or pregnancy. Since pinworm infections are easily spread to others, treat all family members in close contact with the patient.

Common Adverse Reactions Frequency not defined.
Central nervous system: Dizziness, drowsiness, insomnia, headache
Dermatologic: Rash
Gastrointestinal: Anorexia, nausea, vomiting, abdominal cramps, diarrhea, tenesmus
Hepatic: Elevated liver enzymes
Neuromuscular & skeletal: Weakness

Drug Interactions
Decreased Effect: Decreased effect with piperazine

Mechanism of Action Causes the release of acetylcholine and inhibits cholinesterase; acts as a depolarizing neuromuscular blocker, paralyzing the helminths

Pharmacodynamics/Kinetics
Absorption: Oral: Poor
Metabolism: Partially hepatic
Time to peak, serum: 1-3 hours
Excretion: Feces (50% as unchanged drug); urine (7% as unchanged drug)

Dosage Children and Adults (purgation is not required prior to use): Oral:
Roundworm, pinworm, or trichostrongyliasis: 11 mg/kg administered as a single dose; maximum dose: 1 g. **(Note:** For pinworm infection, dosage should be repeated in 2 weeks and all family members should be treated).
Hookworm (unlabeled use): 11 mg/kg administered once daily for 3 days

Administration May be mixed with milk or fruit juice

Monitoring Parameters Stool for presence of eggs, worms, and occult blood, serum AST and ALT

Patient Information May mix drug with milk or fruit juice; strict hygiene is essential to prevent reinfection

Dosage Forms SUSP, oral: (Pin-X®): 144 mg/mL (30 mL, 60 mL); (Reese's® Pinworm Medicine): 144 mg/mL (30 mL). **TAB** (Reese's® Pinworm Medicine): 180 mg

Pyrazinamide *(peer a ZIN a mide)*

Related Information
Antimicrobial Drugs of Choice *on page 1440*
Tuberculosis Treatment Guidelines *on page 1466*

Synonyms Pyrazinoic Acid Amide

Therapeutic Category Antitubercular Agent

Use Adjunctive treatment of tuberculosis in combination with other antituberculosis agents

Pregnancy Risk Factor C

Contraindications Hypersensitivity to pyrazinamide or any component of the formulation; acute gout; severe hepatic damage

Warnings/Precautions Use with caution in patients with renal failure, chronic gout, diabetes mellitus, or porphyria

Common Adverse Reactions 1% to 10%:
Central nervous system: Malaise
Gastrointestinal: Nausea, vomiting, anorexia
Neuromuscular & skeletal: Arthralgia, myalgia

Drug Interactions
Increased Effect/Toxicity: Combination therapy with rifampin and pyrazinamide has been associated with severe and fatal hepatotoxic reactions.

Mechanism of Action Converted to pyrazinoic acid in susceptible strains of *Mycobacterium* which lowers the pH of the environment; exact mechanism of action has not been elucidated

Pharmacodynamics/Kinetics Bacteriostatic or bactericidal depending on drug's concentration at infection site

Absorption: Well absorbed
Distribution: Widely into body tissues and fluids including liver, lung, and CSF
Relative diffusion from blood into CSF: Adequate with or without inflammation (exceeds usual MICs)
CSF:blood level ratio: Inflamed meninges: 100%
Protein binding: 50%
Metabolism: Hepatic
Half-life elimination: 9-10 hours
Time to peak, serum: Within 2 hours
Excretion: Urine (4% as unchanged drug)

Dosage Oral (calculate dose on ideal body weight rather than total body weight): **Note:** A four-drug regimen (isoniazid, rifampin, pyrazinamide, and either streptomycin or ethambutol) is preferred for the initial, empiric treatment of TB. When the drug susceptibility results are available, the regimen should be altered as appropriate. For the treatment of latent TB infection (LTBI), combination pyrazinamide/rifampin therapy should not generally be offered (*MMWR* Aug 8, 2003).

Children and Adults:
Daily therapy: 15-30 mg/kg/day (maximum: 2 g/day)
Directly observed therapy (DOT):
Twice weekly: 50-70 mg/kg (maximum: 4 g)
Three times/week: 50-70 mg/kg (maximum: 3 g)
Elderly: Start with a lower daily dose (15 mg/kg) and increase as tolerated
Dosing adjustment in renal impairment: Cl$_{cr}$ <50 mL/minute: Avoid use or reduce dose to 12-20 mg/kg/day
Dosing adjustment in hepatic impairment: Reduce dose

Monitoring Parameters Periodic liver function tests, serum uric acid, sputum culture, chest x-ray 2-3 months into treatment and at completion

Patient Information Report fever, loss of appetite, malaise, nausea, vomiting, darkened urine, pale stools; do not stop taking without consulting a physician

Dosage Forms TAB: 500 mg

♦ **Pyrazinoic Acid Amide** *see Pyrazinamide on page 1064*

Pyrethrins and Piperonyl Butoxide
(pye RE thrins & pi PER oh nil byo TOKS ide)

U.S. Brand Names A-200® Maximum Strength [OTC]; Pronto® [OTC]; Pyrinyl Plus® [OTC]; RID® Maximum Strength [OTC]; Tisit® [OTC]; Tisit® Blue Gel [OTC]

Synonyms Piperonyl Butoxide and Pyrethrins

Therapeutic Category Antiparasitic Agent, Topical; Pediculocide; Shampoo, Pediculocide

Use Treatment of *Pediculus humanus* infestations (head lice, body lice, pubic lice and their eggs)

Pregnancy Risk Factor C

Contraindications Hypersensitivity to pyrethrins, ragweed, chrysanthemums, or any component of the formulation

Warnings/Precautions For external use only; do not use in eyelashes or eyebrows

Common Adverse Reactions Frequency not defined.
Dermatologic: Pruritus
Local: Burning, stinging, irritation with repeat use

Mechanism of Action Pyrethrins are derived from flowers that belong to the chrysanthemum family. The mechanism of action on the neuronal membranes of lice is similar to that of DDT. Piperonyl butoxide is usually added to pyrethrin to enhance the product's activity by decreasing the metabolism of pyrethrins in arthropods.

Pharmacodynamics/Kinetics
Onset of action: ~30 minutes
Absorption: Minimal
Metabolism: Via ester hydrolysis and hydroxylation

Dosage Application of pyrethrins:
Topical products:
Apply enough solution to completely wet infested area, including hair
Allow to remain on area for 10 minutes
Wash and rinse with large amounts of warm water
(Continued)

Pyrethrins and Piperonyl Butoxide *(Continued)*

Use fine-toothed comb to remove lice and eggs from hair

Shampoo hair to restore body and luster

Treatment may be repeated if necessary once in a 24-hour period

Repeat treatment in 7-10 days to kill newly hatched lice

Solution for furniture, bedding: Spray on entire area to be treated; allow to dry before use. Intended for use on items which cannot be laundered or dry cleaned. **Not for use on humans or animals.**

Administration For external use only; avoid touching eyes, mouth, or other mucous membranes.

Patient Information For external use only; avoid touching eyes, mouth, or other mucous membranes; do not use in eyelashes or eyebrows; contact prescriber if irritation occurs or if condition does not improve in 2-3 days

Dosage Forms FOAM, topical [mousse]: Pyrethrum 0.33% and piperonyl 4% (156 g). **GEL:** Pyrethrum 0.33% and piperonyl 3% (30 g). **LIQ, topical:** Pyrethrum 0.33% and piperonyl 2% (60 mL, 120 mL). **SHAMPOO:** Pyrethrum 0.33% and piperonyl 3% (60 mL, 120 mL), pyrethrum 0.33% and piperonyl 4% (60 mL, 120 mL, 240 mL). **SOLN, spray** [for furniture, garments, bedding; not for human or animal use]: Pyrethrum 0.4% and piperonyl 2% (150 mL)

♦ **2-Pyridine Aldoxime Methochloride** *see Pralidoxime on page 1025*

♦ **Pyridium®** *see Phenazopyridine on page 987*

Pyridostigmine *(peer id oh STIG meen)*

U.S. Brand Names Mestinon®; Mestinon® Timespan®; Regonol® [DSC]

Synonyms Pyridostigmine Bromide

Therapeutic Category Acetylcholinesterase Inhibitor; Antidote, Neuromuscular Blocking Agent; Cholinergic Agent

Use Symptomatic treatment of myasthenia gravis; antidote for nondepolarizing neuromuscular blockers

Military use: Pretreatment for Soman nerve gas exposure

Pregnancy Risk Factor B

Contraindications Hypersensitivity to pyridostigmine, bromides, or any component of the formulation; GI or GU obstruction

Warnings/Precautions Use with caution in patients with epilepsy, asthma, bradycardia, hyperthyroidism, cardiac arrhythmias, or peptic ulcer; adequate facilities should be available for cardiopulmonary resuscitation when testing and adjusting dose for myasthenia gravis; have atropine and epinephrine ready to treat hypersensitivity reactions; overdosage may result in cholinergic crisis, this must be distinguished from myasthenic crisis; anticholinesterase insensitivity can develop for brief or prolonged periods. Safety and efficacy in pediatric patients have not been established. Regonol® injection contains 1% benzyl alcohol as the preservative (not intended for use in newborns!)

Common Adverse Reactions Frequency not defined.

Cardiovascular: Arrhythmias (especially bradycardia), hypotension, decreased carbon monoxide, tachycardia, AV block, nodal rhythm, nonspecific ECG changes, cardiac arrest, syncope, flushing

Central nervous system: Convulsions, dysarthria, dysphonia, dizziness, loss of consciousness, drowsiness, headache

Dermatologic: Skin rash, thrombophlebitis (I.V.), urticaria

Gastrointestinal: Hyperperistalsis, nausea, vomiting, salivation, diarrhea, stomach cramps, dysphagia, flatulence, abdominal pain

Genitourinary: Urinary urgency

Neuromuscular & skeletal: Weakness, fasciculations, muscle cramps, spasms, arthralgias, myalgia

Ocular: Small pupils, lacrimation, amblyopia

Respiratory: Increased bronchial secretions, laryngospasm, bronchiolar constriction, respiratory muscle paralysis, dyspnea, respiratory depression, respiratory arrest, bronchospasm

Miscellaneous: Diaphoresis (increased), anaphylaxis, allergic reactions

Drug Interactions

Increased Effect/Toxicity: Increased effect of depolarizing neuromuscular blockers (succinylcholine). Increased toxicity with edrophonium. Increased bradycardia/hypotension with beta-blockers.

Decreased Effect: Neuromuscular blockade reversal effect of pyridostigmine may be decreased by aminoglycosides, quinolones, tetracyclines, bacitracin, colistin, polymyxin B, sodium colistimethate, quinidine, elevated serum magnesium concentrations.

Mechanism of Action Inhibits destruction of acetylcholine by acetylcholinesterase which facilitates transmission of impulses across myoneural junction

Pharmacodynamics/Kinetics

Onset of action: Oral, I.M.: 15-30 minutes; I.V. injection: 2-5 minutes

Duration: Oral: Up to 6-8 hours (due to slow absorption); I.V.: 2-3 hours

Absorption: Oral: Very poor

Distribution: 19 ± 12 L

Metabolism: Hepatic

Bioavailability: 10% to 20%

Half-life elimination: 1-2 hours; Renal failure: ≤6 hours

Excretion: Urine (80% to 90% as unchanged drug)

Dosage

Myasthenia gravis:

Oral:

Children: 7 mg/kg/24 hours divided into 5-6 doses

Adults: Highly individualized dosing ranges: 60-1500 mg/day, usually 600 mg/day divided into 5-6 doses, spaced to provide maximum relief

Sustained release formulation: Highly individualized dosing ranges: 180-540 mg once or twice daily (doses separated by at least 6 hours); **Note:** Most clinicians reserve sustained release dosage form for bedtime dose only.

I.M., slow I.V. push:

Children: 0.05-0.15 mg/kg/dose

Adults: To supplement oral dosage pre- and postoperatively during labor and postpartum, during myasthenic crisis, or when oral therapy is impractical: ~1/30th of oral dose; observe patient closely for cholinergic reactions

or

I.V. infusion: Initial: 2 mg/hour with gradual titration in increments of 0.5-1 mg/hour, up to a maximum rate of 4 mg/hour

Pretreatment for Soman nerve gas exposure (military use): Oral: Adults: 30 mg every 8 hours beginning several hours prior to exposure; discontinue at first sign of nerve agent exposure, then begin atropine and pralidoxime

Reversal of nondepolarizing muscle relaxants: **Note:** Atropine sulfate (0.6-1.2 mg) I.V. immediately prior to pyridostigmine to minimize side effects: I.V.:

Children: Dosing range: 0.1-0.25 mg/kg/dose*

Adults: 0.1-0.25 mg/kg/dose; 10-20 mg is usually sufficient*

*Full recovery usually occurs ≤15 minutes, but ≥30 minutes may be required

Dosage adjustment in renal dysfunction: Lower dosages may be required due to prolonged elimination; no specific recommendations have been published

Administration Do **not** crush sustained release tablet.

Patient Information Side effects are generally due to exaggerated pharmacologic effects; most common side effects are salivation and muscle fasciculations; report nausea, vomiting, muscle weakness, severe abdominal pain, or difficulty breathing

Dosage Forms INJ, solution (Mestinon®): 5 mg/mL (2 mL); (Regonol® [DSC]): 5 mg/mL (2 mL, 5 mL) . **SYR** (Mestinon®): 60 mg/5 mL (480 mL). **TAB:** 30 mg, 60 mg; (Mestinon®): 60 mg. **TAB, sustained release** (Mestinon® Timespan®): 180 mg

♦ **Pyridostigmine Bromide** *see* Pyridostigmine *on page 1066*

Pyridoxine (peer i DOKS een)

Related Information

Anticonvulsants by Seizure Type *on page 1358*

Epilepsy *on page 1477*

U.S. Brand Names Aminoxin® [OTC]

Synonyms Pyridoxine Hydrochloride; Vitamin B₆

Therapeutic Category Antidote, Cycloserine Toxicity; Antidote, Hydralazine Toxicity; Antidote, Isoniazid Toxicity; Vitamin, Water Soluble

Use Prevention and treatment of vitamin B₆ deficiency, pyridoxine-dependent seizures in infants; adjunct to treatment of acute toxicity from isoniazid, cycloserine, or hydralazine overdose

Pregnancy Risk Factor A/C (dose exceeding RDA recommendation)

Contraindications Hypersensitivity to pyridoxine or any component of the formulation

Warnings/Precautions Dependence and withdrawal may occur with doses >200 mg/day

Common Adverse Reactions Frequency not defined.

Central nervous system: Headache, seizures (following very large I.V. doses), sensory neuropathy

Endocrine & metabolic: Decreased serum folic acid secretions

Gastrointestinal: Nausea

Hepatic: Increased AST

Neuromuscular & skeletal: Paresthesia

Miscellaneous: Allergic reactions

Drug Interactions

Decreased Effect: Pyridoxine may decrease serum levels of levodopa, phenobarbital, and phenytoin (patients taking levodopa without carbidopa should avoid supplemental vitamin B₆ >5 mg per day, which includes multivitamin preparations).

Mechanism of Action Precursor to pyridoxal, which functions in the metabolism of proteins, carbohydrates, and fats; pyridoxal also aids in the release of liver and muscle-stored glycogen and in the synthesis of GABA (within the central nervous system) and heme

Pharmacodynamics/Kinetics

Absorption: Enteral, parenteral: Well absorbed

Metabolism: Via 4-pyridoxic acid (active form) and other metabolites

Half-life elimination: 15-20 days

Excretion: Urine

Dosage

Recommended daily allowance (RDA):

Children:

1-3 years: 0.9 mg

4-6 years: 1.3 mg

7-10 years: 1.6 mg

(Continued)

PYRIMETHAMINE

Pyridoxine *(Continued)*

Adults:
Male: 1.7-2.0 mg
Female: 1.4-1.6 mg
Pyridoxine-dependent Infants:
Oral: 2-100 mg/day
I.M., I.V., S.C.: 10-100 mg
Dietary deficiency: Oral:
Children: 5-25 mg/24 hours for 3 weeks, then 1.5-2.5 mg/day in multiple vitamin product
Adults: 10-20 mg/day for 3 weeks
Drug-induced neuritis (eg, isoniazid, hydralazine, penicillamine, cycloserine): Oral:
Children:
Treatment: 10-50 mg/24 hours
Prophylaxis: 1-2 mg/kg/24 hours
Adults:
Treatment: 100-200 mg/24 hours
Prophylaxis: 25-100 mg/24 hours
Treatment of seizures and/or coma from acute isoniazid toxicity, a dose of pyridoxine hydrochloride equal to the amount of INH ingested can be given I.M./I.V. in divided doses together with other anticonvulsants; if the amount INH ingested is not known, administer 5 g I.V. pyridoxine
Treatment of acute hydralazine toxicity, a pyridoxine dose of 25 mg/kg in divided doses I.M./I.V. has been used

Reference Range Over 50 ng/mL (SI: 243 nmol/L) (varies considerably with method). A broad range is ~25-80 ng/mL (SI: 122-389 nmol/L). HPLC method for pyridoxal phosphate has normal range of 3.5-18 ng/mL (SI: 17-88 nmol/L).

Patient Information Dietary sources of pyridoxine include red meats, bananas, potatoes, yeast, lima beans, whole grain cereals; do not exceed recommended doses

Dosage Forms CAP: 250 mg. **INJ, solution:** 100 mg/mL (1 mL). **TAB:** 25 mg, 50 mg, 100 mg, 250 mg, 500 mg. **TAB, enteric coated:** 20 mg

- **Pyridoxine, Folic Acid, and Cyanocobalamin** *see* Folic Acid, Cyanocobalamin, and Pyridoxine *on page 555*
- **Pyridoxine Hydrochloride** *see* Pyridoxine *on page 1067*

Pyrimethamine *(peer i METH a meen)*

Related Information
Malaria Treatment *on page 1464*

U.S. Brand Names Daraprim®

Therapeutic Category Antimalarial Agent; Antiprotozoal

Use Prophylaxis of malaria due to susceptible strains of plasmodia; used in conjunction with quinine and sulfadiazine for the treatment of uncomplicated attacks of chloroquine-resistant *P. falciparum* malaria; used in conjunction with fast-acting schizonticide to initiate transmission control and suppression cure; synergistic combination with sulfonamide in treatment of toxoplasmosis

Pregnancy Risk Factor C

Contraindications Hypersensitivity to pyrimethamine or any component of the formulation; chloroguanide; resistant malaria; megaloblastic anemia secondary to folate deficiency

Warnings/Precautions When used for more than 3-4 days, it may be advisable to administer leucovorin to prevent hematologic complications; monitor CBC and platelet counts every 2 weeks; use with caution in patients with impaired renal or hepatic function or with possible G6PD

Common Adverse Reactions Frequency not defined.
Cardiovascular: Arrhythmias (large doses)
Central nervous system: Depression, fever, insomnia, lightheadedness, malaise, seizures
Dermatologic: Abnormal skin pigmentation, dermatitis, erythema multiforme, rash, Stevens-Johnson syndrome
Gastrointestinal: Anorexia, abdominal cramps, vomiting, diarrhea, xerostomia, atrophic glossitis
Hematologic: Megaloblastic anemia, leukopenia, pancytopenia, thrombocytopenia, pulmonary eosinophilia
Miscellaneous: Anaphylaxis

Drug Interactions
Cytochrome P450 Effect: Inhibits CYP2C8/9 (moderate), 2D6 (moderate)
Increased Effect/Toxicity: Increased effect with sulfonamides (synergy), methotrexate, and TMP/SMZ.
Decreased Effect: Pyrimethamine effectiveness is decreased by acid.

Mechanism of Action Inhibits parasitic dihydrofolate reductase, resulting in inhibition of vital tetrahydrofolic acid synthesis

Pharmacodynamics/Kinetics
Onset of action: ~1 hour
Absorption: Well absorbed
Distribution: Widely, mainly in blood cells, kidneys, lungs, liver, and spleen; crosses into CSF; crosses placenta; enters breast milk
Protein binding: 80% to 87%
Metabolism: Hepatic

Half-life elimination: 80-95 hours
Time to peak, serum: 1.5-8 hours
Excretion: Urine (20% to 30% as unchanged drug)

Dosage
Malaria chemoprophylaxis (for areas where chloroquine-resistant *P. falciparum* exists): Begin prophylaxis 2 weeks before entering endemic area:
  Children: 0.5 mg/kg once weekly; not to exceed 25 mg/dose
  or
  Children:
    <4 years: 6.25 mg once weekly
    4-10 years: 12.5 mg once weekly
  Children >10 years and Adults: 25 mg once weekly
  Dosage should be continued for all age groups for at least 6-10 weeks after leaving endemic areas
Chloroquine-resistant *P. falciparum* malaria (when used in conjunction with quinine and sulfadiazine):
  Children:
    <10 kg: 6.25 mg/day once daily for 3 days
    10-20 kg: 12.5 mg/day once daily for 3 days
    20-40 kg: 25 mg/day once daily for 3 days
  Adults: 25 mg twice daily for 3 days
Toxoplasmosis:
  Infants for congenital toxoplasmosis: Oral: 1 mg/kg once daily for 6 months with sulfadiazine then every other month with sulfa, alternating with spiramycin.
  Children: Loading dose: 2 mg/kg/day divided into 2 equal daily doses for 1-3 days (maximum: 100 mg/day) followed by 1 mg/kg/day divided into 2 doses for 4 weeks; maximum: 25 mg/day
    With sulfadiazine or trisulfapyrimidines: 2 mg/kg/day divided every 12 hours for 3 days followed by 1 mg/kg/day once daily or divided twice daily for 4 weeks given with trisulfapyrimidines or sulfadiazine
  Adults: 50-75 mg/day together with 1-4 g of a sulfonamide for 1-3 weeks depending on patient's tolerance and response, then reduce dose by 50% and continue for 4-5 weeks **or** 25-50 mg/day for 3-4 weeks
Prophylaxis for first episode of *Toxoplasma gondii*:
  Children ≥1 month of age: 1 mg/kg/day once daily with dapsone, plus oral folinic acid 5 mg every 3 days
  Adolescents and Adults: 50 mg once weekly with dapsone, plus oral folinic acid 25 mg once weekly
Prophylaxis to prevent recurrence of *Toxoplasma gondii*:
  Children ≥1 month of age: 1 mg/kg/day once daily given with sulfadiazine or clindamycin, plus oral folinic acid 5 mg every 3 days
  Adolescents and Adults: 25-50 mg once daily in combination with sulfadiazine or clindamycin, plus oral folinic acid 10-25 mg daily **or** with atovaquone, plus oral folinic acid 10 mg daily

Monitoring Parameters CBC, including platelet counts
Patient Information Take with meals to minimize vomiting; begin malaria prophylaxis at least 1-2 weeks prior to departure; discontinue at first sign of skin rash; report persistent fever, sore throat, bleeding or bruising; regular blood work may be necessary in patients taking high doses
Dosage Forms TAB: 25 mg

• **Pyrimethamine and Sulfadoxine** *see* Sulfadoxine and Pyrimethamine *on page 1172*
• **Pyrinyl Plus® [OTC]** *see* Pyrethrins and Piperonyl Butoxide *on page 1065*
• **Quaternium-18 Bentonite** *see* Bentoquatam *on page 153*

Quazepam (KWAY ze pam)
Related Information
  Benzodiazepines Comparison *on page 1366*
U.S. Brand Names Doral®
Therapeutic Category Benzodiazepine; Hypnotic; Sedative
Use Treatment of insomnia
Restrictions C-IV
Pregnancy Risk Factor X
Dosage Adults: Oral: Initial: 15 mg at bedtime, in some patients the dose may be reduced to 7.5 mg after a few nights
  Elderly: Dosing should be cautious; begin at lower end of dosing range (ie, 7.5 mg)
  Dosage adjustment in hepatic impairment: Dose reduction may be necessary
Dosage Forms TAB: 7.5 mg, 15 mg

• **Quelicin®** *see* Succinylcholine *on page 1166*
• **Questran®** *see* Cholestyramine Resin *on page 269*
• **Questran® Light** *see* Cholestyramine Resin *on page 269*

Quetiapine (kwe TYE a peen)
Related Information
  Antipsychotic Agents Comparison *on page 1364*
U.S. Brand Names Seroquel®
Synonyms Quetiapine Fumarate
  (Continued)

Quetiapine *(Continued)*

Therapeutic Category Antipsychotic Agent, Atypical; Antipsychotic Agent, Dibenzothiazepine

Use Treatment of schizophrenia

Unlabeled/Investigational Use Treatment of mania, bipolar disorder (children and adults); autism, psychosis (children)

Pregnancy Risk Factor C

Contraindications Hypersensitivity to quetiapine or any component of the formulation; severe CNS depression; bone marrow suppression; blood dyscrasias; severe hepatic disease; coma

Warnings/Precautions May induce orthostatic hypotension associated with dizziness, tachycardia, and, in some cases, syncope, especially during the initial dose titration period. Should be used with particular caution in patients with known cardiovascular disease (history of MI or ischemic heart disease, heart failure, or conduction abnormalities), cerebrovascular disease, or conditions that predispose to hypotension. Development of cataracts has been observed in animal studies, therefore, lens examinations should be made upon initiation of therapy and every 6 months thereafter.

Neuroleptic malignant syndrome (NMS) is a potentially fatal symptom complex that has been reported in association with administration of antipsychotic drugs. Clinical manifestations of NMS are hyperpyrexia, muscle rigidity, altered mental status, and evidence of autonomic instability (irregular pulse or blood pressure, tachycardia, diaphoresis, and cardiac dysrhythmia). Management of NMS should include immediate discontinuation of antipsychotic drugs and other drugs not essential to concurrent therapy, intensive symptomatic treatment and medication monitoring, and treatment of any concomitant medical problems for which specific treatment are available.

Tardive dyskinesia; caution in patients with a history of seizures, decreases in total free thyroxine, pre-existing hyperprolactinemia, elevations of liver enzymes, cholesterol levels and/ or triglyceride increases.

Common Adverse Reactions
>10%:
  Central nervous system: Headache, somnolence
  Gastrointestinal: Weight gain
1% to 10%:
  Cardiovascular: Postural hypotension, tachycardia, palpitations
  Central nervous system: Dizziness
  Dermatologic: Rash
  Gastrointestinal: Abdominal pain, constipation, xerostomia, dyspepsia, anorexia
  Hematologic: Leukopenia
  Neuromuscular & skeletal: Dysarthria, back pain, weakness
  Respiratory: Rhinitis, pharyngitis, cough, dyspnea
  Miscellaneous: Diaphoresis

Drug Interactions
  Cytochrome P450 Effect: Substrate of CYP2D6 (minor), 3A4 (major)
  Increased Effect/Toxicity: Quetiapine reduces the metabolism of lorazepam (by 20%). The effects of other centrally-acting drugs, sedatives, or ethanol may be potentiated by quetiapine. Quetiapine may enhance the effects of antihypertensive agents. Although data is not yet available, caution is advised with inhibitors of CYP3A4 (eg, ketoconazole, erythromycin), which may increase levels of quetiapine. Cimetidine increases blood levels of quetiapine (quetiapine's clearance is reduced by by 20%). Metoclopramide may increase risk of extrapyramidal symptoms (EPS).
  Decreased Effect: The metabolism of quetiapine may be increased when administered with enzyme-inducing drugs (phenytoin, rifampin, barbiturates, carbamazepine). Thioridazine increases quetiapine's clearance (by 65%).

Mechanism of Action Mechanism of action of quetiapine, as with other antipsychotic drugs, is unknown. However, it has been proposed that this drug's antipsychotic activity is mediated through a combination of dopamine type 2 (D_2) and serotonin type 2 ($5-HT_2$) antagonism. However, it is an antagonist at multiple neurotransmitter receptors in the brain: serotonin $5-HT_{1A}$ and $5-HT_2$, dopamine D_1 and D_2, histamine H_1, and adrenergic alpha$_1$- and alpha$_2$-receptors; but appears to have no appreciable affinity at cholinergic muscarinic and benzodiazepine receptors.

Antagonism at receptors other than dopamine and $5-HT_2$ with similar receptor affinities may explain some of the other effects of quetiapine. The drug's antagonism of histamine H_1-receptors may explain the somnolence observed with it. The drug's antagonism of adrenergic alpha$_1$-receptors may explain the orthostatic hypotension observed with it.

Pharmacodynamics/Kinetics
  Absorption: Accumulation is predictable upon multiple dosing
  Distribution: V_{dss}: ~2 days; unlikely to interfere with the metabolism of drugs dependent on CYP
  Protein binding, plasma: 83%
  Metabolism: Primarily hepatic; both metabolites are pharmacologically inactive
  Bioavailability: 9% ± 4%; tablet is 100% bioavailable relative to solution
  Half-life elimination: Mean: Terminal: ~6 hours
  Time to peak, plasma: 1.5 hours
  Excretion: Urine (73% as metabolites, <1% as unchanged drug); feces (20%)

Dosage Oral:
Children and Adolescents:
Autism (unlabeled use): 100-350 mg/day (1.6-5.2 mg/kg/day)
Psychosis and mania (unlabeled use): Initial: 25 mg twice daily; titrate as necessary to 450 mg/day
Adults: Schizophrenia/psychoses: Initial: 25 mg twice daily; increase in increments of 25-50 mg 2-3 times/day on the second and third day, if tolerated, to a target dose of 300-400 mg in 2-3 divided doses by day 4. Make further adjustments as needed at intervals of at least 2 days in adjustments of 25-50 mg twice daily. Usual maintenance range: 300-800 mg/day
Elderly: 40% lower mean oral clearance of quetiapine in adults >65 years of age; higher plasma levels expected and, therefore, dosage adjustment may be needed; elderly patients usually require 50-200 mg/day
Dosing comments in hepatic insufficiency: 30% lower mean oral clearance of quetiapine than normal subjects; higher plasma levels expected in hepatically impaired subjects; dosage adjustment may be needed
Monitoring Parameters Vital signs; lipid profile, fasting blood glucose/Hgb A_{1c}; BMI; mental status, abnormal involuntary movement scale (AIMS); patients should have eyes checked for cataracts every 6 months while on this medication
Patient Information May cause headache, drowsiness, dizziness, and/or lightheadedness, especially when the patient stands up or gets up from lying down. If this happens, the patient should sit or lie down immediately. This agent might increase the risk of cataracts; avoid alcohol, overheating, dehydration.
Dosage Forms TAB: 25 mg, 100 mg, 200 mg, 300 mg

♦ **Quetiapine Fumarate** *see Quetiapine on page 1069*
♦ **Quibron®** *see Theophylline and Guaifenesin on page 1210*
♦ **Quibron®-T** *see Theophylline Salts on page 1210*
♦ **Quibron®-T/SR** *see Theophylline Salts on page 1210*
♦ **Quinaglute® Dura-Tabs®** *see Quinidine on page 1073*
♦ **Quinalbarbitone Sodium** *see Secobarbital on page 1128*

Quinapril (KWIN a pril)

Related Information
Angiotensin Agents Comparison *on page 1353*
U.S. Brand Names Accupril®
Synonyms Quinapril Hydrochloride
Therapeutic Category Angiotensin-Converting Enzyme (ACE) Inhibitor; Antihypertensive Agent
Use Management of hypertension; treatment of congestive heart failure
Unlabeled/Investigational Use Treatment of left ventricular dysfunction after myocardial infarction
Pregnancy Risk Factor C/D (2nd and 3rd trimesters)
Contraindications Hypersensitivity to quinapril or any component of the formulation; angioedema related to previous treatment with an ACE inhibitor; bilateral renal artery stenosis; patients with idiopathic or hereditary angioedema; pregnancy (2nd and 3rd trimesters)
Warnings/Precautions Use with caution in patients with renal insufficiency, autoimmune disease, renal artery stenosis; excessive hypotension may be more likely in volume-depleted patients, the elderly, and following the first dose (first dose phenomenon); quinapril should be discontinued if laryngeal stridor or angioedema is observed. Angioedema can occur at any time during treatment (especially following first dose); it may involve head and neck (potentially affecting the airway) or the intestine (presenting with abdominal pain).
Common Adverse Reactions Note: Frequency ranges include data from hypertension and heart failure trials. Higher rates of adverse reactions have generally been noted in patients with CHF. However, the frequency of adverse effects associated with placebo is also increased in this population.

1% to 10%:
Cardiovascular: Hypotension (3%), chest pain (2%), first-dose hypotension (up to 3%)
Central nervous system: Dizziness (4% to 8%), headache (2% to 6%), fatigue (3%)
Dermatologic: Rash (1%)
Endocrine & metabolic: Hyperkalemia (2%)
Gastrointestinal: Vomiting/nausea (1% to 2%), diarrhea (2%)
Neuromuscular & skeletal: Myalgias (2% to 5%), back pain (1%)
Renal: Increased BUN/serum creatinine (2%, transient elevations may occur with a higher frequency), worsening of renal function (in patients with bilateral renal artery stenosis or hypovolemia)
Respiratory: Upper respiratory symptoms, cough (2% to 4%; up to 13% in some studies), dyspnea (2%)
Drug Interactions
Increased Effect/Toxicity: Potassium supplements, co-trimoxazole (high dose), angiotensin II receptor antagonists (candesartan, losartan, irbesartan, etc), or potassium-sparing diuretics (amiloride, spironolactone, triamterene) may result in elevated serum potassium levels when combined with quinapril. ACE inhibitor effects may be increased by phenothiazines or probenecid (increases levels of captopril). ACE inhibitors may increase serum concentrations/effects of digoxin, lithium, and sulfonylureas.

Diuretics have additive hypotensive effects with ACE inhibitors, and hypovolemia increases the potential for adverse renal effects of ACE inhibitors. In patients with compromised renal
(Continued)

Quinapril *(Continued)*

function, coadministration with NSAIDs may result in further deterioration of renal function. Allopurinol and ACE inhibitors may cause a higher risk of hypersensitivity reaction when taken concurrently.

Decreased Effect: Quinapril may reduce the absorption of quinolones and tetracycline antibiotics. Aspirin (high dose) may reduce the therapeutic effects of ACE inhibitors; at low dosages this does not appear to be significant. Rifampin may decrease the effect of ACE inhibitors. Antacids may decrease the bioavailability of ACE inhibitors (may be more likely to occur with captopril); separate administration times by 1-2 hours. NSAIDs, specifically indomethacin, may reduce the hypotensive effects of ACE inhibitors.

Mechanism of Action Competitive inhibitor of angiotensin-converting enzyme (ACE); prevents conversion of angiotensin I to angiotensin II, a potent vasoconstrictor; results in lower levels of angiotensin II which causes an increase in plasma renin activity and a reduction in aldosterone secretion; a CNS mechanism may also be involved in hypotensive effect as angiotensin II increases adrenergic outflow from CNS; vasoactive kallikreins may be decreased in conversion to active hormones by ACE inhibitors, thus reducing blood pressure

Pharmacodynamics/Kinetics

Onset of action: 1 hour

Duration: 24 hours

Absorption: Quinapril: ≥60%

Protein binding: Quinapril: 97%; Quinaprilat: 97%

Metabolism: Rapidly hydrolyzed to quinaprilat, the active metabolite

Half-life elimination: Quinapril: 0.8 hours; Quinaprilat: 3 hours; increases as Cl_{cr} decreases

Time to peak, serum: Quinapril: 1 hour; Quinaprilat: ~2 hours

Excretion: Urine (50% to 60% primarily as quinaprilat)

Dosage

Adults: Oral:

Hypertension: Initial: 10-20 mg once daily, adjust according to blood pressure response at peak and trough blood levels; initial dose may be reduced to 5 mg in patients receiving diuretic therapy if the diuretic is continued (normal dosage range is 20-80 mg/day for hypertension)

Congestive heart failure or post-MI: Initial: 5 mg once daily, titrated at weekly intervals to 20-40 mg daily in 2 divided doses

Elderly: Initial: 2.5-5 mg/day; increase dosage at increments of 2.5-5 mg at 1- to 2-week intervals.

Dosing adjustment in renal impairment: Lower initial doses should be used; after initial dose (if tolerated), administer initial dose twice daily; may be increased at weekly intervals to optimal response:

Hypertension: Initial:

Cl_{cr} >60 mL/minute: Administer 10 mg/day

Cl_{cr} 30-60 mL/minute: Administer 5 mg/day

Cl_{cr} 10-30 mL/minute: Administer 2.5 mg/day

Congestive heart failure: Initial:

Cl_{cr} >30 mL/minute: Administer 5 mg/day

Cl_{cr} 10-30 mL/minute: Administer 2.5 mg/day

Dosing comments in hepatic impairment: In patients with alcoholic cirrhosis, hydrolysis of quinapril to quinaprilat is impaired; however, the subsequent elimination of quinaprilat is unaltered.

Patient Information Do not discontinue medication without advice of prescriber; report sore throat, swelling, palpitations, cough, chest pains, difficulty swallowing, swelling of face, eyes, tongue, lips; hoarseness, sweating, vomiting, or diarrhea; may cause dizziness, lightheadedness during first few days; may also cause changes in taste perception

Dosage Forms TAB: 5 mg, 10 mg, 20 mg, 40 mg

Quinapril and Hydrochlorothiazide

(KWIN a pril & hye droe klor oh THYE a zide)

U.S. Brand Names Accuretic™

Synonyms Hydrochlorothiazide and Quinapril

Therapeutic Category Angiotensin-Converting Enzyme (ACE) Inhibitor/Thiazide Diuretic

Use Treatment of hypertension (not for initial therapy)

Pregnancy Risk Factor C (1st trimester); D (2nd and 3rd trimesters)

Dosage Oral:

Children: Safety and efficacy have not been established.

Adults: Initial:

Patients who have failed quinapril monotherapy:

Quinapril 10 mg/hydrochlorothiazide 12.5 mg **or**

Quinapril 20 mg/hydrochlorothiazide 12.5 mg once daily

Patients with adequate blood pressure control on hydrochlorothiazide 25 mg/day, but significant potassium loss:

Quinapril 10 mg/hydrochlorothiazide 12.5 mg **or**

Quinapril 20 mg/hydrochlorothiazide 12.5 mg once daily

Note: Clinical trials of quinapril/hydrochlorothiazide combinations used quinapril doses of 2.5-40 mg/day and hydrochlorothiazide doses of 6.25-25 mg/day.

Dosage adjustment in renal impairment: Cl_{cr} <30 mL/minute/1.73 m^2 or serum creatinine ≤3 mg/dL: Use is not recommended.

Dosage Forms TAB: 10/25: Quinapril 10 mg and hydrochlorothiazide 12.5 mg; 20/12.5: Quinapril 20 mg and hydrochlorothiazide 12.5 mg; 20/25: Quinapril 20 mg and hydrochlorothiazide 25 mg

◆ **Quinapril Hydrochloride** *see* Quinapril *on page 1071*
◆ **Quinidex® Extentabs®** *see* Quinidine *on page 1073*

Quinidine (KWIN i deen)

Related Information
Malaria Treatment *on page 1464*

U.S. Brand Names Quinaglute® Dura-Tabs®; Quinidex® Extentabs®

Synonyms Quinidine Gluconate; Quinidine Polygalacturonate; Quinidine Sulfate

Therapeutic Category Antiarrhythmic Agent, Class I-A; Antimalarial Agent

Use Prophylaxis after cardioversion of atrial fibrillation and/or flutter to maintain normal sinus rhythm; prevent recurrence of paroxysmal supraventricular tachycardia, paroxysmal AV junctional rhythm, paroxysmal ventricular tachycardia, paroxysmal atrial fibrillation, and atrial or ventricular premature contractions; has activity against *Plasmodium falciparum* malaria

Pregnancy Risk Factor C

Contraindications Hypersensitivity to quinidine or any component of the formulation; thrombocytopenia; thrombocytopenic purpura; myasthenia gravis; heart block greater than first degree; idioventricular conduction delays (except in patients with a functioning artificial pacemaker); those adversely affected by anticholinergic activity; concurrent use of quinolone antibiotics which prolong QT interval, cisapride, amprenavir, or ritonavir

Warnings/Precautions Monitor and adjust dose to prevent QT_c prolongation; watch for proarrhythmic effects. May precipitate or exacerbate CHF. Reduce dosage in hepatic impairment. In patients with atrial fibrillation or flutter, block the AV node before initiating. Correct hypokalemia before initiating therapy. Hypokalemia may worsen toxicity. Use may cause digoxin-induced toxicity (adjust digoxin's dose). Use caution with concurrent use of other antiarrhythmics. Hypersensitivity reactions can occur. Can unmask sick sinus syndrome (causes bradycardia). Has been associated with severe hepatotoxic reactions, including granulomatous hepatitis, increased serum AST and alkaline phosphatase concentrations, and jaundice may occur; use with caution in nursing women and elderly. Hemolysis may occur in patients with G6PD (glucose-6-phosphate dehydrogenase) deficiency.

Common Adverse Reactions
Frequency not defined: Hypotension, syncope

>10%:
Cardiovascular: QT_c prolongation (modest prolongation is common, however, excessive prolongation is rare and indicates toxicity)

Central nervous system: Lightheadedness (15%)

Gastrointestinal: Diarrhea (35%), upper GI distress, bitter taste, diarrhea, anorexia, nausea, vomiting, stomach cramping (22%)

1% to 10%:
Cardiovascular: Angina (6%), palpitation (7%), new or worsened arrhythmias (proarrhythmic effect)

Central nervous system: Syncope (1% to 8%), headache (7%), fatigue (7%), weakness (5%), sleep disturbance (3%), tremor (2%), nervousness (2%), incoordination (1%)

Dermatologic: Rash (5%)

Ocular: Blurred vision

Otic: Tinnitus

Respiratory: Wheezing

Note: Cinchonism, a syndrome which may include tinnitus, high-frequency hearing loss, deafness, vertigo, blurred vision, diplopia, photophobia, headache, confusion, and delirium has been associated with quinidine use. Usually associated with chronic toxicity, this syndrome has also been described after brief exposure to a moderate dose in sensitive patients. Vomiting and diarrhea may also occur as isolated reactions to therapeutic quinidine levels.

Drug Interactions
Cytochrome P450 Effect: Substrate of CYP2C8/9 (minor), 2E1 (minor), 3A4 (major); **Inhibits** CYP2C8/9 (weak), 2D6 (strong), 3A4 (strong)

Increased Effect/Toxicity: Quinidine potentiates nondepolarizing and depolarizing muscle relaxants. Quinidine may increase plasma concentration of digoxin; closely monitor digoxin concentrations. Digoxin dosage may need to be reduced (by 50%) when quinidine is initiated; new steady-state digoxin plasma concentrations occur in 5-7 days. When combined with quinidine, amiloride may cause prolonged ventricular conduction leading to arrhythmias. Urinary alkalinizers (antacids, sodium bicarbonate, acetazolamide) increase quinidine blood levels. Warfarin effects may be increased by quinidine.

Amprenavir, amiodarone, cimetidine, clarithromycin, diltiazem, erythromycin, itraconazole, ketoconazole, nelfinavir, ritonavir, troleandomycin, and verapamil (as well as other inhibitors of cytochrome P450 isoenzyme 3A4 may increase quinidine blood levels). Quinidine may increase blood levels of metoprolol mexiletine, nifedipine, propafenone, propranolol, and timolol.

Effects may be additive with drugs which prolong the QT interval, including amiodarone, amitriptyline, astemizole, bepridil, cisapride (use is contraindicated), disopyramide, erythromycin, haloperidol, imipramine, pimozide, procainamide, sotalol, thioridazine, and some quinolones (sparfloxacin, gatifloxacin, moxifloxacin - concurrent use is contraindicated). (Continued)

Quinidine *(Continued)*

Decreased Effect: Analgesic efficacy of codeine may be reduced. Enzyme inducers (aminoglutethimide, carbamazepine, phenobarbital, phenytoin, primidone, rifabutin, rifampin) may decrease quinidine blood levels.

Mechanism of Action Class 1a antiarrhythmic agent; depresses phase O of the action potential; decreases myocardial excitability and conduction velocity, and myocardial contractility by decreasing sodium influx during depolarization and potassium efflux in repolarization; also reduces calcium transport across cell membrane

Pharmacodynamics/Kinetics

Distribution: V_d: Adults: 2-3.5 L/kg, decreased with congestive heart failure, malaria; increased with cirrhosis; crosses placenta; enters breast milk

Protein binding:

Newborns: 60% to 70%; decreased protein binding with cyanotic congenital heart disease, cirrhosis, or acute myocardial infarction

Adults: 80% to 90%

Metabolism: Extensively hepatic (50% to 90%) to inactive compounds

Bioavailability: Sulfate: 80%; Gluconate: 70%

Half-life elimination, plasma: Children: 2.5-6.7 hours; Adults: 6-8 hours; prolonged with elderly, cirrhosis, and congestive heart failure

Excretion: Urine (15% to 25% as unchanged drug)

Dosage Dosage expressed in terms of the salt: 267 mg of quinidine gluconate = 200 mg of quinidine sulfate.

Children: Test dose for idiosyncratic reaction (sulfate, oral or gluconate, I.M.): 2 mg/kg or 60 mg/m^2

Oral (quinidine sulfate): 15-60 mg/kg/day in 4-5 divided doses or 6 mg/kg every 4-6 hours; usual 30 mg/kg/day or 900 mg/m^2/day given in 5 daily doses

I.V. **not** recommended (quinidine gluconate): 2-10 mg/kg/dose given at a rate ≤10 mg/minute every 3-6 hours as needed

Adults: Test dose: Oral, I.M.: 200 mg administered several hours before full dosage (to determine possibility of idiosyncratic reaction)

Oral (for malaria):

Sulfate: 100-600 mg/dose every 4-6 hours; begin at 200 mg/dose and titrate to desired effect (maximum daily dose: 3-4 g)

Gluconate: 324-972 mg every 8-12 hours

I.M.: 400 mg/dose every 2-6 hours; initial dose: 600 mg (gluconate)

I.V.: 200-400 mg/dose diluted and given at a rate ≤10 mg/minute; may require as much as 500-750 mg

Dosing adjustment in renal impairment: Cl_{cr} <10 mL/minute: Administer 75% of normal dose.

Hemodialysis: Slightly hemodialyzable (5% to 20%); 200 mg supplemental dose posthemodialysis is recommended.

Peritoneal dialysis: Not dialyzable (0% to 5%)

Dosing adjustment/comments in hepatic impairment: Larger loading dose may be indicated, reduce maintenance doses by 50% and monitor serum levels closely.

Administration Administer around-the-clock to promote less variation in peak and trough serum levels

Oral: Do not crush, chew, or break sustained release dosage forms.

Parenteral: When injecting I.M., aspirate carefully to avoid injection into a vessel; maximum I.V. infusion rate: 10 mg/minute

Monitoring Parameters Cardiac monitor required during I.V. administration; CBC, liver and renal function tests, should be routinely performed during long-term administration

Reference Range Therapeutic: 2-5 µg/mL (SI: 6.2-15.4 µmol/L). Patient dependent therapeutic response occurs at levels of 3-6 µg/mL (SI: 9.2-18.5 µmol/L). Optimal therapeutic level is method dependent; >6 µg/mL (SI: >18 µmol/L).

Patient Information Do not crush or chew sustained release preparations. Report rash, fever, unusual bleeding or bruising, ringing in the ears, visual disturbances, or syncope; seek emergency help if palpitations occur.

Dosage Forms INJ, solution: 80 mg/mL (10 mL). **TAB, as sulfate:** 200 mg, 300 mg. **TAB, extended release, as gluconate** (Quinaglute® Dura-Tabs®): 324 mg. **TAB, extended release, as sulfate** (Quinidex® Extentabs®): 300 mg

♦ **Quinidine Gluconate** *see* Quinidine *on page 1073*

♦ **Quinidine Polygalacturonate** *see* Quinidine *on page 1073*

♦ **Quinidine Sulfate** *see* Quinidine *on page 1073*

Quinine *(KWYE nine)*

Related Information

Malaria Treatment *on page 1464*

Synonyms Quinine Sulfate

Therapeutic Category Antimalarial Agent

Use In conjunction with other antimalarial agents, suppression or treatment of chloroquine-resistant *P. falciparum* malaria; treatment of *Babesia microti* infection in conjunction with clindamycin

Unlabeled/Investigational Use Prevention and treatment of nocturnal recumbency leg muscle cramps

Pregnancy Risk Factor X

Contraindications Hypersensitivity to quinine or any component of the formulation; tinnitus, optic neuritis, G6PD deficiency; history of black water fever; thrombocytopenia with quinine or quinidine; pregnancy

Warnings/Precautions Use with caution in patients with cardiac arrhythmias (quinine has quinidine-like activity) and in patients with myasthenia gravis

Common Adverse Reactions Frequency not defined.

Central nervous system: Severe headache

Gastrointestinal: Nausea, vomiting, diarrhea

Ocular: Blurred vision

Otic: Tinnitus

Miscellaneous: Cinchonism (risk of cinchonism is directly related to dose and duration of therapy)

Drug Interactions

Cytochrome P450 Effect: Substrate (minor) of CYP1A2, 2C19, 3A4; **Inhibits** CYP2C8/9 (moderate), 2D6 (strong), 3A4 (weak)

Increased Effect/Toxicity: Beta-blockers + quinine may increase bradycardia. Quinine may enhance warfarin anticoagulant effect. Quinine potentiates nondepolarizing and depolarizing muscle relaxants. Quinine may increase plasma concentration of digoxin. Closely monitor digoxin concentrations. Digoxin dosage may need to be reduced (by one-half) when quinine is initiated. New steady-state digoxin plasma concentrations occur in 5-7 days. Verapamil, amiodarone, alkalinizing agents, and cimetidine may increase quinine serum concentrations.

Decreased Effect: Phenobarbital, phenytoin, and rifampin may decrease quinine serum concentrations.

Mechanism of Action Depresses oxygen uptake and carbohydrate metabolism; intercalates into DNA, disrupting the parasite's replication and transcription; affects calcium distribution within muscle fibers and decreases the excitability of the motor end-plate region; cardiovascular effects similar to quinidine

Pharmacodynamics/Kinetics

Absorption: Readily, mainly from upper small intestine

Protein binding: 70% to 95%

Metabolism: Primarily hepatic

Half-life elimination: Children: 6-12 hours; Adults: 8-14 hours

Time to peak, serum: 1-3 hours

Excretion: Feces and saliva; urine (<5% as unchanged drug)

Dosage Oral:

Children:

Treatment of chloroquine-resistant malaria: 25-30 mg/kg/day in divided doses every 8 hours for 3-7 days with tetracycline (consider risk versus benefit in children <8 years of age)

Babesiosis: 25 mg/kg/day divided every 8 hours for 7 days

Adults:

Treatment of chloroquine-resistant malaria: 650 mg every 8 hours for 3-7 days with tetracycline

Suppression of malaria: 325 mg twice daily and continued for 6 weeks after exposure

Babesiosis: 650 mg every 6-8 hours for 7 days

Leg cramps: 200-300 mg at bedtime

Dosing interval/adjustment in renal impairment:

Cl_{cr} 10-50 mL/minute: Administer every 8-12 hours or 75% of normal dose

Cl_{cr} <10 mL/minute: Administer every 24 hours or 30% to 50% of normal dose

Dialysis: Not removed

Peritoneal dialysis: Dose as for Cl_{cr} <10 mL/minute

Continuous arteriovenous or venovenous hemodiafiltration effects: Dose for Cl_{cr} 10-50 mL/minute

Reference Range Toxic: >10 µg/mL

Patient Information Avoid use of aluminum-containing antacids because of drug absorption problems; swallow dose whole to avoid bitter taste; may cause night blindness. Report rash, fever, unusual bleeding or bruising, ringing in the ears, visual disturbances, or syncope; seek emergency help if palpitations occur.

Dosage Forms CAP: 200 mg, 325 mg. **TAB:** 260 mg

♦ **Quinine Sulfate** *see* Quinine *on page 1074*

♦ **Quinol** *see* Hydroquinone *on page 636*

Quinupristin and Dalfopristin (kwi NYOO pris tin & dal FOE pris tin)

Related Information

Antimicrobial Drugs of Choice *on page 1440*

U.S. Brand Names Synercid®

Synonyms RP-59500; RPistinamycin

Therapeutic Category Antibiotic, Streptogramin

Use Treatment of serious or life-threatening infections associated with vancomycin-resistant *Enterococcus faecium* bacteremia; treatment of complicated skin and skin structure infections caused by methcillin-susceptible *Staphylococcus aureus* or *Streptococcus pyogenes*

Has been studied in the treatment of a variety of infections caused by *Enterococcus faecium* (not *E. fecalis*) including vancomycin-resistant strains. May also be effective in the treatment of serious infections caused by *Staphylococcus* species including those resistant to methicillin.

Pregnancy Risk Factor B

(Continued)

Quinupristin and Dalfopristin *(Continued)*

Contraindications Hypersensitivity to quinupristin, dalfopristin, pristinamycin, or virginiamycin, or any component of the formulation

Warnings/Precautions Use with caution in patients with hepatic or renal dysfunction. May cause pain and phlebitis when infused through a peripheral line (not relieved by hydrocortisone or diphenhydramine). Superinfection may occur. As with many antibiotics, antibiotic-associated colitis and pseudomembranous colitis may occur. May cause arthralgias, myalgias, and hyperbilirubinemia. May inhibit the metabolism of many drugs metabolized by CYP3A4. Concurrent therapy with astemizole and cisapride (which may prolong QT_c interval and lead to arrhythmias) should be avoided.

Common Adverse Reactions

>10%:
   Hepatic: Hyperbilirubinemia (3% to 35%)
   Local: Inflammation at infusion site (38% to 42%), local pain (40% to 44%), local edema (17% to 18%), infusion site reaction (12% to 13%)

1% to 10%:
   Central nervous system: Pain (2% to 3%), headache (2%)
   Dermatologic: Pruritus (2%), rash (3%)
   Endocrine & metabolic: Hyperglycemia (1%)
   Gastrointestinal: Nausea (3% to 5%), diarrhea (3%), vomiting (3% to 4%)
   Hematologic: Anemia (3%)
   Hepatic: Increased LDH (3%), increased GGT (2%)
   Local: Thrombophlebitis (2%)
   Neuromuscular & skeletal: Arthralgia (<1% to 8%), myalgia (<1% to 5%), Increased CPK (2%)

Drug Interactions

Cytochrome P450 Effect: Quinupristin: **Inhibits** CYP3A4 (weak)

Increased Effect/Toxicity: Astemizole and cisapride (which may prolong QT_c interval and lead to arrhythmias) should be avoided. The metabolism of midazolam and nifedipine have been demonstrated to be inhibited *in vitro*. An increase in cyclosporine levels has been documented in patients receiving concomitant therapy. Other medications metabolized by CYP3A4, including protease inhibitors, non-nucleoside reverse transcriptase inhibitors, benzodiazepines, calcium channel blockers, some HMG-CoA reductase inhibitors, immunosuppressive agents, corticosteroids, carbamazepine, quinidine, lidocaine, and disopyramide are predicted to have increased plasma concentrations during concurrent dosing.

Mechanism of Action Quinupristin/dalfopristin inhibits bacterial protein synthesis by binding to different sites on the 50S bacterial ribosomal subunit thereby inhibiting protein synthesis

Pharmacodynamics/Kinetics

Distribution: Quinupristin: 0.45 L/kg; Dalfopristin: 0.24 L/kg
Protein binding: Moderate
Metabolism: To active metabolites via nonenzymatic reactions
Half-life elimination: Quinupristin: 0.85 hour; Dalfopristin: 0.7 hour (mean elimination half-lives, including metabolites: 3 and 1 hours, respectively)
Excretion: Feces (75% to 77% as unchanged drug and metabolites); urine (15% to 19%)

Dosage I.V.:

Children (limited information): Dosages similar to adult dosing have been used in the treatment of complicated skin/soft tissue infections and infections caused by vancomycin-resistant *Enterococcus faecium*
   CNS shunt infection due to vancomycin-resistant *Enterococcus faecium*: 7.5 mg/kg/dose every 8 hours; concurrent intrathecal doses of 1-2 mg/day have been administered for up to 68 days

Adults:
   Vancomycin-resistant *Enterococcus faecium*: 7.5 mg/kg every 8 hours
   Complicated skin and skin structure infection: 7.5 mg/kg every 12 hours

Dosage adjustment in renal impairment: No adjustment required in renal failure, hemodialysis, or peritoneal dialysis

Dosage adjustment in hepatic impairment: Pharmacokinetic data suggest dosage adjustment may be necessary; however, specific recommendations have not been proposed
Elderly: No dosage adjustment is required

Administration Line should be flushed with 5% dextrose in water prior to and following administration. Incompatible with saline. Infusion should be completed over 60 minutes (toxicity may be increased with shorter infusion). Compatible (Y-site injection) with aztreonam, ciprofloxacin, haloperidol, metoclopramide or potassium chloride when admixed in 5% dextrose in water. Also compatible (Y-site injection) with fluconazole (used as undiluted solution). If severe venous irritation occurs following peripheral administration of quinupristin/dalfopristin diluted in 250 mL 5% dextrose in water, consideration should be given to increasing the infusion volume to 500 mL or 750 mL, changing the infusion site, or infusing by a peripherally inserted central catheter (PICC) or a central venous catheter.

Dosage Forms INJ, powder for reconstitution: 500 mg (dalfopristin 350 mg and quinupristin 150 mg)

♦ **Quixin**™ *see* Levofloxacin *on page 734*
♦ **QVAR**™ *see* Beclomethasone *on page 149*
♦ **RabAvert**® *see* Rabies Virus Vaccine *on page 1078*

Rabeprazole (ra BE pray zole)

U.S. Brand Names Aciphex®

Synonyms Pariprazole

Therapeutic Category Gastric Acid Secretion Inhibitor; Proton Pump Inhibitor

Use Short-term (4-8 weeks) treatment and maintenance of erosive or ulcerative gastroesophageal reflux disease (GERD); symptomatic GERD; short-term (up to 4 weeks) treatment of duodenal ulcers; long-term treatment of pathological hypersecretory conditions, including Zollinger-Ellison syndrome; *H. pylori* eradication (in combination with amoxicillin and clarithromycin)

Unlabeled/Investigational Use Maintenance of duodenal ulcer

Pregnancy Risk Factor B

Contraindications Hypersensitivity to rabeprazole, substituted benzimidazoles, or any component of the formulation

Warnings/Precautions Use caution in severe hepatic impairment; relief of symptoms with rabeprazole does not preclude the presence of a gastric malignancy

Common Adverse Reactions 1% to 10%: Central nervous system: Headache

Drug Interactions

Cytochrome P450 Effect: Substrate (major) of CYP2C19, 3A4; **Inhibits** CYP2C19 (moderate), 2DC (weak), 3A4 (weak)

Decreased Effect: CYP2C19 inducers may decrease the levels/effects of rabeprazole; example inducers include aminoglutethimide, carbamazepine, phenytoin, and rifampin. Proton pump inhibitors may decrease the absorption of atazanavir, indinavir, itraconazole, and ketoconazole.

Mechanism of Action Potent proton pump inhibitor; suppresses gastric acid secretion by inhibiting the parietal cell H+/K+ ATP pump

Pharmacodynamics/Kinetics

Onset of action: 1 hour

Duration: 24 hours

Absorption: Oral: Well absorbed within 1 hour

Distribution: 96.3%

Protein binding, serum: 94.8% to 97.5%

Metabolism: Hepatic via CYP3A and 2C19 to inactive metabolites

Bioavailability: Oral: 52%

Half-life elimination (dose dependent): 0.85-2 hours

Time to peak, plasma: 2-5 hours

Excretion: Urine (90% primarily as thioether carboxylic acid); remainder in feces

Dosage Oral: Adults >18 years and Elderly:

GERD: 20 mg once daily for 4-8 weeks; maintenance: 20 mg once daily

Duodenal ulcer: 20 mg/day before breakfast for 4 weeks

H. pylori eradication: 20 mg twice daily for 7 days; to be administered with amoxicillin 1000 mg and clarithromycin 500 mg, also given twice daily for 7 days.

Hypersecretory conditions: 60 mg once daily; dose may need to be adjusted as necessary. Doses as high as 100 mg once daily and 60 mg twice daily have been used.

Dosage adjustment in renal impairment: No dosage adjustment required

Dosage adjustment in hepatic impairment:

Mild to moderate: Elimination decreased; no dosage adjustment required

Severe: Use caution

Administration May be administered with or without food; best if taken before breakfast. Do not crush, split, or chew tablet. May be administered with an antacid.

Patient Information Swallow whole; do not crush, chew, or split tablet. Take before eating.

Dosage Forms TAB, delayed release, enteric coated: 20 mg

Rabies Immune Globulin (Human)

(RAY beez i MYUN GLOB yoo lin, HYU man)

U.S. Brand Names BayRab®; Imogam®

Synonyms RIG

Therapeutic Category Immune Globulin

Use Part of postexposure prophylaxis of persons with rabies exposure who lack a history of pre-exposure or postexposure prophylaxis with rabies vaccine or a recently documented neutralizing antibody response to previous rabies vaccination; although it is preferable to administer RIG with the first dose of vaccine, it can be given up to 8 days after vaccination

Pregnancy Risk Factor C

Contraindications Hypersensitivity to thimerosal or any component of the formulation

Warnings/Precautions Have epinephrine 1:1000 available for anaphylactic reactions. As a product of human plasma, this product may potentially transmit disease; screening of donors, as well as testing and/or inactivation of certain viruses reduces this risk. Use caution in patients with thrombocytopenia or coagulation disorders (I.M. injections may be contraindicated), in patients with isolated IgA deficiency, or in patients with previous systemic hypersensitivity to human immunoglobulins. Not for intravenous administration.

Common Adverse Reactions 1% to 10%:

Central nervous system: Fever (mild)

Local: Soreness at injection site

Mechanism of Action Rabies immune globulin is a solution of globulins dried from the plasma or serum of selected adult human donors who have been immunized with rabies vaccine and (Continued)

Rabies Immune Globulin (Human) *(Continued)*

have developed high titers of rabies antibody. It generally contains 10% to 18% of protein of which not less than 80% is monomeric immunoglobulin G.

Dosage Children and Adults: I.M.: 20 units/kg in a single dose (RIG should always be administered as part of rabies vaccine (HDCV)) regimen (as soon as possible after the first dose of vaccine, up to 8 days); infiltrate ½ of the dose locally around the wound; administer the remainder I.M.

Note: Persons known to have an adequate titer or who have been completely immunized with rabies vaccine should not receive RIG, only booster doses of HDCV

Administration Intramuscular injection only; injection should be made into the gluteal muscle

Dosage Forms INJ, solution: 150 units/mL (2 mL, 10 mL)

Rabies Virus Vaccine *(RAY beez VYE rus vak SEEN)*

U.S. Brand Names Imovax® Rabies; RabAvert®

Synonyms HDCV; Human Diploid Cell Cultures Rabies Vaccine; PCEC; Purified Chick Embryo Cell

Therapeutic Category Vaccine; Vaccine, Inactivated Virus

Use Pre-exposure immunization: Vaccinate persons with greater than usual risk due to occupation or avocation including veterinarians, rangers, animal handlers, certain laboratory workers, and persons living in or visiting countries for longer than 1 month where rabies is a constant threat.

Postexposure prophylaxis: If a bite from a carrier animal is unprovoked, if it is not captured and rabies is present in that species and area, administer rabies immune globulin (RIG) and the vaccine as indicated

Pregnancy Risk Factor C

Contraindications Hypersensitivity to any component of the formulation; developing febrile illness (during pre-exposure therapy only); life-threatening allergic reactions to rabies vaccine or any components of the formulation (however, carefully consider a patient's risk of rabies before continuing therapy)

Warnings/Precautions Report serious reactions to the State Health Department or the manufacturer/distributor, an immune complex reaction is possible 2-21 days following booster doses of HDCV; hypersensitivity reactions may be treated with antihistamines or epinephrine, if severe. Immune response may be decreased in immunosuppressed patients. Imovax® Rabies contains albumin and neomycin. RabAvert® contains amphotericin B, bovine gelatin, chicken protein, chlortetracycline, and neomycin. For I. M. administration only.

Common Adverse Reactions All serious adverse reactions must be reported to the U.S. Department of Health and Human Services (DHHS) Vaccine Adverse Event Reporting System (VAERS) 1-800-822-7967.

Frequency not defined.

Cardiovascular: Edema

Central nervous system: Dizziness, malaise, encephalomyelitis, transverse myelitis, fever, pain, headache, neuroparalytic reactions

Gastrointestinal: Nausea, abdominal pain

Local: Local discomfort, pain at injection site, itching, erythema, swelling or pain

Neuromuscular & skeletal: Myalgia

Mechanism of Action Rabies vaccine is an inactivated virus vaccine which promotes immunity by inducing an active immune response. The production of specific antibodies requires about 7-10 days to develop. Rabies immune globulin or antirabies serum, equine (ARS) is given in conjunction with rabies vaccine to provide immune protection until an antibody response can occur.

Pharmacodynamics/Kinetics

Onset of action: I.M.: Rabies antibody: ~7-10 days

Peak effect: ~30-60 days

Duration: ≥1 year

Dosage

Pre-exposure prophylaxis: 1 mL I.M. on days 0, 7, and 21 to 28. **Note:** Prolonging the interval between doses does not interfere with immunity achieved after the concluding dose of the basic series.

Postexposure prophylaxis: All postexposure treatment should begin with immediate cleansing of the wound with soap and water

Persons not previously immunized as above: Rabies immune globulin 20 units/kg body weight, half infiltrated at bite site if possible, remainder I.M.; and 5 doses of rabies vaccine, 1 mL I.M., one each on days 0, 3, 7, 14, 28

Persons who have previously received postexposure prophylaxis with rabies vaccine, received a recommended I.M. pre-exposure series of rabies vaccine or have a previously documented rabies antibody titer considered adequate: 1 mL of either vaccine I.M. only on days 0 and 3; do not administer RIG

Booster (for occupational or other continuing risk): 1 mL I.M. every 2-5 years or based on antibody titers

Administration For I.M. administration only; give I.M. injections in the deltoid muscle, not the gluteal, in adults and older children; for younger children, use the outer aspect of the thigh.

For patients at risk of hemorrhage following intramuscular injection, the ACIP recommends "it should be administered intramuscularly if, in the opinion of the physician familiar with the patients bleeding risk, the vaccine can be administered with reasonable safety by this route. If the patient receives antihemophilia or other similar therapy, intramuscular vaccination can be scheduled shortly after such therapy is administered. A fine needle (23 gauge or smaller) can be used for the vaccination and firm pressure applied to the site (without rubbing) for at least 2 minutes. The patient should be instructed concerning the risk of hematoma from the injection."

Monitoring Parameters Serum rabies antibody every 6 months-2 years in patients at high risk for exposure

Reference Range Antibody titers ≥115 as determined by rapid fluorescent-focus inhibition test are indicative of adequate response; collect titers on day 28 postexposure

Dosage Forms INJ, powder for reconstitution: (Imovax® Rabies): 2.5 int. units; (RabAvert®): 2.5 int. units

♦ **Radiogardase™** see Ferric Hexacyanoferrate on page 518

♦ **rAHF** see Antihemophilic Factor (Recombinant) on page 105

♦ **R-albuterol** see Levalbuterol on page 726

Raloxifene (ral OKS i feen)

U.S. Brand Names Evista®

Synonyms Keoxifene Hydrochloride; Raloxifene Hydrochloride

Therapeutic Category Selective Estrogen Receptor Modulator (SERM)

Use Prevention and treatment of osteoporosis in postmenopausal women

Pregnancy Risk Factor X

Contraindications Hypersensitivity to raloxifene or any component of the formulation; active thromboembolic disorder; pregnancy (not intended for use in premenopausal women)

Warnings/Precautions History of venous thromboembolism/pulmonary embolism; patients with cardiovascular disease; history of cervical/uterine carcinoma; renal/hepatic insufficiency (however, pharmacokinetic data are lacking); concurrent use of estrogens; women with a history of elevated triglycerides in response to treatment with oral estrogens (or estrogen/progestin)

Common Adverse Reactions Note: Has been associated with increased risk of thromboembolism (DVT, PE) and superficial thrombophlebitis; risk is similar to reported risk of HRT ≥2%:

  Cardiovascular: Chest pain
  Central nervous system: Migraine, depression, insomnia, fever
  Dermatologic: Rash
  Endocrine & metabolic: Hot flashes
  Gastrointestinal: Nausea, dyspepsia, vomiting, flatulence, gastroenteritis, weight gain
  Genitourinary: Vaginitis, urinary tract infection, cystitis, leukorrhea
  Neuromuscular & skeletal: Leg cramps, arthralgia, myalgia, arthritis
  Respiratory: Sinusitis, pharyngitis, cough, pneumonia, laryngitis
  Miscellaneous: Infection, flu syndrome, diaphoresis

Drug Interactions

  Increased Effect/Toxicity: Raloxifene has the potential to interact with highly protein-bound drugs (increase effects of either agent). Use caution with highly protein-bound drugs, warfarin, clofibrate, indomethacin, naproxen, ibuprofen, diazepam, phenytoin, or tamoxifen.

  Decreased Effect: Ampicillin and cholestyramine reduce raloxifene absorption/blood levels.

Mechanism of Action A selective estrogen receptor modulator, meaning that it affects some of the same receptors that estrogen does, but not all, and in some instances, it antagonizes or blocks estrogen; it acts like estrogen to prevent bone loss and improve lipid profiles (decreases total and LDL-cholesterol but does not raise triglycerides), but it has the potential to block some estrogen effects such as those that lead to breast cancer and uterine cancer

Pharmacodynamics/Kinetics

  Onset of action: 8 weeks
  Absorption: ~60%
  Distribution: 2348 L/kg
  Protein binding: >95% to albumin and α-glycoprotein
  Metabolism: Extensive first-pass effect
  Bioavailability: ~2%
  Half-life elimination: 27.7-32.5 hours
  Excretion: Primarily feces; urine (0.2%)

Dosage Adults: Female: Oral: 60 mg/day which may be administered any time of the day without regard to meals

Monitoring Parameters Radiologic evaluation of bone mineral density (BMD) is the best measure of the treatment of osteoporosis; to monitor for the potential toxicities of raloxifene, complete blood counts should be evaluated periodically.

Dosage Forms TAB: 60 mg

♦ **Raloxifene Hydrochloride** see Raloxifene on page 1079

Ramipril (ra MI pril)

Related Information

  Angiotensin Agents Comparison on page 1353

U.S. Brand Names Altace®

Therapeutic Category Angiotensin-Converting Enzyme (ACE) Inhibitor; Antihypertensive Agent

Use Treatment of hypertension, alone or in combination with thiazide diuretics; treatment of congestive heart failure; treatment of left ventricular dysfunction after myocardial infarction; to reduce risk of heart attack, stroke, and death in patients at increased risk for these problems (Continued)

Ramipril *(Continued)*

Pregnancy Risk Factor C/D (2nd and 3rd trimesters)

Contraindications Hypersensitivity to ramipril or any component of the formulation; prior hypersensitivity (including angioedema) to ACE inhibitors; bilateral renal artery stenosis; pregnancy (2nd and 3rd trimesters)

Warnings/Precautions Anaphylactic or anaphylactoid reactions can occur. Use with caution and modify dosage in patients with renal impairment (especially renal artery stenosis), severe CHF. Severe hypotension may occur in the elderly and patients who are sodium and/or volume depleted, initiate lower doses and monitor closely when starting therapy in these patients. Should be discontinued if laryngeal stridor or angioedema of the face, tongue, or glottis is observed. Angioedema can occur at any time during treatment (especially following first dose). Angioedema may involve head and neck (potentially affecting the airway) or the intestine (presenting with abdominal pain). Careful blood pressure monitoring with first dose (hypotension can occur especially in volume depleted patients). Use with caution in hypovolemia; collagen vascular diseases; valvular stenosis (particularly aortic stenosis); hyperkalemia; or before, during, or immediately after anesthesia. Avoid rapid dosage escalation, which may lead to renal insufficiency. Neutropenia/agranulocytosis with myeloid hyperplasia can rarely occur. If patient has renal impairment then a baseline WBC with differential and serum creatinine should be evaluated and monitored closely during the first 3 months of therapy. Hypersensitivity reactions may be seen during hemodialysis with high-flux dialysis membranes (eg, AN69).

Common Adverse Reactions Note: Frequency ranges include data from hypertension and heart failure trials. Higher rates of adverse reactions have generally been noted in patients with CHF. However, the frequency of adverse effects associated with placebo is also increased in this population.

>10%: Respiratory: Cough (increased) (7% to 12%)

1% to 10%:
  Cardiovascular: Hypotension (11%), angina (3%), postural hypotension (2%), syncope (2%)
  Central nervous system: Headache (1% to 5%), dizziness (2% to 4%), fatigue (2%), vertigo (2%)
  Endocrine & metabolic: Hyperkalemia (1% to 10%)
  Gastrointestinal: Nausea/vomiting (1% to 2%)
  Neuromuscular & skeletal: Chest pain (noncardiac) (1%)
  Renal: Renal dysfunction (1%), elevation in serum creatinine (1% to 2%), increased BUN (<1% to 3%); transient elevations of creatinine and/or BUN may occur more frequently
  Respiratory: Cough (estimated 1% to 10%)

Worsening of renal function may occur in patients with bilateral renal artery stenosis or in hypovolemia. In addition, a syndrome which may include fever, myalgia, arthralgia, interstitial nephritis, vasculitis, rash, eosinophilia and positive ANA, and elevated ESR has been reported with ACE inhibitors. Risk of pancreatitis and agranulocytosis may be increased in patients with collagen vascular disease or renal impairment.

Drug Interactions

Increased Effect/Toxicity: Potassium supplements, co-trimoxazole (high dose), angiotensin II receptor antagonists (candesartan, losartan, irbesartan, etc), or potassium-sparing diuretics (amiloride, spironolactone, triamterene) may result in elevated serum potassium levels when combined with ramipril. ACE inhibitor effects may be increased by phenothiazines or probenecid (increases levels of captopril). ACE inhibitors may increase serum concentrations/effects of digoxin, lithium, and sulfonlyureas.

Diuretics have additive hypotensive effects with ACE inhibitors, and hypovolemia increases the potential for adverse renal effects of ACE inhibitors. In patients with compromised renal function, coadministration with NSAIDs may result in further deterioration of renal function. Allopurinol and ACE inhibitors may cause a higher risk of hypersensitivity reaction when taken concurrently.

Decreased Effect: Aspirin (high dose) may reduce the therapeutic effects of ACE inhibitors; at low dosages this does not appear to be significant. Rifampin may decrease the effect of ACE inhibitors. Antacids may decrease the bioavailability of ACE inhibitors (may be more likely to occur with captopril); separate administration times by 1-2 hours. NSAIDs, specifically indomethacin, may reduce the hypotensive effects of ACE inhibitors. More likely to occur in low renin or volume dependent hypertensive patients.

Mechanism of Action Ramipril is an ACE inhibitor which prevents the formation of angiotensin II from angiotensin I and exhibits pharmacologic effects that are similar to captopril. Ramipril must undergo enzymatic saponification by esterases in the liver to its biologically active metabolite, ramiprilat. The pharmacodynamic effects of ramipril result from the high-affinity, competitive, reversible binding of ramiprilat to angiotensin-converting enzyme thus preventing the formation of the potent vasoconstrictor angiotensin II. This isomerized enzyme-inhibitor complex has a slow rate of dissociation, which results in high potency and a long duration of action; a CNS mechanism may also be involved in the hypotensive effect as angiotensin II increases adrenergic outflow from CNS; vasoactive kallikreins may be decreased in conversion to active hormones by ACE inhibitors, thus reducing blood pressure

Pharmacodynamics/Kinetics

Onset of action: 1-2 hours

Duration: 24 hours

Absorption: Well absorbed (50% to 60%)

Distribution: Plasma levels decline in a triphasic fashion; rapid decline is a distribution phase to peripheral compartment, plasma protein and tissue ACE (half-life 2-4 hours); 2nd phase is an apparent elimination phase representing the clearance of free ramiprilat (half-life: 9-18 hours); and final phase is the terminal elimination phase representing the equilibrium phase between tissue binding and dissociation

Metabolism: Hepatic to the active form, ramiprilat

Half-life elimination: Ramiprilat: Effective: 13-17 hours; Terminal: >50 hours

Time to peak, serum: ~1 hour

Excretion: Urine (60%) and feces (40%) as parent drug and metabolites

Dosage Adults: Oral:

Hypertension: 2.5-5 mg once daily, maximum: 20 mg/day

Reduction in risk of MI, stroke, and death from cardiovascular causes: Initial: 2.5 mg once daily for 1 week, then 5 mg once daily for the next 3 weeks, then increase as tolerated to 10 mg once daily (may be given as divided dose)

Heart failure postmyocardial infarction: Initial: 2.5 mg twice daily titrated upward, if possible, to 5 mg twice daily.

Note: The dose of any concomitant diuretic should be reduced. If the diuretic cannot be discontinued, initiate therapy with 1.25 mg. After the initial dose, the patient should be monitored carefully until blood pressure has stabilized.

Dosing adjustment in renal impairment:

Cl_{cr} <40 mL/minute: Administer 25% of normal dose.

Renal failure and hypertension: Administer 1.25 mg once daily, titrated upward as possible.

Renal failure and heart failure: Administer 1.25 mg once daily, increasing to 1.25 mg twice daily up to 2.5 mg twice daily as tolerated.

Administration Capsule is usually swallowed whole, but may be may be mixed in water, apple juice, or applesauce.

Patient Information Report vomiting, diarrhea, excessive perspiration, or dehydration; also sore throat, fever, swelling of face, lips, tongue, or if difficulty in breathing occurs or if persistent cough develops; may cause lightheadedness during first few days of therapy; if a cough develops which is bothersome, consult prescriber. Capsule is usually swallowed whole but may be sprinkled on applesauce or mixed in water or juice.

Dosage Forms CAP: 1.25 mg, 2.5 mg, 5 mg, 10 mg

Ranitidine (ra NI ti deen)

U.S. Brand Names Zantac®; Zantac® 75 [OTC]

Synonyms Ranitidine Hydrochloride

Therapeutic Category Antihistamine, H_2 Blocker; Histamine H_2 Antagonist

Use

Zantac®: Short-term and maintenance therapy of duodenal ulcer, gastric ulcer, gastroesophageal reflux, active benign ulcer, erosive esophagitis, and pathological hypersecretory conditions; as part of a multidrug regimen for *H. pylori* eradication to reduce the risk of duodenal ulcer recurrence

Zantac® 75 [OTC]: Relief of heartburn, acid indigestion, and sour stomach

Unlabeled/Investigational Use Recurrent postoperative ulcer, upper GI bleeding, prevention of acid-aspiration pneumonitis during surgery, and prevention of stress-induced ulcers

Pregnancy Risk Factor B

Contraindications Hypersensitivity to ranitidine or any component of the formulation

Warnings/Precautions Use with caution in patients with hepatic impairment; use with caution in renal impairment, dosage modification required; avoid use in patients with history of acute porphyria (may precipitate attacks); long-term therapy may be associated with vitamin B_{12} deficiency; EFFERdose® formulations contain phenylalanine; safety and efficacy have not been established for pediatric patients <1 month of age

Common Adverse Reactions Frequency not defined.

Cardiovascular: Atrioventricular block, bradycardia, premature ventricular beats, tachycardia, vasculitis

Central nervous system: Agitation, dizziness, depression, hallucinations, headache, insomnia, malaise, mental confusion, somnolence, vertigo

Dermatologic: Alopecia, erythema multiforme, rash

Endocrine & metabolic: Gynecomastia, impotence, increased prolactin levels, loss of libido

Gastrointestinal: Abdominal discomfort/pain, constipation, diarrhea, nausea, pancreatitis, vomiting

Hematologic: Acquired hemolytic anemia, agranulocytosis, aplastic anemia, granulocytopenia, leukopenia, pancytopenia, thrombocytopenia

Hepatic: Hepatic failure, hepatitis

Local: Transient pain, burning or itching at the injection site

Neuromuscular & skeletal: Arthralgia, involuntary motor disturbance, myalgia

Ocular: Blurred vision

Renal: Increased serum creatinine

Miscellaneous: Anaphylaxis, angioneurotic edema, hypersensitivity reactions

Drug Interactions

Cytochrome P450 Effect: Substrate (minor) of CYP1A2, 2C19, 2D6; **Inhibits** CYP1A2 (weak), 2D6 (weak)

Increased Effect/Toxicity: Increased the effect/toxicity of cyclosporine (increased serum creatinine), gentamicin (neuromuscular blockade), glipizide, glyburide, midazolam (increased concentrations), metoprolol, pentoxifylline, phenytoin, quinidine, and triazolam.

Decreased Effect:

Decreased effect: Variable effects on warfarin; antacids may decrease absorption of ranitidine; ketoconazole and itraconazole absorptions are decreased; may produce altered serum levels of procainamide and ferrous sulfate; decreased effect of nondepolarizing

(Continued)

Ranitidine *(Continued)*

muscle relaxants, cefpodoxime, cyanocobalamin (decreased absorption), diazepam, oxaprozin

Decreased toxicity of atropine

Mechanism of Action Competitive inhibition of histamine at H_2-receptors of the gastric parietal cells, which inhibits gastric acid secretion, gastric volume, and hydrogen ion concentration are reduced. Does not affect pepsin secretion, pentagastrin-stimulated intrinsic factor secretion, or serum gastrin.

Pharmacodynamics/Kinetics

Absorption: Oral: 50%

Distribution: Normal renal function: V_d: 1.7 L/kg; Cl_{cr} 25-35 mL/minute: 1.76 L/kg minimally penetrates the blood-brain barrier; enters breast milk

Protein binding: 15%

Metabolism: Hepatic to N-oxide, S-oxide, and N-desmethyl metabolites

Bioavailability: Oral: 48%

Half-life elimination:

Oral: Normal renal function: 2.5-3 hours; Cl_{cr} 25-35 mL/minute: 4.8 hours

I.V.: Normal renal function: 2-2.5 hours

Time to peak, serum: Oral: 2-3 hours; I.M.: ≤15 minutes

Excretion: Urine: Oral: 30%, I.V.: 70% (as unchanged drug); feces (as metabolites)

Dosage

Children 1 month to 16 years:

Duodenal and gastric ulcer:

Oral:

Treatment: 2-4 mg/kg/day divided twice daily; maximum treatment dose: 300 mg/day

Maintenance: 2-4 mg/kg once daily; maximum maintenance dose: 150 mg/day

I.V.: 2-4 mg/kg/day divided every 6-8 hours; maximum: 150 mg/day

GERD and erosive esophagitis:

Oral: 5-10 mg/kg/day divided twice daily; maximum: GERD: 300 mg/day, erosive esophagitis: 600 mg/day

I.V.: 2-4 mg/kg/day divided every 6-8 hours; maximum: 150 mg/day **or as an alternative** Continuous infusion: Initial: 1 mg/kg/dose for one dose followed by infusion of 0.08-0.17 mg/kg/hour or 2-4 mg/kg/day

Children ≥12 years: Prevention of heartburn: Oral: Zantac® 75 [OTC]: 75 mg 30-60 minutes before eating food or drinking beverages which cause heartburn; maximum: 150 mg/24 hours; do not use for more than 14 days

Adults:

Duodenal ulcer: Oral: Treatment: 150 mg twice daily, or 300 mg once daily after the evening meal or at bedtime; maintenance: 150 mg once daily at bedtime

Helicobacter pylori eradication: 150 mg twice daily; requires combination therapy

Pathological hypersecretory conditions:

Oral: 150 mg twice daily; adjust dose or frequency as clinically indicated; doses of up to 6 g/day have been used

I.V.: Continuous infusion for Zollinger-Ellison: 1 mg/kg/hour; measure gastric acid output at 4 hours, if >10 mEq or if patient is symptomatic, increase dose in increments of 0.5 mg/kg/hour; doses of up to 2.5 mg/kg/hour have been used

Gastric ulcer, benign: Oral: 150 mg twice daily; maintenance: 150 mg once daily at bedtime

Erosive esophagitis: Oral: Treatment: 150 mg 4 times/day; maintenance: 150 mg twice daily

Prevention of heartburn: Oral: Zantac® 75 [OTC]: 75 mg 30-60 minutes before eating food or drinking beverages which cause heartburn; maximum: 150 mg in 24 hours; do not use for more than 14 days

Patients not able to take oral medication:

I.M.: 50 mg every 6-8 hours

I.V.: Intermittent bolus or infusion: 50 mg every 6-8 hours

Continuous I.V. infusion: 6.25 mg/hour

Elderly: Ulcer healing rates and incidence of adverse effects are similar in the elderly, when compared to younger patients; dosing adjustments not necessary based on age alone

Dosing adjustment in renal impairment: Adults: Cl_{cr} <50 mL/minute:

Oral: 150 mg every 24 hours; adjust dose cautiously if needed

I.V.: 50 mg every 18-24 hours; adjust dose cautiously if needed

Hemodialysis: Adjust dosing schedule so that dose coincides with the end of hemodialysis

Dosing adjustment/comments in hepatic disease: Patients with hepatic impairment may have minor changes in ranitidine half-life, distribution, clearance, and bioavailability; dosing adjustments not necessary, monitor

Administration

Ranitidine injection may be administered I.M. or I.V.:

I.M.: Injection is administered undiluted

I.V.: Must be diluted; may be administered IVP or IVPB or continuous I.V. infusion

IVP: Ranitidine (usually 50 mg) should be diluted to a total of 20 mL with NS or D_5W and administered over at least 5 minutes

IVPB: Administer over 15-20 minutes

Continuous I.V. infusion: Administer at 6.25 mg/hour and titrate dosage based on gastric pH by continuous infusion over 24 hours

EFFERdose® formulations: Dissolve each dose in 6-8 ounces of water before drinking

Monitoring Parameters AST, ALT, serum creatinine; when used to prevent stress-related GI bleeding, measure the intragastric pH and try to maintain pH >4; signs and symptoms of peptic ulcer disease, occult blood with GI bleeding, monitor renal function to correct dose; monitor for side effects

Patient Information It may take several days before this medicine begins to relieve stomach pain; antacids may be taken with ranitidine unless your prescriber has told you not to use them; wait 30-60 minutes between taking the antacid and ranitidine; may cause drowsiness, impair judgment, or coordination

Dosage Forms CAP: 150 mg, 300 mg. **GRAN, effervescent** (Zantac® EFFERdose®): 150 mg (60s) [DSC]. **INF** [premixed in NaCl 0.45%; preservative free] (Zantac®): 50 mg (50 mL). **INJ, solution** (Zantac®): 25 mg/mL (2 mL, 6 mL, 40 mL). **SYR:** 15 mg/mL (10 mL); (Zantac®): 15 mg/mL (473 mL). **TAB:** 75 mg [OTC], 150 mg, 300 mg; (Zantac®): 150 mg, 300 mg; (Zantac® 75): 75 mg. **TAB, effervescent** (Zantac® EFFERdose®): 150 mg

♦ **Ranitidine Hydrochloride** *see* Ranitidine *on page 1081*
♦ **Rapamune®** *see* Sirolimus *on page 1140*
♦ **Raptiva™** *see* Efalizumab *on page 424*

Rasburicase (ras BYOOR i kayse)

U.S. Brand Names Elitek™

Therapeutic Category Enzyme, Urate-Oxidase (Recombinant)

Use Initial management of uric acid levels in pediatric patients with leukemia, lymphoma, and solid tumor malignancies receiving anticancer therapy expected to result in tumor lysis and elevation of plasma uric acid

Pregnancy Risk Factor C

Contraindications Hypersensitivity, hemolytic or methemoglobinemia reactions to rasburicase or any component of the formulation; glucose-6-phosphatase dehydrogenase (G6PD) deficiency

Warnings/Precautions Hypersensitivity reactions (including anaphylaxis), methemoglobinemia, and severe hemolysis have been reported; discontinue **immediately and permanently** in patients developing any of these reactions. Hemolysis may be associated with G6PD deficiency; patients at higher risk for G6PD deficiency should be screened prior to therapy. Enzymatic degradation of uric acid in blood samples will occur if left at room temperature; specific guidelines for the collection of plasma uric acid samples must be followed. Rasburicase is immunogenic and can elicit an antibody response; studies in healthy volunteers detected neutralizing antibodies from 1-6 weeks after exposure and lasted for up to 494 days. Safety and efficacy have been established for a single treatment course; administration of more than one course is not recommended. Administer concurrently with standard intravenous hydration therapy. Efficacy in adults has not been established.

Common Adverse Reactions As reported in patients receiving rasburicase with antitumor therapy versus active-control:

>10%:
  Central nervous system: Fever (5% to 46%), headache (26%)
  Dermatologic: Rash (13%)
  Gastrointestinal: Vomiting (50%), nausea (27%), abdominal pain (20%), constipation (20%), mucositis (2% to 15%), diarrhea (≤1% to 20%)
1% to 10%:
  Hematologic: Neutropenia with fever (4%), neutropenia (2%)
  Respiratory: Respiratory distress (3%)
  Miscellaneous: Sepsis (3%)

Mechanism of Action Rasburicase is a recombinant urate-oxidase enzyme, which converts uric acid to allantoin (an inactive and soluble metabolite of uric acid); it does not inhibit the formation of uric acid.

Pharmacodynamics/Kinetics
  Distribution: Pediatric patients: 110-127 mL/kg
  Half-life elimination: Pediatric patients: 18 hours

Dosage I.V.: Children: Management of uric acid levels: 0.15 mg/kg or 0.2 mg/kg once daily for 5 days; begin chemotherapy 4-24 hours after the first dose

  Note: Adults and Elderly: Refer to pediatric dosing; insufficient data collected in adult/geriatric patients to determine response to treatment

Administration To be given as an I.V. infusion over 30 minutes; do **not** administer as a bolus infusion. Do **not** filter during infusion. If not possible to administer through a separate line, I.V. line should be flushed with at least 15 mL saline prior to and following rasburicase infusion.

Monitoring Parameters Plasma uric acid levels, CBC

Patient Information This medication can only be given by injection. Notify prescriber immediately for chest pain, difficulty breathing, or itching. May cause headache, nausea, vomiting, constipation, or fever.

Dosage Forms INJ, powder for reconstitution: 1.5 mg

♦ **Rea-Lo® [OTC]** *see* Urea *on page 1282*
♦ **ReAzo [OTC]** *see* Phenazopyridine *on page 987*
♦ **Rebetol®** *see* Ribavirin *on page 1091*
♦ **Rebetron®** *see* Interferon Alfa-2b and Ribavirin *on page 676*
♦ **Rebif®** *see* Interferon Beta-1a *on page 680*
♦ **Recombinant α-L-Iduronidase (Glycosaminoglycan α-L-Iduronohydrolase)** *see* Laronidase *on page 718*
♦ **Recombinant Hirudin** *see* Lepirudin *on page 720*

♦ **Recombinant Human Deoxyribonuclease** *see* Dornase Alfa *on page 403*
♦ **Recombinant Human Follicle Stimulating Hormone** *see* Follitropins *on page 555*
♦ **Recombinant Human Interleukin-11** *see* Oprelvekin *on page 931*
♦ **Recombinant Human Parathyroid Hormone (1-34)** *see* Teriparatide *on page 1200*
♦ **Recombinant Human Platelet-Derived Growth Factor B** *see* Becaplermin *on page 148*
♦ **Recombinant Interleukin-11** *see* Oprelvekin *on page 931*
♦ **Recombinant Plasminogen Activator** *see* Reteplase *on page 1088*
♦ **Recombinate™** *see* Antihemophilic Factor (Recombinant) *on page 105*
♦ **Recombivax HB®** *see* Hepatitis B Vaccine *on page 617*
♦ **Redutemp® [OTC]** *see* Acetaminophen *on page 24*
♦ **Reese's® Pinworm Medicine [OTC]** *see* Pyrantel Pamoate *on page 1064*
♦ **ReFacto®** *see* Antihemophilic Factor (Recombinant) *on page 105*
♦ **Refludan®** *see* Lepirudin *on page 720*
♦ **Regitine® [DSC]** *see* Phentolamine *on page 992*
♦ **Reglan®** *see* Metoclopramide *on page 827*
♦ **Regonol® [DSC]** *see* Pyridostigmine *on page 1066*
♦ **Regranex®** *see* Becaplermin *on page 148*
♦ **Regular Iletin® II** *see* Insulin Preparations *on page 669*
♦ **Reguloid® [OTC]** *see* Psyllium *on page 1063*
♦ **Relafen®** *see* Nabumetone *on page 872*
♦ **Relenza®** *see* Zanamivir *on page 1323*
♦ **Relief® [OTC]** *see* Phenylephrine *on page 993*
♦ **Relpax®** *see* Eletriptan *on page 427*
♦ **Remeron®** *see* Mirtazapine *on page 847*
♦ **Remeron SolTab®** *see* Mirtazapine *on page 847*
♦ **Remicade®** *see* Infliximab *on page 665*

Remifentanil (rem i FEN ta nil)

Related Information
    Narcotic Agonists Comparison *on page 1395*
U.S. Brand Names Ultiva®
Synonyms GI87084B
Therapeutic Category Analgesic, Narcotic
Use Analgesic for use during general anesthesia for continued analgesia in children ≥2 years of age and adults

Unlabeled/Investigational Use Management of pain in mechanically-ventilated patients
Restrictions C-II
Pregnancy Risk Factor C
Contraindications Not for intrathecal or epidural administration, due to the presence of glycine in the formulation; hypersensitivity to remifentanil, fentanyl, or fentanyl analogs, or any component of the formulation; interruption of an infusion will result in offset of effects within 5-10 minutes; the discontinuation of remifentanil infusion should be preceded by the establishment of adequate postoperative analgesia orders, especially for patients in whom postoperative pain is anticipated

Warnings/Precautions Remifentanil is not recommended as the sole agent in general anesthesia, because the loss of consciousness cannot be assured and due to the high incidence of apnea, hypotension, tachycardia and muscle rigidity; it should be administered by individuals specifically trained in the use of anesthetic agents and should not be used in diagnostic or therapeutic procedures outside the monitored anesthesia setting; resuscitative and intubation equipment should be readily available

Common Adverse Reactions
    >10%: Gastrointestinal: Nausea, vomiting
    1% to 10%:
        Cardiovascular: Hypotension, bradycardia, tachycardia, hypertension
        Central nervous system: Dizziness, headache, agitation, fever
        Dermatologic: Pruritus
        Ocular: Visual disturbances
        Respiratory: Respiratory depression, apnea, hypoxia
        Miscellaneous: Shivering, postoperative pain

Drug Interactions
    Increased Effect/Toxicity: Additive effects with other CNS depressants.
Mechanism of Action Binds with stereospecific mu-opioid receptors at many sites within the CNS, increases pain threshold, alters pain reception, inhibits ascending pain pathways
Pharmacodynamics/Kinetics
    Onset of action: I.V.: 1-3 minutes
    Protein binding: 92%
    Metabolism: Rapid via blood and tissue esterases
    Half-life elimination (dose dependent): 10 minutes
    Excretion: Urine
Dosage I.V. continuous infusion:
    Children ≥2 years: Per kg doses are the same as for adult patients
    Adults:
        During induction: 0.5-1 mcg/kg/minute

During maintenance:
  With nitrous oxide (66%): 0.4 mcg/kg/minute (range: 0.1-2 mcg/kg/minute)
  With isoflurane: 0.25 mcg/kg/minute (range: 0.05-2 mcg/kg/minute)
  With propofol: 0.25 mcg/kg/minute (range: 0.05-2 mcg/kg/minute)
Continuation as an analgesic in immediate postoperative period: 0.1 mcg/kg/minute (range: 0.025-0.2 mcg/kg/minute)
Mechanically-ventilated patients: Acute pain (moderate to severe) (unlabeled use): 0.6-15 mcg/kg/hour
Elderly: Elderly patients have an increased sensitivity to effect of remifentanil, doses should be decreased by $\frac{1}{2}$ and titrated

Administration Inject slowly over 3-5 minutes. For final concentration of 50 mcg/mL, may dilute 1 mg in 20 mL, 2 mg in 40 mL, or 5 mg in 100 mL; for final concentration of 25 mcg/mL, dilute 1 mg in 40 mL or 2 mg in 80 mL.

Monitoring Parameters Respiratory and cardiovascular status, blood pressure, heart rate

Dosage Forms INJ, powder for reconstitution: 1 mg, 2 mg, 5 mg

- ◆ **Reminyl**® *see* Galantamine *on page 576*
- ◆ **Remodulin**™ *see* Treprostinil *on page 1257*
- ◆ **Renagel**® *see* Sevelamer *on page 1133*
- ◆ **Renese**® *see* Polythiazide *on page 1016*
- ◆ **Renova**® *see* Tretinoin (Topical) *on page 1260*
- ◆ **ReoPro**® *see* Abciximab *on page 20*

Repaglinide (re pa GLI nide)

Related Information
  Hypoglycemic Drugs & Thiazolidinedione Information *on page 1378*
U.S. Brand Names Prandin®
Therapeutic Category Antidiabetic Agent, Secretogue; Hypoglycemic Agent, Oral; Meglitinide
Use Management of type 2 diabetes mellitus (noninsulin dependent, NIDDM); may be used in combination with metformin or thiazolidinediones
Pregnancy Risk Factor C
Contraindications Hypersensitivity to repaglinide or any component of the formulation; diabetic ketoacidosis, with or without coma (treat with insulin); type 1 diabetes (insulin dependent, IDDM)
Warnings/Precautions Use with caution in patients with hepatic or renal impairment. All oral hypoglycemic agents are capable of producing hypoglycemia. Proper patient selection, dosage, and instructions to the patients are important to avoid hypoglycemic episodes. It may be necessary to discontinue repaglinide and administer insulin if the patient is exposed to stress (fever, trauma, infection, surgery). Safety and efficacy have not been established in pediatric patients.
Common Adverse Reactions
  >10%:
    Central nervous system: Headache (9% to 11%)
    Endocrine & metabolic: Hypoglycemia (16% to 31%)
    Respiratory: Upper respiratory tract infection (10% to 16%)
  1% to 10%:
    Cardiovascular: Chest pain (2% to 3%)
    Gastrointestinal: Nausea (3% to 5%), heartburn (2% to 4%), vomiting (2% to 3%) constipation (2% to 3%), diarrhea (4% to 5%), tooth disorder (<1% to 2%)
    Genitourinary: Urinary tract infection (2% to 3%)
    Neuromuscular & skeletal: Arthralgia (3% to 6%), back pain (5% to 6%), paresthesia (2% to 3%)
    Respiratory: Sinusitis (3% to 6%), rhinitis (3% to 7%), bronchitis (2% to 6%)
    Miscellaneous: Allergy (1% to 2%)
Drug Interactions
  Cytochrome P450 Effect: Substrate of CYP2C8/9 (minor), 3A4 (major)
  Increased Effect/Toxicity: Agents that inhibit CYP3A4 (eg, ketoconazole, miconazole, erythromycin, clarithromycin) may increase repaglinide concentrations. The effect of repaglinide may be potentiated when given concomitantly with other highly protein-bound drugs (ie, phenylbutazone, oral anticoagulants, hydantoins, salicylates, NSAIDs, sulfonamides). Concurrent use of other hypoglycemic agents may increase risk of hypoglycemia. Gemfibrozil may increase the serum concentration of repaglinide (resulting in severe, prolonged hypoglycemia), and the addition of itraconazole may augment the effects of gemfibrozil on repaglinide.
  Decreased Effect: Drugs which induce cytochrome P450 isoenzyme 3A4 may increase metabolism of repaglinide (phenytoin, rifampin, barbiturates, carbamazepine). Certain drugs (thiazides, diuretics, corticosteroids, phenothiazines, thyroid products, estrogens, oral contraceptives, phenytoin, nicotinic acid, sympathomimetics, calcium channel blockers, isoniazid) tend to produce hyperglycemia and may lead to loss of glycemic control.
Mechanism of Action Nonsulfonylurea hypoglycemic agent of the meglitinide class (the nonsulfonylurea moiety of glyburide) used in the management of type 2 diabetes mellitus; stimulates insulin release from the pancreatic beta cells
Pharmacodynamics/Kinetics
  Onset of action: Single dose: Increased insulin levels: ~15-60 minutes
  Duration: 4-6 hours
  (Continued)

Repaglinide *(Continued)*

Absorption: Rapid and complete

Distribution: V_d: 31 L

Protein binding, plasma: >98%

Metabolism: Hepatic via CYP3A4 isoenzyme and glucuronidation to inactive metabolites

Bioavailability: Mean absolute: ~56%

Half-life elimination: 1 hour

Time to peak, plasma: ~1 hour

Excretion: Within 96 hours: Feces (~90%, <2% as parent drug); Urine (~8%)

Dosage Adults: Oral: Should be taken within 15 minutes of the meal, but time may vary from immediately preceding the meal to as long as 30 minutes before the meal

Initial: For patients not previously treated or whose Hb A_{1c} is <8%, the starting dose is 0.5 mg. For patients previously treated with blood glucose-lowering agents whose Hb A_{1c} is ≥8%, the initial dose is 1 or 2 mg before each meal.

Dose adjustment: Determine dosing adjustments by blood glucose response, usually fasting blood glucose. Double the preprandial dose up to 4 mg until satisfactory blood glucose response is achieved. At least 1 week should elapse to assess response after each dose adjustment.

Dose range: 0.5-4 mg taken with meals. Repaglinide may be dosed prandial 2, 3 or 4 times/day in response to changes in the patient's meal pattern. Maximum recommended daily dose: 16 mg.

Patients receiving other oral hypoglycemic agents: When repaglinide is used to replace therapy with other oral hypoglycemic agents, it may be started the day after the final dose is given. Observe patients carefully for hypoglycemia because of potential overlapping of drug effects. When transferred from longer half-life sulfonylureas (eg, chlorpropamide), close monitoring may be indicated for up to ≥1 week.

Combination therapy: If repaglinide monotherapy does not result in adequate glycemic control, metformin or a thiazolidinedione may be added. Or, if metformin or thiazolidinedione therapy does not provide adequate control, repaglinide may be added. The starting dose and dose adjustments for combination therapy are the same as repaglinide monotherapy. Carefully adjust the dose of each drug to determine the minimal dose required to achieve the desired pharmacologic effect. Failure to do so could result in an increase in the incidence of hypoglycemic episodes. Use appropriate monitoring of FPG and Hb A_{1c} measurements to ensure that the patient is not subjected to excessive drug exposure or increased probability of secondary drug failure. If glucose is not achieved after a suitable trial of combination therapy, consider discontinuing these drugs and using insulin.

Dosing adjustment in renal impairment:

Cl_{cr} 40-80 mL/minute (mild to moderate renal dysfunction): Initial dosage adjustment does not appear to be necessary.

Cl_{cr} 20-40 mL/minute: Initiate 0.5 mg with meals; titrate carefully.

Dosing adjustment in hepatic impairment: Use conservative initial and maintenance doses. Use longer intervals between dosage adjustments.

Administration Administer repaglinide 15-30 minutes before meals.

Monitoring Parameters Periodically monitor fasting blood glucose and glycosylated hemoglobin (Hb A_{1c}) levels with a goal of decreasing these levels towards the normal range. During dose adjustment, fasting glucose can be used to determine response.

Reference Range Target range: Adults:

Fasting blood glucose: <120 mg/dL

Glycosylated hemoglobin: <7%

Patient Information Inform patients about the importance of adherence to dietary instructions, of a regular exercise program, and of regular testing of blood glucose and Hb A_{1c}

Explain the risks of hypoglycemia, its symptoms and treatment, and conditions that predispose to its development and concomitant administration of other glucose-lowering drugs to patients and responsible family members

Instruct patients to take repaglinide before meals (2, 3, or 4 times/day prandial). Doses are usually taken within 15 minutes of the meal, but time may vary from immediately preceding the meal to as long as 30 minutes before the meal. Instruct patients who skip a meal (or add an extra meal) to skip (or add) a dose for that meal.

Dosage Forms TAB: 0.5 mg, 1 mg, 2 mg

- ◆ **Repan**® *see* Butalbital, Acetaminophen, and Caffeine *on page 194*
- ◆ **Repronex**® *see* Menotropins *on page 789*
- ◆ **Requip**® *see* Ropinirole *on page 1113*
- ◆ **Rescriptor**® *see* Delavirdine *on page 349*
- ◆ **Rescula**® *see* Unoprostone *on page 1281*
- ◆ **Resectisol**® *see* Mannitol *on page 774*

Reserpine *(re SER peen)*

Therapeutic Category Antihypertensive Agent; Rauwolfia Alkaloid

Use Management of mild to moderate hypertension

Unlabeled/Investigational Use Management of tardive dyskinesia, schizophrenia

Pregnancy Risk Factor C

Dosage Note: When used for management of hypertension, full antihypertensive effects may take as long as 3 weeks.

Oral:

Children: Hypertension: 0.01-0.02 mg/kg/24 hours divided every 12 hours; maximum dose: 0.25 mg/day (not recommended in children)

Adults:

Hypertension: 0.1-0.25 mg/day in 1-2 doses; initial: 0.5 mg/day for 1-2 weeks; maintenance: reduce to 0.1-0.25 mg/day;

Tardive dyskinesia/schizophrenia: Initial: 0.5 mg/day; usual range: 0.1-1 mg

Elderly: Initial: 0.05 mg once daily, increasing by 0.05 mg every week as necessary

Dosing adjustment in renal impairment: Cl_{cr} <10 mL/minute: Avoid use

Dialysis: Not removed by hemo or peritoneal dialysis; supplemental dose is not necessary

Dosage Forms TAB: 0.1 mg, 0.25 mg

♦ **Reserpine, Hydralazine, and Hydrochlorothiazide** *see* Hydralazine, Hydrochlorothiazide, and Reserpine *on page 625*

♦ **Respa-1st®** *see* Guaifenesin and Pseudoephedrine *on page 605*

♦ **Respa-DM®** *see* Guaifenesin and Dextromethorphan *on page 604*

♦ **Respa-GF®** *see* Guaifenesin *on page 603*

♦ **Respaire®-60 SR** *see* Guaifenesin and Pseudoephedrine *on page 605*

♦ **Respaire®-120 SR** *see* Guaifenesin and Pseudoephedrine *on page 605*

♦ **RespiGam® [DSC]** *see* Respiratory Syncytial Virus Immune Globulin (Intravenous) *on page 1087*

Respiratory Syncytial Virus Immune Globulin (Intravenous)

(RES peer rah tor ee sin SISH al VYE rus i MYUN GLOB yoo lin in tra VEE nus)

U.S. Brand Names RespiGam® [DSC]

Synonyms RSV-IGIV

Therapeutic Category Immune Globulin

Use Orphan drug: Prevention of serious lower respiratory infection caused by respiratory syncytial virus (RSV) in children <24 months of age with bronchopulmonary dysplasia (BPD) or a history of premature birth (≤35 weeks gestation)

Pregnancy Risk Factor C

Contraindications Hypersensitivity to any component of the formulation; selective IgA deficiency; history of severe prior reaction to any immunoglobulin preparation

Warnings/Precautions Use caution to avoid fluid overload in patients, particularly infants with bronchopulmonary dysplasia (BPD), when administering RSV-IGIV; hypersensitivity including anaphylaxis or angioneurotic edema may occur; keep epinephrine 1:1000 readily available during infusion; rare occurrences of aseptic meningitis syndrome have been associated with IGIV treatment, particularly with high doses; observe carefully for signs and symptoms and treat promptly.

RespiGam® contains sucrose. Renal dysfunction and /or acute renal failure has been reported with the administration of IVIG; the majority of cases were associated with sucrose-containing IVIG products. Use caution in patients at increased risk of renal failure (including pre-existing renal insufficiency, volume depletion, or concurrent treatment with nephrotoxic drugs). Ensure adequate hydration prior to infusion.

Common Adverse Reactions 1% to 10%:

Cardiovascular: Tachycardia (1%), hypertension (1%), hypotension

Central nervous system: Fever (6%)

Dermatologic: Rash (1%)

Endocrine & metabolic: Fluid overload (1%)

Gastrointestinal: Vomiting (2%), diarrhea (1%), gastroenteritis (1%)

Local: Injection site inflammation (1%)

Respiratory: Respiratory distress (2%), wheezing (2%), rales, hypoxia (1%), tachypnea (1%)

Mechanism of Action RSV-IGIV is a sterile liquid immunoglobulin G containing neutralizing antibody to respiratory syncytial virus. It is effective in reducing the incidence and duration of RSV hospitalization and the severity of RSV illness in high risk infants.

Dosage I.V.: Children <24 months of age: Prevention of respiratory syncytial virus (RSV) infection: 750 mg/kg/month according to the following infusion schedule:

Initial infusion rate for the first 15 minutes: 1.5 mL/kg/hour; after 15 minutes increase to 3.6 mL/kg/hour (maximum infusion rate: 3.6 mL/kg/hour); rate should be decreased in patients at risk of renal dysfunction

Administration Begin infusion within 6 hours and complete within 12 hours after entering vial. Observe for signs of intolerance during and after infusion; administer through an I.V. line using a constant infusion pump and through a separate I.V. line, if possible; if needed, RSV-IGIV may be "piggybacked" into dextrose with or without saline solutions, avoiding dilutions >2:1 with such line configurations. An in-line filter with a pore size >15 micrometers may be used.

Monitoring Parameters Monitor for symptoms of allergic reaction; check vital signs, cardiopulmonary status after each rate increase and thereafter at 30-minute intervals until 30 minutes following completion of the infusion

Dosage Forms INJ, solution [preservative free]: 50 mg/mL (50 mL) [DSC]

♦ **Respi-Tann™** *see* Carbetapentane and Pseudoephedrine *on page 217*

♦ **Restasis™** *see* CycloSPORINE *on page 323*

♦ **Restoril®** *see* Temazepam *on page 1192*

♦ **Retavase®** *see* Reteplase *on page 1088*

Reteplase (RE ta plase)

U.S. Brand Names Retavase®

Synonyms Recombinant Plasminogen Activator; r-PA

Therapeutic Category Fibrinolytic Agent

Use Management of acute myocardial infarction (AMI); improvement of ventricular function; reduction of the incidence of CHF and the reduction of mortality following AMI

Pregnancy Risk Factor C

Contraindications Hypersensitivity to reteplase or any component of the formulation; active internal bleeding; history of cerebrovascular accident; recent intracranial or intraspinal surgery or trauma; intracranial neoplasm, arteriovenous malformations, or aneurysm; known bleeding diathesis; severe uncontrolled hypertension

Warnings/Precautions Concurrent heparin anticoagulation can contribute to bleeding; careful attention to all potential bleeding sites. I.M. injections and nonessential handling of the patient should be avoided. Venipunctures should be performed carefully and only when necessary. If arterial puncture is necessary, use an upper extremity vessel that can be manually compressed. If serious bleeding occurs then the infusion of anistreplase and heparin should be stopped.

For the following conditions the risk of bleeding is higher with use of reteplase and should be weighed against the benefits of therapy: recent major surgery (eg, CABG, obstetrical delivery, organ biopsy, previous puncture of noncompressible vessels), cerebrovascular disease, recent gastrointestinal or genitourinary bleeding, recent trauma including CPR, hypertension (systolic BP >180 mm Hg and/or diastolic BP >110 mm Hg), high likelihood of left heart thrombus (eg, mitral stenosis with atrial fibrillation), acute pericarditis, subacute bacterial endocarditis, hemostatic defects including ones caused by severe renal or hepatic dysfunction, significant hepatic dysfunction, pregnancy, diabetic hemorrhagic retinopathy or other hemorrhagic ophthalmic conditions, septic thrombophlebitis or occluded AV cannula at seriously infected site, advanced age (eg, >75 years), patients receiving oral anticoagulants, any other condition in which bleeding constitutes a significant hazard or would be particularly difficult to manage because of location.

Coronary thrombolysis may result in reperfusion arrhythmias. Follow standard MI management. Rare anaphylactic reactions can occur. Safety and efficacy in pediatric patients have not been established.

Common Adverse Reactions Bleeding is the most frequent adverse effect associated with reteplase. Heparin and aspirin have been administered concurrently with reteplase in clinical trials. The incidence of adverse events is a reflection of these combined therapies, and are comparable with comparison thrombolytics.

>10%: Local: Injection site bleeding (4.6% to 48.6%)

1% to 10%:
    Gastrointestinal: Bleeding (1.8% to 9.0%)
    Genitourinary: Bleeding (0.9% to 9.5%)
    Hematologic: Anemia (0.9% to 2.6%)

Other adverse effects noted are frequently associated with myocardial infarction (and therefore may or may not be attributable to Retavase®) and include arrhythmias, hypotension, cardiogenic shock, pulmonary edema, cardiac arrest, reinfarction, pericarditis, tamponade, thrombosis, and embolism.

Drug Interactions

Increased Effect/Toxicity: The risk of bleeding associated with reteplase may be increased by oral anticoagulants (warfarin), heparin, low molecular weight heparins, and drugs which affect platelet function (eg, NSAIDs, dipyridamole, ticlopidine, clopidogrel, IIb/IIIa antagonists). Concurrent use with aspirin and heparin may increase the risk of bleeding; however, aspirin and heparin were used concomitantly with reteplase in the majority of patients in clinical studies.

Decreased Effect: Aminocaproic acid (antifibrinolytic agent) may decrease effectiveness of thrombolytic agents.

Mechanism of Action Reteplase is a nonglycosylated form of tPA produced by recombinant DNA technology using *E. coli*; it initiates local fibrinolysis by binding to fibrin in a thrombus (clot) and converts entrapped plasminogen to plasmin

Pharmacodynamics/Kinetics

Onset of action: Thrombolysis: 30-90 minutes

Half-life elimination: 13-16 minutes

Excretion: Feces and urine
    Clearance: Plasma: 250-450 mL/minute

Dosage

Children: Not recommended

Adults: 10 units I.V. over 2 minutes, followed by a second dose 30 minutes later of 10 units I.V. over 2 minutes
    Withhold second dose if serious bleeding or anaphylaxis occurs

Administration Reteplase should be reconstituted using the diluent, syringe, needle and dispensing pin provided with each kit and the each reconstituted dose should be administered I.V. over 2 minutes; no other medication should be added to the injection solution

Monitoring Parameters Monitor for signs of bleeding (hematuria, GI bleeding, gingival bleeding)

Dosage Forms INJ, powder for reconstitution [preservative free]: 10.4 units

♦ Retin-A® see Tretinoin (Topical) on page 1260

♦ **Retin-A® Micro** see Tretinoin (Topical) on page 1260
♦ **Retinoic Acid** see Tretinoin (Topical) on page 1260
♦ **Retrovir®** see Zidovudine on page 1324
♦ **Reversol®** see Edrophonium on page 422
♦ **Revex®** see Nalmefene on page 878
♦ **Rēv-Eyes™** see Dapiprazole on page 341
♦ **ReVia®** see Naltrexone on page 880
♦ **Reyataz™** see Atazanavir on page 124
♦ **rFSH-alpha** see Follitropins on page 555
♦ **rFSH-beta** see Follitropins on page 555
♦ **rFVIIa** see Factor VIIa (Recombinant) on page 502
♦ **R-Gene®** see Arginine on page 114
♦ **rGM-CSF** see Sargramostim on page 1124
♦ **r-h α-GAL** see Agalsidase Beta on page 41
♦ **r-hCG** see Chorionic Gonadotropin (Recombinant) on page 273
♦ **Rheumatrex®** see Methotrexate on page 815
♦ **rhFSH-alpha** see Follitropins on page 555
♦ **rhFSH-beta** see Follitropins on page 555
♦ **RhIG** see Rhₒ(D) Immune Globulin on page 1089
♦ **rhIL-11** see Oprelvekin on page 931
♦ **Rhinocort® Aqua®** see Budesonide on page 182
♦ **Rhinosyn® [OTC]** see Chlorpheniramine and Pseudoephedrine on page 263
♦ **Rhinosyn-PD® [OTC]** see Chlorpheniramine and Pseudoephedrine on page 263

Rhₒ(D) Immune Globulin (ar aych oh (dee) i MYUN GLOB yoo lin)

U.S. Brand Names BayRho-D® Full-Dose; BayRho-D® Mini-Dose; MICRhoGAM®; RhoGAM®; WinRho SDF®

Synonyms RhIG; Rho(D) Immune Globulin (Human); RhoIGIV; RhoIVIM

Therapeutic Category Immune Globulin

Use

Suppression of Rh isoimmunization: Use in the following situations when an Rhₒ(D)-negative individual is exposed to Rhₒ(D)-positive blood: During delivery of an Rhₒ(D)-positive infant; abortion; amniocentesis; chorionic villus sampling; ruptured tubal pregnancy; abdominal trauma; transplacental hemorrhage. Used when the mother is Rhₒ(D) negative, the father of the child is either Rhₒ(D) positive or Rhₒ(D) unknown, the baby is either either Rhₒ(D) positive or Rhₒ(D) unknown.

Transfusion: Suppression of Rh isoimmunization in Rhₒ(D)-negative female children and female adults in their childbearing years transfused with Rhₒ(D) antigen-positive RBCs or blood components containing Rhₒ(D) antigen-positive RBCs

Treatment of idiopathic thrombocytopenic purpura (ITP): Used in the following nonsplenectomized Rhₒ(D) positive individuals: Children with acute or chronic ITP, adults with chronic ITP, children and adults with ITP secondary to HIV infection

Pregnancy Risk Factor C

Contraindications Hypersensitivity to immune globulins or any component of the formulation; prior sensitization to Rhₒ(D)

Warnings/Precautions As a product of human plasma, may potentially transmit disease; screening of donors, as well as testing and/or inactivation of certain viruses reduces this risk. Not for replacement therapy in immune globulin deficiency syndromes. Use caution with IgA deficiency, may contain trace amounts of IgA; patients who are IgA deficient may have the potential for developing IgA antibodies, anaphylactic reactions may occur. Administer I.M. injections with caution in patients with thrombocytopenia or coagulation disorders.

ITP: Do not administer I.M. or S.C.; administer dose I.V. only. Safety and efficacy not established in Rhₒ(D) negative or splenectomized patients. Decrease dose with hemoglobin <10 g/dL; use with extreme caution if hemoglobin <8 g/dL

Rhₒ(D) suppression: For use in the mother; do not administer to the neonate.

Common Adverse Reactions Frequency not defined.

Cardiovascular: Hypotension, pallor, vasodilation
Central nervous system: Chills, dizziness, fever, headache, somnolence
Dermatologic: Pruritus, rash
Gastrointestinal: Abdominal pain, diarrhea
Hematologic: Hemoglobin decreased (patients with ITP), intravascular hemolysis (patients with ITP)
Hepatic: LDH increased
Local: Injection site reaction: Discomfort, induration, mild pain, redness, swelling
Neuromuscular & skeletal: Back pain, hyperkinesia, myalgia, weakness
Miscellaneous: Anaphylaxis, diaphoresis

Drug Interactions

Decreased Effect: Rhₒ(D) immune globulin may interfere with the response of live vaccines; vaccines should not be administered within 3 months after Rhₒ(D)

Mechanism of Action

Rh suppression: Suppresses the immune response and antibody formation of Rhₒ(D) negative individuals to Rhₒ(D) positive red blood cells.

(Continued)

Rh₀(D) Immune Globulin *(Continued)*

ITP: Coats the patients Rh₀(D) positive red blood cells with antibody, so that as they are cleared by the spleen, the spleens ability to clear antibody-coated cells is saturated, sparing the platelets.

Pharmacodynamics/Kinetics

Onset of platelet increase: ITP: 1-3 days

Duration: Suppression of Rh isoimmunization: ~12 weeks; Treatment of ITP: 3-4 weeks

Distribution: V_d: I.M.: 8.59 L

Half-life elimination: 21-30 days

Time to peak, plasma: I.M.: 5-10 days

Dosage

ITP: Children and Adults: WinRho SDF®: I.V.:

Initial: 50 mcg/kg as a single injection, or can be given as a divided dose on separate days. If hemoglobin is <10 g/dL: Dose should be reduced to 25-40 mcg/kg.

Subsequent dosing: 25-60 mcg/kg can be used if required to elevate platelet count

Maintenance dosing if patient **did respond** to initial dosing: 25-60 mcg/kg based on platelet and hemoglobin levels:

Maintenance dosing if patient **did not respond** to initial dosing:

Hemoglobin 8-10 g/dL: Redose between 25-40 mcg/kg

Hemoglobin >10 g/dL: Redose between 50-60 mcg/kg

Hemoglobin <8 g/dL: Use with caution

Rh₀(D) suppression: Adults: **Note:** One "full dose" (300 mcg) provides enough antibody to prevent Rh sensitization if the volume of RBC entering the circulation is ≤15 mL. When >15 mL is suspected, a fetal red cell count should be performed to determine the appropriate dose.

Pregnancy:

BayRho-D® Full Dose, RhoGAM®: I.M.: 300 mcg as soon as possible, preferably within 72 hours of delivery

Antenatal prophylaxis: 300 mcg at 28 weeks; following delivery: 300 mcg as soon as possible, preferably within 72 hours

WinRho SDF®: I.M./I.V.: 300 mcg at 28 weeks; if given early in the pregnancy, administer every 12 weeks to ensure adequate levels of passively acquired anti-Rh.

Following delivery: 120 mcg as soon as possible after delivery, preferably within 72 hours; can be given up to 28 days following delivery

Threatened abortion, any time during pregnancy (with continuation of pregnancy):

BayRho-D® Full Dose, RhoGAM®: I.M.: 300 mcg; administer as soon as possible

WinRho SDF®: I.M./I.V.: 300 mcg; administer as soon as possible

Abortion, miscarriage, termination of ectopic pregnancy:

BayRho-D®, RhoGAM®: I.M.: ≥13 weeks gestation: 300 mcg.

BayRho-D Mini Dose®, MICRhoGAM®: <13 weeks gestation: I.M.: 50 mcg

WinRho SDF®: I.M./I.V.: After 34 weeks gestation: 120 mcg; administer immediately or within 72 hours

Amniocentesis, chorionic villus sampling:

BayRho-D®, RhoGAM®: I.M.: At 15-18 weeks gestation or during the 3rd trimester: 300 mcg. If dose is given between 13-18 weeks, repeat at 26-28 weeks and within 72 hours of delivery.

WinRho SDF®: I.M./I.V.: Before 34 weeks gestation: 300 mcg; administer immediately, repeat dose every 12 weeks during pregnancy; After 34 weeks gestation: 120 mcg, administered immediately or within 72 hours

Abdominal trauma, manipulation:

BayRho-D®, RhoGAM®: I.M.: 2nd or 3rd trimester: 300 mcg. If dose is given between 13-18 weeks, repeat at 26-28 weeks and within 72 hours of delivery

WinRho SDF®: I.M./I.V.: After 34 weeks gestation: 120 mcg; administer immediately or within 72 hours

Transfusion:

Children and Adults: WinRho SDF®: Administer within 72 hours after exposure of incompatible blood transfusions or massive fetal hemorrhage.

I.V.: Calculate dose as follows; administer 600 mcg every 8 hours until the total dose is administered:

Exposure to Rh₀(D) positive whole blood: 9 mcg/mL blood

Exposure to Rh₀(D) positive red blood cells: 18 mcg/mL cells

I.M.: Calculate dose as follows; administer 1200 mcg every 12 hours until the total dose is administered:

Exposure to Rh₀(D) positive whole blood: 12 mcg/mL blood

Exposure to Rh₀(D) positive red blood cells: 24 mcg/mL cells

Adults: BayRho-D®, RhoGAM®: I.M.: Multiply the volume of Rh positive whole blood administered by the hematocrit of the donor unit to equal the volume of RBCs transfused. The volume of RBCs is then divided by 15 mL, providing the number of 300 mcg doses (vials/syringes) to administer. If the dose calculated results in a fraction, round up to the next higher whole 300 mcg dose (vial/syringe).

Administration The total volume can be administered in divided doses at different sites at one time or may be divided and given at intervals, provided the total dosage is given within 72 hours of the fetomaternal hemorrhage or transfusion.

I.M.: Administer into the deltoid muscle of the upper arm or anterolateral aspect of the upper thigh; avoid gluteal region due to risk of sciatic nerve injury

I.V.: WinRho SDF®: Infuse over 3-5 minutes; do not administer with other medications

Monitoring Parameters Signs and symptoms of intravascular hemolysis (IVH), anemia, and renal insufficiency

Patient Information This medication is only given by injection. It may be given as a one-time dose, or may need repeated. You may experience pain at the injection site. Notify prescriber if you experience chills, headache, dizziness, fever or rash.

Dosage Forms INJ, solution [preservative free] (BayRho-D® Full-Dose, RhoGam®): 300 mcg [for I.M. use only]; (BayRho-D® Mini-Dose, MICRhoGAM®): 50 mcg [for I.M. use only]. **INJ, powder for reconstitution** [preservative free] (WinRho SDF®): 120 mcg [600 int. units], 300 mcg [1500 int. units], 1000 mcg [5000 int. units] [for I.M. or I.V. use]

- ◆ **Rho(D) Immune Globulin (Human)** *see Rho(D) Immune Globulin on page 1089*
- ◆ **RhoGAM®** *see Rho(D) Immune Globulin on page 1089*
- ◆ **RhoIGIV** *see Rho(D) Immune Globulin on page 1089*
- ◆ **RhoIVIM** *see Rho(D) Immune Globulin on page 1089*
- ◆ **rhPTH(1-34)** *see Teriparatide on page 1200*
- ◆ **rHuEPO-α** *see Epoetin Alfa on page 442*
- ◆ **rhuMAb-E25** *see Omalizumab on page 926*

Ribavirin (rye ba VYE rin)

U.S. Brand Names Copegus™; Rebetol®; Virazole®

Synonyms RTCA; Tribavirin

Therapeutic Category Antiviral Agent; Antiviral Agent, Hepatitis; Antiviral Agent, Inhalation Therapy

Use

Inhalation: Treatment of patients with respiratory syncytial virus (RSV) infections; specially indicated for treatment of severe lower respiratory tract RSV infections in patients with an underlying compromising condition (prematurity, bronchopulmonary dysplasia and other chronic lung conditions, congenital heart disease, immunodeficiency, immunosuppression), and recent transplant recipients

Oral capsule:

In combination with interferon alfa-2b (Intron® A) injection for the treatment of chronic hepatitis C in patients with compensated liver disease who have relapsed after alpha interferon therapy or were previously untreated with alpha interferons

In combination with peginterferon alfa-2b (PEG-Intron®) injection for the treatment of chronic hepatitis C in patients with compensated liver disease who were previously untreated with alpha interferons

Oral solution: In combination with interferon alfa 2b (Intron® A) injection for the treatment of chronic hepatitis C in patients ≥3 years of age with compensated liver disease who were previously untreated with alpha interferons or patients ≥18 years of age who have relapsed after alpha interferon therapy

Oral tablet: In combination with peginterferon alfa-2a (Pegasys®) injection for the treatment of chronic hepatitis C in patients with compensated liver disease who were previously untreated with alpha interferons

Unlabeled/Investigational Use Used in other viral infections including influenza A and B and adenovirus

Pregnancy Risk Factor X

Contraindications Hypersensitivity to ribavirin or any component of the formulation; women of childbearing age who will not use contraception reliably; pregnancy

Additional contraindications for oral formulation: Male partners of pregnant women; $Cl_{cr} < 50$ mL/minute; hemoglobinopathies (eg, thalassemia major, sickle cell anemia); as monotherapy for treatment of chronic hepatitis C; patients with autoimmune hepatitis, anemia, severe heart disease

Warnings/Precautions

Inhalation: Use with caution in patients requiring assisted ventilation or who have COPD or asthma. Monitor for anemia 1-2 weeks post-treatment. Pregnant healthcare workers may consider unnecessary occupational exposure. Healthcare professions or family members who are pregnant or may become pregnant should be counseled about potential risks of exposure and counseled about risk reduction strategies.

Oral: Monitor for anemia 1-2 weeks after initiation. Use caution in cardiac, pulmonary, and elderly patients. Severe psychiatric events have occurred during combination therapy; avoid use in patients with a psychiatric history. Use caution in pulmonary disease; pulmonary symptoms have been associated with administration. Use caution in patients with sarcoidosis (exacerbation reported). Negative pregnancy test required before initiation and monthly thereafter. Avoid pregnancy in female patients and female partners of male patients during therapy. Discontinue therapy in suspected/confirmed pancreatitis. Take renal function into consideration before initiating. Safety and efficacy not established in organ transplant patients, decompensated liver disease, concurrent hepatitis B virus or HIV exposure or pediatric patients <3 years of age.

Common Adverse Reactions

Inhalation:

1% to 10%:

Central nervous system: Fatigue, headache, insomnia

Gastrointestinal: Nausea, anorexia

Hematologic: Anemia

(Continued)

Ribavirin *(Continued)*

Note: Incidence of adverse effects (approximate) in healthcare workers: Headache (51%); conjunctivitis (32%); rhinitis, nausea, rash, dizziness, pharyngitis, and lacrimation (10% to 20%)

Oral (all adverse reactions are documented while receiving combination therapy with interferon alpha-2b; percentages as reported in adults):

>10%:
Central nervous system: Dizziness (17% to 26%), headache (63% to 66%)*, fatigue (60% to 70%)*, fever (32% to 41%)*, insomnia (26% to 39%), irritability (23% to 32%), depression (23% to 36%)*, emotional lability (7% to 12%)*, impaired concentration (10% to 14%)*
Dermatologic: Alopecia (27% to 32%), rash (20% to 28%), pruritus (13% to 21%)
Gastrointestinal: Nausea (38% to 47%), anorexia (21% to 27%), dyspepsia (14% to 16%), vomiting (9% to 12%)*
Hematologic: Decreased hemoglobin (25% to 36%), decreased WBC, absolute neutrophil count <0.5 x 10^9/L (5% to 11%), thrombocytopenia (6% to 14%), hyperbilirubinemia (24% to 34%), hemolysis
Neuromuscular & skeletal: Myalgia (61% to 64%)*, arthralgia (29% to 33%)*, musculoskeletal pain (20% to 28%), rigors (40% to 43%)
Respiratory: Dyspnea (17% to 19%), sinusitis (9% to 12%)*, nasal congestion
Miscellaneous: Flu-like syndrome (13% to 18%)*
*Similar to interferon alone

1% to 10%:
Cardiovascular: Chest pain (5% to 9%)*
Central nervous system: Nervousness (~5%)*
Gastrointestinal: Taste perversion (6% to 8%)
Hematologic: Hemolytic anemia (~10%)
Neuromuscular & skeletal: Weakness (9% to 10%)
*Similar to interferon alone

Incidence of anorexia, headache, fever, suicidal ideation, and vomiting are higher in children.

Drug Interactions

Increased Effect/Toxicity: Concomitant use of ribavirin and nucleoside analogues may increase the risk of developing lactic acidosis (includes adefovir, didanosine, lamivudine, stavudine, zalcitabine, zidovudine). Concurrent use with didanosine has been noted to increase the risk of pancreatitis and/or peripheral neuropathy in addition to lactic acidosis. Suspend therapy if signs/symptoms of toxicity are present.

Decreased Effect: Decreased effect of stavudine and zidovudine (*in vitro*).

Mechanism of Action Inhibits replication of RNA and DNA viruses; inhibits influenza virus RNA polymerase activity and inhibits the initiation and elongation of RNA fragments resulting in inhibition of viral protein synthesis

Pharmacodynamics/Kinetics

Absorption: Inhalation: Systemic; dependent upon respiratory factors and method of drug delivery; maximal absorption occurs with the use of aerosol generator via endotracheal tube; highest concentrations in respiratory tract and erythrocytes
Distribution: Oral capsule: Single dose: V_d 2825 L; distribution significantly prolonged in the erythrocyte (16-40 days), which can be used as a marker for intracellular metabolism
Protein binding: Oral: None
Metabolism: Hepatically and intracellularly (forms active metabolites); may be necessary for drug action
Bioavailability: Oral: 64%
Half-life elimination, plasma:
Children: Inhalation: 6.5-11 hours
Adults: Oral capsule, single dose: 24 hours in healthy adults, 44 hours with chronic hepatitis C infection (increases to ~298 hours at steady state)
Time to peak, serum: Inhalation: At end of inhalation period; Oral capsule: Multiple doses: 3 hours
Excretion: Inhalation: Urine (40% as unchanged drug and metabolites); Oral capsule: Urine (61%), feces (12%)

Dosage

Aerosol inhalation: Infants and children: Use with Viratek® small particle aerosol generator (SPAG-2) at a concentration of 20 mg/mL (6 g reconstituted with 300 mL of sterile water without preservatives). Continuous aerosol administration: 12-18 hours/day for 3 days, up to 7 days in length

Oral capsule or solution:
Children ≥3 years: Chronic hepatitis C (in combination with interferon alfa-2b):
25-36 kg: 400 mg/day (200 mg twice daily)
37-49 kg: 600 mg/day (200 mg in morning and 400 mg in evening)
50-61 kg: 800 mg/day (400 mg twice daily)
>61 kg: Refer to adult dosing
Note: Duration of therapy is 48 weeks in pediatric patients with genotype 1 and 24 weeks in patients with genotype 2,3. Discontinue treatment in any patient if HCV-RNA is not below the limit of detection of the assay after 24 weeks of therapy.
Note: Also refer to Interferon Alfa-2b/Ribavirin combination pack monograph.

Oral capsule:
Adults:
Chronic hepatitis C (in combination with interferon alfa-2b):
≤75 kg: 400 mg in the morning, then 600 mg in the evening

>75 kg: 600 mg in the morning, then 600 mg in the evening

Note: If HCV-RNA is undetectable at 24 weeks, duration of therapy is 48 weeks. In patients who relapse following interferon therapy, duration of dual therapy is 24 weeks.

Note: Also refer to Interferon Alfa-2b/Ribavirin combination pack monograph.

Chronic hepatitis C (in combination with peginterferon alfa-2b): 400 mg twice daily; duration of therapy is 1 year; after 24 weeks of treatment, if serum HCV-RNA is not below the limit of detection of the assay, consider discontinuation.

Oral tablet: Adults:

Chronic hepatitis C, genotype 1,4 (in combination with peginterferon alfa-2a):

<75kg: 1000 mg/day in 2 divided doses for 48 weeks

≥75kg: 1200 mg/day in 2 divided doses for 48 weeks

Chronic hepatitis C, genotype 2,3 (in combination with peginterferon alfa-2a): 800 mg/day in 2 divided doses for 24 weeks

Note: Also refer to Peginterferon Alfa-2a monograph.

Dosage adjustment in renal impairment: Cl$_{cr}$ <50 mL/minute: Oral route is contraindicated

Dosage adjustment for toxicity: Oral: Capsule, solution, tablet:

Patient **without** cardiac history:

Hemoglobin <10 g/dL:

Children: 7.5 mg/kg/day

Adults: Decrease dose to 600 mg/day

Hemoglobin <8.5 g/dL: Children and Adults: Permanently discontinue treatment

Patient **with** cardiac history:

Hemoglobin has ≥2 g/dL decrease during any 4-week period of treatment:

Children: 7.5 mg/kg/day

Adults: Decrease dose to 600 mg/day

Hemoglobin <12 g/dL after 4 weeks of reduced dose: Children and Adults: Permanently discontinue treatment

Administration

Inhalation: Ribavirin should be administered in well-ventilated rooms (at least 6 air changes/hour). In mechanically-ventilated patients, ribavirin can potentially be deposited in the ventilator delivery system depending on temperature, humidity, and electrostatic forces; this deposition can lead to malfunction or obstruction of the expiratory valve, resulting in inadvertently high positive end-expiratory pressures. The use of one-way valves in the inspiratory lines, a breathing circuit filter in the expiratory line, and frequent monitoring and filter replacement have been effective in preventing these problems. Solutions in SPAG-2 unit should be discarded at least every 24 hours and when the liquid level is low before adding newly reconstituted solution. Should not be mixed with other aerosolized medication.

Oral: Administer concurrently with interferon alfa injection.

Capsule, in combination with interferon alfa-2b: May be administered with or without food, but always in a consistent manner in regard to food intake.

Capsule, in combination with peginterferon alfa 2b: Administer with food.

Solution, in combination with interferon alfa-2b: May be administered with or without food, but always in a consistent manner in regard to food intake.

Tablet: Should be administered with food.

Monitoring Parameters

Inhalation: Respiratory function, hemoglobin, reticulocyte count, CBC, I & O

Oral: CBC with differential (pretreatment, 2- and 4 weeks after initiation); pretreatment and monthly pregnancy test for women of childbearing age; LFTs, TSH, HCV-RNA after 24 weeks of therapy; ECG in patients with pre-existing cardiac disease

Patient Information Do not use if you are pregnant.

Dosage Forms CAP (Rebetol®): 200 mg. **POWDER for aerosol** (Virazole®): 6 g. **SOLN, oral** (Rebetol®): 40 mg/mL (100 mL). **TAB** (Copegus™): 200 mg

♦ **Ribavirin and Interferon Alfa-2b Combination Pack** *see* Interferon Alfa-2b and Ribavirin *on page 676*

Riboflavin (RYE boe flay vin)

Synonyms Lactoflavin; Vitamin B$_2$; Vitamin G

Therapeutic Category Vitamin, Water Soluble

Use Prevention of riboflavin deficiency and treatment of ariboflavinosis

Pregnancy Risk Factor A/C (dose exceeding RDA recommendation)

Warnings/Precautions Riboflavin deficiency often occurs in the presence of other B vitamin deficiencies

Common Adverse Reactions Frequency not defined: Genitourinary: Discoloration of urine (yellow-orange)

Drug Interactions

Decreased Effect: Decreased absorption with probenecid.

Mechanism of Action Component of flavoprotein enzymes that work together, which are necessary for normal tissue respiration; also needed for activation of pyridoxine and conversion of tryptophan to niacin

Pharmacodynamics/Kinetics

Absorption: Readily via GI tract, however, food increases extent; decreased with hepatitis, cirrhosis, or biliary obstruction

Metabolism: None

Half-life elimination: Biologic: 66-84 minutes

Excretion: Urine (9%) as unchanged drug

(Continued)

Riboflavin *(Continued)*

Dosage Oral:
Riboflavin deficiency:
  Children: 2.5-10 mg/day in divided doses
  Adults: 5-30 mg/day in divided doses
Recommended daily allowance:
  Children: 0.4-1.8 mg
  Adults: 1.2-1.7 mg

Patient Information Take with food; large doses may cause bright yellow or orange urine
Dosage Forms CAP: 100 mg. **TAB:** 25 mg, 50 mg, 100 mg

♦ **Ridaura®** *see Auranofin on page 136*
♦ **RID® Maximum Strength [OTC]** *see Pyrethrins and Piperonyl Butoxide on page 1065*
♦ **Rid® Spray [OTC]** *see Permethrin on page 984*

Rifabutin *(rif a BYOO tin)*

Related Information
Antimicrobial Drugs of Choice *on page 1440*
Tuberculosis Treatment Guidelines *on page 1466*
U.S. Brand Names Mycobutin®
Synonyms Ansamycin
Therapeutic Category Antibiotic, Miscellaneous; Antitubercular Agent
Use Prevention of disseminated *Mycobacterium avium* complex (MAC) in patients with advanced HIV infection
Unlabeled/Investigational Use Utilized in multidrug regimens for treatment of MAC
Pregnancy Risk Factor B
Contraindications Hypersensitivity to rifabutin, any other rifamycins, or any component of the formulation; rifabutin is contraindicated in patients with a WBC <1000/mm³ or a platelet count <50,000/mm³
Warnings/Precautions Rifabutin as a single agent must not be administered to patients with active tuberculosis since its use may lead to the development of tuberculosis that is resistant to both rifabutin and rifampin; rifabutin should be discontinued in patients with AST >500 units/L or if total bilirubin is >3 mg/dL. Use with caution in patients with liver impairment; modification of dosage should be considered in patients with renal impairment.
Common Adverse Reactions
>10%:
  Dermatologic: Rash (11%)
  Genitourinary: Discoloration of urine (30%)
  Hematologic: Neutropenia (25%), leukopenia (17%)
1% to 10%:
  Central nervous system: Headache (3%)
  Gastrointestinal: Vomiting/nausea (3%), abdominal pain (4%), diarrhea (3%), anorexia (2%), flatulence (2%), eructation (3%)
  Hematologic: Anemia, thrombocytopenia (5%)
  Hepatic: Increased AST/ALT (7% to 9%)
  Neuromuscular & skeletal: Myalgia
Drug Interactions
Cytochrome P450 Effect: Substrate (major) of CYP1A2, 3A4; **Induces** CYP3A4 (strong)
Increased Effect/Toxicity: Concentrations of rifabutin are increased by indinavir (reduce rifabutin to 50% of standard dose) and ritonavir (reduce rifabutin dose to 150 mg every other day). Fluconazole increases rifabutin concentrations.
Decreased Effect: CYP1A2 inducers may decrease the levels/effects of rifabutin; example inducers include aminoglutethimide, carbamazepine, phenobarbital, and rifampin. Rifabutin may decreased plasma concentrations (due to induction of liver enzymes) of verapamil, methadone, digoxin, cyclosporine, corticosteroids, oral anticoagulants, theophylline, barbiturates, chloramphenicol, itraconazole, ketoconazole, oral contraceptives, quinidine, protease inhibitors (indinavir, nelfinavir, ritonavir, saquinavir), non-nucleoside reverse transcriptase inhibitors, halothane, and clarithromycin.
Mechanism of Action Inhibits DNA-dependent RNA polymerase at the beta subunit which prevents chain initiation
Pharmacodynamics/Kinetics
Absorption: Readily, 53%
Distribution: V_d: 9.32 L/kg; distributes to body tissues including the lungs, liver, spleen, eyes, and kidneys
Protein binding: 85%
Metabolism: To active and inactive metabolites
Bioavailability: Absolute: HIV: 20%
Half-life elimination: Terminal: 45 hours (range: 16-69 hours)
Time to peak, serum: 2-4 hours
Excretion: Urine (10% as unchanged drug, 53% as metabolites); feces (10% as unchanged drug, 30% as metabolites)
Dosage Oral:
Children >1 year:
  Prophylaxis: 5 mg/kg daily; higher dosages have been used in limited trials
  Treatment (unlabeled use): Patients not receiving NNRTIs or protease inhibitors:
    Initial phase (2 weeks to 2 months): 10-20 mg/kg daily (maximum: 300 mg).

Second phase: 10-20 mg/kg daily (maximum: 300 mg) or twice weekly
Adults:
  Prophylaxis: 300 mg once daily (alone or in combination with azithromycin)
  Treatment (unlabeled use):
    Patients not receiving NNRTIs or protease inhibitors:
      Initial phase: 5 mg/kg daily (maximum: 300 mg)
      Second phase: 5 mg/kg daily or twice weekly
      Patients receiving nelfinavir, amprenavir, indinavir: Reduce dose to 150 mg/day; no change in dose if administered twice weekly

Dosage adjustment in renal impairment: Cl_{cr} <30 mL/minute: Reduce dose by 50%

Monitoring Parameters Periodic liver function tests, CBC with differential, platelet count

Patient Information May discolor urine, tears, sweat, or other body fluids to a red-orange color; take 1 hour before or 2 hours after a meal on an empty stomach; soft contact lenses may be permanently stained; report any severe or persistent flu-like symptoms, nausea, vomiting, dark urine or pale stools, unusual bleeding or bruising, or any eye problems; can be taken with meals or sprinkled on applesauce

Dosage Forms CAP: 150 mg

♦ **Rifadin**® *see Rifampin on page 1095*

♦ **Rifampicin** *see Rifampin on page 1095*

Rifampin (RIF am pin)

Related Information
  Antimicrobial Drugs of Choice *on page 1440*
  Tuberculosis Prophylaxis *on page 1438*
  Tuberculosis Treatment Guidelines *on page 1466*

U.S. Brand Names Rifadin®; Rimactane®

Synonyms Rifampicin

Therapeutic Category Antibiotic, Miscellaneous; Antitubercular Agent

Use Management of active tuberculosis in combination with other agents; eliminate meningococci from asymptomatic carriers

Unlabeled/Investigational Use Prophylaxis of *Haemophilus influenzae* type b infection; *Legionella* pneumonia; used in combination with other anti-infectives in the treatment of staphylococcal infections

Pregnancy Risk Factor C

Contraindications Hypersensitivity to rifampin, any rifamycins, or any component of the formulation; concurrent use of amprenavir (possibly other protease inhibitors)

Warnings/Precautions Use with caution and modify dosage in patients with liver impairment; observe for hyperbilirubinemia; discontinue therapy if this in conjunction with clinical symptoms or any signs of significant hepatocellular damage develop; since rifampin has enzyme-inducing properties, porphyria exacerbation is possible; use with caution in patients with porphyria; do not use for meningococcal disease, only for short-term treatment of asymptomatic carrier states

Monitor for compliance and effects including hypersensitivity, thrombocytopenia in patients on intermittent therapy; urine, feces, saliva, sweat, tears, and CSF may be discolored to red/orange; do not administer I.V. form via I.M. or S.C. routes; restart infusion at another site if extravasation occurs; remove soft contact lenses during therapy since permanent staining may occur; regimens of 600 mg once or twice weekly have been associated with a high incidence of adverse reactions including a flu-like syndrome

Common Adverse Reactions
Frequency not defined:
  Cardiovascular: Flushing, edema
  Central nervous system: Headache, drowsiness, dizziness, confusion, numbness, behavioral changes, ataxia
  Dermatologic: Pruritus, urticaria, pemphigoid reaction
  Hematologic: Eosinophilia, leukopenia, hemolysis, hemolytic anemia, thrombocytopenia (especially with high-dose therapy)
  Hepatic: Hepatitis (rare)
  Neuromuscular & skeletal: Myalgia, weakness, osteomalacia
  Ocular: Visual changes, exudative conjunctivitis
1% to 10%:
  Dermatologic: Rash (1% to 5%)
  Gastrointestinal (1% to 2%): Epigastric distress, anorexia, nausea, vomiting, diarrhea, cramps, pseudomembranous colitis, pancreatitis
  Hepatic: Increased LFTs (up to 14%)

Drug Interactions

Cytochrome P450 Effect: Substrate (major) of CYP2A6, 2C8/9, 3A4; **Induces** CYP1A2 (strong), 2A6 (strong), 2B6 (strong), 2C8/9 (strong), 2C19 (strong), 3A4 (strong)

Increased Effect/Toxicity: Rifampin levels may be increased when given with co-trimoxazole, probenecid, or ritonavir. Rifampin given with halothane or isoniazid increases the potential for hepatotoxicity. Combination therapy with rifampin and pyrazinamide has been associated with severe and fatal hepatotoxic reactions.

Decreased Effect: Rifampin induces liver enzymes which may decrease the plasma concentration of calcium channel blockers (verapamil, diltiazem, nifedipine), methadone, digoxin, cyclosporine, corticosteroids, haloperidol, oral anticoagulants, theophylline, barbiturates, chloramphenicol, imidazole antifungals (ketoconazole), oral contraceptives, acetaminophen, benzodiazepines, hydantoins, sulfa drugs, enalapril, beta-blockers, clofibrate, (Continued)

Rifampin *(Continued)*

dapsone, antiarrhythmics (disopyramide, mexiletine, quinidine, tocainide), doxycycline, fluoroquinolones, levothyroxine, nortriptyline, tacrolimus, zidovudine, protease inhibitors (ie, amprenavir, atazanavir), and non-nucleoside reverse transcriptase inhibitors. CYP2A6 inducers may decrease the levels/effects of rifampin; example inducers include amobarbital, pentobarbital, phenobarbital, and secobarbital. CYP2C8/9 inducers may decrease the levels/effects of rifampin; example inducers include carbamazepine, phenobarbital, phenytoin, rifapentine, and secobarbital.

Mechanism of Action Inhibits bacterial RNA synthesis by binding to the beta subunit of DNA-dependent RNA polymerase, blocking RNA transcription

Pharmacodynamics/Kinetics

Duration: ≤24 hours

Absorption: Oral: Well absorbed; food may delay or slightly reduce peak

Distribution: Highly lipophilic; crosses blood-brain barrier well

Relative diffusion from blood into CSF: Adequate with or without inflammation (exceeds usual MICs)

CSF:blood level ratio: Inflamed meninges: 25%

Protein binding: 80%

Metabolism: Hepatic; undergoes enterohepatic recirculation

Half-life elimination: 3-4 hours; prolonged with hepatic impairment; End-stage renal disease: 1.8-11 hours

Time to peak, serum: Oral: 2-4 hours

Excretion: Feces (60% to 65%) and urine (~30%) as unchanged drug

Dosage Oral (I.V. infusion dose is the same as for the oral route):

Tuberculosis therapy: Note: A four-drug regimen (isoniazid, rifampin, pyrazinamide, and either streptomycin or ethambutol) is preferred for the initial, empiric treatment of TB. When the drug susceptibility results are available, the regimen should be altered as appropriate.

Infants and Children <12 years:

Daily therapy: 10-20 mg/kg/day usually as a single dose (maximum: 600 mg/day)

Directly observed therapy (DOT): Twice weekly: 10-20 mg/kg (maximum: 600 mg); 3 times/week: 10-20 mg/kg (maximum: 600 mg)

Adults:

Daily therapy: 10 mg/kg/day (maximum: 600 mg/day)

Directly observed therapy (DOT): Twice weekly: 10 mg/kg (maximum: 600 mg); 3 times/week: 10 mg/kg (maximum: 600 mg)

Latent tuberculosis infection (LTBI): As an alternative to isoniazid:

Children: 10-20 mg/kg/day (maximum: 600 mg/day)

Adults: 10 mg/kg/day (maximum: 600 mg/day) for 2 months. **Note:** Combination with pyrazinamide should not generally be offered (*MMWR*, Aug 8, 2003).

H. influenzae **prophylaxis** (unlabeled use):

Infants and Children: 20 mg/kg/day every 24 hours for 4 days, not to exceed 600 mg/dose

Adults: 600 mg every 24 hours for 4 days

Leprosy: Adults:

Multibacillary: 600 mg once monthly for 24 months in combination with ofloxacin and minocycline

Paucibacillary: 600 mg once monthly for 6 months in combination with dapsone

Single lesion: 600 mg as a single dose in combination with ofloxacin 400 mg and minocycline 100 mg

Meningococcal meningitis prophylaxis:

Infants <1 month: 10 mg/kg/day in divided doses every 12 hours for 2 days

Infants ≥1 month and Children: 20 mg/kg/day in divided doses every 12 hours for 2 days

Adults: 600 mg every 12 hours for 2 days

Nasal carriers of *Staphylococcus aureus* (unlabeled use):

Children: 15 mg/kg/day divided every 12 hours for 5-10 days in combination with other antibiotics

Adults: 600 mg/day for 5-10 days in combination with other antibiotics

Synergy for *Staphylococcus aureus* infections (unlabeled use): Adults: 300-600 mg twice daily with other antibiotics

Dosing adjustment in hepatic impairment: Dose reductions may be necessary to reduce hepatotoxicity

Hemodialysis or peritoneal dialysis: Plasma rifampin concentrations are not significantly affected by hemodialysis or peritoneal dialysis.

Administration Administer on an empty stomach (ie, 1 hour prior to, or 2 hours after meals or antacids) to increase total absorption

Monitoring Parameters Periodic (baseline and every 2-4 weeks during therapy) monitoring of liver function (AST, ALT, bilirubin), CBC; hepatic status and mental status, sputum culture, chest x-ray 2-3 months into treatment

Patient Information May discolor urine, tears, sweat, or other body fluids to a red-orange color; take 1 hour before or 2 hours after a meal on an empty stomach; soft contact lenses may be permanently stained; report any severe or persistent flu-like symptoms, nausea, vomiting, dark urine or pale stools, or unusual bleeding or bruising; utilize an alternate form from oral/other systemic contraceptives during therapy; compliance and completion with course of therapy is very important; if you are a diabetic taking oral medications or if you regularly take oral anticoagulant therapy, your medication may need special and careful adjustment.

Dosage Forms CAP: 150 mg, 300 mg; (Rifadin®): 150 mg, 300 mg; (Rimactane®): 300 mg. **INJ, powder for reconstitution** (Rifadin®): 600 mg

Rifapentine (RIF a pen teen)

U.S. Brand Names Priftin®

Therapeutic Category Antitubercular Agent

Use Treatment of pulmonary tuberculosis; rifapentine must always be used in conjunction with at least one other antituberculosis drug to which the isolate is susceptible; it may also be necessary to add a third agent (either streptomycin or ethambutol) until susceptibility is known.

Pregnancy Risk Factor C

Contraindications Hypersensitivity to rifapentine, rifampin, rifabutin, any rifamycin analog, or any component of the formulation

Warnings/Precautions Patients with abnormal liver tests and/or liver disease should only be given rifapentine when absolutely necessary and under strict medical supervision. If signs of liver disease occur or worsen, rifapentine should be discontinued. Experience in treating TB in HIV-infected patients is limited.

Rifapentine may produce a red-orange discoloration of body tissues/fluids including skin, teeth, tongue, urine, feces, saliva, sputum, tears, sweat, and cerebral spinal fluid. Contact lenses may become permanently stained. All patients treated with rifapentine should have baseline measurements of liver function tests and enzymes, bilirubin, and a complete blood count. Patients should be seen and monitored monthly and specifically questioned regarding symptoms associated with adverse reactions. Routine laboratory monitoring in people with normal baseline measurements is generally not necessary.

Common Adverse Reactions

>10%: Endocrine & metabolic: Hyperuricemia (most likely due to pyrazinamide from initiation phase combination therapy)

1% to 10%:

Cardiovascular: Hypertension

Central nervous system: Headache, dizziness

Dermatologic: Rash, pruritus, acne

Gastrointestinal: Anorexia, nausea, vomiting, dyspepsia, diarrhea

Hematologic: Neutropenia, lymphopenia, anemia, leukopenia, thrombocytosis

Hepatic: Increased ALT/AST

Neuromuscular & skeletal: Arthralgia, pain

Renal: Pyuria, proteinuria, hematuria, urinary casts

Respiratory: Hemoptysis

Drug Interactions

Cytochrome P450 Effect: Induces CYP2C8/9 (strong), 3A4 (strong)

Increased Effect/Toxicity: Rifapentine metabolism is mediated by esterase activity, therefore, there is minimal potential for rifapentine metabolism to be affected by other drug therapy.

Decreased Effect: Rifapentine may increase the metabolism of coadministered drugs that are metabolized by these enzymes. Enzymes are induced within 4 days after the first dose and returned to baseline 14 days after discontinuation of rifapentine. The magnitude of enzyme induction is dose and frequency dependent.

Rifampin has been shown to accelerate the metabolism and may reduce activity of the following drugs (therefore, rifapentine may also do the same): Phenytoin, disopyramide, mexiletine, quinidine, tocainide, chloramphenicol, clarithromycin, dapsone, doxycycline, fluoroquinolones, warfarin, fluconazole, itraconazole, ketoconazole, barbiturates, benzodiazepines, beta-blockers, diltiazem, nifedipine, verapamil, corticosteroids, cardiac glycoside preparations, clofibrate, oral or other systemic hormonal contraceptives, haloperidol, HIV protease inhibitors, sulfonylureas, cyclosporine, tacrolimus, levothyroxine, methadone, progestins, quinine, delavirdine, zidovudine, sildenafil, tadalafil, theophylline, vardenafil, amitriptyline, and nortriptyline.

Rifapentine should be used with extreme caution, if at all, in patients who are also taking protease inhibitors.

Patients using oral or other systemic hormonal contraceptives should be advised to change to nonhormonal methods of birth control when receiving concomitant rifapentine.

Mechanism of Action Inhibits DNA-dependent RNA polymerase in susceptible strains of *Mycobacterium tuberculosis* (but not in mammalian cells). Rifapentine is bactericidal against both intracellular and extracellular MTB organisms. MTB resistant to other rifamycins including rifampin are likely to be resistant to rifapentine. Cross-resistance does not appear between rifapentine and other nonrifamycin antimycobacterial agents.

Pharmacodynamics/Kinetics

Absorption: Food increases AUC and C_{max} by 43% and 44% respectively.

Distribution: V_d: ~70.2 L; rifapentine and metabolite accumulate in human monocyte-derived macrophages with intracellular/extracellular ratios of 24:1 and 7:1 respectively

Protein binding: Rifapentine and 25-desacetyl metabolite: 97.7% and 93.2%, primarily to albumin

Metabolism: Hepatic; hydrolyzed by an esterase and esterase enzyme to form the active metabolite 25-desacetyl rifapentine

Bioavailability: ~70%

Half-life elimination: Rifapentine: 14-17 hours; 25-desacetyl rifapentine: 13 hours

Time to peak, serum: 5-6 hours

Excretion: Urine (17% primarily as metabolites)

Dosage

Children: No dosing information available

(Continued)

Rifapentine *(Continued)*

Adults: **Rifapentine should not be used alone**; initial phase should include a 3- to 4-drug regimen

Intensive phase of short-term therapy: 600 mg (four 150 mg tablets) given weekly (every 72 hours); following the intensive phase, treatment should continue with rifapentine 600 mg once weekly for 4 months in combination with INH or appropriate agent for susceptible organisms

Dosing adjustment in renal or hepatic impairment: Unknown

Monitoring Parameters Patients with pre-existing hepatic problems should have liver function tests monitored every 2-4 weeks during therapy

Patient Information May produce a reddish coloration of urine, sweat, sputum, tears, and contact lenses may be permanently stained. Oral or other systemic hormonal contraceptives may not be effective while taking rifapentine; alternative contraceptive measures should be used. Administration of rifapentine with food may decrease GI intolerance. Report fever, decreased appetite, malaise, nausea/vomiting, darkened urine, yellowish discoloration of skin or eyes, chest pain, palpitations, and pain or swelling of the joints. Adherence with the full course of therapy is essential; no doses of therapy should be missed.

Dosage Forms TAB, film coated: 150 mg

+ **rIFN-A** *see* Interferon Alfa-2a *on page 672*

+ **rIFN beta-1a** *see* Interferon Beta-1a *on page 680*

+ **rIFN beta-1b** *see* Interferon Beta-1b *on page 681*

+ **RIG** *see* Rabies Immune Globulin (Human) *on page 1077*

+ **rIL-11** *see* Oprelvekin *on page 931*

+ **Rilutek®** *see* Riluzole *on page 1098*

Riluzole *(RIL yoo zole)*

U.S. Brand Names Rilutek®

Synonyms 2-Amino-6-Trifluoromethoxy-benzothiazole; RP-54274

Therapeutic Category Amyotrophic Lateral Sclerosis (ALS) Agent; Glutamate Inhibitor

Use Orphan drug: Treatment of amyotrophic lateral sclerosis (ALS); riluzole can extend survival or time to tracheostomy

Pregnancy Risk Factor C

Contraindications Severe hypersensitivity reactions to riluzole or any component of the formulation

Warnings/Precautions Among 4000 patients given riluzole for ALS, there were 3 cases of marked neutropenia (ANC <500/mm^3), all seen within the first 2 months of treatment. Use with caution in patients with concomitant renal insufficiency. Use with caution in patients with current evidence or history of abnormal liver function. Monitor liver chemistries.

Common Adverse Reactions

>10%:

Gastrointestinal: Nausea (10% to 21%)

Neuromuscular & skeletal: Weakness (15% to 20%)

Respiratory: Decreased lung function (10% to 16%)

1% to 10%:

Cardiovascular: Hypertension, tachycardia, postural hypotension, edema

Central nervous system: headache, dizziness, somnolence, insomnia, malaise, depression, vertigo, agitation, tremor, circumoral paresthesia

Dermatologic: Pruritus, eczema, alopecia

Gastrointestinal: Abdominal pain, diarrhea, anorexia, dyspepsia, vomiting, stomatitis

Neuromuscular & skeletal: Arthralgia, back pain

Respiratory: Rhinitis, increased cough

Miscellaneous: Aggravation reaction

Drug Interactions

Cytochrome P450 Effect: Substrate of CYP1A2 (major)

Increased Effect/Toxicity: CYP1A2 inhibitors may increase the levels/effects of riluzole; example inhibitors include amiodarone, ciprofloxacin, fluvoxamine, ketoconazole, lomeflox-acin, ofloxacin, and rofecoxib.

Decreased Effect: CYP1A2 inducers may decrease the levels/effects of riluzole; example inducers include aminoglutethimide, carbamazepine, phenobarbital, and rifampin.

Mechanism of Action Inhibitory effect on glutamate release, inactivation of voltage-dependent sodium channels; and ability to interfere with intracellular events that follow transmitter binding at excitatory amino acid receptors

Pharmacodynamics/Kinetics

Absorption: 90%; high fat meal decreases AUC by 20%, peak blood levels by 45%

Protein binding, plasma: 96%, primarily to albumin and lipoproteins

Metabolism: Extensively hepatic to six major and a number of minor metabolites via CYP1A2 dependent hydroxylation and glucuronidation

Bioavailability: Oral: Absolute: 50%

Half-life elimination: 12 hours

Excretion: Urine (90%; 85% as metabolites, 2% as unchanged drug) and feces (5%) within 7 days

Dosage Adults: Oral: 50 mg every 12 hours; no increased benefit can be expected from higher daily doses, but adverse events are increased

Dosage adjustment in smoking: Cigarette smoking is known to induce CYP1A2; patients who smoke cigarettes would be expected to eliminate riluzole faster. There is no information, however, on the effect of, or need for, dosage adjustment in these patients.

Dosage adjustment in special populations: Females and Japanese patients may possess a lower metabolic capacity to eliminate riluzole compared with male and Caucasian subjects, respectively

Dosage adjustment in renal impairment: Use with caution in patients with concomitant renal insufficiency

Dosage adjustment in hepatic impairment: Use with caution in patients with current evidence or history of abnormal liver function indicated by significant abnormalities in serum transaminase, bilirubin or GGT levels. Baseline elevations of several LFTs (especially elevated bilirubin) should preclude use of riluzole.

Monitoring Parameters Monitor serum aminotransferases including ALT levels before and during therapy. Evaluate serum ALT levels every month during the first 3 months of therapy, every 3 months during the remainder of the first year and periodically thereafter. Evaluate ALT levels more frequently in patients who develop elevations. Maximum increases in serum ALT usually occurred within 3 months after the start of therapy and were usually transient when <5 times ULN (upper limits of normal).

In trials, if ALT levels were <5 times ULN, treatment continued and ALT levels usually returned to below 2 times ULN within 2-6 months. Treatment in studies was discontinued, however, if ALT levels exceed 5 times ULN, so that there is no experience with continued treatment of ALS patients once ALT values exceed 5 times ULN.

If a decision is made to continue treatment in patients when the ALT exceeds 5 times ULN, frequent monitoring (at least weekly) of complete liver function is recommended. Discontinue treatment if ALT exceeds 10 times ULN or if clinical jaundice develops.

Patient Information Take at least 1 hour before or 2 hours after a meal to avoid decreased bioavailability. Report any febrile illness to your prescriber. Take riluzole at the same time of the day each day. If a dose is missed, take the next tablet as originally planned.

Dosage Forms TAB: 50 mg

♦ **Rimactane**® *see Rifampin on page 1095*

Rimantadine (ri MAN ta deen)

U.S. Brand Names Flumadine®

Synonyms Rimantadine Hydrochloride

Therapeutic Category Antiviral Agent; Antiviral Agent, Influenza

Use Prophylaxis (adults and children >1 year of age) and treatment (adults) of influenza A viral infection

Pregnancy Risk Factor C

Contraindications Hypersensitivity to drugs of the adamantine class, including rimantadine and amantadine, or any component of the formulation

Warnings/Precautions Use with caution in patients with renal and hepatic dysfunction; avoid use, if possible, in patients with recurrent and eczematoid dermatitis, uncontrolled psychosis, or severe psychoneurosis. An increase in seizure incidence may occur in patients with seizure disorders; discontinue drug if seizures occur; consider the development of resistance during rimantadine treatment of the index case as likely if failure of rimantadine prophylaxis among family contact occurs and if index case is a child; viruses exhibit cross-resistance between amantadine and rimantadine.

Common Adverse Reactions 1% to 10%:

Cardiovascular: Orthostatic hypotension, edema

Central nervous system: Dizziness (2%), confusion, headache (1%), insomnia (2%), difficulty in concentrating, anxiety (1%), restlessness, irritability, hallucinations; incidence of CNS side effects may be less than that associated with amantadine

Gastrointestinal: Nausea (3%), vomiting (2%), xerostomia (2%), abdominal pain (1%), anorexia (2%)

Genitourinary: Urinary retention

Drug Interactions

Increased Effect/Toxicity: Cimetidine increases blood levels/toxicity of rimantadine.

Decreased Effect: Acetaminophen may cause a small reduction in AUC and peak concentration of rimantadine. Peak plasma and AUC concentrations of rimantadine are slightly reduced by aspirin.

Mechanism of Action Exerts its inhibitory effect on three antigenic subtypes of influenza A virus (H1N1, H2N2, H3N2) early in the viral replicative cycle, possibly inhibiting the uncoating process; it has no activity against influenza B virus and is two- to eightfold more active than amantadine

Pharmacodynamics/Kinetics

Onset of action: Antiviral activity: No data exist establishing a correlation between plasma concentration and antiviral effect

Absorption: Tablet and syrup formulations are equally absorbed

Metabolism: Extensively hepatic

Half-life elimination: 25.4 hours; prolonged in elderly

Time to peak: 6 hours

Excretion: Urine (<25% as unchanged drug)

Clearance: Hemodialysis does not contribute to clearance

(Continued)

Rimantadine *(Continued)*

Dosage Oral:

Prophylaxis:

Children <10 years: 5 mg/kg once daily; maximum: 150 mg

Children >10 years and Adults: 100 mg twice daily; decrease to 100 mg/day in elderly or in patients with severe hepatic or renal impairment (Cl_{cr} ≤10 mL/minute)

Treatment: Adults: 100 mg twice daily; decrease to 100 mg/day in elderly or in patients with severe hepatic or renal impairment (Cl_{cr} ≤10 mL/minute)

Administration Initiation of rimantadine within 48 hours of the onset of influenza A illness halves the duration of illness and significantly reduces the duration of viral shedding and increased peripheral airways resistance; continue therapy for 5-7 days after symptoms begin

Monitoring Parameters Monitor for CNS or GI effects in elderly or patients with renal or hepatic impairment

Dosage Forms SYR: 50 mg/5 mL (240 mL). **TAB:** 100 mg

♦ **Rimantadine Hydrochloride** *see* Rimantadine *on page 1099*

Rimexolone (ri MEKS oh lone)

U.S. Brand Names Vexol®

Therapeutic Category Anti-inflammatory Agent, Ophthalmic; Corticosteroid, Ophthalmic

Use Treatment of inflammation after ocular surgery and the treatment of anterior uveitis

Pregnancy Risk Factor C

Contraindications Hypersensitivity to rimexolone or any component of the formulation; fungal, viral, or untreated pus-forming bacterial ocular infections

Warnings/Precautions Prolonged use has been associated with the development of corneal or scleral perforation and posterior subcapsular cataracts; may mask or enhance the establishment of acute purulent untreated infections of the eye; effectiveness and safety have not been established in children

Common Adverse Reactions 1% to 10%: Ocular: Temporary mild blurred vision

Mechanism of Action Decreases inflammation by suppression of migration of polymorphonuclear leukocytes and reversal of increased capillary permeability

Pharmacodynamics/Kinetics

Absorption: Through aqueous humor

Metabolism: Hepatic for any amount of drug absorbed

Excretion: Urine and feces

Dosage Adults: Ophthalmic: Instill 1 drop in conjunctival sac 2-4 times/day up to every 4 hours; may use every 1-2 hours during first 1-2 days

Monitoring Parameters Intraocular pressure and periodic examination of lens (with prolonged use)

Dosage Forms SUSP, ophthalmic: 1% (5 mL, 10 mL)

♦ **Riomet™** *see* Metformin *on page 806*

♦ **Riopan Plus® [OTC]** *see* Magaldrate and Simethicone *on page 768*

♦ **Riopan Plus® Double Strength [OTC]** *see* Magaldrate and Simethicone *on page 768*

Risedronate (ris ED roe nate)

U.S. Brand Names Actonel®

Synonyms Risedronate Sodium

Therapeutic Category Bisphosphonate Derivative

Use Paget's disease of the bone; treatment and prevention of glucocorticoid-induced osteoporosis; treatment and prevention of osteoporosis in postmenopausal women

Pregnancy Risk Factor C

Contraindications Hypersensitivity to risedronate, bisphosphonates, or any component of the formulation; hypocalcemia; abnormalities of the esophagus which delay esophageal emptying such as stricture or achalasia; inability to stand or sit upright for at least 30 minutes; severe renal impairment (Cl_{cr} <30 mL/minute)

Warnings/Precautions Bisphosphonates may cause upper gastrointestinal disorders such as dysphagia, esophageal ulcer, and gastric ulcer. Use caution in patients with renal impairment; hypocalcemia must be corrected before therapy initiation with alendronate; ensure adequate calcium and vitamin D intake, especially for patients with Paget's disease in whom the pretreatment rate of bone turnover may be greatly elevated.

Common Adverse Reactions

Seen in patients taking 30 mg/day for Paget's disease:

>10%:

Central nervous system: Headache (18%)

Dermatologic: Rash (11%)

Gastrointestinal: Diarrhea (20%), abdominal pain (11%)

Neuromuscular & skeletal: Arthralgia (33%)

Miscellaneous: Flu-like syndrome (10%)

1% to 10%:

Cardiovascular: Peripheral edema (8%)

Central nervous system: Chest pain (7%), dizziness (7%)

Gastrointestinal: Nausea (10%), constipation (7%), belching (3%), colitis (3%, placebo 3%)

Neuromuscular & skeletal: Weakness (5%), bone pain (5%, placebo 5%), leg cramps (3%, placebo 3%), myasthenia (3%)

Ocular: Amblyopia (3%, placebo 3%), dry eye (3%)
Otic: Tinnitus (3%, placebo 3%)
Respiratory: Sinusitis (5%), bronchitis (3%, placebo 5%)
Miscellaneous: Neoplasm (3%)

Seen in patient taking 5 mg/day for osteoporosis (events similar to those seen with placebo)
>10%:
Central nervous system: Pain (14%)
Gastrointestinal: Abdominal pain (12%), diarrhea (11%), nausea (11%)
Genitourinary: Urinary tract infection (11%)
Neuromuscular & skeletal: Back pain (26%), arthralgia (24%)
1% to 10%:
Cardiovascular: Hypertension (10%), chest pain (5%), cardiovascular disorder (2%),
angina (2%)
Central nervous system: Depression (7%), dizziness (6%), insomnia (5%), anxiety (4%),
vertigo (3%)
Dermatologic: Rash (8%), bruising (4%), pruritus (3%), skin carcinoma (2%)
Gastrointestinal: Flatulence (5), gastritis (2%), gastrointestinal disorder (2%), rectal
disorder (2%), tooth disorder (2%)
Genitourinary: Cystitis (4%)
Hematologic: Anemia (2%)
Neuromuscular & skeletal: Joint disorder (7%), myalgia (7%), neck pain (5%), asthenia
(5%), bone pain (5%), bone disorder (4%), neuralgia (4%), leg cramps (4%), bursitis
(3%), tendon disorder (3%), hypertonia (2%), paresthesia (2%)
Ocular: Cataract (6%), conjunctivitis (3%)
Otic: Otitis media (2%)
Respiratory: Pharyngitis (6%), rhinitis (6%), dyspnea (4%), pneumonia (3%)
Miscellaneous: Neoplasm(3%), hernia (3%)

Drug Interactions
Decreased Effect: Calcium supplements and antacids interfere with absorption of
risedronate (take at a different time of the day than risedronate).

Mechanism of Action A bisphosphonate which inhibits bone resorption via actions on osteoclasts or on osteoclast precursors; decreases the rate of bone resorption direction, leading to
an indirect decrease in bone formation

Pharmacodynamics/Kinetics
Onset of action: May require weeks
Absorption: Rapid
Distribution: V_d: 6.3 L/kg
Protein binding: ~24%
Metabolism: None
Bioavailability: Poor, ~0.54% to 0.75%
Half-life elimination: Terminal: 480 hours
Excretion: Urine (up to 80%); feces (as unabsorbed drug)

Dosage Risedronate should be taken at least 30 minutes before the first food or drink of the day
other than water. Oral:
Adults (patients should receive supplemental calcium and vitamin D if dietary intake is inade-
quate):
Paget's disease of bone: 30 mg once daily for 2 months
Retreatment may be considered (following post-treatment observation of at least 2
months) if relapse occurs, or if treatment fails to normalize serum alkaline phosphatase.
For retreatment, the dose and duration of therapy are the same as for initial treatment.
No data are available on more than one course of retreatment.
Osteoporosis (postmenopausal) prevention and treatment: 5 mg once daily; efficacy for use
longer than 1 year has not been established; **alternatively,** a dose of 35 mg once weekly
has been demonstrated to be effective
Osteoporosis (glucocorticoid-induced) prevention and treatment: 5 mg once daily
Elderly: Dosage adjustment is not necessary in patients with $Cl_{cr} \geq 30$ mL/minute.

Dosage adjustment in renal impairment: Cl_{cr} <30 mL/minute: **Not** recommended for use
Administration It is imperative to administer risedronate 30-60 minutes before the patient
takes any food, drink, or other medications orally to avoid interference with absorption. The
patient should take risedronate on an empty stomach with a full glass (8 oz) of **plain water** (not
mineral water) and avoid lying down for 30 minutes after swallowing tablet to help delivery to
stomach.

Monitoring Parameters Alkaline phosphatase should be periodically measured; serum
calcium, phosphorus, and possibly potassium due to its drug class; use of absorptiometry may
assist in noting benefit in osteoporosis; monitor pain and fracture rate

Reference Range Calcium (total): Adults: 9.0-11.0 mg/dL (2.05-2.54 mmol/L), may slightly
decrease with aging; phosphorus: 2.5-4.5 mg/dL (0.81-1.45 mmol/L)

Patient Information The expected benefits of risedronate may only be obtained when each
tablet is taken with plain water the first thing in the morning and at least 30 minutes before the
first food, beverage, or medication of the day. Wait >30 minutes to improve risedronate
absorption. Even dosing with orange juice or coffee markedly reduces the absorption of
risedronate. Take risedronate with a full glass of water (6-8 oz/180-240 mL) and do not lie
down (stay fully upright sitting or standing) for at least 30 minutes following administration to
facilitate delivery to the stomach and reduce the potential for esophageal irritation. You may
experience headache (request analgesic), skin rash, abdominal pain, diarrhea, or constipation
(report if persistent). Report unresolved muscle or bone pain, leg cramps, acute abdominal
(Continued)

Risedronate *(Continued)*

pain, chest pain, palpitations, swollen extremities, disturbed vision, excessively dry eyes, ringing in the ears, or persistent flu-like symptoms. Also notify prescriber if experiencing difficulty swallowing, pain when swallowing, or severe or persistent heartburn. Take supplemental calcium and vitamin D if dietary intake is inadequate. Consider weight-bearing exercise along with the modification of certain behavioral factors, such as excessive cigarette smoking or alcohol consumption if these factors exist.

Dosage Forms TAB: 5 mg, 30 mg, 35 mg

♦ **Risedronate Sodium** *see Risedronate on page 1100*

♦ **Risperdal®** *see Risperidone on page 1102*

♦ **Risperdal® Consta™** *see Risperidone on page 1102*

♦ **Risperdal M-Tab™** *see Risperidone on page 1102*

Risperidone *(ris PER i done)*

Related Information

Antipsychotic Agents Comparison *on page 1364*

U.S. Brand Names Risperdal®; Risperdal® Consta™

Synonyms Risperdal M-Tab™

Therapeutic Category Antipsychotic Agent, Benzisoxazole

Use Treatment of schizophrenia; treatment of acute mania or mixed episodes associated with bipolar I disorder (as monotherapy or in combination with lithium or valproate)

Unlabeled/Investigational Use Behavioral symptoms associated with dementia in elderly; treatment of Tourette's disorder; treatment of pervasive developmental disorder and autism in children and adolescents

Pregnancy Risk Factor C

Contraindications Hypersensitivity to risperidone or any component of the formulation

Warnings/Precautions Low to moderately sedating, use with caution in disorders where CNS depression is a feature. Use with caution in Parkinson's disease. Caution in patients with hemodynamic instability; bone marrow suppression; predisposition to seizures; subcortical brain damage; severe cardiac, hepatic, or respiratory disease. Use with caution in renal dysfunction. Esophageal dysmotility and aspiration have been associated with antipsychotic use - use with caution in patients at risk of aspiration pneumonia (ie, Alzheimer's disease). Caution in breast cancer or other prolactin-dependent tumors (may elevate prolactin levels). May alter temperature regulation or mask toxicity of other drugs due to antiemetic effects.

May cause orthostasis; an increased incidence of cerebrovascular events has been associated with risperidone use in elderly demented patients. Use with caution in patients with cardiovascular diseases (eg, heart failure, history of myocardial infarction or ischemia, cerebrovascular disease, conduction abnormalities). Use caution in patients receiving medications for hypertension (orthostatic effects may be exacerbated) or in patients with hypovolemia or dehydration. May alter cardiac conduction; life-threatening arrhythmias have occurred with therapeutic doses of neuroleptics.

May cause anticholinergic effects (confusion, agitation, constipation, xerostomia, blurred vision, urinary retention); therefore, they should be used with caution in patients with decreased gastrointestinal motility, urinary retention, BPH, xerostomia, or visual problems. Conditions which also may be exacerbated by cholinergic blockade include narrow-angle glaucoma (screening is recommended) and worsening of myasthenia gravis. Relative to other neuroleptics, risperidone has a low potency of cholinergic blockade.

May cause extrapyramidal symptoms, including pseudoparkinsonism, acute dystonic reactions, akathisia, and tardive dyskinesia (risk of these reactions is low relative to other neuroleptics, and is dose dependent). May be associated with neuroleptic malignant syndrome (NMS). May rarely cause hyperglycemia - use with caution in patients with diabetes or other disorders of glucose regulation.

Common Adverse Reactions

Frequency not defined: Gastrointestinal: Dysphagia, esophageal dysmotility

>10%:

Central nervous system: Insomnia, agitation, anxiety, headache, extrapyramidal symptoms (dose dependent), dizziness (I.M. injection)

Gastrointestinal: Weight gain

Respiratory: Rhinitis (I.M. injection)

1% to 10%:

Cardiovascular: Hypotension (especially orthostatic), tachycardia

Central nervous system: Sedation, dizziness (oral formulation), restlessness, dystonic reactions, pseudoparkinson, tardive dyskinesia, neuroleptic malignant syndrome, altered central temperature regulation, nervousness, fatigue, somnolence, hallucination, tremor, hypoesthesia, akathisia

Dermatologic: Photosensitivity (rare), rash, dry skin, seborrhea, acne

Endocrine & metabolic: Amenorrhea, galactorrhea, gynecomastia, sexual dysfunction

Gastrointestinal: Constipation, GI upset, xerostomia, dyspepsia, vomiting, abdominal pain, nausea, anorexia, diarrhea, weight changes

Genitourinary: Polyuria

Neuromuscular & skeletal: Myalgia

Ocular: Abnormal vision

Respiratory: Rhinitis (oral formulation), coughing, sinusitis, pharyngitis, dyspnea

Drug Interactions

Cytochrome P450 Effect: Substrate of CYP2D6 (major), 3A4 (minor); **Inhibits** CYP2D6 (weak), 3A4 (weak)

Increased Effect/Toxicity: CYP2D6 inhibitors may increase the levels/effects of risperidone; example inhibitors include chlorpromazine, delavirdine, fluoxetine, miconazole, paroxetine, pergolide, quinidine, quinine, ritonavir, and ropinirole. Risperidone may enhance the hypotensive effects of antihypertensive agents. Clozapine decreases clearance of risperidone. Metoclopramide may increase risk of extrapyramidal symptoms (EPS).

Decreased Effect: Risperidone may antagonize effects of levodopa. Carbamazepine decreases risperidone serum concentrations.

Mechanism of Action Risperidone is a benzisoxazole derivative, mixed serotonin-dopamine antagonist; binds to 5-HT$_2$-receptors in the CNS and in the periphery with a very high affinity; binds to dopamine-D$_2$ receptors with less affinity. The binding affinity to the dopamine-D$_2$ receptor is 20 times lower than the 5-HT$_2$ affinity. The addition of serotonin antagonism to dopamine antagonism (classic neuroleptic mechanism) is thought to improve negative symptoms of psychoses and reduce the incidence of extrapyramidal side effects. Alpha$_1$, alpha$_2$ adrenergic, and histaminergic receptors are also antagonized with high affinity. Risperidone has low to moderate affinity for 5-HT$_{1C}$, 5-HT$_{1D}$, and 5-HT$_{1A}$ receptors, weak affinity for D$_1$ and no affinity for muscarinics or beta$_1$ and beta$_2$ receptors

Pharmacodynamics/Kinetics

Absorption:
Oral: Rapid and well absorbed; food does not affect rate or extent
Injection: <1% absorbed initially; main release occurs at ~3 weeks and is maintained from 4-6 weeks

Distribution: V$_d$: 1-2 L/kg

Protein binding, plasma: Risperidone 90%; 9-hydroxyrisperidone: 77%

Metabolism: Extensively hepatic via CYP2D6 to 9-hydroxyrisperidone (similar pharmacological activity as risperidone); N-dealkylation is a second minor pathway

Bioavailability: Solution: 70%; Tablet: 66%; orally-disintegrating tablets are bioequivalent to tablets

Half-life elimination: Active moiety (risperidone and its active metabolite 9-hydroxyrisperidone)
Oral: 20 hours (mean)
Extensive metabolizers: Risperidone: 3 hours; 9-hydroxyrisperidone: 21 hours
Poor metabolizers: Risperidone: 20 hours; 9-hydroxyrisperidone: 30 hours
Injection: 3-6 days; related to microsphere erosion and subsequent absorption of risperidone

Time to peak, plasma: Oral: Risperidone: Within 1 hour; 9-hydroxyrisperidone: Extensive metabolizers: 3 hours; Poor metabolizers: 17 hours

Excretion: Urine (70%); feces (15%)

Dosage

Oral:
Children and Adolescents:
Pervasive developmental disorder (unlabeled use): Initial: 0.25 mg twice daily; titrate up 0.25 mg/day every 5-7 days; optimal dose range: 0.75-3 mg/day
Autism (unlabeled use): Initial: 0.25 mg at bedtime; titrate to 1 mg/day (0.1 mg/kg/day)
Schizophrenia (unlabeled use): Initial: 0.5 mg once or twice daily; titrate as necessary up to 2-6 mg/day
Bipolar disorder (unlabeled use): Initial: 0.5 mg; titrate to 0.5-3 mg/day
Tourette's disorder (unlabeled use): Initial: 0.5 mg; titrate to 2-4 mg/day

Adults:
Schizophrenia: Recommended starting dose: 0.5-1 mg twice daily; slowly increase to the optimum range of 3-6 mg/day; may be given as a single daily dose once maintenance dose is achieved; daily dosages >10 mg does not appear to confer any additional benefit, and the incidence of extrapyramidal symptoms is higher than with lower doses
Bipolar mania: Recommended starting dose: 2-3 mg once daily; if needed, adjust dose by 1 mg/day in intervals ≥24 hours; dosing range: 1-6 mg/day

Elderly: A starting dose of 0.25-1 mg in 1-2 divided doses, and titration should progress slowly. Additional monitoring of renal function and orthostatic blood pressure may be warranted. If once-a-day dosing in the elderly or debilitated patient is considered, a twice daily regimen should be used to titrate to the target dose, and this dose should be maintained for 2-3 days prior to attempts to switch to a once-daily regimen.

I.M.: Adults: Schizophrenia (Risperdal™ Consta™): 25 mg every 2 weeks; some patients may benefit from larger doses; maximum dose not to exceed 50 mg every 2 weeks. Dosage adjustments should not be made more frequently than every 4 weeks.

Note: Oral risperidone (or other antipsychotic) should be administered with the initial injection of Risperdal® Consta™ and continued for 3 weeks (then discontinued) to maintain adequate therapeutic plasma concentrations prior to main release phase of risperidone from injection site.

Dosing adjustment in renal impairment: Oral: Starting dose of 0.25-0.5 mg twice daily; clearance of the active moiety is decreased by 60% in patients with moderate to severe renal disease compared to healthy subjects.

Dosing adjustment in hepatic impairment: Oral: Starting dose of 0.25-0.5 mg twice daily; the mean free fraction of risperidone in plasma was increased by 35% compared to healthy subjects.

Administration

Oral: Oral solution can be mixed with water, coffee, orange juice, or low-fat milk, but is **not compatible** with cola, grapefruit juice, or tea. May be administered with or without food. (Continued)

Risperidone *(Continued)*

Risperdal® M-Tabs™ should not be removed from blister pack until administered. Using dry hands, place immediately on tongue. Tablet will dissolve within seconds, and may be swallowed with or without liquid. Do not split or chew.

I.M.: Risperdal® Consta™ should be administered into the upper outer quadrant of the gluteal area. Injection should alternate between the two buttocks. Do not combine two different dosage strengths into one single administration.

Monitoring Parameters Vital signs; lipid profile, fasting blood glucose/Hgb A_{1c}; BMI; mental status, abnormal involuntary movement scale (AIMS), extrapyramidal symptoms; orthostatic blood pressure changes for 3-5 days after starting or increasing dose

Patient Information Use exactly as directed (do not increase dose or frequency). It may take several weeks to achieve desired results; do not discontinue without consulting prescriber. Dilute solution with water, milk, or orange juice; do not dilute with beverages containing caffeine, tannin, or pectinate (eg, colas, tea). Avoid concurrent grapefruit juice. Avoid alcohol or caffeine and other prescription or OTC medications not approved by prescriber. Maintain adequate hydration (2-3 L/day of fluids unless instructed to restrict fluid intake). You may experience excess sedation, drowsiness, restlessness, dizziness, or blurred vision (use caution driving or when engaging in tasks requiring alertness until response to drug is known); dry mouth, nausea, or GI upset (small frequent meals, frequent mouth care, chewing gum, or sucking lozenges may help); postural hypotension (use caution climbing stairs or when changing position from lying or sitting to standing); or urinary retention (void before taking medication). Report persistent CNS effects (eg, trembling fingers, altered gait or balance, excessive sedation, seizures, unusual muscle or skeletal movements, anxiety, abnormal thoughts, confusion, personality changes); chest pain, palpitations, rapid heartbeat, severe dizziness; swelling or pain in breasts (male and female), altered menstrual pattern, sexual dysfunction; pain or difficulty on urination; vision changes; skin rash or yellowing of skin; difficulty breathing; or worsening of condition.

Dosage Forms INJ, microspheres for reconstitution, extended release (Risperdal® Consta™): 25 mg, 37.5 mg, 50 mg. **SOLN, oral:** 1 mg/mL (30 mL). **TAB:** 0.25 mg, 0.5 mg, 1 mg, 2 mg, 3 mg, 4 mg. **TAB, orally disintegrating** (Risperdal® M-Tab™): 0.5 mg, 1 mg, 2 mg

◆ **Ritalin®** *see Methylphenidate on page 822*

◆ **Ritalin® LA** *see Methylphenidate on page 822*

◆ **Ritalin-SR®** *see Methylphenidate on page 822*

Ritonavir *(ri TOE na veer)*

Related Information

Antiretroviral Therapy for HIV Infection *on page 1448*

Management of Healthcare Worker Exposures to HBV, HCV, and HIV *on page 1421*

U.S. Brand Names Norvir®

Therapeutic Category Antiretroviral Agent, Protease Inhibitor; Protease Inhibitor

Use Treatment of HIV infection; should always be used as part of a multidrug regimen (at least three antiretroviral agents)

Pregnancy Risk Factor B

Contraindications Hypersensitivity to ritonavir or any component of the formulation; concurrent amiodarone, astemizole, bepridil, cisapride, dihydroergotamine, ergonovine, ergotamine, flecainide, lovastatin, methylergonovine, midazolam, pimozide, propafenone, quinidine, simvastatin, St John's wort, triazolam

Warnings/Precautions Use caution in patients with hepatic insufficiency; safety and efficacy have not been established in children <2 years of age; use caution with benzodiazepines, rifabutin, sildenafil, and certain analgesics (meperidine, piroxicam, propoxyphene). Selected HMG-CoA reductase inhibitors are contraindicated (see Contraindications); atorvastatin should be used at the lowest possible dose, while fluvastatin or pravastatin may be safer alternatives. Avoid concurrent use of St John's wort (may lead to loss of virologic response and/or resistance). Ritonavir may interact with many medications. Careful review is required. Warn patients that redistribution of fat may occur.

Common Adverse Reactions Protease inhibitors cause dyslipidemia which includes elevated cholesterol and triglycerides and a redistribution of body fat centrally to cause increased abdominal girth, buffalo hump, facial atrophy, and breast enlargement. These agents also cause hyperglycemia.

>10%:

Endocrine & metabolic: Triglycerides increased

Gastrointestinal: Diarrhea, nausea, vomiting, taste perversion

Hematologic: Anemia, WBCs decreased

Hepatic: GGT increased

Neuromuscular & skeletal: Weakness

1% to 10%:

Cardiovascular: Vasodilation

Central nervous system: Fever, headache, malaise, dizziness, insomnia, somnolence, thinking abnormally

Dermatologic: Rash

Endocrine & metabolic: Hyperlipidemia, uric acid increased, glucose increased

Gastrointestinal: Abdominal pain, anorexia, constipation, dyspepsia, flatulence, local throat irritation

Hematologic: Neutropenia, eosinophilia, neutrophilia, prolonged PT, leukocytosis

Hepatic: LFTs increased

Neuromuscular & skeletal: CPK increased, myalgia, paresthesia
Respiratory: Pharyngitis
Miscellaneous: Diaphoresis, potassium increased, calcium increased

Drug Interactions

Cytochrome P450 Effect: Substrate of CYP1A2 (minor), 2B6 (minor), 2D6 (major), 3A4 (major); **Inhibits** CYP2C8/9 (weak), 2C19 (weak), 2D6 (strong), 2E1 (weak), 3A4 (strong); **Induces** CYP1A2 (weak), 2C8/9 (weak), 3A4 (weak)

Increased Effect/Toxicity: Concurrent use of amiodarone, bepridil, cisapride, flecainide, pimozide, propafenone, and quinidine is contraindicated. Serum concentrations/toxicity of many benzodiazepines may be increased; midazolam and triazolam are contraindicated. Concurrent use of ergot alkaloids (dihydroergotamine, ergotamine, ergonovine, methylergonovine) with ritonavir is also contraindicated (may cause vasospasm and peripheral ischemia). HMG-CoA reductase inhibitors serum concentrations may be increased by ritonavir, increasing the risk of myopathy/rhabdomyolysis; lovastatin and simvastatin are contraindicated; fluvastatin and pravastatin may be safer alternatives. Serum concentrations of meperidine's neuroexcitatory metabolite (normeperidine) are increased by ritonavir, which may increase the risk of CNS toxicity/seizures. Rifabutin and rifabutin metabolite serum concentrations may be increased by ritonavir; reduce rifabutin dose to 150 mg every other day. Sildenafil serum concentrations may be increased by ritonavir; when used concurrently, do not exceed a maximum sildenafil dose of 25 mg in a 48-hour period. Tadalafil serum concentrations may be increased by ritonavir; maximum tadalafil dose of 10 mg in 72 hours is recommended with strong CYP3A4 inhibitors. Vardenafil serum concentrations may be increased by ritonavir; do not exceed vardenafil dose of 2.5 mg in 72 hours. Saquinavir's serum concentrations are increased by ritonavir; the dosage of both agents should be reduced to 400 mg twice daily. Concurrent therapy with amprenavir may result in increased serum concentrations: dosage adjustment is recommended. Metronidazole or disulfiram may cause disulfiram reaction (oral solution contains 43% ethanol).

CYP2D6 inhibitors may increase the levels/effects of ritonavir; example inhibitors include chlorpromazine, delavirdine, fluoxetine, miconazole, paroxetine, pergolide, quinidine, quinine, and ropinirole. Ritonavir may also increase the serum concentrations of the following drugs (dose decrease may be needed): Benzodiazepines, beta-blockers (metoprolol, timolol), bupropion, calcium channel blockers (diltiazem, nifedipine, verapamil), carbamazepine, clarithromycin, clonazepam, clorazepate, clozapine, cyclosporin, dexamethasone, disopyramide, dronabinol, ethosuximide, itraconazole, ketoconazole, lidocaine, methamphetamine, mexiletine, nefazodone, perphenazine, prednisone, propoxyphene, piroxicam, risperidone, tacrolimus, tramadol, thioridazine, tricyclic antidepressants (including desipramine), and zolpidem. Serum concentrations of rifabutin may be increased by ritonavir; dosage adjustment required. Serum levels/effects of corticosteroids (eg, dexamethasone, fluticasone, prednisone) and immunosuppressants (cyclosporine, sirolimus, tacrolimus; monitor) may be increased by ritonavir.

Decreased Effect: The administration of didanosine (buffered formulation) should be separated from ritonavir by 2.5 hours to limit interaction with ritonavir. Concurrent use of rifampin, rifabutin, dexamethasone, and many anticonvulsants may lower serum concentration of ritonavir. Ritonavir may reduce the concentration of ethinyl estradiol which may result in loss of contraception (including combination products). Theophylline concentrations may be reduced in concurrent therapy. Levels of didanosine and zidovudine may be decreased by ritonavir, however, no dosage adjustment is necessary. In addition, ritonavir may decrease the serum concentrations of the following drugs: Atovaquone, divalproex, lamotrigine, methadone, phenytoin, warfarin.

Mechanism of Action Ritonavir inhibits HIV protease and renders the enzyme incapable of processing of polyprotein precursor which leads to production of noninfectious immature HIV particles

Pharmacodynamics/Kinetics

Absorption: Variable, with or without food
Distribution: High concentrations in serum and lymph nodes
Protein binding: 98% to 99%
Metabolism: Hepatic; five metabolites, low concentration of an active metabolite achieved in plasma (oxidative); see Drug Interactions
Half-life elimination: 3-5 hours
Excretion: Urine (negligible amounts)

Dosage Oral:

Children ≥2 years: 250 mg/m^2 twice daily; titrate dose upward to 400 mg/m^2 twice daily (maximum: 600 mg twice daily)

Adults: 600 mg twice daily; dose escalation tends to avoid nausea that many patients experience upon initiation of full dosing. Escalate the dose as follows: 300 mg twice daily for 1 day, 400 mg twice daily for 2 days, 500 mg twice daily for 1 day, then 600 mg twice daily. Ritonavir may be better tolerated when used in combination with other antiretrovirals by initiating the drug alone and subsequently adding the second agent within 2 weeks.

Note: Dosage adjustments for ritonavir when administered in combination therapy:

Amprenavir: Adjustments necessary for each agent:
Amprenavir 1200 mg with ritonavir 200 mg once daily **or**
Amprenavir 600 mg with ritonavir 100 mg twice daily

Amprenavir plus efavirenz (3-drug regimen): Amprenavir 1200 mg twice daily plus ritonavir 200 mg twice daily plus efavirenz at standard dose

Indinavir: Adjustments necessary for both agents:
Indinavir 800 mg twice daily plus ritonavir 100-200 mg twice daily **or**
Indinavir 400 mg twice daily plus ritonavir 400 mg twice daily

(Continued)

Ritonavir *(Continued)*

Nelfinavir or saquinavir: Ritonavir 400 mg twice daily

Dosing adjustment in renal impairment: None necessary

Dosing adjustment in hepatic impairment: No adjustment required in mild or moderate impairment; however, careful monitoring is required in moderate hepatic impairment (levels may be decreased); caution advised with severe impairment (no data available)

Administration Administer with food. Liquid formulations usually have an unpleasant taste. Consider mixing it with chocolate milk or a liquid nutritional supplement.

Monitoring Parameters Triglycerides, cholesterol, CBC, LFTs, CPK, uric acid, basic HIV monitoring, viral load, and CD4 count, glucose

Patient Information Take with food. Mix liquid formulation with chocolate milk or liquid nutritional supplement. You may experience headache or confusion; if these persist notify prescriber. Diarrhea may be moderate to severe. Notify prescriber if problematic. Report swelling, numbness of tongue, mouth, lips, unresolved vomiting, fever, chills, or extreme fatigue. Do not take any prescription medications, over-the-counter products or herbal products, especially St John's wort, without consulting prescriber.

Dosage Forms CAP: 100 mg. **SOLN:** 80 mg/mL (240 mL)

♦ **Ritonavir and Lopinavir** *see Lopinavir and Ritonavir on page 756*

♦ **Rituxan®** *see Rituximab on page 1106*

Rituximab (ri TUK si mab)

U.S. Brand Names Rituxan®

Synonyms Anti-CD20 Monoclonal Antibody; C2B8; C2B8 Monoclonal Antibody; IDEC-C2B8; Pan-B Antibody

Therapeutic Category Antineoplastic Agent, Monoclonal Antibody; Monoclonal Antibody

Use Treatment of relapsed or refractory CD20 positive, B-cell non-Hodgkin's lymphoma

Pregnancy Risk Factor C

Contraindications Type I hypersensitivity or anaphylactic reactions to murine proteins or any component of the formulation

Warnings/Precautions Rituximab is associated with hypersensitivity reactions which may respond to adjustments in the infusion rate. Hypotension, bronchospasm, and angioedema have occurred as part of an infusion-related symptom complex. Interrupt rituximab infusion for severe reactions and resume at a 50% reduction in rate when symptoms have completely resolved. Treatment of these symptoms with diphenhydramine and acetaminophen is recommended; additional treatment with bronchodilators or I.V. saline may be indicated. In most cases, patients who have experienced nonlife-threatening reactions have been able to complete the full course of therapy. Medications for the treatment of hypersensitivity reactions (eg, epinephrine, antihistamines, corticosteroids) should be available for immediate use in the event of such a reaction during administration. Discontinue infusions in the event of serious or life-threatening cardiac arrhythmias.

Common Adverse Reactions

>10%:

Central nervous system: Headache, fever, chills

Gastrointestinal: Nausea

Hematologic: Leukopenia

Neuromuscular & skeletal: Asthenia

Immunologic: Rituximab-induced B-cell depletion occurred in 70% to 80% of patients and was associated with decreased serum immunoglobulins in a minority of patients. The incidence of infections does not appear to be increased. During the treatment period, 50 patients in the pivotal trial developed infectious events, including six grade 3 events (there were no grade 4 events. The six serious events were not associated with neutropenia).

Infusion-related: An infusion-related symptom complex consisting of fever and chills/rigors occurred in the majority of patients during the first rituximab infusion. Other frequent infusion-related symptoms included nausea, urticaria, fatigue, headache, pruritus, bronchospasm, dyspnea, sensation of tongue or throat swelling (angioedema), rhinitis, vomiting, hypotension, flushing, and pain at disease sites. These reactions generally occurred within 30 minutes to 2 hours of beginning the first infusion, and resolved with slowing or interruption of the infusion and with supportive care (I.V. saline, diphenhydramine, and acetaminophen). The incidence of infusion related events decreased from 80% during the first to ~40% with subsequent infusions. Mild to moderate hypotension requiring interruption of rituximab infusion, with or without the administration of I.V. saline, occurred in 10%. Isolated occurrences of severe reactions requiring epinephrine have been reported in patients receiving rituximab for other indicators. Angioedema was reported in 13% and was serious in one patient.

1% to 10%:

Cardiovascular: Hypotension

Central nervous system: Myalgia, dizziness

Dermatologic: Pruritus, rash, urticaria, angioedema (6%)

Gastrointestinal: Vomiting, abdominal pain

Hematologic: Thrombocytopenia, neutropenia; during the treatment period (up to 30 days following the last dose), the following occurred: Severe thrombocytopenia, severe neutropenia, and severe anemia

Respiratory: Bronchospasm occurred in 8%; 25% of these patients were treated with bronchodilators; rhinitis

Miscellaneous: Throat irritation

Mechanism of Action Rituximab is a monoclonal antibody directed against the CD20 antigen on B-lymphocytes. CD20 regulates cell cycle initiation; and, possibly, functions as a calcium channel. Rituximab binds to the antigen on the cell surface, activating complement-dependent cytotoxicity; and to human Fc receptors, mediating cell killing through an antibody-dependent cellular toxicity.

Pharmacodynamics/Kinetics

Duration: Detectable in serum 3-6 months after completion of treatment; B-cell recovery begins ~6 months following completion of treatment; median B-cell levels return to normal by 12 months following completion of treatment

Absorption: I.V.: Immediate and results in a rapid and sustained depletion of circulating and tissue-based B cells

Half-life elimination:

>100 mg/m^2: 4.4 days (range 1.6-10.5 days)

375 mg/m^2: 50 hours (following first dose) to 174 hours (following fourth dose)

Excretion: Uncertain; may undergo phagocytosis and catabolism in the reticuloendothelial system (RES)

Dosage Adults: I.V. (refer to individual protocols): **Do not administer I.V. push or bolus** (hypersensitivity reactions may occur). Consider premedication (consisting of acetaminophen and diphenhydramine) before each infusion of rituximab. Premedication may attenuate infusion-related events. Because transient hypotension may occur during infusion, give consideration to withholding antihypertensive medications 12 hours prior to rituximab infusion.

I.V. infusion:

375 mg/m^2 once weekly for 4-8 weeks **or**

100 mg/m^2 I.V. day 1, then 375 mg/m^2 3 times/week for 11 doses (cycles may be repeated in patients with refractory or relapsed disease) **or**

250 mg/m^2 I.V. day 1; repeat in 7-9 days with ibritumomab;

Rituximab dose in combination with ibritumomab; (also see Ibritumomab monograph):

Step 1: 250 mg/m^2 at an initial rate of 50 mg/hour. If hypersensitivity or infusion-related events do not occur, increase infusion in increments of 50 mg/hour every 30 minutes, to a maximum of 400 mg/hour. Infusions should be temporarily slowed or interrupted if hypersensitivity or infusion related events occur. The infusion may be resumed at $^1/_2$ the previous rate upon improvement of symptoms.

Step 2: 250 mg/m^2 at an initial rate of 100 mg/hour (50 mg/hour if infusion-related events occurred with the first infusion). If hypersensitivity or infusion-related events do not occur, increase infusion in increments of 100 mg/hour every 30 minutes, to a maximum of 400 mg/hour, as tolerated.

Administration Administer the first infusion at an initial rate of 50 mg/hour. If a reaction occurs, slow or stop the infusion. If the reaction abates, restart the infusion at 50% of the previous rate. Escalate the infusion rate in 50 mg/hour increments every 30 minutes, to a maximum of 400 mg/hour. Subsequent infusions can be administered at an initial rate of 100 mg/hour and increased by 100 mg/hour increments at 30-minute intervals, to a maximum of 400 mg/hour as tolerated.

Monitoring Parameters CBC with differential; peripheral CD20$^+$ cells; HAMA/HACA titers (high levels may increase the risk of allergic reactions)

Reference Range Peripheral CD20+ cells: High level pretreatment (500-1600 cells/µL, malignant or normal) may indicate risk of more severe infusional reactions

Dosage Forms INJ, solution [preservative free]: 10 mg/mL (10 mL, 50 mL)

Rivastigmine (ri va STIG meen)

U.S. Brand Names Exelon®

Synonyms ENA 713; SDZ ENA 713

Therapeutic Category Acetylcholinesterase Inhibitor; Cholinergic Agent

Use Mild to moderate dementia from Alzheimer's disease

Pregnancy Risk Factor B

Contraindications Hypersensitivity to rivastigmine, other carbamate derivatives, or any component of the formulation

Warnings/Precautions Significant nausea, vomiting, anorexia, and weight loss are associated with use; occurs more frequently in women and during the titration phase. If treatment is interrupted for more than several days, reinstate at the lowest daily dose. Use caution in patients with a history of peptic ulcer disease or concurrent NSAID use. Caution in patients undergoing anesthesia who will receive succinylcholine-type muscle relaxation, patients with sick sinus syndrome, bradycardia or supraventricular conduction conditions, urinary obstruction, seizure disorders, or pulmonary conditions such as asthma or COPD. There are no trials evaluating the safety and efficacy in children.

Common Adverse Reactions

>10%:

Central nervous system: Dizziness (21%), headache (17%)

Gastrointestinal: Nausea (47%), vomiting (31%), diarrhea (19%), anorexia (17%), abdominal pain (13%)

2% to 10%:

Cardiovascular: Syncope (3%), hypertension (3%)

Central nervous system: Fatigue (9%), insomnia (9%), confusion (8%), depression (6%), anxiety (5%), malaise (5%), somnolence (5%), hallucinations (4%), aggressiveness (3%)

Gastrointestinal: Dyspepsia (9%), constipation (5%), flatulence (4%), weight loss (3%), eructation (2%)

Genitourinary: Urinary tract infection (7%)

(Continued)

Rivastigmine *(Continued)*

Neuromuscular & skeletal: Weakness (6%), tremor (4%)
Respiratory: Rhinitis (4%)
Miscellaneous: Increased diaphoresis (4%), flu-like syndrome (3%)

>2% (but frequency equal to placebo): Chest pain, peripheral edema, vertigo, back pain, arthralgia, pain, bone fracture, agitation, nervousness, delusion, paranoid reaction, upper respiratory tract infections, infection, coughing, pharyngitis, bronchitis, rash, urinary incontinence.

<2% (Limited to important or life-threatening symptoms; reactions may be at a similar frequency to placebo): Fever, edema, allergy, periorbital or facial edema, hypothermia, hypotension, postural hypotension, cardiac failure, ataxia, convulsions, apraxia, aphasia, dysphonia, hyperkinesia, hypertonia, hypokinesia, migraine, neuralgia, peripheral neuropathy, hypothyroidism, peptic ulcer, gastroesophageal reflux, GI hemorrhage, intestinal obstruction, pancreatitis, colitis, atrial fibrillation, bradycardia, AV block, bundle branch block, sick sinus syndrome, cardiac arrest, supraventricular tachycardia, tachycardia, abnormal hepatic function, cholecystitis, dehydration, arthritis, angina pectoris, myocardial infarction, epistaxis, hematoma, thrombocytopenia, purpura, delirium, emotional lability, psychosis, anemia, bronchospasm, apnea, rashes (maculopapular, eczema, bullous, exfoliative, psoriaform, erythematous), urticaria, acute renal failure, peripheral ischemia, pulmonary embolism, thrombosis, thrombophlebitis, intracranial hemorrhage, conjunctival hemorrhage, diplopia, glaucoma, lymphadenopathy, leukocytosis.

Drug Interactions
Increased Effect/Toxicity:
Beta-blockers without ISA activity may increase risk of bradycardia.
Calcium channel blockers (diltiazem or verapamil) may increase risk of bradycardia.
Cholinergic agonists effects may be increased with rivastigmine.
Cigarette use increases the clearance of rivastigmine by 23%.
Depolarizing neuromuscular blocking agents effects may be increased with rivastigmine.
Digoxin may increase risk of bradycardia.
Decreased Effect: Anticholinergic agents effects may be reduced with rivastigmine.

Mechanism of Action A deficiency of cortical acetylcholine is thought to account for some of the symptoms of Alzheimer's disease; rivastigmine increases acetylcholine in the central nervous system through reversible inhibition of its hydrolysis by cholinesterase

Pharmacodynamics/Kinetics
Absorption: Fasting: Rapid and complete within 1 hour
Distribution: V_d: 1.8-2.7 L/kg
Protein binding: 40%
Metabolism: Extensively via cholinesterase-mediated hydrolysis in the brain; metabolite undergoes N-demethylation and/or sulfate conjugation hepatically; CYP minimally involved; linear kinetics at 3 mg twice daily, but nonlinear at higher doses
Bioavailability: 40%
Half-life elimination: 1.5 hours
Time to peak: 1 hour
Excretion: Urine (97% as metabolites); feces (0.4%)

Dosage Adults: Mild to moderate Alzheimer's dementia: Oral: Initial: 1.5 mg twice daily to start; if dose is tolerated for at least 2 weeks then it may be increased to 3 mg twice daily; increases to 4.5 mg twice daily and 6 mg twice daily should only be attempted after at least 2 weeks at the previous dose; maximum dose: 6 mg twice daily. If adverse events such as nausea, vomiting, abdominal pain, or loss of appetite occur, the patient should be instructed to discontinue treatment for several doses then restart at the same or next lower dosage level; antiemetics have been used to control GI symptoms. If treatment is interrupted for longer than several days, restart the treatment at the lowest dose and titrate as previously described.

Elderly: Clearance is significantly lower in patients older than 60 years of age, but dosage adjustments are not recommended. Titrate dose to individual's tolerance.

Dosage adjustment in renal impairment: Dosage adjustments are not recommended, however, titrate the dose to the individual's tolerance.

Dosage adjustment in hepatic impairment: Clearance is significantly reduced in mild to moderately impaired patients. Although dosage adjustments are not recommended, use lowest possible dose and titrate according to individual's tolerance. May consider waiting >2 weeks between dosage adjustments.

Administration Should be administered with meals (breakfast or dinner). Capsule should be swallowed whole. Liquid form is available for patients who cannot swallow capsules (can be swallowed directly from syringe or mixed with water, milk, or juice). Stir well and drink within 4 hours of mixing.

Monitoring Parameters Cognitive function at periodic intervals

Patient Information Take with meals at breakfast and dinner. Swallow capsule whole. Do not chew, break, or crush capsule. A liquid (solution) is available for patients who cannot swallow capsules. Monitor for nausea, vomiting, loss of appetite, or weight loss; notify prescriber if any of these occur. See instructions for use of oral solution. Can swallow solution directly from syringe or mix with water, juice, or soda. Stir well and drink all of mixture within 4 hours of mixing. Do not mix with other liquids. Avoid concurrent ethanol use.

Dosage Forms CAP: 1.5 mg, 3 mg, 4.5 mg, 6 mg. **SOLN, oral:** 2 mg/mL (120 mL)

Rizatriptan *(rye za TRIP tan)*
Related Information
Antimigraine Drugs Comparison *on page 1363*

U.S. Brand Names Maxalt®; Maxalt-MLT®

Synonyms MK462

Therapeutic Category Antimigraine Agent, Serotonin 5-HT$_{1D}$ Agonist; Serotonin 5-HT$_4$ Receptor Agonist

Use Acute treatment of migraine with or without aura

Pregnancy Risk Factor C

Contraindications Hypersensitivity to rizatriptan or any component of the formulation; documented ischemic heart disease or Prinzmetal's angina; uncontrolled hypertension; basilar or hemiplegic migraine; during or within 2 weeks of MAO inhibitors; during or within 24 hours of treatment with another 5-HT$_1$ agonist, or an ergot-containing or ergot-type medication (eg, methysergide, dihydroergotamine)

Warnings/Precautions Use only in patients with a clear diagnosis of migraine. May cause vasospastic reactions resulting in colonic, peripheral, or coronary ischemia. Use with caution in elderly or patients with hepatic or renal impairment (including dialysis patients), history of hypersensitivity to sumatriptan or adverse effects from sumatriptan, and in patients at risk of coronary artery disease (as predicted by presence of risk factors) unless cardiovascular evaluation provides evidence that the patient is free of cardiovascular disease. In patients with risk factors for coronary artery disease, following adequate evaluation to establish the absence of coronary artery disease, the initial dose should be administered in a setting where response may be evaluated (physician's office or similarly staffed setting). ECG monitoring may be considered. Do not use with ergotamines. May increase blood pressure transiently; may cause coronary vasospasm (less than sumatriptan); avoid in patients with signs/symptoms suggestive of reduced arterial flow (ischemic bowel, Raynaud's) which could be exacerbated by vasospasm.

Patients who experience sensations of chest pain/pressure/tightness or symptoms suggestive of angina following dosing should be evaluated for coronary artery disease or Prinzmetal's angina before receiving additional doses.

Reconsider diagnosis of migraine if no response to initial dose. Long-term effects on vision have not been evaluated.

Common Adverse Reactions 1% to 10%:
Cardiovascular: Systolic/diastolic blood pressure increases (5-10 mm Hg), chest pain (5%), palpitation
Central nervous system: Dizziness, drowsiness, fatigue (13% to 30%, dose related)
Dermatologic: Skin flushing
Endocrine & metabolic: Mild increase in growth hormone, hot flashes
Gastrointestinal: Nausea, abdominal pain, dry mouth (<5%)
Respiratory: Dyspnea

Drug Interactions
Increased Effect/Toxicity: Use within 24 hours of another selective 5-HT$_1$ antagonist or ergot-containing drug should be avoided due to possible additive vasoconstriction. Use with propranolol increased plasma concentration of rizatriptan by 70%. Rarely, concurrent use with SSRIs results in weakness and incoordination; monitor closely. MAO inhibitors and nonselective MAO inhibitors increase concentration of rizatriptan.

Mechanism of Action Selective agonist for serotonin (5-HT$_{1D}$ receptor) in cranial arteries to cause vasoconstriction and reduce sterile inflammation associated with antidromic neuronal transmission correlating with relief of migraine

Pharmacodynamics/Kinetics
Onset of action: ~30 minutes
Duration: 14-16 hours
Protein binding: 14%
Metabolism: Via monoamine oxidase-A; first-pass effect
Bioavailability: 40% to 50%
Half-life elimination: 2-3 hours
Time to peak: 1-1.5 hours
Excretion: Urine (82%, 8% to 16% as unchanged drug); feces (12%)

Dosage Note: In patients with risk factors for coronary artery disease, following adequate evaluation to establish the absence of coronary artery disease, the initial dose should be administered in a setting where response may be evaluated (physician's office or similarly staffed setting). ECG monitoring may be considered.
Oral: 5-10 mg, repeat after 2 hours if significant relief is not attained; maximum: 30 mg in a 24-hour period (use 5 mg dose in patients receiving propranolol with a maximum of 15 mg in 24 hours)
Note: For orally-disintegrating tablets (Maxalt-MLT™): Patient should be instructed to place tablet on tongue and allow to dissolve. Dissolved tablet will be swallowed with saliva.

Monitoring Parameters Headache severity, signs/symptoms suggestive of angina; consider monitoring blood pressure, heart rate, and/or ECG with first dose in patients with likelihood of unrecognized coronary disease, such as patients with significant hypertension, hypercholesterolemia, obese patients, diabetics, smokers with other risk factors or strong family history of coronary artery disease

Patient Information

For orally-disintegrating tablets: Do not remove blister from outer pouch until just before dosing; open blister with dry hands, place tablet on tongue and allow to dissolve. Dissolved tablet will be swallowed with saliva.
(Continued)

Rizatriptan *(Continued)*

For all dosage forms: May repeat dose anytime after 2 hours of the first dose. Do not take a second dose without first consulting your prescriber. Do not take more than 30 mg in a 24-hour period (15 mg maximum in 24 hours if taking propranolol).

Dosage Forms TAB (Maxalt®): 5 mg, 10 mg. **TAB, orally-disintegrating** (Maxalt-MLT®): 5 mg, 10 mg

♦ **rLFN-α2** *see* Interferon Alfa-2b *on page 673*
♦ **RMS**® *see* Morphine Sulfate *on page 861*
♦ **Ro 5488** *see* Tretinoin (Oral) *on page 1258*
♦ **Robafen® AC** *see* Guaifenesin and Codeine *on page 604*
♦ **Robaxin**® *see* Methocarbamol *on page 814*
♦ **Robinul**® *see* Glycopyrrolate *on page 597*
♦ **Robinul® Forte** *see* Glycopyrrolate *on page 597*
♦ **Robitussin**® [OTC] *see* Guaifenesin *on page 603*
♦ **Robitussin® CF [OTC]** *see* Guaifenesin, Pseudoephedrine, and Dextromethorphan *on page 606*
♦ **Robitussin® Cold and Congestion [OTC]** *see* Guaifenesin, Pseudoephedrine, and Dextromethorphan *on page 606*
♦ **Robitussin® Cough and Cold Infant [OTC]** *see* Guaifenesin, Pseudoephedrine, and Dextromethorphan *on page 606*
♦ **Robitussin®-DAC [DSC]** *see* Guaifenesin, Pseudoephedrine, and Codeine *on page 606*
♦ **Robitussin® DM [OTC]** *see* Guaifenesin and Dextromethorphan *on page 604*
♦ **Robitussin® Maximum Strength Cough & Cold [OTC]** *see* Pseudoephedrine and Dextromethorphan *on page 1062*
♦ **Robitussin-PE® [OTC]** *see* Guaifenesin and Pseudoephedrine *on page 605*
♦ **Robitussin® Pediatric Cough & Cold [OTC]** *see* Pseudoephedrine and Dextromethorphan *on page 1062*
♦ **Robitussin® Pediatric Night Relief [OTC]** *see* Chlorpheniramine, Pseudoephedrine, and Dextromethorphan *on page 265*
♦ **Robitussin® Severe Congestion [OTC]** *see* Guaifenesin and Pseudoephedrine *on page 605*
♦ **Robitussin® Sugar Free Cough [OTC]** *see* Guaifenesin and Dextromethorphan *on page 604*
♦ **Rocaltrol**® *see* Calcitriol *on page 200*
♦ **Rocephin**® *see* Ceftriaxone *on page 244*

Rocuronium *(roe kyoor OH nee um)*

Related Information

Neuromuscular Blocking Agents Comparison *on page 1397*

U.S. Brand Names Zemuron®

Synonyms ORG 946; Rocuronium Bromide

Therapeutic Category Neuromuscular Blocker Agent, Nondepolarizing

Use Adjunct to general anesthesia to facilitate both rapid sequence and routine endotracheal intubation and to relax skeletal muscles during surgery; to facilitate mechanical ventilation in ICU patients; does not relieve pain or produce sedation

Pregnancy Risk Factor C

Contraindications Hypersensitivity to rocuronium or any component of the formulation

Warnings/Precautions Use with caution in patients with valvular heart disease, pulmonary disease, hepatic impairment; ventilation must be supported during neuromuscular blockade; certain clinical conditions may result in potentiation or antagonism of neuromuscular blockade:

Potentiation: Electrolyte abnormalities, severe hyponatremia, severe hypocalcemia, severe hypokalemia, hypermagnesemia, neuromuscular diseases, acidosis, acute intermittent porphyria, renal failure, hepatic failure

Antagonism: Alkalosis, hypercalcemia, demyelinating lesions, peripheral neuropathies, diabetes mellitus

Increased sensitivity in patients with myasthenia gravis, Eaton-Lambert syndrome; resistance in burn patients (>30% of body) for period of 5-70 days postinjury; resistance in patients with muscle trauma, denervation, immobilization, infection. Cross-sensitivity with other neuromuscular-blocking agents may occur; use extreme caution in patients with previous anaphylactic reactions.

Common Adverse Reactions >1%: Cardiovascular: Transient hypotension and hypertension

Drug Interactions

Increased Effect/Toxicity: Increased effects are possible with aminoglycosides, beta-blockers, clindamycin, calcium channel blockers, halogenated anesthetics, imipenem, ketamine, lidocaine, loop diuretics (furosemide), macrolides (case reports), magnesium sulfate, procainamide, quinidine, quinolones, tetracyclines, and vancomycin. May increase risk of myopathy when used with high- dose corticosteroids for extended periods.

Decreased Effect: Effect of nondepolarizing neuromuscular blockers may be reduced by carbamazepine (chronic use), corticosteroids (also associated with myopathy - see increased effect), phenytoin (chronic use), sympathomimetics, and theophylline.

Mechanism of Action Blocks acetylcholine from binding to receptors on motor endplate inhibiting depolarization

Pharmacodynamics/Kinetics

Onset of action: Good intubation conditions in 1-2 minutes; maximum neuromuscular blockade within 4 minutes

Duration: ~30 minutes (with standard doses, increases with higher doses)

Metabolism: Minimally hepatic; 17-desacetylrocuronium (5% to 10% activity of parent drug)

Half-life elimination: 60-70 minutes

Excretion: Feces (50%); urine (30%)

Dosage Administer I.V.; dose to effect; doses will vary due to interpatient variability; use ideal body weight for obese patients

Children:

Initial: 0.6 mg/kg under halothane anesthesia produce excellent to good intubating conditions within 1 minute and will provide a median time of 41 minutes of clinical relaxation in children 3 months to 1 year of age, and 27 minutes in children 1-12 years

Maintenance: 0.075-0.125 mg/kg administered upon return of T_1 to 25% of control provides clinical relaxation for 7-10 minutes

Adults:

Tracheal intubation: I.V.:

Initial: 0.6 mg/kg is expected to provide approximately 31 minutes of clinical relaxation under opioid/nitrous oxide/oxygen anesthesia with neuromuscular block sufficient for intubation attained in 1-2 minutes; lower doses (0.45 mg/kg) may be used to provide 22 minutes of clinical relaxation with median time to neuromuscular block of 1-3 minutes; maximum blockade is achieved in <4 minutes

Maximum: 0.9-1.2 mg/kg may be given during surgery under opioid/nitrous oxide/oxygen anesthesia without adverse cardiovascular effects and is expected to provide 58-67 minutes of clinical relaxation; neuromuscular blockade sufficient for intubation is achieved in <2 minutes with maximum blockade in <3 minutes

Maintenance: 0.1, 0.15, and 0.2 mg/kg administered at 25% recovery of control T_1 (defined as 3 twitches of train-of-four) provides a median of 12, 17, and 24 minutes of clinical duration under anesthesia

Rapid sequence intubation: 0.6-1.2 mg/kg in appropriately premedicated and anesthetized patients with excellent or good intubating conditions within 2 minutes

Continuous infusion: Initial: 0.01-0.012 mg/kg/minute only after early evidence of spontaneous recovery of neuromuscular function is evident; infusion rates have ranged from 4-16 mcg/kg/minute

ICU: 10 mcg/kg/minute; adjust dose to maintain appropriate degree of neuromuscular blockade (eg, 1 or 2 twitches on train-of-four)

Dosing adjustment in hepatic impairment: Reductions are necessary in patients with liver disease

Administration Administer I.V. only; may be administered undiluted as a bolus injection or via a continuous infusion using an infusion pump

Monitoring Parameters Peripheral nerve stimulator measuring twitch response, heart rate, blood pressure, assisted ventilation status

Dosage Forms INJ, solution: 10 mg/mL (5 mL, 10 mL)

♦ **Rocuronium Bromide** see Rocuronium on page 1110

Rofecoxib (roe fe COX ib)

Related Information

Nonsteroidal Anti-Inflammatory Agents Comparison on page 1401

U.S. Brand Names Vioxx®

Therapeutic Category Analgesic, Selective COX-II Inhibitor; Anti-inflammatory Agent; Nonsteroidal Anti-inflammatory Drug (NSAID), COX-2 Selective

Use Relief of the signs and symptoms of osteoarthritis; management of acute pain in adults; treatment of primary dysmenorrhea; relief of signs and symptoms of rheumatoid arthritis in adults

Pregnancy Risk Factor C/D (3rd trimester)

Contraindications Hypersensitivity to rofecoxib or any component of the formulation, aspirin, or other NSAIDs; pregnancy (3rd trimester)

Warnings/Precautions Gastrointestinal irritation, ulceration, bleeding, and perforation may occur with NSAIDs (rofecoxib has been associated with rates of these events which are lower than naproxen, a nonselective NSAID); use the lowest effective dose for the shortest duration possible to decrease risk. Use with caution in patients with a history of GI disease (bleeding or ulcers), decreased renal function, hepatic disease, CHF, hypertension, or asthma. Edema, GI irritation, and/or hypertension occur at an increased frequency with chronic use of 50 mg/day. Use with caution in patients with ischemic heart disease; antiplatelet therapies should be considered (rofecoxib is not a substitute for antiplatelet agents). Anaphylactoid reactions may occur, even with no prior exposure to rofecoxib.

Common Adverse Reactions

2% to 10%:

Cardiovascular: Peripheral edema (4%), hypertension (up to 10%)

Central nervous system: Headache (5%), dizziness (3%), weakness (2%)

Gastrointestinal: Diarrhea (7%), nausea (5%), heartburn (4%), epigastric discomfort (4%), dyspepsia (4%), abdominal pain (3%), dry socket (post-dental extraction alveolitis 2%)

Genitourinary: Urinary tract infection (3%)

Neuromuscular & skeletal: Back pain (3%)

Respiratory: Upper respiratory infection (9%), bronchitis (2%), sinusitis (3%)

Miscellaneous: Flu-like syndrome (3%)

(Continued)

Rofecoxib *(Continued)*

0.1% to 2%:

Cardiovascular: Chest pain, upper extremity edema, atrial fibrillation, bradycardia, arrhythmia, palpitation, tachycardia, venous insufficiency, fluid retention

Central nervous system: Anxiety, depression, decreased mental acuity, hypesthesia, insomnia, neuropathy, migraine, paresthesia, somnolence, vertigo, fever, pain

Dermatologic: Alopecia, atopic dermatitis, basal cell carcinoma, contact dermatitis, pruritus, rash, erythema, urticaria, dry skin

Endocrine & metabolic: Weight gain, hypercholesteremia

Gastrointestinal: Reflux, abdominal distension, abdominal tenderness, constipation, dry mouth, esophagitis, flatulence, gastritis, gastroenteritis, hematochezia, hemorrhoids, oral ulceration, dental caries, aphthous stomatitis

Genitourinary: Breast mass, cystitis, dysuria, menopausal disorder, nocturia, urinary retention, vaginitis, pelvic pain

Hematologic: Hematoma

Hepatic: Transaminases increased >3 times ULN (1%)

Neuromuscular & skeletal: Muscle spasm, sciatica, arthralgia, bursitis, cartilage trauma, joint swelling, muscle cramps, muscle weakness, myalgia, tendonitis, traumatic arthropathy, fracture (wrist)

Ocular: Blurred vision, conjunctivitis

Otic: Otic pain, otitis media, tinnitus

Respiratory: Asthma, cough, dyspnea, pneumonia, respiratory infection, pulmonary congestion, rhinitis, epistaxis, laryngitis, dry throat, pharyngitis, tonsillitis, diaphragmatic hernia

Miscellaneous: Allergy, fungal infection, insect bite reaction, syncope, viral syndrome, herpes simplex, herpes zoster, increased diaphoresis

Drug Interactions

Cytochrome P450 Effect: Substrate of CYP2C8/9 (minor); **Inhibits** CYP1A2 (strong); **Induces** CYP3A4 (weak)

Increased Effect/Toxicity: Cimetidine increases AUC of rofecoxib by 23%. Rofecoxib may increase plasma concentrations of methotrexate, lithium, and theophylline. Rofecoxib may be used with low-dose aspirin, however, rates of gastrointestinal bleeding may be increased with coadministration. Rofecoxib may increase the INR in patients receiving warfarin and may increase the risk of bleeding complications.

Decreased Effect: Efficacy of thiazide diuretics, loop diuretics (furosemide), or ACE inhibitors may be diminished by rofecoxib. Rifampin reduces the serum concentration of rofecoxib by ~50% (consider using initial dose of 25 mg/day for osteoarthritis).

Mechanism of Action Inhibits prostaglandin synthesis by decreasing the activity of the enzyme, cyclooxygenase-2 (COX-2), which results in decreased formation of prostaglandin precursors. Rofecoxib does not inhibit cyclooxygenase-1 (COX-1) at therapeutic concentrations.

Pharmacodynamics/Kinetics

Onset of action: 45 minutes

Duration: Up to >24 hours

Distribution: V_{dss} (apparent): 86-91 L

Protein binding: 87%

Metabolism: Hepatic (99%); minor metabolism via CYP2C8/9 isoenzyme; metabolites inactive

Bioavailability: 93%

Half-life elimination: 17 hours

Time to peak: 2-3 hours

Excretion: Urine (72% as metabolites, <1% as unchanged drug); feces (14% as unchanged drug)

Dosage Adult: Oral:

Osteoarthritis: 12.5 mg once daily; may be increased to a maximum of 25 mg once daily

Acute pain and management of dysmenorrhea: 50 mg once daily as needed (use for longer than 5 days has not been studied)

Rheumatoid arthritis: 25 mg once daily

Elderly: No specific adjustment is recommended. However, the AUC in elderly patients may be increased by 34% as compared to younger subjects. Use the lowest recommended dose.

Dosing comment in renal impairment: Use in advanced renal disease is not recommended

Dosing adjustment in hepatic impairment: Moderate hepatic dysfunction (Child-Pugh score 7-9): Maximum dose: 12.5 mg/day

Monitoring Parameters Signs and symptoms of gastrointestinal bleeding

Patient Information Patients should be informed of the signs and symptoms of gastrointestinal bleeding; gastrointestinal bleeding may occur as well as ulceration and perforation; pain may or may not be present. If gastric upset occurs, take with food, milk, or antacid. If gastric upset persists, contact prescriber.

Dosage Forms SUSP, oral: 12.5 mg/5 mL (150 mL); 25 mg/5 mL (150 mL). **TAB:** 12.5 mg, 25 mg, 50 mg

♦ **Roferon-A**® *see* Interferon Alfa-2a *on page 672*

♦ **Rogaine® Extra Strength for Men [OTC]** *see* Minoxidil *on page 845*

♦ **Rogaine® for Men [OTC]** *see* Minoxidil *on page 845*

♦ **Rogaine® for Women [OTC]** *see* Minoxidil *on page 845*

♦ **Rolaids® [OTC]** *see* Calcium Carbonate and Magnesium Hydroxide *on page 204*

♦ **Rolaids® Extra Strength [OTC]** *see* Calcium Carbonate *on page 203*

♦ **Rolaids®, Extra Strength [OTC]** *see* Calcium Carbonate and Magnesium Hydroxide *on page 204*

♦ **Romazicon®** *see* Flumazenil *on page 531*

♦ **Romilar® AC** *see* Guaifenesin and Codeine *on page 604*

♦ **Romycin®** *see* Erythromycin *on page 453*

♦ **Rondec®-DM Drops** *see* Carbinoxamine, Pseudoephedrine, and Dextromethorphan *on page 219*

♦ **Rondec® Drops** *see* Carbinoxamine and Pseudoephedrine *on page 218*

♦ **Rondec® Syrup** *see* Brompheniramine and Pseudoephedrine *on page 181*

♦ **Rondec® Tablets** *see* Carbinoxamine and Pseudoephedrine *on page 218*

♦ **Rondec-TR®** *see* Carbinoxamine and Pseudoephedrine *on page 218*

Ropinirole (roe PIN i role)

Related Information
Parkinson's Agents Comparison *on page 1402*

U.S. Brand Names Requip®

Synonyms Ropinirole Hydrochloride

Therapeutic Category Anti-Parkinson's Agent, Dopamine Agonist; Dopaminergic Agent, Antiparkinson's

Use Treatment of idiopathic Parkinson's disease; in patients with early Parkinson's disease who were not receiving concomitant levodopa therapy as well as in patients with advanced disease on concomitant levodopa

Pregnancy Risk Factor C

Contraindications Hypersensitivity to ropinirole or any component of the formulation

Warnings/Precautions Syncope, sometimes associated with bradycardia, was observed in association with ropinirole in both early Parkinson's disease (without levodopa) patients and advanced Parkinson's disease (with levodopa) patients. Dopamine agonists appear to impair the systemic regulation of blood pressure resulting in postural hypotension, especially during dose escalation. Parkinson's disease patients appear to have an impaired capacity to respond to a postural challenge; use with caution in patients at risk of hypotension (ie, those receiving antihypertensive drugs) or where transient hypotensive episodes would be poorly tolerated (cardiovascular disease or cerebrovascular disease). Parkinson's patients being treated with dopaminergic agonists ordinarily require careful monitoring for signs and symptoms of postural hypotension, especially during dose escalation, and should be informed of this risk. May cause hallucinations. Use with caution in patients with pre-existing dyskinesia, severe hepatic or renal dysfunction.

Patients treated with ropinirole have reported falling asleep while engaging in activities of daily living. Discontinue if significant daytime sleepiness or episodes of falling asleep occur. Pathologic degenerative changes were observed in the retinas of albino rats during studies with this agent, but were not observed in the retinas of albino mice or in other species. The significance of these data for humans remains uncertain.

Although not reported for ropinirole, other dopaminergic agents have been associated with a syndrome resembling neuroleptic malignant syndrome on withdrawal or significant dosage reduction after long-term use. Dopaminergic agents from the ergot class have been associated with fibrotic complications, such as retroperitoneum, lungs, and pleura. No clear association with non-ergot agents (ropinirole) has been established.

Common Adverse Reactions
Early Parkinson's disease (without levodopa):
>10%:
Cardiovascular: Syncope (12%)
Central nervous system: Dizziness (40%), somnolence (40%), fatigue (11%)
Gastrointestinal: Nausea (60%), vomiting (12%)
Miscellaneous: Viral infection (11%)
1% to 10%:
Cardiovascular: Dependent/leg edema (6% to 7%), orthostasis (6%), hypertension (5%), chest pain (4%), flushing (3%), palpitations (3%), peripheral ischemia (3%), hypotension (2%), tachycardia (2%)
Central nervous system: Pain (8%), confusion (5%), hallucinations (5%, dose related), hypoesthesia (4%), amnesia (3%), malaise (3%), vertigo (3%), yawning (3%)
Gastrointestinal: Constipation (>5%), dyspepsia (10%), abdominal pain (6%), xerostomia (5%), anorexia (4%), flatulence (3%)
Genitourinary: Urinary tract infection (5%), impotence (3%)
Hepatic: Elevated alkaline phosphatase (3%)
Neuromuscular & skeletal: Weakness (6%)
Ocular: Abnormal vision (6%), xerophthalmia (2%)
Respiratory: Pharyngitis (6%), rhinitis (4%), sinusitis (4%), dyspnea (3%)
Miscellaneous: Diaphoresis (increased) (6%)

Advanced Parkinson's disease (with levodopa):
>10%:
Central nervous system: Dizziness (26%), somnolence (20%), headache (17%)
Gastrointestinal: Nausea (30%)
Neuromuscular & skeletal: Dyskinesias (34%)
1% to 10%:
Cardiovascular: Syncope (3%), hypotension (2%)
(Continued)

Ropinirole *(Continued)*

Central nervous system: Hallucinations (10%, dose related), aggravated parkinsonism, confusion (9%), pain (5%), paresis (3%), amnesia (5%), anxiety (6%), abnormal dreaming (3%), insomnia

Gastrointestinal: Abdominal pain (9%), vomiting (7%), constipation (6%), diarrhea (5%), dysphagia (2%), flatulence (2%), increased salivation (2%), xerostomia, weight loss (2%)

Genitourinary: Urinary tract infections

Hematologic: Anemia (2%)

Neuromuscular & skeletal: Falls (10%), arthralgia (7%), tremor (6%), hypokinesia (5%), paresthesia (5%), arthritis (3%)

Respiratory: Upper respiratory tract infection (9%), dyspnea (3%)

Miscellaneous: Injury, increased diaphoresis (7%), viral infection, increased drug level (7%)

Other adverse effects (all phase 2/3 trials):

1% to 10%:

Central nervous system: Neuralgia (>1%)

Renal: Elevated BUN (>1%)

Drug Interactions

Cytochrome P450 Effect: Substrate of CYP1A2 (major), 3A4 (minor); **Inhibits** CYP1A2 (weak), 2D6 (strong)

Increased Effect/Toxicity: CYP1A2 inhibitors may increase the levels/effects of ropinirole; example inhibitors include amiodarone, ciprofloxacin, fluvoxamine, ketoconazole, lomeflox-acin, ofloxacin, and rofecoxib. Estrogens may also reduce the metabolism of ropinirole; dosage adjustments may be needed.

Decreased Effect: CYP1A2 inducers may decrease the levels/effects of ropinirole; example inducers include aminoglutethimide, carbamazepine, phenobarbital, and rifampin. Antipsy-chotics, cigarette smoking, and metoclopramide may reduce the effect or serum concentrations of ropinirole.

Mechanism of Action Ropinirole has a high relative *in vitro* specificity and full intrinsic activity at the D_2 and D_3 dopamine receptor subtypes, binding with higher affinity to D_3 than to D_2 or D_4 receptor subtypes; relevance of D_3 receptor binding in Parkinson's disease is unknown. Ropinirole has moderate *in vitro* affinity for opioid receptors. Ropinirole and its metabolites have negligible *in vitro* affinity for dopamine D_1, 5-HT$_1$, 5-HT$_2$, benzodiazepine, GABA, musca-rinic, alpha$_1$-, alpha$_2$-, and beta-adrenoreceptors. Although precise mechanism of action of ropinirole is unknown, it is believed to be due to stimulation of postsynaptic dopamine D_2-type receptors within the caudate-putamen in the brain. Ropinirole caused decreases in systolic and diastolic blood pressure at doses >0.25 mg. The mechanism of ropinirole-induced postural hypotension is believed to be due to D_2-mediated blunting of the noradrenergic response to standing and subsequent decrease in peripheral vascular resistance.

Pharmacodynamics/Kinetics

Absorption: Not affected by food

Distribution: V_d: 525 L

Metabolism: Extensively hepatic via CYP1A2 to inactive metabolites; first-pass effect

Bioavailability: Absolute: 55%

Half-life elimination: ~6 hours

Time to peak: ~1-2 hours; T_{max} increased by 2.5 hours when drug taken with food

Excretion: Clearance: Reduced by 30% in patients >65 years of age

Dosage Adults: Oral: The dosage should be increased to achieve a maximum therapeutic effect, balanced against the principal side effects of nausea, dizziness, somnolence and dyskinesia

Recommended starting dose is 0.25 mg 3 times/day; based on individual patient response, the dosage should be titrated with weekly increments as described below:

• Week 1: 0.25 mg 3 times/day; total daily dose: 0.75 mg

• Week 2: 0.5 mg 3 times/day; total daily dose: 1.5 mg

• Week 3: 0.75 mg 3 times/day; total daily dose: 2.25 mg

• Week 4: 1 mg 3 times/day; total daily dose: 3 mg

After week 4, if necessary, daily dosage may be increased by 1.5 mg per day on a weekly basis up to a dose of 9 mg/day, and then by up to 3 mg/day weekly to a total of 24 mg/day

Removal by hemodialysis is unlikely.

Patient Information Ropinirole can be taken with or without food. Hallucinations can occur and elderly are at a higher risk than younger patients with Parkinson's disease. Postural hypoten-sion may develop with or without symptoms such as dizziness, nausea, syncope, and some-times sweating. Hypotension and/or orthostatic symptoms may occur more frequently during initial therapy or with an increase in dose at any time. Use caution when rising rapidly after sitting or lying down, especially after having done so for prolonged periods and especially at the initiation of treatment with ropinirole. Because of additive sedative effects, caution should be used when taking CNS depressants (eg, benzodiazepines, antipsychotics, antidepres-sants) in combination with ropinirole.

Dosage Forms TAB: 0.25 mg, 0.5 mg, 1 mg, 2 mg, 3 mg, 4 mg, 5 mg

♦ **Ropinirole Hydrochloride** *see* Ropinirole *on page 1113*

Ropivacaine *(roe PIV a kane)*

U.S. Brand Names Naropin®

Synonyms Ropivacaine Hydrochloride

Therapeutic Category Local Anesthetic, Injectable

Use Local anesthetic (injectable) for use in surgery, postoperative pain management, and obstetrical procedures when local or regional anesthesia is needed. It can be administered via local infiltration, epidural block and epidural infusion, or intermittent bolus.

Pregnancy Risk Factor B

Contraindications Hypersensitivity to amide-type local anesthetics (eg, bupivacaine, mepivacaine, lidocaine) or any component of the formulation; septicemia, severe hypotension and for spinal anesthesia, in the presence of complete heart block

Warnings/Precautions Use with caution in patients with liver disease, cardiovascular disease, neurological or psychiatric disorders; it is not recommended for use in emergency situations where rapid administration is necessary

Common Adverse Reactions
>5% (dose and route related):
　Cardiovascular: Hypotension, bradycardia
　Central nervous system: Headache
　Dermatologic: Pruritus
　Gastrointestinal: Nausea, vomiting
　Neuromuscular & skeletal: Back pain, paresthesia
　Miscellaneous: Shivering
1% to 5% (dose related):
　Cardiovascular: Hypertension, tachycardia
　Central nervous system: Dizziness, anxiety, lightheadedness
　Endocrine & metabolic: Hypokalemia
　Neuromuscular & skeletal: Hypoesthesia, rigors, circumoral paresthesia
　Otic: Tinnitus
　Respiratory: Dyspnea

Drug Interactions
　Cytochrome P450 Effect: Substrate (minor) of CYP1A2, 2B6, 2D6, 3A4
　Increased Effect/Toxicity: Other local anesthetics or agents structurally related to the amide-type anesthetics. Increased toxicity possible (but not yet reported) with drugs that decrease cytochrome P450 1A enzyme function. SSRIs may increase ropivacaine levels.

Mechanism of Action Blocks both the initiation and conduction of nerve impulses by decreasing the neuronal membrane's permeability to sodium ions, which results in inhibition of depolarization with resultant blockade of conduction

Pharmacodynamics/Kinetics
Onset of action: Anesthesia (route dependent): 3-15 minutes
Duration (dose and route dependent): 3-15 hours
Metabolism: Hepatic
Half-life elimination: Epidural: 5-7 hours; I.V.: 2.4 hours
Excretion: Urine (86% as metabolites)

Dosage Dose varies with procedure, onset and depth of anesthesia desired, vascularity of tissues, duration of anesthesia, and condition of patient: Adults:

Surgical anesthesia:
　Lumbar epidural: 15-30 mL of 0.5% to 1% solution
　Lumbar epidural block for cesarean section:
　　20-30 mL dose of 0.5% solution
　　15-20 mL dose of 0.75% solution
　Thoracic epidural block: 5-15 mL dose of 0.5% to 0.75% solution
　Major nerve block:
　　35-50 mL dose of 0.5% solution (175-250 mg)
　　10-40 mL dose of 0.75% solution (75-300 mg)
　Field block: 1-40 mL dose of 0.5% solution (5-200 mg)
Labor pain management: Lumbar epidural: Initial: 10-20 mL 0.2% solution; continuous infusion dose: 6-14 mL/hour of 0.2% solution with incremental injections of 10-15 mL/hour of 0.2% solution
Postoperative pain management:
　Lumbar or thoracic epidural: Continuous infusion dose: 6-14 mL/hour of 0.2% solution
　Infiltration/minor nerve block:
　　1-100 mL dose of 0.2% solution
　　1-40 mL dose of 0.5% solution

Dosage Forms INF: 2 mg/mL (100 mL, 200 mL). **INJ, solution:** 2 mg/mL (10 mL, 20 mL); 5 mg/mL (10 mL, 20 mL, 30 mL); 7.5 mg/mL (10 mL, 20 mL); 10 mg/mL (10 mL, 20 mL)

♦ **Ropivacaine Hydrochloride** see Ropivacaine on page 1114
♦ **Rosanil™** see Sulfur and Sulfacetamide on page 1177

Rosiglitazone (roh si GLI ta zone)

Related Information
Hypoglycemic Drugs & Thiazolidinedione Information on page 1378
U.S. Brand Names Avandia®
Therapeutic Category Antidiabetic Agent, Thiazolidinedione; Hypoglycemic Agent, Oral
Use Type 2 diabetes mellitus (noninsulin dependent, NIDDM):
　Monotherapy: Improve glycemic control as an adjunct to diet and exercise
　Combination therapy: In combination with a sulfonylurea, metformin, or insulin when diet, exercise, and a single agent do not result in adequate glycemic control
Pregnancy Risk Factor C
(Continued)

Rosiglitazone *(Continued)*

Contraindications Hypersensitivity to rosiglitazone or any component of the formulation; active liver disease (transaminases >2.5 times the upper limit of normal at baseline); contraindicated in patients who previously experienced jaundice during troglitazone therapy

Warnings/Precautions Should not be used in diabetic ketoacidosis. Mechanism requires the presence of insulin, therefore use in type 1 diabetes is not recommended. Use with caution in premenopausal, anovulatory women; may result in resumption of ovulation, increasing the risk of pregnancy. May result in hormonal imbalance; development of menstrual irregularities should prompt reconsideration of therapy. Use with caution in patients with anemia or depressed leukocyte counts (may reduce hemoglobin, hematocrit, and/or WBC). Use with caution in patients with edema; may increase in plasma volume and/or increase cardiac hypertrophy. Assess for fluid accumulation in patients with unusually rapid weight gain. Avoid use in patients with NYHA Class III or IV heart failure. Discontinue if heart failure develops. Use with caution in patients with elevated transaminases (AST or ALT); see Contraindications and Monitoring. Idiosyncratic hepatotoxicity has been reported with another thiazolidinedione agent (troglitazone). Monitoring should include periodic determinations of liver function.

Common Adverse Reactions Rare cases of hepatocellular injury have been reported in men in their 60s within 2-3 weeks after initiation of rosiglitazone therapy. LFTs in these patients revealed severe hepatocellular injury which responded with rapid improvement of liver function and resolution of symptoms upon discontinuation of rosiglitazone. Patients were also receiving other potentially hepatotoxic medications (*Ann Intern Med*, 2000, 132:121-4; 132:164-6).

>10%: Endocrine & metabolic: Weight gain, increase in total cholesterol, increased LDL-cholesterol, increased HDL-cholesterol

1% to 10%:
   Cardiovascular: Edema (5%)
   Central nervous system: Headache (6%), fatigue (4%)
   Endocrine & metabolic: Hyperglycemia (4%), hypoglycemia (1% to 2%)
   Gastrointestinal: Diarrhea (2%)
   Hematologic: Anemia (2%)
   Neuromuscular & skeletal: Back pain (4%)
   Respiratory: Upper respiratory tract infection (10%), sinusitis (3%)
   Miscellaneous: Injury (8%)

Drug Interactions

Cytochrome P450 Effect: Substrate of CYP2C8/9 (major); **Inhibits** CYP2C8/9 (moderate), 2C19 (weak), 2D6 (weak)

Increased Effect/Toxicity: CYP2C8/9 inhibitors may increase the levels/effects of rosiglitazone; example inhibitors include delavirdine, fluconazole, gemfibrozil, ketoconazole, nicardipine, NSAIDs, pioglitazone, and sulfonamides. Gemfibrozil may increase rosiglitazone levels.

Decreased Effect: CYP2C8/9 inducers may decrease the levels/effects of rosiglitazone; example inducers include carbamazepine, phenobarbital, phenytoin, rifampin, rifapentine, and secobarbital. Bile acid sequestrants may decrease rosiglitazone levels.

Mechanism of Action Thiazolidinedione antidiabetic agent that lowers blood glucose by improving target cell response to insulin, without increasing pancreatic insulin secretion. It has a mechanism of action that is dependent on the presence of insulin for activity.

Pharmacodynamics/Kinetics

Onset of action: Delayed; Maximum effect: Up to 12 weeks
Distribution: V_{dss} (apparent): 17.6 L
Protein binding: 99.8%
Metabolism: Hepatic (99%) via CYP2C8; minor metabolism via CYP2C9
Bioavailability: 99%
Half-life elimination: 3.15-3.59 hours
Time to peak: 1 hour
Excretion: Urine (64%) and feces (23%) as metabolites

Dosage Oral:

Adults: Initial: 4 mg daily as a single daily dose or in divided doses twice daily. If response is inadequate after 12 weeks of treatment, the dosage may be increased to 8 mg daily as a single daily dose or in divided doses twice daily. In clinical trials, the 4 mg twice-daily regimen resulted in the greatest reduction in fasting plasma glucose and Hb A_{1c}. (**Note:** Doses >4 mg in combination with a sulfonylurea or insulin have not been evaluated in clinical trials.)

Elderly: No dosage adjustment is recommended

Dosage adjustment in renal impairment: No dosage adjustment is required

Dosage comment in hepatic impairment: Clearance is significantly lower in hepatic impairment. Therapy should not be initiated if the patient exhibits active liver disease of increased transaminases (>2.5 times the upper limit of normal) at baseline.

Monitoring Parameters Hemoglobin A_{1c} liver enzymes (prior to initiation of therapy, every 2 months for the first year of therapy, then periodically thereafter). Patients with an elevation in ALT >3 times the upper limit of normal should be rechecked as soon as possible. If the ALT levels remain >3 times the upper limit of normal, therapy with rosiglitazone should be discontinued. Monitor serum glucose as recommended by prescriber.

Patient Information May be taken without regard to meals. Follow directions of prescriber. Monitor urine or serum glucose as recommended by prescriber. More frequent monitoring is required during periods of stress, trauma, surgery, pregnancy, increased activity, or exercise. Avoid alcohol. Report chest pain, rapid heartbeat or palpitations, abdominal pain, fever, rash, hypoglycemia reactions, yellowing of skin or eyes, dark urine or light stool, unusual fatigue, or nausea/vomiting.

Dosage Forms TAB: 2 mg, 4 mg, 8 mg

Rosiglitazone and Metformin (roh si GLI ta zone & met FOR min)

U.S. Brand Names Avandamet™

Synonyms Metformin and Rosiglitazone; Metformin Hydrochloride and Rosiglitazone Maleate; Rosiglitazone Maleate and Metformin Hydrochloride

Therapeutic Category Antidiabetic Agent, Combination

Use Management of type 2 diabetes mellitus (noninsulin dependent, NIDDM) in patients who are already treated with the combination of rosiglitazone and metformin, or who are not adequately controlled on metformin alone. Used as an adjunct to diet and exercise to lower the blood glucose when hyperglycemia cannot be controlled satisfactorily by diet and exercise alone

Pregnancy Risk Factor C

Contraindications See individual agents.

Warnings/Precautions See individual agents.

Common Adverse Reactions Also see individual agents. Percentages of adverse effects as reported with the combination product.

>10%:
  Gastrointestinal: Diarrhea (13%)
  Respiratory: Upper respiratory tract infection (16%)

1% to 10%:
  Cardiovascular: Edema (4%)
  Central nervous system: Headache (7%), fatigue (6%)
  Endocrine & metabolic: Hypoglycemia (3%), hyperglycemia (2%)
  Hematologic: Anemia (7%)
  Neuromuscular & skeletal: Arthralgia (5%), back pain (5%)
  Respiratory: Sinusitis (6%)
  Miscellaneous: Viral infection (5%)

Drug Interactions

Cytochrome P450 Effect: Rosiglitazone: **Substrate** of CYP2C8/9 (major); **Inhibits** CYP2C8/9 (moderate), 2C19 (weak), 2D6 (weak)

Increased Effect/Toxicity: See individual agents.

Decreased Effect: See individual agents.

Mechanism of Action See individual agents.

Pharmacodynamics/Kinetics See individual agents.

Dosage Oral:

Adults: Type 2 diabetes mellitus: Initial dose should be based on current dose of rosiglitazone and/or metformin; daily dose should be divided and given with meals

Patients inadequately controlled on **metformin alone**: Initial dose: Rosiglitazone 4 mg/day plus current dose of metformin

Patients inadequately controlled on **rosiglitazone alone**: Initial dose: Metformin 1000 mg/day plus current dose of rosiglitazone

Note: When switching from combination rosiglitazone and metformin as separate tablets: Use current dose

Dose adjustment: Doses may be increased as increments of rosiglitazone 4 mg and/or metformin 500 mg, up to the maximum dose; doses should be titrated gradually.

After a change in the metformin dosage, titration can be done after 1-2 weeks

After a change in the rosiglitazone dosage, titration can be done after 8-12 weeks

Maximum dose: Rosiglitazone 8 mg/metformin 2000 mg daily

Elderly: The initial and maintenance dosing should be conservative, due to the potential for decreased renal function (monitor). Generally, elderly patients should not be titrated to the maximum; do not use in patients ≥80 years unless normal renal function has been established.

Dosage adjustment in renal impairment: Do not use with renal disease or renal dysfunction (serum creatinine ≥1.5 mg/dL in males or ≥1.4 mg/dL in females or abnormal clearance)

Dosage adjustment in hepatic impairment: Do not use with active liver disease or ALT >2.5 times the upper limit of normal

Administration Administer with meals.

Monitoring Parameters Hemoglobin A_{1c}, liver enzymes (prior to initiation of therapy, every 2 months for the first year of therapy, then periodically thereafter). Patients with an elevation in ALT >3 times ULN should be rechecked as soon as possible. If the ALT levels remain >3 times ULN, therapy with rosiglitazone should be discontinued. Serum glucose; vitamin B_{12} and folate if anemia is present.

Reference Range Target range: Adults: Fasting blood glucose: <120 mg/dL; glycosylated hemoglobin: <7%

Patient Information This medication is used to control diabetes; it is not a cure. Other components of treatment plan are important: follow prescribed diet, medication, and exercise regimen. Take exactly as directed; with meal(s) at the same time each day. Do not change dose or discontinue without consulting prescriber. Avoid alcohol while taking this medication; could cause severe reaction. Inform prescriber of all other prescription or OTC medications you are taking; do not introduce new medication without consulting prescriber. Monitor urine or serum glucose as recommended by prescriber. More frequent monitoring is required during periods of stress, trauma, surgery, pregnancy, increased activity or exercise. Maintain regular dietary intake and exercise routine and always carry quick source of sugar with you. You may experience side effects during first weeks of therapy (headache, nausea); consult prescriber if (Continued)

Rosiglitazone and Metformin *(Continued)*

these persist. Report severe or persistent side effects, extended vomiting or flu-like symptoms, skin rash, easy bruising or bleeding, or change in color of urine or stool. Report chest pain, rapid heartbeat or palpitations, abdominal pain, fever, rash, hypoglycemia reactions, yellowing of skin or eyes, dark urine or light stool, or unusual fatigue or nausea/vomiting. Report unusually rapid weight gain; swelling of ankles, legs, or abdomen. Contact your prescriber immediately if you feel very weak, tired or uncomfortable, have unusual muscle pain, trouble breathing, unusual stomach discomfort, are dizzy or lightheaded, or suddenly develop a slow or irregular heartbeat.

Dosage Forms TAB, film coated: 1/500: Rosiglitazone 1 mg and metformin 500 mg; 2/500: Rosiglitazone 2 mg and metformin 500 mg; 4/500: Rosiglitazone 4 mg and metformin 500 mg; 2/1000: Rosiglitazone 2 mg and metformin 1000 mg; 4/1000: Rosiglitazone 4 mg and metformin 1000 mg

♦ **Rosiglitazone Maleate and Metformin Hydrochloride** *see* Rosiglitazone and Metformin *on page 1117*

♦ **Rosula®** *see* Sulfur and Sulfacetamide *on page 1177*

Rosuvastatin *(roe SOO va sta tin)*

Related Information
Lipid-Lowering Agents *on page 1381*

U.S. Brand Names Crestor®

Synonyms Rosuvastatin Calcium

Therapeutic Category Antilipemic Agent, HMG-CoA Reductase Inhibitor; HMG-CoA Reductase Inhibitor

Use Used with dietary therapy for hyperlipidemias to reduce elevations in total cholesterol (TC), LDL-C, apolipoprotein B, and triglycerides (TG) in patients with primary hypercholesterolemia (elevations of 1 or more components are present in Fredrickson type IIa, IIb, and IV hyperlipidemias); treatment of homozygous familial hypercholesterolemia (FH)

Pregnancy Risk Factor X

Contraindications Hypersensitivity to rosuvastatin or any component of the formulation; active liver disease; unexplained persistent elevations of serum transaminases (>3 times ULN); pregnancy; breast-feeding

Warnings/Precautions Secondary causes of hyperlipidemia should be ruled out prior to therapy. Liver function must be monitored by periodic laboratory assessment. Rhabdomyolysis with acute renal failure has occurred. Discontinue in any patient where CPK levels are markedly elevated (>10 times ULN) or if myopathy is diagnosed/suspected. An increased incidence of HMG-CoA reductase inhibitors associated myopathy has been reported during concomitant therapy with fibric acid derivatives, niacin, azole antifungals, and macrolide antibiotics. Temporarily withhold in patients experiencing an acute or serious condition predisposing to renal failure secondary to rhabdomyolysis. Use with caution in patients who consume large amounts of ethanol or have a history of liver disease. Safety and efficacy have not been established in children (limited experience with homozygous FH in patients >8 years of age).

Common Adverse Reactions
2% to 10%:
Cardiovascular: Chest pain, hypertension, peripheral edema
Central nervous system: Headache (6%), depression, dizziness, insomnia, pain
Dermatologic: Rash
Gastrointestinal: Pharyngitis (9%), abdominal pain, constipation, gastroenteritis
Neuromuscular & skeletal: Myalgia (3%), arthritis, arthralgia, hypertonia, paresthesia
Respiratory: Bronchitis, cough
≥1% (Limited to important or life-threatening): Anemia, angina, anxiety, bruising, neuralgia, palpitation, pruritus, vertigo, vomiting

Drug Interactions
Cytochrome P450 Effect: Substrate (minor) of CYP2C9, 3A4
Increased Effect/Toxicity: Cyclosporine may increase serum concentrations of rosuvastatin (up to 10-fold); limit dose to 5 mg/day. Serum concentrations of rosuvastatin may be increased (doubled) during concurrent administration of gemfibrozil; combination should be avoided; limit dose to 10 mg/day. Clofibrate, fenofibrate, or niacin may increase the risk of myopathy and rhabdomyolysis with HMG-CoA reductase inhibitors; the effects on lipids may be additive. The anticoagulant effects of warfarin may be increased by rosuvastatin (monitor). Rosuvastatin increases serum concentrations of hormonal contraceptives (ethinyl estradiol and norgestrel).
Decreased Effect: Plasma concentrations of rosuvastatin may be decreased when given with magnesium/aluminum hydroxide-containing antacids; antacids should be administered at least 2 hours after rosuvastatin. Cholestyramine and colestipol (bile acid sequestrants) may reduce absorption of several HMG-CoA reductase inhibitors; separate administration times by at least 4 hours; cholesterol-lowering effects are additive.

Mechanism of Action Inhibitor of 3-hydroxy-3-methylglutaryl coenzyme A (HMG-CoA) reductase, the rate-limiting enzyme in cholesterol synthesis (reduces the production of mevalonic acid from HMG-CoA); this then results in a compensatory increase in the expression of LDL receptors on hepatocyte membranes and a stimulation of LDL catabolism

Pharmacodynamics/Kinetics
Onset: Within 1 week; maximal at 4 weeks
Distribution: V_d: 134 L
Protein binding: 90%

Metabolism: Hepatic (10%), via CYP2C9 (1 active metabolite identified)
Bioavailability: 20% (high first-pass extraction by liver)
Half-life elimination: 19 hours
Time to peak, plasma: 3-5 hours
Excretion: Feces (90%), primarily as unchanged drug

Dosage Adults: Oral:
Heterozygous familial and nonfamilial hypercholesterolemia; mixed dyslipidemia: Initial: 10 mg once daily (20 mg in patients with severe hypercholesterolemia); after 2 weeks, may be increased to 20 mg once daily; dosing range: 5-40 mg/day (maximum dose: 40 mg once daily)
Homozygous FH: Initial: 20 mg once daily (maximum dose: 40 mg/day)
Dosage adjustment with concomitant medications:
Cyclosporine: Rosuvastatin dose should not exceed 5 mg/day
Gemfibrozil: Rosuvastatin dose should not exceed 10 mg/day
Dosage adjustment in renal impairment:
Mild to moderate impairment: No dosage adjustment required.
Cl_{cr} <30 mL/minute/1.73 m^2: Initial: 5 mg/day; do not exceed 10 mg once daily

Administration May be administered with or without food.

Monitoring Parameters Total cholesterol, LDL, and HDL cholesterol; liver function tests should be determined at baseline (prior to initiation), 3 months following initiation, and 3 months after any increase in dose; baseline CPK (recheck CPK in any patient with symptoms suggestive of myopathy)

Dosage Forms TAB: 5 mg, 10 mg, 20 mg, 40 mg

♦ **Rosuvastatin Calcium** *see* Rosuvastatin *on page 1118*

♦ **Rowasa®** *see* Mesalamine *on page 798*

♦ **Roxanol®** *see* Morphine Sulfate *on page 861*

♦ **Roxanol 100®** *see* Morphine Sulfate *on page 861*

♦ **Roxanol®-T** *see* Morphine Sulfate *on page 861*

♦ **Roxicet™** *see* Oxycodone and Acetaminophen *on page 945*

♦ **Roxicet™ 5/500** *see* Oxycodone and Acetaminophen *on page 945*

♦ **Roxicodone™** *see* Oxycodone *on page 944*

♦ **Roxicodone™ Intensol™** *see* Oxycodone *on page 944*

♦ **RP-6976** *see* Docetaxel *on page 396*

♦ **RP-54274** *see* Riluzole *on page 1098*

♦ **RP-59500** *see* Quinupristin and Dalfopristin *on page 1075*

♦ **r-PA** *see* Reteplase *on page 1088*

♦ **rPDGF-BB** *see* Becaplermin *on page 148*

♦ **RPistinamycin** *see* Quinupristin and Dalfopristin *on page 1075*

♦ **RS-25259** *see* Palonosetron *on page 951*

♦ **RS-25259-197** *see* Palonosetron *on page 951*

♦ **RSV-IGIV** *see* Respiratory Syncytial Virus Immune Globulin (Intravenous) *on page 1087*

♦ **RTCA** *see* Ribavirin *on page 1091*

♦ **RU-486** *see* Mifepristone *on page 839*

♦ **RU-23908** *see* Nilutamide *on page 904*

♦ **RU-38486** *see* Mifepristone *on page 839*

♦ **Rubella, Measles and Mumps Vaccines, Combined** *see* Measles, Mumps, and Rubella Vaccines (Combined) *on page 776*

Rubella Virus Vaccine (Live) (rue BEL a VYE rus vak SEEN, live)

U.S. Brand Names Meruvax® II

Synonyms German Measles Vaccine

Therapeutic Category Vaccine; Vaccine, Live Virus

Use Selective active immunization against rubella; vaccination is routinely recommended for persons from 12 months of age to puberty. All adults, both male and female, lacking documentation of live vaccine on or after first birthday, or laboratory evidence of immunity (particularly women of childbearing age and young adults who work in or congregate in hospitals, colleges, and on military bases) should be vaccinated. Susceptible travelers should be vaccinated.
Note: Trivalent measles - mumps - rubella (MMR) vaccine is the preferred immunizing agent for most children and many adults.

Pregnancy Risk Factor C

Contraindications Hypersensitivity to gelatin or any other component of the vaccine; history of anaphylactic reactions to neomycin; individuals with blood dyscrasias, leukemia, lymphomas, or other malignant neoplasms affecting the bone marrow or lymphatic systems; concurrent immunosuppressive therapy; primary and acquired immunodeficiency states; family history of congenital or hereditary immunodeficiency; active/untreated tuberculosis; current febrile illness or active febrile infection; pregnancy

Warnings/Precautions Immediate treatment for anaphylactic/anaphylactoid reaction should be available during vaccine use. Use with caution in patients with thrombocytopenia and those who develop thrombocytopenia after first dose; thrombocytopenia may worsen. Defer vaccine following blood, plasma, or immune globulin (human) administration; children with HIV infection, who are asymptomatic and not immunosuppressed may be vaccinated.
(Continued)

Rubella Virus Vaccine (Live) *(Continued)*

Common Adverse Reactions All serious adverse reactions must be reported to the U.S. Department of Health and Human Services (DHHS) Vaccine Adverse Event Reporting System (VAERS) 1-800-822-7967.

Frequency not defined.

Cardiovascular: Syncope, vasculitis

Central nervous system: Dizziness, encephalitis, fever, Guillain-Barré syndrome, headache, irritability, malaise, polyneuritis, polyneuropathy

Dermatologic: Angioneurotic edema, erythema multiforme, purpura, rash, Stevens-Johnson syndrome, urticaria

Gastrointestinal: Diarrhea, nausea, sore throat, vomiting

Hematologic: Leukocytosis, thrombocytopenia

Local: Injection site reactions which include burning, induration, pain, redness, stinging, wheal and flare

Neuromuscular & skeletal: Arthralgia/arthritis (variable; highest rates in women, 12% to 26% versus children, up to 3%), myalgia, paresthesia

Ocular: Conjunctivitis, optic neuritis, papillitis, retrobulbar neuritis

Otic: Nerve deafness, otitis media

Respiratory: Bronchial spasm, cough, rhinitis

Miscellaneous: Anaphylactoid reactions, anaphylaxis, regional lymphadenopathy

Drug Interactions

Decreased Effect: The effect of the vaccine may be decreased in individuals who are receiving immunosuppressant drugs (including high-dose systemic corticosteroids). Effect of vaccine may be decreased in given with immune globulin, whole blood or plasma; do not administer with vaccine. Effectiveness may be decreased if given within 30 days of varicella vaccine (effectiveness not decreased when administered simultaneously).

Mechanism of Action Rubella vaccine is a live attenuated vaccine that contains the Wistar Institute RA 27/3 strain, which is adapted to and propagated in human diploid cell culture. Promotes active immunity by inducing rubella hemagglutination-inhibiting antibodies.

Pharmacodynamics/Kinetics Onset of action: Antibodies to vaccine: 2-4 weeks

Dosage Children ≥12 months and Adults: S.C.: 0.5 mL in outer aspect of upper arm; children vaccinated before 12 months of age should be revaccinated. Recommended age for primary immunization is 12-15 months; revaccination with MMR-II is recommended prior to elementary school.

Administration S.C. injection only in outer aspect of upper arm; avoid injection into blood vessel. **Not for I.V. administration.** Federal law requires that the date of administration, the vaccine manufacturer, lot number of vaccine, and the administering person's name, title and address be entered into the patient's permanent medical record.

Patient Information Patient may experience burning or stinging at the injection site; joint pain usually occurs 1-10 weeks after vaccination and persists 1-3 days

Dosage Forms INJ, powder for reconstitution (Wistar RA 27/3 Strain): 1000 TCID$_{50}$

- ♦ **Rubeola Vaccine** *see* Measles Virus Vaccine (Live) *on page 776*
- ♦ **Rubex**® *see* DOXOrubicin *on page 410*
- ♦ **Rubidomycin Hydrochloride** *see* DAUNOrubicin Hydrochloride *on page 346*
- ♦ **Rulox** *see* Aluminum Hydroxide and Magnesium Hydroxide *on page 67*
- ♦ **Rulox No. 1** *see* Aluminum Hydroxide and Magnesium Hydroxide *on page 67*
- ♦ **Rum-K**® *see* Potassium Chloride *on page 1020*
- ♦ **Ryna**® **[OTC] [DSC]** *see* Chlorpheniramine and Pseudoephedrine *on page 263*
- ♦ **Ryna-C**® **[DSC]** *see* Chlorpheniramine, Pseudoephedrine, and Codeine *on page 265*
- ♦ **Rynatan**® *see* Chlorpheniramine and Phenylephrine *on page 262*
- ♦ **Rynatan**® **Pediatric Suspension** *see* Chlorpheniramine and Phenylephrine *on page 262*
- ♦ **Rynatuss**® *see* Chlorpheniramine, Ephedrine, Phenylephrine, and Carbetapentane *on page 263*
- ♦ **Rynatuss**® **Pediatric** *see* Chlorpheniramine, Ephedrine, Phenylephrine, and Carbetapentane *on page 263*
- ♦ **Rythmol**® *see* Propafenone *on page 1049*
- ♦ **Rythmol**® **SR** *see* Propafenone *on page 1049*

Sacrosidase *(sak ROE si dase)*

U.S. Brand Names Sucraid®

Therapeutic Category Enzyme, Gastrointestinal

Use Orphan drug: Oral replacement therapy in sucrase deficiency, as seen in congenital sucrase-isomaltase deficiency (CSID)

Pregnancy Risk Factor C

Contraindications Hypersensitivity to yeast, yeast products, or glycerin

Warnings/Precautions Hypersensitivity reactions to sacrosidase, including bronchospasm, have been reported. Administer initial doses in a setting where acute hypersensitivity reactions may be treated within a few minutes. Skin testing for hypersensitivity may be performed prior to administration to identify patients at risk.

Common Adverse Reactions 1% to 10%: Gastrointestinal: Abdominal pain, vomiting, nausea, diarrhea, constipation

Drug Interactions
Increased Effect/Toxicity: Drug-drug interactions have not been evaluated.
Mechanism of Action Sacrosidase is a naturally-occurring gastrointestinal enzyme which breaks down the disaccharide sucrose to its monosaccharide components. Hydrolysis is necessary to allow absorption of these nutrients.
Pharmacodynamics/Kinetics
  Absorption: Amino acids
  Metabolism: GI tract to individual amino acids
Dosage Oral:
  Infants ≥5 months and Children <15 kg: 8500 int. units (1 mL) per meal or snack
  Children >15 kg and Adults: 17,000 int. units (2 mL) per meal or snack
  Doses should be diluted with 2-4 oz of water, milk, or formula with each meal or snack. Approximately one-half of the dose may be taken before, and the remainder of a dose taken at the completion of each meal or snack.
Administration Do not administer with fruit juices, warm or hot liquids; the solution is fully soluble with water, milk, or formula
Dosage Forms SOLN, oral: 8500 int. units per mL (118 mL)

♦ **Safe Tussin® 30 [OTC]** *see* Guaifenesin and Dextromethorphan *on page 604*
♦ **Saizen®** *see* Human Growth Hormone *on page 620*
♦ **Salagen®** *see* Pilocarpine *on page 1001*
♦ **Salbutamol** *see* Albuterol *on page 45*
♦ **Salflex®** *see* Salsalate *on page 1122*
♦ **Salicylates** *see page 1500*
♦ **Salicylazosulfapyridine** *see* Sulfasalazine *on page 1174*
♦ **Salicylsalicylic Acid** *see* Salsalate *on page 1122*
♦ **SalineX® [OTC]** *see* Sodium Chloride *on page 1146*
♦ **Salk Vaccine** *see* Poliovirus Vaccine (Inactivated) *on page 1013*

Salmeterol (sal ME te role)

Related Information
  Bronchodilators, Comparison of Inhaled Sympathomimetics *on page 1370*
U.S. Brand Names Serevent® [DSC]; Serevent® Diskus®
Synonyms Salmeterol Xinafoate
Therapeutic Category Adrenergic Agonist Agent; Beta₂-Adrenergic Agonist; Bronchodilator
Use Maintenance treatment of asthma and in prevention of bronchospasm (inhalation aerosol in patients >12 years of age; inhalation powder in patients ≥4 years of age) with reversible obstructive airway disease, including patients with symptoms of nocturnal asthma, who require regular treatment with inhaled, short-acting beta₂ agonists; prevention of exercise-induced bronchospasm; maintenance treatment of bronchospasm associated with COPD
Pregnancy Risk Factor C
Contraindications Hypersensitivity to salmeterol, adrenergic amines, or any component of the formulation; need for acute bronchodilation
Warnings/Precautions Salmeterol is not meant to relieve acute asthmatic symptoms. Acute episodes should be treated with short-acting beta₂ agonist. Optimize anti-inflammatory treatment before initiating maintenance treatment with salmeterol. Do not use as a component of chronic therapy without an anti-inflammatory agent. Patient must be instructed to seek medical attention in cases where acute symptoms are not relieved by short-acting beta-agonist (**not** salmeterol) or a previous level of response is diminished. Treatment must not be delayed.

Use caution in patients with cardiovascular disease (arrhythmia or hypertension or CHF), convulsive disorders, diabetes, glaucoma, hyperthyroidism, or hypokalemia. Beta agonists may cause elevation in blood pressure, heart rate, and result in CNS stimulation/excitation. Beta₂ agonists may increase risk of arrhythmia, increase serum glucose, or decrease serum potassium.

In a large, randomized clinical trial (SMART), salmeterol was associated with a small, but statistically significant increase in asthma-related deaths (when added to usual asthma therapy); risk may be greater in African-American patients versus Caucasians.

Do not exceed recommended dose; serious adverse events including fatalities, have been associated with excessive use of inhaled sympathomimetics. Rarely, paradoxical bronchospasm may occur with use of inhaled bronchodilating agents; this should be distinguished from inadequate response. All patients should utilize a spacer device when using a metered-dose inhaler. Safety and efficacy have not been established in children <4 years of age.
Common Adverse Reactions
>10%:
  Central nervous system: Headache
  Endocrine & metabolic: Serum glucose increased, serum potassium decreased
  Respiratory: Pharyngitis
1% to 10%:
  Cardiovascular: Tachycardia, palpitations, elevation or depression of blood pressure, cardiac arrhythmias
  Central nervous system: Nervousness, CNS stimulation, hyperactivity, insomnia, malaise, dizziness
  Gastrointestinal: GI upset, diarrhea, nausea
  Neuromuscular & skeletal: Tremors (may be more common in the elderly), myalgias, back pain, arthralgia
(Continued)

Salmeterol *(Continued)*

Respiratory: Upper respiratory infection, cough, bronchitis

Drug Interactions

Increased Effect/Toxicity:

Increased toxicity (cardiovascular): MAO inhibitors, tricyclic antidepressants

Increased effect: Inhaled corticosteroids: The addition of salmeterol has been demonstrated to improve response to inhaled corticosteroids (as compared to increasing steroid dosage).

Decreased Effect: Beta-adrenergic blockers (eg, propranolol)

Mechanism of Action Relaxes bronchial smooth muscle by selective action on beta$_2$-receptors with little effect on heart rate; because salmeterol acts locally in the lung, therapeutic effect is not predicted by plasma levels

Pharmacodynamics/Kinetics

Onset of action: 5-20 minutes (average 10 minutes)

Peak effect: 2-4 hours

Duration: 12 hours

Protein binding: 94% to 98%

Metabolism: Hepatically hydroxylated

Half-life elimination: 3-4 hours

Dosage

Note: Do **not** use spacer with inhalation powder

Asthma, maintenance and prevention:

Inhalation, aerosol: Children ≥12 years and Adults: 42 mcg (2 puffs) twice daily (12 hours apart)

Inhalation, powder (Serevent® Diskus®): Children ≥4 years and Adults: One inhalation (50 mcg) twice daily

Exercise-induced asthma, prevention:

Inhalation, aerosol: Children ≥12 years and Adults: 42 mcg (2 puffs) 30-60 minutes prior to exercise; additional doses should not be used for 12 hours

Inhalation, powder (Serevent® Diskus®): Children ≥4 years and Adults: One inhalation (50 mcg) at least 30 minutes prior to exercise; additional doses should not be used for 12 hours

COPD (maintenance treatment of associated bronchospasm):

Inhalation, aerosol: Adults: 42 micrograms (2 puffs) twice daily (morning and evening, 12 hours apart)

Inhalation, powder (Serevent® Diskus®): Adults: One inhalation (50 mcg) twice daily, ~12 hours apart

Administration Inhalation: Shake well before use. **Not** to be used for the relief of acute attacks.

Monitoring Parameters FEV$_1$, peak flow, and/or other pulmonary function tests; blood pressure, heart rate; CNS stimulation; serum glucose, serum potassium. Monitor for increased use of short-acting beta$_2$-agonist inhalers; may be marker of a deteriorating asthma condition.

Patient Information Do not use to treat acute symptoms; do not exceed the prescribed dose of salmeterol. Do not stop using inhaled or oral corticosteroids without medical advice even if you "feel better". Shake well before using; avoid spraying in eyes. Remove the canister and rinse the plastic case and cap under warm water and dry daily. Store canister with nozzle end down.

Dosage Forms AERO, oral inhalation (Serevent®) [DSC]: 25 mcg/spray (6.5 g, 13 g). **POWDER,** oral inhalation (Serevent® Diskus®): 50 mcg (28s, 60s)

♦ **Salmeterol and Fluticasone** *see* Fluticasone and Salmeterol *on page 550*

♦ **Salmeterol Xinafoate** *see* Salmeterol *on page 1121*

Salsalate *(SAL sa late)*

Related Information

Salicylates *on page 1500*

U.S. Brand Names Amigesic®; Disalcid® [DSC]; Mono-Gesic®; Salflex®

Synonyms Disalicylic Acid; Salicylsalicylic Acid

Therapeutic Category Analgesic, Salicylate; Anti-inflammatory Agent; Antipyretic; Nonsteroidal Anti-inflammatory Drug (NSAID), Oral; Salicylate

Use Treatment of minor pain or fever; arthritis

Pregnancy Risk Factor C/D (3rd trimester)

Contraindications Hypersensitivity to salsalate or any component of the formulation; GI ulcer or bleeding; pregnancy (3rd trimester)

Warnings/Precautions Use with caution in patients with platelet and bleeding disorders, dehydration, renal dysfunction, erosive gastritis, or peptic ulcer disease, previous nonreaction does not guarantee future safe taking of medication; do not use aspirin in children <16 years of age for chickenpox or flu symptoms due to the association with Reye's syndrome

Common Adverse Reactions

>10%: Gastrointestinal: Nausea, heartburn, stomach pains, dyspepsia

1% to 10%:

Central nervous system: Fatigue

Dermatologic: Rash

Gastrointestinal: Gastrointestinal ulceration

Hematologic: Hemolytic anemia

Neuromuscular & skeletal: Weakness

Respiratory: Dyspnea

Miscellaneous: Anaphylactic shock

Drug Interactions

Increased Effect/Toxicity: Increased effect/toxicity of oral anticoagulants, hypoglycemics, and methotrexate.

Decreased Effect: Decreased effect with urinary alkalinizers, antacids, and corticosteroids. Decreased effect of uricosurics and spironolactone.

Mechanism of Action Inhibits prostaglandin synthesis, acts on the hypothalamus heat-regulating center to reduce fever, blocks prostaglandin synthetase action which prevents formation of the platelet-aggregating substance thromboxane A_2

Pharmacodynamics/Kinetics

Onset of action: Therapeutic: 3-4 days of continuous dosing
Absorption: Complete from small intestine
Metabolism: Hepatically hydrolyzed to two moles of salicylic acid (active)
Half-life elimination: 7-8 hours
Excretion: Primarily urine

Dosage Adults: Oral: 3 g/day in 2-3 divided doses

Dosing comments in renal impairment: In patients with end-stage renal disease undergoing hemodialysis: 750 mg twice daily with an additional 500 mg after dialysis

Patient Information Do not self-medicate with other drug products containing aspirin; use antacids to relieve upset stomach; watch for bleeding gums or any signs of GI bleeding; take with food or milk to minimize GI distress; report ringing in ears or persistent GI pain

Dosage Forms TAB: 500 mg, 750 mg; (Amigesic®, Disalcid® [DSC]): 500 mg, 750 mg; (Mono-Gesic®, Salflex®): 750 mg

- ◆ **Salt** see Sodium Chloride on page 1146
- ◆ **Salt Poor Albumin** see Albumin on page 44
- ◆ **Sal-Tropine™** see Atropine on page 133
- ◆ **Sandimmune®** see CycloSPORINE on page 323
- ◆ **Sandostatin®** see Octreotide on page 920
- ◆ **Sandostatin LAR®** see Octreotide on page 920
- ◆ **Sansert® [DSC]** see Methysergide on page 827
- ◆ **Santyl®** see Collagenase on page 313

Saquinavir (sa KWIN a veer)

Related Information

Antiretroviral Therapy for HIV Infection on page 1448

U.S. Brand Names Fortovase®; Invirase®

Synonyms Saquinavir Mesylate

Therapeutic Category Antiretroviral Agent, Protease Inhibitor; Protease Inhibitor

Use Treatment of HIV infection in selected patients; used in combination with at least two other antiretroviral agents

Pregnancy Risk Factor B

Contraindications Hypersensitivity to saquinavir or any component of the formulation; exposure to direct sunlight without sunscreen or protective clothing; coadministration with cisapride, astemizole, triazolam, midazolam, or ergot derivatives

Warnings/Precautions The indication for saquinavir for the treatment of HIV infection is based on changes in surrogate markers. At present, there are no results from controlled clinical trials evaluating its effect on patient survival or the clinical progression of HIV infection (ie, occurrence of opportunistic infections or malignancies); use caution in patients with hepatic insufficiency; safety and efficacy have not been established in children <16 years of age. May exacerbate pre-existing hepatic dysfunction; use with caution in patients with hepatitis B or C and in cirrhosis. Not recommended for use in patients receiving lovastatin or simvastatin; use caution with atorvastatin or cerivastatin. May be associated with fat redistribution (buffalo hump, increased abdominal girth, breast engorgement, facial atrophy). Avoid concurrent use of St John's wort (may lead to loss of virologic response and/or resistance).

Common Adverse Reactions Protease inhibitors cause dyslipidemia which includes elevated cholesterol and triglycerides and a redistribution of body fat centrally to cause increased abdominal girth, buffalo hump, facial atrophy, and breast enlargement. These agents also cause hyperglycemia.

1% to 10%:
Dermatologic: Rash
Endocrine & metabolic: Hyperglycemia
Gastrointestinal: Diarrhea, abdominal discomfort, nausea, abdominal pain, buccal mucosa ulceration
Neuromuscular & skeletal: Paresthesia, weakness, increased CPK

Drug Interactions

Cytochrome P450 Effect: Substrate of CYP2D6 (minor), 3A4 (major); **Inhibits** CYP2C8/9 (weak), 2C19 (weak), 2D6 (weak), 3A4 (moderate)

Increased Effect/Toxicity:

Decreased effect: Rifampin may decrease saquinavir's plasma levels and AUC by 40% to 80%; other enzyme inducers may induce saquinavir's metabolism (eg, phenobarbital, phenytoin, dexamethasone, carbamazepine); may decrease delavirdine concentrations

Increased effect: Ketoconazole significantly increases plasma levels and AUC of saquinavir; as a known, although not potent inhibitor of the cytochrome P450 system, saquinavir may decrease the metabolism of astemizole, as well as cisapride and ergot derivatives (and result in rare but serious effects including cardiac arrhythmias); other drugs which may

(Continued)

Saquinavir *(Continued)*

have increased adverse effects if coadministered with saquinavir include benzodiaze-pines (midazolam and triazolam), calcium channel blockers, clindamycin, dapsone, ergot alkaloids, and quinidine. Both clarithromycin and saquinavir levels/effects may be increased with coadministration. Delavirdine may increase concentration; ritonavir may increase AUC >17-fold; concurrent administration of nelfinavir results in increase in nelfinavir (18%) and saquinavir (mean: 392%).

Saquinavir increased serum concentrations of simvastatin, lovastatin, and atorvastatin; risk of myopathy/rhabdomyolysis may be increased. Use cautiously with HMG-CoA reductase inhibitors. Avoid use with simvastatin and lovastatin. Use caution with atorvastatin and cerivastatin (fluvastatin and pravastatin are not metabolized by CYP3A4).

Sildenafil serum concentrations are increased in concurrent therapy (limit sildenafil dosage to 25 mg). Tadalafil serum concentrations may be increased by saquinavir; a maximum tadalafil dose of 10 mg in 72 hours is recommended with strong CYP3A4 inhibitors. Vardenafil serum concentrations may be increased by saquinavir; specific dosage adjust-ment guidelines have not been established; recommendations for other strong CYP3A4 inhibitors include vardenafil dose not to exceed 2.5 mg in 24 hours.

Decreased Effect: Nevirapine, rifabutin, rifampin, phenobarbital, phenytoin, dexametha-sone, and carbamazepine may decrease saquinavir concentrations. Saquinavir may decrease delavirdine concentrations.

Mechanism of Action As an inhibitor of HIV protease, saquinavir prevents the cleavage of viral polyprotein precursors which are needed to generate functional proteins in and maturation of HIV-infected cells

Pharmacodynamics/Kinetics

Absorption: Poor; increased with high fat meal; Fortovase® has improved absorption over Invirase®

Distribution: V_d: 700 L; does not distribute into CSF

Protein binding, plasma: ~98%

Metabolism: Extensively hepatic via CYP3A4; extensive first-pass effect

Bioavailability: Invirase®: ~4%; Fortovase®: 12% to 15%

Excretion: Feces (81% to 88%), urine (1% to 3%) within 5 days

Dosage Oral:

Children and Adolescents <16 years: Safety and efficacy have not been established; dosages of 33-50 mg/kg/dose 3 times/day are under study

Adults: **Note:** Fortovase® and Invirase® are not bioequivalent and should not be used inter-changeably; only Fortovase® should be used to initiate therapy:

Fortovase®: Six 200 mg capsules (1200 mg) 3 times/day within 2 hours after a meal in combination with a nucleoside analog

Invirase®: Three 200 mg capsules (600 mg) 3 times/day within 2 hours after a full meal in combination with a nucleoside analog

Note: Dosage adjustment of either Fortovase® or Invirase® in combination with ritonavir: 400 mg twice daily

Note: Dosage adjustments of Fortovase® when administered in combination therapy:

Delavirdine: Fortovase® 800 mg 3 times/day

Lopinavir and ritonavir (Kaletra™): Fortovase® 800 mg twice daily

Nelfinavir: Fortovase® 800 mg 3 times/day or 1200 mg twice daily

Elderly: Clinical studies did not include sufficient numbers of patients ≥65 years of age; use caution due to increased frequency of organ dysfunction

Monitoring Parameters Monitor viral load, CD4 count, triglycerides, cholesterol, glucose

Patient Information Saquinavir is not a cure for HIV infection nor has it been found to reduce the transmission of HIV; opportunistic infections and other illnesses associated with AIDS may still occur; take saquinavir within 2 hours after a full meal; avoid direct sunlight when taking saquinavir. Do not take any prescription medications, over-the-counter products or herbal products, especially St John's wort, without consulting prescriber.

Dosage Forms CAP, as mesylate (Invirase®): 200 mg. **CAP, soft gelatin, as base** (Fortovase®): 200 mg

♦ **Saquinavir Mesylate** *see Saquinavir on page 1123*

♦ **Sarafem™** *see Fluoxetine on page 538*

Sargramostim *(sar GRAM oh stim)*

Related Information

Filgrastim *on page 522*

U.S. Brand Names Leukine®

Synonyms GM-CSF; Granulocyte-Macrophage Colony Stimulating Factor; rGM-CSF

Therapeutic Category Colony-Stimulating Factor

Use

Myeloid reconstitution after autologous bone marrow transplantation: Non-Hodgkin's lymphoma (NHL), acute lymphoblastic leukemia (ALL), Hodgkin's lymphoma, metastatic breast cancer

Myeloid reconstitution after allogeneic bone marrow transplantation

Peripheral stem cell transplantation: Metastatic breast cancer, non-Hodgkin's lymphoma, Hodgkin's lymphoma, multiple myeloma

Orphan drug:

Acute myelogenous leukemia (AML) following induction chemotherapy in older adults to shorten time to neutrophil recovery and to reduce the incidence of severe and life-threatening infections and infections resulting in death

Bone marrow transplant (allogeneic or autologous) failure or engraftment delay
Safety and efficacy of GM-CSF given simultaneously with cytotoxic chemotherapy have not been established. Concurrent treatment may increase myelosuppression.

Pregnancy Risk Factor C

Contraindications Hypersensitivity to sargramostim, yeast-derived products, or any component of the formulation; concurrent myelosuppressive chemotherapy or radiation therapy. The solution for injection contains benzyl alcohol and should not be used in neonates.

Warnings/Precautions Simultaneous administration, or administration 24 hours preceding/following cytotoxic chemotherapy or radiotherapy is not recommended. Use with caution in patients with pre-existing cardiac problems, hypoxia, fluid retention, pulmonary infiltrates or CHF, renal or hepatic impairment.

Rapid increase in peripheral blood counts: If ANC >20,000/mm^3 or platelets >500,000/mm^3, decrease dose by 50% or discontinue drug (counts will fall to normal within 3-7 days after discontinuing drug)

Growth factor potential: Use with caution with myeloid malignancies. Precaution should be exercised in the usage of GM-CSF in any malignancy with myeloid characteristics. GM-CSF can potentially act as a growth factor for any tumor type, particularly myeloid malignancies. Tumors of nonhematopoietic origin may have surface receptors for GM-CSF.

There is a "first-dose effect" (refer to Adverse Reactions for details) which is rarely seen with the first dose and does not usually occur with subsequent doses.

Common Adverse Reactions
>10%:
Cardiovascular: Hypotension, tachycardia, flushing, and syncope may occur with the first dose of a cycle ("first-dose effect"); peripheral edema (11%)
Central nervous system: Headache (26%)
Dermatologic: Rash, alopecia
Endocrine & metabolic: Polydipsia
Gastrointestinal: Diarrhea (52% to 89%), stomatitis, mucositis
Local: Local reactions at the injection site (~50%)
Neuromuscular & skeletal: Myalgia (18%), arthralgia (21%), bone pain
Renal: Increased serum creatinine (14%)
Respiratory: Dyspnea (28%)
1% to 10%:
Cardiovascular: Transient supraventricular arrhythmias; chest pain; capillary leak syndrome; pericardial effusion (4%)
Central nervous system: Headache
Gastrointestinal: Nausea, vomiting
Hematologic: Leukocytosis, thrombocytopenia
Neuromuscular & skeletal: Weakness
Respiratory: Cough; pleural effusion (1%)

Drug Interactions
Increased Effect/Toxicity: Lithium, corticosteroids may potentiate myeloproliferative effects.

Mechanism of Action Stimulates proliferation, differentiation and functional activity of neutrophils, eosinophils, monocytes, and macrophages, as indicated: See table.

Comparative Effects — G-CSF vs GM-CSF

Proliferation/Differentiation	G-CSF (Filgrastim)	GM-CSF (Sargramostim)
Neutrophils	Yes	Yes
Eosinophils	No	Yes
Macrophages	No	Yes
Neutrophil migration	Enhanced	Inhibited

Pharmacodynamics/Kinetics
Onset of action: Increase in WBC: 7-14 days
Duration: WBCs return to baseline within 1 week of discontinuing drug
Half-life elimination: 2 hours
Time to peak, serum: S.C.: 1-2 hours

Dosage
Children and Adults: I.V. infusion over ≥2 hours or S.C.
Existing clinical data suggest that starting GM-CSF between 24 and 72 hours subsequent to chemotherapy may provide optimal neutrophil recover; continue therapy until the occurrence of an absolute neutrophil count of 10,000/µL after the neutrophil nadir
The available data suggest that rounding the dose to the nearest vial size may enhance patient convenience and reduce costs without clinical detriment
Myeloid reconstitution after peripheral stem cell, allogeneic or autologous bone marrow transplant: I.V.: 250 mcg/m^2/day for 21 days to begin 2-4 hours after the marrow infusion on day 0 of autologous bone marrow transplant or ≥24 hours after chemotherapy or 12 hours after last dose of radiotherapy
If a severe adverse reaction occurs, reduce or temporarily discontinue the dose until the reaction abates
If blast cells appear or progression of the underlying disease occurs, disrupt treatment
Interrupt or reduce the dose by half if ANC is >20,000 cells/mm^3
(Continued)

Sargramostim *(Continued)*

Patients should not receive sargramostim until the postmarrow infusion ANC is <500 cells/mm^3

Neutrophil recovery following chemotherapy in AML: I.V.: 250 mcg/m^2/day over a 4-hour period starting approximately day 11 or 4 days following the completion of induction chemotherapy, if day 10 bone marrow is hypoblastic with <5% blasts

If a second cycle of chemotherapy is necessary, administer ~4 days after the completion of chemotherapy if the bone marrow is hypoblastic with <5% blasts

Continue sargramostim until ANC is >1500 cells/mm^3 for consecutive days or a maximum of 42 days

Discontinue sargramostim immediately if leukemic regrowth occurs

If a severe adverse reaction occurs, reduce the dose by 50% or temporarily discontinue the dose until the reaction abates

Mobilization of peripheral blood progenitor cells: I.V.: 250 mcg/m^2/day over 24 hours or S.C. once daily

Continue the same dose through the period of PBPC collection

The optimal schedule for PBPC collection has not been established (usually begun by day 5 and performed daily until protocol specified targets are achieved)

If WBC >50,000 cells/mm^3, reduce the dose by 50%

If adequate numbers of progenitor cells are not collected, consider other mobilization therapy

Postperipheral blood progenitor cell transplantation: I.V.: 250 mcg/m^2/day over 24 hours or S.C. once daily beginning immediately following infusion of progenitor cells and continuing until ANC is >1500 for 3 consecutive days is attained

BMT failure or engraftment delay: I.V.: 250 mcg/m^2/day for 14 days as a 2-hour infusion

The dose can be repeated after 7 days off therapy if engraftment has not occurred

If engraftment still has not occurred, a third course of 500 mcg/m^2/day for 14 days may be tried after another 7 days off therapy; if there is still no improvement, it is unlikely that further dose escalation will be beneficial

If a severe adverse reaction occurs, reduce or temporarily discontinue the dose until the reaction abates

If blast cells appear or disease progression occurs, discontinue treatment

Administration Sargramostim is administered as a subcutaneous injection or intravenous infusion; intravenous infusion should be over at least 2 hours; continuous infusions may be more effective than short infusion or bolus injection. An in-line membrane filter should not be used for intravenous infusion.

Monitoring Parameters Vital signs, weight, CBC with differential, platelets, renal/liver function tests, especially with previous dysfunction, WBC with differential, pulmonary function

Reference Range Excessive leukocytosis: ANC >20,000/mm^3 or WBC >50,000 cells/mm^3

Patient Information You may experience bone pain (request analgesic), nausea and vomiting (small frequent meals may help), hair loss (reversible). Report fever, chills, unhealed sores, severe bone pain, difficulty breathing, swelling or pain at infusion site. Avoid crowds or exposure to infected persons; you will be susceptible to infection.

Dosage Forms INJ, powder for reconstitution: 250 mcg. INJ, solution: 500 mcg/mL (1 mL)

- ◆ **Sarnol®-HC [OTC]** *see* Hydrocortisone *on page 632*
- ◆ **SB-265805** *see* Gemifloxacin *on page 584*
- ◆ **SC 33428** *see* Idarubicin *on page 648*
- ◆ **SCH 13521** *see* Flutamide *on page 546*
- ◆ **S-Citalopram** *see* Escitalopram *on page 455*
- ◆ **Scleromate™** *see* Morrhuate Sodium *on page 863*
- ◆ **Scopace™** *see* Scopolamine *on page 1126*

Scopolamine *(skoe POL a meen)*

Related Information

Cycloplegic Mydriatics Comparison *on page 1375*

U.S. Brand Names Isopto® Hyoscine; Scopace™; Transderm Scōp®

Synonyms Hyoscine; Scopolamine Hydrobromide

Therapeutic Category Anticholinergic Agent; Anticholinergic Agent, Ophthalmic; Anticholinergic Agent, Transdermal; Ophthalmic Agent, Mydriatic

Use Preoperative medication to produce amnesia and decrease salivary and respiratory secretions; to produce cycloplegia and mydriasis; treatment of iridocyclitis; prevention of motion sickness; prevention of nausea/vomiting associated with anesthesia or opiate analgesia (patch); symptomatic treatment of postencephalitic parkinsonism and paralysis agitans (oral); inhibits excessive motility and hypertonus of the gastrointestinal tract in such conditions as the irritable colon syndrome, mild dysentery, diverticulitis, pylorospasm, and cardiospasm

Pregnancy Risk Factor C

Contraindications Hypersensitivity to scopolamine or any component of the formulation; narrow-angle glaucoma; acute hemorrhage; paralytic ileus, GI or GU obstruction; thyrotoxicosis; tachycardia secondary to cardiac insufficiency; myasthenia gravis

Warnings/Precautions Use with caution with hepatic or renal impairment since adverse CNS effects occur more often in these patients; use with caution in infants and children since they may be more susceptible to adverse effects of scopolamine; use with caution in patients with GI obstruction; anticholinergic agents are not well tolerated in the elderly and their use should be avoided when possible

Common Adverse Reactions Frequency not defined.

Ophthalmic: Note: Systemic adverse effects have been reported following ophthalmic administration.
Cardiovascular: Vascular congestion, edema
Central nervous system: Drowsiness
Dermatologic: Eczematoid dermatitis
Ocular: Blurred vision, photophobia, local irritation, increased intraocular pressure, follicular conjunctivitis, exudate
Respiratory: Congestion
Systemic:
Cardiovascular: Orthostatic hypotension, ventricular fibrillation, tachycardia, palpitations
Central nervous system: Confusion, drowsiness, headache, loss of memory, ataxia, fatigue
Dermatologic: Dry skin, increased sensitivity to light, rash
Endocrine & metabolic: Decreased flow of breast milk
Gastrointestinal: Constipation, xerostomia, dry throat, dysphagia, bloated feeling, nausea, vomiting
Genitourinary: Dysuria
Local: Irritation at injection site
Neuromuscular & skeletal: Weakness
Ocular: Increased intraocular pain, blurred vision
Respiratory: Dry nose, diaphoresis (decreased)

Drug Interactions
Increased Effect/Toxicity: Additive adverse effects with other anticholinergic agents.
Decreased Effect: Decreased effect of acetaminophen, levodopa, ketoconazole, digoxin, riboflavin, and potassium chloride in wax matrix preparations.

Mechanism of Action Blocks the action of acetylcholine at parasympathetic sites in smooth muscle, secretory glands and the CNS; increases cardiac output, dries secretions, antagonizes histamine and serotonin

Pharmacodynamics/Kinetics
Onset of action: Oral, I.M.: 0.5-1 hour; I.V.: 10 minutes
Peak effect: 20-60 minutes; may take 3-7 days for full recovery; transdermal: 24 hours
Duration: Oral, I.M.: 4-6 hours; I.V.: 2 hours
Absorption: Well absorbed from all routes
Protein binding, plasma: Reversible
Metabolism: Hepatic
Excretion: Urine

Dosage
Preoperatively:
Children: I.M., S.C.: 6 mcg/kg/dose (maximum: 0.3 mg/dose) or 0.2 mg/m^2 may be repeated every 6-8 hours **or** alternatively:
4-7 months: 0.1 mg
7 months to 3 years: 0.15 mg
3-8 years: 0.2 mg
8-12 years: 0.3 mg
Adults:
I.M., I.V., S.C.: 0.3-0.65 mg; may be repeated every 4-6 hours
Transdermal patch: Apply 2.5 cm^2 patch to hairless area behind ear the night before surgery or 1 hour prior to cesarean section (the patch should be applied no sooner than 1 hour before surgery for best results and removed 24 hours after surgery)
Motion sickness: Transdermal: Children >12 years and Adults: Apply 1 disc behind the ear at least 4 hours prior to exposure and every 3 days as needed; effective if applied as soon as 2-3 hours before anticipated need, best if 12 hours before
Ophthalmic:
Refraction:
Children: Instill 1 drop of 0.25% to eye(s) twice daily for 2 days before procedure
Adults: Instill 1-2 drops of 0.25% to eye(s) 1 hour before procedure
Iridocyclitis:
Children: Instill 1 drop of 0.25% to eye(s) up to 3 times/day
Adults: Instill 1-2 drops of 0.25% to eye(s) up to 4 times/day
Oral: Parkinsonism, spasticity, motion sickness: 0.4-0.8 mg as a range; the dosage may be cautiously increased in parkinsonism and spastic states.

Administration
I.V.: Dilute with an equal volume of sterile water and administer by direct I.V. injection over 2-3 minutes
Transdermal: Topical disc is programmed to deliver *in vivo* 1 mg over 3 days. Once applied, do not remove the patch for 3 full days. Apply to hairless area of skin behind the ear.

Patient Information Report any changes of vision; wait 5 minutes after instilling ophthalmic preparation before using any other drops, do not blink excessively, after instilling ophthalmic preparation, apply pressure to the side of the nose near the eye to minimize systemic absorption; put patch on day before traveling; once applied, do not remove the patch for 3 full days; may cause drowsiness, dizziness, and blurred vision; may impair coordination and judgment; report any CNS effects; apply patch behind ear

Dosage Forms INJ, solution: 0.4 mg/mL (1 mL). **SOLN, ophthalmic** (Isopto® Hyoscine): 0.25% (5 mL, 15 mL). **TAB, soluble** (Scopace™): 0.4 mg. **TRANSDERMAL SYSTEM** (Transderm Scōp®): 1.5 mg (4s)

♦ **Scopolamine and Phenylephrine** *see* Phenylephrine and Scopolamine *on page 994*
♦ **Scopolamine Hydrobromide** *see* Scopolamine *on page 1126*

- **Scopolamine, Hyoscyamine, Atropine, and Phenobarbital** *see Hyoscyamine, Atropine, Scopolamine, and Phenobarbital on page 643*
- **Scot-Tussin® Sugar Free Expectorant [OTC]** *see Guaifenesin on page 603*
- **SDZ ENA 713** *see Rivastigmine on page 1107*
- **SeaMist® [OTC]** *see Sodium Chloride on page 1146*
- **Seasonale®** *see Ethinyl Estradiol and Levonorgestrel on page 484*

Secobarbital (see koe BAR bi tal)
U.S. Brand Names Seconal®
Synonyms Quinalbarbitone Sodium; Secobarbital Sodium
Therapeutic Category Barbiturate; Hypnotic; Sedative
Use Preanesthetic agent; short-term treatment of insomnia
Restrictions C-II
Pregnancy Risk Factor D
Dosage Oral:
  Children:
    Preoperative sedation: 2-6 mg/kg (maximum dose: 100 mg/dose) 1-2 hours before procedure
    Sedation: 6 mg/kg/day divided every 8 hours
  Adults:
    Hypnotic: Usual: 100 mg/dose at bedtime; range 100-200 mg/dose
    Preoperative sedation: 100-300 mg 1-2 hours before procedure
Dosage Forms CAP: 100 mg

- **Secobarbital and Amobarbital** *see Amobarbital and Secobarbital on page 84*
- **Secobarbital Sodium** *see Secobarbital on page 1128*
- **Seconal®** *see Secobarbital on page 1128*
- **Sectral®** *see Acebutolol on page 23*
- **Selective Serotonin Reuptake Inhibitors (SSRIs) Pharmacokinetics** *see page 1403*

Selegiline (se LE ji leen)
Related Information
  Parkinson's Agents Comparison *on page 1402*
U.S. Brand Names Eldepryl®
Synonyms Deprenyl; L-Deprenyl; Selegiline Hydrochloride
Therapeutic Category Antidepressant, Monoamine Oxidase Inhibitor; Anti-Parkinson's Agent, MAO Type B Inhibitor
Use Adjunct in the management of parkinsonian patients in which levodopa/carbidopa therapy is deteriorating
Unlabeled/Investigational Use Early Parkinson's disease; attention-deficit/hyperactivity disorder (ADHD); negative symptoms of schizophrenia; extrapyramidal symptoms; depression; Alzheimer's disease (studies have shown some improvement in behavioral and cognitive performance)
Pregnancy Risk Factor C
Contraindications Hypersensitivity to selegiline or any component of the formulation; concomitant use of meperidine
Warnings/Precautions Increased risk of nonselective MAO inhibition occurs with doses >10 mg/day; it is a monoamine oxidase inhibitor type "B", there should not be a problem with tyramine-containing products as long as the typical doses are employed, however, rare reactions have been reported. Use with tricyclic antidepressants and SSRIs has also been associated with rare reactions and should generally be avoided. Addition to levodopa therapy may result in exacerbation of levodopa adverse effects, requiring a reduction in levodopa dosage. The possibility of a suicide attempt is inherent in major depression and may persist until remission occurs. Use caution in high-risk patients during initiation of therapy. Prescriptions should be written for the smallest quantity consistent with good patient care.
Common Adverse Reactions Frequency not defined.
  Cardiovascular: Orthostatic hypotension, hypertension, arrhythmias, palpitations, angina, tachycardia, peripheral edema, bradycardia, syncope
  Central nervous system: Hallucinations, dizziness, confusion, anxiety, depression, drowsiness, behavior/mood changes, dreams/nightmares, fatigue, delusions
  Dermatologic: Rash, photosensitivity
  Gastrointestinal: Xerostomia, nausea, vomiting, constipation, weight loss, anorexia, diarrhea, heartburn
  Genitourinary: Nocturia, prostatic hyperplasia, urinary retention, sexual dysfunction
  Neuromuscular & skeletal: Tremor, chorea, loss of balance, restlessness, bradykinesia
  Ocular: Blepharospasm, blurred vision
  Miscellaneous: Diaphoresis (increased)
Drug Interactions
  Cytochrome P450 Effect: Substrate of CYP1A2 (minor), 2A6 (minor), 2B6 (major), 2C8/9 (major), 2D6 (minor), 3A4 (minor); **Inhibits** CYP1A2 (weak), 2A6 (weak), 2C8/9 (weak), 2C19 (weak), 2D6 (weak), 2E1 (weak), 3A4 (weak)
  Increased Effect/Toxicity: CYP2B6 inhibitors may increase the levels/effects of selegiline; example inhibitors include desipramine, paroxetine, and sertraline. CYP2C8/9 inhibitors may increase the levels/effects of selegiline; example inhibitors include delavirdine, fluconazole, gemfibrozil, ketoconazole, nicardipine, NSAIDs, and sulfonamides. Concurrent

use of selegiline (high dose) in combination with amphetamines, methylphenidate, dextromethorphan, fenfluramine, meperidine, nefazodone, sibutramine, tramadol, trazodone, tricyclic antidepressants, and venlafaxine may result in serotonin syndrome; these combinations are best avoided. Concurrent use of selegiline with an SSRI may result in mania or hypertension; it is generally best to avoid these combinations. Selegiline (>10 mg/day) in combination with tyramine (cheese, ethanol) may increase the pressor response; avoid high tyramine-containing foods in patients receiving >10 mg/day of selegiline. The toxicity of levodopa (hypertension), lithium (hyperpyrexia), and reserpine may be increased by MAO inhibitors.

Decreased Effect: CYP2B6 inducers may decrease the levels/effects of selegiline; example inducers include carbamazepine, nevirapine, phenobarbital, phenytoin, and rifampin. CYP2C8/9 inducers may decrease the levels/effects of selegiline; example inducers include carbamazepine, phenobarbital, phenytoin, rifampin, rifapentine, and secobarbital.

Mechanism of Action Potent monoamine oxidase (MAO) type-B inhibitor; MAO type B plays a major role in the metabolism of dopamine; selegiline may also increase dopaminergic activity by interfering with dopamine reuptake at the synapse

Pharmacodynamics/Kinetics
Onset of action: Therapeutic: Within 1 hour
Duration: 24-72 hours
Half-life elimination: Steady state: 10 hours
Metabolism: Hepatic to amphetamine and methamphetamine

Dosage Oral:
Children and Adolescents: ADHD (unlabeled use): 5-15 mg/day
Adults: Parkinson's disease: 5 mg twice daily with breakfast and lunch or 10 mg in the morning
Elderly: Parkinson's disease: Initial: 5 mg in the morning, may increase to a total of 10 mg/day

Monitoring Parameters Blood pressure, symptoms of parkinsonism

Patient Information Do not exceed daily doses of 10 mg; report any involuntary movements or CNS agitation; explain the tyramine reaction to patients and tell them to report severe headaches or other unusual symptoms to physician

Dosage Forms CAP (Eldepryl®): 5 mg. **TAB:** 5 mg

♦ **Selegiline Hydrochloride** see Selegiline on page 1128

Selenium (se LEE nee um)
U.S. Brand Names Selepen®
Therapeutic Category Trace Element, Parenteral
Use Trace metal supplement
Pregnancy Risk Factor C
Contraindications Hypersensitivity to selenium or any component of the formulation
Common Adverse Reactions Frequency not defined.
Central nervous system: Lethargy
Dermatologic: Alopecia or hair discoloration
Gastrointestinal: Vomiting following long-term use on damaged skin; abdominal pain, garlic breath
Local: Irritation
Neuromuscular & skeletal: Tremor
Miscellaneous: Diaphoresis
Mechanism of Action Part of glutathione peroxidase which protects cell components from oxidative damage due to peroxidases produced in cellular metabolism
Pharmacodynamics/Kinetics Excretion: Urine, feces, lungs, skin
Dosage I.V. in TPN solutions:
Children: 3 mcg/kg/day
Adults:
Metabolically stable: 20-40 mcg/day
Deficiency from prolonged TPN support: 100 mcg/day for 24 and 21 days
Dosage Forms INJ, solution: 40 mcg/mL (10 mL); (Selepen®): 40 mcg/mL (10 mL, 30 mL).
TAB: 50 mcg, 100 mcg, 200 mcg

Selenium Sulfide (se LEE nee um SUL fide)
U.S. Brand Names Exsel® [DSC]; Head & Shoulders® Intensive Treatment [OTC]; Selsun®; Selsun Blue® 2-in-1 Treatment [OTC]; Selsun Blue® Balanced Treatment [OTC]; Selsun Blue® Medicated Treatment [OTC]; Selsun Blue® Moisturizing Treatment [OTC]
Therapeutic Category Antiseborrheic Agent, Topical; Shampoo; Topical Skin Product
Use Treatment of itching and flaking of the scalp associated with dandruff, to control scalp seborrheic dermatitis; treatment of tinea versicolor
Pregnancy Risk Factor C
Contraindications Hypersensitivity to selenium or any component of the formulation
Warnings/Precautions Do not use on damaged skin to avoid any systemic toxicity; avoid topical use in very young children; safety of topical in infants has not been established
Common Adverse Reactions Frequency not defined.
Central nervous system: Lethargy
Dermatologic: Alopecia or hair discoloration, unusual dryness or oiliness of scalp
Gastrointestinal: Vomiting following long-term use on damaged skin, abdominal pain, garlic breath
Local: Irritation
Neuromuscular & skeletal: Tremor
Miscellaneous: Diaphoresis
(Continued)

Selenium Sulfide *(Continued)*

Mechanism of Action May block the enzymes involved in growth of epithelial tissue

Pharmacodynamics/Kinetics

Absorption: Topical: None through intact skin, but can be absorbed through damaged skin

Excretion: Urine, feces, lungs, skin

Dosage Topical:

Dandruff, seborrhea: Massage 5-10 mL into wet scalp, leave on scalp 2-3 minutes, rinse thoroughly

Tinea versicolor: Apply the 2.5% lotion to affected area and lather with small amounts of water; leave on skin for 10 minutes, then rinse thoroughly; apply every day for 7 days

Administration Shake well before using. May damage jewelry; remove before treatment. For external use only; do not apply to broken or inflamed skin.

Patient Information Topical formulations are for external use only; notify prescriber if condition persists or worsens; avoid contact with eyes; thoroughly rinse after application. May damage jewelry; remove before treatment. If used before or after bleaching, tinting, or permanent waving of the hair, rinse hair thoroughly (at least 5 minutes) to avoid or decrease hair discoloration.

Dosage Forms LOTION, topical: 2.5% (120 mL). **SHAMP, topical:** 1% (210 mL); (Exsel® [DSC], Selsun®): 2.5% (120 mL); (Head & Shoulders® Intensive Treatment): 1% (400 mL); (Selsun Blue® Balanced Treatment, Selsun Blue® Medicated Treatment, Selsun Blue® Moisturizing Treatment, Selsun Blue® 2-in-1 Treatment): 1% (120 mL, 210 mL, 330 mL)

♦ **Selepen®** *see Selenium on page 1129*

♦ **Selsun®** *see Selenium Sulfide on page 1129*

♦ **Selsun Blue® 2-in-1 Treatment [OTC]** *see Selenium Sulfide on page 1129*

♦ **Selsun Blue® Balanced Treatment [OTC]** *see Selenium Sulfide on page 1129*

♦ **Selsun Blue® Medicated Treatment [OTC]** *see Selenium Sulfide on page 1129*

♦ **Selsun Blue® Moisturizing Treatment [OTC]** *see Selenium Sulfide on page 1129*

♦ **Semprex®-D** *see Acrivastine and Pseudoephedrine on page 35*

♦ **Senna and Docusate** *see Docusate and Senna on page 398*

♦ **Senna-S** *see Docusate and Senna on page 398*

♦ **Senokot-S® [OTC]** *see Docusate and Senna on page 398*

♦ **Sensorcaine®** *see Bupivacaine on page 186*

♦ **Sensorcaine®-MPF** *see Bupivacaine on page 186*

♦ **Septra®** *see Sulfamethoxazole and Trimethoprim on page 1173*

♦ **Septra® DS** *see Sulfamethoxazole and Trimethoprim on page 1173*

♦ **Ser-Ap-Es [DSC]** *see Hydralazine, Hydrochlorothiazide, and Reserpine on page 625*

♦ **Serax®** *see Oxazepam on page 939*

♦ **Serentil®** *see Mesoridazine on page 800*

♦ **Serevent® [DSC]** *see Salmeterol on page 1121*

♦ **Serevent® Diskus®** *see Salmeterol on page 1121*

Sermorelin Acetate *(ser moe REL in AS e tate)*

U.S. Brand Names Geref® [DSC]; Geref® Diagnostic

Therapeutic Category Diagnostic Agent, Pituitary Function

Use

Geref® Diagnostic: For evaluation of the ability of the pituitary gland to secrete growth hormone (GH)

Geref® injection: Treatment of idiopathic growth hormone deficiency in children

Orphan drug: Sermorelin has been designated an orphan product for AIDS-associated catabolism or weight loss, and as an adjunct to gonadotropin for ovulation induction.

Pregnancy Risk Factor C

Contraindications Hypersensitivity to sermorelin acetate, mannitol, or any component of the formulation

Warnings/Precautions Not used for the diagnosis of acromegaly. Not recommended for the treatment of GH deficiency due to intracranial lesions. Thyroid status should be evaluated prior to treatment and periodically during therapy with sermorelin.

Common Adverse Reactions Frequency not defined.

Cardiovascular: Tightness in the chest

Central nervous system: Headache, dizziness, hyperactivity, somnolence

Dermatologic: Transient flushing of the face, urticaria

Gastrointestinal: Dysphagia, nausea, vomiting

Local: Pain, redness, and/or swelling at the injection site

Drug Interactions

Decreased Effect: The test should not be conducted in the presence of drugs that directly affect the pituitary secretion of somatotropin. These include preparations that contain or release somatostatin, insulin, glucocorticoids, or cyclooxygenase inhibitors such as ASA or indomethacin. Somatotropin levels may be transiently elevated by clonidine, levodopa, and insulin-induced hypoglycemia. Response to sermorelin may be blunted in patients who are receiving muscarinic antagonists (atropine) or who are hypothyroid or being treated with antithyroid medications such as propylthiouracil. Obesity, hyperglycemia, and elevated plasma fatty acids generally are associated with subnormal GH responses to sermorelin. Exogenous growth hormone therapy should be discontinued at least 1 week before administering the test.

Pharmacodynamics/Kinetics Onset of action: Peak response: Diagnostic: Children 30 ± 27 minutes; Adults: 35 ± 29 minutes

Dosage

Children: Treatment of idiopathic growth hormone deficiency: S.C.: 30 mcg/kg at bedtime; discontinue when epiphyses are fused

Children and Adults: Diagnostic: I.V.: 1 mcg/kg as a single dose in the morning following an overnight fast

Note: Response to diagnostic test may be decreased in patients >40 years

Administration Diagnostic: Venous blood samples for growth hormone determinations should be drawn 15 minutes before and immediately prior to sermorelin administration. Administer a bolus of 1 mcg/kg/body weight sermorelin I.V. over 1-3 minutes at a final concentration not to exceed 100 mcg/mL followed by a 3 mL normal saline flush. Draw venous blood samples for growth hormone determinations at 15, 30, 45, and 60 minutes after sermorelin administration.

Monitoring Parameters Height (every 6 months); thyroid function

Reference Range Peak growth hormone levels of >7-10 mcg/L are rarely achieved upon provocation in patients with classic growth hormone deficiency; a marked growth hormone response in these patients (>10-12 mcg/L) is strongly suggestive of hypothalamic dysfunction, as opposed to pituitary dysfunction

Dosage Forms INJ, powder for reconstitution (Geref® [DSC]): 0.5 mg, 1 mg; (Geref® Diagnostic): 50 mcg

♦ **Seromycin® Pulvules®** *see* CycloSERINE *on page 322*

♦ **Serophene®** *see* ClomiPHENE *on page 296*

♦ **Seroquel®** *see* Quetiapine *on page 1069*

♦ **Serostim®** *see* Human Growth Hormone *on page 620*

Sertraline (SER tra leen)

Related Information

Antidepressant Agents Comparison *on page 1359*

Selective Serotonin Reuptake Inhibitors (SSRIs) Pharmacokinetics *on page 1403*

U.S. Brand Names Zoloft®

Synonyms Sertraline Hydrochloride

Therapeutic Category Antidepressant, Selective Serotonin Reuptake Inhibitor (SSRI)

Use Treatment of major depression; obsessive-compulsive disorder (OCD); panic disorder; post-traumatic stress disorder (PTSD); premenstrual dysphoric disorder (PMDD); social anxiety disorder

Unlabeled/Investigational Use Eating disorders; generalized anxiety disorder (GAD); impulse control disorders

Pregnancy Risk Factor C

Contraindications Hypersensitivity to sertraline or any component of the formulation; use of MAO inhibitors within 14 days; concurrent use of pimozide; concurrent use of sertraline oral concentrate with disulfiram

Warnings/Precautions Do not use in combination with MAO inhibitor or within 14 days of discontinuing treatment or initiating treatment with a MAO inhibitor due to the risk of serotonin syndrome; use with caution in patients with pre-existing seizure disorders, patients in whom weight loss is undesirable, patients with recent myocardial infarction, unstable heart disease, hepatic or renal impairment, patients taking other psychotropic medications, agitated or hyperactive patients as drug may produce or activate mania or hypomania. The possibility of a suicide attempt is inherent in major depression and may persist until remission occurs. Use caution in high-risk patients during initiation of therapy. Prescriptions should be written for the smallest quantity consistent with good patient care. Use oral concentrate formulation with caution in patients with latex sensitivity; dropper dispenser contains dry natural rubber. Monitor growth in pediatric patients. Safety and efficacy in pediatric patients <6 years of age have been established only in the treatment of OCD.

Common Adverse Reactions

>10%:

Central nervous system: Insomnia, somnolence, dizziness, headache, fatigue

Gastrointestinal: Xerostomia, diarrhea, nausea

Genitourinary: Ejaculatory disturbances

1% to 10%:

Cardiovascular: Palpitations

Central nervous system: Agitation, anxiety, nervousness

Dermatologic: Rash

Endocrine & metabolic: Decreased libido

Gastrointestinal: Constipation, anorexia, dyspepsia, flatulence, vomiting, weight gain

Genitourinary: Micturition disorders

Neuromuscular & skeletal: Tremors, paresthesia

Ocular: Visual difficulty, abnormal vision

Otic: Tinnitus

Miscellaneous: Diaphoresis (increased)

Additional adverse reactions reported in pediatric patients (frequency >2%): Aggressiveness, epistaxis, hyperkinesia, purpura, sinusitis, urinary incontinence

Drug Interactions

Cytochrome P450 Effect: Substrate of CYP2B6 (major), 2C8/9 (major), 2C19 (major), 2D6 (minor), 3A4 (major); **Inhibits** CYP1A2 (weak), 2B6(moderate), 2C8/9 (weak), 2C19 (moderate), 2D6 (moderate), 3A4 (moderate)

(Continued)

Sertraline *(Continued)*

Increased Effect/Toxicity: Sertraline should not be used with nonselective MAO inhibitors (phenelzine, isocarboxazid) or other drugs with MAO inhibition (linezolid); fatal reactions have been reported. Wait 5 weeks after stopping sertraline before starting a nonselective MAO inhibitor and 2 weeks after stopping an MAO inhibitor before starting sertraline. Concurrent selegiline has been associated with mania, hypertension, or serotonin syndrome (risk may be reduced relative to nonselective MAO inhibitors). Sertraline may increase serum concentrations of pimozide; concurrent use is contraindicated.

CYP2B6 inhibitors may increase the levels/effects of sertraline; example inhibitors include desipramine and paroxetine. CYP2C8/9 inhibitors may increase the levels/effects of sertraline; example inhibitors include delavirdine, fluconazole, gemfibrozil, ketoconazole, nicardipine, NSAIDs, and sulfonamides. CYP2C19 inhibitors may increase the levels/effects of sertraline; example inhibitors include delavirdine, fluconazole, fluvoxamine, gemfibrozil, isoniazid, omeprazole, and ticlopidine.

Combined used of SSRIs and amphetamines, buspirone, meperidine, nefazodone, serotonin agonists (such as sumatriptan), sibutramine, other SSRIs, sympathomimetics, ritonavir, tramadol, and venlafaxine may increase the risk of serotonin syndrome. Sertraline may increase serum levels/effects of benzodiazepines (alprazolam and diazepam), carbamazepine, carvedilol, clozapine, cyclosporine (and possibly tacrolimus), dextromethorphan, digoxin, haloperidol, HMG-CoA reductase inhibitors (lovastatin and simvastatin - increasing the risk of rhabdomyolysis, despite sertraline's weak inhibition) phenytoin, propafenone, trazodone, tricyclic antidepressants, and valproic acid. Concurrent lithium may increase risk of nephrotoxicity. Risk of hyponatremia may increase with concurrent use of loop diuretics (bumetanide, furosemide, torsemide). Sertraline may increase the hypoprothrombinemic response to warfarin.

Combined use of sumatriptan (and other serotonin agonists) may result in toxicity; weakness, hyper-reflexia, and incoordination have been observed with sumatriptan and SSRIs. In addition, concurrent use may theoretically increase the risk of serotonin syndrome; includes sumatriptan, naratriptan, rizatriptan, and zolmitriptan.

Phenothiazines: CYP3A4 inhibitors (including sertraline) may inhibit the metabolism of thioridazine or mesoridazine, resulting in increased plasma levels and increasing the risk of QT_c interval prolongation. This may lead to serious ventricular arrhythmias, such as torsade de pointes-type arrhythmias and sudden death. Do not use together. Wait at least 5 weeks after discontinuing sertraline prior to starting thioridazine.

Decreased Effect: CYP2B6 inducers may decrease the levels/effects of sertraline; example inducers include carbamazepine, nevirapine, phenobarbital, phenytoin, and rifampin. CYP2C8/9 inducers may decrease the levels/effects of sertraline; example inducers include carbamazepine, phenobarbital, phenytoin, rifampin, rifapentine, and secobarbital. CYP2C19 inducers may decrease the levels/effects of sertraline; example inducers include aminoglutethimide, carbamazepine, phenytoin, and rifampin. Sertraline may decrease the metabolism of tolbutamide; monitor for changes in glucose control.

Mechanism of Action Antidepressant with selective inhibitory effects on presynaptic serotonin (5-HT) reuptake and only very weak effects on norepinephrine and dopamine neuronal uptake. *In vitro* studies demonstrate no significant affinity for adrenergic, cholinergic, GABA, dopaminergic, histaminergic, serotonergic, or benzodiazepine receptors.

Pharmacodynamics/Kinetics

Absorption: Slow

Protein binding: High

Metabolism: Hepatic; extensive first-pass metabolism

Bioavailability: 88%

Half-life elimination: Parent drug: 26 hours; Metabolite N-desmethylsertraline: 66 hours (range: 62-104 hours)

Time to peak, plasma: 4.5-8.4 hours

Excretion: Urine and feces

Dosage Oral:

Children and Adolescents: OCD:

6-12 years: Initial: 25 mg once daily

13-17 years: Initial: 50 mg once daily

Note: May increase daily dose, at intervals of not less than 1 week, to a maximum of 200 mg/day. If somnolence is noted, give at bedtime.

Adults:

Depression/OCD: Oral: Initial: 50 mg/day (see "Note" above)

Panic disorder, PTSD, social anxiety disorder: Initial: 25 mg once daily; increase to 50 mg once daily after 1 week (see "Note" above)

PMDD: 50 mg/day either daily throughout menstrual cycle **or** limited to the luteal phase of menstrual cycle, depending on physician assessment. Patients not responding to 50 mg/day may benefit from dose increases (50 mg increments per menstrual cycle) up to 150 mg/day when dosing throughout menstrual cycle **or** up to 100 mg day when dosing during luteal phase only. If a 100 mg/day dose has been established with luteal phase dosing, a 50 mg/day titration step for 3 days should be utilized at the beginning of each luteal phase dosing period.

Elderly: Depression/OCD: Start treatment with 25 mg/day in the morning and increase by 25 mg/day increments every 2-3 days if tolerated to 50-100 mg/day; additional increases may be necessary; maximum dose: 200 mg/day

Dosage adjustment/comment in renal impairment: Multiple-dose pharmacokinetics are unaffected by renal impairment.
Hemodialysis: Not removed by hemodialysis
Dosage adjustment/comment in hepatic impairment: Sertraline is extensively metabolized by the liver; caution should be used in patients with hepatic impairment; a lower dose or less frequent dosing should be used.

Administration Oral concentrate: Must be diluted before use. Immediately before administration, use the dropper provided to measure the required amount of concentrate; mix with 4 ounces ($^1/_2$ cup) of water, ginger ale, lemon/lime soda, lemonade, or orange juice **only**. Do not mix with any other liquids than these. The dose should be taken immediately after mixing; do not mix in advance. A slight haze may appear after mixing; this is normal. **Note:** Use with caution in patients with latex sensitivity; dropper dispenser contains dry natural rubber.

Monitoring Parameters Monitor nutritional intake and weight

Patient Information If you are currently on another antidepressant drug, please notify your prescriber. Although sertraline has not been shown to increase the effects of alcohol, it is recommended that you refrain from drinking while on this medication. If you are pregnant or intend becoming pregnant while on this drug, please alert your prescriber to this fact. You may experience some weight loss, but it is usually minimal.

Dosage Forms Note: Available as sertraline hydrochloride; mg strength refers to sertraline.
SOLN, oral concentrate: 20 mg/mL (60 mL). **TAB:** 25 mg, 50 mg, 100 mg

♦ **Sertraline Hydrochloride** *see* Sertraline *on page 1131*
♦ **Serutan® [OTC]** *see* Psyllium *on page 1063*
♦ **Serzone®** *see* Nefazodone *on page 887*

Sevelamer (se VEL a mer)

U.S. Brand Names Renagel®
Synonyms Sevelamer Hydrochloride
Therapeutic Category Antidote, Hyperphosphatemia; Phosphate Binder
Use Reduction of serum phosphorous in patients with end-stage renal disease
Pregnancy Risk Factor C
Contraindications Hypersensitivity to sevelamer or any component of the formulation; hypophosphatemia; bowel obstruction
Warnings/Precautions Use with caution in patients with gastrointestinal disorders including dysphagia, swallowing disorders, severe gastrointestinal motility disorders, or major gastrointestinal surgery. May cause reductions in vitamin D, E, K, and folic acid absorption. Long-term studies of carcinogenic potential have not been completed. Capsules should not be taken apart or chewed.

Common Adverse Reactions
>10%:
  Cardiovascular: Hypotension (11%), thrombosis (10%)
  Central nervous system: Headache (10%)
  Endocrine & metabolic: Decreased absorption of vitamins D, E, K and folic acid
  Gastrointestinal: Diarrhea (16%), dyspepsia (5% to 11%), vomiting (12%)
  Neuromuscular & skeletal: Pain (13%)
  Miscellaneous: Infection (15%)
1% to 10%:
  Cardiovascular: Hypertension (9%)
  Gastrointestinal: Nausea (7%), flatulence (4%), diarrhea (4%), constipation (2%)
  Respiratory: Cough (4%)

Drug Interactions
  Decreased Effect: Sevelamer may bind to some drugs in the gastrointestinal tract and decrease their absorption. When changes in absorption of oral medications may have significant clinical consequences (such as antiarrhythmic and antiseizure medications), these medications should be taken at least 1 hour before or 3 hours after a dose of sevelamer.

Mechanism of Action Sevelamer (a polymeric compound) binds phosphate within the intestinal lumen, limiting absorption and decreasing serum phosphate concentrations without altering calcium, aluminum, or bicarbonate concentrations

Pharmacodynamics/Kinetics
  Absorption: None
  Excretion: Feces

Dosage Adults: Oral: Patients not taking a phosphate binder: 800-1600 mg 3 times/day with meals; the initial dose may be based on serum phosphorous:
  (Phosphorous: Initial Dose:)
    >6.0 mg/dL and <7.5 mg/dL: 800 mg 3 times/day
    ≥7.5 mg/dL and <9.0 mg/dL: 1200-1600 mg 3 times/day
    ≥9.0 mg/dL: 1600 mg 3 times/day
  Dosage should be adjusted based on serum phosphorous concentration, with a goal of lowering to <6.0 mg/dL; maximum daily dose studied was equivalent to 30 capsules/day

Administration Must be administered with meals
Monitoring Parameters Serum phosphorus
Patient Information Take as directed, with meals. Do not break or chew capsules or tablets (contents will expand in water). You may experience headache or dizziness (use caution when driving or engaging in tasks requiring alertness until response to drug is known); upset stomach, nausea, or vomiting (frequent small meals, frequent mouth care, or sucking hard candy may help); diarrhea (yogurt or buttermilk may help); hypotension (use caution when
(Continued)

Sevelamer *(Continued)*

rising from sitting or lying position or when climbing stairs or bending over); or mild neuromuscular pain or stiffness (mild analgesic may help). Report persistent adverse reactions.

Dosage Forms CAP: 403 mg. **TAB:** 400 mg, 800 mg

♦ **Sevelamer Hydrochloride** *see Sevelamer on page 1133*

Sevoflurane *(see voe FLOO rane)*

U.S. Brand Names Ultane®

Therapeutic Category General Anesthetic

Use Induction and maintenance of general anesthesia in pediatric and adult patients (inhalation); sevoflurane is less irritating to the airway and therefore is useful to induce general anesthesia

Pregnancy Risk Factor B

Contraindications Previous hypersensitivity to sevoflurane, other halogenated anesthetics, or any component of the formulation; known or suspected susceptibility to malignant hyperthermia

Warnings/Precautions Decrease in blood pressure is dose dependent. Respiration is depressed; hypoxic pulmonary vasoconstriction is blunted which may lead to increased pulmonary shunt. Hypoxemia induced increase in ventilation is abolished at low concentration of sevoflurane. It dilates the cerebral vasculature which can, in certain conditions, increase intracranial pressure. Sevoflurane may trigger malignant hyperthermia. Sevoflurane is degraded in CO_2 absorbers to produce an olefin concentration (compound A), which has caused nephrotoxicity in rats. It is recommended that sevoflurane exposure not exceed 2 MAC-hours at flow rates of 1 to <2 L/minute. Fresh gas flow rates <1 L/minute are not recommended. Use with caution in patients at risk for seizures; seizures have been reported in children and young adults.

Common Adverse Reactions ≥1%:

Cardiovascular: Bradycardia, hypotension, tachycardia, hypertension

Central nervous system: Agitation, headache, somnolence, dizziness, fever, early emergence movement, hypothermia

Gastrointestinal: Nausea (25%) and vomiting (18%), increased salivation

Respiratory: Laryngospasm, airway obstruction, breath holding, increased cough

Miscellaneous: Shivering

Drug Interactions

Cytochrome P450 Effect: Substrate of CYP2A6 (minor), 2B6 (minor), 2E1 (major), 3A4 (minor)

Increased Effect/Toxicity: CYP2E1 inhibitors may increase the levels/effects of sevoflurane; example inhibitors include disulfiram, isoniazid, and miconazole. Administration of 50% N_2O reduces the minimum alveolar concentration (MAC) equivalent dose of sevoflurane by 50% in adults and 25% in children; benzodiazepines and opioids also reduce the MAC of sevoflurane. Sevoflurane may increase the nephrotoxicity of aminoglycosides. Excessive hypotension may occur when combined with antihypertensive drugs. Sevoflurane potentiates the actions of nondepolarizing, neuromuscular-blocking agents.

Pharmacodynamics/Kinetics Sevoflurane has a low blood/gas partition coefficient and therefore is associated with a rapid onset of anesthesia and recovery

Onset of action: Time to induction: Within 2 minutes

Duration: 4-14 minutes

Metabolism: 3% to 5% producing an increase in plasma and urinary fluoride concentration (rarely associated with hepatic or renal injury)

Excretion: Exhaled gases (97%)

Dosage Minimum alveolar concentration (MAC), the concentration at which 50% of patients do not respond to surgical incision, is 2.6% (25 years of age) for sevoflurane. The concentration at which amnesia and loss of awareness occur (MAC - awake) is 0.6%. MAC is reduced in the elderly (50% reduction by age 80).

Dosage adjustment in renal impairment: Safety for use in patients with creatinine >15 mg/dL has not been established.

Dosage adjustment in hepatic impairment: Safety and efficacy have not been established in patients with severe hepatic dysfunction.

Administration Via sevoflurane-specific calibrated vaporizers

Monitoring Parameters Blood pressure, temperature, heart rate, neuromuscular function, oxygen saturation, end-tidal CO_2 and end-tidal sevoflurane concentrations should be monitored prior to and throughout anesthesia.

Dosage Forms LIQ, inhalation: 250 mL

Sibutramine *(si BYOO tra meen)*

Related Information

Obesity Treatment Guidelines for Adults *on page 1482*

U.S. Brand Names Meridia®

Synonyms Sibutramine Hydrochloride Monohydrate

Therapeutic Category Anorexiant

Use Management of obesity, including weight loss and maintenance of weight loss, and should be used in conjunction with a reduced calorie diet

Restrictions C-IV; recommended only for obese patients with a body mass index ≥30 kg/m² or ≥27 kg/m² in the presence of other risk factors such as hypertension, diabetes, and/or dyslipidemia

Pregnancy Risk Factor C

Contraindications Hypersensitivity to sibutramine or any component of the formulation; during or within 2 weeks of MAO inhibitors (eg, phenelzine, selegiline) or concomitant centrally-acting appetite suppressants; anorexia nervosa; uncontrolled or poorly controlled hypertension; congestive heart failure; coronary heart disease; conduction disorders (arrhythmias); stroke; concurrent use of serotonergic agents (eg, SSRIs sumatriptan, dihydroergotamine, dextromethorphan, meperidine, pentazocine, fentanyl, lithium)

Warnings/Precautions Use with caution in severe renal impairment or severe hepatic dysfunction, seizure disorder, hypertension, gallstones, narrow-angle glaucoma, nursing mothers, elderly patients. Primary pulmonary hypertension (PPH), a rare and frequently fatal pulmonary disease, has been reported to occur in patients receiving other agents with serotonergic activity which have been used as anorexiants. Although not reported in clinical trials, it is possible that sibutramine may share this potential, and patients should be monitored closely. Stimulants may unmask tics in individuals with coexisting Tourette's syndrome.

Serious, potentially life-threatening toxicities may occur when thyroid hormones (at dosages above usual daily hormonal requirements) are used in combination with sympathomimetic amines to induce weight loss. Treatment of obesity is not an approved use for thyroid hormone.

Common Adverse Reactions

>10%

Central nervous system: Headache, insomnia

Gastrointestinal: Anorexia, xerostomia, constipation

Respiratory: Rhinitis

1% to 10%

Cardiovascular: Tachycardia, vasodilation, hypertension, palpitations, chest pain, edema

Central nervous system: Migraine, dizziness, nervousness, anxiety, depression, somnolence, CNS stimulation, emotional liability

Dermatologic: Rash

Endocrine & metabolic: Dysmenorrhea

Gastrointestinal: Increased appetite, nausea, dyspepsia, gastritis, vomiting, taste perversion, abdominal pain

Neuromuscular & skeletal: Weakness, arthralgia, back pain

Respiratory: Pharyngitis, sinusitis, cough, laryngitis

Miscellaneous: Diaphoresis, flu-like syndrome, allergic reactions, thirst

Drug Interactions

Cytochrome P450 Effect: Substrate of CYP3A4 (major)

Increased Effect/Toxicity: Serotonergic agents such as buspirone, selective serotonin reuptake inhibitors (eg, citalopram, fluoxetine, fluvoxamine, paroxetine, sertraline), sumatriptan (and similar serotonin agonists), dihydroergotamine, lithium, tryptophan, some opioid/analgesics (eg, meperidine, tramadol), and venlafaxine, when combined with sibutramine may result in serotonin syndrome. Dextromethorphan, MAO inhibitors and other drugs that can raise the blood pressure (eg decongestants, centrally-acting weight loss products, amphetamines, and amphetamine-like compounds) can increase the possibility of sibutramine-associated cardiovascular complications. Sibutramine may increase serum levels of tricyclic antidepressants. Theoretically, inhibitors of CYP3A4 (including ketoconazole, itraconazole, erythromycin) may increase sibutramine levels.

Decreased Effect: Inducers of CYP3A4 (including phenytoin, phenobarbital, carbamazepine, and rifampin) theoretically may reduce sibutramine serum concentrations.

Mechanism of Action Sibutramine blocks the neuronal uptake of norepinephrine and, to a lesser extent, serotonin and dopamine

Pharmacodynamics/Kinetics

Absorption: Rapid

Protein binding, plasma: 94% to 97%

Metabolism: Hepatic; undergoes first-pass metabolism via CYP3A4

Time to peak: Within 3-4 hours

Excretion: Primarily urine (77%); feces

Dosage Adults ≥16 years: Initial: 10 mg once daily; after 4 weeks may titrate up to 15 mg once daily as needed and tolerated (may be used for up to 2 years, per manufacturer labeling)

Monitoring Parameters Do initial blood pressure and heart rate evaluation and then monitor regularly during therapy. If patient has sustained increases in either blood pressure or pulse rate, consider discontinuing or reducing the dose of the drug.

Patient Information Maintain proper medical follow-up and inform prescriber of any potential concomitant medications including over-the-counter products you are taking, especially weight loss products, antidepressants, antimigraine drugs, decongestants, lithium, tryptophan, antitussives, or ergot derivatives

Dosage Forms CAP: 5 mg, 10 mg, 15 mg

♦ **Sibutramine Hydrochloride Monohydrate** *see* Sibutramine *on page 1134*

♦ **Siladryl® Allergy [OTC]** *see* DiphenhydrAMINE *on page 383*

♦ **Silafed® [OTC]** *see* Triprolidine and Pseudoephedrine *on page 1273*

♦ **Silapap® Children's [OTC]** *see* Acetaminophen *on page 24*

♦ **Silapap® Infants [OTC]** *see* Acetaminophen *on page 24*

♦ **Sildec** *see* Carbinoxamine and Pseudoephedrine *on page 218*

Sildenafil (sil DEN a fil)

U.S. Brand Names Viagra®

Synonyms UK92480

Therapeutic Category Phosphodiesterase Enzyme Inhibitor, Selective Type 5

Use Treatment of erectile dysfunction

Unlabeled/Investigational Use Psychotropic-induced sexual dysfunction; primary pulmonary hypertension

Pregnancy Risk Factor B

Contraindications Hypersensitivity to sildenafil or any component of the formulation; concurrent use of organic nitrates (nitroglycerin) in any form (potentiates the hypotensive effects)

Warnings/Precautions There is a degree of cardiac risk associated with sexual activity; therefore, physicians may wish to consider the cardiovascular status of their patients prior to initiating any treatment for erectile dysfunction. Agents for the treatment of erectile dysfunction should be used with caution in patients with anatomical deformation of the penis (angulation, cavernosal fibrosis, or Peyronie's disease), or in patients who have conditions which may predispose them to priapism (sickle cell anemia, multiple myeloma, leukemia).

The safety and efficacy of sildenafil with other treatments for erectile dysfunction have not been studied and are, therefore, not recommended as combination therapy.

A minority of patients with retinitis pigmentosa have generic disorders of retinal phosphodiesterases. There is no safety information on the administration of sildenafil to these patients and sildenafil should be administered with caution.

Common Adverse Reactions

>10%: Central nervous system: Headache

Note: Dyspepsia and abnormal vision (color changes, blurred or increased sensitivity to light) occurred at an incidence of >10% with doses of 100 mg.

1% to 10%:

Cardiovascular: Flushing

Central nervous system: Dizziness

Dermatologic: Rash

Genitourinary: Urinary tract infection

Ophthalmic: Abnormal vision (color changes, blurred or increased sensitivity to light)

Respiratory: Nasal congestion

<2% (Limited to important of life-threatening): Allergic reaction, angina pectoris anorgasmia, asthma, AV block, cardiac arrest, cardiomyopathy, cataract, cerebral thrombosis, colitis, dyspnea, edema, exfoliative dermatitis, eye hemorrhage, gout, heart failure, hyperglycemia, hypotension, migraine, myocardial ischemia, neuralgia, photosensitivity, postural hypotension, priapism, rectal hemorrhage, seizures, shock, syncope, vertigo

Drug Interactions

Cytochrome P450 Effect: Substrate of CYP2C8/9 (minor), 3A4 (major); **Inhibits** CYP1A2 (weak), 2C8/9 (weak), 2C19 (weak), 2D6 (weak), 2E1 (weak), 3A4 (weak)

Increased Effect/Toxicity: Sildenafil potentiates the hypotensive effects of nitrates (amyl nitrate, isosorbide dinitrate, isosorbide mononitrate, nitroglycerin); severe reactions have occurred and concurrent use is contraindicated. Concomitant use of alpha-blockers (doxazosin) may lead to symptomatic hypotension in some patients (sildenafil in doses >25 mg should not be given within 4 hours of administering an alpha-blocker). Sildenafil may potentiate the effect of other antihypertensives. Serum concentrations/toxicity of sildenafil may be increased by inhibitors of CYP3A4, including amprenavir, cimetidine, ciprofloxacin, clarithromycin, clozapine, diltiazem, disulfiram, digoxin, erythromycin, ethanol, fluconazole, fluoxetine, fluvoxamine, grapefruit juice, ritonavir, isoniazid, itraconazole, ketoconazole, labetalol, levodopa, loxapine, metoprolol, metronidazole, miconazole, nefazodone, nelfinavir, omeprazole, phenytoin, rifabutin, rifampin, ritonavir, troleandomycin, valproic acid, and verapamil. Sildenafil may potentiate bleeding in patients receiving heparin. A reduction in sildenafil's dose is recommended when used with ritonavir or indinavir (no more than 25 mg/dose; no more than 25 mg in 48 hours).

Decreased Effect: Enzyme inducers (including phenytoin, carbamazepine, phenobarbital, rifampin) may decrease the serum concentration and efficacy of sildenafil.

Mechanism of Action Does not directly cause penile erections, but affects the response to sexual stimulation. The physiologic mechanism of erection of the penis involves release of nitric oxide (NO) in the corpus cavernosum during sexual stimulation. NO then activates the enzyme guanylate cyclase, which results in increased levels of cyclic guanosine monophosphate (cGMP), producing smooth muscle relaxation and inflow of blood to the corpus cavernosum. Sildenafil enhances the effect of NO by inhibiting phosphodiesterase type 5 (PDE5), which is responsible for degradation of cGMP in the corpus cavernosum; when sexual stimulation causes local release of NO, inhibition of PDE5 by sildenafil causes increased levels of cGMP in the corpus cavernosum, resulting in smooth muscle relaxation and inflow of blood to the corpus cavernosum; at recommended doses, it has no effect in the absence of sexual stimulation.

Pharmacodynamics/Kinetics

Onset of action: ~60 minutes

Duration: 2-4 hours

Absorption: Rapid

Protein binding, plasma: ~96%

Metabolism: Hepatic via CYP3A4 (major) and CYP2C9 (minor route)

Bioavailability: 40%

Half-life elimination: 4 hours

Time to peak: 30-120 minutes

Excretion: Feces (80%); urine (13%)

Dosage Adults: Oral:

Erectile dysfunction: For most patients, the recommended dose is 50 mg taken as needed, approximately 1 hour before sexual activity. However, sildenafil may be taken anywhere from 30 minutes to 4 hours before sexual activity. Based on effectiveness and tolerance, the dose may be increased to a maximum recommended dose of 100 mg or decreased to 25 mg. The maximum recommended dosing frequency is once daily.

Primary pulmonary hypertension (unlabeled use): 25 mg twice daily, titrated based on response. Dosages up to 100 mg 5 times/day have been used (limited data).

Dosage adjustment for patients >65 years of age, hepatic impairment (cirrhosis), severe renal impairment (creatinine clearance <30 mL/minute), or concomitant use of potent cytochrome P450 3A4 inhibitors (erythromycin, ketoconazole, itraconazole, ritonavir, amprenavir): Higher plasma levels have been associated which may result in increase in efficacy and adverse effects and a starting dose of 25 mg should be considered

Administration Administer orally ~1 hour before sexual activity (may be used anytime from 4 hours to 30 minutes before).

Patient Information Discuss with your prescriber the contraindication of sildenafil citrate with concurrent organic nitrates. The use of sildenafil offers no protection against sexually-transmitted diseases. Counseling of patients about the protective measures necessary to guard against transmitted diseases, including the human immunodeficiency virus (HIV), may be considered.

Dosage Forms TAB: 25 mg, 50 mg, 100 mg

- ♦ **Silexin® [OTC]** *see* Guaifenesin and Dextromethorphan *on page 604*
- ♦ **Silfedrine Children's [OTC]** *see* Pseudoephedrine *on page 1061*
- ♦ **Silphen® [OTC]** *see* DiphenhydrAMINE *on page 383*
- ♦ **Silvadene®** *see* Silver Sulfadiazine *on page 1137*

Silver Nitrate (SIL ver NYE trate)

Synonyms $AgNO_3$

Therapeutic Category Antibacterial, Topical; Antibiotic, Ophthalmic; Antibiotic, Topical; Cauterizing Agent, Topical; Topical Skin Product, Antibacterial

Use Cauterization of wounds and sluggish ulcers, removal of granulation tissue and warts; aseptic prophylaxis of burns

Pregnancy Risk Factor C

Contraindications Hypersensitivity to silver nitrate or any component of the formulation; not for use on broken skin, cuts, or wounds

Warnings/Precautions Do not use applicator sticks on the eyes. Prolonged use may result in skin discoloration.

Common Adverse Reactions Frequency not defined.

Dermatologic: Burning and skin irritation, staining of the skin

Endocrine & metabolic: Hyponatremia

Hematologic: Methemoglobinemia

Mechanism of Action Free silver ions precipitate bacterial proteins by combining with chloride in tissue forming silver chloride; coagulates cellular protein to form an eschar; silver ions or salts or colloidal silver preparations can inhibit the growth of both gram-positive and gram-negative bacteria. This germicidal action is attributed to the precipitation of bacterial proteins by liberated silver ions. Silver nitrate coagulates cellular protein to form an eschar, and this mode of action is the postulated mechanism for control of benign hematuria, rhinitis, and recurrent pneumothorax.

Pharmacodynamics/Kinetics

Absorption: Because silver ions readily combine with protein, there is minimal GI and cutaneous absorption of the 0.5% and 1% preparations

Excretion: Highest amounts of silver noted on autopsy have been in kidneys, excretion in urine is minimal

Dosage Children and Adults:

Sticks: Apply to mucous membranes and other moist skin surfaces only on area to be treated 2-3 times/week for 2-3 weeks

Topical solution: Apply a cotton applicator dipped in solution on the affected area 2-3 times/week for 2-3 weeks

Administration Applicators are **not** for ophthalmic use.

Monitoring Parameters With prolonged use, monitor methemoglobin levels

Patient Information Discontinue topical preparation if redness or irritation develop

Dosage Forms APPLICATOR STICKS, topical: Silver nitrate 75% and potassium nitrate 25% (6", 12", 18"). **SOLN, topical:** 10% (30 mL); 25% (30 mL); 50% (30 mL)

Silver Sulfadiazine (SIL ver sul fa DYE a zeen)

Related Information

Sulfonamide Derivatives *on page 1404*

U.S. Brand Names Silvadene®; SSD®; SSD® AF; Thermazene®

Therapeutic Category Antibacterial, Topical; Antibiotic, Topical

Use Prevention and treatment of infection in second and third degree burns

Pregnancy Risk Factor B

Contraindications Hypersensitivity to silver sulfadiazine or any component of the formulation; premature infants or neonates <2 months of age (sulfonamides may displace bilirubin and cause kernicterus); pregnancy (approaching or at term)

(Continued)

Silver Sulfadiazine (Continued)

Warnings/Precautions Use with caution in patients with G6PD deficiency, renal impairment, or history of allergy to other sulfonamides; sulfadiazine may accumulate in patients with impaired hepatic or renal function; fungal superinfection may occur; use of analgesic might be needed before application; systemic absorption is significant and adverse reactions may occur

Common Adverse Reactions Frequency not defined.
Dermatologic: Itching, rash, erythema multiforme, discoloration of skin, photosensitivity
Hematologic: Hemolytic anemia, leukopenia, agranulocytosis, aplastic anemia
Hepatic: Hepatitis
Renal: Interstitial nephritis
Miscellaneous: Allergic reactions may be related to sulfa component

Drug Interactions
Decreased Effect: Topical proteolytic enzymes are inactivated by silver sulfadiazine.

Mechanism of Action Acts upon the bacterial cell wall and cell membrane. Bactericidal for many gram-negative and gram-positive bacteria and is effective against yeast. Active against *Pseudomonas aeruginosa*, *Pseudomonas maltophilia*, *Enterobacter* species, *Klebsiella* species, *Serratia* species, *Escherichia coli*, *Proteus mirabilis*, *Morganella morganii*, *Providencia rettgeri*, *Proteus vulgaris*, *Providencia* species, *Citrobacter* species, *Acinetobacter calcoaceticus*, *Staphylococcus aureus*, *Staphylococcus epidermidis*, *Enterococcus* species, *Candida albicans*, *Corynebacterium diphtheriae*, and *Clostridium perfringens*

Pharmacodynamics/Kinetics
Absorption: Significant percutaneous absorption of silver sulfadiazine can occur especially when applied to extensive burns
Half-life elimination: 10 hours; prolonged with renal impairment
Time to peak, serum: 3-11 days of continuous therapy
Excretion: Urine (~50% as unchanged drug)

Dosage Children and Adults: Topical: Apply once or twice daily with a sterile-gloved hand; apply to a thickness of $^1/_{16}$"; burned area should be covered with cream at all times

Monitoring Parameters Serum electrolytes, urinalysis, renal function tests, CBC in patients with extensive burns on long-term treatment

Patient Information For external use only; bathe daily to aid in debridement (if not contraindicated); apply liberally to burned areas; for external use only; notify prescriber if condition persists or worsens

Dosage Forms CRM, topical: 1% [10 mg/g] (25 g, 85 g, 400 g); (Silvadene®, Thermazene®): 1% (20 g, 50 g, 85 g, 400 g, 1000 g); (SSD®): 1% (25 g, 50 g, 85 g, 400 g); (SSD AF®): 1% (50 g, 400 g)

♦ **Simethicone, Aluminum Hydroxide, and Magnesium Hydroxide** see Aluminum Hydroxide, Magnesium Hydroxide, and Simethicone on page 68

♦ **Simethicone and Magaldrate** see Magaldrate and Simethicone on page 768

♦ **Simply Saline™ [OTC]** see Sodium Chloride on page 1146

♦ **Simulect®** see Basiliximab on page 146

Simvastatin (SIM va stat in)

Related Information
Lipid-Lowering Agents on page 1381

U.S. Brand Names Zocor®

Therapeutic Category Antilipemic Agent, HMG-CoA Reductase Inhibitor; HMG-CoA Reductase Inhibitor

Use Used with dietary therapy for the following:
Secondary prevention of cardiovascular events in hypercholesterolemic patients with established coronary heart disease (CHD) or at high risk for CHD: To reduce cardiovascular morbidity (myocardial infarction, coronary revascularization procedures) and mortality; to reduce the risk of stroke and transient ischemic attacks
Hyperlipidemias: To reduce elevations in total cholesterol, LDL-C, apolipoprotein B, and triglycerides in patients with primary hypercholesterolemia (elevations of 1 or more components are present in Fredrickson type IIa, IIb, III, and IV hyperlipidemias); treatment of homozygous familial hypercholesterolemia
Heterozygous familial hypercholesterolemia (HeFH): In adolescent patients (10-17 years of age, females >1 year postmenarche) with HeFH having LDL-C ≥190 mg/dL or LDL ≥160 mg/dL with positive family history of premature cardiovascular disease (CVD), or 2 or more CVD risk factors in the adolescent patient

Pregnancy Risk Factor X

Contraindications Hypersensitivity to simvastatin or any component of the formulation; acute liver disease; unexplained persistent elevations of serum transaminases; pregnancy; breast-feeding

Warnings/Precautions Secondary causes of hyperlipidemia should be ruled out prior to therapy. Liver function must be monitored by laboratory assessment. Rhabdomyolysis with acute renal failure has occurred. Risk is increased with concurrent use of clarithromycin, danazol, diltiazem, fluvoxamine, indinavir, nefazodone, nelfinavir, ritonavir, verapamil, troleandomycin, cyclosporine, fibric acid derivatives, erythromycin, niacin, or azole antifungals. Weigh the risk versus benefit when combining any of these drugs with simvastatin. Temporarily discontinue in any patient experiencing an acute or serious condition predisposing to renal failure secondary to rhabdomyolysis. Use with caution in patients who consume large amounts of ethanol or have a history of liver disease. Safety and efficacy have not been established in patients <10 years or in premenarcheal girls.

Common Adverse Reactions 1% to 10%:
Gastrointestinal: Constipation (2%), dyspepsia (1%), flatulence (2%)
Neuromuscular & skeletal: CPK elevation (>3x normal on one or more occasions - 5%)
Respiratory: Upper respiratory infection (2%)

Additional class-related events or case reports (not necessarily reported with simvastatin therapy): Alopecia, alteration in taste, anaphylaxis, angioedema, anorexia, anxiety, arthritis, cataracts, chills, cholestatic jaundice, cirrhosis, decreased libido, depression, dermatomyositis, dryness of skin/mucous membranes, dyspnea, elevated transaminases, eosinophilia, erectile dysfunction/impotence, erythema multiforme, facial paresis, fatty liver, fever, flushing, fulminant hepatic necrosis, gynecomastia, hemolytic anemia, hepatitis, hepatoma, hyperbilirubinemia, hypersensitivity reaction, impaired extraocular muscle movement, increased alkaline phosphatase, increased CPK (>10x normal), increased ESR, increased GGT, leukopenia, malaise, memory loss, myopathy, nail changes, nodules, ophthalmoplegia, pancreatitis, paresthesia, peripheral nerve palsy, peripheral neuropathy, photosensitivity, polymyalgia rheumatica, positive ANA, pruritus, psychic disturbance, purpura, rash, renal failure (secondary to rhabdomyolysis), rhabdomyolysis, skin discoloration, Stevens-Johnson syndrome, systemic lupus erythematosus-like syndrome, thrombocytopenia, thyroid dysfunction, toxic epidermal necrolysis, tremor, urticaria, vasculitis, vertigo, vomiting

Drug Interactions
Cytochrome P450 Effect: Substrate of CYP3A4 (major); **Inhibits** CYP2C8/9 (weak), 2D6 (weak)
Increased Effect/Toxicity: Risk of myopathy/rhabdomyolysis may be increased by concurrent use of lipid-lowering agents which may cause rhabdomyolysis (gemfibrozil, fibric acid derivatives, or niacin at doses ≥1 g/day), or during concurrent use of potent CYP3A4 inhibitors (including amiodarone, clarithromycin, cyclosporine, danazol, diltiazem, erythromycin, fluconazole, itraconazole, ketoconazole, nefazodone, verapamil or protease inhibitors such as atazanavir, indinavir, nelfinavir, ritonavir or saquinavir). In large quantities (ie, >1 quart/day), grapefruit juice may also increase simvastatin serum concentrations, increasing the risk of rhabdomyolysis. In general, concurrent use with CYP3A4 inhibitors is not recommended; manufacturer recommends limiting simvastatin dose to 20 mg/day when used with amiodarone or verapamil, and 10 mg/day when used with cyclosporine, gemfibrozil, or fibric acid derivatives. The anticoagulant effect of warfarin may be increased by simvastatin. Cholesterol-lowering effects are additive with bile-acid sequestrants (colestipol and cholestyramine).
Decreased Effect: When taken within 1 before or up to 2 hours after cholestyramine, a decrease in absorption of simvastatin can occur.
Mechanism of Action Simvastatin is a methylated derivative of lovastatin that acts by competitively inhibiting 3-hydroxy-3-methylglutaryl-coenzyme A (HMG-CoA) reductase, the enzyme that catalyzes the rate-limiting step in cholesterol biosynthesis
Pharmacodynamics/Kinetics
Onset of action: >3 days
Peak effect: 2 weeks
Absorption: 85%
Protein binding: ~95%
Metabolism: Hepatic via CYP3A4; extensive first-pass effect
Bioavailability: <5%
Half-life elimination: Unknown
Time to peak: 1.3-2.4 hours
Excretion: Feces (60%); urine (13%)
Dosage Oral: **Note:** Doses should be individualized according to the baseline LDL-cholesterol levels, the recommended goal of therapy, and the patient's response; adjustments should be made at intervals of 4 weeks or more; doses may need adjusted based on concomitant medications
Children 10-17 years (females >1 year postmenarche): HeFH: 10 mg once daily in the evening; range: 10-40 mg/day (maximum: 40 mg/day)
Dosage adjustment for simvastatin with concomitant cyclosporine, fibrates, niacin, amiodarone, or verapamil: Refer to drug-specific dosing in Adults dosing section
Adults:
Homozygous familial hypercholesterolemia: 40 mg once daily in the evening **or** 80 mg/day (given as 20 mg, 20 mg, and 40 mg evening dose)
Prevention of cardiovascular events, hyperlipidemias: 20-40 mg once daily in the evening; range: 5-80 mg/day
Patients requiring only moderate reduction of LDL-cholesterol may be started at 10 mg once daily
Patients requiring reduction of >45% in low-density lipoprotein (LDL) cholesterol may be started at 40 mg once daily in the evening
Patients with CHD or at high risk for CHD: Dosing should be started at 40 mg once daily in the evening; simvastatin may be started simultaneously with diet
Dosage adjustment with concomitant medications:
Cyclosporine: Initial: 5 mg simvastatin, should **not** exceed 10 mg/day
Fibrates or niacin: Simvastatin dose should **not** exceed 10 mg/day
Amiodarone or verapamil: Simvastatin dose should **not** exceed 20 mg/day
Dosing adjustment/comments in renal impairment: Because simvastatin does not undergo significant renal excretion, modification of dose should not be necessary in patients with mild to moderate renal insufficiency.
Severe renal impairment: Cl_{cr} <10 mL/minute: Initial: 5 mg/day with close monitoring.
Administration May be taken without regard to meals.
(Continued)

Simvastatin *(Continued)*

Monitoring Parameters Creatine phosphokinase levels due to possibility of myopathy; serum cholesterol (total and fractionated)

Obtain liver function tests prior to initiation, dose, and thereafter when clinically indicated. Patients titrated to the 80 mg dose should be tested prior to initiation and 3 months after initiating the 80 mg dose. Thereafter, periodic monitoring (ie, semiannually) is recommended for the first year of treatment. Patients with elevated transaminase levels should have a second (confirmatory) test and frequent monitoring until values normalize. Discontinue if increase in ALT/AST is persistently >3 times ULN.

Patient Information Promptly report any unexplained muscle pain, tenderness or weakness, especially if accompanied by malaise or fever; follow prescribed diet; may be taken without regard to meals

Dosage Forms TAB: 5 mg, 10 mg, 20 mg, 40 mg, 80 mg

♦ **Sinemet®** *see* Levodopa and Carbidopa *on page 732*

♦ **Sinemet® CR** *see* Levodopa and Carbidopa *on page 732*

♦ **Sinequan®** *see* Doxepin *on page 407*

♦ **Singulair®** *see* Montelukast *on page 859*

♦ **Sinus-Relief® [OTC]** *see* Acetaminophen and Pseudoephedrine *on page 26*

♦ **Sinutab® Sinus [OTC]** *see* Acetaminophen and Pseudoephedrine *on page 26*

♦ **Sinutab® Sinus Allergy Maximum Strength [OTC]** *see* Acetaminophen, Chlorpheniramine, and Pseudoephedrine *on page 28*

♦ **Sirdalud®** *see* Tizanidine *on page 1234*

Sirolimus *(sir OH li mus)*

U.S. Brand Names Rapamune®

Therapeutic Category Immunosuppressant Agent

Use Prophylaxis of organ rejection in patients receiving renal transplants, in combination with corticosteroids and cyclosporine (cyclosporine may be withdrawn in low-to-moderate immunological risk patients after 2-4 months, in conjunction with an increase in sirolimus dosage)

Unlabeled/Investigational Use Investigational: Immunosuppression in other forms of solid organ transplantation

Pregnancy Risk Factor C

Contraindications Hypersensitivity to sirolimus or any component of the formulation

Warnings/Precautions Immunosuppressive agents, including sirolimus, increase the risk of infection and may be associated with the development of lymphoma. Only physicians experienced in the management of organ transplant patients should prescribe sirolimus. May increase serum lipids (cholesterol and triglycerides). Use with caution in patients with hyperlipidemia. May decrease GFR and increase serum creatinine. Use caution in patients with renal impairment, or when used concurrently with medications which may alter renal function. Monitor renal function closely when combined with cyclosporine; consider dosage adjustment or discontinue in patients with increasing serum creatinine. Has been associated with an increased risk of lymphocele. Avoid concurrent use of ketoconazole or voriconazole; use caution with other CYP3A4 inhibitors. Cases of bronchial anastomotic dehiscence have been reported in lung transplant patients when sirolimus was used as part of an immunosuppressive regimen; most of these reactions were fatal. Use in patients with lung transplants is not recommended. Safety and efficacy of cyclosporine withdrawal in high-risk patients is not currently recommended. Safety and efficacy in children <13 years of age have not been established.

Common Adverse Reactions Incidence of many adverse effects is dose related

>20%:

Cardiovascular: Hypertension (39% to 49%), peripheral edema (54% to 64%), edema (16% to 24%), chest pain (16% to 24%)

Central nervous system: Fever (23% to 34%), headache (23% to 34%), pain (24% to 33%), insomnia (13% to 22%)

Dermatologic: Acne (20% to 31%)

Endocrine & metabolic: Hypercholesterolemia (38% to 46%), hypophosphatemia (15% to 23%), hyperlipidemia (38% to 57%), hypokalemia (11% to 21%)

Gastrointestinal: Abdominal pain (28% to 36%), nausea (25% to 36%), vomiting (19% to 25%), diarrhea (25% to 42%), constipation (28% to 38%), dyspepsia (17% to 25%), weight gain (8% to 21%)

Genitourinary: Urinary tract infection (20% to 33%)

Hematologic: Anemia (23% to 37%), thrombocytopenia (13% to 40%)

Neuromuscular & skeletal: Arthralgia (25% to 31%), weakness (22% to 40%), back pain (16% to 26%), tremor (21% to 31%)

Renal: Increased serum creatinine (35% to 40%)

Respiratory: Dyspnea (22% to 30%), upper respiratory infection (20% to 26%), pharyngitis (16% to 21%)

3% to 20%:

Cardiovascular: Atrial fibrillation, CHF, hypervolemia, hypotension, palpitation, peripheral vascular disorder, postural hypotension, syncope, tachycardia, thrombosis, vasodilation, venous thromboembolism

Central nervous system: Chills, malaise, anxiety, confusion, depression, dizziness, emotional lability, hypesthesia, hypotonia, insomnia, neuropathy, somnolence

Dermatologic: Dermatitis (fungal), hirsutism, pruritus, skin hypertrophy, dermal ulcer, ecchymosis, cellulitis, rash (10% to 20%)

Endocrine & metabolic: Cushing's syndrome, diabetes mellitus, glycosuria, dehydration, hypercalcemia, hyperglycemia, hyperphosphatemia, hypocalcemia, hypoglycemia, hypomagnesemia, hyponatremia, hyperkalemia (12% to 17%)

Gastrointestinal: Enlarged abdomen, anorexia, dysphagia, eructation, esophagitis, flatulence, gastritis, gastroenteritis, gingivitis, gingival hyperplasia, ileus, mouth ulceration, oral moniliasis, stomatitis, weight loss

Genitourinary: Pelvic pain, scrotal edema, testis disorder, impotence

Hematologic: Leukocytosis, polycythemia, TTP, hemolytic-uremic syndrome, hemorrhage, leukopenia (9% to 15%)

Hepatic: Abnormal liver function tests, increased alkaline phosphatase, increased LDH, increased transaminases, ascites

Local: Thrombophlebitis

Neuromuscular & skeletal: Increased CPK, arthrosis, bone necrosis, leg cramps, myalgia, osteoporosis, tetany, hypertonia, paresthesia

Ocular: Abnormal vision, cataract, conjunctivitis

Otic: Ear pain, deafness, otitis media, tinnitus

Renal: Increased BUN, albuminuria, bladder pain, dysuria, hematuria, hydronephrosis, kidney pain, tubular necrosis, nocturia, oliguria, pyuria, nephropathy (toxic), urinary frequency, urinary incontinence, urinary retention

Respiratory: Asthma, atelectasis, bronchitis, cough, epistaxis, hypoxia, lung edema, pleural effusion, pneumonia, rhinitis, sinusitis

Miscellaneous: Abscess, facial edema, flu-like syndrome, hernia, infection, lymphadenopathy, lymphocele, peritonitis, sepsis, diaphoresis

Drug Interactions

Cytochrome P450 Effect: Substrate of CYP3A4 (major); **Inhibits** CYP3A4 (weak)

Increased Effect/Toxicity: Cyclosporine increases sirolimus concentrations during concurrent therapy, and cyclosporine levels may be increased. Diltiazem, ketoconazole, voriconazole, and rifampin increase serum concentrations of sirolimus. Avoid potent CYP3A4 inhibitors (ketoconazole, voriconazole). Other inhibitors of CYP3A4 (eg, calcium channel blockers, antifungal agents, macrolide antibiotics, gastrointestinal prokinetic agents, HIV-protease inhibitors) are likely to increase sirolimus concentrations. Vaccination may be less effective and use of live vaccines should be avoided during sirolimus therapy.

Decreased Effect: Inducers of CYP3A4 (eg, rifampin, phenobarbital, carbamazepine, rifabutin, phenytoin) are likely to decrease serum concentrations of sirolimus.

Mechanism of Action Sirolimus inhibits T-lymphocyte activation and proliferation in response to antigenic and cytokine stimulation. Its mechanism differs from other immunosuppressants. It inhibits acute rejection of allografts and prolongs graft survival.

Pharmacodynamics/Kinetics

Absorption: Rapid

Distribution: 12 L/kg (± 7.52 L/kg)

Protein binding: 92%, primarily to albumin

Metabolism: Extensively hepatic via CYP3A4 and P-glycoprotein

Bioavailability: 14%

Half-life elimination: Mean: 62 hours

Time to peak: 1-3 hours

Excretion: Feces (91%); urine (2.2%)

Dosage Oral:

Children ≥13 years or Adults <40 kg: Loading dose: 3 mg/m² (day 1); followed by a maintenance of 1 mg/m²/day.

Adults ≥40 kg: Loading dose: For *de novo* transplant recipients, a loading dose of 3 times the daily maintenance dose should be administered on day 1 of dosing. Maintenance dose: 2 mg/day. Doses should be taken 4 hours after cyclosporine, and should be taken consistently either with or without food.

Withdrawal of cyclosporine:

Following 2-4 months of combined therapy, withdrawal of cyclosporine may be considered in low-to-moderate risk patients. Cyclosporine withdrawal in not recommended in high immunological risk patients. Cyclosporine should be discontinued over 4-8 weeks, and a necessary increase in the dosage of sirolimus (up to fourfold) should be anticipated due to removal of metabolic inhibition by cyclosporine and to maintain adequate immunosuppressive effects.

Sirolimus dosages should be adjusted to maintain trough concentrations of 12-24 ng/mL. Dosage should be adjusted at intervals of 7-14 days to account for the long half-life of sirolimus. Considerable increases in dosage may require an additional loading dose, calculated as the difference between the target concentration and the current concentration, multiplied by a factor of 3. Loading doses >40 mg may be administered over two days. Serum concentrations should not be used as the sole basis for dosage adjustment (monitor clinical signs/symptoms, tissue biopsy, and laboratory parameters).

Dosage adjustment in renal impairment: No dosage adjustment is necessary in renal impairment

Dosage adjustment in hepatic impairment: Reduce maintenance dose by approximately 33% in hepatic impairment. Loading dose is unchanged.

Administration Amber oral dose syringe should be used to withdraw solution from the bottle. Syringe should then be emptied, or, if a pouch is used, the entire contents should be squeezed out into a glass or plastic cup. The solution in the cup should be mixed with at least 2 ounces of water or orange juice. No other liquids should be used for dilution. Patient should drink diluted solution immediately. The cup should then be refilled with an additional 4 ounces of water or orange juice, stirred vigorously, and the patient should drink the contents at once. Sirolimus (Continued)

Sirolimus *(Continued)*

should be taken 4 hours after cyclosporine oral solution (modified) or cyclosporine capsules (modified)

Monitoring Parameters Monitor sirolimus levels in pediatric patients, patients ≥13 years of age weighing <40 kg, patients with hepatic impairment, or on concurrent potent inhibitors or inducers of CYP3A4, and/or if cyclosporine dosing is markedly reduced or discontinued. Also monitor serum cholesterol and triglycerides, blood pressure, and serum creatinine. Routine therapeutic drug level monitoring is not required in most patients. Serum concentrations should not be used as the sole basis for dosage adjustment, especially during withdrawal of cyclosporine (monitor clinical signs/symptoms, tissue biopsy, and laboratory parameters).

Reference Range Mean serum trough concentrations: 9 ng/mL for the 2 mg/day treatment groups and 17 ng/mL in the 5 mg/day group

Patient Information Do not get pregnant while taking this medication. Use reliable contraception while on this medication and for 3 months after discontinuation. May be taken with or without food but take medication consistently with respect to meals (always take with food or always take on an empty stomach). Wear protective clothing and use sunscreen to limit exposure to sunlight and UV light; decreases risk of skin cancer.

Dosage Forms SOLN, oral [bottle]: 1 mg/mL (60 mL, 150 mL); [unit-dose pouch]: 1 mg/mL (1 mL, 2 mL, 5 mL). **TAB:** 1 mg, 2 mg

- ◆ **SK** *see Streptokinase on page 1161*
- ◆ **SK and F 104864** *see Topotecan on page 1244*
- ◆ **Skelaxin®** *see Metaxalone on page 805*
- ◆ **Skelid®** *see Tiludronate on page 1228*
- ◆ **SKF 104864** *see Topotecan on page 1244*
- ◆ **SKF 104864-A** *see Topotecan on page 1244*

Skin Test Antigens (Multiple) *(skin test AN tee gens, MUL ti pul)*

U.S. Brand Names Multitest CMI®

Therapeutic Category Diagnostic Agent, Hypersensitivity Skin Testing

Use Detection of nonresponsiveness to antigens by means of delayed hypersensitivity skin testing

Pregnancy Risk Factor C

Contraindications Hypersensitivity to skin test antigens; infected or inflamed skin; do not apply at sites involving acneiform, infected or inflamed skin; although severe systemic reactions are rare in diphtheria and tetanus antigens, persons known to have a history of systemic reactions should be tested with this test only after the test heads containing these antigens have been removed

Warnings/Precautions Epinephrine should be available is case of severe reactions. Safety and effectiveness in children <17 years of age have not been established; discard applicator after use, do not reuse.

Common Adverse Reactions 1% to 10%: Local: Irritation

Dosage Select only test sites that permit sufficient surface area and subcutaneous tissue to allow adequate penetration of all eight points, avoid hairy areas. Press loaded unit into the skin with sufficient pressure to puncture the skin and allow adequate penetration of all points, maintain firm contact for at least 5 seconds, during application the device should not be "rocked" back and forth and side to side without removing any of the test heads from the skin sites.

If adequate pressure is applied it will be possible to observe:
1. The puncture marks of the nine tines on each of the eight test heads
2. An imprint of the circular platform surrounding each test head
3. Residual antigen and glycerin at each of the eight sites

If any of the above three criteria are not fully followed, the test results may not be reliable.

Reading should be done in good light, read the test sites at both 24 and 48 hours, the largest reaction recorded from the two readings at each test site should be used. If two readings are not possible, a single 48 hour is recommended. A positive reaction from any of the seven delayed hypersensitivity skin test antigens is **induration** ≥2 mm providing there is no induration at the negative control site. The size of the induration reactions with this test may be smaller than those obtained with other intradermal procedures.

Dosage Forms APPLICATOR, skin test [carton; preloaded]: 7 antigens and a glycerin control

- ◆ **Sleepinal® [OTC]** *see DiphenhydrAMINE on page 383*
- ◆ **Slo-Niacin® [OTC]** *see Niacin on page 897*
- ◆ **Slow FE® [OTC]** *see Ferrous Sulfate on page 520*
- ◆ **Slow-Mag® [OTC]** *see Magnesium Chloride on page 768*

Smallpox Vaccine *(SMAL poks vak SEEN)*

U.S. Brand Names Dryvax®

Synonyms Dried Smallpox Vaccine; Vaccinia Vaccine

Therapeutic Category Vaccine; Vaccine, Inactivated Virus

Use Active immunization against vaccinia virus, the causative agent of smallpox. The ACIP recommends vaccination of laboratory workers at risk of exposure from cultures or contaminated animals which may be a source of vaccinia or related Orthopoxviruses capable of causing infections in humans (monkeypox, cowpox, or variola). Revaccination is recommended every 10 years. The Armed Forces recommend vaccination of certain personnel categories. Recommendations for use in response to bioterrorism are regularly updated by the CDC, and may be found at www.cdc.gov.

Restrictions FDA Licenses Vaccinia Vaccine

In October 2002, the FDA approved the licensing of the current stockpile of smallpox vaccine. This approval allows the vaccine to be distributed and administered in the event of a smallpox attack. The bulk of current supplies have been designated for use by the U.S. military. Additionally, laboratory workers who may be at risk of exposure may require vaccination. Bioterrorism experts have proposed immunization of first responders (including police, fire, and emergency workers), but these plans may not be implemented until additional stocks of vaccine are licensed.

Pregnancy Risk Factor C

Contraindications Hypersensitivity to the vaccine or any component, including polymyxin B, dihydrostreptomycin, chlortetracycline, and neomycin; patients with a history of eczema or patients whose household contacts have acute or chronic exfoliative skin conditions (atopic dermatitis, eczema, burns, impetigo, Varicella zoster, or wounds); immunosuppressed patients and their household contacts, including patients with congenital or acquired immune deficiencies (including HIV, agammaglobulinemia, leukemia, lymphoma, neoplastic disease of the bone marrow or lymphatic system), patients receiving radiation, immunosuppressive drugs, or systemic corticosteroids ≥20 mg/day or ≥2 mg/kg body weight of prednisone for >2 weeks; patients using ocular steroid medications; moderate to severe intercurrent illness; history of Darier disease (or if household contact has active disease); pregnancy or suspected pregnancy (including household contacts of pregnant women); breast-feeding

Note: There are no absolute contraindications regarding vaccination of individuals with a high-risk exposure to smallpox. The decision to vaccinate in an emergency situation must be based on a careful analysis of potential benefits and possible risks.

Warnings/Precautions For vaccination by scarification (multiple punctures into superficial layers of the skin) only. Not for I.M., I.V., or S.C. injection. Packaging contains latex, which may cause hypersensitivity reactions in allergic individuals. Materials used to prepare and vaccinate should be disposed of per manufacturer's recommendations. Virus may be cultured from vaccination sites until scab separates from lesion. Individuals should be instructed to avoid contact with patients at high risk of transmission/adverse effects, including patients with eczema or immunodeficiency during this time. Patients should be advised not to donate blood for 21 days or until the scab has separated; contacts who have inadvertently contracted vaccinia should avoid donating blood for 14 days. Not for use in infants <12 months of age (in emergency conditions) or for use in pediatric patients <18 years of age (nonemergency conditions).

Common Adverse Reactions All serious adverse reactions must be reported to the U.S. Department of Health and Human Services (DHHS) Vaccine Adverse Event Reporting System (VAERS) 1-800-822-7967. In addition, clinicians may enroll patients with adverse reactions in the CDC Registry at 877-554-4625.

Frequency not established for all reactions. Most severe reactions are rare.

Central nervous system: Headache, fatigue, chills, fever (up to 70%; may be ≥102°F in up to 20% in children; frequency in adults may be lower). Rare reactions include: Encephalitis, encephalomyelitis, and encephalopathy

Dermatologic: Rash, secondary pyogenic infections, erythema multiforme

Adverse reactions requiring evaluation or possible treatment: Inadvertent inoculation, generalized vaccinia, eczema vaccinatum, progressive vaccinia, postvaccinial CNS disease, fetal vaccinia

Rare reactions include: Stevens-Johnson syndrome (rare); generalized vaccinia; secondary inoculation of eyelid, face, nose, mouth, genitalia, or rectum (often from autoinoculation from the site of the vaccination and occasionally from contact spread from recently immunized individuals); and rare progressive vaccinia or eczema vaccinatum

Local: Pain at the injection site, satellite lesions, inflammation, lymphadenopathy

Neuromuscular & skeletal: Myalgia

Drug Interactions

Decreased Effect: Smallpox vaccine may suppress tuberculin (PPD) skin test; avoid skin test for ≥1 month after vaccine to prevent false-negative reactions.

Mechanism of Action Live vaccinia virus at a concentration of ~100 million infectious particles per mL. Vaccination results in viral replication, production of neutralizing antibodies, immunity, and cellular hypersensitivity.

Pharmacodynamics/Kinetics Onset: Neutralizing antibodies appear 10-13 days after vaccination.

Dosage Not for I.M., I.V., or S.C. injection: Vaccination by scarification (multiple-puncture technique) only: **Note:** A trace of blood should appear at vaccination site after 15-20 seconds; if no trace of blood is visible, an additional 3 insertions should be made using the same needle, without reinserting the needle into the vaccine bottle.

Adults (children ≥12 months in emergency conditions):

Primary vaccination: Use a single drop of vaccine suspension and 2 or 3 needle punctures (using the same needle) into the superficial skin

Revaccination: Use a single drop of vaccine suspension and 15 needle punctures (using the same needle) into the superficial skin

Dosage adjustment in renal impairment: No dosage adjustment required

Administration Using a bifurcated needle, 1 drop of vaccine is introduced into the superficial layers of the skin using a multiple-puncture technique. The skin over the insertion of the deltoid
(Continued)

Smallpox Vaccine *(Continued)*

muscle or the posterior aspect of the arm over the triceps are the preferred sites for vaccination.

A single-use bifurcated needle should be dipped carefully into the reconstituted vaccine (following removal of rubber stopper). Visually confirm that the needle picks up a drop of vaccine solution. Deposit the drop of vaccine onto clean, dry skin at the vaccination site. Holding the bifurcated needle perpendicular to the skin, punctures are to be made rapidly into the superficial skin of the vaccination site. The puncture strokes should be vigorous enough to allow a trace of blood to appear after approximately 15-20 seconds. Wipe off any remaining vaccine with dry sterile gauze. Dispose of all materials in a biohazard waste container. All materials must be burned, boiled, or autoclaved. If no evidence of vaccine take is apparent after 7 days, the individual may be vaccinated again.

To prevent transmission of the virus, cover vaccination site with gauze and cover gauze with a semipermeable barrier or clothing. Good handwashing prevents inadvertent inoculation.

Monitoring Parameters Monitor vaccination site; inspect after 6-8 days. Evidence of a major reaction (vesicular or pustular lesion or an area of palpable induration surrounding a central lesion) confirms success of vaccination. An equivocal reaction (all responses other than a major reaction) requires revaccination (preferably with another vial or vaccine lot, if available). Consult CDC or state or local health department if response to a second vaccination is equivocal.

Patient Information To avoid transmitting virus, wash hands with soapy water or hand rubs containing ≥60% alcohol immediately after touching vaccination site or after changing vaccination bandages. Place used bandages in sealed plastic bag before disposing.

Dosage Forms INJ, powder for reconstitution [calf liver source]: ~100 million vaccinia virions per mL following reconstitution [contains polymyxin B, neomycin, dihydrostreptomycin sulfate, and chlortetracycline (trace amounts); packed with diluent, venting needle, and 100 bifurcated needles]

- **SMZ-TMP** *see* Sulfamethoxazole and Trimethoprim *on page 1173*
- **Sodium 2-Mercaptoethane Sulfonate** *see* Mesna *on page 799*
- **Sodium 4-Hydroxybutyrate** *see* Sodium Oxybate *on page 1149*

Sodium Acetate *(SOW dee um AS e tate)*

Therapeutic Category Alkalinizing Agent, Parenteral; Electrolyte Supplement, Parenteral; Sodium Salt

Use Sodium source in large volume I.V. fluids to prevent or correct hyponatremia in patients with restricted intake; used to counter acidosis through conversion to bicarbonate

Pregnancy Risk Factor C

Contraindications Alkalosis, hypocalcemia, low sodium diets, edema, cirrhosis

Warnings/Precautions Avoid extravasation, use with caution in patients with hepatic failure

Common Adverse Reactions 1% to 10%:

Cardiovascular: Thrombosis, hypervolemia

Dermatologic: Chemical cellulitis at injection site (extravasation)

Endocrine & metabolic: Hypernatremia, dilution of serum electrolytes, overhydration, hypokalemia, metabolic alkalosis, hypocalcemia

Gastrointestinal: Gastric distension, flatulence

Local: Phlebitis

Respiratory: Pulmonary edema

Miscellaneous: Congestive conditions

Dosage Sodium acetate is metabolized to bicarbonate on an equimolar basis outside the liver; administer in large volume I.V. fluids as a sodium source. Refer to Sodium Bicarbonate monograph.

Maintenance electrolyte requirements of sodium in parenteral nutrition solutions:

Daily requirements: 3-4 mEq/kg/24 hours or 25-40 mEq/1000 kcal/24 hours

Maximum: 100-150 mEq/24 hours

Administration Must be diluted prior to I.V. administration; infusion hypertonic solutions (>154 mEq/L) via a central line; maximum rate of administration: 1 mEq/kg/hour

Dosage Forms INJ, solution: 2 mEq/mL (20 mL, 50 mL, 100 mL, 250 mL); 4 mEq/mL (50 mL, 100 mL)

- **Sodium Acid Carbonate** *see* Sodium Bicarbonate *on page 1144*
- **Sodium Benzoate and Caffeine** *see* Caffeine and Sodium Benzoate *on page 198*
- **Sodium Benzoate and Sodium Phenylacetate** *see* Sodium Phenylacetate and Sodium Benzoate *on page 1150*

Sodium Bicarbonate *(SOW dee um bye KAR bun ate)*

U.S. Brand Names Brioschi® [OTC]; Neut®

Synonyms Baking Soda; NaHCO₃; Sodium Acid Carbonate; Sodium Hydrogen Carbonate

Therapeutic Category Alkalinizing Agent, Oral; Alkalinizing Agent, Parenteral; Antacid; Electrolyte Supplement, Oral; Electrolyte Supplement, Parenteral; Sodium Salt

Use Management of metabolic acidosis; gastric hyperacidity; as an alkalinization agent for the urine; treatment of hyperkalemia; management of overdose of certain drugs, including tricyclic antidepressants and aspirin

Pregnancy Risk Factor C

Contraindications Alkalosis, hypernatremia, severe pulmonary edema, hypocalcemia, unknown abdominal pain

Warnings/Precautions Rapid administration in neonates and children <2 years of age has led to hypernatremia, decreased CSF pressure and intracranial hemorrhage. **Use of I.V. NaHCO₃ should be reserved for documented metabolic acidosis and for hyperkalemia-induced cardiac arrest.** Routine use in cardiac arrest is not recommended. Avoid extravasation, tissue necrosis can occur due to the hypertonicity of $NaHCO_3$. May cause sodium retention especially if renal function is impaired; not to be used in treatment of peptic ulcer; use with caution in patients with CHF, edema, cirrhosis, or renal failure. Not the antacid of choice for the elderly because of sodium content and potential for systemic alkalosis.

Common Adverse Reactions Frequency not defined.

Cardiovascular: Cerebral hemorrhage, CHF (aggravated), edema

Central nervous system: Tetany

Gastrointestinal: Belching, flatulence (with oral), gastric distension

Endocrine & metabolic: Hypernatremia, hyperosmolality, hypocalcemia, hypokalemia, increased affinity of hemoglobin for oxygen-reduced pH in myocardial tissue necrosis when extravasated, intracranial acidosis, metabolic alkalosis, milk-alkali syndrome (especially with renal dysfunction)

Respiratory: Pulmonary edema

Drug Interactions

Increased Effect/Toxicity: Increased toxicity/levels of amphetamines, ephedrine, pseudoephedrine, flecainide, quinidine, and quinine due to urinary alkalinization.

Decreased Effect: Decreased effect/levels of lithium, chlorpropamide, and salicylates due to urinary alkalinization.

Mechanism of Action Dissociates to provide bicarbonate ion which neutralizes hydrogen ion concentration and raises blood and urinary pH

Pharmacodynamics/Kinetics

Onset of action: Oral: Rapid; I.V.: 15 minutes

Duration: Oral: 8-10 minutes; I.V.: 1-2 hours

Absorption: Oral: Well absorbed

Excretion: Urine (<1%)

Dosage

Cardiac arrest: **Routine use of NaHCO₃ is not recommended and should be given only after adequate alveolar ventilation has been established and effective cardiac compressions are provided**

Infants and Children: I.V.: 0.5-1 mEq/kg/dose repeated every 10 minutes or as indicated by arterial blood gases; rate of infusion should not exceed 10 mEq/minute; neonates and children <2 years of age should receive 4.2% (0.5 mEq/mL) solution

Adults: I.V.: Initial: 1 mEq/kg/dose one time; maintenance: 0.5 mEq/kg/dose every 10 minutes or as indicated by arterial blood gases

Metabolic acidosis: Dosage should be based on the following formula if blood gases and pH measurements are available:

Infants and Children:

HCO_3^-(mEq) = 0.3 x weight (kg) x base deficit (mEq/L) **or**

HCO_3^-(mEq) = 0.5 x weight (kg) x [24 - serum HCO_3^- (mEq/L)]

Adults:

HCO_3^-(mEq) = 0.2 x weight (kg) x base deficit (mEq/L) **or**

HCO_3^-(mEq) = 0.5 x weight (kg) x [24 - serum HCO_3^- (mEq/L)]

If acid-base status is not available: Dose for older Children and Adults: 2-5 mEq/kg I.V. infusion over 4-8 hours; subsequent doses should be based on patient's acid-base status

Chronic renal failure: Oral: Initiate when plasma HCO_3^- <15 mEq/L

Children: 1-3 mEq/kg/day

Adults: Start with 20-36 mEq/day in divided doses, titrate to bicarbonate level of 18-20 mEq/L

Hyperkalemia: Adults: I.V.: 1 mEq/kg over 5 minutes

Renal tubular acidosis: Oral:

Distal:

Children: 2-3 mEq/kg/day

Adults: 0.5-2 mEq/kg/day in 4-5 divided doses

Proximal: Children: Initial: 5-10 mEq/kg/day; maintenance: Increase as required to maintain serum bicarbonate in the normal range

Urine alkalinization: Oral:

Children: 1-10 mEq (84-840 mg)/kg/day in divided doses every 4-6 hours; dose should be titrated to desired urinary pH

Adults: Initial: 48 mEq (4 g), then 12-24 mEq (1-2 g) every 4 hours; dose should be titrated to desired urinary pH; doses up to 16 g/day (200 mEq) in patients <60 years and 8 g (100 mEq) in patients >60 years

Antacid: Adults: Oral: 325 mg to 2 g 1-4 times/day

Administration For I.V. administration to infants, use the 0.5 mEq/mL solution or dilute the 1 mEq/mL solution 1:1 with **sterile water**; for direct I.V. infusion in emergencies, administer slowly (maximum rate in infants: 10 mEq/minute); for infusion, dilute to a maximum concentration of 0.5 mEq/mL in dextrose solution and infuse over 2 hours (maximum rate of administration: 1 mEq/kg/hour)

Patient Information Avoid chronic use as an antacid (<2 weeks)

Dosage Forms GRAN, effervescent (Brioschi®): 6 g, 120 g, 240 g. **INJ, solution:** 4.2% [42 mg/mL = 5 mEq/10 mL] (10 mL); 5% [50 mg/mL = 5.95 mEq/10 mL] (500 mL); 7.5% [75 mg/mL = 8.92 mEq/10 mL] (50 mL); 8.4% [84 mg/mL = 10 mEq/10 mL] (10 mL, 50 mL); (Neut®): 4% (Continued)

Sodium Bicarbonate *(Continued)*

[40 mg/mL = 2.4 mEq/5 mL] (5 mL). **INF** [premixed in sterile water]: 5% (500 mL). **POWDER:** 120 g, 480 g. **TAB:** 325 mg [3.8 mEq]; 650 mg [7.6 mEq]

♦ **Sodium Biphosphate, Methenamine, Methylene Blue, Phenyl Salicylate, and Hyoscyamine** *see* Methenamine, Sodium Biphosphate, Phenyl Salicylate, Methylene Blue, and Hyoscyamine *on page 812*

♦ **Sodium Carboxymethylcellulose, Benzocaine, Gelatin, and Pectin** *see* Benzocaine, Gelatin, Pectin, and Sodium Carboxymethylcellulose *on page 155*

Sodium Chloride *(SOW dee um KLOR ide)*

U.S. Brand Names Altamist [OTC]; Ayr® Baby Saline [OTC]; Ayr® Saline [OTC]; Ayr® Saline Mist [OTC]; Breathe Right® Saline [OTC]; Broncho Saline® [OTC]; Entsol® [OTC]; Muro 128® [OTC]; NaSal™ [OTC]; Nasal Moist® [OTC]; Na-Zone® [OTC]; Ocean® [OTC]; Pediamist® [OTC]; Pretz® Irrigation [OTC]; SalineX® [OTC]; SeaMist® [OTC]; Simply Saline™ [OTC]; Wound Wash Saline™ [OTC]

Synonyms NaCl; Normal Saline; Salt

Therapeutic Category Electrolyte Supplement, Oral; Electrolyte Supplement, Parenteral; Lubricant, Ocular; Sodium Salt

Use

Parenteral: Restores sodium ion in patients with restricted oral intake (especially hyponatremia states or low salt syndrome). In general, parenteral saline uses:

Bacteriostatic sodium chloride: Dilution or dissolving drugs for I.M., I.V., or S.C. injections

Concentrated sodium chloride: Additive for parenteral fluid therapy

Hypertonic sodium chloride: For severe hyponatremia and hypochloremia

Hypotonic sodium chloride: Hydrating solution

Normal saline: Restores water/sodium losses

Pharmaceutical aid/diluent for infusion of compatible drug additives

Ophthalmic: Reduces corneal edema

Oral: Restores sodium losses

Inhalation: Restores moisture to pulmonary system; loosens and thins congestion caused by colds or allergies; diluent for bronchodilator solutions that require dilution before inhalation

Intranasal: Restores moisture to nasal membranes

Irrigation: Wound cleansing, irrigation, and flushing

Pregnancy Risk Factor C

Contraindications Hypersensitivity to sodium chloride or any component of the formulation; hypertonic uterus, hypernatremia, fluid retention

Warnings/Precautions Use with caution in patients with CHF, renal insufficiency, liver cirrhosis, hypertension, edema; sodium toxicity is almost exclusively related to how fast a sodium deficit is corrected; both rate and magnitude are extremely important; do not use bacteriostatic sodium chloride in newborns since benzyl alcohol preservatives have been associated with toxicity

Common Adverse Reactions Frequency not defined.

Cardiovascular: Congestive conditions

Endocrine & metabolic: Extravasation, hypervolemia, hypernatremia, dilution of serum electrolytes, overhydration, hypokalemia

Local: Thrombosis, phlebitis, extravasation

Respiratory: Pulmonary edema

Drug Interactions

Decreased Effect: Lithium serum concentrations may be decreased.

Mechanism of Action Principal extracellular cation; functions in fluid and electrolyte balance, osmotic pressure control, and water distribution

Pharmacodynamics/Kinetics

Absorption: Oral, I.V.: Rapid

Distribution: Widely distributed

Excretion: Primarily urine; also sweat, tears, saliva

Dosage

Children: I.V.: Hypertonic solutions (>0.9%) should only be used for the initial treatment of acute serious symptomatic hyponatremia; maintenance: 3-4 mEq/kg/day; maximum: 100-150 mEq/day; dosage varies widely depending on clinical condition

Replacement: Determined by laboratory determinations mEq

Sodium deficiency (mEq/kg) = [% dehydration (L/kg)/100 x 70 (mEq/L)] + [0.6 (L/kg) x (140 - serum sodium) (mEq/L)]

Children ≥2 years and Adults:

Intranasal: 2-3 sprays in each nostril as needed

Irrigation: Spray affected area

Children and Adults: Inhalation: Bronchodilator diluent: 1-3 sprays (1-3 mL) to dilute bronchodilator solution in nebulizer prior to administration

Adults:

GU irrigant: 1-3 L/day by intermittent irrigation

Heat cramps: Oral: 0.5-1 g with full glass of water, up to 4.8 g/day

Replacement I.V.: Determined by laboratory determinations mEq

Sodium deficiency (mEq/kg) = [% dehydration (L/kg)/100 x 70 (mEq/L)] + [0.6 (L/kg) x (140 - serum sodium) (mEq/L)]

To correct acute, serious hyponatremia: mEq sodium = [desired sodium (mEq/L) - actual sodium (mEq/L)] x [0.6 x wt (kg)]; for acute correction use 125 mEq/L as the desired serum sodium; acutely correct serum sodium in 5 mEq/L/dose increments; more gradual correction in increments of 10 mEq/L/day is indicated in the asymptomatic patient

Chloride maintenance electrolyte requirement in parenteral nutrition: 2-4 mEq/kg/24 hours or 25-40 mEq/1000 kcals/24 hours; maximum: 100-150 mEq/24 hours

Sodium maintenance electrolyte requirement in parenteral nutrition: 3-4 mEq/kg/24 hours or 25-40 mEq/1000 kcals/24 hours; maximum: 100-150 mEq/24 hours.

Approximate Deficits of Water and Electrolytes in Moderately Severe Dehydration[1]

Condition	Water (mL/kg)	Sodium (mEq/kg)
Fasting and thirsting	100-120	5-7
Diarrhea		
isonatremic	100-120	8-10
hypernatremic	100-120	2-4
hyponatremic	100-120	10-12
Pyloric stenosis	100-120	8-10
Diabetic acidosis	100-120	9-10

[1]A **negative** deficit indicates total body **excess** prior to treatment.

Adapted from Behrman RE, Kleigman RM, Nelson WE, et al, eds, *Nelson Textbook of Pediatrics*, 14th ed, WB Saunders Co, 1992.

Ophthalmic:

Ointment: Apply once daily or more often

Solution: Instill 1-2 drops into affected eye(s) every 3-4 hours

Administration Infuse hypertonic solutions (>NaCl 0.9%) via central line only; maximum rate of administration: 1 mEq/kg/hour

Monitoring Parameters Serum sodium, potassium, chloride, and bicarbonate levels; I & O, weight

Reference Range Serum/plasma sodium levels:

Neonates:

Full-term: 133-142 mEq/L

Premature: 132-140 mEq/L

Children ≥2 months to Adults: 135-145 mEq/L

Patient Information Blurred vision is common with ophthalmic ointment; may sting eyes when first applied

Dosage Forms GEL, intranasal (Nasal Moist®): 0.65% (30 g). **INJ, solution:** 0.45% (25 mL, 50 mL, 100 mL, 250 mL, 500 mL, 1000 mL, 1500 mL, 2000 mL); 0.9% (1 mL, 2 mL, 3 mL, 5 mL, 10 mL, 20 mL, 25 mL, 30 mL, 50 mL, 100 mL, 150 mL, 250 mL, 500 mL, 1000 mL); 2.5 % (250 mL); 3% (500 mL); 5% (500 mL). **INJ, solution, bacteriostatic:** 0.9% (10 mL, 20 mL, 30 mL). **INJ, solution, concentrate:** 14.6% [2.5 mEq/mL] (20 mL, 40 mL, 250 mL); 23.4% [4 mEq/mL] (30 mL, 50 mL, 100 mL, 200 mL, 250 mL). **INJ, solution** [preservative free]: 0.9% (2 mL, 3 mL, 5 mL, 10 mL, 20 mL, 50 mL, 100 mL). **OINT, ophthalmic** (Muro-128®): 5% (3.5 g). **POWDER, nasal solution:** (Broncho Saline®): 0.9% (90 mL, 240 mL); (Entsol®) 3% (10.5 g). **SOLN, inhalation:** 0.45% (3 mL, 5 mL); 0.9% (3 mL, 5 mL, 15 mL); 3% (15 mL); 10% (15 mL); (Broncho Saline®): 0.9% (90 mL, 240 mL). **SOLN, intranasal:** 0.65% (45 mL); (Altamist): 0.65% (60 mL); (Ayr® Saline, Ayr® Saline Mist): 0.65% (50 mL); (Ayr® Baby Saline, NāSal™): 0.65% (30 mL); (Breathe Right® Saline): 0.65% (44 mL); (Entsol® [preservative free]): 3% (100 mL); (Entsol® Mist): 3% (30 mL); (Enstol® Single Use [preservative free]): 3% (240 mL); (Na-Zone®): 0.75% (60 mL); (NāSal™, SeaMist®): 0.65% (15 mL); (Nasal Moist®): 0.65% (15 mL, 45 mL); (Ocean®): 0.65% (45 mL); (Pediamist®): 0.5% (15 mL); (Pretz® Irrigation): 0.75% (240 mL); (SalineX®): 0.4% (15 mL, 50 mL); (Simply Saline™): 0.9% (44 mL). **SOLN, irrigation:** 0.45% (2000 mL); 0.9% (250 mL, 500 mL, 1000 mL, 1500 mL, 2000 mL, 3000 mL, 4000 mL, 5000 mL); (Wound Wash Saline™): 0.9% (90 mL, 210 mL). **SOLN, ophthalmic:** 5% (15 mL); (Muro-128®): 2% (15 mL), 5% (15 mL, 30 mL). **TAB:** 1 g

Sodium Citrate and Citric Acid (SOW dee um SIT rate & SI trik AS id)

U.S. Brand Names Bicitra®; Cytra-2; Oracit®

Synonyms Modified Shohl's Solution

Therapeutic Category Alkalinizing Agent, Oral

Use Treatment of metabolic acidosis; alkalinizing agent in conditions where long-term maintenance of an alkaline urine is desirable

Pregnancy Risk Factor Not established

Contraindications Hypersensitivity to sodium citrate, citric acid, or any component of the formulation; severe renal insufficiency; sodium-restricted diet

Warnings/Precautions Conversion to bicarbonate may be impaired in patients with hepatic failure, in shock, or who are severely ill. Use caution with cardiac failure, hypertension, impaired renal function, and peripheral or pulmonary edema.

Common Adverse Reactions Frequency not defined. Generally well tolerated with normal renal function.

Central nervous system: Tetany

Endocrine & metabolic: Metabolic alkalosis, hyperkalemia

Gastrointestinal: Diarrhea, nausea, vomiting

(Continued)

Sodium Citrate and Citric Acid *(Continued)*

Drug Interactions

Increased Effect/Toxicity: Increased toxicity/levels of amphetamines, ephedrine, pseudoephedrine, flecainide, quinidine, and quinine due to urinary alkalinization.

Decreased Effect: Decreased effect/levels of lithium, chlorpropamide, and salicylates due to urinary alkalinization.

Pharmacodynamics/Kinetics

Metabolism: Oxidized to sodium bicarbonate

Excretion: Urine (<5% as sodium citrate)

Dosage Oral: Systemic alkalization:

Infants and Children: 2-3 mEq/kg/day in divided doses 3-4 times/day **or** 5-15 mL with water after meals and at bedtime

Adults: 10-30 mL with water after meals and at bedtime

Administration Administer after meals. Dilute with 30-90 mL of water to enhance taste. Chilling solution prior to dosing helps to enhance palatability.

Patient Information Palatability is improved by chilling solution, dilute each dose with 1-3 oz of water and follow with additional water; take after meals to prevent saline laxative effect

Dosage Forms Note: Equivalent to sodium 1 mEq/mL and bicarbonate 1 mEq/mL. **SOLN, oral:** Sodium citrate 500 mg and citric acid 334 mg per 5 mL (480 mL); (Bicitra®, Cytra-2): Sodium citrate 500 mg and citric acid 334 mg per 5 mL (480 mL); (Oracit®): Sodium citrate 490 mg and citric acid 640 mg per 5 mL (15 mL, 30 mL, 480 mL, 3840 mL)

♦ **Sodium Citrate, Citric Acid, and Potassium Citrate** *see* Citric Acid, Sodium Citrate, and Potassium Citrate *on page 287*

♦ **Sodium Edetate** *see* Edetate Disodium *on page 422*

♦ **Sodium Etidronate** *see* Etidronate Disodium *on page 495*

♦ **Sodium Ferric Gluconate** *see* Ferric Gluconate *on page 517*

♦ **Sodium Fluoride** *see* Fluoride *on page 535*

Sodium Hyaluronate *(SOW dee um hye al yoor ON ate)*

U.S. Brand Names Biolon™; Healon®; Healon®5; Healon GV®; Hyalgan®; IPM Wound Gel™ [OTC]; Provisc®; Supartz™; Vitrax®

Synonyms Hyaluronic Acid

Therapeutic Category Ophthalmic Agent, Viscoelastic

Use

Intra-articular injection (Hyalgan®): Treatment of pain in osteoarthritis in knee in patients who have failed nonpharmacologic treatment and simple analgesics

Ophthalmic: Surgical aid in cataract extraction, intraocular implantation, corneal transplant, glaucoma filtration, and retinal attachment surgery

Topical: Management of skin ulcers and wounds

Pregnancy Risk Factor C

Contraindications Hypersensitivity to hyaluronate or any component of the formulation; hypersensitivity to avian proteins (egg products, feathers)

Warnings/Precautions

Intra-articular: Not for use in infected joints

Ophthalmic: Do not overfill the anterior chamber; carefully monitor intraocular pressure

Topical: Cleansing agents other than normal saline are not recommended

Common Adverse Reactions Frequency not defined.

Central nervous system: Headache

Dermatologic: Itching

Local: Injection site: Bruising, pain, rash

Ocular: Postoperative inflammatory reactions (iritis, hypopyon), corneal edema, corneal decompensation, transient postoperative increase in IOP

Mechanism of Action Functions as a tissue lubricant and is thought to play an important role in modulating the interactions between adjacent tissues. Sodium hyaluronate is a polysaccharide which is distributed widely in the extracellular matrix of connective tissue in man. (Vitreous and aqueous humor of the eye, synovial fluid, skin, and umbilical cord.) Sodium hyaluronate forms a viscoelastic solution in water (at physiological pH and ionic strength) which makes it suitable for aqueous and vitreous humor in ophthalmic surgery.

Pharmacodynamics/Kinetics

Distribution: Intravitreous injection: Diffusion occurs slowly

Excretion: Ophthalmic: Via Canal of Schlemm

Dosage Adults:

Intra-articular:

Hyalgan®: Inject 20 mg (2 mL) once weekly for 5 weeks; some patients may benefit with a total of 3 injections

Supartz™: Inject 25 mg (2.5 mL) once weekly for 5 weeks

Ophthalmic: Depends upon procedure (slowly introduce a sufficient quantity into eye)

Topical: Apply to clean dry ulcer or wound, and cover with nonstick dressing; repeat daily. Discontinue if wound size increase after 3-4 applications.

Administration

Intra-articular: Injected directly into the knee joint

Ophthalmic: Drug may become cloudy or form a slight precipitate after administration; clinical significance unknown, but cloudy or precipitated material should be removed by irrigation or aspiration

Topical: Clean wound with normal saline; remove excess moisture with dry gauze; apply gel liberally to wound

Monitoring Parameters Intraocular pressure

Patient Information Following intra-articular administration, avoid strenuous activities or prolonged weight-bearing activities within 48 hours of injection. Following topical administration, notify prescriber if wound size enlarges.

Dosage Forms GEL, topical (IPM Wound Gel™): 2.5% (10 g). **INJ, solution, intra-articular** (Hyalgan®): 10 mg/mL (2 mL). (Supartz™): 10 mg/mL (2.5 mL). **INJ, solution, intraocular** (Biolon™): 10 mg/mL (0.5 mL, 1 mL); (Healon®): 10 mg/mL (0.4 mL, 0.55 mL, 0.85 mL, 2 mL); (Healon®5): 23 mg/mL; (Healon GV®): 14 mg/mL (0.55 mL, 0.85 mL); (Provisc®): 10 mg/mL (0.4 mL, 0.55 mL, 0.8 mL); (Vitrax®): 30 mg/mL (0.65 mL)

♦ **Sodium Hyaluronate-Chrondroitin Sulfate** see Chondroitin Sulfate and Sodium Hyaluronate on page 271

♦ **Sodium Hydrogen Carbonate** see Sodium Bicarbonate on page 1144

Sodium Hypochlorite Solution (SOW dee um hye poe KLOR ite soe LOO shun)

U.S. Brand Names Dakin's Solution

Synonyms Modified Dakin's Solution

Therapeutic Category Disinfectant, Antibacterial (Topical)

Use Treatment of athlete's foot (0.5%); wound irrigation (0.5%); disinfection of utensils and equipment (5%)

Pregnancy Risk Factor C

Contraindications Hypersensitivity to any component of the formulation

Warnings/Precautions For external use only; avoid eye or mucous membrane contact; do not use on open wounds

Common Adverse Reactions Frequency not defined.
Dermatologic: Irritating to skin
Hematologic: Dissolves blood clots, delays clotting

Dosage Topical irrigation

Administration For external use only; do **not** ingest.

Patient Information External use only

Dosage Forms SOLN, topical (Dakin's): 0.25% (480 mL); 0.5% (480 mL, 3840 mL)

♦ **Sodium Hyposulfate** see Sodium Thiosulfate on page 1152

♦ **Sodium L-Triiodothyronine** see Liothyronine on page 749

♦ **Sodium Nafcillin** see Nafcillin on page 875

♦ **Sodium Nitroferricyanide** see Nitroprusside on page 911

♦ **Sodium Nitroprusside** see Nitroprusside on page 911

Sodium Oxybate (SOW dee um ox i BATE)

U.S. Brand Names Xyrem®

Synonyms Gamma Hydroxybutyric Acid; GHB; 4-Hydroxybutyrate; Sodium 4-Hydroxybutyrate

Therapeutic Category Central Nervous System Depressant

Use Orphan drug: Treatment of cataplexy in patients with narcolepsy

Restrictions C-I (illicit use); C-III (medical use)

Sodium oxybate oral solution will be available only to prescribers enrolled in the Xyrem® Success Program™ and dispensed to the patient through the designated centralized pharmacy. Prior to dispensing the first prescription, prescribers will be sent educational materials to be reviewed with the patient and enrollment forms for the postmarketing surveillance program. Patients must be seen at least every 3 months; prescriptions can be written for a maximum of 3 months (the first prescription may only be written for a 1-month supply).

Pregnancy Risk Factor B

Contraindications Hypersensitivity to sodium oxybate or any component of the formulation; ethanol and other CNS depressants; semialdehyde dehydrogenase deficiency

Warnings/Precautions Sodium oxybate is a CNS depressant with abuse potential; it should not be used with ethanol or other CNS depressants. Due to the rapid onset of CNS depressant effects, doses should be administered only at bedtime and while the patient is sitting up in bed. May impair respiratory drive; use caution with compromised respiratory function. Most patients (~80%) in clinical trials were also treated with stimulants; therefore, an independent assessment of the effects of sodium oxybate is lacking. May cause confusion, psychosis, paranoia, hallucinations, agitation, and depression; use caution with history of depression or suicide attempt. May cause sleepwalking, urinary, and/or fecal incontinence. Use caution with hepatic dysfunction. Contains significant amounts of sodium; use caution with heart failure, hypertension, or compromised renal function.

Patients should be instructed not to engage in hazardous activities requiring mental alertness while taking this medication and that CNS effects may carryover to the next day. Seizures, respiratory depression, decreases in level of consciousness, coma and death have been reported when used for nonprescription purposes. Tolerance to sodium oxybate, or withdrawal following its discontinuation, have not been clearly defined in controlled clinical trials, but have been reported at larger doses used for illicit purposes. Safety and efficacy have not been established in patients <16 years of age.

Common Adverse Reactions Percentages reported in controlled clinical trials:
>10%:
Central nervous system: Dizziness (23% to 34%), headache (9% to 31%), pain (9% to 20%), somnolence (12% to 15%), confusion (9% to 14%), sleep disorder (6% to 14%)

(Continued)

Sodium Oxybate *(Continued)*

Dermatologic: Diaphoresis (3% to 11%)
Gastrointestinal: Nausea (6% to 34%), vomiting (6% to 11%)
Genitourinary: Urinary incontinence (5% to 14%, usually nocturnal)
Respiratory: Pharyngitis (11%)
Miscellaneous: Infection (7% to 15%)

1% to 10%:
Cardiovascular: Hypertension (6%), edema
Central nervous system: Dream abnormality (3% to 9%), sleepwalking (7%), depression (6%), amnesia (3% to 6%), anxiety (3% to 6%), thinking abnormality (3% to 6%), insomnia (5%), agitation, ataxia, chills, convulsion, stupor, tremor
Dermatologic: Acne, alopecia, rash
Endocrine & metabolic: Dysmenorrhea (3% to 6%)
Gastrointestinal: Dyspepsia (6% to 9%), diarrhea (6% to 8%), abdominal pain (6%), nausea and vomiting (6%), anorexia, constipation, weight gain
Hepatic: Alkaline phosphatase increased, hypercholesteremia, hypocalcemia
Neuromuscular & skeletal: Hypesthesia (6%), weakness (6% to 8%), myasthenia (3% to 6%), arthritis, leg cramps, myalgia
Ocular: Amblyopia (6%)
Otic: Tinnitus (6%)
Renal: Albuminuria, cystitis, hematuria, metrorrhagia, urinary frequency
Respiratory: Rhinitis (8%), dyspnea
Miscellaneous: Viral infection (3% to 9%), allergic reaction

Drug Interactions
Increased Effect/Toxicity: CNS depressants: CNS depressant effects are potentiated; concomitant use with sodium oxybate is contraindicated.

Mechanism of Action The exact mechanism for the efficacy of sodium oxybate the treatment of cataplexy in patients with narcolepsy is not known.

Pharmacodynamics/Kinetics
Absorption: Rapid
Distribution: 190-384 mL/kg
Protein binding: <1%
Metabolism: Primarily via the Krebs cycle to form water and carbon dioxide; secondarily via beta oxidation; significant first-pass effect; no active metabolites; metabolic pathways are saturable
Bioavailability: 25%
Half-life elimination: 30-60 minutes
Time to peak: 30-75 minutes
Excretion: Primarily pulmonary (as carbon dioxide); urine (<5% unchanged drug)

Dosage Oral:
Children ≥16 years and Adults: Treatment of cataplexy in patients with narcolepsy: Initial: 4.5 g/day, in 2 equal doses; first dose to be given at bedtime after the patient is in bed, and second dose to be given 2.5-4 hours later. Dose may be increased or adjusted in 2-week intervals; average dose: 6-9 g/day (maximum: 9 g/day)
Elderly: Safety and efficacy have not been studied in patients >65 years.
Dosage adjustment in renal impairment: Adjustment not necessary; consider sodium content
Dosage adjustment in hepatic impairment: Decrease starting dose to half and titrate doses carefully in patients with liver dysfunction. Elimination half-life significantly longer in patients with Child's class C liver dysfunction.

Administration Take on an empty stomach; separate last meal (or food) and first dose by several hours; try to take at similar time each day. Doses should be administered while patient is sitting up in bed. Both doses should be prepared prior to bedtime. The first dose is taken at bedtime and the second dose is taken 2.5-4 hours later; an alarm clock may need to be set for the second dose. After taking the dose, patient is to lie down and remain in bed.

Patient Information This medication should only be used by the person it was prescribed for; it is illegal to share with others. Keep in a safe place and prevent access by children or pets. This medication will cause sleep very quickly. It must be taken at bedtime and only after getting in bed. Both doses should be mixed prior to bedtime and stored in the child-resistant containers, which are provided. You may need to set an alarm clock for the second dose. In addition to sleepiness, can cause dizziness, and confusion; these side effects may also carryover to the next day; do not participate in hazardous activities requiring mental alertness until the effects of this medication are fully understood. Do not take with food. May cause nausea and vomiting or bed-wetting. Notify prescriber if you have trouble breathing while asleep, abnormal thinking, depression, loss of consciousness, sleepwalking, or think you may be pregnant. Unused medication may be poured down the drain; empty bottles should be defaced with a marker or pen prior to disposal.

Dosage Forms SOLN, oral: 500 mg/mL (180 mL)

♦ **Sodium PAS** *see* Aminosalicylic Acid *on page 76*

Sodium Phenylacetate and Sodium Benzoate
(SOW dee um fen il AS e tate & SOW dee um BENZ oh ate)
U.S. Brand Names Ucephan®
Synonyms Sodium Benzoate and Sodium Phenylacetate
Therapeutic Category Ammonium Detoxicant

Use Orphan drug: Adjunctive therapy to prevention/treatment of hyperammonemia in patients with urea cycle enzymopathy involving partial or complete deficiencies of carbamoyl-phosphate synthetase, ornithine transcarbamoylase, or argininosuccinate synthetase

Pregnancy Risk Factor C

Dosage Infants and Children: Oral: 2.5 mL (250 mg sodium benzoate and 250 mg sodium phenylacetate)/kg/day divided 3-6 times/day; total daily dose should not exceed 100 mL

Dosage Forms SOLN, oral: Sodium phenylacetate 100 mg and sodium benzoate 100 mg per mL (100 mL)

Sodium Phenylbutyrate (SOW dee um fen il BYOO ti rate)

U.S. Brand Names Buphenyl®

Synonyms Ammonapse

Therapeutic Category Urea Cycle Disorder (UCD) Treatment Agent

Use Orphan drug: Adjunctive therapy in the chronic management of patients with urea cycle disorder involving deficiencies of carbamoylphosphate synthetase, ornithine transcarbamylase, or argininosuccinic acid synthetase

Pregnancy Risk Factor C

Dosage Oral:

Powder: Patients weighing <20 kg: 450-600 mg/kg/day or 9.9-13 g/m^2/day, administered in equally divided amounts with each meal or feeding, four to six times daily; safety and efficacy of doses >20 g/day has not been established

Tablet: Children >20 kg and Adults: 450-600 mg/kg/day or 9.9-13 g/m^2/day, administered in equally divided amounts with each meal; safety and efficacy of doses >20 g/day have not been established

Dosage Forms POWDER, oral solution: 250 mg. **TAB:** 500 mg

♦ **Sodium Phosphate and Potassium Phosphate** see Potassium Phosphate and Sodium Phosphate on page 1024

Sodium Polystyrene Sulfonate (SOW dee um pol ee STYE reen SUL fon ate)

U.S. Brand Names Kayexalate®; Kionex™; SPS®

Therapeutic Category Antidote, Hyperkalemia; Antidote, Potassium

Use Treatment of hyperkalemia

Pregnancy Risk Factor C

Contraindications Hypersensitivity to sodium polystyrene sulfonate or any component of the formulation; hypernatremia

Warnings/Precautions Use with caution in patients with severe CHF, hypertension, edema, or renal failure; avoid using the commercially available liquid product in neonates due to the preservative content; large oral doses may cause fecal impaction (especially in elderly); enema will reduce the serum potassium faster than oral administration, but the oral route will result in a greater reduction over several hours.

Common Adverse Reactions Frequency not defined.

Endocrine & metabolic: Hypokalemia, hypocalcemia, hypomagnesemia, sodium retention

Gastrointestinal: Fecal impaction, constipation, loss of appetite, nausea, vomiting

Drug Interactions

Increased Effect/Toxicity: Systemic alkalosis and seizure has occurred after cation-exchange resins were administered with nonabsorbable cation-donating antacids and laxatives (eg, magnesium hydroxide, aluminum carbonate).

Mechanism of Action Removes potassium by exchanging sodium ions for potassium ions in the intestine before the resin is passed from the body

Pharmacodynamics/Kinetics

Onset of action: 2-24 hours

Absorption: None

Excretion: Completely feces (primarily as potassium polystyrene sulfonate)

Dosage

Children:

Oral: 1 g/kg/dose every 6 hours

Rectal: 1 g/kg/dose every 2-6 hours (In small children and infants, employ lower doses by using the practical exchange ratio of 1 mEq K$^+$/g of resin as the basis for calculation)

Adults: Hyperkalemia:

Oral: 15 g (60 mL) 1-4 times/day

Rectal: 30-50 g every 6 hours

Monitoring Parameters Exchange capacity is 1 mEq/g in vivo, and in vitro capacity is 3.1 mEq/g, therefore, a wide range of exchange capacity exists such that close monitoring of serum electrolytes (potassium, sodium, calcium, magnesium) is necessary; ECG

Reference Range Serum potassium: Adults: 3.5-5.2 mEq/L

Patient Information Mix well in full glass of liquid prior to drinking

Dosage Forms POWDER, suspension, oral/rectal (Kayexalate®): 480 g; (Kionex™): 454 g. **SUSP, oral/rectal:** 15 g/60 mL (60 mL, 120 mL, 200 mL, 500 mL); (SPS®): 15 g/60 mL (60 mL, 120 mL, 480 mL)

♦ **Sodium Sulfacetamide** see Sulfacetamide on page 1169

♦ **Sodium Sulfacetamide and Sulfur** see Sulfur and Sulfacetamide on page 1177

Sodium Thiosulfate (SOW dee um thye oh SUL fate)

U.S. Brand Names Versiclear™

Synonyms Disodium Thiosulfate Pentahydrate; Pentahydrate; Sodium Hyposulfate; Sodium Thiosulphate; Thiosulfuric Acid Disodium Salt

Therapeutic Category Antidote, Arsenic Toxicity; Antidote, Cyanide

Use

Parenteral: Used alone or with sodium nitrite or amyl nitrite in cyanide poisoning or arsenic poisoning; reduce the risk of nephrotoxicity associated with cisplatin therapy

Topical: Treatment of tinea versicolor

Unlabeled/Investigational Use Management of I.V. extravasation

Pregnancy Risk Factor C

Contraindications Hypersensitivity to sodium thiosulfate or any component of the formulation

Warnings/Precautions Safety in pregnancy has not been established; discontinue topical use if irritation or sensitivity occurs; rapid I.V. infusion has caused transient hypotension and ECG changes in dogs; can increase risk of thiocyanate intoxication

Common Adverse Reactions 1% to 10%:

Cardiovascular: Hypotension

Central nervous system: Coma, CNS depression secondary to thiocyanate intoxication, psychosis, confusion

Dermatologic: Contact dermatitis, local irritation

Neuromuscular & skeletal: Weakness

Otic: Tinnitus

Mechanism of Action

Cyanide toxicity: Increases the rate of detoxification of cyanide by the enzyme rhodanese by providing an extra sulfur

Cisplatin toxicity: Complexes with cisplatin to form a compound that is nontoxic to either normal or cancerous cells

Pharmacodynamics/Kinetics

Absorption: Oral: Poor

Distribution: Extracellular fluid

Half-life elimination: 0.65 hour

Excretion: Urine (28.5% as unchanged drug)

Dosage

Cyanide and nitroprusside antidote: I.V.:

Children <25 kg: 50 mg/kg after receiving 4.5-10 mg/kg sodium nitrite; a half dose of each may be repeated if necessary

Children >25 kg and Adults: 12.5 g after 300 mg of sodium nitrite; a half dose of each may be repeated if necessary

Cyanide poisoning: I.V.: Dose should be based on determination as with nitrite, at rate of 2.5-5 mL/minute to maximum of 50 mL.

Variation of sodium nitrite and sodium thiosulfate dose, based on hemoglobin concentration: See table.

Variation of Sodium Nitrite and Sodium Thiosulfate Dose With Hemoglobin Concentration[1]

Hemoglobin (g/dL)	Initial Dose Sodium Nitrite (mg/kg)	Initial Dose Sodium Nitrite 3% (mL/kg)	Initial Dose Sodium Thiosulfate 25% (mL/kg)
7	5.8	0.19	0.95
8	6.6	0.22	1.10
9	7.5	0.25	1.25
10	8.3	0.27	1.35
11	9.1	0.30	1.50
12	10.0	0.33	1.65
13	10.8	0.36	1.80
14	11.6	0.39	1.95

[1]Adapted from Berlin DM Jr, "The Treatment of Cyanide Poisoning in Children," *Pediatrics*, 1970, 46:793.

Cisplatin rescue should be given before or during cisplatin administration: I.V. infusion (in sterile water): 12 g/m^2 over 6 hours or 9 g/m^2 I.V. push followed by 1.2 g/m^2 continuous infusion for 6 hours

Arsenic poisoning: I.V.: 1 mL first day, 2 mL second day, 3 mL third day, 4 mL fourth day, 5 mL on alternate days thereafter

Children and Adults:

Topical: 20% to 25% solution: Apply a thin layer to affected areas twice daily

S.C.: Drug extravasation (unlabeled use):

2% solution: Infiltrate S.C. into the affected area

1/6 M (~4%) solution: 5-10 mL infused through I.V. line and S.C. into the affected area

Administration

I.V.: Inject slowly, over at least 10 minutes; rapid administration may cause hypotension.

Topical: Do not apply to or near eyes.

Monitoring Parameters Monitor for signs of thiocyanate toxicity

SORBITOL

Patient Information Avoid topical application near the eyes, mouth, or other mucous membranes; notify prescriber if condition worsens or burning or irritation occurs; shake well before using

Dosage Forms INJ, solution [preservative free]: 100 mg/mL (10 mL); 250 mg/mL (50 mL).
LOTION (Versiclear™): Sodium thiosulfate 25% and salicylic acid 1% (120 mL)

- **Sodium Thiosulphate** *see* Sodium Thiosulfate *on page 1152*
- **Solagé™** *see* Mequinol and Tretinoin *on page 795*
- **Solaquin® [OTC]** *see* Hydroquinone *on page 636*
- **Solaquin Forte®** *see* Hydroquinone *on page 636*
- **Solaraze™** *see* Diclofenac *on page 367*
- **Solarcaine® [OTC]** *see* Benzocaine *on page 154*
- **Solarcaine® Aloe Extra Burn Relief [OTC]** *see* Lidocaine *on page 742*
- **Soluble Fluorescein** *see* Fluorescein Sodium *on page 534*
- **Solu-Cortef®** *see* Hydrocortisone *on page 632*
- **Solu-Medrol®** *see* MethylPREDNISolone *on page 824*
- **Solurex®** *see* Dexamethasone *on page 356*
- **Solurex L.A.®** *see* Dexamethasone *on page 356*
- **Soma®** *see* Carisoprodol *on page 221*
- **Soma® Compound** *see* Carisoprodol and Aspirin *on page 222*
- **Soma® Compound w/Codeine** *see* Carisoprodol, Aspirin, and Codeine *on page 222*
- **Somatrem** *see* Human Growth Hormone *on page 620*
- **Somatropin** *see* Human Growth Hormone *on page 620*
- **Somavert®** *see* Pegvisomant *on page 968*
- **Sominex® [OTC]** *see* DiphenhydrAMINE *on page 383*
- **Sominex® Maximum Strength [OTC]** *see* DiphenhydrAMINE *on page 383*
- **Somnote™** *see* Chloral Hydrate *on page 254*
- **Sonata®** *see* Zaleplon *on page 1322*

Sorbitol (SOR bi tole)

Related Information
Laxatives, Classification and Properties *on page 1380*

Therapeutic Category Genitourinary Irrigant; Laxative, Miscellaneous

Use Genitourinary irrigant in transurethral prostatic resection or other transurethral resection or other transurethral surgical procedures; diuretic; humectant; sweetening agent; hyperosmotic laxative; facilitate the passage of sodium polystyrene sulfonate through the intestinal tract

Pregnancy Risk Factor C

Contraindications Anuria

Warnings/Precautions Use with caution in patients with severe cardiopulmonary or renal impairment and in patients unable to metabolize sorbitol; large volumes may result in fluid overload and/or electrolyte changes

Common Adverse Reactions Frequency not defined.
Cardiovascular: Edema
Endocrine & metabolic: Fluid and electrolyte losses, hyperglycemia, lactic acidosis
Gastrointestinal: Diarrhea, nausea, vomiting, abdominal discomfort, xerostomia

Mechanism of Action A polyalcoholic sugar with osmotic cathartic actions

Pharmacodynamics/Kinetics
Onset of action: 0.25-1 hour
Absorption: Oral, rectal: Poor
Metabolism: Primarily hepatic to fructose

Dosage Hyperosmotic laxative (as single dose, at infrequent intervals):
Children 2-11 years:
Oral: 2 mL/kg (as 70% solution)
Rectal enema: 30-60 mL as 25% to 30% solution
Children >12 years and Adults:
Oral: 30-150 mL (as 70% solution)
Rectal enema: 120 mL as 25% to 30% solution
Adjunct to sodium polystyrene sulfonate: 15 mL as 70% solution orally until diarrhea occurs (10-20 mL/2 hours) or 20-100 mL as an oral vehicle for the sodium polystyrene sulfonate resin
When administered with charcoal:
Oral:
Children: 4.3 mL/kg of 35% sorbitol with 1 g/kg of activated charcoal
Adults: 4.3 mL/kg of 70% sorbitol with 1 g/kg of activated charcoal every 4 hours until first stool containing charcoal is passed
Topical: 3% to 3.3% as transurethral surgical procedure irrigation

Monitoring Parameters Monitor for fluid overload and/or electrolyte disturbances following large volumes; changes may be delayed due to slow absorption

Dosage Forms SOLN, oral: 70% (480 mL, 3840 mL). **SOLN, genitourinary irrigation:** 3% (1500 mL, 3000 mL), 3.3% (2000 mL, 4000 mL)

- **Soriatane®** *see* Acitretin *on page 33*
- **Sorine®** *see* Sotalol *on page 1154*

SOTALOL

Sotalol (SOE ta lole)

Related Information
 Beta-Blockers Comparison *on page 1368*
U.S. Brand Names Betapace®; Betapace AF®; Sorine®
Synonyms Sotalol Hydrochloride
Therapeutic Category Antiarrhythmic Agent, Class II; Antiarrhythmic Agent, Class III; Beta Blocker, Nonselective
Use Treatment of documented ventricular arrhythmias (ie, sustained ventricular tachycardia), that in the judgment of the physician are life-threatening; maintenance of normal sinus rhythm in patients with symptomatic atrial fibrillation and atrial flutter who are currently in sinus rhythm. Manufacturer states substitutions should not be made for Betapace AF® since Betapace AF® is distributed with a patient package insert specific for atrial fibrillation/flutter.
Pregnancy Risk Factor B
Contraindications Hypersensitivity to sotalol or any component of the formulation; bronchial asthma; sinus bradycardia; second- and third-degree AV block (unless a functioning pacemaker is present); congenital or acquired long QT syndromes; cardiogenic shock; uncontrolled congestive heart failure. Betapace AF® is contraindicated in patients with significantly reduced renal filtration (Cl_{cr} <40 mL/minute).
Warnings/Precautions Must be initiated (or reinitiated) in a setting with continuous monitoring and staff familiar with the recognition and treatment of life-threatening arrhythmias. Patients must be monitored with continuous ECG for a minimum of 3 days (on their maintenance dose). Use cautiously in the renally-impaired (dosage adjustment required). Creatinine clearance must be calculated prior to dosing.

Monitor and adjust dose to prevent QT_c prolongation. Concurrent use with other QT_c-prolonging drugs (including Class I and Class III antiarrhythmics) is generally not recommended; withhold for 3 half-lives. Watch for proarrhythmic effects. Correct electrolyte imbalances before initiating (especially hypokalemia and hyperkalemia). Consider pre-existing conditions such as sick sinus syndrome before initiating. Conduction abnormalities can occur particularly sinus bradycardia. Use cautiously within the first 2 weeks post-MI (experience limited). Administer cautiously in compensated heart failure and monitor for a worsening of the condition. Use caution in patients with PVD (can aggravate arterial insufficiency). Beta-blocker therapy should not be withdrawn abruptly (particularly in patients with CAD), but gradually tapered to avoid acute tachycardia, hypertension, and/or ischemia. Use caution with concurrent use of beta-blockers and either verapamil or diltiazem; bradycardia or heart block can occur. Use cautiously in diabetics because it can mask prominent hypoglycemic symptoms. Can mask signs of thyrotoxicosis. Use care with anesthetic agents which decrease myocardial function.

Common Adverse Reactions
 >10%:
  Cardiovascular: Bradycardia (16%), chest pain (16%), palpitations (14%)
  Central nervous system: Fatigue (20%), dizziness (20%), lightheadedness (12%)
  Neuromuscular & skeletal: Weakness (13%)
  Respiratory: Dyspnea (21%)
 1% to 10%:
  Cardiovascular: Congestive heart failure (5%), peripheral vascular disorders (3%), edema (8%), abnormal ECG (7%), hypotension (6%), proarrhythmia (5%), syncope (5%)
  Central nervous system: Mental confusion (6%), anxiety (4%), headache (8%), sleep problems (8%), depression (4%)
  Dermatologic: Itching/rash (5%)
  Endocrine & metabolic: Decreased sexual ability (3%)
  Gastrointestinal: Diarrhea (7%), nausea/vomiting (10%), stomach discomfort (3% to 6%), flatulence (2%)
  Genitourinary: Impotence (2%)
  Hematologic: Bleeding (2%)
  Neuromuscular & skeletal: Paresthesia (4%), extremity pain (7%), back pain (3%)
  Ocular: Visual problems (5%)
  Respiratory: Upper respiratory problems (5% to 8%), asthma (2%)
Drug Interactions
 Increased Effect/Toxicity: Increased effect/toxicity of beta-blockers with calcium blockers since there may be additive effects on AV conduction or ventricular function. Other agents which prolong QT interval, including Class I antiarrhythmic agents, bepridil, cisapride, erythromycin, haloperidol, pimozide, phenothiazines, tricyclic antidepressants, specific quinolones (including sparfloxacin, gatifloxacin, moxifloxacin), or astemizole may increase the effect of sotalol on the prolongation of QT interval. Amiodarone may cause additive effects on QT_c prolongation as well as decreased heart rate, and has been associated with cardiac arrest in patients receiving some beta-blockers. When used concurrently with clonidine, sotalol may increase the risk of rebound hypertension after or during withdrawal of either agent. Beta-blocker and catecholamine depleting agents (reserpine or guanethidine) may result in additive hypotension or bradycardia. Beta-blockers may increase the action or levels of ethanol, nondepolarizing muscle relaxants, and theophylline although the effects are difficult to predict.
 Decreased Effect: Decreased effect of sotalol may occur with aluminum-magnesium antacids (if taken within 2 hours), aluminum salts, barbiturates, calcium salts, cholestyramine, colestipol, NSAIDs, penicillins (ampicillin), rifampin, salicylates, and sulfinpyrazone due to decreased bioavailability and plasma levels. Beta-blockers may decrease the effect

of sulfonylureas. Beta-agonists such as albuterol, terbutaline may have less of a therapeutic effect when administered concomitantly.

Mechanism of Action

Beta-blocker which contains both beta-adrenoreceptor-blocking (Vaughan Williams Class II) and cardiac action potential duration prolongation (Vaughan Williams Class III) properties

Class II effects: Increased sinus cycle length, slowed heart rate, decreased AV nodal conduction, and increased AV nodal refractoriness

Class III effects: Prolongation of the atrial and ventricular monophasic action potentials, and effective refractory prolongation of atrial muscle, ventricular muscle, and atrioventricular accessory pathways in both the antegrade and retrograde directions

Sotalol is a racemic mixture of *d*- and *l*-sotalol; both isomers have similar Class III antiarrhythmic effects while the *l*-isomer is responsible for virtually all of the beta-blocking activity

Sotalol has both beta$_1$- and beta$_2$-receptor blocking activity

The beta-blocking effect of sotalol is a noncardioselective [half maximal at about 80 mg/day and maximal at doses of 320-640 mg/day]. Significant beta-blockade occurs at oral doses as low as 25 mg/day.

The Class III effects are seen only at oral doses ≥160 mg/day

Pharmacodynamics/Kinetics

Onset of action: Rapid, 1-2 hours

Peak effect: 2.5-4 hours

Duration: 8-16 hours

Absorption: Decreased 20% to 30% by meals compared to fasting

Distribution: Low lipid solubility; enters milk of laboratory animals and is reported to be present in human milk

Protein binding: None

Metabolism: None

Bioavailability: 90% to 100%

Half-life elimination: 12 hours; Children: 9.5 hours; terminal half-life decreases with age <2 years (may by ≥1 week in neonates)

Excretion: Urine (as unchanged drug)

Dosage Sotalol should be initiated and doses increased in a hospital with facilities for cardiac rhythm monitoring and assessment. Proarrhythmic events can occur after initiation of therapy and with each upward dosage adjustment.

Children: Oral: The safety and efficacy of sotalol in children have not been established

Note: Dosing per manufacturer, based on pediatric pharmacokinetic data; wait at least 36 hours between dosage adjustments to allow monitoring of QT intervals

≤2 years: Dosage should be adjusted (decreased) by plotting of the child's age on a logarithmic scale; see graph or refer to manufacturer's package labeling.

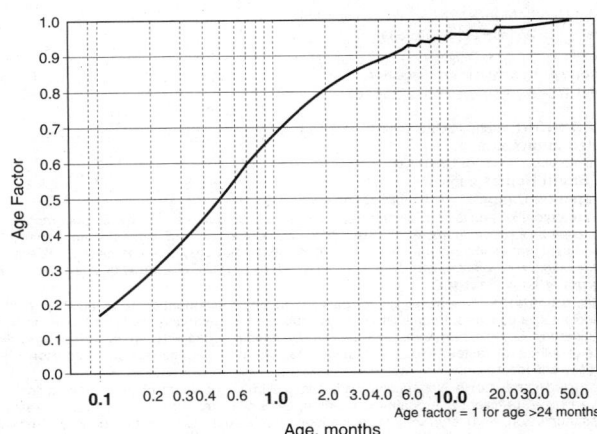

Sotalol Age Factor Nomogram for Patients ≤2 Years of Age

Age factor = 1 for age >24 months

Age, months

Adapted from U.S. Food and Drug Administration.
http://www.fda.gov/cder/foi/label/2001/2115s3lbl.PDF

>2 years: Initial: 90 mg/m²/day in 3 divided doses; may be incrementally increased to a maximum of 180 mg/m²/day

(Continued)

Sotalol *(Continued)*

Adults: Oral:
Ventricular arrhythmias (Betapace®, Sorine®):
Initial: 80 mg twice daily
Dose may be increased gradually to 240-320 mg/day; allow 3 days between dosing increments in order to attain steady-state plasma concentrations and to allow monitoring of QT intervals
Most patients respond to a total daily dose of 160-320 mg/day in 2-3 divided doses.
Some patients, with life-threatening refractory ventricular arrhythmias, may require doses as high as 480-640 mg/day; however, these doses should only be prescribed when the potential benefit outweighs the increased of adverse events.
Atrial fibrillation or atrial flutter (Betapace AF®): Initial: 80 mg twice daily
If the initial dose does not reduce the frequency of relapses of atrial fibrillation/flutter and is tolerated without excessive QT prolongation (not >520 msec) after 3 days, the dose may be increased to 120 mg twice daily. This may be further increased to 160 mg twice daily if response is inadequate and QT prolongation is not excessive.
Elderly: Age does not significantly alter the pharmacokinetics of sotalol, but impaired renal function in elderly patients can increase the terminal half-life, resulting in increased drug accumulation

Dosage adjustment in renal impairment:
Children: Safety and efficacy in children with renal impairment have not been established.
Adults: Impaired renal function can increase the terminal half-life, resulting in increased drug accumulation. Sotalol (Betapace AF®) is contraindicated per the manufacturer for treatment of atrial fibrillation/flutter in patients with a Cl_{cr} <40 mL/minute.
Ventricular arrhythmias (Betapace®, Sorine®):
Cl_{cr} >60 mL/minute: Administer every 12 hours
Cl_{cr} 30-60 mL/minute: Administer every 24 hours
Cl_{cr} 10-30 mL/minute: Administer every 36-48 hours
Cl_{cr} <10 mL/minute: Individualize dose
Atrial fibrillation/flutter (Betapace AF®):
Cl_{cr} >60 mL/minute: Administer every 12 hours
Cl_{cr} 40-60 mL/minute: Administer every 24 hours
Cl_{cr} <40 mL/minute: Use is contraindicated
Dialysis: Hemodialysis would be expected to reduce sotalol plasma concentrations because sotalol is not bound to plasma proteins and does not undergo extensive metabolism; administer dose postdialysis or administer supplemental 80 mg dose; peritoneal dialysis does not remove sotalol; supplemental dose is not necessary

Administration Food may decrease adsorption

Monitoring Parameters Serum magnesium, potassium, ECG

Patient Information Seek emergency help if palpitations occur; do not discontinue abruptly or change dose without notifying prescriber; take on an empty stomach

Dosage Forms TAB: 80 mg, 80 mg [AF], 120 mg, 120 mg [AF], 160 mg, 160 mg [AF], 240 mg; (Betapace®, Sorine®): 80 mg, 120 mg, 160 mg, 240 mg; (Betapace AF®): 80 mg, 120 mg, 160 mg

- ◆ **Sotalol Hydrochloride** *see* Sotalol *on page 1154*
- ◆ **Sotret®** *see* Isotretinoin *on page 696*
- ◆ **SPA** *see* Albumin *on page 44*
- ◆ **Spacol** *see* Hyoscyamine *on page 641*
- ◆ **Spacol T/S** *see* Hyoscyamine *on page 641*

Sparfloxacin *(spar FLOKS a sin)*

Related Information
Antimicrobial Drugs of Choice *on page 1440*

U.S. Brand Names Zagam®

Therapeutic Category Antibiotic, Quinolone

Use Treatment of adults with community-acquired pneumonia caused by *C. pneumoniae, H. influenzae, H. parainfluenzae, M. catarrhalis, M. pneumoniae* or *S. pneumoniae*; treatment of acute bacterial exacerbations of chronic bronchitis caused by *C. pneumoniae, E. cloacae, H. influenzae, H. parainfluenzae, K. pneumoniae, M. catarrhalis, S. aureus* or *S. pneumoniae*

Pregnancy Risk Factor C

Contraindications Hypersensitivity to sparfloxacin, any component of the formulation, or other quinolones; a concurrent administration with drugs which increase the QT interval including: amiodarone, bepridil, bretylium, cisapride, disopyramide, furosemide, procainamide, quinidine, sotalol, albuterol, astemizole, chloroquine, halofantrine, phenothiazines, prednisone, and tricyclic antidepressants

Warnings/Precautions Not recommended in children <18 years of age, other quinolones have caused transient arthropathy in children; CNS stimulation may occur (tremor, restlessness, confusion, and very rarely hallucinations or seizures); use with caution in patients with known or suspected CNS disorder or renal dysfunction; prolonged use may result in superinfection. Moderate to severe photosensitivity reactions may occur in patients exposed to direct or indirect sunlight, or to artificial ultraviolet light. Patients should avoid unnecessary sunlight exposure during treatment and for 5 days following therapy. Pseudomembranous colitis may occur and should be considered in patients who present with diarrhea. Tendon inflammation and/or rupture have been reported with other quinolone antibiotics. Discontinue at first sign of tendon inflammation or pain.

Severe hypersensitivity reactions, including anaphylaxis, have occurred with quinolone therapy. If an allergic reaction occurs (itching, urticaria, dyspnea, facial edema, loss of consciousness, tingling, cardiovascular collapse), discontinue drug immediately. Although quinolones may exacerbate myasthenia gravis, sparfloxacin appears to be an exception; caution is still warranted.

Common Adverse Reactions 1% to 10%:
Cardiovascular: QT_c interval prolongation (1%), vasodilation (1%)
Central nervous system: Insomnia (2%), dizziness (2%), headache (4%)
Dermatologic: Photosensitivity reaction (8%; severe <1%), pruritus (2%)
Gastrointestinal: Diarrhea (5%), dyspepsia (2%), nausea (4%), abdominal pain (2%), vomiting (1%), flatulence (1%), taste perversion (2%)
Hepatic: Increased LFTs

Drug Interactions
Increased Effect/Toxicity: Quinolones cause increased levels of caffeine, warfarin, cyclosporine, and theophylline (although one study indicates that sparfloxacin may not affect theophylline metabolism). Cimetidine, and probenecid increase quinolone levels. An increased incidence of seizures may occur with foscarnet and NSAIDs. Sparfloxacin does not appear to alter warfarin levels, but warfarin effect may be increased due possible effects on gastrointestinal flora. Concurrent use of corticosteroids may increase risk of tendon rupture.
Decreased Effect: Decreased absorption with antacids containing aluminum, magnesium, and/or calcium, sucralfate, didanosine and by products containing zinc and iron salts when administered concurrently. Take >4 hours after sparfloxacin. Phenytoin serum levels may be reduced by quinolones; antineoplastic agents may also decrease serum levels of fluoroquinolones

Mechanism of Action Inhibits DNA-gyrase in susceptible organisms; inhibits relaxation of supercoiled DNA and promotes breakage of double-stranded DNA

Pharmacodynamics/Kinetics
Absorption: Unaffected by food or milk; reduced ~50% by concurrent administration of aluminum- and magnesium-containing antacids
Distribution: Widely throughout the body; V_d: 3.9 L/kg
Protein binding: 45%
Metabolism: Hepatic, primarily by phase II glucuronidation
Half-life elimination: Mean terminal: 20 hours (range: 16-30 hours)
Time to peak, serum: 3-5 hours
Excretion: Urine (50%; ~10% as unchanged drug); feces (50%)

Dosage Adults: Oral:
Loading dose: 400 mg on day 1
Maintenance: 200 mg/day for 10 days total therapy
Dosing adjustment in renal impairment: Cl_{cr} <50 mL/minute: Administer 400 mg on day 1, then 200 mg every 48 hours for a total of 9 days of therapy (total 6 tablets)

Administration May be taken without regard to meals, however, should be administered at the same time each day. Antacids containing aluminum or magnesium; products containing iron, zinc, or calcium; and sucralfate and didanosine should all be given >4 hours after sparfloxacin.

Monitoring Parameters Evaluation of organ system functions (renal, hepatic, ophthalmologic, and hematopoietic) is recommended periodically during therapy; the possibility of crystalluria should be assessed; WBC and signs and symptoms of infection

Patient Information May take with or without food (should be taken at the same time each day). Antacids containing aluminum or magnesium; products containing iron, zinc, or calcium; and sucralfate and didanosine should all be given >4 hours after sparfloxacin. Drink with plenty of fluids; may cause photosensitivity reactions (use sunscreen, wear protective clothing and eyewear, and avoid prolonged or unnecessary exposure to direct sunlight during and for 5 days following therapy); contact your prescriber immediately if signs of allergy occur; do not discontinue therapy until your course has been completed; take a missed dose as soon as possible, unless it is almost time for your next dose

Dosage Forms TAB, film coated: 200 mg

♦ **Spectazole®** *see Econazole on page 420* *on page 420*

Spectinomycin (spek ti noe MYE sin)
U.S. Brand Names Trobicin®
Synonyms Spectinomycin Hydrochloride
Therapeutic Category Antibiotic, Miscellaneous
Use Treatment of uncomplicated gonorrhea
Pregnancy Risk Factor B
Contraindications Hypersensitivity to spectinomycin or any component of the formulation
Mechanism of Action A bacteriostatic antibiotic that selectively binds to the 30s subunits of ribosomes, and thereby inhibiting bacterial protein synthesis
Pharmacodynamics/Kinetics
Duration: Up to 8 hours
Absorption: I.M.: Rapid and almost complete
Distribution: Concentrates in urine; does not distribute well into the saliva
Half-life elimination: 1.7 hours
Time to peak: ~1 hour
Excretion: Urine (70% to 100% as unchanged drug)
(Continued)

Spectinomycin *(Continued)*

Dosage I.M.:

Children:

<45 kg: 40 mg/kg/dose 1 time (ceftriaxone preferred)

≥45 kg: Refer to adult dosing.

Children >8 years who are allergic to PCNS/cephalosporins may be treated with oral tetracycline

Adults:

Uncomplicated urethral, cervical, pharyngeal, or rectal gonorrhea: 2 g deep I.M. or 4 g where antibiotic resistance is prevalent 1 time; 4 g (10 mL) dose should be given as two 5 mL injections, followed by adequate chlamydial treatment (doxycycline 100 mg twice daily for 7 days)

Disseminated gonococcal infection: 2 g every 12 hours

Dosing adjustment in renal impairment: None necessary

Hemodialysis: 50% removed by hemodialysis

Administration For I.M. use only

Dosage Forms INJ, powder for reconstitution: 2 g

- **Spectinomycin Hydrochloride** *see* Spectinomycin *on page 1157*
- **Spectracef™** *see* Cefditoren *on page 233*
- **Spectrex Plus® [OTC]** *see* Bacitracin, Neomycin, Polymyxin B, and Lidocaine *on page 144*

Spironolactone *(speer on oh LAK tone)*

U.S. Brand Names Aldactone®

Therapeutic Category Antihypertensive Agent; Diuretic, Potassium-Sparing

Use Management of edema associated with excessive aldosterone excretion; hypertension; primary hyperaldosteronism; hypokalemia; treatment of hirsutism; cirrhosis of liver accompanied by edema or ascites. The benefits of spironolactone were additive to the benefits of ACE inhibition in patients with severe CHF (further reducing mortality by 30% over 2 years) in RALES - a large controlled clinical trial.

Pregnancy Risk Factor C/D in pregnancy-induced hypertension (per expert analysis)

Contraindications Hypersensitivity to spironolactone or any component of the formulation; anuria; acute renal insufficiency; significant impairment of renal excretory function; hyperkalemia; pregnancy (pregnancy-induced hypertension - per expert analysis)

Warnings/Precautions Avoid potassium supplements, potassium-containing salt substitutes, a diet rich in potassium, or other drugs that can cause hyperkalemia. Monitor for fluid and electrolyte imbalances. Gynecomastia is related to dose and duration of therapy. Diuretic therapy should be carefully used in severe hepatic dysfunction; electrolyte and fluid shifts can cause or exacerbate encephalopathy. Discontinue use prior to adrenal vein catheterization.

Common Adverse Reactions Incidence of adverse events is not always reported. (Mean daily dose: 26 mg)

Cardiovascular: Edema (2%, placebo 2%)

Central nervous system: Disorders (23%, placebo 21%) which may include drowsiness, lethargy, headache, mental confusion, drug fever, ataxia, fatigue

Dermatologic: Maculopapular, erythematous cutaneous eruptions, urticaria, hirsutism, eosinophilia

Endocrine & metabolic: Gynecomastia (men 9%; placebo 1%), breast pain (men 2%; placebo 0.1%), serious hyperkalemia (2%, placebo 1%), hyponatremia, dehydration, hyperchloremic metabolic acidosis in decompensated hepatic cirrhosis, inability to achieve or maintain an erection, irregular menses, amenorrhea, postmenopausal bleeding

Gastrointestinal: Disorders (29%, placebo 29%) which may include anorexia, nausea, cramping, diarrhea, gastric bleeding, ulceration, gastritis, vomiting

Genitourinary: Disorders (12%, placebo 11%)

Hematologic: Agranulocytosis

Hepatic: Cholestatic/hepatocellular toxicity

Renal: Increased BUN concentration

Respiratory: Disorders (32%, placebo 34%)

Miscellaneous: Deepening of the voice, anaphylactic reaction, breast cancer

Drug Interactions

Increased Effect/Toxicity: Concurrent use of spironolactone with other potassium-sparing diuretics, potassium supplements, angiotensin receptor antagonists, co-trimoxazole (high dose), and ACE inhibitors can increase the risk of hyperkalemia, especially in patients with renal impairment. Cholestyramine can cause hyperchloremic acidosis in cirrhotic patients; avoid concurrent use.

Decreased Effect: The effects of digoxin (loss of positive inotropic effect) and mitotane may be reduced by spironolactone. Salicylates and NSAIDs (indomethacin) may decrease the natriuretic effect of spironolactone.

Mechanism of Action Competes with aldosterone for receptor sites in the distal renal tubules, increasing sodium chloride and water excretion while conserving potassium and hydrogen ions; may block the effect of aldosterone on arteriolar smooth muscle as well

Pharmacodynamics/Kinetics

Protein binding: 91% to 98%

Metabolism: Hepatic to multiple metabolites, including canrenone (active)

Half-life elimination: 78-84 minutes

Time to peak, serum: 1-3 hours (primarily as the active metabolite)

Excretion: Urine and feces

Dosage To reduce delay in onset of effect, a loading dose of 2 or 3 times the daily dose may be administered on the first day of therapy. Oral:

Neonates: Diuretic: 1-3 mg/kg/day divided every 12-24 hours
Children:
  Diuretic, hypertension: 1.5-3.5 mg/kg/day **or** 60 mg/m^2/day in divided doses every 6-24 hours
  Diagnosis of primary aldosteronism: 125-375 mg/m^2/day in divided doses
  Vaso-occlusive disease: 7.5 mg/kg/day in divided doses twice daily (not FDA approved)
Adults:
  Edema, hypertension, hypokalemia: 25-200 mg/day in 1-2 divided doses
  Diagnosis of primary aldosteronism: 100-400 mg/day in 1-2 divided doses
  Hirsutism in women: 50-200 mg/day in 1-2 divided doses
  CHF, severe (with ACE inhibitor and a loop diuretic ± digoxin): 25 mg/day, increased or reduced depending on individual response and evidence of hyperkalemia
Elderly: Initial: 25-50 mg/day in 1-2 divided doses, increasing by 25-50 mg every 5 days as needed.
Dosing interval in renal impairment:
  Cl$_{cr}$ 10-50 mL/minute: Administer every 12-24 hours.
  Cl$_{cr}$ <10 mL/minute: Avoid use.
Monitoring Parameters Blood pressure, serum electrolytes (potassium, sodium), renal function, I & O ratios and daily weight throughout therapy
Patient Information Avoid hazardous activity such as driving, until response to drug is known; take with meals or milk; avoid excessive ingestion of foods high in potassium or use of salt substitutes
Dosage Forms TAB: 25 mg, 50 mg, 100 mg

♦ **Spironolactone and Hydrochlorothiazide** *see* Hydrochlorothiazide and Spironolactone *on page 627*

♦ **Sporanox®** *see* Itraconazole *on page 699*

♦ **Sprintec™** *see* Ethinyl Estradiol and Norgestimate *on page 490*

♦ **SPS®** *see* Sodium Polystyrene Sulfonate *on page 1151*

♦ **SSD®** *see* Silver Sulfadiazine *on page 1137*

♦ **SSD® AF** *see* Silver Sulfadiazine *on page 1137*

♦ **SSKI®** *see* Potassium Iodide *on page 1022*

♦ **Stadol®** *see* Butorphanol *on page 196*

♦ **Stadol® NS** *see* Butorphanol *on page 196*

♦ **Stagesic®** *see* Hydrocodone and Acetaminophen *on page 627*

♦ **Stalevo™** *see* Levodopa, Carbidopa, and Entacapone *on page 733*

♦ **Stan-gard®** *see* Fluoride *on page 535*

♦ **Stannous Fluoride** *see* Fluoride *on page 535*

Stanozolol (stan OH zoe lole)

U.S. Brand Names Winstrol®
Therapeutic Category Anabolic Steroid; Androgen
Use Prophylactic use against hereditary angioedema
Restrictions C-III
Pregnancy Risk Factor X
Contraindications Hypersensitivity to stanozolol or any component of the formulation; nephrosis; carcinoma of breast or prostate; pregnancy
Warnings/Precautions May stunt bone growth in children; anabolic steroids may cause peliosis hepatis, liver cell tumors, and blood lipid changes with increased risk of arteriosclerosis; monitor diabetic patients carefully; use with caution in elderly patients, they may be at greater risk for prostatic hyperplasia; use with caution in patients with cardiac, renal, or hepatic disease or epilepsy
Common Adverse Reactions
Male:
Postpubertal:
  >10%:
    Dermatologic: Acne
    Endocrine & metabolic: Gynecomastia
    Genitourinary: Bladder irritability, priapism
  1% to 10%:
    Central nervous system: Insomnia, chills
    Endocrine & metabolic: Decreased libido, hepatic dysfunction
    Gastrointestinal: Nausea, diarrhea
    Genitourinary: Prostatic hyperplasia (elderly)
    Hematologic: Iron deficiency anemia, suppression of clotting factors
Prepubertal:
  >10%:
    Dermatologic: Acne
    Endocrine & metabolic: Virilism
  1% to 10%:
    Central nervous system: Chills, insomnia, factors
    Dermatologic: Hyperpigmentation
    Gastrointestinal: Diarrhea, nausea
(Continued)

Stanozolol *(Continued)*

Hematologic: Iron deficiency anemia, suppression of clotting

Female:
>10%: Endocrine & metabolic: Virilism
1% to 10%:
Central nervous system: Chills, insomnia
Endocrine & metabolic: Hypercalcemia
Gastrointestinal: Nausea, diarrhea
Hematologic: Iron deficiency anemia, suppression of clotting factors
Hepatic: Hepatic dysfunction

Drug Interactions
Increased Effect/Toxicity: ACTH, adrenal steroids may increase risk of edema and acne. Stanozolol enhances the hypoprothrombinemic effects of oral anticoagulants and enhances the hypoglycemic effects of insulin and sulfonylureas (oral hypoglycemics).

Mechanism of Action Synthetic testosterone derivative with similar androgenic and anabolic actions

Pharmacodynamics/Kinetics
Metabolism: Hepatic
Excretion: Urine (90%); feces (6%)

Dosage
Children: Acute attacks:
<6 years: 1 mg/day
6-12 years: 2 mg/day
Adults: Oral: Initial: 2 mg 3 times/day, may then reduce to a maintenance dose of 2 mg/day or 2 mg every other day after 1-3 months
Dosing adjustment in hepatic impairment: Stanozolol is **not** recommended for patients with severe liver dysfunction

Patient Information High protein, high caloric diet is suggested, restrict salt intake; glucose tolerance may be altered in diabetics

Dosage Forms TAB: 2 mg

♦ **Starlix®** *see Nateglinide on page 885*
♦ **Staticin®** *see Erythromycin on page 453*

Stavudine *(STAV yoo deen)*

Related Information
Antiretroviral Therapy for HIV Infection *on page 1448*
Management of Healthcare Worker Exposures to HBV, HCV, and HIV *on page 1421*

U.S. Brand Names Zerit®
Synonyms d4T
Therapeutic Category Antiretroviral Agent, Nucleoside Reverse Transcriptase Inhibitor (NRTI) [Thymidine Analog]
Use Treatment of adults with HIV infection in combination with other antiretroviral agents
Pregnancy Risk Factor C
Contraindications Hypersensitivity to stavudine or any component of the formulation
Warnings/Precautions Use with caution in patients who demonstrate previous hypersensitivity to zidovudine, didanosine, zalcitabine, pre-existing bone marrow suppression, renal insufficiency, or peripheral neuropathy. Peripheral neuropathy may be the dose-limiting side effect. Zidovudine should not be used in combination with stavudine. Lactic acidosis and severe hepatomegaly with steatosis have been reported with stavudine use, including fatal cases. Risk may be increased in obesity, prolonged nucleoside exposure, or in female patients. Suspend therapy in patients with suspected lactic acidosis; consider discontinuation of stavudine if lactic acidosis is confirmed. Pregnant women may be at increased risk of lactic acidosis and liver damage. Severe motor weakness (resembling Guillain-Barré syndrome) has also been reported (including fatal cases, usually in association with lactic acidosis); manufacturer recommends discontinuation if motor weakness develops (with or without lactic acidosis). Pancreatitis (including some fatal cases) has occurred during combination therapy (didanosine with or without hydroxyurea). Risk increased when used in combination regimen with didanosine and hydroxyurea. Suspend therapy with agents toxic to the pancreas (including stavudine, didanosine, or hydroxyurea) in patients with suspected pancreatitis.

Common Adverse Reactions All adverse reactions reported below were similar to comparative agent, zidovudine, except for peripheral neuropathy, which was greater for stavudine.

>10%:
Central nervous system: Headache, chills/fever, malaise, insomnia, anxiety, depression, pain
Dermatologic: Rash
Gastrointestinal: Nausea, vomiting, diarrhea, pancreatitis, abdominal pain
Neuromuscular & skeletal: Peripheral neuropathy (15% to 21%)
1% to 10%:
Hematologic: Neutropenia, thrombocytopenia
Hepatic: Increased hepatic transaminases, increased bilirubin
Neuromuscular & skeletal: Myalgia, back pain, weakness

Drug Interactions

Increased Effect/Toxicity: Drugs associated with peripheral neuropathy (chloramphenicol, cisplatin, dapsone, ethionamide, gold, hydralazine, iodoquinol, isoniazid, lithium, metronidazole, nitrofurantoin, pentamidine, phenytoin, ribavirin, vincristine) may increase risk for stavudine peripheral neuropathy. Risk of neuropathy, pancreatitis, or lactic acidosis and severe hepatomegaly is increased with concurrent use of didanosine and hydroxyurea. Concomitant use of ribavirin and nucleoside analogues may increase the risk of developing lactic acidosis (includes adefovir, didanosine, lamivudine, stavudine, zalcitabine, zidovudine).

Decreased Effect: Zidovudine, ribavirin, and doxorubicin may decrease the activity of stavudine (based on *in vitro* data).

Mechanism of Action Stavudine is a thymidine analog which interferes with HIV viral DNA dependent DNA polymerase resulting in inhibition of viral replication; nucleoside reverse transcriptase inhibitor

Pharmacodynamics/Kinetics

Distribution: V_d: 0.5 L/kg
Bioavailability: 86.4%
Half-life elimination: 1-1.6 hours
Time to peak, serum: 1 hour
Excretion: Urine (40%)

Dosage Oral:
Newborns (Birth to 13 days): 0.5 mg/kg every 12 hours
Children:
>14 days and <30 kg: 1 mg/kg every 12 hours
≥30 kg: 30 mg every 12 hours
Adults:
≥60 kg: 40 mg every 12 hours
<60 kg: 30 mg every 12 hours
Dose may be cut in half if symptoms of peripheral neuropathy occur

Dosing adjustment in renal impairment:
Cl_{cr} >50 mL/minute:
≥60 kg: 40 mg every 12 hours
<60 kg: 30 mg every 12 hours
Cl_{cr} 26-50 mL/minute:
≥60 kg: 20 mg every 12 hours
<60 kg: 15 mg every 12 hours
Hemodialysis:
≥60 kg: 20 mg every 24 hours
<60 kg: 15 mg every 24 hours

Elderly: Older patients should be closely monitored for signs and symptoms of peripheral neuropathy; dosage should be carefully adjusted to renal function

Administration May be administered without regard to meals.

Monitoring Parameters Monitor liver function tests and signs and symptoms of peripheral neuropathy; monitor viral load and CD4 count

Patient Information Take as directed; take for full length of prescription. Maintain adequate hydration and nutrition. Report immediately any tingling, unusual pain, or numbness in extremities. Report fever, chills, unusual fatigue or acute depression, acute abdominal or back pain, persistent muscle pain or weakness, nausea, vomiting, or unusual bruising or bleeding. Risk of adverse reactions may be increased with some combination therapies.

Dosage Forms CAP: 15 mg, 20 mg, 30 mg, 40 mg. **POWDER, oral solution:** 1 mg/mL (200 mL)

- ◆ **Stelazine®** [DSC] *see* Trifluoperazine *on page 1266*
- ◆ **Sterapred®** *see* PredniSONE *on page 1033*
- ◆ **Sterapred® DS** *see* PredniSONE *on page 1033*
- ◆ **STI571** *see* Imatinib *on page 651*
- ◆ **Stimate™** *see* Desmopressin *on page 354*
- ◆ **St. Joseph® Pain Reliever [OTC]** *see* Aspirin *on page 120*
- ◆ **Stop®** *see* Fluoride *on page 535*
- ◆ **Strattera™** *see* Atomoxetine *on page 127*
- ◆ **Streptase®** *see* Streptokinase *on page 1161*

Streptokinase (strep toe KYE nase)

U.S. Brand Names Streptase®
Synonyms SK
Therapeutic Category Fibrinolytic Agent
Use Thrombolytic agent used in treatment of recent severe or massive deep vein thrombosis, pulmonary emboli, myocardial infarction, and occluded arteriovenous cannulas
Pregnancy Risk Factor C
Contraindications Hypersensitivity to anistreplase, streptokinase, or any component of the formulation; active internal bleeding; history of CVA; recent (within 2 months) intracranial or intraspinal surgery or trauma; intracranial neoplasm, arteriovenous malformation, or aneurysm; known bleeding diathesis; severe uncontrolled hypertension
Warnings/Precautions Concurrent heparin anticoagulation can contribute to bleeding; careful attention to all potential bleeding sites. I.M. injections and nonessential handling of the patient should be avoided. Venipunctures should be performed carefully and only when necessary. If
(Continued)

Streptokinase *(Continued)*

arterial puncture is necessary, use an upper extremity vessel that can be manually compressed. If serious bleeding occurs then the infusion of streptokinase and heparin should be stopped. Use with caution in patients >75 years of age, patients with a history of cardiac arrhythmias, septic thrombophlebitis or occluded AV cannula at seriously infected site, patients with a high likelihood of left heart thrombus (eg, mitral stenosis with atrial fibrillation), major surgery within last 10 days, GI bleeding, diabetic hemorrhagic retinopathy, subacute bacterial endocarditis, cerebrovascular disease, recent trauma including cardiopulmonary resuscitation, or severe hypertension (systolic BP >180 mm Hg and/or diastolic BP >110 mm Hg); antibodies to streptokinase remain for 3-6 months after initial dose, use another thrombolytic enzyme (ie, alteplase) if thrombolytic therapy is indicated in patients with prior streptokinase therapy

Coronary thrombolysis may result in reperfusion arrhythmias. Hypotension, occasionally severe, can occur (not from bleeding or anaphylaxis). Follow standard MI management. Rare anaphylactic reactions can occur. Cautious repeat administration in patients who have received anistreplase or streptokinase within 1 year (streptokinase antibody may decrease effectiveness or risk of allergic reactions). Safety and efficacy in pediatric patients have not been established.

Streptokinase is not indicated for restoration of patency of intravenous catheters. Serious adverse events relating to the use of streptokinase in the restoration of patency of occluded intravenous catheters have involved the use of high doses of streptokinase in small volumes (250,000 international units in 2 mL). Uses of lower doses of streptokinase in infusions over several hours, generally into partially occluded catheters, or local instillation into the catheter lumen and subsequent aspiration, have been described in the medical literature. Healthcare providers should consider the risk for potentially life-threatening reactions (eg, hypotension, hypersensitivity reactions, apnea, bleeding) associated with the use of streptokinase in the management of occluded intravenous catheters.

Common Adverse Reactions As with all drugs which may affect hemostasis, bleeding is the major adverse effect associated with streptokinase. Hemorrhage may occur at virtually any site. Risk is dependent on multiple variables, including the dosage administered, concurrent use of multiple agents which alter hemostasis, and patient predisposition (including hypertension). Rapid lysis of coronary artery thrombi by thrombolytic agents may be associated with reperfusion-related atrial and/or ventricular arrhythmias.

>10%:
  Cardiovascular: Hypotension
  Local: Injection site bleeding
1% to 10%:
  Central nervous system: Fever (1% to 4%)
  Dermatologic: Bruising, rash, pruritus
  Gastrointestinal: Gastrointestinal hemorrhage, nausea, vomiting
  Genitourinary: Genitourinary hemorrhage
  Hematologic: Anemia
  Neuromuscular & skeletal: Muscle pain
  Ocular: Eye hemorrhage, periorbital edema
  Respiratory: Bronchospasm, epistaxis
  Miscellaneous: Diaphoresis hemorrhage, gingival hemorrhage

Additional cardiovascular events associated with use in myocardial infarction: Asystole, AV block, cardiac arrest, cardiac tamponade, cardiogenic shock, electromechanical dissociation, heart failure, mitral regurgitation, myocardial rupture, pericardial effusion, pericarditis, pulmonary edema, recurrent ischemia/infarction, thromboembolism, ventricular tachycardia

Drug Interactions
  Increased Effect/Toxicity: The risk of bleeding with streptokinase is increased by oral anticoagulants (warfarin), heparin, low molecular weight heparins, and drugs which affect platelet function (eg, NSAIDs, dipyridamole, ticlopidine, clopidogrel, IIb/IIIa antagonists). Although concurrent use with aspirin and heparin may increase the risk of bleeding. Aspirin and heparin were used concomitantly with streptokinase in the majority of patients in clinical studies of MI.
  Decreased Effect: Antifibrinolytic agents (aminocaproic acid) may decrease effectiveness to thrombolytic agents.

Mechanism of Action Activates the conversion of plasminogen to plasmin by forming a complex, exposing plasminogen-activating site, and cleaving a peptide bond that converts plasminogen to plasmin; plasmin degrades fibrin, fibrinogen and other procoagulant proteins into soluble fragments; effective both outside and within the formed thrombus/embolus

Pharmacodynamics/Kinetics
  Onset of action: Activation of plasminogen occurs almost immediately
  Duration: Fibrinolytic effect: Several hours; Anticoagulant effect: 12-24 hours
  Half-life elimination: 83 minutes
  Excretion: By circulating antibodies and the reticuloendothelial system

Dosage I.V.:
  Children: Safety and efficacy have not been not established. Limited studies have used 3500-4000 units/kg over 30 minutes followed by 1000-1500 units/kg/hour.
  Clotted catheter: I.V.: **Note:** Not recommended due to possibility of allergic reactions with repeated doses: 10,000-25,000 units diluted in NS to a final volume equivalent to catheter volume; instill into catheter and leave in place for 1 hour, then aspirate contents out of catheter and flush catheter with normal saline.

Adults: Antibodies to streptokinase remain for at least 3-6 months after initial dose: Administration requires the use of an infusion pump.

An intradermal skin test of 100 units has been suggested to predict allergic response to streptokinase. If a positive reaction is not seen after 15-20 minutes, a therapeutic dose may be administered.

Guidelines for acute myocardial infarction (AMI): 1.5 million units over 60 minutes
Administration:

Dilute two 750,000 unit vials of streptokinase with 5 mL dextrose 5% in water (D_5W) each, gently swirl to dissolve.

Add this dose of the 1.5 million units to 150 mL D_5W.

This should be infused over 60 minutes; an in-line filter ≥0.45 micron should be used.

Monitor for the first few hours for signs of anaphylaxis or allergic reaction. **Infusion should be slowed if blood pressure falls by 25 mm Hg or terminated if asthmatic symptoms appear**.

Following completion of streptokinase, initiate heparin, if directed, when aPTT returns to less than 2 times the upper limit of control; do not use a bolus, but initiate infusion adjusted to a target aPTT of 1.5-2 times the upper limit of control. If prolonged (>48 hours) heparin is required, infusion may be switched to subcutaneous therapy.

Guidelines for acute pulmonary embolism (APE): 3 million unit dose over 24 hours
Administration:

Dilute four 750,000 unit vials of streptokinase with 5 mL dextrose 5% in water (D_5W) each, gently swirl to dissolve.

Add this dose of 3 million units to 250 mL D_5W, an in-line filter ≥0.45 micron should be used.

Administer 250,000 units (23 mL) over 30 minutes followed by 100,000 units/hour (9 mL/ hour) for 24 hours.

Monitor for the first few hours for signs of anaphylaxis or allergic reaction. **Infusion should be slowed if blood pressure is lowered by 25 mm Hg or if asthmatic symptoms appear**.

Begin heparin 1000 units/hour about 3-4 hours after completion of streptokinase infusion or when PTT is <100 seconds.

Monitor PT, PTT, and fibrinogen levels during therapy.

Thromboses: 250,000 units to start, then 100,000 units/hour for 24-72 hours depending on location.

Cannula occlusion: 250,000 units into cannula, clamp for 2 hours, then aspirate contents and flush with normal saline; **Not recommended; see Warnings/Precautions**

Administration Avoid I.M. injections

Monitoring Parameters Blood pressure, PT, aPTT, platelet count, hematocrit, fibrinogen concentration, signs of bleeding

Reference Range

Partial thromboplastin time (aPTT) activated: 20.4-33.2 seconds
Prothrombin time (PT): 10.9-13.7 seconds (same as control)
Fibrinogen: 200-400 mg/dL

Dosage Forms INJ, powder for reconstitution: 250,000 units; 750,000 units; 1,500,000 units

Streptomycin (strep toe MYE sin)

Related Information

Antimicrobial Drugs of Choice *on page 1440*
Tuberculosis Prophylaxis *on page 1438*
Tuberculosis Treatment Guidelines *on page 1466*

Synonyms Streptomycin Sulfate

Therapeutic Category Antibiotic, Aminoglycoside; Antitubercular Agent

Use Part of combination therapy of active tuberculosis; used in combination with other agents for treatment of streptococcal or enterococcal endocarditis, mycobacterial infections, plague, tularemia, and brucellosis

Pregnancy Risk Factor D

Contraindications Hypersensitivity to streptomycin or any component of the formulation; pregnancy

Warnings/Precautions Use with caution in patients with pre-existing vertigo, tinnitus, hearing loss, neuromuscular disorders, or renal impairment; modify dosage in patients with renal impairment; aminoglycosides are associated with significant nephrotoxicity or ototoxicity; the ototoxicity is directly proportional to the amount of drug given and the duration of treatment; tinnitus or vertigo are indications of vestibular injury and impending bilateral irreversible damage; renal damage is usually reversible

Common Adverse Reactions Frequency not defined.

Cardiovascular: Hypotension
Central nervous system: Neurotoxicity, drowsiness, headache, drug fever, paresthesia
Dermatologic: Skin rash
Gastrointestinal: Nausea, vomiting
Hematologic: Eosinophilia, anemia
Neuromuscular & skeletal: Arthralgia, weakness, tremor
Otic: Ototoxicity (auditory), ototoxicity (vestibular)
Renal: Nephrotoxicity
Respiratory: Difficulty in breathing
(Continued)

Streptomycin *(Continued)*

Drug Interactions

Increased Effect/Toxicity: Increased/prolonged effect with depolarizing and nondepolarizing neuromuscular blocking agents. Concurrent use with amphotericin or loop diuretics may increase nephrotoxicity.

Mechanism of Action Inhibits bacterial protein synthesis by binding directly to the 30S ribosomal subunits causing faulty peptide sequence to form in the protein chain

Pharmacodynamics/Kinetics

Absorption: I.M.: Well absorbed

Distribution: To extracellular fluid including serum, abscesses, ascitic, pericardial, pleural, synovial, lymphatic, and peritoneal fluids; crosses placenta; small amounts enter breast milk

Protein binding: 34%

Half-life elimination: Newborns: 4-10 hours; Adults: 2-4.7 hours, prolonged with renal impairment

Time to peak: Within 1 hour

Excretion: Urine (90% as unchanged drug); feces, saliva, sweat, and tears (<1%)

Dosage

Children:

Tuberculosis:

Daily therapy: 20-40 mg/kg/day (maximum: 1 g/day)

Directly observed therapy (DOT): Twice weekly: 20-40 mg/kg (maximum: 1 g)

DOT: 3 times/week: 25-30 mg/kg (maximum: 1 g)

Adults:

Tuberculosis:

Daily therapy: 15 mg/kg/day (maximum: 1 g)

Directly observed therapy (DOT): Twice weekly: 25-30 mg/kg (maximum: 1.5 g)

DOT: 3 times/week: 25-30 mg/kg (maximum: 1 g)

Enterococcal endocarditis: 1 g every 12 hours for 2 weeks, 500 mg every 12 hours for 4 weeks in combination with penicillin

Streptococcal endocarditis: 1 g every 12 hours for 1 week, 500 mg every 12 hours for 1 week

Tularemia: 1-2 g/day in divided doses for 7-10 days or until patient is afebrile for 5-7 days

Plague: 2-4 g/day in divided doses until the patient is afebrile for at least 3 days

Elderly: 10 mg/kg/day, not to exceed 750 mg/day; dosing interval should be adjusted for renal function; some authors suggest not to give more than 5 days/week or give as 20-25 mg/kg/dose twice weekly

Dosing interval in renal impairment:

Cl$_{cr}$ 10-50 mL/minute: Administer every 24-72 hours

Cl$_{cr}$ <10 mL/minute: Administer every 72-96 hours

Removed by hemo and peritoneal dialysis: Administer dose postdialysis

Administration Inject deep I.M. into large muscle mass; may be administered I.V. over 30-60 minutes

Monitoring Parameters Hearing (audiogram), BUN, creatinine; serum concentration of the drug should be monitored in all patients; eighth cranial nerve damage is usually preceded by high-pitched tinnitus, roaring noises, sense of fullness in ears, or impaired hearing and may persist for weeks after drug is discontinued

Reference Range Therapeutic: Peak: 20-30 µg/mL; Trough: <5 µg/mL; Toxic: Peak: >50 µg/mL; Trough: >10 µg/mL

Patient Information Report any unusual symptom of hearing loss, dizziness, roaring noises, or fullness in ears

Dosage Forms INJ, powder for reconstitution: 1 g

- **Streptomycin Sulfate** *see* Streptomycin *on page 1163*
- **Stresstabs® B-Complex [OTC]** *see* Vitamin B Complex Combinations *on page 1311*
- **Stresstabs® B-Complex + Iron [OTC]** *see* Vitamin B Complex Combinations *on page 1311*
- **Stresstabs® B-Complex + Zinc [OTC]** *see* Vitamin B Complex Combinations *on page 1311*
- **Striant™** *see* Testosterone *on page 1201*
- **Stromectol®** *see* Ivermectin *on page 701*
- **Strong Iodine Solution** *see* Potassium Iodide *on page 1022*

Strontium-89 *(STRON shee um atey nine)*

U.S. Brand Names Metastron®

Synonyms Strontium-89 Chloride

Therapeutic Category Radiopharmaceutical

Use Relief of bone pain in patients with skeletal metastases

Pregnancy Risk Factor D

Contraindications Hypersensitivity to any strontium-containing compounds or any other component of the formulation; pregnancy; breast-feeding

Warnings/Precautions Use caution in patients with bone marrow compromise; incontinent patients may require urinary catheterization. Body fluids may remain radioactive up to one week after injection. Not indicated for use in patients with cancer not involving bone and should be used with caution in patients whose platelet counts fall <60,000 or whose white blood cell counts fall <2400. A small number of patients have experienced a transient increase in bone pain at 36-72 hours postdose; this reaction is generally mild and self-limiting. It should be handled cautiously, in a similar manner to other radioactive drugs. Appropriate safety measures to minimize radiation to personnel should be instituted.

Common Adverse Reactions Most severe reactions of marrow toxicity can be managed by conventional means

Frequency not defined:

Cardiovascular: Flushing (most common after rapid injection)

Central nervous system: Fever and chills (rare)

Hematologic: Thrombocytopenia, leukopenia

Neuromuscular & skeletal: Increase in bone pain may occur (10% to 20% of patients)

Dosage Adults: I.V.: 148 megabecquerel (4 millicurie) administered by slow I.V. injection over 1-2 minutes or 1.5-2.2 megabecquerel (40-60 microcurie)/kg; repeated doses are generally not recommended at intervals <90 days; measure the patient dose by a suitable radioactivity calibration system immediately prior to administration

Monitoring Parameters Routine blood tests

Patient Information Eat and drink normally, there is no need to avoid alcohol or caffeine unless already advised to do so; may be advised to take analgesics until Metastron® begins to become effective; the effect lasts for several months, if pain returns before that, notify medical personnel

Dosage Forms INJ, solution [preservative free]: 10.9-22.6 mg/mL [148 megabecquerel, 4 millicurie] (10 mL)

♦ **Strontium-89 Chloride** *see* Strontium-89 *on page 1164*

♦ **Sublimaze®** *see* Fentanyl *on page 514*

♦ **Suboxone®** *see* Buprenorphine and Naloxone *on page 189*

♦ **Subutex®** *see* Buprenorphine *on page 187*

Succimer (SUKS si mer)

U.S. Brand Names Chemet®

Synonyms DMSA

Therapeutic Category Antidote, Lead Toxicity; Chelating Agent, Oral

Use Orphan drug: Treatment of lead poisoning in children with blood levels >45 μg/dL. It is not indicated for prophylaxis of lead poisoning in a lead-containing environment. Following oral administration, succimer is generally well tolerated and produces a linear dose-dependent reduction in serum lead concentrations. This agent appears to offer advantages over existing lead chelating agents.

Pregnancy Risk Factor C

Contraindications Hypersensitivity to succimer or any component of the formulation

Warnings/Precautions Caution in patients with renal or hepatic impairment; adequate hydration should be maintained during therapy

Common Adverse Reactions

>10%:

Central nervous system: Fever

Gastrointestinal: Nausea, vomiting, diarrhea, appetite loss, hemorrhoidal symptoms, metallic taste

Neuromuscular & skeletal: Back pain

1% to 10%:

Central nervous system: Drowsiness, dizziness

Dermatologic: Rash

Endocrine & metabolic: Serum cholesterol

Gastrointestinal: Sore throat

Hepatic: Elevated AST/ALT, alkaline phosphatase

Respiratory: Nasal congestion, cough

Miscellaneous: Flu-like symptoms

Drug Interactions

Decreased Effect: Not recommended for concomitant administration with edetate calcium disodium or penicillamine.

Mechanism of Action Succimer is an analog of dimercaprol. It forms water soluble chelates with heavy metals which are subsequently excreted renally. Initial data have shown encouraging results in the treatment of mercury and arsenic poisoning. Succimer binds heavy metals; however, the chemical form of these chelates is not known.

Pharmacodynamics/Kinetics

Absorption: Rapid but incomplete

Metabolism: Rapidly and extensively to mixed succimer cysteine disulfides

Half-life elimination: 2 days

Time to peak, serum: ~1-2 hours

Excretion: Urine (~25%) with peak urinary excretion between 2-4 hours (90% as mixed succimer-cysteine disulfide conjugates, 10% as unchanged drug); feces (as unabsorbed drug)

Dosage Children and Adults: Oral: 10 mg/kg/dose every 8 hours for 5 days followed by 10 mg/kg/dose every 12 hours for 14 days

Dosing adjustment in renal/hepatic impairment: Administer with caution and monitor closely

Concomitant iron therapy has been reported in a small number of children without the formation of a toxic complex with iron (as seen with dimercaprol); courses of therapy may be repeated if indicated by weekly monitoring of blood lead levels; lead levels should be stabilized <15 μg/dL; 2 weeks between courses is recommended unless more timely treatment is indicated by lead levels

Monitoring Parameters Blood lead levels, serum aminotransferases

(Continued)

Succimer (Continued)

Patient Information Maintain adequate fluid intake; notify prescriber if rash occurs; capsules may be opened and contents sprinkled on food or put on a spoon

Dosage Forms CAP: 100 mg

Succinylcholine (suks in il KOE leen)

Related Information

Neuromuscular Blocking Agents Comparison *on page 1397*

U.S. Brand Names Anectine® [DSC]; Quelicin®

Synonyms Succinylcholine Chloride; Suxamethonium Chloride

Therapeutic Category Neuromuscular Blocker Agent, Depolarizing

Use Adjunct to general anesthesia to facilitate both rapid sequence and routine endotracheal intubation and to relax skeletal muscles during surgery; to reduce the intensity of muscle contractions of pharmacologically- or electrically-induced convulsions; does not relieve pain or produce sedation

Pregnancy Risk Factor C

Contraindications Hypersensitivity to succinylcholine or any component of the formulation; personal or familial history of malignant hyperthermia; myopathies associated with elevated serum creatine phosphokinase (CPK) values; narrow-angle glaucoma, penetrating eye injuries; disorders of plasma pseudocholinesterase

Warnings/Precautions Use with caution in pediatrics and adolescents secondary to undiagnosed skeletal muscle myopathy and potential for ventricular dysrhythmias and cardiac arrest resulting from hyperkalemia; use with caution in patients with pre-existing hyperkalemia, paraplegia, extensive or severe burns, extensive denervation of skeletal muscle because of disease or injury to the CNS or with degenerative or dystrophic neuromuscular disease; may increase vagal tone

Common Adverse Reactions

>10%:

Ocular: Increased intraocular pressure

Miscellaneous: Postoperative stiffness

1% to 10%:

Cardiovascular: Bradycardia, hypotension, cardiac arrhythmias, tachycardia

Gastrointestinal: Intragastric pressure, salivation

Causes of prolonged neuromuscular blockade: Excessive drug administration; cumulative drug effect; decreased metabolism/excretion (hepatic and/or renal impairment); accumulation of active metabolites; electrolyte imbalance (hypokalemia, hypocalcemia, hypermagnesemia, hypernatremia); hypothermia; drug interactions; increased sensitivity to muscle relaxants (eg, neuromuscular disorders such as myasthenia gravis or polymyositis)

Drug Interactions

Increased Effect/Toxicity:

Increased toxicity: Anticholinesterase drugs (neostigmine, physostigmine, or pyridostigmine) in combination with succinylcholine can cause cardiorespiratory collapse; cyclophosphamide, oral contraceptives, lidocaine, thiotepa, pancuronium, lithium, magnesium salts, aprotinin, chloroquine, metoclopramide, terbutaline, and procaine enhance and prolong the effects of succinylcholine

Prolonged neuromuscular blockade: Inhaled anesthetics, local anesthetics, calcium channel blockers, antiarrhythmics (eg, quinidine or procainamide), antibiotics (eg, aminoglycosides, tetracyclines, vancomycin, clindamycin), immunosuppressants (eg, cyclosporine)

Mechanism of Action Acts similar to acetylcholine, produces depolarization of the motor endplate at the myoneural junction which causes sustained flaccid skeletal muscle paralysis produced by state of accommodation that developes in adjacent excitable muscle membranes

Pharmacodynamics/Kinetics

Onset of action: I.M.: 2-3 minutes; I.V.: Complete muscular relaxation: 30-60 seconds

Duration: I.M.: 10-30 minutes; I.V.: 4-6 minutes with single administration

Metabolism: Rapidly hydrolyzed by plasma pseudocholinesterase

Dosage I.M., I.V.: Dose to effect; doses will vary due to interpatient variability; use ideal body weight for obese patients

I.M.: 2.5-4 mg/kg, total dose should not exceed 150 mg

I.V.:

Children: Initial: 1-2 mg/kg; maintenance: 0.3-0.6 mg/kg every 5-10 minutes as needed; because of the risk of malignant hyperthermia, use of continuous infusions is not recommended in infants and children

Adults: 1-1.5 mg/kg, up to 150 mg total dose

Maintenance: 0.04-0.07 mg/kg every 5-10 minutes as needed

Continuous infusion: 10-100 mcg/kg/minute (or 0.5-10 mg/minute); dilute to concentration of 1-2 mg/mL in D_5W or NS

Note: Initial dose of succinylcholine must be increased when nondepolarizing agent pretreatment used because of the antagonism between succinylcholine and nondepolarizing neuromuscular blocking agents

Dosing adjustment in hepatic impairment: Dose should be decreased in patients with severe liver disease

Administration May be administered by rapid I.V. injection without further dilution; I.M. injections should be made deeply, preferably high into deltoid muscle

Monitoring Parameters Cardiac monitor, blood pressure monitor, and ventilator required during administration; temperature, serum potassium and calcium, assisted ventilator status

Dosage Forms INJ, solution: 20 mg/mL (10 mL); (Anectine® [DSC]): 20 mg/mL (10 mL); (Quelicin®): 20 mg/mL (5 mL, 10 mL); 50 mg/mL (10 mL); 100 mg/mL (10 mL)

- ◆ **Succinylcholine Chloride** *see* Succinylcholine *on page 1166*
- ◆ **Sucraid®** *see* Sacrosidase *on page 1120*

Sucralfate (soo KRAL fate)

U.S. Brand Names Carafate®

Synonyms Aluminum Sucrose Sulfate, Basic

Therapeutic Category Gastrointestinal Agent, Miscellaneous

Use Short-term management of duodenal ulcers; maintenance of duodenal ulcers

Unlabeled/Investigational Use Gastric ulcers; suspension may be used topically for treatment of stomatitis due to cancer chemotherapy and other causes of esophageal and gastric erosions; GERD, esophagitis; treatment of NSAID mucosal damage; prevention of stress ulcers; postsclerotherapy for esophageal variceal bleeding

Pregnancy Risk Factor B

Contraindications Hypersensitivity to sucralfate or any component of the formulation

Warnings/Precautions Successful therapy with sucralfate should not be expected to alter the posthealing frequency of recurrence or the severity of duodenal ulceration; use with caution in patients with chronic renal failure who have an impaired excretion of absorbed aluminum. Because of the potential for sucralfate to alter the absorption of some drugs, separate administration (take other medication 2 hours before sucralfate) should be considered when alterations in bioavailability are believed to be critical

Common Adverse Reactions 1% to 10%: Gastrointestinal: Constipation

Drug Interactions

Decreased Effect: Sucralfate may alter the absorption of digoxin, phenytoin (hydantoins), warfarin, ketoconazole, quinidine, quinolones, tetracycline, theophylline. Because of the potential for sucralfate to alter the absorption of some drugs; separate administration (take other medications at least 2 hours before sucralfate). The potential for decreased absorption should be considered when alterations in bioavailability are believed to be critical.

Mechanism of Action Forms a complex by binding with positively charged proteins in exudates, forming a viscous paste-like, adhesive substance. This selectively forms a protective coating that protects the lining against peptic acid, pepsin, and bile salts.

Pharmacodynamics/Kinetics

Onset of action: Paste formation and ulcer adhesion: 1-2 hours

Duration: Up to 6 hours

Absorption: Oral: <5%

Distribution: Acts locally at ulcer sites; unbound in GI tract to aluminum and sucrose octasulfate

Metabolism: None

Excretion: Urine (small amounts as unchanged compounds)

Dosage Oral:

Children: Dose not established, doses of 40-80 mg/kg/day divided every 6 hours have been used

Stomatitis (unlabeled use): 2.5-5 mL (1 g/10 mL suspension), swish and spit or swish and swallow 4 times/day

Adults:

Stress ulcer prophylaxis: 1 g 4 times/day

Stress ulcer treatment: 1 g every 4 hours

Duodenal ulcer:

Treatment: 1 g 4 times/day on an empty stomach and at bedtime for 4-8 weeks, or alternatively 2 g twice daily; treatment is recommended for 4-8 weeks in adults, the elderly may require 12 weeks

Maintenance: Prophylaxis: 1 g twice daily

Stomatitis (unlabeled use): 1 g/10 mL suspension, swish and spit or swish and swallow 4 times/day

Dosage comment in renal impairment: Aluminum salt is minimally absorbed (<5%), however, may accumulate in renal failure

Administration Tablet may be broken or dissolved in water before ingestion. Administer with water on an empty stomach.

Patient Information Take before meals or on an empty stomach; do not take antacids 30 minutes before or after taking sucralfate

Dosage Forms SUSP, oral: 1 g/10 mL (10 mL); (Carafate®): 1 g/10 mL (420 mL). **TAB** (Carafate®): 1 g

- ◆ **Sucrets® [OTC]** *see* Dyclonine *on page 419*
- ◆ **Sudafed® [OTC]** *see* Pseudoephedrine *on page 1061*
- ◆ **Sudafed® 12 Hour [OTC]** *see* Pseudoephedrine *on page 1061*
- ◆ **Sudafed® 24 Hour [OTC]** *see* Pseudoephedrine *on page 1061*
- ◆ **Sudafed® Children's [OTC]** *see* Pseudoephedrine *on page 1061*
- ◆ **Sudafed® Severe Cold [OTC]** *see* Acetaminophen, Dextromethorphan, and Pseudoephedrine *on page 28*
- ◆ **Sudafed® Sinus & Allergy [OTC]** *see* Chlorpheniramine and Pseudoephedrine *on page 263*
- ◆ **Sudafed® Sinus and Cold [OTC]** *see* Acetaminophen and Pseudoephedrine *on page 26*

- **Sudafed® Sinus Headache [OTC]** *see* Acetaminophen and Pseudoephedrine *on page 26*
- **Sudodrin [OTC]** *see* Pseudoephedrine *on page 1061*
- **SudoGest Sinus [OTC]** *see* Acetaminophen and Pseudoephedrine *on page 26*
- **Sufenta®** *see* Sufentanil *on page 1168*

Sufentanil (soo FEN ta nil)

Related Information
Narcotic Agonists Comparison *on page 1395*
U.S. Brand Names Sufenta®
Synonyms Sufentanil Citrate
Therapeutic Category Analgesic, Narcotic; General Anesthetic
Use Analgesic supplement in maintenance of balanced general anesthesia
Restrictions C-II
Pregnancy Risk Factor C
Contraindications Hypersensitivity to sufentanil or any component of the formulation
Warnings/Precautions Sufentanil can cause severely compromised respiratory depression; use with caution in patients with head injuries, hepatic or renal impairment or with pulmonary disease; sufentanil shares the toxic potential of opiate agonists, precaution of opiate agonist therapy should be observed; rapid I.V. infusion may result in skeletal muscle and chest wall rigidity, impaired ventilation, respiratory distress/arrest; inject slowly over 3-5 minutes; nondepolarizing skeletal muscle relaxant may be required
Common Adverse Reactions
>10%:
Cardiovascular: Bradycardia, hypotension
Central nervous system: Somnolence
Gastrointestinal: Nausea, vomiting
Respiratory: Respiratory depression
1% to 10%:
Cardiovascular: Cardiac arrhythmias, orthostatic hypotension
Central nervous system: CNS depression, confusion
Gastrointestinal: Biliary spasm
Ocular: Blurred vision
Drug Interactions
Cytochrome P450 Effect: Substrate of CYP3A4 (major)
Increased Effect/Toxicity: Additive effect/toxicity with CNS depressants or beta-blockers. May increase response to neuromuscular blocking agents.
Mechanism of Action Binds to opioid receptors throughout the CNS. Once receptor binding occurs, effects are exerted by opening K+ channels and inhibiting Ca++ channels. These mechanisms increase pain threshold, alter pain perception, inhibit ascending pain pathways; short-acting narcotic
Pharmacodynamics/Kinetics
Onset of action: 1-3 minutes
Duration: Dose dependent
Metabolism: Primarily hepatic
Dosage
Children 2-12 years: 10-25 mcg/kg (10-15 mcg/kg most common dose) with 100% O_2, maintenance: up to 1-2 mcg/kg total dose

Adults: Dose should be based on body weight. **Note:** In obese patients (ie, >20% above ideal body weight), use lean body weight to determine dosage.
1-2 mcg/kg with N_2O/O_2 for endotracheal intubation; maintenance: 10-25 mcg as needed
2-8 mcg/kg with N_2O/O_2 more complicated major surgical procedures; maintenance: 10-50 mcg as needed
8-30 mcg/kg with 100% O_2 and muscle relaxant produces sleep; at doses ≥8 mcg/kg maintains a deep level of anesthesia; maintenance: 10-50 mcg as needed
Administration Parenteral: I.V.: Slow I.V. injection or by infusion
Dosage Forms INJ, solution [preservative free]: 50 mcg/mL (1 mL, 2 mL, 5 mL)

- **Sufentanil Citrate** *see* Sufentanil *on page 1168*
- **Sular®** *see* Nisoldipine *on page 906*
- **Sulbactam and Ampicillin** *see* Ampicillin and Sulbactam *on page 96*

Sulconazole (sul KON a zole)

U.S. Brand Names Exelderm®
Synonyms Sulconazole Nitrate
Therapeutic Category Antifungal Agent, Imidazole Derivative; Antifungal Agent, Topical
Use Treatment of superficial fungal infections of the skin, including tinea cruris (jock itch), tinea corporis (ringworm), tinea versicolor, and possibly tinea pedis (athlete's foot, cream only)
Pregnancy Risk Factor C
Contraindications Hypersensitivity to sulconazole or any component of the formulation
Warnings/Precautions Use with caution in nursing mothers; for external use only
Common Adverse Reactions 1% to 10%:
Dermatologic: Itching
Local: Burning, stinging, redness

Drug Interactions
  Cytochrome P450 Effect: Inhibits CYP1A2 (weak), 2A6 (weak), 2C8/9 (weak), 2C19 (weak), 2D6 (weak), 2E1 (weak), 3A4 (weak)
Mechanism of Action Substituted imidazole derivative which inhibits metabolic reactions necessary for the synthesis of ergosterol, an essential membrane component. The end result is usually fungistatic; however, sulconazole may act as a fungicide in *Candida albicans* and parapsilosis during certain growth phases.
Pharmacodynamics/Kinetics
  Absorption: Topical: ~8.7% percutaneously
  Excretion: Primarily urine
Dosage Adults: Topical: Apply a small amount to the affected area and gently massage once or twice daily for 3 weeks (tinea cruris, tinea corporis, tinea versicolor) to 4 weeks (tinea pedis).
Patient Information For external use only; avoid contact with eyes; if burning or irritation develops, notify prescriber
Dosage Forms CRM: 1% (15 g, 30 g, 60 g). **SOLN, topical:** 1% (30 mL)

♦ **Sulconazole Nitrate** *see* Sulconazole *on page 1168*
♦ **Sulf-10®** *see* Sulfacetamide *on page 1169*

Sulfabenzamide, Sulfacetamide, and Sulfathiazole
(sul fa BENZ a mide, sul fa SEE ta mide, & sul fa THYE a zole)
U.S. Brand Names V.V.S.®
Synonyms Triple Sulfa
Therapeutic Category Antibiotic, Vaginal
Use Treatment of *Haemophilus vaginalis* vaginitis
Pregnancy Risk Factor C (avoid if near term)
Contraindications Hypersensitivity to sulfabenzamide, sulfacetamide, sulfathiazole, or any component of the formulation; renal dysfunction; pregnancy (if near term)
Warnings/Precautions Associated with Stevens-Johnson syndrome; if local irritation or systemic toxicity develops, discontinue therapy
Common Adverse Reactions Frequency not defined.
  Dermatologic: Pruritus, urticaria, Stevens-Johnson syndrome
  Local: Local irritation
  Miscellaneous: Allergic reactions
Mechanism of Action Interferes with microbial folic acid synthesis and growth via inhibition of para-aminobenzoic acid metabolism
Pharmacodynamics/Kinetics
  Absorption: Absorption from vagina is variable and unreliable
  Metabolism: Primarily via acetylation
  Excretion: Urine
Dosage Intravaginal: Adults: Female: Cream: Insert one applicatorful into vagina twice daily for 4-6 days; dosage may then be decreased to $1/2$ to $1/4$ of an applicatorful twice daily
Patient Information Complete full course of therapy; notify prescriber if burning, irritation, or signs of a systemic allergic reaction occur
Dosage Forms CRM, vaginal: Sulfabenzamide 3.7%, sulfacetamide 2.86%, and sulfathiazole 3.42% (78 g)

Sulfacetamide (sul fa SEE ta mide)
Related Information
  Sulfonamide Derivatives *on page 1404*
U.S. Brand Names AK-Sulf®; Bleph®-10; Carmol® Scalp; Klaron®; Ocusulf-10; Ovace™; Sulf-10®
Synonyms Sodium Sulfacetamide; Sulfacetamide Sodium
Therapeutic Category Antibiotic, Ophthalmic; Antibiotic, Sulfonamide Derivative
Use
  Ophthalmic: Treatment and prophylaxis of conjunctivitis due to susceptible organisms; corneal ulcers; adjunctive treatment with systemic sulfonamides for therapy of trachoma
  Dermatologic: Scaling dermatosis (seborrheic); bacterial infections of the skin; acne vulgaris
Pregnancy Risk Factor C
Contraindications Hypersensitivity to sulfacetamide, sulfonamides, or any component of the formulation
Warnings/Precautions Severe reactions to sulfonamides have been reported, regardless of route of administration; reactions may include Stevens-Johnson syndrome, toxic epidermal necrolysis, fulminant hepatic necrosis, or blood dyscrasias. Chemical similarities are present among sulfonamides, sulfonylureas, carbonic anhydrase inhibitors, thiazides, and loop diuretics (except ethacrynic acid). Use in patients with sulfonamide allergy is specifically contraindicated in product labeling; however, a risk of cross-reaction exists in patients with allergy to any of these compounds; avoid use when previous reaction has been severe.

  Ophthalmic: Inactivated by purulent exudates containing PABA; use with caution in severe dry eye; ointment may retard corneal epithelial healing. For topical application to the eye only; not for injection. Safety and efficacy have not been established in children <2 months of age.

  Dermatologic: Use caution if applied to denuded or abraded skin. Some products contain sodium metabisulfite which may cause allergic reactions in certain individuals. For external use only; avoid contact with eyes. Safety and efficacy have not been established in children <12 years of age.
  (Continued)

Sulfacetamide *(Continued)*

Common Adverse Reactions Frequency not defined.
    Cardiovascular: Edema
    Dermatologic: Burning, erythema, irritation, itching, stinging, Stevens-Johnson syndrome
    Ocular (following ophthalmic application): Burning, conjunctivitis, conjunctival hyperemia, corneal ulcers, irritation, stinging
    Miscellaneous: Allergic reactions, systemic lupus erythematosus

Drug Interactions
    Decreased Effect: Silver containing products are incompatible with sulfacetamide solutions.

Mechanism of Action Interferes with bacterial growth by inhibiting bacterial folic acid synthesis through competitive antagonism of PABA

Pharmacodynamics/Kinetics
    Half-life elimination: 7-13 hours
    Excretion: When absorbed, primarily urine (as unchanged drug)

Dosage
    Children >2 months and Adults: Ophthalmic:
      Ointment: Apply to lower conjunctival sac 1-4 times/day and at bedtime
      Solution: Instill 1-2 drops several times daily up to every 2-3 hours in lower conjunctival sac during waking hours and less frequently at night; increase dosing interval as condition responds. Usual duration of treatment: 7-10 days
        Trachoma: Instill 2 drops into the conjunctival sac every 2 hours; must be used in conjunction with systemic therapy
    Children >12 years and Adults: Topical:
      Acne: Apply thin film to affected area twice daily
      Seborrheic dermatitis: Apply at bedtime and allow to remain overnight; in severe cases, may apply twice daily. Duration of therapy is usually 8-10 applications; dosing interval may be increased as eruption subsides. Applications once or twice weekly, or every other week may be used to prevent eruptions.
      Secondary cutaneous bacterial infections: Apply 2-4 times/day until infection clears

Administration Topical:
    Scalp lotion: Shampoo hair with a nonirritating shampoo prior to application. Part hair in sections and apply small quantities of lotion to scalp; rub in gently. Brush hair for 2-3 minutes. May discolor white fabric.
    Acne lotion: Shake well before using.

Monitoring Parameters Response to therapy

Patient Information Eye drops will burn upon instillation; wait at least 10 minutes before using another eye preparation; may sting eyes when first applied; do not touch container to eye, ointment will cause blurred vision; notify prescriber if condition does not improve in 3-4 days; may cause sensitivity to sunlight

Dosage Forms LOTION (Carmol® Scalp): 10% (85 g); (Klaron®): 10% (120 mL); (Ovace™): 10% (180 mL, 360 mL). **OINT, ophthalmic** (AK-Sulf®): 10% (3.5 g). **SOLN, ophthalmic:** 10% (15 mL); (Bleph®-10): 10% (5 mL, 15 mL); (Ocusulf-10): 10% (15 mL); (Sulf-10®): 10% (1 mL)

Sulfacetamide and Prednisolone *(sul fa SEE ta mide & pred NIS oh lone)*

U.S. Brand Names Blephamide®; Vasocidin®

Synonyms Prednisolone and Sulfacetamide

Therapeutic Category Antibiotic/Corticosteroid, Ophthalmic; Anti-inflammatory Agent, Ophthalmic

Use Steroid-responsive inflammatory ocular conditions where infection is present or there is a risk of infection; ophthalmic suspension may be used as an otic preparation

Pregnancy Risk Factor C

Dosage Children >2 months and Adults: Ophthalmic:
    Ointment: Apply to lower conjunctival sac 1-4 times/day
    Solution: Instill 1-3 drops every 2-3 hours while awake

Dosage Forms OINT, ophthalmic (Blephamide®): Sulfacetamide 10% and prednisolone acetate 0.2% (3.5 g); (Vasocidin®): Sulfacetamide 10% and prednisolone acetate 0.5% (3.5 g). **SUSP, ophthalmic:** Sulfacetamide 10% and prednisolone sodium phosphate 0.25% (5 mL, 10 mL); (Blephamide®): Sulfacetamide 10% and prednisolone acetate 0.2% (5 mL, 10 mL); (Vasocidin®): Sulfacetamide 10% and prednisolone sodium phosphate: 0.25% (5 mL, 10 mL)

♦ **Sulfacetamide and Sulfur** *see* Sulfur and Sulfacetamide *on page 1177*
♦ **Sulfacetamide Sodium** *see* Sulfacetamide *on page 1169*

Sulfacetamide Sodium and Fluorometholone
(sul fa SEE ta mide SOW dee um & flure oh METH oh lone)

U.S. Brand Names FML-S®

Synonyms Fluorometholone and Sulfacetamide

Therapeutic Category Antibiotic/Corticosteroid, Ophthalmic

Use Steroid-responsive inflammatory ocular conditions where infection is present or there is a risk of infection

Pregnancy Risk Factor C

Dosage Children >2 months and Adults: Ophthalmic: Instill 1-3 drops every 2-3 hours while awake

Dosage Forms SUSP, ophthalmic: Sulfacetamide sodium 10% and fluorometholone 0.1% (5 mL, 10 mL)

♦ **Sulfacet-R**® *see* Sulfur and Sulfacetamide *on page 1177*

SulfaDIAZINE (sul fa DYE a zeen)

Related Information
Sulfonamide Derivatives *on page 1404*

Therapeutic Category Antibiotic, Sulfonamide Derivative

Use Treatment of urinary tract infections and nocardiosis; adjunctive treatment in toxoplasmosis; uncomplicated attack of malaria

Unlabeled/Investigational Use Rheumatic fever prophylaxis

Pregnancy Risk Factor B/D (at term)

Contraindications Hypersensitivity to any sulfa drug or any component of the formulation; porphyria; children <2 months of age unless indicated for the treatment of congenital toxoplasmosis; sunscreens containing PABA; pregnancy (at term)

Warnings/Precautions Use with caution in patients with impaired hepatic function or impaired renal function, G6PD deficiency; dosage modification required in patients with renal impairment; fluid intake should be maintained ≥1500 mL/day, or administer sodium bicarbonate to keep urine alkaline; more likely to cause crystalluria because it is less soluble than other sulfonamides. Chemical similarities are present among sulfonamides, sulfonylureas, carbonic anhydrase inhibitors, thiazides, and loop diuretics (except ethacrynic acid). Use in patients with sulfonamide allergy is specifically contraindicated in product labeling, however, a risk of cross-reaction exists in patients with allergy to any of these compounds; avoid use when previous reaction has been severe.

Common Adverse Reactions Frequency not defined.
Central nervous system: Fever, dizziness, headache
Dermatologic: Lyell's syndrome, Stevens-Johnson syndrome, itching, rash, photosensitivity
Endocrine & metabolic: Thyroid function disturbance
Gastrointestinal: Anorexia, nausea, vomiting, diarrhea
Genitourinary: Crystalluria
Hematologic: Granulocytopenia, leukopenia, thrombocytopenia, aplastic anemia, hemolytic anemia
Hepatic: Hepatitis, jaundice
Renal: Hematuria, acute nephropathy, interstitial nephritis
Miscellaneous: Serum sickness-like reactions

Drug Interactions
Cytochrome P450 Effect: Substrate of CYP2C8/9 (major), 2E1 (minor), 3A4 (minor); **Inhibits** CYP2C8/9 (strong)
Increased Effect/Toxicity: Increased effect of oral anticoagulants and oral hypoglycemic agents.
Decreased Effect: CYP2C8/9 inducers may decrease the levels/effects of sulfadiazine; example inducers include carbamazepine, phenobarbital, phenytoin, rifampin, rifapentine, and secobarbital. Decreased effect with PABA or PABA metabolites of drugs (eg, procaine, proparacaine, tetracaine, sunblock).

Mechanism of Action Interferes with bacterial growth by inhibiting bacterial folic acid synthesis through competitive antagonism of PABA

Pharmacodynamics/Kinetics
Absorption: Well absorbed
Distribution: Throughout body tissues and fluids including pleural, peritoneal, synovial, and ocular fluids; throughout total body water; readily diffused into CSF; enters breast milk
Metabolism: Via N-acetylation
Half-life elimination: 10 hours
Time to peak: Within 3-6 hours
Excretion: Urine (43% to 60% as unchanged drug, 15% to 40% as metabolites)

Dosage Oral:
Asymptomatic meningococcal carriers:
Infants 1-12 months: 500 mg once daily for 2 days
Children 1-12 years: 500 mg twice daily for 2 days
Adults: 1 g twice daily for 2 days
Congenital toxoplasmosis:
Newborns and Children <2 months: 100 mg/kg/day divided every 6 hours in conjunction with pyrimethamine 1 mg/kg/day once daily and supplemental folinic acid 5 mg every 3 days for 6 months
Children >2 months: 25-50 mg/kg/dose 4 times/day
Nocardiosis: 4-8 g/day for a minimum of 6 weeks
Toxoplasmosis:
Children >2 months: Loading dose: 75 mg/kg; maintenance dose: 120-150 mg/kg/day, maximum dose: 6 g/day; divided every 4-6 hours in conjunction with pyrimethamine 2 mg/kg/day divided every 12 hours for 3 days followed by 1 mg/kg/day once daily with supplemental folinic acid
Adults: 2-6 g/day in divided doses every 6 hours in conjunction with pyrimethamine 50-75 mg/day and with supplemental folinic acid
Prevention of recurrent attacks of rheumatic fever (unlabeled use):
>30 kg: 1 g/day
<30 kg: 0.5 g/day

Patient Information Drink plenty of fluids; take on an empty stomach; avoid prolonged exposure to sunlight or wear protective clothing and sunscreen; report rash, difficulty breathing, severe or persistent fever, or sore throat

Dosage Forms TAB: 500 mg

Sulfadoxine and Pyrimethamine (sul fa DOKS een & peer i METH a meen)

U.S. Brand Names Fansidar®

Synonyms Pyrimethamine and Sulfadoxine

Therapeutic Category Antimalarial Agent

Use Treatment of *Plasmodium falciparum* malaria in patients in whom chloroquine resistance is suspected; malaria prophylaxis for travelers to areas where chloroquine-resistant malaria is endemic

Pregnancy Risk Factor C/D (at term)

Contraindications Hypersensitivity to any sulfa drug, pyrimethamine, or any component of the formulation; porphyria, megaloblastic anemia, severe renal insufficiency; children <2 months of age due to competition with bilirubin for protein binding sites; pregnancy (at term)

Warnings/Precautions Use with caution in patients with renal or hepatic impairment, patients with possible folate deficiency, and patients with seizure disorders, increased adverse reactions are seen in patients also receiving chloroquine; fatalities associated with sulfonamides, although rare, have occurred due to severe reactions including Stevens-Johnson syndrome, toxic epidermal necrolysis, hepatic necrosis, agranulocytosis, aplastic anemia and other blood dyscrasias; discontinue use at first sign of rash or any sign of adverse reaction; hemolysis occurs in patients with G6PD deficiency; leucovorin should be administered to reverse signs and symptoms of folic acid deficiency.

Chemical similarities are present among sulfonamides, sulfonylureas, carbonic anhydrase inhibitors, thiazides, and loop diuretics (except ethacrynic acid). Use in patients with sulfonamide allergy is specifically contraindicated in product labeling, however, a risk of cross-reaction exists in patients with allergy to any of these compounds; avoid use when previous reaction has been severe.

Common Adverse Reactions Frequency not defined.
Central nervous system: Ataxia, seizures, headache
Dermatologic: Photosensitivity, Stevens-Johnson syndrome, erythema multiforme, toxic epidermal necrolysis, rash
Endocrine & metabolic: Thyroid function dysfunction
Gastrointestinal: Atrophic glossitis, vomiting, gastritis, anorexia, glossitis
Genitourinary: Crystalluria
Hematologic: Megaloblastic anemia, leukopenia, thrombocytopenia, pancytopenia
Hepatic: Hepatic necrosis, hepatitis
Neuromuscular & skeletal: Tremors
Respiratory: Respiratory failure
Miscellaneous: Hypersensitivity

Drug Interactions
Cytochrome P450 Effect: Pyrimethamine: **Inhibits** CYP2C8/9 (moderate), 2D6 (moderate)
Increased Effect/Toxicity: Hydantoin (phenytoin) levels may be increased. Effect of oral hypoglycemics (rare, but severe) may occur. Combination with methenamine may result in crystalluria; avoid use. May increase methotrexate-induced bone marrow suppression. NSAIDs and salicylates may increase sulfonamide concentrations. Effect of warfarin may be increased.
Decreased Effect: Cyclosporine concentrations may be decreased; monitor levels and renal function. PABA (para-aminobenzoic acid - may be found in some vitamin supplements): interferes with the antibacterial activity of sulfonamides; avoid concurrent use. Pyrimethamine effectiveness decreased by acid.

Mechanism of Action Sulfadoxine interferes with bacterial folic acid synthesis and growth via competitive inhibition of para-aminiobenzoic acid; pyrimethamine inhibits microbial dihydrofolate reductase, resulting in inhibition of tetrahydrofolic acid synthesis

Pharmacodynamics/Kinetics
Absorption: Well absorbed
Distribution: Sulfadoxine: Well distributed like other sulfonamides; Pyrimethamine: Widely distributed, mainly in blood cells, kidneys, lungs, liver, and spleen
Metabolism: Pyrimethamine: Hepatic; Sulfadoxine: None
Half-life elimination: Pyrimethamine: 80-95 hours; Sulfadoxine: 5-8 days
Time to peak, serum: 2-8 hours
Excretion: Urine (as unchanged drug and several unidentified metabolites)

Dosage Children and Adults: Oral:
Treatment of acute attack of malaria: A single dose of the following number of Fansidar® tablets is used in sequence with quinine or alone:
2-11 months: $^1/_4$ tablet
1-3 years: $^1/_2$ tablet
4-8 years: 1 tablet
9-14 years: 2 tablets
>14 years: 3 tablets
Malaria prophylaxis: A single dose should be carried for self-treatment in the event of febrile illness when medical attention is not immediately available:
2-11 months: $^1/_4$ tablet
1-3 years: $^1/_2$ tablet
4-8 years: 1 tablet
9-14 years: 2 tablets
>14 years and Adults: 3 tablets

Monitoring Parameters CBC, including platelet counts, and urinalysis should be performed periodically

Patient Information Begin prophylaxis at least 2 days before departure; drink plenty of fluids; avoid prolonged exposure to the sun; report rash, sore throat, pallor, or glossitis

Dosage Forms TAB: Sulfadoxine 500 mg and pyrimethamine 25 mg

Sulfamethoxazole and Trimethoprim
(sul fa meth OKS a zole & trye METH oh prim)

Related Information
Antimicrobial Drugs of Choice *on page 1440*

U.S. Brand Names Bactrim™; Bactrim™ DS; Septra®; Septra® DS

Synonyms Co-Trimoxazole; SMZ-TMP; Sulfatrim; TMP-SMZ; Trimethoprim and Sulfamethoxazole

Therapeutic Category Antibiotic, Sulfonamide Derivative

Use

Oral treatment of urinary tract infections due to *E. coli*, *Klebsiella* and *Enterobacter* sp, *M. morganii*, *P. mirabilis* and *P. vulgaris*; acute otitis media in children and acute exacerbations of chronic bronchitis in adults due to susceptible strains of *H. influenzae* or *S. pneumoniae*; prophylaxis of *Pneumocystis carinii* pneumonitis (PCP), traveler's diarrhea due to enterotoxigenic *E. coli* or *Cyclospora*

I.V. treatment or severe or complicated infections when oral therapy is not feasible, for documented PCP, empiric treatment of PCP in immune compromised patients; treatment of documented or suspected shigellosis, typhoid fever, *Nocardia asteroides* infection, or other infections caused by susceptible bacteria

Unlabeled/Investigational Use Cholera and salmonella-type infections and nocardiosis; chronic prostatitis; as prophylaxis in neutropenic patients with *P. carinii* infections, in leukemics, and in patients following renal transplantation, to decrease incidence of PCP

Pregnancy Risk Factor C/D (at term - expert analysis)

Contraindications Hypersensitivity to any sulfa drug, trimethoprim, or any component of the formulation; porphyria; megaloblastic anemia due to folate deficiency; infants <2 months of age; marked hepatic damage; severe renal disease; pregnancy (at term)

Warnings/Precautions Use with caution in patients with G6PD deficiency, impaired renal or hepatic function or potential folate deficiency (malnourished, chronic anticonvulsant therapy, or elderly); maintain adequate hydration to prevent crystalluria; adjust dosage in patients with renal impairment. Injection vehicle contains benzyl alcohol and sodium metabisulfite.

Chemical similarities are present among sulfonamides, sulfonylureas, carbonic anhydrase inhibitors, thiazides, and loop diuretics (except ethacrynic acid). Use in patients with sulfonamide allergy is specifically contraindicated in product labeling, however, a risk of cross-reaction exists in patients with allergy to any of these compounds; avoid use when previous reaction has been severe.

Fatalities associated with severe reactions including Stevens-Johnson syndrome, toxic epidermal necrolysis, hepatic necrosis, agranulocytosis, aplastic anemia and other blood dyscrasias; discontinue use at first sign of rash. Elderly patients appear at greater risk for more severe adverse reactions. May cause hypoglycemia, particularly in malnourished, or patients with renal or hepatic impairment. Use with caution in patients with porphyria or thyroid dysfunction. Slow acetylators may be more prone to adverse reactions. Caution in patients with allergies or asthma. May cause hyperkalemia (associated with high doses of trimethoprim). Incidence of adverse effects appears to be increased in patients with AIDS.

Common Adverse Reactions The most common adverse reactions include gastrointestinal upset (nausea, vomiting, anorexia) and dermatologic reactions (rash or urticaria). Rare, life-threatening reactions have been associated with co-trimoxazole, including severe dermatologic reactions and hepatotoxic reactions. Most other reactions listed are rare, however, frequency cannot be accurately estimated.

Cardiovascular: Allergic myocarditis

Central nervous system: Confusion, depression, hallucinations, seizures, aseptic meningitis, peripheral neuritis, fever, ataxia, kernicterus in neonates

Dermatologic: Rashes, pruritus, urticaria, photosensitivity; rare reactions include erythema multiforme, Stevens-Johnson syndrome, toxic epidermal necrolysis, exfoliative dermatitis, and Henoch-Schönlein purpura

Endocrine & metabolic: Hyperkalemia (generally at high dosages), hyperglycemia

Gastrointestinal: Nausea, vomiting, anorexia, stomatitis, diarrhea, pseudomembranous colitis, pancreatitis

Hematologic: Thrombocytopenia, megaloblastic anemia, granulocytopenia, eosinophilia, pancytopenia, aplastic anemia, methemoglobinemia, hemolysis (with G6PD deficiency), agranulocytosis

Hepatic: Elevated serum transaminases, hepatotoxicity (including hepatitis, cholestasis, and hepatic necrosis), hyperbilirubinemia

Neuromuscular & skeletal: Arthralgia, myalgia, rhabdomyolysis

Renal: Interstitial nephritis, crystalluria, renal failure, nephrotoxicity (in association with cyclosporine), diuresis

Respiratory: Cough, dyspnea, pulmonary infiltrates

Miscellaneous: Serum sickness, angioedema, periarteritis nodosa (rare), systemic lupus erythematosus (rare)

(Continued)

Sulfamethoxazole and Trimethoprim *(Continued)*

Drug Interactions

Cytochrome P450 Effect:

Sulfamethoxazole: **Substrate** of CYP2C8/9 (major), 3A4 (minor); **Inhibits** CYP2C8/9 (moderate)

Trimethoprim: **Substrate** (major) of CYP2C8/9, 3A4; **Inhibits** CYP2C8/9 (moderate)

Increased Effect/Toxicity: Sulfamethoxazole/trimethoprim may increase the effect of warfarin and/or oral hypoglycemic agents. Sulfamethoxazole/trimethoprim may increase toxicity of methotrexate. Sulfamethoxazole/trimethoprim may increase the serum levels of procainamide or phenytoin. Concurrent therapy with pyrimethamine (in doses >25 mg/week) may increase the risk of megaloblastic anemia.

ACE Inhibitors, angiotensin receptor antagonists, or potassium-sparing diuretics may increase the risk of hyperkalemia. Concurrent use with cyclosporine may result in an increased risk of nephrotoxicity when used with sulfamethoxazole/trimethoprim. Trimethoprim may increase the serum concentration of dapsone.

Decreased Effect: CYP2C8/9 inducers may decrease the levels/effects of sulfamethoxazole; example inducers include carbamazepine, phenobarbital, phenytoin, rifampin, rifapentine, and secobarbital. Although occasionally recommended to limit or reverse hematologic toxicity of high-dose sulfamethoxazole/trimethoprim, concurrent use has been associated with a decreased effectiveness in treating *Pneumocystis carinii*.

Mechanism of Action Sulfamethoxazole interferes with bacterial folic acid synthesis and growth via inhibition of dihydrofolic acid formation from para-aminobenzoic acid; trimethoprim inhibits dihydrofolic acid reduction to tetrahydrofolate resulting in sequential inhibition of enzymes of the folic acid pathway

Pharmacodynamics/Kinetics See individual agents.

Dosage Dosage recommendations are based on the trimethoprim component

Children >2 months:

Mild to moderate infections: Oral, I.V.: 8 mg TMP/kg/day in divided doses every 12 hours

Serious infection/*Pneumocystis*: I.V.: 20 mg TMP/kg/day in divided doses every 6 hours

Urinary tract infection prophylaxis: Oral: 2 mg TMP/kg/dose daily

Prophylaxis of *Pneumocystis*: Oral, I.V.: 10 mg TMP/kg/day or 150 mg TMP/m^2/day in divided doses every 12 hours for 3 days/week; dose should not exceed 320 mg trimethoprim and 1600 mg sulfamethoxazole 3 days/week

Cholera: Oral, I.V.: 5 mg TMP/kg twice daily for 3 days

Cyclospora: Oral, I.V.: 5 mg TMP/kg twice daily for 7 days

Adults:

Urinary tract infection/chronic bronchitis: Oral: 1 double strength tablet every 12 hours for 10-14 days

Sepsis: I.V.: 20 TMP/kg/day divided every 6 hours

Pneumocystis carinii:

Prophylaxis: Oral: 1 double strength tablet daily or 3 times/week

Treatment: Oral, I.V.: 15-20 mg TMP/kg/day in 3-4 divided doses

Cholera: Oral, I.V.: 160 mg TMP twice daily for 3 days

Cyclospora: Oral, I.V.: 160 mg TMP twice daily for 7 days

Nocardia: Oral, I.V.: 640 mg TMP/day in divided doses for several months (duration is controversial; an average of 7 months has been reported)

Dosing adjustment in renal impairment: Adults:

I.V.:

Cl_{cr} 15-30 mL/minute: Administer 2.5-5 mg/kg every 12 hours

Cl_{cr} <15 mL/minute: Administer 2.5-5 mg/kg every 24 hours

Oral:

Cl_{cr} 15-30 mL/minute: Administer 1 double strength tablet every 24 hours or 1 single strength tablet every 12 hours

Cl_{cr} <15 mL/minute: Not recommended

Administration Infuse over 60-90 minutes, must dilute well before giving; may be given less diluted in a central line; not for I.M. injection; maintain adequate fluid intake to prevent crystalluria

Patient Information Take oral medication with 8 oz of water on an empty stomach (1 hour before or 2 hours after meals) for best absorption; report any skin rashes immediately; finish all medication, do not skip doses

Dosage Forms Note: The 5:1 ratio (SMX:TMP) remains constant in all dosage forms. **INJ, solution:** Sulfamethoxazole 80 mg and trimethoprim 16 mg per mL (5 mL, 10 mL, 30 mL); (Septra®): Sulfamethoxazole 80 mg and trimethoprim 16 mg per mL (10 mL, 20 mL). **SUSP, oral:** Sulfamethoxazole 200 mg and trimethoprim 40 mg per 5 mL (20 mL, 100 mL, 480 mL); (Septra®): Sulfamethoxazole 200 mg and trimethoprim 40 mg per 5 mL (100 mL, 480 mL). **TAB:** Sulfamethoxazole 400 mg and trimethoprim 80 mg; (Bactrim™, Septra®): Sulfamethoxazole 400 mg and trimethoprim 80 mg. **TAB, double strength:** Sulfamethoxazole 800 mg and trimethoprim 160 mg; (Bactrim™ DS, Septra® DS): Sulfamethoxazole 800 mg and trimethoprim 160 mg

♦ **Sulfamylon®** *see* Mafenide *on page 767*

Sulfasalazine *(sul fa SAL a zeen)*

Related Information

Sulfonamide Derivatives *on page 1404*

U.S. Brand Names Azulfidine®; Azulfidine® EN-tabs®

Synonyms Salicylazosulfapyridine

Therapeutic Category 5-Aminosalicylic Acid Derivative; Anti-inflammatory Agent

Use Management of ulcerative colitis; enteric coated tablets are also used for rheumatoid arthritis (including juvenile rheumatoid arthritis) in patients who inadequately respond to analgesics and NSAIDs

Unlabeled/Investigational Use Ankylosing spondylitis, collagenous colitis, Crohn's disease, psoriasis, psoriatic arthritis, juvenile chronic arthritis

Pregnancy Risk Factor B/D (at term)

Contraindications Hypersensitivity to sulfasalazine, sulfa drugs, salicylates, or any component of the formulation; porphyria; GI or GU obstruction; pregnancy (at term)

Warnings/Precautions Use with caution in patients with renal impairment; impaired hepatic function or urinary obstruction, blood dyscrasias severe allergies or asthma, or G6PD deficiency; may cause folate deficiency (consider providing 1 mg/day folate supplement). Chemical similarities are present among sulfonamides, sulfonylureas, carbonic anhydrase inhibitors, thiazides, and loop diuretics (except ethacrynic acid). Use in patients with sulfonamide allergy is specifically contraindicated in product labeling, however, a risk of cross-reaction exists in patients with allergy to any of these compounds; avoid use when previous reaction has been severe. Safety and efficacy have not been established in children <2 years of age.

Common Adverse Reactions

>10%:

Central nervous system: Headache (33%)

Dermatologic: Photosensitivity

Gastrointestinal: Anorexia, nausea, vomiting, diarrhea (33%), gastric distress

Genitourinary: Reversible oligospermia (33%)

<3%:

Dermatologic: Urticaria/pruritus (<3%)

Hematologic: Hemolytic anemia (<3%), Heinz body anemia (<3%)

Additional events reported with sulfonamides and/or 5-ASA derivatives: Cholestatic jaundice, eosinophilia pneumonitis, erythema multiforme, fibrosing alveolitis, hepatic necrosis, Kawasaki-like syndrome, SLE-like syndrome, pericarditis, seizures, transverse myelitis

Drug Interactions

Increased Effect/Toxicity: Sulfasalazine may increase hydantoin levels. Effects of thiopental, oral hypoglycemics, and oral anticoagulants may be increased. Sulfasalazine may increase the risk of myelosuppression with azathioprine, mercaptopurine, or thioguanine (due to TPMT inhibition); may also increase the toxicity of methotrexate. Risk of thrombocytopenia may be increased with thiazide diuretics. Concurrent methenamine may increase risk of crystalluria.

Decreased Effect: Decreased effect with iron, digoxin and PABA or PABA metabolites of drugs (eg, procaine, proparacaine, tetracaine).

Mechanism of Action Acts locally in the colon to decrease the inflammatory response and systemically interferes with secretion by inhibiting prostaglandin synthesis

Pharmacodynamics/Kinetics

Absorption: 10% to 15% as unchanged drug from small intestine

Distribution: Small amounts enter feces and breast milk

Metabolism: Via colonic intestinal flora to sulfapyridine and 5-aminosalicylic acid (5-ASA); following absorption, sulfapyridine undergoes N-acetylation and ring hydroxylation while 5-ASA undergoes N-acetylation

Half-life elimination: 5.7-10 hours

Excretion: Primarily urine (as unchanged drug, components, and acetylated metabolites)

Dosage Oral:

Children ≥2 years: Ulcerative colitis: Initial: 40-60 mg/kg/day in 3-6 divided doses; maintenance dose: 20-30 mg/kg/day in 4 divided doses

Children ≥6 years: Juvenile rheumatoid arthritis: Enteric coated tablet: 30-50 mg/kg/day in 2 divided doses; Initial: Begin with $^1/_4$ to $^1/_3$ of expected maintenance dose; increase weekly; maximum: 2 g/day typically

Adults:

Ulcerative colitis: Initial: 1 g 3-4 times/day, 2 g/day maintenance in divided doses; may initiate therapy with 0.5-1 g/day

Rheumatoid arthritis: Enteric coated tablet: Initial: 0.5-1 g/day; increase weekly to maintenance dose of 2 g/day in 2 divided doses; maximum: 3 g/day (if response to 2 g/day is inadequate after 12 weeks of treatment)

Dosing interval in renal impairment:

Cl$_{cr}$ 10-30 mL/minute: Administer twice daily

Cl$_{cr}$ <10 mL/minute: Administer once daily

Dosing adjustment in hepatic impairment: Avoid use

Administration GI intolerance is common during the first few days of therapy (administer with meals).

Patient Information Maintain adequate fluid intake; take after meals; may cause orange-yellow discoloration of urine and skin; take after meals or with food; do not take with antacids; may permanently stain soft contact lenses yellow; avoid prolonged exposure to sunlight; shake well before using

Dosage Forms TAB (Azulfidine®): 500 mg. **TAB, delayed release, enteric coated** (Azulfidine® EN-tabs®): 500 mg

♦ **Sulfatrim** see Sulfamethoxazole and Trimethoprim on page 1173

Sulfinpyrazone (sul fin PEER a zone)
Synonyms Anturane
Therapeutic Category Antigout Agent; Uricosuric Agent
Use Treatment of chronic gouty arthritis and intermittent gouty arthritis
Unlabeled/Investigational Use To decrease the incidence of sudden death postmyocardial infarction
Pregnancy Risk Factor C/D (near term - expert analysis)
Contraindications Hypersensitivity to sulfinpyrazone, phenylbutazone, other pyrazoles, or any component of the formulation; active peptic ulcer; GI inflammation; blood dyscrasias; pregnancy (near term)
Warnings/Precautions Safety and efficacy not established in children <18 years of age, use with caution in patients with impaired renal function and urolithiasis
Common Adverse Reactions Frequency not defined.
Cardiovascular: Flushing
Central nervous system: Dizziness, headache
Dermatologic: Dermatitis, rash
Gastrointestinal (most frequent adverse effects): Nausea, vomiting, stomach pain
Genitourinary: Polyuria
Hematologic: Anemia, leukopenia, increased bleeding time (decreased platelet aggregation)
Hepatic: Hepatic necrosis
Renal: Nephrotic syndrome, uric acid stones
Drug Interactions
Cytochrome P450 Effect: Substrate of CYP2C8/9 (major), 3A4 (minor); **Inhibits** CYP2C8/9 (moderate); **Induces** CYP3A4 (weak)
Increased Effect/Toxicity: Increased effect of oral hypoglycemics and anticoagulants. Risk of acetaminophen hepatotoxicity is increased, while therapeutic effects may be reduced.
Decreased Effect: CYP2C8/9 inducers may decrease the levels/effects of sulfinpyrazone; example inducers include carbamazepine, phenobarbital, phenytoin, rifampin, rifapentine, and secobarbital. Decreased effect/levels of theophylline, verapamil. Decreased uricosuric activity with salicylates, niacins.
Mechanism of Action Acts by increasing the urinary excretion of uric acid, thereby decreasing blood urate levels; this effect is therapeutically useful in treating patients with acute intermittent gout, chronic tophaceous gout, and acts to promote resorption of tophi; also has antithrombic and platelet inhibitory effects
Pharmacodynamics/Kinetics
Absorption: Rapid and complete
Metabolism: Hepatic to two active metabolites
Half-life elimination: 2.7-6 hours
Time to peak, serum: 1.6 hours
Excretion: Urine (22% to 50% as unchanged drug)
Dosage Adults: Oral: 100-200 mg twice daily; maximum daily dose: 800 mg
Dosing adjustment in renal impairment: Cl_{cr} <50 mL/minute: Avoid use
Monitoring Parameters Serum and urinary uric acid, CBC
Dosage Forms TAB: 100 mg

SulfiSOXAZOLE (sul fi SOKS a zole)
Related Information
Antimicrobial Drugs of Choice *on page 1440*
Sulfonamide Derivatives *on page 1404*
U.S. Brand Names Gantrisin®
Synonyms Sulfisoxazole Acetyl; Sulphafurazole
Therapeutic Category Antibiotic, Sulfonamide Derivative
Use Treatment of urinary tract infections, otitis media, *Chlamydia*; nocardiosis
Pregnancy Risk Factor B/D (near term)
Contraindications Hypersensitivity to sulfisoxazole, any sulfa drug, or any component of the formulation; porphyria; infants <2 months of age (sulfas compete with bilirubin for protein binding sites); patients with urinary obstruction; sunscreens containing PABA; pregnancy (at term)
Warnings/Precautions Use with caution in patients with G6PD deficiency (hemolysis may occur), hepatic or renal impairment; dosage modification required in patients with renal impairment; risk of crystalluria should be considered in patients with impaired renal function. Chemical similarities are present among sulfonamides, sulfonylureas, carbonic anhydrase inhibitors, thiazides, and loop diuretics (except ethacrynic acid). Use in patients with sulfonamide allergy is specifically contraindicated in product labeling, however, a risk of cross-reaction exists in patients with allergy to any of these compounds; avoid use when previous reaction has been severe.
Common Adverse Reactions Frequency not defined.
Cardiovascular: Vasculitis
Central nervous system: Fever, dizziness, headache
Dermatologic: Itching, rash, photosensitivity, Lyell's syndrome, Stevens-Johnson syndrome
Endocrine & metabolic: Thyroid function disturbance
Gastrointestinal: Anorexia, nausea, vomiting, diarrhea
Genitourinary: Crystalluria, hematuria,
Hematologic: Granulocytopenia, leukopenia, thrombocytopenia, aplastic anemia, hemolytic anemia
Hepatic: Jaundice, hepatitis

Renal: Interstitial nephritis
Miscellaneous: Serum sickness-like reactions

Drug Interactions
Cytochrome P450 Effect: Substrate of CYP2C8/9 (major); **Inhibits** CYP2C8/9 (strong)
Increased Effect/Toxicity: Increased effect of oral anticoagulants, methotrexate, and oral hypoglycemic agents. May increase phenytoin levels. Risk of adverse reactions (thrombocytopenia purpura) may be increased by thiazide.
Decreased Effect: Decreased effect with PABA or PABA metabolites of drugs (eg, procaine, proparacaine, tetracaine), thiopental. May decrease cyclosporine levels.

Mechanism of Action Interferes with bacterial growth by inhibiting bacterial folic acid synthesis through competitive antagonism of PABA

Pharmacodynamics/Kinetics
Absorption: Sulfisoxazole acetyl is hydrolyzed in GI tract to sulfisoxazole which is readily absorbed
Distribution: Crosses placenta; enters breast milk
CSF:blood level ratio: Normal meninges: 50% to 80%; Inflamed meninges: 80+%
Protein binding: 85% to 88%
Metabolism: Hepatic via acetylation and glucuronide conjugation to inactive compounds
Half-life elimination: 4-7 hours; prolonged with renal impairment
Time to peak, serum: 2-3 hours
Excretion: Urine (95%, 40% to 60% as unchanged drug) within 24 hours

Dosage Oral: Not for use in patients <2 months of age:
Children >2 months: Initial: 75 mg/kg, followed by 120-150 mg/kg/day in divided doses every 4-6 hours; not to exceed 6 g/day
Adults: Initial: 2-4 g, then 4-8 g/day in divided doses every 4-6 hours
Dosing interval in renal impairment:
Cl$_{cr}$ 10-50 mL/minute: Administer every 8-12 hours
Cl$_{cr}$ <10 mL/minute: Administer every 12-24 hours
Hemodialysis: >50% removed by hemodialysis

Administration Administer around-the-clock to promote less variation in peak and trough serum levels.

Monitoring Parameters CBC, urinalysis, renal function tests, temperature

Patient Information Take with a glass of water on an empty stomach; avoid prolonged exposure to sunlight; report any sore throat, mouth sores, rash, unusual bleeding, or fever; complete full course of therapy

Dosage Forms SUSP, oral, pediatric (Gantrisin®): 500 mg/5 mL (480 mL). **TAB:** 500 mg

- **Sulfisoxazole Acetyl** *see* SulfiSOXAZOLE *on page 1176*
- **Sulfisoxazole and Erythromycin** *see* Erythromycin and Sulfisoxazole *on page 455*
- **Sulfonamide Derivatives** *see page 1404*

Sulfur and Sulfacetamide (SUL fur & sul fa SEE ta mide)

U.S. Brand Names AVAR™; AVAR™ Cleanser; AVAR™ Green; Clenia™; Nocosyn™; Plexion®; Plexion SCT™; Plexion™ TS; Rosanil™; Rosula®; Sulfacet-R®; Zetacet®
Synonyms Sodium Sulfacetamide and Sulfur; Sulfacetamide and Sulfur; Sulfur and Sulfacetamide Sodium
Therapeutic Category Antibiotic, Sulfonamide Derivative; Antiseborrheic Agent, Topical; Topical Skin Product, Acne
Use Aid in the treatment of acne vulgaris, acne rosacea, and seborrheic dermatitis
Pregnancy Risk Factor C
Dosage Topical: Children ≥12 years and Adults: Apply in a thin film 1-3 times/day. Cleansing products should be used 1-2 times/day.
Dosage adjustment in renal impairment: Use is contraindicated.
Dosage Forms CRM: (Clenia™): Sulfur 5% and sulfacetamide sodium 10% (28 g); (Plexion SCT™): Sulfur 5% and sulfacetamide sodium 10% (120 g); (Rosanil™ [cleanser]): Sulfur 5% and sulfacetamide sodium 10% (170 g). **GEL** (AVAR™, AVAR™ Green, Rosula®): Sulfur 5% and sulfacetamide sodium 10% (45 g). **SOAP, liquid:** (Clenia™): Sulfur 5% and sulfacetamide sodium 10% (170 g, 340 g). **LOTION:** Sulfur 5% and sulfacetamide sodium 10% (25 g); (AVAR™ Cleanser): Sulfur 5% and sulfacetamide sodium 10% (228 g); (Nicosyn™, Rosula®): Sulfur 5% and sulfacetamide sodium 10% (45 g); (Plexion™ [cleanser]): Sulfur 5% and sulfacetamide sodium 10% (170 g, 340 g); (Rosula®): Sulfur 5% and sulfacetamide sodium 10% (25 g). **SUSP:** (Plexion™ TS, Zetacet®): Sulfur 5% and sulfacetamide sodium 10% (30 g) [contains benzyl alcohol]

- **Sulfur and Sulfacetamide Sodium** *see* Sulfur and Sulfacetamide *on page 1177*

Sulindac (sul IN dak)

Related Information
Nonsteroidal Anti-Inflammatory Agents Comparison *on page 1401*
U.S. Brand Names Clinoril®
Therapeutic Category Analgesic, Nonsteroidal Anti-inflammatory Drug; Anti-inflammatory Agent; Nonsteroidal Anti-inflammatory Drug (NSAID), Oral
Use Management of inflammatory disease, rheumatoid disorders, acute gouty arthritis, ankylosing spondylitis, bursitis, tendonitis
Pregnancy Risk Factor B/D (3rd trimester)
Contraindications Hypersensitivity to sulindac, any component of the formulation, aspirin or other NSAIDs; pregnancy (3rd trimester)
(Continued)

Sulindac *(Continued)*

Warnings/Precautions Use with caution in patients with CHF, hypertension, dehydration, decreased renal or hepatic function, history of peptic ulcer disease or GI disease (bleeding or ulcers), or those receiving anticoagulants. Elderly are at a high risk for CNS and gastrointestinal adverse effects from NSAIDs. As many as 60% of elderly can develop peptic ulceration and/or hemorrhage asymptomatically.

Use lowest effective dose for shortest period possible. Use of NSAIDs can compromise existing renal function especially when Cl_{cr} is <30 mL/minute. Withhold for at least 4-6 half-lives prior to surgical or dental procedures. May have adverse effects on fetus. Use with caution with dehydration. Use in children is not recommended.

Common Adverse Reactions 1% to 10%:
Cardiovascular: Edema
Central nervous system: Dizziness, headache, nervousness
Dermatologic: Pruritus, rash
Gastrointestinal: GI pain, heartburn, nausea, vomiting, diarrhea, constipation, flatulence, anorexia, abdominal cramps
Otic: Tinnitus

Drug Interactions
Increased Effect/Toxicity: Increased toxicity with probenecid, NSAIDs. Increased toxicity of digoxin, anticoagulants, methotrexate, lithium, aminoglycosides antibiotics (reported in neonates), cyclosporine (increased nephrotoxicity), and potassium-sparing diuretics (hyperkalemia).
Decreased Effect: Decreased effect of diuretics, beta-blockers, hydralazine, and captopril.

Mechanism of Action Inhibits prostaglandin synthesis by decreasing the activity of the enzyme, cyclooxygenase, which results in decreased formation of prostaglandin precursors

Pharmacodynamics/Kinetics
Onset of action: Analgesic: ~1 hour
Duration: 12-24 hours
Absorption: 90%
Metabolism: Hepatic; prodrug requiring metabolic activation to sulfide metabolite (active) for therapeutic effects and to sulfone metabolites (inactive)
Half-life elimination: Parent drug: 7 hours; Active metabolite: 18 hours
Excretion: Urine (50%); feces (25%)

Dosage Maximum therapeutic response may not be realized for up to 3 weeks
Oral:
Children: Dose not established
Adults: 150-200 mg twice daily or 300-400 mg once daily; not to exceed 400 mg/day
Dosing adjustment in hepatic impairment: Dose reduction is necessary

Administration Should be administered with food or milk.

Monitoring Parameters Liver enzymes, BUN, serum creatinine, CBC, blood pressure; signs and symptoms of GI bleeding

Patient Information Take with food or milk; inform dentist or surgeon because of prolonged bleeding time; do not take aspirin; may cause dizziness, drowsiness, impair coordination and judgment

Dosage Forms TAB: 150 mg, 200 mg

♦ **Sulphafurazole** *see* SulfiSOXAZOLE *on page 1176*

Sumatriptan *(soo ma TRIP tan SUKS i nate)*

Related Information
Antimigraine Drugs Comparison *on page 1363*

U.S. Brand Names Imitrex®

Synonyms Sumatriptan Succinate

Therapeutic Category Antimigraine Agent, Serotonin 5-HT$_{1D}$ Agonist; Serotonin 5-HT$_4$ Receptor Agonist

Use Acute treatment of migraine with or without aura
Sumatriptan injection: Acute treatment of cluster headache episodes

Pregnancy Risk Factor C

Contraindications Hypersensitivity to sumatriptan or any component of the formulation; patients with ischemic heart disease or signs or symptoms of ischemic heart disease (including Prinzmetal's angina, angina pectoris, myocardial infarction, silent myocardial ischemia); cerebrovascular syndromes (including strokes, transient ischemic attacks); peripheral vascular syndromes (including ischemic bowel disease); uncontrolled hypertension; use within 24 hours of ergotamine derivatives; use with in 24 hours of another 5-HT$_1$ agonist; concurrent administration or within 2 weeks of discontinuing an MAO inhibitor, specifically MAO type A inhibitors; management of hemiplegic or basilar migraine; prophylactic treatment of migraine; severe hepatic impairment; not for I.V. administration

Warnings/Precautions
Sumatriptan is indicated only in patients ≥18 years of age with a clear diagnosis of migraine or cluster headache
Cardiac events (coronary artery vasospasm, transient ischemia, myocardial infarction, ventricular tachycardia/fibrillation, cardiac arrest and death), cerebral/subarachnoid hemorrhage, and stroke have been reported with 5-HT$_1$ agonist administration
Do not give to patients with risk factors for CAD until a cardiovascular evaluation has been performed; if evaluation is satisfactory, the healthcare provider should administer the first dose and cardiovascular status should be periodically evaluated

Significant elevation in blood pressure, including hypertensive crisis, has also been reported on rare occasions in patients with and without a history of hypertension. Vasospasm-related reactions have been reported other than coronary artery vasospasm. Peripheral vascular ischemia and colonic ischemia with abdominal pain and bloody diarrhea have occurred.

Use with caution in patients with a history of seizure disorder or in patients with a lowered seizure threshold. Safety and efficacy in pediatric patients have not been established

Common Adverse Reactions

>10%:

Central nervous system: Dizziness (injection 12%), warm/hot sensation (injection 11%)

Gastrointestinal: Bad taste (nasal spray 13% to 24%), nausea (nasal spray 11% to 13%), vomiting (nasal spray 11% to 13%)

Local: Injection: Pain at the injection site (59%)

Neuromuscular & skeletal: Tingling (injection 13%)

1% to 10%:

Cardiovascular: Chest pain/tightness/heaviness/pressure (injection 2% to 3%, tablet 1% to 2%)

Central nervous system: Burning (injection 7%), dizziness (nasal spray 1% to 2%, tablet >1%), feeling of heaviness (injection 7%), flushing (injection 7%), pressure sensation (injection 7%), feeling of tightness (injection 5%), numbness (injection 5%), drowsiness (injection 3%, tablet >1%), malaise/fatigue (tablet 2% to 3%, injection 1%), feeling strange (injection 2%), headache (injection 2%, tablet >1%), tight feeling in head (injection 2%), nonspecified pain (tablet 1% to 2%, placebo 1%), vertigo (tablet <1% to 2%, nasal spray 1% to 2%), migraine (tablet >1%), sleepiness (tablet >1%), cold sensation (injection 1%), anxiety (injection 1%)

Gastrointestinal: Nausea (tablet >1%), vomiting (tablet >1%), hyposalivation (tablet >1%), abdominal discomfort (injection 1%), dysphagia (injection 1%)

Neuromuscular & skeletal: Neck, throat, and jaw pain/tightness/pressure (injection 2% to 5%, tablet 2% to 3%), mouth/tongue discomfort (injection 5%), paresthesia (tablet 3% to 5%), weakness (injection 5%), myalgia (injection 2%), muscle cramps (injection 1%)

Ocular: Vision alterations (injection 1%)

Respiratory: Nasal disorder/discomfort (nasal spray 2% to 4%, injection 2%), throat discomfort (injection 3%, nasal spray 1% to 2%)

Miscellaneous: Warm/cold sensation (tablet 2% to 3%, placebo 2%), nonspecified pressure/tightness/heaviness (tablet 1% to 3%, placebo 2%), diaphoresis (injection 2%)

Drug Interactions

Increased Effect/Toxicity: Increased toxicity with ergot-containing drugs, avoid use, wait 24 hours from last ergot containing drug (dihydroergotamine, or methysergide) before administering sumatriptan. MAO inhibitors decrease clearance of sumatriptan increasing the risk of systemic sumatriptan toxic effects. Sumatriptan may enhance CNS toxic effects when taken with selective serotonin reuptake inhibitors (SSRIs) like fluoxetine, fluvoxamine, paroxetine, or sertraline. **Note:** Use cautiously in patients receiving concomitant medications that can lower the seizure threshold.

Mechanism of Action Selective agonist for serotonin (5-HT$_{1D}$ receptor) in cranial arteries to cause vasoconstriction and reduces sterile inflammation associated with antidromic neuronal transmission correlating with relief of migraine

Pharmacodynamics/Kinetics

Onset of action: ~30 minutes

Distribution: V$_d$: 2.4 L/kg

Protein binding: 14% to 21%

Bioavailability: S.C.: 97% ± 16% of that following I.V. injection

Half-life elimination: Injection, tablet: 2.5 hours; Nasal spray: 2 hours

Time to peak, serum: 5-20 minutes

Excretion:

Injection: Urine (38% as indole acetic acid metabolite, 22% as unchanged drug)

Nasal spray: Urine (42% as indole acetic acid metabolite, 3% as unchanged drug)

Tablet: Urine (60% as indole acetic acid metabolite, 3% as unchanged drug); feces (40%)

Dosage Adults:

Oral: A single dose of 25 mg, 50 mg, or 100 mg (taken with fluids). If a satisfactory response has not been obtained at 2 hours, a second dose may be administered. Results from clinical trials show that initial doses of 50 mg and 100 mg are more effective than doses of 25 mg, and that 100 mg doses do not provide a greater effect than 50 mg and may have increased incidence of side effects. Although doses of up to 300 mg/day have been studied, the total daily dose should not exceed 200 mg. The safety of treating an average of >4 headaches in a 30-day period have not been established.

Intranasal: A single dose of 5 mg, 10 mg, or 20 mg administered in one nostril. A 10 mg dose may be achieved by administering a single 5 mg dose in each nostril. If headache returns, the dose may be repeated once after 2 hours, not to exceed a total daily dose of 40 mg. The safety of treating an average of >4 headaches in a 30-day period has not been established.

S.C.: 6 mg; a second injection may be administered at least 1 hour after the initial dose, but not more than 2 injections in a 24-hour period. If side effects are dose-limiting, lower doses may be used.

Dosage adjustment in renal impairment: Dosage adjustment not necessary

Dosage adjustment in hepatic impairment: Bioavailability of oral sumatriptan is increased with liver disease. If treatment is needed, do not exceed single doses of 50 mg. The nasal spray has not been studied in patients with hepatic impairment, however, because the spray does not undergo first-pass metabolism, levels would not be expected to alter. Use of all dosage forms is contraindicated with severe hepatic impairment.

(Continued)

Sumatriptan *(Continued)*

Elderly: Due to increased risk of CAD, decreased hepatic function, and more pronounced blood pressure increases, use of the tablet dosage form in elderly patients is not recommended. Use of the nasal spray has not been studied in the elderly. Pharmacokinetics of injectable sumatriptan in the elderly are similar to healthy patients.

Administration

Oral: Should be taken with fluids as soon as symptoms to appear

Do not administer I.V.; may cause coronary vasospasm

Patient Information Take at first sign of migraine attack. This drug is to be used to relieve your migraine, not to prevent or reduce number of attacks.

Oral: If headache returns or is not fully resolved after first dose, the dose may be repeated after 2 hours. **Do not exceed 200 mg in 24 hours.** Take whole with fluids.

S.C.: If headache returns or is not fully resolved after first dose, the dose may be repeated after 1 hour. **Do not exceed two injections in 24 hours.**

Nasal: Administer dose into one nostril. If headache returns or is not fully resolved after the first dose, the dose may be repeated after 2 hours. Do not exceed 40 mg in 24 hours.

All dosage forms: Do not take within 24 hours of any other migraine medication without first consulting prescriber. You may experience some dizziness (use caution); hot flashes (cool room may help); nausea or vomiting (frequent small meals, frequent mouth care, sucking lozenges, or chewing gum may help); pain at injection site (lasts about 1 hour, will resolve); or excess sweating (will resolve). Report chest tightness or pain; excessive drowsiness; acute abdominal pain; skin rash or burning sensation; muscle weakness, soreness, or numbness; or respiratory difficulty.

Dosage Forms Note: Expressed as sumatriptan base. **INJ, solution:** 12 mg/mL (0.5 mL). **SOLN, intranasal spray:** 5 mg (100 μL unit dose spray device); 20 mg (100 μL unit dose spray device). **TAB:** 25 mg, 50 mg, 100 mg

Tacrine *(TAK reen)*

U.S. Brand Names Cognex®

Synonyms Tacrine Hydrochloride; Tetrahydroaminoacrine; THA

Therapeutic Category Acetylcholinesterase Inhibitor; Cholinergic Agent

Use Treatment of mild to moderate dementia of the Alzheimer's type

Pregnancy Risk Factor C

Contraindications Hypersensitivity to tacrine, acridine derivatives, or any component of the formulation; patients previously treated with tacrine who developed jaundice

Warnings/Precautions The use of tacrine has been associated with elevations in serum transaminases; serum transaminases (specifically ALT) must be monitored throughout therapy; use extreme caution in patients with current evidence of a history of abnormal liver function tests; use caution in patients with urinary tract obstruction (bladder outlet obstruction or prostatic hyperplasia), asthma, and sick-sinus syndrome, bradycardia, or conduction abnormalities (tacrine may cause bradycardia and/or heart block). Also, patients with cardiovascular disease, asthma, or peptic ulcer should use cautiously. Adverse cardiovascular events may also occur in patients without known cardiac disease. Use with caution in patients with a history of seizures. May cause nausea, vomiting, or loose stools. Abrupt discontinuation or dosage decrease may worsen cognitive function. May be associated with neutropenia.

Common Adverse Reactions
>10%:
  Central nervous system: Headache, dizziness
  Gastrointestinal: Nausea, vomiting, diarrhea
  Miscellaneous: Elevated transaminases
1% to 10%:
  Cardiovascular: Flushing
  Central nervous system: Confusion, ataxia, insomnia, somnolence, depression, anxiety, fatigue
  Dermatologic: Rash
  Gastrointestinal: Dyspepsia, anorexia, abdominal pain, flatulence, constipation, weight loss
  Neuromuscular & skeletal: Myalgia, tremor
  Respiratory: Rhinitis

Drug Interactions
Cytochrome P450 Effect: Substrate of CYP1A2 (major); **Inhibits** CYP1A2 (weak)
Increased Effect/Toxicity: CYP1A2 inhibitors may increase the levels/effects of tacrine; example inhibitors include amiodarone, ciprofloxacin, fluvoxamine, ketoconazole, lomefloxacin, ofloxacin, and rofecoxib. Tacrine in combination with other cholinergic agents (eg, ambenonium, edrophonium, neostigmine, pyridostigmine, bethanechol), will likely produce additive cholinergic effects. Tacrine in combination with beta-blockers may produce additive bradycardia. Tacrine may increase the levels/effect of succinylcholine and theophylline. in elevated plasma levels. Fluvoxamine, enoxacin, and cimetidine increase tacrine concentrations via enzyme inhibition (CYP1A2).
Decreased Effect: CYP1A2 inducers may decrease the levels/effects of tacrine; example inducers include aminoglutethimide, carbamazepine, phenobarbital, rifampin, and cigarette smoking, Tacrine may worsen Parkinson's disease and inhibit the effects of levodopa. Tacrine may antagonize the therapeutic effect of anticholinergic agents (benztropine, trihexyphenidyl).

Mechanism of Action Centrally-acting cholinesterase inhibitor. It elevates acetylcholine in cerebral cortex by slowing the degradation of acetylcholine.

Pharmacodynamics/Kinetics
Absorption: Oral: Rapid
Distribution: V_d: Mean: 349 L; reduced by food
Protein binding, plasma: 55%
Metabolism: Extensively by CYP450 to multiple metabolites; first pass effect
Bioavailability: Absolute: 17%
Half-life elimination, serum: 2-4 hours; Steady-state: 24-36 hours
Time to peak, plasma: 1-2 hours

Dosage Adults: Initial: 10 mg 4 times/day; may increase by 40 mg/day adjusted every 6 weeks; maximum: 160 mg/day; best administered separate from meal times.
  Dose adjustment based upon transaminase elevations:
  ALT ≤3 times ULN*: Continue titration
  ALT >3 to ≤5 times ULN*: Decrease dose by 40 mg/day, resume when ALT returns to normal
  ALT >5 times ULN*: Stop treatment, may rechallenge upon return of ALT to normal
  *ULN = upper limit of normal
  Patients with clinical jaundice confirmed by elevated total bilirubin (>3 mg/dL) should not be rechallenged with tacrine

Monitoring Parameters ALT (SGPT) levels and other liver enzymes weekly for at least the first 18 weeks, then monitor once every 3 months

Reference Range In clinical trials, serum concentrations >20 ng/mL were associated with a much higher risk of development of symptomatic adverse effects

Patient Information Effect of tacrine therapy is thought to depend upon its administration at regular intervals, as directed; possibility of adverse effects such as those occurring in close temporal association with the initiation of treatment or an increase in dose (ie, nausea, vomiting, loose stools, diarrhea) and those with a delayed onset (ie, rash, jaundice, changes in the color of stool); inform prescriber of the emergence of new events or any increase in the severity of existing adverse effects; abrupt discontinuation of the drug or a large reduction in total daily dose (80 mg/day or more) may cause a decline in cognitive function and behavioral disturbances; unsupervised increases in the dose may also have serious consequences; do not change dose without consulting prescriber

Dosage Forms CAP: 10 mg, 20 mg, 30 mg, 40 mg

♦ **Tacrine Hydrochloride** see Tacrine on page 1180

Tacrolimus (ta KROE li mus)
U.S. Brand Names Prograf®; Protopic®
Synonyms FK506
Therapeutic Category Immunosuppressant Agent
Use
  Oral/injection: Potent immunosuppressive drug used in liver or kidney transplant recipients
  (Continued)

Tacrolimus *(Continued)*

Topical: Moderate to severe atopic dermatitis in patients not responsive to conventional therapy or when conventional therapy is not appropriate

Unlabeled/Investigational Use Potent immunosuppressive drug used in heart, lung, small bowel transplant recipients; immunosuppressive drug for peripheral stem cell/bone marrow transplantation

Pregnancy Risk Factor C

Contraindications Hypersensitivity to tacrolimus or any component of the formulation

Warnings/Precautions

Oral/injection: Insulin-dependent post-transplant diabetes mellitus (PTDM) has been reported (1% to 20%); risk increases in African-American and Hispanic kidney transplant patients. Increased susceptibility to infection and the possible development of lymphoma may occur after administration of tacrolimus. Nephrotoxicity and neurotoxicity have been reported, especially with higher doses; to avoid excess nephrotoxicity do not administer simultaneously with cyclosporine; monitoring of serum concentrations (trough for oral therapy) is essential to prevent organ rejection and reduce drug-related toxicity; tonic clonic seizures may have been triggered by tacrolimus. Use caution in renal or hepatic dysfunction, dosing adjustments may be required. Delay initiation if postoperative oliguria occurs. Myocardial hypertrophy has been reported (rare). Each mL of injection contains polyoxyl 60 hydrogenated castor oil (HCO-60) (200 mg) and dehydrated alcohol USP 80% v/v. Anaphylaxis has been reported with the injection, use should be reserved for those patients not able to take oral medications.

Topical: Infections at the treatment site should be cleared prior to therapy. Patients with atopic dermatitis are predisposed to skin infections, including eczema herpeticum, varicella zoster, and herpes simplex. Discontinue use in patients with unknown cause of lymphadenopathy or acute infectious mononucleosis. Not recommended for use in patients with Netherton's syndrome. Safety not established in patients with generalized erythroderma.

Common Adverse Reactions

Oral, I.V.:

≥15%:

Cardiovascular: Chest pain, hypertension

Central nervous system: Dizziness, headache, insomnia, tremor (headache and tremor are associated with high whole blood concentrations and may respond to decreased dosage)

Dermatologic: Pruritus, rash

Endocrine & metabolic: Diabetes mellitus, hyperglycemia, hyperkalemia, hyperlipemia, hypomagnesemia, hypophosphesemia

Gastrointestinal: Abdominal pain, constipation, diarrhea, dyspepsia, nausea, vomiting

Genitourinary: Urinary tract infection

Hematologic: Anemia, leukocytosis, thrombocytopenia

Hepatic: Ascites

Neuromuscular & skeletal: Arthralgia, back pain, weakness, paresthesia

Renal: Abnormal kidney function, increased creatinine, oliguria, urinary tract infection, increased BUN

Respiratory: Atelectasis, dyspnea, increased cough

3% to 15% (Limited to important or life-threatening symptoms):

Cardiovascular: Abnormal ECG, angina pectoris, deep thrombophlebitis, hemorrhage, hypotension, postural hypotension, thrombosis

Central nervous system: Agitation, amnesia, anxiety, confusion, depression, encephalopathy, hallucinations, psychosis, somnolence

Dermatologic: Acne, alopecia, exfoliative dermatitis, hirsutism, photosensitivity reaction, skin discoloration

Endocrine & metabolic: Cushing's syndrome, decreased bicarbonate, decreased serum iron, diabetes mellitus, hypercalcemia, hypercholesterolemia, hyperphosphatemia

Gastrointestinal: Dysphagia, esophagitis, GI perforation/hemorrhage, ileus

Hematologic: Coagulation disorder, decreased prothrombin, leukopenia

Hepatic: Cholangitis, jaundice, hepatitis

Neuromuscular & skeletal: Incoordination, myasthenia, neuropathy, osteoporosis

Respiratory: Asthma, pneumothorax, pulmonary edema

Miscellaneous: Abscess, allergic reaction, flu-like syndrome, peritonitis, sepsis

Postmarketing and/or case reports: Acute renal failure, anaphylaxis, coma, deafness, delirium, hearing loss, hemolytic-uremic syndrome, leukoencephalopathy, lymphoproliferative disorder (related to EBV), myocardial hypertrophy (associated with ventricular dysfunction), pancreatitis, seizures, Stevens-Johnson syndrome, thrombocytopenic purpura, torsade de pointes

Topical:

>10%:

Central nervous system: Headache (5% to 20%), fever (1% to 21%)

Dermatologic: Skin burning (43% to 58%), pruritus (41% to 46%), erythema (12% to 28%)

Respiratory: Increased cough (18% children)

Miscellaneous: Flu-like syndrome (23% to 28%), allergic reaction (4% to 12%)

Drug Interactions

Cytochrome P450 Effect: Substrate of CYP3A4 (major); **Inhibits** CYP3A4 (weak)

Increased Effect/Toxicity: Amphotericin B and other nephrotoxic antibiotics have the potential to increase tacrolimus-associated nephrotoxicity. Agents which may increase tacrolimus plasma concentrations resulting in toxicity are erythromycin, clarithromycin, clotrimazole, fluconazole, itraconazole, ketoconazole, diltiazem, nicardipine, verapamil, bromocriptine, cimetidine, cisapride, danazol, metoclopramide, methylprednisolone, and cyclosporine (synergistic immunosuppression). Voriconazole may increase tacrolimus serum concentrations; decrease tacrolimus dosage by 66% when initiating voriconazole.

Decreased Effect:

Antacids: Impaired tacrolimus absorption (separate administration by at least 2 hours).

Agents which may decrease tacrolimus plasma concentrations and reduce the therapeutic effect include rifampin, rifabutin, phenytoin, phenobarbital, and carbamazepine.

St John's wort may reduce tacrolimus serum concentrations (avoid concurrent use).

Mechanism of Action Suppresses cellular immunity (inhibits T-lymphocyte activation), possibly by binding to an intracellular protein, FKBP-12

Pharmacodynamics/Kinetics

Absorption: Better in resected patients with a closed stoma; unlike cyclosporine, clamping of the T-tube in liver transplant patients does not alter trough concentrations or AUC

Oral: Incomplete and variable; food within 15 minutes of administration decreases absorption (27%)

Topical: Serum concentrations range from undetectable to 20 ng/mL (<5 ng/mL in majority of adult patients studied)

Protein binding: 99%

Metabolism: Extensively hepatic via CYP3A4 to eight possible metabolites (major metabolite, 31-demethyl tacrolimus, shows same activity as tacrolimus *in vitro*)

Bioavailability: Oral: Adults: 7% to 28%, Children: 10% to 52%; Topical: <0.5%; Absolute: Unknown

Half-life elimination: Variable, 21-61 hours in healthy volunteers

Time to peak: 0.5-4 hours

Excretion: Feces (~92%); feces/urine (<1% as unchanged drug)

Dosage

Children:

Liver transplant: Patients without pre-existing renal or hepatic dysfunction have required and tolerated higher doses than adults to achieve similar blood concentrations. It is recommended that therapy be initiated at high end of the recommended adult I.V. and oral dosing ranges; dosage adjustments may be required.

Oral: Initial dose: 0.15-0.20 mg/kg/day in 2 divided doses, given every 12 hours; begin oral dose no sooner than 6 hours post-transplant; adjunctive therapy with corticosteroids is recommended; if switching from I.V. to oral, the oral dose should be started 8-12 hours after stopping the infusion

Typical whole blood trough concentrations: Months 1-12: 5-20 ng/mL

I.V.: **Note:** I.V. route should only be used in patients not able to take oral medications, anaphylaxis has been reported. Initial dose: 0.03-0.05 mg/kg/day as a continuous infusion; begin no sooner than 6 hours post-transplant; adjunctive therapy with corticosteroids is recommended; continue only until oral medication can be tolerated

Children ≥2 years: Moderate to severe atopic dermatitis: Topical: Apply 0.03% ointment to affected area twice daily; rub in gently and completely; continue applications for 1 week after symptoms have cleared

Adults:

Kidney transplant:

Oral: Initial dose: 0.2 mg/kg/day in 2 divided doses, given every 12 hours; initial dose may be given within 24 hours of transplant, but should be delayed until renal function has recovered; African-American patients may require larger doses to maintain trough concentration

Typical whole blood trough concentrations: Months 1-3: 7- 20 ng/mL; months 4-12: 5-15 ng/mL

I.V.: **Note:** I.V. route should only be used in patients not able to take oral medications, anaphylaxis has been reported. Initial dose: 0.03-0.05 mg/kg/day as a continuous infusion; begin no sooner than 6 hours post-transplant, starting at lower end of the dosage range; adjunctive therapy with corticosteroids is recommended; continue only until oral medication can be tolerated

Liver transplant:

Oral: Initial dose: 0.1-0.15 mg/kg/day in 2 divided doses, given every 12 hours; begin oral dose no sooner than 6 hours post-transplant; adjunctive therapy with corticosteroids is recommended; if switching from I.V. to oral, the oral dose should be started 8-12 hours after stopping the infusion

Typical whole blood trough concentrations: Months 1-12: 5-20 ng/mL

I.V.: **Note:** I.V. route should only be used in patients not able to take oral medications, anaphylaxis has been reported. Initial dose: 0.03-0.05 mg/kg/day as a continuous infusion; begin no sooner than 6 hours post-transplant starting at lower end of the dosage range; adjunctive therapy with corticosteroids is recommended; continue only until oral medication can be tolerated

Prevention of graft-vs-host disease: I.V.: 0.03 mg/kg/day as continuous infusion

Moderate to severe atopic dermatitis: Topical: Apply 0.03% or 0.1% ointment to affected area twice daily; rub in gently and completely; continue applications for 1 week after symptoms have cleared

Dosing adjustment in renal impairment: Evidence suggests that lower doses should be used; patients should receive doses at the lowest value of the recommended I.V. and oral dosing ranges; further reductions in dose below these ranges may be required

Tacrolimus therapy should usually be delayed up to 48 hours or longer in patients with postoperative oliguria

Hemodialysis: Not removed by hemodialysis; supplemental dose is not necessary

(Continued)

Tacrolimus *(Continued)*

Peritoneal dialysis: Significant drug removal is unlikely based on physiochemical characteristics

Dosing adjustment in hepatic impairment: Use of tacrolimus in liver transplant recipients experiencing post-transplant hepatic impairment may be associated with increased risk of developing renal insufficiency related to high whole blood levels of tacrolimus. The presence of moderate-to-severe hepatic dysfunction (serum bilirubin >2 mg/dL) appears to affect the metabolism of FK506. The half-life of the drug was prolonged and the clearance reduced after I.V. administration. The bioavailability of FK506 was also increased after oral administration. The higher plasma concentrations as determined by ELISA, in patients with severe hepatic dysfunction are probably due to the accumulation of FK506 metabolites of lower activity. These patients should be monitored closely and dosage adjustments should be considered. Some evidence indicates that lower doses could be used in these patients.

Administration I.V.: Administer by I.V. continuous infusion only (use infusion pump). Dilute with 5% dextrose injection or 0.9% sodium chloride injection to a final concentration between 0.004 mg/mL and 0.02 mg/mL. Use glass or polyethylene containers, do not use PVC containers. Do not use PVC tubing when administering dilute solutions

Monitoring Parameters Renal function, hepatic function, serum electrolytes, glucose and blood pressure, measure 3 times/week for first few weeks, then gradually decrease frequency as patient stabilizes. Whole blood concentrations should be used for monitoring (trough for oral therapy). Signs/symptoms of anaphylactic reactions during infusion should also be monitored.

Reference Range

Liver transplant: Whole blood trough concentration: 5-20 ng/mL

Kidney transplant: whole blood trough concentrations:

Months 1-3: 7-20 ng/mL

Months 4-12: 5-15 ng/mL

Patient Information You will be susceptible to infection (avoid crowds and people with infections or contagious diseases). May lead to diabetes mellitus, notify prescriber if you develop increased urination, increased thirst, or increased hunger. If you are diabetic, monitor glucose levels closely (may alter glucose levels). You may experience nausea, vomiting, loss of appetite (frequent small meals, frequent mouth care may help); diarrhea (boiled milk, yogurt, or buttermilk may help); constipation (increased exercise or dietary fruit, fluid, or fiber may help, if not consult prescriber); muscle or back pain (mild analgesics may be recommended). Report chest pain; acute headache or dizziness; symptoms of respiratory infection, cough, or difficulty breathing; unresolved gastrointestinal effects; fatigue, chills, fever, unhealed sores, white plaques in mouth, irritation in genital area; unusual bruising or bleeding; pain or irritation on urination or change in urinary patterns; rash or skin irritation; or other unusual effects related to this medication.

Oral: Take as directed, preferably 30 minutes before or 30 minutes after meals. Do not take within 2 hours before or after antacids. Do not alter dose and do not discontinue without consulting prescriber. Maintain adequate hydration (2-3 L/day of fluids unless instructed to restrict fluid intake) during entire course of therapy.

Topical: For external use only. Avoid exposure to sunlight or tanning beds. Apply to clean, dry skin. Do not cover with occlusive dressings. Burning and itching are most common in the first few days of use and improve as atopic dermatitis improves. Wash hands after use, unless hands are an area of treatment.

Dosage Forms CAP (Prograf®): 0.5 mg, 1 mg, 5 mg. **INJ, solution** (Prograf®): 5 mg/mL (1 mL). **OINT, topical** (Protopic®): 0.03% (30 g, 60 g, 100 g); 0.1% (30 g, 60 g, 100 g)

Tadalafil *(tah DA la fil)*

U.S. Brand Names Cialis®

Synonyms GF196960

Therapeutic Category Phosphodiesterase Enzyme Inhibitor, Selective Type 5

Use Treatment of erectile dysfunction

Pregnancy Risk Factor B

Contraindications Hypersensitivity to tadalafil or any component of the formulation; concurrent use of organic nitrates (nitroglycerin) in any form; concurrent use of alpha-adrenergic antagonists (except tamsulosin 0.4 mg/day)

Warnings/Precautions There is a degree of cardiac risk associated with sexual activity; therefore, physicians may wish to consider the cardiovascular status of their patients prior to initiating any treatment for erectile dysfunction. Use caution in patients with left ventricular outflow obstruction (aortic stenosis or IHSS); may be more sensitive to hypotensive actions. Use caution in patients receiving strong CYP3A4 inhibitors, the elderly, or those with hepatic impairment or renal impairment; dosage adjustment/limitation is needed. Use caution in patients with peptic ulcer disease.

Agents for the treatment of erectile dysfunction should be used with caution in patients with anatomical deformation of the penis (angulation, cavernosal fibrosis, or Peyronie's disease), or in patients who have conditions which may predispose them to priapism (sickle cell anemia, multiple myeloma, leukemia). All patients should be instructed to seek medical attention if erection persists >4 hours. The safety and efficacy of tadalafil with other treatments for erectile dysfunction have not been studied and are, therefore, not recommended as combination therapy.

Safety and efficacy have not been studied in patients with the following conditions, therefore, use in these patients is not recommended: Arrhythmias, hypotension, uncontrolled hypertension, unstable angina or angina during intercourse, cardiac failure (NYHA Class II or greater), recent myocardial infarction, or stroke within the last 6 months. A minority of patients with retinitis pigmentosa have generic disorders of retinal phosphodiesterases. There is no safety information on the administration of tadalafil to these patients; administer with caution.

Common Adverse Reactions
>10%:
    Central nervous system: Headache (11% to 15%)
    Gastrointestinal: Dyspepsia (4% to 10%)
2% to 10%:
    Cardiovascular: Flushing (2% to 3%)
    Neuromuscular & skeletal: CPK increased (2%), back pain (3% to 6%), myalgia (1% to 3%)
    Respiratory: Nasal congestion (2% to 3%)
    Miscellaneous: Limb pain (1% to 3%)

Drug Interactions
Cytochrome P450 Effect: Substrate of CYP3A4 (major)

Mechanism of Action Does not directly cause penile erections, but affects the response to sexual stimulation. The physiologic mechanism of erection of the penis involves release of nitric oxide (NO) in the corpus cavernosum during sexual stimulation. NO then activates the enzyme guanylate cyclase, which results in increased levels of cyclic guanosine monophosphate (cGMP), producing smooth muscle relaxation and inflow of blood to the corpus cavernosum. Tadalafil enhances the effect of NO by inhibiting phosphodiesterase type 5 (PDE5), which is responsible for degradation of cGMP in the corpus cavernosum; when sexual stimulation causes local release of NO, inhibition of PDE5 by tadalafil causes increased levels of cGMP in the corpus cavernosum, resulting in smooth muscle relaxation and inflow of blood to the corpus cavernosum. At recommended doses, it has no effect in the absence of sexual stimulation.

Pharmacodynamics/Kinetics
Onset: Within 1 hour
Duration: Up to 36 hours
Distribution: V_d: 63 L
Protein binding: 94%
Metabolism: Hepatic, via CYP3A4 to metabolites (inactive)
Half-life elimination: 17.5 hours
Time to peak, plasma: 2 hours
Excretion: Feces (61%, as metabolites); urine (36%, as metabolites)

Dosage Oral: Adults: Erectile dysfunction: 10 mg prior to anticipated sexual activity (dosing range: 5-20 mg); to be given as one single dose and not given more than once daily. **Note:** Erectile function may be improved for up to 36 hours following a single dose; adjust dose.
Elderly: No adjustment is recommended
    Dosing adjustment with concomitant medications: CYP3A4 inhibitors: Dose reduction of tadalafil is recommended with strong CYP3A4 inhibitors. The dose of tadalafil should not exceed 10 mg, and tadalafil should not be taken more frequently than once every 72 hours. Examples of such inhibitors include azole antifungals, clarithromycin, diclofenac, doxycycline, erythromycin, grapefruit juice, imatinib, isoniazid, nefazodone, nicardipine, propofol, protease inhibitors, quinidine, and verapamil.
    Dosage adjustment in renal impairment:
        Cl_{cr} 31-50 mL/minute: Initial dose 5 mg once daily; maximum dose 10 mg not to be given more frequently than every 48 hours.
        Cl_{cr} <30 mL/minute or hemodialysis: Maximum dose 5 mg.
    Dosage adjustment in hepatic impairment:
        Mild-to-moderate hepatic impairment (Child-Pugh class A or B): Dose should not exceed 10 mg once daily
        Severe hepatic impairment: Use is not recommended

Administration May be administered with or without food, prior to anticipated sexual activity.

Patient Information Patients should inform prescribers of all prescriptions, OTC medications, grapefruit juice, or herbal products they are taking, and should not take any new medication during therapy without consulting prescriber. Should be used as directed prior to anticipated sexual activity. May be taken without regard to meals. Do not combine with other approaches to treating erectile dysfunction without consulting prescriber. Patients may experience headache, flushing, or blurred vision (caution when driving at night or in poorly lit environments until response is known). Instruct patients to immediately report chest pain; acute head pain; respiratory difficulty; allergic response (chills, fever, respiratory difficulty, rash); genital swelling; or other adverse reactions. Contact prescriber immediately if erection persists >4 hours. **Note:** This medication does not provide protection against sexually-transmitted diseases, including HIV.

Dosage Forms TAB: 5 mg, 10 mg, 20 mg

♦ **Tagamet®** *see* Cimetidine *on page 276*
♦ **Tagamet® HB 200 [OTC]** *see* Cimetidine *on page 276*
♦ **Talwin®** *see* Pentazocine *on page 977*
♦ **Talwin® NX** *see* Pentazocine *on page 977*
♦ **TAM** *see* Tamoxifen *on page 1186*
♦ **Tambocor™** *see* Flecainide *on page 525*
♦ **Tamiflu®** *see* Oseltamivir *on page 934*

Tamoxifen (ta MOKS i fen)

U.S. Brand Names Nolvadex®

Synonyms ICI-46474; NSC-180973; TAM; Tamoxifen Citrate

Therapeutic Category Antineoplastic Agent, Estrogen Receptor Antagonist; Estrogen Receptor Antagonist

Use Palliative or adjunctive treatment of advanced breast cancer; reduce the incidence of breast cancer in women at high risk; reduce risk of invasive breast cancer in women with ductal carcinoma *in situ* (DCIS); metastatic male breast cancer; treatment of melanoma, desmoid tumors

Unlabeled/Investigational Use Treatment of mastalgia, gynecomastia, pancreatic carcinoma; induction of ovulation; treatment of precocious puberty in females, secondary to McCune-Albright syndrome

Pregnancy Risk Factor D

Contraindications Hypersensitivity to tamoxifen or any component of the formulation; concurrent warfarin therapy (when used for cancer risk reduction); pregnancy

Warnings/Precautions Serious, life-threatening, or fatal events (including endometrial cancer, uterine sarcoma, stroke, pulmonary embolism) have occurred in women taking tamoxifen. Healthcare providers should discuss the potential benefits versus the potential risks of these serious events with women considering tamoxifen therapy to reduce their risk of developing breast cancer. Use with caution in patients with leukopenia, thrombocytopenia, or hyperlipidemias; ovulation may be induced; "hot flashes" may be countered by Bellergal-S® tablets or clonidine; decreased visual acuity, retinopathy and corneal changes have been reported with use for more than 1 year at doses above recommended; hypercalcemia in patients with bone metastasis; hepatocellular carcinomas have been reported in animal studies. Endometrial hyperplasia and polyps have occurred.

Common Adverse Reactions Note: Differences in the frequency of some adverse events may be related to use for a specific indication.

Frequency not defined: Depression, dizziness, headache, hypercalcemia, lightheadedness, peripheral edema, pruritus vulvae, taste disturbance, vaginal dryness

>10%:

Cardiovascular: Fluid retention (32%)

Central nervous system: Mood changes (up to 12%; may include depression)

Dermatologic: Skin changes (19%)

Endocrine & metabolic: Hot flashes (64% to 80%), weight loss (23%)

Gastrointestinal: Nausea (26%)

Genitourinary: Vaginal bleeding (up to 23%), vaginal discharge (30% to 55%), menstrual irregularities (25%)

Neuromuscular & skeletal: Bone pain, tumor pain, and local disease flare (including increase in lesion size and erythema) during treatment of metastatic breast cancer (generally resolves with continuation)

1% to 10%:

Dermatologic: Alopecia (<1% to 5%)

Gastrointestinal: Constipation (up to 4%)

Hematologic: Thrombocytopenia (<1% to 2%)

Hepatic: SGOT increased (2%), serum bilirubin increased (2%)

Renal: Serum creatinine increased (up to 2%)

Miscellaneous: Infection/sepsis (up to 6%), allergic reaction (up to 3%)

Drug Interactions

Cytochrome P450 Effect: Substrate of CYP2A6 (minor), 2B6 (minor), 2C8/9 (major), 2D6 (major), 2E1 (minor), 3A4 (major); **Inhibits** CYP2B6 (weak), 2C8/9 (weak), 3A4 (weak)

Increased Effect/Toxicity: Allopurinol and tamoxifen results in exacerbation of allopurinol-induced hepatotoxicity. Cyclosporine serum levels may be increased when taken with tamoxifen. Bromocriptine may increase serum levels of tamoxifen. Concomitant use of warfarin is contraindicated when used for risk reduction; results in significant enhancement of the anticoagulant effects of warfarin. CYP2C8/9 inhibitors may increase the levels/effects of tamoxifen; example inhibitors include delavirdine, fluconazole, gemfibrozil, ketoconazole, nicardipine, NSAIDs, pioglitazone, and sulfonamides. CYP2D6 inhibitors may increase the levels/effects of tamoxifen; example inhibitors include chlorpromazine, delavirdine, fluoxetine, miconazole, paroxetine, pergolide, quinidine, quinine, ritonavir, and ropinirole. CYP3A4 inhibitors may increase the levels/effects of tamoxifen; example inhibitors include azole antifungals, ciprofloxacin, clarithromycin, diclofenac, doxycycline, erythromycin, imatinib, isoniazid, nefazodone, nicardipine, propofol, protease inhibitors, quinidine, and verapamil.

Decreased Effect: CYP2C8/9 inducers may decrease the levels/effects of tamoxifen; example inducers include carbamazepine, phenobarbital, phenytoin, rifampin, rifapentine, and secobarbital. CYP3A4 inducers may decrease the levels/effects of tamoxifen; example inducers include aminoglutethimide, carbamazepine, nafcillin, nevirapine, phenobarbital, phenytoin, and rifamycins. verapamil. Letrozole serum levels may be reduced by tamoxifen.

Mechanism of Action Competitively binds to estrogen receptors on tumors and other tissue targets, producing a nuclear complex that decreases DNA synthesis and inhibits estrogen effects; nonsteroidal agent with potent antiestrogenic properties which compete with estrogen for binding sites in breast and other tissues; cells accumulate in the G_0 and G_1 phases; therefore, tamoxifen is cytostatic rather than cytocidal.

Pharmacodynamics/Kinetics

Absorption: Well absorbed

Distribution: High concentrations found in uterus, endometrial and breast tissue

Protein binding: 99%

Metabolism: Hepatic (via CYP3A4) to major metabolites, desmethyltamoxifen and 4-hydroxytamoxifen; undergoes enterohepatic recirculation

Half-life elimination: Distribution: 7-14 hours; Elimination: 5-7 days; Metabolites: 14 days

Time to peak, serum: 5 hours

Excretion: Feces (26% to 51%); urine (9% to 13%)

Dosage Oral (refer to individual protocols):

Children: Female: Precocious puberty and McCune-Albright syndrome (unlabeled use): A dose of 20 mg/day has been reported in patients 2-10 years of age; safety and efficacy have not been established for treatment of longer than 1 year duration

Adults:

Breast cancer:

Metastatic (males and females) or adjuvant therapy (females): 20-40 mg/day

Prevention (high-risk females): 20 mg/day for 5 years

DCIS (females): 20 mg once daily for 5 years

Note: Higher dosages (up to 700 mg/day) have been investigated for use in modulation of multidrug resistance (MDR), but are not routinely used in clinical practice

Induction of ovulation (unlabeled use): 5-40 mg twice daily for 4 days

Monitoring Parameters Monitor WBC and platelet counts, serum calcium, LFTs; abnormal vaginal bleeding

Patient Information Take as directed, morning and night, and maintain adequate hydration (2-3 L/day of fluids unless instructed to restrict fluid intake). You may experience menstrual irregularities, vaginal bleeding, hot flashes, hair loss, loss of libido (these will subside when treatment is completed). Bone pain may indicate a good therapeutic response (consult prescriber for mild analgesics). For nausea/vomiting, small frequent meals, chewing gum, or sucking lozenges may help. You may experience photosensitivity (use sunscreen, wear protective clothing and eyewear, and avoid direct sunlight). Report unusual bleeding or bruising, severe weakness, sedation, mental changes, swelling or pain in calves, difficulty breathing, or any changes in vision.

Dosage Forms TAB: 10 mg, 20 mg

♦ **Tamoxifen Citrate** *see* Tamoxifen *on page 1186*

Tamsulosin (tam SOO loe sin)

U.S. Brand Names Flomax®

Synonyms Tamsulosin Hydrochloride

Therapeutic Category Alpha-Adrenergic Blocking Agent, Oral

Use Treatment of signs and symptoms of benign prostatic hyperplasia (BPH)

Pregnancy Risk Factor B

Contraindications Hypersensitivity to tamsulosin or any component of the formulation; concurrent use with phosphodiesterase-5 (PDE-5) inhibitors including sildenafil (>25 mg), tadalafil (if tamsulosin dose >0.4 mg/day), or vardenafil

Warnings/Precautions Not intended for use as an antihypertensive drug. May cause orthostasis, syncope or dizziness. Patients should avoid situations where injury may occur as a result of syncope. Rule out prostatic carcinoma before beginning therapy with tamsulosin.

Common Adverse Reactions

>10%:

Cardiovascular: Studies specific for orthostatic hypotension: Overall, at least one positive test was observed in 16% of patients receiving 0.4 mg and 19% of patients receiving the 0.8 mg dose. "First-dose" orthostatic hypotension following a 0.4 mg dose was reported as 7% at 4 hours postdose and 6% at 8 hours postdose.

Central nervous system: Headache (19% to 21%), dizziness (15% to 17%)

Genitourinary: Abnormal ejaculation (8% to 18%)

Respiratory: Rhinitis (13% to 18%)

1% to 10%:

Cardiovascular: Chest pain (~4%)

Central nervous system: Somnolence (3% to 4%), insomnia (1% to 2%), vertigo (0.6% to 1%)

Endocrine & metabolic: Libido decreased (1% to 2%)

Gastrointestinal: Diarrhea (4% to 6%), nausea (3% to 4%), stomach discomfort (2% to 3%), bitter taste (2% to 3%)

Neuromuscular & skeletal: Weakness (8% to 9%), back pain (7% to 8%)

Ocular: Amblyopia (0.2% to 2%)

Respiratory: Pharyngitis (5% to 6%), cough (3% to 5%), sinusitis (2% to 4%)

Miscellaneous: Infection (9% to 11%), tooth disorder (1% to 2%)

Drug Interactions

Cytochrome P450 Effect: Substrate (major) of CYP2D6, 3A4

Increased Effect/Toxicity: CYP2D6 inhibitors may increase the levels/effects of tamsulosin; example inhibitors include chlorpromazine, delavirdine, fluoxetine, miconazole, paroxetine, pergolide, quinidine, quinine, ritonavir, and ropinirole. Alpha-adrenergic blockers and calcium channel blockers may increase risk of hypotension. Risk of first-dose orthostatic hypotension may increase with beta-blockers. Cimetidine may decrease tamsulosin clearance. Blood pressure-lowering effects are additive with sildenafil (use with extreme caution), tadalafil (may be used when tamsulosin dose is ≤0.4 mg/day), and vardenafil (use is contraindicated by the manufacturer).

Mechanism of Action Tamsulosin is an antagonist of alpha$_{1A}$ adrenoreceptors in the prostate. Smooth muscle tone in the prostate is mediated by alpha$_{1A}$ adrenoreceptors; blocking them leads to relaxation of smooth muscle in the bladder neck and prostate causing an improvement

(Continued)

Tamsulosin *(Continued)*

of urine flow and decreased symptoms of BPH. Approximately 75% of the alpha$_1$ receptors in the prostate are of the alpha$_{1A}$ subtype.

Pharmacodynamics/Kinetics

Absorption: >90%

Protein binding: 94% to 99%, primarily to alpha$_1$ acid glycoprotein (AAG)

Metabolism: Hepatic via CYP; metabolites undergo extensive conjugation to glucuronide or sulfate

Bioavailability: Fasting: 30% increase

Distribution: V$_d$: 16 L

Steady-state: By the fifth day of once-daily dosing

Half-life elimination: Healthy volunteers: 9-13 hours; Target population: 14-15 hours

Time to peak: Fasting: 4-5 hours; With food: 6-7 hours

Excretion: Urine (76%, <10% as unchanged drug); feces (21%)

Dosage Oral: Adults: 0.4 mg once daily ~30 minutes after the same meal each day; dose may be increased after 2-4 weeks to 0.8 mg once daily in patients who fail to respond. If therapy is interrupted for several days, restart with 0.4 mg once daily.

Dosage adjustment in renal impairment:

Cl$_{cr}$ ≥10 mL/minute: No adjustment needed

Cl$_{cr}$ <10 mL/minute: Not studied

Administration Capsules should be swallowed whole; do not crush, chew, or open.

Patient Information May rarely cause priapism (persistent, painful erection); notify prescriber immediately if this should occur. Capsules should be swallowed whole, do not crush, chew or open. Symptoms related to postural hypotension (ie, dizziness) may occur; do not drive, operate machinery, or perform hazardous activities.

Dosage Forms CAP: 0.4 mg

- **Tamsulosin Hydrochloride** *see Tamsulosin on page 1187*
- **Tanafed®** *see Chlorpheniramine and Pseudoephedrine on page 263*
- **Tanafed DM™** *see Chlorpheniramine, Pseudoephedrine, and Dextromethorphan on page 265*
- **Tanafed DMX™** *see Chlorpheniramine, Pseudoephedrine, and Dextromethorphan on page 265*
- **Tanafed DP™** *see Chlorpheniramine and Pseudoephedrine on page 263*
- **Tao®** *see Troleandomycin on page 1275*
- **TAP-144** *see Leuprolide on page 724*
- **Tapazole®** *see Methimazole on page 813*
- **Targretin®** *see Bexarotene on page 164*
- **Tarka®** *see Trandolapril and Verapamil on page 1252*
- **Tasmar®** *see Tolcapone on page 1239*
- **TAT** *see Tetanus Antitoxin on page 1203*
- **Tavist® Allergy [OTC]** *see Clemastine on page 290*
- **Taxol®** *see Paclitaxel on page 948*
- **Taxotere®** *see Docetaxel on page 396*

Tazarotene *(taz AR oh teen)*

U.S. Brand Names Avage™; Tazorac®

Therapeutic Category Keratolytic Agent

Use Topical treatment of facial acne vulgaris; topical treatment of stable plaque psoriasis of up to 20% body surface area involvement; mitigation (palliation) of facial skin wrinkling, facial mottled hyper/hypopigmentation, and benign facial lentigines

Pregnancy Risk Factor X

Contraindications Hypersensitivity to tazarotene, other retinoids or vitamin A derivatives (isotretinoin, tretinoin, etretinate), or any component of the formulation; use in women of childbearing potential who are unable to comply with birth control requirements; pregnancy (negative pregnancy test required)

Warnings/Precautions Women of childbearing potential must use adequate contraceptive measures because of potential teratogenicity. May cause photosensitivity; exposure to sunlight should be avoided unless deemed medically necessary, and in such cases, exposure should be minimized (including use of sunscreens/protective clothing) during use of tazarotene. Risk may be increased by concurrent therapy with known photosensitizers (thiazides, tetracyclines, fluoroquinolones, phenothiazines, sulfonamides). For external use only; avoid contact with eyes, eyelids, and mouth. Not for use on eczematous, broken, or sunburned skin; not for treatment of lentigo maligna. Avoid application over extensive areas; specifically, safety and efficacy of gel applied over >20% of BSA have not been established. Safety and efficacy in children <12 years of age have not been established.

Common Adverse Reactions Percentage of incidence varies with formulation and/or strength:

>10%: Dermatologic: Burning/stinging, desquamation, dry skin, erythema, pruritus, skin pain, worsening of psoriasis

1% to 10%: Dermatologic: Contact dermatitis, discoloration, fissuring, hypertriglyceridemia, inflammation, irritation, localized bleeding, rash

Frequency not defined:

Dermatologic: Photosensitization

Neuromuscular & skeletal: Peripheral neuropathy

Drug Interactions

Increased Effect/Toxicity: Increased toxicity may occur with sulfur, benzoyl peroxide, salicylic acid, resorcinol, or any product with strong drying effects (including alcohol-containing compounds) due to increased drying actions. May augment phototoxicity of sensitizing medications (thiazides, tetracyclines, fluoroquinolones, phenothiazines, sulfonamides).

Mechanism of Action Synthetic, acetylenic retinoid which modulates differentiation and proliferation of epithelial tissue and exerts some degree of anti-inflammatory and immunological activity

Pharmacodynamics/Kinetics

Duration: Therapeutic: Psoriasis: Effects have been observed for up to 3 months after a 3-month course of topical treatment

Absorption: Minimal following cutaneous application (≤6% of dose)

Distribution: Retained in skin for prolonged periods after topical application.

Protein binding: >99%

Metabolism: Prodrug, rapidly metabolized via esterases to an active metabolite (tazarotenic acid) following topical application and systemic absorption; tazarotenic acid undergoes further hepatic metabolism

Half-life elimination: 18 hours

Excretion: Urine and feces (as metabolites)

Dosage Topical: **Note:** In patients experiencing excessive pruritus, burning, skin redness, or peeling, discontinue until integrity of the skin is restored, or reduce dosing to an interval the patient is able to tolerate.

Children ≥12 years and Adults:

Acne: Tazorac® cream/gel 0.1%: Cleanse the face gently. After the skin is dry, apply a thin film of tazarotene (2 mg/cm^2) once daily, in the evening, to the skin where the acne lesions appear; use enough to cover the entire affected area

Psoriasis: Tazorac® gel 0.05% or 0.1%: Apply once daily, in the evening, to psoriatic lesions using enough (2 mg/cm^2) to cover only the lesion with a thin film to no more than 20% of body surface area. If a bath or shower is taken prior to application, dry the skin before applying. Unaffected skin may be more susceptible to irritation, avoid application to these areas.

Children ≥17 years and Adults: Palliation of fine facial wrinkles, facial mottled hyper/hypopigmentation, benign facial lentigines: Avage™: Apply a pea-sized amount once daily to clean dry face at bedtime; lightly cover entire face including eyelids if desired. Emollients or moisturizers may be applied before or after; if applied before tazarotene, ensure cream or lotion has absorbed into the skin and has dried completely.

Adults: Psoriasis: Tazorac® cream 0.05% or 0.1%: Apply once daily, in the evening, to psoriatic lesions using enough (2 mg/cm^2) to cover only the lesion with a thin film to no more than 20% of body surface area. If a bath or shower is taken prior to application, dry the skin before applying. Unaffected skin may be more susceptible to irritation, avoid application to these areas.

Elderly: No differences in safety or efficacy were seen when administered to patients >65 years of age; may experience increased sensitivity

Administration Do not apply to eczematous or sunburned skin; apply thin film to affected areas; avoid eyes and mouth

Monitoring Parameters Disease severity in plaque psoriasis during therapy (reduction in erythema, scaling, induration); routine blood chemistries (including transaminases) are suggested during long-term topical therapy; pregnancy test prior to treatment of female patients

Patient Information Do not take this medication if you have had an allergic reaction to tazarotene. Do not use tazarotene if you are pregnant or planning to become pregnant. Tazarotene may cause birth defects or be harmful to an unborn baby if used during pregnancy. This may be more likely if the medicine is used on large areas of skin. Your prescriber will tell you how much medicine to use and how often. Do not use more of the medication than your prescriber ordered. Using too much of the medication can cause red, peeling, or irritated skin. Wash your hands before and after using this medication (unless treating psoriasis lesions on your hands). Use this medication on your skin only. Do not put the medication in your eyes or in your mouth. If you do get the medication in your eyes, rinse them with large amounts of cool water. Tell your prescriber if you have eye pain or redness that does not go away.

Acne patients: Gently wash and dry your face. Apply a thin layer of medication to cover the acne. Your acne should start to clear up in about 4 weeks.

Psoriasis patients: If using the medication after bathing or showering, make sure your skin is completely dry before applying the medication. Apply a thin layer to lesions.

Wash off any medication that gets on skin areas that do not need to be treated. The medication can irritate skin that does not need treatment. Do not bandage or cover the treated skin. Ask your prescriber or pharmacist before taking any other medication, including over-the-counter products. Talk with your prescriber or pharmacist before using medicated cosmetics or shampoos, abrasive soaps or cleansers, products with alcohol, spice, or lime in them, other acne medicines, hair removal products, or products that dry your skin.

This medication may make your skin sensitive to sunlight and cause a rash or sunburn. Avoid spending long periods of time in direct sunlight and protect your skin with clothing and a strong sunscreen when you are outdoors. Do not use a sunlamp or tanning booth. Call your prescriber if you have blistering or crusting skin, severe redness, pain, or swelling on the areas that you use the medication.
(Continued)

Tazarotene *(Continued)*

Dosage Forms CRM (Avage™): 0.1% (15 g, 30 g); (Tazorac®): 0.05% (15 g, 30 g, 60 g); 0.1% (15 g, 30 g, 60 g). **GEL** (Tazorac®): 0.05% (30 g, 100 g); 0.1% (30 g, 100 g)

♦ **Tazicef®** *see* Ceftazidime *on page 241*
♦ **Tazidime®** *see* Ceftazidime *on page 241*
♦ **Tazorac®** *see* Tazarotene *on page 1188*
♦ **Taztia XT™** *see* Diltiazem *on page 380*
♦ **3TC** *see* Lamivudine *on page 712*
♦ **3TC, Abacavir, and Zidovudine** *see* Abacavir, Lamivudine, and Zidovudine *on page 19*
♦ **T-Cell Growth Factor** *see* Aldesleukin *on page 47*
♦ **TCGF** *see* Aldesleukin *on page 47*
♦ **TCN** *see* Tetracycline *on page 1206*
♦ **Td** *see* Diphtheria and Tetanus Toxoid *on page 386*
♦ **TDF** *see* Tenofovir *on page 1195*

Tegaserod (teg a SER od)

U.S. Brand Names Zelnorm™
Synonyms HTF919; Tegaserod Maleate
Therapeutic Category Serotonin 5-HT$_4$ Receptor Agonist
Use Short-term treatment of constipation-predominate irritable bowel syndrome (IBS) in women
Pregnancy Risk Factor B
Contraindications Hypersensitivity to tegaserod or any component of the formulation; severe renal impairment; moderate or severe hepatic impairment; history of bowel obstruction, symptomatic gallbladder disease, suspected sphincter of Oddi dysfunction, or abdominal adhesions. Treatment should **not** be started in patients with diarrhea or in those who experience diarrhea frequently.
Warnings/Precautions Discontinue immediately with new or sudden worsening abdominal pain. Diarrhea may occur after the start of treatment, most cases reported as a single episode within the first week of therapy, and may resolve with continued dosing. Patients who develop severe diarrhea, or diarrhea with severe cramping, abdominal pain, or dizziness should consult healthcare provider. Use caution with mild hepatic impairment. Safety and efficacy have not been established in males or patients <18 years of age.
Common Adverse Reactions
>10%:
Central nervous system: Headache (15%)
Gastrointestinal: Abdominal pain (12%)
1% to 10%:
Central nervous system: Dizziness (4%), migraine (2%)
Gastrointestinal: Diarrhea (9%), nausea (8%), flatulence (6%)
Neuromuscular & skeletal: Back pain (5%), arthropathy (2%), leg pain (1%)
Mechanism of Action Tegaserod is a partial neuronal 5-HT$_4$ receptor agonist. Its action at the receptor site leads to stimulation of the peristaltic reflex and intestinal secretion, and moderation of visceral sensitivity.
Pharmacodynamics/Kinetics
Distribution: V_d: 368 ± 223 L
Protein binding: 98% primarily to α_1-acid glycoprotein
Metabolism: GI: Hydrolysis in the stomach; Hepatic: Oxidation, conjugation, and glucuronidation; metabolite (negligible activity); significant first-pass effect
Bioavailability: Fasting: 10%
Half-life elimination: I.V.: 11 ± 5 hours
Time to peak: 1 hour
Excretion: Feces (~66% as unchanged drug); urine (~33% as metabolites)
Dosage Oral:
Adults: Female: IBS with constipation: 6 mg twice daily, before meals, for 4-6 weeks; may consider continuing treatment for an additional 4-6 weeks in patients who respond initially.
Elderly: Dosing adjustment not recommended
Dosage adjustment in renal impairment: C_{max} and AUC of the inactive metabolite are increased with renal impairment.
Mild to moderate impairment: No dosage adjustment recommended
Severe impairment: Use is contraindicated
Dosage adjustment in hepatic impairment: C_{max} and AUC of tegaserod are increased with hepatic impairment.
Mild impairment: No dosage adjustment recommended; however, use caution
Moderate to severe impairment: Use is contraindicated
Administration Administer 30 minutes before meals.
Patient Information Diarrhea may occur during therapy, usually within the first week of treatment, and should resolve. Notify prescriber of severe diarrhea; diarrhea with severe cramping, or dizziness; new or worsening abdominal pain. Do not take if having diarrhea or if you experience diarrhea frequently.
Dosage Forms TAB: 2 mg, 6 mg

♦ **Tegaserod Maleate** *see* Tegaserod *on page 1190*
♦ **Tegretol®** *see* Carbamazepine *on page 214*
♦ **Tegretol®-XR** *see* Carbamazepine *on page 214*

Telmisartan (tel mi SAR tan)

Related Information
 Angiotensin Agents Comparison *on page 1353*
U.S. Brand Names Micardis®
Therapeutic Category Angiotensin II Receptor Antagonist (ARB); Antihypertensive Agent
Use Treatment of hypertension; may be used alone or in combination with other antihypertensive agents
Pregnancy Risk Factor C (1st trimester); D (2nd and 3rd trimesters)
Contraindications Hypersensitivity to telmisartan or any component of the formulation; hypersensitivity to other A-II receptor antagonists; bilateral renal artery stenosis; pregnancy (2nd and 3rd trimesters)
Warnings/Precautions Avoid use or use a smaller dose in patients who are volume depleted; correct depletion first. Deterioration in renal function can occur with initiation. Use with caution in unilateral renal artery stenosis and pre-existing renal insufficiency; significant aortic/mitral stenosis. Use with caution in patients who have biliary obstructive disorders or hepatic dysfunction.
Common Adverse Reactions May be associated with worsening of renal function in patients dependent on renin-angiotensin-aldosterone system.

 1% to 10%:
  Cardiovascular: Hypertension (1%), chest pain (1%), peripheral edema (1%)
  Central nervous system: Headache (1%), dizziness (1%), pain (1%), fatigue (1%)
  Gastrointestinal: Diarrhea (3%), dyspepsia (1%), nausea (1%), abdominal pain (1%)
  Genitourinary: Urinary tract infection (1%)
  Neuromuscular & skeletal: Back pain (3%), myalgia (1%)
  Respiratory: Upper respiratory infection (7%), sinusitis (3%), pharyngitis (1%), cough (2%)
  Miscellaneous: Flu-like syndrome (1%)

Drug Interactions
 Cytochrome P450 Effect: Inhibits CYP2C19 (weak)
 Increased Effect/Toxicity: Telmisartan may increase serum digoxin concentrations. Potassium salts/supplements, co-trimoxazole (high dose), ACE inhibitors, and potassium-sparing diuretics (amiloride, spironolactone, triamterene) may increase the risk of hyperkalemia with telmisartan.
 Decreased Effect: Telmisartan decreased the trough concentrations of warfarin during concurrent therapy, however, INR was not changed.
Mechanism of Action Angiotensin II acts as a vasoconstrictor. In addition to causing direct vasoconstriction, angiotensin II also stimulates the release of aldosterone. Once aldosterone is released, sodium as well as water are reabsorbed. The end result is an elevation in blood pressure. Telmisartan is a nonpeptide AT1 angiotensin II receptor antagonist. This binding prevents angiotensin II from binding to the receptor thereby blocking the vasoconstriction and the aldosterone secreting effects of angiotensin II.
Pharmacodynamics/Kinetics Orally active, not a prodrug
 Onset of action: 1-2 hours
  Peak effect: 0.5-1 hours
 Duration: Up to 24 hours
 Protein binding: >99.5%
 Metabolism: Hepatic via conjugation to inactive metabolites; not metabolized via CYP
 Bioavailability (dose dependent): 42% to 58%
 Half-life elimination: Terminal: 24 hours
 Excretion: Feces (97%)
  Clearance: Total body: 800 mL/minute
Dosage Adults: Oral: Initial: 40 mg once daily; usual maintenance dose range: 20-80 mg/day. Patients with volume depletion should be initiated on the lower dosage with close supervision.
 Dosage adjustment in hepatic impairment: Supervise patients closely.
Monitoring Parameters Supine blood pressure, electrolytes, serum creatinine, BUN, urinalysis, symptomatic hypotension, and tachycardia
Patient Information Patients of childbearing age should be informed about the consequences of 2nd and 3rd trimester exposure to drugs that act on the renin-angiotensin system, and that these consequences do not appear to have resulted from intrauterine drug exposure that has been limited to the 1st trimester. Patients should report pregnancy to their prescriber as soon as possible.
Dosage Forms TAB: 20 mg, 40 mg, 80 mg

♦ **Telmisartan and HCTZ** *see* Telmisartan and Hydrochlorothiazide *on page 1191*

Telmisartan and Hydrochlorothiazide

 (tel mi SAR tan & hye droe klor oh THYE a zide)
U.S. Brand Names Micardis® HCT
Synonyms HCTZ and Telmisartan; Hydrochlorothiazide and Telmisartan; Telmisartan and HCTZ
Therapeutic Category Angiotensin II Antagonist/Thiazide Diuretic Combination; Antihypertensive Agent, Combination
Use Treatment of hypertension; combination product should not be used for initial therapy
Pregnancy Risk Factor C (1st trimester); D (2nd and 3rd trimesters)
Dosage Adults: Oral: Replacement therapy: Combination product can be substituted for individual titrated agents. Initiation of combination therapy when monotherapy has failed to achieve desired effects:
 (Continued)

Telmisartan and Hydrochlorothiazide *(Continued)*

Patients currently on telmisartan: Initial dose if blood pressure is not currently controlled on monotherapy of 80 mg telmisartan: Telmisartan 80 mg/hydrochlorothiazide 12.5 mg once daily; may titrate up to telmisartan 160 mg/hydrochlorothiazide 25 mg if needed

Patients currently on HCTZ: Initial dose if blood pressure is not currently controlled on monotherapy of 25 mg once daily, or is controlled and experiencing hypokalemia: Telmisartan 80 mg/hydrochlorothiazide 12.5 mg once daily; may titrate up to telmisartan 160 mg/hydrochlorothiazide 25 mg if blood pressure remains uncontrolled after 2-4 weeks of therapy

Dosage adjustment in renal impairment:
Cl_{cr} >30 mL/minute: Usual recommended dose
Cl_{cr} <30 mL/minute: Not recommended

Dosage adjustment in hepatic impairment: Dosing should be started at telmisartan 40 mg/hydrochlorothiazide 12.5 mg; do **not** use in patients with severe hepatic impairment

Elderly: No dosing adjustment needed based on age; monitor renal and hepatic function

Dosage Forms TAB: 40/12.5: Telmisartan 40 mg and hydrochlorothiazide 12.5 mg; 80/12.5: Telmisartan 80 mg and hydrochlorothiazide 12.5 mg

Temazepam (te MAZ e pam)

Related Information

Benzodiazepines Comparison *on page 1366*

U.S. Brand Names Restoril®

Therapeutic Category Benzodiazepine; Hypnotic; Sedative

Use Short-term treatment of insomnia

Unlabeled/Investigational Use Treatment of anxiety; adjunct in the treatment of depression; management of panic attacks

Restrictions C-IV

Pregnancy Risk Factor X

Contraindications Hypersensitivity to temazepam or any component of the formulation (cross-sensitivity with other benzodiazepines may exist); narrow-angle glaucoma (not in product labeling, however, benzodiazepines are contraindicated); pregnancy

Warnings/Precautions Should be used only after evaluation of potential causes of sleep disturbance. Failure of sleep disturbance to resolve after 7-10 days may indicate psychiatric or medical illness. A worsening of insomnia or the emergence of new abnormalities of thought or behavior may represent unrecognized psychiatric or medical illness and requires immediate and careful evaluation.

Use with caution in elderly or debilitated patients, patients with hepatic disease (including alcoholics), or renal impairment. Use with caution in patients with respiratory disease, or impaired gag reflex. Avoid use inpatients with sleep apnea.

Causes CNS depression (dose-related) resulting in sedation, dizziness, confusion, or ataxia which may impair physical and mental capabilities. Patients must be cautioned about performing tasks which require mental alertness (eg, operating machinery or driving). Use with caution in patients receiving other CNS depressants or psychoactive agents. Effects with other sedative drugs or ethanol may be potentiated. Benzodiazepines have been associated with falls and traumatic injury and should be used with extreme caution in patients who are at risk of these events (especially the elderly).

Use caution in patients with suicidal risk. Use with caution in patients with a history of drug dependence. Benzodiazepines have been associated with dependence and acute withdrawal symptoms on discontinuation or reduction in dose (may occur after as little as 10 days). Acute withdrawal, including seizures, may be precipitated after administration of flumazenil to patients receiving long-term benzodiazepine therapy.

Benzodiazepines have been associated with anterograde amnesia. Paradoxical reactions, including hyperactive or aggressive behavior, have been reported with benzodiazepines, particularly in adolescent/pediatric or psychiatric patients. Does not have analgesic, antidepressant, or antipsychotic properties.

Common Adverse Reactions

1% to 10%:
Central nervous system: Confusion, dizziness, drowsiness, fatigue, anxiety, headache, lethargy, hangover, euphoria, vertigo
Dermatologic: Rash
Endocrine & metabolic: Decreased libido
Gastrointestinal: Diarrhea
Neuromuscular & skeletal: Dysarthria, weakness
Ocular: Blurred vision
Miscellaneous: Diaphoresis

Drug Interactions

Cytochrome P450 Effect: Substrate (minor) of CYP2B6, 2C8/9, 2C19, 3A4

Increased Effect/Toxicity: Temazepam potentiates the CNS depressant effects of narcotic analgesics, barbiturates, phenothiazines, ethanol, antihistamines, MAO inhibitors, sedative-hypnotics, and cyclic antidepressants. Serum levels of temazepam may be increased by inhibitors of CYP3A4, including cimetidine, ciprofloxacin, clarithromycin, clozapine, diltiazem, disulfiram, digoxin, erythromycin, ethanol, fluconazole, fluoxetine, fluvoxamine, grapefruit juice, isoniazid, itraconazole, ketoconazole, labetalol, levodopa, loxapine, metoprolol, metronidazole, miconazole, nefazodone, omeprazole, phenytoin, rifabutin, rifampin, troleandomycin, valproic acid, and verapamil.

Decreased Effect: Oral contraceptives may increase the clearance of temazepam. Temazepam may decrease the antiparkinsonian efficacy of levodopa. Theophylline and other CNS stimulants may antagonize the sedative effects of temazepam. Carbamazepine, rifampin, rifabutin may enhance the metabolism of temazepam and decrease its therapeutic effect.

Mechanism of Action Binds to stereospecific benzodiazepine receptors on the postsynaptic GABA neuron at several sites within the central nervous system, including the limbic system, reticular formation. Enhancement of the inhibitory effect of GABA on neuronal excitability results by increased neuronal membrane permeability to chloride ions. This shift in chloride ions results in hyperpolarization (a less excitable state) and stabilization.

Pharmacodynamics/Kinetics
Distribution: V_d: 1.4 L/kg
Protein binding: 96%
Metabolism: Hepatic
Half-life elimination: 9.5-12.4 hours
Time to peak, serum: 2-3 hours
Excretion: Urine (80% to 90% as inactive metabolites)

Dosage Oral:
Adults: 15-30 mg at bedtime
Elderly or debilitated patients: 15 mg

Monitoring Parameters Respiratory and cardiovascular status

Reference Range Therapeutic: 26 ng/mL after 24 hours

Patient Information Avoid alcohol and other CNS depressants; avoid activities needing good psychomotor coordination until CNS effects are known; drug may cause physical or psychological dependence; avoid abrupt discontinuation after prolonged use

Dosage Forms CAP: 15 mg, 30 mg; (Restoril®): 7.5 mg, 15 mg, 30 mg

♦ **Temodar®** *see* Temozolomide *on page 1193*
♦ **Temovate®** *see* Clobetasol *on page 293*
♦ **Temovate E®** *see* Clobetasol *on page 293*

Temozolomide (te moe ZOE loe mide)

U.S. Brand Names Temodar®
Synonyms NSC-362856; TMZ
Therapeutic Category Antineoplastic Agent, Alkylating Agent
Use Treatment of adult patients with refractory (first relapse) anaplastic astrocytoma who have experienced disease progression on nitrosourea and procarbazine
Unlabeled/Investigational Use Glioma, melanoma
Pregnancy Risk Factor D
Contraindications Hypersensitivity to temozolomide or any component of the formulation; hypersensitivity to dacarbazine (since both drugs are metabolized to MTIC); pregnancy
Warnings/Precautions Elderly patients and women have a higher incidence of myelosuppression. Safety/efficacy in pediatrics not established. Use caution in patients with severe hepatic or renal impairment. The U.S. Food and Drug Administration (FDA) currently recommends that procedures for proper handling and disposal of antineoplastic agents be considered.

Common Adverse Reactions
>10%:
Cardiovascular: Peripheral edema (11%)
Central nervous system: Headache (41%), fatigue (34%), convulsions (23%), hemiparesis (29%), dizziness (19%), fever (11%), coordination abnormality (11%), amnesia (10%), insomnia (10%), somnolence. In the case of CNS malignancies, it is difficult to distinguish the relative contributions of temozolomide and progressive disease to CNS symptoms.
Gastrointestinal: Nausea (53%), vomiting (42%), constipation (33%), diarrhea (16%)
Hematologic: Neutropenia (grade 3-4, 14%), thrombocytopenia (grade 3-4 19%)
Neuromuscular & skeletal: Weakness (13%)
1% to 10%:
Central nervous system: Ataxia (8%), confusion (5%), anxiety (7%), depression (6%)
Dermatologic: Rash (8%), pruritus (8%)
Endocrine & metabolic: Hypercorticism (8%), breast pain (6%), weight gain (5%)
Gastrointestinal: Dysphagia (7%), abdominal pain (9%), anorexia (9%)
Genitourinary: Increased micturition frequency (6%)
Hematologic: Anemia (8%; grade 3-4, 4%)
Neuromuscular & skeletal: Paresthesia (9%), back pain (8%), myalgia (5%)
Ocular: Diplopia (5%), vision abnormality (5%)
Respiratory: Pharyngitis (8%), sinusitis (6%), cough (5%)

Drug Interactions
Decreased Effect: Although valproic acid reduces the clearance of temozolomide by 5%, the clinical significance of this is unknown.
Mechanism of Action Like dacarbazine, temozolomide is converted to the active alkylating metabolite MTIC [(methyl-triazene-1-yl)-imidazole-4-carboxamide]. Unlike dacarbazine, however, this conversion is spontaneous, nonenzymatic, and occurs under physiologic conditions in all tissues to which the drug distributes.

Pharmacodynamics/Kinetics
Distribution: V_d: Parent drug: 0.4 L/kg
Protein binding: 15%
Metabolism: Prodrug, hydrolyzed to the active form, MTIC; MTIC is eventually eliminated as CO_2 and 5-aminoimidazole-4-carboxamide (AIC), a natural constituent in urine
Bioavailability: 100%
(Continued)

Temozolomide *(Continued)*

Half-life elimination: Mean: Parent drug: 1.8 hours

Time to peak: Empty stomach: 1 hour

Excretion: Urine (5% to 7% of total)

Dosage Oral (refer to individual protocols):

Adults: Usual dose: 150-200 mg/m^2/day for 5 days; repeat every 28 days. This monthly-cycle regimen may be preceded by a 6-7 week regimen of 75 mg/m^2/day.

Elderly: Patients ≥70 years of age had a higher incidence of grade 4 neutropenia and thrombocytopenia in the first cycle of therapy than patients <70 years of age

Dosage adjustment in renal impairment: No guidelines exist. Caution should be used when administered to patients with severe renal impairment (Cl$_{cr}$ <39 mL/minute).

Dosage adjustment in hepatic impairment: Caution should be used when administering to patients with severe hepatic impairment

Administration Capsules should not be opened or chewed but swallowed whole with a glass of water. May be administered on an empty stomach to reduce nausea and vomiting. Bedtime administration may be advised.

Monitoring Parameters CBC

Patient Information Swallow capsules whole with a glass of water. Take on an empty stomach at similar times each day. If you have nausea and vomiting, contact prescriber for medicine to decrease this. Male and female patients who take temozolomide should protect against pregnancy (use effective contraception). Do not breast-feed while on medicine.

Dosage Forms CAP: 5 mg, 20 mg, 100 mg, 250 mg

Tenecteplase *(ten EK te plase)*

U.S. Brand Names TNKase™

Therapeutic Category Fibrinolytic Agent

Use Thrombolytic agent used in the management of acute myocardial infarction for the lysis of thrombi in the coronary vasculature to restore perfusion and reduce mortality.

Pregnancy Risk Factor C

Contraindications Hypersensitivity to tenecteplase or any component of the formulation; active internal bleeding; history of stroke; intracranial/intraspinal surgery or trauma within 2 months; intracranial neoplasm; arteriovenous malformation or aneurysm; bleeding diathesis; severe uncontrolled hypertension

Warnings/Precautions Stop antiplatelet agents and heparin if serious bleeding occurs. Avoid I.M. injections and nonessential handling of the patient for a few hours after administration. Monitor for bleeding complications. Venipunctures should be performed carefully and only when necessary. If arterial puncture is necessary, then use an upper extremity that can be easily compressed manually. For the following conditions, the risk of bleeding is higher with use of tenecteplase and should be weighed against the benefits: Recent major surgery, cerebrovascular disease, recent GI or GU bleed, recent trauma, uncontrolled hypertension (systolic BP ≥180 mm Hg and/or diastolic BP ≥110 mm Hg), suspected left heart thrombus, acute pericarditis, subacute bacterial endocarditis, hemostatic defects, severe hepatic dysfunction, pregnancy, hemorrhagic diabetic retinopathy or other hemorrhagic ophthalmic conditions, septic thrombophlebitis or occluded arteriovenous cannula at seriously infected site, advanced age (see Usual Dosing, Elderly), anticoagulants, recent administration of GP IIb/IIIa inhibitors. Coronary thrombolysis may result in reperfusion arrhythmias. Caution with readministration of tenecteplase. Safety and efficacy have not been established in pediatric patients. Cholesterol embolism has rarely been reported.

Common Adverse Reactions As with all drugs which may affect hemostasis, bleeding is the major adverse effect associated with tenecteplase. Hemorrhage may occur at virtually any site. Risk is dependent on multiple variables, including the dosage administered, concurrent use of multiple agents which alter hemostasis, and patient predisposition. Rapid lysis of coronary artery thrombi by thrombolytic agents may be associated with reperfusion-related arterial and/or ventricular arrhythmias. The incidence of stroke and bleeding increase in patients >65 years.

>10%:

Hematologic: Bleeding (22% minor: ASSENT-2 trial)

Local: Hematoma (12% minor)

1% to 10%:

Central nervous system: Stroke (2%)

Gastrointestinal: GI hemorrhage (1% major, 2% minor), epistaxis (2% minor)

Genitourinary: GU bleeding (4% minor)

Hematologic: Bleeding (5% major: ASSENT-2 trial)

Local: Bleeding at catheter puncture site (4% minor), hematoma (2% major)

Respiratory: Pharyngeal bleeding (3% minor)

Additional cardiovascular events associated with use in myocardial infarction: Cardiogenic shock, arrhythmias, AV block, pulmonary edema, heart failure, cardiac arrest, recurrent myocardial ischemia, myocardial reinfarction, myocardial rupture, cardiac tamponade, pericarditis, pericardial effusion, mitral regurgitation, thrombosis, embolism, electromechanical dissociation, hypotension, fever, nausea, vomiting

Drug Interactions

Increased Effect/Toxicity: Drugs which affect platelet function (eg, NSAIDs, dipyridamole, ticlopidine, clopidogrel, IIb/IIIa antagonists) may potentiate the risk of hemorrhage; use with caution.

Heparin and aspirin: Use with aspirin and heparin may increase bleeding. However, aspirin and heparin were used concomitantly with tenecteplase in the majority of patients in clinical studies.

Warfarin or oral anticoagulants: Risk of bleeding may be increased during concurrent therapy.

Decreased Effect: Aminocaproic acid (antifibrinolytic agent) may decrease effectiveness.

Mechanism of Action Initiates fibrinolysis by binding to fibrin and converting plasminogen to plasmin.

Pharmacodynamics/Kinetics
Distribution: V_d is weight related and approximates plasma volume
Metabolism: Primarily hepatic
Half-life elimination: 90-130 minutes
Excretion: Clearance: Plasma: 99-119 mL/minute

Dosage I.V.:
Adult: Recommended total dose should not exceed 50 mg and is based on patient's weight; administer as a bolus over 5 seconds
If patient's weight:
<60 kg, dose: 30 mg
≥60 to <70 kg, dose: 35 mg
≥70 to <80 kg, dose: 40 mg
≥80 to <90 kg, dose: 45 mg
≥90 kg, dose: 50 mg
All patients received 150-325 mg of aspirin as soon as possible and then daily. Intravenous heparin was initiated as soon as possible and aPTT was maintained between 50-70 seconds.

Dosage adjustment in renal impairment: No formal recommendations for renal impairment

Dosage adjustment in hepatic impairment: Severe hepatic failure is a relative contraindication. Recommendations were not made for mild to moderate hepatic impairment.

Elderly: Although dosage adjustments are not recommended, the elderly have a higher incidence of morbidity and mortality with the use of tenecteplase. The 30-day mortality in the ASSENT-2 trial was 2.5% for patients <65 years, 8.5% for patients 65-74 years, and 16.2% for patients ≥75 years. The intracranial hemorrhage rate was 0.4% for patients <65, 1.6% for patients 65-74 years, and 1.7% for patients ≥75. The risks and benefits of use should be weighted carefully in the elderly.

Administration Tenecteplase should be reconstituted using the supplied 10 cc syringe with TwinPak™ dual cannula device and 10 mL sterile water for injection. Do not shake when reconstituting. Slight foaming is normal and will dissipate if left standing for several minutes. The reconstituted solution is 5 mg/mL. Any unused solution should be discarded. Tenecteplase is **incompatible** with dextrose solutions. Dextrose-containing lines must be flushed with a saline solution before and after administration. Administer as a single I.V. bolus over 5 seconds. Avoid I.M. injections and nonessential handling of patient.

Monitoring Parameters CBC, aPTT, signs and symptoms of bleeding, ECG monitoring

Patient Information This medication can only be administered I.V. You will have a tendency to bleed easily following its use; use caution to prevent injury (use electric razor, soft toothbrush), and use caution when using sharp objects (eg, scissors, knives). Strict bedrest should be maintained to reduce the risk of bleeding. If bleeding occurs, apply pressure to bleeding spot until bleeding stops completely. Report unusual bruising or bleeding; blood in urine, stool, or vomitus; bleeding gums; changes in vision; difficulty breathing; or chest pain/pressure.

Dosage Forms INJ, powder for reconstitution, recombinant: 50 mg

♦ **Tenex**® see Guanfacine on page 607

Teniposide (ten i POE side)

U.S. Brand Names Vumon
Synonyms EPT; VM-26
Therapeutic Category Antineoplastic Agent, Miscellaneous
Use Treatment of acute lymphocytic leukemia, small cell lung cancer
Pregnancy Risk Factor D
Dosage I.V.:
Children: 130 mg/m²/week, increasing to 150 mg/m² after 3 weeks and up to 180 mg/m² after 6 weeks
Acute lymphoblastic leukemia (ALL): 165 mg/m² twice weekly for 8-9 doses **or** 250 mg/m² weekly for 4-8 weeks
Adults: 50-180 mg/m² once or twice weekly for 4-6 weeks or 20-60 mg/m²/day for 5 days
Small cell lung cancer: 80-90 mg/m²/day for 5 days every 4-6 weeks

Dosage adjustment in renal/hepatic impairment: Data is insufficient, but dose adjustments may be necessary in patient with significant renal or hepatic impairment

Dosage adjustment in Down syndrome patients: Reduce initial dosing; administer the first course at half the usual dose. Patients with both Down syndrome and leukemia may be especially sensitive to myelosuppressive chemotherapy.

Dosage Forms INJ, solution: 10 mg/mL (5 mL)

Tenofovir (te NOE fo veer)

Related Information
Antiretroviral Therapy for HIV Infection on page 1448
U.S. Brand Names Viread®
Synonyms PMPA; TDF; Tenofovir Disoproxil Fumarate
(Continued)

Tenofovir *(Continued)*

Therapeutic Category Antiretroviral Agent, Reverse Transcriptase Inhibitor (Nucleotide)

Use Management of HIV infections in combination with at least two other antiretroviral agents

Pregnancy Risk Factor B

Contraindications Hypersensitivity to tenofovir or any component of the formulation

Warnings/Precautions Lactic acidosis and severe hepatomegaly with steatosis have been reported with nucleoside analogues, including fatal cases; use with caution in patients with risk factors for liver disease (risk may be increased in obese patients or prolonged exposure) and suspend treatment in any patient who develops clinical or laboratory findings suggestive of lactic acidosis (transaminase elevation may/may not accompany hepatomegaly and steatosis).

Use caution in renal impairment (Cl$_{cr}$ <50 mL/minute; dosage adjustment required. May cause osteomalacia and/or renal toxicity; monitor renal function and possible bone abnormalities during therapy. Use caution in hepatic impairment. All patients with HIV should be tested for HBV prior to initiation of treatment. Safety and efficacy of tenofovir during co-infection of HIV and HBV have not been established; exacerbations of HBV have been reported following tenofovir discontinuation. Safety and efficacy have not been established in pediatric patients.

Common Adverse Reactions Clinical trials involved addition to prior antiretroviral therapy. Frequencies listed are treatment-emergent adverse effects noted at higher frequency than in the placebo group.

>10%: Gastrointestinal: Nausea (11%)

1% to 10%:
- Endocrine & metabolic: Glycosuria (3%, frequency equal to placebo); other metabolic effects (hyperglycemia, hypertriglyceridemia) noted at frequencies less than placebo
- Gastrointestinal: Diarrhea (9%), vomiting (5%), flatulence (4%), abdominal pain (3%, frequency equal to placebo), anorexia (3%)
- Hematologic: Neutropenia (1%, frequency equal to placebo)
- Hepatic: Increased transaminases (2% to 4%)
- Neuromuscular & skeletal: Weakness (8%, frequency equal to placebo)

Drug Interactions

Cytochrome P450 Effect: Inhibits CYP1A2 (weak)

Increased Effect/Toxicity: Concurrent use has been noted to increase serum concentrations/exposure to didanosine and its metabolites, potentially increasing the risk of didanosine toxicity (pancreatitis, peripheral neuropathy, or lactic acidosis); use caution and monitor closely; suspend therapy if signs/symptoms of toxicity are present. Drugs which may compete for renal tubule secretion (including acyclovir, cidofovir, ganciclovir, valacyclovir, valganciclovir) may increase the serum concentrations of tenofovir. Drugs causing nephrotoxicity may reduce elimination of tenofovir. Lopinavir/ritonavir may increase serum concentrations of tenofovir.

Decreased Effect: Serum levels of lopinavir and/or ritonavir may be decreased by tenofovir. Tenofovir may decrease serum concentrations of atazanavir, resulting in a loss of virologic response (specific atazanavir dosing recommendations provided by manufacturer).

Mechanism of Action Tenofovir disoproxil fumarate (TDF) is an analog of adenosine 5'-monophosphate; it interferes with the HIV viral RNA dependent DNA polymerase resulting in inhibition of viral replication. TDF is first converted intracellularly by hydrolysis to tenofovir and subsequently phosphorylated to the active tenofovir diphosphate; nucleotide reverse transcriptase inhibitor.

Pharmacodynamics/Kinetics

Distribution: 1.2-1.3 L/kg

Protein binding: 7% to serum proteins

Metabolism: Tenofovir disoproxil fumarate (TDF) is converted intracellularly by hydrolysis (by nonCYP enzymes) to tenofovir, then phosphorylated to the active tenofovir diphosphate

Bioavailability: 25% (fasting); increases ~40% with high-fat meal

Time to peak, serum: Fasting: 1 hour; With food: 2 hours

Excretion: Urine (70% to 80%) via filtration and active secretion, primarily as unchanged tenofovir

Dosage Oral: Adults: HIV infection: 300 mg once daily

Dosage adjustment in renal impairment:

Cl$_{cr}$ 30-49 mL/minute: 300 mg every 48 hours

Cl$_{cr}$ 10-29 mL/minute: 300 mg twice weekly

Cl$_{cr}$ <10 mL/minute without dialysis: No recommendation available.

Hemodialysis: 300 mg every 7 days or after ~12 hours of dialysis

Administration May be administered with or without food.

Monitoring Parameters CBC with differential, reticulocyte count, serum creatine kinase, CD4 count, HIV RNA plasma levels, renal and hepatic function tests, bone density (long-term), serum phosphorus

Patients with HIV and HVB co-infection should be monitored for several months following tenofovir discontinuation.

Patient Information Tenofovir is not a cure for AIDS. Take as directed, with or without food. Do not take with other medications. Take precautions to avoid transmission to others. Report unresolved nausea or vomiting; abdominal pain; tingling, numbness, or pain of toes or fingers; skin rash or irritation; or muscle weakness or tremors. Notify prescriber if you are pregnant or plan to be pregnant. HIV infected mothers are discouraged from breast-feeding to prevent potential transmission of HIV.

Dosage Forms TAB: 300 mg

♦ **Tenofovir Disoproxil Fumarate** *see Tenofovir on page 1195*

♦ **Tenoretic**® *see* Atenolol and Chlorthalidone *on page 127*
♦ **Tenormin**® *see* Atenolol *on page 126*
♦ **Tenuate**® *see* Diethylpropion *on page 372*
♦ **Tenuate**® **Dospan**® *see* Diethylpropion *on page 372*
♦ **Tequin**® *see* Gatifloxacin *on page 579*
♦ **Terazol**® **3** *see* Terconazole *on page 1200*
♦ **Terazol**® **7** *see* Terconazole *on page 1200*

Terazosin (ter AY zoe sin)

U.S. Brand Names Hytrin®
Therapeutic Category Alpha-Adrenergic Blocking Agent, Oral; Antihypertensive Agent
Use Management of mild to moderate hypertension; alone or in combination with other agents such as diuretics or beta-blockers; benign prostate hyperplasia (BPH)
Pregnancy Risk Factor C
Contraindications Hypersensitivity to quinazolines (doxazosin, prazosin, terazosin) or any component of the formulation; concurrent use with phosphodiesterase-5 (PDE-5) inhibitors including sildenafil (>25 mg), tadalafil, or vardenafil
Warnings/Precautions Marked orthostatic hypotension, syncope, and loss of consciousness may occur with first dose ("first dose phenomenon"). This reaction is more likely to occur in patients receiving beta-blockers, diuretics, low sodium diets, or first doses >1 mg/dose in adults; avoid rapid increase in dose; use with caution in patients with renal impairment.
Common Adverse Reactions Asthenia, postural hypotension, dizziness, somnolence, nasal congestion/rhinitis, and impotence were the only events noted in clinical trials to occur at a frequency significantly greater than placebo (p <0.05).

>10%: Central nervous system: Dizziness, headache, muscle weakness
1% to 10%:
    Cardiovascular: Edema, palpitations, chest pain, peripheral edema (3%), orthostatic hypotension (2.7% to 3.9%), tachycardia
    Central nervous system: Fatigue, nervousness, drowsiness
    Gastrointestinal: Dry mouth
    Genitourinary: Urinary incontinence
    Ocular: Blurred vision
    Respiratory: Dyspnea, nasal congestion

Drug Interactions
Increased Effect/Toxicity: Terazosin's hypotensive effect is increased with beta-blockers, diuretics, ACE inhibitors, calcium channel blockers, other antihypertensive medications, sildenafil (use with extreme caution at a dose ≤25 mg), tadalafil (use is contraindicated by the manufacturer), and vardenafil (use is contraindicated by the manufacturer).
Decreased Effect: Decreased antihypertensive response with NSAIDs. Alpha-blockers reduce the response to pressor agents (norepinephrine).
Mechanism of Action Alpha$_1$-specific blocking agent with minimal alpha$_2$ effects; this allows peripheral postsynaptic blockade, with the resultant decrease in arterial tone, while preserving the negative feedback loop which is mediated by the peripheral presynaptic alpha$_2$-receptors; terazosin relaxes the smooth muscle of the bladder neck, thus reducing bladder outlet obstruction
Pharmacodynamics/Kinetics
Onset of action: 1-2 hours
Absorption: Rapid
Protein binding: 90% to 95%
Metabolism: Extensively hepatic
Half-life elimination: 9.2-12 hours
Time to peak, serum: ~1 hour
Excretion: Feces (60%); urine (40%)
Dosage Oral: Adults:
Hypertension: Initial: 1 mg at bedtime; slowly increase dose to achieve desired blood pressure, up to 20 mg/day; usual dose: 1-5 mg/day
Dosage reduction may be needed when adding a diuretic or other antihypertensive agent; if drug is discontinued for greater than several days, consider beginning with initial dose and retitrate as needed; dosage may be given on a twice daily regimen if response is diminished at 24 hours and hypotensive is observed at 2-4 hours following a dose
Benign prostatic hyperplasia: Initial: 1 mg at bedtime, increasing as needed; most patients require 10 mg day; if no response after 4-6 weeks of 10 mg/day, may increase to 20 mg/day
Monitoring Parameters Standing and sitting/supine blood pressure, especially following the initial dose at 2-4 hours following the dose and thereafter at the trough point to ensure adequate control throughout the dosing interval; urinary symptoms
Patient Information Report any gain of body weight or painful, persistent erection; fainting sometimes occurs after the first dose; rise slowly from prolonged sitting or standing
Dosage Forms CAP (Hytrin®): 1 mg, 2 mg, 5 mg, 10 mg. **TAB:** 1 mg, 2 mg, 5 mg, 10 mg

Terbinafine (TER bin a feen)

Related Information
Antifungal Agents Comparison *on page 1362*
U.S. Brand Names Lamisil®; Lamisil® AT™ [OTC]
Synonyms Terbinafine Hydrochloride
(Continued)

Terbinafine *(Continued)*

Therapeutic Category Antifungal Agent, Oral; Antifungal Agent, Systemic; Antifungal Agent, Topical

Use Active against most strains of *Trichophyton mentagrophytes*, *Trichophyton rubrum*; may be effective for infections of *Microsporum gypseum* and *M. nanum*, *Trichophyton verrucosum*, *Epidermophyton floccosum*, *Candida albicans*, and *Scopulariopsis brevicaulis*

Oral: Onychomycosis of the toenail or fingernail due to susceptible dermatophytes

Topical: Antifungal for the treatment of tinea pedis (athlete's foot), tinea cruris (jock itch), and tinea corporis (ringworm) [OTC/prescription formulations]; tinea versicolor [prescription formulations]

Pregnancy Risk Factor B

Contraindications Hypersensitivity to terbinafine, naftifine, or any component of the formulation; pre-existing liver or renal disease (≤50 mL/minute GFR)

Warnings/Precautions While rare, the following complications have been reported and may require discontinuation of therapy: Changes in the ocular lens and retina, pancytopenia, neutropenia, Stevens-Johnson syndrome, toxic epidermal necrolysis. Rare cases of hepatic failure (including fatal cases) have been reported following oral treatment of onychomycosis. Not recommended for use in patients with active or chronic liver disease. Discontinue if symptoms or signs of hepatobiliary dysfunction or cholestatic hepatitis develop. If irritation/sensitivity develop with topical use, discontinue therapy. **Use caution in writing and/or filling prescription/orders. Confusion between Lamictal® (lamotrigine) and Lamisil® (terbinafine) has occurred.**

Common Adverse Reactions

Oral: 1% to 10%:

Central nervous system: Headache, dizziness, vertigo

Dermatologic: Rash, pruritus, and alopecia with oral therapy

Gastrointestinal: Nausea, diarrhea, dyspepsia, abdominal pain, appetite decrease, taste disturbance

Hematologic: Lymphocytopenia

Hepatic: Liver enzyme elevations

Ocular: Visual disturbance

Miscellaneous: Allergic reaction

Topical: 1% to 10%:

Dermatologic: Pruritus, contact dermatitis, irritation, burning, dryness

Local: Irritation, stinging

Drug Interactions

Cytochrome P450 Effect: Substrate of CYP3A4 (major); **Inhibits** CYP2D6 (strong); **Induces** CYP3A4 (weak)

Increased Effect/Toxicity: Terbinafine clearance is decreased by cimetidine (33%); caffeine clearance is decreased by terbinafine (19%); effects of drugs metabolized by CYP2D6 (including beta-blockers, SSRIs, MAO inhibitors, tricyclic antidepressants) may be increased; warfarin effects may be increased

Decreased Effect: Cyclosporine clearance is increased (~15%) with concomitant terbinafine; rifampin increases terbinafine clearance (100%); rifampin increases the metabolism of terbinafine (decreases serum concentration)

Mechanism of Action Synthetic alkylamine derivative which inhibits squalene epoxidase, a key enzyme in sterol biosynthesis in fungi. This results in a deficiency in ergosterol within the fungal cell wall and results in fungal cell death.

Pharmacodynamics/Kinetics

Absorption: Topical: Limited (<5%); Oral: >70%

Distribution: V_d: 2000 L; distributed to sebum and skin predominantly

Protein binding, plasma: >99%

Metabolism: Hepatic; no active metabolites; first-pass effect; little effect on CYP

Bioavailability: Oral: 40%

Half-life elimination:

Topical: 22-26 hours

Oral: Terminal half-life: 200-400 hours; very slow release of drug from skin and adipose tissues occurs

Time to peak, plasma: 1-2 hours

Excretion: Urine (70% to 75%)

Dosage

Children ≥12 years and Adults:

Topical cream, solution:

Athlete's foot (tinea pedis): Apply to affected area twice daily for at least 1 week, not to exceed 4 weeks [OTC/prescription formulations]

Ringworm (tinea corporis) and jock itch (tinea cruris): Apply cream to affected area once or twice daily for at least 1 week, not to exceed 4 weeks; apply solution once daily for 7 days [OTC formulations]

Adults:

Oral:

Superficial mycoses: Fingernail: 250 mg/day for up to 6 weeks; toenail: 250 mg/day for 12 weeks; doses may be given in two divided doses

Systemic mycosis: 250-500 mg/day for up to 16 months

Topical solution: Tinea versicolor: Apply to affected area twice daily for 1 week [prescription formulation]

Dosing adjustment in renal impairment: Oral administration: Although specific guidelines are not available, dose reduction in significant renal insufficiency (GFR <50 mL/minute) is recommended

Dosing adjustment in hepatic impairment: Clearance is decreased by ~50% with hepatic cirrhosis

Monitoring Parameters CBC and LFTs at baseline and repeated if use is for >6 weeks

Patient Information Topical: Avoid contact with eyes, nose, or mouth during treatment; nursing mothers should not use on breast tissue; advise physician if eyes or skin becomes yellow or if irritation, itching, or burning develops. Do not use occlusive dressings concurrent with therapy. Full clinical effect may require several months due to the time required for a new nail to grow.

Dosage Forms CRM (Lamisil® AT™): 1% (15 g, 30 g). **SOLN, topical spray** (Lamisil®, Lamisil® AT™): 1% (30 mL). **TAB** (Lamisil®): 250 mg

♦ **Terbinafine Hydrochloride** *see Terbinafine on page 1197*

Terbutaline (ter BYOO ta leen)
Related Information
Bronchodilators, Comparison of Inhaled Sympathomimetics *on page 1370*
U.S. Brand Names Brethine®
Synonyms Brethaire [DSC]; Bricanyl [DSC]
Therapeutic Category Beta$_2$-Adrenergic Agonist; Bronchodilator; Sympathomimetic Agent; Tocolytic Agent
Use Bronchodilator in reversible airway obstruction and bronchial asthma; tocolytic agent
Unlabeled/Investigational Use Tocolytic agent (management of preterm labor)
Pregnancy Risk Factor B
Contraindications Hypersensitivity to terbutaline or any component of the formulation; cardiac arrhythmias associated with tachycardia; tachycardia caused by digitalis intoxication
Warnings/Precautions When used for tocolysis, there is some risk of maternal pulmonary edema, which has been associated with the following risk factors, excessive hydration, multiple gestation, occult sepsis and underlying cardiac disease. To reduce risk, limit fluid intake to 2.5-3 L/day, limit sodium intake, maintain maternal pulse to <130 beats/minute.

Use caution in patients with cardiovascular disease (arrhythmia or hypertension or CHF), convulsive disorders, diabetes, glaucoma, hyperthyroidism, or hypokalemia. Beta agonists may cause elevation in blood pressure, heart rate, and result in CNS stimulation/excitation. Beta$_2$ agonists may increase risk of arrhythmia, increase serum glucose, or decrease serum potassium.

When used as a bronchodilator, optimize anti-inflammatory treatment before initiating maintenance treatment with terbutaline. Do not use as a component of chronic therapy without an anti-inflammatory agent. Only the mildest form of asthma (Step 1 and/or exercise-induced) would not require concurrent use based upon asthma guidelines. Patient must be instructed to seek medical attention in cases where acute symptoms are not relieved or a previous level of response is diminished. The need to increase frequency of use may indicate deterioration of asthma, and treatment must not be delayed.

Do not exceed recommended dose; serious adverse events including fatalities, have been associated with excessive use of inhaled sympathomimetics. Rarely, paradoxical bronchospasm may occur with use of inhaled bronchodilating agents; this should be distinguished from inadequate response.

Common Adverse Reactions
>10%:
Central nervous system: Nervousness, restlessness
Endocrine & metabolic: Serum glucose increased, serum potassium decreased
Neuromuscular & skeletal: Trembling
1% to 10%:
Cardiovascular: Tachycardia, hypertension
Central nervous system: Dizziness, drowsiness, headache, insomnia
Gastrointestinal: Xerostomia, nausea, vomiting, bad taste in mouth
Neuromuscular & skeletal: Muscle cramps, weakness
Miscellaneous: Diaphoresis

Drug Interactions
Increased Effect/Toxicity: Increased toxicity with MAO inhibitors, tricyclic antidepressants.
Decreased Effect: Decreased effect with beta-blockers.
Mechanism of Action Relaxes bronchial smooth muscle by action on beta$_2$-receptors with less effect on heart rate

Pharmacodynamics/Kinetics
Onset of action: Oral: 30-45 minutes; S.C.: 6-15 minutes
Protein binding: 25%
Metabolism: Hepatic to inactive sulfate conjugates
Bioavailability: S.C. doses are more bioavailable than oral
Half-life elimination: 11-16 hours
Excretion: Urine

Dosage
Children <12 years: Bronchoconstriction:
Oral: Initial: 0.05 mg/kg/dose 3 times/day, increased gradually as required; maximum: 0.15 mg/kg/dose 3-4 times/day or a total of 5 mg/24 hours
S.C.: 0.005-0.01 mg/kg/dose to a maximum of 0.3 mg/dose every 15-20 minutes for 3 doses
(Continued)

Terbutaline *(Continued)*

Children >12 years and Adults: Bronchoconstriction:
Oral:
12-15 years: 2.5 mg every 6 hours 3 times/day; not to exceed 7.5 mg in 24 hours
>15 years: 5 mg/dose every 6 hours 3 times/day; if side effects occur, reduce dose to 2.5 mg every 6 hours; not to exceed 15 mg in 24 hours
S.C.: 0.25 mg/dose repeated in 15-30 minutes for one time only; a total dose of 0.5 mg should not be exceeded within a 4-hour period inhalations
Adults: Premature labor (tocolysis; unlabeled use):
Acute: I.V. 2.5-10 mcg/minute; increased gradually every 10-20 minutes; effective maximum dosages from 17.5-30 mcg/minute have been used with caution. Duration of infusion is at least 12 hours.
Maintenance: Oral: 2.5-10 mg every 4-6 hours for as long as necessary to prolong pregnancy depending on patient tolerance
Dosing adjustment/comments in renal impairment:
Cl_{cr} 10-50 mL/minute: Administer at 50% of normal dose
Cl_{cr} <10 mL/minute: Avoid use
Administration
I.V.: Use infusion pump.
Oral: Administer around-the-clock to promote less variation in peak and trough serum levels
Monitoring Parameters Serum potassium, glucose; heart rate, blood pressure, respiratory rate; monitor for signs and symptoms of pulmonary edema (when used as a tocolytic); monitor FEV_1, peak flow, and/or other pulmonary function tests (when used as bronchodilator)
Patient Information Precede administration of aerosol adrenocorticoid by 15 minutes; report any decreased effectiveness of drug; do not exceed recommended dose or frequency; may take last dose at 6 PM to avoid insomnia
Dosage Forms INJ, solution: 1 mg/mL (1 mL). **TAB:** 2.5 mg, 5 mg

Terconazole *(ter KONE a zole)*

U.S. Brand Names Terazol® 3; Terazol® 7
Synonyms Triaconazole
Therapeutic Category Antifungal Agent, Vaginal
Use Local treatment of vulvovaginal candidiasis
Pregnancy Risk Factor C
Contraindications Hypersensitivity to terconazole or any component of the formulation
Warnings/Precautions Should be discontinued if sensitization or irritation occurs. Microbiological studies (KOH smear and/or cultures) should be repeated in patients not responding to terconazole in order to confirm the diagnosis and rule out other pathogens.
Common Adverse Reactions 1% to 10%:
Central nervous system; Fever, chills
Gastrointestinal: Abdominal pain
Genitourinary: Vulvar/vaginal burning, dysmenorrhea
Mechanism of Action Triazole ketal antifungal agent; involves inhibition of fungal cytochrome P450. Specifically, terconazole inhibits cytochrome P450-dependent 14-alpha-demethylase which results in accumulation of membrane disturbing 14-alpha-demethylsterols and ergosterol depletion.
Pharmacodynamics/Kinetics Absorption: Extent of systemic absorption after vaginal administration may be dependent on presence of a uterus; 5% to 8% in women who had a hysterectomy versus 12% to 16% in nonhysterectomy women
Dosage Adults: Female:
Terazol® 3 vaginal cream: Insert 1 applicatorful intravaginally at bedtime for 3 consecutive days
Terazol® 7 vaginal cream: Insert 1 applicatorful intravaginally at bedtime for 7 consecutive days
Terazol® 3 vaginal suppository: Insert 1 suppository intravaginally at bedtime for 3 consecutive days
Patient Information Insert high into vagina; complete full course of therapy; contact prescriber if itching or burning occurs
Dosage Forms CRM, vaginal (Terazol® 7): 0.4% (45 g); (Terazol® 3): 0.8% (20 g). **SUPP, vaginal** (Terazol® 3): 80 mg (3s)

Teriparatide *(ter i PAR a tide)*

U.S. Brand Names Forteo™
Synonyms Parathyroid Hormone (1-34); Recombinant Human Parathyroid Hormone (1-34); rhPTH(1-34)
Therapeutic Category Parathyroid Hormone Analog
Use Treatment of osteoporosis in postmenopausal women at high risk of fracture; treatment of primary or hypogonadal osteoporosis in men at high risk of fracture
Pregnancy Risk Factor C
Contraindications Hypersensitivity to teriparatide or any component of the formulation
Warnings/Precautions In animal studies, teriparatide has been associated with an increase in osteosarcoma; risk was dependent on both dose and duration. Avoid use in patients with an increased risk of osteosarcoma (including Paget's disease, prior radiation, unexplained elevation of alkaline phosphatase, or in patients with open epiphyses). Do not use in patients with a history of skeletal metastases, hyperparathyroidism, or pre-existing hypercalcemia. Exclude

metabolic bone disease other than osteoporosis prior to initiating therapy. Use caution in patients with active or recent urolithiasis. Use caution in patients at risk of orthostasis (including concurrent antihypertensive therapy), or in patients who may not tolerate transient hypotension (cardiovascular or cerebrovascular disease). Use caution in patients with renal or hepatic impairment (limited data available concerning safety and efficacy). Not approved for use in pediatric patients.

Common Adverse Reactions 1% to 10%:
Cardiovascular: Chest pain (3%), syncope (3%)
Central nervous system: Dizziness (8%), depression (4%), vertigo (4%)
Dermatologic: Rash (5%)
Endocrine & metabolic: Hypercalcemia (transient increases noted 4-6 hours postdose in 11% of women and 6% of men)
Gastrointestinal: Nausea (9%), dyspepsia (5%), vomiting (3%), tooth disorder (2%)
Genitourinary: Hyperuricemia (3%)
Neuromuscular & skeletal: Arthralgia (10%), weakness (9%), leg cramps (3%)
Respiratory: Rhinitis (10%), pharyngitis (6%), dyspnea (4%), pneumonia (4%)
Miscellaneous: Antibodies to teriparatide (3% of women in long-term treatment; hypersensitivity reactions or decreased efficacy were not associated in preclinical trials)

Drug Interactions
Increased Effect/Toxicity: Digitalis serum concentrations are not affected, however, transient hypercalcemia may increase risk of digitalis toxicity (case reports).

Mechanism of Action Teriparatide is a recombinant formulation of endogenous parathyroid hormone (PTH), containing a 34-amino-acid sequence which is identical to the N-terminal portion of this hormone. The pharmacologic activity of teriparatide is similar to the physiologic activity of PTH, stimulating osteoblast function, increasing gastrointestinal calcium absorption, increasing renal tubular reabsorption of calcium. Treatment with teriparatide increases bone mineral density, bone mass, and strength. In postmenopausal women, it has been shown to decrease osteoporosis-related fractures.

Pharmacodynamics/Kinetics
Distribution: V_d: 0.12 L/kg
Metabolism: Hepatic (nonspecific proteolysis)
Bioavailability: 95%
Half-life elimination: Serum: I.V.: 5 minutes; S.C.: 1 hour
Excretion: Urine (as metabolites)

Dosage S.C.: Adults: 20 mcg once daily; **Note:** Initial administration should occur under circumstances in which the patient may sit or lie down, in the event of orthostasis.
Dosage adjustment in renal impairment: No dosage adjustment required. Bioavailability and half-life increase with Cl_{cr} <30 mL/minute.

Administration Administer by subcutaneous injection into the thigh or abdominal wall. Initial administration should occur under circumstances in which the patient may sit or lie down, in the event of orthostasis.

Monitoring Parameters Serum calcium, serum phosphorus; blood pressure

Patient Information Use injector pen as instructed. Initial doses should be administered under circumstances which allow the patient to sit or lie down in the event of dizziness/lightheadedness. Inject subcutaneously into the skin of the upper thigh or abdominal wall. Injector may be used for up to 28 days following the first injection. Store in refrigerator, do not freeze. Pen should be discarded after 28 days, even if solution remains in the pen. Report any rash, symptomatic hypotension (lightheadedness/dizziness, especially when sitting up or standing), or persistent weakness to prescriber.

Dosage Forms INJ, solution [prefilled syringe]: 250 mcg/mL (3 mL)

◆ **Terramycin® I.M.** *see* Oxytetracycline *on page 947*
◆ **Terramycin® w/Polymyxin B Ophthalmic** *see* Oxytetracycline and Polymyxin B *on page 947*
◆ **Teslac®** *see* Testolactone *on page 1201*
◆ **TESPA** *see* Thiotepa *on page 1219*
◆ **Tessalon®** *see* Benzonatate *on page 155*
◆ **Testim™** *see* Testosterone *on page 1201*
◆ **Testoderm®** *see* Testosterone *on page 1201*
◆ **Testoderm® with Adhesive** *see* Testosterone *on page 1201*

Testolactone (tes toe LAK tone)

U.S. Brand Names Teslac®
Therapeutic Category Androgen; Antineoplastic Agent, Androgen
Use Palliative treatment of advanced or disseminated breast carcinoma
Restrictions C-III
Pregnancy Risk Factor C
Dosage Adults: Female: Oral: 250 mg 4 times/day for at least 3 months; desired response may take as long as 3 months
Dosage Forms TAB: 50 mg

◆ **Testopel®** *see* Testosterone *on page 1201*

Testosterone (tes TOS ter one)

U.S. Brand Names Androderm®; AndroGel®; Delatestryl®; Depo®-Testosterone; Striant™; Testim™; Testoderm®; Testoderm® with Adhesive; Testopel®
Synonyms Testosterone Cypionate; Testosterone Enanthate
(Continued)

Testosterone *(Continued)*

Therapeutic Category Androgen

Use

Injection: Androgen replacement therapy in the treatment of delayed male puberty; male hypogonadism (primary or hypogonadotropic); inoperable female breast cancer (enanthate only)

Pellet: Androgen replacement therapy in the treatment of delayed male puberty; male hypogonadism (primary or hypogonadotropic)

Buccal, topical: Male hypogonadism (primary or hypogonadotropic)

Restrictions C-III

Pregnancy Risk Factor X

Contraindications Hypersensitivity to testosterone or any component of the formulation (including soy); severe renal or cardiac disease; benign prostatic hyperplasia with obstruction; undiagnosed genital bleeding; males with carcinoma of the breast or prostate; pregnancy

Warnings/Precautions When used to treat delayed male puberty, perform radiographic examination of the hand and wrist every 6 months to determine the rate of bone maturation. May accelerate bone maturation without producing compensating gain in linear growth. Has both androgenic and anabolic activity, the anabolic action may enhance hypoglycemia. Use caution in elderly patients or patients with other demographic factors which may increase the risk of prostatic carcinoma; careful monitoring is required. May cause fluid retention; use caution in patients with cardiovascular disease or other edematous conditions. Prolonged use has been associated with serious hepatic effects (hepatitis, hepatic neoplasms, cholestatic hepatitis, jaundice). May potentiate sleep apnea in some male patients (obesity or chronic lung disease). Gels and buccal system have not been evaluated in males <18 years of age; safety and efficacy of injection have not been established in males <12 years of age.

Common Adverse Reactions Frequency not defined.

Cardiovascular: Flushing, edema

Central nervous system: Excitation, aggressive behavior, sleeplessness, anxiety, mental depression, headache

Dermatologic: Hirsutism (increase in pubic hair growth), acne

Endocrine & metabolic: Menstrual problems (amenorrhea), virilism, breast soreness, gynecomastia, hypercalcemia, hypoglycemia

Gastrointestinal: Nausea, vomiting, GI irritation

Following buccal administration: Bitter taste, gum edema, gum or mouth irritation, gum tenderness, taste perversion

Genitourinary: Prostatic hyperplasia, prostatic carcinoma, impotence, testicular atrophy, epididymitis, priapism, bladder irritability

Hepatic: Hepatic dysfunction, cholestatic hepatitis, hepatic necrosis

Hematologic: Leukopenia, polycythemia, suppression of clotting factors

Miscellaneous: Hypersensitivity reactions

Drug Interactions

Cytochrome P450 Effect: Substrate (minor) of CYP2B6, 2C8/9, 2C19, 3A4; **Inhibits** CYP3A4 (weak)

Increased Effect/Toxicity: Warfarin and testosterone: Effects of oral anticoagulants may be enhanced. Testosterone may increase levels of oxyphenbutazone. May enhance fluid retention from corticosteroids.

Mechanism of Action Principal endogenous androgen responsible for promoting the growth and development of the male sex organs and maintaining secondary sex characteristics in androgen-deficient males

Pharmacodynamics/Kinetics

Duration (route and ester dependent): I.M.: Cypionate and enanthate esters have longest duration, ≤2-4 weeks

Absorption: Transdermal gel: ~10% of dose

Distribution: Crosses placenta; enters breast milk

Protein binding: 98% bound to sex hormone-binding globulin (40%) and albumin

Metabolism: Hepatic; forms metabolites

Half-life elimination: 10-100 minutes

Excretion: Urine (90%); feces (6%)

Dosage

Adolescents: I.M.:

Male hypogonadism:

Initiation of pubertal growth: 40-50 mg/m²/dose (cypionate or enanthate ester) monthly until the growth rate falls to prepubertal levels

Terminal growth phase: 100 mg/m²/dose (cypionate or enanthate ester) monthly until growth ceases

Maintenance virilizing dose: 100 mg/m²/dose (cypionate or enanthate ester) twice monthly

Delayed male puberty: 40-50 mg/m²/dose monthly (cypionate or enanthate ester) for 6 months

Adolescents and Adults: Pellet (for subcutaneous implantation): Delayed male puberty, male hypogonadism: 150-450 mg every 3-6 months

Adults:

I.M.:

Female: Inoperable breast cancer: Testosterone enanthate: 200-400 mg every 2-4 weeks

Male: Long-acting formulations: Testosterone enanthate (in oil)/testosterone cypionate (in oil):
Hypogonadism: 50-400 mg every 2-4 weeks
Delayed puberty: 50-200 mg every 2-4 weeks for a limited duration
Transdermal: Primary male hypogonadism **or** hypogonadotropic hypogonadism:
Testoderm®: Apply 6 mg patch daily to scrotum (if scrotum is inadequate, use a 4 mg daily system)
Androderm®: Apply two systems nightly to clean, dry area on the back, abdomen, upper arms, or thighs for 24 hours for a total of 5 mg day
AndroGel®, Testim™: 5 g (to deliver 50 mg of testosterone with 5 mg systemically absorbed) applied once daily (preferably in the morning) to clean, dry, intact skin of the shoulder and upper arms. AndroGel® may also be applied to the abdomen. Dosage may be increased to a maximum of 10 g (100 mg). **Do not apply testosterone gel to the genitals**.
Oral (buccal): Hypogonadism or hypogonadotropic hypogonadism: 30 mg twice daily (every 12 hours) applied to the gum region above the incisor tooth

Dosing adjustment/comments in hepatic disease: Reduce dose
Administration
I.M.: Warm to room temperature; shaking vial will help redissolve crystals that have formed after storage. Administer by deep I.M. injection into the upper outer quadrant of the gluteus maximus.
Oral: Striant™: One mucoadhesive for buccal application (buccal system) should be applied to a comfortable area above the incisor tooth. Apply flat side of system to gum. Rotate to alternate sides of mouth with each application. Hold buccal system firmly in place for 30 seconds to ensure adhesion. The buccal system should adhere to gum for 12 hours. If the buccal system falls out, replace with a new system. If the system falls out within 4 hours of next dose, the new buccal system should remain in place until the time of the following scheduled dose. System will soften and mold to shape of gum as it absorbs moisture from mouth. Do not chew or swallow the buccal system. The buccal system will not dissolve; gently remove by sliding downwards from gum; avoid scratching gum.
Transdermal:
Androderm®: Apply to clean, dry area of skin on the arm, back, or upper buttocks.
Testoderm®: Apply to clean, dry scrotal skin. Dry shave scrotal hair for optimal skin contact. Do not use chemical depilatories.
AndroGel®, Testim™: Apply (preferably in the morning) to clean, dry, intact skin of the shoulder and upper arms (AndroGel® may also be applied to the abdomen). Upon opening the packet(s), the entire contents should be squeezed into the palm of the hand and immediately applied to the application site(s). Alternatively, a portion may be squeezed onto palm of hand and applied, repeating the process until entire packet has been applied. Application sites should be allowed to dry for a few minutes prior to dressing. Hands should be washed with soap and water after application. **Do not apply testosterone gel to the genitals**.
Monitoring Parameters Periodic liver function tests, PSA, cholesterol, hemoglobin and hematocrit; radiologic examination of wrist and hand every 6 months (when using in prepubertal children)
Gel: Morning serum testosterone levels 14 days after start of therapy
Reference Range Testosterone, urine: Male: 100-1500 ng/24 hours; Female: 100-500 ng/24 hours
Patient Information Virilization may occur in female patients; report menstrual irregularities; male patients report persistent penile erections. All patients should report persistent GI distress, diarrhea, or jaundice. Gels are flammable; avoid smoking or exposure to fire/flame during use.
Dosage Forms BUCCAL, mucoadhesive [buccal system]: (Striant™): 30 mg. **GEL, topical** (AndroGel®): 25 mg/2.5 g (30s); 50 mg/5 g (30s); (Testim™): 50 mg/5 g (30s). **INJ, in oil, as cypionate** (Depo® Testosterone): 100 mg/mL (10 mL); 200 mg/mL (1 mL, 10 mL). **INJ, in oil, as enanthate** (Delatestryl®): 200 mg/mL (1 mL, 5 mL). **PELLET, for subcutaneous implantation** (Testopel®): 75 mg (1 pellet/vial). **TRANSDERMAL SYSTEM** (Androderm®): 2.5 mg/day (60s); 5 mg/day (30s); (Testoderm®): 4 mg/day (30s); 6 mg/day (30s); 5 mg/day (30s); (Testoderm® with Adhesive): 6 mg/day (30s)

♦ **Testosterone and Estradiol** *see* Estradiol and Testosterone *on page 464*
♦ **Testosterone Cypionate** *see* Testosterone *on page 1201*
♦ **Testosterone Enanthate** *see* Testosterone *on page 1201*
♦ **Testred®** *see* MethylTESTOSTERone *on page 826*
♦ **Tetanus and Diphtheria Toxoid** *see* Diphtheria and Tetanus Toxoid *on page 386*

Tetanus Antitoxin (TET a nus an tee TOKS in)
Synonyms TAT
Therapeutic Category Antitoxin
Use Tetanus prophylaxis or treatment of active tetanus only when tetanus immune globulin (TIG) is not available; tetanus immune globulin (Hyper-Tet®) is the preferred tetanus immunoglobulin for the treatment of active tetanus; may be given concomitantly with tetanus toxoid adsorbed when immediate treatment is required, but active immunization is desirable
Pregnancy Risk Factor D
Contraindications Hypersensitivity to equine-derived preparations or any component of the formulation; pregnancy
(Continued)

Tetanus Antitoxin (Continued)

Warnings/Precautions Tetanus antitoxin is not the same as tetanus immune globulin; sensitivity testing should be conducted in all individuals regardless of clinical history; have epinephrine 1:1000 available

Common Adverse Reactions ≥10%: Skin eruptions, erythema, urticaria, local pain, numbness, arthralgia, serum sickness may develop up to several weeks after injection, anaphylaxis

Mechanism of Action Provides passive immunization; solution of concentrated globulins containing antitoxic antibodies obtained from horse serum after immunization against tetanus toxin

Dosage
Prophylaxis: I.M., S.C.:
Children <30 kg: 1500 units
Children and Adults ≥30 kg: 3000-5000 units
Treatment: Children and Adults: Inject 10,000-40,000 units into wound; administer 40,000-100,000 units

Dosage Forms INJ, equine: Not less than 400 units/mL (12.5 mL, 50 mL)

Tetanus Immune Globulin (Human)
(TET a nus i MYUN GLOB yoo lin HYU man)

U.S. Brand Names BayTet™

Synonyms TIG

Therapeutic Category Immune Globulin

Use Passive immunization against tetanus; tetanus immune globulin is preferred over tetanus antitoxin for treatment of active tetanus; part of the management of an unclean, wound in a person whose history of previous receipt of tetanus toxoid is unknown or who has received less than three doses of tetanus toxoid; elderly may require TIG more often than younger patients with tetanus infection due to declining antibody titers with age

Pregnancy Risk Factor C

Contraindications Hypersensitivity to tetanus immune globulin, thimerosal, or any component of the formulation

Warnings/Precautions Have epinephrine 1:1000 available for anaphylactic reactions. Use caution in patients with isolated immunoglobulin A deficiency or a history of systemic hypersensitivity to human immunoglobulins. As a product of human plasma, this product may potentially transmit disease; screening of donors, as well as testing and/or inactivation of certain viruses reduces this risk. Use caution in patients with thrombocytopenia or coagulation disorders (I.M. injections may be contraindicated). Not for intravenous administration.

Common Adverse Reactions
>10%: Local: Pain, tenderness, erythema at injection site
1% to 10%:
Central nervous system: Fever (mild)
Dermatologic: Urticaria, angioedema
Neuromuscular & skeletal: Muscle stiffness
Miscellaneous: Anaphylaxis reaction

Mechanism of Action Passive immunity toward tetanus

Pharmacodynamics/Kinetics Absorption: Well absorbed

Dosage I.M.:
Prophylaxis of tetanus:
Children: 4 units/kg; some recommend administering 250 units to small children
Adults: 250 units
Treatment of tetanus:
Children: 500-3000 units; some should infiltrate locally around the wound
Adults: 3000-6000 units

Administration Do not administer I.V.; I.M. use only

Dosage Forms INJ, solution [prefilled syringe; preservative free]: 250 units/mL (1 mL)

Tetanus Toxoid (Adsorbed) (TET a nus TOKS oyd, ad SORBED)

Therapeutic Category Toxoid

Use Selective induction of active immunity against tetanus in selected patients. **Note:** Tetanus and diphtheria toxoids for adult use (Td) is the preferred immunizing agent for most adults and for children after their seventh birthday. Young children should receive trivalent DTwP or DTaP (diphtheria/tetanus/pertussis - whole cell or acellular), as part of their childhood immunization program, unless pertussis is contraindicated, then TD is warranted.

Pregnancy Risk Factor C

Contraindications Hypersensitivity to tetanus toxoid or any component of the formulation (may use the fluid tetanus toxoid to immunize the rare patient who is hypersensitive to aluminum adjuvant); avoid use with chloramphenicol or if neurological signs or symptoms occurred after prior administration; poliomyelitis outbreaks require deferral of immunizations; acute respiratory infections or other active infections may dictate deferral of administration of routine primary immunizing but not emergency doses

Warnings/Precautions Not equivalent to tetanus toxoid fluid; the tetanus toxoid adsorbed is the preferred toxoid for immunization and Td, TD or DTaP/DTwP are the preferred adsorbed forms; avoid injection into a blood vessel; have epinephrine (1:1000) available; not for use in treatment of tetanus infection nor for immediate prophylaxis of unimmunized individuals; immunosuppressive therapy or other immunodeficiencies may diminish antibody response, however, it is recommended for routine immunization of symptomatic and asymptomatic

HIV-infected patients; deferral of immunization until immunosuppression is discontinued or administration of an additional dose >1 month after treatment is recommended; allergic reactions may occur; epinephrine 1:1000 must be available; use in pediatrics should be deferred until >1 year of age when a history of a CNS disorder is present; elderly may not mount adequate antibody titers following immunization

Common Adverse Reactions
>10%: Local: Induration/redness at injection site
1% to 10%:
Central nervous system: Chills, fever
Local: Sterile abscess at injection site
Miscellaneous: Allergic reaction

Mechanism of Action Tetanus toxoid preparations contain the toxin produced by virulent tetanus bacilli (detoxified growth products of *Clostridium tetani*). The toxin has been modified by treatment with formaldehyde so that it has lost toxicity but still retains ability to act as antigen and produce active immunity; the aluminum salt, a mineral adjuvant, delays the rate of absorption and prolongs and enhances its properties; duration ~10 years.

Pharmacodynamics/Kinetics Duration: Primary immunization: ~10 years

Dosage Adults: I.M.:
Primary immunization: 0.5 mL; repeat 0.5 mL at 4-8 weeks after first dose and at 6-12 months after second dose
Routine booster doses are recommended only every 5-10 years

Administration Inject intramuscularly in the area of the vastus lateralis (midthigh laterally) or deltoid

For patients at risk of hemorrhage following intramuscular injection, the ACIP recommends "it should be administered intramuscularly if, in the opinion of the physician familiar with the patients bleeding risk, the vaccine can be administered with reasonable safety by this route. If the patient receives antihemophilia or other similar therapy, intramuscular vaccination can be scheduled shortly after such therapy is administered. A fine needle (23 gauge or smaller) can be used for the vaccination and firm pressure applied to the site (without rubbing) for at least 2 minutes. The patient should be instructed concerning the risk of hematoma from the injection."

Patient Information A nodule may be palpable at the injection site for a few weeks. DT, Td and T vaccines cause few problems; they may cause mild fever or soreness, swelling, and redness where the shot was given. These problems usually last 1-2 days, but this does not happen nearly as often as with DTP vaccine. Sometimes, adults who get these vaccines can have a lot of soreness and swelling where the shot was given.

Dosage Forms INJ, suspension: Tetanus 5 Lf units per 0.5 mL (5 mL)

Tetanus Toxoid (Fluid) (TET a nus TOKS oyd FLOO id)

Synonyms Tetanus Toxoid Plain
Therapeutic Category Toxoid
Use Indicated as booster dose in the active immunization against tetanus in the rare adult or child who is allergic to the aluminum adjuvant (a product containing adsorbed tetanus toxoid is preferred); not indicated for primary immunization
Unlabeled/Investigational Use Anergy testing (no longer recommended)
Pregnancy Risk Factor C
Contraindications Hypersensitivity to tetanus toxoid or any component of the formulation
Warnings/Precautions Epinephrine 1:1000 should be readily available; skin test responsiveness may be delayed or reduced in elderly patients. Patients who are immunocompromised may have reduced response; may be used in patients with HIV infection. May defer elective immunization during febrile illness or acute infection; defer elective immunization during outbreaks of poliomyelitis. In patients with a history of severe local reaction (Arthus-type) following previous dose, do not give further routine or emergency doses of tetanus and diphtheria toxoids for 10 years. Use caution in patients on anticoagulants, with thrombocytopenia, or bleeding disorders (bleeding may occur following intramuscular injection). Contains thimerosal; vial stopper contains natural latex rubber. Safety and efficacy in children <6 weeks of age have not been established; this product is not indicated for use in children <7 years of age.

Common Adverse Reactions All serious adverse reactions must be reported to the U.S. Department of Health and Human Services (DHHS) Vaccine Adverse Event Reporting System (VAERS) 1-800-822-7967.

Frequency not defined.
Cardiovascular: Hypotension
Central nervous system: Brachial neuritis, fever, Guillain-Barré syndrome, malaise
Dermatologic: Rash, urticaria
Gastrointestinal: Nausea
Local: Edema, induration (with or without tenderness), redness, warmth
Neuromuscular & skeletal: Arthralgia
Miscellaneous: Anaphylaxis, Arthus-type hypersensitivity reactions (severe local reaction developing 2-8 hours following injection)

Drug Interactions
Increased Effect/Toxicity: Increased bleeding and bruising may occur from I.M. injection in patients on anticoagulants.
Decreased Effect: Decreased effect of vaccine may occur with corticosteroids (greater than physiologic doses) or immunosuppressive agents
Mechanism of Action Tetanus toxoid preparations contain the toxin produced by virulent tetanus bacilli (detoxified growth products of *Clostridium tetani*). The toxin has been modified
(Continued)

Tetanus Toxoid (Fluid) *(Continued)*

by treatment with formaldehyde so that is has lost toxicity but still retains ability to act as antigen and produce active immunity.

Dosage

Primary immunization: Not indicated for this use.

Booster doses: I.M., S.C.: 0.5 mL every 10 years

Anergy testing (unlabeled use; no longer recommended for this indication): Intradermal: 0.1 mL; doses that have been used range from 0.1 mL of a 1:10 dilution to 0.1 mL of the undiluted product

Administration

I.M. Shake well prior to use. Administer I.M. in lateral aspect of mid-thigh or deltoid muscle of upper arm

For patients at risk of hemorrhage following intramuscular injection, the ACIP recommends "it should be administered intramuscularly if, in the opinion of the physician familiar with the patients bleeding risk, the vaccine can be administered with reasonable safety by this route. If the patient receives antihemophilia or other similar therapy, intramuscular vaccination can be scheduled shortly after such therapy is administered. A fine needle (23 gauge or smaller) can be used for the vaccination and firm pressure applied to the site (without rubbing) for at least 2 minutes. The patient should be instructed concerning the risk of hematoma from the injection."

S.C.: Shake well prior to use. Administer in area of the lateral aspect of mid-thigh or deltoid.

S.C. route may be preferred in patients with thrombocytopenia or coagulation disorders.

Dosage Forms INJ, solution: Tetanus 4 Lf units per 0.5 mL (7.5 mL)

♦ **Tetanus Toxoid Plain** *see* Tetanus Toxoid (Fluid) *on page 1205*

Tetracaine *(TET ra kane)*

U.S. Brand Names AK-T-Caine™; Cēpacol Viractin® [OTC]; Opticaine®; Pontocaine®

Synonyms Amethocaine Hydrochloride; Tetracaine Hydrochloride

Therapeutic Category Local Anesthetic, Ester Derivative; Local Anesthetic, Injectable; Local Anesthetic, Ophthalmic; Local Anesthetic, Oral; Local Anesthetic, Topical

Use Spinal anesthesia; local anesthesia in the eye for various diagnostic and examination purposes; topically applied to nose and throat for various diagnostic procedures; topical gel [OTC] for treatment of pain associated with cold sores and fever blisters; **approximately 10 times more potent than procaine**

Pregnancy Risk Factor C

Dosage

Children ≥2 years and Adults: Topical gel [OTC]: Cold sores and fever blisters: Apply to affected area up to 3-4 times/day for up to 7 days

Adults:

Ophthalmic solution (not for prolonged use): Instill 1-2 drops

Spinal anesthesia:

High, medium, low, and saddle blocks: 0.2% to 0.3% solution

Prolonged (2-3 hours): 1% solution

Subarachnoid injection: 5-20 mg

Saddle block: 2-5 mg; a 1% solution should be diluted with equal volume of CSF before administration

Topical mucous membranes (2% solution): Apply as needed; dose should not exceed 20 mg

Dosage Forms Gel (Cēpacol Viractin®): 2% (7.1 g). **INJ, solution** (Pontocaine®): 1% [10 mg/mL] (2 mL). **INJ, solution** [premixed in dextrose 6%] (Pontocaine®): 0.3% [3 mg/mL] (5 mL). **INJ, powder for reconstitution** (Pontocaine®): 20 mg. **SOLN, ophthalmic:** 0.5% [5 mg/mL] (15 mL); (AK-T-Caine™, Opticaine®): 0.5% (15 mL); (Pontocaine®): 0.5% (15 mL, 59 mL). **SOLN, topical** (Pontocaine®): 2% [20 mg/mL] (30 mL, 118 mL)

♦ **Tetracaine Hydrochloride** *see* Tetracaine *on page 1206*

♦ **Tetracaine Hydrochloride, Benzocaine, Butyl Aminobenzoate, and Benzalkonium Chloride** *see* Benzocaine, Butyl Aminobenzoate, Tetracaine, and Benzalkonium Chloride *on page 154*

♦ **Tetracosactide** *see* Cosyntropin *on page 315*

Tetracycline *(tet ra SYE kleen)*

Related Information

Antimicrobial Drugs of Choice *on page 1440*

Malaria Treatment *on page 1464*

U.S. Brand Names Sumycin®; Wesmycin®

Synonyms Achromycin; TCN; Tetracycline Hydrochloride

Therapeutic Category Acne Product; Antibiotic, Ophthalmic; Antibiotic, Tetracycline Derivative; Antibiotic, Topical

Use Treatment of susceptible bacterial infections of both gram-positive and gram-negative organisms; also infections due to *Mycoplasma*, *Chlamydia*, and *Rickettsia*; indicated for acne, exacerbations of chronic bronchitis, and treatment of gonorrhea and syphilis in patients that are allergic to penicillin; as part of a multidrug regimen for *H. pylori* eradication to reduce the risk of duodenal ulcer recurrence

Pregnancy Risk Factor D

Contraindications Hypersensitivity to tetracycline or any component of the formulation; do not administer to children ≤8 years of age; pregnancy

Warnings/Precautions Use of tetracyclines during tooth development may cause permanent discoloration of the teeth and enamel, hypoplasia and retardation of skeletal development and bone growth with risk being the greatest for children <4 years and those receiving high doses; use with caution in patients with renal or hepatic impairment (eg, elderly); dosage modification required in patients with renal impairment since it may increase BUN as an antianabolic agent; pseudotumor cerebri has been reported with tetracycline use (usually resolves with discontinuation); outdated drug can cause nephropathy; superinfection possible; use protective measure to avoid photosensitivity

Common Adverse Reactions Frequency not defined.

Cardiovascular: Pericarditis

Central nervous system: Intracranial pressure increased, bulging fontanels in infants, pseudotumor cerebri, paresthesia

Dermatologic: Photosensitivity, pruritus, pigmentation of nails, exfoliative dermatitis

Endocrine & metabolic: Diabetes insipidus syndrome

Gastrointestinal: Discoloration of teeth and enamel hypoplasia (young children), nausea, diarrhea, vomiting, esophagitis, anorexia, abdominal cramps, antibiotic-associated pseudomembranous colitis, staphylococcal enterocolitis, pancreatitis

Hematologic: Thrombophlebitis

Hepatic: Hepatotoxicity

Renal: Acute renal failure, azotemia, renal damage

Miscellaneous: Superinfections, anaphylaxis, hypersensitivity reactions, candidal superinfection

Drug Interactions

Cytochrome P450 Effect: Substrate of CYP3A4 (major); **Inhibits** CYP3A4 (moderate)

Increased Effect/Toxicity: Methoxyflurane anesthesia when concurrent with tetracycline may cause fatal nephrotoxicity. Warfarin with tetracyclines may cause increased anticoagulation.

Decreased Effect: Calcium, magnesium- or aluminum-containing antacids, iron, zinc, sodium bicarbonate, sucralfate, didanosine, or quinapril may decrease tetracycline absorption. Therapeutic effect of penicillins may be reduced with coadministration of tetracycline. Although anecdotal reports suggest oral contraceptive efficacy could be reduced by tetracyclines, this has been refuted by more rigorous scientific and clinical data.

Mechanism of Action Inhibits bacterial protein synthesis by binding with the 30S and possibly the 50S ribosomal subunit(s) of susceptible bacteria; may also cause alterations in the cytoplasmic membrane

Pharmacodynamics/Kinetics

Absorption: Oral: 75%

Distribution: Small amount appears in bile

Relative diffusion from blood into CSF: Good only with inflammation (exceeds usual MICs)

CSF:blood level ratio: Inflamed meninges: 25%

Protein binding: ~65%

Half-life elimination: Normal renal function: 8-11 hours; End-stage renal disease: 57-108 hours

Time to peak, serum: Oral: 2-4 hours

Excretion: Urine (60% as unchanged drug); feces (as active form)

Dosage Oral:

Children >8 years: 25-50 mg/kg/day in divided doses every 6 hours

Adults: 250-500 mg/dose every 6 hours

Helicobacter pylori eradication: 500 mg 2-4 times/day depending on regimen; requires combination therapy with at least one other antibiotic and an acid-suppressing agent (proton pump inhibitor or H$_2$ blocker)

Dosing interval in renal impairment:

Cl$_{cr}$ 50-80 mL/minute: Administer every 8-12 hours

Cl$_{cr}$ 10-50 mL/minute: Administer every 12-24 hours

Cl$_{cr}$ <10 mL/minute: Administer every 24 hours

Dialysis: Slightly dialyzable (5% to 20%) via hemo- and peritoneal dialysis or via continuous arteriovenous or venovenous hemofiltration; no supplemental dosage necessary

Dosing adjustment in hepatic impairment: Avoid use or maximum dose is 1 g/day

Administration Should be administered on an empty stomach (ie, 1 hour prior to, or 2 hours after meals) to increase total absorption. Administer at least 1-2 hours prior to, or 4 hours after antacid because aluminum and magnesium cations may chelate with tetracycline and reduce its total absorption.

Monitoring Parameters Renal, hepatic, and hematologic function test, temperature, WBC, cultures and sensitivity, appetite, mental status

Patient Information Take 1 hour before or 2 hours after meals with adequate amounts of fluid; avoid prolonged exposure to sunlight or sunlamps; avoid taking antacids, iron, or dairy products within 2 hours of taking tetracyclines; report persistent nausea, vomiting, yellow coloring of skin or eyes, dark urine, or pale stools

Dosage Forms CAP: 250 mg, 500 mg; (Wesmycin®): 250 mg. **SUSP, oral** (Sumycin®): 125 mg/5 mL (480 mL). **TAB** (Sumycin®): 250 mg, 500 mg

Thalidomide (tha LI doe mide)

U.S. Brand Names Thalomid®

Therapeutic Category Immunosuppressant Agent

Use Treatment and maintenance of cutaneous manifestations of erythema nodosum leprosum

Unlabeled/Investigational Use Treatment of Crohn's disease; treatment or prevention of graft-versus-host reactions after bone marrow transplantation; AIDS-related aphthous stomatitis; Behçet's syndrome; Waldenström's macroglobulinemia; Langerhans cell histiocytosis; may be effective in rheumatoid arthritis, discoid lupus erythematosus, and erythema multiforme

Restrictions Thalidomide is approved for marketing only under a special distribution program. This program, called the "System for Thalidomide Education and Prescribing Safety" (STEPS™), has been approved by the FDA. Prescribing and dispensing of thalidomide is restricted to prescribers and pharmacists registered with the program. Prior to dispensing, an authorization number must be obtained (1-888-423-5436) from Celgene (write authorization number on prescription). No more than a 4-week supply should be dispensed. Blister packs should be dispensed intact (do not repackage capsules). Prescriptions must be filled within 7 days.

Pregnancy Risk Factor X

Contraindications Hypersensitivity to thalidomide or any component of the formulation; neuropathy (peripheral); pregnancy or women in childbearing years unless alternative therapies are inappropriate and adequate precautions are taken to avoid pregnancy; patient unable to comply with STEPS™ program.

Warnings/Precautions Effective contraception must be used for at least 4 weeks before initiating therapy, during therapy, and for 4 weeks following discontinuation of thalidomide. Males (even those vasectomized) must use a latex condom during any sexual contact with women of childbearing age. May cause sedation, patients must be warned to use caution when performing tasks which require alertness. Use caution in patients with renal or hepatic impairment, neurological disorders, cardiovascular disease, or constipation.

Thalidomide has been associated with the development of peripheral neuropathy, which may be irreversible. Consider immediate discontinuation, if clinically appropriate, in patients who develop neuropathy. Use caution in patients with a history of seizures, concurrent therapy with drugs which alter seizure threshold, or conditions which predispose to seizures. May cause neutropenia; discontinue therapy if absolute neutrophil count decrease to <750/mm³. Use caution in patients with HIV infection; has been associated with increased viral loads.

May cause orthostasis and/or bradycardia; use with caution in patients with cardiovascular disease or in patients who would not tolerate transient hypotensive episodes. Thrombotic events have been reported in patients receiving thalidomide, generally in patients with other risk factors for thrombosis (neoplastic disease, inflammatory disease, or concurrent therapy with other drugs which may cause thrombosis). Safety and efficacy have not been established in children <12 years of age.

Common Adverse Reactions

Controlled clinical trials: ENL:

>10%:

Central nervous system: Somnolence (37.5%), headache (12.5%)

Dermatologic: Rash (20.8%)

1% to 10%:

Cardiovascular: Peripheral edema

Central nervous system: Dizziness (4.2%), vertigo (8.3%), chills, malaise (8.3%),

Dermatologic: Dermatitis (fungal) (4.2%), nail disorder (4.2%), pruritus (8.3%), rash (maculopapular) (4.2%)

Gastrointestinal (4.2%): Constipation, diarrhea, nausea, moniliasis, tooth pain, abdominal pain

Genitourinary: Impotence (8.2%)

Neuromuscular & skeletal: Asthenia (8.3%), pain (8.3%), back pain (4.2%), neck pain (4.2%), neck rigidity (4.2%), tremor (4.2%)

Respiratory (4.2%): Pharyngitis, rhinitis, sinusitis

HIV-seropositive:

General: An increased viral load has been noted in patients treated with thalidomide. This is of uncertain clinical significance - see monitoring

>10%:

Central nervous system: Somnolence (36% to 37%), dizziness (18.7% to 19.4%), fever (19.4% to 21.9%), headache (16.7% to 18.7%)

Dermatologic: Rash (25%), maculopapular rash (16.7% to 18.7%), acne (3.1% to 11.1%)

Gastrointestinal: AST increase (2.8% to 12.5%), diarrhea (11.1% to 18.7%), nausea (≤12.5%), oral moniliasis (6.3% to 11.1%)

Hematologic: Leukopenia (16.7% to 25%), anemia (5.6% to 12.5%)

Neuromuscular & skeletal: Paresthesia (5.6% to 15.6%), weakness (5.6% to 21.9%)

Miscellaneous: Diaphoresis (≤12.5%), lymphadenopathy (5.6% to 12.5%)

1% to 10%:

Cardiovascular: Peripheral edema (3.1% to 8.3%)

Central nervous system: Nervousness (2.8% to 9.4%), insomnia (≤9.4%), agitation (≤9.4%), chills (≤9.4%), neuropathy (up to 8% in HIV-seropositive patients)

Dermatologic: Dermatitis (fungal) (5.6% to 9.4%), nail disorder (≤3.1%), pruritus (2.8% to 6.3%)

Gastrointestinal: Anorexia (2.8% to 9.4%), constipation (2.8% to 9.4%), dry mouth (8.3% to 9.4%), flatulence (8.3% to 9.4%), multiple abnormalities LFTs (≤9.4%), abdominal pain (2.8% to 3.1%)

Neuromuscular & skeletal: Back pain (≤5%), pain (≤3.1%)

Respiratory: Pharyngitis (6.3% to 8.3%), sinusitis (3.1% to 8.3%)

Miscellaneous: Accidental injury (≤5.6%), infection (6.3% to 8.3%)

Drug Interactions

Increased Effect/Toxicity: Thalidomide may enhance the sedative activity of other drugs such as ethanol, barbiturates, reserpine, and chlorpromazine. Drugs which may cause peripheral neuropathy should be used with caution in patients receiving thalidomide. Women using any drug which may decrease the serum concentrations and/or efficacy of hormonal contraceptives must use 2 other methods of contraception or abstain from heterosexual contact.

Mechanism of Action A derivative of glutethimide; mode of action for immunosuppression is unclear; inhibition of neutrophil chemotaxis and decreased monocyte phagocytosis may occur; may cause 50% to 80% reduction of tumor necrosis factor - alpha

Pharmacodynamics/Kinetics

Distribution: V_d: 120 L

Protein binding: 55% to 66%

Metabolism: Nonenzymatic hydrolysis in plasma; forms multiple metabolites

Half-life elimination: 5-7 hours

Time to peak, plasma: 2-6 hours

Excretion: Urine (<1%)

Dosage Oral:

Cutaneous ENL:

Initiate dosing at 100-300 mg/day taken once daily at bedtime with water (at least 1 hour after evening meal)

Patients weighing <50 kg: Initiate at lower end of the dosing range

Severe cutaneous reaction or previously requiring high dose may be initiated at 400 mg/day; doses may be divided, but taken 1 hour after meals

Dosing should continue until active reaction subsides (usually at least 2 weeks), then tapered in 50 mg decrements every 2-4 weeks

Patients who flare during tapering or with a history or requiring prolonged maintenance should be maintained on the minimum dosage necessary to control the reaction. Efforts to taper should be repeated every 3-6 months, in increments of 50 mg every 2-4 weeks.

Behçet's syndrome (unlabeled use): 100-400 mg/day

Graft-vs-host reactions (unlabeled use): 100-1600 mg/day; usual initial dose: 200 mg 4 times/day for use up to 700 days

AIDS-related aphthous stomatitis (unlabeled use): 200 mg twice daily for 5 days, then 200 mg/day for up to 8 weeks

Discoid lupus erythematosus (unlabeled use): 100-400 mg/day; maintenance dose: 25-50 mg

Administration Avoid extensive handling of capsules; capsules should remain in blister pack until ingestion. If exposed to the powder content from broken capsules or body fluids from patients receiving thalidomide, the exposed area should be washed with soap and water.

Monitoring Parameters WBC with differential; signs of neuropathy monthly for the first 3 months, then periodically during treatment; consider monitoring of sensory nerve application potential amplitudes (at baseline and every 6 months) to detect asymptomatic neuropathy. In HIV-seropositive patients: viral load after 1 and 3 months, then every 3 months. Pregnancy testing is required within 24 hours of initiation of therapy, weekly during the first 4 weeks, then every 4 weeks in women with regular menstrual cycles or every 2 weeks in women with irregular menstrual cycles.

Reference Range Therapeutic plasma thalidomide levels in graft-vs-host reactions are 5-8 µg/mL, although it has been suggested that lower plasma levels (0.5-1.5 µg/mL) may be therapeutic; peak serum thalidomide level after a 200 mg dose: 1.2 µg/mL

Patient Information Thalidomide must be obtained via "STEPS™ Program" through Boston University. Effective contraception must be used for at least 1 month prior to beginning therapy, during therapy, and continued for 1 month after thalidomide has been discontinued. Two reliable forms of contraception must be used. Males must use a latex condom during sexual contact with women of childbearing age. Thalidomide may cause drowsiness and/or orthostatic hypotension. Patients should not donate blood. Patients should report signs of tingling, numbness, or pain in hands or feet.

Dosage Forms CAP: 50 mg

♦ **Theolair**™ *see* Theophylline Salts *on page 1210*

♦ **Theolair-SR**® **[DSC]** *see* Theophylline Salts *on page 1210*

♦ **Theolate** *see* Theophylline and Guaifenesin *on page 1210*

Theophylline and Guaifenesin (thee OFF i lin & gwye FEN e sin)

U.S. Brand Names Elixophyllin-GG®; Quibron®; Theolate

Synonyms Guaifenesin and Theophylline

Therapeutic Category Theophylline Derivative

Use Symptomatic treatment of bronchospasm associated with bronchial asthma, chronic bronchitis, and pulmonary emphysema

Pregnancy Risk Factor C

Dosage Adults: Oral: 16 mg/kg/day or 400 mg theophylline/day, in divided doses, every 6-8 hours

Dosage Forms CAP (Quibron®): Theophylline 150 mg and guaifenesin 90 mg. **LIQ** (Elixophyllin-GG®): Theophylline 100 mg and guaifenesin 100 mg per 15 mL (240 mL, 480 mL); (Theolate): Theophylline 150 mg and guaifenesin 90 mg per 15 mL (480 mL)

♦ **Theophylline Anhydrous** *see* Theophylline Salts *on page 1210*

♦ **Theophylline Ethylenediamine** *see* Theophylline Salts *on page 1210*

Theophylline Salts (thee OFF i lin salts)

U.S. Brand Names Elixophyllin®; Quibron®-T; Quibron®-T/SR; Theo-24®; Theochron®; Theolair™; Theolair-SR® [DSC]; T-Phyl®; Uniphyl®

Synonyms Aminophylline; Theophylline Anhydrous; Theophylline Ethylenediamine

Therapeutic Category Bronchodilator; Theophylline Derivative

Use Bronchodilator in reversible airway obstruction due to asthma, chronic bronchitis, and emphysema; for neonatal apnea/bradycardia

Pregnancy Risk Factor C

Contraindications Hypersensitivity to theophylline, ethylenediamine, or any component of the formulation

Warnings/Precautions If a patient develops signs and symptoms of theophylline toxicity (eg, persistent, repetitive vomiting), a serum theophylline level should be measured and subsequent doses held. Due to potential saturation of theophylline clearance at serum levels in or (in some patients) less than the therapeutic range, dosage adjustment should be made in small increments (maximum: 25%). Due to wider interpatient variability, theophylline serum level measurements must be used to optimize therapy and prevent serious toxicity. Use with caution in patients with peptic ulcer, hyperthyroidism, seizure disorders, hypertension, and patients with cardiac arrhythmias (excluding bradyarrhythmias).

Drug Interactions

Cytochrome P450 Effect:

    Aminophylline: **Substrate** of CYP1A2 (major), 2E1 (minor), 3A4 (minor)

    Theophylline: **Substrate** of CYP1A2 (major), 2C8/9 (minor), 2D6 (minor), 2E1 (major), 3A4 (major); **Inhibits** CYP1A2 (weak)

Increased Effect/Toxicity:

    Aminophylline: CYP1A2 inhibitors may increase the levels/effects of aminophylline; common inhibitors include amiodarone, fluvoxamine, ketoconazole, quinolone antibiotics, and rofecoxib.

    Theophylline: Changes in diet may affect the elimination of theophylline. The following may increase serum theophylline levels: propranolol, allopurinol (>600 mg/day), erythromycin, cimetidine, troleandomycin, ciprofloxacin (other quinolone antibiotics), oral contraceptives, beta-blockers, calcium channel blockers, corticosteroids, disulfiram, ephedrine, influenza virus vaccine, interferon, macrolides, mexiletine, thiabendazole, thyroid hormones, carbamazepine, isoniazid, and loop diuretics. Other inhibitors of cytochrome P450 1A2 may increase theophylline levels.

Decreased Effect:

    Aminophylline: CYP1A2 inducers may decrease the levels/effects of aminophylline; common inducers include aminoglutethimide, carbamazepine, phenobarbital, and rifampin.

    Theophylline: Changes in diet may affect the elimination of theophylline. Charcoal-broiled foods may increase elimination, reducing half-life by 50%. The following factors decrease theophylline serum levels: Smoking (cigarettes, marijuana), high protein/low carbohydrate diet, charcoal, phenytoin, phenobarbital, carbamazepine, rifampin, ritonavir, I.V. isoproterenol, aminoglutethimide, barbiturates, hydantoins, ketoconazole, sulfinpyrazone, isoniazid, loop diuretics, and sympathomimetics.

Mechanism of Action Causes bronchodilatation, diuresis, CNS and cardiac stimulation, and gastric acid secretion by blocking phosphodiesterase which increases tissue concentrations of cyclic adenine monophosphate (cAMP) which in turn promotes catecholamine stimulation of lipolysis, glycogenolysis, and gluconeogenesis and induces release of epinephrine from adrenal medulla cells

Pharmacodynamics/Kinetics Theophylline:

Absorption: Oral: Dosage form dependent

Distribution: 0.45 L/kg based on ideal body weight

Protein binding: 40%, primarily to albumin

Metabolism: Children >1 year and Adults: Hepatic; involves CYP1A2, 2E1 and 3A4; forms active metabolites (caffeine and 3-methylxanthine)

Half-life elimination: Highly variable and dependent upon age, liver function, cardiac function, lung disease, and smoking history

Time to peak, serum:

Oral: Immediate release: 1-2 hours

I.V.: Within 30 minutes

Excretion: Urine

Neonates: 50% unchanged

Children >3 months and Adults: 10% unchanged

Dosage Use ideal body weight for obese patients

I.V.: Initial: Maintenance infusion rates:

Infants 6-52 weeks: 0.008 (age in weeks) + 0.21 mg/kg/hour theophylline

Children >1 year and Adults:

Treatment of acute bronchospasm: I.V.: Loading dose (in patients not currently receiving aminophylline or theophylline): 6 mg/kg (based on aminophylline) given I.V. over 20-30 minutes; administration rate should not exceed 25 mg/minute (aminophylline). See table.

Approximate I.V. Theophylline Dosage for Treatment of Acute Bronchospasm

Group	Dosage for Next 12 h[1]	Dosage After 12 h[1]
Infants 6 wk - 6 mo	0.5 mg/kg/h	
Children 6 mo - 1 y	0.6-0.7 mg/kg/h	
Children 1-9 y	0.95 mg/kg/h (1.2 mg/kg/h)	0.79 mg/kg/h (1 mg/kg/h)
Children 9-16 y and young adult smokers	0.79 mg/kg/h (1 mg/kg/h)	0.63 mg/kg/h (0.8 mg/kg/h)
Healthy, nonsmoking adults	0.55 mg/kg/h (0.7 mg/kg/h)	0.39 mg/kg/h (0.5 mg/kg/h)
Older patients and patients with cor pulmonale	0.47 mg/kg/h (0.6 mg/kg/h)	0.24 mg/kg/h (0.3 mg/kg/h)
Patients with congestive heart failure or liver failure	0.39 mg/kg/h (0.5 mg/kg/h)	0.08-0.16 mg/kg/h (0.1-0.2 mg/kg/h)

[1]Equivalent hydrous aminophylline dosage indicated in parentheses.

Approximate I.V. maintenance dosages are based upon continuous infusions; bolus dosing (often used in children <6 months of age) may be determined by multiplying the hourly infusion rate by 24 hours and dividing by the desired number of doses/day; see table on next page.

Dosage should be adjusted according to serum level measurements during the first 12- to 24-hour period; see table on next page.

Oral theophylline: Initial dosage recommendation: Loading dose (to achieve a serum level of about 10 mcg/mL; loading doses should be given using a rapidly absorbed oral product **not** a sustained release product):

If no theophylline has been administered in the previous 24 hours: 4-6 mg/kg theophylline

If theophylline has been administered in the previous 24 hours: administer 1/2 loading dose or 2-3 mg/kg theophylline can be given in emergencies when serum levels are not available

(Continued)

Theophylline Salts *(Continued)*

Maintenance Dose for Acute Symptoms

Population Group	Oral Theophylline (mg/kg/day)	I.V. Aminophylline
Premature infant or newborn - 6 wk (for apnea/bradycardia)	4	5 mg/kg/day
6 wk - 6 mo	10	12 mg/kg/day or continuous I.V. infusion[1]
Infants 6 mo - 1 y	12-18	15 mg/kg/day or continuous I.V. infusion[1]
Children 1-9 y	20-24	1 mg/kg/h
Children 9-12 y, and adolescent daily smokers of cigarettes or marijuana, and otherwise healthy adult smokers <50 y	16	0.9 mg/kg/h
Adolescents 12-16 y (nonsmokers)	13	0.7 mg/kg/h
Otherwise healthy nonsmoking adults (including elderly patients)	10 (not to exceed 900 mg/day)	0.5 mg/kg/h
Cardiac decompensation, cor pulmonale, and/or liver dysfunction	5 (not to exceed 400 mg/day)	0.25 mg/kg/h

[1]For continuous I.V. infusion divide total daily dose by 24 = mg/kg/h.

Dosage Adjustment After Serum Theophylline Measurement

Serum Theophylline		Guidelines
Within normal limits	10-20 mcg/mL	Maintain dosage if tolerated. Recheck serum theophylline concentration at 6- to 12-month intervals.[1]
Too high	20-25 mcg/mL	Decrease doses by about 10%. Recheck serum theophylline concentration after 3 days and then at 6- to 12-month intervals.[1]
	25-30 mcg/mL	Skip next dose and decrease subsequent doses by about 25%. Recheck serum theophylline.
	>30 mcg/mL	Skip next 2 doses and decrease subsequent doses by 50%. Recheck serum theophylline.
Too low	7.5-10 mcg/mL	Increase dose by about 25%.[2] Recheck serum theophylline concentration after 3 days and then at 6- to 12-month intervals.[1]
	5-7.5 mcg/mL	Increase dose by about 25% to the nearest dose increment[2] and recheck serum theophylline for guidance in further dosage adjustment (another increase will probably be needed, but this provides a safety check).

[1]Finer adjustments in dosage may be needed for some patients.

[2]Dividing the daily dose into 3 doses administered at 8-hour intervals may be indicated if symptoms occur repeatedly at the end of a dosing interval.

From Weinberger M and Hendeles L, "Practical Guide to Using Theophylline," *J Resp Dis*, 1981,2:12-27.

Oral Theophylline Dosage for Bronchial Asthma[1]

Age (y)	Initial 3 Days	Second 3 Days	Steady-State Maintenance
<1	0.2 x (age in weeks) + 5		0.3 x (age in weeks) + 8
1-9	16 up to a maximum of 400 mg/24 h	20	22
9-12	16 up to a maximum of 400 mg/24 h	16 up to a maximum of 600 mg/24 h	20 up to a maximum of 800 mg/24 h
12-16	16 up to a maximum of 400 mg/24 h	16 up to a maximum of 600 mg/24 h	18 up to a maximum of 900 mg/24 h
Adults	400 mg/24 h	600 mg/24 h	900 mg/24 h

[1]Dose in mg/kg/24 hours of theophylline.

On the average, for every 1 mg/kg theophylline given, blood levels will rise 2 mcg/mL
Ideally, defer the loading dose if a serum theophylline concentration can be obtained rapidly.
However, if this is not possible, exercise clinical judgment. If the patient is not experiencing theophylline toxicity, this is unlikely to result in dangerous adverse effects.
See table on previous page.

Increasing dose: The dosage may be increased in approximately 25% increments at 2- to 3-day intervals so long as the drug is tolerated or until the maximum dose is reached

Maintenance dose: In newborns and infants, a fast-release oral product can be used. The total daily dose can be divided every 12 hours in newborns and every 6-8 hours in infants. In children and healthy adults, a slow-release product can be used. The total daily dose can be divided every 8-12 hours.

Administration

Aminophylline: Dilute with I.V. fluid to a concentration of 1 mg/mL and infuse over 20-30 minutes; maximum concentration: 25 mg/mL; maximum rate of infusion: 0.36 mg/kg/minute, and no greater than 25 mg/minute. I.M. administration is not recommended. Oral and I.V. should be administered around-the-clock rather than 4 times/day, 3 times/day, etc (ie, 12-6-12-6, not 9-1-5-9) to promote less variation in peak and trough serum levels.

Theophylline: Oral: Long-acting preparations should be taken with a full glass of water, swallowed whole, or cut in half if scored. Do **not** crush. Extended release capsule forms may be opened and the contents sprinkled on soft foods; do **not** chew beads.

Patient Information Oral preparations may be taken with a full glass of water; capsule forms may be opened and sprinkled on soft foods; do not chew beads; notify physician if nausea, vomiting, severe GI pain, restlessness, or irregular heartbeat occurs; do not drink or eat large quantities of caffeine-containing beverages or food (colas, coffee, chocolate); remain in bed for 15-20 minutes after inserting suppository; do not chew or crush enteric coated or sustained release products; take at regular intervals; notify physician if insomnia, nervousness, irritability, palpitations, seizures occur; do not change brands or doses without consulting physician

♦ **Theracort® [OTC]** *see* Hydrocortisone *on page 632*

♦ **TheraCys®** *see* BCG Vaccine *on page 148*

♦ **Thera-Flu® Cold and Sore Throat Night Time [OTC]** *see* Acetaminophen, Chlorpheniramine, and Pseudoephedrine *on page 28*

♦ **Thera-Flur-N®** *see* Fluoride *on page 535*

♦ **Thera-Flu® Severe Cold Non-Drowsy [OTC] [DSC]** *see* Acetaminophen, Dextromethorphan, and Pseudoephedrine *on page 28*

♦ **Theragran® Heart Right™ [OTC]** *see* Vitamins (Multiple/Oral) *on page 1312*

♦ **Theragran-M® Advanced Formula [OTC]** *see* Vitamins (Multiple/Oral) *on page 1312*

♦ **Theramycin Z®** *see* Erythromycin *on page 453*

♦ **Therapeutic Multivitamins** *see* Vitamins (Multiple/Oral) *on page 1312*

♦ **Thermazene®** *see* Silver Sulfadiazine *on page 1137*

Thiabendazole (thye a BEN da zole)

U.S. Brand Names Mintezol®

Synonyms Tiabendazole

Therapeutic Category Anthelmintic

Use Treatment of strongyloidiasis, cutaneous larva migrans, visceral larva migrans, dracunculiasis, trichinosis, and mixed helminthic infections

Unlabeled/Investigational Use Cutaneous larva migrans (topical application)

Pregnancy Risk Factor C

Contraindications Hypersensitivity to thiabendazole or any component of the formulation; not for use as prophylactic treatment of enterobiasis (pinworm) infestation

Warnings/Precautions Use with caution in patients with renal or hepatic impairment, malnutrition or anemia, or dehydration. Causes sedation; caution must be used in performing tasks which require alertness. Not suitable treatment for mixed infections with ascaris. Ophthalmic changes may occur and persist >1 year. Safety and efficacy are limited in children <14 kg (30 lb).

Common Adverse Reactions Frequency not defined.

Central nervous system: Seizures, hallucinations, delirium, dizziness, drowsiness, headache, chills

Dermatologic: Rash, Stevens-Johnson syndrome, pruritus, angioedema

Endocrine & metabolic: Hyperglycemia

Gastrointestinal: Anorexia, diarrhea, nausea, vomiting, drying of mucous membranes, abdominal pain

Genitourinary: Malodor of urine, hematuria, crystalluria, enuresis

Hematologic: Leukopenia

Hepatic: Jaundice, cholestasis, hepatic failure, hepatotoxicity

Neuromuscular & skeletal: Numbness, incoordination

Ocular: Abnormal sensation in eyes, blurred vision, dry eyes, Sicca syndrome, vision decreased, xanthopsia

Otic: Tinnitus

Renal: Nephrotoxicity

Miscellaneous: Anaphylaxis, hypersensitivity reactions, lymphadenopathy

Drug Interactions

Cytochrome P450 Effect: Substrate of CYP1A2 (minor); **Inhibits** CYP1A2 (strong)

Increased Effect/Toxicity: Increased levels of theophylline and other xanthines.

Mechanism of Action Inhibits helminth-specific mitochondrial fumarate reductase

(Continued)

Thiabendazole *(Continued)*

Pharmacodynamics/Kinetics
Absorption: Rapid and well absorbed
Metabolism: Rapidly hepatic; metabolized to 5-hydroxy form
Half-life elimination: 1.2 hours
Time to peak, plasma: Oral suspension: Within 1-2 hours
Excretion: Urine (90%) and feces (5%) primarily as conjugated metabolites

Dosage Purgation is not required prior to use; drinking of fruit juice aids in expulsion of worms by removing the mucous to which the intestinal tapeworms attach themselves.

Children and Adults:
Oral: 50 mg/kg/day divided every 12 hours (if >68 kg: 1.5 g/dose); maximum dose: 3 g/day
Treatment duration:
Strongyloidiasis, ascariasis, uncinariasis: For 2 consecutive days
Cutaneous larva migrans: For 2 consecutive days; if active lesions are still present 2 days after completion, a second course of treatment is recommended.
Visceral larva migrans: For 7 consecutive days
Trichinosis: For 2-4 consecutive days; optimal dosage not established
Dracunculosis: 50-75 mg/kg/day divided every 12 hours for 3 days
Topical (unlabeled): Cutaneous larva migrans: Apply directly to larval tracks 2-3 times/day for up to 2 weeks; application frequencies may range from 2-6 times/day. **Note:** Not available as a topical formulation; oral suspension (10% to 15%) has been used topically, as well as a number of extemporaneous formulations.

Dosing comments in renal/hepatic impairment: Use with caution

Patient Information Take after meals, chew chewable tablet well; may decrease alertness, avoid driving or operating machinery; drinking of fruit juice aids in expulsion of worms by removing the mucous to which the intestinal tapeworms attach themselves

Dosage Forms SUSP, oral: 500 mg/5 mL (120 mL). **TAB, chewable:** 500 mg

- **Thiamazole** *see* Methimazole *on page 813*
- **Thiamilate® [OTC]** *see* Thiamine *on page 1214*

Thiamine *(THYE a min)*

U.S. Brand Names Thiamilate® [OTC]

Synonyms Aneurine Hydrochloride; Thiamine Hydrochloride; Thiaminium Chloride Hydrochloride; Vitamin B_1

Therapeutic Category Vitamin, Water Soluble

Use Treatment of thiamine deficiency including beriberi, Wernicke's encephalopathy syndrome, and peripheral neuritis associated with pellagra, alcoholic patients with altered sensorium; various genetic metabolic disorders

Pregnancy Risk Factor A/C (dose exceeding RDA recommendation)

Contraindications Hypersensitivity to thiamine or any component of the formulation

Warnings/Precautions Use with caution with parenteral route (especially I.V.) of administration

Mechanism of Action An essential coenzyme in carbohydrate metabolism by combining with adenosine triphosphate to form thiamine pyrophosphate

Pharmacodynamics/Kinetics
Absorption: Oral: Adequate; I.M.: Rapid and complete
Excretion: Urine (as unchanged drug and as pyrimidine after body storage sites become saturated)

Dosage
Recommended daily allowance:
<6 months: 0.3 mg
6 months to 1 year: 0.4 mg
1-3 years: 0.7 mg
4-6 years: 0.9 mg
7-10 years: 1 mg
11-14 years: 1.1-1.3 mg
>14 years: 1-1.5 mg
Thiamine deficiency (beriberi):
Children: 10-25 mg/dose I.M. or I.V. daily (if critically ill), or 10-50 mg/dose orally every day for 2 weeks, then 5-10 mg/dose orally daily for 1 month
Adults: 5-30 mg/dose I.M. or I.V. 3 times/day (if critically ill); then orally 5-30 mg/day in single or divided doses 3 times/day for 1 month
Wernicke's encephalopathy: Adults: Initial: 100 mg I.V., then 50-100 mg/day I.M. or I.V. until consuming a regular, balanced diet
Dietary supplement (depends on caloric or carbohydrate content of the diet):
Infants: 0.3-0.5 mg/day
Children: 0.5-1 mg/day
Adults: 1-2 mg/day
Note: The above doses can be found in multivitamin preparations
Metabolic disorders: Oral: Adults: 10-20 mg/day (dosages up to 4 g/day in divided doses have been used)

Administration Parenteral form may be administered by I.M. or slow I.V. injection

Reference Range Therapeutic: 1.6-4 mg/dL

Patient Information Dietary sources include legumes, pork, beef, whole grains, yeast, fresh vegetables; a deficiency state can occur in as little 3 weeks following total dietary absence

Dosage Forms INJ, solution: 100 mg/mL (2 mL). TAB: 50 mg, 100 mg, 250 mg, 500 mg.
TAB, enteric coated (Thiamilate®): 20 mg

♦ Thiamine Hydrochloride *see* Thiamine *on page 1214*
♦ Thiaminium Chloride Hydrochloride *see* Thiamine *on page 1214*

Thiethylperazine (thye eth il PER a zeen)

U.S. Brand Names Torecan®
Synonyms Thiethylperazine Maleate
Therapeutic Category Antiemetic; Phenothiazine Derivative
Use Relief of nausea and vomiting
Unlabeled/Investigational Use Treatment of vertigo
Pregnancy Risk Factor X
Contraindications Hypersensitivity to thiethylperazine or any component of the formulation (cross-sensitivity to other phenothiazines may exist); comatose states; pregnancy
Warnings/Precautions Reduce or discontinue if extrapyramidal symptoms occur; safety and efficacy in children <12 years of age have not been established; postural hypotension may occur after I.M. injection; the injectable form contains sulfite which may cause allergic reactions in some patients; use caution in patients with narrow-angle glaucoma
Common Adverse Reactions
>10%:
  Central nervous system: Drowsiness, dizziness
  Gastrointestinal: Xerostomia
  Respiratory: Dry nose
1% to 10%:
  Cardiovascular: Tachycardia, orthostatic hypotension
  Central nervous system: Confusion, convulsions, extrapyramidal symptoms, tardive dyskinesia, fever, headache
  Hematologic: Agranulocytosis
  Hepatic: Cholestatic jaundice
  Otic: Tinnitus
Drug Interactions
  Increased Effect/Toxicity: Increased effect with CNS depressants (eg, anesthetics, opiates, tranquilizers, alcohol), lithium, atropine, epinephrine, MAO inhibitors, TCAs
Mechanism of Action Blocks postsynaptic mesolimbic dopaminergic receptors in the brain; exhibits a strong alpha-adrenergic blocking effect and depresses the release of hypothalamic and hypophyseal hormones; acts directly on chemoreceptor trigger zone and vomiting center; may also inhibit impulses from peripheral autonomic afferents to the vomiting center
Pharmacodynamics/Kinetics
  Onset of action: Antiemetic: ~30 minutes
  Duration: ~4 hours
Dosage Children >12 years and Adults:
  Oral, I.M., I.V.: 10 mg 1-6 times/day as needed
  Hemodialysis: Not dialyzable (0% to 5%)
  Dosing comments in hepatic impairment: Use with caution
Administration Inject I.M. deeply into large muscle mass, patient should be lying down and remain so for at least 1 hour after administration; although not generally recommended, thiethylperazine can be given as an I.V. infusion over 15-30 minutes; should **not** be given I.V. push; S.C. administration not recommended
Patient Information May cause drowsiness, impair judgment and coordination; may cause photosensitivity; avoid excessive sunlight; report involuntary movements or feelings of restlessness
Dosage Forms INJ, solution [DSC]: 5 mg/mL (2 mL). **TAB:** 10 mg

♦ Thiethylperazine Maleate *see* Thiethylperazine *on page 1215*

Thioguanine (thye oh GWAH neen)

Synonyms 2-Amino-6-Mercaptopurine; NSC-752; TG; 6-TG; 6-Thioguanine; Tioguanine
Therapeutic Category Antineoplastic Agent, Antimetabolite (Purine)
Use Treatment of acute myelogenous (nonlymphocytic) leukemia; treatment of chronic myelogenous leukemia and granulocytic leukemia
Pregnancy Risk Factor D
Contraindications Hypersensitivity to thioguanine or any component of the formulation; pregnancy
Warnings/Precautions The U.S. Food and Drug Administration (FDA) currently recommends that procedures for proper handling and disposal of antineoplastic agents be considered. Use with caution and reduce dose of thioguanine in patients with renal or hepatic impairment; thioguanine is potentially carcinogenic and teratogenic; myelosuppression may be delayed. Caution with history of previous therapy resistance with either thioguanine or mercaptopurine (there is usually complete cross resistance between these two).
Common Adverse Reactions
>10%:
  Hematologic: Myelosuppressive:
    WBC: Moderate
    Platelets: Moderate
    Onset (days): 7-10
    Nadir (days): 14
(Continued)

Thioguanine *(Continued)*

Recovery (days): 21
1% to 10%:
 Dermatologic: Skin rash
 Endocrine & metabolic: Hyperuricemia
 Gastrointestinal: Mild nausea or vomiting, anorexia, stomatitis, diarrhea
 Neuromuscular & skeletal: Unsteady gait

Drug Interactions
 Increased Effect/Toxicity: Allopurinol can be used in full doses with thioguanine unlike mercaptopurine. Use with busulfan may cause hepatotoxicity and esophageal varices. Aminosalicylates (olsalazine, mesalamine, sulfasalazine) may inhibit TPMT, increasing toxicity/myelosuppression of thioguanine.

Mechanism of Action Purine analog that is incorporated into DNA and RNA resulting in the blockage of synthesis and metabolism of purine nucleotides

Pharmacodynamics/Kinetics
 Absorption: 30% (highly variable)
 Distribution: Crosses placenta
 Metabolism: Rapidly and extensively hepatic to 2-amino-6-methylthioguanine (active) and inactive compounds
 Half-life elimination: Terminal: 11 hours
 Time to peak, serum: Within 8 hours
 Excretion: Urine

Dosage Total daily dose can be given at one time; is sometimes ordered as 6-thioguanine, with 6 being part of the drug name and not a unit or strength

 Oral (refer to individual protocols):
  Infants and Children <3 years: Combination drug therapy for acute nonlymphocytic leukemia: 3.3 mg/kg/day in divided doses twice daily for 4 days
  Children and Adults: 2-3 mg/kg/day calculated to nearest 20 mg or 75-200 mg/m^2/day in 1-2 divided doses for 5-7 days or until remission is attained

  Dosing comments in renal or hepatic impairment: Reduce dose

Monitoring Parameters CBC with differential and platelet count, liver function tests, hemoglobin, hematocrit, serum uric acid

Patient Information You may experience nausea and vomiting, diarrhea, or loss of appetite (frequent small meals may help/request medication) or weakness or lethargy (use caution when driving or engaging in tasks requiring alertness until response to drug is known). Use good oral care to reduce incidence of mouth sores. May cause headache (request medication). Report signs or symptoms of infection (eg, fever, chills, sore throat, burning urination, fatigue), bleeding (eg, tarry stools, easy bruising), vision changes, unresolved mouth sores, nausea or vomiting, CNS changes (hallucinations), or respiratory difficulty. Avoid crowds or exposure to infected persons; you will be susceptible to infection. The drug may cause permanent sterility and may cause birth defects. Contraceptive measures should be used during therapy. The drug may be excreted in breast milk, therefore, an alternative form of feeding your baby should be used.

Dosage Forms INJ, powder for reconstitution: 75 mg [investigational in U.S.]. **TAB** [scored]: 40 mg

♦ **6-Thioguanine** *see* Thioguanine *on page 1215*

Thiopental *(thye oh PEN tal)*

U.S. Brand Names Pentothal®
Synonyms Thiopental Sodium
Therapeutic Category Anticonvulsant, Barbiturate; Barbiturate; General Anesthetic; Sedative
Use Induction of anesthesia; adjunct for intubation in head injury patients; control of convulsive states; treatment of elevated intracranial pressure
Restrictions C-III
Pregnancy Risk Factor C
Contraindications Hypersensitivity to thiopental, barbiturates, or any component of the formulation; status asthmaticus; severe cardiovascular disease; porphyria (variegate or acute intermittent); should not be administered by intra-arterial injection
Warnings/Precautions Laryngospasm or bronchospasms may occur; use with extreme caution in patients with reactive airway diseases (asthma or COPD). Use with caution when the hypnotic may be prolonged or potentiated (excessive premedication, Addison's disease, hepatic or renal dysfunction, myxedema, increased blood urea, severe anemia, or myasthenia gravis). Potential for drug dependency exists, abrupt cessation may precipitate withdrawal, including status epilepticus in epileptic patients. Use caution in patients with unstable aneurysms, cardiovascular disease, renal impairment, or hepatic disease. Use caution in elderly, debilitated, or pediatric patients. May cause paradoxical responses, including agitation and hyperactivity, particularly in acute pain and pediatric patients. Effects with other sedative drugs or ethanol may be potentiated. May cause respiratory depression or hypotension; use with caution in hemodynamically unstable patients (hypotension or shock) or patients with respiratory disease. Repeated dosing or continuous infusions may cause cumulative effects. Extravasation or intra-arterial injection causes necrosis due to pH of 10.6, ensure patient has intravenous access.
Common Adverse Reactions Frequency not defined.
 Cardiovascular: Bradycardia, hypotension, syncope

Central nervous system: Drowsiness, lethargy, CNS excitation or depression, impaired judgment, "hangover" effect, confusion, somnolence, agitation, hyperkinesia, ataxia, nervousness, headache, insomnia, nightmares, hallucinations, anxiety, dizziness, shivering

Dermatologic: Rash, exfoliative dermatitis, Stevens-Johnson syndrome

Gastrointestinal: Nausea, vomiting, constipation

Hematologic: Agranulocytosis, thrombocytopenia, megaloblastic anemia, immune hemolytic anemia (rare)

Local: Pain at injection site, thrombophlebitis with I.V. use

Renal: Oliguria

Respiratory: Laryngospasm, respiratory depression, apnea (especially with rapid I.V. use), hypoventilation, apnea, sneezing, coughing, bronchospasm

Miscellaneous: Gangrene with inadvertent intra-arterial injection, anaphylaxis, anaphylactic reactions

Drug Interactions

Increased Effect/Toxicity: In chronic use, barbiturates are potent inducers of CYP isoenzymes resulting in multiple interactions with medication groups. When used for limited periods, thiopental is not likely to interact via this mechanism. Sedative effects and/or respiratory depression with barbiturates may be additive with other CNS depressants; includes ethanol, sedatives, antidepressants, narcotic analgesics, and benzodiazepines. Felbamate may inhibit the metabolism of barbiturates and barbiturates may increase the metabolism of felbamate. Barbiturates may enhance the nephrotoxic effects of methoxyflurane

Mechanism of Action Short-acting barbiturate with sedative, hypnotic, and anticonvulsant properties. Barbiturates depress the sensory cortex, decrease motor activity, alter cerebellar function, and produce drowsiness, sedation, and hypnosis. In high doses, barbiturates exhibit anticonvulsant activity; barbiturates produce dose-dependent respiratory depression.

Pharmacodynamics/Kinetics

Onset of action: Anesthetic: I.V.: 30-60 seconds

Duration: 5-30 minutes

Distribution: V_d: 1.4 L/kg

Protein binding: 72% to 86%

Metabolism: Hepatic, primarily to inactive metabolites but pentobarbital is also formed

Half-life elimination: 3-11.5 hours; decreased in children

Dosage I.V.:

Induction anesthesia:

Infants: 5-8 mg/kg

Children 1-12 years: 5-6 mg/kg

Adults: 3-5 mg/kg

Maintenance anesthesia:

Children: 1 mg/kg as needed

Adults: 25-100 mg as needed

Increased intracranial pressure: Children and Adults: 1.5-5 mg/kg/dose; repeat as needed to control intracranial pressure

Seizures:

Children: 2-3 mg/kg/dose; repeat as needed

Adults: 75-250 mg/dose; repeat as needed

Dosing adjustment in renal impairment: Cl_{cr} <10 mL/minute: Administer at 75% of normal dose

Note: Accumulation may occur with chronic dosing due to lipid solubility; prolonged recovery may result from redistribution of thiopental from fat stores

Administration Rapid I.V. injection may cause hypotension or decreased cardiac output

Monitoring Parameters Respiratory rate, heart rate, blood pressure

Reference Range Therapeutic: Hypnotic: 1-5 µg/mL (SI: 4.1-20.7 µmol/L); Coma: 30-100 µg/mL (SI: 124-413 µmol/L); Anesthesia: 7-130 µg/mL (SI: 29-536 µmol/L); Toxic: >10 µg/mL (SI: >41 µmol/L)

Dosage Forms INJ, powder for reconstitution: 500 mg, 2.5 g, 5 g; (Pentothal®): 250 mg, 400 mg, 500 mg, 1 g, 2.5 g, 5 g

♦ **Thiopental Sodium** see Thiopental on page 1216

♦ **Thiophosphoramide** see Thiotepa on page 1219

♦ **Thioplex®** see Thiotepa on page 1219

Thioridazine (thye oh RID a zeen)

Related Information

Antipsychotic Agents Comparison on page 1364

U.S. Brand Names Mellaril® [DSC]; Thioridazine Intensol™

Synonyms Thioridazine Hydrochloride

Therapeutic Category Antipsychotic Agent, Phenothiazine; Antipsychotic Agent, Phenothiazine, Piperidine; Phenothiazine Derivative

Use Management of schizophrenic patients who fail to respond adequately to treatment with other antipsychotic drugs, either because of insufficient effectiveness or the inability to achieve an effective dose due to intolerable adverse effects from those medications

Unlabeled/Investigational Use Psychosis

Pregnancy Risk Factor C

Contraindications Hypersensitivity to thioridazine or any component of the formulation (cross-reactivity between phenothiazines may occur); severe CNS depression; circulatory

(Continued)

Thioridazine *(Continued)*

collapse; severe hypotension; bone marrow suppression; blood dyscrasias; coma; in combination with other drugs that are known to prolong the QT_c interval; in patients with congenital long QT syndrome or a history of cardiac arrhythmias; concurrent use with medications that inhibit the metabolism of thioridazine (fluoxetine, paroxetine, fluvoxamine, propranolol, pindolol); patients known to have genetic defect leading to reduced levels of activity of CYP2D6

Warnings/Precautions Oral formulations may cause stomach upset; may cause thermoregulatory changes; use caution in patients with narrow-angle glaucoma; doses of 1 g/day frequently cause pigmentary retinopathy; thioridazine has dose-related effects on ventricular repolarization leading to QT_c prolongation, a potentially life-threatening effect. As a result, it should be reserved for patients whose schizophrenia has failed to respond to adequate trials of other antipsychotic drugs. Use with caution in Parkinson's disease; hemodynamic instability; bone marrow suppression; predisposition to seizures; subcortical brain damage; severe cardiac, hepatic, renal, or respiratory disease. Esophageal dysmotility and aspiration have been associated with antipsychotic use - use with caution in patients at risk of pneumonia (ie, Alzheimer's disease). Caution in breast cancer or other prolactin-dependent tumors (may elevate prolactin levels). May alter temperature regulation or mask toxicity of other drugs due to antiemetic effects.

Phenothiazines may cause anticholinergic effects (confusion, agitation, constipation, xerostomia, blurred vision, urinary retention); therefore, they should be used with caution in patients with decreased gastrointestinal motility, urinary retention, BPH, xerostomia, or visual problems. Conditions which also may be exacerbated by cholinergic blockade include narrow-angle glaucoma (screening is recommended) and worsening of myasthenia gravis. Relative to other neuroleptics, thioridazine has a high potency of cholinergic blockade.

May cause extrapyramidal reactions, including pseudoparkinsonism, acute dystonic reactions, akathisia, and tardive dyskinesia (risk of these reactions is low relative to other neuroleptics). May be associated with neuroleptic malignant syndrome (NMS).

Common Adverse Reactions Frequency not defined.

Cardiovascular: Hypotension, orthostatic hypotension, peripheral edema, ECG changes

Central nervous system: EPS (pseudoparkinsonism, akathisia, dystonias, tardive dyskinesia), dizziness, drowsiness, neuroleptic malignant syndrome (NMS), impairment of temperature regulation, lowering of seizures threshold, seizure

Dermatologic: Increased sensitivity to sun, rash, discoloration of skin (blue-gray)

Endocrine & metabolic: Changes in menstrual cycle, changes in libido, breast pain, galactorrhea, amenorrhea

Gastrointestinal: Constipation, weight gain, nausea, vomiting, stomach pain, xerostomia, nausea, vomiting, diarrhea

Genitourinary: Difficulty in urination, ejaculatory disturbances, urinary retention, priapism

Hematologic: Agranulocytosis, leukopenia

Hepatic: Cholestatic jaundice, hepatotoxicity

Neuromuscular & skeletal: Tremor

Ocular: Pigmentary retinopathy, blurred vision, cornea and lens changes

Respiratory: Nasal congestion

Drug Interactions

Cytochrome P450 Effect: Substrate of CYP2C19 (minor), 2D6 (major); **Inhibits** CYP1A2 (weak), 2C8/9 (weak), 2D6 (moderate), 2E1 (weak)

Increased Effect/Toxicity: Concurrent use of phenothiazines with an antihypertensive may produce additive hypotensive effects (particularly orthostasis). Concurrent use of beta-blockers may increase the risk of arrhythmia; propranolol and pindolol are **contraindicated**. Phenothiazines inhibit the ability of bromocriptine to lower serum prolactin concentrations. Serum concentrations of carvedilol or valproic acid may be increased by phenothiazines. The sedative effects of CNS depressants or ethanol may be additive with phenothiazines. Phenothiazines and trazodone may produce additive hypotensive effects Concurrent use of phenothiazines and tricyclic antidepressants may produce increased toxicity or altered therapeutic response. Metoclopramide may increase risk of extrapyramidal symptoms (EPS).

QT_c-prolonging agents: Effects on QT_c interval may be additive with phenothiazines, increasing the risk of malignant arrhythmias; includes type Ia antiarrhythmics, TCAs, and some quinolone antibiotics (sparfloxacin, moxifloxacin and gatifloxacin). **These agents are contraindicated with thioridazine.** Potassium depleting agents may increase the risk of serious arrhythmias with thioridazine (includes many diuretics, aminoglycosides, and amphotericin).

CYP2D6 inhibitors may increase the levels/effects of thioridazine; example inhibitors include chlorpromazine, delavirdine, fluoxetine, miconazole, paroxetine, pergolide, quinidine, quinine, ritonavir, and ropinirole. **Thioridazine is contraindicated with inhibitors of this enzyme. Concurrent use with fluvoxamine is contraindicated.**

Phenothiazines may produce neurotoxicity with lithium; this is a rare effect. Rare cases of respiratory paralysis have been reported with concurrent use of phenothiazines and polypeptide antibiotics. Naltrexone in combination with thioridazine has been reported to cause lethargy and somnolence. Phenylpropanolamine has been reported to result in cardiac arrhythmias when combined with thioridazine.

Decreased Effect: Aluminum salts may decrease the absorption of phenothiazines. The efficacy of amphetamines may be diminished by antipsychotics; in addition, amphetamines may increase psychotic symptoms; avoid concurrent use. Anticholinergics may inhibit the therapeutic response to phenothiazines and excess anticholinergic effects may occur (includes benztropine, trihexyphenidyl, biperiden, and drugs with significant anticholinergic activity). Chlorpromazine (and possibly other low potency antipsychotics) may diminish the pressor effects of epinephrine. The antihypertensive effects of guanethidine or guanadrel may be inhibited by phenothiazines. Phenothiazines may inhibit the antiparkinsonian effect of levodopa. Enzyme inducers may enhance the hepatic metabolism of phenothiazines; larger doses may be required; includes rifampin, rifabutin, barbiturates, phenytoin, and cigarette smoking.

Mechanism of Action Blocks postsynaptic mesolimbic dopaminergic receptors in the brain; exhibits a strong alpha-adrenergic blocking effect and depresses the release of hypothalamic and hypophyseal hormones

Pharmacodynamics/Kinetics
Duration: 4-5 days
Half-life elimination: 21-25 hours
Time to peak, serum: ~1 hour

Dosage Oral:
Children >2-12 years: Range: 0.5-3 mg/kg/day in 2-3 divided doses; usual: 1 mg/kg/day; maximum: 3 mg/kg/day
Behavior problems: Initial: 10 mg 2-3 times/day, increase gradually
Severe psychoses: Initial: 25 mg 2-3 times/day, increase gradually
Children >12 years and Adults:
Schizophrenia/psychoses: Initial: 50-100 mg 3 times/day with gradual increments as needed and tolerated; maximum: 800 mg/day in 2-4 divided doses; if >65 years, initial dose: 10 mg 3 times/day
Depressive disorders/dementia: Initial: 25 mg 3 times/day; maintenance dose: 20-200 mg/day
Elderly: Behavioral symptoms associated with dementia: Oral: Initial: 10-25 mg 1-2 times/day; increase at 4- to 7-day intervals by 10-25 mg/day; increase dose intervals (qd, bid, etc) as necessary to control response or side effects. Maximum daily dose: 400 mg; gradual increases (titration) may prevent some side effects or decrease their severity.
Hemodialysis: Not dialyzable (0% to 5%)

Administration Oral concentrate must be diluted in 2-4 oz of liquid (eg, water, fruit juice, carbonated drinks, milk, or pudding) before administration. Do not take antacid within 2 hours of taking drug. Thioridazine concentrate is not compatible with carbamazepine suspension; schedule dosing at least 1-2 hours apart from each other. **Note:** Avoid skin contact with oral suspension or solution; may cause contact dermatitis.

Monitoring Parameters Baseline and periodic ECG; vital signs; serum potassium, lipid profile, fasting blood glucose/Hgb A_{1c}; BMI; mental status, abnormal involuntary movement scale (AIMS); periodic eye exam; do not initiate if QT_c >450 msec

Reference Range Toxic: >1 mg/mL; lethal: 2-8 mg/dL

Patient Information Oral concentrate must be diluted in 2-4 oz of liquid (water, fruit juice, carbonated drinks, milk, or pudding); do not take antacid within 1 hour of taking drug; avoid excess sun exposure; may cause drowsiness, restlessness, avoid alcohol and other CNS depressants; do not alter dosage or discontinue without consulting prescriber; yearly eye exams are necessary; might discolor urine (pink or reddish brown)

Dosage Forms SOLN, oral concentrate (Thioridazine Intensol™): 30 mg/mL (120 mL); 100 mg/mL (120 mL). **TAB:** 10 mg, 15 mg, 25 mg, 50 mg, 100 mg, 150 mg, 200 mg

♦ **Thioridazine Hydrochloride** *see* Thioridazine *on page 1217*
♦ **Thioridazine Intensol™** *see* Thioridazine *on page 1217*
♦ **Thiosulfuric Acid Disodium Salt** *see* Sodium Thiosulfate *on page 1152*

Thiotepa (thye oh TEP a)

U.S. Brand Names Thioplex®
Synonyms TESPA; Thiophosphoramide; Triethylenethiophosphoramide; TSPA
Therapeutic Category Antineoplastic Agent, Alkylating Agent
Use Treatment of superficial tumors of the bladder; palliative treatment of adenocarcinoma of breast or ovary; lymphomas and sarcomas; controlling intracavitary effusions caused by metastatic tumors; I.T. use: CNS leukemia/lymphoma, CNS metastases

Pregnancy Risk Factor D

Contraindications Hypersensitivity to thiotepa or any component of the formulation; severe myelosuppression with leukocyte count <3000/mm^3 or platelet count <150,000 mm^3, except in stem cell transplant; pregnancy

Warnings/Precautions The U.S. Food and Drug Administration (FDA) currently recommends that procedures for proper handling and disposal of antineoplastic agents be considered. The drug is potentially mutagenic, carcinogenic, and teratogenic. Reduce dosage in patients with hepatic, renal, or bone marrow damage.

Common Adverse Reactions
>10%:
Hematopoietic: Dose-limiting toxicity which is dose-related and cumulative; moderate to severe leukopenia and severe thrombocytopenia have occurred. Anemia and pancytopenia may become fatal, so careful hematologic monitoring is required; intravesical administration may cause bone marrow suppression as well.
Hematologic: Myelosuppressive:
WBC: Moderate
Platelets: Severe
Onset: 7-10 days
(Continued)

Thiotepa *(Continued)*

Nadir: 14 days
Recovery: 28 days
Local: Pain at injection site
1% to 10%:
Central nervous system: Dizziness, fever, headache
Dermatologic: Alopecia, rash, pruritus, hyperpigmentation with high-dose therapy
Endocrine & metabolic: Hyperuricemia
Gastrointestinal: Anorexia, nausea and vomiting rarely occur
Emetic potential: Low (<10%)
Genitourinary: Hemorrhagic cystitis
Renal: Hematuria
Miscellaneous: Tightness of the throat, allergic reactions

Drug Interactions

Cytochrome P450 Effect: Inhibits CYP2B6 (weak)

Increased Effect/Toxicity: Other alkylating agents or irradiation used concomitantly with thiotepa intensifies toxicity rather than enhancing therapeutic response. Prolonged muscular paralysis and respiratory depression may occur when neuromuscular blocking agents are administered. Succinylcholine and other neuromuscular blocking agents' action can be prolonged due to thiotepa inhibiting plasma pseudocholinesterase.

Mechanism of Action

Alkylating agent that reacts with DNA phosphate groups to produce cross-linking of DNA strands leading to inhibition of DNA, RNA, and protein synthesis; mechanism of action has not been explored as thoroughly as the other alkylating agents, it is presumed that the aziridine rings open and react as nitrogen mustard; reactivity is enhanced at a lower pH

Pharmacodynamics/Kinetics

Absorption: Intracavitary instillation: Unreliable (10% to 100%) through bladder mucosa; I.M.: variable
Metabolism: Extensively hepatic
Half-life elimination: Terminal (dose-dependent clearance): 109 minutes
Excretion: Urine (as metabolites and unchanged drug)

Dosage

Refer to individual protocols; dosing must be based on the clinical and hematologic response of the patient
Children: Sarcomas: I.V.: 25-65 mg/m² as a single dose every 21 days
Adults:
I.M., I.V., S.C.: 30-60 mg/m² once per week
I.V. doses of 0.3-0.4 mg/kg by rapid I.V. administration every 1-4 weeks, or 0.2 mg/kg or 6-8 mg/m²/day for 4-5 days every 2-4 weeks
High-dose therapy for bone marrow transplant: I.V.: 500 mg/m²; up to 900 mg/m²
I.M. doses of 15-30 mg in various schedules have been given
Intracavitary: 0.6-0.8 mg/kg
Intrapericardial dose: Usually 15-30 mg

Dosing comments/adjustment in renal impairment: Use with extreme caution, reduced dose may be warranted. Less than 3% of alkylating species are detected in the urine in 24 hours.

Intrathecal: Doses of 1-10 mg/m² administered 1-2 times/week in concentrations of 1 mg/mL diluted with preservative-free sterile water for injection
Intravesical: Used for treatment of carcinoma of the bladder; patients should be dehydrated for 8-12 hours prior to treatment; instill 60 mg (in 30-60 mL of NS) into the bladder and retain for a minimum of 2 hours. Patient should be positioned every 15 minutes for maximal area exposure. Instillations usually once a week for 4 weeks. Monitor for bone marrow suppression.
Intratumor: Use a 22-gauge needle to inject thiotepa directly into the tumor. Initial dose: 0.6-0.8 mg/kg (diluted to 10 mg/mL) are used every 1-4 weeks; maintenance dose: 0.07-0.8 mg/kg are administered at 1- to 4-week intervals
Ophthalmic: 0.05% solution in LR has been instilled into the eye every 3 hours for 6-8 weeks for the prevention of pterygium recurrence

Administration

Thiotepa is usually administered intravenously, either as a short bolus or push, or a 1-hour infusion; or as an intravesical infusion. The drug is occasionally administered as intracavitary, intramuscular, or intrathecal injections. Intrathecal doses are usually diluted to a concentration of 1 mg/mL in preservative-free sterile water or normal saline. Bladder irrigations should be diluted in 50-100 mL of sterile water or normal saline, and retained for at least 2 hours. The patient should be repositioned every 15 minutes for maximal exposure.

Monitoring Parameters

CBC with differential and platelet count, uric acid, urinalysis

Patient Information

This drug can only be administered I.V. You will require regular blood tests to assess response to therapy. Avoid alcohol and aspirin or aspirin-containing medications unless approved by prescriber. Maintain adequate hydration (2-3 L/day of fluids unless instructed to restrict fluid intake) to prevent kidney damage. For nausea and vomiting, small frequent meals, chewing gum, or sucking lozenges may help, antiemetics may be prescribed. You may experience amenorrhea or changed sperm production, rash, hair loss, or loss of appetite (maintaining adequate nutrition is important). You may have increased sensitivity to infection (avoid crowds and infected persons). Report unusual bleeding or bruising, persistent fever or chills, sore throat, sores in mouth or vagina, blackened stool, or difficulty breathing. The drug may cause permanent sterility and may cause birth defects. The drug may be excreted in breast milk, therefore, an alternative form of feeding your baby should be used. Contraceptive measures are recommended during therapy.

Dosage Forms

INJ, powder for reconstitution: 15 mg

Thiothixene (thye oh THIKS een)

Related Information
Antipsychotic Agents Comparison *on page 1364*

U.S. Brand Names Navane®

Synonyms Tiotixene

Therapeutic Category Antipsychotic Agent, Thioxanthene Derivative; Phenothiazine Derivative

Use Management of schizophrenia

Unlabeled/Investigational Use Psychotic disorders

Pregnancy Risk Factor C

Contraindications Hypersensitivity to thiothixene or any component of the formulation; severe CNS depression; circulatory collapse; blood dyscrasias; coma

Warnings/Precautions Safety in children <12 years of age has not been established. May be sedating. Use with caution in Parkinson's disease; hemodynamic instability; predisposition to seizures; subcortical brain damage; bone marrow suppression; severe cardiac, hepatic, renal, or respiratory disease. Esophageal dysmotility and aspiration have been associated with antipsychotic use - use with caution in patients at risk of pneumonia (ie, Alzheimer's disease). Caution in breast cancer or other prolactin-dependent tumors (may elevate prolactin levels). May alter temperature regulation or mask toxicity of other drugs due to antiemetic effects. May alter cardiac conduction - life-threatening arrhythmias have occurred with therapeutic doses of neuroleptics. May cause orthostatic hypotension - use with caution in patients at risk of this effect or those who would tolerate transient hypotensive episodes (cerebrovascular disease, cardiovascular disease, or other medications which may predispose).

Phenothiazines may cause anticholinergic effects (confusion, agitation, constipation, xerostomia, blurred vision, urinary retention); therefore, they should be used with caution in patients with decreased gastrointestinal motility, urinary retention, BPH, xerostomia, or visual problems. Conditions which also may be exacerbated by cholinergic blockade include narrow-angle glaucoma (screening is recommended) and worsening of myasthenia gravis. Relative to other neuroleptics, thiothixene has a low potency of cholinergic blockade.

May cause extrapyramidal reactions, including pseudoparkinsonism, acute dystonic reactions, akathisia, and tardive dyskinesia (risk of these reactions is high relative to other neuroleptics). May be associated with neuroleptic malignant syndrome (NMS) or pigmentary retinopathy.

Common Adverse Reactions Frequency not defined.
Cardiovascular: Hypotension, tachycardia, syncope, nonspecific ECG changes
Central nervous system: Extrapyramidal signs (pseudoparkinsonism, akathisia, dystonias, lightheadedness, tardive dyskinesia), dizziness, drowsiness, restlessness, agitation, insomnia
Dermatologic: Discoloration of skin (blue-gray), rash, pruritus, urticaria, photosensitivity
Endocrine & metabolic: Changes in menstrual cycle, changes in libido, breast pain, galactorrhea, lactation, amenorrhea, gynecomastia, hyperglycemia, hypoglycemia
Gastrointestinal: Weight gain, nausea, vomiting, stomach pain, constipation, xerostomia, increased salivation
Genitourinary: Difficulty in urination, ejaculatory disturbances, impotence
Hematologic: Leukopenia, leukocytes
Neuromuscular & skeletal: Tremors
Ocular: Pigmentary retinopathy, blurred vision
Respiratory: Nasal congestion
Miscellaneous: Diaphoresis

Drug Interactions
Cytochrome P450 Effect: Substrate of CYP1A2 (major); **Inhibits** CYP2D6 (weak)

Increased Effect/Toxicity: CYP1A2 inhibitors may increase the levels/effects of thiothixene; example inhibitors include amiodarone, ciprofloxacin, fluvoxamine, ketoconazole, lomefloxacin, ofloxacin, and rofecoxib. Thiothixene and CNS depressants (ethanol, narcotics) may produce additive CNS depressant effects. Thiothixene may increase the effect/toxicity of antihypertensives, benztropine (and other anticholinergic agents), lithium, trazodone, and TCAs. Thiothixene's concentrations may be increased by chloroquine, sulfadoxine-pyrimethamine, and propranolol. Metoclopramide may increase risk of extrapyramidal symptoms (EPS).

Decreased Effect: CYP1A2 inducers may decrease the levels/effects of thiothixene; example inducers include aminoglutethimide, carbamazepine, phenobarbital, and rifampin. Thiothixene inhibits the activity of guanadrel, guanethidine, levodopa, and bromocriptine. Benztropine (and other anticholinergics) may inhibit the therapeutic response to thiothixene. Thiothixene and low potency antipsychotics may reverse the pressor effects of epinephrine.

Mechanism of Action Elicits antipsychotic activity by postsynaptic blockade of CNS dopamine receptors resulting in inhibition of dopamine-mediated effects; also has alpha-adrenergic blocking activity

Pharmacodynamics/Kinetics
Metabolism: Extensively hepatic
Half-life elimination: >24 hours with chronic use

Dosage Oral:
Children <12 years (unlabeled): Schizophrenia/psychoses: 0.25 mg/kg/24 hours in divided doses (dose not well established; use not recommended)

(Continued)

Thiothixene *(Continued)*

Children >12 years and Adults:

Mild to moderate psychosis: 2 mg 3 times/day, up to 20-30 mg/day; more severe psychosis: Initial: 5 mg 2 times/day, may increase gradually, if necessary; maximum: 60 mg/day

Rapid tranquilization of the agitated patient (administered every 30-60 minutes): 5-10 mg; average total dose for tranquilization: 15-30 mg

Hemodialysis: Not dialyzable (0% to 5%)

Administration Oral (concentrate) solution: Dilute immediately before administration with water, fruit juice, milk, etc. **Note:** Avoid skin contact with oral medication; may cause contact dermatitis.

Monitoring Parameters Vital signs; lipid profile, fasting blood glucose/Hgb A_{1c}; BMI; mental status, abnormal involuntary movement scale (AIMS), extrapyramidal symptoms (EPS)

Patient Information May cause drowsiness, restlessness, avoid alcohol and other CNS depressants; do not alter dosage or discontinue without consulting prescriber

Dosage Forms CAP: 1 mg, 2 mg, 5 mg, 10 mg; (Navane®): 1 mg, 2 mg, 5 mg, 10 mg, 20 mg.
SOLN, oral concentrate: 5 mg/mL (120 mL)

♦ **Thonzonium, Neomycin, Colistin, and Hydrocortisone** *see* Neomycin, Colistin, Hydrocortisone, and Thonzonium *on page 892*

♦ **Thorazine® [DSC]** *see* ChlorproMAZINE *on page 266*

♦ **Thrombate III®** *see* Antithrombin III *on page 107*

♦ **Thymocyte Stimulating Factor** *see* Aldesleukin *on page 47*

♦ **Thymoglobulin®** *see* Antithymocyte Globulin (Rabbit) *on page 109*

♦ **Thyrogen®** *see* Thyrotropin Alpha *on page 1223*

Thyroid *(THYE roid)*

U.S. Brand Names Armour® Thyroid; Nature-Throid® NT; Westhroid®

Synonyms Desiccated Thyroid; Thyroid Extract; Thyroid USP

Therapeutic Category Thyroid Product

Use Replacement or supplemental therapy in hypothyroidism; pituitary TSH suppressants (thyroid nodules,. thyroiditis, multinodular goiter, thyroid cancer), thyrotoxicosis, diagnostic suppression tests

Pregnancy Risk Factor A

Contraindications Hypersensitivity to beef or pork or any component of the formulation; recent myocardial infarction; thyrotoxicosis uncomplicated by hypothyroidism; uncorrected adrenal insufficiency

Warnings/Precautions Ineffective for weight reduction. High doses may produce serious or even life-threatening toxic effects particularly when used with some anorectic drugs. Use cautiously in patients with pre-existing cardiovascular disease (angina, CHD), elderly since they may be more likely to have compromised cardiovascular function. Chronic hypothyroidism predisposes patients to coronary artery disease. Desiccated thyroid contains variable amounts of T_3, T_4, and other triiodothyronine compounds which are more likely to cause cardiac signs or symptoms due to fluctuating levels. Should avoid use in the elderly for this reason. Drug of choice is levothyroxine in the minds of many clinicians.

Drug Interactions

Increased Effect/Toxicity: Thyroid may potentiate the hypoprothrombinemic effect of oral anticoagulants. Tricyclic antidepressants (TAD) coadministered with thyroid hormone may increase potential for toxicity of both drugs.

Decreased Effect: Thyroid hormones increase the therapeutic need for oral hypoglycemics or insulin. Cholestyramine can bind thyroid and reduce its absorption. Phenytoin may decrease thyroxine serum levels. Thyroid hormone may decrease effect of oral sulfonylureas.

Mechanism of Action The primary active compound is T_3 (triiodothyronine), which may be converted from T_4 (thyroxine) and then circulates throughout the body to influence growth and maturation of various tissues; exact mechanism of action is unknown; however, it is believed the thyroid hormone exerts its many metabolic effects through control of DNA transcription and protein synthesis; involved in normal metabolism, growth, and development; promotes gluconeogenesis, increases utilization and mobilization of glycogen stores and stimulates protein synthesis, increases basal metabolic rate

Pharmacodynamics/Kinetics

Absorption: T_4: 48% to 79%; T_3: 95%; desiccated thyroid contains thyroxine, liothyronine, and iodine (primarily bound)

Metabolism: Thyroxine: Largely converted to liothyronine

Half-life elimination, serum: Liothyronine: 1-2 days; Thyroxine: 6-7 days

Recommended Pediatric Dosage for Congenital Hypothyroidism

Age	Daily Dose (mg)	Daily Dose/kg (mg)
0-6 mo	15-30	4.8-6
6-12 mo	30-45	3.6-4.8
1-5 y	45-60	3-3.6
6-12 y	60-90	2.4-3
>12 y	>90	1.2-1.8

Dosage Oral:

Children: See table on previous page.

Adults: Initial: 15-30 mg; increase with 15 mg increments every 2-4 weeks; use 15 mg in patients with cardiovascular disease or myxedema. Maintenance dose: Usually 60-120 mg/ day; monitor TSH and clinical symptoms.

Thyroid cancer: Requires larger amounts than replacement therapy

Dosage Forms CAP: 15 mg, 30 mg, 60 mg, 90 mg, 120 mg, 180 mg, 240 mg. **TAB:** 30 mg, 32.5 mg, 60 mg, 65 mg, 120 mg, 130 mg, 180 mg; (Armour® Thyroid): 15 mg, 30 mg, 60 mg, 90 mg, 120 mg, 180 mg, 240 mg, 300 mg; (Nature-Throid® NT, Westhroid®): 32.4 mg, 64.8 mg, 129.6 mg, 194.4 mg

♦ **Thyroid Extract** *see* Thyroid *on page 1222*

♦ **Thyroid USP** *see* Thyroid *on page 1222*

♦ **Thyrolar®** *see* Liotrix *on page 749*

Thyrotropin Alpha (thye roe TROH pin AL fa)

U.S. Brand Names Thyrogen®

Synonyms Human Thyroid Stimulating Hormone; TSH

Therapeutic Category Diagnostic Agent

Use As an adjunctive diagnostic tool for serum thyroglobulin (Tg) testing with or without radioiodine imaging in the follow-up of patients with well-differentiated thyroid cancer

Potential clinical use:

1. Patients with an undetectable Tg on thyroid hormone suppressive therapy to exclude the diagnosis of residual or recurrent thyroid cancer
2. Patients requiring serum Tg testing and radioiodine imaging who are unwilling to undergo thyroid hormone withdrawal testing and whose treating physician believes that use of a less sensitive test is justified
3. Patients who are either unable to mount an adequate endogenous TSH response to thyroid hormone withdrawal or in whom withdrawal is medically contraindicated

Pregnancy Risk Factor C

Contraindications Hypersensitivity to thyrotropin alpha or any component of the formulation

Warnings/Precautions Caution should be exercised when administered to patients who have been previously treated with bovine TSH and, in particular, to those patients who have experienced hypersensitivity reactions to bovine TSH

Considerations in the use of Thyrogen®:

1. There remains a meaningful risk of a diagnosis of thyroid cancer or of an underestimating the extent of disease when Thyrogen®-stimulated Tg testing is performed and in combination with radioiodine imaging
2. Thyrogen® Tg levels are generally lower than, and do not correlate with, Tg levels after thyroid hormone withdrawal
3. Newly detectable Tg level or a Tg level rising over time after Thyrogen® or a high index of suspicion of metastatic disease, even in the setting of a negative or low-stage Thyrogen® radioiodine scan, should prompt further evaluation such as thyroid hormone withdrawal to definitively establish the location and extent of thyroid cancer.
4. Decision to perform a Thyrogen® radioiodine scan in conjunction with a Thyrogen® serum Tg test and whether or when to withdraw a patient from thyroid hormones are complex. Pertinent factors in this decision include the sensitivity of the Tg assay used, the Thyrogen® Tg level obtained, and the index of suspicion of recurrent or persistent local or metastatic disease.
5. Thyrogen® is not recommended to stimulate radioiodine uptake for the purposes of ablative radiotherapy of thyroid cancer
6. The signs and symptoms of hypothyroidism which accompany thyroid hormone withdrawal are avoided with Thyrogen® use

Common Adverse Reactions 1% to 10%:

Central nervous system: Headache, chills, fever, dizziness

Gastrointestinal: Nausea, vomiting

Neuromuscular & skeletal: Weakness, paresthesia

Miscellaneous: Flu-like syndrome

Mechanism of Action An exogenous source of human TSH that offers an additional diagnostic tool in the follow-up of patients with a history of well-differentiated thyroid cancer. Binding of thyrotropin alpha to TSH receptors on normal thyroid epithelial cells or on well-differentiated thyroid cancer tissue stimulates iodine uptake and organification and synthesis and secretion of thyroglobulin, triiodothyronine, and thyroxine.

Pharmacodynamics/Kinetics

Half-life elimination: 25 ± 10 hours

Time to peak: Mean: 3-24 hours after injection

Dosage Children >16 years and Adults: I.M.: 0.9 mg every 24 hours for 2 doses or every 72 hours for 3 doses

For radioiodine imaging, radioiodine administration should be given 24 hours following the final Thyrogen® injection. Scanning should be performed 48 hours after radioiodine administration (72 hours after the final injection of Thyrogen®).

For serum testing, serum Tg should be obtained 72 hours after final injection.

Administration I.M. injection into the buttock

Dosage Forms INJ, powder for reconstitution [kit]: 1.1 mg [supplied as two vials of Thyrogen® and two 10 mL vials of SWFI]

♦ **Tiabendazole** *see* Thiabendazole *on page 1213*

Tiagabine (tye AG a been)

Related Information

Anticonvulsants by Seizure Type *on page 1358*

U.S. Brand Names Gabitril®

Synonyms Tiagabine Hydrochloride

Therapeutic Category Anticonvulsant, Miscellaneous

Use Adjunctive therapy in adults and children ≥12 years of age in the treatment of partial seizures

Unlabeled/Investigational Use Bipolar disorder

Pregnancy Risk Factor C

Contraindications Hypersensitivity to tiagabine or any component of the formulation

Warnings/Precautions Anticonvulsants should not be discontinued abruptly because of the possibility of increasing seizure frequency; tiagabine should be withdrawn gradually to minimize the potential of increased seizure frequency, unless safety concerns require a more rapid withdrawal. Rarely, nonconvulsive status epilepticus has been reported following abrupt discontinuation or dosage reduction.

Use with caution in patients with hepatic impairment. Experience in patients not receiving enzyme-inducing drugs has been limited - caution should be used in treating any patient who is not receiving one of these medications. Weakness, sedation, and confusion may occur with tiagabine use. Patients must be cautioned about performing tasks which require mental alertness (eg, operating machinery or driving). Effects with other sedative drugs or ethanol may be potentiated. May cause potentially serious rash, including Stevens-Johnson syndrome.

Common Adverse Reactions

>10%:

Central nervous system: Dizziness, somnolence

Gastrointestinal: Nausea

Neuromuscular & skeletal: Weakness

1% to 10%:

Central nervous system: Nervousness, difficulty with concentration, insomnia, ataxia, confusion, speech disorder, depression, emotional lability, abnormal gait, hostility

Dermatologic: Rash, pruritus

Gastrointestinal: Diarrhea, vomiting, increased appetite

Neuromuscular & skeletal: Tremor, paresthesia

Ocular: Nystagmus

Otic: Hearing impairment

Respiratory: Pharyngitis, cough

Drug Interactions

Cytochrome P450 Effect: Substrate of 3A4 (major)

Increased Effect/Toxicity: Valproate increased free tiagabine concentrations by 40%.

Decreased Effect: Primidone, phenobarbital, phenytoin, and carbamazepine increase tiagabine clearance by 60%.

Mechanism of Action The exact mechanism by which tiagabine exerts antiseizure activity is not definitively known; however, *in vitro* experiments demonstrate that it enhances the activity of gamma aminobutyric acid (GABA), the major neuroinhibitory transmitter in the nervous system; it is thought that binding to the GABA uptake carrier inhibits the uptake of GABA into presynaptic neurons, allowing an increased amount of GABA to be available to postsynaptic neurons; based on *in vitro* studies, tiagabine does not inhibit the uptake of dopamine, norepinephrine, serotonin, glutamate, or choline

Pharmacodynamics/Kinetics

Absorption: Rapid (within 1 hour); prolonged with food

Protein binding: 96%, primarily to albumin and α_1-acid glycoprotein

Metabolism: Hepatic via CYP (primarily 3A4)

Bioavailability: Oral: Absolute: 90%

Half-life elimination: 6.7 hours

Time to peak, plasma: 45 minutes

Excretion: Feces (63%) and urine (25%, 2% as unchanged drug); primarily as metabolites

Dosage Oral (administer with food):

Children 12-18 years: 4 mg once daily for 1 week; may increase to 8 mg daily in 2 divided doses for 1 week; then may increase by 4-8 mg weekly to response or up to 32 mg daily in 2-4 divided doses

Adults: 4 mg once daily for 1 week; may increase by 4-8 mg weekly to response or up to 56 mg daily in 2-4 divided doses

Monitoring Parameters A reduction in seizure frequency is indicative of therapeutic response to tiagabine in patients with partial seizures; complete blood counts, renal function tests, liver function tests, and routine blood chemistry should be monitored periodically during therapy

Reference Range Maximal plasma level after a 24 mg/dose: 552 ng/mL

Patient Information Use exactly as directed; take orally with food, usually beginning at 4 mg once daily, and usually in addition to other antiepilepsy drugs. The dose will be increased based on age and medical condition, up to 2-4 times/day. Do not interrupt or discontinue treatment without consulting your prescriber or pharmacist. If told to stop this medication, it should be discontinued gradually.

Dosage Forms TAB: 2 mg, 4 mg, 12 mg, 16 mg

♦ **Tiagabine Hydrochloride** *see* Tiagabine *on page 1224*

♦ **Tiazac®** *see* Diltiazem *on page 380*

♦ **Ticar®** *see* Ticarcillin *on page 1225*

Ticarcillin (tye kar SIL in)

Related Information

Antimicrobial Drugs of Choice *on page 1440*

Community-Acquired Pneumonia in Adults *on page 1457*

U.S. Brand Names Ticar®

Synonyms Ticarcillin Disodium

Therapeutic Category Antibiotic, Penicillin

Use Treatment of susceptible infections such as septicemia, acute and chronic respiratory tract infections, skin and soft tissue infections, and urinary tract infections due to susceptible strains of *Pseudomonas*, and other gram-negative bacteria

Pregnancy Risk Factor B

Contraindications Hypersensitivity to ticarcillin, any component of the formulation, or penicillins

Warnings/Precautions Due to sodium load and adverse effects (anemia, neuropsychological changes), use with caution and modify dosage in patients with renal impairment; serious and occasionally severe or fatal hypersensitivity (anaphylactoid) reactions have been reported in patients on penicillin therapy (especially with a history of beta-lactam hypersensitivity and/or a history of sensitivity to multiple allergens); use with caution in patients with seizures

Common Adverse Reactions Frequency not defined.

Central nervous system: Confusion, convulsions, drowsiness, fever, Jarisch-Herxheimer reaction

Dermatologic: Rash

Endocrine & metabolic: Electrolyte imbalance

Gastrointestinal: *Clostridium difficile* colitis

Hematologic: Bleeding, eosinophilia, hemolytic anemia, leukopenia, neutropenia, positive Coombs' reaction, thrombocytopenia

Hepatic: Hepatotoxicity, jaundice

Local: Thrombophlebitis

Neuromuscular & skeletal: Myoclonus

Renal: Interstitial nephritis (acute)

Miscellaneous: Anaphylaxis, hypersensitivity reactions

Drug Interactions

Increased Effect/Toxicity: Probenecid may increase penicillin levels. Neuromuscular blockers may have an increased duration of action (neuromuscular blockade). Penicillins may increase the exposure to methotrexate during concurrent therapy; monitor.

Decreased Effect: Tetracyclines may decrease penicillin effectiveness. Aminoglycosides may cause physical inactivation of aminoglycosides in the presence of high concentrations of ticarcillin and potential toxicity in patients with mild-moderate renal dysfunction. Although anecdotal reports suggest oral contraceptive efficacy could be reduced by penicillins, this has been refuted by more rigorous scientific and clinical data.

Mechanism of Action Inhibits bacterial cell wall synthesis by binding to one or more of the penicillin binding proteins (PBPs); which in turn inhibits the final transpeptidation step of peptidoglycan synthesis in bacterial cell walls, thus inhibiting cell wall biosynthesis. Bacteria eventually lyse due to ongoing activity of cell wall autolytic enzymes (autolysins and murein hydrolases) while cell wall assembly is arrested.

Pharmacodynamics/Kinetics

Absorption: I.M.: 86%

Distribution: Blister fluid, lymph tissue, and gallbladder; low concentrations into CSF increasing with inflamed meninges, otherwise widely distributed; crosses placenta; enters breast milk (low concentrations)

Protein binding: 45% to 65%

Half-life elimination:

Neonates: <1 week old: 3.5-5.6 hours; 1-8 weeks old: 1.3-2.2 hours

Children 5-13 years: 0.9 hour

Adults: 66-72 minutes; prolonged with renal and/or hepatic impairment

Time to peak, serum: I.M.: 30-75 minutes

Excretion: Almost entirely urine (as unchanged drug and metabolites); feces (3.5%)

Dosage Ticarcillin is generally given I.V., I.M. injection is only for the treatment of uncomplicated urinary tract infections and dose should not exceed 2 g/injection when administered I.M.

Neonates: I.M., I.V.:

Postnatal age <7 days:

<2000 g: 75 mg/kg/dose every 12 hours

>2000 g: 75 mg/kg/dose every 8 hours

Postnatal age >7 days:

<1200 g: 75 mg/kg/dose every 12 hours

1200-2000 g: 75 mg/kg/dose every 8 hours

>2000 g: 75 mg/kg/dose every 6 hours

Infants and Children:

Systemic infections: I.V.: 200-300 mg/kg/day in divided doses every 4-6 hours

Urinary tract infections: I.M., I.V.: 50-100 mg/kg/day in divided doses every 6-8 hours

Maximum dose: 24 g/day

Adults: I.M., I.V.: 1-4 g every 4-6 hours, usual dose: 3 g I.V. every 4-6 hours

Dosing adjustment in renal impairment: Adults:

Cl_{cr} 30-60 mL/minute: 2 g every 4 hours or 3 g every 8 hours

Cl_{cr} 10-30 mL/minute: 2 g every 8 hours or 3 g every 12 hours

Cl_{cr} <10 mL/minute: 2 g every 12 hours

(Continued)

Ticarcillin *(Continued)*

Moderately dialyzable (20% to 50%)

Continuous arteriovenous or venovenous hemodiafiltration effects: Dose as for Cl_{cr} 10-50 mL/minute

Administration Administer 1 hour apart from aminoglycosides

Monitoring Parameters Serum electrolytes, bleeding time, and periodic tests of renal, hepatic, and hematologic function; monitor for signs of anaphylaxis during first dose

Dosage Forms INJ, powder for reconstitution: 3 g, 20 g

Ticarcillin and Clavulanate Potassium

(tye kar SIL in & klav yoo LAN ate poe TASS ee um)

Related Information

Antimicrobial Drugs of Choice *on page 1440*

Community-Acquired Pneumonia in Adults *on page 1457*

U.S. Brand Names Timentin®

Synonyms Ticarcillin and Clavulanic Acid

Therapeutic Category Antibiotic, Anaerobic; Antibiotic, Penicillin & Beta-lactamase Inhibitor

Use Treatment of infections of lower respiratory tract, urinary tract, skin and skin structures, bone and joint, and septicemia caused by susceptible organisms. Clavulanate expands activity of ticarcillin to include beta-lactamase producing strains of *S. aureus, H. influenzae, Bacteroides* species, and some other gram-negative bacilli

Pregnancy Risk Factor B

Contraindications Hypersensitivity to ticarcillin, clavulanate, any penicillin, or any component of the formulation

Warnings/Precautions Not approved for use in children <12 years of age; use with caution and modify dosage in patients with renal impairment; use with caution in patients with a history of allergy to cephalosporins and in patients with CHF due to high sodium load

Common Adverse Reactions Frequency not defined.

Central nervous system: Confusion, convulsions, drowsiness, fever, Jarisch-Herxheimer reaction

Dermatologic: Rash, erythema multiforme, toxic epidermal necrolysis, Stevens-Johnson syndrome

Endocrine & metabolic: Electrolyte imbalance

Gastrointestinal: *Clostridium difficile* colitis

Hematologic: Bleeding, hemolytic anemia, leukopenia, neutropenia, positive Coombs' reaction, thrombocytopenia

Hepatic: Hepatotoxicity, jaundice

Local: Thrombophlebitis

Neuromuscular & skeletal: Myoclonus

Renal: Interstitial nephritis (acute)

Miscellaneous: Anaphylaxis, hypersensitivity reactions

Drug Interactions

Increased Effect/Toxicity: Probenecid may increase penicillin levels. Neuromuscular blockers may have an increased duration of action (neuromuscular blockade). Penicillins may increase the exposure to methotrexate during concurrent therapy; monitor.

Decreased Effect: Tetracyclines may decrease penicillin effectiveness. Aminoglycosides may cause physical inactivation of aminoglycosides in the presence of high concentrations of ticarcillin and potential toxicity in patients with mild-moderate renal dysfunction. Although anecdotal reports suggest oral contraceptive efficacy could be reduced by penicillins, this has been refuted by more rigorous scientific and clinical data.

Mechanism of Action Inhibits bacterial cell wall synthesis by binding to one or more of the penicillin binding proteins (PBPs); which in turn inhibits the final transpeptidation step of peptidoglycan synthesis in bacterial cell walls, thus inhibiting cell wall biosynthesis. Bacteria eventually lyse due to ongoing activity of cell wall autolytic enzymes (autolysins and murein hydrolases) while cell wall assembly is arrested.

Pharmacodynamics/Kinetics

Ticarcillin: See Ticarcillin monograph.

Clavulanic acid:

Protein binding: 9% to 30%

Metabolism: Hepatic

Half-life elimination: 66-90 minutes

Excretion: Urine (45% as unchanged drug)

Clearance: Does not affect clearance of ticarcillin

Dosage I.V.:

Children and Adults <60 kg: 200-300 mg of ticarcillin component/kg/day in divided doses every 4-6 hours

Children >60 kg and Adults: 3.1 g (ticarcillin 3 g plus clavulanic acid 0.1 g) every 4-6 hours; maximum: 24 g/day

Urinary tract infections: 3.1 g every 6-8 hours

Dosing adjustment in renal impairment:

Cl_{cr} 30-60 mL/minute: Administer 2 g every 4 hours or 3.1 g every 8 hours

Cl_{cr} 10-30 mL/minute: Administer 2 g every 8 hours or 3.1 g every 12 hours

Cl_{cr} <10 mL/minute: Administer 2 g every 12 hours

Moderately dialyzable (20% to 50%)

Continuous arteriovenous or venovenous hemodiafiltration effects: Dose as for Cl_{cr} 10-50 mL/minute

Peritoneal dialysis: 3.1 g every 12 hours
Hemodialysis: 2 g every 12 hours; supplemented with 3.1 g after each dialysis

Dosing adjustment in hepatic dysfunction: Cl_{cr} <10 mL/minute: 2 g every 24 hours
Administration Infuse over 30 minutes; administer 1 hour apart from aminoglycosides
Monitoring Parameters Observe for signs and symptoms of anaphylaxis during first dose.
Dosage Forms INF [premixed, frozen]: Ticarcillin 3 g and clavulanate potassium 0.1 g (100 mL). **INJ, powder for reconstitution:** Ticarcillin 3 g and clavulanate potassium 0.1 g (3.1 g, 31 g)

- **Ticarcillin and Clavulanic Acid** see Ticarcillin and Clavulanate Potassium on page 1226
- **Ticarcillin Disodium** see Ticarcillin on page 1225
- **TICE® BCG** see BCG Vaccine on page 148
- **Ticlid®** see Ticlopidine on page 1227

Ticlopidine (tye KLOE pi deen)

U.S. Brand Names Ticlid®
Synonyms Ticlopidine Hydrochloride
Therapeutic Category Antiplatelet Agent; Platelet Aggregation Inhibitor
Use Platelet aggregation inhibitor that reduces the risk of thrombotic stroke in patients who have had a stroke or stroke precursors. **Note:** Due to its association with life-threatening hematologic disorders, ticlopidine should be reserved for patients who are intolerant to aspirin, or who have failed aspirin therapy. Adjunctive therapy (with aspirin) following successful coronary stent implantation to reduce the incidence of subacute stent thrombosis.
Unlabeled/Investigational Use Protection of aortocoronary bypass grafts, diabetic microangiopathy, ischemic heart disease, prevention of postoperative DVT, reduction of graft loss following renal transplant
Pregnancy Risk Factor B
Contraindications Hypersensitivity to ticlopidine or any component of the formulation; active pathological bleeding such as PUD or intracranial hemorrhage; severe liver dysfunction; hematopoietic disorders (neutropenia, thrombocytopenia, a past history of TTP)
Warnings/Precautions Use with caution in patients who may be at risk of increased bleeding. Consider discontinuing 10-14 days before elective surgery. Use caution in mixing with other antiplatelet drugs. Use with caution in patients with severe liver disease (experience is limited). May cause life-threatening hematologic reactions, including neutropenia, agranulocytosis, thrombotic thrombocytopenia purpura (TTP), and aplastic anemia. Routine monitoring is required (see Monitoring Parameters). Monitor for signs and symptoms of neutropenia including WBC count. Discontinue if the absolute neutrophil count falls to <1200/mm³ or if the platelet count falls to <80,000/mm³.
Common Adverse Reactions As with all drugs which may affect hemostasis, bleeding is associated with ticlopidine. Hemorrhage may occur at virtually any site. Risk is dependent on multiple variables, including the use of multiple agents which alter hemostasis and patient susceptibility.

>10%:
  Endocrine & metabolic: Increased total cholesterol (increases of ~8% to 10% within 1 month of therapy)
  Gastrointestinal: Diarrhea (13%)
1% to 10%:
  Central nervous system: Dizziness (1%)
  Dermatologic: Rash (5%), purpura, pruritus (1%)
  Gastrointestinal: Nausea (7%), dyspepsia (7%), gastrointestinal pain (4%), vomiting (2%), flatulence (2%), anorexia (1%)
  Hematologic: Neutropenia (2%)
  Hepatic: Abnormal liver function test (1%)
Drug Interactions
  Cytochrome P450 Effect: Substrate of CYP3A4 (major); **Inhibits** CYP1A2 (weak), 2C8/9 (weak), 2C19 (strong), 2D6 (moderate), 2E1 (weak), 3A4 (weak)
  Increased Effect/Toxicity: Ticlopidine may increase effect/toxicity of aspirin, anticoagulants, theophylline, and NSAIDs. Cimetidine may increase ticlopidine blood levels. Phenytoin blood levels may be increased by ticlopidine (case reports).
  Decreased Effect: Decreased effect of ticlopidine with antacids (decreased absorption). Ticlopidine may decrease the effect of digoxin, cyclosporine.
Mechanism of Action Ticlopidine is an inhibitor of platelet function with a mechanism which is different from other antiplatelet drugs. The drug significantly increases bleeding time. This effect may not be solely related to ticlopidine's effect on platelets. The prolongation of the bleeding time caused by ticlopidine is further increased by the addition of aspirin in ex vivo experiments. Although many metabolites of ticlopidine have been found, none have been shown to account for in vivo activity.
Pharmacodynamics/Kinetics
  Onset of action: ~6 hours
    Peak effect: 3-5 days; serum levels do not correlate with clinical antiplatelet activity
  Metabolism: Extensively hepatic; has at least one active metabolite
  Half-life elimination: 24 hours
Dosage Oral: Adults:
  Stroke prevention: 250 mg twice daily with food
  Coronary artery stenting (initiate after successful implantation): 250 mg twice daily with food (in combination with antiplatelet doses of aspirin) for up to 30 days
  (Continued)

Ticlopidine *(Continued)*

Administration Oral: Administer with food.

Monitoring Parameters Signs of bleeding; CBC with differential every 2 weeks starting the second week through the third month of treatment; more frequent monitoring is recommended for patients whose absolute neutrophil counts have been consistently declining or are 30% less than baseline values. The peak incidence of TTP occurs between 3-4 weeks, the peak incidence of neutropenia occurs at approximately 4-6 weeks, and the incidence of aplastic anemia peaks after 4-8 weeks of therapy. Few cases have been reported after 3 months of treatment. Liver function tests (alkaline phosphatase and transaminases) should be performed in the first 4 months of therapy if liver dysfunction is suspected.

Dosage Forms TAB: 250 mg

♦ **Ticlopidine Hydrochloride** *see* Ticlopidine *on page 1227*

♦ **TIG** *see* Tetanus Immune Globulin (Human) *on page 1204*

♦ **Tigan**® *see* Trimethobenzamide *on page 1269*

♦ **Tikosyn**™ *see* Dofetilide *on page 398*

♦ **Tilade**® *see* Nedocromil *on page 887*

Tiludronate *(tye LOO droe nate)*

U.S. Brand Names Skelid®

Synonyms Tiludronate Disodium

Therapeutic Category Bisphosphonate Derivative

Use Treatment of Paget's disease of the bone in patients who have a level of serum alkaline phosphatase (SAP) at least twice the upper limit of normal, or who are symptomatic, or who are at risk for future complications of their disease

Pregnancy Risk Factor C

Contraindications Hypersensitivity to bisphosphonates or any component of the formulation

Warnings/Precautions Not recommended in patients with severe renal impairment (Cl_{cr} <30 mL/minute). Use with caution in patients with active upper GI problems (eg, dysphagia, symptomatic esophageal diseases, gastritis, duodenitis, ulcers).

Common Adverse Reactions The following events occurred >2% and at a frequency greater than placebo:

1% to 10%:
Cardiovascular: Chest pain (3%), edema (3%)
Central nervous system: Dizziness (4%), paresthesia (4%)
Dermatologic: Rash (3%), skin disorder (3%)
Gastrointestinal: Nausea (9%), diarrhea (9%), heartburn (5%), vomiting (4%), flatulence (3%)
Neuromuscular & skeletal: Arthrosis (3%)
Ocular: cataract (3%), conjunctivitis (3%), glaucoma (3%)
Respiratory: Rhinitis (5%), sinusitis (5%), coughing (3%), pharyngitis (3%)

Drug Interactions

Increased Effect/Toxicity: Administration of indomethacin increases bioavailability of tiludronate two- to fourfold.

Decreased Effect: Concurrent administration of calcium salts, aluminum- or magnesium-containing antacids, and aspirin markedly decrease absorption/bioavailability (by 50% to 60%) of tiludronate if given within 2 hours of a dose.

Mechanism of Action Inhibition of normal and abnormal bone resorption. Inhibits osteoclasts through at least two mechanisms: disruption of the cytoskeletal ring structure, possibly by inhibition of protein-tyrosine-phosphatase, thus leading to the detachment of osteoclasts from the bone surface area and the inhibition of the osteoclast proton pump.

Pharmacodynamics/Kinetics

Onset of action: Delayed, may require several weeks
Absorption: Rapid
Distribution: Widely to bone and soft tissue
Protein binding: 90%, primarily to albumin
Metabolism: Little, if any
Bioavailability: 6%; reduced by food
Half-life elimination: Healthy volunteers: 50 hours; Pagetic patients: 150 hours
Time to peak, plasma: ~2 hours
Excretion: Urine (60% as unchanged drug) within 13 days

Dosage Tiludronate should be taken with 6-8 oz of plain water and not taken within 2 hours of food

Adults: Oral: 400 mg (2 tablets of tiludronic acid) daily for a period of 3 months; allow an interval of 3 months to assess response

Dosing adjustment in renal impairment: Cl_{cr} <30 mL/minute: **Not recommended**

Dosing adjustment in hepatic impairment: Adjustment is not necessary

Administration Administer as a single oral dose, take with 6-8 oz of plain water. Beverages other than plain water (including mineral water), food, and some medications (see Drug Interactions) are likely to reduce the absorption of tiludronate. Do not take within 2 hours of food. Take calcium or mineral supplements at least 2 hours before or after tiludronate. Take aluminum- or magnesium-containing antacids at least 2 hours after taking tiludronate. Do not take tiludronate within 2 hours of indomethacin.

Patient Information Take tiludronate with 6-8 oz of plain water. Do not take within 2 hours of food. Maintain adequate vitamin D and calcium intake. Do not take calcium supplements, aspirin, and indomethacin within 2 hours before or after tiludronate. Take aluminum- or magnesium-containing antacids, if needed, at least 2 hours after tiludronate.

Dosage Forms TAB, tiludronic acid: 200 mg

♦ **Tiludronate Disodium** *see Tiludronate on page 1228*

♦ **Timentin®** *see Ticarcillin and Clavulanate Potassium on page 1226*

Timolol (TYE moe lole)

Related Information

Beta-Blockers Comparison *on page 1368*
Glaucoma Drug Therapy Comparison *on page 1481*

U.S. Brand Names Betimol®; Blocadren®; Timoptic®; Timoptic® OcuDose®; Timoptic-XE®

Synonyms Timolol Hemihydrate; Timolol Maleate

Therapeutic Category Antianginal Agent; Antihypertensive Agent; Antimigraine Agent, Prophylaxis; Beta Blocker, Nonselective; Beta-Adrenergic Blocker, Ophthalmic

Use Ophthalmic dosage form used in treatment of elevated intraocular pressure such as glaucoma or ocular hypertension; oral dosage form used for treatment of hypertension and angina, to reduce mortality following myocardial infarction, and for prophylaxis of migraine

Pregnancy Risk Factor C (manufacturer); D (2nd and 3rd trimesters - expert analysis)

Contraindications Hypersensitivity to timolol or any component of the formulation; sinus bradycardia; sinus node dysfunction; heart block greater than first degree (except in patients with a functioning artificial pacemaker); cardiogenic shock; uncompensated cardiac failure; bronchospastic disease; pregnancy (2nd and 3rd trimesters)

Warnings/Precautions Administer cautiously in compensated heart failure and monitor for a worsening of the condition. Beta-blocker therapy should not be withdrawn abruptly (particularly in patients with CAD), but gradually tapered to avoid acute tachycardia, hypertension, and/or ischemia. Use caution with concurrent use of beta-blockers and either verapamil or diltiazem; bradycardia or heart block can occur. Beta-blockers can aggravate symptoms in patients with PVD. Patients with bronchospastic disease should generally not receive beta-blockers - monitor closely if used in patients with potential risk of bronchospasm. Use cautiously in diabetics because it can mask prominent hypoglycemic symptoms. Can mask signs of thyrotoxicosis. Can cause fetal harm when administered in pregnancy. Use cautiously in severe renal impairment: marked hypotension can occur in patients maintained on hemodialysis. Use care with anesthetic agents which decrease myocardial function. Can worsen myasthenia gravis. Similar reactions found with systemic administration may occur with topical administration.

Common Adverse Reactions

Ophthalmic:

>10%: Ocular: Conjunctival hyperemia

1% to 10%: Ocular: Anisocoria, corneal punctate keratitis, keratitis, corneal staining, decreased corneal sensitivity, eye pain, vision disturbances

Systemic:

>10%:

Central nervous system: Drowsiness, insomnia
Endocrine & metabolic: Decreased sexual ability

1% to 10%:

Cardiovascular: Bradycardia, palpitations, edema, CHF, reduced peripheral circulation
Central nervous system: Mental depression
Gastrointestinal: Diarrhea or constipation, nausea, vomiting, stomach discomfort
Respiratory: Bronchospasm
Miscellaneous: Cold extremities

Drug Interactions

Cytochrome P450 Effect: Substrate of CYP2D6 (major); **Inhibits** CYP2D6 (weak)

Increased Effect/Toxicity: CYP2D6 inhibitors may increase the levels/effects of timolol; example inhibitors include chlorpromazine, delavirdine, fluoxetine, miconazole, paroxetine, pergolide, quinidine, quinine, ritonavir, and ropinirole. The heart rate-lowering effects of timolol are additive with other drugs which slow AV conduction (digoxin, verapamil, diltiazem). Reserpine increases the effects of timolol. Concurrent use of timolol may increase the effects of alpha-blockers (prazosin, terazosin), alpha-adrenergic stimulants (epinephrine, phenylephrine), and the vasoconstrictive effects of ergot alkaloids. Timolol may mask the tachycardia from hypoglycemia caused by insulin and oral hypoglycemics. In patients receiving concurrent therapy, the risk of hypertensive crisis is increased when either clonidine or the beta-blocker is withdrawn. Beta-blockers may increase the action or levels of ethanol, disopyramide, nondepolarizing muscle relaxants, and theophylline although the effects are difficult to predict.

Decreased Effect: Decreased effect of timolol with aluminum salts, barbiturates, calcium salts, cholestyramine, colestipol, NSAIDs, penicillins (ampicillin), rifampin, salicylates, and sulfinpyrazone due to decreased bioavailability and plasma levels. Beta-blockers may decrease the effect of sulfonylureas. Beta-blockers may affect the action or levels of ethanol, disopyramide, nondepolarizing muscle relaxants, and theophylline, although the effects are difficult to predict.

Mechanism of Action Blocks both beta$_1$- and beta$_2$-adrenergic receptors, reduces intraocular pressure by reducing aqueous humor production or possibly outflow; reduces blood pressure by blocking adrenergic receptors and decreasing sympathetic outflow, produces a negative chronotropic and inotropic activity through an unknown mechanism

Pharmacodynamics/Kinetics

Onset of action: Hypotensive: Oral: 15-45 minutes

(Continued)

Timolol *(Continued)*

Peak effect: 0.5-2.5 hours
Duration: ~4 hours; Ophthalmic: Intraocular: 24 hours
Protein binding: 60%
Metabolism: Extensively hepatic; extensive first-pass effect
Half-life elimination: 2-2.7 hours; prolonged with renal impairment
Excretion: Urine (15% to 20% as unchanged drug)

Dosage

Children and Adults: Ophthalmic:

Solution: Initial: 0.25% solution, instill 1 drop twice daily; increase to 0.5% solution if response not adequate; decrease to 1 drop/day if controlled; do not exceed 1 drop twice daily of 0.5% solution

Gel-forming solution (Timoptic-XE®): Instill 1 drop (either 0.25% or 0.5%) once daily

Adults: Oral:

Hypertension: Initial: 10 mg twice daily, increase gradually every 7 days, usual dosage: 20-40 mg/day in 2 divided doses; maximum: 60 mg/day

Prevention of myocardial infarction: 10 mg twice daily initiated within 1-4 weeks after infarction

Migraine headache: Initial: 10 mg twice daily, increase to maximum of 30 mg/day

Administration Administer other topically-applied ophthalmic medications at least 10 minutes before Timoptic-XE®; wash hands before use; invert closed bottle and shake once before use; remove cap carefully so that tip does not touch anything; hold bottle between thumb and index finger; use index finger of other hand to pull down the lower eyelid to form a pocket for the eye drop and tilt head back; place the dispenser tip close to the eye and gently squeeze the bottle to administer 1 drop; remove pressure after a single drop has been released; **do not allow the dispenser tip to touch the eye**; replace cap and store bottle in an upright position in a clean area; do **not** enlarge hole of dispenser; do **not** wash tip with water, soap, or any other cleaner

Monitoring Parameters Blood pressure, apical and radial pulses, fluid I & O, daily weight, respirations, mental status, circulation in extremities before and during therapy

Patient Information Apply gentle pressure to lacrimal sac during and immediately following instillation (1 minute) to avoid systemic absorption; stop drug if breathing difficulty occurs

Dosage Forms Gel-forming solution, ophthalmic, as maleate (Timoptic-XE®): 0.25% (2.5 mL, 5 mL); 0.5% (2.5 mL, 5 mL). **SOLN, ophthalmic, as hemihydrate** (Betimol®): 0.25% (5 mL, 10 mL, 15 mL); 0.5% (5 mL, 10 mL, 15 mL). **SOLN, ophthalmic, as maleate**: 0.25% (5 mL, 10 mL, 15 mL); 0.5% (5 mL, 10 mL, 15 mL); (Timoptic®): 0.25% (5 mL, 10 mL); 0.5% (5 mL, 10 mL). **SOLN, ophthalmic, as maleate** [preservative free] (Timoptic® OcuDose®): 0.25% (0.2 mL); 0.5% (0.2 mL). **TAB, as maleate** (Blocadren®): 5 mg, 10 mg, 20 mg

◆ **Timolol and Dorzolamide** *see* Dorzolamide and Timolol *on page 404*
◆ **Timolol Hemihydrate** *see* Timolol *on page 1229*
◆ **Timolol Maleate** *see* Timolol *on page 1229*
◆ **Timoptic®** *see* Timolol *on page 1229*
◆ **Timoptic® OcuDose®** *see* Timolol *on page 1229*
◆ **Timoptic-XE®** *see* Timolol *on page 1229*
◆ **Tinactin® Antifungal [OTC]** *see* Tolnaftate *on page 1241*
◆ **Tinactin® Antifungal Jock Itch [OTC]** *see* Tolnaftate *on page 1241*
◆ **Tinaderm [OTC]** *see* Tolnaftate *on page 1241*
◆ **Tine Test** *see* Tuberculin Tests *on page 1279*
◆ **Ting® [OTC]** *see* Tolnaftate *on page 1241*

Tinzaparin *(tin ZA pa rin)*

Related Information

Anticoagulants, Injectable *on page 1357*

U.S. Brand Names Innohep®

Synonyms Tinzaparin Sodium

Therapeutic Category Anticoagulant, Low Molecular Weight Heparin; Low Molecular Weight Heparin

Use Treatment of acute symptomatic deep vein thrombosis, with or without pulmonary embolism, in conjunction with warfarin sodium

Pregnancy Risk Factor B

Contraindications Hypersensitivity to tinzaparin sodium, heparin, sulfites, benzyl alcohol, pork products, or any component of the formulation; active major bleeding; heparin-induced thrombocytopenia (current or history of)

Warnings/Precautions

Patients with recent or anticipated neuraxial anesthesia (epidural or spinal anesthesia) are at risk of spinal or epidural hematoma and subsequent paralysis. Consider risk versus benefit prior to neuraxial anesthesia; risk is increased by concomitant agents that may alter hemostasis, as well as traumatic or repeated epidural or spinal puncture, and indwelling epidural catheters. Patient should be observed closely for signs and symptoms of neurological impairment. Not to be used interchangeably (unit for unit) with heparin or any other low molecular weight heparins.

Monitor patient closely for signs or symptoms of bleeding. Certain patients are at increased risk of bleeding. Risk factors include bacterial endocarditis; congenital or acquired bleeding disorders; active ulcerative or angiodysplastic GI diseases; severe uncontrolled hypertension; hemorrhagic stroke; use shortly after brain, spinal, or ophthalmologic surgery; patients treated concomitantly with platelet inhibitors; recent GI bleeding; thrombocytopenia or platelet defects; severe liver disease; hypertensive or diabetic retinopathy; or in patients undergoing invasive procedures.

Safety and efficacy in pediatric patients has not been established. Use with caution in the elderly (delayed elimination may occur). Patients with severe renal impairment may show reduced elimination of tinzaparin

Heparin can cause hyperkalemia by affecting aldosterone; similar reactions could occur with LMWHs. Monitor for hyperkalemia. Discontinue therapy if platelets are <100,000/mm^3. For subcutaneous injection only, do not mix with other injections or infusions. Clinical experience is limited in patients with BMI >40 kg.

Common Adverse Reactions As with all anticoagulants, bleeding is the major adverse effect of tinzaparin. Hemorrhage may occur at virtually any site. Risk is dependent on multiple variables.

>10%:
  Hepatic: Increased ALT (13%)
  Local: Injection site hematoma (16%)

1% to 10%:
  Cardiovascular: Angina pectoris, chest pain (2%), hypertension, hypotension, tachycardia
  Central nervous system: Confusion, dizziness, fever (2%), headache (2%), insomnia, pain (2%)
  Dermatologic: Bullous eruption, pruritus, rash (1%), skin disorder
  Gastrointestinal: Constipation (1%), dyspepsia, flatulence, nausea (2%), nonspecified gastrointestinal disorder, vomiting (1%)
  Genitourinary: Dysuria, urinary retention, urinary tract infection (4%)
  Hematologic: Anemia, hematoma, hemorrhage (2%), thrombocytopenia (1%)
  Hepatic: Increased AST (9%)
  Local: Deep vein thrombosis, injection site hematoma
  Neuromuscular & skeletal: Back pain (2%)
  Renal: Hematuria (1%)
  Respiratory: Dyspnea (1%), epistaxis (2%), pneumonia, pulmonary embolism (2%), respiratory disorder
  Miscellaneous: Impaired healing, infection, unclassified reactions

Drug Interactions

Increased Effect/Toxicity: Drugs which affect platelet function (eg, aspirin, NSAIDs, dipyridamole, ticlopidine, clopidogrel, sulfinpyrazone, dextran) may potentiate the risk of hemorrhage. Thrombolytic agents increase the risk of hemorrhage.

Warfarin: Risk of bleeding may be increased during concurrent therapy. Tinzaparin is commonly continued during the initiation of warfarin therapy to assure anticoagulation and to protect against possible transient hypercoagulability

Mechanism of Action Standard heparin consists of components with molecular weights ranging from 4000-30,000 daltons with a mean of 16,000 daltons. Heparin acts as an anticoagulant by enhancing the inhibition rate of clotting proteases by antithrombin III, impairing normal hemostasis and inhibition of factor Xa. Low molecular weight heparins have a small effect on the activated partial thromboplastin time and strongly inhibit factor Xa. The primary inhibitory activity of tinzaparin is through antithrombin. Tinzaparin is derived from porcine heparin that undergoes controlled enzymatic depolymerization. The average molecular weight of tinzaparin ranges between 5500 and 7500 daltons which is distributed as (<10%) 2000 daltons (60% to 72%) 2000-8000 daltons, and (22% to 36%) >8000 daltons. The antifactor Xa activity is approximately 100 int. units/mg.

Pharmacodynamics/Kinetics
Onset of action: 2-3 hours
Distribution: 3-5 L
Half-life elimination: 3-4 hours
Metabolism: Partially metabolized by desulphation and depolymerization
Bioavailability: 87%
Time to peak: 4-5 hours
Excretion: Urine

Dosage S.C.:
Adults: 175 anti-Xa int. units/kg of body weight once daily. Warfarin sodium should be started when appropriate. Administer tinzaparin for at least 6 days and until patient is adequately anticoagulated with warfarin.
  Note: To calculate the volume of solution to administer per dose: Volume to be administered (mL) = patient weight (kg) x 0.00875 mL/kg (may be rounded off to the nearest 0.05 mL)
Elderly: No significant differences in safety or response were seen when used in patients ≥65 years of age. However, increased sensitivity to tinzaparin in elderly patients may be possible due to a decline in renal function.
Dosage adjustment in renal impairment: Patients with severe renal impairment had a 24% decrease in clearance, use with caution.
Dosage adjustment in hepatic impairment: No specific dosage adjustment has been recommended.

Administration Patient should be lying down or sitting. Administer by deep S.C. injection, alternating between the left and right anterolateral and left and right posterolateral abdominal wall. Vary site daily. The entire needle should be introduced into the skin fold formed by the thumb and forefinger. Hold the skin fold until injection is complete. To minimize bruising, do not rub the injection site.

Monitoring Parameters CBC including platelet count and hematocrit or hemoglobin, and stool for occult blood; the monitoring of PT and/or aPTT is not necessary. Patients receiving both
(Continued)

Tinzaparin (Continued)

warfarin and tinzaparin should have their INR drawn just prior to the next scheduled dose of tinzaparin.

Patient Information This drug can only be administered by S.C. injection. You may have a tendency to bleed easily while taking this drug; brush teeth with soft brush; floss with waxed floss; use electric razor; avoid scissors or sharp knives and potentially harmful activities. Report chest pain; persistent constipation; persistent erection; unusual bleeding or bruising (bleeding gums, nosebleed, blood in urine, dark stool); pain in joints or back; or numbness, tingling, swelling, or pain at injection site.

Dosage Forms INJ, solution: 20,000 anti-Xa int. units/mL (2 mL)

♦ **Tinzaparin Sodium** see Tinzaparin on page 1230

Tioconazole (tye oh KONE a zole)

U.S. Brand Names 1-Day™ [OTC]; Vagistat®-1 [OTC]

Therapeutic Category Antifungal Agent, Imidazole Derivative; Antifungal Agent, Vaginal

Use Local treatment of vulvovaginal candidiasis

Pregnancy Risk Factor C

Contraindications Hypersensitivity to tioconazole or any component of the formulation

Warnings/Precautions For vaginal use only. Petrolatum-based vaginal products may damage rubber or latex condoms or diaphragms. Separate use by 3 days.

Common Adverse Reactions Frequency not defined.

Central nervous system: Headache

Gastrointestinal: Abdominal pain

Dermatologic: Burning, desquamation

Genitourinary: Discharge, dyspareunia, dysuria, irritation, itching, nocturia, vaginal pain, vaginitis, vulvar swelling

Drug Interactions

Cytochrome P450 Effect: Inhibits CYP1A2 (weak), 2A6 (weak), 2C8/9 (weak), 2C19 (weak), 2D6 (weak), 2E1 (weak)

Mechanism of Action A 1-substituted imidazole derivative with a broad antifungal spectrum against a wide variety of dermatophytes and yeasts, including *Trichophyton mentagrophytes*, *T. rubrum*, *T. erinacei*, *T. tonsurans*, *Microsporum canis*, *Microsporum gypseum*, and *Candida albicans*. Both agents appear to be similarly effective against *Epidermophyton floccosum*.

Pharmacodynamics/Kinetics

Onset of action: Some improvement: Within 24 hours; Complete relief: Within 7 days

Absorption: Intravaginal: Systemic (small amounts)

Distribution: Vaginal fluid: 24-72 hours

Excretion: Urine and feces

Dosage Adults: Vaginal: Insert 1 applicatorful in vagina, just prior to bedtime, as a single dose

Administration Insert high into vagina

Patient Information Insert high into vagina; contact prescriber if itching or burning continues; May interact with condoms and vaginal contraceptive diaphragms (ie, weaken latex); do not rely on these products for 3 days following treatment

Dosage Forms OINT, vaginal: 6.5% (4.6 g)

♦ **Tioguanine** see Thioguanine on page 1215

♦ **Tiotixene** see Thiothixene on page 1221

♦ **TipTapToe [OTC]** see Tolnaftate on page 1241

Tirofiban (tye roe FYE ban)

Related Information

Glycoprotein Antagonists on page 1376

U.S. Brand Names Aggrastat®

Synonyms MK383; Tirofiban Hydrochloride

Therapeutic Category Antiplatelet Agent, Glycoprotein IIb/IIIa Inhibitor; Glycoprotein IIb/IIIa Inhibitor; Platelet Aggregation Inhibitor

Use In combination with heparin, is indicated for the treatment of acute coronary syndrome, including patients who are to be managed medically and those undergoing PTCA or atherectomy. In this setting, it has been shown to decrease the rate of a combined endpoint of death, new myocardial infarction or refractory ischemia/repeat cardiac procedure.

Pregnancy Risk Factor B

Contraindications Hypersensitivity to tirofiban or any component of the formulation; active internal bleeding or a history of bleeding diathesis within the previous 30 days; history of intracranial hemorrhage, intracranial neoplasm, arteriovenous malformation, or aneurysm; history of thrombocytopenia following prior exposure; history of CVA within 30 days or any history of hemorrhagic stroke; major surgical procedure or severe physical trauma within the previous month; history, symptoms, or findings suggestive of aortic dissection; severe hypertension (systolic BP >180 mm Hg and/or diastolic BP >110 mm Hg); concomitant use of another parenteral GP IIb/IIIa inhibitor; acute pericarditis

Warnings/Precautions Bleeding is the most common complication encountered during this therapy; most major bleeding occurs at the arterial access site for cardiac catheterization. Caution in patients with platelets <150,000/mm³; patients with hemorrhagic retinopathy; chronic dialysis patients; when used in combination with other drugs impacting on coagulation. To minimize bleeding complications, care must be taken in sheath insertion/removal. Sheath hemostasis should be achieved at least 4 hours before hospital discharge. Other trauma and vascular punctures should be minimized. Avoid obtaining vascular access through a noncompressible site (eg, subclavian or jugular vein). Patients with severe renal insufficiency require dosage reduction. Do not administer in the same I.V. line as diazepam.

Common Adverse Reactions Bleeding is the major drug-related adverse effect. Patients received background treatment with aspirin and heparin. Major bleeding was reported in 1.4% to 2.2%; minor bleeding in 10.5% to 12%; transfusion was required in 4% to 4.3%.

>1% (nonbleeding adverse events):

Cardiovascular: Bradycardia (4%), coronary artery dissection (5%), edema (2%)

Central nervous system: Dizziness (3%), fever (>1%), headache (>1%), vasovagal reaction (2%)

Gastrointestinal: Nausea (>1%)

Genitourinary: Pelvic pain (6%)

Hematologic: Thrombocytopenia: <90,000/mm^3 (1.5%), <50,000/mm^3 (0.3%)

Neuromuscular & skeletal: Leg pain (3%)

Miscellaneous: Diaphoresis (2%)

Drug Interactions

Increased Effect/Toxicity: Use of tirofiban with aspirin and heparin is associated with an increase in bleeding over aspirin and heparin alone; however, efficacy of tirofiban is improved. Risk of bleeding is increased when used with thrombolytics, oral anticoagulants, NSAIDs, dipyridamole, ticlopidine, and clopidogrel. Avoid concomitant use of other IIb/IIIa antagonists. Cephalosporins which contain the MTT side chain may theoretically increase the risk of hemorrhage.

Decreased Effect: Levothyroxine and omeprazole decrease tirofiban levels; however, the clinical significance of this interaction remains to be demonstrated.

Mechanism of Action A reversible antagonist of fibrinogen binding to the GP IIb/IIIa receptor, the major platelet surface receptor involved in platelet aggregation. When administered intravenously, it inhibits *ex vivo* platelet aggregation in a dose- and concentration-dependent manner. When given according to the recommended regimen, >90% inhibition is attained by the end of the 30-minute infusion. Platelet aggregation inhibition is reversible following cessation of the infusion.

Pharmacodynamics/Kinetics

Distribution: 35% unbound

Metabolism: Minimally hepatic

Half-life elimination: 2 hours

Excretion: Urine (65%) and feces (25%) primarily as unchanged drug

Clearance: Elderly: Reduced by 19% to 26%

Dosage Adults: I.V.: Initial rate of 0.4 mcg/kg/minute for 30 minutes and then continued at 0.1 mcg/kg/minute; dosing should be continued through angiography and for 12-24 hours after angioplasty or atherectomy. See table.

Tirofiban Dosing
(Using 50 mcg/mL Concentration)

Patient Weight (kg)	Patients With Normal Renal Function		Patients With Renal Dysfunction	
	30-Min Loading Infusion Rate (mL/h)	Maintenance Infusion Rate (mL/h)	30-Min Loading Infusion Rate (mL/h)	Maintenance Infusion Rate (mL/h)
30-37	16	4	8	2
38-45	20	5	10	3
46-54	24	6	12	3
55-62	28	7	14	4
63-70	32	8	16	4
71-79	36	9	18	5
80-87	40	10	20	5
88-95	44	11	22	6
96-104	48	12	24	6
105-112	52	13	26	7
113-120	56	14	28	7
121-128	60	15	30	8
128-137	64	16	32	8
138-145	68	17	34	9
146-153	72	18	36	9

Dosing adjustment in severe renal impairment: Cl$_{cr}$ <30 mL/minute: Reduce dose to 50% of normal rate.

Administration Intended for intravenous delivery using sterile equipment and technique. Do not add other drugs or remove solution directly from the bag with a syringe. Do not use plastic containers in series connections; such use can result in air embolism by drawing air from the first container if it is empty of solution. Discard unused solution 24 hours following the start of infusion. May be administered through the same catheter as heparin. Tirofiban injection must be diluted to a concentration of 50 mcg/mL (premixed solution does not require dilution). Infuse over 30 minutes.

(Continued)

Tirofiban (Continued)

Monitoring Parameters Platelet count. Hemoglobin and hematocrit should be monitored prior to treatment, within 6 hours following loading infusion, and at least daily thereafter during therapy. Platelet count may need to be monitored earlier in patients who received prior glycoprotein IIb/IIIa antagonists. Persistent reductions of platelet counts <90,000/mm³ may require interruption or discontinuation of infusion. Because tirofiban requires concurrent heparin therapy, aPTT levels should also be followed. Monitor vital signs and laboratory results prior to, during, and after therapy. Assess infusion insertion site during and after therapy (every 15 minutes or as institutional policy). Observe and teach patient bleeding precautions (avoid invasive procedures and activities that could result in injury). Monitor closely for signs of unusual or excessive bleeding (eg, CNS changes, blood in urine, stool, or vomitus, unusual bruising or bleeding). Breast-feeding is contraindicated.

Dosage Forms INF [premixed in sodium chloride]: 50 mcg/mL (100 mL, 250 mL). **INJ, solution:** 250 mcg/mL (25 mL, 50 mL)

- ◆ **Tirofiban Hydrochloride** see Tirofiban on page 1232
- ◆ **Tisit® [OTC]** see Pyrethrins and Piperonyl Butoxide on page 1065
- ◆ **Tisit® Blue Gel [OTC]** see Pyrethrins and Piperonyl Butoxide on page 1065
- ◆ **Titralac ™ [OTC]** see Calcium Carbonate on page 203
- ◆ **Titralac™ Extra Strength [OTC]** see Calcium Carbonate on page 203

Tizanidine (tye ZAN i deen)

U.S. Brand Names Zanaflex®

Synonyms Sirdalud®

Therapeutic Category Alpha-Adrenergic Agonist

Use Skeletal muscle relaxant used for treatment of muscle spasticity

Unlabeled/Investigational Use Tension headaches, low back pain, and trigeminal neuralgia

Pregnancy Risk Factor C

Contraindications Hypersensitivity to tizanidine or any component of the formulation

Warnings/Precautions Reduce dose in patients with liver or renal disease; use with caution in patients with hypotension or cardiac disease. Tizanidine clearance is reduced by more than 50% in elderly patients with renal insufficiency (Cl_{cr} <25 mL/minute) compared to healthy elderly subjects; this may lead to a longer duration of effects and, therefore, should be used with caution in renally impaired patients.

Common Adverse Reactions

>10%:
- Cardiovascular: Hypotension
- Central nervous system: Sedation, daytime drowsiness, somnolence
- Gastrointestinal: Xerostomia

1% to 10%:
- Cardiovascular: Bradycardia, syncope
- Central nervous system: Fatigue, dizziness, anxiety, nervousness, insomnia
- Dermatologic: Pruritus, skin rash
- Gastrointestinal: Nausea, vomiting, dyspepsia, constipation, diarrhea
- Hepatic: Elevation of liver enzymes
- Neuromuscular & skeletal: Muscle weakness, tremor

Drug Interactions

Increased Effect/Toxicity:

Increased effect: Oral contraceptives

Increased toxicity: Additive hypotensive effects may be seen with diuretics, other alpha adrenergic agonists, or antihypertensives; CNS depression with alcohol, baclofen or other CNS depressants

Mechanism of Action An alpha₂-adrenergic agonist agent which decreases excitatory input to alpha motor neurons; an imidazole derivative chemically-related to clonidine, which acts as a centrally acting muscle relaxant with alpha₂-adrenergic agonist properties; acts on the level of the spinal cord

Pharmacodynamics/Kinetics
- Duration: 3-6 hours
- Bioavailability: 40%
- Half-life elimination: 2.5 hours
- Time to peak, serum: 1-5 hours

Dosage

Adults: 2-4 mg 3 times/day

Usual initial dose: 4 mg, may increase by 2-4 mg as needed for satisfactory reduction of muscle tone every 6-8 hours to a maximum of three doses in any 24 hour period

Maximum dose: 36 mg/day

Dosing adjustment in renal/hepatic impairment: May require dose reductions or less frequent dosing

Monitoring Parameters Monitor liver function (aminotransferases) at baseline, 1, 3, 6 months and then periodically thereafter; monitor ophthalmic function

Dosage Forms TAB: 2 mg, 4 mg

- ◆ **TMP** see Trimethoprim on page 1270
- ◆ **TMP-SMZ** see Sulfamethoxazole and Trimethoprim on page 1173
- ◆ **TMZ** see Temozolomide on page 1193
- ◆ **TNKase™** see Tenecteplase on page 1194

♦ **TOBI**® *see Tobramycin on page 1235*

♦ **TobraDex**® *see Tobramycin and Dexamethasone on page 1237*

Tobramycin (toe bra MYE sin)

Related Information
Aminoglycoside Dosing and Monitoring *on page 1350*
Antimicrobial Drugs of Choice *on page 1440*
Prevention of Wound Infection & Sepsis in Surgical Patients *on page 1436*

U.S. Brand Names AKTob®; Nebcin®; TOBI®; Tobrex®

Synonyms Tobramycin Sulfate

Therapeutic Category Antibiotic, Aminoglycoside; Antibiotic, Ophthalmic

Use Treatment of documented or suspected infections caused by susceptible gram-negative bacilli including *Pseudomonas aeruginosa*; topically used to treat superficial ophthalmic infections caused by susceptible bacteria. Tobramycin solution for inhalation is indicated for the management of cystic fibrosis patients (>6 years of age) with *Pseudomonas aeruginosa*.

Pregnancy Risk Factor D (injection, inhalation); B (ophthalmic)

Contraindications Hypersensitivity to tobramycin, other aminoglycosides, or any component of the formulation; pregnancy (injection/inhalation)

Warnings/Precautions Use with caution in patients with renal impairment; pre-existing auditory or vestibular impairment; and in patients with neuromuscular disorders; dosage modification required in patients with impaired renal function (I.M. & I.V.). Aminoglycosides are associated with significant nephrotoxicity or ototoxicity; the ototoxicity is directly proportional to the amount of drug given and the duration of treatment; tinnitus or vertigo are indications of vestibular injury; ototoxicity is often irreversible; renal damage is usually reversible.

Common Adverse Reactions
Injection: Frequency not defined:
Central nervous system: Confusion, disorientation, dizziness, fever, headache, lethargy, vertigo

Dermatologic: Exfoliative dermatitis, itching, rash, urticaria

Endocrine & metabolic: Serum calcium, magnesium, potassium, and/or sodium decreased

Gastrointestinal: Diarrhea, nausea, vomiting

Hematologic: Anemia, eosinophilia, granulocytopenia, leukocytosis, leukopenia, thrombocytopenia

Hepatic: ALT, AST, bilirubin, and/or LDH increased

Local: Pain at the injection site

Otic: Hearing loss, tinnitus, ototoxicity (auditory), ototoxicity (vestibular), roaring in the ears

Renal: BUN increased, cylindruria, serum creatinine increased, oliguria, proteinuria

Inhalation:
>10%:
Gastrointestinal: Sputum discoloration (21%)
Respiratory: Voice alteration (13%)
1% to 10%:
Central nervous system: Malaise (6%)
Otic: Tinnitus (3%)

Drug Interactions
Increased Effect/Toxicity: Increased antimicrobial effect of tobramycin with extended spectrum penicillins (synergistic). Neuromuscular blockers may have an increased duration of action (neuromuscular blockade). Amphotericin B, cephalosporins, and loop diuretics may increase the risk of nephrotoxicity.

Mechanism of Action Interferes with bacterial protein synthesis by binding to 30S and 50S ribosomal subunits resulting in a defective bacterial cell membrane

Pharmacodynamics/Kinetics
Absorption: I.M.: Rapid and complete

Distribution: V_d: 0.2-0.3 L/kg; Pediatrics: 0.2-0.7 L/kg; to extracellular fluid including serum, abscesses, ascitic, pericardial, pleural, synovial, lymphatic, and peritoneal fluids; crosses placenta; poor penetration into CSF, eye, bone, prostate

Protein binding: <30%

Half-life elimination:
Neonates: ≤1200 g: 11 hours; >1200 g: 2-9 hours
Adults: 2-3 hours; directly dependent upon glomerular filtration rate
Adults with impaired renal function: 5-70 hours

Time to peak, serum: I.M.: 30-60 minutes; I.V.: ~30 minutes

Excretion: Normal renal function: Urine (~90% to 95%) within 24 hours

Dosage Individualization is critical because of the low therapeutic index

Use of ideal body weight (IBW) for determining the mg/kg/dose appears to be more accurate than dosing on the basis of total body weight (TBW)

In morbid obesity, dosage requirement may best be estimated using a dosing weight of IBW + 0.4 (TBW - IBW)

Initial and periodic peak and trough plasma drug levels should be determined, particularly in critically ill patients with serious infections or in disease states known to significantly alter aminoglycoside pharmacokinetics (eg, cystic fibrosis, burns, or major surgery). Two to three serum level measurements should be obtained after the initial dose to measure the half-life in order to determine the frequency of subsequent doses.
(Continued)

Tobramycin *(Continued)*

Once daily dosing: Higher peak serum drug concentration to MIC ratios, demonstrated aminoglycoside postantibiotic effect, decreased renal cortex drug uptake, and improved cost-time efficiency are supportive reasons for the use of once daily dosing regimens for aminoglycosides. Current research indicates these regimens to be as effective for nonlife-threatening infections, with no higher incidence of nephrotoxicity, than those requiring multiple daily doses. Doses are determined by calculating the entire day's dose via usual multiple dose calculation techniques and administering this quantity as a single dose. Doses are then adjusted to maintain mean serum concentrations above the MIC(s) of the causative organism(s). (Example: 2.5-5 mg/kg as a single dose; expected Cp$_{max}$: 10-20 mcg/mL and Cp$_{min}$: <1 mcg/mL). Further research is needed for universal recommendation in all patient populations and gram-negative disease; exceptions may include those with known high clearance (eg, children, patients with cystic fibrosis, or burns who may require shorter dosage intervals) and patients with renal function impairment for whom longer than conventional dosage intervals are usually required.

Some clinicians suggest a daily dose of 4-7 mg/kg for all patients with normal renal function. This dose is at least as efficacious with similar, if not less, toxicity than conventional dosing; see "Aminoglycoside Dosing and Monitoring" *on page 1350* in the Appendix

I.M., I.V.:
Infants and Children <5 years: 2.5 mg/kg/dose every 8 hours
Children >5 years: 1.5-2.5 mg/kg/dose every 8 hours
Note: Some patients may require larger or more frequent doses if serum levels document the need (ie, cystic fibrosis or febrile granulocytopenic patients).
Adults:
Severe life-threatening infections: 2-2.5 mg/kg/dose
Urinary tract infection: 1.5 mg/kg/dose
Synergy (for gram-positive infections): 1 mg/kg/dose
Ophthalmic: Children ≥2 months and Adults: Instill 1-2 drops of solution every 4 hours; apply ointment 2-3 times/day; for severe infections apply ointment every 3-4 hours, or solution 2 drops every 30-60 minutes initially, then reduce to less frequent intervals
Inhalation: Cystic fibrosis:
Standard aerosolized tobramycin:
Children: 40-80 mg 2-3 times/day
Adults: 60-80 mg 3 times/day
High-dose regimen: Children ≥6 years and Adults: 300 mg every 12 hours (do not administer doses less than 6 hours apart); administer in repeated cycles of 28 days on drug followed by 28 days off drug

Dosing interval in renal impairment: I.M., I.V.:
Cl$_{cr}$ ≥60 mL/minute: Administer every 8 hours
Cl$_{cr}$ 40-60 mL/minute: Administer every 12 hours
Cl$_{cr}$ 20-40 mL/minute: Administer every 24 hours
Cl$_{cr}$ 10-20 mL/minute: Administer every 48 hours
Cl$_{cr}$ <10 mL/minute: Administer every 72 hours
Hemodialysis: Dialyzable; 30% removal of aminoglycosides occurs during 4 hours of HD - administer dose after dialysis and follow levels
Continuous arteriovenous or venovenous hemofiltration: Dose as for Cl$_{cr}$ of 10-40 mL/minute and follow levels
Administration in CAPD fluid:
Gram-negative infection: 4-8 mg/L (4-8 mcg/mL) of CAPD fluid
Gram-positive infection (ie, synergy): 3-4 mg/L (3-4 mcg/mL) of CAPD fluid
Administration IVPB/I.M.: Dose as for Cl$_{cr}$ <10 mL/minute and follow levels

Dosing adjustment/comments in hepatic disease: Monitor plasma concentrations
Administration
I.V.: Infuse over 30-60 minutes; give penicillins or cephalosporins at least 1 hour apart from tobramycin. Flush with saline before and after administration.
Inhalation (TOBI®): To be inhaled over ~15 minutes using a handheld nebulizer.
Ophthalmic solution: Allow 5 minutes between application of "multiple-drop" therapy.
Monitoring Parameters Urinalysis, urine output, BUN, serum creatinine, peak and trough plasma tobramycin levels; be alert to ototoxicity; hearing should be tested before and during treatment
Reference Range
Timing of serum samples: Draw peak 30 minutes after 30-minute infusion has been completed or 1 hour following I.M. injection or beginning of infusion; draw trough immediately before next dose
Therapeutic levels:
Peak:
Serious infections: 6-8 µg/mL (SI: 12-17 mg/L)
Life-threatening infections: 8-10 µg/mL (SI: 17-21 mg/L)
Urinary tract infection: 4-6 µg/mL (SI: 7-12 mg/L)
Synergy against gram-positive organisms: 3-5 µg/mL
Trough:
Serious infections: 0.5-1 µg/mL
Life-threatening infections: 1-2 µg/mL
Monitor serum creatinine and urine output; obtain drug levels after the third dose unless otherwise directed

Inhalation: Serum levels are ~1 µg/mL one hour following a 300 mg dose in patients with normal renal function.

Patient Information Report symptoms of superinfection; for eye drops - no other eye drops 5-10 minutes before or after tobramycin; report any dizziness or sensations of ringing or fullness in ears

Dosage Forms INJ, solution: 10 mg/mL (2 mL, 6 mL, 8 mL); 40 mg/mL (2 mL, 30 mL, 50 mL); (Nebcin®): 40 mg/mL (2 mL, 30 mL); (Nebcin® Pediatric): 10 mg/mL (2 mL). **INJ, powder for reconstitution** (Nebcin®): 1.2 g. **OINT, ophthalmic** (Tobrex®): 0.3% (3.5 g). **SOLN, for nebulization** [preservative free] (TOBI®): 60 mg/mL (5 mL). **SOLN, ophthalmic** (AKTob®, Tobrex®): 0.3% (5 mL)

Tobramycin and Dexamethasone (toe bra MYE sin & deks a METH a sone)
U.S. Brand Names TobraDex®
Synonyms Dexamethasone and Tobramycin
Therapeutic Category Antibiotic/Corticosteroid, Ophthalmic
Use Treatment of external ocular infection caused by susceptible gram-negative bacteria and steroid responsive inflammatory conditions of the palpebral and bulbar conjunctiva, lid, cornea, and anterior segment of the globe
Pregnancy Risk Factor B
Dosage Children and Adults: Ophthalmic: Instill 1-2 drops of solution every 4 hours; apply ointment 2-3 times/day; for severe infections apply ointment every 3-4 hours, or solution 2 drops every 30-60 minutes initially, then reduce to less frequent intervals
Dosage Forms OINT, ophthalmic: Tobramycin 0.3% and dexamethasone 0.1% (3.5 g). **SUSP, ophthalmic:** Tobramycin 0.3% and dexamethasone 0.1% (2.5 mL, 5 mL, 10 mL)

♦ **Tobramycin Sulfate** *see* Tobramycin *on page 1235*
♦ **Tobrex®** *see* Tobramycin *on page 1235*

Tocainide (toe KAY nide)
U.S. Brand Names Tonocard® [DSC]
Synonyms Tocainide Hydrochloride
Therapeutic Category Antiarrhythmic Agent, Class I-B
Use Suppression and prevention of symptomatic life-threatening ventricular arrhythmias
Unlabeled/Investigational Use Trigeminal neuralgia
Pregnancy Risk Factor C
Contraindications Hypersensitivity to tocainide, any component of the formulation, or any local anesthetics of the amide type; second- or third-degree heart block (except in patients with a functioning artificial pacemaker)
Warnings/Precautions May exacerbate some arrhythmias (ie, atrial fibrillation/flutter); use with caution in CHF patients; administer with caution in patients with pre-existing bone marrow failure, cytopenia, severe renal or hepatic disease; bone marrow depression can rarely occur during the first 3 months of therapy
Common Adverse Reactions
>10%:
  Central nervous system: Dizziness (8% to 15%)
  Gastrointestinal: Nausea (14% to 15%)
1% to 10%:
  Cardiovascular: Tachycardia (3%), bradycardia/angina/palpitations (0.5% to 1.8%), hypotension (3%)
  Central nervous system: Nervousness (0.5% to 1.5%), confusion (2% to 3%), headache (4.6%), anxiety, incoordination, giddiness, vertigo
  Dermatologic: Rash (0.5% to 8.4%)
  Gastrointestinal: Vomiting (4.5%), diarrhea (4% to 5%), anorexia (1% to 2%), loss of taste
  Neuromuscular & skeletal: Paresthesia (3.5% to 9%), tremor (dose-related: 2.9% to 8.4%), ataxia (dose-related: 2.9% to 8.4%), hot and cold sensations
  Ocular: Blurred vision (~1.5%), nystagmus (1%)

Note: Rare, potentially severe hematologic reactions, have occurred (generally within the first 12 weeks of therapy). These may include agranulocytosis, bone marrow depression, aplastic anemia, hypoplastic anemia, hemolytic anemia, anemia, leukopenia, neutropenia, thrombocytopenia, and eosinophilia.
Drug Interactions
  Cytochrome P450 Effect: Inhibits CYP1A2 (weak)
  Increased Effect/Toxicity: Tocainide may increase serum levels of caffeine and theophylline.
  Decreased Effect: Decreased tocainide plasma levels with cimetidine, phenobarbital, phenytoin, rifampin, and other hepatic enzyme inducers.
Mechanism of Action Class 1B antiarrhythmic agent; suppresses automaticity of conduction tissue, by increasing electrical stimulation threshold of ventricle, His-Purkinje system, and spontaneous depolarization of the ventricles during diastole by a direct action on the tissues; blocks both the initiation and conduction of nerve impulses by decreasing the neuronal membrane's permeability to sodium ions, which results in inhibition of depolarization with resultant blockade of conduction
Pharmacodynamics/Kinetics
  Absorption: Oral: 99% to 100%
  Distribution: V_d: 1.62-3.2 L/kg
  Protein binding: 10% to 20%
  (Continued)

Tocainide *(Continued)*

Metabolism: Hepatic to inactive metabolites; negligible first-pass effect
Half-life elimination: 11-14 hours; Renal and hepatic impairment: 23-27 hours
Time to peak, serum: 30-160 minutes
Excretion: Urine (40% to 50% as unchanged drug)

Dosage Adults: Oral: 1200-1800 mg/day in 3 divided doses, up to 2400 mg/day

Dosing adjustment in renal impairment: Cl_{cr} <30 mL/minute: Administer 50% of normal dose or 600 mg once daily.
Hemodialysis: Moderately dialyzable (20% to 50%)
Dosing adjustment in hepatic impairment: Maximum daily dose: 1200 mg
Reference Range Therapeutic: 5-12 µg/mL (SI: 22-52 µmol/L)
Patient Information Report any unusual bleeding, fever, sore throat, or any breathing difficulties; do not discontinue or alter dose without notifying prescriber; may cause drowsiness, dizziness, impair judgment, and coordination
Dosage Forms TAB [DSC]: 400 mg, 600 mg

♦ **Tocainide Hydrochloride** *see* Tocainide *on page 1237*
♦ **Tofranil®** *see* Imipramine *on page 655*
♦ **Tofranil-PM®** *see* Imipramine *on page 655*

TOLAZamide *(tole AZ a mide)*

Related Information
Hypoglycemic Drugs & Thiazolidinedione Information *on page 1378*
Sulfonamide Derivatives *on page 1404*
U.S. Brand Names Tolinase®
Therapeutic Category Antidiabetic Agent, Sulfonylurea; Hypoglycemic Agent, Oral; Sulfonylurea Agent
Use Adjunct to diet for the management of mild to moderately severe, stable, type 2 diabetes mellitus (noninsulin dependent, NIDDM)
Pregnancy Risk Factor D
Dosage Oral (doses >1000 mg/day normally do not improve diabetic control):
Adults:
Initial: 100-250 mg/day with breakfast or the first main meal of the day
Fasting blood sugar <200 mg/dL: 100 mg/day
Fasting blood sugar >200 mg/dL: 250 mg/day
Patient is malnourished, underweight, elderly, or not eating properly: 100 mg/day
Adjust dose in increments of 100-250 mg/day at weekly intervals to response. If >500 mg/day is required, give in divided doses twice daily; maximum daily dose: 1 g (doses >1 g/day are not likely to improve control)
Conversion from insulin → tolazamide
10 units day = 100 mg/day
20-40 units/day = 250 mg/day
>40 units/day = 250 mg/day and 50% of insulin dose
Doses >500 mg/day should be given in 2 divided doses
Dosing adjustment in renal impairment: Conservative initial and maintenance doses are recommended because tolazamide is metabolized to active metabolites, which are eliminated in the urine
Dosing comments in hepatic impairment: Conservative initial and maintenance doses and careful monitoring of blood glucose are recommended
Dosage Forms TAB: 100 mg, 250 mg, 500 mg; (Tolinase®): 100 mg, 250 mg

Tolazoline *(tole AZ oh leen)*

U.S. Brand Names Priscoline® [DSC]
Synonyms Benzazoline Hydrochloride; Tolazoline Hydrochloride
Therapeutic Category Alpha-Adrenergic Blocking Agent, Parenteral
Use Treatment of persistent pulmonary vasoconstriction and hypertension of the newborn (persistent fetal circulation), peripheral vasospastic disorders
Pregnancy Risk Factor C
Dosage
Neonates: Initial: I.V.: 1-2 mg/kg over 10-15 minutes via scalp vein or upper extremity; maintenance: 1-2 mg/kg/hour; use lower maintenance doses in patients with decreased renal function. Also used in neonates for acute vasospasm "cath toes" at 0.25 mg/kg/hour (no load); maximum dose: 6-8 mg/kg/hour.
Dosing interval in renal impairment in newborns: Urine output <0.9 mL/kg/hour: Decrease dose to 0.08 mg/kg/hour for every 1 mg/kg of loading dose
Adults: Peripheral vasospastic disorder: I.M., I.V., S.C.: 10-50 mg 4 times/day
Dosage Forms INJ, solution [DSC]: 25 mg/mL (4 mL)

♦ **Tolazoline Hydrochloride** *see* Tolazoline *on page 1238*

TOLBUTamide *(tole BYOO ta mide)*

Related Information
Hypoglycemic Drugs & Thiazolidinedione Information *on page 1378*
Sulfonamide Derivatives *on page 1404*
U.S. Brand Names Orinase Diagnostic® [DSC]; Tol-Tab®
Synonyms Tolbutamide Sodium

Therapeutic Category Antidiabetic Agent, Sulfonylurea; Diagnostic Agent, Hypoglycemia; Diagnostic Agent, Insulinoma; Hypoglycemic Agent, Oral; Sulfonylurea Agent

Use Adjunct to diet for the management of mild to moderately severe, stable, type 2 diabetes mellitus (noninsulin dependent, NIDDM)

Pregnancy Risk Factor D

Dosage Divided doses may improve gastrointestinal tolerance

Adults:

Oral: Initial: 1-2 g/day as a single dose in the morning or in divided doses throughout the day. Total doses may be taken in the morning; however, divided doses may allow increased gastrointestinal tolerance. Maintenance dose: 0.25-3 g/day; however, a maintenance dose >2 g/day is seldom required.

I.V. bolus: 1 g over 2-3 minutes

Elderly: Oral: Initial: 250 mg 1-3 times/day; usual: 500-2000 mg; maximum: 3 g/day

Dosing adjustment in renal impairment: Adjustment is not necessary

Hemodialysis: Not dialyzable (0% to 5%)

Dosing adjustment in hepatic impairment: Reduction of dose may be necessary in patients with impaired liver function

Dosage Forms INJ, powder for reconstitution (Orinase Diagnostic® [DSC]): 1 g. **TAB** (Tol-Tab®): 500 mg

♦ **Tolbutamide Sodium** see TOLBUTamide on page 1238

Tolcapone (TOLE ka pone)

Related Information

Parkinson's Agents Comparison on page 1402

U.S. Brand Names Tasmar®

Therapeutic Category Anti-Parkinson's Agent, COMT Inhibitor; Reverse COMT Inhibitor

Use Adjunct to levodopa and carbidopa for the treatment of signs and symptoms of idiopathic Parkinson's disease

Pregnancy Risk Factor C

Contraindications Hypersensitivity to tolcapone or any component of the formulation

Warnings/Precautions Note: Due to reports of fatal liver injury associated with use of this drug, the manufacturer is advising that tolcapone be reserved for use only in patients who do not have severe movement abnormalities and who do not respond to or who are not appropriate candidates for other available treatments. Before initiating therapy with tolcapone, the risks should be discussed with the patient, and the patient can provide written informed consent (form available from Roche).

It is not recommended that patients receive tolcapone concomitantly with nonselective MAO inhibitors (see Drug Interactions). Selegiline is a selective MAO-B inhibitor and can be taken with tolcapone.

Patients receiving tolcapone are predisposed to orthostatic hypotension, diarrhea (usually within the first 6-12 weeks of therapy), transient hallucinations (most commonly within the first 2 weeks of therapy), and new onset or worsened dyskinesia. Use with caution in patients with severe renal failure. Tolcapone is secreted into maternal milk in rats and may be excreted into human milk; until more is known, tolcapone should be considered **incompatible** with breast-feeding.

Common Adverse Reactions

>10%:

Cardiovascular: Orthostatic hypotension

Central nervous system: Sleep disorder, excessive dreaming, somnolence, headache

Gastrointestinal: Nausea, diarrhea, anorexia

Neuromuscular & skeletal: Dyskinesia, dystonia, muscle cramps

1% to 10%:

Central nervous system: Hallucinations, fatigue, loss of balance, hyperkinesia

Gastrointestinal: Vomiting, constipation, xerostomia, abdominal pain, flatulence, dyspepsia

Genitourinary: Urine discoloration

Neuromuscular & skeletal: Paresthesia, stiffness

Miscellaneous: Diaphoresis (increased)

Drug Interactions

Cytochrome P450 Effect: Inhibits CYP2C8/9 (weak)

Increased Effect/Toxicity: Tolcapone may increase the effect/levels of methyldopa, dobutamine, apomorphine, and isoproterenol due to inhibition of catechol-O-methyl transferase enzymes (COMT).

Mechanism of Action Tolcapone is a selective and reversible inhibitor of catechol-o-methyltransferase (COMT)

Pharmacodynamics/Kinetics

Absorption: Rapid

Protein binding: >99.0%

Metabolism: Glucuronidation

Bioavailability: 65%

Half-life elimination: 2-3 hours

Time to peak: ~2 hours

Excretion: Urine and feces (40%)

Dosage Adults: Oral: Initial: 100-200 mg 3 times/day; levodopa therapy may need to be decreased upon initiation of tolcapone

(Continued)

Tolcapone *(Continued)*

Monitoring Parameters Blood pressure, symptoms of Parkinson's disease, liver enzymes at baseline and then every 2 weeks for the first year of therapy, every 4 weeks for the next 6 months, then every 8 weeks thereafter. If the dose is increased to 200 mg 3 times/day, reinitiate LFT monitoring at the previous frequency. Discontinue therapy if the ALT or AST exceeds the upper limit of normal or if the clinical signs and symptoms suggest the onset of liver failure.

Patient Information Take exactly as directed (may be prescribed in conjunction with levodopa/carbidopa); do not change dosage or discontinue without consulting prescriber. Therapeutic effects may take several weeks or months to achieve and you may need frequent monitoring during first weeks of therapy. Best to take 2 hours before or after a meal; however, may be taken with meals if GI upset occurs. Take at same time each day. Maintain adequate hydration (2-3 L/day). Do not use alcohol, prescription or OTC sedatives, or CNS depressants without consulting prescriber. Urine or perspiration may appear darker. You may experience drowsiness, dizziness, confusion, or vision changes (use caution when driving, climbing stairs, or engaging in hazardous tasks). Orthostatic hypotension (use caution when changing position - rising to standing from sitting or lying); increased susceptibility to heat stroke, decreased perspiration (use caution in hot weather - maintain adequate fluids and reduce exercise activity); constipation (increased exercise, fluids, or dietary fruit and fiber may help); dry skin or nasal passages (consult prescriber for appropriate relief); nausea, vomiting, loss of appetite, or stomach discomfort (small frequent meals, chewing gum, or sucking on lozenges may help). Report unresolved constipation or vomiting; chest pain or irregular heartbeat; difficulty breathing; acute headache or dizziness; CNS changes (hallucination, loss of memory, nervousness, etc); painful or difficult urination; abdominal pain or blood in stool; increased muscle spasticity, rigidity, or involuntary movements; skin rash; or significant worsening of condition.

Dosage Forms TAB: 100 mg, 200 mg

♦ **Tolectin®** *see Tolmetin on page 1240*

♦ **Tolectin® DS** *see Tolmetin on page 1240*

♦ **Tolinase®** *see TOLAZamide on page 1238*

Tolmetin *(TOLE met in)*

Related Information
Nonsteroidal Anti-Inflammatory Agents Comparison *on page 1401*

U.S. Brand Names Tolectin®; Tolectin® DS

Synonyms Tolmetin Sodium

Therapeutic Category Analgesic, Nonsteroidal Anti-inflammatory Drug; Anti-inflammatory Agent; Nonsteroidal Anti-inflammatory Drug (NSAID), Oral

Use Treatment of rheumatoid arthritis and osteoarthritis, juvenile rheumatoid arthritis

Pregnancy Risk Factor C/D (3rd trimester or at term)

Contraindications Hypersensitivity to tolmetin, any component of the formulation, aspirin, or other NSAIDs; pregnancy (3rd trimester or near term)

Warnings/Precautions Use with caution in patients with upper GI disease, impaired renal function, CHF, dehydration, hypertension, and patients receiving anticoagulants; if GI upset occurs with tolmetin, take with antacids other than sodium bicarbonate. Withhold for at least 4-6 half-lives prior to surgical or dental procedures.

Common Adverse Reactions 1% to 10%:
Cardiovascular: Chest pain, hypertension, edema
Central nervous system: Headache, dizziness, drowsiness, depression
Dermatologic: Skin irritation
Endocrine & metabolic: Weight gain/loss
Gastrointestinal: Heartburn, abdominal pain, diarrhea, flatulence, vomiting, constipation, gastritis, peptic ulcer, nausea
Genitourinary: Urinary Tract Infection
Hematologic: Elevated BUN, transient decreases in hemoglobin/hematocrit
Ocular: Visual disturbances
Otic: Tinnitus

Drug Interactions
Increased Effect/Toxicity: Increased toxicity of digoxin, methotrexate, cyclosporine, lithium, insulin, sulfonylureas, potassium-sparing diuretics, and aspirin.
Decreased Effect: Decreased effect with aspirin. Decreased effect of thiazides and furosemide.

Mechanism of Action Inhibits prostaglandin synthesis by decreasing the activity of the enzyme, cyclooxygenase, which results in decreased formation of prostaglandin precursors

Pharmacodynamics/Kinetics
Onset of action: Analgesic: 1-2 hours; Anti-inflammatory: Days to weeks
Absorption: Well absorbed
Bioavailability: Reduced 16% with food or milk
Half-life elimination: Biphasic: Rapid: 1-2 hours; Slow: 5 hours
Time to peak, serum: 30-60 minutes
Excretion: Urine (as inactive metabolites or conjugates) within 24 hours

Dosage Oral:
Children ≥2 years:
Anti-inflammatory: Initial: 20 mg/kg/day in 3 divided doses, then 15-30 mg/kg/day in 3 divided doses

Analgesic: 5-7 mg/kg/dose every 6-8 hours
Adults: 400 mg 3 times/day; usual dose: 600 mg to 1.8 g/day; maximum: 2 g/day
Monitoring Parameters Occult blood loss, CBC, liver enzymes, BUN, serum creatinine, periodic liver function test
Patient Information Take with food, milk, or water; may cause drowsiness, impair judgment or coordination
Dosage Forms CAP (Tolectin® DS): 400 mg. **TAB:** 200 mg, 600 mg; (Tolectin®): 600 mg

♦ **Tolmetin Sodium** *see Tolmetin on page 1240*

Tolnaftate (tole NAF tate)

U.S. Brand Names Absorbine Jr.® Antifungal [OTC]; Aftate® Antifungal [OTC]; Blis-To-Sol® [OTC]; Dermasept Antifungal [OTC]; Fungi-Guard [OTC]; Gold Bond® Antifungal [OTC]; Tinactin® Antifungal [OTC]; Tinactin® Antifungal Jock Itch [OTC]; Tinaderm [OTC]; Ting® [OTC]; TipTapToe [OTC]
Therapeutic Category Antifungal Agent, Topical
Use Treatment of tinea pedis, tinea cruris, tinea corporis
Pregnancy Risk Factor C
Contraindications Hypersensitivity to tolnaftate or any component of the formulation; nail and scalp infections
Warnings/Precautions For external use only; apply to clean, dry skin; keep away from eyes
Common Adverse Reactions Frequency not defined.
Dermatologic: Pruritus, contact dermatitis
Local: Irritation, stinging
Mechanism of Action Distorts the hyphae and stunts mycelial growth in susceptible fungi
Pharmacodynamics/Kinetics Onset of action: 24-72 hours
Dosage Children ≥2 years and Adults: Topical: Wash and dry affected area; spray aerosol or apply 1-3 drops of solution or a small amount of cream, gel, or powder and rub into the affected areas 2 times/day
Note: May use for up to 4 weeks for tinea pedis or tinea corporis, and up to 2 weeks for tinea cruris
Patient Information Avoid contact with the eyes; apply to clean dry area; consult the prescriber if a skin irritation develops or if the skin infection worsens or does not improve after 10 days of therapy; does not stain skin or clothing
Dosage Forms AERO, liquid, topical (Aftate®, Tinactin® Antifungal): 1% (120 mL); (Ting®): 1% (90 mL). **AERO, powder, topical** (Aftate®): 1% (105 g); (Tinactin® Antifungal): 1% (45 g, 90 g, 100 g, 150 g); (Tinactin® Antifungal Jock Itch): 1% (100 g); (Ting®): 1% (90 g). **CRM, topical:** 1% (15 g, 30 g); (Fungi-Guard, Tinactin® Antifungal Jock Itch): 1% (15 g); (Tinactin® Antifungal): 1% (15 g, 30 g). **GEL, topical** (Absorbine Jr.® Antifungal): 1% (21 g). **LIQ, topical:** (Blis-To-Sol®): 1% (30 mL, 55 mL); Dermasept Antifungal: 1% (30 mL). **POWDER, topical:** 1% (45 g). **SOLN, topical:** 1% (10 mL); (Absorbine Jr.® Antifungal): 1% (60 mL); (Tinaderm): 1% (10 mL). **SWAB, topical [liquid filled swabstick]:** (Gold Bond® Antifungal): 1% (24s); (TipTapToe): 1% (72s)

♦ **Tol-Tab®** *see TOLBUTamide on page 1238*

Tolterodine (tole TER oh deen)

U.S. Brand Names Detrol®; Detrol® LA
Synonyms Tolterodine Tartrate
Therapeutic Category Anticholinergic Agent
Use Treatment of patients with an overactive bladder with symptoms of urinary frequency, urgency, or urge incontinence
Pregnancy Risk Factor C
Contraindications Hypersensitivity to tolterodine or any component of the formulation; urinary retention; gastric retention; uncontrolled narrow-angle glaucoma; myasthenia gravis
Warnings/Precautions Use with caution in patients with bladder flow obstruction, may increase the risk of urinary retention. Use with caution in patients with gastrointestinal obstructive disorders (ie, pyloric stenosis), may increase the risk of gastric retention. Use with caution in patients with controlled (treated) narrow-angle glaucoma; metabolized in the liver and excreted in the urine and feces, dosage adjustment is required for patients with renal or hepatic impairment. Patients on CYP3A4 inhibitors require lower dose. Safety and efficacy in pediatric patients have not been established.
Common Adverse Reactions As reported with immediate release tablet, unless otherwise specified
>10%: Gastrointestinal: Dry mouth (35%; extended release capsules 23%)
1% to 10%:
Cardiovascular: Chest pain (2%)
Central nervous system: Headache (7%; extended release capsules 6%), somnolence (3%; extended release capsules 3%), fatigue (4%; extended release capsules 2%), dizziness (5%; extended release capsules 2%), anxiety (extended release capsules 1%)
Dermatologic: Dry skin (1%)
Gastrointestinal: Abdominal pain (5%; extended release capsules 4%), constipation (7%; extended release capsules 6%), dyspepsia (4%; extended release capsules 3%), diarrhea (4%), weight gain (1%)
Genitourinary: Dysuria (2%; extended release capsules 1%)
Neuromuscular & skeletal: Arthralgia (2%)
(Continued)

1241

Tolterodine *(Continued)*

Ocular: Abnormal vision (2%; extended release capsules 1%), dry eyes (3%; extended release capsules 3%)

Respiratory: Bronchitis (2%), sinusitis (extended release capsules 2%)

Drug Interactions

Cytochrome P450 Effect: Substrate of CYP2C8/9 (minor), 2C19 (minor), 2D6 (major), 3A4 (major)

Increased Effect/Toxicity: CYP2D6 inhibitors may increase the levels/effects of tolterodine; example inhibitors include chlorpromazine, delavirdine, fluoxetine, miconazole, paroxetine, pergolide, quinidine, quinine, ritonavir, and ropinirole. No dosage adjustment was needed in patients coadministered tolterodine and fluoxetine.

Serum level and/or toxicity of tolterodine may be increased by drugs which inhibit CYP3A4, particularly in patients who are poor metabolizers via CYP2D6; effect was seen with ketoconazole. Other inhibitors include amiodarone, cimetidine, clarithromycin, cyclosporine, erythromycin, delavirdine, diltiazem, dirithromycin, disulfiram, fluoxetine, fluvoxamine, grapefruit juice, indinavir, itraconazole, nefazodone, nevirapine, propoxyphene, quinupristin-dalfopristin, ritonavir, saquinavir, verapamil, vinblastine, zafirlukast, zileuton.

Mechanism of Action Tolterodine is a competitive antagonist of muscarinic receptors. In animal models, tolterodine demonstrates selectivity for urinary bladder receptors over salivary receptors. Urinary bladder contraction is mediated by muscarinic receptors. Tolterodine increases residual urine volume and decreases detrusor muscle pressure.

Pharmacodynamics/Kinetics

Absorption: Immediate release tablet: Rapid

Distribution: I.V.: V_d: 113 ± 27 L

Protein binding: Highly bound to alpha$_1$-acid glycoprotein

Metabolism: Extensively hepatic, primarily via CYP2D6 (some metabolites share activity) and 3A4 usually (minor pathway). In patients with a genetic deficiency of CYP2D6, metabolism via 3A4 predominates. Forms three active metabolites.

Bioavailability: Immediate release tablet: 77%; increased with food

Half-life elimination:

Immediate release tablet: Extensive metabolizers: ~2 hours; Poor metabolizers: ~10 hours

Extended release capsule: Extensive metabolizers: ~7 hours; Poor metabolizers: ~18 hours

Time to peak: Immediate release tablet: 1-2 hours; Extended release tablet: 2-6 hours

Excretion: Urine (77% as unchanged drug, 5% to 14% as metabolites, <1% as metabolites in poor metabolizers); feces (17%, <1% as unchanged drug, <2.5% in poor metabolizers)

Dosage

Children: Safety and efficacy in pediatric patients have not been established

Adults: Treatment of overactive bladder: Oral:

Immediate release tablet: 2 mg twice daily; the dose may be lowered to 1 mg twice daily based on individual response and tolerability

Dosing adjustment in patients concurrently taking CYP3A4 inhibitors: 1 mg twice daily

Extended release capsule: 4 mg once a day; dose may be lowered to 2 mg daily based on individual response and tolerability

Dosing adjustment in patients concurrently taking CYP3A4 inhibitors: 2 mg daily

Elderly: Safety and efficacy in patients >64 years was found to be similar to that in younger patients; no dosage adjustment is needed based on age

Dosing adjustment in renal impairment: Use with caution (studies conducted in patients with Cl_{cr} 10-30 mL/minute):

Immediate release tablet: 1 mg twice daily

Extended release capsule: 2 mg daily

Dosing adjustment in hepatic impairment:

Immediate release tablet: 1 mg twice daily

Extended release capsule: 2 mg daily

Administration Extended release capsule: Swallow whole; do not crush, chew, or open

Patient Information Take as directed, preferably with food. Do not crush, chew, or open extended release capsule; swallow whole. You may experience headache (a mild analgesic may help); blurred vision, dizziness, nervousness, or sleepiness (use caution when driving, climbing stairs, or engaging in tasks requiring alertness until response to drug is known); abdominal discomfort, diarrhea, constipation, nausea or vomiting (small frequent meals, increased exercise, adequate fluid intake may help). Report back pain, muscle spasms, alteration in gait, or numbness of extremities; unresolved or persistent constipation, diarrhea, or vomiting; or symptoms of upper respiratory infection or flu. Report immediately any chest pain or palpitations; difficulty urinating or pain on urination.

Dosage Forms CAP, extended release (Detrol® LA): 2 mg, 4 mg. **TAB** (Detrol®): 1 mg, 2 mg

Topiramate (toe PYRE a mate)

Related Information
Anticonvulsants by Seizure Type *on page 1358*

U.S. Brand Names Topamax®

Therapeutic Category Anticonvulsant, Miscellaneous

Use In adults and pediatric patients, adjunctive therapy for partial onset seizures and adjunctive therapy of primary generalized tonic-clonic seizures; treatment of seizures associated with Lennox-Gastaut syndrome

Unlabeled/Investigational Use Bipolar disorder, infantile spasms, neuropathic pain, migraine, cluster headache

Pregnancy Risk Factor C

Contraindications Hypersensitivity to topiramate or any component of the formulation

Warnings/Precautions Avoid abrupt withdrawal of topiramate therapy, it should be withdrawn slowly to minimize the potential of increased seizure frequency; the risk of kidney stones is about 2-4 times that of the untreated population, the risk of this event may be reduced by increasing fluid intake. May be associated (rarely) with severe oligohydrosis and hyperthermia, most frequently in children; use caution and monitor closely during strenuous exercise, during exposure to high environmental temperature, or in patients receiving drugs with anticholinergic activity.

Topiramate may decrease serum bicarbonate concentrations, due to inhibition of carbonic anhydrase and increased renal bicarbonate loss. Decreased serum bicarbonate may occur commonly (up to 67% of patients), while treatment-emergent metabolic acidosis is less common. Risk may be increased in patients with a predisposing condition (renal, respiratory and/or hepatic impairment), ketogenic diet, or concurrent treatment with other drugs which may cause acidosis. Serum bicarbonate should be monitored, as well as potential complications of chronic acidosis (nephrolithiasis, osteomalacia, and reduced growth rates in children). Dose reduction or discontinuation (by tapering dose) should be considered in patients with persistent or severe metabolic acidosis. If treatment is continued, alkali supplementation should be considered.

Use cautiously in patients with hepatic or renal impairment and during pregnancy. Has been associated with secondary angle-closure glaucoma in adults and children, typically within 1 month of initiation. Discontinue in patients with acute onset of decreased visual acuity or ocular pain. Safety and efficacy have not been established in children <2 years of age.

Common Adverse Reactions
>10%:
  Central nervous system: Dizziness, ataxia, somnolence, psychomotor slowing, nervousness, memory difficulties, speech problems, fatigue
  Endocrine & metabolic: Serum bicarbonate decreased (up to 67%; marked reductions to <17 mEq/L have been reported in up to 11% of patients)
  Gastrointestinal: Nausea
  Neuromuscular & skeletal: Paresthesia, tremor
  Ocular: Nystagmus, diplopia, abnormal vision
  Respiratory: Upper respiratory infections
1% to 10%:
  Cardiovascular: Chest pain, edema
  Central nervous system: Language problems, abnormal coordination, confusion, depression, difficulty concentrating, hypoesthesia, hallucination, psychosis, suicide attempt
  Endocrine & metabolic: Hot flashes; metabolic acidosis (hyperchloremia, nonanion gap); dehydration
  Gastrointestinal: Dyspepsia, abdominal pain, anorexia, constipation, xerostomia, gingivitis, weight loss, diarrhea, vomiting
  Genitourinary: Impotence, dysuria
  Neuromuscular & skeletal: Myalgia, weakness, back pain, leg pain, rigors, hypertonia, arthralgia
  Ocular: Conjunctivitis
  Otic: Hearing decreased
  Renal: Nephrolithiasis, renal calculus
  Respiratory: Pharyngitis, sinusitis, epistaxis
  Miscellaneous: Flu-like symptoms

Drug Interactions
Cytochrome P450 Effect: Inhibits CYP2C19 (weak); **Induces** CYP3A4 (weak)

Increased Effect/Toxicity: Concomitant administration with other CNS depressants will increase its sedative effects. Coadministration with other carbonic anhydrase inhibitors may increase the chance of nephrolithiasis and/or hyperthermia (includes acetazolamide). Topiramate may increase phenytoin concentration by 25%. Concurrent administration with anticholinergic drugs may increase the risk of oligohydrosis and/or hyperthermia (includes drugs with high anticholinergic activity such as antihistamines, cyclic antidepressants, and antipsychotics); use caution.

Decreased Effect: Phenytoin can decrease topiramate levels by as much as 48%, carbamazepine reduces it by 40%, and valproic acid reduces topiramate by 14%. Digoxin levels and ethinyl estradiol blood levels are decreased when coadministered with topiramate. Topiramate may decrease valproic acid concentration by 11%.

Mechanism of Action Mechanism is not fully understood, it is thought to decrease seizure frequency by blocking sodium channels in neurons, enhancing GABA activity and by blocking glutamate activity
(Continued)

Topiramate *(Continued)*

Pharmacodynamics/Kinetics
Absorption: Good; unaffected by food
Protein binding: 13% to 17%
Metabolism: Minimally hepatic via hydroxylation, hydrolysis, glucuronidation
Bioavailability: 80%
Half-life elimination: Mean: Adults: 21 hours; shorter in pediatric patients; clearance is 50% higher in pediatric patients
Time to peak, serum: ~2-4 hours
Excretion: Urine (~70% as unchanged drug)
Dialyzable: ~30%

Dosage Oral:
Children 2-16 years: Partial seizures (adjunctive therapy), primary generalized tonic-clonic seizures (adjunctive therapy), or seizure associated with Lennox-Gastaut syndrome: Initial dose titration should begin at 25 mg (or less, based on a range of 1-3 mg/kg/day) nightly for the first week; dosage may be increased in increments of 1-3 mg/kg/day (administered in 2 divided doses) at 1- or 2-week intervals to a total daily dose of 5-9 mg/kg/day.

Adults:
Partial onset seizures (adjunctive therapy), primary generalized tonic-clonic seizures (adjunctive therapy): Initial: 25-50 mg/day; titrate in increments of 25-50 mg until an effective daily dose is reached; the daily dose may be increased by 25 mg at weekly intervals for the first 4 weeks; thereafter, the daily dose may be increased by 25-50 mg weekly to an effective daily dose (usually at least 400 mg); usual maximum dose: 1600 mg/day

> **Note:** A more rapid titration schedule has been previously recommended (ie, 50 mg/week), and may be attempted in some clinical situations; however, this may reduce the patient's ability to tolerate topiramate.

Migraine, cluster headache (unlabeled uses): Initial: 25 mg/day, titrated at weekly intervals in 25 mg increments, up to 200 mg/day

Dosing adjustment in renal impairment: Cl_{cr} <70 mL/minute: Administer 50% dose and titrate more slowly
Hemodialysis: Supplemental dose may be needed during hemodialysis

Dosing adjustment in hepatic impairment: Clearance may be reduced

Administration Oral: May be administered without regard to meals
Capsule sprinkles: May be swallowed whole or opened to sprinkle the contents on soft food (drug/food mixture should not be chewed).
Tablet: Because of bitter taste, tablets should not be broken.

Monitoring Parameters Seizure frequency, hydration status; electrolytes (recommended monitoring includes serum bicarbonate at baseline and periodically during treatment); monitor for symptoms of acute acidosis and complications of long-term acidosis (nephrolithiasis, osteomalacia, and reduced growth rates in children)

Patient Information While using this medication, do not use alcohol and other prescription or OTC medications (especially pain medications, sedatives, antihistamines, or hypnotics) without consulting prescriber. Maintain adequate hydration (2-3 L/day of fluids) unless advised by prescriber to restrict fluids. Maintain hydration prior to and during exposure to high temperatures or during vigorous exercise. Use caution when driving or engaging in tasks requiring alertness until response to drug is known. Adults should be aware of and follow state laws about driving with a seizure disorder.

Dosage Forms CAP, sprinkle: 15 mg, 25 mg. **TAB:** 25 mg, 100 mg, 200 mg

◆ **TOPO** *see Topotecan on page 1244*
◆ **Toposar®** *see Etoposide on page 497*

Topotecan *(toe poe TEE kan)*
U.S. Brand Names Hycamtin®
Synonyms Hycamptamine; NSC-609699; SK and F 104864; SKF 104864; SKF 104864-A; TOPO; Topotecan Hydrochloride; TPT
Therapeutic Category Antineoplastic Agent, Natural Source (Plant) Derivative; Antineoplastic Agent, Topoisomerase Inhibitor
Use Treatment of ovarian cancer, small cell lung cancer
Unlabeled/Investigational Use Investigational: Treatment of nonsmall cell lung cancer, sarcoma (pediatrics)
Pregnancy Risk Factor D
Contraindications Hypersensitivity to topotecan or any component of the formulation; severe bone marrow depression; pregnancy; breast-feeding
Warnings/Precautions The U.S. Food and Drug Administration (FDA) currently recommends that procedures for proper handling and disposal of antineoplastic agents be considered; monitor bone marrow function. Use caution in renal impairment.
Common Adverse Reactions
>10%:
Central nervous system: Headache, fatigue, fever, pain
Dermatologic: Alopecia (reversible), rash
Gastrointestinal: Nausea, vomiting, diarrhea, constipation, abdominal pain, stomatitis, anorexia
Hematologic: Myelosuppressive: Principle dose-limiting toxicity; white blood cell count nadir is 8-11 days and is more frequent than thrombocytopenia (at lower doses); recover is usually within 21 days and cumulative toxicity has not been noted.

Neuromuscular & skeletal: Weakness
Respiratory: Dyspnea (22%), cough
1% to 10%:
Hepatic: Transient increases in liver enzymes
Neuromuscular & skeletal: Paresthesia

Drug Interactions

Increased Effect/Toxicity: Concurrent administration of TPT and G-CSF in clinical trials results in severe myelosuppression. If G-CSF is to be used, manufacturer recommends that it should not be initiated until 24 hours after the completion of treatment with topotecan. Concurrent *in vitro* exposure to TPT and the topoisomerase II inhibitor etoposide results in no altered effect; sequential exposure results in potentiation. Concurrent exposure to TPT and 5-azacytidine results in potentiation both *in vitro* and *in vivo*. Myelosuppression was more severe when given in combination with cisplatin.

Mechanism of Action Binds to topoisomerase I and stabilizes the cleavable complex so that religation of the cleaved DNA strand cannot occur. This results in the accumulation of cleavable complexes and single-strand DNA breaks. Topotecan acts in S phase.

Pharmacodynamics/Kinetics

Absorption: Oral: ~30%
Distribution: V_{dss} of the lactone is high (mean: 87.3 L/mm²; range: 25.6-186 L/mm²), suggesting wide distribution and/or tissue sequestering
Protein binding: 35%
Metabolism: Undergoes a rapid, pH-dependent opening of the lactone ring to yield a relatively inactive hydroxy acid in plasma
Half-life elimination: 2-3 hours
Excretion: Urine (30%) within 24 hours

Dosage Adults (refer to individual protocols):
Metastatic ovarian cancer and small cell lung cancer:
IVPB: 1.5 mg/m²/day for 5 days; repeated every 21 days (neutrophil count should be >1500/mm³ and platelet count should be >100,000/mm³)
I.V. continuous infusion: 0.2-0.7 mg/m²/day for 7-21 days
Dosage adjustment for hematological effects: If neutrophil count <1500/mm³, reduce dose by 0.25 mg/m²/day for 5 days for next cycle

Dosing adjustment in renal impairment:
Cl$_{cr}$ 20-39 mL/minute: Administer 50% of normal dose
Cl$_{cr}$ <20 mL/minute: Do not use, insufficient data available
Hemodialysis: Supplemental dose is not necessary
CAPD effects: Unknown
CAVH effects: Unknown

Dosing adjustment in hepatic impairment: Bilirubin 1.5-10 mg/dL: Adjustment is not necessary

Administration Administer IVPB over 30 minutes or by 24-hour continuous infusion.

Monitoring Parameters CBC with differential and platelet count and renal function tests

Patient Information This medication can only be administered I.V. and frequent blood tests may be necessary to monitor effects of the drug. Report pain, swelling, or irritation at infusion site. Do not use alcohol, prescription, and/or OTC medications without consulting prescriber. Maintain adequate hydration (2-3 L/day of fluids unless instructed to restrict fluid intake); maintain good oral hygiene (use a soft toothbrush or cotton applicators several times a day and rinse mouth frequently). You may experience nausea, vomiting, or loss of appetite (frequent small meals, frequent mouth care, sucking lozenges, or chewing gum may help, or consult prescriber). Hair loss may occur (reversible). You will be susceptible to infection; avoid crowds and infected persons and do not receive any vaccinations unless approved by prescriber. Report persistent fever or chills, unhealed sores, oral or vaginal sores, foul-smelling urine, painful urination, easy bruising or bleeding, yellowing of eyes or skin, and change in color of urine or stool. The drug may cause permanent sterility and may cause birth defects. Contraceptive measures should be used during therapy. The drug may be excreted in breast milk, therefore, an alternative form of feeding your baby should be used.

Dosage Forms INJ, powder for reconstitution: 4 mg (base)

♦ **Topotecan Hydrochloride** *see* Topotecan *on page 1244*
♦ **Toprol-XL®** *see* Metoprolol *on page 829*
♦ **Toradol®** *see* Ketorolac *on page 706*
♦ **Torecan®** *see* Thiethylperazine *on page 1215*

Toremifene (TORE em i feen)

U.S. Brand Names Fareston®

Synonyms FC1157a; Toremifene Citrate

Therapeutic Category Antineoplastic Agent, Estrogen Receptor Antagonist; Estrogen Receptor Antagonist

Use Treatment of advanced breast cancer; management of desmoid tumors and endometrial carcinoma

Pregnancy Risk Factor D

Contraindications Hypersensitivity to toremifene or any component of the formulation; pregnancy

Warnings/Precautions Hypercalcemia and tumor flare have been reported in some breast cancer patients with bone metastases during the first weeks of treatment. Tumor flare is a syndrome of diffuse musculoskeletal pain and erythema with increased size of tumor lesions that later regress. It is often accompanied by hypercalcemia. Tumor flare does not imply
(Continued)

Toremifene *(Continued)*

treatment failure or represent tumor progression. Institute appropriate measures if hypercalcemia occurs, and if severe, discontinue treatment. Drugs that decrease renal calcium excretion (eg, thiazide diuretics) may increase the risk of hypercalcemia in patients receiving toremifene. Use cautiously in patients with anemia, hepatic failure, or thromboembolic disease.

Common Adverse Reactions
>10%:
Endocrine & metabolic: Vaginal discharge, hot flashes
Gastrointestinal: Nausea, vomiting
Miscellaneous: Diaphoresis
1% to 10%:
Cardiovascular: Thromboembolism: Tamoxifen has been associated with the occurrence of venous thrombosis and pulmonary embolism; arterial thrombosis has also been described in a few case reports; cardiac failure, myocardial infarction, edema
Central nervous system: Dizziness
Endocrine & metabolic: Hypercalcemia may occur in patients with bone metastases; galactorrhea and vitamin deficiency, menstrual irregularities
Genitourinary: Vaginal bleeding or discharge, endometriosis, priapism, possible endometrial cancer
Ocular: Ophthalmologic effects (visual acuity changes, cataracts, or retinopathy), corneal opacities, dry eyes

Drug Interactions
Cytochrome P450 Effect: Substrate of CYP1A2 (minor), 3A4 (major)
Increased Effect/Toxicity: Enzyme inhibitors (such as ketoconazole or erythromycin) may increase blood levels of toremifene. Concurrent therapy with warfarin results in significant enhancement of anticoagulant effects; has been speculated that a ↓ in antitumor effect of tamoxifen may also occur due to alterations in the percentage of active tamoxifen metabolites.
Decreased Effect: Phenobarbital, phenytoin, and carbamazepine increase the rate of toremifene metabolism and lower blood levels.

Mechanism of Action Nonsteroidal, triphenylethylene derivative. Competitively binds to estrogen receptors on tumors and other tissue targets, producing a nuclear complex that decreases DNA synthesis and inhibits estrogen effects. Nonsteroidal agent with potent antiestrogenic properties which compete with estrogen for binding sites in breast and other tissues; cells accumulate in the G_0 and G_1 phases; therefore, toremifene is cytostatic rather than cytocidal.

Pharmacodynamics/Kinetics
Absorption: Well absorbed
Distribution: V_d: 580 L
Protein binding, plasma: >99.5%, primarily to albumin
Metabolism: Extensively hepatic, principally by CYP3A4 to N-demethyltoremifene, which is also antiestrogenic but with weak *in vivo* antitumor potency
Half-life elimination: ~5 days
Time to peak, serum: ~3 hours
Excretion: Primarily feces; urine (10%) during a 1-week period

Dosage Refer to individual protocols.
Adults: Oral: 60 mg once daily, generally continued until disease progression is observed
Dosage adjustment in renal impairment: No dosage adjustment necessary
Dosage adjustment in hepatic impairment: Toremifene is extensively metabolized in the liver and dosage adjustments may be indicated in patients with liver disease; however, no specific guidelines have been developed

Administration Orally, usually as a single daily dose; occasionally in 2 or 3 divided doses

Monitoring Parameters Obtain periodic complete blood counts, calcium levels, and liver function tests. Closely monitor patients with bone metastases for hypercalcemia during the first few weeks of treatment. Leukopenia and thrombocytopenia have been reported rarely; monitor leukocyte and platelet counts during treatment.

Patient Information Take as directed, without regard to food. You may experience an initial "flare" of this disease (increased bone pain and hot flashes) which will subside with continued use. You may experience nausea, vomiting, or loss of appetite (frequent mouth care, frequent small meals, chewing gum, or sucking lozenges may help); dizziness (use caution when driving, climbing stairs, or engaging in tasks requiring alertness until response to drug is known); or loss of hair (reversible). Report vomiting that occurs immediately after taking medication; chest pain, palpitations or swollen extremities; vaginal bleeding, hot flashes, or excessive perspiration; chest pain, unusual coughing, or difficulty breathing; or any changes in vision or dry eyes.

Dosage Forms TAB: 60 mg

♦ **Toremifene Citrate** *see* Toremifene *on page 1245*

Torsemide *(TORE se mide)*
Related Information
Sulfonamide Derivatives *on page 1404*
U.S. Brand Names Demadex®
Therapeutic Category Antihypertensive Agent; Diuretic, Loop
Use Management of edema associated with congestive heart failure and hepatic or renal disease; used alone or in combination with antihypertensives in treatment of hypertension; I.V. form is indicated when rapid onset is desired

Pregnancy Risk Factor B

Contraindications Hypersensitivity to torsemide, any component of the formulation, or any sulfonylureas; anuria

Warnings/Precautions Excessive diuresis may result in dehydration, acute hypotensive or thromboembolic episodes and cardiovascular collapse; rapid injection, renal impairment, or excessively large doses may result in ototoxicity; SLE may be exacerbated; sudden alterations in electrolyte balance may precipitate hepatic encephalopathy and coma in patients with hepatic cirrhosis and ascites; monitor carefully for signs of fluid or electrolyte imbalances, especially hypokalemia in patients at risk for such (eg, digitalis therapy, history of ventricular arrhythmias, elderly, etc), hyperuricemia, hypomagnesemia, or hypocalcemia; use caution with exposure to ultraviolet light. Ototoxicity is associated with rapid I.V. administration of other loop diuretics and has been seen with oral torsemide. Do not administer intravenously in less than 2 minutes; single doses should not exceed 200 mg.

Chemical similarities are present among sulfonamides, sulfonylureas, carbonic anhydrase inhibitors, thiazides, and loop diuretics (except ethacrynic acid). Use in patients with sulfonylurea allergy is specifically contraindicated in product labeling, however, a risk of cross-reaction exists in patients with allergy to any of these compounds; avoid use when previous reaction has been severe.

Common Adverse Reactions 1% to 10%:
Cardiovascular: Edema (1.1%), EKG abnormality (2%), chest pain (1.2%)
Central nervous system: Headache (7.3%), dizziness (3.2%), insomnia (1.2%), nervousness (1%)
Endocrine & metabolic: Hyperglycemia, hyperuricemia, hypokalemia
Gastrointestinal: Diarrhea (2%), constipation (1.8%), nausea (1.8%), dyspepsia (1.6%), sore throat (1.6%)
Genitourinary: Excessive urination (6.7%)
Neuromuscular & skeletal: Weakness (2%), arthralgia (1.8%), myalgia (1.6%)
Respiratory: Rhinitis (2.8%), cough increase (2%)

Drug Interactions

Cytochrome P450 Effect: Substrate of CYP2C8/9 (major); **Inhibits** CYP2C19 (weak)

Increased Effect/Toxicity: Torsemide-induced hypokalemia may predispose to digoxin toxicity and may increase the risk of arrhythmia with drugs which may prolong QT interval, including type Ia and type III antiarrhythmic agents, cisapride, and some quinolones (spar-floxacin, gatifloxacin, and moxifloxacin). The risk of toxicity from lithium and salicylates (high dose) may be increased by loop diuretics. Hypotensive effects and/or adverse renal effects of ACE inhibitors and NSAIDs are potentiated by bumetanide-induced hypovolemia. The effects of peripheral adrenergic-blocking drugs or ganglionic blockers may be increased by bumetanide.

Torsemide may increase the risk of ototoxicity with other ototoxic agents (aminoglycosides, cis-platinum), especially in patients with renal dysfunction. Synergistic diuretic effects occur with thiazide-type diuretics. Diuretics tend to be synergistic with other antihypertensive agents, and hypotension may occur.

Decreased Effect: Torsemide action may be reduced with probenecid. Diuretic action may be impaired in patients with cirrhosis and ascites if used with salicylates. Glucose tolerance may be decreased when used with sulfonylureas. CYP2C8/9 inducers may decrease the levels/effects of torsemide; example inducers include carbamazepine, phenobarbital, phenytoin, rifampin, rifapentine, and secobarbital. Torsemide efficacy may be decreased with NSAIDs.

Mechanism of Action Inhibits reabsorption of sodium and chloride in the ascending loop of Henle and distal renal tubule, interfering with the chloride-binding cotransport system, thus causing increased excretion of water, sodium, chloride, magnesium, and calcium; does not alter GFR, renal plasma flow, or acid-base balance

Pharmacodynamics/Kinetics
Onset of action: Diuresis: 30-60 minutes
Peak effect: 1-4 hours
Duration: ~6 hours
Absorption: Oral: Rapid
Protein binding, plasma: ~97% to 99%
Metabolism: Hepatic (80%) via CYP
Bioavailability: 80% to 90%
Half-life elimination: 2-4; Cirrhosis: 7-8 hours
Excretion: Urine (20% as unchanged drug)

Dosage Adults: Oral, I.V.:
Congestive heart failure: 10-20 mg once daily; may increase gradually for chronic treatment by doubling dose until the diuretic response is apparent (for acute treatment, I.V. dose may be repeated every 2 hours with double the dose as needed)
Chronic renal failure: 20 mg once daily; increase as described above
Hepatic cirrhosis: 5-10 mg once daily with an aldosterone antagonist or a potassium-sparing diuretic; increase as described above
Hypertension: 2.5-5 mg once daily; increase to 10 mg after 4-6 weeks if an adequate hypotensive response is not apparent; if still not effective, an additional antihypertensive agent may be added

Administration I.V. injections should be administered over ≥2 minutes; the oral form may be administered regardless of meal times; patients may be switched from the I.V. form to the oral and vice-versa with no change in dose; no dosage adjustment is needed in the elderly or patients with hepatic impairment
(Continued)

Torsemide *(Continued)*

To administer as a continuous infusion: 50 mg or 200 mg torsemide should be diluted in 250 mL or 500 mL of compatible solution in plastic containers

Monitoring Parameters Renal function, electrolytes, and fluid status (weight and I & O), blood pressure

Patient Information May be taken with food or milk; rise slowly from a lying or sitting position to minimize dizziness, lightheadedness or fainting; also use extra care when exercising, standing for long periods of time, and during hot weather; take dose in the morning or early in the evening to prevent nocturia; use caution with exposure to ultraviolet light

Dosage Forms INJ, solution: 10 mg/mL (2 mL, 5 mL). **TAB:** 5 mg, 10 mg, 20 mg, 100 mg

Tositumomab and Iodine I 131 Tositumomab

(toe si TYOO mo mab & EYE oh dyne eye one THUR tee one toe si TYOO mo mab)

U.S. Brand Names Bexxar®

Synonyms Anti-CD20-Murine Monoclonal Antibody I-131; B1; B1 Antibody; 131 I Anti-B1 Antibody; 131 I-Anti-B1 Monoclonal Antibody; Iodine I 131 Tositumomab and Tositumomab; Tositumomab I-131

Therapeutic Category Antineoplastic Agent, Monoclonal Antibody; Radiopharmaceutical

Use Treatment of relapsed or refractory CD20 positive, follicular, non-Hodgkin's lymphoma

Pregnancy Risk Factor X

Contraindications Hypersensitivity to murine proteins or any component of the formulation; pregnancy; breast-feeding

Warnings/Precautions Hypersensitivity reactions (including anaphylaxis) have been reported. Patients should be screened for human antimouse antibodies (HAMA); may be at increased risk of allergic or serious hypersensitivity reactions. Hematologic toxicity was reported to be the most common adverse effect with 27% patients requiring supportive care. Severe or life-threatening cytopenias (NCI CTC grade 3 or 4) have been reported in a large number of patients; may be prolonged and severe. Secondary malignancies have been reported following use. Treatment may lead to hypothyroidism; patients should receive thyroid-blocking medications prior to the start of therapy. Patients should be premedicated to prevent infusion related reactions. For a single course of therapy only; multiple courses or use in combination with other chemotherapy or irradiation have not been studied. Safety has not been established in patients with >25% lymphoma marrow involvement, platelet count <100,000 cells/mm^3 or neutrophil count <1500 cells/mm^3. Use caution with cardiovascular disease, renal, or hepatic impairment. Safety and efficacy have not been established with impaired renal function or in pediatric patients.

Common Adverse Reactions

>10%:

Central nervous system: Fever (37%), pain (19%), chills (18%), headache (16%)

Dermatologic: Rash (17%)

Gastrointestinal: Nausea (36%), abdominal pain (15%), vomiting (15%), anorexia (14%), diarrhea (12%)

Hematologic:

Neutropenia (grade 3 or 4, 63%); thrombocytopenia (grade 3 or 4, 53%)

Time to nadir: 4-7 weeks

Duration: 30 days (>90 days in 5% to 7% of patients)

Neuromuscular & skeletal: Weakness (46%), myalgia (13%)

Respiratory: Cough (21%), pharyngitis (12%), dyspnea (11%)

Miscellaneous: Infusion-related reactions (26%, occurred within 14 days of infusion, included bronchospasm, chills, dyspnea, fever, hypotension, nausea, rigors, diaphoresis), infection (21%), HAMA-positive seroconversion (11%)

1% to 10%:

Cardiovascular: Hypotension (10%), peripheral edema (9%), chest pain (7%), vasodilation (5%)

Central nervous system: Dizziness (5%), somnolence (5%)

Dermatologic: Pruritus (10%), diaphoresis (8%)

Endocrine & metabolic: Hypothyroidism (7%)

Gastrointestinal: Constipation (6%), dyspepsia (6%), weight loss (6%)

Local: Injection site hypersensitivity

Neuromuscular & skeletal: Arthralgia (10%), back pain (8%), neck pain (6%)

Respiratory: Rhinitis (10%), pneumonia (6%), laryngismus

Miscellaneous: Hypersensitivity reaction (6%), secondary leukemia/myelodysplastic syndrome (3%), anaphylactoid reaction, secondary malignancies, serum sickness

Drug Interactions

Increased Effect/Toxicity: No formal drug interaction studies have been conducted.

Decreased Effect: No formal drug interaction studies have been conducted.

Mechanism of Action Tositumomab is a murine IgG2a lambda monoclonal antibody which binds to the CD20 antigen, expressed on B-lymphocytes and on >90% of B-cell non-Hodgkin's lymphomas. Iodine I 131 tositumomab is a radio-iodinated derivative of tositumomab covalently linked to iodine 131. The possible actions of the regimen include apoptosis, complement-dependent cytotoxicity, antibody-dependent cellular cytotoxicity, and cell death. Administration results in depletion of CD20 positive cells.

Pharmacodynamics/Kinetics

Distribution: Tositumomab: V_d increased with high tumor burden, splenomegaly, or bone marrow involvement

Half-life elimination: Tositumomab:
  Elimination: 36-48 hours
  Terminal half-life decreased with high tumor burden, splenomegaly, or bone marrow involvement
  Clearance: Blood: 68.2 mg/hour
  Excretion: Iodine-131: Urine (98%) and decay

Dosage I.V.: Adults: Dosing consists of four components administered in 2 steps. Thyroid protective agents (SSKI, Lugol's solution or potassium iodide), acetaminophen and diphenhydramine should be given with treatment. Refer to Additional Information.

Step 1: Dosimetric step (Day 0):
  Tositumomab 450 mg in NS 50 mL administered over 60 minutes
  Iodine I 131 tositumomab (containing I-131 5.0 mCi and tositumomab 35mg) in NS 30 mL administered over 20 minutes
  Note: Whole body dosimetry and biodistribution should be determined on Day 0; days 2, 3, or 4; and day 6 or 7 prior to administration of Step 2. If biodistribution is not acceptable, do not administer the therapeutic step. On day 6 or 7, calculate the patient specific activity of iodine I 131 tositumomab to deliver 75 cGy TBD or 65 cGy TBD (in mCi).

Step 2: Therapeutic step (Day 7):
  Tositumomab 450 mg in NS 50 mL administered over 60 minutes
  Iodine I 131 tositumomab:
    Platelets ≥150,000/mm³: Iodine I 131 calculated to deliver 75 cGy total body irradiation and tositumomab 35 mg over 20 minutes
    Platelets ≥100,000/mm³ and <150,000/mm³: Iodine I 131 calculated to deliver 65 cGy total body irradiation and tositumomab 35 mg over 20 minutes

Administration I.V.: Reduce the rate of infusion by 50% for mild-to-moderate infusion-related toxicities; interrupt for severe toxicity. Once severe toxicity has resolved, infusion may be restarted at half the previous rate. The same IV tubing set with an in-line filter should be used for the entire dosimetric or therapeutic step. Changing filters may result in loss of drug. Prior to infusion, patients should be premedicated and a thyroid-protective agent should be started.

Monitoring Parameters CBC with differential (prior to therapy and at least weekly); TSH (prior to therapy and yearly); serum creatinine (immediately prior to administration)

Following infusion of the iodine I 131 tositumomab dosimetric dose, the total body gamma camera counts and whole body images should be taken within 1 hour of the infusion and prior to urination, and 2-4 days after the infusion and following urination, and 6-7 days after the infusion and following urination.

Patient Information This medication is given only by injection. Follow instructions to limit exposure of radioactivity to family and friends. Notify prescriber if pregnant or if pregnancy occurs within 12 months after completion of therapy; effective birth control should be used by male and female patients during treatment and for 12 months following therapy. Breast-feeding is not recommended; discontinue and change to formula feedings prior to therapy.

Dosage Forms Note: Not all components are shipped from the same facility. When ordering, ensure that all will arrive on the same day.
  KIT [dosimetric package] (Bexxar®): Tositumomab 225 mg/16.1 mL [2 vials], tositumomab 35 mg/2.5 mL [1 vial], and iodine I 131 tositumomab 0.1 mg/mL and 0.61mCi/mL (20 mL) [1 vial]. **KIT [therapeutic package]** (Bexxar®): Tositumomab 225 mg/16.1 mL [2 vials], tositumomab 35 mg/2.5 mL [1 vial], and iodine I 131 tositumomab 1.1 mg/mL and 5.6 mCi/mL (20 mL) [1 or 2 vials]

Tramadol (TRA ma dole)

U.S. Brand Names Ultram®
Synonyms Tramadol Hydrochloride
Therapeutic Category Analgesic, Non-narcotic
Use Relief of moderate to moderately-severe pain
Pregnancy Risk Factor C
Contraindications Hypersensitivity to tramadol, opioids, or any component of the formulation; opioid-dependent patients; acute intoxication with alcohol, hypnotics, centrally-acting analgesics, opioids, or psychotropic drugs
Warnings/Precautions Should be used only with extreme caution in patients receiving MAO inhibitors. May cause CNS depression and/or respiratory depression, particularly when combined with other CNS depressants. Use with caution and reduce dosage when administered to patients receiving other CNS depressants. An increased risk of seizures may occur in
(Continued)

Tramadol *(Continued)*

patients receiving serotonin reuptake inhibitors (SSRIs or anorectics), tricyclic antidepressants, other cyclic compounds (including cyclobenzaprine, promethazine), neuroleptics, MAO inhibitors, or drugs which may lower seizure threshold. Patients with a history of seizures, or with a risk of seizures (head trauma, metabolic disorders, CNS infection, or malignancy, or during ethanol/drug withdrawal) are also at increased risk.

Elderly patients and patients with chronic respiratory disorders may be at greater risk of adverse events. Use with caution in patients with increased intracranial pressure or head injury. Use tramadol with caution and reduce dosage in patients with liver disease or renal dysfunction and in patients with myxedema, hypothyroidism, or hypoadrenalism. Not recommended during pregnancy or in nursing mothers. Tolerance or drug dependence may result from extended use; abrupt discontinuation should be avoided. Safety and efficacy in pediatric patients have not been established.

Common Adverse Reactions Incidence of some adverse effects may increase over time
>10%:
   Central nervous system: Dizziness, headache, somnolence, vertigo
   Gastrointestinal: Constipation, nausea
1% to 10%:
   Cardiovascular: Vasodilation
   Central nervous system: Agitation, anxiety, confusion, coordination impaired, emotional lability, euphoria, hallucinations, malaise, nervousness, sleep disorder, tremor
   Dermatologic: Pruritus, rash
   Endocrine & metabolic: Menopausal symptoms
   Gastrointestinal: Abdominal pain, anorexia, diarrhea, dry mouth, dyspepsia, flatulence, vomiting
   Genitourinary: Urinary frequency, urinary retention
   Neuromuscular & skeletal: Hypertonia, spasticity, weakness
   Ocular: Miosis, visual disturbance
   Miscellaneous: Diaphoresis

Drug Interactions
   Cytochrome P450 Effect: Substrate of CYP2D6 (major), 3A4 (minor)
   Increased Effect/Toxicity: Amphetamines may increase the risk of seizures with tramadol. Cimetidine increases the half-life of tramadol by 20% to 25%. SSRIs may increase the risk of seizures with tramadol. Tricyclic antidepressants may increase the risk of seizures. Linezolid may be associated with increased risk of seizures (due to MAO inhibition). MAO inhibitors may increases the risk of seizures. It is not clear if drugs with selective MAO type B inhibition are safer than nonselective agents. Avoid drugs with MAO activity (ie, linezolid). Naloxone may increase the risk of seizures in tramadol overdose. Neuroleptic agents may increase the risk of tramadol-associated seizures and may have additive CNS depressant effects. Opioids may increase the risk of seizures, and may have additive CNS depressant effects. Quinidine (and other inhibitors of CYP2D6) may increase the tramadol serum concentrations.
   Decreased Effect: CYP2D6 inhibitors may decrease the effects of tramadol; example inhibitors include chlorpromazine, delavirdine, fluoxetine, miconazole, paroxetine, pergolide, quinidine, quinine, ritonavir, and ropinirole. Carbamazepine may decrease analgesic efficacy of tramadol (half-life decreases 33% to 50%) and may increase the risk of seizures in patients requiring anticonvulsants.

Mechanism of Action Binds to μ-opiate receptors in the CNS causing inhibition of ascending pain pathways, altering the perception of and response to pain; also inhibits the reuptake of norepinephrine and serotonin, which also modifies the ascending pain pathway

Pharmacodynamics/Kinetics
   Onset of action: ~1 hour
   Duration of action: 9 hours
   Absorption: Rapid and complete
   Distribution: V_d: 2.5-3 L/kg
   Protein binding, plasma: 20%
   Metabolism: Extensively hepatic via demethylation, glucuronidation, and sulfation; has pharmacologically active metabolite formed by CYP2D6
   Bioavailability: 75%
   Half-life elimination: Tramadol: ~6 hours; Active metabolite: 7 hours; prolonged in elderly, hepatic or renal impairment
   Time to peak: 2 hours
   Excretion: Urine (as metabolites)

Dosage Oral:
   Adults: Moderate to severe chronic pain: 50-100 mg every 4-6 hours, not to exceed 400 mg/day
      For patients not requiring rapid onset of effect, tolerability may be improved by starting dose at 25 mg/day and titrating dose by 25 mg every 3 days, until reaching 25 mg 4 times/day. Dose may then be increased by 50 mg every 3 days as tolerated, to reach dose of 50 mg 4 times/day.
   Elderly: >75 years: 50-100 mg every 4-6 hours (not to exceed 300 mg/day); see dosing adjustments for renal and hepatic impairment

   Dosing adjustment in renal impairment: Cl_{cr} <30 mL/minute: Administer 50-100 mg dose every 12 hours (maximum: 200 mg/day)
   Dosing adjustment in hepatic impairment: Cirrhosis: Recommended dose: 50 mg every 12 hours

Monitoring Parameters Pain relief, respiratory rate, blood pressure, and pulse; signs of tolerance or abuse

Reference Range 100-300 ng/mL; however, serum level monitoring is not required

Patient Information Avoid driving or operating machinery until the effect of drug wears off. Report cravings to your prescriber immediately.

Dosage Forms TAB: 50 mg

♦ **Tramadol Hydrochloride** *see* Tramadol *on page 1249*

♦ **Tramadol Hydrochloride and Acetaminophen** *see* Acetaminophen and Tramadol *on page 27*

♦ **Trandate®** *see* Labetalol *on page 710*

Trandolapril (tran DOE la pril)

Related Information
Angiotensin Agents Comparison *on page 1353*

U.S. Brand Names Mavik®

Therapeutic Category Angiotensin-Converting Enzyme (ACE) Inhibitor; Antihypertensive Agent

Use Management of hypertension alone or in combination with other antihypertensive agents; treatment of left ventricular dysfunction after myocardial infarction

Unlabeled/Investigational Use As a class, ACE inhibitors are recommended in the treatment of systolic congestive heart failure

Pregnancy Risk Factor C/D (2nd and 3rd trimesters)

Contraindications Hypersensitivity to trandolapril or any component of the formulation; history of angioedema-related to previous treatment with an ACE inhibitor; bilateral renal artery stenosis; pregnancy (2nd and 3rd trimesters)

Warnings/Precautions Neutropenia, agranulocytosis, angioedema, decreased renal function (hypertension, renal artery stenosis, CHF), hepatic dysfunction (elimination, activation), proteinuria, first-dose hypotension (hypovolemia, CHF, dehydrated patients at risk, eg, diuretic use, elderly), elderly (due to renal function changes); use with caution and modify dosage in patients with renal impairment (Cl_{cr} <30 mL/minute); use with caution in patients with collagen vascular disease, CHF, hypovolemia, valvular stenosis, hyperkalemia (>5.7 mEq/L), anesthesia

Patients taking diuretics are at risk for developing hypotension on initial dosing; to prevent this, discontinue diuretics 2-3 days prior to initiating trandolapril; may restart diuretics if blood pressure is not controlled by trandolapril alone

Common Adverse Reactions Note: Frequency ranges include data from hypertension and heart failure trials. Higher rates of adverse reactions have generally been noted in patients with CHF. However, the frequency of adverse effects associated with placebo is also increased in this population.

>1%:
  Cardiovascular: Hypotension (<1% to 11%), bradycardia (<1% to 4.7%), intermittent claudication (3.8%), stroke (3.3%)
  Central nervous system: Dizziness (1.3% to 23%), syncope (5.9%), asthenia (3.3%)
  Endocrine & metabolic: Elevated uric acid (15%), hyperkalemia (5.3%), hypocalcemia (4.7%)
  Gastrointestinal: Dyspepsia (6.4%), gastritis (4.2%)
  Neuromuscular & skeletal: Myalgia (4.7%)
  Renal: Elevated BUN (9%), elevated serum creatinine (1.1% to 4.7%) Respiratory: Cough (1.9% to 35%)

Drug Interactions

Increased Effect/Toxicity: Potassium supplements, co-trimoxazole (high dose), angiotensin II receptor antagonists (candesartan, losartan, irbesartan, etc), or potassium-sparing diuretics (amiloride, spironolactone, triamterene) may result in elevated serum potassium levels when combined with trandolapril. ACE inhibitor effects may be increased by phenothiazines or probenecid (increases levels of captopril). ACE inhibitors may increase serum concentrations/effects of digoxin, lithium, and sulfonlyureas.

Diuretics have additive hypotensive effects with ACE inhibitors, and hypovolemia increases the potential for adverse renal effects of ACE inhibitors. In patients with compromised renal function, coadministration with NSAIDs may result in further deterioration of renal function. Allopurinol and ACE inhibitors may cause a higher risk of hypersensitivity reaction when taken concurrently.

Decreased Effect: Aspirin (high dose) may reduce the therapeutic effects of ACE inhibitors; at low dosages this does not appear to be significant. Rifampin may decrease the effect of ACE inhibitors. Antacids may decrease the bioavailability of ACE inhibitors (may be more likely to occur with captopril); separate administration times by 1-2 hours. NSAIDs, specifically indomethacin, may reduce the hypotensive effects of ACE inhibitors. More likely to occur in low renin or volume dependent hypertensive patients.

Mechanism of Action Trandolapril is an ACE inhibitor which prevents the formation of angiotensin II from angiotensin I. Trandolapril must undergo enzymatic hydrolysis, mainly in liver, to its biologically active metabolite, trandolaprilat. A CNS mechanism may also be involved in the hypotensive effect as angiotensin II increases adrenergic outflow from the CNS. Vasoactive kallikrein's may be decreased in conversion to active hormones by ACE inhibitors, thus, reducing blood pressure.

Pharmacodynamics/Kinetics
Onset of action: 1-2 hours
(Continued)

Trandolapril *(Continued)*

Peak effect: Reduction in blood pressure: 6 hours
Duration: Prolonged; 72 hours after single dose
Absorption: Rapid
Distribution: Trandolaprilat (active metabolite) is very lipophilic in comparison to other ACE inhibitors
Protein binding: 80%
Metabolism: Hepatically hydrolyzed to active metabolite, trandolaprilat
Half-life elimination:
Trandolapril: 6 hours; Trandolaprilat: Effective: 10 hours, Terminal: 24 hours
Elimination: As metabolites in urine:
Time to peak: Parent: 1 hour; Active metabolite trandolaprilat: 4-10 hours
Excretion: Urine (as metabolites)
Clearance: Reduce dose in renal failure; creatinine clearances ≤30 mL/minute result in accumulation of active metabolite

Dosage Adults: Oral:
Hypertension: Initial dose in patients not receiving a diuretic: 1 mg/day (2 mg/day in black patients). Adjust dosage according to the blood pressure response. Make dosage adjustments at intervals of ≥1 week. Most patients have required dosages of 2-4 mg/day. There is a little experience with doses >8 mg/day. Patients inadequately treated with once daily dosing at 4 mg may be treated with twice daily dosing. If blood pressure is not adequately controlled with trandolapril monotherapy, a diuretic may be added.
Heart failure postmyocardial infarction or left ventricular dysfunction postmyocardial infarction: Initial: 1 mg/day; titrate patients (as tolerated) towards the target dose of 4 mg/day. If a 4 mg dose is not tolerated, patients can continue therapy with the greatest tolerated dose.
Dosing adjustment in renal impairment: Cl$_{cr}$ ≤30 mL/minute: Recommended starting dose: 0.5 mg/day.
Dosing adjustment in hepatic impairment: Cirrhosis: Recommended starting dose: 0.5 mg/day.
Monitoring Parameters Serum potassium, renal function, serum creatinine, BUN, CBC
Patient Information Do not discontinue medication without advice of prescriber; report sore throat, swelling, palpitations, cough, chest pains, difficulty swallowing, swelling of face, eyes, tongue, lips, hoarseness, sweating, vomiting, or diarrhea; may cause dizziness, lightheadedness during first few days; may also cause changes in taste perception; do not use salt substitutes containing potassium without consulting a physician
Dosage Forms TAB: 1 mg, 2 mg, 4 mg

Trandolapril and Verapamil *(tran DOE la pril & ver AP a mil)*
U.S. Brand Names Tarka®
Synonyms Verapamil and Trandolapril
Therapeutic Category Angiotensin-Converting Enzyme (ACE) Inhibitor/Calcium Channel Blocker Combination; Antihypertensive Agent, Combination
Use Combination drug for the treatment of hypertension, however, not indicated for initial treatment of hypertension; replacement therapy in patients receiving separate dosage forms (for patient convenience); when monotherapy with one component fails to achieve desired antihypertensive effect, or when dose-limiting adverse effects limit upward titration of monotherapy
Pregnancy Risk Factor C/D (2nd and 3rd trimesters)
Dosage Dose is individualized
Dosage Forms TAB, combination [trandolapril component is immediate release, verapamil component is sustained release]: Trandolapril 1 mg and verapamil 240 mg; trandolapril 2 mg and verapamil 180 mg; trandolapril 2 mg and verapamil 240 mg; trandolapril 4 mg and verapamil 240 mg

Tranexamic Acid *(tran eks AM ik AS id)*
U.S. Brand Names Cyklokapron®
Therapeutic Category Antihemophilic Agent; Hemostatic Agent
Use Short-term use (2-8 days) in hemophilia patients during and following tooth extraction to reduce or prevent hemorrhage
Unlabeled/Investigational Use Has been used as an alternative to aminocaproic acid for subarachnoid hemorrhage
Pregnancy Risk Factor B
Dosage Children and Adults: I.V.: 10 mg/kg immediately before surgery, then 25 mg/kg/dose orally 3-4 times/day for 2-8 days
Alternatively:
Oral: 25 mg/kg 3-4 times/day beginning 1 day prior to surgery
I.V.: 10 mg/kg 3-4 times/day in patients who are unable to take oral
Dosing adjustment/interval in renal impairment:
Cl$_{cr}$ 50-80 mL/minute: Administer 50% of normal dose or 10 mg/kg twice daily I.V. or 15 mg/kg twice daily orally
Cl$_{cr}$ 10-50 mL/minute: Administer 25% of normal dose or 10 mg/kg/day I.V. or 15 mg/kg/day orally
Cl$_{cr}$ <10 mL/minute: Administer 10% of normal dose or 10 mg/kg/dose every 48 hours I.V. or 15 mg/kg/dose every 48 hours orally
Dosage Forms INJ, solution: 100 mg/mL (10 mL). **TAB:** 500 mg

Tranylcypromine (tran il SIP roe meen)

Related Information
Antidepressant Agents Comparison *on page 1359*

U.S. Brand Names Parnate®

Synonyms Transamine Sulphate; Tranylcypromine Sulfate

Therapeutic Category Antidepressant, Monoamine Oxidase Inhibitor

Use Treatment of major depressive episode without melancholia

Unlabeled/Investigational Use Post-traumatic stress disorder

Pregnancy Risk Factor C

Contraindications Hypersensitivity to tranylcypromine or any component of the formulation; uncontrolled hypertension; pheochromocytoma; hepatic or renal disease; cerebrovascular defect; cardiovascular disease (CHF); concurrent use of sympathomimetics (and related compounds); CNS depressants, ethanol, meperidine, bupropion, buspirone, dexfenfluramine, dextromethorphan, guanethidine, and serotonergic drugs (including SSRIs) - do not use within 5 weeks of fluoxetine discontinuation or 2 weeks of other antidepressant discontinuation; general anesthesia (discontinue 10 days prior to elective surgery); local vasoconstrictors; spinal anesthesia (hypotension may be exaggerated); foods which are high in tyramine, tryptophan, or dopamine, chocolate, or caffeine.

Warnings/Precautions Safety in children <16 years of age has not been established; use with caution in patients who are hyperactive, hyperexcitable, or who have glaucoma, suicidal tendencies, hyperthyroidism, or diabetes; avoid use of meperidine within 2 weeks of phenelzine use. Toxic reactions have occurred with dextromethorphan. Hypertensive crisis may occur with tyramine, tryptophan, or dopamine-containing foods. Should not be used in combination with other antidepressants. Hypotensive effects of antihypertensives (beta-blockers, thiazides) may be exaggerated. May cause orthostatic hypotension (especially at dosages >30 mg/day) - use with caution in patients with hypotension or patients who would not tolerate transient hypotensive episodes - effects may be additive when used with other agents known to cause orthostasis (phenothiazines). Has been associated with activation of hypomania and/or mania in bipolar patients. May worsen psychotic symptoms in some patients. The possibility of a suicide attempt is inherent in major depression and may persist until remission occurs. Use caution in high-risk patients during initiation of therapy. Prescriptions should be written for the smallest quantity consistent with good patient care. Use with caution in patients at risk of seizures, or in patients receiving other drugs which may lower seizure threshold. Discontinue at least 48 hours prior to myelography. Use with caution in patients receiving disulfiram. Use with caution in patients with renal impairment.

The MAO inhibitors are effective and generally well tolerated by older patients. It is the potential interactions with tyramine or tryptophan-containing foods and other drugs, and their effects on blood pressure that have limited their use.

Common Adverse Reactions Frequency not defined.

Cardiovascular: Orthostatic hypotension, edema

Central nervous system: Dizziness, headache, drowsiness, sleep disturbances, fatigue, hyper-reflexia, twitching, ataxia, mania, akinesia, confusion, disorientation, memory loss

Dermatologic: Rash, pruritus, urticaria, localized scleroderma, cystic acne (flare), alopecia

Endocrine & metabolic: Sexual dysfunction (anorgasmia, ejaculatory disturbances, impotence), hypernatremia, hypermetabolic syndrome, SIADH

Gastrointestinal: Xerostomia, constipation, weight gain

Genitourinary: Urinary retention, incontinence

Hematologic: Leukopenia, agranulocytosis

Hepatic: Hepatitis

Neuromuscular & skeletal: Weakness, tremor, myoclonus

Ocular: Blurred vision, glaucoma

Miscellaneous: Diaphoresis

Drug Interactions

Cytochrome P450 Effect: Inhibits CYP1A2 (moderate), 2A6 (strong), 2C8/9 (weak), 2C19 (moderate), 2D6 (moderate), 2E1 (weak), 3A4 (weak)

Increased Effect/Toxicity: In general, the combined use of tranylcypromine with TCAs, venlafaxine, trazodone, dexfenfluramine, sibutramine, lithium, meperidine, fenfluramine, dextromethorphan, and SSRIs should be avoided due to the potential for severe adverse reactions (serotonin syndrome, death). Tranylcypromine in combination with amphetamines, other stimulants (methylphenidate), levodopa, metaraminol, buspirone, bupropion, reserpine, and decongestants (pseudoephedrine) may result in severe hypertensive reactions. MAO inhibitors (including tranylcypromine) may inhibit the metabolism of barbiturates and prolong their effect. Foods (eg, cheese) and beverages (eg, ethanol) containing tyramine should be avoided; hypertensive crisis may result. Tranylcypromine may increase the pressor response of norepinephrine and may prolong neuromuscular blockade produced by (Continued)

Tranylcypromine *(Continued)*

succinylcholine. Tramadol may increase the risk of seizures and serotonin syndrome in patients receiving an MAO inhibitor. Tranylcypromine may produce additive hypoglycemic effect in patients receiving hypoglycemic agents and may produce delirium in patients receiving disulfiram. Tryptophan combined use with an MAO inhibitor has been reported to cause disorientation, confusion, anxiety, delirium, agitation, hypomanic signs, ataxia, and myoclonus; concurrent use is contraindicated.

Decreased Effect: Tranylcypromine inhibits the antihypertensive response to guanadrel or guanethidine.

Mechanism of Action Thought to act by increasing endogenous concentrations of epinephrine, norepinephrine, dopamine and serotonin through inhibition of the enzyme (monoamine oxidase) responsible for the breakdown of these neurotransmitters

Pharmacodynamics/Kinetics
Onset of action: Therapeutic: 2-3 weeks continued dosing
Half-life elimination: 90-190 minutes
Time to peak, serum: ~2 hours
Excretion: Urine

Dosage Adults: Oral: 10 mg twice daily, increase by 10 mg increments at 1- to 3-week intervals; maximum: 60 mg/day

Dosing comments in hepatic impairment: Use with care and monitor plasma levels and patient response closely

Monitoring Parameters Blood pressure, mental status

Patient Information Tablets may be crushed; avoid alcohol; do not discontinue abruptly; avoid foods high in tyramine (eg, aged cheeses, Chianti wine, raisins, liver, bananas, chocolate, yogurt, sour cream); discuss list of drugs and foods to avoid with pharmacist or prescriber; arise slowly from prolonged sitting or lying

Dosage Forms TAB: 10 mg

♦ **Tranylcypromine Sulfate** *see Tranylcypromine on page 1253*

Trastuzumab *(tras TU zoo mab)*

U.S. Brand Names Herceptin®

Therapeutic Category Antineoplastic Agent, Monoclonal Antibody; Monoclonal Antibody

Use
Single agent for the treatment of patients with metastatic breast cancer whose tumors overexpress the HER-2/*neu* protein and who have received one or more chemotherapy regimens for their metastatic disease
Combination therapy with paclitaxel for the treatment of patients with metastatic breast cancer whose tumors overexpress the HER-2/*neu* protein and who have not received chemotherapy for their metastatic disease

Unlabeled/Investigational Use Treatment of ovarian, gastric, colorectal, endometrial, lung, bladder, prostate, and salivary gland tumors

Pregnancy Risk Factor B

Contraindications Hypersensitivity to trastuzumab, Chinese hamster ovary cell proteins, or any component of the formulation. No specific contraindications noted in product labeling. However, patients experiencing severe hypersensitivity reactions have been reported to have repeat episodes despite pretreatment with antihistamines and corticosteroids.

Warnings/Precautions Congestive heart failure associated with trastuzumab may be severe and has been associated with disabling cardiac failure, death, mural thrombus, and stroke. Left ventricular function should be evaluated in all patients prior to and during treatment with trastuzumab. Discontinuation should be strongly considered in patients who develop a clinically significant decrease in ejection fraction during therapy. Combination therapy which includes anthracyclines and cyclophosphamide increases the incidence and severity of cardiac dysfunction. Extreme caution should be used when treating patients with pre-existing cardiac disease or dysfunction, and in patients with previous exposure to anthracyclines. Advanced age may also predispose to cardiac toxicity. Hypersensitivity to hamster ovary cell proteins or any component of this product.

Serious adverse events, including hypersensitivity reaction (anaphylaxis), infusion reactions (including fatalities), and pulmonary events (including adult respiratory distress syndrome) have been associated with trastuzumab. Most of these events occur within 24 hours of infusion, however, delayed reactions have occurred. Use with caution in pre-existing pulmonary disease. Discontinuation of trastuzumab should be strongly considered in any patient who develops anaphylaxis, angioedema, or acute respiratory distress syndrome. Retreatment of patients who experienced severe hypersensitivity reactions has been attempted (with premedication). Some patients tolerated retreatment, while others experienced a second severe reaction. When used in combination with myelosuppressive chemotherapy, trastuzumab may increase the incidence of neutropenia (moderate-to-severe) and febrile neutropenia.

Common Adverse Reactions Note: The most common adverse effects are infusion-related, occurring in up to 40% of patients, consisting of fever and chills (mild to moderate, often with other systemic symptoms). Treatment with acetaminophen, diphenhydramine, and/or meperidine is usually effective.

>10%:
Central nervous system: Pain (47%), fever (36%), chills (32%), headache (26%)
Dermatologic: Rash (18%)

Gastrointestinal: Nausea (33%), diarrhea (25%), vomiting (23%), abdominal pain (22%), anorexia (14%)

Neuromuscular & skeletal: Weakness (42%), back pain (22%)

Respiratory: Cough (26%), dyspnea (22%), rhinitis (14%), pharyngitis (12%)

Miscellaneous: Infection (20%); infusion reaction (40%, chills and fever most common)

1% to 10%:

Cardiovascular: Peripheral edema (10%), CHF (7%), tachycardia (5%)

Central nervous system: Insomnia (14%), dizziness (13%), paresthesia (9%), depression (6%), peripheral neuritis (2%), neuropathy (1%)

Dermatologic: Herpes simplex (2%), acne (2%)

Genitourinary: Urinary tract infection (5%)

Hematologic: Anemia (4%), leukopenia (3%)

Neuromuscular & skeletal: Bone pain (7%), arthralgia (6%)

Respiratory: Sinusitis (9%)

Miscellaneous: Flu syndrome (10%), accidental injury (6%), allergic reaction (3%)

Drug Interactions

Increased Effect/Toxicity: Paclitaxel may result in a decrease in clearance of trastuzumab, increasing serum concentrations. Combined use with anthracyclines or cyclophosphamide may increase the incidence/severity of cardiac dysfunction. Trastuzumab may increase the incidence of neutropenia and/or febrile neutropenia when used in combination with myelosuppressive chemotherapy.

Mechanism of Action Trastuzumab is a monoclonal antibody which binds to the extracellular domain of the human epidermal growth factor receptor 2 protein (HER2); it mediates antibody-dependent cellular cytotoxicity against cells which overproduce HER2

Pharmacodynamics/Kinetics

Distribution: V_d: 44 mL/kg

Half-life elimination: Mean: 5.8 days (range: 1-32 days)

Dosage I.V. infusion: Adults:

Initial loading dose: 4 mg/kg intravenous infusion over 90 minutes

Maintenance dose: 2 mg/kg intravenous infusion over 90 minutes (can be administered over 30 minutes if prior infusions are well tolerated) weekly until disease progression

Dosing adjustment in renal impairment: Data suggest that the disposition of trastuzumab is not altered based on age or serum creatinine (up to 2 mg/dL); however, no formal interaction studies have been performed

Dosing adjustment in hepatic impairment: No data is currently available

Administration Administered by I.V. infusion; loading doses are infused over 90 minutes; maintenance doses may be infused over 30 minutes if tolerated.

Monitoring Parameters Signs and symptoms of cardiac dysfunction; monitor vital signs during infusion

Dosage Forms INJ, powder for reconstitution: 440 mg

♦ **Trasylol**® see Aprotinin on page 111
♦ **Travatan**® see Travoprost on page 1255

Travoprost (TRA voe prost)

Related Information

Glaucoma Drug Therapy Comparison on page 1481

U.S. Brand Names Travatan®

Therapeutic Category Ophthalmic Agent, Prostaglandin Derivative; Prostaglandin, Ophthalmic

Use Reduction of elevated intraocular pressure in patients with open-angle glaucoma or ocular hypertension who are intolerant of the other IOP-lowering medications or insufficiently responsive (failed to achieve target IOP determined after multiple measurements over time) to another IOP-lowering medication

Pregnancy Risk Factor C

Contraindications Hypersensitivity to travoprost or any component of the formulation; pregnancy

Warnings/Precautions May permanently change/increase brown pigmentation of the iris, the eyelid skin, and eyelashes. In addition, may increase the length and/or number of eyelashes (may vary between eyes); changes occur slowly and may not be noticeable for months or years. Bacterial keratitis, caused by inadvertent contamination of multiple-dose ophthalmic solutions, has been reported. Use caution in patients with intraocular inflammation, aphakic patients, pseudophakic patients with a torn posterior lens capsule, or patients with risk factors for macular edema. Contains benzalkonium chloride which may be adsorbed by contact lenses; remove contacts prior to administration and wait 15 minutes before reinserting. Contact with contents of vial should be avoided in women who are pregnant or attempting to become pregnant; in case of accidental exposure to the skin, wash the exposed area with soap and water immediately. Safety and efficacy have not been determined for use in patients with renal or hepatic impairment, angle-closure-, inflammatory-, or neovascular glaucoma. Safety and efficacy in pediatric patients have not been established.

Common Adverse Reactions

>10%: Ocular: Hyperemia (35% to 50%)

5% to 10%: Ocular: Decreased visual acuity, eye discomfort, foreign body sensation, pain, pruritus

1% to 5%:

Cardiovascular: Angina pectoris, bradycardia, hypotension, hypertension

Central nervous system: Depression, pain, anxiety, headache

(Continued)

Travoprost *(Continued)*

Endocrine & metabolic: Hypercholesterolemia

Gastrointestinal: Dyspepsia

Genitourinary: Prostate disorder, urinary incontinence

Neuromuscular & skeletal: Arthritis, back pain, chest pain

Ocular (1% to 4%): Abnormal vision, blepharitis, blurred vision, conjunctivitis, dry eye, iris discoloration, keratitis, lid margin crusting, photophobia, subconjunctival hemorrhage, cataract, tearing, periorbital skin discoloration (darkening), eyelash darkening, eyelash growth increased

Respiratory: Bronchitis, sinusitis

Mechanism of Action A selective FP prostanoid receptor agonist which lowers intraocular pressure by increasing outflow

Pharmacodynamics/Kinetics

Onset of action: ~2 hours

Peak effect: 12 hours

Duration: Plasma levels decrease to <10 pg/mL within 1 hour

Absorption: Absorbed via cornea

Metabolism: Hydrolyzed by esterases in the cornea to active free acid; systemically; the free acid is metabolized to inactive metabolites

Dosage Ophthalmic: Adults: Glaucoma (open angle) or ocular hypertension: Instill 1 drop into affected eye(s) once daily in the evening; do not exceed once-daily dosing (may decrease IOP-lowering effect). If used with other topical ophthalmic agents, separate administration by at least 5 minutes.

Administration May be used with other eye drops to lower intraocular pressure. If using more than one ophthalmic product, wait at least 5 minutes in between application of each medication. Remove contact lenses prior to administration and wait 15 minutes before reinserting.

Patient Information Wash hands before instilling. Sit or lie down to instill. Open eye, look at ceiling, and instill prescribed amount of solution. Apply gentle pressure to inner corner of eye. Do not let tip of applicator touch eye; do not contaminate tip of applicator (contamination may cause eye infection leading to possible eye damage or vision loss). Contact prescriber concerning continued use of drops if eye infection develops, trauma occurs to the eye, and prior to eye surgery. This product contains benzalkonium chloride which may be adsorbed by contact lenses; remove contacts prior to administration and wait 15 minutes before reinserting. May cause permanent changes in eye color (increases the amount of brown pigment in the iris), eyelid, and eyelashes. May also increase the length and/or number of eyelashes. Changes may occur slowly (months to years). May be used with other eye drops to lower intraocular pressure. If using more than one eye drop medicine, wait at least 5 minutes in between application of each medication. Notify prescriber if conjunctivitis or eyelid reactions occur with use of this product.

Dosage Forms SOLN, ophthalmic: 0.004% (2.5 mL)

Trazodone (TRAZ oh done)

Related Information

Antidepressant Agents Comparison *on page 1359*

U.S. Brand Names Desyrel®

Synonyms Trazodone Hydrochloride

Therapeutic Category Antidepressant, Serotonin Reuptake Inhibitor/Antagonist (SRIA)

Use Treatment of depression

Unlabeled/Investigational Use Potential augmenting agent for antidepressants, hypnotic

Pregnancy Risk Factor C

Contraindications Hypersensitivity to trazodone or any component of the formulation

Warnings/Precautions Safety and efficacy in children <18 years of age have not been established; monitor closely and use with extreme caution in patients with cardiac disease or arrhythmias. Very sedating, but little anticholinergic effects; therapeutic effects may take up to 4 weeks to occur; therapy is normally maintained for several months after optimum response is reached to prevent recurrence of depression. The possibility of a suicide attempt is inherent in major depression and may persist until remission occurs. Use caution in high-risk patients during initiation of therapy. Prescriptions should be written for the smallest quantity consistent with good patient care.

Common Adverse Reactions

>10%:

Central nervous system: Dizziness, headache, sedation

Gastrointestinal: Nausea, xerostomia

1% to 10%:

Cardiovascular: Syncope, hypertension, hypotension, edema

Central nervous system: Confusion, decreased concentration, fatigue, incoordination

Gastrointestinal: Diarrhea, constipation, weight gain/loss

Neuromuscular & skeletal: Tremor, myalgia

Ocular: Blurred vision

Respiratory: Nasal congestion

Drug Interactions

Cytochrome P450 Effect: Substrate of CYP2D6 (minor), 3A4 (major); **Inhibits** CYP2D6 (moderate), 3A4 (weak)

Increased Effect/Toxicity: Trazodone, in combination with other serotonergic agents (buspirone, MAO inhibitors), may produce additive serotonergic effects, including serotonin syndrome. Trazodone, in combination with other psychotropics (low potency antipsychotics), may result in additional hypotension. Trazodone, in combination with ethanol, may result in additive sedation and impairment of motor skills. Fluoxetine may inhibit the metabolism of trazodone resulting in elevated plasma levels.

Decreased Effect: Trazodone inhibits the hypotensive response to clonidine.

Mechanism of Action Inhibits reuptake of serotonin, causes adrenoreceptor subsensitivity, and induces significant changes in 5-HT presynaptic receptor adrenoreceptors. Trazodone also significantly blocks histamine (H_1) and alpha$_1$-adrenergic receptors.

Pharmacodynamics/Kinetics
Onset of action: Therapeutic: 1-3 weeks
Protein binding: 85% to 95%
Metabolism: Hepatic
Half-life elimination: 7-8 hours, two compartment kinetics
Time to peak, serum: 30-100 minutes; delayed with food (up to 2.5 hours)
Excretion: Primarily urine; secondarily feces

Dosage Oral: Therapeutic effects may take up to 6 weeks to occur; therapy is normally maintained for 6-12 months after optimum response is reached to prevent recurrence of depression

Children 6-12 years: Depression: Initial: 1.5-2 mg/kg/day in divided doses; increase gradually every 3-4 days as needed; maximum: 6 mg/kg/day in 3 divided doses
Adolescents: Depression: Initial: 25-50 mg/day; increase to 100-150 mg/day in divided doses
Adults:
Depression: Initial: 150 mg/day in 3 divided doses (may increase by 50 mg/day every 3-7 days); maximum: 600 mg/day
Sedation/hypnotic (unlabeled use): 25-50 mg at bedtime (often in combination with daytime SSRIs); may increase up to 200 mg at bedtime
Elderly: 25-50 mg at bedtime with 25-50 mg/day dose increase every 3 days for inpatients and weekly for outpatients, if tolerated; usual dose: 75-150 mg/day

Reference Range
Plasma levels do not always correlate with clinical effectiveness
Therapeutic: 0.5-2.5 µg/mL
Potentially toxic: >2.5 µg/mL
Toxic: >4 µg/mL

Patient Information Take shortly after a meal or light snack, can be given as bedtime dose if drowsiness occurs; avoid alcohol; be aware of possible photosensitivity reaction; report any prolonged or painful erection

Dosage Forms TAB: 50 mg, 100 mg, 150 mg, 300 mg

♦ **Trazodone Hydrochloride** *see* Trazodone *on page 1256*
♦ **Trecator®-SC** *see* Ethionamide *on page 494*
♦ **Trelstar™ Depot** *see* Triptorelin *on page 1274*
♦ **Trelstar™ LA** *see* Triptorelin *on page 1274*
♦ **Trental®** *see* Pentoxifylline *on page 981*

Treprostinil (tre PROST in il)

U.S. Brand Names Remodulin™
Synonyms Treprostinil Sodium
Therapeutic Category Vasodilator
Use Treatment of pulmonary arterial hypertension (PAH) in patients with NYHA Class II-IV symptoms to decrease exercise-associated symptoms
Pregnancy Risk Factor B
Contraindications Hypersensitivity to treprostinil or any component of formulation
Warnings/Precautions Administer via continuous S.C. infusion only; use caution in hepatic insufficiency, dose modification may be warranted; use caution in renal impairment; abrupt withdrawal/large dosage reductions may worsen symptoms of PAH; therapy should be initiated in monitored setting and under the supervision of clinicians experienced in diagnosis and management of PAH. Safety and efficacy have not been established in patients ≤16 years of age.

Common Adverse Reactions >10%:
Cardiovascular: Vasodilation (11%)
Central nervous system: Headache (27%)
Dermatologic: Rash (14%)
Gastrointestinal: Diarrhea (25%), nausea (22%)
Local: Infusion site pain (85%), infusion site reaction (83%)
Miscellaneous: Jaw pain (13%)

Drug Interactions
Increased Effect/Toxicity: Concomitant use of treprostinil with other agents that inhibit platelet aggregation (eg, NSAIDs, ASA, antiplatelet agents) or promote anticoagulation (eg, warfarin) may increase the risk of bleeding.

Mechanism of Action Treprostinil is a direct dilator of both pulmonary and systemic arterial vascular beds; also inhibits platelet aggregation.

Pharmacodynamics/Kinetics
Absorption: S.C.: Rapidly and completely
Distribution: 14 L/70 kg lean body weight
Protein binding: 91%
Metabolism: Hepatic (enzymes unknown); forms metabolites
Bioavailability: 100%
(Continued)

Treprostinil *(Continued)*

Half-life elimination: Terminal: 2-4 hours

Excretion: Urine (4% as unchanged drug; 64% as metabolites); feces (13%)

Dosage S.C. infusion:

Adults: PAH: Initial: 1.25 ng/kg/minute continuous; if dose cannot be tolerated, reduce to 0.625 ng/kg/minute. Increase at rate not >1.25 ng/kg/minute per week for first 4 weeks, and not >2.5 ng/kg/minute per week for remainder of therapy. Limited experience with doses >40 ng/kg/minute.

Note: Dose must be carefully and individually titrated (symptom improvement with minimal adverse effects).

Elderly: Limited experience in patients >65 years; refer to adult dosing; use caution

Dosage adjustment in renal impairment: No specific dosage adjustment recommended; use with caution.

Dosage adjustment in hepatic impairment:

Mild to moderate: Initial: 0.625 ng/kg/minute; increase with caution.

Severe: No data available.

Administration Administer via continuous S.C. infusion using an appropriately-designed infusion pump. Patients must be assessed regarding their ability to manage such a delivery system.

Monitoring Parameters Dyspnea, fatigue, activity tolerance

Dosage Forms INJ, solution: 1 mg/mL (20 mL); 2.5 mg/mL (20 mL); 5 mg/mL (20 mL); 10 mg/mL (20 mL)

♦ **Treprostinil Sodium** *see* Treprostinil *on page 1257*

♦ **Tretinoin and Mequinol** *see* Mequinol and Tretinoin *on page 795*

♦ **Tretinoin, Fluocinolone Acetonide, and Hydroquinone** *see* Fluocinolone, Hydroquinone, and Tretinoin *on page 533*

Tretinoin (Oral) (TRET i noyn, oral)

U.S. Brand Names Vesanoid®

Synonyms All-*trans*-Retinoic Acid; ATRA; NSC-122758; Ro 5488; tRA; *trans*-Retinoic Acid

Therapeutic Category Antineoplastic Agent, Miscellaneous; Retinoic Acid Derivative; Vitamin A Derivative

Use Induction of remission in patients with acute promyelocytic leukemia (APL), French American British (FAB) classification M3 (including the M3 variant)

Pregnancy Risk Factor D

Contraindications Sensitivity to parabens, vitamin A, other retinoids, or any component of the formulation; pregnancy

Warnings/Precautions Patients with acute promyelocytic leukemia (APL) are at high risk and can have severe adverse reactions to tretinoin. Administer under the supervision of a physician who is experienced in the management of patients with acute leukemia and in a facility with laboratory and supportive services sufficient to monitor drug tolerance and to protect and maintain a patient compromised by drug toxicity, including respiratory compromise.

About 25% of patients with APL, who have been treated with tretinoin, have experienced a syndrome called the retinoic acid-APL (RA-APL) syndrome which is characterized by fever, dyspnea, weight gain, radiographic pulmonary infiltrates and pleural or pericardial effusions. This syndrome has occasionally been accompanied by impaired myocardial contractility and episodic hypotension. It has been observed with or without concomitant leukocytosis. Endotracheal intubation and mechanical ventilation have been required in some cases due to progressive hypoxemia, and several patients have expired with multiorgan failure. The syndrome usually occurs during the first month of treatment, with some cases reported following the first dose.

Management of the syndrome has not been defined, but high-dose steroids given at the first suspicion of RA-APL syndrome appear to reduce morbidity and mortality. At the first signs suggestive of the syndrome, immediately initiate high-dose steroids (dexamethasone 10 mg I.V.) every 12 hours for 3 days or until resolution of symptoms, regardless of the leukocyte count. The majority of patients do not require termination of tretinoin therapy during treatment of the RA-APL syndrome.

During treatment, ~40% of patients will develop rapidly evolving leukocytosis. Rapidly evolving leukocytosis is associated with a higher risk of life-threatening complications.

If signs and symptoms of the RA-APL syndrome are present together with leukocytosis, initiate treatment with high-dose steroids immediately. Consider adding full-dose chemotherapy (including an anthracycline, if not contraindicated) to the tretinoin therapy on day 1 or 2 for patients presenting with a WBC count of >5 x 10^9/L or immediately, for patients presenting with a WBC count of <5 x 10^9/L, if the WBC count reaches ≥6 x 10^9/L by day 5, or ≥10 x 10^9/L by day 10 or ≥15 x 10^9/L by day 28.

Not to be used in women of childbearing potential unless the woman is capable of complying with effective contraceptive measures; therapy is normally begun on the second or third day of next normal menstrual period; two reliable methods of effective contraception must be used during therapy and for 1 month after discontinuation of therapy, unless abstinence is the chosen method. Within one week prior to the institution of tretinoin therapy, the patient should have blood or urine collected for a serum or urine pregnancy test with a sensitivity of at least 50 mIU/L. When possible, delay tretinoin therapy until a negative result from this test is obtained. When a delay is not possible, place the patient on two reliable forms of contraception. Repeat pregnancy testing and contraception counseling monthly throughout the period of treatment.

Initiation of therapy with tretinoin may be based on the morphological diagnosis of APL. Confirm the diagnosis of APL by detection of the t(15;17) genetic marker by cytogenetic studies. If these are negative, PML/RARα fusion should be sought using molecular diagnostic techniques. The response rate of other AML subtypes to tretinoin has not been demonstrated.

Retinoids have been associated with pseudotumor cerebri (benign intracranial hypertension), especially in children. Early signs and symptoms include papilledema, headache, nausea, vomiting and visual disturbances.

Up to 60% of patients experienced hypercholesterolemia or hypertriglyceridemia, which were reversible upon completion of treatment.

Elevated liver function test results occur in 50% to 60% of patients during treatment. Carefully monitor liver function test results during treatment and give consideration to a temporary withdrawal of tretinoin if test results reach >5 times the upper limit of normal.

Common Adverse Reactions Virtually all patients experience some drug-related toxicity, especially headache, fever, weakness and fatigue. These adverse effects are seldom permanent or irreversible nor do they usually require therapy interruption

>10%:
  Cardiovascular: Arrhythmias, flushing, hypotension, hypertension, peripheral edema, chest discomfort, edema
  Central nervous system: Dizziness, anxiety, insomnia, depression, confusion, malaise, pain
  Dermatologic: Burning, redness, cheilitis, inflammation of lips, dry skin, pruritus, photosensitivity
  Endocrine & metabolic: Increased serum concentration of triglycerides
  Gastrointestinal: GI hemorrhage, abdominal pain, other GI disorders, diarrhea, constipation, dyspepsia, abdominal distention, weight gain/loss, xerostomia
  Hematologic: Hemorrhage, disseminated intravascular coagulation
  Local: Phlebitis, injection site reactions
  Neuromuscular & skeletal: Bone pain, arthralgia, myalgia, paresthesia
  Ocular: Itching of eye
  Renal: Renal insufficiency
  Respiratory: Upper respiratory tract disorders, dyspnea, respiratory insufficiency, pleural effusion, pneumonia, rales, expiratory wheezing, dry nose
  Miscellaneous: Infections, shivering
1% to 10%:
  Cardiovascular: Cardiac failure, cardiac arrest, myocardial infarction, enlarged heart, heart murmur, ischemia, stroke, myocarditis, pericarditis, pulmonary hypertension, secondary cardiomyopathy, cerebral hemorrhage, pallor
  Central nervous system: Intracranial hypertension, agitation, hallucination, agnosia, aphasia, cerebellar edema, cerebellar disorders, convulsions, coma, CNS depression, encephalopathy, hypotaxia, no light reflex, neurologic reaction, spinal cord disorder, unconsciousness, dementia, forgetfulness, somnolence, slow speech, hypothermia
  Dermatologic: Skin peeling on hands or soles of feet, rash, cellulitis
  Endocrine & metabolic: Fluid imbalance, acidosis
  Gastrointestinal: Hepatosplenomegaly, ulcer
  Genitourinary: Dysuria, polyuria, enlarged prostate
  Hepatic: Ascites, hepatitis
  Neuromuscular & skeletal: Tremor, leg weakness, hyporeflexia, dysarthria, facial paralysis, hemiplegia, flank pain, asterixis, abnormal gait
  Ocular: Dry eyes, photophobia
  Renal: Acute renal failure, renal tubular necrosis
  Respiratory: Lower respiratory tract disorders, pulmonary infiltration, bronchial asthma, pulmonary/larynx edema, unspecified pulmonary disease
  Miscellaneous: Face edema, lymph disorders
Drug Interactions
  Cytochrome P450 Effect: Substrate (minor) of CYP2A6, 2B6, 2C8/9; **Inhibits** CYP2C8/9 (weak); **Induces** CYP2E1 (weak)
  Increased Effect/Toxicity: Ketoconazole increases the mean plasma AUC of tretinoin. Other drugs which inhibit CYP3A4 would be expected to increase tretinoin concentrations, potentially increasing toxicity.
Mechanism of Action Tretinoin appears to bind one or more nuclear receptors and inhibits clonal proliferation and/or granulocyte differentiation
Pharmacodynamics/Kinetics
  Protein binding: >95%
  Metabolism: Hepatic via CYP; primary metabolite: 4-oxo-all-*trans*-retinoic acid
  Half-life elimination: Terminal: Parent drug: 0.5-2 hours
  Time to peak, serum: 1-2 hours
  Excretion: Urine (63%); feces (30%)
Dosage Oral: Children and Adults:
  Remission induction: 45 mg/m^2/day in 2-3 divided doses for up to 30 days after complete remission (maximum duration of treatment: 90 days)
  Remission maintenance: 45-200 mg/m^2/day in 2-3 divided doses for up to 12 months. **Note:** Optimal consolidation or maintenance regimens have not been determined. All patients (Continued)

Tretinoin (Oral) *(Continued)*

should therefore receive a standard consolidation or maintenance chemotherapy regimen for APL after induction therapy with tretinoin unless otherwise contraindicated.

Administration Administer with meals; do not crush capsules

Monitoring Parameters Monitor the patient's hematologic profile, coagulation profile, liver function test results and triglyceride and cholesterol levels frequently

Patient Information Take with food; do not crush, chew, or dissolve capsules. You will need frequent blood tests while taking this medication. Maintain adequate hydration (2-3 L/day of fluids unless instructed to restrict fluid intake), avoid alcohol and foods containing vitamin A, and foods with high fat content. You may experience lethargy, dizziness, visual changes, confusion, anxiety (avoid driving or engaging in tasks requiring alertness until response to drug is known). For nausea/vomiting, loss of appetite, or dry mouth, small frequent meals, chewing gum, or sucking lozenges may help. You may experience photosensitivity (use sunscreen, wear protective clothing and eyewear, and avoid direct sunlight). You may experience dry, itchy, skin, and dry or irritated eyes (avoid contact lenses). Report persistent vomiting or diarrhea, difficulty breathing, unusual bleeding or bruising, acute GI pain, bone pain, or vision changes immediately.

Dosage Forms CAP: 10 mg

Tretinoin (Topical) (TRET i noyn, TOP i kal)

U.S. Brand Names Altinac™; Avita®; Renova®; Retin-A®; Retin-A® Micro

Synonyms Retinoic Acid; *trans*-Retinoic Acid; Vitamin A Acid

Therapeutic Category Acne Product; Retinoic Acid Derivative; Vitamin A Derivative

Use Treatment of acne vulgaris; photodamaged skin; palliation of fine wrinkles, mottled hyper-pigmentation, and tactile roughness of facial skin as part of a comprehensive skin care and sun avoidance program

Unlabeled/Investigational Use Some skin cancers

Pregnancy Risk Factor C

Contraindications Hypersensitivity to tretinoin or any component of the formulation; sunburn

Warnings/Precautions Use with caution in patients with eczema; avoid excessive exposure to sunlight and sunlamps; avoid contact with abraded skin, mucous membranes, eyes, mouth, angles of the nose. Palliation of fine wrinkles, mottled hyperpigmentation, and tactile rough-ness of facial skin: Do not use the 0.05% cream for longer than 48 weeks or the 0.02% cream for longer than 52 weeks. Not for use on moderate- to heavily-pigmented skin. Gel is flam-mable; do not expose to high temperatures or flame.

Common Adverse Reactions

>10%: Dermatologic: Excessive dryness, erythema, scaling of the skin, pruritus

1% to 10%:

Dermatologic: Hyperpigmentation or hypopigmentation, photosensitivity, initial acne flare-up

Local: Edema, blistering, stinging

Drug Interactions

Cytochrome P450 Effect: Substrate (minor) of CYP2A6, 2B6, 2C8/9; **Inhibits** CYP2C8/9 (weak); **Induces** CYP2E1 (weak)

Increased Effect/Toxicity: Topical application of sulfur, benzoyl peroxide, salicylic acid, resorcinol, or any product with strong drying effects potentiates adverse reactions with tretinoin.

Photosensitizing medications (thiazides, tetracyclines, fluoroquinolones, phenothiazines, sulfonamides) augment phototoxicity and should not be used when treating palliation of fine wrinkles, mottled hyperpigmentation, and tactile roughness of facial skin.

Mechanism of Action Keratinocytes in the sebaceous follicle become less adherent which allows for easy removal; inhibits microcomedone formation and eliminates lesions already present

Pharmacodynamics/Kinetics

Absorption: Minimal

Metabolism: Hepatic for the small amount absorbed

Excretion: Urine and feces

Dosage Topical:

Children >12 years and Adults: Acne vulgaris: Begin therapy with a weaker formulation of tretinoin (0.025% cream, 0.04% microsphere gel, or 0.01% gel) and increase the concentra-tion as tolerated; apply once daily to acne lesions before retiring or on alternate days; if stinging or irritation develop, decrease frequency of application

Adults ≥18: Palliation of fine wrinkles, mottled hyperpigmentation, and tactile roughness of facial skin: Pea-sized amount of the 0.02% or 0.05% cream applied to entire face once daily in the evening

Elderly: Use of the 0.02% cream in patients 65-71 years of age showed similar improvement in fine wrinkles as seen in patients <65 years. Safety and efficacy of the 0.02% cream have not been established in patients >71 years of age. Safety and efficacy of the 0.05% cream have not been established in patients >50 years of age.

Administration Palliation of fine wrinkles, mottled hyperpigmentation, and tactile roughness of facial skin: Cream: Prior to application, gently wash face with a mild soap. Pat dry. Wait 20-30 minutes to apply cream. Avoid eyes, ears, nostrils, and mouth.

Patient Information For once-daily use, do not overuse. Avoid increased intake of vitamin A. Thoroughly wash hands before applying. Wash area to be treated at least 30 minutes before applying. Do not wash face more frequently than 2-3 times a day. Avoid using topical prepara-tions that contain alcohol or harsh chemicals during treatment. You may experience increased sensitivity to sunlight; protect skin with sunblock (minimum SPF 15), wear protective clothing, or avoid direct sunlight. Stop treatment and inform prescriber if rash, skin irritation, redness, scaling, or excessive dryness occurs. When used for hyperpigmentation and tactile redness of facial skin, wrinkles will not be eliminated. Must be used in combination with a comprehensive skin care program.

Gel: Flammable; do not expose to flame and do not smoke during use.

Dosage Forms CRM, topical: 0.025% (20 g, 45 g); 0.05% (20 g, 45 g); 0.1% (20 g, 45 g); (Altinac™): 0.025% (20 g, 45 g); 0.05% (20 g, 45 g); 0.1% (20 g, 45 g); (Avita®): 0.025% (20 g, 45 g); (Renova®): 0.02% (40 g); 0.05% (40 g, 60 g); (Retin-A®): 0.025% (20 g, 45 g); 0.05% (20 g, 45 g); 0.1% (20 g, 45 g). **Gel, topical:** 0.025% (15 g, 45 g); (Avita®): 0.025% (15 g, 45 g); (Retin-A®): 0.01% (15 g, 45 g); 0.025% (15 g, 45 g); (Retin-A® Micro) [microsphere gel]: 0.04% (20 g, 45 g); 0.1% (20 g, 45 g). **LIQ, topical** (Retin-A®): 0.05% (28 mL)

♦ **Trexall**™ see Methotrexate on page 815

♦ **Triacetyloleandomycin** see Troleandomycin on page 1275

♦ **Triacin-C® [DSC]** see Triprolidine, Pseudoephedrine, and Codeine on page 1274

♦ **Triaconazole** see Terconazole on page 1200

Triamcinolone (trye am SIN oh lone)

Related Information
Corticosteroids Comparison on page 1372

U.S. Brand Names Aristocort®; Aristocort® A; Aristocort® Forte; Aristospan®; Azmacort®; Kenalog®; Kenalog-10®; Kenalog-40®; Kenalog® in Orabase®; Nasacort® [DSC]; Nasacort® AQ; Triderm®; Tri-Nasal®

Synonyms Triamcinolone Acetonide, Aerosol; Triamcinolone Acetonide, Parenteral; Triamcinolone Diacetate, Oral; Triamcinolone Diacetate, Parenteral; Triamcinolone Hexacetonide; Triamcinolone, Oral

Therapeutic Category Anti-inflammatory Agent; Anti-inflammatory Agent, Inhalant; Corticosteroid, Inhalant; Corticosteroid, Intranasal; Corticosteroid, Systemic; Corticosteroid, Topical (Medium Potency); Corticosteroid, Topical (High Potency); Glucocorticoid

Use
Nasal inhalation: Management of seasonal and perennial allergic rhinitis in patients ≥6 years of age

Oral inhalation: Control of bronchial asthma and related bronchospastic conditions

Oral topical: Adjunctive treatment and temporary relief of symptoms associated with oral inflammatory lesions and ulcerative lesions resulting from trauma

Systemic: Adrenocortical insufficiency, rheumatic disorders, allergic states, respiratory diseases, systemic lupus erythematosus (SLE), and other diseases requiring anti-inflammatory or immunosuppressive effects

Topical: Inflammatory dermatoses responsive to steroids

Pregnancy Risk Factor C

Contraindications Hypersensitivity to triamcinolone or any component of the formulation; systemic fungal infections; serious infections (except septic shock or tuberculous meningitis); primary treatment of status asthmaticus; fungal, viral, or bacterial infections of the mouth or throat (oral topical formulation)

Warnings/Precautions May cause suppression of hypothalamic-pituitary-adrenal (HPA) axis, particularly in younger children or in patients receiving high doses for prolonged periods. Particular care is required when patients are transferred from systemic corticosteroids to inhaled products due to possible adrenal insufficiency or withdrawal from steroids, including an increase in allergic symptoms. Patients receiving 20 mg per day of prednisone (or equivalent) may be most susceptible. Fatalities have occurred due to adrenal insufficiency in asthmatic patients during and after transfer from systemic corticosteroids to aerosol steroids; aerosol steroids do **not** provide the systemic steroid needed to treat patients having trauma, surgery, or infections. Withdrawal and discontinuation of the corticosteroid should be done slowly and carefully

Use with caution in patients with hypothyroidism, cirrhosis, nonspecific ulcerative colitis and patients at increased risk for peptic ulcer disease. Corticosteroids should be used with caution in patients with diabetes, hypertension, osteoporosis, glaucoma, cataracts, or tuberculosis. Use caution in hepatic impairment. Do not use occlusive dressings on weeping or exudative lesions and general caution with occlusive dressings should be observed; discontinue if skin irritation or contact dermatitis should occur; do not use in patients with decreased skin circulation; avoid the use of high potency steroids on the face.

Because of the risk of adverse effects, systemic corticosteroids should be used cautiously in the elderly, in the smallest possible dose, and for the shortest possible time. Azmacort® (metered dose inhaler) comes with its own spacer device attached and may be easier to use in older patients.

Orally-inhaled and intranasal corticosteroids may cause a reduction in growth velocity in pediatric patients; appears to be related to dose and duration of exposure. The growth of pediatric patients receiving inhaled corticosteroids, should be monitored routinely (eg, via stadiometry). Titrate to the lowest effective dose.

May suppress the immune system, patients may be more susceptible to infection. Use with caution in patients with systemic infections or ocular herpes simplex. Avoid exposure to chickenpox and measles.
(Continued)

Triamcinolone *(Continued)*

Oral topical: Discontinue if local irritation or sensitization should develop. If significant regeneration or repair of oral tissues has not occurred in seven days, re-evaluation of the etiology of the oral lesion is advised.

Common Adverse Reactions

Systemic: Frequency not defined:

Cardiovascular: CHF, hypertension

Central nervous system: Convulsions, fever, headache, intracranial pressure increased, vertigo

Dermatologic: Bruising, facial erythema, petechiae, photosensitivity, rash, thin/fragile skin, wound healing impaired

Endocrine & metabolic: Adrenocortical/pituitary unresponsiveness (particularly during stress), carbohydrate tolerance decreased, cushingoid state, diabetes mellitus (manifestations of latent disease), fluid retention, growth suppression (children), hypokalemic alkalosis, menstrual irregularities, negative nitrogen balance, potassium loss, sodium retention

Gastrointestinal: Abdominal distention, diarrhea, dyspepsia, nausea, oral *Monilia* (oral inhaler), pancreatitis, peptic ulcer, ulcerative esophagitis, weight gain

Local: Skin atrophy (at the injection site)

Neuromuscular & skeletal: Femoral/humeral head aseptic necrosis, muscle mass decreased, muscle weakness, osteoporosis, pathologic fracture of long bones, steroid myopathy, vertebral compression fractures

Ocular: Cataracts, intraocular pressure increased, exophthalmos, glaucoma

Respiratory: Cough increased (nasal spray), epistaxis (nasal inhaler/spray), pharyngitis (nasal spray/oral inhaler), sinusitis (oral inhaler), voice alteration (oral inhaler)

Miscellaneous: Anaphylaxis, diaphoresis increased, suppression to skin tests

Topical: Frequency not defined:

Dermatologic: Itching, allergic contact dermatitis, dryness, folliculitis, skin infection (secondary), itching, hypertrichosis, acneiform eruptions, hypopigmentation, skin maceration, skin atrophy, striae, miliaria, perioral dermatitis, atrophy of oral mucosa

Local: Burning, irritation

Drug Interactions

Increased Effect/Toxicity: Salicylates or NSAIDs coadministered oral corticosteroids may increase risk of GI ulceration.

Decreased Effect: Decreased effect with barbiturates and phenytoin. Rifampin increased metabolism of triamcinolone. Vaccine and toxoid effects may be reduced.

Mechanism of Action Decreases inflammation by suppression of migration of polymorphonuclear leukocytes and reversal of increased capillary permeability; suppresses the immune system by reducing activity and volume of the lymphatic system; suppresses adrenal function at high doses

Pharmacodynamics/Kinetics

Duration: Oral: 8-12 hours

Absorption: Topical: Systemic

Time to peak: I.M.: 8-10 hours

Half-life elimination: Biologic: 18-36 hours

Dosage The lowest possible dose should be used to control the condition; when dose reduction is possible, the dose should be reduced gradually. Parenteral dose is usually $1/3$ to $1/2$ the oral dose given every 12 hours. In life-threatening situations, parenteral doses larger than the oral dose may be needed.

Triamcinolone Dosing

	Acetonide	Diacetate	Hexacetonide
Intrasynovial	2.5-40 mg	5-40 mg	
Intralesional	1-30 mg (usually 1 mg per injection site); 10 mg/mL suspension usually used	5-48 mg (not >25 mg per lesion)	Up to 0.5 mg/sq inch affected area
Sublesional	1-30 mg		
Systemic I.M.	2.5-60 mg/dose (usual adult dose: 60 mg; may repeat with 20-100 mg dose when symptoms recur)	~40 mg/wk	
Intra-articular	2.5-40 mg	2-40 mg	2-20 mg average
large joints	5-15 mg		10-20 mg
small joints	2.5-5 mg		2-6 mg
Tendon sheaths	2.5-10 mg		
Intradermal	1 mg/site		

Injection:
Acetonide:
  Intra-articular, intrabursal, tendon sheaths: Adults: Initial: Smaller joints: 2.5-5 mg, larger joints: 5-15 mg
  Intradermal: Adults: Initial: 1 mg
  I.M.: Range: 2.5-60 mg/day
      Children 6-12 years: Initial: 40 mg
      Children >12 years and Adults: Initial: 60 mg
Diacetate: Adults:
  Intra-articular, Intrasynovial: Range: 5-40 mg; duration of effect varies from 1 week to 2 months, although more frequent dosing may be needed in acutely-inflamed joints
      Average dose: Knee: 25 mg, finger: 2-5 mg
  Intralesional, sublesional: Range: 5-48 mg, dependent upon size of lesion
      Maximum: 12.5 mg/injection site, 25 mg/lesion, 75 mg/week
      Usual treatment course: 2-3 injections at 1- to 2-week intervals
  I.M.: Initial range: 3-48 mg/day; average dose: 40 mg/week
Hexacetonide: Adults:
  Intralesional, sublesional: Up to 0.5 mg/square inch of affected skin
  Intra-articular: Range: 2-20 mg

Intranasal: Perennial allergic rhinitis, seasonal allergic rhinitis:
  Nasal spray:
      Children 6-11 years: 110 mcg/day as 1 spray in each nostril once daily.
      Children ≥12 years and Adults: 220 mcg/day as 2 sprays in each nostril once daily
  Nasal inhaler:
      Children 6-11 years: Initial: 220 mcg/day as 2 sprays in each nostril once daily
      Children ≥12 years and Adults: Initial: 220 mcg/day as 2 sprays in each nostril once daily; may increase dose to 440 mcg/day (given once daily or divided and given 2 or 4 times/day)

Oral: Adults:
  Acute rheumatic carditis: Initial: 20-60 mg/day; reduce dose during maintenance therapy
  Acute seasonal or perennial allergic rhinitis: 8-12 mg/day
  Adrenocortical insufficiency: Range 4-12 mg/day
  Bronchial asthma: 8-16 mg/day
  Dermatological disorders, contact/atopic dermatitis: Initial: 8-16 mg/day
  Ophthalmic disorders: 12-40 mg/day
  Rheumatic disorders: Range: 8-16 mg/day
  SLE: Initial: 20-32 mg/day, some patients may need initial doses ≥48 mg; reduce dose during maintenance therapy

Oral inhalation: Asthma:
  Children 6-12 years: 100-200 mcg 3-4 times/day **or** 200-400 mcg twice daily; maximum dose: 1200 mg/day
  Children >12 years and Adults: 200 mcg 3-4 times/day **or** 400 mcg twice daily; maximum dose: 1600 mcg/day

Oral topical: Oral inflammatory lesions/ulcers: Press a small dab (about ¼ inch) to the lesion until a thin film develops. A larger quantity may be required for coverage of some lesions. For optimal results use only enough to coat the lesion with a thin film; do not rub in.

Topical:
  Cream, Ointment: Apply thin film to affected areas 2-4 times/day
  Spray: Apply to affected area 3-4 times/day

Administration
  Injection: Avoid injecting into a previously infected joint; do not inject into unstable joints
      I.M.: Inject deep in large muscle mass, avoid deltoid.
      S.C.: Avoid subcutaneous administration.
  Nasal spray, inhalation: Shake well prior to use. Gently blow nose to clear nostrils.
  Oral inhalation: Shake well prior to use. Rinse mouth and throat after using inhaler to prevent candidiasis. Use spacer device provided with Azmacort®.
  Oral topical: Apply small dab to lesion until a thin film develops; do not rub in. Apply at bedtime or after meals if applications are needed throughout the day.
  Tablet: Once-daily doses should be given in the morning.
  Topical: Apply a thin film sparingly and avoid topical application on the face. Do not use on open skin or wounds. Do not occlude area unless directed.

Patient Information Report any change in body weight. Do not discontinue or decrease the drug without contacting your prescriber. Carry an identification card or bracelet advising that you are on steroids. May take with meals to decrease GI upset.

Nasal inhaler: Do not use intranasal product if you have a nasal infection, nasal injury, or recent nasal surgery. If using two products, consult prescriber in which order to use the two products. Clear nasal passages before administration (use decongestant as needed). Follow package insert instructions for use. Do not exceed maximum dosage. Report unusual cough or spasm; persistent nasal bleeding, burning, or irritation; or worsening of condition.

Oral inhaler: Shake gently before use. Use at regular intervals, no more frequently than directed. Not for use during acute asthmatic attack. Follow directions that accompany product. Rinse mouth and throat after use to prevent candidiasis. Sit when using. Take deep breaths for 3-5 minutes. Hold breath for 5-10 seconds after use, and wait 1-3 minutes between inhalations. Follow package insert instructions for use. Do not exceed maximum dosage. If also using inhaled bronchodilator, use before triamcinolone.
(Continued)

Triamcinolone *(Continued)*

Oral topical: Dab small amount to lesion, do not rub in. Notify health care provider if improvement is not seen within 7 days.

Topical: For external use only. Not for eyes or mucous membranes or open wounds. Apply in very thin layer to occlusive dressing. Apply dressing to area being treated. Avoid prolonged or excessive use around sensitive tissues, genital, or rectal areas. Inform prescriber if condition worsens (swelling, redness, irritation, pain, open sores) or fails to improve.

Dosage Forms AERO, for nasal inhalation, as acetonide (Nasacort® [DSC]): 55 mcg/inhalation (10 g). **AERO, for nasal inhalation, as acetonide** [spray] (Nasacort® AQ): 55 mcg/inhalation (16.5 g); (Tri-Nasal®): 50 mcg/inhalation (15 mL). **AERO, for oral inhalation, as acetonide** (Azmacort®): 100 mcg per actuation (20 g). **AERO, topical, as acetonide** (Kenalog®): 0.2 mg/2-second spray (63 g). **CRM, as acetonide:** 0.025% (15 g, 80 g); 0.1% (15 g, 80 g, 454 g, 2270 g); 0.5% (15 g); (Aristocort® A): 0.025% (15 g, 60 g); 0.1% (15 g, 60 g); 0.5% (15 g); (Kenalog®): 0.1% (15 g, 60 g, 80 g); 0.5% (20 g); (Triderm®): 0.1% (30 g, 85 g). **INJ, suspension, as acetonide** (Kenalog-10®): 10 mg/mL (5 mL) [not for I.V. or I.M. use]; (Kenalog-40®): 40 mg/mL (1 mL, 5 mL, 10 mL) [not for I.V. or intradermal use]. **INJ, suspension, as diacetate** (Aristocort®): 25 mg/mL (5 mL) [not for I.V. use]; (Aristocort® Forte): 40 mg/mL (1 mL, 5mL) [not for I.V. use]. **INJ, suspension, as hexacetonide** (Aristospan®): 5 mg/mL (5 mL); 20 mg/mL (1 mL, 5 mL) [not for I.V. use]. **LOTION, as acetonide** (Kenalog®): 0.025% (60 mL); 0.1% (60 mL). **OINT, topical, as acetonide:** 0.025% (80 g); 0.1% (15 g, 80 g, 454 g); (Aristocort® A, Kenalog®): 0.1% (15 g, 60 g). **PASTE, oral, topical, as acetonide** (Kenalog® in Orabase®): 0.1% (5 g). **TAB** (Aristocort®): 4 mg

♦ **Triamcinolone Acetonide, Aerosol** *see* Triamcinolone *on page 1261*
♦ **Triamcinolone Acetonide, Parenteral** *see* Triamcinolone *on page 1261*
♦ **Triamcinolone and Nystatin** *see* Nystatin and Triamcinolone *on page 920*
♦ **Triamcinolone Diacetate, Oral** *see* Triamcinolone *on page 1261*
♦ **Triamcinolone Diacetate, Parenteral** *see* Triamcinolone *on page 1261*
♦ **Triamcinolone Hexacetonide** *see* Triamcinolone *on page 1261*
♦ **Triamcinolone, Oral** *see* Triamcinolone *on page 1261*
♦ **Triaminic® Allergy Congestion [OTC]** *see* Pseudoephedrine *on page 1061*
♦ **Triaminic® Cold and Allergy [OTC]** *see* Chlorpheniramine and Pseudoephedrine *on page 263*
♦ **Triaminic® Cold and Night Time Cough [OTC]** *see* Chlorpheniramine, Pseudoephedrine, and Dextromethorphan *on page 265*
♦ **Triaminic® Cough and Sore Throat Formula [OTC]** *see* Acetaminophen, Dextromethorphan, and Pseudoephedrine *on page 28*

Triamterene *(trye AM ter een)*

U.S. Brand Names Dyrenium®
Therapeutic Category Antihypertensive Agent; Diuretic, Potassium-Sparing
Use Alone or in combination with other diuretics in treatment of edema and hypertension; decreases potassium excretion caused by kaliuretic diuretics
Pregnancy Risk Factor B (manufacturer); D (expert analysis)
Dosage Adults: Oral: 100-300 mg/day in 1-2 divided doses; maximum dose: 300 mg/day; usual dosage range (JNC 7): 50-100 mg/day
Dosing comments in renal impairment: Cl_{cr} <10 mL/minute: Avoid use.
Dosing adjustment in hepatic impairment: Dose reduction is recommended in patients with cirrhosis.
Dosage Forms CAP: 50 mg, 100 mg

♦ **Triamterene and Hydrochlorothiazide** *see* Hydrochlorothiazide and Triamterene *on page 627*
♦ **Triavil®** *see* Amitriptyline and Perphenazine *on page 81*

Triazolam *(trye AY zoe lam)*

Related Information
Benzodiazepines Comparison *on page 1366*
U.S. Brand Names Halcion®
Therapeutic Category Benzodiazepine; Hypnotic; Sedative
Use Short-term treatment of insomnia
Restrictions C-IV
Pregnancy Risk Factor X
Contraindications Hypersensitivity to triazolam or any component of the formulation (cross-sensitivity with other benzodiazepines may exist); concurrent therapy with atazanavir, ketoconazole, itraconazole, nefazodone, and ritonavir; pregnancy
Warnings/Precautions Should be used only after evaluation of potential causes of sleep disturbance. Failure of sleep disturbance to resolve after 7-10 days may indicate psychiatric or medical illness. A worsening of insomnia or the emergence of new abnormalities of thought or behavior may represent unrecognized psychiatric or medical illness and requires immediate and careful evaluation. Prescription should be written for a maximum of 7-10 days and should not be prescribed in quantities exceeding a 1-month supply. Abrupt discontinuation after sustained use (generally >10 days) may cause withdrawal symptoms.

An increase in daytime anxiety may occur after as few as 10 days of continuous use, which may be related to withdrawal reaction in some patients. Anterograde amnesia may occur at a higher rate with triazolam than with other benzodiazepines. Use with caution in elderly or debilitated patients, patients with hepatic disease (including alcoholics), or renal impairment. Use with caution in patients with respiratory disease or impaired gag reflex. Avoid use in patients with sleep apnea.

Causes CNS depression (dose-related) resulting in sedation, dizziness, confusion, or ataxia which may impair physical and mental capabilities. Patients must be cautioned about performing tasks which require mental alertness (eg, operating machinery or driving). Use with caution in patients receiving other CNS depressants or psychoactive agents. Effects with other sedative drugs or ethanol may be potentiated. Benzodiazepines have been associated with falls and traumatic injury and should be used with extreme caution in patients who are at risk of these events (especially the elderly).

Use caution with potent CYP3A4 inhibitors, as they may significantly decreased the clearance of triazolam. Use caution in patients with suicidal risk. Use with caution in patients with a history of drug dependence. Benzodiazepines have been associated with dependence and acute withdrawal symptoms on discontinuation or reduction in dose. Acute withdrawal, including seizures, may be precipitated after administration of flumazenil to patients receiving long-term benzodiazepine therapy.

Paradoxical reactions, including hyperactive or aggressive behavior have been reported with benzodiazepines, particularly in adolescent/pediatric or psychiatric patients. Does not have analgesic, antidepressant, or antipsychotic properties.

Common Adverse Reactions
>10%: Central nervous system: Drowsiness, anteriograde amnesia
1% to 10%:
Central nervous system: Headache, dizziness, nervousness, lightheadedness, ataxia
Gastrointestinal: Nausea, vomiting

Drug Interactions
Cytochrome P450 Effect: Substrate of CYP3A4 (major); **Inhibits** CYP2C8/9 (weak)
Increased Effect/Toxicity: Triazolam levels may be increased by cimetidine, ciprofloxacin, clarithromycin, clozapine, CNS depressants, diltiazem, disulfiram, digoxin, erythromycin, ethanol, fluconazole, fluoxetine, fluvoxamine, grapefruit juice, isoniazid, itraconazole, ketoconazole, labetalol, levodopa, loxapine, metoprolol, metronidazole, miconazole, nefazodone, omeprazole, phenytoin, ranitidine, rifabutin, rifampin, troleandomycin, valproic acid, and verapamil. Concurrent use of some protease inhibitors (including atazanavir, ritonavir and amprenavir) is contraindicated. Oral contraceptives may decrease the clearance and increase the half-life of triazolam (monitor for increased triazolam effect).
Decreased Effect: Carbamazepine, rifampin, and rifabutin may enhance the metabolism of triazolam and decrease its therapeutic effect.
Mechanism of Action Binds to stereospecific benzodiazepine receptors on the postsynaptic GABA neuron at several sites within the central nervous system, including the limbic system, reticular formation. Enhancement of the inhibitory effect of GABA on neuronal excitability results by increased neuronal membrane permeability to chloride ions. This shift in chloride ions results in hyperpolarization (a less excitable state) and stabilization.

Pharmacodynamics/Kinetics
Onset of action: Hypnotic: 15-30 minutes
Duration: 6-7 hours
Distribution: V_d: 0.8-1.8 L/kg
Protein binding: 89%
Metabolism: Extensively hepatic
Half-life elimination: 1.7-5 hours
Excretion: Urine as unchanged drug and metabolites

Dosage Oral (onset of action is rapid, patient should be in bed when taking medication):
Children <18 years: Dosage not established
Adults:
Hypnotic: 0.125-0.25 mg at bedtime (maximum dose: 0.5 mg/day)
Preprocedure sedation (dental): 0.25 mg taken the evening before oral surgery; or 0.25 mg 1 hour before procedure
Elderly: Insomnia (short-term use): 0.0625-0.125 mg at bedtime; maximum dose: 0.25 mg/day (see Geriatric Considerations)
Dosing adjustment/comments in hepatic impairment: Reduce dose or avoid use in cirrhosis
Administration May take with food. Tablet may be crushed or swallowed whole. Onset of action is rapid, patient should be in bed when taking medication.
Monitoring Parameters Respiratory and cardiovascular status
Patient Information Avoid alcohol and other CNS depressants; avoid activities needing good psychomotor coordination until CNS effects are known; drug may cause physical or psychological dependence; avoid abrupt discontinuation after prolonged use
Dosage Forms TAB: 0.125 mg, 0.25 mg

♦ Tribavirin *see Ribavirin on page 1091*

Trichlormethiazide (trye klor meth EYE a zide)
Related Information
Sulfonamide Derivatives *on page 1404*
U.S. Brand Names Naqua®
Therapeutic Category Antihypertensive Agent; Diuretic, Thiazide
(Continued)

Trichlormethiazide *(Continued)*

Use Management of mild to moderate hypertension; treatment of edema in congestive heart failure and nephrotic syndrome

Pregnancy Risk Factor D

Dosage Adults: Oral: 1-4 mg/day; initially doses may be given twice daily.

Dosing adjustment in renal impairment: Reduced dosage is necessary.

Dosage Forms TAB: 4 mg

◆ **Trichloroacetaldehyde Monohydrate** *see Chloral Hydrate on page 254*

◆ **Trichloromonofluoromethane and Dichlorodifluoromethane** *see Dichlorodifluoromethane and Trichloromonofluoromethane on page 367*

◆ **TriCor®** *see Fenofibrate on page 511*

◆ **Tricosal** *see Choline Magnesium Trisalicylate on page 270*

◆ **Triderm®** *see Triamcinolone on page 1261*

◆ **Tridesilon®** *see Desonide on page 356*

Trientine *(TRYE en teen)*

U.S. Brand Names Syprine®

Synonyms Trientine Hydrochloride

Therapeutic Category Antidote, Copper Toxicity; Chelating Agent, Oral

Use Treatment of Wilson's disease in patients intolerant to penicillamine

Pregnancy Risk Factor C

Contraindications Hypersensitivity to trientine or any component of the formulation; rheumatoid arthritis, biliary cirrhosis, cystinuria

Warnings/Precautions May cause iron-deficiency anemia; monitor closely; use with caution in patients with reactive airway disease

Common Adverse Reactions Frequency not defined.

Central nervous system: Dystonia, malaise

Dermatologic: Thickening and fissuring of skin

Endocrine & metabolic: Iron deficiency

Gastrointestinal: Epigastric pain, heartburn

Hematologic: Anemia

Local: Tenderness

Neuromuscular & skeletal: Muscle cramps, muscular spasm, myasthenia gravis

Miscellaneous: Systemic lupus erythematosus

Drug Interactions

Decreased Effect: Iron and possibly other mineral supplements may decrease effect.

Mechanism of Action Trientine hydrochloride is an oral chelating agent structurally dissimilar from penicillamine and other available chelating agents; an effective oral chelator of copper used to induce adequate cupriuresis

Dosage Oral (administer on an empty stomach):

Children <12 years: 500-750 mg/day in divided doses 2-4 times/day; maximum: 1.5 g/day

Adults: 750-1250 mg/day in divided doses 2-4 times/day; maximum dose: 2 g/day

Patient Information Take 1 hour before or 2 hours after meals and at least 1 hour apart from any drug, food, or milk; do not chew capsule, swallow whole followed by a full glass of water; notify prescriber of any fever or skin changes; any skin exposed to the contents of a capsule should be promptly washed with water

Dosage Forms CAP: 250 mg

◆ **Trientine Hydrochloride** *see Trientine on page 1266*

Triethanolamine Polypeptide Oleate-Condensate

(trye eth a NOLE a meen pol i PEP tide OH lee ate-KON den sate)

U.S. Brand Names Cerumenex®

Therapeutic Category Otic Agent, Cerumenolytic

Use Removal of ear wax (cerumen)

Pregnancy Risk Factor C

Dosage Children and Adults: Otic: Fill ear canal, insert cotton plug; allow to remain 15-30 minutes; flush ear with lukewarm water as a single treatment; if a second application is needed for unusually hard impactions, repeat the procedure

Dosage Forms SOLN, otic: 10% (6 mL, 12 mL)

◆ **Triethylenethiophosphoramide** *see Thiotepa on page 1219*

Trifluoperazine *(trye floo oh PER a zeen)*

Related Information

Antipsychotic Agents Comparison *on page 1364*

U.S. Brand Names Stelazine® [DSC]

Synonyms Trifluoperazine Hydrochloride

Therapeutic Category Antianxiety Agent; Antipsychotic Agent, Phenothiazine; Antipsychotic Agent, Phenothiazine, Piperazine; Phenothiazine Derivative

Use Treatment of schizophrenia

Unlabeled/Investigational Use Management of psychotic disorders

Pregnancy Risk Factor C

Contraindications Hypersensitivity to trifluoperazine or any component of the formulation (cross-reactivity between phenothiazines may occur); severe CNS depression; bone marrow suppression; blood dyscrasias; severe hepatic disease; coma

Warnings/Precautions Safety in children <6 months of age has not been established; use with caution in patients with cardiovascular disease, seizures, hepatic dysfunction, narrow-angle glaucoma, or bone marrow suppression; watch for hypotension when administering I.M. or I.V.; use with caution in patients with myasthenia gravis or Parkinson's disease

Common Adverse Reactions Frequency not defined.

Cardiovascular: Hypotension, orthostatic hypotension, cardiac arrest

Central nervous system: Extrapyramidal signs (pseudoparkinsonism, akathisia, dystonias, tardive dyskinesia), dizziness, headache, neuroleptic malignant syndrome (NMS), impairment of temperature regulation, lowering of seizures threshold

Dermatologic: Increased sensitivity to sun, rash, discoloration of skin (blue-gray)

Endocrine & metabolic: Changes in menstrual cycle, changes in libido, breast pain, hyperglycemia, hypoglycemia, gynecomastia, lactation, galactorrhea

Gastrointestinal: Constipation, weight gain, nausea, vomiting, stomach pain, xerostomia

Genitourinary: Difficulty in urination, ejaculatory disturbances, urinary retention, priapism

Hematologic: Agranulocytosis, leukopenia, pancytopenia, thrombocytopenic purpura, eosinophilia, hemolytic anemia, aplastic anemia

Hepatic: Cholestatic jaundice, hepatotoxicity

Neuromuscular & skeletal: Tremor

Ocular: Pigmentary retinopathy, cornea and lens changes

Respiratory: Nasal congestion

Drug Interactions

Cytochrome P450 Effect: Substrate of CYP1A2 (major)

Increased Effect/Toxicity: CYP1A2 inhibitors may increase the levels/effects of trifluoperazine; example inhibitors include amiodarone, ciprofloxacin, fluvoxamine, ketoconazole, lomefloxacin, ofloxacin, and rofecoxib. Trifluoperazine's effects on CNS depression may be additive when trifluoperazine is combined with CNS depressants (narcotic analgesics, ethanol, barbiturates, cyclic antidepressants, antihistamines, or sedative-hypnotics). Trifluoperazine may increase the effects/toxicity of anticholinergics, antihypertensives, lithium (rare neurotoxicity), trazodone, or valproic acid. Concurrent use with TCA may produce increased toxicity or altered therapeutic response. Chloroquine and propranolol may increase trifluoperazine concentrations. Hypotension may occur when trifluoperazine is combined with epinephrine. May increase the risk of arrhythmia when combined with antiarrhythmics, cisapride, pimozide, sparfloxacin, or other drugs which prolong QT interval. Metoclopramide may increase risk of extrapyramidal symptoms (EPS).

Decreased Effect: CYP1A2 inducers may decrease the levels/effects of trifluoperazine; example inducers include aminoglutethimide, carbamazepine, phenobarbital, and rifampin. Phenothiazines inhibit the effects of levodopa, guanadrel, guanethidine, and bromocriptine. Benztropine (and other anticholinergics) may inhibit the therapeutic response to trifluoperazine and excess anticholinergic effects may occur. Cigarette smoking may enhance the hepatic metabolism of trifluoperazine. Trifluoperazine and possibly other low potency antipsychotics may reverse the pressor effects of epinephrine.

Mechanism of Action Blocks postsynaptic mesolimbic dopaminergic receptors in the brain; exhibits alpha-adrenergic blocking effect and depresses the release of hypothalamic and hypophyseal hormones

Pharmacodynamics/Kinetics

Metabolism: Extensively hepatic

Half-life elimination: >24 hours with chronic use

Dosage

Children 6-12 years: Schizophrenia/psychoses:

Oral: Hospitalized or well-supervised patients: Initial: 1 mg 1-2 times/day, gradually increase until symptoms are controlled or adverse effects become troublesome; maximum: 15 mg/day

I.M.: 1 mg twice daily

Adults:

Schizophrenia/psychoses:

Outpatients: Oral: 1-2 mg twice daily

Hospitalized or well-supervised patients: Initial: 2-5 mg twice daily with optimum response in the 15-20 mg/day range; do not exceed 40 mg/day

I.M.: 1-2 mg every 4-6 hours as needed up to 10 mg/24 hours maximum

Nonpsychotic anxiety: Oral: 1-2 mg twice daily; maximum: 6 mg/day; therapy for anxiety should not exceed 12 weeks; do not exceed 6 mg/day for longer than 12 weeks when treating anxiety; agitation, jitteriness, or insomnia may be confused with original neurotic or psychotic symptoms

Elderly:

Schizophrenia/psychoses:

Oral: Refer to adult dosing. Dose selection should start at the low end of the dosage range and titration must be gradual.

I.M.: Initial: 1 mg every 4-6 hours; increase at 1 mg increments; do not exceed 6 mg/day

Behavioral symptoms associated with dementia behavior: Oral: Initial: 0.5-1 mg 1-2 times/day; increase dose at 4- to 7-day intervals by 0.5-1 mg/day; increase dosing intervals (bid, tid, etc) as necessary to control response or side effects. Maximum daily dose: 40 mg. Gradual increases (titration) may prevent some side effects or decrease their severity.

Hemodialysis: Not dialyzable (0% to 5%)

Administration Administer I.M. injection deep in upper outer quadrant of buttock

(Continued)

Trifluoperazine *(Continued)*

Monitoring Parameters Vital signs; lipid profile, fasting blood glucose/Hgb A$_{1c}$; BMI; mental status, abnormal involuntary movement scale (AIMS)

Reference Range Therapeutic response and blood levels have not been established

Patient Information This drug usually requires several weeks for a full therapeutic response to be seen. Avoid excessive exposure to sunlight tanning lamps.

Dosage Forms INJ, solution (Stelazine®): 2 mg/mL (10 mL) [DSC]. **TAB:** 1 mg, 2 mg, 5 mg, 10 mg; (Stelazine®): 5 mg [DSC]

♦ **Trifluoperazine Hydrochloride** *see* Trifluoperazine *on page 1266*

♦ **Trifluorothymidine** *see* Trifluridine *on page 1268*

Trifluridine *(trye FLURE i deen)*

U.S. Brand Names Viroptic®

Synonyms F$_3$T; Trifluorothymidine

Therapeutic Category Antiviral Agent; Antiviral Agent, Ophthalmic

Use Treatment of primary keratoconjunctivitis and recurrent epithelial keratitis caused by herpes simplex virus types I and II

Pregnancy Risk Factor C

Contraindications Hypersensitivity to trifluridine or any component of the formulation

Warnings/Precautions Mild local irritation of conjunctival and cornea may occur when instilled but usually transient effects

Common Adverse Reactions 1% to 10%: Local: Burning, stinging

Mechanism of Action Interferes with viral replication by incorporating into viral DNA in place of thymidine, inhibiting thymidylate synthetase resulting in the formation of defective proteins

Pharmacodynamics/Kinetics Absorption: Ophthalmic: Systemic absorption negligible, corneal penetration adequate

Dosage Adults: Instill 1 drop into affected eye every 2 hours while awake, to a maximum of 9 drops/day, until re-epithelialization of corneal ulcer occurs; then use 1 drop every 4 hours for another 7 days; do **not** exceed 21 days of treatment; if improvement has not taken place in 7-14 days, consider another form of therapy

Patient Information Notify prescriber if improvement is not seen after 7 days, condition worsens, or if irritation occurs; do not discontinue without notifying the physician, do not exceed recommended dosage

Dosage Forms SOLN, ophthalmic: 1% (7.5 mL)

Trihexyphenidyl *(trye heks ee FEN i dil)*

Related Information

Parkinson's Agents Comparison *on page 1402*

Synonyms Artane; Benzhexol Hydrochloride; Trihexyphenidyl Hydrochloride

Therapeutic Category Anticholinergic Agent; Anti-Parkinson's Agent, Anticholinergic

Use Adjunctive treatment of Parkinson's disease; treatment of drug-induced extrapyramidal symptoms

Pregnancy Risk Factor C

Contraindications Hypersensitivity to trihexyphenidyl or any component of the formulation; narrow-angle glaucoma; pyloric or duodenal obstruction; stenosing peptic ulcers; bladder neck obstructions; achalasia; myasthenia gravis

Warnings/Precautions Use with caution in hot weather or during exercise, especially when administered concomitantly with other atropine-like drugs to chronically-ill patients, alcoholics, patients with CNS disease, or persons doing manual labor in a hot environment. Elderly patients require strict dosage regulation. Use with caution in patients with tachycardia, cardiac arrhythmias, hypertension, hypotension, prostatic hyperplasia or any tendency toward urinary retention, liver or kidney disorders, and obstructive disease of the GI or GU tract. May exacerbate mental symptoms when used to treat extrapyramidal symptoms. When given in large doses or to susceptible patients, may cause weakness.

Common Adverse Reactions Frequency not defined.

Cardiovascular: Tachycardia

Central nervous system: Confusion, agitation, euphoria, drowsiness, headache, dizziness, nervousness, delusions, hallucinations, paranoia

Dermatologic: Dry skin, increased sensitivity to light, rash

Gastrointestinal: Constipation, xerostomia, dry throat, ileus, nausea, vomiting, parotitis

Genitourinary: Urinary retention

Neuromuscular & skeletal: Weakness

Ocular: Blurred vision, mydriasis, increase in intraocular pressure, glaucoma, blindness (long-term use in narrow-angle glaucoma)

Respiratory: Dry nose

Miscellaneous: Diaphoresis (decreased)

Drug Interactions

Increased Effect/Toxicity: Central and/or peripheral anticholinergic syndrome can occur when administered with amantadine, rimantadine, narcotic analgesics, phenothiazines and other antipsychotics (especially with high anticholinergic activity), tricyclic antidepressants, MAO inhibitors, quinidine and some other antiarrhythmics, and antihistamines. CNS depressants (cannabinoids, ethanol, barbiturates, and narcotic analgesics) may have additive effects with trihexyphenidyl; an abuse potential exits.

Decreased Effect: May increase gastric degradation of levodopa and decrease the amount of levodopa absorbed by delaying gastric emptying; the opposite may be true for digoxin. Therapeutic effects of cholinergic agents (tacrine, donepezil, rivastigmine, galantamine) and neuroleptics may be antagonized.

Mechanism of Action Exerts a direct inhibitory effect on the parasympathetic nervous system. It also has a relaxing effect on smooth musculature; exerted both directly on the muscle itself and indirectly through parasympathetic nervous system (inhibitory effect)

Pharmacodynamics/Kinetics

Onset of action: Peak effect: ~1 hour

Half-life elimination: 3.3-4.1 hours

Time to peak, serum: 1-1.5 hours

Excretion: Primarily urine

Dosage Adults: Oral: Initial: 1-2 mg/day, increase by 2 mg increments at intervals of 3-5 days; usual dose: 5-15 mg/day in 3-4 divided doses

Monitoring Parameters IOP monitoring and gonioscopic evaluations should be performed periodically

Patient Information Take after meals or with food if GI upset occurs; do not discontinue drug abruptly; report adverse GI effects, rapid or pounding heartbeat, confusion, eye pain, rash, fever or heat intolerance. Observe caution when performing hazardous tasks or those that require alertness such as driving, as may cause drowsiness. Avoid alcohol and other CNS depressants. May cause dry mouth - adequate fluid intake or hard sugar free candy may relieve. Difficult urination or constipation may occur - notify physician if effects persist; may increase susceptibility to heat stroke.

Dosage Forms ELIX: 2 mg/5 mL (480 mL). TAB: 2 mg, 5 mg

♦ **Trihexyphenidyl Hydrochloride** see Trihexyphenidyl on page 1268

♦ **TriHIBit®** see Diphtheria, Tetanus Toxoids, and Acellular Pertussis Vaccine and *Haemophilus influenzae* b Conjugate Vaccine on page 390

♦ **Tri-K®** see Potassium Acetate, Potassium Bicarbonate, and Potassium Citrate on page 1018

♦ **Trilafon® [DSC]** see Perphenazine on page 985

♦ **Trileptal®** see Oxcarbazepine on page 940

♦ **Tri-Levlen®** see Ethinyl Estradiol and Levonorgestrel on page 484

♦ **Trilisate®** see Choline Magnesium Trisalicylate on page 270

♦ **Tri-Luma™** see Fluocinolone, Hydroquinone, and Tretinoin on page 533

Trimethobenzamide (trye meth oh BEN za mide)

U.S. Brand Names Tigan®

Synonyms Trimethobenzamide Hydrochloride

Therapeutic Category Anticholinergic Agent; Antiemetic

Use Treatment of nausea and vomiting

Pregnancy Risk Factor C

Contraindications Hypersensitivity to trimethobenzamide, benzocaine (or similar local anesthetics), or any component of the formulation; injection contraindicated in children; suppositories contraindicated in premature infants or neonates

Warnings/Precautions May mask emesis due to Reye's syndrome or mimic CNS effects of Reye's syndrome in patients with emesis of other etiologies; use in patients with acute vomiting should be avoided

Common Adverse Reactions Frequency not defined.

Cardiovascular: Hypotension

Central nervous system: Coma, depression, disorientation, dizziness, drowsiness, EPS, headache, opisthotonos, Parkinson-like syndrome, seizures

Hematologic: Blood dyscrasias

Hepatic: Jaundice

Neuromuscular & skeletal: Muscle cramps

Ocular: Blurred vision

Miscellaneous: Hypersensitivity reactions

Mechanism of Action Acts centrally to inhibit the medullary chemoreceptor trigger zone

Pharmacodynamics/Kinetics

Onset of action: Antiemetic: Oral: 10-40 minutes; I.M.: 15-35 minutes

Duration: 3-4 hours

Absorption: Rectal: ~60%

Bioavailability: Oral: 100%

Half-life elimination: 7-9 hours

Time to peak: Oral: 45 minutes; I.M.: 30 minutes

Excretion: Urine (30% to 50%)

Dosage Rectal use is contraindicated in neonates and premature infants

Children:

<14 kg: Oral, rectal: 100 mg 3-4 times/day

14-40 kg: Oral, rectal: 100-200 mg 3-4 times/day

Adults:

Oral: 250-300 mg 3-4 times/day

I.M., rectal: 200 mg 3-4 times/day

Administration Administer I.M. only; inject deep into upper outer quadrant of gluteal muscle

Patient Information May cause drowsiness, impair judgment and coordination; report any restlessness or involuntary movements

(Continued)

Trimethobenzamide *(Continued)*

Dosage Forms CAP: 250 mg [DSC] (Tigan®): 300 mg. **INJ, solution:** 100 mg/mL (2 mL); (Tigan®): 100 mg/mL (2 mL, 20 mL). **SUPP, rectal** (Tigan®): 100 mg, 200 mg

♦ **Trimethobenzamide Hydrochloride** *see* Trimethobenzamide *on page 1269*

Trimethoprim (trye METH oh prim)

U.S. Brand Names Primsol®; Proloprim®
Synonyms TMP
Therapeutic Category Antibiotic, Miscellaneous
Use Treatment of urinary tract infections due to susceptible strains of *E. coli, P. mirabilis, K. pneumoniae, Enterobacter* sp and coagulase-negative *Staphylococcus* including *S. saprophyticus*; acute otitis media in children; acute exacerbations of chronic bronchitis in adults; in combination with other agents for treatment of toxoplasmosis, *Pneumocystis carinii*; treatment of superficial ocular infections involving the conjunctiva and cornea
Pregnancy Risk Factor C
Contraindications Hypersensitivity to trimethoprim or any component of the formulation; megaloblastic anemia due to folate deficiency
Warnings/Precautions Use with caution in patients with impaired renal or hepatic function or with possible folate deficiency
Common Adverse Reactions Frequency not defined.
　Central nervous system: Aseptic meningitis (rare), fever
　Dermatologic: Maculopapular rash (3% to 7% at 200 mg/day; incidence higher with larger daily doses), erythema multiforme (rare), exfoliative dermatitis (rare), pruritus (common), phototoxic skin eruptions, Stevens-Johnson syndrome (rare), toxic epidermal necrolysis (rare)
　Endocrine & metabolic: Hyperkalemia, hyponatremia
　Gastrointestinal: Epigastric distress, glossitis, nausea, vomiting
　Hematologic: Leukopenia, megaloblastic anemia, methemoglobinemia, neutropenia, thrombocytopenia
　Hepatic: Liver enzyme elevation, cholestatic jaundice (rare)
　Renal: BUN and creatinine increased
　Miscellaneous: Anaphylaxis, hypersensitivity reactions
Drug Interactions
　Cytochrome P450 Effect: Substrate (major) of CYP2C8/9, 3A4; **Inhibits** CYP2C8/9 (moderate)
　Increased Effect/Toxicity: Increased effect/toxicity/levels of phenytoin. Concurrent use with ACE inhibitors increases risk of hyperkalemia. Increased myelosuppression with methotrexate. May increase levels of digoxin. Concurrent use with dapsone may increase levels of dapsone and trimethoprim. Concurrent use with procainamide may increase levels of procainamide and trimethoprim.
　Decreased Effect: CYP2C8/9 inducers may decrease the levels/effects of trimethoprim; example inducers include carbamazepine, phenobarbital, phenytoin, rifampin, rifapentine, and secobarbital.
Mechanism of Action Inhibits folic acid reduction to tetrahydrofolate, and thereby inhibits microbial growth
Pharmacodynamics/Kinetics
　Absorption: Readily and extensive
　Distribution: Widely into body tissues and fluids (middle ear, prostate, bile, aqueous humor, CSF); crosses placenta; enters breast milk
　Protein binding: 42% to 46%
　Metabolism: Partially hepatic
　Half-life elimination: 8-14 hours; prolonged with renal impairment
　Time to peak, serum: 1-4 hours
　Excretion: Urine (60% to 80%) as unchanged drug
Dosage Oral:
　Children: 4 mg/kg/day in divided doses every 12 hours
　Adults: 100 mg every 12 hours or 200 mg every 24 hours; in the treatment of *Pneumocystis carinii* pneumonia; dose may be as high as 15-20 mg/kg/day in 3-4 divided doses
　Dosing interval in renal impairment:
　　Cl$_{cr}$ 15-30 mL/minute: Administer 100 mg every 18 hours or 50 mg every 12 hours
　　Cl$_{cr}$ <15 mL/minute: Administer 100 mg every 24 hours or avoid use
　　Hemodialysis: Moderately dialyzable (20% to 50%)
Administration Administer with milk or food.
Reference Range Therapeutic: Peak: 5-15 mg/L; Trough: 2-8 mg/L
Patient Information Take with milk or food; report any skin rash, persistent or severe fatigue, fever, sore throat, or unusual bleeding or bruising; complete full course of therapy
Dosage Forms SOLN, oral (Primsol®): 50 mg (base)/5 mL (480 mL). **TAB:** 100 mg; (Proloprim®): 100 mg, 200 mg

Trimethoprim and Polymyxin B (trye METH oh prim & pol i MIKS in bee)

U.S. Brand Names Polytrim®
Synonyms Polymyxin B and Trimethoprim
Therapeutic Category Antibiotic, Ophthalmic
Use Treatment of surface ocular bacterial conjunctivitis and blepharoconjunctivitis
Pregnancy Risk Factor C
Dosage Instill 1-2 drops in eye(s) every 4-6 hours

Elderly: No overall differences observed between elderly and other adults

Dosage Forms SOLN, ophthalmic: Trimethoprim 1 mg and polymyxin B 10,000 units per mL (10 mL)

♦ **Trimethoprim and Sulfamethoxazole** *see* Sulfamethoxazole and Trimethoprim *on page 1173*

Trimetrexate Glucuronate (tri me TREKS ate gloo KYOOR oh nate)

U.S. Brand Names Neutrexin®

Synonyms NSC-352122

Therapeutic Category Antineoplastic Agent, Folate Antagonist; Antineoplastic Agent, Miscellaneous; Antiprotozoal

Use Alternative therapy for the treatment of moderate-to-severe *Pneumocystis carinii* pneumonia (PCP) in immunocompromised patients, including patients with acquired immunodeficiency syndrome (AIDS), who are intolerant of, or are refractory to, co-trimoxazole therapy or for whom co-trimoxazole and pentamidine are contraindicated. **Concurrent folinic acid (leucovorin) must always be administered.**

Unlabeled/Investigational Use Treatment of nonsmall cell lung cancer, metastatic colorectal cancer, metastatic head and neck cancer, pancreatic adenocarcinoma

Pregnancy Risk Factor D

Contraindications Hypersensitivity to trimetrexate, methotrexate, leucovorin, or any component of the formulation; severe existing myelosuppression; pregnancy

Warnings/Precautions The U.S. Food and Drug Administration (FDA) currently recommends that procedures for proper handling and disposal of antineoplastic agents be considered. Appropriate safety equipment is recommended for preparation, administration, and disposal of antineoplastics. If trimetrexate contacts the skin, immediately wash with soap and water. **Must be administered with concurrent leucovorin to avoid potentially serious or life-threatening toxicities.** Leucovorin therapy must extend for 72 hours past the last dose of trimetrexate. Hypersensitivity/allergic-type reactions have been reported, primarily when given as a bolus infusion, at higher than recommended doses for PCP, or in combination with fluorouracil or leucovorin. Use with caution in patients with mild myelosuppression, severe hepatic or renal dysfunction, hypoproteinemia, hypoalbuminemia, or previous extensive myelosuppressive therapies.

Common Adverse Reactions
>10%:
Hematologic: Neutropenia
Hepatic: LFTs increased
1% to 10%:
Central nervous system: Seizures, fever
Dermatologic: Rash
Gastrointestinal: Stomatitis, nausea, vomiting
Hematologic: Thrombocytopenia, anemia
Neuromuscular & skeletal: Peripheral neuropathy
Renal: Increased serum creatinine
Miscellaneous: Flu-like illness, hypersensitivity reactions, anaphylactoid reactions

Drug Interactions
Increased Effect/Toxicity: Cimetidine, clotrimazole, and ketoconazole may decrease trimetrexate metabolism, resulting in increased serum levels. Trimetrexate may increase toxicity (infections) of live virus vaccines.

Mechanism of Action Trimetrexate is a folate antimetabolite that inhibits DNA synthesis by inhibition of dihydrofolate reductase (DHFR); DHFR inhibition reduces the formation of reduced folates and thymidylate synthetase, resulting in inhibition of purine and thymidylic acid synthesis.

Pharmacodynamics/Kinetics
Distribution: V_d: 0.62 L/kg
Metabolism: Extensively hepatic
Half-life elimination: 15-17 hours

Dosage Note: Concurrent leucovorin 20 mg/m² every 6 hours must be administered daily (oral or I.V.) during treatment and for 72 hours past the last dose of trimetrexate glucuronate.

Adults: I.V.:
Pneumocystis carinii: 45 mg/m² once daily for 21 days; **alternative dosing based on weight:**
<50 kg:Trimetrexate glucuronate 1.5 mg/kg/day; leucovorin 0.6 mg/kg 4 times/day
50-80 kg:Trimetrexate glucuronate 1.2 mg/kg/day; leucovorin 0.5 mg/kg/4 times/day
>80 kg: Trimetrexate glucuronate 1 mg/kg/day; leucovorin 0.5 mg/kg/4 times/day
Note: Oral doses of leucovorin should be rounded up to the next higher 25 mg increment.
Antineoplastic (unlabeled use): 6-16 mg/m² once daily for 5 days every 21-28 days **or** 150-200 mg/m² every 2 weeks

Dosage adjustment in hepatic impairment: Although it may be necessary to reduce the dose in patients with liver dysfunction, no specific recommendations exist.

Administration Reconstituted solution should be filtered (0.22 µM) prior to further dilution; final solution should be clear, hue will range from colorless to pale yellow; trimetrexate forms a precipitate instantly upon contact with chloride ion or leucovorin, therefore it should not be added to solutions containing sodium chloride or other anions; trimetrexate and leucovorin solutions **must** be administered separately; intravenous lines should be flushed with at least 10 mL of D_5W between trimetrexate and leucovorin
(Continued)

Trimetrexate Glucuronate *(Continued)*

Monitoring Parameters Check and record patient's temperature daily; absolute neutrophil counts (ANC), platelet count, renal function tests (serum creatinine, BUN), hepatic function tests (ALT, AST, alkaline phosphatase)

Patient Information Report promptly any fever, rash, flu-like symptoms, numbness or tingling in the extremities, nausea, vomiting, abdominal pain, mouth sores, increased bruising or bleeding, black tarry stools

Dosage Forms INJ, powder for reconstitution: 25 mg, 200 mg

Trimipramine *(trye MI pra meen)*

Related Information

Antidepressant Agents Comparison *on page 1359*

U.S. Brand Names Surmontil®

Synonyms Trimipramine Maleate

Therapeutic Category Antidepressant, Tricyclic (Tertiary Amine)

Use Treatment of depression

Pregnancy Risk Factor C

Contraindications Hypersensitivity to trimipramine, any component of the formulation, or other dibenzodiazepines; use of MAO inhibitors within 14 days; use in a patient during the acute recovery phase of MI

Warnings/Precautions Often causes sedation, resulting in impaired performance of tasks requiring alertness (eg, operating machinery or driving). Sedative effects may be additive with other CNS depressants and/or ethanol. The degree of sedation is very high relative to other antidepressants. May worsen psychosis in some patients or precipitate a shift to mania or hypomania in patients with bipolar disease. May increase the risks associated with electroconvulsive therapy. This agent should be discontinued, when possible, prior to elective surgery. Therapy should not be abruptly discontinued in patients receiving high doses for prolonged periods. Use with caution in patients with hepatic or renal dysfunction and in elderly patients.

May cause orthostatic hypotension (risk is high relative to other antidepressants) - use with caution in patients at risk of hypotension or in patients where transient hypotensive episodes would be poorly tolerated (cardiovascular disease or cerebrovascular disease). The degree of anticholinergic blockade produced by this agent is very high relative to other cyclic antidepressants - use caution in patients with urinary retention, benign prostatic hypertrophy, narrow-angle glaucoma, xerostomia, visual problems, constipation, or history of bowel obstruction. May cause alteration in glucose regulation - use with caution in patients with diabetes.

The possibility of a suicide attempt is inherent in major depression and may persist until remission occurs. Use caution in high-risk patients during initiation of therapy. Prescriptions should be written for the smallest quantity consistent with good patient care. Use with caution in patients with a history of cardiovascular disease (including previous MI, stroke, tachycardia, or conduction abnormalities). The risk conduction abnormalities with this agent is high relative to other antidepressants. Use caution in patients with a previous seizure disorder or condition predisposing to seizures such as brain damage, alcoholism, or concurrent therapy with other drugs which lower the seizure threshold. Use with caution in hyperthyroid patients or those receiving thyroid supplementation.

Common Adverse Reactions Frequency not defined.

Cardiovascular: Arrhythmias, hypotension, hypertension, tachycardia, palpitations, heart block, stroke, myocardial infarction

Central nervous system: Headache, exacerbation of psychosis, confusion, delirium, hallucinations, nervousness, restlessness, delusions, agitation, insomnia, nightmares, anxiety, seizures, drowsiness

Dermatologic: Photosensitivity, rash, petechiae, itching

Endocrine & metabolic: Sexual dysfunction, breast enlargement, galactorrhea, SIADH

Gastrointestinal: Xerostomia, constipation, increased appetite, nausea, unpleasant taste, weight gain, diarrhea, heartburn, vomiting, anorexia, trouble with gums, decreased lower esophageal sphincter tone may cause GE reflux

Genitourinary: Difficult urination, urinary retention, testicular edema

Hematologic: Agranulocytosis, eosinophilia, purpura, thrombocytopenia

Hepatic: Cholestatic jaundice, increased liver enzymes

Neuromuscular & skeletal: Tremors, numbness, tingling, paresthesia, incoordination, ataxia, peripheral neuropathy, extrapyramidal symptoms

Ocular: Blurred vision, eye pain, disturbances in accommodation, mydriasis, increased intraocular pressure

Otic: Tinnitus

Miscellaneous: Allergic reactions

Drug Interactions

Cytochrome P450 Effect: Substrate (major) of CYP2C19, 2D6, 3A4

Increased Effect/Toxicity: Trimipramine increases the effects of amphetamines, anticholinergics, other CNS depressants (sedatives, hypnotics, or ethanol), chlorpropamide, tolazamide, and warfarin. When used with MAO inhibitors, hyperpyrexia, hypertension, tachycardia, confusion, seizures, and **deaths have been reported** (serotonin syndrome). Serotonin syndrome has also been reported with ritonavir (rare). CYP2D6 inhibitors may increase the levels/effects of trimipramine; example inhibitors include chlorpromazine, delavirdine, fluoxetine, miconazole, paroxetine, pergolide, quinidine, quinine, ritonavir, and ropinirole. Cimetidine, grapefruit juice, indinavir, methylphenidate, diltiazem, and verapamil increase the serum concentrations of TCAs. CYP2C19 inhibitors may increase the levels/

effects of trimipramine; example inhibitors include delavirdine, fluconazole, fluvoxamine, gemfibrozil, isoniazid, omeprazole, and ticlopidine. Use of lithium with a TCA may increase the risk for neurotoxicity. Phenothiazines may increase concentration of some TCAs and TCAs may increase concentration of phenothiazines. Pressor response to I.V. epinephrine, norepinephrine, and phenylephrine may be enhanced in patients receiving TCAs (**Note:** Effect is unlikely with epinephrine or levonordefrin dosages typically administered as infiltration in combination with local anesthetics). Combined use of beta-agonists or drugs which prolong QT_c (including quinidine, procainamide, disopyramide, cisapride, sparfloxacin, gatifloxacin, moxifloxacin) with TCAs may predispose patients to cardiac arrhythmias.

Decreased Effect: CYP2C19 inducers may decrease the levels/effects of trimipramine; example inducers include aminoglutethimide, carbamazepine, phenytoin, and rifampin. Trimipramine inhibits the antihypertensive response to bethanidine, clonidine, debrisoquin, guanadrel, guanethidine, guanabenz, and guanfacine. Cholestyramine and colestipol may bind TCAs and reduce their absorption; monitor for altered response.

Mechanism of Action Increases the synaptic concentration of serotonin and/or norepinephrine in the central nervous system by inhibition of their reuptake by the presynaptic neuronal membrane

Pharmacodynamics/Kinetics
Distribution: V_d: 17-48 L/kg
Protein binding: 95%; free drug: 3% to 7%
Metabolism: Hepatic; significant first-pass effect
Bioavailability: 18% to 63%
Half-life elimination: 16-40 hours
Excretion: Urine

Dosage Oral:
Adults: 50-150 mg/day as a single bedtime dose up to a maximum of 200 mg/day outpatient and 300 mg/day inpatient
Elderly: Adequate studies have not been done in the elderly. In general, dosing should be cautious, starting at the lower end of dosing range.

Monitoring Parameters Blood pressure and pulse rate prior to and during initial therapy; evaluate mental status; monitor weight; ECG in older adults

Patient Information Avoid unnecessary exposure to sunlight; avoid alcohol; do not discontinue medication abruptly; may cause urine to turn blue-green; may cause drowsiness; can use sugarless gum or hard candy for dry mouth; full effect may not occur for 4-6 weeks

Dosage Forms CAP: 25 mg, 50 mg, 100 mg

♦ **Trimipramine Maleate** *see* Trimipramine *on page 1272*
♦ **Trimox®** *see* Amoxicillin *on page 86*
♦ **Tri-Nasal®** *see* Triamcinolone *on page 1261*
♦ **Tri-Norinyl®** *see* Ethinyl Estradiol and Norethindrone *on page 487*
♦ **Trinsicon®** *see* Vitamin B Complex Combinations *on page 1311*
♦ **Triostat®** *see* Liothyronine *on page 749*
♦ **Tripedia®** *see* Diphtheria, Tetanus Toxoids, and Acellular Pertussis Vaccine *on page 389*

Tripelennamine (tri pel ENN a meen)

U.S. Brand Names PBZ®; PBZ-SR®
Synonyms Tripelennamine Citrate; Tripelennamine Hydrochloride
Therapeutic Category Antihistamine
Use Perennial and seasonal allergic rhinitis and other allergic symptoms including urticaria
Pregnancy Risk Factor B
Dosage Oral:
Infants and Children: 5 mg/kg/day in 4-6 divided doses, up to 300 mg/day maximum
Adults: 25-50 mg every 4-6 hours, extended release tablets 100 mg morning and evening up to 100 mg every 8 hours
Dosage Forms TAB: 50 mg

♦ **Tripelennamine Citrate** *see* Tripelennamine *on page 1273*
♦ **Tripelennamine Hydrochloride** *see* Tripelennamine *on page 1273*
♦ **Triphasil®** *see* Ethinyl Estradiol and Levonorgestrel *on page 484*
♦ **Triple Antibiotic®** *see* Bacitracin, Neomycin, and Polymyxin B *on page 143*
♦ **Triple Care® Antifungal [OTC]** *see* Miconazole *on page 834*
♦ **Triple Sulfa** *see* Sulfabenzamide, Sulfacetamide, and Sulfathiazole *on page 1169*

Triprolidine and Pseudoephedrine (trye PROE li deen & soo doe e FED rin)

U.S. Brand Names Actifed® Cold and Allergy [OTC]; Allerfrim® [OTC]; Allerphed® [OTC]; Aphedrid™ [OTC]; Aprodine® [OTC]; Genac® [OTC]; Silafed® [OTC]; Tri-Sudo® [OTC]; Uni-Fed® [OTC]
Synonyms Pseudoephedrine and Triprolidine
Therapeutic Category Alpha/Beta Agonist; Antihistamine
Use Temporary relief of nasal congestion, decongest sinus openings, running nose, sneezing, itching of nose or throat and itchy, watery eyes due to common cold, hay fever, or other upper respiratory allergies
Pregnancy Risk Factor C
(Continued)

Triprolidine and Pseudoephedrine *(Continued)*

Dosage Oral:

Children:

Syrup:

4 months to 2 years: 1.25 mL 3-4 times/day

2-4 years: 2.5 mL 3-4 times/day

4-6 years: 3.75 mL 3-4 times/day

6-12 years: 5 mL every 4-6 hours; do not exceed 4 doses in 24 hours

Tablet: ½ every 4-6 hours; do not exceed 4 doses in 24 hours

Children >12 years and Adults:

Syrup: 10 mL every 4-6 hours; do not exceed 4 doses in 24 hours

Tablet: 1 every 4-6 hours; do not exceed 4 doses in 24 hours

Dosage Forms SYR: Triprolidine 1.25 mg and pseudoephedrine 30 mg per 5 mL (120 mL); (Allerfrim®): Triprolidine 1.25 mg and pseudoephedrine 30 mg per 5 mL (120 mL, 480 mL); (Allerphed®, Aprodine®): Triprolidine 1.25 mg and pseudoephedrine 30 mg per 5 mL (120 mL); (Silafed®): Triprolidine 1.25 mg and pseudoephedrine 30 mg per 5 mL (120 mL, 240 mL). **TAB** (Actifed® Cold and Allergy, Allerfrim®, Aphedrid™, Aprodine®, Genac®, Tri-Sudo®, Uni-Fed®): Triprolidine 2.5 mg and pseudoephedrine 60 mg

◆ **Triprolidine, Codeine, and Pseudoephedrine** *see* Triprolidine, Pseudoephedrine, and Codeine *on page 1274*

Triprolidine, Pseudoephedrine, and Codeine

(trye PROE li deen, soo doe e FED rin, & KOE deen)

U.S. Brand Names Triacin-C® [DSC]

Synonyms Codeine, Pseudoephedrine, and Triprolidine; Pseudoephedrine, Triprolidine, and Codeine Pseudoephedrine, Codeine, and Triprolidine; Triprolidine, Codeine, and Pseudoephedrine; Triprolidine, Pseudoephedrine, and Codeine, Triprolidine, and Pseudoephedrine

Therapeutic Category Antihistamine/Decongestant/Antitussive

Use Symptomatic relief of upper respiratory symptoms and cough

Restrictions C-V (CDSA-I)

Pregnancy Risk Factor C

Dosage Oral:

Children:

2-6 years: 2.5 mL 4 times/day

7-12 years: 5 mL 4 times/day **or** ½ tablet 4 times/day

Children >12 years and Adults: 10 mL 4 times/day **or** 1 tablet 4 times/day

Dosage Forms SYR: Triprolidine 1.25 mg, pseudoephedrine 30 mg, and codeine 10 mg per 5 mL; (CoActifed®, CoVan®, ratio-Cotridin): Triprolidine hydrochloride 2 mg, pseudoephedrine hydrochloride 30 mg, and codeine phosphate 10 mg per 5 mL [available in Canada; not available in U.S.]. **TAB** (CoActifed®): Triprolidine hydrochloride 4 mg, pseudoephedrine hydrochloride 60 mg, and codeine phosphate 20 mg (50s) [available in Canada; not available in U.S.]

◆ **Triprolidine, Pseudoephedrine, and Codeine, Triprolidine, and Pseudoephedrine** *see* Triprolidine, Pseudoephedrine, and Codeine *on page 1274*

◆ **Triptoraline** *see* Triptorelin *on page 1274*

Triptorelin (trip toe REL in)

U.S. Brand Names Trelstar™ Depot; Trelstar™ LA

Synonyms AY-25650; CL-118,532; D-Trp(6)-LHRH; Triptoraline; Triptorelin Pamoate; Tryptoreline

Therapeutic Category Luteinizing Hormone-Releasing Hormone Analog

Use Palliative treatment of advanced prostate cancer as an alternative to orchiectomy or estrogen administration

Unlabeled/Investigational Use Treatment of endometriosis, growth hormone deficiency, hyperandrogenism, *in vitro* fertilization, ovarian carcinoma, pancreatic carcinoma, precocious puberty, uterine leiomyomata

Pregnancy Risk Factor X

Contraindications Hypersensitivity to triptorelin or any component of the formulation, other LHRH agonists or LHRH; pregnancy

Warnings/Precautions Transient increases in testosterone can lead to worsening symptoms (bone pain, hematuria, bladder outlet obstruction) of prostate cancer during the first few weeks of therapy. Cases of spinal cord compression have been reported with LHRH agonists. Hypersensitivity reactions including angioedema and anaphylaxis have rarely occurred. Safety and efficacy not established in pediatric population.

Common Adverse Reactions As reported with Trelstar™ Depot and Trelstar™ LA; frequency of effect may vary by product:

>10%:

Central nervous system: Headache (30% to 60%)

Endocrine & metabolic: Hot flashes (95% to 100%), glucose increased, hemoglobin decreased, RBC count decreased

Hepatic: Alkaline phosphatase increased, ALT increased, AST increased

Neuromuscular & skeletal: Skeletal pain (12% to 13%)

Renal: BUN increased

1% to 10%:
  Cardiovascular: Leg edema (6%), hypertension (4%), chest pain (2%), peripheral edema (1%)
  Central nervous system: Dizziness (1% to 3%), pain (2% to 3%), emotional lability (1%), fatigue (2%), insomnia (2%)
  Dermatologic: Rash (2%), pruritus (1%)
  Endocrine & metabolic: Alkaline phosphatase increased (2%), breast pain (2%), gynocomastia (2%), libido decreased (2%), tumor flare (8%)
  Gastrointestinal: Nausea (3%), anorexia (2%), constipation (2%), dyspepsia (2%), vomiting (2%), abdominal pain (1%), diarrhea (1%)
  Genitourinary: Dysuria (5%), impotence (2% to 7%), urinary retention (1%), urinary tract infection (1%)
  Hematologic: Anemia (1%)
  Local: Injection site pain (4%)
  Neuromuscular & skeletal: Leg pain (2% to 5%), back pain (3%), arthralgia (2%), leg cramps (2%), myalgia (1%), weakness (1%)
  Ocular: Conjunctivitis (1%), eye pain (1%)
  Respiratory: Cough (2%), dyspnea (1%), pharyngitis (1%)
  Postmarketing and/or case reports: Anaphylaxis, angioedema, hypersensitivity reactions, spinal cord compression, renal dysfunction

Drug Interactions
  Increased Effect/Toxicity: Not studied. Hyperprolactinemic drugs (dopamine antagonists such as antipsychotics, and metoclopramide) are contraindicated.
  Decreased Effect: Not studied. Hyperprolactinemic drugs (dopamine antagonists such as antipsychotics, and metoclopramide) are contraindicated.

Mechanism of Action Causes suppression of ovarian and testicular steroidogenesis due to decreased levels of LH and FSH with subsequent decrease in testosterone (male) and estrogen (female) levels. After chronic and continuous administration, usually 2-4 weeks after initiation, a sustained decrease in LH and FSH secretion occurs.

Pharmacodynamics/Kinetics
  Absorption: Oral: Not active
  Distribution: V_d: 30-33 L
  Protein binding: None
  Metabolism: Unknown; unlikely to involve CYP; no known metabolites
  Half-life elimination: 2.8 ± 1.2 hours
    Moderate to severe renal impairment: 6.5-7.7 hours
    Hepatic impairment: 7.6 hours
  Time to peak: 1-3 hours
  Excretion: Urine (42% as intact peptide); hepatic

Dosage I.M.: Adults: Prostate cancer:
  Trelstar™ Depot: 3.75 mg once every 28 days
  Trelstar™ LA: 11.25 mg once every 84 days
  Dosage adjustment in renal/hepatic impairment: Although this drug is excreted renally, no guidelines for adjustments are available.

Administration Must be administered under the supervision of a physician. Administer by I.M. injection into the buttock; alternate injection sites.
  Debioclip™: Follow manufacturer's instructions for mixing prior to use.

Monitoring Parameters Serum testosterone levels, prostate-specific antigen

Patient Information Use as directed. Do not miss monthly appointment for injection. You may experience disease flare (increased bone pain), blood in urine, and urinary retention during early treatment (usually resolves within 1 week). Hot flashes are common; you may feel flushed and hot (wearing layers of clothes or summer clothes and cool environment may help). If it becomes annoying and bothersome, let prescriber know. Report irregular or rapid heartbeat, unresolved nausea or vomiting, numbness of extremities, breast swelling or pain, difficulty breathing, or infection at injection sites.

Dosage Forms INJ, powder for reconstitution [also available packaged with Debioclip™ (prefilled syringe containing sterile water)]: (Trelstar™ Depot): 3.75 mg; (Trelstar™ LA): 11.25 mg

♦ **Triptorelin Pamoate** see Triptorelin on page 1274
♦ **Tris Buffer** see Tromethamine on page 1276
♦ **Trisenox™** see Arsenic Trioxide on page 115
♦ **Tris(hydroxymethyl)aminomethane** see Tromethamine on page 1276
♦ **Tri-Sudo® [OTC]** see Triprolidine and Pseudoephedrine on page 1273
♦ **Tri-Vent™ DM** see Guaifenesin, Pseudoephedrine, and Dextromethorphan on page 606
♦ **Tri-Vent™ HC** see Hydrocodone, Carbinoxamine, and Pseudoephedrine on page 632
♦ **Trivora®** see Ethinyl Estradiol and Levonorgestrel on page 484
♦ **Trizivir®** see Abacavir, Lamivudine, and Zidovudine on page 19
♦ **Trobicin®** see Spectinomycin on page 1157
♦ **Trocaine® [OTC]** see Benzocaine on page 154

Troleandomycin (troe lee an doe MYE sin)

U.S. Brand Names Tao®
Synonyms Triacetyloleandomycin
Therapeutic Category Antibiotic, Macrolide
Use Antibiotic with spectrum of activity similar to erythromycin
  (Continued)

Troleandomycin *(Continued)*

Pregnancy Risk Factor C

Contraindications Hypersensitivity to troleandomycin, other macrolides, or any component of the formulation; concomitant use with ergot derivatives, pimozide, astemizole, or cisapride

Warnings/Precautions Use with caution in patients with impaired hepatic function; chronic hepatitis may occur in patients with long or repetitive courses

Common Adverse Reactions Frequency not defined.

Gastrointestinal: Abdominal cramping and discomfort (dose-related), nausea, vomiting, diarrhea, rectal burning

Dermatologic: Urticaria, rashes

Hepatic: Cholestatic jaundice

Drug Interactions

Cytochrome P450 Effect: Substrate of CYP3A4 (major); **Inhibits** CYP3A4 (moderate)

Increased Effect/Toxicity: Avoid concomitant use of the following with troleandomycin due to increased risk of malignant arrhythmias: Astemizole, cisapride, gatifloxacin, moxifloxacin, pimozide, sparfloxacin, thioridazine. Other agents that prolong the QT_c interval, including type Ia (eg, quinidine) and type III antiarrhythmic agents, and selected antipsychotic agents (eg, mesoridazine, thioridazine) should be used with extreme caution.

Troleandomycin may increase the serum concentrations (and possibly the toxicity) of the following agents: Alfentanil (and possibly other narcotic analgesics), benzodiazepines (alprazolam, diazepam, midazolam, triazolam), buspirone, calcium channel blockers, dihydropyridine (felodipine), carbamazepine, cilostazol, clozapine, colchicine, cyclosporine, digoxin, disopyramide, ergot alkaloids (eg, bromocriptine), HMG-CoA reductase inhibitors (except fluvastatin, pravastatin), loratadine, methylprednisolone, rifabutin, tacrolimus, theophylline, valproate, vinblastine, vincristine, zopiclone. Sildenafil serum levels may be increased by troleandomycin (consider reduction in sildenafil dosage). Tadalafil serum concentrations may be increased by troleandomycin; a maximum tadalafil dose of 10 mg in 72 hours is recommended with strong CYP3A4 inhibitors. Vardenafil serum concentrations may be increased by troleandomycin; specific dosage adjustment guidelines have not been established; recommendations for other strong CYP3A4 inhibitors include vardenafil dose not to exceed 2.5 mg in 24 hours.

The effects of neuromuscular-blocking agents and warfarin have been potentiated by troleandomycin. Troleandomycin serum concentrations may be increased by amprenavir (and possibly other protease inhibitors).

Decreased Effect: Troleandomycin may decrease the serum concentrations of zafirlukast. Troleandomycin may antagonize the therapeutic effects of clindamycin and lincomycin.

Mechanism of Action Decreases methylprednisolone clearance from a linear first order decline to a nonlinear decline in plasma concentration. Troleandomycin also has an undefined action independent of its effects on steroid elimination. Inhibits RNA-dependent protein synthesis at the chain elongation step; binds to the 50S ribosomal subunit resulting in blockage of transpeptidation.

Pharmacodynamics/Kinetics

Time to peak, serum: ~2 hours

Excretion: Urine (10% to 25% as active drug); feces

Dosage Oral:

Children 7-13 years: 25-40 mg/kg/day divided every 6 hours (125-250 mg every 6 hours)

Adults: 250-500 mg 4 times/day (around-the-clock every 6 hours)

Administration Administer around-the-clock every 6 hours.

Monitoring Parameters Hepatic function tests

Patient Information Complete full course of therapy; report persistent or severe abdominal pain, nausea, vomiting, jaundice, darkened urine, or fever

Dosage Forms CAP: 250 mg

Tromethamine *(troe METH a meen)*

U.S. Brand Names THAM®

Synonyms Tris Buffer; Tris(hydroxymethyl)aminomethane

Therapeutic Category Alkalinizing Agent, Parenteral

Use Correction of metabolic acidosis associated with cardiac bypass surgery or cardiac arrest; to correct excess acidity of stored blood that is preserved with acid citrate dextrose; to prime the pump-oxygenator during cardiac bypass surgery; indicated in infants needing alkalinization after receiving maximum sodium bicarbonate (8-10 mEq/kg/24 hours); (advantage of THAM® is that it alkalinizes without increasing pCO_2 and sodium)

Pregnancy Risk Factor C

Contraindications Uremia or anuria; chronic respiratory acidosis (neonates); salicylate intoxication (neonates)

Warnings/Precautions Reduce dose and monitor pH carefully in renal impairment; drug should not be given for a period of longer than 24 hours unless for a life-threatening situation

Common Adverse Reactions 1% to 10%:

Cardiovascular: Venospasm

Local: Tissue irritation, necrosis with extravasation

Mechanism of Action Acts as a proton acceptor, which combines with hydrogen ions to form bicarbonate buffer, to correct acidosis

Pharmacodynamics/Kinetics

Absorption: 30% of dose is not ionized

Excretion: Urine (>75%) within 3 hours

Dosage

Neonates and Infants: Metabolic acidosis associated with RDS: Initial: Approximately 1 mL/kg for each pH unit below 7.4; additional doses determined by changes in PaO_2, pH, and pCO_2; **Note:** Although THAM® solution does not raise pCO_2 when treating metabolic acidosis with concurrent respiratory acidosis, bicarbonate may be preferred because the osmotic effects of THAM® are greater.

Adults: Dose depends on buffer base deficit; when deficit is known: tromethamine (mL of 0.3 M solution) = body weight (kg) x base deficit (mEq/L); when base deficit is not known: 3-6 mL/kg/dose I.V. (1-2 mEq/kg/dose)

Metabolic acidosis with cardiac arrest:

I.V.: 3.5-6 mL/kg (1-2 mEq/kg/dose) into large peripheral vein; 500-1000 mL if needed in adults

I.V. continuous drip: Infuse slowly by syringe pump over 3-6 hours

Acidosis associated with cardiac bypass surgery: Average dose: 9 mL/kg (2.7 mEq/kg); 500 mL is adequate for most adults; maximum dose: 500 mg/kg in ≤1 hour

Excess acidity of acid citrate dextrose priming blood: 14-70 mL of 0.3 molar solution added to each 500 mL of blood

Dosing comments in renal impairment: Use with caution and monitor for hyperkalemia and ECG

Administration Maximum concentration: 0.3 molar; infuse slowly over at least 1 hour

If extravasation occurs, aspirate as much fluid as possible, then infiltrate area with procaine 1% to which hyaluronidase has been added

Monitoring Parameters Serum electrolytes, arterial blood gases, serum pH, blood sugar, ECG monitoring, renal function tests

Reference Range Blood pH: 7.35-7.45

Dosage Forms INJ, solution (THAM®): 18 g [0.3 molar] (500 mL)

♦ **Tropicacyl®** see Tropicamide on page 1277

Tropicamide (troe PIK a mide)

Related Information

Cycloplegic Mydriatics Comparison on page 1375

U.S. Brand Names Mydriacyl®; Opticyl®; Tropicacyl®

Synonyms Bistropamide

Therapeutic Category Ophthalmic Agent, Mydriatic

Use Short-acting mydriatic used in diagnostic procedures; as well as preoperatively and postoperatively; treatment of some cases of acute iritis, iridocyclitis, and keratitis

Pregnancy Risk Factor C

Dosage Ophthalmic: Children and Adults (individuals with heavily pigmented eyes may require larger doses):

Cycloplegia: Instill 1-2 drops (1%); may repeat in 5 minutes

Exam must be performed within 30 minutes after the repeat dose; if the patient is not examined within 20-30 minutes, instill an additional drop

Mydriasis: Instill 1-2 drops (0.5%) 15-20 minutes before exam; may repeat every 30 minutes as needed

Dosage Forms SOLN, ophthalmic: 0.5% (15 mL); 1% (2 mL, 3 mL, 15 mL); (Mydriacyl®): 0.5% (15 mL); 1% (3 mL, 15 mL); (Opticyl®, Tropicacyl®): 0.5% (15 mL); 1% (15 mL)

Trovafloxacin (TROE va floks a sin)

U.S. Brand Names Trovan® [DSC]

Synonyms Alatrofloxacin Mesylate; CP-99,219-27

Therapeutic Category Antibiotic, Quinolone

Use Should be used only in life- or limb-threatening infections

Treatment of nosocomial pneumonia, community-acquired pneumonia, complicated intra-abdominal infections, gynecologic/pelvic infections, complicated skin and skin structure infections

Pregnancy Risk Factor C

Contraindications History of hypersensitivity to trovafloxacin, alatrofloxacin, quinolone antimicrobial agents, or any component of the formulation

Warnings/Precautions For use only in serious life- or limb-threatening infections. Initiation of therapy must occur in an inpatient healthcare facility. May alter GI flora resulting in pseudomembranous colitis due to *Clostridium difficile*; use with caution in patients with seizure disorders or severe cerebral atherosclerosis; photosensitivity; CNS stimulation may occur which may lead to tremor, restlessness, confusion, hallucinations, paranoia, depression, nightmares, insomnia, or lightheadedness. Hepatic reactions have resulted in death. Risk of hepatotoxicity is increased if therapy exceeds 14 days. Tendon inflammation and/or rupture have been reported with other quinolone antibiotics. Discontinue at first sign of tendon inflammation or pain. Quinolones may exacerbate myasthenia gravis.

Severe hypersensitivity reactions, including anaphylaxis, have occurred with quinolone therapy. If an allergic reaction occurs (itching, urticaria, dyspnea, facial edema, loss of consciousness, tingling, cardiovascular collapse), discontinue drug immediately. Prolonged use may result in superinfection; pseudomembranous colitis may occur and should be considered in all patients who present with diarrhea.

(Continued)

Trovafloxacin (Continued)

Common Adverse Reactions Note: Fatalities have occurred in patients developing hepatic necrosis.

1% to 10% (range reported in clinical trials):

Central nervous system: Dizziness (2% to 11%), lightheadedness (<1% to 4%), headache (1% to 5%)

Dermatologic: Rash (<1% to 2%), pruritus (<1% to 2%)

Gastrointestinal: Nausea (4% to 8%), abdominal pain (<1% to 1%), vomiting, diarrhea

Genitourinary: Vaginitis (<1% to 1%)

Hepatic: Increased LFTs

Local: Injection site reaction, pain, or inflammation

Drug Interactions

Increased Effect/Toxicity: Concurrent use of corticosteroids may increase risk of tendon rupture.

Decreased Effect: Coadministration with antacids containing aluminum or magnesium, citric acid/sodium citrate, sucralfate, and iron markedly reduces absorption of trovafloxacin. Separate oral administration by at least 2 hours. Coadministration of intravenous morphine also reduces absorption. Separate I.V. morphine by 2 hours (when trovafloxacin is taken in fasting state) or 4 hours (when taken with food). Do not administer multivalent cations (eg, calcium, magnesium) through the same intravenous line.

Mechanism of Action Inhibits DNA-gyrase in susceptible organisms; inhibits relaxation of supercoiled DNA and promotes breakage of double-stranded DNA

Pharmacodynamics/Kinetics

Distribution: Concentration in most tissues greater than plasma or serum

Protein binding: 76%

Metabolism: Hepatic conjugation; glucuronidation 13%, acetylation 9%

Bioavailability: 88%

Half-life elimination: 9-12 hours

Time to peak, serum: Oral: Within 2 hours

Excretion: Feces (43% as unchanged drug); urine (6% as unchanged drug)

Dosage Adults:

Nosocomial pneumonia: I.V.: 300 mg single dose followed by 200 mg/day orally for a total duration of 10-14 days

Community-acquired pneumonia: Oral, I.V.: 200 mg/day for 7-14 days

Complicated intra-abdominal infections, including postsurgical infections/gynecologic and pelvic infections: I.V.: 300 mg as a single dose followed by 200 mg/day orally for a total duration of 7-14 days

Skin and skin structure infections, complicated, including diabetic foot infections: Oral, I.V.: 200 mg/day for 10-14 days

Dosage adjustment in renal impairment: No adjustment is necessary

Dosage adjustment for hemodialysis: None required; trovafloxacin not sufficiently removed by hemodialysis

Dosage adjustment in hepatic impairment:

Mild to moderate cirrhosis:

Initial dose for normal hepatic function: 300 mg I.V.; 200 mg I.V. or oral; 100 mg oral

Reduced dose: 200 mg I.V.; 100 mg I.V. or oral; 100 mg oral

Severe cirrhosis: No data available

Administration

Oral: Administer without regard to meals.

I.V.: Not for I.M. or S.C.; administer IVPB over 60 minutes

Monitoring Parameters Periodic assessment of liver function tests should be considered

Patient Information Drink fluids liberally; do not take antacids containing magnesium or aluminum or products containing iron or zinc simultaneously or within 4 hours before or 2 hours after taking dose. May cause dizziness or lightheadedness; observe caution while driving or performing other tasks requiring alertness, coordination, or physical dexterity. CNS stimulation may occur (eg, tremor, restlessness, confusion). Avoid excessive sunlight/artificial ultraviolet light; discontinue drug if phototoxicity occurs. Avoid re-exposure to ultraviolet light. Reactions may recur up to several weeks after stopping therapy.

Dosage Forms INJ, solution [alatrofloxacin]: 5 mg/mL (40 mL, 60 mL). **TAB** [trovafloxacin]: 100 mg, 200 mg

♦ **Trovan® [DSC]** *see* Trovafloxacin *on page 1277*

♦ **Trusopt®** *see* Dorzolamide *on page 404*

Trypsin, Balsam Peru, and Castor Oil

(TRIP sin, BAL sam pe RUE, & KAS tor oyl)

U.S. Brand Names Granulex®

Synonyms Balsam Peru, Trypsin, and Castor Oil; Castor Oil, Trypsin, and Balsam Peru

Therapeutic Category Protectant, Topical

Use Treatment of decubitus ulcers, varicose ulcers, debridement of eschar, dehiscent wounds and sunburn

Dosage Topical: Apply a minimum of twice daily or as often as necessary

Dosage Forms AERO, topical: Trypsin 0.12 mg, balsam Peru 87 mg, and castor oil 788 mg per gram (60 g, 120 g)

♦ **Tryptoreline** *see* Triptorelin *on page 1274*

♦ **TSH** *see* Thyrotropin Alpha *on page 1223*

- ◆ **TSPA** *see* Thiotepa *on page 1219*
- ◆ **TST** *see* Tuberculin Tests *on page 1279*
- ◆ **T-Stat®** *see* Erythromycin *on page 453*
- ◆ **T-Tab®** *see* Clorazepate *on page 303*
- ◆ **Tuberculin Purified Protein Derivative** *see* Tuberculin Tests *on page 1279*
- ◆ **Tuberculin Skin Test** *see* Tuberculin Tests *on page 1279*

Tuberculin Tests (too BER kyoo lin tests)

U.S. Brand Names Aplisol®; Tubersol®

Synonyms Mantoux; PPD; Tine Test; TST; Tuberculin Purified Protein Derivative; Tuberculin Skin Test

Therapeutic Category Diagnostic Agent, Skin Test

Use Skin test in diagnosis of tuberculosis, cell-mediated immunodeficiencies

Pregnancy Risk Factor C

Contraindications 250 TU strength should not be used for initial testing

Warnings/Precautions Do not administer I.V. or S.C.; epinephrine (1:1000) should be available to treat possible allergic reactions

Common Adverse Reactions Frequency not defined.
   Dermatologic: Ulceration, necrosis, vesiculation
   Local: Pain at injection site

Mechanism of Action Tuberculosis results in individuals becoming sensitized to certain antigenic components of the *M. tuberculosis* organism. Culture extracts called tuberculins are contained in tuberculin skin test preparations. Upon intracutaneous injection of these culture extracts, a classic delayed (cellular) hypersensitivity reaction occurs. This reaction is characteristic of a delayed course (peak occurs >24 hours after injection, induration of the skin secondary to cell infiltration, and occasional vesiculation and necrosis). Delayed hypersensitivity reactions to tuberculin may indicate infection with a variety of nontuberculosis mycobacteria, or vaccination with the live attenuated mycobacterial strain of *M. bovis* vaccine, BCG, in addition to previous natural infection with *M. tuberculosis*.

Pharmacodynamics/Kinetics
   Onset of action: Delayed hypersensitivity reactions: 5-6 hours
   Peak effect: 48-72 hours
   Duration: Reactions subside over a few days

Dosage Children and Adults: Intradermal: 0.1 mL about 4" below elbow; use $1/4$" to $1/2$" or 26- or 27-gauge needle; significant reactions are ≥5 mm in diameter
   Interpretation of induration of tuberculin skin test injections: Positive: ≥10 mm; inconclusive: 5-9 mm; negative: <5 mm
   Interpretation of induration of Tine test injections: Positive: >2 mm and vesiculation present; inconclusive: <2 mm (give patient Mantoux test of 5 TU/0.1 mL - base decisions on results of Mantoux test); negative: <2 mm or erythema of any size (no need for retesting unless person is a contact of a patient with tuberculosis or there is clinical evidence suggestive of the disease)

Administration Select a site without acne or hair

Patient Information Return to physician for reaction interpretation at 48-72 hours

Dosage Forms INJ, solution: 5 TU/0.1 mL (1 mL, 5 mL)

- ◆ **Tuberculosis Prophylaxis** *see page 1438*
- ◆ **Tuberculosis Treatment Guidelines** *see page 1466*
- ◆ **Tubersol®** *see* Tuberculin Tests *on page 1279*
- ◆ **Tuinal® [DSC]** *see* Amobarbital and Secobarbital *on page 84*
- ◆ **Tums® [OTC]** *see* Calcium Carbonate *on page 203*
- ◆ **Tums® 500 [OTC]** *see* Calcium Carbonate *on page 203*
- ◆ **Tums® E-X [OTC]** *see* Calcium Carbonate *on page 203*
- ◆ **Tums® Extra Strength Sugar Free [OTC]** *see* Calcium Carbonate *on page 203*
- ◆ **Tums® Smooth Dissolve [OTC]** *see* Calcium Carbonate *on page 203*
- ◆ **Tums® Ultra [OTC]** *see* Calcium Carbonate *on page 203*
- ◆ **Tussafed®** *see* Carbinoxamine, Pseudoephedrine, and Dextromethorphan *on page 219*
- ◆ **Tussigon®** *see* Hydrocodone and Homatropine *on page 630*
- ◆ **Tussionex®** *see* Hydrocodone and Chlorpheniramine *on page 630*
- ◆ **Tussi-Organidin® DM NR** *see* Guaifenesin and Dextromethorphan *on page 604*
- ◆ **Tussi-Organidin® NR** *see* Guaifenesin and Codeine *on page 604*
- ◆ **Tussi-Organidin® S-NR** *see* Guaifenesin and Codeine *on page 604*
- ◆ **Tusstat®** *see* DiphenhydrAMINE *on page 383*
- ◆ **Twilite® [OTC]** *see* DiphenhydrAMINE *on page 383*
- ◆ **Twinrix®** *see* Hepatitis A Inactivated and Hepatitis B (Recombinant) Vaccine *on page 615*
- ◆ **Tylenol® [OTC]** *see* Acetaminophen *on page 24*
- ◆ **Tylenol® 8 Hour [OTC]** *see* Acetaminophen *on page 24*
- ◆ **Tylenol® Allergy Sinus [OTC]** *see* Acetaminophen, Chlorpheniramine, and Pseudoephedrine *on page 28*
- ◆ **Tylenol® Arthritis Pain [OTC]** *see* Acetaminophen *on page 24*
- ◆ **Tylenol® Children's [OTC]** *see* Acetaminophen *on page 24*
- ◆ **Tylenol® Cold Day Non-Drowsy [OTC]** *see* Acetaminophen, Dextromethorphan, and Pseudoephedrine *on page 28*

- ◆ **Tylenol® Cold, Infants [OTC]** *see* Acetaminophen and Pseudoephedrine *on page 26*
- ◆ **Tylenol® Extra Strength [OTC]** *see* Acetaminophen *on page 24*
- ◆ **Tylenol® Flu Non-Drowsy Maximum Strength [OTC]** *see* Acetaminophen, Dextromethorphan, and Pseudoephedrine *on page 28*
- ◆ **Tylenol® Infants [OTC]** *see* Acetaminophen *on page 24*
- ◆ **Tylenol® Junior Strength [OTC]** *see* Acetaminophen *on page 24*
- ◆ **Tylenol® PM Extra Strength [OTC]** *see* Acetaminophen and Diphenhydramine *on page 26*
- ◆ **Tylenol® Severe Allergy [OTC]** *see* Acetaminophen and Diphenhydramine *on page 26*
- ◆ **Tylenol® Sinus, Children's [OTC]** *see* Acetaminophen and Pseudoephedrine *on page 26*
- ◆ **Tylenol® Sinus Day Non-Drowsy [OTC]** *see* Acetaminophen and Pseudoephedrine *on page 26*
- ◆ **Tylenol® Sore Throat [OTC]** *see* Acetaminophen *on page 24*
- ◆ **Tylenol® With Codeine** *see* Acetaminophen and Codeine *on page 25*
- ◆ **Tylox®** *see* Oxycodone and Acetaminophen *on page 945*
- ◆ **Typhim Vi®** *see* Typhoid Vaccine *on page 1280*

Typhoid Vaccine (TYE foid vak SEEN)

U.S. Brand Names Typhim Vi®; Vivotif Berna®

Synonyms Typhoid Vaccine Live Oral Ty21a

Therapeutic Category Vaccine; Vaccine, Inactivated Bacteria

Use Typhoid vaccine: Live, attenuated Ty21a typhoid vaccine should not be administered to immunocompromised persons, including those known to be infected with HIV. Parenteral inactivated vaccine is a theoretically safer alternative for this group.

Parenteral: Promotes active immunity to typhoid fever for patients intimately exposed to a typhoid carrier or foreign travel to a typhoid fever endemic area

Oral: For immunization of children >6 years of age and adults who expect intimate exposure of or household contact with typhoid fever, travelers to areas of world with risk of exposure to typhoid fever, and workers in microbiology laboratories with expected frequent contact with *S. typhi*

Pregnancy Risk Factor C

Contraindications Acute respiratory or other active infections, previous sensitivity to typhoid vaccine, congenital or acquired immunodeficient state, acute febrile illness, acute GI illness (oral), other active infection, persistent diarrhea or vomiting (oral)

Warnings/Precautions Postpone use in presence of acute infection; use during pregnancy only when clearly needed, immune deficiency conditions; not all recipients of typhoid vaccine will be fully protected against typhoid fever. Travelers should take all necessary precautions to avoid contact or ingestion of potentially contaminated food or water sources. Unless a complete immunization schedule is followed, an optimum immune response may not be achieved.

Common Adverse Reactions All serious adverse reactions must be reported to the U.S. Department of Health and Human Services (DHHS) Vaccine Adverse Event Reporting System (VAERS) 1-800-822-7967.

Oral: 1% to 10%:

Central nervous system: Headache, fever

Dermatologic: Rash

Gastrointestinal: Abdominal discomfort, stomach cramps, diarrhea, nausea, vomiting

Injection:

>10%:

Central nervous system: Headache (13% to 20%), fever (3% to 11%), malaise (4% to 24%)

Dermatologic: Local tenderness (13% to 98%), induration (5% to 15%), pain at injection site (7% to 41%)

1% to 10%:

Central nervous system: Fever ≥100°F (2%)

Gastrointestinal: Nausea (2% to 8%), diarrhea (3% to 4%), vomiting (2%)

Local: Erythema at injection site (4% to 5%)

Neuromuscular & skeletal: Myalgia (3% to 7%)

Mechanism of Action Virulent strains of *Salmonella typhi* cause disease by penetrating the intestinal mucosa and entering the systemic circulation via the lymphatic vasculature. One possible mechanism of conferring immunity may be the provocation of a local immune response in the intestinal tract induced by oral ingesting of a live strain with subsequent aborted infection. The ability of *Salmonella typhi* to produce clinical disease (and to elicit an immune response) is dependent on the bacteria having a complete lipopolysaccharide. The live attenuate Ty21a strain lacks the enzyme UDP-4-galactose epimerase so that lipopolysaccharide is only synthesized under conditions that induce bacterial autolysis. Thus, the strain remains avirulent despite the production of sufficient lipopolysaccharide to evoke a protective immune response. Despite low levels of lipopolysaccharide synthesis, cells lyse before gaining a virulent phenotype due to the intracellular accumulation of metabolic intermediates.

Pharmacodynamics/Kinetics

Onset of action: Immunity to *Salmonella typhi*: Oral: ~1 week

Duration: Immunity: Oral: ~5 years; Parenteral: ~3 years

Dosage Immunization:

Oral: Children ≥6 years and Adults:

Primary immunization: One capsule on alternate days (day 1, 3, 5, and 7) for a total of 4 doses; all doses should be complete at least 1 week prior to potential exposure

Booster immunization: Repeat full course of primary immunization every 5 years

I.M. (Typhim Vi®): Children ≥2 years and Adults: 0.5 mL given at least 2 weeks prior to expected exposure

Re-immunization: 0.5 mL; optimal schedule has not been established; a single dose every 2 years is currently recommended for repeated or continued exposure

Administration Typhim Vi® may be given I.M. and is indicated for children ≥2 years of age; administer as a single 0.5 mL (25 mcg) injection in deltoid muscle

Patient Information Oral capsule should be taken 1 hour before a meal with cold or lukewarm drink, (swallow capsule whole, do not chew); systemic adverse effects may persist for 1-2 days. Take all 4 doses exactly as directed on alternate days to obtain a maximal response.

Dosage Forms CAP, enteric coated (Vivotif Berna®): Viable *S. typhi* Ty21a colony-forming units 2-6 x 10⁹ and nonviable *S. typhi* Ty21a colony-forming units 50 x 10⁹. **INJ, solution** (Typhim Vi®): Purified Vi capsular polysaccharide 25 mcg/0.5 mL (0.5 mL)

- ◆ **Typhoid Vaccine Live Oral Ty21a** *see Typhoid Vaccine on page 1280*
- ◆ **U-90152S** *see Delavirdine on page 349*
- ◆ **UCB-P071** *see Cetirizine on page 250*
- ◆ **Ucephan®** *see Sodium Phenylacetate and Sodium Benzoate on page 1150*
- ◆ **UK** *see Urokinase on page 1283*
- ◆ **UK92480** *see Sildenafil on page 1136*
- ◆ **UK109496** *see Voriconazole on page 1313*
- ◆ **Ultane®** *see Sevoflurane on page 1134*
- ◆ **Ultiva®** *see Remifentanil on page 1084*
- ◆ **Ultracet™** *see Acetaminophen and Tramadol on page 27*
- ◆ **Ultram®** *see Tramadol on page 1249*
- ◆ **Ultra Mide®** *see Urea on page 1282*
- ◆ **Ultraprin [OTC]** *see Ibuprofen on page 645*
- ◆ **Ultrase®** *see Pancrelipase on page 953*
- ◆ **Ultrase® MT** *see Pancrelipase on page 953*
- ◆ **Ultravate®** *see Halobetasol on page 609*
- ◆ **Unasyn®** *see Ampicillin and Sulbactam on page 96*
- ◆ **Uni-Fed® [OTC]** *see Triprolidine and Pseudoephedrine on page 1273*
- ◆ **Uniphyl®** *see Theophylline Salts on page 1210*
- ◆ **Uniretic®** *see Moexipril and Hydrochlorothiazide on page 856*
- ◆ **Unisom® Maximum Strength SleepGels® [OTC]** *see DiphenhydrAMINE on page 383*
- ◆ **Unithroid®** *see Levothyroxine on page 740*
- ◆ **Univasc®** *see Moexipril on page 855*
- ◆ **Unna's Boot** *see Zinc Gelatin on page 1327*
- ◆ **Unna's Paste** *see Zinc Gelatin on page 1327*

Unoprostone (yoo noe PROS tone)

Related Information

Glaucoma Drug Therapy Comparison *on page 1481*

U.S. Brand Names Rescula®

Synonyms Unoprostone Isopropyl

Therapeutic Category Ophthalmic Agent, Prostaglandin Derivative; Prostaglandin, Ophthalmic

Use To lower intraocular pressure (IOP) in patients with open-angle glaucoma or ocular hypertension; should be used in patients who are not tolerant of, or failed treatment with other IOP-lowering medications

Pregnancy Risk Factor C

Contraindications Hypersensitivity to unoprostone, benzalkonium chloride, or any component of the formulation

Warnings/Precautions May cause permanent changes in eye color (increases the amount of brown pigment in the iris); long-term consequences and potential injury to eye are not known. Bacterial keratitis, caused by inadvertent contamination of multiple-dose ophthalmic solutions, has been reported. Use caution in patients with intraocular inflammation. Contains benzalkonium chloride which may be adsorbed by contact lenses; remove contacts prior to administration and wait 15 minutes before reinserting. Safety and efficacy have not been determined for use in patients with renal or hepatic impairment, angle closure, inflammatory or neovascular glaucoma. Safety and efficacy in pediatric patients have not been established.

Common Adverse Reactions

>10%: Ocular: Burning/stinging (10% to 25%), dry eyes (10% to 25%), injection (10% to 25%), ophthalmic itching (10% to 25%), increased length of eyelashes (10% to 14%)

1% to 10%:

Cardiovascular: Hypertension

Central nervous system: Dizziness, headache, insomnia, pain

Endocrine & metabolic: Diabetes mellitus

Neuromuscular & skeletal: Back pain

Ocular: Abnormal vision (5% to 10%), eyelid disorder (5% to 10%), foreign body sensation (5% to 10%), lacrimation disorder (5% to 10%), decreased length of eyelashes (7%), blepharitis, cataract, conjunctivitis, corneal lesion, eye discharge, eye hemorrhage, eye pain, irritation, keratitis, photophobia, vitreous disorder

Respiratory: Bronchitis, increased cough, pharyngitis, rhinitis, sinusitis

(Continued)

Unoprostone *(Continued)*

Miscellaneous: Flu-like syndrome (6%), accidental injury, allergic reaction

Drug Interactions

Increased Effect/Toxicity: Specific drug interactions have not been reported. When using more than one ophthalmic product, wait at least 5 minutes between application of each medication.

Mechanism of Action The exact mechanism of action is unknown; however, unoprostone decreases IOP by increasing the outflow of aqueous humor. Cardiovascular and pulmonary function were not affected in clinical studies. IOP was decreased by 3-4 mm Hg in patients with a mean baseline IOP of 23 mm Hg.

Pharmacodynamics/Kinetics

Absorption: Through cornea and conjunctival epithelium

Metabolism: Hydrolyzed by esterases unoprostone-free acid

Half-life elimination: 14 minutes

Excretion: Urine (as metabolites)

Dosage Ophthalmic: Adults: Instill 1 drop into affected eye(s) twice daily

Dosage adjustment in renal impairment: Use with caution, no dosing adjustment reported.

Dosage adjustment in hepatic impairment: Use with caution, no dosing adjustment reported.

Elderly: No differences in safety and efficacy have been reported in the elderly.

Administration May be used with other eye drops to lower intraocular pressure; if using more than one product, wait at least 5 minutes between application of each medication. Remove contact lenses prior to administration and wait 15 minutes before reinserting.

Patient Information Wash hands before instilling solution. Sit or lie down to instill. Open eye, look at ceiling, and instill prescribed amount of solution. Apply gentle pressure to inner corner of eye. Do not let tip of applicator touch eye; do not contaminate tip of applicator (contamination may cause eye infection leading to possible eye damage or vision loss). Contact prescriber concerning continued use of drops if eye infection develops, trauma occurs to the eye, and prior to eye surgery. This product contains benzalkonium chloride which may be adsorbed by contact lenses; remove contacts prior to administration and wait 15 minutes before reinserting. May cause permanent changes in eye color (increases the amount of brown pigment in the iris); long-term consequences and potential injury to eye are not known. Changes to eye color may occur slowly (months to years). May be used with other eye drops to lower intraocular pressure; if using more than one product, wait at least 5 minutes between application of each medication. Notify prescriber if conjunctivitis or eyelid reactions occur with use of this product.

Dosage Forms SOLN, ophthalmic: 0.15% (5 mL)

♦ **Unoprostone Isopropyl** *see* Unoprostone *on page 1281*

Urea *(yoor EE a)*

U.S. Brand Names Amino-Cerv™; Aquacare® [OTC]; Aquaphilic® With Carbamide [OTC]; Carmol® 10 [OTC]; Carmol® 20 [OTC]; Carmol® 40; Carmol® Deep Cleaning; DPM™ [OTC]; Gormel® [OTC]; Lanaphilic® [OTC]; Nutraplus® [OTC]; Rea-Lo® [OTC]; Ultra Mide®; Ureacin® [OTC]; Vanamide™

Synonyms Carbamide

Therapeutic Category Diuretic, Osmotic; Keratolytic Agent; Topical Skin Product

Use

Topical: Keratolytic agent to soften nails or skin; OTC: Moisturizer for dry, rough skin

Vaginal: Treatment of cervicitis

Pregnancy Risk Factor C

Dosage Adults:

Hyperkeratotic conditions, dry skin: Topical: Apply 1-3 times/day

Cervicitis: Vaginal: Insert 1 applicatorful in vagina at bedtime for 2-4 weeks

Dosage Forms CRM: (Aquacare®): 10% (75 g); (Carmol® 20): 20% (90 g); (DPM™): 20% (118 g); (Gormel®): 20% (75 g, 120 g, 454 g, 2270 g); (Nutraplus®): 10% (90 g, 454 g); (Rea-Lo®): 30% (60 g, 240 g); (Ureacin®-20): 20% (120 g); (Vanamide™): 40% (85 g, 199 g). **CRM, vaginal** (Amino-Cerv™): 8.34% (82.5 g). **GEL** (Carmol® 40): 40% (15 mL). **LOTION:** (Aquacare®): 10% (240 mL); (Carmol® 10): 10% (180 mL); (Carmol® 40): 40% (240 mL); (Nutraplus®): 10% (240 mL, 480 mL); (Rea-Lo®): 15% (120 mL); (Ultra Mide®): 25% (120 mL, 240 mL); (Ureacin®-10): 10% (240 mL)

Urea and Hydrocortisone *(yoor EE a & hye droe KOR ti sone)*

U.S. Brand Names Carmol-HC®

Synonyms Hydrocortisone and Urea

Therapeutic Category Topical Skin Product

Use Inflammation of corticosteroid-responsive dermatoses

Pregnancy Risk Factor C

Dosage Apply thin film and rub in well 1-4 times/day. Therapy should be discontinued when control is achieved; if no improvement is seen, reassessment of diagnosis may be necessary.

Dosage Forms CRM: Urea 10% and hydrocortisone 1% (30 g)

♦ **Ureacin® [OTC]** *see* Urea *on page 1282*

♦ **Urea Peroxide** *see* Carbamide Peroxide *on page 216*

♦ **Urecholine®** *see* Bethanechol *on page 163*

♦ **Urex®** *see* Methenamine *on page 811*

♦ **Urimar-T** *see* Methenamine, Sodium Biphosphate, Phenyl Salicylate, Methylene Blue, and Hyoscyamine *on page 812*

♦ **Urimax**® *see* Methenamine, Sodium Biphosphate, Phenyl Salicylate, Methylene Blue, and Hyoscyamine *on page 812*

♦ **Urispas**® *see* Flavoxate *on page 525*

♦ **Uristat**® **[OTC]** *see* Phenazopyridine *on page 987*

♦ **Urofollitropin** *see* Follitropins *on page 555*

Urokinase (yoor oh KIN ase)

U.S. Brand Names Abbokinase®

Synonyms UK

Therapeutic Category Fibrinolytic Agent

Use Thrombolytic agent for the lysis of acute massive pulmonary emboli or pulmonary emboli with unstable hemodynamics

Unlabeled/Investigational Use Thrombolytic agent used in treatment of recent severe or massive deep vein thrombosis, myocardial infarction, and occluded I.V. or dialysis cannulas

Pregnancy Risk Factor B

Contraindications Hypersensitivity to urokinase or any component of the formulation; active internal bleeding; history of CVA; recent (within 2 months) intracranial or intraspinal surgery or trauma; intracranial neoplasm, arteriovenous malformation, or aneurysm; known bleeding diathesis; severe uncontrolled hypertension

Warnings/Precautions Concurrent heparin anticoagulation can contribute to bleeding; careful attention to all potential bleeding sites. I.M. injections and nonessential handling of the patient should be avoided. Venipunctures should be performed carefully and only when necessary. If arterial puncture is necessary, use an upper extremity vessel that can be manually compressed. If serious bleeding occurs, then the infusion of urokinase and heparin should be stopped.

For the following conditions the risk of bleeding is higher with use of anistreplase and should be weighed against the benefits of therapy: recent (within 10 days) major surgery (eg, CABG, obstetrical delivery, organ biopsy, previous puncture of noncompressible vessels), cerebrovascular disease, recent (within 10 days) gastrointestinal or genitourinary bleeding, recent trauma (within 10 days) including CPR, hypertension (systolic BP >180 mm Hg and/or diastolic BP >110 mm Hg), high likelihood of left heart thrombus (eg, mitral stenosis with atrial fibrillation), acute pericarditis, subacute bacterial endocarditis, hemostatic defects including ones caused by severe renal or hepatic dysfunction, significant hepatic dysfunction, pregnancy, diabetic hemorrhagic retinopathy or other hemorrhagic ophthalmic conditions, septic thrombophlebitis or occluded AV cannula at seriously infected site, advanced age (eg, >75 years), patients receiving oral anticoagulants, any other condition in which bleeding constitutes a significant hazard or would be particularly difficult to manage because of location.

Coronary thrombolysis may result in reperfusion arrhythmias. Follow standard MI management. Rare anaphylactoid reactions can occur. Safety and efficacy in pediatric patients have not been established.

Common Adverse Reactions As with all drugs which may affect hemostasis, bleeding is the major adverse effect associated with urokinase. Hemorrhage may occur at virtually any site. Risk is dependent on multiple variables, including the dosage administered, concurrent use of multiple agents which alter hemostasis, and patient predisposition.

>10%: Local: Injection site: Bleeding (5% decrease in hematocrit reported in 37% patients; most bleeding occurring at external incisions or injection sites, but also reported in other areas)

Drug Interactions

Increased Effect/Toxicity: Oral anticoagulants (warfarin), heparin, low molecular weight heparins, and drugs which affect platelet function (eg, NSAIDs, dipyridamole, ticlopidine, clopidogrel, IIb/IIIa antagonists) may potentiate the risk of hemorrhage.

Decreased Effect: Aminocaproic acid (an antifibrinolytic agent) may decrease the effectiveness of thrombolytic therapy.

Mechanism of Action Promotes thrombolysis by directly activating plasminogen to plasmin, which degrades fibrin, fibrinogen, and other procoagulant plasma proteins

Pharmacodynamics/Kinetics

Onset of action: I.V.: Fibrinolysis occurs rapidly

Duration: ≥4 hours

Distribution: 11.5 L

Half-life elimination: 6.4-18.8 minutes

Excretion: Urine and feces (small amounts)

Dosage

Children and Adults: Deep vein thrombosis (unlabeled use): I.V.: Loading: 4400 units/kg over 10 minutes, then 4400 units/kg/hour for 12 hours

Adults:

Acute pulmonary embolism: I.V.: Loading: 4400 int. units/kg over 10 minutes; maintenance: 4400 int. units/kg/hour for 12 hours. Following infusion, anticoagulation treatment is recommended to prevent recurrent thrombosis. Do not start anticoagulation until aPTT has decreased to less than twice the normal control value. If heparin is used, do not administer loading dose. Treatment should be followed with oral anticoagulants.

Myocardial infarction (unlabeled use): Intracoronary: 750,000 units over 2 hours (6000 units/minute over up to 2 hours)

(Continued)

Urokinase *(Continued)*

Occluded I.V. catheters (unlabeled use):

5000 units in each lumen over 1-2 minutes, leave in lumen for 1-4 hours, then aspirate; may repeat with 10,000 units in each lumen if 5000 units fails to clear the catheter; **do not infuse into the patient**; volume to instill into catheter is equal to the volume of the catheter

I.V. infusion: 200 units/kg/hour in each lumen for 12-48 hours at a rate of at least 20 mL/hour

Dialysis patients: 5000 units is administered in each lumen over 1-2 minutes; leave urokinase in lumen for 1-2 days, then aspirate

Administration Solution may be filtered using a 0.22 or 0.45 micron filter during I.V. therapy. Administer using a pump which can deliver a total volume of 195 mL. The loading dose should be administered at 90 mL/hour over 10 minutes. The maintenance dose should be administered at 15 mL/hour over 12 hours. I.V. tubing should be flushed with NS or D_5W to ensure total dose is administered.

Monitoring Parameters Blood pressure; pulse; CBC, platelet count, aPTT, urinalysis

Dosage Forms INJ, powder for reconstitution: 250,000 units 250,000 int. units [contains human albumin 250 mg and mannitol 25 mg]

♦ **Uro-KP-Neutral®** *see Potassium Phosphate and Sodium Phosphate on page 1024*

♦ **Urolene Blue®** *see Methylene Blue on page 821*

♦ **Uro-Mag® [OTC]** *see Magnesium Oxide on page 771*

♦ **Uroxatral™** *see Alfuzosin on page 54*

♦ **Urso®** *see Ursodiol on page 1284*

♦ **Ursodeoxycholic Acid** *see Ursodiol on page 1284*

Ursodiol *(ER soe dye ole)*

U.S. Brand Names Actigall®; Urso®

Synonyms Ursodeoxycholic Acid

Therapeutic Category Gallstone Dissolution Agent

Use Actigall®: Gallbladder stone dissolution; prevention of gallstones in obese patients experiencing rapid weight loss; Urso®: Primary biliary cirrhosis

Unlabeled/Investigational Use Liver transplantation

Pregnancy Risk Factor B

Dosage Adults: Oral:

Gallstone dissolution: 8-10 mg/kg/day in 2-3 divided doses; use beyond 24 months is not established; obtain ultrasound images at 6-month intervals for the first year of therapy; 30% of patients have stone recurrence after dissolution

Gallstone prevention: 300 mg twice daily

Primary biliary cirrhosis: 13-15 mg/kg/day in 4 divided doses (with food)

Dosage Forms CAP (Actigall®): 300 mg. **TAB, film coated (Urso®):** 250 mg

♦ **UTI Relief® [OTC]** *see Phenazopyridine on page 987*

♦ **Uvadex®** *see Methoxsalen on page 818*

♦ **Vaccinia Vaccine** *see Smallpox Vaccine on page 1142*

♦ **Vagifem®** *see Estradiol on page 459*

♦ **Vagi-Gard® [OTC]** *see Povidone-Iodine on page 1025*

♦ **Vagistat®-1 [OTC]** *see Tioconazole on page 1232*

Valacyclovir *(val ay SYE kloe veer)*

U.S. Brand Names Valtrex®

Synonyms Valacyclovir Hydrochloride

Therapeutic Category Antiviral Agent

Use Treatment of herpes zoster (shingles) in immunocompetent patients; treatment of first-episode genital herpes; episodic treatment of recurrent genital herpes; suppression of recurrent genital herpes and reduction of heterosexual transmission of genital herpes in immunocompetent patients; suppression of genital herpes in HIV-infected individuals; treatment of herpes labialis (cold sores)

Pregnancy Risk Factor B

Contraindications Hypersensitivity to valacyclovir, acyclovir, or any component of the formulation

Warnings/Precautions Thrombotic thrombocytopenic purpura/hemolytic uremic syndrome has occurred in immunocompromised patients; use caution and adjust the dose in elderly patients or those with renal insufficiency; safety and efficacy in prepubertal patients have not been established

Common Adverse Reactions

>10%: Central nervous system: Headache (14% to 35%)

1% to 10%:

Central nervous system: Dizziness (2% to 4%), depression (0% to 7%)

Endocrine: Dysmenorrhea (≤1% to 8%)

Gastrointestinal: Abdominal pain (2% to 11%), vomiting (<1% to 6%), nausea (6% to 15%)

Hematologic: Leukopenia (≤1%), thrombocytopenia (≤1%)

Hepatic: AST increased (1% to 4%)

Neuromuscular & skeletal: Arthralgia (≤1 to 6%)

Drug Interactions

Increased Effect/Toxicity: Valacyclovir and acyclovir have increased CNS side effects with zidovudine and probenecid.

Decreased Effect: Cimetidine and/or probenecid has decreased the rate but not the extent of valacyclovir conversion to acyclovir leading to decreased effectiveness of valacyclovir.

Mechanism of Action Valacyclovir is rapidly and nearly completely converted to acyclovir by intestinal and hepatic metabolism. Acyclovir is converted to acyclovir monophosphate by virus-specific thymidine kinase then further converted to acyclovir triphosphate by other cellular enzymes. Acyclovir triphosphate inhibits DNA synthesis and viral replication by competing with deoxyguanosine triphosphate for viral DNA polymerase and being incorporated into viral DNA.

Pharmacodynamics/Kinetics

Absorption: Rapid

Distribution: Acyclovir is widely distributed throughout the body including brain, kidney, lungs, liver, spleen, muscle, uterus, vagina, and CSF

Protein binding: 13.5% to 17.9%

Metabolism: Hepatic; valacyclovir is rapidly and nearly completely converted to acyclovir and L-valine by first-pass effect; acyclovir is hepatically metabolized to a very small extent by aldehyde oxidase and by alcohol and aldehyde dehydrogenase (inactive metabolites)

Bioavailability: ~55% once converted to acyclovir

Half-life elimination: Normal renal function: Adults: Acyclovir: 2.5-3.3 hours, Valacyclovir: ~30 minutes; End-stage renal disease: Acyclovir: 14-20 hours

Excretion: Urine, primarily as acyclovir (88%); **Note:** Following oral administration of radiolabeled valacyclovir, 46% of the label is eliminated in the feces (corresponding to nonabsorbed drug), while 47% of the radiolabel is eliminated in the urine.

Dosage Oral:

Adolescents and Adults: Herpes labialis (cold sores): 2 g twice daily for 1 day (separate doses by ~12 hours)

Adults:

Herpes zoster (shingles): 1 g 3 times/day for 7 days

Genital herpes:

Initial episode: 1 g twice daily for 10 days

Recurrent episode: 500 mg twice daily for 3 days

Reduction of transmission: 500 mg once daily (source partner)

Suppressive therapy:

Immunocompetent patients: 1000 mg once daily (500 mg once daily in patients with <9 recurrences per year)

HIV-infected patients (CD4 ≥100 cells/mm^3): 500 mg twice daily

Dosing interval in renal impairment:

Herpes zoster: Adults:

Cl_{cr} 30-49 mL/minute: 1 g every 12 hours

Cl_{cr} 10-29 mL/minute: 1 g every 24 hours

Cl_{cr} <10 mL/minute: 500 mg every 24 hours

Genital herpes: Adults:

Initial episode:

Cl_{cr} 10-29 mL/minute: 1 g every 24 hours

Cl_{cr} <10 mL/minute: 500 mg every 24 hours

Recurrent episode: Cl_{cr} <10-29 mL/minute: 500 mg every 24 hours

Suppressive therapy: Cl_{cr} <10-29 mL/minute:

For usual dose of 1 g every 24 hours, decrease dose to 500 mg every 24 hours

For usual dose of 500 mg every 24 hours, decrease dose to 500 mg every 48 hours

HIV-infected patients: 500 mg every 24 hours

Herpes labialis: Adolescents and Adults:

Cl_{cr} 30-49 mL/minute: 1 g every 12 hours for 2 doses

Cl_{cr} 10-29 mL/minute: 500 mg every 12 hours for 2 doses

Cl_{cr} <10 mL/minute: 500 mg as a single dose

Hemodialysis: Dialyzable (~33% removed during 4-hour session); administer dose postdialysis

Chronic ambulatory peritoneal dialysis/continuous arteriovenous hemofiltration dialysis: Pharmacokinetic parameters are similar to those in patients with ESRD; supplemental dose not needed following dialysis

Administration If GI upset occurs, administer with meals.

Monitoring Parameters Urinalysis, BUN, serum creatinine, liver enzymes, and CBC

Patient Information

Herpes zoster: Therapy is most effective when started within 48 hours of onset of zoster rash

Recurrent genital herpes: Therapy should be initiated within 24 hours after the onset of signs or symptoms

Dosage Forms CAPLET: 500 mg, 1000 mg

♦ **Valacyclovir Hydrochloride** *see* Valacyclovir *on page 1284*

♦ **Valcyte**™ *see* Valganciclovir *on page 1287*

Valdecoxib (val de KOKS ib)

Related Information

Nonsteroidal Anti-Inflammatory Agents Comparison *on page 1401*

U.S. Brand Names Bextra®

(Continued)

Valdecoxib *(Continued)*

Therapeutic Category Analgesic, Selective COX-II Inhibitor; Anti-inflammatory Agent; Nonsteroidal Anti-inflammatory Drug (NSAID), COX-2 Selective

Use Relief of signs and symptoms of osteoarthritis and adult rheumatoid arthritis; treatment of primary dysmenorrhea

Pregnancy Risk Factor C/D (3rd trimester)

Contraindications Hypersensitivity to valdecoxib, sulfonamides, or any component of the formulation; patients who have experienced asthma, urticaria, or allergic-type reactions to aspirin or NSAIDs; pregnancy (3rd trimester)

Warnings/Precautions Gastrointestinal irritation, ulceration, bleeding, and perforation may occur with NSAIDs. Use with caution in patients with a history of GI bleeding, ulcers, or risk factor for GI bleeding. Anaphylactic/anaphylactoid reactions may occur, even with no prior exposure to valdecoxib. Serious dermatologic reactions have been reported; discontinue in any patients who develop rash or any signs of hypersensitivity. Use with caution in patients with decreased renal function, hepatic disease, CHF, hypertension, dehydration, or asthma. Use caution in patients with known or suspected deficiency of cytochrome P450 isoenzyme 2C9. Use in patients with severe hepatic impairment (Child-Pugh Class C) is not recommended. Safety and efficacy have not been established for patients <18 years of age.

Common Adverse Reactions 2% to 10%:
Cardiovascular: Peripheral edema (2% to 3%), hypertension (2%)
Central nervous system: Headache (5% to 9%), dizziness (3%)
Dermatologic: Rash (1% to 2%)
Gastrointestinal: Dyspepsia (8% to 9%), abdominal pain (7% to 8%), nausea (6% to 7%), diarrhea (5% to 6%), flatulence (3% to 4%), abdominal fullness (2%)
Neuromuscular & skeletal: Back pain (2% to 3%), myalgia (2%)
Otic: Earache, tinnitus
Respiratory: Upper respiratory tract infection (6% to 7%), sinusitis (2% to 3%)
Miscellaneous: Influenza-like symptoms (2%)

Drug Interactions

Cytochrome P450 Effect: Substrate (minor) of CYP2C8/9, 3A4; **Inhibits** CYP2C8/9 (weak), 2C19 (weak)

Increased Effect/Toxicity: Anticoagulants and antiplatelet drugs may increase risk of bleeding. Warfarin efficacy may increase. Corticosteroids may increase risk of GI ulceration. CYP2C8/9 and 3A4 inhibitors may increase valdecoxib levels. Cyclosporine, dextromethorphan, lithium levels increased. Serum concentrations/toxicity of methotrexate may be increased.

Decreased Effect: ACE inhibitors, angiotensin II antagonists, hydralazine, loop and thiazide diuretics effects reduced.

Mechanism of Action Inhibits prostaglandin synthesis by decreasing the activity of the enzyme, cyclooxygenase-2 (COX-2), which results in decreased formation of prostaglandin precursors. Does not affect platelet function.

Pharmacodynamics/Kinetics
Onset of action: Dysmenorrhea: 60 minutes
Distribution: V_d: 86 L
Protein binding: 98%
Metabolism: Extensively hepatic via CYP3A4 and 2C9; glucuronidation
Bioavailability: 83%
Half-life elimination: 8-11 hours
Time to peak: 2.25-3 hours
Excretion: Primarily urine (as metabolites)

Dosage Oral: Adults:
Osteoarthritis and rheumatoid arthritis: 10 mg once daily; **Note:** No additional benefits seen with 20 mg/day
Primary dysmenorrhea: 20 mg twice daily as needed
Dosage adjustment in renal impairment: Not recommended for use in advanced disease
Dosage adjustment in hepatic impairment: Not recommended for use in advanced liver dysfunction (Child-Pugh Class C)

Administration Avoid dehydration. Encourage patient to drink plenty of fluids.

Monitoring Parameters If used in patients with advanced renal disease, monitor serum creatinine closely; signs and symptoms of GI bleeding

Patient Information Do not take more than recommended dose. May be taken with food to reduce GI upset. Avoid alcohol, aspirin, and OTC medication unless approved by prescriber. Drink plenty of fluids unless advised not to. You may experience dizziness, headache; abdominal pain, nausea, vomiting, gastric distress (small frequent meals, frequent mouth care, sucking lozenges, or chewing gum may help). GI bleeding, ulceration, or perforation can occur with or without pain. Stop taking medication and report immediately stomach pain or cramping, unusual bleeding or bruising, or blood in vomitus, stool, or urine. Report any skin rash; unusual fatigue, lethargy, yellowing of skin or eyes, itching, abdominal tenderness, flu-like symptoms, easy bruising or bleeding; sudden weight gain; fluid build up, changes in urination pattern; or respiratory difficulty.

Dosage Forms TAB: 10 mg, 20 mg

♦ **23-Valent Pneumococcal Polysaccharide Vaccine** *see* Pneumococcal Polysaccharide Vaccine (Polyvalent) *on page 1011*

Valganciclovir (val gan SYE kloh veer)

U.S. Brand Names Valcyte™

Synonyms Valganciclovir Hydrochloride

Therapeutic Category Antiviral Agent

Use Treatment of cytomegalovirus (CMV) retinitis in patients with acquired immunodeficiency syndrome (AIDS); prevention of CMV disease in high-risk patients (donor CMV positive/recipient CMV negative) undergoing kidney, heart, or kidney/pancreas transplantation

Pregnancy Risk Factor C

Contraindications Hypersensitivity to valganciclovir, ganciclovir, acyclovir, or any component of the formulation; absolute neutrophil count <500/mm^3; platelet count <25,000/mm^3; hemoglobin <8 g/dL

Warnings/Precautions Dosage adjustment or interruption of valganciclovir therapy may be necessary in patients with neutropenia and/or thrombocytopenia and patients with impaired renal function. Ganciclovir may adversely affect spermatogenesis and fertility; due to its mutagenic potential, contraceptive precautions for female and male patients need to be followed during and for at least 90 days after therapy with the drug. Due to differences in bioavailability, valganciclovir tablets cannot be substituted for ganciclovir capsules on a one-to-one basis. Not indicated for use in liver transplant patients (higher incidence of tissue-invasive CMV relative to oral ganciclovir was observed in trials). Safety and efficacy not established in pediatric patients.

Common Adverse Reactions

>10%:

Central nervous system: Fever (31%), headache (9% to 22%), insomnia (16%)

Gastrointestinal: Diarrhea (16% to 41%), nausea (8% to 30%), vomiting (21%), abdominal pain (15%)

Hematologic: Granulocytopenia (11% to 27%), anemia (8% to 26%)

Ocular: Retinal detachment (15%)

1% to 10%:

Central nervous system: Peripheral neuropathy (9%), paresthesia (8%), seizures (<5%), psychosis, hallucinations (<5%), confusion (<5%), agitation (<5%)

Hematologic: Thrombocytopenia (8%), pancytopenia (<5%), bone marrow depression (<5%), aplastic anemia (<5%), bleeding (potentially life-threatening due to thrombocytopenia <5%)

Renal: Decreased renal function (<5%)

Miscellaneous: Local and systemic infections, including sepsis (<5%); allergic reaction (<5%)

Drug Interactions

Increased Effect/Toxicity: Reported for ganciclovir: Immunosuppressive agents may increase hematologic toxicity of ganciclovir. Imipenem/cilastatin may increase seizure potential. Oral ganciclovir increases blood levels of zidovudine, although zidovudine decreases steady-state levels of ganciclovir. Since both drugs have the potential to cause neutropenia and anemia, some patients may not tolerate concomitant therapy with these drugs at full dosage. Didanosine levels are increased with concurrent ganciclovir. Other nephrotoxic drugs (eg, amphotericin and cyclosporine) may have additive nephrotoxicity with ganciclovir.

Decreased Effect: Reported for ganciclovir: A decrease in blood levels of ganciclovir AUC may occur when used with didanosine.

Mechanism of Action Valganciclovir is rapidly converted to ganciclovir in the body. The bioavailability of ganciclovir from valganciclovir is increased 10-fold compared to the oral ganciclovir. A dose of 900 mg achieved systemic exposure of ganciclovir comparable to that achieved with the recommended doses of intravenous ganciclovir of 5 mg/kg. Ganciclovir is phosphorylated by a substrate which competitively inhibits the binding of deoxyguanosine triphosphate to DNA polymerase resulting in inhibition of viral DNA synthesis.

Pharmacodynamics/Kinetics

Absorption: Well absorbed; high-fat meal increases AUC by 30%

Distribution: Ganciclovir: V_d: 15.26 L/1.73 m^2; widely to all tissues including CSF and ocular tissue

Protein binding: 1% to 2%

Metabolism: Converted to ganciclovir by intestinal mucosal cells and hepatocytes

Bioavailability: With food: 60%

Half-life elimination: Ganciclovir: 4.08 hours; prolonged with renal impairment; Severe renal impairment: Up to 68 hours

Excretion: Urine (primarily as ganciclovir)

Dosage Oral: Adults:

CMV retinitis:

Induction: 900 mg twice daily for 21 days (with food)

Maintenance: Following induction treatment, or for patients with inactive CMV retinitis who require maintenance therapy: Recommended dose: 900 mg once daily (with food)

Prevention of CMV disease following transplantation: 900 mg once daily (with food) beginning within 10 days of transplantation; continue therapy until 100 days post-transplantation

Dosage adjustment in renal impairment:

Induction dose:

Cl_{cr} 40-59 mL/minute: 450 mg twice daily

Cl_{cr} 25-39 mL/minute: 450 mg once daily

Cl_{cr} 10-24 mL/minute: 450 mg every 2 days

(Continued)

Valganciclovir *(Continued)*

Maintenance dose:

Cl_{cr} 40-59 mL/minute: 450 mg once daily

Cl_{cr} 25-39 mL/minute: 450 mg every 2 days

Cl_{cr} 10-24 mL/minute: 450 mg twice weekly

Note: Valganciclovir is not recommended in patients receiving hemodialysis. For patients on hemodialysis (Cl_{cr} <10 mL/minute), it is recommended that ganciclovir be used (dose adjusted as specified for ganciclovir).

Administration Avoid direct contact with broken or crushed tablets. Consideration should be given to handling and disposal according to guidelines issued for antineoplastic drugs. However, there is no consensus on the need for these precautions.

Monitoring Parameters Retinal exam (at least every 4-6 weeks), CBC, platelet counts, serum creatinine

Patient Information Valganciclovir is not a cure for CMV retinitis; for oral administration, take as directed (with food) and maintain adequate hydration (2-3 L/day of fluids unless instructed to restrict fluid intake). Swallow tablets whole, do not break or crush. Avoid handling broken or crushed tablets. Wash area thoroughly if contact occurs. Report fever, chills, unusual bleeding or bruising, infection, or unhealed sores or white plaques in mouth.

Dosage Forms TAB: 450 mg

♦ **Valganciclovir Hydrochloride** *see Valganciclovir on page 1287*

♦ **Valium®** *see Diazepam on page 364*

♦ **Valorin [OTC]** *see Acetaminophen on page 24*

♦ **Valorin Extra [OTC]** *see Acetaminophen on page 24*

♦ **Valproate Semisodium** *see Valproic Acid and Derivatives on page 1288*

♦ **Valproate Sodium** *see Valproic Acid and Derivatives on page 1288*

♦ **Valproic Acid** *see Valproic Acid and Derivatives on page 1288*

Valproic Acid and Derivatives *(val PROE ik AS id & dah RIV ah tives)*

Related Information

Anticonvulsants by Seizure Type *on page 1358*

Epilepsy *on page 1477*

Febrile Seizures *on page 1478*

U.S. Brand Names Depacon®; Depakene®; Depakote® Delayed Release; Depakote® ER; Depakote® Sprinkle®

Synonyms Dipropylacetic Acid; Divalproex Sodium; DPA; 2-Propylpentanoic Acid; 2-Propylvaleric Acid; Valproate Semisodium; Valproate Sodium; Valproic Acid

Therapeutic Category Anticonvulsant, Miscellaneous; Antimanic Agent; Antimigraine Agent, Prophylaxis

Use Monotherapy and adjunctive therapy in the treatment of patients with complex partial seizures; monotherapy and adjunctive therapy of simple and complex absence seizures; adjunctive therapy patients with multiple seizure types that include absence seizures

Mania associated with bipolar disorder (Depakote®)

Migraine prophylaxis (Depakote®, Depakote® ER)

Unlabeled/Investigational Use Behavior disorders in Alzheimer's disease

Pregnancy Risk Factor D

Contraindications Hypersensitivity to valproic acid, derivatives, or any component of the formulation; hepatic dysfunction; urea cycle disorders; pregnancy

Warnings/Precautions Hepatic failure resulting in fatalities has occurred in patients; children <2 years of age are at considerable risk; other risk factors include organic brain disease, mental retardation with severe seizure disorders, congenital metabolic disorders, and patients on multiple anticonvulsants. Hepatotoxicity has been reported after 3 days to 6 months of therapy. Monitor patients closely for appearance of malaise, weakness, facial edema, anorexia, jaundice, and vomiting; may cause severe thrombocytopenia, inhibition of platelet aggregation and bleeding; tremors may indicate overdosage; use with caution in patients receiving other anticonvulsants.

Cases of life-threatening pancreatitis, occurring at the start of therapy or following years of use, have been reported in adults and children. Some cases have been hemorrhagic with rapid progression of initial symptoms to death.

May cause teratogenic effects such as neural tube defects (eg, spina bifida). Use in women of childbearing potential requires that benefits of use in mother be weighed against the potential risk to fetus, especially when used for conditions not associated with permanent injury or risk of death (eg, migraine).

Hyperammonemic encephalopathy, sometimes fatal, has been reported following the initiation of valproate therapy in patients with known or suspected urea cycle disorders (UCD), particularly those with ornithine transcarbamylase deficiency. Although a rare genetic disorder, UCD evaluation should be considered for the following patients, prior to the start of therapy: History of unexplained encephalopathy or coma; encephalopathy associated with protein load; pregnancy or postpartum encephalopathy; unexplained mental retardation; history of elevated plasma ammonia or glutamine; history of cyclical vomiting and lethargy; episodic extreme irritability, ataxia; low BUN or protein avoidance; family history of UCD or unexplained infant deaths (particularly male); signs or symptoms of UCD (hyperammonemia, encephalopathy, respiratory alkalosis). Patients who develop symptoms of hyperammonemic encephalopathy during therapy with valproate should receive prompt evaluation for UCD and valproate should be discontinued.

Hyperammonemia may occur with therapy and may be present with normal liver function tests. Ammonia levels should be measured in patients who develop unexplained lethargy and vomiting, or changes in mental status. Discontinue therapy if ammonia levels are increased and evaluate for possible UCD.

In vitro studies have suggested valproate stimulates the replication of HIV and CMV viruses under experimental conditions. The clinical consequence of this is unknown, but should be considered when monitoring affected patients.

Anticonvulsants should not be discontinued abruptly because of the possibility of increasing seizure frequency; valproate should be withdrawn gradually to minimize this risk, unless safety concerns require a more rapid withdrawal. Concomitant use with clonazepam may induce absence status.

Hyperammonemia may occur, even in the absence of overt liver function abnormalities. Asymptomatic elevations require continued surveillance; symptomatic elevations should prompt modification or discontinuation of valproate therapy. CNS depression may occur with valproate use. Patients must be cautioned about performing tasks which require mental alertness (operating machinery or driving). Effects with other sedative drugs or ethanol may be potentiated.

Common Adverse Reactions

Adverse reactions reported when used as monotherapy for complex partial seizures:

>10%:

Central nervous system: Somnolence (18% to 30%), dizziness (13% to 18%), insomnia (9% to 15%), nervousness (7% to 11%)

Dermatologic: Alopecia (13% to 24%)

Gastrointestinal: Nausea (26% to 34%), diarrhea (19% to 23%), vomiting (15% to 23%), abdominal pain (9% to 12%), dyspepsia (10% to 11%), anorexia (4% to 11%)

Hematologic: Thrombocytopenia (1% to 24%)

Neuromuscular & skeletal: Tremor (19% to 57%), weakness (10% to 21%)

Respiratory: Respiratory tract infection (13% to 20%), pharyngitis (2% to 8%), dyspnea (1% to 5%)

1% to 10%

Cardiovascular: Hypertension, palpitation, peripheral edema (3% to 8%), tachycardia, chest pain

Central nervous system: Amnesia (4% to 7%), abnormal dreams, anxiety, confusion, depression (4% to 5%), malaise, personality disorder

Dermatologic: Bruising (4% to 5%), dry skin, petechia, pruritus, rash

Endocrine & metabolic: Amenorrhea, dysmenorrhea

Gastrointestinal: Eructation, flatulence, hematemesis, increased appetite, pancreatitis, periodontal abscess, taste perversion, weight gain (4% to 9%)

Genitourinary: Urinary frequency, urinary incontinence, vaginitis

Hepatic: AST and ALT increased

Neuromuscular & skeletal: Abnormal gait, arthralgia, back pain, hypertonia, incoordination, leg cramps, myalgia, myasthenia, paresthesia, twitching

Ocular: Amblyopia/blurred vision (4% to 8%), abnormal vision, nystagmus (1% to 7%)

Otic: Deafness, otitis media, tinnitus (1% to 7%)

Respiratory: Epistaxis, increased cough, pneumonia, sinusitis

Additional adverse effects: Frequency not defined:

Cardiovascular: Bradycardia

Central nervous system: Aggression, ataxia, behavioral deterioration, cerebral atrophy (reversible), dementia, emotional upset, encephalopathy (rare), fever, hallucinations, headache, hostility, hyperactivity, hypesthesia, incoordination, Parkinsonism, psychosis, vertigo

Dermatologic: Cutaneous vasculitis, erythema multiforme, photosensitivity, Stevens-Johnson syndrome, toxic epidermal necrolysis (rare)

Endocrine & metabolic: Breast enlargement, galactorrhea, hyperammonemia, hyponatremia, inappropriate ADH secretion, irregular menses, parotid gland swelling, polycystic ovary disease (rare), abnormal thyroid function tests

Genitourinary: Enuresis, urinary tract infection

Hematologic: Anemia, aplastic anemia, bone marrow suppression, eosinophilia, hematoma formation, hemorrhage, hypofibrinogenemia, intermittent porphyria, leukopenia, lymphocytosis, macrocytosis, pancytopenia

Hepatic: Bilirubin increased, hyperammonemic encephalopathy (in patients with UCD)

Neuromuscular & skeletal: Asterixis, bone pain, dysarthria

Ocular: Diplopia, "spots before the eyes"

Renal: Fanconi-like syndrome (rare, in children)

Miscellaneous: Anaphylaxis, decreased carnitine, hyperglycinemia, lupus

Drug Interactions

Cytochrome P450 Effect: For valproic acid: **Substrate** (minor) of CYP2A6, 2B6, 2C8/9, 2C19, 2E1; **Inhibits** CYP2C8/9 (weak), 2C19 (weak), 2D6 (weak), 3A4 (weak); **Induces** CYP2A6 (weak)

Increased Effect/Toxicity: Absence seizures have been reported in patients receiving VPA and clonazepam. Valproic acid may increase, decrease, or have no effect on carbamazepine and phenytoin levels. Valproic acid may increase serum concentrations of carbamazepine - epoxide (active metabolite). Valproic acid may increase serum concentrations of
(Continued)

Valproic Acid and Derivatives *(Continued)*

diazepam, lamotrigine, nimodipine, and phenobarbital, and tricyclic antidepressants. Chlorpromazine (and possibly other phenothiazines), macrolide antibiotics (clarithromycin, erythromycin, troleandomycin), felbamate, and isoniazid may inhibit the metabolism of valproic acid. Aspirin or other salicylates may displace valproic acid from protein-binding sites, leading to acute toxicity.

CYP2C18/19 inhibitors: May increase serum concentrations of valproic acid; inhibitors include cimetidine, felbamate, fluoxetine, and fluvoxamine

Decreased Effect: Valproic acid may displace clozapine from protein binding site resulting in decreased clozapine serum concentrations. Carbamazepine, lamotrigine, and phenytoin may induce the metabolism of valproic acid. Cholestyramine (and possibly colestipol) may bind valproic acid in GI tract, decreasing absorption. Acyclovir may reduce valproic acid levels. Mefloquine may decrease serum concentration of valproic acid.

Mechanism of Action Causes increased availability of gamma-aminobutyric acid (GABA), an inhibitory neurotransmitter, to brain neurons or may enhance the action of GABA or mimic its action at postsynaptic receptor sites

Pharmacodynamics/Kinetics

Distribution: Total valproate: 11 L/1.73 m^2; free valproate 92 L/1.73 m^2

Protein binding (dose dependent): 80% to 90%

Metabolism: Extensively hepatic via glucuronide conjugation and mitochondrial beta-oxidation. The relationship between dose and total valproate concentration is nonlinear; concentration does not increase proportionally with the dose, but increases to a lesser extent due to saturable plasma protein binding. The kinetics of unbound drug are linear.

Bioavailability: Extended release: 90% of I.V. dose and 81% to 90% of delayed release dose

Half-life elimination: (increased in neonates and with liver disease): Children: 4-14 hours; Adults: 9-16 hours

Time to peak, serum: 1-4 hours; Divalproex (enteric coated): 3-5 hours

Excretion: Urine (30% to 50% as glucuronide conjugate, 3% as unchanged drug)

Dosage

Seizures:

Children >10 years and Adults:

Oral: Initial: 10-15 mg/kg/day in 1-3 divided doses; increase by 5-10 mg/kg/day at weekly intervals until therapeutic levels are achieved; maintenance: 30-60 mg/kg/day. Adult usual dose: 1000-2500 mg/day. **Note:** Regular release and delayed release formulations are usually given in 2-4 divided doses/day, extended release formulation (Depakote® ER) is usually given once daily. Conversion to Depakote® ER from a stable dose of Depakote® may require an increase in the total daily dose between 8% and 20% to maintain similar serum concentrations.

Children receiving more than one anticonvulsant (ie, polytherapy) may require doses up to 100 mg/kg/day in 3-4 divided doses

I.V.: Administer as a 60-minute infusion (≤20 mg/minute) with the same frequency as oral products; switch patient to oral products as soon as possible. Alternatively, rapid infusions have been given: ≤15 mg/kg over 5-10 minutes (1.5-3 mg/kg/minute).

Rectal (unlabeled): Dilute syrup 1:1 with water for use as a retention enema; loading dose: 17-20 mg/kg one time; maintenance: 10-15 mg/kg/dose every 8 hours

Mania: Adults: Oral: 750-1500 mg/day in divided doses; dose should be adjusted as rapidly as possible to desired clinical effect; a loading dose of 20 mg/kg may be used; maximum recommended dosage: 60 mg/kg/day

Migraine prophylaxis: Adults: Oral:

Extended release tablets: 500 mg once daily for 7 days, then increase to 1000 mg once daily; adjust dose based on patient response; usual dosage range 500-1000 mg/day

Delayed release tablets: 250 mg twice daily; adjust dose based on patient response, up to 1000 mg/day

Elderly: Elimination is decreased in the elderly. Studies of elderly patients with dementia show a high incidence of somnolence. In some patients, this was associated with weight loss. Starting doses should be lower and increases should be slow, with careful monitoring of nutritional intake and dehydration. Safety and efficacy for use in patients >65 years have not been studied for migraine prophylaxis.

Dosing adjustment in renal impairment: A 27% reduction in clearance of unbound valproate is seen in patients with Cl$_{cr}$ <10 mL/minute. Hemodialysis reduces valproate concentrations by 20%, therefore no dose adjustment is needed in patients with renal failure. Protein binding is reduced, monitoring only total valproate concentrations may be misleading.

Dosing adjustment/comments in hepatic impairment: Reduce dose. Clearance is decreased with liver impairment. Hepatic disease is also associated with decreased albumin concentrations and 2- to 2.6-fold increase in the unbound fraction. Free concentrations of valproate may be elevated while total concentrations appear normal.

Administration

Depakote® ER: Swallow whole, do not crush or chew. Patients who need dose adjustments smaller than 500 mg/day for migraine prophylaxis should be changed to Depakote® delayed release tablets. Sprinkle capsules may be swallowed whole or open cap and sprinkle on small amount (1 teaspoonful) of soft food and use immediately (do not store or chew).

Depacon®: Following dilution to final concentration, administer over 60 minutes at a rate of ≤20 mg/minute. Alternatively, single doses up to 15 mg/kg have been administered as a rapid infusion over 5-10 minutes (1.5-3 mg/kg/minute).

Monitoring Parameters Liver enzymes, CBC with platelets

Reference Range

Therapeutic:

Epilepsy: 50-100 μg/mL (SI: 350-690 μmol/L)

Mania: 50-125 μg/mL (SI: 350-860 μmol/L)

Toxic: >200 μg/mL (SI: >1390 μmol/L)

Seizure control: May improve at levels >100 μg/mL (SI: 690 μmol/L), but toxicity may occur at levels of 100-150 μg/mL (SI: 690-1040 μmol/L)

Mania: Clinical response seen with trough levels between 50-125 μg/mL; risk of toxicity increases at levels >125 μg/mL

Patient Information When used to treat generalized seizures, patient instructions are determined by patient's condition and ability to understand.

Oral: Take as directed; do not alter dose or timing of medication. Do not increase dose or take more than recommended. Do not crush or chew capsule or enteric-coated pill. While using this medication, do not use alcohol and other prescription or OTC medications (especially pain medications, sedatives, antihistamines, or hypnotics) without consulting prescriber. Maintain adequate hydration (2-3 L/day of fluids unless instructed to restrict fluid intake). Diabetics should monitor serum glucose closely (valproic acid will alter results of urine ketones). Report alterations in menstrual cycle; abdominal cramps, unresolved diarrhea, vomiting, or constipation; skin rash; unusual bruising or bleeding; blood in urine, stool or vomitus; malaise; weakness; facial swelling; yellowing of skin or eyes; excessive sedation; or restlessness.

Dosage Forms CAP, as valproic acid (Depakene®): 250 mg. **CAP, sprinkles, as divalproex sodium** (Depakote® Sprinkle®): 125 mg. **INJ, solution, as valproate sodium** (Depacon®): 100 mg/mL (5 mL). **SYR, as valproic acid:** 250 mg/5 mL (5 mL, 480 mL); (Depakene®): 250 mg/5 mL (480 mL). **TAB, delayed release, as divalproex sodium** (Depakote®): 125 mg, 250 mg, 500 mg. **TAB, extended release, as divalproex sodium** (Depakote® ER): 250 mg, 500 mg

Valrubicin (val ROO bi sin)

U.S. Brand Names Valstar®

Synonyms AD3L; N-trifluoroacetyladriamycin-14-valerate

Therapeutic Category Antineoplastic Agent, Anthracycline

Use Intravesical therapy of BCG-refractory carcinoma *in situ* of the urinary bladder

Pregnancy Risk Factor C

Contraindications Hypersensitivity to anthracyclines, Cremophor® EL, or any component of the formulation; concurrent urinary tract infection or small bladder capacity (unable to tolerate a 75 mL instillation)

Warnings/Precautions Complete response observed in only 1 of 5 patients, delay of cystectomy may lead to development of metastatic bladder cancer, which is lethal. If complete response is not observed after 3 months or disease recurs, cystectomy must be reconsidered. Do not administer if mucosal integrity of bladder has been compromised or bladder perforation is present. Following TURP, status of bladder mucosa should be evaluated prior to initiation of therapy. Administer under the supervision of a physician experienced in the use of intravesical chemotherapy. Aseptic technique must be used during administration. All patients of reproductive age should use an effective method of contraception during the treatment period. Irritable bladder symptoms may occur during instillation and retention. Caution in patients with severe irritable bladder symptoms. Do not clamp urinary catheter. Red-tinged urine is typical for the first 24 hours after instillation. Prolonged symptoms or discoloration should prompt contact with the physician.

Valrubicin preparation should be performed in a class II laminar flow biologic safety cabinet. Personnel should be wearing surgical gloves and a closed front surgical gown with knit cuffs. Appropriate safety equipment is recommended for preparation, administration, and disposal of antineoplastics. If valrubicin contacts the skin, wash and flush thoroughly with water.

Common Adverse Reactions

>10%: Genitourinary: Frequency (61%), dysuria (56%), urgency (57%), bladder spasm (31%), hematuria (29%), bladder pain (28%), urinary incontinence (22%), cystitis (15%), urinary tract infection (15%)

1% to 10%:

Cardiovascular: Chest pain (2%), vasodilation (2%), peripheral edema (1%)

Central nervous system: Headache (4%), malaise (4%), dizziness (3%), fever (2%)

Dermatologic: Rash (3%)

Endocrine & metabolic: Hyperglycemia (1%)

Gastrointestinal: Abdominal pain (5%), nausea (5%), diarrhea (3%), vomiting (2%), flatulence (1%)

Genitourinary: Nocturia (7%), burning symptoms (5%), urinary retention (4%), urethral pain (3%), pelvic pain (1%), hematuria (microscopic) (3%)

Hematologic: Anemia (2%)

Neuromuscular & skeletal: Weakness (4%), back pain (3%), myalgia (1%)

Respiratory: Pneumonia (1%)

Drug Interactions

Increased Effect/Toxicity: No specific drug interactions studies have been performed. Systemic exposure to valrubicin is negligible, and interactions are unlikely.

Decreased Effect: No specific drug interactions studies have been performed. Systemic exposure to valrubicin is negligible, and interactions are unlikely.

Mechanism of Action Blocks function of DNA topoisomerase II; inhibits DNA synthesis, causes extensive chromosomal damage, and arrests cell development; unlike other anthracyclines, does not appear to intercalate DNA

(Continued)

Valrubicin *(Continued)*

Pharmacodynamics/Kinetics

Absorption: Well absorbed into bladder tissue, negligible systemic absorption. Trauma to mucosa may increase absorption, and perforation greatly increases absorption with significant systemic myelotoxicity.

Metabolism: Negligible after intravesical instillation and 2 hour retention

Excretion: Urine when expelled from urinary bladder (98.6% as intact drug; 0.4% as N-trifluoroacetyladriamycin)

Dosage Adults: Intravesical: 800 mg once weekly for 6 weeks

Dosing adjustment in renal impairment: No specific adjustment recommended

Dosing adjustment in hepatic impairment: No specific adjustment recommended

Administration Valrubicin is administered as an intravesicular bladder lavage, usually in 75 mL of 0.9% sodium chloride injection. The drug is retained in the bladder for 2 hours, then voided. Due to the Cremophor® EL diluent, valrubicin should be administered through non-PVC tubing.

Monitoring Parameters Cystoscopy, biopsy, and urine cytology every 3 months for recurrence or progression

Patient Information This medication will be instilled into your bladder through a catheter to be retained for as long as possible. Your urine will be red tinged for the next 24 hours; report promptly if this continues for a longer period. You may experience altered urination patterns (frequency, dysuria, or incontinence), some bladder pain, pain on urination, or pelvic pain; report if these persist. Diabetics should monitor glucose levels closely (may cause hyperglycemia). It is important that you maintain adequate hydration (2-3 L/day of fluids unless instructed to restrict fluid intake). You may experience some dizziness (use caution when driving or engaging in tasks requiring alertness until response to drug is known); or nausea, vomiting, or taste disturbance (small frequent meals, frequent mouth care, chewing gum, or sucking lozenges may help). Report chest pain or palpitations; persistent dizziness; swelling of extremities; persistent nausea, vomiting, diarrhea, or abdominal pain; muscle weakness, pain, or tremors; unusual cough or difficulty breathing; or other adverse effects related to this medication.

Dosage Forms INJ, solution: 40 mg/mL (5 mL)

Valsartan *(val SAR tan)*

Related Information

Angiotensin Agents Comparison *on page 1353*

U.S. Brand Names Diovan®

Therapeutic Category Angiotensin II Receptor Antagonist (ARB); Antihypertensive Agent

Use Alone or in combination with other antihypertensive agents in treating essential hypertension; treatment of heart failure (NYHA Class II-IV) in patients intolerant to angiotensin converting enzyme (ACE) inhibitors

Pregnancy Risk Factor C/D (2nd and 3rd trimesters)

Contraindications Hypersensitivity to valsartan or any component of the formulation; hypersensitivity to other A-II receptor antagonists; bilateral renal artery stenosis; pregnancy (2nd and 3rd trimesters)

Warnings/Precautions Use extreme caution with concurrent administration of potassium-sparing diuretics or potassium supplements, in patients with mild to moderate hepatic dysfunction (adjust dose), in those who may be sodium/water depleted (eg, on high-dose diuretics), and in the elderly; avoid use in patients with CHF, unilateral renal artery stenosis, aortic/mitral valve stenosis, coronary artery disease, or hypertrophic cardiomyopathy, if possible

Common Adverse Reactions

Hypertension: Similar incidence to placebo; independent of race, age, and gender.

>1%:

Central nervous system: Dizziness (2% to 8%), fatigue (2%)

Endocrine & metabolic: Serum potassium increased (4.4%)

Gastrointestinal: Abdominal pain (2%)

Hematologic: Neutropenia (1.9%)

Respiratory: Cough (2.6% versus 1.5% in placebo)

Miscellaneous: Viral infection (3%)

>1% but frequency ≤ placebo: Headache, upper respiratory infection, cough, diarrhea, rhinitis, sinusitis, nausea, pharyngitis, edema, arthralgia

Heart failure:

>10%: Central nervous system: Dizziness (17%)

1% to 10%:

Cardiovascular: Hypotension (7%), postural hypotension (2%)

Central nervous system: Fatigue (3%)

Endocrine & metabolic: Hyperkalemia (2%)

Gastrointestinal: Diarrhea (5%)

Neuromuscular & skeletal: Arthralgia (3%), back pain (3%)

Renal: Creatinine elevated >50% (4%)

Drug Interactions

Cytochrome P450 Effect: Inhibits CYP2C8/9 (weak)

Increased Effect/Toxicity: Valsartan blood levels may be increased by cimetidine and monoxidine; clinical effect is unknown. Concurrent use of potassium salts/supplements, co-trimoxazole (high dose), ACE inhibitors, and potassium-sparing diuretics (amiloride, spironolactone, triamterene) may increase the risk of hyperkalemia.

Decreased Effect: Phenobarbital, ketoconazole, troleandomycin, sulfaphenazole

Mechanism of Action As a prodrug, valsartan produces direct antagonism of the angiotensin II (AT2) receptors, unlike the ACE inhibitors. It displaces angiotensin II from the AT1 receptor and produces its blood pressure lowering effects by antagonizing AT1-induced vasoconstriction, aldosterone release, catecholamine release, arginine vasopressin release, water intake, and hypertrophic responses. This action results in more efficient blockade of the cardiovascular effects of angiotensin II and fewer side effects than the ACE inhibitors.

Pharmacodynamics/Kinetics
Onset of action: Peak antihypertensive effect: 2-4 weeks
Distribution: V_d: 17 L (adults)
Protein binding: 95%, primarily albumin
Metabolism: To inactive metabolite
Bioavailability: 25% (range 10% to 35%)
Half-life elimination: 6 hours
Time to peak, serum: 2-4 hours
Excretion: Feces (83%) and urine (13%) as unchanged drug

Dosage Adults: Oral:
Hypertension: Initial: 80 mg or 160 mg once daily (in patients who are not volume depleted); majority of effect within 2 weeks, maximal effects in 4-6 weeks; dose may be increased to achieve desired effect; maximum recommended dose: 320 mg/day
Heart failure: Initial: 40 mg twice daily; titrate dose to 80-160 mg twice daily, as tolerated; maximum daily dose: 320 mg. **Note:** Do not use with ACE inhibitors and beta blockers.

Dosing adjustment in renal impairment: No dosage adjustment necessary if Cl_{cr} >10 mL/minute.
Dosing adjustment in hepatic impairment (mild - moderate): ≤80 mg/day
Dialysis: Not significantly removed

Administration Administer with or without food.

Monitoring Parameters Baseline and periodic electrolyte panels, renal and liver function tests, urinalysis; symptoms of hypotension or hypersensitivity

Patient Information Do not stop taking this medication unless instructed by a physician, do not take this medication during pregnancy or lactation; take a missed dose as soon as possible unless it is almost time for your next dose; call your prescriber immediately if you have symptoms of allergy or develop side effects including headache and dizziness

Dosage Forms CAP [DSC]: 80 mg, 160 mg, 320 mg; **TAB:** 40 mg, 80 mg, 160 mg, 320 mg

Valsartan and Hydrochlorothiazide
(val SAR tan & hye droe klor oh THYE a zide)

U.S. Brand Names Diovan HCT®
Synonyms Hydrochlorothiazide and Valsartan
Therapeutic Category Angiotensin II Antagonist/Thiazide Diuretic Combination; Antihypertensive Agent, Combination
Use Treatment of hypertension (not indicated for initial therapy)
Pregnancy Risk Factor C/D (2nd and 3rd trimester)
Dosage Oral: Adults: Dose is individualized (combination substituted for individual components); dose may be titrated after 3-4 weeks of therapy.
Usual recommended starting dose of valsartan: 80 mg or 160 mg once daily when used as monotherapy in patients who are not volume depleted
Dosage adjustment in renal impairment: Cl_{cr} ≤30 mL/minute: Use of combination not recommended. Contraindicated in patients with anuria.
Dosage adjustment in hepatic impairment: Use with caution
Dosage Forms TAB: 80 mg/12.5 mg: Valsartan 80 mg and hydrochlorothiazide 12.5 mg; 160 mg/12.5 mg: Valsartan 160 mg and hydrochlorothiazide 12.5 mg; 160 mg/25 mg: Valsartan 160 mg and hydrochlorothiazide 25 mg

♦ **Valstar®** see Valrubicin on page 1291
♦ **Valtrex®** see Valacyclovir on page 1284
♦ **Vanamide™** see Urea on page 1282
♦ **Vancenase® AQ 84 mcg [DSC]** see Beclomethasone on page 149
♦ **Vancenase® Pockethaler® [DSC]** see Beclomethasone on page 149
♦ **Vanceril® [DSC]** see Beclomethasone on page 149
♦ **Vancocin®** see Vancomycin on page 1293

Vancomycin (van koe MYE sin)
Related Information
Antimicrobial Drugs of Choice on page 1440
Community-Acquired Pneumonia in Adults on page 1457
Prevention of Bacterial Endocarditis on page 1429
Prevention of Wound Infection & Sepsis in Surgical Patients on page 1436
U.S. Brand Names Vancocin®
Synonyms Vancomycin Hydrochloride
Therapeutic Category Antibiotic, Miscellaneous
Use Treatment of patients with infections caused by staphylococcal species and streptococcal species; used orally for staphylococcal enterocolitis or for antibiotic-associated pseudomembranous colitis produced by C. difficile
Pregnancy Risk Factor C
(Continued)

Vancomycin *(Continued)*

Contraindications Hypersensitivity to vancomycin or any component of the formulation; avoid in patients with previous severe hearing loss

Warnings/Precautions Use with caution in patients with renal impairment or those receiving other nephrotoxic or ototoxic drugs; dosage modification required in patients with impaired renal function (especially elderly)

Common Adverse Reactions

Oral:

>10%: Gastrointestinal: Bitter taste, nausea, vomiting

1% to 10%:

Central nervous system: Chills, drug fever

Hematologic: Eosinophilia

Parenteral:

>10%:

Cardiovascular: Hypotension accompanied by flushing

Dermatologic: Erythematous rash on face and upper body (red neck or red man syndrome - infusion rate related)

1% to 10%:

Central nervous system: Chills, drug fever

Dermatologic: Rash

Hematologic: Eosinophilia, reversible neutropenia

Drug Interactions

Increased Effect/Toxicity: Increased toxicity with other ototoxic or nephrotoxic drugs. Increased neuromuscular blockade with most neuromuscular blocking agents.

Mechanism of Action Inhibits bacterial cell wall synthesis by blocking glycopeptide polymerization through binding tightly to D-alanyl-D-alanine portion of cell wall precursor

Pharmacodynamics/Kinetics

Absorption: Oral: Poor; I.M.: Erratic; Intraperitoneal: ~38%

Distribution: Widely in body tissues and fluids. except for CSF

Relative diffusion from blood into CSF: Good only with inflammation (exceeds usual MICs)

CSF:blood level ratio: Normal meninges: Nil; Inflamed meninges: 20% to 30%

Protein binding: 10% to 50%

Half-life elimination: Biphasic: Terminal:

Newborns: 6-10 hours

Infants and Children 3 months to 4 years: 4 hours

Children >3 years: 2.2-3 hours

Adults: 5-11 hours; significantly prolonged with renal impairment

End-stage renal disease: 200-250 hours

Time to peak, serum: I.V.: 45-65 minutes

Excretion: I.V.: Urine (80% to 90% as unchanged drug); Oral: Primarily feces

Dosage Initial dosage recommendation: I.V.:

Neonates:

Postnatal age ≤7 days:

<1200 g: 15 mg/kg/dose every 24 hours

1200-2000 g: 10 mg/kg/dose every 12 hours

>2000 g: 15 mg/kg/dose every 12 hours

Postnatal age >7 days:

<1200 g: 15 mg/kg/dose every 24 hours

≥1200 g: 10 mg/kg/dose divided every 8 hours

Infants >1 month and Children:

40 mg/kg/day in divided doses every 6 hours

Prophylaxis for bacterial endocarditis:

Dental, oral, or upper respiratory tract surgery: 20 mg/kg 1 hour prior to the procedure

GI/GU procedure: 20 mg/kg plus gentamicin 2 mg/kg 1 hour prior to surgery

Infants >1 month and Children with staphylococcal central nervous system infection: 60 mg/kg/day in divided doses every 6 hours

Adults:

With normal renal function: 1 g **or** 10-15 mg/kg/dose every 12 hours

Prophylaxis for bacterial endocarditis:

Dental, oral, or upper respiratory tract surgery: 1 g 1 hour before surgery

GI/GU procedure: 1 g plus 1.5 mg/kg gentamicin 1 hour prior to surgery

Dosing interval in renal impairment (vancomycin levels should be monitored in patients with any renal impairment):

Cl_{cr} >60 mL/minute: Start with 1 g or 10-15 mg/kg/dose every 12 hours

Cl_{cr} 40-60 mL/minute: Start with 1 g or 10-15 mg/kg/dose every 24 hours

Cl_{cr} <40 mL/minute: Will need longer intervals; determine by serum concentration monitoring

Hemodialysis: Not dialyzable (0% to 5%); generally not removed; exception minimal-moderate removal by some of the newer high-flux filters; dose may need to be administered more frequently; monitor serum concentrations

Continuous ambulatory peritoneal dialysis (CAPD): Not significantly removed; administration via CAPD fluid: 15-30 mg/L (15-30 mcg/mL) of CAPD fluid

Continuous arteriovenous hemofiltration: Dose as for Cl_{cr} 10-40 mL/minute

Antibiotic lock technique (for catheter infections): 2 mg/mL in SWI/NS or D_5W; instill 3-5 mL into catheter port as a flush solution instead of heparin lock (**Note:** Do not mix with any other solutions)

Intrathecal: Vancomycin is available as a powder for injection and may be diluted to 1-5 mg/mL concentration in preservative-free 0.9% sodium chloride for administration into the CSF

Neonates: 5-10 mg/day
Children: 5-20 mg/day
Adults: Up to 20 mg/day
Oral: Pseudomembranous colitis produced by *C. difficile*:
Neonates: 10 mg/kg/day in divided doses
Children: 40 mg/kg/day in divided doses, added to fluids
Adults: 125 mg 4 times/day for 10 days

Administration Administer vancomycin by I.V. intermittent infusion over at least 60 minutes at a final concentration not to exceed 5 mg/mL. If a maculopapular rash appears on the face, neck, trunk, and/or upper extremities (Red man syndrome), slow the infusion rate to over $1\frac{1}{2}$ to 2 hours and increase the dilution volume. Hypotension, shock, and cardiac arrest (rare) have also been reported with too rapid of infusion. Reactions are often treated with antihistamines and possibly steroids.

Extravasation treatment: Monitor I.V. site closely; extravasation will cause serious injury with possible necrosis and tissue sloughing. Rotate infusion site frequently.

Monitoring Parameters Periodic renal function tests, urinalysis, serum vancomycin concentrations, WBC, audiogram

Reference Range
Timing of serum samples: Draw peak 1 hour after 1-hour infusion has completed; draw trough just before next dose
Therapeutic levels: Peak: 25-40 µg/mL; Trough: 5-12 µg/mL
Toxic: >80 µg/mL (SI: >54 µmol/L)

Patient Information Report pain at infusion site, dizziness, fullness or ringing in ears with I.V. use; nausea or vomiting with oral use

Dosage Forms CAP (Vancocin®): 125 mg, 250 mg. **INF** [premixed in iso-osmotic dextrose]: 500 mg (100 mL); 1 g (200 mL). **INJ, powder for reconstitution:** 500 mg, 1 g, 5 g, 10 g; (Vancocin® [DSC]): 500 mg, 1 g, 10 g. **POWDER, oral solution** (Vancocin®): 1 g, 10 g

♦ **Vancomycin Hydrochloride** *see* Vancomycin *on page 1293*

♦ **Vanex Forte™-D** *see* Chlorpheniramine, Phenylephrine, and Methscopolamine *on page 264*

♦ **Vaniqa™** *see* Eflornithine *on page 426*

♦ **Vanoxide-HC®** *see* Benzoyl Peroxide and Hydrocortisone *on page 155*

♦ **Vanquish® Extra Strength Pain Reliever [OTC]** *see* Acetaminophen, Aspirin, and Caffeine *on page 27*

♦ **Vantin®** *see* Cefpodoxime *on page 239*

♦ **VAQTA®** *see* Hepatitis A Vaccine *on page 615*

Vardenafil (var DEN a fil)

U.S. Brand Names Levitra®

Synonyms Vardenafil Hydrochloride

Therapeutic Category Phosphodiesterase Enzyme Inhibitor, Selective Type 5

Use Treatment of erectile dysfunction

Pregnancy Risk Factor B

Contraindications Hypersensitivity to vardenafil or any component of the formulation; concurrent use of organic nitrates (nitroglycerin; scheduled dosing or as needed); concomitant use of alpha blockers

Warnings/Precautions There is a degree of cardiac risk associated with sexual activity; therefore, physicians may wish to consider the patient's cardiovascular status prior to initiating any treatment for erectile dysfunction. Use caution in patients with anatomical deformation of the penis (angulation, cavernosal fibrosis, or Peyronie's disease) and in patients who have conditions which may predispose them to priapism (sickle cell anemia, multiple myeloma, leukemia). Patients should be instructed to seek medical attention if erection persists >4 hours.

Not recommended for use in patients with congenital QT prolongation or those taking Class Ia or III antiarrhythmics. Use caution with effective CYP3A4 inhibitors, the elderly, or those with hepatic impairment (Child-Pugh class B); dosage adjustment is needed.

Safety and efficacy have not been studied in patients with the following conditions, therefore, use in these patients is not recommended at this time: Hypotension, uncontrolled hypertension, unstable angina, severe cardiac failure; a life-threatening arrhythmia, myocardial infarction,or stroke within the last 6 months; severe hepatic impairment (Child-Pugh class C); end-stage renal disease requiring dialysis; retinitis pigmentosa or other degenerative retinal disorders. The safety and efficacy of vardenafil with other treatments for erectile dysfunction have not been studied and are not recommended as combination therapy.

Common Adverse Reactions
>10%:
Cardiovascular: Flushing (11%)
Central nervous system: Headache (15%)
2% to 10%:
Central nervous system: Dizziness (2%)
Gastrointestinal: Dyspepsia (4%), nausea (2%)
Neuromuscular & skeletal: CPK increased (2%)
Respiratory: Rhinitis (9%), sinusitis (3%)
Miscellaneous: Flu-like syndrome (3%)
(Continued)

Vardenafil *(Continued)*

Drug Interactions

  Cytochrome P450 Effect: Substrate of CYP2C (minor), 3A5 (minor), 3A4 (major)

  Increased Effect/Toxicity: The concentrations/effects of vardenafil may be increased by effective CYP3A4 inhibitors, erythromycin, protease inhibitors, and imidazole derivatives. Alpha blockers and nitroglycerin may lead to excessive hypotension; concomitant use is contraindicated.

Mechanism of Action Does not directly cause penile erections, but affects the response to sexual stimulation. The physiologic mechanism of erection of the penis involves release of nitric oxide (NO) in the corpus cavernosum during sexual stimulation. NO then activates the enzyme guanylate cyclase, which results in increased levels of cyclic guanosine monophosphate (cGMP), producing smooth muscle relaxation and inflow of blood to the corpus cavernosum. Vardenafil enhances the effect of NO by inhibiting phosphodiesterase type 5 (PDE5), which is responsible for degradation of cGMP in the corpus cavernosum; when sexual stimulation causes local release of NO, inhibition of PDE5 by vardenafil causes increased levels of cGMP in the corpus cavernosum, resulting in smooth muscle relaxation and inflow of blood to the corpus cavernosum; at recommended doses, it has no effect in the absence of sexual stimulation.

Pharmacodynamics/Kinetics

  Absorption: Rapid

  Distribution: V_d: 208 L; <0.01% found in semen 1.5 hours after dose

  Metabolism: Hepatic via CYP3A4 (major), CYP2C and 3A5 (minor); forms metabolite (active)

  Bioavailability: 15%; Elderly (≥65 years): 52%; Hepatic impairment (Child-Pugh class B): 160%

  Half-life elimination: Terminal: Vardenafil and metabolite: 4-5 hours

  Time to peak, plasma: 0.5-2 hours

  Excretion: Feces (91% to 95% as metabolites); urine (2% to 6%)

  Clearance: 56 L/hour

Dosage Oral: Adults: Erectile dysfunction: 10 mg 60 minutes prior to sexual activity; dosing range: 5-20 mg; to be given as one single dose and not given more than once daily

  Dosing adjustment with concomitant medications:

    Erythromycin: Maximum vardenafil dose: 5 mg/24 hours

    Indinavir: Maximum vardenafil dose: 2.5 mg/24 hours

    Itraconazole:

      200 mg/day: Maximum vardenafil dose: 5 mg/24 hours

      400 mg/day: Maximum vardenafil dose: 2.5 mg/24 hours

    Ketoconazole:

      200 mg/day: Maximum vardenafil dose: 5 mg/24 hours

      400 mg/day: Maximum vardenafil dose: 2.5 mg/24 hours

    Ritonavir: Maximum vardenafil dose: 2.5 mg/72 hours

  Elderly: ≥65 years: Initial: 5 mg 60 minutes prior to sexual activity; to be given as one single dose and not given more than once daily

  Dosage adjustment in renal impairment: Dose adjustment not needed for mild, moderate, or severe impairment; use has not been studied in patients on renal dialysis

  Dosage adjustment in hepatic impairment: Child-Pugh class B: Initial: 5 mg 60 minutes prior to sexual activity (maximum dose: 10 mg); to be given as one single dose and not given more than once daily

Administration May be administered with or without food, 60 minutes prior to sexual activity.

Patient Information Inform prescriber of all other medications you are taking; serious side effects can result when vardenafil is used with nitrates and some other medications. Do not combine vardenafil with other approaches to treating erectile dysfunction without consulting prescriber. **Note:** Vardenafil provides no protection against sexually-transmitted diseases, including HIV. You may experience headache, flushing, or abnormal vision (color changes, blurred or increased sensitivity to light); use caution when driving at night or in poorly lit environments. Report immediately acute allergic reactions; chest pain or palpitations; persistent dizziness; sign of urinary tract infection; skin rash; difficulty breathing; genital swelling; or other adverse reactions. If erection lasts >4 hours, contact prescriber immediately; permanent damage to the penis can occur.

Dosage Forms TAB, film-coated: 2.5 mg, 5 mg, 10 mg, 20 mg

♦ **Vardenafil Hydrochloride** *see* Vardenafil *on page 1295*

Varicella Virus Vaccine *(var i SEL a VYE rus vak SEEN)*

U.S. Brand Names Varivax®

Synonyms Chicken Pox Vaccine; Varicella-Zoster Virus (VZV) Vaccine

Therapeutic Category Vaccine; Vaccine, Live Virus

Use Immunization against varicella in children ≥12 months of age and adults. The American Association of Pediatrics recommends that the chickenpox vaccine should be given to all healthy children between 12 months and 18 years; children between 12 months and 13 years who have not been immunized or who have not had chickenpox should receive 1 vaccination while children 13-18 years of age require 2 vaccinations 4-8 weeks apart; the vaccine has been added to the childhood immunization schedule for infants 12-28 months of age and children 11-12 years of age who have not been vaccinated previously or who have not had the disease; it is recommended to be given with the measles, mumps, and rubella (MMR) vaccine

Pregnancy Risk Factor C

Contraindications Hypersensitivity to any component of the vaccine, including gelatin; a history of anaphylactoid reaction to neomycin; individuals with blood dyscrasias, leukemia, lymphomas, or other malignant neoplasms affecting the bone marrow or lymphatic systems;

those receiving immunosuppressive therapy; primary and acquired immunodeficiency states; a family history of congenital or hereditary immunodeficiency; active untreated tuberculosis; current febrile illness; pregnancy; I.V. injection

Warnings/Precautions Immediate treatment for anaphylactoid reaction should be available during vaccine use; defer vaccination for at least 5 months following blood or plasma transfusions, immune globulin (IgG), or VZIG (avoid IgG or IVIG use for 2 months following vaccination); salicylates should be avoided for 5 weeks after vaccination; vaccinated individuals should not have close association with susceptible high risk individuals (newborns, pregnant women, immunocompromised persons) following vaccination

Common Adverse Reactions All serious adverse reactions must be reported to the U.S. Department of Health and Human Services (DHHS) Vaccine Adverse Event Reporting System (VAERS) 1-800-822-7967.

As reported in ≥1% of patients, unless otherwise specified

>10%:

Central nervous system: Fever (10% to 15%)

Local: Injection site reaction (19% to 24%)

1% to 10%:

Central nervous system: Chills, fatigue, headache, irritability, malaise, nervousness, sleep disturbance

Dermatologic: Generalized varicella-like rash (4% to 5%), contact rash, dermatitis, diaper rash, dry skin, eczema, heat rash, itching

Gastrointestinal: Abdominal pain, appetite decreased, cold/canker sore, constipation, nausea, vomiting

Hematologic: Lymphadenopathy

Local: Varicella-like rash at the injection site (3%)

Neuromuscular & skeletal: Arthralgia, myalgia, stiff neck

Otic: Otitis

Respiratory: Cough, lower/upper respiratory illness

Miscellaneous: Allergic reactions, teething

Drug Interactions

Increased Effect/Toxicity: Salicylates may increase the risk of Reye's following varicella vaccination (avoid salicylate use for 6 weeks following vaccination).

Decreased Effect: The effect of the vaccine may be decreased and the risk of varicella disease in individuals who are receiving immunosuppressant drugs (including high dose systemic corticosteroids) may be increased. Effect of vaccine may be decreased in given within 5 months of immune globulins. Effectiveness of varicella vaccine may be decreased if given within 30 days of MMR vaccine (effectiveness not decreased when administered simultaneously).

Mechanism of Action As a live, attenuated vaccine, varicella virus vaccine offers active immunity to disease caused by the varicella-zoster virus

Pharmacodynamics/Kinetics

Onset of action: Seroconversion: ~4-6 weeks

Duration: Lowest breakthrough rates (0.2% to 2.9%) in the first 2 years following postvaccination, slightly higher rates in third through fifth year

Dosage S.C.:

Children 12 months to 12 years: 0.5 mL

Children 12 years to Adults: 2 doses of 0.5 mL separated by 4-8 weeks

Administration Do not administer I.V.; inject S.C. into the outer aspect of the upper arm, if possible. Federal law requires that the date of administration, the vaccine manufacturer, lot number of vaccine, and the administering person's name, title and address be entered into the patient's permanent medical record.

Monitoring Parameters Rash, fever

Patient Information Report any adverse reactions to the prescriber or Vaccine Adverse Event Reporting System (1-800-822-7967). Some side effects may occur 1-6 weeks after the shot. Common side effects include soreness or swelling in the area where the shot is given, mild rash, fever. Do not take aspirin for 6 weeks after getting the vaccine. Do not use in pregnancy and do not get pregnant for 3 months after getting this vaccine.

Dosage Forms INJ, powder for reconstitution [preservative free]: 1350 plaque-forming units (PFU)

Varicella-Zoster Immune Globulin (Human)

(var i SEL a- ZOS ter i MYUN GLOB yoo lin HYU man)

Synonyms VZIG

Therapeutic Category Immune Globulin

Use Passive immunization of susceptible immunodeficient patients after exposure to varicella; most effective if begun within 96 hours of exposure; there is no evidence VZIG modifies established varicella-zoster infections.

Restrict administration to those patients meeting the following criteria:

Neoplastic disease (eg, leukemia or lymphoma)

Congenital or acquired immunodeficiency

Immunosuppressive therapy with steroids, antimetabolites or other immunosuppressive treatment regimens

Newborn of mother who had onset of chickenpox within 5 days before delivery or within 48 hours after delivery

Premature (≥28 weeks gestation) whose mother has no history of chickenpox

Premature (<28 weeks gestation or ≤1000 g VZIG) regardless of maternal history

(Continued)

Varicella-Zoster Immune Globulin (Human) *(Continued)*

One of the following types of exposure to chickenpox or zoster patient(s) may warrant administration:

Continuous household contact

Playmate contact (>1 hour play indoors)

Hospital contact (in same 2-4 bedroom or adjacent beds in a large ward or prolonged face-to-face contact with an infectious staff member or patient)

Susceptible to varicella-zoster

Age <15 years; administer to immunocompromised adolescents and adults and to other older patients on an individual basis

An acceptable alternative to VZIG prophylaxis is to treat varicella, if it occurs, with high-dose I.V. acyclovir

Age is the most important risk factor for reactivation of varicella zoster; persons <50 years of age have incidence of 2.5 cases per 1000, whereas those 60-79 have 6.5 cases per 1000 and those >80 years have 10 cases per 1000

Pregnancy Risk Factor C

Contraindications Not for prophylactic use in immunodeficient patients with history of varicella, unless patient's immunosuppression is associated with bone marrow transplantation; **not** recommended for nonimmunodeficient patients, including pregnant women, because the severity of chickenpox is much less than in immunosuppressed patients; allergic response to gamma globulin or anti-immunoglobulin; sensitivity to thimerosal; persons with IgA deficiency; do not administer to patients with thrombocytopenia or coagulopathies

Warnings/Precautions VZIG is not indicated for prophylaxis or therapy of normal adults who are exposed to or who develop varicella; it is not indicated for treatment of herpes zoster. Do not inject I.V.

Common Adverse Reactions 1% to 10%: Local: Discomfort at the site of injection (pain, redness, edema)

Mechanism of Action The exact mechanism has not been clarified but the antibodies in varicella-zoster immune globulin most likely neutralize the varicella-zoster virus and prevent its pathological actions

Dosage High risk susceptible patients who are exposed again more than 3 weeks after a prior dose of VZIG should receive another full dose; there is no evidence VZIG modifies established varicella-zoster infections.

I.M.: Administer by deep injection in the gluteal muscle or in another large muscle mass. Inject 125 units/10 kg (22 lb); maximum dose: 625 units (5 vials); minimum dose: 125 units; do not administer fractional doses. Do not inject I.V.

VZIG dose based on weight: See table.

VZIG Dose Based on Weight

Weight of Patient		Dose	
kg	lb	Units	No. of Vials
0-10	0-22	125	1
10.1-20	22.1-44	250	2
20.1-30	44.1-66	375	3
30.1-40	66.1-88	500	4
>40	>88	625	5

Administration Do not inject I.V.; administer deep I.M. into the gluteal muscle or other large muscle mass. For patients ≤10 kg, administer 1.25 mL at a single site; for patients >10 kg, administer no more than 2.5 mL at a single site. Administer entire contents of each vial

Dosage Forms INJ, solution: 125 units (1.25 mL); 625 units (6.25 mL)

♦ **Varicella-Zoster Virus (VZV) Vaccine** *see* Varicella Virus Vaccine *on page 1296*

♦ **Varivax**® *see* Varicella Virus Vaccine *on page 1296*

♦ **Vascor**® **[DSC]** *see* Bepridil *on page 157*

♦ **Vaseretic**® *see* Enalapril and Hydrochlorothiazide *on page 432*

♦ **Vasocidin**® *see* Sulfacetamide and Prednisolone *on page 1170*

♦ **VasoClear**® **[OTC]** *see* Naphazoline *on page 881*

♦ **Vasocon-A**® **[OTC]** *see* Naphazoline and Antazoline *on page 882*

♦ **Vasodilan**® *see* Isoxsuprine *on page 698*

Vasopressin *(vay soe PRES in)*

U.S. Brand Names Pitressin®

Synonyms ADH; Antidiuretic Hormone; 8-Arginine Vasopressin; Vasopressin Tannate

Therapeutic Category Antidiuretic Hormone Analog; Hormone, Posterior Pituitary; Vesicant

Use Treatment of diabetes insipidus; prevention and treatment of postoperative abdominal distention; differential diagnosis of diabetes insipidus

Unlabeled/Investigational Use Adjunct in the treatment of GI hemorrhage and esophageal varices; pulseless ventricular tachycardia (VT)/ventricular fibrillation (VF); vasodilatory shock (septic shock); out-of-hospital asystole

Pregnancy Risk Factor C

Dosage

Diabetes insipidus (highly variable dosage; titrated based on serum and urine sodium and osmolality in addition to fluid balance and urine output):

I.M., S.C.:

Children: 2.5-10 units 2-4 times/day as needed

Adults: 5-10 units 2-4 times/day as needed (dosage range 5-60 units/day)

Continuous I.V. infusion: Children and Adults: 0.5 milliunit/kg/hour (0.0005 unit/kg/hour); double dosage as needed every 30 minutes to a maximum of 0.01 unit/kg/hour

Intranasal: Administer on cotton pledget, as nasal spray, or by dropper

Abdominal distention: Adults: I.M.: 5 units stat, 10 units every 3-4 hours

GI hemorrhage (unlabeled use): I.V. infusion: Dilute in NS or D_5W to 0.1-1 unit/mL

Children: Initial: 0.002-0.005 units/kg/minute; titrate dose as needed; maximum: 0.01 unit/kg/minute; continue at same dosage (if bleeding stops) for 12 hours, then taper off over 24-48 hours

Adults: Initial: 0.2-0.4 unit/minute, then titrate dose as needed, if bleeding stops; continue at same dose for 12 hours, taper off over 24-48 hours

Out-of-hospital asystole (unlabeled use): Adults: I.V.: 40 units; if spontaneous circulation is not restored in 3 minutes, then repeat dose

Pulseless VT/VF (ACLS protocol): I.V.: 40 units (as a single dose only); if no I.V. access, administer 40 units diluted with NS (to a total volume of 10 mL) endotracheally

Vasodilatory shock/septic shock (unlabeled use): Adults: I.V.: Vasopressin has been used in doses of 0.01-0.1 units/minute for the treatment of septic shock. Doses >0.05 units/minute may have more cardiovascular side effects. Most case reports have used 0.04 units/minute continuous infusion as a fixed dose.

Dosing adjustment in hepatic impairment: Some patients respond to much lower doses with cirrhosis

Dosage Forms INJ, solution, aqueous: 20 pressor units/mL (0.5 mL, 1 mL, 10 mL); (Pitressin®): 20 pressor units/mL (1 mL)

♦ **Vasopressin Tannate** *see* Vasopressin *on page 1298*

♦ **Vasotec®** *see* Enalapril *on page 429*

♦ **Vasotec® I.V.** *see* Enalapril *on page 429*

♦ **VCR** *see* VinCRIStine *on page 1306*

♦ **V-Dec-M®** *see* Guaifenesin and Pseudoephedrine *on page 605*

Vecuronium (ve KYOO roe ni um)

Related Information

Neuromuscular Blocking Agents Comparison *on page 1397*

U.S. Brand Names Norcuron®

Synonyms ORG NC 45

Therapeutic Category Neuromuscular Blocker Agent, Nondepolarizing

Use Adjunct to general anesthesia to facilitate endotracheal intubation and to relax skeletal muscles during surgery; to facilitate mechanical ventilation in ICU patients; does not relieve pain or produce sedation

Pregnancy Risk Factor C

Contraindications Hypersensitivity to vecuronium or any component of the formulation

Warnings/Precautions Ventilation must be supported during neuromuscular blockade; certain clinical conditions may result in potentiation or antagonism of neuromuscular blockade:

Potentiation: Electrolyte abnormalities, severe hyponatremia, severe hypocalcemia, severe hypokalemia, hypermagnesemia, neuromuscular diseases, acidosis, acute intermittent porphyria, renal failure, hepatic failure

Antagonism: Alkalosis, hypercalcemia, demyelinating lesions, peripheral neuropathies, diabetes mellitus

Increased sensitivity in patients with myasthenia gravis, Eaton-Lambert syndrome; resistance in burn patients (>30% of body) for period of 5-70 days postinjury; resistance in patients with muscle trauma, denervation, immobilization, infection; use with caution in patients with hepatic or renal impairment; does not counteract bradycardia produced by anesthetics/vagal stimulation. Cross-sensitivity with other neuromuscular-blocking agents may occur; use extreme caution in patients with previous anaphylactic reactions.

Drug Interactions

Increased Effect/Toxicity: Increased effects are possible with aminoglycosides, beta-blockers, clindamycin, calcium channel blockers, halogenated anesthetics, imipenem, ketamine, lidocaine, loop diuretics (furosemide), macrolides (case reports), magnesium sulfate, procainamide, quinidine, quinolones, tetracyclines, and vancomycin. May increase risk of myopathy when used with high- dose corticosteroids for extended periods.

Mechanism of Action Blocks acetylcholine from binding to receptors on motor endplate inhibiting depolarization

Pharmacodynamics/Kinetics

Onset of action:

Good intubation conditions: Within 2.5-3 minutes

Maximum neuromuscular blockade: Within 3-5 minutes

Duration: 20-40 minutes

Metabolism: Active metabolite: 3-desacetyl vecuronium ($1/2$ the activity of parent drug)

Half-life elimination: 51-80 minutes

Excretion: Primarily feces (40% to 75%); urine (30% as unchanged drug and metabolites)

(Continued)

Vecuronium (Continued)

Dosage Administer I.V.; dose to effect; doses will vary due to interpatient variability; use ideal body weight for obese patients

Surgery:

Neonates: 0.1 mg/kg/dose; maintenance: 0.03-0.15 mg/kg every 1-2 hours as needed

Infants >7 weeks to 1 year: Initial: 0.08-0.1 mg/kg/dose; maintenance: 0.05-0.1 mg/kg every 60 minutes as needed

Children >1 year and Adults: Initial: 0.08-0.1 mg/kg or 0.04-0.06 mg/kg after initial dose of succinylcholine for intubation; maintenance: 0.01-0.015 mg/kg 25-40 minutes after initial dose, then 0.01-0.015 mg/kg every 12-15 minutes (higher doses will allow less frequent maintenance doses); may be administered as a continuous infusion at 0.8-2 mcg/kg/ minute

Pretreatment/priming: Adults: 10% of intubating dose given 3-5 minutes before initial dose

ICU: Adults: 0.05-0.1 mg/kg bolus followed by 0.8-1.7 mcg/kg/minute once initial recovery from bolus observed or 0.1-0.2 mg/kg/dose every 1 hour

Note: Children (1-10 years) may require slightly higher initial doses and slightly more frequent supplementation; infants >7 weeks to 1 year may be more sensitive to vecuronium and have a longer recovery time

Dosing adjustment in renal impairment: Prolongation of blockade

Dosing adjustment in hepatic impairment: Dose reductions are necessary in patients with cirrhosis or cholestasis

Administration Concentration of 1 mg/mL may be administered by rapid I.V. injection. May further dilute reconstituted vial to 0.1-0.2 mg/mL in a compatible solution for I.V. infusion. Concentration of 1 mg/mL may be used for I.V. infusion in fluid-restricted patients.

Monitoring Parameters Blood pressure, heart rate

Dosage Forms INJ, powder for reconstitution: 10 mg, 20 mg

- ◆ **Veetids®** see Penicillin V Potassium on page 975
- ◆ **Velban® [DSC]** see VinBLAStine on page 1304
- ◆ **Velcade™** see Bortezomib on page 173
- ◆ **Velosef®** see Cephradine on page 249
- ◆ **Velosulin® BR (Buffered) [DSC]** see Insulin Preparations on page 669

Venlafaxine (VEN la faks een)

Related Information

Antidepressant Agents Comparison on page 1359

U.S. Brand Names Effexor®; Effexor® XR

Therapeutic Category Antidepressant, Serotonin/Norepinephrine Reuptake Inhibitor (SNRI)

Use Treatment of depression, generalized anxiety disorder (GAD), social anxiety disorder

Unlabeled/Investigational Use Obsessive-compulsive disorder (OCD), chronic fatigue syndrome; hot flashes; neuropathic pain; attention-deficit/hyperactivity disorder (ADHD) and autism in children

Pregnancy Risk Factor C

Contraindications Hypersensitivity to venlafaxine or any component of the formulation; use of MAO inhibitors within 14 days; should not initiate MAO inhibitor within 7 days of discontinuing venlafaxine

Warnings/Precautions May cause sustained increase in blood pressure; may cause increase in anxiety, nervousness, insomnia; may cause weight loss (use with caution in patients where weight loss is undesirable). Venlafaxine has been associated with the development of SIADH and hyponatremia. May worsen psychosis in some patients or precipitate a shift to mania or hypomania in patients with bipolar disease. May increase the risks associated with electroconvulsive therapy. The possibility of a suicide attempt is inherent in major depression and may persist until remission occurs. Use caution in high-risk patients during initiation of therapy. Prescriptions should be written for the smallest quantity consistent with good patient care. The risks of cognitive or motor impairment, as well as the potential for anticholinergic effects are very low. May cause or exacerbate sexual dysfunction. Abrupt discontinuation or dosage reduction after extended (≥6 weeks) therapy may lead to agitation, dysphoria, nervousness, anxiety, and other symptoms. When discontinuing therapy, dosage should be tapered gradually over at least a 2-week period. Use caution in patients with increased intraocular pressure or at risk of acute narrow-angle glaucoma.

Common Adverse Reactions

≥10%:

Central nervous system: Headache (25%), somnolence (23%), dizziness (19%), insomnia (18%), nervousness (13%)

Gastrointestinal: Nausea (37%), xerostomia (22%), constipation (15%), anorexia (11%)

Genitourinary: Abnormal ejaculation/orgasm (12%)

Neuromuscular & skeletal: Weakness (12%)

Miscellaneous: Diaphoresis (12%)

1% to 10%:

Cardiovascular: Vasodilation (4%), hypertension (dose-related; 3% in patients receiving <100 mg/day, up to 13% in patients receiving >300 mg/day), tachycardia (2%), chest pain (2%), postural hypotension (1%)

Central nervous system: Anxiety (6%), abnormal dreams (4%), yawning (3%), agitation (2%), confusion (2%), abnormal thinking (2%), depersonalization (1%), depression (1%)

Dermatologic: Rash (3%), pruritus (1%)

Endocrine & metabolic: Decreased libido

Gastrointestinal: Diarrhea (8%), vomiting (6%), dyspepsia (5%), flatulence (3%), taste perversion (2%), weight loss (1%)

Genitourinary: Impotence (6%), urinary frequency (3%), impaired urination (2%), orgasm disturbance (2%), urinary retention (1%)

Neuromuscular & skeletal: Tremor (5%), hypertonia (3%), paresthesia (3%), twitching (1%)

Ocular: Blurred vision (6%), mydriasis (2%)

Otic: Tinnitus (2%)

Miscellaneous: Infection (6%), chills (3%), trauma (2%)

Drug Interactions

Cytochrome P450 Effect: Substrate of CYP2C8/9 (minor), 2C19 (minor), 2D6 (major), 3A4 (major); **Inhibits** CYP2B6 (weak), 2D6 (weak), 3A4 (weak)

Increased Effect/Toxicity: Concurrent use of MAO inhibitors (phenelzine, isocarboxazid), or drugs with MAO inhibitor activity (linezolid) may result in serotonin syndrome; should not be used within 2 weeks of each other. Selegiline may have a lower risk of this effect, particularly at low dosages, due to selectivity for MAO type B. In addition, concurrent use of buspirone, lithium, meperidine, nefazodone, selegiline, serotonin agonists (sumatriptan, naratriptan), sibutramine, SSRIs, trazodone, or tricyclic antidepressants may increase the risk of serotonin syndrome. Serum levels of haloperidol may be increased by venlafaxine. Inhibitors of CYP3A4 may increase the serum levels and/or toxicity of venlafaxine. CYP2D6 inhibitors may increase the levels/effects of venlafaxine; example inhibitors include chlorpromazine, delavirdine, fluoxetine, miconazole, paroxetine, pergolide, quinidine, quinine, ritonavir, and ropinirole.

Decreased Effect: Serum levels of indinavir may be reduced by venlafaxine (AUC reduced by 28%) - clinical significance not determined. Enzyme inducers (carbamazepine, phenytoin, phenobarbital) may reduce the serum concentrations of venlafaxine.

Mechanism of Action Venlafaxine and its active metabolite o-desmethylvenlafaxine (ODV) are potent inhibitors of neuronal serotonin and norepinephrine reuptake and weak inhibitors of dopamine reuptake

Pharmacodynamics/Kinetics

Absorption: Oral: 92% to 100%; food has no significant effect on the absorption of venlafaxine or formation of the active metabolite O-desmethylvenlafaxine (ODV)

Distribution: At steady state: Venlafaxine 7.5 ± 3.7 L/kg, ODV 5.7 ± 1.8 L/Kg

Protein binding: Bound to human plasma protein: Venlafaxine 27%, ODV 30%

Metabolism: Hepatic via CYP2D6 to active metabolite, O-desmethylvenlafaxine (ODV); other metabolites include N-desmethylvenlafaxine and N,O-didesmethylvenlafaxine

Bioavailability: Absolute: ~45%

Half-life elimination: Venlafaxine: 3-7 hours; ODV: 9-13 hours; Steady-state, plasma: Venlafaxine/ODV: Within 3 days of multiple dose therapy; prolonged with cirrhosis (Adults: Venlafaxine: ~30%, ODV: ~60%) and with dialysis (Adults: Venlafaxine: ~180%, ODV: ~142%)

Time to peak:

Immediate release: Venlafaxine: 2 hours, ODV: 3 hours

Extended release: Venlafaxine: 5.5 hours, ODV: 9 hours

Excretion: Urine (~87%, 5% as unchanged drug, 29% as unconjugated ODV, 26% as conjugated ODV, 27% as minor metabolites) within 48 hours

Clearance at steady state: Venlafaxine: 1.3 ± 0.6 L/hour/kg, ODV: 0.4 ± 0.2 L/hour/kg

Clearance decreased with:

Cirrhosis: Adults: Venlafaxine: ~50%, ODV: ~30%

Severe cirrhosis: Adults: Venlafaxine: ~90%

Renal impairment (Cl$_{cr}$ 10-70 mL/minute): Adults: Venlafaxine: ~24%

Dialysis: Adults: Venlafaxine: ~57%, ODV: ~56%; due to large volume of distribution, a significant amount of drug is not likely to be removed.

Dosage Oral:

Children and Adolescents:

ADHD (unlabeled use): Initial: 12.5 mg/day

Children <40 kg: Increase by 12.5 mg/week to maximum of 50 mg/day in 2 divided doses

Children ≥40 kg: Increase by 25 mg/week to maximum of 75 mg/day in 3 divided doses.

Mean dose: 60 mg or 1.4 mg/kg administered in 2-3 divided doses

Autism (unlabeled use): Initial: 12.5 mg/day; adjust to 6.25-50 mg/day

Adults:

Depression: Immediate-release tablets: 75 mg/day, administered in 2 or 3 divided doses, taken with food; dose may be increased in 75 mg/day increments at intervals of at least 4 days, up to 225-375 mg/day

Depression, GAD, social anxiety disorder: Extended-release capsules: 75 mg once daily taken with food; for some new patients, it may be desirable to start at 37.5 mg/day for 4-7 days before increasing to 75 mg once daily; dose may be increased by up to 75 mg/day increments every 4 days as tolerated, up to a maximum of 225 mg/day

Note: When discontinuing this medication after more than 1 week of treatment, it is generally recommended that the dose be tapered. If venlafaxine is used for 6 weeks or longer, the dose should be tapered over 2 weeks when discontinuing its use.

Dosing adjustment in renal impairment: Cl$_{cr}$ 10-70 mL/minute: Decrease dose by 25%; decrease total daily dose by 50% if dialysis patients; dialysis patients should receive dosing after completion of dialysis

Dosing adjustment in moderate hepatic impairment: Reduce total daily dosage by 50%

Administration Administer with food.

(Continued)

Venlafaxine (Continued)

Extended release capsule: Swallow capsule whole; do not crush or chew. Alternatively, contents may be sprinkled on a spoonful of applesauce and swallowed immediately without chewing; followed with a glass of water to ensure complete swallowing of the pellets.

Monitoring Parameters Blood pressure should be regularly monitored, especially in patients with a high baseline blood pressure

Reference Range Peak serum level of 163 ng/mL (325 ng/mL of ODV metabolite) obtained after a 150 mg oral dose

Patient Information Avoid alcohol; use caution when operating hazardous machinery; if a rash or shortness of breath occurs while using venlafaxine, contact prescriber immediately. Extended release capsule should be swallowed whole; do not crush or chew. Alternatively, contents may be sprinkled on a spoonful of applesauce and swallowed immediately without chewing; followed with a glass of water to ensure complete swallowing of the pellets.

Dosage Forms CAP, extended release (Effexor® XR): 37.5 mg, 75 mg, 150 mg. **TAB** (Effexor®): 25 mg, 37.5 mg, 50 mg, 75 mg, 100 mg

♦ **Venoglobulin®-S** see Immune Globulin (Intravenous) on page 659

♦ **Ventolin® [DSC]** see Albuterol on page 45

♦ **Ventolin® HFA** see Albuterol on page 45

♦ **VePesid®** see Etoposide on page 497

Verapamil (ver AP a mil)

Related Information
Calcium Channel Blockers Comparison on page 1371

U.S. Brand Names Calan®; Calan® SR; Covera-HS®; Isoptin® SR; Verelan®; Verelan® PM

Synonyms Iproveratril Hydrochloride; Verapamil Hydrochloride

Therapeutic Category Antianginal Agent; Antiarrhythmic Agent, Class IV; Antihypertensive Agent; Calcium Channel Blocker

Use Orally for treatment of angina pectoris (vasospastic, chronic stable, unstable) and hypertension; I.V. for supraventricular tachyarrhythmias (PSVT, atrial fibrillation, atrial flutter)

Unlabeled/Investigational Use Migraine; hypertrophic cardiomyopathy; bipolar disorder (manic manifestations)

Pregnancy Risk Factor C

Contraindications Hypersensitivity to verapamil or any component of the formulation; severe left ventricular dysfunction; hypotension (systolic pressure <90 mm Hg) or cardiogenic shock; sick sinus syndrome (except in patients with a functioning artificial pacemaker); second- or third-degree AV block (except in patients with a functioning artificial pacemaker); atrial flutter or fibrillation and an accessory bypass tract (WPW, Lown-Ganong-Levine syndrome)

Warnings/Precautions Use with caution in sick-sinus syndrome, severe left ventricular dysfunction, hepatic or renal impairment, hypertrophic cardiomyopathy (especially obstructive), abrupt withdrawal may cause increased duration and frequency of chest pain; avoid I.V. use in neonates and young infants due to severe apnea, bradycardia, or hypotensive reactions; elderly may experience more constipation and hypotension. Monitor ECG and blood pressure closely in patients receiving I.V. therapy particularly in patients with supraventricular tachycardia. May prolong recovery from nondepolarizing neuromuscular-blocking agents.

Common Adverse Reactions

>10%: Gastrointestinal: Gingival hyperplasia (19%)

1% to 10%:

Cardiovascular: Bradycardia (1.4% oral, 1.2% I.V.); first-, second-, or third-degree AV block (1.2% oral, unknown I.V.); CHF (1.8% oral); hypotension (2.5% oral, 3% I.V.); peripheral edema (1.9% oral); symptomatic hypotension (1.5% I.V.); severe tachycardia (1% I.V.)

Central nervous system: Dizziness (3.3% oral, 1.2% I.V.), fatigue (1.7% oral), headache (2.2% oral, 1.2% I.V.)

Dermatologic: Rash (1.2% oral)

Gastrointestinal: Constipation (12% up to 42% in clinical trials), nausea (2.7% oral, 0.9% I.V.)

Respiratory: Dyspnea (1.4% oral)

Drug Interactions

Cytochrome P450 Effect: Substrate of CYP1A2 (minor), 2B6 (minor), 2C8/9 (minor), 2C18 (minor), 2E1 (minor), 3A4 (major); **Inhibits** CYP1A2 (weak), 2C8/9 (weak), 2D6 (weak), 3A4 (moderate)

Increased Effect/Toxicity: Use of verapamil with amiodarone, beta-blockers, or flecainide may lead to bradycardia and decreased cardiac output. Aspirin and concurrent verapamil use may increase bleeding times. Azole antifungals, cimetidine, erythromycin may inhibit verapamil metabolism, increasing serum concentrations/effect of verapamil. Lithium neurotoxicity may result when verapamil is added. Effect of nondepolarizing neuromuscular blocker is prolonged by verapamil. Grapefruit juice may increase verapamil serum concentrations. Blood pressure-lowering effects may be additive with sildenafil, tadalafil, and vardenafil (use caution).

Cisapride and astemizole levels may be increased by verapamil, potentially resulting in life-threatening arrhythmias; avoid concurrent use. Serum concentrations of the following drugs may be increased by verapamil: Alfentanil, buspirone, carbamazepine, cyclosporine, digoxin, doxorubicin, ethanol, HMG-CoA reductase inhibitors (atorvastatin, cerivastatin, lovastatin, simvastatin), midazolam, prazosin, quinidine, tacrolimus, and theophylline.

Decreased Effect: Rifampin or phenobarbital may decrease verapamil serum concentrations by increased hepatic metabolism. Lithium levels may be decreased by verapamil. Nafcillin decreases plasma concentration of verapamil.

Mechanism of Action Inhibits calcium ion from entering the "slow channels" or select voltage-sensitive areas of vascular smooth muscle and myocardium during depolarization; produces a relaxation of coronary vascular smooth muscle and coronary vasodilation; increases myocardial oxygen delivery in patients with vasospastic angina; slows automaticity and conduction of AV node.

Pharmacodynamics/Kinetics

Onset of action: Peak effect: Oral: Immediate release: 2 hours; I.V.: 1-5 minutes

Duration: Oral: Immediate release tablets: 6-8 hours; I.V.: 10-20 minutes

Protein binding: 90%

Metabolism: Hepatic via multiple CYP isoenzymes; extensive first-pass effect

Bioavailability: Oral: 20% to 30%

Half-life elimination: Infants: 4.4-6.9 hours; Adults: Single dose: 2-8 hours, Multiple doses: Up to 12 hours; prolonged with hepatic cirrhosis

Excretion: Urine (70%, 3% to 4% as unchanged drug); feces (16%)

Dosage

Children: SVT:

I.V.:

<1 year: 0.1-0.2 mg/kg over 2 minutes; repeat every 30 minutes as needed

1-15 years: 0.1-0.3 mg/kg over 2 minutes; maximum: 5 mg/dose, may repeat dose in 15 minutes if adequate response not achieved; maximum for second dose: 10 mg/dose

Oral (dose not well established):

1-5 years: 4-8 mg/kg/day in 3 divided doses **or** 40-80 mg every 8 hours

>5 years: 80 mg every 6-8 hours

Adults:

SVT: I.V.: 2.5-5 mg (over 2 minutes); second dose of 5-10 mg (~0.15 mg/kg) may be given 15-30 minutes after the initial dose if patient tolerates, but does not respond to initial dose; maximum total dose: 20 mg

Angina: Oral: Initial dose: 80-120 mg 3 times/day (elderly or small stature: 40 mg 3 times/day); range: 240-480 mg/day in 3-4 divided doses

Hypertension: Oral: 80 mg 3 times/day or 240 mg/day (sustained release); range: 240-480 mg/day; 120 mg/day in the elderly or small patients (no evidence of additional benefit in doses >360 mg/day).

Note: One time per day dosing is recommended at bedtime with Covera-HS®.

Dosing adjustment in renal impairment: Cl_{cr} <10 mL/minute: Administer at 50% to 75% of normal dose.

Dialysis: Not dialyzable (0% to 5 %) via hemo- or peritoneal dialysis; supplemental dose is not necessary.

Dosing adjustment/comments in hepatic disease: Reduce dose in cirrhosis, reduce dose to 20% to 50% of normal and monitor ECG.

Administration

Oral: Administer sustained release product with food or milk; sprinkling contents of capsules onto food does not affect absorption; should be dosed 1-2 times/day; **do not crush sustained release drug product.** Other oral formulations may be given with or without food.

I.V.: Rate of infusion: Over 2 minutes.

Monitoring Parameters Monitor blood pressure closely

Reference Range Therapeutic: 50-200 ng/mL (SI: 100-410 nmol/L) for parent; under normal conditions norverapamil concentration is the same as parent drug. Toxic: >90 µg/mL

Patient Information Sustained release products should be taken with food and not crushed; limit caffeine intake; notify prescriber if angina pain is not reduced when taking this drug, or if irregular heartbeat or shortness of breath occurs

Dosage Forms CAP, extended release: 120 mg, 180 mg, 240 mg; (Verelan® PM): 100 mg, 200 mg, 300 mg. **CAPLET, sustained release** (Calan® SR): 120 mg, 180 mg, 240 mg. **CAP, sustained release** (Verelan®): 120 mg, 180 mg, 240 mg, 360 mg. **INJ, solution:** 2.5 mg/mL (2 mL, 4 mL). **TAB** (Calan®): 40 mg, 80 mg, 120 mg. **TAB, extended release:** 120 mg, 180 mg, 240 mg; (Covera HS®): 180 mg, 240 mg. **TAB, sustained release** (Isoptin® SR): 120 mg, 180 mg, 240 mg

- **Vibra-Tabs**® *see* Doxycycline *on page 413*
- **Vicks**® **44D Cough & Head Congestion [OTC]** *see* Pseudoephedrine and Dextromethorphan *on page 1062*
- **Vicks**® **44E [OTC]** *see* Guaifenesin and Dextromethorphan *on page 604*
- **Vicks**® **Children's NyQuil**® **[OTC]** *see* Chlorpheniramine, Pseudoephedrine, and Dextromethorphan *on page 265*
- **Vicks**® **DayQuil**® **Multi-Symptom Cold and Flu [OTC]** *see* Acetaminophen, Dextromethorphan, and Pseudoephedrine *on page 28*
- **Vicks**® **Pediatric 44**®**m [OTC]** *see* Chlorpheniramine, Pseudoephedrine, and Dextromethorphan *on page 265*
- **Vicks**® **Pediatric Formula 44E [OTC]** *see* Guaifenesin and Dextromethorphan *on page 604*
- **Vicks**® **Sinex**® **Nasal Spray [OTC]** *see* Phenylephrine *on page 993*
- **Vicks**® **Sinex**® **UltraFine Mist [OTC]** *see* Phenylephrine *on page 993*
- **Vicodin**® *see* Hydrocodone and Acetaminophen *on page 627*
- **Vicodin**® **ES** *see* Hydrocodone and Acetaminophen *on page 627*
- **Vicodin**® **HP** *see* Hydrocodone and Acetaminophen *on page 627*
- **Vicodin Tuss**® *see* Hydrocodone and Guaifenesin *on page 630*
- **Vicon Forte**® *see* Vitamins (Multiple/Oral) *on page 1312*
- **Vicon Plus**® **[OTC]** *see* Vitamins (Multiple/Oral) *on page 1312*
- **Vicoprofen**® *see* Hydrocodone and Ibuprofen *on page 630*

Vidarabine (vye DARE a been)
U.S. Brand Names Vira-A® [DSC]
Synonyms Adenine Arabinoside; Ara-A; Arabinofuranosyladenine; Vidarabine Monohydrate
Therapeutic Category Antiviral Agent; Antiviral Agent, Ophthalmic
Use Treatment of acute keratoconjunctivitis and epithelial keratitis due to herpes simplex virus type 1 and 2; superficial keratitis caused by herpes simplex virus
Pregnancy Risk Factor C
Contraindications Hypersensitivity to vidarabine or any component of the formulation; sterile trophic ulcers
Warnings/Precautions Not effective against RNA virus, adenoviral ocular infections, bacterial fungal or chlamydial infections of the cornea, or trophic ulcers; temporary visual haze may be produced; neoplasia has occurred with I.M. vidarabine-treated animals; although *in vitro* studies have been inconclusive, they have shown mutagenesis
Common Adverse Reactions Frequency not defined: Ocular: Burning eyes, lacrimation, keratitis, photophobia, foreign body sensation, uveitis
Drug Interactions
Increased Effect/Toxicity: Allopurinol (may increase vidarabine levels).
Mechanism of Action Inhibits viral DNA synthesis by blocking DNA polymerase
Dosage Children and Adults: Ophthalmic: Keratoconjunctivitis: Instill ½" of ointment in lower conjunctival sac 5 times/day every 3 hours while awake until complete re-epithelialization has occurred, then twice daily for an additional 7 days
Administration Administer by I.V. infusion over 12 to 24 hours; vidarabine must be filtered with a 0.45 micron or smaller pore size inline filter; administer at a final concentration not to exceed 0.45 mg/mL to prevent precipitation. However, concentrations up to 0.7 mg/mL have been administered to fluid-restricted patients.
Patient Information Do not use eye make-up when on this medication for ophthalmic infection; use sunglasses if photophobic reaction occurs; may cause blurred vision; notify prescriber if improvement not seen after 7 days or if condition worsens
Dosage Forms OINT, ophthalmic: 3% (3.5 g) [DSC]

- **Vidarabine Monohydrate** *see* Vidarabine *on page 1304*
- **Vi-Daylin**® **+ Iron Liquid [OTC]** *see* Vitamins (Multiple/Oral) *on page 1312*
- **Vi-Daylin**® **Liquid [OTC]** *see* Vitamins (Multiple/Oral) *on page 1312*
- **Videx**® *see* Didanosine *on page 370*
- **Videx**® **EC** *see* Didanosine *on page 370*
- **Vigamox**™ *see* Moxifloxacin *on page 864*

VinBLAStine (vin BLAS teen)
U.S. Brand Names Velban® [DSC]
Synonyms NSC-49842; Vinblastine Sulfate; VLB
Therapeutic Category Antineoplastic Agent; Antineoplastic Agent, Natural Source (Plant) Derivative; Antineoplastic Agent, Vesicant; Antineoplastic Agent, Vinca Alkaloid; Vesicant
Use Treatment of Hodgkin's and non-Hodgkin's lymphoma, testicular, lung, head and neck, breast, and renal carcinomas, Mycosis fungoides, Kaposi's sarcoma, histiocytosis, choriocarcinoma, and idiopathic thrombocytopenic purpura
Pregnancy Risk Factor D
Contraindications For I.V. use only; **I.T. use may result in death**; hypersensitivity to vinblastine or any component of the formulation; severe bone marrow suppression or presence of bacterial infection not under control prior to initiation of therapy; pregnancy
Warnings/Precautions The U.S. Food and Drug Administration (FDA) currently recommends that procedures for proper handling and disposal of antineoplastic agents be considered. Vinblastine is a moderate vesicant; avoid extravasation; extravasation may cause tissue damage and pain. Discontinue immediately if extravasation occurs (remaining portion of dose

to be infused through another vein). Dosage modification required in patients with impaired liver function and neurotoxicity. Using small amounts of drug daily for long periods may cause neurotoxicity and is therefore not advised. For I.V. use only. **Intrathecal administration may result in death.** Monitor closely for shortness of breath or bronchospasm in patients receiving mitomycin C.

Common Adverse Reactions
>10%:

Dermatologic: Alopecia

Endocrine & metabolic: SIADH

Gastrointestinal: Diarrhea (less common), stomatitis, anorexia, metallic taste

Hematologic: May cause severe bone marrow suppression and is the dose-limiting toxicity of VLB (unlike vincristine); severe granulocytopenia and thrombocytopenia may occur following the administration of VLB and nadir 5-10 days after treatment

Myelosuppression (primarily leukopenia, may be dose limiting)

Onset: 4-7 days

Nadir: 5-10 days

Recovery: 4-21 days

1% to 10%:

Cardiovascular: Hypertension, Raynaud's phenomenon

Central nervous system: Depression, malaise, headache, seizures

Dermatologic: Rash, photosensitivity, dermatitis

Endocrine & metabolic: Hyperuricemia

Gastrointestinal: Constipation, abdominal pain, nausea (mild), vomiting (mild), paralytic ileus, stomatitis

Genitourinary: Urinary retention

Neuromuscular & skeletal: Jaw pain, myalgia, paresthesia

Respiratory: Bronchospasm

Drug Interactions
Cytochrome P450 Effect: Substrate of CYP2D6 (minor), 3A4 (major); **Inhibits** CYP2D6 (weak), 3A4 (weak)

Increased Effect/Toxicity: Vinblastine levels may be increased when given with drugs that inhibit cytochrome P450 3A4 enzyme substrate. Previous or simultaneous use with mito-mycin-C has resulted in acute shortness of breath and severe bronchospasm within minutes or several hours after *Vinca* alkaloid injection and may occur up to 2 weeks after the dose of mitomycin. Mitomycin-C in combination with administration of VLB may cause acute short-ness of breath and severe bronchospasm, onset may be within minutes or several hours after VLB injection.

Decreased Effect: Phenytoin plasma levels may be reduced with concomitant combination chemotherapy with vinblastine. Alpha-interferon enhances interferon toxicity; phenytoin may ↓ plasma levels.

Mechanism of Action
Vinblastine binds to tubulin and inhibits microtubule formation, there-fore, arresting the cell at metaphase by disrupting the formation of the mitotic spindle; it is specific for the M and S phases. Vinblastine may also interfere with nucleic acid and protein synthesis by blocking glutamic acid utilization.

Pharmacodynamics/Kinetics
Distribution: V_d: 27.3 L/kg; binds extensively to tissues; does not penetrate CNS or other fatty tissues; distributes to liver

Protein binding: 99%

Metabolism: Hepatic to active metabolite

Half-life elimination: Biphasic: Initial: 0.164 hours; Terminal: 25 hours

Excretion: Feces (95%); urine (<1% as unchanged drug)

Dosage
Refer to individual protocols.

Children and Adults: I.V.: 4-20 mg/m² (0.1-0.5 mg/kg) every 7-10 days **or** 5-day continuous infusion of 1.5-2 mg/m²/day **or** 0.1-0.5 mg/kg/week

Dosing adjustment in hepatic impairment:

Serum bilirubin 1.5-3.0 mg/dL or AST 60-180 units: Administer 50% of normal dose

Serum bilirubin 3.0-5.0 mg/dL: Administer 25% of dose

Serum bilirubin >5.0 mg/dL or AST >180 units: Omit dose

Administration
FATAL IF GIVEN INTRATHECALLY. Administer vinblastine I.V., usually as a slow (2-3 minutes) push, or a bolus (5- to 15-minute) infusion. It is occasionally given as a 24-hour continuous infusion. Avoid extravasation; may cause sloughing. Solution should be administered only by qualified personnel. Do not allow to come in contact with skin; if contact occurs, wash well with soap and water.

Extravasation management: Mix 250 units hyaluronidase with 6 mL of NS. Inject the hyalu-ronidase solution subcutaneously through 6 clockwise injections into the infiltrated area using a 25-gauge needle; change the needle with each new injection. Apply heat immediately for 1 hour. Repeat 4 times/day for 3-5 days. Elevate extremity. Application of cold or hydrocortisone is contraindicated.

Monitoring Parameters
CBC with differential and platelet count, serum uric acid, hepatic function tests

Patient Information
This medication can only be administered by infusion, usually on a cyclic basis. Maintain adequate hydration (2-3 L/day of fluids unless instructed to restrict fluid intake) and nutrition (small frequent meals will help). You will most likely lose your hair (reversible after therapy); experience nausea or vomiting (request antiemetic); photosensitivity (use sunscreen, wear protective clothing and eyewear, and avoid direct sunlight); or feel weak or lethargic (use caution when driving or engaging in tasks requiring alertness until response to drug is known). Use good oral care to reduce incidence of mouth sores. You will be more susceptible to (Continued)

VinBLAStine *(Continued)*

infection; avoid crowds or exposure to infection. Report numbness or tingling in fingers or toes (use care to prevent injury); signs of infection (eg, fever, chills, sore throat, burning urination, fatigue); unusual bleeding (eg, tarry stools, easy bruising, blood in stool, urine, or mouth); unresolved mouth sores; skin rash or itching; or difficulty breathing. The drug may cause permanent sterility and may cause birth defects. Contraceptive measures are recommended during therapy. The drug may be excreted in breast milk, therefore, an alternative form of feeding your baby should be used.

Dosage Forms INJ, powder for reconstitution: 10 mg. **INJ, solution:** 1 mg/mL (10 mL)

♦ **Vinblastine Sulfate** *see* VinBLAStine *on page 1304*
♦ **Vincasar PFS®** *see* VinCRIStine *on page 1306*

VinCRIStine *(vin KRIS teen)*

U.S. Brand Names Oncovin® [DSC]; Vincasar PFS®

Synonyms LCR; Leurocristine Sulfate; NSC-67574; VCR; Vincristine Sulfate

Therapeutic Category Antineoplastic Agent, Natural Source (Plant) Derivative; Antineoplastic Agent, Vesicant; Antineoplastic Agent, Vinca Alkaloid; Vesicant

Use Treatment of leukemias, Hodgkin's disease, non-Hodgkin's lymphomas, Wilms' tumor, neuroblastoma, rhabdomyosarcoma

Pregnancy Risk Factor D

Contraindications Hypersensitivity to vincristine or any component of the formulation; **for I.V. use only, fatal if given intrathecally**; patients with demyelinating form of Charcot-Marie-Tooth syndrome; pregnancy

Warnings/Precautions The U.S. Food and Drug Administration (FDA) currently recommends that procedures for proper handling and disposal of antineoplastic agents be considered. Dosage modification required in patients with impaired hepatic function or who have pre-existing neuromuscular disease; avoid extravasation; use with caution in the elderly; avoid eye contamination; observe closely for shortness of breath, bronchospasm, especially in patients treated with mitomycin C. For I.V. use only; **intrathecal administration results in death**; administer allopurinol to prevent uric acid nephropathy; not to be used with radiation.

Common Adverse Reactions
>10%:
  Dermatologic: Alopecia occurs in 20% to 70% of patients
  Extravasation: VCR is a vesicant and can cause tissue irritation and necrosis if infiltrated; if extravasation occurs, follow institutional policy, which may include hyaluronidase and hot compresses
    Vesicant chemotherapy
1% to 10%:
  Cardiovascular: Orthostatic hypotension or hypertension, hypertension, hypotension
  Central nervous system: Motor difficulties, seizures, headache, CNS depression, cranial nerve paralysis, fever
  Dermatologic: Rash
  Endocrine & metabolic: Hyperuricemia
    SIADH: Rarely occurs, but may be related to the neurologic toxicity; may cause symptomatic hyponatremia with seizures; the increase in serum ADH concentration usually subsides within 2-3 days after onset
  Gastrointestinal: Constipation and possible paralytic ileus secondary to neurologic toxicity; oral ulceration, abdominal cramps, anorexia, metallic taste, bloating, nausea (mild), vomiting, weight loss, diarrhea
  Local: Phlebitis
  Neurologic: Alterations in mental status such as depression, confusion, or insomnia; constipation, paralytic ileus, and urinary tract disturbances may occur. All patients should be on a prophylactic bowel management regimen. Cranial nerve palsies, headaches, jaw pain, optic atrophy with blindness have been reported. Intrathecal administration of VCR has uniformly caused death; VCR should **never** be administered by this route. Neurologic effects of VCR may be additive with those of other neurotoxic agents and spinal cord irradiation.
  Neuromuscular & skeletal: Jaw pain, leg pain, myalgia, cramping, numbness, weakness
    Peripheral neuropathy: Frequently the dose-limiting toxicity of VCR. Most frequent in patients >40 years of age; occurs usually after an average of 3 weekly doses, but may occur after just one dose. Manifested as loss of the deep tendon reflexes in the lower extremities, numbness, tingling, pain, paresthesias of the fingers and toes (stocking glove sensation), and "foot drop" or "wrist drop"
  Ocular: Photophobia

Drug Interactions
  Cytochrome P450 Effect: Substrate of CYP3A4 (major); **Inhibits** CYP3A4 (weak)
  Increased Effect/Toxicity: Vincristine levels may be increased when given with drugs that inhibit cytochrome P450 3A enzyme (itraconazole has been shown to increase onset and severity of neuromuscular adverse effects of vincristine). Digoxin plasma levels and renal excretion may decrease with combination chemotherapy including vincristine. Vincristine should be given 12-24 hours before asparaginase to minimize toxicity (may decrease the hepatic clearance of vincristine). Acute pulmonary reactions may occur with mitomycin-C. Previous or simultaneous use with mitomycin-C has resulted in acute shortness of breath and severe bronchospasm within minutes or several hours after *Vinca* alkaloid injection and may occur up to 2 weeks after the dose of mitomycin.

Decreased Effect: Digoxin and phenytoin levels may decrease with combination chemotherapy.

Mechanism of Action Binds to tubulin and inhibits microtubule formation; therefore arresting the cell at metaphase by disrupting the formation of the mitotic spindle; it is specific for the M and S phases. Vincristine may also interfere with nucleic acid and protein synthesis by blocking glutamic acid utilization.

Pharmacodynamics/Kinetics

Absorption: Oral: Poor

Distribution: V_d: 163-165 L/m^2; Poor penetration into CSF; rapidly removed from bloodstream and tightly bound to tissues; penetrates blood-brain barrier poorly

Protein binding: 75%

Metabolism: Extensively hepatic

Half-life elimination: Terminal: 24 hours

Excretion: Feces (~80%); urine (<1% as unchanged drug)

Dosage Note: Doses are often capped at 2 mg; however, this may reduce the efficacy of the therapy and may not be advisable. Refer to individual protocols; orders for single doses >2.5 mg or >5 mg/treatment cycle should be verified with the specific treatment regimen and/or an experienced oncologist prior to dispensing. I.V.:

Children ≤10 kg or BSA <1 m^2: Initial therapy: 0.05 mg/kg once weekly then titrate dose; maximum single dose: 2 mg

Children >10 kg or BSA ≥1 m^2: 1-2 mg/m^2, may repeat once weekly for 3-6 weeks; maximum single dose: 2 mg

Neuroblastoma: I.V. continuous infusion with doxorubicin: 1 mg/m^2/day for 72 hours

Adults: 0.4-1.4 mg/m^2, may repeat every week **or**

0.4-0.5 mg/day continuous infusion for 4 days every 4 weeks **or**

0.25-0.5 mg/m^2/day for 5 days every 4 weeks

Dosing adjustment in hepatic impairment:

Serum bilirubin 1.5-3.0 mg/dL or AST 60-180 units: Administer 50% of normal dose

Serum bilirubin 3.0-5.0 mg/dL: Administer 25% of dose

Serum bilirubin >5.0 mg/dL or AST >180 units: Omit dose

Administration FATAL IF GIVEN INTRATHECALLY.

I.V.: Usually administered as slow (1-2 minutes) push or as short (10-15 minutes) infusion; 24-hour continuous infusions are occasionally used

Intralesional injection has been reported for Kaposi's sarcoma.

Extravasation management: Mix 250 units hyaluronidase with 6 mL of NS. Inject the hyaluronidase solution subcutaneously through 6 clockwise injections into the infiltrated area using a 25-gauge needle. Change the needle with each new injection. Elevate extremity. Apply heat immediately for 1 hour. Repeat 4 times/day for 3-5 days. Application of cold or hydrocortisone is contraindicated.

Monitoring Parameters Serum electrolytes (sodium), hepatic function tests, neurologic examination, CBC, serum uric acid

Patient Information This medication can only be administered by infusion, usually on a cyclic basis. Maintain adequate hydration (2-3 L/day of fluids unless instructed to restrict fluid intake) and nutrition (small frequent meals will help). You will most likely lose your hair (reversible after therapy); experience constipation (request medication); or feel weak or lethargic (use caution when driving or engaging in tasks requiring alertness until response to drug is known). Use good oral care to reduce incidence of mouth sores. You will be more susceptible to infection; avoid crowds or exposure to infection. Report pain, numbness, or tingling in fingers or toes (use care to prevent injury); alterations in mental status (eg, confusion, insomnia, headaches, jaw pain, loss of vision); signs of infection (eg, fever, chills, sore throat, burning urination, fatigue); unusual bleeding (eg, tarry stools, easy bruising, or blood in stool, urine, or mouth), unresolved mouth sores; skin rash or itching; nausea; vomiting; abdominal pain; bloating; or difficulty breathing. Contraceptive measures are recommended during therapy.

Dosage Forms INJ, solution: 1 mg/mL (1 mL, 2 mL)

♦ Vincristine Sulfate *see* VinCRIStine *on page 1306*

Vinorelbine (vi NOR el been)

U.S. Brand Names Navelbine®

Synonyms Dihydroxydeoxynorvinkaleukoblastine; NVB; Vinorelbine Tartrate

Therapeutic Category Antineoplastic Agent, Natural Source (Plant) Derivative; Antineoplastic Agent, Vesicant; Antineoplastic Agent, Vinca Alkaloid; Vesicant

Use Treatment of nonsmall cell lung cancer

Unlabeled/Investigational Use Treatment of breast cancer, ovarian carcinoma, Hodgkin's disease, non-Hodgkin's lymphoma

Pregnancy Risk Factor D

Contraindications For I.V. use only; **I.T. use may result in death**; hypersensitivity to vinorelbine or any component of the formulation; severe bone marrow suppression (granulocyte counts <1000 cells/mm^3); pregnancy

Warnings/Precautions The U.S. Food and Drug Administration (FDA) currently recommends that procedures for proper handling and disposal of antineoplastic agents be considered. Avoid extravasation; dosage modification required in patients with impaired liver function and neurotoxicity. Frequently monitor patients for myelosuppression both during and after therapy. Granulocytopenia is dose-limiting. **Intrathecal administration may result in death**. Use with caution in patients with cachexia or ulcerated skin.

(Continued)

Vinorelbine *(Continued)*

Acute shortness of breath and severe bronchospasm have been reported, most commonly when administered with mitomycin. Fatal cases of interstitial pulmonary changes and ARDS have also been reported. May cause severe constipation (grade 3-4), paralytic ileus, intestinal obstruction, necrosis, and/or perforation.

Common Adverse Reactions

>10%:

Central nervous system: Fatigue (27%)

Dermatologic: Alopecia (12%)

Gastrointestinal: Nausea (44%, severe <2%) and vomiting (20%) are most common and are easily controlled with standard antiemetics; constipation (35%), diarrhea (17%)

Emetic potential: Moderate (30% to 60%)

Hematologic: May cause severe bone marrow suppression and is the dose-limiting toxicity of vinorelbine; severe granulocytopenia (90%) may occur following the administration of vinorelbine; leukopenia (92%), anemia (83%)

Myelosuppressive:

WBC: Moderate - severe

Onset: 4-7 days

Nadir: 7-10 days

Recovery: 14-21 days

Hepatic: Elevated SGOT (67%), elevated total bilirubin (13%)

Local: Injection site reaction (28%), injection site pain (16%)

Neuromuscular & skeletal: Weakness (36%), peripheral neuropathy (20% to 25%)

1% to 10%:

Cardiovascular: Chest pain (5%)

Gastrointestinal: Paralytic ileus (1%)

Hematologic: Thrombocytopenia (5%)

Local: Extravasation: Vesicant and can cause tissue irritation and necrosis if infiltrated; if extravasation occurs, follow institutional policy, which may include hyaluronidase and hot compresses; phlebitis (7%)

Vesicant chemotherapy

Neuromuscular & skeletal: Mild to moderate peripheral neuropathy manifested by paresthesia and hyperesthesia, loss of deep tendon reflexes (<5%); myalgia (<5%), arthralgia (<5%), jaw pain (<5%)

Respiratory: Dyspnea (3% to 7%)

Drug Interactions

Cytochrome P450 Effect: Substrate of CYP2D6 (minor), 3A4 (major); **Inhibits** CYP2D6 (weak), 3A4 (weak)

Increased Effect/Toxicity: Previous or simultaneous use with mitomycin-C has resulted in acute shortness of breath and severe bronchospasm within minutes or several hours after *Vinca* alkaloid injection and may occur up to 2 weeks after the dose of mitomycin.

Cisplatin: Incidence of granulocytopenia is significantly higher than with single-agent vinorelbine.

Mechanism of Action Semisynthetic vinca alkaloid which binds to tubulin and inhibits microtubule formation, therefore, arresting the cell at metaphase by disrupting the formation of the mitotic spindle; it is specific for the M and S phases. Vinorelbine may also interfere with nucleic acid and protein synthesis by blocking glutamic acid utilization.

Pharmacodynamics/Kinetics

Absorption: Unreliable; must be given I.V.

Distribution: V_d: 25.4-40.1 L/kg; binds extensively to human platelets and lymphocytes (79.6% to 91.2%)

Protein binding: 80% to 90%

Metabolism: Extensively hepatic to two metabolites, deacetylvinorelbine (active) and vinorelbine N-oxide

Bioavailability: Oral: 26% to 45%

Half-life elimination: Triphasic: Terminal: 27.7-43.6 hours

Excretion: Feces (46%); urine (18%, 10% to 12% as unchanged drug)

Clearance: Plasma: Mean: 0.97-1.26 L/hour/kg

Dosage Refer to individual protocols.

Adults: I.V.:

Single-agent therapy: 30 mg/m² every 7 days

Combination therapy with cisplatin: 25 mg/m² every 7 days (with cisplatin 100 mg/m² every 4 weeks); **Alternatively:** 30 mg/m² in combination with cisplatin 120 mg/m² on days 1 and 29, then every 6 weeks

Dosage adjustment in hematological toxicity: Granulocyte counts should be ≥1000 cells/mm³ prior to the administration of vinorelbine. Adjustments in the dosage of vinorelbine should be based on granulocyte counts obtained on the day of treatment as follows:

Granulocytes ≥1500 cells/mm³ on day of treatment: Administer 100% of starting dose

Granulocytes 1000-1499 cells/mm³ on day of treatment: Administer 50% of starting dose

Granulocytes <1000 cells/mm³ on day of treatment: Do not administer. Repeat granulocyte count in one week; if 3 consecutive doses are held because granulocyte count is <1000 cells/mm³, discontinue vinorelbine

For patients who, during treatment, have experienced fever and/or sepsis while granulocytopenic or had 2 consecutive weekly doses held due to granulocytopenia, subsequent doses of vinorelbine should be:

75% of starting dose for granulocytes ≥1500 cells/mm³

37.5% of starting dose for granulocytes 1000-1499 cells/mm^3

Dosage adjustment in renal impairment: No dose adjustments are required for renal insufficiency.

Dosing adjustment in hepatic impairment: Vinorelbine should be administered with caution in patients with hepatic insufficiency. In patients who develop hyperbilirubinemia during treatment with vinorelbine, the dose should be adjusted for total bilirubin as follows:
Serum bilirubin ≤2 mg/dL: Administer 100% of starting dose
Serum bilirubin 2.1-3 mg/dL: Administer 50% of starting dose
Serum bilirubin >3 mg/dL: Administer 25% of starting dose

Dosing adjustment in patients with concurrent hematologic toxicity and hepatic impairment: Administer the lower doses determined from the above recommendations

Administration FATAL IF GIVEN INTRATHECALLY. Administer as a direct intravenous push or rapid bolus, over 6-10 minutes (up to 30 minutes). Longer infusions may increase the risk of pain and phlebitis. Intravenous doses should be followed by 150-250 mL of saline or dextrose to reduce the incidence of phlebitis and inflammation. **CENTRAL LINE ONLY** for IVPB administration. Avoid extravasation; may cause sloughing.

Extravasation management: Mix 250 units hyaluronidase with 6 mL of NS. Inject the hyaluronidase solution subcutaneously through 6 clockwise injections into the infiltrated area using a 25-gauge needle. Change the needle with each new injection. Elevate extremities. Apply heat immediately for 1 hour. Repeat 4 times/day for 3-5 days. Application of cold or hydrocortisone is contraindicated.

Monitoring Parameters CBC with differential and platelet count, hepatic function tests

Patient Information This medication can only be administered by infusion, usually on a cyclic basis. Maintain adequate hydration (2-3 L/day of fluids unless instructed to restrict fluid intake) and nutrition (small frequent meals will help). You will most likely lose your hair (reversible after therapy); experience nausea or vomiting (request medication); feel weak or lethargic (use caution when driving or engaging in tasks requiring alertness until response to drug is known). Use good oral care to reduce incidence of mouth sores. You will be more susceptible to infection; avoid crowds or exposure to infection. Report weakness, skeletal pain, or tremors; signs of infection (eg, fever, chills, sore throat, burning urination, fatigue); unusual bleeding (eg, tarry stools, easy bruising, blood in stool, urine, or mouth); numbness, pain, or tingling of fingers or toes; unresolved mouth sores; skin rash or itching; uncontrolled nausea, vomiting, or abdominal pain; or difficulty breathing. The drug may cause permanent sterility and may cause birth defects. Contraceptive measures are recommended during therapy. The drug is excreted in breast milk, therefore, an alternative form of feeding your baby should be used.

Dosage Forms INJ, solution [preservative free]: 10 mg/mL (1 mL, 5 mL)

- ◆ **Vinorelbine Tartrate** *see* Vinorelbine *on page 1307*
- ◆ **Viokase®** *see* Pancrelipase *on page 953*
- ◆ **Viosterol** *see* Ergocalciferol *on page 449*
- ◆ **Vioxx®** *see* Rofecoxib *on page 1111*
- ◆ **Vira-A® [DSC]** *see* Vidarabine *on page 1304*
- ◆ **Viracept®** *see* Nelfinavir *on page 889*
- ◆ **Viramune®** *see* Nevirapine *on page 896*
- ◆ **Virazole®** *see* Ribavirin *on page 1091*
- ◆ **Viread®** *see* Tenofovir *on page 1195*
- ◆ **Virilon®** *see* MethylTESTOSTERone *on page 826*
- ◆ **Viroptic®** *see* Trifluridine *on page 1268*
- ◆ **Viscoat®** *see* Chondroitin Sulfate and Sodium Hyaluronate *on page 271*
- ◆ **Visine-A™ [OTC]** *see* Naphazoline and Pheniramine *on page 882*
- ◆ **Vistaril®** *see* HydrOXYzine *on page 640*
- ◆ **Vistide®** *see* Cidofovir *on page 274*
- ◆ **Vita-C® [OTC]** *see* Ascorbic Acid *on page 117*
- ◆ **Vitacon Forte** *see* Vitamins (Multiple/Oral) *on page 1312*

Vitamin A (VYE ta min aye)

U.S. Brand Names Aquasol A®; Palmitate-A® [OTC]

Synonyms Oleovitamin A

Therapeutic Category Vitamin, Fat Soluble

Use Treatment and prevention of vitamin A deficiency; parenteral (I.M.) route is indicated when oral administration is not feasible or when absorption is insufficient (malabsorption syndrome)

Pregnancy Risk Factor A/X (dose exceeding RDA recommendation)

Contraindications Hypersensitivity to vitamin A or any component of the formulation; hypervitaminosis A; pregnancy (dose exceeding RDA)

Warnings/Precautions Evaluate other sources of vitamin A while receiving this product; patients receiving >25,000 units/day should be closely monitored for toxicity. Parenteral vitamin A: In low birth weight infants, polysorbates have been associated with thrombocytopenia, renal dysfunction, hepatomegaly, cholestasis, ascites, hypotension, and metabolic acidosis (E-Ferol syndrome).

Common Adverse Reactions 1% to 10%:
Central nervous system: Irritability, vertigo, lethargy, malaise, fever, headache
Dermatologic: Drying or cracking of skin
Endocrine & metabolic: Hypercalcemia
Gastrointestinal: Weight loss
Ocular: Visual changes
(Continued)

Vitamin A *(Continued)*

Miscellaneous: Hypervitaminosis A

Drug Interactions

Increased Effect/Toxicity: Retinoids may have additive adverse effects.

Decreased Effect: Cholestyramine resin decreases absorption of vitamin A. Neomycin and mineral oil may also interfere with vitamin A absorption.

Mechanism of Action Needed for bone development, growth, visual adaptation to darkness, testicular and ovarian function, and as a cofactor in many biochemical processes

Pharmacodynamics/Kinetics

Absorption: Vitamin A in dosages **not** exceeding physiologic replacement is well absorbed after oral administration; water miscible preparations are absorbed more rapidly than oil preparations; large oral doses, conditions of fat malabsorption, low protein intake, or hepatic or pancreatic disease reduces oral absorption

Distribution: Large amounts concentrate for storage in the liver; enters breast milk

Metabolism: Conjugated with glucuronide; undergoes enterohepatic recirculation

Excretion: Feces

Dosage

RDA:

<1 year: 375 mcg

1-3 years: 400 mcg

4-6 years: 500 mcg*

7-10 years: 700 mcg*

>10 years: 800-1000 mcg*

Male: 1000 mcg

Female: 800 mcg

* mcg retinol equivalent (0.3 mcg retinol = 1 unit vitamin A)

Vitamin A supplementation in measles (recommendation of the World Health Organization): Children: Oral: Administer as a single dose; repeat the next day and at 4 weeks for children with ophthalmologic evidence of vitamin A deficiency:

6 months to 1 year: 100,000 units

>1 year: 200,000 units

Note: Use of vitamin A in measles is recommended only for patients 6 months to 2 years of age hospitalized with measles and its complications **or** patients >6 months of age who have any of the following risk factors and who are not already receiving vitamin A: immunodeficiency, ophthalmologic evidence of vitamin A deficiency including night blindness, Bitot's spots or evidence of xerophthalmia, impaired intestinal absorption, moderate to severe malnutrition including that associated with eating disorders, or recent immigration from areas where high mortality rates from measles have been observed

Note: Monitor patients closely; dosages >25,000 units/kg have been associated with toxicity

Severe deficiency with xerophthalmia: Oral:

Children 1-8 years: 5000-10,000 units/kg/day for 5 days or until recovery occurs

Children >8 years and Adults: 500,000 units/day for 3 days, then 50,000 units/day for 14 days, then 10,000-20,000 units/day for 2 months

Deficiency (without corneal changes): Oral:

Infants <1 year: 100,000 units every 4-6 months

Children 1-8 years: 200,000 units every 4-6 months

Children >8 years and Adults: 100,000 units/day for 3 days then 50,000 units/day for 14 days

Deficiency: I.M.: **Note:** I.M. route is indicated when oral administration is not feasible or when absorption is insufficient (malabsorption syndrome):

Infants: 7500-15,000 units/day for 10 days

Children 1-8 years: 17,500-35,000 units/day for 10 days

Children >8 years and Adults: 100,000 units/day for 3 days, followed by 50,000 units/day for 2 weeks

Note: Follow-up therapy with an oral therapeutic multivitamin (containing additional vitamin A) is recommended:

Low Birth Weight Infants: Additional vitamin A is recommended, however, no dosage amount has been established

Children ≤8 years: 5000-10,000 units/day

Children >8 years and Adults: 10,000-20,000 units/day

Malabsorption syndrome (prophylaxis): Children >8 years and Adults: Oral: 10,000-50,000 units/day of water miscible product

Dietary supplement: Oral:

Infants up to 6 months: 1500 units/day

Children:

6 months to 3 years: 1500-2000 units/day

4-6 years: 2500 units/day

7-10 years: 3300-3500 units/day

Children >10 years and Adults: 4000-5000 units/day

Administration Do not give by I.V. push.

Reference Range 1 RE = 1 retinol equivalent; 1 RE = 1 µg retinol or 6 µg beta-carotene; Normal levels of Vitamin A in serum = 80-300 units/mL

Patient Information Avoid use of mineral oil when taking drug; take with food; report nausea, vomiting, anorexia, malaise, drying or cracking of skin or lips, irritability, headache, or hair loss

Dosage Forms CAP [softgel]: 10,000 units, 25,000 units. **INJ, solution** (Aquasol A®): 50,000 units/mL (2 mL). **TAB** (Palmitate-A®): 5000 units, 15,000 units

♦ **Vitamin A Acid** *see* Tretinoin (Topical) *on page 1260*

Vitamin A and Vitamin D (VYE ta min aye & VYE ta min dee)

U.S. Brand Names A and D® Ointment [OTC]; Baza® Clear [OTC]; Clocream® [OTC]; Sween Cream® [OTC]

Synonyms Cod Liver Oil

Therapeutic Category Topical Skin Product

Use Temporary relief of discomfort due to chapped skin, diaper rash, minor burns, abrasions, as well as irritations associated with ostomy skin care

Pregnancy Risk Factor B

Dosage Topical: Apply locally with gentle massage as needed

Dosage Forms CAP: Vitamin A 1250 int. units and vitamin D 135 int. units; Vitamin A 5000 int. units and vitamin D 400 int. units; Vitamin A 10,000 int. units and vitamin D 400 int. units; Vitamin A 25,000 int. units and vitamin D 400 int. units. **CRM** (Sween Cream®): 14 g, 57 g, 142 g, 255 g. **OINT:** 5 g, 60 g, 120 g, 454 g; (A and D® Ointment): 45 g, 120 g, 454 g; (Baza® Clear): 15 g, 50 g, 150 g, 240 g; (Clocream®): 30 g

♦ **Vitamin B₁** *see* Thiamine *on page 1214*
♦ **Vitamin B₂** *see* Riboflavin *on page 1093*
♦ **Vitamin B₃** *see* Niacin *on page 897*
♦ **Vitamin B₃** *see* Niacinamide *on page 899*
♦ **Vitamin B₆** *see* Pyridoxine *on page 1067*
♦ **Vitamin B₁₂** *see* Cyanocobalamin *on page 318*
♦ **Vitamin B₁₂** *see* Hydroxocobalamin *on page 637*

Vitamin B Complex Combinations

(VYE ta min bee KOM pleks kom bi NAY shuns)

U.S. Brand Names Allbee® C-800 [OTC]; Allbee® C-800 + Iron [OTC]; Allbee® with C [OTC]; Apatate® [OTC]; Diatx™; DiatxFe™; Gevrabon® [OTC]; NephPlex® Rx; Nephrocaps®; Nephron FA®; Nephro-Vite®; Nephro-Vite® Rx; Stresstabs® B-Complex [OTC]; Stresstabs® B-Complex + Iron [OTC]; Stresstabs® B-Complex + Zinc [OTC]; Surbex-T® [OTC]; Trinsicon®; Z-Bec® [OTC]

Synonyms B Complex Combinations; B Vitamin Combinations

Therapeutic Category Vitamin

Use Supplement for use in the wasting syndrome in chronic renal failure, uremia, impaired metabolic functions of the kidney, dialysis; labeled for OTC use as a dietary supplement

Pregnancy Risk Factor A (RDA recommended doses)

Dosage Oral: Adults:

Dietary supplement: One tablet daily
    Aptate® liquid: One teaspoonful daily, 1 hour prior to mid-day meal
    Gevabron® liquid: Two tablespoonsful (30 mL) once daily; shake well before use
Renal patients: One tablet or capsule daily between meals; take after treatment if on dialysis
    Nephron FA®: Two tablets once daily, between meals

Dosage Forms Content varies depending on product used.

♦ **Vitamin C** *see* Ascorbic Acid *on page 117*
♦ **Vitamin D₂** *see* Ergocalciferol *on page 449*

Vitamin E (VYE ta min ee)

U.S. Brand Names Aqua Gem E® [OTC]; Aquasol E® [OTC]; E-Gems® [OTC]; Key-E® [OTC]; Key-E® Kaps [OTC]

Synonyms *d*-Alpha Tocopherol; *dl*-Alpha Tocopherol

Therapeutic Category Vitamin, Fat Soluble; Vitamin, Topical

Use Prevention and treatment hemolytic anemia secondary to vitamin E deficiency, dietary supplement

Unlabeled/Investigational Use To reduce the risk of bronchopulmonary dysplasia or retrolental fibroplasia in infants exposed to high concentrations of oxygen; prevention and treatment of tardive dyskinesia and Alzheimer's disease

Pregnancy Risk Factor A/C (dose exceeding RDA recommendation)

Contraindications Hypersensitivity to vitamin E or any component of the formulation; I.V. route

Warnings/Precautions May induce vitamin K deficiency; necrotizing enterocolitis has been associated with oral administration of large dosages (eg, >200 units/day) of a hyperosmolar vitamin E preparation in low birth weight infants

Drug Interactions

Increased Effect/Toxicity: Vitamin E may alter the effect of vitamin K actions on clotting factors resulting in an increase hypoprothrombinemic response to warfarin; monitor.

Decreased Effect: Vitamin E may impair the hematologic response to iron in children with iron-deficiency anemia; monitor.

Mechanism of Action Prevents oxidation of vitamin A and C; protects polyunsaturated fatty acids in membranes from attack by free radicals and protects red blood cells against hemolysis

Pharmacodynamics/Kinetics

Absorption: Oral: Depends on presence of bile; reduced in conditions of malabsorption, in low birth weight premature infants, and as dosage increases; water miscible preparations are better absorbed than oil preparations

Distribution: To all body tissues, especially adipose tissue, where it is stored

Metabolism: Hepatic to glucuronides

(Continued)

Vitamin E *(Continued)*

Excretion: Feces

Dosage One unit of vitamin E = 1 mg *dl*-alpha-tocopherol acetate. Oral:

Recommended daily allowance (RDA):

Premature infants ≤3 months: 17 mg (25 units)

Infants:

≤6 months: 3 mg (4.5 units)

7-12 months: 4 mg (6 units)

Children:

1-3 years: 6 mg (9 units); upper limit of intake should not exceed 200 mg/day

4-8 years: 7 mg (10.5 units); upper limit of intake should not exceed 300 mg/day

9-13 years: 11 mg (16.5 units); upper limit of intake should not exceed 600 mg/day

14-18 years: 15 mg (22.5 units); upper limit of intake should not exceed 800 mg/day

Adults: 15 mg (22.5 units); upper limit of intake should not exceed 1000 mg/day

Pregnant female:

≤18 years: 15 mg (22.5 units); upper level of intake should not exceed 800 mg/day

19-50 years: 15 mg (22.5 units); upper level of intake should not exceed 1000 mg/day

Lactating female:

≤18 years: 19 mg (28.5 units); upper level of intake should not exceed 800 mg/day

19-50 years: 19 mg (28.5 units); upper level of intake should not exceed 1000 mg/day

Vitamin E deficiency:

Children (with malabsorption syndrome): 1 unit/kg/day of water miscible vitamin E (to raise plasma tocopherol concentrations to the normal range within 2 months and to maintain normal plasma concentrations)

Adults: 60-75 units/day

Prevention of vitamin E deficiency: Adults: 30 units/day

Prevention of retinopathy of prematurity or BPD secondary to O_2 therapy (AAP considers this use investigational and routine use is not recommended):

Retinopathy prophylaxis: 15-30 units/kg/day to maintain plasma levels between 1.5-2 μg/mL (may need as high as 100 units/kg/day)

Cystic fibrosis, beta-thalassemia, sickle cell anemia may require higher daily maintenance doses:

Children:

Cystic fibrosis: 100-400 units/day

Beta-thalassemia: 750 units/day

Adults:

Sickle cell: 450 units/day

Alzheimer's disease: 1000 units twice daily

Tardive dyskinesia: 1600 units/day

Monitoring Parameters Monitor plasma tocopherol concentrations (normal range: 6-14 mcg/mL)

Reference Range Therapeutic: 0.8-1.5 mg/dL (SI: 19-35 μmol/L), some method variation

Patient Information Drops can be placed directly in the mouth or mixed with cereal, fruit juice, or other food; take only the prescribed dose. Vitamin E toxicity appears as blurred vision, diarrhea, dizziness, flu-like symptoms, nausea, headache; swallow capsules whole, do not crush or chew

Dosage Forms CAP: 100 units, 200 units, 400 units, 500 units, 600 units, 1000 units; (Aqua Gem E®, Key-E Kaps®): 200 units, 400 units; (E-Gems®): 30 units, 100 units, 600 units, 800 units, 1000 units, 1200 units. **CRM:** 100 units/g (60 g); (Key-E®): 30 units/g (60 g, 120 g, 480 g). **OIL:** 100 units/0.25 mL (60 mL); 1150 units/0.25 mL (30 mL, 60 mL, 120 mL); (E-Gem®): 100 units/10 drops (15 mL, 60 mL). **OINT, topical** (Key-E®): 30 units/g (60 g, 120 g, 480 g). **POWDER** (Key-E®): 700 units/dose (15 g, 75 g, 1000 g). **SOLN, oral drops** (Aquasol E®): 15 units/0.3 mL (12 mL, 30 mL). **SUPP** (Key-E®): 30 units (12s, 24s). **SPRAY** (Key-E®): 30 units/3 seconds (105 g). **TAB:** 100 units, 200 units, 400 units, 500 units, 800 units; (Key-E®): 100 units, 200 units, 400 units

♦ **Vitamin G** *see* Riboflavin *on page 1093*

♦ **Vitamin K₁** *see* Phytonadione *on page 1000*

Vitamins (Multiple/Oral) *(VYE ta mins, MUL ti pul/OR al)*

Related Information

Multivitamin Products *on page 1382*

U.S. Brand Names Centrum® [OTC]; Centrum® Performance™ [OTC]; Centrum® Silver® [OTC]; Geritol® Tonic [OTC]; Iberet® [OTC]; Iberet®-500 [OTC]; Iberet-Folic-500®; One-A-Day® 50 Plus Formula [OTC]; One-A-Day® Active Formula [OTC]; One-A -Day® Essential Formula [OTC]; One-A-Day® Maximum Formula [OTC]; One-A- Day® Men's Formula [OTC]; One-A-Day® Today [OTC]; One-A-Day® Women's Formula [OTC]; Theragran® Heart Right™ [OTC]; Theragran-M® Advanced Formula [OTC]; Vicon Forte®; Vicon Plus® [OTC]; Vi-Daylin® + Iron Liquid [OTC]; Vi-Daylin® Liquid [OTC]; Vitacon Forte

Synonyms Multiple Vitamins; Therapeutic Multivitamins; Vitamins, Multiple (Oral); Vitamins, Multiple (Therapeutic); Vitamins, Multiple With Iron

Therapeutic Category Vitamin

Use Prevention/treatment of vitamin and mineral deficiencies; labeled for OTC use as a dietary supplement

Pregnancy Risk Factor A (at RDA recommended dose)

Contraindications Hypersensitivity to any component of the formulation; pre-existing hypervitaminosis

Warnings/Precautions RDA values are not requirements, but are recommended daily intakes of certain essential nutrients; use with caution in patients with severe renal or hepatic dysfunction or failure. Adult preparations may contain amounts of ethanol or iron which should not be used in children.

Common Adverse Reactions Refer to individual vitamin monographs.

Dosage Oral: Adults: Daily dose of adult preparations varies by product. Generally, 1 tablet or capsule or 5-15 mL of liquid per day. Consult package labeling. Prescription doses may be higher for burn or cystic fibrosis patients.

Administration May administer with food to decrease stomach upset.

Reference Range Recommended daily allowances are published by Food and Nutrition Board, National Research Council - National Academy of Sciences and are revised periodically. RDA quantities apply only to healthy persons and are not intended to cover therapeutic nutrition requirements in disease or other abnormal states (ie, metabolic disorders, weight reduction, chronic disease, drug therapy).

Patient Information Do not take more than the recommended dose. May take with food to decrease stomach upset. May cause constipation.

Dosage Forms CAP: (Vitacon Forte, Vicon Plus®). **CAPLET:** (Theragran® Heart Right™, Theragran-M® Advanced Formula). **LIQ:** (Centrum®, Geritol® Tonic, Iberet®, Iberet®-500, Vi-Daylin®, ViDaylin® + Iron). **TAB:** (Centrum®, Centrum® Performance™, Centrum® Silver®, Iberet®-500, Iberet-Folic-500®, One-A-Day® 50 Plus Formula, One-A-Day® Active Formula, One-A-Day® Essential Formula, One-A-Day® Maximum Formula, One-A-Day® Men's Formula, One-A-Day® Today, One-A-Day® Women's Formula). **TAB, chewable:** (Centrum®)

Voriconazole (vor i KOE na zole)

Related Information
Antifungal Agents Comparison *on page 1362*

U.S. Brand Names VFEND®

Synonyms UK109496

Therapeutic Category Antifungal Agent, Oral; Antifungal Agent, Parental; Antifungal Agent, Systemic

Use Treatment of invasive aspergillosis; treatment of esophageal candidiasis; treatment of serious fungal infections caused by *Scedosporium apiospermum* and *Fusarium* spp (including *Fusarium solani*) in patients intolerant of, or refractory to, other therapy

Pregnancy Risk Factor D

Contraindications Hypersensitivity to voriconazole or any component of the formulation (cross-reaction with other azole antifungal agents may occur but has not been established, use caution); coadministration of CYP3A4 substrates which may lead to QT$_c$ prolongation (cisapride, pimozide, or quinidine); coadministration with barbiturates (long acting), carbamazepine, ergot alkaloids, rifampin, rifabutin, and sirolimus; pregnancy (unless risk:benefit justifies use)

Warnings/Precautions Visual changes are commonly associated with treatment. Patients should be warned to avoid tasks which depend on vision, including operating machinery or driving. Changes are reversible on discontinuation following brief exposure/treatment regimens (≤28 days).

Serious hepatic reactions (including hepatitis, cholestasis, and fulminant hepatic failure) have occurred during treatment, primarily in patients with serious concomitant medical conditions. However, hepatotoxicity has occurred in patients with no identifiable risk factors. Use caution in patients with pre-existing hepatic impairment (dose adjustment required).

Voriconazole tablets contain lactose; avoid administration in hereditary galactose intolerance, Lapp lactase deficiency, or glucose-galactose malabsorption. Suspension contains sucrose; use caution with fructose intolerance, sucrose-isomaltase deficiency, or glucose-galactose malabsorption. Avoid/limit use of intravenous formulation in patients with renal impairment; intravenous formulation contains excipient sulfobutyl ether beta-cyclodextrin (SBECD), which (Continued)

Voriconazole *(Continued)*

may accumulate in renal insufficiency. Infusion-related reactions may occur with intravenous dosing. Consider discontinuation of infusion if reaction is severe.

Use caution in patients with an increased risk of arrhythmia (concurrent QT_c-prolonging drugs, hypokalemia, cardiomyopathy, or prior cardiotoxic therapy).

Avoid use in pregnancy, unless an evaluation of the potential benefit justifies possible risk to the fetus. Safety and efficacy have not been established in children <12 years of age.

Common Adverse Reactions Note: Includes adverse reactions reported from all trials, including trials conducted in immunocompromised patients; cause:effect relationship not established for many reactions

>10%: Ocular: Visual changes (photophobia, color changes, increased or decreased visual acuity, or blurred vision occur in ~30%)

1% to 10%:

Cardiovascular: Tachycardia (3%), hypertension (2%), hypotension (2%), vasodilation (2%), peripheral edema (1%)

Central nervous system: Fever (6%), chills (4%), headache (3%), hallucinations (3%), dizziness (1%)

Dermatologic: Rash (6%), pruritus (1%)

Endocrine & metabolic: Hypokalemia (2%), hypomagnesemia (1%)

Gastrointestinal: Nausea (6%), vomiting (5%), abdominal pain (2%), diarrhea (1%), xerostomia (1%)

Hematologic: Thrombocytopenia (1%)

Hepatic: Alkaline phosphatase increased (4%), serum transaminases increased (2%), AST increased (2%), ALT increased (2%), cholestatic jaundice (1%)

Renal: Acute renal failure (1%)

Drug Interactions

Cytochrome P450 Effect: Substrate of CYP2C8/9 (major), 2C19 (major), 3A4 (minor); **Inhibits** CYP2C8/9 (weak), 2C19 (weak), 3A4 (moderate)

Increased Effect/Toxicity: Voriconazole may increase the serum concentrations of cisapride, pimozide leading to malignant arrhythmias; use in contraindicated. Concurrent use of QT_c-prolonging agents (including class Ia and III antiarrhythmics) may increase risk of arrhythmias. Serum levels of ergot alkaloids may be increased by voriconazole, leading to ergot toxicity; concurrent use is contraindicated. Rifabutin serum levels are increased by voriconazole; concurrent use is contraindicated. Serum concentrations of busulfan, docetaxel, and dofetilide may be increased; avoid concurrent use.

Serum concentrations of immunosuppressants (cyclosporine, sirolimus, and tacrolimus) may be increased; concurrent use of sirolimus is contraindicated. Decrease cyclosporine dosage by 50% when initiating voriconazole, decreased tacrolimus dosage by 66% when initiating voriconazole.

Serum levels of voriconazole may be increased by efavirenz or delavirdine. Indinavir did not appear to alter voriconazole serum concentrations during concurrent treatment; other protease inhibitors may result in increased voriconazole concentrations.

Voriconazole may increase the serum concentrations of benzodiazepines (oxidatively metabolized), buspirone, calcium channel blockers, methylprednisolone, quinidine, sulfonylureas, trimetrexate, vinca alkaloids, or zolpidem. In addition, the anticoagulant effect of warfarin may be increased. Serum concentrations of HMG-CoA reductase inhibitors may be increased (except pravastatin and fluvastatin); increasing the risk of myopathy/rhabdomyolysis. Changes in gastric acidity (due to H_2 antagonists or proton pump inhibitors) do not appear to significantly affect voriconazole absorption. However, voriconazole may significantly increase serum levels of omeprazole. For omeprazole dosages >40 mg/day, reduce omeprazole dosage by 50%. Serum levels of other proton pump inhibitors may also be increased.

Decreased Effect: CYP2C8/9 inducers may decrease the levels/effects of voriconazole; example inducers include carbamazepine, phenobarbital, phenytoin, rifampin, rifapentine, and secobarbital. CYP2C19 inducers may decrease the levels/effects of voriconazole; example inducers include aminoglutethimide, carbamazepine, phenytoin, and rifampin. Rifampin decreases voriconazole's serum concentration to levels which are no longer effective; avoid concurrent use. When used with phenytoin, prospective adjustment of voriconazole dosage is recommended. Serum levels of voriconazole may be decreased by efavirenz or nevirapine.

Mechanism of Action Interferes with fungal cytochrome P450 activity, decreasing ergosterol synthesis (principal sterol in fungal cell membrane) and inhibiting fungal cell membrane formation.

Pharmacodynamics/Kinetics

Absorption: Well absorbed after oral administration

Distribution: V_d: 4.6 L/kg

Protein binding: 58%

Metabolism: Hepatic, via CYP2C19 (major pathway) and CYP2C9 and CYP3A4 (less significant); saturable (may demonstrate nonlinearity)

Bioavailability: 96%

Half-life elimination: Variable, dose-dependent

Time to peak: 1-2 hours

Excretion: Urine (as inactive metabolites)

Dosage

Children <12 years: No data available

Children ≥12 years and Adults:

Invasive aspergillosis and other serious fungal infections: I.V.: Initial: Loading dose: 6 mg/kg every 12 hours for 2 doses; followed by maintenance dose of 4 mg/kg every 12 hours

Conversion to oral dosing:

Patients <40 kg: 100 mg every 12 hours; increase to 150 mg every 12 hours in patients who fail to respond adequately

Patients ≥40 kg: 200 mg every 12 hours; increase to 300 mg every 12 hours in patients who fail to respond adequately

Esophageal candidiasis: Oral:

Patients <40 kg: 100 mg every 12 hours

Patients ≥40 kg: 200 mg every 12 hours

Note: Treatment should continue for a minimum of 14 days, and for at least 7 days following resolution of symptoms.

Dosage adjustment in patients unable to tolerate treatment:

I.V.: Dose may be reduced to 3 mg/kg every 12 hours

Oral: Dose may be reduced in 50 mg increments to a minimum dosage of 200 mg every 12 hours in patients weighing ≥40 kg (100 mg every 12 hours in patients <40 kg)

Dosage adjustment in patients receiving concomitant phenytoin:

I.V.: Increase maintenance dosage to 5 mg/kg every 12 hours

Oral: Increase dose from 200 mg to 400 mg every 12 hours in patients ≥40 kg (100 mg to 200 mg every 12 hours in patients <40 kg)

Dosage adjustment in renal impairment: In patients with Cl_{cr} <50 mL/minute, accumulation of the intravenous vehicle (SBECD) occurs. After initial loading dose, oral voriconazole should be administered to these patients, unless an assessment of the benefit:risk to the patient justifies the use of I.V. voriconazole. Monitor serum creatinine and change to oral voriconazole therapy when possible.

Dosage adjustment in hepatic impairment:

Mild-to-moderate hepatic dysfunction (Child-Pugh Class A and B): Following standard loading dose, reduce maintenance dosage by 50%

Severe hepatic impairment: Should only be used if benefit outweighs risk; monitor closely for toxicity

Administration

Oral: Administer 1 hour before or 1 hour after a meal.

I.V.: Infuse over 1-2 hours (rate not to exceed 3 mg/kg/hour)

Monitoring Parameters Hepatic function, visual function, renal function

Dosage Forms INJ, powder for reconstitution: 200 mg. **POWDER, oral suspension:** 200 mg/5 mL (70 mL). **TAB:** 50 mg, 200 mg

Warfarin (WAR far in)

U.S. Brand Names Coumadin®; Jantoven™

Synonyms Warfarin Sodium

Therapeutic Category Anticoagulant, Coumarin Derivative

Use Prophylaxis and treatment of venous thrombosis, pulmonary embolism and thromboembolic disorders; atrial fibrillation with risk of embolism and as an adjunct in the prophylaxis of systemic embolism after myocardial infarction

Unlabeled/Investigational Use Prevention of recurrent transient ischemic attacks and to reduce risk of recurrent myocardial infarction

Pregnancy Risk Factor X

Contraindications Hypersensitivity to warfarin or any component of the formulation; hemorrhagic tendencies; hemophilia; thrombocytopenia purpura; leukemia; recent or potential surgery of the eye or CNS; major regional lumbar block anesthesia or surgery resulting in large, open surfaces; patients bleeding from the GI, respiratory, or GU tract; threatened abortion; aneurysm; ascorbic acid deficiency; history of bleeding diathesis; prostatectomy; continuous tube drainage of the small intestine; polyarthritis; diverticulitis; emaciation; malnutrition; cerebrovascular hemorrhage; eclampsia/pre-eclampsia; blood dyscrasias; severe uncontrolled or malignant hypertension; severe hepatic disease; pericarditis or pericardial effusion; subacute bacterial endocarditis; visceral carcinoma; following spinal puncture and other diagnostic or therapeutic procedures with potential for significant bleeding; history of warfarin-induced necrosis; an unreliable, noncompliant patient; alcoholism; patient who has a history of falls or is a significant fall risk; pregnancy

Warnings/Precautions

Do not switch brands once desired therapeutic response has been achieved

Use with caution in patients with active tuberculosis or diabetes

Concomitant use with vitamin K may decrease anticoagulant effect; monitor carefully

(Continued)

Warfarin *(Continued)*

Concomitant use with NSAIDs or aspirin may cause severe GI irritation and also increase the risk of bleeding due to impaired platelet function

Salicylates may further increase warfarin's effect by displacing it from plasma protein binding sites

Patients with protein C or S deficiency are at increased risk of skin necrosis syndrome

Before committing an elderly patient to long-term anticoagulation therapy, their risk for bleeding complications secondary to falls, drug interactions, living situation, and cognitive status should be considered. The risk for bleeding complications decreases with the duration of therapy and may increase with advancing age.

If a patient is to undergo an invasive surgical procedure (dental to actual minor/major surgery), warfarin should be stopped 3 days before the scheduled surgery date and the INR/PT should be checked prior to the procedure

Common Adverse Reactions As with all anticoagulants, bleeding is the major adverse effect of warfarin. Hemorrhage may occur at virtually any site. Risk is dependent on multiple variables, including the intensity of anticoagulation and patient susceptibility.

Additional adverse effects are often related to idiosyncratic reactions, and the frequency cannot be accurately estimated.

Cardiovascular: Vasculitis, edema, hemorrhagic shock

Central nervous system: Fever, lethargy, malaise, asthenia, pain, headache, dizziness, stroke

Dermatologic: Rash, dermatitis, bullous eruptions, urticaria, pruritus, alopecia

Gastrointestinal: Anorexia, nausea, vomiting, stomach cramps, abdominal pain, diarrhea, flatulence, gastrointestinal bleeding, taste disturbance, mouth ulcers

Genitourinary: Priapism, hematuria

Hematologic: Hemorrhage, leukopenia, unrecognized bleeding sites (eg, colon cancer) may be uncovered by anticoagulation, retroperitoneal hematoma, agranulocytosis

Hepatic: Increased transaminases, hepatic injury, jaundice,

Neuromuscular & skeletal: Paresthesia, osteoporosis

Respiratory: Hemoptysis, epistaxis, pulmonary hemorrhage, tracheobronchial calcification

Miscellaneous: Hypersensitivity/allergic reactions

Skin necrosis/gangrene, due to paradoxical local thrombosis, is a known but rare risk of warfarin therapy. Its onset is usually within the first few days of therapy and is frequently localized to the limbs, breast or penis. The risk of this effect is increased in patients with protein C or S deficiency.

"Purple toes syndrome," caused by cholesterol microembolization, also occurs rarely. Typically, this occurs after several weeks of therapy, and may present as a dark, purplish, mottled discoloration of the plantar and lateral surfaces. Other manifestations of cholesterol microembolization may include rash; livedo reticularis; gangrene; abrupt and intense pain in lower extremities; abdominal, flank, or back pain; hematuria; renal insufficiency; hypertension; cerebral ischemia; spinal cord infarction; or other symptom of vascular compromise.

Enhanced Anticoagulant Effects

Decrease Vitamin K	Displace Anticoagulant	Inhibit Metabolism	Other
Oral antibiotics: Can ↑/↓ INR. Check INR 3 days after a patient begins antibiotics to see the INR value and adjust the warfarin dose accordingly	Chloral hydrate Clofibrate Diazoxide Ethacrynic acid Miconazole (including intravaginal use) Nalidixic acid Salicylates Sulfonamides Sulfonylureas	Allopurinol Amiodarone Azole antifungals Capecitabine Chloramphenicol Chlorpropamide Cimetidine Ciprofloxacin Co-trimoxazole Disulfiram Ethanol (acute ingestion)[1] Flutamide Isoniazid Metronidazole Norfloxacin Ofloxacin Omeprazole Phenytoin Propafenone Propoxyphene Quinidine "Statins"[2] Sulfinpyrazone Sulfonamides Tamoxifen Tolbutamide Zafirlukast Zileuton	Acetaminophen Anabolic steroids Capecitabine Celecoxib Clarithromycin Clofibrate Danazol Erythromycin Gemfibrozil Glucagon Influenza vaccine Propranolol Propylthiouracil Ranitidine Rofecoxib SSRIs Sulindac Tetracycline Thyroid drugs Vitamin E (≥400 int. units)

[1]The hypoprothrombinemic effect of oral anticoagulants has been reported to be both increased and decreased during chronic and excessive alcohol ingestion. Data are insufficient to predict the direction of this interaction in alcoholic patients.

[2]Particularly lovastatin and fluvastatin; others (atorvastatin, pravastatin) rarely associated with increased PT.

Drug Interactions

Cytochrome P450 Effect: Substrate of CYP1A2 (minor), 2C8/9 (major), 2C19 (minor), 3A4 (minor); **Inhibits** CYP2C8/9 (moderate), 2C19 (weak)

Increased Effect/Toxicity: CYP2C8/9 inhibitors may increase the levels/effects of warfarin; example inhibitors include delavirdine, fluconazole, gemfibrozil, ketoconazole, nicardipine, NSAIDs, and sulfonamides.

Also see tables on previous page and below.

Increased Bleeding Tendency

Inhibit Platelet Aggregation	Inhibit Procoagulant Factors	Ulcerogenic Drugs
Cephalosporins	Antimetabolites	Adrenal corticosteroids
Clopidogrel	Quinidine	Indomethacin
Dipyridamole	Quinine	Potassium products
Indomethacin	Salicylates	Salicylates
Penicillin, parenteral		
Salicylates		
Sulfinpyrazone		
Ticlopidine		

Use of these agents with oral anticoagulants may increase the chances of hemorrhage.

Decreased Effect: CYP2C8/9 inducers may decrease the levels/effects of warfarin; example inducers include carbamazepine, phenobarbital, phenytoin, rifampin, rifapentine, and secobarbital. Also see table.

Decreased Anticoagulant Effects

Induction of Enzymes		Increased Procoagulant Factors	Decreased Drug Absorption	Other
Barbiturates	Nafcillin	Estrogens	Aluminum hydroxide	Ethchlorvynol
Carbamazepine	Phenytoin	Oral contraceptives	Cholestyramine[1]	Griseofulvin
Glutethimide	Rifampin	Vitamin K (including	Colestipol[1]	Spironolactone[2]
Griseofulvin		nutritional supplements)		Sucralfate

Decreased anticoagulant effect may occur when these drugs are administered with oral anticoagulants.

[1]Cholestyramine and colestipol may increase the anticoagulant effect by binding vitamin K in the gut; yet, the decreased drug absorption appears to be of more concern.

[2]Diuretic-induced hemoconcentration with subsequent concentration of clotting factors has been reported to decrease the effects of oral anticoagulants.

Mechanism of Action Interferes with hepatic synthesis of vitamin K-dependent coagulation factors (II, VII, IX, X)

Pharmacodynamics/Kinetics

Onset of action: Anticoagulation: Oral: 36-72 hours

Peak effect: Full therapeutic effect: 5-7 days; INR may increase in 36-72 hours

Duration: 2-5 days

Absorption: Oral: Rapid

Metabolism: Hepatic

Half-life elimination: 20-60 hours; Mean: 40 hours; highly variable among individuals

Dosage

Oral:

Infants and Children: 0.05-0.34 mg/kg/day; infants <12 months of age may require doses at or near the high end of this range; consistent anticoagulation may be difficult to maintain in children <5 years of age

Adults: Initial dosing must be individualized. Consider the patient (hepatic function, cardiac function, age, nutritional status, concurrent therapy, risk of bleeding) in addition to prior dose response (if available) and the clinical situation. Start 5-10 mg daily for 2 days. Adjust dose according to INR results; usual maintenance dose ranges from 2-10 mg daily (individual patients may require loading and maintenance doses outside these general guidelines).

Note: Lower starting doses may be required for patients with hepatic impairment, poor nutrition, CHF, elderly, or a high risk of bleeding. Higher initial doses may be reasonable in selected patients (ie, receiving enzyme-inducing agents and with low risk of bleeding).

I.V. (administer as a slow bolus injection): 2-5 mg/day

Dosing adjustment/comments in hepatic disease: Monitor effect at usual doses; the response to oral anticoagulants may be markedly enhanced in obstructive jaundice (due to reduced vitamin K absorption) and also in hepatitis and cirrhosis (due to decreased production of vitamin K-dependent clotting factors); prothrombin index should be closely monitored

Administration

Oral: Do not take with food. Take at the same time each day.

I.V.: Administer as a slow bolus injection over 1-2 minutes; avoid all I.M. injections

Monitoring Parameters Prothrombin time, hematocrit, INR

Reference Range

Therapeutic: 2-5 µg/mL (SI: 6.5-16.2 µmol/L)

Prothrombin time should be 1½ to 2 times the control or INR should be ↑ 2 to 3 times based upon indication

Normal prothrombin time: 10-13 seconds

INR ranges based upon indication: See table on next page.

(Continued)

Warfarin *(Continued)*

INR Ranges Based Upon Indication

Indication	Targeted INR Range	Targeted INR
Acute myocardial infarction with risk factor[1]	2.0-3.0	2.5
Atrial fibrillation (moderate- to high-risk patients)	2.0-3.0	2.5
Bileaflet or tilting disk mechanical aortic valve (NSR, NL LA)	2.0-3.0	2.5
Bileaflet mechanical aortic valve with atrial fibrillation	2.5-3.5	3
Bileaflet mechanical aortic valve with atrial fibrillation with ASA 80-100 mg/day	2.0-3.0	2.5
Bileaflet or tilting disk mechanical mitral valve	2.5-3.5	3
Bileaflet or tilting disk mechanical mitral valve with ASA 80-100 mg/day	2.0-3.0	2.5
Bioprosthetic mitral or aortic valve[2]	2.0-3.0	2.5
Bioprosthetic mitral or aortic valve with atrial fibrillation	2.0-3.0	2.5
Cardioembolic cerebral ischemic events	2.0-3.0	2.5
Mechanical heart valve (caged ball, caged disk) with ASA 80-100 mg/day	2.5-3.5	3
Mechanical prosthetic valve with systemic embolism despite adequate anticoagulation[3]	2.5-3.5	3
Rheumatic mitral valve disease and NSR (left atrial diameter >5.5 cm)	2.0-3.0	2.5
Venous thromboembolism	2.0-3.0	2.5

[1]Up to 3 months of therapy following heparin or LMWH in patients with anterior Q-wave infarction, severe left-ventricular dysfunction, mural thrombus on 2D echo, atrial fibrillation, history of systemic or pulmonary embolism, congestive heart failure.

[2]Maintained for 3 months; chronic low-dose aspirin (80 mg/day) after warfarin therapy.

[3]Add ASA 80-100 mg/day.

For complete discussion, *Chest,* 2001, 119 (Suppl):1S-370S

> Warfarin levels are not used for monitoring degree of anticoagulation. They may be useful if a patient with unexplained coagulopathy is using the drug surreptitiously or if it is unclear whether clinical resistance is due to true drug resistance or lack of drug intake.
>
> Normal prothrombin time (PT): 10.9-12.9 seconds. Healthy premature newborns have prolonged coagulation test screening results (eg, PT, aPTT, TT) which return to normal adult values at approximately 6 months of age. Healthy prematures, however, do not develop spontaneous hemorrhage or thrombotic complications because of a balance between procoagulants and inhibitors
>
> The World Health Organization (WHO), in cooperation with other regulatory-advisory bodies, has developed system of standardizing the reporting of PT values through the determination of the International Normalized Ratio (INR). The INR involves the standardization of the PT by the generation of two pieces of information: the PT ratio and the International Sensitivity Index (ISI)
>
> Therapeutic ranges are now available or being developed to assist practicing physicians in their treatment of patients with a wide variety of thrombotic disorders

Patient Information
Call your prescriber immediately if you have any of the following:
> A fever or developing illness, including vomiting, diarrhea, or infection
> Pain, swelling, discomfort or any other unusual symptoms
> Prolonged bleeding from cuts, nosebleeds
> Unusual bleeding from gums when brushing teeth
> Increased menstrual flow or vaginal bleeding
> Red or dark brown urine
> Red or tarry-black stools
> Unusual bruising for unknown reasons
> Pregnancy or planned pregnancy

Call your prescriber immediately if you have serious fall or trauma. Discuss any new medications with your prescriber or pharmacist; talk to your prescriber before starting, changing, or discontinuing any medication (including OTC medications). Notify you prescriber immediately with any severe diarrhea (alters absorption of vitamin K) to discuss the need to check INR. Try to keep the same general diet and avoid excessive amounts of alcohol. Carry Medi-Alert® ID identifying drug usage. If you forget to take a pill one day, let your prescriber know. **Do not take another pill to "catch up."** Consult physician before undergoing dental work or elective surgery. Concomitant use of aspirin or nonsteroidal anti-inflammatory medicine, such as Motrin® or Advil®, is **not recommended** unless discussed with your prescriber. It is important to strictly adhere to the prescribed dosing schedule. Dosage is highly individual and may need to be adjusted several times based on lab test results.

Dosage Forms INJ, powder for reconstitution (Coumadin®): 5 mg. **TAB** (Coumadin®, Jantoven™): 1 mg, 2 mg, 2.5 mg, 3 mg, 4 mg, 5 mg, 6 mg, 7.5 mg, 10 mg

- **Wesmycin®** *see* Tetracycline *on page 1206*
- **Westcort®** *see* Hydrocortisone *on page 632*
- **Westhroid®** *see* Thyroid *on page 1222*
- **Wigraine®** *see* Ergotamine *on page 450*
- **WinRho SDF®** *see* Rh₀(D) Immune Globulin *on page 1089*
- **Winstrol®** *see* Stanozolol *on page 1159*
- **Wound Wash Saline™ [OTC]** *see* Sodium Chloride *on page 1146*
- **WR2721** *see* Amifostine *on page 70*
- **WR-139007** *see* Dacarbazine *on page 332*
- **WR-139013** *see* Chlorambucil *on page 255*
- **WR-139021** *see* Carmustine *on page 222*
- **Wycillin [DSC]** *see* Penicillin G Procaine *on page 974*
- **Wytensin® [DSC]** *see* Guanabenz *on page 606*
- **Xalatan®** *see* Latanoprost *on page 719*
- **Xanax®** *see* Alprazolam *on page 59*
- **Xanax XR®** *see* Alprazolam *on page 59*
- **Xeloda®** *see* Capecitabine *on page 209*
- **Xenical®** *see* Orlistat *on page 932*
- **Xigris®** *see* Drotrecogin Alfa *on page 418*
- **Xolair®** *see* Omalizumab *on page 926*
- **Xopenex®** *see* Levalbuterol *on page 726*
- **Xylocaine®** *see* Lidocaine *on page 742*
- **Xylocaine® MPF** *see* Lidocaine *on page 742*
- **Xylocaine® MPF With Epinephrine** *see* Lidocaine and Epinephrine *on page 745*
- **Xylocaine® Viscous** *see* Lidocaine *on page 742*
- **Xylocaine® With Epinephrine** *see* Lidocaine and Epinephrine *on page 745*
- **Xyrem®** *see* Sodium Oxybate *on page 1149*
- **Y-90 Zevalin** *see* Ibritumomab *on page 643*
- **Yasmin®** *see* Ethinyl Estradiol and Drospirenone *on page 478*

Yellow Fever Vaccine (YEL oh FEE ver vak SEEN)

U.S. Brand Names YF-VAX®

Therapeutic Category Vaccine; Vaccine, Live Virus

Use Induction of active immunity against yellow fever virus, primarily among persons traveling or living in areas where yellow fever infection exists. (Some countries require a valid international Certification of Vaccination showing receipt of vaccine; if a pregnant woman is to be vaccinated only to satisfy an international requirement, efforts should be made to obtain a waiver letter.) The WHO requires revaccination every 10 years to maintain traveler's vaccination certificate.

Pregnancy Risk Factor D

Contraindications Hypersensitivity to egg or chick embryo protein, or any component of the formulation; children <9 months of age unless in high risk area; children <4 months of age; pregnancy

Warnings/Precautions Do not use in immunodeficient persons or patients receiving immunosuppressants (eg, steroids, radiation). Patients who are immunosuppressed have a theoretical risk of encephalitis with yellow fever vaccine administration; consider waiving vaccine. Patients on low-dose or short-term corticosteroids, or with asymptomatic HIV infection are not considered immunosuppressant and may receive the vaccine. Have epinephrine available in persons with previous history of egg allergy if the vaccine must be used. Avoid use in infants <9 months and pregnant women unless travel to high-risk areas are unavoidable; avoid use in infants <4 months of age due to risk of encephalitis.

Common Adverse Reactions All serious adverse reactions must be reported to the U.S. Department of Health and Human Services (DHHS) Vaccine Adverse Event Reporting System (VAERS) 1-800-822-7967.

1% to 10%:

Central nervous system: Fever, malaise (7-14 days after administration 2% to 5%), headache (2% to 5%)

Neuromuscular & skeletal: Myalgia (2% to 5%)

Dosage Adults: One dose (0.5 mL) S.C. 10 days to 10 years before travel, booster every 10 years; see Warnings/Precautions

Administration For S.C. injection only. Do not administer I.M. or I.V.; use within 1 hour of reconstitution.

Monitoring Parameters Monitor for adverse effects up to 10 days after vaccination.

Patient Information Immunity develops by the tenth day and WHO requires revaccination every 10 years to maintain travelers' vaccination certificates

Dosage Forms INJ, powder for reconstitution [preservative free; diluent provided]: Not less than 5.04 Log₁₀ plaque-forming units (PFU) [single-dose vial]; not less than 25.2 Log₁₀ plaque-forming units (PFU) [5-dose vial]

- **YF-VAX®** *see* Yellow Fever Vaccine *on page 1319*
- **YM-08310** *see* Amifostine *on page 70*
- **Yodoxin®** *see* Iodoquinol *on page 683*
- **Z4942** *see* Ifosfamide *on page 649*

♦ **Zaditor**™ *see Ketotifen on page 708*

Zafirlukast (za FIR loo kast)

U.S. Brand Names Accolate®

Synonyms ICI 204, 219

Therapeutic Category Leukotriene Receptor Antagonist

Use Prophylaxis and chronic treatment of asthma in adults and children ≥5 years of age

Pregnancy Risk Factor B

Contraindications Hypersensitivity to zafirlukast or any component of the formulation

Warnings/Precautions The clearance of zafirlukast is reduced in patients with stable alcoholic cirrhosis such that the C_{max} and AUC are approximately 50% to 60% greater than those of normal adults.

Zafirlukast is not indicated for use in the reversal of bronchospasm in acute asthma attacks, including status asthmaticus. Therapy with zafirlukast can be continued during acute exacerbations of asthma.

An increased proportion of zafirlukast patients >55 years of age reported infections as compared to placebo-treated patients. These infections were mostly mild or moderate in intensity and predominantly affected the respiratory tract. Infections occurred equally in both sexes, were dose-proportional to total milligrams of zafirlukast exposure and were associated with coadministration of inhaled corticosteroids.

Rare hepatic events have been reported, including hepatitis, hyperbilirubinemia, and hepatic failure. Female patients may be at greater risk. Discontinue **immediately** if liver dysfunction is suspected. If hepatic dysfunction is suspected (due to clinical signs/symptoms) liver function tests should be measured immediately. Do not resume or restart if hepatic function tests are consistent with dysfunction.

Rare cases of eosinophilic vasculitis (Churg-Strauss) have been reported in patients receiving zafirlukast (usually, but not always, associated with reduction in concurrent steroid dosage). No causal relationship established.

Common Adverse Reactions

>10%: Central nervous system: Headache (12.9%)

1% to 10%:

    Central nervous system: Dizziness, pain, fever

    Gastrointestinal: Nausea, diarrhea, abdominal pain, vomiting, dyspepsia

    Hepatic: SGPT elevation

    Neuromuscular & skeletal: Back pain, myalgia, weakness

Drug Interactions

    Cytochrome P450 Effect: Substrate of CYP2C8/9 (major); **Inhibits** CYP1A2 (weak), 2C8/9 (moderate), 2C19 (weak), 2D6 (weak), 3A4 (weak)

    Increased Effect/Toxicity: Zafirlukast concentrations are increased by aspirin. Warfarin effect may be increased with zafirlukast. Zafirlukast may increase theophylline levels.

    Decreased Effect: CYP2C8/9 inducers may decrease the levels/effects of zafirlukast; example inducers include carbamazepine, phenobarbital, phenytoin, rifampin, rifapentine, and secobarbital. Zafirlukast concentrations may be reduced by erythromycin.

Mechanism of Action Zafirlukast is a selectively and competitive leukotriene-receptor antagonist (LTRA) of leukotriene D4 and E4 (LTD4 and LTE4), components of slow-reacting substance of anaphylaxis (SRSA). Cysteinyl leukotriene production and receptor occupation have been correlated with the pathophysiology of asthma, including airway edema, smooth muscle constriction and altered cellular activity associated with the inflammatory process, which contribute to the signs and symptoms of asthma.

Pharmacodynamics/Kinetics

    Protein binding: >99%, primarily to albumin

    Metabolism: Extensively hepatic via CYP2C9

    Bioavailability: Reduced 40% with food

    Half-life elimination: 10 hours

    Time to peak, serum: 3 hours

    Excretion: Urine (10%); feces

Dosage Oral:

    Children <5 years: Safety and effectiveness have not been established

    Children 5-11 years: 10 mg twice daily

    Children ≥12 years and Adults: 20 mg twice daily

    Elderly: The mean dose (mg/kg) normalized AUC and C_{max} increase and plasma clearance decreases with increasing age. In patients >65 years of age, there is a two- to threefold greater C_{max} and AUC compared to younger adults.

    Dosing adjustment in renal impairment: There are no apparent differences in the pharmacokinetics between renally impaired patients and normal subjects.

    Dosing adjustment in hepatic impairment: In patients with hepatic impairment (ie, biopsy-proven cirrhosis), there is a 50% to 60% greater C_{max} and AUC compared to normal subjects.

Administration Administer at least 1 hour before or 2 hours after a meal

Patient Information Take regularly as prescribed, even during symptom-free periods. This medication should be taken on an empty stomach (1 hour before or 2 hours after meals). Do not use to treat acute episodes of asthma. Do not decrease the dose or stop taking any other antiasthma medications unless instructed by a physician. Nursing women should not take zafirlukast. Contact prescriber immediately if experiencing right upper abdominal pain, nausea, fatigue, itching, flu-like symptoms; swelling of the eyes, face, neck, or throat; worsening of condition or anorexia.

Dosage Forms TAB: 10 mg, 20 mg

♦ **Zagam**® *see Sparfloxacin on page 1156*

Zalcitabine (zal SITE a been)

Related Information
Antiretroviral Therapy for HIV Infection *on page 1448*

U.S. Brand Names Hivid®

Synonyms ddC; Dideoxycytidine

Therapeutic Category Antiretroviral Agent, Nucleoside Reverse Transcriptase Inhibitor (NRTI) [Cytosine Analog]

Use In combination with at least two other antiretrovirals in the treatment of patients with HIV infection; it is not recommended that zalcitabine be given in combination with didanosine, stavudine, or lamivudine due to overlapping toxicities, virologic interactions, or lack of clinical data

Pregnancy Risk Factor C

Contraindications Hypersensitivity to zalcitabine or any component of the formulation

Warnings/Precautions Careful monitoring of pancreatic enzymes and liver function tests in patients with a history of pancreatitis, increased amylase, those on parenteral nutrition or with a history of ethanol abuse; discontinue use immediately if pancreatitis is suspected; lactic acidosis and severe hepatomegaly and failure have rarely occurred with zalcitabine resulting in fatality (stop treatment if lactic acidosis or hepatotoxicity occurs); some cases may possibly be related to underlying hepatitis B; use with caution in patients on digitalis, CHF, renal failure, hyperphosphatemia; zalcitabine can cause severe peripheral neuropathy; avoid use, if possible, in patients with pre-existing neuropathy

Common Adverse Reactions
>10%:
  Central nervous system: Fever (5% to 17%), malaise (2% to 13%)
  Neuromuscular & skeletal: Peripheral neuropathy (28%)
1% to 10%:
  Central nervous system: Headache (2%), dizziness (1%), fatigue (4%), seizures (1.3%)
  Dermatologic: Rash (2% to 11%), pruritus (3% to 5%)
  Endocrine & metabolic: Hypoglycemia (2% to 6%), hyponatremia (4%), hyperglycemia (1% to 6%)
  Gastrointestinal: Nausea (3%), dysphagia (1% to 4%), anorexia (4%), abdominal pain (3% to 8%), vomiting (1% to 3%), diarrhea (<1% to 10%), weight loss, oral ulcers (3% to 7%), increased amylase (3% to 8%)
  Hematologic: Anemia (occurs as early as 2-4 weeks), granulocytopenia (usually after 6-8 weeks)
  Hepatic: Abnormal hepatic function (9%), hyperbilirubinemia (2% to 5%)
  Neuromuscular & skeletal: Myalgia (1% to 6%), foot pain
  Respiratory: Pharyngitis (2%), cough (6%), nasal discharge (4%)

Drug Interactions
Increased Effect/Toxicity: Amphotericin, foscarnet, and aminoglycosides may potentiate the risk of developing peripheral neuropathy or other toxicities associated with zalcitabine by interfering with the renal elimination of zalcitabine. Other drugs associated with peripheral neuropathy include chloramphenicol, cisplatin, dapsone, disulfiram, ethionamide, glutethimide, gold, hydralazine, iodoquinol, isoniazid, metronidazole, nitrofurantoin, phenytoin, ribavirin, and vincristine. Concomitant use with zalcitabine may increase risk of peripheral neuropathy. Concomitant use of zalcitabine with didanosine is not recommended. Concomitant use of ribavirin and nucleoside analogues may increase the risk of developing lactic acidosis (includes adefovir, didanosine, lamivudine, stavudine, zalcitabine, zidovudine).

Decreased Effect: It is not recommended that zalcitabine be given in combination with didanosine, stavudine, or lamivudine due to overlapping toxicities, virologic interactions, or lack of clinical data. Doxorubicin and lamivudine have been shown *in vitro* to decrease zalcitabine phosphorylation. Magnesium/aluminum-containing antacids and metoclopramide may decrease the absorption of zalcitabine.

Mechanism of Action Purine nucleoside analog, zalcitabine or 2',3'-dideoxycytidine (ddC) is converted to active metabolite ddCTP; lack the presence of the 3'-hydroxyl group necessary for phosphodiester linkages during DNA replication. As a result viral replication is prematurely terminated. ddCTP acts as a competitor for binding sites on the HIV-RNA dependent DNA polymerase (reverse transcriptase) to further contribute to inhibition of viral replication.

Pharmacodynamics/Kinetics
Absorption: Well, but variable; decreased 39% with food
Distribution: Minimal data available; variable CSF penetration
Protein binding: <4%
Metabolism: Intracellularly to active triphosphorylated agent
Bioavailability: >80%
Half-life elimination: 2.9 hours; Renal impairment: ≤8.5 hours
Excretion: Urine (>70% as unchanged drug)

Dosage Oral:
Neonates: Dose unknown
Infants and Children <13 years: Safety and efficacy have not been established; suggested usual dose: 0.01 mg/kg every 8 hours; range: 0.005-0.01 mg/kg every 8 hours
(Continued)

Zalcitabine *(Continued)*

Adolescents and Adults: 0.75 mg 3 times/day
Dosing adjustment in renal impairment: Adults:
Cl$_{cr}$ 10-40 mL/minute: 0.75 mg every 12 hours
Cl$_{cr}$ <10 mL/minute: 0.75 mg every 24 hours
Moderately dialyzable (20% to 50%)

Monitoring Parameters Renal function, viral load, liver function tests, CD4 counts, CBC, serum amylase, triglycerides, calcium

Patient Information Zalcitabine is not a cure; if numbness or tingling occurs, or if persistent, severe abdominal pain, nausea, or vomiting occur, notify prescriber. Women of childbearing age should use effective contraception while on zalcitabine; take on an empty stomach, if possible.

Dosage Forms TAB: 0.375 mg, 0.75 mg

Zaleplon (ZAL e plon)

U.S. Brand Names Sonata®

Therapeutic Category Hypnotic

Use Short-term (7-10 days) treatment of insomnia (has been demonstrated to be effective for up to 5 weeks in controlled trial)

Restrictions C-IV

Pregnancy Risk Factor C

Contraindications Hypersensitivity to zaleplon or any component of the formulation

Warnings/Precautions Symptomatic treatment of insomnia should be initiated only after careful evaluation of potential causes of sleep disturbance. Failure of sleep disturbance to resolve after 7-10 days may indicate psychiatric and/or medical illness.

Use with caution in patients with depression, particularly if suicidal risk may be present. Use with caution in patients with a history of drug dependence. Abrupt discontinuance may lead to withdrawal symptoms. May impair physical and mental capabilities. Patients must be cautioned about performing tasks which require mental alertness (operating machinery or driving). Use with caution in patients receiving other CNS depressants or psychoactive medications. Effects with other sedative drugs or ethanol may be potentiated.

Use with caution in the elderly, those with compromised respiratory function, or renal and hepatic impairment. Because of the rapid onset of action, zaleplon should be administered immediately prior to bedtime or after the patient has gone to bed and is having difficulty falling asleep.

Common Adverse Reactions
1% to 10%:
Cardiovascular: Peripheral edema, chest pain
Central nervous system: Amnesia, anxiety, depersonalization, dizziness, hallucinations, hypesthesia, somnolence, vertigo, malaise, depression, lightheadedness, impaired coordination, fever, migraine
Dermatologic: Photosensitivity reaction, rash, pruritus
Gastrointestinal: Abdominal pain, anorexia, colitis, dyspepsia, nausea, constipation, xerostomia
Genitourinary: Dysmenorrhea
Neuromuscular & skeletal: Paresthesia, tremor, myalgia, weakness, back pain, arthralgia
Ocular: Abnormal vision, eye pain
Otic: Hyperacusis
Miscellaneous: Parosmia

Drug Interactions
Cytochrome P450 Effect: Substrate of CYP3A4 (minor)
Increased Effect/Toxicity: Zaleplon potentiates the CNS effects of CNS depressants, including alcohol, anticonvulsants, antipsychotics, barbiturates, benzodiazepines, narcotic agonists, and other sedative agents. Cimetidine increases concentrations of zaleplon. Avoid concurrent use or use 5 mg zaleplon as starting dose in patient receiving cimetidine.
Decreased Effect: CYP3A4 inducers (eg, phenytoin, carbamazepine, phenobarbital) could lead to ineffectiveness of zaleplon.

Mechanism of Action Zaleplon is unrelated to benzodiazepines, barbiturates, or other hypnotics. However, it interacts with the benzodiazepine GABA receptor complex. Nonclinical studies have shown that it binds selectively to the brain omega-1 receptor situated on the alpha subunit of the GABA-A receptor complex.

Pharmacodynamics/Kinetics
Onset of action: Rapid
Peak effect: ~1 hour
Duration: 6-8 hours
Absorption: Rapid and almost complete
Distribution: V$_d$: 1.4 L/kg
Protein binding: 60% ± 15%
Metabolism: Extensive, primarily via aldehyde oxidase to form 5-oxo-zaleplon and to a lesser extent by CYP3A4 to desethylzaleplon; all metabolites are pharmacologically inactive
Bioavailability: 30%
Half-life elimination: 1 hour
Time to peak, serum: 1 hour
Excretion: Urine (primarily metabolites, <1% as unchanged drug)
Clearance: Plasma: Oral: 3 L/hour/kg

Dosage Oral:
Adults: 10 mg at bedtime (range: 5-20 mg); has been used for up to 5 weeks of treatment in controlled trial setting
Elderly: 5 mg at bedtime
Dosage adjustment in renal impairment: No adjustment for mild to moderate renal impairment; use in severe renal impairment has not been adequately studied
Dosage adjustment in hepatic impairment: Mild to moderate impairment: 5 mg; not recommended for use in patients with severe hepatic impairment

Administration Immediately before bedtime or when the patient is in bed and cannot fall asleep

Patient Information Take exactly as directed; immediately before bedtime, or when you cannot fall asleep. Do not alter dosage or frequency; may be habit forming. Avoid alcohol and other prescription or OTC medications (especially medications to relieve pain, induce sleep, reduce anxiety, treat or prevent cold, coughs, or allergies) unless approved by prescriber. You may experience drowsiness, dizziness, somnolence, vertigo, lightheadedness, blurred vision (avoid driving or engaging in activities that require alertness until response to drug is known); photosensitivity (avoid exposure to direct sunlight, wear protective clothing, and sunscreen); nausea or GI discomfort (small frequent meals, good mouth care, chewing gum, or sucking hard candy may help); constipation (increase exercise or dietary fiber and fluids); menstrual disturbances (reversible when drug is discontinued). Discontinue drug and report any severe CNS disturbances (hallucinations, acute nervousness or anxiety, persistent sleepiness or lethargy, impaired coordination, amnesia, or impaired thought processes); skin rash or irritation; eye pain or major vision changes; difficulty breathing; chest pain; ear pain; muscle weakness or pain.

Dosage Forms CAP: 5 mg, 10 mg

♦ **Zanaflex**® *see* Tizanidine *on page 1234*

Zanamivir (za NA mi veer)

U.S. Brand Names Relenza®

Therapeutic Category Antiviral Agent, Influenza; Antiviral Agent, Inhalation Therapy; Neuraminidase Inhibitor

Use Treatment of uncomplicated acute illness due to influenza virus in adults and children ≥7 years of age; should not be used in patients with underlying airway disease. Treatment should only be initiated in patients who have been symptomatic for no more than 2 days.

Unlabeled/Investigational Use Investigational: Prophylaxis against influenza A/B infections

Pregnancy Risk Factor C

Contraindications Hypersensitivity to zanamivir or any component of the formulation

Warnings/Precautions Patients must be instructed in the use of the delivery system. No data are available to support the use of this drug in patients who begin treatment after 48 hours of symptoms, as a prophylactic treatment for influenza, or in patients with significant underlying medical conditions. Not recommended for use in patients with underlying respiratory disease, such as asthma or COPD, due to lack of efficacy and risk of serious adverse effects. Bronchospasm, decreased lung function, and other serious adverse reactions, including those with fatal outcomes, have been reported. For a patient with an underlying airway disease where a medical decision has been made to use zanamivir, a fast-acting bronchodilator should be made available, and used prior to each dose. Not a substitute for the flu shot. Consider primary or concomitant bacterial infections. Powder for oral inhalation contains lactose.

Common Adverse Reactions Most adverse reactions occurred at a frequency which was equal to the control (lactose vehicle).

>1.5%:
Central nervous system: Headache (2%), dizziness (2%)
Gastrointestinal: Nausea (3%), diarrhea (3% adults, 2% children), vomiting (1% adults, 2% children)
Respiratory: Sinusitis (3%), bronchitis (2%), cough (2%), other nasal signs and symptoms (2%), infection (ear, nose, and throat; 2% adults, 5% children)

Drug Interactions
Increased Effect/Toxicity: No clinically significant pharmacokinetic interactions are predicted.
Decreased Effect: No clinically significant pharmacokinetic interactions are predicted.

Mechanism of Action Zanamivir inhibits influenza virus neuraminidase enzymes, potentially altering virus particle aggregation and release.

Pharmacodynamics/Kinetics
Absorption: Inhalation: 4% to 17%
Protein binding, plasma: <10%
Metabolism: None
Half-life elimination, serum: 2.5-5.1 hours
Excretion: Urine (as unchanged drug); feces (unabsorbed drug)

Dosage Children ≥7 years and Adults: 2 inhalations (10 mg total) twice daily for 5 days. Two doses should be taken on the first day of dosing, regardless of interval, while doses should be spaced by approximately 12 hours on subsequent days.
Prophylaxis (investigational use): 2 inhalations (10 mg) once daily for duration of exposure period (6 weeks has been used in clinical trial)

Administration Inhalation: Must be used with Diskhaler® delivery device. Patients who are scheduled to use an inhaled bronchodilator should use their bronchodilator prior to zanamivir.

Patient Information Use delivery device exactly as directed; complete full 5-day regimen, even if symptoms improve sooner. If you have asthma or COPD you may be at risk for
(Continued)

Zanamivir *(Continued)*

bronchospasm; see prescriber for appropriate bronchodilator before using zanamivir. Stop using this medication and contact your prescriber if you experience shortness of breath, increased wheezing, or other signs of bronchospasm. You may experience dizziness or headache (use caution when driving or engaging in hazardous tasks until response to drug is known). Report unresolved diarrhea, vomiting, or nausea; acute fever or muscle pain; or other acute and persistent adverse effects.

Dosage Forms POWDER, oral inhalation: 5 mg/blister (20s) [4 blisters per Rotadisk®, 5 Rotadisk® per package]

Zidovudine *(zye DOE vyoo deen)*

Related Information

Antiretroviral Therapy for HIV Infection *on page 1448*
Management of Healthcare Worker Exposures to HBV, HCV, and HIV *on page 1421*
Prevention of Perinatal HIV-1 Transmission *on page 1434*

U.S. Brand Names Retrovir®

Synonyms Azidothymidine; AZT; Compound S; ZDV

Therapeutic Category Antiretroviral Agent, Nucleoside Reverse Transcriptase Inhibitor (NRTI) [Thymidine Analog]

Use Management of patients with HIV infections in combination with at least two other antiretroviral agents; for prevention of maternal/fetal HIV transmission as monotherapy

Unlabeled/Investigational Use Postexposure prophylaxis for HIV exposure as part of a multidrug regimen

Pregnancy Risk Factor C

Contraindications Life-threatening hypersensitivity to zidovudine or any component of the formulation

Warnings/Precautions Associated with hematologic toxicity [granulocytopenia, severe anemia requiring transfusions, or (rarely) pancytopenia]. Use with caution in patients with bone marrow compromise; dosage adjustment may be required in patients who develop anemia or neutropenia. Lactic acidosis and severe hepatomegaly with steatosis have been reported, including fatal cases; use with caution in patients with risk factors for liver disease and suspend treatment in any patient who develops clinical or laboratory findings suggestive of lactic acidosis. Prolonged use has been associated with symptomatic myopathy. Reduce dose in patients with renal impairment.

Common Adverse Reactions

>10%:

Central nervous system: Severe headache (42%), fever (16%)
Dermatologic: Rash (17%)
Gastrointestinal: Nausea (46% to 61%), anorexia (11%), diarrhea (17%), pain (20%), vomiting (6% to 25%)
Hematologic: Anemia (23% in children), leukopenia, granulocytopenia (39% in children)

Neuromuscular & skeletal: Weakness (19%)
1% to 10%:
Central nervous system: Malaise (8%), dizziness (6%), insomnia (5%), somnolence (8%)
Dermatologic: Hyperpigmentation of nails (bluish-brown)
Gastrointestinal: Dyspepsia (5%)
Hematologic: Changes in platelet count
Neuromuscular & skeletal: Paresthesia (6%)

Drug Interactions

Cytochrome P450 Effect: Substrate (minor) of CYP2A6, 2C8/9, 2C19, 3A4

Increased Effect/Toxicity: Coadministration of zidovudine with drugs that are nephrotoxic (amphotericin B), cytotoxic (flucytosine, vincristine, vinblastine, doxorubicin, interferon), inhibit glucuronidation or excretion (acetaminophen, cimetidine, indomethacin, lorazepam, probenecid, aspirin), or interfere with RBC/WBC number or function (acyclovir, ganciclovir, pentamidine, dapsone). Clarithromycin may increase blood levels of zidovudine (although total body exposure was unaffected, peak plasma concentrations were increased). Valproic acid significantly increases zidovudine's blood levels (believed due to inhibition first pass metabolism). Concomitant use of ribavirin and nucleoside analogues may increase the risk of developing lactic acidosis (includes adefovir, didanosine, lamivudine, stavudine, zalcitabine, zidovudine).

Decreased Effect: *In vitro* evidence suggests zidovudine's antiretroviral activity may be antagonized by doxorubicin and ribavirin; avoid concurrent use. Zidovudine may decrease the antiviral activity of stavudine (based on *in vitro* data); avoid concurrent use.

Mechanism of Action

Zidovudine is a thymidine analog which interferes with the HIV viral RNA dependent DNA polymerase resulting in inhibition of viral replication; nucleoside reverse transcriptase inhibitor

Pharmacodynamics/Kinetics

Absorption: Oral: 66% to 70%

Distribution: Significant penetration into the CSF; crosses placenta
Relative diffusion from blood into CSF: Adequate with or without inflammation (exceeds usual MICs)
CSF:blood level ratio: Normal meninges: ~60%

Protein binding: 25% to 38%

Metabolism: Hepatic via glucuronidation to inactive metabolites; extensive first-pass effect

Half-life elimination: Terminal: 60 minutes

Time to peak, serum: 30-90 minutes

Excretion:
Oral: Urine (72% to 74% as metabolites, 14% to 18% as unchanged drug)
I.V.: Urine (45% to 60% as metabolites, 18% to 29% as unchanged drug)

Dosage

Prevention of maternal-fetal HIV transmission:

Neonatal: **Note:** Dosing should begin 6-12 hours after birth and continue for the first 6 weeks of life.

Oral:
Full-term infants: 2 mg/kg/dose every 6 hours
Infants ≥30 weeks and <35 weeks gestation at birth: 2 mg/kg/dose every 12 hours; at 2 weeks of age, advance to 2 mg/kg/dose every 8 hours
Infants <30 weeks gestation at birth: 2 mg/kg/dose every 12 hours; at 4 weeks of age, advance to 2 mg/kg/dose every 8 hours

I.V.: Infants unable to receive oral dosing:
Full term: 1.5 mg/kg/dose every 6 hours
Infants ≥30 weeks and <35 weeks gestation at birth: 1.5 mg/kg/dose every 12 hours; at 2 weeks of age, advance to 1.5 mg/kg/dose every 8 hours
Infants <30 weeks gestation at birth: 1.5 mg/kg/dose every 12 hours; at 4 weeks of age, advance to 1.5 mg/kg/dose every 8 hours

Maternal (may delay treatment until after 10-12 weeks gestation): Oral (per AIDSinfo 2003 guidelines): 200 mg 3 times/day or 300 mg twice daily until start of labor
During labor and delivery, administer zidovudine I.V. at 2 mg/kg over 1 hour followed by a continuous I.V. infusion of 1 mg/kg/hour until the umbilical cord is clamped

Children 3 months to 12 years for HIV infection:
Oral: 160 mg/m²/dose every 8 hours; dosage range: 90 mg/m²/dose to 180 mg/m²/dose every 6-8 hours; some Working Group members use a dose of 180 mg/m² every 12 hours when using in drug combinations with other antiretroviral compounds, but data on this dosing in children is limited
I.V. continuous infusion: 20 mg/m²/hour
I.V. intermittent infusion: 120 mg/m²/dose every 6 hours

Adults:
Oral: 300 mg twice daily or 200 mg 3 times/day
I.V.: 1-2 mg/kg/dose (infused over 1 hour) administered every 4 hours around-the-clock (6 doses/day)
Prevention of HIV following needlesticks (unlabeled use): 200 mg 3 times/day plus lamivudine 150 mg twice daily; a protease inhibitor (eg, indinavir) may be added for high risk exposures; begin therapy within 2 hours of exposure if possible
Patients should receive I.V. therapy only until oral therapy can be administered

Dosing interval in renal impairment: Cl_{cr} <10 mL/minute: May require minor dose adjustment
(Continued)

Zidovudine *(Continued)*

Hemodialysis: At least partially removed by hemo- and peritoneal dialysis; administer dose after hemodialysis or administer 100 mg supplemental dose; during CAPD, dose as for Cl_{cr} <10 mL/minute

Continuous arteriovenous or venovenous hemodiafiltration effects: Administer 100 mg every 8 hours

Dosing adjustment in hepatic impairment: Reduce dose by 50% or double dosing interval in patients with cirrhosis

Administration

Oral: Administer around-the-clock to promote less variation in peak and trough serum levels; may be administered without regard to food

I.M.: Do not administer I.M.

I.V.: Avoid rapid infusion or bolus injection

Neonates: Infuse over 30 minutes

Adults: Infuse over 1 hour

Monitoring Parameters Monitor CBC and platelet count at least every 2 weeks, MCV, serum creatinine kinase, viral load, and CD4 count; observe for appearance of opportunistic infections

Patient Information Zidovudine is not a cure for AIDS. Take as directed; may be taken without regard to food. Take around-the-clock; do not take with other medications. Take precautions to avoid transmission to others. You may experience headache or insomnia; if these persist notify prescriber. Report unresolved nausea or vomiting; signs of infection (eg, fever, chills, sore throat, burning urination, flu-like symptoms, fatigue); unusual bleeding (eg, tarry stools, easy bruising, or blood in stool, urine, or mouth); pain, tingling, or numbness of toes or fingers; skin rash or irritation; or muscles weakness or tremors.

Dosage Forms CAP: 100 mg. **INJ, solution:** 10 mg/mL (20 mL). **SYR:** 50 mg/5 mL (240 mL). **TAB:** 300 mg

♦ **Zidovudine, Abacavir, and Lamivudine** *see* Abacavir, Lamivudine, and Zidovudine *on page 19*

Zidovudine and Lamivudine *(zye DOE vyoo deen & la MI vyoo deen)*

U.S. Brand Names Combivir®

Synonyms AZT + 3TC; Lamivudine and Zidovudine

Therapeutic Category Antiretroviral Agent, Reverse Transcriptase Inhibitor (Combination)

Use Treatment of HIV infection when therapy is warranted based on clinical and/or immunological evidence of disease progression. Combivir® given twice daily, provides an alternative regimen to lamivudine 150 mg twice daily plus zidovudine 600 mg/day in divided doses; this drug form reduces capsule/tablet intake for these two drugs to 2 per day instead of up to 8.

Pregnancy Risk Factor C

Dosage Children >12 years and Adults: Oral: One tablet twice daily

Dosage Forms TAB: Zidovudine 300 mg and lamivudine 150 mg

♦ **Zilactin®-B [OTC]** *see* Benzocaine *on page 154*

♦ **Zilactin® Baby [OTC]** *see* Benzocaine *on page 154*

♦ **Zilactin-L® [OTC]** *see* Lidocaine *on page 742*

Zileuton *(zye LOO ton)*

U.S. Brand Names Zyflo™ [DSC]

Therapeutic Category 5-Lipoxygenase Inhibitor

Use Prophylaxis and chronic treatment of asthma in children ≥12 years of age and adults

Pregnancy Risk Factor C

Contraindications Hypersensitivity to zileuton or any component of the formulation; active liver disease or transaminase elevations greater than or equal to three times the upper limit of normal (≥3 times ULN)

Warnings/Precautions Elevations of one or more liver function tests may occur during therapy. These laboratory abnormalities may progress, remain unchanged or resolve with continued therapy. Use with caution in patients who consume substantial quantities of ethanol or have a past history of liver disease. Zileuton is not indicated for use in the reversal of bronchospasm in acute asthma attacks, including status asthmaticus. Zileuton can be continued during acute exacerbations of asthma.

Common Adverse Reactions

>10%:

Central nervous system: Headache (24.6%)

Hepatic: ALT elevation (12%)

1% to 10%:

Cardiovascular: Chest pain

Central nervous system: Pain, dizziness, fever, insomnia, malaise, nervousness, somnolence

Gastrointestinal: Dyspepsia, nausea, abdominal pain, constipation, flatulence

Hematologic: Low white blood cell count

Neuromuscular & skeletal: Myalgia, arthralgia, weakness

Ocular: Conjunctivitis

Drug Interactions

Cytochrome P450 Effect: Substrate (minor) of CYP1A2, 2C8/9, 3A4; **Inhibits** CYP1A2 (weak)

Increased Effect/Toxicity: Zileuton increases concentrations/effects of of beta-blockers (propranolol), theophylline, and warfarin. Potentially, it may increase levels of many drugs, including cisapride, due to inhibition of CYP3A4.

Mechanism of Action Specific inhibitor of 5-lipoxygenase and thus inhibits leukotriene (LTB4, LTC4, LTD4 and LTE4) formation. Leukotrienes are substances that induce numerous biological effects including augmentation of neutrophil and eosinophil migration, neutrophil and monocyte aggregation, leukocyte adhesion, increased capillary permeability and smooth muscle contraction.

Pharmacodynamics/Kinetics
  Absorption: Rapid
  Distribution: 1.2 L/kg
  Protein binding: 93%
  Metabolism: Several metabolites in plasma and urine; metabolized by CYP1A2, 2C9, and 3A4
  Bioavailability: Unknown
  Half-life elimination: 2.5 hours
  Time to peak, serum: 1.7 hours
  Excretion: Urine (~95% primarily as metabolites); feces (~2%)

Dosage Oral:
  Children ≥12 years of age and Adults: 600 mg 4 times/day with meals and at bedtime
  Elderly: Zileuton pharmacokinetics were similar in healthy elderly subjects (>65 years) compared with healthy younger adults (18-40 years)
  Dosing adjustment in renal impairment: Dosing adjustment is not necessary in renal impairment or renal failure (even during dialysis)
  Dosing adjustment in hepatic impairment: Contraindicated in patients with active liver disease

Administration May be administered without regard to meals (ie, with or without food)

Monitoring Parameters Evaluate hepatic transaminases at initiation of and during therapy with zileuton. Monitor serum ALT before treatment begins, once-a-month for the first 3 months, every 2-3 months for the remainder of the first year, and periodically thereafter for patients receiving long-term zileuton therapy. If symptoms of liver dysfunction (right upper quadrant pain, nausea, fatigue, lethargy, pruritus, jaundice or "flu-like" symptoms) develop or transaminase elevations >5 times ULN occur, discontinue therapy and follow transaminase levels until normal.

Patient Information Inform patients that zileuton is indicated for the chronic treatment of asthma and to take regularly as prescribed even during symptom-free periods. Zileuton is not a bronchodilator; do not use to treat acute episodes of asthma. When taking zileuton, do not decrease the dose or stop taking any other antiasthma medications unless instructed by a physician. While using zileuton, seek medical attention if short-acting bronchodilators are needed more often than usual or if more than the maximum number of inhalations of short-acting bronchodilator treatment prescribed for a 24-period are needed. The most serious side effect of zileuton is elevation of liver enzyme tests. While taking zileuton, patients must have liver enzyme tests monitored on a regular basis. If patients experience signs or symptoms of liver dysfunction (right upper quadrant pain, nausea, fatigue, lethargy, pruritus, jaundice, or "flu-like" symptoms), contact prescriber immediately. Zileuton can interact with other drugs. While taking zileuton, consult a physician before starting or stopping any prescription or nonprescription medicines.

Dosage Forms TAB: 600 mg

♦ **Zinacef®** see Cefuroxime on page 245
♦ **Zinc Acetate** see Zinc Supplements on page 1327
♦ **Zinca-Pak® Zincate®** see Zinc Supplements on page 1327
♦ **Zinc Carbonate** see Zinc Supplements on page 1327
♦ **Zinc Chloride** see Zinc Supplements on page 1327
♦ **Zincfrin® [OTC]** see Phenylephrine and Zinc Sulfate on page 995

Zinc Gelatin (zink JEL ah tin)

U.S. Brand Names Gelucast®
Synonyms Dome Paste Bandage; Unna's Boot; Unna's Paste; Zinc Gelatin Boot
Therapeutic Category Topical Skin Product
Use As a protectant and to support varicosities and similar lesions of the lower limbs
Dosage Apply externally as an occlusive boot
Dosage Forms BANDAGE: 3" x 10 yards; 4" x 10 yards

♦ **Zinc Gelatin Boot** see Zinc Gelatin on page 1327
♦ **Zinc Gluconate** see Zinc Supplements on page 1327
♦ **Zinc Sulfate** see Zinc Supplements on page 1327
♦ **Zinc Sulfate and Phenylephrine** see Phenylephrine and Zinc Sulfate on page 995

Zinc Supplements (zink SUP la ments)

U.S. Brand Names Cold-Eeze® [OTC]; Eye-Sed® [OTC]; Orazinc® [OTC]; Verazinc® [OTC]; Zinca-Pak® Zincate®
Synonyms Zinc Acetate; Zinc Carbonate; Zinc Chloride; Zinc Gluconate; Zinc Sulfate
Therapeutic Category Mineral, Oral; Mineral, Parenteral; Trace Element
Use Cofactor for replacement therapy to different enzymes helps maintain normal growth rates, normal skin hydration and senses of taste and smell; zinc supplement (oral and parenteral) for treatment and prevention of zinc deficiency states; may improve wound healing in those who
(Continued)

Zinc Supplements *(Continued)*

are deficient; promote wound healing in patients with pressure sores; lozenges are used to diminish symptoms and duration of the common cold; maintenance treatment of Wilson's disease (zinc acetate)

Pregnancy Risk Factor C (A for zinc acetate)

Contraindications Hypersensitivity to zinc salts or any component

Warnings/Precautions Do not administer undiluted by direct injection into a peripheral vein because of potential for phlebitis, tissue irritation, and potential to increase renal loss of minerals from a bolus injection. Administration of zinc in absence of copper may decrease plasma copper levels. Excessive dose may increase HDL and impair immune system function.

Drug Interactions

Decreased Effect: Decreased penicillamine and tetracycline effect. Iron may decrease the uptake of zinc. Bran products, dairy products reduce absorption of zinc.

Mechanism of Action Provides for normal growth and tissue repair; cofactor for more than 70 enzymes which are important to carbohydrate and protein metabolism; helps to maintain normal growth and tissue repair, normal skin hydration, and senses of taste and smell; in Wilson's disease, zinc cation inhibits the absorption of dietary copper by inducing the synthesis of metallothionein, a metal-binding protein present in the intestinal mucosa, which binds metals, including copper, forming a nontoxic complex that is not absorbed systematically but excreted in the stool; ophthalmic astringent and weak antiseptic due to precipitation of protein and clearing mucus from outer surface of the eye

Pharmacodynamics/Kinetics

Absorption: Poor from GI tract (20% to 30%)

Excretion: Feces and traces in urine

Dosage Clinical response may not occur for up to 6-8 weeks.

RDA: Oral:

Infants <12 months: 5 mg **elemental** zinc/day

Children 1-10 years: 10 mg **elemental** zinc/day

Children ≥11 years: Male: 15 mg **elemental** zinc/day; Female: 12 mg **elemental** zinc/day

Adults: Male: 15 mg **elemental** zinc/day; Female: 12 mg **elemental** zinc/day

Zinc deficiency: Oral:

Infants and Children: 0.5-1 mg **elemental** zinc/kg/day divided 1-3 times/day; larger doses may be needed if impaired intestinal absorption or an excessive loss of zinc (eg, excessive, prolonged diarrhea)

Adults: 25-50 mg **elemental** zinc/dose (110-220 mg zinc sulfate) 3 times/day

Supplement to parenteral nutrition support (clinical response may not occur for up to 6-8 weeks): I.V. (all doses are mcg of **elemental** zinc):

Premature Infants: 400 mcg/kg/day

Term Infants <3 months: 300 mcg/kg/day

Infants ≥3 months and Children ≤5 years: 100 mcg/kg/day (maximum: 5 mg/day)

Children >5 years and Adolescents: 2-5 mg/day

Adults:

Stable metabolically: 2.5-4 mg **elemental** zinc/day; catabolic state: Increase by an additional 2 mg/day (eg, 4.5-6 mg **elemental** zinc/day)

Stable with fluid loss from small bowel: Additional 12.2 mg **elemental** zinc/L parenteral nutrition or 17.1 mg **elemental** zinc/kg of stool or ileostomy output

Wound healing: Oral: Adults: 50 mg **elemental** zinc (220 mg zinc sulfate) 3 times daily in patients with low serum zinc levels (<110 mcg/dL)

Common cold: Zinc gluconate glycine: Adults:

Lozenge: Completely dissolve lozenge (13.3 mg ionic zinc) in mouth. Do not chew. Repeat every 3-4 hours as needed (recommendation: 6 lozenges/day) until symptoms are gone.

Gum: Chew a stick of gum (13.3 mg ionic zinc) for at least 10 minutes. Repeat every 3-4 hours as needed (recommendation 6 sticks per day) until symptoms are gone.

Tablet: Completely dissolve tablet (4.3 mg ionic zinc) in mouth. Do not chew. Repeat every hour as needed (maximum 16 tablets/day) until symptoms are gone.

Monitoring Parameters Patients on TPN therapy should have periodic serum copper and serum zinc levels; alkaline phosphatase, taste acuity, mental depression, wound healing (if indicated), growth (if indicated), skin integrity; Wilson's disease: 24-hour urinary copper excretion, neuropsychiatric evaluations, LFTs

Patient Information Take as directed; do not take more than recommended. Take with food; however, avoid foods high in calcium, phosphorous, or phytate. Stop medication and contact prescriber if you develop severe nausea or vomiting or acute indigestion; easy bruising or bleeding; persistent dizziness; or unusual respiratory difficulty.

Zinc gluconate glycine: Dissolve lozenge or tablet slowing in mouth. **Do not chew or swallow tablets whole.** Chew each stick of gum for at least 10 minutes.

♦ **Zinecard**® *see* Dexrazoxane *on page 361*

Ziprasidone *(zi PRAY si done)*

Related Information

Antipsychotic Agents Comparison *on page 1364*

U.S. Brand Names Geodon®

Synonyms Zeldox; Ziprasidone Hydrochloride; Ziprasidone Mesylate

Therapeutic Category Antipsychotic Agent, Benzylisothiazolylpiperazine

Use Treatment of schizophrenia

Unlabeled/Investigational Use Tourette's syndrome

Pregnancy Risk Factor C

Contraindications Hypersensitivity to ziprasidone or any component of the formulation; history (or current) prolonged QT; congenital long QT syndrome; recent myocardial infarction; history of arrhythmias; uncompensated heart failure; concurrent use of other QT_c-prolonging agents including amiodarone, arsenic trioxide, chlorpromazine, cisapride, class Ia antiarrhythmics (quinidine, procainamide), dofetilide, dolasetron, droperidol, halofantrine, levomethadyl, mefloquine, mesoridazine, pentamidine, pimozide, some quinolone antibiotics (moxifloxacin, sparfloxacin, gatifloxacin), sotalol, tacrolimus, and thioridazine

Warnings/Precautions May result in QT_c prolongation (dose-related), which has been associated with the development of malignant ventricular arrhythmias (torsade de pointes). Avoid hypokalemia, hypomagnesemia. Use caution in patients with bradycardia. Discontinue in patients found to have persistent QT_c intervals >500 msec. Patients with symptoms of dizziness, palpitations, or syncope should receive further cardiac evaluation. May cause orthostatic hypotension; use with caution in patients at risk of this effect or those who would tolerate transient hypotensive episodes.

May cause extrapyramidal symptoms, including tardive dyskinesia. Disturbances of temperature regulation and/or neuroleptic malignant syndrome (NMS) have been reported with antipsychotics. Use with caution in patients at risk of seizures, including those receiving medications which may lower seizure threshold. Elderly patients may be at increased risk of seizures due to an increased prevalence of predisposing factors.

Other atypical antipsychotics have been associated with development of hyperglycemia (limited documentation with ziprasidone); use caution in patients with diabetes or other disorders of glucose regulation.

Cognitive and/or motor impairment (sedation) is common with ziprasidone. Use with caution in disorders where CNS depression is a feature. Use with caution in Parkinson's disease. Esophageal dysmotility and aspiration have been associated with antipsychotic use; use with caution in patients at risk of aspiration pneumonia (ie, Alzheimer's disease). Caution in breast cancer or other prolactin-dependent tumors (may elevate prolactin levels). Ziprasidone has been associated with a fairly high incidence of rash (5%); discontinue if alternative etiology is not identified. Safety and efficacy have not been established in pediatric patients.

Common Adverse Reactions Note: Although minor QT_c prolongation (mean 10 msec at 160 mg/day) may occur more frequently (incidence not specified), clinically relevant prolongation (>500 msec) was rare (0.06%).

>10%:
  Central nervous system: Somnolence (8% to 20%), headache (3% to 13%)
  Gastrointestinal: Nausea (4% to 12%)
1% to 10%:
  Cardiovascular: Bradycardia (2%), hypertension (2%), tachycardia (2%), postural hypotension (1% to 5%), vasodilation (1%)
  Central nervous system: Akathisia (2% to 8%), dizziness (3% to 10%), extrapyramidal symptoms (2% to 5%), dystonia (4%), hypertonia (3%), insomnia (3%), agitation (2%), anxiety (2%), speech disorder (2%), psychosis (1%)
  Dermatologic: Rash (with urticaria, 4% to 5%), fungal dermatitis (2%), furunculosis (2%)
  Endocrine & metabolic: Dysmenorrhea (2%)
  Gastrointestinal: Constipation (2% to 9%), dyspepsia (1% to 8%), diarrhea (3% to 5%), xerostomia (1% to 4%), vomiting (3%), abdominal pain (2%), anorexia (2%), weight gain (10%), rectal hemorrhage (2%)
  Genitourinary: Priapism (1%)
  Local: Pain at injection site (7% to 9%)
  Neuromuscular & skeletal: Weakness (2% to 5%), paresthesia (2%), cogwheel rigidity (1%), hypertonia (1%), myalgia (1%)
  Ocular: Abnormal vision (3%)
  Respiratory: Respiratory disorder (8%, primarily cold symptoms, upper respiratory infection), rhinitis (1% to 4%), cough increased (3%)
  Miscellaneous: Accidental injury (4%), diaphoresis (2%)

Drug Interactions

  Cytochrome P450 Effect: Substrate (minor) of CYP1A2, 3A4; **Inhibits** CYP2D6 (weak), 3A4 (weak)

  Increased Effect/Toxicity:
    Ketoconazole may increase serum concentrations of ziprasidone. Other CYP3A4 inhibitors may share this potential. Inhibitors include amiodarone, clarithromycin, erythromycin, delavirdine, diltiazem, dirithromycin, disulfiram, fluoxetine, fluvoxamine, grapefruit juice, indinavir, itraconazole, ketoconazole, nefazodone, nevirapine, propoxyphene, quinupristin-dalfopristin, ritonavir, saquinavir, verapamil, zafirlukast, zileuton
    Concurrent use with QT_c-prolonging agents may result in additive effects on cardiac conduction, potentially resulting in malignant or lethal arrhythmias. Concurrent use is contraindicated. Includes amiodarone, arsenic trioxide, chlorpromazine, cisapride; class Ia antiarrhythmics (quinidine, procainamide); dofetilide, dolasetron, droperidol, halofantrine, levomethadyl, mefloquine, mesoridazine, pentamidine, pimozide; some quinolone antibiotics (moxifloxacin, sparfloxacin, gatifloxacin); sotalol, tacrolimus, and thioridazine. Potassium- or magnesium-depleting agents (diuretics, aminoglycosides, cyclosporine, and amphotericin B) may increase the risk of QT_c prolongation. Antihypertensive agents may increase the degree of orthostatic hypotension. CNS depressants may increase the degree of sedation caused by ziprasidone. Metoclopramide may increase risk of extrapyramidal symptoms (EPS).
  (Continued)

Ziprasidone *(Continued)*

Decreased Effect: Carbamazepine may decrease serum concentrations of ziprasidone. Other enzyme-inducing agents may share this potential. Amphetamines may decrease the efficacy of ziprasidone. Ziprasidone may inhibit the efficacy of levodopa.

Mechanism of Action The exact mechanism of action is unknown. However, *in vitro* radioligand studies show that ziprasidone has high affinity for D_2, $5\text{-}HT_{2A}$, $5\text{-}HT_{1A}$, $5\text{-}HT_{2C}$ and $5\text{-}HT_{1D}$, moderate affinity for alpha$_1$ adrenergic and histamine H_1 receptors, and low affinity for alpha$_2$ adrenergic, beta adrenergic, $5\text{-}HT_3$, $5\text{-}HT_4$, cholinergic, mu, sigma, or benzodiazepine receptors. Ziprasidone moderately inhibits the reuptake of serotonin and norepinephrine.

Pharmacodynamics/Kinetics

Absorption: Well absorbed

Distribution: V_d: 1.5 L/kg

Protein binding: 99%, primarily to albumin and alpha-1-acid glycoprotein

Metabolism: Extensively hepatic, primarily via aldehyde oxidase; less than $\frac{1}{3}$ of total metabolism via CYP3A4 and CYP1A2 (minor)

Bioavailability: Oral (with food): 60% (up to twofold increase with food); I.M.: 100%

Half-life elimination: Oral: 7 hours; I.M.: 2-5 hours

Time to peak: Oral: 6-8 hours; I.M.: ≤60 minutes

Excretion: Feces (66%) and urine (20%) as metabolites; little as unchanged drug (1% urine, 4% feces)

Dosage

Oral:

Children and Adolescents: Tourette's syndrome (unlabeled use): 5-40 mg/day

Adults: Psychosis: Initial: 20 mg twice daily (with food)

Adjustment: Increases (if indicated) should be made no more frequently than every 2 days; ordinarily patients should be observed for improvement over several weeks before adjusting the dose

Maintenance: Range 20-100 mg twice daily; however, dosages >80 mg twice daily are generally not recommended

I.M.: Adults: Psychosis: 10 mg every 2 hours **or** 20 mg every 4 hours; maximum: 40 mg/day; oral therapy should replace I.M. administration as soon as possible

Elderly: No dosage adjustment is recommended; consider initiating at a low end of the dosage range, with slower titration

Dosage adjustment in renal impairment:

Oral: No dosage adjustment is recommended

I.M.: Cyclodextrin, an excipient in the I.M. formulation, is cleared by renal filtration; use with caution.

Dosage adjustment in hepatic impairment: No dosage adjustment is recommended

Administration Oral: Administer with food.

Monitoring Parameters Vital signs; serum potassium and magnesium, lipid profile, fasting blood glucose/Hgb A_{1c}; BMI; mental status, abnormal involuntary movement scale (AIMS). The value of routine ECG screening or monitoring has not been established. Potential for extrapyramidal symptoms.

Patient Information Use exactly as directed (do not change dose or frequency). Ziprasidone should be taken with food. It may take 2-3 weeks to achieve desired results; do not discontinue without consulting prescriber. Avoid excess alcohol, caffeine, grapefruit and grapefruit juice, other prescription or OTC medications not approved by prescriber. Maintain adequate hydration (2-3 L/day of fluids unless instructed to restrict fluid intake). You may experience excess sedation, drowsiness, restlessness, dizziness, or blurred vision (use caution driving or when engaging in tasks requiring alertness until response to drug is known); dry mouth, nausea, or GI upset (small frequent meals, frequent mouth care, chewing gum, or sucking lozenges may help); postural hypotension (use caution climbing stairs or when changing position from lying or sitting to standing); or urinary retention (void before taking medication). Report persistent CNS effects (eg, trembling fingers, altered gait or balance, excessive sedation, seizures, unusual muscle or skeletal movements, anxiety, abnormal thoughts, confusion, personality changes); chest pain, palpitations, rapid heartbeat, severe dizziness; swelling or pain in breasts (male and female), altered menstrual pattern, sexual dysfunction; pain or difficulty on urination; vision changes; skin rash or yellowing of skin; difficulty breathing; or worsening of condition.

Dosage Forms CAP: 20 mg, 40 mg, 60 mg, 80 mg. **INJ, powder for reconstitution:** 20 mg

Zoledronic Acid *(ZOE le dron ik AS id)*

U.S. Brand Names Zometa®

Synonyms CGP-42446; Zoledronate

Therapeutic Category Antidote, Hypercalcemia; Bisphosphonate Derivative

Use Treatment of hypercalcemia and bone metastases of solid tumors

Unlabeled/Investigational Use Investigational: Prevention of bone metastases from breast or prostate cancer; treatment of metabolic bone diseases

Pregnancy Risk Factor D

Contraindications Hypersensitivity to zoledronic acid, other bisphosphonates, or any component of the formulation; pregnancy

Warnings/Precautions Renal toxicity has been reported with doses >4 mg or infusions administered over <15 minutes. Renal function should be assessed prior to and after treatment; if decreased after treatment, additional treatments should be withheld until renal function returns to within 10% of baseline. Use caution in patients with previous renal impairment. Use is not recommended in patients with severe renal impairment (serum creatinine >3 mg/dL) and bone metastases (limited data). Adequate hydration is required during treatment (urine output ~2 L/day); avoid overhydration, especially in patients with heart failure; diuretics should not be used before correcting hypovolemia. Use caution in patients with aspirin-sensitive asthma (may cause bronchoconstriction), hepatic dysfunction, and the elderly. Safety and efficacy in pediatric patients have not been established.

Common Adverse Reactions
>10%:
Cardiovascular: Leg edema (up to 19%)
Central nervous system: Fatigue (36%), fever (30% to 44%), headache (up to 18%), insomnia (15%), anxiety (9% to 14%), dizziness (14%), agitation (13%), depression (12%)
Dermatologic: Alopecia (11%)
Endocrine & metabolic: Hypophosphatemia (13%), hypokalemia (12%), dehydration (up to 12%)
Gastrointestinal: Nausea (29% to 45%), constipation (27% to 28%), vomiting (14% to 30%), diarrhea (17% to 22%), abdominal pain (12% to 16%)
Genitourinary: Urinary tract infection (11% to 14%)
Hematologic: Anemia (22% to 29%), neutropenia (11%)
Neuromuscular & skeletal: Myalgia (21%), paresthesias (18%), arthralgia (up to 18%) skeletal pain (12%)
Respiratory: Dyspnea (22% to 24%), coughing (12% to 19%)
Miscellaneous: Moniliasis (12%)
1% to 10%:
Cardiovascular: Hypotension (10%), chest pain
Central nervous system: Hypoesthesia (10%)
Dermatologic: Dermatitis (10%)
Endocrine & metabolic: Hypomagnesemia (up to 10%), hypocalcemia, hypophosphatemia (9%), hypermagnesemia (Grade 3: 2%)
Gastrointestinal: Anorexia (9%), mucositis, dysphagia
Genitourinary: Urinary tract infection (14%)
Hematologic: Thrombocytopenia, pancytopenia, granulocytopenia
Neuromuscular & skeletal: Rigors (10%), weakness
Renal: Serum creatinine increased
Respiratory: Pleural effusion, upper respiratory tract infection (8%)
Symptoms of hypercalcemia include polyuria, nephrolithiasis, anorexia, nausea, vomiting, constipation, weakness, fatigue, confusion, stupor, and coma. These may not be drug-related adverse events, but related to the underlying metabolic condition.

Drug Interactions
Increased Effect/Toxicity: Aminoglycosides may also lower serum calcium levels; loop diuretics increase risk of hypocalcemia; thalidomide increases renal toxicity

Mechanism of Action A bisphosphonate which inhibits bone resorption via actions on osteoclasts or on osteoclast precursors; inhibits osteoclastic activity and skeletal calcium release induced by tumors. Decreases serum calcium and phosphorus, and increases their elimination.

Pharmacodynamics/Kinetics
Onset of action: Maximum effect may not been seen for 7 days
Distribution: Binds to bone
Protein binding: ~22%
Half-life elimination: Triphasic; Terminal: 146 hours
Excretion: Urine (39% ± 16% as unchanged drug) within 24 hours; feces (<3%)

Dosage I.V.: Adults:
Hypercalcemia of malignancy (albumin-corrected serum calcium ≥12 mg/dL): 4 mg (maximum) given as a single dose infused over **no less than 15 minutes**; patients should be adequately hydrated prior to treatment (restoring urine output to ~2 L/day). Monitor serum calcium and wait at least 7 days before considering retreatment. Dosage adjustment may be needed in patients with decreased renal function following treatment.
Multiple myeloma or metastatic bone lesions from solid tumors: 4 mg given over 15 minutes every 3-4 weeks
Note: Patients should receive a daily calcium supplement and multivitamin containing vitamin D

Dosage adjustment in renal impairment: Specific dosing guidelines are not available. Patients with hypercalcemia of malignancy and pretreatment serum creatinine ≥4.5 mg/dL were excluded from clinical trials. Patients with bone metastases and pretreatment serum creatinine >3 mg/dL were excluded from clinical trials.
Dosage adjustment in hepatic impairment: Specific guidelines are not available.
(Continued)

Zoledronic Acid *(Continued)*

Dosage adjustment for toxicity:

Hypercalcemia of malignancy: Evidence of renal deterioration: Evaluate risk versus benefit.

Bone metastases: Evidence of renal deterioration: Discontinue further dosing until renal function returns to baseline: renal deterioration defined as follows:

Normal baseline creatinine: Increase of 0.5 mg/dL

Abnormal baseline creatinine: Increase of 1 mg/dL

Administration In order to prevent renal toxicity, infuse solution over at least 15 minutes. Infuse in a line separate from other medications. Patients should be appropriately hydrated prior to treatment.

Monitoring Parameters Monitor serum creatinine prior to each dose. Serum electrolytes, phosphate, magnesium, and hemoglobin/hematocrit should be evaluated regularly. Monitor serum calcium to assess response and avoid over-treatment.

Patient Information This medication can only be administered intravenously. Avoid food high in calcium or vitamins during infusion or for 2-3 hours after completion. You may experience some nausea or vomiting (small frequent meals, good mouth care, sucking lozenges, or chewing gum may help) or recurrent bone pain (consult prescriber for analgesic). Report unusual muscle twitching or spasms, severe diarrhea/constipation, acute bone pain, or other persistent adverse effects.

Dosage Forms INJ, powder for reconstitution: 4 mg. **INJ, solution:** 4 mg/5 mL (5 mL)

Zolmitriptan *(zohl mi TRIP tan)*

Related Information

Antimigraine Drugs Comparison *on page 1363*

U.S. Brand Names Zomig®; Zomig-ZMT™

Synonyms 311C90

Therapeutic Category Antimigraine Agent, Serotonin 5-HT$_{1D}$ Agonist; Serotonin 5-HT$_4$ Receptor Agonist

Use Acute treatment of migraine with or without aura

Pregnancy Risk Factor C

Contraindications Hypersensitivity to zolmitriptan or any component of the formulation; ischemic heart disease or Prinzmetal's angina; signs or symptoms of ischemic heart disease; uncontrolled hypertension; symptomatic Wolff-Parkinson-White syndrome or arrhythmias associated with other cardiac accessory conduction pathway disorders; use with ergotamine derivatives (within 24 hours of); use within 24 hours of another 5-HT$_1$ agonist; concurrent administration or within 2 weeks of discontinuing an MAO inhibitor; management of hemiplegic or basilar migraine

Warnings/Precautions Zolmitriptan is indicated only in patient populations with a clear diagnosis of migraine. Not for prophylactic treatment of migraine headaches. Cardiac events (coronary artery vasospasm, transient ischemia, myocardial infarction, ventricular tachycardia/fibrillation, cardiac arrest, and death) have been reported with 5-HT$_1$ agonist administration. Should not be given to patients who have risk factors for CAD (eg, hypertension, hypercholesterolemia, smoker, obesity, diabetes, strong family history of CAD, menopause, male >40 years of age) without adequate cardiac evaluation. Patients with suspected CAD should have cardiovascular evaluation to rule out CAD before considering zolmitriptan's use; if cardiovascular evaluation negative, first dose would be safest if given in the healthcare provider's office. Periodic evaluation of those without cardiovascular disease, but with continued risk factors should be done. Significant elevation in blood pressure, including hypertensive crisis, has also been reported on rare occasions in patients with and without a history of hypertension. Vasospasm-related reactions have been reported other than coronary artery vasospasm. Peripheral vascular ischemia and colonic ischemia with abdominal pain and bloody diarrhea have occurred. Use with caution in patients with hepatic impairment. Zomig-ZMT™ tablets contain phenylalanine. Safety and efficacy not established in patients <18 years of age.

Common Adverse Reactions Percentages noted from oral preparations.

1% to 10%:

Cardiovascular: Chest pain (2% to 4%), palpitations (up to 2%)

Central nervous system: Dizziness (6% to 10%), somnolence (5% to 8%), pain (2% to 3%), vertigo (≤2%)

Gastrointestinal: Nausea (4% to 9%), xerostomia (3% to 5%), dyspepsia (1% to 3%), dysphagia (≤2%)

Neuromuscular & skeletal: Paresthesia (5% to 9%), weakness (3% to 9%), warm/cold sensation (5% to 7%), hypesthesia (1% to 2%), myalgia (1% to 2%), myasthenia (up to 2%)

Miscellaneous: Neck/throat/jaw pain (4% to 10%), diaphoresis (up to 3%), allergic reaction (up to 1%)

Drug Interactions

Cytochrome P450 Effect: Substrate of CYP1A2 (minor)

Increased Effect/Toxicity: Ergot-containing drugs may lead to vasospasm; cimetidine, MAO inhibitors, oral contraceptives, propranolol increase levels of zolmitriptan; concurrent use with SSRIs and sibutramine may lead to serotonin syndrome.

Mechanism of Action Selective agonist for serotonin (5-HT$_{1B}$ and 5-HT$_{1D}$ receptors) in cranial arteries to cause vasoconstriction and reduce sterile inflammation associated with antidromic neuronal transmission correlating with relief of migraine

Pharmacodynamics/Kinetics

Onset of action: 0.5-1 hour

Absorption: Well absorbed

Distribution: V_d: 7 L/kg

Protein binding: 25%

Metabolism: Converted to an active N-desmethyl metabolite (2-6 times more potent than zolmitriptan)

Half-life elimination: 2.8-3.7 hours

Bioavailability: 40%

Time to peak, serum: Tablet: 1.5 hours; Orally-disintegrating tablet and nasal spray: 3 hours

Excretion: Urine (~60% to 65% total dose); feces (30% to 40%)

Dosage Oral:

Children: Safety and efficacy have not been established

Adults: Migraine:

Tablet: Initial: ≤2.5 mg at the onset of migraine headache; may break 2.5 mg tablet in half

Orally-disintegrating tablet: Initial: 2.5 mg at the onset of migraine headache

Nasal spray: Initial: 1 spray (5 mg) at the onset of migraine headache

Note: Use the lowest possible dose to minimize adverse events. If the headache returns, the dose may be repeated after 2 hours; do not exceed 10 mg within a 24-hour period. Controlled trials have not established the effectiveness of a second dose if the initial one was ineffective

Elderly: No dosage adjustment needed but elderly patients are more likely to have underlying cardiovascular disease and should have careful evaluation of cardiovascular system before prescribing.

Dosage adjustment in renal impairment: No dosage adjustment recommended. There is a 25% reduction in zolmitriptan's clearance in patients with severe renal impairment (Cl_{cr} 5-25 mL/minute)

Dosage adjustment in hepatic impairment: Administer with caution in patients with liver disease, generally using doses <2.5 mg. Patients with moderate-to-severe hepatic impairment may have decreased clearance of zolmitriptan, and significant elevation in blood pressure was observed in some patients.

Administration Administer as soon as migraine headache starts.

Tablet: May be broken

Orally-disintegrating tablet: Must be taken whole; do not break, crush or chew; place on tongue and allow to dissolve; administration with liquid is not required

Nasal spray: Blow nose gently prior to use. After removing protective cap, instill device into nostril. Block opposite nostril; breathe in gently through nose while pressing plunger of spray device. One dose (5 mg) is equal to 1 spray in 1 nostril.

Patient Information Take a single dose with fluids as soon as symptoms of migraine appear; a second dose may be taken if symptoms return, but no sooner than 2 hours following the first dose. For a given attack, if there is no response to the first tablet, do not take a second tablet without first consulting prescriber. Do not take >10 mg in any 24-hour period. If the patient has risk factors for heart disease (high blood pressure, high cholesterol, obesity, diabetes, smoking, strong family history of heart disease, postmenopausal woman, or a male >40 years of age), tell prescriber. This agent is intended to relieve migraine, but not to prevent or reduce the number of attacks. Use only to treat an actual migraine attack. Do not use this agent if you are pregnant, think you may be pregnant, are trying to become pregnant, or are not using adequate contraception, unless you have discussed this with your prescriber. If pain or tightness in the chest or throat occurs when using this agent, discuss with prescriber before using more. If the chest pain is severe or does not go away, call prescriber immediately. If shortness of breath; wheezing; heart throbbing; swelling of eyelids, face or lips; skin rash, skin lumps or hives occur, tell prescriber immediately. Do not take any more unless the prescriber instructs you to do so. If feelings of tingling, heat, flushing (redness of face lasting a short time), heaviness, pressure, drowsiness, dizziness, tiredness, or sickness develop, tell your prescriber.

Dosage Forms SOLN, nasal spray [single dose] (Zomig®): 5 mg/0.1 mL (0.1 mL). **TAB** (Zomig®): 2.5 mg, 5 mg. **TAB, orally-disintegrating** (Zomig-ZMT™): 2.5 mg, 5 mg

♦ **Zoloft®** see Sertraline cn page 1131

Zolpidem (zole PI dem)

U.S. Brand Names Ambien®

Synonyms Zolpidem Tartrate

Therapeutic Category Hypnotic; Sedative

Use Short-term treatment of insomnia

Restrictions C-IV

Pregnancy Risk Factor B

Contraindications Hypersensitivity to zolpidem or any component of the formulation

Warnings/Precautions Should be used only after evaluation of potential causes of sleep disturbance. Failure of sleep disturbance to resolve after 7-10 days may indicate psychiatric or medical illness. Use with caution in patients with depression. Behavioral changes have been associated with sedative-hypnotics. Causes CNS depression, which may impair physical and mental capabilities. Effects with other sedative drugs or ethanol may be potentiated. Closely monitor elderly or debilitated patients for impaired cognitive or motor performance; not recommended for use in children <18 years of age. Avoid use in patients with sleep apnea or a history of sedative-hypnotic abuse.

Common Adverse Reactions 1% to 10%:

Cardiovascular: Palpitations

Central nervous system: Headache, drowsiness, dizziness, lethargy, lightheadedness, depression, abnormal dreams, amnesia

(Continued)

Zolpidem (Continued)

Dermatologic: Rash
Gastrointestinal: Nausea, diarrhea, xerostomia, constipation
Respiratory: Sinusitis, pharyngitis

Drug Interactions

Cytochrome P450 Effect: Substrate of CYP1A2 (minor), 2C8/9 (minor), 2C19 (minor), 2D6 (minor), 3A4 (major)

Increased Effect/Toxicity: Use of zolpidem in combination with other centrally-acting drugs may produce additive CNS depression. Concurrent use of drugs which inhibit cytochrome P450 3A4 (including erythromycin, clarithromycin, diltiazem, itraconazole, ketoconazole, nefazodone, and verapamil) may increase the levels of zolpidem.

Decreased Effect: Rifampin may reduce levels and effect of zolpidem. Other enzyme inducers may have a similar effect.

Mechanism of Action Structurally dissimilar to benzodiazepine, however, has much or all of its actions explained by its effects on benzodiazepine (BZD) receptors, especially the omega-1 receptor (with a high affinity ratio of the alpha 1/alpha 5 subunits); retains hypnotic and much of the anxiolytic properties of the BZD, but has reduced effects on skeletal muscle and seizure threshold.

Pharmacodynamics/Kinetics

Onset of action: 30 minutes
Duration: 6-8 hours
Absorption: Rapid
Distribution: Very low amounts enter breast milk
Protein binding: 92%
Metabolism: Hepatic to inactive metabolites
Half-life elimination: 2-2.6 hours; Cirrhosis: Up to 9.9 hours

Dosage Duration of therapy should be limited to 7-10 days
Adults: Oral: 10 mg immediately before bedtime; maximum dose: 10 mg
Elderly: 5 mg immediately before bedtime
Hemodialysis: Not dialyzable

Dosing adjustment in hepatic impairment: Decrease dose to 5 mg

Administration Ingest immediately before bedtime due to rapid onset of action

Monitoring Parameters Daytime alertness; respiratory and cardiac status

Reference Range 80-150 ng/mL

Patient Information Avoid alcohol and other CNS depressants while taking this medication; for fastest onset, take on an empty stomach; may cause drowsiness

Dosage Forms TAB: 5 mg, 10 mg

◆ **Zolpidem Tartrate** see Zolpidem on page 1333
◆ **Zometa®** see Zoledronic Acid on page 1330
◆ **Zomig®** see Zolmitriptan on page 1332
◆ **Zomig-ZMT™** see Zolmitriptan on page 1332
◆ **Zonalon®** see Doxepin on page 407
◆ **Zone-A®** see Pramoxine and Hydrocortisone on page 1028
◆ **Zone-A Forte®** see Pramoxine and Hydrocortisone on page 1028
◆ **Zonegran®** see Zonisamide on page 1334

Zonisamide (zoe NIS a mide)

Related Information

Anticonvulsants by Seizure Type on page 1358

U.S. Brand Names Zonegran®

Therapeutic Category Anticonvulsant, Miscellaneous

Use Adjunct treatment of partial seizures in children >16 years of age and adults with epilepsy

Unlabeled/Investigational Use Bipolar disorder

Pregnancy Risk Factor C

Contraindications Hypersensitivity to zonisamide, sulfonamides, or any component of the formulation

Warnings/Precautions Rare, but potentially fatal sulfonamide reactions have occurred following the use of zonisamide. These reactions include Stevens-Johnson syndrome and toxic epidermal necrolysis, usually appearing within 2-16 weeks of drug initiation. Discontinue zonisamide if rash develops. Chemical similarities are present among sulfonamides, sulfonylureas, carbonic anhydrase inhibitors, thiazides, and loop diuretics (except ethacrynic acid). Use in patients with sulfonamide allergy is specifically contraindicated in product labeling, however, a risk of cross-reaction exists in patients with allergy to any of these compounds; avoid use when previous reaction has been severe.

Decreased sweating (oligohydrosis) and hyperthermia requiring hospitalization have been reported in children. Discontinue zonisamide in patients who develop acute renal failure or a significant sustained increase in creatinine/BUN concentration. Kidney stones have been reported. Use cautiously in patients with renal or hepatic dysfunction. Significant CNS effects include psychiatric symptoms, psychomotor slowing, and fatigue or somnolence. Fatigue and somnolence occur within the first month of treatment, most commonly at doses of 300-500 mg/day. Abrupt withdrawal may precipitate seizures; discontinue or reduce doses gradually. Safety and efficacy in children <16 years of age has not been established.

Common Adverse Reactions Adjunctive Therapy: Frequencies noted in patients receiving other anticonvulsants:

>10%:
    Central nervous system: Somnolence (17%), dizziness (13%)
    Gastrointestinal: Anorexia (13%)
1% to 10%:
    Central nervous system: Headache (10%), agitation/irritability (9%), fatigue (8%), tiredness (7%), ataxia (6%), confusion (6%), decreased concentration (6%), memory impairment (6%), depression (6%), insomnia (6%), speech disorders (5%), mental slowing (4%), anxiety (3%), nervousness (2%), schizophrenic/schizophreniform behavior (2%), difficulty in verbal expression (2%), status epilepticus (1%), tremor (1%), convulsion (1%), hyperesthesia (1%), incoordination (1%)
    Dermatologic: Rash (3%), bruising (2%), pruritus (1%)
    Gastrointestinal: Nausea (9%), abdominal pain (6%), diarrhea (5%), dyspepsia (3%), weight loss (3%), constipation (2%), dry mouth (2%), taste perversion (2%), vomiting (1%)
    Neuromuscular & skeletal: Paresthesia (4%), weakness (1%), abnormal gait (1%)
    Ocular: Diplopia (6%), nystagmus (4%), amblyopia (1%)
    Otic: Tinnitus (1%)
    Respiratory: Rhinitis (2%), pharyngitis (1%), increased cough (1%)
    Miscellaneous: Flu-like syndrome (4%) accidental injury (1%)

Drug Interactions
    Cytochrome P450 Effect: Substrate of CYP2C19 (minor), 3A4 (major)
    Increased Effect/Toxicity: Sedative effects may be additive with other CNS depressants; monitor for increased effect; includes barbiturates, benzodiazepines, narcotic analgesics, ethanol, and other sedative agents. Serum level and/or toxicity of zonisamide may be increased by CYP3A4 inhibitors; inhibitors include amiodarone, cimetidine, clarithromycin, erythromycin, delavirdine, diltiazem, dirithromycin, disulfiram, fluoxetine, fluvoxamine, grapefruit juice, indinavir, itraconazole, ketoconazole, metronidazole, nefazodone, nevirapine, propoxyphene, quinupristin-dalfopristin, ritonavir, saquinavir, verapamil, zafirlukast, zileuton; monitor for increased response.

Decreased Effect:
    Note: Zonisamide did NOT affect steady state levels of carbamazepine, phenytoin, or valproate; zonisamide half-life is decreased by carbamazepine, phenytoin, phenobarbital, and valproate
    Enzyme inducers: May increase the metabolism of zonisamide, reducing its effectiveness; inducers include phenytoin, carbamazepine, phenobarbital, and rifampin

Mechanism of Action The exact mechanism of action is not known. May stabilize neuronal membranes and suppress neuronal hypersynchronization through action at sodium and calcium channels. Does not affect GABA activity.

Pharmacodynamics/Kinetics
    Distribution: V_d: 1.45 L/kg
    Protein binding: 40%
    Metabolism: Hepatic via CYP3A4; forms N-acetyl zonisamide and 2-sulfamoylacetyl phenol (SMAP)
    Half-life elimination: 63 hours
    Time to peak: 2-6 hours
    Excretion: Urine (62%, 35% as unchanged drug, 65% as metabolites); feces (3%)

Dosage Oral:
    Children >16 years and Adults:
        Adjunctive treatment of partial seizures: Initial: 100 mg/day; dose may be increased to 200 mg/day after 2 weeks. Further dosage increases to 300 mg/day and 400 mg/day can then be made with a minimum of 2 weeks between adjustments, in order to reach steady state at each dosage level. Doses of up to 600 mg/day have been studied, however, there is no evidence of increased response with doses above 400 mg/day.
        Mania (unlabeled use): Initial: 100-200 mg/day; maximum: 600 mg/day (Kanba, 1994)
    Elderly: Data from clinical trials is insufficient for patients >65 years; begin dosing at the low end of the dosing range.
    Dosage adjustment in renal/hepatic impairment: Slower titration and frequent monitoring are indicated in patients with renal or hepatic disease. There is insufficient experience regarding dosing/toxicity in patients with estimated GFR <50 mL/minute. Marked renal impairment (Cl_{cr} <20 mL/minute) was associated with a 35% increase in AUC.

Administration Capsules should be swallowed whole. Dose may be administered once or twice daily. Doses of 300 mg/day and higher are associated with increased side effects. Steady-state levels are reached in 14 days.

Monitoring Parameters Monitor BUN and serum creatinine

Patient Information May cause drowsiness, especially at higher doses. Do not drive a car or operate other complex machinery until effects on performance can be determined. Avoid alcohol and other CNS depressants. Contact prescriber immediately if seizures worsen or for any of the following: skin rash; sudden back pain, abdominal pain, blood in the urine; fever, sore throat, oral ulcers or easy bruising. Contact prescriber before becoming pregnant or breast-feeding. Swallow capsules whole, do not bite or break. It is important to drink 6-8 glasses of water each day while using this medication. Do not stop taking this or other seizure medications without talking to your healthcare professional first.

Dosage Forms CAP: 25 mg, 50 mg, 100 mg

♦ **Zorbtive™** see Human Growth Hormone on page 620

♦ **ZORprin®** see Aspirin on page 120

♦ **Zosyn®** see Piperacillin and Tazobactam Sodium on page 1006

♦ **Zovia™** see Ethinyl Estradiol and Ethynodiol Diacetate on page 480

- **Zovirax®** *see* Acyclovir *on page 35*
- **Zyban®** *see* BuPROPion *on page 189*
- **Zydone®** *see* Hydrocodone and Acetaminophen *on page 627*
- **Zyflo™ [DSC]** *see* Zileuton *on page 1326*
- **Zyloprim®** *see* Allopurinol *on page 56*
- **Zymar™** *see* Gatifloxacin *on page 579*
- **Zyprexa®** *see* Olanzapine *on page 923*
- **Zyprexa® Zydis®** *see* Olanzapine *on page 923*
- **Zyrtec®** *see* Cetirizine *on page 250*
- **Zyvox™** *see* Linezolid *on page 747*

APPENDIX TABLE OF CONTENTS

APPENDIX TABLE OF CONTENTS *(Continued)*

ABBREVIATIONS, ACRONYMS, AND SYMBOLS

Abbreviation	Meaning
aa, aā	of each
AA	Alcoholics Anonymous
ABG	arterial blood gases
ac	before meals or food
ACA	Adult Children of Alcoholics
ACLS	advanced cardiac life support
ad	to, up to
a.d.	right ear
ADHD	attention-deficit/hyperactivity disorder
ADLs	activities of daily living
ad lib	at pleasure
AIDS	acquired immune deficiency syndrome
AIMS	Abnormal Involuntary Movement Scale
a.l.	left ear
ALS	amyotrophic lateral sclerosis
AM	morning
AMA	against medical advice
amp	ampul
amt	amount
aq	water
aq. dest.	distilled water
ARC	AIDS-related complex
ARDS	adult respiratory distress syndrome
ARF	acute renal failure
a.s.	left ear
ASAP	as soon as possible
a.u.	each ear
AUC	area under the curve
BDI	Beck Depression Inventory
bid	twice daily
BLS	basic life support
bm	bowel movement
BMI	body mass index
bp	blood pressure
BPH	benign prostatic hyperplasia
BPRS	Brief Psychiatric Rating Scale
BSA	body surface area
c	a gallon
c̄	with
CA	cancer
CABG	coronary artery bypass graft
CAD	coronary artery disease
cal	calorie
cap	capsule
CBT	cognitive behavioral therapy
cc	cubic centimeter
CCL	creatinine clearance
CF	cystic fibrosis
CGI	Clinical Global Impression
CIE	chemotherapy-induced emesis
cm	centimeter
CIV	continuous I.V. infusion
CNS	central nervous system
comp	compound
cont	continue
COPD	chronic obstructive pulmonary disease
CRF	chronic renal failure
CT	computed tomography
d	day

ABBREVIATIONS, ACRONYMS, AND SYMBOLS *(Continued)*

Abbreviation	Meaning
DBP	diastolic blood pressure
d/c	discontinue
dil	dilute
disp	dispense
div	divide
DOE	dyspnea on exertion
DSM-IV	Diagnostic and Statistical Manual
DTs	delirium tremens
dtd	give of such a dose
DVT	deep vein thrombosis
Dx	diagnosis
ECT	electroconvulsive therapy
EEG	electroencephalogram
EKG	electrocardiogram
elix, el	elixir
emp	as directed
EPS	extrapyramidal side effects
ESRD	end stage renal disease
et	and
EtOH	alcohol
ex aq	in water
f, ft	make, let be made
FDA	Food and Drug Administration
FMS	fibromyalgia syndrome
g	gram
GA	Gamblers Anonymous
GAD	generalized anxiety disorder
GAF	Global Assessment of Functioning Scale
GABA	gamma-aminobutyric acid
GERD	gastroesophageal reflux disease
GFR	glomerular filtration rate
GITS	gastrointestinal therapeutic system
gr	grain
gtt	a drop
GVHD	graft versus host disease
h	hour
HAM-A	Hamilton Anxiety Scale
HAM-D	Hamilton Depression Scale
hs	at bedtime
HSV	herpes simplex virus
HTN	hypertension
IBD	inflammatory bowel disease
IBS	irritable bowel syndrome
ICH	intracranial hemorrhage
IHSS	idiopathic hypertrophic subaortic stenosis
I.M.	intramuscular
IOP	intraocular pressure
IU	international unit
I.V.	intravenous
kcal	kilocalorie
kg	kilogram
KIU	kallikrein inhibitor unit
L	liter
LAMM	L-α-acetyl methadol
liq	a liquor, solution
LVH	left ventricular hypertrophy
M	mix; Molar
MADRS	Montgomery Asbery Depression Rating Scale
MAOIs	monamine oxidase inhibitors
mcg	microgram
MDEA	3,4-methylene-dioxy amphetamine
m. dict	as directed

Abbreviation	Meaning
MDMA	3,4-methylene-dioxy methamphetamine
mEq	milliequivalent
mg	milligram
mixt	a mixture
mL	milliliter
mm	millimeter
mM	millimolar
MMSE	mini mental status examination
MPPP	l-methyl-4-proprionoxy-4-phenyl pyridine
MR	mental retardation
MRI	magnetic resonance imaging
MS	multiple sclerosis
NF	National Formulary
NKA	no known allergies
NMS	neuroleptic malignant syndrome
no.	number
noc	in the night
non rep	do not repeat, no refills
NPO	nothing by mouth
NSAID	nonsteroidal anti-inflammatory drug
NV	nausea and vomiting
O, Oct	a pint
OA	osteoarthritis
OCD	obsessive-compulsive disorder
o.d.	right eye
o.l.	left eye
o.s.	left eye
o.u.	each eye
PANSS	Positive and Negative Symptom Scale
PAT	paroxysmal atrial tachycardia
pc, post cib	after meals
PCP	phencyclidine
PD	Parkinson's disease
PE	pulmonary embolus
per	through or by
PID	pelvic inflammatory disease
PM	afternoon or evening
P.O.	by mouth
PONV	postoperative nausea and vomiting
P.R.	rectally
prn	as needed
PSVT	paroxysmal supraventricular tachycardia
PTA	prior to admission
PTSD	post-traumatic stress disorder
PUD	peptic ulcer disease
pulv	a powder
PVD	peripheral vascular disease
q	every
qad	every other day
qd	every day
qh	every hour
qid	four times a day
qod	every other day
qs	a sufficient quantity
qs ad	a sufficient quantity to make
qty	quantity
qv	as much as you wish
RA	rheumatoid arthritis
REM	rapid eye movement
Rx	take, a recipe
rep	let it be repeated
s̄	without
sa	according to art
SAH	subarachnoid hemorrhage

ABBREVIATIONS, ACRONYMS, AND SYMBOLS *(Continued)*

Abbreviation	Meaning
sat	saturated
SBE	subacute bacterial endocarditis
SBP	systolic blood pressure
S.C.	subcutaneous
SIADH	syndrome of inappropriate antidiuretic hormone secretion
sig	label, or let it be printed
SL	sublingual
SLE	systemic lupus erythematosus
SOB	shortness of breath
sol	solution
solv	dissolve
s̄s̄	one-half
sos	if there is need
SSKI	saturated solution of potassium iodide
SSRIs	selective serotonin reuptake inhibitors
stat	at once, immediately
STD	sexually transmitted disease
supp	suppository
SVT	supraventricular tachycardia
Sx	symptom
syr	syrup
tab	tablet
tal	such
TCA	tricyclic antidepressant
TD	tardive dyskinesia
tid	three times a day
TKO	to keep open
TPN	total parenteral nutrition
tr, tinct	tincture
trit	triturate
tsp	teaspoonful
Tx	treatment
ULN	upper limits of normal
ung	ointment
URI	upper respiratory infection
USAN	United States Adopted Names
USP	United States Pharmacopeia
UTI	urinary tract infection
u.d., ut dict	as directed
v.o.	verbal order
VTE	venous thromboembolism
VZV	varicella zoster virus
w.a.	while awake
x3	3 times
x4	4 times
YBOC	Yale Brown Obsessive-Compulsive Scale
YMRS	Young Mania Rating Scale

APOTHECARY / METRIC EQUIVALENTS

Approximate Liquid Measures
Basic equivalent: 1 fluid ounce = 30 mL

Examples:

1 gallon	3800 mL	1 gallon	128 fluid ounces
1 quart	960 mL	1 quart	32 fluid ounces
1 pint	480 mL	1 pint	16 fluid ounces
8 fluid oz	240 mL	15 minims	1 mL
4 fluid oz	120 mL	10 minims	0.6 mL

Approximate Household Equivalents

1 teaspoonful	5 mL	1 tablespoonful	15 mL

Weights

Basic equivalents:

1 oz	30 g	15 gr	1 g

Examples:

4 oz	120 g	1 gr	60 mg
2 oz	60 g	1/100 gr	600 mcg
10 gr	600 mg	1/150 gr	400 mcg
7½ gr	500 mg	1/200 gr	300 mcg
16 oz	1 lb		

Metric Conversions

Basic equivalents:

1 g	1000 mg	1 mg	1000 mcg

Examples:

5 g	5000 mg	5 mg	5000 mcg
0.5 g	500 mg	0.5 mg	500 mcg
0.05 g	50 mg	0.05 mg	50 mcg

Exact Equivalents

1 g	=	15.43 gr	0.1 mg	=	1/600 gr
1 mL	=	16.23 minims	0.12 mg	=	1/500 gr
1 minim	=	0.06 mL	0.15 mg	=	1/400 gr
1 gr	=	64.8 mg	0.2 mg	=	1/300 gr
1 pint (pt)	=	473.2 mL	0.3 mg	=	1/200 gr
1 oz	=	28.35 g	0.4 mg	=	1/150 gr
1 lb	=	453.6 g	0.5 mg	=	1/120 gr
1 kg	=	2.2 lbs	0.6 mg	=	1/100 gr
1 qt	=	946.4 mL	0.8 mg	=	1/80 gr
			1 mg	=	1/65 gr

Solids[1]

¼ grain	=	15 mg
½ grain	=	30 mg
1 grain	=	60 mg
1½ grains	=	90 mg
5 grains	=	300 mg
10 grains	=	600 mg

[1]Use exact equivalents for compounding and calculations requiring a high degree of accuracy.

AVERAGE WEIGHTS AND SURFACE AREAS

**Average Weight and Surface Area of Preterm Infants,
Term Infants, and Children**

Age	Average Weight (kg)[1]	Approximate Surface Area (m²)
Weeks Gestation		
26	0.9-1	0.1
30	1.3-1.5	0.12
32	1.6-2	0.15
38	2.9-3	0.2
40 (term infant at birth)	3.1-4	0.25
Months		
3	5	0.29
6	7	0.38
9	8	0.42
Year		
1	10	0.49
2	12	0.55
3	15	0.64
4	17	0.74
5	18	0.76
6	20	0.82
7	23	0.90
8	25	0.95
9	28	1.06
10	33	1.18
11	35	1.23
12	40	1.34
Adults	70	1.73

[1]Weights from age 3 months and older are rounded off to the nearest kilogram.

BODY MASS INDEX (BMI)

$$\text{BMI} = \frac{\text{weight (kg)}}{[\text{height (m)}]^2}$$

See "Obesity Treatment Guidelines for Adults" in Therapy Recommendations section.

BODY SURFACE AREA OF ADULTS AND CHILDREN

Calculating Body Surface Area in Children

In a child of average size, find weight and corresponding surface area on the boxed scale to the left; or, use the nomogram to the right. Lay a straightedge on the correct height and weight points for the child, then read the intersecting point on the surface area scale.

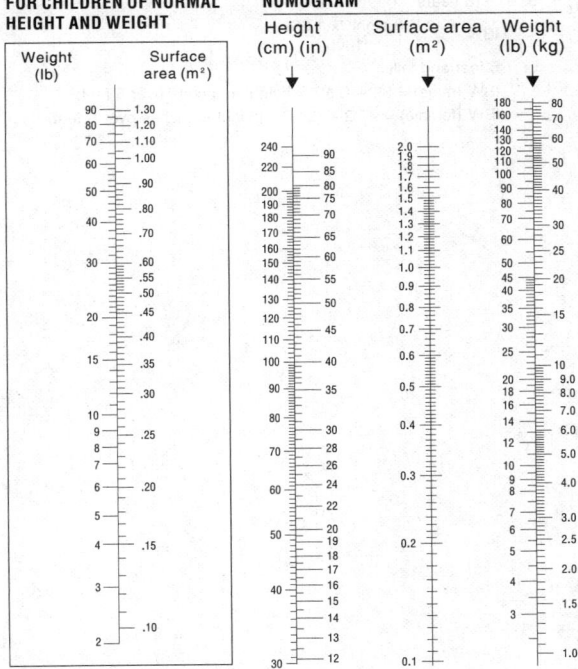

FOR CHILDREN OF NORMAL HEIGHT AND WEIGHT

NOMOGRAM

BODY SURFACE AREA FORMULA
(Adult and Pediatric)

$$\text{BSA (m}^2) = \sqrt{\frac{\text{Ht (in)} \times \text{Wt (lb)}}{3131}} \quad \text{or, in metric:} \quad \text{BSA (m}^2) = \sqrt{\frac{\text{Ht (cm)} \times \text{Wt (kg)}}{3600}}$$

References
  Lam TK and Leung DT, "More on Simplified Calculation of Body Surface Area," *N Engl J Med*, 1988, 318(17):1130 (Letter).
  Mosteller RD, "Simplified Calculation of Body Surface Area", *N Engl J Med*, 1987, 317(17):1098 (Letter).

IDEAL BODY WEIGHT CALCULATION

Adults (18 years and older) (IBW is in kg)

IBW (male) = 50 + (2.3 x height in inches over 5 feet)

IBW (female) = 45.5 + (2.3 x height in inches over 5 feet)

Children (IBW is in kg; height is in cm)

a. 1-18 years

$$IBW = \frac{(height^2 \times 1.65)}{1000}$$

b. 5 feet and taller

IBW (male) = 39 + (2.27 x height in inches over 5 feet)

IBW (female) = 42.2 + (2.27 x height in inches over 5 feet)

POUNDS / KILOGRAMS CONVERSION

1 pound = 0.45359 kilograms
1 kilogram = 2.2 pounds

lb	=	kg	lb	=	kg	lb	=	kg
1		0.45	70		31.75	140		63.50
5		2.27	75		34.02	145		65.77
10		4.54	80		36.29	150		68.04
15		6.80	85		38.56	155		70.31
20		9.07	90		40.82	160		72.58
25		11.34	95		43.09	165		74.84
30		13.61	100		45.36	170		77.11
35		15.88	105		47.63	175		79.38
40		18.14	110		49.90	180		81.65
45		20.41	115		52.16	185		83.92
50		22.68	120		54.43	190		86.18
55		24.95	125		56.70	195		88.45
60		27.22	130		58.91	200		90.72
65		29.48	135		61.24			

TEMPERATURE CONVERSION

Celsius to Fahrenheit = ($°$C x 9/5) + 32 = $°$F
Fahrenheit to Celsius = ($°$F − 32) x 5/9 = $°$C

$°$C	=	$°$F	$°$C	=	$°$F	$°$C	=	$°$F
100.0		212.0	39.0		102.2	36.8		98.2
50.0		122.0	38.8		101.8	36.6		97.9
41.0		105.8	38.6		101.5	36.4		97.5
40.8		105.4	38.4		101.1	36.2		97.2
40.6		105.1	38.2		100.8	36.0		96.8
40.4		104.7	38.0		100.4	35.8		96.4
40.2		104.4	37.8		100.1	35.6		96.1
40.0		104.0	37.6		99.7	35.4		95.7
39.8		103.6	37.4		99.3	35.2		95.4
39.6		103.3	37.2		99.0	35.0		95.0
39.4		102.9	37.0		98.6	0		32.0
39.2		102.6						

CREATININE CLEARANCE ESTIMATING METHODS IN PATIENTS WITH STABLE RENAL FUNCTION

These formulas provide an acceptable estimate of the patient's creatinine clearance **except** in the following instances.

- Patient's serum creatinine is changing rapidly (either up or down).
- Patients are markedly emaciated.

In above situations, certain assumptions have to be made.

- In patients with rapidly rising serum creatinines (ie, >0.5-0.7 mg/dL/day), it is best to assume that the patient's creatinine clearance is probably <10 mL/minute.
- In emaciated patients, although their actual creatinine clearance is less than their calculated creatinine clearance (because of decreased creatinine production), it is not possible to easily predict how much less.

Infants

Estimation of creatinine clearance using serum creatinine and body length (to be used when an adequate timed specimen cannot be obtained). **Note:** This formula may not provide an accurate estimation of creatinine clearance for infants younger than 6 months of age and for patients with severe starvation or muscle wasting.

$Cl_{cr} = K \times L/S_{cr}$

where:

Cl_{cr} = creatinine clearance in mL/minute/1.73 m²

K = constant of proportionality that is age specific

Age	K
Low birth weight ≤1 y	0.33
Full-term ≤1 y	0.45
2-12 y	0.55
13-21 y female	0.55
13-21 y male	0.70

L = length in cm

S_{cr} = serum creatinine concentration in mg/dL

Reference

Schwartz GJ, Brion LP, and Spitzer A, "The Use of Plasma Creatinine Concentration for Estimating Glomerular Filtration Rate in Infants, Children and Adolescents," *Ped Clin N Amer*, 1987, 34:571-90.

Children (1-18 years)

Method 1: (Traub SL and Johnson CE, *Am J Hosp Pharm*, 1980, 37:195-201)

Equation:

$$Cl_{cr} = \frac{0.48 \times (height)}{S_{cr}}$$

where

Cl_{cr} = creatinine clearance in mL/min/1.73 m²

S_{cr} = serum creatinine in mg/dL

Height = height in cm

Method 2: Nomogram (Traub SL and Johnson CE, *Am J Hosp Pharm*, 1980, 37:195-201)

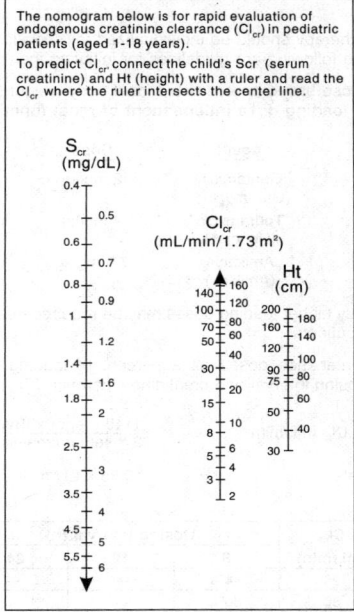

The nomogram below is for rapid evaluation of endogenous creatinine clearance (Cl_{cr}) in pediatric patients (aged 1-18 years).

To predict Cl_{cr}, connect the child's Scr (serum creatinine) and Ht (height) with a ruler and read the Cl_{cr} where the ruler intersects the center line.

Adults (18 years and older)

Method 1: (Cockroft DW and Gault MH, *Nephron*, 1976, 16:31-41)

Estimated creatinine clearance (Cl_{cr}) (mL/min):

$$\text{Male} = \frac{(140 - \text{age})\ \text{IBW (kg)}}{72 \times S_{cr}}$$

$$\text{Female} = \text{estimated } Cl_{cr} \text{ male} \times 0.85$$

Note: The use of the patient's ideal body weight (IBW) is recommended for the above formula except when the patient's actual body weight is less than ideal. Use of the IBW is especially important in obese patients.

Method 2: (Jelliffe RW, *Ann Intern Med*, 1973, 79:604)

Estimated creatinine clearance (Cl_{cr}) (mL/min/1.73 m^2):

$$\text{Male} = \frac{98 - 0.8\ (\text{age} - 20)}{\text{serum creatinine}}$$

$$\text{Female} = \text{estimated } Cl_{cr} \text{ male} \times 0.90$$

AMINOGLYCOSIDE DOSING AND MONITORING

All aminoglycoside therapy should be individualized for specific patients in specific clinical situation. The following are guidelines for initiating therapy.

1. Loading dose based on estimated ideal body weight (IBW). **All patients require a loading dose independent of renal function**.

Agent	Dose
Gentamicin (Garamycin®)	2 mg/kg
Tobramycin (Nebcin®)	2 mg/kg
Amikacin (Amikin®)	7.5 mg/kg

Significantly higher loading doses may be required in severely ill intensive care unit patients.

2. Initial maintenance doses as a percent of loading dose according to desired dosing interval and creatinine clearance (Cl$_{cr}$):

$$\text{Male Cl}_{cr} \text{ (mL/min)} = \frac{(140 - \text{age}) \times \text{IBW}}{72 \times \text{serum creatinine}}$$

$$\text{Female} = 0.85 \times \text{Cl}_{cr} \text{ males}$$

Cl$_{cr}$ (mL/min)	Dosing Interval (h)		
	8	12	24
90	84%	—	—
80	80%	—	—
70	76%	88%	—
60	—	84%	—
50	—	79%	—
40	—	72%	92%
30	—	—	86%
25	—	—	81%
20	—	—	75%

Patients >65 years of age should not receive initial aminoglycoside maintenance dosing more often than every 12 hours.

3. Serum concentration monitoring

   a. Serum concentration monitoring is necessary for **safe** and **effective** therapy, particularly in patients with serious infections and those with risk factors for toxicity.

   b. Peak serum concentrations should be drawn 30 minutes after the completion of a 30-minute infusion. Trough serum concentrations should be drawn within 30 minutes prior to the administered dose.

   c. Serum concentrations should be drawn after 5 half-lives, usually around the third dose or thereafter.

4. Desired measured serum concentrations

	Peak (mcg/mL)	Trough (mcg/mL)
Gentamicin	6-10	0.5-2.0
Tobramycin	6-10	0.5-2.0
Amikacin	20-30	<5

5. For patients receiving hemodialysis:
   - administer the **same** loading dose
   - administer $2/3$ of the loading dose after each dialysis
   - **serum concentrations must be monitored**
   - watch for ototoxicity from accumulation of drug

6. For individual clinical situations the prescribing physician should feel free to consult Infectious Disease, the Pharmacology Service, or the Pharmacy.

"Once Daily" Aminoglycosides

High dose, "once daily" aminoglycoside therapy for treatment of gram-negative bacterial infections has been studied and remains controversial. The pharmacodynamics of aminoglycosides reveal dose-dependent killing which suggests an efficacy advantage of "high" peak serum concentrations. It is also suggested that allowing troughs to fall to unmeasurable levels decreases the risk of nephrotoxicity without detriment to efficacy. Because of a theoretical saturation of tubular cell uptake of aminoglycosides, decreasing the number of times the drug is administered in a particular time period may play a role in minimizing the risk of nephrotoxicity. Ototoxicity has not been sufficiently formally evaluated through audiometry or vestibular testing comparing "once daily" to standard therapy. Over 100 letters, commentaries, studies and reviews have been published on the topic of "once daily" aminoglycosides with varying dosing regimens, monitoring parameters, inclusion and exclusion criteria, and results (most of which have been favorable for the "once daily" regimens). The caveats of this simplified method of dosing are several, including assurance that creatinine clearances be calculated, that all patients are not candidates and should not be considered for this regimen, and that "once daily" is a semantic misnomer.

Because of the controversial nature of this method, it is beyond the scope of this book to present significant detail and dosing regimen recommendations. Considerable experience with two methods warrants mention. The Hartford Hospital has experience with over 2000 patients utilizing a 7 mg/kg dose, a dosing scheme for various creatinine clearance estimates, and a serum concentration monitoring nomogram.[1] Providence Medical Center utilizes a 5 mg/kg dosing regimen but only in patients with excellent renal function; serum concentrations are monitored 4-6 hours prior to the dose administered.[2] Two excellent reviews discuss the majority of studies and controversies regarding these dosing techniques.[3,4] An editorial accompanies one of the reviews and is worth examination.[5]

"Once daily" dosing may be a safe and effective method of providing aminoglycoside therapy to a large number of patients who require these efficacious yet toxic agents. As with any method of aminoglycoside administration, dosing must be individualized and the caveats of the method considered.

Footnotes

1. Nicolau DP, Freeman CD, Belliveau PP, et al, "Experience With a Once-Daily Aminoglycoside Program Administered to 2,184 Patients," *Antimicrob Agents Chemother*, 1995, 39:650-5.

2. Gilbert DN, "Once-Daily Aminoglycoside Therapy," *Antimicrob Agents Chemother*, 1991, 35:399-405.

3. Preston SL and Briceland LL, "Single Daily Dosing of Aminoglycosides," *Pharmacotherapy*, 1995, 15:297-316.

4. Bates RD and Nahata MC, "Once-Daily Administration of Aminoglycosides," *Ann Pharmacother*, 1994, 28:757-66.

5. Rotschafer JC and Rybak MJ, "Single Daily Dosing of Aminoglycosides: A Commentary," *Ann Pharmacother*, 1994, 28:797-801.

AMINOGLYCOSIDE DOSING AND MONITORING *(Continued)*

Aminoglycoside Penetration Into Various Tissues

Site	Extent of Distribution
Eye	Poor
CNS	Poor (<25%)
Pleural	Excellent
Bronchial secretions	Poor
Sputum	Fair (10%-50%)
Pulmonary tissue	Excellent
Ascitic fluid	Variable (43%-132%)
Peritoneal fluid	Poor
Bile	Variable (25%-90%)
Bile with obstruction	Poor
Synovial fluid	Excellent
Bone	Poor
Prostate	Poor
Urine	Excellent
Renal tissue	Excellent

From Neu HC, "Pharmacology of Aminoglycosides," *The Aminoglycosides*, Whelton E and Neu HC, eds, New York, NY: Marcel Dekker, Inc, 1981.

ANGIOTENSIN AGENTS

Comparison of Indications and Adult Dosages

Drug	Hypertension	CHF	Renal Dysfunction	Dialyzable	Strengths (mg)
Benazepril (Lotensin®)	10-40 mg/day	LV dysfunction (post-MI): 20-40 mg/day in 1-2 divided doses	Cl_{cr} <30 mL/min: 5 mg/day initially Maximum: 40 mg qd	Yes	Tablets 5, 10, 20, 40
Candesartan[1] (Atacand®)	4-32 mg qd qd-bid Maximum: 32 mg qd	4-32 mg once daily (not FDA approved)	No dosage adjustment necessary	No	Tablets 4, 8, 16, 32
Captopril (Capoten®)	25-150 mg qd bid-tid Maximum: 450 mg qd	6.25-100 mg tid Maximum: 450 mg qd	Cl_{cr} 10-50 mL/min: 75% of usual dose Cl_{cr} <10 mL/min: 50% of usual dose	Yes	Tablets 12.5, 25, 50, 100
Enalapril (Vasotec®)	5-40 mg qd qd-bid Maximum: 40 mg qd	2.5-20 mg bid Maximum: 20 mg bid	Cl_{cr} 30-80 mL/min: 5 mg/day initially Cl_{cr} <30 mL/min: 2.5 mg/day initially	Yes	Tablets 2.5, 5, 10, 20
Enalaprilat[2]	0.625 mg, 1.25 mg, 2.5 mg q6h Maximum: 5 mg q6h		Cl_{cr} <30 mL/min: 0.625 mg	Yes	2.5 mg/2 mL vial
Eprosartan[1] (Teveten®)	400-800 mg qd qd-bid	Not FDA approved	No dosage adjustment necessary	Unknown	Tablets 400, 600
Fosinopril (Monopril®)	10-40 mg qd Maximum: 80 mg qd	10-40 mg qd	No dosage reduction necessary	Not well dialyzed	Tablets 10, 20, 40
Irbesartan[1] (Avapro®)	150 mg qd Maximum: 300 mg qd	Not FDA approved	No dosage reduction necessary	No	Tablets 75, 150, 300
Lisinopril (Prinivil®, Zestril®)	10-40 mg qd Maximum: 40 mg qd	5-40 mg qd	Cl_{cr} 10-30 mL/min: 5 mg/day initially Cl_{cr} <10 mL/min: 2.5 mg/day initially	Yes	Tablets 2.5, 5, 10, 20, 30, 40
Losartan[1] (Cozaar®)	25-100 mg qd or bid	Not FDA approved	No dosage adjustment necessary	No	Tablets 25, 50, 100
Moexipril (Univasc®)	7.5-30 mg qd qd-bid Maximum: 30 mg qd	Not FDA approved	Cl_{cr} <30 mL/min: 3.75 mg/day initially Maximum: 15 mg/day	Unknown	Tablets 7.5, 15
Olmesartan (Benicar™)	5-40 mg qd	Not FDA approved	No dosage adjustment necessary	Unknown	Tablets 5, 20, 40
Perindopril (Aceon®)	4-16 mg qd	4 mg qd	Cl_{cr} 30-60 mL/min: 2 mg qd Cl_{cr} 15-29 mL/min: 2 mg qod Cl_{cr} <15 mL/min: 2 mg on dialysis days	Yes	Tablets 2, 4, 8

ANGIOTENSIN AGENTS (Continued)

Comparison of Indications and Adult Dosages (continued)

Drug	Hypertension	CHF	Renal Dysfunction	Dialyzable	Strengths (mg)
Quinapril (Accupril®)	10-80 mg qd qd-bid	5-20 mg bid	Cl_{cr} 30-60 mL/min: 5 mg/day initially Cl_{cr} <10 mL/min: 2.5 mg qd initially	Not well dialyzed	Tablets 5, 10, 20, 40
Ramipril (Altace™)	2.5-20 mg qd qd-bid	2.5-10 mg qd	Cl_{cr} <40 mL/min: 1.25 mg/day Maximum: 5 mg qd	Unknown	Capsules 1.25, 2.5, 5, 10
Telmisartan[1] (Micardis®)	20-80 mg qd	Not FDA approved	No dosage reduction necessary	No	Tablets 20, 40, 80
Trandolapril (Mavik®)	2-4 mg qd Maximum: 8 mg/d qd-bid	LV dysfunction (post-MI): 1-4 mg qd	Cl_{cr} <30 mL/min: 0.5 mg/day initially	No	Tablets 1 mg, 2 mg, 4 mg
Valsartan[1] (Diovan®)	80-160 mg qd Maximum: 320 mg/day	40-160 mg bid	Decrease dose only if Cl_{cr} <10 mL/minute	No	Tablets 80, 160, 320

Dosage is based on 70 kg adult with normal hepatic and renal function.

[1]Angiotensin II antagonist.

[2]Enalaprilat is the only available ACE inhibitor in a parenteral formulation.

Comparative Pharmacokinetics

Drug	Prodrug	Absorption (%)	Serum t₁/₂ (h) Normal Renal Function	Serum Protein Binding (%)	Elimination	Onset of BP Lowering Action (h)	Peak BP Lowering Effects (h)	Duration of BP Lowering Effects (h)
Benazepril	Yes	37		~97	Renal (32%), biliary (~12%)	1	2-4	24
Benazeprilat			10-11 (effective)	~95%				
Captopril	No	60-75 (fasting)	1.9 (elimination)	25-30	Renal	0.25-0.5	1-1.5	~6
Enalapril	Yes	55-75	2	50-60	Renal (60%-80%), fecal	1	4-6	12-24
Enalaprilat			11 (effective)					
Fosinopril		36			Renal (~50%), biliary (~50%)	1		24
Fosinoprilat			12 (effective)	>99				
Moexipril	Yes		1	90	Fecal (53%), renal (8%)		1-2	>24
Moexiprilat			2-10	50				
Perindopril	Yes		1.5-3	60	Renal		3-7	
Perindoprilat			3-10 (effective)	10-20				
Quinapril	Yes	>60	0.8	97	Renal (~60%) as metabolite, fecal	1	2-4	24
Quinaprilat			2					
Ramipril	Yes	50-60	1-2	73	Renal (60%), fecal (40%)	1-2	3-6	24
Ramiprilat			13-17 (effective)	56				
Trandolapril	Yes		6	80	Renal (33%), fecal (66%)	1-2	6	≥24
Trandolaprilat			10	65-94				

ANGIOTENSIN AGENTS *(Continued)*

Comparative Pharmacokinetics of Angiotensin II Receptor Antagonists

	Candesartan (Atacand®)	Eprosartan (Teveten®)	Irbesartan (Avapro®)	Losartan (Cozaar®)	Olmesartan (Benicar™)	Telmisartan (Micardis®)	Valsartan (Diovan™)
Prodrug	Yes[1]	No	No	Yes[2]	Yes	No	No
Time to peak	3-4 h	1-2 h	1.5-2	1 h / 3-4 h[2]	1-2 h	0.5-1 h	2-4 h
Bioavailability	15%	13%	60%-80%	33%	26%	42%-58%	25%
Food – area-under-the-curve	No effect	No effect	No effect	9%-10%	No effect	9.6%-20%	9%-40%
Elimination half-life	9 h	5-9 h	11-15 h	1.5-2 h / 6-9 h[2]	13 h	24 h	6 h
Elimination altered in renal dysfunction	Yes[3]	No	No	No	Yes	No	No
Precautions in severe renal dysfunction	Yes	Yes	Yes	Yes	Yes	Yes	Yes
Elimination altered in hepatic dysfunction	No	No	No	Yes	Yes	Yes	Yes
Precautions in hepatic dysfunction	No	Yes	No	No	No	Yes	No
Protein binding	>99%	98%	90%	~99%	99%	>99.5%	95%

[1] Candesartan cilexetil: Active metabolite candesartan.
[2] Losartan: Active metabolite E-3174.
[3] Dosage adjustments are not necessary.

ANTICOAGULANTS, INJECTABLE

Name	Use	Limitation	Dose (S.C. unless otherwise noted)	Average MW (in daltons)
Low Molecular Weight Heparins				
Dalteparin (Fragmin®)	Prophylaxis	Abdominal surgery[1] Abdominal surgery[2]	2500 units/d 5000 units/d	4000-6000
		Hip surgery[1]	5000 units/d postoperatively	
	Treatment	DVT[3]	100 units/kg bid 200 units/kg qd	4000-6000
		Unstable[4] angina Non-Q-wave MI	120 units/kg (max: 10,000 units) q12h for 5-8 d	
Enoxaparin (Lovenox®)	Prophylaxis	Hip or knee replacement	30 mg twice daily[5]	3500-5500
		High-risk hip replacement or abdominal surgery	40 mg once daily	
	Treatment	DVT or PE	1 mg/kg q12h	
		Acute coronary	1 mg/kg q12h	
Tinzaparin (Innohep®)	Treatment	DVT or PE	175 anti-Xa int. units/kg/day	5500-7500
Heparin				
Heparin (Hep-Lock®)	Prophylaxis	Risk of thromboembolic disease	5000 units q8-12h	3000-30,000
	Treatment	Thrombosis or embolization	80 units/kg IVP then 20,000-40,000 units daily as continuous I.V. infusion	
	Treatment[3]	Unstable angina[3]	80 units/kg IVP then 20,000-40,000 units daily as continuous I.V. infusion	
Heparinoid				
Danaparoid (Orgaran®)	Prophylaxis	Hip replacement	750 units bid	6500
	Treatment[3]		2000 units q12h	
Selective Anti-Xa Inhibitor				
Fondaparinux[6] (Arixtra®)	Prophylaxis	Hip fracture Hip or knee replacement	2.5 mg once daily	1728

[1]Patients with low risk of DVT.
[2]Patients with high risk of DVT.
[3]Not FDA approved.
[4]Patients >60 years of age may require a lower dose of heparin.
[5]Patients weighing <100 lb or ≥65 years of age may receive 0.5 mg/kg/dose every 12 hours.
[6]Synthetic pentasaccharide.

ANTICONVULSANTS BY SEIZURE TYPE

Seizure Type	Age	Commonly Used	Alternatives
Primary generalized tonic-clonic	1 mo - 6 y	Carbamazepine, phenytoin, phenobarbital	Valproate
	6-11 y	Carbamazepine	Valproate, phenytoin, phenobarbital, lamotrigine, primidone
Primary generalized tonic-clonic with absence or with myoclonic	1 mo - 18 y	Valproate	Phenytoin, phenobarbital, carbamazepine, primidone
Partial seizures (with or without secondary generalization)	1-12 mo	Phenobarbital	Carbamazepine, phenytoin
	1-6 y	Carbamazepine	Phenytoin, phenobarbital, valproate, lamotrigine, gabapentin, oxcarbazepine (>4 y), primidone
	>6 y	Carbamazepine	Lamotrigine, levetiracetam, oxcarbazepine, phenytoin, phenobarbital, tiagabine, topiramate, valproate, primidone, zonisamide (>16 y)
Absence seizures	<10 y	Ethosuximide, valproate	Clonazepam, acetazolamide, lamotrigine
	>10 y	Valproate	Ethosuximide, acetazolamide, clonazepam
Juvenile myoclonic		Valproate	Phenobarbital, primidone, clonazepam; consider: carbamazepine, phenytoin, acetazolamide
Progressive myoclonic		Valproate	Valproate plus clonazepam, phenobarbital
Lennox-Gastaut and related syndromes		Valproate	lamotrigine, phenobarbital, clonazepam, ethosuximide; consider: steroids, ketogenic diet
Infantile spasms		ACTH, steroids	Valproate; consider: clonazepam, vigabatrin, pyridoxine
Neonatal seizures		Phenobarbital	Phenytoin; consider: clonazepam, primidone, valproate, pyridoxine

ANTIDEPRESSANT AGENTS

Comparison of Usual Dosage, Mechanism of Action, and Adverse Effects

Drug	Initial Dose	Usual Dosage (mg/d)	Dosage Forms	ACH	Drowsiness	Orthostatic Hypotension	Conduction Abnormalities[1]	GI Distress	Weight Gain	Comments
Tricyclic Antidepressants and Related Compounds										
Amitriptyline (Elavil®, Vanatrip®)	25-75 mg qhs	100-300	T, I	4+	4+	3+	3+	1	4+	Also used in chronic pain, migraine, and as a hypnotic; contraindicated with cisapride
Amoxapine	50 mg bid	100-400	T	2+	2+	2+	2+	0	2+	May cause extrapyramidal symptom (EPS)
Clomipramine[2] (Anafranil®)	25-75 mg qhs	100-250	C	4+	4+	2+	3+	1+	4+	Approved for OCD
Desipramine (Norpramin®)	25-75 mg qhs	100-300	T	1+	2+	2+	2+	0	1+	Blood levels useful for therapeutic monitoring
Doxepin (Sinequan®, Zonalon®)	25-75 mg qhs	100-300	C, L	3+	4+	2+	2+	0	4+	
Imipramine (Tofranil®, Tofranil-PM®)	25-75 mg qhs	100-300	T, C	3+	3+	4+	3+	1+	4+	Blood levels useful for therapeutic monitoring
Maprotiline (Ludiomil®)	25-75 mg qhs	100-225	T	2+	3+	2+	2+	0	2+	
Nortriptyline (Aventyl® Pamelor®)	25-50 mg qhs	50-150	C, L	2+	2+	1+	2+	0	1+	Blood levels useful for therapeutic monitoring
Protriptyline (Vivactil®)	15 mg qAM	15-60	T	2+	1+	2+	3+	1+	1+	
Trimipramine (Surmontil®)	25-75 mg qhs	100-300	C	4+	4+	3+	3+	0	4+	

ANTIDEPRESSANT AGENTS (Continued)

Comparison of Usual Dosage, Mechanism of Action, and Adverse Effects (continued)

Drug	Initial Dose	Usual Dosage (mg/d)	Dosage Forms	Adverse Effects						Comments
				ACH	Drowsiness	Orthostatic Hypotension	Conduction Abnormalities	GI Distress	Weight Gain	
Selective Serotonin Reuptake Inhibitors[3]										
Citalopram (Celexa™)	20 mg qAM	20–60	T	0	0	0	0	$3+^4$	1+	
Escitalopram (Lexapro™)	10 mg qAM	10–20	T	0	0	0	0	3+	1+	S-enantiomer of citalopram
Fluoxetine (Prozac®, Prozac® Weekly™, Sarafem™)	10–20 mg qAM	20–80	C, L, T	0	0	0	0	$3+^4$	1+	CYP2B6 and 2D6 inhibitor
Fluvoxamine (Luvox®)[2]	50 mg qhs	100–300	T	0	0	0	0	$3+^4$	1+	Contraindicated with pimozide, thioridazine, mesoridazine, CYP1A2, 2B6, 2C19, and 3A4 inhibitors
Paroxetine (Paxil®, Paxil® CR™)	10–20 mg qAM	20–50	T, L	1+	1+	0	0	$3+^4$	2+	CYP2B6 and 2D6 inhibitor
Sertraline (Zoloft®)	25–50 mg qAM	50–200	T	0	0	0	0	$3+^4$	1+	CYP2B6 and 2C19 inhibitor
Dopamine-Reuptake Blocking Compounds										
Bupropion (Wellbutrin® Wellbutrin SR®, Wellbutrin XL™, Zyban®)	100 mg bid-tid IR[5] 150 mg qAM-bid SR[6]	300–450[7]	T	0	0	0	1+/0	1+	0	Contraindicated with seizures, bulimia, and anorexia; low incidence of sexual dysfunction IR: A 6-h interval between doses preferred SR: An 8-h interval between doses preferred
Serotonin / Norepinephrine Reuptake Inhibitors[8]										
Venlafaxine (Effexor®, Effexor® XR)	25 mg bid-tid IR 37.5 mg qd XR	75–375	T	1+	1+	0	1+	$3+^4$	0	High-dose is useful to treat refractory depression; frequency of hypertension increases with dosage >225 mg/d

Comparison of Usual Dosage, Mechanism of Action, and Adverse Effects (continued)

Drug	Initial Dose	Usual Dosage (mg/d)	Dosage Forms	Adverse Effects						Comments
				ACH	Drowsiness	Orthostatic Hypotension	Conduction Abnormalities	GI Distress	Weight Gain	
5HT2 Receptor Antagonist Properties										
Nefazodone (Serzone®)	100 mg bid	300–600	T	1+	1+	2+	1+	1+	0	Contraindicated with carbamazepine, pimozide, astemizole, cisapride, and terfenadine; caution with triazolam and alprazolam; low incidence of sexual dysfunction
Trazodone (Desyrel®)	50 mg tid	150–600	T	0	4+	3+	1+	1+	2+	
Noradrenergic Antagonist										
Mirtazapine (Remeron®, Remeron® SolTab™)	15 mg qhs	15–45	T	1+	3+	1+	1+	0	3+	Dose >15 mg/d less sedating, low incidence of sexual dysfunction
Monoamine Oxidase Inhibitors										
Isocarboxazid (Marplan®)	10 mg tid	10–30	T	2+	2+	2+	1+	1+	2+	Diet must be low in tyramine; contraindicated with sympathomimetics and other antidepressants
Phenelzine (Nardil®)	15 mg tid	15–90	T	2+	2+	2+	0	1+	3+	
Tranylcypromine (Parnate®)	10 mg bid	10–60	T	2+	1+	2+	1+	1+	2+	

ACH = anticholinergic effects (dry mouth, blurred vision, urinary retention, constipation); 0 - 4+ = absent or rare -relatively common. T = tablet, L = liquid, I = injectable, C = capsule; IR = immediate release, SR = sustained release.

Important note: A 1-week supply taken all at once in a patient receiving the maximum dose can be fatal.

[1]Not approved by FDA for depression. Approved for OCD.

[2]Flat dose response curve, headache, nausea, and sexual dysfunction are common side effects for SSRIs.

[3]Nausea is usually mild and transient.

[4]IR: 100 mg bid, may be increased to 100 mg tid no sooner than 3 days after beginning therapy.

[5]SR: 150 mg qAM, may be increased to 150 mg bid as early as day 4 of dosing.

[6]To minimize seizure risk, do not exceed IR 150 mg/dose or SR 200 mg/dose.

[7]Do not use with sibutramine; relatively safe in overdose.

ANTIFUNGAL AGENTS

Activities of Various Agents Against Specific Fungi

Fungus	Amphotericin B[1]	Caspofungin	Fluconazole	Flucytosine
Aspergillus	FA	FA	N	?
Blastomyces dermatitidis	FA	?	A	N
Candida albicans	FA	FA	FA	FA
Candida krusei	FA	A	?	A
Candida tropicalis	FA	A	?	A
Coccidioides immitis	FA	?	A	N
Cryptococcus sp	FA	N	FA	FA
Dermatophytes	A	?	A	?
Fusarium	A	N	N	N
Histoplasma capsulatum	FA	A?	A	N
Penicillium	A	?	?	A
Pseudoallescheria boydii	?	A	N	N
Sporothrix schenckii	A	?	?	?
Torulopsis glabrata	A	A	?	A
Zygomycetes (Mucor, Rhizopus)	A	N	N	N

Fungus	Griseofulvin	Itraconazole	Ketoconazole	Miconazole
Aspergillus	N	FA	N	N
Blastomyces dermatitidis	N	FA	FA	N
Candida albicans	N	FA	FA	FA
Candida krusei	N	A	?	?
Candida tropicalis	N	?	?	?
Coccidioides immitis	N	A	FA	A
Cryptococcus sp	N	A	A	A
Dermatophytes	FA	A	A	N
Fusarium	N	N	N	N
Histoplasma capsulatum	N	FA	FA	N
Penicillium	N	?	N	N
Pseudoallescheria boydii	N	N	N	N
Sporothrix schenckii	N	?	N	?
Torulopsis glabrata	N	?	?	?
Zygomycetes (Mucor, Rhizopus)	N	N	N	N

Fungus	Nystatin	Terbinafine	Voriconazole
Aspergillus	A	N	FA
Blastomyces dermatitidis	A	N	A
Candida albicans	FA	A	A
Candida krusei	A	?	A
Candida tropicalis	A	?	A
Coccidioides immitis	N	N	A
Cryptococcus sp	N	N	A
Dermatophytes	N	FA	?
Fusarium	N	N	FA
Histoplasma capsulatum	N	N	A
Penicillium	N	N	?
Pseudoallescheria boydii	N	N	FA
Sporothrix schenckii	N	N	?
Torulopsis glabrata	A	?	A
Zygomycetes (Mucor, Rhizopus)	N	N	N?

FA = FDA approved indication.

A = active.

? = unknown or questionable.

N = not active.

[1]Various lipid products have differing indications, but all have activity against the same organisms.

ANTIMIGRAINE DRUGS

5-HT$_1$ Receptor Agonists: Pharmacokinetic Differences

Pharmacokinetic Parameter	Almotriptan (Axert®) Oral (6.25 mg)	Eletriptan (Relpax®) Tablets	Frovatriptan (Frova®) Oral	Naratriptan (Amerge®) Oral	Rizatriptan (Maxalt®, Maxalt-MLT®) Tablets	Rizatriptan Disintegrating Tablets	Sumatriptan (Imitrex®) S.C. (6 mg)	Sumatriptan Oral (100 mg)	Sumatriptan Nasal (20 mg)	Zolmitriptan (Zomig®, Zomig-ZMT™) Oral (5 mg)	Zolmitriptan Oral (10 mg)
Onset	<60 min	<2 h	<2 h	1-3 h	30-120 min	30-120 min	10 min	30-60 min	<60 min	45 min	
Duration	Short	Short	Long	Long	Short	Short	Short	Short	Short	Short	
Time to peak serum concentration (h)	1-3	1.5-2	2-4	2-4	1-1.5	1.6-2.5	5-20	1.5-2.5	1	1.5	2-3.5
Average bioavailability (%)	70	50	20-30	70	45	—	96	14	17	40-46	46-49
Volume of distribution (L)	180-200	138	210-280	170	110-140	110-140	170	170	NA	—	402
Half-life (h)	3-4	4	26	6	2-3	2-3	2	2-2.5[1]	2	2.8-3.4	2.5-3.7
Fraction excreted unchanged in urine (%)	40	—	32	50	14	14	22	22	—	8	8

[1] With extended dosing, the half-life extends to 7 hours.

ANTIPSYCHOTIC AGENTS

Antipsychotic Agent	Dosage Forms	I.M./P.O. Potency	Equiv Dosages (approx) (mg)	Usual Adult Daily Maint Dose (mg)	Sedation (Incidence)	Extrapyramidal Side Effects	Anticholinergic Side Effects	Orthostatic Hypotension	Comments
Aripiprazole (Abilify™)	Tab		4	10-30	Low	Very low	Very low	Very low	Low weight gain; activating
Chlorpromazine (Thorazine®)	Conc, Inj, Supp, Syr, Tab	4:1	100	200-1000	High	Moderate	Moderate	Moderate/high	
Clozapine (Clozaril®)	Tab		100	75-900	High	Very low	High	High	~1% incidence of agranulocytosis; weekly-biweekly CBC required; potential for weight gain, lipid abnormalities, and diabetes
Fluphenazine (Permitil®, Prolixin®, Prolixin Decanoate®, Prolixin Enanthate®)	Conc, Elix, Inj, Tab	2:1	2	0.5-20	Low	High	Low	Low	
Haloperidol (Haldol®, Haldol Decanoate)	Conc, Inj, Tab	2:1	2	0.5-20	Low	High	Low	Low	
Loxapine (Loxitane®, Loxitane® C, Loxitane® I.M.)	Cap, Conc, Inj		10	25-250	Moderate	Moderate	Low	Low	
Mesoridazine (Serentil®)	Inj, Liq, Tab	3:1	50	30-400	High	Low	High	Moderate	Prolongs QTc; use only in treatment of refractory illness
Molindone (Moban®)	Conc, Tab		15	15-225	Low	Moderate	Low	Low	May cause less weight gain
Olanzapine (Zyprexa®, Zyprexa Zydis®)	Tab		4	5-20	Moderate/high	Low	Moderate	Moderate	Potential for weight gain, lipid abnormalities, diabetes
Perphenazine (Trilafon®)	Conc, Inj, Tab		10	16-64	Low	Moderate	Low	Low	
Pimozide (Orap™)	Tab		2	1-20	Moderate	High	Moderate	Low	Contraindicated with CYP3A inhibitors

Antipsychotic Agent	Dosage Forms	I.M./P.O. Potency	Equiv Dosages (approx) (mg)	Usual Adult Daily Maint Dose (mg)	Sedation (Incidence)	Extrapyramidal Side Effects	Anticholinergic Side Effects	Orthostatic Hypotension	Comments
Quetiapine (Seroquel®)	Tab		125	50–800	Moderate/high	Very low	Moderate	Moderate	Moderate weight gain; potential for lipid abnormalities; diabetes
Risperidone (Risperdal®)	Sol, Tab		1	0.5–6	Low/moderate	Low	Very low	Moderate	Low to moderate weight gain; potential for diabetes
Thioridazine (Mellaril®)	Conc; Tab		100	200–800	High	Low	High	Moderate/high	May cause irreversible retinitis pigmentosa at doses >800 mg/d; prolongs QTc; use only in treatment of refractory illness
Thiothixene (Navane®)	Cap, Conc, Powder for inj	4:1	4	5–40	Low	High	Low	Low/moderate	
Trifluoperazine (Stelazine® [DSC])	Conc, Inj, Tab		5	2–40	Low	High	Low	Low	
Ziprasidone (Geodon®)	Cap, Powder for inj	2:1	40	40–160	Low/moderate	Low	Very low	Low/moderate	Low weight gain; contraindicated with QTc-prolonging agents

BENZODIAZEPINES

Agent	Dosage Forms	Relative Potency	Peak Blood Levels (oral) (h)	Protein Binding (%)	Volume of Distribution (L/kg)	Major Active Metabolite	Half-Life (parent) (h)	Half-Life[1] (metabolite) (h)	Usual Initial Dose	Adult Oral Dosage Range
Anxiolytic										
Alprazolam (Alprazolam Intensol®, Xanax®)	Sol, Tab	0.5	1-2	80	0.9-1.2	No	12-15	—	0.25-0.5 tid	0.75-4 mg/d
Chlordiazepoxide (Librium®)	Cap, Powd for inj	10	2-4	90-98	0.3	Yes	5-30	24-96	5-25 mg tid-qid	15-100 mg/d
Diazepam (Diastat® Rectal Delivery System, Diazepam Intensol®, Valium®)	Gel, Inj, Sol, Tab	5	0.5-2	98	1.1	Yes	20-80	50-100	2-10 mg bid-qid	4-40 mg/d
Lorazepam (Ativan®, Lorazepam Intensol®)[2]	Inj, Sol, Tab	1	1-6	88-92	1.3	No	10-20	—	0.5-2 mg tid-qid	2-4 mg/d
Oxazepam (Serax®)	Cap, Tab	15-30	2-4	86-99	0.6-2	No	5-20	—	10-30 mg tid-qid	30-120 mg/d
Sedative / Hypnotic										
Estazolam (ProSom®)	Tab	0.3	2	93	—	No	10-24	—	1 mg qhs	1-2 mg
Flurazepam (Dalmane®)	Cap	5	0.5-2	97	—	Yes	Not significant	40-114	15 mg qhs	15-60 mg
Quazepam (Doral®)	Tab	5	2	95	5	Yes	25-41	28-114	15 mg qhs	7.5-15 mg
Temazepam (Restoril®)	Cap	5	2-3	96	1.4	No	10-40	—	15-30 mg qhs	15-30 mg
Triazolam (Halcion®)	Tab	0.1	1	89-94	0.8-1.3	No	2.3	—	0.125-0.25 qhs	0.125-0.25 mg

Agent	Dosage Forms	Relative Potency	Peak Blood Levels (oral) (h)	Protein Binding (%)	Volume of Distribution (L/kg)	Major Active Metabolite	Half-Life (parent) (h)	Half-Life[1] (metabolite) (h)	Usual Initial Dose	Adult Oral Dosage Range
Miscellaneous										
Clonazepam (Klonopin®)	Tab	0.25-0.5	1-2	86	1.8-4	No	18-50 h	—	0.5 mg tid	1.5-20 mg/d
Clorazepate (Tranxene®)	Tab	7.5	1-2	80-95	—	Yes	Not significant	50-100 h	7.5-15 mg bid-qid	15-60 mg
Midazolam (Versed®)	Inj, Syr		0.4-0.7[3]	95	0.8-6.6	No	2-5 h	—	NA	

[1]Significant metabolite.

[2]Reliable bioavailability when given I.M.

[3]I.V. only.

NA = not available.

BETA-BLOCKERS

Agent	Adrenergic Receptor Blocking Activity	Lipid Solubility	Protein Bound (%)	Half-Life (h)	Bioavail- ability (%)	Primary (Secondary) Route of Elimination	Indications	Usual Dosage
Acebutolol (Sectral®)	beta$_1$	Low	15-25	3-4	40 7-fold[1]	Hepatic (renal)	Hypertension, arrhythmias	P.O.: 400-1200 mg/d
Atenolol (Tenormin®)	beta$_1$	Low	<5-10	6-9[2]	50-60 4-fold[1]	Renal (hepatic)	Hypertension, angina pectoris, acute MI	P.O.: 50-200 mg/d I.V.: 5 mg x 2 doses
Betaxolol (Kerlone®)	beta$_1$	Low	50-55	14-22	84-94	Hepatic (renal)	Hypertension	P.O.: 10-20 mg/d
Bisoprolol (Zebeta®)	beta$_1$	Low	26-33	9-12	80	Renal (hepatic)	Hypertension, heart failure	P.O.: 2.5-5 mg
Carteolol (Cartrol®)	beta$_1$ beta$_2$	Low	20-30	6	80-85	Renal	Hypertension	P.O.: 2.5-10 mg/d
Carvedilol (Coreg®)	beta$_1$ beta$_2$ alpha$_1$	ND	98	7-10	25-35	Bile into feces	Hypertension, heart failure (mild to severe)	P.O.: 6.25 mg twice daily
Esmolol (Brevibloc®)	beta$_1$	Low	55	0.15	NA 5-fold[1]	Red blood cell	Supraventricular tachycardia, sinus tachycardia	I.V. infusion: 25-300 mcg/kg/min
Labetalol (Normodyne®, Trandate®)	alpha$_1$ beta$_1$ beta$_2$	Moderate	50	5.5-8	18-30 10-fold[1]	Renal (hepatic)	Hypertension	P.O.: 200-2400 mg/d I.V.: 20-80 mg at 10-min intervals up to a maximum of 300 mg **or** continuous infusion of 2 mg/min
Metoprolol (Lopressor®, Toprol-XL®)	beta$_1$	Moderate	10-12	3-7	50 10-fold[1] (Toprol XL®: 77)	Hepatic/renal	Hypertension, angina pectoris, acute MI, heart failure (mild to moderate; XL formulation only)	P.O.: 100-450 mg/d I.V.: Post-MI 15 mg Angina: 15 mg then 2-5 mg/hour Arrhythmias: 0.2 mg/kg
Nadolol (Corgard®)	beta$_1$ beta$_2$	Low	25-30	20-24	30 5- to 8-fold[1]	Renal	Hypertension, angina pectoris	P.O.: 40-320 mg/d
Penbutolol (Levatol®)	beta$_1$ beta$_2$	High	80-98	5	≅100	Hepatic (renal)	Hypertension	P.O.: 20-80 mg/d
Pindolol	beta$_1$ beta$_2$	Moderate	57	3-4[2]	90 4-fold[1]	Hepatic (renal)	Hypertension	P.O.: 20-60 mg/d

Agent	Adrenergic Receptor Blocking Activity	Lipid Solubility	Protein Bound (%)	Half-Life (h)	Bioavailability (%)	Primary (Secondary) Route of Elimination	Indications	Usual Dosage
Propranolol (Inderal®, various)	beta$_1$ beta$_2$	High	90	3-5[2]	30 20-fold[1]	Hepatic	Hypertension, angina pectoris, arrhythmias	P.O.: 40-480 mg/d I.V.: Reflex tachycardia 1-10 mg
Propranolol long-acting (Inderal-LA®)	beta$_1$ beta$_2$	High	90	9-18	20- to 30-fold[1]	Hepatic	Hypertrophic subaortic stenosis, prophylaxis (post-MI)	P.O.: 180-240 mg/d
Sotalol (Betapace®, Betapace AF®, Sorine®)	beta$_1$ beta$_2$	Low	0	12	90-100	Renal	Ventricular arrhythmias/ tachyarrhythmias	P.O.: 160-320 mg/d
Timolol (Blocadren®)	beta$_1$ beta$_2$	Low to moderate	<10	4	75 7-fold[1]	Hepatic (renal)	Hypertension, prophylaxis (post-MI)	P.O.: 20-60 mg/d P.O.: 20 mg/d

Dosage is based on 70 kg adult with normal hepatic and renal function.

Note: All beta$_1$-selective agents will inhibit beta$_2$ receptors at higher doses.

[1]Interpatient variations in plasma levels.

[2]Half-life increased to 16-27 hours in creatinine clearance of 15-35 mL/minutes and >27 hours in creatinine clearance <15 mL/minutes.

BRONCHODILATORS

Comparison of Inhaled Sympathomimetic Bronchodilators

Drug	Adrenergic Receptor	Onset (min)	Duration Activity (h)
Albuterol (Proventil®, Ventolin®)	$Beta_1 < Beta_2$	<5	3-8
Epinephrine (various)	Alpha and $Beta_1$ and $Beta_2$	1-5	1-3
Formoterol (Foradil®)	$Beta_1 < Beta_2$	3-5	12
Isoetharine (various)	$Beta_1 < Beta_2$	<5	1-3
Isoproterenol (Isuprel®)	$Beta_1$ and $Beta_2$	2-5	0.5-2
Levalbuterol (Xopenex®)	$Beta_1 < Beta_2$	10-17	5-6
Metaproterenol (Alupent®)	$Beta_1 < Beta_2$	5-30	2-6
Pirbuterol (Maxair™)	$Beta_1 < Beta_2$	<5	5
Salmeterol (Serevent®)	$Beta_1 < Beta_2$	5-14	12
Terbutaline (Brethine®)	$Beta_1 < Beta_2$	5-30	3-6

CALCIUM CHANNEL BLOCKERS

Comparative Pharmacokinetics

Agent	Bioavailability (%)	Protein Binding (%)	Onset (min)	Peak (h)	Half-Life (h)	Volume of Distribution	Route of Metabolism	Route of Excretion
Dihydropyridines								
Amlodipine (Norvasc®)	52-88	97	6 h	6-9	33.8	21 L/kg	Liver, inactive metabolites, not a significant first-pass metabolism/presystemic metabolism	Bile, gut wall
Felodipine (Plendil®)	10-25	>99	3-5 h	2.5-5	10-36	10.3 L/kg	Liver, inactive metabolites, extensive metabolism by several pathways including cytochrome P450, extensive first-pass metabolism/presystemic metabolism	70% urine, 10% feces
Isradipine (DynaCirc®)	15-24	97	120	0.5-2.5	8	2.9 L/kg	Liver, inactive metabolites, extensive first-pass metabolism	90% urine, 10% feces
Nicardipine (Cardene®)	35	>95	20	0.5-2	2-4	ND	Liver, saturable first-pass metabolism	60% urine, 35% feces
Nifedipine (prototype) (Adalat® CC, Procardia®/Procardia XL®)	Immediate/sustained release 45-70/86	92-98	20	Immediate/sustained release 0.5/6	2-5	ND	Liver, inactive metabolites	60%-80% urine, feces, bile
Nimodipine (Nimotop®)	13	>95	ND	≤1	1-2	0.43 L/kg	Liver, inactive metabolites, high first-pass metabolism	Urine
Nisoldipine (Sular®)	4-8	>99	ND	6-12	7-12	4-5 L/kg	Liver, 1 active metabolite (10%), presystemic metabolism	70%-75% kidney, 6%-12% feces
Phenylalkylamines								
Verapamil (prototype) (Calan®, Isoptin®)	20-35	83-92	30	1-2.2	3-7	4.5-7 L/kg	Liver	70% urine, 16% feces
Benzothiazepines								
Diltiazem (prototype) (Cardizem®/Cardizem® CD, Dilacor® XR)	40-67	70-80	30-60	Immediate/sustained release 2-3/6-11	Immediate/sustained release 3.5-6/5-7	ND	Liver; drugs which inhibit/induce hepatic microsomal enzymes may alter disposition	Urine
Miscellaneous								
Bepridil (Vascor®)	59	>99	60	2-3	24	ND	Liver	70% urine, 22% feces

CORTICOSTEROIDS

Corticosteroids, Systemic Equivalencies

Glucocorticoid	Pregnancy Category	Approximate Equivalent Dose (mg)	Routes of Administration	Relative Anti-inflammatory Potency	Relative Mineralocorticoid Potency	Protein Binding (%)	Half-life Plasma (min)	Half-life Biologic (h)
Short-Acting								
Cortisone	D	25	P.O., I.M.	0.8	2	90	30	8-12
Hydrocortisone	C	20	I.M., I.V.	1	2	90	80-118	8-12
Intermediate-Acting								
Methylprednisolone[1]	—	4	P.O., I.M., I.V.	5	0	—	78-188	18-36
Prednisolone	B	5	P.O., I.M., I.V., intra-articular, intradermal, soft tissue injection	4	1	90-95	115-212	18-36
Prednisone	B	5	P.O.	4	1	70	60	18-36
Triamcinolone[1]	C	4	P.O., I.M., intra-articular, intradermal, intrasynovial, soft tissue injection	5	0	—	200+	18-36
Long-Acting								
Betamethasone	C	0.6-0.75	P.O., I.M., intra-articular, intradermal, intrasynovial, soft tissue injection	25	0	64	300+	36-54
Dexamethasone	C	0.75	P.O., I.M., I.V., intra-articular, intradermal, soft tissue injection	25-30	0	—	110-210	36-54
Mineralocorticoids								
Fludrocortisone	C	—	P.O.	10	125	42	210+	18-36

[1]May contain propylene glycol as an excipient in injectable forms.

GUIDELINES FOR SELECTION AND USE OF TOPICAL CORTICOSTEROIDS

The quantity prescribed and the frequency of refills should be monitored to reduce the risk of adrenal suppression. In general, short courses of high-potency agents are preferable to prolonged use of low potency. After control is achieved, control should be maintained with a low potency preparation.

1. Low-to-medium potency agents are usually effective for treating thin, acute, inflammatory skin lesions; whereas, high or super-potent agents are often required for treating chronic, hyperkeratotic, or lichenified lesions.

2. Since the stratum corneum is thin on the face and intertriginous areas, low-potency agents are preferred but a higher potency agent may be used for 2 weeks.

3. Because the palms and soles shave a thick stratum corneum, high or super-potent agents are frequently required.

4. Low potency agents are preferred for infants and the elderly. Infants have a high body surface area to weight ratio; elderly patients have thin, fragile skin.

5. The vehicle in which the topical corticosteroid is formulated influences the absorption and potency of the drug. Ointment bases are preferred for thick, lichenified lesions; they enhance penetration of the drug. Creams are preferred for acute and subacute dermatoses; they may be used on moist skin areas or intertriginous areas. Solutions, gels, and sprays are preferred for the scalp or for areas where a nonoil-based vehicle is needed.

6. In general, super-potent agents should not be used for longer than 3 weeks unless the lesion is limited to a small body area. Medium-to-high potency agents usually cause only rare adverse effects when treatment is limited to 3 months or less, and use on the face and intertriginous areas are avoided. If long-term treatment is needed, intermittent vs continued treatment is recommended.

7. Most preparations are applied once or twice daily. More frequent application may be necessary for the palms or soles because the preparation is easily removed by normal activity and penetration is poor due to a thick stratum corneum. Every-other-day or weekend-only application may be effective for treating some chronic conditions.

Corticosteroids, Topical

Steroid		Vehicle
Very High Potency		
0.05%	Augmented betamethasone dipropionate	Ointment
0.05%	Clobetasol propionate	Cream, ointment
0.05%	Diflorasone diacetate	Ointment
0.05%	Halobetasol propionate	Cream, ointment
High Potency		
0.1%	Amcinonide	Cream, ointment, lotion
0.05%	Betamethasone dipropionate, augmented	Cream
0.05%	Betamethasone dipropionate	Cream, ointment
0.1%	Betamethasone valerate	Ointment
0.05%	Desoximetasone	Gel
0.25%	Desoximetasone	Cream, ointment
0.05%	Diflorasone diacetate	Cream, ointment
0.2%	Fluocinolone acetonide	Cream
0.05%	Fluocinonide	Cream, ointment, gel
0.1%	Halcinonide	Cream, ointment
0.5%	Triamcinolone acetonide	Cream, ointment

CORTICOSTEROIDS *(Continued)*

Corticosteroids, Topical *(continued)*

Steroid		Vehicle
Intermediate Potency		
0.025%	Betamethasone benzoate	Cream, gel, lotion
0.05%	Betamethasone dipropionate	Lotion
0.1%	Betamethasone valerate	Cream
0.1%	Clocortolone pivalate	Cream
0.05%	Desoximetasone	Cream
0.025%	Fluocinolone acetonide	Cream, ointment
0.05%	Flurandrenolide	Cream, ointment, lotion, tape
0.005%	Fluticasone propionate	Ointment
0.05%	Fluticasone propionate	Cream
0.1%	Hydrocortisone butyrate[1]	Ointment, solution
0.2%	Hydrocortisone valerate[1]	Cream, ointment
0.1%	Mometasone furoate[1]	Cream, ointment, lotion
0.1%	Prednicarbate	Cream, ointment
0.025%	Triamcinolone acetonide	Cream, ointment, lotion
0.1%	Triamcinolone acetonide	Cream, ointment, lotion
Low Potency		
0.05%	Alclometasone dipropionate[1]	Cream, ointment
0.05%	Desonide	Cream
0.01%	Dexamethasone	Aerosol
0.04%	Dexamethasone	Aerosol
0.1%	Dexamethasone sodium phosphate	Cream
0.01%	Fluocinolone acetonide	Cream, solution
0.25%	Hydrocortisone[1]	Lotion
0.5%	Hydrocortisone[1]	Cream, ointment, lotion, aerosol
0.5%	Hydrocortisone acetate[1]	Cream, ointment
1%	Hydrocortisone acetate[1]	Cream, ointment
1%	Hydrocortisone	Cream, ointment, lotion, solution
2.5%	Hydrocortisone	Cream, ointment, lotion

[1] Not fluorinated.

CYCLOPLEGIC MYDRIATICS

Agent	Peak Mydriasis	Peak Cycloplegia	Time to Recovery
Atropine	30-40 min	1-3 h	>14 d
Cyclopentolate	25-75 min	25-75 min	24 h
Homatropine	30-90 min	30-90 min	6 h-4 d
Scopolamine	20-30 min	30 min-1 h	5-7 d
Tropicamide	20-40 min	20-35 min	1-6 h

FOSPHENYTOIN AND PHENYTOIN

Comparison of Parenteral Fosphenytoin and Phenytoin

	Fosphenytoin (Cerebyx®)	Phenytoin (Dilantin®)
Parenteral dosage forms available	50 mg PE/mL in 2 mL and 10 mL vials	50 mg phenytoin sodium/mL in 2 mL and 5 mL vials
Intravenous Administration	Recommended	Recommended
Loading dose	10-20 mg PE[1]/kg	10-15 mg/kg
Maintenance dose	4-7 mg/kg/day	100 mg I.V. q6-8h (oral form available)
Maximum infusion rate	Up to 150 mg PE/min	Up to 50 mg/min
Minimum infusion time for 1000 mg	6.7 min	20 min
Compatible with saline	Yes	Yes
Compatible with D_5W	Yes	No
Saline flush recommended after infusion	No	Yes
Intramuscular Administration	Recommended	Not recommended
Loading dose	10-20 mg PE/kg	10-15 mg/kg
Maintenance dose	4-7 mg/kg	Not recommended

[1]PE = phenytoin equivalents. See Fosphenytoin monograph for more details.

GLYCOPROTEIN ANTAGONISTS

Comparison of Glycoprotein IIb / IIIa Receptor Antagonists

	Abciximab (ReoPro®)	Tirofiban (Aggrastat®)	Eptifibatide (Integrilin®)
Type	Monoclonal antibody	Nonpeptide	Peptide
Mechanism of action	Steric hindrance and conformational changes	Mimics native protein sequence in receptor	Mimics native protein sequence in receptor
Biologic half-life	12-24 h	4-8 h	4-8 h
Reversible with platelet infusions	Yes	No (effect dissipates within 4-8 h)	No (effect dissipates within 4-8 h)
Speed of reversibility (return of platelet function)	Slow (>48 h)	Fast (2 h)	Fast (2 h)
Vitronectin activity	Yes	No	No
FDA-approved labeling			
Percutaneous coronary intervention (PCI)	Yes	No	Yes
Coronary stents	Yes	No	No
Unstable angina pre-PCI	When PCI planned	When PCI planned	When PCI planned
Unstable angina, medical stabilization	No	Yes	Yes
FDA-approved dosing for percutaneous coronary intervention	0.25 mg/kg bolus followed by 0.125 mcg/kg/min infusion (max: 10 mcg/min) x 12 h	Not approved for use in planned PCI	180 mcg/kg bolus immediately before the initiation of PCI, followed by 2 mcg/kg/min infusion until discharge or 18-24 hours. Repeat bolus 10 minutes after initial bolus.
FDA-approved dosing for unstable angina stabilization	0.25 mg/kg bolus followed by 10 mcg/min infusion x 18-24 h, concluding 1 h post-PCI	0.4 mcg/kg/min x 30 min followed by 0.1 mcg/kg/min infusion through angiography or 12-24 h after subsequent PCI	180 mcg/kg/bolus followed by 2 mcg/kg/min infusion until discharge, CABG procedure or up to 72 h
How supplied – volume of injectable (total drug contents/vial)	5 mL vial (10 mg)	50 mL vial (12.5 mg) 500 mL premixed solution (25 mg)	10 mL vial (20 mg) 100 mL vial (75 mg)
Storage requirements	Refrigerate, do not freeze and do not shake	Can store at room temperature, do not freeze, protect from light during storage	Refrigerate and protect from light until administered

HEMODYNAMIC SUPPORT, INTRAVENOUS

Drug	Hemodynamic Effects			
	CO	TPR	Mean BP	Renal Perfusion
Dobutamine (Dobutrex®)	↑	↓	↑	0
Dopamine (Intropin®)	↑	+/−[1]	0/↑[1]	↑[1]
Epinephrine (Adrenalin®)	↑	↓	↑	↓
Inamrinone	↑	↓	0	↑
Isoproterenol (Isuprel®)	↑	↓	↓	+/−[2]
Metaraminol (Aramine®)	↓	↑	↑	↓
Milrinone (Primacor®)	↑	↓	0	↑
Norepinephrine (Levophed®)	0/↓	↑	↑	↓
Phenylephrine (Neo-Synephrine®)	↓	↑	↑	↓

↑ = increase ↓ = decrease, 0 = no change.

[1] Dose dependent.

[2] In patients with cardiogenic or septic shock, renal perfusion commonly increases; however, in the normal patient, renal perfusion may be reduced with isoproterenol.

Drug	Hemodynamic Effects			
	α1	β1	β2	Dopamine
Dobutamine	+	++++	++	0
Dopamine	++++	++++	++	++
Epinephrine	++++	++++	++	++
Isoproterenol	0	++++	++++	0
Norepinephrine	++++	++++	0	0

Usual Hemodynamic Effects of Intravenous Agents Commonly Used for the Treatment of Acute/Severe Heart Failure

Drug	Dose	HR	MAP	PCWP	CO	SVR
Dobutamine	2.5-20 mcg/kg/min	0/↑	0/↑	↓	↑	↓
Dopamine	1-3 mcg/kg/min	0	0	0	0/↑	↓
	3-10 mcg/kg/min	↑	↑	0	↑	0
	>10 mcg/kg/min	↑	↑	↑	↑	↑
Furosemide (Lasix®)	20-80 mg, repeated as needed up to 4-6 times/day	0	0	↓	0	0
Inamrinone	5-10 mcg/kg/min	0/↑	0/↓	↓	↑	↓
Milrinone	0.375-0.75 mcg/kg/min	0/↑	0/↓	↓	↑	↓
Nesiritide	2 mcg/kg bolus; 0.01-0.03 mcg/kg/min infusion	0	↓	↓	0/↑	↓
Nitroglycerin	0.1-2 mcg/kg/min	0/↑	0/↓	↓	0/↑	0/↓
Nitroprusside (Nitropress®)	0.25-3 mcg/kg/min	0/↑	0/↓	↓	↑	↓

HR = heart rate, MAP = mean arterial pressure, PCWP = pulmonary capillary wedge pressure, CO = cardiac output, SVR = systemic vascular resistance.

↑ = increase, ↓ = decrease, 0 = no change.

HYPOGLYCEMIC DRUGS AND THIAZOLIDINEDIONE INFORMATION

Contraindications to Therapy and Potential Adverse Effects of Oral Antidiabetic Agents

	Sulfonylureas/ Meglitinide	Metformin (Glucophage®)	Acarbose (Precose®)/ Miglitol (Glyset®)	Pioglitazone (Actos®)/ Rosiglitazone (Avandia®)
Contraindications				
Insulin dependency	A	A	A[1]	
Pregnancy/lactation	A	A	A	
Hypersensitivity to the agent	A	A	A	A
Hepatic impairment	R	A	R	A
Renal impairment	R	A	R	
Congestive heart failure		A		R
Chronic lung disease		A		
Peripheral vascular disease		A		
Steroid-induced diabetes	R	R		
Inflammatory bowel disease		A	A	
Major recurrent illness	R	A		
Surgery	R	A		
Alcoholism	R	A		A
Adverse Effects				
Hypoglycemia	Yes	No	No	No
Body weight gain	Yes	No	No	Yes
Hypersensitivity	Yes	No	No	No
Drug interactions	Yes	No	No	Yes/No
Lactic acidosis	No	Yes	No	No
Gastrointestinal disturbances	No	Yes	No	No

[1]Can be used in conjunction with insulin. A = absolute; R = relative.

Comparative Pharmacokinetics

Drug	Duration of Action (h)	Daily Dose and Frequency (mg)	Metabolism
First Generation Sulfonylurea Agents			
Acetohexamide	12-24	250-1500 bid	Hepatic (60%) with active metabolite
Chlorpropamide (Diabinese®)	24-72	100-500 qd	Renal excretion (30%) and hepatic metabolism with active metabolites
Tolazamide (Tolinase®)	10-24	100-1000 qd or bid	Hepatic with active metabolites
Tolbutamide (Orinase®)	6-24	500-3000 qd-tid	Hepatic
Second Generation Sulfonylurea Agents			
Glimepiride (Amaryl®)	24	1-4 mg qd	Hepatic
Glipizide (Glucotrol®)	12-24	2.5-40 mg qd or bid	Hepatic
Glipizide GITS	24	5-10 qd	Hepatic
Glyburide (DiaBeta®, Glynase®, Micronase®)	16-24	1.25-20 qd or bid	Hepatic with active metabolites
Biguanine			
Metformin (Glucophage®)	12-24	1000-2550 mg/day bid or tid	None; excreted unchanged in urine
Alpha-Glucosidase Inhibitors			
Acarbose (Precose®)	8-12	150-300 mg/day tid	GI tract
Miglitol (Glyset®)	8	50 mg 3 times/day	Renal excretion
Meglitinides			
Nateglinide (Starlix®)	<4	120 mg 3 times/day before meals	Hepatic with active metabolites
Repaglinide (Prandin®)	<4 (single dose)	0.4-4 mg administered with meals 2, 3, or 4 times/day	Hepatic to inactive metabolites

Comparative Thiazolidinedione Pharmacokinetics

Parameter	Pioglitazone (Actos®)	Rosiglitazone (Avandia®)
Absorption	Food slightly delays but does not alter the extent of absorption	Absolute bioavailability is 99% Food ↓ C_{max} and delays T_{max}, but not change in AUC
C_{max}	156-342 ng/mL	–
T_{max}	2 hours	1 hour
Distribution	0.63 ± 0.41 L/kg	17.6 L
Plasma protein binding	>99% to serum albumin	99.8% to serum albumin
Metabolism	Extensive liver metabolism by hydroxylation and oxidation. Some metabolites are pharmacologically active. CYP2C8 and CYP3A4 metabolism	Extensive metabolism via N-demethylation and hydroxylation with no unchanged drug excreted in the urine CYP2C8 and some CYP2C9 metabolism
Excretion	Urine (15% to 30%) and bile	Urine (64%) and feces (23%)
Half-life	3-6 hours (pioglitazone) 16-24 hours (pioglitazone and metabolites)	3.15-3.59 hours
Effect of hemodialysis	Not removed	Not removed

Approved Indications for Thiazolidinedione Derivatives

Indication	Pioglitazone (Actos®)	Rosiglitazone (Avandia®)
Monotherapy	x	x
Combination Therapy – Dual Therapy		
Combination with sulfonylureas	x	x
Combination therapy with Glucophage® (metformin)	x	x
Combination therapy with insulin	x	x
Combination Therapy – Triple Therapy		
Combination therapy with sulfonylureas and Glucophage® (metformin)	–	–

Comparative Lipid Effects

Parameter	Pioglitazone (Actos®)	Rosiglitazone (Avandia®)
LDL	No significant change	↑ up to 12.1%
HDL	↑ up to 13%	↑ up to 18.5%
Total cholesterol	No significant change	↑
Total cholesterol/HDL ratio	–	–
LDL/HDL ratio	–	No change
Triglycerides	↓ up to 28%	Variable effects

LAXATIVES, CLASSIFICATION AND PROPERTIES

Laxative	Onset of Action	Site of Action	Mechanism of Action
Saline			
Magnesium citrate Magnesium hydroxide (Phillips'® Milk of Magnesia)	30 min to 3 h	Small and large intestine	Attract/retain water in intestinal lumen increasing intraluminal pressure; cholecystokinin release
Sodium phosphate/ biphosphate enema (Fleet® Enema)	2-15 min	Colon	
Irritant / Stimulant			
Cascara Casanthranol Senna (Senokot®)	6-10 h	Colon	Direct action on intestinal mucosa; stimulate myenteric plexus; alter water and electrolyte secretion
Bisacodyl (Dulcolax®) tablets, suppositories	15 min to 1 h	Colon	
Castor oil	2-6 h	Small intestine	
Cascara aromatic fluid extract	6-10 h	Colon	
Bulk-Producing			
Methylcellulose (Citrucel®) Psyllium (Metamucil®) Malt soup extract (Maltsupex®) Calcium polycarbophil (Mitrolan®, FiberCon®)	12-24 h (up to 72 h)	Small and large intestine	Holds water in stool; mechanical distention; malt soup extract reduces fecal pH
Lubricant			
Mineral oil	6-8 h	Colon	Lubricates intestine; retards colonic absorption of fecal water; softens stool
Surfactants / Stool Softener			
Docusate sodium (Colace®) Docusate calcium (Surfak®) Docusate potassium	24-72 h	Small and large intestine	Detergent activity; facilitates admixture of fat and water to soften stool
Miscellaneous and Combination Laxatives			
Glycerin suppository	15-30 min	Colon	Local irritation; hyperosmotic action
Lactulose	24-48 h	Colon	Delivers osmotically active molecules to colon
Docusate/senna (Peri-Colace®)	8-12 h	Small and large intestine	Senna – mild irritant; docusate – stool softener
Polyethylene glycol-electrolyte solution (GoLYTELY®)	30-60 min	Small and large intestine	Nonabsorbable solution which acts as an osmotic agent
Sorbitol 70%	24-48 h	Colon	Delivers osmotically active molecules to colon

LIPID-LOWERING AGENTS

Effects on Lipoproteins

Drug	Total Cholesterol (%)	LDLC (%)	HDLC (%)	TG (%)
Bile-acid resins	↓20-25	↓20-35	→	↑5-20
Fibric acid derivatives	↓10	↓10 (↑)	↑10-25	↓40-55
HMG-CoA RI (statins)	↓15-35	↓20-40	↑2-15	↓7-25
Nicotinic acid	↓25	↓20	↑20	↓40
Probucol	↓10-15	↓<10	↓30	→

Lipid-Lowering Agents

Drug	Dose/Day	Effect on LDL (%)	Effect on HDL (%)	Effect on TG (%)
HMG-CoA Reductase Inhibitors				
Atorvastatin	10 mg	-39	+6	-13
	20 mg	-43	+5	-20
	40 mg	-50	+5	-32
	80 mg	-60	+5	-37
Fluvastatin	20 mg	-22	+2	-5
	40 mg	-25	+3	-12
	80 mg	-36	+4	-12
Lovastatin	20 mg	-27	+7	-8
	40 mg	-32	+5	-2
	80 mg	-42	+8	-13
Pravastatin	10 mg	-22	+5	-3
	20 mg	-32	+3	-15
	40 mg	-34	+6	-10
Rosuvastatin	10 mg	-52	+14	-10
	20 mg	-55	+8	-23
	40 mg	-63	+10	-28
Simvastatin	5 mg	-26	+7	-12
	10 mg	-30	+5	-17
	20 mg	-38	+10	-15
	40 mg	-41	+8	-24
	80 mg	-47		
Bile Acid Sequestrants				
Cholestyramine	4-24 g	-15 to -30	+3 to +5	+0 to +20
Colestipol	7-30 g	-15 to -30	+3 to +5	+0 to +20
Colesevelam	6 tablets	-10	+10 to +25	-40 to -55
Fibric Acid Derivative				
Clofibrate	500 mg 4 times	-10	+10 to +25	-40 to -55
Fenofibrate	67-200 mg	-20 to -25	+1 to -34	-30 to -50
Gemfibrozil	600 mg twice daily	-5 to -10[1]	+10 to +20	-40 to -60
Niacin	1.5-6 g	-21 to -27	+10 to +35	-10 to -50
2-Azetidinone				
Ezetimibe	10 mg	-16 to -18	+1 to +4	-5 to -6

[1]May increase LDL in some patients.

Recommended Liver Function Monitoring for HMG-CoA Reductase Inhibitors

Agent	Initial and After Elevation in Dose	6 Weeks[1]	12 Weeks[1]	Periodically
Atorvastatin (Lipitor®)	x		x	x
Fluvastatin (Lescol®)	x		x	x
Lovastatin (Mevacor®)	x	x	x	x
Pravastatin (Pravachol®)	x			x
Simvastatin (Zocor®)	x			x

[1]After initiation of therapy or any elevation in dose.

MULTIVITAMIN PRODUCTS

Injectable Formulations

Product	A (int. units)	B₁ (mg)	B₂ (mg)	B₆ (mg)	B₁₂ (mcg)	C (mg)	D (int. units)	E (int. units)	K (mcg)	Additional Information
Solution										
Infuvite® Adult (per 10 mL)	3300	6	3.6	6	5	200	200	10	150	Supplied as two 5 mL vials. Biotin 60 mcg, folic acid 600 mcg, niacinamide 40 mg, dexpanthenol 15 mg
Infuvite® Pediatric (per 5 mL)	2300	1.6	1.4	1	1	80	400	7	200	Supplied as one 4 mL vial and one 1 mL vial. Biotin 20 mcg, folic acid 140 mcg, niacinamide 17 mg, dexpanthenol 5 mg
M.V.I.®-12 (per 10 mL)	3300	3	3.6	4	12.5	100	200	10	–	Supplied as two 5 mL vials or a single 2-chambered 10 mL vial. Biotin 60 mcg, folic acid 400 mcg, niacinamide 40 mg, dexpanthenol 15 mg
Powder for Reconstitution										
M.V.I.® Pediatric	2300	1.2	1.4	1	1	80	400	7	200	Biotin 20 mcg, folic acid 140 mcg, niacinamide 17 mg, dexpanthenol 5 mg, aluminum, polysorbate 80

Adult Formulations

Product	A (int. units)	B₁ (mg)	B₂ (mg)	B₆ (mg)	B₁₂ (mcg)	C (mg)	D (int. units)	E (int. units)	Additional Information
Liquid									
Centrum® [OTC] (per 15 mL)	2500	1.5	1.7	2	6	60	400	30	Biotin 300 mcg, Cr 25 mcg, Fe 9 mg, iodine 150 mcg, Mn 2 mg, Mo 25 mg, niacin 20 mg, pantothenic acid 10 mg, Zn 3 mg; alcohol 5.4%, sodium benzoate (240 mL)
Geritol® Tonic [OTC] (per 15 mL)		2.5	2.5	0.5					Chlorine bitartrate 50 mg, Fe 18 mg, methionine 25 mg, niacin 50 mg, pantothenic acid 2 mg; sugars 7 g, alcohol 12%, benzoic acid (120 mL, 360 mL)
Iberet® [OTC] (per 5 mL)		1.2	1.35	0.925	5.63	33.8			Fe 23.6 mg, niacin 6.8 mg, pantothenic acid 2.4 mg; alcohol (240 mL)
Iberet®-500 [OTC] (per 5 mL)		1.2	1.35	0.925	5.63	125			Fe 23.6 mg, niacin 6.8 mg, pantothenic acid 2.4 mg; alcohol (240 mL)
Vi-Daylin® [OTC] (per 5 mL)	2500	1.05	1.2	1.05	4.5	60	400	15	Niacin 13.5 mg; alcohol <0.5%, benzoic acid; lemon/orange flavor (240 mL, 480 mL)
Vi-Daylin® + Iron [OTC] (per 5 mL)	2500	1.05	1.2	1.05	4.5	60	400	15	Fe 10 mg, niacin 13.5 mg; alcohol <0.5%, benzoic acid; lemon/orange flavor (240 mL, 480 mL)
Caplet									
Theragran® Heart Right™ [OTC]	5000	3	3.4	16	30	120	400	400	Alpha-carotene, beta-carotene, biotin 30 mcg, Ca 55 mg, Cr 50 mcg, cryptoxanthin, Cu 1.5 mg, Fe 4 mg, folic acid as folate 0.6 mg, iodine 150 mcg, lutein, lycopene, Mg 150 mg, Mn 2 mg, Mo 75 mcg, niacin 20 mg, pantothenic acid 10 mg, Se 70 mcg, vit K 14 mcg, zeaxanthin, Zn 15 mg
Theragran-M® Advanced Formula [OTC]	5000	3	3.4	6	12	90	400	60	Biotin 30 mcg, boron 150 mcg, Ca 40 mg, chloride 7.5 mg, Cr 50 mcg, Cu 2 mg, Fe 9 mg, folic acid 0.4 mg, iodine 150 mcg, Mg 100 mg, Mn 2 mg, Mo 75 mcg, niacin 20 mg, nickel 5 mcg, pantothenic acid 10 mg, phosphorus 31 mg, potassium 7.5 mg, Se 70 mcg, silicon 2 mg, tin 10 mcg, vanadium 10 mcg, vit K 28 mcg, Zn 15 mg
Capsule									
Vicon Forte®	8000	10	5	2	10	150		50	Folic acid 1 mg, Mg 70 mg, Mn 4 mg, niacinamide 25 mg, Zn 80 mg
Vicon Plus® [OTC]	3400	9.3	4.6	1.5		140		45	Mg 5 mg, Mn 1 mg, niacin 24 mg, pantothenic acid 11 mg, Zn 10 mg
Vitacon Forte	8000	10	5	2	10	150		50	Folic acid 1 mg, Mg 70 mg, Mn 4 mg, niacinamide 25 mg, Zn 80 mg

MULTIVITAMIN PRODUCTS (Continued)

Adult Formulations (continued)

Product	A (int. units)	B$_1$ (mg)	B$_2$ (mg)	B$_6$ (mg)	B$_{12}$ (mcg)	C (mg)	D (int. units)	E (int. units)	Additional Information
						Tablet			
Centrum® [OTC]	5000	1.5	1.7	2	6	60	400	30	Biotin 30 mcg, boron 150 mcg, Ca 162 mg, chloride 72 mg, Cr 120 mcg, Cu 2 mg, Fe 18 mg, folic acid 0.4 mg, iodine 150 mcg, lutein 250 mcg, Mg 100 mg, Mo 75 mcg, niacin 20 mg, nickel 5 mcg, pantothenic acid 10 mg, phosphorus 109 mg, potassium 80 mg, Se 20 mcg, silicon 2 mg, tin 10 mcg, vanadium 10 mcg, vit K 25 mcg, Zn 15 mg
Centrum® Performance™ [OTC]	5000	4.5	5.1	6	18	120	400	60	Biotin 40 mcg, boron 60 mcg, chloride 72 mg, folic acid 0.4 mg, Ca 100 mg, Cr 120 mcg, Cu 2 mg, Fe 18 mg, ginkgo biloba leaf 60 mg, ginseng root 50 mg, iodine 150 mcg, Mg 40 mg, Mn 4 mg, Mo 75 mcg, niacin 40 mg, nickel 5 mcg, pantothenic acid 10 mg, phosphorus 48 mg, potassium 80 mg, Se 70 mcg, silicon 4 mg, tin 10 mcg, vanadium 10 mcg, vit K 25 mcg, Zn 15 mg
Centrum® Silver® [OTC]	5000	1.5	1.7	3	25	60	400	45	Biotin 30 mcg, boron 150 mcg, Ca 200 mg, chloride 72 mg, Cr 150 mcg, Cu 2 mg, folic acid 0.4 mg, iodine 150 mcg, lutein 250 mcg, Mg 100 mg, Mn 2 mg, Mo 75 mcg, niacin 20 mg, nickel 5 mcg, pantothenic acid 10 mg, phosphorus 48 mg, potassium 80 mg, Se 20 mcg, silicon 2 mg, vanadium 10 mcg, vit K 10 mcg, Zn 15 mg
Iberet®-500 [OTC]		4.96	5.4	3.7	22.5	500			Fe 95 mg (controlled release), niacin 27.2 mg, pantothenic acid 8.28 mg, sodium 65 mg
Iberet-Folic-500® [OTC]		6	6	5	25	500			Fe 105 mg (controlled release), folic acid 0.8 mg, niacinamde 30 mg, pantothenic acid 10 mg
Olay® Vitamins Complete Women's [OTC]	5000	1.5	1.7	2	6	120	400	50	Biotin 30 mcg, boron 150 mcg, Ca 250 mg, chloride 36 mg, coenzyme Q$_{10}$ 2 mg, Cr 120 mcg, Cu 5 mg, Fe 18 mg, folic acid 0.4 mg, iodine 150 mcg, lutein 250 mg, Mg 100 mg, Mn 2 mg, Mo 25 mcg, niacin 20 mg, nickel 5 mcg, pantothenic acid 10 mg, phosphorus 77 mg, potassium 40 mg, Se 25 mcg, silicon 2 mg, vanadium 10 mcg, Zn 15 mg
Olay® Vitamins Complete Women's 50+ [OTC]	5000	3	3.4	4	25	120	400	60	Biotin 30 mcg, boron 150 mcg, Ca 250 mg, chloride 72 mg, coenzyme Q$_{10}$ 2 mg, Cr 120 mcg, Cu 5 mg, folic acid 0.4 mg, iodine 150 mcg, lutein 250 mg, Mg 120 mg, Mn 2 mg, Mo 25 mcg, niacin 20 mg, nickel 5 mcg, pantothenic acid 10 mg, phosphorus 48 mg, potassium 80 mg, Se 50 mcg, silicon 2 mg, Zn 22 mg

Adult Formulations (continued)

Product	A (int. units)	B₁ (mg)	B₂ (mg)	B₆ (mg)	B₁₂ (mcg)	C (mg)	D (int. units)	E (int. units)	Additional Information
One-A-Day® 50 Plus Formula [OTC]	5000	4.5	3.4	6	30	120	400	60	Biotin 30 mcg, Ca 120 mg, chloride 34 mg, Cr 180 mcg, Cu 2 mg, folic acid 0.4 mg, iodine 150 mcg, Mg 100 mg, Mn 4 mg, Mo 93.75 mcg, niacin 20 mg, pantothenic acid 15 mg, potassium 37.5 mg, Se 150 mcg, vit K 20 mcg, Zn 22.5 mg
One-A-Day® Active Formula [OTC]	5000	4.5	5.1	6	18	120	400	60	American ginseng 55 mg, biotin 40 mcg, boron 150 mcg, Ca 110 mg, chloride 180 mg, Cr 100 mcg, Cu 2 mg, Fe 9 mg, folic acid 0.4 mg, iodine 150 mcg, Mg 40 mg, Mn 2 mg, Mo 25 mcg, niacin 40 mg, nickel 5 mcg, pantothenic acid 10 mg, phosphorus 48 mg, potassium 200 mg, Se 45 mcg, silicon 6 mg, tin 10 mcg, vanadium 10 mcg, vit K 25 mcg, Zn 15 mg
One-A-Day® Essential Formula [OTC]	5000	1.5	1.7	2	6	60	400	30	Folic acid 0.4 mg, niacin 20 mg, pantothenic acid 10 mg
One-A-Day® Maximum Formula [OTC]	5000	1.5	1.7	2	6	60	400	30	Biotin 30 mcg, boron 150 mcg, Ca 162 mg, chloride 72 mg, Cr 65 mcg, Cu 2 mg, Fe 18 mg, folic acid 0.4 mg, iodine 150 mcg, Mg 100 mg, Mn 3.5 mg, Mo 160 mcg, niacin 20 mg, nickel 5 mcg, pantothenic acid 10 mg, phosphorus 109 mg, potassium 80 mg, Se 20 mcg, silicon 2 mg, tin 10 mcg, vanadium 10 mcg, vit K 25 mcg, Zn 15 mg
One-A-Day® Men's Formula [OTC]	5000	2.25	2.55	3	9	90	400	45	Chloride 34 mg, Cr 150 mcg, Cu 2 mg, folic acid 0.4 mcg, iodine 150 mcg, Mg 100 mg, Mn 3.5 mg, niacin 20 mg, pantothenic acid 10 mg, potassium 37.5 mg, Se 87.5 mcg, Zn 15 mg
One-A-Day® Today [OTC]	3000	1.1	1.7	3	18	75	400	33	Biotin 30 mcg, Ca 240 mg, Cr 120 mcg, Cu 2 mg, folic acid 0.4 mg, Mg 120 mg, Mn 2 mg, niacin 14 mg, pantothenic acid 5 mg, potassium 100 mg, Se 70 mcg, soy extract 10 mg, vit K 20 mcg, Zn 15 mg
One-A-Day® Women's Formula [OTC]	2500	1.5	1.7	2	6	60	400	30	Ca 450 mg, Fe 18 mg, folic acid 0.4 mg, Mg 50 mg, niacin 10 mg, pantothenic acid 5 mg, Zn 15 mg
Tablet, Chewable									
Centrum® [OTC]	5000	1.5	1.7	2	6	60	400	30	Biotin 45 mcg, Ca 108 mg, Cr 20 mcg, Cu 2 mg, Fe 18 mg, folic acid 0.4 mg, iodine 150 mcg, Mg 40 mg, Mn 1 mg, Mo 20 mcg, niacin 20 mg, pantothenic acid 10 mg, Zn 15 mg

Ca = calcium, Cr = chromium, Cu = copper, Fe = iron, Mg = magnesium, Mn = manganese, Mo = molybdenum, Se = selenium, Zn = zinc.

MULTIVITAMIN PRODUCTS *(Continued)*

Pediatric Formulations

Product	A (int. units)	B₁ (mg)	B₂ (mg)	B₆ (mg)	B₁₂ (mcg) Drops	C (mg)	D (int. units)	E (int. units)	Additional Information
ADEKs [OTC] (per mL)	1500	0.5	0.6	0.6	4	45	400	40	Beta carotene 1 mg, biotin 15 mcg, niacin 6 mg, vit K 0.1 mg, Zn 5 mg; alcohol free, dye free (60 mL)
Poly-Vi-Flor® 0.25 mg (per mL)	1500	0.5	0.6	0.4	2	35	400	5	Fluoride 0.25 mg, niacin 8 mg; fruit flavor (50 mL)
Poly-Vi-Flor® 0.5 mg (per mL)	1500	0.5	0.6	0.4	2	35	400	5	Fluoride 0.5 mg, niacin 8 mg; fruit flavor (50 mL)
Poly-Vi-Flor® With Iron 0.25 mg (per mL)	1500	0.5	0.6	0.4		35	400	5	Fluoride 0.25 mg, iron 10 mg, niacin 8 mg; fruit flavor (50 mL)
Poly-Vi-Sol® [OTC] (per mL)	1500	0.5	0.6	0.4	2	35	400	5	Niacin 8 mg (50 mL)
Poly-Vi-Sol® With Iron [OTC] (per mL)	1500	0.5	0.6	0.4		35	400	5	Iron 10 mg, niacin 8 mg (50 mL)
Soluvite-F® (per 0.6 mL)	1500					35	400		Fluoride 0.25 mg; alcohol free, dye free, orange flavor (57 mL)
Tri-Vi-Flor® 0.25 mg (per mL)	1500					35	400		Fluoride 0.25 mg; fruit flavor (50 mL)
Tri-Vi-Flor® With Iron 0.25 mg (per mL)	1500					35	400		Fluoride 0.25 mg, iron 10 mg; fruit flavor (50 mL)
Tri-Vi-Sol® [OTC] (per mL)	1500					35	400		Fruit flavor (50 mL)
Tri-Vi-Sol® With Iron [OTC] (per mL)	1500					35	400		Iron 10 mg; fruit flavor (50 mL)
Vi-Daylin® [OTC] (per mL)	1500	0.5	0.6	0.4	1.5	35	400	5	Niacin 8 mg; alcohol <0.5%, sugar free, fruit flavor (50 mL)
Vi-Daylin® + Iron [OTC] (per mL)	1500	0.5	0.6	0.4		35	400	5	Iron 10 mg, niacin 8 mg; alcohol <0.5%, sugar free, fruit flavor (50 mL)
Vi-Daylin® ADC [OTC] (per mL)	1500					35	400		Alcohol <0.5%, sugar free, fruit flavor (50 mL)
Vi-Daylin® ADC + Iron [OTC] (per mL)	1500					35	400		Iron 10 mg; benzoic acid, sugar free, fruit flavor (50 mL)
Vi-Daylin®/F (per mL)	1500	0.5	0.6	0.4		35	400	5	Fluoride 0.25 mg, niacin 8 mg; alcohol <0.1%, benzoic acid, sugar free, fruit flavor (50 mL)
Vi-Daylin®/F + Iron (per mL)	1500	0.5	0.6	0.4		35	400	5	Fluoride 0.25 mg, iron 10 mg, niacin 8 mg; alcohol <0.1%, benzoic acid, sugar free, fruit flavor (50 mL)

Pediatric Formulations (continued)

Product	A (int. units)	B₁ (mg)	B₂ (mg)	B₆ (mg)	B₁₂ (mcg)	C (mg)	D (int. units)	E (int. units)	Additional Information
Vi-Daylin®/F ADC (per mL)	1500					35	400		**Fluoride 0.25 mg:** sugar free, fruit flavor (50 mL)
Vi-Daylin®/F ADC + Iron (per mL)	1500					35	400		**Fluoride 0.25 mg,** iron 10 mg; sugar free, fruit flavor (50 mL)
Gum									
Vitaball®	5000	1.5	1.7	2	6	60	400	30	Biotin 45 mcg, folic acid 400 mcg, niacinamide 20 mg, pantothenic acid 10 mg; bubble gum, cherry, grape, and watermelon flavors
Tablet, Chewable									
ADEKs® [OTC]	4000	1.2	1.3	1.5	12	60	400	150	Beta carotene 3 mg, biotin 50 mcg, folic acid 0.2 mg, niacin 10 mg, pantothenic acid 10 mg, vit K 150 mcg, Zn 7.5 mg; dye free
Centrum® Kids Rugrats™ Complete [OTC]	5000	1.5	1.7	2	6	60	400	30	Biotin 45 mcg, Ca 108 mg, Cr 20 mcg, Cu 2 mg, Fe 18 mg, folic acid 0.4 mg, iodine 150 mcg, Mg 40 mg, Mn 1 mg, Mo 20 mcg, niacin 20 mg, pantothenic acid 10 mg, phosphorus 50 mg, vit K 10 mg, Zn 15 mg; cherry, fruit punch, and orange flavors
Centrum® Kids Rugrats™ Extra C [OTC]	5000	1.5	1.7	1	5	250	400	15	Ca 108 mg, Cu 0.5 mg, folic acid 0.3 mg, niacin 13.5 mg, phosphorus 50 mg, sodium 15 mg, Zn 4 mg; cherry, fruit punch, and orange flavors
Centrum® Kids Rugrats™ Extra Calcium [OTC]	5000	1.5	1.7	1	5	60	400	15	Ca 200 mg, Cu 0.5 mg, folic acid 0.3 mg, niacin 13.5 mg, phosphorus 50 mg, Zn 4 mg; cherry, fruit punch, and orange flavors
Flintstones® Complete [OTC]	5000	1.5	1.7	2	6	60	400	30	Biotin 40 mcg, Ca 100 mg, Cu 2 mg, Fe 18 mg, folic acid 0.4 mg, iodine 150 mcg, Mg 20 mg, niacin 20 mg, pantothenic acid 10 mg, phosphorus 100 mg, Zn 15 mg; **phenylalanine 4.56 mg:** cherry, grape, and orange flavors
Flintstones® Original [OTC]	2500	1.05	1.2	1.05	4.5	60	400	15	Folic acid 0.3 mg, niacin 13.5 mg

MULTIVITAMIN PRODUCTS (Continued)

Pediatric Formulations (continued)

Product	A (int. units)	B_1 (mg)	B_2 (mg)	B_6 (mg)	B_{12} (mcg)	C (mg)	D (int. units)	E (int. units)	Additional Information
Flintstones® Plus Calcium [OTC]	2500	1.05	1.2	1.05	4.5	60	400	15	Ca 200 mg, folic acid 0.3 mg, niacin 13.5 mg; phenylalanine <4 mg; cherry, grape, and orange flavors
Flintstones® Plus Extra C [OTC]	2500	1.05	1.2	1.05	4.5	250	400	15	Folic acid 0.3 mg, niacin 13.5 mg; grape, orange, peach-apricot, raspberry, and strawberry flavors
Flintstones® Plus Iron [OTC]	2500	1.05	1.2	1.05	4.5	60	400	15	Fe 15 mg, folic acid 0.3 mg, niacin 13.5 mg; grape, orange, peach-apricot, raspberry, and strawberry flavors
My First Flintstones® [OTC]	2500	1.05	1.2	1.05	4.5	60	400	15	Folic acid 0.3 mg, niacin 13.5 mg; cherry, grape, and orange flavors
One-A-Day® Kids Bugs Bunny and Friends Complete [OTC]	5000	1.5	1.7	2	6	60	400	30	Biotin 40 mcg, Ca 100 mg, Cu 2 mg, Fe 18 mg, folic acid 0.4 mg, iodine 150 mcg, Mg 20 mg, niacin 20 mg, pantothenic acid 10 mg, phosphorus 100 mg, Zn 15 mg; sugar free, fruity flavors
One-A-Day® Kids Bugs Bunny and Friends Plus Extra C [OTC]	2500	1.05	1.2	1.05	4.5	250	400	15	Folic acid 0.3 mg, niacin 13.5 mg, phenylalanine; sugar free, fruity flavors
One-A-Day® Kids Extreme Sports [OTC]	5000	1.5	1.2	2	6	60	400	30	Biotin 40 mcg, Ca 100 mg, Cu 2 mg, Fe 18 mg, folic acid 0.4 mg, iodine 150 mcg, Mg 20 mg, niacin 20 mg, pantothenic acid 10 mg, phosphorus 100 mg, Zn 15 mg
One-A-Day® Kids Scooby-Doo! Complete [OTC]	5000	1.5	1.7	2	6	60	400	30	Biotin 40 mcg, Ca 100 mg, Cu 2 mg, Fe 18 mg, folic acid 0.4 mg, iodine 150 mcg, Mg 20 mg, niacin 20 mg, pantothenic acid 10 mg, phosphorus 100 mg, Zn 15 mg; fruity flavors
One-A-Day® Kids Scooby-Doo! Plus Calcium [OTC]	2500	1.05	1.2	1.05	4.5	60	400	15	Ca 200 mg, folic acid 0.3 mg, niacin 13.5 mg; fruity flavors

Ca = calcium; Cr = chromium, Cu = copper, Fe = iron, Mg = magnesium, Mn = manganese, Mo = molybdenum, Zn = zinc.

Prenatal Formulations

Product	A (int. units)	B₁ (mg)	B₂ (mg)	B₆ (mg)	B₁₂ (mcg)	C (mg)	D (int. units)	E (int. units)	Additional Information
Caplet									
StrongStart™	1000	3	3	20	12	100	400	30	Ca 200 mg, Fe 29 mg, folic acid 1 mg, niacinamide 15 mg, pantothenic acid 7 mg, Zn 20 mg; docusate sodium 25 mg
Capsule									
Anemagen™ OB		1.6	1.8	20	12	60	400	30	Ca 200 mg, Fe 28 mg, folic acid 1 mg; docusate calcium 25 mg
Chromagen OB®		1.6	1.8	20	12	60	400	30	Ca 200 mg, Fe 28 mg, folic acid 1 mg, Mn 2 mg, niacinamide 5 mg, Zn 25 mg; docusate calcium 25 mg
Powder									
Obegyn™ (per 4 level tsp/8.25 g)	2500 (as palmitate) 2500 (as beta-carotene)	1.7	2	10	12	120	400	60	Biotin 300 mcg, Ca 455 mg, Cu 2 mg, Fe 18 mg, folic acid 1 mg, iodine 150 mcg, Mg 150 mg, niacin 20 mg, pantothenic acid 10 mg, Zn 25 mg; **phenylalanine 84 mg/8.25 g**; orange flavor (495 g/60 doses)
Tablet									
Advanced NatalCare®	2700	3	3.4	20	12	120	400	30	Ca 200 mg, Cu 2 mg, Fe 90 mg, folic acid 1 mg, Mg 30 mg, niacinamide 20 mg, Zn 25 mg; docusate sodium 50 mg
Citracal® Prenatal Rx	2700	3	3.4	20	12	120	400	30	Ca 125 mg, Cu 2 mg, Fe 27 mg, folic acid 1 mg, iodine 150 mcg, niacinamide 20 mg, Zn 25 mg; docusate sodium 50 mg
Duet®	3000	1.8	4	25	12	120	400	30	Ca 200 mg, Cu 2 mg, Fe 29 mg, folic acid 1 mg, Mg 25 mg, niacinamide 20 mg, Zn 25 mg
NatalCare® GlossTabs™	2700	3	3.4	20	12	120	400	10	Biotin 30 mcg, Ca 200 mg, Cu 2 mg, Fe 90 mg, folic acid 1 mg, Mg 30 mg, niacinamide 20 mg, pantothenic acid 6 mg, Zn 15 mg; docusate sodium 50 mg
NatalCare® PIC	400	2.43	3	1.64		50	400		Ca 125 mg, folic acid 1 mg, niacinamide 10 mg, polysaccharide-iron complex 60 mg, Zn 18 mg
NatalCare® PIC Forte	5000	3	3.4	4	12	80	400	30	Ca 250 mg, Cu 2 mg, folic acid 1 mg, iodine 200 mcg, Mg 10 mg, niacinamide 20 mg, polysaccharide-iron complex 60 mg, Zn 25 mg

MULTIVITAMIN PRODUCTS *(Continued)*

Prenatal Formulations *(continued)*

Product	A (int. units)	B₁ (mg)	B₂ (mg)	B₆ (mg)	B₁₂ (mcg)	C (mg)	D (int. units)	E (int. units)	Additional Information
NatalCare® Plus	4000	1.84	3	10	12	120	400	22	Ca 200 mg, Cu 2 mg, Fe 27 mg, folic acid 1 mg, niacinamide 20 mg, Zn 25 mg
NatalCare® Rx	4000	1.5	1.6	4	2.5	80	400	15	Biotin 30 mcg, Ca 200 mg, Cu 3 mg, folate 1 mg, iodine 54 mcg, Mg 100 mg, niacin 17 mg, pantothenic acid 7 mg, Zn 25 mg
NatalCare™ Three	3000	1.8	4	25	12	120	400	22	Ca 200 mg, Cu 2 mg, Fe 28 mg, folic acid 1 mg, Mg 25 mg, niacinamide 20 mg, Zn 25 mg
NataFort®	1000	2	3	10	12	120	400	11	Fe 60 mg, folic acid 1 mg, niacinamide 20 mg
NataTab™ CFe	4000	3	3	3	8	120	400	30	Ca 200 mg, Fe 50 mg, folic acid 1 mg, iodine 150 mcg, niacin 20 mg, Zn 15 mg
NataTab™ FA	4000	3	3	6	8	120	400	30	Ca 200 mg, Fe 29 mg, folic acid 1 mg, iodine 150 mcg, niacin 20 mg, Zn 15 mg
NataTab™ Rx	4000	3	3	3	8	120	400	30	Biotin 30 mcg, Ca 200 mg, Cu 3 mg, Fe 29 mg, folic acid 1 mg, iodine 150 mcg, Mg 100 mg, niacin 20 mg, pantothenic acid 7 mg, Zn 15 mg
Nestabs® CBF	4000	3	3	3	8	120	400	30	Ca 200 mg, Fe 50 mg, folic acid 1 mg, iodine 150 mcg, niacin 20 mg, Zn 15 mg
Nestabs® FA	4000	3	3	6	8	120	400	30	Ca 200 mg, Fe 29 mg, folic acid 1 mg, iodine 150 mcg, niacin 20 mg, Zn 15 mg
Nestabs® RX	4000	3	3	3	8	120	400	30	Biotin 30 mcg, Ca 200 mg, Cu 3 mg, Fe 29 mg, folic acid 1 mg, iodine 150 mcg, Mg 100 mg, niacin 20 mg, pantothenic acid 7 mg, Zn 15 mg
Niferex®-PN	4000	2.43	3	1.64	3	50	400		Ca 125 mg, folic acid 1 mg, niacinamide 10 mg, polysaccharide-iron complex 60 mg, Zn 18 mg
Niferex®-PN Forte	5000	3	3.4	4	12	80	400	30	Ca 250 mg, Cu 2 mg, folic acid 1 mg, iodine 200 mcg, Mg 10 mg, niacinamide 20 mg, polysaccharide-iron complex 60 mg, Zn 25 mg
Pramilet® FA	4000	3	2	3	3	60	400		Ca 250 mg, calcium pantothenate 1 mg, Cu 0.15 mg, Fe 40 mg, folic acid 1 mg, iodine 100 mcg, Mg 10 mg, niacinamide 10 mg, Zn 0.085 mg

Prenatal Formulations (continued)

Product	A (int. units)	B₁ (mg)	B₂ (mg)	B₆ (mg)	B₁₂ (mcg)	C (mg)	D (int. units)	E (int. units)	Additional Information
Prenatal MR 90 Fe™	4000	3	3.4	20	12	120	400	30	Ca 250 mg, Cu 2 mg, Fe 90 mg, folic acid 1 mg, iodine 150 mcg, niacinamide 20 mg, Zn 25 mg; docusate sodium 50 mg
Prenatal MRT with Selenium	5000	3	3.4	10	12	120	400	30	Biotin 30 mcg, Ca 200 mg, Cr 25 mcg, Cu 2 mg, Fe 27 mg, folic acid 1 mg, iodine 150 mcg, Mg 25 mg, Mn 5 mg, Mo 25 mcg, niacinamide 20 mg, pantothenic acid 10 mg, Se 20 mcg, Zn 25 mg
Prenatal Plus	4000	1.8	3	10	12	120	400	22	Ca 200 mg, Cu 2 mg, Fe 27 mg, folic acid 1 mg, niacinamide 20 mg, Zn 25 mg
Prenatal Rx	4000	1.5	1.6	4	2.5	80	400	15	Biotin 30 mcg, Ca 200 mg, Cu 3 mg, Fe 60 mg, folic acid 1 mg, Mg 100 mg, niacinamide 17 mg, pantothenic acid 7 mg, Zn 25 mg
Prenatal Z	3000	1.5	1.6	2.2	2.2	70	400	10	Ca 200 mg, Fe 65 mg, folic acid 1 mg, iodine 175 mcg, Mg 100 mg, niacin 17 mg, Zn 15 mg
Prenate GT™	2700	3	3.4	20	12	120	400	10	Biotin 30 mcg, Ca 200 mg, Cu 2 mg, Fe 90 mg, folic acid 1 mg, Mg 30 mg, niacinamide 20 mg, pantothenic acid 6 mg, Zn 15 mg; docusate sodium 50 mg
Stuartnatal® Plus 3™	3000	1.8	4	25	12	120	400	22	Ca 200 mg, Cu 2 mg, Fe 28 mg, folic acid 1 mg, Mg 25 mg, niacinamide 20 mg, Zn 25 mg
Stuart Prenatal®	4000	1.8	1.7	2.6	8	120	400	30	Ca 200 mg, Fe 28 mg, folic acid 0.8 mg, niacin 20 mg, Zn 25 mg
Ultra NatalCare®	2700	3	3.4	20	12	120	400	30	Ca 200 mg, Cu 2 mg, Fe 90 mg, folic acid 1 mg, iodine 150 mcg, niacinamide 20 mg, Zn 25 mg; docusate sodium 50 mg

MULTIVITAMIN PRODUCTS *(Continued)*

Prenatal Formulations *(continued)*

Product	A (int. units)	B₁ (mg)	B₂ (mg)	B₆ (mg)	B₁₂ (mcg)	C (mg)	D (int. units)	E (int. units)	Additional Information
					Tablet, Chewable				
Duet®	3000	1.8	4	25	12	120	400	30	Ca 100 mg, Cu 2 mg, Fe 29 mg, folic acid 1 mg, Mg 25 mg, niacinamide 20 mg, Zn 25 mg; **phenylalanine 15 mg/ tablet**
NataChew™	1000	2	3	10	12	120	400	11	Fe 29 mg, folic acid 1 mg, niacinamide 20 mg; peanut extract, wildberry flavor
StrongStart™	1000	3	3	20	12	100	400	30	Ca 200 mg, Fe 20 mg, folic acid 1 mg, niacinamide 15 mg, pantothenic acid 7 mg, Zn 20 mg; **phenylalanine 6 mg/ tablet**

Cr = chromium, Cu = copper, Fe = iron, Mg = magnesium, Mn = manganese, Mo = molybdenum, Se = selenium, Zn = zinc.

Vitamin B Complex Combinations

Product	B₁ (mg)	B₂ (mg)	B₆ (mg)	B₁₂ (mcg)	C (mg)	E (int. units)	Additional Information
Caplet							
Allbee® with C [OTC]	15	10.2	5		300		Niacinamide 50 mg, pantothenic acid 10 mg
Allbee® C-800 [OTC]	15	17	25	12	800	45	Niacinamide 100 mg, pantothenic acid 25 mg
Allbee® C-800 + Iron [OTC]	15	17	25	12	800	45	Fe 27 mg, folic acid 0.4 mg, niacinamide 100 mg, pantothenic acid 25 mg
Capsule							
Trinsicon®				15			C 75 mg, Fe 110 mg, folic acid 0.5 mg, liver-stomach concentrate (containing intrinsic factor and other vitamin B complex factors) 240 mg
Liquid							
Apatate® [OTC] (per 5 mL) [OTC]	15		0.5	25			Cherry flavor (120 mL)
Gevrabon® [OTC] (per 30 mL) [OTC]	5	2.5	1	1			Choline 10 mg, Fe 15 mg, iodine 100 mcg, Mg 2 mg, Mn 2 mg, niacinamide 60 mg, pantothenic acid 10 mg, Zn 2 mg; alcohol, benzoic acid; sherry wine flavor (480 mL)
Softgel							
Nephrocaps®	1.5	1.7	10	6	100		Biotin 150 mcg, folic acid 1 mcg, niacinamide 20 mg, pantothenic acid 5 mg
Tablet							
Diatx™	1.5	1.5	50		60		Biotin 300 mcg, cobalamin 1 mg, folacin 1 mg, niacinamide 20 mg, pantothenic acid 10 mg [dye free, lactose free, sugar free]
DiatxFe™	1.5	1.5	50		60		Biotin 300 mcg, cobalamin 1 mg, ferrous fumarate 304 mg, folacin 5 mg, niacinamide 20 mg, pantothenic acid 10 mg [dye free, lactose free, sugar free]
NephPlex® Rx	1.5	1.7	10	6	60		Biotin 300 mcg, folic acid 1 mg, niacinamide 20 mg, pantothenic acid 10 mg, zinc 12.5 mg
Nephro-Vite®	1.5	1.7	10	6	60		Biotin 300 mcg, folic acid 0.8 mcg, niacinamide 20 mg, pantothenic acid 10 mg
Nephro-Vite® Rx	1.5	1.7	10	6	60		Biotin 300 mcg, folic acid 1 mg, niacinamide 20 mg, pantothenic acid 10 mg
Nephron FA®	1.5	1.7	10	6	40		Biotin 300 mcg, docusate sodium 75 mg, ferrous fumarate 200 mg, folic acid 1 mg, pantothenic acid 10 mg
Olay® Vitamins Essential Folic Acid w/B₁₂ Complex [OTC]		25	25	200		200	Folic acid 600 mcg, selenium 50 mcg
Olay® Vitamins Super B-Stress Defense [OTC]	10	10	5	12	500	30	Biotin 100 mcg, folic acid 400 mcg, niacin 100 mg, pantothenic acid 20 mg
Stresstabs® B-Complex [OTC]	10	10	5	12	500	30	Biotin 45 mcg, folic acid 0.4 mcg, niacinamide 100 mg, pantothenic acid 20 mg

MULTIVITAMIN PRODUCTS (Continued)

Vitamin B Complex Combinations (continued)

Product	B$_1$ (mg)	B$_2$ (mg)	B$_6$ (mg)	B$_{12}$ (mcg)	C (mg)	E (int. units)	Additional Information
Stresstabs® B-Complex + Iron [OTC]	10	10	5	12	500	30	Biotin 45 mcg, Fe 18 mg, folic acid 0.4 mcg, niacinamide 100 mg, pantothenic acid 20 mg
Stresstabs® B-Complex + Zinc [OTC]	10	10	5	12	500	30	Biotin 45 mcg, Cu 3 mg, folic acid 0.4 mcg, niacinamide 100 mg, pantothenic acid 20 mg, Zn 23.9 mg
Surbex-T® [OTC]	15	10	5	10	500		Ca 20 mg, niacinamide 100 mg
Z-Bec® [OTC]	15	10.2	10	6	600	45	Niacinamide 100 mg, pantothenic acid 25 mg, Zn 22.5 mg
Tablet, Chewable							
Apatate® [OTC]	15		0.5	25			Cherry flavor

Ca = calcium, Cu = copper, Fe = iron, Mg = magnesium, Mn = manganese, Zn = zinc.

NARCOTIC AGONISTS

Comparative Pharmacokinetics

Drug	Onset (min)	Peak (h)	Duration (h)	Half-Life (h)	Average Dosing Interval (h)	Equianalgesic Doses[1] (mg) I.M.	Equianalgesic Doses[1] (mg) Oral
Alfentanil	Immediate	ND	ND	1-2	—	ND	NA
Buprenorphine	15	1	4-8	2-3		0.4	—
Butorphanol	I.M.: 30-60; I.V.: 4-5	0.5-1	3-5	2.5-3.5	3 (3-6)	2	—
Codeine	P.O.: 30-60; I.M.: 10-30	0.5-1	4-6	3-4	3 (3-6)	120	200
Fentanyl	I.M.: 7-15 I.V.: Immediate	ND	1-2	1.5-6	1 (0.5-2)	0.1	NA
Hydrocodone	ND	ND	4-8	3.3-4.4	6 (4-8)	ND	ND
Hydromorphone	P.O.: 15-30	0.5-1	4-6	2-4	4 (3-6)	1.5	7.5
Levorphanol	P.O.: 10-60	0.5-1	4-8	12-16	6 (6-24)	2 (A) 1 (C)	4 (A) 1 (C)
Meperidine	P.O./I.M./S.C.: 10-15 I.V.: ≤5	0.5-1	2-4	3-4	3 (2-4)	75	300
Methadone	P.O.: 30-60; I.V.: 10-20	0.5-1	4-6 (acute); >8 (chronic)	15-30	8 (6-12)	10 (A) 2-4 (C)	20 (A) 2-4 (C)
Morphine	P.O.: 15-60 I.V.: ≤5	P.O./I.M./S.C.: 0.5-1; I.V.: 0.3	3-6	2-4	4 (3-6)	10	60[2] (A) 30 (C)
Nalbuphine	I.M.: 30; I.V.: 1-3	1	3-6	5	—	10	—
Oxycodone	P.O.: 10-15	0.5-1	4-6	3-4	4 (3-6)	NA	20
Oxymorphone	5-15	0.5-1	3-6	—	—	1	10[3]
Pentazocine	15-20	0.25-1	3-4	2-3	3 (3-6)	ND	ND
Propoxyphene	P.O.: 30-60	2-2.5	4-6	3.5-15	6 (4-8)	ND	130[4]-200[5]
Remifentanil	1-3	<0.3	0.1-0.2	0.15-0.3	—	ND	ND
Sufentanil	1.3-3	ND	ND	2.5-3	—	0.02	NA

ND = no data available. NA = not applicable. (A) = acute, (C) = chronic.

[1] Based on acute, short-term use. Chronic administration may alter pharmacokinetics and decrease the oral parenteral ratio. The morphine oral-parenteral ratio decreases to ~1.5-2.5:1 upon chronic dosing.

[2] Extensive survey data suggest that the relative potency of I.M.:P.O. morphine of 1:6 changes to 1:2-3 with chronic dosing.

[3] Rectal

[4] HCl salt

[5] Napsylate salt

Adapted from *Principles of Analgesic Use in the Treatment of Acute Pain and Cancer Pain*, 4th ed, Skokie, IL: The American Pain Society, 1999.

NARCOTIC AGONISTS (Continued)

Comparative Pharmacology

Drug	Analgesic	Antitussive	Constipation	Respiratory Depression	Sedation	Emesis
Phenanthrenes						
Codeine	+	+++	+	+	+	+
Hydrocodone	+	+++		+		
Hydromorphone	++	+++	+	++	+	+
Levorphanol	++	++	++	++	++	+
Morphine	++	+++	++	++	++	++
Oxycodone	++	+++	++	++	++	++
Oxymorphone	++	+	++	+++		+++
Phenylpiperidines						
Alfentanil	++					
Fentanyl	++			+		
Meperidine	++	+	+	++	+	+
Remifentanil	++			++	+	
Sufentanil	+++			++	+++	++
Diphenylheptanes						
Methadone	++	++	++	++	+	+
Propoxyphene	+			+	+	+
Agonist / Antagonist						
Buprenorphine	++	N/A	++	+++	++	++
Butorphanol	++	N/A	+++	+++	++	+
Dezocine	++		+	++	+	++
Nalbuphine	++	N/A	+++	+++	++	++
Pentazocine	++	N/A	+	++	++ or stimulation	++

NEUROMUSCULAR BLOCKING AGENTS

Suggested Dosing Guidelines for the Use of Neuromuscular Blocking Agents in the Intensive Care Unit

Agent	Intermittent Injection	Continuous Infusion
Short Duration		
Mivacurium (Mivacron®)	0.15-0.25 mg/kg followed by 0.1 mg/kg every 15 minutes	1-15 mcg/kg/min
Intermediate Duration		
Atracurium (Tracrium®)	0.4-0.5 mg/kg every 25-35 minutes	0.4-1 mg/kg/h
Cisatracurium (Nimbex®)	0.15-0.2 mg/kg every 40-60 minutes	0.03-0.6 mg/kg/h
Rocuronium (Zemuron®)	0.6 mg/kg every 30 minutes	0.6 mg/kg/h
Vecuronium (Norcuron®)	0.1 mg/kg every 35-45 minutes	0.05-0.1 mg/kg/h
Long Duration		
Doxacurium (Nuromax®)	0.025 mg/kg every 2-3 hours	0.015-0.045 mg/kg/h
Pancuronium	0.1 mg/kg every 90-100 minutes	0.05-0.1 mg/kg/h

NEUROMUSCULAR BLOCKING AGENTS (Continued)

Pharmacokinetic and Pharmacodynamic Properties of Neuromuscular Blocking Agents

Agent	Clearance (mL/kg/min)	V_{dss} (L/kg)	Half-life (min)	ED95[1] (mg/kg)	Initial Adult Dose[2,3] (mg/kg)	Onset (min)	Clinical Duration of Action of Initial Dose (min)	Administration as an Intraoperative Infusion (mcg/kg/min)
Ultra-Short Duration								
Succinylcholine	Unknown	Unknown	Unknown	0.2	1-1.5	0.5-1	4-8	10-100
Short Duration								
Mivacurium	50-100[2]	0.2	2[4]	0.07	0.15-0.25	1.5-3	12-20	1-15
Intermediate Duration								
Atracurium	5-7	0.2	20	0.2	0.4-0.5	2-3	20-45	4-12
Cisatracurium	4.6	0.15	22-29	0.05	0.15-0.2	2-3	40-60	1-3
Rocuronium	4	0.17-0.29	60-70	0.3	0.6-1.2	1-1.5	31-67	4-16
Vecuronium	4.5	0.16-0.27	51-80	0.05	0.08-0.1	2-3	20-40	0.8-2
Long Duration								
Doxacurium	1-2.5	0.2	100-200	0.025	0.05-0.08	4-6	100-160	n/a
Pancuronium	1-2	0.18-0.26	107-169	0.07	0.08-0.1	3-5	60-100	n/a

[1]ED95: Effective dose causing 95% blockade.

[2]Initial dose (intubation dose) is usually 2 x ED95 with the exception of cisatracurium where the recommended initial dose is 3-4 x ED95.

[3]Prior administration of succinylcholine generally enhances the magnitude and duration of nondepolarizing NMB agents; initial doses should be lower.

[4]Values reflect contribution of cis-trans and trans-trans isomers only.

NICOTINE PRODUCTS

Dosage Form	Brand Name	Dosing	Recommended Treatment Duration	Strengths Available
Lozenge	Commit™ (OTC)	Patients who smoke their first cigarette within 30 minutes of waking should use the 4 mg strength; otherwise the 2 mg strength is recommended. 1-6 wk: One lozenge q1-2h 7-9 wk: One lozenge q2-4h 10-12 wk: One lozenge q4-8h	~12 wk	2 mg, 4 mg
Chewing gum	Nicorette® (OTC)	Chew 1 piece q1-2h for 6 wk, then decrease to 1 piece q2-4h for 3 wk, then 1 piece q4-8h for 3 wk, then discontinue.	~12 wk	2 mg, 4 mg
Transdermal	Nicoderm CQ® (OTC)	One 21 mg/d patch qd for 6 wk, then one 14 mg/d patch qd for 2 wk, then one 7 mg/d patch qd for 2 wk, then discontinue. Low-dose regimen[1]: One 14 mg/d patch qd for 6 wk, then one 7 mg/d patch qd for 2 wk, then discontinue.	~10 wk	Patch: 21 mg/d 14 mg/d 7 mg/d
	Nicotrol®	One 15 mg patch qd, worn for 16 h/d and removed for 8 h/d for a total of 6 wk, then discontinue.	~6 wk	15 mg/16 h patch
	ProStep®	One 22 mg patch qd for 6 wks. If patient smokes ≤15 cigarettes/day, start one 11 mg patch qd for 6 wks.	~6 wk	Patch: 22 mg/d 11 mg/d
Nasal spray	Nicotrol® NS	One dose is 2 sprays (1 spray in each nostril). Initial dose: 1-2 sprays q1h, should not exceed 10 sprays (5 doses)/h or 80 sprays (40 doses)/d.	~12 wk	10 mL spray 0.5/mg spray (200 actuations)
Inhaler	Nicotrol®	Inhaler releases 4 mg nicotine (the equivalent of 2 cigarettes smoked) for 20 min of active inhaler puffing. Usual dose: 6-16 cartridges/d for up to 12 wk, then reduce dose gradually over ensuing 12 wk, then discontinue.	~18-24 wk	10 mg/cartridge: releases 4 mg/cartridge

[1]Transdermal low-dose regimens are intended for patients <100 lb, smoke <10 cigarettes/day, and/or have a history of cardiovascular disease.

NITRATES

Nitrates[1]	Dosage Form	Onset (min)	Duration
Nitroglycerin	I.V.	1-2	3-5 min
	Sublingual	1-3	30-60 min
	Translingual spray	2	30-60 min
	Oral, sustained release	40	4-8 h
	Topical ointment	20-60	2-12 h
	Transdermal	40-60	18-24 h
Isosorbide dinitrate	Sublingual and chewable	2-5	1-2 h
	Oral	20-40	4-6 h
	Oral, sustained release	Slow	8-12 h
Isosorbide mononitrate	Oral	60-120	5-12 h

[1]Hemodynamic and antianginal tolerance often develops within 24-48 hours of continuous nitrate administration.

Adapted from Corwin S and Reiffel JA, "Nitrate Therapy for Angina Pectoris," *Arch Intern Med*, 1985, 145:538-43 and Franciosa JA, "Nitroglycerin and Nitrates in Congestive Heart Failure," *Heart and Lung*, 1980, 9(5):873-82.

NONSTEROIDAL ANTI-INFLAMMATORY AGENTS

Comparative Dosages and Pharmacokinetics

Drug	Maximum Recommended Daily Dose (mg)	Time to Peak Levels (h)[1]	Half-life (h)
Acetic Acids			
Diclofenac potassium immediate release (Cataflam®)	200	1	1-2
Diclofenac sodium delayed release (Voltaren®)	225	2-3	1-2
Etodolac (Lodine®)	1200	1-2	7.3
Indomethacin (Indocin®)	200	1-2	4.5
Indomethacin SR	150	2-4	4.5-6
Ketorolac (Toradol®)	I.M.: 120[2] P.O.: 40	0.5-1	3.8-8.6
Sulindac (Clinoril®)	400	2-4	7.8 (16.4)[3]
Tolmetin (Tolectin®)	2000	0.5-1	1-1.5
Fenamates (Anthranilic Acids)			
Meclofenamate	400	0.5-1	2 (3.3)[4]
Mefenamic acid (Ponstel®)	1000	2-4	2-4
Propionic Acids			
Fenoprofen (Nalfon®)	3200	1-2	2-3
Flurbiprofen (Ansaid®)	300	1.5	5.7
Ibuprofen (various)	3200	1-2	1.8-2.5
Ketoprofen (Orudis®, others)	300	0.5-2	2-4
Naproxen (Naprosyn®)	1500	2-4	12-15
Naproxen sodium (Anaprox®, others)	1375	1-2	12-13
Oxaprozin (Daypro®)	1800	3-5	42-50
Nonacidic Agent			
Nabumetone (Relafen®)	2000	3-6	24
Salicylic Acid Derivative			
Diflunisal (Dolobid®)	1500	2-3	8-12
Salsalate	3000	2-3	7-8
COX-2 Inhibitors			
Celecoxib (Celebrex®)	400	3	11
Rofecoxib (Vioxx®)	50	2-3	17
Valdecoxib (Bextra®)	40	2.25-3	8-11
Oxicam			
Meloxicam (MOBIC®)	15	4-5	15-20
Piroxicam (Feldene®)	20	3-5	30-86

Dosage is based on 70 kg adult with normal hepatic and renal function.

[1]Food decreases the rate of absorption and may delay the time to peak levels.

[2]150 mg on the first day.

[3]Half-life of active sulfide metabolite.

[4]Half-life with multiple doses.

PARKINSON'S AGENTS

Drugs Used for the Treatment of Parkinson's Disease

Drug	Receptor Affinity	Initial Dose	Titration Schedule	Usual Daily Dosage Range	Recommended Dosing Schedule
Amantadine (Symmetrel®)	NMDA receptor antagonist and inhibits neuronal reuptake of dopamine	100 mg every other day	100 mg/dose every week, up to 300 mg 3 times/d	100-200 mg	Twice daily
Benztropine (Cogentin®)	Cholinergic receptors, also has antihistamine effects	0.5-2 mg/d in 1-4 divided doses	0.5 mg/dose every 5-6 d	2-6 mg	1-2 times/d
Bromocriptine (Parlodel®)	Moderate affinity for D_2 and D_3 dopamine receptors	1.25 mg twice daily	2.5 mg/d every 2-4 wk	2.5-100 mg	3 times/d
Cabergoline (Dostinex®)[1]	Selective to D_2 dopamine receptors	0.5 mg once daily	0.25-0.5 mg/d every 4 wk	0.5-5 mg	Once daily
Entacapone (Comtan®)	COMT enzyme inhibitor	200 mg 3 times/d	Titrate down the doses of levodopa/carbidopa as required	600-1600 mg	3 times/d; up to 8 times/d
Levodopa/carbidopa (Sinemet® CR)	Converts to dopamine; binds to all CNS dopamine receptors	10-25/100 mg 2-4 times/d	0.5-1 tablet (10 or 25/100 mg) every 1-2 d	50/200 to 200/2000 mg (3-8 tablets)	3 times/d or twice daily (for controlled release)
Pergolide (Permax®)	Low affinity for D_1 and maximal affinity for D_2 and D_3 dopamine receptors	0.05 mg/night	0.1-0.15 mg/d every 3 d for 12 d, then 0.25 mg/d every 3 d	0.05-5 mg	3 times/d
Pramipexole (Mirapex®)	High affinity for D_2 and D_3 dopamine receptors	0.125 mg 3 times/d	0.125 mg/dose every 5-7 d	1.5-4.5 mg	3 times/d
Ropinirole (Requip®)	High affinity for D_2 and D_3 dopamine receptors	0.25 mg 3 times/d	0.25 mg/dose weekly for 4 wk, then 1.5 mg/d every week up to 9 mg/d; 3 mg/d up to a max of 24 mg/d	0.75-24 mg	3 times/d
Selegiline (Eldepryl®)	No receptor effects, inhibits monoamine oxidase	5-10 mg twice daily	Titrate down the doses of levodopa/carbidopa as required	5-10 mg	Twice daily
Tolcapone (Tasmar®)	COMT enzyme inhibitor	100 mg 3 times/d	Titrate down the doses of levodopa/carbidopa as required	300-600 mg	3 times/d
Trihexyphenidyl	Cholinergic receptors; also some direct effect	1-2 mg/d	2 mg/d at intervals of 3-5 d	5-15 mg	3-4 times/d

[1]Cabergoline is not FDA approved for the treatment of Parkinson's disease.

SELECTIVE SEROTONIN REUPTAKE INHIBITORS (SSRIs) PHARMACOKINETICS

SSRI	Half-life (h)	Metabolite Half-life	Peak Plasma Level (h)	% Protein Bound	Bioavailability (%)	Initial Dose
Citalopram (Celexa™)	35	S-desmethyl-citalopram 59 hours	4	80	80	20 mg qAM
Escitalopram (Lexapro™)	27-32	S-desmethyl-citalopram 59 hours	5	56	80	10 mg qAM
Fluoxetine (Prozac®, Prozac® Weekly™, Sarafem™)	Initial: 24-72 Chronic: 96-144	Norfluoxetine: 4-16 days	6-8	95	72	10-20 mg qAM
Fluvoxamine	16	N/A	3	80	53	50 mg qhs
Paroxetine (Paxil®, Paxil® CR™)	21	N/A	5	95	>90	10-20 mg qAM
Sertraline (Zoloft®)	26	N-desmethyl-sertraline: 62-104 hours	5-8	98	88	25-50 mg qAM

SULFONAMIDE DERIVATIVES

The following table lists commonly prescribed drugs which are either sulfonamide derivatives or are structurally similar to sulfonamides. Please note that the list may not be all inclusive.

Commonly Prescribed Drugs

Classification	Specific Drugs
Antimicrobial Agents	Mafenide acetate (Sulfamylon®) Silver sulfadiazine (Silvadene®) Sodium sulfacetamide Sulfadiazine Sulfamethoxazole (ie, Bactrim™ and co-trimoxazole) Sulfisoxazole (Gantrisin®)
Diuretics, Carbonic Anhydrase Inhibitors	Acetazolamide (Diamox®) Dichlorphenamide (Daranide®) Methazolamide (Neptazane®)
Diuretics, Loop	Bumetanide (Bumex®) Furosemide (Lasix®) Torsemide (Demadex®)
Diuretics, Thiazide	Bendroflumethiazide (Naturetin®) Chlorothiazide (Diuril®) Chlorthalidone (Thalitone®) Hydrochlorothiazide (various and combinations, eg, Dyazide®, Maxzide®) Indapamide (Lozol®) Methyclothiazide (Enduron®) Metolazone (Mykrox®, Zaroxolyn®) Polythiazide (Renese®) Trichlormethiazide (Naqua®)
Hypoglycemic Agents, Oral	Acetohexamide Chlorpropamide (Diabinese®) Glimepiride (Amaryl®) Glipizide (Glucotrol®) Glyburide (DiaBeta®, Glynase®, Micronase®) Tolazamide (Tolinase®) Tolbutamide (Orinase®, Tol-Tab®)
Other Agents	Celecoxib (Celebrex®) Sulfasalazine (Azulfidine®)

CYTOCHROME P450 ENZYMES: SUBSTRATES, INHIBITORS, AND INDUCERS

INTRODUCTION

Most drugs are eliminated from the body, at least in part, by being chemically altered to less lipid-soluble products (ie, metabolized), and thus are more likely to be excreted via the kidneys or the bile. Phase I metabolism includes drug hydrolysis, oxidation, and reduction, and results in drugs that are more polar in their chemical structure, while Phase II metabolism involves the attachment of an additional molecule onto the drug (or partially metabolized drug) in order to create an inactive and/or more water soluble compound. Phase II processes include (primarily) glucuronidation, sulfation, glutathione conjugation, acetylation, and methylation.

Virtually any of the Phase I and II enzymes can be inhibited by some xenobiotic or drug. Some of the Phase I and II enzymes can be induced. Inhibition of the activity of metabolic enzymes will result in increased concentrations of the substrate (drug), whereas induction of the activity of metabolic enzymes will result in decreased concentrations of the substrate. For example, the well-documented enzyme-inducing effects of phenobarbital may include a combination of Phase I and II enzymes. Phase II glucuronidation may be increased via induced UDP-glucuronosyltransferase (UGT) activity, whereas Phase I oxidation may be increased via induced cytochrome P450 (CYP) activity. However, for most drugs, the primary route of metabolism (and the primary focus of drug-drug interaction) is Phase I oxidation, and specifically, metabolism.

CYP enzymes may be responsible for the metabolism (at least partial metabolism) of approximately 75% of all drugs, with the CYP3A subfamily responsible for nearly half of this activity. Found throughout plant, animal, and bacterial species, CYP enzymes represent a superfamily of xenobiotic metabolizing proteins. There have been several hundred CYP enzymes identified in nature, each of which has been assigned to a family (1, 2, 3, etc), subfamily (A, B, C, etc), and given a specific enzyme number (1, 2, 3, etc) according to the similarity in amino acid sequence that it shares with other enzymes. Of these many enzymes, only a few are found in humans, and even fewer appear to be involved in the metabolism of xenobiotics (eg, drugs). The key human enzyme subfamilies include CYP1A, CYP2A, CYP2B, CYP2C, CYP2D, CYP2E, and CYP3A.

CYP enzymes are found in the endoplasmic reticulum of cells in a variety of human tissues (eg, skin, kidneys, brain, lungs), but their predominant sites of concentration and activity are the liver and intestine. Though the abundance of CYP enzymes throughout the body is relatively equally distributed among the various subfamilies, the relative contribution to drug metabolism is (in decreasing order of magnitude) CYP3A4 (nearly 50%), CYP2D6 (nearly 25%), CYP2C8/9 (nearly 15%), then CYP1A2, CYP2C19, CYP2A6, and CYP2E1. Owing to their potential for numerous drug-drug interactions, those drugs that are identified in preclinical studies as substrates of CYP3A enzymes are often given a lower priority for continued research and development in favor of drugs that appear to be less affected by (or less likely to affect) this enzyme subfamily.

Each enzyme subfamily possesses unique selectivity toward potential substrates. For example, CYP1A2 preferentially binds medium-sized, planar, lipophilic molecules, while CYP2D6 preferentially binds molecules that possess a basic nitrogen atom. Some CYP subfamilies exhibit polymorphism (ie, multiple allelic variants that manifest differing catalytic properties). The best described polymorphisms involve CYP2C9, CYP2C19, and CYP2D6. Individuals possessing "wild type" gene alleles exhibit normal functioning CYP capacity. Others, however, possess allelic variants that leave the person with a subnormal level of catalytic potential (so called "poor metabolizers"). Poor metabolizers would be more likely to experience toxicity from drugs metabolized by the affected enzymes (or less effects if the enzyme is responsible for converting a prodrug to it's active form as in the case of codeine). The percentage of people classified as poor metabolizers varies by enzyme and population group. As an example, approximately 7% of Caucasians and only about 1% of Orientals appear to be CYP2D6 poor metabolizers.

CYTOCHROME P450 ENZYMES: SUBSTRATES, INHIBITORS, AND INDUCERS *(Continued)*

CYP enzymes can be both inhibited and induced by other drugs, leading to increased or decreased serum concentrations (along with the associated effects), respectively. Induction occurs when a drug causes an increase in the amount of smooth endoplasmic reticulum, secondary to increasing the amount of the affected CYP enzymes in the tissues. This "revving up" of the CYP enzyme system may take several days to reach peak activity, and likewise, may take several days, even months, to return to normal following discontinuation of the inducing agent.

CYP inhibition occurs via several potential mechanisms. Most commonly, a CYP inhibitor competitively (and reversibly) binds to the active site on the enzyme, thus preventing the substrate from binding to the same site, and preventing the substrate from being metabolized. The affinity of an inhibitor for an enzyme may be expressed by an inhibition constant (Ki) or IC50 (defined as the concentration of the inhibitor required to cause 50% inhibition under a given set of conditions). In addition to reversible competition for an enzyme site, drugs may inhibit enzyme activity by binding to sites on the enzyme other than that to which the substrate would bind, and thereby cause a change in the functionality or physical structure of the enzyme. A drug may also bind to the enzyme in an irreversible (ie, "suicide") fashion. In such a case, it is not the concentration of drug at the enzyme site that is important (constantly binding and releasing), but the number of molecules available for binding (once bound, always bound).

Although an inhibitor or inducer may be known to affect a variety of CYP subfamilies, it may only inhibit one or two in a clinically important fashion. Likewise, although a substrate is known to be at least partially metabolized by a variety of CYP enzymes, only one or two enzymes may contribute significantly enough to its overall metabolism to warrant concern when used with potential inducers or inhibitors. Therefore, when attempting to predict the level of risk of using two drugs that may affect each other via altered CYP function, it is important to identify the relative effectiveness of the inhibiting/inducing drug on the CYP subfamilies that significantly contribute to the metabolism of the substrate. The contribution of a specific CYP pathway to substrate metabolism should be considered not only in light of other known CYP pathways, but also other nonoxidative pathways for substrate metabolism (eg, glucuronidation) and transporter proteins (eg, P-glycoprotein) that may affect the presentation of a substrate to a metabolic pathway.

HOW TO USE THE TABLES

The following CYP SUBSTRATES, INHIBITORS, and INDUCERS tables provide a comprehensive perspective on drugs that are affected by, or affect, cytochrome P450 (CYP) enzymes.

The CYP Substrates table contains a list of drugs reported to be metabolized, at least in part, by one or more CYP enzymes. An enzyme that appears to play a clinically significant (major) role in a drug's metabolism is marked with a filled circle "●", and an enzyme whose role appears to be clinically insignificant (minor) is marked with an open circle "○". The designation of clinically significant is the result of a two-phase review. The first phase considered the clinical relevance of a substrate's concentration being increased twofold, or decreased by one-half. If either of these changes (which might occur in the presence of an effective enzyme inhibitor or inducer) was considered to present a clinically significant concern, the drug was subjected to a second phase. The second phase considered the contribution of each CYP enzyme to the overall metabolism of the drug. The enzyme pathway was considered clinically relevant if it was responsible for at least 30% of the metabolism of the drug.

The CYP Inhibitors table contains a list of drugs that are reported to inhibit one or more CYP enzymes. Enzymes that are strongly inhibited by a drug are marked with a filled circle "●;". Enzymes that are moderately inhibited are marked with a half-filled circle "◑". Enzymes that are weakly inhibited are marked with an open circle "○". The designations are the result of the authors' review of published clinical reports, available Ki data, and assessments published by other experts in the field. As it pertains to Ki values set in a ratio with achievable serum drug concentrations ([I]) under normal dosing conditions, the following parameters were employed: [I]/Ki ≥1 = strong; [I]/Ki 0.1-1 = moderate; [I]/Ki <0.1 = weak.

The CYP Inducers table contains a list of drugs that are reported to induce one or more CYP enzymes. Enzymes that appear to be effectively induced by a drug are marked with a filled circle "●", and enzymes that do not appear to be effectively induced are marked with an open circle "○". The designations are the result of the authors' review of published clinical reports and assessments published by other experts in the field.

In general, clinically significant interactions are more likely to occur between substrates and either inhibitors or inducers of the same enzyme(s), all of which have been marked with a filled circle "●". However, these assessments possess a degree of subjectivity on behalf of the authors, at times based on limited indications regarding the significance of CYP effects of particular agents. The authors have attempted to balance a conservative, clinically-sensitive presentation of the data with a desire to avoid the numbing effect of a "beware of everything" approach. Even so, other potential interactions (ie, those involving enzymes marked with an open circle "○") may warrant consideration in some cases. It is important to note that information related to CYP metabolism of drugs is expanding at a rapid pace, and thus, the contents of this table should only be considered to represent a "snapshot" of the information available at the time of publication.

Selected Readings

Bjornsson TD, Callaghan JT, Einolf HJ, et al, "The Conduct of *in vitro* and *in vivo* Drug-Drug Interaction Studies: A PhRMA Perspective," *J Clin Pharmacol*, 2003, 43(5):443-69.

Drug-Drug Interactions, Rodrigues AD, ed, New York, NY: Marcel Dekker, Inc, 2002.

Levy RH, Thummel KE, Trager WF, et al, eds, *Metabolic Drug Interactions*, Philadelphia, PA: Lippincott Williams & Wilkins, 2000.

Michalets EL, "Update: Clinically Significant Cytochrome P-450 Drug Interactions," *Pharmacotherapy*, 1998, 18(1):84-112.

Thummel KE and Wilkinson GR, "*In vitro* and *in vivo* Drug Interactions Involving Human CYP3A," *Annu Rev Pharmacol Toxicol*, 1998, 38:389-430.

Zhang Y and Benet LZ, "The Gut as a Barrier to Drug Absorption: Combined Role of Cytochrome P450 3A and P-Glycoprotein," *Clin Pharmacokinet*, 2001, 40(3):159-68.

Selected Websites

http://www.gentest.com

http://www.imm.ki.se/CYPalleles

http://medicine.iupui.edu/flockhart

http://www.mhc.com/Cytochromes

CYTOCHROME P450 ENZYMES: SUBSTRATES, INHIBITORS, AND INDUCERS *(Continued)*

CYP Substrates

Drug	1A2	2A6	2B6	2C8/9	2C19	2D6	2E1	3A4
Acetaminophen	○	○		○		○	○	○
Albendazole	○							●
Albuterol								●
Alfentanil								●
Almotriptan						○		○
Alosetron	○			●				○
Alprazolam								●
Aminophylline	●						○	○
Amiodarone	○			●	○	○		○
Amitriptyline	○		○	○	○	●		○
Amlodipine								●
Amoxapine						●		
Amphetamine						○		
Amprenavir				○				●
Aprepitant	○				○			●
Argatroban								○
Aripiprazole						●		●
Aspirin				○				
Atazanavir								●
Atomoxetine					○	●		
Atorvastatin								●
Azelastine	○				○	○		○
Azithromycin								○
Benzphetamine			○					●
Benztropine						○		
Betaxolol	●					●		
Bexarotene								○
Bezafibrate								○
Bisoprolol						○		●
Bortezomib	○			○	○	○		●
Bosentan				●				●
Brinzolamide								○
Bromazepam								●
Bromocriptine								●
Budesonide								○
Bupivacaine	○				○	○		○
Buprenorphine								●
BuPROPion	○	○	●	○		○	○	○
BusPIRone						○		●
Busulfan								●
Caffeine	●			○		○	○	○
Candesartan				○				
Capsaicin							○	
Captopril						●		
Carbamazepine				○				●
Carisoprodol					●			
Carteolol						○		
Carvedilol	○			●		●	○	○
Celecoxib				○				○
Cerivastatin								●
Cetirizine								○
Cevimeline						○		○
Chlordiazepoxide								●

CYP Substrates *(continued)*

Drug	1A2	2A6	2B6	2C8/9	2C19	2D6	2E1	3A4
Chloroquine						●		●
Chlorpheniramine						○		●
ChlorproMAZINE	○					●		○
ChlorproPAMIDE				○				
Chlorzoxazone	○	○				○	●	○
Cilostazol	○				○	○		○
Cisapride	○	○	○	○	○			●
Citalopram					●	○		●
Clarithromycin								●
Clobazam								●
Clofibrate								○
ClomiPRAMINE	●				●	●		○
Clonazepam								●
Clopidogrel	○							○
Clorazepate								●
Clozapine	●	○		○	○	○		○
Cocaine								●
Codeine[1]						●		○
Colchicine								●
Cyclobenzaprine	●					○		○
Cyclophosphamide[2]		○	●	○	○			●
CycloSPORINE								●
Dacarbazine	●						●	●
Dantrolene								●
Dapsone				○	○		○	●
Delavirdine						○		●
Desipramine	○					●		
Desogestrel					●			
Dexamethasone								○
Dexmedetomidine		●						
Dextroamphetamine						●		
Dextromethorphan		○		○	○	●	○	○
Diazepam	○		○	○	●			●
Diclofenac	○		○	○	○	○		○
Digitoxin								●
Digoxin								○
Dihydrocodeine[1]						●		
Dihydroergotamine								●
Diltiazem				○		○		●
Dirithromycin								○
Disopyramide								●
Disulfiram	○	○	○			○	○	○
Docetaxel								●
Dofetilide								○
Dolasetron				○				○
Domperidone								○
Donepezil						○		○
Dorzolamide				○				○
Doxepin	●					●		●
DOXOrubicin						●		●
Doxycycline								●
Drospirenone								○
Dutasteride								○
Efavirenz			●					●
Eletriptan								●
Enalapril								●

CYTOCHROME P450 ENZYMES: SUBSTRATES, INHIBITORS, AND INDUCERS *(Continued)*

CYP Substrates *(continued)*

Drug	1A2	2A6	2B6	2C8/9	2C19	2D6	2E1	3A4
Enflurane							●	
Eplerenone								●
Ergoloid mesylates								●
Ergonovine								●
Ergotamine								●
Erythromycin			○					●
Escitalopram					●			●
Esomeprazole					●			○
Estazolam								○
Estradiol	●	○	○	○	○	○	○	●
Estrogens, conjugated A/synthetic	●	○	○	○	○	○	○	●
Estrogens, conjugated equine	●	○	○	○	○	○	○	●
Estrogens, conjugated esterified	●		○	○			○	●
Estrone	●		○	○			○	●
Estropipate	●		○	○			○	●
Ethinyl estradiol								●
Ethosuximide								●
Etonogestrel								○
Etoposide	○						○	●
Exemestane								○
Felbamate							○	●
Felodipine								●
Fenofibrate								○
Fentanyl								●
Fexofenadine								○
Finasteride								○
Flecainide	○					●		
Fluoxetine	○		○	●	○	●	○	○
Fluphenazine						●		
Flurazepam								●
Flurbiprofen				○				
Flutamide	●							●
Fluticasone								○
Fluvastatin				○		○		○
Fluvoxamine	●					●		
Formoterol		○		○	○	○		
Fosamprenavir (as amprenavir)				○				●
Fosphenytoin (as phenytoin)			●		●			○
Frovatriptan	○							
Fulvestrant								●
Galantamine						○		○
Gefitinib								●
Gemfibrozil								○
Glimepiride				●				
GlipiZIDE				●				
Granisetron								○
Guanabenz	●							
Halazepam								○
Halofantrine				○		○		●

CYP Substrates *(continued)*

Drug	1A2	2A6	2B6	2C8/9	2C19	2D6	2E1	3A4
Haloperidol	○					●		●
Halothane		○	○	○		○	●	○
Hydrocodone[1]						●		
Hydrocortisone								○
Ibuprofen				○	○			
Ifosfamide[3]		○	○	○	○			●
Imatinib	○			○	○	○		●
Imipramine	○		○		●	●		○
Imiquimod	○							○
Indinavir						○		●
Indomethacin				○	○			
Irbesartan				○				
Irinotecan			●					●
Isoflurane							●	
Isoniazid							●	
Isosorbide								●
Isosorbide dinitrate								●
Isosorbide mononitrate								●
Isradipine								●
Itraconazole								○
Ivermectin								○
Ketamine			●	●				●
Ketoconazole								●
Labetalol						●		
Lansoprazole				○	●			●
Letrozole		○						●
Levobupivacaine	○							○
Levomethadyl acetate hydrochloride			○					●
Levonorgestrel								●
Lidocaine	○	○	○	○		●		●
Lomustine						●		
Lopinavir								○
Loratadine						○		○
Losartan				●				●
Lovastatin								●
Maprotiline						●		
MedroxyPROGESTERone								●
Mefenamic acid				○				
Mefloquine								●
Meloxicam				○				○
Mephenytoin			○	●	●			
Mephobarbital			○	○	●			
Mestranol[4]				●				●
Methadone				○	○	○		●
Methamphetamine						●		
Methoxsalen		○						
Methsuximide					●			
Methylergonovine								●
Methylphenidate						●		
MethylPREDNISolone								○
Methysergide								●
Metoclopramide	○					○		
Metoprolol					○	●		
Mexiletine	●					●		
Miconazole								●

CYTOCHROME P450 ENZYMES: SUBSTRATES, INHIBITORS, AND INDUCERS *(Continued)*

CYP Substrates *(continued)*

Drug	1A2	2A6	2B6	2C8/9	2C19	2D6	2E1	3A4
Midazolam			○					●
Mifepristone								○
Miglustat								●
Mirtazapine	●			○		●		●
Moclobemide					●	●		
Modafinil								●
Mometasone furoate								○
Montelukast				●				●
Moricizine								●
Morphine sulfate						○		
Naproxen	○			○				
Nateglinide				●				
Nefazodone						●		●
Nelfinavir				○	●	○		●
Nevirapine			○			○		●
NiCARdipine	○			○		○		●
Nicotine	○	○	○	○	○	○	○	○
NIFEdipine						○		●
Nilutamide					●			
Nimodipine								●
Nisoldipine								●
Nitrendipine								●
Norelgestromin								○
Norethindrone								●
Norgestrel								●
Nortriptyline	○				○	●		○
Olanzapine	○					○		
Omeprazole		○		○	●	○		○
Ondansetron	○			○		○	○	●
Orphenadrine	○		○			○		○
Oxybutynin								○
Oxycodone[1]						●		
Paclitaxel				●				●
Palonosetron	○					○		○
Pantoprazole					●			○
Paroxetine						●		
Pentamidine					●			
Pergolide								●
Perphenazine	○			○	○	●		○
Phencyclidine								●
Phenobarbital				○	●		○	
Phenytoin				●	●			○
Pimecrolimus								○
Pimozide	●							●
Pindolol						●		
Pioglitazone				●				●
Pipecuronium				○				
Piroxicam				○				
Pravastatin								○
Prazepam								○
PrednisoLONE								○
PredniSONE								○
Primaquine								●

CYP Substrates *(continued)*

Drug	1A2	2A6	2B6	2C8/9	2C19	2D6	2E1	3A4
Procainamide						●		
Progesterone	○	○		○	●	○		●
Proguanil	○				○			○
Promethazine			●			●		
Propafenone	○					●		○
Propofol	○	○	●	●	○	○	○	○
Propranolol	●				●	●		○
Quazepam								○
Quetiapine						○		●
Quinidine				○			○	●
Quinine	○				○			○
Rabeprazole					●			●
Ranitidine	○				○	○		
Repaglinide				○				●
Rifabutin	●							●
Rifampin		●		●				●
Riluzole	●							
Risperidone						●		○
Ritonavir	○		○			●		●
Rofecoxib				○				
Ropinirole	●							○
Ropivacaine	○		○			○		○
Rosiglitazone				●				
Rosuvastatin				○				○
Saquinavir						○		●
Selegiline	○	○	●	●		○		○
Sertraline			●	●	●	○		●
Sevoflurane		○	○				●	○
Sibutramine								●
Sildenafil				○				●
Simvastatin								●
Sirolimus								●
Spiramycin								●
Sufentanil								●
SulfaDIAZINE				●			○	○
Sulfamethoxazole				●				○
Sulfinpyrazone				●				○
SulfiSOXAZOLE				●				
Suprofen				○				
Tacrine	●							
Tacrolimus								●
Tamoxifen		○	○	●		●	○	●
Tamsulosin						●		●
Telithromycin	○							●
Temazepam			○	○	○			○
Teniposide								●
Terbinafine								●
Testosterone			○	○	○			○
Tetracycline								●
Theophylline	●			○		○	●	●
Thiabendazole	○							
Thioridazine					○	●		
Thiothixene	●							
Tiagabine								●
Ticlopidine								●
Timolol						●		

CYTOCHROME P450 ENZYMES: SUBSTRATES, INHIBITORS, AND INDUCERS (Continued)

CYP Substrates (continued)

Drug	1A2	2A6	2B6	2C8/9	2C19	2D6	2E1	3A4
TOLBUTamide				●	○			
Tolcapone		○						○
Tolterodine				○	○	●		●
Toremifene	○							●
Torsemide				●				
Tramadol[1]						●		○
Trazodone						○		●
Tretinoin		○	○	○				
Triazolam								●
Trifluoperazine	●							
Trimethadione				○	○		●	○
Trimethoprim				●				●
Trimipramine					●	●		●
Troleandomycin								●
Valdecoxib				○				○
Valproic acid		○	○	○	○		○	
Vardenafil								●
Venlafaxine				○	○	●		●
Verapamil	○		○	○			○	●
VinBLAStine						○		●
VinCRIStine								●
Vinorelbine						○		●
Voriconazole				●	●			○
Warfarin	○			●	○			○
Yohimbine						○		
Zafirlukast				●				
Zaleplon								○
Zidovudine		○		○	○			○
Zileuton	○			○				○
Ziprasidone	○							○
Zolmitriptan	○							
Zolpidem	○			○	○	○		●
Zonisamide					○			●
Zopiclone				●				●
Zuclopenthixol						●		

[1]This opioid analgesic is bioactivated in vivo via CYP2D6. Inhibiting this enzyme would decrease the effects of the analgesic. The active metabolite might also affect, or be affected by, CYP enzymes.
[2]Cyclophosphamide is bioactivated in vivo to acrolein via CYP2B6 and 3A4. Inhibiting these enzymes would decrease the effects of cyclophosphamide.
[3]Ifosfamide is bioactivated in vivo to acrolein via CYP3A4. Inhibiting this enzyme would decrease the effects of ifosfamide.
[4]Mestranol is bioactivated in vivo to ethinyl estradiol via CYP2C8/9. See Ethinyl Estradiol for additional CYP information.

CYP Inhibitors

Drug	1A2	2A6	2B6	2C8/9	2C19	2D6	2E1	3A4
Acebutolol						○		
Acetaminophen								○
AcetaZOLAMIDE								○
Albendazole	○							
Alosetron	○						○	
Amiodarone	●	◐	○	◐	○	◐		◐
Amitriptyline	○			○	○	○	○	
Amlodipine	◐	○	○	○		○		○
Amphetamine						○		
Amprenavir					○			●
Anastrozole	○			○				○
Aprepitant				○				○
Atazanavir	○			○				●
Atorvastatin								○
Azelastine			○	○	○	○		○
Azithromycin								○
Bepridil						○		
Betamethasone								○
Betaxolol						○		
Biperiden						○		
Bortezomib	○			○	◐	○		○
Bromazepam							○	
Bromocriptine	○							○
Buprenorphine	○	○			○	○		
BuPROPion						○		
Caffeine	●							◐
Candesartan				○				
Celecoxib						○		
Cerivastatin								○
Chloramphenicol				○				○
Chloroquine						◐		
Chlorpheniramine						○		
ChlorproMAZINE						●	○	
Chlorzoxazone							○	○
Cholecalciferol				○	○	○		
Cimetidine	◐			○	◐	◐	○	◐
Ciprofloxacin	●							○
Cisapride						○		○
Citalopram	○		○		○	○		
Clarithromycin	○							●
Clemastine						○		○
Clofazimine								○
Clofibrate		○						
ClomiPRAMINE						◐		
Clopidogrel				○				
Clotrimazole	○	○	○	○	○	○	○	◐
Clozapine	○			○	○	◐	○	○
Cocaine						●		○
Codeine						○		
Cyclophosphamide								○
CycloSPORINE				○				◐
Danazol								○
Delavirdine	○			●	●	●		○
Desipramine		◐	◐			◐	○	◐
Dexmedetomidine	○			○		●		○
Dextromethorphan						○		

CYTOCHROME P450 ENZYMES: SUBSTRATES, INHIBITORS, AND INDUCERS *(Continued)*

CYP Inhibitors *(continued)*

Drug	1A2	2A6	2B6	2C8/9	2C19	2D6	2E1	3A4
Diazepam					○			○
Diclofenac	◑			○			○	●
Dihydroergotamine								○
Diltiazem				○		○		◑
Dimethyl sulfoxide				○	○			
DiphenhydrAMINE						◑		
Disulfiram	○	○	○	○		○	●	○
Docetaxel								○
Dolasetron						○		
DOXOrubicin			◑			○		○
Doxycycline								●
Drospirenone	○			○	○			○
Econazole							○	
Efavirenz				○	○			○
Enoxacin	●							●
Entacapone	○	○		○	○	○	○	○
Eprosartan				○				
Ergotamine								○
Erythromycin	○							◑
Escitalopram						○		
Estradiol	○							
Estrogens, conjugated A/synthetic	○							
Estrogens, conjugated equine	○							
Ethinyl estradiol	○		○		○			○
Ethotoin					○			
Etoposide				○				○
Felbamate					○			
Felodipine				○		○		○
Fentanyl								○
Fexofenadine						○		
Flecainide						○		
Fluconazole	○			●	●			◑
Fluoxetine	◑		○	○	◑	●		○
Fluphenazine	○			○		○	○	
Flurazepam							○	
Flurbiprofen				●				
Flutamide	○							
Fluvastatin	○			◑		○		○
Fluvoxamine	●		○	○	●	○		○
Fosamprenavir (as amprenavir)					○			●
Gefitinib					○	○		
Gemfibrozil	◑			●	●			
Glyburide								○
Grapefruit juice								◑
Halofantrine						○		
Haloperidol						◑		◑
HydrALAZINE								○
HydrOXYzine						○		
Ibuprofen				●				
Ifosfamide								○
Imatinib				○		○		●

CYP Inhibitors (continued)

Drug	1A2	2A6	2B6	2C8/9	2C19	2D6	2E1	3A4
Imipramine	○				○	◐	○	
Indinavir				○	○	○		●
Indomethacin				●	○			
Interferon alfa-2a	○							
Interferon alfa-2b	○							
Interferon gamma-1b	○						○	
Irbesartan				◐		○		○
Isoflurane			○					
Isoniazid	○	◐		◐	●	◐	◐	●
Isradipine								○
Itraconazole								●
Ketoconazole	●	◐	○	●	◐	◐		◐
Ketoprofen				○				
Labetalol						○		
Lansoprazole				○	◐	○		○
Leflunomide				○				
Letrozole		○			○			
Lidocaine	●					◐		◐
Lomefloxacin	●							
Lomustine						○		○
Loratadine					◐	○		
Losartan	○			◐	○			○
Lovastatin				○		○		○
Mefenamic acid				●				
Mefloquine						○		○
Meloxicam				○				
Mephobarbital					○			
Mestranol	○		○		○			○
Methadone						◐		○
Methimazole	○	○	○	○	○	◐	○	○
Methotrimeprazine						○		
Methoxsalen	●	●		○	○	○	○	○
Methsuximide					○			
Methylphenidate						○		
MethylPREDNISolone								○
Metoclopramide						○		
Metoprolol						○		
Metronidazole				○				◐
Metyrapone		○						
Mexiletine	●							
Miconazole	◐	●	○	●	●	●	◐	●
Midazolam				○				○
Mifepristone						○		○
Mirtazapine	○							○
Mitoxantrone								○
Moclobemide	○				○	○		
Modafinil	○	○		○	●		○	○
Montelukast				○				
Nalidixic acid	●							
Nateglinide				○				
Nefazodone	○		○			○		●
Nelfinavir	○		○	○	○	○		●
Nevirapine	○					○		○
NiCARdipine				●	◐	◐		●
Nicotine		○					○	
NIFEdipine	◐			○		○		○

1417

CYTOCHROME P450 ENZYMES: SUBSTRATES, INHIBITORS, AND INDUCERS (Continued)

CYP Inhibitors (continued)

Drug	1A2	2A6	2B6	2C8/9	2C19	2D6	2E1	3A4
Nilutamide					○			
Nisoldipine	○							○
Nitrendipine								○
Nizatidine								○
Norfloxacin	●							◐
Nortriptyline						○	○	
Ofloxacin	●							
Olanzapine	○			○	○	○		○
Omeprazole	○			◐	●	○		○
Ondansetron	○			○		○		
Orphenadrine	○	○	○	○	○	○	○	○
Oxcarbazepine					○			
Oxprenolol						○		
Oxybutynin						○		○
Pantoprazole				◐				
Paroxetine	○		◐	○	○	●		○
Peginterferon alfa-2a	○							
Peginterferon alfa-2b	○							
Pentamidine				○	○	○		○
Pentoxifylline	○							
Pergolide						●		○
Perphenazine	○					○		
Phencyclidine								○
Pilocarpine		○					○	○
Pimozide						○	○	○
Pindolol						○		
Pioglitazone				●	○	◐		
Piroxicam				●				
Pravastatin				○		○		○
Praziquantel						○		
PrednisoLONE								○
Primaquine	●					○		○
Probenecid					○			
Progesterone				○	○			○
Promethazine						○		
Propafenone	○			○		○		
Propofol	◐			○	◐	○	○	●
Propoxyphene				○		○		○
Propranolol	○					○		
Pyrimethamine				◐		◐		
Quinidine				○		●		●
Quinine				◐		●		○
Quinupristin								○
Rabeprazole					◐	○		○
Ranitidine	○					○		
Risperidone						○		○
Ritonavir				○	○	●	○	●
Rofecoxib	●							
Ropinirole	○					●		
Rosiglitazone				◐	○	○		
Saquinavir				○	○	○		◐
Selegiline	○	○		○	○	○	○	○
Sertraline	○		◐	○	◐	◐		◐

CYP Inhibitors *(continued)*

Drug	1A2	2A6	2B6	2C8/9	2C19	2D6	2E1	3A4
Sildenafil	○			○	○	○	○	○
Simvastatin				○		○		
Sirolimus								○
Sulconazole	○	○		○	○	○	○	○
SulfaDIAZINE				●				
Sulfamethoxazole				◐				
Sulfinpyrazone				◐				
SulfiSOXAZOLE				●				
Tacrine	○							
Tacrolimus								○
Tamoxifen			○	○				○
Telithromycin						○		●
Telmisartan					○			
Teniposide				○				○
Tenofovir	○							
Terbinafine						●		
Testosterone								○
Tetracycline								◐
Theophylline	○							
Thiabendazole	●							
Thioridazine	○			○		◐	○	
Thiotepa			○					
Thiothixene						○		
Ticlopidine	○			○	●	◐	○	○
Timolol						○		
Tioconazole	○	○		○	○	○	○	
Tocainide	○							
TOLBUTamide				●				
Tolcapone				○				
Topiramate					○			
Torsemide					○			
Tranylcypromine	◐	●		○	◐	◐	○	○
Trazodone						◐		○
Tretinoin				○				
Triazolam				○				
Trimethoprim				◐				
Tripelennamine						◐		
Triprolidine						○		
Troleandomycin								◐
Valdecoxib				○	○			
Valproic acid				○	○	○		○
Valsartan				○				
Venlafaxine			○			○		○
Verapamil	○			○		○		◐
VinBLAStine						○		○
VinCRIStine								○
Vinorelbine						○		○
Voriconazole				○	○			◐
Warfarin				◐	○			
Yohimbine						○		
Zafirlukast	○			◐	○	○		○
Zileuton	○							
Ziprasidone						○		○

CYTOCHROME P450 ENZYMES: SUBSTRATES, INHIBITORS, AND INDUCERS *(Continued)*

CYP Inducers

Drug	1A2	2A6	2B6	2C8/9	2C19	2D6	2E1	3A4
Aminoglutethimide	●				●			●
Amobarbital		●						
Aprepitant				○				○
Azatadine								○
Bexarotene								○
Bosentan				○				○
Calcitriol								○
Carbamazepine	●		●	●	●			●
Clofibrate			○					○
Colchicine				○			○	○
Cyclophosphamide			○	○				
Dexamethasone		○	○	○				○
Dicloxacillin								○
Efavirenz (in liver only)			○					○
Estradiol								○
Estrogens, conjugated A/synthetic								○
Estrogens, conjugated equine								○
Felbamate								○
Fosphenytoin (as phenytoin)			●	●	●			●
Griseofulvin	○			○				○
Hydrocortisone								○
Ifosfamide				○				
Insulin preparations	○							
Isoniazid (after D/C)							○	
Lansoprazole	○							
MedroxyPROGESTERone								○
Mephobarbital		○						
Metyrapone								○
Modafinil	○		○					○
Moricizine	○							○
Nafcillin								●
Nevirapine			●					●
Norethindrone					○			
Omeprazole	○							
Oxcarbazepine								●
Paclitaxel								○
Pantoprazole	○							○
Pentobarbital		●						●
Phenobarbital	●	●	●	●				●
Phenytoin			●	●	●			●
Pioglitazone								○
PredniSONE					○			○
Primaquine	○							
Primidone[1]	●		●	●				●
Rifabutin								●
Rifampin	●	●	●	●	●			●
Rifapentine				●				●
Ritonavir (long-term)	○			○				○
Rofecoxib								○
Secobarbital		●		●				
Sulfinpyrazone								○
Terbinafine								○
Topiramate								○
Tretinoin							○	
Troglitazone								○
Valproic acid		○						

[1]Primidone is partially metabolized to phenobarbital. See Phenobarbital for additional CYP information.

MANAGEMENT OF HEALTHCARE WORKER EXPOSURES TO HBV, HCV, AND HIV

Adapted from "U.S. Public Health Service Guidelines for the Management of Occupational Exposures to HBV, HCV, and HIV and Recommendations for Postexposure Prophylaxis," *MMWR Morb Mortal Wkly Rep*, 2001, 50(RR-11).

Factors to Consider in Assessing the Need for Follow-up of Occupational Exposures

- **Type of exposure**
  - Percutaneous injury
  - Mucous membrane exposure
  - Nonintact skin exposure
  - Bites resulting in blood exposure to either person involved
- **Type and amount of fluid/tissue**
  - Blood
  - Fluids containing blood
  - Potentially infectious fluid or tissue (semen; vaginal secretions; and cerebrospinal, synovial, pleural, peritoneal, pericardial, and amniotic fluids)
  - Direct contact with concentrated virus
- **Infectious status of source**
  - Presence of HB_sAg
  - Presence of HCV antibody
  - Presence of HIV antibody
- **Susceptibility of exposed person**
  - Hepatitis B vaccine and vaccine response status
  - HBV, HCV, HIV immune status

Evaluation of Occupational Exposure Sources

Known sources

- Test known sources for HB_sAg, anti-HCV, and HIV antibody
  - Direct virus assays for routine screening of source patients are **not** recommended
  - Consider using a rapid HIV-antibody test
  - If the source person is **not** infected with a bloodborne pathogen, baseline testing or further follow-up of the exposed person is **not** necessary
- For sources whose infection status remains unknown (eg, the source person refuses testing), consider medical diagnoses, clinical symptoms, and history of risk behaviors
- Do not test discarded needles for bloodborne pathogens

Unknown sources

- For unknown sources, evaluate the likelihood of exposure to a source at high risk for infection
  - Consider the likelihood of bloodborne pathogen infection among patients in the exposure setting

MANAGEMENT OF HEALTHCARE WORKER EXPOSURES TO HBV, HCV, AND HIV *(Continued)*

Recommended Postexposure Prophylaxis for Exposure to Hepatitis B Virus

Vaccination and Antibody Response Status of Exposed Workers[1]	Treatment		
	Source HB$_s$Ag[2]-Positive	Source HB$_s$Ag[2]-Negative	Source Unknown or Not Available for Testing
Unvaccinated	HBIG[3] x 1 and initiate HB vaccine series[4]	Initiate HB vaccine series	Initiate HB vaccine series
Previously vaccinated			
Known responder[5]	No treatment	No treatment	No treatment
Known nonresponder[6]	HBIG x 1 and initiate revaccination or HBIG x 2[7]	No treatment	If known high risk source, treat as if source was HB$_s$Ag-positive
Antibody response unknown	Test exposed person for anti-HB$_s$[8] 1. If adequate,[5] no treatment is necessary 2. If inadequate,[6] administer HBIG x 1 and vaccine booster	No treatment	Test exposed person for anti-HB$_s$ 1. If adequate,[4] no treatment is necessary 2. If inadequate,[4] administer vaccine booster and recheck titer in 1-2 months

[1]Persons who have previously been infected with HBV are immune to reinfection and do not require postexposure prophylaxis.

[2]Hepatitis B surface antigen.

[3]Hepatitis B immune globulin; dose is 0.06 mL/kg intramuscularly.

[4]Hepatitis B vaccine.

[5]A responder is a person with adequate levels of serum antibody to HB$_s$Ag (ie, anti-HB$_s$ ≥10 mIU/mL).

[6]A nonresponder is a person with inadequate response to vaccination (ie, serum anti-HB$_s$ <10 mIU/mL).

[7]The option of giving one dose of HBIG and reinitiating the vaccine series is preferred for nonresponders who have not completed a second 3-dose vaccine series. For persons who previously completed a second vaccine series but failed to respond, two doses of HBIG are preferred.

[8]Antibody to HB$_s$Ag.

Recommended HIV Postexposure Prophylaxis for Percutaneous Injuries

Exposure Type	Infection Status of Source			
	HIV-Positive Class 1[1]	HIV-Positive Class 2[1]	Unknown HIV Status[2]	Unknown Source[3]	HIV-Negative
Less severe[4]	Recommend basic 2-drug PEP	Recommend expanded 3-drug PEP	Generally, no PEP warranted; however, consider basic 2-drug PEP[5] for source with HIV risk factors[6]	Generally, no PEP warranted; however, consider basic 2-drug PEP[5] in settings where exposure to HIV-infected persons is likely	No PEP warranted
More severe[7]	Recommend expanded 3-drug PEP	Recommend expanded 3-drug PEP	Generally, no PEP warranted; however consider basic 2-drug PEP[5] for source with HIV risk factors[6]	Generally, no PEP warranted; however, consider basic 2-drug PEP[5] in settings where exposure to HIV-infected persons is likely	No PEP warranted

[1]HIV-Positive, Class 1 – asymptomatic HIV infection or known low viral load (eg, <1500 RNA copies/mL). HIV-Positive Class 2 – symptomatic HIV infection, AIDS, acute seroconversion, or known high viral load. If drug resistance is a concern, obtain expert consultation. Initiation of postexposure prophylaxis (PEP) should not be delayed pending expert consultation, and, because expert consultation alone cannot substitute for face-to-face counseling, resources should be available to provide immediate evaluation and follow-up care for all exposures.

[2]Source of unknown HIV status (eg, deceased source person with no samples available for HIV testing).

[3]Unknown source (eg, a needle from a sharps disposal container).

[4]Less severe (eg, solid needle and superficial injury).

[5]The designation "consider PEP" indicates the PEP is optional and should be based on an individualized decision between the exposed person and the treating clinician.

[6]If PEP is offered and taken and the source is later determined to be HIV-negative, PEP should be discontinued.

[7]More severe (eg, large-bore hollow needle, deep puncture, visible blood on device, or needle used in patient's artery or vein).

MANAGEMENT OF HEALTHCARE WORKER EXPOSURES TO HBV, HCV, AND HIV *(Continued)*

Recommended HIV Postexposure Prophylaxis for Mucous Membrane Exposures and Nonintact Skin[1] Exposures

Exposure Type	Infection Status of Source			
	HIV-Positive Class 1[2]	HIV-Positive Class 2[2]	Unknown HIV Status[3]	Unknown Source[4]	HIV-Negative
Small volume[5]	Consider basic 2-drug PEP[6]	Recommend basic 2-drug PEP	Generally, no PEP warranted; however, consider basic 2-drug PEP[6] for source with HIV risk factors[7]	Generally, no PEP warranted; however, consider basic 2-drug PEP[6] in settings where exposure to HIV-infected persons is likely	No PEP warranted
Large volume[8]	Recommend basic 2-drug PE	Recommend expanded 3-drug PEP	Generally, no PEP warranted; however consider basic 2-drug PEP[6] for source with HIV risk factors[7]	Generally, no PEP warranted; however, consider basic 2-drug PEP[6] in settings where exposure to HIV-infected persons is likely	No PEP warranted

[1]For skin exposures, follow-up is indicated only if there is evidence of compromised skin integrity (eg, dermatitis, abrasion, or open wound).

[2]HIV-Positive, Class 1 – asymptomatic HIV infection or known low viral load (eg, <1500 RNA copies/mL). HIV-Positive Class 2 – symptomatic HIV infection, AIDS, acute seroconversion, or known high viral load. If drug resistance is a concern, obtain expert consultation. Initiation of postexposure prophylaxis (PEP) should not be delayed pending expert consultation, and, because expert consultation alone cannot substitute for face-to-face counseling, resources should be available to provide immediate evaluation and follow-up care for all exposures.

[3]Source of unknown HIV status (eg, deceased source person with no samples available for HIV testing).

[4]Unknown source (eg, splash from inappropriately disposed blood).

[5]Small volume (eg, a few drops).

[6]The designation "consider PEP" indicates the PEP is optional and should be based on an individualized decision between the exposed person and the treating clinician.

[7]If PEP is offered and taken and the source is later determined to be HIV-negative, PEP should be discontinued.

[8]Large volume (eg, major blood splash).

Situations for Which Expert[1] Consultation for HIV Postexposure Prophylaxis Is Advised

- **Delayed (ie, later than 24-36 hours) exposure report**
  - The interval after which there is no benefit from postexposure prophylaxis (PEP) is undefined

- **Unknown source (eg, needle in sharps disposal container or laundry)**
  - Decide use of PEP on a case-by-case basis
  - Consider the severity of the exposure and the epidemiologic likelihood of HIV exposure
  - Do not test needles or sharp instruments for HIV

- **Known or suspected pregnancy in the exposed person**
  - Does not preclude the use of optimal PEP regimens
  - Do not deny PEP solely on the basis of pregnancy

- **Resistance of the source virus to antiretroviral agents**
  - Influence of drug resistance on transmission risk is unknown
  - Selection of drugs to which the source person's virus is unlikely to be resistant is recommended, if the source person's virus is unknown or suspected to be resistant to ≥1 of the drugs considered for the PEP regimen
  - Resistance testing of the source person's virus at the time of the exposure is not recommended

- **Toxicity of the initial PEP regimen**
  - Adverse symptoms, such as nausea and diarrhea, are common with PEP
  - Symptoms can often be managed without changing the PEP regimen by prescribing antimotility and/or antiemetic agents
  - Modification of dose intervals (ie, administering a lower dose of drug more frequently throughout the day, as recommended by the manufacturer), in other situations, might help alleviate symptoms

[1]Local experts and/or the National Clinicians' Postexposure Prophylaxis Hotline (PEPline 1-888-448-4911).

MANAGEMENT OF HEALTHCARE WORKER EXPOSURES TO HBV, HCV, AND HIV *(Continued)*

Occupational Exposure Management Resources

National Clinicians' Postexposure Prophylaxis Hotline (PEPline)
Run by University of California-San Francisco/San Francisco General Hospital staff; supported by the Health Resources and Services Administration Ryan White CARE Act, HIV/AIDS Bureau, AIDS Education and Training Centers, and CDC

Phone: (888) 448-4911
Internet: http://www.ucsf.edu/hivcntr

Needlestick!
A website to help clinicians manage and document occupational blood and body fluid exposures. Developed and maintained by the University of California, Los Angeles (UCLA), Emergency Medicine Center, UCLA School of Medicine, and funded in part by CDC and the Agency for Healthcare Research and Quality.

Internet: http://
www.needlestick.mednet.ucla.edu

Hepatitis Hotline

Phone: (888) 443-7232
Internet: http://www.cdc.gov/hepatitis

Reporting to CDC:
Occupationally acquired HIV infections and failures of PEP

Phone: (800) 893-0485

HIV Antiretroviral Pregnancy Registry

Phone: (800) 258-4263
Fax: (800) 800-1052
Address: 1410 Commonwealth Drive, Suite 215
Wilmington, NC 28405
Internet: http://www.glaxowellcome.com/preg_reg/antiretroviral

Food and Drug Administration
Report unusual or severe toxicity to antiretroviral agents

Phone: (800) 332-1088
Address: MedWatch
HF-2, FDA
5600 Fishers Lane
Rockville, MD 20857
Internet: http://www.fda.gov/medwatch

HIV/AIDS Treatment Information Service

Internet: http://www.aidsinfo.nih.gov

Management of Occupational Blood Exposures

Provide immediate care to the exposure site
- Wash wounds and skin with soap and water
- Flush mucous membranes with water

Determine risk associated with exposure by:
- Type of fluid (eg, blood, visibly bloody fluid, other potentially infectious fluid or tissue, and concentrated virus)
- Type of exposure (ie, percutaneous injury, mucous membrane or nonintact skin exposure, and bites resulting in blood exposure)

Evaluate exposure source
- Assess the risk of infection using available information
- Test known sources for HB_sAg, anti-HCV, and HIV antibody (consider using rapid testing)
- For unknown sources, assess risk of exposure to HBV, HCV, or HIV infection
- Do not test discarded needle or syringes for virus contamination

Evaluate the exposed person
- Assess immune status for HBV infection (ie, by history of hepatitis B vaccination and vaccine response)

Give PEP for exposures posing risk of infection transmission
- HBV: See Recommended Postexposure Prophylaxis for Exposure to Hepatitis B Virus Table
- HCV: PEP not recommended
- HIV: See Recommended HIV Postexposure Prophylaxis for Percutaneous Injuries Table and Recommended HIV Postexposure Prophylaxis for Mucous Membrane Exposures and Nonintact Skin Exposures Table
  - Initiate PEP as soon as possible, preferably within hours of exposure
  - Offer pregnancy testing to all women of childbearing age not known to be pregnant
  - Seek expert consultation if viral resistance is suspected
  - Administer PEP for 4 weeks if tolerated

Perform follow-up testing and provide counseling
- Advise exposed persons to seek medical evaluation for any acute illness occurring during follow-up

HBV exposures
- Perform follow-up anti-HB_s testing in persons who receive hepatitis B vaccine
  - Test for anti-HB_s 1-2 months after last dose of vaccine
  - Anti-HB_s response to vaccine cannot be ascertained if HBIG was received in the previous 3-4 months

HCV exposures
- Perform baseline and follow-up testing for anti-HCV and alanine amino-transferase (ALT) 4-6 months after exposures
- Perform HCV RNA at 4-6 months if earlier diagnosis of HCV infection is desired
- Confirm repeatedly reactive anti-HCV enzyme immunoassays (EIAs) with supplemental tests

HIV exposures
- Perform HIV antibody testing for at least 6 months postexposure (eg, at baseline, 6 weeks, 3 months, and 6 months)
- Perform HIV antibody testing if illness compatible with an acute retroviral syndrome occurs
- Advise exposed persons to use precautions to prevent secondary transmission during the follow-up period
- Evaluate exposed persons taking PEP within 72 hours after exposure and monitor for drug toxicity for at least 2 weeks

MANAGEMENT OF HEALTHCARE WORKER EXPOSURES TO HBV, HCV, AND HIV *(Continued)*

Basic and Expanded HIV Postexposure Prophylaxis Regimens

Basic Regimens

- Zidovudine (Retrovir™; ZDV; AZT) + Lamivudine (Epivir™; 3TC); available as Combivir™
  - ZDV: 600 mg daily, in two or three divided doses, and
  - 3TC: 150 mg twice daily

Alternative Basic Regimens

- Lamivudine (3TC) + Stavudine (Zerit™; d4T)
  - 3TC: 150 mg twice daily, and
  - d4T: 40 mg twice daily (if body weight is <60 kg, 30 mg twice daily)
- Didanosine (Videx™, chewable/dispersible buffered tablet; Videx™ EC, delayed-release capsule; ddI) + Stavudine (d4T)
  - ddI: 400 mg daily on an empty stomach (if body weight is <60 kg, 125 mg twice daily)
  - d4T: 40 mg twice daily (if body weight is <60 kg, 30 mg twice daily)

Expanded Regimen

Basic regimen plus one of the following:

- Indinavir (Crixivan™; IDV)
  - 800 mg every 8 hours, on an empty stomach
- Nelfinavir (Viracept™; NFV)
  - 750 mg three times daily, with meals or snack, or
  - 1250 mg twice daily, with meals or snack
- Efavirenz (Sustiva™; EFV)
  - 600 mg daily, at bedtime
  - Should not be used during pregnancy because of concerns about teratogenicity
- Abacavir (Ziagen™; ABC); available at Trizivir™, a combination of ZDV, 3TC, and ABC
  - 300 mg twice daily

Antiretroviral Agents for Use at PEP Only With Expert Consultation

- Ritonavir (Norvir™; RTV)
- Amprenavir (Agenerase™; AMP)
- Delavirdine (Rescriptor™; DLV)
- Lopinavir/Ritonavir (Kaletra™)
  - 400/100 mg twice daily

Antiretroviral Agents Generally Not Recommended For Use as PEP

- Nevirapine (Viramune™; NVP)
  - 200 mg daily for 2 weeks, then 200 mg twice daily

PREVENTION OF BACTERIAL ENDOCARDITIS

Recommendations by the American Heart Association
(*JAMA*, 1997, 277:1794-801)

Consensus Process - The recommendations were formulated by the writing group after specific therapeutic regimens were discussed. The consensus statement was subsequently reviewed by outside experts not affiliated with the writing group and by the Science Advisory and Coordinating Committee of the American Heart Association. These guidelines are meant to aid practitioners but are not intended as the standard of care or as a substitute for clinical judgment.

Table 1. Cardiac Conditions[1]

Endocarditis Prophylaxis Recommended

High-Risk Category

    Prosthetic cardiac valves, including bioprosthetic and homograft valves

    Previous bacterial endocarditis

    Complex cyanotic congenital heart disease (eg, single ventricle states, transposition of the great arteries, tetralogy of Fallot)

    Surgically constructed systemic pulmonary shunts or conduits

Moderate-Risk Category

    Most other congenital cardiac malformations (other than above and below)

    Acquired valvar dysfunction (eg, rheumatic heart disease)

    Hypertrophic cardiomyopathy

    Mitral valve prolapse with valvar regurgitation and/or thickened leaflets

Endocarditis Prophylaxis Not Recommended

Negligible-Risk Category (no greater risk than the general population)

    Isolated secundum atrial septal defect

    Surgical repair of atrial septal defect, ventricular septal defect, or patent ductus arteriosus (without residua beyond 6 months)

    Previous coronary artery bypass graft surgery

    Mitral valve prolapse without valvar regurgitation

    Physiologic, functional, or innocent heart murmurs

    Previous Kawasaki disease without valvar dysfunction

    Previous rheumatic fever without valvar dysfunction

    Cardiac pacemakers (intravascular and epicardial) and implanted defibrillators

[1]This table lists selected conditions but is not meant to be all-inclusive.

PREVENTION OF BACTERIAL ENDOCARDITIS *(Continued)*

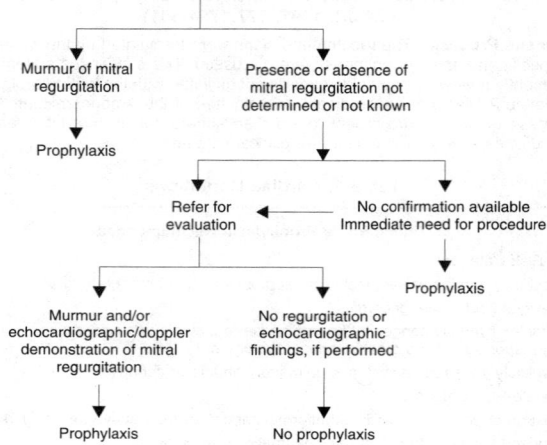

Patient With Suspected Mitral Valve Prolapse

- Murmur of mitral regurgitation → Prophylaxis
- Presence or absence of mitral regurgitation not determined or not known
  - Refer for evaluation
  - No confirmation available / Immediate need for procedure → Prophylaxis
    - Murmur and/or echocardiographic/doppler demonstration of mitral regurgitation → Prophylaxis
    - No regurgitation or echocardiographic findings, if performed → No prophylaxis

Table 2. Dental Procedures and Endocarditis Prophylaxis

Endocarditis Prophylaxis Recommended[1]

Dental extractions

Periodontal procedures including surgery, scaling and root planing, probing, and recall maintenance

Dental implant placement and reimplantation of avulsed teeth

Endodontic (root canal) instrumentation or surgery only beyond the apex

Subgingival placement of antibiotic fibers or strips

Initial placement of orthodontic bands but not brackets

Intraligamentary local anesthetic injections

Prophylactic cleaning of teeth or implants where bleeding is anticipated

Endocarditis Prophylaxis Not Recommended

Restorative dentistry[2] (operative and prosthodontic) with or without retraction cord[3]

Local anesthetic injections (nonintraligamentary)

Intracanal endodontic treatment; post placement and buildup[3]

Placement of rubber dams[3]

Postoperative suture removal

Placement of removable prosthodontic or orthodontic appliances

Taking of oral impressions[3]

Fluoride treatments

Taking of oral radiographs

Orthodontic appliance adjustment

Shedding of primary teeth

[1]Prophylaxis is recommended for patients with high- and moderate-risk cardiac conditions.

[2]This includes restoration of decayed teeth (filling cavities) and replacement of missing teeth.

[3]Clinical judgment may indicate antibiotic use in selected circumstances that may create significant bleeding.

Table 3. Recommended Standard Prophylactic Regimen for Dental, Oral, or Upper Respiratory Tract Procedures in Patients Who Are at Risk

Endocarditis Prophylaxis Recommended

Respiratory Tract
    Tonsillectomy and/or adenoidectomy
    Surgical operations that involve respiratory mucosa
    Bronchoscopy with a rigid bronchoscope
Gastrointestinal Tract[1]
    Sclerotherapy for esophageal varices
    Esophageal stricture dilation
    Endoscopic retrograde cholangiography with biliary obstruction
    Biliary tract surgery
    Surgical operations that involve intestinal mucosa
Genitourinary Tract
    Prostatic surgery
    Cystoscopy
    Urethral dilation

Endocarditis Prophylaxis Not Recommended

Respiratory Tract
    Endotracheal intubation
    Bronchoscopy with a flexible bronchoscope, with or without biopsy[2]
    Tympanostomy tube insertion
Gastrointestinal Tract
    Transesophageal echocardiography[2]
    Endoscopy with or without gastrointestinal biopsy[2]
Genitourinary Tract
    Vaginal hysterectomy[2]
    Vaginal delivery[2]
    Cesarean section
    In uninfected tissues:
        Urethral catheterization
        Uterine dilatation and curettage
        Therapeutic abortion
        Sterilization procedures
        Insertion or removal of intrauterine devices
Other
    Cardiac catheterization, including balloon angioplasty
    Implanted cardiac pacemakers, implanted defibrillators, and coronary stents
    Incision or biopsy or surgically scrubbed skin
    Circumcision

[1]Prophylaxis is recommended for high-risk patients, optional for medium-risk patients.
[2]Prophylaxis is optional for high-risk patients.

PREVENTION OF BACTERIAL ENDOCARDITIS *(Continued)*

Table 4. Prophylactic Regimens for Dental, Oral, Respiratory Tract, or Esophageal Procedures

Situation	Agent	Regimen[1]	
		Adults	Children
Standard general prophylaxis	Amoxicillin	2 g P.O. 1 h before procedure	50 mg/kg P.O. 1 h before procedure
Unable to take oral medications	Ampicillin	2 g I.M./I.V. within 30 min before procedure	50 mg/kg I.M./I.V. within 30 min before procedure
Allergic to penicillin	Clindamycin or	600 mg P.O. 1 h before procedure	20 mg/kg P.O. 1 h before procedure
	Cephalexin[2] or cefadroxil[2] or	2 g P.O 1 h before procedure	50 mg/kg P.O. 1 h before procedure
	Azithromycin or clarithromycin	500 mg P.O. 1 h before procedure	15 mg/kg P.O. 1 h before procedure
Allergic to penicillin and unable to take oral medications	Clindamycin or	600 mg I.V. within 30 min before procedure	20 mg/kg I.V. within 30 min before procedure
	Cefazolin[2]	1 g I.M./I.V. within 30 min before procedure	25 mg/kg I.M./I.V. within 30 min before procedure

[1]Total children's dose should not exceed adult dose.

[2]Cephalosporins should not be used in individuals with immediate-type hypersensitivity reaction (urticaria, angioedema, or anaphylaxis) to penicillins.

Table 5. Prophylactic Regimens for Genitourinary / Gastrointestinal (Excluding Esophageal) Procedures

Situation	Agents	Regimen[1,2]	
		Adults	Children
High-risk[3] patients	Ampicillin plus gentamicin	Ampicillin 2 g I.M. or I.V. plus gentamicin 1.5 mg/kg (not to exceed 120 mg) within 30 min of starting the procedure; 6 h later, ampicillin 1 g I.M./I.V. or amoxicillin 1 g orally	Ampicillin 50 mg/kg I.M./I.V. (not to exceed 2 g) plus gentamicin 1.5 mg/kg within 30 min of starting the procedure; 6 h later, ampicillin 25 mg/kg I.M./I.V. or amoxicillin 25 mg/kg orally
High-risk[3] patients allergic to ampicillin/amoxicillin	Vancomycin plus gentamicin	Vancomycin 1 g I.V. over 1-2 h plus gentamicin 1.5 mg/kg I.M./I.V. (not to exceed 120 mg); complete injection/infusion within 30 min of starting the procedure	Vancomycin 20 mg/kg I.V. over 1-2 h plus gentamicin 1.5 mg/kg I.M./I.V.; complete injection/infusion within 30 min of starting the procedure
Moderate-risk[4] patients	Amoxicillin or ampicillin	Amoxicillin 2 g orally 1 h before procedure, or ampicillin 2 g I.M./I.V within 30 min of starting the procedure	Amoxicillin 50 mg/kg orally 1 h before procedure, or ampicillin 50 mg/kg I.M./I.V. within 30 min of starting the procedure

Table 5. Prophylactic Regimens for Genitourinary / Gastrointestinal (Excluding Esophageal) Procedures *(continued)*

Situation	Agents	Regimen[1,2]	
		Adults	Children
Moderate-risk[4] patients allergic to ampicillin/amoxicillin	Vancomycin	Vancomycin 1 g I.V. over 1-2 h; complete infusion within 30 min of starting the procedure	Vancomycin 20 mg/kg I.V. over 1-2 h; complete infusion within 30 min of starting the procedure

[1]Total children's dose should not exceed adult dose.

[2]No second dose of vancomycin or gentamicin is recommended.

[3]High-risk: Patients are those who have prosthetic valves, a previous history of endocarditis (even in the absence of other heart disease, complex cyanotic congenital heart disease, or surgically constructed systemic pulmonary shunts or conduits).

[4]Moderate-risk: Individuals with certain other underlying cardiac defects. Congenital cardiac conditions include the following uncorrected conditions: Patent ductus arteriosus, ventricular septal defect, ostium primum atrial septal defect, coarctation of the aorta, and bicuspid aortic valve. Acquired valvar dysfunction and hypertrophic cardiomyopathy are also moderate risk conditions.

PREVENTION OF PERINATAL HIV-1 TRANSMISSION

Adapted from "U.S. Public Health Service Task Force Recommendations for Use of Antiretroviral Drugs in Pregnant Women Infected With HIV-1 for Maternal Health and for Reducing Perinatal HIV-1 Transmission in the United States." (http://AIDSinfo.nih.gov)

Pediatric AIDS Clinical Trials Group (PACTG) 076 Zidovudine (ZDV) Regimen

Time of ZDV Administration	Regimen
Antepartum	Oral administration of 100 mg ZDV 5 times/day,[1] initiated at 14-34 weeks gestation and continued throughout the pregnancy
Intrapartum	During labor, intravenous administration of ZDV in a 1-hour initial dose of 2 mg/kg body weight, followed by a continuous infusion of 1 mg/kg body weight/hour until delivery
Postpartum	Oral administration of ZDV to the newborn (ZDV syrup at 2 mg/kg body weight/dose every 6 hours) for the first 6 weeks of life, beginning at 8-12 hours after birth.[2]

[1]Oral ZDV administered as 200 mg 3 times/day or 300 mg bid is currently used in general clinical practice and is an acceptable alternative regimen to 100 mg orally 5 times/day.

[2]Intravenous dosage for full-term infants who cannot tolerate oral intake is 1.5 mg/kg body weight intravenously every 6 hours. ZDV dosing for infants <35 weeks gestation at birth is 1.5 mg/kg/dose intravenously, or 2 mg/kg/dose orally, every 12 hours, advancing to every 8 hours at 2 weeks of age if >30 weeks gestation at birth or at 4 weeks of age if <30 weeks gestation at birth.

Clinical Scenarios and Recommendations for the Use of Antiretroviral Drugs to Reduce Perinatal Human Immunodeficiency Virus (HIV-1) Transmission

SCENARIO #1
HIV-1-infected pregnant women who have not received prior antiretroviral therapy

- Pregnant women with HIV-1 infection must receive standard clinical, immunologic, and virologic evaluation. Recommendations for initiation and choice of antiretroviral therapy should be based on the same parameters used for persons who are not pregnant, although the known and unknown risks and benefits of such therapy during pregnancy must be considered and discussed.

- The three-part ZDV chemoprophylaxis regimen, initiated after the first trimester, should be recommended for all HIV-1-infected pregnant women regardless of antenatal HIV-1 RNA copy number to reduce the risk for perinatal transmission.

- The combination of ZDV chemoprophylaxis with additional antiretroviral drugs for treatment of HIV-1 infection is recommended for infected women whose clinical, immunologic, or virologic status requires treatment or who have HIV-1 RNA over 1000 copies/mL regardless of clinical or immunologic status.

- Women who are in the first trimester of pregnancy may consider delaying initiation of therapy until after 10-12 weeks gestation.

SCENARIO #2
HIV-1-infected women receiving antiretroviral therapy during the current pregnancy

- HIV-1-infected women receiving antiretroviral therapy in whom pregnancy is identified after the first trimester should continue therapy. ZDV should be a component of the antenatal antiretroviral treatment regimen after the first trimester whenever possible, although this may not always be feasible.

- For women receiving antiretroviral therapy in whom pregnancy is recognized during the first trimester, the woman should be counseled regarding the benefits and potential risks of antiretroviral administration during this period, and continuation of therapy should be considered. If therapy is discontinued during the first trimester, all drugs should be stopped and reintroduced simultaneously to avoid the development of drug resistance.

- Regardless of the antepartum antiretroviral regimen, ZDV administration is recommended during the intrapartum period and for the newborn.

SCENARIO #3
HIV-1-infected women in labor who have had no prior therapy

Several effective regimens are available. These include:

- single-dose nevirapine at the onset of labor followed by a single dose of nevirapine for the newborn at age 48 hours

- oral ZDV and 3TC during labor, followed by 1 week of oral ZDV/3TC for the newborn

- intrapartum intravenous ZDV followed by 6 weeks of ZDV for the newborn

- two-dose nevirapine regimen combined with intrapartum intravenous ZDV and 6-week ZDV for the newborn

In the immediate postpartum period, the woman should have appropriate assessments (eg, CD4$^+$ count and HIV-1 RNA copy number) to determine whether antiretroviral therapy is recommended for her own health.

SCENARIO #4
Infants born to mothers who have received no antiretroviral therapy during pregnancy or intrapartum

- The 6-week neonatal ZDV component of the ZDV chemoprophylactic regimen should be discussed with the mother and offered for the newborn.

- ZDV should be initiated as soon as possible after delivery – preferably within 6-12 hours of birth.

- Some clinicians may choose to use ZDV in combination with other antiretroviral drugs, particularly if the mother is known or suspected to have ZDV-resistant virus. However, the efficacy of this approach for prevention of transmission has not been proven in clinical trials, and appropriate dosing regimens for neonates are incompletely defined for many drugs.

- In the immediate postpartum period, the woman should undergo appropriate assessments (eg, CD4$^+$ count and HIV-1 RNA copy number) to determine whether antiretroviral therapy is required for her own health. The infant should undergo early diagnostic testing so that if HIV-1-infected, treatment can be initiated as soon as possible.

Note: Discussion of treatment options and recommendations should be noncoercive, and the final decision regarding the use of antiretroviral drugs is the responsibility of the woman. A decision to not accept treatment with ZDV or other drugs should not result in punitive action or denial of care. Use of ZDV should not be denied to a woman who wishes to minimize exposure of the fetus to other antiretroviral drugs and who, therefore, chooses to receive only ZDV during pregnancy to reduce the risk for perinatal transmission.

PREVENTION OF WOUND INFECTION AND SEPSIS IN SURGICAL PATIENTS

Nature of Operation	Likely Pathogens	Recommended Drugs	Adult Dosage Before Surgery[1]
Cardiac			
Prosthetic valve, coronary artery bypass, other open-heart surgery, pacemaker or defibrillator implant	*S. aureus*, *S. epidermidis*, *Corynebacterium*, enteric gram-negative bacilli	Cefazolin	1-2 g I.V.[2]
		or cefuroxime	1-5 g I.V.[2]
		or vancomycin[3]	1 g I.V.
Gastrointestinal			
Esophageal, gastroduodenal	Enteric gram-negative bacilli, gram-positive cocci	*High risk[4] only:* cefazolin[5]	1-2 g I.V.
Biliary tract	Enteric gram-negative bacilli, enterococci, clostridia	*High risk[6] only:* cefazolin[5]	1-2 g I.V.
Colorectal	Enteric gram-negative bacilli, anaerobes, enterococci	*Oral:* neomycin + erythromycin base[7]	1-2 g I.V.
		Parenteral:	
		Cefoxitin	1-2 g I.V.
		or cefotetan	1-2 g I.V.
		+ metronidazole	0.5 g I.V.
Appendectomy, nonperforated	Enteric gram-negative bacilli, anaerobes, enterococci	Cefoxitin	1-2 g I.V.
		or cefotetan	1-2 g I.V.
Genitourinary	Enteric gram-negative bacilli, enterococci	*High risk[8] only:* Ciprofloxacin	500 mg P.O. or 400 mg I.V.
Gynecologic and Obstetric			
Vaginal or abdominal hysterectomy	Enteric gram-negatives, anaerobes, group B streptococci, enterococci	Cefazolin	1-2 g I.V.
		or cefotetan	1-2 g I.V.
		or cefoxitin	1 g I.V.
Cesarean section	Same as for hysterectomy	*High risk[9] only:* Cefazolin	1 g I.V. after cord clamping
Abortion	Same as for hysterectomy	*First trimester, high-risk[10] only:* Aqueous penicillin G	2 mill units I.V.
		or doxycycline	300 mg P.O.[11]
		Second trimester: Cefazolin	1 g I.V.
Head and Neck			
Incisions through oral or pharyngeal mucosa	Anaerobes, enteric gram-negative bacilli, *S. aureus*	Clindamycin	600-900 mg I.V.
		± gentamicin	1.5 mg/kg I.V.
		or cefazolin	1-2 g I.V.
Neurosurgery			
Craniotomy	*S. aureus*, *S. epidermidis*	Cefazolin	1-2 g I.V.
		or vancomycin[3]	1 g I.V.
Ophthalmic	*S. aureus*, *S. epidermidis*, streptococci, enteric gram-negative bacilli, *Pseudomonas*	Gentamicin, tobramycin, ciprofloxacin, ofloxacin or neomycin-gramicidin-polymyxin B	Multiple drops topically over 2-24 h
		Cefazolin	100 mg subconjunctivally

Nature of Operation	Likely Pathogens	Recommended Drugs	Adult Dosage Before Surgery[1]
Orthopedic			
Total joint replacement, internal fixation of fractures	S. aureus, S. epidermidis	Cefazolin	1-2 g I.V.
		or vancomycin[3]	1 g I.V.
Thoracic (Noncardiac)	S. aureus, S. epidermidis, streptococci, enteric gram-negative bacilli	Cefazolin	1-2 g I.V.
		or cefuroxime	1-5 g I.V.
		or vancomycin[3]	1 g I.V.
Vascular			
Arterial surgery involving a prosthesis, the abdominal aorta, or a groin incision	S. aureus, S. epidermidis, enteric gram-negative bacilli	Cefazolin	1-2 g I.V.
		or vancomycin[3]	1 g I.V.
Lower extremity amputation for ischemia	S. aureus, S. epidermidis, enteric gram-negative bacilli, clostridia	Cefazolin[5]	1-2 g I.V.
		or vancomycin[3]	1 g I.V.
CONTAMINATED SURGERY[12]			
Ruptured viscus	Enteric gram-negative bacilli, anaerobes, enterococci	Cefoxitin	1-2 g I.V. q6h
		or cefotetan	1-2 g I.V. q12h
		± gentamicin	1.5 mg/kg I.V. q8h
		or clindamycin	600 mg I.V. q6h
		+ gentamicin	1.5 mg/kg I.V. q8h
Traumatic wound	S. aureus, Group A strep, clostridia	Cefazolin[13]	1-2 g I.V. q8h

[1]Parenteral prophylactic antimicrobials can be given as a single intravenous dose completed 30 minutes or less before the operation. For prolonged operations, additional intraoperative doses should be given q4-8h for the duration of the procedure.

[2]Some consultants recommend an additional dose when patients are removed from bypass during open-heart surgery.

[3]For hospitals in which methicillin-resistant S. aureus and S. epidermidis are a frequent cause of postoperative wound infection, or for patients allergic to penicillins or cephalosporin. Rapid I.V. administration may cause hypotension, which could be especially dangerous during induction of anesthesia. Even if the drug is given over 60 minutes, hypotension may occur; treatment with diphenhydramine (Benadryl® and others) and further slowing of the infusion rate may be helpful. For procedures in which enteric gram-negative bacilli are likely pathogens, such as vascular surgery involving a groin incision, cefazolin or cefuroxime should be included in the prophylaxis regimen for patients not allergic to cephalosporins.

[4]Morbid obesity, esophageal obstruction, decreased gastric acidity, or gastrointestinal motility.

[5]Some Medical Letter consultants favor cefoxitin for better anaerobic coverage in this setting.

[6]Age >70 years, acute cholecystitis, nonfunctioning gallbladder, obstructive jaundice, or common duct stones.

[7]After appropriate diet and catharsis, 1 g of each at 1 PM, 2 PM, and 11 PM the day before an 8 AM operation.

[8]Urine culture positive or unavailable, preoperative catheter, transrectal prostatic biopsy.

[9]Active labor or premature rupture of membranes.

[10]Patients with previous pelvic inflammatory disease, previous gonorrhea or multiple sex partners.

[11]Divided into 100 mg 1 hour before the abortion and 200 mg 30 minutes after.

[12]For contaminated or "dirty" surgery, therapy should usually be continued for about 5 days. Ruptured viscus in postoperative setting (dehiscence) requires antibacterials to include coverage of nosocomial pathogens.

[13]For bite wounds, in which likely pathogens may also include oral anaerobes, Eikenella corrodens (human), or Pasteurella multocida (dog and cat), some Medical Letter consultants recommend use of amoxicillin/clavulanic acid (Augmentin®) or ampicillin/sulbactam (Unasyn®) (Smith PF, Meadowcroft AM, and May DB, "Treating Mammalian Bite Wounds," J Clin Pharm Ther, 2000, 25(2):85-99. For penetrating intracranial wounds, including gunshot injuries, a broad-spectrum antimicrobial such as ampicillin/sulbactam is recommended (Bayston R, de Louvois J, Brown EM, et al, "Use of Antibiotics in Penetrating Craniocerebral Injuries. 'Infection in Neurosurgery' Working Party of British Society for Antimicrobial Chemotherapy, Lancet, 2000, 355(9217):1813-7.

Adapted with permission from "Antimicrobial Prophylaxis in Surgery," Med Lett Drugs Ther, 2001, 43(1116-1117):96-7.

TUBERCULOSIS

Tuberculin Skin Test Recommendations[1]

Children for whom immediate skin testing is indicated:

- Contacts of persons with confirmed or suspected infectious tuberculosis (contact investigation); this includes children identified as contacts of family members or associates in jail or prison in the last 5 years

- Children with radiographic or clinical findings suggesting tuberculosis

- Children immigrating from endemic countries (eg, Asia, Middle East, Africa, Latin America)

- Children with travel histories to endemic countries and/or significant contact with indigenous persons from such countries

Children who should be tested annually for tuberculosis[2]:

- Children infected with HIV or living in household with HIV-infected persons

- Incarcerated adolescents

Children who should be tested every 2-3 years[2]:

- Children exposed to the following individuals: HIV-infected, homeless, residents of nursing homes, institutionalized adolescents or adults, users of illicit drugs, incarcerated adolescents or adults, and migrant farm workers. Foster children with exposure to adults in the preceding high-risk groups are included.

Children who should be considered for tuberculin skin testing at ages 4-6 and 11-16 years:

- Children whose parents immigrated (with unknown tuberculin skin test status) from regions of the world with high prevalence of tuberculosis; continued potential exposure by travel to the endemic areas and/or house-hold contact with persons from the endemic areas (with unknown tuber-culin skin test status) should be an indication for repeat tuberculin skin testing

- Children without specific risk factors who reside in high-prevalence areas; in general, a high-risk neighborhood or community does not mean an entire city is at high risk; rates in any area of the city may vary by neighborhood, or even from block to block; physicians should be aware of these patterns in determining the likelihood of exposure; public health officials or local tuberculosis experts should help clinicians identify areas that have appreciable tuberculosis rates

Children at increased risk of progression of infection to disease: Those with other medical risk factors, including diabetes mellitus, chronic renal failure, malnutri-tion, and congenital or acquired immunodeficiencies deserve special consideration. Without recent exposure, these persons are not at increased risk of acquiring tuber-culosis infection. Underlying immune deficiencies associated with these conditions theoretically would enhance the possibility for progression to severe disease. Initial histories of potential exposure to tuberculosis should be included on all of these patients. If these histories or local epidemiologic factors suggest a possibility of exposure, immediate and periodic tuberculin skin testing should be considered. An initial Mantoux tuberculin skin test should be performed before initiation of immuno-suppressive therapy in any child with an underlying condition that necessitates immunosuppressive therapy.

---

[1]BCG immunization is not a contraindication to tuberculin skin testing.

[2]Initial tuberculin skin testing is at the time of diagnosis or circumstance, beginning as early as at age 3 months.

Tuberculosis Prophylaxis

Specific Circumstances/ Organism	Comments	Regimen
Category I. Exposure		
(Household members and other close contacts of potentially infectious cases) (Exposee tuberculin test negative)[1]		
Neonate	Rx essential	INH (10 mg/kg/d) for 3 months, then repeat tuberculin test (TBnT). If mother's smear negative and infant's TBnT negative and chest x-ray (CXR) are normal, stop INH. In the United Kingdom, BCG is then given (*Lancet*, 1990, 2:1479), unless mother is HIV-positive. If infant's repeat TBnT is positive and/or CXR abnormal (hilar adenopathy and/or infiltrate), administer INH + RIF (10-20 mg/kg/d) (or streptomycin) for a total of 6 months. If mother is being treated, separation from mother is not indicated.
Children <5 y	Rx indicated	As for neonate first 3 months. If repeat TBnT is negative, stop. If repeat TBnT is positive, continue INH for a total of 9 months. If INH is not given initially, repeat TBnT at 3 months; if positive, treat with INH for 9 months (see Category II below).
Older children and adults	No Rx	Repeat TBnT at 3 months, if positive, treat with INH for 6 months (see Category II below)
Category II. Infection Without Disease		
(Positive tuberculin test)[1]		
Regardless of age (see INH Preventive Therapy)	Rx indicated	INH (5 mg/kg/d, maximum: 300 mg/d for adults, 10 mg/kg/d not to exceed 300 mg/d for children). Results with 6 months of treatment are nearly as effective as 12 months (65% vs 75% reduction in disease). *Am Thoracic Society* (6 months), *Am Acad Pediatrics*, 1991 (9 months). If CXR is abnormal, treat for 12 months. In HIV-positive patient, treatment for a minimum of 12 months, some suggest longer. Monitor transaminases monthly (*MMWR Morb Mortal Wkly Rep* 1989, 38:247).
Age <35 y	Rx indicated	Reanalysis of earlier studies favors INH prophylaxis for 6 months (if INH-related hepatitis case fatality rate is <1% and TB case fatality is ≥6.7%, which appears to be the case, monitor transaminases monthly (*Arch Int Med*, 1990, 150:2517).
INH-resistant organisms likely	Rx indicated	Data on efficacy of alternative regimens is currently lacking. Regimens include ETB + RIF daily for 6 months. PZA + RIF daily for 2 months, then INH + RIF daily until sensitivities from index case (if available) known, then if INH-CR, discontinue INH and continue RIF for 9 months, otherwise INH + RIF for 9 months (this latter is *Am Acad Pediatrics*, 1991 recommendation).
INH + RIF resistant organisms likely	Rx indicated	Efficacy of alternative regimens is unknown; PZA (25-30 mg/kg/d P.O.) + ETB (15-25 mg/kg/d P.O.) (at 25 mg/kg ETB, monitoring for retrobulbar neuritis required), for 6 months unless HIV-positive, then 12 months; PZA + ciprofloxacin (750 mg P.O. bid) or ofloxacin (400 mg P.O. bid) x 6-12 months (*MMWR Morb Mortal Wkly Rep*, 1992, 41(RR11):68).

INH = isoniazid; RIF = rifampin; KM = kanamycin; ETB = ethambutol
SM = streptomycin; CXR = chest x-ray; Rx = treatment
See also guidelines for interpreting PPD in "Skin Testing for Delayed Hypersensitivity."
[1]Tuberculin test (TBnT). The standard is the Mantoux test, 5 TU PPD in 0.1 mL diluent stabilized with Tween 80. Read at 48-72 hours measuring maximum diameter of induration. A reaction ≥5 mm is defined as positive in the following: positive HIV or risk factors, recent close case contacts, CXR consistent with healed TBc. ≥10 mm is positive in foreign-born in countries of high prevalence, injection drug users, low income populations, nursing home residents, patients with medical conditions which increase risk (see above, preventive treatment). ≥15 mm is positive in all others (*Am Rev Resp Dis*, 1990, 142:725). Two-stage TBnT: Use in individuals to be tested regularly (ie, healthcare workers). TBn reactivity may decrease over time but be boosted by skin testing. If unrecognized, individual may be incorrectly diagnosed as recent converter. If first TBnT is reactive but <10 mm, repeat 5 TU in 1 week, if then ≥10 mm = positive, not recent conversion (*Am Rev Resp Dis*, 1979, 119:587).

ANTIMICROBIAL DRUGS OF CHOICE

The following table lists the antibacterial drugs of choice for various infecting organisms. This table is reprinted with permission from "The Choice of Antibacterial Drugs," *Med Lett Drugs Ther*, 2001, 43(1111-1112):69-78. Users should not assume that all antibiotics which are appropriate for a given organism are listed or that those not listed are inappropriate. The infection caused by the organism may encompass varying degrees of severity, and since the antibiotics listed may not be appropriate for the differing degrees of severity, or because of other patient-related factors, it cannot be assumed that the antibiotics listed for any specific organism are interchangeable. This table should not be used by itself without first referring to *The Medical Letter*, an infectious disease manual, or the infectious disease department. Therefore, only use this table as a tool for obtaining more information about the therapies available.

Infecting Organism	Drug of First Choice	Alternative Drugs
GRAM-POSITIVE COCCI		
Enterococcus[1]		
endocarditis or other severe infection	Penicillin G or ampicillin + gentamicin or streptomycin[2]	Vancomycin + gentamicin or streptomycin[2]; linezolid; quinupristin/dalfopristin
uncomplicated urinary tract infection	Ampicillin or amoxicillin	Nitrofurantoin; a fluoroquinolone[3]; fosfomycin
Staphylococcus aureus or *epidermidis*		
methicillin-sensitive	A penicillinase-resistant penicillin[4]	A cephalosporin[5,6]; vancomycin; amoxicillin/clavulanic acid; ticarcillin/clavulanic acid; piperacillin/tazobactam; ampicillin/sulbactam; imipenem or meropenem; clindamycin; a fluoroquinolone[3]
methicillin-resistant[7]	Vancomycin ± gentamicin ± rifampin	Linezolid; quinupristin/dalfopristin; a fluoroquinolone[3]; a tetracycline[8]; trimethoprim-sulfamethoxazole
Streptococcus pyogenes (group A[9]) and groups C and G	Penicillin G or V[10]	Clindamycin; erythromycin; a cephalosporin[5,6]; vancomycin; clarithromycin[11]; azithromycin
Streptococcus, group B	Penicillin G or ampicillin	A cephalosporin[5,6]; vancomycin; erythromycin
Streptococcus, viridans group[1]	Penicillin G ± gentamicin	A cephalosporin[5,6]; vancomycin
Streptococcus bovis	Penicillin G	A cephalosporin[5,6]; vancomycin
Streptococcus, anaerobic or *Peptostreptococcus*	Penicillin G	Clindamycin; a cephalosporin[5,6]; vancomycin
Streptococcus pneumoniae[12] (pneumococcus), penicillin-susceptible (MIC <0.1 mcg/mL)	Penicillin G or V[10]; amoxicillin	A cephalosporin[5,6]; erythromycin; azithromycin; clarithromycin[11]; levofloxacin[13]; gatifloxacin[13] or moxifloxacin[13]; meropenem; imipenem; trimethoprim-sulfamethoxazole; clindamycin; a tetracycline[8]
penicillin-intermediate resistance (MIC 0.1-≤2 mcg/mL)	Penicillin G I.V. (12 million units/day for adults); ceftriaxone or cefotaxime	Levofloxacin[13]; gatifloxacin[13] or moxifloxacin[13]; vancomycin; clindamycin
penicillin-high level resistance (MIC ≥2 mcg/mL)	**Meningitis:** Vancomycin + ceftriaxone or cefotaxime ± rifampin	Meropenem; imipenem

Infecting Organism	Drug of First Choice	Alternative Drugs
	Other Infections: Vancomycin + ceftriaxone or cefotaxime; or levofloxacin,[13] gatifloxacin[13] or moxifloxacin[13]	Linezolid; quinupristin/dalfopristin
GRAM-NEGATIVE COCCI		
Moraxella (Branhamella) catarrhalis	Cefuroxime[5]; a fluoroquinolone[3]	Trimethoprim-sulfamethoxazole; amoxicillin/clavulanic acid; erythromycin; a tetracycline[8]; cefotaxime[5]; ceftizoxime[5]; ceftriaxone[5]; cefuroxime axetil[5]; cefixime[5]; cefpodoxime[5]; clarithromycin[11]; azithromycin
*Neisseria gonorrhoeae (gonococcus)[14]	Ceftriaxone[5] or cefixime[5]; or ciprofloxacin,[13] gatifloxacin[13] or ofloxacin[13]	Cefotaxime[5]; penicillin G
Neisseria meningitidis[15] (meningococcus)	Penicillin G	Cefotaxime[5]; ceftizoxime[5]; ceftriaxone[5]; chloramphenicol[16]; a sulfonamide[17]; a fluoroquinolone[3]
GRAM-POSITIVE BACILLI		
Bacillus anthracis (anthrax)	Penicillin G	Ciprofloxacin[13]; erythromycin; a tetracycline[8]
Bacillus cereus, subtilis	Vancomycin	Imipenem or meropenem; clindamycin
Clostridium perfringens[18]	Penicillin G; clindamycin	Metronidazole; imipenem or meropenem; chloramphenicol[16]
Clostridium tetani[19]	Metronidazole	Penicillin G; a tetracycline[8]
Clostridium difficile[20]	Metronidazole	Vancomycin (oral)
Corynebacterium diphtheriae[21]	Erythromycin	Penicillin G
Corynebacterium, JK group	Vancomycin	Penicillin G + gentamicin; erythromycin
*Erysipelothrix rhusiopathiae	Penicillin G	Erythromycin, a cephalosporin[5,6]; a fluoroquinolone[3]
Listeria monocytogenes	Ampicillin ± gentamicin	Trimethoprim-sulfamethoxazole
ENTERIC GRAM-NEGATIVE BACILLI		
*Bacteroides	Metronidazole or clindamycin	Imipenem or meropenem; amoxicillin/clavulanic acid; ticarcillin/clavulanic acid; piperacillin/tazobactam; ampicillin/sulbactam; cefoxitin[5]; cefotetan[5]; chloramphenicol[16]; cefmetazole[5]; penicillin G; gatifloxacin[13] or moxifloxacin[13]
*Campylobacter fetus	Imipenem or meropenem	Gentamicin
*Campylobacter jejuni	Erythromycin or azithromycin	A fluoroquinolone[2]; a tetracycline[8]; gentamicin
*Citrobacter freundii	Imipenem or meropenem[22]	A fluoroquinolone[3]; amikacin; a tetracycline[8]; trimethoprim-sulfamethoxazole; cefotaxime[5,22]; ceftizoxime[5,22]; ceftriaxone[5,22]; cefepime[5,22] or ceftazidime[5,22]

ANTIMICROBIAL DRUGS OF CHOICE (Continued)

Infecting Organism	Drug of First Choice	Alternative Drugs
Enterobacter	Imipenem or meropenem[22]	Gentamicin, tobramycin or amikacin; trimethoprim-sulfamethoxazole; ciprofloxacin[13]; ticarcillin[23]; mezlocillin[23] or piperacillin[23]; aztreonam[22]; cefotaxime[5,22]; ceftizoxime[5,22]; ceftriaxone[5,22]; cefepime[5,22] or ceftazidime[5,22]
Escherichia coli[24]	Cefotaxime, ceftizoxime, ceftriaxone, cefepime or ceftazidime[5,22]	Ampicillin ± gentamicin, tobramycin or amikacin; carbenicillin[23]; ticarcillin[23]; mezlocillin[23] or piperacillin[23]; gentamicin, tobramycin or amikacin; amoxicillin/clavulanic acid[22]; ticarcillin/clavulanic acid[23]; piperacillin/tazobactam[23]; ampicillin/sulbactam[22]; trimethoprim/sulfamethoxazole; imipenem or meropenem[22]; aztreonam[22]; a fluoroquinolone[3]; another cephalosporin[5,6]
Helicobacter pylori[25]	Omeprazole + amoxicillin + clarithromycin; or tetracycline HCl[8] + metronidazole + bismuth subsalicylate	Tetracycline HCl[8] + clarithromycin[11] + bismuth subsalicylate; amoxicillin + metronidazole + bismuth subsalicylate; amoxicillin + clarithromycin[11]
Klebsiella pneumoniae[24]	Cefotaxime, ceftizoxime, ceftriaxone, cefepime or ceftazidime[5,22]	Imipenem or meropenem[22]; gentamicin, tobramycin or amikacin; amoxicillin/clavulanic acid[22]; ticarcillin/clavulanic acid[23]; piperacillin/tazobactam[23]; ampicillin/sulbactam[22]; trimethoprim-sulfamethoxazole; aztreonam[22]; a fluoroquinolone[3]; mezlocillin[23] or piperacillin[23]; another cephalosporin[5,6]
Proteus mirabilis[24]	Ampicillin[26]	A cephalosporin[5,6,22]; ticarcillin[23]; mezlocillin[23] or piperacillin[23]; gentamicin, tobramycin, or amikacin; trimethoprim-sulfamethoxazole; imipenem or meropenem[22]; aztreonam[23]; a fluoroquinolone[3]; chloramphenicol[16]
Proteus, indole-positive (including *Providencia rettgeri*, *Morganella morganii*, and *Proteus vulgaris*)	Cefotaxime, ceftizoxime, ceftriaxone, cefepime, or ceftazidime[5,22]	Imipenem or meropenem[22]; gentamicin, tobramycin, or amikacin; carbenicillin[23]; ticarcillin[23]; mezlocillin[23] or piperacillin[23]; amoxicillin/clavulanic acid[22]; ticarcillin/clavulanic acid[23]; piperacillin/tazobactam[23]; ampicillin/sulbactam[22]; aztreonam[22]; trimethoprim-sulfamethoxazole; a fluoroquinolone[3]
Providencia stuartii	Cefotaxime, ceftizoxime, ceftriaxone, cefepime, or ceftazidime[5,22]	Imipenem or meropenem[22]; ticarcillin/clavulanic acid[23]; piperacillin/tazobactam[23]; gentamicin, tobramycin, or amikacin; carbenicillin[23]; ticarcillin,[23] mezlocillin,[23] or piperacillin[23]; aztreonam[22]; trimethoprim-sulfamethoxazole; a fluoroquinolone[3]

Infecting Organism	Drug of First Choice	Alternative Drugs
*Salmonella typhi[27] (typhoid fever)	A fluoroquinolone[3] or ceftriaxone[5]	Chloramphenicol[16]; trimethoprim-sulfamethoxazole; ampicillin; amoxicillin; azithromycin[28]
*other Salmonella[29]	Cefotaxime[5] or ceftriaxone[5] or a fluoroquinolone[3]	Ampicillin or amoxicillin; trimethoprim-sulfamethoxazole; chloramphenicol[16]
*Serratia	Imipenem or meropenem[22]	Gentamicin or amikacin; cefotaxime, ceftizoxime, ceftriaxone, cefepime, or ceftazidime[5,22]; aztreonam[22]; trimethoprim-sulfamethoxazole; carbenicillin[30], ticarcillin[30], mezlocillin[30] or piperacillin[30]; a fluoroquinolone[3]
*Shigella	A fluoroquinolone[3]	Azithromycin; trimethoprim-sulfamethoxazole; ampicillin; ceftriaxone[5]
*Yersinia enterocolitica	Trimethoprim-sulfamethoxazole	A fluoroquinolone[3]; gentamicin, tobramycin, or amikacin; cefotaxime or ceftizoxime[5]

OTHER GRAM-NEGATIVE BACILLI

Infecting Organism	Drug of First Choice	Alternative Drugs
*Acinetobacter	Imipenem or meropenem[22]	An aminoglycoside; ciprofloxacin[13]; trimethoprim-sulfamethoxazole; ticarcillin,[23] mezlocillin[23], or piperacillin[23]; ceftazidime[22]; minocycline[8]; doxycycline[8]; sulbactam[31]; polymyxin
*Aeromonas	Trimethoprim-sulfamethoxazole	Gentamicin or tobramycin; imipenem; a fluoroquinolone[3]
Bartonella henselae or quintana (bacillary angiomatosis)	Erythromycin	Doxycycline[8]; azithromycin
Bartonella henselae[32] (cat scratch bacillus)	Azithromycin	Ciprofloxacin[13]; erythromycin; trimethoprim-sulfamethoxazole; gentamicin; rifampin
Bordetella pertussis (whooping cough)	Erythromycin	Azithromycin or clarithromycin[11]; trimethoprim-sulfamethoxazole
*Brucella	A tetracycline[8] + rifampin	A tetracycline[8] + streptomycin or gentamicin; chloramphenicol[16] ± streptomycin; trimethoprim-sulfamethoxazole ± gentamicin; ciprofloxacin[13] + rifampin
*Burkholderia cepacia	Trimethoprim-sulfamethoxazole	Ceftazidime[5]; chloramphenicol[16]; imipenem
Burkholderia (Pseudomonas) mallei (glanders)	Streptomycin + a tetracycline[8]	Streptomycin + chloramphenicol[16]; imipenem
*Burkholderia (Pseudomonas) pseudomallei (melioidosis)	Imipenem; ceftazidime[5]	Meropenem; chloramphenicol[16] + doxycycline[8] + trimethoprim-sulfamethoxazole; amoxicillin/clavulanic acid
Calymmatobacterium granulomatis (granuloma inguinale)	Trimethoprim-sulfamethoxazole	Doxycycline[8] or ciprofloxacin[13] ± gentamicin
Capnocytophaga canimorsus[33]	Penicillin G	Cefotaxime[5]; ceftizoxime[5]; ceftriaxone[5]; imipenem or meropenem; vancomycin; a fluoroquinolone[3]; clindamycin
*Eikenella corrodens	Ampicillin	An erythromycin; a tetracycline[8]; amoxicillin/clavulanic acid; ampicillin/sulbactam; ceftriaxone[5]
*Francisella tularensis (tularemia)	Streptomycin	Gentamicin; a tetracycline[8]; chloramphenicol[16]; ciprofloxacin[13]

ANTIMICROBIAL DRUGS OF CHOICE (Continued)

Infecting Organism	Drug of First Choice	Alternative Drugs
*Fusobacterium	Penicillin G	Metronidazole; clindamycin; cefoxitin[5]; chloramphenicol[16]
Gardnerella vaginalis (bacterial vaginosis)	Oral metronidazole[34]	Topical clindamycin or metronidazole; oral clindamycin
*Haemophilus ducreyi (chancroid)	Azithromycin or ceftriaxone	Ciprofloxacin[13] or erythromycin
*Haemophilus influenzae		
meningitis, epiglottitis, arthritis, and other serious infections	Cefotaxime or ceftriaxone[5]	Cefuroxime[5] (not for meningitis); chloramphenicol[16]; meropenem
upper respiratory infections and bronchitis	Trimethoprim-sulfamethoxazole	Cefuroxime[5]; amoxicillin/clavulanic acid; cefuroxime axetil[5]; cefpodoxime[5]; cefaclor[5]; cefotaxime[5]; ceftizoxime[5]; ceftriaxone[5]; cefixime[5]; a tetracycline[8]; clarithromycin[11]; azithromycin; a fluoroquinolone[3]; ampicillin or amoxicillin
Legionella species	Azithromycin or a fluoroquinolone[3] ± rifampin	Doxycycline[8] ± rifampin; trimethoprim-sulfamethoxazole; erythromycin
Leptotrichia buccalis	Penicillin G	A tetracycline[8]; clindamycin; erythromycin
Pasteurella multocida	Penicillin G	A tetracycline[8]; a cephalosporin[5,6]; amoxicillin/clavulanic acid; ampicillin/sulbactam
*Pseudomonas aeruginosa		
urinary tract infection	Ciprofloxacin[13]	Levofloxacin[13]; carbenicillin, ticarcillin, piperacillin, or mezlocillin; ceftazidime[5]; cefepime[5]; imipenem or meropenem; aztreonam; tobramycin; gentamicin; amikacin
other infections	Ticarcillin, mezlocillin, or piperacillin + tobramycin, gentamicin, or amikacin[35]	Ceftazidime[5], imipenem, meropenem, aztreonam, cefepime[5] + tobramycin, gentamicin, or amikacin; ciprofloxacin[13]
Spirillum minus (rat bite fever)	Penicillin G	A tetracycline[8]; streptomycin
*Stenotrophomonas maltophilia	Trimethoprim-sulfamethoxazole	Minocycline[8]; a fluoroquinolone[3]
Streptobacillus moniliformis (rat bite fever, Haverhill fever)	Penicillin G	A tetracycline[8]; streptomycin
Vibrio cholerae (cholera)[36]	A tetracycline[8]	A fluoroquinolone[3]; trimethoprim-sulfamethoxazole
Vibrio vulnificus	A tetracycline[8]	Cefotaxime[5]
Yersinia pestis (plague)	Streptomycin ± a tetracycline[8]	Chloramphenicol[16]; gentamicin; trimethoprim-sulfamethoxazole
ACID-FAST BACILLI		
*Mycobacterium tuberculosis	Isoniazid + rifampin + pyrazinamide ± ethambutol or streptomycin[16]	A fluoroquinolone[3]; cycloserine[16]; capreomycin[16] or kanamycin[16] or amikacin[16]; ethionamide[16]; para-aminosalicylic acid[16]; ± clofazimine[16]
*Mycobacterium kansasii	Isoniazid + rifampin ± ethambutol or streptomycin[16]	Clarithromycin[11] or azithromycin; ethionamide[16]; cycloserine[16]

Infecting Organism	Drug of First Choice	Alternative Drugs
Mycobacterium avium complex	Clarithromycin[11] or azithromycin + ethambutol ± rifabutin	Ciprofloxacin[13]; amikacin[16]
prophylaxis	Clarithromycin[11] or azithromycin ± rifabutin	
Mycobacterium fortuitum/ chelonae complex	Amikacin + clarithromycin[11]	Cefoxitin[5]; rifampin; a sulfonamide; doxycycline[8]; ethambutol; linezolid
Mycobacterium marinum (balnei)[37]	Minocycline[8]	Trimethoprim-sulfamethoxazole; rifampin; clarithromycin[11]; doxycycline[8]
Mycobacterium leprae (leprosy)	Dapsone + rifampin ± clofazimine	Minocycline[8]; ofloxacin[13]; sparfloxacin[13]; clarithromycin[11]

ACTINOMYCETES

Actinomyces israelii (actinomycosis)	Penicillin G	A tetracycline[8]; erythromycin; clindamycin
Nocardia	Trimethoprim-sulfamethoxazole	Sulfisoxazole; amikacin[16]; a tetracycline[8]; imipenem or meropenem; cycloserine[16]; linezolid
Rhodococcus equi	Vancomycin ± a fluoroquinolone[3], rifampin, imipenem or meropenem; amikacin	Erythromycin
Tropheryma whippelii (agent of Whipple's disease)	Trimethoprim-sulfamethoxazole	Penicillin G; a tetracycline[8]

CHLAMYDIAE

Chlamydia psittaci (psittacosis, ornithosis)	A tetracycline[8]	Chloramphenicol[16]
Chlamydia trachomatis		
(trachoma)	Azithromycin	A tetracycline[8] (topical plus oral); a sulfonamide (topical plus oral)
(inclusion conjunctivitis)	Erythromycin (oral or I.V.)	A sulfonamide
(pneumonia)	Erythromycin	A sulfonamide
(urethritis, cervicitis)	Azithromycin or doxycycline[8]	Erythromycin; ofloxacin[13]; amoxicillin
(lymphogranuloma venereum)	A tetracycline[8]	Erythromycin
Chlamydia pneumoniae (TWAR strain)	Erythromycin; a tetracycline[8]; clarithromycin[11] or azithromycin	A fluoroquinolone[3]

EHRLICHIA

Ehrlichia chaffeensis	Doxycycline[8]	Chloramphenicol[16]
Ehrlichia ewingii	Doxycycline[8]	
Ehrlichia phagocytophila	Doxycycline[8]	Rifampin

MYCOPLASMA

Mycoplasma pneumoniae	Erythromycin; a tetracycline[8]; clarithromycin[11] or azithromycin	A fluoroquinolone[3]
Ureaplasma urealyticum	Erythromycin	A tetracycline[8]; clarithromycin[11]; azithromycin; ofloxacin[13]

ANTIMICROBIAL DRUGS OF CHOICE (Continued)

Infecting Organism	Drug of First Choice	Alternative Drugs
RICKETTSIA – Rocky Mountain spotted fever, endemic typhus (murine), epidemic typhus (louse-borne), scrub typhus (*Orientia tsutsugamushi*), trench fever, Q fever	Doxycycline[8]	Chloramphenicol[16]; a fluoroquinolone[3]; rifampin
SPIROCHETES		
Borrelia burgdorferi (Lyme disease)[38]	Doxycycline[8]; amoxicillin; cefuroxime axetil[5]	Ceftriaxone[5]; cefotaxime[5]; penicillin G; azithromycin; clarithromycin[11]
Borrelia recurrentis (relapsing fever)	A tetracycline[8]	Penicillin G
Leptospira	Penicillin G	A tetracycline[8]
Treponema pallidum (syphilis)	Penicillin G[10]	A tetracycline[8]; ceftriaxone[5]
Treponema pertenue (yaws)	Penicillin G	A tetracycline[8]

*Resistance may be a problem; susceptibility tests should be used to guide therapy.

[1] Disk sensitivity testing may not provide adequate information; beta-lactamase assays, "E" tests, and dilution tests for susceptibility should be used in serious infections.

[2] Aminoglycoside resistance is increasingly common among enterococci; treatment options include ampicillin 2 g I.V. q4h, continuous infusion of ampicillin, a combination of ampicillin plus a fluoroquinolone, or a combination of ampicillin, imipenem, and vancomycin.

[3] Among the fluoroquinolones, levofloxacin, gatifloxacin, and moxifloxacin have excellent *in vitro* activity against *S. pneumoniae*, including penicillin- and cephalosporin-resistant strains. Levofloxacin, gatifloxacin, and moxifloxacin also have good activity against many strains of *S. aureus*, but resistance has become frequent among methicillin-resistant strains. Ciprofloxacin has the greatest activity against *Pseudomonas aeruginosa*. For urinary tract infections, norfloxacin, lomefloxacin, or enoxacin can be used. For tuberculosis, levofloxacin, ofloxacin, ciprofloxacin, gatifloxacin, or moxifloxacin could be used. Ciprofloxacin, ofloxacin, levofloxacin, and gatifloxacin are available for intravenous use. None of these agents are recommended for children or pregnant women.

[4] For oral use against staphylococci, cloxacillin or dicloxacillin is preferred; for severe infections, a parenteral formulation of nafcillin or oxacillin should be used. Ampicillin, amoxicillin, carbenicillin, ticarcillin, and piperacillin are not effective against penicillinase-producing staphylococci. The combinations of clavulanic acid with amoxicillin or ticarcillin, sulbactam with ampicillin, and tazobactam with piperacillin may be active against these organisms.

[5] The cephalosporins have been used as alternatives to penicillins in patients allergic to penicillins, but such patients may also have allergic reactions to cephalosporins.

[6] For parenteral treatment of staphylococcal or nonenterococcal streptococcal infections, a first-generation cephalosporin such as cefazolin can be used. For oral therapy, cephalexin or cephradine can be used. The second-generation cephalosporins cefamandole, cefprozil, cefuroxime, cefotetan, cefmetazole, cefoxitin, and loracarbef are more active than the first-generation drugs against gram-negative bacteria. Cefuroxime is active against ampicillin-resistant strains of *H. influenzae*. Cefoxitin, cefotetan, and cefmetazole are the most active of the cephalosporins against *B. fragilis*, but cefotetan and cefmetazole have been associated with prothrombin deficiency. The third-generation cephalosporins cefotaxime, cefoperazone, ceftizoxime, ceftriaxone, and ceftazidime, and the fourth-generation cefepime have greater activity than the second-generation drugs against enteric gram-negative bacilli. Ceftazidime has poor activity against many gram-positive cocci and anaerobes, and ceftizoxime has poor activity against penicillin-resistant *S. pneumoniae*. Cefepime has *in vitro* activity against gram-positive cocci similar to cefotaxime and ceftriaxone and somewhat greater activity against enteric gram-negative bacilli. The activity of cefepime against *Pseudomonas aeruginosa* is similar to that of ceftazidime. Cefixime, cefpodoxime, cefdinir, and cefibuten are oral cephalosporins with more activity than second-generation cephalosporins against facultative gram-negative bacilli; they have no useful activity against anaerobes or *P. aeruginosa*, and cefixime and cefibuten have no useful activity against staphylococci. With the exception of cefoperazone (which, like cefamandole, can cause bleeding), ceftazidime and cefepime, the activity of all currently available cephalosporins against *P. aeruginosa* is poor or inconsistent.

[7] Many strains of coagulase-positive staphylococci and coagulase-negative staphylococci are resistant to penicillinase-resistant penicillins; these strains are also resistant to cephalosporins, imipenem, and meropenem, and are often resistant to fluoroquinolones, trimethoprim/ sulfamethoxazole, and clindamycin.

[8] Tetracyclines are generally not recommended for pregnant women or children younger than 8 years old.

[9] For serious soft-tissue infection due to group A streptococci, clindamycin may be more effective than penicillin. Group A streptococci may, however, be resistant to clindamycin; therefore, some *Medical Letter* consultants suggest using both clindamycin and penicillin, with or without I.V. immune globulin, to treat serious soft-tissue infections. Group A streptococci may also be resistant to erythromycin, azithromycin, and clarithromycin.

[10]Penicillin V (or amoxicillin) is preferred for oral treatment of infections caused by nonpenicillinase-producing streptococci. For initial therapy of severe infections, penicillin G, administered parenterally, is first choice. For somewhat longer action in less severe infections due to group A streptococci, pneumococci or *Treponema pallidum*, procaine penicillin G, an intramuscular formulation, can be given once or twice daily, but is seldom used now. Benzathine penicillin G, a slowly absorbed preparation, is usually given in a single monthly injection for prophylaxis of rheumatic fever, once for treatment of group A streptococcal pharyngitis and once or more for treatment of syphilis.

[11]Not recommended for use in pregnancy.

[12]Some strains of *S. pneumoniae* are resistant to erythromycin, clindamycin, trimethoprim-sulfamethoxazole, clarithromycin, azithromycin and chloramphenicol, and resistance to the newer fluoroquinolones is increasing. Nearly all strains tested so far are susceptible to linezolid and quinupristin/dalfopristin *in vitro* (Patel R, Rouse MS, Piper KE, et al, "*In Vitro* Activity of Linezolid Against Vancomycin-Resistant Enterococci, Methicillin-Resistant *Staphylococcus aureus* and Penicillin-Resistant *Streptococcus pneumoniae*," *Diagn Microbiol Infect Dis*, 1999, 34(2):119-22; Verhaegen J and Verbist L, "*In Vitro* Activities of 16 Non-beta-lactam Antibiotics Against Penicillin-Susceptible and Penicillin-Resistant *Streptococcus pneumoniae*," *J Antimicrob Chemother*, 1999, 43(4):563-7.

[13]Usually not recommended for use in children or pregnant women.

[14]Patients with gonorrhea should be treated presumptively for coinfection with *C. trachomatis* with azithromycin or doxycycline.

[15]Rare strains of *N. meningitidis* are resistant or relatively resistant to penicillin. A fluoroquinolone or rifampin is recommended for prophylaxis after close contact with infected patients.

[16]Because of the possibility of serious adverse effects, this drug should be used only for severe infections when less hazardous drugs are ineffective.

[17]Sulfonamide-resistant strains are frequent in the U.S.A; sulfonamides should be used only when susceptibility is established by susceptibility tests.

[18]Debridement is primary. Large doses of penicillin G are required. Hyperbaric oxygen therapy may be a useful adjunct to surgical debridement in management of the spreading, necrotizing type of infection.

[19]For prophylaxis, a tetanus toxoid booster and, for some patients, tetanus immune globulin (human) are required.

[20]In order to decrease the emergence of vancomycin-resistant enterococci in hospitals and to reduce costs, most clinicians now recommend use of metronidazole first in treatment of patients with *C. difficile* colitis, with oral vancomycin used only for seriously ill patients or those who do not respond to metronidazole.

[21]Antitoxin is primary; antimicrobials are used only to halt further toxin production and to prevent the carrier state.

[22]In severely ill patients, most *Medical Letter* consultants would add gentamicin, tobramycin, or amikacin.

[23]In severely ill patients, most *Medical Letter* consultants would add gentamicin, tobramycin, or amikacin (but see footnote 35).

[24]For an acute, uncomplicated urinary tract infection, before the infecting organism is known, the drug of first choice is trimethoprim-sulfamethoxazole.

[25]Eradication of *H. pylori* with various antibacterial combinations, given concurrently with an H_2-receptor blocker or proton pump inhibitor, has led to rapid healing of active peptic ulcers and low recurrence rates (Mégraud F and Marshall BJ, "How to Treat *Helicobacter pylori*. First-line, Second-line, and Future Therapies," *Gastroenterol Clin North Am*, 2000, 29(4):759-73.

[26]Large doses (6 g or more daily) are usually necessary for systemic infections. In severely ill patients, some *Medical Letter* consultants would add gentamicin, tobramycin, or amikacin.

[27]A fluoroquinolone or amoxicillin is the drug of choice for *S. typhi* carriers.

[28]Frenck RW Jr, Nakhla I, Sultan Y, et al, "Azithromycin Versus Ceftriaxone for the Treatment of Uncomplicated Typhoid Fever in Children," *Clin Infect Dis*, 2000, 31(5):1134-8.

[29]Most cases of *Salmonella* gastroenteritis subside spontaneously without antimicrobial therapy. Immunosuppressed patients, young children, and the elderly may benefit the most from antibacterials.

[30]In severely ill patients, most *Medical Letter* consultants would add gentamicin or amikacin (but see footnote 35).

[31]Sulbactam may be useful to treat multidrug resistant *Acinetobacter*. It is only available in combination with ampicillin as Unasyn®. *Medical Letter* consultants recommend 3 g I.V. q4h.

[32]Role of antibiotics is not clear (Conrad DA, "Treatment of Cat-Scratch Disease," *Curr Opin Pediatr*, 2001, 13(1):56-9.

[33]Pers C, Gahrn-Hansen B, Frederiksen W, et al, "*Capnocytophaga canimorsus* Septicemia in Denmark, 1982-1995: Review of 39 Cases," *Clin Infect Dis*, 1996, 23(1):71-5.

[34]Metronidazole is effective for bacterial vaginosis even though it is not usually active *in vitro* against *Gardnerella*.

[35]Neither gentamicin, tobramycin, netilmicin, or amikacin should be mixed in the same bottle with carbenicillin, ticarcillin, mezlocillin, or piperacillin for intravenous administration. When used in high doses or in patients with renal impairment, these penicillins may inactivate the aminoglycosides.

[36]Antibiotic therapy is an adjunct to and not a substitute for prompt fluid and electrolyte replacement.

[37]Most infections are self-limited without drug treatment.

[38]For treatment of erythema migrans, facial nerve palsy, mild cardiac disease, and some cases of arthritis, oral therapy is satisfactory; for more serious neurologic or cardiac disease or arthritis, parenteral therapy with ceftriaxone, cefotaxime, or penicillin G is recommended (*Medical Letter*, 2000, 42:37).

ANTIRETROVIRAL THERAPY FOR HIV INFECTION

Report of the NIH Panel to Define Principles of Therapy of HIV Infection

GUIDELINES FOR THE USE OF ANTIRETROVIRAL AGENTS IN HIV-1-INFECTED ADULTS AND ADOLESCENTS

Adapted from the Panel on Clinical Practices for Treatment of HIV Infection Convened by the Department of Health and Human Services (DHHS), November 10, 2003 (http://aidsinfo.nih.gov)

Indications for Plasma HIV RNA Testing[1]

Clinical Indication	Information	Use
Syndrome consistent with acute HIV infection	Establishes diagnosis when HIV antibody test is negative or indeterminate	Diagnosis[2]
Initial evaluation of newly diagnosed HIV infection	Baseline viral load "set point"	Decision to start or defer therapy
Every 3-4 months in patients not on therapy	Changes in viral load	Decision to start therapy
2-8 weeks after initiation of antiretroviral therapy	Initial assessment of drug efficacy	Decision to continue or change therapy
3-4 months after start of therapy	Maximal effect of therapy	Decision to continue or change therapy
Every 3-4 months in patients on therapy	Durability of antiretroviral effect	Decision to continue or change therapy
Clinical event or significant decline in CD4+ T cells	Association with changing or stable viral load	Decision to continue, initiate, or change therapy

[1]Acute illness (eg, bacterial pneumonia, tuberculosis, HSV, PCP) and immunizations can cause increases in plasma HIV RNA for 2-4 weeks; viral load testing should not be performed during this time. Plasma HIV RNA results should usually be verified with a repeat determination before starting or making changes in therapy.

[2]Diagnosis of HIV infection determined by HIV RNA testing should be confirmed by standard methods (eg, Western blot serology) performed 2-4 months after the initial indeterminate or negative test.

Potential Benefits and Risks of Early vs Delayed Therapy Initiation for the Asymptomatic HIV-Infected Patient[1]

Potential Benefits and Risks of Early Therapy[1]

Potential Benefits of Early Therapy

- Earlier suppression of viral replication
- Preservation of immune function
- Prolongation of disease-free survival
- Lower risk of resistance with complete viral suppression
- Possible decrease in the risk of HIV transmission[2]

Potential Risks of Early Therapy

- Drug-related adverse effects on quality of life
- Drug-related serious toxicities
- Early development of drug resistance due to suboptimal viral suppression
- Risk of transmission of virus resistant to antiretroviral drugs (if suboptimal suppression)
- Limitation of future treatment options
- Unknown durability of current available therapy

Potential Benefits and Risks of Delayed Therapy[1]

Potential Benefits of Delayed Therapy

- Avoid negative effects on quality of life
- Avoid drug-related adverse events
- Preserve future treatment options
- Delay in development of drug resistance

Potential Risks of Delayed Therapy

- Possible risk of irreversible immune system compromise
- Possible greater difficulty in viral suppression
- Possible increased risk of HIV transmission

[1]See table "Indications for Initiating Antiretroviral Therapy for the Chronically HIV-1-Infected Patient," for consensus recommendations regarding when to initiate therapy.

[2]The risk of viral transmission still exists; antiretroviral therapy cannot substitute for primary HIV prevention measures (eg, use of condoms and safer sex practices).

Indications for Initiating Antiretroviral Therapy for the Chronically HIV-1-Infected Patient

The optimal time to initiate therapy is unknown among persons with asymptomatic disease and CD4+ T cell count of >200 cells/mm³. This table provides general guidance rather than absolute recommendations for an individual patient. All decisions regarding initiating therapy should be made on the basis of prognosis as determined by the CD4+ T cell count and level of plasma HIV RNA, the potential benefits and risks of therapy, and the willingness of the patient to accept therapy.

Clinical Category	CD4+ T Cell Count	Plasma HIV RNA	Recommendation
Symptomatic (AIDS or severe symptoms)	Any value	Any value	Treat
Asymptomatic, AIDS	CD4+ T cells <200/mm³	Any value	Treat
Asymptomatic	CD4+ T cells >200/mm³ but ≤350/mm³	Any value	Treatment should be offered, although controversial.[1]
Asymptomatic	CD4+ T cells >350/mm³	>55,000 (by RT-PCR or bDNA)[2]	Some experienced clinicians recommend initiating therapy, recognizing that the 3-year risk for untreated patients to develop AIDS is >30%; in the absence of increased levels of plasma HIV RNA, other clinicians recommend deferring therapy and monitoring the CD4+ T cell count and level of plasma HIV RNA more frequently; clinical outcome data after initiating therapy are lacking.
Asymptomatic	CD4+ T cells >350/mm³	<55,000 (by RT-PCR or bDNA)[2]	Most experienced clinicians recommend deferring therapy and monitoring the CD4+ T cell count, recognizing that the 3-year risk for untreated patients to experience AIDS is <15%.

[1]Clinical benefit has been demonstrated in controlled trials only for patients with CD4+ T cells <200/mm³; however, the majority of clinicians would offer therapy at a CD4+ T cell threshold <350/mm³. A recent evaluation of data from the Multicenter AIDS Cohort Study (MACS) of 231 persons with CD4+ T cell counts >200 and <350 cells/mm³ demonstrated that of 40 (17%) persons with plasma HIV RNA <10,000 copies/mL, none progressed to AIDS by 3 years (source: Phair JP, Mellors JW, Detels R, et al, "Virologic and Immunologic Values Allowing Safe Deferral of Antiretroviral Therapy," AIDS, 2002, 16(18):2455-9). Of 28 persons (29%) with plasma viremia of 10,000-20,000 copies/mL, 4% and 11% progressed to AIDS at 2 and 3 years respectively. Plasma HIV RNA was calculated as RT-PCR values from measured bDNA values.

[2]Although a 2- to 2.5-fold difference existed between RT-PCR and the first bDNA assay (version 2.0), with the 3.0 version bDNA assay, values obtained by bDNA and RT-PCR are similar except at the lower end of the linear range (<1500 copies/mL).

ANTIRETROVIRAL THERAPY FOR HIV INFECTION
(Continued)

Antiretroviral Regimens Recommended for Treatment of HIV-1 Infection in Antiretroviral Naive Patients

This table is a guide to treatment regimens for patients who have no previous experience with HIV therapy. Regimens should be individualized based on the advantages and disadvantages of each combination such as pill burden, dosing frequency, toxicities, and drug-drug interactions, and patient variables, such as pregnancy, comorbid conditions, and level of plasma HIV-RNA. Regimens are designated as "preferred" for use in treatment-naive patients when clinical trial data suggest optimal efficacy and durability with acceptable tolerability and ease of use. Alternative regimens refer to regimens for which clinical trial data show efficacy, but it is considered alternative due to disadvantages compared to the preferred regimens in terms of antiviral activity, demonstrated durable effect, tolerability or ease of use. In some cases, based on individual patient characteristics, a regimen listed as an alternative regimen in the table may actually be the preferred regimen for a selected patient. Of note, the designation of regimens as "preferred" or "alternative" may change as new safety and efficacy data emerge, which, in the opinion of the Panel, warrants reassignment of regimens in these categories. Revisions will be updated on an ongoing basis. Clinicians initiating antiretroviral regimens in the HIV-1-infected pregnant patient should refer to "Recommendations for Use of Antiretroviral Drugs in Pregnant HIV-1-Infected Women for Maternal Health and Interventions to Reduce Perinatal HIV-1 Transmission in the United States," at http://www.aidsinfo.nih.gov/guidelines.

NNRTI-Based Regimens	
Preferred Regimens	Efavirenz + lamivudine + (zidovudine or tenofovir DF or stavudine[1]) – except for pregnant women or women with pregnancy potential
Alternative Regimens	Efavirenz + emtricitabine + (zidovudine or tenofovir DF or stavudine[1]) – except for pregnant women or women with pregnancy potential[2]
	Efavirenz + (lamivudine or emtricitabine) + didanosine – except for pregnant women or women with pregnancy potential[2]
	Nevirapine + (lamivudine or emtricitabine) + (zidovudine or stavudine[1] or didanosine)
PI-Based Regimens	
Preferred Regimens	Lopinavir/ritonavir (coformulated as Kaletra™) + lamivudine + (zidovudine or stavudine)
Alternative Regimens	Amprenavir/ritonavir[3] + (lamivudine or emtricitabine) + (zidovudine or stavudine)
	Atazanavir + (lamivudine or emtricitabine) + (zidovudine or stavudine[1])
	Indinavir + (lamivudine or emtricitabine) + (zidovudine or stavudine[1])
	Indinavir/ritonavir[3] + (lamivudine or emtricitabine) + (zidovudine or stavudine[1])
	Lopinavir/ritonavir (coformulated as Kaletra™) + emtricitabine + (zidovudine or stavudine[1])
	Nelfinavir[4] + (lamivudine or emtricitabine) + (zidovudine or stavudine[1])
	Saquinavir (soft or hard gel capsule)/ritonavir[3] + (lamivudine or emtricitabine) + (zidovudine or stavudine[1])
Triple NRTI Regimen – only when an NNRTI- or a PI-based regimen cannot or should not be used as first line therapy	
Only as alternative to NNRTI- or PI-based regimen	Abacavir + lamivudine + zidovudine (or stavudine[1])

[1]Higher incidence of lipoatrophy, hyperlipidemia, and mitochondrial toxicities reported with stavudine than with other NRTIs.

[2]Women with child bearing potential implies women who want to conceive or those who are not using effective contraception.

[3]Low-dose (100-400 mg) ritonavir.

[4]Nelfinavir available in 250 mg or 625 mg tablet.

Antiretroviral Regimens or Components That Should Not Be Offered at Any Time

	Rationale	Exception
Antiretroviral Regimens Not Recommended		
Monotherapy	• Rapid development of resistance • Inferior antiretroviral activity when compared to combination with three or more antiretrovirals	Pregnant women with HIV-RNA <1000 copies/mL using zidovudine monotherapy for prevention of perinatal HIV transmission[1] and not for HIV treatment for the mother
Two-agents drug combinations	• Rapid development of resistance • Inferior antiretroviral activity when compared to combination with three or more antiretrovirals	For patients currently on this treatment, it is reasonable to continue if virologic goals are achieved
Abacavir + tenofovir + lamivudine – (combination as a triple NRTI regimen)	High rate of early virologic nonresponse seen when this triple NRTI combination was used as initial regimen in treatment naive patients	No exception
Tenofovir + didanosine + lamivudine – (combination as a triple NRTI regimen)	High rate of early virologic nonresponse seen when this triple NRTI combination was used as initial regimen in treatment naive patients	No exception
Antiretroviral Components Not Recommended as Part of Antiretroviral Regimen		
Saquinavir hard gel capsule (Invirase®) as **single** protease inhibitor	• Poor oral bioavailability (4%) • Inferior antiretroviral activity when compared to other protease inhibitors	No exception
Stavudine + didanosine	• High incidence of toxicities – peripheral neuropathy, pancreatitis, and hyperlactatemia • Reports of serious, even fatal, cases of lactic acidosis with hepatic steatosis with or without pancreatitis in pregnant women	When no other antiretroviral options are available and potential benefits outweigh the risks[1]
Efavirenz in pregnancy	Teratogenic in nonhuman primate	When no other antiretroviral options are available and potential benefits outweigh the risks[1]
Amprenavir oral solution in: • pregnant women • children <4 y • patients with renal or hepatic failure • patients treated with metronidazole or disulfiram	Oral liquid contains large amount of the excipient propylene glycol, which may be toxic in the patients at risk	No exception
Stavudine + zidovudine	Antagonistic	No exception
Stavudine + zalcitabine	Additive peripheral neuropathy	No exception
Didanosine + zalcitabine	Additive peripheral neuropathy	No exception
Atazanavir + indinavir	Potential additive hyperbilirubinemia	No exception
Emtricitabine + lamivudine	• Similar resistance profile • No potential benefit	No exception
Hydroxyurea	• Decreased CD4 count • Increased ddI-associated side effects – such as pancreatitis and peripheral neuropathy • Inconsistent evidence of improved viral suppression • Contraindicated in pregnancy (Pregnancy Category D)	No exception

[1]When constructing an antiretroviral regimen for an HIV-infected pregnant women, please consult "Public Health Service Task Force Recommendations for the Use of Antiretroviral Drugs in Pregnant HIV-1-Infected Women for Maternal Health and Interventions to Reduce Perinatal HIV-1 Transmission in the United States" in http://www.aidsinfo.nih.gov/guidelines.

ANTIRETROVIRAL THERAPY FOR HIV INFECTION
(Continued)

Goals of HIV Therapy and Tools to Achieve Them

Goals of Therapy

- Maximal and durable suppression of viral load
- Restoration and/or preservation of immunologic function
- Improvement of quality of life
- Reduction of HIV-related morbidity and mortality

Tools to Achieve Goals of Therapy

- Maximize adherence to the antiretroviral regimen
- Rational sequencing of drugs
- Preservation of future treatment options
- Use of resistance testing in selected clinical settings

GUIDELINES FOR THE USE OF ANTIRETROVIRAL AGENTS IN PEDIATRIC HIV INFECTION

Adapted from The Working Group on Antiretroviral Therapy and Medical Management of HIV-Infected Children Convened by the National Pediatric and Family HIV Resource Center (NPHRC), The Health Resources and Services Administration (HRSA), and The National Institutes of Health (NIH), November 26, 2003 (http://aidsinfo.nih.gov)

1994 Revised Human Immunodeficiency Virus Pediatric Classification System: Immune Categories Based on Age-specific CD4[+] T-lymphocyte and Percentage[1]

Immune Category	<12 (mo)		1-5 (y)		6-12 (y)	
	No./μL	%	No./μL	%	No./μL	%
Category 1 (no suppression)	≥1500	≥25	≥1000	≥25	≥500	≥25
Category 2 (moderate suppression)	750-1499	15-24	500-999	15-24	200-499	15-24
Category 3 (severe suppression)	<750	<15	<500	<15	<200	<15

[1]Modified from CDC, "1994 Revised Classification System for Human Immunodeficiency Virus Infection in Children Less Than 13 Years of Age," *MMWR Recomm Rep*, 1994, 43(RR-12):1-10.

1994 Revised Human Immunodeficiency Virus Pediatric Classification System: Clinical Categories[1]

Category N: Not Symptomatic

Children who have no signs or symptoms considered to be the result of HIV infection or who have only **one** of the conditions listed in category A

Category A: Mildly Symptomatic

Children with **two** or more of the following conditions, but none of the conditions listed in categories B and C:

- Lymphadenopathy ($\geq$0.5 cm at more than two sites; bilateral = one site)
- Hepatomegaly
- Splenomegaly
- Dermatitis
- Parotitis
- Recurrent or persistent upper respiratory infection, sinusitis, or otitis media

Category B: Moderately Symptomatic

Children who have symptomatic conditions other than those listed for category A or category C that are attributed to HIV infection. Examples of conditions in clinical category B include, but are not limited to, the following:

- Anemia (<8 g/dL), neutropenia (<1000/mm^3), or thrombocytopenia (<100,000/mm^3) persisting $\geq$30 days
- Bacterial meningitis, pneumonia, or sepsis (single episode)
- Candidiasis, oropharyngeal (ie, thrush) persisting for >2 months in children aged >6 months
- Cardiomyopathy
- Cytomegalovirus infection with onset before age 1 month
- Diarrhea, recurrent or chronic
- Hepatitis
- Herpes simplex virus (HSV) stomatitis, recurrent (ie, more than two episodes within 1 year)
- HSV bronchitis, pneumonitis, or esophagitis with onset before age 1 month
- Herpes zoster (ie, shingles) involving at least two distinct episodes or more than one dermatome
- Leiomyosarcoma
- Lymphoid interstitial pneumonia (LIP) or pulmonary lymphoid hyperplasia complex
- Nephropathy
- Nocardiosis
- Fever lasting >1 month
- Toxoplasmosis with onset before age 1 month
- Varicella, disseminated (ie, complicated chickenpox)

Category C: Severely Symptomatic

Children who have any condition listed in the 1987 surveillance case definition for acquired immunodeficiency syndrome, with the exception of LIP (which is a category B condition).

[1]Modified from CDC, "1994 Revised Classification System for Human Immunodeficiency Virus Infection in Children Less Than 13 Years of Age," *MMWR Recomm Rep*, 1994, 43(RR-12):1-10.

ANTIRETROVIRAL THERAPY FOR HIV INFECTION
(Continued)

Association of Baseline CD4⁺ T-Lymphocyte Percentage With Long-Term Risk for Death in Human Immunodeficiency Virus (HIV)-Infected Children[1]

Baseline (%)	No. Patients[2]	Deaths[3]	
		No.	%
<5	33	32	97
5-9	29	22	76
10-14	30	13	43
15-19	41	18	44
20-24	52	13	25
25-29	49	15	31
30-34	48	5	10
≥35	92	30	33

[1]Data from the National Institute of Child Health and Human Development Intravenous Immunoglobulin Clinical Trial.

[2]Includes 374 patients for whom baseline CD4⁺ T-lymphocyte percentage data were available.

[3]Mean follow-up: 5.1 years.

Adapted from Mofenson L, Korelitz J, Meyer WA, et al, "The Relationship Between Serum Human Immunodeficiency Virus Type 1 (HIV-1) RNA Level, CD4 Lymphocyte Percent and Long-Term Mortality Risk in HIV-1 Infected Children," *J Infect Dis*, 1997, 175:1029-38.

Indications for Initiation of Antiretroviral Therapy in Children <12 Months of Age Infected With Human Immunodeficiency Virus (HIV) Infection

This table provides general guidance rather than absolute recommendations for an individual patient. Factors to be considered in decisions about initiation of therapy include the risk of disease progression as determined by CD4⁺ percentage, the potential benefits and risks of therapy, and the ability of the caregiver to adhere to administration of the therapeutic regimen. Issues associated with adherence should be fully assessed, discussed, and addressed with the caregivers for the HIV-infected infant before the decision to initiate therapy is made.

Clinical Category		CD4⁺ Cell Percentage	Plasma HIV RNA Copy Number[1]	Recommendation
Symptomatic (clinical category A, B, or C)	**or**	<25% (immune category 2 or 3)	Any value	Treat
Asymptomatic (clinical category N)	**and**	≥25% (immune category 1)	Any value	Consider treatment[2]

[1]Plasma HIV RNA levels are higher in HIV-infected infants than older infected children and adults, and may be difficult to interpret in infants <12 months of age because overall HIV RNA levels are high and there is overlap in HIV RNA levels between infants who have and those who do not have rapid disease progression.

[2]Because HIV infection progresses more rapidly in infants than older children or adults, some experts would treat all HIV-infected infants <6 months or <12 months of age, regardless of clinical, immunologic, or virologic parameters.

Indications for Initiation of Antiretroviral Therapy in Children ≥1 Year of Age Infected With Human Immunodeficiency Virus (HIV)

This table provides general guidance rather than absolute recommendations for an individual patient. Factors to be considered in decisions about initiation of therapy include the risk of disease progression as determined by CD4+ percentage and plasma HIV RNA copy number, the potential benefits and risks of therapy, and the ability of the caregiver to adhere to administration of the therapeutic regimen. Issues associated with adherence should be fully assessed, discussed, and addressed with the child, if age-appropriate, and caregiver before the decision to initiate therapy is made.

Clinical Category		CD4+ Cell Percentage		Plasma HIV RNA Copy Number[1]	Recommendation
AIDS (clinical category C)	or	<15% (immune category 3)		Any value	Treat
Mild-moderate symptoms (clinical category A or B)	or	15%-25%[1] (immune category 2)	or	≥100,000 copies/mL[2]	Consider treatment
Asymptomatic (clinical category N)	and	>25% (immune category 1)	and	<100,000 copies/mL[2]	Many experts would defer therapy and closely monitor clinical, immune, and viral parameters

[1]Many experts would initiate therapy if CD4+ cell percentage is between 15% to 20%, and defer therapy with increased monitoring frequency in children with CD4+ cell percentage 21% to 25%.

[2]There is controversy among pediatric HIV experts regarding the plasma HIV RNA threshold warranting consideration of therapy in children in the absence of clinical or immune abnormalities; some experts would consider initiation of therapy in asymptomatic children if plasma HIV RNA levels were between 50,000 to 100,000 copies/mL.

Recommended Antiretroviral Regimens for Initial Therapy for Human Immunodeficiency Virus (HIV) Infection in Children

Protease Inhibitor-Based Regimens

Strongly recommended	Two NRTIs[1] *plus* lopinavir/ritonavir *or* nelfinavir *or* ritonavir
Alternative	Two NRTIs[1] *plus* amprenavir (children ≥4 years old)[2] *or* indinavir

Non-nucleoside Reverse Transcriptase Inhibitor-Based Regimens

Strongly recommended	Children >3 years: Two NRTIs[1] *plus* efavirenz[3] (with or without nelfinavir)
	Children ≤3 years or who can't swallow capsules: Two NRTIs[1] *plus* nevirapine[3]
Alternative	Two NRTIs[1] *plus* nevirapine[3] (children >3 years)

Nucleoside Analogue-Based Regimens

Strongly recommended	None
Alternative	Zidovudine *plus* lamivudine *plus* abacavir
Use in special circumstances	Two NRTIs[1]

Regimens That Are Not Recommended

Monotherapy[4]

Certain two NRTI combinations[1]

Two NRTIs *plus* saquinavir soft or hard gel capsule as a sole protease inhibitor[5]

Insufficient Data to Recommend

Two NRTIs[1] *plus* delavirdine

Dual protease inhibitors, including saquinavir soft or hard gel capsule with low dose ritonavir, with the exception of lopinavir/ritonavir[4]

NRTI **plus** NNRTI **plus** protease inhibitor[6]

Tenofovir-containing regimens

Enfuvirtide (T-20)-containing regimens

Emtricitabine (FTC)-containing regimens

Atazanavir-containing regimens

NRTI = nucleoside analogue reverse transcriptase inhibitor.
NNRTI = non-nucleoside analogue reverse transcriptase inhibitor.
See footnotes on next page.

ANTIRETROVIRAL THERAPY FOR HIV INFECTION
(Continued)

[1]Dual NRTI combination recommendations:
   Strongly recommended choices: Zidovudine plus didanosine or lamivudine; or stavudine plus lamivudine.
   Alternative choices: Abacavir plus zidovudine or lamivudine; or didanosine plus lamivudine.
   Use in special circumstances: Stavudine plus didanosine; or zalcitabine plus zidovudine.
   Insufficient data: Tenofovir- or emtricitabine-containing regimens.
   Not recommended: Zalcitabine plus didanosine, stavudine, or lamivudine; or zidovudine plus stavudine.

[2]Amprenavir should not be administered to children <4 years of age due to the propylene glycol and vitamin E content of the oral liquid preparation and lack or pharmacokinetic data in this age group.

[3]Efavirenz is currently available only in capsule form, although a liquid formulation is currently under study to determine appropriate dosage in HIV-infected children <3 years of age; nevirapine would be the preferred NNRTI for children <3 years of age or who require a liquid formulation.

[4]Except for zidovudine chemoprophylaxis administered to HIV-exposed infants during the first 6 weeks of life to prevent perinatal HIV transmission; if an infant is confirmed as HIV-infected while receiving zidovudine prophylaxis, therapy should either be discontinued or changed to a combination antiretroviral drug regimen.

[5]With the exception of lopinavir/ritonavir, data on the pharmacokinetics and safety of dual protease inhibitor combinations (eg, low dose ritonavir pharmacologic boosting of saquinavir, indinavir, or nelfinavir) are limited, use of dual protease inhibitors as a component of initial therapy is not recommended, although such regimens may have utility as secondary treatment regimens for children who have failed initial therapy. Saquinavir soft and hard gel capsule require low dose ritonavir boosting to achieve adequate levels in children, but pharmacokinetic data on appropriate dosing not yet available.

[6]With the exception of efavirenz plus nelfinavir plus 1 or 2 NRTIs, which has been studied in HIV-infected children and shown to have virologic and immunologic efficacy in a clinical trial.

Considerations for Changing Antiretroviral Therapy for Human Immunodeficiency Virus (HIV)-Infected Children

Virologic Considerations[1]

- Less than a minimally acceptable virologic response after 8-12 weeks of therapy. For children receiving aggressive antiretroviral therapy, such a response is defined as a less than tenfold (1.0 $\log_{10}$) decrease from baseline HIV RNA levels.
- HIV RNA not suppressed to undetectable levels after 4-6 months of antiretroviral therapy.[2]
- Repeated detection of HIV RNA in children who initially had undetectable levels in response to antiretroviral therapy.[3]
- A reproducible increase in HIV RNA copy number among children who have had a substantial HIV RNA response, but still have low levels of detectable HIV RNA. Such an increase would warrant change in therapy if, after achieving a virologic nadir, a greater than threefold (>0.5 $\log_{10}$) increase in copy number for children ≥2 years of age and greater than fivefold (>0.7 $\log_{10}$) increase is observed for children <2 years of age.

Immunologic Considerations

- Change in immunologic classification.[4]
- For children with CD4+ T-cell percentages of <15% (ie, those in immune category 3), a persistent decline of 5 percentiles or more in CD4+ T-cell percentage (eg, from 15% to 10%).
- A rapid and substantial decrease in absolute CD4+ T-cell count (ie, a >30% decline in <6 months).

Clinical Considerations

- Progressive neurodevelopmental deterioration.
- Growth failure defined as persistent decline in weight-growth velocity despite adequate nutritional support and without other explanation.
- A disease progression defined as advancement from one pediatric clinical category to another (ie, from clinical category A to clinical category B).[5]

[1]At least two measurements (taken 1 week apart) should be performed before considering a change in therapy.

[2]The initial HIV RNA level of the child at the start of therapy and the level achieved with therapy should be considered when contemplating potential drug changes. For example, an immediate change in therapy may not be warranted if there is a sustained 1.5-2.0 $\log_{10}$ decrease in HIV RNA copy number, even if RNA remains detectable at low levels.

[3]Continued observation with more frequent evaluation of HIV RNA levels should be considered if the HIV RNA increase is limited (ie, <5000 copies/mL). The presence of repeatedly detectable and increasing RNA levels suggests the development of resistance mutations.

[4]Minimal changes in CD4+ T-cell percentile that may result in change in immunologic category (ie, from 26% to 24%, or 16% to 14%) may not be as concerning as a rapid substantial change in CD4+ T-cell percentile within the same immunologic category (ie, a drop from 35% to 25%).

[5]In patients with stable immunologic and virologic parameters, progression from one clinical category to another may not represent an indication to change therapy. Thus, in patients whose disease progression is not associated with neurologic deterioration or growth failure, virologic and immunologic considerations are important in deciding whether to change therapy.

COMMUNITY-ACQUIRED PNEUMONIA IN ADULTS

The initial site of treatment should be based on a 3-step process:

1. assessment of pre-existing conditions that compromise safety of home care
2. calculation of the pneumonia PORT (Pneumonia Outcome Research Team) Severity Index with recommendation for home care for risk classes I, II, and III, and
3. clinical judgment

Algorithm

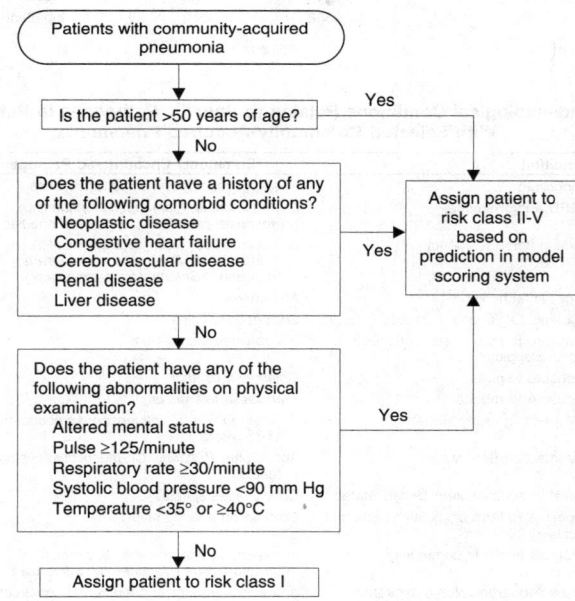

Stratification of Risk Score

Risk	Risk Class	Based on
	I	Algorithm
Low	II	≤70 total points
	III	71-90 total points
Moderate	IV	91-130 total points
High	V	>130 total points

COMMUNITY-ACQUIRED PNEUMONIA IN ADULTS
(Continued)

Risk-Class Mortality Rates for Patients With Pneumonia

Risk Class	No. of Points	Validation Cohort		Recommended Site of Care
		No. of Patients	Mortality (%)	
I	No predictors	3034	0.1	Outpatient
II	≤70	5778	0.6	Outpatient
III	71-90	6790	2.8	Outpatient or brief inpatient
IV	91-130	13,104	8.2	Inpatient
V	>130	9333	29.2	Inpatient

Epidemiological Conditions Related to Specific Pathogens in Patients With Selected Community-Acquired Pneumonia

Condition	Commonly Encountered Pathogens
Alcoholism	*Streptococcus pneumoniae*, anaerobes
COPD and/or smoker	*S. pneumoniae, Haemophilus influenzae, Moraxella catarrhalis, Legionella* species
Nursing home residency	*S. pneumoniae*, gram-negative bacilli, *H. influenzae, Staphylococcus aureus*, anaerobes, *Chlamydia pneumoniae*
Poor dental hygiene	Anaerobes
Epidemic Legionnaires' disease	*Legionella* species
Exposure to bats or soil enriched with bird droppings	*Histoplasma capsulatum*
Exposure to birds	*Chlamydia psittaci*
Exposure to rabbits	*Francisella tularensis*
HIV infection (early stage)	*S. pneumoniae, H. influenzae, Mycobacterium tuberculosis*
HIV infection (late stage)	Above plus *P. carinii, Cryptococcus, Histoplasma* species
Travel to southwestern United States	*Coccidioides* species
Exposure to farm animals or parturient cats	*Coxiella burnetii* (Q fever)
Influenza active in community	Influenza, *S. pneumoniae, S. aureus, Streptococcus pyogenes, H. influenzae*
Suspected large-volume aspiration	Anaerobes (chemical pneumonitis, obstruction)
Structural disease of the lung (bronchiectasis, cystic fibrosis, etc)	*Pseudomonas aeruginosa, Burkholderia (Pseudomonas) cepacia, S. aureus*
Injection drug use	*S. aureus*, anaerobes, *M. tuberculosis, S. pneumoniae*
Airway obstruction	Anaerobes, *S. pneumoniae, H. influenzae, S. aureus*

COPD = chronic obstructive pulmonary disease.

Scoring System: Assignment to Risk Classes II-V

Patient Characteristic	Points Assigned[1]
Demographic factors	
Age	
Male	No. of years
Female	No. of years -10
Nursing home resident	+10
Comorbid illnesses	
Neoplastic disease[2]	+30
Liver disease[3]	+20
Congestive heart failure[4]	+10
Cerebrovascular disease[5]	+10
Renal disease[6]	+10
Physical examination findings	
Altered mental status[7]	+20
Respiratory rate >30 breaths/minute	+20
Systolic blood pressure <90 mm Hg	+20
Temperature <35°C or >40°C	+15
Pulse >125 beats/minute	+10
Laboratory or radiographic findings	
Arterial pH <7.35	+30
BUN >30 mg/dL	+20
Sodium <130 mEq/L	+20
Glucose >250 mg/dL	+10
Hematocrit <30%	+10
pO_2 <60 mm Hg[8]	+10
Pleural effusion	+10

[1]A total point score for a given patient is obtained by adding the patient's age in years (age -10, for females) and the points for each applicable patient characteristic.

[2]Any cancer, except basal or squamous cell cancer of the skin, that was active at the time of presentation or diagnosed within 1 year of presentation.

[3]A clinical or histologic diagnosis of cirrhosis or other form of chronic liver disease such as chronic active hepatitis.

[4]Systolic or diastolic ventricular dysfunction documented by history and physical examination, as well as chest radiography, echocardiography, Muga scanning, or left ventriculography.

[5]A clinical diagnosis of stroke, transient ischemic attack, or stroke documented by MRI or computed axial tomography.

[6]A history of chronic renal disease or abnormal blood urea nitrogen (BUN) and creatinine values documented in the medical record.

[7]Disorientation (to person, place, or time; not known to be chronic), stupor, or coma.

[8]In the Pneumonia Patient Outcome Research Team cohort study, an oxygen saturation value <90% on pulse oximetry or intubation before admission was also considered abnormal.

COMMUNITY-ACQUIRED PNEUMONIA IN ADULTS
(Continued)

Flow Chart Approach to Treating Outpatients and Inpatients with Community-Acquired Pneumonia

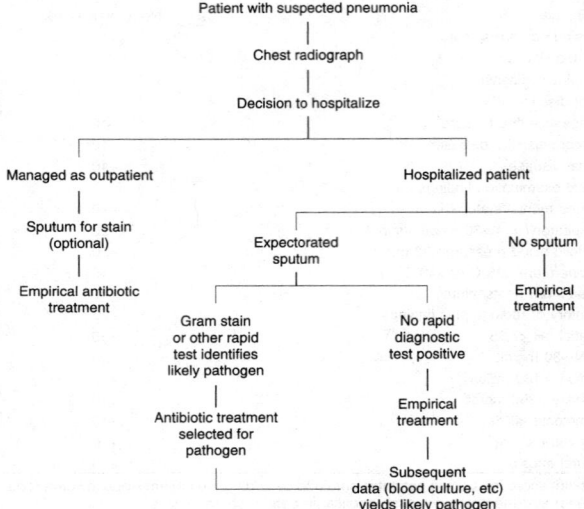

Community-Acquired Pneumonia

Possible factors to be considered when patients fail to respond or their conditions deteriorate after initiation of empirical therapy

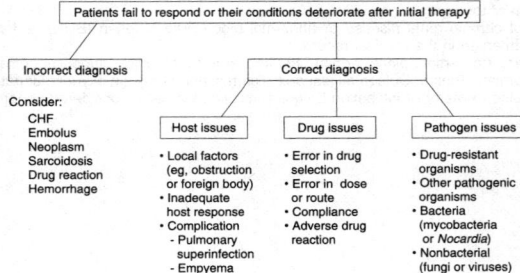

Initial Empiric Therapy for Suspected Bacterial Community-Acquired Pneumonia (CAP) in Immunocompetent Adults

Patient Variable	Preferred Treatment Options
Outpatient	
Previously healthy	
No recent antibiotic therapy	A macrolide[1] or doxycycline
Recent antibiotic therapy[2]	A respiratory fluoroquinolone[3] alone, an advanced macrolide[4] plus high-dose amoxicillin,[5] or an advanced macrolide plus high dose amoxicillin-clavulanate[6]
Comorbidities (COPD, diabetes, renal or congestive heart failure, or malignancy)	
No recent antibiotic therapy	An advanced macrolide[4] or a respiratory fluoroquinolone
Recent antibiotic therapy	A respiratory fluoroquinolone[3] alone or an advanced macrolide plus a β-lactam[7]
Suspected aspiration with infection	Amoxicillin-clavulanate or clindamycin
Influenza with bacterial superinfection	A β-lactam[7] or a respiratory fluoroquinolone
Inpatient	
Medical ward	
No recent antibiotic therapy	A respiratory fluoroquinolone alone or an advanced macrolide plus a β-lactam[8]
Recent antibiotic therapy	An advanced macrolide plus a β-lactam or a respiratory fluoroquinolone alone (regimen selected will depend on nature of recent antibiotic therapy)
ICU	
Pseudomonas infection is not an issue	A β-lactam[8] plus either an advanced macrolide or a respiratory fluoroquinolone
Pseudomonas infection is not an issue but patient has a β-lactam allergy	A respiratory fluoroquinolone, with or without clindamycin
Pseudomonas infection is not an issue[9]	Either (1) an antipseudomonal agent[10] plus ciprofloxacin, or (2) an antipseudomonal agent plus an aminoglycoside[11] plus a respiratory fluoroquinolone or a macrolide
Pseudomonas infection is an issue but the patient has a β-lactam allergy	Either (1) aztreonam plus levofloxacin,[12] or (2) aztreonam plus moxifloxacin or gatifloxacin, with or without an aminoglycoside
Nursing home	
Receiving treatment in nursing home	A respiratory fluoroquinolone alone or amoxicillin-clavulanate plus an advanced macrolide
Hospitalized	Same as for medical ward and ICU

COPD = chronic obstructive pulmonary disease; ICU = intensive care unit.

[1]Erythromycin, azithromycin, or clarithromycin.

[2]That is, the patient was given a course of antibiotic(s) for treatment of any infection within the past 3 months, excluding the current episode of infection. Such treatment is a risk factor for drug-resistant *Streptococcus pneumoniae* and possibly for infection with gram-negative bacilli. Depending on the class of antibiotics recently given, one or other of the suggested options may be selected. Recent use of a fluoroquinolone should dictate selection of a nonfluoroquinolone regimen, and vice versa.

[3]Moxifloxacin, gatifloxacin, levofloxacin, or gemifloxacin (oral gemifloxacin only, which was approved by the U.S. Food and Drug Administration on 4 April 2003 and which is the only fluoroquinolone approved for multidrug-resistant *S. pneumoniae*; not yet marketed).

[4]Azithromycin or clarithromycin.

[5]Dosage, 1 g P.O. 3 times/day.

[6]Dosage, 2 g P.O. twice daily.

[7]High-dose amoxicillin, high-dose amoxicillin-clavulanate, cefpodoxime, cefprozil, or cefuroxime.

[8]Cefotaxime, ceftriaxone, ampicillin-sulbactam, or ertapenem; ertapenem was recently approved for such use (in once daily parenteral treatment), but there is little experience thus far.

[9]The antipseudomonal agents chosen reflect this concern. Risk factors for *Pseudomonas* infection include severe structural lung disease (eg, bronchiectasis), and recent antibiotic therapy or stay in hospital (especially in the ICU). For patients with CAP in the ICU, coverage for *S. pneumoniae* and *Legionella* species must always be assured. Piperacillin-tazobactam, imipenem, meropenem, and cefepime are excellent β-lactams and are adequate for most *S. pneumoniae* and *Haemophilus influenzae* infections. They may be preferred when there is concern for relatively unusual CAP pathogens, such as *Pseudomonas aeruginosa*, *Klebsiella* species, and other gram-negative bacteria.

[10]Piperacillin, piperacillin-tazobactam, imipenem, meropenem, or cefepime.

[11]Data suggest that elderly patients receiving aminoglycosides have worse outcomes.

[12]Dosage for hospitalized patients, 750 mg every day.

COMMUNITY-ACQUIRED PNEUMONIA IN ADULTS
(Continued)

ANTIMICROBIAL TREATMENT

Pathogen-Specific Therapy

S. pneumoniae: Susceptibility of *S. pneumoniae* isolates to cefotaxime and ceftriaxone in nonmeningeal infections should be defined as an MIC ≤1 µg/mL, intermediate should be defined as an MIC 2 µg/mL, and resistant should be defined as an MIC ≥4 µg/mL (A-III). Cefotaxime or ceftriaxone are the preferred parenteral agents for treatment of pneumococcal pneumonia without meningitis for strains with reduced susceptibility to penicillin but with MICs of cefotaxime or ceftriaxone <2 µg/mL (B-III). Amoxicillin is the preferred antibiotic for oral treatment of pneumococcal pneumonia involving susceptible strains (B-II).

Initial empiric therapy prior to availability of culture data for a patient ill enough to require admission to a hospital ward can be with a β-lactam plus macrolide combination or a respiratory fluoroquinolone alone (A-I). If sufficiently ill to need ICU management and if *Pseudomonas* infection is not a concern, a combination of a β-lactam plus either a macrolide or a respiratory fluoroquinolone should be used (B-III). Once culture data are available and it is known that the patient has pneumococcal pneumonia with bacteremia without evidence to support infection with a copathogen, treatment will depend upon *in vitro* susceptibility results. If the isolate is penicillin susceptible, a β-lactam (penicillin G or amoxicillin) alone may be used (B-II). If the isolate is penicillin resistant, cefotaxime, ceftriaxone, or a respiratory fluoroquinolone or other agent indicated by *in vitro* testing may be used (A-III).

Legionella: Treatment for legionnaires' disease is appropriate when there is epidemiologic evidence of this disease, despite negative diagnostic test results (B-III). The preferred treatment for legionnaires' disease for hospitalized patients is azithromycin or a fluoroquinolone (moxifloxacin, gatifloxacin, and levofloxacin; gemifloxacin is only available as an oral formulation) (B-II). For patients who do not require hospitalization, acceptable antibiotics include erythromycin, doxycycline, azithromycin, clarithromycin, or a fluoroquinolone (A-II). Treatment should be initiated as rapidly as is feasible (A-II).

Influenza: Early treatment (within 48 hours after onset of symptoms) is effective in the treatment of influenza A using amantadine, rimantadine, oseltamivir, or zanamivir and is effective in the treatment influenza B using oseltamivir and zanamivir (B-I). Use of these drugs is not recommended for uncomplicated influenza with a duration of symptoms of >48 hours (D-I), but these drugs may be used to reduce viral shedding in hospitalized patients or for influenza pneumonia (C-III).

Herpes viruses: Pneumonia caused by varicella zoster virus or herpes simplex virus should be treated with parenteral acyclovir (A-II).

Other viruses: There is no antiviral agent with established efficacy for the treatment of adults with pulmonary infections involving parainfluenza virus, respiratory syncytial virus, adenovirus, metapneumovirus, the SARS agent, or Hantavirus (D-I).

Pathogen-Directed Antimicrobial Therapy for Community-Acquired Pneumonia

Organism	Preferred Antimicrobial	Alternative Antimicrobial
Streptococcus pneumoniae		
Penicillin susceptible (MIC, <2 mcg/mL)	Penicillin G, amoxicillin	Cephalosporins (cefazolin, cefuroxime, cefotaxime, ceftriaxone, or cefepime), oral cephalosporins (cefpodoxime, cefprozil, or cefuroxime), imipenem or meropenem, macrolides,[1] clindamycin, fluoroquinolone,[2] doxycycline, ampicillin ± sulbactam or piperacillin ± tazobactam
Penicillin resistant (MIC, ≥2 mcg/mL)	Agents based on *in vitro* susceptibility tests, including cefotaxime and ceftriaxone, fluoroquinolone,[2] vancomycin	—
Haemophilus influenzae	Cephalosporins (2nd or 3rd generation), doxycycline, beta-lactam/beta-lactamase inhibitor, azithromycin, TMP-SMZ	Fluoroquinolone,[2] clarithromycin
Moraxella catarrhalis	Cephalosporin (2nd or 3rd generation), TMP-SMZ, macrolide, beta-lactam/beta-lactamase inhibitor	Fluoroquinolone[2]
Anaerobe	Beta-lactam/beta-lactamase inhibitor, clindamycin	Imipenem
Staphylococcus aureus[3]		
Methicillin-susceptible	Nafcillin/oxacillin ± rifampin or gentamicin[3]	Cefazolin or cefuroxime, vancomycin, clindamycin, TMP-SMZ
Methicillin-resistant	Vancomycin ± rifampin or gentamicin	Linezolid
Enterobacteriaceae (coliforms: *Escherichia coli, Klebsiella, Proteus, Enterobacter*)	Cephalosporin (3rd generation) ± aminoglycoside, carbapenem	Aztreonam, beta-lactam/ beta-lactamase inhibitor, fluoroquinolone[2]
Pseudomonas aeruginosa[3]	Aminoglycoside + antipseudomonal beta-lactam: ticarcillin, piperacillin, mezlocillin, ceftazidime, cefepime, aztreonam, or carbapenem	Aminoglycoside + ciprofloxacin, ciprofloxacin + antipseudomonal beta-lactam
Legionella	Macrolide[1] ± rifampin, fluoroquinolone[2] (including ciprofloxacin)	Doxycycline ± rifampin
Mycoplasma pneumoniae	Doxycycline, macrolide[1]	Fluoroquinolone[2]
Chlamydia pneumoniae	Doxycycline, macrolide[1]	Fluoroquinolone[2]
Chlamydia psittaci	Doxycycline	Erythromycin, chloramphenicol
Nocardia	TMP-SMZ, sulfonamide ± minocycline or amikacin	Imipenem ± amikacin, doxycycline or minocycline
Coxiella burnetii (Q fever)	Tetracycline	Chloramphenicol
Influenza virus	Amantadine or rimantadine (influenza A), zanamivir or oseltamivir (influenza A or B)	—
Hantavirus	Supportive care	—

Note: TMP-SMZ = trimethoprim-sulfamethoxazole.

[1]Erythromycin, clarithromycin, azithromycin, or dirithromycin; *S. pneumoniae*, especially strains with reduced susceptibility to penicillin, should have verified *in vitro* susceptibility.

[2]Levofloxacin, gatifloxacin, moxifloxacin, trovafloxacin, or other fluoroquinolone with enhanced activity against *S. pneumoniae*; ciprofloxacin is appropriate for *Legionella, C. pneumoniae*, fluoroquinolone-susceptible *S. aureus*, and most gram-negative bacilli; ciprofloxacin may not be as effective as other quinolones against *S. pneumoniae*.

[3]*In vitro* susceptibility tests are required for optimal treatment; against *Enterobacter* species, the preferred antibiotics are fluoroquinolones and carbapenems.

References

Bartlett JG, Breiman RF, Mandell LA, et al, "Community-Acquired Pneumonia in Adults: Guidelines for Management. The Infectious Diseases Society of America," *Clin Infect Dis*, 1998, 26(4):811-38.

Bartlett JG, Dowell SF, Mandell LA, et al, "Practice Guidelines for the Management of Community-Acquired Pneumonia in Adults. The Infectious Diseases Society of America," *Clin Infect Dis*, 2000, 31(2):347-82.

Mandell LA, Bartlett JG, Dowell SF, et al, "Update of Practice Guidelines for the Management of Community-Acquired Pneumonia in Immunocompetent Adults," *Clin Infect Dis*, 2003, 37(11):1405-33.

MALARIA TREATMENT

Drug of Choice	Adult Dosage	Pediatric Dosage
Chloroquine-Resistance *Plasmodium falciparum*[1]		
ORAL		
Quinine sulfate	650 mg q8h x 3-7 d[2]	25 mg/kg/d in 3 doses x 3-7 d[2]
plus doxycycline[3,4]	100 mg bid x 7 d	2 mg/kg/d x 7 d
or plus tetracycline[3,4]	250 mg qid x 7 d	6.25 mg/kg qid x 7 d
or plus pyrimethamine-sulfadoxine[5]	3 tablets at once on last day of quinine	<1 y: $^1/_4$ tablet 1-3 y: $^1/_2$ tablet 4-8 y: 1 tablet 9-14 y: 2 tablets
or plus clindamycin[3,6]	900 mg tid x 5 d	20-40 mg/kg/d in 3 doses x 5 d
OR		
Atovaquone/proguanil[7]	2 adult tablets bid x 3 d	11-20 kg: 1 adult tablet/day x 3 d 21-30 kg: 2 adult tablets/day x 3 d 31-40 kg: 3 adult tablets/day x 3 d >40 kg: 2 adult tablets bid x 3 d
***Alternatives:*[8]**		
Mefloquine[9,10]	750 mg followed by 500 mg 12 h later	<45 kg: 15 mg/kg P.O. followed by 10 mg/kg P.O. 8-12 h later
Halofantrine[11]	500 mg q6h x 3 doses; repeat in 1 week[12]	<40 kg: 8 mg/kg q6h x 3 doses; repeat in 1 week[12]
OR		
Artesunate[13]*	4 mg/kg/d x 3 d	
plus mefloquine[9,10]	750 mg followed by 500 mg 12 h later	15 mg/kg followed 8-12 h later by 10 mg/kg
Chloroquine-Resistant *P. vivax*[14]		
Quinine sulfate	650 mg q8h x 3-7 d[2]	25 mg/kg/d in 3 doses x 3-7 d[2]
plus doxycycline[3,4]	100 mg bid x 7 d	2 mg/kg/d x 7 d
OR		
Mefloquine[9,10]	750 mg followed by 500 mg 12 h later	15 mg/kg followed 8-12 h later by 10 mg/kg
Alternatives:		
Halofantrine[11,15]*	500 mg q6h x 3 doses	8 mg/kg q6h x 3 doses
Chloroquine	25 mg base/kg in 3 doses over 48 h	
plus primaquine[16]	2.5 mg base/kg in 3 doses over 48 h	
All *Plasmodium* Except Chloroquine-Resistant *P. falciparum*[1] and Chloroquine-Resistant *P. vivax*[14]		
ORAL		
Chloroquine phosphate[17]	1 g (600 mg base), then 500 mg (300 mg base) 6 h later, then 500 mg (300 mg base) at 24 and 48 h	10 mg base/kg (max 600 mg base), then 5 mg base/kg 6 h later, then 5 mg base/kg at 24 and 48 h
All *Plasmodium*[18]		
PARENTERAL		
Quinidine gluconate[19]	10 mg/kg loading dose (max 600 mg) in normal saline slowly over 1-2 h, followed by continuous infusion of 0.02 mg/kg/min until oral therapy can be started	Same as adult dose
OR		
Quinine dihydrochloride[19]	20 mg/kg loading dose I.V. in 5% dextrose over 4 h, followed by 10 mg/kg over 2-4 h q8h (max: 1800 mg/d) until oral therapy can be started	Same as adult dose
Alternative		
Artemether[20]*	3.2 mg/kg I.M., then 1.6 mg/kg daily x 5-7 d	Same as adult dose
Prevention of Relapses: *P. vivax* and *P. ovale* Only		
Primaquine phosphate[16,21]	26.3 mg (15 mg base)/d x 14 d **or** 79 mg (45 mg base)/wk x 8 wk	0.3 mg base/kg/d x 14 d

*Availability problems.

[1]Chloroquine-resistant *P. falciparum* occur in all malarious areas except Central America west of the Panama Canal Zone, Mexico, Haiti, the Dominican Republic, and most of the Middle East (chloroquine resistance has been reported in Yemen, Oman, Saudi Arabia, and Iran).

[2]In Southeast Asia, relative resistance to quinine has increased and the treatment should be continued for 7 days.

[3]An approved drug, but considered investigational for this condition by the U.S. Food and Drug Administration.

[4]Use of tetracyclines is contraindicated in pregnancy and in children <8 years of age.
[5]Fansidar® tablets contain 25 mg pyrimethamine and 500 mg sulfadoxine. Resistance to pyrimethamine-sulfadoxine has been reported from Southeast Asia, the Amazon Basin, sub-Saharan Africa, Bangladesh, and Oceania.
[6]For use in pregnancy.
[7]Atovaquone plus proguanil is available as a fixed-dose combination tablet: adult tablets (250 mg atovaquone/100 mg proguanil, Malarone™) and pediatric tablets (62.5 mg atovaquone/25 mg proguanil, Malarone™ Pediatric). To enhance absorption, it should be taken within 45 minutes after eating (Looareesuwan S, Chulay JD, Canfield CJ, "Malarone™ (Atovaquone and Proguanil Hydrochloride): A Review of Its Clinical Development for Treatment of Malaria, Malarone Clinical Trials Study Group," *Am J Trop Med Hyg*, 1999, 60(4):533-41). Although approved for once daily dosing, to decrease nausea and vomiting the dose for treatment is usually divided in two.
[8]For treatment of multiple-drug-resistant *P. falciparum* in Southeast Asia, especially Thailand, where resistance to mefloquine and halofantrine is frequent, a 7-day course of quinine and tetracycline is recommended (Watt G, Loesuttivibool L, Shanks GD, et al, "Quinine With Tetracycline for the Treatment of Drug-Resistant *Falciparum malariae* in Thailand," *Am J Trop Med Hyg*, 1992, 47(1):108-11). Artesunate plus mefloquine (Luxemburger C, ter Kuile FO, Nosten F, et al, "Single Day Mefloquine-Artesunate Combination in the Treatment of Multi-drug Resistant *Falciparum malariae*," *Trans R Soc Trop Med Hyg*, 1994, 88(2):213-7), artemether plus mefloquine (Karbwang J et al, *Trans R Soc Trop Med Hyg*, 1995, 89:296), mefloquine plus doxycycline or atovaquone/proguanil may also be used to treat multiple-drug-resistant *P. falciparum*.
[9]At this dosage, adverse effects including nausea, vomiting, diarrhea, dizziness, disturbed sense of balance, toxic psychosis, and seizures can occur. Mefloquine is teratogenic in animals and should not be used for treatment of malaria in pregnancy. It should not be given together with quinine, quinidine, or halofantrine, and caution is required in using quinine, quinidine, or halofantrine to treat patients with malaria who have taken mefloquine for prophylaxis. The pediatric dosage has not been approved by the FDA. Resistance to mefloquine has been reported in some areas, such as the Thailand-Myanmar and Cambodia borders and in the Amazon basin, where 25 mg/kg should be used.
[10]In the U.S.A., a 250 mg tablet of mefloquine contains 228 mg mefloquine base. Outside the U.S.A., each 275 mg tablet contains 250 mg base.
[11]May be effective in multiple-drug-resistant *P. falciparum* malaria, but treatment failures and resistance have been reported, and the drug has caused lengthening of the PR and QTc intervals and fatal cardiac arrhythmias. It should not be used for patients with cardiac conduction defects or with other drugs that may affect the QT interval, such as quinine, quinidine, and mefloquine. Cardiac monitoring is recommended. Variability in absorption is a problem; halofantrine should not be taken 1 hour before to 2 hours after meals because food increases its absorption. It should not be used in pregnancy.
[12]A single 250 mg dose can be used for repeat treatment in mild to moderate infections (Touze JE, Perret JL, Nicolas X, et al, "Efficacy of Low-Dose Halofantrine for Second Treatment of Uncomplicated *P. falciparum* malaria," *Lancet*, 1997, 349(9047):255-6.
[13]Na-Bangchang K, Tippanangkosol P, Ubalee R, et al, "Comparative Clinical Trial of Four Regimens of Dihydroartemisinin-Mefloquine in Multidrug-Resistant *Falciparum malaria*," *Trop Med Int Health*, 1999, 4(9):602-10.
[14]*P. vivax* with decreased susceptibility to chloroquine is a significant problem in Papua-New Guinea and Indonesia. There are also a few reports of resistance from Myanmar, India, Thailand, the Solomon Islands, Vanuatu, Guyana, Brazil, Colombia, and Peru.
[15]Baird JK, Basri H, Subianto B, et al, "Treatment of Chloroquine-Resistant *Plasmodium vivax* With Chloroquine and Primaquine or Halofantrine," *J Infect Dis*, 1995, 171(6):1678-82.
[16]Primaquine phosphate can cause hemolytic anemia, especially in patients whose red cells are deficient in glucose-6-phosphate dehydrogenase. This deficiency is most common in African, Asian, and Mediterranean peoples. Patients should be screened for G-6-PD deficiency before treatment. Primaquine should not be used during pregnancy.
[17]If chloroquine phosphate is not available, hydroxychloroquine sulfate is as effective; 400 mg of hydroxychloroquine sulfate is equivalent to 500 mg of chloroquine phosphate.
[18]Exchange transfusion has been helpful for some patients with high-density (>10%) parasitemia, altered mental status, pulmonary edema, or renal complications (Miller KD, Greenberg AE, and Campbell CC, "Treatment of Severe Malaria in the United States With a Continuous Infusion of Quinidine Gluconate and Exchange Transfusion," *N Engl J Med*, 1989, 321(2):65-7).
[19]Continuous EKG, blood pressure and glucose monitoring are recommended, especially in pregnant women and young children. For problems with quinidine availability, call the manufacturer (Eli Lilly, 800-821-0538) or the CDC Malaria Hotline (770-488-7788). Quinidine may have greater antimalarial activity than quinine. The loading dose should be decreased or omitted in those patients who have received quinine or mefloquine. If >48 hours of parenteral treatment is required, the quinine or quinidine dose should be reduced by 1/3 to 1/2.
[20]Artemether-Quinine Meta-Analysis Study Group, "A Meta-Analysis Using Individual Patient Data of Trials Comparing Artemether With Quinine in the Treatment of Severe *Falciparum* Malaria," *Trans R Soc Trop Med Hyg*, 2001, 95(6):637-50. Not available in the United States.
[21]Relapses have been reported with this regimen, and should be treated with a second 14-day course of 30 mg base/day. In Southeast Asia and Somalia the higher dose (30 mg base/day) should be used initially.

Adapted from "Report of the Committee on Infectious Diseases," *2003, Red Book*®, 26th ed, 756-9.

TUBERCULOSIS TREATMENT GUIDELINES

Recommended Treatment Regimens for Drug-Susceptible Tuberculosis in Infants, Children, and Adolescents

Infection or Disease Category	Regimen	Remarks
Latent tuberculosis infection (positive tuberculin skin test, no disease):		
• Isoniazid-susceptible	9 months of isoniazid once a day	If daily therapy is not possible, directly observed therapy twice a week may be used for 9 months.
• Isoniazid-resistant	6 months of rifampin once a day	
• Isoniazid-rifampin-resistant[1]	Consult a tuberculosis specialist	
Pulmonary and extrapulmonary (except meningitis)	2 months of isoniazid, rifampin, and pyrazinamide daily, followed by 4 months of isoniazid and rifampin[2]	If possible drug resistance is a concern, another drug (ethambutol or aminoglycoside) is added to the initial 3-drug therapy until drug susceptibilities are determined. Directly observed therapy is highly desirable.
		If hilar adenopathy only, a 6-month course of isoniazid and rifampin is sufficient.
		Drugs can be given 2 or 3 times/week under directly observed therapy in the initial phase if nonadherence is likely.
Meningitis	2 months of isoniazid, rifampin, pyrazinamide, and aminoglycoside or ethionamide, once a day, followed by 7-10 months of isoniazid and rifampin once a day or twice a week (9-12 months total)	A fourth drug, usually an aminoglycoside, is given with initial therapy until drug susceptibility is known.
		For patients who may have acquired tuberculosis in geographic areas where resistance to streptomycin is common, capreomycin, kanamycin, or amikacin may be used instead of streptomycin.

[1]Duration of therapy is longer for human immunodeficiency virus (HIV)-infected people, and additional drugs may be indicated.

[2]Medications should be administered daily for the first 2 weeks to 2 months of treatment and then can be administered 2-3 times/week by directly observed therapy.

Adapted from "Report of the Committee on Infectious Diseases," *2003 Red Book*®, 26th ed, 649.

Commonly Used Drugs for the Treatment of Tuberculosis in Infants, Children, and Adolescents

Drugs	Dosage Forms	Daily Dose (mg/kg)	Twice a Week Dose (mg/kg per dose)	Maximum Dose	Adverse Reactions
Ethambutol	Tablets 100 mg 400 mg	15-25	50	2.5 g	Optic neuritis (usually reversible), decreased red-green color discrimination, gastrointestinal tract disturbances, hypersensitivity
Isoniazid[1]	Scored tablets 100 mg 300 mg Syrup 10 mg/mL	10-15[2]	20-30	Daily, 300 mg Twice a week, 900 mg	Mild hepatic enzyme elevation, hepatitis,[2] peripheral neuritis, hypersensitivity
Pyrazinamide[1]	Scored tablets 500 mg	20-40	50	2 g	Hepatotoxic effects, hyperuricemia
Rifampin[1]	Capsules 150 mg 300 mg Syrup formulated in syrup from capsules	10-20	10-20	600 mg	Orange discoloration of secretions or urine, staining of contact lenses, vomiting, hepatitis, influenza-like reaction, thrombocytopenia; oral contraceptives may be ineffective

[1]Rifamate® (Aventis Pharmaceuticals, Bridgewater, NJ) is a capsule containing 150 mg of isoniazid and 300 mg of rifampin. Two capsules provide the usual adult (>50 kg) daily doses of each drug. Rifater® is a capsule containing 50 mg of isoniazid, 120 mg of rifampin, and 300 mg of pyrazinamide. Isoniazid and rifampin also are available for parenteral administration.

[2]When isoniazid in a dosage exceeding 10 mg/kg/day is used in combination with rifampin, the incidence of hepatotoxic effects may be increased.

Adapted from "Report of the Committee on Infectious Diseases," *2003 Red Book®*, 26th ed, 650.

Rifampin is a bactericidal agent. It is metabolized by the liver and affects the pharmacokinetics of many other drugs, affecting their serum concentrations. Mycobacterium tuberculosis, initially resistant to rifampin, remains relatively uncommon in most areas of the United States. Rifampin is excreted in bile and urine and can cause orange urine, sweat and tears. It can also cause discoloration of soft contact lenses and render oral contraceptives ineffective. Hepatotoxicity occurs rarely. Blood dyscrasia accompanied by influenza-like symptoms can occur if doses are taken sporadically.

TUBERCULOSIS TREATMENT GUIDELINES *(Continued)*

Less Commonly Used Drugs for Treatment of Drug-Resistant Tuberculosis in Infants, Children, and Adolescents[1]

Drugs	Dosage Forms	Daily Dose (mg/kg)	Maximum Dose	Adverse Reactions
Capreomycin	Vials 1 g	15-30 I.M.	1 g	Ototoxic and nephrotoxic effects
Ciprofloxacin[2]	Tablets 250 mg 500 mg 750 mg	Adults 500-1500 mg total per day (twice daily)	1.5 g	Theoretic effect on growing cartilage, gastrointestinal tract disturbances, rash, headache
Cycloserine	Capsules 250 mg	10-20	1 g	Psychosis, personality changes, seizures, rash
Ethionamide	Tablets 250 mg	15-20, given in 2-3 divided doses	1 g	Gastrointestinal tract disturbances, hepatotoxic effects, hypersensitive reactions
Kanamycin	Vials 75 mg/2 mL 500 mg/2 mL 1 g/3 mL	15-30 I.M.	1 g	Auditory and vestibular toxic effects, nephrotoxic effects
Levofloxacin[2]	Tablets 250 mg 500 mg Vials 25 mg/mL	Adults 500-1000 mg once daily	1 g	Theoretic effect on growing cartilage, gastrointestinal tract disturbances, rash, headache
Para-amino-salicylic acid (PAS)	Packets 3 mg	200-300 (2-4 times/day)	10 g	Gastrointestinal tract disturbances, hypersensitivity, hepatotoxic effects
Streptomycin (I.M.)	Vials 1 g 4 g	20-40	1 g	Auditory and vestibular toxic effects, nephrotoxic effects, rash

[1]These drugs should be used in consultation with a specialist in tuberculosis.

[2]Fluoroquinolones currently are not licensed for use in people <18 years of age; their use in younger patients necessitates assessment of the potential risks and benefits.

Adapted from "Report of the Committee on Infectious Diseases," *2003 Red Book*®, 26th ed, 651.

TB Drugs in Special Situations

Drug	Pregnancy[1]	CNS TB Disease	Renal Insufficiency
Isoniazid	Safe	Good penetration	Normal clearance
Rifampin	Safe	Fair penetration Penetrates inflamed meninges (10% to 20%)	Normal clearance
Pyrazinamide	Avoid	Good penetration	Clearance reduced Decrease dose or prolong interval
Ethambutol	Safe	Penetrates inflamed meninges only (4% to 64%)	Clearance reduced Decrease dose or prolong interval
Streptomycin	Avoid	Penetrates inflamed meninges only	Clearance reduced Decrease dose or prolong interval
Capreomycin	Avoid	Penetrates inflamed meninges only	Clearance reduced Decrease dose or prolong interval
Kanamycin	Avoid	Penetrates inflamed meninges only	Clearance reduced Decrease dose or prolong interval
Ethionamide	Do not use	Good penetration	Normal clearance
Para-aminosalicylic acid	Safe	Penetrates inflamed meninges only (10% to 50%)	Incomplete data on clearance
Cycloserine	Avoid	Good penetration	Clearance reduced Decrease dose or prolong interval
Ciprofloxacin	Do not use	Fair penetration (5% to 10%) Penetrates inflamed meninges (50% to 90%)	Clearance reduced Decrease dose or prolong interval
Ofloxacin	Do not use	Fair penetration (5% to 10%) Penetrates inflamed meninges (50% to 90%)	Clearance reduced Decrease dose or prolong interval
Amikacin	Avoid	Penetrates inflamed meninges only	Clearance reduced Decrease dose or prolong interval
Clofazimine	Avoid	Penetration unknown	Clearance probably normal

[1]Safe = the drug has not been demonstrated to have teratogenic effects.

Avoid = data on the drug's safety are limited, or the drug is associated with mild malformations (as in the aminoglycosides).

Do not use = studies show an association between the drug and premature labor, congenital malformations, or teratogenicity.

TUBERCULOSIS TREATMENT GUIDELINES *(Continued)*

Recommendations for Coadministering Different Antiretroviral Drugs With the Antimycobacterial Drugs Rifabutin and Rifampin

Antiretroviral	Use in Combination with Rifabutin	Use in Combination with Rifampin	Comments
Saquinavir[1] Hard-gel capsules (HGC)	Possibly[2], if antiretroviral regimen also includes ritonavir	Possibly, if antiretroviral regimen also includes ritonavir	Coadministration of saquinavir SGC with usual-dose rifabutin (300 mg/day or 2-3 times/week) is a possibility. However, the pharmacokinetic data and clinical experience for this combination are limited.
Soft-gel capsules (SGC)	Probably[3]	Possibly, if antiretroviral regimen also includes ritonavir	The combination of saquinavir SGC or saquinavir HGC and ritonavir, coadministered with 1) usual-dose rifampin (600 mg/day or 2-3 times/week), or 2) reduced-dose rifabutin (150 mg 2-3 times/week) is a possibility. However, the pharmacokinetic data and clinical experience for these combinations are limited. Coadministration of saquinavir or saquinavir SGC with rifampin is not recommended because rifampin markedly decreases concentrations of saquinavir.
Ritonavir	Probably	Probably	If the combination of ritonavir and rifabutin is used, then a substantially reduced-dose rifabutin regimen (150 mg 2-3 times/week) is recommended. Coadministration of ritonavir with usual-dose rifampin (600 mg/day or 2-3 times/week) is a possibility, though pharmacokinetic data and clinical experience are limited.
Indinavir	Yes	No	There is limited, but favorable, clinical experience with coadministration of indinavir[4] with a reduced daily dose of rifabutin (150 mg) or with the usual dose of rifabutin (300 mg 2-3 times/week). Coadministration of indinavir with rifampin is not recommended because rifampin markedly decreases concentrations of indinavir.
Nelfinavir	Yes	No	There is limited, but favorable, clinical experience with coadministration of nelfinavir[5] with a reduced daily dose of rifabutin (150 mg) or with the usual dose of rifabutin (300 mg 2-3 times/week). Coadministration of nelfinavir with rifampin is not recommended because rifampin markedly decreases concentrations of nelfinavir.
Amprenavir	Yes	No	Coadministration of amprenavir with a reduced daily dose of rifabutin (150 mg) or with the usual dose of rifabutin (300 mg 2-3 times/week) is a possibility, but there is no published clinical experience. Coadministration of amprenavir with rifampin is not recommended because rifampin markedly decreases concentrations of amprenavir.

Recommendations for Coadministering Different Antiretroviral Drugs With the Antimycobacterial Drugs Rifabutin and Rifampin
(continued)

Antiretroviral	Use in Combination with Rifabutin	Use in Combination with Rifampin	Comments
Nevirapine	Yes	Possibly	Coadministration of nevirapine with usual-dose rifabutin (300 mg/day or 2-3 times/week) is a possibility based on pharmacokinetic study data. However, there is no published clinical experience for this combination. Data are insufficient to assess whether dose adjustments are necessary when rifampin is coadministered with nevirapine. Therefore, rifampin and nevirapine should be used only in combination if clearly indicated and with careful monitoring.
Delavirdine	No	No	Contraindicated because of the marked decrease in concentrations of delavirdine when administered with either rifabutin or rifampin.
Efavirenz	Probably	Probably	Coadministration of efavirenz with increased-dose rifabutin (450 mg/day or 600 mg/day, or 600 mg 2-3 times/week) is a possibility, though there is no published clinical experience. Coadministration of efavirenz[6] with usual-dose rifampin (600 mg/day or 2-3 times/week) is a possibility, though there is no published clinical experience.

[1]Usual recommended doses are 400 mg twice daily for each of these protease inhibitors and 400 mg of ritonavir.

[2]Despite limited data and clinical experience, the use of this combination is potentially successful.

[3]Based on available data and clinical experience, the successful use of this combination is likely.

[4] Usual recommended dose is 800 mg every 8 hours; some experts recommend increasing the indinavir dose to 1000 mg every 8 hours if indinavir is used in combination with rifabutin.

[5]Usual recommended dose is 750 mg 3 times/day or 1250 mg twice daily; some experts recommend increasing the nelfinavir dose to 1000 mg if the 3-times/day dosing is used and nelfinavir is used in combination with rifabutin.

[6]Usual recommended dose is 600 mg/day; some experts recommend increasing the efavirenz dose to 800 mg/day if efavirenz is used in combination with rifampin.

Updated March 2000 from www.aidsinfo.nih.gov -"Updated Guidelines for the Use of Rifabutin or Rifampin for the Treatment and Prevention of Tuberculosis Among HIV-Infected Patients Taking Protease Inhibitors or Non-nucleoside Reverse Transcriptase Inhibitors," *MMWR*, March 10, 2000, 49(09):185-9.

TUBERCULOSIS TREATMENT GUIDELINES *(Continued)*

Criteria for Tuberculin Positivity, by Risk Group

Reaction ≥5 mm of Induration	Reaction ≥10 mm of Induration	Reaction ≥15 mm of Induration
HIV-positive persons	Recent immigrants (ie, within the last 5 years) from high prevalence countries	Persons with no risk factors for TB
Recent contacts of tuberculosis (TB) case patients	Injection drug users	
Fibrotic changes on chest radiograph consistent with prior TB	Residents and employees[1] of the following high risk congregate settings: prisons and jails, nursing homes and other long-term facilities for the elderly, hospitals and other healthcare facilities, residential facilities for patients with AIDS, and homeless shelters	
Patients with organ transplant and other immunosuppressed patients (receiving the equivalent of ≥15 mg/day of prednisone for 1 month of more)[2]	Mycobacteriology laboratory personnel	
	Persons with the following clinical conditions that place them at high risk: silicosis, diabetes mellitus, chronic renal failure, some hematologic disorders (eg, leukemias and lymphomas), other specific malignancies (eg, carcinoma of the head or neck and lung), weight loss of ≥10% of ideal body weight, gastrectomy, and jejunoileal bypass	
	Children <4 years of age or infants, children, and adolescents exposed to adults at high-risk	

[1]For persons who are otherwise at low risk and are tested at the start of employment, a reaction of ≥15 mm induration is considered positive.

[2]Risk of TB in patients treated with corticosteroids increases with higher dose and longer duration.

Modified from *MMWR Morb Mortal Wkly Rep*, 2000, 49(RR-6).

Revised Drug Regimens for Treatment of Latent Tuberculosis Infection (LTBI) in Adults

Drug	Interval and Duration	Comments[1]	Rating[2] (Evidence)[3]	
			HIV⁻	HIV⁺
Isoniazid	Daily for 9 months[4,5]	In HIV-infected patients, isoniazid may be administered concurrently with nucleoside reverse transcriptase inhibitors (NRTIs), protease inhibitors, or non-nucleoside reverse transcriptase inhibitors (NNRTIs)	A (II)	A (II)
	Twice weekly for 9 months[4,5]	Directly observed therapy (DOT) must be used with twice-weekly dosing	B (II)	B (II)
Isoniazid	Daily for 6 months[5]	Not indicated for HIV-infected persons, those with fibrotic lesions on chest radiographs, or children	B (I)	C (I)
	Twice weekly for 6 months[5]	DOT must be used with twice-weekly dosing	B (II)	C (I)
Rifampin[6]	Daily for 4 months	Used for persons who are contacts of patients with isoniazid-resistant, rifampin-susceptible TB	B (II)	B (III)
		In HIV-infected persons, most protease inhibitors or delavirdine should not be administered concurrently with rifampin. Rifabutin with appropriate dose adjustments can be used with protease inhibitors (saquinavir should be augmented with ritonavir) and NNRTIs (except delavirdine). Clinicians should consult web-based updates for the latest specific recommendations.		
Rifampin plus pyrazinamide (RZ)	Daily for 2 months	RZ generally should not be offered for treatment of LTBI for HIV-infected or HIV-negative persons	D (II)	D (II)
	Twice weekly for 2-3 months		D (III)	D (III)

[1]Interactions with human immunodeficiency virus (HIV)-related drugs are updated frequently and are available at http://www.aidsinfo.nih.gov/guidelines.

[2]Strength of recommendation:

A. Both strong evidence of efficacy and substantial clinical benefit support recommendation for use. Should always be offered.

B. Moderate evidence for efficacy or strong evidence for efficacy but only limited clinical benefit supports recommendation for use. Should generally be offered.

C. Evidence for efficacy is insufficient to support a recommendation for or against use, or evidence for efficacy might not outweigh adverse consequences (eg, drug toxicity, drug interactions) or cost of the treatment or alternative approaches. Optional.

D. Moderate evidence for lack of efficacy or for adverse outcome supports a recommendation against use. Should generally not be offered.

E. Good evidence for lack of efficacy or for adverse outcome support a recommendation against use. Should never be offered.

[3]Quality of evidence supporting the recommendation:

I. Evidence from at least one properly randomized controlled trial.

II. Evidence from at least one well-designed clinical trial without randomization from cohort or case-controlled analytic studies (preferably from more than one center), from multiple time-series studies, or from dramatic results from uncontrolled experiments.

III. Evidence from opinions or respected authorities based on clinical experience, descriptive studies, or reports of expert committees.

[4]Recommended regimen for persons <18 years of age.

[5]Recommended regimens for pregnant women.

[6]The substitution of rifapentine for rifampin is not recommended because rifapentine's safety and effectiveness have not been established for patients with LTBI.

Adapted from CDC and American Thoracic Society, "Update: Adverse Event Data and Revised American Thoracic Society/CDC Recommendations Against the Use of Rifampin and Pyrazinamide for Treatment of Latent Tuberculosis Infection – United States, 2003," *MMWR Morb Mortal Wkly Rep*, 2003, 52(31):735-9.

TUBERCULOSIS TREATMENT GUIDELINES *(Continued)*

Recommendations, Rankings, and Performance Indicators for Treatment of Patients With Tuberculosis (TB)

Recommendation	Ranking[1] (Evidence)[2]	Performance Indicator
Obtain bacteriologic confirmation and susceptibility testing for patients with TB or suspected of having TB	A (II)	90% of adults with or suspected of having TB have 3 cultures for mycobacteria obtained before initiation of antituberculosis therapy (50% of children 0-12 y)
Place persons with suspected or confirmed smear-positive pulmonary or laryngeal TB in respiratory isolation until noninfectious	A (II)	90% of persons with sputum smear-positive TB remain in respiratory isolation until smear converts to negative
Begin treatment of patients with confirmed or suspected TB disease with one of the following drug combinations, depending on local resistance patterns: INH + RIF + PZA **or** INH + RIF + PZA + EMB **or** INH + RIF + PZA + SM	A (III)	90% of all patients with TB are started on INH + RIF + PZA + EMB or SM in geographic areas where >4% of TB isolates are resistant to INH
Report each case of TB promptly to the local public health department	A (III)	100% of persons with active TB are reported to the local public health department within 1 week of diagnosis
Perform HIV testing for all patients with TB	A (III)	80% of all patients with TB have HIV status determined within 2 months of a diagnosis of TB
Treat patients with TB caused by a susceptible organism for 6 months, using an ATS/CDC-approved regimen	A (I)	90% of all patients with TB complete 6 months of therapy with 12 months of beginning treatment
Re-evaluate patients with TB who are smear positive at 3 months for possible nonadherence or infection with drug-resistant bacilli	A (III)	90% of all patients with TB who are smear positive at 3 months have sputum culture/susceptibility testing performed within 1 month of the 3-month visit
Add ≥2 new antituberculosis agents when TB treatment failure is suspected	A (II)	100% of patients with TB with suspected treatment failure are prescribed ≥2 new antituberculosis agents
Perform tuberculin skin testing on all patients with a history of ≥1 of the following: HIV infection, I.V. drug use, homelessness, incarceration, or contact with a person with pulmonary TB	A (II)	80% of persons in the indicated population groups receive tuberculin skin test and return for reading
Administer treatment for latent TB infection to all persons with latent TB infection, unless it can be documented that they received such treatment previously	A (I)	75% of patients with positive tuberculin skin tests who are candidates for treatment for latent TB infection complete a course of therapy within 12 months of initiation

Note: ATS/CDC = American Thoracic Society and Centers for Disease Control and Prevention; EMB = ethambutol; INH = isoniazid; PZA = pyrazinamide; RIF = rifampin; SM = streptomycin.

[1]Strength of recommendation: A = preferred; B = acceptable alternative; C = offer when A and B cannot be given.

[2]Quality of evidence: I = randomized clinical trial data; II = data from clinical trials that are not randomized or were conducted in other populations; III = expert opinion.

Adapted from the Infectious Diseases Society of America, *Clinical Infectious Diseases,* 2000, 31:633-9.

ASTHMA

ESTIMATED COMPARATIVE <u>DAILY</u> DOSAGES FOR INHALED CORTICOSTEROIDS

Adults

Drug	Low Dose	Medium Dose	High Dose
Beclomethasone dipropionate	168-504 mcg	504-840 mcg	>840 mcg
42 mcg/puff	4-12 puffs	12-20 puffs	>20 puffs
84 mcg/puff	2-6 puffs	6-10 puffs	>10 puffs
Beclomethasone dipropionate HFA	80-240 mcg	240-640 mcg	>640 mcg
40 mcg/puff	2-6 puffs	6-16 puffs	>16 puffs
80 mcg/puff	1-3 puffs	3-8 puffs	>8 puffs
Budesonide Turbuhaler	200-600 mcg	600-1200 mcg	>1200 mcg
200 mcg/inhalation	1-3 inhalations	3-6 inhalations	>6 inhalations
Flunisolide	500-1000 mcg	1000-2000 mcg	>2000 mcg
250 mcg/puff	2-4 puffs	4-8 puffs	>8 puffs
Fluticasone	88-264 mcg	264-660 mcg	>660 mcg
MDI: 44, 110, 220 mcg/puff			
DPI: 50, 100, 250 mcg/dose			
Triamcinolone acetonide	400-1000 mcg	1000-2000 mcg	>2000 mcg
100 mcg/puff	4-10 puffs	10-20 puffs	>20 puffs

Children

Drug	Low Dose	Medium Dose	High Dose
Beclomethasone dipropionate	84-336 mcg	336-672 mcg	>672 mcg
42 mcg/puff	2-8 puffs	8-16 puffs	>16 puffs
84 mcg/puff	1-4 puffs	4-8 puffs	>8 puffs
Beclomethasone dipropionate HFA	80-160 mcg	160-320 mcg	>320 mcg
40 mcg/puff	2-4 puffs	4-8 puffs	>8 puffs
80 mcg/puff	1-2 puffs	2-4 puffs	>4 puffs
Budesonide Turbuhaler	200-400 mcg	400-800 mcg	>800 mcg
200 mcg/inhalation	1-2 inhalations	2-4 inhalations	>4 inhalations
Inhalation suspension for nebulization	0.5 mg	1 mg	2 mg
Flunisolide	500-750 mcg	1000-1250 mcg	>1250 mcg
250 mcg/puff	2-3 puffs	4-5 puffs	>5 puffs
Fluticasone	88-176 mcg	176-440 mcg	>440 mcg
MDI: 44, 110, 220 mcg/puff			
DPI: 50, 100, 250 mcg/dose			
Triamcinolone acetonide	400-800 mcg	800-1200 mcg	>1200 mcg
100 mcg/puff	4-8 puffs	8-12 puffs	>12 puffs

Notes:

- **The most important determinant of appropriate dosing is the clinician's judgment of the patient's response to therapy.** The clinician must monitor the patient's response on several clinical parameters and adjust the dose accordingly. The stepwise approach to therapy emphasizes that once control of asthma is achieved, the dose of mediation should be carefully titrated to the minimum dose required to maintain control, thus reducing the potential for adverse effect.

ASTHMA *(Continued)*

- The reference point for the range in the dosages for children is data on the safety on inhaled corticosteroids in children, which, in general, suggest that the dose ranges are equivalent to beclomethasone dipropionate 200-400 mcg/day (low dose), 400-800 mcg/day (medium dose), and >800 mcg/day (high dose).
- Some dosages may be outside package labeling.
- Metered-dose inhaler (MDI) dosages are expressed as the actuator dose (the amount of drug leaving the actuator and delivered to the patient), which is the labeling required in the United States. This is different from the dosage expressed as the valve dose (the amount of drug leaving the valve, all of which is not available to the patient), which is used in many European countries and in some of the scientific literature. Dry powder inhaler (DPI) doses (eg, Turbuhaler) are expressed as the amount of drug in the inhaler following activation.

EPILEPSY

Antiepileptic Drugs for Children and Adolescents by Seizure Type and Epilepsy Syndrome

Seizure Type or Epilepsy Syndrome	First Line Therapy	Alternatives
Partial seizures (with or without secondary generalization)	Carbamazepine	Valproate, phenytoin, gabapentin, lamotrigine, vigabatrin, phenobarbital, primidone; consider clonazepam, clorazepate, acetazolamide, oxcarbazepine
Generalized tonic-clonic seizures	Valproate or carbamazepine	Phenytoin, phenobarbital, primidone; consider clonazepam
Childhood absence epilepsy		
Before 10 years of age	Ethosuximide or valproate	Methsuximide, acetazolamide, clonazepam, lamotrigine
After 10 years of age	Valproate	Ethosuximide, methsuximide, acetazolamide, clonazepam, lamotrigine; consider adding carbamazepine, phenytoin, or phenobarbital for generalized tonic-clonic seizures if valproate not tolerated
Juvenile myoclonic epilepsy	Valproate	Phenobarbital, primidone, clonazepam; consider carbamazepine, phenytoin, methsuximide, acetazolamide
Progressive myoclonic epilepsy	Valproate	Valproate plus clonazepam, phenobarbital
Lennox-Gastaut and related syndromes	Valproate	Clonazepam, phenobarbital, lamotrigine, ethosuximide, felbamate; consider methsuximide, ACTH or steroids, pyridoxine, ketogenic diet, topiramate
Infantile spasms	ACTH or steroids	Valproate; consider clonazepam, vigabatrin (especially with tuberous sclerosis), pyridoxine
Benign epilepsy of childhood with centrotemporal spikes	Carbamazepine or valproate	Phenytoin; consider phenobarbital, primidone
Neonatal seizures	Phenobarbital	Phenytoin; consider clonazepam, primidone, valproate, pyridoxine

Adapted from Bourgeois BFD, "Antiepileptic Drugs in Pediatric Practice," *Epilepsia*, 1995, 36(Suppl 2):S34-S45.

EPILEPSY *(Continued)*

FEBRILE SEIZURES

A febrile seizure is defined as a seizure occurring for no reason other than an elevated temperature. It does not have an infectious or metabolic origin within the CNS (ie, it is not caused by meningitis or encephalitis). Fever is usually >102°F rectally, but the more rapid the rise in temperature, the more likely a febrile seizure may occur. About 4% of children develop febrile seizures at one time in their life, usually occurring between 3 months and 5 years of age with the majority occurring at 6 months to 3 years of age. There are three types of febrile seizures:

1. **Simple** febrile seizures are nonfocal febrile seizures of less than 15 minutes duration. They do not occur in multiples.

2. **Complex** febrile seizures are febrile seizures that are either focal, have a focal component, are longer than 15 minutes in duration, or are multiple febrile seizures that occur within 30 minutes.

3. **Febrile status epilepticus** is a febrile seizure that is a generalized tonic-clonic seizure lasting longer than 30 minutes.

Note: Febrile seizures should not be confused with true epileptic seizures associated with fever or "seizure with fever." "Seizure with fever" includes seizures associated with acute neurologic illnesses (ie, meningitis, encephalitis).

Long-term prophylaxis with phenobarbital may reduce the risk of subsequent febrile seizures. The 1980 NIH Consensus paper stated that after the first febrile seizure, long-term prophylaxis should be considered under any of the following:

1. Presence of abnormal neurological development or abnormal neurological exam

2. Febrile seizure was complex in nature: duration >15 minutes focal febrile seizure followed by transient or persistent neurological abnormalities

3. Positive family history of afebrile seizures (epilepsy)

Also consider long-term prophylaxis in certain cases if:

1. the child has multiple febrile seizures
2. the child is <12 months of age

Anticonvulsant prophylaxis is usually continued for 2 years or 1 year after the last seizure, whichever is longer. With the identification of phenobarbital's adverse effects on learning and cognitive function, many physicians will not start long-term phenobarbital prophylaxis after the first febrile seizure unless the patient has more than one of the above risk factors. Most physicians would start long-term prophylaxis if the patient has a second febrile seizure.

Daily administration of phenobarbital and therapeutic phenobarbital serum concentrations ≥15 mcg/mL decrease recurrence rates of febrile seizures. Valproic acid is also effective in preventing recurrences of febrile seizures, but is usually reserved for patients who have significant adverse effects to phenobarbital. The administration of rectal diazepam (as a solution or suppository) at the time of the febrile illness has been shown to be as effective as daily phenobarbital in preventing recurrences of febrile seizures. However, these rectal dosage forms are not available in the United States. Some centers in the U.S. are using the injectable form of diazepam rectally. The solution for injection is filtered prior to use if drawn from an ampul. A recent study suggests that oral diazepam, 0.33 mg/kg/dose given every 8 hours only when the child has a fever, may reduce the risk of recurrent febrile seizures (see Rosman, et al). **Note**: A more recent study by Uhari (1995) showed that lower doses of diazepam, 0.2 mg/kg/dose, were not effective.) Carbamazepine and phenytoin are not effective in preventing febrile seizures.

References

Berg AT, Shinnar S, Hauser WA, et al, "Predictors of Recurrent Febrile Seizures: A Meta-Analytic Review," *J Pediatr*, 1990, 116(3):329-37.

Camfield PR, Camfield CS, Gordon K, et al, "Prevention of Recurrent Febrile Seizures," *J Pediatr*, 1995, 126(6):929-30.

NIH Consensus Statement, "Febrile Seizures: A Consensus of Their Significance, Evaluation and Treatment," *Pediatrics*, 1980, 66(6):1009-12.

Rosman NP, Colton T, Labazzo J, et al, "A Controlled Trial of Diazepam Administration During Febrile Illnesses to Prevent Recurrence of Febrile Seizures," *N Engl J Med*, 1993, 329(2):79-84.

Uhari M, Rantala H, Vainionpaa L, et al, "Effects of Acetaminophen and of Low Intermittent Doses of Diazepam on Prevention of Recurrences of Febrile Seizures," *J Pediatr*, 1995, 126(6):991-5.

CONVULSIVE STATUS EPILEPTICUS

Recommendations of the Epilepsy Foundation of America's Working Group on Status Epilepticus

(*JAMA*, 1993, 270:854-9)

Convulsive status epilepticus is an emergency that is associated with high morbidity and mortality. The outcome largely depends on etiology, but prompt and appropriate pharmacological therapy can reduce morbidity and mortality. Etiology varies in children and adults and reflects the distribution of disease in these age groups. Antiepileptic drug administration should be initiated whenever a seizure has lasted 10 minutes. Immediate concerns include supporting respiration, maintaining blood pressure, gaining intravenous access, and identifying and treating the underlying cause. Initial therapeutic and diagnostic measures are conducted simultaneously. The goal of therapy is rapid termination of clinical and electrical seizure activity; the longer a seizure continues, the greater the likelihood of an adverse outcome. Several drug protocols now in use will terminate status epilepticus. Common to all patients is the need for a clear plan, prompt administration of appropriate drugs in adequate doses, and attention to the possibility of apnea, hypoventilation, or other metabolic abnormalities.

Figure 1. Algorithm for the Initial Management of Status Epilepticus

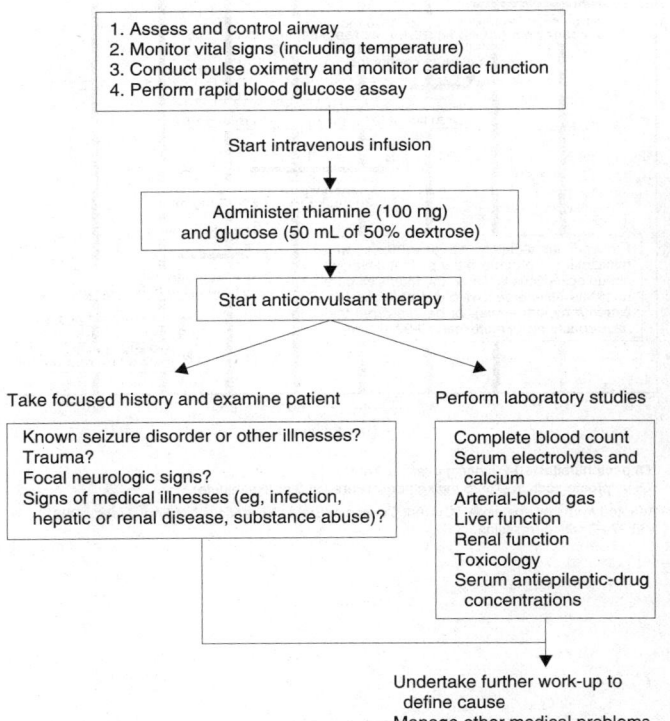

Adapted from Lowenstein A, "Current Concepts: Status Epilepticus," *N Engl J Med*, 1998, 338:970-6 with permission.

EPILEPSY *(Continued)*

Figure 2. Antiepileptic Drug Therapy for Status Epilepticus

I.V. denotes intravenous and PE denotes phenytoin equivalents. The horizontal bars indicate the approximate duration of drug infusions.

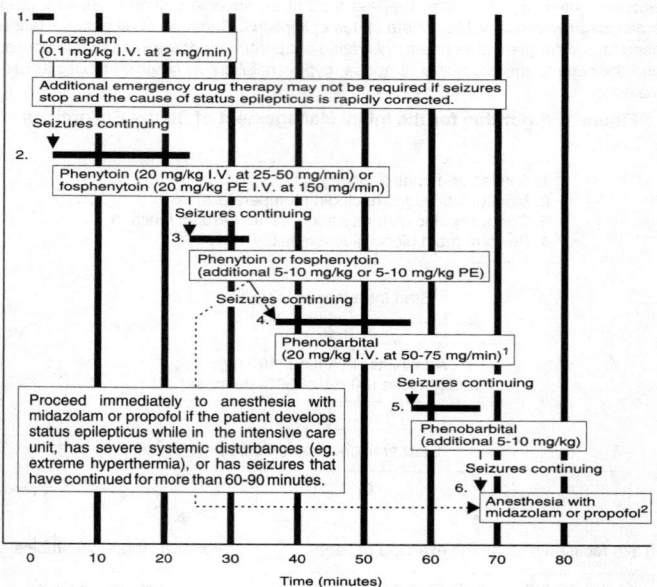

[1]Or pentobarbital (10-20 mg/kg over 1-2 hours).
[2]Or valproate sodium (15-25 mg/kg administered at 3 mg/kg/minute).

Adapted from Lowenstein A, "Current Concepts: Status Epilepticus," *N Engl J Med*, 1998, 338:970-6 with permission.

GLAUCOMA DRUG THERAPY

Ophthalmic Agent (Brand)	Reduces Aqueous Humor Production	Increases Aqueous Humor Outflow[1]	Average Duration of Action	Strengths Available
Cholinesterase Inhibitors				
Echothiophate (Phospholine Iodide®)	No data	Significant	2 wk	0.03% to 0.25%
Physostigmine	No data	Significant	24 h	0.25%
Direct-Acting Cholinergic Miotics				
Carbachol (Carbastat®)	Some activity	Significant	8 h	0.75% to 3%
Pilocarpine (various)	Some activity	Significant	5 h	0.5%, 1%, 2%, 3%, 4%
Sympathomimetics				
Apraclonidine (Iopidine®)	Moderate	Moderate	4 h	0.5%, 1%
Brimonidine (Alphagan®, Alphagan® P)	Moderate	Moderate	12 h	0.2%
Dipivefrin (Propine®)	Some activity	Moderate	12 h	0.1%
Epinephrine (Epifrin®)	Some activity	Moderate	18 h	0.25% to 2%
Beta-Blockers				
Betaxolol (Betoptic® S)	Significant	Some activity	12 h	0.5%
Carteolol (Ocupress®)	Yes	No	12 h	1%
Levobetaxolol (Betaxon®)	Significant	No data	12 h	0.5%
Levobunolol (Betagan®)	Significant	Some activity	18 h	0.5%
Metipranolol (OptiPranolol®)	Significant	Some activity	18 h	0.3%
Timolol (Betimol®, Timoptic®)	Significant	Some activity	18 h	0.25%, 0.5%
Carbonic Anhydrase Inhibitors				
Acetazolamide (Diamox®)	Significant	No data	10 h	250 mg tab; 500 mg cap
Brinzolamide (Azopt®)	Yes	No data	8 h	1%
Dorzolamide (Trusopt®)	Yes	No	8 h	2%
Methazolamide (Neptazane®)	Significant	No data	14 h	50 mg
Prostaglandin Agonists				
Bimatoprost (Lumigan®)		Yes	≥24 h	0.03%
Latanoprost (Xalatan®)		Yes	≥24 h	0.005%
Travoprost (Travatan®)		Yes	20 h	0.004%
Unoprostone (Rescula®)		Yes	12 h	0.15%

[1]All miotic drugs significantly affect accommodation.

OBESITY TREATMENT GUIDELINES FOR ADULTS

SUMMARY OF CLINICAL PRACTICE GUIDELINES
National Heart, Lung, and Blood Institute

Note: Weight loss treatment for children and adolescents is not covered by these guidelines.

ASSESSMENT

Assessment of weight involves evaluating body mass index, waist circumference, and the patient's risk factors.

A. Body Mass Index (BMI)

　　1.　BMI should be calculated for all adults (see table). Those with normal BMI should be reassessed in 2 years. A very muscular person may have a high BMI without the additional health risks.

　　2.　Overweight is defined as a BMI of 25-29.9 kg/m^2.

　　3.　Obesity is defined as a BMI of ≥30 kg/m^2.

B. Abdominal Fat

　　1.　Excess abdominal fat, not proportional to total body fat, is an independent predictor for risk and morbidity.

　　2.　Waist circumference for men >40 inches or women >35 inches is an increased risk for those with a BMI of 25-34.9.

C. Risk Factors

　　1.　Coronary heart disease or other atherosclerotic diseases, type 2 diabetes, and sleep apnea are factors associated with a very high risk of developing disease complications and mortality.

　　2.　Other obesity-associated diseases: Gynecological abnormalities, osteoarthritis, gallstones, stress incontinence.

　　3.　Cardiovascular risk factors: Cigarette smoking, hypertension, high-risk LDL-cholesterol, low HDL-cholesterol, impaired fasting glucose, family history of premature CHD.

　　4.　Other risk factors: Physical inactivity, high serum triglycerides.
　　　　Weight loss is recommended for those who are obese and for those who are classified as overweight or have a high waist circumference and two or more risk factors.

Body Mass Index (BMI), kg/m^2
Height (feet, inches)

Weight (lb)	5'0"	5'3"	5'6"	5'9"	6'0"	6'3"
140	27	25	23	21	19	18
150	29	27	24	22	20	19
160	31	28	26	24	22	20
170	33	30	28	25	23	21
180	35	32	29	27	25	23
190	37	34	31	28	26	24
200	39	36	32	30	27	25
210	41	37	34	31	29	26
220	43	39	36	33	30	28
230	45	41	37	34	31	29
240	47	43	39	36	33	30
250	49	44	40	37	34	31

Note: For BMI calculations see "Body Mass Index" in Abbreviations and Measurements section.

TREATMENT

Patients who are overweight or obese, but are not candidates for weight loss or do not wish to lose weight, should be counseled to avoid further weight gain.

A. Goals of Treatment

   1. Prevent further weight gain.

   2. Reduce body weight. The initial goal is to reduce body weight by 10% from baseline over the suggested time period of 6 months.

   3. Maintain a lower body weight, long term.

B. Nonpharmacologic treatment should include:

   1. An individually-planned diet which includes a decrease in fat as well as total calories.

   2. An increase in physical activity. Physical activity should be gradually increased to a goal of 30 minutes per day of moderate-intensity activity.

   3. Behavior therapy, which should include tools to help overcome individual barriers to weight loss.

      Nonpharmacologic treatment should be tried for 6 months before starting physician-prescribed drug therapy.

C. Drug Therapy

   In select patients with BMI ≥30, or BMI ≥27 with 2 or more risk factors, who did not lose weight or maintain weight loss, drug therapy can be started along with dietary therapy and physical activity.

D. Surgery

   Patients with severe clinical obesity, BMI ≥40 or BMI ≥35 with coexisting conditions, can be considered for weight loss surgery when other methods have failed. Lifelong surveillance after surgery is necessary.

Medications for the Treatment of Obesity

Generic (Trade) Name	Therapeutic Category / Mechanism of Action	Usual Adult Dosage
Orlistat (Xenical®)	Lipase inhibitor; a reversible inhibitor of gastric and pancreatic lipases thus inhibiting absorption of dietary fats by 30% (at doses of 120 mg 3 times/day)	120 mg 3 times/day with each main meal containing fat (during or up to 1 hour after the meal); omit dose if meal is occasionally missed or contains no fat.
Amphetamine	The amphetamines are noncatecholamine sympathomimetic amines with CNS stimulant activity. The anorexigenic effect is probably secondary to the CNS-stimulating effect; the site of action is probably the hypothalamic feeding center.	Long-acting capsule: 10 or 15 mg/day, up to 30 mg/day; Immediate release tablets: 5-30 mg/day in divided doses
Benzphetamine (Didrex®)	Anorexiant; noncatechol sympathomimetic amines with pharmacologic actions similar to ephedrine; anorexigenic effect is probably secondary to the CNS-stimulating effect; the site of action is probably the hypothalamic feeding center	25-50 mg 2-3 times/day, preferably twice daily (midmorning and midafternoon); maximum dose: 50 mg 3 times/day

OBESITY TREATMENT GUIDELINES FOR ADULTS
(Continued)

Medications for the Treatment of Obesity *(continued)*

Generic (Trade) Name	Therapeutic Category / Mechanism of Action	Usual Adult Dosage
Diethylpropion (Tenuate®; Tenuate® Dospan®)	Anorexiant; pharmacological and chemical properties similar to those of amphetamines. The mechanism of action of diethylpropion in reducing appetite appears to be secondary to CNS effects, specifically stimulation of the hypothalamus to release catecholamines into the central nervous system; anorexiant effects are mediated via norepinephrine and dopamine metabolism. An increase in physical activity and metabolic effects (inhibition of lipogenesis and enhancement of lipolysis) may also contribute to weight loss.	Tablet: 25 mg 3 times/day before meals or food Tablet, controlled release: 75 mg at midmorning
Methamphetamine (Desoxyn®)	A sympathomimetic amine related to ephedrine and amphetamine with CNS stimulant activity	5 mg, 30 minutes before each meal; long-acting formulation: 10-15 mg in morning; treatment duration should not exceed a few weeks
Phentermine (Adipex-P®, Ionamin®)	Anorexiant; structurally similar to dextroamphetamine and is comparable to dextroamphetamine as an appetite suppressant, but is generally associated with a lower incidence and severity of CNS side effects. Stimulates the hypothalamus to result in decreased appetite; anorexiant effects are most likely mediated via norepinephrine and dopamine metabolism. However, other CNS effects or metabolic effects may be involved.	8 mg 3 times/day 30 minutes before meals or food or 15-37.5 mg/day before breakfast or 10-14 hours before retiring
Sibutramine (Meridia™)	Anorexiant; blocks the neuronal uptake of norepinephrine and, to a lesser extent, serotonin and dopamine	Initial: 10 mg once daily; after 4 weeks may titrate up to 15 mg once daily as needed and tolerated

MANAGEMENT OF OVERDOSAGES

Antidote	Poison/Drug	Indications	Dosage	Comments
Acetylcysteine (Mucomyst®)	Acetaminophen	Unknown quantity ingested and <24 hours have elapsed since the time of ingestion or unable to obtain serum acetaminophen levels within 12 hours of ingestion. >7.5 g acetaminophen acutely ingested. Serum acetaminophen level >140 mcg/mL at 4 hours postingestion. Ingested dose >140 mg/kg.	Dilute to 5% solutions with carbonated beverage, fruit juice, or water and administer orally. **Loading:** 140 mg/kg for 1 dose **Maintenance:** 70 mg/kg for 17 doses, starting 4 hours after the loading dose and given every 4 hours	SGOT, SGPT, bilirubin, prothrombin time, creatinine, BUN, blood sugar, and electrolytes should be obtained daily if a toxic serum acetaminophen level has been determined. **Note:** Activated charcoal has been shown to absorb acetylcysteine *in vitro* and may do so in patients. Serum acetaminophen levels may not peak until 4 hours postingestion, and therefore, serum levels should not be drawn earlier.
Amyl nitrate, sodium nitrate, sodium thiosulfate (cyanide antidote package)	Cyanide	Begin treatment at the first sign of toxicity if exposure is known or strongly expected.	Break ampul of amyl nitrate and allow patient to inhale for 15 seconds, then take away for 15 seconds. Use a fresh ampul every 3 minutes. Continue until injection of sodium nitrate (3% solution) 300 mg (0.15-0.33 mL/kg over 5 minutes in pediatric patients) can be injected at 2.5-5 mL/min. Then immediately inject 12.5 g 25% sodium thiosulfate, slow I.V. (1.65 mL/kg in children)	If symptoms return, treatment may be repeated at half the normal dosages. For pediatric dosing see package insert. Do **not** use methylene blue to reduce elevated methemoglobin levels. Oxygen therapy may be useful when combined with sodium thiosulfate therapy.
Antivenin (*Crotalidae*) polyvalent (equine origin)	Pit viper bites (rattlesnakes, cotton-mouths, copperheads)	Mild, moderate, or severe symptoms and history of envenomation by a pit viper **Mild:** Local swelling (progressive), pain, no systemic systems **Moderate:** Ecchymosis and swelling beyond the bite site, some systemic symptoms and/or lab changes **Severe:** Profound edema involving entire extremity, cyanosis, serious systemic involvement, significant lab changes	**Mild:** 3-5 vials of antivenin in 250-500 mL NS **Moderate:** 6-10 vials of antivenin in 500 mL NS **Severe:** Minimum of 10 vials in 500-1000 mL NS Administer over 4-6 hours. Additional antivenin should be given on the basis of clinical response and continuing assessment of severity of the poisoning.	Draw blood for type and crossmatch, hematocrit, BUN, electrolytes, CBC, platelets, coagulation profile. Do **not** administer heparin for possible allergic reaction. A tetanus shot should also be given.

MANAGEMENT OF OVERDOSAGES *(Continued)*

Antidote	Poison/Drug	Indications	Dosage	Comments
Atropine	Organophosphate and carbamate insecticides, mushrooms containing muscarine (inocybe or clitocybe)	Myoclonic seizures, severe hallucinations, weakness, arrhythmias, excessive salivation, involuntary urination, and defecation	**Children:** I.V.: 0.05 mg/kg **Adults:** I.V.: 1-2 mg Repeat dosage every 10 minutes until patient is atropinized (normal pulse, dilated pupils, absence of rales, dry mouth)	Caution should be used in patients with narrow-angle glaucoma, cardiovascular disease, or pregnancy. Plasma and/or erythrocyte cholinesterase levels will be depressed from normal. Atropine should only be used when indicated; otherwise, use may result in anticholinergic poisoning. For organophosphate poisoning, large doses of atropine may be required.
Calcium EDTA (calcium disodium versenate)	Lead	Symptomatic patients or asymptomatic children with blood levels >50 mcg/dL	50-75 mg/kg/day deep I.M. or slow I.V. infusion in 3-6 divided doses for up to 5 days	If urine flow is not established, hemodialysis must accompany calcium EDTA dosing. In most cases, the I.M. route is preferred.
Calcium gluconate	Hydrofluoric acid (HF), magnesium	Calcium gluconate gel 2.5% for dermal exposures of HF <20% concentration. S.C. injections of calcium gluconate for dermal exposures of HF in >20% concentration or failure to respond to calcium gluconate gel.	Massage 2.5% gel into exposed area for 15 minutes. Infiltrate each square centimeter of exposed area with 0.5 mL of 10% calcium gluconate S.C. using a 30-gauge needle. 1 mL/kg I.V. of a 10% solution for magnesium toxicity (intra-arterial injection).	Injections of calcium gluconate should not be used in digital area. With exposures to dilute concentrations of HF, symptoms may take several hours to develop. Calcium gluconate gel is not currently available. Contact your regional poison control center for compounding instructions.
Deferoxamine (Desferal®)	Iron	Serum iron >350 mcg/dL. Inability to obtain serum iron in a reasonable time and patient is symptomatic.	**Mild symptoms:** I.M.: 10 mg/kg up to 1 g every 8 hours **Severe symptoms:** I.V.: 10-15 mg/kg/hour not to exceed 6 g in 24 hours; rates up to 35 mg/kg have been given.	Passing of vin rose-colored urine indicates free iron was present. Therapy should be discontinued when urine returns to normal color. Monitor for hypotension, especially when giving deferoxamine I.V.

Antidote	Poison/Drug	Indications	Dosage	Comments
Digoxin immune fab (ovine), (Digibind®)	Digoxin, digitoxin, oleander, foxglove, lily-of-the-valley (?), red squill (?)	Life-threatening cardiac arrhythmias, progressive bradyarrhythmias, second or third degree heart block unresponsive to atropine, serum digoxin level >5 ng/mL, potassium levels >5 mEq/L, or ingestion >10 mg in adults (or 4 mg in children).	Multiply serum digoxin concentration at steady-state level by 5.6 and multiply the result by the patient's weight in kilograms, divide this by 1000 and divide the result by 0.6. This gives the dose in number of vials to use. For other dosing methods, see package insert.	Monitor potassium levels, continuous EKG. **Note:** Digibind® interferes with serum digoxin/digitoxin levels.
Dimercaprol (BAL in oil®)	Arsenic, lead, mercury, gold, trivalent antimony, methyl bromide, methyl iodide	Any symptoms due to arsenic exposure. All patients with symptoms or asymptomatic children with blood levels >70 mcg/dL. Any symptoms due to mercury and patient unable to take D-penicillamine.	3-5 mg/kg/dose deep I.M. every 4 hours until GI symptoms subside and patient switched to D-penicillamine. 3-5 mg/kg/dose deep I.M. every 4 hours for 2 days then every 4-12 hours for up to 7 additional days. 3-5 mg/kg/dose deep I.M. every 4 hours for 48 hours, then 3 mg/kg/dose every 6 hours, then 3 mg/kg/dose every 12 hours for 7 or more days.	Patients receiving dimercaprol should be monitored for hypertension, tachycardia, hyperpyrexia, and urticaria. Used in conjunction with calcium EDTA in lead poisoning.
Ethanol	Ethylene glycol or methanol	Ethylene glycol or methanol blood levels >20 mg/dL. Blood levels not readily available and suspected ingestion of toxic amounts. Any symptomatic patient with a history of ethylene glycol or methanol ingestion.	**Loading dose:** I.V.: 7.5-10 mL/kg 10% ethanol in D_5W over 1 hour **Maintenance dose:** I.V.: 1.4 mL/kg/ hour of 10% ethanol in D_5W. Maintain blood ethanol level of 100-200 mg/dL.	Monitor blood glucose, especially in children, as ethanol may cause hypoglycemia. Do not use 5% ethanol in D_5W as excessive amounts of fluid would be required to maintain adequate ethanol blood levels. If dialysis is performed, adjustment of ethanol dosing is required.
Flumazenil (Romazicon®)	Benzodiazepine	As adjunct to conventional management/diagnosis of benzodiazepine overdose.	I.V.: 0.2 mg over 30 seconds; wait another 30 seconds, and then give an additional 0.3 mg over 30 seconds. Additional doses of 0.5 mg over 30 seconds at 1-minute intervals up to a cumulative dose of 3 mg.	Onset of reversal usually within 1-2 minutes. Contraindicated in patients with epilepsy, increased intracranial pressure, or coingestion of seizuregenic agents (ie, cyclic antidepressant).

MANAGEMENT OF OVERDOSAGES (Continued)

Antidote	Poison/Drug	Indications	Dosage	Comments
Glucagon	Propranolol: Hypoglycemic agents	Propranolol-induced cardiac dysfunction. Treatment of hypoglycemia.	S.C., I.M., or I.V.: 0.5-1 mg May repeat after 15 minutes	Requires liver glycogen stores for hyperglycemic response. Intravenous glucose must also be given in treatment of hypoglycemia.
Leucovorin (citrovorum factor, folinic acid)	Methotrexate, trimethoprim, pyrimethamine, methanol, trimetrexate	Methotrexate-induced bone marrow depression (methotrexate serum level >1 x 10^{-5} mmol/L); may also be useful in pyrimethamine-trimethoprim bone marrow depression	Dose should be equal to or greater than the dose of methotrexate ingested. Usually 10-100 mg/m^2 is given I.V. or orally every 6 hours for 72 hours.	Most effective if given within 1 hour after exposure. May not be effective to prevent liver toxicity. Monitor methotrexate levels. May enhance the toxicity of fluorouracil.
Methylene blue	Methemoglobin inducers (ie, nitrites, phenazopyridine)	Cyanosis Methemoglobin level >30% in an asymptomatic patient	I.V.: 1-2 mg/kg (0.1-0.2 mL/kg) per dose over 2-3 minutes. May repeat doses as needed clinically. Injection can be given as 1% solution or diluted in normal saline.	Treatment can result in falsely elevated methemoglobin levels when measured by a co-oximeter. Large doses (>15 mg/kg) may cause hemolysis.
Naloxone (Narcan®)	Opiates (eg, heroin, morphine, codeine)	Coma or respiratory depression from unknown cause or from opiate overdose	Give 0.4-2.0 mg I.V. bolus. Doses may be repeated if there is no response, up to 10 mg.	For prolonged intoxication, a continuous infusion may be used.
D-penicillamine (Cuprimine®)	Arsenic, lead, mercury	Following BAL therapy in symptomatic acutely poisoned patients. Asymptomatic patients with excess lead burden. Patient symptomatic from mercury exposure or excessive levels	100 mg/kg/day up to 2 g in 4 divided doses for 5 days **Children:** 100 mg/kg/day up to 1 g/day in 4 divided doses. Given for 3-10 days. **Adults:** P.O.: 250 mg 4 times/day	Possible contraindication for patients with penicillin allergy. Monitor heavy metal levels daily in severely poisoned patients. Monitor CBC and renal function in patients receiving chronic D-penicillamine therapy. Dosages given are for short-term acute therapy only.

Antidote	Poison/Drug	Indications	Dosage	Comments
Physostigmine salicylate	Atropine and anticholinergic agents, cyclic antidepressants, intrathecal baclofen	Myoclonic seizures, severe arrhythmias Refractory seizures or arrhythmias unresponsive to conventional therapies	**Children:** Slow I.V. push: 0.5 mg. Repeat as required for life-threatening symptoms **Adults:** Slow I.V. push: 0.5-2 mg Same as above	Dramatic reversal of anticholinergic symptoms after I.V. use. Should not be used just to keep patient awake. **Contraindications:** Asthma, gangrene; physostigmine use in cyclic antidepressant-induced cardiac toxicity it controversial. **Extreme caution** is advised — should be considered only in the presence of life-threatening anticholinergic symptoms.
Pralidoxime (2-PAM, Protopam®)	Organophosphate, insecticides, tacrine	An adjunct to atropine therapy for treatment of profound muscle weakness, respiratory depression, muscle twitching	**Children:** 25-50 mg/kg in 250 mL saline over 30 minutes **Adults:** I.V.: 2 g at 0.5 g/minute or infused in 250 mL NS over 30 minutes	Most effective when used in initial 24-36 hours after the exposure. Dosage may be repeated in 1 hour followed by every 8 hours if indicated.
Phytonadione (vitamin K₁)	Coumarin derivatives, indandione derivatives	Large acute ingestion of warfarin rodenticides; chronic exposure or greater than normal prothrombin time	**Children:** vitamin K: 1-5 mg. With severe toxicity, vitamin K₁ may be given I.V. **Adults:** I.M.: 10 mg	Vitamin K therapy is relatively contraindicated for patients with prosthetic heart valves unless toxicity is life-threatening.
Protamine sulfate	Heparin	Severe hemorrhage	Maximum rate of 5 mg/minute up to a total dose of 200 mg in 2 hours. 1 mg of protamine neutralizes 90 units of beef lung heparin or 115 units of pork intestinal heparin.	Monitor partial thromboplastin time or activated coagulation time. Effect may be immediate and can last for 2 hours. Monitor for hypotension.
Pyridoxine (vitamin B₆)	Isoniazid monomethyl-hydrazine-containing mushrooms (Gyromitra); acrylamide, hydrazine	Unknown overdose or ingested isoniazid (INH) amount >80 mg/kg	I.V. pyridoxine in the amount of INH ingested or 5 g if amount is unknown given over 30-60 minutes.	Cumulative dose of pyridoxine is arbitrarily limited to 40 g in adults and 20 g in children.
Succimer (Chemet®)	Lead, arsenic, mercury	Asymptomatic children with venous blood lead 45-69 mcg/dL. Not FDA approved for adult lead exposure or other metals.	**P.O.:** 10 mg/kg or 350 mg/m² every 8 hours for 5 days. Reduce to 10 mg/kg or 350 mg/m² every 12 hours for an additional 2 weeks.	Monitor liver function; emits "rotten egg" sulfur odor.

Adapted from Rush Poison Control Center, Rush-Presbyterian-St Luke's Medical Center, Chicago, IL 60612.

OVERDOSE AND TOXICOLOGY — SYMPTOMS and TREATMENT

Drug or Drug Class	Signs/Symptoms	Treatment/Comments
Acetaminophen	Generally asymptomatic	Assess severity of ingestion; adult doses ≥140 mg/kg are thought to be toxic. Obtain serum concentration ≥4 hours postingestion and use acetaminophen nomogram to evaluate need for acetylcysteine. Gastric decontamination within 2-4 hours after ingestion. May administer activated charcoal for one dose, this may decrease absorption of acetylcysteine if given within 1 hour of acetylcysteine. For unknown ingested quantities and for significant ingestion give acetylcysteine orally (diluted 1:4 with juice or carbonated beverage); initial: 140 mg/kg then give 70 mg/kg every 4 hours for 17 doses. I.V. protocols are used in some institutions.
Alpha-adrenergic blocking agents	Hypotension, drowsiness	Give activated charcoal, additional treatment if symptomatic; use I.V. fluids, dopamine, or norepinephrine to treat hypotension. Epinephrine may worsen hypotension due to beta effects.
Aminoglycosides	Ototoxicity, nephrotoxicity, neuromuscular toxicity	Hemodialysis or peritoneal dialysis may be useful in patients with decreased renal function; calcium may reverse the neuromuscular toxicity.
Amphetamines and other CNS stimulants	Seizures, hyperactivity, coma, hypertension	There is no specific antidote for amphetamines and other stimulant intoxication and the bulk of the treatment is supportive. Hyperactivity and agitation usually respond to reduced sensory input, however with extreme agitation, haloperidol (2-5 mg I.M. for adults) may be required. Hyperthermia is best treated with external cooling measures, or when severe or unresponsive, muscle paralysis with pancuronium may be needed. Hypertension is usually transient and generally does not require treatment unless severe. For diastolic blood pressures >110 mm Hg, a nitroprusside infusion should be initiated. Seizures usually respond to diazepam IVP and/or phenytoin maintenance regimens.

Drug or Drug Class	Signs/Symptoms	Treatment/Comments
Anticholinergics, antihistamines	Coma, hallucinations, delirium, tachycardia, dry skin, urinary retention, dilated pupils	For life-threatening arrhythmias or seizures. Adults: 2 mg/dose physostigmine, may repeat 1-2 mg in 20 minutes and give 1-4 mg slow I.V. over 5-10 minutes if signs and symptoms recur (relatively contraindicated if QRS >0.1 msec).
Barbiturates	Respiratory depression, circulatory collapse, bradycardia, hypotension, hypothermia, slurred speech, confusion, coma	Repeated oral doses of activated charcoal given every 3-6 hours will increase clearance. Adults: 30-60 g. Assure GI motility, adequate hydration, and renal function. Urinary alkalinization with I.V. sodium bicarbonate will increase renal elimination of longer-acting barbiturates (eg, phenobarbital). Charcoal hemoperfusion may be required in severe overdose.
Benzodiazepines (including zolpidem)	Respiratory depression, apnea (after rapid I.V.), hypoactive reflexes, hypotension, slurred speech, unsteady gait, coma	Dialysis is of limited value; support blood pressure and respiration until symptoms subside. Flumazenil: Initial dose: 0.2 mg given I.V. over 30 seconds. If further response is desired after 30 seconds, give 0.3 mg over another 30 seconds. Further doses of 0.5 mg can be given over 30 seconds at 1-minute intervals up to a total of 3 mg. Continuous infusions may be used in rare instances since duration of benzodiazepines is longer than flumazenil.
Beta-adrenergic blockers	Hypotension, bronchospasm, bradycardia, hypoglycemia, seizures	Activated charcoal; treat symptomatically; glucagon, atropine, isoproterenol, dobutamine, or cardiac pacing may be needed to treat bradycardia, conduction defects, or hypotension.
Carbamazepine	Dizziness, drowsiness, ataxia, involuntary movements, opisthotonos, seizures, nausea, vomiting, agitation, nystagmus, coma, urinary retention, respiratory depression, tachycardia, arrhythmias	Use supportive therapy, general poisoning management as needed. Use repeated oral doses of activated charcoal given every 3-6 hours to decrease serum concentrations. Charcoal hemoperfusion may be needed. Treat hypotension with I.V. fluids, dopamine, or norepinephrine. Monitor EKG. Diazepam may control convulsions but may exacerbate respiratory depression.
Cardiac glycosides	Hyperkalemia may develop rapidly and result in life-threatening cardiac arrhythmias, progressive bradyarrhythmias, second or third degree heart block unresponsive to atropine, ventricular fibrillation, asystole	Obtain serum drug level, induce emesis or perform gastric lavage. Give activated charcoal to reduce further absorption. Atropine may reverse heart block. Digoxin immune Fab (digoxin specific antibody fragments) is used in serious cases. Each 40 mg of digoxin immune Fab binds with 0.6 mg of digoxin.

OVERDOSE AND TOXICOLOGY — SYMPTOMS and TREATMENT *(Continued)*

Drug or Drug Class	Signs/Symptoms	Treatment/Comments
Cholinergic	Nausea, vomiting, diarrhea, miosis, CNS depression, excessive salivation, excessive sweating, muscle weakness	Suction oral secretions, decontaminate skin, atropinize patient. Atropine dose must be individualized. Adults: Initial atropine dose: 1 mg; titrate dose upward. Pralidoxime (2-PAM) may need to be added for moderate to severe intoxications.
Cyanide	Myocardial depression, lactic acidosis, hypotension, respiratory depression, shock and cyanosis despite high oxygen saturation	Cyanide antidote kit: 1) Inhale vapor from 0.3 mL amyl nitrate ampul until I.V. sodium nitrite available; 2) sodium nitrite 300 mg I.V. then 3) sodium thiosulfate 12.5 g I.V. over 10 minutes
Heparin	Severe hemorrhage	1 mg of protamine sulfate will neutralize approximately 90 units of heparin sodium (bovine) or 115 units of heparin sodium (porcine) or 100 units of heparin calcium (porcine).
Hydantoin derivatives	Nausea, vomiting, nystagmus, slurred speech, ataxia, coma	Gastric lavage or emesis; repeated oral doses of activated charcoal may increase clearance of phenytoin. Use 0.5-1 g/kg (30-60 g/dose) activated charcoal every 3-6 hours until nontoxic serum concentration is obtained. Assure adequate GI motility, supportive therapy.
Iron	Lethargy, nausea, vomiting, green or tarry stools, hypotension, weak rapid pulse, metabolic acidosis, shock, coma, hepatic necrosis, renal failure, local GI erosions	If immediately after ingestion and not already vomiting, give ipecac or lavage with saline solution. Give deferoxamine mesylate I.V. at 15 mg/kg/hour in cases of severe poisoning (serum iron >350 µg/mL) until the urine color is normal, the patient is asymptomatic, or a maximum daily dose of 8 g is reached. Urine output should be maintained >2 mL/kg/hour to avoid hypovolemic shock.
Isoniazid	Nausea, vomiting, blurred vision, CNS depression, intractable seizures, coma, metabolic acidosis	Control seizures with diazepam. Give pyridoxine I.V. equal dose to the suspected overdose of isoniazid or up to 5 g empirically. Give activated charcoal.
Magnesium Salts	Symptoms usually present with serum level >4 mEq/L	Serum magnesium >4: Deep tendon reflexes may be depressed; ≥10: Deep tendon reflexes may disappear, respiratory paralysis may occur, heart block may occur; >12 mEq/L may be fatal, serum level ≥10 mEq/L may cause complete heart block. I.V. calcium (5-10 mEq) 1-2 g calcium gluconate will reverse respiratory depression or heart block; in extreme cases, peritoneal dialysis or hemodialysis may be required.

Drug or Drug Class	Signs/Symptoms	Treatment/Comments
MAO inhibitors	Tachycardia, palpitations, muscle twitching, seizures, insomnia, restlessness, transient hypertension, hypotension, drowsiness, hyperpyrexia, coma	Competent supportive care is the most important treatment. Both hyper- or hypotension can occur with intoxication. Hypotension may respond to I.V. fluids or vasopressors and hypertension usually responds to an alpha-adrenergic blocker. While treating the hypertension, care is warranted to avoid sudden drops in blood pressure, since this may worsen the MAO inhibitor toxicity, Muscle irritability and seizures often respond to diazepam, while hyperthermia is best treated with antipyretics and cooling blankets. Cardiac arrhythmias are best treated with phenytoin and procainamide.
Methotrexate	Nausea, vomiting, alopecia, melena, renal failure	Antidote is leucovorin; administer as soon as toxicity is seen; administer 10 mg/m^2 orally or parenterally; follow with 10 mg/m^2 orally every 6 hours for 72 hours. After 24 hours following methotrexate administration, if the serum creatinine is ≥50% premethotrexate serum creatinine, increase leucovorin dose to 100 mg/m^2 every 3 hours until serum MTX level is <5 x 10^{-8}M. Hydration and alkalinization may be used to prevent precipitation of MTX or MTX metabolites in the renal tubules. Toxicity in low-dose range is negligible, but can result from overdose. Neither peritoneal nor hemodialysis have been shown to increase elimination. Leucovorin should be administered intravenously, never intrathecally, for overdoses of intrathecal methotrexate.
Nonsteroidal anti-inflammatory drugs	Dizziness, abdominal pain, sweating, apnea, nystagmus, cyanosis, hypotension, coma, seizures (rarely)	Induce emesis. Give activated charcoal via NG tube. Fluid therapy is commonly effective in managing the hypotension that may occur following an acute NSAIDs overdose, except when this is due to an acute blood loss. Seizures tend to be very short-lived and often do not require drug treatment; although, recurrent seizures should be treated with I.V. diazepam. Since many of the NSAIDs undergo enterohepatic cycling, multiple doses of charcoal may be needed to reduce the potential for delayed toxicities. Provide symptomatic and supportive care.

OVERDOSE AND TOXICOLOGY — SYMPTOMS and TREATMENT *(Continued)*

Drug or Drug Class	Signs/Symptoms	Treatment/Comments
Opioids and morphine analogs (including tramadol)	Respiratory depression, miosis, hypothermia, bradycardia, circulatory collapse, pulmonary edema, apnea	Establish airway and adequate ventilation. Give naloxone 0.4 mg and titrate to a maximum of 10 mg. Additional doses may be needed every 20-60 minutes. May need to institute continuous infusion, as duration of action of opiates can be longer than duration of action of naloxone.
Organophosphates (insecticides, pyridostigmine, neostigmine)	Bronchospasm, diarrhea, diaphoresis, ventricular dysrhythmia, fasciculations, flaccid paralysis, lethargy, coma	Atropine 2-5 mg every 15 minutes until symptoms abate (0.05 mg/kg children). If severe, may add pralidoxime 1-2 g over 15-30 minutes (20-50 mg/kg children); may repeat every 8-12 hours or continuous infusion 0.5 g/hour (10-20 mg/kg/hour children).
Phenothiazines	Deep, unarousable sleep, anticholinergic symptoms, extrapyramidal signs, diaphoresis, rigidity, tachycardia, cardiac dysrhythmias, hypotension	Activated charcoal; do **not** dialyze. Use I.V. benztropine mesylate 1-2 mg/dose slowly over 3-6 minutes for extrapyramidal signs. Use I.V. fluids and norepinephrine to treat hypotension. Avoid epinephrine which may cause hypotension due to phenothiazine-induced alpha-adrenergic blockade and unopposed epinephrine B_2 action. Use benzodiazepines for seizure management and to decrease rigidity.
Potassium salts	Muscle weakness, paralysis, peaked T waves, flattened P waves, prolongation of QRS complex, ventricular arrhythmias	Removal of potassium can be accomplished by various means; removal through the GI tract with Kayexalate® administration; by way of the kidney through diuresis, mineralocorticoid administration, or increased sodium intake; by hemodialysis or peritoneal dialysis, or by shifting potassium back into the cells by insulin, glucose infusion, or sodium bicarbonate; calcium chloride reverses cardiac effects.
Salicylates	Nausea, vomiting, respiratory alkalosis, hyperthermia, dehydration, hyperapnea, tinnitus, headache, dizziness, metabolic acidosis, coma, hypoglycemia, seizures	Induce emesis or gastric lavage immediately. Give several doses of activated charcoal, rehydrate, and use sodium bicarbonate to correct metabolic acidosis and enhance renal elimination by alkalinizing the urine. Control hyperthermia by cooling blankets or sponge baths. Correct coagulopathy with vitamin K I.V. and platelet transfusions as necessary. Hypoglycemia may be treated with I.V. dextrose. Seizures should be treated with I.V. benzodiazepines (diazepam 5-10 mg I.V.). Give supplemental potassium after renal function has been determined to be adequate. Monitor electrolytes; obtain stat serum salicylate level and follow.

Drug or Drug Class	Signs/Symptoms	Treatment/Comments
Sulfonylureas and Insulin	Low blood sugar, tingling of lips and tongue, nausea, yawning, confusion, agitation, tachycardia, sweating, convulsions, stupor, coma	Intoxications with sulfonylureas can cause hypoglycemia and are best managed with glucose administration (oral for milder hypoglycemia or by injection in more severe forms). For insulin overdose, glucagon administration may be necessary.
Tricyclic antidepressants	Agitation, confusion, hallucinations, urinary retention, hypothermia, hypotension, tachycardia, arrhythmias, seizures	Give activated charcoal ± lavage. Use sodium bicarbonate for QRS >0.1 msec; alkalinization by hyperventilation has been used in patients on mechanical ventilation; I.V. fluids and norepinephrine may be used for hypotension; benzodiazepines may be used for seizure management.
Warfarin	Internal or external hemorrhage, hematuria	For moderate overdoses, give oral, S.C., or I.D., or slow I.V. (I.V. associated with anaphylactoid reactions) phytonadione; usual dose: 2.5-10 mg, adjust per prothrombin time. For severe hemorrhage, give fresh frozen plasma or whole blood. See Warfarin monograph.
Xanthine derivatives	Vomiting, abdominal pain, bloody diarrhea, tachycardia, extrasystoles, tachypnea, tonic/clonic seizures	Give activated charcoal orally. Repeated oral doses of activated charcoal increase clearance. Use 0.5-1 g/kg (30-60 g/dose) of activated charcoal every 1-4 hours (depending on the severity of ingestion) until nontoxic serum concentrations are obtained. Assure adequate GI motility, supportive therapy. Charcoal hemoperfusion or hemodialysis can also be effective in decreasing serum concentrations and should be used if the serum concentration approaches 90-100 mcg/mL in acute overdoses.

SALICYLATES

Toxic Symptoms	Treatment
Overdose	Induce emesis with ipecac, and/or lavage with saline, followed with activated charcoal
Dehydration	I.V. fluids with KCl (no D_5W only)
Metabolic acidosis (must be treated)	Sodium bicarbonate
Hyperthermia	Cooling blankets or sponge baths
Coagulopathy/hemorrhage	Vitamin K I.V.
Hypoglycemia (with coma, seizures, or change in mental status)	Dextrose 25 g I.V.
Seizures	Diazepam 5-10 mg I.V.

TOXICOLOGY INFORMATION

Initial Stabilization of the Patients

The recommended treatment plan for the poisoned patient is not unlike general treatment plans taught in advanced cardiac life support (ACLS) or advanced trauma life support (ATLS) courses. In this manner, the initial approach to the poisoned patient should be essentially similar in every case, irrespective of the toxin ingested, just as the initial approach to the trauma patient is the same irrespective of the mechanism of injury. This approach, which can be termed as routine poison management, essentially includes the following aspects.

- Stabilization: ABCs (airway, breathing, circulation; administration of glucose, thiamine, oxygen, and naloxone
- History, physical examination leading toward the identification of class of toxin (toxidrome recognition)
- Prevention of absorption (decontamination)
- Specific antidote, if available
- Removal of absorbed toxin (enhancing excretion)
- Support and monitoring for adverse effects

Drug	Effect	Comment
25-50 g **dextrose** (D_{50}W) intravenously to reverse the effects of drug-induced hypoglycemia (adult) 1 mL/kg D_{50}W diluted 1:1 (child)	This can be especially effective in patients with limited glycogen stores (ie, neonates and patients with cirrhosis)	Extravasation into the extremity of this hyperosmolar solution can cause Volkmann's contractures
50-100 mg intravenous **thiamine**	Prevent Wernicke's encephalopathy	A water-soluble vitamin with low toxicity; rare anaphylactoid reactions have been reported
Initial dosage of **naloxone** should be 2 mg in adult patients preferably by the intravenous route, although intramuscular, subcutaneous, intralingual, and endotracheal routes may also be utilized. Pediatric dose is 0.1 mg/kg from birth until 5 years of age	Specific opioid antagonist without any agent properties	It should be noted that some semisynthetic opiates (such as meperidine or propoxyphene) may require higher initial doses for reversal, so that a total dose of 6-10 mg is not unusual for the adults. If the patient responds to a bolus dose and then relapses to a lethargic or comatose state, a naloxone drip can be considered. This can be accomplished by administering two-thirds of the bolus dose that revives the patient per hour or injecting 4 mg naloxone in 1 L crystalloid solution and administering at a rate of 100 mL/hour 0.4 mg/hour)
Oxygen, utilized in 100% concentration	Useful for carbon monoxide, hydrogen, sulfide, and asphyxiants	While oxygen is antidotal for carbon monoxide intoxication, the only relative toxic contraindication is in paraquat intoxication (in that it can promote pulmonary fibrosis)
Flumazenil	Benzodiazepine antagonist	Not routinely recommended due to increased risk of seizures

TOXICOLOGY INFORMATION *(Continued)*

Laboratory Evaluation of Overdose

Unknown ingestion: Electrolytes, anion gap, serum osmolality, arterial blood gases, serum drug concentration

Known ingestion: Labs tailored to agent

Toxins Affecting the Anion Gap

Drugs Causing Increased Anion Gap (>12 mEq/L)

Nonacidotic

Carbenicillin	Sodium salts

Metabolic Acidosis

Acetaminophen (ingestion >75-100 g)	Isoniazid
Acetazolamide	Ketamine
Amiloride	Ketoprofen
Ascorbic acid	Metaldehyde
Benzalkonium chloride	Metformin
Benzyl alcohol	Methanol
Beta-adrenergic drugs	Methenamine mandelate
Bialaphos	Monochloracetic acid
2-Butanone	Nalidixic acid
Carbon monoxide	Naproxen
Centrimonium bromide	Niacin
Chloramphenicol	Papaverine
Colchicine	Pennyroyal oil
Cyanide	Pentachlorophenol
Dapsone	Phenelzine
Dimethyl sulfate	Phenformin (off the market)
Dinitrophenol	Phenol
Endosulfan	Phenylbutazone
Epinephrine (I.V. overdose)	Phosphoric acid
Ethanol	Potassium chloroplatinite
Ethylene dibromide	Propylene glycol
Ethylene glycol	Salicylates
Fenoprofen	Sorbitol (I.V.)
Fluoroacetate	Strychnine
Formaldehyde	Surfactant herbicide
Fructose (I.V.)	Tetracycline (outdated)
Glycol ethers	Theophylline
Hydrogen sulfide	Tienilic acid
Ibuprofen (ingestion >300 mg/kg)	Toluene
Inorganic acid	Tranylcypromine
Iodine	Vacor
Iron	Verapamil

Drugs Causing Decreased Anion Gap (<6 mEq/L)

Acidosis

Ammonium chloride	Lithium
Bromide	Polymyxin B
Iodide	Tromethamine

Drugs Causing Increased Osmolar Gap
(by freezing-point depression, gap is >10 mOsm)

Ethanol[1]

Ethylene glycol[1]

Glycerol

Hypermagnesemia (>9.5 mEq/L)

Isopropanol[1] (acetone)

Iodine (questionable)

Mannitol

Methanol[1]

Propylene glycol

Severe alcoholic ketoacidosis or
    lactic acidosis

Sorbitol[1]

[1]Toxins increasing both anion and osmolar gap.

Toxins Associated With Oxygen Saturation Gap
(>5% difference between measured and calculated value)

Carbon monoxide

Cyanide (questionable)

Hydrogen sulfide (possible)

Methemoglobin

Acetaminophen Toxicity

The Toxicology Laboratory is also very useful for determining levels of toxin in body fluids. Often these drug levels will guide therapy. For example, use of the Rumack-Matthew nomogram for acute acetaminophen poisoning can direct N-acetylcysteine therapy if the serum acetaminophen level falls above the treatment line.

Acetaminophen Toxicity Nomogram

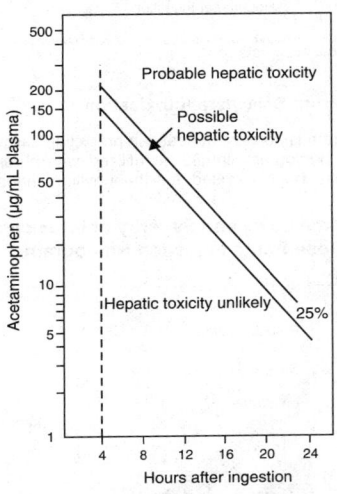

The Rumack-Matthew nomogram, relating expected severity of liver toxicity to serum acetaminophen concentrations.

From Smilkstein MJ, Bronstein AC, Linden C, et al, "Acetaminophen Overdose: A 48-Hour Intravenous N-Acetylcysteine Treatment Protocol," *Ann Emerg Med*, 1991, 20(10):1058, with permission.

TOXICOLOGY INFORMATION *(Continued)*

Ibuprofen Toxicity Nomogram

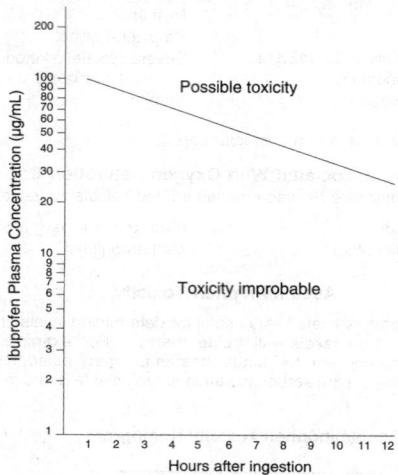

Adapted from Hall AH, Smolinske SC, Stover B, et al, "Ibuprofen Overdose in Adults," *J Toxicol Clin Toxicol*, 1992, 30:34.

Serum Salicylate Intoxication

Similarly, the Done nomogram is somewhat useful in predicting salicylate toxicity in pediatric patients. Neither nomogram should be utilized with chronic ingestions. Recently, a nomogram has been devised for theophylline ingestion; see the following nomogram.

Serum Salicylate Level and Severity of Intoxication
Single Dose Acute Ingestion Nomogram

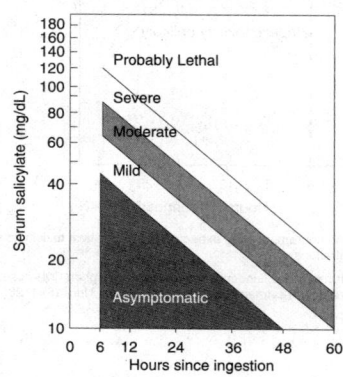

Done nomogram for salicylate poisoning. Note that this nomogram is not accurate for chronic ingestions nor for acute ingestions with enteric coated tabs. Clinical laboratory signs and symptoms are best indicators for assessments. (From Done AK, "Salicylate Intoxication: Significance of Measurements of Salicylate in Blood in Cases of Acute Ingestions," *Pediatrics*, 1960, 26:800; copyright American Academy of Pediatrics, 1960.)

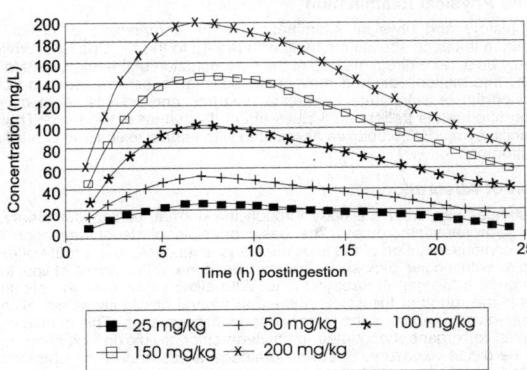

Serum Theophylline Overdose

Nonsmokers

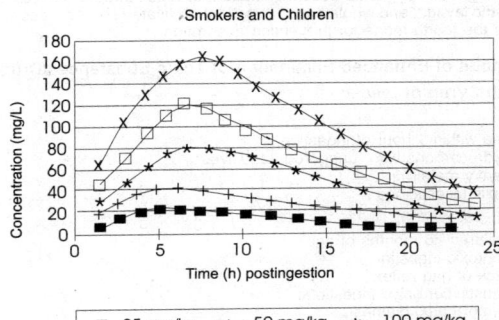

Serum Theophylline Overdose

Smokers and Children

Nomogram for overdose of sustained-release theophylline in 1) nonsmoking adults, and 2) smokers and children. (Courtesy of Frank Paloucek, PharmD, College of Pharmacy, University of Illinois, Chicago.)

TOXICOLOGY INFORMATION *(Continued)*

History and Physical Examination

While the history and physical examination is the cornerstone of clinical patient management, it takes on special meaning with regard to the toxic patient. While taking a history may be a more direct method of the determination of the toxin, quite often is is not reliable. Information obtained may prove minimal in some cases and could be considered partial or inaccurate in suicide gestures and addicts. A quick physical examination often leads to important clues about the nature of the toxin. These clues can be specific symptom complexes associated with certain toxins and can be referred to as "toxidromes".

Prevention of Absorption

Toxic substances can enter the body through the dermal, ocular, pulmonary, parenteral, and gastrointestinal routes. The basic principle of decontamination involves appropriate copious irrigation of the toxic substances relatable to the route of exposure. For example, with ocular exposure, this can be done with normal saline for 30-40 minutes through a Morgan therapeutic lens. With alkali exposures, the pH should be checked until the runoff of the solution is either neutral or slightly acidic. Skin decontamination involves removal of the toxin with nonabrasive soap. This should especially be considered for organophosphates, methylene chloride, dioxin, radiation, hydrocarbons, and herbicide exposure. Separate drainage areas should be obtained for the contaminated runoff.

Since >80% of incidents of accidental poisoning in children occur through the gastrointestinal tract, a thorough knowledge of gastric decontamination is essential. There are essentially four modes of gastric decontamination, of which three are physical removal (emesis, gastric lavage, and whole bowel irrigation). Activated charcoal associated with a cathartic is the fourth mode for preventing absorption.

Methods of Enhanced Elimination of Toxic Substances/Drugs

Emesis with Syrup of Ipecac

Indications

- Use within 1 hour of ingestion
- Hydrocarbons with "dangerous additives"
- Heavy metals
- Toxic insecticides

Contraindications

- Children <6 months of age
- Nontoxic ingestion
- Lack of gag reflex
- Caustic/corrosive ingestions
- Hemorrhagic diathesis
- Sharp object ingestion
- Prior vomiting
- Ingestion of pure petroleum distillate

Dose: + 15 mL H_2O

Children:	6-12 months: 10 mL	
	1-5 years: 15 mL	
	>5 years: 30 mL	
Adults:	30 mL	

Note: Ipecac use is becoming less frequently recommended since <30% of the stomach is usually emptied and its use may delay the use of activated charcoal.

Gastric Lavage

Indications

- Use within 1 hour of ingestion
- Comatose patient with significant ingestion without contraindications
- Failure to respond to ipecac
- Large quantities of toxins

Contraindications

- Seizures
- Nontoxic ingestion
- Significant hemorrhagic diathesis
- Caustic ingestions, hydrocarbons
- Usually unable to use large enough tube in children <12 years of age

Note: Lavage is not routinely recommended except for recent and very large ingestions of noncontraindicated toxins since it is believed to actually push a significant portion of drug into the intestine and may delay administration of activated charcoal.

Enhancement of Elimination

Only recently has this aspect of poison management received more than cursory attention in practice and in the literature. The standard practice for enhancement of elimination consisted primarily of forced diuresis in order to excrete the toxin. However, the past 10 years experience has produced a radical change in the approach to this and therefore, a more focused methodology to eliminating absorbed toxins. Essentially, there are three methods by which absorbed toxins may be eliminated: recurrent adsorption with multiple dosings of activated charcoal, use of forced diuresis in combination with possible alkalinization of the urine, and use of dialysis or charcoal hemoperfusion.

Activated Charcoal Indications

Indications

- Single dose for agents known to be bound
- Multiple dose for drugs with favorable characteristics: Small volume of distribution (<1 L/kg), low plasma protein binding, biliary or gastric secretion, active metabolites that recirculate, drugs that exhibit a large free fraction (eg, dapsone, carbamazepine, digitalis, methotrexate, phenobarbital, salicylates, theophylline, tricyclic antidepressants), unchanged, lipophilic, long half-life

Recently, multiple dosing of activated charcoal ("pulse dosing") has been advocated as a method for removal of absorbed drug. This procedure has been demonstrated to be efficacious in drugs that re-enter the gastrointestinal tract through enterohepatic circulation (ie, digitoxin, carbamazepine, glutethimide) and with drugs that diffuse from the systemic circulation into the gastrointestinal tract due to formation of a concentration gradient ("the infinite sink" hypothesis).

Toxins Eliminated by Multiple Dosing of Activated Charcoal (MDAC)

Acetaminophen	Meprobamate
Amitriptyline	Methotrexate
Amoxapine	Methyprylon
Baclofen (?)	Nadolol
Benzodiazepines (?)	Nortriptyline
Bupropion (?)	Phencyclidine
Carbamazepine[1]	Phenobarbital[1]
Chlordecone	Phenylbutazone
Cyclosporine	Phenytoin (?)
Dapsone	Piroxicam
Diazepam	Propoxyphene
Digoxin	Propranolol
Disopyramide	Salicylates (?)[1]
Glutethimide	Theophylline[1]
Maprotiline	Valproic acid[1]

[1]Only agents routinely recommended for removal with MDAC.

Contraindications

- Absence of hypoactive bowel sounds
- Caustic ingestions
- Drugs without effect: Acids, alkalis, alcohols, boric acid, cyanide, iron, heavy metals, lithium, insecticides

Dose

Children and Adults: 50-100 g initially or 1 g/kg weight; repeat doses of 25 g or 0.5 g/kg every 2-4 hours

Most effective at 1-hour postingestion but can remove at >1-hour postingestion

Doses subsequent to first may be admixed with water rather than a cathartic such as sorbitol to avoid diarrhea and consequent electrolyte disturbances.

TOXICOLOGY INFORMATION *(Continued)*

Whole Bowel Irrigation – propylene glycol based solutions

Initial dose of charcoal is necessary prior to use. Avoid pretreatment with ipecac.

Indications

- Iron, lead, lithium
- Agents not bound by charcoal
- Modified or sustained release dosage forms
- Body packers

Contraindications

- Bowel perforation
- Obstruction
- Ileus
- Gastrointestinal bleed

Dose

Maximum: 5-10 L
Toddlers/preschool: 250-500 mL/hour or 35 mL/kg
Adults: 1-2 L/hour
Terminate when rectal effluent = infusate = clear

Urinary Ion Trapping – to alkalinize the urine

Indications

- Salicylates
- Phenobarbital

Toxins Eliminated by Forced Saline Diuretics	Toxins Eliminated by Alkaline Diuresis
Bromidex	2,4-D chlorphenoxyacetic acid
Chromium	Fluoride
Cimetidine (?)	Isoniazid (?)
Cis-platinum	Mephobarbital
Cyclophosphamide	Methotrexate
Hydrazine	Phenobarbital
Iodide	Primidone
Iodine	Quinolones antibiotic
Isoniazid (?)	Salicylates
Lithium	Uranium
Methyl iodide	
Potassium chloroplatinite	
Thallium	

Dose

Sodium bicarbonate 1-2 mEq/kg every 3-4 hours or 100 mEq $NaHCO_3$ in 1 L $D_5\frac{1}{4}NS$ at 200 mL/hour (desired urine pH: 7.6-7.8)

A urine flow of 3-5 mL/kg/hour should be achieved with a combination of isotonic fluids or diuretics. Although several drugs can exhibit enhanced elimination through an acidic urine (quinine, amphetamines, PCP, nicotine, bismuth, ephedrine, flecainide), the practice of acidifying the urine should be discouraged in that it can produce metabolic acidosis and promote renal failure in the presence of rhabdomyolysis. **Note:** Use caution in alkalinizing urine of children to avoid fluid overdose.

Hemodialysis

Indications

Drugs with favorable characteristics

- Low molecular weight (<500 daltons)
- Ionically charged
- H_2O soluble
- Low plasma protein binding (<70%-80%)
- Small volume of distribution (<1 L/kg)
- Low tissue binding
- Methanol, ethylene glycol, boric acid

Drugs and Toxins Removed by Hemodialysis

Acetaminophen
Acyclovir
Amanita phalloides (?)
Amantadine (?)
Ammonium chloride
Amphetamine
Anilines
Atenolol
Boric acid
Bromides
Bromisoval
Calcium
Captopril (?)
Carbromal
Carisoprodol
Chloral hydrate
Chlorpropamide
Chromium
Cimetidine (?)
Cyclophosphamide
Dapsone
Disopyramide
Enalapril (?)
Ethanol
Ethylene glycol
Famotidine (?)
Fluoride
Folic acid
Formaldehyde
Foscarnet sodium
Gabapentin
Glycol ethers
Hydrazine (?)
Hydrochlorothiazide

Iodides
Isoniazid
Isopropanol
Ketoprofen
Lithium
Magnesium
Meprobamate
Metal-chelate compounds
Metformin (?)
Methanol
Methaqualone
Methotrexate
Methyldopa
Methylprylone
Monochloroacetic acid
Nadolol
Oxalic acid
Phenelzine (?)
Phenobarbital
Phosphoric acid
Potassium
Procainamide
Quinidine
Ranitidine (?)
Rifabutin
Salicylates
Sotalol
Strychnine
Thallium
Theophylline
Thiocyanates
Tranylcypromine sulfate (?)
Verapamil (?)

Hemoperfusion

Indications

Drugs with favorable characteristics:
- Affinity for activated charcoal
- Tissue binding
- High rate of equilibration from peripheral tissues to blood

Examples: Barbiturates, carbamazepine, ethchlorvynol, methotrexate, phenytoin, theophylline

Drugs and Toxins Removed by Hemoperfusion (Charcoal)

Aconitine
Amanita phalloides (?)
Atenolol (?)
Bromisoval
Bromoethylbutyramide
Caffeine
Carbamazepine
Carbon tetrachloride (?)
Carbromal
Chloral hydrate (trichloroethanol)
Chloramphenicol
Chlorpropamide
Colchicine (?)
Creosote (?)
Dapsone
Diltiazem (?)
Disopyramide
Ethchlorvynol
Ethylene oxide
Glutethimide
Lindane

Meprobamate
Methaqualone
Methotrexate
Methsuximide
Methyprylon (?)
Metoprolol (?)
Nadolol (?)
Oxalic acid (?)
Paraquat
Phenelzine (?)
Phenobarbital
Phenytoin
Podophyllin (?)
Procainamide (?)
Quinidine (?)
Rifabutin (?)
Sotalol (?)
Thallium
Theophylline
Verapamil (?)

Exchange transfusion is another mode of extracorporeal removal of toxins that can be utilized in neonatal infant drug toxicity. It may be especially useful for barbiturate, iron, caffeine, sodium nitrite, or theophylline overdose.

TOXIDROMES

Overdose Signs and Symptoms

Toxin	Vital Signs	Mental Status	Symptoms	Physical Exam	Laboratories
Acetaminophen	Normal	Normal	Anorexia, nausea, vomiting	RUQ tenderness, jaundice	Elevated LFTs
Cocaine	Hypertension, tachycardia, hyperthermia	Anxiety, agitation, delirium	Hallucinations	Mydriasis, tremor, diaphoresis, seizures, perforated nasal septum	EKG abnormalities, increased CPK
Cyclic antidepressants	Tachycardia, hypotension, hyperthermia	Decreased, including coma	Confusion, dizziness	Mydriasis, dry mucous membranes, distended bladder, decreased bowel sounds, flushed, seizures	Long QRS complex, cardiac dysrhythmias
Iron	Early: Normal Late: Hypotension, tachycardia	Normal; lethargic if hypotensive	Nausea, vomiting, diarrhea, abdominal pain, hematemesis	Abdominal tenderness	Heme + stool and vomit, metabolic acidosis, EKG and x-ray findings, elevated serum iron (early); child: hyperglycemia, leukocytosis
Opioids	Hypotension, bradycardia, hypoventilation, hypothermia	Decreased, including coma	Intoxication	Miosis, absent bowel sounds	Abnormal ABGs
Salicylates	Hyperventilation, hyperthermia	Agitation; lethargy, including coma	Tinnitus, nausea, vomiting, confusion	Diaphoresis, tender abdomen	Anion gap metabolic acidosis, respiratory alkalosis, abnormal LFTs, and coagulation studies
Theophylline	Tachycardia, hypotension, hyperventilation, hyperthermia	Agitation, lethargy, including coma	Nausea, vomiting, diaphoresis, tremor, confusion	Seizures, arrhythmias	Hypokalemia, hyperglycemia, metabolic acidosis, abnormal EKG

Examples of Toxidromes

Toxidromes	Pattern	Example of Drugs	Treatment Approach
Anticholinergic	Fever, ileus, flushing, tachycardia, urinary retention, inability to sweat, visual blurring, and mydriasis. Central manifestations include myoclonus, choreoathetosis, toxic psychosis with lilliputian hallucinations, seizures, and coma.	Antihistamines Baclofen Benztropine Jimson weed Methylpyroline Phenothiazines Propantheline Tricyclic antidepressants	Physostigmine for life-threatening symptoms only; may predispose to arrhythmias[1]
Cholinergic	Characterized by salivation, lacrimation, urination, defecation, gastrointestinal cramps, and emesis ("sludge"). Bradycardia and bronchoconstriction may also be seen.	Carbamate Organophosphates Pilocarpine	• Atropine[1] • Pralidoxime for organophosphate insecticides[1]
Extrapyramidal	Choreoathetosis, hyperreflexia, trismus, opisthotonos, rigidity, and tremor	Haloperidol Phenothiazines	• Diphenhydramine • Benztropine
Hallucinogenic	Perceptual distortions, synthesis, depersonalization, and derealization	Amphetamines Cannabinoids Cocaine Indole alkaloids Phencyclidine	Benzodiazepine
Narcotic	Altered mental status, unresponsiveness, shallow respirations, slow respiratory rate or periodic breathing, miosis, bradycardia, hypothermia	Opiates Dextromethorphan Pentazocine Propoxyphene	Naloxone[1]

TOXIDROMES *(Continued)*

Examples of Toxidromes *(continued)*

Toxidromes	Pattern	Example of Drugs	Treatment Approach
Sedative/Hypnotic	Manifested by sedation with progressive deterioration of central nervous system function. Coma, stupor, confusion, apnea, delirium, or hallucinations may accompany this pattern.	Anticonvulsants Antipsychotics Barbiturates Benzodiazepines Ethanol Ethchlorvynol Fentanyl Glutethimide Meprobamate Methadone Methocarbamol Opiates Quinazolines Propoxyphene Tricyclic antidepressants	• Naloxone[1] • Flumazenil; usually not recommended due to increased risk of seizures[1] • Urinary alkalinization (barbiturates)
Seizuregenic	May mimic stimulant pattern with hyperthermia, hyperreflexia, and tremors being prominent signs	Anticholinergics Camphor Chlorinated hydrocarbons Cocaine Isoniazid Lidocaine Lindane Nicotine Phencyclidine Strychnine Xanthines	• Antiseizure medications • Pyridoxine for isoniazid[1] • Extracorporeal removal of drug (ie, lindane, camphor, xanthines) • Physostigmine for anticholinergic agents[1]

Examples of Toxidromes *(continued)*

Toxidromes	Pattern	Example of Drugs	Treatment Approach
Serotonin	Confusion, myoclonus, hyperreflexia, diaphoresis, tremor, facial flushing, diarrhea, fever, trismus	Clomipramine Fluoxetine Isoniazid L-tryptophan Paroxetine Phenelzine Sertraline Tranylcypromine Drug combinations include: • MAO inhibitors with L-tryptophan • Fluoxetine or meperidine • Fluoxetine with carbamazepine or sertraline • Clomipramine and meclobemide • Trazadol and buspirone • Paroxetine and dextromethorphan	Withdrawal of drug/benzodiazepine
Solvent	Lethargy, confusion, dizziness, headache, restlessness, incoordination, derealization, depersonalization	Acetone Chlorinated hydrocarbons Hydrocarbons Naphthalene Trichloroethane Toluene	Avoid catecholamines

TOXIDROMES *(Continued)*

Examples of Toxidromes *(continued)*

Toxidromes	Pattern	Example of Drugs	Treatment Approach
Stimulant	Restlessness, excessive speech and motor activity, tachycardia, tremor, and insomnia — may progress to seizure. Other effects noted include euphoria, mydriasis, anorexia, and paranoia.	Amphetamines Caffeine (xanthines) Cocaine Ephedrine/pseudoephedrine Methylphenidate Nicotine Phencyclidine	Benzodiazepines
Uncoupling of oxidative phosphylation	Hyperthermia, tachypnea, diaphoresis, metabolic acidosis (usually)	Aluminum phosphide Aspirin/salicylates 2,4-Dichlorophenol Di-n-Butyl phthalate Dinitrophenols Dinitro-o-cresols Hexachlorobutadiene Phosphorus Pentachlorophenol Tin (?) Zinc phosphide	Sodium bicarbonate to treat metabolic acidosis; patient cooling techniques; avoidance of atropine or salicylate agents; hemodialysis may be required for acidosis treatment

[1]See the Poison Control Center Antidote Chart.

From Nice A, Leikin JB, Maturen A, et al, "Toxidrome Recognition to Improve Efficiency of Emergency Urine Drug Screens," *Ann Emerg Med*, 1988, 17:676-80.

THERAPEUTIC CATEGORY & KEY WORD INDEX

Anti-inflammatory Agent, Inhalant

Anti-inflammatory Agent, Ophthalmic

Anti-inflammatory Agent, Rectal

Anti-inflammatory/Beta$_2$-Adrenergic Agonist

Antilipemic Agent, 2-Azetidinone

Antilipemic Agent, Bile Acid Sequestrant

Antilipemic Agent, Fibric Acid

Antilipemic Agent, HMG-CoA Reductase Inhibitor

(Continued)

NOTES

NOTES

NOTES

NOTES

NOTES

Other books offered by
LEXI-COMP

DRUG INFORMATION HANDBOOK

Perfect Bound / Book Size: 4.5" x 9"
International edition also available
by Lacy, Armstrong, Goldman, Lance

Specifically compiled and designed for the healthcare
professional requiring quick access to concisely-stated
comprehensive data concerning clinical use of
medications. This is an ideal portable drug information
resource, providing the reader with up to 34 key points of
data concerning clinical use and dosing of the medication.
Material provided in the Appendix section is recognized
by many users to be, by itself, well worth the purchase of
the handbook.

PEDIATRIC DOSAGE HANDBOOK

Perfect Bound / Book Size: 4.375" x 8"
International edition also available
by Taketomo, Hodding, Kraus

Special considerations must frequently be taken into account
when dosing medications for the pediatric patient. This highly
regarded quick reference handbook is a compilation of
recommended pediatric doses based on current literature, as well
as the practical experience of the authors and their many
colleagues who work every day in the pediatric clinical setting.
Includes neonatal dosing, drug administration, and (in select
monographs) extemporaneous preparations for medications used
in pediatric medicine.

GERIATRIC DOSAGE HANDBOOK

Perfect Bound / Book Size: 4.375" x 8"
by Semla, Beizer, Higbee

Many physiologic changes occur with aging, some of which affect
the pharmacokinetics or pharmacodynamics of medications.
Strong consideration should also be given to the effect of
decreased renal or hepatic functions in the elderly, as well as the
probability of the geriatric patient being on multiple drug
regimens. Healthcare professionals working with nursing homes
and assisted living facilities will find the drug information
contained in this handbook to be an invaluable source of helpful
information. An International Brand Name Index with names
from 58 different countries is also included.

2000 "Book of the Year"
American Journal of Nursing

To order call toll free anywhere in the U.S.: 1-800-837-LEXI (5394)
Outside of the U.S. call: 330-650-6506 or online at www.lexi.com

PHARMACOGENOMICS HANDBOOK

Perfect Bound / Book Size: 4.25" x 7"

by Humma, Ellingrod, Kolesar

This exciting new title by Lexi-Comp, introduces Pharmacogenomics to the forward-thinking healthcare professional and student! It presents information concerning key genetic variations that may influence drug disposition and/or sensitivity. Brief introductions to fundamental concepts in genetics and genomics are provided in order to bring the reader up-to-date on these rapidly emerging sciences. This book provides a foundation for all clinicians who will be called on to integrate rapidly expanding genomic knowledge into the management of drug therapy. A great introduction to pharmacogenetic principles as well as a concise reference on key polymorphisms known to influence drug response!

DRUG-INDUCED NUTRIENT DEPLETION HANDBOOK

Perfect Bound / Book Size: 4.25" x 7"

by Pelton, LaValle, Hawkins, Krinsky

A complete and up-to-date listing of all drugs known to deplete the body of nutritional compounds.

This book is alphabetically organized and provides extensive cross-referencing to related information in the various sections of the book. Drug monographs identify the nutrients depleted and provide cross-references to the nutrient monographs for more detailed information on effects of depletion, biological function & effect, side effects & toxicity, RDA, dosage range, and dietary sources. this book also contains a studies & abstracts section, a valuable appendix, and alphabetical & pharmacological indexes.

NATURAL THERAPEUTICS POCKET GUIDE

Perfect Bound / Book Size: 4.375" x 8"

by Krinsky, LaValle, Hawkins, Pelton, Ashbrook Willis

Provides condition-specific information on common uses of natural therapies. Each condition discussed includes the following: review of condition, decision tree, list of commonly recommended herbals, nutritional supplements, homeopathic remedies, lifestyle modifications, and special considerations.

Provides herbal/nutritional/nutraceutical monographs with over 10 fields including references, reported uses, dosage, pharmacology, toxicity, warnings & interactions, and cautions & contraindications. The Appendix includes: drug-nutrient depletion, herb-drug interactions, drug-nutrient interaction, herbal medicine use in pediatrics, unsafe herbs, and reference of top herbals.

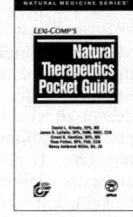

To order call toll free anywhere in the U.S.: 1-800-837-LEXI (5394)
Outside of the U.S. call: 330-650-6506 or online at www.lexi.com

Other books offered by
LEXI-COMP

DRUG INFORMATION HANDBOOK FOR ADVANCED PRACTICE NURSING

Perfect Bound / Book Size: 4.5" x 9"

by Turkoski, Lance, Bonfiglio

Designed specifically to meet the needs of nurse practitioners, clinical nurse specialists, nurse midwives, and graduate nursing students. The handbook is a unique resource for detailed, accurate information, which is vital to support the advanced practice nurse's role in patient drug therapy management. Over 4750 U.S., Canadian, and Mexican medications are covered in the 1000 monographs. Drug data is presented in an easy-to-use, alphabetically-organized format covering up to 46 key points of information (including dosing for pediatrics, adults, and geriatrics). Appendix contains over 230 pages of valuable comparison tables and additional information. Also included are two indexes, Pharmacologic Category and Controlled Substance, which facilitate comparison between agents.

1999 "Book of the Year"
American Journal of Nursing

DRUG INFORMATION HANDBOOK FOR NURSING

Perfect Bound / Book Size: 4.5" x 9"

by Turkoski, Lance, Bonfiglio

Registered professional nurses and upper-division nursing students involved with drug therapy will find this handbook provides quick access to drug data in a concise easy-to-use format. Over 4000 U.S., Canadian, and Mexican medications are covered with up to 43 key points of information in each monograph. The handbook contains basic pharmacology concepts and nursing issues such as patient factors that influence drug therapy (ie, pregnancy, age, weight, etc) and general nursing issues (ie, assessment, administration, monitoring, and patient education). The Appendix contains over 230 pages of valuable information.

ANESTHESIOLOGY & CRITICAL CARE DRUG HANDBOOK

Perfect Bound / Book Size: 4.375" x 8"

by Donnelly, Cunningham, Baughman

Contains the most commonly used drugs in the perioperative and critical care setting and also Special Issues and Topics including: Allergic Reaction, Anesthesia for Cardiac Patients in Noncardiac Surgery, Anesthesia for Obstetric Patients in Nonobstetric Surgery, Anesthesia for Patients With Liver Disease, Chronic Pain Management, Chronic Renal Failure, Conscious Sedation, Perioperative Management of Patients on Antiseizure Medication, and Substance Abuse and Anesthesia. The Appendix includes Abbreviations & Measurements, Anesthesiology Information, Assessment of Liver & Renal Function, Comparative Drug Charts, Infectious Disease-Prophylaxis & Treatment, Laboratory Values, Therapy Re-commendations, Toxicology information, *and much more*. International Brand Name Index with names from over 58 different countries is also included.

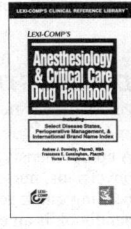

To order call toll free anywhere in the U.S.: 1-800-837-LEXI (5394)
Outside of the U.S. call: 330-650-6506 or online at www.lexi.com

Other books offered by
LEXI-COMP

CLINICIAN'S GUIDE TO INTERNAL MEDICINE—A Practical Approach

Perfect Bound / Book Size: 4.375" x 8"
by Desai

Provides quick access to essential information covering diagnosis, treatment, and management of commonly encountered patient problems in Internal Medicine. This up-to-date and clinically-relevant information is in an easy-to-read format and is easily accessible. Provides practical approaches that are not readily available in standard textbooks. Contains algorithms to help you establish the diagnosis and select the appropriate therapy. There are numerous tables and boxes that summarize diagnostic and therapeutic strategies. An ideal reference for use at the point-of-care. This is a reference companion that will provide you with the tools necessary to tackle even the most challenging problems in Internal Medicine.

CLINICIAN'S GUIDE TO DIAGNOSIS —A Practical Approach

Perfect Bound / Book Size: 4.375" x 8"
by Desai

Symptoms are what prompt patients to seek medical care. In the evaluation of a patient's symptom, it is not unusual for healthcare professionals to ask "What do I do next?" This is precisely the question for which this book provides the answer. It will lead you from symptom to diagnosis through a series of steps designed to mimic the logical thought processes of seasoned clinicians. For the young clinician, this is an ideal book to help bridge the gap between the classroom and actual patient care. For the experienced clinician, this concise handbook offers rapid answers to the questions that are commonly encountered on a day-to-day basis. Let this guide become your companion, providing you with the tools necessary to tackle even the most challenging symptoms.

CLINICIAN'S GUIDE TO LABORATORY MEDICINE—A Practical Approach

Perfect Bound / Book Size: 4.375" x 8" Pocket Guide: 4.25" x 7"
by Desai, Isa-Pratt

When faced with the patient presenting with abnormal laboratory tests, the clinician can now turn to the *Clinician's Guide to Laboratory Medicine: A Practical Approach*. This source is unique in its ability to lead the clinician from laboratory test abnormality to clinical diagnosis. Written for the busy clinician, this concise handbook will provide rapid answers to the questions that busy clinicians face in the care of their patients. No longer does the clinician have to struggle in an effort to find this information - it's all here. Included is a **FREE copy of** *Clinician's Guide to Laboratory Medicine - Pocket*. Great to carry in your pocket! Perfect for use "in the trenches."

FREE
Pocket Guide

To order call toll free anywhere in the U.S.: 1-800-837-LEXI (5394)
Outside of the U.S. call: 330-650-6506 or online at www.lexi.com

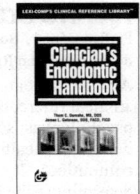
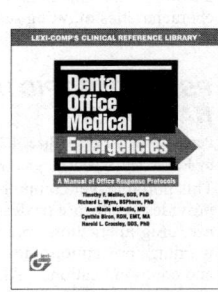

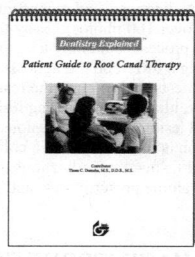
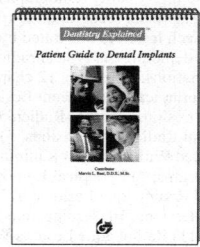

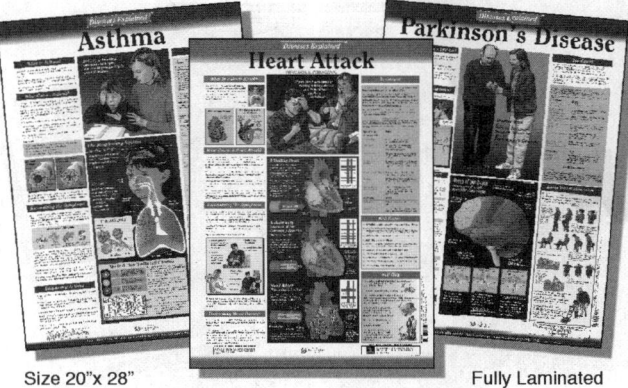

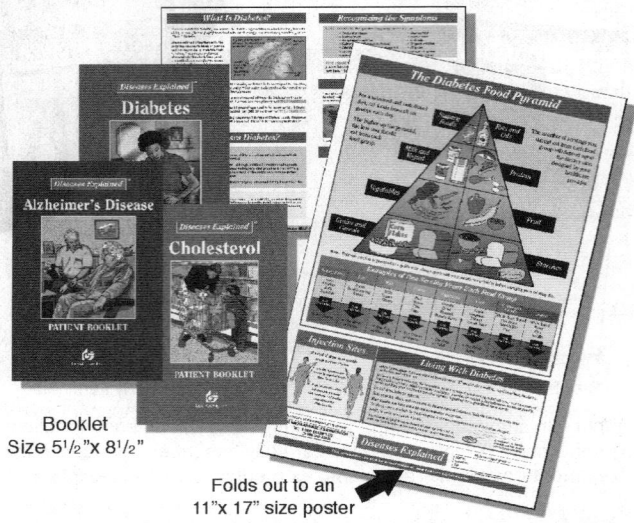

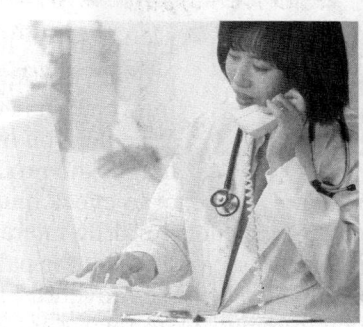

LEXI-COMP ON-HAND SOFTWARE LIBRARY

For Palm OS® and
Windows™ Powered Pocket PC Devices

 ™ Lexi-Comp's handheld software solutions provide quick, portable access to clinical information needed at the point-of-care. Whether you need laboratory test or diagnostic procedure information, to validate a dose, or to check multiple medications and natural products for drug interactions, Lexi-Comp has the information you need in the palm of your hand. Lexi-Comp also provides advanced linking technology to allow you to hyperlink to related information topics within a title or to the same topic in another title for more extensive information. No longer will you have to exit 5MCC to look up a dose in Lexi-Drugs or lab test information in Lexi-Diagnostic Medicine — seamlessly link between all databases to **save valuable time**.

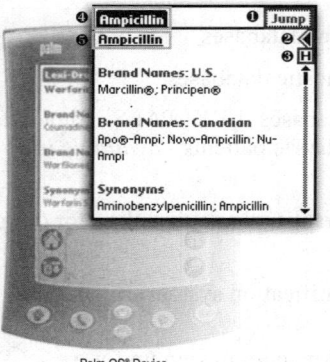

Palm OS® Device

New Navigational Tools:

❶ **"Jump"** provides a drop down list of available fields to easily navigate through information.

❷ **Back arrow** returns to the index from a monograph or to the "Installed Books" menu from the Index.

❸ **"H"** provides a linkable History to return to any of the last 12 Topics viewed during your session.

❹ **Title bar:** Tap the monograph or topic title bar to activate a menu to "Edit a Note" or return to the "Installed Books" menu.

❺ **Linking:** Link to another companion database by clicking the topic or monograph title link or within a database noted by various hyperlinked (colorized and underlined) text.

To order call toll free anywhere in the U.S.: 1-800-837-LEXI (5394)
Outside of the U.S. call: 330-650-6506 or online at www.lexi.com